Oxford Dictionary of English

THIRD EDITION

Edited by
Angus Stevenson

First edition edited by
Judy Pearsall
Patrick Hanks

OXFORD
UNIVERSITY PRESS

OXFORD
UNIVERSITY PRESS

Great Clarendon Street, Oxford OX2 6DP

Oxford University Press is a department of the University of Oxford.
It furthers the University's objective of excellence in research, scholarship,
and education by publishing worldwide in

Oxford New York
Auckland Cape Town Dar es Salaam Hong Kong Karachi
Kuala Lumpur Madrid Melbourne Mexico City Nairobi
New Delhi Shanghai Taipei Toronto

With offices in

Argentina Austria Brazil Chile Czech Republic France Greece
Guatemala Hungary Italy Japan Poland Portugal Singapore
South Korea Switzerland Thailand Turkey Ukraine Vietnam

First edition 1998
Second edition 2003
Second edition, revised 2005
Third edition 2010

British Library Cataloguing in Publication Data
Data available

Library of Congress Cataloging in Publication Data
Data available

Typeset in Parable, Frutiger, and OUP Argo by Datagrafix, Inc.
Printed in Italy by L.E.G.O. S.p.A., Lavis (TN)

ISBN 978-0-19-957112-3

10 9 8 7 6 5 4 3 2

Introduction

The *Oxford Dictionary of English* has been compiled according to principles which are quite different from those of traditional dictionaries. Evidence of real language use is now available in sufficient quantity to allow us to construct a picture of English that is more accurate than has been possible before. The approach to structuring and organizing within individual dictionary entries has been rethought, as has the approach to the selection and presentation of information in every aspect of the dictionary: definitions, choice of examples, grammar, word histories, and every other category. The aim of this introduction is to give you background information for using this dictionary and, in particular, to explain some of the thinking behind the new approaches.

What makes an Oxford dictionary?

The information presented in the *Oxford Dictionary of English* is based on close analysis of how words behave in real, natural language. Behind every dictionary entry are examples of the word in use—often hundreds and thousands of them—which have been analysed to give information about typical usage, about distribution (whether typically British or typically US, for example), about register (whether informal or derogatory, for example), about currency (whether archaic or dated, for example), and about subject (whether used only in Medicine, Finance, Chemistry, or Sport, for example).

The Oxford English Corpus

The first edition of the *Oxford Dictionary of English* (then called the *New Oxford Dictionary of English*) was the first English dictionary intended primarily for native speakers that was compiled by analysis of a corpus. A corpus is a collection of texts of written (or spoken) language presented in electronic form. It provides the evidence of how language is used in real situations, from which lexicographers can write accurate and meaningful dictionary entries. Whereas compilers of previous dictionaries were able to base their work on only a limited selection of citations, lexicographers on the *New Oxford Dictionary of English* could analyse hundreds or thousands of examples of each word to see how real language behaves today.

The corpus used on the first edition was the British National Corpus, a database of 100 million words. Revisions made to to this third edition, and new material added to it, have been derived largely from analysis of the new Oxford English Corpus, which contains more than two billion words. All content dates from 2000 at the earliest, and the corpus is regularly updated with the latest material, allowing a true picture of language change to build up.

The Oxford English Corpus represents all types of English, from fiction and specialist journals to everyday newspapers and magazines, and from official reports to the language of Internet message boards and chat rooms. And, as English is a global language, used by an estimated one third of the world's population, the Oxford English Corpus contains language from all parts of the world—not only from the UK and the United States but also from Australia, the Caribbean, Canada, India, Singapore, and South Africa. It is the largest English corpus of its type: the most representative slice of the English language available.

Meanings of words and phrases change and so do spellings, despite the existence of 'standard' or 'correct' spelling. A strength of the corpus is that it contains not only published works in which the text has been edited (and made to conform to standard spellings and grammar) but also unpublished and unedited writing like emails and blogs. Some of the most inventive uses and deliberate exploitations of language, not to mention common-or-garden mistakes, start out in this kind of informal and unselfconscious language, so tracking them is an essential part of tracking the language as a whole.

Analysing the corpus lets us identify items that occur there but are not covered in the dictionary, and so helps us to draw up a shortlist of potential new entries. It tells us which words are commoner than they were ten years ago, and which are rarer; and which words are increasingly being used in a different way, or in a different sense. It also lets us define familiar, established words more accurately, by telling us more about them. For example, the corpus shows that the verb **cause** typically has as its object something bad—like *death, damage, chaos, disturbance, problems*, etc. Most dictionaries define the word neutrally, for example as 'make (something) happen', but armed with the corpus information we have redefined it as 'make (something, especially something bad) happen'. Similarly, **decline** is often defined simply as 'become smaller, fewer, or less', but a look at the corpus shows us that the typical subject is something regarded as good, such as standards, output, or income—when something such as crime decreases it doesn't decline, it falls.

Concordances show at a glance that some combinations of words (called 'collocations') occur together much more often than others. For example, in the concordance on page x, 'end in', 'end the', and 'end up' all occur quite often. But are any of these combinations important enough to be given special treatment in the dictionary?

Recent research has focused on identifying combinations that are not merely frequent but also statistically significant. In the Oxford English Corpus the two words 'end the' occur very frequently together, but they do not form a statistically significant unit, since the word 'the' is the commonest in the language. The combinations **end up** and **end in**, on the other hand, are shown to be more significant and tell us something about the way the verb **end** behaves in normal use. Of course, a dictionary for general use cannot go into detailed statistical analysis of word combinations, but it can present examples

weblog	; I would say his book is mostly nonsense from beginning to	**end**	, but I 'll return to this) , molding the details and structures
news	mutually assured destruction . </p><p> There the similarities	**end**	. Niall Stokes 's shock tactics earned some mild rebukes on
news	confection , designed to distract us from the truth : that we will	**end**	. Totally . " </p><p> Gloomy ? Definitely . Yet there is also
weblog	impossible to breath , unyielding in their stubborn refusal ever to	**end**	. Was a time I tried for that , tried to find the measure of
news	couple of days . " </p><p> · SALTIRES hero Paul Hoffmann hopes to	**end**	a personal jinx and help Uddingston keep the Coronel Scottish
sport	" added Collingwood who hit the winning runs at Edgbaston to	**end**	a run of 14 - straight one-day defeats for England against
computing	will drop off the charts , the denial of service attack will	**end**	and the author - if he has any sense - will hide under his
news	tirelessly to forge an agreement with the Chinese authorities to	**end**	bear farming . </p><p> In 1998 she set up the Animals Asia Foundation
news	Society criticized Mr Hain for agreeing to its suggestion to	**end**	candidates standing in both constituency and top-up list elections
news	as we did not use any PA equipment in those days , we used to	**end**	each evening triumphant but hoarse and shattered . </p><p> One
sport	twice against Charlton in London to provide a fitting victory to	**end**	Fergie 's big week . </p><p> " It means a lot to us that the
sport	yearssome slump . </p><p> So it will surprise nobody if Woods doesn't	**end**	his barren run in golf 's biggest events with his fourth Masters
society	suggesting that simply dumping vast amounts of steel in Africa could	**end**	hunger . </p><p> The most critical issues are the sheer poverty
weblog	looking at similar measures . Something like 10 % of burglaries	**end**	in convictions . The perceived clear-up rate for motoring offences
humanities	a crisis ' , wrote Diderot as Maupeou struck , ' which will	**end**	in slavery or in freedom ; if it is slavery , it will be a
news	administration . </p><p> " We don't reject anyone but what we are going to	**end**	in this country from now on is graft and impunity , " Reuters
life_and_leisure	yet to decide their holiday destination , added : " We always	**end**	in Vegas - we never start there because you have to wash your
weblog	life , if I wanted I could go and step in front of a bus and	**end**	it " or something to that effect . That 's nice in theory but
sport	an invitation for next month 's race . </p><p> Mapei decided to	**end**	its sponsorship of the world 's biggest professional cycling
business	essential to the development of core products and eventually to	**end**	products ; </p><p> essential to the implementation of the strategic
news	revealed after a government minister hinted at new legislation to	**end**	selective education . </p><p> Trafford is the only borough in
news	the waitress moved off into the night she predicted they would	**end**	soon . </p><p> " The weather is changing . It 's getting colder
weblog	as ever remains with Israel , as does the responsibility to	**end**	the conflict by ending the occupation . </p><p> In the near term
news	judges and sheriffs , with details expected before Easter to	**end**	the culture of secrecy which dominates judicial appointments
news	train . ' </p><p> Others are suggesting major political reform to	**end**	the tribal areas ' special status and consequent isolation
humanities	, Balck was an exceptionally inspiring commander who was to	**end**	the war as an army group general . Having succeeded in crossing
news	matched in any other sport . " </p><p> The Claymores are aiming to	**end**	their ten-game tour around Europe on a victorious note , and
military	</p><p> The ambitions of the Kwantung Army 's officers did not	**end**	there . A truce was signed with China in 1933 , which created
news	is difficult to avoid the conclusion that one or other will	**end**	this case by walking away from Old Trafford , with all the
weblog	very winnable tie away at Bolton in the next round . </p><p> To	**end**	this round-up , the very definition of a dour cup tie . Sixth
life_and_leisure	Well , they are going to drop an ' A ' bomb which we hope will	**end**	this war . " </p><p> A lot of people said the bomb should never
news	BPISG) . </p><p> The aim of the review , which is scheduled to	**end**	tomorrow with the result coming any time over the next few
arts	years in development and Down recognises that companies can	**end**	up " endlessly scratching " without ever taking the leap into
news	sure Ilkley 's tourist-drawing central shopping streets do not	**end**	up armed to the teeth with as much off-putting security paraphernalia
computing	SRGG show up and join the crowd , but they (almost) always	**end**	up being fairly normal people who also game after a year or
news	frontbencher . </p><p> But the risk is that the Lib Dems could	**end**	up being seen as a party of the left , especially following
sport	where I would find it . </p><p> The last thing I wanted was to	**end**	up diving from a second-rate centre on tired coral reefs .
news	and if they get too full of the importance of the place , they	**end**	up doing a worse job . " </p><p> The man who describes himself
computing	stories on this site . Once you use the clusters a few times , you	**end**	up getting to what you 're looking for faster than with advanced
weblog	on the fire dump , which is where most of these planes will	**end**	up given their age and general condition . </p><p> UN - 76497
life_and_leisure	And there are ways of doing it without that so that we don't	**end**	up in a brave new world . The thing that I 'm saying about
news	and that details are input accurately if they don't want to	**end**	up in a dark room being grilled by border officials . " </p>
news	chance to change their ways , so , as Sgt Foster said , if they	**end**	up in serious trouble they have no one to blame but themselves
news	scored more goals - a factor which will count if both teams	**end**	up on the same points . Now , courtesy of a recent victory
life_and_leisure	law and end up pregnant at 13 or so . Because i bet they 'll	**end**	up regretting the whole episode and maybe even hating the poor
weblog	have to think about a little person who grows very fast so you	**end**	up saying ' Oh , I can't buy that tiny and cute little jacket
news	paying prescription charges , they do . </p><p> Some Scots do	**end**	up selling their homes to care for their elderly relatives
society	house . </p><p> There are fewer and fewer council flats , so you	**end**	up shovelling rents into private landlords ' pockets . </p><p>
news	so they won't nip you . With a ready-cooked lobster you might	**end**	up with a dry , rubbery texture rather than deliciously succulent
news	then aged for three years in casks made from white oak . You	**end**	up with a spirit which is neither white nor dark , but delicately

Figure 1 Extract from a short concordance from the Oxford English Corpus, showing the word 'end'.

that are typical of normal usage. In the *Oxford Dictionary of English* particularly significant or important patterns are highlighted, in bold or in bold italics, e.g.

> **end**
>
> [no obj.] (**end in**) have as its final part or result: *the match ended in a draw*.
>
> [no obj.] (**end up**) eventually come to a specified place or situation: ***I ended up in*** *Eritrea* | *you could* ***end up with*** *a higher income*.

For further details, see the section on *Grammar*.

The Oxford Reading Programme

The citation database created by the Oxford Reading Programme is an ongoing research project in which readers around the world select short extracts from a huge variety of specialist and non-specialist sources in all varieties of English. This database currently stands at around 100 million words, and tens of thousands of new citations are added every year.

Illustrative examples

The *Oxford Dictionary of English* contains many more examples of words in use than any other comparable dictionary. Generally, the examples are there to show typical uses of the word or sense. All examples are authentic, in that they represent actual usage. In the past dictionaries used made-up examples, partly because not enough authentic text was available and partly through an assumption that invented examples were somehow better in that they could be tailored to the precise needs of the dictionary entry. Such a view finds little favour today, and it is now generally recognized that the 'naturalness' provided by authentic examples is of the utmost importance in providing an accurate picture of language in use.

Word trends

Through our analysis of the Oxford English Corpus for the third edition we have been able to identify some high-profile words whose use has changed significantly since the beginning of the century. Thus, for example, *terror* is now commonly used as shorthand for *terrorism*, and *web* primarily relates to the Internet rather than to spiders. Some of these findings have been presented in a new feature called Word Trends, which give an informal account of the word's development.

The structure of an entry

If a word has more than one part of speech, the first part of speech shown is the primary one for that word: thus, for **bag** and **balloon** the senses of the noun are given before those for the verb, while for **babble** and **bake** the senses of the verb are given before those of the noun.

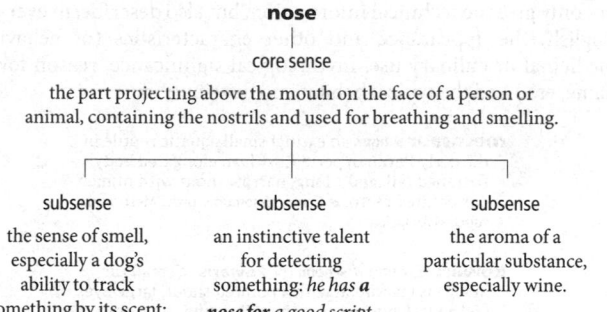

nose

core sense

the part projecting above the mouth on the face of a person or animal, containing the nostrils and used for breathing and smelling.

subsense	subsense	subsense
the sense of smell, especially a dog's ability to track something by its scent: *a dog with a keen nose.*	an instinctive talent for detecting something: *he has a **nose** for a good script.*	the aroma of a particular substance, especially wine.

The general principle on which the senses in the *Oxford Dictionary of English* are organized is that each word or part of speech has at least one **core sense** or **core meaning**, to which a number of subsenses may be attached. If there is more than one core meaning, this is introduced by a bold sense number. Core meanings represent typical, central uses of the word in question in modern standard English, as established by analysis of the Oxford English Corpus and our other language databases. The core meaning is the one accepted by native speakers as the most literal and central in ordinary modern usage. This is not necessarily the same as the oldest meaning, because word meanings change over time. Nor is it necessarily the most frequent meaning, because sometimes the most frequently used modern sense of a word is a figurative or extended one.

The core sense also acts as a gateway to other, related subsenses. These subsenses are grouped under the core sense, each one being introduced by a solid square symbol.

> **nose** ▶ noun **1** the part projecting above the mouth on the face of a person or animal, containing the nostrils and used for breathing and smelling. ■ [in sing.] the sense of smell, especially a dog's ability to track something by its scent: *a dog with a keen nose.* ■ [in sing.] an instinctive talent for detecting something: *he has a **nose** for a good script.* ■ the aroma of a particular substance, especially wine.

There is a logical relationship between each subsense and the core sense under which it appears. The organization of senses according to this logical relationship is designed to help the user, not only in being able to navigate the entry more easily and find relevant senses more readily, but also in building up an understanding of how senses in the language relate to one another and how the language is constructed on this model. The main types of relationship of core sense to subsense are as follows:

(a) figurative or metaphorical extension of the core sense, e.g.

	barbed
core sense	having a barb or barbs: *barbed arrows.*
subsense	(of a remark or joke) deliberately hurtful: *a fair degree of barbed wit.*

	boiling point
core sense	the temperature at which a liquid boils and turns to vapour.
subsense	the point at which anger or excitement breaks out into violent expression: *emotions had reached boiling point and could spill over into violence.*

(b) specialized case of the core sense, e.g.

	ball
core sense	a single throw, kick, or hit of the ball in a game, in particular:
subsense	*Cricket* a delivery of the ball by the bowler to the batsman.
subsense	*Baseball* a pitch delivered outside the strike zone which the batter does not attempt to hit.

	demand
core sense	an insistent and peremptory request, made as of right.
subsense	[mass noun] the desire of consumers, clients, employers, etc. for a particular commodity, service, or other item: *a recent slump in demand.*

(c) other extension or shift in meaning, retaining one or more elements of the core sense, e.g.

	bamboo
core sense	[mass noun] a giant woody grass which is grown chiefly in the tropics.
subsense	the hollow jointed stem of this plant, used as a cane or to make furniture and implements.

	management
core sense	the process of dealing with or controlling things or people: *the management of the economy / businesses were slow to adopt the key elements of environmental risk management.*
subsense	[treated as sing. or pl.] the people managing a company or organization, regarded collectively: *management were extremely cooperative.*

	ambassador
core sense	an accredited diplomat sent by a state as its permanent representative in a foreign country.
subsense	a representative or promoter of a specified activity: *he is a good ambassador for the industry.*

Many entries have just one core sense. However, some entries are more complex and have different strands of meaning, each constituting a core sense. In this case, each core sense is introduced by a bold sense number, and each potentially has its own block of subsenses relating to it.

> **belt** ▶ noun **1** a strip of leather or other material worn, typically round the waist, to support or hold in clothes or to carry weapons. ■ short for SEAT BELT. ■ a belt worn as a sign of rank or achievement: *he was awarded the victor's belt.* ■ a belt of a specified colour, marking the attainment of a particular level in judo, karate, or similar sports: [as modifier] *brown-belt level.* ■ a person who has reached such a level: *Shaun became a brown belt in judo.* ■ (**the belt**) the punishment of being struck with a belt.
> **2** a strip of material used in various technical applications, in particular: ■ a continuous band of material used in machinery for transferring motion from one wheel to another. ■ a conveyor belt. ■ a flexible strip carrying machine-gun cartridges.

Specialist vocabulary

One of the most important uses of a dictionary is to provide explanations of terms in specialized fields which are unfamiliar to a general reader. Yet in many traditional dictionaries the definitions have been written by specialists as if for other specialists, and as a result the definitions are often opaque and difficult for the general reader to understand.

One of the primary aims of the *Oxford Dictionary of English* has been to break down the barriers to understanding specialist vocabulary. The challenge has been, on the one hand, to give information which is comprehensible, relevant, and readable, suitable for the general reader, while on the other hand maintaining the high level of technical information and accuracy suitable for the more specialist reader.

This has been achieved in some cases, notably entries for plants and animals and chemical substances, by separating out technical information from the rest of the definition:

> **balloonfish** ▸ **noun** (pl. **same** or **balloonfishes**) a tropical porcupine fish which lives in shallow water and can inflate itself when threatened. • *Diodon holocanthus*, family Diodontidae.

> **benzopyrene** /ˌbɛnzə(ʊ)ˈpʌɪriːn/ ▸ **noun** [mass noun] Chemistry a compound which is the major carcinogen present in cigarette smoke, and also occurs in coal tar. • A polycyclic aromatic hydrocarbon; chem. formula: $C_{20}H_{12}$.

In other cases it is achieved by giving additional explanatory information within the definition itself:

> **curling** ▸ **noun** [mass noun] a game played on ice, especially in Scotland and Canada, in which large round flat stones are slid across the surface towards a mark. Members of a team use brooms to sweep the surface of the ice in the path of the stone to control its speed and direction.

> **curling** ▸ **noun** [mass noun] a game played on ice, especially in Scotland and Canada, in which large round flat stones are slid across the surface towards a mark. Members of a team use brooms to sweep the surface of the ice in the path of the stone to control its speed and direction.

> **cuttlebone** ▸ **noun** the flattened oval internal skeleton of the cuttlefish, which is made of white lightweight chalky material. It is used as a dietary supplement for cage birds and for making casts for precious metal items.

As elsewhere, the purpose is to give information which is relevant and interesting, aiming not just to define the word but also to describe and explain its context in the real world. Additional information of this type, where it is substantial, is given in the form of separate boxed features:

> **earth** ▸ **noun 1** (also **Earth**) the planet on which we live; the world: *the diversity of life **on earth**.* ■ the surface of the world as distinct from the sky or the sea: *the pilot brought the plane gently back to earth.* ■ the present abode of humankind, as distinct from heaven or hell.
>
> The earth is the third planet from the sun in the solar system, orbiting between Venus and Mars at an average distance of 149.6 million km from the sun, and has one natural satellite, the moon. It has an equatorial diameter of 12,756 km, an average density 5.5 times that of water, and is believed to have formed about 4,600 million years ago. The earth, which is three-quarters covered by oceans and has a dense atmosphere of nitrogen and oxygen, is the only planet known to support life.

> **Eocene** /ˈiːə(ʊ)siːn/ ▸ **adjective** Geology relating to or denoting the second epoch of the Tertiary period, between the Palaeocene and Oligocene epochs. ■ (as noun **the Eocene**) the Eocene epoch or the system of rocks deposited during it.
>
> The Eocene epoch lasted from 56.5 to 35.4 million years ago. It was a time of rising temperatures, and there was an abundance of mammals, including the first horses, bats, and whales.

An especially important feature of the *Oxford Dictionary of English* is the coverage of animals and plants. In-depth research and a thorough review have been carried out for animals and plants throughout the world and, as a result, a large number of entries have been included which have never before been included in general dictionaries. The style and presentation of these entries follow the general principles for specialist vocabulary in the *Oxford Dictionary of English*: the entries not only give the technical information, but also describe, in everyday English, the appearance and other characteristics (of behaviour, medicinal or culinary use, mythological significance, reason for the name, etc.) and the typical habitat and distribution:

> **mesosaur** ▸ **noun** an extinct small aquatic reptile of the early Permian period, with an elongated body, flattened tail, and a long, narrow snout with numerous pointed teeth. • Genus *Mesosaurus*, order Mesosauria, subclass Anapsida.

> **kowari** /kəˈwɑːri/ ▸ **noun** (pl. **kowaris**) a small carnivorous marsupial with a pointed snout, large eyes, and a black bushy tip to the tail, found in central Australia. • *Dasycercus byrnei*, family Dasyuridae.

> **hiba** /ˈhiːbə/ ▸ **noun** a Japanese conifer with evergreen scale-like leaves which form flattened sprays of foliage, widely planted as an ornamental and yielding durable timber. • *Thujopsis dolabrata*, family Cupressaceae.

Encyclopedic material

The *Oxford Dictionary of English* includes all those terms forming part of the enduring common knowledge of English speakers, regardless of whether they are classified as 'words' or 'proper names'. Names such as *Shakespeare* and *England* are as much part of the language as words such as *drama* or *language*, and belong in a large dictionary.

The proper-name entries are designed to provide not just the basic facts (such as birth and death dates, full name, and nationality), but also a brief context giving information about, for example, a person's life and why he or she is important. For a few really important encyclopedic entries—for example, countries—a fuller treatment is given and additional information is given in a separate boxed note.

Grammar

In recent years grammar has begun to enjoy greater prominence than in previous decades. It is once again being taught explicitly in state schools throughout Britain and elsewhere. In addition there is a recognition that different meanings of a word are closely associated with different lexical and syntactic patterns. The *Oxford Dictionary of English* records and exemplifies the most important of these patterns at the relevant senses of each word, thus giving guidance on language use as well as word meaning.

For example, with the word **bomb**, it is possible to distinguish the main senses of the verb simply on the basis of the grammar: whether the verb takes a direct object, no direct object, or no direct object plus an obligatory adverbial:

core sense	attack *(a place or object)* with a bomb or bombs: *they bombed *the city* at dawn.*
grammar	[with obj.]

(the asterisks match the direct object in the example with the bracketed item in the definition)

core sense	*informal* (of a film, play, or other event) fail badly: *it just became another big-budget film that bombed.*
grammar	[no obj.]

elegantly, and to give information about some of the less well-founded assertions about 'correctness' that are sometimes made.

This reappraisal has involved looking carefully at evidence of actual usage (in the Oxford English Corpus and other sources) in order to find out where mistakes are actually being made, and where confusion and ambiguity actually arise. The issues on which journalists and others tend to comment have been reassessed and a judgement made about whether their comments are justified.

Since the 15th century traditionalists have been objecting to particular senses of certain English words and phrases, for example 'aggravate', 'due to', and 'hopefully'. Certain grammatical structures, too, have been singled out for adverse comment, notably the split infinitive and the use of a preposition at the end of a clause. Some of these objections are founded on very dubious arguments, for example the notion that English grammatical structures should precisely parallel those of Latin or that meaning change of any kind is inherently suspect.

> **USAGE** There is a traditional view, first set forth by the 17th-century poet and dramatist John Dryden, that it is incorrect to put a preposition at the end of a sentence, as in *where do you come **from**?* or *she's not a writer I've ever come **across***. The rule was formulated on the basis that, since in Latin a preposition cannot come after the word it governs or is linked with, the same should be true of English. The problem is that English is not like Latin in this respect, and in many cases (particularly in questions and with phrasal verbs) the attempt to move the preposition produces awkward, unnatural-sounding results. Winston Churchill famously objected to the rule, saying, *'This is the sort of English **up with** which I will not **put**.'* In standard English the placing of a preposition at the end of a sentence is widely accepted, provided the use sounds natural and the meaning is clear.

> **USAGE** **Due to** in the sense 'because of', as in *he had to retire **due to** an injury*, has been condemned as incorrect on the grounds that **due** is an adjective and should not be used as a preposition; **owing to** is often recommended as a better alternative. However, the prepositional use, first recorded at the end of the 19th century, is now common in all types of literature and is regarded as part of standard English.

> **USAGE** **Aggravate** in the sense 'annoy or exasperate' dates back to the 17th century and has been so used by respected writers ever since. This use is still regarded as incorrect by some traditionalists on the grounds that it is too radical a departure from the etymological meaning of 'make heavy'. It is, however, comparable to meaning changes in hundreds of other words which have long been accepted without comment.

The usage notes in the *Oxford Dictionary of English* take the view that English is English, not Latin, and that English is, like all languages, subject to change. Good usage is usage that gets the writer's message across, not usage that conforms to some arbitrary rules that fly in the face of historical fact or current evidence. The prescriptions of pundits in the past have had remarkably little practical effect on the way the language is actually used. A good dictionary reports the language as it is, not as the editors (or anyone else) would wish it to be, and the usage notes must give guidance that accords with observed facts about present-day usage.

This is not to imply that the issues are straightforward or that there are simple solutions, however, and it is certainly not intended to advocate an 'anything goes' approach to writing and speaking. Much of the debate about use of language is highly political and controversy is, occasionally, inevitable. Changing social attitudes have stigmatized long-established uses such as the word 'man' to denote the human race in general, for example, and have highlighted the absence of a gender-neutral singular pronoun meaning both 'he' and 'she' (for which purpose 'they' is increasingly being used). Similarly, words such as 'race' and 'native' are now associated with particular problems of sensitivity in use, and the ways that disability is referred to have come under close examination. The usage notes in the *Oxford Dictionary of English* offer information and practical advice on such issues.

> **USAGE** Traditionally the word **man** has been used to refer not only to adult males but also to human beings in general, regardless of sex. There is a historical explanation for this: in Old English the principal sense of **man** was 'a human being', and the words **wer** and **wif** were used to refer specifically to 'a male person' and 'a female person' respectively. Subsequently, **man** replaced **wer** as the normal term for 'a male person', but at the same time the older sense 'a human being' remained in use.
> In the second half of the twentieth century the generic use of **man** to refer to 'human beings in general' (as in *reptiles were here long before man appeared on the earth*) became problematic; the use is now often regarded as sexist or at best old-fashioned. In some contexts, alternative terms such as **the human race** or **humankind** may be used. Fixed phrases and sayings such as *time and tide wait for no **man*** can be easily rephrased, e.g. *time and tide wait for **nobody***. Alternatives for terms such as **manpower** or the verb **man** exist: for example, **staff** or **employees**, and **to staff** or **to operate**.

> **USAGE** In contexts such as *a **native** of Boston* or *New York in the summer was too hot even for the **natives*** the noun **native** is quite acceptable. But when it is used to mean 'a non-white original inhabitant of a country', as in *this dance is a favourite with the **natives***, it is more problematic. This meaning has an old-fashioned feel and, because of its associations with a colonial European outlook, it may cause offence.

> **USAGE** The word **disabled** came to be used as the standard term in referring to people with physical or mental disabilities in the second half of the 20th century, and it remains the most generally accepted term in both British and US English today. It superseded outmoded, now often offensive, terms such as **crippled**, **defective**, and **handicapped** and has not been overtaken itself by newer coinages such as **differently abled** or **physically challenged**.
> Although the usage is very widespread, some people regard the use of the adjective as a plural noun (as in *the needs of the disabled*) as dehumanizing because it tends to treat people with disabilities as an undifferentiated group, defined merely by their capabilities. To avoid offence, a more acceptable term would be **people with disabilities**.

Word Histories

The etymologies in standard dictionaries explain the language from which a word was brought into English, the period at which it is first recorded in English, and the development of modern word forms. While the *Oxford Dictionary of English* does this, it also goes further. It explains sense development as well as morphological (or form) development. Information is presented clearly and with a minimum of technical terminology, and the perspective taken is that of the general reader who would like to know about word origins but who is not a philological specialist. In this context, the history of how and why a particular meaning developed from an apparently quite different older meaning is likely to be at least as interesting as, for example, what the original form was in Latin or Greek.

For example, the word history for the word **oaf** shows how the present meaning developed from the meaning 'elf', while the entry for **conker** shows how the word may be related both to 'conch' and 'conquer' (explaining how the original game of conkers was played with snail shells rather than the nut of the horse chestnut):

> **oaf** ▸ **noun** a man who is rough or clumsy and unintelligent.
> – ORIGIN early 17th cent.: variant of obsolete *auf*, from Old Norse *álfr* 'elf'. The original meaning was 'elf's child, changeling', later 'idiot child' and 'half-wit', generalized in the current sense.

conker ▸ noun Brit. the hard, shiny dark brown nut of a horse chestnut tree. ■ (**conkers**) [treated as sing.] a children's game in which each has a conker on the end of a string and takes turns in trying to break another's with it.
– ORIGIN mid 19th cent. (a dialect word denoting a snail shell, with which the game, or a form of it, was originally played): perhaps from **CONCH**, but associated with (and frequently spelled) **CONQUER** in the 19th and early 20th cents: an alternative name was *conquerors*.

Additional special features of the *Oxford Dictionary of English* include 'internal etymologies' and 'folk etymologies'. Internal etymologies are given within entries to explain the origin of particular senses, phrases, or idioms. For example, how did the meaning of **red herring** come about? Why do we call something a **flash in the pan**?

red herring ▸ noun **1** a dried smoked herring, which is turned red by the smoke.
2 a clue or piece of information which is or is intended to be misleading or distracting: *the argument about women's choices is largely a red herring.* [so named from the practice of using the scent of red herring in training hounds.]

– PHRASES **flash in the pan** a thing or person whose sudden but brief success is not repeated or repeatable: *our start to the season was just a flash in the pan.* [with allusion to priming of a firearm, the flash arising from an explosion of gunpowder within the lock.]

The *Oxford Dictionary of English* presents the information in a straightforward, user-friendly fashion immediately following the relevant definition.

In a similar vein, folk etymologies—those explanations which are unfounded but nevertheless well known to many people—have traditionally just been ignored in dictionaries. The *Oxford Dictionary of English* gives an account of widely held but often erroneous folk etymologies, explaining competing theories and assessing their relative merits where applicable.

posh informal ▸ adjective elegant or stylishly luxurious: *a posh hotel | I'll have to look posh.* ■ Brit. typical of or belonging to the upper class: *she had a posh accent.*
▸ adverb Brit. in an upper-class way: *trying to talk posh.*
▸ noun [mass noun] Brit. the quality of being elegant, stylish, or upper class: *we finally bought a colour TV, which seemed the height of posh.*
▸ verb [with obj.] (**posh something up**) Brit. smarten something up: *the sealing wax with which she poshed up Muriel's dancing shoes.*
– DERIVATIVES **poshly** adverb, **poshness** noun.
– ORIGIN early 20th cent.: perhaps from slang *posh*, denoting a dandy. There is no evidence to support the folk etymology that *posh* is formed from the initials of *port out starboard home* (referring to the more comfortable accommodation, out of the heat of the sun, on ships between England and India).

snob ▸ noun a person with an exaggerated respect for high social position or wealth who seeks to associate with social superiors and looks down on those regarded as socially inferior. ■ [with adj. or noun modifier] a person who believes that their tastes in a particular area are superior to those of other people: *a musical snob.*
– DERIVATIVES **snobbism** noun, **snobby** adjective (**snobbier**, **snobbiest**).
– ORIGIN late 18th cent. (originally dialect in the sense 'cobbler'): of unknown origin; early senses conveyed a notion of 'lower status or rank', later denoting a person seeking to imitate those of superior social standing or wealth. Folk etymology connects the word with Latin *sine nobilitate* 'without nobility' but the first recorded sense has no connection with this.

Researching word histories is similar in some respects to archaeology: the evidence is often partial or not there at all, and etymologists must make informed decisions using the evidence available, however inadequate it may be. From time to time new evidence becomes available, and the known history of a word may need to be reconsidered. In this, the *Oxford Dictionary of English* has been able to draw on the extensive expertise and ongoing research of the *Oxford English Dictionary*.

Pronunciations

Generally speaking, native speakers of English do not need information about the pronunciation for ordinary, everyday words such as **bake, baby, beach, bewilder, boastful,** or **budget**. For this reason, no pronunciations are given for such words (or their compounds and derivatives) in the *Oxford Dictionary of English*. Words such as **baba ganoush, baccalaureate, beatific, bijouterie, bucolic,** and **buddleia**, on the other hand, are less familiar and may give problems. Similarly, difficulties are often encountered in pronouncing names of people and places, especially foreign ones, such as **Chechnya, Kieslowski,** and **Althusser**.

In the *Oxford Dictionary of English* the principle followed is that pronunciations are given where they are likely to cause problems for the native speaker of English, in particular for foreign words, foreign names, scientific and other specialist terms, rare words, words with unusual stress patterns, and words where there are alternative pronunciations or where there is a dispute about the standard pronunciation.

The *Oxford Dictionary of English* uses the International Phonetic Alphabet (IPA) to represent the standard accent of English as spoken in the south of England (sometimes called Received Pronunciation or RP). The transcriptions reflect pronunciation as it actually is in modern English, unlike some longer-established systems, which reflect the standard pronunciation of broadcasters and public schools in the 1930s. It is recognized that, although the English of southern England is the pronunciation given, many variations are heard in standard speech in other parts of the English-speaking world.

The symbols used for English words, with their values, are given below. In multisyllable words the symbol ˈ is used to show that the following syllable is stressed (as in kəˈbal); the symbol ˌ indicates a secondary stress (as in ˌkaləˈbriːs).

Consonants: *b, d, f, h, k, l, m, n, p, r, s, t, v, w,* and *z* have their usual English values. Other symbols are used as follows:

ɡ	***g**et*	x	lo***ch***	ð	***th**is*	j	***y**es*
tʃ	***ch**ip*	ŋ	ri***ng***	ʃ	***sh**e*		
dʒ	***j**ar*	θ	***th**in*	ʒ	deci***s**ion*		

Vowels

short vowels		*long vowels (ː indicates length)*		*diphthongs*		*triphthongs*	
a	c***a**t*	ɑː	***ar**m*	ʌɪ	m***y***	ʌɪə	***fire***
ɛ	b***e**d*	ɛː	h***air***	aʊ	h***ow***	aʊə	s***our***
ə	***a**go*	əː	h***er***	eɪ	d***ay***		
ɪ	s***i**t*	iː	s***ee***	əʊ	n***o***		
i	cos***y***	ɔː	s***aw***	ɪə	n***ear***		
ɒ	h***o**t*	uː	t***oo***	ɔɪ	b***oy***		
ʌ	r***u**n*			ʊə	p***oor***		
ʊ	p***u**t*						

(ə) before /l/, /m/, or /n/ indicates that the syllable may be realized with a syllabic **l**, **m**, or **n**, rather than with a vowel and consonant, e.g. /ˈbʌt(ə)n/ rather than /ˈbʌtən/.

(r) indicates an *r* that is sometimes sounded when a vowel follows, as in drawer, cha-chaing.

Foreign pronunciations

Foreign words and phrases, whether naturalized or not, are always given an anglicized pronunciation. The anglicized pronunciation represents the normal pronunciation used by native speakers of standard English (who may not be speakers of other languages) when using the word in an English context. A foreign pronunciation is also given for words taken from other languages (principally French, Dutch, German, Italian, Russian, and Spanish) where this is appreciably different from the anglicized form and where the other language is familiar to a reasonable number of English speakers.

Where the native form of a foreign place name is given in addition to the anglicized form, only the foreign pronunciation of this form is given, e.g.

Wisła /ˈviswa/ Polish name for **Vistula**.

Foreign-language transcriptions are based on current national standards. Regional variations have not been given, except in the case of Spanish transcriptions, where both Castilian and American Spanish variants are given (if distinct). Transcriptions are broad, and many symbols, identical to those used for transcribing English, have similar values to those of RP. In a few cases, where there is no English equivalent to a foreign sound, a symbol has been added to the inventory. The additional symbols used to represent foreign pronunciations are given on the right.

Consonants

ç	(German)	Ehrli*ch*, gemütli*ch*
ɲ	(French) (Italian) (Portuguese) (Spanish)	Monsei*gn*eur, Auver*gn*e, Daubi*gn*y Emilia-Roma*gn*a Mi*nh*o Espa*ñ*a, Bu*ñ*uel
β	(Spanish)	Bil*b*ao
ɣ	(Spanish)	Bur*g*os
ʀ	French 'r'	Anve*r*s, A*r*les
r	all other values of 'r' in other featured languages	(German) B*r*aunschweig (Italian) Albe*r*ti (Russian) G*r*ozny (Spanish) Algeci*r*as, zar*z*uela

Vowels

SHORT VOWELS		LONG VOWELS (ː *indicates length*)	
ɐ	(German) Abitu*r*	aː	(Dutch) Den H*aa*g (German) *Aa*chen
ɑ	(Dutch) Nederl*a*nd	eː	(German) W*eh*rmach (Dutch) N*e*derland (Irish) G*ae*ltacht
e	(French) abb*é* (Italian) Cr*o*ce (Spanish) Albac*e*te	oː	(German) verb*o*ten (Hungarian) Brass*ó*
o	(French) *au*berge (Italian) Pali*o* (Spanish) C*o*rtes		
ɔ	(French) B*o*nnard (German) durchk*o*mponiert (Greek) Dhíl*o*s (Hungarian) Br*a*ssó (Italian) B*o*rgia		
œ	(French) Past*eu*r		
ø	(French) à d*eux*	øː	(German) Gasth*ö*fe
u	(French) Anj*ou* (Italian) D*u*ccio (Spanish) As*u*nción		
y	(French) cr*u*	yː	(German) gem*ü*tlich
ʏ	(German) M*ü*nchen		
ʲ	(Irish) Dái*l* (Russian) Arkhan*ge*lsk		
ᵓ	(French) *H*orta		
ɥ	(French) app*u*i		

NASALIZED VOWELS (˜ *indicates nasality*)		DIPHTHONGS	
ã	p*in*cette } used for anglicized French pronunciations	aɪ	(German) Gl*ei*chschaltung
ɒ̃	cord*on* bleu		
ɑ̃	(French) D*a*nton, Lac Lem*an*		
ɛ̃	(French) Ami*en*s, Rod*in*		
œ̃	(French) Verd*un*		
ɔ̃	(French) arr*on*dissement		

How to use this dictionary

New part of speech (indicated by ▶)

Part of speech

Core sense

Subsenses (introduced by ■)

ear[1] ▶ **noun** the organ of hearing and balance in humans and other vertebrates, especially the external part of this. ■ an organ sensitive to sound in other animals. ■ [in sing.] an ability to recognize, appreciate, and reproduce sounds, especially music or language: ***an ear for rhythm and melody***. ■ used to refer to a person's willingness to listen to others: *she offers a sympathetic ear to worried pet owners*.

Encyclopedic information

> The ear of a mammal is composed of three parts. The outer or external ear consists of a fleshy external flap and a tube leading to the eardrum or tympanum. The middle ear is an air-filled cavity connected to the throat, containing three small linked bones that transmit vibrations from the eardrum to the inner ear. The inner ear is a complex fluid-filled labyrinth including the spiral cochlea (where vibrations are converted to nerve impulses) and the three semicircular canals (forming the organ of balance).

Label (showing level of formality)

Phrase

Example (showing typical use)

– PHRASES **be all ears** informal be listening eagerly. **bring something (down) about one's ears** bring misfortune on oneself: *she brought her world crashing about her ears*. **one's ears are burning** one is subconsciously aware of being talked about or criticized. **grin** (or **smile**) **from ear to ear** smile broadly. **have something coming out of one's ears** informal have a substantial amount of something: *that man's got money coming out of his ears*. **have someone's ear** have access to and influence with someone: *he claimed to have the prime minister's ear*. **have** (or **keep**) **an ear to the ground** be well informed about events and trends. **in one ear and out the other** heard but quickly forgotten: *whatever he tells me seems to go in one ear and out the other*. **listen with half an ear** not give one's full attention. **be out on one's ear** informal be dismissed ignominiously. **reach someone's ears** be heard or heard about by someone: *the sound of running feet reached my ears | one of those stories reached our ears*. **up to one's ears in** informal very busy with: *I'm up to my ears in work here*.

– DERIVATIVES **eared adjective** [in combination] *long-eared*, **earless adjective**.

– ORIGIN Old English *ēare*, of Germanic origin; related to Dutch *oor* and German *Ohr*, from an Indo-European root shared by Latin *auris* and Greek *ous*.

Homonym number (indicates different word with the same spelling)

ear[2] ▶ **noun** the seed-bearing head or spike of a cereal plant. ■ N. Amer. a head of maize.

– ORIGIN Old English *ēar*, of Germanic origin; related to Dutch *aar* and German *Ähre*.

Common pattern (indicated within the example)

Label (showing regional distribution)

Phrasal verb

earn ▶ **verb** [with obj.] **1** obtain (money) in return for labour or services: *he earns his living as a lorry driver* | [with two objs] *earn yourself a few pounds*. ■ [with two objs] (of an activity) cause (someone) to obtain (money): *this latest win earned them $50,000 in prize money*. ■ (of capital invested) gain (money) as interest or profit.
2 gain deservedly in return for one's behaviour or achievements: *through the years she has earned affection and esteem*.
– PHRASES **earn one's corn** Brit. informal put in a lot of effort to show that one deserves one's wages. **earn one's keep** work in return for food and accommodation. ■ be worth the time or money spent on one.
– PHRASAL VERBS **earn something out** (of an author, book, recording artist, etc.) generate sufficient income through sales to equal the amount paid in an advance or royalty.
– ORIGIN Old English *earnian*, of West Germanic origin, from a base shared by Old English *esne* 'labourer'.

Pronunciation (for selected words)

Encyclopedic entry (biography)

Earp /əːp/, Wyatt (Berry Stapp) (1848–1929), American gambler and marshal. He is famous for the gunfight at the OK Corral (1881), in which Wyatt with his brothers and his friend Doc Holliday fought the Clanton brothers at Tombstone, Arizona.

Label (showing currency)

Word history

ebullient /ɪˈbʌljənt, -ˈbʊl-/ ▶ **adjective** **1** cheerful and full of energy: *she sounded ebullient and happy*.
2 archaic (of liquid or matter) boiling or agitated as if boiling: *misted and ebullient seas*.
– DERIVATIVES **ebulliently** **adverb**.
– ORIGIN late 16th cent. (in the sense 'boiling'): from Latin *ebullient-* 'boiling up', from the verb *ebullire*, from *e-* (variant of *ex-*) 'out' + *bullire* 'to boil'.

Subject label

ecdysis /ˈɛkdɪsɪs, ɛkˈdʌɪsɪs/ ▶ **noun** [mass noun] Zoology the process of shedding the old skin (in reptiles) or casting off the outer cuticle (in insects and other arthropods).
– DERIVATIVES **ecdysial** /ɛkˈdɪzɪəl/ **adjective**.
– ORIGIN mid 19th cent.: from Greek *ekdusis*, from *ekduein* 'put off', from *ek-* 'out, off' + *duein* 'put'.

Technical information

Alternative name

echidna /ɪˈkɪdnə/ ▶ **noun** a spiny insectivorous egg-laying mammal with a long snout and claws, native to Australia and New Guinea. Also called SPINY ANTEATER. ● Family Tachyglossidae, order Monotremata: two genera and species.
– ORIGIN mid 19th cent.: modern Latin, from Greek *ekhidna* 'viper', also the name of a mythical creature which gave birth to the Hydra; compare with *ekhinos* 'sea urchin, hedgehog'.

Encyclopedic entry (place name)

Ecuador /ˈɛkwədɔː/, Spanish /ekwaˈðoɾ/ an equatorial republic in South America, on the Pacific coast; pop. 14,573,100 (est. 2009); languages, Spanish (official), Quechua; capital, Quito.

Additional information (in separate block)

> Ranges and plateaux of the Andes separate the coastal plain from the tropical forests of the Amazon basin. Formerly part of the Inca empire, Ecuador was conquered by the Spanish in 1534 and remained part of Spain's American empire until, after the first uprising against Spanish rule in 1809, independence was gained in 1822.

– DERIVATIVES **Ecuadorian** (also **Ecuadorean**) **adjective & noun**.

Grammatical information (in square brackets)

Verb inflections

Typical form (in bold)

Typical pattern (in bold)

edit ▸ **verb** (**edits, editing, edited**) [with obj.] **1** prepare (written material) for publication by correcting, condensing, or otherwise modifying it: *Volume I was edited by J. Johnson.* ▪ choose material for (a film or radio or television programme) and arrange it to form a coherent whole: (as adj. **edited**) *edited highlights of the match.* ▪ change (text) on a computer. ▪ (**edit something out**) remove unnecessary or inappropriate material from a text, film, or radio or television programme.
2 be editor of (a newspaper or magazine).
▸ **noun** a change or correction made as a result of editing.
– ORIGIN late 18th cent. (as a verb): partly a back-formation from **EDITOR**, reinforced by French *éditer* 'to edit' (from *édition* 'edition').

Plural form

Derivatives (in alphabetical order)

elf ▸ **noun** (pl. **elves**) a supernatural creature of folk tales, typically represented as a small, delicate, elusive figure in human form with pointed ears, magical powers, and a capricious nature.
– DERIVATIVES **elfish** adjective, **elven** adjective (literary), **elvish** adjective.
– ORIGIN Old English, of Germanic origin; related to German *Alp* 'nightmare'.

Cross-reference entry

eon ▸ **noun** US spelling of **AEON**.

Variant spelling

epicentre (US **epicenter**) ▸ **noun** the point on the earth's surface vertically above the focus of an earthquake. ▪ the central point of something, typically a difficult or unpleasant situation: *the epicentre of labour militancy was the capital itself.*
– DERIVATIVES **epicentral** adjective.
– ORIGIN late 19th cent.: from Greek *epikentros* 'situated on a centre', from *epi* 'upon' + *kentron* 'centre'.

A[1] (also **a**) ▶ **noun** (pl. **As** or **A's**) **1** the first letter of the alphabet. ■ denoting the first in a set of items, categories, sizes, etc. ■ denoting the first of two or more hypothetical people or things: *suppose A had killed B.* ■ the highest class of academic mark. ■ (in the UK) denoting the most important category of road, other than a motorway: *the A34 | busy A-roads.* ■ denoting the highest-earning socio-economic category for marketing purposes, including top management and senior professional personnel. ■ **(a)** Chess denoting the first file from the left, as viewed from White's side of the board. ■ (usu. **a**) the first constant to appear in an algebraic expression. ■ Geology denoting the uppermost soil horizon, especially the topsoil. ■ the human blood type (in the ABO system) containing the A antigen and lacking the B. ■ (with numeral) denoting a series of international standard paper sizes each twice the area of the next, as *A0, A1, A2, A3, A4*, etc., A4 being 210 × 297 mm.
2 a shape like that of a capital A: [in combination] *an A-shape.*
3 Music the sixth note of the diatonic scale of C major. The A above middle C is usually used as the basis for tuning and in modern music has a standard frequency of 440 Hz. ■ a key based on a scale with A as its keynote.
– PHRASES **from A to B** from one's starting point to one's destination: *most road atlases will get you from A to B.* **from A to Z** over the entire range; completely.

A[2] ▶ **abbreviation** ■ (in card games) ace: *you cash ♥AK.* ■ against (heading the column in a table of sports results which shows the goals or points scored against each club). ■ informal A level. ■ ampere(s). ■ **(Å)** ångstrom(s). ■ answer: *Q: What is a hung parliament? A: One in which no single party has an overall majority.* ■ (in names of sports clubs) Athletic: *Dunfermline A.* ■ attack (in designations of US aircraft types). ■ Austria (international vehicle registration).

a[1] (**an** before a vowel sound) [called the indefinite article] ▶ **determiner 1** used when mentioning someone or something for the first time in a text or conversation: *a man came out of the room | it has been an honour to meet you.* Compare with **THE**. ■ used with units of measurement to mean one such unit: *a hundred | a quarter of an hour.* ■ [with negative] one single; any: *I simply haven't a thing to wear.* ■ used when mentioning the name of someone not known to the speaker: *a Mr Smith telephoned.* ■ someone like (the name specified): *you're no better than a Hitler.*
2 used to indicate membership of a class of people or things: *he is a lawyer | this car is a BMW.*
3 in, to, or for each; per (used when expressing rates or ratios): *typing 60 words a minute | a move to raise petrol prices by 3p a litre.*
– ORIGIN Middle English: weak form of Old English *ān* 'one'.

> **USAGE** On the question of using a or an before words beginning with h, see **USAGE** at **AN**.

a[2] ▶ **abbreviation** ■ (in travel timetables) arrives: *Penzance a 0915.* ■ [in combination] (in units of measurement) atto- (10^{-18}). ■ Brit. (with reference to sporting fixtures) away: *March 15 Sheffield United (a).* ■ (used before a date) before: *a1200.* [from Latin *ante.*]
▶ **symbol** *(a)* Physics acceleration.

a-[1] (often **an-** before a vowel) ▶ **prefix** not; without: *atheistic | acephalous.*
– ORIGIN from Greek.

a-[2] ▶ **prefix** to; towards: *aside | ashore.* ■ in the process of (an activity): *a-hunting.* ■ in a specified state: *aflutter.* ■ on: *afoot.* ■ in: *nowadays.*
– ORIGIN Old English, unstressed form of **ON**.

a-[3] ▶ **prefix** variant spelling of **AD-** assimilated before *sc, sp*, and *st* (as in *ascend, aspire*, and *astringent*).

a-[4] ▶ **prefix 1** of: *anew.*
2 utterly: *abash.*
– ORIGIN sense 1 is an unstressed form of **OF**; sense 2 is from Anglo-Norman French *a-* (Old French *e-, es-*), from Latin *ex.*

-a[1] ▶ **suffix** forming: **1** ancient or Latinized modern names of animals and plants: *primula.*
2 names of oxides: *baryta.*
3 geographical names: *Africa.*
4 ancient or Latinized modern feminine forenames: *Lydia.*
5 nouns from Italian, Portuguese, and Spanish: *duenna | stanza.*
– ORIGIN representing a Greek, Latin, or Romance feminine singular.

-a[2] ▶ **suffix** forming plural nouns: **1** from Greek or Latin neuter plurals corresponding to a singular in *-um* or *-on* (such as *addenda, phenomena*).
2 in names (often from modern Latin) of zoological groups: *Insectivora.*

-a[3] ▶ **suffix** informal **1** of: *coupla.*
2 have: *mighta.*
3 to: *oughta.*
– ORIGIN representing a casual pronunciation.

A1 ▶ **adjective** informal very good or well; excellent: *guitar, A1 condition.*

A2 level ▶ **noun** (in the UK except Scotland) an examination or pass at A2 level, representing the second component of an A-level qualification.

A3 ▶ **noun** [mass noun] a standard European size of paper, 420 × 297 mm: [as modifier] *A3 posters.*

A4 ▶ **noun** [mass noun] a standard European size of paper, 297 × 210 mm: [as modifier] *an A4 page.*

A5 ▶ **noun** [mass noun] a standard European size of paper, 210 × 148 mm: [as modifier] *a little A5 booklet.*

AA ▶ **abbreviation** ■ Alcoholics Anonymous. ■ anti-aircraft. ■ (in the UK and South Africa) Automobile Association.

aa /ˈɑːɑː/ ▶ **noun** [mass noun] Geology basaltic lava forming very rough, jagged masses with a light frothy texture. Often contrasted with **PAHOEHOE**.
– ORIGIN mid 19th cent.: from Hawaiian *'a-'a.*

AAA ▶ **abbreviation** ■ (in the UK) Amateur Athletic Association. ■ American Automobile Association. ■ Australian Automobile Association.

AAAS ▶ **abbreviation** American Association for the Advancement of Science.

Aachen /ˈɑːx(ə)n, ˈɑːk(ə)n/, German /ˈaːxn/ an industrial city and spa in western Germany, in North Rhine-Westphalia; pop. 258,800 (est. 2006). French name **AIX-LA-CHAPELLE**.

AAD ▶ **abbreviation** analogue analogue digital, indicating that a musical recording was made and mastered in analogue form before being stored digitally.

Aalborg /ˈɔːlbɔːg/ (also **Ålborg**) an industrial city and port in north Jutland, Denmark; pop. 101,497 (2009).

AAM ▶ **abbreviation** air-to-air missile.

A & E ▶ **abbreviation** accident and emergency.

A & M ▶ **abbreviation** Hymns Ancient and Modern.

A & R ▶ **abbreviation** artist(s) and repertoire (or recording), used to denote employees of a record company who select and sign new artists.

aapa /ˈɑːpə/ ▶ **noun** Indian an elder sister.
– ORIGIN from Urdu *āpa.*

aardvark /ˈɑːdvɑːk/ ▶ **noun** a nocturnal badger-sized burrowing mammal of Africa, with long ears, a tubular snout, and a long extensible tongue, feeding on ants and termites. Also called **ANTBEAR**. ● *Orycteropus afer*, the only member of the family Orycteropidae and order Tubulidentata.
– ORIGIN late 18th cent.: from South African Dutch, from *aarde* 'earth' + *vark* 'pig'.

aardwolf /ˈɑːdwʊlf/ ▶ **noun** (pl. **aardwolves**) a black-striped nocturnal African mammal that feeds mainly on termites. ● *Proteles cristatus*, family Hyaenidae.
– ORIGIN mid 19th cent.: from South African Dutch, from *aarde* 'earth' + *wolf* 'wolf'.

aargh /ɑː/ ▶ **exclamation** used as an expression of anguish, horror, rage, or other strong emotion, often with humorous intent.
– ORIGIN late 18th cent.: lengthened form of **AH**, expressing a prolonged cry.

Aarhus /ˈɔːhuːs/ (also **Århus**) a city on the coast of east Jutland, Denmark; pop. 239,865 (2009).

Aaron /ˈɛːrən/ (in the Bible) brother of Moses and traditional founder of the Jewish priesthood (see Exod. 28:1).

Aaron's beard ▶ **noun** a name given to the rose of Sharon and some other plants.
– ORIGIN early 19th cent.: alluding to **AARON**, whose beard 'went down to the skirts of his garments' (Ps. 133:2), because of the prominent hairy stamens or the long runners which some of these plants put out.

Aaron's rod ▶ **noun** the common or great mullein.
– ORIGIN mid 18th cent.: alluding to **AARON**, whose staff was said to have flowered (Num. 17:8).

AARP ▶ **abbreviation** American Association of Retired Persons.

A'asia ▶ **abbreviation** Australasia.

AB[1] ▶ **noun** a human blood type (in the ABO system) containing both the A and B antigens. In blood transfusion, a person with blood of this group is a potential universal recipient.

AB[2] ▶ **abbreviation** ■ able seaman. ■ Alberta (in official postal use). ■ US Bachelor of Arts. [from Latin *Artium Baccalaureus.*]

Ab[1] (also **Av**) ▶ **noun** (in the Jewish calendar) the eleventh month of the civil and fifth of the religious year, usually coinciding with parts of July and August.
– ORIGIN from Hebrew *'āḇ.*

Ab[2] ▶ **abbreviation** Biology antibody.

ab ▶ **noun** (usu. **abs**) informal an abdominal muscle.

ab- (also **abs-**) ▶ **prefix** away; from: *abaxial | abdicate.*
– ORIGIN from Latin.

ABA ▸ **abbreviation** ■ (in the UK) Amateur Boxing Association. ■ (in the US) American Bar Association. ■ (in the US) American Booksellers' Association.

abaca /ˈabəkə/ ▸ **noun** a large herbaceous Asian plant of the banana family, yielding Manila hemp. ● *Musa textilis*, family Musaceae.
■ [mass noun] Manila hemp.
– ORIGIN mid 18th cent.: via Spanish from Tagalog *abaká*.

aback ▸ **adverb 1** archaic towards or situated to the rear; back.
2 Sailing with the sail pressed backwards against the mast by a headwind.
– PHRASES **take someone aback** shock or surprise someone: *he was taken aback by her directness.*
– ORIGIN Old English *on bæc* (see A-², BACK). The term came to be treated as a single word in nautical use.

abacus /ˈabəkəs/ ▸ **noun** (pl. **abacuses**) **1** a simple device for calculating, consisting of a frame with rows of wires or grooves along which beads are slid.
2 Architecture the flat slab on top of a capital, supporting the architrave.
– ORIGIN late Middle English (denoting a board strewn with sand on which to draw figures): from Latin, from Greek *abax, abak-* 'slab, drawing board', of Semitic origin; probably related to Hebrew *'ābāq* 'dust'.

Abadan /ˌabəˈdɑːn/ a major port and oil-refining centre on an island of the same name on the Shatt al-Arab waterway in western Iran; pop. 219,772 (2006).

Abaddon /əˈbad(ə)n/ a name for the Devil (Rev. 9:11) or for hell.
– ORIGIN late Middle English: via Greek from Hebrew *'ăbaddōn* 'destruction'. Its use for 'hell' arose in the late 17th cent.

abaft /əˈbɑːft/ Nautical ▸ **adverb** in or behind the stern of a ship.
▸ **preposition** nearer the stern than; behind.
– ORIGIN Middle English (in the sense 'backwards'): from A-² (expressing motion) + archaic *baft* 'in the rear'.

Abakan /ˌabəˈkɑːn/ an industrial city in south central Russia, capital of the republic of Khakassia; pop. 163,200 (est. 2008). Former name (until 1931) UST-ABAKANSKOE.

abalone /ˌabəˈləʊni/ ▸ **noun** an edible mollusc of warm seas, with a shallow ear-shaped shell lined with mother-of-pearl and pierced with a line of respiratory holes. Also called ORMER, EAR SHELL. ● Genus *Haliotis*, family Haliotidae, class Gastropoda.
– ORIGIN mid 19th cent. (originally North American): from American Spanish *abulones*, plural of *abulón*, from *aulón*, the name in an American Indian language of Monterey Bay, California.

abandon ▸ **verb** [with obj.] **1** cease to support or look after (someone); desert: *her natural mother had abandoned her at an early age.* ■ leave (a place or vehicle) empty or uninhabited, without intending to return: *derelict houses were abandoned.* ■ (**abandon someone/thing to**) condemn someone or something to (a specified fate) by ceasing to take an interest in them: *an attempt to persuade businesses not to abandon the area to inner-city deprivation.*
2 give up completely (a practice or a course of action): *he had clearly abandoned all pretence of trying to succeed.* ■ discontinue (a scheduled event) before completion: *fans invaded the pitch and the match was abandoned.*
3 (**abandon oneself to**) allow oneself to indulge in (a desire or impulse): *she abandoned herself to his kiss.*
▸ **noun** [mass noun] complete lack of inhibition or restraint: *she sings and sways with total abandon.*
– PHRASES **abandon ship** leave a ship because it is sinking. ■ hurriedly leave an organization or enterprise: *he would rather abandon ship now than resign in shame in two years.*
– ORIGIN late Middle English: from Old French *abandoner*, from *a-* (from Latin *ad* 'to, at') + *bandon* 'control' (related to BAN¹). The original sense was 'bring under control', later 'give in to the control of, surrender to' (sense 3 of the verb).

abandoned ▸ **adjective 1** having been deserted or left: *an abandoned car | abandoned pets.*
2 unrestrained; uninhibited: *a wild, abandoned dance.*

abandonment ▸ **noun** [mass noun] the action or fact of abandoning or being abandoned: *she had a feeling of utter abandonment and loneliness.*

abase /əˈbeɪs/ ▸ **verb** [with obj.] (usu. **abase oneself**) behave in a way that belittles or degrades (someone): *I watched my colleagues abasing themselves before the board of trustees.*
– ORIGIN late Middle English: from Old French *abaissier*, from *a-* (from Latin *ad* 'to, at') + *baissier* 'to lower', based on late Latin *bassus* 'short of stature'. The spelling has been influenced by BASE².

abasement /əˈbeɪsm(ə)nt/ ▸ **noun** [mass noun] the action or fact of abasing or being abased; humiliation or degradation.

abash ▸ **verb** [with obj.] (usu. as adj. **abashed**) make (someone) feel embarrassed, disconcerted, or ashamed: *Harriet looked slightly abashed.*
– DERIVATIVES **abashment** noun.
– ORIGIN Middle English: from Anglo-Norman French *abaiss-*; compare with Old French *esbaiss-*, lengthened stem of *esbair*, from *es-* 'utterly' + *bair* 'astound'.

abate /əˈbeɪt/ ▸ **verb** [no obj.] (of something unpleasant or severe) become less intense or widespread: *the storm suddenly abated.* ■ [with obj.] make (something) less intense: *nothing abated his crusading zeal.* ■ [with obj.] Law reduce or remove (a nuisance).
– ORIGIN Middle English (in the legal sense): from Old French *abatre* 'to fell', from *a-* (from Latin *ad* 'to, at') + *batre* 'to beat' (from Latin *battere, battuere* 'to beat').

abatement /əˈbeɪtm(ə)nt/ ▸ **noun** [mass noun] **1** the action of abating or being abated; ending or subsiding: *this trend shows no sign of abatement.*
2 Law the reduction or removal of a nuisance: [as modifier] *it was resolved to serve an abatement notice.*

abatis /ˈabətɪs/ ▸ **noun** (pl. **abatises**) historical a defence made of felled trees placed lengthwise over each other with the boughs pointing outwards.
– ORIGIN mid 18th cent.: from French, literally 'felled (trees)', from Old French *abatre* 'to fell' (see ABATE).

abattoir /ˈabətwɑː/ ▸ **noun** Brit. a slaughterhouse.
– ORIGIN early 19th cent.: from French, from *abattre* 'to fell'.

abaxial /abˈaksɪəl/ ▸ **adjective** Botany facing away from the stem of a plant (in particular denoting the lower surface of a leaf). The opposite of ADAXIAL.

abaya /əˈbeɪjə/ ▸ **noun** a full-length, sleeveless outer garment worn by some Arab women.
– ORIGIN mid 19th cent.: from Arabic *'abāya*.

Abba /ˈabə/ ▸ **noun 1** (in the New Testament) God as father. ■ (in the Syrian Orthodox and Coptic Churches) a title given to bishops and patriarchs.
2 (**abba**) Indian father (often as a familiar form of address in Muslim families).
– ORIGIN via Greek from Aramaic *'abbā* 'father'; sense 2 is from Hindi *abbā*, from Arabic *ab*.

abbacy /ˈabəsi/ ▸ **noun** (pl. **abbacies**) the office or period of office of an abbot or abbess.
– ORIGIN late Middle English: from ecclesiastical Latin *abbacia*, from *abbas, abbat-* (see ABBOT).

Abbas¹ /əˈbas/, Ferhat (1899–1989), Algerian nationalist leader. President of the provisional government of the Algerian republic from 1958, he was appointed first President of independent Algeria in 1962 but fell from favour the following year.

Abbas² /əˈbɑːs/, Mahmoud (b.1935), Palestinian statesman; also known as **Abu Mazen**. He was appointed first Prime Minister of the Palestinian Authority in 2003 and in 2005 was elected President, following the death of Yasser Arafat.

Abbasid /əˈbasɪd, ˈabəsɪd/ ▸ **adjective** relating to a dynasty of caliphs who ruled in Baghdad from 750 to 1258.
▸ **noun** a member of the Abbasid dynasty.
– ORIGIN named after *Abbas* (566–652), the prophet Muhammad's uncle and founder of the dynasty.

abbatial /əˈbeɪʃ(ə)l/ ▸ **adjective** relating to an abbey, abbot, or abbess.
– ORIGIN late 17th cent.: from medieval Latin *abbatialis*, from *abbas, abbat-* (see ABBOT).

abbé /ˈabeɪ/, French /abe/ ▸ **noun** (in France) an abbot or other cleric.
– ORIGIN mid 16th cent.: French, from ecclesiastical Latin *abbas, abbat-* (see ABBOT).

abbess /ˈabɛs/ ▸ **noun** a woman who is the head of an abbey of nuns.
– ORIGIN Middle English: from Old French *abbesse* 'female abbot', from ecclesiastical Latin *abbatissa*, from *abbas, abbat-* (see ABBOT).

Abbevillian /abˈvɪlɪən/ ▸ **adjective** Archaeology, dated relating to or denoting the first Palaeolithic culture in Europe, now usually referred to as the Lower Acheulian. ■ (as noun **the Abbevillian**) the Abbevillian culture or period.
– ORIGIN 1930s: from French *Abbevillien* 'from *Abbeville*', a town in northern France where tools from this culture were discovered.

abbey ▸ **noun** (pl. **abbeys**) the building or buildings occupied by a community of monks or nuns. ■ a church that was formerly an abbey.
– ORIGIN Middle English: from Old French *abbeie*, from medieval Latin *abbatia* 'abbacy', from *abbas, abbat-* (see ABBOT).

abbot ▸ **noun** a man who is the head of an abbey of monks.
– ORIGIN Old English *abbod*, from ecclesiastical Latin *abbas, abbat-*, from Greek *abbas* 'father', from Aramaic *'abbā* (see ABBA).

abbreviate /əˈbriːvɪeɪt/ ▸ **verb** [with obj.] shorten (a word, phrase, or text): *'network' is often* ***abbreviated to*** *'net'.*
– ORIGIN late Middle English: from late Latin *abbreviat-* 'shortened', from the verb *abbreviare*, from Latin *brevis* 'short'.

abbreviated /əˈbriːvɪeɪtɪd/ ▸ **adjective** shortened; cut short: *an abbreviated version of the earlier work | we intended to run an abbreviated event.*

abbreviation ▸ **noun** a shortened form of a word or phrase. ■ [mass noun] the process of abbreviating something.

ABC¹ ▸ **noun 1** the alphabet.
2 an alphabetical guide: *an ABC of British locomotives.* ■ the rudiments of a subject: *the business had been learning the ABC of its trade.*
– PHRASES **(as) easy** (or **simple**) **as ABC** extremely easy.

ABC² ▸ **abbreviation** ■ American Broadcasting Company. ■ Australian Broadcasting Corporation.

ABC Islands an acronym for the islands of Aruba, Bonaire, and Curaçao.

ABD ▸ **abbreviation** N. Amer. all but dissertation, used to denote a student who has completed all other parts of a doctorate.

abdabs (also **habdabs**) ▸ **plural noun** Brit. informal nervous anxiety or irritation: *that idea gives most lawyers* ***the screaming abdabs.***
– ORIGIN 1940s: of unknown origin.

abdicate /ˈabdɪkeɪt/ ▸ **verb 1** [no obj.] (of a monarch) renounce one's throne: *in 1918 Kaiser Wilhelm abdicated as German emperor* | [with obj.] *Ferdinand abdicated the throne in favour of the emperor's brother.*
2 [with obj.] fail to fulfil or undertake (a responsibility or duty): *the government was accused of abdicating its responsibility.*
– ORIGIN mid 16th cent.: from Latin *abdicat-* 'renounced', from the verb *abdicare*, from *ab-* 'away, from' + *dicare* 'declare'.

abdication /ˌabdɪˈkeɪʃ(ə)n/ ▸ **noun 1** an act of abdicating or renouncing the throne: *Edward VIII did not marry until after his abdication.*
2 failure to fulfil a responsibility or duty: *we are witnessing an* ***abdication of responsibility*** *on the part of European governments.*

abdomen /ˈabdəmən, abˈdəʊmən/ ▸ **noun** the part of the body of a vertebrate containing the digestive and reproductive organs; the belly. ■ Zoology the hinder part of the body of an arthropod, especially the segments of an insect's body behind the thorax.
– ORIGIN mid 16th cent.: from Latin.

abdominal /abˈdɒmɪn(ə)l/ ▸ **adjective** relating to the abdomen: *abdominal pain.*
▸ **noun** (usu. **abdominals**) an abdominal muscle.
– DERIVATIVES **abdominally** adverb.

abdominoplasty /abˈdɒmɪnə(ʊ)ˌplasti/ ▸ **noun** (pl. **abdominoplasties**) Medicine a surgical operation involving the removal of excess flesh from the abdomen.

abducens nerve /abˈdjuːs(ə)nz/ ▸ **noun** Anatomy each of the sixth pair of cranial nerves, supplying the muscles concerned with the lateral movement of the eyeballs.
– ORIGIN early 19th cent.: *abducens* (modern Latin, 'leading away'), from the Latin verb *abducere*.

abduct ▸ **verb** [with obj.] **1** take (someone) away illegally by force or deception; kidnap: *the millionaire who disappeared may have been abducted.*
2 Physiology (of a muscle) move (a limb or part) away from the midline of the body or from another part. The opposite of ADDUCT¹.
– ORIGIN early 17th cent.: from Latin *abduct-* 'led away', from the verb *abducere*, from *ab-* 'away, from' + *ducere* 'to lead'.

abductee ▸ **noun** a person who has been abducted.

abduction ▸ **noun** [mass noun] **1** the action of forcibly taking someone away against their will: *they organized the abduction of Mr Cordes on his way to the airport* | [count noun] *abductions by armed men in plain clothes.* ■ (in legal use) the illegal removal of a child from its parents or guardians.
2 Physiology the movement of a limb or other part away from the midline of the body, or from another part. The opposite of **ADDUCTION** (see **ADDUCT**[1]).

abductor ▸ **noun 1** a person who abducts another person.
2 (also **abductor muscle**) Anatomy a muscle whose contraction moves a limb or part away from the midline of the body, or from another part. Compare with **ADDUCTOR**.
– ORIGIN early 17th cent. (as a term in anatomy): modern Latin (see **ABDUCT**).

Abdul Hamid II /ˌabdʊl ˈhamɪd/ (1842–1918), Ottoman sultan 1876–1909. An autocratic ruler, he was deposed after the revolt of the Young Turks.

Abdullah ibn Hussein /abˌdʊlə ˌɪb(ə)n hʊˈseɪn/ (1882–1951), king of Jordan 1946–51. He served as emir of Transjordan from 1921, becoming king of Jordan on its independence.

Abdul Rahman /ˌabdʊl ˈrɑːmən/, Tunku (1903–90), Malayan statesman, first Prime Minister of independent Malaya 1957–63 and of Malaysia 1963–70.

abeam ▸ **adverb** on a line at right angles to a ship's or an aircraft's length. ■ (**abeam of**) opposite the middle of (a ship or aircraft): *she was lying almost abeam of us* | [as prep.] *before I knew it, I was abeam the ship.*
– ORIGIN mid 19th cent.: from **A-**[2] (expressing general direction) + **BEAM**.

abecedarian /ˌeɪbiːsiːˈdɛːrɪən/ ▸ **adjective** arranged alphabetically: *in abecedarian sequence.*
– ORIGIN mid 17th cent.: from late Latin *abecedarius* 'alphabetical' (from the names of the letters *a, b, c, d*) + **-AN**.

abed ▸ **adverb** archaic in bed.

Abel[1] /ˈeɪb(ə)l/ (in the Bible) the second son of Adam and Eve, murdered by his brother Cain.

Abel[2] /ˈɑːb(ə)l/, Niels Henrik (1802–29), Norwegian mathematician. He proved that equations of the fifth degree cannot be solved by conventional algebraic methods, and made advances in the fields of power series and elliptic functions.

Abelard /ˈabəlɑː(d)/, Peter (1079–1142), French scholar, theologian, and philosopher. He is famous for his tragic love affair with his pupil Héloïse (see **HÉLOÏSE**).

abelia /əˈbiːlɪə/ ▸ **noun** an East Asian shrub of the honeysuckle family, typically having small tubular pink or white flowers. ● Genus *Abelia*, family Caprifoliaceae.
– ORIGIN modern Latin; named after Clarke Abel (1780–1826), English botanist.

abelian /əˈbiːlɪən/ ▸ **adjective** Mathematics (of a group) having members related by a commutative operation (i.e. $a*b = b*a$).
– ORIGIN mid 19th cent.: from N. H. *Abel* (see **ABEL**[2]) + **-IAN**.

Abenaki /ˌabəˈnaki/ ▸ **noun & adjective** variant spelling of **ABNAKI**.

Abeokuta /ˌabɪəʊˈkuːtə/ a city in SW Nigeria, capital of the state of Ogun; pop. 487,600 (est. 2005).

Aberdeen[1] a city and seaport in NE Scotland; pop. 166,900 (est. 2009). It is a centre of the offshore North Sea oil industry.

Aberdeen[2], George Hamilton Gordon, 4th Earl of (1784–1860), British Conservative statesman, Prime Minister 1852–5.

Aberdeen Angus ▸ **noun** an animal of a Scottish breed of hornless black beef cattle.
– ORIGIN mid 19th cent.: from **ABERDEENSHIRE** and **ANGUS**[1], where the breed originated.

Aberdeenshire a council area and former county of NE Scotland. Between 1975 and 1996 it was part of Grampian region.

Aberdonian /ˌabəˈdəʊnɪən/ ▸ **adjective** of Aberdeen.
▸ **noun** a person from Aberdeen.
– ORIGIN mid 17th cent.: from medieval Latin *Aberdonia* 'Aberdeen' + **-AN**.

Aberfan /ˌabəˈvan/ a village in South Wales where, in 1966, a slag heap collapsed, overwhelming houses and a school and killing 28 adults and 116 children.

aberrant /əˈbɛr(ə)nt/ ▸ **adjective** departing from an accepted standard. ■ chiefly Biology diverging from the normal type: *aberrant chromosomes.*
– DERIVATIVES **aberrance** noun, **aberrancy** noun, **aberrantly** adverb.
– ORIGIN mid 16th cent.: from Latin *aberrant-* 'wandering away', from the verb *aberrare*, from *ab-* 'away, from' + *errare* 'to stray'.

aberration /ˌabəˈreɪʃ(ə)n/ ▸ **noun** a departure from what is normal, usual, or expected, typically an unwelcome one: *they described the outbreak of violence in the area as an aberration.* ■ Biology a characteristic that deviates from the normal type: *colour aberrations.* ■ Optics the failure of rays to converge at one focus because of a defect in a lens or mirror. ■ Astronomy the apparent displacement of a celestial object from its true position, caused by the relative motion of the observer and the object.
– DERIVATIVES **aberrational** adjective.
– ORIGIN late 16th cent.: from Latin *aberratio(n-)*, from *aberrare* 'to stray' (see **ABERRANT**).

Abertawe /ˌaberˈtawe/ Welsh name for **SWANSEA**.

abet /əˈbɛt/ ▸ **verb** (**abets, abetting, abetted**) [with obj.] encourage or assist (someone) to do something wrong, in particular to commit a crime: *he was not guilty of murder, but guilty of* ***aiding and abetting*** *others.* ■ encourage or assist someone to commit (a crime): *we are* ***aiding and abetting*** *this illegal traffic.*
– DERIVATIVES **abetment** noun, **abettor** (also **abetter**) noun.
– ORIGIN late Middle English (in the sense 'urge to do something good or bad'): from Old French *abeter*, from *a-* (from Latin *ad* 'to, at') + *beter* 'hound, urge on'.

abeyance /əˈbeɪəns/ ▸ **noun** [mass noun] a state of temporary disuse or suspension: *matters were* ***held in abeyance*** *pending further enquiries.* ■ Law the position of being without, or of waiting for, an owner or claimant.
– DERIVATIVES **abeyant** adjective.
– ORIGIN late 16th cent. (in the legal sense): from Old French *abeance* 'aspiration to a title', from *abeer* 'aspire after', from *a-* 'towards' + *beer* 'to gape'.

ABH ▸ **abbreviation** actual bodily harm.

abhinaya /əb(h)ɪˈnɑːjə/ ▸ **noun** [mass noun] (in Indian dance) expressive techniques used to convey a theme, mood, or idea.
– ORIGIN Sanskrit, from *abhi* 'towards' + *ni* 'carry', literally 'carry towards (an audience)'.

abhor /əbˈhɔː/ ▸ **verb** (**abhors, abhorring, abhorred**) [with obj.] regard with disgust and hatred: *he abhorred sexism in every form.*
– DERIVATIVES **abhorrer** noun.
– ORIGIN late Middle English: from Latin *abhorrere*, from *ab-* 'away from' + *horrere* 'to shudder'.

abhorrence /əbˈhɒr(ə)ns/ ▸ **noun** [mass noun] a feeling of revulsion; disgusted loathing: *the thought of marrying him filled her with abhorrence.*

abhorrent ▸ **adjective** inspiring disgust and loathing; repugnant: *racism was* ***abhorrent to*** *us all.*
– ORIGIN late 16th cent.: from Latin *abhorrent-* 'shuddering away from in horror', from the verb *abhorrere* (see **ABHOR**).

abide ▸ **verb 1** [no obj.] (**abide by**) accept or act in accordance with (a rule, decision, or recommendation).
2 [with obj.] (**can/could not abide**) informal be unable to tolerate: *if there is one thing I cannot abide it is a lack of discipline.*
3 [no obj.] (of a feeling or memory) continue without fading or being lost. ■ archaic live; dwell.
– DERIVATIVES **abidance** noun.
– ORIGIN Old English *ābīdan* 'wait', from *ā-* 'onwards' + *bīdan* (see **BIDE**).

abiding ▸ **adjective** (of a feeling or memory) lasting a long time; enduring: *he had an abiding respect for her.*
– DERIVATIVES **abidingly** adverb [as submodifier] *an abidingly mysterious quality.*

Abidjan /ˌabɪˈdʒɑːn/ the chief port of Côte d'Ivoire (Ivory Coast), the capital 1935–83; pop. 4,000,000 (est. 2009).

abigail ▸ **noun** archaic a lady's maid.
– ORIGIN mid 17th cent.: from the name of a character in *The Scornful Lady* by Beaumont and Fletcher, possibly in allusion to 1 Sam. 25: 23–24: 'And when Abigail saw David, she ... fell at his feet, and said, "... hear the words of thine handmaid".'

ability ▸ **noun** (pl. **abilities**) **1** [in sing., with infinitive] possession of the means or skill to do something: *the manager had lost his ability to motivate the players.*
2 [mass noun] talent, skill, or proficiency in a particular area: *a man of exceptional ability* | [count noun] *pupils of all abilities.*
– ORIGIN late Middle English: from Old French *ablete*, from Latin *habilitas*, from *habilis* 'able'.

-ability ▸ **suffix** forming nouns of quality corresponding to adjectives ending in *-able* (such as *suitability* corresponding to *suitable*).
– ORIGIN from French *-abilité* or Latin *-abilitas*.

ab initio /ˌab ɪˈnɪʃɪəʊ/ ▸ **adverb & adjective** formal or Law from the beginning: [as adv.] *the agreement should be declared void ab initio.*
– ORIGIN Latin.

abiogenesis /ˌeɪbʌɪə(ʊ)ˈdʒɛnɪsɪs/ ▸ **noun** technical term for **SPONTANEOUS GENERATION**.
– DERIVATIVES **abiogenic** adjective.
– ORIGIN late 19th cent.: from **A-**[1] 'not' + Greek *bios* 'life' + **GENESIS**.

abiotic /ˌeɪbʌɪˈɒtɪk/ ▸ **adjective** physical rather than biological; not derived from living organisms. ■ devoid of life; sterile.

Abitur /ˌabɪˈtʊə/, German /ˌabiˈtuːɐ/ ▸ **noun** (in Germany) a set of examinations taken in the final year of secondary school.
– ORIGIN from German, abbreviation of *Abiturientenexamen* 'leavers' examination'.

abject /ˈabdʒɛkt/ ▸ **adjective 1** (of something bad) experienced or present to the maximum degree: *his letter plunged her into abject misery* | *abject poverty.* ■ (of a situation or condition) extremely unpleasant and degrading: *the abject condition of the peasants.*
2 (of a person or their behaviour) completely without pride or dignity; self-abasing: *an abject apology.*
– DERIVATIVES **abjection** noun, **abjectly** adverb, **abjectness** noun.
– ORIGIN late Middle English (in the sense 'rejected'): from Latin *abjectus*, past participle of *abicere* 'reject', from *ab-* 'away' + *jacere* 'to throw'.

abjure /əbˈdʒʊə, əbˈdʒɔː/ ▸ **verb** [with obj.] formal solemnly renounce (a belief, cause, or claim): *MPs were urged to abjure their Jacobite allegiance.*
– PHRASES **abjure the realm** historical swear an oath to leave a country forever.
– DERIVATIVES **abjuration** noun.
– ORIGIN late Middle English: from Latin *abjurare*, from *ab-* 'away' + *jurare* 'swear'.

Abkhaz /abˈkɑːz/ ▸ **noun** (pl. **same**) **1** a member of a people living mainly in Abkhazia.
2 [mass noun] the North Caucasian language of the Abkhaz.
▸ **adjective** relating to Abkhazia, its people, or their language.

Abkhazia /abˈkɑːzɪə/ an autonomous territory in NW Georgia, west of the Caucasus mountains on the Black Sea; pop. 215,972 (2003); capital, Sokhumi. In 1992 Abkhazia unilaterally declared itself independent, sparking armed conflict with Georgia, and the following year drove Georgian forces from its territory.
– DERIVATIVES **Abkhazian** /abˈkɑːzɪən, abˈkeɪzjən/ adjective & noun.

ablation /əˈbleɪʃ(ə)n/ ▸ **noun** [mass noun] **1** the surgical removal of body tissue.
2 the removal of snow and ice from a glacier or iceberg by melting or evaporation. ■ the erosion of rock, typically by wind action. ■ the loss of surface material from a spacecraft or meteorite through evaporation or melting caused by friction with the atmosphere.
– DERIVATIVES **ablate** verb.
– ORIGIN late Middle English (in the general sense 'taking away, removal'): from late Latin *ablatio(n-)*, from Latin *ablat-* 'taken away', from *ab-* 'away' + *lat-* 'carried' (from the verb *ferre*).

ablative /ˈablətɪv/ ▸ **adjective 1** Grammar denoting a case (especially in Latin) of nouns and pronouns and words in grammatical agreement with them indicating an agent, instrument, or source, expressed by 'by', 'with', or 'from' in English.
2 (of surgical treatment) involving ablation.
3 relating to or subject to ablation through melting or evaporation: *the spacecraft's ablative heat shield.*
▸ **noun** Grammar a word in the ablative case. ■ (**the ablative**) the ablative case.
– ORIGIN late Middle English: from Old French *ablative* (feminine of *ablatif*), Latin *ablativus*, from *ablat-* 'taken away' (see **ABLATION**).

ablative absolute ▸ **noun** a construction in Latin which consists of a noun and participle or adjective in the ablative case and functions as a sentence adverb, for example *Deo volente* 'God willing'.

A

ablaut /ˈablaʊt/ ▸ **noun** [mass noun] alternation in the vowels of related word forms, especially in Germanic strong verbs (e.g. in *sing, sang, sung*).
– ORIGIN mid 19th cent.: from German, from *ab* 'off' + *Laut* 'sound'.

ablaze ▸ **adjective** [predic.] burning fiercely: *his clothes were ablaze* | [as complement] *farm buildings were set ablaze.* ■ very brightly coloured or lighted: *New England is* **ablaze with** *colour in autumn.* ■ filled with anger or another strong emotion: *his eyes were* **ablaze with** *excitement.*

able ▸ **adjective** (**abler, ablest**) **1** [with infinitive] having the power, skill, means, or opportunity to do something: *he was able to read Greek at the age of eight* | *they would never be able to afford such a big house.* **2** having considerable skill, proficiency, or intelligence: *the dancers were technically very able.*
– ORIGIN late Middle English (also in the sense 'easy to use, suitable'): from Old French *hable*, from Latin *habilis* 'handy', from *habere* 'to hold'.

-able ▸ **suffix** forming adjectives meaning: **1** able to be: *calculable.* **2** due to be: *payable.* **3** subject to: *taxable.* **4** relevant to or in accordance with: *fashionable.* **5** having the quality to: *suitable* | *comfortable.*
– ORIGIN from French *-able* or Latin *-abilis*; originally found in words only from these forms but later used to form adjectives directly from English verbs ending in *-ate*, e.g. *educable* from *educate*; subsequently used to form adjectives from verbs of all types (influenced by the unrelated word **ABLE**), e.g. *bearable, saleable.*

able-bodied ▸ **adjective** fit and healthy; not physically disabled.

abled ▸ **adjective** having a full range of physical or mental abilities; not disabled. See also **DIFFERENTLY ABLED.**
– ORIGIN 1980s: back-formation from **DISABLED.**

ableism /ˈeɪblɪz(ə)m/ (also **ablism**) ▸ **noun** [mass noun] discrimination in favour of able-bodied people.
– DERIVATIVES **ableist adjective.**

able seaman ▸ **noun** a rank of sailor in the Royal Navy above ordinary seaman and below leading seaman.

abloom ▸ **adjective** [predic.] covered in flowers.

ablush ▸ **adjective** [predic.] literary blushing.

ablution /əˈbluːʃ(ə)n/ ▸ **noun** (usu. **ablutions**) formal or humorous an act of washing oneself: *the women performed their ablutions.* ■ a ceremonial act of washing parts of the body or sacred containers. ■ (**the ablutions**) Brit. (in army slang) a building or room containing washing facilities and toilets.
– DERIVATIVES **ablutionary adjective.**
– ORIGIN late Middle English: from Latin *ablutio(n-)*, from *abluere*, from *ab-* 'away' + *luere* 'wash'. The original use was as a term in chemistry and alchemy meaning 'purification by using liquids', hence 'purification of the body by washing' (mid 16th cent.).

ably ▸ **adverb** skilfully; competently: *Steven has summed up our concerns very ably.*

-ably ▸ **suffix** forming adverbs corresponding to adjectives ending in *-able* (such as *suitably* corresponding to *suitable*).

ABM ▸ **abbreviation** anti-ballistic missile.

Abnaki /abˈnaki/ (also **Abenaki** /abəˈnaki/) ▸ **noun** (pl. **same** or **Abnakis**) **1** a member of an American Indian people of Maine and southern Quebec. **2** [mass noun] either or both of the two extinct Algonquian languages (**Eastern Abnaki** and **Western Abnaki**) of the Abnaki.
▸ **adjective** relating to the Abnaki or their language.
– ORIGIN from French *Abénaqui*, from Montagnais *ouabanăkionek* 'people of the eastern land'.

abnegate /ˈabnɪgeɪt/ ▸ **verb** [with obj.] formal renounce or reject (something desired or valuable): *he attempts to abnegate personal responsibility.*
– ORIGIN early 17th cent.: from Latin *abnegat-* 'renounced', from the verb *abnegare*, from *ab-* 'away, off' + *negare* 'deny'.

abnegation ▸ **noun** [mass noun] the action of renouncing or rejecting something: *abnegation of political power.* ■ self-denial.
– ORIGIN Middle English: from Latin *abnegatio(n-)*, from the verb *abnegare* (see **ABNEGATE**).

Abney level /ˈabni/ ▸ **noun** Surveying a kind of clinometer consisting of a sighting tube, spirit level, and graduated scale.
– ORIGIN late 19th cent.: named after Sir William *Abney* (1844–1920), English scientist.

abnormal ▸ **adjective** deviating from what is normal or usual, typically in a way that is undesirable or worrying: *the illness is recognizable from the patient's abnormal behaviour.*
– DERIVATIVES **abnormally adverb.**
– ORIGIN mid 19th cent.: alteration (by association with Latin *abnormis* 'monstrous') of 16th-cent. *anormal*, from French, variant of *anomal*, via Latin from Greek *anōmalos* (see **ANOMALOUS**).

abnormality ▸ **noun** (pl. **abnormalities**) an abnormal feature, characteristic, or occurrence: *babies with congenital abnormalities.* ■ [mass noun] the quality or state of being abnormal.

Abo /ˈabəʊ/ Austral. informal, offensive ▸ **noun** (pl. **Abos**) an Aborigine.
▸ **adjective** Aboriginal.
– ORIGIN early 20th cent.: abbreviation.

Åbo /ˈɔːbuː/ Swedish name for **TURKU.**

aboard ▸ **adverb & preposition** on or into (a ship, aircraft, train, or other vehicle): [as adv.] *the plane crashed, killing all 158 people aboard* | figurative *he came aboard as IBM's new chairman* | [as prep.] *I climbed aboard the yacht.* ■ on or on to (a horse): [as adv.] *with Richard Migliore aboard, he won the cup at a gallop.* ■ Baseball on base: [as adv.] *putting their first batter aboard.*
– PHRASES **all aboard!** a call warning passengers to get on a ship, train, or bus that is about to depart.
– ORIGIN late Middle English: from **A-**[2] (expressing motion) + **BOARD**, reinforced by Old French *à bord.*

abode[1] ▸ **noun** formal or literary a place of residence; a house or home: *my humble abode.* ■ [mass noun] residence: *their right of abode in Britain.* ■ archaic a stay; a sojourn.
– PHRASES **of no fixed abode** (of a person) having no permanent residence: *both defendants were said to be of no fixed abode.*
– ORIGIN Middle English (in the sense 'act of waiting'): verbal noun from **ABIDE.**

abode[2] ▸ **verb** archaic past of **ABIDE.**

abolish ▸ **verb** [with obj.] formally put an end to (a system, practice, or institution): *the tax was abolished in 1977.*
– DERIVATIVES **abolisher noun, abolishment noun.**
– ORIGIN late Middle English: from Old French *aboliss-*, lengthened stem of *abolir*, from Latin *abolere* 'destroy'.

abolition ▸ **noun** [mass noun] the action of abolishing a system, practice, or institution: *the abolition of the death penalty.*
– ORIGIN early 16th cent.: from Latin *abolitio(n-)*, from *abolere* 'destroy'.

abolitionist ▸ **noun** a person who favours the abolition of a practice or institution, especially capital punishment or (formerly) slavery.
– DERIVATIVES **abolitionism noun.**

abomasum /ˌabəʊˈmeɪsəm/ ▸ **noun** (pl. **abomasa** /-sə/) Zoology the fourth stomach of a ruminant, which receives food from the omasum and passes it to the small intestine.
– ORIGIN late 17th cent.: modern Latin, from *ab-* 'away, from' + *omasum* (see **OMASUM**).

A-bomb ▸ **noun** short for **ATOM BOMB.**

Abomey /əˈbəʊmeɪ, ˌabə(ʊ)ˈmeɪ/ a town in southern Benin, capital of the former kingdom of Dahomey; pop. 87,941 (2006).

abominable ▸ **adjective** causing moral revulsion: *the uprising was suppressed with abominable cruelty.* ■ very bad; terrible: *what an abominable mess!*
– ORIGIN Middle English: via Old French from Latin *abominabilis*, from *abominari* (see **ABOMINATE**). The term was once widely believed to be from **AB-** 'away from' + Latin *homine* (from *homo* 'human being'), thus 'inhuman, beastly', and frequently spelled *abhominable* until the 17th cent.

Abominable Snowman ▸ **noun** (pl. **Abominable Snowmen**) another term for **YETI.**

abominably ▸ **adverb** very unpleasantly or unfairly: *he had treated her abominably.* ■ very badly: *his head hurt abominably.*

abominate /əˈbɒmɪneɪt/ ▸ **verb** [with obj.] formal detest; loathe: *they abominated the very idea of monarchy.*
– DERIVATIVES **abominator noun.**
– ORIGIN mid 17th cent.: from Latin *abominat-* 'deprecated', from the verb *abominari*, from *ab-* 'away, from' + *omen, omin-* 'omen'.

abomination ▸ **noun** a thing that causes disgust or loathing: *concrete abominations masquerading as hotels.* ■ a feeling of hatred: *a Calvinist abomination of indulgence.*
– ORIGIN Middle English: from Latin *abominatio(n-)*, from the verb *abominari* (see **ABOMINATE**).

aboral /abˈɔːr(ə)l/ ▸ **adjective** Zoology relating to or denoting the side or end that is furthest from the mouth, especially in animals that lack clear upper and lower sides such as echinoderms. ■ moving or leading away from the mouth.
– DERIVATIVES **aborally adverb.**

aboriginal ▸ **adjective** inhabiting or existing in a land from the earliest times or from before the arrival of colonists; indigenous. ■ (**Aboriginal**) relating to the Australian Aborigines or their languages.
▸ **noun 1** an aboriginal inhabitant of a place. ■ (**Aboriginal**) a person belonging to one of the indigenous peoples of Australia. **2** (**Aboriginal**) [mass noun] any of the numerous Australian Aboriginal languages.
– DERIVATIVES **Aboriginality noun.**
– ORIGIN mid 17th cent.: from Latin *aborigines* 'original inhabitants' (see **ABORIGINE**) + **-AL.**

aborigine /abəˈrɪdʒɪniː/ ▸ **noun** a person, animal, or plant that has been in a country or region from earliest times. ■ (**Aborigine**) an aboriginal inhabitant of Australia.
– ORIGIN mid 19th cent.: back-formation from the 16th-cent. plural *aborigines* 'original inhabitants' (in classical times referring to those of Italy and Greece), from the Latin phrase *ab origine* 'from the beginning'.

> **USAGE** Both **Aboriginal** and **Aborigine** may be used as nouns referring to a member of an Australian Aboriginal people, but **Aborigine** is the commoner and is often preferred, especially in the plural.

aborning /əˈbɔːnɪŋ/ ▸ **adverb** chiefly N. Amer. while being born or produced: *the idea died aborning.*
– ORIGIN 1930s: from *a-* 'in the process of' + *borning*, verbal noun from *born* (North American dialect usage) 'to be born'.

abort ▸ **verb** [with obj.] **1** carry out or undergo the abortion of (a fetus). ■ [no obj.] (of a pregnant woman or female animal) have a miscarriage, with loss of the fetus. ■ [no obj.] Biology (of an embryonic organ or organism) remain undeveloped; fail to mature. **2** bring to a premature end because of a problem or fault: *the flight crew aborted the take-off.*
▸ **noun** informal or technical an act of aborting a flight, space mission, or other enterprise: *an abort because of bad weather.* ■ an aborted enterprise.
– ORIGIN mid 16th cent.: from Latin *aboriri* 'miscarry', from *ab-* 'away, from' + *oriri* 'be born'.

abortifacient /əˌbɔːtɪˈfeɪʃ(ə)nt/ Medicine ▸ **adjective** (chiefly of a drug) causing abortion.
▸ **noun** an abortifacient drug.

abortion ▸ **noun 1** [mass noun] the deliberate termination of a human pregnancy, most often performed during the first 28 weeks: *concerns such as abortion and euthanasia* | [count noun] *illegal abortions.* ■ the expulsion of a fetus from the womb by natural causes before it is able to survive independently. ■ Biology the arrest of the development of a seed, fruit, or other organ. **2** an object or undertaking that is unpleasant or badly made or carried out.
– ORIGIN mid 16th cent.: from Latin *abortio(n-)*, from *aboriri* 'miscarry' (see **ABORT**).

abortionist ▸ **noun** derogatory a person who carries out abortions.

abortion mill ▸ **noun** N. Amer. informal used pejoratively by opponents of abortion to refer to an abortion clinic.

abortive ▸ **adjective 1** failing to produce the intended result: *the rebel officers who led the abortive coup were shot.* **2** Biology, dated (of an organ or organism) rudimentary; arrested in development: *abortive medusae.* **3** rare causing or resulting in abortion.
– DERIVATIVES **abortively adverb.**
– ORIGIN Middle English (as a noun denoting a stillborn child or animal): via Old French from Latin *abortivus*, from *aboriri* 'miscarry' (see **ABORT**).

abortus fever /əˈbɔːtəs/ ▸ **noun** [mass noun] the commonest form of undulant fever in humans. ● This disease is caused by the bacterium *Brucella abortus*, which is also the chief cause of brucellosis in cattle.
– ORIGIN 1920s: from Latin *abortus* 'miscarriage'.

ABO system ▶ noun a system of four basic types (A, AB, B, and O) into which human blood may be classified, based on the presence or absence of certain inherited antigens.

Aboukir Bay, Battle of /ˌabuːˈkɪə/ (also **Abukir Bay**) a naval battle in 1798 off Aboukir Bay at the mouth of the Nile, in which the British under Nelson defeated the French fleet. Also called **NILE, BATTLE OF THE**.

aboulia ▶ noun variant spelling of **ABULIA**.

abound ▶ verb [no obj.] exist in large numbers or amounts: *rumours of a further scandal abound.* ■ (**abound in/with**) have in large numbers or amounts: *this area abounds with caravan sites.*
– ORIGIN Middle English (in the sense 'overflow, be abundant'): from Old French *abunder*, from Latin *abundare* 'overflow', from *ab-* 'from' + *undare* 'surge' (from *unda* 'a wave').

abounding ▶ adjective very plentiful; abundant: *his abounding creative talent.*

about ▶ preposition **1** on the subject of; concerning: *I was thinking about you | a book about ancient Greece | it's **all about** having fun.* ■ so as to affect: *there's nothing we can do about it.*
2 chiefly Brit. used to indicate movement within a particular area: *she looked about the room.*
3 chiefly Brit. used to express location in a particular place: *rugs were strewn about the hall | he produced a knife from somewhere about his person.* ■ used to describe a quality apparent in a person: *there was a look about her that said everything.*
▶ adverb **1** chiefly Brit. used to indicate movement within an area: *men were floundering about | finding my way about.*
2 chiefly Brit. used to express location in a particular place: *there was a lot of flu about.*
3 (used with a number or quantity) approximately: *reduced by about 5 per cent | he's about 35.*
– PHRASES **be about to do something** intend to do something, or be close to doing something, very soon: *the ceremony was about to begin.* **be not about to do something** be unwilling to do something: *he is not about to step down after so long.* **be on about** see **ON**. **know what one is about** informal be sensible, self-possessed, and aware of how to deal with difficult situations.
– ORIGIN Old English *onbūtan*, from *on* 'in, on' + *būtan* 'outside of' (see **BUT²**).

about-turn (also chiefly N. Amer. **about-face**) Brit. ▶ noun (chiefly in military contexts) a turn made so as to face the opposite direction: *he did an about-turn and marched out of the tent.* ■ a complete change of opinion or policy: *the government made an about-turn over the bill.*
▶ verb [no obj.] turn so as to face the opposite direction.
▶ exclamation (**about turn!**) a military command to make an about-turn.
– ORIGIN late 19th cent. (originally as a military command): shortening of *right about turn*

above ▶ preposition **1** in extended space over and not touching: *a display of fireworks above the town | a cable runs above the duct.* ■ extending upwards over: *she held her arms above her head.* ■ higher than and to one side of; overlooking: *in the hills above the capital | on the wall above the altar.*
2 at a higher level or layer than: *from his flat above the corner shop | bruises above both eyes.* ■ higher in grade or rank than: *at a level above the common people.* ■ considered of higher status or worth than; too good for: *she **married above her**.* ■ in preference to: *the firm cynically chose profit above car safety.* ■ at a higher volume or pitch than: *he seldom spoke above a whisper | the doorbell went unheard above the din.*
3 higher than (a specified amount, rate, or norm): *the food was well above average | above sea level.*
▶ adverb at a higher level or layer: *place a quantity of mud in a jar with water above.* ■ higher in grade or rank: *an officer of the rank of superintendent or above.* ■ higher than a specified amount, rate, or norm: *boats of 31 ft or above.* ■ (in printed text) mentioned earlier or further up on the same page: *the two cases described above | see above left |* [as adj.] *at the above address |* [as noun] *since writing **the above**, I have reconsidered.*
– PHRASES **above all (else)** more so than anything else: *he was concerned above all to speak the truth.* **above and beyond** in excess of the expectations or demands of: *she was always there to help us out in difficult times, **above and beyond the call of duty**.* ■ in addition to: *you might consider giving employees an extra day or two off each quarter, above and beyond sick days.* **above oneself** conceited; arrogant: *he's getting a bit above himself.* **above the law** in a position where one can avoid being bound by the laws that govern ordinary people: *the army was above the law and enjoyed complete impunity.* **from above** from overhead: *branches rained from above.* ■ from a position of higher rank or authority: *mass culture is imposed from above.* **not be above** be capable of stooping to (an unworthy act): *he was not above practical jokes.* **up above** above one's head; overhead: *we heard a sudden rumbling **from up above**.*
ORIGIN Old English *abufan* (as an adverb), from *a-* 'on' + *bufan* (from *bi* 'by' + *ufan* 'above').

above board ▶ adjective & adverb legitimate, honest, and open: [as adj.] *certain transactions were not totally above board |* [as adv.] *the accountants acted completely above board.*

ab ovo /ab ˈəʊvəʊ/ ▶ adverb from the very beginning.
– ORIGIN Latin, literally 'from the egg'.

Abp ▶ abbreviation Archbishop.

abracadabra ▶ exclamation a word said by conjurors when performing a magic trick.
▶ noun [mass noun] informal language used to give the impression of arcane knowledge or power: *I get so fed up with all the mumbo jumbo and abracadabra.*
– ORIGIN late 17th cent. (as a mystical word engraved and used as a charm to ward off illness): from Latin, first recorded in a 2nd-cent. poem by Q. Serenus Sammonicus, from a Greek base.

abrade /əˈbreɪd/ ▶ verb [with obj.] scrape or wear away by friction or erosion: *it was a landscape slowly abraded by a fine, stinging dust.*
– DERIVATIVES **abrader** noun.
– ORIGIN late 17th cent.: from Latin *abradere*, from *ab-* 'away, from' + *radere* 'to scrape'.

Abraham /ˈeɪbrəham/ (in the Bible) the Hebrew patriarch from whom all Jews trace their descent (Gen. 11:27–25:10). In Gen. 22 he is ordered by God to sacrifice his son Isaac as a test of faith, a command later revoked.

Abraham, Plains of see **PLAINS OF ABRAHAM**.

Abrahams /ˈeɪbrəhamz/, Harold (Maurice) (1899–1978), English athlete. In 1924 he became the first Englishman to win the 100 metres in the Olympic Games. His story was the subject of the film *Chariots of Fire* (1981).

abrasion /əˈbreɪʒ(ə)n/ ▶ noun [mass noun] the process of scraping or wearing something away: *the metal is resistant to abrasion.* ■ [count noun] an area damaged by scraping or wearing away: *there were cuts and abrasions to the lips and jaw.*
– ORIGIN mid 17th cent.: from Latin *abrasio(n-)*, from the verb *abradere* (see **ABRADE**).

abrasive /əˈbreɪsɪv/ ▶ adjective **1** (of a substance or material) capable of polishing or cleaning a hard surface by rubbing or grinding. ■ tending to rub or graze the skin: *the trees were abrasive to the touch.*
2 showing little concern for the feelings of others; harsh: *her abrasive and arrogant personal style won her few friends.*
▶ noun a substance used for grinding, polishing, or cleaning a hard surface.
– DERIVATIVES **abrasively** adverb, **abrasiveness** noun.
– ORIGIN mid 19th cent. (as a noun): from Latin *abras-* 'abraded', from the verb *abradere* (see **ABRADE**), + **-IVE**.

abrazo /əˈbrɑːzəʊ, əˈbrasəʊ/ ▶ noun (pl. **abrazos**) US an embrace.
– ORIGIN Spanish.

abreact /ˌabrɪˈakt/ ▶ verb [with obj.] Psychoanalysis release (an emotion) by abreaction.
– ORIGIN early 20th cent.: back-formation from **ABREACTION**.

abreaction ▶ noun [mass noun] Psychoanalysis the expression and consequent release of a previously repressed emotion, achieved through reliving the experience that caused it (typically through hypnosis or suggestion).
– DERIVATIVES **abreactive** adjective.
– ORIGIN early 20th cent.: from **AB-** 'away from' + **REACTION**, translating German *Abreagierung*.

abreast ▶ adverb **1** side by side and facing the same way: *the path was wide enough for two people to walk abreast | they were riding three abreast.*
2 (usu. **abreast of**) alongside or level with something: *the cart came abreast of the Americans in their rickshaw.* ■ up to date with the latest news, ideas, or information: *keeping abreast of developments.*
– ORIGIN late Middle English: from **A-²** 'in' + **BREAST**.

abridge ▶ verb [with obj.] **1** (often as adj. **abridged**) shorten (a book, film, speech, etc.) without losing the sense: *an abridged text of his speech.*
2 Law curtail (a right or privilege).
– DERIVATIVES **abridger** noun.
– ORIGIN Middle English (in the sense 'deprive of'): from Old French *abregier*, from late Latin *abbreviare* 'cut short' (see **ABBREVIATE**).

abridgement (also chiefly US **abridgment**) ▶ noun [mass noun] **1** the action of abridging a text. ■ [count noun] a shortened version of a larger work.
2 Law curtailment of rights.
– ORIGIN late Middle English: from Old French *abregement*, from the verb *abreg(i)er* (see **ABRIDGE**).

abroad chiefly Brit. ▶ adverb **1** in or to a foreign country or countries: *we usually **go abroad** for a week in May | competition from companies at home and abroad.*
2 in different directions; over a wide area: *millions of seeds are annually scattered abroad.* ■ (of a feeling or rumour) widely current: *there is a new buccaneering spirit abroad.* ■ freely moving about: *hospital inmates abroad on the streets of the town.*
3 archaic out of doors: *few people ventured abroad from their warm houses.*
4 archaic wide of the mark; in error.
▶ noun [mass noun] foreign countries considered collectively: *servicemen returning from abroad.*
– ORIGIN Middle English: from **A-²** 'on' + **BROAD**.

abrogate /ˈabrəgeɪt/ ▶ verb [with obj.] formal repeal or do away with (a law, right, or formal agreement): *a proposal to abrogate temporarily the right to strike.*
– ORIGIN early 16th cent.: from Latin *abrogat-* 'repealed', from the verb *abrogare*, from *ab-* 'away, from' + *rogare* 'propose a law'.

abrogation /abrəˈgeɪʃ(ə)n/ ▶ noun [mass noun] formal the repeal or abolition of a law, right, or agreement.

abrupt ▶ adjective **1** sudden and unexpected: *I was surprised by the abrupt change of subject | the match came to an abrupt end.*
2 brief to the point of rudeness; curt: *you were rather abrupt with that young man.* ■ (of a style of speech or writing) not flowing smoothly; disjointed.
3 steep; precipitous: *the abrupt double peak.*
– DERIVATIVES **abruptly** adverb, **abruptness** noun.
– ORIGIN late 16th cent.: from Latin *abruptus* 'broken off, steep', past participle of *abrumpere*, from *ab-* 'away, from' + *rumpere* 'break'.

abruption ▶ noun [mass noun] technical the sudden breaking away of a portion from a mass. ■ (also **placental abruption**) Medicine separation of the placenta from the wall of the womb during pregnancy, especially when it occurs prematurely.
– ORIGIN early 17th cent.: from Latin *abruptio(n-)*, from *abrumpere* 'break off' (see **ABRUPT**).

Abruzzi /əˈbrʊtsi/ (also **Abruzzo** /-tsəʊ/) a mountainous region of east central Italy; capital, Aquila.

ABS ▶ abbreviation ■ acrylonitrile-butadiene-styrene, a hard composite plastic used to make car bodies and cases for computers and other appliances. ■ anti-lock braking system (for motor vehicles).

abs- ▶ prefix variant spelling of **AB-** before *c*, *q*, and *t* (as in *abscond*, *abstain*).

abscess ▶ noun a swollen area within body tissue, containing an accumulation of pus.
– DERIVATIVES **abscessed** adjective.
– ORIGIN mid 16th cent.: from Latin *abscessus* 'a going away', from the verb *abscedere*, from *ab-* 'away from' + *cedere* 'go', referring to the elimination of infected matter via the pus.

abscisic acid /abˈsɪsɪk/ ▶ noun [mass noun] Biochemistry a plant hormone which promotes leaf detachment, induces seed and bud dormancy, and inhibits germination.
– ORIGIN 1960s: *abscisic* from *abscisin* (the earlier name for the hormone), from **ABSCISSION**.

abscissa /abˈsɪsə/ ▶ noun (pl. **abscissae** /-siː/ or **abscissas**) Mathematics (in a system of coordinates) the distance from a point to the vertical or *y*-axis, measured parallel to the horizontal or *x*-axis; the *x*-coordinate. Compare with **ORDINATE**.
– ORIGIN early 17th cent. (denoting the part of a line between a point on it and the point of intersection with an ordinate): from modern Latin *abscissa* (*linea*) 'cut-off (line)', feminine past participle of *abscindere* (see **ABSCISSION**).

abscission /abˈsɪʃ(ə)n/ ▶ noun [mass noun] Botany the natural detachment of parts of a plant, typically dead leaves and ripe fruit.
– DERIVATIVES **abscise** /əbˈsʌɪz/ verb.
– ORIGIN early 17th cent.: from Latin *abscissio(n-)*, from *abscindere*, from *ab-* 'off' + *scindere* 'to cut'.

abscond /əbˈskɒnd, ab-/ ▶ verb [no obj.] leave hurriedly and secretly, typically to escape from custody or

avoid arrest: *the barman absconded with a week's takings | 176 detainees absconded.* ■ (of a person on bail) fail to surrender oneself for custody at the appointed time.
– DERIVATIVES **absconder** noun.
– ORIGIN mid 16th cent. (in the sense 'hide, conceal oneself'): from Latin *abscondere* 'hide', from *ab-* 'away, from' + *condere* 'stow'.

abseil /ˈabseɪl, -zʌɪl/ Brit. ▸ **verb** [no obj., with adverbial of direction] descend a rock face or other near-vertical surface by using a doubled rope coiled round the body and fixed at a higher point: (as noun **abseiling**) *facilities for abseiling and rock climbing.*
▸ **noun** a descent made by abseiling.
– DERIVATIVES **abseiler** noun.
– ORIGIN 1930s: from German *abseilen*, from *ab* 'down' + *Seil* 'rope'.

absence ▸ **noun** [mass noun] the state of being away from a place or person: *the letter had arrived during his absence | I supervised the rehearsal* ***in the absence of*** *the director.* ■ [count noun] an occasion or period of being away from a place or person: *repeated absences from school.* ■ (**absence of**) the non-existence or lack of: *she found his total absence of facial expression disconcerting.*
– PHRASES **absence makes the heart grow fonder** proverb you feel more affection for those you love when parted from them. **absence of mind** failure to concentrate on or remember what one is doing.
– ORIGIN late Middle English: from Old French, from Latin *absentia*, from *absens, absent-* (see **ABSENT**).

absent ▸ **adjective** /ˈabs(ə)nt/ **1** not present in a place, at an occasion, or as part of something: *most pupils were* ***absent from*** *school at least once | absent colleagues | wings are absent in several species of crane flies.*
2 (of an expression or manner) showing that someone is not paying attention to what is being said or done: *she looked up with an absent smile.*
▸ **verb** /abˈsɛnt/ [with obj.] (**absent oneself**) stay or go away: *halfway through the meal, he* ***absented himself from*** *the table.*
▸ **preposition** formal, N. Amer. without: *absent a willingness to negotiate, you can't have collective bargaining.*
– ORIGIN Middle English: via Old French from Latin *absens, absent-* 'being absent', present participle of *abesse*, from *ab-* 'from, away' + *esse* 'to be'.

absentee ▸ **noun** a person who is expected or required to be present at a place or event but is not.

absentee ballot ▸ **noun** North American term for **POSTAL VOTE.**

absenteeism ▸ **noun** [mass noun] the practice of regularly staying away from work or school without good reason.

absentee landlord ▸ **noun** a landlord who does not live at and rarely visits the property they let.

absently /ˈabs(ə)ntli/ ▸ **adverb** in an absent-minded way; vaguely: *Keira toyed absently with her fork.*

absent-minded ▸ **adjective** having or showing a forgetful or inattentive disposition: *an absent-minded smile.*
– DERIVATIVES **absent-mindedly** adverb, **absent-mindedness** noun.

absinth /ˈabsɪnθ/ ▸ **noun 1** the shrub wormwood. ■ [mass noun] an essence made from wormwood.
2 (usu. **absinthe**) [mass noun] a potent green aniseed-flavoured liqueur, originally made with wormwood (which is now banned because of its toxicity).
– ORIGIN late Middle English: from French *absinthe*, via Latin from Greek *apsinthion* 'wormwood'.

absit omen /ˌabsɪt ˈəʊmən/ ▸ **exclamation** used when referring to something undesirable, in the hope that the thing mentioned will not occur.
– ORIGIN Latin, literally 'may this (evil) omen be absent'.

absolute /ˈabsəluːt/ ▸ **adjective 1** not qualified or diminished in any way; total: *absolute secrecy | absolute silence.* ■ used for emphasis when expressing an opinion: *the policy is absolute folly.* ■ (of powers or rights) not subject to any limitation; unconditional: *no one dare challenge her absolute authority | the right to life is absolute.* ■ (of a ruler) having unrestricted power: *Dom Miguel proclaimed himself absolute monarch.* ■ Law (of a decree) final: *the decree of nullity was made absolute.* See also **DECREE ABSOLUTE.**
2 viewed or existing independently and not in relation to other things; not relative or comparative: *absolute moral standards.*
3 Grammar (of a construction) syntactically independent of the rest of the sentence, as in *dinner being over, we left the table.* ■ (of a transitive verb) used without an expressed object (e.g. *guns kill*). ■ (of an adjective) used without an expressed noun (e.g. *the brave*).
▸ **noun** Philosophy a value or principle which is regarded as universally valid or which may be viewed without relation to other things: *good and evil are presented as absolutes.* ■ (**the absolute**) that which exists without being dependent on anything else. ■ (**the Absolute**) ultimate reality; God.
– DERIVATIVES **absoluteness** noun.
– ORIGIN late Middle English: from Latin *absolutus* 'freed, unrestricted', past participle of *absolvere* (see **ABSOLVE**).

absolute alcohol ▸ **noun** [mass noun] ethanol containing less than one per cent of water by weight.

absolutely ▸ **adverb 1** with no qualification, restriction, or limitation; totally: *she trusted him absolutely |* [as submodifier] *you're absolutely right.* ■ used to emphasize a strong or exaggerated statement: *he absolutely adores that car |* [as submodifier] *Dad was absolutely furious.* ■ [with negative] none whatsoever: *she had absolutely no idea what he was talking about.* ■ [as exclamation] informal used to express and emphasize one's assent or agreement: *'Did they give you a free hand when you joined the band?' 'Absolutely!'*
2 not viewed in relation to other things: *white-collar crime increased both absolutely and in comparison with other categories.*
3 Grammar (of a verb) without a stated object.

absolute magnitude ▸ **noun** Astronomy the magnitude (brightness) of a celestial object as it would be seen at a standard distance of 10 parsecs. Compare with **APPARENT MAGNITUDE.**

absolute majority ▸ **noun** a majority over all rivals combined; more than half.

absolute music ▸ **noun** [mass noun] instrumental music not intended to represent or illustrate something else. Compare with **PROGRAMME MUSIC.**

absolute pitch ▸ **noun** [mass noun] Music another term for **PERFECT PITCH.** ■ pitch according to a fixed standard defined by the frequency of the sound vibration.

absolute privilege ▸ **noun** see **PRIVILEGE.**

absolute temperature ▸ **noun** a temperature measured from absolute zero in kelvins. (Symbol: **T**)

absolute title ▸ **noun** [mass noun] Law the guarantee of title to the ownership of a property or lease.

absolute unit ▸ **noun** a unit of measurement which is defined in terms of the fundamental units of a system (mass, length, and time), and is not based on arbitrary definitions.

absolute value ▸ **noun 1** Mathematics the magnitude of a real number without regard to its sign. Also called **MODULUS.** • The absolute value of a complex number $a + ib$ is the positive square root of $a^2 + b^2$.
2 technical the actual magnitude of a numerical value or measurement, irrespective of its relation to other values.

absolute zero ▸ **noun** the lowest temperature that is theoretically possible, at which the motion of particles which constitutes heat would be minimal. It is zero on the Kelvin scale, equivalent to −273.15°C.

absolution ▸ **noun** [mass noun] formal release from guilt, obligation, or punishment. ■ ecclesiastical declaration that a person's sins have been forgiven: *she had been granted* ***absolution for*** *her sins.*
– ORIGIN Middle English: via Old French from Latin *absolutio(n-)*, from the verb *absolvere* (see **ABSOLVE**).

absolutism ▸ **noun** [mass noun] the holding of absolute principles in political, philosophical, or theological matters.
– DERIVATIVES **absolutist** noun & adjective.

absolutize (also **absolutise**) ▸ **verb** [with obj.] chiefly Philosophy & Theology make or treat (something) as absolute.
– DERIVATIVES **absolutization** noun.

absolve /əbˈzɒlv/ ▸ **verb** [with obj.] declare (someone) free from guilt, obligation, or punishment: *the pardon* ***absolved*** *them* ***of*** *any crimes.* ■ (in church use) give absolution for (a sin).
– ORIGIN late Middle English: from Latin *absolvere* 'set free, acquit', from *ab-* 'from' + *solvere* 'loosen'.

absonant /ˈabs(ə)nənt/ ▸ **adjective** archaic discordant or unreasonable.
– ORIGIN mid 16th cent.: from Latin *ab-* 'away, from' + *sonant-* 'sounding' (from the verb *sonare*), on the pattern of words such as *dissonant*.

absorb /əbˈzɔːb, -ˈsɔːb/ ▸ **verb** [with obj.] **1** take in or soak up (energy or a liquid or other substance) by chemical or physical action: *buildings can be designed to absorb and retain heat | steroids are* ***absorbed into*** *the bloodstream.* ■ take in and understand fully (information, ideas, or experience): *she absorbed the information in silence.* ■ take control of (a smaller or less powerful entity) and make it a part of a larger one: *the family firm was* ***absorbed into*** *a larger group.* ■ use or take up (time or resources): *arms spending absorbs roughly two per cent of the national income.* ■ take up and reduce the effect or intensity of (sound or an impact): *deep-pile carpets absorbed all sound of the outside world.*
2 (often **be absorbed in**) take up the attention of (someone); interest greatly: *she sat in an armchair, absorbed in a book | the work absorbed him and continued to make him happy.*
– DERIVATIVES **absorbability** noun, **absorbable** adjective, **absorbedly** adverb, **absorber** noun.
– ORIGIN late Middle English: from Latin *absorbere*, from *ab-* 'from' + *sorbere* 'suck in'.

absorbance ▸ **noun** Physics a measure of the capacity of a substance to absorb light of a specified wavelength. It is equal to the logarithm of the reciprocal of the transmittance.

absorbed dose ▸ **noun** Physics the quantity of ionizing radiation absorbed by a body, measured (usually in grays) as the energy absorbed per unit mass.

absorbent ▸ **adjective** (of a material) able to soak up liquid easily: *absorbent kitchen paper.*
▸ **noun** a substance that soaks up liquid easily.
– DERIVATIVES **absorbency** noun.

absorbent cotton ▸ **noun** North American term for **COTTON WOOL.**

absorbing ▸ **adjective** intensely interesting; engrossing: *an absorbing account of their marriage.*
– DERIVATIVES **absorbingly** adverb.

absorptiometer /əbˌzɔːpʃɪˈɒmɪtə, -ˌsɔːp-/ ▸ **noun** Physics an instrument for measuring the absorption of light or other radiation.
– DERIVATIVES **absorptiometric** adjective, **absorptiometry** noun.

absorption /əbˈzɔːpʃ(ə)n, -ˈsɔːp-/ ▸ **noun** [mass noun] **1** the process by which one thing absorbs or is absorbed by another: *the country's* ***absorption into*** *the Ottoman Empire | shock absorption.*
2 the state of being engrossed in something: *her* ***absorption in*** *the problems of the Third World.*
– DERIVATIVES **absorptive** adjective, **absorptivity** noun.
– ORIGIN late 16th cent. (in the sense 'the swallowing up of something'): from Latin *absorptio(n-)*, from *absorbere* 'swallow up' (see **ABSORB**).

absorption costing ▸ **noun** [mass noun] a method of calculating the cost of a product or enterprise by taking into account indirect expenses (overheads) as well as direct costs.

absorption nebula ▸ **noun** Astronomy another term for **DARK NEBULA.**

absorption spectrum ▸ **noun** Physics a spectrum of electromagnetic radiation transmitted through a substance, showing dark lines or bands due to absorption at specific wavelengths. Compare with **EMISSION SPECTRUM.**

absquatulate /əbˈskwɒtjʊleɪt/ ▸ **verb** [no obj., with adverbial] humorous, chiefly N. Amer. leave abruptly: *some overthrown dictator who had absquatulated to the USA.*
– DERIVATIVES **absquatulation** noun.
– ORIGIN mid 19th cent.: blend (simulating a Latin form) of **ABSCOND**, *squattle* 'squat down', and **PERAMBULATE.**

abstain ▸ **verb** [no obj.] **1** restrain oneself from doing or enjoying something: *she intends to* ***abstain from*** *sex before marriage.* ■ refrain from drinking alcohol: *most pregnant women abstain or drink very little.*
2 formally decline to vote either for or against a proposal or motion: *forty-one voted with the Opposition, and some sixty more abstained.*
– DERIVATIVES **abstainer** noun.
– ORIGIN late Middle English: from Old French *abstenir*, from Latin *abstinere*, from *ab-* 'from' + *tenere* 'hold'.

abstemious /əbˈstiːmɪəs/ ▸ **adjective** indulging only very moderately in something, especially food and drink: *'We only had a bottle.' 'Very abstemious of you.'*
– DERIVATIVES **abstemiously** adverb, **abstemiousness** noun.
– ORIGIN early 17th cent.: from Latin *abstemius*, (from *ab-* 'from' + a word related to *temetum* 'alcoholic drink') + **-OUS.**

A

abstention /əbˈstɛnʃ(ə)n/ ▶ **noun 1** an instance of declining to vote for or against a proposal or motion: *a resolution passed by 126 votes to none, with six abstentions.*
2 [mass noun] restraint in one's consumption; abstinence.
– DERIVATIVES **abstentionism noun.**
– ORIGIN early 16th cent. (denoting the action of keeping back or restraining): from late Latin *abstentio(n-)*, from the verb *abstinere* (see **ABSTAIN**).

abstinence /ˈabstɪnəns/ ▶ **noun** [mass noun] the practice of restraining oneself from indulging in something, typically alcohol or sex: *I started drinking again after six years of abstinence* | ***abstinence from*** *premarital intercourse.*
– ORIGIN Middle English: from Old French, from Latin *abstinentia*, from the verb *abstinere* (see **ABSTAIN**).

abstinent ▶ **adjective** refraining from an activity or from the consumption of something, especially alcohol: *the patients are best advised to be totally* ***abstinent from*** *alcohol.*
– DERIVATIVES **abstinently adverb.**
– ORIGIN late Middle English: via Old French from Latin *abstinent-* 'abstaining', from the verb *abstinere* (see **ABSTAIN**).

abstract ▶ **adjective** /ˈabstrakt/ **1** existing in thought or as an idea but not having a physical or concrete existence: *abstract concepts such as love or beauty.* ■ dealing with ideas rather than events: *the novel was too abstract and esoteric to sustain much attention.* ■ not based on a particular instance; theoretical: *we have been discussing the problem in a very abstract manner.* ■ (of a noun) denoting an idea, quality, or state rather than a concrete object.
2 relating to or denoting art that does not attempt to represent external reality, but rather seeks to achieve its effect using shapes, colours, and textures.
▶ **verb** /əbˈstrakt/ [with obj.] **1** (**abstract something from**) consider something theoretically or separately from (something else): *to abstract science and religion from their historical context can lead to anachronism.*
2 (usu. **abstract something from**) extract or remove (something): *applications to abstract more water from streams.* ■ (**abstract oneself**) withdraw: *as our relationship deepened you seemed to abstract yourself.*
3 make a written summary of (an article or book): *staff who abstract material for an online database.*
▶ **noun** /ˈabstrakt/ **1** a summary of the contents of a book, article, or speech: *an abstract of her speech.*
2 an abstract work of art: *a big unframed abstract.*
– PHRASES **in the abstract** in a general way; without reference to specific instances.
– DERIVATIVES **abstractly adverb, abstractor noun.**
– ORIGIN Middle English: from Latin *abstractus*, literally 'drawn away', past participle of *abstrahere*, from *ab-* 'from' + *trahere* 'draw off'.

abstracted ▶ **adjective** lacking concentration on what is happening around one: *she seemed abstracted and unaware of her surroundings* | *an abstracted smile.*
– DERIVATIVES **abstractedly adverb.**

abstract expressionism ▶ **noun** [mass noun] a development of abstract art which originated in New York in the 1940s and 1950s and aimed at subjective emotional expression with particular emphasis on the spontaneous creative act (e.g. action painting). Leading figures were Jackson Pollock and Willem de Kooning.
– DERIVATIVES **abstract expressionist noun & adjective.**

abstraction ▶ **noun** [mass noun] **1** the quality of dealing with ideas rather than events: *topics will vary in degrees of abstraction.* ■ [count noun] something which exists only as an idea: *the question can no longer be treated as an academic abstraction.*
2 freedom from representational qualities in art: *geometric abstraction has been a mainstay in her work.* ■ [count noun] an abstract work of art.
3 a state of preoccupation: *she sensed his momentary abstraction.*
4 the process of considering something independently of its associations or attributes: *the question cannot be considered* ***in abstraction from*** *the historical context in which it was raised.*
5 the process of removing something, especially water from a river or other source.
– ORIGIN late Middle English: from Latin *abstractio(n-)*, from the verb *abstrahere* 'draw away' (see **ABSTRACT**).

abstractionism ▶ **noun** [mass noun] the principles and practice of abstract art. ■ the presentation of ideas in abstract terms.
– DERIVATIVES **abstractionist noun & adjective.**

abstract of title ▶ **noun** Law a summary giving details of the title deeds and documents that prove an owner's right to dispose of land, together with any encumbrances that relate to the property.

abstruse /əbˈstruːs/ ▶ **adjective** difficult to understand; obscure: *an abstruse philosophical inquiry.*
– DERIVATIVES **abstrusely adverb, abstruseness noun.**
– ORIGIN late 16th cent.: from Latin *abstrusus* 'put away, hidden', from *abstrudere* 'conceal', from *ab-* 'from' + *trudere* 'to push'.

absurd ▶ **adjective** wildly unreasonable, illogical, or inappropriate: *the allegations are patently absurd.* ■ arousing amusement or derision; ridiculous: *short skirts and knee socks looked absurd on such a tall girl.*
▶ **noun** (**the absurd**) an absurd state of affairs: *the incidents that followed bordered on the absurd.*
– ORIGIN mid 16th cent.: from Latin *absurdus* 'out of tune', hence 'irrational'; related to *surdus* 'deaf, dull'.

absurdism ▶ **noun** [mass noun] the belief that human beings exist in a purposeless, chaotic universe.
– DERIVATIVES **absurdist adjective & noun.**

absurdity ▶ **noun** (pl. **absurdities**) [mass noun] the quality or state of being ridiculous or wildly unreasonable: *Duncan laughed at the absurdity of the situation* | [count noun] *the absurdities of haute cuisine.*
– ORIGIN late Middle English (in the sense 'dissonance'): from Latin *absurditas*, from *absurdus* (see **ABSURD**).

absurdly ▶ **adverb** in an absurd way; ridiculously: *he brags absurdly about his horse.* ■ [as submodifier] to a very surprising extent: *the share price is absurdly low.*

ABTA ▶ **abbreviation** (in the UK) Association of British Travel Agents.

abubble ▶ **adjective** [predic.] full of excitement and enthusiasm: *he was* ***abubble with*** *the news.*

Abu Dhabi /ˌabuː ˈdɑːbi/ the largest of the seven member states of the United Arab Emirates, lying between Oman and the Gulf coast; pop. 2,061,100 (est. 2009). The former sheikhdom joined the federation of the United Arab Emirates in 1971. ■ the capital of this state; pop. 896,800 (est. 2009). It is also the federal capital of the United Arab Emirates.

Abuja /əˈbuːdʒə/ a newly built city in central Nigeria, replacing Lagos as the national capital in 1991; pop. 776,300 (est. 2006).

Abukir Bay, Battle of see **ABOUKIR BAY, BATTLE OF.**

abulia /əˈbuːlɪə/ (also **aboulia**) ▶ **noun** [mass noun] Psychiatry an absence of willpower or an inability to act decisively, a symptom of schizophrenia or other mental illness.
– ORIGIN mid 19th cent.: coined from **A-**[1] 'without' + Greek *boulē* 'the will'.

Abu Musa /ˌabuː ˈmuːsə/ a small island in the Persian Gulf. Formerly held by the emirate of Sharjah, it has been occupied by Iran since 1971.

Abuna /əˈbuːnə/ ▶ **noun** a title given to the Patriarch of the Ethiopian Orthodox Church.
– ORIGIN Amharic, from Arabic *'abūnā* 'our father'.

abundance /əˈbʌnd(ə)ns/ ▶ **noun 1** a very large quantity of something: *the tropical island boasts* ***an abundance of*** *wildlife.* ■ [mass noun] the state or condition of having a copious quantity of something; plentifulness: *vines and figs grew* ***in abundance*** | *she was blessed with talent and charm* ***in abundance.*** ■ [mass noun] plentifulness of the good things of life; prosperity: *the growth of industry promised wealth and abundance.* ■ the quantity or amount of something present in a particular area, volume, or sample: *estimates of the abundance of harp seals.*
2 (in solo whist) a bid by which a player undertakes to make nine or more tricks.
– ORIGIN Middle English: from Latin *abundantia*, from *abundant-* 'overflowing', from the verb *abundare* (see **ABOUND**).

abundant ▶ **adjective** existing or available in large quantities; plentiful: *there was abundant evidence to support the theory.* ■ (**abundant in**) having plenty of: *the riverbanks were abundant in beautiful wild plants.*
– ORIGIN late Middle English: from Latin *abundant-* 'abounding', from the verb *abundare* (see **ABOUND**).

abundantly ▶ **adverb** in large quantities; plentifully: *the plant grows abundantly in the wild.* ■ [as submodifier] extremely: *my boss* ***made it abundantly clear*** *that if I didn't like it, I should look for another job.*

abura /əˈbjuːrə/ ▶ **noun** a West African tree which yields soft pale timber, and leaves that are used in herbal medicine. ● *Mitragyna stipulosa*, family Rubiaceae.
– ORIGIN early 20th cent.: from Yoruba.

abuse ▶ **verb** /əˈbjuːz/ [with obj.] **1** use (something) to bad effect or for a bad purpose; misuse: *the judge abused his power by imposing the fines.* ■ make excessive and habitual use of (alcohol or drugs, especially illegal ones).
2 treat with cruelty or violence, especially regularly or repeatedly: *riders who abuse their horses should be prosecuted.* ■ assault (someone, especially a woman or child) sexually: *he was a depraved man who had abused his two young daughters* | (as adj. **abused**) *abused children.* ■ (**abuse oneself**) euphemistic masturbate. ■ use or treat in such a way as to cause damage or harm: *he had been abusing his body for years.*
3 speak to (someone) in an insulting and offensive way: *the referee was abused by players from both teams.*
▶ **noun** /əˈbjuːs/ [mass noun] **1** the improper use of something: *alcohol abuse* | [count noun] ***an abuse of*** *public funds.* ■ unjust or corrupt practice: *protection against fraud and abuse* | [count noun] *human rights abuses.*
2 cruel and violent treatment of a person or animal: *a black eye and other signs of physical abuse.* ■ violent treatment involving sexual assault, especially on a regular basis.
3 insulting and offensive language: *waving his fists and* ***hurling abuse at*** *the driver.*
– DERIVATIVES **abuser noun** *drug abusers.*
– ORIGIN late Middle English: via Old French from Latin *abus-* 'misused', from the verb *abuti*, from *ab-* 'away' (i.e. 'wrongly') + *uti* 'to use'.

Abu Simbel /ˌabuː ˈsɪmb(ə)l/ the site of two huge rock-cut temples in southern Egypt, built during the reign of Ramses II in the 13th century BC and commemorating him and his first wife Nefertari. Following the building of the High Dam at Aswan, the monument was rebuilt higher up the hillside.

abusive ▶ **adjective 1** extremely offensive and insulting: *the goalkeeper was sent off for using abusive language* | *he became quite abusive and swore at her.*
2 engaging in or characterized by habitual violence and cruelty: *abusive parents* | *an abusive relationship.*
3 involving injustice or illegality: *the abusive and predatory practices of businesses.*
– DERIVATIVES **abusively adverb, abusiveness noun.**

abustle ▶ **adjective** [predic.] bustling; busy: *the pier was* ***abustle with*** *voyagers and well-wishers.*

abut /əˈbʌt/ ▶ **verb** (**abuts, abutting, abutted**) [with obj.] (of a building or an area of land) be next to or have a common boundary with: *gardens abutting Great Prescott Street* | [no obj.] *a park* ***abutting on*** *an area of waste land.* ■ touch or lean on: *masonry may crumble where a roof abuts it.*
– ORIGIN late Middle English: the sense 'have a common boundary' from Anglo-Latin *abuttare*, from *a-* (from Latin *ad* 'to, at') + Old French *but* 'end'; the sense 'lean upon' (late 16th cent.) from Old French *abouter*, from *a-* (from Latin *ad* 'to, at') + *bouter* 'strike, butt', of Germanic origin.

abutilon /əˈbjuːtɪlɒn/ ▶ **noun** a herbaceous plant or shrub of warm climates, typically bearing showy yellow, red, or mauve flowers and sometimes used for fibre. ● Genus *Abutilon*, family Malvaceae.
– ORIGIN modern Latin, from Arabic *ūbūtīlūn* 'Indian mallow'.

abutment ▶ **noun** a structure built to support the lateral pressure of an arch or span, e.g. at the ends of a bridge. ■ [mass noun] the process of supporting something with an abutment. ■ a point at which something abuts against something else.

abutter ▶ **noun** chiefly US the owner of an adjoining property.

abuzz ▶ **adjective** [predic.] filled with a continuous humming sound: *the room was* ***abuzz with*** *mosquitoes* | figurative *the city was* ***abuzz with*** *rumours.*

ABV ▶ **abbreviation** alcohol by volume.

abysm /əˈbɪz(ə)m/ ▶ **noun** literary an abyss: *the abysm from which nightmares crawl.*
– ORIGIN Middle English: from Old French *abisme*, medieval Latin *abysmus*, alteration of late Latin *abyssus* 'bottomless pit', the ending being assimilated to the Greek ending *-ismos*.

abysmal ▶ **adjective 1** informal extremely bad; appalling: *the quality of her work is abysmal.*
2 literary very deep.

– DERIVATIVES **abysmally** adverb [as submodifier] *a boy who is abysmally lazy.*
– ORIGIN mid 17th cent. (used literally as in sense 2): from **ABYSM**. Sense 1 dates from the early 19th cent.

abyss /əˈbɪs/ ▶ noun a deep or seemingly bottomless chasm: *a rope led down into the dark abyss.* ■ a wide or profound difference between people; a gulf: *the abyss between the two nations.* ■ the regions of hell conceived of as a bottomless pit: *Satan's dark abyss.* ■ (**the abyss**) a catastrophic situation seen as likely to occur: *teetering on the edge of the abyss of a total political wipeout.*
– ORIGIN late Middle English (in the sense 'infernal pit'): via late Latin from Greek *abussos* 'bottomless', from *a-* 'without' + *bussos* 'depth'.

abyssal ▶ adjective chiefly technical relating to or denoting the depths or bed of the ocean, especially between about 3000 and 6000 metres down. ■ Geology another term for **PLUTONIC** (sense 1).
– ORIGIN mid 17th cent.: from late Latin *abyssalis* 'belonging to an abyss' (see **ABYSS**).

Abyssinia /ˌabɪˈsɪnɪə/ former name for **ETHIOPIA**.

Abyssinian ▶ adjective historical relating to Abyssinia or its people.
▶ noun **1** historical a native of Abyssinia.
2 (also **Abyssinian cat**) a cat of a breed having long ears and short brown hair flecked with grey.

AC ▶ abbreviation ■ (also **a.c.**) alternating current. ■ (also **ac**) air conditioning: *a sedan with power steering and AC.* ■ Aircraftman. ■ appellation contrôlée: *AC Sauvignon and Chardonnay.* ■ athletic club. ■ (**ac.**) N. Amer. acre: *a 22-ac. site.* ■ before Christ. [from Latin *ante Christum.*] ■ Companion of the Order of Australia.

Ac ▶ symbol the chemical element actinium.

a/c ▶ abbreviation ■ account. [from the obsolete phrase *account current*, denoting a continuous account detailing sums paid and received.] ■ (also **A/C**) air conditioning.

ac- ▶ prefix variant spelling of **AD-** assimilated before *c*, *k*, and *q* (as in *accept, acquit*, and *acquiesce*).

-ac ▶ suffix forming adjectives which are often also (or only) used as nouns, such as *maniac*. Compare with **-ACAL**.
– ORIGIN via Latin *-acus* or French *-aque* from Greek *-akos*.

acacia /əˈkeɪʃə, -sɪə/ (also **acacia tree**) ▶ noun a tree or shrub of warm climates which bears spikes or clusters of yellow or white flowers and is typically thorny. Also called **WATTLE**[1], especially in Australia.
● Genus *Acacia*, family Leguminosae: numerous species.
– ORIGIN late Middle English: via Latin from Greek *akakia*.

academe /ˈakədiːm/ ▶ noun [mass noun] the academic environment or community; academia: *bridging the gap between industry and academe* | *a lifetime in the groves of academe.*
– ORIGIN late 16th cent. (in the sense 'academy'): from Latin *academia*, reinforced by Greek *Akadēmos* (see **ACADEMY**).

academia /ˌakəˈdiːmɪə/ ▶ noun [mass noun] the environment or community concerned with the pursuit of research, education, and scholarship: *he spent his working life in academia.*
– ORIGIN 1950s: from Latin (see **ACADEMY**).

academic ▶ adjective **1** relating to education and scholarship: *academic achievement* | *he had no academic qualifications.* ■ relating to an educational or scholarly institution or environment: *students resplendent in academic dress.* ■ (of an institution or a course of study) placing a greater emphasis on reading and study than on technical or practical work: *a very academic school aiming to get pupils into Oxford or Cambridge.* ■ (of a person) interested in or excelling at scholarly pursuits and activities: *Ben is not an academic child but he tries hard.* ■ (of an art form) conventional, especially in an idealized or excessively formal way: *academic painting.*
2 not of practical relevance; of only theoretical interest: *the debate has been largely academic.*
▶ noun a teacher or scholar in a university or other institute of higher education.
– DERIVATIVES **academically** adverb.
– ORIGIN mid 16th cent.: from French *académique* or medieval Latin *academicus*, from *academia* (see **ACADEMY**).

academical ▶ adjective relating to a college or university: *the academical year.*
▶ noun (**academicals**) Brit. dated formal university attire.

academician /əˌkadəˈmɪʃ(ə)n/ ▶ noun **1** a member of an academy, especially the Royal Academy of Arts or the Académie française.
2 N. Amer. an academic or intellectual.
– ORIGIN mid 18th cent.: from French *académicien*, from medieval Latin *academicus* (see **ACADEMIC**).

academicism /ˌakəˈdɛmɪsɪz(ə)m/ (also **academism**) ▶ noun [mass noun] adherence to formal or conventional rules and traditions in art or literature.

academic year ▶ noun the period of the year during which students attend school or university, usually reckoned from the beginning of the autumn term to the end of the summer term.

Académie française /əˌkadəmi frɒ̃ˈseɪz/, French /akademi frɑ̃sɛz/ a French literary academy responsible for the standard form of the French language and for compiling and revising a definitive dictionary of the French language.

academy ▶ noun (pl. **academies**) **1** a place of study or training in a special field: *a police academy.* ■ Brit. an inner-city school which is funded partly by the government and partly by a private individual or organization. ■ US & Scottish a secondary school, in the US typically a private one. ■ (**the Academy**) the teaching school founded by Plato.
2 a society or institution of distinguished scholars and artists or scientists that aims to promote and maintain standards in its particular field: *the Royal Academy of Arts.*
– ORIGIN late Middle English (denoting the garden where Plato taught): from French *académie* or Latin *academia*, from Greek *akadēmeia*, from *Akadēmos*, the hero after whom Plato's garden was named.

Academy Award ▶ noun an award given by the Academy of Motion Picture Arts and Sciences (Hollywood, US) presented annually since 1928 for achievement in the film industry in various categories; an Oscar.

Acadia /əˈkeɪdɪə/ a former French colony established in 1604 in the territory now forming Nova Scotia in Canada. It was contested by France and Britain until it was eventually ceded to Britain in 1763; French-speaking Acadians were deported to other parts of North America, especially Louisiana.
– ORIGIN from *Acadie*, the French name for Nova Scotia.

Acadian chiefly historical ▶ noun a native or inhabitant of Acadia. ■ chiefly Canadian a French-speaking descendant of the early French settlers in Acadia. ■ US a descendant of the Acadians deported to Louisiana in the 18th century; a Cajun.
▶ adjective relating to Acadia or its people.

açai /aˈsʌɪiː, asʌɪˈiː/ ▶ noun (pl. **same**) a South American palm tree producing small edible blackish-purple berries. ● Genus *Euterpe*, especially *E. oleracea*.
– ORIGIN mid 19th cent.: from Portuguese *açaí*, from Tupi-Guarani *asaí*.

acajou /ˈakəʒuː/ ▶ noun another term for **CASHEW**.
– ORIGIN late 16th cent.: from French, via Portuguese from Tupi *acajú*.

-acal ▶ suffix forming adjectives such as *maniacal*, often from nouns ending in *-ac* (as in *maniacal* from *maniac*).

acalculia /ˌeɪkalˈkjuːlɪə/ ▶ noun [mass noun] Medicine loss of the ability to perform simple calculations, typically resulting from disease or injury of the parietal lobe of the brain.
– ORIGIN early 20th cent.: from **A-**[1] 'not' + Latin *calculare* 'calculate' + **-IA**[1].

acanthamoeba /əˌkanθəˈmiːbə/ ▶ noun (pl. **acanthamoebae** /-ˈmiːbiː/) an amoeba of a genus which includes a number that can cause opportunistic infections in humans. ● Genus *Acanthamoeba*, phylum Rhizopoda.

acantho- /əˈkanθəʊ/ (also **acanth-** before a vowel) ▶ combining form having thorn-like characteristics.
– ORIGIN from Greek *akantha* 'thorn'.

Acanthocephala /əˌkanθə(ʊ)ˈsɛfələ, -ˈkɛf-/ ▶ plural noun Zoology a small phylum of parasitic invertebrates that comprises the thorny-headed worms.
– DERIVATIVES **acanthocephalan** adjective & noun, **acanthocephalid** adjective & noun.
– ORIGIN modern Latin (plural), from **ACANTHO-** 'thorn-like' + Greek *kephalē* 'head'.

acanthodian /əˌkanˈθəʊdɪən/ ▶ noun a small spiny-finned fossil fish of a group found chiefly in the Devonian period. ● Class (or subclass) Acanthodii.
– ORIGIN mid 19th cent.: from modern Latin *Acanthodii* (from **ACANTHO-**) + **-AN**.

acanthus /əˈkanθəs/ ▶ noun a herbaceous plant or shrub with bold flower spikes and spiny decorative leaves, found in warm regions of the Old World.
● Genus *Acanthus*, family Acanthaceae: many species, including bear's breeches.
■ Architecture a conventionalized representation of an acanthus leaf, used especially as a decoration for Corinthian column capitals.
– ORIGIN via Latin from Greek *akanthos*, from *akantha* 'thorn', from *akē* 'sharp point'; the architectural term dates from the mid 18th cent.

a cappella /ˌa kəˈpɛlə, ˌɑː/ ▶ adjective & adverb (with reference to choral music) sung without instrumental accompaniment: [as adj.] *an a cappella Mass* | [as adv.] *the consorts usually perform a cappella.*
– ORIGIN Italian, literally 'in chapel style'.

Acapulco /akəˈpʊlkəʊ/ a port and resort in southern Mexico, on the Pacific coast; pop. 616,384 (2005). Full name **Acapulco de Juárez** /deɪ ˈhwɑːrɛz/, Spanish /ðe ˈxwares, -reθ/.

acara /əˈkɑːrə/ ▶ noun a small deep-bodied freshwater fish native to Central and South America, having elongated dorsal and anal fins. ● Genera *Aequidens* and *Cichlisoma*, family Cichlidae: several species.
– ORIGIN from Portuguese *acaré*, from Tupi.

Acari /əˈkɑːri/ (also **Acarina** /ˌakəˈrʌɪnə/) ▶ plural noun Zoology a large order (or subclass) of small arachnids which comprises the mites and ticks. They are distinguished by an apparent lack of body divisions.
– DERIVATIVES **acarid** /ˈakərɪd/ noun & adjective.
– ORIGIN modern Latin (plural), from *acarus*, from Greek *akari* 'mite'.

acaricide /ˈakərɪsʌɪd/ ▶ noun a substance poisonous to mites or ticks.
– ORIGIN late 19th cent.: from Greek *akari* 'mite, tick' + **-CIDE**.

acarine /ˈakərʌɪn/ Zoology ▶ noun a small arachnid of the order Acari; a mite or tick.
▶ adjective relating to or denoting acarines.

acaroid /ˈakərɔɪd/ (also **acaroid resin**) ▶ noun [mass noun] a resin obtained in Australia from some kinds of grass tree, used in making varnish.
– ORIGIN mid 19th cent.: of unknown origin.

acarology /ˌakəˈrɒlədʒi/ ▶ noun [mass noun] the study of mites and ticks.
– DERIVATIVES **acarologist** noun.
– ORIGIN early 20th cent.: from Greek *akari* 'mite, tick' + **-LOGY**.

ACAS /ˈeɪkas/ ▶ abbreviation (in the UK) Advisory, Conciliation, and Arbitration Service.

acatalectic /əˌkatəˈlɛktɪk/ Prosody ▶ adjective (of a line of verse) having the full number of syllables.
▶ noun a line of verse of such a type.

acausal ▶ adjective not governed or operating by the laws of cause and effect.

accede /əkˈsiːd/ ▶ verb [no obj.] (usu. **accede to**) formal **1** agree to a demand, request, or treaty: *the authorities did not accede to the strikers' demands.*
2 assume an office or position: *Elizabeth I acceded to the throne in 1558.* ■ become a member of an organization: *Albania acceded to the IMF in 1990.*
– ORIGIN late Middle English (in the general sense 'come forward, approach'): from Latin *accedere*, from *ad-* 'to' + *cedere* 'give way, yield'.

accelerando /əkˌsɛləˈrandəʊ, əˌtʃɛl-/ Music ▶ adverb & adjective (especially as a direction) with a gradual increase of speed.
▶ noun (pl. **accelerandos** or **accelerandi** /-di/) an accelerando passage.
– ORIGIN Italian.

accelerant ▶ noun a substance used to aid the spread of fire.
▶ adjective technical accelerating or causing acceleration.

accelerate /əkˈsɛləreɪt/ ▶ verb [no obj.] (especially of a vehicle) begin to move more quickly: *the car accelerated towards her.* ■ increase in rate, amount, or extent: *inflation started to accelerate* | [with obj.] *the key question is whether stress accelerates ageing.* ■ Physics undergo a change in velocity.
– DERIVATIVES **accelerative** adjective.
– ORIGIN early 16th cent. (in the sense 'hasten the occurrence of'): from Latin *accelerat-* 'hastened', from the verb *accelerare*, from *ad-* 'towards' + *celer* 'swift'.

accelerated learning ▶ noun [mass noun] **1** an intensive method of study which enables material to be learnt in a relatively short time.
2 a programme of learning which allows academically able children to progress through school more rapidly than others.

acceleration ▸ **noun** [mass noun] a vehicle's capacity to gain speed: *the three-litre model has spectacular acceleration.* ■ increase in speed or rate: *the acceleration of the industrialization process.* ■ Physics the rate of change of velocity per unit of time.
– ORIGIN late 15th cent.: from Latin *acceleratio(n-)*, from *accelerare* 'hasten' (see ACCELERATE).

accelerator ▸ **noun** something which brings about acceleration, in particular: ■ a device, typically a foot pedal, which controls the speed of a vehicle's engine. ■ Physics an apparatus for accelerating charged particles to high velocities.

accelerometer /əkˌseləˈrɒmɪtə/ ▸ **noun** an instrument for measuring the acceleration of a moving or vibrating body.

accent ▸ **noun** /ˈaks(ə)nt, -sɛnt/ **1** a distinctive way of pronouncing a language, especially one associated with a particular country, area, or social class: *a strong American accent.*
2 a distinct emphasis given to a syllable or word in speech by stress or pitch. ■ a mark on a letter, typically a vowel, to indicate pitch, stress, or vowel quality: *a circumflex accent.* ■ Music an emphasis on a particular note or chord.
3 [in sing.] a special or particular emphasis: *the accent is on participation.* ■ a feature which gives a distinctive visual emphasis to something.
▸ **verb** /akˈsɛnt/ [with obj.] emphasize (a particular feature): *fabrics which accent the background colours in the room.* ■ Music play (a note or beat) with emphasis.
– DERIVATIVES **accentual** adjective.
– ORIGIN late Middle English (in the sense 'intonation'): from Latin *accentus* 'tone, signal, or intensity' (from *ad-* 'to' + *cantus* 'song'), translating Greek *prosōidia* 'a song sung to music, intonation'.

accented ▸ **adjective 1** spoken with or characterized by a particular accent: *he spoke in slightly accented English.*
2 (of a word or syllable) stressed.

accentor /əkˈsɛntə/ ▸ **noun** a small Eurasian songbird with generally drab-coloured plumage. ● Family Prunellidae and genus *Prunella*: several species, including the dunnock.
– ORIGIN early 19th cent.: from late Latin, from *ad-* 'to' + *cantor* 'singer'.

accentuate /əkˈsɛntʃʊeɪt, -tjʊ-/ ▸ **verb** [with obj.] make more noticeable or prominent: *his jacket unfortunately accentuated his paunch.*
– ORIGIN mid 18th cent.: from medieval Latin *accentuat-* 'accented', from the verb *accentuare*, from *accentus* 'tone' (see ACCENT).

accentuation ▸ **noun** [mass noun] the action or fact of accentuating or of being accentuated. ■ the pattern of relative prominence of syllables in a phrase or utterance.
– ORIGIN late 15th cent.: in early use from medieval Latin *accentuatio(n-)*; in later use (early 19th cent.) from ACCENTUATE.

accept ▸ **verb** [with obj.] **1** consent to receive or undertake (something offered): *he accepted a pen as a present | she accepted a temporary post as a clerk.* ■ give an affirmative answer to (an offer or proposal); say yes to: *he would accept their offer and see what happened | [no obj.] Tim offered Brian a lift home and he accepted.* ■ dated say yes to a proposal of marriage from (a man). ■ receive as adequate, valid, or suitable: *the college accepted her as a student | credit cards are widely accepted.* ■ regard favourably or with approval; welcome: *the Irish never accepted him as one of them.* ■ (of a thing) be designed to allow (something) to be inserted or applied: *vending machines that accepted 100-yen coins for cans of beer.*
2 believe or come to recognize (a proposition) as valid or correct: *this tentative explanation came to be accepted by the men | [with clause] it is accepted that ageing is a continuous process.* ■ take upon oneself (a responsibility or liability); acknowledge: *Jenkins is willing to accept his responsibility | [with clause] he accepts that he made a mistake.*
3 tolerate or submit to (something unpleasant or undesired): *they accepted the need to cut overheads.*
– DERIVATIVES **accepter** noun.
– ORIGIN late Middle English: from Latin *acceptare*, frequentative of *accipere* 'take something to oneself', from *ad-* 'to' + *capere* 'take'.

acceptable ▸ **adjective 1** able to be agreed on; suitable: *the electoral arrangements must be* ***acceptable to*** *the people.* ■ moderately good; satisfactory: *an acceptable substitute for champagne.* ■ pleasing; welcome: *some coffee would be most acceptable.*
2 able to be tolerated or allowed: *pollution in the city had reached four times the acceptable level.*
– PHRASES **the acceptable face of ——** the tolerable manifestation or aspect of (something usually considered suspect or immoral): *the film's breezy domesticity is the acceptable face of sentimental guff.*
– DERIVATIVES **acceptability** noun **acceptably** adverb.
– ORIGIN late Middle English: from Old French, from late Latin *acceptabilis*, from *acceptare* (see ACCEPT).

acceptance ▸ **noun** [mass noun] **1** the action of consenting to receive or undertake something offered: *charges involving the acceptance of bribes.* ■ [count noun] a draft or bill of exchange that is accepted by being signed: *a banker's acceptance.*
2 the process or fact of being received as adequate, valid, or suitable: *you must wait for acceptance into the village.*
3 agreement with or belief in an idea or explanation: *acceptance of the teaching of the Church.* ■ willingness to tolerate a difficult situation: *a mood of resigned acceptance.*
– ORIGIN mid 16th cent.: from Old French, from *accepter* (see ACCEPT).

acceptant ▸ **adjective** (**acceptant of**) rare willingly accepting (something).
– ORIGIN late 16th cent.: from French, 'accepting', present participle of *accepter.*

acceptation /ˌaksɛpˈteɪʃ(ə)n/ ▸ **noun** a particular sense or the generally recognized meaning (**common acceptation**) of a word or phrase.
– ORIGIN late Middle English (originally in the sense 'favourable reception, approval'): from late Latin *acceptatio(n-)*, from the verb *acceptare* (see ACCEPT). The current sense dates from the early 17th cent.

accepted ▸ **adjective** generally believed or recognized to be valid or correct: *he wasn't handsome in the accepted sense.*

acceptor ▸ **noun** a person or thing that accepts something, in particular: ■ Chemistry an atom or molecule which is able to bind to or accept an electron or other species. ■ Physics such an atom forming a positive hole in a semiconductor.

access ▸ **noun 1** [mass noun] (often **access to**) the means or opportunity to approach or enter a place: *the staircase gives access to the top floor | wheelchair access.* ■ the right or opportunity to use or benefit from something: *do you* ***have access to*** *a computer? | awards to help people* ***gain access to*** *training.* ■ the right or opportunity to approach or see someone: *we were denied access to our grandson.* ■ the process of obtaining or retrieving information stored in a computer's memory. ■ [as modifier] denoting broadcasting produced by minority and specialist interest groups, rather than by professionals: *access television.*
2 [in sing.] literary an attack or outburst of an emotion: *I was suddenly overcome with* ***an access of*** *rage.*
▸ **verb** [with obj.] **1** approach or enter (a place): *single rooms have private facilities accessed via the balcony.*
2 obtain or retrieve (computer data or a file).
– ORIGIN Middle English (in the sense 'sudden attack of illness'): from Latin *accessus*, from the verb *accedere* 'to approach' (see ACCEDE). Sense 1 of the noun is first recorded in the early 17th cent.

accessary ▸ **noun** variant spelling of ACCESSORY (sense 2 of the noun).

access charge (also **access fee**) ▸ **noun** a charge made for the use of computer or local telephone-network facilities.

access course ▸ **noun** Brit. an educational course enabling those without traditional qualifications to become eligible for higher education.

accessible ▸ **adjective 1** (of a place) able to be reached or entered: *the town is* ***accessible by*** *bus | this room is not* ***accessible to*** *elderly people.* ■ able to be easily obtained or used: *making learning opportunities more* ***accessible to*** *adults.* ■ easily understood or appreciated: *an accessible account of his theories.* ■ able to be reached, entered, or used by people who have a disability: *features such as non-slip floors and accessible entrances.*
2 (of a person, especially one in a position of authority) friendly and easy to talk to; approachable: *he is more accessible than most tycoons.*
– DERIVATIVES **accessibility** noun, **accessibly** adverb.
– ORIGIN late Middle English: from late Latin *accessibilis*, from Latin *access-* 'approached', from the verb *accedere* (see ACCEDE).

WORD TRENDS Although the frequency of use of **accessible** has remained fairly static in the last few decades, the way it is being used has changed significantly. A new sense referring specifically to the way in which something can be used or accessed by people with a disability emerged in 1970. Though US in origin, the sense is now just as common in the UK, with the Disability Discrimination Act of 1995 containing numerous provisions for **accessibility**. Used most literally, it refers to the ease with which disabled people can physically enter a place, or use a service: *they're actively trying to expand the accessible bus network | there are fully accessible toilets on all three floors.* **Accessible** is also used to refer to computing tools and websites that can easily be used by people with disabilities.

accession ▸ **noun 1** [mass noun] the attainment or acquisition of a position of rank or power: *the Queen's* ***accession to*** *the throne.* ■ the action or process of formally joining or being accepted by an institution or group: *the* ***accession*** *of Spain and Portugal* ***to*** *the EU.* ■ the formal acceptance of a treaty or agreement: ***accession to*** *the Treaty of Rome was effected in 1971.*
2 a new item added to an existing collection of books, paintings, or artefacts. ■ an amount added to an existing quantity of something.
▸ **verb** [with obj.] record the addition of (a new item) to a library, museum, or other collection.
– ORIGIN late 16th cent. (in the general sense 'something added'): from Latin *accessio(n-)*, from the verb *accedere* 'approach, come to' (see ACCEDE).

accessorize (also **accessorise**) ▸ **verb** [with obj.] provide (a garment) with a fashion accessory: *sequinned catsuits were accessorized with cork-heeled shoes.*

accessory ▸ **noun** (pl. **accessories**) **1** a thing which can be added to something else in order to make it more useful, versatile, or attractive: *optional accessories include a battery charger and shoulder strap.* ■ a small article or item of clothing carried or worn to complement a garment or outfit: *she wore the suit with perfectly matching accessories—hat, bag, shoes.*
2 (also **accessary**) Law someone who gives assistance to the perpetrator of a crime without taking part in it: *she was charged as an* ***accessory to*** *murder.*
▸ **adjective** chiefly technical contributing to or aiding an activity or process in a minor way; subsidiary or supplementary: *functionally the maxillae are a pair of accessory jaws.*
– PHRASES **accessory before** (or **after**) **the fact** Law, dated a person who incites or assists someone to commit an arrestable offence (or knowingly aids someone who has committed such an offence).
– DERIVATIVES **accessorial** adjective (chiefly Law).
– ORIGIN late Middle English: from medieval Latin *accessorius* 'additional thing', from Latin *access-* 'increased', from the verb *accedere* (see ACCEDE).

accessory cell ▸ **noun** Physiology any of various cells of the immune system that interact with T lymphocytes in the initiation of the immune response.

accessory mineral ▸ **noun** Geology a constituent mineral present in small quantity and not taken into account in identifying a rock.

accessory nerve ▸ **noun** Anatomy each of the eleventh pair of cranial nerves, supplying certain muscles in the neck and shoulder.

access provider ▸ **noun** another term for SERVICE PROVIDER.

acciaccatura /əˌtʃakəˈtjʊərə/ ▸ **noun** (pl. **acciaccaturas** or **acciaccature**) Music a grace note performed as quickly as possible before an essential note of a melody.
– ORIGIN Italian, from *acciaccare* 'to crush'.

accidence /ˈaksɪd(ə)ns/ ▸ **noun** [mass noun] dated the part of grammar that deals with the inflections of words.
– ORIGIN early 16th cent.: from late Latin *accidentia* (translation of Greek *parepomena* 'things happening alongside'), neuter plural of the present participle of *accidere* 'happen' (see ACCIDENT).

accident ▸ **noun 1** an unfortunate incident that happens unexpectedly and unintentionally, typically resulting in damage or injury: *he had an accident at the factory | [mass noun] if you are unable to work owing to accident or sickness.* ■ a crash involving road or other vehicles: *four people were killed in a road accident.* ■ euphemistic an incidence of incontinence by a child or animal.
2 an event that happens by chance or that is without apparent or deliberate cause: *the pregnancy was an accident |* ***it is no accident that*** *Manchester has produced more than its fair share of professional comics.* ■ [mass noun] the working of fortune; chance: *members belong to the House of Lords through hereditary right or* ***accident of birth.***
3 Philosophy (in Aristotelian thought) a property of a thing which is not essential to its nature.
– PHRASES **accident and emergency** Brit. a hospital department concerned with the provision of immediate treatment to people who are seriously injured in

A

an accident or who are suddenly taken seriously ill. **an accident waiting to happen** informal a potentially disastrous situation, typically caused by negligent or faulty procedures. **accidents will happen in the best regulated families** proverb however careful you try to be, it is inevitable that some unfortunate or unforeseen events will occur: *problems like these should not occur, but accidents will happen.* **by accident** unintentionally; by chance: *she didn't get where she is today by accident.*
– ORIGIN late Middle English (in the general sense 'an event'): via Old French from Latin *accident-* 'happening', from the verb *accidere*, from *ad-* 'towards, to' + *cadere* 'to fall'.

accidental ▸ adjective **1** happening by chance, unintentionally, or unexpectedly: *a verdict of accidental death | the damage might have been accidental.*
2 incidental; subsidiary: *the location is accidental and contributes nothing to the poem.*
3 Philosophy (in Aristotelian thought) relating to or denoting properties which are not essential to a thing's nature.
▸ noun **1** Music a sign indicating a momentary departure from the key signature by raising or lowering a note.
2 Ornithology another term for VAGRANT.
– ORIGIN late Middle English (in sense 2 of the adjective and sense 3 of the adjective): from late Latin *accidentalis*, from Latin *accident-* 'happening' (see ACCIDENT).

accidentally ▸ adverb by chance; inadvertently: *his gun went off accidentally.*

accident-prone ▸ adjective tending to be involved in a greater than average number of accidents.

accidie /ˈaksɪdi/ ▸ noun [mass noun] literary spiritual or mental sloth; apathy.
– ORIGIN Middle English: via Old French from medieval Latin *accidia*, alteration of ACEDIA. Obsolete after the 16th cent., the term was revived in the late 19th cent.

accipiter /akˈsɪpɪtə/ ▸ noun Ornithology a hawk of a group distinguished by short, broad wings and relatively long legs, adapted for fast flight in wooded country. ● *Accipiter* and related genera, family Accipitridae: numerous species, including the goshawk.
– ORIGIN from Latin, 'hawk, bird of prey'.

accipitrine /akˈsɪpɪtrʌɪn/ ▸ adjective Ornithology relating to or denoting birds of a family that includes most diurnal birds of prey other than falcons, New World vultures, and the osprey. ● Family Accipitridae; treated as a subfamily (Accipitrinae) in this sense when the osprey is included in this family.
– ORIGIN mid 19th cent.: from French, from Latin *accipiter* 'bird of prey'.

acclaim ▸ verb [with obj.] praise enthusiastically and publicly: *the conference was* ***acclaimed as*** *a considerable success.*
▸ noun [mass noun] enthusiastic and public praise: *she has won acclaim for her commitment to democracy.*
– ORIGIN early 17th cent. (in the sense 'express approval'): from Latin *acclamare*, from *ad-* 'to' + *clamare* 'to shout'. The change in the ending was due to association with CLAIM. Current senses date from the 17th cent.

acclaimed ▸ adjective publicly praised; celebrated: *the band released their critically acclaimed debut in 1994.*

acclamation ▸ noun [mass noun] loud and enthusiastic approval: *the tackle brought the supporters to their feet in acclamation.*
– PHRASES **by acclamation 1** (of election, agreement, etc.) by overwhelming vocal approval and without ballot. **2** Canadian (of election) by virtue of being the sole candidate.
– ORIGIN mid 16th cent.: from Latin *acclamatio(n-)*, from *acclamare* 'shout at', later 'shout in approval' (see ACCLAIM).

acclimate /ˈaklɪmeɪt, əˈklʌɪmət/ ▸ verb [no obj.] (often **acclimate to**) chiefly N. Amer. acclimatize: *helping freshmen to acclimate to college life.* ■ Biology respond physiologically or behaviourally to a change in a single environmental factor. Compare with ACCLIMATIZE. ■ [with obj.] Botany & Horticulture harden off (a plant).
– DERIVATIVES **acclimation** noun.
– ORIGIN late 18th cent.: from French *acclimater*, from *a-* (from Latin *ad* 'to, at') + *climat* 'climate'.

acclimatize (also **acclimatise**) ▸ verb [no obj.] (often **acclimatize to** or **be/become acclimatized to**) become accustomed to a new climate or new conditions; adjust: *it's unknown whether people will acclimatize to increasingly warm weather.* ■ Biology respond physiologically or behaviourally to changes in a complex of environmental factors. Compare with ACCLIMATE. ■ [with obj.] Botany & Horticulture harden off (a plant).
– DERIVATIVES **acclimatization** noun.
– ORIGIN mid 19th cent.: from French *acclimater* 'acclimatize' + -IZE.

acclivity /əˈklɪvɪti/ ▸ noun (pl. **acclivities**) an upward slope.
– DERIVATIVES **acclivitous** adjective.
– ORIGIN early 17th cent.: from Latin *acclivitas*, from *acclivis*, from *ad-* 'towards' + *clivus* 'a slope'.

accolade /ˈakəleɪd, ˌakəˈleɪd/ ▸ noun **1** an award or privilege granted as a special honour or as an acknowledgement of merit: *the hotel has won numerous accolades.* ■ an expression of praise or admiration.
2 a touch on a person's shoulders with a sword at the bestowing of a knighthood.
– ORIGIN early 17th cent.: from French, from Provençal *acolada*, literally 'embrace around the neck (when bestowing knighthood)', from Latin *ad-* 'at, to' + *collum* 'neck'.

accommodate ▸ verb [with obj.] **1** (of a building or other area) provide lodging or sufficient space for: *the cottages accommodate up to six people.*
2 fit in with the wishes or needs of: *any language must accommodate new concepts.* ■ [no obj.] (**accommodate to**) adapt to: *making users accommodate to the realities of today's marketplace.*
– DERIVATIVES **accommodative** adjective.
– ORIGIN mid 16th cent.: from Latin *accommodat-* 'made fitting', from the verb *accommodare*, from *ad-* 'to' + *commodus* 'fitting'.

accommodating ▸ adjective fitting in with someone's wishes or demands in a helpful way.
– DERIVATIVES **accommodatingly** adverb.

accommodation ▸ noun **1** [mass noun] Brit. a room, group of rooms, or building in which someone may live or stay: *they were living in temporary accommodation.* ■ (**accommodations**) chiefly N. Amer. lodgings, sometimes also including board: *the company offers a number of guest house accommodations in Oberammergau.* ■ the available space for occupants in a building, vehicle, or vessel: *there was lifeboat accommodation for 1,178 people.* ■ the provision of a room or lodgings: *the building is used exclusively for the accommodation of guests.*
2 a convenient arrangement; a settlement or compromise: *the prime minister was seeking an accommodation with Labour.*
3 [mass noun] the process of adapting or adjusting to someone or something: ***accommodation to*** *a separate political entity was not possible.* ■ [mass noun] the automatic adjustment of the focus of the eye by flattening or thickening of the lens.
– ORIGIN early 17th cent.: from Latin *accommodatio(n-)*, from *accommodare* 'fit one thing to another' (see ACCOMMODATE).

accommodation address ▸ noun Brit. an address for correspondence used by a person who wishes to conceal or does not have a permanent address.

accommodationist ▸ noun US a person or political group that seeks compromise with an opposing point of view.

accommodation ladder ▸ noun a ladder or flight of steps up the side of a ship allowing access from a small boat or a quayside.

accompaniment ▸ noun **1** a musical part which supports or partners an instrument, voice, or group: *she sang to a guitar accompaniment |* [mass noun] *sonatas for piano with violin accompaniment.* ■ a piece of music played as a complement or background to an activity: *lush string accompaniments to romantic scenes in films | we filed out* ***to the accompaniment of*** *the organ.*
2 something that supplements or complements something else: *these biscuits are a lovely* ***accompaniment to*** *tea.*
– ORIGIN early 18th cent.: from French *accompagnement*, from *accompagner* 'accompany'.

accompanist ▸ noun a person who provides a musical accompaniment to another musician or to a singer.

accompany ▸ verb (**accompanies, accompanying, accompanied**) [with obj.] **1** go somewhere with (someone) as a companion or escort: *the two sisters were to accompany us to London.*
2 be present or occur at the same time as (something else): *the illness is often accompanied by nausea |* (as adj. **accompanying**) *the accompanying documentation.* ■ provide a complement or addition to: *home-cooked ham accompanied by brown bread.*
3 play a musical accompaniment for.
– ORIGIN late Middle English: from Old French *accompagner*, from *a-* (from Latin *ad* 'to, at') + *compagne*, from Old French *compaignon* 'companion'. The spelling change was due to association with COMPANY.

accomplice /əˈkʌmplɪs, əˈkɒm-/ ▸ noun a person who helps another commit a crime.
– ORIGIN mid 16th cent.: alteration (probably by association with ACCOMPANY) of Middle English *complice* 'an associate', via Old French from late Latin *complex, complic-* 'allied', from *com-* 'together' + the root of *plicare* 'to fold'.

accomplish ▸ verb [with obj.] achieve or complete successfully: *the planes accomplished their mission.*
– ORIGIN late Middle English: from Old French *acompliss-*, lengthened stem of *acomplir*, based on Latin *ad-* 'to' + *complere* 'to complete'.

accomplished ▸ adjective highly trained or skilled in a particular activity: *an accomplished pianist.* ■ well educated and having good social skills.

accomplishment ▸ noun something that has been achieved successfully: *the reduction of inflation was a remarkable accomplishment.* ■ [mass noun] the successful achievement of a task: *the accomplishment of planned objectives.* ■ an activity that a person can do well: *typing was another of her accomplishments.* ■ [mass noun] skill or ability in an activity: *a poet of considerable accomplishment.*

accord ▸ verb **1** [with obj.] give or grant someone (power, status, or recognition): *the powers* ***accorded to*** *the head of state |* [with two objs] *the national assembly accorded the General more power.*
2 [no obj.] (**accord with**) (of a concept or fact) be harmonious or consistent with.
▸ noun an official agreement or treaty. ■ [mass noun] agreement or harmony: *the government and the rebels are* ***in accord*** *on one point.*
– PHRASES **in accord with** according to. **of one's own accord** voluntarily or without outside intervention: *he would not seek treatment of his own accord | the rash may go away of its own accord.* **with one accord** in a united way.
– ORIGIN Old English, from Old French *acorder* 'reconcile, be of one mind', from Latin *ad-* 'to' + *cor, cord-* 'heart'; influenced by CONCORD.

accordance ▸ noun (in phrase **in accordance with**) in a manner conforming with: *the ballot was held in accordance with trade union rules.*
– ORIGIN Middle English: from Old French *acordance*, from *acorder* 'bring to an agreement' (see ACCORD).

accordant ▸ adjective archaic agreeing or compatible: *I found the music* ***accordant with*** *the words of the service.*
– ORIGIN Middle English: from Old French *acordant*, from *acorder* 'bring to an agreement' (see ACCORD).

according ▸ adverb **1** (usu. **according to**) as stated by or in: *the outlook for investors is not bright, according to financial experts.* ■ in a manner corresponding or conforming to: *cook the rice according to the instructions.* ■ in proportion or relation to: *salary will be fixed according to experience.*
2 (**according as**) formal depending on whether.

accordingly ▸ adverb **1** in a way that is appropriate to the particular circumstances: *we have to discover what his plans are and act accordingly.*
2 [sentence adverb] as a result; therefore: *there was no breach of the rules; accordingly, there will be no disciplinary inquiry.*

accordion /əˈkɔːdɪən/ ▸ noun a musical instrument played by stretching and squeezing with the hands to work a central bellows that blows air over metal reeds, the melody and chords being sounded by buttons or keys. Compare with CONCERTINA. ■ [as modifier] folding like the bellows of an accordion: *an accordion pleat.*
– DERIVATIVES **accordionist** noun.
– ORIGIN mid 19th cent.: from German *Akkordion*, from Italian *accordare* 'to tune'.

accost ▸ verb [with obj.] approach and address (someone) boldly or aggressively: *reporters accosted him in the street.*
– ORIGIN late 16th cent. (originally in the sense 'lie or go alongside'): from French *accoster*, from Italian *accostare*, from Latin *ad-* 'to' + *costa* 'rib, side'.

accouchement /əˈkuːʃmɒ̃/ ▸ noun [mass noun] archaic the action of giving birth to a baby.
– ORIGIN late 18th cent.: French, from *accoucher* 'act as midwife', from *a-* (from Latin *ad* 'to, at') + *coucher* 'put to bed' (see COUCH[1]).

accoucheur /ˌakuːˈʃəː/ ▶ noun a male midwife.
– ORIGIN mid 18th cent.: French, from *accoucher* (see ACCOUCHEMENT).

account ▶ noun **1** a report or description of an event or experience: *a detailed account of what has been achieved.*
2 a record or statement of financial expenditure and receipts relating to a particular period or purpose: *the barman was doing his accounts.* ■ chiefly Brit. a bill for goods or services provided over a period: *there's no money to pay the tradesmen's accounts this month.*
3 an arrangement by which a body holds funds on behalf of a client or supplies goods or services to them on credit: *a bank account | I began buying things **on account**.* ■ a client having an account with a supplier: *selling bibles to established accounts in the North.* ■ a contract to do work for a client: *another agency was awarded the account.* ■ Stock Exchange, Brit. a fixed period on a stock exchange, at the end of which payment must be made for stock that has been bought.
4 [mass noun] importance: *money was **of no account** to her.*
5 an interpretation or rendering of a piece of music: *a lively account of Offenbach's score.*
▶ verb **1** [with obj. and complement] consider or regard in a specified way: *her visit could not be accounted a success | he **accounted himself** the unluckiest man alive.*
2 [no obj.] archaic give or receive an account for money received: *after 1292 he **accounted to** the Westminster exchequer.*
– PHRASES **by** (or **from**) **all accounts** according to what one has heard or read: *by all accounts he is a pretty nice guy.* **call** (or **bring**) **someone to account** require someone to explain a mistake or poor performance. **give a good** (or **bad**) **account of oneself** make a favourable (or unfavourable) impression through one's performance. **keep an account of** keep a record of. **leave something out of account** fail or decline to consider a factor. **money of account** denominations of money used in reckoning but not current as coins. **on someone's account** for a specified person's benefit: *don't bother on my account.* **on account of** because of: *they had closed early on account of the snow.* **on no account** under no circumstances: *on no account let anyone know we're interested.* **on one's own account** for one's own purposes; for oneself: *he began trading on his own account.* ■ alone; unaided: *he'll be investigating on his own account.* **settle** (or **square**) **accounts with** have revenge on. **take something into account** (or **take account of**) consider something along with other factors before reaching a decision. **there's no accounting for tastes** (or **taste**) proverb it's impossible to explain why different people like different things, especially those things which the speaker considers unappealing. **turn something to** (**good**) **account** turn something to one's advantage.
– PHRASAL VERBS **account for 1** give a satisfactory record of (something, typically money, that one is responsible for). ■ provide or serve as a satisfactory explanation for: *he was brought before the Board to account for his behaviour.* ■ know the fate or whereabouts of (someone or something), especially after an accident: *everyone was accounted for after the floods.* **2** succeed in killing, destroying, or defeating: *a mishit drive accounted for Jones, who had scored 32.* **3** supply or make up (a specified amount or proportion): *social security accounts for about a third of total public spending.*
– ORIGIN Middle English (in the sense 'counting', 'to count'): from Old French *acont* (noun), *aconter* (verb), based on *conter* 'to count'.

accountability ▶ noun [mass noun] the fact or condition of being accountable; responsibility: *lack of accountability has corroded public respect for business and political leaders.*

accountable ▶ adjective **1** required or expected to justify actions or decisions; responsible: *ministers are **accountable to** Parliament | parents cannot be **held accountable for** their children's actions.*
2 able to be explained or understood.
– DERIVATIVES **accountably** adverb.

accountancy ▶ noun [mass noun] the profession or duties of an accountant.

accountant ▶ noun a person whose job is to keep or inspect financial accounts.
– ORIGIN Middle English: from Law French, present participle of Old French *aconter* (see ACCOUNT). The original use was as an adjective meaning 'liable to give an account', hence denoting a person who must do so.

account executive ▶ noun a business executive who manages the interests of a particular client, typically in advertising.

accounting ▶ noun [mass noun] the process or work of keeping financial accounts.

accounts payable ▶ plural noun money owed by a company to its creditors.

accounts receivable ▶ plural noun money owed to a company by its debtors.

accoutre /əˈkuːtə/ (US also **accouter**) ▶ verb (**accoutres, accoutring, accoutred**; US **accouters, accoutering, accoutered**) [with obj.] clothe or equip in something noticeable or impressive.
– ORIGIN mid 16th cent.: from French *accoutrer*, from Old French *acoustrer*, from *a-* (from Latin *ad* 'to, at') + *cousture* 'sewing'.

accoutrement /əˈkuːtəm(ə)nt, -trə-/ (US also **accouterment**) ▶ noun (usu. **accoutrements**) an additional item of dress or equipment: *the accoutrements of religious ritual.*
– ORIGIN mid 16th cent.: from French, from *accoutrer* 'clothe, equip' (see ACCOUTRE).

Accra /əˈkrɑː/ the capital of Ghana, a port on the Gulf of Guinea; pop. 1,970,400 (est. 2005).

accra /ˈakrə, əˈkrɑː/ (also **akara**) ▶ noun (in West Africa and the Caribbean) a fritter made with black-eyed peas or a similar pulse, or, especially in Trinidad, mashed fish.
– ORIGIN from Yoruba *àkàrà* 'bean cake'.

accredit ▶ verb (**accredits, accrediting, accredited**) [with obj.] **1** give credit to (someone) for something: *he was **accredited with** being one of the world's fastest sprinters.* ■ (**accredit something to**) attribute an action, saying, or quality to: *the discovery of distillation is usually accredited to the Arabs.*
2 (of an official body) give authority or sanction to (someone or something) when recognized standards have been met: *institutions that do not meet the standards will not be accredited for teacher training* | (as adj. **accredited**) *an accredited practitioner.*
3 give official authorization for (someone, typically a diplomat or journalist) to be in a particular place or to hold a particular post: *no journalist **accredited to** the UN has ever been expelled.*
– DERIVATIVES **accreditation** noun, **accreditor** noun.
– ORIGIN early 17th cent. (in sense 2): from French *accréditer*, from *a-* (from Latin *ad* 'to, at') + *crédit* 'credit'.

accrete /əˈkriːt/ ▶ verb [no obj.] grow by accumulation or coalescence: *ice that had accreted grotesquely into stalactites.* ■ [with obj.] form (a composite whole) by gradual accumulation: *the collection of art he had accreted was to be sold.* ■ Astronomy (with reference to matter or a body) come or bring together under the influence of gravitation.
– ORIGIN late 18th cent.: from Latin *accret-* 'grown', from the verb *accrescere*, from *ad-* 'to' + *crescere* 'grow'.

accretion ▶ noun [mass noun] growth or increase by the gradual accumulation of additional layers or matter: *the accretion of sediments in coastal mangroves* | figurative *the growing accretion of central government authority.* ■ [count noun] a thing formed or added by gradual growth or increase: *the city has a historic core surrounded by recent accretions.* ■ Astronomy the coming together and cohesion of matter under the influence of gravitation to form larger bodies.
– DERIVATIVES **accretive** adjective.
– ORIGIN early 17th cent.: from Latin *accretio(n-)*, from *accrescere* 'become larger' (see ACCRETE).

accretionary prism (also **accretionary wedge**) ▶ noun Geology a mass of sedimentary material scraped off a region of oceanic crust during subduction and piled up at the edge of a continental crustal plate.

accretion disc ▶ noun Astronomy a rotating disc of matter formed by accretion around a massive body (such as a black hole) under the influence of gravitation.

accrue /əˈkruː/ ▶ verb (**accrues, accruing, accrued**) [no obj.] (of a benefit or sum of money) be received by someone in regular or increasing amounts over time: *financial benefits will **accrue from** restructuring* | (as adj. **accrued**) *the accrued interest.* ■ [with obj.] accumulate or receive (payments or benefits) over time: *they accrue entitlements to holiday pay.* ■ [with obj.] make provision for (a charge) at the end of a financial period for work that has been done but not yet invoiced.
– DERIVATIVES **accrual** noun.
– ORIGIN late Middle English: from Old French *acreue*, past participle of *acreistre* 'increase', from Latin *accrescere* 'become larger' (see ACCRETE).

acculturate /əˈkʌltʃəreɪt/ ▶ verb assimilate to a different culture, typically the dominant one: [no obj.] *those who have **acculturated to** the United States* | [with obj.] *the next weeks were spent acculturating the field staff.*
– DERIVATIVES **acculturation** noun, **acculturative** adjective.
– ORIGIN 1930s: from AC- + CULTURE + -ATE³. The noun *acculturation* dates from the late 19th cent.

accumulate /əˈkjuːmjʊleɪt/ ▶ verb [with obj.] gather together or acquire an increasing number or quantity of: *investigators have yet to accumulate enough evidence.* ■ gradually gather or acquire (a resulting whole): *her goal was to accumulate a huge fortune.* ■ [no obj.] gather; build up: *the toxin accumulated in their bodies.*
– ORIGIN late 15th cent.: from Latin *accumulat-* 'heaped up', from the verb *accumulare*, from *ad-* 'to' + *cumulus* 'a heap'.

accumulation ▶ noun [mass noun] the acquisition or gradual gathering of something: *the accumulation of wealth.* ■ [count noun] a mass or quantity of something that has gradually gathered or been acquired: *the accumulation of paperwork on her desk.*

accumulative /əˈkjuːmjʊlətɪv/ ▶ adjective gathering or growing by gradual increases: *the accumulative effects of pollution.*

accumulator ▶ noun a person or thing that accumulates, in particular: ■ Brit. a large rechargeable electric cell. ■ Brit. a bet placed on a series of races (or other events), the winnings and stake from each being placed on the next: *an eight-horse accumulator.* ■ Computing a register used to contain the results of an arithmetical or logical operation.

accuracy ▶ noun (pl. **accuracies**) [mass noun] the quality or state of being correct or precise: *we have confidence in the accuracy of the statistics.* ■ technical the degree to which the result of a measurement, calculation, or specification conforms to the correct value or a standard: *the accuracy of radiocarbon dating* | [count noun] *accuracies of 50–70 per cent.* Compare with PRECISION.

accurate /ˈakjʊrət/ ▶ adjective **1** (especially of information, measurements, or predictions) correct in all details; exact: *accurate information about the illness is essential.* ■ (of an instrument or method) capable of giving accurate information: *an accurate thermometer.* ■ providing a faithful representation of someone or something: *the portrait is an accurate likeness of Mozart.*
2 (with reference to a weapon, missile, or shot) capable of or successful in reaching the intended target: *reliable, accurate rifles | a player who can deliver long accurate passes to the wingers.*
– DERIVATIVES **accurately** adverb.
– ORIGIN late 16th cent.: from Latin *accuratus* 'done with care', past participle of *accurare*, from *ad-* 'towards' + *cura* 'care'.

accursed /əˈkəːsɪd, əˈkəːst/ ▶ adjective literary **1** under a curse: *the Angel of Death walks this accursed house.*
2 [attrib.] used to express strong dislike of or anger at someone or something: *this accursed country!*
– ORIGIN Middle English: past participle of obsolete *accurse*, from *a-* (expressing intensity) + CURSE.

accurst ▶ adjective archaic spelling of ACCURSED.

accusal ▶ noun less common term for ACCUSATION.

accusation ▶ noun a charge or claim that someone has done something illegal or wrong: *accusations of bribery.* ■ [mass noun] the action or process of accusing someone: *there was accusation in Brian's voice.*
– ORIGIN late Middle English: from Old French, from Latin *accusatio(n-)*, from *accusare* 'call to account' (see ACCUSE).

accusative /əˈkjuːzətɪv/ Grammar ▶ adjective (in Latin, Greek, German, and some other languages) denoting a case of nouns, pronouns, and adjectives which expresses the object of an action or the goal of motion.
▶ noun a word in the accusative case. ■ (**the accusative**) the accusative case.
– ORIGIN late Middle English: from Latin (*casus*) *accusativus*, literally 'relating to an accusation or (legal) case', translating Greek (*ptōsis*) *aitiatikē* '(the case) showing cause'.

accusatorial /əˌkjuːzəˈtɔːrɪəl/ ▶ adjective Law (of a trial or legal procedure) involving accusation by a prosecutor and a verdict reached by an impartial judge or jury. Compare with ADVERSARIAL, INQUISITORIAL.

A

accusatory /əˈkjuːzət(ə)ri/ ▶ **adjective** indicating or suggesting that one believes a person has done something wrong: *he pointed an accusatory finger in her direction.*

accuse ▶ **verb** [with obj.] (often **accuse someone of**) charge (someone) with an offence or crime: *he was accused of murdering his wife's lover.* ■ claim that (someone) has done something wrong: *he was accused of favouritism.*
– DERIVATIVES **accuser** noun.
– ORIGIN Middle English: from Old French *acuser*, from Latin *accusare* 'call to account', from *ad-* 'towards' + *causa* 'reason, motive, lawsuit'.

accused ▶ **noun** (**the accused**) [treated as sing. or pl.] a person or group of people who are charged with or on trial for a crime.

accusing ▶ **adjective** (of an expression, gesture, or tone of voice) indicating a belief in someone's guilt or culpability: *she stared at him with accusing eyes.*
– DERIVATIVES **accusingly** adverb.

accustom ▶ **verb** [with obj.] (**accustom someone/thing to**) make someone or something accept (something) as normal or usual: *I accustomed my eyes to the lenses* | [with obj. and infinitive] *sixth-form education is supposed to accustom pupils to think for themselves.* ■ (**be accustomed to**) be used to: *I am not accustomed to having my word questioned.*
– ORIGIN late Middle English: from Old French *acostumer*, from *a-* (from Latin *ad* 'to, at') + *costume* 'custom'.

accustomed ▶ **adjective** [attrib.] customary; usual: *his accustomed route.*

AC/DC ▶ **adjective 1** alternating current/direct current.
2 informal bisexual.

ace ▶ **noun 1** a playing card with a single spot on it, ranked as the highest card in its suit in most card games: *the ace of diamonds* | figurative *life had started dealing him aces again.*
2 informal a person who excels at a particular sport or other activity: *a motorcycle ace.* ■ a pilot who has shot down many enemy aircraft.
3 (in tennis and similar games) a service that an opponent is unable to return and thus wins a point. ■ Golf, informal a hole in one.
▶ **adjective** informal very good: *an ace swimmer* | [as exclamation] *Ace! You've done it!*
▶ **verb** [with obj.] informal **1** (in tennis and similar games) serve an ace against (an opponent). ■ Golf score an ace on (a hole) or with (a shot).
2 N. Amer. achieve high marks in (a test or exam): *I aced my grammar test.* ■ (**ace someone out**) outdo someone in a competitive situation.
– PHRASES **an ace up one's sleeve** (or N. Amer. **in the hole**) a plan or piece of information kept secret until it becomes necessary to use it. **hold all the aces** have all the advantages. **play one's ace** use one's best resource: *deciding to play her ace, Emily showed the letter to Vic.* **within an ace of** Brit. very close to: *they came within an ace of death.*
– ORIGIN Middle English (denoting the 'one' on dice): via Old French from Latin *as* 'unity, a unit'.

-acea ▶ **suffix** Zoology forming the names of zoological groups: *Crustacea.*
– ORIGIN from Latin, 'of the nature of', neuter plural adjectival ending.

-aceae ▶ **suffix** Botany forming the names of families of plants: *Liliaceae.*
– ORIGIN from Latin, 'of the nature of', feminine plural adjectival ending.

-acean ▶ **suffix** Zoology forming the singular of group names ending in *-acea* (such as *crustacean* from *Crustacea*).
– ORIGIN from Latin *-aceus* 'of the nature of' + **-AN**.

acedia /əˈsiːdɪə/ ▶ **noun** literary another term for **ACCIDIE**.
– ORIGIN early 17th cent.: via late Latin from Greek *akēdia* 'listlessness', from *a-* 'without' + *kēdos* 'care'.

acellular ▶ **adjective** Biology not consisting of, divided into, or containing cells. ■ (especially of protozoa) consisting of one cell only.

acentric ▶ **adjective** without a centre; not centralized. ■ Genetics (of a chromosome) having no centromere.

-aceous ▶ **suffix 1** Botany forming adjectives from family names ending in *-aceae* (such as *ericaceous* from *Ericaceae*).
2 chiefly Biology & Geology forming adjectives describing similarity, especially in shape, texture, or colour: *arenaceous* | *olivaceous.*
– ORIGIN from Latin *-aceus* 'of the nature of' + **-OUS**.

acephalous /eɪˈsɛf(ə)ləs, -ˈkɛf-/ ▶ **adjective 1** lacking a head.
2 having no leader or chief: *an acephalous society.*
3 Prosody (typically of a hexameter beginning with a short syllable) lacking a syllable or syllables in the first foot.
– ORIGIN mid 18th cent.: via medieval Latin from Greek *akephalos* 'headless' (from *a-* 'without' + *kephalē* 'head') + **-OUS**.

acer /ˈeɪsə/ ▶ **noun** a Eurasian or North American deciduous tree or shrub of a genus which includes the maples and the European sycamore. ● Genus *Acer*, family Aceraceae: numerous species.
– ORIGIN from Latin, 'maple'.

acerb /əˈsəːb/ ▶ **adjective** literary, chiefly US another term for **ACERBIC**.
– ORIGIN early 17th cent.: from Latin *acerbus* 'sour-tasting'.

acerbic ▶ **adjective 1** (especially of a comment or style of speaking) sharp and forthright: *his acerbic wit.*
2 archaic or technical tasting sour or bitter.
– DERIVATIVES **acerbically** adverb, **acerbity** noun.
– ORIGIN mid 19th cent.: from Latin *acerbus* 'sour-tasting' + **-IC**.

acesulfame /ˌasɪˈsʌlfeɪm/ ▶ **noun** [mass noun] a white crystalline compound used as a low-calorie artificial sweetener, typically in the form of a potassium salt (**acesulfame-K**). ● A sulphur-containing heterocyclic compound; chem. formula: $C_4H_5NO_4S$.
– ORIGIN 1980s: of unknown origin.

acet- ▶ **combining form** variant spelling of **ACETO-** shortened before a vowel (as in *acetaldehyde*).

acetabulum /ˌasɪˈtabjʊləm/ ▶ **noun** (pl. **acetabula** /-lə/) **1** Anatomy the socket of the hip bone, into which the head of the femur fits.
2 Zoology any cup-shaped structure, especially a sucker.
– DERIVATIVES **acetabular** adjective.
– ORIGIN late Middle English (denoting a vinegar cup, hence a cup-shaped cavity): from Latin, from *acetum* 'vinegar' + *-abulum*, denoting a container.

acetal /ˈasɪtal/ ▶ **noun** Chemistry an organic compound formed by the condensation of two alcohol molecules with an aldehyde molecule. ● Acetals have the general formula $R^1CH(OR^2)_2$, where R^1 and R^2 are alkyl groups.
– ORIGIN mid 19th cent.: from **ACETIC ACID** + *al* from **ALCOHOL**.

acetaldehyde /ˌasɪtˈaldɪhʌɪd/ ▶ **noun** [mass noun] Chemistry a colourless volatile liquid aldehyde obtained by oxidizing ethanol. ● Alternative name: **ethanal**; chem. formula: CH_3CHO.

acetamide /əˈsiːtəmʌɪd, əˈsɛt-/ ▶ **noun** [mass noun] Chemistry the amide of acetic acid, a crystalline solid with a characteristic musty odour. ● Alternative name: **ethanamide**; chem. formula: CH_3CONH_2.
– ORIGIN mid 19th cent.: from **ACETYL** + **AMIDE**.

acetaminophen /əˌsiːtəˈmɪnəfɛn, əˌsɛtə-/ ▶ **noun** North American term for **PARACETAMOL**.
– ORIGIN 1960s: from para-*acetylaminophen*ol.

acetanilide /ˌasɪˈtanɪlʌɪd/ ▶ **noun** [mass noun] Chemistry a crystalline solid prepared by acetylation of aniline, used in dye manufacture. ● Chem. formula: $C_6H_5NHCOCH_3$.
– ORIGIN mid 19th cent.: from *acet(yl)* + *anil(ine)* + **-IDE**.

acetate /ˈasɪteɪt/ ▶ **noun 1** Chemistry a salt or ester of acetic acid, containing the anion CH_3COO^- or the group $-OOCCH_3$.
2 [mass noun] cellulose acetate, especially as used to make textile fibres or plastic: [as modifier] *acetate silk.* ■ [count noun] a transparency made of cellulose acetate film. ■ [count noun] a direct-cut recording disc coated with cellulose acetate.

acetic acid /əˈsiːtɪk, əˈsɛt-/ ▶ **noun** [mass noun] Chemistry the acid that gives vinegar its characteristic taste. The pure acid is a colourless viscous liquid or glassy solid. ● Alternative name: **ethanoic acid**; chem. formula: CH_3COOH.
– ORIGIN late 18th cent.: *acetic* from French *acétique*, from Latin *acetum* 'vinegar'.

acetic anhydride ▶ **noun** [mass noun] Chemistry the anhydride of acetic acid, a colourless pungent liquid used in making synthetic fibres. ● Chem. formula: $(CH_3CO)_2O$.

aceto- (also **acet-** before a vowel) ▶ **combining form** Chemistry representing **ACETIC ACID** or **ACETYL**.

acetobacter /əˌsiːtə(ʊ)ˈbaktə, ˌasɪtəʊ-/ ▶ **noun** [mass noun] bacteria that oxidize organic compounds to acetic acid, as in vinegar formation. ● Genus *Acetobacter*; Gram-negative oval or rod-shaped bacteria.
– ORIGIN modern Latin (genus name), from **ACETO-** + **BACTERIUM**.

acetogenic /əˌsiːtə(ʊ)ˈdʒɛnɪk, ˌasɪtəʊ-/ ▶ **adjective** (of bacteria) forming acetate or acetic acid as a product of metabolism.

acetonaemia /ˌasɪtə(ʊ)ˈniːmɪə/ ▶ **noun** another term for **KETOSIS**.

acetone /ˈasɪtəʊn/ ▶ **noun** [mass noun] Chemistry a colourless volatile liquid ketone made by oxidizing isopropanol, used as an organic solvent and synthetic reagent. ● Alternative name: **propanone**; chem. formula: CH_3COCH_3.
– ORIGIN mid 19th cent.: from **ACETIC ACID** + **-ONE**.

acetonitrile /əˌsiːtə(ʊ)ˈnʌɪtrʌɪl, ˌasɪtəʊ-/ ▶ **noun** [mass noun] Chemistry an odoriferous toxic liquid, used as a solvent in high-performance liquid chromatography. ● Alternative name: **methyl cyanide**; chem. formula: $CH_3C{\equiv}N$.

acetous /əˈsiːtəs/ ▶ **adjective** producing or resembling vinegar: *acetous fermentation.*
– ORIGIN late Middle English (rare before the late 18th cent.): from late Latin *acetosus* 'sour', from Latin *acetum* 'vinegar'.

acetyl /ˈasɪtʌɪl, -tɪl/ ▶ **noun** [as modifier] Chemistry of or denoting the acyl radical $-C(O)CH_3$, derived from acetic acid: *acetyl chloride* | *an acetyl group.*

acetylate /əˈsɛtɪleɪt/ ▶ **verb** [with obj.] (often as adj. **acetylated**) Chemistry introduce an acetyl group into (a molecule or compound): *the acetylated forms of chloramphenicol.*
– DERIVATIVES **acetylation** noun.

acetylcholine /ˌasɪtʌɪlˈkəʊliːn, -tɪl-/ ▶ **noun** [mass noun] Biochemistry a compound which occurs throughout the nervous system, in which it functions as a neurotransmitter.

acetylcholinesterase /ˌasɪtʌɪlˌkəʊlɪnˈɛstəreɪz, -tɪl-/ ▶ **noun** [mass noun] Biochemistry an enzyme that causes rapid hydrolysis of acetylcholine. Its action serves to stop excitation of a nerve after transmission of an impulse.

acetyl coenzyme A ▶ **noun** [mass noun] Biochemistry the acetyl ester of coenzyme A, involved as an acetylating agent in many biochemical processes.

acetylene /əˈsɛtɪliːn/ ▶ **noun** Chemistry a colourless pungent-smelling hydrocarbon gas, which burns with a bright flame, used in welding and formerly in lighting. ● Alternative name: **ethyne**; chem. formula: C_2H_2.
– ORIGIN mid 19th cent.: from **ACETIC ACID** + **-YL** + **-ENE**.

acetylide /əˈsɛtɪlʌɪd/ ▶ **noun** Chemistry a salt-like compound formed from acetylene and a metal, containing the anion $(C{\equiv}C)^{2-}$ or $HC{\equiv}C^-$. Acetylides are typically unstable or explosive.

acetylsalicylic acid /ˌasɪtʌɪlˌsalɪˈsɪlɪk, -tɪl-/ ▶ **noun** systematic chemical name for **ASPIRIN**.

ach /ɑːx/ ▶ **exclamation** dialect (chiefly Scottish) form of **AH**: *ach well, win some lose some.*
– ORIGIN late 15th cent.: Scottish Gaelic, Dutch, and German.

achaar ▶ **noun** variant spelling of **ACHAR**.

Achaea /əˈkiːə/ a region of ancient Greece on the north coast of the Peloponnese.

Achaean ▶ **adjective** relating to Achaea in ancient Greece. ■ literary (especially in Homeric contexts) Greek.
▶ **noun** an inhabitant of Achaea. ■ literary (especially in Homeric contexts) a Greek.

> The Achaeans were among the earliest Greek-speaking inhabitants of Greece, being established there well before the 12th century BC. Some scholars identify them with the Mycenaeans of the 14th–13th centuries BC. The Greek protagonists in the Trojan War are regularly called Achaeans in the *Iliad*, though this may have referred only to the leaders.

Achaemenid /əˈkiːmənɪd/ (also **Achaemenian** /ˌakɪˈmiːnɪən/) ▶ **adjective** relating to the dynasty ruling in Persia from Cyrus I to Darius III (553–330 BC).
▶ **noun** a member of the Achaemenid dynasty.
– ORIGIN from Greek *Akhaimenēs* 'Achaemenes' (the reputed ancestor of the dynasty) + **-ID³**.

achalasia /ˌakəˈleɪzɪə/ ▶ **noun** [mass noun] Medicine a condition in which the muscles of the lower part of the oesophagus fail to relax, preventing food from passing into the stomach.
– ORIGIN early 20th cent.: from **A-¹** 'without, not' + Greek *khalasis* 'loosening' (from *khalan* 'relax') + **-IA¹**.

achar /əˈtʃɑː, ˈatʃɑː/ (also **achaar**) ▶ **noun** [mass noun] (in Indian cookery) a type of pickle in which the food is preserved in spiced oil: *mango achar.*
– ORIGIN from Hindi *acār*, from Persian.

acharnement /əˈʃɑːnmɒ̃/ ▶ **noun** [mass noun] archaic bloodthirsty fury or ferocity.

– ORIGIN French, from *acharner* 'give a taste of flesh to a dog, falcon, etc.', from *charn*, archaic variant of *chair*, from Latin *caro, carn-* 'flesh'.

acharya /əˈtʃɑːrə/ ▸ **noun** (in South Asia) a Hindu or Buddhist spiritual teacher or leader. ▪ an influential mentor.
– ORIGIN early 19th cent.: from Sanskrit *ācārya* 'master, teacher'.

Achates /əˈkeɪtiːz/ Greek & Roman Mythology a companion of Aeneas. His loyalty to his friend was so exemplary as to become proverbial, hence the term *fidus Achates* ('faithful Achates').

ache ▸ **noun 1** a continuous or prolonged dull pain in a part of one's body: *the ache in her head worsened | a handful of salt in the bath water is good for* ***aches and pains*** | [mass noun] *he had stomach ache.*
2 [in sing.] an emotion experienced with painful or bittersweet intensity: *an ache in her heart.*
▸ **verb** [no obj.] **1** suffer from a continuous dull pain: *my legs ached from the previous day's exercise | I'm aching all over.*
2 feel intense sadness or compassion: *she sat still and silent, her heart aching | she looked so tired that my heart* ***ached for*** *her.*
3 feel an intense desire for: *she* ***ached for*** *his touch* | [with infinitive] *he was aching to get his hands on the ball.*
– ORIGIN Old English *æce* (noun), *acan* (verb). In Middle and early modern English the noun was spelled *atche* and rhymed with 'batch' and the verb was spelled and pronounced as it is today. The noun began to be pronounced like the verb around 1700. The modern spelling is largely due to Dr Johnson, who mistakenly assumed its derivation to be from Greek *akhos* 'pain'.

Achebe /əˈtʃeɪbi/, Chinua (b.1930), Nigerian novelist, poet, short-story writer, and essayist; born *Albert Chinualumgu*. His novels, such as *Things Fall Apart* (1958), show traditional African society in confrontation with European customs and values.

achene /əˈkiːn/ ▸ **noun** Botany a small, dry one-seeded fruit that does not open to release the seed.
– ORIGIN mid 19th cent.: from modern Latin *achaenium*, derived irregularly from *a-* 'not' + Greek *khainein* 'to gape'.

Achernar /ˈeɪkənɑː/ Astronomy the ninth brightest star in the sky and the brightest in the constellation Eridanus, visible only in the southern hemisphere.
– ORIGIN from Arabic, 'end of the river (i.e. Eridanus)'.

Acheron /ˈakərɒn/ Greek Mythology one of the rivers of Hades. ▪ literary hell.
– ORIGIN Latin, from Greek *Akherōn*.

Acheson /ˈatʃɪs(ə)n/, Dean (Gooderham) (1893–1971), American statesman, Secretary of State 1949–53. He was instrumental in the formation of NATO, and implemented the Marshall Plan and the Truman Doctrine.

Acheulian /əˈʃuːlɪən/ (also **Acheulean**) ▸ **adjective** Archaeology relating to or denoting the main Lower Palaeolithic culture in Europe (preceding the Mousterian) and a similar culture in Africa. It is represented by hand-axe industries, which are dated as a whole to about 1,500,000–150,000 years ago. See also **ABBEVILLIAN**. ▪ (as noun **the Acheulian**) the Acheulian culture or period.
– ORIGIN early 20th cent.: from French *Acheuléen*, from *St-Acheul* near Amiens in northern France, where objects from this culture were found.

achha /aˈtʃhɑː/ ▸ **exclamation** Indian **1** okay; all right.
2 is that so? (used in responses to indicate the speaker's surprise, joy, or doubt).
– ORIGIN from Hindi *acchā*.

achieve ▸ **verb** [with obj.] successfully bring about or reach (a desired objective or result) by effort, skill, or courage: *he achieved his ambition to become a press photographer | the killings achieved nothing* | [no obj.] *people striving to achieve.*
– DERIVATIVES **achievable** adjective.
– ORIGIN Middle English (in the sense 'complete successfully'): from Old French *achever* 'come or bring to a head', from *a chief* 'to a head'.

achievement ▸ **noun 1** a thing done successfully with effort, skill, or courage: *to reach this stage is a great achievement.*
2 [mass noun] the process or fact of achieving something: *the achievement of professional recognition | a sense of achievement.*
3 Heraldry a representation of a coat of arms with all the adjuncts to which a bearer of arms is entitled.

achiever ▸ **noun** a person who achieves a high or specified level of success.

achillea /ˌakɪˈliːə, əˈkɪlɪə/ ▸ **noun** a Eurasian and North African plant of a genus that includes the yarrow, typically having heads of small white or yellow flowers and fern-like leaves. ● Genus *Achillea*, family Compositae: numerous species.
– ORIGIN via Latin from Greek *Akhilleios*, denoting a plant supposed to have been used medicinally by Achilles.

Achilles /əˈkɪliːz/ Greek Mythology a hero of the Trojan War, son of Peleus and Thetis. During his infancy his mother plunged him in the Styx, thus making his body invulnerable except for the heel by which she held him. During the Trojan War Achilles killed Hector but was later wounded in the heel by an arrow shot by Paris and died.

Achilles heel ▸ **noun** a weakness or vulnerable point.
– ORIGIN early 19th cent.: alluding to the vulnerability of **ACHILLES**.

Achilles tendon ▸ **noun** the tendon connecting calf muscles to the heel.

achimenes /əˈkɪmɪniːz/ ▸ **noun** (pl. **same**) a Central American plant with tubular or trumpet-shaped flowers. ● Genus *Achimenes*, family Gesneriaceae.
– ORIGIN modern Latin, either from Greek *akhaimenis*, denoting a different plant (euphorbia), or from *a-* 'not' + *kheimanein* 'expose to the cold'.

Achinese /ˈatʃɪniːz/ ▸ **noun** (pl. **same**) **1** a member of a people living in northern Sumatra.
2 [mass noun] the Indonesian language of the Achinese.
▸ **adjective** relating to the Achinese or their language.
– ORIGIN from *Acheh, Atjeh*, a territory in northern Sumatra, + *-n-* + **-ESE**.

aching ▸ **adjective 1** having an ache in a part of one's body: *the cool air was a relief to my aching head.*
2 feeling intense or wistful sadness; sorrowful: *an aching feeling of nostalgia.*
– DERIVATIVES **achingly** adverb [as submodifier] *a sound which was achingly familiar to me.*

achiote /ˌatʃɪˈɒti/ ▸ **noun** North American term for **ANNATTO**.
– ORIGIN mid 17th cent.: from Spanish, from Nahuatl *achiotl*.

achiral /eɪˈkʌɪr(ə)l/ ▸ **adjective** Chemistry (chiefly of a molecule) symmetric in such a way that it can be superimposed on its mirror image; not chiral.

achkan /ˈatʃkən/ ▸ **noun** a knee-length coat buttoned in front, worn by men from South Asia.
– ORIGIN from Hindi *ackan*.

achlorhydria /ˌeɪklɔːˈhʌɪdrɪə, ˌaklɔː-/ ▸ **noun** [mass noun] Medicine absence of hydrochloric acid in the gastric secretions.
– ORIGIN late 19th cent.: from **A-**[1] 'without' + **CHLOR-** + **HYDRO-** + **-IA**[1].

Acholi /əˈtʃəʊli/ ▸ **noun** (pl. **same**) **1** a member of a farming and pastoral people of northern Uganda and southern Sudan.
2 [mass noun] the Nilotic language of the Acholi.
▸ **adjective** relating to the Acholi or their language.
– ORIGIN the name in Acholi.

achondrite /əˈkɒndrʌɪt/ ▸ **noun** a stony meteorite containing no small mineral granules (chondrules).
– DERIVATIVES **achondritic** adjective.
– ORIGIN early 20th cent.: from **A-**[1] 'without' + **CHONDRITE**.

achondroplasia /əˌkɒndrə(ʊ)ˈpleɪzɪə, eɪ-/ ▸ **noun** [mass noun] a hereditary condition in which the growth of long bones by ossification of cartilage is retarded, resulting in very short limbs and sometimes a face which is small in relation to the skull.
– DERIVATIVES **achondroplasic** adjective, **achondroplastic** adjective.
– ORIGIN late 19th cent.: from **A-**[1] 'without' + Greek *khondros* 'cartilage' + *plasis* 'moulding' + **-IA**[1].

achromat /ˈakrə(ʊ)mat/ ▸ **noun** a lens that transmits light without separating it into constituent colours.

achromatic /ˌakrə(ʊ)ˈmatɪk/ ▸ **adjective 1** relating to, using, or denoting lenses that transmit light without separating it into constituent colours.
2 literary without colour: *the achromatic gloom.*
– ORIGIN late 18th cent.: via French from Greek *a-* 'without' + *khrōmatikos* (from *khrōma* 'colour').

achy (also **achey**) ▸ **adjective** (**achier, achiest**) suffering from continuous dull pain: *she felt tired and achy.*
– DERIVATIVES **achiness** noun.

acicular /əˈsɪkjʊlə/ ▸ **adjective** technical (chiefly of crystals) needle-shaped.
– ORIGIN early 18th cent.: from late Latin *acicula* 'small needle' (diminutive of *acus*) + **-AR**[1].

acid ▸ **noun 1** a substance with particular chemical properties including turning litmus red, neutralizing alkalis, and dissolving some metals; typically, a corrosive or sour-tasting liquid of this kind. Often contrasted with **ALKALI** and **BASE**[1]. ▪ [mass noun] bitter or cutting remarks or tone of voice: *she was unable to quell the acid in her voice.*
2 Chemistry a molecule or other species which can donate a proton or accept an electron pair in reactions.
3 [mass noun] informal the drug LSD.

> Acids are compounds which release hydrogen ions (H^+) when dissolved in water. Any solution with a pH of less than 7 is acidic, strong acids such as sulphuric or hydrochloric acid having a pH as low as 1 or 2.

▸ **adjective 1** containing acid or having the properties of an acid; having a pH of less than 7: *acid soils.* Often contrasted with **ALKALINE** or **BASIC**.
2 sharp-tasting or sour: *acid fruit.* ▪ (of a person's remarks or tone) bitter or cutting: *she was stung into acid defiance.* ▪ (of a colour) strikingly intense or bright: *an acid green.*
3 Geology (of rock, especially lava) containing a relatively high proportion of silica. ▪ Metallurgy relating to or denoting steel-making processes involving silica-rich refractories and slags.
– PHRASES **put the acid on** Austral./NZ informal seek to extract a loan or favour from (someone). [*acid* from **ACID TEST**, referring to possible resistance (because gold resists nitric acid).]
– DERIVATIVES **acidy** adjective.
– ORIGIN early 17th cent. (in the sense 'sour-tasting'): from Latin *acidus*, from *acere* 'be sour'.

acid drop ▸ **noun** Brit. a kind of boiled sweet with a sharp taste.

acid-fast ▸ **adjective** Microbiology denoting bacteria that cannot be decolorized by an acid after staining, which is characteristic of the mycobacteria that cause tuberculosis and leprosy.

acid head ▸ **noun** informal a habitual user of the drug LSD.

acid house ▸ **noun** [mass noun] a kind of popular synthesized dance music with a fast repetitive beat, popular in the 1980s and associated with the taking of drugs such as Ecstasy.

acidic ▸ **adjective 1** having the properties of an acid, or containing acid; having a pH below 7. Often contrasted with **ALKALINE** and **BASIC**.
2 sharp-tasting or sour: *acidic wine.* ▪ (of a person's remarks or tone) bitter or cutting: *the occasional acidic comment.* ▪ (of a colour) strikingly intense or bright: *an acidic yellow.*
3 Geology (of rock, especially lava) relatively rich in silica. ▪ Metallurgy relating to or denoting steel-making processes involving silica-rich refractories and slags.

acidify /əˈsɪdɪfʌɪ/ ▸ **verb** (**acidifies, acidifying, acidified**) make or become acid: [with obj.] *pollutants can acidify surface water.*
– DERIVATIVES **acidification** noun.

acidity ▸ **noun** [mass noun] **1** the level of acid in substances such as water, soil, or wine. ▪ the level of acid in the gastric juices, typically when excessive and causing discomfort.
2 bitterness or sharpness in a person's remarks or tone: *the cutting acidity in his voice.*

acid jazz ▸ **noun** [mass noun] a kind of popular dance music incorporating elements of jazz, funk, soul, and hip hop.
– ORIGIN apparently coined from **ACID HOUSE** and popularized by the *Acid Jazz* record label founded in 1988.

acidly ▸ **adverb** with bitterness or sarcasm: *'Is it up to you to make that decision?' she asked acidly.*

acidophil /əˈsɪdə(ʊ)fɪl/ ▸ **noun** Physiology an acidophilic white blood cell.

acidophilic /ˌasɪdə(ʊ)ˈfɪlɪk, əˌsɪd-/ ▸ **adjective** Biology
1 (of a cell or its contents) readily stained with acid dyes.
2 (of a microorganism or plant) growing best in acidic conditions.

acidophilus /ˌasɪˈdɒfɪləs/ ▸ **noun** [mass noun] a bacterium that is used to make yogurt and to supplement the intestinal flora. ● *Lactobacillus acidophilus*; a Gram-positive rod-shaped bacterium.
– ORIGIN 1920s: modern Latin, literally 'acid-loving'.

acidosis /ˌasɪˈdəʊsɪs/ ▸ **noun** [mass noun] Medicine an excessively acid condition of the body fluids or tissues.
– DERIVATIVES **acidotic** adjective.

A

acid rain ▸ **noun** [mass noun] rainfall made so acidic by atmospheric pollution that it causes environmental harm, chiefly to forests and lakes. The main cause is the industrial burning of coal and other fossil fuels, the waste gases from which contain sulphur and nitrogen oxides which combine with atmospheric water to form acids.

acid rock ▸ **noun** [mass noun] a style of rock music popular chiefly in the late 1960s, associated with or inspired by hallucinogenic drugs.

acid salt ▸ **noun** Chemistry a salt formed by incomplete replacement of the hydrogen of an acid, e.g. potassium hydrogen sulphate ($KHSO_4$).

acid test ▸ **noun** [in sing.] a conclusive test of the success or value of something: *gritstone is the acid test of a climber's ability*.
– ORIGIN figuratively, from the original use denoting a test for gold using nitric acid.

acidulate /əˈsɪdjʊleɪt/ ▸ **verb** [with obj.] (usu. as adj. **acidulated**) make slightly acidic: *acidulated water*.
– ORIGIN mid 18th cent.: from Latin *acidulus* (from *acidus* 'sour') + **-ATE³**.

acidulous /əˈsɪdjʊləs/ ▸ **adjective** sharp-tasting; sour. ■ (of a person's remarks or tone) bitter; cutting.
– ORIGIN mid 18th cent.: from Latin *acidulus* (from *acidus* 'sour') + **-OUS**.

acinus /ˈasɪnəs/ ▸ **noun** (pl. **acini** /-nʌɪ/) Anatomy **1** a small sac-like cavity in a gland, surrounded by secretory cells.
2 a region of the lung supplied with air from one of the terminal bronchioles.
– DERIVATIVES **acinar** adjective.
– ORIGIN mid 18th cent.: Latin, literally 'a kernel'.

-acious ▸ **suffix** (forming adjectives) inclined to; having as a capacity: *audacious* | *capacious*.
– ORIGIN from Latin *-ax*, *-ac-* (especially forming adjectives from verbal stems) + **-OUS**.

-acity ▸ **suffix** forming nouns of quality or state corresponding to adjectives ending in *-acious* (such as *audacity* corresponding to *audacious*).
– ORIGIN from French *-acité* or Latin *-acitas*.

ack-ack ▸ **noun** [mass noun] [usu. as modifier] Military, informal anti-aircraft gunfire: *a quick burst of ack-ack fire*.
– ORIGIN signallers' name for the letters *AA*; *ack* for *A* was replaced in military use by *able* in 1942.

ackee /ˈaki/ (also **akee**) ▸ **noun** a tropical West African tree which is cultivated for its fruit and has been introduced into the Caribbean and elsewhere. ● *Blighia sapida*, family Sapindaceae.
■ [mass noun] the fruit of the ackee, which is eaten as a vegetable but is poisonous until fully ripe.
– ORIGIN late 18th cent.: from Kru *ākee*.

ack emma ▸ **adverb** Brit. dated informal term for **A.M.**
– ORIGIN First World War: signallers' name for these letters.

ackers /ˈakəz/ ▸ **plural noun** Brit. informal money.
– ORIGIN 1930s (originally used by British troops in Egypt as a name for the piastre): probably an alteration of Arabic *fakka* 'small change, coins'.

acknowledge ▸ **verb 1** [reporting verb] accept or admit the existence or truth of: [with obj.] *the plight of the refugees was acknowledged by the authorities* | [with clause] *the government* ***acknowledged that*** *the tax was unfair* | [with direct speech] *'That's true,' she acknowledged.*
2 [with obj.] recognize the importance or quality of: *the art world has begun to acknowledge his genius* | *the hotel is widely* ***acknowledged as*** *one of Cornwall's finest*. ■ express gratitude for or appreciation of: *he received a letter acknowledging his services*. ■ accept the validity or legitimacy of: *Henry acknowledged Richard as his heir*.
3 [with obj.] show that one has noticed or recognized (someone) by making a gesture or greeting: *she refused to acknowledge my presence*. ■ confirm (receipt of something).
– DERIVATIVES **acknowledgeable** adjective.
– ORIGIN late 15th cent.: from the obsolete Middle English verb *knowledge*, influenced by obsolete *acknow* 'acknowledge, confess'.

acknowledged ▸ **adjective** recognized as being good or important: *he's an acknowledged expert in the field*. ■ accepted as valid or legitimate: *Prince Louis's acknowledged heir*.

acknowledgement (also chiefly US **acknowledgment**) ▸ **noun** [mass noun] **1** acceptance of the truth or existence of something: *there was no acknowledgement of the family's trauma*.
2 recognition of the importance or quality of something. ■ the expression of gratitude or appreciation for something: *he received an award* ***in acknowledgement of*** *his work*. ■ the action of showing that one has noticed someone or something: *he touched his hat* ***in acknowledgement***. ■ [count noun] a letter confirming receipt of something.
3 (**acknowledgements**) a statement printed at the beginning of a book expressing the author's or publisher's gratitude to others.

ACL ▸ **abbreviation** anterior cruciate ligament.

aclinic line /əˈklɪnɪk/ ▸ **noun** another term for **MAGNETIC EQUATOR**.
– ORIGIN mid 19th cent.: *aclinic* from Greek *aklinēs*, from *a-* 'not' + *klinein* 'to bend'.

ACLU ▸ **abbreviation** American Civil Liberties Union.

acme /ˈakmi/ ▸ **noun** [in sing.] the point at which something is at its best or most highly developed: *physics is the acme of scientific knowledge*.
– ORIGIN late 16th cent.: from Greek *akmē* 'highest point'. Until the 18th cent. it was often consciously used as a Greek word and written in Greek letters.

Acmeist /ˈakmiːɪst/ ▸ **adjective** relating to or denoting an early 20th-century movement in Russian poetry which rejected the values of symbolism in favour of formal technique and clarity of exposition. Notable members were Anna Akhmatova and Osip Mandelstam.
▸ **noun** a member of the Acmeist movement.
– DERIVATIVES **Acmeism** noun.

acne ▸ **noun** [mass noun] a skin condition characterized by red pimples on the skin, especially on the face, due to inflamed or infected sebaceous glands and prevalent chiefly among adolescents.
– DERIVATIVES **acned** adjective.
– ORIGIN mid 19th cent.: via modern Latin from Greek *aknas*, a misreading of *akmas*, accusative plural of *akmē* 'highest point, peak, or facial eruption'; compare with **ACME**.

acne rosacea ▸ **noun** another term for **ROSACEA**.

Acol /ˈakɒl/ ▸ **noun** Bridge a British system of bidding designed to enable partners with weaker hands to find suitable contracts.
– ORIGIN 1930s: from *Acol* Road in Hampstead, London, the address of a house in which the system was devised.

acolyte /ˈakəlʌɪt/ ▸ **noun** a person assisting a priest in a religious service or procession. ■ an assistant or follower.
– ORIGIN Middle English: from Old French *acolyt* or ecclesiastical Latin *acolytus*, from Greek *akolouthos* 'follower'.

Aconcagua /ˌakɒnˈkɑːɡwə/ an extinct volcano in the Andes, on the border between Chile and Argentina, rising to 6,960 m (22,834 ft). It is the highest mountain in the western hemisphere.

aconite /ˈakənʌɪt/ ▸ **noun 1** a poisonous plant of the buttercup family, bearing hooded pink or purple flowers and found in temperate regions of the northern hemisphere. ● Genus *Aconitum*, family Ranunculaceae: many species, including monkshood and wolfsbane.
■ [mass noun] an extract of aconite, used as a poison or in pharmacy.
2 (also **winter aconite**) a small herbaceous Eurasian plant, cultivated for its yellow flowers in early spring. ● Genus *Eranthis*, family Ranunculaceae: several species.
– ORIGIN mid 16th cent.: via French and Latin from Greek *akoniton*.

aconitine /əˈkɒnɪtiːn/ ▸ **noun** [mass noun] Chemistry a poisonous alkaloid obtained from monkshood and related plants.

acorn ▸ **noun** the fruit of the oak, a smooth oval nut in a rough cup-like base.
– ORIGIN Old English *æcern*, of Germanic origin; related to Dutch *aker*, also to **ACRE**, later associated with **OAK** and **CORN¹**.

acorn barnacle ▸ **noun** a stalkless barnacle that attaches itself to a variety of surfaces including rocks, ships, and marine animals. ● Genus *Balanus*, family Balanidae.

acorn squash ▸ **noun** a winter squash of a variety with ridged dark green to orange rind and yellow flesh.

acorn worm ▸ **noun** a burrowing worm-like marine animal of shallow waters. Its body consists of a proboscis, a collar, and a long trunk with gill slits, and contains a structure resembling a notochord. ● Class Enteropneusta, phylum Hemichordata.

acotyledon /əˌkɒtɪˈliːd(ə)n/ ▸ **noun** Botany a plant with no distinct seed leaves, especially a fern or moss.
– DERIVATIVES **acotyledonous** adjective.
– ORIGIN mid 18th cent.: from modern Latin plural *acotyledones* (see **A-¹**, **COTYLEDON**).

acouchi /əˈkuːʃi/ ▸ **noun** (pl. **acouchis**) a large forest rodent resembling an agouti, found in the Amazon basin. ● Genus *Myoprocta*, family Dasyproctidae: two species.
– ORIGIN late 18th cent.: from French, from Tupi.

acoustic /əˈkuːstɪk/ ▸ **adjective 1** relating to sound or the sense of hearing: *dogs have a much greater acoustic range than humans*. ■ (of building materials) used for soundproofing or modifying sound: *acoustic tiles*. ■ (of a device or system) utilizing sound energy in its operation. ■ (of an explosive mine or other weapon) able to be set off by sound waves.
2 (of popular music or musical instruments) not having electrical amplification: *an acoustic guitar*.
▸ **noun 1** (also **acoustics**) the properties or qualities of a room or building that determine how sound is transmitted in it: *the Symphony Hall has perfect acoustics*.
2 (**acoustics**) [treated as sing.] the branch of physics concerned with the properties of sound.
3 a guitar without electrical amplification.
– DERIVATIVES **acoustical** adjective, **acoustically** adverb.
– ORIGIN mid 17th cent.: from Greek *akoustikos*, from *akouein* 'hear'.

acoustic coupler ▸ **noun** a modem which converts digital signals into audible signals and vice versa so that they can be transmitted and received over telephone lines.

acoustician /ˌakuːˈstɪʃ(ə)n/ ▸ **noun** an expert in the branch of physics concerned with the properties of sound.

acoustic impedance ▸ **noun** Physics the ratio of the pressure over an imaginary surface in a sound wave to the rate of particle flow across the surface.

acoustic shock ▸ **noun** [mass noun] damaged hearing suffered by the user of an earphone as a result of sudden excessive noise in the device.

acquaint ▸ **verb** [with obj.] (**acquaint someone with**) make someone aware of or familiar with: *new staff should be acquainted with fire exit routes* | *you need to acquaint yourself with the house style*. ■ (**be acquainted**) know someone slightly: *I am not* ***acquainted with*** *any young lady of that name* | *I'll leave you two to* ***get acquainted***.
– ORIGIN Middle English: from Old French *acointier* 'make known', from late Latin *accognitare*, from Latin *accognoscere*, from *ad-* 'to' + *cognoscere* 'come to know'.

acquaintance ▸ **noun 1** [mass noun] knowledge or experience of something: *the pupils had little* ***acquaintance with*** *the language*. ■ slight knowledge of or friendship with someone: *I renewed my* ***acquaintance with*** *Herbert*.
2 a person one knows slightly, but who is not a close friend: *a wide circle of friends and acquaintances*.
■ [mass noun] acquaintances considered collectively: *his extensive acquaintance included Oscar Wilde and Yeats*.
– PHRASES **make the acquaintance of** (or **make someone's acquaintance**) meet someone for the first time and come to know them slightly.
– DERIVATIVES **acquaintanceship** noun.
– ORIGIN Middle English (in the sense 'mutual knowledge, being acquainted'): from Old French *acointance*, from *acointier* 'make known' (see **ACQUAINT**).

acquaintance rape ▸ **noun** [mass noun] chiefly N. Amer. rape by a person who is known to the victim.

acquiesce /ˌakwɪˈɛs/ ▸ **verb** [no obj.] accept something reluctantly but without protest: *Sara* ***acquiesced in*** *his decision*.
– ORIGIN early 17th cent.: from Latin *acquiescere*, from *ad-* 'to, at' + *quiescere* 'to rest'.

acquiescence ▸ **noun** [mass noun] the reluctant acceptance of something without protest: *in silent acquiescence, she rose to her feet*.

acquiescent ▸ **adjective** ready to accept something without protest, or to do what someone else wants: *his acquiescent mood*.
– ORIGIN early 17th cent.: from Latin *acquiescent-* 'remaining at rest', from the verb *acquiescere* (see **ACQUIESCE**).

acquire ▸ **verb** [with obj.] **1** buy or obtain (an asset or object) for oneself: *I managed to acquire all the books I needed*.
2 learn or develop (a skill, habit, or quality): *I've acquired a taste for whisky*. ■ come to have (a particular reputation) as a result of one's behaviour or activities.

– PHRASES **an acquired taste** a thing that one comes to like over time: *pumpkin pie is an acquired taste.*
– DERIVATIVES **acquirable** adjective, **acquiree** noun (Finance), **acquirer** noun.
– ORIGIN late Middle English *acquere*, from Old French *aquerre*, based on Latin *acquirere* 'get in addition', from *ad-* 'to' + *quaerere* 'seek'. The English spelling was modified (*c.*1600) by association with the Latin word.

acquired character (also **acquired characteristic**) ▶ noun Biology a modification or change in an organ or tissue that is due to use, disuse, or environmental effects during an organism's lifetime.

acquired immune deficiency syndrome ▶ noun see **AIDS**.

acquirement ▶ noun [mass noun] the action of acquiring something: *the acquirement of self control.* ■ [count noun] something acquired, typically a skill.

acquisition /ˌakwɪˈzɪʃ(ə)n/ ▶ noun **1** an asset or object bought or obtained, typically by a library or museum. ■ a purchase of one company by another. ■ [mass noun] the buying or obtaining of assets or objects: *western culture places a high value on material acquisition.*
2 [mass noun] the learning or developing of a skill, habit, or quality: *the acquisition of management skills.*
– ORIGIN late Middle English (in the sense 'act of acquiring something'): from Latin *acquisitio(n-)*, from the verb *acquirere* (see **ACQUIRE**).

acquisition accounting ▶ noun [mass noun] a procedure in accounting in which the value of the assets of a company is changed from book to fair market level after a takeover.

acquisitive ▶ adjective excessively interested in acquiring money or material things.
– DERIVATIVES **acquisitively** adverb.
– ORIGIN mid 19th cent.: from French *acquisitif, -ive*, from late Latin *acquisitivus*. from Latin *acquisit-* 'acquired', from the verb *acquirere* (see **ACQUIRE**).

acquisitiveness ▶ noun [mass noun] excessive interest in acquiring money or material things: *a culture of acquisitiveness permeated his administration.*

acquit ▶ verb (**acquits, acquitting, acquitted**) **1** [with obj.] free (someone) from a criminal charge by a verdict of not guilty: *she was acquitted on all counts | the jury* ***acquitted*** *Bream* ***of*** *murder.*
2 (**acquit oneself**) conduct oneself or perform in a specified way: *the goalkeeper acquitted himself well.* ■ (**acquit oneself of**) archaic discharge (a duty or responsibility).
– ORIGIN Middle English (originally in the sense 'pay a debt, discharge a liability'): from Old French *acquiter*, from medieval Latin *acquitare* 'pay a debt', from *ad-* 'to' + *quitare* 'set free'.

acquittal ▶ noun a judgement or verdict that a person is not guilty of the crime with which they have been charged.

acquittance ▶ noun Law a written receipt attesting the settlement of a fine or debt.
– ORIGIN Middle English: from Old French, from *aquiter* 'discharge (a debt)' (see **ACQUIT**).

acrasia ▶ noun variant spelling of **AKRASIA**.

Acre 1 /ˈeɪkə/ an industrial seaport of Israel; pop. 46,300 (est. 2008). Also called **Akko**.
2 /ˈɑːkrə/ a state of western Brazil, on the border with Peru; capital, Rio Branco.

acre /ˈeɪkə/ ▶ noun a unit of land area equal to 4,840 square yards (0.405 hectare). ■ (**acres of**) informal a large extent or amount of something: *acres of space.*
– DERIVATIVES **acred** adjective [in combination] *a many-acred park.*
– ORIGIN Old English *æcer* (denoting the amount of land a yoke of oxen could plough in a day), of Germanic origin; related to Dutch *akker* and German *Acker* 'field', from an Indo-European root shared by Sanskrit *ajra* 'field', Latin *ager*, and Greek *agros*.

acreage /ˈeɪk(ə)rɪdʒ/ ▶ noun [mass noun] an area of land, typically when used for agricultural purposes, but not necessarily measured in acres: *a 35 per cent increase in net acreage* | [count noun] *a modest acreage.*

acre-foot ▶ noun (pl. **acre-feet**) a unit of volume equal to the volume of a sheet of water one acre (0.405 hectare) in area and one foot (30.48 cm) in depth; 43,560 cubic feet (1233.5 cubic metres).

acrid /ˈakrɪd/ ▶ adjective unpleasantly bitter or pungent: *acrid smoke | an acrid smell.*
– DERIVATIVES **acridity** noun, **acridly** adverb.
– ORIGIN early 18th cent.: formed irregularly from Latin *acer, acri-* 'sharp, pungent' + **-ID**[1], probably influenced by *acid.*

acridine /ˈakrɪdiːn/ ▶ noun [mass noun] Chemistry a colourless solid compound obtained from coal tar, used in the manufacture of dyes and drugs. ● Chem. formula: $C_{13}H_9N$.
– ORIGIN late 19th cent.: coined in German from **ACRID** + **-INE**[4].

acriflavine /ˌakrɪˈfleɪvɪn, -iːn/ ▶ noun [mass noun] a bright orange-red dye derived from acridine, used as an antiseptic.
– ORIGIN early 20th cent.: formed irregularly from **ACRIDINE** + Latin *flavus* 'yellow' + **-INE**[4].

Acrilan /ˈakrɪlan/ ▶ noun [mass noun] trademark a synthetic acrylic textile fibre.
– ORIGIN 1950s: from **ACRYLIC** + Latin *lana* 'wool'.

acrimonious /ˌakrɪˈməʊnɪəs/ ▶ adjective (typically of speech or discussion) angry and bitter: *an acrimonious dispute about wages.*
– DERIVATIVES **acrimoniously** adverb.
– ORIGIN early 17th cent. (in the sense 'bitter, pungent'): from **ACRIMONY** + **-OUS**.

acrimony /ˈakrɪməni/ ▶ noun [mass noun] bitterness or ill feeling: *the AGM dissolved into acrimony.*
– ORIGIN mid 16th cent. (in the sense 'bitter taste or smell'): from French *acrimonie* or Latin *acrimonia*, from *acer, acri-* 'pungent, acrid'.

acrobat ▶ noun an entertainer who performs spectacular gymnastic feats.
– ORIGIN early 19th cent.: from French *acrobate*, from Greek *akrobatēs*, from *akrobatos* 'walking on tiptoe', from *akron* 'tip' + *bainein* 'to walk'.

acrobatic ▶ adjective performing, involving, or adept at spectacular gymnastic feats: *an acrobatic dive.*
– DERIVATIVES **acrobatically** adverb.

acrobatics ▶ plural noun [usu. treated as sing.] spectacular gymnastic feats.

acrocyanosis /ˌakrə(ʊ)sʌɪəˈnəʊsɪs/ ▶ noun [mass noun] Medicine a condition marked by bluish or purple colouring of the hands and feet, caused by slow circulation.
– ORIGIN late 19th cent.: from Greek *akron* 'tip' + **CYANOSIS**.

acrolect /ˈakrə(ʊ)lɛkt/ ▶ noun Linguistics the most prestigious dialect or variety of a particular language. Contrasted with **BASILECT**.
– DERIVATIVES **acrolectal** adjective.
– ORIGIN 1960s: from Greek *akron* 'summit' + *-lect* as in *dialect.*

acromegaly /ˌakrə(ʊ)ˈmɛgəli/ ▶ noun [mass noun] Medicine abnormal growth of the hands, feet, and face, caused by overproduction of growth hormone by the pituitary gland.
– DERIVATIVES **acromegalic** /-mɪˈgalɪk/ adjective.
– ORIGIN late 19th cent.: coined in French from Greek *akron* 'tip, extremity' + *megas, megal-* 'great'.

acronym /ˈakrənɪm/ ▶ noun an abbreviation formed from the initial letters of other words and pronounced as a word (e.g. *ASCII, NASA*).
– ORIGIN 1940s: from Greek *akron* 'end, tip' + **-ONYM**.

acropetal /əˈkrɒpɪt(ə)l/ ▶ adjective Botany (of growth or development) upwards from the base or point of attachment. The opposite of **BASIPETAL**. ■ (of the movement of dissolved substances) outwards towards the shoot and root apices.
– DERIVATIVES **acropetally** adverb.
– ORIGIN late 19th cent.: from Greek *akron* 'tip' + Latin *petere* 'seek' + **-AL**.

acrophobia /ˌakrəˈfəʊbɪə/ ▶ noun [mass noun] extreme or irrational fear of heights.
– DERIVATIVES **acrophobic** adjective.
– ORIGIN late 19th cent.: from Greek *akron* 'summit' + **-PHOBIA**.

acropolis /əˈkrɒpəlɪs/ ▶ noun a citadel or fortified part of an ancient Greek city, typically one built on a hill. ■ (**the Acropolis**) the ancient citadel at Athens, containing the Parthenon and other notable buildings, mostly dating from the 5th century BC.
– ORIGIN Greek, from *akron* 'summit' + *polis* 'city'.

across ▶ preposition & adverb **1** from one side to the other of (a place, area, etc.): [as prep.] *I ran across the street | travelling across Europe* | [as adv.] *he had swum across.* ■ [as adv.] used with an expression of measurement: *mounds some 30 metres across.*
2 expressing position or orientation: [as prep.] *they lived across the street from one another | the bridge across the river* | [as adv.] *he looked across at me | halfway across, Jenny jumped.*
3 [as adv.] referring to a crossword answer which reads horizontally: *19 across.*
– PHRASES **across the board 1** applying to all: *the cutbacks might be across the board.* **2** US (in horse racing) denoting a bet in which equal amounts are staked on the same horse to win, place, or show in a race. **across from** opposite: *she sat across from me.* **be** (or **get**) **across something** fully understand all the details of an issue or situation.
– ORIGIN Middle English (as an adverb meaning 'in the form of a cross'): from Old French *a croix, en croix* 'in or on a cross', later regarded as being from **A-**[2] + **CROSS**.

acrostic /əˈkrɒstɪk/ ▶ noun a poem, word puzzle, or other composition in which certain letters in each line form a word or words.
– ORIGIN late 16th cent.: from French *acrostiche*, from Greek *akrostikhis*, from *akron* 'end' + *stikhos* 'row, line of verse'. The change in the ending was due to association with **-IC**.

Acrux /ˈeɪkrʌks/ Astronomy the star Alpha Crucis, which is the brightest star in the southern constellation Crux and the twelfth brightest in the sky.
– ORIGIN from *A* for alpha + **CRUX**.

acrylamide /əˈkrɪləmʌɪd/ ▶ noun [mass noun] Chemistry a colourless crystalline solid which readily forms water-soluble polymers. ● The amide of acrylic acid; chem. formula: $CH_2{=}CHCONH_2$.
– ORIGIN late 19th cent.: from **ACRYLIC** + **AMIDE**.

acrylate /ˈakrɪleɪt/ ▶ noun Chemistry a salt or ester of acrylic acid.

acrylic /əˈkrɪlɪk/ ▶ adjective (of synthetic resins and textile fibres) made from polymers of acrylic acid or acrylates: *a red acrylic jumper.* ■ (of paint) based on acrylic resin as a medium: *acrylic colours.*
▶ noun **1** [mass noun] an acrylic textile fibre: *a sweater in four-ply acrylic.*
2 (often **acrylics**) an acrylic paint.
– ORIGIN mid 19th cent.: from the liquid aldehyde *acrolein* (from Latin *acer, acri-* 'pungent' + *ol(eum)* 'oil' + **-IN**[1]) + **-YL** + **-IC**.

acrylic acid ▶ noun [mass noun] Chemistry a pungent liquid organic acid which can be polymerized to make synthetic resins. ● Alternative name: **propenoic acid**; chem. formula: $CH_2CH{=}COOH$.

acrylonitrile /ˌakrɪlə(ʊ)ˈnʌɪtrʌɪl/ ▶ noun [mass noun] Chemistry a pungent, toxic liquid, used in making artificial fibres and other polymers. ● The nitrile of acrylic acid; chem. formula: $CH_2{=}CHCN$.

ACT ▶ abbreviation ■ advance corporation tax. ■ Australian Capital Territory.

act ▶ verb [no obj.] **1** take action; do something: *they urged Washington to act* | [with infinitive] *governments must act to reduce pollution.* ■ (**act on**) take action according to or in the light of: *I shall certainly act on his suggestion.* ■ (**act for**) take action in order to bring about: *one's ability to act for community change.* ■ (**act for/on behalf of**) represent (someone) on a contractual, legal, or paid basis: *he chose a solicitor to act for him.* ■ (**act from/out of**) be motivated by: *you acted from greed.*
2 [with adverbial] behave in the way specified: *they challenged a man who was seen acting suspiciously | he* ***acts as if*** *he owned the place | try to* ***act like*** *civilized adults.*
3 (**act as**) fulfil the function or serve the purpose of: *they need volunteers to act as foster-parents | a day-care centre which will act as a meeting place.*
4 take effect; have a particular effect: *bacteria act on proteins and sugar.*
5 perform a role in a play, film, or television: *she acted in her first professional role at the age of six* | [with obj.] *he acted the role of the king.* ■ [with complement] behave so as to appear to be; pretend to be: *I acted dumb at first.* ■ [with obj.] (**act something out**) perform a narrative as if it were a play: *encouraging pupils to act out the stories.* ■ [with obj.] (**act something out**) Psychoanalysis express repressed emotion or impulses in overt behaviour as a defensive substitute for conscious recall, typical of some behavioural disorders.
▶ noun **1** a thing done; a deed: *a criminal act | the act of writing down one's thoughts | an act of heroism.* ■ (**Acts** or **Acts of the Apostles**) a New Testament book immediately following the Gospels and relating the history of the early Church.
2 [in sing.] a pretence: *she was putting on an act and laughing a lot.* ■ [with adj. or noun modifier] a particular type of behaviour or routine: *he did his Sir Galahad act.*
3 (usu. **Act** or **Act of Parliament**) a written law passed by Parliament, Congress, etc.: *the 1989 Children Act.* ■ a document attesting a legal transaction. ■ (**acts**) dated the recorded decisions or proceedings of a committee or an academic body.

A

4 a main division of a play, ballet, or opera: *the first act.* ▪ a set performance: *her one-woman poetry act.* ▪ a performing group: *an act called the Apple Blossom Sisters.*
– PHRASES **act of God** an instance of uncontrollable natural forces in operation. **act of grace** a privilege or concession that cannot be claimed as a right. **catch someone in the act** surprise someone in the process of doing something wrong: *the thieves were caught in the act.* **clean up one's act** behave in a more acceptable manner. **get one's act together** informal galvanize oneself into organizing one's affairs effectively. **get** (or **be**) **in on the act** informal become (or be) involved in a particular activity, in order to gain an advantage. **a hard** (or **tough**) **act to follow** an achievement or performance which sets a standard regarded as being hard for others to measure up to. **in the act of** in the process of: *they photographed him in the act of reading other people's mail.*
– PHRASAL VERBS **act up 1** informal (of a thing) fail to function properly: *the plane's engine was acting up.* ▪ behave badly. **2** be promoted to a more senior position on a temporary basis.
– DERIVATIVES **actable** adjective.
– ORIGIN late Middle English: from Latin *actus* 'event, thing done', *act-* 'done', from the verb *agere*, reinforced by the French noun *acte*.

Actaeon /akˈtiːən, ˈaktɪən/ Greek Mythology a hunter who, because he accidentally saw Artemis bathing, was changed by her into a stag and killed by his own hounds.

actant /ˈaktənt/ ▶ noun **1** Grammar a noun or noun phrase involved in the action expressed by a verb. **2** (in literary theory) a person, creature, or object playing any of a set of active roles in a narrative.

ACTH ▶ abbreviation Biochemistry adrenocorticotrophic hormone.

actin /ˈaktɪn/ ▶ noun [mass noun] Biochemistry a protein which forms (together with myosin) the contractile filaments of muscle cells, and is also involved in motion in other types of cell.
– ORIGIN 1940: from Greek *aktis, aktin-* 'ray' + **-IN**[1].

acting ▶ noun [mass noun] the art or occupation of performing fictional roles in plays, films, or television: *she studied acting in New York* | [as modifier] *an acting career.*
▶ adjective [attrib.] temporarily doing the duties of another person: *the acting supervisor.*

acting pilot officer ▶ noun a rank in the RAF above warrant officer and below pilot officer.

actinian /akˈtɪnɪən/ ▶ noun Zoology a sea anemone.
– ORIGIN mid 18th cent.: from the modern Latin genus name *Actinia* (from Greek *aktis, aktin-* 'ray') + **-AN**.

actinic /akˈtɪnɪk/ ▶ adjective technical (of light or lighting) able to cause photochemical reactions, as in photography, through having a significant short wavelength or ultraviolet component.
– DERIVATIVES **actinism** noun.
– ORIGIN mid 19th cent.: from Greek *aktis, aktin-* 'ray' + **-IC**.

actinide /ˈaktɪnʌɪd/ ▶ noun Chemistry any of the series of fifteen metallic elements from actinium (atomic number 89) to lawrencium (atomic number 103) in the periodic table. They are all radioactive, the heavier members being extremely unstable and not of natural occurrence.
– ORIGIN 1940s: from **ACTINIUM** + **-IDE**, on the pattern of *lanthanide*.

actinium /akˈtɪnɪəm/ ▶ noun [mass noun] the chemical element of atomic number 89, a radioactive metallic element of the actinide series. It is rare in nature, occurring as an impurity in uranium ores. (Symbol: **Ac**)
– ORIGIN early 20th cent.: from Greek *aktis, aktin-* 'ray' + **-IUM**.

actinolite /akˈtɪnəlʌɪt/ ▶ noun [mass noun] a green mineral of the amphibole group containing calcium, magnesium, and iron and occurring chiefly in metamorphic rocks and as a form of asbestos.
– ORIGIN late 18th cent.: from Greek *aktis, aktin-* 'ray' + *lithos* 'stone' (because of the ray-like crystals).

actinometer /ˌaktɪˈnɒmɪtə/ ▶ noun Physics an instrument for measuring the intensity of radiation, especially ultraviolet radiation.
– ORIGIN mid 19th cent.: from Greek *aktis, aktin-* 'ray' + **-METER**.

actinomorphic /ˌaktɪnə(ʊ)ˈmɔːfɪk/ ▶ adjective Biology characterized by radial symmetry, such as a starfish or the flower of a daisy. Compare with **ZYGOMORPHIC**.
– DERIVATIVES **actinomorphy** noun.
– ORIGIN late 19th cent.: from Greek *aktis, aktin-* 'ray' + *morphē* 'form' + **-IC**.

actinomycete /ˌaktɪnə(ʊ)ˈmʌɪsiːt/ ▶ noun a bacterium of an order of typically non-motile filamentous forms. They include streptomycetes, and were formerly regarded as fungi. ● Order Actinomycetales; Gram-positive.
– ORIGIN 1920s (originally only in the plural): modern Latin, from Greek *aktis, aktin-* 'ray' + *mukētes*, plural of *mukēs* 'fungus'.

action ▶ noun **1** [mass noun] the fact or process of doing something, typically to achieve an aim: *ending child labour will require action on many levels.* ▪ the way in which something such as a chemical has an effect or influence: *the seeds require the catalytic action of water to release heat.* ▪ short for **INDUSTRIAL ACTION**. ▪ the events represented in a story or play: *the action is set in a country house.* ▪ informal exciting or notable activity: *the weekend sporting action begins on Saturday* | *people in media want to be where the action is.* ▪ [as exclamation] used by a film director as a command to begin: *lights, camera, action.*
2 a thing done; an act: *she frequently questioned his actions.* ▪ a gesture or movement.
3 the way in which something works or moves: *the weapon has a smooth action.* ▪ the mechanism that makes a machine or instrument work.
4 [mass noun] armed conflict: *servicemen listed as missing in action during the war.* ▪ [count noun] a military engagement: *a rearguard action.*
5 legal proceedings; a lawsuit: *a civil action for damages.*
▶ verb [with obj.] take action on; deal with: *your request will be actioned.*
– PHRASES **action at a distance** Physics, chiefly historical the exertion of force by one body on another separated from the first by empty space. **actions speak louder than words** proverb what someone actually does means more than what they say they will do. **go into action** start work or activity. **in action** in operation; working: *watching him in action, normal workers are left in awe.* **man of action** a man whose life is characterized by physical activity or deeds rather than by words or intellectual matters. **out of action** temporarily unable to work or function: *a heart attack put him out of action.* **put into action** put into effect; carry out: *ideas need to be put into action.* **take action** do something official or concerted to achieve an aim or deal with a problem: *if there is a breach of regulations, we will take action.*
– ORIGIN late Middle English: via Old French from Latin *actio(n-)*, from *agere* 'do, act'.

actionable ▶ adjective **1** Law giving sufficient reason to take legal action: *an actionable assertion.* **2** able to be done or acted on; having practical value: *insightful and actionable information on the effect advertising is having on your brand.*

actioner ▶ noun informal a film predominantly consisting of exciting action and adventure.

action figure ▶ noun a doll representing a character known for vigorous activity, such as a soldier or superhero.

action for declarator ▶ noun see **DECLARATOR**.

action group ▶ noun a body formed to campaign politically on a particular issue.

action-packed ▶ adjective informal full of activity or excitement: *an action-packed programme of events.*

action painting ▶ noun [mass noun] a style of abstract painting in which paint is randomly splashed, thrown, or poured on to the canvas. It was made famous by Jackson Pollock, and formed part of the more general movement of abstract expressionism.

action point ▶ noun a specific proposal for action to be taken, typically one arising from a discussion or meeting.

action potential ▶ noun Physiology the change in electrical potential associated with the passage of an impulse along the membrane of a muscle cell or nerve cell.

action replay ▶ noun Brit. a playback of part of a television broadcast, typically a slow-motion replay of an incident in a sporting event. ▪ informal an exact repetition of an action or event.

action research ▶ noun [mass noun] studies carried out in the course of an activity or occupation, typically in the field of education, to improve the methods and approach of those involved.

action stations ▶ plural noun the positions taken up by military personnel in preparation for action (often as a command or signal to prepare for action).

Actium, Battle of /ˈaktɪəm/ a naval battle which took place in 31 BC off the promontory of Actium in western Greece, in the course of which Octavian defeated Mark Antony.

activate ▶ verb [with obj.] make (something) active or operative: *fumes from cooking are enough to activate the alarm.* ▪ convert (a substance, molecule, etc.) into a reactive form.
– DERIVATIVES **activation** noun, **activator** noun.

activated carbon (also **activated charcoal**) ▶ noun [mass noun] charcoal that has been heated or otherwise treated to increase its adsorptive power.

activated sludge ▶ noun [mass noun] aerated sewage containing aerobic microorganisms which help to break it down.

activation analysis ▶ noun [mass noun] Chemistry a technique of analysis in which atoms of a particular element in a sample are made radioactive, typically by irradiation with neutrons, and their concentration is then determined radiologically.

activation energy ▶ noun Chemistry the minimum quantity of energy which the reacting species must possess in order to undergo a specified reaction.

active ▶ adjective **1** engaging or ready to engage in physically energetic pursuits: *although he was seventy he was still robust and active.* ▪ moving or tending to move about vigorously or frequently: *I couldn't feel the baby moving, and it was normally very active.* ▪ characterized by busy or lively activity: *they enjoyed an active social life.* ▪ (of a person's mind or imagination) alert and lively.
2 participating or engaged in a particular sphere or activity: *sexually active teenagers* | *she was an active member of the society.* ▪ [predic.] (of a person or animal) pursuing their usual occupation or activity at a particular place or time: *tigers are active mainly at night.*
3 in operation; working: *the old watermill was active until 1960.* ▪ (of an electric circuit) capable of modifying its state or characteristics automatically in response to input or feedback. ▪ (of a volcano) that is erupting or has erupted in historical times. ▪ (of a disease) in which the symptoms are manifest; not in remission or latent. ▪ having a chemical or biological effect on something: *active ingredients.*
4 Grammar denoting a voice of verbs in which the subject is typically the person or thing performing the action and which can take a direct object (e.g. *she loved him* as opposed to the passive form *he was loved*).
▶ noun Grammar an active form of a verb.
– DERIVATIVES **actively** adverb, **activeness** noun.
– ORIGIN Middle English (in the sense 'preferring action to contemplation'): from Latin *activus*, from *act-* 'done', from the verb *agere*.

active birth ▶ noun [mass noun] childbirth during which the mother is encouraged to move around freely and assume any position which feels comfortable.

active carbon (also **active charcoal**) ▶ noun another term for **ACTIVATED CARBON**.

active citizen ▶ noun a person who actively takes responsibility and initiative in areas of public concern such as crime prevention and the local community.
– DERIVATIVES **active citizenship** noun.

active duty ▶ noun [mass noun] the playing of a direct role in the operational work of the police or armed forces as opposed to doing administrative work.

active immunity ▶ noun [mass noun] Physiology the immunity which results from the production of antibodies by the immune system in response to the presence of an antigen. Compare with **PASSIVE IMMUNITY**.

active layer ▶ noun Geography the seasonally thawed surface layer above permafrost.

active list ▶ noun a list of the officers in an armed service who are liable to be called on for duty.

active matrix ▶ noun Electronics a display system in which each pixel is individually controlled.

active service ▶ noun [mass noun] direct participation in military operations as a member of the armed forces.

active site ▶ noun Biochemistry a region on an enzyme that binds to a protein or other substance during a reaction.

active transport ▶ noun [mass noun] Biology the movement of ions or molecules across a cell membrane into a region of higher concentration, assisted by enzymes and requiring energy.

activewear ▶ noun [mass noun] casual, comfortable clothing suitable for sport or exercise.

activism ▶ noun [mass noun] the policy or action of using vigorous campaigning to bring about political or social change.
– DERIVATIVES **activist** noun & adjective.

activity ▶ noun (pl. **activities**) **1** [mass noun] the condition in which things are happening or being done: *there has been a sustained level of activity in the economy*. ▪ busy or vigorous action or movement: *the room was a **hive of activity**.*
2 (usu. **activities**) a thing that a person or group does or has done: *the firm's marketing activities*. ▪ a recreational pursuit or pastime: *a range of sporting activities*.
3 Chemistry a thermodynamic quantity representing the effective concentration of a particular component in a solution or other system, equal to its concentration multiplied by an **activity coefficient**.
– ORIGIN late Middle English: from French *activité* or late Latin *activitas*, from Latin *act-* 'done', from the verb *agere*.

act of contrition ▶ noun (in the Roman Catholic Church) a penitential prayer. ▪ something done to make amends for an offence.

Act of Parliament ▶ noun see **ACT** (sense 3 of the noun).

Act of Settlement, Act of Uniformity, etc. see **SETTLEMENT, ACT OF; UNIFORMITY, ACT OF,** etc.

act of state ▶ noun an act passed by the executive power of a state, typically one relating to foreign affairs or foreign citizens.

actomyosin /ˌaktə(ʊ)ˈmʌɪəsɪn/ ▶ noun [mass noun] Biochemistry a complex of actin and myosin of which the contractile protein filaments of muscle tissue are composed.
– ORIGIN 1940s: from **ACTIN** + **MYOSIN**.

actor ▶ noun **1** a person whose profession is acting on the stage, in films, or on television. ▪ a person who behaves in a way that is not genuine: *in war one must be a good actor*.
2 a participant in an action or process: *employers are key actors within industrial relations*.
– DERIVATIVES **actorish** adjective.
– ORIGIN late Middle English (originally denoting an agent or administrator): from Latin, 'doer, actor', from *agere* 'do, act'.

> **USAGE** In the time of Shakespeare female roles were played by boys or men, and women did not appear on stage in England until after the Restoration of 1660. Female performers were then called either **actors** or **actresses**—it was only later that **actor** became restricted to men—and it seems that we are returning to the original situation. Although there is still an awards category at the Oscars called Best Actress, some people are again using the gender-neutral term **actor** for both sexes. See also **USAGE** at **-ESS**[1].

actorly ▶ adjective characteristic of an actor or actress: *he seems to lack the actorly range that the role requires*. ▪ affected or excessively dramatic: *she eschews the actorly flourishes of her co-star*.

Actors' Studio an acting workshop in New York City, founded in 1947 by Elia Kazan and others, and a leading centre of method acting.

actress ▶ noun a female actor.

> **USAGE** See **USAGE** at **ACTOR**.

actressy ▶ adjective (of a woman) self-consciously theatrical or emotionally volatile: *her actressy manner*.

actual /ˈaktʃʊəl, -tjʊəl/ ▶ adjective **1** existing in fact; real: *the estimate was much less than the actual cost*. ▪ used to emphasize the important aspect of something: *the book could be condensed into half the space, but what of the actual content?*
2 existing now; current: *using actual income to measure expected income*.
– PHRASES **in actual fact** used to emphasize a comment that modifies or contradicts a previous statement: *people talk as if he was a monster—in actual fact he was a very kind guy*. **your actual ——** informal the real, genuine, or important thing specified: *is this a drop of your actual feminine intuition?*
– ORIGIN Middle English: from Old French *actuel* 'active, practical', from late Latin *actualis*, from *actus* (see **ACT**).

actual bodily harm (abbrev.: **ABH**) ▶ noun [mass noun] Law minor injury, such as bruising, inflicted on a person by the deliberate action of another, considered less serious than grievous bodily harm.

actuality ▶ noun (pl. **actualities**) [mass noun] the state of existing in reality: *the building looked as impressive **in actuality** as it did in magazines*. ▪ (**actualities**) existing conditions or facts: *the grim actualities of prison life*.
– ORIGIN late Middle English (in the sense 'activity'): from Old French *actualite* or medieval Latin *actualitas*, from *actualis* 'active, practical', from *actus* (see **ACT**).

actualize (also **actualise**) ▶ verb [with obj.] make a reality of: *he had actualized his dream and achieved the world record*.
– DERIVATIVES **actualization** noun.

actually ▶ adverb **1** as the truth or facts of a situation: *we must pay attention to what young people are actually doing*.
2 [sentence adverb] used to emphasize that something someone has said or done is surprising: *he actually expected me to be pleased about it!* ▪ used when expressing a contradictory or unexpected opinion or correcting someone: *'Tom's happy anyway.' 'He isn't, actually, not any more.'* ▪ used to introduce a new topic or to add information to a previous statement: *he had a thick Cockney accent—he sounded like my grandad actually*.

actuary /ˈaktʃʊəri, tjʊ-/ ▶ noun (pl. **actuaries**) a person who compiles and analyses statistics and uses them to calculate insurance risks and premiums.
– DERIVATIVES **actuarial** adjective, **actuarially** (also **actuarily**) adverb.
– ORIGIN mid 16th cent. (originally denoting a clerk or registrar of a court): from Latin *actuarius* 'bookkeeper', from *actus* (see **ACT**). The current sense dates from the mid 19th cent.

actuate /ˈaktʃʊeɪt, -tjʊ-/ ▶ verb **1** [with obj.] make (a machine or device) operate: *the pendulum actuates an electrical switch*.
2 make (someone) act in a particular way; motivate: *the defendants were actuated by malice*.
– DERIVATIVES **actuation** noun, **actuator** noun.
– ORIGIN late 16th cent.: from medieval Latin *actuat-* 'carried out, caused to operate', from the verb *actuare*, from Latin *actus* (see **ACT**). The original sense was 'carry out in practice', later 'stir into activity, enliven'; sense 1 dates from the mid 17th cent.

actus reus /ˌaktəs ˈreɪəs/ ▶ noun [mass noun] Law action or conduct which is a constituent element of a crime, as opposed to the mental state of the accused. Compare with **MENS REA**.
– ORIGIN Latin, literally 'guilty act'.

acuity /əˈkjuːɪti/ ▶ noun [mass noun] sharpness or keenness of thought, vision, or hearing: *intellectual acuity | visual acuity*.
– ORIGIN late Middle English: from Old French *acuite* or medieval Latin *acuitas*, from Latin *acuere* 'sharpen' (see **ACUTE**).

aculeate /əˈkjuːlɪət/ ▶ adjective **1** Entomology (of an insect) having a sting.
2 Botany sharply pointed; prickly.
▶ noun Entomology a stinging insect of a group that includes the bees, wasps, and ants. ● Section Aculeata, suborder Apocrita, order Hymenoptera.
– ORIGIN mid 17th cent.: from Latin *aculeatus*, from *aculeus* 'a sting', diminutive of *acus* 'needle'.

acumen /ˈakjʊmən, əˈkjuːmən/ ▶ noun [mass noun] the ability to make good judgements and take quick decisions: *she hides a shrewd business acumen*.
– ORIGIN late 16th cent.: from Latin, 'sharpness, point', from *acuere* 'sharpen' (see **ACUTE**).

acuminate /əˈkjuːmɪnət/ ▶ adjective Biology (of a plant or animal structure, e.g. a leaf) tapering to a point.
– ORIGIN late 16th cent.: from late Latin *acuminatus* 'pointed', from *acuminare* 'sharpen to a point', from *acuere* 'sharpen' (see **ACUTE**).

acupoint /ˈakjʊpɔɪnt/ ▶ noun any of the supposed energy points on the body where acupuncture needles are inserted or manual pressure is applied during acupressure.

acupressure /ˈakjʊˌprɛʃə/ ▶ noun [mass noun] a form of alternative therapy in which manual pressure is used to stimulate specific points on the body along what are considered to be lines of energy.
– ORIGIN 1950s: blend of **ACUPUNCTURE** and **PRESSURE**.

acupuncture /ˈakjʊˌpʌŋ(k)tʃə/ ▶ noun [mass noun] a system of complementary medicine in which fine needles are inserted in the skin at specific points along what are considered to be lines of energy (meridians), used in the treatment of various physical and mental conditions.
– DERIVATIVES **acupuncturist** noun.
– ORIGIN late 17th cent.: from Latin *acu* 'with a needle' + **PUNCTURE**.

acushla /əˈkʊʃlə/ ▶ noun Irish dated an affectionate form of address.
– ORIGIN mid 19th cent.: from Irish *a chuisle* (*moi chroi*) 'O pulse (of my heart)!'.

acutance /əˈkjuːt(ə)ns/ ▶ noun [mass noun] the sharpness of a photographic or printed image.

acute ▶ adjective **1** (of an unpleasant or unwelcome situation or phenomenon) present or experienced to a severe or intense degree: *an acute housing shortage | the problem is acute and getting worse*. ▪ (of a disease or its symptoms) severe but of short duration: *acute appendicitis*. Often contrasted with **CHRONIC**.
2 having or showing a perceptive understanding or insight; shrewd: *an acute awareness of changing fashions*. ▪ (of a physical sense or faculty) highly developed; keen: *an acute sense of smell*.
3 (of an angle) less than 90°. ▪ having a sharp end; pointed.
4 (of a sound) high; shrill.
▶ noun short for **ACUTE ACCENT**.
– DERIVATIVES **acuteness** noun.
– ORIGIN late Middle English (describing a disease or its symptoms): from Latin *acutus*, past participle of *acuere* 'sharpen', from *acus* 'needle'.

acute abdomen ▶ noun Medicine a condition of severe abdominal pain, usually requiring emergency surgery, caused by acute disease of or injury to the internal organs.

acute accent ▶ noun a mark (´) placed over certain letters in some languages to indicate a feature such as altered sound quality (e.g. in *fiancée*).

acutely ▶ adverb [as submodifier] **1** (with reference to something unpleasant or unwelcome) intensely: *the whole situation was acutely embarrassing*.
2 in a way that shows a perceptive understanding or insight: *we are all **acutely aware** of the fragility of our world*.

acute rheumatism ▶ noun another term for **RHEUMATIC FEVER**.

ACW ▶ abbreviation aircraftwoman.

-acy ▶ suffix forming nouns of state or quality: *celibacy | lunacy*.
– ORIGIN variant of **-CY**, from Latin *-atia* (medieval Latin *-acia*), or from Greek *-ateia*.

acyclic /eɪˈsʌɪklɪk, -ˈsɪk-/ ▶ adjective **1** not displaying or forming part of a cycle. ▪ (of a woman) not having a menstrual cycle.
2 Chemistry (of a compound or molecule) containing no rings of atoms.

acyclovir /eɪˈsʌɪklə(ʊ)ˌvɪə/ ▶ noun [mass noun] Medicine an antiviral drug used chiefly in the treatment of herpes and AIDS. Also called **ZOVIRAX** (trademark).
– ORIGIN 1970s: from *acycl(ic)* + *vir(al DNA)*.

acyl /ˈeɪsʌɪl, ˈasɪl/ ▶ noun [as modifier] Chemistry denoting a radical of general formula –C(O)R, where R is an alkyl group, derived from a carboxylic acid.
– ORIGIN late 19th cent.: coined in German, from Latin *acidus* (see **ACID**) + **-YL**.

acylate /ˈeɪsʌɪleɪt, ˈasɪl-/ ▶ verb [with obj.] Chemistry introduce an acyl group into (a molecule or compound).
– DERIVATIVES **acylation** noun.

AD ▶ abbreviation Anno Domini (used to indicate that a date comes the specified number of years after the traditional date of Christ's birth).

> **USAGE** AD is normally written in small capitals and should be placed before the numerals, as in *AD 375* (not *375 AD*). The reason for this is that AD is an abbreviation of *anno domini*, which means 'in the year of our Lord'. However, when the date is spelled out, it is normal to write *the third century AD* (**not** *AD the third century*). Compare with **BC**.

ad ▶ noun informal **1** an advertisement.
2 Tennis advantage.
– ORIGIN mid 19th cent.: abbreviation.

ad- ▶ prefix denoting motion or direction to: *advance | adduce*. ▪ denoting reduction or change into: *adapt | adulterate*. ▪ denoting addition, increase, or intensification: *adjunct*.
– ORIGIN from Latin *ad* 'to'; in the 16th cent. the use of *ad-* and its variants was extended to replace *a-* from a different origin such as Latin *ab-* (e.g. *advance*, from French *avancer* based on late Latin *abante* 'in front').

A

A/D ▶ **abbreviation** Electronics analogue to digital.

-ad¹ /ad, əd/ ▶ **suffix** forming nouns: **1** in collective numerals: *myriad* | *triad*.
2 in names of females in classical mythology: *dryad* | *naiad*.
3 in names of poems and similar compositions: *Iliad* | *jeremiad*.
4 in names of members of some taxonomic groupings: *bromeliad*.
– ORIGIN from the Greek ending *-as, -ad-*.

-ad² /əd/ ▶ **suffix** forming nouns such as *ballad, salad*. Compare with **-ADE¹**.
– ORIGIN from French *-ade*.

Ada /ˈeɪdə/ ▶ **noun** [mass noun] a high-level computer programming language used chiefly in real-time computerized control systems, e.g. for aircraft navigation.
– ORIGIN 1980s: named after *Ada* Lovelace (see **LOVELACE¹**).

adage /ˈadɪdʒ/ ▶ **noun** a proverb or short statement expressing a general truth.
– ORIGIN mid 16th cent.: from French, from Latin *adagium* 'saying', based on an early form of *aio* 'I say'.

adagio /əˈdɑː(d)ʒɪəʊ/ Music ▶ **adverb & adjective** (especially as a direction) in slow time.
▶ **noun** (pl. **adagios**) a movement, passage, or composition marked to be performed adagio.
– ORIGIN Italian, from *ad agio* 'at ease'.

Adam¹ (in the biblical and Koranic traditions) the name of the first man. According to the Book of Genesis, Adam was created by God as the progenitor of the human race and lived with Eve in the Garden of Eden.
– PHRASES **not know someone from Adam** not know or be completely unable to recognize the person in question.
– ORIGIN from Hebrew *'āḏām* 'man', later taken to be a name.

Adam², Robert (1728–92), Scottish architect. He was influenced by neoclassical theory and, assisted by his brother **James** (1730–94), he initiated a lighter, more decorative style than the Palladianism favoured by the British architecture of the previous half-century.

adamant ▶ **adjective** refusing to be persuaded or to change one's mind: *he is adamant that he is not going to resign*.
▶ **noun** [mass noun] archaic a legendary rock or mineral to which many properties were attributed, formerly associated with diamond or lodestone.
– DERIVATIVES **adamance** noun, **adamancy** noun, **adamantly** adverb.
– ORIGIN Old English (as a noun), from Old French *adamaunt-*, via Latin from Greek *adamas, adamant-*, 'untameable, invincible' (later used to denote the hardest metal or stone, hence diamond), from *a-* 'not' + *daman* 'to tame'. The phrase *to be adamant* dates from the 1930s, although adjectival use had been implied in such collocations as 'an adamant heart' since the 16th cent.

adamantine /ˌadəˈmantʌɪn/ ▶ **adjective** literary unable to be broken: *adamantine chains* | figurative *her adamantine will*.

Adams¹, Ansel (Easton) (1902–84), American photographer, noted for his black-and-white photographs of American landscapes.

Adams², John (1735–1826), American Federalist statesman, 2nd President of the US 1797–1801; father of John Quincy Adams. He helped draft the Declaration of Independence (1776).

Adams³, John Couch (1819–92), English astronomer. In 1843 he calculated the position of a supposed planet beyond Uranus; similar calculations performed by Le Verrier resulted in the discovery of Neptune three years later.

Adams⁴, John Quincy (1767–1848), American statesman, 6th President of the US 1825–9; eldest son of John Adams.

Adam's ale ▶ **noun** [mass noun] dated, humorous water.

Adam's apple ▶ **noun** a projection at the front of the neck formed by the thyroid cartilage of the larynx, often prominent in men.
– ORIGIN mid 18th cent.: so named from the notion that a piece of the forbidden fruit became lodged in Adam's throat.

Adam's Bridge a line of shoals lying between NW Sri Lanka and the SE coast of Tamil Nadu in India, separating the Palk Strait from the Gulf of Mannar.

Adam's needle ▶ **noun** another term for **YUCCA**.

Adam's Peak a mountain in south central Sri Lanka, rising to 2,243 m (7,360 ft). A rock near the top bears a depression resembling a footprint, which is the focus of religious pilgrimages.

Adana /ˈadənə/ a town in southern Turkey, capital of a province of the same name; pop. 1,366,000 (est. 2007).

adapt ▶ **verb** [with obj.] make (something) suitable for a new use or purpose; modify: *hospitals have had to be adapted for modern medical practice* | [with obj. and infinitive] *the policies can be adapted to suit individual needs*. ■ [no obj.] become adjusted to new conditions: *a large organization can be slow to* ***adapt to*** *change*. ■ alter (a text) to make it suitable for filming, broadcasting, or the stage: *the film was* ***adapted from*** *a Turgenev short story*.
– ORIGIN late Middle English: from French *adapter*, from Latin *adaptare*, from *ad-* 'to' + *aptare* (from *aptus* 'fit').

adaptable ▶ **adjective** able to adjust to new conditions: *rats are highly* ***adaptable to*** *change*. ■ able to be modified for a new use or purpose: *telephone links that are adaptable for modems*.
– DERIVATIVES **adaptability** noun, **adaptably** adverb.

adaptation ▶ **noun** [mass noun] the action or process of adapting or being adapted: *the adaptation of teaching strategy to meet students' needs* | [count noun] *adaptations to the school curriculum*. ■ [count noun] a film, television drama, or stage play that has been adapted from a written work: *a three-part adaptation of Hard Times*. ■ Biology the process of change by which an organism or species becomes better suited to its environment.
– ORIGIN early 17th cent.: from French, from late Latin *adaptatio(n-)*, from Latin *adaptare* (see **ADAPT**).

adaptationism ▶ **noun** [mass noun] Biology the axiom or assumption that each feature of an organism is the result of evolutionary adaptation for a particular function.
– DERIVATIVES **adaptationist** noun & adjective.

adaption ▶ **noun** another term for **ADAPTATION**.

adaptive ▶ **adjective** chiefly technical characterized by or given to adaptation: *mutation is ultimately essential for adaptive evolution in all populations*.
– DERIVATIVES **adaptively** adverb, **adaptivity** /adapˈtɪvɪti/ noun.

adaptive radiation ▶ **noun** [mass noun] Biology the diversification of a group of organisms into forms filling different ecological niches.

adaptogen /əˈdaptədʒ(ə)n/ ▶ **noun** (in herbal medicine) a natural substance considered to help the body adapt to stress.
– DERIVATIVES **adaptogenic** adjective.
– ORIGIN 1960s: from Russian (see **ADAPT, -GEN**).

adaptor (also **adapter**) ▶ **noun 1** a device for connecting pieces of equipment that cannot be connected directly. ■ a device for connecting several electric plugs to one socket.
2 a person who adapts a text to make it suitable for filming, broadcasting, or the stage.

Adar /aˈdɑː/ ▶ **noun** (in the Jewish calendar) the sixth month of the civil and twelfth of the religious year, usually coinciding with parts of February and March. It is known in leap years as **Second Adar**. ■ an intercalary month preceding Adar in leap years, also called **First Adar**.
– ORIGIN from Hebrew *'ăḏār*.

ADAS /ˈeɪdas/ ▶ **abbreviation** Agricultural Development and Advisory Service, set up in Britain in 1971.

adaxial /adˈaksɪəl/ ▶ **adjective** Botany facing towards the stem of a plant (in particular denoting the upper surface of a leaf). The opposite of **ABAXIAL**.

ADC ▶ **abbreviation** ■ aide-de-camp. ■ analogue to digital converter.

ADD ▶ **abbreviation** ■ analogue digital digital, indicating that a music recording was made in analogue format before being mastered and stored digitally. ■ attention deficit disorder.

add ▶ **verb** [with obj.] **1** join (something) to something else so as to increase the size, number, or amount: *a new wing was* ***added to*** *the building* | *some box offices now* ***add on*** *a convenience charge* | (as adj. **added**) *one vitamin tablet daily will give added protection*. ■ [no obj.] (**add up**) increase in amount, number, or degree: *watch those air miles add up!*
2 put in (an additional element, ingredient, etc.): *chlorine is* ***added to*** *the water to kill bacteria* | (as adj. **added**) *the fruit juice contains no added sugar*. ■ contribute (an enhancing quality) to something: *the suite will* ***add*** *a touch of class* ***to*** *your bedroom*.
3 put together (two or more numbers or amounts) to calculate their total value: *they* ***added*** *all the figures* ***up*** | ***add*** *the two numbers* ***together***. ■ [no obj.] (**add up to**) amount to: *this adds up to a total of 400 calories* | figurative *these isolated incidents don't add up to a true picture of the situation*. ■ [no obj.] [usu. with negative] (**add up**) informal seem reasonable or consistent; make sense: *many things in her story didn't add up*.
4 [reporting verb] say as a further remark: [with direct speech] *'I hope we haven't been too much trouble,' she added politely* | [with obj.] *we would like to add our congratulations*.
– ORIGIN late Middle English: from Latin *addere*, from *ad-* 'to' + the base of *dare* 'put'.

adda /ˈadˌdɑː/ ▶ **noun** Indian **1** a place where people gather for conversation. ■ an illicit drinking place. ■ [mass noun] informal conversation among a group of people.
2 a junction point for public transport.
– ORIGIN from Hindi *aḍḍā*, originally in the sense 'perch for tame birds'.

addax /ˈadaks/ ▶ **noun** a large antelope with a mainly greyish and white coat, native to the deserts of North Africa. ● *Addax nasomaculatus*, family Bovidae.
– ORIGIN late 17th cent.: from Latin, from an African word recorded by Pliny.

added value ▶ **noun & adjective** another term for **VALUE ADDED**.

addendum /əˈdɛndəm/ ▶ **noun** (pl. **addenda** /-də/) **1** an item of additional material added at the end of a book or other publication.
2 Engineering the radial distance from the pitch circle of a cogwheel or wormwheel to the crests of the teeth or ridges. Compare with **DEDENDUM**.
– ORIGIN late 17th cent.: Latin, 'that which is to be added', gerundive of *addere* (see **ADD**).

adder¹ ▶ **noun** a small venomous Eurasian snake which has a dark zigzag pattern on its back and bears live young. It is the only poisonous snake in Britain. Also called **VIPER**. ● *Vipera berus*, family Viperidae.
■ used in names of similar or related snakes, e.g. **death adder, puff adder**.
– ORIGIN Old English *nædre* 'serpent, adder', of Germanic origin; related to Dutch *adder* and German *Natter*. The initial *n* was lost in Middle English by wrong division of *a naddre*; compare with **APRON, AUGER**, and **UMPIRE**.

adder² ▶ **noun** Electronics a unit which adds together two input variables. A **full adder** can add a bit carried from another addition as well as the two inputs, whereas a **half adder** can only add the inputs together.

adder's tongue (US also **adder-tongue**) ▶ **noun 1** a fern having a single pointed oval frond and a straight spore-bearing stem. ● Genus *Ophioglossum*, family Ophioglossaceae, in particular *O. vulgatum*.
2 North American term for **DOG'S-TOOTH VIOLET**.

addict /ˈadɪkt/ ▶ **noun** a person who is addicted to a particular substance, typically an illegal drug. ■ [with modifier] informal an enthusiastic devotee of a specified thing or activity: *a self-confessed chocolate addict*.
– ORIGIN early 20th cent.: from the obsolete verb *addict*, which was a back-formation from **ADDICTED**.

addicted /əˈdɪktɪd/ ▶ **adjective** (usu. **addicted to**) physically and mentally dependent on a particular substance: *she became addicted to alcohol and diet pills*. ■ informal enthusiastically devoted to a particular thing or activity: *he's addicted to computers*.
– ORIGIN mid 16th cent.: from the obsolete adjective *addict* 'bound or devoted (to someone)', from Latin *addict-* 'assigned', from the verb *addicere*, from *ad-* 'to' + *dicere* 'say'.

addiction /əˈdɪkʃ(ə)n/ ▶ **noun** [mass noun] the fact or condition of being addicted to a particular substance, thing, or activity: *he committed the offence to finance his drug addiction*.
– ORIGIN late 16th cent. (denoting a person's inclination or proclivity): from Latin *addictio(n-)*, from *addicere* 'assign' (see **ADDICTED**).

addictive /əˈdɪktɪv/ (also informal **addicting**) ▶ **adjective** (of a substance or activity) causing or likely to cause someone to become addicted to it: *a highly addictive drug*. ■ relating or susceptible to addiction: *he has an addictive personality*.
– DERIVATIVES **addictively** adverb.

add-in ▶ **noun** a device or piece of software that can be added to a computer to give extra features or functions.

Addington, Henry, 1st Viscount Sidmouth (1757–1844), British Tory statesman, Prime Minister 1801–4 and Home Secretary (1812–21).

Addis Ababa /ˌadɪs ˈabəbə/ (also **Adis Abeba**) the capital of Ethiopia, situated at an altitude of about 2,440 m (8,000 ft); pop. 3,101,000 (est. 2007).

Addison, Joseph (1672–1719), English essayist, poet, dramatist, and Whig politician, noted for his simple, unornamented prose style. In 1711 he founded the *Spectator* with Sir Richard Steele.

Addisonian /ˌadɪˈsəʊnɪən/ ▶ **adjective 1** relating to or characteristic of the writing of Joseph Addison. **2** Medicine relating to or characterized by Addison's disease.

Addisonian anaemia ▶ **noun** another term for PERNICIOUS ANAEMIA.

Addison's disease ▶ **noun** [mass noun] a disease characterized by progressive anaemia, low blood pressure, great weakness, and bronze discoloration of the skin. It is caused by inadequate secretion of hormones by the adrenal cortex.
– ORIGIN mid 19th cent.: named after Thomas *Addison* (1793–1860), the English physician who described the disease.

addition ▶ **noun** [mass noun] **1** the action or process of adding something to something else: *the hotel has been extended with the addition of more rooms.* ■ [count noun] a person or thing added or joined: *you will find the coat a useful* ***addition to*** *your wardrobe.* **2** the process of calculating the total of two or more numbers or amounts. ■ Mathematics the process of combining matrices, vectors, or other quantities under specific rules to obtain their sum or resultant.
– PHRASES **in addition** as an extra person or thing: *members of the board were paid a small allowance* ***in addition to*** *their normal salary.*
– ORIGIN late Middle English: from Latin *additio(n-)*, from the verb *addere* (see ADD).

additional ▶ **adjective** added, extra, or supplementary to what is already present or available: *we require additional information.*

additionally ▶ **adverb** as an extra factor or circumstance: *brokers finance themselves additionally by short-term borrowing.* ■ [sentence adverb] used to introduce a new fact or argument: *additionally, 50 hours of practical experience will be necessary.*

additional member system ▶ **noun** a type of proportional representation in which each elector votes separately for a party and for a representative.

addition reaction ▶ **noun** Chemistry a reaction in which one molecule combines with another to form a larger molecule with no other products.

additive ▶ **noun** a substance added to something in small quantities to improve or preserve it: *many foods contain chemical additives.*
▶ **adjective** characterized by, relating to, or produced by addition: *the combination of these factors has an additive effect.* ■ technical relating to the reproduction of colours by the superimposition of primary colours.
– ORIGIN late 17th cent. (as an adjective): from late Latin *additivus*, from Latin *addit-* 'added', from the verb *addere* (see ADD). The noun dates from the 1940s.

addle ▶ **verb 1** [with obj.] chiefly humorous make (someone) unable to think clearly; confuse: *being in love must have addled your brain.* **2** [no obj.] (of an egg) become rotten, producing no chick.
▶ **adjective 1** [in combination] not clear or cogent; muddled: *the film is addle-brained.* **2** archaic (of an egg) rotten.
– ORIGIN Middle English (in sense 2 of the adjective): from Old English *adela* 'liquid filth', of Germanic origin; related to Dutch *aal* and German *Adel* 'mire, puddle'.

addled ▶ **adjective 1** unable to think clearly; confused: *this might just be my addled brain playing tricks* | [in combination] *a drug-addled frat boy.* **2** (of an egg) rotten.

Addled Parliament the Parliament of James I of England (James VI of Scotland), so known because it refused to accede to the king's requests and was dissolved without having passed any legislation.

add-on ▶ **noun** something that has been or can be added to an existing object or arrangement: [as modifier] *cars with add-on extras.* ■ an accessory device designed to increase the capability of a computer or hi-fi system.

addorsed /əˈdɔːst/ ▶ **adjective** Heraldry placed back to back.
– ORIGIN late 16th cent.: from Latin *ad* 'to' + *dorsum* 'back' + -ED².

addra gazelle /ˈadrə/ ▶ **noun** another term for DAMA GAZELLE.
– ORIGIN *addra* probably a local African word.

address ▶ **noun 1** the particulars of the place where someone lives or an organization is situated: *they exchanged addresses and agreed to keep in touch.* ■ the place where someone lives or an organization is situated: *our officers called at the address.* ■ Computing a string of characters which identifies a destination for email messages or the location of a website. ■ Computing a binary number which identifies a particular location in a data storage system or computer memory. **2** a formal speech delivered to an audience: *an address to the European Parliament.* ■ [mass noun] archaic a person's manner of speaking to someone else: *his address was abrupt and unceremonious.* ■ (**addresses**) archaic courteous or amorous approaches to someone: *he persecuted her with his addresses.* **3** [mass noun] dated skill, dexterity, or readiness: *he rescued me with the most consummate address.*
▶ **verb** [with obj.] **1** write the name and address of the intended recipient on (an envelope, letter, or parcel): *I* ***addressed*** *my letter* ***to*** *him personally* | (as adj. **addressed**) *please enclose a stamped addressed envelope.* **2** speak to (a person or an assembly): *she addressed the open-air meeting.* ■ (**address someone as**) name someone (in the specified way) when talking to them: *she addressed my father as 'Mr Stevens'.* ■ (**address something to**) say or write remarks or a protest to: *address your complaints to the Trading Standards Board.* **3** think about and begin to deal with (an issue or problem): *a fundamental problem has still to be addressed.* **4** Golf take up one's stance and prepare to hit (the ball).
– PHRASES **form of address** a name or title used in speaking or writing to a person of a specified rank or function.
– DERIVATIVES **addresser** noun.
– ORIGIN Middle English (as a verb in the senses 'set upright' and 'guide, direct', hence 'write directions for delivery on' and 'direct spoken words to'): from Old French, based on Latin *ad-* 'towards' + *directus* (see DIRECT). The noun is of mid 16th-cent. origin in the sense 'act of approaching or speaking to someone'.

addressable ▶ **adjective** Computing relating to or denoting a memory unit in which all locations can be separately accessed by a particular program.

addressee /ˌadrɛˈsiː/ ▶ **noun** the person to whom something is addressed.

adduce /əˈdjuːs/ ▶ **verb** [with obj.] cite as evidence: *a number of factors are adduced to explain the situation.*
– DERIVATIVES **adducible** adjective.
– ORIGIN late Middle English: from Latin *adducere*, from *ad-* 'towards' + *ducere* 'to lead'.

adduct¹ /əˈdʌkt/ ▶ **verb** [with obj.] (of a muscle) move (a limb or other part of the body) towards the midline of the body or towards another part. The opposite of ABDUCT.
– DERIVATIVES **adduction** noun.
– ORIGIN mid 19th cent.: back-formation from late Middle English *adduction*, from late Latin *adductio(n-)* 'bringing forward', from the verb *adducere* 'bring in' (see ADDUCE).

adduct² /ˈadʌkt/ ▶ **noun** Chemistry the product of an addition reaction between two compounds.
– ORIGIN 1940s: from German *Addukt* (blend of *Addition* and *Produkt*).

adductor /əˈdʌktə/ (also **adductor muscle**) ▶ **noun** Anatomy a muscle whose contraction moves a limb or other part of the body towards the midline of the body or towards another part. Compare with ABDUCTOR.
– ORIGIN early 17th cent.: modern Latin, from Latin *adduct-* 'brought in', from the verb *adducere* (see ADDUCE).

addy ▶ **noun** (pl. **addies**) informal an email address.

-ade¹ ▶ **suffix** forming nouns: **1** denoting an action that is completed: *barricade* | *blockade*. **2** denoting the body concerned in an action or process: *brigade* | *cavalcade*. **3** denoting the product or result of an action or process: *arcade* | *marmalade*.
– ORIGIN from French, via Portuguese, Provençal, and Spanish *-ada* or via Italian *-ata*, from Latin *-atus* (past participial suffix of verbs ending in *-are*).

-ade² ▶ **suffix** forming nouns such as *decade*.
– ORIGIN variant of -AD¹, from French *-ade*, from Greek *-as*, *-ad-*.

-ade³ ▶ **suffix** forming nouns: **1** equivalent in sense to nouns ending in -ADE¹: *brocade*. **2** denoting a person: *renegade*.
– ORIGIN from Spanish or Portuguese *-ado*, masculine form of *-ada* (see -ADE¹).

Adelaide /ˈadəleɪd/ a city in Australia, the capital and chief port of the state of South Australia; pop. 1,172,105 (2008).

-adelic ▶ **suffix** forming adjectives denoting musical genres or styles that incorporate psychedelic music with another element: *sampladelic*.
– ORIGIN from PSYCHEDELIC.

Adélie Land /aˈdeɪli/ (also **Adélie Coast**) a section of the Antarctic continent south of the 60th parallel, between Wilkes Land and King George V Land.

Aden /ˈeɪd(ə)n/ a port in Yemen at the mouth of the Red Sea; pop. 588,900 (est. 2004). Aden was formerly under British rule, first as part of British India (from 1839), then from 1935 as a Crown Colony. It was capital of the former South Yemen from 1967 until 1990.

Aden, Gulf of a part of the eastern Arabian Sea lying between the south coast of Yemen and the Horn of Africa.

Adenauer /ˈadmaʊə/, German /ˈaːdənaʊɐ/, Konrad (1876–1967), German statesman, first Chancellor of the Federal Republic of Germany 1949–63. As Chancellor, he presided over the political and economic transformation of his country.

adenine /ˈadɪniːn/ ▶ **noun** [mass noun] Biochemistry a compound which is one of the four constituent bases of nucleic acids. A purine derivative, it is paired with thymine in double-stranded DNA. ● Alternative name: **6-aminopurine**; chem. formula: $C_5H_5N_5$.
– ORIGIN late 19th cent.: coined in German from Greek *adēn* 'gland' + -INE⁴.

adeno- ▶ **combining form** relating to a gland or glands: *adenocarcinoma*.
– ORIGIN from Greek *adēn* 'gland'.

adenocarcinoma /ˌadɪnəʊˌkɑːsɪˈnəʊmə/ ▶ **noun** (pl. **adenocarcinomas** or **adenocarcinomata** /-mətə/) Medicine a malignant tumour formed from glandular structures in epithelial tissue.

adenoids /ˈadɪnɔɪdz/ ▶ **plural noun** a mass of enlarged lymphatic tissue between the back of the nose and the throat, often hindering speaking and breathing in young children.
– DERIVATIVES **adenoidal** adjective.
– ORIGIN late 19th cent.: *adenoid* from Greek *adēn* 'gland' + -OID.

adenoma /ˌadɪˈnəʊmə/ ▶ **noun** (pl. **adenomas** or **adenomata** /-mətə/) Medicine a benign tumour formed from glandular structures in epithelial tissue.
– DERIVATIVES **adenomatous** adjective.
– ORIGIN late 19th cent.: modern Latin, from Greek *adēn* 'gland'.

adenosine /əˈdɛnə(ʊ)siːn/ ▶ **noun** [mass noun] Biochemistry a compound consisting of adenine combined with ribose, present in all living tissue in combined form as nucleotides.
– ORIGIN early 20th cent.: blend of ADENINE and RIBOSE.

adenosine deaminase /diːˈamɪneɪz/ ▶ **noun** [mass noun] Biochemistry an enzyme which catalyses the deamination of adenosine to inosine.

adenosine monophosphate (abbrev.: **AMP**) ▶ **noun** another term for ADENYLIC ACID.

adenosine triphosphate (abbrev.: **ATP**) ▶ **noun** [mass noun] Biochemistry a compound consisting of an adenosine molecule bonded to three phosphate groups, present in all living tissue. The breakage of one phosphate linkage (to form **adenosine diphosphate, ADP**) provides energy for physiological processes such as muscular contraction.

adenovirus /ˈadɪnəʊˌvʌɪrəs/ ▶ **noun** Medicine any of a group of DNA viruses first discovered in adenoid tissue, most of which cause respiratory diseases.
– DERIVATIVES **adenoviral** adjective.

adenylate /əˈdɛnɪleɪt/ ▶ **noun** Chemistry a salt or ester of adenylic acid.

adenylate cyclase /əˌdɛnɪleɪt ˈsʌɪkleɪz, ˈsɪk-/ ▶ **noun** [mass noun] Biochemistry an enzyme that catalyses the formation of cyclic adenylic acid from adenosine triphosphate.

adenylic acid /ˌadɪˈnɪlɪk/ ▶ **noun** [mass noun] Biochemistry a compound consisting of an adenosine molecule bonded to one acidic phosphate group, present in

most DNA and RNA. It typically exists in a cyclic form with the phosphate bonded to the nucleoside at two points.
– ORIGIN late 19th cent.: *adenylic* from ADENINE + -YL + -IC.

adept ▶ adjective /əˈdɛpt, ˈadɛpt/ very skilled or proficient at something: *she is **adept at** cutting through red tape | an adept negotiator.*
▶ noun /ˈadɛpt/ a person who is skilled or proficient at something: *he is an adept at imitation.*
– DERIVATIVES **adeptly** adverb, **adeptness** noun.
– ORIGIN mid 17th cent.: from Latin *adeptus* 'achieved', past participle of *adipisci* 'obtain, attain'.

adequacy ▶ noun [mass noun] the state or quality of being adequate: *the adequacy of testing procedures.*

adequate ▶ adjective satisfactory or acceptable in quality or quantity: *this office is perfectly **adequate for** my needs | adequate resources and funding.*
– DERIVATIVES **adequately** adverb.
– ORIGIN early 17th cent.: from Latin *adaequatus* 'made equal to', past participle of the verb *adaequare*, from *ad-* 'to' + *aequus* 'equal'.

à deux /ɑː ˈdəː/, French /a dø/ ▶ adverb for or involving two people: *dinner à deux.*
– ORIGIN French.

ADF ▶ abbreviation automatic direction finder, a device used by pilots to aid navigation.

ad fin. /ad ˈfɪn/ ▶ adverb at or near the end of a piece of writing.
– ORIGIN from Latin *ad finem* 'at the end'.

ADH ▶ abbreviation Biochemistry antidiuretic hormone.

adhan /ədˈhɑːn/ ▶ noun variant spelling of AZAN.

ADHD ▶ abbreviation attention deficit hyperactivity disorder.

adhere /ədˈhɪə/ ▶ verb [no obj.] (**adhere to**) **1** stick fast to (a surface or substance): *paint won't adhere well to a greasy surface.*
2 believe in and follow the practices of: *I do not adhere to any organized religion.* ■ closely follow, observe, or represent: *the account adhered firmly to fact.*
– ORIGIN late 15th cent.: from Latin *adhaerere*, from *ad-* 'to' + *haerere* 'to stick'.

adherent ▶ noun someone who supports a particular party, person, or set of ideas: *he was a strong adherent of monetarism.*
▶ adjective sticking fast to an object or surface.
– DERIVATIVES **adherence** noun.
– ORIGIN late Middle English: from Old French *adherent*, from Latin *adhaerent-* 'sticking to', from the verb *adhaerere* (see ADHERE).

adhesion /ədˈhiːʒ(ə)n/ ▶ noun [mass noun] **1** the action or process of adhering to a surface or object: *the adhesion of the gum strip to the paper.* ■ the frictional grip of wheels, shoes, etc. on a surface: *the sole unit provides good adhesion for walking on all surfaces.* ■ Physics the sticking together of particles of different substances.
2 Medicine an abnormal adhering of surfaces due to inflammation or injury.
– ORIGIN late 15th cent.: from French *adhésion*, from Latin *adhaesio(n-)*, from the verb *adhaerere* (see ADHERE).

adhesive /ədˈhiːsɪv, -zɪv/ ▶ adjective able to stick fast to a surface or object; sticky: *an adhesive label.*
▶ noun a substance used for sticking objects or materials together; glue.
– DERIVATIVES **adhesively** adverb, **adhesiveness** noun.
– ORIGIN late 17th cent. (in the sense 'tending to adhere or cling to'): from French *adhésif, -ive*, from the verb *adhérer*, from Latin *adhaerere* 'stick to' (see ADHERE).

adhibit /ədˈhɪbɪt/ ▶ verb (**adhibits, adhibiting, adhibited**) [with obj.] formal apply or affix (something) to something else.
– DERIVATIVES **adhibition** noun.
– ORIGIN early 16th cent. (in the sense 'take in, include'): from Latin *adhibit-* 'brought in', from the verb *adhibere*, from *ad-* 'to' + *habere* 'hold, have'.

ad hoc /ad ˈhɒk/ ▶ adjective & adverb created or done for a particular purpose as necessary: [as adj.] *the discussions were on an ad hoc basis* | [as adv.] *the group was constituted ad hoc.*
– ORIGIN Latin, literally 'to this'.

adhocracy /adˈhɒkrəsi/ ▶ noun [mass noun] a system of flexible and informal organization and management in place of rigid bureaucracy.
– ORIGIN 1970s: blend of AD HOC and -CRACY.

ad hominem /ad ˈhɒmɪnɛm/ ▶ adverb & adjective **1** relating to or associated with a particular person: [as adv.] *the office was created ad hominem for Fenton.*
2 (of an argument or reaction) directed against a person rather than the position they are maintaining: [as adj.] *an ad hominem response.*
– ORIGIN Latin, literally 'to the person'.

adiabatic /ˌeɪdʌɪəˈbatɪk, ˌadɪə-/ Physics ▶ adjective relating to or denoting a process or condition in which heat does not enter or leave the system concerned. ■ impassable to heat.
▶ noun a curve or formula representing adiabatic phenomena.
– DERIVATIVES **adiabatically** adverb.
– ORIGIN late 19th cent.: from Greek *adiabatos* 'impassable', from *a-* 'not' + *dia* 'through' + *batos* 'passable' (from *bainein* 'go'), + -IC.

adiabatic lapse rate ▶ noun Meteorology the rate at which atmospheric temperature decreases with increasing altitude in conditions of thermal equilibrium.

adieu /əˈdjuː/ chiefly literary ▶ exclamation goodbye.
▶ noun (pl. **adieus** or **adieux** /əˈdjuːz/) a goodbye: *he whispered a fond adieu.*
– ORIGIN late Middle English: from Old French, from *a* 'to' + *Dieu* 'God'; compare with ADIOS.

Adi Granth /ˌɑːdɪ ˈgrʌnt/ another term for GURU GRANTH SAHIB.
– ORIGIN from Sanskrit *ādigrantha*, literally 'first book', based on *grantha* 'literary composition', from *granth* 'to tie'.

ad infinitum /ˌad ɪnfɪˈnʌɪtəm/ ▶ adverb again and again in the same way; forever: *registration is for seven years and may be renewed ad infinitum.*
– ORIGIN Latin, literally 'to infinity'.

ad interim /ad ˈɪntərɪm/ ▶ adverb for an intervening or temporary period of time.
▶ adjective temporary.
– ORIGIN Latin, from *ad* 'to' and *interim* 'meanwhile', used as a noun.

adios /ˌadɪˈɒs/ ▶ exclamation & noun Spanish term for GOODBYE.
– ORIGIN Spanish *adiós*, from *a* 'to' + *Dios* 'God'; compare with ADIEU.

adipate /ˈadɪpeɪt/ ▶ noun Chemistry a salt or ester of adipic acid.

adipic acid /əˈdɪpɪk/ ▶ noun [mass noun] Chemistry a crystalline fatty acid obtained from natural fats and used especially in the manufacture of nylon. ● Alternative name: **hexanedioic acid**; chem. formula: $HOOC(CH_2)_4COOH$.
– ORIGIN mid 19th cent.: from Latin *adeps, adip-* 'fat' (because the acid was first prepared by oxidizing fats) + -IC.

adipocere /ˌadɪpə(ʊ)ˈsɪə/ ▶ noun [mass noun] a greyish waxy substance formed by the decomposition of soft tissue in dead bodies subjected to moisture.
– ORIGIN early 19th cent.: from French *adipocire*, from Latin *adeps, adip-* 'fat' + French *cire* 'wax' (from Latin *cera*).

adipocyte /ˈadɪpə(ʊ)sʌɪt/ ▶ noun Biology a cell specialized for the storage of fat, found in connective tissue.
– ORIGIN 1930s: from ADIPOSE + -CYTE.

adipose /ˈadɪpəʊs, -z/ ▶ adjective technical (especially of body tissue) used for the storage of fat.
– DERIVATIVES **adiposity** noun.
– ORIGIN mid 18th cent.: from modern Latin *adiposus*, from *adeps, adip-* 'fat'.

adipose fin ▶ noun Zoology a small, rayless, fleshy dorsal fin present in certain fishes, notably in the salmon family.

Adirondack chair /ˌadɪˈrɒndak/ ▶ noun N. Amer. an armchair constructed from wide wooden slats, for outdoor use.

Adirondack Mountains /ˌadɪˈrɒndak/ (also **the Adirondacks**) a range of mountains in New York State, source of the Hudson and Mohawk Rivers.

Adis Abeba variant spelling of ADDIS ABABA.

adit /ˈadɪt/ ▶ noun a horizontal passage leading into a mine for the purposes of access or drainage.
– ORIGIN early 17th cent.: from Latin *aditus* 'approach, entrance', from *adit-* 'approached', from the verb *adire*, from *ad-* 'towards' + *ire* 'go'.

Adivasi /ˌɑːdɪˈvɑːsi/ ▶ noun (pl. **Adivasis**) a member of any of the aboriginal tribal peoples living in India before the arrival of the Aryans in the second millennium BC. ■ a descendant of any of the Adivasi peoples.
– ORIGIN from modern Sanskrit *ādivāsī*, from Sanskrit *ādi* 'earliest' + *vāsi* 'inhabitant'.

Adj. ▶ abbreviation adjutant.

adjacent /əˈdʒeɪs(ə)nt/ ▶ adjective **1** next to or adjoining something else: *adjacent rooms | the area **adjacent to** the station.*
2 Geometry (of a pair of angles) formed on the same side of a straight line when intersected by another line.
– DERIVATIVES **adjacency** noun.
– ORIGIN late Middle English: from Latin *adjacent-* 'lying near to', from *adjacere*, from *ad-* 'to' + *jacere* 'lie down'.

adjective ▶ noun Grammar a word naming an attribute of a noun, such as *sweet, red*, or *technical*.
– DERIVATIVES **adjectival** adjective, **adjectivally** adverb.
– ORIGIN late Middle English: from Old French *adjectif, -ive*, from Latin *adject-* 'added', from the verb *adicere*, from *ad-* 'towards' + *jacere* 'throw'. The term was originally used in the phrase *noun adjective*, translating Latin *nomen adjectivum*, a translation of Greek *onoma epitheton* 'attributive name'.

adjigo /ˈadʒɪgəʊ/ (also **adjiko** /ˈadʒɪkəʊ/) ▶ noun (pl. **adjigos**) a yam with edible tubers, native to parts of SW Australia. ● *Dioscorea hastifolia*, family Dioscoreaceae.
– ORIGIN mid 19th cent.: probably from Nhanta (an Aboriginal language) *ajuga* 'vegetable food'.

adjoin ▶ verb [with obj.] be next to and joined with (a building, room, or piece of land): *the dining room adjoins a conservatory.* ■ archaic or technical add or join something to.
– ORIGIN Middle English: from Old French *ajoindre*, from Latin *adjungere*, from *ad-* 'to' + *jungere* 'to join'.

adjoining ▶ adjective (of a building, room, or piece of land) next to or joined with: *I was in an adjoining room and could hear voices | they ended up buying the adjoining land.*

adjoint Mathematics ▶ adjective relating to or denoting a function or quantity related to a given function or quantity by a particular process of transposition. ■ denoting a matrix that is the transpose of the complex conjugates or the cofactors of a given square matrix.
▶ noun an adjoint matrix, function, or quantity.
– ORIGIN late 19th cent.: from French, literally 'joined to', from *adjoindre* (see ADJOIN).

adjourn /əˈdʒəːn/ ▶ verb [with obj.] break off (a meeting, legal case, or game) with the intention of resuming it later: *the meeting was adjourned until December 4* | [no obj.] *let's adjourn and reconvene at 2 o'clock.* ■ [no obj., with adverbial] (of a group of people) go somewhere for rest or refreshment: *they **adjourned to** a local pub.* ■ put off or postpone (a resolution or sentence): *sentence was adjourned for a social inquiry report.*
– ORIGIN Middle English (in the sense 'summon someone to appear on a particular day'): from Old French *ajorner*, from the phrase *a jorn (nome)* 'to an (appointed) day'.

adjournment ▶ noun an act or period of adjourning or being adjourned: *she sought an adjournment of the trial | I suggest we have a short adjournment.*

adjournment debate ▶ noun (in the UK) a debate in the House of Commons on the motion that the House be adjourned, used as an opportunity for raising various matters.

Adjt ▶ abbreviation adjutant.

adjudge ▶ verb [with obj. and complement] consider or declare to be true or the case: *she was adjudged guilty.* ■ (**adjudge something to**) (in legal use) award something judicially to: *the court adjudged legal damages to her.* ■ [with obj. and infinitive] (in legal use) condemn (someone) to pay a penalty: *the defaulter was adjudged to pay the whole amount.*
– ORIGIN late Middle English: from Old French *ajuger*, from Latin *adjudicare*, from *ad-* 'to' + *judicare*, from *judex, judic-* 'a judge'.

adjudicate /əˈdʒuːdɪkeɪt/ ▶ verb [no obj.] make a formal judgement on a disputed matter: *the Committee **adjudicates on** all betting disputes* | [with obj.] *the case was adjudicated in the High Court.* ■ act as a judge in a competition: *we asked him to adjudicate at the local flower show.* ■ [with obj. and complement] pronounce or declare judicially: *he was adjudicated bankrupt.*
– DERIVATIVES **adjudicative** adjective.
– ORIGIN early 18th cent. (in the sense 'award judicially'): from Latin *adjudicat-* 'awarded judicially', from the verb *adjudicare* (see ADJUDGE). The noun *adjudication* (as a Scots legal term) dates from the early 17th cent.

adjudication ▸ noun [mass noun] the action or process of adjudicating: *the matter may have to go to court for adjudication.* ■ [count noun] a formal judgement on a disputed matter: *an adjudication had found a degree of unwarranted infringement of privacy.*

adjudicator ▸ noun a person who adjudicates: *the proposal to close the school will have to go before an adjudicator.*

adjunct /ˈadʒʌŋ(k)t/ ▸ noun **1** a thing added to something else as a supplementary rather than an essential part: *computer technology is an* ***adjunct to*** *learning.* ■ a person who is another's assistant or subordinate.
2 Grammar a word or phrase that constitutes an optional element or is considered of secondary importance in a sentence, for example *on the table* in *we left some flowers on the table.* ■ (in systemic grammar) an obligatory or optional adverbial functioning as a constituent of clause structure.
▸ adjective [attrib.] connected or added to something: *other adjunct therapies include immunotherapy.* ■ N. Amer. (of an academic post) attached to the staff of a university in a temporary or assistant capacity: *an adjunct professor of entomology.*
– DERIVATIVES **adjunctive** adjective.
– ORIGIN early 16th cent. (as an adjective meaning 'joined on, subordinate'): from Latin *adjunctus*, past participle of *adjungere* (see **ADJOIN**).

adjunction ▸ noun [mass noun] **1** Mathematics the joining of two sets which without overlapping jointly constitute a larger set, or the relation between two such sets.
2 Logic the asserting in a single formula of two previously asserted formulae.
– ORIGIN late 16th cent.: from Latin *adjunctio(n)-*, from the verb *adjungere* (see **ADJOIN**).

adjure /əˈdʒʊə, əˈdʒɔː/ ▸ verb [with obj. and infinitive] formal urge or request (someone) solemnly or earnestly to do something: *I adjure you to tell me the truth.*
– DERIVATIVES **adjuration** noun.
– ORIGIN late Middle English (in the sense 'put a person on oath'): from Latin *adjurare*, from *ad-* 'to' + *jurare* 'swear' (from *jus, jur-* 'oath').

adjust ▸ verb **1** [with obj.] alter or move (something) slightly in order to achieve the desired fit, appearance, or result: *he smoothed his hair and adjusted his tie | a single control adjusts the water flow.* ■ [no obj.] permit small alterations or movements so as to achieve a desired fit, appearance, or result: *a harness that* ***adjusts to*** *the correct fit.* ■ [no obj.] adapt or become used to a new situation: *she must be allowed to grieve and to adjust in her own way | his eyes had* ***adjusted to*** *semi-darkness.*
2 [with obj.] assess (loss or damages) when settling an insurance claim.
– PHRASES **do not adjust your set** used to tell someone that information is true, although it appears strange or incorrect: *yes, the candidate is from Montana. Do not adjust your set.*
– DERIVATIVES **adjuster** noun.
– ORIGIN early 17th cent. (in the senses 'harmonize discrepancies' and 'assess loss or damages'): from obsolete French *adjuster*, from Old French *ajoster* 'to approximate', based on Latin *ad-* 'to' + *juxta* 'near'.

adjustable ▸ adjective able to be adjusted: *the car has fully adjustable seats and steering wheel.*
– DERIVATIVES **adjustability** noun.

adjustment ▸ noun a small alteration or movement made to achieve a desired fit, appearance, or result: *I've made a few adjustments to my diet | only slight adjustments to the boat are necessary.* ■ [mass noun] the process of adapting or becoming used to a new situation: *for many couples there may need to be a period of adjustment.*

adjutant /ˈadʒʊt(ə)nt/ ▸ noun **1** a military officer who acts as an administrative assistant to a senior officer.
2 (also **adjutant stork** or **adjutant bird**) a large black-and-white stork with a massive bill and a bare head and neck, found in India and SE Asia. ● Genus *Leptoptilos*, family Ciconiidae: two species.
– DERIVATIVES **adjutancy** noun.
– ORIGIN early 17th cent. (in the sense 'assistant, helper'): from Latin *adjutant-* 'being of service to', from *adjutare*, frequentative of *adjuvare* 'assist' (see **ADJUVANT**).

adjutant general ▸ noun (pl. **adjutants general**) (in the British army) a high-ranking administrative officer. ■ (in the US army) the chief administrative officer.

adjuvant /ˈadʒʊv(ə)nt/ Medicine ▸ adjective (of therapy) applied after initial treatment for cancer, especially to suppress secondary tumour formation.
▸ noun a substance which enhances the body's immune response to an antigen.
– ORIGIN late 16th cent.: from Latin *adjuvant-* 'helping towards', from the verb *adjuvare*, from *ad-* 'towards' + *juvare* to 'help'.

adland ▸ noun [mass noun] informal the business world of advertising and advertisers.

Adler /ˈadlə/, German /ˈaːdlɐ/, Alfred (1870–1937), Austrian psychologist and psychiatrist. Adler disagreed with Freud's idea that mental illness was caused by sexual conflicts in infancy, arguing that society and culture were significant factors. He introduced the concept of the inferiority complex.
– DERIVATIVES **Adlerian** /adˈlɪərɪən/ adjective & noun.

ad-lib ▸ verb (**ad-libs, ad-libbing, ad-libbed**) [no obj.] speak or perform without previously preparing one's words: *Charles had to ad-lib because he'd forgotten his script.*
▸ adverb & adjective (also **ad lib**) **1** spoken or performed without previous preparation: [as adj.] *an ad-lib commentary* | [as adv.] *I spoke ad lib.* ■ Music (especially as a direction) with free rhythm and expression.
2 as much and as often as desired: [as adv.] *the price includes meals and drinks ad lib.*
▸ noun an ad-lib remark or speech.
– ORIGIN early 19th cent. (as an adverb): abbreviation of **AD LIBITUM**.

ad libitum /ad ˈlɪbɪtəm/ ▸ adverb & adjective more formal term for **AD-LIB**.
– ORIGIN Latin, literally 'according to pleasure'.

ad litem /ad ˈlʌɪtɛm/ ▸ adjective Law appointed to act in a lawsuit on behalf of a child or other person who is not considered capable of representing themselves.
– ORIGIN Latin, literally 'for the lawsuit'.

Adm. ▸ abbreviation Admiral.

adman ▸ noun (pl. **admen**) informal a person who works in advertising.

admeasurement ▸ noun [mass noun] archaic the action of ascertaining and apportioning just shares in something.
– ORIGIN early 16th cent.: from Old French *amesurement*, from the verb *amesurer*, from medieval Latin *admensurare*, based on Latin *metiri* 'to measure'.

admin ▸ noun [mass noun] informal, chiefly Brit. the administration of a business, organization, etc.: *day-to-day admin* | [as modifier] *admin staff.*
– ORIGIN 1940s: abbreviation.

adminicle /ədˈmɪnɪk(ə)l/ ▸ noun Scots Law a document giving evidence as to the existence or contents of another, missing document.
– ORIGIN mid 16th cent.: from Latin *adminiculum* 'prop, support'.

administer ▸ verb [with obj.] **1** manage and be responsible for the running of (a business, organization, etc.): *each school was administered separately.* ■ be responsible for the implementation or use of (law or resources): *a Health and Safety agency would administer new regulations.*
2 dispense or apply (a remedy or drug): *paramedic crews are capable of administering drugs.* ■ deal out or inflict (punishment): *retribution was administered to those found guilty.*
3 (of a priest) perform the rites of (a sacrament).
4 archaic or Law direct the taking of (an oath).
– DERIVATIVES **administrable** adjective.
– ORIGIN late Middle English: via Old French from Latin *administrare*, from *ad-* 'to' + *ministrare* (see **MINISTRATION**).

administrate ▸ verb less common term for **ADMINISTER** (sense 1).
– ORIGIN mid 16th cent.: from Latin *administrat-* 'managed', from the verb *administrare* (see **ADMINISTER**).

administration ▸ noun **1** [mass noun] the process or activity of running a business, organization, etc.: *the day-to-day administration of the company | a career in arts administration.* ■ (**the administration**) the people responsible for running a business, organization, etc.: *the university administration took their demands seriously.* ■ Law the management and disposition of the property of a deceased person, debtor, or insolvent company, by a legally appointed administrator: *the company* ***went into administration.***
2 [mass noun] the management of public affairs; government: *the inhabitants of the island voted to remain under French administration.* ■ [count noun] the government in power: *successive Conservative administrations enjoyed a comfortable majority.* ■ [count noun] chiefly N. Amer. the term of office of a political leader or government: *the early years of the Reagan Administration.* ■ [count noun] (in the US) a department or agency of the government: *the US Food and Drug Administration.*
3 [mass noun] the action of dispensing, giving, or applying something: *the oral administration of the antibiotic | the administration of justice.*
– ORIGIN Middle English: from Latin *administratio(n-)*, from the verb *administrare* (see **ADMINISTER**).

administrative ▸ adjective relating to the running of a business, organization, etc.: *administrative problems | administrative staff.*
– DERIVATIVES **administratively** adverb.
– ORIGIN mid 18th cent.: from Latin *administrativus*, from *administrat-* 'managed', from the verb *administrare* (see **ADMINISTRATE**).

administrator ▸ noun **1** a person responsible for carrying out the administration of a business or organization. ■ Law a person legally appointed to manage and dispose of the estate of a deceased person, debtor, or insolvent company.
2 a person who dispenses or administers something: *administrators of justice.*

administratrix /ədˌmɪnɪˈstreɪtrɪks/ ▸ noun (pl. **administratrixes, administratrices** /-trɪsiːz/) Law a female administrator of an estate.

admirable ▸ adjective arousing or deserving respect and approval: *he has one admirable quality—he is totally honest.*
– DERIVATIVES **admirably** adverb.
– ORIGIN late Middle English: via Old French from Latin *admirabilis* 'to be wondered at', from *admirari* (see **ADMIRE**).

admiral ▸ noun **1** the most senior commander of a fleet or navy. ■ (**Admiral**) a naval officer of the second most senior rank, above vice admiral and below Admiral of the Fleet or Fleet Admiral. ■ short for **VICE ADMIRAL** or **REAR ADMIRAL**.
2 [with modifier] a butterfly which has dark wings with bold red or white markings. See **RED ADMIRAL, WHITE ADMIRAL**.
– ORIGIN Middle English (denoting an emir or Saracen commander): from Old French *amiral*, *admirail*, via medieval Latin from Arabic *ʼamīr* 'commander' (from *ʼamara* 'to command'). The ending *-al* was from Arabic *-al-* 'of the', used in titles (e.g. *ʼamīr-al-ʼumarā* 'ruler of rulers'), later assimilated to the familiar Latinate suffix **-AL**.

Admiral of the Fleet ▸ noun the highest rank of admiral in the Royal Navy.

Admiral's Cup a yacht-racing competition held every two years since 1957 between international teams of three yachts.

Admiralty ▸ noun (pl. **Admiralties**) **1** (in the UK) the government department that administered the Royal Navy, now incorporated in the Ministry of Defence and current only in titles.
2 (**admiralty**) [mass noun] Law the jurisdiction of courts of law over cases concerning ships or the sea and other navigable waters.
– ORIGIN late Middle English: from Old French *admiralte*, from *admirail* 'emir, leader' (see **ADMIRAL**)

Admiralty Islands a group of about forty islands in the western Pacific, part of Papua New Guinea.

admiration ▸ noun [mass noun] respect and warm approval: *I have the greatest* ***admiration for*** *all those involved in the project.* ■ (**the admiration of**) something regarded as impressive or worthy of respect: *her house was the admiration of everyone.*
– ORIGIN late Middle English (in the sense 'marvelling, wonder'): from Latin *admiratio(n-)*, from the verb *admirari* (see **ADMIRE**).

admire ▸ verb [with obj.] regard with respect or warm approval: *I admire your courage* | (as adj. **admiring**) *she couldn't help but notice his admiring glance.* ■ look at (something impressive or attractive) with pleasure: *we were just admiring your garden.*
– DERIVATIVES **admiringly** adverb.
– ORIGIN late 16th cent.: from Latin *admirari*, from *ad-* 'at' + *mirari* 'wonder'.

admirer ▸ noun someone who has a particular regard for someone or something: *he was a great admirer of Henry James.* ■ a man who is attracted to a particular woman: *she's got a secret admirer.*

admissible ▸ adjective **1** acceptable or valid, especially as evidence in a court of law: *the tape recording was admissible as evidence.*

2 having the right to be admitted to a place: *foreigners were admissible only as temporary workers.*
– DERIVATIVES **admissibility** noun.
– ORIGIN early 17th cent.: from medieval Latin *admissibilis*, from Latin *admittere* (see **ADMIT**).

admission ▸ noun 1 a statement acknowledging the truth of something: *an admission of guilt | a tacit admission that things had gone wrong.*
2 [mass noun] the process or fact of entering or being allowed to enter a place or organization: *the evening before her admission to hospital | the country's admission to the UN.* ■ the fee charged for entry to a public place: *admission is £1 for adults and 50p for children.* ■ (**admissions**) the number of people entering a place: *cinema admissions have been rising recently.* ■ [count noun] a person admitted to hospital for treatment: *there was a substantial reduction in hospital admissions.*
– ORIGIN late Middle English: from Latin *admissio(n-)*, from the verb *admittere* (see **ADMIT**).

admit ▸ verb (**admits, admitting, admitted**) 1 [reporting verb] confess to be true or to be the case: [with clause] *the Home Office finally admitted that several prisoners had been injured* | [with direct speech] *'I am feeling pretty tired,' Jane admitted.* ■ [with obj.] confess to (a crime or fault, or one's responsibility for it): *he was sentenced to prison after admitting 47 charges of burglary* | [no obj.] *the paramilitaries* ***admitted to*** *the illegal possession of arms.* ■ [with obj.] acknowledge (a failure or fault): *after searching for an hour, she finally had to* ***admit defeat.***
2 [with obj.] (usu. **admit to**) allow (someone) to enter a place: *old-age pensioners are admitted free to the museum.* ■ receive (a patient) into a hospital for treatment: *she was admitted to hospital suffering from a chest infection.* ■ allow (a person, country, etc.) to join an organization: *Canada was admitted to the League of Nations.* ■ allow (someone) to share in a privilege: *he was admitted to the freedom of the city in 1583.*
3 [with obj.] accept as valid: *the courts can refuse to admit police evidence which has been illegally obtained.*
4 [no obj.] (**admit of**) allow the possibility of: *the need to inform him was too urgent to admit of further delay.*
– ORIGIN late Middle English: from Latin *admittere*, from *ad-* 'to' + *mittere* 'send'.

admittance ▸ noun [mass noun] 1 the process or fact of entering or being allowed to enter a place or institution: *people were unable to* ***gain admittance*** *to the hall.*
2 Physics a measure of electrical conduction, numerically equal to the reciprocal of the impedance.

admittedly ▸ adverb [sentence adverb] used to express a concession or recognition that something is the case: *admittedly, the salary was not wonderful.*

admix ▸ verb [with obj.] technical mix (something) with something else.
– ORIGIN late Middle English: back-formation from the obsolete adjective 'admixt', from Latin *admixtus* 'mixed together', past participle of *admiscere*, from *ad-* 'to' + *miscere* 'to mix'.

admixture ▸ noun a mixture. ■ something mixed with something else: *green with an admixture of black.* ■ [mass noun] the action of adding an ingredient to something else.
– ORIGIN early 17th cent. (in the sense 'act of admixing'): from **AD-** (expressing addition) + **MIXTURE**.

admonish ▸ verb [with obj.] reprimand firmly: *she admonished me for appearing at breakfast unshaven.* ■ [with obj. and infinitive] advise or urge (someone) earnestly: *she admonished him to drink no more than one glass of wine.* ■ archaic warn (someone) of something to be avoided: *he admonished the people against the evil of such practices.*
– DERIVATIVES **admonishment** noun.
– ORIGIN Middle English *amonest* 'urge, exhort', from Old French *amonester*, based on Latin *admonere* 'urge by warning'. Later, the final *-t* of *amonest* was taken to indicate the past tense, and the present tense changed on the pattern of verbs such as *abolish*; the prefix became *ad-* in the 16th cent. by association with the Latin form.

admonition ▸ noun a firm warning or reprimand: *he received numerous admonitions for his behaviour.*

admonitory /əd'mɒnɪt(ə)ri/ ▸ adjective giving or conveying a warning or reprimand: *the sergeant lifted an admonitory finger.*
– ORIGIN late 16th cent.: from medieval Latin *admonitorius*, from *admonit-* 'urged', from Latin *admonere* (see **ADMONISH**).

ADN ▸ abbreviation Yemen (international vehicle registration).
– ORIGIN from **ADEN**.

adnate /'adneɪt/ ▸ adjective Botany joined by having grown together.
– ORIGIN mid 17th cent.: from Latin *adnatus*, variant of *agnatus* (see **AGNATE**), by association with **AD-**.

ad nauseam /ad 'nɔːzɪam, -sɪam/ ▸ adverb used to refer to the fact that something has been done or repeated so often that it has become annoying or tiresome: *he repeated the phrase ad nauseam.*
– ORIGIN Latin, literally 'to sickness'.

adnexa /ad'nɛksə/ ▸ plural noun Anatomy the parts adjoining an organ.
– DERIVATIVES **adnexal** adjective.
– ORIGIN late 19th cent.: Latin, neuter plural of *adnexus* 'joined', from *adnectere* 'fasten to'.

adnominal /əd'nɒmɪn(ə)l/ ▸ adjective Grammar attached to or modifying a noun.
– ORIGIN mid 19th cent.: from Latin *adnomen* 'added name' + **-AL**.

Adnyamathanha /'adnjə,mʌdənə/ ▸ noun [mass noun] an Aboriginal language of South Australia.

ado ▸ noun [mass noun] a state of agitation or fuss: *this is* ***much ado*** *about almost nothing.* ■ dated trouble or difficulty: *I hastened there without delay or ado.*
– PHRASES **without further** (or **more**) **ado** without any fuss or delay; immediately.
– ORIGIN late Middle English (originally in the sense 'action, business'): from northern Middle English *at do* 'to do', from Old Norse *at* (used to mark an infinitive) and **DO**[1].

-ado /'ɑːdəʊ, 'eɪ-/ ▸ suffix forming nouns such as *bravado, desperado.* Compare with **-ADE**[3].
– ORIGIN from Spanish and Portuguese *-ado*, or refashioning of Italian *-ata*, Spanish *-ada*, based on Latin *-atus* (past participial suffix of verbs ending in *-are*).

adobe /ə'dəʊbi, ə'dəʊb/ ▸ noun [mass noun] a kind of clay used as a building material. ■ [count noun] a brick formed from adobe. ■ [count noun] US a building constructed from adobe clay or bricks.
– ORIGIN mid 18th cent.: from Spanish, from *adobar* 'to plaster', from Arabic *aṭ-ṭūb*, from *al* 'the' + *ṭūb* 'bricks'.

adobo /ə'dəʊbəʊ/ ▸ noun (pl. **adobos**) [mass noun] 1 a Filipino dish of chicken or pork stewed in vinegar, garlic, soy sauce, bay leaves, and peppercorns. ■ the marinade in which this is cooked.
2 (also **adobo sauce**) a paste or marinade made from chillies, vinegar, herbs, and spices, used in Mexican cookery to flavour meat or fish.
– ORIGIN Spanish, literally 'marinade'.

adolescence ▸ noun [mass noun] the period following the onset of puberty during which a young person develops from a child into an adult.
– ORIGIN late Middle English: from French, from Latin *adolescentia*, from *adolescere* 'grow to maturity' (see **ADOLESCENT**).

adolescent ▸ adjective (of a young person) in the process of developing from a child into an adult. ■ relating to or characteristic of adolescence: *his adolescent years | adolescent problems.*
▸ noun an adolescent boy or girl.
– ORIGIN late Middle English (as a noun): via French from Latin *adolescent-* 'coming to maturity', from *adolescere*, from *ad-* 'to' + *alescere* 'grow, grow up', from *alere* 'nourish'. The adjective dates from the late 18th cent.

Adonai /,adɒ'nʌɪ, -'neɪʌɪ/ ▸ noun a Hebrew name for God.
– ORIGIN from Hebrew *'ăḏōnāy*; see also **JEHOVAH**.

Adonis /ə'dəʊnɪs/ Greek Mythology a beautiful youth loved by both Aphrodite and Persephone. He was killed by a boar, but Zeus decreed that he should spend the winter of each year in the underworld with Persephone and the summer months with Aphrodite. ■ (as noun **an Adonis**) an extremely handsome young man.

Adonis blue ▸ noun a small Eurasian butterfly, the male of which has vivid sky-blue wings. ● *Lysandra bellargus*, family Lycaenidae.

adopt ▸ verb [with obj.] 1 legally take (another's child) and bring it up as one's own: *there are many people eager to adopt a baby.*
2 choose to take up or follow (an idea, method, or course of action): *this approach has been adopted by many big banks.* ■ choose and move to (a country or city) as one's permanent place of residence.
3 take on or assume (an attitude or position): *he adopted a patronizing tone.* ■ Brit. choose (someone) as a candidate for office: *she was recently adopted as Labour candidate for the constituency.* ■ formally approve or accept (a report or suggestion): *the committee voted 5–1 to adopt the proposal.*
4 Brit. (of a local authority) accept responsibility for the maintenance of (a road).
– DERIVATIVES **adoptable** adjective, **adoptee** noun, **adopter** noun.
– ORIGIN late 15th cent.: via French from Latin *adoptare*, from *ad-* 'to' + *optare* 'choose'.

adoption ▸ noun [mass noun] the action or fact of adopting or being adopted: *she gave up her children for adoption | the widespread adoption of agricultural technology.*
– ORIGIN Middle English: from Latin *adoptio(n-)*, from *ad-* 'to' + *optio(n-)* 'choosing' (see **OPTION**).

adoptive ▸ adjective (of a child or parent) in that relationship by adoption: *adoptive parents.* ■ denoting a country or city which a person has chosen as their permanent place of residence.
– DERIVATIVES **adoptively** adverb.
– ORIGIN late Middle English: via Old French from Latin *adoptivus*, from *adoptare* 'select for oneself' (see **ADOPT**).

adorable ▸ adjective inspiring great affection or delight: *I have four adorable Siamese cats.*
– DERIVATIVES **adorability** noun, **adorableness** noun, **adorably** adverb.
– ORIGIN early 17th cent. (in the sense 'worthy of divine worship'): from French, from Latin *adorabilis*, from the verb *adorare* (see **ADORE**).

adoral /ad'ɔːr(ə)l/ ▸ adjective Zoology relating to or denoting the side or end where the mouth is situated.
– DERIVATIVES **adorally** adverb.
– ORIGIN late 19th cent.: from **AD-** 'at' + **ORAL**.

adoration ▸ noun [mass noun] 1 deep love and respect: *he gave her a look of adoration.*
2 worship; veneration: *the Adoration of the Magi.*

adore ▸ verb [with obj.] 1 love and respect (someone) deeply: *he adored his mother.* ■ informal like very much: *she adores Mexican cuisine* | (as adj. **adoring**) *a gift from an adoring fan.*
2 worship; venerate.
– DERIVATIVES **adorer** noun, **adoringly** adverb.
– ORIGIN late Middle English: via Old French from Latin *adorare* 'to worship', from *ad-* 'to' + *orare* 'speak, pray'.

adorn ▸ verb [with obj.] make more beautiful or attractive: *pictures and prints adorned his walls.*
– DERIVATIVES **adorner** noun.
– ORIGIN late Middle English: via Old French from Latin *adornare*, from *ad-* 'to' + *ornare* 'deck, add lustre'.

adornment ▸ noun a thing which adorns or decorates; an ornament: *the necktie is no longer a necessary male adornment.* ■ [mass noun] the action of adorning something: *precious stones have been used for the purposes of adornment for over 7,000 years.*

Adorno /ə'dɔːnəʊ/, German /a'dɔrnəʊ/, Theodor Wiesengrund (1903–69), German philosopher, sociologist, and musicologist; born *Theodor Wiesengrund*. A member of the Frankfurt School, Adorno argued that philosophical authoritarianism is inevitably oppressive and that all theories should be rejected.

ADP ▸ abbreviation Biochemistry adenosine diphosphate.

ad personam /,ad pəː'səʊnam/ ▸ adverb formal on an individual basis.
– ORIGIN Latin.

adpressed ▸ adjective Botany lying closely against the adjacent part, or against the ground.
– ORIGIN early 19th cent.: from Latin *adpress-* 'pressed near', from *adprimere*, from *ad* 'to, at' + *premere* 'to press', + **-ED**[2].

ADR ▸ abbreviation ■ alternative dispute resolution. ■ (in the US) American depositary receipt.

Adrar des Iforas /a,drɑː deɪz ɪ'fɔːrɑː/ a massif region in the central Sahara, on the border between Mali and Algeria.

ad rem /ad 'rɛm/ ▸ adverb & adjective formal relevant to what is being done or discussed at the time.
– ORIGIN late 16th cent.: Latin, literally 'to the matter'.

adrenal /ə'driːn(ə)l/ ▸ adjective relating to or denoting a pair of ductless glands situated above the kidneys. Each consists of a core region (**adrenal medulla**) secreting adrenalin and noradrenaline, and an outer region (**adrenal cortex**) secreting corticosteroids.

▶ noun (usu. **adrenals**) an adrenal gland.
– ORIGIN late 19th cent.: from AD- + RENAL.

adrenalin /əˈdrɛn(ə)lɪn/ (also **adrenaline**, US **Adrenalin** (trademark)) ▶ noun [mass noun] a hormone secreted by the adrenal glands that increases rates of blood circulation, breathing, and carbohydrate metabolism and prepares muscles for exertion. Also called EPINEPHRINE.
– ORIGIN early 20th cent.: from ADRENAL + -IN[1].

adrenalized /əˈdrɛnəlʌɪzd/ (also **adrenalised**) ▶ adjective affected with adrenalin. ■ informal excited, charged, or tense: *they possess an adrenalized vigour that distinguishes them from other bands.*

adrenergic /ˌadrɪˈnəːdʒɪk/ ▶ adjective Physiology relating to or denoting nerve cells in which adrenalin, noradrenaline, or a similar substance acts as a neurotransmitter. Contrasted with CHOLINERGIC.
– ORIGIN 1930s: from ADRENALIN + Greek *ergon* 'work' + -IC.

adrenocorticotrophic hormone /əˌdriːnə(ʊ)ˌkɔːtɪkə(ʊ)ˈtrəʊfɪk, -ˈtrɒfɪk/ (also **adrenocorticotropic hormone** /-ˈtrəʊpɪk, -ˈtrɒpɪk/) (abbrev.: **ACTH**) ▶ noun [mass noun] Biochemistry a hormone secreted by the pituitary gland and stimulating the adrenal cortex.
– ORIGIN 1930s: from *adreno-* and *cortico-* (combining forms of ADRENAL and CORTEX) + -TROPHIC or -TROPIC.

adrenocorticotrophin /əˌdriːnə(ʊ)ˌkɔːtɪkə(ʊ)ˈtrəʊfɪn, -ˈtrɒfɪn/ (also **adrenocorticotropin** /-pɪn/) ▶ noun another term for ADRENOCORTICOTROPHIC HORMONE.

adret /ˈadreɪ/ ▶ noun a mountain slope which faces the sun. Compare with UBAC.
– ORIGIN from French, from dialect variants of *à* 'to' and *droit* 'straight'.

Adrian IV (*c.*1100–59), pope 1154–9; born *Nicholas Breakspear*. He is the only Englishman to have held this office.

Adriatic /ˌeɪdrɪˈatɪk/ ▶ adjective relating to the region comprising the Adriatic Sea and its coasts and islands.
▶ noun (**the Adriatic**) the Adriatic Sea or its coasts and islands.

Adriatic, Marriage of the see MARRIAGE OF THE ADRIATIC.

Adriatic Sea an arm of the Mediterranean Sea between the Balkans and the Italian peninsula.

adrift ▶ adjective & adverb **1** (of a boat or its passengers) floating without being either moored or steered: [as adv.] *a cargo ship* ***went adrift*** | [as predic. adj.] *the seamen are adrift in lifeboats.* ■ without purpose, direction, or guidance: [as adv.] *she found herself* ***cast adrift*** *in a land full of strangers* | [as predic. adj.] *the film industry was adrift in a sea of debt.* ■ [as adv.] informal no longer fixed in position: *one of my fillings has* ***come adrift***.
2 [as predic. adj.] Brit. informal failing to reach a target or winning position: *the team are three points* ***adrift of*** *the leaders.*
– ORIGIN late 16th cent.: from A-[2] 'on, in' + DRIFT.

adroit /əˈdrɔɪt/ ▶ adjective clever or skilful: *he was* ***adroit at*** *tax avoidance.*
– DERIVATIVES **adroitly** adverb.
– ORIGIN mid 17th cent.: from French, from *à droit* 'according to right, properly'.

adroitness ▶ noun [mass noun] cleverness or skill: *he lacks political adroitness.*

adscititious /ˌadsɪˈtɪʃəs/ ▶ adjective archaic forming an addition or supplement; not integral.
– ORIGIN early 17th cent.: from Latin *adscit-* 'admitted, adopted', from *adsciscere*, + -ITIOUS[1], on the pattern of *adventitious*.

ADSL ▶ abbreviation asymmetric digital subscriber line, a technology for transmitting digital information over standard telephone lines which allows high-speed transmission of signals from the telephone network to an individual subscriber, but a slower rate of transmission from the subscriber to the network.

adsorb /ədˈzɔːb, -ˈsɔːb/ ▶ verb [with obj.] (of a solid) hold (molecules of a gas or liquid or solute) as a thin film on the outside surface or on internal surfaces within the material: *the dye is* ***adsorbed on to*** *the fibre.*
– DERIVATIVES **adsorption** noun, **adsorptive** adjective.
– ORIGIN late 19th cent.: blend of AD- (expressing adherence) + ABSORB.

adsorbate ▶ noun a substance adsorbed.

adsorbent ▶ noun a substance which adsorbs another.
▶ adjective able to adsorb substances.

adstratum /ˈadstrɑːtəm, adˈstrɑːtəm/ ▶ noun (pl. **adstrata**) Linguistics a language or group of elements within it that is responsible for changes in a neighbouring language.
– DERIVATIVES **adstrate** adjective.
– ORIGIN 1930s: modern Latin, from Latin *ad* 'to' + *stratum* 'something laid down'.

ADT ▶ abbreviation Atlantic Daylight Time (see ATLANTIC TIME).

aduki /əˈduːki/ ▶ noun variant spelling of ADZUKI.

adulate /ˈadjʊleɪt/ ▶ verb [with obj.] praise (someone) excessively.
– DERIVATIVES **adulator** noun.
– ORIGIN mid 18th cent.: from Latin *adulat-* 'fawned on', from the verb *adulari*.

adulation /adjʊˈleɪʃ(ə)n/ ▶ noun [mass noun] excessive admiration or praise: *he found it difficult to cope with the adulation of the fans.*
– ORIGIN late Middle English: from Latin *adulatio(n)-*, from *adulari* 'fawn on'.

adulatory /ˌadʒʊˈleɪt(ə)ri/ ▶ adjective excessively praising or admiring: *an adulatory review* | *the tone here is adulatory and uncritical.*

Adullamite /əˈdʌləmʌɪt/ ▶ noun a member of a dissident political group (originally applied to a group of British MPs who seceded from the Liberal party in 1866).
– ORIGIN adopted in allusion to the cave of Adullam, where those discontented with the rule of Saul came to join David (1 Sam. 22:1-2).

adult /ˈadʌlt, əˈdʌlt/ ▶ noun a person who is fully grown or developed. ■ a fully developed animal. ■ Law a person who has reached the age of majority.
▶ adjective fully grown or developed: *an adult woman.* ■ of or for adult people: *adult education.* ■ emotionally and mentally mature: *an effort to be adult and civilized.* ■ suitable only for adults (used euphemistically to refer to a sexually explicit film, book, or magazine).
– DERIVATIVES **adulthood** noun, **adultly** adverb.
– ORIGIN mid 16th cent.: from Latin *adultus*, past participle of *adolescere* 'grow to maturity' (see ADOLESCENT).

adulterant ▶ noun a substance used to adulterate another.
▶ adjective used in adulterating something.
– ORIGIN mid 18th cent.: from Latin *adulterant-* 'corrupting', from the verb *adulterare* (see ADULTERATE).

adulterate ▶ verb /əˈdʌltəreɪt/ [with obj.] render (something) poorer in quality by adding another substance: *the brewer is said to adulterate his beer.*
▶ adjective /əˈdʌlt(ə)rət/ archaic not pure or genuine: *adulterate remedies.*
– DERIVATIVES **adulteration** noun.
– ORIGIN early 16th cent. (as an adjective): from Latin *adulterat-* 'corrupted', from the verb *adulterare*.

adulterer ▶ noun a person who commits adultery.
– ORIGIN early 16th cent.: from the obsolete verb *adulter* 'commit adultery', from Latin *adulterare* 'debauch, corrupt', replacing an earlier Middle English noun *avouterer*, from Old French *avoutrer* 'commit adultery'.

adulteress ▶ noun a female adulterer.

adulterine /əˈdʌlt(ə)rʌɪn/ ▶ adjective **1** (of a child) born as the result of an adulterous relationship.
2 archaic illegal, unlicensed, or spurious: *an adulterine castle.*
– ORIGIN mid 18th cent. (in the sense 'due to adulteration'): from Latin *adulterinus*, from *adulterare* 'debauch, corrupt'.

adulterous ▶ adjective of or involving adultery: *an adulterous affair.*
– DERIVATIVES **adulterously** adverb.
– ORIGIN mid 16th cent.: from the obsolete noun *adulter* 'adulterer' (see ADULTERY) + -OUS.

adultery ▶ noun [mass noun] voluntary sexual intercourse between a married person and a person who is not their spouse: *she was* ***committing adultery*** *with a much younger man.*
– ORIGIN late 15th cent.: from the obsolete noun *adulter*, from Latin *adulter* 'adulterer', replacing an earlier form *avoutrie*, from Old French *avouterie*.

adultescent /adʌlˈtɛs(ə)nt/ ▶ noun informal a middle-aged person whose clothes, interests, and activities are typically associated with youth culture.
– ORIGIN 1990s: blend of ADULT and ADOLESCENT.

adumbrate /ˈadʌmbreɪt/ ▶ verb [with obj.] formal **1** represent in outline: *Hobhouse had already adumbrated the idea of a welfare state.* ■ indicate faintly: *the walls were only adumbrated by the meagre light.*
2 foreshadow (a future event).
3 overshadow: *her happy reminiscences were adumbrated by consciousness of something else.*
– DERIVATIVES **adumbration** noun.
– ORIGIN late 16th cent.: from Latin *adumbrat-* 'shaded', from the verb *adumbrare*, from *ad-* 'to' (as an intensifier) + *umbrare* 'cast a shadow' (from *umbra* 'shade').

adust /əˈdʌst/ ▶ adjective archaic **1** scorched; burnt.
2 gloomy; melancholic.
– ORIGIN late Middle English: from French *aduste* or Latin *adustus* 'burnt', from *adurere*, from *ad* 'to' (as an intensifier) + *urere* 'to burn'.

Advaita /ʌdˈvʌɪtʌ/ ▶ noun [mass noun] Hinduism a Vedantic doctrine that identifies the individual self (atman) with the ground of reality (brahman). It is associated especially with the Indian philosopher Shankara (*c.*788–820).
– ORIGIN Sanskrit, literally 'non-duality'.

ad valorem /ˌad vəˈlɔːrɛm/ ▶ adverb & adjective (of the levying of tax or customs duties) in proportion to the estimated value of the goods or transaction concerned.
– ORIGIN Latin, 'according to the value'.

advance ▶ verb **1** [no obj.] move forwards in a purposeful way: *he advanced towards the dispatch box* | *the troops* ***advanced on*** *the capital.* ■ move forward in time: *as the nineteenth century advanced.* ■ [with obj.] change the date of (an event) so as to occur earlier than planned: *I advanced the schedule by several weeks.*
2 make or cause to make progress: [no obj.] *our knowledge is advancing all the time* | [with obj.] *it was a chance to advance his own interests.* ■ [no obj.] (of shares) increase in price.
3 [with obj.] put forward (a theory or suggestion): *the hypothesis I wish to advance in this article.*
4 [with two objs] lend (money) to (someone): *the building society advanced them a loan.* ■ pay (money) to (someone) before it is due: *he advanced me a month's salary.*
▶ noun **1** a forward movement: *the rebels' advance on Madrid was well under way* | figurative *the advance of civilization.*
2 a development or improvement: ***advances in*** *engineering techniques* | [mass noun] *decades of great scientific advance.* ■ an increase in amount or price: *share prices showed significant advances.*
3 an amount of money paid before it is due or for work only partly completed: *the author was paid a £250,000 advance.* ■ a loan: *an advance from the bank.*
4 (usu. **advances**) an approach made to someone with the aim of initiating sexual or amorous relations: *her tutor* ***made advances to*** *her.*
▶ adjective [attrib.] done, sent, or supplied beforehand: *advance notice.*
– PHRASES **in advance** ahead in time: *you need to book weeks in advance.* **in advance of** ahead of; before: *we went on ahead in advance of the main group.*
– DERIVATIVES **advancer** noun.
– ORIGIN Middle English: from Old French *avance* (noun), *avancer* (verb), from late Latin *abante* 'in front', from *ab* 'from' + *ante* 'before'. The initial *a-* was erroneously assimilated to AD- in the 16th cent.

Advance Australia Fair the national anthem of Australia, composed *c.*1878 by P. D. McCormick (*c.*1834–1916), a Scot, under the pen name 'Amicus'. It officially replaced 'God Save the Queen' in 1984.

advanced ▶ adjective far on or ahead in development or progress: *negotiations are at an advanced stage.*

advanced gas-cooled reactor ▶ noun a nuclear reactor in which the coolant is carbon dioxide, with uranium oxide fuel clad in steel and using graphite as a moderator.

advance directive ▶ noun a living will which gives durable power of attorney to a surrogate decision-maker, remaining in effect during the incompetency of the person making it.

advanced level ▶ noun [mass noun] (in the UK except Scotland) the higher of the two main levels of the GCE examination. Compare with ORDINARY LEVEL.

advanced subsidiary level ▶ noun [mass noun] (in the UK except Scotland) a GCE examination at a level between GCSE and advanced level.

advance guard (also **advanced guard**) ▶ noun a body of soldiers preceding and making preparations for the main body of an army.

A

advance man ▶ **noun** N. Amer. a person who visits a location before the arrival of an important visitor to make the appropriate arrangements.

advancement ▶ **noun 1** [mass noun] the process of promoting a cause or plan: *their lives were devoted to the advancement of science.* ■ the promotion of a person in rank or status: *opportunities for career advancement.*
2 [count noun] a development or improvement: *technological advancements.*
– ORIGIN Middle English: from Old French *avancement*, from *avancer* 'to advance'.

advantage ▶ **noun** a condition or circumstance that puts one in a favourable or superior position: *companies with a computerized database are* ***at an advantage*** | *she had an* ***advantage over*** *her mother's generation.* ■ [mass noun] the opportunity to gain something; benefit or profit: *you could learn something* ***to your advantage*** | *he saw some advantage in the proposal.* ■ a favourable or desirable feature: *the village's proximity to the town is an advantage.* ■ Tennis a score marking a point interim between deuce and winning the game.
▶ **verb** [with obj.] put in a favourable or superior position.
– PHRASES **have the advantage of** dated be in a stronger position than. **take advantage of 1** exploit for one's own benefit: *people tend to take advantage of a placid nature.* ■ dated (of a man) seduce (a woman). **2** make good use of the opportunities offered by: *take full advantage of the facilities available.* **to advantage** in a way which displays or makes good use of the best aspects of something: *her shoes showed off her legs to advantage* | *plan your space* ***to its best advantage.*** **turn something to advantage** (or **to one's advantage**) handle or respond to something in such a way as to benefit from it.
– ORIGIN Middle English: from Old French *avantage*, from *avant* 'in front', from late Latin *abante* (see ADVANCE).

advantaged ▶ **adjective** having a comparatively favourable position in terms of economic or social circumstances: *children from less advantaged homes.*

advantageous /advən'teɪdʒəs/ ▶ **adjective** involving or creating favourable circumstances that increase the chances of success or effectiveness; beneficial: *the scheme is* ***advantageous to*** *your company* | *we are in an advantageous position.*
– DERIVATIVES **advantageously** adverb.

advection /əd'vɛkʃ(ə)n/ ▶ **noun** [mass noun] the transfer of heat or matter by the flow of a fluid, especially horizontally in the atmosphere or the sea.
– DERIVATIVES **advect** verb, **advective** adjective.
– ORIGIN early 20th cent.: from Latin *advectio(n-)*, from *advehere* 'bring', from *ad-* 'to' + *vehere* 'carry'.

advent /'adv(ə)nt, -vɛnt/ ▶ **noun** [in sing.] **1** the arrival of a notable person or thing: *the advent of television.*
2 (**Advent**) the first season of the Church year, leading up to Christmas and including the four preceding Sundays. ■ (**Advent**) Christian Theology the coming or second coming of Christ.
– ORIGIN Old English, from Latin *adventus* 'arrival', from *advenire*, from *ad-* 'to' + *venire* 'come'.

Advent calendar ▶ **noun** a piece of card incorporating small numbered flaps, one of which is opened on each day of Advent to reveal a picture appropriate to the season.

Adventist ▶ **noun** a member of any of various Christian sects emphasizing belief in the imminent second coming of Christ. See also SEVENTH-DAY ADVENTIST.
– DERIVATIVES **Adventism** noun.

adventitia /,adven'tɪʃə/ ▶ **noun** [mass noun] the outermost layer of the wall of a blood vessel.
– DERIVATIVES **adventitial** adjective.
– ORIGIN late 19th cent.: shortening of modern Latin *tunica adventitia* 'additional sheath'.

adventitious /,adv(ə)n'tɪʃəs/ ▶ **adjective** happening as a result of an external factor or chance rather than design or inherent nature: *adventitious similarities.* ■ coming from outside; not native: *the adventitious population.* ■ Biology formed accidentally or in an unusual anatomical position: *adventitious lobes may appear between the primaries.* ■ Botany (of a root, shoot, etc.) produced in an unusual part of a plant.
– DERIVATIVES **adventitiously** adverb.
– ORIGIN early 17th cent.: from Latin *adventicius* 'coming to us from abroad' (from *advenire* 'arrive') + **-ous** (see also **-ITIOUS²**).

Advent Sunday ▶ **noun** the first Sunday in Advent, falling on or near 30 November.

adventure ▶ **noun** an unusual and exciting or daring experience: *her recent adventures in Italy.* ■ [mass noun] excitement associated with danger or the taking of risks: *she travelled the world in search of adventure.* ■ a reckless or potentially hazardous action or enterprise: *in any military adventure, the first casualty is truth.* ■ archaic a commercial venture.
▶ **verb** [no obj.] dated engage in daring or risky activity: *they had* ***adventured into*** *the forest.* ■ [with obj.] put (one's money or life) at risk: *he adventured £300 in the purchase of land.*
– ORIGIN Middle English: from Old French *aventure* (noun), *aventurer* (verb), based on Latin *adventurus* 'about to happen', from *advenire* 'arrive'.

adventure game ▶ **noun** a type of computer game in which the participant plays a fantasy role in an episodic adventure story.

adventure playground ▶ **noun** Brit. a playground containing objects or structures such as ropes, slides, and tunnels, for children to play on or in.

adventurer ▶ **noun** a person who enjoys or seeks adventure. ■ a person willing to take risks or use dishonest methods for personal gain: *a political adventurer.* ■ archaic a financial speculator. ■ archaic a mercenary soldier.
– ORIGIN late 15th cent. (denoting a gambler): from French *aventurier*, from *aventurer* 'venture upon' (see ADVENTURE).

adventuresome ▶ **adjective** given to adventures or to running risks; adventurous: *three adventuresome, energetic boys.*

adventuress ▶ **noun** a female adventurer.

adventurism ▶ **noun** [mass noun] the willingness to take risks in business or politics; actions or attitudes regarded as reckless or potentially hazardous.
– DERIVATIVES **adventurist** noun & adjective.

adventurous ▶ **adjective** willing to take risks or to try out new methods, ideas, or experiences: *an adventurous traveller.* ■ involving new ideas or methods: *they wanted more adventurous meals.* ■ full of excitement: *my life couldn't be more adventurous.*
– DERIVATIVES **adventurously** adverb, **adventurousness** noun.
– ORIGIN Middle English: from Old French *aventureus*, from *aventure* (see ADVENTURE).

adverb ▶ **noun** Grammar a word or phrase that modifies the meaning of an adjective, verb, or other adverb, expressing manner, place, time, or degree (e.g. *gently, here, now, very*). Some adverbs, for example **sentence adverbs**, can also be used to modify whole sentences.
– ORIGIN late Middle English: from Latin *adverbium*, from *ad-* 'to' (expressing addition) + *verbum* 'word, verb'.

adverbial Grammar ▶ **noun** a word or phrase functioning as a major clause constituent and typically expressing place (*in the garden*), time (*in May*), or manner (*in a strange way*).
▶ **adjective** relating to or functioning as an adverb or adverbial.
– DERIVATIVES **adverbially** adverb.

adversarial /,advə'sɛːrɪəl/ ▶ **adjective** involving or characterized by conflict or opposition: *the adversarial nature of the two-party system.* ■ Law (of a trial or legal proceedings) in which the parties in a dispute have the responsibility for finding and presenting evidence. Compare with ACCUSATORIAL, INQUISITORIAL.
– DERIVATIVES **adversarially** adverb.

adversary /'advəs(ə)ri/ ▶ **noun** (pl. **adversaries**) one's opponent in a contest, conflict, or dispute: *Davis beat his old adversary in the quarter-finals.*
▶ **adjective** /'advəs(ə)ri, ad'vəːsəri/ another term for ADVERSARIAL.
– ORIGIN Middle English: from Old French *adversarie*, from Latin *adversarius* 'opposed, opponent', from *adversus* (see ADVERSE).

adversative /əd'vəːsətɪv/ ▶ **adjective** Grammar (of a word or phrase) expressing opposition or antithesis.
– ORIGIN late Middle English: from French *adversatif, -ive* or late Latin *adversativus*, from Latin *adversari* 'oppose', from *adversus* (see ADVERSE).

adverse /'advəːs/ ▶ **adjective** preventing success or development; harmful; unfavourable: *taxes are having an adverse effect on production* | *adverse weather conditions.*
– DERIVATIVES **adversely** adverb.
– ORIGIN late Middle English: from Old French *advers*, from Latin *adversus* 'against, opposite', past participle of *advertere*, from *ad-* 'to' + *vertere* 'to turn'. Compare with AVERSE.

> **USAGE** The two words **adverse** and **averse** are related in origin but they do not have the same meaning. **Adverse** means 'unfavourable or harmful' and is normally used of conditions and effects rather than people, as in ***adverse*** *weather conditions.* **Averse**, on the other hand, is used of people, nearly always with **to**, and means 'having a strong dislike or opposition to something', as in *I am not* ***averse*** *to helping out.* A common error is to use **adverse** instead of **averse**, as in *he is not* ***adverse to*** *making a profit.*

adversity ▶ **noun** (pl. **adversities**) [mass noun] a difficult or unpleasant situation: *resilience in the face of adversity* | [count noun] *she overcame many adversities.*
– ORIGIN Middle English: from Old French *adversite*, from Latin *adversitas*, from *advertere* 'turn towards'.

advert¹ /'advəːt/ ▶ **noun** Brit. informal an advertisement.
– ORIGIN mid 19th cent.: abbreviation.

advert² /əd'vəːt/ ▶ **verb** [no obj.] (**advert to**) formal refer to in speaking or writing: *I have already adverted to the solar revolution.*
– ORIGIN late Middle English: from Old French *avertir*, from Latin *advertere* 'turn towards' (see ADVERSE). The original sense was 'turn one's attention to', later 'bring to someone's attention'.

advertise ▶ **verb** [with obj.] describe or draw attention to (a product, service, or event) in a public medium in order to promote sales or attendance: *a billboard advertising beer.* ■ publicize information about (a vacancy): *for every job we advertise we get a hundred applicants* | [no obj.] *he* ***advertised for*** *dancers in the trade papers.* ■ make (a quality or fact) known: *Meryl coughed briefly to advertise her presence.* ■ archaic notify (someone) of something: *some prisoners* ***advertised*** *the French* ***of*** *this terrible danger.*
– DERIVATIVES **advertiser** noun.
– ORIGIN late Middle English: from Old French *advertiss-*, lengthened stem of *advertir*, from Latin *advertere* 'turn towards' (see ADVERT²).

advertisement ▶ **noun** a notice or announcement in a public medium promoting a product, service, or event or publicizing a job vacancy: ***advertisements for*** *alcoholic drinks.* ■ (**advertisement for**) informal a person or thing regarded as a means of recommending something: *unhappy clients are not a good advertisement for the firm.*
– ORIGIN late Middle English (denoting a statement calling attention to something): from Old French *advertissement*, from the verb *advertir* (see ADVERTISE).

advertising ▶ **noun** [mass noun] the activity or profession of producing advertisements for commercial products or services: *her father was in advertising* | [as modifier] *an advertising agency.*

Advertising Standards Authority (abbrev.: **ASA**) (in the UK) an independent regulatory body set up in 1962 to monitor standards within advertising and to ensure that advertisements comply with the requirement that they be legal, decent, honest, and truthful.

advertorial /,advəː'tɔːrɪəl/ ▶ **noun** a newspaper or magazine advertisement giving information about a product in the style of an editorial or objective journalistic article.
– ORIGIN 1960s (originally US): blend of ADVERTISEMENT and EDITORIAL.

advice ▶ **noun 1** [mass noun] guidance or recommendations offered with regard to prudent action: *my advice is to see your doctor* | *he should* ***take advice*** *from his accountant.*
2 a formal notice of a financial transaction: *remittance advices.*
3 [mass noun] (also **advices**) archaic information; news.
– ORIGIN Middle English: from Old French *avis*, based on Latin *ad* 'to' + *visum*, past participle of *videre* 'to see'. The original sense was 'way of looking at something, judgement', hence later 'an opinion given'.

advisability ▶ **noun** [mass noun] the quality of being advisable or sensible; wisdom: *many questioned the advisability of this policy.*

advisable ▶ **adjective** (of a course of action) to be recommended; sensible: *it is advisable to carry one of the major credit cards* | *early booking is advisable.*

advise ▶ **verb** [reporting verb] offer suggestions about the best course of action to someone: [with obj. and infinitive] *I advised him to go home* | [with obj.] *he advised caution* | [no obj.] *we* ***advise against*** *sending cash by post.* ■ [with obj.] recommend: *sleeping pills are not advised.* ■ [with obj.] inform (someone) about a fact or situation in a formal or official way: *you will be* ***advised of*** *the requirements* | [with obj. and clause] *the lawyer advised the court that his client wished to give evidence.*
– ORIGIN Middle English: from Old French *aviser*, based on Latin *ad-* 'to' + *visere*, frequentative of

videre 'to see'. The original senses included 'look at' and 'consider', hence 'consult with others'.

advised ▸ adjective acting in a way that would be recommended; sensible; wise: *you **would be advised** to check on increases to your pension.*

advisedly ▸ adverb deliberately and after consideration: *I've used the term 'old' advisedly.*

advisement ▸ noun [mass noun] archaic or N. Amer. careful consideration. ■ advice or counsel.
– PHRASES **take something under advisement** N. Amer. reserve judgement while considering something.
– ORIGIN Middle English: from Old French *avisement*, from *aviser* 'look at' (see ADVISE).

adviser (also **advisor**) ▸ noun a person who gives advice in a particular field: *the military adviser to the President.*

> **USAGE** The spellings **adviser** and **advisor** are both correct. **Adviser** is more common, but **advisor** is also widely used, especially in North America. **Adviser** may be seen as less formal, while **advisor** often suggests an official position.

advisory ▸ adjective having or consisting in the power to make recommendations but not to take action enforcing them: *the Commission acts in an advisory capacity.* ■ recommended but not compulsory: *the EC has put forward an advisory maximum figure.*
▸ noun (pl. **advisories**) an official announcement or warning.

> **WORD TRENDS** Many words once labelled as specifically North American are now just as common in British English—and **advisory** is a prime example. Typically used as an adjective, it first emerged as a noun in the 1930s in reference to a severe weather warning issued by a meteorological office, and was considered to be a specifically American usage until recently. The use became more widely known when stickers bearing the words *Parental Advisory: Explicit Contents* began to be fixed to some CDs of rock and rap music in the early 1990s. The Oxford English Corpus shows that the noun is now just as likely to be used in British English, in contexts such as travel advice: *Thailand is the latest country to be given a thumbs-down travel advisory from the British Foreign Office.*

advocaat /ˈadvəkɑː/ ▸ noun [mass noun] a liqueur made with eggs, sugar, and brandy.
– ORIGIN 1930s: from Dutch, literally 'advocate' (being originally considered a lawyer's drink).

advocacy /ˈadvəkəsi/ ▸ noun [mass noun] **1** public support for or recommendation of a particular cause or policy: *his outspoken **advocacy of** the agreement has won no friends.*
2 the profession or work of a legal advocate.
– ORIGIN late Middle English: via Old French from medieval Latin *advocatia*, from *advocare* 'summon, call to one's aid' (see ADVOCATE).

advocate ▸ noun /ˈadvəkət/ **1** a person who publicly supports or recommends a particular cause or policy: *he was an untiring **advocate of** economic reform.*
2 a person who puts a case on someone else's behalf: *care managers can become advocates for their clients.* ■ a professional pleader in a court of justice. ■ Scottish and South African term for BARRISTER.
▸ verb /ˈadvəkeɪt/ [with obj.] publicly recommend or support: *voters supported candidates who advocated an Assembly.*
– DERIVATIVES **advocation** noun.
– ORIGIN Middle English: from Old French *avocat*, from Latin *advocatus*, past participle (used as a noun) of *advocare* 'call (to one's aid)', from *ad-* 'to' + *vocare* 'to call'.

advocate depute ▸ noun (pl. **advocates depute**) (in Scotland) any of a number of officers who assist the Lord Advocate in prosecutions.

advocate general ▸ noun (pl. **advocates general**) any of a number of officers assisting the judges in the European Court of Justice.

advowson /ədˈvaʊz(ə)n/ ▸ noun Brit. (in ecclesiastical law) the right to recommend a member of the Anglican clergy for a vacant benefice, or to make such an appointment.
– ORIGIN Middle English (in the sense 'patronage of a religious house or benefice', with the obligation to defend it and speak for it): from Old French *avoeson*, from Latin *advocatio(n-)*, from *advocare* 'summon' (see ADVOCATE).

advt ▸ abbreviation advertisement.

adware ▸ noun [mass noun] Computing software that automatically displays or downloads advertising material (often unwanted) when a user is online.

Adygea /ˈɑːdɪɡeɪə, ˌɑːdɪˈjeɪə/ an autonomous republic in the NW Caucasus in SW Russia, with a largely Muslim population; pop. 408,500 (est. 2009); capital, Maikop. Full name **Adygei Autonomous Republic** /ˈɑːdɪɡeɪ, ˌɑːdɪˈjeɪ/.

Adyghe /ˈadɪɡeɪ, ˌɑːdɪˈɡeɪ/ (also **Adygei**) ▸ noun (pl. same) **1** a member of a mainly Sunni Muslim people of the NW Caucasus, especially Adygea. Also called CIRCASSIAN.
2 [mass noun] the North Caucasian language of the Adyghe, with about 100,000 speakers in the Caucasus and 100,000 elsewhere.
▸ adjective relating to the Adyghe or their language.

adytum /ˈadɪtəm/ ▸ noun (pl. **adyta** /-tə/) the innermost sanctuary of an ancient Greek temple.
– ORIGIN Latin, from Greek *aduton*, neuter singular of *adutos* 'impenetrable', from *a-* 'not' + *duein* 'enter'.

adze /adz/ (US **adz**) ▸ noun a tool similar to an axe, with an arched blade at right angles to the handle, used for cutting or shaping large pieces of wood.
▸ verb (**adz, adzing, adzed**) [with obj.] cut away the surface of (a piece of wood) with an adze.
– ORIGIN Old English *adesa*, of unknown origin.

adzuki /ədˈzuːki/ (also **adzuki bean, aduki**) ▸ noun (pl. **adzukis**) **1** a small, round dark-red edible bean.
2 the bushy Asian plant which produces the adzuki bean. ● *Vigna angularis*, family Leguminosae.
– ORIGIN early 18th cent.: from Japanese *azuki*.

AE ▸ abbreviation auto-exposure.

Æ (also **æ**) ▸ noun a letter used in Old English to represent a vowel intermediate between a and e and from the 16th century onwards used in Latin or Latinized Greek words, representing an original diphthong ae or ai (see ASH[2]).

-ae /iː, ʌɪ/ ▸ suffix forming plural nouns: **1** used in names of animal and plant families and other groups: *Felidae | Gymnospermae.*
2 used instead of *-as* in the plural of many non-naturalized or unfamiliar nouns ending in *-a* derived from Latin or Greek: *striae | larvae.*
– ORIGIN Latin plural suffix, or representing the Greek plural ending *-ai*.

AEA ▸ abbreviation (in the UK) Atomic Energy Authority.

aedile /ˈiːdʌɪl/ ▸ noun Roman History either of two (later four) Roman magistrates responsible for public buildings and originally also for the public games and the supply of corn to the city.
– DERIVATIVES **aedileship** noun.
– ORIGIN mid 16th cent.: from Latin *aedilis* 'concerned with buildings', from *aedes* 'building'.

Aegean /iːˈdʒiːən, ɪ-/ ▸ adjective relating to the region comprising the Aegean Sea and its coasts and islands.
▸ noun (**the Aegean**) the Aegean Sea or its region.
– ORIGIN early 17th cent.: via Latin from Greek *Aigaios* + -EAN.

Aegean Islands a group of islands in the Aegean Sea, forming a region of Greece. The principal islands of the group are Chios, Samos, Lesbos, the Cyclades, and the Dodecanese.

Aegean Sea a part of the Mediterranean Sea lying between Greece and Turkey, bounded to the south by Crete and Rhodes and linked to the Black Sea by the Dardanelles, the Sea of Marmara, and the Bosporus.

aegis /ˈiːdʒɪs/ ▸ noun **1** [in sing.] the protection, backing, or support of a particular person or organization: *the negotiations were conducted **under the aegis of** the UN.*
2 (in classical art and mythology) an attribute of Zeus and Athene (or their Roman counterparts Jupiter and Minerva) usually represented as a goatskin shield.
– ORIGIN early 17th cent. (denoting armour or a shield, especially that of a god): via Latin from Greek *aigis* 'shield of Zeus'.

Aegisthus /ɪˈɡɪsθəs/ Greek Mythology the son of Thyestes and lover of Agamemnon's wife Clytemnestra.

aegrotat /ʌɪˈɡrə(ʊ)tat, ˈiː-, iːˈɡrə(ʊ)-/ ▸ noun Brit. a certificate stating that a university student is too ill to attend an examination. ■ an examination pass awarded to a student having an aegrotat.
– ORIGIN late 18th cent.: Latin, literally 'he is sick'.

Aelfric /ˈalfrɪk/ (*c.*955–*c.*1020), Anglo-Saxon monk, writer, and grammarian; known as **Grammaticus**. Notable works: *Lives of the Saints* (993–6).

-aemia (also **-haemia**, US **-emia** or **-hemia**) ▸ combining form in nouns denoting that a substance is present in the blood: *septicaemia | leukaemia.*
– ORIGIN modern Latin, from Greek *-aimia*, from *haima* 'blood'.

Aeneas /ɪˈniːəs/ Greek & Roman Mythology a Trojan leader, son of Anchises and Aphrodite, and legendary ancestor of the Romans. When Troy fell to the Greeks he escaped and after wandering for many years eventually reached Italy. The story of his voyage is recounted in Virgil's *Aeneid*.

Aeneid /ɪˈniːɪd, ˈiːnɪɪd/ a Latin epic poem in twelve books by Virgil which relates the travels and experiences of Aeneas after the fall of Troy.

aeolian /iːˈəʊlɪən/ (US **eolian**) ▸ adjective chiefly Geology relating to or arising from the action of the wind.
– ORIGIN early 17th cent.: from the name AEOLUS + -IAN.

aeolian harp ▸ noun a stringed instrument that produces musical sounds when a current of air passes through it.

Aeolian Islands ancient name for LIPARI ISLANDS.

Aeolian mode /iːˈəʊlɪən/ ▸ noun Music the mode represented by the natural diatonic scale A–A (containing a minor 3rd, 6th, and 7th).
– ORIGIN late 18th cent.: from Latin *Aeolius*, 'from *Aeolis*' (an ancient coastal district of Asia Minor) + -AN.

Aeolus /ˈiːələs/ Greek Mythology the god of the winds.
– ORIGIN from Greek *Aiolos*, from *aiolos* 'swift, changeable'.

aeon /ˈiːɒn/ (US or technical also **eon**) ▸ noun **1** (often **aeons**) an indefinite and very long period of time: *he reached the crag aeons before I arrived.* ■ Astronomy & Geology a unit of time equal to a thousand million years. ■ Geology a major division of geological time, subdivided into eras: *the Precambrian aeon.*
2 Philosophy (in Neoplatonism, Platonism, and Gnosticism) a power existing from eternity; an emanation or phase of the supreme deity.
– ORIGIN mid 17th cent.: via ecclesiastical Latin from Greek *aiōn* 'age'.

aepyornis /ˌiːpɪˈɔːnɪs/ ▸ noun another term for ELEPHANT BIRD.
– ORIGIN mid 19th cent.: modern Latin, from Greek *aipus* 'high' + *ornis* 'bird'.

AER ▸ abbreviation annual equivalence rate, the notional rate of interest on loans or credit payable if the interest was paid and added each year.

aerate /ˈɛːreɪt/ ▸ verb [with obj.] introduce air into (a material): *aerate the lawn using a garden fork.*
– DERIVATIVES **aeration** noun, **aerator** noun.
– ORIGIN late 18th cent.: from Latin *aer* 'air' + -ATE[3], influenced by French *aérer*.

aerated ▸ adjective **1** (of a liquid) made effervescent by being charged with carbon dioxide or some other gas.
2 Brit. informal agitated, angry, or overexcited: *don't get so aerated!*

aerenchyma /ɛːˈrɛŋkɪmə/ ▸ noun [mass noun] Botany a soft plant tissue containing air spaces, found especially in many aquatic plants.
– DERIVATIVES **aerenchymatous** adjective.
– ORIGIN late 19th cent.: from Greek *aēr* 'air' + *enkhuma* 'infusion'.

aerial /ˈɛːrɪəl/ ▸ noun **1** Brit. a rod, wire, or other structure by which signals are transmitted or received as part of a radio or television transmission or receiving system.
2 (**aerials**) a type of freestyle skiing in which the skier jumps from a ramp and carries out manoeuvres in the air.
▸ adjective [attrib.] existing, happening, or operating in the air: *an aerial battle | an intrepid aerial adventurer.* ■ coming or carried out from the air, especially using aircraft: *aerial bombardment of civilian targets | aerial photography.* ■ (of a part of a plant) growing above ground. ■ (of a bird) spending much of its time in flight. ■ of or in the atmosphere; atmospheric.
– DERIVATIVES **aeriality** noun, **aerially** adverb.
– ORIGIN late 16th cent. (in the sense 'thin as air, imaginary'): via Latin *aerius* from Greek *aerios* (from *aēr* 'air') + -AL.

aerialist ▸ noun a person who performs acrobatics high above the ground on a tightrope or trapezes.

aerial perspective ▸ noun [mass noun] Art the technique of representing more distant objects as fainter and more blue.

aerie ▸ noun US spelling of EYRIE.

aero ▸ adjective [attrib.] informal **1** aeronautical: *an aero club.*

A

2 aerodynamic: *we softened the lines for a more aero look.*
– ORIGIN early 20th cent. (in sense 1): abbreviation.

aero- /ˈɛːrəʊ/ ▸ combining form **1** relating to air: *aerobe | aerobics.*
2 relating to aircraft: *aerotowing | aerodrome.*
– ORIGIN from Greek *aēr* 'air'.

aerobatics ▸ plural noun [usu. treated as sing.] loops, rolls, and other feats of spectacular flying performed in one or more aircraft to entertain an audience on the ground.
– DERIVATIVES **aerobatic** adjective.
– ORIGIN First World War: from AERO- + a shortened form of ACROBATICS.

aerobe /ˈɛːrəʊb/ ▸ noun a microorganism which grows in the presence of air or requires oxygen for growth.
– ORIGIN late 19th cent.: coined in French from Greek *aēr* + *bios* 'life'.

aerobic /ɛːˈrəʊbɪk/ ▸ adjective Biology relating to, involving, or requiring free oxygen: *simple aerobic bacteria.* ■ relating to or denoting exercise taken to improve the efficiency of the body's cardiovascular system in absorbing and transporting oxygen.
– DERIVATIVES **aerobically** adverb.
– ORIGIN late 19th cent.: from AERO- + Greek *bios* 'life' + -IC.

aerobicized /ɛːˈrəʊbɪsʌɪzd/ (also **aerobicised**) ▸ adjective (of a person's body) toned by aerobic exercise: *a 53-year-old aerobicized divorcee who looks more like a cheerleader than a grandmother.*

aerobics ▸ plural noun [often treated as sing.] vigorous exercises designed to increase cardiovascular efficiency.
– DERIVATIVES **aerobicist** noun.

aerobiology ▸ noun [mass noun] the study of airborne microorganisms, pollen, spores, and seeds, especially as agents of infection.

aerobrake ▸ verb [no obj.] technical cause a spacecraft to slow down by flying through a planet's rarefied atmosphere to produce aerodynamic drag.
▸ noun a mechanism for aerobraking.

aerodrome ▸ noun Brit. a small airport or airfield.

aerodynamic ▸ adjective relating to aerodynamics: *aerodynamic forces.* ■ of or having a shape which reduces the drag from air moving past: *the plane has a more aerodynamic shape.*
– DERIVATIVES **aerodynamically** adverb.

aerodynamics ▸ plural noun [treated as sing.] the study of the properties of moving air and the interaction between the air and solid bodies moving through it. ■ [treated as pl.] the properties of a solid object regarding the manner in which air flows around it.
– DERIVATIVES **aerodynamicist** noun.

aeroelasticity ▸ noun [mass noun] the science of the interaction between aerodynamic forces and non-rigid structures.
– DERIVATIVES **aeroelastic** adjective.

aerofoil ▸ noun Brit. a structure with curved surfaces designed to give the most favourable ratio of lift to drag in flight, used as the basic form of the wings, fins, and tailplanes of most aircraft.

aerogel ▸ noun a solid material of extremely low density, produced by removing the liquid component from a conventional gel.

aerogramme (US **aerogram**) ▸ noun another term for AIR LETTER.

aerolite ▸ noun a meteorite made of stone.

aeromagnetic ▸ adjective relating to or denoting the measurement of the earth's magnetic field using airborne instruments.

aeromedical ▸ adjective **1** relating to the use of aircraft for medical purposes such as transporting patients to hospital.
2 relating to medical issues associated with air travel.

aeromodelling ▸ noun [mass noun] the hobby of building and flying model aircraft.
– DERIVATIVES **aeromodeller** noun.

aeronaut ▸ noun dated a traveller in a hot-air balloon, airship, or other flying craft.
– ORIGIN late 18th cent.: from French *aéronaute*, from Greek *aēr* 'air' + *nautēs* 'sailor'.

aeronautics ▸ plural noun [treated as sing.] the science or practice of building or flying aircraft.
– DERIVATIVES **aeronautic** adjective, **aeronautical** adjective.
– ORIGIN early 19th cent.: from modern Latin *aeronautica* 'matters relating to aeronautics', from Greek (see AERONAUT).

aeronomy /ɛːˈrɒnəmi/ ▸ noun [mass noun] the study of the upper atmosphere.

aerophagy /ɛːˈrɒfədʒi/ ▸ noun [mass noun] Medicine the swallowing of air.

aerophone ▸ noun Music a wind instrument.

aeroplane ▸ noun Brit. a powered flying vehicle with fixed wings and a weight greater than that of the air it displaces.
– ORIGIN late 19th cent.: from French *aéroplane*, from *aéro-* 'air' + Greek *-planos* 'wandering'.

aeroponics /ˌɛːrə(ʊ)ˈpɒnɪks/ ▸ plural noun [treated as sing.] a plant-cultivation technique in which the roots hang suspended in the air while nutrient solution is delivered to them in the form of a fine mist.
– DERIVATIVES **aeroponic** adjective, **aeroponically** adverb.
– ORIGIN 1950s: blend of AERO- and HYDROPONICS.

aeroshell ▸ noun a casing which protects a spacecraft during re-entry.

aerosol ▸ noun a substance enclosed under pressure and released as a fine spray by means of a propellant gas. ■ a container holding an aerosol. ■ Chemistry a colloidal suspension of particles dispersed in air or gas.
– ORIGIN 1920s: from AERO- + SOL².

aerosolize (also **aerosolise**) ▸ verb [with obj.] (often as adj. **aerosolized**) convert into a fine spray or colloidal suspension in air: *the drug is being tested in an aerosolized form.*

aerospace ▸ noun [mass noun] the branch of technology and industry concerned with both aviation and space flight.

aerostat /ˈɛːrəstat/ ▸ noun an airship or hot-air balloon.
– ORIGIN late 18th cent.: from French *aérostat*, from Greek *aēr* 'air' + *statos* 'standing'.

aerotowing ▸ noun [mass noun] the towing of a glider by a powered aircraft to a height suitable for launching.

Aertex /ˈɛːtɛks/ ▸ noun [mass noun] trademark a cellular cotton fabric used for leisurewear and underwear.
– ORIGIN late 19th cent.: from *aer-* as in AERATE and TEXTILE.

Aeschines /ˈiːskɪniːz/ (*c.*390–*c.*314 BC), Athenian orator and statesman. He opposed Demosthenes' efforts to unite the Greek city-states against Macedon, with which he attempted to make peace.

Aeschylus /ˈiːskɪləs/ (*c.*525–*c.*456 BC), Greek dramatist. Aeschylus is best known for his trilogy the *Oresteia* (458 BC, consisting of the tragedies *Agamemnon*, *Choephoroe*, and *Eumenides*), which tells the story of Agamemnon's murder at the hands of his wife Clytemnestra and the vengeance of their son Orestes.

Aesculapian /ˌiːskjʊˈleɪpɪən/ ▸ adjective archaic relating to medicine or physicians.
– ORIGIN late 16th cent.: from Latin *Aesculapius*, the name of the Roman god of medicine, + -IAN.

Aesculapian snake ▸ noun a long, slender olive-brown to greyish snake found in Europe and SW Asia. In ancient times it was protected owing to its mythical link with the god of medicine, Aesculapius. ● *Elaphe longissima*, family Colubridae.

Æsir /ˈiːsə/ Scandinavian Mythology the Norse gods and goddesses collectively, including Odin, Thor, and Balder.

Aesop /ˈiːsɒp/ (6th century BC), Greek storyteller. The moral animal fables associated with him were probably collected from many sources, and initially communicated orally. Aesop is said to have lived as a slave on the island of Samos.

aesthete /ˈiːsθiːt, ˈɛs-/ (US also **esthete**) ▸ noun a person who is appreciative of and sensitive to art and beauty.
– ORIGIN late 19th cent.: from Greek *aisthētēs* 'a person who perceives', or from AESTHETIC, on the pattern of the pair *athlete, athletic*.

aesthetic /iːsˈθɛtɪk, ɛs-/ (US also **esthetic**) ▸ adjective concerned with beauty or the appreciation of beauty: *the pictures give great aesthetic pleasure.* ■ giving or designed to give pleasure through beauty: *the law applies to both functional and aesthetic objects.*
▸ noun [in sing.] a set of principles underlying the work of a particular artist or artistic movement: *the Cubist aesthetic.*
– DERIVATIVES **aesthetically** adverb.
– ORIGIN late 18th cent. (in the sense 'relating to perception by the senses'): from Greek *aisthētikos*, from *aisthēta* 'perceptible things', from *aisthesthai* 'perceive'. The sense 'concerned with beauty' was coined in German in the mid 18th cent. and adopted into English in the early 19th cent., but its use was controversial until much later in the century.

aesthetician (US also **esthetician**) ▸ noun **1** a person who is knowledgeable about aesthetics.
2 N. Amer. a beautician.

aestheticism (US also **estheticism**) ▸ noun [mass noun] an approach to art exemplified by the Aesthetic Movement.

aestheticize (US also **estheticize**) ▸ verb [with obj.] represent as beautiful or artistically pleasing.

Aesthetic Movement a literary and artistic movement which flourished in England in the 1880s, devoted to 'art for art's sake' and rejecting the notion that art should have a social or moral purpose. Its chief exponents included Oscar Wilde, Max Beerbohm, Aubrey Beardsley, and others associated with the journal the *Yellow Book*.

aesthetics (US also **esthetics**) ▸ plural noun [usu. treated as sing.] a set of principles concerned with the nature and appreciation of beauty. ■ the branch of philosophy which deals with questions of beauty and artistic taste.

aestival /ˈiːstɪv(ə)l, iːˈstʌɪv(ə)l, ˈɛst-, ɛˈstʌɪv(ə)l/ (US also **estival**) ▸ adjective technical belonging to or appearing in summer.
– ORIGIN late Middle English: from Latin *aestivalis*, from *aestivus*, from *aestus* 'heat'.

aestivate /ˈiːstɪveɪt, ˈɛst-/ (US **estivate**) ▸ verb [no obj.] Zoology (of an insect, fish, or amphibian) spend a hot or dry period in a prolonged state of torpor or dormancy.
– ORIGIN early 17th cent. (in the sense 'pass the summer'): from Latin *aestivat-*, from *aestivare* 'spend the summer', from *aestus* 'heat'.

aestivation /ˌiːstɪˈveɪʃ(ə)n, ˌɛst-/ (US **estivation**) ▸ noun [mass noun] **1** Zoology prolonged torpor or dormancy of an insect, fish, or amphibian during a hot or dry period.
2 Botany the arrangement of petals and sepals in a flower bud before it opens. Compare with VERNATION.

aet. (also **aetat.**) ▸ abbreviation formal of or at the age of; aged: *Mary Freemantle died 19 May 1746 aet. 77.*
– ORIGIN abbreviation of Latin *aetatis*, genitive singular of *aetas* 'age'.

a.e.t. ▸ abbreviation after extra time (in a soccer match).

aether ▸ noun variant spelling of ETHER (sense 2, sense 3).

aetiology /ˌiːtɪˈɒlədʒi/ (US **etiology**) ▸ noun [mass noun] **1** Medicine the cause, set of causes, or manner of causation of a disease or condition. ■ the causation of diseases and disorders as a subject of investigation.
2 the investigation or attribution of the cause or reason for something, often expressed in terms of historical or mythical explanation.
– DERIVATIVES **aetiologic** adjective, **aetiological** adjective, **aetiologically** adverb.
– ORIGIN mid 16th cent.: via medieval Latin from Greek *aitiologia*, from *aitia* 'a cause' + *-logia* (see -LOGY).

AF ▸ abbreviation ■ audio frequency. ■ autofocus.

af- ▸ prefix variant spelling of AD- assimilated before *f* (as in *affiliate, affirm*).

AFAIK ▸ abbreviation informal as far as I know: *none of his stories have been filmed, AFAIK.*

Afar /ˈɑːfɑː/ ▸ noun (pl. **same** or **Afars**) **1** a member of a people living in Djibouti and NE Ethiopia. Also called DANAKIL.
2 [mass noun] the Cushitic language of the Afar, with about 700,000 speakers.
▸ adjective relating to the Afar or their language.
– ORIGIN from Afar *qafar*.

afar ▸ adverb literary at or to a distance: *for months he had loved her **from afar**.*
– ORIGIN Middle English *of feor* 'from far'.

afara /əˈfɑːrə/ ▸ noun a tall West African hardwood tree with a characteristic shape resembling a pagoda. Also called LIMBA. ● *Terminalia superba*, family Combretaceae.
– ORIGIN 1920s: from Yoruba.

Afars and Issas, French Territory of the /ˈɑːfɑːz, ˈiːsɑːz/ former name (1946–77) for the Republic of DJIBOUTI.

AFC ▸ abbreviation ■ (in the UK) Air Force Cross, awarded for bravery while flying but not in active service against an enemy. ■ (in the UK) Association Football Club. ■ automatic frequency control, a system in radios and television which keeps them tuned to an incoming signal.

AFDC ▸ abbreviation (in the US) Aid to Families with Dependent Children, a welfare benefit paid by the federal government.

afeared ▸ adjective archaic or dialect afraid.
– ORIGIN Old English, from *āfǣran* 'frighten', from *ā-* (expressing intensity) + *fǣran* (see FEAR); used commonly by Shakespeare, but rarely after 1700 in written form.

afebrile ▸ adjective Medicine not feverish.
– ORIGIN late 19th cent.: from A-[1] 'not' + FEBRILE.

affability ▸ noun [mass noun] the quality of being affable; geniality: *an air of benign affability.*

affable ▸ adjective friendly, good-natured, or easy to talk to: *an affable and agreeable companion.*
– DERIVATIVES **affably** adverb.
– ORIGIN late Middle English: via Old French from Latin *affabilis*, from the verb *affari*, from *ad-* 'to' + *fari* 'speak'.

affair ▸ noun **1** an event or sequence of events of a specified kind or that has previously been referred to: *the board admitted responsibility for the affair* | *I wanted the funeral to be a family affair.* ■ a matter that is a particular person's concern or responsibility: *what you do in your spare time is your affair.* ■ (**affairs**) matters of public interest and importance: *commissions were created to advise on foreign affairs.* ■ (**affairs**) business and financial dealings: *his time was spent in winding up his affairs.*
2 a love affair: *his wife is having an affair.*
3 [with adj.] informal an object of a particular type: *her dress was a black low-cut affair.*
– PHRASES **put one's affairs in order** ensure that one's financial and legal arrangements are properly organized, especially in preparation for one's death: *before he died he put his affairs in order and updated his will.*
– ORIGIN Middle English: from Old French *afaire*, from *à faire* 'to do'; compare with ADO.

affaire /aˈfɛː/, French /afɛʀ/ (also **affaire de** or **du cœur** /də ˈkəː, djuː/, French /də, dy kœʀ/) ▸ noun a love affair.
– ORIGIN early 19th cent.: French, literally 'affair (of the heart)'.

affairé /aˈfɛːreɪ/, French /afeʀe/ ▸ adjective busy; involved.
– ORIGIN French, from *affaire*, from *à* 'to' + *faire* 'do'.

affect[1] /əˈfɛkt/ ▸ verb [with obj.] have an effect on; make a difference to: *the dampness began to affect my health* | [with clause] *your attitude will* ***affect how*** *successful you are.* ■ touch the feelings of; move emotionally: *he was visibly affected by the tragedy.*
– ORIGIN late Middle English (in the sense 'attack as a disease'): from French *affecter* or Latin *affect-* 'influenced, affected', from the verb *afficere* (see AFFECT[2]).

> **USAGE** Affect and effect are quite different in meaning, though frequently confused. Affect is primarily a verb meaning 'make a difference to', as in *their gender need not affect their career*. Effect, on the other hand, is used both as a noun and a verb, meaning 'a result' as a noun (*move the cursor until you get the* ***effect*** *you want*) or 'bring about a result' as a verb (*growth in the economy can only be* ***effected*** *by stringent economic controls*).

affect[2] /əˈfɛkt/ ▸ verb [with obj.] pretend to have or feel (something): *as usual I affected a supreme unconcern* | [with infinitive] *a book that affects to loathe the modern world.* ■ use, wear, or assume (something) pretentiously or so as to make an impression on others: *an Anglophile who had affected a British accent.*
– ORIGIN late Middle English: from French *affecter* or Latin *affectare* 'aim at', frequentative of *afficere* 'work on, influence', from *ad-* 'at, to' + *facere* 'do'. The original sense was 'like, love', hence '(like to) use, assume, etc.'.

affect[3] /ˈafɛkt/ ▸ noun [mass noun] Psychology emotion or desire as influencing behaviour.
– DERIVATIVES **affectless** adjective, **affectlessness** noun.
– ORIGIN late 19th cent.: coined in German from Latin *affectus* 'disposition', from *afficere* 'to influence' (see AFFECT[2]).

affectation ▸ noun [mass noun] behaviour, speech, or writing that is pretentious and designed to impress: *the affectation of a man who measures every word for effect* | [count noun] *she called the room her boudoir, which he thought an affectation.* ■ [count noun] a studied display of real or pretended feeling: *an affectation of calm.*
– ORIGIN mid 16th cent.: from Latin *affectatio(n-)*, from the verb *affectare* (see AFFECT[2]).

affected ▸ adjective **1** influenced or touched by an external factor: *affected areas.*
2 pretentious and designed to impress: *the gesture appeared both affected and stagy.*
3 [predic.] archaic disposed or inclined in a specified way: *you might become differently affected towards him.*
– DERIVATIVES **affectedly** adverb.

affecting ▸ adjective touching the emotions; moving: *a highly affecting account of her experiences in prison.*
– DERIVATIVES **affectingly** adverb.

affection ▸ noun [mass noun] **1** a gentle feeling of fondness or liking: *she felt* ***affection for*** *the wise old lady* | [count noun] *he won a place in her affections.*
2 archaic the action or process of affecting or being affected. ■ [count noun] a condition or disease: *an affection of the skin.* ■ [count noun] a mental state; an emotion.
– DERIVATIVES **affectional** adjective.
– ORIGIN Middle English: via Old French from Latin *affectio(n-)*, from *afficere* 'to influence' (see AFFECT[2]).

affectionate ▸ adjective readily feeling or showing fondness or tenderness: *his affectionate nature.* ■ expressing fondness: *an affectionate kiss.*
– DERIVATIVES **affectionately** adverb.
– ORIGIN late 15th cent. (in the sense 'disposed, inclined towards'): from French *affectionné* 'beloved' or medieval Latin *affectionatus* 'devoted', from *affectio(n-)*, from *afficere* 'to influence' (see AFFECT[2]).

affective ▸ adjective Psychology relating to moods, feelings, and attitudes. ■ denoting or relating to mental disorders in which disturbance of mood is the primary symptom.
– DERIVATIVES **affectively** adverb, **affectivity** noun.
– ORIGIN late Middle English: via French from late Latin *affectivus*, from *afficere* (see AFFECT[2]).

Affenpinscher /ˈafənˌpɪnʃə/ ▸ noun a dog of a small breed resembling the griffon.
– ORIGIN German, from *Affe* 'monkey' + *Pinscher* 'terrier'.

afferent /ˈaf(ə)r(ə)nt/ ▸ adjective Physiology conducting or conducted inwards or towards something (for nerves, the central nervous system; for blood vessels, the organ supplied). The opposite of EFFERENT.
▸ noun an afferent nerve fibre or vessel.
– ORIGIN mid 19th cent.: from Latin *afferent-* 'bringing towards', from the verb *afferre*, from *ad-* 'to' + *ferre* 'bring'.

affiance /əˈfʌɪəns/ ▸ verb (**be affianced**) literary be engaged to marry: *Edward was* ***affianced to*** *Lady Eleanor Butler* | (as adj. **affianced**) *an affianced couple.*
– ORIGIN late 15th cent.: from Old French *afiancer*, from *afier* 'promise, entrust', from medieval Latin *affidare* 'declare on oath', from *ad-* 'towards' + *fides* 'trust'.

affiant /əˈfʌɪənt/ ▸ noun US Law a person who makes an affidavit.
– ORIGIN early 19th cent.: from French, present participle of *afier*, from medieval Latin *affidare* 'declare on oath' (see AFFIANCE).

affidavit /ˌafɪˈdeɪvɪt/ ▸ noun Law a written statement confirmed by oath or affirmation, for use as evidence in court.
– ORIGIN mid 16th cent.: from medieval Latin, literally 'he has stated on oath', from *affidare*.

affiliate ▸ verb /əˈfɪlɪeɪt/ [with obj.] (usu. **be affiliated to/with**) officially attach or connect (a subsidiary group or a person) to an organization: *they are national associations affiliated to larger organizations.* ■ (of an organization) admit as a member: *the main party agreed to affiliate four Conservative associations.* ■ [no obj.] officially join or become attached to an organization: *almost all students* ***affiliate to*** *the Students' Union.*
▸ noun /əˈfɪlɪət/ a person or organization officially attached to a larger body.
– DERIVATIVES **affiliative** adjective.
– ORIGIN mid 18th cent.: from medieval Latin *affiliat-* 'adopted as a son', from the verb *affiliare*, from *ad-* 'towards' + *filius* 'son'.

affiliated ▸ adjective (of a subsidiary group or a person) officially attached or connected to an organization: *affiliated union members* | *Microsoft and its affiliated companies.*

affiliation ▸ noun [mass noun] the state or process of affiliating or being affiliated: *the group has no* ***affiliation to*** *any preservation society* | [count noun] *his political affiliations.*
– ORIGIN late 18th cent.: from French, from medieval Latin *affiliatio(n-)*, from the verb *affiliare* (see AFFILIATE).

affiliation order ▸ noun English Law, historical a legal order that the man judged to be the father of an illegitimate child must help to support it.

affinal /əˈfʌɪn(ə)l/ ▸ adjective Anthropology concerning or having a family relationship by marriage.
– ORIGIN mid 19th cent.: from Latin *affinis* 'related' (see AFFINITY) + -AL.

affine /əˈfʌɪn/ ▸ adjective Mathematics allowing for or preserving parallel relationships.
▸ noun Anthropology a relative by marriage.
– ORIGIN early 16th cent. (as a noun): from Old French *afin* or Latin *affinis* 'related' (see AFFINITY). The mathematical sense dates from the early 20th cent.

affined ▸ adjective archaic related or connected.
– ORIGIN late 16th cent.: from Latin *affinis* 'related' (see AFFINITY) + -ED[1].

affinity ▸ noun (pl. **affinities**) **1** a natural liking for and understanding of someone or something: *he had a special affinity with horses.* ■ a similarity of characteristics suggesting a relationship, especially a resemblance in structure between animals, plants, or languages: *a semantic affinity between two words.* ■ [mass noun] relationship, especially by marriage as opposed to blood ties.
2 chiefly Biochemistry the degree to which a substance tends to combine with another.
– ORIGIN Middle English (in the sense 'relationship by marriage'): via Old French from Latin *affinitas*, from *affinis* 'related' (literally 'bordering on'), from *ad-* 'to' + *finis* 'border'.

affinity card ▸ noun a cheque card or credit card for which the bank donates a portion of the money spent using the card to a specific charity or other organization.

affinity group ▸ noun chiefly US a group of people linked by a common interest or purpose.

affirm ▸ verb **1** [reporting verb] state emphatically or publicly: [with obj.] *he affirmed the country's commitment to peace* | [with clause] *they affirmed that policies were to be judged by their contribution to social justice.* ■ [with obj.] declare one's support for; uphold; defend: *the referendum affirmed the republic's right to secede.* ■ [with obj.] Law accept or confirm the validity of (a judgement or agreement); ratify. ■ [no obj.] Law make a formal declaration rather than taking an oath.
2 [with obj.] offer (someone) emotional support or encouragement: *there are five common ways parents fail to affirm their children* | *good teachers know that students need to be both affirmed and challenged.*
– DERIVATIVES **affirmatory** adjective, **affirmer** noun.
– ORIGIN Middle English (in the sense 'make firm'): via Old French from Latin *affirmare*, from *ad-* 'to' + *firmus* 'strong'.

affirmation ▸ noun [mass noun] **1** the action or process of affirming something: *he nodded in affirmation* | [count noun] *an affirmation of basic human values.* ■ [count noun] Law a formal declaration by a person who declines to take an oath.
2 emotional support or encouragement: *the lack of one or both parents' affirmation leaves some children emotionally crippled.*
– ORIGIN late Middle English: from Latin *affirmatio(n-)*, from the verb *affirmare* (see AFFIRM).

affirmative ▸ adjective **1** agreeing with or consenting to a statement or request: *an affirmative answer.* ■ Grammar & Logic stating that a fact is so; making an assertion: *affirmative sentences.* Contrasted with NEGATIVE and INTERROGATIVE. ■ (of a vote) expressing approval or agreement. ■ relating to or denoting proposed legislation which must receive a parliamentary vote in its favour before it can come into force.
2 offering emotional support: *the family is usually a source of encouragement from which affirmative influences come.*
▸ noun a statement of agreement with or consent to an assertion or request: *he accepted her reply as an affirmative.* ■ Grammar a word used in making assertions or to express consent. ■ Logic a statement asserting that something is true of the subject of a proposition. ■ (**the affirmative**) a position of agreement or confirmation: *his answer veered towards the affirmative.*
▸ exclamation chiefly N. Amer. expressing agreement with or consent to a statement or request; yes.
– PHRASES **in the affirmative** so as to accept or agree to a statement or request: *he answered the question in the affirmative.*
– DERIVATIVES **affirmatively** adverb.

A

– ORIGIN late Middle English (in the sense 'assertive, positive'): via Old French from late Latin *affirmativus*, from *affirmare* 'assert' (see AFFIRM).

affirmative action ▸ noun [mass noun] chiefly N. Amer. action favouring those who tend to suffer from discrimination; positive discrimination.

affix ▸ verb /əˈfɪks/ [with obj.] stick, attach, or fasten (something) to something else: *panels to which he affixes copies of fine old prints.* ■ [no obj.] be able to be fixed: *the strings **affix to** the back of the bridge.*
▸ noun /ˈafɪks/ Grammar an addition to the base form or stem of a word in order to modify its meaning or create a new word. Compare with PREFIX, SUFFIX, INFIX.
– DERIVATIVES **affixation** noun.
– ORIGIN late Middle English: from Old French *affixer* or medieval Latin *affixare*, frequentative of Latin *affigere*, from *ad-* 'to' + *figere* 'to fix'.

afflatus /əˈfleɪtəs/ ▸ noun formal a divine creative impulse or inspiration.
– ORIGIN mid 17th cent.: from Latin, from the verb *afflare*, from *ad-* 'to' + *flare* 'to blow'.

afflict ▸ verb [with obj.] (of a problem or illness) cause pain or trouble to; affect adversely: *his younger child was afflicted with a skin disease* | *serious ills afflict the industry* | (as plural noun **the afflicted**) *he comforted the afflicted.* ■ Astrology (of a celestial body) be in a stressful aspect with (another celestial body or a point on the ecliptic): *Jupiter is afflicted by Mars in opposition.*
– DERIVATIVES **afflictive** adjective (archaic).
– ORIGIN late Middle English (in the sense 'deject, humiliate'): from Latin *afflictare* 'knock about, harass', or from *afflict-* 'knocked down, weakened': both from the verb *affligere*, from *ad-* 'to' + *fligere* 'to strike, dash'.

affliction ▸ noun a cause of pain or harm: *a crippling affliction of the nervous system.* ■ [mass noun] the state of being in pain: *poor people in great affliction.* ■ Astrology an instance of one celestial body afflicting another.
– ORIGIN Middle English (originally in the sense 'infliction of pain or humiliation', specifically 'religious self-mortification'): via Old French from Latin *afflictio(n-)*, from the verb *affligere* (see AFFLICT).

affluence ▸ noun [mass noun] the state of having a great deal of money; wealth: *a sign of our growing affluence.*

affluent ▸ adjective **1** (especially of a group or area) having a great deal of money; wealthy: *the affluent societies of the western world.*
2 archaic (of water) flowing freely or in great quantity.
▸ noun archaic a tributary stream.
– DERIVATIVES **affluently** adverb.
– ORIGIN late Middle English (in sense 2 of the adjective): via Old French from Latin *affluent-* 'flowing towards, flowing freely', from the verb *affluere*, from *ad-* 'to' + *fluere* 'to flow'.

affluential informal ▸ adjective rich and socially influential: *the daughter of an affluential businessman.*
▸ noun a rich and socially influential person.
– ORIGIN 1970s: blend of AFFLUENT and INFLUENTIAL.

affluenza /ˈafluːˈɛnzə/ ▸ noun [mass noun] a psychological malaise supposedly affecting young wealthy people, symptoms of which include a lack of motivation, feelings of guilt, and a sense of isolation.
– ORIGIN 1970s: blend of AFFLUENT and INFLUENZA.

afflux /ˈaflʌks/ ▸ noun archaic a flow of something, especially water or air.
– ORIGIN early 17th cent.: from medieval Latin *affluxus*, from *affluere* 'flow freely' (see AFFLUENT).

afforce ▸ verb [with obj.] rare reinforce (a body of people) with new members.
– ORIGIN Middle English (in the sense 'to force'): from Old French *aforcier*, from *a-* (from Latin *ad* 'to, at') + *force* (from Latin *fortis* 'strong').

afford ▸ verb [with obj.] **1** (**can/could afford**) have enough money to pay for: *the best that I could afford was a first-floor room* | [with infinitive] *we could never have afforded to heat the place.* ■ have (a resource such as money or time) available or to spare: *it was taking up more time than he could afford.* ■ [with infinitive] be able to do something without risk of adverse consequences: *only aristocrats could afford to stoop to such practices.*
2 provide or supply (an opportunity or facility): *the rooftop terrace affords beautiful views* | [with two objs] *they were afforded the luxury of bed and breakfast.*
– ORIGIN late Old English *geforthian*, from *ge-* (prefix implying completeness) + *forthian* 'to further', from FORTH. The original sense was 'promote, perform, accomplish', later 'manage, be in a position to do'.

affordable ▸ adjective inexpensive; reasonably priced: *affordable homes.*
– DERIVATIVES **affordability** noun, **affordably** adverb [as submodifier] *affordably priced hotel rooms.*

afforest /əˈfɒrɪst/ ▸ verb [with obj.] convert (land) into forest, especially for commercial exploitation. ■ Brit. historical bring (woodland) under the jurisdiction of forest law for the purpose of hunting.
– DERIVATIVES **afforestation** noun.
– ORIGIN early 16th cent.: from medieval Latin *afforestare*, from *ad-* 'to' (expressing change) + *foresta* 'forest'.

affranchise ▸ verb [with obj.] archaic release from servitude.
– ORIGIN late 15th cent.: from Old French *afranchiss-*, lengthened stem of *afranchir*, from *a-* (from Latin *ad* 'to, at') + *franc* 'free'.

affray ▸ noun Law, dated an instance of group fighting in a public place that disturbs the peace: *Lowe was charged with causing an affray* | [mass noun] *a person guilty of affray.*
– ORIGIN Middle English (in the general sense 'disturbance, fray'): from Anglo-Norman French *afrayer* 'disturb, startle', based on an element of Germanic origin related to Old English *frithu* 'peace, safety' (compare with German *Friede* 'peace').

affricate /ˈafrɪkət/ ▸ noun Phonetics a phoneme which combines a plosive with an immediately following fricative or spirant sharing the same place of articulation, e.g. *ch* as in *chair* and *j* as in *jar*.
– ORIGIN late 19th cent.: from Latin *affricatus*, past participle of *affricare*, from *ad-* 'to' + *fricare* 'to rub'.

affright archaic ▸ verb [with obj.] frighten (someone): *ghosts could never affright her.*
▸ noun [mass noun] fright: *the deer gazed at us in affright.*
– ORIGIN late Middle English: in early use from *āfyrhted* 'frightened' in Old English; later by vague form association with FRIGHT.

affront ▸ noun an action or remark that causes outrage or offence: *he took his son's desertion as a personal affront* | *the sackings were **an affront to** justice.*
▸ verb [with obj.] (usu. **be affronted**) offend the modesty or values of: *she was affronted by his familiarity.*
– ORIGIN Middle English (as a verb): from Old French *afronter* 'to slap in the face, insult', based on Latin *ad frontem* 'to the face'.

affronté /əˈfrʌnti/ (also **affronty**) ▸ adjective [predic. or postpositive] Heraldry (of an animal's head) facing the observer.
– ORIGIN mid 16th cent. (as *affronty*): French, past participle of *affronter* 'to face'.

AFG ▸ abbreviation Afghanistan (international vehicle registration).

Afghan /ˈafgan/ ▸ noun **1** a native or inhabitant of Afghanistan, or a person of Afghan descent.
2 another term for PASHTO.
3 (**afghan**) a woollen blanket or shawl, typically one knitted or crocheted in strips or squares.
4 short for AFGHAN COAT or AFGHAN HOUND.
▸ adjective relating to Afghanistan, its people, or their language.
– ORIGIN from Pashto *afghānī*.

Afghan coat ▸ noun Brit. a kind of sheepskin coat with the skin outside, typically having a shaggy border.

Afghan hound ▸ noun a tall hunting dog of a breed with long silky hair.

afghani /afˈgɑːni/ ▸ noun (pl. **afghanis**) the basic monetary unit of Afghanistan, equal to 100 puls.
– ORIGIN from Pashto *afghānī*.

Afghanistan /afˈganɪstɑːn, -stan/ a mountainous landlocked republic in central Asia; pop. 28,395,700 (est. 2009); official languages, Pashto and Dari (the local form of Persian); capital, Kabul.

> Part of the Indian Mogul empire, Afghanistan became independent in the mid 18th century, and in the 19th and early 20th centuries was a focal point for conflicting Russian and British interests on the North-West Frontier. Afghanistan was invaded by the Soviet Union in 1979; after Soviet forces withdrew in 1988–9 the country was thrown into turmoil with various Islamic groups struggling for power. In 1996 the Taliban gained control of Kabul and set up an Islamic state: this was overthrown in 2001 by US-led forces in conjunction with Afghan groups following the attacks on the World Trade Center and the Pentagon on 11 September 2001. A new government was formed, but instability continued in many areas of the country.

aficionado /əˌfɪsjəˈnɑːdəʊ, -ˌfɪʃjə-/ ▸ noun (pl. **aficionados**) a person who is very knowledgeable and enthusiastic about an activity, subject, or pastime: *a crossword aficionado.*
– ORIGIN mid 19th cent. (denoting a devotee of bullfighting): from Spanish, 'amateur', past participle of *aficionar* 'become fond of' used as a noun, based on Latin *affectio(n-)* '(favourable) disposition towards' (see AFFECTION).

afield ▸ adverb **1** to or at a distance: *competitors from as far afield as Aberdeen.*
2 in the field (in reference to hunting): *the satisfaction of a day afield.*
– ORIGIN Middle English (in sense 2): from A-² 'on, in' + FIELD.

afire ▸ adverb & adjective literary on fire; burning: [as predic. adj.] *the whole mill was afire.*

AFK ▸ abbreviation informal away from the keyboard: *I'll generally be AFK, though I plan on hitting an Internet cafe on Thursday.*

AFL ▸ abbreviation Australian Football League.

aflame ▸ adverb & adjective in flames; burning: [as adv.] *pour brandy over the steaks and then set aflame.*

aflatoxin /ˌafləˈtɒksɪn/ ▸ noun Chemistry any of a class of toxic compounds produced by certain moulds found in food, which can cause liver damage and cancer. ● These are produced by fungi of the *Aspergillus flavus* group, subdivision Deuteromycotina.
– ORIGIN 1960s: from elements of the modern Latin taxonomic name (see above) + TOXIN.

AFL-CIO ▸ abbreviation American Federation of Labor and Congress of Industrial Organizations.

afloat ▸ adjective & adverb **1** floating in water; not sinking: [as adv.] *they trod water to keep afloat* | [as predic. adj.] *the canoes were still afloat.* ■ on board a ship or boat: [as predic. adj.] *he hopes to find a second-hand craft and be afloat by the end of the month.*
2 out of debt or difficulty: [as adv.] *professional management will be needed to keep firms afloat.*
– ORIGIN Old English *on flote* (see A-², FLOAT), influenced in Middle English by Old Norse *á flot(i)* and Old French *en flot*.

aflood ▸ adjective flooded or submerged: *a market aflood with dumped food.*

aflutter ▸ adjective [predic.] in a state of tremulous excitement: *he has the physique that could send a thousand female hearts aflutter.*

AFM ▸ abbreviation (in the UK) Air Force Medal, awarded for bravery.

afoot ▸ adverb & adjective **1** in preparation or progress; happening or beginning to happen: [as predic. adj.] *plans are afoot for a festival.*
2 chiefly N. Amer. on foot: [as adv.] *they were forced to go afoot.*

afore ▸ preposition archaic or dialect before: *he died the day afore yesterday.*
– ORIGIN Old English *onforan* (see A-², FORE).

afore- ▸ prefix before; previously.

aforementioned ▸ adjective denoting a thing or person previously mentioned: *songs from the aforementioned album.*

aforesaid ▸ adjective another term for AFOREMENTIONED.

aforethought ▸ adjective see MALICE AFORETHOUGHT.

a fortiori /ˌeɪ fɔːtɪˈɔːrʌɪ, ˌɑː, -riː/ ▸ adverb & adjective used to express a conclusion for which there is stronger evidence than for a previously accepted one: [as adv.] *they reject all absolute ideas of justice, and a fortiori the natural-law position.*
– ORIGIN early 17th cent.: Latin, from *a fortiori argumento* 'from stronger argument'.

afoul ▸ adverb N. Amer. into conflict or difficulty with.

afraid ▸ adjective [predic.] feeling fear or anxiety; frightened: *I'm **afraid of** dogs* | *she tried to think about the future without feeling afraid.* ■ worried that something undesirable will occur or be done: *she was **afraid that** he would be angry.* ■ [with infinitive] unwilling or reluctant to do something for fear of the consequences: *I'm often afraid to go out on the streets.* ■ (**afraid for**) anxious about the well-being or safety of: *William was suddenly afraid for her.*
– PHRASES **I'm afraid** [with clause] used to express polite or formal apology or regret: *I'm afraid I don't understand.*
– ORIGIN Middle English: past participle of the obsolete verb *affray*, from Anglo-Norman French *afrayer* (see AFFRAY).

A-frame ▸ noun a frame shaped like a capital letter A. ■ N. Amer. a house built around a timber A-frame.

afreet /ˈafriːt/ (also **afrit**) ▶ **noun** (in Arabian and Muslim mythology) a powerful jinn or demon.
– ORIGIN late 18th cent.: from Arabic *ʻifrīt*.

afresh ▶ **adverb** in a new or different way: *she left the job to start afresh*.

Africa the second-largest continent, a southward projection of the Old World land mass divided roughly in two by the equator and surrounded by sea except where the Isthmus of Suez joins it to Asia.

African ▶ **noun** a person from Africa, especially a black person. ■ a person of black African descent.
▶ **adjective** relating to Africa or people of African descent.
– ORIGIN from Latin *Africanus*, from *Africa* (*terra*) '(land) of the *Afri*', an ancient people of North Africa.

Africana /ˌafrɪˈkɑːnə/ ▶ **plural noun** books, artefacts, and other collectors' items connected with Africa, especially southern Africa.

African American chiefly US ▶ **noun** a black American.
▶ **adjective** relating to black Americans.

USAGE See USAGE at BLACK.

African daisy ▶ **noun** a plant of the daisy family, cultivated for its bright flowers. ● *Dimorphotheca* and other genera, family Compositae.

Africander /ˌafrɪˈkandə/ ▶ **noun** variant spelling of AFRIKANDER.

African elephant ▶ **noun** the elephant native to Africa, which is larger than the Indian elephant and has larger ears and a two-lipped trunk. ● *Loxodonta africana*, family Elephantidae.

African Eve hypothesis ▶ **noun** another term for EVE HYPOTHESIS.

African grey parrot ▶ **noun** another term for GREY PARROT.

African horse sickness ▶ **noun** a notifiable viral disease of horses, which is usually fatal. It is transmitted by biting insects and occurs chiefly in Africa, the Middle East, and the Mediterranean.

Africanism ▶ **noun 1** a feature of language or culture regarded as characteristically African.
2 [mass noun] the belief that black Africans and their culture should predominate in Africa.
– DERIVATIVES **Africanist** noun & adjective.

Africanize (also **Africanise**) ▶ **verb** [with obj.] **1** make African in character: (as adj. **Africanized**) *an Africanized form of Cajun music*. ■ (in Africa) restructure (an organization) by replacing white employees with black Africans.
2 (usu. as adj. **Africanized**) hybridize (honeybees of European stock) with bees of African stock, producing an aggressive strain.
– DERIVATIVES **Africanization** noun.

African lynx ▶ **noun** another term for CARACAL.

African National Congress (abbrev.: **ANC**) a South African political party and black nationalist organization. Having been banned by the South African government 1960–90, the ANC was victorious in the country's first democratic elections in 1994 and its leader Nelson Mandela became the country's President.

African Union an association of African states formed in 2002 from the Organization of African Unity.

African violet ▶ **noun** a small East African plant with heart-shaped velvety leaves and violet, pink, or white flowers. ● Genus *Saintpaulia*, family Gesneriaceae: several species, in particular *S. ionantha*, a popular houseplant.

Afrikaans /ˌafrɪˈkɑːns/ ▶ **noun** [mass noun] a language of southern Africa, derived from the form of Dutch brought to the Cape by Protestant settlers in the 17th century. It is an official language of South Africa, spoken by around 6 million people as their first language.
▶ **adjective** relating to the Afrikaner people, their way of life, or their language.
– ORIGIN the name in Afrikaans, from Dutch, literally 'African'.

Afrika Korps /ˈafrɪkə ˌkɔː/ a German army force sent to North Africa in 1941 under General Rommel.

Afrikander /ˌafrɪˈkɑːndə/ (also **Africander**) ▶ **noun** an animal of a South African breed of sheep or longhorn cattle.
– ORIGIN early 19th cent. (an early form of AFRIKANER, having the same senses): via Afrikaans from South African Dutch.

Afrikaner /ˌafrɪˈkɑːnə/ ▶ **noun 1** an Afrikaans-speaking white person in South Africa, especially one descended from the Dutch and Huguenot settlers of the 17th century.
2 S. African a gladiolus native to southern Africa. ● *Gladiolus* and related genera, family Iridaceae.
– DERIVATIVES **Afrikanerdom** noun.
ORIGIN Afrikaans, from South African Dutch *Africander*, from Dutch *Afrikaan* 'an African' + the personal suffix *-der*, on the pattern of *Hollander* 'Dutchman'.

Afrikanerbond /ˌafrɪˈkɑːnəbɒnd, -bɒnt/ a society in South Africa promoting the interests of Afrikaners.

Afrikaner Broederbond former name for AFRIKANERBOND.
– ORIGIN Afrikaans, from *broeder* 'brother' + *bond* 'league'.

afrit ▶ **noun** variant spelling of AFREET.

Afro ▶ **noun** (pl. **Afros**) a hairstyle consisting of a mass of very tight curls that stick out all round the head, like the natural hair of some black people.
– ORIGIN 1930s: independent usage of AFRO-, or an abbreviation of AFRICAN.

Afro- ▶ **combining form** African; African and ...: *Afro-Asiatic* | *Afro-Belizean*. ■ relating to Africa: *Afrocentric*.
– ORIGIN from Latin *Afer, Afr-* 'African'.

Afro-American chiefly N. Amer. ▶ **adjective & noun** another term for AFRICAN AMERICAN.

Afro-Asiatic ▶ **adjective** relating to or denoting a family of languages spoken in the Middle East and North Africa. They can be divided into five groups: Semitic, Omotic, Berber, Cushitic, and Chadic. Ancient Egyptian was also a member of this family. Also called HAMITO-SEMITIC.

Afrobeat ▶ **noun** [mass noun] a style of popular music incorporating elements of African music and jazz, soul, and funk.

Afro-Caribbean ▶ **noun** a person of African descent living in or coming from the Caribbean.
▶ **adjective** relating to Afro-Caribbeans.

Afrocentric ▶ **adjective** regarding African or black culture as pre-eminent.
– DERIVATIVES **Afrocentrism** noun, **Afrocentrist** noun.

afrormosia /ˌafrɔːˈməʊzɪə/ ▶ **noun 1** [mass noun] the valuable timber of a tropical tree, resembling teak and used for furniture.
2 the tree that yields afrormosia timber, occurring mainly in West Africa. ● Genus *Pericopsis* (formerly *Afrormosia*), family Leguminosae: several species, especially *P. elata* and *P. laxiflora*.
– ORIGIN 1920s: modern Latin, from AFRO- + the related genus name *Ormosia*, formed irregularly from Greek *hormos* 'necklace' (because necklaces were strung with the seeds).

Afrotropical ▶ **adjective** another term for ETHIOPIAN (sense 2 of the adjective).

aft /ɑːft/ ▶ **adverb & adjective** at, near, or towards the stern of a ship or tail of an aircraft: [as adv.] *Travis made his way aft* | [as adj.] *the aft cargo compartment*.
– ORIGIN early 17th cent.: probably from obsolete *baft* (see ABAFT), influenced by Low German and Dutch *achter* 'abaft, after'.

after ▶ **preposition 1** in the time following (an event or another period of time): *shortly after their marriage they moved to Colorado* | *after a while he returned* | *he'd gone out with his secretary for an after-work drink*. ■ in phrases indicating something happening continuously or repeatedly: ***day after day** we kept studying*. ■ N. Amer. past (used in specifying a time): *I strolled in about ten minutes after two*. ■ during the time following the departure or action of: *she cooks for him and cleans up after him*.
2 behind: *she went out, shutting the door after her*. ■ (with reference to looking or speaking) in the direction of someone who is moving further away: *she stared after him*.
3 in pursuit or quest of: *chasing after something you can't have*.
4 next to and following in order or importance: *in their order of priorities health **comes after** housing*.
5 in allusion to (someone or something with the same or a related name): *they named her Pauline, after Barbara's mother*. ■ in imitation of: *a drawing after Millet's The Reapers*.
▶ **conjunction & adverb** during the period of time following (an event): [as conjunction] *bath-time ended in a flood after the taps were left running* | [as adv.] *Duke Frederick died soon after*.
▶ **adjective** [attrib.] **1** archaic later: *he was sorry in after years*.
2 nearer the stern of a ship: *the after cabin*.
– PHRASES **after all** in spite of any indications or expectations to the contrary: *I rang and told her I couldn't come after all*. **after hours** after normal working or licensed opening hours. **after you** a polite formula used to suggest that someone goes in front of or takes a turn before oneself. **be after doing something** Irish be on the point of doing something or have just done it: *the pigs were after breaking loose*.
– ORIGIN Old English *æfter*, of Germanic origin; related to Dutch *achter*.

afterbirth ▶ **noun** [mass noun] the placenta and fetal membranes discharged from the womb after the birth of offspring.

afterburner ▶ **noun** an auxiliary burner in which extra fuel is burned in the exhaust of a jet engine, to increase thrust.

aftercare ▶ **noun** [mass noun] **1** care of a patient after a stay in hospital or of a person on release from prison.
2 support or advice offered to a customer following the purchase of a product or service.

afterdamp ▶ **noun** [mass noun] choking gas left after an explosion of firedamp in a mine, rich in carbon monoxide.

afterdeck ▶ **noun** an open deck toward the stern of a ship.

after-effect ▶ **noun** an effect that follows after the primary action of something: *he was suffering the after-effects of the drug*.

afterglow ▶ **noun** [in sing.] light or radiance remaining in the sky after the sun has set. ■ good feelings remaining after a pleasurable or successful experience: *basking in the afterglow of victory*.

after-image ▶ **noun** an impression of a vivid image retained by the eye after the stimulus has ceased.

afterlife ▶ **noun** [in sing.] (in some religions) life after death: *most Christians believe in an afterlife*.

aftermarket ▶ **noun** chiefly N. Amer. the market for spare parts, accessories, and components for motor vehicles. ■ Stock Exchange the market for shares and bonds after their original issue.

aftermath ▶ **noun 1** the consequences or after-effects of a significant unpleasant event: *food prices soared **in the aftermath of** the drought*.
2 Farming new grass growing after mowing or harvest.
– ORIGIN late 15th cent. (in sense 2): from AFTER (as an adjective) + dialect *math* 'mowing', of Germanic origin; related to German *Mahd*.

aftermost ▶ **adjective** [attrib.] nearest the stern of a ship or tail of an aircraft.
– ORIGIN late 18th cent.: from AFTER (as an adjective) + -MOST.

afternoon ▶ **noun** the time from noon or lunchtime to evening: *I telephoned **this afternoon** | I'll be back at three in the afternoon | she worked on Tuesday afternoons*.
▶ **adverb** (**afternoons**) informal in the afternoon; every afternoon.
▶ **exclamation** informal short for GOOD AFTERNOON.

afterpains ▶ **plural noun** pains after childbirth caused by contraction of the womb.

after-party ▶ **noun** a party held after another event, especially a concert or another party.

afters ▶ **plural noun** Brit. informal **1** the sweet course following the main course of a meal; pudding.
2 (in soccer) a confrontation between players after a foul or other incident: *they were both yellow-carded for a spot of afters before half-time*.

aftershave ▶ **noun** [mass noun] an astringent scented lotion for applying to the skin after shaving.

aftershock ▶ **noun** a smaller earthquake following the main shock of a large earthquake.

aftersun ▶ **adjective** denoting a product applied to the skin after exposure to the sun.

aftertaste ▶ **noun** a taste remaining in the mouth after eating or drinking something: *the wine had a bitter aftertaste* | figurative *we concluded many exchanges in uneasy fashion, leaving behind a sour aftertaste*.

afterthought ▶ **noun** something that is thought of or added later: *as an afterthought she said 'Thank you'*.

aftertouch ▶ **noun** [mass noun] a facility on an electronic music keyboard by which an effect is produced by depressing a key after striking it.

A

afterwards (US also **afterward** /-wəd/) ▶ **adverb** at a later or future time: *the offender was arrested shortly afterwards*.
– ORIGIN Old English *æftewearde*, from *æftan* 'aft' + **-WARDS**, influenced by **AFTER**.

afterword ▶ **noun** a concluding section in a book.

afterworld ▶ **noun** a world entered after death.

AG ▶ **abbreviation** ■ Adjutant General. ■ Aktiengesellschaft, used in the names of German joint-stock companies. ■ Attorney General.

Ag¹ ▶ **symbol** the chemical element silver.
– ORIGIN from Latin *argentum*.

Ag² ▶ **abbreviation** Biochemistry antigen.

ag¹ /ag/ N. Amer. informal ▶ **adjective** short for **AGRICULTURAL**. ▶ **noun** short for **AGRICULTURE**.

ag² /ax, ʌx/ ▶ **exclamation** S. African used to express a range of emotions from irritation or grief to pleasure: *ag man, there's nothing anyone can do*.
– ORIGIN Afrikaans, from Dutch *ach* (see **ACH**).

ag- ▶ **prefix** variant spelling of **AD-** assimilated before *g* (as in *aggravate*, *aggression*).

Aga /ˈɑːgə/ ▶ **noun** Brit. trademark a type of heavy heat-retaining stove or range used for cooking and heating.
– ORIGIN 1930s: from the Swedish name *(Svenskaa) A(ktiebolaget) Ga(sackumulator)* 'Swedish Gas Accumulator Company', the original manufacturer.

aga /ˈɑːgə/ ▶ **noun** chiefly historical (in Muslim countries, especially under the Ottoman Empire) a military commander or official.
– ORIGIN mid 16th cent.: from Turkish *ağa* 'master, lord', from Mongolian *aqa*.

Agadir /ˌagəˈdɪə/ a seaport and resort on the Atlantic coast of Morocco; pop. 487,954 (2004).

again /əˈgɛn, əˈgeɪn/ ▶ **adverb** another time; once more: *it was great to meet old friends again*. ■ returning to a previous position or condition: *he rose, tidied the bed, and sat down again*. ■ in addition to what has already been mentioned: *the wages were low but they made half as much again in tips*. ■ [sentence adverb] used to introduce a further point for consideration, supporting or contrasting with what has just been said: *I never saw any signs, but* **then again**, *maybe I wasn't looking*. ■ used to ask someone to repeat something: *what was your name again?*
– PHRASES **again and again** repeatedly.
– ORIGIN Old English *ongēan*, *ongægn*, etc., of Germanic origin; related to German *entgegen* 'opposite'.

against /əˈgɛnst, əˈgeɪnst/ ▶ **preposition 1** in opposition to: *the fight against crime* | *he decided against immediate publication* | *swimming against the tide*. ■ with reference to legal action: *the first victim gave evidence against him*. ■ with reference to a sporting contest: *the championship match against Somerset*.
2 in anticipation of and preparation for (a problem or difficulty): *he gritted his teeth against the pain* | *makeshift barricades against tank attacks*. ■ (in betting) in anticipation of the failure of: *the odds were 5–1 against England*. ■ in resistance to; as protection from: *he turned up his collar against the wind*. ■ in relation to (an amount of money owed, due, or lent) so as to reduce, cancel, or secure it: *money was advanced against the value of the property*.
3 in conceptual contrast to: *the benefits must be weighed against the costs*. ■ in visual contrast to: *he was silhouetted against the light of the stair window*.
4 in or into physical contact with (something), so as to be supported by or collide with it: *she stood with her back against the door* | *frustration made him bang his head against the wall*.
– PHRASES **against one's wishes** when one is unwilling or has refused: *if any photos or information are included here against your wishes, please let me know and they will be removed immediately*. **against the law** (or **rules**) illegal or unlawful: *cockfighting has been against the law in South Carolina for 120 years* | *it was against the rules to have a guy in a girl's room*. **have something against someone** dislike or bear a grudge towards someone: *I have nothing against you personally*.
– ORIGIN Middle English: from **AGAIN** + *-s* (adverbial genitive) + *-t* probably by association with superlatives (as in *amongst*).

Aga Khan /ˌɑːgə ˈkɑːn/ ▶ **noun** the title of the spiritual leader of the Nizari sect of Ismaili Muslims. The first Aga Khan was given his title in 1818 by the shah of Persia. The present (fourth) Aga Khan (**Karim al-Hussain Shah**, b.1937) inherited the title in 1957.

agal /aˈgɑːl/ ▶ **noun** a headband worn by Bedouin Arab men to keep the keffiyeh in place.
– ORIGIN mid 19th cent.: representing a Bedouin pronunciation of Arabic *ʿiqāl* 'bond, hobble'.

agama /əˈgɑːmə/ ▶ **noun** an Old World lizard with a large head and a long tail, typically showing a marked difference in colour and form between the sexes. ● Genus *Agama*, family Agamidae: many species.
– DERIVATIVES **agamid** noun & adjective.
– ORIGIN late 18th cent.: perhaps from Carib (the name was originally applied to a West Indian lizard).

A game ▶ **noun** informal, chiefly US used in reference to performing to the very best of one's ability: *she'll bring her A game tonight—she understands how important it is*.

Agamemnon /ˌagəˈmɛmnən/ Greek Mythology king of Mycenae and brother of Menelaus, commander-in-chief of the Greek expedition against Troy. On his return home from Troy he was murdered by his wife Clytemnestra and her lover Aegisthus; his murder was avenged by his son Orestes and daughter Electra.

agamic /əˈgamɪk/ ▶ **adjective** Biology asexual; reproducing asexually: *winged agamic females*.
– ORIGIN mid 19th cent.: from Greek *agamos* 'unmarried' + **-IC**.

agammaglobulinaemia /eɪˌgaməˌglɒbjʊlɪˈniːmɪə/ (also **agammaglobulinemia**) ▶ **noun** [mass noun] Medicine lack of gamma globulin in the blood plasma, causing immune deficiency.

agamospermy /ˈagəmə(ʊ)ˌspəːmi/ ▶ **noun** [mass noun] Botany asexual reproduction in which seeds are produced from unfertilized ovules.
– DERIVATIVES **agamospermous** adjective.
– ORIGIN 1930s: from Greek *agamos* 'unmarried' + *sperma* 'seed'.

agapanthus /ˌagəˈpanθəs/ ▶ **noun** a South African plant of the lily family, with blue or white flowers growing in rounded clusters. ● Genus *Agapanthus*, family Liliaceae (or Alliaceae).
– ORIGIN modern Latin, from Greek *agapē* 'love' + *anthos* 'flower'.

agape¹ /əˈgeɪp/ ▶ **adjective** [predic.] (of a person's mouth) wide open in surprise or wonder.
– ORIGIN mid 17th cent.: from **A-²** 'on' + **GAPE**.

agape² /ˈagəpi/ ▶ **noun** [mass noun] Theology Christian love, as distinct from erotic love or simple affection. ■ [count noun] a communal meal held in Christian fellowship.
– ORIGIN early 17th cent.: from Greek *agapē* 'brotherly love'.

agar /ˈeɪgɑː/ (also **agar-agar** /eɪgɑːrˈeɪgɑː/) ▶ **noun** [mass noun] a gelatinous substance obtained from certain red seaweeds and used in biological culture media and as a thickener in foods.
– ORIGIN early 19th cent.: from Malay.

agarbatti /ˈagəːˌbʌtiː/ ▶ **noun** (pl. **same** or **agarbattis**) Indian term for **JOSS STICK**.
– ORIGIN from Hindi *agarbattī*.

agaric /ˈag(ə)rɪk, əˈgarɪk/ ▶ **noun** a fungus with a fruiting body that resembles a mushroom, having a convex or flattened cap with gills on the underside. ● Order Agaricales, class Hymenomycetes, in particular the mushroom family Agaricaceae.
– ORIGIN late Middle English (originally denoting various bracket fungi with medicinal or other uses): from Latin *agaricum*, from Greek *agarikon* 'tree fungus'.

agarose /ˈagərəʊz, -s/ ▶ **noun** [mass noun] Biochemistry a substance which is the main constituent of agar and is used especially in gels for electrophoresis. It is a polysaccharide mainly containing galactose residues.

Agartala /ˈʌgətəˌlɑː/ a city in the far north-east of India, capital of the state of Tripura, situated near the border with Bangladesh; pop. 218,000 (est. 2009).

Agassiz /ˈagəsi/, Jean Louis Rodolphe (1807–73), Swiss-born American zoologist, geologist, and palaeontologist. In 1837 Agassiz was the first to propose that much of Europe had once been in the grip of an ice age.

agate /ˈagət/ ▶ **noun** [mass noun] an ornamental stone consisting of a hard variety of chalcedony (quartz), typically banded in appearance. ■ [count noun] a coloured toy marble resembling a banded gemstone.
– ORIGIN late 15th cent.: from French, via Latin from Greek *akhatēs*.

agave /əˈgeɪvi/ ▶ **noun** a succulent plant with rosettes of narrow spiny leaves and tall flower spikes, native to the southern US and tropical America. ● Genus *Agave*, family Agavaceae: numerous species, including the century plant.
– ORIGIN Latin, from Greek *Agauē*, the name of one of the daughters of Cadmus in Greek mythology, from *agauos* 'illustrious'.

AGC ▶ **abbreviation** Electronics automatic gain control.

age ▶ **noun 1** the length of time that a person has lived or a thing has existed: *he died from a heart attack at the age of 51* | *he must be nearly 40 years of age*. ■ a particular stage in someone's life: *children of primary school age*. ■ [mass noun] the state of being old: *fine wine improves with age*.
2 a distinct period of history: *an age of technological growth*. ■ Geology a division of time that is a subdivision of an epoch, corresponding to a stage in chronostratigraphy. ■ (**ages**/**an age**) Brit. informal a very long time: *I haven't seen her for ages*.
▶ **verb** (**ages**, **ageing** or **aging**, **aged**) [no obj.] grow old or older: *the tiredness we feel as we age*. ■ [with obj.] cause to appear old or older: *he even tried ageing the painting with a spoonful of coffee*. ■ (with reference to an alcoholic drink, cheese, etc.) mature or allow to mature: [no obj.] *the wine ages in open vats or casks* | [with obj.] *a cheese that has been aged for four months*. ■ [with obj.] determine how old (something) is: *we didn't have a clue how to age these animals*.
– PHRASES **act** (or **be**) **one's age** [usu. in imperative] behave in a manner appropriate to someone of one's age and not to someone younger. **come of age** reach adult status (in UK law at 18, formerly 21). ■ (of a movement or activity) become fully established: *space travel will then finally come of age*. **of an age 1** old enough to be able or expected to do something: *the sons are of an age to marry*. **2** (of two or more people or things) of a similar age: *the children all seemed of an age*. **through the ages** throughout history: *the influence of Greek culture through the ages*.
– ORIGIN Middle English: from Old French, based on Latin *aetas*, *aetat-*, from *aevum* 'age, era'.

-age ▶ **suffix** forming nouns: **1** denoting an action: *leverage* | *voyage*. ■ the product of an action: *spillage* | *wreckage*. ■ a function; a sphere of action: *homage* | *peerage*.
2 denoting an aggregate or number of: *mileage* | *percentage*. ■ fees payable for; the cost of using: *postage* | *tonnage*. ■ informal denoting a large number of something (typically forming nouns whose plurals are correctly formed with -s): *decibelage* | *kissage*.
3 denoting a place or abode: *vicarage* | *village*.
– ORIGIN from Old French, based on Latin *-aticum*, neuter form of the adjectival ending *-aticus*.

aged ▶ **adjective 1** /eɪdʒd/ [predic. or postpositive] having lived for a specified length of time; of a specified age: *young people aged 14 to 18* | *he died aged 60*. ■ (of a horse or farm animal) over a certain defined age of maturity, typically 6 to 12 years for horses, 3 or 4 years for cattle.
2 /ˈeɪdʒɪd/ having lived or existed for a long time; very old: *aged men with white hair*.
3 /eɪdʒd/ having been subjected to ageing: *replica guitar with aged finish*.

age gap ▶ **noun** a difference in age between people, especially as a potential source of misunderstanding.

age group ▶ **noun** a number of people or things classed together as being of similar age: *that attitude is widespread in my age group*.

age hardening ▶ **noun** [mass noun] spontaneous hardening of a metal which occurs if it is quenched and then stored at ambient temperature or treated with mild heat.
– DERIVATIVES **age-hardened** adjective.

ageing (also **aging**) ▶ **noun** [mass noun] the process of growing old: *the external signs of ageing*. ■ the process of change in the properties of a material occurring over a period, either spontaneously or through deliberate action.
▶ **adjective** (of a person) growing old; elderly: *an ageing population*. ■ (of a thing) reaching the end of useful life: *the world's ageing fleet of oil tankers*.

ageism ▶ **noun** [mass noun] prejudice or discrimination on the grounds of a person's age.
– DERIVATIVES **ageist** adjective & noun.

ageless ▶ **adjective** not ageing or appearing to age. ■ lasting for a long time or forever: *the town retains an ageless charm*.
– DERIVATIVES **agelessness** noun.

age-long ▶ **adjective** [attrib.] having existed for a very long time: *the will to change age-long habits*.

agency ▶ **noun 1** [often with adj. or noun modifier] a business or organization providing a particular service on behalf of another business, person, or group: *an advertising agency* | *aid agencies*. ■ a department or body providing a specific service for a government

or other organization: *the Environmental Protection Agency.*
2 [mass noun] action or intervention producing a particular effect: *canals carved* **by the agency of** *running water.* ■ [count noun] a thing or person that acts to produce a particular result: *the movies could be an agency moulding the values of the public.*
– ORIGIN mid 17th cent.: from medieval Latin *agentia*, from *agent-* 'doing' (see **AGENT**).

agenda /ə'dʒɛndə/ ▶ **noun 1** a list of items to be discussed at a formal meeting: *the question of nuclear weapons had been removed from the agenda.* ■ a plan of things to be done or problems to be addressed: *he vowed to put jobs at the top of his agenda | the government had its own agenda.* ■ the underlying intentions or motives of a particular person or group: *Miller has his own agenda and it has nothing to do with football.*
2 N. Amer. an appointment diary.
– PHRASES **on the agenda** likely or needing to be dealt with or done: *his release was not on the agenda.* **set the agenda** influence or determine a programme of action: *he has set the agenda for future work in this field.*
– ORIGIN early 17th cent. (in the sense 'things to be done'): from Latin, neuter plural of *agendum*, gerundive of *agere* 'do'.

USAGE Although **agenda** is the plural of **agendum** in Latin, in standard modern English it is normally used as a singular noun with a standard plural form (**agendas**). See also **USAGE** at **DATA** and **MEDIA**[1]

agent ▶ **noun 1** a person who acts on behalf of another, in particular: ■ a person who manages business, financial, or contractual matters for an actor, performer, writer, etc. ■ a person or company that provides a particular service, typically one that involves organizing transactions between two other parties: *a travel agent.* ■ a person who works secretly to obtain information for a government or other official body: *a trained intelligence agent.*
2 a person or thing that takes an active role or produces a specified effect: *agents of environmental change | bleaching agents.* ■ Grammar the doer of an action, typically expressed as the subject of an active verb or in a *by* phrase with a passive verb. ■ Computing an independently operating Internet program, typically one that performs background tasks such as information retrieval or processing on behalf of a user or other program.
– DERIVATIVES **agentive** adjective (Grammar).
– ORIGIN late Middle English (in the sense 'someone or something that produces an effect'): from Latin *agent-* 'doing', from *agere*.

agent general ▶ **noun** (pl. **agents general**) the representative of an Australian state or Canadian province in London or another major foreign city.

agent noun ▶ **noun** a noun denoting someone or something that performs the action of a verb, usually ending in *-er* or *-or*, e.g. *worker, accelerator.*

Agent Orange ▶ **noun** [mass noun] a defoliant chemical used by the US in the Vietnam War.

agent provocateur /ˌaʒɒ̃ prəˌvɒkə'təː/, French /aʒɑ̃ pʀɔvɔkatœʀ/ ▶ **noun** (pl. **agents provocateurs** pronunc. **same**) a person employed to induce others to break the law so that they can be convicted.
– ORIGIN late 19th cent.: French, literally 'provocative agent'.

age of consent ▶ **noun** the age at which a person's consent to sexual intercourse is valid in law.

age of discretion ▶ **noun** the age at which someone is considered able to manage their own affairs or take responsibility for their actions.

age of reason ▶ **noun** [mass noun] **1** the Enlightenment.
2 (especially in the Roman Catholic Church) the age at which a child is held capable of discerning right from wrong.

age-old ▶ **adjective** having existed for a very long time: *the age-old quest for knowledge.*

Aggadah ▶ **noun** variant spelling of **HAGGADAH**.

agglomerate ▶ **verb** /ə'glɒməreɪt/ collect or form into a mass or group: [with obj.] *he is seeking to agglomerate the functions of the Home Office* | [no obj.] *these small particles soon agglomerate together.*
▶ **noun** /ə'glɒmərət/ a mass or collection of things: *a multimedia agglomerate.* ■ [mass noun] Geology a volcanic rock consisting of large fragments bonded together.
▶ **adjective** /ə'glɒmərət/ collected or formed into a mass.
– DERIVATIVES **agglomerative** adjective.
– ORIGIN late 17th cent.: from Latin *agglomerat-* 'added to', from the verb *agglomerare*, from *ad-* 'to' + *glomerare* (from *glomus* 'ball').

agglomeration /əglɒmə'reɪʃ(ə)n/ ▶ **noun** a mass or collection of things; an assemblage: *the arts centre is an agglomeration of theatres, galleries, shops, restaurants and bars.*

agglutinate /ə'gluːtɪneɪt/ ▶ **verb** firmly stick or be stuck together to form a mass: (as adj **agglutinated**) *rhinoceros horns are agglutinated masses of hair.* ■ Biology (with reference to bacteria or red blood cells) clump together. ■ [with obj.] Linguistics (of a language) combine (word elements) to express compound ideas.
– DERIVATIVES **agglutination** noun.
– ORIGIN mid 16th cent.: from Latin *agglutinat-* 'caused to adhere', from the verb *agglutinare*, from *ad-* 'to' + *glutinare* (from *gluten* 'glue').

agglutinative /ə'gluːtɪnətɪv/ ▶ **adjective** Linguistics (of a language, e.g. Hungarian, Turkish, Korean, and Swahili) tending to express concepts in complex words consisting of many elements, rather than by inflection or by using isolated elements. Contrasted with **ANALYTIC** and **SYNTHETIC**.

agglutinin /ə'gluːtɪnɪn/ ▶ **noun** Biology an antibody, lectin, or other substance that causes agglutination.
– ORIGIN late 19th cent.: from **AGGLUTINATE** + **-IN**[1].

aggradation /ˌagrə'deɪʃ(ə)n/ ▶ **noun** [mass noun] Geology the deposition of material by a river, stream, or current.
– ORIGIN late 19th cent.: from **AG-** (expressing increase) + *(de)gradation.*

aggrandize /ə'grandʌɪz/ (also **aggrandise**) ▶ **verb** [with obj.] increase the power, status, or wealth of: *an action intended to aggrandize the Frankish dynasty.* ■ enhance the reputation of (someone) beyond what is justified by the facts: *he hoped to aggrandize himself by dying a hero's death.*
– DERIVATIVES **aggrandizement** noun, **aggrandizer** noun.
– ORIGIN mid 17th cent. (in the general sense 'increase, magnify'): from French *agrandiss-*, lengthened stem of *agrandir*, probably from Italian *aggrandire*, from Latin *grandis* 'large'. The ending was changed by association with verbs ending in **-IZE**.

aggravate ▶ **verb** [with obj.] **1** make (a problem, injury, or offence) worse or more serious: *military action would only aggravate the situation.*
2 informal annoy or exasperate: (as adj. **aggravating**) *she found him thoroughly aggravating and unprofessional.*
– DERIVATIVES **aggravatingly** adverb.
– ORIGIN mid 16th cent.: from Latin *aggravat-* 'made heavy', from the verb *aggravare*, from *ad-* (expressing increase) + *gravis* 'heavy'.

USAGE **Aggravate** in the sense 'annoy or exasperate' dates back to the 17th century and has been so used by respected writers ever since. This use is still regarded as incorrect by some traditionalists on the grounds that it is too radical a departure from the etymological meaning of 'make heavy'. It is, however, comparable to meaning changes in hundreds of other words which have long been accepted without comment.

aggravated ▶ **adjective** [attrib.] Law (of an offence) made more serious by attendant circumstances: *aggravated burglary.* ■ (of a penalty) made more severe in recognition of the seriousness of an offence: *aggravated damages.*

aggravation ▶ **noun** [mass noun] **1** the state of becoming worse or more serious; exacerbation: *the patient experienced an aggravation of symptoms.*
2 informal annoyance or exasperation: *the whole business has caused me a lot of aggravation.* ■ aggressive behaviour; harassment.

aggregate ▶ **noun** /'agrɪgət/ **1** a whole formed by combining several separate elements: *the council was an aggregate of three regional assemblies.* ■ the total score of a player or team in a fixture comprising more than one game or round: *he set the pace with a one-over-par aggregate of 151* | [mass noun] *the result put the sides level* **on aggregate**.
2 a material or structure formed from a mass of fragments or particles loosely compacted together. ■ [mass noun] pieces of broken or crushed stone or gravel used to make concrete and in building.
▶ **adjective** /'agrɪgət/ [attrib.] formed or calculated by the combination of several separate elements; total: *the aggregate amount of grants made.* ■ Botany (of a group of species) comprising several very similar species formerly regarded as a single species. ■ Economics denoting the total supply or demand for goods and services in an economy at a particular time.
▶ **verb** /'agrɪgeɪt/ form or group into a class or cluster: [with obj.] *socio-occupational groups aggregate men sharing similar kinds of occupation* | [no obj.] *the butterflies aggregate in dense groups.*
– PHRASES **in (the) aggregate** in total; as a whole: *10,000 tonnes in aggregate.*
– DERIVATIVES **aggregation** noun, **aggregative** /'agrɪgətɪv/ adjective.
– ORIGIN late Middle English: from Latin *aggregat-* 'herded together', from the verb *aggregare*, from *ad-* 'towards' + *grex, greg-* 'a flock'.

aggregate fruit ▶ **noun** Botany a fruit formed from several carpels derived from the same flower, e.g. a raspberry.

aggregator ▶ **noun** Computing a website or program that collects related items of content and displays them or links to them.

aggression ▶ **noun** [mass noun] feelings of anger or antipathy resulting in hostile or violent behaviour; readiness to attack or confront: *his chin was jutting with aggression | territorial aggression between individuals of the same species.* ■ the action of attacking without provocation: *he called for an end to foreign aggression against his country.* ■ forcefulness: *the sheer volume and aggression of his playing*
– ORIGIN early 17th cent. (in the sense 'an attack'): from Latin *aggressio(n-)*, from *aggredi* 'to attack', from *ad-* 'towards' + *gradi* 'proceed, walk'.

aggressive ▶ **adjective** ready or likely to attack or confront; characterized by or resulting from aggression: *he's very uncooperative and aggressive.* ■ behaving or done in a determined and forceful way: *we needed more growth to pursue our aggressive acquisition strategy.*
– DERIVATIVES **aggressively** adverb, **aggressiveness** noun.
– ORIGIN early 19th cent.: from Latin *aggress-* 'attacked' (from the verb *aggredi*) + **-IVE**; compare with French *agressif, -ive.*

aggressor ▶ **noun** a person or country that attacks another first.
– ORIGIN mid 17th cent.: from late Latin, from *aggredi* 'to attack' (see **AGGRESSION**).

aggrieved ▶ **adjective** feeling resentment at having been unfairly treated: *they were aggrieved at the outcome.*
– ORIGIN Middle English (in the sense 'distressed'): past participle of *aggrieve*, from Old French *agrever* 'make heavier', based on Latin *aggravare* (see **AGGRAVATE**).

aggro ▶ **noun** [mass noun] Brit. informal aggressive, violent behaviour. ■ problems and difficulties.
– ORIGIN 1960s: abbreviation of *aggravation* (see **AGGRAVATE**), or of **AGGRESSION**.

aghast /ə'gɑːst/ ▶ **adjective** [predic.] filled with horror or shock: *she winced,* **aghast at** *his cruelty.*
– ORIGIN late Middle English: past participle of the obsolete verb *agast, gast* 'frighten', from Old English *gǣsten*. The spelling with *gh* (originally Scots) became general by about 1700, probably influenced by **GHOST**; compare with **GHASTLY**.

Aghios Nikolaos /ˌagɪɒs ˌnɪkə'lʌɪɒs/ a fishing port and holiday resort on the north coast of Crete, east of Heraklion; pop. 11,100 (est. 2009). Greek name **Áyios Nikólaos**.

agile ▶ **adjective** able to move quickly and easily: *Ruth was as agile as a monkey.* ■ able to think and understand quickly: *his vague manner concealed an agile mind.*
– DERIVATIVES **agilely** adverb, **agility** noun.
– ORIGIN late Middle English: via French from Latin *agilis*, from *agere* 'do'.

agin /ə'gɪn/ ▶ **preposition** dialect form of **AGAINST**.
– ORIGIN early 19th cent.: variant of the obsolete preposition *again*, with the same meaning.

Agincourt, Battle of /'adʒɪnˌkɔː, -ˌkɔːt/ a battle in northern France in 1415 during the Hundred Years War, in which the English under Henry V defeated a large French army. The victory, achieved largely by use of the longbow, allowed Henry to occupy Normandy.

aging ▶ **adjective & noun** variant spelling of **AGEING**.

agio /'adʒɪəʊ/ ▶ **noun** (pl. **agios**) the percentage charged on the exchange of one currency, or one form of money, into another that is more valuable.
– ORIGIN late 17th cent.: from Italian *agio, aggio*, literally 'ease, convenience'.

A

agist[1] /əˈdʒɪst/ ▶ **verb** [with obj.] take in and feed (livestock) for payment.
– DERIVATIVES **agister** noun, **agistment** noun.
– ORIGIN late Middle English (in the sense 'use or allow the use of land for pasture'): from Old French *agister*, from *a-* (from Latin *ad* 'to, at') + *gister*, from *giste* 'lodging'.

agist[2] /ˈeɪdʒɪst/ ▶ **adjective & noun** variant spelling of **AGEIST** (see **AGEISM**).

agitate ▶ **verb** [with obj.] **1** make (someone) troubled or nervous: *the thought of questioning Toby agitated him extremely.*
2 stir or disturb (something, especially a liquid) briskly: *agitate the water to disperse the oil.*
3 [no obj.] campaign to arouse public concern about an issue in the hope of prompting public action: *they agitated for a reversal of the decision.*
– ORIGIN late Middle English (in the sense 'drive away'): from Latin *agitat-* 'agitated, driven', from *agitare*, frequentative of *agere* 'do, drive'.

agitated ▶ **adjective** feeling or appearing troubled or nervous: *there's no point getting agitated.*
– DERIVATIVES **agitatedly** adverb.

agitation ▶ **noun** [mass noun] **1** a state of anxiety or nervous excitement: *she was wringing her hands in agitation.*
2 brisk stirring or disturbance of a liquid.
3 the arousing of public concern about an issue and pressing for action on it: *widespread agitation for social reform.* ■ [count noun] Indian a public demonstration.
– ORIGIN mid 16th cent. (in the sense 'action, being active'): from Latin *agitatio(n-)*, from the verb *agitare* (see **AGITATE**).

agitato /ˌadʒɪˈtɑːtəʊ/ ▶ **adverb & adjective** Music (especially as a direction) agitated in manner: *allegro agitato.*
– ORIGIN Italian, literally 'agitated'.

agitator ▶ **noun 1** a person who urges others to protest or rebel: *a political agitator.*
2 an apparatus for stirring liquid.

agitprop /ˈadʒɪtprɒp, ˈag-/ ▶ **noun** [mass noun] political (originally communist) propaganda, especially in art or literature.
– ORIGIN 1930s: Russian, blend of *agitatsiya* 'agitation' and *propaganda* 'propaganda'.

agleam ▶ **adjective** [predic.] gleaming: *his eyes were agleam with the intensity of his fervour.*

aglet /ˈaglət/ ▶ **noun** a metal or plastic tube fixed round each end of a shoelace.
– ORIGIN late Middle English: from French *aiguillette* 'small needle', diminutive of *aiguille* (see **AIGUILLE**).

agley /əˈgleɪ, əˈgliː/ ▶ **adverb** Scottish askew; awry.
– ORIGIN late 18th cent.: from **A-**[2] 'on' + Scots *gley* 'squint', of unknown origin.

aglow ▶ **adjective** [predic.] glowing: *she was aglow with health.*

AGM ▶ **abbreviation** Brit. annual general meeting.

agma /ˈagmə/ ▶ **noun** Phonetics the speech sound of 'ng' as in *thing*, a velar nasal consonant represented by the symbol /ŋ/ in the International Phonetic Alphabet.
– ORIGIN 1950s: from late Greek, from Greek, literally 'fragment'.

agnail /ˈagneɪl/ ▶ **noun** another term for **HANGNAIL**.

agnate /ˈagneɪt/ chiefly Law ▶ **noun** a person descended from the same male ancestor as another specified or implied person, especially through the male line.
▶ **adjective** descended from the same male ancestor. Compare with **COGNATE** (sense 2 of the adjective).
– DERIVATIVES **agnatic** /-ˈnatɪk/ adjective, **agnation** noun.
– ORIGIN late 15th cent. (as a noun): from Latin *agnatus*, from *ad-* 'to' + *gnatus*, *natus* 'born'.

Agnatha /agˈneɪθə/ ▶ **plural noun** Zoology a group of primitive jawless vertebrates which includes the lampreys, hagfishes, and many fossil fishlike forms. Compare with **CYCLOSTOME**. ● Superclass Agnatha: the living forms are in the classes Myxini (hagfishes) and Cephalaspidomorphi (lampreys).
– DERIVATIVES **agnathan** noun & adjective.
– ORIGIN from modern Latin *Agnatha*, from **A-**[1] 'without' + Greek *gnathos* 'jaw'.

Agnes, St[1] (died *c.*304), Roman martyr, said to have been a Christian virgin who refused to marry. She is the patron saint of virgins and her emblem is a lamb (Latin *agnus*). Feast day, 21 January.

Agnes, St[2] (*c.*1211–82), patron saint of Bohemia. She was canonized in 1989. Feast day, 2 March.

Agnesi /anˈjeɪzi/, Maria Gaetana (1718–99), Italian mathematician and philosopher, regarded as the first female mathematician of the Western world. Her major work, produced in 1748, was a comprehensive treatment of algebra and analysis.

Agni /ˈagni/ the Vedic god of fire, the priest of the gods and the god of the priests.

agnolotti /ˌanjəˈlɒti/ ▶ **plural noun** pasta squares stuffed with a variety of fillings, like small ravioli.
– ORIGIN Italian.

agnosia /agˈnəʊsɪə/ ▶ **noun** [mass noun] Medicine inability to interpret sensations and hence to recognize things, typically as a result of brain damage.
– ORIGIN early 20th cent.: coined in German from Greek *agnōsia* 'ignorance'.

agnostic /agˈnɒstɪk/ ▶ **noun** a person who believes that nothing is known or can be known of the existence or nature of God.
▶ **adjective** relating to agnostics or agnosticism. ■ (in a non-religious context) having a doubtful or noncommittal attitude towards something: *until now I've been fairly agnostic about electoral reform.*
– DERIVATIVES **agnosticism** noun.
– ORIGIN mid 19th cent.: from **A-**[1] 'not' + **GNOSTIC**.

Agnus Dei /ˌagnʊs ˈdeɪiː, ˌanjʊs, ˈdiːʌɪ/ ▶ **noun 1** a figure of a lamb bearing a cross or flag, as an emblem of Christ.
2 Christian Church an invocation beginning with the words 'Lamb of God' forming a set part of the Mass.
– ORIGIN late Middle English: from Latin, literally 'Lamb of God'.

ago ▶ **adverb** before the present; earlier (used with a measurement of time): *he went five minutes ago | two years ago his parents moved house | as long ago as 1942 | not long ago he came across a rattlesnake outside his house.*
– ORIGIN Middle English *ago*, *agone*, past participle of the obsolete verb *ago* 'pass', used to express passage of time.

> **USAGE** When **ago** is followed by a clause, the clause should be introduced by **that** rather than **since**, e.g. *it was sixty years ago **that** I left this place* (not *it was sixty years ago **since** I left this place*). The use of **since** is not correct in standard English.

agog ▶ **adjective** [predic.] very eager or curious to hear or see something: *I'm **all agog** | Papa was **agog with** curiosity.*
– ORIGIN mid 16th cent.: from Old French *en gogues*, from *en* 'in' + the plural of *gogue* 'fun'.

agogic /əˈgɒdʒɪk/ Music ▶ **adjective** relating to or denoting accentuation within musical phrases by slight lengthening of notes.
▶ **noun** (**agogics**) [usu. treated as sing.] the use of agogic accents.
– ORIGIN late 19th cent.: coined in German from Greek *agōgos* 'leading', from *agein* 'to lead', + **-IC**.

agogo /əˈgəʊgəʊ/ ▶ **noun** a small bell made of two joined metal cones, used as a percussion instrument in African and Latin music.
– ORIGIN from Yoruba.

a gogo /ə ˈgəʊgəʊ/ ▶ **adjective** [postpositive] informal in abundance; galore: *Gershwin à gogo—all the hits.*
– ORIGIN 1960s: from French *à gogo*, from Old French *gogue* 'fun'.

agonic line /əˈgɒnɪk/ ▶ **noun** an imaginary line round the earth passing through both the north pole and the north magnetic pole, at any point on which a compass needle points to true north.
– ORIGIN mid 19th cent.: from Greek *agōnios*, *agōnos* (from *a-* 'without' + *gonia* 'angle') + **-IC**.

agonist /ˈagənɪst/ ▶ **noun 1** Biochemistry a substance which initiates a physiological response when combined with a receptor. Compare with **ANTAGONIST**.
2 Anatomy a muscle whose contraction moves a part of the body directly. Compare with **ANTAGONIST**.
3 another term for **PROTAGONIST**.
– DERIVATIVES **agonism** noun.
– ORIGIN early 20th cent.: from Greek *agōnistēs* 'contestant' (a sense reflected in English in the early 17th cent.), from *agōn* 'contest'.

agonistic ▶ **adjective 1** polemical; combative: *an agonistic exchange.* ■ Zoology (of animal behaviour) associated with conflict.
2 Biochemistry relating to or acting as an agonist.
– DERIVATIVES **agonistically** adverb.
– ORIGIN mid 17th cent.: via late Latin from Greek *agōnistikos*, from *agōnistēs* 'contestant' (see **AGONIST**).

agonize (also **agonise**) ▶ **verb** [no obj.] undergo great mental anguish through worrying about something: *I didn't agonize over the problem.* ■ [with obj.] cause mental anguish to.
– ORIGIN late 16th cent.: from French *agoniser* or late Latin *agonizare*, from Greek *agōnizesthai* 'contend', from *agōn* 'contest'.

agonized (also **agonised**) ▶ **adjective** manifesting, suffering, or characterized by great physical or mental pain: *she gave an agonized cry | months of agonized discussion.*

agonizing (also **agonising**) ▶ **adjective** causing great physical or mental pain: *an agonizing death | there is an agonizing choice to make.*
– DERIVATIVES **agonizingly** adverb [as submodifier] *agonizingly slow steps.*

agony ▶ **noun** (pl. **agonies**) [mass noun] extreme physical or mental suffering: *he crashed to the ground in agony.* ■ the final stages of a difficult or painful death: *his last agony.*
– ORIGIN late Middle English (originally denoting mental anguish alone): via Old French and late Latin from Greek *agōnia*, from *agōn* 'contest'. The sense of physical suffering dates from the early 17th cent.

agony aunt (or **agony uncle**) ▶ **noun** Brit. informal a person who answers letters in an agony column.

agony column ▶ **noun** Brit. informal a column in a newspaper or magazine offering advice on personal problems to readers who write in.

agora[1] /ˈagɒrə/ ▶ **noun** (pl. **agorae** /-riː/ or **agoras**) (in ancient Greece) a public open space used for assemblies and markets.
– ORIGIN from Greek.

agora[2] /ˌagəˈrɑː/ ▶ **noun** (pl. **agorot** or **agoroth** /ˌagəˈrəʊt, -rəʊθ/) a monetary unit of Israel, equal to one hundredth of a shekel.
– ORIGIN from Hebrew *'ăgōrāh* 'small coin'.

agoraphobia /ˌag(ə)rəˈfəʊbɪə/ ▶ **noun** [mass noun] extreme or irrational fear of open or public places.
– DERIVATIVES **agoraphobe** noun, **agoraphobic** adjective & noun.
– ORIGIN late 19th cent.: from Greek *agora* 'place of assembly, marketplace' + **-PHOBIA**.

agouti /əˈguːti/ ▶ **noun** (pl. **same** or **agoutis**) a large long-legged burrowing rodent related to the guinea pig, native to Central and South America. ● Genera *Cuniculus* and *Dasyprocta*, family Dasyproctidae: several species.
■ [mass noun] fur in which each hair has alternate dark and light bands, producing a grizzled appearance. ■ a rodent, especially a mouse, having agouti fur.
– ORIGIN mid 16th cent.: via French or from Spanish *aguti*, from Tupi *akutí*.

AGR ▶ **abbreviation** advanced gas-cooled (nuclear) reactor.

Agra /ˈɑːgrə/ a city on the River Jumna in Uttar Pradesh state, northern India; pop. 1,638,200 (est. 2009). Founded in 1566, Agra was the capital of the Mogul empire until 1658. It is the site of the Taj Mahal.

agrammatism /əˈgramətɪz(ə)m/ ▶ **noun** [mass noun] Medicine a tendency to form sentences without the correct inflectional structure as a result of brain damage, as in Broca's aphasia.

agranulocytosis /əˌgranjʊlə(ʊ)sʌɪˈtəʊsɪs/ ▶ **noun** [mass noun] Medicine a deficiency of granulocytes in the blood, causing increased vulnerability to infection.
– ORIGIN early 20th cent.: from **A-**[1] + **GRANULOCYTE** + **-OSIS**.

agraphia /əˈgrafɪə, eɪ-/ ▶ **noun** [mass noun] Medicine inability to write, as a language disorder resulting from brain damage.
– ORIGIN mid 19th cent.: from **A-**[1] 'without' + Greek *-graphia* 'writing'.

agrarian /əˈgrɛːrɪən/ ▶ **adjective** relating to cultivated land or the cultivation of land. ■ relating to landed property: *the agrarian reforms.*
▶ **noun** a person who advocates a redistribution of landed property.
– ORIGIN early 17th cent. (originally denoting a Roman law for the division of conquered lands): from Latin *agrarius*, from *ager*, *agr-* 'field'.

Agrarian Revolution the transformation of British agriculture during the 18th century, characterized by the enclosure of common land and the introduction of technological innovations such as the seed drill and the rotation of crops.

agree ▶ **verb** (**agrees**, **agreeing**, **agreed**) [no obj.] **1** have the same opinion about something; concur: *I completely **agree with** your recent editorial | we both **agreed on** issues such as tougher penalties for*

criminals | [with direct speech] *'Yes, dreadful, isn't it,' she agreed.* ■ (**agree with**) approve of (something) with regard to its moral correctness: *I don't agree with random drugs testing in schools.*
2 (**agree to** or **to do something**) say that one will do something which has been suggested by another person: *she had agreed to go and see a movie with him.* ■ [with obj.] reach agreement about (something) after negotiation: *if they had agreed a price the deal would have gone through* | [no obj.] *the commission **agreed on** a proposal to limit imports.*
3 (**agree with**) be consistent with: *your body language does not agree with what you are saying.* ■ Grammar have the same number, gender, case, or person as: *the verb agrees with the final noun.* ■ [usu. with negative] be healthy or appropriate for (someone): *she's eaten something which did not agree with her.*
– PHRASES **agree to differ** see DIFFER.
– ORIGIN late Middle English: from Old French *agreer*, based on Latin *ad-* 'to' + *gratus* 'pleasing'.

agreeable ▸ **adjective 1** quite enjoyable and pleasurable; pleasant: *a cheerful and agreeable companion.*
2 [predic.] willing to agree to something: *they were **agreeable to** its publication.* ■ (of a course of action) acceptable: *a compromise which might be **agreeable to** both coal owners and unions.*
– DERIVATIVES **agreeableness** noun, **agreeably** adverb [as submodifier] *an agreeably warm day.*
– ORIGIN late Middle English: from Old French *agreable*, from *agreer* 'make agreeable to' (see AGREE).

agreed ▸ **adjective** [attrib.] discussed or negotiated and then accepted by all parties: *the agreed date.* ■ (of two or more parties) holding the same view or opinion on something: *all the republics are **agreed on** the necessity of a common defence policy* | [with clause] *we are agreed that what is needed is a catchy title.*

agreement ▸ **noun** [mass noun] harmony or accordance in opinion or feeling: *the governments failed to **reach agreement*** | *the two officers nodded **in agreement**.* ■ [count noun] a negotiated and typically legally binding arrangement between parties as to a course of action: *a trade agreement* | *a verbal agreement to sell.* ■ the absence of incompatibility between two things; consistency: *agreement between experimental observations and theory.* ■ Grammar the condition of having the same number, gender, case, and/or person as another word.
– ORIGIN late Middle English: from Old French, from *agreer* 'make agreeable to' (see AGREE).

agrestic /ə'grɛstɪk/ ▸ **adjective** chiefly literary relating to the country; rural or rustic.
– ORIGIN early 17th cent.: from Latin *agrestis*, from *ager, agr-* 'field' + -IC.

agri- ▸ **noun** variant form of AGRO-.

agribusiness ▸ **noun** [mass noun] **1** agriculture conducted on strictly commercial principles. ■ [count noun] an organization engaged in agribusiness.
2 the group of industries dealing with agricultural produce and services required in farming.

agrichemical ▸ **noun & adjective** variant form of AGROCHEMICAL.

Agricola /ə'grɪkələ/, Gnaeus Julius (AD 40–93), Roman general and governor of Britain 78–84. As governor he completed the subjugation of Wales and defeated the Scottish Highland tribes.

agricultural ▸ **adjective 1** relating to agriculture: *agricultural land* | *an agricultural worker.*
2 Brit. informal (in a sporting context) clumsy: *Keith took an agricultural swing at the ball.*
– DERIVATIVES **agriculturalist** noun, **agriculturally** adverb.

agriculture ▸ **noun** [mass noun] the science or practice of farming, including cultivation of the soil for the growing of crops and the rearing of animals to provide food, wool, and other products.
– DERIVATIVES **agriculturist** noun.
– ORIGIN late Middle English: from Latin *agricultura*, from *ager, agr-* 'field' + *cultura* 'growing, cultivation'.

agrimony /'agrɪməni/ ▸ **noun** (pl. **agrimonies**) a plant of the rose family which bears slender flower spikes and hooked fruits, found in north temperate regions.
● Genus *Agrimonia*, family Rosaceae: several species.
– ORIGIN late Middle English: directly or (in early use) via Old French from Latin *agrimonia*, alteration of *argemonia*, from Greek *argemōnē* 'poppy'.

agrion /'agrɪɒn/ ▸ **noun** a large damselfly that has a body with a metallic sheen. Also called DEMOISELLE.
● Genus *Agrion* (or *Calopteryx*), family Calopterygidae: numerous species.
– ORIGIN Greek, neuter of *agrios* 'wild'.

Agrippa /ə'grɪpə/, Marcus Vipsanius (63–12 BC), Roman general. Augustus' adviser and son-in-law, he played an important part in the naval victories over Mark Antony.

agriscience ▸ **noun** [mass noun] the application of science to agriculture.
– DERIVATIVES **agriscientist** noun.

agritourism ▸ **noun** [mass noun] tourism in which tourists stay with local people in rural areas abroad.

agro- /'agrəʊ/ (also **agri-**) ▸ **combining form** agricultural: *agro-industry* | *agrobiology.* ■ agriculture and ...: *agroforestry.*
– ORIGIN from Greek *agros* 'field'.

agrobiology ▸ **noun** [mass noun] the branch of biology that deals with soil science and plant nutrition and its application to crop production.
– DERIVATIVES **agrobiological** adjective, **agrobiologist** noun.

agrochemical (also **agrichemical**) ▸ **noun** a chemical used in agriculture, such as a pesticide or a fertilizer.
▸ **adjective** relating to agrochemicals or their use: *the dangers of agrochemical pollution.*

agroecosystem ▸ **noun** an ecosystem on agricultural land.

agroforestry ▸ **noun** [mass noun] agriculture incorporating the cultivation of trees.

agro-industry ▸ **noun** [mass noun] industry connected with agriculture. ■ agriculture developed along industrial lines.
– DERIVATIVES **agro-industrial** adjective.

agronomy /ə'grɒnəmi/ ▸ **noun** [mass noun] the science of soil management and crop production.
– DERIVATIVES **agronomic** adjective, **agronomical** adjective, **agronomically** adverb, **agronomist** noun.
– ORIGIN early 19th cent.: from French *agronomie*, from *agronome* 'agriculturist', from Greek *agros* 'field' + *-nomos* 'arranging' (from *nemoein* 'arrange').

Agro Pontino /,agrəʊ pɒn'tiːnəʊ/ Italian name for PONTINE MARSHES.

agrostology /,agrə'stɒlədʒi/ ▸ **noun** [mass noun] the branch of botany concerned with grasses.
– ORIGIN mid 19th cent.: from Greek *agrōstis* (denoting a kind of grass) + -LOGY.

agroterrorism ▸ **noun** [mass noun] terrorist acts intended to disrupt or damage a country's agriculture, especially the use of a biological agent against crops or livestock.
– DERIVATIVES **agroterrorist** noun.

aground ▸ **adjective & adverb** (with reference to a ship) on or on to the bottom in shallow water: [as adv.] *the ships must slow to avoid **running aground*** | [as predic. adj.] *a cargo ship aground in the Pentland Firth.*
– ORIGIN Middle English (in the sense 'on the ground'): from A-[2] 'on' + GROUND[1].

aguardiente /ə,gwɑːdɪ'ɛnteɪ/, Spanish /aɣwar'ðjente/ ▸ **noun** [mass noun] a distilled liquor resembling brandy, especially as made in South America from sugar cane.
– ORIGIN from Spanish, from *agua* 'water' + *ardiente* 'fiery'.

Aguascalientes /,agwəska'ljɛnteɪz/ a state of central Mexico. ■ the capital of Aguascalientes, a health resort noted for its hot springs; pop. 663,671 (2005).
– ORIGIN Spanish, literally 'hot waters'.

ague /'eɪgjuː/ ▸ **noun** [mass noun] archaic malaria or another illness involving fever and shivering. ■ [count noun] a fever or shivering fit.
– DERIVATIVES **agued** adjective, **aguish** adjective.
– ORIGIN Middle English: via Old French from medieval Latin *acuta (febris)* 'acute (fever)'.

Agulhas, Cape /ə'gʌləs/ the most southerly point of the continent of Africa, in the province of Western Cape, South Africa.

Agulhas Current an ocean current flowing southward along the east coast of Africa.

AH ▸ **abbreviation** in the year of the Hegira (used in the Muslim calendar for reckoning years from Muhammad's departure from Mecca in AD 622); of the Muslim era: *a Koran dated 556 AH.*
– ORIGIN from Latin *anno Hegirae*.

ah ▸ **exclamation** used to express a range of emotions including surprise, pleasure, sympathy, and realization: *ah, there you are!*
– ORIGIN Middle English: from Old French.

AHA ▸ **abbreviation** alpha-hydroxy acid.

aha ▸ **exclamation** used to express satisfaction, triumph, or surprise.
– ORIGIN Middle English: from AH + HA[1].

Ahaggar Mountains /ɑː'hɑːgə/ another name for HOGGAR MOUNTAINS.

ahead ▸ **adverb 1** further forward in space; in the line of one's forward motion: *the road ahead* | *he was striding ahead towards the stream.* ■ further forward in time; in the near future: *he contemplated the day ahead* | *we have to plan ahead.*
2 in the lead: *he was slightly ahead on points.*
3 higher in number, amount, or value than previously: *profits were slightly ahead.*
– PHRASES **ahead of** in front of or before. ■ in store for; awaiting: *we have a long drive ahead of us.* ■ earlier than: *elimination of trade barriers came five years **ahead of schedule**.* **ahead of time** in advance: *being prepared with appropriate graphics ahead of time is a great policy.* **ahead of one's** (or **its**) **time** innovative and radical by the standards of the time. **get ahead of oneself** act or plan prematurely or overconfidently: *I am getting ahead of myself; let's return to the beginning.*
– ORIGIN mid 16th cent. (originally in nautical use): from A-[2] 'in, at' + HEAD.

ahem ▸ **exclamation** used to represent the noise made when clearing the throat, typically to attract attention or express disapproval or embarrassment.
– ORIGIN mid 18th cent.: lengthened form of HEM[2]

Ahern /ə'həːn/, Bertie (b.1951), Irish Fianna Fáil statesman, Taoiseach (Prime Minister) 1997–2008; full name *Patrick Bartholomew Ahern.*

ahi /'ɑːhi/ ▸ **noun** (in Hawaii) a large tuna, especially as an item of food.
– ORIGIN Hawaiian *'ahi.*

ahimsa /ə'hɪmsɑː/ ▸ **noun** [mass noun] (in the Hindu, Buddhist, and Jainist tradition) respect for all living things and avoidance of violence towards others.
– ORIGIN Sanskrit, from *a* 'non-, without' + *hiṃsā* 'violence'.

ahistorical ▸ **adjective** lacking historical perspective or context.
– DERIVATIVES **ahistorically** adverb.

Ahmadabad /'ɑːmədəbad/ (also **Ahmedabad**) an industrial city in the state of Gujarat in western India; pop. 3,913,800 (est. 2009).

aholehole /ə,həʊlɪ'həʊli/ ▸ **noun** a small silvery fish occurring only in the shallow waters around the Hawaiian islands, where it is a food fish. ● *Kuhlia sandvicensis*, family Kuhliidae.
– ORIGIN from Hawaiian.

-aholic (also **-oholic**) ▸ **suffix** denoting a person addicted to something: *shopaholic* | *workaholic.*
– ORIGIN on the pattern of *(alc)oholic.*

ahoy ▸ **exclamation** Nautical or humorous a call used in hailing: *ahoy there!* | *land ahoy!*
– ORIGIN mid 18th cent.: from AH + HOY[1].

Ahriman /'ɑːrɪmən/ the evil spirit in the doctrine of Zoroastrianism, the opponent of Ahura Mazda.

Ahura Mazda /ə,hʊərə 'mazdə/ the creator god of Zoroastrianism, the force for good and the opponent of Ahriman. Also called ORMAZD.
– ORIGIN Avestan, literally 'wise deity'.

Ahvaz /ɑː'vɑːz/ (also **Ahwaz** /ɑː'wɑːz/) a town in western Iran; pop. 985,614 (2006).

Ahvenanmaa /'ɑːvənəmɑː/ Finnish name for ÅLAND ISLANDS.

AI ▸ **abbreviation** ■ Amnesty International. ■ artificial insemination. ■ artificial intelligence.

ai /'ɑːi/ ▸ **noun** (pl. **ais**) the three-toed sloth.
– ORIGIN early 17th cent.: from Tupi, imitative of its cry.

AID ▸ **abbreviation** artificial insemination by donor.

aid ▸ **noun 1** [mass noun] help, typically of a practical nature: *he saw the pilot slumped in his cockpit and **went to his aid*** | *she walked **with the aid of** a Zimmer frame.* ■ financial or material help given to a country or area in need: *700,000 tons of food aid* | [as modifier] *an aid agency.* ■ [count noun] a source of help or assistance: *exercise is an important **aid to** recovery after heart attacks* | *a teaching aid.*
2 historical a grant of subsidy or tax to a king or queen.
▸ **verb** [with obj.] help or support (someone or something) in the achievement of something: *women were aided in childbirth by midwives* | [no obj.] *research was conducted to **aid in** making decisions.* ■ promote or encourage (something): *diet and exercise aid healthy skin.*
– PHRASES **aid and abet** see ABET. **in aid of** chiefly Brit. in support of; for the purpose of raising money for: *a charity show in aid of Leukaemia Research.* **what's**

(all) this in aid of? Brit. informal what is the purpose of this?
– ORIGIN late Middle English: from Old French *aide* (noun), *aidier* (verb), based on Latin *adjuvare*, from *ad-* 'towards' + *juvare* 'to help'.

Aidan, St /ˈeɪd(ə)n/ (d. AD 651), Irish missionary. While a monk in the monastery at Iona he set out to Christianize Northumbria, founding a church and monastery at Lindisfarne in 635 and becoming its first bishop.

aid climbing ▶ **noun** [mass noun] rock climbing using the assistance of objects such as pegs placed in the rock. Compare with FREE CLIMBING.

aide /eɪd/ ▶ **noun** an assistant to an important person, especially a political leader. ■ short for AIDE-DE-CAMP.

aide-de-camp /ˌeɪddəˈkɒ̃/ ▶ **noun** (pl. **aides-de-camp** pronunc. **same**) a military officer acting as a confidential assistant to a senior officer.
– ORIGIN late 17th cent.: from French, 'camp adjutant'.

aide-memoire /ˌeɪd mɛmˈwɑː/, French /ɛd mɛmwaʀ/ ▶ **noun** (pl. **aides-memoires** or **aides-memoire** pronunc. **same**) **1** an aid to the memory, especially a book or note.
2 an informal diplomatic message.
– ORIGIN mid 19th cent.: from French *aide-mémoire*, from *aider* 'to help' and *mémoire* 'memory'.

AIDS (also **Aids**) ▶ **noun** [mass noun] a disease in which there is a severe loss of the body's cellular immunity, greatly lowering the resistance to infection and malignancy.

> AIDS was first identified in the early 1980s and now affects millions of people. The cause is a virus (called the human immunodeficiency virus or HIV) transmitted in blood and in sexual fluids, and although the incubation period may be long and treatment can slow the course of the disease there is currently no cure or vaccine. In the developed world the disease first spread among homosexuals, intravenous drug users, and recipients of infected blood transfusions, before reaching the wider population. This has tended to overshadow a greater epidemic in parts of Africa, where transmission is mainly through heterosexual contact.

– ORIGIN 1980s: acronym from *acquired immune deficiency syndrome*.

AIDS-related complex ▶ **noun** [mass noun] the symptoms of a person who is affected with the AIDS virus but does not necessarily develop the disease.

aigrette /ˈeɪɡrɛt, eɪˈɡrɛt/ ▶ **noun** a headdress consisting of a white egret's feather or other decoration such as a spray of gems.
– ORIGIN mid 18th cent.: from French, 'egret'.

aiguille /ˈeɪɡwiːl/ ▶ **noun** a sharp pinnacle of rock in a mountain range.
– ORIGIN mid 18th cent.: from French, literally 'needle', from medieval Latin *acucula* 'little needle', diminutive of Latin *acus*.

aiguillette /ˌeɪɡwɪˈlɛt/ ▶ **noun** an ornament on some military and naval uniforms, consisting of braided loops hanging from the shoulder and on dress uniforms ending in points that resemble pencils.
– ORIGIN mid 16th cent.: from French, literally 'small needle', diminutive of *aiguille*.

AIH ▶ **abbreviation** artificial insemination by husband.

aikido /ʌɪˈkiːdəʊ/ ▶ **noun** [mass noun] a Japanese form of self-defence and martial art that uses locks, holds, throws, and the opponent's own movements.
– ORIGIN 1950s: from Japanese *aikidō*, literally 'way of adapting the spirit', from *ai* 'together, unify' + *ki* 'spirit' + *dō* 'way'.

ail ▶ **verb** [with obj.] archaic trouble or afflict (someone) in mind or body: *exercise is good for whatever ails one.*
– ORIGIN Old English *eglian, eglan*, from *egle* 'troublesome', of Germanic origin; related to Gothic *agls* 'disgraceful'.

ailanthus /eɪˈlanθəs/ ▶ **noun** a tall large-leaved deciduous tree grown as an ornamental or shade tree. Native to Asia and Australasia, it has been naturalized in North America and Europe. ● Genus *Ailanthus*, family Simaroubaceae: several species, in particular the tree of heaven.
– ORIGIN modern Latin, from French *ailante*, from Ambonese *ailanto*, literally 'tree of heaven' (the ending being influenced by names ending with *-anthus*, from Greek *anthos* 'flower').

aileron /ˈeɪlərɒn/ ▶ **noun** a hinged surface in the trailing edge of an aeroplane wing, used to control the roll of an aircraft about its longitudinal axis.
– ORIGIN early 20th cent.: from French, literally 'small wing', diminutive of *aile*, from Latin *ala* 'wing'.

ailing ▶ **adjective** in poor health: *I went to see my ailing mother* | figurative *the ailing economy.*

ailment ▶ **noun** an illness, typically a minor one.

ailurophile /ʌɪˈljʊərəˌfʌɪl/ ▶ **noun** a cat lover.
– ORIGIN 1930s: from Greek *ailuros* 'cat' + -PHILE.

ailurophobia /ˌʌɪljʊərəˈfəʊbɪə/ ▶ **noun** [mass noun] extreme or irrational fear of cats.
– DERIVATIVES **ailurophobe** noun.

AIM ▶ **abbreviation** (in the UK) Alternative Investment Market.

aim ▶ **verb 1** [with obj.] point or direct (a weapon or camera) at a target: ***aim** the camcorder **at** some suitable object* | [no obj.] ***aim for** the middle of the target.* ■ direct (a missile or blow) at someone or something: *she had **aimed** the bottle **at** Gary's head.* ■ (**aim something at**) direct information, a product, or an action towards (a particular group): *the TV campaign is aimed at the 16–24 age group.*
2 [no obj.] have the intention of achieving: *the programme will **aim at** deepening understanding* | [with infinitive] *we aim to give you the best possible service.*
▶ **noun 1** a purpose or intention; a desired outcome: *our primary aim is to achieve financial discipline.*
2 [in sing.] the directing of a weapon or missile at a target: *his aim was perfect.*
– PHRASES **aim high** be ambitious. **take aim** point a weapon or camera at a target.
– ORIGIN Middle English: from Old French *amer*, variant of *esmer* (from Latin *aestimare* 'assess, estimate'), reinforced by *aemer, aesmer* (from late Latin *adaestimare*, intensified form of *aestimare*).

aimless ▶ **adjective** without purpose or direction: *an aimless existence.*
– DERIVATIVES **aimlessly** adverb, **aimlessness** noun.

ain't informal ▶ **contraction** am not; are not; is not: *if it ain't broke, don't fix it.* [first representing London dialect.] ■ has not; have not: *they ain't got nothing to say.* [from dialect *hain't*.]

> **USAGE** The use of **ain't** was widespread in the 18th century, typically as a contraction for **am not**. It is still perfectly normal in many dialects and informal speech in both Britain and North America. Today, however, it does not form part of standard English and should never be used in formal or written contexts. See also USAGE at AREN'T.

Aintab /ˈʌɪntɑːb/ former name (until 1921) for GAZIANTEP.

Aintree /ˈeɪntriː/ a suburb of Liverpool, site of a racecourse over which the Grand National is run.

Ainu /ˈeɪnuː/ ▶ **noun** (pl. **same** or **Ainus**) **1** a member of an aboriginal people of northern Japan, physically distinct (with light skin colour and round eyes) from the majority population.
2 [mass noun] the language of the Ainu people, perhaps related to Altaic. It is no longer in everyday use.
▶ **adjective** relating to the Ainu or their language.
– ORIGIN the name in Ainu, literally 'man, person'.

aioli /ʌɪˈəʊli/ ▶ **noun** [mass noun] mayonnaise seasoned with garlic.
– ORIGIN French *aïoli*, from Provençal *ai* 'garlic' + *oli* 'oil'.

air ▶ **noun 1** [mass noun] the invisible gaseous substance surrounding the earth, a mixture mainly of oxygen and nitrogen. ■ air regarded as necessary for breathing: *the air was stale* | *the doctor told me to get some fresh air.* ■ the free or unconfined space above the surface of the earth: *he celebrated by tossing his hat high in the air.* ■ [usu. as modifier] referring to the use of aircraft: *air travel* | *all goods must come in **by air**.* ■ the earth's atmosphere as a medium for transmitting radio waves: *radio stations have successfully sold products **over the air**.* ■ one of the four elements in ancient and medieval philosophy and in astrology (considered essential to the nature of the signs of Gemini, Aquarius, and Libra): [as modifier] *an air sign.* ■ [count noun] a breeze or light wind.
2 an impression of a quality or manner given by someone or something: *she answered with a faint air of boredom* | *he leaned over with a confidential air.* ■ (**airs**) an annoyingly affected and condescending manner: *he began to **put on airs** and think he could boss us around.*
3 Music a tune or short melodious song.
4 a jump off the ground on a snowboard.
▶ **verb** [with obj.] **1** express (an opinion or grievance) publicly: *a meeting in which long-standing grievances were aired.* ■ broadcast (a programme) on radio or television: *the programmes were aired on India's state TV network.* ■ archaic parade or show (something) ostentatiously.
2 Brit. expose (a room) to the open air in order to ventilate it: *the window sashes were lifted regularly to air the room.* ■ warm (washed laundry) to remove dampness.
– PHRASES **airs and graces** Brit. derogatory an affectation of superiority. **in the air** felt by a number of people to be happening or about to happen: *panic was in the air* | *you can tell there's an election in the air.* **on** (or **off**) **the air** being (or not being) broadcast on radio or television. **take the air** go out of doors. **up in the air** (of a plan or issue) still to be settled; unresolved. **walk** (or **tread**) **on air** feel elated.
– ORIGIN Middle English (in sense 1 of the noun): from Old French *air*, from Latin *aer*, from Greek *aēr*, denoting the gas. Sense 2 of the noun is from French *air*, probably from Old French *aire* 'site, disposition', from Latin *ager, agr-* 'field' (influenced by sense 1). Sense 3 of the noun comes from Italian *aria* (see ARIA).

airbag ▶ **noun** a safety device fitted inside a road vehicle, consisting of a cushion designed to inflate rapidly and protect passengers from impact in the event of a collision.

air ball ▶ **noun** Basketball a shot which misses the basket and backboard entirely.

airband ▶ **noun** a range of frequencies allocated for radio communications involving aircraft.

airbase ▶ **noun** a base for the operation of military aircraft.

air bearing ▶ **noun** a bearing in which moving surfaces are kept apart by a layer of air provided by jets.

airbed ▶ **noun** Brit. an inflatable mattress.

air bladder ▶ **noun** an air-filled bladder or sac found in certain animals and plants. ■ another term for SWIM BLADDER.

airboat ▶ **noun** a shallow-draught boat powered by an aircraft engine, for use in swamps.

airborne ▶ **adjective** transported by air: *airborne pollutants.* ■ (of an aircraft) in the air after taking off.

air brake ▶ **noun 1** a brake worked by air pressure.
2 a movable flap or other device on an aircraft to reduce its speed.

airbrick ▶ **noun** Brit. a brick perforated with small holes for ventilation.

air bridge ▶ **noun** Brit. a movable bridge placed against an aircraft door to allow passengers to embark or disembark.

airbrush ▶ **noun** an artist's device for spraying paint by means of compressed air.
▶ **verb** [with obj.] paint with an airbrush. ■ alter or conceal (a photograph or a detail in one) using an airbrush. ■ represent or describe as better or more beautiful than in reality: *many lived through the disasters and know that the past has been airbrushed.*

airburst ▶ **noun** an explosion in the air, especially of a nuclear bomb or large meteorite.

air chief marshal ▶ **noun** a high rank of officer in the RAF, above air marshal and below Marshal of the RAF.

air commodore ▶ **noun** a rank of officer in the RAF, above group captain and below air vice-marshal.

air con ▶ **noun** short for AIR CONDITIONING.

air conditioning ▶ **noun** [mass noun] a system for controlling the humidity, ventilation, and temperature in a building or vehicle, typically to maintain a cool atmosphere in warm conditions.
– DERIVATIVES **air-conditioned** adjective, **air conditioner** noun.

air corridor ▶ **noun** a route to which aircraft are restricted, especially over a foreign country.

air cover ▶ **noun** [mass noun] protection by aircraft for land-based or naval operations in war situations.

aircraft ▶ **noun** (pl. **same**) an aeroplane, helicopter, or other machine capable of flight.

aircraft carrier ▶ **noun** a large warship with a deck from which aircraft can take off and land.

aircraftman (or **aircraftwoman**) ▶ **noun** (pl. **aircraftmen** or **aircraftwomen**) the lowest rank in the RAF, below leading aircraftman.

aircrew ▶ **noun** (pl. **aircrews**) [treated as sing. or pl.] the crew staffing an aircraft. ■ (pl. **same**) a member of an aircrew.

air cushion ▶ **noun** the layer of air supporting a hovercraft or similar vehicle.

air dam ▶ **noun** a streamlining device below the front bumper of a vehicle; a front spoiler.

air-dash ▸ verb [no obj.] Indian travel to a desination by air at short notice: *he had air-dashed to Chennai from Bikaner last night.*

air date ▸ noun the date on which a particular television or radio programme is scheduled to be broadcast.

airdrome ▸ noun US term for AERODROME.

airdrop ▸ noun an act of dropping supplies, troops, or equipment by parachute from an aircraft.
▸ verb (**airdrops, airdropping, airdropped**) [with obj.] drop (supplies, troops, etc.) by parachute.

air-dry ▸ verb make or become dry through contact with unheated air.
▸ adjective not giving off any moisture on exposure to air.

Airedale /ˈɛːdeɪl/ ▸ noun a large terrier of a rough-coated black-and-tan breed.
– ORIGIN late 19th cent.: from *Airedale*, a district in Yorkshire, where the dog was bred.

airer ▸ noun Brit. a frame or stand for airing or drying clothes.

airfare ▸ noun the price to be paid by an aircraft passenger for a particular journey.

airfield ▸ noun an area of land set aside for the take-off, landing, and maintenance of aircraft.

air filter ▸ noun a device for filtering particles from the air passing through it, especially one protecting the air inlet of an internal-combustion engine.

airflow ▸ noun the flow of air, especially that encountered by a moving aircraft or vehicle.

airfoil ▸ noun North American term for AEROFOIL.

air force ▸ noun a branch of the armed forces concerned with fighting or defence in the air.

Air Force One the official aircraft of the President of the United States.

airframe ▸ noun the body of an aircraft as distinct from its engine.

airfreight ▸ noun [mass noun] the carriage of goods by aircraft. ■ goods in transit, or to be carried, by aircraft.
▸ verb [with obj.] carry or send (goods) by aircraft.

air freshener ▸ noun a substance or device for making the air in a room smell fresh.

airglow ▸ noun [mass noun] a glow in the night sky caused by radiation from the upper atmosphere.

air guitar ▸ noun informal an imaginary guitar 'played' by someone miming to rock music: *we like our audiences to sing along and play air guitar.*

airgun ▸ noun **1** a gun which fires pellets using compressed air.
2 (also **hot-air gun**) a tool used to strip paint by means of a stream of very hot air.

airhead[1] ▸ noun Military a base close to the area of active operations where supplies and troops can be received and evacuated by air.
– ORIGIN Second World War: on the pattern of *bridgehead*.

airhead[2] ▸ noun informal a silly or foolish person.

air horn ▸ noun a powerful horn which produces sound by means of compressed air.

air hostess ▸ noun Brit. a stewardess in a passenger aircraft.

airily ▸ adverb in a way that shows that one is not treating something as serious; casually: *he was airily dismissive of the question.*

airing ▸ noun **1** an exposure to warm or fresh air, for the purpose of ventilating or removing dampness from something: *somebody had given the place a thorough airing* | [as modifier] *an airing cupboard.* ■ a walk or outing to take air or exercise: *taking the baby out for an airing.*
2 a public expression of an opinion or subject: *these are ideas I feel might be worth an airing.* ■ a transmission of a television or radio programme.

air-kiss ▸ verb [with obj.] purse the lips as if kissing (someone), without making contact.
▸ noun (**air kiss**) a simulated kiss, without contact.

air layering ▸ noun [mass noun] Horticulture a form of layering in which the branch is potted or wrapped in a moist growing medium to promote root growth.

airless ▸ adjective stuffy; not ventilated: *a dusty, airless basement.* ■ without wind or breeze; still: *a hot, airless night.*
– DERIVATIVES **airlessness** noun.

air letter ▸ noun a sheet of light paper folded and sealed to form a letter for sending by airmail.

airlift ▸ noun an act of transporting supplies by aircraft, typically in a blockade or other emergency.
▸ verb [with obj.] transport (troops or supplies) by aircraft.

airline ▸ noun **1** an organization providing a regular public service of air transport on one or more routes.
2 (usu. **air line**) a pipe supplying air.

airliner ▸ noun a large passenger aircraft.

airlock ▸ noun **1** a stoppage of the flow in a pump or pipe, caused by an air bubble.
2 a compartment with controlled pressure and parallel sets of doors, to permit movement between areas at different pressures.

airmail ▸ noun [mass noun] a system of transporting mail by aircraft, typically overseas: *instructions were sent by airmail.*
▸ verb [with obj.] send (mail) by aircraft.

airman (or **airwoman**) ▸ noun (pl. **airmen** or **airwomen**) a pilot or member of the crew of an aircraft, especially in an air force. ■ a member of the RAF below commissioned rank. ■ a member of the US air force of the lowest rank, below staff sergeant. ■ a member of the US navy whose general duties are concerned with aircraft.

airmanship ▸ noun [mass noun] skill in flying an aircraft.

air marshal ▸ noun a high rank of officer in the RAF, above air vice-marshal and below air chief marshal.

air mass ▸ noun Meteorology a body of air with horizontally uniform levels of temperature, humidity, and pressure.

air mattress ▸ noun North American term for AIRBED.

air mile ▸ noun a nautical mile used as a measure of distance flown by aircraft. ■ (**Air Miles**) trademark points (equivalent to miles of free air travel) accumulated by buyers of airline tickets and other products and redeemable against the cost of air travel with a particular airline.

airmobile /ɛːˈməʊbʌɪl/ ▸ adjective (of troops) moved about by air.

air officer ▸ noun any rank of officer in the RAF above that of group captain.

air pistol ▸ noun a pistol which fires pellets using compressed air.

airplane ▸ noun chiefly N. Amer. an aeroplane.

air plant ▸ noun a tropical American plant that grows on trees as an epiphyte, with long, narrow leaves that absorb water and nutrients from the atmosphere.
• Genus *Tillandsia*, family Bromeliaceae: several species.

airplay ▸ noun [mass noun] broadcasting time devoted to a particular record, performer, or musical genre.

air pocket ▸ noun a cavity containing air. ■ a region of low pressure causing an aircraft to lose height suddenly.

airport ▸ noun a complex of runways and buildings for the take-off, landing, and maintenance of civil aircraft, with facilities for passengers. ■ [as modifier] relating to or denoting light popular fiction such as is offered for sale to travellers in airports: *an airport thriller.*

air power ▸ noun [mass noun] the ability to defend or attack by means of aircraft.

air pump ▸ noun a device for pumping air into or out of an enclosed space.

air quality ▸ noun the degree to which the air in a particular place is pollution-free.

air quotes ▸ plural noun informal a pair of quotation marks gestured by a speaker's fingers in the air, to indicate that what is being said is ironic or mocking, or is not a turn of phrase the speaker would typically employ.

air rage ▸ noun [mass noun] sudden violent anger or aggressive behaviour provoked in a passenger on board an aircraft by the stress associated with air travel.

air raid ▸ noun an attack in which bombs are dropped from aircraft on to a ground target.

air-raid shelter ▸ noun a building or structure designed to protect people from bombs dropped during air raids.

air rank ▸ noun [mass noun] the rank attained by air officers.

air rifle ▸ noun a rifle which fires pellets using compressed air.

air sac ▸ noun a lung compartment containing air; an alveolus. ■ an extension of a bird's lung cavity into a bone or other part of the body.

airscrew ▸ noun Brit. an aircraft propeller.

air-sea rescue ▸ noun chiefly Brit. a rescue of a person from the sea using aircraft.

air shaft ▸ noun a straight, typically vertical passage admitting air into a mine, tunnel, or building.

airship ▸ noun a power-driven aircraft that is kept buoyant by a body of gas (usually helium, formerly hydrogen) which is lighter than air.

air shot ▸ noun informal a missed attempt to hit or kick a ball.

air show ▸ noun a show at which aircraft perform aerial displays.

airsick ▸ adjective affected with nausea due to travel in an aircraft.
– DERIVATIVES **airsickness** noun.

airside ▸ noun the side of an airport terminal beyond passport and customs control. Contrasted with LANDSIDE.

airspace ▸ noun [mass noun] the air available to aircraft to fly in, especially the part subject to the jurisdiction of a particular country. ■ room available in the atmosphere immediately above the earth: *temples and mosques fight for airspace with skyscrapers.* ■ Law the right of a private landowner to the space above his land and any structures on it.

airspeed ▸ noun [mass noun] the speed of an aircraft relative to the air through which it is moving. Compare with GROUND SPEED.

air station ▸ noun an airfield operated by a navy or marine corps.

airstream ▸ noun a current of air.

air strike ▸ noun an attack made by aircraft.

airstrip ▸ noun a strip of ground set aside for the take-off and landing of aircraft.

airtight ▸ adjective not allowing air to escape or pass through: *an airtight box.* ■ having no weaknesses; unassailable: *she had an airtight alibi.*

airtime ▸ noun [mass noun] time during which a broadcast is being transmitted. ■ the time during which a mobile phone is in use.

air-to-air ▸ adjective directed or operating from one aircraft to another in flight.

air-to-ground ▸ adjective directed or operating from an aircraft in flight to the land surface.

air-to-surface ▸ adjective directed or operating from an aircraft in flight to the surface of the sea or other body of water.

air traffic control ▸ noun [mass noun] the ground-based personnel and equipment concerned with controlling and monitoring air traffic within a particular area.
– DERIVATIVES **air traffic controller** noun.

air vice-marshal ▸ noun a high rank of officer in the RAF, above air commodore and below air marshal.

airwaves ▸ plural noun the radio frequencies used for broadcasting: *football pervades the airwaves.*

airway ▸ noun **1** the passage by which air reaches a person's lungs. ■ a tube for supplying air to a person's lungs in an emergency.
2 a recognized route followed by aircraft. ■ (**Airways**) in names of airlines: *British Airways.*
3 a ventilating passage in a mine.

airwoman ▸ noun see AIRMAN.

airworthy ▸ adjective (of an aircraft) safe to fly.
– DERIVATIVES **airworthiness** noun.

airy ▸ adjective (**airier, airiest**) **1** (of a room or building) spacious, well lit, and well ventilated. ■ delicate, as though filled with or made of air: *airy clouds.* ■ giving an impression of light gracefulness and elegance: *her airy presence filled the house.*
2 not treating something as serious; casual: *her airy unconcern for economy.*
– DERIVATIVES **airiness** noun.

airy-fairy ▸ adjective informal, chiefly Brit. impractical and foolishly idealistic: *love might seem an airy-fairy, romantic concept.*

aisle /ʌɪl/ ▸ noun a passage between rows of seats in a building such as a church or theatre, an aircraft, or train: *the musical had the audience dancing in the aisles.* ■ a passage between cabinets and shelves of goods in a supermarket or other building. ■ Architecture (in a church) a lower part parallel to the nave, choir, or transept, from which it is divided by pillars.

– PHRASES **lead someone up the aisle** get married to someone.
– DERIVATIVES **aisled** adjective.
– ORIGIN late Middle English *ele*, *ile*, from Old French *ele*, from Latin *ala* 'wing'. The spelling change in the 17th cent. was due to confusion with *isle* and influenced by French *aile* 'wing'.

ait /eɪt/ (also **eyot**) ▶ noun [in place names] Brit. a small island in a river: *Raven's Ait*.
– ORIGIN Old English *iggath*, *īgeth*, based on *īeg* 'island' + a diminutive suffix.

aitch ▶ noun the letter H.
– PHRASES **drop one's aitches** fail to pronounce the letter *h* at the beginning of words, a characteristic feature of certain dialects.
– ORIGIN mid 16th cent.: from Old French *ache*.

aitchbone ▶ noun the buttock or rump bone of cattle. ■ a cut of beef lying over the aitchbone.
– ORIGIN late 15th cent., from dialect *nache* 'rump', from Old French, based on Latin *natis* 'buttock(s)', + BONE. The initial *n* in *a nache bone* was lost by wrong division; compare with ADDER[1].

Aitken /ˈeɪtkɪn/, William Maxwell, see BEAVERBROOK.

Aix-en-Provence /ˌɛksɑ̃prɒˈvɒ̃s/, French /ɛksɑ̃pʀɔvɑ̃s/ a city in Provence in southern France; pop. 145,721 (2006).

Aix-la-Chapelle /ɛkslaʃapɛl/ French name for AACHEN.

Aizawl /ˈʌɪdʒəl/ a city in the far north-east of India, capital of the state of Mizoram; pop. 295,900 (est. 2009).

Ajaccio /əˈdʒaksɪəʊ/, French /aʒaksjo/ a port on the west coast of Corsica; pop. 64,432 (2007). It is the capital of the southern department of Corse-du-Sud.

Ajanta Caves /əˈdʒʌntə/ a series of caves in the state of Maharashtra, south central India, containing Buddhist frescoes and sculptures dating from the 1st century BC to the 7th century AD.

ajar[1] ▶ adverb & adjective (of a door or other opening) slightly open: [as adv.] *the home help had left the window ajar* | [as predic. adj.] *the door to the sitting room was ajar*.
– ORIGIN late 17th cent.: from A-[2] 'on' + obsolete *char* (Old English *cerr*) 'a turn, return'.

ajar[2] ▶ adverb archaic in a jarring state; unharmonious.
– ORIGIN mid 19th cent.: from A-[2] 'in, at' + JAR[2].

Ajax /ˈeɪdʒaks/ Greek Mythology **1** a Greek hero of the Trojan war, son of Telamon, king of Salamis. He was proverbial for his size and strength.
2 a Greek hero, son of Oileus, king of Locris.

Ajman /adʒˈmɑːn/ one of the seven member states of the United Arab Emirates; pop. 387,300 (est. 2009).

Ajmer /ʌdʒˈmɪə/ a city in NW India, in Rajasthan; pop. 549,600 (est. 2009).

ajowan /ˈadʒəwɒn/ ▶ noun an annual plant with feathery leaves and white flowers, native to India.
● *Trachyspermum ammi*, family Umbelliferae.
■ [mass noun] the aromatic seeds of the ajowan plant, used as a culinary spice. ■ [mass noun] the essential oil of the ajowan plant.
– ORIGIN from Hindi *ajvāyn*.

ajuga /əˈdʒuːɡə/ ▶ noun a plant of a genus that includes bugle. ● Genus *Ajuga*, family Labiatae.
– ORIGIN modern Latin, from medieval Latin *ajuga*.

AK ▶ abbreviation Alaska (in official postal use).

AK-47 ▶ noun a type of assault rifle originally manufactured in the Soviet Union.
– ORIGIN 1970s: abbreviation of Russian *Avtomat Kalashnikov 1947*, the designation of the original model designed by Mikhail T. Kalashnikov (born 1919).

aka ▶ abbreviation also known as: *John Merrick, aka the Elephant Man*.

Akali /aˈkɑːli/ ▶ noun (pl. **Akalis**) a member of a Sikh political group.
– ORIGIN from Punjabi *akālī*, literally 'follower of the Immortal One'.

Akan /ˈɑːk(ə)n/ ▶ noun (pl. **same**) **1** a member of a people inhabiting southern Ghana and adjacent parts of Côte d'Ivoire (Ivory Coast).
2 [mass noun] the language of the Akan, belonging to the Kwa group and having over 4 million speakers. Its main dialects are Ashanti and Fante. Also called TWI.
▶ adjective relating to the Akan or their language.
– ORIGIN the name in Akan.

akara /əˈkarə/ ▶ noun variant spelling of ACCRA.

akasha /əˈkɑːʃə/ ▶ noun (in Indian religion) a supposed all-pervading field in the ether in which a record of past events is imprinted.
– DERIVATIVES **akashic** adjective.
– ORIGIN from Sanskrit *ākāśa*.

Akbar /ˈakbɑː/, Jalaludin Muhammad (1542–1605), Mogul emperor of India 1556–1605; known as **Akbar the Great**. Akbar expanded the Mogul empire to incorporate northern India and established an efficient and enlightened administration.

akebia /əˈkiːbɪə/ ▶ noun an East Asian climbing shrub with purplish flowers and deeply divided leaves.
● Genus *Akebia*, family Lardizabalaceae.
– ORIGIN 1837: modern Latin, coined by J. Decaisne, French botanist, from Japanese *akebi*.

akee ▶ noun variant spelling of ACKEE.

Akela /ɑːˈkeɪlə/ ▶ noun informal the adult leader of a group of Cub Scouts (officially termed **Cub Scout Leader**).
– ORIGIN 1920s: from the name of the leader of a wolf pack in Kipling's *Jungle Books* (1894–5).

Akhenaten /ˌakəˈnɑːt(ə)n/ (also **Akhenaton** or **Ikhnaton**) (14th century BC), Egyptian pharaoh of the 18th dynasty, reigned 1379–1362 BC; came to the throne as *Amenhotep IV*. The husband of Nefertiti, he introduced the monotheistic solar cult of Aten and moved the capital from Thebes to the newly built city of Akhetaten.

Akhetaten /ˌakəˈtɑːt(ə)n/ an ancient Egyptian capital built by Akhenaten in *c.*1375 BC when he established the new worship of the sun disc Aten, but abandoned after his death. See also TELL EL-AMARNA.

Akihito /ɑkɪˈhiːtəʊ/ (b.1933), son of Emperor Hirohito, emperor of Japan since 1989; full name *Tsugu Akihito*.

akimbo /əˈkɪmbəʊ/ ▶ adverb with hands on the hips and elbows turned outwards: *she stood with* **arms akimbo**, *frowning at the small boy*. ■ (with reference to limbs) flung out widely or haphazardly.
– ORIGIN late Middle English: from *in kenebowe* in Middle English, probably from Old Norse.

akin ▶ adjective [predic.] of similar character: *something akin to gratitude overwhelmed her* | *genius and madness are akin*. ■ related by blood.
– ORIGIN mid 16th cent.: contracted form of *of kin*.

akinesia /ˌeɪkɪˈniːsɪə, a-/ ▶ noun [mass noun] Medicine loss or impairment of the power of voluntary movement.
– DERIVATIVES **akinetic** adjective.
– ORIGIN mid 19th cent.: from Greek *akinēsia* 'quiescence', from *a-* 'without' + *kinēsis* 'motion'.

Akita /əˈkiːtə/ ▶ noun a spitz (dog) of a Japanese breed.
– ORIGIN early 20th cent.: from *Akita*, the name of a district in northern Japan.

Akkad /ˈakad, aˈkad/ the capital city which gave its name to an ancient kingdom traditionally founded by Sargon in north central Mesopotamia. Its site is lost.

Akkadian /əˈkeɪdɪən, -ˈkad-/ ▶ noun **1** an inhabitant of Akkad.
2 [mass noun] the extinct language of Akkad, written in cuneiform, with two dialects, Assyrian and Babylonian, widely used from about 3500 BC. It is the oldest Semitic language for which records exist.
▶ adjective relating to Akkad or its language.

Akko /ˈakəʊ/ another name for ACRE (sense 1).

Ak-Mechet /ˌakmɛˈtʃɛt/ former name for SIMFEROPOL.

Akmola /akˈmɒla/ former name for ASTANA.

akrasia /əˈkreɪzɪə, əˈkrasɪə/ (also **acrasia**) ▶ noun [mass noun] chiefly Philosophy the state of mind in which someone acts against their better judgement through weakness of will.
– DERIVATIVES **akratic** adjective.
– ORIGIN early 19th cent.: from Greek, from *a-* 'without' + *kratos* 'power, strength'. The term is used especially with reference to Aristotle's *Nicomachean Ethics*.

Akron /ˈakrən/ a city in NE Ohio; pop. 207,510 (est. 2008).

aks ▶ verb variant spelling of AX.

Aksai Chin /ˌaksʌɪ ˈtʃɪn/ a region of the Himalayas occupied by China since 1950, but claimed by India as part of Kashmir.

Aksum /ˈɑːksəm/ (also **Axum**) a town in the province of Tigray in northern Ethiopia. It was a religious centre and the capital of a powerful kingdom between the 1st and 6th centuries AD.
– DERIVATIVES **Aksumite** adjective & noun.

Akubra /əˈkuːbrə/ ▶ noun Austral. trademark a type of broad-brimmed hat traditionally worn by farmers and cattlemen.
– ORIGIN early 20th cent.: from the name of the manufacturer, perhaps from an Aboriginal language.

akvavit /ˈakvəvɪt/ ▶ noun variant spelling of AQUAVIT.

AL ▶ abbreviation ■ Alabama (in official postal use). ■ Albania (international vehicle registration). ■ American League (in baseball).

Al ▶ symbol the chemical element aluminium.

al- ▶ prefix variant spelling of AD- assimilated before *-l* (as in *alleviate*, *allocate*).

-al ▶ suffix **1** (forming adjectives) relating to; of the kind of: ■ from Latin words: *annual* | *infernal*. ■ from Greek words: *historical* | *comical*. ■ from English nouns: *tidal*.
2 forming nouns chiefly denoting verbal action: *arrival* | *transmittal*.
– ORIGIN Sense 1 from French *-el* or Latin *-alis*; sense 2 from French *-aille* or from Latin *-alis* functioning as a noun ending.

ALA ▶ abbreviation all letters answered (used in personal advertisements).

Ala. ▶ abbreviation Alabama.

à la /ɑː lɑː, a la/ ▶ preposition (of a dish) cooked or prepared in a specified way: *fish cooked à la meunière*. ■ informal in the style or manner of: *afternoon talk shows à la Oprah*.
– ORIGIN French, from À LA MODE.

alaap ▶ noun variant spelling of ALAP.

Alabama /ˌaləˈbamə/ a state in the south-eastern US, on the Gulf of Mexico; pop. 4,661,900 (est. 2008); capital, Montgomery. It became the 22nd state in 1819.
– DERIVATIVES **Alabaman** adjective & noun.

alabaster /ˈaləbɑːstə, -bastə, ˌaləˈbɑːstə, -ˈbastə/ ▶ noun [mass noun] a translucent form of gypsum or calcite, typically white, often carved into ornaments.
▶ adjective made of alabaster. ■ literary like alabaster in whiteness and smoothness: *her alabaster cheeks flushed with warmth*.
– ORIGIN late Middle English: via Old French from Latin *alabaster*, *alabastrum*, from Greek *alabastos*, *alabastros*.

à la carte /ɑː lɑː ˈkɑːt, a la/, French /a la kaʀt/ ▶ adjective (in a restaurant) referring to food that can be ordered as separate items, rather than part of a set meal: *an à la carte menu*.
– ORIGIN early 19th cent.: French, literally 'according to the (menu) card'.

alack (also **alack-a-day**) ▶ exclamation archaic used to express regret or dismay.
– ORIGIN late Middle English: probably from AH + LACK.

alacrity /əˈlakrɪti/ ▶ noun [mass noun] brisk and cheerful readiness: *she accepted the invitation with alacrity*.
– ORIGIN late Middle English: from Latin *alacritas*, from *alacer* 'brisk'.

Aladdin /əˈladɪn/ the hero of a story in the *Arabian Nights*, who finds an old lamp which, when rubbed, summons a genie who obeys the will of the owner.

Aladdin's cave ▶ noun a place filled with a great number and variety of strange or precious items: *the market is an Aladdin's cave of goodies*.

Alagoas /ˌaləˈɡəʊəs/ a state in eastern Brazil, on the Atlantic coast; capital, Maceió.

Alain-Fournier /ˌalɛ̃ˈfʊənɪeɪ/, French /alɛ̃fuʀnje/ (1886–1914), French novelist; pseudonym of *Henri-Alban Fournier*. A literary columnist, he completed only one novel, *Le Grand Meaulnes* (1913), before his death in the First World War.

alameda /ˌaləˈmeɪdə/ ▶ noun (in Spain and Spanish-speaking areas) a public walkway or promenade, shaded with trees.
– ORIGIN late 18th cent.: Spanish.

Alamein see EL ALAMEIN, BATTLE OF.

Alamo /ˈaləməʊ/ (**the Alamo**) a mission in San Antonio, Texas, site of a siege in 1836 by Mexican forces, in which all 180 defenders were killed.

à la mode /ɑː lɑː ˈməʊd, a la/ ▶ adverb & adjective **1** in fashion; up to date: [as adj.] *corduroy is extremely à la mode this season*.
2 (of beef) braised in wine.
3 N. Amer. served with ice cream.
– ORIGIN late 16th cent.: French, literally 'in the fashion'.

Åland Islands /ˈɔːlənd/ a group of islands in the Gulf of Bothnia, forming an autonomous region of

Finland; capital, Mariehamn (known in Finnish as Maarianhamina). Finnish name **Ahvenanmaa**.

alanine /ˈaləniːn/ ▶ **noun** [mass noun] Biochemistry an amino acid which is a constituent of most proteins. ● Chem. formula: $CH_3CH(NH_2)COOH$.
– ORIGIN mid 19th cent.: coined in German as *Alanin*, from **aldehyde** + *-an* (for ease of pronunciation) + **-ine**[4].

alannah /əˈlanə/ (also **alanna**) ▶ **noun** Irish my child (used as an affectionate form of address).
– ORIGIN mid 19th cent.: from Irish *a leanbh* 'O child'.

Al-Anon /ˌaləˈnɒn/ a mutual support organization for the families and friends of alcoholics, especially those of members of Alcoholics Anonymous.

alap /ɑːˈlɑːp/ (also **alaap**) ▶ **noun** (in Indian music) the improvised section of a raga, forming a prologue to the formal expression.
– ORIGIN from Hindi *ālāp*.

Alar /ˈeɪlɑː/ ▶ **noun** [mass noun] trademark a growth retardant sprayed on fruit and vegetables to enhance the quality of the crop.
– ORIGIN 1960s: of unknown origin.

alar /ˈeɪlə/ ▶ **adjective** Zoology or Anatomy relating to or resembling a wing or wings. ■ Botany another term for **axillary**.
– ORIGIN mid 19th cent.: from Latin *alaris*, from *ala* 'wing'.

Alarcón /ˌalɑːˈkɒn/, Pedro Antonio de (1833–91), Spanish novelist and short-story writer. Notable works: *The Three-Cornered Hat* (1874).

Alarcón y Mendoza see **Ruiz de Alarcón y Mendoza**.

Alaric /ˈalərɪk/ (*c.*370–410), king of the Visigoths 395–410. He invaded Italy in 408 and captured Rome in 410.

alarm ▶ **noun** [mass noun] an anxious awareness of danger: *the boat tilted and the boatmen cried out in* ***alarm*** | *he views the right-wing upsurge in Europe* ***with alarm***. ■ [in sing.] a warning of danger: *I hammered on several doors to* ***raise the alarm*** | *Oliver smelled smoke and* ***gave the alarm***. ■ [count noun] a warning sound or device: *a burglar alarm*. ■ [count noun] an alarm clock.
▶ **verb 1** [with obj.] make (someone) feel frightened, disturbed, or in danger: *the government was alarmed by an outbreak of unrest*.
2 (**be alarmed**) be fitted or protected with an alarm: *this door is locked and alarmed between 11 p.m. and 6 a.m.*
– ORIGIN late Middle English (as an exclamation meaning 'to arms!'): from Old French *alarme*, from Italian *allarme*, from *all' arme!* 'to arms!'.

alarm bell ▶ **noun** a bell rung as a warning of danger: *the alarm bell rang out* | figurative *the proposal has set* ***alarm bells ringing***.

alarm call ▶ **noun 1** a warning cry made by a bird or other animal when startled.
2 a telephone call made by prior arrangement to wake the person called.

alarm clock ▶ **noun** a clock with a device that can be made to sound at the time set in advance, used to wake someone up.

alarming ▶ **adjective** worrying or disturbing: *our countryside is disappearing at an alarming rate*.
– DERIVATIVES **alarmingly adverb** *the water swirls alarmingly* | [as submodifier] *an alarmingly high rate*.

alarmist ▶ **noun** someone who exaggerates a danger and so causes needless worry or panic.
▶ **adjective** creating needless worry or panic: *alarmist rumours*.
– DERIVATIVES **alarmism noun**.

alarum /əˈlɑːrəm/ ▶ **noun** archaic term for **alarm**.
– PHRASES **alarums and excursions** humorous confused activity and uproar.

alas ▶ **exclamation** archaic or humorous used to express grief, pity, or concern: *alas, my funds have some limitations*.
– ORIGIN Middle English: from Old French *a las, a lasse*, from *a* 'ah' + *las(se)* (from Latin *lassus* 'weary').

Alas. ▶ **abbreviation** Alaska.

Alaska the largest state of the US, in the extreme north-west of North America, with coasts on the Arctic Ocean, Bering Sea, and North Pacific; pop. 686,293 (est. 2008); capital, Juneau. The territory was purchased from Russia in 1867 and became the 49th state of the US in 1959.
– DERIVATIVES **Alaskan adjective & noun**.

Alaska, Gulf of a part of the NE Pacific between the Alaska Peninsula and the Alexander Archipelago.

Alaska Peninsula a peninsula on the south coast of Alaska. It extends south-westwards into the NE Pacific and is continued in the Aleutian Islands.

alate /ˈeɪleɪt/ ▶ **adjective** Botany & Entomology (chiefly of insects or seeds) having wings or wing-like appendages.
– ORIGIN mid 17th cent.: from Latin *alatus*, from *ala* 'wing'.

alb /alb/ ▶ **noun** a white vestment reaching to the feet, worn by clergy and servers in some Christian Churches.
– ORIGIN Old English *albe*, from ecclesiastical Latin *tunica* (or *vestis*) *alba* 'white garment', from Latin *albus* 'white'.

alba /ˈalbə/ ▶ **noun** a shrub rose of a variety with grey-green leaves and pinkish-white, sweet-scented flowers.
– ORIGIN mid 19th cent.: from Latin *alba*, feminine of *albus* 'white', from the name *rosa alba*, an old white garden rose.

Albacete /ˌalbəˈseɪti/, Spanish /albaˈθete, -ˈsete/ a city in a province of the same name in SE Spain; pop. 166,090 (2008).

albacore /ˈalbəkɔː/ ▶ **noun** a tuna of warm seas, which travels in large schools and is of commercial importance as a food fish. ● Two species in the family Scombridae.
– ORIGIN late 16th cent.: from Portuguese *albacora*, from Arabic *al-bakūra*, perhaps from *al* 'the' + *bakūr* 'premature, precocious'.

Alba Iulia /ˌalbə ˈjuːlɪə/ a city in west central Romania, to the north of the Transylvanian Alps; pop. 66,747 (2006). Founded by the Romans in the 2nd century AD, it was the capital of Transylvania.

Alban, St /ˈɔːlbən/ (3rd century), the first British Christian martyr, a native of Verulamium (now St Albans). He was put to death for sheltering a fugitive priest. Feast day, 22 June.

Albania /alˈbeɪnɪə/ a republic in SE Europe, bordering on the Adriatic Sea; pop. 3,639,500 (est. 2009); official language, Albanian; capital, Tirana.

> Previously part of the Byzantine and later the Ottoman Empire, Albania gained independence in 1912. It became a Stalinist regime under Enver Hoxha after the Second World War, remaining extremely isolationist in policy and outlook until the communists lost power in 1992. Following a period of political instability a democratically elected government was brought to power in 2001.

Albanian ▶ **noun 1** a native or inhabitant of Albania, or a person of Albanian descent.
2 [mass noun] the language of Albania, with about 6 million speakers. It forms a separate branch of Indo-European, and has two distinct dialects, Tosk and Gheg.
▶ **adjective** relating to Albania or its people or their language.

Albany /ˈɔːlbəni/ the state capital of New York, on the Hudson River; pop. 93,539 (est. 2008).

albatross /ˈalbətrɒs/ ▶ **noun** (pl. **albatrosses**) **1** a very large, chiefly white oceanic bird with long, narrow wings, found mainly in the southern oceans. ● Family Diomedeidae: genera *Diomedea* and *Phoebetria*.
■ a source of frustration or guilt; an encumbrance (in allusion to Coleridge's *The Rime of the Ancient Mariner*): *an albatross of a marriage*.
2 Golf another term for **double eagle**.
– ORIGIN late 17th cent.: alteration (influenced by Latin *albus* 'white') of 16th-cent. *alcatras*, applied to various seabirds including the frigate bird and pelican, from Spanish and Portuguese *alcatraz*, from Arabic *al-ġaṭṭās* 'the diver'.

albedo /alˈbiːdəʊ/ ▶ **noun** (pl. **albedos**) chiefly Astronomy the proportion of the incident light or radiation that is reflected by a surface, typically that of a planet or moon.
– ORIGIN mid 19th cent.: ecclesiastical Latin, 'whiteness', from Latin *albus* 'white'.

Albee /ˈɔːlbiː, ˈal-/, Edward Franklin (b.1928), American dramatist. He was initially associated with the Theatre of the Absurd, but *Who's Afraid of Virginia Woolf?* (1962) marked a more naturalistic departure.

albeit /ɔːlˈbiːɪt/ ▶ **conjunction** though: *he was making progress, albeit rather slowly*.
– ORIGIN late Middle English: from the phrase *all be it* 'although it be (that)'.

Albena /alˈbeɪnə/ a resort town in Bulgaria, on the coast of the Black Sea.

albert (also **albert chain**) ▶ **noun** Brit. a watch chain with a bar at one end for attaching to a buttonhole.
– ORIGIN mid 19th cent.: named after *Prince Albert* (see **Albert, Prince**).

Albert, Lake a lake in the Rift Valley of east central Africa, on the border between the Democratic Republic of the Congo (Zaire) and Uganda. It is linked to Lake Edward by the Semliki River and to the White Nile by the Albert Nile. African name **Mobutu Sese Seko, Lake**.
– ORIGIN named after the Prince Consort by the English explorer Samuel Baker, who in 1864 was the first European to sight it.

Albert, Prince Albert Francis Charles Augustus Emmanuel (1819–61), consort to Queen Victoria and prince of Saxe-Coburg-Gotha.

Alberta a prairie province in western Canada, bounded on the south by the US and on the west by the Rocky Mountains; capital, Edmonton; pop. 3,290,350 (2006).
– DERIVATIVES **Albertan noun & adjective**.

Alberti /alˈbɛːti/, Italian /alˈberti/, Leon Battista (1404–72), Italian architect, humanist, painter, and art critic. His book *On Painting* (1435) was the first account of the theory of perspective in the Renaissance.

Albert Nile the upper part of the Nile, flowing through NW Uganda between Lake Albert and the Ugandan–Sudanese border.

Albertus Magnus, St /alˌbəːtəs ˈmagnəs/ (*c.*1200–80), Dominican theologian, philosopher, and scientist; known as **Doctor Universalis**. A teacher of St Thomas Aquinas, he was a pioneer in the study of Aristotle and contributed significantly to the comparison of Christian theology and pagan philosophy. Feast day, 15 November.

albescent /alˈbɛs(ə)nt/ ▶ **adjective** literary growing or shading into white: *albescent mist*.
– ORIGIN early 18th cent.: from Latin *albescere* 'become white', from *albus* 'white'.

Albi /ˈalbi/ a town in southern France; pop. 51,199 (2006). The Albigensian movement originated there.

Albigenses /ˌalbɪˈgɛnsiːz, -ˈdʒɛn-/ ▶ **plural noun** a heretical Catharist sect of southern France in the 12th–13th centuries, believing in a form of Manichaean dualism with an extremely strict moral and social code.
– DERIVATIVES **Albigensian adjective & noun**.
– ORIGIN from medieval Latin, from *Albiga*, the Latin name of **Albi** in southern France.

albino /alˈbiːnəʊ/ ▶ **noun** (pl. **albinos**) a person or animal having a congenital absence of pigment in the skin and hair (which are white) and the eyes (which are usually pink). ■ informal an abnormally white animal or plant: [as modifier] *an albino tiger*.
– DERIVATIVES **albinism** /ˈalbɪnɪz(ə)m/ **noun**.
– ORIGIN early 18th cent.: from Portuguese (originally denoting albinos among African blacks) and Spanish, from *albo* (from Latin *albus* 'white') + the suffix *-ino* (see **-ine**[1]).

Albinoni /ˌalbɪˈnəʊni/, Tomaso (1671–1751), Italian composer. The *Adagio in G* with which he is popularly associated was in fact composed by Remo Giazotto, based on a manuscript fragment by Albinoni.

Albinus /alˈbiːnəs/ another name for **Alcuin**.

Albion /ˈalbɪən/ ▶ **noun** a literary term for Britain or England, often used when referring to ancient or historical times.
– ORIGIN Old English, from Latin, probably of Celtic origin and related to Latin *albus* 'white' (in allusion to the white cliffs of Dover). The phrase *perfidious Albion* (mid 19th cent.) translates the French *la perfide Albion*, alluding to alleged treachery to other nations.

albite /ˈalbʌɪt/ ▶ **noun** [mass noun] a sodium-rich mineral of the feldspar group, typically white, occurring in silicate rocks.
– ORIGIN early 19th cent.: from Latin *albus* 'white' + **-ite**[1].

albizzia /alˈbɪzɪə/ ▶ **noun** a leguminous tree or shrub of warm climates, with feathery leaves and plume-like flowers that typically resemble bottlebrushes. ● Genus *Albizia*, family Leguminosae.
– ORIGIN modern Latin, named after Filippo degli Albizzi, a Tuscan nobleman who introduced the silk tree *A. julibrizzen* into Italy in the mid 18th cent.

Ålborg variant spelling of **Aalborg**.

album ▶ **noun 1** a blank book for the insertion of photographs, stamps, or pictures: *the wedding pictures had pride of place in the family album*.

A

2 a collection of recordings issued as a single item on CD, record, or cassette.
– ORIGIN early 17th cent.: from Latin, neuter of *albus* 'white' used as a noun meaning 'a blank tablet'. Taken into English from the German use of the Latin phrase *album amicorum* 'album of friends' (a blank book in which autographs, drawings, poems, etc. were collected), it was originally used consciously as a Latin word.

albumen /'albjʊmɪn/ ▶ **noun** [mass noun] egg white, or the protein contained in it.
– ORIGIN late 16th cent.: from Latin, 'egg white', from *albus* 'white'.

albumin /'albjʊmɪn/ ▶ **noun** [mass noun] Biochemistry a simple form of protein that is soluble in water and coagulable by heat, such as that found in egg white, milk, and (in particular) blood serum.
– ORIGIN mid 19th cent.: from French *albumine*, based on Latin *albumen*, *albumin-* (see **ALBUMEN**).

albuminoid /al'bju:mɪnɔɪd/ ▶ **noun** another term for **SCLEROPROTEIN**.

albuminous /al'bju:mɪnəs/ ▶ **adjective** consisting of, resembling, or containing albumen.

albuminuria /,albjʊmɪ'njʊərɪə/ ▶ **noun** [mass noun] Medicine the presence of albumin in the urine, typically as a symptom of kidney disease.

Albuquerque[1] /'albə,kə:ki/ the largest city in the state of New Mexico; pop. 521,999 (est. 2008).

Albuquerque[2] /'albə,kə:ki/, Alfonso de (1453–1515), Portuguese colonial statesman. He conquered Goa (1510) and made it the capital of the Portuguese empire in the east.

Alcaeus /al'si:əs/ (*c.*620–*c.*580 BC), Greek lyric poet. He invented a new form of lyric metre, the alcaic; he also wrote political odes, drinking songs, and love songs. His works were a model for Horace and the verse of the Renaissance.

alcahest ▶ **noun** variant spelling of **ALKAHEST**.

alcaic /al'keɪɪk/ Prosody ▶ **adjective** using or denoting a verse metre occurring in four-line stanzas.
▶ **plural noun** (**alcaics**) alcaic verse.
– ORIGIN mid 17th cent.: via late Latin from Greek *alkaikos*, from *Alkaios* (see **ALCAEUS**).

Alcalá de Henares /,alka'lɑ: deɪ ɛ'nɑ:rɛs/ a city in central Spain, on the River Henares, 25 km (15 miles) north-east of Madrid; pop. 203,645 (2008).

alcalde /al'kaldeɪ/ ▶ **noun** a magistrate or mayor in a Spanish, Portuguese, or Latin American town.
– ORIGIN mid 16th cent.: Spanish, from Arabic *al-qāḍī* 'the judge' (see **CADI**).

Alcatraz /'alkətraz/ a rocky island in San Francisco Bay, California. Between 1934 and 1963 it was the site of a top-security federal prison.
– ORIGIN from Spanish *alcatraz* 'pelicans', which were once common there.

alcazar /,alkə'zɑ:/ ▶ **noun** a Spanish palace or fortress of Moorish origin.
– ORIGIN early 17th cent.: from Spanish *alcázar*, from Arabic *al-qaṣr* 'the castle'.

Alcestis /al'sɛstɪs/ Greek Mythology wife of Admetus, king of Pherae in Thessaly. She saved her husband's life by consenting to die on his behalf.

alchemilla /,alkə'mɪlə/ ▶ **noun** a plant of a genus that includes lady's mantle and its relatives. ● Genus *Alchemilla*, family Rosaceae.
– ORIGIN modern Latin, from a medieval Latin diminutive of *alchimia* 'alchemy', from the belief that dew from the leaves of the plant could turn base metals into gold.

alchemy /'alkɪmi/ ▶ **noun** [mass noun] the medieval forerunner of chemistry, concerned with the transmutation of matter, in particular with attempts to convert base metals into gold or find a universal elixir. ■ a seemingly magical process of transformation, creation, or combination: *finding the person who's right for you requires a very subtle alchemy.*
– DERIVATIVES **alchemic** /al'kɛmɪk/ adjective, **alchemical** adjective, **alchemist** noun, **alchemize** (also **alchemise**) verb.
– ORIGIN late Middle English: via Old French and medieval Latin from Arabic *al-kīmiyā'*, from *al* 'the' + *kīmiyā'* (from Greek *khēmia*, *khēmeia* 'art of transmuting metals').

Alcheringa /,altʃə'rɪŋgə/ (also **Alchera** /'altʃərə/) ▶ **noun** (in the mythology of some Australian Aborigines) the 'golden age' when the first ancestors were created. Also called **DREAMTIME**.
– ORIGIN late 19th cent.: from Arrernte *aljerre-nge* 'in the Dreamtime'.

Alcian blue /'alsɪən/ ▶ **noun** [mass noun] trademark a water-soluble copper-containing blue dye used as a histological stain for glycosaminoglycans.
– ORIGIN 1940s: *Alcian* perhaps from (*phth*)*al*(*o*)*cyan*(*ine*) with a phonetic respelling.

Alcibiades /,alsɪ'bʌɪədi:z/ (*c.*450–404 BC), Athenian general and statesman. He led the unsuccessful Athenian expeditions against Sparta and Sicily during the Peloponnesian War but fled to Sparta after being charged with sacrilege.

alcid /'alsɪd/ ▶ **noun** Ornithology a bird of the auk family (Alcidae); an auk.
– ORIGIN late 19th cent.: from modern Latin *Alcidae* (plural), from the genus name *Alca*, from Old Norse *álka* 'razorbill'; compare with **AUK**.

Alclad /'alklad/ ▶ **noun** [mass noun] trademark a composite material consisting of sheets of aluminium alloy coated with pure aluminium or a different alloy to increase corrosion resistance.
– ORIGIN 1920s: from *al*(*uminium*) + **CLAD[2]**.

Alcock /'ɔ:lkɒk/, Sir John William (1892–1919), English aviator. Together with Sir Arthur Whitten Brown he made the first non-stop transatlantic flight (16 hours 27 minutes) on 14–15 June 1919.

alcohol ▶ **noun** [mass noun] a colourless volatile flammable liquid which is the intoxicating constituent of wine, beer, spirits, and other drinks, and is also used as an industrial solvent and as fuel. ● Alternative names: **ethanol**, **ethyl alcohol**; chem. formula: C_2H_5OH. ■ drink containing alcohol: *he has not taken alcohol in twenty-five years.* ■ [count noun] Chemistry any organic compound whose molecule contains one or more hydroxyl groups attached to a carbon atom.
– ORIGIN mid 16th cent.: French (earlier form of *alcool*), or from medieval Latin, from Arabic *al-kuḥl* 'the kohl'. In early use the term referred to powders, specifically kohl, and especially those obtained by sublimation; later 'a distilled or rectified spirit' (mid 17th cent.).

alcohol-free ▶ **adjective** (of a drink) not containing alcohol: *alcohol-free lager.* ■ not serving or consuming alcoholic drinks.

alcoholic ▶ **adjective 1** containing or relating to alcohol: *alcoholic liquor.* ■ caused by the excessive consumption of alcohol: *alcoholic liver disease.* **2** suffering from alcoholism.
▶ **noun** a person suffering from alcoholism.

Alcoholics Anonymous (abbrev.: **AA**) a self-help organization for people fighting alcoholism, founded in the US in 1935 and now having branches worldwide.

alcoholism ▶ **noun** [mass noun] addiction to the consumption of alcoholic drink; alcohol dependency.

alcopop ▶ **noun** Brit. informal a ready-mixed drink that resembles a soft drink but contains alcohol.

Alcott /'ɔ:lkɒt/, Louisa May (1832–88), American novelist. She is best known for the novel *Little Women* (1868–9), based on her New England childhood. Alcott was involved in diverse reform movements, including women's suffrage.

alcove ▶ **noun** a recess in the wall of a room or garden.
– ORIGIN late 16th cent.: from French *alcôve*, from Spanish *alcoba*, from Arabic *al-qubba* 'the vault'.

Alcuin /'alkwɪn/ (*c.*735–804) English scholar, theologian, and adviser to Charlemagne; also known as **Albinus**. He is credited with the transformation of Charlemagne's court into a cultural centre in the period known as the Carolingian Renaissance.

Aldabra /al'dabrə/ a coral island group in the Indian Ocean, north-west of Madagascar. Formerly part of the British Indian Ocean Territory, it became an outlying dependency of the Seychelles in 1976.

Aldebaran /al'dɛbərən/ Astronomy the brightest star in the constellation Taurus. It is a binary star of which the main component is a red giant.
– ORIGIN Arabic, 'the follower (of the Pleiades)'.

Aldeburgh /'ɔ:ldbrə/ a town on the coast of Suffolk, England; pop. 2,700 (est. 2005). It is the setting for a music festival established by Benjamin Britten.

aldehyde /'aldɪhʌɪd/ ▶ **noun** Chemistry an organic compound containing the group –CHO, formed by the oxidation of alcohols. Typical aldehydes include methanal (formaldehyde) and ethanal (acetaldehyde).
– DERIVATIVES **aldehydic** /,aldɪ'hɪdɪk/ **adjective**.
– ORIGIN mid 19th cent.: shortened from Latin *alcohol dehydrogenatum* 'alcohol deprived of hydrogen'.

al dente /al 'dɛnteɪ, -ti/ ▶ **adjective & adverb** (of food, typically pasta) cooked so as to be still firm when bitten.
– ORIGIN Italian, literally 'to the tooth'.

alder /'ɔ:ldə/ (also **alder tree**) ▶ **noun** a widely distributed tree of the birch family which has toothed leaves and bears male catkins and woody female cones. ● Genus *Alnus*, family Betulaceae: many species.
– ORIGIN Old English *alor*, *aler*, of Germanic origin; related to German *Erle*; forms spelled with *d* are recorded from the 14th cent.

alder buckthorn ▶ **noun** a deciduous Eurasian shrub which bears glossy leaves and black berries. ● *Frangula alnus* (or *Rhamnus frangula*), family Rhamnaceae.

alderfly ▶ **noun** (pl. **alderflies**) a brownish fly-like insect that lives near water and has predatory aquatic larvae. ● Family Sialidae, order Neuroptera: several genera.

alderman ▶ **noun** (pl. **aldermen**) chiefly historical a co-opted member of an English county or borough council, next in status to the Mayor. ■ (also **alderperson** or **alderwoman**) N. Amer. & Austral. an elected member of a city council.
– DERIVATIVES **aldermanic** adjective, **aldermanship** noun.
– ORIGIN Old English *aldormann* (originally in the general sense 'a man of high rank'), from *aldor*, *ealdor* 'chief, patriarch' (from *ald* 'old') + **MAN**. Later the sense 'warden of a guild' arose; then, as the guilds became identified with the ruling municipal body, 'local magistrate, municipal officer'.

Aldermaston /'ɔ:ldə,mɑ:st(ə)n/ a village near Reading in southern England, site of the Atomic Weapons Research Establishment.

Alderney /'ɔ:ldəni/ an island in the English Channel, to the north-east of Guernsey; pop. 2,200 (est. 2002). It is the third largest of the Channel Islands.

Aldershot /'ɔ:ldəʃɒt/ a town in southern England, in Hampshire; pop. 57,500 (est. 2009).

aldicarb /'aldɪkɑ:b/ ▶ **noun** [mass noun] a systemic agricultural pesticide used against some mites, insects, and nematode worms.
– ORIGIN 1970s: blend of **ALDEHYDE** + *carbamide* (from **CARBO-** + **AMIDE**).

Aldine /'aldʌɪn/ ▶ **adjective** relating to the Italian printer Aldus Manutius, or to certain display typefaces.
– ORIGIN early 19th cent.: from Latin *Aldinus*, from *Aldus*, the printer's given name.

Aldis lamp /'ɔ:ldɪs/ ▶ **noun** trademark a handheld lamp for signalling in Morse code.
– ORIGIN First World War: named after Arthur C. W. *Aldis* (1878–1953), its British inventor.

aldol /'aldɒl/ ▶ **noun** [mass noun] Chemistry a viscous liquid obtained when acetaldehyde dimerizes in dilute alkali or acid. ● Chem. formula: $CH_3CH(OH)CH_2CHO$.
– ORIGIN late 19th cent.: from *al*(*dehyde*) + **-OL**.

aldosterone /al'dɒstərəʊn/ ▶ **noun** [mass noun] Biochemistry a corticosteroid hormone which stimulates absorption of sodium by the kidneys and so regulates water and salt balance.
– ORIGIN 1950s: blend of **ALDEHYDE** and **STEROID**, + **-ONE**.

aldosteronism /,aldə(ʊ)'stɛrənɪz(ə)m/ ▶ **noun** [mass noun] Medicine a condition in which there is excessive secretion of aldosterone, which disturbs the balance of sodium, potassium, and water in the blood and so leads to high blood pressure.

Aldrin /'ɔ:ldrɪn/, Buzz (b.1930), American astronaut; full name *Edwin Eugene Aldrin*. In 1969 he took part in the first moon landing, the Apollo 11 mission, becoming the second person to set foot on the moon, after Neil Armstrong.

aldrin /'ɔ:ldrɪn/ ▶ **noun** [mass noun] a toxic synthetic insecticide, now generally banned. ● A chlorinated polycyclic hydrocarbon; chem. formula: $C_{12}H_8Cl_6$.
– ORIGIN 1940s: from the name of K. *Alder* (see **DIELS–ALDER REACTION**) + **-IN[1]**.

Aldus Manutius /,ɔ:ldəs mə'nju:ʃɪəs/ (1450–1515), Italian scholar, printer, and publisher; Latinized name of *Teobaldo Manucci*; also known as **Aldo Manuzio**. He printed fine first editions of many Greek and Latin classics.

ale ▶ **noun** [mass noun] chiefly Brit. any beer other than lager, stout, or porter: *a draught of ale* | [count noun] *traditional cask-conditioned ales.* ■ N. Amer. beer brewed by top fermentation. ■ historical a drink made like beer but without the addition of hops.

– ORIGIN Old English *alu*, *ealu*, of Germanic origin; related to Old Norse *ǫl*. Formerly the word referred especially to the paler varieties of beer.

aleatory /ˈeɪlɪət(ə)ri, ˈal-/ (also **aleatoric** /ˌeɪlɪəˈtɒrɪk, ˌal-/) ▶ **adjective** depending on the throw of a die or on chance; random. ■ relating to or denoting music or other forms of art involving elements of random choice (sometimes using statistical or computer techniques) during their composition, production, or performance.
– ORIGIN late 17th cent.: from Latin *aleatorius*, from *aleator* 'dice player', from *alea* 'die', + **-Y**[1].

alecost /ˈeɪlkɒst/ ▶ **noun** another term for **COSTMARY**.
– ORIGIN late 16th cent.: from **ALE** + *cost*.

Alecto /əˈlɛktəʊ/ (also **Allecto**) Greek Mythology one of the Furies.

alee /əˈliː/ ▶ **adjective & adverb** Nautical on the side of a ship that is sheltered from the wind. ■ (of the helm) moved round to leeward in order to tack a vessel or to bring its bows up into the wind.
– ORIGIN late Middle English: from **A-**[2] 'on' + **LEE**.

alehouse ▶ **noun** dated an inn or public house.

Aleksandropol /ˌalɪkˈsɑːndrəpɒl/ (also **Alexandropol**) former name (1840–1924) for **GYUMRI**.

Aleksandrovsk /ˌalɪkˈsɑːndrəfsk/ former name (until 1921) for **ZAPORIZHZHYA**.

alembic /əˈlɛmbɪk/ ▶ **noun** a distilling apparatus, now obsolete, consisting of a gourd-shaped container and a cap with a long beak for conveying the products to a receiver.
– ORIGIN Middle English: via Old French from medieval Latin *alembicus*, from Arabic *al-ʾanbīq*, from *al-* 'the' + *ʾanbīq* 'still' (from Greek *ambix*, *ambik-* 'cup, cap of a still').

Alentejo /ˌalɛnˈteɪʒuː/ a region and former province of east central Portugal.

aleph /ˈɑːlɛf/ ▶ **noun** the first letter of the Hebrew alphabet.
– ORIGIN Middle English: from Hebrew *ʾālep*, literally 'ox' (the character in Phoenician and ancient Hebrew possibly being derived from a hieroglyph of an ox's head).

Aleppo /əˈlɛpəʊ/ a city in northern Syria; pop. 1,693,800 (est. 2009). Arabic name **HALAB**.

Aleppo gall ▶ **noun** a hard nut-like gall that forms on the valonia oak (formerly known as the **Aleppo oak**) in response to the developing larva of a gall wasp. It is used as a source of gallic acid and tannin. ● The wasp is *Cynips tinctoria*, family Cynipidae.

alerce /əˈləːsi/ ▶ **noun** a cypress tree that is valued for its timber. ● Several species in the family Cupressaceae.
– ORIGIN mid 19th cent.: from Spanish, 'larch'.

alert ▶ **adjective** quick to notice any unusual and potentially dangerous or difficult circumstances; vigilant: *an alert police officer discovered a lorry full of explosive | schools need to be constantly **alert to** this problem.* ■ able to think clearly; intellectually active: *she remained active and alert until well into her eighties.*
▶ **noun** [mass noun] the state of being watchful for possible danger: *security forces are **on the alert for** an upsurge in violence.* ■ [count noun] an announcement or signal warning of danger: *a bomb alert.* ■ [count noun] a period of vigilance following a warning of danger: *traffic was halted during the alert.* ■ [count noun] a signal on an electronic device that prompts the user to do something or attracts their attention: *a vibrating alert is a discreet alternative to ringtones.*
▶ **verb** [with obj.] warn (someone) of a danger or problem: *he **alerted** people **to** the dangers of smoking | police were alerted after three men drove away without paying.*
– DERIVATIVES **alertly** adverb.
– ORIGIN late 16th cent. (originally in military use): from French *alerte*, from Italian *all' erta* 'to the watchtower'.

alertness ▶ **noun** [mass noun] the quality of being alert: *a lack of mental alertness.*

-ales /ˈeɪliːz/ ▶ **suffix** Botany forming the names of orders of plants: *Rosales.*
– ORIGIN from the plural of the Latin adjectival suffix *-alis* (see **-AL**).

alethic /əˈliːθɪk/ ▶ **adjective** Philosophy denoting modalities of truth, such as necessity, contingency, or impossibility.
– ORIGIN 1950s: from Greek *alētheia* 'truth' + **-IC**.

Aletschhorn /ˈalɛtʃˌhɔːn/ a mountain in Switzerland, in the Bernese Alps, rising to 4,195 m (13,763 ft). Its glaciers are among the largest in Europe.

aleurone /əˈljʊərəʊn/ ▶ **noun** [mass noun] Botany protein stored as granules in the cells of plant seeds.
– ORIGIN mid 19th cent.: from Greek *aleuron* 'flour'.

Aleut /əˈljuːt, ˈalɪuːt/ ▶ **noun 1** a member of a people inhabiting the Aleutian Islands, other islands in the Bering Sea, and parts of western Alaska.
2 [mass noun] the language of the Aleuts, related to Eskimo but now almost extinct.
▶ **adjective** relating to the Aleuts or their language.
– ORIGIN of unknown origin.

Aleutian Islands /əˈl(j)uːʃ(ə)n/ (also **the Aleutians**) a chain of volcanic islands in US possession, extending south-west from the Alaska Peninsula.

A level ▶ **noun** Brit. short for **ADVANCED LEVEL**. ■ an A-level exam or pass.

alevin /ˈaləvɪn/ ▶ **noun** a newly spawned salmon or trout still carrying the yolk.
– ORIGIN mid 19th cent.: from French, based on Latin *allevare* 'raise up'.

alewife ▶ **noun** (pl. **alewives**) a NW Atlantic fish of the herring family, which swims up rivers to spawn. ● *Alosa pseudoharengus*, family Clupeidae.
– ORIGIN mid 17th cent.: possibly from earlier *alewife* 'woman who keeps an ale house', with reference to the fish's large belly.

Alexander[1] (356–323 BC), king of Macedon 336–323, son of Philip II; known as **Alexander the Great**. He conquered Persia, Egypt, Syria, Mesopotamia, Bactria, and the Punjab; in Egypt he founded the city of Alexandria.

Alexander[2] the name of three kings of Scotland:
■ **Alexander I** (*c*.1077–1124), son of Malcolm III, reigned 1107–24. ■ **Alexander II** (1198–1249), son of William I of Scotland, reigned 1214–49. ■ **Alexander III** (1241–86), son of Alexander II, reigned 1249–86.

Alexander[3] the name of three tsars of Russia:
■ **Alexander I** (1777–1825), reigned 1801–25.
■ **Alexander II** (1818–81), son of Nicholas I, reigned 1855–81; known as **Alexander the Liberator**. His reforms included limited emancipation of the serfs.
■ **Alexander III** (1845–94), son of Alexander II, reigned 1881–94. He reversed many of his father's reforms, resulting in a dangerous situation in Russia.

Alexander[4], Harold (Rupert Leofric George), 1st Earl Alexander of Tunis (1891–1969), British Field Marshal and Conservative statesman, holding commands during the Second World War.

Alexander Archipelago a group of about 1,100 islands off the coast of SE Alaska.

Alexander Nevsky /ˈnjɛfski/ (also **Nevski**) (*c*.1220–63), prince of Novgorod 1236–63; canonized as **St Alexander Nevsky**. He defeated the Swedes on the banks of the River Neva in 1240. Feast day, 30 August or 23 November.

alexanders ▶ **plural noun** [treated as sing.] a European plant of the parsley family with yellowish flowers, formerly eaten as a salad vegetable. ● *Smyrnium olusatrum*, family Umbelliferae.
– ORIGIN Old English *alexandre*, from medieval Latin *alexandrum*.

Alexander technique ▶ **noun** a system designed to promote well-being by retraining one's awareness and habits of posture to ensure minimum effort and strain.
– ORIGIN 1930s: named after Frederick Matthias *Alexander* (1869–1955), the Australian-born actor and elocutionist who developed it.

Alexandretta /ˌalɪgzɑːnˈdrɛtə/ former name for **ISKENDERUN**.

Alexandria /ˌalɪgˈzɑːndrɪə/ the chief port of Egypt; pop. 4,084,700 (est. 2006). Alexandria was a major centre of Hellenistic culture and was renowned for its extensive library (burned down in the late 3rd century BC).

Alexandrian ▶ **adjective** relating to Alexandria in Egypt. ■ belonging to the schools of literature and philosophy of ancient Alexandria. ■ (of a writer) derivative or imitative of previous writers and fond of obscure learning.

alexandrine /ˌalɪgˈzɑːndrɪn, -ʌɪn/ Prosody ▶ **adjective** (of a line of verse) having six iambic feet.
▶ **noun** (usu. **alexandrines**) an alexandrine line.
– ORIGIN late 16th cent.: from French *alexandrin*, from *Alexandre* (see **ALEXANDER**[1]), the subject of an Old French poem in this metre.

alexandrite /ˌalɪgˈzɑːndrʌɪt/ ▶ **noun** [mass noun] a gem variety of chrysoberyl which appears green in daylight and red in artificial light.
– ORIGIN mid 19th cent.: from the name of Tsar *Alexander* II of Russia (see **ALEXANDER**[3]) + **-ITE**[1].

Alexandropol variant spelling of **ALEKSANDROPOL**.

alexia /əˈlɛksɪə, eɪ-/ ▶ **noun** [mass noun] Medicine inability to recognize or read written words or letters, typically as a result of brain damage. Compare with **DYSLEXIA**.
– ORIGIN late 19th cent.: from **A-**[1] 'without' + Greek *lexis* 'speech', from *legein* 'speak', which was confused with Latin *legere* 'read'.

alfalfa /alˈfalfə/ ▶ **noun** [mass noun] a leguminous plant with clover-like leaves and bluish flowers, native to SW Asia and widely grown for fodder. Also called **LUCERNE**. ● *Medicago sativa*, family Leguminosae.
– ORIGIN mid 19th cent.: from Spanish, from Arabic *al-fasfaṣa*, a green fodder.

al-Fatah see **FATAH**.

alfisol /ˈalfɪsɒl/ ▶ **noun** Soil Science a soil of an order comprising leached basic or slightly acid soils with a clay-enriched B horizon.
– ORIGIN 1960s: from the arbitrary element *Alfi-* + **-SOL**.

alfoil ▶ **noun** [mass noun] Austral. trademark tinfoil.
– ORIGIN from **ALUMINIUM** + **FOIL**[1].

Alfonso XIII /alˈfɒnsəʊ/ (1886–1941), king of Spain 1886–1931, forced into exile after elections indicating a preference for a republic.

Alfred (849–99), king of Wessex 871–99; known as **Alfred the Great**. Alfred's military resistance saved SW England from Viking occupation. A great reformer, he is credited with the foundation of the English navy and with a revival of learning.

Alfredo /alˈfreɪdəʊ/ ▶ **adjective** denoting a sauce for pasta incorporating butter, cream, garlic, and Parmesan cheese: [postpositive] *fettuccine Alfredo.*
– ORIGIN named after *Alfredo* di Lelio, the Italian chef and restaurateur who invented the sauce.

al fresco /al ˈfrɛskəʊ/ ▶ **adverb & adjective** in the open air: [as adj.] *an al fresco supper.*
– ORIGIN mid 18th cent.: Italian, literally 'in the fresh (air)'.

al-Fujayrah another name for **FUJAIRAH**.

Alfvén /ˈalvɛn/, Hannes Olof Gösta (1908–95), Swedish theoretical physicist. His work was important for controlled thermonuclear fusion. Nobel Prize for Physics (1970).

Alfvén wave ▶ **noun** Physics a transverse magnetohydrodynamic wave travelling in the direction of the magnetic field in a magnetized plasma. The velocity of such waves (the **Alfvén velocity** or **speed**) is characteristic for a plasma of given properties.

alga /ˈalgə/ ▶ **noun** (pl. **algae** /ˈaldʒiː, ˈalgiː/) a simple, non-flowering, and typically aquatic plant of a large assemblage that includes the seaweeds and many single-celled forms. Algae contain chlorophyll but lack true stems, roots, leaves, and vascular tissue. ● Divisions Chlorophyta (**green algae**), Heterokontophyta (**brown algae**), and Rhodophyta (**red algae**); some (or all) are frequently placed in the kingdom Protista.
– DERIVATIVES **algal** adjective.
– ORIGIN mid 16th cent.: from Latin, 'seaweed'.

algal bloom ▶ **noun** a rapid growth of microscopic algae or cyanobacteria in water, often resulting in a coloured scum on the surface.

Algarve /alˈgɑːv/ (**the Algarve**) the southernmost province of Portugal, on the Atlantic coast; capital, Faro.

algebra /ˈaldʒɪbrə/ ▶ **noun** [mass noun] the part of mathematics in which letters and other general symbols are used to represent numbers and quantities in formulae and equations. ■ a system of algebra based on given axioms.
– DERIVATIVES **algebraist** /ˌaldʒɪˈbreɪɪst/ **noun**.
– ORIGIN late Middle English: from Italian, Spanish, and medieval Latin, from Arabic *al-jabr* 'the reunion of broken parts', 'bone-setting', from *jabara* 'reunite, restore'. The original sense, 'the surgical treatment of fractures', probably came via Spanish, in which it survives; the mathematical sense comes from the title of a book, *ʿilm al-jabr wa'l-muqābala* 'the science of restoring what is missing and equating like with like', by the mathematician al-Ḵwārizmī (see **ALGORITHM**).

algebraic ▶ **adjective** relating to or involving algebra. ■ denoting a mathematical expression or equation in which a finite number of symbols are combined using only the operations of addition, subtraction, multiplication, division, and exponentiation with

constant rational exponents. Compare with TRANSCENDENTAL.
– DERIVATIVES **algebraical** adjective, **algebraically** adverb.

Algeciras /ˌaldʒɪˈsɪərəs/, Spanish /alxeˈθiras, -ˈsiras/ a ferry port and resort in southern Spain; pop. 115,333 (2008).

Algeria /alˈdʒɪərɪə/ a republic on the Mediterranean coast of North Africa; pop. 34,178,200 (est. 2009); official language, Arabic; capital, Algiers.

> Algeria was colonized by France in the mid 19th century and was for a time closely integrated with metropolitan France, but following civil war in the 1950s the country achieved independence in 1962. A brief period of multi-party democracy was ended by a military takeover in 1992 after the fundamentalist Islamic Salvation Front had won the first round of the national elections; violent civil strife ensued until 2000, when the armed segment of the Islamic Salvation Front was dissolved.

– DERIVATIVES **Algerian** adjective & noun.

-algia ▶ combining form denoting pain in a specified part of the body: *neuralgia | myalgia*.
– DERIVATIVES **-algic** combining form in corresponding adjectives.
– ORIGIN from Greek *algos* 'pain'.

algicide /ˈaldʒɪsʌɪd, ˈalgɪ-/ ▶ noun a substance which is poisonous to algae.

Algiers /alˈdʒɪəz/ the capital of Algeria and one of the leading Mediterranean ports of North Africa; pop. 2,203,700 (est. 2009).

alginate ▶ noun Chemistry a salt of alginic acid.

alginic acid /alˈdʒɪnɪk/ ▶ noun [mass noun] Chemistry an insoluble gelatinous carbohydrate found (chiefly as salts) in many brown seaweeds. The sodium salt is used as a thickener in foods and many other materials.
– ORIGIN late 19th cent.: *alginic* from ALGA + -IN[1] + -IC.

ALGOL /ˈalgɒl/ ▶ noun [mass noun] an early high-level computer programming language devised to carry out scientific calculations.
– ORIGIN 1950s: from *algo(rithmic)* + the initial letter of LANGUAGE.

Algol /ˈalgɒl/ Astronomy a variable star in the constellation Perseus, regarded as the prototype of eclipsing binary stars.
– ORIGIN from Arabic *al ġūl* 'the ghoul'.

algolagnia /ˌalgə(ʊ)ˈlagnɪə/ ▶ noun [mass noun] Psychiatry desire for sexual gratification through inflicting pain on oneself or others; sadomasochism.
– ORIGIN early 20th cent.: coined in German from Greek *algos* 'pain' + *lagneia* 'lust'.

algology /əlˈgɒlədʒi/ ▶ noun [mass noun] the study of algae.
– DERIVATIVES **algological** adjective, **algologist** noun.

Algonquian /alˈgɒŋkwɪən, -kɪ-/ (also **Algonkian** /-kɪən/) ▶ adjective denoting or relating to a large family of North American Indian languages formerly spoken across a vast area from the Atlantic seaboard to the Great Lakes and the Great Plains, and including Ojibwa, Cree, Blackfoot, Cheyenne, and Delaware. Many words in English have been adopted from these languages, e.g. *moccasin*, *moose*, and *toboggan*.
▶ noun **1** [mass noun] the Algonquian family of languages. **2** a speaker of any of the Algonquian languages.
– ORIGIN from ALGONQUIN + -IAN.

Algonquin /alˈgɒŋkwɪn/ (also **Algonkin**) ▶ noun **1** a member of an American Indian people living in Canada along the Ottawa River and its tributaries and westward to the north of Lake Superior. **2** [mass noun] the Algonquian language of the Algonquin people, with about 3,000 speakers.
▶ adjective relating to the Algonquin people or their language.
– ORIGIN French, contraction of obsolete *Algoumequin*, from a Micmac word meaning 'at the place of spearing fish and eels'.

algorithm /ˈalgərɪð(ə)m/ ▶ noun a process or set of rules to be followed in calculations or other problem-solving operations, especially by a computer: *a basic **algorithm for** division*.
– DERIVATIVES **algorithmic** adjective, **algorithmically** adverb.
– ORIGIN late 17th cent. (denoting the Arabic or decimal notation of numbers): variant (influenced by Greek *arithmos* 'number') of Middle English *algorism*, via Old French from medieval Latin *algorismus*. The Arabic source, *al-Kwārizmī* 'the man of Kwārizm' (now Khiva), was a name given to the 9th-cent. mathematician Abū Ja'far Muhammad ibn Mūsa, author of widely translated works on algebra and arithmetic.

alguacil /ˌalgwaˈθiːl/, Spanish /ˌalɣwaˈθil, -ˈsil/ ▶ noun (pl. **alguaciles** /ˌalgwaˈθiːlɪz/, Spanish /ˌalɣwaˈθiles, -ˈsiles/) each of a pair of mounted constables acting as an official at a bullfight.
– ORIGIN Spanish, from Arabic *al-wazīr* 'the helper, aide, or vizier'.

alhaji /alˈhadʒi/ ▶ noun (pl. **alhajis**; fem. **alhaja**) (in West Africa) a Muslim who has been to Mecca as a pilgrim (often used as a title).
– ORIGIN Hausa, from Arabic *al* 'the' + *hājī* 'pilgrim'.

Alhambra /alˈhambrə/ a fortified Moorish palace, the last stronghold of the Muslim kings of Granada, built between 1248 and 1354 near Granada in Spain.

al-Hudayda /ˌalhuːˈdeɪdə/ Arabic name for HODEIDA.

Ali[1], Muhammad, see MUHAMMAD ALI[1].

Ali[2], Muhammad, see MUHAMMAD ALI[2].

-alia ▶ suffix (forming plural nouns) denoting items associated with a particular area of activity or interest: *kitchenalia*.
– ORIGIN from Latin, neuter plural ending of adjectives ending in *-alis*.

alias /ˈeɪlɪəs/ ▶ adverb used to indicate that a named person is also known or more familiar under another specified name: *Eric Blair, alias George Orwell*.
▶ noun **1** a false or assumed identity: *a spy operating **under the alias** Barsad*. ■ Computing an alternative name or label that refers to a file, command, address, or other item, and can be used to locate or access it. **2** Physics & Telecommunications each of a set of signal frequencies which, when sampled at a given uniform rate, would give the same set of sampled values, and thus might be incorrectly substituted for one another when reconstructing the original signal.
▶ verb [with obj.] Physics & Telecommunications misidentify (a signal frequency), introducing distortion or error.
– ORIGIN late Middle English: from Latin, 'at another time, otherwise'.

aliasing ▶ noun [mass noun] **1** Physics & Telecommunications the misidentification of a signal frequency, introducing distortion or error. **2** Computing the use of aliases to designate files, commands, addresses, or other items. **3** Computing the distortion of a reproduced image so that curved or inclined lines appear inappropriately jagged, caused by the mapping of a number of points to the same pixel.

Ali Baba /ˌali ˈbɑːbə/ the hero of a story supposed to be from the *Arabian Nights*, who discovered the magic formula ('Open Sesame!') which opened a cave where forty thieves kept their treasure.

alibi /ˈalɪbʌɪ/ ▶ noun (pl. **alibis**) a claim or piece of evidence that one was elsewhere when an act, typically a criminal one, is alleged to have taken place: *she has an alibi for the whole of yesterday evening*. ■ informal an excuse or pretext: *a catch-all alibi for failure and inadequacy*.
▶ verb (**alibis**, **alibiing**, **alibied**) [with obj.] informal provide an alibi for.
– ORIGIN late 17th cent. (as an adverb in the sense 'elsewhere'): from Latin, 'elsewhere'. The noun use dates from the late 18th cent.

> **USAGE** The word **alibi**, which in Latin means 'elsewhere', has been used since the 18th century to mean 'an assertion by a person that he or she was elsewhere'. In the 20th century a new sense arose (originally in the US) with the meaning 'an excuse'. This use is a fairly common and natural extension of the core meaning, but is still regarded as incorrect by some traditionalists.

Alicante /ˌalɪˈkanti, -teɪ/ a seaport on the Mediterranean coast of SE Spain, the capital of a province of the same name; pop. 331,750 (2008).

Alice band ▶ noun a flexible band worn by women and girls to hold back the hair.
– ORIGIN *Alice*, from the name of the heroine of two books by Lewis Carroll.

Alice Springs a railway terminus and supply centre serving the outback of Northern Territory, Australia; pop. 27,481 (2008).

alicyclic /ˌalɪˈsʌɪklɪk, -ˈsɪk-/ Chemistry ▶ adjective relating to or denoting organic compounds which combine cyclic structure with aliphatic properties, e.g. cyclohexane and other saturated cyclic hydrocarbons. Compare with AROMATIC.
▶ noun an alicyclic compound.
– ORIGIN late 19th cent.: blend of ALIPHATIC and CYCLIC.

alidade /ˈalɪdeɪd/ ▶ noun a sighting device or pointer for determining directions or measuring angles, used in surveying and (formerly) astronomy.
– ORIGIN late Middle English: directly or (in modern use) via French and Spanish from Arabic *al-ʿiḍāda* 'the revolving radius', probably based on *aḍud* 'upper arm'.

alien ▶ adjective **1** belonging to a foreign country: *an alien culture*. ■ (of a plant or animal species) introduced from another country and later naturalized. **2** unfamiliar and disturbing or distasteful: *principles that are **alien to** them | they found the world of further education a little alien*. **3** supposedly from another world; extraterrestrial: *alien beings | an alien spacecraft*.
▶ noun **1** a foreigner, especially one who is not a naturalized citizen of the country where he or she is living: *an enemy alien*. ■ a plant or animal species originally introduced from another country and later naturalized. **2** a hypothetical or fictional being from another world.
– DERIVATIVES **alienness** noun.
– ORIGIN Middle English: via Old French from Latin *alienus* 'belonging to another', from *alius* 'other'.

alienable ▶ adjective Law able to be transferred to new ownership.
– DERIVATIVES **alienability** noun.

alienage ▶ noun [mass noun] chiefly Law the state or condition of being an alien.

alienate ▶ verb [with obj.] **1** make (someone) feel isolated or estranged: *an urban environment which would alienate its inhabitants* | (as adj. **alienated**) *an alienated, angst-ridden twenty-two-year-old*. ■ make (someone) become unsympathetic or hostile: *the association does not wish to alienate its members*. **2** Law transfer ownership of (property rights) to another person or group.
– PHRASES **alienate someone's affections** US Law induce someone to transfer their affection from a person (such as a spouse) with legal rights or claims on them.
– ORIGIN early 16th cent.: from Latin *alienat-* 'estranged', from the verb *alienare*, from *alienus* 'of another' (see ALIEN).

alienation ▶ noun [mass noun] **1** the state or experience of being alienated: *a sense of **alienation from** our environment | unemployment may generate a sense of political alienation*. ■ (in Marxist theory) a condition of workers in a capitalist economy, resulting from a lack of identity with the products of their labour and a sense of being controlled or exploited. ■ Psychiatry a state of depersonalization or loss of identity in which the self seems unreal, thought to be caused by difficulties in relating to society and the resulting prolonged inhibition of emotion. ■ (also **alienation effect**) Theatre an effect, sought by some dramatists, whereby the audience remains objective and does not identify with the actors. **2** Law the transfer of the ownership of property rights.
– ORIGIN late Middle English: from Latin *alienatio(n-)*, from the verb *alienare* 'estrange', from *alienus* (see ALIEN). The term *alienation effect* (1940s) is a translation of German *Verfremdungseffekt*.

alienist ▶ noun former term for PSYCHIATRIST.
– ORIGIN mid 19th cent.: from French *aliéniste*, based on Latin *alienus* 'of another' (see ALIEN).

aliform /ˈeɪlɪfɔːm/ ▶ adjective wing-shaped.
– ORIGIN early 18th cent.: from modern Latin *aliformis*, from Latin *ala* 'wing' + *-formis* (see -FORM).

Aligarh /ˌɑːlɪˈgɑː/ a city in northern India, in Uttar Pradesh; pop. 846,400 (est. 2009). The city comprises the ancient fort of Aligarh and the former city of Koil.

Alighieri /ˌalɪˈgjɛːri/, Dante, see DANTE.

alight[1] ▶ verb [no obj., with adverbial of place] formal descend from a train, bus, or other form of transport: *visitors should alight at the Fort Road stop*. ■ (of a bird) descend from the air and settle: *one bird alighted on the arm of my chair*.
– PHRASAL VERBS **alight on** find by chance; notice: *her eyes alighted on the item in question*.
– ORIGIN Old English *ālīhtan*, from *ā-* (as an intensifier) + *līhtan* 'descend' (see LIGHT[3]).

alight[2] ▶ adverb & adjective on fire; burning: [as adj.] *the house was alight when the firemen arrived* | [as adv.] *flammable liquid was set alight*. ■ shining brightly: [as adj.] *a single lamp was alight* | figurative *the boy's face was alight with excitement*.

A

– PHRASES **set the world alight** informal achieve something which causes great excitement and makes one famous.
– ORIGIN late Middle English: probably from the phrase *on a light* (= lighted) *fire*.

align ▶ **verb 1** [with obj.] place or arrange (things) in a straight line: *the desks are aligned in straight rows facing forwards*. ■ put (things) into correct or appropriate relative positions: *the fan blades are carefully aligned* | figurative *aligning domestic prices with prices in world markets*. ■ [no obj.] lie in a straight line, or in correct relative positions: *the pattern of the border at the joint should align perfectly*.
2 (**align oneself with**) give support to (a person, organization, or cause): *newspapers usually align themselves with certain political parties*. ■ [no obj.] come together in agreement or alliance: *all of them must now align against the foe*.
– ORIGIN late 17th cent.: from French *aligner*, from *à ligne* 'into line'.

alignment ▶ **noun 1** [mass noun] arrangement in a straight line or in correct relative positions: *the tiles had slipped out of alignment*. ■ [count noun] the route or course of a railway or road. ■ [count noun] Archaeology a linear arrangement of stones.
2 a position of agreement or alliance: *the uncertain nature of political alignments*.
– ORIGIN late 18th cent.: from French *alignement*, from *aligner* (see ALIGN).

alike ▶ **adjective** [predic.] (of two or more people or things) similar to each other: *the brothers were very much alike* | *the houses all looked alike*.
▶ **adverb** in the same or a similar way: *the girls dressed alike in black trousers and jackets*. ■ used to show that something applies equally to a number of specified subjects: *he talked in a friendly manner to staff and patients alike*.
– ORIGIN Old English *gelīc*, of Germanic origin; related to Dutch *gelijk* and German *gleich*, reinforced in Middle English by Old Norse *álíkr* (adjective) and *álíka* (adverb).

aliment /ˈalɪm(ə)nt/ ▶ **noun** [mass noun] **1** archaic food; nourishment.
2 Scots Law maintenance; alimony.
– ORIGIN late 15th cent.: from Latin *alimentum*, from *alere* 'nourish'.

alimentary ▶ **adjective** relating to nourishment or sustenance.
– ORIGIN late 16th cent.: from Latin *alimentarius*, from *alimentum* 'nourishment' (see ALIMENT).

alimentary canal ▶ **noun** the whole passage along which food passes through the body from mouth to anus during digestion.

alimentation ▶ **noun** [mass noun] formal the provision of nourishment or other necessities of life.
– ORIGIN late 16th cent. (in the sense 'maintenance, support'): from medieval Latin *alimentatio(n-)*, from late Latin *alimentare* 'to feed', from *alimentum* 'nourishment' (see ALIMENT).

alimony /ˈalɪməni/ ▶ **noun** [mass noun] chiefly N. Amer. a husband's (or wife's) provision for a spouse after separation or divorce; maintenance.
– ORIGIN early 17th cent. (in the sense 'nourishment, means of subsistence'): from Latin *alimonia* 'nutriment', from *alere* 'nourish'.

A-line ▶ **adjective** (of a garment) slightly flared from a narrow waist or shoulders: *A-line skirts*.

aliphatic /ˌalɪˈfatɪk/ Chemistry ▶ **adjective** relating to or denoting organic compounds in which carbon atoms form open chains (as in the alkanes), not aromatic rings.
▶ **noun** an aliphatic compound.
– ORIGIN late 19th cent. (originally used of the fatty acids): from Greek *aleiphar, aleiphat-* 'fat' + -IC.

aliquot /ˈalɪkwɒt/ ▶ **noun** a portion of a larger whole, especially a sample taken for chemical analysis or other treatment. ■ (also **aliquot part** or **portion**) Mathematics a quantity which can be divided into another an integral number of times.
▶ **verb** [with obj.] divide (a whole) into aliquots.
– ORIGIN late 16th cent.: from French *aliquote*, from Latin *aliquot* 'some, so many', from *alius* 'one of two' + *quot* 'how many'.

alisphenoid /ˌalɪˈsfiːnɔɪd/ (also **alisphenoid bone**) ▶ **noun** Anatomy & Zoology a wing-like cartilaginous bone within a mammal's skull forming part of the socket of the eye.
– ORIGIN mid 19th cent.: from Latin *ala* 'wing' + SPHENOID.

A-list (or **B-list**) ▶ **noun** a real or imaginary list of the most (or second most) celebrated or sought-after individuals, especially in show business: [as modifier] *an A-list celebrity*.

aliterate /eɪˈlɪt(ə)rət/ ▶ **adjective** unwilling to read, although able to do so.
▶ **noun** an aliterate person.
– DERIVATIVES **aliteracy** noun.

alive ▶ **adjective** [predic.] **1** (of a person, animal, or plant) living, not dead: *hopes of finding anyone still alive were fading* | *he was kept alive by a feeding tube*. ■ continuing in existence or use: *keeping hope alive* | *fortunately the old recipes are very much alive*.
2 alert and active; animated: *Ken **comes alive** when he hears his music played*. ■ having interest and meaning: *we hope we will make history **come alive** for the children*.
3 (**alive to**) aware of and interested in; responsive to: *she was always alive to new ideas*.
4 (**alive with**) swarming or teeming with: *in spring those cliffs are alive with auks and gulls*.
– PHRASES **alive and kicking** informal prevalent and very active: *bigotry is still alive and kicking*. **alive and well** still existing or active (often used to deny rumours or beliefs that something has disappeared or declined): *the sports car industry is alive and well*.
– DERIVATIVES **aliveness** noun.
– ORIGIN Old English *on līfe*, literally 'in life'.

aliyah /ˈalɪjə/ ▶ **noun** (pl. **aliyoth** /ˈalɪjəʊt/) Judaism **1** [mass noun] immigration to Israel: *students **making aliyah***.
2 the honour of being called upon to read from the Torah: *I was called up for an aliyah*.
– ORIGIN from Hebrew *'ălīyyāh* 'ascent'.

alizarin /əˈlɪz(ə)rɪn/ ▶ **noun** [mass noun] Chemistry a red pigment present in madder root, used in dyeing. ● Chem. formula: $C_{14}H_8O_4$.
– ORIGIN mid 19th cent.: from French *alizarine*, from *alizari* 'madder', from Arabic *al-'iṣāra* 'pressed juice', from *'aṣara* 'to press fruit'.

al-Jizah /al ˈdʒiːzə/ Arabic name for GIZA.

alkahest /ˈalkəhɛst/ (also **alcahest**) ▶ **noun** historical the hypothetical universal solvent sought by alchemists.
– ORIGIN mid 17th cent.: sham Arabic, probably invented by Paracelsus.

alkali /ˈalkəlʌɪ/ ▶ **noun** (pl. **alkalis**) a compound with particular chemical properties including turning litmus blue and neutralizing or effervescing with acids; typically, a caustic or corrosive substance of this kind such as lime or soda. Often contrasted with ACID and BASE[1]. ■ [as modifier] chiefly N. Amer. alkaline.

> Alkalis release hydroxide ions (OH^-) when dissolved in water. Any solution with a pH of more than 7 is alkaline.

– ORIGIN late Middle English (denoting a saline substance derived from the ashes of various plants, including glasswort): from medieval Latin, from Arabic *al-qalī* 'calcined ashes (of the glasswort etc.)', from *qalā* 'fry, roast'.

alkalic /alˈkalɪk/ ▶ **adjective** Geology (of a rock or mineral) richer in sodium and/or potassium than is usual for its type.

alkali feldspar ▶ **noun** Geology any of the group of feldspars rich in sodium and/or potassium.

alkali metal ▶ **noun** Chemistry any of the elements lithium, sodium, potassium, rubidium, caesium, and francium, occupying Group IA (1) of the periodic table. They are very reactive, electropositive, monovalent metals forming strongly alkaline hydroxides.

alkaline ▶ **adjective** having the properties of an alkali, or containing alkali; having a pH greater than 7. Often contrasted with ACIDIC and BASIC.
– DERIVATIVES **alkalinity** noun.

alkaline earth (also **alkaline earth metal**) ▶ **noun** any of the elements beryllium, magnesium, calcium, strontium, barium, and radium, occupying Group IIA (2) of the periodic table. They are reactive, electropositive, divalent metals, and form basic oxides which react with water to form comparatively insoluble hydroxides.

alkalize (also **alkalise**) ▶ **verb** [with obj.] treat with alkali.

alkaloid /ˈalkəlɔɪd/ ▶ **noun** Chemistry any of a class of nitrogenous organic compounds of plant origin which have pronounced physiological actions on humans. They include many drugs (morphine, quinine) and poisons (atropine, strychnine).
– ORIGIN early 19th cent.: coined in German from ALKALI.

alkalosis /ˌalkəˈləʊsɪs/ ▶ **noun** [mass noun] Medicine an excessively alkaline condition of the body fluids or tissues, which may cause weakness or cramp.

alkane /ˈalkeɪn/ ▶ **noun** Chemistry any of the series of saturated hydrocarbons including methane, ethane, propane, and higher members. ● Alkanes have the general formula: C_nH_{2n+2}.
– ORIGIN late 19th cent.: from ALKYL + -ANE[2].

alkanet /ˈalkənɛt/ ▶ **noun** a Eurasian plant of the borage family, typically having a hairy stem and blue flowers. ● *Anchusa* and other genera, family Boraginaceae: several species, including the European *A. officinalis*.
– ORIGIN Middle English: from colloquial Arabic *al-ḥannat* (classical Arabic *al-ḥinnā'*) 'the henna shrub'.

alkene /ˈalkiːn/ ▶ **noun** Chemistry any of the series of unsaturated hydrocarbons containing a double bond, including ethylene and propene. ● Alkenes have the general formula: C_nH_{2n}.
– ORIGIN late 19th cent.: from ALKYL + -ENE.

alky (also **alkie**) ▶ **noun** (pl. **alkies**) informal an alcoholic.

alkyd /ˈalkɪd/ ▶ **noun** Chemistry any of a group of synthetic polyester resins derived from various alcohols and acids.
– ORIGIN 1920s: blend of ALKYL and ACID.

alkyl /ˈalkʌɪl, -kɪl/ ▶ **noun** [as modifier] Chemistry of or denoting a hydrocarbon radical derived from an alkane by removal of a hydrogen atom.
– ORIGIN late 19th cent.: German, from *Alkohol* 'alcohol' + -YL.

alkylate /ˈalkɪleɪt/ ▶ **verb** [with obj.] (usu. as adj. **alkylating** or **alkylated**) Chemistry introduce an alkyl radical into (a compound): *alkylating agents*.
– DERIVATIVES **alkylation** noun.

alkyne /ˈalkʌɪn/ ▶ **noun** Chemistry any of the series of unsaturated hydrocarbons containing a triple bond, including acetylene. ● Alkynes have the general formula: C_nH_{2n-2}.
– ORIGIN early 20th cent.: from ALKYL + -YNE.

all ▶ **predeterminer, determiner, & pronoun** used to refer to the whole quantity or extent of a particular group or thing: [as predeterminer] *all the people I met* | *she left all her money to him* | [as determiner] *10 per cent of all cars sold* | *he slept all day* | [as pronoun] *carry **all of** the blame* | *we all have different needs*. ■ [determiner] any whatever: *he denied all knowledge of it*. ■ [determiner] used to emphasize the greatest possible amount of a quality: *they were in all probability completely unaware* | *with all due respect*. ■ [pronoun] [with clause] the only thing (used for emphasis): *all I want is to be left alone*. ■ [pronoun] (used to refer to surroundings or a situation in general) everything: *all was well* | *all is not lost yet*.
▶ **adverb 1** completely: *dressed all in black* | *she's been all round the world* | *all by himself*. ■ informal used to emphasize a temporary quality: *my ankle's gone all wobbly* | *he was **all of a dither***.
2 (in games) used after a number to indicate an equal score: *after extra time it was still two all*.
– PHRASES **all along** all the time; from the beginning: *she'd known all along*. **all and sundry** everyone: *he has borne a lot of unfair criticism from all and sundry*. **all but 1** very nearly: *the subject was all but forgotten*. **2** all except: *we have support from all but one of the networks*. **all comers** chiefly informal anyone who chooses to take part in an activity, typically a competition: *the champion took on all comers*. **all for** informal strongly in favour of: *I was all for tolerance*. **all get-out** see AS —— AS ALL GET-OUT at GET-OUT. **all in** informal exhausted: *he was all in by half-time*. See also ALL-IN. **all in all** on the whole: *all in all it's been a good year*. **all kinds** (or **sorts**) **of** many different kinds of: *he gets into all kinds of trouble*. **all manner of** see MANNER. **all of** as much as (often used ironically of an amount or quantity considered small by the speaker): *the show lasted all of six weeks*. **all of a sudden** see SUDDEN. **all-or-none** another way of saying ALL-OR-NOTHING. ■ Physiology (of a response) having a strength independent of the strength of the stimulus that caused it. **all-or-nothing** having no middle position or compromise available: *an all-or-nothing decision*. **all out** using all one's strength or resources: *going all out to win* | [as adj.] *an all-out effort*. **all over 1** completely finished: *it's all over between us*. **2** informal everywhere: *there were bodies all over*. ■ with reference to all parts of the body: *I was shaking all over*. **3** informal typical of the person mentioned: *that's our management all over!* **4** informal effusively attentive to: *James was all over her*. **all over the place** (or N. Amer. also **all over the map**, Brit. also **shop**) informal everywhere: *we've been all over the place looking for you*. ■ in a state of disorder: *my hair was*

A

all over the place. **all round** (US **all around**) **1** in all respects: *it was a bad day all round* | [as modifier] *a man of all-round ability.* **2** for or by each person: *drinks all round.* **all sorts of** see ALL KINDS OF above. **all's well that ends well** proverb if the outcome of a situation is happy, this compensates for any previous difficulty or unpleasantness. **all that** —— see THAT. **all the same** see SAME. **all the** —— see THE (sense 6). **all there** [usu. with negative] informal in full possession of one's mental faculties: *he's not quite all there.* **all the time** see TIME. **all together** all in one place or in a group; all at once: *they arrived all together.* Compare with ALTOGETHER. **all told** in total: *they tried a dozen times all told.* **all the way** informal without limit or reservation: *I'm with you all the way.* —— **and all** used to emphasize something additional that is being referred to: *she threw her coffee over him, mug and all.* ■ informal as well: *get one for me and all.* **at all** [with negative or in questions] (used for emphasis) in any way; to any extent: *I don't like him at all.* ■ Irish added at the end of an utterance for emphasis: *what is the matter with you at all?* **be all one to** make no difference to: *simple cases or hard cases, it's all one to me.* **be all that** US informal be very attractive or good: *He thinks he's all that—Yeah, God's gift.* **be all up with** see UP. **be all very well** informal used to criticize or reject a favourable or consoling remark: *your proposal is all very well in theory, but in practice it will not pay.* **for all** —— in spite of ——: *for all its clarity and style, the book is not easy reading.* **in all** in total number; altogether: *there were about 5,000 people in all.* **on** (or **on to**) **all fours** on (or on to) hands and knees or (of an animal) on all four legs rather than just the hind ones. **one's all** one's whole strength or resources: *I want to **give my all to** what I am doing now.*

– ORIGIN Old English *all, eall*, of Germanic origin; related to Dutch *al* and German *all*.

alla breve /ˌalə ˈbreɪvi, ˈbrɛveɪ/ ▸ **noun** Music a time signature indicating two or four minim beats in a bar.
– ORIGIN Italian, literally 'according to the breve'.

alla cappella /kəˈpɛlə/ ▸ **adjective & adverb** another term for A CAPPELLA.

Allah /ˈalə, əlˈlɑː/ the name of God among Muslims (and Arab Christians).
– ORIGIN from Arabic *'allāh*, contraction of *al-'ilāh* 'the god'.

Allahabad /ˈaləhəˌbad/ a city in the state of Uttar Pradesh, north central India; pop. 1,125,000 (est. 2009). Situated at the confluence of the sacred Jumna and Ganges Rivers, it is a place of Hindu pilgrimage.

allamanda /ˌaləˈmandə/ ▸ **noun** any of a number of tropical shrubs or climbers which bear showy yellow or purple flowers. ● Several species, particularly in the genus *Allamanda* (family Apocynaceae).
– ORIGIN modern Latin, named after Jean-Nicholas-Sébastien *Allamand* (1713–87), Swiss naturalist.

all-American ▸ **adjective** **1** possessing qualities characteristic of US ideals, such as honesty, industriousness, and health: *his all-American wholesomeness.* **2** drawn only from America or the US: *an all-American anthology.* ■ involving or representing the whole of America or the US: *an all-American final.* ■ (also **all-America**) US (of a sports player) honoured as one of the best amateur competitors in the US.
▸ **noun** (also **all-America**) US a sports player honoured as one of the best amateurs in the US.

allanite /ˈalənʌɪt/ ▸ **noun** [mass noun] a brownish-black mineral of the epidote group, consisting of a silicate of rare earth metals, aluminium, and iron.
– ORIGIN early 19th cent.: named after Thomas *Allan* (1777–1833), Scottish mineralogist, + -ITE[1].

allantoin /əˈlantəʊɪn/ ▸ **noun** [mass noun] Biochemistry a crystalline compound formed in the nitrogen metabolism of many mammals (excluding primates). ● A cyclic compound related to hydantoin; chem. formula: $C_4H_6N_4O_3$.
– ORIGIN mid 19th cent.: from ALLANTOIS (because it was discovered in the allantoic fluid of cows) + -IN[1].

allantois /əˈlantəʊɪs/ ▸ **noun** (pl. **allantoides** /-ɪdiːz/) the fetal membrane lying below the chorion in many vertebrates, formed as an outgrowth of the embryo's gut. In birds and reptiles it grows to surround the embryo; in eutherian mammals it forms part of the placenta.
– DERIVATIVES **allantoic** adjective, **allantoid** adjective.
– ORIGIN mid 17th cent.: modern Latin, based on Greek *allantoeidēs* 'sausage-shaped'.

allargando /ˌalɑːˈgandəʊ/ Music ▸ **adverb & adjective** (especially as a direction) getting slower and broader.
▸ **noun** (pl. **allargandi** /-di/ or **allargandos**) an allargando passage.
– ORIGIN Italian, 'broadening'.

all-around ▸ **adjective** US term for ALL-ROUND.

allay /əˈleɪ/ ▸ **verb** [with obj.] diminish or put at rest (fear, suspicion, or worry): *the report attempted to educate the public and allay fears.* ■ relieve or alleviate (pain or hunger): *some stale figs partly allayed our hunger.*
– ORIGIN Old English *ālecgan* 'lay down or aside'.

All Blacks the New Zealand international rugby union team, so called because of their black strip.

all-clear ▸ **noun** a signal that danger or difficulty is over: *she was **given the all-clear** to travel home.*

all-day ▸ **adjective** lasting or available throughout the day: *an all-day excursion to Blackpool.*

Allecto variant spelling of ALECTO.

allée /ˈaleɪ/ ▸ **noun** an alley in a formal garden or park, bordered by trees or bushes.
– ORIGIN mid 18th cent.: French.

allegation ▸ **noun** a claim or assertion that someone has done something illegal or wrong, typically one made without proof: *he made allegations of corruption against the administration* | ***allegations that** the army was operating a shoot-to-kill policy.*
– ORIGIN late Middle English: from Latin *allegatio(n-)*, from *allegare* 'allege'.

allege /əˈlɛdʒ/ ▸ **verb** [reporting verb] claim or assert that someone has done something illegal or wrong, typically without proof: [with clause] ***he alleged that** he had been assaulted* | [with obj. and infinitive] *he is alleged to have assaulted five men.*
– ORIGIN Middle English (in the sense 'declare on oath'): from Old French *esligier*, based on Latin *lis, lit-* 'lawsuit'; confused in sense with Latin *allegare* 'allege'.

alleged ▸ **adjective** [attrib.] said, without proof, to have taken place or to have a specified illegal or undesirable quality: *the alleged conspirators.*

allegedly ▸ **adverb** [sentence adverb] used to convey that something is claimed to be the case or have taken place, although there is no proof: *he was allegedly a leading participant in the coup attempt* | [as submodifier] *allegedly obscene material.*

Allegheny Mountains /ˌaləˈgeɪni/ (also **the Alleghenies**) a mountain range of the Appalachian system in the eastern US.

allegiance ▸ **noun** [mass noun] loyalty or commitment to a superior or to a group or cause: *those wishing to receive citizenship must **swear allegiance to** the republic* | [count noun] *a complex pattern of cross-party allegiances.*
– ORIGIN late Middle English: from Anglo-Norman French, variant of Old French *ligeance*, from *lige, liege* (see LIEGE), perhaps by association with Anglo-Latin *alligantia* 'alliance'.

allegorical ▸ **adjective** constituting or containing allegory: *an allegorical painting.*
– DERIVATIVES **allegoric** adjective, **allegorically** adverb.

allegorize (also **allegorise**) ▸ **verb** [with obj.] interpret or represent symbolically: *the picture is interpreted as allegorizing an alienated society.*
– DERIVATIVES **allegorization** noun.

allegory ▸ **noun** (pl. **allegories**) a story, poem, or picture which can be interpreted to reveal a hidden meaning, typically a moral or political one: *Pilgrim's Progress is an allegory of the spiritual journey.* ■ a symbol.
– DERIVATIVES **allegorist** noun.
– ORIGIN late Middle English: from Old French *allegorie*, via Latin from Greek *allēgoria*, from *allos* 'other' + *-agoria* 'speaking'.

allegretto /ˌalɪˈgrɛtəʊ/ Music ▸ **adverb & adjective** (especially as a direction) at a fairly brisk speed.
▸ **noun** (pl. **allegrettos**) a movement or passage marked to be performed allegretto.
– ORIGIN Italian, diminutive of ALLEGRO.

Allegri /aˈlɛgri, -ˈleɪ-/, Gregorio (1582–1652), Italian priest and composer, noted especially for his *Miserere*, written for performance in the Sistine Chapel.

allegro /əˈlɛgrəʊ, -ˈleɪg-/ Music ▸ **adverb & adjective** (especially as a direction) at a brisk speed.
▸ **noun** (pl. **allegros**) a movement, passage, or composition marked to be performed allegro.
– ORIGIN Italian, literally 'lively, gay'.

allele /ˈaliːl/ ▸ **noun** Genetics each of two or more alternative forms of a gene that arise by mutation and are found at the same place on a chromosome. Also called ALLELOMORPH.
– DERIVATIVES **allelic** adjective.
– ORIGIN 1930s: from German *Allel*, abbreviation of ALLELOMORPH.

allelochemical /əˌliːləʊˈkɛmɪk(ə)l/ ▸ **noun** a chemical produced by a living organism that exerts a detrimental physiological effect on individuals of another species when released into the environment.
– ORIGIN 1970s: from Greek *allēl-* 'one another' + CHEMICAL.

allelomorph /əˈliːləʊmɔːf/ ▸ **noun** another term for ALLELE.
– DERIVATIVES **allelomorphic** adjective.
– ORIGIN early 20th cent.: from Greek *allēl-* 'one another' + *morphē* 'form'.

allelopathy /ˌaliːˈlɒpəθi/ ▸ **noun** [mass noun] Ecology the chemical inhibition of one plant (or other organism) by another, due to the release into the environment of substances acting as germination or growth inhibitors.
– DERIVATIVES **allelopathic** /əˌliːlə(ʊ)ˈpaθɪk/ adjective.
– ORIGIN 1950s: from Greek *allēl-* 'one another' + -PATHY.

alleluia /ˌalɪˈluːjə/ ▸ **exclamation & noun** variant spelling of HALLELUJAH.

allemande /ˈalmɑːnd/ ▸ **noun** any of a number of German dances, in particular an elaborate court dance popular in the 16th century. ■ the music for an allemande, especially as a movement of a suite. ■ a figure in country dancing in which adjacent dancers link arms or join hands and make a full or partial turn.
– ORIGIN late 17th cent.: from French, 'German (dance)'.

all-embracing ▸ **adjective** including or covering everything or everyone; comprehensive: *the all-embracing term 'folk art' appears to be increasingly inadequate.*

Allen[1], Ethan (1738–89), American soldier. He fought the British in the War of Independence and led the irregular force the Green Mountain Boys in their campaign to gain independence for the state of Vermont.

Allen[2], Woody (b.1935), American film director, writer, and actor; born *Allen Stewart Konigsberg*. Allen stars in most of his own films, many of which have won Oscars and which humorously explore themes of neurosis and sexual inadequacy. Notable works: *Play it Again, Sam* (1972) and *Annie Hall* (1977).

Allenby /ˈalənbi/, Edmund Henry Hynman, 1st Viscount (1861–1936), British soldier. Commander of the Egyptian Expeditionary Force against the Turks, he captured Jerusalem in 1917 and defeated the Turkish forces at Megiddo in 1918.

Allende /aˈjɛndeɪ/, Salvador (1908–73), Chilean statesman, President 1970–3. The first avowed Marxist to win a presidency in a free election, Allende was overthrown and killed in a military coup led by General Pinochet.

Allen key (US **Allen wrench**) ▸ **noun** Brit. trademark a spanner designed to fit into and turn an Allen screw.
– ORIGIN 1960s: from the name of the manufacturer, the *Allen* Manufacturing Company, of Hartford, Connecticut.

Allen screw ▸ **noun** trademark a screw with a hexagonal socket in the head.
– ORIGIN 1930s: from the name of the manufacturer (see ALLEN KEY).

Allenstein /ˈalənˌʃtaɪn/ German name for OLSZTYN.

allergen /ˈalədʒ(ə)n/ ▸ **noun** a substance that causes an allergic reaction.
– DERIVATIVES **allergenic** adjective, **allergenicity** noun.
– ORIGIN early 20th cent.: blend of ALLERGY and -GEN.

allergic /əˈləːdʒɪk/ ▸ **adjective** caused by or relating to an allergy: *an allergic reaction to penicillin.* ■ [predic.] having an allergy to a substance: *one and a half per cent of the population is **allergic to** bee venom.* ■ (**allergic to**) informal having a strong dislike for: *I'm allergic to the hype.*

allergist ▸ **noun** a medical practitioner specializing in the diagnosis and treatment of allergies.

allergy /ˈalədʒi/ ▸ **noun** (pl. **allergies**) a damaging immune response by the body to a substance, especially a particular food, pollen, fur, or dust, to which

it has become hypersensitive. ■ informal a strong dislike: *their allergy to free enterprise.*
– ORIGIN early 20th cent.: from German *Allergie*, from Greek *allos* 'other', on the pattern of *Energie* 'energy'.

Allerød /ˈalərəːd/ ▶ **noun** (**the Allerød**) Geology the second climatic stage of the late-glacial period in northern Europe, between the two Dryas stages (about 12,000 to 10,800 years ago). It was an interlude of warmer weather marked by the spread of birch.
– ORIGIN 1920s: place name near Copenhagen in Denmark.

alleviate /əˈliːvɪeɪt/ ▶ **verb** [with obj.] make (suffering, deficiency, or a problem) less severe: *he couldn't prevent her pain, only alleviate it | measures to alleviate unemployment.*
– DERIVATIVES **alleviation** noun, **alleviative** adjective, **alleviator** noun.
– ORIGIN late Middle English: from late Latin *alleviat-* 'lightened', from the verb *alleviare*, from Latin *allevare*, from *ad-* 'to' + *levare* 'raise', influenced by *levis* 'light'.

alley[1] ▶ **noun** (pl. **alleys**) a narrow passageway between or behind buildings. ■ a path lined with trees, bushes, or stones. ■ [with modifier] a long, narrow area in which games such as skittles and bowling are played: *a skittle alley.* ■ Tennis, N. Amer. either of the two side strips between the service court and the sidelines which count as part of the court in a doubles match. ■ Baseball the area between the outfielders in left-centre or right-centre field.
– ORIGIN late Middle English: from Old French *alee* 'walking or passage', from *aler* 'go', from Latin *ambulare* 'to walk'.

alley[2] ▶ **noun** (pl. **alleys**) variant spelling of **ALLY[2]**.

alley cat ▶ **noun** a cat that lives wild in a town.

alley-oop ▶ **exclamation** used to encourage or draw attention to the performance of an acrobatic feat.
▶ **noun** (also **alley-oop pass**) Basketball a high pass caught by a leaping teammate who tries to dunk the ball before landing.
– ORIGIN early 20th cent.: perhaps from French *allez!* 'go on!' + a supposedly French pronunciation of **UP**.

alleyway ▶ **noun** another term for **ALLEY[1]**.

All Fools' Day ▶ **noun** another term for **APRIL FOOL'S DAY**.

All Hallows ▶ **noun** another term for **ALL SAINTS' DAY**.

allheal ▶ **noun** any of a number of plants used in herbal medicine and traditionally considered to be effective in treating a variety of conditions, in particular common valerian.

alliaceous /ˌalɪˈeɪʃəs/ ▶ **adjective** Botany relating to or denoting plants of a group that comprises the onions and other alliums.
– ORIGIN late 18th cent.: from Latin *allium* 'garlic' + **-ACEOUS**; compare with the modern Latin taxonomic family name *Alliaceae*.

alliance ▶ **noun** a union or association formed for mutual benefit, especially between countries or organizations: *a defensive alliance between Australia and New Zealand | divisions within the alliance.* ■ a relationship based on similarity of interests, nature, or qualities: *an alliance between medicine and morality.* ■ [mass noun] the state of being joined or associated: *his party is **in alliance with** the Greens.* ■ Ecology a group of closely related plant associations.
– ORIGIN Middle English: from Old French *aliance*, from *alier* 'to ally' (see **ALLY[1]**).

allicin /ˈalɪsɪn/ ▶ **noun** [mass noun] Chemistry a pungent oily liquid with antibacterial properties, present in garlic. ● Chem. formula: $(C_3H_5S)_2O$.
– ORIGIN 1940s: from Latin *allium* 'garlic' + **-IN[1]**.

allied /ˈalʌɪd, əˈlʌɪd/ ▶ **adjective** joined by or relating to members of an alliance: *allied territories | the allied fleet.* ■ (usu. **Allied**) relating to Britain and her allies in the First and Second World Wars and after: *the liberation of Paris by Allied troops.* ■ (**allied to/with**) in combination or working together with: *skilled craftsmanship allied to advanced technology.* ■ connected; related: *members of the medical and allied professions.*

Allier /ˈalɪeɪ/, French /alje/ a river of central France which rises in the Cévennes and flows 410 km (258 miles) north-west to meet the Loire.

alligator ▶ **noun** a large semiaquatic reptile similar to a crocodile but with a broader and shorter head, native to the Americas and China. ● Genus *Alligator*, family Alligatoridae, order Crocodylia: the **American alligator** (*A. mississippiensis*) and the **Chinese alligator** (*A. sinensis*). ■ [mass noun] the skin of the alligator or material resembling it.
– ORIGIN late 16th cent.: from Spanish *el lagarto* 'the lizard', probably based on Latin *lacerta*.

alligator clip ▶ **noun** chiefly N. Amer. another term for **CROCODILE CLIP**.

alligator fish ▶ **noun** a small, slender bottom-dwelling fish of the NW Atlantic, with an armour of bony plates and two curved spines on the snout. ● *Aspidophoroides monopterygius*, family Agonidae.

alligator lizard ▶ **noun** a heavily built slow-moving lizard native to North America and Mexico. ● Genus *Gerrhonotus*, family Anguidae: several species.

alligator pear ▶ **noun** North American term for **AVOCADO**.

alligator snapper (also **alligator snapping turtle**) ▶ **noun** a large snapping turtle occurring in fresh water around the Gulf of Mexico. ● *Macroclemys temminckii*, family Chelydridae.

all-important ▶ **adjective** vitally important; crucial: *the town's all-important tourist industry.*

all-in ▶ **adjective** Brit. inclusive of everything: *an all-in fee.*

all-inclusive ▶ **adjective** including everything or everyone. ■ denoting or relating to a holiday in which all or most meals, drinks, and activities are included in the overall price.

all-in-one ▶ **adjective** [attrib.] combining two or more items or functions in a single unit: *an all-in-one shampoo/conditioner.*
▶ **noun** a garment that takes the place of two or more other garments.

all-in wrestling ▶ **noun** [mass noun] Brit. wrestling with few or no restrictions.

allis shad /ˈalɪs/ ▶ **noun** a European shad (fish) with a deep blue back and silvery sides. Also called **KING OF THE HERRINGS**. ● *Alosa alosa*, family Clupeidae.
– ORIGIN late 16th cent.: *allis* from Old French *alose*, from late Latin *alausa*.

alliterate /əˈlɪtəreɪt/ ▶ **verb** [no obj.] (of a phrase or line of verse) contain words which begin with the same sound or letter: *his first and last names alliterated.* ■ use words beginning with the same sound or letter.
– ORIGIN late 18th cent.: back-formation from **ALLITERATION**.

alliteration ▶ **noun** [mass noun] the occurrence of the same letter or sound at the beginning of adjacent or closely connected words.
– ORIGIN early 17th cent.: from medieval Latin *alliteratio(n-)*, from Latin *ad-* (expressing addition) + *littera* 'letter'.

alliterative /əˈlɪt(ə)rətɪv/ ▶ **adjective** relating to or marked by alliteration.
– DERIVATIVES **alliteratively** adverb.

allium /ˈalɪəm/ ▶ **noun** (pl. **alliums**) a bulbous plant of a genus that includes the onion and its relatives (e.g. garlic, leek, and chives). ● Genus *Allium*, family Liliaceae (or Alliaceae).
– ORIGIN Latin, 'garlic'.

all-night ▶ **adjective** [attrib.] lasting, open, or operating throughout the night: *an all-night party.*

all-nighter ▶ **noun** informal an event or activity that continues throughout the night.

allo- /ˈaləʊ/ ▶ **combining form** other; different: *allopatric | allotrope.*
– ORIGIN from Greek *allos* 'other'.

allocate ▶ **verb** [with obj.] distribute (resources or duties) for a particular purpose: *in past years we didn't **allocate** enough funds **to** infrastructure maintenance | [with two objs] students are allocated accommodation on a yearly basis.*
– DERIVATIVES **allocable** adjective, **allocator** noun.
– ORIGIN mid 17th cent.: from medieval Latin *allocat-* 'allotted', from the verb *allocare*, from *ad-* 'to' + *locare* (see **LOCATE**).

allocation ▶ **noun** [mass noun] the action or process of allocating or sharing out something: *more efficient allocation of resources | ticket allocation.* ■ [count noun] an amount of a resource assigned to a particular recipient.
– DERIVATIVES **allocative** adjective (chiefly Economics).
– ORIGIN late Middle English: from medieval Latin *allocatio(n-)*, from the verb *allocare* (see **ALLOCATE**).

allochthonous /əˈlɒkθənəs/ ▶ **adjective** Geology denoting a deposit or formation that originated at a distance from its present position. Often contrasted with **AUTOCHTHONOUS**.
– ORIGIN early 20th cent.: from **ALLO-** 'other' + Greek *khthōn* 'earth' + **-OUS**.

allocution /ˌaləˈkjuːʃ(ə)n/ ▶ **noun** a formal speech giving advice or a warning.
– ORIGIN early 17th cent.: from Latin *allocutio(n-)*, from *alloqui* 'speak to', from *ad-* 'to' + *loqui* 'speak'.

allodium /əˈləʊdɪəm/ (also **allod**) ▶ **noun** (pl. **allodia** /əˈləʊdɪə/) historical an estate held in absolute ownership, without acknowledgement to a superior.
– DERIVATIVES **allodial** adjective.
– ORIGIN early 17th cent.: from medieval Latin *al(l)odium*, used frequently in the Domesday Book, from a Germanic cognate of **ALL** + *ōd* 'estate'.

allogamy /əˈlɒgəmi/ ▶ **noun** [mass noun] Botany the fertilization of a flower by pollen from another flower, especially one on a different plant. Compare with **AUTOGAMY**.
– DERIVATIVES **allogamous** adjective.
– ORIGIN late 19th cent.: from **ALLO-** 'other, different' + Greek *-gamia* (from *gamos* 'marriage').

allogeneic /ˌaləʊ)dʒɪˈniːɪk, -dʒɪˈneɪɪk/ ▶ **adjective** Medicine relating to or denoting tissues or cells which are genetically dissimilar and hence immunologically incompatible, although from individuals of the same species. Compare with **XENOGENEIC**.
– ORIGIN 1960s: from **ALLO-** 'different' + Greek *genea* 'race, stock' + **-IC**.

allogenic /ˌaləˈdʒɛnɪk/ ▶ **adjective 1** Geology (of a mineral or sediment) transported to its present position from elsewhere. Often contrasted with **AUTHIGENIC**. **2** Ecology (of a successional change) caused by non-living factors in the environment.

allograft /ˈaləgrɑːft/ ▶ **noun** a tissue graft from a donor of the same species as the recipient but not genetically identical. Compare with **HOMOGRAFT**.

allograph /ˈaləgrɑːf/ ▶ **noun** Linguistics each of two or more alternative forms of a letter of an alphabet or other grapheme, for example the capital, lower case, italic, and various handwritten forms of a letter. ■ Phonetics each of two or more letters or letter combinations representing a single phoneme in different words. Allographs of the phoneme /f/ include the (f) of 'fake' and the (ph) of 'phase'.
– DERIVATIVES **allographic** adjective.
– ORIGIN 1950s: from **ALLO-** 'other, different' + **GRAPHEME**.

allometry /əˈlɒmɪtri/ ▶ **noun** [mass noun] Biology the growth of body parts at different rates, resulting in a change of body proportions. ■ the study of allometry.
– DERIVATIVES **allometric** adjective.

allomorph /ˈaləmɔːf/ ▶ **noun** Linguistics any of two or more actual representations of a morpheme, such as the plural endings /s/ (as in *bats*), /z/ (as in *bugs*), and /ɪz/ (as in *buses*).
– DERIVATIVES **allomorphic** adjective.
– ORIGIN 1940s: from **ALLO-** 'other, different' + **MORPHEME**.

allopath /ˈaləpaθ/ ▶ **noun** a person who practises allopathy.

allopathy /əˈlɒpəθi/ ▶ **noun** [mass noun] the treatment of disease by conventional means, i.e. with drugs having effects opposite to the symptoms. Often contrasted with **HOMEOPATHY**.
– DERIVATIVES **allopathic** adjective, **allopathist** noun.

allopatric /ˌaləˈpatrɪk/ ▶ **adjective** Biology (of animals or plants, especially of related species or populations) occurring in separate non-overlapping geographical areas. Compare with **SYMPATRIC**. ■ (of speciation) taking place as a result of allopatric separation.
– DERIVATIVES **allopatry** noun.
– ORIGIN 1940s: from **ALLO-** 'other' + Greek *patra* 'fatherland' + **-IC**.

allophone[1] /ˈaləfəʊn/ ▶ **noun** Phonetics any of the various phonetic realizations of a phoneme in a language, which do not contribute to distinctions of meaning. For example, in English an aspirated *p* (as in *pin*) and unaspirated *p* (as in *spin*) are allophones of /p/, whereas in ancient Greek the distinction was phonemic.
– DERIVATIVES **allophonic** adjective.
– ORIGIN 1930s: from **ALLO-** 'other, different' + **PHONEME**.

allophone[2] /ˈaləfəʊn/ ▶ **noun** Canadian (especially in Quebec) an immigrant whose first language is neither French nor English.
– ORIGIN 1970s: from **ALLO-**, on the pattern of **FRANCOPHONE**.

allopurinol /ˌaləʊ)ˈpjʊərɪnɒl/ ▶ **noun** [mass noun] Medicine a synthetic drug which inhibits uric acid formation, used to treat gout and related conditions.
– ORIGIN 1960s: from **ALLO-** 'other' + **PURINE** + **-OL**.

A

All Ordinaries index (on the Australian stock exchanges) an index based on the weighted average of selected ordinary share prices.

allosaurus /ˌaləˈsɔːrəs/ ▶ **noun** a large bipedal carnivorous dinosaur of the late Jurassic period. ● Genus *Allosaurus*, suborder Theropoda, order Saurischia.
– ORIGIN modern Latin, from Greek *allos* 'other' + *sauros* 'lizard'.

allosteric /ˌaləˈstɛrɪk, -ˈstɪərɪk/ ▶ **adjective** Biochemistry relating to or denoting the alteration of the activity of an enzyme by means of a conformational change induced by a different molecule.

allot ▶ **verb** (**allots, allotting, allotted**) [with obj.] give or apportion (something) to someone: *equal time was allotted to each* | [with two objs] *I was allotted a little room in the servant's block.*
– ORIGIN late 15th cent.: from Old French *aloter*, from *a-* (from Latin *ad* 'to') + *loter* 'divide into lots'.

allotment ▶ **noun 1** Brit. a plot of land rented by an individual for growing vegetables or flowers. ■ US, chiefly historical a piece of land made over by the government to an American Indian.
2 [mass noun] the action of allotting something. ■ [count noun] an amount allotted to a person.

allotrope /ˈalətrəʊp/ ▶ **noun** Chemistry each of two or more different physical forms in which an element can exist. Graphite, charcoal, and diamond are all allotropes of carbon.
– ORIGIN late 19th cent.: back-formation from ALLOTROPY.

allotropy /əˈlɒtrəpi/ ▶ **noun** [mass noun] Chemistry the existence of two or more different physical forms of a chemical element.
– DERIVATIVES **allotropic** adjective.
– ORIGIN mid 19th cent.: from Greek *allotropos* 'of another form', from *allo-* 'other' + *tropos* 'manner' (from *trepein* 'to turn').

allottee ▶ **noun** a person to whom something is allotted, especially land or shares.

all-over ▶ **adjective** [attrib.] covering the whole of something: *she returned with an all-over tan.*

allow ▶ **verb** [with obj.] **1** let (someone) have or do something: [with obj. and infinitive] *the dissident was allowed to leave the country* | [with two objs] *she was allowed a higher profile.* ■ [with obj. and adverbial of direction] let (someone) enter a place or go in a particular direction: *the river was patrolled and few people were allowed across.* ■ declare or decide that (an event or activity) is legal or acceptable: *political advertising on television is not allowed.*
2 give the necessary time or opportunity for: *they agreed to a ceasefire to allow talks with the government* | [with obj. and infinitive] *he stopped to allow his eyes to adjust.* ■ [no obj.] (**allow for**) make provision or provide scope for: *the house was demolished to allow for road widening.* ■ [no obj.] (**allow for**) take (something) into consideration when making plans or calculations: *income rose by 11 per cent allowing for inflation.* ■ provide or set aside for a particular purpose: *allow an hour or so for driving.*
3 [reporting verb] admit the truth of; concede: [with clause] *he allowed that the penalty appeared too harsh for the crime* | [with direct speech] *'Could happen,' she allowed indifferently.* ■ [with clause] N. Amer. informal or dialect be of the opinion; assert: *Lincoln allowed that he himself could never support the man.*
– PHRASES **allow me** said when making a polite request or offering help: *please allow me to introduce myself* | *"Here, allow me," came a woman's voice from behind him.*
– DERIVATIVES **allowedly** adverb.
– ORIGIN Middle English (originally in the senses 'commend, sanction' and 'assign as a right'): from Old French *alouer*, from Latin *allaudare* 'to praise', reinforced by medieval Latin *allocare* 'to place' (see ALLOCATE).

allowable ▶ **adjective 1** allowed, especially within a set of regulations; permissible: *the loan deal has been extended to the maximum allowable three months.*
2 Brit. (of an amount of money) able to be earned or received free of tax: *tax is payable after deduction of allowable expenses.*
– DERIVATIVES **allowably** adverb.

allowance ▶ **noun 1** the amount of something that is permitted, especially within a set of regulations or for a specified purpose: *your baggage allowance.* ■ Brit. an amount of money that can be earned or received free of tax: *a personal allowance.* ■ Horse Racing a deduction in the weight that a horse is required to carry in a race.
2 a sum of money paid regularly to a person to meet needs or expenses: *the elderly receive a heating allowance every winter.* ■ chiefly N. Amer. a small amount of money given regularly to a child by its parents.
3 [mass noun] archaic tolerance: *the allowance of slavery in the South.*
▶ **verb** [with obj.] archaic give (someone) a sum of money as an allowance.
– PHRASES **make allowance(s) for 1** take into consideration when planning something. **2** treat leniently on account of mitigating circumstances.
– ORIGIN late Middle English: from Old French *alouance*, from *alouer* (see ALLOW).

alloxan /əˈlɒks(ə)n/ ▶ **noun** [mass noun] Chemistry an acidic compound obtained by the oxidation of uric acid and isolated as an efflorescent crystalline hydrate.
● Chem. formula: $C_4H_2N_2O_4$.
– ORIGIN mid 19th cent.: from *all(antoin)* + *ox(alic)* + -AN.

alloy ▶ **noun** /ˈalɔɪ/ a metal made by combining two or more metallic elements, especially to give greater strength or resistance to corrosion: *an alloy of nickel, bronze, and zinc* | [as modifier] *alloy wheels.* ■ an inferior metal mixed with a precious one.
▶ **verb** /əˈlɔɪ/ [with obj.] mix (metals) to make an alloy: *alloying tin with copper to make bronze.*
– ORIGIN late 16th cent.: from Old French *aloi* (noun) and French *aloyer* (verb), both from Old French *aloier, aleier* 'combine', from Latin *alligare* 'bind'. In early use the term denoted the comparative purity of gold or silver; the sense 'mixture of metals' arose in the mid 17th cent.

all-party ▶ **adjective** [attrib.] Brit. involving all political parties: *the measure received all-party support.*

all-pervasive (also **all-pervading**) ▶ **adjective** occurring or having an effect through or into every part of something: *the all-pervasive excitement.*

all-points bulletin (abbrev.: **APB**) ▶ **noun** (in the US) a radio message sent to every officer in a police force giving details of a suspected criminal or stolen vehicle.

all-powerful ▶ **adjective** having complete power: *an all-powerful dictator.*

all-purpose ▶ **adjective** having a great many uses: *an all-purpose kitchen knife.*

all right ▶ **adjective** [predic.] of a satisfactory or acceptable quality: *the tea was all right.* ■ in a satisfactory mental or physical state: *do you feel all right to walk home?* ■ permissible; allowable: *it's all right for you to go now.*
▶ **adverb 1** in a satisfactory manner or to a satisfactory extent; fairly well: *we get on all right.*
2 used to emphasize how certain one is about something: *'Are you sure it's him?' 'It's him all right.'*
▶ **exclamation** expressing or asking for assent, agreement, or acceptance: *all right, I'll tell you.*
– PHRASES **it's all right for——** used to suggest that someone is luckier than you: *it was all right for them! They didn't have to put up with the brat trailing after them* | *"It's all right for some," Grandad huffed.* **it'll be all right on the night** used to say that a performance or event will be successful even if the preparations have not gone well: *the organizers assure everyone that it will all be all right on the night.*

all-round ▶ **adjective** [attrib.] Brit. **1** having a great many abilities or uses; versatile: *an all-round artist.* ■ in many or all respects: *his all-round excellence.*
2 on or from every side or in every direction: *the car's large glass area provides excellent all-round vision.*

all-rounder ▶ **noun** Brit. a versatile person or thing, especially a cricketer who can both bat and bowl well.

All Saints' Day ▶ **noun** a Christian festival in honour of all the saints in heaven, held (in the Western Church) on 1 November.

all-seater ▶ **adjective** Brit. (of a sports stadium) having a seat for every spectator and no standing places.

allseed ▶ **noun** any of a number of plants producing a large number of seeds for their size. ● Species in several families, in particular the small *Radiola linoides* (family Linaceae) of Europe.

All Souls' Day ▶ **noun** a Catholic commemoration with prayers for the souls of the dead, held on 2 November.

allspice ▶ **noun 1** [mass noun] the dried aromatic fruit of a Caribbean tree, used whole or ground as a culinary spice and in the production of certain liqueurs such as Benedictine.
2 a tree of the myrtle family from which allspice is obtained. Also called PIMENTO or JAMAICA PEPPER.
● *Pimenta dioica*, family Myrtaceae.
3 an aromatic North American tree or shrub. ● Genus *Calycanthus*, family Calycanthaceae.

all-star ▶ **adjective** [attrib.] composed wholly of outstanding performers or players: *an all-star cast.*
▶ **noun** N. Amer. a member of an all-star group or team.

Allston /ˈɔːlst(ə)n/, Washington (1779–1843), American landscape painter, the first major artist of the American romantic movement.

all-terrain vehicle ▶ **noun** a small open motor vehicle with one seat and three or more wheels fitted with large tyres, designed for use on rough ground.

all-ticket ▶ **adjective** denoting an event, especially a sports match, for which spectators must buy tickets in advance.

all-time ▶ **adjective** [attrib.] unsurpassed: *her all-time favourite* | *interest rates hit an all-time high.*

allude ▶ **verb** [no obj.] (**allude to**) suggest or call attention to indirectly; hint at: *she had a way of alluding to Jean but never saying her name.* ■ mention without discussing at length: *we will allude briefly to the main points.* ■ (of an artist or a work of art) recall (an earlier work or style) in such a way as to suggest a relationship with it.
– ORIGIN late 15th cent. (in the sense 'hint at, suggest'): from Latin *allus-*, *alludere*, from *ad-* 'towards' + *ludere* 'to play'.

all-up weight ▶ **noun** chiefly Brit. the total weight of an aircraft with passengers, cargo, and fuel.

allure ▶ **noun** [mass noun] the quality of being powerfully and mysteriously attractive or fascinating: *people for whom gold holds no allure.*
▶ **verb** [with obj.] powerfully attract or charm; tempt: *will sponsors really be allured by such opportunities?*
– DERIVATIVES **allurement** noun.
– ORIGIN late Middle English (in the sense 'tempt, entice'): from Old French *aleurier* 'attract', from *a-* (from Latin *ad* 'to') + *luere* 'a lure' (originally a falconry term).

alluring ▶ **adjective** powerfully and mysteriously attractive or fascinating; seductive: *the town offers alluring shops and restaurants.*
– DERIVATIVES **alluringly** adverb.

allus /ˈɔːləz, ˈaləz/ ▶ **adverb** non-standard spelling of ALWAYS.
– ORIGIN mid 19th cent.: representing a regional pronunciation.

allusion ▶ **noun** an expression designed to call something to mind without mentioning it explicitly; an indirect or passing reference: *an allusion to Shakespeare* | *a classical allusion.* ■ [mass noun] the practice of making allusions.
– ORIGIN mid 16th cent. (denoting a pun, metaphor, or parable): from French, or from late Latin *allusio(n-)*, from the verb *alludere* (see ALLUDE).

allusive ▶ **adjective** using or containing suggestion rather than explicit mention: *allusive references to the body* | *a highly allusive poet.*
– DERIVATIVES **allusively** adverb, **allusiveness** noun.

alluvial /əˈl(j)uːvɪəl/ ▶ **adjective** relating to or derived from alluvium: *rich alluvial soils.*

alluvion /əˈl(j)uːvɪən/ ▶ **noun** [mass noun] chiefly Law the action of the sea or a river in adding to the area of land by deposition. Compare with AVULSION.
– ORIGIN mid 16th cent. (originally denoting a flood, especially one carrying suspended material which is then deposited): from French, from Latin *alluvio(n-)*, from *ad-* 'towards' + *luere* 'to wash'.

alluvium /əˈl(j)uːvɪəm/ ▶ **noun** [mass noun] a deposit of clay, silt, and sand left by flowing floodwater in a river valley or delta, typically producing fertile soil.
– ORIGIN mid 17th cent.: Latin, neuter of *alluvius* 'washed against', from *ad-* 'towards' + *luere* 'to wash'.

all-weather ▶ **adjective** in or suitable for all types of weather: *an all-weather soccer pitch.*

all-wheel drive ▶ **noun** North American term for FOUR-WHEEL DRIVE.

ally[1] /ˈalʌɪ/ ▶ **noun** (pl. **allies**) a state formally cooperating with another for a military or other purpose. ■ a person or organization that cooperates with or helps another in a particular activity: *he was forced to dismiss his closest political ally.* ■ (**the Allies**) the countries that fought with Britain in the First and Second World Wars.
▶ **verb** also /əˈlʌɪ/ (**allies, allying, allied**) [with obj.] (**ally something to/with**) combine or unite a resource or commodity with (another) for mutual benefit: *he*

allied his racing experience with his father's business acumen. ■ (**ally oneself with**) side with or support: *he allied himself with the forces of change.*
– ORIGIN Middle English (as a verb): from Old French *alier*, from Latin *alligare* 'bind together', from *ad-* 'to' + *ligare* 'to bind'; the noun is partly via Old French *alie* 'allied'. Compare with ALLOY.

ally[2] /ˈali/ (also **alley**) ▸ noun (pl. **allies**) a toy marble made of marble, alabaster, or glass.
– ORIGIN early 18th cent.: perhaps a diminutive of ALABASTER.

-ally ▸ suffix forming adverbs from adjectives ending in *-al* (such as *radically* from *radical*). Compare with -AL, -LY[2], -ICALLY.

allyl /ˈalʌɪl, -lɪl/ ▸ noun [as modifier] Chemistry of or denoting the unsaturated hydrocarbon radical $-CH_2CH{=}CH_2$: *allyl alcohol.*
– DERIVATIVES **allylic** adjective.
– ORIGIN mid 19th cent.: from Latin *allium* 'garlic' + -YL.

Alma-Ata /ˌalmə əˈtɑː/ variant spelling of ALMATY.

al-Madinah /ˌalmaˈdiːnə/ Arabic name for MEDINA.

Almagest /ˈalmədʒɛst/ ▸ noun (**the Almagest**) an Arabic version of Ptolemy's astronomical treatise. ■ (in the Middle Ages) any celebrated textbook on astrology and alchemy.
– ORIGIN late Middle English: from Old French *almageste*, based on Arabic, from *al* 'the' + Greek *megistē* 'greatest (composition)'.

alma mater /ˌalmə ˈmɑːtə, ˈmeɪt-/ ▸ noun (**one's Alma Mater**) the university, school, or college that one formerly attended.
– ORIGIN mid 17th cent. (in the general sense 'someone or something providing nourishment'): Latin, literally 'generous mother'.

almanac /ˈɔːlmənak, ˈɒl-/ (also, especially in titles, **almanack**) ▸ noun an annual calendar containing important dates and statistical information such as astronomical data and tide tables. ■ a handbook, typically published annually, containing information of general interest or on a sport or pastime.
– ORIGIN late Middle English: via medieval Latin from Greek *almenikhiaka*, of unknown origin.

Almanach de Gotha /ˌɔːlmənak də ˈɡəʊtə, ˌɒl-/ an annual publication giving information about European royalty, nobility, and diplomats, published in Gotha 1763–1944 and revived in 1968.

almandine /ˈalməndiːn, -dʌɪn/ ▸ noun [mass noun] a kind of garnet with a violet tint.
– ORIGIN late Middle English: from obsolete French, alteration of *alabandine*, from medieval Latin *alabandina (gemma)*, 'jewel from *Alabanda*', an ancient city in Asia Minor where these stones were cut.

Alma-Tadema /ˌalməˈtadəmə/, Sir Lawrence (1836–1912), Dutch-born British painter. He is best known for lush genre scenes set in the ancient world.

Almaty /ˈalmɑːti/ (also **Alma-Ata**) the former capital of the central Asian republic of Kazakhstan; pop. 1,247,900 (est. 2006). Former name (until 1921) VERNY.

Almería /ˌalməˈrɪə/ a town in a province of the same name in Andalusia, Spain; pop. 187,521 (2008).

almighty ▸ adjective having complete power; omnipotent: *I swear by almighty God.* ■ informal very great; enormous: *the silence was broken by an almighty roar.*
▸ noun (**the Almighty**) a name or title for God.
– ORIGIN Old English *ælmihtig* (see ALL, MIGHTY).

almirah /alˈmʌɪrə/ ▸ noun Indian a free-standing cupboard or wardrobe.
– ORIGIN from Hindi *almārī*, via Portuguese from Latin *armarium* 'closet, chest'.

Almirante Brown /ˌalmɪˈranti/ a city in eastern Argentina, forming part of the conurbation of Buenos Aires; pop. 568,500 (est. 2008).

Almohad /ˈalməhad/ (also **Almohade** /-heɪd/) ▸ noun (pl. **Almohads**) a member of a Berber Muslim movement and dynasty that conquered the Spanish and North African empire of the Almoravids in the 12th century.
– ORIGIN Spanish, ultimately from Arabic *al-muwaḥḥidun* 'believers in one God'.

almond ▸ noun **1** the oval edible nut-like seed (kernel) of the almond tree, growing in a woody shell.
2 (also **almond tree**) the tree that produces almonds, related to the peach and plum. Native to western Asia, it is widely cultivated in warm climates. ● *Prunus dulcis*, family Rosaceae.
– ORIGIN Middle English: from Old French *alemande*, from medieval Latin *amandula*, from Greek *amugdalē*.

almond eyes ▸ plural noun eyes that are narrow and oval with pointed ends.

almond oil ▸ noun [mass noun] oil expressed from bitter almonds, used for cosmetic preparations, flavouring, and medicinal purposes.

almond paste ▸ noun [mass noun] marzipan.

almoner /ˈɑːmənə, ˈalm-/ ▸ noun historical an official distributor of alms.
– ORIGIN Middle English: from Old French *aumonier*, based on medieval Latin *eleemosynarius*, from *eleemosyna* 'alms' (see ALMS).

almonry /ˈɑːmənri, ˈalm-/ ▸ noun (pl. **almonries**) a building or place where alms were formerly distributed.
– ORIGIN late Middle English: from Old French *au(l)mosnerie*, from medieval Latin *eleemosynarius* (see ALMONER).

Almoravid /alˈmɔːrəvɪd/ (also **Almoravide** /-vʌɪd/) ▸ noun (pl. **Almoravids**) a member of a federation of Muslim Berber peoples that established an empire in Morocco, Algeria, and Spain in the 11th century, but were in turn driven out by the Almohads.
– ORIGIN Spanish, from Arabic *al-murābit*, literally 'one who is bound'.

almost ▸ adverb not quite; very nearly: *he almost knocked Georgina over* | *the place was almost empty* | *blues, jazz—he can play almost anything.*
– ORIGIN Old English *æl mæst* 'for the most part' (see ALL, MOST).

alms /ɑːmz/ ▸ plural noun (in historical contexts) money or food given to poor people.
– ORIGIN Old English *ælmysse, ælmesse*, from Christian Latin *eleemosyna*, from Greek *eleēmosunē* 'compassion', from *eleēmōn* 'compassionate', from *eleos* 'mercy'.

almshouse ▸ noun a house founded by charity, offering accommodation for poor people.

almucantar /ˌalməˈkantə/ ▸ noun **1** Astronomy a circle on the celestial sphere parallel to the horizon; a parallel of altitude.
2 a telescope mounted on a float resting on mercury, used to determine stellar altitude and azimuth.
– ORIGIN Middle English: from medieval Latin *almucantarath* or obsolete French *almucantara*, from Arabic *al-muqanṭarāt* 'lines of celestial latitude', based on *al* 'the' + *qanṭara* 'arch'.

al-Nakba /alˈnakbə/ ▸ noun the Palestinian term for the events of 1948, when many Palestinians were displaced by the creation of the new state of Israel.
– ORIGIN Arabic, literally 'the disaster'.

aloe /ˈaləʊ/ ▸ noun **1** a succulent plant with a rosette of thick tapering leaves and bell-shaped or tubular flowers on long stems, native to the Old World. ● Genus *Aloe*, family Liliaceae (or Aloaceae).
■ (**aloes** or **bitter aloes**) [mass noun] a strong laxative obtained from the bitter juice of various kinds of aloe. ■ (also **American aloe**) another term for CENTURY PLANT.
2 (also **aloes wood**) [mass noun] the fragrant heartwood of a tropical Asian tree. ● The tree belongs to the genus *Aquilaria*, family Thymelaeaceae, in particular *A. agallocha*.
■ the resin obtained from aloes wood, used in perfume, incense, and medicine.
– ORIGIN Old English *alewe, alwe* (denoting the fragrant resin or heartwood of certain oriental trees), via Latin from Greek *aloē*; reinforced in late Middle English by Old French *aloes* 'aloe', hence frequently used in the plural.

aloe vera /ˈvɪərə/ ▸ noun **1** [mass noun] a gelatinous substance obtained from a kind of aloe, used especially in cosmetics as an emollient.
2 the plant that yields aloe vera, grown chiefly in the Caribbean area and the southern US. ● *Aloe vera*, family Liliaceae (or Aloaceae).
– ORIGIN early 20th cent.: modern Latin, literally 'true aloe', probably in contrast to the American agave, which closely resembles aloe vera: both plants were formerly classified together in the lily family.

aloft ▸ adjective & adverb up in or into the air; overhead: [as predic. adj.] *the congregation sways, hands aloft* | [as adv.] *she held her glass aloft.* ■ up the mast or into the rigging of a ship.
– ORIGIN Middle English: from Old Norse *á lopt, á lopti*, from *á* 'in, on, to' + *lopt* 'air'.

alogical ▸ adjective opposed to or lacking in logic.

aloha /əˈləʊhə/ ▸ exclamation & noun a Hawaiian word used when greeting or parting from someone.
– ORIGIN early 19th cent.: from Maori *aroha* 'love, affection, pity'.

aloha shirt ▸ noun a loose, brightly patterned Hawaiian shirt.

Aloha State informal name for HAWAII.

alone ▸ adjective & adverb **1** having no one else present; on one's own: [as predic. adj.] *she was alone that evening* | [as adv.] *he lives alone.* ■ without others' help or participation; single-handed: [as adv.] *team members are more effective than individuals working alone* | [as predic. adj.] *they were not alone in dissenting from the advice.* ■ [as adj.] isolated and lonely: *she was terribly alone and exposed.*
2 [as adv.] indicating that something is confined to the specified subject or recipient: *he is answerable to Parliament alone* | *it was a smile for him alone.* ■ used to emphasize that only one factor out of several is being considered and that the whole is greater or more extreme: *there were fifteen churches in the town centre alone.*
– PHRASES **go it alone** informal act by oneself without assistance. **leave** (or **let**) **someone/thing alone** **1** abandon or desert someone or something. **2** stop disturbing or interfering with someone or something.
– DERIVATIVES **aloneness** noun.
– ORIGIN Middle English: from ALL + ONE.

along ▸ preposition & adverb **1** moving in a constant direction on (a more or less horizontal surface): [as prep.] *soon we were driving along a narrow road* | *he saw Gray run along the top of the wall* | [as adv.] *we continued to plod along.* ■ used to refer to the passage of time or the making of progress: [as prep.] *you'll pick up some valuable tips along the way* | [as adv.] *they asked how the construction was coming along.*
2 [prep.] extending in a more or less horizontal line on: *cars were parked along the grass verge* | *the path along the cliff.*
3 [adverb] in or into company with others: *he had brought along a friend of his.*
– PHRASES **along with** in company with or at the same time as: *I was chosen, along with twelve other artists.* **be** (or **come**) **along** arrive: *she'll be along soon.*
– ORIGIN Old English *andlang*, of West Germanic origin; related to LONG[1].

alongshore ▸ adverb along or by the shore: *currents flowing alongshore.*

alongside ▸ preposition (N. Amer. also **alongside of**) close to the side of; next to: *she was sitting alongside him* | [as adv.] *the boat came alongside.* ■ together and in cooperation with: *a care assistant was working alongside him.* ■ at the same time as or in coexistence with: *they aim to encourage coverage of disabled sport alongside able-bodied achievement.*

aloo /ˈɑːluː, ˈaluː/ (also **alu**) ▸ noun [mass noun] Indian potato: *aloo jeera.*
– ORIGIN from Hindi, Urdu, and Sanskrit *ālū*.

aloof ▸ adjective not friendly or forthcoming; cool and distant: *they were courteous but faintly aloof* | *an aloof and somewhat austere figure.* ■ conspicuously uninvolved: *he stayed aloof from the bickering.*
– DERIVATIVES **aloofly** adverb, **aloofness** noun.
– ORIGIN mid 16th cent.: from A-[2] (expressing direction) + LUFF. The term was originally an adverb in nautical use, meaning 'away and to windward!', i.e. with the ship's head kept close to the wind away from a lee shore etc. towards which it might drift. From this arose the sense 'at a distance'.

alopecia /ˌaləˈpiːʃə/ ▸ noun [mass noun] Medicine the partial or complete absence of hair from areas of the body where it normally grows; baldness.
– ORIGIN late Middle English: via Latin from Greek *alōpekia*, literally 'fox mange', from *alōpēx* 'fox'.

Alor Setar /ˌɑːlɔː səˈtɑː/ the capital of the state of Kedah in Malaysia, near the west coast of the central Malay Peninsula; pop. 223,200 (est. 2009).

aloud ▸ adverb **1** audibly; not silently or in a whisper: *he read the letter aloud.*
2 archaic loudly: *he wept aloud.*
– ORIGIN Middle English: from A-[2] (expressing manner) + LOUD.

alow /əˈləʊ/ ▸ adverb archaic or dialect below; downwards. ■ Nautical, archaic on or near the deck of a ship.
– ORIGIN late Middle English: from A-[2] 'on' + LOW[1].

ALP ▸ abbreviation Australian Labor Party.

A

alp ▶ **noun** a high mountain, especially a snow-capped one. ■ (in Switzerland) an area of green pasture on a mountainside.
– ORIGIN late Middle English: singular of **Alps**.

alpaca /alˈpakə/ ▶ **noun** (pl. **same** or **alpacas**) a long-haired domesticated South American mammal related to the llama, valued for its wool. ● *Lama pacos*, family Camelidae, probably descended from the wild guanaco. ■ [mass noun] the wool of the alpaca. ■ [mass noun] fabric made from alpaca wool: [as modifier] *an alpaca jersey*.
– ORIGIN late 18th cent.: from Spanish, from Aymara *allpaca*.

alpargata /ˌalpɑːˈɡɑːtə/ ▶ **noun** a light canvas shoe with a plaited fibre sole; an espadrille.
– ORIGIN early 19th cent.: from Spanish.

alpenglow /ˈalpənɡləʊ/ ▶ **noun** [mass noun] the rosy light of the setting or rising sun seen on high mountains.
– ORIGIN late 19th cent.: a partial translation of German *Alpenglühen*, literally 'Alp glow'.

alpenhorn /ˈalpənhɔːn/ (also **alphorn**) ▶ **noun** a very long valveless wooden wind instrument played like a horn and used for signalling in the Alps.
– ORIGIN late 19th cent.: from German, literally 'Alp horn'.

alpenstock /ˈalpənstɒk/ ▶ **noun** an iron-tipped stick used by hillwalkers and formerly by mountaineers.
– ORIGIN early 19th cent.: from German, literally 'Alp stick'.

alpha /ˈalfə/ ▶ **noun 1** the first letter of the Greek alphabet (Α, α), transliterated as 'a'. ■ [as modifier] denoting the first of a series of items or categories, e.g. forms of a chemical compound: *the α and β chains of haemoglobin*. ■ Brit. a first-class mark given for an examination paper or piece of school or college work: *he had been awarded alpha double plus*. ■ [as modifier] denoting the dominant animal or person in a particular group: *Turner soon proved to be the alpha male*. ■ short for **alpha test**. ■ (**Alpha**) [followed by Latin genitive] Astronomy the first (typically the brightest) star in a constellation: *Alpha Orionis*. ■ [as modifier] relating to alpha decay or alpha particles: *an alpha emitter*.
2 a code word representing the letter A, used in radio communication.
▶ **symbol** ■ (α) a plane angle. ■ (α) angular acceleration. ■ (α) Astronomy right ascension.
– PHRASES **alpha and omega** ■ the beginning and the end (used by Christians as a title for Jesus). ■ the essence or most important features.
– ORIGIN via Latin from Greek.

alphabet ▶ **noun** a set of letters or symbols in a fixed order used to represent the basic set of speech sounds of a language, especially the set of letters from A to Z. ■ the basic elements in a system which combine to form complex entities: *DNA's 4-letter alphabet*.

> The origin of the alphabet goes back to the Phoenician system of the 2nd millennium BC, from which the modern Hebrew and Arabic systems are ultimately derived. The Greek alphabet, which emerged in 1000–900 BC, developed two branches, Cyrillic (which became the script of Russian) and Etruscan (from which derives the Roman alphabet used in the West).

– ORIGIN early 16th cent.: from late Latin *alphabetum*, from Greek *alpha*, *bēta*, the first two letters of the Greek alphabet.

alphabetical ▶ **adjective** relating to an alphabet: *alphabetical characters*. ■ in the order of the letters of the alphabet: *an alphabetical index | in alphabetical order*.
– DERIVATIVES **alphabetic** adjective, **alphabetically** adverb.

alphabetize /ˈalfəbətʌɪz/ (also **alphabetise**) ▶ **verb** [with obj.] arrange in alphabetical order: *the listings are arranged by state and alphabetized by city*.
– DERIVATIVES **alphabetization** noun.

alphabet soup ▶ **noun** [mass noun] informal a confusing or confused mixture of things: *the alphabet soup of European security institutions*.
– ORIGIN early 20th cent.: alluding to a kind of clear soup containing pasta in the shapes of letters.

alpha blocker ▶ **noun** Medicine any of a class of drugs which prevent the stimulation of the adrenergic receptors responsible for increased blood pressure.

Alpha Centauri /ˌalfə sɛnˈtɔːrʌɪ/ Astronomy the third-brightest star in the sky, in the constellation Centaurus, visible only to observers in the southern hemisphere. It is the nearest bright star to the solar system (distance 4.34 light years), and is a visual binary. Also called **Rigil Kentaurus**.

alphafetoprotein /ˌalfəˌfiːtəʊˈprəʊtiːn/ ▶ **noun** [mass noun] Medicine a protein produced by a fetus which is present in amniotic fluid and the bloodstream of the mother. Levels of the protein can be measured to detect certain congenital defects such as spina bifida and Down's syndrome.

alpha-hydroxy acid ▶ **noun** Chemistry an organic acid containing a hydroxyl group bonded to the carbon atom adjacent to the carboxylic acid group. A number of such compounds are used in skincare preparations for their exfoliating properties.

alphanumeric ▶ **adjective** consisting of or using both letters and numerals: *alphanumeric data*.
▶ **noun** a character that is either a letter or a number.
– DERIVATIVES **alphanumerical** adjective.

alpha particle ▶ **noun** Physics a helium nucleus emitted by some radioactive substances, originally regarded as a ray.

alpha radiation ▶ **noun** [mass noun] ionizing radiation consisting of alpha particles, emitted by some substances undergoing radioactive decay.

alpha rhythm ▶ **noun** [mass noun] Physiology the normal electrical activity of the brain when conscious and relaxed, consisting of oscillations (**alpha waves**) with a frequency of 8 to 13 hertz.

alpha test ▶ **noun** a trial of machinery, software, or other products carried out by a developer before a product is made available for beta testing.
▶ **verb** (**alpha-test**) [with obj.] subject (a product) to an alpha test.

alphorn /ˈalphɔːn/ ▶ **noun** another term for **alpenhorn**.

alpine ▶ **adjective** relating to high mountains: *alpine and subalpine habitats*. ■ (**Alpine**) relating to the Alps: *Alpine guides*. ■ Skiing relating to or denoting skiing downhill: *an alpine ski team*. Often contrasted with **Nordic**.
▶ **noun 1** a plant native to mountain districts, often suitable for growing in rock gardens.
2 a North American butterfly which has brownish-black wings with orange-red markings. ● Genus *Erebia*, subfamily Satyrinae, family Nymphalidae.
– ORIGIN late Middle English: from Latin *Alpinus*, from *Alpes* 'Alps' (see **alp**).

alpinist ▶ **noun** a climber of high mountains, especially in the Alps.

alprazolam /alˈpreɪzə(ʊ)lam/ ▶ **noun** [mass noun] Medicine a drug of the benzodiazepine group, used in the treatment of anxiety.
– ORIGIN 1970s: from *al-* of unknown origin + *p(henyl)* + *(t)r(i)azol(e)* + *(-azep)am*.

Alps a mountain system in Europe extending in a curve from the coast of SE France through NW Italy, Switzerland, Liechtenstein, southern Germany, and Austria into Slovenia. The highest peak of the Alps, Mont Blanc, rises to a height of 4,807 m (15,771 ft).
– ORIGIN late Middle English: via French from Latin *Alpes*, from Greek *Alpeis*, of unknown origin.

al-Qaeda /alˈkʌɪdə, ˌalkɑːˈiːdə/ (also **al-Qaida**) a militant Islamic fundamentalist group.
– ORIGIN Arabic *al-qā'ida*, literally 'the base'.

al-Qahira /alˈkɑːhiːrɑː/ (also **el-Qahira**) Arabic name for **Cairo**.

already ▶ **adverb 1** before or by now or the time in question: *Anna has suffered a great deal already*. ■ as surprisingly soon or early as this: *it was already past four o' clock*.
2 N. Amer. informal used after a word or phrase to express impatience: *enough already with these crazy kids and their wacky dances!*
– ORIGIN Middle English: from **all** (as an adverb) + **ready**; sense 2 is influenced by Yiddish use.

alright ▶ **adjective, adverb, & exclamation** variant spelling of **all right**.

> **USAGE** The merging of **all** and **right** to form the one-word spelling **alright** is not recorded until the end of the 19th century (unlike other similar merged spellings such as **altogether** and **already**, which date from much earlier). There is no logical reason for insisting on **all right** as two words, when other single-word forms such as **altogether** have long been accepted. Nevertheless it is still considered by many people to be unacceptable in formal writing.

Alsace /alˈsas/, French /alzas/ a region of NE France, on the borders with Germany and Switzerland. Alsace was annexed by Prussia, along with part of Lorraine (forming **Alsace-Lorraine**), after the Franco-Prussian War of 1870–1, and restored to France after the First World War.

Alsatian ▶ **noun 1** Brit. a large dog of a breed typically used as guard dogs or for police work. Also called **German shepherd**.
2 a native or inhabitant of Alsace.
▶ **adjective** relating to Alsace or its inhabitants.
– ORIGIN from medieval Latin *Alsatia* 'Alsace' + **-an**.

alsike /ˈalsɪk/ (also **alsike clover**) ▶ **noun** a tall clover which is widely grown for fodder, native to Europe and naturalized in North America. ● *Trifolium hybridum*, family Leguminosae.
– ORIGIN mid 19th cent.: named after *Alsike* in Sweden; Linnaeus mentions the plant growing there.

also ▶ **adverb** in addition; too: *a brilliant linguist, he was also interested in botany | dyslexia, also known as word blindness* | [sentence adverb] *also, a car's very expensive to run*.
– ORIGIN Old English *alswā* 'quite so, in that manner, similarly' (see **all**, **so**[1]).

also-ran ▶ **noun** (pl. **also-rans**) a loser in a race or other contest, especially by a large margin. ■ informal an undistinguished or unsuccessful person or thing.
– ORIGIN late 19th cent.: originally applied to racehorses that did not finish in the first three.

alstroemeria /ˌalstrəˈmɪərɪə/ ▶ **noun** a South American plant with showy lily-like flowers, cultivated as an ornamental. ● Genus *Alstroemeria*, family Liliaceae: several species.
– ORIGIN late 18th cent.: modern Latin, named after Klas von *Alstroemer* (1736–96), Swedish naturalist.

alt. (also **alt-**) ▶ **combining form** denoting a version of something, especially popular music, that is regarded as outside the mainstream of its genre: *alt.country*.
– ORIGIN 1990s: abbreviation of **alternative**, influenced by the *alt.* prefix of some Internet newsgroups.

Alta ▶ **abbreviation** Alberta.

Altai /ˈaltʌɪ/ (also **Altay**) a krai (administrative territory) of Russia in SW Siberia, on the border with Kazakhstan; capital, Barnaul.

Altaic /alˈteɪɪk/ ▶ **adjective 1** relating to the Altai Mountains.
2 denoting or belonging to a phylum or superfamily of languages which includes the Turkic, Mongolian, Tungusic, and Manchu languages. They are characterized by agglutination and vowel harmony.
▶ **noun** [mass noun] the Altaic family of languages.

Altai Mountains a mountain system of central Asia extending about 1,600 km (1,000 miles) eastwards from Kazakhstan into western Mongolia and northern China.

Altair /ˈaltɛː/ Astronomy the brightest star in the constellation Aquila.
– ORIGIN Arabic, literally 'flying eagle'.

Altamira /ˌaltəˈmɪərə/ the site of a cave with Palaeolithic rock paintings, south of Santander in northern Spain, discovered in 1879.

altar /ˈɔːltə, ˈɒl-/ ▶ **noun** the table in a Christian church at which the bread and wine are consecrated in communion services. ■ a table or flat-topped block used as the focus for a religious ritual, especially for making sacrifices or offerings to a deity.
– PHRASES **lead someone to the altar** marry a woman. **sacrifice someone/thing on/at the altar of** make someone or something suffer in the interests of: *no businessman is going to sacrifice his company on the altar of such altruism*.
– ORIGIN Old English *altar*, *alter*, based on late Latin *altar*, *altarium*, from Latin *altus* 'high'.

altar boy ▶ **noun** a boy who acts as a priest's assistant during a service, especially in the Roman Catholic Church.

altarpiece ▶ **noun** a painting or other work of art designed to be set above and behind an altar.

Altay variant spelling of **Altai**.

altazimuth /alˈtazɪməθ/ ▶ **noun 1** (also **altazimuth mount** or **mounting**) Astronomy a telescope mounting that moves in azimuth (about a vertical axis) and in altitude (about a horizontal axis). Compare with **equatorial mount**. ■ (also **altazimuth telescope**) a telescope on an altazimuth mounting.
2 a surveying instrument for measuring vertical and horizontal angles, resembling a theodolite but larger and more precise.
– ORIGIN mid 19th cent.: blend of **altitude** and **azimuth**.

alt.country (also **alt-country**) ▶ **noun** [mass noun] a style of country music that is influenced by alternative rock.

Altdorfer /ˈaltdɔːfə/, German /ˈaltdɔrfɐ/, Albrecht (*c*.1485–1538), German painter and engraver. He was one of the first modern European landscape painters and was principal artist of the Danube School.

alter /'ɔːltə, 'ɒl-/ ▶ **verb** change in character or composition, typically in a comparatively small but significant way: [with obj.] *Eliot was persuaded to alter the passage* | [no obj.] *our outward appearance alters as we get older* | (as adj. **altered**) *an altered state.* ■ [with obj.] make structural changes to (a building): *plans to alter the dining hall.* ■ [with obj.] N. Amer. & Austral. castrate or spay (a domestic animal).
– DERIVATIVES **alterable** adjective.
– ORIGIN late Middle English: from Old French *alterer*, from late Latin *alterare*, from Latin *alter* 'other'.

alteration ▶ **noun** [mass noun] the action or process of altering or being altered: *careful alteration of old buildings* | [count noun] *alterations had to be made.*
– DERIVATIVES **alterative** adjective.
– ORIGIN late Middle English: from Old French, or from late Latin *alteratio(n-)*, from the verb *alterare* (see ALTER).

altercate /'ɔːltəkeɪt, 'ɒl-/ ▶ **verb** [no obj.] archaic dispute or argue noisily and publicly.
– ORIGIN mid 16th cent.: from Latin *altercat-* 'wrangled', from *altercari*.

altercation ▶ **noun** a noisy argument or disagreement, especially in public: *I had an altercation with the ticket collector.*
– ORIGIN late Middle English: from Latin *altercatio(n-)*, from the verb *altercari* (see ALTERCATE).

altered state ▶ **noun** a state of mind that differs from the normal state of consciousness, typically one induced by drugs, hypnosis, or mental disorder.

alter ego /ˌaltər 'ɛɡəʊ, ˌɒlt-, 'iːɡ-/ ▶ **noun** (pl. **alter egos**) a person's secondary or alternative personality. ■ an intimate and trusted friend.
– ORIGIN mid 16th cent.: Latin, 'other self'.

alterity /al'tɛrɪti, ɒl-/ ▶ **noun** [mass noun] formal the state of being other or different; otherness.
– ORIGIN mid 17th cent.: from late Latin *alteritas*, from *alter* 'other'.

alternant /ɔːl'təːnənt, ɒl-/ ▶ **noun** an alternative form of a word or other linguistic unit; a variant.
▶ **adjective** changing from one to the other; alternating.
– ORIGIN mid 17th cent.: from Latin *alternant-* 'doing things by turns', from the verb *alternare* (see ALTERNATE).

alternate ▶ **verb** /'ɔːltəneɪt, 'ɒl-/ [no obj.] occur in turn repeatedly: *bouts of depression* ***alternate with*** *periods of elation* | (as adj. **alternating**) *a season of alternating hot days and cool nights.* ■ [with obj.] do or perform in turn repeatedly: *some adults who wish to* ***alternate*** *work* ***with*** *education.* ■ change repeatedly between two contrasting conditions: *the government* ***alternated between*** *the Labour and Conservative parties.*
▶ **adjective** /ɔːl'təːnət, ɒl-/ [attrib.] **1** every other; every second: *she was asked to attend on alternate days.* ■ (of two things) each following and succeeded by the other in a regular pattern: *alternate bouts of intense labour and of idleness.* ■ Botany (of leaves or shoots) placed alternately on the two sides of the stem.
2 chiefly N. Amer. another term for ALTERNATIVE: *a novel set in an alternate universe.*
▶ **noun** /ɔːl'təːnət, ɒl-/ N. Amer. a person who acts as a deputy or substitute.
– DERIVATIVES **alternately** adverb, **alternation** noun.
– ORIGIN early 16th cent. (earlier (late Middle English) as *alternation*): from Latin *alternat-* 'done by turns', from *alternare*, from *alternus* 'every other', from *alter* 'other'.

> **USAGE** In both British and American English the adjective **alternate** means 'every other or every second', as in *they meet on* ***alternate*** *Sundays*, or '(of two things) each following and succeeded by the other in a regular pattern', as in ***alternate*** *layers of potato and sauce.* **Alternative** means 'available as another possibility or choice' (*an* ***alternative*** *route; some European countries follow an* ***alternative*** *approach*). In American usage, however, **alternate** can also be used to mean 'available as another choice': *an* ***alternate*** *plan called for construction to begin immediately rather than waiting for spring.* This American use of **alternate** is still regarded as incorrect by many people in Britain.

alternate angles ▶ **plural noun** Mathematics two angles, formed when a line crosses two other lines, that lie on opposite sides of the transversal line and on opposite relative sides of the other lines. If the two lines crossed are parallel, the alternate angles are equal.

alternating current (abbrev.: **AC** or **ac**) ▶ **noun** an electric current that reverses its direction many times a second at regular intervals, typically used in power supplies. Compare with DIRECT CURRENT.

alternation of generations ▶ **noun** [mass noun] Biology a pattern of reproduction occurring in the life cycles of many lower plants and some invertebrates, involving a regular alternation between two distinct forms. The generations are alternately sexual and asexual (as in ferns) or dioecious and parthenogenetic (as in some jellyfishes).

alternative ▶ **adjective 1** [attrib.] (of one or more things) available as another possibility or choice: *the various alternative methods for resolving disputes.* ■ (of two things) mutually exclusive: *the facts fit two alternative scenarios.*
2 of or relating to activities that depart from or challenge traditional norms: *an alternative lifestyle.*
▶ **noun** one of two or more available possibilities: *audio cassettes are an interesting* ***alternative to*** *reading* | *she had no alternative but to break the law.*
– ORIGIN mid 16th cent. (in the sense 'alternating, alternate'): from French *alternatif, -ive* or medieval Latin *alternativus*, from Latin *alternare* 'interchange' (see ALTERNATE).

> **USAGE** Some traditionalists maintain that you can only have a maximum of two alternatives, because the word **alternative** comes from Latin *alter* 'other (of two)') and that uses where there are more than two alternatives are wrong. Such uses are, however, normal in modern standard English. See also **USAGE** at **ALTERNATE**.

alternative comedy ▶ **noun** [mass noun] a style of comedy rejecting established (especially racist or sexist) stereotypes and sometimes having a political component.

alternative dispute resolution ▶ **noun** [mass noun] chiefly N. Amer. the use of methods such as mediation or arbitration to resolve a dispute without resort to litigation.

alternative energy ▶ **noun** [mass noun] energy fuelled in ways that do not use up the earth's natural resources or otherwise harm the environment, especially by avoiding the use of fossil fuels or nuclear power.

alternative fuel ▶ **noun** a fuel other than petrol or diesel for powering motor vehicles, such as natural gas, methanol, or electricity.

alternatively ▶ **adverb** [sentence adverb] as another option or possibility: *alternatively, you may telephone us direct if you wish.*

alternative medicine ▶ **noun** [mass noun] any of a range of medical therapies that are not regarded as orthodox by the medical profession, such as herbalism, naturopathy, and crystal healing. See also COMPLEMENTARY MEDICINE.

Alternative Service Book ▶ **noun** a book containing the public liturgy of the Church of England published in 1980 for use as the alternative to the Book of Common Prayer.

alternator ▶ **noun** a dynamo that generates an alternating current.

Althing /'ɔːlθɪŋ, 'ɒl-/ the bicameral legislative assembly of Iceland.
– ORIGIN Icelandic, from Old Norse.

althorn /'althɔːn/ ▶ **noun** a musical instrument of the saxhorn family, especially the alto or tenor saxhorn in E flat.
– ORIGIN mid 19th cent.: from German, from *alt* 'high' (from Latin *altus*) + *Horn* 'horn'.

although ▶ **conjunction** in spite of the fact that; even though: *although the sun was shining it wasn't that warm* | *although small, the room has a spacious feel.* ■ however; but: *he says he has the team shirt, although I've never seen him wear it.*
– ORIGIN Middle English: from ALL (as an adverb) + THOUGH.

> **USAGE** The form **although** can be replaced by **though**, the only difference being that **although** tends to be more formal than **though**. Some uses of **though** are not interchangeable with **although**, however: for example, adverbial uses (*it was nice of him to phone,* ***though***) and uses in phrases with 'as' or 'even' (*she doesn't look* ***as though*** *she's listening*).

Althusser /'altʊseː/, French /altysɛʀ/, Louis (1918–90), French philosopher. In giving a reinterpretation of traditional Marxism in the light of structuralist theories his work had a significant influence on literary and cultural theory.

altimeter /'altɪmiːtə/ ▶ **noun** an instrument for determining altitude attained, especially a barometric or radar device fitted in an aircraft.
– ORIGIN early 20th cent.: from Latin *altus* 'high' + -METER.

altimetry /al'tɪmɪtri/ ▶ **noun** [mass noun] the measurement of height or altitude.
– DERIVATIVES **altimetric** adjective.
– ORIGIN late Middle English: from medieval Latin *altimetria*.

altiplano /ˌaltɪ'plɑːnəʊ/ ▶ **noun** (pl. **altiplanos**) the high tableland of central South America.
– ORIGIN early 20th cent.: from Spanish.

altissimo /al'tɪsɪməʊ/ ▶ **adjective** Music very high in pitch: *the extreme altissimo range of his horn.*
– ORIGIN Italian, superlative of *alto* 'high'.

altitude ▶ **noun** [mass noun] the height of an object or point in relation to sea level or ground level: *flight data including airspeed and altitude* | [count noun] *flying at altitudes over 15,000 feet.* ■ great height: *the mechanism can freeze at altitude.* ■ Astronomy the apparent height of a celestial object above the horizon, measured in angular distance. ■ Geometry the length of the perpendicular line from a vertex to the opposite side of a figure.
– DERIVATIVES **altitudinal** adjective.
– ORIGIN late Middle English: from Latin *altitudo*, from *altus* 'high'.

altitude sickness ▶ **noun** [mass noun] illness caused by ascent to high altitude, characterized by hyperventilation, nausea, and exhaustion resulting from shortage of oxygen.

Alt key ▶ **noun** Computing a key on a keyboard which, when pressed simultaneously with another key, gives the latter an alternative function.
– ORIGIN late 20th cent.: abbreviation of *alt(ernative) key*.

Altman /'ɔːltm(ə)n, 'ɒlt-/, Robert (1925–2006), American film director. He made his name with *MASH* (1970), a black comedy set in the Korean war. Other notable films include *The Player* (1992).

alto /'altəʊ/ ▶ **noun** (pl. **altos**) **1** (especially in church music) the highest adult male singing voice (sometimes distinguished from the countertenor voice as using falsetto). ■ the lowest female singing voice; contralto. ■ a person with an alto voice. ■ a part written for an alto voice.
2 [as modifier] denoting the member of a family of instruments pitched second or third highest: *alto flute.* ■ an alto saxophone.
– DERIVATIVES **altoist** noun.
– ORIGIN late 16th cent.: from Italian *alto (canto)* 'high (song)'.

alto clef ▶ **noun** a clef placing middle C on the middle line of the stave, used chiefly for viola music.

altocumulus ▶ **noun** (pl. **altocumuli**) [mass noun] cloud forming a layer of rounded masses with a level base, occurring at medium altitude (typically 2 to 7 km, 6,500 to 23,000 ft).
– ORIGIN late 19th cent.: from modern Latin *alto-* (from Latin *altus* 'high') + CUMULUS.

altogether ▶ **adverb** completely; totally: *I stopped seeing her altogether* | [as submodifier] *I'm not altogether sure that I'd trust him.* ■ including everything or everyone; in total: *he had married several times and had forty-six children altogether.* ■ [sentence adverb] taking everything into consideration; on the whole: *altogether it was a great evening.*
– PHRASES **in the altogether** informal without any clothes on; naked.
– ORIGIN Old English (see ALL, TOGETHER).

> **USAGE** Note that **altogether** and **all together** do not mean the same thing. **Altogether** means 'in total', as in *there are six bedrooms* ***altogether***, whereas **all together** means 'all in one place' or 'all at once', as in *it was good to have a group of friends* ***all together***; *they came in* ***all together***.

alto-relievo /ˌaltəʊrɪ'liːvəʊ/ ▶ **noun** (pl. **alto-relievos**) [mass noun] another term for HIGH RELIEF at RELIEF (sense 4).
– ORIGIN mid 17th cent.: from Italian *alto-rilievo*.

altostratus ▶ **noun** [mass noun] cloud forming a continuous uniform layer which resembles stratus but occurs at medium altitude (typically 2 to 7 km, 6,500 to 23,000 ft).
– ORIGIN late 19th cent.: from modern Latin *alto-* (from Latin *altus* 'high') + STRATUS.

altricial /əl'trɪʃ(ə)l/ ▶ **adjective** Zoology (of a young bird or other animal) hatched or born in an undeveloped

A

state and requiring care and feeding by the parents. Also called **NIDICOLOUS**. Often contrasted with **PRECOCIAL**. ■ (of a particular species) having altricial young.
– ORIGIN late 19th cent.: from Latin *altrix, altric-*, feminine of *altor* 'nourisher', from *alere* 'nourish'.

altruism /ˈaltrʊɪz(ə)m/ ▶ **noun** [mass noun] disinterested and selfless concern for the well-being of others. ■ Zoology behaviour of an animal that benefits another at its own expense.
– DERIVATIVES **altruist** noun.
– ORIGIN mid 19th cent.: from French *altruisme*, from Italian *altrui* 'somebody else', from Latin *alteri huic* 'to this other'.

altruistic ▶ **adjective** showing a disinterested and selfless concern for the well-being of others; unselfish: *it was an entirely altruistic act.*
– DERIVATIVES **altruistically** adverb.

ALU ▶ **abbreviation** Computing arithmetic logic unit.

alu /ˈɑːluː/ ▶ **noun** (pl. **alus**) variant spelling of **ALOO**.

aludel /ˈaljʊdɛl/ ▶ **noun** a pear-shaped earthenware or glass pot, open at both ends to enable a series to be fitted one above another, formerly used in sublimation and other chemical processes.
– ORIGIN late Middle English: from Old French *alutel*, via Spanish from Arabic *al-'uṯāl* 'the sublimation vessel'.

alula /ˈaljʊlə/ ▶ **noun** (pl. **alulae** /ˈaljʊliː/) technical term for **BASTARD WING**.
– ORIGIN late 18th cent.: modern Latin, literally 'small wing', diminutive of *ala*.

alum /ˈaləm/ (also **potash alum**) ▶ **noun** [mass noun] Chemistry a colourless astringent compound which is a hydrated double sulphate of aluminium and potassium, used in solution in dyeing and tanning. ● Chem. formula: $AlK(SO_4)_2.12H_2O$.
■ [count noun] any of a number of analogous crystalline double sulphates of a monovalent metal (or group) and a trivalent metal.
– ORIGIN late Middle English: via Old French from Latin *alumen, alumin-* related to *aluta* 'tawed leather'.

alumina /əˈluːmɪnə/ ▶ **noun** [mass noun] a white solid that is a major constituent of many rocks, especially clays, and is found crystallized as corundum, sapphire, and other minerals. ● Alternative name: **aluminium oxide**; chem. formula: Al_2O_3.
– ORIGIN late 18th cent.: from Latin *alumen* (see **ALUM**), on the pattern of words such as *magnesia*.

aluminium (US **aluminum**) ▶ **noun** [mass noun] the chemical element of atomic number 13, a light silvery-grey metal. (Symbol: **Al**)

> Aluminium is the most abundant metal in the earth's crust and is obtained mainly from bauxite. Its resistance to corrosion, lightness, and strength (especially in alloys) have led to widespread use in domestic utensils, engineering parts, and aircraft construction.

– ORIGIN early 19th cent.: from **ALUMINA** + **-IUM**.

aluminium bronze ▶ **noun** [mass noun] an alloy of copper and aluminium.

aluminize /əˈluːmɪnʌɪz/ (also **aluminise**) ▶ **verb** [with obj.] (usu. as adj. **aluminized**) coat with aluminium.

aluminosilicate /əˌluːmɪnə(ʊ)ˈsɪlɪkeɪt/ ▶ **noun** Chemistry a silicate in which aluminium replaces some of the silicon, especially a rock-forming mineral such as a feldspar or a clay mineral.

aluminous /əˈluːmɪnəs/ ▶ **adjective** (chiefly of minerals and rocks) containing alumina or aluminium.
– ORIGIN late Middle English: from Latin *aluminosus*, from *alumen, alumin-* (see **ALUM**).

aluminum /əˈluːmɪnəm/ ▶ **noun** US spelling of **ALUMINIUM**.

alumna /əˈlʌmnə/ ▶ **noun** (pl. **alumnae** /-niː/) a female former pupil or student of a particular school, college, or university.
– ORIGIN late 19th cent.: from Latin, feminine of *alumnus* (see **ALUMNUS**).

alumnus /əˈlʌmnəs/ ▶ **noun** (pl. **alumni** /-nʌɪ/) a male former pupil or student of a particular school, college, or university: *a Harvard alumnus.*
– ORIGIN mid 17th cent.: from Latin, 'nursling, pupil', from *alere* 'nourish'.

> **USAGE** In the singular, **alumnus** nearly always means a male, but the plural **alumni** can be used to refer to pupils or students of either sex.

alum root ▶ **noun** chiefly N. Amer. another term for **HEUCHERA**.

al-Uqsur /al ˈʊksʊə/ variant spelling of **EL-UQSUR**.

Alvarez /alˈvɑːrɛz/, Luis Walter (1911–88), American physicist. In 1980 Alvarez and his son identified iridium in sediment from the Cretaceous–Tertiary boundary and proposed that this resulted from a catastrophic meteorite impact that may have resulted in the extinction of the dinosaurs.

alveolar /alˈvɪələ, ˌalvɪˈəʊlə/ ▶ **adjective 1** Anatomy relating to an alveolus.
2 Phonetics (of a consonant) pronounced with the tip of the tongue on or near this ridge (e.g. *n, s, d, t*).
▶ **noun** Phonetics an alveolar consonant.

alveolitis /ˌalvɪə(ʊ)ˈlʌɪtɪs/ ▶ **noun** [mass noun] Medicine inflammation of the air sacs of the lungs.

alveolus /ˌalvɪˈəʊləs, alˈvɪələs/ ▶ **noun** (pl. **alveoli** /-lʌɪ, -liː/) chiefly Anatomy a small cavity, pit, or hollow, in particular: ■ any of the many tiny air sacs of the lungs which allow for rapid gaseous exchange. ■ the bony socket for the root of a tooth. ■ an acinus (sac-like cavity) in a gland.
– DERIVATIVES **alveolate** /alˈvɪələt/ adjective.
– ORIGIN late 17th cent.: from Latin, 'small cavity', diminutive of *alveus*.

alway ▶ **adverb** archaic form of **ALWAYS**.

always ▶ **adverb 1** at all times; on all occasions: *the sun always rises in the east.* ■ throughout a long period of the past: *Isabel had always been in rude health.* ■ for all future time; forever: *she will always be missed.* ■ repeatedly and annoyingly: *she is always making derogatory remarks.*
2 as a last resort; failing all else: *if the marriage doesn't work out, we can always get divorced.*
– PHRASES **as always** as usual; as always happens: *opinions, as always, were divided* | *as always, I think that consumers are looking for a product that tastes good.*
– ORIGIN Middle English: genitive case of *all way*, the inflection probably giving the sense 'at every time' as opposed to 'at one uninterrupted time': the difference between the two is no longer distinct.

alyssum /ˈalɪs(ə)m, əˈlɪs(ə)m/ ▶ **noun** (pl. **alyssums**) a herbaceous Eurasian plant which typically bears small white or yellow flowers. Some kinds are cultivated in gardens. ● Genera *Alyssum* and *Lobularia*, family Cruciferae: many species.
– ORIGIN mid 16th cent. (used loosely to denote various medicinal herbs): modern Latin, from Latin *alysson*, from Greek *alusson*, from *a-* 'without' + *lussa* 'rabies' (referring to early herbalist use).

Alzheimer's disease /ˈaltshʌɪməz/ ▶ **noun** [mass noun] progressive mental deterioration that can occur in middle or old age, due to generalized degeneration of the brain. It is the commonest cause of premature senility.
– ORIGIN early 20th cent.: named after Alois *Alzheimer* (1864–1915), the German neurologist who first identified it.

AM ▶ **abbreviation** ■ amplitude modulation. ■ (**A.M.**) Hymns Ancient and Modern. ■ US Master of Arts. [Latin *artium magister*.] ■ Member of the Order of Australia.
▶ **noun** (pl. **AMs**) an Assembly Member (i.e. a Member of the Welsh Assembly).

Am ▶ **symbol** the chemical element americium.

am first person singular present of **BE**.

a.m. ▶ **abbreviation** before noon (used after times of day between midnight and noon not expressed using the twenty-four-hour clock): *at 7.45 a.m.*
– ORIGIN from Latin *ante meridiem*.

amacrine cell /ˈaməkrʌɪn, -krɪn/ ▶ **noun** Anatomy a small nerve cell within the retina which has dendrites but no axon.
– ORIGIN early 20th cent.: from **A-**[1] 'not' + Greek *makros* 'large' + *is, in-* 'sinew or strip'.

amadavat /ˈamədəvat/ ▶ **noun** variant spelling of **AVADAVAT**.

amadou /ˈamәduː/ ▶ **noun** [mass noun] historical a spongy substance made by drying certain bracket fungi and formerly used as an absorbent in medicine, as tinder, and for drying fishing flies.
– ORIGIN late 18th cent.: from French, from Latin *amator* 'lover' (because it easily ignites).

amah /ˈɑːmə/ ▶ **noun** a nursemaid or maid in East Asia or India.
– ORIGIN from Portuguese *ama* 'nurse'.

amakhosi /ˌamaˈkɒsi/ ▶ **plural noun** S. African tribal leaders regarded collectively.
– ORIGIN Zulu and Xhosa, plural of *inkosi* 'ruler, chief'.

Amal /əˈmɑːl/ a Lebanese Shiite Muslim organization founded in 1975 and having political and paramilitary wings.
– ORIGIN from Arabic *amal* 'hope'.

Amalfi /əˈmalfi/ a port and resort on the west coast of Italy, on the Gulf of Salerno; pop. 5,391 (2008).

amalgam /əˈmalgəm/ ▶ **noun** a mixture or blend: *a curious amalgam of the traditional and the modern.* ■ Chemistry an alloy of mercury with another metal, especially one used for dental fillings.
– ORIGIN late 15th cent.: from French *amalgame* or medieval Latin *amalgama*, from Greek *malagma* 'an emollient'.

amalgamate /əˈmalgəmeɪt/ ▶ **verb** combine or unite to form one organization or structure: [with obj.] *he* ***amalgamated*** *his company* ***with*** *another* | [no obj.] *numerous small British railway companies amalgamated.* ■ [with obj.] Chemistry alloy (a metal) with mercury.
– ORIGIN early 17th cent.: from medieval Latin *amalgamat-* 'formed into a soft mass', from the verb *amalgamare*, from *amalgama* (see **AMALGAM**).

amalgamation ▶ **noun** [mass noun] the action, process, or result of combining or uniting: *the threat of* ***amalgamation with*** *another college* | [count noun] *an amalgamation of two separate companies.*
– ORIGIN early 17th cent.: from medieval Latin *amalgamare* (see **AMALGAMATE**).

Amalthea /ˌaməlˈθɪə/ Astronomy a satellite of Jupiter, the third closest to the planet, being reddish in colour and heavily cratered (262 km long and 146 km across).
– ORIGIN from the name of a goat in Greek Mythology, which suckled the infant Zeus.

amanuensis /əˌmanjʊˈɛnsɪs/ ▶ **noun** (pl. **amanuenses** /-siːz/) a literary or artistic assistant, in particular one who takes dictation or copies manuscripts.
– ORIGIN early 17th cent.: Latin, from (*servus*) *a manu* '(slave) at hand(writing), secretary' + *-ensis* 'belonging to'.

Amapá /ˌaməˈpɑː/ a state of northern Brazil, on the Atlantic coast, lying between the Amazon delta and the border with French Guiana; capital, Macapá. It is a region of dense rainforest.

amaranth /ˈamәranθ/ ▶ **noun 1** a plant of a chiefly tropical family that includes love-lies-bleeding. ● Family Amaranthaceae: several genera, especially *Amaranthus*.
2 a purple colour.
– DERIVATIVES **amaranthine** /ˌaməˈranθʌɪn/ adjective.
– ORIGIN mid 16th cent.: from French *amarante* or modern Latin *amaranthus*, alteration (on the pattern of plant names ending in *-anthus*, from Greek *anthos* 'flower') of Latin *amarantus*, from Greek *amarantos* 'not fading'.

amaretti /ˌaməˈrɛti/ ▶ **plural noun** Italian almond-flavoured biscuits.
– ORIGIN Italian, based on *amaro* 'bitter'; compare with **AMARETTO**.

amaretto /ˌaməˈrɛtəʊ/ ▶ **noun** [mass noun] (pl. **amarettos**) a brown almond-flavoured liqueur produced in Italy.
– ORIGIN Italian, diminutive of *amaro* 'bitter' (with reference to bitter almonds).

Amarna, Tell el- /ˌtɛl ɛl əˈmɑːnə/ see **TELL EL-AMARNA**.

amaryllis /ˌaməˈrɪlɪs/ ▶ **noun** a bulbous plant with showy trumpet-shaped flowers and strap-shaped leaves. ● Two plants of the family Liliaceae (or Amaryllidaceae): the South African *Amaryllis belladonna* (also called **BELLADONNA LILY**), and (popularly) a tropical South American plant of the genus *Hippeastrum*, grown as a houseplant.
– ORIGIN modern Latin, from Latin *Amaryllis* (from Greek *Amarullis*), a name for a country girl in pastoral poetry.

amass ▶ **verb** [with obj.] gather together or accumulate (a large amount or number of material or things) over a period of time: *he amassed a fortune estimated at close to a million pounds.* ■ [no obj.] archaic gather together in a crowd or group: *the soldiers were amassing from all parts of Spain.*
– DERIVATIVES **amasser** noun.
– ORIGIN late 15th cent.: from French *amasser* or medieval Latin *amassare*, based on Latin *massa* 'lump' (see **MASS**).

Amaterasu /əˌmɑːtəˈrɑːsuː/ the principal deity of the Japanese Shinto religion, the sun goddess and ancestor of Jimmu, the founder of the imperial dynasty.

amateur /ˈamətə, -tʃə, -tjʊə, ˌaməˈtəː/ ▶ **noun** a person who engages in a pursuit, especially a sport, on an unpaid basis. ■ a person who is contemptibly inept

at a particular activity: *that bunch of stumbling amateurs.*
▶ **adjective** engaging or engaged in without payment; non-professional: *an amateur archaeologist | amateur athletics.* ■ done in an inept or unskilful way: *it's all so amateur!*
– DERIVATIVES **amateurism** noun.
– ORIGIN late 18th cent.: from French, from Italian *amatore*, from Latin *amator* 'lover', from *amare* 'to love'.

amateurish ▶ **adjective** done in an unskilful or inept way: *her amateurish interviewing technique.*
– DERIVATIVES **amateurishly** adverb, **amateurishness** noun.

Amati /əˈmɑːti/ a family of Italian violin-makers from Cremona. In the 16th and 17th centuries three generations of the Amatis developed the basic proportions of the violin, viola, and cello.

amatol /ˈamətɒl/ ▶ **noun** [mass noun] a high explosive consisting of a mixture of TNT and ammonium nitrate.
– ORIGIN early 20th cent.: formed irregularly from *am(monium)* + *tol(uene)*.

amatory /ˈamət(ə)ri/ ▶ **adjective** relating to or induced by sexual love or desire: *his amatory exploits.*
– ORIGIN late 16th cent.: from Latin *amatorius*, from *amator* (see AMATEUR).

Amatriciana /ˌamətrɪʃiˈɑːnə/ ▶ **adjective** denoting a spicy pasta sauce made with tomatoes, pancetta or bacon, and basil.
– ORIGIN from Italian *all'Amatriciana* 'in the style of Amatrice', from *Amatrice*, a town in central Italy, + the suffix *-ana*.

amaurosis /ˌamɔːˈrəʊsɪs/ ▶ **noun** [mass noun] Medicine partial or total blindness without visible change in the eye, typically due to disease of the optic nerve, spinal cord, or brain.
– DERIVATIVES **amaurotic** adjective.
– ORIGIN mid 17th cent.: from Greek *amaurōsis*, from *amauroun* 'darken', from *amauros* 'dim'.

amaze ▶ **verb** [with obj.] surprise (someone) greatly; fill with astonishment: *he was* ***amazed at*** *how modern everything was* | [with obj. and clause] *she was amazed that Paul should notice her.*
– ORIGIN Old English *āmasian*, of unknown origin.

amazement ▶ **noun** [mass noun] a feeling of great surprise or wonder: *she shook her head* ***in amazement*** | ***to her amazement****, Bill was keen.*

amazing ▶ **adjective** causing great surprise or wonder; astonishing: *an amazing number of people registered* | *it is amazing how short memories are.* ■ informal very impressive; excellent: *she makes the most amazing cakes.*
– DERIVATIVES **amazingly** adverb [sentence adverb] *amazingly, Alan escaped with a few cuts and bruises.*

Amazon[1] /ˈaməz(ə)n/ a river in South America, flowing over 6,683 km (4,150 miles) through Peru, Colombia, and Brazil into the Atlantic Ocean. It drains two fifths of the continent and in terms of water flow it is the largest river in the world.
– DERIVATIVES **Amazonian** adjective.
– ORIGIN the river bore various names after it was first encountered by Europeans in 1500 and was finally called *Amazon* after a legendary race of female warriors believed to live on its banks.

Amazon[2] /ˈaməz(ə)n/ ▶ **noun 1** a member of a legendary race of female warriors believed by the ancient Greeks to exist in Scythia or elsewhere on the edge of the known world. ■ a very tall and strong or athletic woman.
2 (**amazon**) a parrot, typically green, found in Central and South America. ● Genus *Amazona*, family Psittacidae: numerous species.
– DERIVATIVES **Amazonian** /aməˈzəʊnɪən/ **adjective**.
– ORIGIN late Middle English: via Latin from Greek *Amazōn*, explained by the Greeks as 'without a breast' (as if from *a-* 'without' + *mazos* 'breast'), referring to the fable that the Amazons cut off the right breast so as not to interfere with the use of a bow, but probably a folk etymology of an unknown foreign word.

amazon ant ▶ **noun** a small reddish ant which captures the pupae of other ant colonies to raise as slaves. ● Genus *Polyergus*, family Formicidae.

Amazonas /ˌaməˈzəʊnəs/ a state of NW Brazil; capital, Manaus. It is crossed by the Amazon and its numerous tributaries.

Amazon dolphin ▶ **noun** another term for BOTO.

Amazonia /ˌaməˈzəʊnɪə/ the area around the River Amazon in South America, principally in Brazil, but also extending into Peru, Colombia, and Bolivia. The region comprises approximately one third of the world's remaining tropical rainforest. ■ a national park protecting 10,000 sq. km (3,850 sq. miles) of tropical rainforest in the state of Pará, northern Brazil.

ambassador ▶ **noun** an accredited diplomat sent by a state as its permanent representative in a foreign country: *the French* ***ambassador to*** *Portugal.* ■ a representative or promoter of a specified activity: *he is a good ambassador for the industry.*
– DERIVATIVES **ambassadorial** adjective, **ambassadorship** noun.
– ORIGIN late Middle English: from French *ambassadeur*, from Italian *ambasciator*, based on Latin *ambactus* 'servant'.

ambassador-at-large ▶ **noun** N. Amer. an ambassador with special duties not appointed to a particular country.

ambassador extraordinary ▶ **noun** a diplomat sent by one state or monarch on a diplomatic mission to another.

ambassador plenipotentiary ▶ **noun** an ambassador with full powers to sign treaties or otherwise act for the state or monarch.

ambassadress ▶ **noun** a female ambassador.

ambatch /ˈambatʃ/ ▶ **noun** a tropical African tree of the pea family, with light spongy timber that is used for rafts and floats. ● *Aeschynomene elaphroxylon*, family Leguminosae.
– ORIGIN mid 19th cent.: of Ethiopic origin.

Ambato /amˈbɑːtəʊ/ a market town in the Andes of central Ecuador; pop. 209,000 (est. 2008).

amber ▶ **noun** [mass noun] hard translucent fossilized resin originating from extinct coniferous trees of the Tertiary period, typically yellowish in colour. It has been used in jewellery since antiquity. ■ a honey-yellow colour typical of amber: [as modifier] *amber eyes.* ■ a yellow light used as a cautionary signal between green for 'go' and red for 'stop': *the lights were at amber.*
– ORIGIN late Middle English (also in the sense 'ambergris'): from Old French *ambre*, from Arabic *'anbar* 'ambergris', later 'amber'.

amber fluid (also **amber liquid**) ▶ **noun** [mass noun] Austral. informal beer.

ambergris /ˈambəgrɪs, -iːs/ ▶ **noun** [mass noun] a wax-like substance that originates as a secretion in the intestines of the sperm whale, found floating in tropical seas and used in perfume manufacture.
– ORIGIN late Middle English: from Old French *ambre gris* 'grey amber', as distinct from *amber jaune* 'yellow amber' (the resin).

amberjack ▶ **noun** a large marine game fish which occurs in inshore tropical and subtropical waters of the Atlantic and South Pacific. ● Genus *Seriola*, family Carangidae: several species.
– ORIGIN late 19th cent.: from AMBER (because of its yellowish tail) + JACK[1].

ambidextrous /ˌambɪˈdɛkstrəs/ ▶ **adjective** able to use the right and left hands equally well. ■ (of an implement) designed to be used by left-handed and right-handed people with equal ease.
– DERIVATIVES **ambidexterity** noun, **ambidextrously** adverb, **ambidextrousness** noun.
– ORIGIN mid 17th cent.: from late Latin *ambidexter* (from Latin *ambi-* 'on both sides' + *dexter* 'right-handed') + -OUS.

ambience /ˈambɪəns/ (also **ambiance**) ▶ **noun** the character and atmosphere of a place: *the relaxed ambience of the cocktail lounge is popular with guests.* ■ quality or character given to a sound recording by the space in which the sound occurs.
– ORIGIN late 19th cent.: from AMBIENT + -ENCE, or from French *ambiance*, from *ambiant* 'surrounding'.

ambient /ˈambɪənt/ ▶ **adjective 1** relating to the immediate surroundings of something: *the liquid is stored at below ambient temperature.* ■ relating to ambient music.
2 relating to or denoting advertising that makes use of sites or objects other than the established media (e.g. by placing slogans on the back of bus tickets).
– ORIGIN late 16th cent.: from French *ambiant* or Latin *ambient-* 'going round', from *ambire*.

ambient music ▶ **noun** [mass noun] a style of gentle, largely electronic instrumental music with no persistent beat, used to create or enhance a mood or atmosphere.

ambiguity /ambɪˈgjuːɪti/ ▶ **noun** (pl. **ambiguities**) [mass noun] the quality of being open to more than one interpretation; inexactness: *we can detect no ambiguity in this section of the Act* | [count noun] *ambiguities in such questions are potentially very dangerous.*
– ORIGIN late Middle English: from Old French *ambiguite* or Latin *ambiguitas*, from *ambiguus* 'doubtful' (see AMBIGUOUS).

ambiguous /amˈbɪgjʊəs/ ▶ **adjective** open to more than one interpretation; not having one obvious meaning: *ambiguous phrases.* ■ not clear or decided: *the election result was ambiguous.*
– DERIVATIVES **ambiguously** adverb, **ambiguousness** noun.
– ORIGIN early 16th cent. (in the sense 'indistinct, obscure'): from Latin *ambiguus* 'doubtful' (from *ambigere* 'waver, go around', from *ambi-* 'both ways' + *agere* 'to drive') + -OUS.

ambisexual /ˌambɪˈsɛkʃʊəl, -sjʊəl/ ▶ **adjective** bisexual or androgynous.
▶ **noun** an ambisexual person.
– DERIVATIVES **ambisexually** adverb.
– ORIGIN 1930s: from Latin *ambi-* 'on both sides' + SEXUAL.

ambisonic ▶ **adjective** denoting or relating to a high-fidelity audio system that reproduces the directional and acoustic properties of recorded sound using two or more channels.
▶ **noun** (**ambisonics**) [treated as sing.] ambisonic reproduction or systems.
– ORIGIN 1970s: from Latin *ambi-* 'on both sides' + SONIC.

ambit /ˈambɪt/ ▶ **noun** [in sing.] the scope, extent, or bounds of something: *a full discussion of this complex issue was beyond the ambit of one book.*
– ORIGIN late Middle English (in the sense 'precincts, environs'): from Latin *ambitus* 'circuit', from *ambire* 'go round'.

ambition ▶ **noun** a strong desire to do or achieve something: *her ambition was to become a model* | *he achieved his ambition of making a fortune.* ■ [mass noun] desire and determination to achieve success: *young men and women with ambition.*
– ORIGIN Middle English: via Old French from Latin *ambitio(n-)*, from *ambire* 'go around (canvassing for votes)'.

ambitious ▶ **adjective** having or showing a strong desire and determination to succeed: *a ruthlessly ambitious woman.* ■ (of a plan or piece of work) intended to satisfy high aspirations and therefore difficult to achieve: *an ambitious enterprise.*
– DERIVATIVES **ambitiously** adverb, **ambitiousness** noun.
– ORIGIN late Middle English: from Old French *ambitieux* or Latin *ambitiosus*, from *ambitio* (see AMBITION).

ambivalence ▶ **noun** [mass noun] the state of having mixed feelings or contradictory ideas about something or someone: *government ambivalence towards the arts.*

ambivalent /amˈbɪv(ə)l(ə)nt/ ▶ **adjective** having mixed feelings or contradictory ideas about something or someone: *some loved her, some hated her, few were ambivalent about her* | *an ambivalent attitude to Europe.*
– DERIVATIVES **ambivalently** adverb.
– ORIGIN early 20th cent.: from *ambivalence* (from German *Ambivalenz*), on the pattern of *equivalent*.

ambivert /ˈambɪvəːt/ ▶ **noun** Psychology a person who has a balance of extrovert and introvert features in their personality.
– DERIVATIVES **ambiversion** noun.
– ORIGIN 1920s: from Latin *ambi-* 'on both sides', on the pattern of *extrovert* and *introvert*.

amble ▶ **verb** [no obj., with adverbial of direction] walk or move at a slow, relaxed pace: *they ambled along the riverbank.*
▶ **noun** a walk at a slow, relaxed pace, especially for pleasure: *a peaceful riverside amble.*
– DERIVATIVES **ambler** noun.
– ORIGIN Middle English (originally denoting a horse's gait): from Old French *ambler*, from Latin *ambulare* 'to walk'.

amblyopia /ˌamblɪˈəʊpɪə/ ▶ **noun** [mass noun] Medicine impaired or dim vision without obvious defect or change in the eye.
– DERIVATIVES **amblyopic** adjective.
– ORIGIN early 18th cent.: from Greek *ambluōpia* 'short-sightedness', from *ambluōpos* (adjective), from *amblus* 'dull' + *ōps*, *ōp-* 'eye'.

ambo /ˈambəʊ/ ▶ **noun** (pl. **ambos** or **ambones** /-ˈbəʊniːz/) (in an early Christian church) an oblong pulpit with steps at each end.

– ORIGIN mid 17th cent.: via medieval Latin from Greek *ambōn* 'rim' (in medieval Greek 'pulpit').

Ambon /amˈbɒn/ (also **Amboina** /-ˈbɔɪnə/) a mountainous island in eastern Indonesia, one of the Molucca Islands. ■ a port on this island, the capital of the Molucca Islands; pop. 204,200 (est. 2005).
– DERIVATIVES **Ambonese** (also **Amboinese**) noun & adjective.

amboyna /amˈbɔɪnə/ (also **amboyna wood**) ▶ **noun** [mass noun] the decorative timber of a rapidly growing SE Asian tree, used for cabinetmaking. ● The tree is *Pterocarpus indicus*, family Leguminosae.
– ORIGIN mid 19th cent.: named after *Amboina* Island (see **AMBON**).

Ambrose, St /ˈambrəʊz/ (*c*.339–97), Doctor of the Church, bishop of Milan. A champion of orthodoxy, he also encouraged developments in church music. Feast day, 7 December.
– DERIVATIVES **Ambrosian** adjective.

ambrosia /amˈbrəʊzɪə/ ▶ **noun** [mass noun] **1** Greek & Roman Mythology the food of the gods. ■ something very pleasing to taste or smell: *the tea was ambrosia after the slop I'd been suffering*.
2 a fungal product used as food by ambrosia beetles.
3 another term for **BEE BREAD**.
– DERIVATIVES **ambrosial** adjective.
– ORIGIN mid 16th cent.: via Latin from Greek, 'elixir of life', from *ambrotos* 'immortal'.

ambrosia beetle ▶ **noun** a small wood-boring beetle whose adults and larvae (called **pinhole borers**) feed on ambrosia produced by fungus in the wood. ● Genus *Platypus* (family Platypodidae), and *Xyleborus* and other genera (family Scolytidae).

ambry /ˈambri/ ▶ **noun** variant spelling of **AUMBRY**.

ambulacrum /ˌambjʊˈleɪkrəm, -ˈlakrəm/ ▶ **noun** (pl. **ambulacra** /-ˈleɪkrə, -ˈlakrə/) Zoology (in an echinoderm) each of the radially arranged bands, together with their underlying structures, through which the double rows of tube feet protrude.
– DERIVATIVES **ambulacral** adjective.
– ORIGIN early 19th cent.: Latin, 'avenue', from *ambulare* 'to walk'.

ambulance ▶ **noun** a vehicle equipped for taking sick or injured people to and from hospital, especially in emergencies.
▶ **verb** [with obj. and adverbial of direction] convey in an ambulance: *he was ambulanced to accident and emergency*.
– ORIGIN early 19th cent.: French, from *hôpital ambulant* 'mobile (horse-drawn) field hospital', from Latin *ambulant-* 'walking' (see **AMBULANT**).

ambulance chaser ▶ **noun** derogatory, chiefly N. Amer. a lawyer who specializes in bringing cases seeking damages for personal injury.
– ORIGIN late 19th cent.: from the reputation gained by certain lawyers for attending accidents and encouraging victims to sue.

ambulant /ˈambjʊl(ə)nt/ ▶ **adjective** Medicine (of a patient) able to walk about; not confined to bed.
– ORIGIN early 17th cent.: from Latin *ambulant-* 'walking', from *ambulare*.

ambulate /ˈambjʊleɪt/ ▶ **verb** [no obj.] formal or technical walk; move about.
– DERIVATIVES **ambulation** noun.
– ORIGIN early 17th cent.: from Latin *ambulat-* 'walked', from the verb *ambulare*.

ambulatory /ˈambjʊlət(ə)ri/ ▶ **adjective** relating to or adapted for walking. ■ another term for **AMBULANT**. ■ movable; mobile: *an ambulatory ophthalmic service*.
▶ **noun** (pl. **ambulatories**) a place for walking, especially an aisle or cloister in a church or monastery.
– ORIGIN mid 16th cent. (as a noun): from Latin *ambulatorius*, from *ambulare* 'to walk'.

Ambulocetus /ˌambjʊlə(ʊ)ˈsiːtəs/ ▶ **noun** a cetacean of the Eocene epoch that had fore and hind limbs and could walk on land.
– ORIGIN modern Latin, from Latin *ambulare* 'to walk' + *cetus* 'whale'.

ambuscade /ˌambəˈskeɪd/ ▶ **noun** dated an ambush.
▶ **verb** [with obj.] archaic ambush (someone).
– ORIGIN late 16th cent.: from French *embuscade*, from Italian *imboscata*, Spanish *emboscada*, or Portuguese *embuscada*, based on a late Latin word meaning 'to place in a wood'; related to **BUSH**[1].

ambush ▶ **noun** a surprise attack by people lying in wait in a concealed position: *seven members of a patrol were killed in an ambush* | [mass noun] *there might be terrorists waiting in ambush*.
▶ **verb** [with obj.] make a surprise attack on (someone) from a concealed position: *they were ambushed and taken prisoner by the enemy*. ■ confront (someone) suddenly and unexpectedly with unwelcome questions: *Tory representatives were ambushed by camera crews*.
– ORIGIN Middle English (in the sense 'place troops in hiding in order to surprise an enemy'): from Old French *embusche* (noun), *embuschier* (verb), based on a late Latin word meaning 'to place in a wood'; related to **BUSH**[1].

ambush marketing ▶ **noun** [mass noun] the practice by which a rival company attempts to associate its products with an event that already has official sponsors.

am-dram ▶ **noun** [treated as sing. or pl.] informal amateur dramatics.

ameba ▶ **noun** (pl. **amebae** or **amebas**) US spelling of **AMOEBA**.

amebiasis ▶ **noun** US spelling of **AMOEBIASIS**.

amelanchier /ˌaməˈlaŋkɪə/ ▶ **noun** a shrub of a genus that includes juneberry and snowy mespilus, typically bearing white flowers. ● Genus *Amelanchier*, family Rosaceae.
– ORIGIN from French dialect *amelancier* 'medlar'.

ameliorate /əˈmiːlɪəreɪt/ ▶ **verb** [with obj.] formal make (something bad or unsatisfactory) better: *the reform did much to ameliorate living standards*.
– DERIVATIVES **ameliorative** adjective.
– ORIGIN mid 18th cent.: alteration of **MELIORATE**, influenced by French *améliorer*, from *meilleur* 'better'.

amelioration ▶ **noun** [mass noun] formal the act of making something better; improvement: *progress brings with it the amelioration of the human condition*.

amen /ɑːˈmɛn, eɪ-/ ▶ **exclamation** uttered at the end of a prayer or hymn, meaning 'so be it'. ■ used to express agreement or assent: *amen to that!*
▶ **noun** an utterance of 'amen'.
– ORIGIN Old English, from ecclesiastical Latin, from Greek *amēn*, from Hebrew *'āmēn* 'truth, certainty', used adverbially as expression of agreement, and adopted in the Septuagint as a solemn expression of belief or affirmation.

amenable /əˈmiːnəb(ə)l/ ▶ **adjective** open and responsive to suggestion; easily persuaded or controlled: *parents who have amenable children*. ■ (**amenable to**) capable of being acted upon in a particular way; susceptible: *cardiac failure not amenable to medical treatment*.
– DERIVATIVES **amenability** noun, **amenably** adverb.
– ORIGIN late 16th cent. (in the sense 'liable to answer to a law or tribunal'): an Anglo-Norman French legal term, from Old French *amener* 'bring to' from *a-* (from Latin *ad*) 'to' + *mener* 'bring' (from late Latin *minare* 'drive animals', from Latin *minari* 'threaten').

amen corner ▶ **noun** US the part of a Methodist meeting house formerly occupied by worshippers who responded to the preacher's utterances with occasional shouts of 'Amen!'.

amend ▶ **verb** [with obj.] **1** make minor changes to (a text, piece of legislation, etc.) in order to make it fairer or more accurate, or to reflect changing circumstances: *the rule was amended to apply only to non-members*.
2 improve the texture or fertility of (soil). ■ archaic put right: *a few things had gone wrong, but these had been amended*.
– DERIVATIVES **amendable** adjective, **amender** noun.
– ORIGIN Middle English: from Old French *amender*, based on Latin *emendare* (see **EMEND**).

amende honorable /əˌmɒ̃d ɒnɔːˈrɑːbl(ə)/, French /amɑ̃d ɔnɔʀabl/ ▶ **noun** (pl. **amendes honorables** pronunc. **same**) literary a public or open apology, typically with some form of reparation.
– ORIGIN French, literally 'honourable reparation'.

amendment ▶ **noun** a minor change or addition designed to improve a text, piece of legislation, etc.: *an amendment to existing bail laws*. ■ (**Amendment**) an article added to the US Constitution: *the First Amendment*. ■ something which is added to soil in order to improve its texture or fertility.
– ORIGIN Middle English (in the sense 'improvement, correction'): from Old French *amendement*, from *amender* (see **AMEND**).

amends ▶ **plural noun** (in phrase **make amends**) compensate or make up for a wrongdoing: *try to make amends for the rude way you spoke to Lucy*.
– PHRASES **offer of amends** Law an offer to publish a correction and an apology for an act of libel.
– ORIGIN Middle English: from Old French *amendes* 'penalties, fine', plural of *amende* 'reparation', from *amender* (see **AMEND**).

Amenhotep /ˌɑːmɛnˈhəʊtɛp/ the name of four Egyptian pharaohs of the 18th dynasty; Greek name *Amenophis*. ■ **Amenhotep I** (16th century BC), son of Ahmose I (founder of the 18th dynasty), reigned 1546–1526. ■ **Amenhotep II** (15th century BC), son of Tuthmosis III, reigned 1450–1425. ■ **Amenhotep III** (15th–14th centuries BC), son of Tuthmosis IV, reigned 1417–1379. He embarked on an extensive building programme centred on his capital, Thebes, including the colossi of Memnon and the Luxor temple. ■ **Amenhotep IV** see **AKHENATEN**.

amenity /əˈmiːnɪti, -ˈmɛn-/ ▶ **noun** (pl. **amenities**) a desirable or useful feature or facility of a building or place: *the property is situated in a convenient location, close to all local amenities*. ■ [mass noun] the pleasantness or attractiveness of a place: *developments which would clash with amenity*.
– ORIGIN late Middle English: from Old French *amenite* or Latin *amoenitas*, from *amoenus* 'pleasant'.

amenorrhoea /əˌmɛnəˈriːə/ (US **amenorrhea**) ▶ **noun** [mass noun] an abnormal absence of menstruation.
– ORIGIN early 19th cent.: from **A-**[1] 'without' + **MENORRHOEA**.

ament /ˈeɪmɛnt, əˈmɛnt/ ▶ **noun** Botany a catkin.
– ORIGIN mid 18th cent.: from Latin *amentum* 'thong'.

amentia /eɪˈmɛnʃə, ə-/ ▶ **noun** [mass noun] Medicine, dated severe congenital mental disability.
– ORIGIN late Middle English: from Latin, literally 'madness', from *amens*, *ament-* 'mad', from *a-* 'without' + *mens* 'the mind'.

Amerasian /ˌaməˈreɪʃ(ə)n, -ʒ(ə)n/ ▶ **adjective** having one American and one Asian parent.
▶ **noun** a person with one American and one Asian parent.

amercement /əˈməːsmənt/ ▶ **noun** English Law, historical a fine.
– DERIVATIVES **amerce** verb.
– ORIGIN late Middle English: from Anglo-Norman French *amerciment*, based on *estre amercie* 'be at the mercy of another' (with respect to the amount of a fine), from *a merci* 'at (the) mercy'.

America (also **the Americas**) a land mass of the western hemisphere consisting of the continents of North and South America joined by the Isthmus of Panama. ■ used as a name for the United States.

> America was originally inhabited by American Indians and Inuit peoples. The NE coastline of North America was visited by Norse seamen in the early 11th century, but for the modern world America was first reached by Christopher Columbus, who arrived in the Caribbean in 1492 and the South American mainland in 1498.

– ORIGIN the name *America* dates from the early 16th cent. and is believed to derive from the Latin form (*Americus*) of the name of Amerigo Vespucci, who sailed along the west coast of South America in 1501.

American ▶ **adjective** relating to or characteristic of the United States or its inhabitants: *the election of a new American president*. ■ relating to the continents of America: *the American continent south of the tropic of Cancer*.
▶ **noun 1** a native or citizen of the United States. ■ a native or inhabitant of any of the countries of North, South, or Central America.
2 [mass noun] the English language as it is used in the United States; American English.
– PHRASES **the American dream** the ideal by which equality of opportunity is available to any American, allowing the highest aspirations and goals to be achieved.
– DERIVATIVES **Americanism** noun, **Americanness** noun.

Americana /əˌmɛrɪˈkɑːnə/ ▶ **plural noun** things associated with America, especially the United States.

American aloe ▶ **noun** another term for **CENTURY PLANT**.

American Civil War the war between the northern US states (usually known as the Union) and the Confederate States of America, 1861–5.

> The war was fought over the issues of slavery and states' rights. The pro-slavery Southern states seceded from the Federal Union following the election of Abraham Lincoln on an anti-slavery platform, but were defeated by the North after failing to gain foreign recognition.

American depositary receipt (also **American depositary share**) ▶ **noun** (in the US) a negotiable certificate of title to a number of shares in a non-US company which are deposited in an overseas bank.

American English ▸ **noun** [mass noun] the English language as spoken and written in the US.

> As well as differences from British English in spelling, pronunciation, and grammar, there are specifically American uses of words and meanings, principally: adoptions from languages with which the early settlers came in contact (*moccasin, prairie*), changes in meaning (*corn, vest*), survivals of 17th- and 18th-century English (*gotten*), and different words for the same referent (*elevator* for *lift*).

American Federation of Labor a federation of North American trade unions, merged in 1955 with the Congress of Industrial Organizations to form the American Federation of Labor and Congress of Industrial Organizations (AFL–CIO).

American football ▸ **noun** [mass noun] a kind of football played with an oval ball on a field marked out as a gridiron. Points are scored mainly through touchdowns and field goals. Each side has eleven players on the field at any time. In the US called simply **FOOTBALL**.

American Independence, War of the war of 1775–83 in which the American colonists won independence from British rule. Called in the US and Canada the **AMERICAN REVOLUTION**.

> The war was triggered by resentment of the economic policies of Britain, particularly the right of Parliament to tax the colonies, and by the exclusion of the colonists from participation in political decisions affecting their interests. Following disturbances such as the Boston Tea Party of 1773, fighting broke out in 1775; a year later the Declaration of Independence was signed. The Americans gained the support of France and Spain, and French sea power eventually played a crucial role in the decisive surrender of a British army at Yorktown in 1781.

American Indian ▸ **noun** a member of any of the groups of indigenous peoples of North, Central, and South America, especially those of North America.
▸ **adjective** relating to American Indians.

> **USAGE** The term **American Indian** has been steadily replaced in the US, especially in official contexts, by **Native American** (first recorded in the 1950s and becoming prominent in the 1970s). The latter is preferred by some as being a more accurate and respectful description (the word **Indian** recalling Columbus' assumption that, on reaching America, he had reached the east coast of India), as well as avoiding the stereotype of cowboys and Indians in the stories of the Wild West. **American Indian** is still widespread in general use even in the US, however, partly because it is not normally regarded as offensive by American Indians themselves. Nevertheless, since the category **American Indian** is very broad, it is preferable, where possible, to name the specific people, such as **Apache**, **Comanche**, or **Sioux**.

Americanize (also **Americanise**) ▸ **verb** [with obj.] (often as adj. **Americanized**) make American in character or nationality.
– DERIVATIVES **Americanization** /-ˈzeɪʃ(ə)n/ **noun**.

American Legion (in the US) an association of ex-servicemen formed in 1919.

Americano /əmɛriˈkɑːnəʊ/ (also **café Americano**) ▸ **noun** (pl. **Americanos**) a drink of espresso coffee diluted with hot water.
– ORIGIN 1970s: American Spanish, literally 'American (coffee)'.

American organ ▸ **noun** a type of reed organ resembling the harmonium but in which air is sucked (not blown) through reeds.

American plan ▸ **noun** North American term for **FULL BOARD**. Often contrasted with **EUROPEAN PLAN**.

American Revolution US and Canadian term for **AMERICAN INDEPENDENCE, WAR OF**.

American Saddle Horse ▸ **noun** a light, strong horse of a breed developed in America to be comfortable to ride over long distances.

American Samoa an unincorporated overseas territory of the US comprising a group of islands in the southern Pacific Ocean, to the east of Samoa and south of the Kiribati group; pop. 65,600 (est. 2009); capital, Fagatogo. In 1899 the US acquired rights to the islands by agreement with Germany and Britain, and in April 1900 the two main islands were ceded to the US by their chiefs. Further islands were handed over in succeeding years.

American Sign Language ▸ **noun** [mass noun] a form of sign language developed in the US for the use of deaf people, consisting of over 4,000 signs.

American Standard Version ▸ **noun** an English translation of the Bible published in the US in 1901, based on the Revised Version of 1881–95 with additional work by American scholars.

America's Cup an international yachting race held every three to four years.

americium /ˌaməˈrɪsjəm/ ▸ **noun** [mass noun] the chemical element of atomic number 95, a radioactive metal of the actinide series. Americium does not occur naturally and was first made by bombarding plutonium with neutrons. (Symbol: **Am**)
– ORIGIN 1940s: from **AMERICA** (where it was first made) + **-IUM**.

Amerindian /ˌaməˈrɪndɪən/ (also **Amerind** /ˈamərɪnd/) ▸ **adjective & noun** another term for **AMERICAN INDIAN**, used chiefly in anthropological and linguistic contexts.
– ORIGIN late 19th cent.: blend of **AMERICAN** and **INDIAN**.

Ameslan /ˈamɪslan/ ▸ **noun** another term for **AMERICAN SIGN LANGUAGE**.
– ORIGIN 1970s: acronym.

Ames test /eɪmz/ ▸ **noun** Medicine a test to determine the mutagenic activity of chemicals by observing whether they cause mutations in sample bacteria.
– ORIGIN 1970s: named after Bruce N. *Ames* (born 1928), the American biochemist who devised it.

amethyst /ˈaməθɪst/ ▸ **noun** a precious stone consisting of a violet or purple variety of quartz. ■ a violet or purple colour: [as modifier] *an amethyst dress*.
– DERIVATIVES **amethystine** /-ˈθɪstiːn/ **adjective**.
– ORIGIN Middle English: via Old French from Latin *amethystus*, from Greek *amethustos* 'not drunken' (because the stone was believed to prevent intoxication).

amethyst deceiver ▸ **noun** an edible woodland mushroom with a lilac cap and stem, found in both Eurasia and North America. ● *Laccaria amethystea*, family Tricholomataceae, class Hymenomycetes.

Amex ▸ **abbreviation** ■ trademark American Express. ■ American Stock Exchange.

Amhara /amˈhɑːrə/ ▸ **noun** (pl. **same** or **Amharas**) a member of a Semitic people of central Ethiopia.
– ORIGIN from *Amhara*, the name of a region of central Ethiopia.

Amharic /amˈharɪk/ ▸ **noun** [mass noun] the official language of Ethiopia, a Semitic language descended from Ge'ez and spoken by about 9 million people.
▸ **adjective** relating to Amharic.

amiability ▸ **noun** [mass noun] the quality of having a friendly and pleasant manner; geniality: *his good-natured amiability*.

amiable ▸ **adjective** having or displaying a friendly and pleasant manner: *the amiable young man greeted me enthusiastically*.
– DERIVATIVES **amiableness** **noun**, **amiably** **adverb**.
– ORIGIN late Middle English (originally in the senses 'kind', and 'lovely, lovable'): via Old French from late Latin *amicabilis* 'amicable'. The current sense, influenced by modern French *aimable* 'trying to please', dates from the mid 18th cent.

amianthus /ˌamɪˈanθəs/ ▸ **noun** [mass noun] a variety of asbestos with fine silky fibres which can be woven.
– ORIGIN early 17th cent.: from Latin *amiantus*, from Greek *amiantos* 'undefiled' (i.e. purified of stains by fire, it being incombustible), from *a-* 'not' + *miainein* 'defile'. The spelling was changed from the Latin on the pattern of plant names ending in *-anthus*, from Greek *anthos* 'flower'.

amicable /ˈamɪkəb(ə)l/ ▸ **adjective** characterized by friendliness and absence of discord: *an amicable settlement of the dispute | the meeting was relatively amicable*.
– DERIVATIVES **amicability** **noun**, **amicableness** **noun**, **amicably** **adverb**.
– ORIGIN late Middle English (in the sense 'pleasant, benign', applied to things): from late Latin *amicabilis*, from Latin *amicus* 'friend'.

amicable numbers ▸ **plural noun** Mathematics a pair of numbers, each of which is the sum of the factors of the other (e.g. 220 and 284).

amice /ˈamɪs/ ▸ **noun 1** a white linen cloth worn on the neck and shoulders, under the alb, by a priest celebrating the Eucharist.
2 a cap, hood, or cape worn by members of certain religious orders.
– ORIGIN late Middle English: sense 1 from medieval Latin *amicia*, *amisia*, of unknown origin; sense 2 from Old French *aumusse*, from medieval Latin *almucia*, of unknown origin.

amicus /aˈmʌɪkəs/ (in full **amicus curiae** /ˈkjʊərɪiː/) ▸ **noun** (pl. **amici** /-siː/, **amici curiae**) an impartial adviser to a court of law in a particular case.
– ORIGIN early 17th cent.: modern Latin, literally 'friend', (in full) 'friend of the court'.

amid ▸ **preposition** surrounded by; in the middle of: *our dream home, set amid magnificent rolling countryside*. ■ in an atmosphere or against a background of: *talks broke down amid accusations of a hostile takeover bid*.
– ORIGIN Middle English *amidde(s)* (see **A**[2], **MID**[1]).

Amidah /əˈmiːdə/ ▸ **noun** Judaism a prayer consisting of a varying number of blessings recited while the worshippers stand.
– ORIGIN late 19th cent.: Hebrew, literally 'standing'.

amide /ˈeɪmʌɪd, ˈamʌɪd/ ▸ **noun** Chemistry an organic compound containing the group $-C(O)NH_2$, derived from ammonia by replacement of a hydrogen atom by an acyl group. ■ a compound derived from ammonia by replacement of a hydrogen atom by a metal, containing the anion NH_2^-.
– ORIGIN mid 19th cent.: from **AMMONIA** + **-IDE**.

amidships (also **amidship**) ▸ **adverb & adjective** in the middle of a ship, either longitudinally or laterally: [as adv.] *the destroyer rammed her amidships* | [as adj.] *an amidships engine room*.
– ORIGIN late 17th cent.: from **A-**[2] (expressing position or direction) + **MIDSHIP**, influenced by **AMID**.

amidst ▸ **preposition** chiefly literary variant of **AMID**.

Amiens /ˈamɪənz/, French /amjɛ̃/ a town in northern France; pop. 139,271 (2006).

amigo /əˈmiːgəʊ/ ▸ **noun** (pl. **amigos**) N. Amer. informal used to address or refer to a friend, chiefly in Spanish-speaking areas.
– ORIGIN mid 19th cent.: Spanish.

Amin /aˈmiːn/, Idi (1925–2003), Ugandan soldier and head of state 1971–9; full name *Idi Amin Dada*. Amin overthrew President Obote in a coup, and was deposed after a period of rule characterized by the murder of political opponents and the expulsion of non-Africans.

Amindivi Islands /ˌamɪnˈdiːvi/ the northernmost group of islands in the Indian territory of Lakshadweep in the Indian Ocean.

amine /ˈeɪmiːn/ ▸ **noun** Chemistry an organic compound derived from ammonia by replacement of one or more hydrogen atoms by organic radicals.
– ORIGIN mid 19th cent.: from **AMMONIA** + **-INE**[4].

amino /əˈmiːnəʊ, əˈmʌɪnəʊ/ ▸ **noun** [as modifier] Chemistry the group $-NH_2$, present in amino acids, amides, and many amines.
– ORIGIN late 19th cent.: from **AMINE**.

amino acid ▸ **noun** Biochemistry a simple organic compound containing both a carboxyl ($-COOH$) and an amino ($-NH_2$) group.

> Amino acids occur naturally in plant and animal tissues and form the basic constituents of proteins. There are about twenty common amino acids, of which the simplest is glycine (H_2NCH_2COOH).

amir /əˈmɪə/ ▸ **noun** variant spelling of **EMIR**.
– ORIGIN late 16th cent.: from Persian and Urdu, from Arabic *'amīr* 'commander', from *'amara* 'to command'; compare with **EMIR**.

Amirante Islands /ˈamɪrant, ˌamɪˈranti/ a group of coral islands in the Indian Ocean, forming part of the Seychelles.

Amis[1] /ˈeɪmɪs/, Sir Kingsley (1922–95), English novelist. He achieved popular success with his first novel *Lucky Jim* (1954); his later novels include *The Old Devils* (Booker Prize, 1986) and *The Folks that Live on the Hill* (1990).

Amis[2] /ˈeɪmɪs/, Martin (Louis) (b.1949), English novelist, son of Kingsley Amis. Notable works: *The Rachel Papers* (1973), *Money* (1984), and *Time's Arrow* (1991).

Amish /ˈamɪʃ, ˈɑː-, ˈeɪ-/ ▸ **plural noun** the members of a strict Mennonite sect founded by the Swiss preacher Jakob Amman (or Amen) (*c.*1645–*c.*1730). Now living mainly in Pennsylvania and Ohio, the Amish migrated to North America from *c.*1720.
▸ **adjective** relating to the Amish.
– ORIGIN mid 19th cent.: apparently from German *amisch*, from the name Jakob *Amman*.

amiss ▸ **adjective** [predic.] not quite right; inappropriate or out of place: *there was* ***something amiss*** *about his calculations*.
▸ **adverb** wrongly or inappropriately: *the prime minister may have constructed his cabinet a little amiss*.

– PHRASES **take something amiss** Brit. be offended by something that is said, especially through misinterpreting the intentions behind it. **something would not go** (or **come**) **amiss** Brit. the specified thing would be welcome and useful: *you look as if a good meal wouldn't go amiss.*
– ORIGIN Middle English: probably from Old Norse *á mis* 'so as to miss', from *á* 'on' + *mis* (related to MISS[1]).

amitotic /ˌeɪmʌɪˈtɒtɪk, ˌamʌɪ-/ ▶ **adjective** Biology relating to or denoting the division of a cell nucleus without mitosis.
– DERIVATIVES **amitosis** noun, **amitotically** adverb.

amitriptyline /ˌamɪˈtrɪptɪliːn/ ▶ **noun** [mass noun] Medicine an antidepressant drug of the tricyclic group, with a mild tranquillizing action.
– ORIGIN 1960s: from *ami(ne)* + TRI- + *(he)ptyl* + -INE[4].

amity /ˈamɪti/ ▶ **noun** [mass noun] formal friendly relations.
– ORIGIN late Middle English: from Old French *amitie*, based on Latin *amicus* 'friend'.

amma /ˈʌmɑː/ ▶ **noun** Indian informal one's mother (often used as a familiar form of address).
– ORIGIN probably derived from a child's word, perhaps influenced by AMAH.

Amman /əˈmɑːn/ the capital of Jordan; pop. 1,307,017 (2004).

ammeter /ˈamɪtə/ ▶ **noun** an instrument for measuring electric current in amperes.
– ORIGIN late 19th cent.: from AMPERE + -METER.

ammo /ˈaməʊ/ ▶ **noun** informal term for AMMUNITION.

Ammon Greek and Roman form of AMUN.

ammonia /əˈməʊnɪə/ ▶ **noun** [mass noun] a colourless gas with a characteristic pungent smell, which dissolves in water to give a strongly alkaline solution.
● Chem. formula: NH_3.
■ a solution of ammonia, used as a cleaning fluid.
– ORIGIN late 18th cent.: modern Latin, from *sal ammoniacus* (see SAL AMMONIAC).

ammoniacal /ˌamə(ʊ)ˈnʌɪək(ə)l/ ▶ **adjective** of or containing ammonia.
– ORIGIN mid 18th cent.: from Middle English *ammoniac*, via Old French from Latin *ammoniacus*. This represented the Greek word *ammōniakos* 'of Ammon', used as a name for the salt and gum obtained near the temple of *Jupiter Ammon* at Siwa in Egypt. Compare with SAL AMMONIAC.

ammoniated ▶ **adjective** combined or treated with ammonia.

ammonite /ˈamənʌɪt/ ▶ **noun** an ammonoid fossil, especially one of a later type found chiefly in the Jurassic and Cretaceous periods, typically with intricately frilled suture lines. Compare with CERATITE and GONIATITE. ● Typified by ammonoids of the order Ammonitida.
– ORIGIN mid 18th cent.: from modern Latin *ammonites*, from medieval Latin *cornu Ammonis* 'horn of Ammon', from the fossil's resemblance to the ram's horn associated with Jupiter Ammon (see AMMONIACAL).

ammonium /əˈməʊnɪəm/ ▶ **noun** [as modifier] Chemistry the cation NH_4^+, present in solutions of ammonia and in salts derived from ammonia.
– ORIGIN early 19th cent.: from AMMONIA + -IUM.

ammonium carbonate ▶ **noun** [mass noun] Chemistry a white crystalline solid which slowly decomposes, giving off ammonia, and is an ingredient of sal volatile.
● Chem. formula: $(NH_4)_2CO_3$. Commercial forms often contain other, related salts.

ammonium chloride ▶ **noun** [mass noun] Chemistry a white crystalline salt used chiefly in dry cells, as a mordant, and as soldering flux. Also called SAL AMMONIAC. ● Chem. formula: NH_4Cl.

ammonium nitrate ▶ **noun** [mass noun] Chemistry a white crystalline solid used as a fertilizer and as a component of some explosives. ● Chem. formula: NH_4NO_3.

ammonoid /ˈamənɔɪd/ Palaeontology ▶ **noun** an extinct cephalopod mollusc with a flat-coiled spiral shell, found commonly as a fossil in marine deposits from the Devonian to the Cretaceous periods. ● Subclass Ammonoidea, class Cephalopoda: numerous families. See AMMONITE, CERATITE, and GONIATITE.
▶ **adjective** relating to the ammonoids.
– ORIGIN mid 19th cent.: from modern Latin *Ammonoidea*, based on AMMON (see AMMONITE).

ammunition ▶ **noun** [mass noun] a supply or quantity of bullets and shells. ■ considerations that can be used to support one's case in debate: *these figures provide ammunition to the argument for more resources.*
– ORIGIN late 16th cent.: from obsolete French *amunition*, alteration (by wrong division) of *la munition* 'the munition' (see MUNITION).

amnesia /amˈniːzɪə/ ▶ **noun** [mass noun] a partial or total loss of memory.
– DERIVATIVES **amnesiac** noun & adjective, **amnesic** adjective & noun.
– ORIGIN late 18th cent.: from Greek *amnēsia* 'forgetfulness'.

amnesty ▶ **noun** (pl. **amnesties**) an official pardon for people who have been convicted of political offences: *an amnesty for political prisoners.* ■ an undertaking by the authorities to take no action against specified offences during a fixed period: *a month-long weapons amnesty.*
▶ **verb** (**amnesties**, **amnestying**, **amnestied**) [with obj.] grant an official pardon to.
– ORIGIN late 16th cent.: via Latin from Greek *amnēstia* 'forgetfulness'.

Amnesty International an independent international organization in support of human rights, especially for prisoners of conscience. The organization was awarded the Nobel Peace Prize in 1977.

amnio /ˈamnɪəʊ/ ▶ **noun** (pl. **amnios**) informal term for AMNIOCENTESIS.

amniocentesis /ˌamnɪəʊsɛnˈtiːsɪs/ ▶ **noun** (pl. **amniocenteses** /-siːz/) a process in which amniotic fluid is sampled using a hollow needle inserted into the uterus, to screen for abnormalities in the developing fetus.
– ORIGIN 1950s: from AMNION + Greek *kentēsis* 'pricking' (from *kentein* 'to prick').

amnion /ˈamnɪən/ ▶ **noun** (pl. **amnions** or **amnia**) the innermost membrane that encloses the embryo of a mammal, bird, or reptile.
– ORIGIN mid 17th cent.: from Greek, 'caul', diminutive of *amnos* 'lamb'.

amniote /ˈamnɪəʊt/ ▶ **noun** Zoology an animal whose embryo develops in an amnion and chorion and has an allantois; a mammal, bird, or reptile.
– ORIGIN late 19th cent.: from modern Latin *Amniota*, back-formation from AMNIOTIC.

amniotic ▶ **adjective** relating to the amnion.
– ORIGIN early 19th cent.: formed irregularly from obsolete *amnios* 'amnion' + -OTIC, perhaps via French *amniotique*.

amniotic fluid ▶ **noun** [mass noun] the fluid surrounding a fetus within the amnion.

amn't /ˈam(ə)nt/ chiefly Scottish & Irish ▶ **contraction** am not.

amoeba /əˈmiːbə/ (US also **ameba**) ▶ **noun** (pl. **amoebas** or **amoebae** /-biː/) a single-celled animal which catches food and moves about by extending finger-like projections of protoplasm. Amoebas are either free-living in damp environments or parasitic.
● Many families and genera in the phylum Rhizopoda, kingdom Protista, including the aquatic *Amoeba proteus*.
– DERIVATIVES **amoebic** adjective, **amoeboid** adjective.
– ORIGIN mid 19th cent.: modern Latin, from Greek *amoibē* 'change, alternation'.

amoebiasis /ˌamiːˈbʌɪəsɪs/ (US also **amebiasis**) ▶ **noun** [mass noun] Medicine infection with amoebas, especially as causing dysentery.
– ORIGIN early 20th cent.: from AMOEBA + -ASIS.

amok /əˈmɒk/ (also **amuck**) ▶ **adverb** (in phrase **run amok**) behave uncontrollably and disruptively: *stone-throwing anarchists were running amok.*
– ORIGIN mid 17th cent.: via Portuguese *amouco*, from Malay *amok* 'rushing in a frenzy'. Early use was as a noun denoting a Malay in a homicidal frenzy.

Amon variant spelling of AMUN.

among (chiefly Brit. also **amongst**) ▶ **preposition 1** situated more or less centrally in relation to (several other things): *flowers hidden among the roots of the trees | you're among friends.*
2 being a member or members of (a larger set): *a British woman was among the 54 victims of the disaster | snakes are among the animals most feared by man.*
3 occurring in or shared by (some members of a group or community): *a drop in tooth decay among children | members of the government bickered **among** themselves.*
4 indicating a division, choice, or differentiation involving three or more participants: *the old king called the three princesses to divide his kingdom among them | the State Council would elect a temporary president from among its members.*
– ORIGIN Old English *ongemang* (from *on* 'in' + *gemang* 'assemblage, mingling'). The *-st* of *amongst* represents *-s* (adverbial genitive) + *-t* probably by association with superlatives (as in *against*).

amontillado /əˌmɒntɪˈlɑːdəʊ, -ˈjɑː-/ ▶ **noun** (pl. **amontillados**) [mass noun] a medium dry sherry.
– ORIGIN Spanish, from *Montilla*, the name of a town in southern Spain where the original wine was produced.

amoral /eɪˈmɒr(ə)l/ ▶ **adjective** lacking a moral sense; unconcerned with the rightness or wrongness of something: *an amoral attitude to sex.*
– DERIVATIVES **amoralism** noun, **amoralist** noun, **amorality** noun, **amorally** adverb.

> **USAGE** Amoral is distinct in meaning from **immoral**: while **immoral** means 'not conforming to accepted standards of morality', **amoral** implies 'not concerned with morality'. The difference is illustrated in the following two examples: *the client pays for the **amoral** expertise of the lawyer; the council judged the film to be **immoral** and obscene.*

amoretto /ˌaməˈrɛtəʊ/ ▶ **noun** (pl. **amoretti** /-ti/) a representation of Cupid in a work of art.
– ORIGIN Italian, diminutive of *amore* 'love', from Latin *amor*.

amorist /ˈamərɪst/ ▶ **noun** a person who is in love or who writes about love.
– ORIGIN late 16th cent.: from Latin *amor* or French *amour* 'love' + -IST.

Amorite /ˈamərʌɪt/ ▶ **noun** a member of a seminomadic people living in Mesopotamia, Palestine, and Syria in the 3rd millennium BC, founders of the ancient city of Mari on the Euphrates and the first dynasty of Babylon.
▶ **adjective** relating to the Amorites.
– ORIGIN from Hebrew *'ĕmōrī* + -ITE[1].

amoroso[1] /ˌaməˈrəʊzəʊ, -səʊ/ ▶ **adverb & adjective** Music (especially as a direction) in a loving or tender manner.
– ORIGIN Italian, from medieval Latin *amorosus* (see AMOROUS).

amoroso[2] /ˌaməˈrəʊzəʊ, -səʊ/ ▶ **noun** [mass noun] a dark, sweet sherry.
– ORIGIN from Spanish, literally 'amorous', from medieval Latin *amorosus* (see AMOROUS).

amorous ▶ **adjective** showing, feeling, or relating to sexual desire: *she rejected his amorous advances.*
– DERIVATIVES **amorously** adverb, **amorousness** noun.
– ORIGIN Middle English: via Old French from medieval Latin *amorosus*, from Latin *amor* 'love'.

amorphous /əˈmɔːfəs/ ▶ **adjective** without a clearly defined shape or form: *an amorphous, characterless conurbation.* ■ lacking a clear structure or focus: *an amorphous and leaderless legislature.* ■ Mineralogy & Chemistry (of a solid) not crystalline, or not apparently crystalline.
– DERIVATIVES **amorphously** adverb, **amorphousness** noun.
– ORIGIN mid 18th cent.: from modern Latin *amorphus*, from Greek *amorphos* 'shapeless' (from *a-* 'without' + *morphē* 'form') + -OUS.

amortize /əˈmɔːtʌɪz/ (also **amortise**) ▶ **verb** [with obj.] gradually write off the initial cost of (an asset) over a period. ■ reduce or pay off (a debt) with regular payments. ■ historical transfer (land) to a corporation in mortmain.
– DERIVATIVES **amortization** noun.
– ORIGIN late Middle English (in the senses 'deaden' and 'transfer (land) to a corporation in mortmain'): from Old French *amortiss-*, lengthened stem of *amortir*, based on Latin *ad* 'to, at' + *mors, mort-* 'death'.

Amos /ˈeɪmɒs/ a Hebrew minor prophet (*c.*760 BC), a shepherd of Tekoa, near Jerusalem. ■ a book of the Bible containing the prophecies of Amos.

amosite /ˈeɪməsʌɪt/ ▶ **noun** [mass noun] an iron-rich amphibole asbestos, mined in South Africa.
– ORIGIN early 20th cent.: from the initial letters of Asbestos Mines of South Africa + -ITE[1].

amount ▶ **noun** a quantity of something, especially the total of a thing or things in number, size, value, or extent: *sport gives an enormous **amount** of pleasure to many people | the substance is harmless if taken in small amounts.* ■ a sum of money: *they have spent a colossal amount rebuilding the stadium.*
▶ **verb** [no obj.] (**amount to**) come to be (the total) when added together: *losses amounted to over 10 million pounds.* ■ be regarded or classified as; be the equivalent of: *their actions amounted to a conspiracy | what*

this guy was doing clearly did amount to persecution. ■ develop into; become: *you'll never amount to anything.*
– PHRASES **any amount of** a great deal or number of: *the second half produced any amount of action.* **no amount of** not even the greatest possible amount of: *no amount of talk is going to change anything.*
– ORIGIN Middle English (as a verb): from Old French *amunter*, from *amont* 'upward', literally 'uphill', from Latin *ad montem*. The noun use dates from the early 18th cent.

amour /əˈmʊə/ ▶ **noun** a love affair or lover, especially one that is secret: *he is enraged at this revelation of his past amours.*
– ORIGIN Middle English (originally in the sense 'love, affection'): via Old French from Latin *amor* 'love'. The current sense dates from the late 16th cent.

amour courtois /əˌmʊə kɔːˈtwʌ/, French /amuʀ kuʀtwa/ ▶ **noun** another term for **COURTLY LOVE**.
– ORIGIN French.

amour fou /əˌmʊə ˈfuː/, French /amuʀ fu/ ▶ **noun** [mass noun] uncontrollable or obsessive passion.
– ORIGIN 1970s: French, 'insane love'.

amour propre /aˌmʊə ˈprɒpr(ə)/, French /amuʀ pʀɔpʀ/ ▶ **noun** [mass noun] a sense of one's own worth; self-respect: *Pablo's amour propre must have been tested by his short stature.*
– ORIGIN French.

amoxycillin /əˌmɒksɪˈsɪlɪn/ (also **amoxicillin**) ▶ **noun** [mass noun] Medicine a semi-synthetic penicillin closely related to ampicillin and with similar properties, but more readily absorbed when taken orally.
– ORIGIN 1970s: from **AMINO** + **OXY-**[2] + **PENICILLIN**.

Amoy /əˈmɔɪ/ another name for **XIAMEN**.

AMP ▶ **abbreviation** Biochemistry adenosine monophosphate.

amp[1] ▶ **noun** short for **AMPERE**.

amp[2] informal ▶ **noun** short for **AMPLIFIER**.
▶ **verb** [with obj.] **1** (often **amp something up**) play (music) through electric amplification: *their willingness to amp up traditional songs virtually began the folk-rock genre.*
2 (as adj. **amped** or **amped up**) N. Amer. full of nervous energy, especially through taking amphetamines or similar drugs.

Ampakine /ˈampəkʌɪn/ ▶ **noun** (trademark in the US) any of a class of synthetic compounds which facilitate transmission of nerve impulses in the brain and appear to improve memory and learning capacity.
– ORIGIN 1990s: from *AMPA* (an acronym denoting certain receptors in the brain) + Greek *kinein* 'to move'.

ampelographer /ˌampəˈlɒɡrəfə/ ▶ **noun** an expert in the study and classification of cultivated varieties of grape.
– DERIVATIVES **ampelography** noun.
– ORIGIN late 19th cent.: via French from Greek *ampelos* 'vine' + **-GRAPHER**.

ampelopsis /ˌampɪˈlɒpsɪs/ ▶ **noun** (pl. **same**) a bushy climbing plant of the vine family. ● Genus *Ampelopsis*, family Vitaceae: two species.
– ORIGIN modern Latin, from Greek *ampelos* 'vine' + *opsis* 'appearance'.

amperage /ˈamp(ə)rɪdʒ/ ▶ **noun** the strength of an electric current in amperes.

ampere /ˈampɛː/ (abbrev.: **A**) ▶ **noun** a unit of electric current equal to a flow of one coulomb per second.
● The SI base unit of electric current, 1 ampere is precisely defined as that constant current which, if maintained in two straight parallel conductors of infinite length, of negligible circular cross section, and placed 1 metre apart in a vacuum, would produce between these conductors a force of 2×10^{-7} newton per metre.
– ORIGIN late 19th cent.: named after A-M **AMPÈRE**.

Ampère /ˈampɛː/, French /ɑ̃pɛʀ/, André-Marie (1775–1836), French physicist, mathematician, and philosopher, who analysed the relationship between magnetic force and electric current.

ampersand /ˈampəsand/ ▶ **noun** the sign & (standing for *and*, as in *Smith & Co.*, or the Latin *et*, as in *&c.*).
– ORIGIN mid 19th cent.: alteration of *and per se and*, '& by itself is *and*', formerly chanted as an aid to learning the sign.

amphetamine /amˈfɛtəmiːn, -ɪn/ ▶ **noun** [mass noun] a synthetic, addictive, mood-altering drug, used illegally as a stimulant: *the amphetamine put him on a high for an hour* | [count noun] *he was jailed for three months for possessing amphetamines.* ● Chem. formula: $C_6H_5CH_2CH(CH_3)NH_2$.
– ORIGIN 1930s: abbreviation of its chemical name, *a(lpha-)m(ethyl) phe(ne)t(hyl)amine*.

amphi- /ˈamfi/ ▶ **combining form 1** both: *amphibian.* ■ of both kinds: *amphipod.* ■ on both sides: *amphiprostyle.*
2 around: *amphitheatre.*
– ORIGIN from Greek.

amphibian ▶ **noun** a cold-blooded vertebrate animal of a class that comprises the frogs, toads, newts, salamanders, and caecilians. They are distinguished by having an aquatic gill-breathing larval stage followed (typically) by a terrestrial lung-breathing adult stage. ● Class Amphibia: orders Urodela (newts and salamanders), Anura (frogs and toads), and Gymnophiona (caecilians).
▶ **adjective** relating to amphibians.
– ORIGIN mid 17th cent. (in the sense 'having two modes of existence or of doubtful nature'): from modern Latin *amphibium* 'an amphibian', from Greek *amphibion* (noun use of *amphibios* 'living both in water and on land', from *amphi* 'both' + *bios* 'life').

amphibious /amˈfɪbɪəs/ ▶ **adjective** relating to, living in, or suited for both land and water: *an amphibious vehicle.* ■ (of a military operation) involving forces landed from the sea: *an amphibious assault.*
– DERIVATIVES **amphibiously** adverb.
– ORIGIN mid 17th cent.: from modern Latin *amphibium*, from Greek *amphibion* (see **AMPHIBIAN**) + **-OUS**.

amphibole /ˈamfɪbəʊl/ ▶ **noun** [mass noun] any of a class of rock-forming silicate or aluminosilicate minerals typically occurring as fibrous or columnar crystals.
– ORIGIN early 19th cent.: from French, from Latin *amphibolus* 'ambiguous' (because of the varied structure of these minerals), from Greek *amphibolos*, from *amphi-* 'both, on both sides' + *ballein* 'to throw'.

amphibolite /amˈfɪbəlʌɪt/ ▶ **noun** [mass noun] Geology a granular metamorphic rock consisting mainly of hornblende and plagioclase.

amphibology /ˌamfɪˈbɒlədʒi/ ▶ **noun** (pl. **amphibologies**) a phrase or sentence that is grammatically ambiguous, such as *She sees more of her children than her husband.*
– ORIGIN late Middle English: from Old French *amphibologie*, from late Latin *amphibologia*, from Latin *amphibolia*, from Greek *amphibolos* 'ambiguous' (see **AMPHIBOLE**).

amphiboly /amˈfɪbəli/ ▶ **noun** (pl. **amphibolies**) another term for **AMPHIBOLOGY**.

amphibrach /ˈamfɪbrak/ ▶ **noun** Prosody a metrical foot consisting of a stressed syllable between two unstressed syllables or (in Greek and Latin) a long syllable between two short syllables.
– ORIGIN late 16th cent. (originally in the Latin forms *amphibrachus*, *amphibrachys*): via Latin from Greek *amphibrakhus* 'short at both ends'.

amphimixis /ˌamfɪˈmɪksɪs/ ▶ **noun** [mass noun] Botany sexual reproduction involving the fusion of two different gametes to form a zygote. Often contrasted with **APOMIXIS**.
– DERIVATIVES **amphimictic** adjective.
– ORIGIN late 19th cent.: from **AMPHI-** + Greek *mixis* 'mingling'.

amphioxus /ˌamfɪˈɒksəs/ ▶ **noun** a small lancelet which is caught for food in parts of Asia. ● Genus *Branchiostoma* (formerly *Amphioxus*), family Branchiostomidae.
– ORIGIN mid 19th cent.: modern Latin, from **AMPHI-** + Greek *oxus* 'sharp'.

amphipathic /ˌamfɪˈpaθɪk/ (also **amphiphilic** /ˌamfɪˈfɪlɪk/) ▶ **adjective** Biochemistry (of a molecule, especially a protein) having both hydrophilic and hydrophobic parts.
– ORIGIN 1930s: from **AMPHI-** + Greek *pathikos* (from *pathos* 'experience').

amphipod /ˈamfɪpɒd/ ▶ **noun** Zoology a crustacean of the chiefly marine order Amphipoda.

Amphipoda /ˌamfɪˈpəʊdə/ ▶ **plural noun** Zoology an order of chiefly marine crustaceans with a laterally compressed body and a large number of leg-like appendages.
– ORIGIN modern Latin (plural), from **AMPHI-** 'of both kinds' (because some legs are specialized for swimming and some for feeding) + Greek *pous*, *pod-* 'foot'.

amphiprostyle /amˈfɪprəstʌɪl/ ▶ **adjective** (of a classical building) having a portico at each end but not at the sides.
– ORIGIN early 18th cent.: via Latin from Greek *amphiprostulos*, from *amphi-* 'both, on both sides' + *prostulos* 'having pillars in front' (see **PROSTYLE**).

amphisbaena /ˌamfɪsˈbiːnə/ ▶ **noun** a mythical serpent with a head at each end.
– ORIGIN late Middle English: via Latin from Greek *amphisbaina*, from *amphis* 'both ways' + *bainein* 'go'.

Amphisbaenia /ˌamfɪsˈbiːnɪə/ ▶ **plural noun** Zoology a group of reptiles which comprises the worm lizards. ● Suborder Amphisbaenia, order Squamata.
– DERIVATIVES **amphisbaenian** noun & adjective.
– ORIGIN modern Latin, from Greek *amphisbaina*, from *amphis* 'both' + *bainein* 'go, walk'.

amphitheatre (US **amphitheater**) ▶ **noun** (especially in Greek and Roman architecture) an open, circular or oval building with a central space for the presentation of dramatic or sporting events surrounded by tiers of seats for spectators. ■ a semicircular seating gallery in a theatre.
– ORIGIN late Middle English: via Latin from Greek *amphitheatron*, from *amphi* 'on both sides' + *theatron* (see **THEATRE**).

Amphitrite /ˌamfɪˈtrʌɪti/ Greek Mythology a sea goddess, wife of Poseidon and mother of Triton.

amphiuma /ˌamfɪˈjuːmə/ ▶ **noun** a fully aquatic eel-like amphibian with very small limbs, occurring in stagnant water and swamps in the south-eastern US. ● Family Amphiumidae and genus *Amphiuma*: three species.
– ORIGIN modern Latin, probably formed irregularly from **AMPHI-** 'both' + Greek *pneuma* 'breath'.

amphora /ˈamf(ə)rə/ ▶ **noun** (pl. **amphorae** /-riː/ or **amphoras**) a tall ancient Greek or Roman jar or jug with two handles and a narrow neck.
– ORIGIN Latin, from Greek *amphoreus*, or from French *amphore*.

amphoteric /ˌamfəˈtɛrɪk/ ▶ **adjective** Chemistry (of a compound, especially a metal oxide or hydroxide) able to react both as a base and as an acid.
– ORIGIN mid 19th cent.: from Greek *amphoteros*, comparative of *amphō* 'both', + **-IC**.

ampicillin /ˌampɪˈsɪlɪn/ ▶ **noun** [mass noun] Medicine a semi-synthetic form of penicillin used to treat infections of the urinary and respiratory tracts.
– ORIGIN 1960s: blend of **AMINO** and a contraction of **PENICILLIN**.

ample ▶ **adjective** (**ampler**, **amplest**) enough or more than enough; plentiful: *there is ample time for discussion* | *an ample supply of consumer goods.* ■ large and accommodating: *he leaned back in his ample chair.* ■ (of a person's figure) full or broad: *she stood with her hands on her ample hips.*
– DERIVATIVES **ampleness** noun, **amply** adverb.
– ORIGIN late Middle English: via French from Latin *amplus* 'large, capacious, abundant'.

amplexus /amˈplɛksəs/ ▶ **noun** [mass noun] Zoology the mating position of frogs and toads, in which the male clasps the female about the back.
– ORIGIN 1930s: from Latin, 'an embrace'.

amplifier ▶ **noun** an electronic device for increasing the amplitude of electrical signals, used chiefly in sound reproduction. ■ a device of this kind combined with a loudspeaker, used to amplify electric guitars and other musical instruments.

amplify ▶ **verb** (**amplifies**, **amplifying**, **amplified**) [with obj.] **1** increase the volume of (sound), especially using an amplifier: (as adj. **amplified**) *amplified pop music.* ■ increase the amplitude of (an electrical signal or other oscillation). ■ make (something) more marked or intense: *urban policy initiatives amplified social polarization.*
2 enlarge upon or add detail to (a story or statement): *the notes amplify information contained in the statement.*
3 Genetics make multiple copies of (a gene or DNA sequence).
– DERIVATIVES **amplification** noun.
– ORIGIN late Middle English (in the general sense 'increase, augment'): from Old French *amplifier*, from Latin *amplificare*, from *amplus* 'large, abundant'.

amplitude ▶ **noun** [mass noun] **1** Physics the maximum extent of a vibration or oscillation, measured from the position of equilibrium. ■ the maximum difference of an alternating electric current or potential from the average value.
2 Astronomy the angular distance of a celestial object from the true east or west point of the horizon at rising or setting.
3 breadth, range, or magnitude: *the amplitude of the crime of manslaughter lies beneath murder.*
4 Mathematics the angle between the real axis of an Argand diagram and a vector representing a complex number.
– ORIGIN mid 16th cent. (in the senses 'physical extent' and 'grandeur'): from Latin *amplitudo*, from *amplus* 'large, abundant'.

amplitude modulation (abbrev.: **AM**) ▶ **noun** [mass noun] the modulation of a wave by varying its amplitude, used especially as a means of broadcasting an audio signal by combining it with a radio carrier wave. Often contrasted with **FREQUENCY MODULATION**.

ampoule /ˈampuːl/ (US also **ampul** or **ampule** /ˈampjuːl/) ▶ **noun** a small sealed glass capsule containing a liquid, especially a measured quantity ready for injecting.
– ORIGIN early 20th cent.: from French, from Latin *ampulla* (see **AMPULLA**).

ampulla /amˈpʊlə/ ▶ **noun** (pl. **ampullae** /-liː/) **1** a roughly spherical Roman flask with two handles. ■ a flask for sacred uses such as holding the oil for anointing the sovereign at a coronation.
2 Anatomy & Zoology a cavity, or the dilated end of a vessel, shaped like a Roman ampulla.
– ORIGIN late Middle English: from Latin, diminutive of *ampora*, variant of *amphora* (see **AMPHORA**).

amputate /ˈampjʊteɪt/ ▶ **verb** [with obj.] cut off (a limb) by surgical operation: *surgeons had to amputate her left hand*.
– DERIVATIVES **amputation** noun, **amputator** noun.
– ORIGIN mid 16th cent.: from Latin *amputat-* 'lopped off', from *amputare*, from *am-* (for *amb-* 'about') + *putare* 'to prune'.

amputee ▶ **noun** a person who has had a limb amputated.

AMRAAM /ˈamram/ ▶ **abbreviation** advanced medium range air-to-air missile.

amrit /ˈʌmrɪt/ ▶ **noun** [mass noun] a syrup considered by Sikhs to be divine, and which they drink at religious observances including baptism.
– ORIGIN from Sanskrit *amṛta* 'immortal'.

Amritsar /ʌmˈrɪtsə/ a city in the state of Punjab in NW India; pop. 1,194,700 (est. 2009). It became the centre of the Sikh faith and the site of its holiest temple, the Golden Temple. It was the scene of a riot in 1919, in which 400 people were killed by British troops.

Amsterdam /ˌamstəˈdam, ˈamstədam/ the capital and largest city of the Netherlands; pop. 747,093 (2008). It is built on some ninety islands separated by canals. Although Amsterdam is the capital, the country's seat of government and administrative centre is at The Hague.

AMT ▶ **abbreviation** (in the US) alternative minimum tax, introduced to prevent companies and individuals using deductions and credits to pay no tax.

amtrac /ˈamtrak/ (also **amtrak**) ▶ **noun** US an amphibious tracked vehicle used for landing assault troops on a shore.
– ORIGIN Second World War: blend of **AMPHIBIOUS** and **TRACTOR**.

Amtrak /ˈamtrak/ trademark a federal passenger railway service in the US, operated by the National Railroad Passenger Corporation.

amu ▶ **abbreviation** atomic mass unit.

amuck /əˈmʌk/ ▶ **adverb** variant spelling of **AMOK**.

Amu Darya /ˌɑːmuː ˈdɑːrɪə/ a river of central Asia, rising in the Pamirs and flowing 2,400 km (1,500 miles) into the Aral Sea. In classical times it was known as the Oxus.

amulet /ˈamjʊlɪt/ ▶ **noun** an ornament or small piece of jewellery thought to give protection against evil, danger, or disease.
– ORIGIN late 16th cent.: from Latin *amuletum*, of unknown origin.

Amun /ˈamən/ (also **Amon**) Egyptian Mythology a supreme god of the ancient Egyptians, identified with the sun god Ra, and in Greek and Roman times with Zeus and Jupiter (under the name **Ammon**).

Amundsen /ˈɑːmʊnds(ə)n/, Roald (1872–1928), Norwegian explorer. Amundsen was the first to navigate the North-West Passage (1903–6), during which expedition he located the site of the magnetic north pole. In 1911 he became the first to reach the South Pole.

Amur /əˈmʊə/ a river of NE Asia, forming for the greater part of its length the boundary between Russia and China. Its length is about 4,350 km (2,737 miles). Chinese name **HEILONG**.

amuse ▶ **verb** [with obj.] **1** cause (someone) to find something funny: *he made faces to amuse her* | (as adj. **amused**) *people looked on with amused curiosity*.
2 provide interesting and enjoyable occupation for (someone); entertain: *they amused themselves digging through an old encyclopedia*.
– DERIVATIVES **amusedly** adverb (sense 1).
– ORIGIN late 15th cent. (in the sense 'delude, deceive'): from Old French *amuser* 'entertain, deceive', from *a-* (expressing causal effect) + *muser* 'stare stupidly'. Current senses date from the mid 17th cent.

amuse-bouche /əˌmjuːzˈbuːʃ, -muːz-/ ▶ **noun** (pl. **amuse-bouches** or **same**) another term for **AMUSE-GUEULE**.
– ORIGIN French, literally 'amuse mouth'.

amuse-gueule /əˌmjuːzˈgəːl/ ▶ **noun** (pl. **amuse-gueules** or **same**) a small savoury item of food served as an appetizer before a meal.
– ORIGIN French, literally 'amuse mouth'.

amusement ▶ **noun** [mass noun] **1** the state or experience of finding something funny: *we looked with amusement at our horoscopes*.
2 the provision or enjoyment of entertainment: *an evening's amusement*. ■ [count noun] something that causes laughter or provides entertainment: *she was like an adult planning amusements for a child*.
3 [count noun] Brit. a roundabout, game machine, etc. for providing entertainment at a fairground or resort.
– ORIGIN early 17th cent. (in the sense 'musing, diversion of the attention'): from French, from the verb *amuser* (see **AMUSE**).

amusement arcade ▶ **noun** Brit. an indoor area containing coin-operated game machines.

amusement park ▶ **noun** a large outdoor area with fairground rides, shows, and other entertainments.

amusing ▶ **adjective** causing laughter and providing entertainment: *such a likeable, amusing man!*
– DERIVATIVES **amusingly** adverb.

amygdala /əˈmɪgdələ/ ▶ **noun** (pl. **amygdalae** /əˈmɪgdəliː/) Anatomy a roughly almond-shaped mass of grey matter inside each cerebral hemisphere, involved with the experiencing of emotions.
– ORIGIN Late Middle English: via Latin from Greek *amugdalē* 'almond'.

amygdale /əˈmɪgdeɪl/ ▶ **noun** Geology a vesicle in an igneous rock, containing secondary minerals.
– ORIGIN late 19th cent.: from French, from Latin *amygdala* (see **AMYGDALA**).

amygdalin /əˈmɪgd(ə)lɪn/ ▶ **noun** [mass noun] Chemistry a bitter crystalline compound found in bitter almonds and the stones of peaches, apricots, and other fruit.
– ORIGIN mid 19th cent.: from Latin *amygdala* 'almond' + **-IN**[1].

amygdaloid /əˈmɪgdəlɔɪd/ ▶ **adjective** technical shaped like an almond.
▶ **noun** (also **amygdaloid nucleus**) Anatomy another term for **AMYGDALA**.

amygdaloidal ▶ **adjective** Geology relating to or containing amygdales.

amyl /ˈeɪmʌɪl, ˈamɪl/ ▶ **noun** [as modifier] Chemistry of or denoting the straight-chain pentyl radical $-C_5H_{11}$. ■ [mass noun] informal short for **AMYL NITRITE**.
– ORIGIN mid 19th cent.: from Latin *amylum* 'starch' + **-YL**.

amylase /ˈamɪleɪz/ ▶ **noun** [mass noun] Biochemistry an enzyme, found chiefly in saliva and pancreatic fluid, that converts starch and glycogen into simple sugars.

amyl nitrate ▶ **noun** [mass noun] Chemistry a colourless synthetic liquid used as an additive in diesel fuel to improve its ignition properties. ● Chem. formula: $C_5H_{11}NO_3$.

> **USAGE** **Amyl nitrate** and **amyl nitrite** are distinct substances. The street drug is **amyl nitrite**, but is often incorrectly called **amyl nitrate**.

amyl nitrite ▶ **noun** [mass noun] a yellowish volatile synthetic liquid used medicinally as a vasodilator. It is rapidly absorbed by the body on inhalation, and is sometimes used for its stimulatory effects. ● Chem. formula: $C_5H_{11}NO_2$.

amyloid /ˈamɪlɔɪd/ ▶ **noun** [mass noun] Medicine a starch-like protein which is deposited in the liver, kidneys, spleen, or other tissues in certain diseases. ■ another term for **AMYLOIDOSIS**.

amyloidosis /ˌamɪlɔɪˈdəʊsɪs/ ▶ **noun** [mass noun] Medicine deposition of amyloid in the body.

amylopectin /ˌamɪləʊˈpɛktɪn/ ▶ **noun** [mass noun] Biochemistry the non-crystallizable form of starch, consisting of branched polysaccharide chains.

amylose /ˈamɪləʊs, ˈamɪləʊz/ ▶ **noun** [mass noun] Biochemistry the crystallizable form of starch, consisting of long unbranched polysaccharide chains.

amyotrophic lateral sclerosis ▶ **noun** another term for **LOU GEHRIG'S DISEASE**.

amyotrophy /ˌamɪˈɒtrəfi/ ▶ **noun** [mass noun] Medicine muscular atrophy.
– DERIVATIVES **amyotrophic** adjective.
– ORIGIN late 19th cent.: from **A-**[1] 'not' + Greek *mus, muo-* 'muscle' + Greek *trophē* 'nourishment'.

Amytal /ˈamɪt(ə)l/ ▶ **noun** [mass noun] trademark a barbiturate drug used as a sedative and a hypnotic. ● Chem. formula: $C_{11}H_{18}N_2O_3$.
– ORIGIN 1920s: from **AMYL** + *-t-* (for ease of pronunciation) + **-AL**.

an ▶ **determiner** the form of the indefinite article (see **A**[1]) used before words beginning with a vowel sound.

> **USAGE** Is it '**a** historical document' or '**an** historical document'? '**A** hotel' or '**an** hotel'? There is still some divergence of opinion over which form of the indefinite article should be used before words that begin with **h-** and have an unstressed first syllable. In the 18th and 19th centuries people often did not pronounce the initial **h** for these words, and so **an** was commonly used. Today the **h** is pronounced, and so it is logical to use **a** rather than **an**. However, the indefinite article **an** is still encountered before the **h** in both British and American English, particularly with **historical**: in the Oxford English Corpus around a quarter of examples of **historical** are preceded with **an** rather than **a**.

an-[1] ▶ **prefix** variant spelling of **A-**[1] before a vowel (as in *anaemia*).

an-[2] ▶ **prefix** variant spelling of **AD-** assimilated before *n* (as in *annihilate, annotate*).

an-[3] ▶ **prefix** variant spelling of **ANA-** shortened before a vowel (as in *aneurysm*).

-an ▶ **suffix 1** forming adjectives and nouns, especially from: ■ names of places: *Cuban*. ■ names of systems: *Anglican*. ■ names of zoological classes or orders: *crustacean*. ■ names of founders: *Lutheran*.
2 /an/ Chemistry forming names of organic compounds, chiefly polysaccharides: *dextran*.
– ORIGIN from Latin *-anus, -ana, -anum*.

ana /ˈɑːnə/ ▶ **noun** archaic **1** [treated as pl.] anecdotes or literary gossip about a person.
2 [treated as sing.] a collection of a person's memorable sayings.
– ORIGIN mid 18th cent.: from **-ANA**.

ana- (usu. **an-** before a vowel) ▶ **prefix 1** up: *anabatic*.
2 back: *anamnesis*.
3 again: *anabiosis*.
– ORIGIN from Greek *ana* 'up'.

-ana ▶ **suffix** (forming plural nouns) denoting things associated with a person, place, or field of interest: *Americana* | *Victoriana*.
– ORIGIN from Latin, neuter plural of *-anus*, adjectival ending.

Anabaptism /ˌanəˈbaptɪz(ə)m/ ▶ **noun** [mass noun] the doctrine that baptism should only be administered to believing adults, held by a radical Protestant sect of the 16th century.
– DERIVATIVES **Anabaptist** noun & adjective.
– ORIGIN mid 16th cent.: via ecclesiastical Latin from Greek *anabaptismos*, from *ana-* 'over again' + *baptismos* 'baptism'.

anabasis /aˈnabəsɪs/ ▶ **noun** (pl. **anabases** /-siːz/) rare a military advance into the interior of a country (with reference to that of Cyrus the Younger into Asia in 401 BC, as narrated by Xenophon in his work *Anabasis*).
– ORIGIN from Greek, 'ascent', from *anabainein* 'walk up', from *ana-* 'up' + *bainein* 'go'.

anabatic /ˌanəˈbatɪk/ ▶ **adjective** Meteorology (of a wind) caused by local upward motion of warm air.
– ORIGIN early 20th cent.: from Greek *anabatikos*, from *anabatēs* 'a person who ascends', from *anabainein* 'walk up'.

anabiosis /ˌanəbʌɪˈəʊsɪs/ ▶ **noun** [mass noun] Zoology a temporary state of suspended animation or greatly reduced metabolism.
– DERIVATIVES **anabiotic** /-ˈɒtɪk/ adjective.
– ORIGIN late 19th cent.: from Greek *anabiōsis*, from *anabioein* 'return to life'.

anabolic /ˌanəˈbɒlɪk/ ▶ **adjective** Biochemistry relating to or promoting anabolism.

anabolic steroid ▶ **noun** a synthetic steroid hormone which resembles testosterone in promoting the growth of muscle. Such hormones are used medicinally to treat some forms of weight loss and (illegally) by some athletes and sports players to enhance physical performance.

anabolism /əˈnabəlɪz(ə)m/ ▶ **noun** [mass noun] Biochemistry the synthesis of complex molecules in living organ-

isms from simpler ones together with the storage of energy; constructive metabolism.
– ORIGIN late 19th cent.: from Greek *anabolē* 'ascent', from *ana-* 'up' + *ballein* 'to throw'.

anabranch /ˈanəbrɑːn(t)ʃ/ ▶ **noun** chiefly Austral. a stream that leaves a river and re-enters it further along its course.
– ORIGIN mid 19th cent.: from *ana(stomosing)* (present participle of **ANASTOMOSE**) + **BRANCH**.

anachronic /ˌanəˈkrɒnɪk/ ▶ **adjective** relating to or involving anachronism.
– ORIGIN early 19th cent.: from **ANACHRONISM**, on the pattern of pairs such as *synchronism, synchronic*.

anachronism /əˈnakrəˌnɪz(ə)m/ ▶ **noun** a thing belonging or appropriate to a period other than that in which it exists, especially a thing that is conspicuously old-fashioned: *the town is a throwback to medieval times, an anachronism that has survived the passing years.* ■ [mass noun] the action of attributing something to a period to which it does not belong.
– DERIVATIVES **anachronistic** adjective, **anachronistically** adverb.
– ORIGIN mid 17th cent.: from Greek *anakhronismos*, from *ana-* 'backwards' + *khronos* 'time'.

anaclitic /ˌanəˈklɪtɪk/ ▶ **adjective** Psychoanalysis relating to or characterized by a strong emotional dependence on another or others: *anaclitic depression.*
– ORIGIN 1920s: from Greek *anaklitos* 'for reclining', from *anaklinein* 'recline'.

anacoluthon /ˌanəkəˈluːθɒn, -θ(ə)n/ ▶ **noun** (pl. **anacolutha** /-θə/) a sentence or construction in which the expected grammatical sequence is absent, for example *while in the garden, the door banged shut.*
– DERIVATIVES **anacoluthic** adjective.
– ORIGIN early 18th cent.: via late Latin from Greek *anakolouthon*, from *an-* 'not' + *akolouthos* 'following'.

anaconda /ˌanəˈkɒndə/ ▶ **noun** a semiaquatic snake of the boa family which may grow to a great size, native to tropical South America. ● Genus *Eunectes*, family Boidae: several species.
– ORIGIN mid 18th cent. (originally denoting a kind of Sri Lankan snake): unexplained alteration of Latin *anacandaia* 'python', from Sinhalese *henakaňdayā* 'whip snake', from *hena* 'lightning' + *kaňda* 'stem'.

Anacreon /əˈnakrɪən/ (*c.*570–478 BC), Greek lyric poet, best known for his celebrations of love and wine.
– DERIVATIVES **anacreontic** adjective & noun.

anacronym /ənˈakrənɪm/ ▶ **noun** an acronym of which the constituent letters are taken from words that are unfamiliar to most people (e.g. *Nicam, scuba*).
– ORIGIN 1980s: from Greek *an-* 'without' + **ACRONYM**.

anacrusis /ˌanəˈkruːsɪs/ ▶ **noun** (pl. **anacruses** /-siːz/)
1 Prosody one or more unstressed syllables at the beginning of a verse.
2 Music one or more unstressed notes before the first bar line of a piece or passage.
– ORIGIN mid 19th cent.: modern Latin, from Greek *anakrousis* 'prelude', from *ana-* 'up' + *krousis*, from *krouein* 'to strike'.

anadromous /əˈnadrəməs/ ▶ **adjective** Zoology (of a fish such as the salmon) migrating up rivers from the sea to spawn. The opposite of **CATADROMOUS**.
– ORIGIN mid 18th cent.: from Greek *anadromos* (from *ana-* 'up' + *dromos* 'running') + **-OUS**.

anaemia /əˈniːmɪə/ (US **anemia**) ▶ **noun** [mass noun] a condition in which there is a deficiency of red cells or of haemoglobin in the blood, resulting in pallor and weariness.
– ORIGIN early 19th cent.: via modern Latin from Greek *anaimia*, from *an-* 'without' + *haima* 'blood'.

anaemic (US **anemic**) ▶ **adjective** suffering from anaemia. ■ lacking in colour, spirit, or vitality.

anaerobe /ˈanərəʊb, əˈnɛːrəʊb/ ▶ **noun** Biology a microorganism that is able to, or can only, live in the absence of oxygen.
– ORIGIN late 19th cent.: from **AN-¹** + **AEROBE**.

anaerobic ▶ **adjective** Biology relating to or requiring an absence of free oxygen: *anaerobic bacteria.* ■ relating to or denoting exercise which does not improve the efficiency of the body's cardiovascular system in absorbing and transporting oxygen.
– DERIVATIVES **anaerobically** adverb.

anaesthesia /ˌanɪsˈθiːzɪə/ (US **anesthesia**) ▶ **noun** [mass noun] insensitivity to pain, especially as artificially induced by the administration of gases or the injection of drugs before surgical operations.
– ORIGIN early 18th cent.: modern Latin, from Greek *anaisthēsia*, from *an-* 'without' + *aisthēsis* 'sensation'.

anaesthesiology /ˌanɪsˌθiːzɪˈɒlədʒi/ (US **anesthesiology**) ▶ **noun** [mass noun] the branch of medicine concerned with anaesthesia and anaesthetics.
– DERIVATIVES **anaesthesiologist** noun.

anaesthetic /ˌanɪsˈθɛtɪk/ (US **anesthetic**) ▶ **noun 1** a substance that induces insensitivity to pain.
2 (**anaesthetics**) [treated as sing.] the study or practice of anaesthesia.
▶ **adjective** inducing or relating to insensitivity to pain.
– ORIGIN mid 19th cent.: from Greek *anaisthētos* 'insensible', related to *anaisthēsia* (see **ANAESTHESIA**), + **-IC**.

anaesthetist /əˈniːsθətɪst/ (US **anesthetist**) ▶ **noun** a medical specialist who administers anaesthetics.

anaesthetize /əˈniːsθətʌɪz/ (also **anaesthetise**, US **anesthetize**) ▶ **verb** [with obj.] administer an anaesthetic to (a person or animal), especially so as to induce a loss of consciousness. ■ deprive of feeling or awareness: *the feeling of numb unreality persisted and anaesthetized me.*
– DERIVATIVES **anaesthetization** noun.

anagen /ˈanədʒ(ə)n/ ▶ **noun** [mass noun] Physiology the growing phase of a hair follicle. Often contrasted with **TELOGEN**.
– ORIGIN 1920s: from **ANA-** + **-GEN**.

anagenesis /ˌanəˈdʒɛnɪsɪs/ ▶ **noun** [mass noun] Biology species formation without branching of the evolutionary line of descent.
– DERIVATIVES **anagenetic** adjective.
– ORIGIN late 19th cent.: from **ANA-** and **GENESIS**.

anaglyph /ˈanəglɪf/ ▶ **noun 1** Photography a stereoscopic photograph with the two images superimposed and printed in different colours, usually red and green, producing a stereo effect when viewed with appropriate filters over each eye.
2 an object, such as a cameo, embossed or carved in low relief.
– DERIVATIVES **anaglyphic** adjective.
– ORIGIN late 16th cent. (in sense 2): from Greek *anagluphē*, from *ana-* 'up' + *gluphē* (from *gluphein* 'carve'). Sense 1 dates from the late 19th cent.

Anaglypta /ˌanəˈglɪptə/ ▶ **noun** [mass noun] trademark a type of thick embossed wallpaper, designed to be painted over.
– ORIGIN late 19th cent.: from Latin *anaglypta* 'work in low relief'.

anagram /ˈanəgram/ ▶ **noun** a word, phrase, or name formed by rearranging the letters of another, such as *spar*, formed from *rasp.*
– DERIVATIVES **anagrammatic** adjective, **anagrammatical** adjective.
– ORIGIN late 16th cent.: from French *anagramme* or modern Latin *anagramma*, from Greek *ana-* 'back, anew' + *gramma* 'letter'.

anagrammatize /ˌanəˈgramətʌɪz/ (also **anagrammatise**) ▶ **verb** [with obj.] make an anagram of (a word, phrase, or name).
– DERIVATIVES **anagrammatization** noun.

Anaheim /ˈanəhʌɪm/ a city in California, on the SE side of the Los Angeles conurbation; pop. 335,288 (est. 2008). It is the site of the amusement park Disneyland.

anal /ˈeɪn(ə)l/ ▶ **adjective** relating to or situated near the anus. ■ Psychoanalysis (in Freudian theory) relating to or denoting a stage of infantile psychosexual development in which defecation is the major source of sensuous pleasure and the anus forms the centre of self-awareness. ■ informal anal-retentive: *he's anal about things like that.*
– DERIVATIVES **anally** adverb.
– ORIGIN mid 18th cent.: from modern Latin *analis*, from Latin *anus* (see **ANUS**).

analects /ˈanəlɛkts/ (also **analecta** /ˌanəˈlɛktə/) ▶ **plural noun** a collection of short literary or philosophical extracts.
– ORIGIN late Middle English: via Latin from Greek *analekta* 'things gathered up', from *analegein* 'pick up', from *ana-* 'up' + *legein* 'gather'.

analeptic /ˌanəˈlɛptɪk/ Medicine ▶ **adjective** (chiefly of a drug) tending to restore a person's health or strength; restorative.
▶ **noun** a restorative drug. ■ a drug that stimulates the central nervous system.
– ORIGIN late 16th cent.: via late Latin from Greek *analēptikos* 'restorative'.

anal fin ▶ **noun** Zoology an unpaired fin located on the underside of a fish posterior to the anus.

analgesia /ˌan(ə)lˈdʒiːzɪə/ ▶ **noun** [mass noun] Medicine the inability to feel pain. ■ medication that acts to relieve pain.
– ORIGIN early 18th cent.: from Greek *analgēsia* 'painlessness', from *an-* 'not' + *algein* 'feel pain'.

analgesic /ˌan(ə)lˈdʒiːzɪk, -sɪk/ Medicine ▶ **adjective** (of a drug) acting to relieve pain.
▶ **noun** an analgesic drug.

analogize /əˈnalədʒʌɪz/ (also **analogise**) ▶ **verb** [with obj.] make a comparison of (something) with something else to assist understanding.

analogous /əˈnaləgəs/ ▶ **adjective** comparable in certain respects, typically in a way which makes clearer the nature of the things compared: *they saw the relationship between a ruler and his subjects as* ***analogous to*** *that of father and children.* ■ Biology (of organs) performing a similar function but having a different evolutionary origin, such as the wings of insects and birds. Often contrasted with **HOMOLOGOUS**.
– DERIVATIVES **analogously** adverb.
– ORIGIN mid 17th cent.: via Latin from Greek *analogos* 'proportionate' + **-OUS**.

analogue /ˈanəlɒg/ (US also **analog**) ▶ **noun** a person or thing seen as comparable to another: *an interior analogue of the exterior world.* ■ Chemistry a compound with a molecular structure closely similar to that of another.
▶ **adjective** relating to or using signals or information represented by a continuously variable physical quantity such as spatial position, voltage, etc. Often contrasted with **DIGITAL** (sense 1). ■ (of a clock or watch) showing the time by means of hands or a pointer rather than displayed digits.
– ORIGIN early 19th cent.: from French, from Greek *analogon*, neuter of *analogos* 'proportionate'.

analogue to digital converter ▶ **noun** a device for converting analogue signals to digital form.

analogy /əˈnalədʒi/ ▶ **noun** (pl. **analogies**) a comparison between one thing and another, typically for the purpose of explanation or clarification: *an* ***analogy between*** *the workings of nature and those of human societies* | [mass noun] *he interprets logical functions* ***by analogy with*** *machines.* ■ a correspondence or partial similarity. ■ a thing which is comparable to something else in significant respects. ■ [mass noun] Logic a process of arguing from similarity in known respects to similarity in other respects. ■ [mass noun] Linguistics a process by which new words and inflections are created on the basis of regularities in the form of existing ones. ■ [mass noun] Biology the resemblance of function between organs that have a different evolutionary origin.
– DERIVATIVES **analogic** adjective, **analogical** adjective, **analogically** adverb.
– ORIGIN late Middle English (in the sense 'appropriateness, correspondence'): from French *analogie*, Latin *analogia* 'proportion', from Greek, from *analogos* 'proportionate'.

analphabetic ▶ **adjective 1** representing sounds by composite signs rather than by single letters or symbols.
2 completely illiterate.

anal-retentive Psychoanalysis ▶ **adjective** excessively orderly and fussy (supposedly owing to conflict over toilet-training in infancy).
▶ **noun** a person who is excessively orderly and fussy.
– DERIVATIVES **anal retention** noun, **anal retentiveness** noun.

anal-sadistic ▶ **adjective** Psychoanalysis displaying abnormal aggressive and destructive tendencies supposedly caused by fixation at the anal stage of development.

analysand /əˈnalɪzand/ ▶ **noun** a person undergoing psychoanalysis.

analyse (US **analyze**) ▶ **verb** [with obj.] **1** examine (something) methodically and in detail, typically in order to explain and interpret it: *we need to analyse our results more clearly.* ■ discover or reveal (something) through close examination: [with clause] *he tried to analyse exactly what was going on.* ■ identify and measure the chemical constituents of (a substance or specimen). ■ Grammar resolve (a sentence) into its grammatical elements; parse.
2 psychoanalyse (someone).
– DERIVATIVES **analysable** adjective, **analyser** noun.
– ORIGIN late 16th cent.: influenced by French *analyser*, from medieval Latin *analysis* (see **ANALYSIS**).

analysis /əˈnalɪsɪs/ ▶ **noun** (pl. **analyses** /-siːz/)
1 [mass noun] detailed examination of the elements or structure of something: *statistical analysis* | [count noun] *an analysis of popular culture.* ■ the process of separating something into its constituent elements. Often contrasted with **SYNTHESIS**. ■ the identification and measurement of the chemical constituents of

A

a substance or specimen. ■ Mathematics the part of mathematics concerned with the theory of functions and the use of limits, continuity, and the operations of calculus.
2 short for **PSYCHOANALYSIS**.
– PHRASES **in the final** (or **last**) **analysis** when everything has been considered (used to suggest that a statement expresses the basic truth about a complex situation): *in the final analysis it is a question of political history*.
– ORIGIN late 16th cent.: via medieval Latin from Greek *analusis*, from *analuein* 'unloose', from *ana-* 'up' + *luein* 'loosen'.

analyst ▸ **noun** a person who conducts analysis. ■ a psychoanalyst.
– ORIGIN mid 17th cent.: from French *analyste*, from the verb *analyser* (see **ANALYSE**).

analyte /ˈanəlʌɪt/ ▸ **noun** Chemistry a substance whose chemical constituents are being identified and measured.

analytic ▸ **adjective** another term for **ANALYTICAL**. ■ Logic true by virtue of the meaning of the words or concepts used to express it, so that its denial would be a self-contradiction. Compare with **SYNTHETIC**. ■ Linguistics (of a language, e.g. Chinese and English) tending not to alter the form of its words but to use word order to express grammatical structure. Contrasted with **SYNTHETIC** and **AGGLUTINATIVE**.
– ORIGIN early 17th cent.: via Latin from Greek *analutikos*, from *analuein* 'unloose'.

analytical ▸ **adjective** relating to or using analysis or logical reasoning.
– DERIVATIVES **analytically** adverb.

analytical geometry ▸ **noun** [mass noun] geometry using coordinates.

analytical philosophy (also **analytic philosophy**) ▸ **noun** [mass noun] a method of approaching philosophical problems through analysis of the terms in which they are expressed, associated with Anglo-American philosophy of the early 20th century.

analytical psychology ▸ **noun** [mass noun] the psychoanalytical system of psychology developed and practised by Carl Gustav Jung.

analyze ▸ **verb** US spelling of **ANALYSE**.

anamnesis /ˌanəmˈniːsɪs/ ▸ **noun** (pl. **anamneses** /-siːz/) [mass noun] **1** recollection, especially of a supposed previous existence.
2 [count noun] Medicine a patient's account of their medical history.
3 Christian Church the part of the Eucharist in which the Passion, Resurrection, and Ascension of Christ are recalled.
– ORIGIN late 16th cent.: from Greek *anamnēsis* 'remembrance'.

anamnestic /ˌanəmˈnɛstɪk/ ▸ **adjective** Medicine denoting an enhanced reaction of the body's immune system to an antigen which is related to one previously encountered.

anamorphosis /ˌanəˈmɔːfəsɪs/ ▸ **noun** (pl. **anamorphoses** /ˌanəˈmɔːfəsiːz/) a distorted projection or drawing which appears normal when viewed from a particular point or with a suitable mirror or lens. ■ [mass noun] the process by which such images are produced.
– DERIVATIVES **anamorphic** adjective.
– ORIGIN early 18th cent.: from Greek *anamorphōsis* 'transformation', from *ana-* 'back, again' + *morphosis* 'a shaping' (from *morphoun* 'to shape', from *morphē* 'shape, form').

ananda /ɑːˈnʌndə/ ▸ **noun** [mass noun] (in Hinduism, Buddhism, and Jainism) extreme happiness, one of the highest states of being.
– ORIGIN from Sanskrit *ānanda* 'blessedness, bliss'.

Anangu /ˈɑːnɑːŋuː/ ▸ **noun** (pl. **same**) Austral. an Aborigine, especially one from central Australia.
– ORIGIN from Western Desert (an Aboriginal language), literally 'person'.

Ananias /ˌanəˈnʌɪəs/ two figures in the New Testament, the husband of Sapphira, struck dead because he lied (Acts 5), and the Jewish high priest before whom St Paul was brought (Acts 23).

anapaest /ˈanəpiːst, -pɛst/ (US **anapest**) ▸ **noun** Prosody a metrical foot consisting of two short or unstressed syllables followed by one long or stressed syllable.
– DERIVATIVES **anapaestic** /-ˈpiːstɪk, -ˈpɛstɪk/ **adjective**.
– ORIGIN late 16th cent.: via Latin from Greek *anapaistos* 'reversed', from *ana-* 'back' + *paiein* 'strike' (because it is the reverse of a dactyl).

anaphase /ˈanəfeɪz/ ▸ **noun** [mass noun] Genetics the third stage of cell division, between metaphase and telophase, during which the chromosomes move away from one another to opposite poles of the spindle.

anaphor /ˈanəfə, -fɔː/ ▸ **noun** Grammar a word or phrase that refers back to an earlier word or phrase (e.g. in *my cousin said she was coming*, *she* is used as an anaphor for *my cousin*).
– ORIGIN 1970s: back-formation from **ANAPHORA**.

anaphora /əˈnaf(ə)rə/ ▸ **noun** [mass noun] **1** Grammar the use of a word referring back to a word used earlier in a text or conversation, to avoid repetition, for example the pronouns *he*, *she*, *it*, and *they* and the verb *do* in *I like it and so do they*. Compare with **CATAPHORA**.
2 Rhetoric the repetition of a word or phrase at the beginning of successive clauses.
3 Christian Church the part of the Eucharist which contains the consecration, anamnesis, and communion.
– DERIVATIVES **anaphoric** /ˌanəˈfɒrɪk/ **adjective**, **anaphorically** /ˌanəˈfɒrɪk(ə)li/ **adverb**.
– ORIGIN late 16th cent.: sense 1, sense 2 via Latin from Greek, 'repetition', from *ana-* 'back' + *pherein* 'to bear'; sense 3 from late Greek.

anaphrodisiac /əˌnafrəˈdɪzɪak/ Medicine ▸ **adjective** (chiefly of a drug) tending to reduce sexual desire.
▸ **noun** an anaphrodisiac drug.

anaphylactic /ˌanəfɪˈlaktɪk/ ▸ **adjective** Medicine relating to or caused by anaphylaxis.

anaphylactic shock ▸ **noun** [mass noun] Medicine an extreme, often life-threatening allergic reaction to an antigen to which the body has become hypersensitive.

anaphylaxis /ˌanəfɪˈlaksɪs/ ▸ **noun** [mass noun] Medicine an acute allergic reaction to an antigen (e.g. a bee sting) to which the body has become hypersensitive.
– ORIGIN early 20th cent.: modern Latin, from Greek *ana-* 'again' + *phulaxis* 'guarding'.

anaptyxis /ˌanəpˈtɪksɪs/ ▸ **noun** [mass noun] Phonetics the insertion of a vowel between two consonants to aid pronunciation, as in *he went thataway*.
– DERIVATIVES **anaptyctic** adjective.
– ORIGIN late 19th cent.: modern Latin, from Greek *anaptuxis* 'unfolding', from *ana-* 'back, again' + *ptuxis* 'folding'.

anarch /ˈanɑːk/ archaic ▸ **noun** an anarchist.
▸ **adjective** anarchic.
– ORIGIN mid 17th cent.: from Greek *anarkhos* 'without a chief' (see **ANARCHY**).

anarchic /əˈnɑːkɪk/ ▸ **adjective** with no controlling rules or principles to give order: *an anarchic and bitter civil war*. ■ (of comedy or humour) uncontrolled by convention: *his anarchic wit*.
– DERIVATIVES **anarchical** adjective, **anarchically** adverb.

anarchism ▸ **noun** [mass noun] belief in the abolition of all government and the organization of society on a voluntary, cooperative basis without recourse to force or compulsion. ■ a political force or movement based on belief in anarchism.
– ORIGIN mid 17th cent.: from Greek *anarkhos* 'without a chief' (see **ANARCHY**) + **-ISM**; later influenced by French *anarchisme*.

anarchist ▸ **noun** a person who believes in or tries to bring about anarchy.
▸ **adjective** relating to or supporting anarchy or anarchists: *an anarchist newspaper*.
– DERIVATIVES **anarchistic** adjective.
– ORIGIN mid 17th cent.: from Greek *anarkhos* 'without a chief' (see **ANARCHY**) + **-IST**; later influenced by French *anarchiste*.

anarchy ▸ **noun** [mass noun] **1** a state of disorder due to absence or non-recognition of authority or other controlling systems: *he must ensure public order in a country threatened with anarchy*.
2 absence of government and absolute freedom of the individual, regarded as a political ideal.
– ORIGIN mid 16th cent.: via medieval Latin from Greek *anarkhia*, from *anarkhos*, from *an-* 'without' + *arkhos* 'chief, ruler'.

Anasazi /ˌanəˈsɑːzi/ ▸ **noun** (pl. **same** or **Anasazis**) a member of an ancient American Indian people of the south-western US, who flourished between *c.*200 BC and AD 1500. The earliest phase of their culture is known as the Basket Maker period; the present-day Pueblo culture developed from a later stage.
– ORIGIN from Navajo, 'ancient one' or 'enemy ancestor'.

anastigmat /əˈnastɪgmat/ ▸ **noun** an anastigmatic lens system.

anastigmatic /ˌanastɪgˈmatɪk/ ▸ **adjective** (of a lens system) constructed so that the astigmatism of each element is cancelled out.
– ORIGIN late 19th cent.: from **AN-**[1] 'not' + *astigmatic* (see **ASTIGMATISM**).

anastomose /əˈnastəməʊz/ ▸ **verb** Medicine link or be linked by anastomosis.
– ORIGIN late 17th cent.: coined in French from Greek *anastomōsis* (see **ANASTOMOSIS**).

anastomosis /əˌnastəˈməʊsɪs/ ▸ **noun** (pl. **anastomoses** /-siːz/) technical a cross-connection between adjacent channels, tubes, fibres, or other parts of a network. ■ Medicine a connection made surgically between adjacent blood vessels, parts of the intestine, or other channels of the body.
– DERIVATIVES **anastomotic** adjective & noun.
– ORIGIN late 16th cent.: modern Latin, from Greek *anastomōsis*, from *anastomoun* 'provide with a mouth'.

anastrophe /əˈnastrəfi/ ▸ **noun** [mass noun] Rhetoric the inversion of the usual order of words or clauses.
– ORIGIN mid 16th cent.: from Greek *anastrophē* 'turning back', from *ana-* 'back' + *strephein* 'to turn'.

anathema /əˈnaθəmə/ ▸ **noun 1** [mass noun] something or someone that one vehemently dislikes: *racial hatred was* **anathema to** *her*.
2 a formal curse by a pope or a council of the Church, excommunicating a person or denouncing a doctrine. ■ literary a strong curse.
– ORIGIN early 16th cent.: from ecclesiastical Latin, 'excommunicated person, excommunication', from Greek *anathema* 'thing dedicated', (later) 'thing devoted to evil, accursed thing', from *anatithenai* 'to set up'.

anathematize /əˈnaθəmətʌɪz/ (also **anathematise**) ▸ **verb** [with obj.] curse; condemn: *he anathematized them as 'bloody scroungers'*.
– ORIGIN mid 16th cent.: from French *anathématiser*, from Latin *anathematizare*, from Greek *anathematizein*, from *anathema* (see **ANATHEMA**).

Anatolia /ˌanəˈtəʊlɪə/ the western peninsula of Asia, bounded by the Black Sea, the Aegean, and the Mediterranean, that forms the greater part of Turkey.

Anatolian ▸ **adjective** relating to Anatolia, its inhabitants, or their ancient languages.
▸ **noun 1** a native or inhabitant of Anatolia.
2 [mass noun] an extinct group of ancient languages constituting a branch of the Indo-European language family and including Hittite, Luwian, Lydian, and Lycian.

anatomical ▸ **adjective** relating to bodily structure: *anatomical abnormalities*. ■ relating to the study of anatomy: *anatomical lectures*.
– DERIVATIVES **anatomic** adjective, **anatomically** adverb.
– ORIGIN late 16th cent.: from late Latin *anatomicus*, from *anatomia* (see **ANATOMY**), + **-AL**.

anatomist ▸ **noun** an expert in anatomy.
– ORIGIN mid 16th cent.: from French *anatomiste*, from a medieval Latin derivative of *anatomizare* (see **ANATOMIZE**).

anatomize (also **anatomise**) ▸ **verb** [with obj.] dissect (a body). ■ examine and analyse in detail: *successful comedy is notoriously difficult to anatomize*.
– ORIGIN late Middle English: from medieval Latin *anatomizare*, from *anatomia* (see **ANATOMY**).

anatomy ▸ **noun** (pl. **anatomies**) **1** [mass noun] the branch of science concerned with the bodily structure of humans, animals, and other living organisms, especially as revealed by dissection and the separation of parts. ■ [count noun] the bodily structure of an organism: *descriptions of the cat's anatomy and behaviour*. ■ [count noun] informal a person's body.
2 a study of the structure or internal workings of something: *a detailed anatomy of a society and its institutions*.
– ORIGIN late Middle English: from Old French *anatomie* or late Latin *anatomia*, from Greek, from *ana-* 'up' + *tomia* 'cutting' (from *temnein* 'to cut').

anatto ▸ **noun** variant spelling of **ANNATTO**.

Anaxagoras /ˌanakˈsagərəs/ (*c.*500–*c.*428 BC), Greek philosopher, teaching in Athens. He believed that all matter was infinitely divisible and motionless until animated by mind (*nous*).

Anaximander /aˌnaksɪˈmandə/ (*c.*610–*c.*545 BC), Greek scientist, who lived at Miletus. He believed the earth to be cylindrical and poised in space, and is reputed to have taught that life began in water and that humans originated from fish.

Anaximenes /ˌanakˈsɪmɪniːz/ (*fl.* 6th century), Greek philosopher and scientist, who lived at Miletus. Anaximenes believed the earth to be flat and shallow, a view of astronomy that was a retrograde step from that of Anaximander.

ANC ▶ **abbreviation** African National Congress.

-ance ▶ **suffix** forming nouns: **1** denoting a quality or state or an instance of one: *allegiance | extravagance | perseverance*.
2 denoting an action: *appearance | utterance*.
– ORIGIN from French *-ance*, from Latin *-antia*, *-entia* (from present participial stems *-ant-*, *-ent-*).

ancestor ▶ **noun** a person, typically one more remote than a grandparent, from whom one is descended: *he could trace his ancestors back to James the First*. ■ an early type of animal or plant from which others have evolved. ■ an early version of a machine, system, etc.: *this instrument is an ancestor of the lute*.
– ORIGIN Middle English: from Old French *ancestre*, from Latin *antecessor*, from *antecedere*, from *ante* 'before' + *cedere* 'go'.

ancestral ▶ **adjective** of, belonging to, or inherited from an ancestor or ancestors: *the family's ancestral home*.
– DERIVATIVES **ancestrally** **adverb**.
– ORIGIN late Middle English: from Old French *ancestrel*, from *ancestre* (see **ANCESTOR**).

ancestress ▶ **noun** a female ancestor.

ancestry ▶ **noun** (pl. **ancestries**) **1** one's family or ethnic descent: *he was proud of his Irish ancestry*. ■ the evolutionary or genetic line of descent of an animal or plant: *the ancestry of the rose is extremely complicated*.
2 the origin or background of something: *the book traces the ancestry of women's poetry*.
– ORIGIN Middle English: alteration of Old French *ancesserie*, from *ancestre* (see **ANCESTOR**).

Anchises /anˈkʌɪsiːz/ Greek & Roman Mythology the father of the Trojan hero Aeneas.

ancho /ˈantʃəʊ/ (also **ancho chilli**) ▶ **noun** (pl. **anchos**) a large aromatic variety of chilli, used (usually dried) in dishes of Mexican origin or style.
– ORIGIN from Mexican Spanish (*chile*) *ancho*, 'wide (chilli)'.

anchor ▶ **noun** **1** a heavy object attached to a cable or chain and used to moor a ship to the sea bottom, typically having a metal shank with a pair of curved, barbed flukes at one end. ■ (**anchors**) Brit. informal the brakes of a car.
2 a person or thing which provides stability or confidence in an otherwise uncertain situation: *the European Community is the economic anchor of the New Europe*.
3 [usu. as modifier] a large and prestigious department store prominently sited in a new shopping centre: *an anchor tenant*.
4 chiefly N. Amer. an anchorman or anchorwoman.
▶ **verb** [with obj.] **1** moor (a ship) to the sea bottom with an anchor: *the ship was anchored in the lee of the island* | [no obj., with adverbial of place] *we anchored in the harbour*. ■ secure firmly in position: *the tail is used as a hook with which the fish* ***anchors itself to*** *coral*. ■ provide with a firm basis or foundation: *it is important that policy be anchored to some acceptable theoretical basis*.
2 chiefly N. Amer. present and coordinate (a television or radio programme).
– PHRASES **at anchor** (of a ship) moored by means of an anchor. **drop anchor** (of a ship) let down the anchor and moor. **weigh** (or **raise**) **anchor** (of a ship) take up the anchor when ready to start sailing.
– ORIGIN Old English *ancor*, *ancra*, via Latin from Greek *ankura*; reinforced in Middle English by Old French *ancre*. The current form is from *anchora*, an erroneous Latin spelling. The verb (from Old French *ancrer*) dates from Middle English.

Anchorage the largest city in Alaska, a seaport on an inlet of the Pacific Ocean; pop. 279,243 (est. 2008).

anchorage ▶ **noun** **1** an area off the coast which is suitable for a ship to anchor.
2 [mass noun] the action of securing something to a base or the state of being secured: *the plant needs firm anchorage*.
3 historical an anchorite's dwelling place.

anchor escapement ▶ **noun** a form of escapement in clocks and watches in which the teeth of the crown wheel or balance wheel act on the pallets by recoil.

anchoress ▶ **noun** historical a female anchorite.

anchorite /ˈaŋkərʌɪt/ ▶ **noun** historical a religious recluse.
– DERIVATIVES **anchoritic** **adjective**.
– ORIGIN late Middle English: from medieval Latin *anchorita* (ecclesiastical Latin *anchoreta*), from ecclesiastical Greek *anakhōrētēs*, from *anakhōrein* 'retire', from *ana-* 'back' + *khōra*, *khōr-* 'a place'.

anchorman ▶ **noun** (pl. **anchormen**) **1** (also **anchorwoman** or **anchorperson**) a person who presents and coordinates a live television or radio programme involving other contributors. ■ the central or most dependable contributor to something: *the anchorman of the Hampshire batting*.
2 the member of a relay team who runs the last leg.

anchoveta /ˌantʃə(ʊ)ˈvɛtə/ ▶ **noun** an anchovy found off the Pacific coasts of South America, of great commercial importance to Peru. ● *Engraulis ringens*, family Engraulidae.
– ORIGIN 1940s: from Spanish, diminutive of *anchova* (see **ANCHOVY**).

anchovy /ˈantʃəvi, anˈtʃəʊvi/ ▶ **noun** (pl. **anchovies**) a small shoaling fish of commercial importance as a food fish and as bait. It is strongly flavoured and is usually preserved in salt and oil. ● Genus *Engraulis*, family Engraulidae: several species.
– ORIGIN late 16th cent.: from Spanish and Portuguese *anchova*, of unknown origin.

anchusa /aŋˈkjuːzə, anˈtʃuːsə/ ▶ **noun** an Old World plant of the borage family, which is widely cultivated for its bright, typically blue, flowers. ● Genus *Anchusa*, family Boraginaceae.
– ORIGIN via Latin from Greek *ankhousa*.

ancien régime /ˌɒsɪã reɪˈʒiːm/, French /ɑ̃sjɛ̃ ʁeʒim/ ▶ **noun** (pl. **anciens régimes** pronunc. **same**) a political or social system that has been displaced by another. ■ (**Ancien Régime**) the political and social system in France before the Revolution of 1789.
– ORIGIN French, literally 'old rule'.

ancient[1] ▶ **adjective** belonging to the very distant past and no longer in existence: *the ancient civilizations of the Mediterranean*. ■ having been in existence for a very long time: *ancient forests*. ■ humorous showing or feeling signs of age or wear: *an ancient pair of jeans | you make me feel ancient*.
▶ **noun** archaic or humorous an old man: *a solitary ancient in a tweed jacket*.
– PHRASES **the Ancient of Days** a biblical title for God. **the ancients** the people of ancient times, especially the Greeks and Romans of classical antiquity. ■ the classical Greek and Roman authors.
– DERIVATIVES **ancientness** **noun**.
– ORIGIN late Middle English: from Old French *ancien*, based on Latin *ante* 'before'.

ancient[2] ▶ **noun** archaic a standard, flag, or ensign.
– ORIGIN mid 16th cent.: alteration of **ENSIGN** by association with *ancien*, an early form of **ANCIENT**[1].

ancient demesne ▶ **noun** [mass noun] land recorded in Domesday Book as belonging to the Crown.

ancient history ▶ **noun** [mass noun] the history of the ancient civilizations of the Mediterranean area and the Near East up to the fall of the Western Roman Empire in AD 476. ■ informal something that is already long familiar and no longer new, interesting, or relevant: *the New Wave is ancient history now*.
– DERIVATIVES **ancient historian** **noun**.

ancient lights ▶ **plural noun** [treated as sing.] English Law the right of access to light of a property, established by custom and used to prevent the construction of buildings on adjacent property which would obstruct such access.
– ORIGIN mid 18th cent.: from *lights* meaning 'light from the sky'. In England the sign 'Ancient Lights' was often placed on a house, adjacent to a site where a high building might be erected.

anciently ▶ **adverb** long ago: *the area was anciently called Dalriada*.

ancient monument ▶ **noun** Brit. an old building or site that is preserved by an official agency.

ancient world ▶ **noun** the region around the Mediterranean and the Near East before the fall of the Western Roman Empire in AD 476.

ancillary /anˈsɪləri/ ▶ **adjective** providing necessary support to the primary activities or operation of an organization, system, etc.: *ancillary staff*. ■ in addition to something else, but not as important: *paragraph 19 was merely* ***ancillary to*** *paragraph 16*.
▶ **noun** (pl. **ancillaries**) a person whose work provides necessary support to the primary activities of an organization, system, etc.: *the employment of specialist teachers and ancillaries*. ■ something which functions in a supplementary or supporting role.
– ORIGIN mid 17th cent.: from Latin *ancillaris*, from *ancilla* 'maidservant'.

ancon /ˈaŋkɒn, -k(ə)n/ ▶ **noun** (pl. **ancones** /aŋˈkəʊniːz/) Architecture **1** a console, typically consisting of two volutes, that supports or appears to support a cornice.
2 each of a pair of projections on either side of a block of stone or other material, used for lifting it.
– ORIGIN early 18th cent. (denoting the corner or quoin of a wall or rafter): via Latin from Greek *ankōn* 'bend, elbow'.

Ancona[1] /aŋˈkəʊnə/ a port on the Adriatic coast of central Italy, capital of Marche region; pop. 102,047 (2008).

Ancona[2] /ənˈkəʊnə/ ▶ **noun** a chicken of a breed with black-and-white mottled plumage.

-ancy ▶ **suffix** (forming nouns) denoting a quality or state: *buoyancy | expectancy*. Compare with **-ANCE**.
– ORIGIN from Latin *-antia* (see also **-ENCY**).

ancylostomiasis /ˌaŋkɪlə(ʊ)stə(ʊ)ˈmʌɪəsɪs, ˌansɪ-/ (also **ankylostomiasis**) ▶ **noun** [mass noun] Medicine hookworm infection of the small intestine, often leading to anaemia. ● The worm is typically *Ancylostoma duodenale*, class Phasmida.
– ORIGIN late 19th cent.: from modern Latin *Ancylostoma* (from Greek *ankulos* 'crooked' + *stoma* 'mouth') + **-IASIS**.

Ancyra /anˈsʌɪrə/ ancient Roman name for **ANKARA**.

AND ▶ **abbreviation** Andorra (international vehicle registration).

and ▶ **conjunction** **1** used to connect words of the same part of speech, clauses, or sentences, that are to be taken jointly: *bread and butter | they can read and write | a hundred and fifty*. ■ used to connect two clauses when the second refers to something that happens after the first: *he turned round and walked out*. ■ used to connect two clauses, the second of which refers to something that results from the first: *there was a flash flood and by the next morning the town was under water*. ■ connecting two identical comparatives, to emphasize a progressive change: *getting better and better*. ■ connecting two identical words, implying great duration or great extent: *I cried and cried*. ■ used to connect two identical words to indicate that things of the same name or class have different qualities: *all human conduct is determined or caused—but there are causes and causes*. ■ used to connect two numbers to indicate that they are being added together: *six and four makes ten*. ■ archaic used to connect two numbers, implying succession: *a line of men marching two and two*.
2 used to introduce an additional comment or interjection: *if it came to a choice—and this was the worst thing—she would turn her back on her parents*. ■ used to introduce a question in connection with what someone else has just said: *'I found the letter in her bag.' 'And did you steam it open?'* ■ used to introduce a statement about a new topic: *and now to the dessert*.
3 informal used after some verbs and before another verb to indicate intention, instead of 'to': *I would try and do what he said*. See usage below.
▶ **noun** (**AND**) Electronics a Boolean operator which gives the value one if and only if all the operands are one, and otherwise has a value of zero. ■ (also **AND gate**) a circuit which produces an output signal only when signals are received simultaneously through all input connections.
– PHRASES **and/or** either or both of two stated possibilities: *audio and/or video components*.
– ORIGIN Old English *and*, *ond*, of Germanic origin; related to Dutch *en* and German *und*.

USAGE **1** It is still widely taught and believed that conjunctions such as **and** (and also **but** and **because**) should not be used to start a sentence, the argument being that a sentence starting with **and** expresses an incomplete thought and is therefore incorrect. Writers down the centuries have readily ignored this advice, however, using **and** to start a sentence, typically for rhetorical effect, as in the following example: *What are the government's chances of winning in court?* ***And*** *what are the consequences?*
2 A small number of verbs, notably **try**, **come**, and **go** can be followed by **and** with another verb, as in sentences like *we're going to* ***try and*** *explain it to them* or *why don't you* ***come and*** *see the film?* The structures in these verbs correspond to the use of the infinitive **to**, as in *we're going to* ***try to*** *explain it to them or why don't you* ***come to*** *see the film?* Since these structures are grammatically odd—for example, the use is normally only idiomatic with the

A

infinitive of the verb and not with other forms (i.e. it is not possible to say *I tried and explained it to them*)—they are regarded as wrong by some traditionalists. However, these uses are extremely common and can certainly be regarded as part of standard English.
3 For information about whether it is more correct to say *both **the boys** and **the girls*** or *both **the boys** and **girls***, see USAGE at BOTH
4 Where items in a list are separated by **and**, the following verb needs to be in the plural: see USAGE at OR[1].

-and ▸ **suffix** (forming nouns) denoting a person or thing to be treated in a specified way: *analysand*.
– ORIGIN from Latin gerundive ending *-andus*.

Andalusia /ˌandəˈluːsɪə/ the southernmost region of Spain, bordering on the Atlantic and the Mediterranean; capital, Seville. The region was under Moorish rule from 711 to 1492. Spanish name **Andalucía** /andaluˈθia, -ˈsia/.

Andalusian /ˌandəˈluːzɪən, -sɪən/ ▸ **adjective** relating to Andalusia or its people or their dialect.
▸ **noun 1** a native or inhabitant of Andalusia.
2 [mass noun] the dialect of Spanish spoken in Andalusia.
3 a light horse of a strong breed from Andalusia.

andalusite /ˌandəˈluːsʌɪt/ ▸ **noun** [mass noun] a grey, green, brown, or pink aluminosilicate mineral occurring mainly in metamorphic rocks as elongated rhombic prisms, sometimes of gem quality.
– ORIGIN early 19th cent.: from the name of the Spanish region of ANDALUSIA + -ITE[1].

Andaman and Nicobar Islands /ˈandəmən, ˈnɪkəbɑː/ two groups of islands in the Bay of Bengal, constituting a Union Territory in India; pop. 423,700 (est. 2009); capital, Port Blair.

andante /anˈdanteɪ/ Music ▸ **adverb & adjective** (especially as a direction) in a moderately slow tempo.
▸ **noun** a movement, passage, or composition marked to be performed andante.
– ORIGIN Italian, literally 'going', present participle of *andare*.

andantino /ˌandanˈtiːnəʊ/ Music ▸ **adverb & adjective** (especially as a direction) lighter than andante, and usually quicker.
▸ **noun** (pl. **andantinos**) a movement or passage marked to be performed andantino.
– ORIGIN Italian, diminutive of ANDANTE.

Andean /anˈdiːən, ˈandɪən/ ▸ **adjective** relating to the Andes.
▸ **noun** a native or inhabitant of the Andes.

Andersen, Hans Christian (1805–75), Danish author. He is famous for his fairy tales, published from 1835, such as 'The Snow Queen', 'The Ugly Duckling', and 'The Little Match Girl'. Although rooted in Danish folklore, the stories were also shaped by Andersen's own psychological alienation.

Anderson[1], Carl David (1905–91), American physicist. In 1932 he discovered the positron—the first antiparticle known. Nobel Prize for Physics (1936, shared with Victor Francis Hess).

Anderson[2], Elizabeth Garrett (1836–1917), English physician. She established a dispensary for women and children in London (renamed the Elizabeth Garrett Anderson Hospital) and was the first woman elected to the BMA (1873).

Anderson shelter ▸ **noun** historical a small prefabricated air-raid shelter of a type built in the UK during the Second World War.
– ORIGIN 1930s: named after Sir John *Anderson*, the Home Secretary in 1939–40 when the shelter was adopted.

Andes /ˈandiːz/ a major mountain system running the length of the Pacific coast of South America. Its highest peak is Aconcagua, which rises to a height of 6,960 m (22,834 ft).

andesite /ˈandɪzʌɪt, -sʌɪt/ ▸ **noun** [mass noun] Geology a dark, fine-grained, brown or greyish intermediate volcanic rock which is a common constituent of lavas in some areas.
– DERIVATIVES **andesitic** adjective.
– ORIGIN mid 19th cent.: named after the ANDES mountains, where it is found + -ITE[1].

Andhra Pradesh /ˌɑːndrə prəˈdeʃ/ a state in SE India, on the Bay of Bengal; capital, Hyderabad.

andiron /ˈandʌɪən/ ▸ **noun** a metal stand, typically one of a pair, for supporting wood burning in a fireplace.
– ORIGIN Middle English: from Old French *andier*, of unknown origin. The ending was altered by association with IRON.

Andorra /anˈdɔːrə/ a small autonomous principality in the southern Pyrenees, between France and Spain; pop. 83,900 (est. 2009); official languages, Catalan and French; capital, Andorra la Vella. Its independence dates from the late 8th century, when Charlemagne is said to have granted the Andorrans self-government for their help in defeating the Moors.
– DERIVATIVES **Andorran** adjective & noun.

andosol /ˈandəsɒl/ (also **andisol**) ▸ **noun** Soil Science a black or dark brown soil formed from volcanic material, with an A horizon rich in organic material.

andouille /ɒ̃ˈduːj/ ▸ **noun** [mass noun] chiefly N. Amer. a type of pork sausage, served typically as an hors d'oeuvre.
– ORIGIN French.

andradite /ˈandrədʌɪt/ ▸ **noun** [mass noun] a mineral of the garnet group, containing calcium and iron. It occurs as yellow, green, brown, or black crystals, sometimes of gem quality.
– ORIGIN mid 19th cent.: named after J. B. de *Andrada e Silva* (*c.*1763–1838), Brazilian geologist, + -ITE[1].

Andrew, Prince, Andrew Albert Christian Edward, Duke of York (b.1960), second son of Elizabeth II. He married Sarah Ferguson in 1986 but the couple divorced in 1996; they have two children, Princess Beatrice (b.1988) and Princess Eugenie (b.1990).

Andrew, St, an Apostle, the brother of St Peter. The X-shaped cross became associated with his name during the Middle Ages because he is said to have died by crucifixion on such a cross. St Andrew is the patron saint of Scotland and Russia. Feast day, 30 November.

Andrews, Thomas (1813–85), Irish physical chemist. He discovered the critical temperature of carbon dioxide, and showed that ozone is an allotrope of oxygen.

andro- ▸ **combining form** of men; male: *androcentric*.
– ORIGIN from Greek *anēr, andr-* 'man'.

androcentric /ˌandrə(ʊ)ˈsɛntrɪk/ ▸ **adjective** focused or centred on men: *in the radical feminist view science is sexist and androcentric*.
– DERIVATIVES **androcentrism** noun.

Androcles /ˈandrəkliːz/ a runaway slave in a story by Aulus Gellius (2nd century AD) who extracted a thorn from the paw of a lion, which later recognized him and refrained from attacking him when he faced it in the arena.

androcracy /anˈdrɒkrəsi/ ▸ **noun** (pl. **androcracies**) a social system ruled or dominated by men.
– DERIVATIVES **androcratic** adjective.

androecium /anˈdriːsɪəm/ ▸ **noun** (pl. **androecia** /-sɪə/) Botany the stamens of a flower collectively.
– DERIVATIVES **androecial** adjective.
– ORIGIN mid 19th cent.: modern Latin, from ANDRO- + Greek *oikion* 'house'.

androgen /ˈandrədʒ(ə)n/ ▸ **noun** Biochemistry a male sex hormone, such as testosterone.
– DERIVATIVES **androgenic** adjective.
– ORIGIN 1930s: from ANDRO- + -GEN.

androgenize /anˈdrɒdʒənʌɪz/ (also **androgenise**) ▸ **verb** [with obj.] (usu. as adj. **androgenized**) treat with or expose to male hormones, typically with the result that male sexual characteristics are produced.
– DERIVATIVES **androgenization** noun.

androgyne /ˈandrədʒʌɪn/ ▸ **noun** an androgynous individual. ■ a hermaphrodite.
– ORIGIN mid 16th cent.: via Latin from Greek *androgunos*, from *anēr, andr-* 'man' + *gunē* 'woman'.

androgynous /anˈdrɒdʒɪnəs/ ▸ **adjective** partly male and partly female in appearance; of indeterminate sex. ■ having the physical characteristics of both sexes; hermaphrodite.
– DERIVATIVES **androgyny** noun.
– ORIGIN early 17th cent.: from Latin *androgynus* (see ANDROGYNE) + -OUS.

android /ˈandrɔɪd/ ▸ **noun** (in science fiction) a robot with a human appearance.
– ORIGIN early 18th cent.: from modern Latin *androides*, from ANDRO- + -OID.

andrology /anˈdrɒlədʒi/ ▸ **noun** [mass noun] the branch of physiology and medicine which deals with diseases and conditions specific to men.
– DERIVATIVES **andrologist** noun.

Andromache /anˈdrɒməki/ Greek Mythology the wife of Hector. She became the slave of Neoptolemus (son of Achilles) after the fall of Troy.

Andromeda /anˈdrɒmɪdə/ **1** Greek Mythology an Ethiopian princess whose mother Cassiopeia boasted that she herself (or, in some stories, her daughter) was more beautiful than the Nereids. In revenge Poseidon sent a sea monster to ravage the country; to placate him Andromeda was fastened to a rock and exposed to the monster, from which she was rescued by Perseus.
2 Astronomy a large northern constellation between Perseus and Pegasus, with few bright stars. It is chiefly notable for the **Andromeda Galaxy** (or **Great Nebula of Andromeda**), a conspicuous spiral galaxy probably twice as massive as our own and located two million light years away.

andromeda /anˈdrɒmɪdə/ ▸ **noun** a bog rosemary, especially (**marsh andromeda**) the common bog rosemary.

andropause ▸ **noun** a collection of symptoms, including fatigue and a decrease in libido, experienced by some older men and attributed to a gradual decline in testosterone levels.
– ORIGIN 1960s: from ANDRO-, on the pattern of MENOPAUSE.

Andropov[1] /anˈdrɒpɒf/ former name (1984–9) for RYBINSK.

Andropov[2] /anˈdrɒpɒf/, Yuri (Vladimirovich) (1914–84), Soviet statesman, General Secretary of the Communist Party of the USSR 1982–4 and President 1983–4. As President he initiated the reform process carried through by Mikhail Gorbachev, his chosen successor.

androstenedione /ˌandrɒstiːnˈdaɪəʊn/ ▸ **noun** [mass noun] an androgenic steroid from which testosterone and certain oestrogens are derived in humans.
– ORIGIN 1930s: from ANDROSTERONE + -ENE + DI-[1] + -ONE.

androsterone /ˌandrə(ʊ)ˈstɪərəʊn, anˈdrɒstərəʊn/ ▸ **noun** [mass noun] Biochemistry a relatively inactive male sex hormone produced by metabolism of testosterone.
– ORIGIN 1930s: from ANDRO- + STEROL + -ONE.

-androus ▸ **combining form** Botany having male organs or stamens of a specified number: *polyandrous*.
– ORIGIN from modern Latin *-andrus* (from Greek *-andros*, from *anēr, andr-* 'man') + -OUS.

-ane[1] ▸ **suffix** variant spelling of -AN, usually with a distinction of sense (such as *humane* compared with *human*) but sometimes with no corresponding form in *-an* (such as *mundane*).

-ane[2] ▸ **suffix** Chemistry forming names of saturated hydrocarbons: *methane* | *propane*.
– ORIGIN on the pattern of words such as *-ene, -ine*.

anecdotage /ˈanɪkdəʊtɪdʒ/ ▸ **noun** [mass noun] **1** anecdotes collectively: *a number of reports cannot be dismissed as anecdotage*.
2 humorous old age, especially in someone who is inclined to be garrulous. [from a blend of ANECDOTE and DOTAGE.]

anecdotal ▸ **adjective** (of an account) not necessarily true or reliable, because based on personal accounts rather than facts or research: *while there was much anecdotal evidence there was little hard fact*. ■ characterized by or fond of telling anecdotes: *her book is anecdotal and chatty*. ■ (of a painting) depicting small narrative incidents.
– DERIVATIVES **anecdotalist** noun, **anecdotally** adverb.

anecdote /ˈanɪkdəʊt/ ▸ **noun** a short amusing or interesting story about a real incident or person: *he told anecdotes about his job*. ■ an account regarded as unreliable or hearsay: [mass noun] *his wife's death has long been the subject of rumour and anecdote*. ■ [mass noun] the depiction of a minor narrative incident in a painting.
– ORIGIN late 17th cent.: from French, or via modern Latin from Greek *anekdota* 'things unpublished', from *an-* 'not' + *ekdotos*, from *ekdidōnai* 'publish'.

anechoic /ˌanɪˈkəʊɪk/ ▸ **adjective** technical free from echo: *an anechoic chamber*. ■ (of a coating or material) tending to deaden sound.

anele /əˈniːl/ ▸ **verb** [with obj.] archaic anoint (someone), especially as part of the Christian rite of giving extreme unction to the dying.
– ORIGIN Middle English: from *an-* 'on' + archaic *elien* 'to oil' (from Old English *ele*, from Latin *oleum* 'oil').

anemia ▸ **noun** US spelling of ANAEMIA.

anemic ▸ **adjective** US spelling of ANAEMIC.

anemometer /ˌanɪˈmɒmɪtə/ ▸ **noun** an instrument for measuring the speed of the wind, or of any current of gas.
– DERIVATIVES **anemometric** adjective, **anemometry** noun.

– ORIGIN early 18th cent.: from Greek *anemos* 'wind' + **-METER**.

anemone /ə'nɛməni/ ▸ **noun 1** a plant of the buttercup family which typically has brightly coloured flowers and deeply divided leaves. ● Genus *Anemone*, family Ranunculaceae: numerous species, including the common Eurasian **wood anemone** (*A. nemorosa*).
2 short for **SEA ANEMONE**.
– ORIGIN mid 16th cent.: from Latin, said to be from Greek *anemōnē* 'windflower', literally 'daughter of the wind', from *anemos* 'wind', thought to be so named because the flowers open only when the wind blows.

anemone fish ▸ **noun** another term for **CLOWNFISH**.

anemophilous /ˌanɪ'mɒfɪləs/ ▸ **adjective** Botany (of a plant) wind-pollinated.
– DERIVATIVES **anemophily** noun.
– ORIGIN late 19th cent.: from Greek *anemos* 'wind' + *-philous* (see **-PHILIA**).

anencephalic /ˌanɛnsɪ'falɪk, -kɛ'falɪk/ Medicine ▸ **adjective** having part or all of the cerebral hemispheres and the rear of the skull congenitally absent.
▸ **noun** an anencephalic fetus or infant.
– DERIVATIVES **anencephaly** noun.
– ORIGIN mid 19th cent.: from Greek *anenkephalos* 'without brain' + **-IC**.

anent /ə'nɛnt/ ▸ **preposition** chiefly archaic or Scottish concerning; about: *I'll say a few words anent the letter*
– ORIGIN Old English *on efen* 'in line with, in company with'.

-aneous ▸ **suffix** forming adjectives from Latin words: *cutaneous | spontaneous*.
– ORIGIN from the Latin suffix *-aneus*.

anergia /a'nəːdʒɪə/ ▸ **noun** [mass noun] Psychiatry abnormal lack of energy.
– ORIGIN late 19th cent.: modern Latin, from Greek *an-* 'without' + *ergon* 'work'.

anergy /'anədʒi/ ▸ **noun** [mass noun] Medicine absence of the normal immune response to a particular antigen or allergen.
– DERIVATIVES **anergic** /ə'nəːdʒɪk/ **adjective**.
– ORIGIN early 20th cent.: from German *Anergie*, from Greek *an-* 'not', on the pattern of *Allergie* 'allergy'.

aneroid /'anərɔɪd/ ▸ **adjective** relating to or denoting a barometer that measures air pressure by the action of the air in deforming the elastic lid of an evacuated box.
▸ **noun** an aneroid barometer.
– ORIGIN mid 19th cent.: coined in French from Greek *a-* 'without' + *nēros* 'water'.

anesthesia etc. ▸ **noun** US spelling of **ANAESTHESIA** etc.

aneuploid /'anjʊplɔɪd/ ▸ **adjective** Genetics not euploid.
– DERIVATIVES **aneuploidy** noun.

aneurysm /'anjʊrɪz(ə)m/ (also **aneurism**) ▸ **noun** Medicine an excessive localized swelling of the wall of an artery.
– DERIVATIVES **aneurysmal** adjective.
– ORIGIN late Middle English: from Greek *aneurusma* 'dilatation', from *aneurunein* 'widen out'.

anew ▸ **adverb** chiefly literary in a new or different and typically more positive way: *her career had begun anew, with a lucrative Japanese modelling contract*. ■ once more; again: *tears filled her eyes anew*.

anfractuous /an'fraktjʊəs/ ▸ **adjective** rare sinuous or circuitous.
– DERIVATIVES **anfractuosity** noun.
– ORIGIN late 16th cent.: from late Latin *anfractuosus*, from Latin *anfractus* 'a bending'.

angary /'aŋgəri/ ▸ **noun** [mass noun] Law the right of a country at war to seize or destroy neutral property out of military necessity, provided that compensation is paid.
– ORIGIN late 19th cent.: from French *angarie* 'chore, imposition', from Italian or Latin *angaria* 'forced service', from Greek *angareia*, from *angaros* 'courier' (being liable to serve as the King's messenger), from Persian.

angel ▸ **noun 1** a spiritual being believed to act as an attendant, agent, or messenger of God, conventionally represented in human form with wings and a long robe: *God sent an angel to talk to Gideon | the Angel of Death*. ■ an attendant spirit, especially a benevolent one: *there was an angel watching over me*. See also **GUARDIAN ANGEL**. ■ (in traditional Christian angelology) a being of the lowest order of the ninefold celestial hierarchy. ■ **(Angel)** short for **HELL'S ANGEL**.
2 a person of exemplary conduct or virtue: *women were then seen as angels or whores | I know I'm no angel*. ■ used in similes or comparisons to refer to a person's outstanding beauty, qualities, or abilities: *you sang like an angel*. ■ used in approval to a person who is kind or helpful: *be an angel and let us come in*. ■ used as a term of endearment: *I miss you too, angel*.
3 informal a financial backer of a theatrical or business enterprise.
4 a former English coin minted between the reigns of Edward IV and Charles I and bearing the figure of the archangel Michael killing a dragon.
5 (angels) aviation slang an aircraft's altitude (often used with a numeral indicating thousands of feet): *we rendezvous at angels nine*.
6 informal an unexplained radar echo.
– PHRASES **on the side of the angels** on the side of what is right: *we're not in the business of polluting the environment, we're on the side of the angels*.
– ORIGIN Old English *engel*, ultimately via ecclesiastical Latin from Greek *angelos* 'messenger'; superseded in Middle English by forms from Old French *angele*.

angel cake (N. Amer. also **angel food cake**) ▸ **noun** a very light, pale sponge cake made of flour, egg whites, and no fat, typically baked in a ring shape and covered with soft icing.

angel dust ▸ **noun** [mass noun] informal **1** the hallucinogenic drug phencyclidine hydrochloride.
2 another term for **CLENBUTEROL**.

Angeleno /ˌandʒə'liːnəʊ/ (also **Los Angeleno**, **Angelino**) ▸ **noun** (pl. **Angelenos**) a native or inhabitant of Los Angeles: [as modifier] *Angeleno sports fans*.
– ORIGIN late 19th cent.: from American Spanish.

Angel Falls a waterfall in the Guiana Highlands of SE Venezuela. It is the highest waterfall in the world, with an uninterrupted descent of 978 m (3,210 ft). The falls were discovered in 1935 by the American aviator and prospector James Angel (*c*.1899–1956).

angelfish ▸ **noun** (pl. **same** or **angelfishes**) any of a number of laterally compressed deep-bodied fishes with extended dorsal and anal fins, typically brightly coloured or boldly striped: ● a freshwater fish native to the Amazon basin (genus *Pterophyllum*, family Cichlidae), in particular *P. scalare*. ● a marine or reef-dwelling fish (several genera in the family Chaetodontidae). ● another term for **BATFISH** (sense 2).

angel hair (also **angel's hair**) ▸ **noun** [mass noun] a type of pasta consisting of very fine long strands.

angelic ▸ **adjective** relating to angels: *the angelic hosts*. ■ (of a person) exceptionally beautiful, innocent, or kind: *she looks remarkably young and angelic*.
– DERIVATIVES **angelical** adjective, **angelically** adverb.
– ORIGIN late Middle English: from French *angélique*, via late Latin from Greek *angelikos*, from *angelos* (see **ANGEL**).

angelica /an'dʒɛlɪkə/ ▸ **noun** a tall aromatic plant of the parsley family, with large leaves and yellowish-green flowers. It is used in cooking and herbal medicine. ● Genus *Angelica*, family Umbelliferae: many species, especially the cultivated *A. archangelica*.
■ [mass noun] the candied stalk of angelica, used in confectionery and cake decoration.
– ORIGIN early 16th cent.: from medieval Latin (*herba*) *angelica* 'angelic (herb)', so named because it was believed to be efficacious against poisoning and disease.

angelica tree ▸ **noun** a tree of the ginseng family, with large leaves and black berries. ● Genus *Aralia*, family Araliaceae.

Angelic Doctor the nickname of St Thomas Aquinas.

Angelico /an'dʒɛlɪkəʊ/, Fra (*c*.1400–55), Italian painter and Dominican friar; born *Guido di Pietro*; monastic name *Fra Giovanni da Fiesole*. Notable works: the frescoes in the convent of San Marco, Florence (*c*.1438–47).

Angelino ▸ **noun** variant spelling of **ANGELENO**.

Angelman syndrome ▸ **noun** [mass noun] a rare congenital disorder characterized by mental disability and a tendency to jerky movement, caused by the absence of certain genes normally present on the copy of chromosome 15 inherited from the mother.
– ORIGIN 1970s: named after Harold *Angelman* (1915–96), the British doctor who described the condition.

angelology ▸ **noun** [mass noun] theological doctrine concerning angels.

Angelou /'andʒəluː/, Maya (b.1928), American novelist and poet, acclaimed for the first volume of her autobiography, *I Know Why the Caged Bird Sings* (1970), which recounts her harrowing experiences as a black child in the American South.

angel shark ▸ **noun** a large, active bottom-dwelling cartilaginous fish with broad wing-like pectoral fins. ● Family Squatinidae and genus *Squatina*: several species, in particular *S. squatina* (also called **MONKFISH**).

angels on horseback ▸ **plural noun** Brit. an appetizer consisting of oysters individually wrapped in bacon and served on toast.

angel's trumpet ▸ **noun** a South American shrub or small tree with large pendulous trumpet-shaped flowers, cultivated as an ornamental and in some regions consumed for its narcotic properties. ● Genus *Brugmansia*, family Solanaceae; often placed in the genus *Datura*.

Angelus /'andʒ(ə)ləs/ ▸ **noun** a Roman Catholic devotion commemorating the Incarnation of Jesus and including the Hail Mary, said at morning, noon, and sunset. ■ a ringing of church bells announcing the Angelus.
– ORIGIN mid 17th cent.: from the Latin phrase *Angelus domini* 'the angel of the Lord', the opening words of the devotion.

angel wings ▸ **plural noun** [treated as sing.] a large white edible piddock (mollusc) which occurs in the Caribbean and on the east coast of North America. ● *Barnea costata*, family Pholadidae.

anger ▸ **noun** [mass noun] a strong feeling of annoyance, displeasure, or hostility: *the colonel's anger at his daughter's disobedience*.
▸ **verb** [with obj.] fill (someone) with anger; provoke anger in: *she was angered by his terse answer* | [with obj. and clause] *he was angered that he had not been told*.
– ORIGIN Middle English: from Old Norse *angr* 'grief', *angra* 'vex'. The original use was in the Old Norse senses; current senses date from late Middle English.

Angers /'ɒ̃ʒeɪ/, French /ɑ̃ʒe/ a town in western France, capital of the former province of Anjou; pop. 156,965 (2006).

Angevin /'andʒəvɪn/ ▸ **noun** a native, inhabitant, or ruler of Anjou. ■ any of the Plantagenet kings of England, especially those who were also counts of Anjou (Henry II, Richard I, and John).
▸ **adjective** relating to Anjou. ■ relating to or denoting the Plantagenets.
– ORIGIN from French, from medieval Latin *Andegavinus*, from *Andegavum* 'Angers' (see **ANGERS**).

angina /an'dʒʌɪnə/ ▸ **noun** [mass noun] **1** (also **angina pectoris** /'pɛkt(ə)rɪs/) a condition marked by severe pain in the chest, often also spreading to the shoulders, arms, and neck, owing to an inadequate blood supply to the heart. [Latin *pectoris* 'of the chest'.]
2 [with modifier] any of a number of disorders in which there is an intense localized pain: *Ludwig's angina*.
– DERIVATIVES **anginal** adjective.
– ORIGIN mid 16th cent.: from Latin, 'quinsy', from Greek *ankhonē* 'strangling'.

angio- /'andʒɪəʊ/ ▸ **combining form 1** relating to blood vessels: *angiography*.
2 relating to seed vessels: *angiosperm*.
– ORIGIN from Greek *angeion* 'vessel'.

angiogenesis ▸ **noun** [mass noun] Physiology the development of new blood vessels.

angiogram /'andʒɪə(ʊ)gram/ ▸ **noun** an X-ray photograph of blood or lymph vessels, made by angiography.

angiography /ˌandʒɪ'ɒgrəfi/ ▸ **noun** [mass noun] radiography of blood or lymph vessels, carried out after introduction of a radiopaque substance.
– DERIVATIVES **angiographic** adjective, **angiographically** adverb.

angioma /ˌandʒɪ'əʊmə/ ▸ **noun** (pl. **angiomas** or **angiomata** /-mətə/) Medicine an abnormal growth produced by the dilatation or new formation of blood vessels.
– ORIGIN late 19th cent.: from Greek *angeion* 'vessel' + **-OMA**.

angioneurotic ▸ **adjective** Medicine (of oedema) marked by swelling and itching of areas of skin, usually allergic in origin.

angioplasty /'andʒɪə(ʊ)ˌplasti/ ▸ **noun** (pl. **angioplasties**) [mass noun] Medicine surgical repair or unblocking of a blood vessel, especially a coronary artery.

angiosperm ▸ **noun** Botany a plant of a large group that comprises those that have flowers and produce seeds enclosed within a carpel, including herbaceous plants, shrubs, grasses, and most trees. Compare with **GYMNOSPERM**. ● Subdivision Angiospermae, division Spermatophyta.
– DERIVATIVES **angiospermous** /-'spəːməs/ **adjective**.

angiotensin /ˌandʒɪə(ʊ)ˈtɛnsɪn/ ▸ **noun** [mass noun] Biochemistry a protein whose presence in the blood promotes aldosterone secretion and tends to raise blood pressure.
– ORIGIN 1950s: from **ANGIO-** + *(hyper)tens(ion)* + **-IN**[1].

Angkor /ˈaŋkɔː/ the capital of the ancient kingdom of Khmer in NW Cambodia, noted for its temples, especially the Angkor Wat (mid 12th century); the site was rediscovered in 1860.

Angle ▸ **noun** a member of a Germanic people, originally inhabitants of what is now Schleswig-Holstein, who came to England in the 5th century AD. The Angles founded kingdoms in Mercia, Northumbria, and East Anglia and gave their name to England and the English.
– ORIGIN from Latin *Anglus*, (plural) *Angli* 'the people of *Angul*', a district of Schleswig (now in northern Germany), so named because of its shape; of Germanic origin, related to Old English *angul* (see **ANGLE**[2]). Compare with **ENGLISH**.

angle[1] ▸ **noun 1** the space (usually measured in degrees) between two intersecting lines or surfaces at or close to the point where they meet. ■ a corner, especially an external projection or an internal recess of a part of a building or other structure: *a skylight in the angle of the roof*. ■ a measure of the inclination of one line or surface with respect to another: *sloping at an angle of 33° to the horizontal*. ■ a position from which something is viewed or along which it travels or acts, typically as measured by its inclination from an implicit horizontal or vertical baseline: *from this angle Maggie could not see Naomi's face*.
2 a particular way of approaching or considering an issue or problem: *discussing the problems from every conceivable angle* | *he always had a fresh* ***angle on*** *life*.
3 [often with modifier] Astrology each of the four cardinal points of a chart, from which the first, fourth, seventh, and tenth houses extend anticlockwise respectively.
4 [mass noun] angle iron or a similar constructional material made of another metal.
▸ **verb** [with obj. and adverbial of direction] direct or incline at an angle: *he angled his chair so that he could watch her*. ■ [no obj., with adverbial of direction] move or be inclined at an angle: *still the rain angles down*. ■ [with obj.] present (information) to reflect a particular view or have a particular focus: *angle your answer so that it is relevant to the job for which you are applying*.
– PHRASES **at an angle** in a direction or at an inclination markedly different from parallel, vertical, or horizontal with respect to an implicit baseline: *she wore her beret at an angle* | *an armchair was drawn up* ***at an angle to*** *his desk*. **from all angles** from every direction or point of view: *they come shooting at us from all angles*.
– ORIGIN late Middle English: from Old French, from Latin *angulus* 'corner'.

angle[2] ▸ **verb** [no obj.] **1** fish with a rod and line.
2 seek something desired by indirectly prompting someone to offer it: *Ralph had begun to* ***angle for*** *an invitation*.
▸ **noun** archaic a fish hook.
– ORIGIN Old English *angul* (noun); the verb dates from late Middle English.

angle bead ▸ **noun** a strip of metal or wood fixed to a corner before it is plastered to reinforce and protect it.

angle bracket ▸ **noun 1** either of a pair of marks in the form < >, used to enclose words or figures so as to separate them from their context.
2 another term for **BRACKET** (sense 3 of the noun).

angled ▸ **adjective 1** placed or inclined at an angle to something else: *he sent an angled shot into the net*. ■ (of information) presented so as to reflect a particular view or to have a particular focus.
2 [in combination] having an angle or angles of a specified type or number: *a right-angled bend*.

angle grinder ▸ **noun** a device with a rotating abrasive disc, used to grind, polish, or cut metal and other materials.

angle iron ▸ **noun** [mass noun] a constructional material consisting of pieces of iron or steel with an L-shaped cross section, able to be bolted together. ■ [count noun] a piece of metal of this kind.

angle of attack ▸ **noun** Aeronautics the angle between the line of the chord of an aerofoil and the relative airflow.

angle of incidence ▸ **noun** Physics the angle which an incident line or ray makes with a perpendicular to the surface at the point of incidence.

angle of reflection ▸ **noun** Physics the angle made by a reflected ray with a perpendicular to the reflecting surface.

angle of refraction ▸ **noun** Physics the angle made by a refracted ray with a perpendicular to the refracting surface.

angle of repose ▸ **noun** the steepest angle at which a sloping surface formed of loose material is stable.

anglepoise ▸ **noun** trademark a type of desk lamp with a jointed arm and counterbalancing springs that hold it in any position to which it is adjusted: [as modifier] *an anglepoise lamp*.

angler ▸ **noun** a person who fishes with a rod and line. ■ short for **ANGLERFISH**.

anglerfish ▸ **noun** (pl. **same** or **anglerfishes**) a fish that lures prey with a fleshy lobe on a filament arising from the snout, typically with a very large head and wide mouth, and a small body and tail. ● Order Lophiiformes: several families. Some rest motionless on the seabed, in particular those of the family Lophiidae; many others are deep-sea fish.

Anglesey /ˈaŋg(ə)lsi/ an island and (since 1996) county of NW Wales, separated from the mainland by the Menai Strait; pop. 70,000 (est. 2009). Welsh name **YNYS MÔN**.

angle shades ▸ **plural noun** [treated as sing.] a European moth with wings patterned in muted green, red, and pink. ● *Phlogophora meticulosa*, family Noctuidae.

angle wings ▸ **plural noun** [treated as sing.] a North American butterfly that is related to and resembles the comma. ● Genus *Polygonia*, subfamily Nymphalinae, family Nymphalidae: several species.

Anglian /ˈaŋglɪən/ ▸ **adjective 1** relating to the ancient Angles.
2 Geology relating to or denoting a Pleistocene glaciation in Britain, identified with the Elsterian of northern Europe (and perhaps the Mindel of the Alps). ■ (as noun **the Anglian**) the Anglian glaciation or the system of deposits laid down during it.
– ORIGIN from Latin *Angli* (see **ANGLE**) + **-IAN**.

Anglican ▸ **adjective** relating to or denoting the Church of England or any Church in communion with it.
▸ **noun** a member of any of the Anglican Churches.
– DERIVATIVES **Anglicanism** noun.
– ORIGIN early 17th cent.: from medieval Latin *Anglicanus* (its adoption suggested by *Anglicana ecclesia* 'the English church' in the Magna Carta), from Latin *Anglicus*, from *Angli* (see **ANGLE**).

Anglican chant ▸ **noun** [mass noun] a method of singing unmetrical psalms and canticles to short harmonized melodies, the first note being extended to accommodate as many syllables as necessary.

Anglican Communion the group of Christian Churches derived from or related to the Church of England, including the Episcopal Church in the US and other national, provincial, and independent Churches. The body's senior bishop is the Archbishop of Canterbury.

anglice /ˈaŋglɪsi/ ▸ **adverb** formal in English.
– ORIGIN from medieval Latin, from Latin *Anglus* (see **ANGLE**).

Anglicism ▸ **noun** a word or phrase that is peculiar to British English: *this new autobiography is studded with Anglicisms like lorries, plimsolls, and doing a bunk*. ■ [mass noun] the quality of being typically English or of favouring English things.
– ORIGIN mid 17th cent.: from Latin *Anglicus*, from *Angli* (see **ANGLE**) + **-ISM**.

anglicize (also **anglicise**) ▸ **verb** [with obj.] make English in form or character: *he anglicized his name to Goodman* | (as adj. **anglicized**) *an anglicized form of a Navajo word*.
– DERIVATIVES **anglicization** noun.

angling ▸ **noun** [mass noun] Brit. the sport or pastime of fishing with a rod and line.

Anglo ▸ **noun** (pl. **Anglos**) **1** chiefly N. Amer. a white English-speaking person of British or northern European origin, in particular (in the US) as distinct from a Hispanic American or (in Canada) as distinct from a French-speaker. ■ Indian, often offensive an Anglo-Indian.
2 Brit. informal a person selected for a Scottish, Irish, or Welsh national sports team who plays for an English club.
– ORIGIN early 19th cent.: independent usage of **ANGLO-**.

Anglo- ▸ **combining form** English: *anglophone*. ■ of English origin: *Anglo-Saxon*. ■ English and ...: *Anglo-Latin*. ■ British and ...: *Anglo-Indian*.
– ORIGIN modern Latin, from Latin *Anglus* 'English'.

Anglo-Boer War S. African either of the Boer Wars, but typically the second. See **BOER WARS**.

Anglo-Catholic ▸ **adjective** relating to Anglo-Catholicism.
▸ **noun** a member of an Anglo-Catholic Church.

Anglo-Catholicism ▸ **noun** [mass noun] a tradition within the Anglican Church which is close to Catholicism in its doctrine and worship and is broadly identified with High Church Anglicanism. As a movement, Anglo-Catholicism grew out of the Oxford Movement of the 1830s and 1840s.

Anglo-Celt ▸ **noun** a person of British or Irish descent (used chiefly outside Britain and Ireland).
– DERIVATIVES **Anglo-Celtic** adjective.

Anglocentric ▸ **adjective** centred on or considered in terms of England or Britain: *an Anglocentric, white view of Australian history*.

Anglo-Indian ▸ **adjective** relating to both Britain and India: *Anglo-Indian business cooperation*. ■ of Indian descent but born or living in Britain. ■ of mixed British and Indian parentage. ■ chiefly historical of British descent or birth but living or having lived long in India.
▸ **noun** an Anglo-Indian person.

Anglo-Irish ▸ **adjective** relating to both Britain and Ireland (or specifically the Republic of Ireland). ■ of English descent but born or resident in Ireland. ■ of mixed English and Irish parentage.

Anglo-Irish Agreement an agreement made between Britain and the Republic of Ireland in 1985, admitting the Republic to discussions on Northern Irish affairs and providing for greater cooperation between the security forces in border areas.

Anglo-Irish Treaty an agreement signed in 1921 by representatives of the British government and the provisional Irish Republican government, by which Ireland was partitioned and the Irish Free State created in 1922.

Anglo-Latin ▸ **noun** [mass noun] the form of Latin used in medieval England.
▸ **adjective** relating to Anglo-Latin.

Anglomania ▸ **noun** [mass noun] excessive admiration of English customs.
– DERIVATIVES **Anglomaniac** noun.

Anglo-Norman French (also **Anglo-Norman**) ▸ **noun** [mass noun] the variety of Norman French used in England after the Norman Conquest. It remained the language of the English nobility for several centuries.
▸ **adjective** relating to Anglo-Norman French.

Anglophile ▸ **noun** a person who is fond of or greatly admires England or Britain.
– DERIVATIVES **Anglophilia** noun.

Anglophobe ▸ **noun** a person who greatly hates or fears England or Britain.
– DERIVATIVES **Anglophobia** noun.

anglophone ▸ **adjective** English-speaking: *the population is largely anglophone*.
▸ **noun** an English-speaking person.
– ORIGIN early 20th cent. (as a noun; rare before the 1960s): from **ANGLO-** + **-PHONE**, on the pattern of *francophone*.

Anglo-Saxon ▸ **adjective** relating to or denoting the Germanic inhabitants of England from their arrival in the 5th century up to the Norman Conquest. ■ of English descent. ■ informal (of an English word or expression) plain, in particular vulgar: *using a lot of good old Anglo-Saxon expletives*.
▸ **noun 1** a Germanic inhabitant of England between the 5th century and the Norman Conquest. ■ a person of English descent. ■ chiefly N. Amer. any white, English-speaking person.
2 [mass noun] the Old English language. ■ informal plain English, in particular vulgar slang.
– ORIGIN from modern Latin *Anglo-Saxones* (plural), medieval Latin *Angli Saxones*.

Anglosphere /ˈaŋglə(ʊ)sfɪə/ ▸ **noun** (**the Anglosphere**) the countries where English is the main native language, considered collectively.

Angola /aŋˈgəʊlə/ a republic on the west coast of southern Africa; pop. 12,799,300 (est. 2009); languages, Portuguese (official), Bantu languages; capital, Luanda.

Angola was a Portuguese possession from the end of the 16th century until it achieved independence in 1975. Independence was followed by years of civil war between the

A

ruling Marxist MPLA and the UNITA movement; this was halted by the signing of a ceasefire in 2002.

– DERIVATIVES **Angolan** adjective & noun.

Angora /aŋ'gɔːrə/ former name (until 1930) for ANKARA.

angora /aŋ'gɔːrə/ ▶ noun [often as modifier] a cat, goat, or rabbit of a long-haired breed: *angora rabbits.* ■ [mass noun] a yarn or fabric made from the hair of the angora goat or rabbit: *an angora cardigan.*
– ORIGIN early 19th cent. (denoting a long-haired breed): from the place name ANGORA.

angora wool ▶ noun [mass noun] a mixture of sheep's wool and angora rabbit hair.

Angostura /ˌaŋgə'stjʊərə/ former name (until 1846) for CIUDAD BOLÍVAR.

angostura /ˌaŋgə'stjʊərə/ (also **angostura bark**) ▶ noun [mass noun] an aromatic bitter bark from certain South American trees, used as a flavouring, and formerly as a tonic and to reduce fever. ● The trees are *Angostura febrifuga* and *Galipea officinalis*, family Rutaceae. ■ short for ANGOSTURA BITTERS.
– ORIGIN late 18th cent.: from the place name ANGOSTURA.

Angostura bitters ▶ plural noun trademark a kind of tonic first made in Angostura.

angrez /ʌŋ'reɪz/ Indian informal ▶ noun (pl. **same**) an English person.
▶ adjective English.
– ORIGIN Hindi, 'Englishman'.

Angrezi /ʌŋ'reɪzi/ Indian informal ▶ noun [mass noun] the English language.
▶ adjective English.

angry ▶ adjective (**angrier**, **angriest**) feeling or showing strong annoyance, displeasure, or hostility; full of anger: *why are you angry with me?* | *I'm angry that she didn't call me.* ■ (of the sea or sky) stormy, turbulent, or threatening: *the wild, angry sea.* ■ (of a wound or sore) red and inflamed.
– DERIVATIVES **angrily** adverb.

angry white male ▶ noun chiefly US a right-wing or anti-liberal white man, especially a working-class one.

angry young man ▶ noun a young man dissatisfied with and outspoken against existing social and political structures. ■ (**Angry Young Men**) a number of British playwrights and novelists of the early 1950s whose work was marked by irreverence towards the Establishment and disgust at the survival of class distinctions and privilege. Notable members of the group were John Osborne and Kingsley Amis.

angst /aŋst/ ▶ noun [mass noun] a feeling of deep anxiety or dread, typically an unfocused one about the human condition or the state of the world in general: *angst-ridden sixth-formers.*
– DERIVATIVES **angsty** adjective.
– ORIGIN 1920s: from German, 'fear'.

Ångström /'ɒŋstrəːm/, Anders Jonas (1814–74), Swedish physicist. He proposed a relationship between the emission and absorption spectra of chemical elements, and measured optical wavelengths in the unit later named in his honour.

angstrom /'aŋstrəm/ (also **ångström** /'ɒŋstrəːm/, **angstrom unit**) (abbrev.: **Å**) ▶ noun a unit of length equal to one hundred-millionth of a centimetre, 10^{-10} metre, used mainly to express wavelengths and interatomic distances.
– ORIGIN late 19th cent.: named after A. J. ÅNGSTRÖM.

Anguilla /aŋ'gwɪlə/ the most northerly of the Leeward Islands in the Caribbean; pop. 14,400 (est. 2009); languages, English (official), English Creole; capital, The Valley. Formerly a British colony, and briefly united with St Kitts and Nevis (1967), the island is now a self-governing British overseas territory.
– DERIVATIVES **Anguillan** adjective & noun.

anguilliform /aŋ'gwɪlɪfɔːm/ ▶ adjective rare shaped like or resembling an eel. ■ Zoology relating to a large order of fishes (Anguilliformes) that comprises the eels.
– ORIGIN late 17th cent.: from Latin *anguilla* 'eel' + -IFORM.

anguine /'aŋgwɪn/ ▶ adjective rare of or resembling a snake.
– ORIGIN mid 17th cent.: from Latin *anguinus*, from *anguis* 'snake'.

anguish ▶ noun [mass noun] severe mental or physical pain or suffering: *she shut her eyes in anguish* | *Philip gave a cry of anguish.*
▶ verb [no obj.] be extremely distressed about something: *I spent the next two weeks anguishing about whether I'd made the right decision.*
– ORIGIN Middle English: via Old French from Latin *angustia* 'tightness', (plural) 'straits, distress', from *angustus* 'narrow'.

anguished ▶ adjective experiencing or expressing severe mental or physical pain or suffering: *he gave an anguished cry.*
– ORIGIN early 17th cent.: past participle of ANGUISH (verb) in the rare sense 'distress with severe mental or physical pain', from Old French *anguissier*, from ecclesiastical Latin *angustiare* 'to distress', from Latin *angustia*.

angular /'aŋgjʊlə/ ▶ adjective **1** having angles or sharp corners: *angular chairs* | *Adam's angular handwriting.* ■ (of a person or part of their body) lean and having a prominent bone structure: *her angular face.*
2 Physics denoting physical properties or quantities measured with reference to or by means of an angle, especially those associated with rotation: *angular acceleration.*
3 Astrology relating to or denoting any of the houses that begin at the four cardinal points of a chart.
– DERIVATIVES **angularity** noun, **angularly** adverb.
– ORIGIN late Middle English (as an astrological term): from Latin *angularis*, from *angulus* (see ANGLE[1]).

angular diameter ▶ noun Astronomy the apparent diameter of a planet or other celestial object measured by the angle which it subtends at the point of observation.

angular frequency ▶ noun Physics the frequency of a steadily recurring phenomenon expressed in radians per second. A frequency in hertz can be converted to an angular frequency by multiplying it by 2π. (Symbol: ω)

angular momentum ▶ noun Physics the quantity of rotation of a body, which is the product of its moment of inertia and its angular velocity.

angular velocity ▶ noun Physics the rate of change of angular position of a rotating body.

angulate ▶ verb [with obj.] technical hold, bend, or distort (a part of the body) so as to form an angle or angles. ■ Skiing incline (the upper body) sideways and outwards during a turn.
– DERIVATIVES **angulation** noun.
– ORIGIN late 15th cent. (as *angulated*, used chiefly as a botanical or zoological term): from Latin *angulatus*, past participle of *angulare*, from *angulus* 'angle'. The skiing term dates from the 1970s.

Angus[1] /'aŋgəs/ a council area of NE Scotland; administrative centre, Forfar. It was known from the 16th century until 1928 as Forfarshire, and between 1975 and 1996 was part of Tayside region.

Angus[2] /'aŋgəs/ ▶ noun short for ABERDEEN ANGUS.

angwantibo /əŋ'gwɒntɪbəʊ/ ▶ noun (pl. **angwantibos**) a small rare nocturnal primate of west central Africa, related to the potto. ● *Arctocebus calabarensis*, family Lorisidae.
– ORIGIN mid 19th cent.: from Efik.

anharmonic ▶ adjective Physics relating to or denoting motion that is not simple harmonic.
– DERIVATIVES **anharmonicity** noun.

anhedonia /ˌanhɪ'dəʊnɪə/ ▶ noun [mass noun] Psychiatry inability to feel pleasure in normally pleasurable activities.
– DERIVATIVES **anhedonic** adjective.
– ORIGIN late 19th cent.: from French *anhédonie*, from Greek *an-* 'without' + *hēdonē* 'pleasure'.

anhedral /an'hiːdr(ə)l, -'hɛd-/ ▶ adjective Crystallography (of a crystal) having no plane faces.
▶ noun [mass noun] Aeronautics downward inclination of an aircraft's wing. Compare with DIHEDRAL.
– ORIGIN late 19th cent. (as an adjective): from AN-[1] 'not' + *-hedral* (see -HEDRON).

anhinga /an'hɪŋgə/ ▶ noun chiefly N. Amer. another term for DARTER (sense 1).
– ORIGIN mid 18th cent.: from Portuguese, from Tupi *áyinga.*

Anhui /an'hweɪ/ (also **Anhwei**) a province in eastern China; capital, Hefei.

anhydride /an'hʌɪdrʌɪd/ ▶ noun Chemistry the compound obtained by removing the elements of water from a particular acid. ■ [usu. with modifier] an organic compound containing the group −C(O)OC(O)−, derived from a carboxylic acid.
– ORIGIN mid 19th cent.: from Greek *anudros* (see ANHYDROUS) + -IDE.

anhydrite /an'hʌɪdrʌɪt/ ▶ noun [mass noun] a white mineral consisting of anhydrous calcium sulphate. It typically occurs in evaporite deposits.
– ORIGIN early 19th cent.: from Greek *anudros* (see ANHYDROUS) + -ITE[1].

anhydrous /an'hʌɪdrəs/ ▶ adjective Chemistry (of a substance, especially a crystalline compound) containing no water.
– ORIGIN early 19th cent.: from Greek *anudros* (from *an-* 'without' + *hudōr* 'water') + -OUS.

ani /'ɑːni/ ▶ noun (pl. **anis**) a glossy black long-tailed bird of the cuckoo family, with a large deep bill, found in Central and South America. ● Genus *Crotophaga*, family Cuculidae: three species.
– ORIGIN early 19th cent.: from Spanish *ani*, Portuguese *anum*, from Tupi *anū*.

aniline /'anɪliːn, -lɪn/ ▶ noun [mass noun] Chemistry a colourless oily liquid present in coal tar. It is used in the manufacture of dyes, drugs, and plastics, and was the basis of the earliest synthetic dyes. ● Chem. formula: $C_6H_5NH_2$.
– ORIGIN mid 19th cent.: from *anil* 'indigo' (from which it was originally obtained), via French and Portuguese from Arabic *an-nīl* (from Sanskrit *nīlī*, from *nīla* 'dark blue').

aniline dye ▶ noun chiefly historical a synthetic dye, especially one made from aniline.

anilingus /ˌeɪnɪ'lɪŋgəs/ ▶ noun [mass noun] sexual stimulation of the anus by the tongue or mouth.
– ORIGIN 1960s: from Latin *anus* 'anus' on the pattern of *cunnilingus*.

anima /'anɪmə/ ▶ noun Psychoanalysis **1** (in Jungian psychology) the feminine part of a man's personality. Often contrasted with ANIMUS (sense 3).
2 the part of the psyche which is directed inwards, in touch with the subconscious. Often contrasted with PERSONA.
– ORIGIN 1920s: from Latin, 'mind, soul'.

animadversion /ˌanɪməd'vəːʃ(ə)n/ ▶ noun [mass noun] formal criticism or censure: *her animadversion against science.* ■ [count noun] a comment or remark, especially a critical one.
– ORIGIN mid 16th cent.: from French, or from Latin *animadversio(n-)*, from the verb *animadvertere* (see ANIMADVERT).

animadvert /ˌanɪməd'vəːt/ ▶ verb [no obj.] (**animadvert on/upon/against**) formal pass criticism or censure on; speak out against: *we shall be obliged to animadvert most severely upon you in our report.*
– ORIGIN late Middle English (in the sense 'pay attention to'): from Latin *animadvertere*, from *animus* 'mind' + *advertere* (from *ad-* 'towards' + *vertere* 'to turn').

animal ▶ noun a living organism which feeds on organic matter, typically having specialized sense organs and nervous system and able to respond rapidly to stimuli. ■ any such living organism other than a human being: *are humans superior to animals, or just different?* ■ a mammal, as opposed to a bird, reptile, fish, or insect: *the snowfall seemed to have chased all birds, animals, and men indoors.* ■ a person without human attributes or civilizing influences, especially someone who is very cruel, violent, or repulsive: *those men have to be animals—what they did to that boy was savage.* ■ [with adj. or noun modifier] a particular type of person or thing: *a regular party animal* | *I am a political animal.*

Animals are generally distinguished from plants by being unable to synthesize organic molecules from inorganic ones, so that they have to feed on plants or on other animals. They are typically able to move about, though this ability is sometimes restricted to a particular stage in the life cycle. The great majority of animals are invertebrates, of which there are some thirty phyla; the vertebrates constitute but a single subphylum.

▶ adjective **1** relating to or characteristic of animals: *the evolution of animal life* | *animal welfare.* ■ of animals as distinct from plants: *tissues of animal and vegetable protein.* ■ characteristic of the physical and instinctive needs of animals; of the flesh rather than the spirit or intellect: *a crude surrender to animal lust.*
2 Biology relating to or denoting the pole or extremity of an embryo that contains the more active cytoplasm in the early stages of development. The opposite of VEGETAL.
– ORIGIN Middle English: the noun from Latin *animal*, based on Latin *animalis* 'having breath' from *anima* 'breath'; the adjective via Old French from Latin *animalis*.

A

animalcule /ˌanɪˈmalkjuːl/ ▶ **noun** archaic a microscopic animal.
– DERIVATIVES **animalcular** adjective.
– ORIGIN late 16th cent.: from modern Latin *animalculum*, from *animal* 'an animal' + **-CULE**.

animalism ▶ **noun** [mass noun] **1** behaviour that is characteristic of animals, particularly in being physical and instinctive.
2 religious worship of animals.
– DERIVATIVES **animalistic** adjective.

animalist ▶ **noun** an animal liberationist.

animality ▶ **noun** [mass noun] animal nature or character: *a pre-human condition of animality*. ■ physical, instinctive behaviour or qualities: *what attracted me to her was her animality*.

animalize (also **animalise**) ▶ **verb** [with obj.] make into or like an animal.
– DERIVATIVES **animalization** noun.

animal liberation ▶ **noun** [mass noun] the freeing of animals from exploitation and cruel treatment by humans.
– DERIVATIVES **animal liberationist** noun.

animal magnetism ▶ **noun** [mass noun] **1** a quality of sexual attractiveness: *he had an animal magnetism that women found irresistible*.
2 historical a supposed emanation to which the action of mesmerism was ascribed.

animal rights ▶ **plural noun** the rights of animals to live free from human exploitation and abuse: [as modifier] *animal rights activists*.

animal spirits ▶ **plural noun** natural exuberance.

animate ▶ **verb** /ˈanɪmeɪt/ [with obj.] **1** bring to life: *Prometheus stole fire from heaven to animate his clay men*. ■ give inspiration, encouragement, or renewed vigour to: *she has animated the government with a sense of political direction*.
2 give (a film or character) the appearance of movement using animation techniques.
▶ **adjective** /ˈanɪmət/ alive or having life: *gods in a wide variety of forms, both animate and inanimate*.
– DERIVATIVES **animator** noun.
– ORIGIN late Middle English: from Latin *animat-* 'instilled with life', from the verb *animare*, from *anima* 'life, soul'.

animated ▶ **adjective 1** full of life or excitement; lively: *an animated conversation*.
2 (of a film) made using animation techniques: *an animated version of the classic fairy tale*.
– DERIVATIVES **animatedly** adverb.

animated stick ▶ **noun** a stick insect of the eastern Australian coast, which is one of the world's longest insects at up to 25 cm. ● *Acrophylla titan*, family Phasmatidae, order Phasmida.

animateur /ˌanɪməˈtəː/ ▶ **noun** a person who enlivens or encourages something, especially a promoter of artistic projects.
– ORIGIN 1950s: French, from medieval Latin *animator*.

animatic /ˌanɪˈmatɪk/ ▶ **noun** a preliminary version of a film, produced by shooting successive sections of a storyboard and adding a soundtrack.
– ORIGIN 1970s: from *animat(ed)* + **-IC**, or a blend of **ANIMATED** and **SCHEMATIC**.

animation ▶ **noun** [mass noun] **1** the state of being full of life or vigour; liveliness: *they started talking with animation*. ■ chiefly archaic the state of being alive.
2 the technique of photographing successive drawings or positions of puppets or models to create an illusion of movement when the film is shown as a sequence. ■ (also **computer animation**) the manipulation of electronic images by means of a computer in order to create moving images.

animato /ˌanɪˈmɑːtəʊ/ Music ▶ **adverb & adjective** (especially as a direction) in an animated manner.
▶ **noun** (pl. **animatos** or **animati** /ˌanɪˈmɑːti/) a passage marked to be performed animato.
– ORIGIN Italian.

animatronics /ˌanɪməˈtrɒnɪks/ ▶ **plural noun** [treated as sing.] the technique of making and operating lifelike robots, typically for use in film or other entertainment.
– DERIVATIVES **animatronic** adjective.
– ORIGIN 1970s: blend of **ANIMATED** and **ELECTRONICS**.

anime /ˈanɪmeɪ, ˈanɪmə/ ▶ **noun** [mass noun] Japanese film and television animation, typically having a science-fiction theme and sometimes including violent or explicitly sexual material. Compare with **MANGA**.
– ORIGIN 1980s: Japanese.

animism /ˈanɪmɪz(ə)m/ ▶ **noun** [mass noun] **1** the attribution of a living soul to plants, inanimate objects, and natural phenomena.
2 the belief in a supernatural power that organizes and animates the material universe.
– DERIVATIVES **animist** noun, **animistic** adjective.
– ORIGIN mid 19th cent.: from Latin *anima* 'life, soul' + **-ISM**.

animosity /ˌanɪˈmɒsɪti/ ▶ **noun** (pl. **animosities**) [mass noun] strong hostility: *he no longer felt any animosity towards her*.
– ORIGIN late Middle English (originally in the sense 'spirit, courage'): from Old French *animosite* or late Latin *animositas*, from *animosus* 'spirited', from Latin *animus* 'spirit, mind'. The current sense dates from the early 17th cent.

animus /ˈanɪməs/ ▶ **noun 1** [mass noun] hostility or ill feeling: *the author's animus towards her*.
2 [mass noun] motivation to do something: *the reformist animus came from within the Party*.
3 Psychoanalysis (in Jungian psychology) the masculine part of a woman's personality. Often contrasted with **ANIMA**.
– ORIGIN early 19th cent.: from Latin, 'spirit, mind'.

anion /ˈanʌɪən/ ▶ **noun** Chemistry a negatively charged ion, i.e. one that would be attracted to the anode in electrolysis. The opposite of **CATION**.
– DERIVATIVES **anionic** adjective.
– ORIGIN mid 19th cent.: from **ANODE** or **ANA-**, + **ION**.

anise /ˈanɪs/ ▶ **noun 1** a Mediterranean plant of the parsley family, cultivated for its aromatic seeds which are used in cooking and herbal medicine. ● *Pimpinella anisum*, family Umbelliferae. See also **ANISEED**.
2 an Asian or American tree or shrub which bears fruit with an aniseed-like odour. ● Genus *Illicium*, family Illiciaceae: many species, especially **star anise** (*I. verum*), used in Chinese cooking.
– ORIGIN Middle English: via Old French from Latin *anisum*, from Greek *anison* 'anise, dill'.

anise cap ▶ **noun** a pale greenish mushroom which has a funnel-shaped cap and smells strongly of aniseed. ● *Clitocybe odora*, family Tricholomataceae, class Hymenomycetes.

aniseed ▶ **noun** [mass noun] the seed of the anise, used in cooking and herbal medicine.
– ORIGIN late Middle English: from **ANISE** + **SEED**.

anisette /ˌanɪˈzɛt/ ▶ **noun** [mass noun] a liqueur flavoured with aniseed.
– ORIGIN mid 19th cent.: from French, diminutive of *anis* 'anise'.

anisogamy /ˌanʌɪˈsɒgəmi/ ▶ **noun** [mass noun] Biology sexual reproduction by the fusion of dissimilar gametes. Compare with **ISOGAMY**.
– DERIVATIVES **anisogamous** adjective.
– ORIGIN late 19th cent.: from Greek *anisos* 'unequal' + *-gamy* (from *gamos* 'marriage').

Anisoptera /ˌanʌɪˈzɒptərə/ ▶ **plural noun** Entomology a group of insects which comprises the dragonflies. Compare with **ZYGOPTERA**. ● Suborder Anisoptera, order Odonata.
– DERIVATIVES **anisopteran** noun & adjective.
– ORIGIN modern Latin (plural), from Greek *anisos* 'unequal' + *pteron* 'wing'.

anisotropic /ˌanʌɪsə(ʊ)ˈtrɒpɪk/ ▶ **adjective** Physics (of an object or substance) having a physical property which has a different value when measured in different directions. An example is wood, which is stronger along the grain than across it. Often contrasted with **ISOTROPIC**. ■ (of a property or phenomenon) varying in magnitude according to the direction of measurement.
– DERIVATIVES **anisotropically** adverb, **anisotropy** /-ˈsɒtrəpi/ noun.
– ORIGIN late 19th cent.: from Greek *anisos* 'unequal' + *tropos* 'turn' + **-IC**.

Anjou /ˈɑ̃ʒuː/, French /ɑ̃ʒu/ a former province of western France, on the Loire. It was an English possession from 1154 until 1204.

Ankara /ˈaŋkərə/ the capital of Turkey since 1923; pop. 3,763,600 (est. 2007). Prominent in Roman times as Ancyra, it later declined in importance until chosen by Kemal Atatürk in 1923 as his seat of government. Former name (until 1930) **ANGORA**.

ankh /aŋk/ ▶ **noun** an object or design resembling a cross but having a loop instead of the top arm, used in ancient Egypt as a symbol of life.
– ORIGIN late 19th cent.: from Egyptian, literally 'life, soul'.

ankle ▶ **noun** the joint connecting the foot with the leg. ■ the narrow part of the leg between the ankle joint and the calf: *her slim ankles | the men are ankle-deep in mud*.
▶ **verb** [no obj.] **1** [with adverbial of direction] US informal walk: *we can ankle off to a new locale*. ■ [with obj.] leave: *he ankled the series to do a movie*.
2 (usu. as noun **ankling**) flex the ankles while cycling in order to increase pedalling efficiency.
– DERIVATIVES **ankled** adjective.
– ORIGIN Old English *ancleow*, of Germanic origin; superseded in Middle English by forms from Old Norse; related to Dutch *enkel* and German *Enkel*, from an Indo-European root shared by **ANGLE**[1].

ankle-biter ▶ **noun** humorous, chiefly N. Amer. & Austral./NZ a child.

ankle bone ▶ **noun** the chief bone of the ankle joint; the talus.

ankle sock ▶ **noun** a sock that reaches just above the ankle.

anklet ▶ **noun 1** an ornament worn round an ankle.
2 chiefly N. Amer. an ankle sock.
– ORIGIN early 19th cent.: from **ANKLE** + **-LET**, on the pattern of *bracelet*.

ankus /ˈaŋkəs/ ▶ **noun** Indian a goad for elephants.
– ORIGIN via Hindi from Sanskrit *aṅkuśa*.

ankylosaur /ˈaŋkɪləsɔː/ ▶ **noun** a heavily built quadrupedal herbivorous dinosaur of the Cretaceous period, armoured with bony plates. ● Infraorder Ankylosauria, order Ornithischia: several genera, in particular *Ankylosaurus*.
– ORIGIN early 20th cent.: from modern Latin *Ankylosaurus*, from Greek *ankulos* (see **ANKYLOSIS**) + *sauros* 'lizard'.

ankylose /ˈaŋkɪləʊz/ ▶ **verb** (**be/become ankylosed**) Medicine (of bones or a joint) be or become stiffened or united by ankylosis.
– ORIGIN late 18th cent.: back-formation from **ANKYLOSIS**, on the pattern of words such as *anastomose*.

ankylosing spondylitis ▶ **noun** [mass noun] Medicine a form of spinal arthritis, chiefly affecting young males, that eventually causes ankylosis of vertebral and sacroiliac joints.

ankylosis /ˌaŋkɪˈləʊsɪs/ ▶ **noun** [mass noun] Medicine abnormal stiffening and immobility of a joint due to fusion of the bones.
– DERIVATIVES **ankylotic** adjective.
– ORIGIN early 18th cent.: from Greek *ankulōsis*, from *ankuloun* 'to crook', from *ankulos* 'crooked'.

ankylostomiasis /ˌaŋkɪlə(ʊ)stə(ʊ)ˈmʌɪəsɪs/ ▶ **noun** variant spelling of **ANCYLOSTOMIASIS**.

anlage /ˈanlɑːgə/ ▶ **noun** (pl. **anlagen** /-g(ə)n/) Biology the rudimentary basis of a particular organ or other part, especially in an embryo.
– ORIGIN late 19th cent.: from German, 'foundation, basis'.

anna /ˈanə/ ▶ **noun** a former monetary unit of India and Pakistan, equal to one sixteenth of a rupee.
– ORIGIN from Hindi *ānā*.

Annaba /ˈanəbə/ a port of NE Algeria; pop. 205,600 (est. 2009). The modern town is adjacent to the site of Hippo Regius, a prominent city in Roman Africa and the home and bishopric of St Augustine of Hippo from 396 to 430. Former name **BÔNE**.

an-Najaf /an/ another name for **NAJAF**.

annal /ˈan(ə)l/ ▶ **noun** a record of the events of one year: *the annal for 1032*. ■ a record of one item in a chronicle.
– ORIGIN late 17th cent.: back-formation from **ANNALS**.

annalist ▶ **noun** a person who writes annals.
– DERIVATIVES **annalistic** adjective, **annalistically** adverb.

annals ▶ **plural noun** a record of events year by year: *eighth-century Northumberland annals*. ■ historical records: *the annals of the police courts* | figurative *the deed will live forever in the annals of infamy*. ■ (**Annals**) used in titles of learned journals: *Annals of Neurobiology*.
– ORIGIN mid 16th cent.: from Latin *annales (libri)* 'yearly (books)', from *annus* 'year'.

Annan /aˈnan, ˈan(ə)n/, Kofi (Atta) (b.1938), Ghanaian diplomat, Secretary General of the United Nations 1997–2007.

Annapolis /əˈnapəlɪs/ the state capital of Maryland, on Chesapeake Bay; pop. 36,524 (est. 2008). It is the home of the US Naval Academy.

Annapurna /ˌanəˈpəːnə/ a ridge of the Himalayas, in north central Nepal. Its highest peak rises to 8,078 m (26,503 ft).

Anna's hummingbird ▶ **noun** a North American hummingbird which lives chiefly in California. The male has an iridescent rose-red head and throat. ● *Calypte anna*, family Trochilidae.
– ORIGIN mid 19th cent.: named after *Anna*, the wife of Prince François Massena (*c.*1795–1863), Duc de Ravoli, who obtained the original specimen.

annates /ˈaneɪts/ ▶ **plural noun** chiefly historical a year's revenue of a Roman Catholic see or benefice, paid to the Pope by a bishop or other cleric on his appointment.
– ORIGIN early 16th cent.: from French, from medieval Latin *annata* 'year's proceeds', from *annus* 'year'.

annatto /əˈnatəʊ/ (also **anatto**) ▶ **noun** (pl. **annattos**) **1** [mass noun] an orange-red dye obtained from the seed coat of a tropical fruit, used for colouring foods. **2** the tropical American tree from which this fruit is obtained. ● *Bixa orellana*, family Bixaceae.
– ORIGIN early 17th cent.: from Carib.

Anne (1665–1714), queen of England and Scotland (known as Great Britain from 1707) and Ireland 1702–14. The last of the Stuart monarchs, daughter of the Catholic James II (but herself a Protestant), she succeeded her brother-in-law William III to the throne. None of her children survived into adulthood, and by the Act of Settlement (1701) the throne passed to the House of Hanover on her death.

Anne, Princess, Anne Elizabeth Alice Louise, the Princess Royal (b.1950), daughter of Elizabeth II. She is a skilled horsewoman (riding for Great Britain in the 1976 Olympics) and is president of Save the Children Fund. Her two children are Peter (b.1977) and Zara Philips (b.1981), by her former husband Captain Mark Philips.

Anne, St, traditionally the mother of the Virgin Mary, first mentioned by name in the apocryphal gospel of James (2nd century). She is the patron saint of Brittany and the province of Quebec in Canada. Feast day, 26 July.

anneal /əˈniːl/ ▶ **verb** [with obj.] **1** heat (metal or glass) and allow it to cool slowly, in order to remove internal stresses and toughen it. **2** Biochemistry recombine (DNA) in the double-stranded form.
– DERIVATIVES **annealer** noun.
– ORIGIN Old English *onǣlan*, from *on* + *ǣlan* 'burn, bake' from *āl* 'fire, burning'. The original sense was 'set on fire', hence (in late Middle English) 'subject to fire, alter by heating'.

Anne Boleyn see **BOLEYN**.

annelid /ˈan(ə)lɪd/ Zoology ▶ **noun** a segmented worm of the phylum Annelida, such as an earthworm or leech.
▶ **adjective** relating to or denoting annelids.
– DERIVATIVES **annelidan** noun & adjective.

Annelida /əˈnɛlɪdə/ ▶ **plural noun** Zoology a large phylum that comprises the segmented worms, which include earthworms, lugworms, ragworms, and leeches.
– ORIGIN modern Latin (plural), from French *(animaux) annelés* 'ringed (animals)', from Old French *anel* 'a ring', from Latin *anellus*, diminutive of *anulus* 'a ring'.

Anne of Cleves /kliːvz/ (1515–57), fourth wife of Henry VIII. Arranged for political purposes, the marriage was dissolved after only six months; Henry, initially deceived by a flattering portrait of Anne by Holbein, took an instant dislike to her.

annex ▶ **verb** /əˈnɛks/ [with obj.] **1** add as an extra or subordinate part, especially to a document: *the first ten amendments were* **annexed to** *the Constitution in 1791.* ■ archaic add or attach as a condition or consequence. **2** add (territory) to one's own territory by appropriation: *the left bank of the Rhine was annexed by France in 1797.*
▶ **noun** /ˈanɛks/ (chiefly Brit. also **annexe**) (pl. **annexes**) **1** a building joined to or associated with a main building, providing additional space or accommodation. **2** an addition to a document: *an annex to the report.*
– ORIGIN late Middle English: from Old French *annexer*, from Latin *annectere* 'connect', from *ad-* 'to' + *nectere* 'tie, fasten'.

annexation ▶ **noun** [mass noun] the action of annexing something, especially territory: *the annexation of Austria by Nazi Germany in 1938.*
– DERIVATIVES **annexationist** noun & adjective.

annihilate /əˈnʌɪleɪt/ ▶ **verb** [with obj.] **1** destroy utterly; obliterate: *a simple bomb of this type could annihilate them all | a crusade to annihilate evil.* ■ defeat utterly: *the stronger force annihilated its opponent virtually without loss.* **2** Physics convert (a subatomic particle) into radiant energy.
– DERIVATIVES **annihilator** noun.
– ORIGIN late Middle English (originally as an adjective meaning 'destroyed, annulled'): from late Latin *annihilatus* 'reduced to nothing', from the verb *annihilare*, from *ad-* 'to' + *nihil* 'nothing'. The sense 'destroy utterly' dates from the mid 16th cent.

annihilation ▶ **noun** [mass noun] **1** complete destruction or obliteration: *the threat of global annihilation.* ■ total defeat: *a show of independence is its only hope of avoiding annihilation in next year's elections.* **2** Physics the conversion of matter into energy, especially the mutual conversion of a particle and an antiparticle into electromagnetic radiation.
– ORIGIN mid 16th cent.: from late Latin *annihilatio(n-)*, from the verb *annihilare* (see **ANNIHILATE**).

anniversary ▶ **noun** (pl. **anniversaries**) the date on which an event took place or an institution was founded in a previous year: *the 50th anniversary of the Battle of Britain | the 75th anniversary of the RAF.* ■ the date on which a couple were married in a previous year: *he even forgot our tenth anniversary!*
– ORIGIN Middle English: from Latin *anniversarius* 'returning yearly', from *annus* 'year' + *versus* 'turning'.

Annobón /ˈanəbɒn/ an island of Equatorial Guinea, in the Gulf of Guinea. Former name (1973–9) **PAGALU**.

Anno Domini /ˌanəʊ ˈdɒmɪnʌɪ/ ▶ **adverb** full form of **AD**.
▶ **noun** [mass noun] informal advancing age: *since retirement Anno Domini has restricted my activities.*
– ORIGIN Latin, 'in the year of the Lord'.

annotate /ˈanəteɪt/ ▶ **verb** [with obj.] add notes to (a text or diagram) giving explanation or comment: (as adj. **annotated**) *an annotated bibliography.*
– DERIVATIVES **annotatable** adjective, **annotative** adjective, **annotator** noun.
– ORIGIN late 16th cent.: from Latin *annotat-* 'marked', from the verb *annotare*, from *ad-* 'to' + *nota* 'a mark'.

annotation ▶ **noun** a note by way of explanation or comment added to a text or diagram: *marginal annotations.* ■ [mass noun] the action of annotating a text or diagram: *annotation of prescribed texts.*
– ORIGIN late Middle English: from French, or from Latin *annotatio(n-)*, from the verb *annotare* (see **ANNOTATE**).

announce ▶ **verb** [reporting verb] make a formal public statement about a fact, occurrence, or intention: [with clause] *the President's office announced that the siege would be lifted* | [with obj.] *he announced his retirement from international football* | [with direct speech] *'I have a confession to make,' she announced.* ■ make known the arrival of (a guest) at a formal social occasion. ■ give information about (transport) in a station or airport via a public address system: *they were announcing her train.*
– ORIGIN late 15th cent.: from French *annoncer*, from Latin *annuntiare*, from *ad-* 'to' + *nuntiare* 'declare, announce' (from *nuntius* 'messenger').

announcement ▶ **noun** a formal public statement about a fact, occurrence, or intention: *the minister was about to* **make an announcement**. ■ [mass noun] the action of making an announcement: *the announcement of the decision of the European Parliament.* ■ a notice appearing in a newspaper or public place and announcing something such as a birth, death, or marriage. ■ a piece of information given over a public address system.

announcer ▶ **noun** a person who announces something, in particular someone who introduces or gives information about programmes on radio or television.

annoy ▶ **verb** [with obj.] **1** make (someone) a little angry; irritate: *the decision really annoyed him.* **2** archaic harm or attack repeatedly: *a gallant Saxon, who annoyed this Coast.*
– DERIVATIVES **annoyer** noun.
– ORIGIN Middle English (in the sense 'be hateful to'): from Old French *anoier* (verb), *anoi* (noun), based on Latin *in odio* in the phrase *mihi in odio est* 'it is hateful to me'.

annoyance ▶ **noun** [mass noun] the feeling or state of being annoyed; irritation: *there was annoyance at government interference | he turned his charm on Tara,* **much to** *Hegarty's* **annoyance**. ■ [count noun] a thing that annoys someone; a nuisance.
– ORIGIN late Middle English: from Old French *anoiance*, from *anoier* (see **ANNOY**).

annoyed ▶ **adjective** slightly angry; irritated: *Kelly was* **annoyed with** *him | he was* **annoyed at** *being woken up so early.*
– DERIVATIVES **annoyedly** adverb.

annoying ▶ **adjective** causing irritation or annoyance: *annoying habits | unsolicited calls are annoying.*
– DERIVATIVES **annoyingly** adverb [as submodifier] *the car is annoyingly noisy.*

annual ▶ **adjective** occurring once every year: *the sponsored walk became an annual event | an annual report.* ■ calculated over or covering a period of a year: *an annual rate of increase | his basic annual income.* ■ (of a plant) living only for a year or less, perpetuating itself by seed. Compare with **BIENNIAL**, **PERENNIAL**.
▶ **noun 1** a book or magazine that is published once a year under the same title but with different contents. **2** an annual plant.
– ORIGIN late Middle English: from Old French *annuel*, from late Latin *annualis*, based on Latin *annus* 'year'.

annual general meeting ▶ **noun** Brit. a yearly meeting of the members or shareholders of a club, company, or other organization, especially for holding elections and reporting on the year's events.

annualized (also **annualised**) ▶ **adjective** (of a rate of interest, inflation, or return on an investment) recalculated as an annual rate.

annually ▶ **adverb** once a year; every year: *the prize is awarded annually | sales are increasing by about 17% annually.*

annual ring ▶ **noun** a ring in the cross section of the stem or root of a temperate woody plant, produced by one year's growth.

annuitant /əˈnjuːɪt(ə)nt/ ▶ **noun** formal a person who receives an annuity.
– ORIGIN early 18th cent.: from **ANNUITY**, on the pattern of *accountant*.

annuity ▶ **noun** (pl. **annuities**) a fixed sum of money paid to someone each year, typically for the rest of their life. ■ a form of insurance or investment entitling the investor to a series of annual sums.
– DERIVATIVES **annuitize** (also **annuitise**) verb.
– ORIGIN late Middle English: from French *annuité*, from medieval Latin *annuitas*, from Latin *annuus* 'yearly', from *annus* 'year'.

annul /əˈnʌl/ ▶ **verb** (**annuls**, **annulling**, **annulled**) [with obj.] declare invalid (an official agreement, decision, or result): *the elections were annulled by the general amid renewed protests.* ■ declare (a marriage) to have had no legal existence.
– ORIGIN late Middle English: from Old French *anuller*, from late Latin *annullare*, from *ad-* 'to' + *nullum* 'nothing'.

annular /ˈanjʊlə/ ▶ **adjective** technical ring-shaped.
– DERIVATIVES **annularly** adverb.
– ORIGIN late 16th cent.: from French *annulaire* or Latin *annularis*, from *anulus*, *annulus* 'a ring'.

annular eclipse ▶ **noun** an eclipse of the sun in which the edge of the sun remains visible as a bright ring around the moon.

annulate /ˈanjʊlət/ ▶ **adjective** chiefly Zoology having rings; marked with or formed of rings.
– DERIVATIVES **annulated** adjective, **annulation** noun.
– ORIGIN early 19th cent.: from Latin *annulatus*, from *anulus*, *annulus* 'a ring'.

annulet /ˈanjʊlɪt/ ▶ **noun 1** Architecture a small fillet or band encircling a column. **2** Heraldry a charge in the form of a small ring.
– ORIGIN late Middle English (in the general sense 'small ring'): from Old French *anelet*, from Latin *anulus*, *annulus* 'ring' + **-ET**[1]. The spelling change in the 16th cent. was due to association with the Latin.

annulment ▶ **noun** [mass noun] the act of annulling something: *the applicant sought the annulment of the decision* | [count noun] *grounds for an annulment.*

annulus /ˈanjʊləs/ ▶ **noun** (pl. **annuli** /-lʌɪ, -liː/) technical a ring-shaped object, structure, or region. ■ Mathematics a plane figure consisting of the area between a pair of concentric circles.
– ORIGIN mid 16th cent.: from Latin *anulus*, *annulus*.

annunciate /əˈnʌnsɪeɪt/ ▶ **verb** [with obj.] archaic announce (something).

A

– ORIGIN late Middle English (originally as a past participle): from medieval Latin *annunciat-*, variant spelling of Latin *annuntiat-* 'announced', from the verb *annuntiare*.

annunciation ▶ **noun 1** (usu. **the Annunciation**) the announcement of the Incarnation by the angel Gabriel to Mary (Luke 1:26–38). ■ a Church festival commemorating the Annunciation, held on 25 March (Lady Day).
2 ■ [mass noun] formal or archaic the announcement of something: *the annunciation of a set of rules applying to the relationships between states.*
– ORIGIN Middle English: from Old French *annonciation*, from late Latin *annuntiatio(n-)*, from the verb *annuntiare* (see **ANNUNCIATE**).

annunciator ▶ **noun** a bell, light, or other device that provides information on the state or condition of something by indicating which of several electric circuits has been activated.

annus horribilis /ˌanəs hɒˈriːbɪlɪs/ ▶ **noun** a year of disaster or misfortune.
– ORIGIN modern Latin, suggested by **ANNUS MIRABILIS**.

annus mirabilis /mɪˈrɑːbɪlɪs/ ▶ **noun** a remarkable or auspicious year.
– ORIGIN modern Latin, 'wonderful year'.

anoa /əˈnəʊə/ ▶ **noun** (pl. **same** or **anoas**) a small deer-like water buffalo, native to Sulawesi. ● Genus *Bubalus*, family Bovidae: two species.
– ORIGIN mid 19th cent.: a local word.

anode /ˈanəʊd/ ▶ **noun** the positively charged electrode by which the electrons leave an electrical device. The opposite of **CATHODE**. ■ the negatively charged electrode of an electrical device, such as a primary cell, that supplies current.
– DERIVATIVES **anodal** adjective, **anodic** adjective.
– ORIGIN mid 19th cent.: from Greek *anodos* 'way up', from *ana* 'up' + *hodos* 'way'.

anodize /ˈanədʌɪz/ (also **anodise**) ▶ **verb** [with obj.] (usu. as adj. **anodized**) coat (a metal, especially aluminium) with a protective oxide layer by an electrolytic process in which the metal forms the anode.
– DERIVATIVES **anodizer** noun.

anodyne /ˈanədʌɪn/ ▶ **adjective** not likely to cause offence or disagreement and somewhat dull: *anodyne music.*
▶ **noun** a painkilling drug or medicine.
– ORIGIN mid 16th cent.: via Latin from Greek *anōdunos* 'painless', from *an-* 'without' + *odunē* 'pain'.

anogenital /ˌeɪnəʊˈdʒɛnɪt(ə)l/ ▶ **adjective** Medicine & Anatomy relating to the anus and genitals.

anoint ▶ **verb** [with obj.] smear or rub with oil, typically as part of a religious ceremony: *high priests were **anointed with** oil | bodies were anointed after death for burial.* ■ (**anoint something with**) smear or rub something with (any other substance): *Kuna Indians anoint the tips of their arrows with poison.* ■ ceremonially confer divine or holy office upon (a priest or monarch) by smearing or rubbing with oil: [with obj. and complement] *Samuel anointed him king.* ■ nominate or choose (someone) as successor to or leading candidate for a position: (as adj. **anointed**) *his officially anointed heir.*
– PHRASES **Anointing of the Sick** (in the Roman Catholic Church) the sacramental anointing of the ill or infirm with blessed oil; unction. **God's** (or **the Lord's**) **anointed** a monarch ruling by divine right.
– DERIVATIVES **anointer** noun, **anointment** noun.
– ORIGIN Middle English: from Old French *enoint* 'anointed', past participle of *enoindre*, from Latin *inungere*, from *in-* 'upon' + *ungere* 'anoint, smear with oil'.

anole /əˈnəʊli/ ▶ **noun** a small, mainly arboreal American lizard with a throat fan that (in the male) is typically brightly coloured. Anoles have some ability to change colour. ● Genus *Anolis*, family Iguanidae: numerous species.
– ORIGIN early 18th cent.: from Carib.

anomalistic /əˌnɒməˈlɪstɪk/ ▶ **adjective 1** of the nature of an anomaly; anomalous: *the production is stylistically anomalistic.*
2 Astronomy relating to the anomaly of a planet.

anomalistic month ▶ **noun** Astronomy a month measured between successive perigees of the moon (approximately 27½ days).

anomalistic year ▶ **noun** Astronomy a year measured between successive perihelia of the earth (approximately 365¼ days).

anomalous /əˈnɒm(ə)ləs/ ▶ **adjective** deviating from what is standard, normal, or expected: *an anomalous situation | sentences which are grammatically anomalous.*
– DERIVATIVES **anomalously** adverb, **anomalousness** noun.
– ORIGIN mid 17th cent.: via late Latin from Greek *anōmalos* (from *an-* 'not' + *homalos* 'even') + **-OUS**.

anomaly /əˈnɒm(ə)li/ ▶ **noun** (pl. **anomalies**) **1** something that deviates from what is standard, normal, or expected: *there are a number of anomalies in the present system* | [with clause] *the apparent **anomaly that** those who produced the wealth were the poorest* | [mass noun] *the position abounds in anomaly.*
2 Astronomy the angular distance of a planet or satellite from its last perihelion or perigee.
– ORIGIN late 16th cent.: via Latin from Greek *anōmalia*, from *anōmalos* (see **ANOMALOUS**).

anomia /əˈnəʊmɪə/ ▶ **noun** [mass noun] Medicine a form of aphasia in which the patient is unable to recall the names of everyday objects.
– DERIVATIVES **anomic** adjective.
– ORIGIN early 20th cent.: formed irregularly from **A-**¹ 'without, not' + Latin *nomen* 'name' + **-IA**¹.

anomie /ˈanəmi/ (also **anomy**) ▶ **noun** [mass noun] lack of the usual social or ethical standards in an individual or group: *the theory that high-rise architecture leads to anomie in the residents.*
– DERIVATIVES **anomic** /əˈnɒmɪk/ adjective.
– ORIGIN 1930s: from French, from Greek *anomia*, from *anomos* 'lawless'.

anon ▶ **adverb** archaic or informal soon; shortly: *I'll see you anon.*
– ORIGIN Old English *on ān* 'into one', *on āne* 'in one'. The original sense was 'in or into one state, course, etc.', which developed into the temporal sense 'at once'.

anon. ▶ **abbreviation** anonymous.

anonym ▶ **noun 1** an anonymous person or publication.
2 a pseudonym.
– ORIGIN early 19th cent.: from French *anonyme*, from Greek *anōnumos* (see **ANONYMOUS**).

anonymity /anəˈnɪmɪti/ ▶ **noun** [mass noun] the condition of being anonymous: *the official spoke on condition of anonymity.* ■ lack of outstanding, individual, or unusual features; impersonality: *the anonymity of big city life definitely has its advantages.*

anonymize (also **anonymise**) ▶ **verb** [with obj.] (usu. as adj. **anonymized**) remove identifying particulars or details from (something, especially medical test results) for statistical or other purposes: *anonymized testing of routine blood samples.*
– ORIGIN 1970s: from **ANONYMOUS** + **-IZE**.

anonymous /əˈnɒnɪməs/ ▶ **adjective** (of a person) not identified by name; of unknown name: *the donor's wish to remain anonymous | an anonymous phone call.* ■ having no outstanding, individual, or unusual features; unremarkable or impersonal: *his impeccable, slightly anonymous Chelsea flat.*
– DERIVATIVES **anonymously** adverb.
– ORIGIN late 16th cent.: via late Latin from Greek *anōnumos* 'nameless' (from *an-* 'without' + *onoma* 'name') + **-OUS**.

anonymous FTP ▶ **noun** [mass noun] Computing an implementation of an FTP server that allows anyone who can use FTP to log on to the system, using a general username and without a password check.

anopheles /əˈnɒfɪliːz/ (also **anopheles mosquito**) ▶ **noun** a mosquito of a genus which is particularly common in warmer countries and includes the mosquitoes that transmit the malarial parasite to humans. Compare with **CULEX**. ● Genus *Anopheles*, subfamily Anophelinae, family Culicidae.
– DERIVATIVES **anopheline** /əˈnɒfɪlʌɪn, -liːn/ adjective & noun.
– ORIGIN late 19th cent.: modern Latin, from Greek *anōphelēs* 'unprofitable, useless'.

Anoplura /ˌanə(ʊ)ˈplʊərə/ ▶ **plural noun** Entomology an order of insects that comprises the sucking lice. Also called **SIPHUNCULATA**. See also **PHTHIRAPTERA**.
– DERIVATIVES **anopluran** noun & adjective.
– ORIGIN modern Latin (plural), from *anoplos* 'unarmed' + *oura* 'tail'.

anorak ▶ **noun 1** a waterproof jacket, typically with a hood, of a kind originally used in polar regions.
2 Brit. informal, derogatory a studious or obsessive person with unfashionable and largely solitary interests.
– DERIVATIVES **anorakish** adjective, **anoraky** adjective.
– ORIGIN 1920s: from Greenland Eskimo *anoraq*. The British English informal sense dates from the 1980s and derives from the anoraks worn by trainspotters, regarded as typifying this kind of person.

anorectal /ˌeɪnəʊˈrɛkt(ə)l/ ▶ **adjective** Medicine & Anatomy relating to the anus and rectum.
– ORIGIN late 19th cent.: from French *ano-rectal*, from Latin *ano-* (combining form of **ANUS**) + *rectal* (see **RECTAL**).

anorexia /ˌanəˈrɛksɪə/ ▶ **noun** [mass noun] lack or loss of appetite for food (as a medical condition). ■ (also **anorexia nervosa**) an emotional disorder characterized by an obsessive desire to lose weight by refusing to eat.
– ORIGIN late 16th cent.: via late Latin from Greek, from *an-* 'without' + *orexis* 'appetite'.

anorexic (also **anorectic**) ▶ **adjective** relating to, characterized by, or suffering from anorexia. ■ informal extremely thin.
▶ **noun 1** a person suffering from anorexia.
2 (**anorectic**) a medicine which produces a loss of appetite.

anorgasmia /ˌanɔːˈgazmɪə/ ▶ **noun** [mass noun] Medicine persistent inability to achieve orgasm despite responding to sexual stimulation.
– DERIVATIVES **anorgasmic** adjective.
– ORIGIN 1970s: from **AN-**¹ + **ORGASM** + **-IA**¹.

anorthite /əˈnɔːθʌɪt/ ▶ **noun** [mass noun] a calcium-rich mineral of the feldspar group, typically white, occurring in many basic igneous rocks.
– ORIGIN mid 19th cent.: from **AN-**¹ + Greek *orthos* 'straight' + **-ITE**¹.

anorthosite /əˈnɔːθəsʌɪt/ ▶ **noun** [mass noun] Geology a granular igneous rock composed largely of labradorite or another plagioclase.
– ORIGIN mid 19th cent.: from French *anorthose* 'plagioclase' + **-ITE**¹.

anosmia /əˈnɒzmɪə/ ▶ **noun** [mass noun] Medicine the loss of the sense of smell, either total or partial. It may be caused by head injury, infection, or blockage of the nose.
– DERIVATIVES **anosmic** adjective.
– ORIGIN early 19th cent.: from **AN-**² + Greek *osmē* 'smell'.

another ▶ **determiner & pronoun 1** used to refer to an additional person or thing of the same type as one already mentioned or known about; one more; a further: [as determiner] *have another drink | I didn't say another word* | [as pronoun] *she was to become **another** of his stars.* ■ [as determiner] used with a proper name to indicate someone or something's similarity to the person or event specified: *this will not be another Vietnam.*
2 used to refer to a different person or thing from one already mentioned or known about: [as determiner] *come back another day | his wife left him for another man* | [as pronoun] *moving from one place to another.* ■ [as determiner] used to refer to someone sharing an attribute in common with the person already mentioned: *his kiss with another man caused a tabloid rumpus.*
– ORIGIN Middle English: as *an other* until the 16th cent.

A. N. Other ▶ **pronoun** Brit. used when listing a group or team to refer to a person who is not named or whose selection has not been confirmed.

another place ▶ **noun** Brit. the other House of Parliament (used in the Commons to refer to the Lords, and vice versa).

anothery (also **anotherie**) ▶ **noun** Austral. informal another one: *I'll have anothery.*

Anouilh /ˈɒnwiː/, French /anuj/, Jean (1910–87), French dramatist. He wrote many plays but is best known for his reworking of the Greek myth of Antigone in *Antigone* (1944).

ANOVA /aˈnəʊvə/ ▶ **noun** [mass noun] analysis of variance, a statistical method in which the variation in a set of observations is divided into distinct components.
– ORIGIN 1960s: acronym.

anovulant /aˈnɒvjʊl(ə)nt/ Medicine ▶ **adjective** (chiefly of a drug) preventing ovulation.
▶ **noun** an anovulant drug.
– ORIGIN 1960s: from **AN-**¹ + *ovul(ation)* + **-ANT**.

anovulatory /ˌanɒvjʊˈleɪt(ə)ri/ ▶ **adjective** Medicine (of a menstrual cycle) in which ovulation does not occur.

anoxia /aˈnɒksɪə/ ▶ **noun** [mass noun] technical an absence of oxygen. ■ Medicine an absence or deficiency of oxygen reaching the tissues; severe hypoxia.
– DERIVATIVES **anoxic** adjective.
– ORIGIN 1930s: from **AN-**¹ + *ox(ygen)* + **-IA**¹.

ANS ▶ **abbreviation** autonomic nervous system.

ansatz /ˈansats/ ▸ **noun** Mathematics an assumption about the form of an unknown function which is made in order to facilitate solution of an equation or other problem.
– ORIGIN 1940s: from German *Ansatz* 'approach, attempt'.

Anschluss /ˈanʃlʊs/ the annexation of Austria by Germany in 1938. Hitler had forced the resignation of the Austrian Chancellor by demanding that he admit Nazis into his cabinet. The new Chancellor, a pro-Nazi, invited German troops to enter the country on the pretext of restoring law and order.
– ORIGIN German, from *anschliessen* 'to join'.

Anselm, St /ˈanselm/ (*c.*1033–1109), Italian-born philosopher and theologian, Archbishop of Canterbury 1093–1109. He worked to free the Church from secular control and believed that the best way to defend the faith was by intellectual reasoning. His writings include *Cur Deus Homo?*, a mystical study on the Atonement. Feast day, 21 April.

anserine /ˈansərʌɪn/ ▸ **adjective** of or like a goose.
– ORIGIN mid 19th cent.: from Latin *anserinus*, from *anser* 'goose'.

Anshan /anˈʃan/ a city in Liaoning, China; pop. 1,293,000 (est. 2006). Anshan is situated close to major iron-ore deposits and China's largest iron and steel complex is nearby.

ANSI ▸ **abbreviation** American National Standards Institute.

answer ▸ **noun 1** a thing that is said, written, or done as a reaction to a question, statement, or situation: *he knocked and entered without waiting for an answer* | *I hurried along the passage* ***in answer to*** *the doorbell's ring.* ■ a thing written or said in reaction to a question in a test or quiz: *write your answers on a postcard.* ■ the correct solution to a question in a test or quiz: *the answer is 280°.*
2 a solution to a problem or dilemma: *the* ***answer to*** *poverty and unemployment is a properly funded range of services.*
3 [in sing.] (**answer to**) a person or thing regarded as the equivalent to a better-known one from another place: *the press called her Britain's answer to Marilyn Monroe.*
▸ **verb 1** [reporting verb] say or write something as a reaction to someone or something: [with direct speech] *'Of course I can,' she answered* | [with clause] *she answered that she would take nothing but the ring* | [with obj.] *she tried to answer his questions truthfully* | [no obj.] *Steve was about to answer, but Hazel spoke first.* ■ [with obj.] provide the required response to (a question in a test or quiz): *answer the questions below for a chance to win a holiday.* ■ [no obj.] (**answer back**) respond impudently or disrespectfully to someone, especially when being criticized or told to do something.
2 [with obj.] act in reaction to (a sound such as a telephone ringing or a knock or ring on a door): *Digby answered the door* | [no obj.] *she rang Edward's house, hoping the housekeeper would answer.*
3 [no obj.] (**answer to**) be responsible or report to (someone): *I answer to the Assistant Commissioner of Specialist Operations.*
4 [with obj.] defend oneself against (a charge, accusation, or criticism): *he said he would return to Spain to answer all charges.* ■ [no obj.] (**answer to**) be required to explain or justify oneself to (someone): *you will have the police to answer to.* ■ [no obj.] (**answer for**) be responsible or to blame for: *the dust mite* ***has a lot to answer for****, especially if you are asthmatic.*
5 [with obj.] be suitable for fulfilling (a need); satisfy: *entrepreneurship is necessary to answer the needs of national and international markets.*
– PHRASES **answer the description of** correspond to a description, especially one of a suspect issued by the police. **the answer to someone's prayers** the thing that someone really wants: *the opportunity for a commission in the army seemed an answer to their prayers.* **answer to (the name of)** often humorous be called: *an attractive woman answering to the name of Suzanne.* **have** (or **know**) **all the answers** informal be overconfident about one's knowledge of something.
– DERIVATIVES **answerer** noun.
– ORIGIN Old English *andswaru* (noun), *andswarian* (verb), of Germanic origin; from a base shared by **SWEAR**.

answerable ▸ **adjective 1** (**answerable to**) required to explain or justify one's actions to; responsible or having to report to: *the Attorney General is answerable only to Parliament for his decisions.* ■ (**answerable for**) responsible for: *an employer is answerable for the negligence of his employees.*
2 (of a question) able to be answered: *straightforward and answerable questions.*

answering machine ▸ **noun** a tape recorder or digital device which supplies a recorded answer to a telephone call and can record a message from the caller.

answering service ▸ **noun** a business that receives and answers telephone calls for its clients.

answerphone ▸ **noun** Brit. a telephone answering machine.

ant ▸ **noun** a small insect typically having a sting and living in a complex social colony with one or more breeding queens. It is wingless except for fertile adults, which form large mating swarms, and is proverbial for its industriousness. ● Family Formicidae, order Hymenoptera: several subfamilies.
– PHRASES **have ants in one's pants** informal be fidgety or restless.
– ORIGIN Old English *ǣmete* of West Germanic origin; related to German *Ameise*. Compare with **EMMET**.

ant- ▸ **prefix** variant spelling of **ANTI-**. shortened before a vowel or *h* (as in *Antarctic*).

-ant ▸ **suffix 1** (forming adjectives) denoting attribution of an action or state: *arrogant* | *pendant.*
2 (forming nouns) denoting an agent: *deodorant* | *propellant.*
– ORIGIN from French or Latin present participial verb stems (see also **-ENT**).

Antabuse /ˈantəbjuːs/ ▸ **noun** trademark for **DISULFIRAM**.
– ORIGIN 1940s: from **ANTI-** + **ABUSE**.

antacid /anˈtasɪd/ ▸ **adjective** (chiefly of a medicine) preventing or correcting acidity, especially in the stomach.
▸ **noun** an antacid medicine.

Antaeus /anˈtiːəs/ Greek Mythology a giant, the son of Poseidon and Earth, who compelled all comers to wrestle with him, overcoming and killing them all until he was defeated by Hercules.

antagonism /anˈtag(ə)nɪz(ə)m/ ▸ **noun** [mass noun] active hostility or opposition: *the* ***antagonism between*** *them* | *his* ***antagonism towards*** *the local people* | [count noun] *petty antagonisms and jealousies.*
– ORIGIN early 19th cent.: from French *antagonisme*, from Greek *antagōnizesthai* 'struggle against' (see **ANTAGONIST**).

antagonist ▸ **noun 1** a person who actively opposes or is hostile to someone or something; an adversary.
2 Biochemistry a substance which interferes with or inhibits the physiological action of another. Compare with **AGONIST**.
3 Anatomy a muscle whose action counteracts that of another specified muscle. Compare with **AGONIST**.
– ORIGIN late 16th cent.: from French *antagoniste* or late Latin *antagonista*, from Greek *antagōnistēs*, from *antagōnizesthai* 'struggle against' (see **ANTAGONIZE**).

antagonistic ▸ **adjective 1** showing or feeling active opposition or hostility towards someone or something: *he was* ***antagonistic to*** *the government's reforms* | *an antagonistic group of bystanders.*
2 Biochemistry & Physiology relating to an antagonist or its action.
– DERIVATIVES **antagonistically** adverb.

antagonize (also **antagonise**) ▸ **verb** [with obj.] **1** cause (someone) to become hostile: *the aim was to antagonize visiting supporters.*
2 Biochemistry (of a substance) act as an antagonist of (a substance or its action).
– ORIGIN mid 18th cent. (in the sense 'struggle against'): from Greek *antagōnizesthai*, from *ant-* 'against' + *agōnizesthai* 'struggle' (from *agōn* 'contest').

Antakya /ʌnˈtʌkjʌ/ Turkish name for **ANTIOCH**.

Antalya /anˈtaljə/ a port in southern Turkey; pop. 775,200 (est. 2007).

Antananarivo /ˌantəˌnanəˈriːvəʊ/ the capital of Madagascar, situated in the central plateau; pop. 1,697,000 (est. 2007). Former name (until 1975) **TANANARIVE**.

Antarctic ▸ **adjective** relating to the south polar region or Antarctica. ■ Botany relating to or denoting a phytogeographical kingdom comprising New Zealand, southern parts of Chile and Argentina, and islands in the South Atlantic and southern Indian Ocean.
▸ **noun** (**the Antarctic**) the Antarctic region.
– ORIGIN late Middle English: from Old French *antartique* or Latin *antarcticus*, from Greek *antarktikos* 'opposite to the north', from *ant-* 'against' + *arktikos* (see **ARCTIC**).

Antarctica a continent round the South Pole, situated mainly within the Antarctic Circle and almost entirely covered by ice sheets.

Antarctic Circle the parallel of latitude 66° 33′ south of the equator. It marks the southernmost point at which the sun is visible on the southern winter solstice and the northernmost point at which the midnight sun can be seen on the southern summer solstice.

Antarctic Convergence the zone of the Antarctic Ocean where the cold, nutrient-laden Antarctic surface water sinks beneath the warmer waters to the north.

Antarctic Ocean the sea surrounding Antarctica, consisting of parts of the South Atlantic, the South Pacific, and the southern Indian Ocean. Also called **SOUTHERN OCEAN**.

Antarctic Peninsula a mountainous peninsula of Antarctica between the Bellingshausen Sea and the Weddell Sea, extending northwards towards Cape Horn and the Falkland Islands.

Antares /anˈtɑːriːz/ Astronomy the brightest star in the constellation Scorpius. It is a binary star of which the main component is a red supergiant.
– ORIGIN Greek, literally 'simulating Mars (in colour)'.

antbear ▸ **noun** another term for **AARDVARK**.

antbird ▸ **noun** an insectivorous, long-legged, short-tailed bird which typically has dark grey plumage in the male, found mainly in the tropical forests of South America. ● Family Formicariidae: several genera.

ante /ˈanti/ ▸ **noun** a stake put up by a player in poker or brag before receiving cards.
▸ **verb** (**antes**, **anteing**, **anted**) [with obj.] (**ante something up**) put up an amount as an ante in poker or brag and similar games. ■ N. Amer. informal pay an amount of money in advance: *he anted up $925,000 of his own money* | [no obj.] *the owners have to ante up if they want to attract the best talent.*
– PHRASES **up** (or **raise**) **the ante** increase what is at stake or under discussion, especially in a conflict or dispute: *he decided to up the ante in the trade war.*
– ORIGIN early 19th cent.: from Latin, literally 'before'.

ante- /ˈanti/ ▸ **prefix** before; preceding: *antechapel* | *antecedent.*
– ORIGIN from Latin *ante* 'before'.

anteater ▸ **noun** a mammal that feeds on ants and termites, with a long snout and sticky tongue. ● Most anteaters are edentates of the Central and South American family Myrmecophagidae, which includes the **giant anteater** and the tamanduas. The echidna, numbat, and pangolin are alternatively known as **spiny**, **banded**, and **scaly anteater** respectively.

antebellum /ˌantɪˈbɛləm/ ▸ **adjective** [attrib.] occurring or existing before a particular war, especially the US Civil War: *the conventions of the antebellum South.*
– ORIGIN mid 19th cent.: from Latin, from *ante* 'before' and *bellum* 'war'.

antecedent /ˌantɪˈsiːd(ə)nt/ ▸ **noun 1** a thing that existed before or logically precedes another: *some antecedents to the African novel might exist in Africa's oral traditions.*
2 (**antecedents**) a person's ancestors or family and social background: *her early life and antecedents have been traced.*
3 Grammar an earlier word, phrase, or clause to which another word (especially a following relative pronoun) refers back.
4 Logic the statement contained in the 'if' clause of a conditional proposition.
▸ **adjective 1** preceding in time or order; previous or pre-existing: *antecedent events.*
2 Grammar denoting or counting as an antecedent.
– DERIVATIVES **antecedence** noun, **antecedently** adverb.
– ORIGIN late Middle English: from Old French or from Latin *antecedent-* 'going before', from *antecedere*, from *ante* 'before' + *cedere* 'go'.

antechamber ▸ **noun** a small room leading to a main one.
– ORIGIN mid 17th cent. (as *antichamber*): from French *antichambre*, from Italian *anticamera*, from *anti-* 'preceding' + *camera* (see **CHAMBER**).

antechapel ▸ **noun** (especially in Oxford and Cambridge colleges) a distinct part of a chapel between the entrance and the nave or choir.

antechinus /ˌantɪˈkʌɪnəs/ ▸ **noun** a marsupial mouse of shrew-like habits and appearance, found

in Australia, New Guinea, and Tasmania. ● Genera *Antechinus* and *Parantechinus*, family Dasyuridae: several species.
– ORIGIN modern Latin, from Greek *anti-* 'simulating' + *ekhinos* 'sea urchin, hedgehog' (from its bristly fur).

antedate ▶ **verb** [with obj.] precede in time; come before (something) in date: *a civilization that antedated the Roman Empire.* ■ indicate or discover that (a document, event, or word) should be assigned to an earlier date: *there are no references to him that would antedate his birth.*

antediluvian /ˌantɪdɪˈluːvɪən/ ▶ **adjective** of or belonging to the time before the biblical Flood: *gigantic bones of antediluvian animals.* ■ chiefly humorous ridiculously old-fashioned: *they maintain antediluvian sex-role stereotypes.*
– ORIGIN mid 17th cent.: from **ANTE-** + Latin *diluvium* 'deluge' + **-AN**.

antelope ▶ **noun** (pl. **same** or **antelopes**) a swift-running deer-like ruminant with smooth hair and upward-pointing horns, of a group native to Africa and Asia that includes the gazelles, impala, gnus, and elands. ● Many genera and species, in the family Bovidae. ■ N. Amer. another term for **PRONGHORN**.
– ORIGIN late Middle English (originally the name of a fierce mythical creature with long serrated horns, said to live on the banks of the Euphrates): via Old French and medieval Latin from late Greek *antholops*, of unknown origin and meaning.

ante-mortem ▶ **adjective & adverb** before death: [as adj.] *the ante-mortem instructions of the dead leader.*
– ORIGIN Latin 'before death'.

antenatal Brit. ▶ **adjective** before birth; during or relating to pregnancy: *antenatal care.*
▶ **noun** informal a medical examination during pregnancy.
– DERIVATIVES **antenatally** adverb.

antenna ▶ **noun** (pl. **antennae** /-niː/) **1** Zoology either of a pair of long, thin sensory appendages on the heads of insects, crustaceans, and some other arthropods. ■ (**antennae**) the faculty of instinctively detecting and interpreting subtle signs: *he has the political antennae of a party whip.*
2 (pl. also **antennas**) chiefly N. Amer. or technical another term for **AERIAL**: *a TV antenna.*
– DERIVATIVES **antennal** adjective.
– ORIGIN mid 17th cent.: from Latin, alteration of *antemna* 'yard' (of a ship), used in the plural to translate Greek *keraioi* 'horns (of insects)', used by Aristotle.

antennule /anˈtɛnjuːl/ ▶ **noun** Zoology a small antenna, especially either of the first pair of antennae in a crustacean.
– ORIGIN mid 19th cent.: diminutive of **ANTENNA**.

antenuptial ▶ **adjective** chiefly Brit. another term for **PRENUPTIAL**.
– ORIGIN early 19th cent.: from late Latin *antenuptialis* (see **ANTE-, NUPTIAL**).

antepartum /antɪˈpɑːtəm/ ▶ **adjective** Medicine occurring not long before childbirth.
– ORIGIN late 19th cent.: from Latin, 'before birth'.

antepenult /ˌantɪpɪˈnʌlt/ ▶ **noun** Linguistics the last syllable but two in a word, e.g. *-ul-* in *antepenultimate*.

antepenultimate ▶ **adjective** last but two in a series; third last: *the antepenultimate item on the agenda.*

ante-post ▶ **adjective** [attrib.] Brit. (of a bet on a horse race) placed at odds fixed at the time, and before the runners are known, on a horse thought likely to be entered.
– ORIGIN early 20th cent.: from **ANTE-** + **POST**[1].

anterior ▶ **adjective** **1** technical nearer the front, especially in the front of the body, or nearer to the head or forepart: *the veins* ***anterior to*** *the heart.* The opposite of **POSTERIOR**. ■ Botany (of a part of a flower or leaf) situated further away from the main stem. ■ Phonetics pronounced with an obstruction located in front of the palato-alveolar region of the mouth, e.g. *b, p, d, t*.
2 formal coming before in time; earlier: *an incident anterior to her troubles.*
– DERIVATIVES **anteriority** noun, **anteriorly** adverb.
– ORIGIN mid 16th cent.: from French *antérieur* or Latin *anterior*, comparative of *ante* 'before'.

antero- /ˈantərəʊ/ ▶ **combining form** chiefly Anatomy representing **ANTERIOR**: *anteroposterior.*

anterograde ▶ **adjective** directed forwards in time. ■ of or denoting a form of amnesia which involves inability to remember information encountered after its onset.
– ORIGIN late 19th cent.: from **ANTERIOR**, on the pattern of *retrograde*.

anterolateral ▶ **adjective** chiefly Anatomy both anterior and lateral.

anteroom ▶ **noun** an antechamber, typically serving as a waiting room. ■ Military a large room in an officers' mess, typically adjacent to the dining room.

anteroposterior ▶ **adjective** chiefly Anatomy relating to or directed towards both front and back.

anteverted /ˈantɪvəːtɪd/ ▶ **adjective** Anatomy & Medicine (of an organ of the body, especially the womb) inclined forward.
– ORIGIN mid 19th cent.: from Latin *antevertere*, from *ante* 'before' + *vertere* 'to turn' + **-ED**[2].

ant heap ▶ **noun** another term for **ANTHILL**.

anthelion /antˈhiːlɪən, anˈθiːl-/ ▶ **noun** (pl. **anthelia** /-lɪə/) a luminous halo round a shadow projected by the sun on to a cloud or fog bank. ■ a parhelion seen opposite the sun in the sky.
– ORIGIN late 17th cent.: from Greek *anthēlion*, neuter of *anthēlios* 'opposite to the sun', from *anth-* (variant of *anti-* 'against') + *hēlios* 'sun'.

anthelmintic /ˌanθ(ə)lˈmɪntɪk/ Medicine ▶ **adjective** (chiefly of medicines) used to destroy parasitic worms.
▶ **noun** an anthelmintic medicine.
– ORIGIN late 17th cent. (as an adjective): from *anth-* (variant of *anti* 'against') + Greek *helmins, helminth-* 'worm' + **-IC**.

anthem ▶ **noun** **1** a rousing or uplifting song identified with a particular group, body, or cause: *the song became the anthem for hippy activists.* ■ (also **national anthem**) a solemn patriotic song officially adopted by a country as an expression of national identity.
2 a musical setting of a religious text to be sung by a choir during a church service, especially in Anglican or Protestant Churches.
– ORIGIN Old English *antefn, antifne* (denoting a composition sung antiphonally), from late Latin *antiphona* (see **ANTIPHON**). The spelling with *th*, which began in the 16th cent., was on the pattern of similar words such as *Antony, Anthony*.

anthemic /anˈθiːmɪk/ ▶ **adjective** (of a song) like an anthem in being rousing or uplifting.

anthemion /anˈθiːmɪən/ ▶ **noun** (pl. **anthemia** /-mɪə/) an ornamental design of alternating motifs resembling clusters of narrow leaves or honeysuckle petals.
– ORIGIN mid 19th cent.: from Greek, literally 'flower'.

anther ▶ **noun** Botany the part of a stamen that contains the pollen.
– ORIGIN early 18th cent.: from French *anthère* or modern Latin *anthera*, from Greek *anthēra* 'flowery', from *anthos* 'flower'.

antheridium /ˌanθəˈrɪdɪəm/ ▶ **noun** (pl. **antheridia** /-dɪə/) Botany the male sex organ of algae, mosses, ferns, fungi, and other non-flowering plants.
– DERIVATIVES **antheridial** adjective.
– ORIGIN mid 19th cent.: modern Latin, from *anthera* (see **ANTHER**) + *-idium* (from the Greek diminutive suffix *-idion*).

antherozoid /ˌanθ(ə)rə(ʊ)ˈzəʊɪd/ ▶ **noun** Botany another term for **SPERMATOZOID**.
– ORIGIN mid 19th cent.: from **ANTHER** + **ZOOID**.

anthesis /anˈθiːsɪs/ ▶ **noun** [mass noun] Botany the flowering period of a plant, from the opening of the flower bud.
– ORIGIN mid 19th cent.: from Greek *anthēsis* 'flowering', from *anthein* 'to blossom'.

anthill ▶ **noun** a nest in the form of a mound built by ants or termites.

antho- /ˈanθəʊ/ ▶ **combining form** relating to flowers: *anthophilous.*
– ORIGIN from Greek *anthos* 'flower'.

anthocyanin /ˌanθə(ʊ)ˈsʌɪənɪn/ ▶ **noun** [mass noun] Chemistry a blue, violet, or red flavonoid pigment found in plants.
– ORIGIN mid 19th cent.: from German *Anthocyan*, from Greek *anthos* 'flower' + *kuanos* 'blue' + **-IN**[1].

anthologize (also **anthologise**) ▶ **verb** [with obj.] (usu. as adj. **anthologized**) include (an author or work) in an anthology: *the most anthologized of today's poets.*
– DERIVATIVES **anthologization** noun.

anthology ▶ **noun** (pl. **anthologies**) a published collection of poems or other pieces of writing. ■ a collection of songs or musical compositions issued in one album.
– DERIVATIVES **anthologist** noun.
– ORIGIN mid 17th cent.: via French or medieval Latin from Greek *anthologia*, from *anthos* 'flower' + *-logia* 'collection' (from *legein* 'gather'). In Greek, the word originally denoted a collection of the 'flowers' of verse, i.e. small choice poems or epigrams, by various authors.

Anthony, St /ˈantəni, ˈanθəni/ (also **Antony**) (*c.*251–356), Egyptian hermit, the founder of monasticism. Feast day, 17 January.

Anthony of Padua, St (also **Antony**) (1195–1231), Portuguese Franciscan friar. His devotion to the poor is commemorated by alms known as St Anthony's bread; he is invoked to find lost articles. Feast day, 13 June.

anthophilous /anˈθɒfɪləs/ ▶ **adjective** Zoology (of insects or other animals) frequenting flowers.

Anthozoa /ˌanθəˈzəʊə/ ▶ **plural noun** Zoology a large class of sedentary marine coelenterates that includes the sea anemones and corals. They are either solitary or colonial, and have a central mouth surrounded by tentacles.
– ORIGIN modern Latin (plural), from Greek *anthos* 'flower' + *zōia* 'animals'.

anthozoan Zoology ▶ **noun** a member of a large class of marine coelenterates (the Anthozoa), such as a sea anemone or coral.
▶ **adjective** relating to or denoting anthozoans.

anthracene /ˈanθrəsiːn/ ▶ **noun** [mass noun] Chemistry a colourless crystalline aromatic hydrocarbon obtained by the distillation of crude oils and used in chemical manufacture. ● A tricyclic compound; chem. formula: $C_{14}H_{10}$.
– ORIGIN mid 19th cent.: from Greek *anthrax, anthrak-* 'coal' + **-ENE**.

anthracite /ˈanθrəsʌɪt/ ▶ **noun** [mass noun] coal of a hard variety that contains relatively pure carbon and burns with little flame and smoke. ■ a dark grey colour.
– ORIGIN late 16th cent. (denoting a gem described by Pliny and said to resemble coals, supposedly hydrophane (a type of opal)): from Greek *anthrakitēs*, from *anthrax, anthrak-* 'coal'.

anthracnose /anˈθraknəʊs/ ▶ **noun** [mass noun] a mainly fungal disease of plants, causing dark lesions. ● This is usually caused by fungi of the subdivision Deuteromycotina.
– ORIGIN late 19th cent.: coined in French from Greek *anthrax, anthrak-* 'coal' + *nosos* 'disease'.

anthranilate /ˌanθrəˈnʌɪleɪt/ ▶ **noun** Chemistry a salt or ester of anthranilic acid.

anthranilic acid /ˌanθrəˈnɪlɪk/ ▶ **noun** [mass noun] Chemistry a colourless or yellow crystalline compound first obtained by alkaline hydrolysis of indigo. ● Chem. formula: $NH_2C_6H_4COOH$.
– ORIGIN mid 19th cent.: *anthranilic* from Greek *anthrax* 'coal' + *anil* (being any imine derived from aniline) + **-IC**.

anthraquinone /ˌanθrəˈkwɪnəʊn/ ▶ **noun** [mass noun] Chemistry a yellow crystalline compound obtained by oxidation of anthracene. It is the basis of many natural and synthetic dyes. ● Chem. formula: $C_{14}H_8O_2$.
– ORIGIN late 19th cent.: from *anthra(cene)* + **QUINONE**.

anthrax /ˈanθraks/ ▶ **noun** [mass noun] a serious bacterial disease of sheep and cattle, typically affecting the skin and lungs. It can be transmitted to humans, causing severe skin ulceration (see **MALIGNANT PUSTULE**) or a form of pneumonia (**wool-sorters' disease**).
– ORIGIN late Middle English: Latin, 'carbuncle' (the earliest sense in English), from Greek *anthrax, anthrak-* 'coal, carbuncle', with reference to the skin ulceration in humans.

anthropic principle /anˈθrɒpɪk/ ▶ **noun** the cosmological principle that theories of the universe are constrained by the necessity to allow human existence.
– ORIGIN 1970s: *anthropic* from Greek *anthrōpikos*, from *anthrōpos* 'human being'.

anthropo- /ˈanθrəpəʊ/ ▶ **combining form** human; of a human being: *anthropometry.* ■ relating to humankind: *anthropology.*
– ORIGIN from Greek *anthrōpos* 'human being'.

anthropocentric ▶ **adjective** regarding humankind as the central or most important element of existence, especially as opposed to God or animals.
– DERIVATIVES **anthropocentrically** adverb, **anthropocentrism** noun.

anthropogenic /ˌanθrəpəˈdʒɛnɪk/ ▶ **adjective** (chiefly of environmental pollution and pollutants) originating in human activity.
– DERIVATIVES **anthropogenically** adverb.

anthropoid ▸ adjective resembling a human being in form: *anthropoid gods*. ▪ Zoology relating to the group of higher primates, which includes monkeys, apes, and humans. ▪ Zoology (of an ape) belonging to the family of great apes.
▸ noun Zoology a higher primate, especially an ape or ape-man. ● Suborder Anthropoidea, order Primates.
– ORIGIN mid 19th cent.: from Greek *anthrōpoeidēs*, from *anthrōpos* 'human being' + -OID.

anthropology /ˌanθrəˈpɒlədʒi/ ▸ noun [mass noun] the study of humankind, in particular: ▪ (also **cultural** or **social anthropology**) the comparative study of human societies and cultures and their development. ▪ (also **physical anthropology**) the science of human zoology, evolution, and ecology.
– DERIVATIVES **anthropological** adjective, **anthropologically** adverb, **anthropologist** noun.

anthropometrics ▸ plural noun [treated as sing.] anthropometry, especially as it relates to the design of furniture and machinery.

anthropometry /ˌanθrəˈpɒmɪtri/ ▸ noun [mass noun] the scientific study of the measurements and proportions of the human body.
– DERIVATIVES **anthropometric** adjective.

anthropomorphic /anθrəpəˈmɔːfɪk/ ▸ adjective relating to or characterized by anthropomorphism. ▪ having human characteristics: *anthropomorphic bears and monkeys*.
– DERIVATIVES **anthropomorphically** adverb.
– ORIGIN early 19th cent.: from Greek *anthrōpomorphos* (see ANTHROPOMORPHOUS) + -IC.

anthropomorphism /ˌanθrəpəˈmɔːfɪz(ə)m/ ▸ noun [mass noun] the attribution of human characteristics or behaviour to a god, animal, or object.
– DERIVATIVES **anthropomorphize** (also **anthropomorphise**) verb.

anthropomorphous ▸ adjective (of a god, animal, or object) human in form or nature.
– ORIGIN mid 18th cent.: from Greek *anthrōpomorphos* (from *anthrōpos* 'human being' + *morphē* 'form') + -OUS.

anthropopathy /ˌanθrəˈpɒpəθi/ ▸ noun [mass noun] the attribution of human emotions to a god.

anthropophagus /ˌanθrəˈpɒfəgəs/ ▸ noun (pl. **anthropophagi** /ˌanθrəˈpɒfəgʌɪ/) (especially in legends or fables) a cannibal.
– ORIGIN mid 16th cent.: Latin, from Greek *anthrōpophagos* 'man-eating', from *anthrōpos* 'human being' + *-phagos* (see -PHAGOUS).

anthropophagy /ˌanθrəˈpɒfədʒi/ ▸ noun [mass noun] the eating of human flesh by human beings.
– DERIVATIVES **anthropophagous** /-gəs/ adjective.
– ORIGIN mid 17th cent.: from Greek *anthrōpophagia*, from *anthrōpophagos* (see ANTHROPOPHAGUS).

anthroposophy /ˌanθrəˈpɒsəfi/ ▸ noun [mass noun] a formal educational, therapeutic, and creative system established by Rudolf Steiner, seeking to use mainly natural means to optimize physical and mental health and well-being.
– DERIVATIVES **anthroposophical** adjective.
– ORIGIN early 20th cent.: from ANTHROPO- + Greek *sophia* 'wisdom'.

anthurium /anˈθ(j)ʊərɪəm/ ▸ noun (pl. **anthuriums**) a tropical American plant which is widely grown for its ornamental foliage or brightly coloured flowering spathes. ● Genus *Anthurium*, family Araceae.
– ORIGIN modern Latin, from Greek *anthos* 'flower' + *oura* 'tail'.

anti informal ▸ preposition opposed to; against: *I'm anti the abuse of drink and the hassle that it causes*.
▸ adjective [predic.] opposed: *the local councils are anti*.
▸ noun (pl. **antis**) a person opposed to a particular policy, activity, or idea: *the threat to field sports from the antis is a serious one*.
– ORIGIN late 18th cent. (as a noun): independent usage of ANTI-.

anti- (also **ant-**) ▸ prefix **1** opposed to; against: *antiaircraft*. ▪ preventing: *antibacterial*. ▪ relieving: *antipruritic*. ▪ the opposite of: *anticlimax*. ▪ acting as a rival: *antipope*. ▪ unlike the conventional form: *anti-hero*.
2 Physics the antiparticle of a specified particle: *antiproton*.
– ORIGIN from Greek *anti* 'against'.

anti-abortion ▸ adjective opposing or legislating against medically induced abortion.
– DERIVATIVES **anti-abortionist** noun & adjective.

anti-aircraft ▸ adjective (especially of a gun or missile) used to attack enemy aircraft.

anti-American ▸ adjective hostile to the interests of the United States.
– DERIVATIVES **anti-Americanism** noun.

anti-apartheid ▸ adjective opposed to a policy or system of apartheid.

antibacterial ▸ adjective active against bacteria.

Antibes /ɒ̃ˈtiːb/, French /ɑ̃tib/ a fishing port and resort in SE France; pop. 76,925 (2006).

antibiosis /ˌantɪbʌɪˈəʊsɪs/ ▸ noun [mass noun] Biology an antagonistic association between two organisms (especially microorganisms), in which one is adversely affected. Compare with SYMBIOSIS.
– ORIGIN late 19th cent.: from ANTI- + a shortened form of SYMBIOSIS.

antibiotic ▸ noun a medicine (such as penicillin or its derivatives) that inhibits the growth of or destroys microorganisms.
▸ adjective relating to antibiotics.
– ORIGIN mid 19th cent. (in the sense 'doubting the possibility of life in a particular environment'): from ANTI- + Greek *biōtikos* 'fit for life' (from *bios* 'life').

antibody ▸ noun (pl. **antibodies**) a blood protein produced in response to and counteracting a specific antigen. Antibodies combine chemically with substances which the body recognizes as alien, such as bacteria, viruses, and foreign substances in the blood.
– ORIGIN early 20th cent.: from ANTI- + BODY, translating German *Antikorper*, from *anti-* 'against' + *Körper* 'body'.

antic ▸ adjective archaic grotesque or bizarre.
– ORIGIN early 16th cent.: from Italian *antico* 'antique', used to mean 'grotesque'.

anti-capitalist ▸ adjective opposed to capitalism.
▸ noun a person who is opposed to capitalism.
– DERIVATIVES **anti-capitalism** noun.

anticathode ▸ noun Physics the target (or anode) of an X-ray tube which is struck by electrons from the cathode and from which X-rays are emitted.

anti-choice ▸ adjective chiefly N. Amer. opposed to granting choice, especially the right to choose abortion.

anticholinergic /ˌantɪˌkəʊlɪˈnəːdʒɪk/ Medicine ▸ adjective (chiefly of a drug) inhibiting the physiological action of acetylcholine, especially as a neurotransmitter.
▸ noun an anticholinergic drug.

Antichrist ▸ noun (**the Antichrist**) a postulated personal opponent of Christ expected by the early Church to appear before the end of the world. ▪ a person or force seen as opposing Christ or the Christian Church.
– ORIGIN Old English, via Old French or ecclesiastical Latin from Greek *antikhristos*, from *anti* 'against' + *Khristos* (see CHRIST).

anti-Christian ▸ adjective **1** opposed to Christianity or Christian values.
2 relating to the Antichrist.

anticipate ▸ verb [with obj.] **1** regard as probable; expect or predict: *she anticipated scorn on her return to the theatre* | [with clause] *it was anticipated that the rains would slow the military campaign*. ▪ guess or be aware of (what will happen) and take action in order to be prepared: *they failed to anticipate a full-scale invasion*. ▪ look forward to: *Stephen was eagerly anticipating the break from the routine of business*.
2 act as a forerunner or precursor of: *he anticipated Bates's theories on mimicry and protective coloration*. ▪ come or take place before (an event or process expected or scheduled for a later time).
– DERIVATIVES **anticipative** adjective, **anticipator** noun.
– ORIGIN mid 16th cent. (in the senses 'to take something into consideration', 'mention something before the proper time'): from Latin *anticipat-* 'acted in advance', from *anticipare*, based on *ante-* 'before' + *capere* 'take'.

anticipation ▸ noun [mass noun] the action of anticipating something; expectation or prediction: *her eyes sparkled with anticipation* | *they manned the telephones **in anticipation of** a flood of calls*. ▪ Music the introduction in a composition of part of a chord which is about to follow in full.
– ORIGIN late Middle English: from Latin *anticipatio(n-)*, from the verb *anticipare* (see ANTICIPATE).

anticipatory /antɪsɪˈpeɪt(ə)ri/ ▸ adjective happening, performed, or felt in anticipation of something: *an anticipatory flash of excitement*.

anticlerical chiefly historical ▸ adjective opposed to the power or influence of the clergy, especially in politics.
▸ noun a person holding anticlerical views.
– DERIVATIVES **anticlericalism** noun.

anticlimax ▸ noun a disappointing end to an exciting or impressive series of events: *the rest of the journey was an anticlimax by comparison* | [mass noun] *a sense of anticlimax and incipient boredom*.
– DERIVATIVES **anticlimactic** adjective, **anticlimactically** adverb.

anticline /ˈantɪklʌɪn/ ▸ noun Geology a ridge or fold of stratified rock in which the strata slope downwards from the crest. Compare with SYNCLINE.
– DERIVATIVES **anticlinal** adjective.
– ORIGIN mid 19th cent.: from ANTI- + Greek *klinein* 'lean', on the pattern of *incline*.

anticlockwise ▸ adverb & adjective Brit. in the opposite direction to the way in which the hands of a clock move round: [as adv.] *stopcocks are opened by turning them anticlockwise* | [as adj.] *an anticlockwise direction*.

anticoagulant ▸ adjective having the effect of retarding or inhibiting the coagulation of the blood.
▸ noun an anticoagulant substance.

anticodon /ˌantɪˈkəʊdɒn/ ▸ noun Biochemistry a sequence of three nucleotides forming a unit of genetic code in a transfer RNA molecule, corresponding to a complementary codon in messenger RNA.

anti-communist ▸ adjective opposed to communism.
▸ noun a person who is opposed to communism.

anticompetitive ▸ adjective (of regulations, practices, etc.) tending to suppress economic competition: *several industries are already under investigation after complaints of anticompetitive behaviour*.

anti-constitutional ▸ adjective violating a political constitution: *anti-constitutional activity*.

anticonvulsant ▸ adjective (chiefly of a drug) used to prevent or reduce the severity of epileptic fits or other convulsions.
▸ noun an anticonvulsant drug.

Anti-Corn-Law League a pressure group formed in Britain in 1838 to campaign for the repeal of the Corn Laws, under the leadership of Richard Cobden and John Bright.

antics ▸ plural noun foolish, outrageous, or amusing behaviour: *the antics of our political parties*.
– ORIGIN early 16th cent.: from ANTIC.

anticyclone ▸ noun a weather system with high barometric pressure at its centre, around which air slowly circulates in a clockwise (northern hemisphere) or anticlockwise (southern hemisphere) direction. Anticyclones are associated with calm, fine weather.
– DERIVATIVES **anticyclonic** adjective.

anti-democratic ▸ adjective in conflict with the principles of democracy: *these anti-democratic measures have severely curtailed political freedom*.

antidepressant ▸ adjective (chiefly of a drug) used to alleviate depression.
▸ noun an antidepressant drug.

antidiarrhoeal ▸ adjective (of a drug) used to alleviate diarrhoea.
▸ noun an antidiarrhoeal drug.

antidisestablishmentarianism /ˌantɪdɪsɪˌstablɪʃm(ə)nˈtɛːrɪənɪz(ə)m/ ▸ noun [mass noun] rare opposition to the disestablishment of the Church of England.
– DERIVATIVES **antidisestablishmentarian** noun & adjective.

> **USAGE** Antidisestablishmentarianism is very occasionally found in genuine use, but it is most often cited as an example of a very long word. Other similar curiosities are FLOCCINAUCINIHILIPILIFICATION and PNEUMONOULTRAMICROSCOPICSILICOVOLCANOCONIOSIS (the longest word in this dictionary). The longest word to be encountered in Britain is the Welsh place name *Llanfairpwllgwyngyllgogerychwyrndrobwllllantysiliogogogoch*, which is generally abbreviated to Llanfair PG; this name was created in the 19th century.

antidiuretic hormone ▸ noun another term for VASOPRESSIN.

antidote ▸ noun a medicine taken or given to counteract a particular poison. ▪ something that counteracts an unpleasant feeling or situation: *laughter is a good **antidote to** stress*.
– DERIVATIVES **antidotal** adjective.

A

– ORIGIN late Middle English: via Latin, from Greek *antidoton*, neuter of *antidotos* 'given against', from *anti-* 'against' + *didonai* 'give'.

antidromic /ˌantɪˈdrəʊmɪk/ ▸ adjective Physiology (of an impulse) travelling in the opposite direction to that normal in a nerve fibre. The opposite of **ORTHODROMIC**.
– ORIGIN early 20th cent.: from **ANTI-** + Greek *dromos* 'running' + **-IC**.

anti-emetic ▸ adjective (chiefly of a drug) preventing vomiting.
▸ noun an anti-emetic drug.

anti-establishment ▸ adjective against the establishment or established authority.

antifeedant ▸ noun a naturally occurring substance in certain plants which adversely affects insects or other animals which eat them.
– ORIGIN 1960s: from **ANTI-** + **FEED** + **-ANT**.

antiferromagnetic ▸ adjective Physics denoting or exhibiting a form of magnetism characterized by an antiparallel alignment of adjacent electron spins in a crystal lattice. Compare with **FERRIMAGNETIC**.

antifouling ▸ noun [mass noun] treatment of a boat's hull with a paint or similar substance designed to prevent fouling.

anti-fraud ▸ adjective designed to prevent fraudulent practices: *new anti-fraud measures will save the taxpayer millions in lost revenue*.

antifreeze ▸ noun [mass noun] a liquid, typically one based on ethylene glycol, which can be added to water to lower the freezing point, chiefly used in the radiator of a motor vehicle.

anti-g ▸ adjective short for **ANTIGRAVITY**.
– ORIGIN 1940s: from **ANTI-** + *g*, the symbol for acceleration due to gravity.

antigen ▸ noun a toxin or other foreign substance which induces an immune response in the body, especially the production of antibodies.
– DERIVATIVES **antigenic** adjective.
– ORIGIN early 20th cent.: via German from French *antigène* (see **ANTI-**, **-GEN**).

antigenic determinant ▸ noun Biochemistry another term for **EPITOPE**.

antiglobalization (also **antiglobalisation**) ▸ noun [mass noun] opposition to the increase in the global power and influence of businesses, especially multinational corporations.

Antigone /anˈtɪɡəni/ Greek Mythology daughter of Oedipus and Jocasta, the subject of a tragedy by Sophocles. She was sentenced to death for defying her uncle Creon, king of Thebes, but she took her own life before the sentence could be carried out, and Creon's son Haemon, who was engaged to her, killed himself over her body.

antigorite /anˈtɪɡərʌɪt/ ▸ noun [mass noun] a mineral of the serpentine group, occurring typically as thin green plates.
– ORIGIN mid 19th cent.: from *Antigorio*, a valley in Piedmont, Italy, + **-ITE**[1].

antigravity ▸ noun [mass noun] Physics a hypothetical force opposing gravity.
▸ adjective designed to counteract the effects of high acceleration.

Antigua /anˈtiːɡwə/ **1** one of the islands that make up the country of Antigua and Barbuda. **2** (also **Antigua Guatemala**) a town in the central highlands of Guatemala; pop. 54,100 (est. 2009).

Antigua and Barbuda /bɑːˈbuːdə/ a country consisting of three islands (Antigua, Barbuda, and Redonda) in the Leeward Islands in the Eastern Caribbean; pop. 85,600 (est. 2009); languages, English (official), Creole; capital, St John's (on Antigua). Discovered in 1493 by Columbus and settled by the English in 1632, Antigua became a British colony with Barbuda as its dependency; the islands gained independence within the Commonwealth in 1981.
– DERIVATIVES **Antiguan** adjective & noun.

anti-hero ▸ noun (pl. **anti-heroes**) a central character in a story, film, or drama who lacks conventional heroic attributes.

anti-heroine ▸ noun a female anti-hero.

antihistamine ▸ noun a drug or other compound that inhibits the physiological effects of histamine, used especially in the treatment of allergies.

anti-infective ▸ adjective (of a drug) used to prevent infection.
▸ noun an anti-infective drug.

anti-inflammatory ▸ adjective (chiefly of a drug) used to reduce inflammation.
▸ noun (pl. **anti-inflammatories**) an anti-inflammatory drug.

anti-knock ▸ noun [mass noun] a substance (such as tetraethyl lead) added to petrol to inhibit pre-ignition.

Anti-Lebanon Mountains a range of mountains running north to south along the border between Lebanon and Syria, east of the Lebanon range.

Antilles /anˈtɪliːz/ a group of islands, forming the greater part of the West Indies. The **Greater Antilles**, extending roughly east to west, comprise Cuba, Jamaica, Hispaniola (Haiti and the Dominican Republic), and Puerto Rico; the **Lesser Antilles**, to the south-east, include the Virgin Islands, Leeward Islands, Windward Islands, and various small islands to the north of Venezuela. See also **NETHERLANDS ANTILLES**.

anti-lock ▸ adjective (of brakes) designed so as to prevent the wheels locking and the vehicle skidding if applied suddenly.

antilog ▸ noun short for **ANTILOGARITHM**.

antilogarithm ▸ noun the number of which a given number is the logarithm.

antilogy /anˈtɪlədʒi/ ▸ noun (pl. **antilogies**) archaic a contradiction in terms or ideas.
– ORIGIN early 17th cent.: from French *antilogie*, from Greek *antilogia*, from *anti-* 'against' + *-logia* (see **-LOGY**).

antimacassar /ˌantɪməˈkasə/ ▸ noun a piece of cloth put over the back of a chair to protect it from grease and dirt or as an ornament.
– ORIGIN mid 19th cent.: from **ANTI-** + **MACASSAR**.

anti-magnetic ▸ adjective (especially of watches) resistant to magnetization.

antimalarial ▸ adjective (of a drug) used to prevent malaria.
▸ noun an antimalarial drug.

antimatter ▸ noun [mass noun] Physics matter consisting of elementary particles which are the antiparticles of those making up normal matter.

antimetabolite ▸ noun Physiology a substance that interferes with the normal metabolic processes within cells, typically by combining with enzymes.

antimicrobial ▸ adjective active against microbes.
▸ noun an antimicrobial substance.

anti-monarchist ▸ noun an opponent of monarchy.

antimony /ˈantɪməni/ ▸ noun [mass noun] the chemical element of atomic number 51, a brittle silvery-white semimetal. (Symbol: **Sb**)

> Antimony was known from ancient times; the naturally occurring black sulphide was used as the cosmetic kohl. The element is used in alloys, usually with lead, such as pewter, type metal, and Britannia metal.

– DERIVATIVES **antimonial** adjective, **antimonic** adjective, **antimonious** adjective.
– ORIGIN late Middle English (denoting stibnite, the most common ore of the metal): from medieval Latin *antimonium*, of unknown origin. The current sense dates from the early 19th cent.

anti-national ▸ adjective opposed to national interests or nationalism.

anting ▸ noun [mass noun] Ornithology behaviour seen in some birds, in which the bird either picks up ants and rubs them on the feathers or stands with the wings spread and allows the ants to crawl over it. It is probable that the ants' secretions help to keep the feathers in good condition.

antinode ▸ noun Physics the position of maximum displacement in a standing wave system.

anti-noise ▸ noun [mass noun] sound generated for the purpose of reducing noise by interference.

antinomian /antɪˈnəʊmɪən/ ▸ adjective relating to the view that Christians are released by grace from the obligation of observing the moral law.
▸ noun a person holding such a view.
– DERIVATIVES **antinomianism** noun.
– ORIGIN mid 17th cent.: from medieval Latin *Antinomi*, the name of a 16th-cent. sect in Germany alleged to hold this view, from Greek *anti-* 'opposite, against' + *nomos* 'law'.

antinomy /anˈtɪnəmi/ ▸ noun (pl. **antinomies**) a contradiction between two beliefs or conclusions that are in themselves reasonable; a paradox.
– ORIGIN late 16th cent. (in the sense 'a conflict between two laws'): from Latin *antinomia*, from Greek, from *anti* 'against' + *nomos* 'law'.

antinovel ▸ noun a novel in which the conventions and traditions of the genre are studiously avoided.

anti-nuclear ▸ adjective opposed to the development of nuclear weapons or nuclear power.

Antioch /ˈantɪɒk/ **1** a city in southern Turkey, near the Syrian border; pop. 186,200 (est. 2007). Antioch was the ancient capital of Syria under the Seleucid kings, who founded it *c.*300 BC. Turkish name **ANTAKYA**.
2 a city in ancient Phrygia.

Antiochus /anˈtʌɪəkəs/ the name of eight Seleucid kings, notably: ■ **Antiochus III** (*c.*242–187 BC), reigned 223–187 BC; known as **Antiochus the Great**. He restored and expanded the Seleucid empire. ■ **Antiochus IV** (*c.*215–163 BC), son of Antiochus III, reigned 175–163 BC; known as **Antiochus Epiphanes**. His firm control of Judaea and his attempt to Hellenize the Jews resulted in the revival of Jewish nationalism and the Maccabean revolt.

antioxidant ▸ noun a substance that inhibits oxidation, especially one used to counteract the deterioration of stored food products. ■ a substance such as vitamin C or E that removes potentially damaging oxidizing agents in a living organism.

antiparallel ▸ adjective Physics parallel but moving or oriented in opposite directions.

antiparticle ▸ noun Physics a subatomic particle having the same mass as a given particle but opposite electric or magnetic properties. Every kind of subatomic particle has a corresponding antiparticle, e.g. the positron has the same mass as the electron but an equal and opposite charge.

antipasto /ˌantɪˈpastəʊ/ ▸ noun (pl. **antipasti** /-ti/) (in Italian cookery) an hors d'oeuvre.
– ORIGIN Italian, from *anti-* 'before' + *pasto* (from Latin *pastus* 'food').

antipathetic ▸ adjective showing or feeling a strong aversion: *it is human nature to be **antipathetic to** change*.
– ORIGIN mid 19th cent.: from **ANTIPATHY**, on the pattern of *pathetic*.

antipathy /anˈtɪpəθi/ ▸ noun (pl. **antipathies**) [mass noun] a deep-seated feeling of aversion: *his fundamental **antipathy to** capitalism*.
– ORIGIN late 16th cent. (in the sense 'opposition of feeling, nature, or disposition'): from French *antipathie*, or via Latin from Greek *antipatheia*, from *antipathēs* 'opposed in feeling', from *anti* 'against' + *pathos* 'feeling'.

anti-personnel ▸ adjective (of weapons, especially bombs) designed to kill or injure people rather than to damage buildings or equipment.

antiperspirant ▸ noun [mass noun] a substance that is applied to the skin, especially under the arms, to prevent or reduce perspiration.

antiphon /ˈantɪf(ə)n/ ▸ noun (in traditional Western Christian liturgy) a short sentence sung or recited before or after a psalm or canticle. ■ a musical setting of an antiphon.
– ORIGIN late Middle English: via ecclesiastical Latin from Greek *antiphōna* 'harmonies', neuter plural of *antiphōnos* 'responsive', from *anti* 'in return' + *phōnē* 'sound'.

antiphonal /anˈtɪfən(ə)l/ ▸ adjective (of music, especially church music, or a section of a church liturgy) sung, recited, or played alternately by two groups.
▸ noun another term for **ANTIPHONARY**.
– DERIVATIVES **antiphonally** adverb.

antiphonary /anˈtɪf(ə)nəri/ ▸ noun (pl. **antiphonaries**) (in the Western Christian Church) a book of plainsong for the Divine Office.
– ORIGIN early 17th cent.: from ecclesiastical Latin *antiphonarium*, from *antiphōna* (see **ANTIPHON**).

antiphony /anˈtɪf(ə)ni/ ▸ noun [mass noun] antiphonal singing, playing, or chanting.

anti-piracy ▸ adjective **1** designed to prevent the unauthorized use or reproduction of copyright material: *the music industry's anti-piracy campaign*. **2** designed to prevent or thwart piracy at sea: *anti-piracy patrols*.

antipodal /anˈtɪpəd(ə)l/ ▸ adjective relating to or situated on the opposite side of the earth. ■ (**antipodal to**) diametrically opposed to.

antipode /ˈantɪpəʊd/ ▸ noun the direct opposite of something: *the pole and its antipode*.
– ORIGIN early 17th cent.: back-formation from **ANTIPODES**.

Antipodean /ˌantɪpəˈdiːən/ ▸ adjective relating to Australia or New Zealand (used by inhabitants of the northern hemisphere): *Antipodean wines*.

A

▶ **noun** a person from Australia or New Zealand (used by inhabitants of the northern hemisphere).
– ORIGIN mid 17th cent.: formed irregularly from **ANTIPODES** + **-AN**.

antipodes /anˈtɪpədiːz/ ▶ **plural noun 1** (**the Antipodes**) Australia and New Zealand (used by inhabitants of the northern hemisphere).
2 the direct opposite of something: *voting and violence are antipodes*.
– ORIGIN late Middle English: via French or late Latin from Greek *antipodes* 'having the feet opposite', from *anti* 'against, opposite' + *pous, pod-* 'foot'. The term originally denoted the inhabitants of opposite sides of the earth.

antipope ▶ **noun** a person established as pope in opposition to one held by others to be canonically chosen.
– ORIGIN late Middle English *antipape*, via French from medieval Latin *antipapa* (on the pattern of *Antichrist*). The change in the ending in the 17th cent. was due to association with **POPE**[1].

antiproton ▶ **noun** Physics the negatively charged antiparticle of a proton.

antipruritic /ˌantɪprʊˈrɪtɪk/ ▶ **adjective** (chiefly of a drug) used to relieve itching.
▶ **noun** an antipruritic drug.
– ORIGIN late 19th cent.: from **ANTI-** + *pruritic* (see **PRURITUS**).

antipsychotic ▶ **adjective** (chiefly of a drug) used to treat psychotic disorders.
▶ **noun** an antipsychotic drug.

antipyretic ▶ **adjective** (chiefly of a drug) used to prevent or reduce fever.
▶ **noun** an antipyretic drug.

antiquarian /ˌantɪˈkwɛːrɪən/ ▶ **adjective 1** relating to or dealing in antiques or rare books.
2 relating to the study of antiquities.
▶ **noun** a person who studies or collects antiques or antiquities.
– DERIVATIVES **antiquarianism noun**.
– ORIGIN early 17th cent.: from Latin *antiquarius* (see **ANTIQUARY**).

antiquark ▶ **noun** Physics the antiparticle of a quark.

antiquary /ˈantɪkwəri/ ▶ **noun** (pl. **antiquaries**) another term for **ANTIQUARIAN**.
– ORIGIN mid 16th cent.: from Latin *antiquarius*, from *antiquus* (see **ANTIQUE**).

antiquated ▶ **adjective** old-fashioned or outdated: *this antiquated central heating system*.
– ORIGIN late 16th cent. (in the sense 'old, of long standing'): from ecclesiastical Latin *antiquare* 'make old', from *antiquus* (see **ANTIQUE**).

antique ▶ **noun** a collectable object such as a piece of furniture or work of art that has a high value because of its age and quality.
▶ **adjective 1** having a high value because of age and quality: *an antique clock*. ■ intended to resemble the appearance of high-quality old furniture: *bookshelves with an antique finish*.
2 belonging to ancient times: *statues of antique gods*. ■ old-fashioned or outdated: *antique work practices*. ■ humorous showing signs of great age or wear: *the kitchen had an antique cooker*.
▶ **verb** (**antiques, antiquing, antiqued**) [with obj.] make (something) resemble an antique by artificial means.
– ORIGIN late 15th cent. (as an adjective): from Latin *antiquus, anticus* 'former, ancient', from *ante* 'before'.

antiquity ▶ **noun** (pl. **antiquities**) [mass noun] **1** the ancient past, especially the period of classical and other human civilizations before the Middle Ages: *the great civilizations of antiquity*.
2 [count noun] (usu. **antiquities**) an object, building, or work of art from the ancient past: *a collection of Islamic antiquities*.
3 great age: *a church of great antiquity*.
– ORIGIN Middle English: from Old French *antiquite*, from Latin *antiquitas*, from *antiquus* 'old, former' (see **ANTIQUE**).

anti-racism ▶ **noun** [mass noun] the policy or practice of opposing racism and promoting racial tolerance.
– DERIVATIVES **anti-racist noun & adjective**.

antiretroviral /ˌantɪˈrɛtrəʊˌvʌɪrəl/ ▶ **adjective** denoting or relating to a class of drugs which inhibit the activity of retroviruses such as HIV.
▶ **noun** an antiretroviral drug.

anti-roll bar ▶ **noun** a rubber-mounted bar fitted in the suspension of a vehicle to increase its stability, especially when cornering.

antirrhinum /ˌantɪˈrʌɪnəm/ ▶ **noun** (pl. **antirrhinums**) a plant of a genus that includes the snapdragon. ● Genus *Antirrhinum*, family Scrophulariaceae.
– ORIGIN from Latin, from Greek *antirrhinon*, from *anti-* 'counterfeiting' + *rhis, rhin-* 'nose', from the resemblance of the flower to an animal's snout.

antiscorbutic Medicine ▶ **adjective** (chiefly of a drug) having the effect of preventing or curing scurvy.
▶ **noun** an antiscorbutic food or drug.

anti-Semitism ▶ **noun** [mass noun] hostility to or prejudice against Jews.
– DERIVATIVES **anti-Semite noun**, **anti-Semitic adjective**.

antisense ▶ **adjective** Genetics having a sequence of nucleotides complementary to (and hence capable of binding to) a coding (or sense) sequence, which may be either that of the strand of a DNA double helix which undergoes transcription, or that of a messenger RNA molecule.

antisepsis ▶ **noun** [mass noun] the practice of using antiseptics to eliminate the microorganisms that cause disease. Compare with **ASEPSIS**.

antiseptic ▶ **adjective 1** preventing the growth of disease-causing microorganisms.
2 scrupulously clean or pure, especially so as to be bland or characterless: *their squeaky-clean home epitomizes this antiseptic respectability*.
▶ **noun** an antiseptic compound or preparation.
– DERIVATIVES **antiseptically adverb**.

antiserum ▶ **noun** (pl. **antisera**) a blood serum containing antibodies against specific antigens, injected to treat or protect against specific diseases.

antisocial ▶ **adjective 1** contrary to the laws and customs of society, in a way that causes annoyance and disapproval in others: *children's antisocial behaviour*. ■ Psychiatry sociopathic.
2 not sociable or wanting the company of others.
– DERIVATIVES **antisocially adverb**.

> **USAGE** On the difference in use between **antisocial**, **unsocial**, and **unsociable**, see **USAGE** at **UNSOCIABLE**.

antispasmodic ▶ **adjective** (chiefly of a drug) used to relieve spasm of involuntary muscle.
▶ **noun** an antispasmodic drug.

anti-static ▶ **adjective** preventing the build-up of static electricity or reducing its effects.

Antisthenes /anˈtɪsθəniːz/ (*c.*445–*c.*360 BC), Greek philosopher and teacher, regarded as the founder of the school of Cynics. A pupil and friend of Socrates, he believed that happiness is based on virtuous action rather than ease and pleasure, and that virtue, once acquired, cannot be lost.

antistrophe /anˈtɪstrəfi/ ▶ **noun** the second section of an ancient Greek choral ode or of one division of it. Compare with **STROPHE**.
– ORIGIN mid 16th cent. (as a term in rhetoric denoting the repetition of words in reverse order): via late Latin from Greek *antistrophē*, from *antistrephein* 'turn against', from *anti* 'against' + *strephein* 'to turn'.

antisymmetric ▶ **adjective** Mathematics & Physics unaltered in magnitude but changed in sign by exchange of two variables or by a particular symmetry operation.

anti-tank ▶ **adjective** for use against enemy tanks.

antiterror ▶ **adjective** denoting political activities or measures designed to prevent or thwart terrorism: *the government introduced tough new antiterror laws*.

antiterrorism ▶ **noun** [mass noun] political activities or measures designed to prevent or thwart terrorism.
– DERIVATIVES **antiterrorist adjective**.

anti-tetanus ▶ **adjective** preventing or effective against tetanus: *an anti-tetanus injection*.

antithesis /anˈtɪθəsɪs/ ▶ **noun** (pl. **antitheses** /-siːz/) **1** a person or thing that is the direct opposite of someone or something else: *love is the antithesis of selfishness*. ■ a contrast or opposition between two things: *the **antithesis between** occult and rational mentalities*. ■ [mass noun] a rhetorical or literary device in which an opposition or contrast of ideas is expressed.
2 [mass noun] (in Hegelian philosophy) the negation of the thesis as the second stage in the process of dialectical reasoning. Compare with **SYNTHESIS**.
– ORIGIN late Middle English (originally denoting the substitution of one grammatical case for another): from late Latin, from Greek *antitithenai* 'set against', from *anti* 'against' + *tithenai* 'to place'. The earliest current sense, denoting a rhetorical or literary device, dates from the early 16th cent.

antithetical /ˌantɪˈθɛtɪk(ə)l/ ▶ **adjective 1** directly opposed or contrasted; mutually incompatible: *people whose religious beliefs are **antithetical to** mine*.
2 connected with, containing, or using the rhetorical device of antithesis.
– DERIVATIVES **antithetic adjective**, **antithetically adverb**.
– ORIGIN late 16th cent. (in sense 2): from Greek *antithetikos*, from *antithetos* 'placed in opposition', from *antitithenai* 'set against'.

antitoxin ▶ **noun** Physiology an antibody that counteracts a toxin.
– DERIVATIVES **antitoxic adjective**.

antitrades (also **antitrade winds**) ▶ **plural noun** steady winds that blow in the opposite direction to and overlie the trade winds.

antitrust ▶ **adjective** [attrib.] (of legislation, chiefly in the US) preventing or controlling trusts or other monopolies, and so promoting fair competition in business.

antitussive ▶ **adjective** (especially of a drug) used to prevent or relieve a cough.
▶ **noun** an antitussive drug.

antitype ▶ **noun** a person or thing that represents the opposite of someone or something else: *the antitype of female virtue*.
– DERIVATIVES **antitypical adjective**.
– ORIGIN early 17th cent.: from late Latin *antitypus*, from Greek *antitupos* 'corresponding as an impression to the die', from *anti* 'against, opposite' + *tupos* 'type, a stamp'.

antivenin /ˌantɪˈvɛnɪn/ ▶ **noun** an antiserum containing antibodies against specific poisons, especially those in the venom of snakes, spiders, and scorpions.
– DERIVATIVES **antivenom noun**.
– ORIGIN late 19th cent.: from **ANTI-** + *ven(om)* + **-IN**[1].

antiviral ▶ **adjective 1** Medicine (chiefly of a drug or treatment) effective against viruses.
2 Computing (of software) designed to detect, remove, or offer protection against computer viruses.
▶ **noun** Medicine an antiviral drug or medicine.

antivirus ▶ **adjective** [attrib.] Computing (of software) designed to detect and destroy computer viruses.

antivivisection ▶ **adjective** [attrib.] opposed to the use of live animals for scientific research.
– DERIVATIVES **antivivisectionist noun & adjective**.

anti-war ▶ **adjective** opposed to war in general or to the conduct of a specific war: *his speech was interrupted by anti-war protesters*.

anti-Western ▶ **adjective** hostile to the interests of Europe and North America, especially the United States.

antler ▶ **noun** each of the branched horns on the head of an adult deer (typically a male one), which are made of bone and are grown and cast annually. ■ each of the branches on an antler.
– DERIVATIVES **antlered adjective**.
– ORIGIN late Middle English (originally denoting the lowest (forward-directed) branch of the antler): from Anglo-Norman French, variant of Old French *antoillier*, of unknown origin.

Antlia /ˈantlɪə/ Astronomy a small and faint southern constellation (the Air Pump), between Hydra and Vela.
– ORIGIN Latin, from Greek.

ant lion ▶ **noun** an insect that resembles a dragonfly, with predatory larvae that construct conical pits into which insect prey, especially ants, fall. ● Family Myrmeleontidae, order Neuroptera.

Antofagasta /ˌantəfəˈgastə/ a port in northern Chile, capital of a region of the same name; pop. 341,900 (est. 2006).

Antonine /ˈantənʌɪn/ ▶ **adjective** relating to the Roman emperors Antoninus Pius and Marcus Aurelius or their rules (AD 138–80).
▶ **plural noun** (**the Antonines**) the Antonine emperors.

Antonine Wall a defensive fortification about 59 km (37 miles) long, built (*c.*140 AD) across the narrowest part of southern Scotland between the Firth of Forth and the Firth of Clyde. It was intended to mark the frontier of the Roman province of Britain.

Antoninus Pius /ˌantəˈnʌɪnəs ˈpʌɪəs/ (86–161), Roman emperor 138–61. The adopted son and successor of Hadrian, he had a generally peaceful and harmonious reign.

Antonioni /anˌtəʊnɪˈəʊni/, Michelangelo (1912–2007), Italian film director. Notable films: *L'avventura* (1960), *Blow-Up* (1966), and *Zabriskie Point* (1970).

A

antonomasia /ˌantənəˈmeɪzɪə, anˌtɒnə-/ ▶ **noun** [mass noun] **1** Linguistics the substitution of an epithet or title for a proper name (e.g. *the Maid of Orleans* for Joan of Arc).
2 the use of a proper name to express a general idea (e.g. *a Scrooge* for a miser).
– ORIGIN mid 16th cent.: via Latin from Greek, from *antonomazein* 'name instead', from *anti-* 'against, instead' + *onoma* 'a name'.

Anton Piller order ▶ **noun** English Law a court order which requires the defendant in proceedings to permit the plaintiff or his or her legal representatives to enter the defendant's premises in order to obtain evidence essential to the plaintiff's case.
– ORIGIN 1970s: named after *Anton Piller*, German manufacturers of electric motors, who were involved in legal proceedings (1975) in which such an order was granted.

Antony /ˈantəni/, Mark (*c.*83–30 BC), Roman general and triumvir; Latin name *Marcus Antonius*. A supporter of Julius Caesar, he was appointed one of the triumvirate after Caesar's murder. Following the battle of Philippi he took charge of the Eastern Empire, where he established his association with Cleopatra. Quarrels with Octavian led finally to his defeat at the battle of Actium and to his suicide.

Antony, St see **Anthony, St**.

antonym /ˈantənɪm/ ▶ **noun** a word opposite in meaning to another (e.g. *bad* and *good*).
– DERIVATIVES **antonymous** adjective, **antonymy** noun.
– ORIGIN mid 19th cent.: from French *antonyme*, from *ant-* (from Greek *anti-* 'against') + Greek *onuma* 'a name'.

Antony of Padua, St see **Anthony of Padua, St**.

antrectomy /anˈtrɛktəmi/ ▶ **noun** [mass noun] surgical removal of the walls of an antrum, especially the antrum of the stomach.

Antrim one of the Six Counties of Northern Ireland, since 1973 an administrative district. ■ a town in this district, on the NE shore of Lough Neagh; pop. 22,000 (est. 2009).

Antron /ˈantrɒn/ ▶ **noun** [mass noun] trademark a type of strong, light nylon fibre used chiefly in making carpets and upholstery.
– ORIGIN 1960s: an invented name.

antrum /ˈantrəm/ ▶ **noun** (pl. **antra** /-trə/) Anatomy a natural chamber or cavity in a bone or other anatomical structure. ■ the pyloric end of the stomach.
– DERIVATIVES **antral** adjective.
– ORIGIN early 19th cent.: from Latin, from Greek *antron* 'cave'.

ants' eggs ▶ **plural noun** the pupae of ants, especially when used as food for pet fish.

antsy /ˈantsi/ ▶ **adjective** (**antsier**, **antsiest**) N. Amer. informal agitated, impatient, or restless: *Dick **got antsy** the day he put to sea.*
– ORIGIN mid 19th cent.: probably from the phrase *have ants in one's pants* (see **ant**).

ant-thrush ▶ **noun** any of a number of thrush-sized ant-eating birds: ● a large antbird (three genera in the family Formicariidae). ● an African thrush (genus *Neocossyphus*). ● another term for **pitta²**.

Antung /anˈtʊŋ/ former name for **Dandong**.

Antwerp /ˈantwəːp/ a port in northern Belgium, on the Scheldt; pop. 472,071 (2008). By the 16th century it had become a leading European commercial and financial centre. Flemish name **Antwerpen**, French name **Anvers**. ■ a province of Belgium of which Antwerp is the capital.

Anubis /əˈnjuːbɪs/ Egyptian Mythology the god of mummification, protector of tombs, typically represented as having a dog's head.

Anura /əˈnjʊərə/ ▶ **plural noun** Zoology an order of tailless amphibians that comprises the frogs and toads. Also called **Salientia** or **Batrachia**. ■ (**anura**) amphibians of this order; frogs and toads.
– ORIGIN modern Latin (plural), from **an-¹** 'without' + Greek *oura* 'tail'.

Anuradhapura /əˌnʊrɑːdəˈpʊərə/ a city in north central Sri Lanka, capital of a district of the same name; pop. 81,500 (est. 2007). The ancient capital of Sri Lanka, it is a centre of Buddhist pilgrimage.

anuran Zoology ▶ **noun** a tailless amphibian of the order Anura; a frog or toad.
▶ **adjective** relating to or denoting anurans.

anuria /əˈnjʊərɪə/ ▶ **noun** [mass noun] Medicine failure of the kidneys to produce urine.
– DERIVATIVES **anuric** adjective.
– ORIGIN mid 19th cent.: from **an-¹** + **-uria**.

anus /ˈeɪnəs/ ▶ **noun** Anatomy & Zoology the opening at the end of the alimentary canal through which solid waste matter leaves the body.
– ORIGIN late Middle English: from Latin, originally 'a ring'.

Anvers /ɑ̃vɛʀ/ French name of **Antwerp**.

anvil ▶ **noun 1** a heavy iron block with a flat top and concave sides, on which metal can be hammered and shaped.
2 the horizontally extended upper part of a cumulonimbus cloud.
3 Anatomy another term for **incus**.
– ORIGIN Old English *anfilte*, from the Germanic base of **on** + a verbal stem meaning 'beat'.

anxiety ▶ **noun** (pl. **anxieties**) [mass noun] **1** a feeling of worry, nervousness, or unease about something with an uncertain outcome: *he felt a surge of anxiety* | [count noun] *anxieties about the moral decline of today's youth.* ■ Psychiatry a nervous disorder marked by excessive uneasiness and apprehension, typically with compulsive behaviour or panic attacks.
2 [with infinitive] strong desire or concern to do something or for something to happen: *the housekeeper's eager anxiety to please.*
– ORIGIN early 16th cent.: from French *anxiété* or Latin *anxietas*, from *anxius* (see **anxious**).

anxiolytic /ˌaŋzɪəˈlɪtɪk/ Medicine ▶ **adjective** (chiefly of a drug) used to reduce anxiety.
▶ **noun** a drug used to relieve anxiety.
– ORIGIN 1960s: from **anxiety** + **-lytic**.

anxious ▶ **adjective 1** feeling or showing worry, nervousness, or unease about something with an uncertain outcome: *she was extremely anxious about her exams* | *an anxious look.* ■ [attrib.] (of a situation or period of time) causing or characterized by worry or nervousness: *there were some anxious moments.*
2 very eager or concerned to do something or for something to happen: *the company was **anxious to** avoid any trouble* | [with clause] *my parents were anxious that I get an education.*
– DERIVATIVES **anxiously** adverb, **anxiousness** noun.
– ORIGIN early 17th cent.: from Latin *anxius* (from *angere* 'to choke') + **-ous**.

any ▶ **determiner & pronoun 1** [usu. with negative or in questions] used to refer to one or some of a thing or number of things, no matter how much or how many: [as determiner] *I don't have any choice* | *do you have any tips to pass on?* | [as pronoun] *someone asked him for a match, but Joe didn't have any* | *you don't know **any of** my friends.* ■ anyone: *the city council ceased payments to any but the aged.*
2 whichever of a specified class might be chosen: [as determiner] *these constellations are visible at any hour of the night* | [as pronoun] *the illness may be due to **any of** several causes.*
▶ **adverb** [usu. with negative or in questions] [as submodifier] at all; in some degree (used for emphasis): *he wasn't any good at basketball* | *why look any further?* | *no one would be **any the wiser**.* ■ US informal at all (used alone, not qualifying another word): *I didn't hurt you any.*
– PHRASES **any amount of** see **amount**. **any more** (also **anymore**) [usu. with negative or in questions] to any further extent; any longer: *she refused to listen any more.* **any old** see **old**. **any road** (**up**) chiefly N. English informal term for **anyway**: *any road, I'm sure you'll make a go of it.* **any time** (also **anytime**) at whatever time: *she can come any time.* **any time** (or **day** or **minute** etc.) **now** informal very soon: *we'll get them back any day now.* **be not having any** (**of it**) informal be uninterested or disagree: *I tried to make polite conversation, but he wasn't having any.*
– ORIGIN Old English *ǣnig* (see **one**, **-y¹**), of Germanic origin; related to Dutch *eenig* and German *einig*.

> **USAGE** When used as a pronoun **any** can be used with either a singular or a plural verb, depending on the context: *we needed more sugar but there **wasn't any** left* (**singular verb**) or ***are any** of the new videos available?* (**plural verb**).

anybody ▶ **pronoun** anyone: *there wasn't anybody around.*
– PHRASES **anybody's guess** see **guess**.

anyhow ▶ **adverb 1** another term for **anyway**.
2 in a careless or haphazard way: *two suitcases flung anyhow.*

anymore ▶ **adverb** chiefly N. Amer. variant of **any more** at **any**.

anyone ▶ **pronoun 1** [usu. with negative or in questions] any person or people: *there wasn't anyone there* | *does anyone remember him?* | *I was afraid to tell anyone.* ■ [without negative] used for emphasis: *anyone could do it.*
2 a person of importance or authority: *they are read by anyone who's anyone.*
– PHRASES **be anyone's** informal be open to sexual advances from anyone: *three shandies and he's anyone's.* **anyone's game** an evenly balanced contest: *it was still anyone's game at half-time.*

> **USAGE** The two-word form **any one** is not the same as the one-word form **anyone** and the two forms cannot be used interchangeably. **Any one** means 'any single (person or thing)', as in: *not more than twelve new members are admitted in **any one** year.*

anyplace ▶ **adverb** N. Amer. informal term for **anywhere**: *Miami is hotter than anyplace else.*

anything ▶ **pronoun** [usu. with negative or in questions] used to refer to a thing, no matter what: *nobody was saying anything* | *have you found anything?* | *he inquired whether there was anything he could do.* ■ [without negative] used for emphasis: *I was ready for anything.* ■ used to indicate a range: *he trains anything from seven to eight hours a day.*
– PHRASES **anything but** not at all (used for emphasis): *he is anything but racist.* **anything like ——** [with negative] at all like —— (used for emphasis): *it doesn't taste anything like wine.* (**as**) **—— as anything** informal extremely ——: *she said it out loud, clear as anything.* **or anything** [usu. with negative or in questions] informal added as a general reference to other things similar to the thing mentioned: *no strings attached, you don't have to join up or anything.*

anytime ▶ **adverb** variant of **any time** at **any**.

Anytown ▶ **noun** a real or fictional place regarded as being typical of a small US town: *a basketball arena straight out of a high school in Anytown, USA.*

anyway ▶ **adverb 1** used to confirm or support a point or idea just mentioned: *I told you, it's all right, and anyway, it was my fault* | *it's too late now anyway.* ■ used in questions to emphasize the speaker's wish to obtain the truth: *'What are you doing here, anyway?'*
2 used to end a conversation, to change the subject, or to resume a subject after interruption: *'Anyway, Dot, I must dash.'* ■ used to pass over less significant aspects of an account in order to focus on what is important: *'Poor John always enjoyed a drink. Anyway, he died last year.'*
3 used to indicate that something happened or will happen in spite of something else: *nobody invited Miss Honey to sit down but she sat down anyway.*

anyways ▶ **adverb** N. Amer. informal or dialect form of **anyway**: *you wouldn't understand all them long words anyways.*

anywhere ▶ **adverb** [usu. with negative or in questions] in or to any place: *he couldn't be found anywhere.* ■ [without negative] used for emphasis: *I could go anywhere in the world.* ■ used to indicate a range: *he could get **anywhere from** three to seven years.*
▶ **pronoun** any place: *he doesn't have anywhere to live.*
– PHRASES **anywhere near** [with negative or in questions] at all near (used for emphasis): *I wouldn't dream of letting a surgeon anywhere near my eyes.* ■ remotely close to in extent, level, or scope: *imitations rarely look anywhere near as good as the real thing.*

anywheres ▶ **adverb & pronoun** chiefly N. Amer. informal or dialect form of **anywhere**: [as adv.] *I'll see if I can see your clothes anywheres.*

anywise ▶ **adverb** archaic in any manner or way.
– ORIGIN Old English *on ǣnige wīsan* 'in any wise'.

Anzac ▶ **noun** a soldier in the Australian and New Zealand Army Corps (1914–18). ■ informal a person from Australia or New Zealand, especially a member of the armed services.
– ORIGIN acronym.

Anzac Day ▶ **noun** (in Australia and New Zealand) the day on which the Anzac landing at Gallipoli in 1915 is annually commemorated, 25 April.

Anzus /ˈanzəs/ an alliance between Australia, New Zealand, and the US, established in 1951 and designed to protect those countries in the Pacific area from armed attack. Also called **Pacific Security Treaty**.

AO ▶ **abbreviation** Officer of the Order of Australia.

AOB ▶ **abbreviation** any other business (at the end of an agenda for a meeting).

AOC ▶ **abbreviation** appellation d'origine contrôlée (see **appellation contrôlée**).

ao dai /ˈaʊ ˌdʌɪ/ ▶ **noun** (pl. **ao dais**) a Vietnamese woman's long-sleeved tunic with ankle-length panels at front and back, worn over trousers.
– ORIGIN 1960s: Vietnamese.

A-OK (also **A-okay**) N. Amer. informal ▶ **adjective** in good order or condition; all right.
▶ **adverb** in a good manner or way; all right.
– ORIGIN 1960s (originally an astronauts' term): from *a*ll systems *OK*.

AONB ▶ **abbreviation** (in the UK) Area of Outstanding Natural Beauty.

AOR ▶ **noun** [mass noun] a style of popular music in which a hard rock background is combined with softer or more melodic elements.
– ORIGIN 1970s (originally US): from *album-oriented rock* or *adult-oriented rock*.

Aoraki/Mount Cook /aʊˈraki/ official name for Mount Cook (see **Cook, Mount**).

aorist /ˈeɪərɪst, ˈɛːr-/ Grammar ▶ **noun** a past tense of a verb (especially in Greek), which does not contain any reference to duration or completion of the action.
▶ **adjective** relating to or denoting this tense.
– DERIVATIVES **aoristic** adjective.
– ORIGIN late 16th cent.: from Greek *aoristos* 'indefinite', from *a-* 'not' + *horizein* 'define, limit'.

aorta /eɪˈɔːtə/ ▶ **noun** the main artery of the body, supplying oxygenated blood to the circulatory system. In humans it passes over the heart from the left ventricle and runs down in front of the backbone.
– DERIVATIVES **aortic** adjective.
– ORIGIN mid 16th cent.: from Greek *aortē* (used in the plural by Hippocrates for the branches of the windpipe, and by Aristotle for the great artery), from *aeirein* 'raise'.

Aosta /ɑːˈɒstə/ a city in NW Italy, capital of Valle d'Aosta region; pop. 34,979 (2008).

Aotearoa /aʊˌteɪəˈrəʊə/ Maori name for **New Zealand**.
– ORIGIN Maori, literally 'land of the long white cloud'.

aoudad /ˈɑːʊdad/ ▶ **noun** another term for **Barbary sheep**.
– ORIGIN early 19th cent.: from French, from Berber *udād*.

à outrance /ɑː ˈuːtrɒ̃s/, French /a utʀɑ̃s/ ▶ **adverb** literary to the death or the very end: *a duel à outrance*.
– ORIGIN French, literally 'to the utmost'.

Aozou Strip /aʊˈzuː/ (also **Aouzou Strip**) a narrow corridor of disputed desert land in northern Chad, stretching the full length of the border between Chad and Libya.

AP ▶ **abbreviation** Associated Press.

ap-[1] ▶ **prefix** variant spelling of **ad-** assimilated before *p* (as in *apposite*, *apprehend*).

ap-[2] ▶ **prefix** variant spelling of **apo-** shortened before a vowel or *h* (as in *aphelion*).

apace ▶ **adverb** literary swiftly; quickly: *work continues apace*.
– ORIGIN late Middle English: from Old French *a pas* 'at (a considerable) pace'.

Apache /əˈpatʃi/ ▶ **noun** (pl. **same** or **Apaches**) **1** a member of an American Indian people living chiefly in New Mexico and Arizona. Under the leadership of Geronimo, the Apache were the last American Indian people to be conquered by the European settlers.
2 [mass noun] any of the Athabaskan languages of the Apache, which have about 14,000 speakers altogether, though some are virtually extinct.
▶ **adjective** relating to the Apache or their language.
– ORIGIN from Mexican Spanish, probably from Zuni *Apachu*, literally 'enemy'.

apache /əˈpaʃ/, French /apaʃ/ ▶ **noun** (pl. **apaches** pronunc. **same**) a violent street ruffian, originally in Paris.
– ORIGIN early 20th cent.: French, from **Apache**, by association with the reputed ferocity of the American Indian people.

apanage ▶ **noun** variant spelling of **appanage**.

apart ▶ **adverb 1** (of two or more people or things) separated by a specified distance in time or space: *two stone gateposts some thirty feet apart | studies from as far apart as America and Iceland* | figurative *the two sides remained far apart on the issue of cruise missiles*. ■ no longer living together or close emotionally: *alcoholism had driven us apart*.
2 to or on one side; at a distance from the main body: *Isabel stepped away from Joanna and stood apart*.
■ used after a noun to indicate that someone or something has qualities which mark them out from other people or things: *wrestlers were a breed apart*.
■ used to indicate that one is dismissing something from consideration or moving from one tone or topic to another: *Alaska apart, much of America's energy business concentrates on producing gas | joking apart, they do a really remarkable job*.
3 so as to be shattered; into pieces: *he leapt out of the car just before it was blown apart*.
– PHRASES **apart from 1** except for: *the whole world seemed to be sleeping, apart from Barbara*. **2** in addition to; as well as: *quite apart from all the work, he had such financial problems*.
– DERIVATIVES **apartness** noun.
– ORIGIN late Middle English: from Old French, from Latin *a parte* 'at the side'.

apartheid /əˈpɑːtheɪt, əˈpɑːtʌɪd/ ▶ **noun** [mass noun] historical (in South Africa) a policy or system of segregation or discrimination on grounds of race.

> Adopted as a slogan in the 1948 election by the successful Afrikaner National Party, apartheid extended and institutionalized existing racial segregation. Despite rioting and terrorism at home and isolation abroad from the 1960s onwards, the white regime maintained the apartheid system with only minor relaxation until February 1991.

– ORIGIN 1940s: from Afrikaans, literally 'separateness', from Dutch *apart* 'separate' + *-heid* (equivalent of **-hood**).

aparthotel (also **apartotel**) ▶ **noun** a type of hotel providing self-catering apartments as well as ordinary hotel facilities.
– ORIGIN 1960s: from Spanish *Apartotel*, the name of a company specializing in this type of accommodation, from a blend of *apartamento* 'apartment' and *hotel*.

apartment ▶ **noun** Brit. a flat, typically one that is well appointed or used for holidays: *self-catering holiday apartments*. ■ N. Amer. any flat: *the family lived in a rented apartment*. ■ N. Amer. a block of apartments.
■ (**apartments**) a set of private rooms in a very large house: *the Imperial apartments*.
– ORIGIN mid 17th cent. (denoting a private suite of rooms): from French *appartement*, from Italian *appartamento*, from *appartare* 'to separate', from *a parte* 'apart'.

apartment building (also **apartment block** or chiefly US **apartment house**) ▶ **noun** a block of apartments.

apartment hotel ▶ **noun** N. Amer. a hotel with furnished suites of rooms including kitchen facilities, available for long-term or short-term rental.

apathetic ▶ **adjective** showing or feeling no interest, enthusiasm, or concern: *an apathetic electorate*.
– DERIVATIVES **apathetically** adverb.
– ORIGIN mid 18th cent.: from **apathy**, on the pattern of *pathetic*.

apathy /ˈapəθi/ ▶ **noun** [mass noun] lack of interest, enthusiasm, or concern: *widespread apathy among students*.
– ORIGIN early 17th cent.: from French *apathie*, via Latin from Greek *apatheia*, from *apathēs* 'without feeling', from *a-* 'without' + *pathos* 'suffering'.

apatite /ˈapətʌɪt/ ▶ **noun** [mass noun] a widely occurring pale green to purple mineral, consisting of calcium phosphate with some fluorine, chlorine, and other elements. It is used in the manufacture of fertilizers.
– ORIGIN early 19th cent.: coined in German from Greek *apatē* 'deceit' (from the mineral's diverse forms and colours).

apatosaurus /əˌpatəˈsɔːrəs/ ▶ **noun** a huge herbivorous dinosaur of the late Jurassic period, with a long neck and tail. Formerly called **brontosaurus**. ● Genus *Apatosaurus* (formerly *Brontosaurus*), infraorder Sauropoda, order Saurischia.
– ORIGIN modern Latin, from Greek *apatē* 'deceit' + *sauros* 'lizard'.

APB ▶ **abbreviation** US all-points bulletin.

APC ▶ **abbreviation** armoured personnel carrier.

ape ▶ **noun 1** a large primate that lacks a tail, including the gorilla, chimpanzees, orang-utan, and gibbons.
● Families Pongidae and Hylobatidae.
■ used in names of macaque monkeys with short tails, e.g. **Barbary ape**. ■ (in general use) any monkey.
2 an unintelligent or clumsy person.
3 archaic an inferior imitator or mimic: *cunning is but the ape of wisdom*.
▶ **verb** [with obj.] (**apes, aping, aped**) imitate (someone or something), especially in an absurd or unthinking way: *new architecture can respect the old without aping its style*.
– PHRASES **go ape** (or vulgar slang, chiefly N. Amer. **apeshit**) informal become very angry or excited.
– DERIVATIVES **apelike** adjective.
– ORIGIN Old English *apa*, of Germanic origin; related to Dutch *aap* and German *Affe*.

APEC ▶ **abbreviation** Asia Pacific Economic Cooperation, a regional economic forum established in 1989, including the US, Japan, China, Australia, Indonesia, Hong Kong, and Thailand.

Apeldoorn /ˈap(ə)ldɔːn/ a town in the east central Netherlands; pop. 155,108 (2008). It is the site of the summer residence of the Dutch royal family.

Apelles /əˈpɛliːz/ (4th century BC), Greek painter. He is now known only from written sources, but was highly acclaimed throughout the ancient world.

apeman ▶ **noun** (pl. **apemen**) an extinct apelike primate believed to be related or ancestral to present-day humans.

Apennines /ˈapɪnʌɪnz/ a mountain range running 1,400 km (880 miles) down the length of Italy, from the north-west to the southern tip of the peninsula.

aperçu /ˌapɛːˈsjuː/ ▶ **noun** (pl. **aperçus**) a comment or brief reference which makes an illuminating or entertaining point.
– ORIGIN early 19th cent.: from French, past participle of *apercevoir* 'perceive'.

aperient /əˈpɪərɪənt/ Medicine ▶ **adjective** (chiefly of a drug) used to relieve constipation.
▶ **noun** a drug used to relieve constipation.
– ORIGIN early 17th cent.: from Latin *aperient-* 'opening', from *aperire*.

aperiodic ▶ **adjective** technical not periodic; irregular.
■ Physics denoting a potentially oscillating or vibrating system (such as an instrument with a pointer) that is damped to prevent oscillation or vibration.
– DERIVATIVES **aperiodicity** noun.

aperitif /əˈpɛrɪtiːf, əˌpɛrɪˈtiːf/ ▶ **noun** an alcoholic drink taken before a meal to stimulate the appetite.
– ORIGIN late 19th cent.: from French *apéritif*, from medieval Latin *aperitivus*, based on Latin *aperire* 'to open'.

aperture /ˈapətʃə, -tj(ʊ)ə/ ▶ **noun** an opening, hole, or gap. ■ a space through which light passes in an optical or photographic instrument, especially the variable opening by which light enters a camera.
– DERIVATIVES **apertural** adjective.
– ORIGIN late Middle English: from Latin *apertura*, from *apert-* 'opened', from *aperire* 'to open'.

aperture priority ▶ **noun** [mass noun] Photography a system used in some automatic cameras in which the aperture is selected by the user and the appropriate shutter speed is controlled automatically. Compare with **shutter priority**.

apery /ˈeɪpəri/ ▶ **noun** [mass noun] archaic the action of imitating the behaviour or manner of someone, especially in an absurd or unthinking way.

apetalous /eɪˈpɛt(ə)ləs, ə-/ ▶ **adjective** Botany (of a flower) having no petals.
– ORIGIN early 18th cent.: from modern Latin *apetalus*, from Greek *apetalos* 'leafless' (from *a-* 'without' + *petalon* 'leaf') + **-ous**.

Apex /ˈeɪpɛks/ ▶ **noun** [mass noun] a system of reduced fares for scheduled airline flights and railway journeys which must be booked and paid for before a certain period in advance of departure.
– ORIGIN 1970s: from Advance Purchase Excursion.

apex /ˈeɪpɛks/ ▶ **noun** (pl. **apexes** or **apices** /ˈeɪpɪsiːz/)
1 the top or highest part of something, especially one forming a point: *the apex of the roof* | figurative *the central bank is at the apex of the financial system*.
■ Geometry the highest point in a plane or solid figure, relative to a base line or plane. ■ Botany the growing point of a shoot.
2 the highest point of achievement; a climax: *the apex of his career was in 1966 when he hoisted aloft the World Cup for England*.
3 Motor Racing the point in turning a corner when the vehicle is closest to the edge of the track.
▶ **verb 1** [no obj.] reach a high point or climax.
2 [with obj.] Motor Racing turn (a corner) very close to the edge of the track.
– ORIGIN early 17th cent.: from Latin, 'peak, tip'.

Apgar score /ˈapgɑː/ ▶ **noun** Medicine a measure of the physical condition of a newborn infant. It is obtained by adding points (2, 1, or 0) for heart rate, respiratory effort, muscle tone, response to stimulation, and skin coloration; a score of ten represents the best possible condition.

– ORIGIN 1960s: named after Virginia *Apgar* (1909–74), the American anaesthesiologist who devised this method of assessment in 1953.

aphasia /əˈfeɪzɪə/ ▶ **noun** [mass noun] Medicine inability (or impaired ability) to understand or produce speech, as a result of brain damage. Compare with **APHONIA**.
– DERIVATIVES **aphasic** adjective & noun.
– ORIGIN mid 19th cent.: from Greek, from *aphatos* 'speechless', from *a-* 'not' + *phanai* 'speak'.

aphelion /apˈhiːlɪən/ ▶ **noun** (pl. **aphelia** /-lɪə/) Astronomy the point in the orbit of a planet, asteroid, or comet at which it is furthest from the sun: *Mars is at* ***aphelion***. The opposite of **PERIHELION**.
– ORIGIN mid 17th cent.: alteration of modern Latin *aphelium* (by substitution of the Greek inflection *-on*), from Greek *aph' hēlion* 'from the sun'.

apheresis /ˌeɪfəˈriːsɪs/ ▶ **noun** [mass noun] (pl. **aphereses** /-siːz/) **1** Linguistics omission of the initial sound of a word, as when *he is* is pronounced *he's*.
2 Medicine a technique by which a particular substance or component is removed from the blood, the main volume being returned to the body.
– ORIGIN mid 16th cent.: via late Latin from Greek *aphairesis*, from *aphairein* 'take away', from *apo* 'from' + *hairein* 'take'.

aphesis /ˈafɪsɪs/ ▶ **noun** [mass noun] Linguistics the gradual loss of an unstressed vowel at the beginning of a word (e.g. of *e* from *esquire* to form *squire*).
– DERIVATIVES **aphetic** /əˈfɛtɪk/ adjective, **aphetically** adverb.
– ORIGIN late 19th cent.: from Greek, literally 'letting go', from *apo* 'from' + *hienai* 'let go, send'.

aphicide /ˈeɪfɪsʌɪd/ ▶ **noun** an insecticide used against aphids.

aphid /ˈeɪfɪd/ ▶ **noun** a small bug which feeds by sucking sap from plants; a blackfly or greenfly. Aphids reproduce rapidly, sometimes producing live young without mating, and large numbers can cause extensive damage to plants. ● Superfamily Aphidoidea, suborder Homoptera.
– ORIGIN late 19th cent.: back-formation from *aphides*, plural of **APHIS**.

aphis /ˈeɪfɪs/ ▶ **noun** (pl. **aphides** /-diːz/) an aphid, especially one of the genus *Aphis* (which includes the common greenfly and blackfly).
– ORIGIN late 18th cent.: modern Latin, from Greek, perhaps a misreading of *koris* 'bug' (interpreting the characters κορ 'kor' as αφ 'aph').

aphonia /eɪˈfəʊnɪə, ə-/ (also **aphony** /ˈaf(ə)ni/) ▶ **noun** [mass noun] Medicine inability to speak through disease of or damage to the larynx or mouth. Compare with **APHASIA**.
– ORIGIN late 17th cent.: modern Latin, from Greek *aphōnia*, from *aphōnos* 'voiceless', from *a-* 'without' + *phōnē* 'voice'.

aphorism /ˈafərɪz(ə)m/ ▶ **noun** a pithy observation which contains a general truth. ■ a concise statement of a scientific principle, typically by a classical author.
– DERIVATIVES **aphorist** noun, **aphoristic** adjective, **aphoristically** adverb, **aphorize** (also **aphorise**) verb.
– ORIGIN early 16th cent.: from French *aphorisme* or late Latin *aphorismus*, from Greek *aphorismos* 'definition', from *aphorizein* 'define'.

aphrodisiac /ˌafrəˈdɪzɪak/ ▶ **noun** a food, drink, or other thing that stimulates sexual desire: *power is the ultimate aphrodisiac.*
▶ **adjective** of the nature of an aphrodisiac; stimulating sexual desire: *the aphrodisiac effects of ylang-ylang oil.*
– DERIVATIVES **aphrodisiacal** adjective.
– ORIGIN early 18th cent.: from Greek *aphrodisiakos*, from *aphrodisios*, from *Aphroditē* (see **APHRODITE**).

Aphrodisias /ˌafrəˈdɪsɪəs/ an ancient city of western Asia Minor, site of a temple dedicated to Aphrodite. Now in ruins, it is situated 80 km (50 miles) west of Aydin, in modern Turkey.

Aphrodite /ˌafrəˈdʌɪti/ Greek Mythology the goddess of beauty, fertility, and sexual love. She is variously described as the daughter of Zeus and Dione, or as being born from the sea. Roman equivalent **VENUS**.
– ORIGIN Greek, literally 'foam-born', from *aphros* 'foam'.

aphtha /ˈafθə/ ▶ **noun** (pl. **aphthae** /ˈafθiː/) Medicine a small ulcer occurring in groups in the mouth or on the tongue. ■ [mass noun] a condition in which such ulcers occur.
– DERIVATIVES **aphthous** adjective.
– ORIGIN mid 17th cent.: via Latin from Greek, connected with *haptein* 'set on fire'.

API ▶ **abbreviation** Computing application programming interface.

Apia /ˈapɪə/ the capital of Samoa; pop. 43,000 (est. 2007).

apian /ˈeɪpɪən/ ▶ **adjective** relating to bees.
– ORIGIN early 19th cent.: from Latin *apianus*, from *apis* 'bee'.

apiary /ˈeɪpɪəri/ ▶ **noun** (pl. **apiaries**) a place where bees are kept; a collection of beehives.
– DERIVATIVES **apiarian** adjective, **apiarist** noun.
– ORIGIN mid 17th cent.: from Latin *apiarium*, from *apis* 'bee'.

apical /ˈeɪpɪk(ə)l, ˈap-/ ▶ **adjective** **1** technical relating to or denoting an apex.
2 Phonetics (of a consonant) formed with the tip of the tongue at or near the front teeth or the alveolar ridge, for example *th* or trilled *r*.
– ORIGIN early 19th cent.: from Latin *apex*, *apic-* (see **APEX**) + **-AL**.

apices plural form of **APEX**.

Apicomplexa /ˌeɪpɪkɒmˈplɛksə/ another term for **SPOROZOA**.

apiculture /ˈeɪpɪˌkʌltʃə/ ▶ **noun** technical term for **BEEKEEPING**.
– DERIVATIVES **apicultural** adjective, **apiculturist** noun.
– ORIGIN mid 19th cent.: from Latin *apis* 'bee' + **CULTURE**, on the pattern of words such as *agriculture*.

apiece ▶ **adverb** to, for, or by each one of a group (used after a noun or an amount): *we sold 385 prints at £10 apiece.*
– ORIGIN late Middle English: from **A**[1] + **PIECE**.

Apis /ˈɑːpɪs, ˈap-/ Egyptian Mythology a god depicted as a bull, symbolizing fertility and strength in war.

apish /ˈeɪpɪʃ/ ▶ **adjective** **1** resembling or likened to an ape.
2 foolish or silly.
– DERIVATIVES **apishly** adverb, **apishness** noun.

aplanat /ˈaplənat/ ▶ **noun** Physics a reflecting or refracting surface which is free from spherical aberration.
– DERIVATIVES **aplanatic** adjective.
– ORIGIN late 19th cent.: coined in German from Greek *aplanētos*, from *a-* 'not' + *planan* 'wander'.

aplasia /əˈpleɪzɪə/ ▶ **noun** [mass noun] Medicine the failure of an organ or tissue to develop or to function normally.
– DERIVATIVES **aplastic** adjective.
– ORIGIN late 19th cent.: from **A-**[1] 'without' + Greek *plasis* 'formation'.

aplastic anaemia ▶ **noun** [mass noun] Medicine deficiency of all types of blood cell caused by failure of bone marrow development.

aplenty ▶ **adjective** [postpositive] in abundance: *there is passion aplenty in the events described.*

aplomb /əˈplɒm/ ▶ **noun** [mass noun] self-confidence or assurance, especially when in a demanding situation: *Diana passed the test* ***with aplomb***.
– ORIGIN late 18th cent. (in the sense 'perpendicularity, steadiness'): from French, from *à plomb* 'according to a plumb line'.

apnoea /apˈniːə/ (US **apnea**) ▶ **noun** [mass noun] Medicine temporary cessation of breathing, especially during sleep: *thousands suffer from* ***sleep apnoea***.
– DERIVATIVES **apnoeic** adjective.
– ORIGIN early 18th cent.: modern Latin, from Greek *apnoia*, from *apnous* 'breathless'.

apo- /ˈapəʊ/ ▶ **prefix** **1** away from: *apocrine.* ■ separate: *apocarpous.*
2 Astronomy denoting the furthest point in the orbit of a body in relation to the primary: *apolune.* Compare with **PERI-**.
– ORIGIN from Greek *apo* 'from, away, quite, un-'.

Apoc. ▶ **abbreviation** ■ Apocalypse. ■ Apocrypha.

apocalypse /əˈpɒkəlɪps/ ▶ **noun** **1** (often **the Apocalypse**) the complete final destruction of the world, as described in the biblical book of Revelation. ■ (**the Apocalypse**) (especially in the Vulgate Bible) the book of Revelation.
2 an event involving destruction or damage on a catastrophic scale: *the apocalypse of World War II.*
– PHRASES **the Four Horsemen of the Apocalypse** four allegorical mounted figures, commonly identified as Pestilence (or Conquest), War, Famine, and Death, whose arrival heralds the end of the world, as described in the biblical book of Revelation. ■ used to refer to people or phenomena seen as agents of imminent catastrophe: *in 2003, the airline industry survived the four horsemen of the apocalypse.*
– ORIGIN Old English, via Old French and ecclesiastical Latin from Greek *apokalupsis*, from *apokaluptein* 'uncover, reveal', from *apo-* 'un-' + *kaluptein* 'to cover'.

apocalyptic ▶ **adjective** describing or prophesying the complete destruction of the world: *the apocalyptic visions of ecologists.* ■ momentous or catastrophic: *the struggle between the two countries is assuming apocalyptic proportions.* ■ of or resembling the biblical Apocalypse: *apocalyptic imagery.*
– DERIVATIVES **apocalyptically** adverb.
– ORIGIN early 17th cent. (as a noun denoting the writer of the Apocalypse, St John): from Greek *apokaluptikos*, from *apokaluptein* 'uncover' (see **APOCALYPSE**).

apocarpous /ˌapəˈkɑːpəs/ ▶ **adjective** Botany (of a flower, fruit, or ovary) having distinct carpels that are not joined together. Often contrasted with **SYNCARPOUS**.
– ORIGIN mid 19th cent.: from **APO-** + Greek *karpos* 'fruit' + **-OUS**.

apochromat /ˈapəkrəmat/ ▶ **noun** Physics a lens or lens system that reduces spherical and chromatic aberration.
– DERIVATIVES **apochromatic** adjective.
– ORIGIN early 20th cent.: from **APO-** + **CHROMATIC**.

apocope /əˈpɒkəpi/ ▶ **noun** [mass noun] Linguistics omission of the final sound of a word, as when *cup of tea* is pronounced as *cuppa tea*.
– ORIGIN mid 16th cent.: from late Latin, from Greek *apokoptein* 'cut off', from *apo-* 'from' + *koptein* 'to cut'.

Apocr. ▶ **abbreviation** Apocrypha.

apocrine /ˈapəkrʌɪn, -krɪn/ ▶ **adjective** Physiology relating to or denoting multicellular glands which release some of their cytoplasm in their secretions, especially the sweat glands associated with hair follicles in the armpits and pubic regions. Compare with **ECCRINE**.
– ORIGIN early 20th cent.: from **APO-** + Greek *krinein* 'to separate'.

Apocrypha /əˈpɒkrɪfə/ ▶ **plural noun** [treated as sing. or pl.] biblical or related writings not forming part of the accepted canon of Scripture. ■ (**apocrypha**) writings or reports not considered genuine.
– ORIGIN late Middle English: from ecclesiastical Latin *apocrypha (scripta)* 'hidden (writings)', from Greek *apokruphos*, from *apokruptein* 'hide away'.

apocryphal ▶ **adjective** (of a story or statement) of doubtful authenticity, although widely circulated as being true. ■ of or belonging to the Apocrypha.
– DERIVATIVES **apocryphally** adverb.

apodictic /ˌapəˈdɪktɪk/ (also **apodeictic** /-ˈdʌɪktɪk/) ▶ **adjective** formal clearly established or beyond dispute.
– ORIGIN mid 17th cent.: via Latin from Greek *apodeiktikos*, from *apodeiknunai* 'show off, demonstrate'.

apodosis /əˈpɒdəsɪs/ ▶ **noun** (pl. **apodoses** /-siːz/) Grammar the main clause of a conditional sentence (e.g. *I would agree* in *if you asked me I would agree*). Often contrasted with **PROTASIS**.
– ORIGIN early 17th cent.: via late Latin from Greek, from *apodidonai* 'give back'.

apodous /ˈapədəs/ ▶ **adjective** Zoology without feet or having only rudimentary feet.
– ORIGIN early 19th cent.: from Greek *apous*, *apod-* 'footless' (from *a-* 'without' + *pous*, *pod-* 'foot') + **-OUS**.

apogee /ˈapədʒiː/ ▶ **noun** **1** the highest point in the development of something; a climax or culmination: *a film which was the apogee of German expressionist cinema.*
2 Astronomy the point in the orbit of the moon or a satellite at which it is furthest from the earth. The opposite of **PERIGEE**.
– ORIGIN late 16th cent.: from French *apogée* or modern Latin *apogaeum*, from Greek *apogaion (diastēma)*, '(distance) away from earth', from *apo* 'from' + *gaia*, *gē* 'earth'.

apolar ▶ **adjective** chiefly Biochemistry having no electrical polarity.

apolitical ▶ **adjective** not interested or involved in politics: *he took an apolitical stance.*

Apollinaire /əˌpɒlɪˈnɛː/, French /apɔlinɛʀ/, Guillaume (1880–1918), French poet; pseudonym of *Wilhelm Apollinaris de Kostrowitzki*. He coined the term *surrealist* and was acknowledged by the surrealist poets as their precursor. Notable works: *Les Alcools* (1913) and *Calligrammes* (1918).

Apollinaris /əˌpɒlɪˈnɛːrɪs/ (*c.*310–*c.*390), bishop of Laodicea in Asia Minor. He upheld the heretical doctrine that Christ had a human body and soul but no human spirit, this being replaced by the divine Logos.
– DERIVATIVES **Apollinarian** adjective & noun.

Apollo 1 Greek Mythology a god, son of Zeus and Leto and brother of Artemis. He is associated with music, poetic inspiration, archery, prophecy, medicine, pastoral life, and the sun.
2 the American space programme for landing astronauts on the moon. *Apollo 8* was the first mission to orbit the moon (1968), *Apollo 11* was the first to land astronauts (1969), and five further landings took place up to 1972.

apollo ▶ noun (pl. **apollos**) a large butterfly which has creamy-white wings marked with black and red spots, found chiefly on the mountains of mainland Europe. ● *Parnassius apollo*, family Papilionidae.
– ORIGIN mid 19th cent.: from **APOLLO**.

Apollonian /ˌapəˈləʊnɪən/ ▶ adjective **1** Greek Mythology relating to the god Apollo.
2 relating to the rational, ordered, and self-disciplined aspects of human nature. Compare with **DIONYSIAC**.

Apollonius[1] /ˌapəˈləʊnɪəs/ (*c.*260–190 BC), Greek mathematician; known as **Apollonius of Perga**. He examined and redefined conic sections and was the first to use the terms *ellipse*, *parabola*, and *hyperbola* for these classes of curve.

Apollonius[2] /ˌapəˈləʊnɪəs/ (3rd century BC), Greek poet and grammarian; known as **Apollonius of Rhodes**. He is known for his *Argonautica*, an epic poem in Homeric style dealing with the expedition of the Argonauts.

Apollyon /əˈpɒljən/ a name for the Devil (Rev. 9:11).
– ORIGIN from late Latin (Vulgate), from Greek *Apolluōn* (translating **ABADDON**), from *apollunai*, from *apo-* 'quite' + *ollunai* 'destroy'.

apologetic ▶ adjective **1** expressing or showing regretful acknowledgement of an offence or failure: *she was very apologetic about the whole incident* | *an apologetic smile*.
2 constituting a formal defence or justification of a theory or doctrine.
– DERIVATIVES **apologetically** adverb.
– ORIGIN late Middle English (as a noun denoting a formal justification): from French *apologétique* or late Latin *apologeticus*, from Greek *apologētikos*, from *apologeisthei* 'speak in one's own defence', from *apologia* (see **APOLOGY**). The current sense dates from the mid 19th cent.

apologetics ▶ plural noun [treated as sing. or pl.] reasoned arguments or writings in justification of something, typically a theory or religious doctrine: *apologetics for the slave trade are quite out of order*.
– ORIGIN mid 18th cent.: from **APOLOGETIC**.

apologia /ˌapəˈləʊdʒɪə/ ▶ noun a formal written defence of one's opinions or conduct: *an apologia for book-banning*.
– ORIGIN late 18th cent.: from Latin (see **APOLOGY**).

apologist ▶ noun a person who offers an argument in defence of something controversial: *an enthusiastic apologist for fascism in the 1920s*.
– ORIGIN mid 17th cent.: from French *apologiste*, from Greek *apologizesthai* 'give an account' (see **APOLOGIZE**).

apologize (also **apologise**) ▶ verb [no obj.] express regret for something that one has done wrong: *I must apologize for disturbing you like this* | *we apologize to him for our error*.
– ORIGIN late 16th cent. (in the sense 'make a defensive argument'): from Greek *apologizesthai* 'give an account', from *apologos* (see **APOLOGUE**). In English the verb has always been used as if it were a direct derivative of *apology*.

apologue /ˈapəlɒɡ/ ▶ noun a moral fable, especially one with animals as characters.
– ORIGIN mid 16th cent.: from French, via Latin from Greek *apologos* 'story'.

apology ▶ noun (pl. **apologies**) **1** a regretful acknowledgement of an offence or failure: *we owe you an apology* | *my apologies for the delay*. ■ (**apologies**) a formal expression of regret at being unable to attend a meeting or social function: *Robert can't come and sends his apologies*.
2 (**an apology for**) a very poor or inadequate example of: *we were shown into an apology for a bedroom*.
3 another term for **APOLOGIA**.
– PHRASES **with apologies to** used to introduce a parody or adaptation of a particular person's work: *here, with apologies to Rudyard Kipling, is a more apt version of 'If'*.
– ORIGIN mid 16th cent. (denoting a formal defence against an accusation): from French *apologie*, or via late Latin from Greek *apologia* 'a speech in one's own defence', from *apo* 'away' + *-logia* (see **-LOGY**).

apolune /ˈapə(ʊ)luːn/ ▶ noun [mass noun] the point at which a spacecraft in lunar orbit is furthest from the moon. The opposite of **PERILUNE**.
– ORIGIN 1960s: from **APO-** + Latin *luna* 'moon', on the pattern of *apogee*.

apomict /ˈapəmɪkt/ ▶ noun Botany a plant which reproduces by apomixis.

apomixis /ˌapəˈmɪksɪs/ ▶ noun [mass noun] Botany asexual reproduction in plants, in particular agamospermy. Often contrasted with **AMPHIMIXIS**.
– DERIVATIVES **apomictic** adjective.
– ORIGIN early 20th cent.: from **APO-** + Greek *mixis* 'mingling'.

apomorphine /ˌapəˈmɔːfiːn/ ▶ noun [mass noun] Medicine a white crystalline compound used as an emetic and in the treatment of parkinsonism. ● A morphine derivative; chem. formula: $C_{17}H_{17}NO_2$.

aponeurosis /ˌapənjʊˈrəʊsɪs/ ▶ noun (pl. **aponeuroses** /-siːz/) Anatomy a sheet of pearly white fibrous tissue which takes the place of a tendon in sheet-like muscles having a wide area of attachment.
– DERIVATIVES **aponeurotic** adjective.
– ORIGIN late 17th cent.: modern Latin, from Greek *aponeurōsis*, from *apo* 'off, away' + *neuron* 'sinew' + **-OSIS**.

apophatic /ˌapəˈfatɪk/ ▶ adjective Theology (of knowledge of God) obtained through negating concepts that might be applied to him. The opposite of **CATAPHATIC**.
– ORIGIN mid 19th cent.: from Greek *apophatikos* 'negative', from *apophasis* 'denial', from *apo-* 'other than' + *phanai* 'speak'.

apophthegm /ˈapəθɛm/ (US **apothegm**) ▶ noun a concise saying or maxim; an aphorism.
– DERIVATIVES **apophthegmatic** /-θɛɡˈmatɪk/ adjective.
– ORIGIN mid 16th cent.: from French *apophthegme* or modern Latin *apothegma*, from Greek, from *apophthengesthai* 'speak out'.

apophyllite /əˈpɒfɪlʌɪt/ ▶ noun [mass noun] a mineral occurring typically as white glassy prisms, usually as a secondary mineral in volcanic rocks. It is a hydrated silicate and fluoride of calcium and potassium.
– ORIGIN early 19th cent.: from **APO-** + Greek *phullon* 'leaf' + **-ITE**[1].

apophysis /əˈpɒfɪsɪs/ ▶ noun (pl. **apophyses**) **1** Zoology & Anatomy a natural protuberance from a bone, or inside the shell or exoskeleton of a sea urchin or insect, for the attachment of muscles.
2 Botany a swelling at the base of the sporangium in some mosses.
3 Geology a small offshoot extending from an igneous intrusion into the surrounding rock.
– DERIVATIVES **apophyseal** adjective.
– ORIGIN late 16th cent.: modern Latin, from Greek *apophusis* 'offshoot', from *apo-* 'from, away' + *phusis* 'growth'.

apoplectic /ˌapəˈplɛktɪk/ ▶ adjective **1** informal overcome with anger; furious: *Mark was apoplectic with rage at the decision*.
2 dated relating to or denoting apoplexy (stroke): *an apoplectic attack*.
– DERIVATIVES **apoplectically** adverb.
– ORIGIN early 17th cent.: from French *apoplectique* or late Latin *apoplecticus*, from Greek *apoplēktikos*, from *apoplēssein* 'disable by a stroke'.

apoplexy /ˈapəplɛksi/ ▶ noun (pl. **apoplexies**) [mass noun] **1** dated unconsciousness or incapacity resulting from a cerebral haemorrhage or stroke.
2 informal extreme anger: *the decision has aroused apoplexy among environmentalists*.
– ORIGIN late Middle English: from Old French *apoplexie*, from late Latin *apoplexia*, from Greek *apoplēxia*, from *apoplēssein* 'disable by a stroke'.

apoprotein /ˌapəˈprəʊtiːn/ ▶ noun Biochemistry a protein which together with a prosthetic group forms a particular biochemical molecule such as a hormone or enzyme.

apoptosis /ˌapə(p)ˈtəʊsɪs/ ▶ noun [mass noun] Physiology the death of cells which occurs as a normal and controlled part of an organism's growth or development. Also called **PROGRAMMED CELL DEATH**.
– DERIVATIVES **apoptotic** /-ˈtɒtɪk/ adjective.
– ORIGIN 1970s: from Greek *apoptōsis* 'falling off', from *apo* 'from' + *ptōsis* 'falling, a fall'.

aporia /əˈpɔːrɪə, əˈpɒrɪə/ ▶ noun an irresolvable internal contradiction or logical disjunction in a text, argument, or theory. ■ [mass noun] Rhetoric the expression of doubt.
– DERIVATIVES **aporetic** adjective.
– ORIGIN mid 16th cent.: via late Latin from Greek, from *aporos* 'impassable', from *a-* 'without' + *poros* 'passage'.

aposematic /ˌapə(ʊ)sɪˈmatɪk/ ▶ adjective Zoology denoting coloration or markings serving to warn or repel predators.
– DERIVATIVES **aposematism** noun.
– ORIGIN late 19th cent.: from **APO-** 'away from' + Greek *sēma* 'sign' + **-ATIC**.

aposiopesis /ˌapə(ʊ)ˌsʌɪəˈpiːsɪs/ ▶ noun (pl. **aposiopeses** /-siːz/) [mass noun] Rhetoric the device of suddenly breaking off in speech.
– DERIVATIVES **aposiopetic** adjective.
– ORIGIN late 16th cent.: via Latin from Greek *aposiōpēsis*, from *aposiōpan* 'be silent'.

apostasy /əˈpɒstəsi/ ▶ noun [mass noun] the abandonment or renunciation of a religious or political belief or principle.
– ORIGIN Middle English: from ecclesiastical Latin *apostasia*, from a late Greek alteration of Greek *apostasis* 'defection'.

apostate /ˈapəsteɪt/ ▶ noun a person who renounces a religious or political belief or principle.
▶ adjective abandoning a religious or political belief or principle: *an apostate Roman Catholic*.
– DERIVATIVES **apostatical** adjective.
– ORIGIN Middle English: from ecclesiastical Latin *apostata*, from Greek *apostatēs* 'apostate, runaway slave'.

apostatize /əˈpɒstətʌɪz/ (also **apostatise**) ▶ verb [no obj.] renounce a religious or political belief or principle.
– ORIGIN mid 16th cent.: from medieval Latin *apostatizare*, from *apostata* (see **APOSTATE**).

a posteriori /eɪ, ɑː, pɒˌstɛrɪˈɔːrʌɪ, pɒˌstɪə-/ ▶ adjective relating to or denoting reasoning or knowledge which proceeds from observations or experiences to the deduction of probable causes. ■ (in general use) of the nature of an afterthought or subsequent rationalization.
▶ adverb in a way based on reasoning from known facts or past events rather than by making assumptions or predictions. ■ [sentence adverb] with hindsight; as an afterthought.
– ORIGIN early 17th cent.: Latin, 'from what comes after'.

apostle ▶ noun (**Apostle**) each of the twelve chief disciples of Jesus Christ. ■ an important early Christian teacher or pioneering missionary. ■ a vigorous and pioneering advocate or supporter of a particular policy, idea, or cause: *a man once known as the apostle of free-market economics*.

> The twelve Apostles were Peter, Andrew, James, John, Philip, Bartholomew, Thomas, Matthew, James (the Less), Judas (or Thaddaeus), Simon, and Judas Iscariot. After the suicide of Judas Iscariot his place was taken by Matthias.

– DERIVATIVES **apostleship** noun.
– ORIGIN Old English *apostol*, via ecclesiastical Latin from Greek *apostolos* 'messenger', from *apostellein* 'send forth'.

apostlebird ▶ noun a gregarious Australian bird of the mud-nester family, with grey, brown, and black plumage and a robust black bill. ● *Struthidea cinerea*, family Corcoracidae (or Grallinidae).
■ Austral. any of a number of other gregarious birds, especially babblers.
– ORIGIN early 20th cent.: named from the supposed habit of these birds of going about in flocks of twelve.

Apostles' Creed a statement of Christian belief used in the Western Church, dating from the 4th century and traditionally ascribed to the twelve Apostles.

Apostle spoon ▶ noun a teaspoon with the figure of an Apostle or saint on the handle.

apostolate /əˈpɒstəleɪt/ ▶ noun (chiefly in Roman Catholic contexts) the position or authority of an apostle or a religious leader. ■ a group of apostles or religious leaders. ■ a form of evangelistic activity or work.
– ORIGIN late Middle English: from ecclesiastical Latin *apostolatus*, from *apostulus* (see **APOSTLE**).

A

apostolic /ˌapəˈstɒlɪk/ ▸ adjective **1** relating to the Apostles: *apostolic writings*.
2 relating to the Pope, especially when he is regarded as the successor to St Peter: *an apostolic nuncio*.
– ORIGIN Middle English: from French *apostolique* or ecclesiastical Latin *apostolicus*, from Greek *apostolikos*, from *apostolos* (see APOSTLE).

Apostolic Fathers ▸ plural noun the Christian leaders immediately succeeding the Apostles.

apostolic succession ▸ noun (in Christian thought) the uninterrupted transmission of spiritual authority from the Apostles through successive popes and bishops, taught by the Roman Catholic Church but denied by most Protestants.

apostrophe¹ /əˈpɒstrəfi/ ▸ noun a punctuation mark (') used to indicate either possession (e.g. *Harry's book; boys' coats*) or the omission of letters or numbers (e.g. *can't; he's; 1 Jan. '99*).
– ORIGIN mid 16th cent. (denoting the omission of one or more letters): via late Latin, from Greek *apostrophos* 'accent of elision', from *apostrephein* 'turn away', from *apo* 'from' + *strephein* 'to turn'.

> **USAGE** Many people are uncertain when to use an apostrophe, and this confusion is probably increased by the fact that it is often omitted in company names (e.g. *Barclays Bank*). The apostrophe should be used when indicating possession (*Sue's cat*) or the omission of letters or numbers (*he's gone, 1 Jan. '09*). It should not be used in forming the plural of ordinary words, as in *apple's and pear's* or *I saw two dog's*, or in possessive pronouns such as **hers**, **yours**, or **theirs**. See also **USAGE** at **ITS**.

apostrophe² /əˈpɒstrəfi/ ▸ noun Rhetoric an exclamatory passage in a speech or poem addressed to a person (typically one who is dead or absent) or thing (typically one that is personified).
– ORIGIN mid 16th cent.: via Latin from Greek *apostrophē* 'turning away', from *apostrephein* 'turn away' (see APOSTROPHE¹).

apostrophize /əˈpɒstrəfʌɪz/ (also **apostrophise**) ▸ verb [with obj.] **1** Rhetoric address an exclamatory passage in a speech or poem to (someone or something).
2 punctuate (a word) with an apostrophe.

apothecaries' measure (also **apothecaries' weight**) ▸ noun [mass noun] historical systems of units formerly used in pharmacy for liquid volume (or weight). They were based respectively on the fluid ounce (= 8 drachms or 480 minims) and the ounce troy (= 8 drachms or 24 scruples or 480 grains).

apothecary /əˈpɒθɪk(ə)ri/ ▸ noun (pl. **apothecaries**) archaic a person who prepared and sold medicines and drugs.
– ORIGIN late Middle English: via Old French from late Latin *apothecarius*, from Latin *apotheca*, from Greek *apothēkē* 'storehouse'.

apothegm ▸ noun US spelling of APOPHTHEGM.

apothem /ˈapəθɛm/ ▸ noun Geometry a line from the centre of a regular polygon at right angles to any of its sides.
– ORIGIN late 19th cent.: from Greek *apotithenai* 'put aside, deposit', from *apo* 'away' + *tithenai* 'to place'.

apotheosis /əˌpɒθɪˈəʊsɪs/ ▸ noun (pl. **apotheoses** /-siːz/) **1** the highest point in the development of something; a culmination or climax: *his appearance as Hamlet was the apotheosis of his career*.
2 the elevation of someone to divine status.
– ORIGIN late 16th cent.: via ecclesiastical Latin from Greek *apotheōsis*, from *apotheoun* 'make a god of', from *apo* 'from' + *theos* 'god'.

apotheosize /əˈpɒθɪəsʌɪz/ (also **apotheosise**) ▸ verb [with obj.] elevate to, or as if to, the rank of a god; idolize.

apotropaic /ˌapətrəˈpeɪɪk/ ▸ adjective supposedly having the power to avert evil influences or bad luck: *apotropaic statues*.
– DERIVATIVES **apotropaically** adverb.
– ORIGIN late 19th cent.: from Greek *apotropaios* 'averting evil', from *apotrepein* 'turn away or from' + -IC.

app ▸ noun Computing short for APPLICATION (sense 5).

appal (US **appall**) ▸ verb (**appals, appalling, appalled**) [with obj.] (usu. **be appalled**) greatly dismay or horrify: *bankers are* ***appalled at*** *the economic incompetence of some ministers* | (as adj. **appalled**) *Alison looked at me, appalled*.
– ORIGIN Middle English: from Old French *apalir* 'grow pale', from *a-* (from Latin *ad* 'to, at') + *palir* 'to pale'. The original sense was 'grow pale', later 'make pale', hence 'horrify' (late Middle English).

Appalachian Mountains /ˌapəˈleɪ(t)ʃ(ə)n/ (also **the Appalachians**) a mountain system of eastern North America, stretching from Quebec and Maine in the North to Georgia and Alabama in the South. Its highest peak is Mount Mitchell in North Carolina, which rises to 2,037 m (6,684 ft).

Appalachian Trail a 3,200-km (about 2,000-mile) footpath through the Appalachian Mountains from Mount Katahdin in Maine to Springer Mountain in Georgia.

appalling ▸ adjective horrifying; shocking: *the cat suffered appalling injuries during the attack*. ■ informal shockingly bad; awful: *his conduct was appalling*.
– DERIVATIVES **appallingly** adverb.

Appaloosa /ˌapəˈluːsə/ ▸ noun a horse of a North American breed having dark spots on a light background.
– ORIGIN 1920s: from *Opelousas* in Louisiana, or *Palouse*, a river in Idaho.

appanage /ˈap(ə)nɪdʒ/ (also **apanage**) ▸ noun historical a provision made for the maintenance of the younger children of kings and princes, consisting of a gift of land, an official position, or money. ■ archaic a benefit or right belonging to someone; a perquisite: *the appanages of her rank*.
– ORIGIN early 17th cent.: from French, based on medieval Latin *appanare* 'provide with the means of subsistence', from *ad-* 'to' + *panis* 'bread'.

apparat /ˌapəˈrɑːt/ ▸ noun [in sing.] chiefly historical the administrative system of a communist party, especially in a communist country.
– ORIGIN Russian, from German, literally 'apparatus'.

apparatchik /ˌapəˈratʃɪk/ ▸ noun (pl. **apparatchiks** or **apparatchiki** /-kiː/) **1** chiefly historical a member of a Communist Party apparat.
2 derogatory or humorous an official in a large political organization: *Tory apparatchiks*.
– ORIGIN 1940s: from Russian, from *apparat* (see APPARAT).

apparatus /ˌapəˈreɪtəs/ ▸ noun (pl. **apparatuses**) **1** [mass noun] the technical equipment or machinery needed for a particular activity or purpose: *firemen wearing breathing apparatus*.
2 the complex structure of a particular organization or system: *the apparatus of government*.
3 (also **critical apparatus**) a collection of notes, variant readings, and other matter accompanying a printed text.
– ORIGIN early 17th cent.: Latin, from *apparare* 'make ready for', from *ad-* 'towards' + *parare* 'make ready'.

apparatus criticus /ˈkrɪtɪkəs/ ▸ noun (pl. **apparatus critici** /ˈkrɪtɪsʌɪ/) another term for APPARATUS (sense 3).

apparel ▸ noun [mass noun] formal or US clothing.
■ (**apparels**) embroidered ornamentation on ecclesiastical vestments.
▸ verb (**apparels, apparelling, apparelled**; US **apparels, appareling, appareled**) [with obj.] archaic clothe (someone): *all the vestments in which they used to apparel their Deities*.
– ORIGIN Middle English (as a verb in the sense 'make ready or fit'; as a noun 'furnishings, equipment'): from Old French *apareillier*, based on Latin *ad-* 'to' (expressing change) + *par* 'equal'.

apparent ▸ adjective **1** clearly visible or understood; obvious: *for no apparent reason she laughed* | [with clause] *it became apparent that he was talented*.
2 seeming real or true, but not necessarily so: *his apparent lack of concern*.
– ORIGIN late Middle English: from Old French *aparant*, from Latin *apparent-* 'appearing', from the verb *apparere* (see APPEAR).

apparent horizon ▸ noun see HORIZON (sense 1).

apparently ▸ adverb [sentence adverb] as far as one knows or can see: *the child nodded, apparently content with the promise*.

apparent magnitude ▸ noun Astronomy the magnitude of a celestial object as it is actually measured from the earth. Compare with ABSOLUTE MAGNITUDE.

apparent time ▸ noun another term for MEAN SOLAR TIME.

apparent wind ▸ noun the wind as it is experienced on board a moving sailing vessel, as a result of the combined effects of the true wind and the boat's speed.

apparition ▸ noun a ghost or ghostlike image of a person. ■ a remarkable or unexpected appearance of someone or something: *an apparition of the Virgin Mary*.
– DERIVATIVES **apparitional** adjective.
– ORIGIN late Middle English (in the sense 'the action of appearing'): from Latin *apparitio(n-)* 'attendance', from the verb *apparere* (see APPEAR).

appeal ▸ verb [no obj.] **1** make a serious, urgent, or heartfelt request: *police are* ***appealing for*** *information about the incident* | *she* ***appealed to*** *Germany for political asylum*. ■ (**appeal to**) try to persuade someone to do something by calling on (a particular principle or quality): *I appealed to his sense of justice*. ■ Cricket (of the bowler or fielders) call on the umpire to declare a batsman out, traditionally with a shout of 'How's that?'.
2 Law apply to a higher court for a reversal of the decision of a lower court: *he said he would* ***appeal against*** *the conviction*. ■ [with obj.] chiefly N. Amer. apply to a higher court for a reversal of (the decision of a lower court): *they have 48 hours to appeal the decision*.
3 be attractive or interesting: *the range of topics will* ***appeal to*** *youngsters*.
▸ noun **1** a serious, urgent, or heartfelt request: *his mother made an appeal for the return of the ring*.
■ Cricket a shout of 'How's that?' or a similar call by a bowler or fielder to an umpire to declare a batsman out. ■ [mass noun] entreaty: *a look of appeal on his face*.
■ an attempt to persuade someone do to something by calling on a particular principle or quality: *an appeal to their common cultural values*.
2 Law an application to a higher court for a decision to be reversed: *he has 28 days in which to lodge an appeal* | [mass noun] *the right of appeal*.
3 a request for donations to support a charity or cause: *a public appeal to raise £120,000*.
4 [mass noun] the quality of being attractive or interesting: *the popular appeal of football*.
– DERIVATIVES **appealer** noun.
– ORIGIN Middle English (in legal contexts): from Old French *apel* (noun), *apeler* (verb), from Latin *appellare* 'to address', based on *ad-* 'to' + *pellere* 'to drive'.

appealable ▸ adjective Law (of a case or ruling) able to be referred to a higher court for review.

appeal court ▸ noun a court that hears appeals, especially (**the Appeal Court**) the Court of Appeal.

appealing ▸ adjective **1** attractive or interesting: *village life is somehow more appealing*.
2 showing or expressing a desire for help or sympathy: *an appealing look*.
– DERIVATIVES **appealingly** adverb.

appear ▸ verb [no obj.] **1** come into sight; become visible or noticeable, especially without apparent cause: *smoke appeared on the horizon*. ■ come into existence or use: *the major life forms appeared on earth*. ■ be published or offered for sale: *the paperback edition didn't appear for another two years*. ■ feature or be shown: *the symbol* ***appears in*** *many paintings of the period*. ■ informal arrive at a place: *by ten o'clock Bill still hadn't appeared*.
2 present oneself formally in a court or tribunal: *he* ***appeared on*** *six charges of theft*.
3 perform publicly in a film, play, etc.: *he* ***appeared on*** *Broadway*.
4 seem; give the impression of being: [with infinitive] *she appeared not to know what was happening* | [with clause] *it appears unlikely that interest rates will fall*.
– ORIGIN Middle English: from Old French *apareir*, from Latin *apparere*, from *ad-* 'towards' + *parere* 'come into view'.

appearance ▸ noun **1** [mass noun] the way that someone or something looks: *she checked her appearance in the mirror*. ■ [count noun] an impression given by someone or something: *she read it with every appearance of interest*.
2 an act of performing or participating in a public event: *he is well known for his television appearances*.
3 an act of arriving or becoming visible: *the sudden appearance of her daughter startled her*. ■ a process of coming into existence or use: *the appearance of the railway*.
– PHRASES **keep up appearances** maintain an impression of wealth or well-being. **make** (or **put in**) **an appearance** attend an event briefly, especially as a matter of courtesy. **to** (or **by**) **all appearances** as far as can be seen: *to all appearances, it had been a normal day*.
– ORIGIN late Middle English: from Old French *aparance, aparence*, from late Latin *apparentia*, from Latin *apparere* (see APPEAR).

appearance money ▸ noun [mass noun] money paid to secure the appearance of a celebrity, especially a sports player, at a particular event.

A

appease ▸ **verb** [with obj.] **1** pacify or placate (someone) by acceding to their demands: *amendments have been added to appease local pressure groups*.
2 assuage or satisfy (a demand or a feeling): *we give to charity because it appeases our guilt*.
– DERIVATIVES **appeaser** noun.
– ORIGIN Middle English: from Old French *apaisier*, from *a-* (from Latin *ad* 'to, at') + *pais* 'peace'.

appeasement ▸ **noun** [mass noun] the action or process of appeasing: *a policy of appeasement*.

appellant /əˈpɛl(ə)nt/ ▸ **noun** Law a person who applies to a higher court for a reversal of the decision of a lower court.
– ORIGIN late Middle English: from French *apelant*, literally 'appealing', from the verb *apeler* (see APPEAL).

appellate /əˈpɛlət/ ▸ **adjective** [attrib.] Law (especially of a court) concerned with or dealing with applications for decisions to be reversed.
– ORIGIN late Middle English (originally in the sense 'appealed against, accused'): from Latin *appellatus* 'appealed against', from the verb *appellare* (see APPEAL). The current sense dates from the mid 18th cent.

appellation[1] /ˌapəˈleɪʃ(ə)n/ ▸ **noun** formal a name or title.
– ORIGIN late Middle English: via Old French from Latin *appellatio(n-)*, from the verb *appellare* (see APPEAL).

appellation[2] /ˌapəˈlasjɔ̃/, French /apɛlasjɔ̃/ ▸ **noun** an appellation contrôlée. ▪ a wine bearing such a guarantee. ▪ the district in which such wine is produced.
– ORIGIN abbreviation of *appellation (d'origine) contrôlée*.

appellation contrôlée /apəˌlasjɔ̃ kənˈtrəʊleɪ/, French /apɛlasjɔ̃ kɔ̃tʀɔle/ (also **appellation d'origine** /ˌdɒrɪˈʒiːn/, French /dɔʀiʒin/ **contrôlée**) ▸ **noun** a description awarded to French wine guaranteeing that it was produced in the region specified, using vines and production methods which satisfy the regulating body.
– ORIGIN French, literally 'controlled appellation'.

appellative /əˈpɛlətɪv/ ▸ **adjective** formal relating to or denoting the giving of a name.
▸ **noun** a common noun, such as 'doctor', 'mother', or 'sir', used as a vocative.
– ORIGIN late Middle English: from late Latin *appellativus*, from *appellat-* 'addressed', from the verb *appellare* (see APPEAL).

appellee /ˌapəˈliː, əˌpɛˈliː/ ▸ **noun** Law, chiefly US the defending party in a case taken to a higher court.
– ORIGIN mid 16th cent.: from French *appelé*, past participle of *appeler* 'call'. from Latin *appellare* 'to address' (see APPEAL).

append ▸ **verb** [with obj.] add (something) to the end of a written document: *the results of the survey are* ***appended to*** *this chapter*.
– ORIGIN late Middle English: from Latin *appendere* 'hang on', from *ad-* 'to' + *pendere* 'hang'.

appendage ▸ **noun 1** a thing that is added or attached to something larger or more important: *they treat Scotland as a mere appendage of England*.
2 Biology a projecting part of an invertebrate or other living organism, with a distinct appearance or function: *a pair of feathery appendages through which oxygen is absorbed*.

appendant formal ▸ **adjective** attached or added, especially in a subordinate capacity.
▸ **noun** a subordinate person or thing.
– ORIGIN late Middle English (in legal contexts): from Old French *apendant*, from *apendre* 'depend on, belong to', from Latin *appendere* (see APPEND).

appendectomy /ˌap(ə)nˈdɛktəmi/ (Brit. also **appendicectomy** /əˌpɛndɪˈsɛktəmi/) ▸ **noun** (pl. **appendectomies**) a surgical operation to remove the appendix.

appendicitis ▸ **noun** [mass noun] a serious medical condition in which the appendix becomes inflamed and painful.

appendicular /ˌap(ə)nˈdɪkjʊlə/ ▸ **adjective** Anatomy relating to a limb or limbs.
– ORIGIN mid 17th cent.: from Latin *appendicula* 'small appendage', diminutive of *appendix*, + -AR[1].

appendix /əˈpɛndɪks/ ▸ **noun** (pl. **appendixes** or **appendices** /-siːz/) **1** Anatomy a tube-shaped sac attached to and opening into the lower end of the large intestine in humans and some other mammals. In humans the appendix is small and has no known function, but in rabbits, hares, and some other herbivores it is involved in the digestion of cellulose. Also called VERMIFORM APPENDIX.
2 a section or table of subsidiary matter at the end of a book or document.
– ORIGIN mid 16th cent. (in sense 2): from Latin, from *appendere* 'hang upon' (see APPEND). Sense 1 dates from the early 17th cent.

USAGE Appendix typically has the plural **appendixes** in the anatomical sense, and **appendices** when referring to a part of a book or document.

apperception ▸ **noun** [mass noun] Psychology, dated the mental process by which a person makes sense of an idea by assimilating it to the body of ideas he or she already possesses.
– DERIVATIVES **apperceptive** adjective.
– ORIGIN mid 18th cent.: from French *aperception* or modern Latin *aperceptio(n-)*, from Latin *ad-* 'to' + *percipere* 'perceive'.

appertain /ˌapəˈteɪn/ ▸ **verb** [no obj.] **1** (**appertain to**) relate to; concern: *the answers generally appertain to improvements in standard of service*.
2 be appropriate or applicable: *the institutional arrangements which appertain under the system*.
– ORIGIN late Middle English: from Old French *apertenir*, from late Latin *appertinere*, from *ad-* 'to' + Latin *pertinere* 'to pertain'.

appestat /ˈapɪstat/ ▸ **noun** Physiology the region of the hypothalamus of the brain which is believed to control a person's appetite for food.
– ORIGIN 1950s: from APPETITE, probably on the pattern of *thermostat*.

appetency /ˈapɪt(ə)nsi/ (also **appetence**) ▸ **noun** (pl. **appetencies**) rare a longing or desire. ▪ a natural tendency or affinity.
– ORIGIN early 17th cent.: from Latin *appetentia*, from *appetere* 'seek after' (see APPETITE).

appetite ▸ **noun** a natural desire to satisfy a bodily need, especially for food: *he has a healthy appetite* | [mass noun] *they suffered from loss of appetite*. ▪ a strong desire or liking for something: *her appetite for life*.
– ORIGIN Middle English: from Old French *apetit* (modern *appétit*), from Latin *appetitus* 'desire for', from *appetere* 'seek after', from *ad-* 'to' + *petere* 'seek'.

appetitive /əˈpɛtɪtɪv/ ▸ **adjective** characterized by a natural desire to satisfy bodily needs: *the appetitive behaviour of animals*.
– ORIGIN mid 16th cent.: from French *appétitif* or medieval Latin *appetitivus*, from *appetire* 'seek after' (see APPETITE).

appetizer (also **appetiser**) ▸ **noun** a small dish of food or a drink taken before a meal or the main course of a meal to stimulate one's appetite.

appetizing (also **appetising**) ▸ **adjective** stimulating one's appetite: *the appetizing aroma of sizzling bacon*.
– DERIVATIVES **appetizingly** adverb.
– ORIGIN mid 17th cent.: from French *appétissant*, irregular formation from *appétit* (see APPETITE).

Appian Way /ˈapɪən/ the principal road southward from Rome in classical times, named after the censor Appius Claudius Caecus, who in 312 BC built the section to Capua; it was later extended to Brindisi. Latin name VIA APPIA.

applaud ▸ **verb** [no obj.] show approval or praise by clapping: *the crowd whistled and applauded* | [with obj.] *his speech was loudly applauded*. ▪ [with obj.] show strong approval of (a person or action); praise: *Jill applauded the decision*.
– ORIGIN late 15th cent.: from Latin *applaudere*, from *ad-* 'to' + *plaudere* 'to clap', reinforced by French *applaudir*.

applause ▸ **noun** [mass noun] approval or praise expressed by clapping: *they gave him* ***a round of applause***.
– ORIGIN late Middle English: from medieval Latin *applausus*, from the verb *applaudere* (see APPLAUD).

applause line ▸ **noun** US a statement in a political speech calculated to win a favourable response from an audience: *an urgent plea for health-care reform is still a reliable applause line*.

apple ▸ **noun 1** the round fruit of a tree of the rose family, which typically has thin green or red skin and crisp flesh. ▪ used in names of unrelated fruits or other plant growths that resemble apples in some way, e.g. **custard apple**, **oak apple**.
2 (also **apple tree**) the tree bearing apples, with hard pale timber that is used in carpentry and to smoke food. ● Genus *Malus*, family Rosaceae: numerous hybrids and cultivars.
– PHRASES **the apple never falls far from the tree** proverb salient family characteristics are usually inherited. **the apple of one's eye** a person of whom one is extremely fond and proud. [originally denoting the pupil of the eye, considered to be a globular solid body, extended as a symbol of something cherished.] **apples and oranges** N. Amer. (of two people or things) irreconcilably or fundamentally different. **apples and pears** Brit. rhyming slang stairs. **a rotten** (or **bad**) **apple** informal a bad or corrupt person in a group, especially one whose behaviour is likely to have a detrimental influence on the others. [with reference to the effect that a rotten apple has on fruit with which it is in contact.] **she's apples** Austral./NZ informal used to indicate that everything is in good order and there is nothing to worry about: *'Is the fire safe?' 'Yeah, she's apples.'* [from *apples and spice* or *apples and rice*, rhyming slang for 'nice'.] **upset the apple cart** spoil a plan or disturb the status quo.
– ORIGIN Old English *æppel*, of Germanic origin; related to Dutch *appel* and German *Apfel*.

apple butter ▸ **noun** [mass noun] N. Amer. a paste of spiced stewed apple used as a spread or condiment, typically made with cider.

apple-cheeked ▸ **adjective** (of a person) having round rosy cheeks.

apple green ▸ **noun** [mass noun] a bright green.

Apple Isle (also **Apple Island**) Austral. informal name for TASMANIA.
– DERIVATIVES **Apple Islander** noun.
– ORIGIN so named because it is a region popularly associated with apple-growing.

applejack ▸ **noun** [mass noun] N. Amer. an alcoholic drink distilled from fermented cider.
– ORIGIN early 19th cent.: from APPLE + JACK[1].

apple pie ▸ **noun 1** a pie made with apples.
2 [mass noun] N. Amer. used to represent a cherished ideal of homeliness: *to say I'm fed up with the Olympics is like being against* ***motherhood and apple pie***.
– PHRASES **apple-pie bed** a bed which, as a practical joke, has been made with one of the sheets folded back on itself so that a person's legs cannot be stretched out. **apple-pie order** perfect order or neatness: *everything was in apple-pie order*. **as American as apple pie** N. Amer. typically American in character.

apple-polisher ▸ **noun** N. Amer. informal a toady.
– DERIVATIVES **apple-polishing** noun.

applesauce ▸ **noun** [mass noun] N. Amer. informal nonsense: *Oh, applesauce! I will be glad when it's all over*.

applet /ˈaplɪt/ ▸ **noun** Computing a very small application, especially a utility program performing one or a few simple functions.
– ORIGIN 1990s: blend of APPLICATION and -LET.

Appleton, Sir Edward Victor (1892–1965), English physicist. He discovered a region of ionized gases (the Appleton layer) in the atmosphere above the Heaviside or E layer, and won the Nobel Prize for Physics in 1947.

applewood ▸ **noun** (**applewoods**) [mass noun] the timber of the apple tree.

appley ▸ **adjective** (especially of white wine) smelling or tasting of apples.

appliance ▸ **noun 1** a device or piece of equipment designed to perform a specific task: *electrical and gas appliances*.
2 a fire engine.
3 [mass noun] Brit. the action or process of bringing something into operation: *the appliance of science could increase crop yields*.

applianced ▸ **adjective** US (of a kitchen) having or fitted with appliances.

applicable ▸ **adjective** relevant or appropriate: *the same considerations are equally* ***applicable to*** *accident claims*.
– DERIVATIVES **applicability** noun, **applicably** adverb.
– ORIGIN mid 16th cent. (in the sense 'compliant'): from Old French, or from medieval Latin *applicabilis*, from the verb *applicare* (see APPLY).

applicant ▸ **noun** a person who makes a formal application for something, especially a job.
– ORIGIN early 19th cent.: from APPLICATION + -ANT.

application ▸ **noun 1** a formal request to an authority: *an application for leave* | [mass noun] *licences are available* ***on application*** | [as modifier] *an application form*.
2 [mass noun] the action of putting something into operation: *the application of general rules to particular cases* | [count noun] *massage has far-reaching medical applications*. ▪ practical use or relevance: *this principle has no application to the present case*.

A

3 [mass noun] the action of applying something to a surface: *paints suitable for application on fabric* | [count noun] *a fresh application of make-up.* ■ a medicinal substance applied to the skin.
4 [mass noun] sustained effort; hard work: *the job takes a great deal of patience and application.*
5 (also **application program**) Computing a program or piece of software designed to fulfil a particular purpose: *a database application.*
– DERIVATIVES **applicational** adjective.
– ORIGIN Middle English: via Old French from Latin *applicatio(n-)*, from the verb *applicare* (see APPLY).

application programming interface ▶ noun Computing a system of tools and resources in an operating system, enabling developers to create software applications.

applicative /ˈaplɪkeɪtɪv, əˈplɪkətɪv/ ▶ adjective relating to or involving the application of a subject or idea; practical or applied: *applicative algebra.*
– ORIGIN mid 17th cent.: from Latin *applicat-* 'set close or in contact, fastened to', from the verb *applicare* (see APPLY).

applicator ▶ noun a device used for inserting something or for applying a substance to a surface.
– ORIGIN mid 17th cent.: from Latin *applicat-* 'fastened to' (from the verb *applicare*) + -OR[1].

applied ▶ adjective [attrib.] (of a subject of study) put to practical use as opposed to being theoretical: *applied chemistry.* Compare with PURE.

applied linguistics ▶ plural noun [treated as sing.] the branch of linguistics concerned with practical applications of language studies, for example language teaching, translation, and speech therapy.

applied mathematics ▶ plural noun see MATHEMATICS.

appliqué /əˈpliːkeɪ/ ▶ noun [mass noun] ornamental needlework in which pieces of fabric are sewn or stuck on to a larger piece to form a picture or pattern.
▶ verb (**appliqués**, **appliquéing**, **appliquéd**) [with obj.] (usu. **be appliquéd with**) sew or stick pieces of fabric on to (a garment or larger piece of fabric) to form pictures or patterns: *the coat is appliquéd with exotic-looking cloth* | (as adj. **appliquéd**) *19th-century appliquéd silks.*
– ORIGIN mid 18th cent.: from French, past participle of *appliquer* 'apply', from Latin *applicare* (see APPLY).

apply ▶ verb (**applies**, **applying**, **applied**) **1** [no obj.] make a formal application or request: *you need to* ***apply to*** *the local authority for a grant* | [with infinitive] *a number of people have applied to vote by proxy.* ■ put oneself forward formally as a candidate for a job: *she had* ***applied for*** *a number of positions.*
2 [no obj.] be applicable or relevant: *prices do not* ***apply to*** *public holiday periods* | *normal rules apply.* ■ [with obj.] bring or put into operation or use: *the oil industry has failed to apply appropriate standards of care.*
3 [with obj.] put or spread (a substance) on a surface: *the sealer can be* ***applied to*** *new wood.* ■ use; exert: *smooth over with a cloth, applying even pressure.*
4 (**apply oneself**) give one's full attention to a task; work hard.
– DERIVATIVES **applier** noun.
– ORIGIN late Middle English: from Old French *aplier*, from Latin *applicare* 'fold, fasten to', from *ad-* 'to' + *plicare* 'to fold'.

appoggiatura /əˌpɒdʒəˈtjʊərə/ ▶ noun (pl. **appoggiaturas** or **appoggiature**) Music a grace note which delays the next note of the melody, taking half or more of its written time value.
– ORIGIN Italian, from *appoggiare* 'lean upon, rest'.

appoint ▶ verb [with obj.] **1** assign a job or role to (someone): *she has been* ***appointed to*** *the board* | *they* ***appointed*** *her* ***as*** *personnel manager.*
2 determine or decide on (a time or a place): *they appointed a day in May for the meeting.* ■ archaic decree: *such laws are appointed by God.*
3 Law decide the disposition of (property of which one is not the owner) under powers granted by the owner: *trustees appoint the capital to the beneficiaries.*
– DERIVATIVES **appointee** noun, **appointer** noun.
– ORIGIN late Middle English: from Old French *apointer*, from *a point* 'to a point'.

appointed ▶ adjective **1** (of a time or place) decided on beforehand; designated: *she arrived at the appointed time.*
2 (of a building or room) equipped or furnished in a specified way: *a luxuriously appointed lounge.*

appointive ▶ adjective N. Amer. (of a job) relating to or filled by appointment rather than election.

appointment ▶ noun **1** an arrangement to meet someone at a particular time and place: *she made an appointment with my receptionist.*
2 an act of assigning a job or position to someone: *his appointment as President.* ■ a job or position: *she took up an appointment as head of communications.* ■ a person appointed to a job or position.
3 (**appointments**) furniture or fittings: *the room was spartan in its appointments.*
– PHRASES **by appointment** having previously made an arrangement to do something: *visits are by appointment only.* **by appointment to the Queen** (in the UK) used by manufacturers to indicate that their products are sold to the queen and are therefore of guaranteed quality. **power of appointment** **1** power to select the holder of a particular job or position. **2** Law power to decide the disposal of property, in exercise of a right conferred by the owner.
– ORIGIN Middle English: from Old French *apointement*, from *apointer* (see APPOINT).

apport /əˈpɔːt/ ▶ noun a material object produced supposedly by occult means, especially at a seance.
– ORIGIN late 19th cent.: from French *apport* 'something brought', from *apporter* 'bring to'.

apportion ▶ verb [with obj.] divide up and share out: *voting power will be apportioned according to contribution.* ■ assign: *they did not* ***apportion*** *blame or liability* ***to*** *any one individual.*
– DERIVATIVES **apportionable** adjective.
– ORIGIN late 16th cent.: from Old French *apportionner* or medieval Latin *apportionare*, from *ad-* 'to' + *portionare* 'divide into portions'.

apportionment ▶ noun [mass noun] the action or result of apportioning something: *the apportionment of blame.* ■ the determination of the proportional number of members each US state sends to the House of Representatives, based on population figures.

appose /əˈpəʊz/ ▶ verb [with obj.] technical place (something) side by side with or close to something else: *the specimen was* ***apposed to*** *X-ray film.*
– ORIGIN late 16th cent.: from Latin *apponere*, on the pattern of words such as *compose*, *expose*.

apposite /ˈapəzɪt/ ▶ adjective apt in the circumstances or in relation to something: *an apposite quotation* | *the observations are* ***apposite to*** *the discussion.*
– DERIVATIVES **appositely** adverb, **appositeness** noun.
– ORIGIN late 16th cent.: from Latin *appositus*, past participle of *apponere* 'apply', from *ad-* 'towards' + *ponere* 'put'.

apposition ▶ noun [mass noun] **1** chiefly technical the positioning of things side by side or close together.
2 Grammar a relationship between two or more words or phrases in which the two units are grammatically parallel and have the same referent (e.g. *my friend Sue*; *the first US president, George Washington*).
– DERIVATIVES **appositional** adjective & noun.
– ORIGIN late Middle English: from late Latin *appositio(n-)*, from *apponere* 'to apply' (see APPOSITE).

appositive ▶ adjective & noun Grammar another term for APPOSITIONAL (see APPOSITION).
– ORIGIN late 17th cent.: from late Latin *appositivus* 'subsidiary'.

appraisal ▶ noun an act of assessing something or someone: *she carried out a thorough appraisal* | [mass noun] *the report has been subject to appraisal.* ■ a formal assessment, typically in an interview, of the performance of an employee over a particular period.

appraisal drilling ▶ noun [mass noun] drilling undertaken to establish the quality, quantity, and other characteristics of oil or gas in a newly discovered field.

appraise ▶ verb [with obj.] assess the value or quality of: *there is a need to appraise existing techniques* | (as adj. **appraising**) *she cast an appraising eye over the notes.* ■ assess the performance of (an employee) formally. ■ (of an official valuer) set a price on; value: *they appraised the painting at £200,000.*
– DERIVATIVES **appraisable** adjective, **appraisee** noun, **appraisement** noun, **appraiser** noun, **appraisingly** adverb, **appraisive** adjective.
– ORIGIN late Middle English (in the sense 'set a price on'): alteration of APPRIZE, by association with PRAISE. The current sense dates from the mid 19th cent.

> **USAGE** The verb **appraise** is frequently confused with **apprise**. **Appraise** means 'assess (someone or something)', as in *a need to* ***appraise*** *existing techniques*, or 'value', as in *have the gold watch appraised by an expert*, while **apprise** means 'inform (someone)' and is often used in the structure **apprise someone of something**, as in *psychiatrists were* ***apprised of*** *his condition*. People often incorrectly use **appraise** rather than **apprise**, as in *once* ***appraised of*** *the real facts, there was only one person who showed any opposition*.

appreciable ▶ adjective large or important enough to be noticed: *pupils may have to travel appreciable distances.*
– ORIGIN early 19th cent.: from French *appréciable*, from *apprécier* (see APPRECIATE).

appreciably ▶ adverb to an appreciable extent; considerably: *profits have grown appreciably over the last four years* | [as submodifier] *an appreciably higher risk.*

appreciate /əˈpriːʃɪeɪt, -sɪ-/ ▶ verb [with obj.] **1** recognize the full worth of: *she feels that he does not appreciate her.* ■ be grateful for (something): *I'd appreciate any information you could give me.*
2 understand (a situation) fully; grasp the full implications of: *they failed to appreciate the pressure he was under* | [with clause] *I appreciate that you cannot be held totally responsible.*
3 [no obj.] rise in value or price: *the dollar* ***appreciated against*** *the euro by 15 per cent.*
– DERIVATIVES **appreciator** noun, **appreciatory** /-ʃ(ɪ)ət(ə)ri/ adjective.
– ORIGIN mid 16th cent.: from late Latin *appretiat-* 'set at a price, appraised', from the verb *appretiare*, from *ad-* 'to' + *pretium* 'price'.

appreciation ▶ noun [mass noun] **1** recognition and enjoyment of the good qualities of someone or something: *I smiled in appreciation* | [count noun] *he had a fine appreciation of drawing.* ■ gratitude: *they would be the first to show their appreciation.* ■ [count noun] a written assessment of an artist or piece of work, typically a favourable one.
2 a full understanding of a situation: *the bank's lack of appreciation of their problems.*
3 [mass noun] increase in monetary value: *the appreciation of the dollar against the pound.*
– ORIGIN late Middle English: from French *appréciation*, from late Latin *appretiatio(n-)*, from the verb *appretiare* 'set at a price, appraise' (see APPRECIATE).

appreciative ▶ adjective feeling or showing gratitude or pleasure: *an appreciative audience* | *the team are very* ***appreciative of*** *your support.*
– DERIVATIVES **appreciatively** adverb, **appreciativeness** noun.

apprehend ▶ verb [with obj.] **1** arrest (someone) for a crime: *a warrant was issued but he has not been apprehended.*
2 understand or perceive: *we enter a field of vision we could not otherwise apprehend.* ■ archaic anticipate (something) with uneasiness or fear.
– ORIGIN late Middle English (originally in the sense 'grasp, get hold of (physically or mentally)'): from French *appréhender* or Latin *apprehendere*, from *ad-* 'towards' + *prehendere* 'lay hold of'.

apprehensible ▶ adjective archaic or literary capable of being understood or perceived: *a bat whirred, apprehensible only from the displacement of air.*
– ORIGIN early 17th cent.: from late Latin *apprehensibilis*, from Latin *apprehendere* (see APPREHEND).

apprehension ▶ noun [mass noun] **1** anxiety or fear that something bad or unpleasant will happen: *he felt sick with apprehension* | [count noun] *she had some apprehensions about the filming.*
2 understanding; grasp: *his first apprehension of such large issues.*
3 the action of arresting someone: *they acted with intent to prevent lawful apprehension.*
– ORIGIN late Middle English (in the sense 'learning, acquisition of knowledge'): from late Latin *apprehensio(n-)*, from *apprehendere* 'seize, grasp' (see APPREHEND).

apprehensive ▶ adjective **1** anxious or fearful that something bad or unpleasant will happen: *he felt apprehensive about going home.*
2 rare relating to perception or understanding.
– DERIVATIVES **apprehensively** adverb, **apprehensiveness** noun.
– ORIGIN late Middle English (in sense 2): from French *appréhensif* or medieval Latin *apprehensivus*, from Latin *apprehendere* 'seize, grasp' (see APPREHEND).

apprentice ▶ noun a person who is learning a trade from a skilled employer, having agreed to work for a fixed period at low wages: [as modifier] *an apprentice electrician.*
▶ verb [with obj.] (usu. **be apprenticed to**) employ (someone) as an apprentice: *Edward was apprenticed*

to a printer. ■ [no obj.] N. Amer. serve as an apprentice: *she apprenticed with midwives in San Francisco.*
– ORIGIN Middle English: from Old French *aprentis* (from *apprendre* 'learn', from Latin *apprehendere* 'apprehend'), on the pattern of words ending in *-tis*, *-tif*, from Latin *-tivus* (see -IVE).

apprenticeship ▶ **noun** the position of an apprentice: *he served his apprenticeship as a fitter.*

appress /əˈprɛs/ ▶ **verb** [with obj.] (usu. **be appressed**) technical press (something) close to something else: *the two cords can be closely* ***appressed to*** *one another.*
– ORIGIN early 17th cent.: from Latin *appress-* 'pressed close', from the verb *apprimere*, from *ad-* 'to' + *premere* 'to press'.

apprise /əˈprʌɪz/ ▶ **verb** [with obj.] inform or tell (someone): *I thought it right to* ***apprise*** *Chris* ***of*** *what had happened.*
– ORIGIN late 17th cent.: from French *appris*, *apprise*, past participle of *apprendre* 'learn, teach', from Latin *apprehendere* (see APPREHEND).

USAGE The verb **apprise** is frequently confused with **appraise**. See **USAGE** at **APPRAISE**.

apprize /əˈprʌɪz/ (also **apprise**) archaic ▶ **verb** [with obj.] **1** put a price on; appraise: *the sheriff was to apprize the value of the lands.*
2 value highly; esteem: *how highly your Highness apprizeth peace.*
– ORIGIN late Middle English: from Old French *aprisier*, from *a-* (from Latin *ad* 'to, at') + *prisier* 'to price, prize', from *pris* (see PRICE). The change in the ending in the 17th cent. was due to association with PRIZE[1].

appro ▶ **noun** (in phrase **on appro**) Brit. informal on approval.

approach ▶ **verb** [with obj.] **1** come near or nearer to (someone or something) in distance or time: *the train approached the main line* | [no obj.] *winter was approaching* | (as adj. **approaching**) *an approaching car.* ■ come close to (a number, level, or standard) in quality or quantity: *the population will approach 12 million by the end of the decade.* ■ archaic bring nearer: *all those changes shall serve to approach him the faster to the blest mansion.*
2 speak to (someone) for the first time about a proposal or request: *the department had been approached about funding.*
3 start to deal with (a situation or problem) in a certain way: *one must approach the matter with caution.*
▶ **noun 1** a way of dealing with a situation or problem: *we need a whole new* ***approach to*** *the job.*
2 an initial proposal or request made to someone: *the landowner made an approach to the developer.* ■ (**approaches**) dated behaviour intended to propose personal or sexual relations with someone: *feminine resistance to his approaches.*
3 [in sing.] the action of coming near or nearer to someone or something in distance or time: *the approach of winter.* ■ (**approach to**) an approximation to something: *the past is impossible to recall with any approach to accuracy.* ■ the part of an aircraft's flight in which it descends gradually towards an airfield or runway for landing. ■ (usu. **approaches**) a road, sea passage, or other way leading to a place: *the northern* ***approaches to*** *London.*
– ORIGIN Middle English: from Old French *aprochier*, *aprocher*, from ecclesiastical Latin *appropiare* 'draw near', from *ad-* 'to' + *propius* (comparative of *prope* 'near').

approachable ▶ **adjective 1** friendly and easy to talk to: *managers should be approachable.*
2 (of a place) able to be reached from a particular direction or by a particular means: *the site is approachable from the roundabout.*
– DERIVATIVES **approachability** noun.

approach road ▶ **noun** Brit. a road leading up to a particular place or feature.

approach shot ▶ **noun** Golf a stroke which sends the ball from the fairway on to or nearer the green.

approbate /ˈaprəbeɪt/ ▶ **verb** [with obj.] US rare approve formally; sanction: *a letter approbating the affair.*
– ORIGIN late Middle English: from Latin *approbat-* 'approved', from the verb *approbare*, from *ad-* 'to' + *probare* 'try, test' (from *probus* 'good').

approbation ▶ **noun** [mass noun] formal approval or praise: *a term of approbation.*
– DERIVATIVES **approbative** adjective, **approbatory** adjective.
– ORIGIN late Middle English: via Old French from Latin *approbatio(n-)*, from the verb *approbare* (see APPROBATE).

appropriate ▶ **adjective** /əˈprəʊprɪət/ suitable or proper in the circumstances: *this isn't the appropriate time or place* | *a measure* ***appropriate to*** *a wartime economy.*
▶ **verb** /əˈprəʊprɪeɪt/ [with obj.] **1** take (something) for one's own use, typically without the owner's permission: *the accused had appropriated the property.*
2 devote (money or assets) to a special purpose: *there can be problems in* ***appropriating*** *funds* ***for*** *legal expenses.*
– DERIVATIVES **appropriately** adverb [sentence adverb] *appropriately, the first recital will be given at the festival*, **appropriateness** noun, **appropriator** noun.
– ORIGIN late Middle English: from late Latin *appropriatus*, past participle of *appropriare* 'make one's own', from *ad-* 'to' + *proprius* 'own, proper'.

appropriation ▶ **noun 1** [mass noun] the action of appropriating something: *dishonest appropriation of property.* ■ the deliberate reworking of images and styles from earlier, well-known works of art.
2 a sum of money allocated officially for a particular use.
– ORIGIN late Middle English: from late Latin *appropriatio(n-)*, from *appropriare* 'make one's own' (see APPROPRIATE).

appropriationist ▶ **noun** often derogatory an artist whose work contains reworkings of well-known images by other artists: [as modifier] *appropriationist art.*

approval ▶ **noun** [mass noun] the action of approving something: *the road schemes have been given approval* | [count noun] *they have delayed the launch to await project approvals.* ■ the belief that someone or something is good or acceptable: *step-parents need to win a child's approval.*
– PHRASES **on approval** (of goods) supplied on condition that they may be returned if not satisfactory. **seal** (or **stamp**) **of approval** an official statement or indication that something is accepted or regarded favourably.

approve ▶ **verb** [with obj.] **1** officially agree to or accept as satisfactory: *the budget was approved by parliament* | (as adj. **approved**) *places on approved courses.* ■ [no obj.] believe that someone or something is good or acceptable: *I don't* ***approve of*** *romance* | *they would not approve.*
2 archaic prove; show: *he* ***approved himself*** *ripe for military command.*
– ORIGIN Middle English: from Old French *aprover*, from Latin *approbare* (see APPROBATE). The original sense was 'prove, demonstrate', later 'corroborate, confirm', hence 'pronounce to be satisfactory' (late Middle English).

approved school ▶ **noun** Brit. historical a residential institution for young offenders.

approving ▶ **adjective** showing or feeling approval of someone or something: *the wine drew approving comments from across the table.*
– DERIVATIVES **approvingly** adverb.

approx. ▶ **abbreviation** approximate(ly).

approximant ▶ **noun 1** Mathematics a function, series, or other expression which is an approximation to the solution of a problem.
2 Phonetics a consonant produced by bringing one articulator (the tongue or lips) close to another without actually touching it, as in English *r* and *w*.

approximate ▶ **adjective** /əˈprɒksɪmət/ close to the actual, but not completely accurate or exact: *the approximate time of death.*
▶ **verb** /əˈprɒksɪmeɪt/ [no obj.] come close or be similar to something in quality, nature, or quantity: *a leasing agreement* ***approximating to*** *ownership* | [with obj.] *reality can be approximated by computational techniques.* ■ [with obj.] estimate or calculate (a quantity) fairly accurately: *I had to approximate the weight of my horse.*
– DERIVATIVES **approximative** adjective.
– ORIGIN late Middle English (in the adjectival sense 'close, similar'): from late Latin *approximatus*, past participle of *approximare*, from *ad-* 'to' + *proximus* 'very near'. The verb (originally meaning 'bring close') arose in the mid 17th cent.; the current adjectival sense dates from the early 19th cent.

approximately ▶ **adverb** used to show that something is almost, but not completely, accurate or exact; roughly: *a journey of approximately two hours.*

approximation ▶ **noun** a value or quantity that is nearly but not exactly correct: *these figures are only approximations.* ■ a thing that is similar to something else, but is not exactly the same: *the band smashed up their equipment in an approximation of rock star behaviour.*

appurtenance /əˈpəːt(ɪ)nəns/ ▶ **noun** (usu. **appurtenances**) an accessory or other item associated with a particular activity or style of living: *the appurtenances of consumer culture.*
– ORIGIN Middle English: from Old French *apertenance*, based on late Latin *appertinere* 'belong to' (see APPERTAIN).

appurtenant ▶ **adjective** belonging; pertinent: *properties* ***appurtenant to*** *the main building.*
– ORIGIN late Middle English: from Old French *apartenant* 'appertaining', from the verb *apartenir* (see APPERTAIN).

APR ▶ **abbreviation** annual or annualized percentage rate (used typically of interest on loans or credit).

Apr. ▶ **abbreviation** April.

apraxia /əˈpraksɪə/ ▶ **noun** [mass noun] Medicine inability to perform particular purposive actions, as a result of brain damage.
– DERIVATIVES **apraxic** adjective.
– ORIGIN late 19th cent.: from German *Apraxie*, from Greek *apraxia* 'inaction'.

après- /ˈapreɪ/ ▶ **prefix** informal, humorous coming after in time, typically specifying a period following an activity: *après-shopping.*
– ORIGIN French, 'after', used in combinations on the pattern of *après-ski*.

après-ski ▶ **noun** [mass noun] the social activities and entertainment following a day's skiing.
– DERIVATIVES **après-skiing** noun.
– ORIGIN 1950s: from French, literally 'after skiing'.

apricot /ˈeɪprɪkɒt/ ▶ **noun 1** a juicy, soft fruit of an orange-yellow colour resembling a small peach. ■ [mass noun] an orange-yellow colour like the skin of a ripe apricot.
2 (also **apricot tree**) the tree bearing apricots.
● *Prunus armeniaca*, family Rosaceae.
– ORIGIN mid 16th cent.: from Portuguese *albricoque* or Spanish *albaricoque*, from Spanish Arabic *al* 'the' + *barqūq* (via late Greek from Latin *praecoquum*, variant of *praecox* 'early-ripe'); influenced by Latin *apricus* 'ripe' and French *abricot*.

April ▶ **noun** the fourth month of the year, in the northern hemisphere usually considered the second month of spring: *the prison was to close in April* | *the show opens next April.*
– ORIGIN Old English, from Latin *Aprilis*.

April Fool ▶ **noun** a person who is the victim of a trick or hoax on April Fool's Day. ■ a trick or hoax on April Fool's Day.

April Fool's Day (also **April Fools' Day**) ▶ **noun** 1 April, in many Western countries traditionally an occasion for playing tricks. This custom has been observed for hundreds of years, but its origin is unknown. Also called **ALL FOOLS' DAY**.

a priori /ˌeɪ prʌɪˈɔːrʌɪ, ˌɑː priːˈɔːri/ ▶ **adjective** relating to or denoting reasoning or knowledge which proceeds from theoretical deduction rather than from observation or experience: *a priori assumptions about human nature.*
▶ **adverb** in a way based on theoretical deduction rather than empirical observation: *sexuality may be a factor but it cannot be assumed a priori.*
– DERIVATIVES **apriorism** /eɪˈprʌɪərɪz(ə)m/ noun.
– ORIGIN late 16th cent.: Latin, 'from what is before'.

apron ▶ **noun 1** a protective garment worn over the front of one's clothes and tied at the back. ■ a similar garment worn as part of official dress, as by a bishop or Freemason. ■ a sheet of lead worn to shield the body during an X-ray examination.
2 a small area adjacent to another larger area or structure: *a tiny* ***apron of*** *garden.* ■ a hard-surfaced area on an airfield used for manoeuvring or parking aircraft. ■ (also **apron stage**) a projecting strip of stage for playing scenes in front of the curtain. ■ US an area of asphalt where the drive of a house meets the road. ■ the narrow strip of a boxing ring lying outside the ropes.
3 Geology an extensive outspread deposit of sediment, typically at the foot of a glacier or mountain.
4 [often as modifier] an endless conveyor made of overlapping plates: *apron feeders bring coarse ore to a grinding mill.*
– PHRASES **tied to someone's apron strings** too much under someone's influence and control.
– ORIGIN Middle English *naperon*, from Old French, diminutive of *nape*, *nappe* 'tablecloth', from Latin *mappa* 'napkin'. The *n* was lost by wrong division of *a napron*; compare with ADDER[1].

A

aproned ▸ adjective wearing an apron: *aproned waiters in white caps.*

apropos /ˌaprəˈpəʊ, ˈaprəpəʊ/ ▸ preposition with reference to; concerning: *she remarked **apropos of** the initiative, 'It's not going to stop the abuse.'*
▸ adjective [predic.] very appropriate to a particular situation: *the song feels **apropos to** a midnight jaunt.*
– PHRASES **apropos of nothing** having no relevance to any previous discussion or situation.
– ORIGIN mid 17th cent.: from French *à propos* '(with regard) to (this) purpose'.

apsara /ˈʌpsərɑː/ (also **apsaras** /ˈʌpsərɑːs/) ▸ noun (pl. **apsaras** or **apsarases**) (in Hindu mythology) a celestial nymph, typically the wife of a heavenly musician.
– ORIGIN from Hindi *apsarā*, from Sanskrit *apsarās*.

apse /aps/ ▸ noun **1** a large semicircular or polygonal recess in a church, arched or with a domed roof and typically at the church's eastern end.
2 another term for **APSIS**.
– DERIVATIVES **apsidal** /ˈapsɪd(ə)l/ adjective.
– ORIGIN early 19th cent. (in sense 2): from Latin *apsis* (see **APSIS**).

apsis /ˈapsɪs/ ▸ noun (pl. **apsides** /-diːz/) either of two points on the orbit of a planet or satellite that are nearest to or furthest from the body round which it moves.
– DERIVATIVES **apsidal** adjective.
– ORIGIN early 17th cent. (denoting the orbit of a planet): via Latin from Greek *apsis*, *hapsis* 'arch, vault', perhaps from *haptein* 'fasten, join'.

apt ▸ adjective **1** appropriate or suitable in the circumstances: *the theme could not be more apt.*
2 [predic., with infinitive] having a tendency to do something: *he is apt to be swayed by irrational considerations.*
3 quick to learn: *she proved an apt pupil.*
– DERIVATIVES **aptly** adverb.
– ORIGIN late Middle English (in the sense 'suited, appropriate'): from Latin *aptus* 'fitted', past participle of *apere* 'fasten'.

apt. ▸ abbreviation N. Amer. apartment.

apterous /ˈapt(ə)rəs/ ▸ adjective Entomology (of an insect) having no wings.
– ORIGIN late 18th cent.: from Greek *apteros* (from *a-* 'without' + *pteron* 'wing') + **-OUS**.

Apterygota /apˈtɛrɪˌgəʊtə/ ▸ plural noun Entomology a group of insects which includes the bristletails and springtails, having a primitive body form without wings and no distinct larval stage. Compare with **PTERYGOTA**. • Subclass Apterygota, class Insecta (or Hexapoda): several orders, some of which are sometimes excluded from the Insecta.
– ORIGIN modern Latin *Apterygota*, from Greek *a-* 'not' + *pterugōtos* 'winged'.

apterygote ▸ noun Entomology a primitive wingless insect of the group Apterygota, which includes the bristletails and springtails.

aptitude ▸ noun a natural ability to do something: *children with an **aptitude for** painting and drawing.* ■ a natural tendency: *his **aptitude for** deceit.*
– ORIGIN late Middle English: via Old French from late Latin *aptitudo*, from *aptus* (see **APT**).

aptitude test ▸ noun a test designed to determine a person's ability in a particular skill or field of knowledge.

aptness ▸ noun [mass noun] the quality of being appropriate or suitable: *the aptness of the punishment.*

APU ▸ abbreviation auxiliary power unit, a device used on aircraft to provide power while on the ground and to start the main engines.

Apuleius /ˌapjʊˈliːəs/ (born *c.*123 AD), Roman writer, born in Africa. His writings are characterized by an exuberant and bizarre use of language. Notable works: *Metamorphoses* (*The Golden Ass*).

Apulia /əˈpjuːlɪə/ a region of SE Italy, extending into the 'heel' of the peninsula; capital, Bari. Italian name **PUGLIA**.
– DERIVATIVES **Apulian** noun & adjective.

Apus /ˈeɪpəs/ Astronomy a faint southern constellation (the Bird of Paradise), close to the south celestial pole.
– ORIGIN Latin, denoting a kind of bird, from Greek *apous*.

Aqaba /ˈakəbə/ Jordan's only port, at the head of the Gulf of Aqaba; pop. 79,839 (2004).

Aqaba, Gulf of a part of the Red Sea extending northwards between the Sinai and Arabian peninsulas.

aqua¹ /ˈakwə/ ▸ noun [mass noun] a light bluish-green colour; aquamarine.
– ORIGIN 1930s: abbreviation of **AQUAMARINE**.

aqua² /ˈakwə/ ▸ noun [mass noun] (especially in pharmaceutical and commercial use) water.
– ORIGIN Latin.

aqua- /ˈakwə/ ▸ combining form relating to water: *aquaculture.* ■ relating to water sports or aquatic entertainment: *aquarobics*.
– ORIGIN from Latin *aqua* 'water'.

aqua aura ▸ noun [mass noun] quartz or other mineral to which a thin film of gold has been applied, giving it a blue iridescent colour.
– ORIGIN 1990s: from Latin *aqua* 'water' + *aura*, representing Latin *aurum* 'gold'.

aquacade /ˌakwəˈkeɪd/ ▸ noun US a spectacle involving swimming and diving, usually with musical accompaniment.

aquaculture ▸ noun [mass noun] Botany the rearing of aquatic animals or the cultivation of aquatic plants for food.
– ORIGIN mid 19th cent.: from Latin *aqua* 'water' + **CULTURE**, on the pattern of words such as *agriculture*.

aqua fortis /ˈfɔːtɪs/ ▸ noun archaic term for **NITRIC ACID**.
– ORIGIN late 15th cent.: from Latin, literally 'strong water'.

aqualung ▸ noun a portable breathing apparatus for divers, consisting of cylinders of compressed air strapped on the diver's back, feeding air automatically through a mask or mouthpiece.
– ORIGIN 1950s (originally a proprietary name in the US): from Latin *aqua* 'water' + **LUNG**.

aquamanile /ˌakwəməˈnʌɪli, -ˈniːli/ ▸ noun a water container or ewer, typically in the form of a mammal or bird, used in medieval times.
– ORIGIN late 19th cent.: from late Latin, from Latin *aquaemanalis*, literally 'ewer of water'.

aquamarine ▸ noun a precious stone consisting of a light bluish-green variety of beryl. ■ a light bluish-green colour: [as modifier] *the aquamarine water.*
– ORIGIN early 18th cent.: from Latin *aqua marina* 'seawater'.

aquanaut ▸ noun a person who swims under water using an aqualung.
– ORIGIN late 19th cent.: from Latin *aqua* 'water' + Greek *nautēs* 'sailor'.

aquaplane ▸ noun a board for riding on water, pulled by a speedboat.
▸ verb [no obj.] (of a vehicle) slide uncontrollably on a wet surface: *the plane is believed to have aquaplaned on the runway.*
– ORIGIN early 20th cent. (originally US): from Latin *aqua* 'water' + **PLANE**¹.

aquaplaning ▸ noun [mass noun] the sport of riding on an aquaplane.

aqua regia /ˈriːdʒə/ ▸ noun [mass noun] Chemistry a mixture of concentrated nitric and hydrochloric acids. It is a highly corrosive liquid able to attack gold and other resistant substances.
– ORIGIN early 17th cent.: Latin, literally 'royal water'.

aquarelle /ˌakwəˈrɛl/ ▸ noun [mass noun] the technique of painting with thin, transparent watercolours (as distinct from gouache). ■ [count noun] a painting of this kind.
– ORIGIN mid 19th cent.: from French, from Italian *acquarella* 'watercolour', diminutive of *acqua*, from Latin *aqua* 'water'.

Aquarian /əˈkwɛːrɪən/ Astrology ▸ noun a person born under the sign of Aquarius.
▸ adjective relating to the sign of Aquarius. ■ relating to the Age of Aquarius.

aquarist /ˈakwərɪst/ ▸ noun a person who keeps an aquarium.

aquarium ▸ noun (pl. **aquaria** /-rɪə/ or **aquariums**) a transparent tank of water in which live fish and other water creatures and plants are kept. ■ a building containing tanks of live fish of different species.
– ORIGIN mid 19th cent.: from Latin, neuter of *aquarius* 'of water', on the pattern of *vivarium*.

Aquarius /əˈkwɛːrɪəs/ **1** Astronomy a large constellation (the Water Carrier or Water Bearer), said to represent a man pouring water from a jar. It contains no bright stars but has several planetary nebulae.
2 Astrology the eleventh sign of the zodiac, which the sun enters about 21 January. ■ **(an Aquarius)** a person born when the sun is in this sign.
– PHRASES **Age of Aquarius** an astrological age which is about to begin, marked by the precession of the vernal equinox into Aquarius, believed by some to herald worldwide peace and harmony.
– ORIGIN Latin *aquarius* 'of water', used as a noun to mean 'water carrier'.

aquarobics /ˌakwəˈrəʊbɪks/ ▸ plural noun [often treated as sing.] aerobic exercises performed in water.
– ORIGIN 1980s: blend of **AQUA-** and **AEROBICS**.

aquatic /əˈkwatɪk, -ˈkwɒt-/ ▸ adjective relating to water. ■ (of a plant or animal) growing or living in or near water.
▸ noun **1** an aquatic plant or animal, especially one suitable for a pond or aquarium.
2 (aquatics) sports played in or on water.
– ORIGIN late 15th cent. (in the sense 'watery, rainy'): from Old French *aquatique* or Latin *aquaticus*, from *aqua* 'water'.

aquatint ▸ noun a print resembling a watercolour, made by etching a copper plate with nitric acid and using resin and varnish to produce areas of tonal shading. ■ [mass noun] the technique or process of producing aquatints.
▸ verb [with obj.] produce (a print) in this way.
– ORIGIN late 18th cent.: from French *aquatinte*, from Italian *acqua tinta* 'coloured water'.

aquavit /ˌakwəˈviːt/ (also **akvavit**) ▸ noun [mass noun] an alcoholic spirit made from potatoes or other starchy plants.
– ORIGIN late 19th cent.: from Norwegian, Swedish, and Danish *akvavit* (see **AQUA VITAE**).

aqua vitae /ˈvʌɪtiː, ˈviːtʌɪ/ ▸ noun [mass noun] strong alcoholic spirit, especially brandy.
– ORIGIN late Middle English: from Latin, literally 'water of life'; compare with **AQUAVIT**, **EAU DE VIE**, **USQUEBAUGH**, and **WHISKY**.

aqueduct /ˈakwɪdʌkt/ ▸ noun **1** a bridge or viaduct carrying a waterway over a valley or other gap. ■ an artificial channel for conveying water.
2 Anatomy a small duct in the body containing fluid.
– ORIGIN mid 16th cent.: from obsolete French (now *aqueduc*), from Latin *aquae ductus* 'conduit', from *aqua* 'water' + *ducere* 'to lead'.

aqueduct of Sylvius /ˈsɪlvɪəs/ ▸ noun Anatomy a fluid-filled canal which runs through the midbrain connecting the third and fourth ventricles. Also called **CEREBRAL AQUEDUCT**.

aqueous /ˈeɪkwɪəs/ ▸ adjective of or containing water: *an aqueous solution of potassium permanganate.* ■ like water; watery: *an eerie, aqueous light.*
– ORIGIN mid 17th cent.: from medieval Latin *aqueus*, from Latin *aqua* 'water'.

aqueous humour ▸ noun [mass noun] the clear fluid filling the space in the front of the eyeball between the lens and the cornea. Compare with **VITREOUS HUMOUR**.

aquifer /ˈakwɪfə/ ▸ noun a body of permeable rock which can contain or transmit groundwater.
– ORIGIN early 20th cent.: from Latin *aqui-* (from *aqua* 'water') + *-fer* 'bearing'.

Aquila¹ /ˈakwɪlə, əˈkwɪlə/ Astronomy a small northern constellation (the Eagle), said to represent the eagle that carried Ganymede to Olympus. It contains the bright star Altair, and some rich star fields of the Milky Way.
– ORIGIN Latin.

Aquila² /ˈakwɪlə/ a city in east central Italy, capital of Abruzzi region; pop. 72,988 (2008). Italian name **L'AQUILA**.

aquilegia /ˌakwɪˈliːdʒə/ ▸ noun a plant of the buttercup family, which bears showy flowers with backward-pointing spurs. Native to temperate regions of the northern hemisphere, it is widely grown in gardens. • Genus *Aquilegia*, family Ranunculaceae. See also **COLUMBINE**.
– ORIGIN from medieval Latin, probably from Latin *aquilegus* 'water-collecting'.

aquiline /ˈakwɪlʌɪn/ ▸ adjective like an eagle. ■ (of a person's nose) hooked or curved like an eagle's beak.
– ORIGIN mid 17th cent.: from Latin *aquilinus*, from *aquila* 'eagle'.

Aquinas, St Thomas /əˈkwʌɪnəs/ (1225–74), Italian philosopher, theologian, and Dominican friar; known as **the Angelic Doctor**.

> He is regarded as the greatest figure of scholasticism; one of his most important achievements was the introduction of the work of Aristotle to Christian western Europe. His works include commentaries on Aristotle as well as the *Summa Contra Gentiles*, intended as a manual for missionaries, and *Summa Theologiae*, the greatest achievement of medieval systematic theology. He also devised the official Roman Catholic tenets. Feast day, 28 January.

Aquitaine¹ /ˌakwɪˈteɪn/, French /akitɛn/ a region and former province of SW France, on the Bay of Biscay, centred on Bordeaux. It became an English possession by the marriage of Eleanor of Aquitaine to Henry II, and remained so until 1453.

Aquitaine², Eleanor of, see ELEANOR OF AQUITAINE.

aquiver /əˈkwɪvə/ ▶ adjective [predic.] quivering; trembling: *her face was aquiver with pleasure.*

AR ▶ abbreviation ■ US Arkansas (in official postal use). ■ Autonomous Republic.

Ar ▶ symbol the chemical element argon.

ar- ▶ prefix variant spelling of AD- assimilated before *r* (as in *arrive, arrogate*).

-ar¹ ▶ suffix **1** (forming adjectives) of the kind specified; relating to: *lunar* | *molecular*.
2 forming nouns such as *scholar*.
– ORIGIN from Old French *-aire, -ier*, or from Latin *-aris*.

-ar² ▶ suffix forming nouns such as *pillar*.
– ORIGIN via Old French from Latin *-are* (neuter of *-aris*).

-ar³ ▶ suffix forming nouns such as *bursar, exemplar, vicar*.
– ORIGIN from Old French *-aire, -ier*, or from Latin *-arius, -arium*.

-ar⁴ ▶ suffix alteration of -ER¹, -OR¹ (as in *liar, pedlar*).

ARA ▶ abbreviation Associate of the Royal Academy.

Ara /ˈɑːrə/ Astronomy a small and faint southern constellation (the Altar), in the Milky Way near Scorpius.
– ORIGIN Latin.

Arab /ˈarəb, ˈeɪrab/ ▶ noun **1** a member of a Semitic people, originally from the Arabian peninsula and neighbouring territories, inhabiting much of the Middle East and North Africa.
2 a horse of a breed originating in Arabia, with a distinctive high-set tail.
▶ adjective relating to Arabian people: *Arab countries.*
– ORIGIN via Latin and Greek from Arabic *ʻarab*.

arabesque /ˌarəˈbɛsk/ ▶ noun **1** Ballet a posture in which one leg is extended backwards at right angles, the torso bent forwards, and the arms outstretched, one forwards and one backwards.
2 an ornamental design consisting of intertwined flowing lines, originally found in ancient Islamic art: [as modifier] *arabesque scrolls.*
3 Music a passage or composition with fanciful ornamentation of the melody.
– ORIGIN mid 17th cent.: from French, from Italian *arabesco* 'in the Arabic style', from *arabo* 'Arab'.

Arabia /əˈreɪbɪə/ (also **Arabian peninsula**) a peninsula of SW Asia, largely desert, lying between the Red Sea and the Persian Gulf and bounded on the north by Jordan and Iraq. The original homeland of the Arabs and the historic centre of Islam, it comprises the states of Saudi Arabia, Yemen, Oman, Bahrain, Kuwait, Qatar, and the United Arab Emirates.

Arabian ▶ adjective relating to Arabia or its inhabitants.
▶ noun historical a native or inhabitant of Arabia. ■ an Arab horse.

Arabian camel ▶ noun the domesticated one-humped camel, probably native to the deserts of North Africa and SW Asia. See also DROMEDARY.
● *Camelus dromedarius*, family Camelidae.

Arabian Desert the desert in eastern Egypt, between the Nile and the Red Sea. Also called the EASTERN DESERT.

Arabian Gulf another name for PERSIAN GULF.

Arabian Nights a collection of stories and romances written in Arabic, called in full *The Arabian Nights' Entertainment*. The king of Samarkand has killed all his wives after one night's marriage until he marries Scheherazade, who saves her life by entertaining him with stories. The stories include the tales of Aladdin and Sinbad the Sailor. Also called THOUSAND AND ONE NIGHTS.

Arabian peninsula another name for ARABIA.

Arabian Sea the north-western part of the Indian Ocean, between Arabia and India.

Arabic ▶ noun [mass noun] the Semitic language of the Arabs, spoken by some 150 million people throughout the Middle East and North Africa.
▶ adjective relating to the literature or language of Arab people.

> Arabic is written from right to left in a cursive script of twenty-eight consonants, the vowels being indicated by additional signs. The classical or literary language is based largely on that of the Koran; colloquial Arabic has many dialects. The script has been adapted for various languages, including Persian, Urdu, Malay, and (formerly) Turkish.

– DERIVATIVES **Arabicization** (also **Arabicisation**) noun, **Arabicize** (also **Arabicise**) verb.
– ORIGIN Middle English: via Latin *arabicus* from Greek *arabikos*, from *Araps, Arab-* 'Arab', from the Arabic (see ARAB).

arabica /əˈrabɪkə/ ▶ noun **1** [mass noun] coffee or coffee beans from the most widely grown coffee plant.
2 the bush that produces these beans, native to the Old World tropics. ● *Coffea arabica*, family Rubiaceae. See also ROBUSTA.
– ORIGIN 1920s: from Latin, feminine of *arabicus* (see ARABIC).

Arabic numeral ▶ noun any of the numerals 0, 1, 2, 3, 4, 5, 6, 7, 8, and 9. Arabic numerals reached western Europe (replacing Roman numerals) through Arabia by about AD 1200 but probably originated in India.

arabinose /ˈarəbɪnəʊz, -s/ ▶ noun [mass noun] Chemistry a sugar of the pentose class which is a constituent of many plant gums.
– ORIGIN late 19th cent.: from ARABICA + -IN¹ + -OSE².

arabis /ˈarəbɪs/ ▶ noun a low-growing herbaceous plant which typically bears white or pink flowers, frequently grown in rock gardens. Also called ROCK CRESS or WALL CRESS. ● Genus *Arabis*, family Cruciferae.
– ORIGIN via medieval Latin from Greek, feminine of *Araps, Arab-* (see ARABIC).

Arabism ▶ noun **1** [mass noun] Arab culture or identity. ■ support for Arab nationalism or political interests.
2 an Arabic linguistic usage, word, or phrase.
– DERIVATIVES **Arabist** noun & adjective.

Arabize (also **Arabise**) ▶ verb [with obj.] (usu. as adj. **Arabized**) give (someone or something) an Arab or Arabic character: *an Arabized script.*
– DERIVATIVES **Arabization** noun.

arable ▶ adjective (of land) used or suitable for growing crops. ■ (of crops) able to be grown on such land. ■ concerned with growing such crops: *arable farming.*
▶ noun [mass noun] arable land or crops.
– ORIGIN late Middle English: from Old French, or from Latin *arabilis*, from *arare* 'to plough'.

Arab League another name for LEAGUE OF ARAB STATES.

Araby /ˈarəbi/ archaic term for ARABIA.
– ORIGIN late Middle English: from Old French *Arabie*, from Latin *Arabia*, from Greek.

Aracajú /ˌarəkəˈʒuː/ a port in eastern Brazil, on the Atlantic coast, capital of the state of Sergipe; pop. 520,303 (2007).

aracari /ˌarəˈsɑːri, ˌarəˈkɑːri/ (also **araçari** /-ˈsɑːri/) ▶ noun (pl. **aracaris**) a small toucan with a serrated bill, and typically with a green back and wings, yellow underside, and red rump. ● Genus *Pteroglossus*, family Ramphastidae: several species.
– ORIGIN early 19th cent.: via Portuguese from Tupi *arasa'ri*.

arachidonic acid /əˌrakɪˈdɒnɪk/ ▶ noun [mass noun] Biochemistry a polyunsaturated fatty acid present in animal fats. It is important in metabolism, especially in the synthesis of prostaglandins and leukotrienes, and is an essential constituent of the diet. ● Alternative name: **eicosa-5,8,11,14-enoic acid**; chem. formula: $C_{19}H_{31}COOH$.
– ORIGIN early 20th cent.: *arachidonic* formed irregularly from *arachidic* (a saturated fatty acid) from Latin *arachis*, see ARACHIS OIL, + -ONE + -IC.

arachis oil /ˈarəkɪs/ ▶ noun another term for PEANUT OIL.
– ORIGIN mid 19th cent.: modern Latin *arachis*, from Greek *arak(h)os, -kis*, a leguminous plant.

Arachne /əˈrakni/ Greek Mythology a woman of Colophon in Lydia, a skilful weaver who challenged Athene to a contest. Athene destroyed Arachne's work and Arachne tried to hang herself, but Athene changed her into a spider.
– ORIGIN from Greek *arakhnē* 'spider'.

arachnid /əˈraknɪd/ Zoology ▶ noun an arthropod of the class Arachnida, such as a spider or scorpion.
▶ adjective relating to or denoting arachnids.

Arachnida /əˈraknɪdə/ ▶ plural noun Zoology a class of chelicerate arthropods that includes spiders, scorpions, mites, and ticks. They have become adapted for a terrestrial life and possess both lungs and tracheae, and many have silk or poison glands.
– ORIGIN modern Latin (plural), from Greek *arakhnē* 'spider'.

arachnoid /əˈraknɔɪd/ ▶ adjective like a spider or arachnid.
▶ noun (also **arachnoid membrane**) Anatomy a fine, delicate membrane, the middle one of the three membranes or meninges that surround the brain and spinal cord, situated between the dura mater and the pia mater.
– ORIGIN mid 18th cent.: from modern Latin *arachnoides*, from Greek *arakhnoeidēs* 'like a cobweb', from *arakhnē* 'spider'.

arachnophobia /əˌraknəˈfəʊbɪə/ ▶ noun [mass noun] extreme or irrational fear of spiders.
– DERIVATIVES **arachnophobe** noun, **arachnophobic** adjective.
– ORIGIN 1920s: modern Latin, from Greek *arakhnē* 'spider' + -PHOBIA.

Arafat /ˈarəfat/, Yasser (1929–2004), Palestinian statesman, chairman of the Palestine Liberation Organization 1968–2004 and Palestinian President 1996–2004. He became leader of the new Palestine National Authority in 1994, following the signing of a PLO–Israeli peace accord for which he shared the 1994 Nobel Peace Prize with Yitzhak Rabin and Shimon Peres.

Arafura Sea /ˌarəˈfʊərə/ a sea lying between northern Australia, the islands of east Indonesia, and New Guinea.

Aragon¹ /ˈarəg(ə)n/ an autonomous region of NE Spain, bounded on the north by the Pyrenees and on the east by Catalonia and Valencia; capital, Saragossa. Formerly an independent kingdom, it was united with Catalonia in 1137 and with Castile in 1479. Spanish name **Aragón**.

Aragon², Catherine of, see CATHERINE OF ARAGON.

aragonite /ˈarəg(ə)nʌɪt/ ▶ noun [mass noun] a mineral consisting of calcium carbonate and typically occurring as colourless prisms in deposits from hot springs.
– ORIGIN early 19th cent.: from the place name ARAGON¹ + -ITE¹.

arak /əˈrak/ ▶ noun variant spelling of ARRACK.

aralia /əˈreɪlɪə/ ▶ noun a plant of a very diverse group of trees and shrubs native to America and Asia. Several kinds are cultivated for their foliage and tiny flowers, and some are used in herbal medicine. ● Genus *Aralia*, family Araliaceae: several species, including the Japanese angelica tree (*A. elata*).
– ORIGIN modern Latin, of unknown origin.

Aral Sea /ˈarəl/ an inland sea in central Asia, on the border between Kazakhstan and Uzbekistan. Its area was reduced to two thirds of its original size between 1960 and 1990, after water was diverted for irrigation, with serious consequences for the environment of the area.

Aramaean /ˌarəˈmiːən/ (also **Aramean**) ▶ noun a member of an ancient Aramaic-speaking people inhabiting Aram (modern Syria) and most of Mesopotamia in the 11th–8th centuries BC.
▶ adjective relating to Aram or the Aramaeans.
– ORIGIN from Latin *Aramaeus* (from Greek *Aramaios*: see ARAMAIC) + -AN.

Aramaic /ˌarəˈmeɪɪk/ ▶ noun [mass noun] a branch of the Semitic family of languages, especially the language of Syria used as a lingua franca in the Near East from the 6th century BC. It replaced Hebrew locally as the language of the Jews, and though displaced by Arabic in the 7th century AD, it still has about 200,000 speakers in scattered communities.
▶ adjective relating to this language.
– ORIGIN mid 19th cent.: from Greek *Aramaios* 'of Aram' (the biblical name of Syria) + -IC.

arame /ˈarəmi/ ▶ noun [mass noun] an edible Pacific seaweed with broad brown leaves which is used in Japanese cookery. ● *Ecklonia bicyclis*, class Phaeophyceae.

aramid /ˈarəmɪd/ ▶ noun any of a class of synthetic polyamides that are formed from aromatic monomers, and yield fibres of exceptional strength and thermal stability.
– ORIGIN 1970s: from AROMATIC + POLYAMIDE.

Aran /ˈar(ə)n/ ▶ adjective [attrib.] denoting a type of knitwear or garment with traditional patterns, typically involving raised cable stitch and large diamond designs.
– ORIGIN 1960s: from the ARAN ISLANDS.

Aranda /əˈrʌntə, aˈruːndə/ ▶ noun & adjective variant form of ARRERNTE.

A

araneid /əˈreɪnɪɪd/ ▶ noun Zoology an invertebrate of an order that comprises the spiders. ● Order Araneae, in particular the family Araneidae.
– ORIGIN late 19th cent.: from modern Latin *Araneida* (former order name), from *aranea* 'spider'.

Aran Islands a group of three islands, Inishmore, Inishmaan, and Inisheer, off the west coast of the Republic of Ireland.

Aranyaka /ˌarəˈnjakə/ ▶ noun each of a set of Hindu sacred treatises based on the Brahmanas, composed in Sanskrit *c.*700 BC. Intended only for initiates, the Aranyakas contain mystical and philosophical material and explications of esoteric rites.

Arapaho /əˈrapəhəʊ/ ▶ noun (pl. **same** or **Arapahos**)
1 a member of a North American Indian people living chiefly on the Great Plains, especially in Wyoming.
2 [mass noun] the Algonquian language of the Arapaho, now almost extinct.
▶ adjective relating to the Arapaho or their language.
– ORIGIN from Crow *alappahó*, literally 'many tattoo marks'.

arapaima /ˌarəˈpʌɪmə/ ▶ noun a very large edible freshwater fish native to tropical South America. ● *Arapaima gigas*, family Osteoglossidae.
– ORIGIN mid 19th cent.: from Tupi.

Ararat, Mount /ˈarərat/ a pair of volcanic peaks in eastern Turkey, near the borders with Armenia and Iran. The higher peak, which rises to 5,165 m (16,946 ft), is the traditional site of the resting place of Noah's ark after the Flood (Gen. 8:4).

arational ▶ adjective not based on or governed by logical reasoning.

Araucanian /ˌarɔːˈkeɪnɪən/ ▶ noun **1** a member of a group of American Indian peoples of Chile and adjacent parts of Argentina, including the Mapuche.
2 [mass noun] the language of the Araucanians, constituting a distinct language family sometimes linked to Penutian.
▶ adjective relating to or denoting the Araucanians or their language. See also **MAPUCHE**.
– ORIGIN from Spanish *Araucania*, a region in Chile, + **-AN**.

araucaria /ˌarɔːˈkɛːrɪə/ ▶ noun an evergreen conifer of a genus that includes the monkey puzzle, having stiff sharp leaves. ● Genus *Araucaria*, family Araucariaceae.
– ORIGIN modern Latin, from Spanish *Arauco*, the name of a province of Araucania, Chile.

Arawak /ˈarəwak/ ▶ noun (pl. **same** or **Arawaks**) **1** a member of a group of indigenous peoples of the Greater Antilles and northern and western South America. They were forced out of the Antilles by the Caribs shortly before Spanish expansion in the Caribbean.
2 [mass noun] any of the languages of the Arawak.
▶ adjective relating to the Arawak or their languages.
– ORIGIN from Carib *aruac*.

Arawakan /ˌarəˈwak(ə)n/ ▶ adjective denoting or belonging to a widely scattered family of South American Indian languages, most of which are now extinct or nearly so.
▶ noun [mass noun] this family of languages.

arb /ɑːb/ ▶ noun informal short for **ARBITRAGEUR**.

arbalest /ˈɑːbəlɛst/ (also **arblast**) ▶ noun historical a crossbow with a special mechanism for drawing back and releasing the string.
– ORIGIN Old English *arblast*, from Old French *arbaleste*, from late Latin *arcubalista*, from Latin *arcus* 'bow' + *ballista* (see **BALLISTA**).

arbiter /ˈɑːbɪtə/ ▶ noun a person who settles a dispute or has ultimate authority in a matter: *the Secretary of State is the final arbiter*. ■ a person whose views or actions have influence in a particular sphere: *an arbiter of taste*.
– ORIGIN late Middle English: from Latin, 'judge, supreme ruler'.

arbiter elegantiarum /ˌɛlɪgantɪˈɑːrəm/ (also **arbiter elegantiae** /ˌɛlɪˈgantɪʌɪ/) ▶ noun a judge of artistic taste and etiquette.
– ORIGIN Latin, 'judge of elegance', used by Tacitus to describe **PETRONIUS**, arbiter of taste at Nero's court.

arbitrage /ˈɑːbɪtrɪdʒ, ˌɑːbɪˈtrɑːʒ/ Economics ▶ noun [mass noun] the simultaneous buying and selling of securities, currency, or commodities in different markets or in derivative forms in order to take advantage of differing prices for the same asset.
▶ verb [no obj.] buy and sell assets using arbitrage.
– ORIGIN late Middle English (originally denoting the exercise of individual judgement): from French, from *arbitrer* 'give judgement', from Latin *arbitrari* (see **ARBITRATE**). The current sense dates from the late 19th cent.

arbitrageur /ˌɑːbɪtrɑːˈʒəː/ (also **arbitrager** /ˈɑːbɪtrɪdʒə/) ▶ noun a person who engages in arbitrage.
– ORIGIN late 19th cent.: from French, from *arbitrer* 'give judgement', from Latin *arbitrari* (see **ARBITRATE**).

arbitral /ˈɑːbɪtr(ə)l/ ▶ adjective relating to or resulting from the use of an arbitrator to settle a dispute.
– ORIGIN late 15th cent.: from late Latin *arbitralis*, from *arbiter* 'judge, supreme ruler'.

arbitrament /ɑːˈbɪtrəm(ə)nt/ ▶ noun [mass noun] the settling of a dispute by an arbitrator. ■ [count noun] an authoritative decision made by an arbitrator.
– ORIGIN late Middle English: from Old French *arbitrement*, from medieval Latin *arbitramentum*, from *arbitrari* (see **ARBITRATE**).

arbitrary /ˈɑːbɪt(rə)ri/ ▶ adjective **1** based on random choice or personal whim, rather than any reason or system: *an arbitrary decision*.
2 (of power or a ruling body) unrestrained and autocratic in the use of authority: *a country under arbitrary government*.
3 Mathematics (of a constant or other quantity) of unspecified value.
– DERIVATIVES **arbitrarily** adverb, **arbitrariness** noun.
– ORIGIN late Middle English (in the sense 'dependent on one's will or pleasure, discretionary'): from Latin *arbitrarius*, from *arbiter* 'judge, supreme ruler', perhaps influenced by French *arbitraire*.

arbitrate /ˈɑːbɪtreɪt/ ▶ verb [no obj.] (of an independent person or body) reach an authoritative judgement or settlement: *the board has the power to arbitrate in disputes* | [with obj.] *the insurance ombudsman arbitrates insurance matters*.
– ORIGIN mid 16th cent.: from Latin *arbitrat-* 'judged', from *arbitrari*, from *arbiter* 'judge, supreme ruler'.

arbitration ▶ noun [mass noun] the use of an arbitrator to settle a dispute.
– PHRASES **go to arbitration** use an arbitrator to settle a dispute.

arbitrator ▶ noun an independent person or body officially appointed to settle a dispute.

arbitress ▶ noun archaic a female arbiter.

arblast /ˈɑːblɑːst/ ▶ noun variant spelling of **ARBALEST**.

arbor[1] /ˈɑːbə/ ▶ noun an axle or spindle on which something revolves. ■ a device holding a tool in a lathe.
– ORIGIN mid 17th cent.: from French *arbre* 'tree, axis'. The spelling change was due to association with Latin *arbor* 'tree'.

arbor[2] ▶ noun US spelling of **ARBOUR**.

Arbor Day ▶ noun a day dedicated annually to public tree planting in the US, Australia, and other countries.
– ORIGIN from Latin *arbor* 'tree'.

arboreal /ɑːˈbɔːrɪəl/ ▶ adjective living in trees: *arboreal rodents*. ■ relating to trees.
– DERIVATIVES **arboreality** noun.
– ORIGIN mid 17th cent.: from Latin *arboreus*, from *arbor* 'tree', + **-AL**.

arborescent /ˌɑːbəˈrɛs(ə)nt/ ▶ adjective chiefly Botany tree-like in growth or appearance.
– DERIVATIVES **arborescence** noun.
– ORIGIN late 17th cent.: from Latin *arborescent-* 'growing into a tree', from *arborescere*, from *arbor* 'tree'.

arboretum /ˌɑːbəˈriːtəm/ ▶ noun (pl. **arboretums** or **arboreta** /-tə/) a botanical garden devoted to trees.
– ORIGIN early 19th cent.: from Latin, 'a place with trees', from *arbor* 'tree'.

arboriculture /ˈɑːb(ə)rɪˌkʌltʃə, ɑːˈbɔː-/ ▶ noun [mass noun] the cultivation of trees and shrubs.
– DERIVATIVES **arboricultural** adjective, **arboriculturist** noun.
– ORIGIN early 19th cent.: from Latin *arbor* 'tree' + **CULTURE**, on the pattern of words such as *agriculture*.

Arborio /ɑːˈbɔːrɪəʊ/ ▶ noun [mass noun] a variety of round-grained rice produced in Italy and used in making risotto.
– ORIGIN Italian.

arborist /ˈɑːbərɪst/ ▶ noun a tree surgeon.

arborization /ˌɑːb(ə)rʌɪˈzeɪʃ(ə)n/ (also **aborisation**) ▶ noun Anatomy a fine branching structure at the end of a nerve fibre.

arbor vitae /ˌɑːbə ˈvʌɪtiː, ˈviːtʌɪ/ ▶ noun another term for **THUJA**.
– ORIGIN mid 16th cent.: from Latin, literally 'tree of life', probably with reference to its medicinal use.

arbour /ˈɑːbə/ (US **arbor**) ▶ noun a shady garden alcove with the sides and roof formed by trees or climbing plants trained over a framework.
– DERIVATIVES **arboured** adjective.
– ORIGIN Middle English (also denoting a lawn or flower bed): from Old French *erbier*, from *erbe* 'grass, herb', from Latin *herba*. The phonetic change to *ar-* (common in words having *er-* before a consonant) was assisted by association with Latin *arbor* 'tree'.

arbovirus /ˈɑːbə(ʊ),vʌɪrəs/ ▶ noun Medicine any of a group of viruses which are transmitted by mosquitoes, ticks, or other arthropods. They include the virus of yellow fever.
– ORIGIN 1950s: from *ar(thropod)-bo(rne)* + **VIRUS**.

Arbus /ˈɑːbəs/, Diane (1923–71), American photographer. She is best known for her disturbing images of people on the streets of US cities.

Arbuthnot /ɑːˈbʌθnət/, John (1667–1735), Scottish physician and writer. His satirical *History of John Bull* (1712) was the origin of John Bull as the personification of the typical Englishman.

arbutus /ɑːˈbjuːtəs, ˈɑːbjʊtəs/ ▶ noun an evergreen tree or shrub of a genus that includes the strawberry tree. See also **TRAILING ARBUTUS**. ● Genus *Arbutus*, family Ericaceae.
– ORIGIN from Latin.

ARC ▶ abbreviation ■ historical (in the UK) Agricultural Research Council. ■ Medicine AIDS-related complex.

arc /ɑːk/ ▶ noun **1** a part of a curve, especially a part of the circumference of a circle. ■ a shape or structure resembling this: *the huge arc of the sky*. ■ a curving trajectory: *he swung his torch in a wide arc*. ■ [as modifier] Mathematics indicating the inverse of a trigonometrical function. [from the former method of defining trigonometrical functions by arcs.]
2 a luminous electrical discharge between two electrodes or other points.
3 (in a novel, play, or film) the development or resolution of the narrative or principal theme: *his transformation provides the emotional arc of the story*.
▶ verb (**arcs, arcing** /ˈɑːkɪŋ/, **arced** /ɑːkt/) [no obj.] **1** [with adverbial of direction] move with a curving trajectory: *the ball arced across the room*.
2 (usu. as noun **arcing**) form an electric arc: *check that switches operate properly with no sign of arcing*.
– PHRASES **minute of arc** see **MINUTE**[1] (sense 2). **second of arc** see **SECOND**[2] (sense 2).
– ORIGIN late Middle English (denoting the path of a celestial object, especially the sun, from horizon to horizon): via Old French from Latin *arcus* 'bow, curve'.

arcade ▶ noun **1** a covered passage with arches along one or both sides. ■ a covered walk with shops along one or both sides. ■ Architecture a series of arches supporting a wall, or set along it.
2 short for **AMUSEMENT ARCADE**.
– DERIVATIVES **arcaded** adjective, **arcading** noun.
– ORIGIN late 17th cent.: from French, from Provençal *arcada* or Italian *arcata*, based on Latin *arcus* 'bow'.

Arcadia /ɑːˈkeɪdɪə/ a mountainous district in the Peloponnese of southern Greece. In poetic fantasy it represents a pastoral paradise and in Greek mythology it is the home of Pan.

Arcadian ▶ noun a native of Arcadia. ■ literary an idealized country dweller.
▶ adjective relating to Arcadia. ■ literary relating to an ideal pastoral paradise.
– ORIGIN late 16th cent.: from Latin *Arcadius*, from Greek *Arkadia* (see **ARCADIA**).

Arcady /ˈɑːkədi/ ▶ noun literary an ideal rustic paradise.
– ORIGIN late 16th cent.: from Greek *Arkadia* (see **ARCADIA**).

arcana /ɑːˈkeɪnə/ ▶ plural noun [treated as sing. or pl.] (sing. **arcanum**) **1** secrets or mysteries: *the arcana of his profession*.
2 either of the two groups of cards in a tarot pack: the twenty-two trumps (the **major arcana**) and the fifty-six suit cards (the **minor arcana**).
– ORIGIN mid 16th cent.: from Latin, neuter plural of *arcanus* (see **ARCANE**).

arcane /ɑːˈkeɪn/ ▶ adjective understood by few; mysterious or secret: *arcane procedures for electing people*.
– DERIVATIVES **arcanely** adverb.
– ORIGIN mid 16th cent.: from Latin *arcanus*, from *arcere* 'to shut up', from *arca* 'chest'.

arc cosine (abbrev.: **arcos**) ▶ noun a mathematical function that is the inverse of the cosine function.

Arc de Triomphe /ˌɑːk də ˈtriːɒmf/, French /aʀk də tʀijɔ̃f/ a ceremonial arch standing at the top of the Champs-Élysées in Paris, commissioned by Napoleon to commemorate his victories in 1805–6. Inspired by the Arch of Constantine in Rome, it was completed in 1836.

arc eye ▶ **noun** [mass noun] Medicine a painful eye condition caused by damage to the cornea from ultraviolet radiation during arc welding.

arch[1] ▶ **noun** a curved symmetrical structure spanning an opening and typically supporting the weight of a bridge, roof, or wall above it. ■ an arch forming a monument or ornamental feature: *a triumphal arch.* ■ a shape resembling an arch: *the delicate arch of his eyebrows.* ■ the inner side of the foot.
▶ **verb** [no obj., with adverbial of place] have the curved shape of an arch: *a beautiful bridge that arched over a canal.* ■ form or cause to form the curved shape of an arch: [no obj.] *her eyebrows arched in surprise* | [with obj.] *she arched her back.*
– ORIGIN Middle English: from Old French *arche*, based on Latin *arcus* 'bow'.

arch[2] ▶ **adjective** deliberately or affectedly playful and teasing: *a somewhat arch tone of voice.*
– DERIVATIVES **archly** adverb, **archness** noun.
– ORIGIN mid 17th cent.: from **ARCH-**, by association with the sense 'rogue' in combinations such as *arch-scoundrel.*

arch- ▶ **combining form** chief; principal: *archbishop* | *archdiocese.* ■ pre-eminent of its kind; out-and-out: *arch-enemy.*
– ORIGIN via Latin from Greek *arkhi-*, from *arkhos* 'chief'.

-arch /ɑːk/ ▶ **combining form** (forming nouns) denoting a ruler or leader: *monarch.*
– ORIGIN Greek *arkhos* 'ruling', from *arkhein* 'to rule'.

archaea /ɑːˈkiːə/ ▶ **plural noun** Biology microorganisms which are similar to bacteria in size and simplicity of structure but radically different in molecular organization. They are now believed to constitute an ancient group which is intermediate between the bacteria and eukaryotes. Also called **ARCHAEBACTERIA**.
– DERIVATIVES **archaean** (also **archaeal**) adjective & noun.
– ORIGIN modern Latin (plural), from Greek *arkhaios* 'primitive'.

Archaean /ɑːˈkiːən/ (US **Archean**) ▶ **adjective** Geology relating to or denoting the aeon that constitutes the earlier (or middle) part of the Precambrian, in which there was no life on the earth. It precedes the Proterozoic aeon and (in some schemes) is preceded by the Priscoan aeon. Also called **THE AZOIC**. ■ (as noun **the Archaean**) the Archaean aeon or the system of rocks deposited during it.

The Archaean extended from the origin of the earth (see **PRECAMBRIAN**) to about 2,500 million years ago. In schemes which include the Priscoan aeon, the Archaean began about 4,000 million years ago.

– ORIGIN late 19th cent.: from Greek *arkhaios* 'ancient' + **-AN**.

archaebacteria /ˌɑːkɪbakˈtɪərɪə/ ▶ **plural noun** (sing. **archaebacterium**) another term for **ARCHAEA**.
– DERIVATIVES **archaebacterial** adjective.

archaeo- /ˈɑːkɪəʊ/ ▶ **combining form** relating to archaeology or prehistoric times: *archaeoastronomy.*
– ORIGIN from Greek *arkhaios* 'ancient'.

archaeoastronomy ▶ **noun** [mass noun] the investigation of the astronomical knowledge of prehistoric cultures. Also called **ASTRO-ARCHAEOLOGY**.

archaeology (US also **archeology**) ▶ **noun** [mass noun] the study of human history and prehistory through the excavation of sites and the analysis of artefacts and other physical remains.
– DERIVATIVES **archaeologic** adjective, **archaeological** adjective, **archaeologically** adverb, **archaeologist** noun, **archaeologize** (also **archaeologise**) verb.
– ORIGIN early 17th cent. (in the sense 'ancient history'): from modern Latin *archaeologia*, from Greek *arkhaiologia* 'ancient history', from *arkhaios* 'ancient'. The current sense dates from the mid 19th cent.

archaeomagnetism ▶ **noun** [mass noun] magnetism possessed by components of clay and rocks which have in the past been heated above a certain temperature. The orientation and intensity of this remanent magnetism was fixed by the earth's magnetic field when the material cooled, and can be used to study the earth's magnetism and as a method of geological and archaeological dating.
– DERIVATIVES **archaeomagnetic** adjective.

archaeometry /ˌɑːkɪˈɒmətri/ ▶ **noun** [mass noun] the application of scientific techniques to the dating of archaeological remains.
– DERIVATIVES **archaeometric** adjective.

archaeopteryx /ˌɑːkɪˈɒptərɪks/ ▶ **noun** the oldest known fossil bird, of the late Jurassic period. It had feathers, wings, and hollow bones like a bird, but teeth, a bony tail, and legs like a small coelurosaur dinosaur. ● *Archaeopteryx lithographica*, subclass Archaeornithes.
– ORIGIN from **ARCHAEO-** 'ancient' + Greek *pterux* 'wing'.

archaic /ɑːˈkeɪɪk/ ▶ **adjective** very old or old-fashioned: *prisons are run on archaic methods.* ■ (of a word or a style of language) no longer in everyday use but sometimes used to impart an old-fashioned flavour. ■ of an early period of art or culture, especially the 7th–6th centuries BC in Greece: *the archaic temple at Corinth.*
– DERIVATIVES **archaically** adverb.
– ORIGIN mid 19th cent.: from French *archaïque*, from Greek *arkhaikos*, from *arkhaios*, from *arkhē* 'beginning'.

archaism /ˈɑːkeɪɪz(ə)m/ ▶ **noun** a thing that is very old or old-fashioned, especially an archaic word or style of language or art: *conscious archaisms inspired by French harpsichord music.* ■ [mass noun] the use or conscious imitation of archaic styles or features in language or art.
– DERIVATIVES **archaistic** adjective.
– ORIGIN mid 17th cent.: from modern Latin *archaismus*, from Greek *arkhaismos*, from *arkhaizein* 'imitate archaic styles', from *arkhaios* 'ancient', from *arkhē* 'beginning'.

archaize /ˈɑːkeɪʌɪz/ (also **archaise**) ▶ **verb** [with obj.] give (an artistic work) an old-fashioned flavour by using archaic words or styles. ■ [no obj.] use archaic words or styles in an artistic work.
– ORIGIN mid 19th cent.: from Greek *arkhaizein*, from *arkhaios* 'ancient' (see **ARCHAEAN**).

archaizing (also **archaising**) ▶ **adjective** consciously imitating a word or a style of language or art that is very old or old-fashioned.

Archangel /ˈɑːkeɪndʒ(ə)l/ a port of NW Russia, on the White Sea; pop. 348,700 (est. 2008). It is named after the monastery of the Archangel Michael situated there. Russian name **ARKHANGELSK**.

archangel /ˈɑːkeɪndʒ(ə)l, ɑːkˈeɪn-/ ▶ **noun 1** an angel of greater than ordinary rank. ■ (in traditional Christian angelology) a being of the eighth-highest order of the ninefold celestial hierarchy.
2 (also **yellow archangel**) a yellow-flowered Eurasian dead-nettle found in woodland. ● *Lamiastrum galeobdolon* (or *Galeobdolon luteum*), family Labiatae.
– DERIVATIVES **archangelic** adjective.
– ORIGIN Middle English, from Anglo-Norman French *archangele*, via ecclesiastical Latin from ecclesiastical Greek *arkhangelos*, from *arkhi-* 'chief' + *angelos* 'messenger, angel'.

archbishop ▶ **noun** the chief bishop responsible for a large district.
– ORIGIN Old English, from **ARCH-** 'chief' + *biscop* (see **BISHOP**), replacing earlier *heah-biscop* 'high-bishop'.

archbishopric ▶ **noun** the office of an archbishop. ■ an archdiocese.
– ORIGIN Old English *arcebiscoprice* (see **ARCH-**, **BISHOPRIC**).

archdeacon ▶ **noun** a senior Christian cleric (in the early Church a deacon, in the modern Anglican Church a priest) to whom a bishop delegates certain responsibilities.
– ORIGIN Old English *arce-*, *ercediacon*, from ecclesiastical Latin *archidiaconus*, from ecclesiastical Greek *arkhidiakonos*, from *arkhi-* 'chief' + *diakonos* (see **DEACON**).

archdeaconry ▶ **noun** (pl. **archdeaconries**) the district for which an archdeacon is responsible. ■ the residence of an archdeacon. ■ the office of an archdeacon.

archdiocese ▶ **noun** the district for which an archbishop is responsible.
– DERIVATIVES **archdiocesan** adjective.

archduchess ▶ **noun** historical **1** the wife or widow of an archduke.
2 a daughter of the Emperor of Austria.

archduke ▶ **noun** a chief duke, in particular (formerly) the son of the Emperor of Austria.
– DERIVATIVES **archducal** adjective, **archduchy** noun.
– ORIGIN early 16th cent.: from Old French *archeduc*, from Merovingian Latin *archidux*, *archiduc-*, from *archi-* 'chief' + *dux*, *duc-* (see **DUKE**).

Archean ▶ **adjective** US spelling of **ARCHAEAN**.

arched ▶ **adjective** constructed with or in the form of an arch or arches: *high arched windows.*

archegonium /ˌɑːkɪˈɡəʊnɪəm/ ▶ **noun** (pl. **archegonia** /-ɪə/) Botany the female sex organ in mosses, liverworts, ferns, and most conifers.
– ORIGIN mid 19th cent.: modern Latin, from Greek *arkhegonos*, from *arkhe-* 'chief' + *gonos* 'race'.

arch-enemy ▶ **noun** a person who is extremely opposed or hostile to someone or something: *the twins were arch-enemies.* ■ (**the Arch-enemy**) the Devil.

archenteron /ɑːˈkɛntərɒn/ ▶ **noun** Embryology the rudimentary alimentary cavity of an embryo at the gastrula stage.
– ORIGIN late 19th cent.: from Greek *arkhē* 'beginning' + *enteron* 'intestine'.

archeology ▶ **noun** US spelling of **ARCHAEOLOGY**.

archer ▶ **noun** a person who shoots with a bow and arrows, especially at a target as a sport. ■ (**the Archer**) the zodiacal sign or constellation Sagittarius.
– ORIGIN Middle English: from Old French *archier*, based on Latin *arcus* 'bow'.

archerfish ▶ **noun** (pl. **same** or **archerfishes**) a freshwater fish that knocks insect prey off overhanging vegetation by shooting water at it from its mouth. It is native to Asia, Australia, and the Philippines. ● Genus *Toxotes*, family Toxotidae: several species, in particular *T. jaculator*.

archery ▶ **noun** [mass noun] shooting with a bow and arrows, especially at a target as a sport.
– ORIGIN late Middle English: from Old French *archerie*, from *archier* (see **ARCHER**).

arches ▶ **plural noun** [treated as sing.] used in names of moths with curving arch-like patterns on the wings, such as **dark arches**. ● Several genera in the families Noctuidae and Notodontidae.

archetypal /ˌɑːkɪˈtʌɪp(ə)l/ ▶ **adjective 1** very typical of a certain kind of person or thing: *the archetypal country doctor.* ■ relating to or denoting an original which has been imitated: *archetypal myths.*
2 relating to or denoting Jungian archetypes.
3 recurrent as a symbol or motif in literature, art, or mythology: *an archetypal journey representing the quest for identity.*
– DERIVATIVES **archetypally** adverb.

archetype /ˈɑːkɪtʌɪp/ ▶ **noun 1** a very typical example of a certain person or thing: *he was the archetype of the old-style football club chairman.* ■ an original which has been imitated; a prototype: *an instrument which was the archetype of the early flute.*
2 Psychoanalysis (in Jungian theory) a primitive mental image inherited from the earliest human ancestors, and supposed to be present in the collective unconscious.
3 a recurrent symbol or motif in literature, art, or mythology: *mythological archetypes of good and evil.*
– DERIVATIVES **archetypical** adjective, **archetypically** adverb.
– ORIGIN mid 16th cent.: via Latin from Greek *arkhetupon* 'something moulded first as a model', from *arkhe-* 'primitive' + *tupos* 'a model'.

archidiaconal /ˌɑːkɪdʌɪˈak(ə)n(ə)l/ ▶ **adjective** relating to an archdeacon.
– ORIGIN late Middle English: from medieval Latin *archidiaconalis*, from *archi-* 'chief' + *diaconalis* (see **DIACONAL**).

archiepiscopal /ˌɑːkɪɪˈpɪskəp(ə)l/ ▶ **adjective** relating to an archbishop.
– DERIVATIVES **archiepiscopacy** noun (pl. **archiepiscopacies**), **archiepiscopate** noun.
– ORIGIN early 17th cent.: via ecclesiastical Latin from Greek *arkhiepiskopos* 'archbishop' (from *arkhi-* 'chief' + *episkopos* 'bishop') + **-AL**.

Archilochus /ɑːˈkɪləkəs/ (8th or 7th century BC), Greek poet. Acclaimed in his day as equal in stature to Homer and Pindar, he wrote satirical verse and fables and is credited with the invention of iambic metre.

archimandrite /ˌɑːkɪˈmandrʌɪt/ ▶ **noun** the superior of a large monastery or group of monasteries in the Orthodox Church. ■ an honorary title given to a monastic priest.
– ORIGIN mid 17th cent.: via ecclesiastical Latin, from ecclesiastical Greek *arkhimandritēs*, from *arkhi-* 'chief' + *mandra* 'monastery'.

A

Archimedean screw /ˌɑːkɪˈmiːdɪən/ ▶ **noun** a device invented by Archimedes for raising water by means of a helix rotating within a tube.

Archimedes /ˌɑːkɪˈmiːdiːz/ (*c.*287–212 BC), Greek mathematician and inventor, of Syracuse. He is famous for his discovery of Archimedes' principle (legend has it that he made this discovery while taking a bath, and ran through the streets shouting 'Eureka!'); among his mathematical discoveries are the ratio of the radius of a circle to its circumference, and formulas for the surface area and volume of a sphere and of a cylinder.
– DERIVATIVES **Archimedean** adjective.

Archimedes' principle Physics a law stating that a body totally or partially immersed in a fluid is subject to an upward force equal in magnitude to the weight of fluid it displaces.

archipelago /ˌɑːkɪˈpɛləɡəʊ/ ▶ **noun** (pl. **archipelagos** or **archipelagoes**) an extensive group of islands. ■ a sea or stretch of water having many islands.
– ORIGIN early 16th cent.: from Italian *arcipelago*, from Greek *arkhi-* 'chief' + *pelagos* 'sea'. The word was originally used as a proper name (*the Archipelago* 'the Aegean Sea'): the general sense arose because the Aegean Sea is notable for its large numbers of islands.

Archipiélago de Colón /arkiˈpjelaɣəʊ ðe kəʊˈləʊn/ official Spanish name for **GALAPAGOS ISLANDS**.

architect ▶ **noun** a person who designs buildings and in many cases also supervises their construction. ■ a person who is responsible for inventing or realizing a particular idea or project: *the architects of the reform programme*.
▶ **verb** [with obj.] Computing design and configure (a program or system).
– ORIGIN mid 16th cent.: from French *architecte*, from Italian *architetto*, via Latin from Greek *arkhitektōn*, from *arkhi-* 'chief' + *tektōn* 'builder'.

architectonic /ˌɑːkɪtɛkˈtɒnɪk/ ▶ **adjective 1** relating to architecture or architects.
2 (of an artistic composition) having a clearly defined structure, especially one that is artistically pleasing: *the painting's architectonic harmony*.
▶ **noun** (**architectonics**) [usu. treated as sing.] **1** the scientific study of architecture.
2 musical, literary, or artistic structure.
– DERIVATIVES **architectonically** adverb.
– ORIGIN mid 17th cent.: via Latin from Greek *arkhitektonikos*, from *arkhitektōn* (see **ARCHITECT**).

architecture ▶ **noun** [mass noun] **1** the art or practice of designing and constructing buildings. ■ the style in which a building is designed and constructed, especially with regard to a specific period, place, or culture: *Georgian architecture*.
2 the complex or carefully designed structure of something: *the chemical architecture of the human brain*. ■ the conceptual structure and logical organization of a computer or computer-based system.
– DERIVATIVES **architectural** adjective, **architecturally** adverb.
– ORIGIN mid 16th cent.: from Latin *architectura*, from *architectus* (see **ARCHITECT**).

architrave /ˈɑːkɪtreɪv/ ▶ **noun 1** (in classical architecture) a main beam resting across the tops of columns.
2 the moulded frame around a doorway or window. ■ a moulding round the exterior of an arch.
– ORIGIN mid 16th cent.: from French, from Italian, from *archi-* 'chief' + *-trave* from Latin *trabs*, *trab-* 'a beam'.

archive /ˈɑːkʌɪv/ ▶ **noun** (usu. **archives**) a collection of historical documents or records providing information about a place, institution, or group of people: [as modifier] *a section of archive film*. ■ the place where historical documents or records are kept. ■ a complete record of the data in part or all of a computer system, stored on an infrequently used medium.
▶ **verb** [with obj.] place or store (something) in an archive. ■ Computing transfer (data) to a less frequently used storage medium such as magnetic tape.
– DERIVATIVES **archival** adjective.
– ORIGIN early 17th cent. (in the sense 'place where records are kept'): from French *archives* (plural), from Latin *archiva*, *archia*, from Greek *arkheia* 'public records', from *arkhē* 'government'. The verb dates from the late 19th cent.

archivist /ˈɑːkɪvɪst/ ▶ **noun** a person who maintains and is in charge of archives.

archivolt /ˈɑːkɪvəʊlt/ ▶ **noun** a band of mouldings round the lower curve of an arch. ■ the lower curve of an arch from impost to impost of the columns.
– ORIGIN mid 17th cent.: from French *archivolte* or Italian *archivolto*, based on Latin *arcus* 'bow, arch' + *volvere* 'to roll'.

archlute ▶ **noun** a bass lute with an extended neck which supports unstopped bass strings.
– ORIGIN mid 17th cent.: from French *archiluth*, from *archi-* 'chief' + *luth* 'lute'.

archon /ˈɑːkən/ ▶ **noun** each of the nine chief magistrates in ancient Athens.
– DERIVATIVES **archonship** noun.
– ORIGIN late 16th cent.: from Greek *arkhōn* 'ruler', noun use of the present participle of *arkhein* 'to rule'.

archosaur /ˈɑːkəsɔː/ ▶ **noun** Zoology & Palaeontology a reptile of a large group that includes the dinosaurs and pterosaurs and is represented today only by the crocodilians. ● Subdivision Archosauria, subclass Diapsida.
– ORIGIN 1930s: from modern Latin *Archosauria*, from Greek *arkhos* 'chief' or *arkhōn* 'ruler' + **-SAUR**.

archpriest ▶ **noun** a chief priest.

arch-rival ▶ **noun** the chief rival of a person, team, or organization.

archway ▶ **noun** a curved structure forming a passage or entrance.

-archy /ˈɑːki/ ▶ **combining form** (forming nouns) denoting a type of rule or government, corresponding to nouns ending in *-arch*: *monarchy*.
– ORIGIN representing Greek *arkh(e)ia* 'government, leadership', formed as **-ARCH**: see **-Y³**.

arc lamp (also **arc light**) ▶ **noun** a light source using an electric arc.

arc minute ▶ **noun** see **MINUTE¹** (sense 2).

arco /ˈɑːkəʊ/ ▶ **adverb & adjective** Music (especially as a direction) played on a violin or other stringed instrument using the bow. Often contrasted with **PIZZICATO**.

arcology /ɑːˈkɒlədʒi/ ▶ **noun** (pl. **arcologies**) an ideal integrated city contained within a massive vertical structure, allowing maximum conservation of the surrounding environment.
– ORIGIN 1969: blend of **ARCHITECTURE** and **ECOLOGY**.

arcos ▶ **abbreviation** arc cosine.

arc second (also **second of arc**) ▶ **noun** see **SECOND²**.

arc sine (abbrev.: **arcsin**) ▶ **noun** a mathematical function that is the inverse of the sine function.

arc tangent (abbrev.: **arctan**) ▶ **noun** a mathematical function that is the inverse of the tangent function.

Arctic ▶ **adjective 1** relating to the regions around the North Pole: *an Arctic explorer*. ■ (of animals or plants) living or growing in the region around the North Pole.
2 (**arctic**) informal (of weather conditions) very cold.
▶ **noun 1** (**the Arctic**) the regions around the North Pole.
2 N. Amer. a thick waterproof overshoe extending to the ankle or above.
3 (**arctic**) a drab-coloured hairy butterfly of the arctic and subarctic regions of the New World. ● Genus *Oenis*, subfamily Satyrinae, family Nymphalidae.
– ORIGIN late Middle English: via Old French from Latin *arcticus*, *arcticus*, from Greek *arktikos*, from *arktos* 'bear, Ursa Major, pole star'.

Arctic charr ▶ **noun** see **CHARR**.

Arctic Circle the parallel of latitude 66° 33′ north of the equator. It marks the northernmost point at which the sun is visible on the northern winter solstice and the southernmost point at which the midnight sun can be seen on the northern summer solstice.

Arctic fox ▶ **noun** a small fox with a thick coat that turns white in winter, found on the tundra of North America and Eurasia. ● *Alopex lagopus*, family Canidae.

Arctic hare ▶ **noun** a hare whose coat turns white in winter, found in the arctic areas of North America. ● *Lepus arcticus*, family Leporidae; sometimes treated as the same species as the mountain hare of Eurasia.

Arctic Ocean the sea that surrounds the North Pole, lying within the Arctic Circle. Much of the sea is covered with pack ice throughout the year.

Arctic tern ▶ **noun** a red-billed tern which breeds in the Arctic and adjacent areas, migrating to Antarctic regions to overwinter. ● *Sterna paradisaea*, family Sternidae.

Arctogaea /ˌɑːktəˈdʒiːə/ (US **Arctogea**) Zoology a major zoogeographical area comprising the Palaearctic, Nearctic, Ethiopian, and Oriental regions.
– DERIVATIVES **Arctogaean** adjective.
– ORIGIN modern Latin, from Greek *arktos* 'northern' + *gaia* 'earth'.

arctophile /ˈɑːktəfʌɪl/ ▶ **noun** a person who collects or is very fond of teddy bears.
– DERIVATIVES **arctophily** /ɑːkˈtɒfɪli/ noun.
– ORIGIN 1970s: from Greek *arctos* 'bear' + **-PHILE**.

Arcturus /ɑːkˈtjʊərəs/ Astronomy the fourth-brightest star in the sky, and the brightest in the constellation Boötes. It is an orange giant.
– ORIGIN from Greek *arktos* 'bear' + *ouros* 'guardian' (because of its position in line with the tail of Ursa Major).

arcuate /ˈɑːkjʊət/ ▶ **adjective** technical shaped like a bow; curved.
– ORIGIN late Middle English: from Latin *arcuatus*, past participle of *arcuare* 'to curve', from *arcus* 'bow, curve'.

arcus senilis /ˌɑːkəs sɪˈnʌɪlɪs/ ▶ **noun** Medicine a narrow opaque band encircling the cornea, common in old age.
– ORIGIN Latin, literally 'senile bow'.

arc welding ▶ **noun** [mass noun] a technique in which metals are welded using the heat generated by an electric arc.

-ard ▶ **suffix** forming nouns such as *bollard*, *wizard*. ■ forming nouns having a depreciatory sense: *drunkard* | *dullard*.
– ORIGIN from Old French, from German *-hard* 'hard, hardy'.

Ardennes /ɑːˈdɛn/ a forested upland region extending over parts of SE Belgium, NE France, and Luxembourg. It was the scene of fierce fighting in both world wars.

ardent /ˈɑːd(ə)nt/ ▶ **adjective 1** very enthusiastic or passionate: *an ardent supporter of the conservative cause*.
2 archaic or literary burning; glowing: *the ardent flames*.
– DERIVATIVES **ardency** noun, **ardently** adverb.
– ORIGIN Middle English: from Old French *ardant* from Latin *ardens*, *ardent-*, from *ardere* 'to burn'.

Ard Fheis /ɑːd ˈɛʃ/, Irish /ɑːrd ˈeʃ/ ▶ **noun** (pl. **Ard Fheiseann**) an Irish party political conference.
– ORIGIN Irish, from *ard* 'chief' + *feis* 'convention'.

Ardizzone /ˌɑːdɪˈzəʊni/, Edward (Jeffrey Irving) (1900–79), British artist, best known as an illustrator and writer of children's books. He was appointed an official war artist in the Second World War.

Ardnamurchan /ˌɑːdnəˈməːk(ə)n/ a peninsula on the coast of Highland region in western Scotland.

ardour /ˈɑːdə/ (US **ardor**) ▶ **noun** [mass noun] great enthusiasm or passion: *the rebuff did little to dampen his ardour*.
– ORIGIN late Middle English: via Old French from Latin *ardor*, from *ardere* 'to burn'.

arduous /ˈɑːdjʊəs/ ▶ **adjective** involving or requiring strenuous effort; difficult and tiring: *an arduous journey*.
– DERIVATIVES **arduously** adverb, **arduousness** noun.
– ORIGIN mid 16th cent.: from Latin *arduus* 'steep, difficult' + **-OUS**.

are¹ second person singular present and first, second, third person plural present of **BE**.

are² /ɑː/ ▶ **noun** historical a metric unit of measurement, equal to 100 square metres.
– ORIGIN late 18th cent.: from French, from Latin *area* (see **AREA**).

area ▶ **noun 1** a region or part of a town, a country, or the world: *rural areas of Britain* | *people living in the area are at risk*. ■ [with modifier] a space allocated for a specific use: *the dining area*. ■ a part of an object or surface: *areas of the body*. ■ (**the area**) Soccer short for **PENALTY AREA**.
2 the extent or measurement of a surface or piece of land: *the area of a triangle* | [mass noun] *the room is twelve square feet in area*.
3 a subject or range of activity or interest: *the key areas of science*.
4 [usu. as modifier] a sunken enclosure giving access to the basement of a building: *the area steps*.
– DERIVATIVES **areal** adjective.
– ORIGIN mid 16th cent. (in the sense 'space allocated for a specific purpose'): from Latin, literally 'vacant piece of level ground'.

area code ▶ **noun** another term for **DIALLING CODE**.

area dean ▶ **noun** see **DEAN¹** (sense 1).

areaway ▶ **noun** N. Amer. a sunken enclosure giving access to the basement of a building. ■ a passageway between buildings.

areca /ˈarɪkə, əˈriːkə/ (also **areca palm**) ▶ **noun** a tropical Asian palm. ● Genus *Areca*, family Palmae: several species, in particular *A. catechu*.
– ORIGIN via Portuguese from Malayalam *āḍekka*.

A

areca nut ▸ noun the astringent seed of an areca palm (*Areca catechu*), which is often chewed with betel leaves. Also called **BETEL NUT**.

areg plural form of **ERG²**.

areligious /eɪrɪˈlɪdʒəs/ ▸ adjective not influenced by or practising religion: *areligious rationalism was the prevalent trend.*

arena ▸ noun **1** a level area surrounded by seating, in which sports, entertainments, and other public events are held.
2 a place or scene of activity, debate, or conflict: *he has re-entered the political arena.*
– ORIGIN early 17th cent.: from Latin *harena, arena* 'sand, sand-strewn place of combat'.

arenaceous /ˌarɪˈneɪʃəs/ ▸ adjective Geology consisting of sand or sand-like particles. ■ Biology (of animals or plants) living or growing in sand.
– ORIGIN mid 17th cent.: from Latin *arenaceus*, from *arena, harena* 'sand'.

arenavirus /əˈriːnəˌvʌɪrəs/ ▸ noun Medicine any of a group of RNA viruses (including that causing Lassa fever) which appear under an electron microscope to contain sand-like granules.
– ORIGIN 1970s: from Latin *arenosus* 'sandy' (from *arena* 'sand') + **VIRUS**.

aren't ▸ contraction are not: *they aren't here.* ■ am not (only used in questions). *I'm right, aren't I?* | *why aren't I being given a pay rise?*

> **USAGE** The contraction **aren't** is used in standard English to mean 'am not' in questions, as in *I'm right, **aren't** I?* The more logical form **amn't** is now non-standard and restricted to Scottish, Irish, and dialect use. Outside questions, it is incorrect to use **aren't** to mean 'am not' (for example, *I **aren't** going* is clearly wrong).

areola /əˈriːələ/ ▸ noun (pl. **areolae** /-liː/) Anatomy a small circular area, in particular the ring of pigmented skin surrounding a nipple. ■ Biology any of the small spaces between lines or cracks on a leaf or an insect's wing. ■ Medicine a reddened patch around a spot or papule.
– DERIVATIVES **areolar** adjective, **areolate** adjective.
– ORIGIN mid 17th cent. (in the sense 'small space or interstice'): from Latin, literally 'small open space', diminutive of *area* (see **AREA**).

areole /ˈɛːrɪəʊl/ ▸ noun Biology an areola, especially a small area bearing spines or hairs on a cactus.
– ORIGIN mid 19th cent.: from French *aréole*, from Latin (see **AREOLA**).

areology /ˌɛːrɪˈɒlədʒi/ ▸ noun [mass noun] the study of the planet Mars.
– DERIVATIVES **areological** adjective.
– ORIGIN late 19th cent.: from **ARES** + **-OLOGY**.

Areopagus /ˌarɪˈɒpəgəs/ (in ancient Athens) a hill on which was sited the highest governmental council and later a judicial court.
– ORIGIN from Greek *Areios pagos* 'hill of Ares'; the name for the site came to denote the court itself.

Arequipa /ˌarɛˈkiːpə/ a city in the Andes of southern Peru; pop. 784,700 (est. 2007).

Ares /ˈɛːriːz/ Greek Mythology the Greek war god, son of Zeus and Hera. Roman equivalent **MARS**.

arête /əˈrɛt, əˈreɪt/ ▸ noun a sharp mountain ridge.
– ORIGIN early 19th cent.: from French, from Latin *arista* 'ear of corn, fish bone, spine'.

arf (usu. **arf arf**) ▸ exclamation used to imitate or represent laughter or a dog's bark.

'arf ▸ noun, predeterminer, pronoun, adjective, & adverb non-standard spelling of **HALF**, used to represent southern English (especially Cockney) speech.

argali /ˈɑːg(ə)li/ ▸ noun (pl. **same**) the largest wild sheep, which has massive horns and is found in mountainous areas of Asia. ● *Ovis ammon*, family Bovidae.
– ORIGIN late 18th cent.: from Mongolian.

argan /ˈɑːg(ə)n/ ▸ noun an evergreen Moroccan tree or shrub which has hard, heavy wood and yields seeds whose oil is used in cosmetics and cooking. ● *Argania spinosa*, family Sapotaceae.
– ORIGIN Moroccan Arabic, from Berber *argān*.

Argand diagram /ˈɑːgand/ ▸ noun Mathematics a diagram on which complex numbers are represented geometrically using Cartesian axes, the horizontal coordinate representing the real part of the number and the vertical coordinate the complex part.
– ORIGIN early 20th cent.: named after J. R. *Argand* (1768–1822), French mathematician.

Argand lamp ▸ noun historical an oil or gas lamp fitted with a cylindrical burner which allowed air to pass both inner and outer surfaces of the flame.
– ORIGIN late 18th cent.: named after Aimé *Argand* (1755–1803), French physicist.

argent /ˈɑːdʒ(ə)nt/ ▸ adjective literary & Heraldry silver; silvery white: *the argent moon.*
▸ noun [mass noun] Heraldry silver as a heraldic tincture.
– ORIGIN late Middle English (denoting silver coins): via Old French from Latin *argentum* 'silver'.

argentiferous /ˌɑːdʒ(ə)nˈtɪf(ə)rəs/ ▸ adjective (of rocks or minerals) containing silver.
– ORIGIN late 18th cent.: from Latin *argentum* 'silver' + **-FEROUS**.

Argentina /ˌɑːdʒənˈtiːnə/ a republic occupying much of the southern part of South America; pop. 40,913,600 (est. 2009); official language, Spanish; capital, Buenos Aires. Also called **the Argentine** /ˈɑːdʒənˌtʌɪn, -ˌtiːn/.

> Colonized by the Spanish in the 16th century, Argentina declared its independence in 1816. It emerged as a democratic republic in the mid 19th century, but has periodically fallen under military rule. Having long claimed the Falkland Islands, Argentina invaded them in 1982 but was defeated and expelled by British forces.

– DERIVATIVES **Argentine** adjective & noun, **Argentinian** adjective & noun.

argentine /ˈɑːdʒ(ə)ntʌɪn/ ▸ adjective archaic of or resembling silver.
▸ noun a small marine fish with a silvery sheen. ● Family Argentinidae: two genera and several species, in particular *Argentina silus* of the North Atlantic.
– ORIGIN late Middle English: from Old French *argentin, argentine*, from *argent* 'silver', from Latin *argentum*.

Argentine ant ▸ noun a small South American ant that has become established in parts of Europe and Africa. ● *Iridomyrmex humilis*, family Formicidae.

argh ▸ exclamation variant spelling of **AARGH**.

argillaceous /ˌɑːdʒɪˈleɪʃəs/ ▸ adjective Geology (of rocks or sediment) consisting of or containing clay.
– ORIGIN late 17th cent.: from Latin *argillaceus* (from *argilla* 'clay') + **-OUS**.

argillite /ˈɑːdʒɪlʌɪt/ ▸ noun [mass noun] Geology a sedimentary rock that does not split easily, formed from consolidated clay.
– ORIGIN late 18th cent.: from Latin *argilla* 'clay' + **-ITE¹**.

arginine /ˈɑːdʒɪniːn/ ▸ noun [mass noun] Biochemistry a basic amino acid which is a constituent of most proteins. It is an essential nutrient in the diet of vertebrates. ● Chem. formula: $HN{=}C(NH_2)NH(CH_2)_3CH(NH_2)COOH$.
– ORIGIN late 19th cent.: from German *Arginin*, perhaps from Greek *arginoeis* 'bright shining, white'.

Argive /ˈɑːgʌɪv, -dʒʌɪv/ ▸ adjective relating to the ancient city of Argos. ■ (especially in Homer) Greek.
▸ noun a citizen of Argos. ■ (especially in Homer) a Greek person.
– ORIGIN from Latin *Argivus*, from Greek *Argeios* 'relating to Argos'.

argle-bargle ▸ noun [mass noun] **1** copious but meaningless talk or writing; waffle: *bureaucratic argle-bargle.*
2 another term for **ARGY-BARGY**.
– ORIGIN early 19th cent.: reduplication of dialect *argle*, a late 16th-cent. alteration of **ARGUE**.

Argo /ˈɑːgəʊ/ (in full **Argo Navis**) Astronomy, historical a large southern constellation (the ship *Argo*), which is now divided into the constellations Carina, Puppis, and Vela.
– ORIGIN Latin.

argol /ˈɑːg(ə)l/ ▸ noun [mass noun] tartar obtained from wine fermentation.
– ORIGIN Middle English: from Anglo-Norman French *argoile*, of unknown origin.

argon /ˈɑːgɒn/ ▸ noun [mass noun] the chemical element of atomic number 18, an inert gaseous element of the noble gas group. Argon is the commonest noble gas, making up nearly one per cent of the earth's atmosphere. (Symbol: **Ar**)
– ORIGIN late 19th cent.: from Greek, neuter of *argos* 'idle', from *a-* 'without' + *ergon* 'work'.

argonaut /ˈɑːg(ə)nɔːt/ ▸ noun a small floating octopus, the female of which has webbed sail-like arms and secretes a thin coiled papery shell in which the eggs are laid. Also called **PAPER NAUTILUS**. ● Genus *Argonauta*, order Octopoda.

Argonauts /ˈɑːgənɔːts/ Greek Mythology a group of heroes who accompanied Jason on board the ship *Argo* in the quest for the Golden Fleece.
– ORIGIN *argonaut* from Greek *argonautēs* 'sailor in the ship *Argo*'.

Argos /ˈɑːgɒs/ a city in the NE Peloponnese of Greece; pop. 23,600 (est. 2009). One of the oldest cities of ancient Greece, it dominated the Peloponnese and the western Aegean in the 7th century BC.

argosy /ˈɑːgəsi/ ▸ noun (pl. **argosies**) literary a large merchant ship, originally one from Ragusa (now Dubrovnik) or Venice.
– ORIGIN late 16th cent.: apparently from Italian *Ragusea (nave)* '(vessel) of *Ragusa*'.

argot /ˈɑːgəʊ/ ▸ noun the jargon or slang of a particular group or class: *teenage argot.*
– ORIGIN mid 19th cent. (originally denoting the jargon or slang of criminals): from French, of unknown origin.

arguable ▸ adjective **1** able to be argued or asserted: [with clause] *it was arguable that the bank had no authority to honour the cheques.*
2 open to disagreement; not obviously correct: *a highly arguable assumption.*

arguably ▸ adverb [sentence adverb] it may be argued (used to qualify the statement of an opinion or belief): *she is arguably the greatest woman tennis player of all time.*

argue ▸ verb (**argues, arguing, argued**) **1** [reporting verb] give reasons or cite evidence in support of an idea, action, or theory, typically with the aim of persuading others to share one's view: [with clause] *sociologists argue that inequalities in industrial societies are being reduced* | [no obj.] *he **argued for** extra resources* | [with direct speech] *'It stands to reason,' she argued.* ■ [with obj.] (**argue someone into/out of**) persuade someone to do or not to do (something) by giving reasons: *I tried to argue him out of it.*
2 [no obj.] exchange or express diverging or opposite views, typically in a heated or angry way: *the two men started arguing in a local pub* | figurative *I wasn't going to **argue with** a gun* | [with obj.] *she was too tired to **argue the point**.*
– PHRASES **argue the toss** informal, chiefly Brit. dispute a decision or choice already made.
– DERIVATIVES **arguer** noun.
– ORIGIN Middle English: from Old French *arguer*, from Latin *argutari* 'prattle', frequentative of *arguere* 'make clear, prove, accuse'.

argufy /ˈɑːgjʊfʌɪ/ ▸ verb (**argufies, argufying, argufied**) [no obj.] humorous or dialect argue or quarrel, typically about something trivial: *It won't do to argufy, I tell you.*
– ORIGIN late 17th cent.: fanciful formation from **ARGUE**; compare with *speechify*.

argument ▸ noun **1** an exchange of diverging or opposite views, typically a heated or angry one: *I've had an **argument with** my father* | *heated arguments over public spending* | [mass noun] *there was some argument about the decision.*
2 a reason or set of reasons given in support of an idea, action or theory: *there is a strong argument for submitting a formal appeal* | [with clause] *he rejected the argument that keeping the facility would be costly.*
3 Mathematics & Logic an independent variable associated with a function or proposition and determining its value. For example, in the expression $y = F(x_1, x_2)$, the arguments of the function F are x_1 and x_2, and the value is y.
4 another term for **AMPLITUDE** (sense 4).
5 Linguistics any of the noun phrases in a clause that are related directly to the verb, typically the subject, direct object, and indirect object.
6 archaic a summary of the subject matter of a book.
– PHRASES **for the sake of argument** as a basis for discussion or reasoning.
– ORIGIN Middle English (in the sense 'process of reasoning'): via Old French from Latin *argumentum*, from *arguere* 'make clear, prove, accuse'.

argumentation ▸ noun [mass noun] the action or process of reasoning systematically in support of an idea, action, or theory: *lines of argumentation used to support his thesis.*
– ORIGIN late Middle English: via Old French from Latin *argumentatio(n-)*, from *argumentat-* 'conducted as an argument', from *argumentari*.

argumentative ▸ adjective **1** given to arguing: *an argumentative child.*
2 using or characterized by systematic reasoning: *the highest standards of argumentative rigour.*

A

– DERIVATIVES **argumentatively** adverb, **argumentativeness** noun.
– ORIGIN late Middle English: from Old French *argumentatif, -ive* or late Latin *argumentativus*, from *argumentari* 'conduct an argument'.

argument from design ▶ noun Christian Theology the argument that God's existence is demonstrable from the evidence of design in the universe.

argus /ˈɑːɡəs/ ▶ noun **1** (also **argus pheasant**) a large long-tailed pheasant with generally brown plumage, found in SE Asia and Indonesia. ● Two species in the family Phasianidae: the **great argus** (*Argusianus argus*) and the **crested argus** (*Rheinartia ocellata*), which has the longest tail feathers of any bird.
2 a small brown or bluish Eurasian butterfly which has eye-like markings near the wing margins. ● *Aricia* and other genera, family Lycaenidae.
3 (also **argus fish**) a silvery deep-bodied fish with round spots, found throughout the tropical Indo-Pacific region in both fresh and salt water. ● *Scatophagus argus*, family Scatophagidae.
– ORIGIN late Middle English: from Latin, from Greek *Argos*, the name of a mythical watchman with a hundred eyes.

Argus-eyed ▶ adjective literary vigilant.

argute /ɑːˈɡjuːt/ ▶ adjective rare shrewd.
– ORIGIN late 16th cent.: from Latin *argutus* 'made clear, proved, accused', from *arguere*.

argy-bargy /ˌɑːdʒɪˈbɑːdʒi, ˌɑːɡɪˈbɑːɡi/ ▶ noun (pl. **argy-bargies**) [mass noun] informal, chiefly Brit. noisy quarrelling or wrangling: *a bit of argy-bargy between actor and director* | [count noun] *an argy-bargy over the price*.
– ORIGIN late 19th cent. (originally Scots): rhyming jingle based on ARGUE.

argyle /ɑːˈɡʌɪl/ ▶ noun [usu. as modifier] a pattern composed of diamonds of various colours on a plain background, used in knitted garments such as sweaters and socks.
– ORIGIN 1940s: from *Argyll*, a family name and a former county of Scotland. The pattern is based on the tartan of the *Argyll* branch of the Campbell clan.

Argyll and Bute /ɑːˈɡʌɪl, bjuːt/ a council area in the west of Scotland, created in 1996; administrative centre, Lochgilphead.

Argyllshire a former county on the west coast of Scotland. It was divided between Strathclyde and Highland regions in 1975 and in 1996 became part of Argyll and Bute.

arhat /ˈɑːhat/ ▶ noun (in Buddhism and Jainism) a saint of one of the highest ranks.
– ORIGIN from Sanskrit, literally 'meritorious'.

Århus variant spelling of AARHUS.

arhythmic ▶ adjective variant spelling of ARRHYTHMIC.

aria /ˈɑːrɪə/ ▶ noun Music a long accompanied song for a solo voice, typically one in an opera or oratorio.
– ORIGIN early 18th cent.: from Italian, from Latin *aer* 'air'.

Ariadne /ˌarɪˈadni/ Greek Mythology the daughter of King Minos of Crete and Pasiphaë. She helped Theseus to escape from the Minotaur's labyrinth by giving him a ball of thread, which he unravelled as he went in and used to trace his way out again after killing the Minotaur.

Arian[1] /ˈɛːrɪən/ (also **Arien**) ▶ noun a person born under the sign of Aries.
▶ adjective relating to a person born under the sign of Aries.

Arian[2] /ˈɛːrɪən/ ▶ noun an adherent of the doctrine of Arianism.
▶ adjective of or concerning Arianism.

-arian ▶ suffix (forming adjectives and corresponding nouns) having a concern or belief in a specified thing: *humanitarian* | *vegetarian*.
– ORIGIN from the Latin suffix *-arius*.

Arianism ▶ noun [mass noun] Christian Theology the main heresy denying the divinity of Christ, originating with the Alexandrian priest Arius (*c.*250–*c.*336). Arianism maintained that the son of God was created by the Father and was therefore neither coeternal nor consubstantial with the Father.

arid /ˈarɪd/ ▶ adjective **1** (of land or a climate) having little or no rain; too dry or barren to support vegetation: *the arid plains north of Cape Town*.
2 lacking in interest, excitement, or meaning: *his arid years in suburbia*.
– DERIVATIVES **aridity** noun, **aridly** adverb, **aridness** noun.
– ORIGIN mid 17th cent.: from French *aride* or Latin *aridus*, from *arere* 'be dry or parched'.

aridisol /əˈrɪdɪsɒl/ ▶ noun Soil Science a soil of an order comprising typically saline or alkaline soils with very little organic matter, characteristic of arid regions.

Ariel /ˈɛːrɪəl/ **1** Astronomy a satellite of Uranus discovered in 1851, the twelfth closest to the planet and the fourth largest (diameter 1,160 km).
2 a series of six American and British satellites devoted to studies of the ionosphere and X-ray astronomy (1962–79).
– ORIGIN the name of a fairy in Shakespeare's *The Tempest*.

ariel /ˈɛːrɪəl/ ▶ noun a gazelle found in the Middle East and North Africa. ● Genus *Gazella*, family Bovidae: possibly the mountain gazelle (*G. gazella*) or the dorcas gazelle (*G. dorcas*).
– ORIGIN mid 19th cent.: from Arabic *'aryal*.

Arien ▶ noun & adjective variant spelling of ARIAN[1].

Aries /ˈɛːriːz/ **1** Astronomy a small constellation (the Ram), said to represent the ram whose Golden Fleece was sought by Jason and the Argonauts.
2 Astrology the first sign of the zodiac, which the sun enters at the vernal equinox (about 20 March). ■ (**an Aries**) (pl. **same**) a person born when the sun is in this sign.
– PHRASES **First Point of Aries** Astronomy the point on the celestial sphere where the path of the sun crosses the celestial equator from south to north in March, marking the zero point of right ascension. Owing to precession of the equinoxes it has moved from Aries into Pisces, and is now approaching Aquarius . Also called VERNAL EQUINOX.
– ORIGIN Latin.

aright ▶ adverb dialect correctly; properly: *I wondered if I'd heard aright*.
– ORIGIN Old English *on riht, ariht* (see A-[2] 'in', RIGHT).

aril /ˈarɪl/ ▶ noun Botany an extra seed covering, typically coloured and hairy or fleshy, e.g. the red fleshy cup around a yew seed.
– DERIVATIVES **arillate** adjective.
– ORIGIN mid 18th cent.: from modern Latin *arillus*, of unknown origin; perhaps related to medieval Latin *arilli* 'dried grape stones'.

arioso /ˌarɪˈəʊzəʊ, -səʊ/ Music ▶ noun [mass noun] (especially in opera and oratorio) a style of vocal performance more melodic than recitative but less formal than an aria. ■ [count noun] (pl. **ariosos**) a passage in this style.
▶ adjective & adverb in such a style or manner.
– ORIGIN Italian, from ARIA.

Ariosto /ˌarɪˈɒstəʊ/, Ludovico (1474–1533), Italian poet noted for his romantic epic *Orlando Furioso* (final version 1532).

-arious ▶ suffix forming adjectives such as *gregarious, vicarious*.
– ORIGIN from the Latin suffix *-arius* + -OUS.

arise ▶ verb (past **arose**; past participle **arisen**) [no obj.]
1 (of a problem, opportunity, or situation) emerge; become apparent: *new difficulties had arisen*. ■ come into being; originate: *the practice arose in the nineteenth century*. ■ (**arise from/out of**) occur as a result of: *motorists are liable for damages arising out of accidents*.
2 formal or literary get or stand up: *he arose at 9.30*.
– ORIGIN Old English *ārīsan*, from *ā-* 'away' (as an intensifier) + the verb RISE.

arisings ▶ plural noun materials forming the secondary or waste products of industrial operations.

Aristarchus[1] /ˌarɪˈstɑːkəs/ (3rd century BC), Greek astronomer; known as **Aristarchus of Samos**. Founder of an important school of Hellenic astronomy, he was aware of the rotation of the earth around the sun and so was able to account for the seasons.

Aristarchus[2] /ˌarɪˈstɑːkəs/ (*c.*217–145 BC), Greek scholar; known as **Aristarchus of Samothrace**. The librarian at Alexandria, he is noted for his editions of the writings of Homer and other Greek authors.

Aristides /ˌarɪˈstʌɪdiːz/ (5th century BC), Athenian statesman and general; known as **Aristides the Just**. He commanded the Athenian army at the battle of Plataea.

Aristippus /əˈrɪstɪpəs, ˌarɪˈstɪpəs/ (late 5th century BC), Greek philosopher; known as **Aristippus the Elder**. He was a pupil of Socrates and is generally considered the founder of the Cyrenaic school.

aristo /əˈrɪstəʊ/ ▶ noun (pl. **aristos**) informal term for ARISTOCRAT.

aristocracy ▶ noun (pl. **aristocracies**) (usu. **the aristocracy**) [treated as sing. or pl.] the highest class in certain societies, typically comprising people of noble birth holding hereditary titles and offices: *members of the aristocracy*. ■ a form of government in which power is held by the nobility. ■ a state in which governing power is held by the nobility.
– ORIGIN late 15th cent.: from Old French *aristocratie*, from Greek *aristokratia*, from *aristos* 'best' + *-kratia* 'power'. The term originally denoted the government of a state by its best citizens, later by the rich and well born, hence the sense 'nobility', regardless of the form of government (mid 17th cent.).

aristocrat /ˈarɪstəkrat, əˈrɪst-/ ▶ noun a member of the aristocracy.
– ORIGIN late 18th cent.: from French *aristocrate* (a word of the French Revolution), from *aristocratie* (see ARISTOCRACY).

aristocratic ▶ adjective of, belonging to, or typical of the aristocracy: *an aristocratic family*.
– DERIVATIVES **aristocratically** adverb.
– ORIGIN early 17th cent.: from French *aristocratique*, from Greek *aristokratikos*, from *aristokratia* (see ARISTOCRACY).

Aristophanes /ˌarɪˈstɒfəniːz/ (*c.*450–*c.*385 BC), Greek comic dramatist. His surviving plays are characterized by exuberant language and the satirization of leading contemporary figures. Notable works: *Lysistrata*, the *Birds*, the *Frogs*.

Aristotelian /ˌarɪstəˈtiːlɪən/ ▶ adjective relating to Aristotle or his philosophy.
▶ noun a student of Aristotle or an adherent of his philosophy.

Aristotelian logic ▶ noun [mass noun] the traditional system of logic expounded by Aristotle and developed in the Middle Ages, concerned chiefly with deductive reasoning as expressed in syllogisms.

Aristotle /ˈarɪstɒt(ə)l/ (384–322 BC), Greek philosopher and scientist.

> A pupil of Plato and tutor to Alexander the Great, he founded a school (the Lyceum) outside Athens. He is one of the most influential thinkers in the history of Western thought and his work was central to Islamic and Christian medieval philosophy. His surviving works cover a vast range of subjects, including logic, ethics, metaphysics, politics, natural science, and physics.

Aristotle's lantern ▶ noun Zoology a conical structure of calcareous plates and muscles supporting the rasping teeth of a sea urchin.

Arita /əˈriːtə/ ▶ noun [mass noun] a type of Japanese porcelain characterized by asymmetric decoration.
– ORIGIN late 19th cent.: named after *Arita*, a town in Japan, where it is made.

arithmetic ▶ noun /əˈrɪθmətɪk/ [mass noun] the branch of mathematics dealing with the properties and manipulation of numbers: *the laws of arithmetic*. ■ the use of numbers in counting and calculation: *arithmetic had never been her strong point*.
▶ adjective /ˌarɪθˈmɛtɪk/ [attrib.] relating to arithmetic: *arithmetic calculations*.
– DERIVATIVES **arithmetical** adjective, **arithmetically** adverb, **arithmetician** noun.
– ORIGIN Middle English: from Old French *arismetique*, based on Latin *arithmetica*, from Greek *arithmētikē* (*tekhnē*) '(art) of counting', from *arithmos* 'number'.

arithmetic logic unit ▶ noun a unit in a computer which carries out arithmetic and logical operations.

arithmetic mean ▶ noun the average of a set of numerical values, as calculated by adding them together and dividing by the number of terms in the set.

arithmetic progression (also **arithmetic series**) ▶ noun a sequence of numbers in which each differs from the preceding one by a constant quantity (e.g. 1, 2, 3, 4, etc.; 9, 7, 5, 3, etc.).

arithmetic unit ▶ noun another term for ARITHMETIC LOGIC UNIT.

arithmetize /əˈrɪθmətʌɪz/ (also **arithmetise**) ▶ verb [with obj.] express arithmetically; reduce to arithmetical form.

-arium /ˈɛːrɪəm/ ▶ suffix forming nouns usually denoting a place: *planetarium* | *vivarium*.
– ORIGIN from Latin, neuter of *-arius*, adjectival ending.

Ariz. ▶ abbreviation Arizona.

Arizona a state of the south-western US, on the border with Mexico; pop. 6,500,180 (est. 2008); capital, Phoenix. It became the 48th state of the US in 1912.
– DERIVATIVES **Arizonan** noun & adjective.

Arjuna /ˈɑːdʒʊnə/ Hinduism a Kshatriya prince in the Mahabharata, one of the two main characters in the Bhagavadgita.

ark ▶ noun **1** (**the ark**) (in the Bible) the ship built by Noah to save his family and two of every kind of animal from the Flood; Noah's ark. ■ archaic a ship or boat.
2 short for **Ark of the Covenant**. ■ (also **Holy Ark**) a chest or cupboard housing the Torah scrolls in a synagogue.
3 (also **ark shell**) a small bivalve mollusc which attaches itself to rocks with byssus threads. ● Order Arcoidea: *Arca* and other genera.
– PHRASES **be out of** (or **have gone out with**) **the ark** Brit. informal be very old-fashioned.
– ORIGIN Old English *ærc*, from Latin *arca* 'chest'.

Ark. ▶ abbreviation Arkansas.

Arkansas /ˈɑːkənsɔː/ a state of the south central US; pop. 2,855,390 (est. 2008); capital, Little Rock. It became the 25th state of the US in 1836.
– DERIVATIVES **Arkansan** noun & adjective.

Arkhangelsk /arˈxangʲilʲsk/ Russian name for **Archangel**.

Ark of the Covenant (also **Ark of the Testimony**) the wooden chest which contained the tablets of the laws of the ancient Israelites. Carried by the Israelites on their wanderings in the wilderness, it was later placed by Solomon in the Temple at Jerusalem.

arkose /ˈɑːkəʊs, -z/ ▶ noun [mass noun] Geology a coarse-grained sandstone which is at least 25 per cent feldspar.
– DERIVATIVES **arkosic** adjective.
– ORIGIN mid 19th cent.: from French, probably from Greek *arkhaios* 'ancient'.

Arkwright, Sir Richard (1732–92), English inventor and industrialist. In 1767 he patented a water-powered spinning machine capable of producing yarn strong enough to be used as warp.

Arles /ɑːl/, French /aʀl/ a city in SE France; pop. 53,058 (2006). It was the capital of the medieval kingdom of Arles, formed in the 10th century by the union of Provence and Burgundy.

Arlington /ˈɑːlɪŋtən/ **1** a county in northern Virginia, forming a suburb of Washington. It is the site of the Pentagon.
2 an industrial city in northern Texas, between Dallas and Fort Worth; pop. 374,417 (est. 2008).

Arlon /ɑːˈlɒ̃/, French /aʀlɔ̃/ a town in SE Belgium, capital of the province of Luxembourg; pop. 26,929 (2008).

arm¹ ▶ noun **1** each of the two upper limbs of the human body from the shoulder to the hand: *she held the baby in her arms*. ■ a flexible limb of an invertebrate animal, e.g. an octopus. ■ a sleeve of a garment. ■ used to refer to the holding of a person's arm in support or companionship: *as they walked he offered her his arm | he arrived with a pretty girl on his arm*. ■ used to refer to something powerful or protective: *they have extended the arm of friendship to developing countries*.
2 a thing resembling an arm in form or function, in particular: ■ a side part of a chair or other seat on which a sitter can rest their arm. ■ a narrow strip of water or land projecting from a larger body.
3 a branch or division of a company or organization: *the political arm of the separatist group*. ■ each of the types of troops of which an army is composed, such as infantry or artillery. [also understood as a figurative use of **arm²**.]
4 Mathematics each of the lines enclosing an angle.
– PHRASES **arm in arm** (of two or more people) with arms linked. **as long as one's** (or **someone's**) **arm** informal very long: *I have a list of vices as long as your arm*. **at arm's length 1** away from the body, with one's arm fully extended: *I held the telephone at arm's length*. **2** avoiding intimacy or close contact: *he has long fought to keep the government at arm's length from big business*. **cost an arm and a leg** informal be extremely expensive. **give one's right arm** informal used to convey how much one would like to have or do something: *I'd give my right arm to go with them*. **in arms** (of a baby) too young to walk: *a babe in arms*. **the long** (or **strong**) **arm of the law** the far-reaching power of the law. **put the arm on** N. Amer. informal attempt to force or coerce (someone) to do something: *she started putting the arm on them for donations*. **under one's arm** between one's arm and one's body: *Meryl tucked the papers under her arm*. **with open arms** with great affection or enthusiasm: *schools have welcomed such arrangements with open arms*. **within** (or **beyond**) **arm's reach** near (or not near) enough to reach by extending one's arm: *he came closer, almost within arm's reach | the bookshelf is within arm's reach of my computer*.
– DERIVATIVES **armful** noun (pl. **armfuls**), **armless** adjective, **armload** noun.
ORIGIN Old English *arm*, *earm*, of Germanic origin; related to Dutch *arm* and German *Arm*.

arm² ▶ verb [with obj.] **1** supply or provide with weapons: *the security forces are **armed with** automatic rifles*. ■ supply or provide with equipment, tools, or other items in preparation or readiness for something: *she **armed them with** brushes and mops*.
2 activate the fuse of (a bomb, missile, or other explosive device) so that it is ready to explode.
– ORIGIN Middle English: from Old French *armer* (verb), from Latin *armare*, from *arma* 'armour, arms'.

armada /ɑːˈmɑːdə/ ▶ noun a fleet of warships. ■ (**the Armada** or **the Spanish Armada**) a Spanish naval invasion force sent against England in 1588 by Philip II of Spain. It was defeated by the English fleet and almost completely destroyed by storms off the Hebrides.
– ORIGIN mid 16th cent.: from Spanish, from *armata*, feminine past participle of Latin *armare* 'to arm'.

armadillo /ˌɑːməˈdɪləʊ/ ▶ noun (pl. **armadillos**) a nocturnal insectivorous mammal that has large claws for digging and a body covered in bony plates. Armadillos are native to Central and South America and one kind is spreading into the southern US. ● Family Dasypodidae, order Xenarthra (or Edentata): several genera.
– ORIGIN late 16th cent.: from Spanish, diminutive of *armado* 'armed man', from Latin *armatus*, past participle of *armare* 'to arm'.

Armageddon /ˌɑːməˈgɛd(ə)n/ ▶ noun (in the New Testament) the last battle between good and evil before the Day of Judgement. ■ the place where the Armageddon will be fought. ■ a dramatic and catastrophic conflict, especially one seen as likely to destroy the world or the human race: *nuclear Armageddon*.
– ORIGIN Greek, from Hebrew *har měgiddōn* 'hill of Megiddo' (Rev. 16:16).

Armagh /ɑːˈmɑː/ one of the Six Counties of Northern Ireland, since 1973 an administrative district. ■ the chief town of Armagh; pop. 15,100 (est. 2009).

Armagnac /ˈɑːmənjak/ ▶ noun [mass noun] a type of brandy traditionally made in Aquitaine in SW France.
– ORIGIN from the former name of a district in Aquitaine.

Armalite /ˈɑːməlʌɪt/ ▶ noun trademark a type of light automatic rifle.

armament /ˈɑːməm(ə)nt/ ▶ noun [mass noun] (also **armaments**) military weapons and equipment. ■ the process of equipping military forces for war. ■ [count noun] archaic a military force equipped for war.
– ORIGIN late 17th cent. (in the sense 'force equipped for war'): from Latin *armamentum*, from *armare* 'to arm' (see **arm²**).

armamentarium /ˌɑːməmɛnˈtɛːrɪəm/ ▶ noun (pl. **armamentaria** /-rɪə/) the medicines, equipment, and techniques available to a medical practitioner.
– ORIGIN late 19th cent.: from Latin, 'arsenal, armoury'.

Armani /ɑːˈmɑːni/, Italian /arˈmani/, Giorgio (b.1935), Italian fashion designer.

armature /ˈɑːmətʃə, -tj(ʊ)ə/ ▶ noun **1** the rotating coil or coils of a dynamo or electric motor. ■ any moving part of an electrical machine in which a voltage is induced by a magnetic field. ■ a piece of iron or other object acting as a keeper for a magnet.
2 an open framework on which a sculpture is moulded with clay or similar material. ■ a framework or formal structure, especially of a literary work: *Shakespeare's plots have served as the armature for many novels*.
3 Biology the protective covering of an animal or plant. ■ [mass noun] archaic armour.
– ORIGIN late Middle English: from French, from Latin *armatura* 'armour', from *armare* 'to arm' (see **arm²**). The original sense was 'armour', hence 'protective covering' (sense 3, early 18th cent.), later 'keeper of a magnet', source of sense 1 (mid 19th cent.).

armband ▶ noun a band worn around a person's upper arm to hold up a shirtsleeve or as a form of identification. ■ an inflatable plastic band worn around a person's upper arm as a swimming aid.

arm candy ▶ noun informal a sexually attractive companion accompanying a person, especially a celebrity, at social events.

armchair ▶ noun a large, comfortable chair with side supports for a person's arms. ■ [as modifier] lacking or not involving practical or direct experience of a particular subject or activity: *an armchair traveller*.

Armco /ˈɑːmkəʊ/ ▶ noun [mass noun] trademark a very pure soft iron, used in particular for roadside crash barriers.
– ORIGIN early 20th cent.: acronym from *American Rolling Mill Company*.

armed ▶ adjective **1** equipped with or carrying a firearm or firearms: *heavily armed troops*. ■ involving the use of firearms: *armed robbery*.
2 Heraldry having claws, a beak, etc. of a specified tincture.
– PHRASES **armed to the teeth** formidably armed.

armed forces (also **armed services**) ▶ plural noun a country's army, navy, and air force.

Armenia /ɑːˈmiːnɪə/ a landlocked country in the Caucasus of SW Asia; pop. 2,967,000 (est. 2009); official language, Armenian; capital, Yerevan.

> The Armenian homeland fell under Turkish rule from the 16th century, and with the decline of the Ottomans was divided between Turkey, Iran, and Russia. In 1915 the Turks forcibly deported 1,750,000 Armenians to the deserts of Syria and Mesopotamia; more than 600,000 were killed or died on forced marches. Russian Armenia was absorbed into the Soviet Union in 1922, gaining independence as a member of the Commonwealth of Independent States in 1991.

Armenian /ɑːˈmiːnɪən/ ▶ noun **1** a native of Armenia, or a person of Armenian descent.
2 [mass noun] the Indo-European language of Armenia, spoken by around 4 million people and written in a distinctive alphabet of thirty-eight letters.
▶ adjective relating to Armenia or to the Armenian Church.

Armenian Church (also **Armenian Apostolic Orthodox Church**) an independent Christian Church established in Armenia since *c.*300 and influenced by Roman and Byzantine as well as Syrian traditions. A small Armenian Catholic Church also exists (see **Uniate**).

armhole ▶ noun each of two openings in a garment through which the wearer puts their arms.

armiger /ˈɑːmɪdʒə/ ▶ noun a person entitled to heraldic arms.
– DERIVATIVES **armigerous** adjective.
– ORIGIN mid 16th cent.: Latin, literally 'bearing arms', from *arma* 'arms' + *gerere* 'to bear'.

armillaria /ˌɑːmɪˈlɛːrɪə/ ▶ noun a fungus of a genus that includes the honey fungus, found chiefly in woodland. Its mycelia can grow for a considerable distance, enabling individuals of parasitic species to invade more than one tree. ● Genus *Armillaria*, family Tricholomataceae, class Hymenomycetes: many species, including *A. bulbosa*, a single individual of which may span several hectares.
– ORIGIN modern Latin: from Latin *armilla* 'bracelet' (because of the bracelet-like frill on the fruiting bodies).

armillary sphere ▶ noun a model of the celestial globe constructed from rings and hoops representing the equator, the tropics, and other celestial circles, and able to revolve on its axis.
– ORIGIN mid 17th cent.: from modern Latin *armillaris* 'relating to an *armilla*', an astronomical instrument consisting of a hoop fixed in the plane of the equator (sometimes crossed by one in the plane of the meridian), used by the ancient astronomers to show the recurrence of equinoxes and solstices; from Latin *armilla* 'bracelet'.

Arminian /ɑːˈmɪnɪən/ ▶ adjective relating to the doctrines of Jacobus Arminius (Latinized name of Jakob Hermandszoon, 1560–1609), a Dutch Protestant theologian who rejected the Calvinist doctrine of predestination. His teachings had a considerable influence on Methodism.
▶ noun an adherent of Arminian doctrines.
– DERIVATIVES **Arminianism** noun.

armistice /ˈɑːmɪstɪs/ ▶ noun an agreement made by opposing sides in a war to stop fighting for a certain time; a truce.
– ORIGIN early 18th cent.: from French, or from modern Latin *armistitium*, from *arma* 'arms' (see **arm²**) + *-stitium* 'stoppage'.

Armistice Day ▶ noun the anniversary of the armistice of 11 November 1918, now replaced by Remembrance Sunday in the UK and Veterans Day in the US.

A

armlet ▸ noun a band or bracelet worn round the upper part of a person's arm.

armlock ▸ noun a method of restraining someone by holding their arm tightly behind their back.

armoire /ɑːˈmwɑː/ ▸ noun a cupboard or wardrobe, typically one that is ornate or antique.
– ORIGIN late 16th cent.: from French, from Old French *armarie* (see AUMBRY).

armor ▸ noun US spelling of ARMOUR.

armored ▸ adjective US spelling of ARMOURED.

armorer ▸ noun US spelling of ARMOURER.

armorial /ɑːˈmɔːrɪəl/ ▸ adjective relating to heraldry or heraldic devices: *armorial bearings*.
– ORIGIN late Middle English: from Old French *armoierie* (see ARMOURY).

Armorica /ɑːˈmɒrɪkə/ an ancient region of NW France between the Seine and the Loire.

Armorican ▸ adjective relating to Armorica. ■ Geology another term for HERCYNIAN.

armory[1] /ˈɑːməri/ ▸ noun [mass noun] heraldry.
– ORIGIN late Middle English: from Old French *armoierie* (see ARMOURY).

armory[2] ▸ noun US spelling of ARMOURY.

armour (US **armor**) ▸ noun [mass noun] **1** the metal coverings formerly worn to protect the body in battle: *knights in armour* | *a suit of armour*.
2 (also **armour plate**) the tough metal layer covering a military vehicle or ship to defend it from attack. ■ military vehicles collectively: *infantry, armour, and logistic units*.
3 the protective layer or shell of some animals and plants.
4 a person's emotional, social, or other defences: *his armour of self-confidence*.
▸ verb [with obj.] provide (someone) with emotional, social, or other defences: *the knowledge **armoured** him **against** her*.
– DERIVATIVES **armour-plated** adjective.
– ORIGIN Middle English: from Old French *armure*, from Latin *armatura*, from *armare* 'to arm' (see ARM[2]).

armoured (US **armored**) ▸ adjective **1** covered with or protected by armour: *armoured vehicles*.
2 (of some animals and plants) having a protective layer or shell: *armoured fish*.

armoured personnel carrier ▸ noun an armoured military vehicle used to transport troops.

armourer (US **armorer**) ▸ noun **1** a maker, supplier, or repairer of weapons or armour.
2 an official in charge of the arms of a warship or regiment.
– ORIGIN Middle English: from Old French *armurier*, from *armure* (see ARMOUR).

armoury (US **armory**) ▸ noun (pl. **armouries**) **1** a place where arms are kept. ■ a supply of arms: *Britain's nuclear armoury expanded*. ■ US a place where arms are manufactured.
2 an array of resources available for a particular purpose: *his armoury of comic routines*.
3 N. Amer. a place where militia units drill and train.
– ORIGIN Middle English (in the sense 'armour'): from Old French *armoirie, armoierie*, from *armoier* 'to blazon', from *arme* 'weapon' (see ARMS). The change in the second syllable in the 17th cent. was due to association with ARMOUR.

armpit ▸ noun a hollow under the arm at the shoulder. Also called AXILLA. ■ informal, chiefly N. Amer. a place regarded as extremely unpleasant: *they call the region the armpit of America*.
– PHRASES **up to one's armpits** chiefly US deeply involved in a particular unpleasant situation or enterprise: *the country is **up to its armpits** in drug trafficking*.

armrest ▸ noun a padded or upholstered arm of a chair or other seat on which a sitter can comfortably rest their arm.

arms ▸ plural noun **1** weapons; armaments: *arms and ammunition* | [as modifier] *arms exports*.
2 distinctive emblems or devices originally borne on shields in battle and now forming the heraldic insignia of families, corporations, or countries.
– PHRASES **a call to arms** a call to defend or make ready for confrontation. **in arms** armed; prepared to fight. **take up arms** begin fighting. **under arms** equipped and ready for war or battle. **up in arms** protesting vigorously about something: *teachers are **up in arms about** new school tests*.
– ORIGIN Middle English: from Old French *armes*, from Latin *arma*.

arms control ▸ noun [mass noun] international disarmament or arms limitation, especially by mutual consent.

arm's-length ▸ adjective [attrib.] avoiding intimacy or close contact: *they maintained an arm's-length relationship*.

arms race ▸ noun a competition between nations for superiority in the development and accumulation of weapons.

Armstrong[1], (Daniel) Louis (1900–71), American jazz musician; known as **Satchmo**. A major influence on Dixieland jazz, he was a trumpet and cornet player as well as a bandleader and a distinctive singer.

Armstrong[2], Neil (Alden) (b.1930), American astronaut. He commanded the Apollo 11 mission, during which he became the first man to set foot on the moon (20 July 1969).

arm-twisting ▸ noun [mass noun] informal the action of pressurizing someone into doing something they are unwilling do do: *a day of arm-twisting by government whips*.
– DERIVATIVES **arm-twist** verb.

arm-wrestling ▸ noun [mass noun] a trial of strength in which two people sit opposite each other with one elbow resting on a table, clasp each other's hands, and try to force each other's arm down on to the table.
– DERIVATIVES **arm-wrestle** verb.

army ▸ noun (pl. **armies**) **1** [treated as sing. or pl.] an organized military force equipped for fighting on land: *the two armies were in position* | [as modifier] *army officers*. ■ (**the army**) the part of a country's military force trained to fight on land: *he joined the army at 16*.
2 (**an army of**/**armies of**) a large number of people or things: *an army of photographers*.
– PHRASES **you and whose army?** informal used as an expression of disbelief in someone's ability to carry out a threat: *'One word to him and I'll have you.' 'You and whose army?'*
– ORIGIN late Middle English: from Old French *armee*, from *armata*, feminine past participle of Latin *armare* 'to arm'.

army ant ▸ noun a blind nomadic tropical ant that forages in large columns, preying chiefly on insects and spiders. Also called DRIVER ANT. ● Subfamily Dorylinae, family Formicidae.

army disposal ▸ noun Australian term for ARMY SURPLUS.

army issue ▸ noun [mass noun] [usu. as modifier] equipment or clothing supplied by the army.

Army List ▸ noun (in the UK) an official list of commissioned officers.

army-navy ▸ adjective US denoting the type of shop which specializes in military surplus equipment, or the goods sold there.

army surplus ▸ noun [mass noun] goods and equipment which are surplus to the army's requirements: [as modifier] *an army surplus store*.

army worm ▸ noun any of a number of insect larvae which occur in destructive swarms, in particular: ● the caterpillars of some moths, which feed on cereals and other crops and move en masse when the food is exhausted (*Spodoptera* and other genera, family Noctuidae). ● the small maggots of certain fungus gnats, which move in large numbers within secreted slime (genus *Sciara*, family Mycetophilidae).

Arne /ɑːn/, Thomas (1710–78), English composer noted for 'Rule, Britannia' (whose words are attributed to James Thomson) and for his settings of Shakespearean songs.

Arnel /ˈɑːnɛl/ ▸ noun [mass noun] trademark a synthetic fibre or fabric made from cellulose triacetate.

Arnhem /ˈɑːnəm/ a town in the eastern Netherlands, situated on the River Rhine, capital of the province of Gelderland; pop. 143,582 (2008). During the Second World War, in September 1944, Allied airborne troops made a landing nearby but were overwhelmed by German forces.

Arnhem Land a peninsula in Northern Territory, Australia, whose chief town is Nhulunbuy. In 1976 Arnhem Land was declared an Aboriginal reservation.

arnica /ˈɑːnɪkə/ ▸ noun a plant of the daisy family which bears yellow, daisy-like flowers, found in cooler regions of the northern hemisphere. ● Genus *Arnica*, family Compositae: many species, especially mountain tobacco (*A. montana*) of central Europe.
■ [mass noun] a preparation of the arnica plant used medicinally, especially for the treatment of bruises.
– ORIGIN mid 18th cent.: modern Latin, of unknown origin.

Arno /ˈɑːnəʊ/ a river which rises in the Apennines of northern Italy and flows westwards 240 km (150 miles) through Florence and Pisa to the Ligurian Sea.

Arnold[1], Sir Malcolm (Henry) (1921–2006), English composer and trumpeter, noted especially for his orchestral works and film scores.

Arnold[2], Matthew (1822–88), English poet, essayist, and social critic. In works such as *Culture and Anarchy* (1869) he criticized the Victorian age in terms of its materialism, philistinism, and complacency. Notable poems: 'The Scholar Gipsy' (1853), 'Dover Beach' (1867).

aroha /ˈɑːrɒhə/ ▸ noun [mass noun] NZ love; affection. ■ sympathy.
– ORIGIN Maori.

aroid /ˈɛːrɔɪd/ (also **aroid lily**) ▸ noun Botany a plant of the arum family (Araceae).
– ORIGIN late 19th cent.: from ARUM + -OID.

arolla /əˈrɒlə/ (also **arolla pine**) ▸ noun a tall pine tree of the Alps and Carpathian Mountains, frequently planted in dense clumps as an avalanche break. ● *Pinus cembra*, family Pinaceae. Alternative name: **Swiss stone pine**.
– ORIGIN late 19th cent.: from Swiss French *arol(l)e*.

aroma ▸ noun a distinctive, typically pleasant smell: *the tantalizing aroma of fresh coffee*. ■ a subtle, pervasive quality or atmosphere: *the aroma of officialdom*.
– ORIGIN Middle English (usually in the plural denoting fragrant plants or spices): via Latin from Greek *arōma* 'spice'.

aromatherapy ▸ noun [mass noun] the use of aromatic plant extracts and essential oils for healing and cosmetic purposes.
– DERIVATIVES **aromatherapeutic** adjective, **aromatherapist** noun.

aromatic ▸ adjective **1** having a pleasant and distinctive smell: *a massage with aromatic oils*.
2 Chemistry relating to or denoting organic compounds containing a planar unsaturated ring of atoms which is stabilized by an interaction of the bonds forming the ring, e.g. benzene and its derivatives. Compare with ALICYCLIC.
▸ noun **1** a substance or plant emitting a pleasant and distinctive smell.
2 Chemistry an aromatic compound.
– DERIVATIVES **aromatically** adverb, **aromaticity** noun (Chemistry).
– ORIGIN late Middle English: via Old French from late Latin *aromaticus*, from Greek *arōmatikos*, from *arōma* (see AROMA).

aromatize (also **aromatise**) ▸ verb [with obj.] **1** Chemistry convert (a compound) into an aromatic structure.
2 give (something) a pleasant and distinctive smell.
– DERIVATIVES **aromatization** noun.
– ORIGIN late Middle English: from Old French *aromatiser*, from late Latin *aromatizare*, from Greek *arōmatizein* 'to spice'.

aronia /əˈrəʊnɪə/ ▸ noun a plant of the genus *Aronia* in the rose family, especially (in gardening) a chokeberry.
– ORIGIN modern Latin, from Greek *arōnia* 'medlar'.

arose past of ARISE.

around ▸ adverb **1** located or situated on every side: *the mountains towering all around*.
2 so as to face in the opposite direction: *Guy seized her by the shoulders and turned her around*.
3 in or to many places throughout a locality: *word got around that he was on the verge of retirement*.
4 aimlessly or unsystematically; here and there: *one of them was glancing nervously around*.
5 present, living, in the vicinity, or in active use: *there was no one around* | *maize has been around for a long time*.
6 (used with a number or quantity) approximately: *software costs would be around £1,500* | *I returned to my hotel around 3 a.m.*
▸ preposition **1** on every side of: *the palazzo is built around a courtyard* | *the hills around the city*. ■ (of something abstract) having (the thing mentioned) as a focal point: *our entire culture is built around those loyalties*.
2 in or to many places throughout (a community or locality): *cycling around the village* | *a number of large depots around the country*.

3 following an approximately circular route: *he walked around the airfield | it can drill around corners.*
4 so as to encircle or embrace (someone or something): *he put his arm around her.*
– PHRASES **have been around** informal have a lot of varied experience and understanding of the world.
– ORIGIN Middle English: from **A-**[2] 'in, on' + **ROUND**.

> **USAGE** On the difference in use between **round** and **around**, see **USAGE** at **ROUND**.

arousal ▶ **noun** [mass noun] the action or fact of arousing or being aroused: *sexual arousal in dreams is common.*

arouse ▶ **verb** [with obj.] **1** evoke or awaken (a feeling, emotion, or response): *something about the man aroused the guard's suspicions | the letter **aroused in** him a sense of urgency.* ■ excite or provoke (someone) to anger or strong emotions: *an ability to influence the audience and to arouse the masses.* ■ excite (someone) sexually: *his touch, which had so aroused her moments before, unnerved her now* | (as adj. **aroused**) *she told him how aroused she was.*
2 awaken (someone) from sleep: *she had been aroused from deep slumber.*
– DERIVATIVES **arousable** adjective.
– ORIGIN late 16th cent.: from **ROUSE**, on the pattern of the pair of *rise, arise*.

ARP ▶ **abbreviation** Brit. historical air-raid precautions.

Arp /ɑːp/, French /aʀp/, Jean (1887–1966), French painter, sculptor, and poet; also known as **Hans Arp**. He was a co-founder of the Dada movement and is noted for his three-dimensional abstract curvilinear sculptures in marble and bronze.

arpeggiate /ɑːˈpɛdʒɪeɪt/ ▶ **verb** [with obj.] Music play (a chord) as a series of ascending or descending notes.
– DERIVATIVES **arpeggiation** noun, **arpeggiator** noun.

arpeggio /ɑːˈpɛdʒɪəʊ/ ▶ **noun** (pl. **arpeggios**) Music the notes of a chord played in rapid succession, either ascending or descending.
– ORIGIN Italian, from *arpeggiare* 'play the harp', from *arpa* 'harp'.

arpeggione /ɑːˌpɛdʒɪˈəʊneɪ, -ni/ ▶ **noun** an early 19th-century stringed instrument resembling a guitar in shape and having six strings and frets, but played with a bow like a cello.
– ORIGIN late 19th cent.: from German, from **ARPEGGIO**.

arquebus /ˈɑːkwɪbəs/ (also **harquebus**) ▶ **noun** historical an early type of portable gun supported on a tripod or a forked rest.
– ORIGIN mid 16th cent.: from French *harquebuse*, based on Middle Low German *hakebusse*, from *hake* 'hook' + *busse* 'gun'.

arr. ▶ **abbreviation** ■ (of a piece of music) arranged by: *Variations on a theme of Corelli (arr. Wild).* ■ (with reference to the arrival time of a bus, train, or aircraft) arrives.

arrabbiata /ˌarəˈbjɑːtə/ ▶ **adjective** denoting a spicy pasta sauce made with tomatoes and chilli peppers.
– ORIGIN Italian, literally 'angry', feminine past participle of *arrabbiare* 'make angry'.

arrack /ˈarək, əˈrak/ (also **arak**) ▶ **noun** [mass noun] an alcoholic spirit made in Eastern countries from the sap of the coco palm or from rice.
– ORIGIN early 17th cent.: from Arabic *ʿaraq* 'sweat', from the phrase *ʿaraq al-tamr*, denoting an alcoholic spirit made from dates.

arrah /ˈarə/ ▶ **exclamation** Irish expressing excitement or strong emotion: *'Arrah, don't be talking nonsense,' Elmer exclaimed.*
– ORIGIN late 17th cent.: from Irish *ara, arú*.

arraign /əˈreɪn/ ▶ **verb** call or bring (someone) before a court to answer a criminal charge: *her sister was **arraigned on** charges of attempted murder.* ■ find fault with; censure: *social workers were relieved it was not they who were arraigned in the tabloids.*
– ORIGIN late Middle English: from Old French *araisnier*, based on Latin *ad-* 'to' + *ratio(n-)* 'reason, account'.

arraignment ▶ **noun** [mass noun] the action of arraigning someone in court: *he's scheduled for arraignment in New York on Thursday* | [count noun] *she pleaded not guilty at her arraignment.*

Arran an island in the Firth of Clyde, in the west of Scotland.

arrange ▶ **verb** [with obj.] **1** put (things) in a neat, attractive, or required order: *she had just finished arranging the flowers | the columns are **arranged in** 12 rows.*
2 organize or make plans for (a future event): *they hoped to arrange a meeting* | [no obj.] *my aunt **arranged for** the furniture to be stored.* ■ [no obj.] reach agreement about an action or event in advance: *I **arranged with** my boss to have the time off* | [with infinitive] *they arranged to meet at eleven o'clock.* ■ ensure that (something) is done or provided by organizing it in advance: *accommodation can be arranged if required.*
3 Music adapt (a composition) for performance with instruments or voices other than those originally specified: *songs **arranged for** viola and piano.*
4 archaic settle (a dispute or claim).
– DERIVATIVES **arrangeable** adjective, **arranger** noun.
– ORIGIN late Middle English: from Old French *arangier*, from *a-* (from Latin *ad* 'to, at') + *rangier* 'put in order' (see **RANGE**).

arranged marriage ▶ **noun** a marriage planned and agreed by the families or guardians of the couple concerned.

arrangement ▶ **noun 1** [mass noun] the action, process, or result of arranging or being arranged: *the arrangement of the furniture in the room.* ■ [count noun] a thing that has been arranged in a neat or attractive way: *flower arrangements | an intricate arrangement of gravel paths.*
2 (usu. **arrangements**) a plan or preparation for a future event: *all the arrangements for the wedding were made.* ■ an agreement with someone to do something: *the travel agents have an **arrangement with** the hotel* | [mass noun] ***by special arrangement***, *students can take a course in other degree programmes.*
3 Music a composition arranged for performance with instruments or voices differing from those originally specified: *Mozart's symphonies in **arrangements for** cello and piano.*
4 archaic a settlement of a dispute or claim.

arrant /ˈar(ə)nt/ ▶ **adjective** [attrib.] dated complete, utter: *what arrant nonsense!*
– DERIVATIVES **arrantly** adverb.
– ORIGIN Middle English: variant of **ERRANT**, originally in phrases such as *arrant thief* ('outlawed, roving thief').

Arras /ˈarəs/, French /aʀas/ a town in NE France; pop. 43,663 (2006). In medieval times it was a centre for the manufacture of tapestries.

arras /ˈarəs/ ▶ **noun** a wall hanging made of a rich tapestry fabric, typically used to conceal an alcove.
– ORIGIN late Middle English (originally denoting the fabric itself): named after the French town of **ARRAS**.

array /əˈreɪ/ ▶ **noun 1** an impressive display or range of a particular type of thing: *there is a vast array of literature on the topic | a bewildering array of choices.*
2 an ordered arrangement, in particular: ■ an arrangement of troops. ■ Mathematics an arrangement of quantities or symbols in rows and columns; a matrix. ■ Computing an indexed set of related elements.
3 [mass noun] literary elaborate or beautiful clothing: *he was clothed in fine array.*
4 Law a list of jurors impanelled.
▶ **verb 1** [with obj. and adverbial of place] display or arrange (things) in a particular way: *the manifesto immediately divided the forces arrayed against him.*
2 [with obj.] (usu. **be arrayed in**) dress someone in (the clothes specified): *they were arrayed in Hungarian national dress.*
3 [with obj.] Law impanel (a jury).
– ORIGIN Middle English (in the senses 'preparedness' and 'place in readiness'): from Old French *arei* (noun), *areer* (verb), based on Latin *ad-* 'towards' + a Germanic base meaning 'prepare'.

arré /ˈəreɪ/ ▶ **exclamation** Indian used to express annoyance, surprise, or interest, or to attract someone's attention.
– ORIGIN via Hindi from Sanskrit *are*, an interjection for calling to a person of inferior rank.

arrears ▶ **plural noun** money that is owed and should have been paid earlier.
– PHRASES **in arrears** (also chiefly Law **in arrear**) **1** behind with paying money that is owed: *two out of three tenants are in arrears.* ■ (of payments made or due for wages, rent, etc.) at the end of each period in which work is done or a tenancy is occupied: *you will be paid monthly in arrears.* **2** (of a competitor in a sports race or match) having a lower score or weaker performance than other competitors: *she finished ten metres in arrears.*
– DERIVATIVES **arrearage** noun.
– ORIGIN Middle English (first used in the phrase *in arrear*): from *arrear* (adverb) 'behind, overdue', from Old French *arere*, from medieval Latin *adretro*, from *ad-* 'towards' + *retro* 'backwards'.

Arrernte /əˈrʌntə, aˈruːndə/ ▶ **noun** (pl. **same**) **1** a member of an Aboriginal people of central Australia.
2 [mass noun] the language of the Arrernte, now with fewer than 2,000 speakers.
▶ **adjective** relating to the Arrernte or their language.
– ORIGIN the name in Arrernte.

arrest ▶ **verb** [with obj.] **1** seize (someone) by legal authority and take them into custody: *the police **arrested** him **for** possession of marijuana | two youths aged 16 were arrested.* ■ seize and detain (a ship) by legal authority.
2 stop or check (progress or a process): *the spread of the disease can be arrested.* ■ [no obj.] suffer a heart attack: *they were trying to resuscitate a patient who had arrested.*
3 attract the attention of (someone): *the church's stillness arrested her.*
▶ **noun 1** [mass noun] the action of seizing someone and taking them into custody: *I have a warrant for your arrest | they **placed** her **under arrest*** | [count noun] *at least 69 arrests were made.*
2 a stoppage or sudden cessation of motion: *a respiratory arrest.*
– PHRASES **arrest of judgement** Law the suspension of proceedings in a criminal trial between the verdict and the sentence on the grounds of a material irregularity in the course of the trial.
– ORIGIN late Middle English: from Old French *arester*, based on Latin *ad-* 'at, to' + *restare* 'remain, stop'.

arrestable offence ▶ **noun** Law, Brit. an offence for which there is a fixed mandatory penalty or which carries a sentence of at least five years' imprisonment (e.g. theft).

arrestee ▶ **noun** chiefly N. Amer. a person who has been or is being legally arrested.

arrester (also **arrestor**) ▶ **noun** a device which prevents or stops a specified thing: *a spark arrester.* ■ a device on an aircraft carrier that slows down aircraft after landing by means of a hook and cable.

arresting ▶ **adjective** striking; eye-catching: *at 6 ft 6 in he was an arresting figure.*
– DERIVATIVES **arrestingly** adverb.

arrestment ▶ **noun** Scots Law an attachment of property for the satisfaction of a debt.

Arretine /ˈarətʌɪn/ ▶ **adjective** denoting Samian ware (Roman pottery), especially that made at Arretium (modern Arezzo) in central Italy.
– ORIGIN late 18th cent.: from the name of the city + **-INE**[1].

arrhythmia /eɪˈrɪðmɪə/ (also **arhythmia**) ▶ **noun** [mass noun] Medicine a condition in which the heart beats with an irregular or abnormal rhythm.
– ORIGIN late 19th cent.: from Greek *arruthmia* 'lack of rhythm', from *a-* 'without' + *rhuthmos* (see **RHYTHM**).

arrhythmic (also **arhythmic**) ▶ **adjective** not rhythmic; without rhythm or regularity: *the arrhythmic phrasing of the music.* ■ Medicine relating to or suffering from cardiac arrhythmia.
– DERIVATIVES **arrhythmical** adjective, **arrhythmically** adverb.

arrière-pensée /ˌarɪɛː ˈpɒ̃seɪ/, French /aʀjɛʀ pɑ̃se/ ▶ **noun** a concealed thought or intention; an ulterior motive.
– ORIGIN French, literally 'behind thought'.

arris /ˈarɪs/ ▶ **noun** Architecture a sharp edge formed by the meeting of two flat or curved surfaces.
– ORIGIN late 17th cent.: alteration of early modern French *areste* 'sharp ridge', earlier form of **ARÊTE**.

arris rail ▶ **noun** a fence rail with a triangular cross section.

arrival ▶ **noun** [mass noun] the action or process of arriving: *Ruth's arrival in New York | he was dead **on arrival** at hospital.* ■ [count noun] a person who has arrived somewhere: *hotel staff greeted the late arrivals.* ■ the emergence or appearance of a new development or product: *the arrival of democracy.* ■ [count noun] a newly emerged development or product: *sociology is a relatively new arrival on the academic scene.*
– ORIGIN late Middle English: from Anglo-Norman French *arrivaille*, from Old French *arriver* (see **ARRIVE**).

arrive ▶ **verb** [no obj.] **1** reach a place at the end of a journey or a stage in a journey: *we **arrived at** his house and knocked at the door | the team **arrived in** New Delhi on July 30 | they had recently **arrived from***

A

Turkey. ■ (of a thing) be brought or delivered: *the invitation arrived a few days later.*
2 (of an event or a particular moment) happen or come: *we will be in touch with them when the time arrives.* ■ (of a new development or product) come into existence or use: *microcomputers arrived at the start of the 1970s.*
3 (**arrive at**) reach (a conclusion or decision): *they arrived at the same conclusion.*
4 (of a baby) be born: *he will feel jealous when a new baby arrives.*
5 informal achieve success or recognition.
– ORIGIN Middle English (in the sense 'reach the shore after a voyage'): from Old French *ariver*, based on Latin *ad-* 'to' + *ripa* 'shore'.

arrivederci /əriːvəˈdɛːtʃi, arivɛˈdɛrtʃi/ ▶ **exclamation** goodbye until we meet again.
– ORIGIN Italian, 'until we see each other again'.

arriviste /ˌariːˈviːst/ ▶ **noun** an ambitious or ruthlessly self-seeking person.
– DERIVATIVES **arrivisme** /ˌariːˈviːzm(ə)/ **noun**.
– ORIGIN early 20th cent.: from French, from *arriver* (see **ARRIVE**).

arrogance ▶ **noun** [mass noun] the quality of being arrogant: *the arrogance of this man is astounding.*

arrogant ▶ **adjective** having or revealing an exaggerated sense of one's own importance or abilities: *he's arrogant and opinionated | a typically arrogant assumption.*
– DERIVATIVES **arrogantly adverb**.
– ORIGIN late Middle English: via Old French from Latin *arrogant-* 'claiming for oneself', from the verb *arrogare* (see **ARROGATE**).

arrogate /ˈarəgeɪt/ ▶ **verb** [with obj.] take or claim (something) for oneself without justification: *they* ***arrogate to themselves*** *the ability to divine the nation's true interests.*
– DERIVATIVES **arrogation noun**.
– ORIGIN mid 16th cent.: from Latin *arrogat-* 'claimed for oneself', from the verb *arrogare*, from *ad-* 'to' + *rogare* 'ask'.

arrondissement /aˈrɒndiːsmɑ̃, ˌarɒnˈdiːsmɑ̃/, French /arɔ̃dismɑ̃/ ▶ **noun** a subdivision of a French department, for local government administration. ■ an administrative district of certain large French cities, in particular Paris.
– ORIGIN French, from *arrondir* 'make round'.

arrow ▶ **noun** a weapon consisting of a thin, straight stick with a sharp point, designed to be shot from a bow. ■ a mark or sign resembling an arrow, used to show direction or position: *we followed a series of arrows.*
▶ **verb** [no obj., with adverbial of direction] move or appear to move swiftly and directly: *lights* ***arrowed down*** *into the airport.*
– DERIVATIVES **arrowed adjective**, **arrowy adjective**.
– ORIGIN Old English *arewe*, *arwe*, from Old Norse.

arrowgrass ▶ **noun** [mass noun] a grass-like marsh plant with a slender spike of tiny flowers. ● Genus *Triglochin*, family Juncaginaceae.

arrowhead ▶ **noun 1** the pointed end of an arrow.
2 Geometry a quadrilateral in which one internal angle is more than 180°.
3 a Eurasian water plant with arrow-shaped leaves above the water surface. ● Genus *Sagittaria*, family Alismataceae: several species.

arrowroot ▶ **noun** a herbaceous Caribbean plant from which a starch is prepared. ● *Maranta arundinacea*, family Marantaceae.
■ [mass noun] the fine-grained starch obtained from arrowroot, used in cookery and medicine.
– ORIGIN late 17th cent.: alteration of Arawak *aru-aru* (literally 'meal of meals') by association with **ARROW** and **ROOT**[1], the tubers being used to absorb poison from arrow wounds.

arrow slit ▶ **noun** (especially in a medieval fortified building) a narrow vertical slit in a wall for shooting or looking through or to admit light and air.

arrow worm ▶ **noun** a slender transparent worm-like animal with fins, having spines on the head for grasping prey. It is common in marine plankton. Also called **CHAETOGNATH**. ● Phylum Chaetognatha.

arroyo /əˈrɔɪəʊ/ ▶ **noun** (pl. **arroyos**) a steep-sided gully formed by the action of fast-flowing water in an arid or semi-arid region, found chiefly in the south-western US.
– ORIGIN mid 19th cent.: from Spanish.

arroz /aˈrɒs/, Spanish /aˈrəθ, aˈrəs/ ▶ **noun** Spanish word for **RICE**, used in the names of various dishes.

arse Brit. vulgar slang ▶ **noun 1** a person's buttocks or anus.
2 a stupid, irritating, or contemptible person.
▶ **verb 1** [no obj.] (**arse about/around**) behave in a stupid way; waste time.
2 [with obj.] (**arse something up**) make a botched attempt at something.
3 (**can't be arsed**) not want to do something because one has no interest in or enthusiasm for it.
– PHRASES **arse about face** contrary to what is usual, expected, or logical. **arse over tit** so as to fall over in a sudden or dramatic way. **get off one's arse** stop being lazy. **my arse!** used to convey that one does not believe something that has just been said. **not know one's arse from one's elbow** be totally ignorant or incompetent. **talk out of one's arse** talk rubbish. **up your arse!** used to express contempt for someone or something.
– ORIGIN Old English *ærs*, of Germanic origin; related to Dutch *aars* and German *Arsch*.

arse bandit ▶ **noun** Brit. vulgar slang a male homosexual.

arsehole ▶ **noun** Brit. vulgar slang **1** the anus.
2 a stupid, irritating, or contemptible person.

arse-kissing ▶ **noun** another term for **ARSE-LICKING**.

arse-licking ▶ **noun** [mass noun] vulgar slang the action or practice of behaving obsequiously in order to gain favour.
– DERIVATIVES **arse-licker noun**.

arsenal ▶ **noun** a collection of weapons and military equipment: *Britain's nuclear arsenal.* ■ a place where weapons and military equipment are stored or made. ■ an array of resources available for a certain purpose: *we have an arsenal of computers at our disposal.*
– ORIGIN early 16th cent. (denoting a dock for the construction and repair of ships): from French, or from obsolete Italian *arzanale*, based on Arabic *dār-aṣ-ṣinā'a*, from *dār* 'house' + *al-* '(of) the' + *sinā'a* 'art, industry'.

arsenate /ˈɑːs(ə)neɪt/ ▶ **noun** Chemistry a salt or ester of any oxyacid of arsenic.

arsenic ▶ **noun** /ˈɑːs(ə)nɪk/ [mass noun] the chemical element of atomic number 33, a brittle steel-grey semimetal. (Symbol: **As**)

> Arsenic compounds (and their poisonous properties) have been known since ancient times, and the metallic form was isolated in the Middle Ages. Arsenic occurs naturally in orpiment, realgar, and other minerals, and rarely as the free element. Arsenic is used in semiconductors and some specialized alloys; its toxic compounds are widely used as herbicides and pesticides.

▶ **adjective** /ɑːˈsɛnɪk/ relating to arsenic. ■ Chemistry of arsenic with a valency of five; of arsenic(V). Compare with **ARSENIOUS**.
– ORIGIN late Middle English (denoting yellow orpiment, arsenic sulphide): via Old French from Latin *arsenicum*, from Greek *arsenikon* 'yellow orpiment', identified with *arsenikos* 'male', but in fact from Arabic *al-zarnīḵ* 'the orpiment', based on Persian *zar* 'gold'.

arsenic acid ▶ **noun** [mass noun] Chemistry a weakly acidic crystalline solid with oxidizing properties, formed when arsenic reacts with nitric acid. ● Chem. formula: H_3AsO_4.

arsenical /ɑːˈsɛnɪk(ə)l/ ▶ **adjective** of or containing arsenic.
▶ **noun** an arsenical drug or other compound.

arsenide ▶ **noun** Chemistry a binary compound of arsenic with a metallic element.

arsenious /ɑːˈsiːnɪəs/ ▶ **adjective** Chemistry of arsenic with a valency of three; of arsenic(III). Compare with **ARSENIC**.

arsenopyrite /ˌɑːs(ə)nəʊˈpʌɪrʌɪt/ ▶ **noun** [mass noun] a silvery-grey mineral consisting of an arsenide and sulphide of iron and cobalt.

arsey ▶ **adjective** (**arsier**, **arsiest**) informal **1** Brit. bad-tempered or uncooperative.
2 Austral. very lucky. [alteration of slang *tin arse* 'lucky person', from *tin* 'money', figuratively 'luck'.]

arsine /ˈɑːsiːn/ ▶ **noun** [mass noun] Chemistry a poisonous gas smelling slightly of garlic, made by the reaction of some arsenides with acids. ● Alternative name: **arsenic trihydride**; chem. formula: AsH_3.
– ORIGIN late 19th cent.: from **ARSENIC**, on the pattern of *amine*.

arsis /ˈɑːsɪs/ ▶ **noun** (pl. **arses** /-siːz/) Prosody a stressed syllable or part of a metrical foot in Greek or Latin verse. Often contrasted with **THESIS** (sense 3).
– ORIGIN late Middle English: via late Latin from Greek, literally 'lifting', from *airein* 'raise'.

arson ▶ **noun** [mass noun] the criminal act of deliberately setting fire to property: *police are treating the fire as arson* | [as modifier] *an arson attack.*
– ORIGIN late 17th cent.: an Anglo-Norman French legal term, from medieval Latin *arsio(n-)*, from Latin *ardere* 'to burn'.

arsonist ▶ **noun** a person who commits arson: *police believe arsonists were responsible for both fires.*

arsphenamine /ɑːsˈfɛnəmiːn, -ɪn/ ▶ **noun** [mass noun] Medicine a synthetic organic arsenic compound formerly used to treat syphilis and other diseases. See also **EHRLICH**.
– ORIGIN early 20th cent.: blend of **ARSENIC**, **PHENYL**, and **AMINE**.

arsy-versy ▶ **adjective & adverb** informal in a confused, disordered, or perversely contrary state or manner: [as adj.] *they got things all arsy-versy.*
– ORIGIN mid 16th cent.: from **ARSE** + Latin *versus* 'turned', the addition of **-Y**[1] to both elements forming a jingle.

art[1] ▶ **noun 1** [mass noun] the expression or application of human creative skill and imagination, typically in a visual form such as painting or sculpture, producing works to be appreciated primarily for their beauty or emotional power: *the art of the Renaissance | great art is concerned with moral imperfections | she studied art in Paris.* ■ works produced by such skill and imagination: *his collection of modern art* | [as modifier] *an art critic.* ■ creative activity resulting in the production of paintings, drawings, or sculpture: *she's good at art.*
2 (**the arts**) the various branches of creative activity, such as painting, music, literature, and dance: *the visual arts* | [in sing.] *the art of photography.*
3 (**arts**) subjects of study primarily concerned with human creativity and social life, such as languages, literature, and history (as contrasted with scientific or technical subjects): *the belief that the arts and sciences were incompatible | the Faculty of Arts.*
4 a skill at doing a specified thing, typically one acquired through practice: *the art of conversation.*
– PHRASES **art for art's sake** used to convey the idea that the chief or only aim of a work of art is the self-expression of the individual artist who creates it. **art is long, life is short** proverb there is so much knowledge to acquire that a lifetime is not sufficient.
– ORIGIN Middle English: via Old French from Latin *ars*, *art-*.

art[2] archaic or dialect second person singular present of **BE**.

art. ▶ **abbreviation** article.

Artaud /ɑːˈtəʊ/, French /artəʊ/, Antonin (1896–1948), French actor, director, and poet. He developed the concept of the non-verbal Theatre of Cruelty, which concentrated on the use of sound, mime, and lighting, expounding his theory in a series of essays *Le Théâtre et son double* (1938).

Artaxerxes /ˌɑːtəˈzəːksiːz/ the name of three kings of ancient Persia: ■ **Artaxerxes I** son of Xerxes I, reigned 464–424 BC. ■ **Artaxerxes II** son of Darius II, reigned 404–358 BC. ■ **Artaxerxes III** son of Artaxerxes II, reigned 358–338 BC.

art deco /ˈdɛkəʊ/ ▶ **noun** [mass noun] the predominant decorative art style of the 1920s and 1930s, characterized by precise and boldly delineated geometric shapes and strong colours and used most notably in household objects and in architecture.
– ORIGIN 1960s: shortened from French *art décoratif* 'decorative art', from the 1925 *Exposition des Arts décoratifs* in Paris.

artefact /ˈɑːtɪfakt/ (US **artifact**) ▶ **noun 1** an object made by a human being, typically one of cultural or historical interest: *gold and silver artefacts.*
2 something observed in a scientific investigation or experiment that is not naturally present but occurs as a result of the preparative or investigative procedure.
– DERIVATIVES **artefactual adjective**.
– ORIGIN early 19th cent.: from Latin *arte* 'by or using art' + *factum* 'something made' (neuter past participle of *facere* 'make').

artel /ɑːˈtɛl/ ▶ **noun** (pl. **artels**, **arteli**) historical (in pre-revolutionary Russia) a cooperative association of craftsmen living and working together.
– ORIGIN from Russian *artel'*.

Artemis /ˈɑːtɪmɪs/ Greek Mythology a goddess, daughter of Zeus and sister of Apollo. She was a huntress and is typically depicted with a bow and arrows. Roman equivalent **DIANA**.

artemisia /ˌɑːtɪˈmɪzɪə/ ▶ **noun** an aromatic or bitter-tasting plant of a genus that includes wormwood,

mugwort, and sagebrush. Several kinds are used in herbal medicine and many are cultivated for their feathery grey foliage. ● Genus *Artemisia*, family Compositae.
– ORIGIN Middle English: via Latin from Greek, 'wormwood', named after the goddess **Artemis**, to whom it was sacred.

artemisinin /ˌɑːtɪˈmiːsɪnɪn/ ▶ **noun** [mass noun] a terpene-based antimalarial substance used in Chinese medicine. ● The drug is obtained from *Artemisia annua*, family Compositae.
– ORIGIN 1970s: blend of **artemisia** and **quinine**.

Arte Povera /ˌɑːteɪ ˈpɒvərə/ ▶ **noun** [mass noun] an artistic movement that originated in Italy in the 1960s, combining aspects of conceptual, minimalist, and performance art, and making use of worthless or common materials such as earth or newspaper, in the hope of subverting the commercialization of art.
– ORIGIN 1960s: Italian, literally 'impoverished art', from *arte* 'art' + *povera* (feminine of *povero* 'needy').

arterial /ɑːˈtɪərɪəl/ ▶ **adjective 1** relating to an artery or arteries.
2 denoting an important route in a system of roads, railway lines, or rivers: *one of the main arterial routes from York.*
– ORIGIN late Middle English: from medieval Latin *arterialis*, from Latin *arteria* (see **artery**).

arterialize (also **arterialise**) ▶ **verb** [with obj.] (usu. as adj. **arterialized**) convert venous into arterial (blood) by oxygenation, especially in the lungs.
– DERIVATIVES **arterialization** noun.

arterio- ▶ **combining form** relating to the arteries: *arteriosclerosis.*
– ORIGIN from Greek *artēria* (see **artery**).

arteriography /ɑːˌtɪərɪˈɒɡrəfi/ ▶ **noun** [mass noun] Medicine radiography of an artery, carried out after injection of a radiopaque substance.

arteriole /ɑːˈtɪərɪəʊl/ ▶ **noun** Anatomy a small branch of an artery leading into capillaries.
– DERIVATIVES **arteriolar** adjective.
– ORIGIN mid 19th cent.: from French *artériole*, diminutive of *artère* (see **artery**).

arteriosclerosis /ɑːˌtɪərɪəʊsklɪəˈrəʊsɪs, -sklə-/ ▶ **noun** [mass noun] Medicine the thickening and hardening of the walls of the arteries, occurring typically in old age.
– DERIVATIVES **arteriosclerotic** adjective.

arteriovenous /ɑːˌtɪərɪəʊˈviːnəs/ ▶ **adjective** Anatomy relating to or affecting an artery and a vein.

arteritis ▶ **noun** [mass noun] Medicine inflammation of the walls of an artery.

artery ▶ **noun** (pl. **arteries**) **1** any of the muscular-walled tubes forming part of the circulation system by which blood (mainly that which has been oxygenated) is conveyed from the heart to all parts of the body. Compare with **vein** (sense 1).
2 an important route in a system of roads, rivers, or railway lines: *George Street, main artery of Edinburgh's Golden Mile.*
– ORIGIN late Middle English: from Latin *arteria*, from Greek *artēria*, probably from *airein* 'raise'.

artesian /ɑːˈtiːzɪən, -ʒ(ə)n/ ▶ **adjective** relating to or denoting a well bored perpendicularly into water-bearing strata lying at an angle, so that natural pressure produces a constant supply of water with little or no pumping.
– ORIGIN mid 19th cent.: from French *artésien* 'from Artois' (see **Artois**), where such wells were first made.

Artex /ˈɑːtɛks/ ▶ **noun** [mass noun] trademark a kind of plaster applied to walls and ceilings to give a textured finish.
▶ **verb** [with obj.] cover (a wall or ceiling) with Artex.
– ORIGIN 1950s: blend of **art**[1] and **texture**.

art form ▶ **noun** a conventionally established form of artistic composition, such as the novel, sonata, or sonnet. ■ any activity regarded as a medium of imaginative or creative self-expression: *he elevates stage managing to an art form.*

artful ▶ **adjective 1** clever or skilful, especially in a crafty or cunning way: *her artful wiles.*
2 showing creative skill or taste: *an artful photograph of a striking woman.*
– DERIVATIVES **artfully** adverb, **artfulness** noun.

art history ▶ **noun** [mass noun] the academic study of the history and development of painting, sculpture, and the other visual arts.
– DERIVATIVES **art historian** noun.

art house ▶ **noun** a cinema which specializes in showing films that are artistic or experimental rather than merely entertaining.

arthralgia /ɑːˈθraldʒə/ ▶ **noun** [mass noun] Medicine pain in a joint.
– ORIGIN mid 19th cent.: from Greek *arthron* 'joint' + **-algia**.

arthritis /ɑːˈθrʌɪtɪs/ ▶ **noun** [mass noun] a disease causing painful inflammation and stiffness of the joints.
– DERIVATIVES **arthritic** adjective & noun.
– ORIGIN mid 16th cent.: via Latin from Greek, from *arthron* 'joint'. *Arthritic* was already used in late Middle English.

arthro- ▶ **combining form** of a joint; relating to joints: *arthroscope.*
– ORIGIN from Greek *arthron* 'joint'.

arthrodesis /ɑːˈθrɒdɪsɪs/ ▶ **noun** [mass noun] surgical immobilization of a joint by fusion of the bones.
– ORIGIN early 20th cent.: from **arthro-** + Greek *desis* 'binding together'.

arthropod /ˈɑːθrəpɒd/ ▶ **noun** Zoology an invertebrate animal of the large phylum Arthropoda, such as an insect, spider, or crustacean.

Arthropoda /ˌɑːθrəˈpəʊdə/ ▶ **plural noun** Zoology a large phylum of invertebrate animals that includes insects, spiders, crustaceans, and their relatives. They have a segmented body, an external skeleton, and jointed limbs, and are sometimes placed in different phyla.
– ORIGIN modern Latin (plural), from Greek *arthron* 'joint' + *pous, pod-* 'foot'.

arthroscope /ˈɑːθrəskəʊp/ ▶ **noun** Medicine an instrument through which the interior of a joint may be inspected or operated on.
– DERIVATIVES **arthroscopic** adjective, **arthroscopy** noun.

Arthur[1] a legendary king of Britain, historically perhaps a 5th- or 6th-century Romano-British chieftain or general. Stories of his life, the exploits of his knights, and the Round Table of his court at Camelot were developed by Malory, Chrétien de Troyes, and other medieval writers and became the subject of many legends.
– DERIVATIVES **Arthurian** /ɑːˈθjʊərɪən/ adjective.

Arthur[2], Chester Alan (1830–86), American Republican statesman, 21st President of the US 1881–5.

artic /ˈɑːtɪk/ ▶ **noun** Brit. informal an articulated lorry.
– ORIGIN 1950s: abbreviation.

artichoke /ˈɑːtɪtʃəʊk/ ▶ **noun 1** (also **globe artichoke**) a European plant cultivated for its large thistle-like flower heads. ● *Cynara scolymus*, family Compositae.
■ the unopened flower head of the artichoke, of which the heart and the fleshy bases of the bracts are edible.
2 Brit. short for **Jerusalem artichoke**.
– ORIGIN mid 16th cent.: from northern Italian *articiocco*, from Spanish *alcarchofa*, from Arabic *al-ḵaršūfa*.

article ▶ **noun 1** a particular item or object: *small household articles | articles of clothing.*
2 a piece of writing included with others in a newspaper, magazine, or other publication: *an article about middle-aged executives.*
3 a separate clause or paragraph of a legal document or agreement, typically one outlining a single rule or regulation.
4 (**articles**) Brit. a period of training with a firm as a solicitor, architect, surveyor, or accountant: *he is already in articles | it may be worth taking articles in a specialized firm.* ■ the terms on which crew members take service on a ship.
5 Grammar the definite or indefinite article. See also **determiner** (sense 2).
▶ **verb** [with obj.] Brit. bind (a trainee solicitor, architect, surveyor, or accountant) to undergo a period of training with a firm in order to become qualified: *he was articled to a firm of solicitors in York.*
– PHRASES **an article of faith** a firmly held belief. **article of virtu** see **virtu**. **the finished article** something that is complete and ready for use. **the genuine article** a person or thing considered to be an authentic and excellent example of their kind.
– ORIGIN Middle English (denoting a separate clause of the Apostles' Creed): from Old French, from Latin *articulus* 'small connecting part', diminutive of *artus* 'joint'.

articled clerk ▶ **noun** Brit. a trainee solicitor.

articular /ɑːˈtɪkjʊlə/ ▶ **adjective** relating to a joint or the joints: *articular cartilage.*
– ORIGIN late Middle English: from Latin *articularis*, from *articulus* 'small connecting part' (see **article**).

articulate ▶ **adjective** /ɑːˈtɪkjʊlət/ **1** having or showing the ability to speak fluently and coherently: *she was not very articulate.*
2 technical having joints or jointed segments. ■ Zoology denoting a brachiopod which has projections and sockets that form a hinge joining the two halves of the shell.
▶ **verb** /ɑːˈtɪkjʊleɪt/ [with obj.] **1** pronounce (something) clearly and distinctly: *he articulated each word with precision.* ■ express (an idea or feeling) fluently and coherently: *they were unable to articulate their emotions.*
2 [no obj.] form a joint: *the mandible is a solid piece articulating with the head.* ■ (**be articulated**) be connected by joints.
– DERIVATIVES **articulable** adjective, **articulacy** noun, **articulately** adverb, **articulateness** noun.
– ORIGIN mid 16th cent.: from Latin *articulatus*, past participle of *articulare* 'divide into joints, utter distinctly', from *articulus* 'small connecting part' (see **article**).

articulated ▶ **adjective** Brit. having two or more sections connected by a flexible joint: *an articulated lorry | the trilobite's thorax has a number of articulated segments.*

articulation ▶ **noun** [mass noun] **1** the formation of clear and distinct sounds in speech: *the articulation of vowels and consonants.* ■ the action of putting into words an idea or feeling: *it would involve the articulation of a theory of the just war.* ■ Phonetics the formation of a speech sound by constriction of the air flow in the vocal organs at a particular place (e.g. the tongue, teeth, or palate) and in a particular way (as a plosive, affricate, etc.).
2 Music clarity in the production of successive notes.
3 the state of being jointed: *the area of articulation of the lower jaw.* ■ [count noun] a specified joint: *the leg articulation.*
– ORIGIN late Middle English (in the senses 'joint', 'joining'): from Latin *articulatio(n-)*, from the verb *articulare* (see **articulate**).

articulator ▶ **noun 1** a person who puts forward or expresses an idea.
2 any of the vocal organs above the larynx, including the tongue, lips, teeth, and hard palate.

articulatory /ɑːˈtɪkjʊlət(ə)ri, ɑːˌtɪkjʊˈleɪt(ə)ri/ ▶ **adjective** relating to the formation of speech sounds.

artifact ▶ **noun** US spelling of **artefact**.

artifice /ˈɑːtɪfɪs/ ▶ **noun** [mass noun] clever or cunning devices or expedients, especially as used to trick or deceive others: *an industry dominated by artifice |* [count noun] *the style is not free from the artifices of the period.*
– ORIGIN late Middle English (in the sense 'workmanship'): from Old French, from Latin *artificium*, based on *ars, art-* 'art' + *facere* 'make'.

artificer /ɑːˈtɪfɪsə/ ▶ **noun 1** a skilled mechanic in the armed forces.
2 archaic a skilled craftsman or inventor.
– ORIGIN late Middle English: from Anglo-Norman French, probably an alteration of Old French *artificien*, from *artifice* (see **artifice**).

artificial ▶ **adjective 1** made or produced by human beings rather than occurring naturally, especially as a copy of something natural: *her skin glowed in the artificial light | an artificial limb | artificial flowers.* ■ (of a situation or concept) not existing naturally; contrived or false: *the artificial division of people into age groups.*
2 (of a person or their behaviour) insincere or affected: *she gave an artificial smile.*
3 Bridge (of a bid) conventional as opposed to natural.
– DERIVATIVES **artificiality** noun, **artificially** adverb.
– ORIGIN late Middle English: from Old French *artificiel* or Latin *artificialis*, from *artificium* 'handicraft' (see **artifice**).

artificial horizon ▶ **noun** a gyroscopic instrument or a fluid surface, typically one of mercury, used to provide the pilot of an aircraft with a horizontal reference plane for navigational measurement when the natural horizon is obscured.

artificial insemination (abbrev.: **AI**) ▶ **noun** [mass noun] the medical or veterinary procedure of injecting semen into the vagina or uterus.

artificial intelligence (abbrev.: **AI**) ▶ **noun** [mass noun] the theory and development of computer systems able to perform tasks normally requiring human intelligence, such as visual perception,

A

speech recognition, decision-making, and translation between languages.

artificial kidney ▶ noun a machine or other mechanical device which performs the functions of the human kidney.

artificial life ▶ noun [mass noun] the simulation by computer programs or computerized systems of the behaviour, population dynamics, or other characteristics of living organisms.

artificial respiration ▶ noun [mass noun] the restoration or initiation of someone's breathing by manual, mechanical, or mouth-to-mouth methods.

artificial silk ▶ noun old-fashioned term for VISCOSE.

artillery /ɑːˈtɪləri/ ▶ noun (pl. **artilleries**) [mass noun] large-calibre guns used in warfare on land: *tanks and heavy artillery*. ■ a military detachment or branch of the armed forces that uses large-calibre guns.
– DERIVATIVES **artillerist** noun.
– ORIGIN late Middle English: from Old French *artillerie*, from *artiller*, alteration of *atillier* 'equip, arm', probably a variant of *atirier*, from *a-* (from Latin *ad* 'to, at') + *tire* 'rank, order'.

artilleryman ▶ noun (pl. **artillerymen**) a member of a regiment of artillery.

artiodactyl /ɑːtɪə(ʊ)ˈdaktʌɪl, -tɪl/ Zoology ▶ noun a mammal of the order Artiodactyla, such as a cow, sheep, camel, or pig.
▶ adjective relating to or denoting artiodactyls.

Artiodactyla /ˌɑːtɪə(ʊ)ˈdaktɪlə/ ▶ plural noun Zoology an order of mammals that comprises the even-toed ungulates. Compare with PERISSODACTYLA.
– ORIGIN modern Latin (plural), from Greek *artios* 'even' + *daktulos* 'finger, toe'.

artisan /ˌɑːtɪˈzan, ˈɑːtɪzan/ ▶ noun a worker in a skilled trade, especially one that involves making things by hand.
– DERIVATIVES **artisanal** /ɑːˈtɪzən(ə)l/ adjective.
– ORIGIN mid 16th cent.: from French, from Italian *artigiano*, based on Latin *artitus*, past participle of *artire* 'instruct in the arts', from *ars, art-* 'art'.

artist ▶ noun **1** a person who creates paintings or drawings as a profession or hobby. ■ a person who practises or performs any of the creative arts, such as a sculptor, film-maker, actor, or dancer. ■ a person skilled at a particular task or occupation: *a surgeon who is an artist with the scalpel*.
2 [with modifier] informal a person who habitually practises a specified reprehensible activity: *rip-off artists*.
– ORIGIN early 16th cent. (denoting a master of the liberal arts): from French *artiste*, from Italian *artista*, from *arte* 'art', from Latin *ars, art-*.

artiste /ɑːˈtiːst/ ▶ noun a professional entertainer, especially a singer or dancer: *cabaret artistes*.
– ORIGIN early 19th cent.: from French (see ARTIST).

artistic ▶ adjective having or revealing natural creative skill: *my lack of artistic ability*. ■ relating to or characteristic of art or artists: *a denial of artistic freedom*. ■ aesthetically pleasing: *computer programs which produce artistic designs*.
– DERIVATIVES **artistically** adverb.

artistic director ▶ noun the person with overall responsibility for the selection and interpretation of the works performed by a theatre, ballet, or opera company.

artistry ▶ noun [mass noun] creative skill or ability: *the artistry of the pianist*.

artist's fungus ▶ noun a bracket fungus with a reddish-brown upper surface and a pale lower surface on which scratches remain visible as dark marks, found in both Eurasia and North America.
● *Ganoderma applanatum*, family Ganodermataceae, class Hymenomycetes.

artist's impression ▶ noun a sketch or drawing of someone or something, produced when no photograph is available.

artless ▶ adjective without guile or deception: *an artless, naive girl* | *artless sincerity*. ■ without effort or pretentiousness; natural and simple: *an artless literary masterpiece*. ■ without skill or finesse: *her awkward, artless prose*.
– DERIVATIVES **artlessly** adverb.

art nouveau /ˌɑː(t) nuːˈvəʊ/ ▶ noun [mass noun] a style of decorative art, architecture, and design prominent in western Europe and the USA from about 1890 until the First World War and characterized by intricate linear designs and flowing curves based on natural forms.
– ORIGIN early 20th cent.: from French, literally 'new art'.

Artois /ɑːˈtwʌ/, French /aʀtwa/ a region and former province of NE France.

art paper ▶ noun [mass noun] Brit. high-quality paper coated with china clay or a similar substance to give it a smooth surface.

arts and crafts ▶ plural noun decorative design and handicraft.

Arts and Crafts Movement an English decorative arts movement of the second half of the 19th century which sought to revive the ideal of craftsmanship in an age of increasing mechanization and mass production. William Morris was its most prominent member.

art therapy ▶ noun [mass noun] a form of psychotherapy involving the encouragement of free self-expression through painting, drawing, or modelling, used as a remedial or diagnostic activity.

artwork ▶ noun [mass noun] illustrations, photographs, or other non-textual material prepared for inclusion in a publication. ■ paintings, drawings, or other artistic works: *a collection of artwork from tribal cultures* | [count noun] *each artwork is reproduced in colour on a full page*.

arty (chiefly N. Amer. also **artsy**) ▶ adjective (**artier, artiest; artsier, artsiest**) informal making a strong, affected, or pretentious display of being artistic or interested in the arts: *television people and arty types* | *a very arty film*.
– DERIVATIVES **artily** adverb, **artiness** noun.

arty-crafty (chiefly N. Amer. also **artsy-craftsy**) ▶ adjective informal interested or involved in making decorative artistic objects, especially ones perceived as quaint or homespun: *he mixed with the arty-crafty set*.

arty-farty (chiefly N. Amer. also **artsy-fartsy**) ▶ adjective informal, derogatory associated with or showing an interest in the arts: *you'll have to forget that arty-farty nonsense here*.

Aruba /əˈruːbə/ an island in the Caribbean Sea, close to the Venezuelan coast; pop. 103,100 (est. 2009); capital, Oranjestad. Formerly part of the Netherlands Antilles, it separated from that group in 1986 to become a self-governing territory of the Netherlands.

arugula /əˈruːgjʊlə/ (also **rucola, rugola**) ▶ noun [mass noun] N. Amer. the rocket plant, used in cookery.
– ORIGIN 1970s: from Italian dialect, ultimately a diminutive of Latin *eruca* 'down-stemmed plant'.

arum /ˈɛːrəm/ ▶ noun a European plant which has arrow-shaped leaves and a broad leafy spathe enclosing a club-shaped spadix. Pollination is by small flies which are temporarily trapped by the plant. ● Genus *Arum*, family Araceae (the **arum family**): several species, in particular the common **wild arum** or cuckoo pint.
– ORIGIN late Middle English: from Latin, from Greek *aron*.

arum lily ▶ noun chiefly Brit. a tall lily-like African plant which bears a large showy spathe. Also called CALLA LILY, especially in North America. ● Genus *Zantedeschia*, family Araceae: several species, in particular *Z. aethiopica*.

Arunachal Pradesh /ɑːrəˌnɑːtʃəl prəˈdɛʃ/ a mountainous state in the far north-east of India, lying on the borders of Tibet to the north and Burma (Myanmar) to the east; capital, Itanagar. It became a state of India in 1986.

Arunta /əˈrʌntə, aˈruːndə/ ▶ noun & adjective variant form of ARRERNTE.

ARV ▶ abbreviation antiretroviral (drug).

arvo /ˈɑːvəʊ/ ▶ noun (pl. **arvos**) Austral./NZ informal afternoon: *on Monday arvo*.
– ORIGIN 1930s: abbreviation of AFTERNOON (with voicing of the *f*) + -O.

-ary[1] ▶ suffix **1** forming adjectives such as *budgetary, primary*.
2 forming nouns such as *dictionary, granary*.
– ORIGIN from French *-aire* or Latin *-arius* 'connected with'.

-ary[2] ▶ suffix forming adjectives such as *capillary, military*.
– ORIGIN from French *-aire* or Latin *-aris* 'relating to'.

Aryabhata I /ˌarɪəˈbɑːtə/, (476–c.550), Indian astronomer and mathematician. His surviving work, the *Aryabhatiya* (499), has sections dealing with mathematics, the measurement of time, planetary models, the sphere, and eclipses.

Aryan /ˈɛːrɪən/ ▶ adjective relating to or denoting a people speaking an Indo-European language who invaded northern India in the 2nd millennium BC, displacing the Dravidian and other aboriginal peoples. ■ old-fashioned term for PROTO-INDO-EUROPEAN or INDO-IRANIAN. ■ (in Nazi ideology) relating to or denoting people of Caucasian race not of Jewish descent.

> The idea that there was an 'Aryan' race corresponding to the parent Indo-European language was proposed by certain 19th-century writers, and was taken up by Hitler and other proponents of racist ideology, but it has been generally rejected by scholars.

▶ noun a member of the ancient Aryan people. ■ [mass noun] the language of the Aryan people. ■ (in Nazi ideology) a person of Caucasian race not of Jewish descent.
– ORIGIN from Sanskrit *ārya* 'noble' + -AN.

aryl /ˈarʌɪl, -rɪl/ ▶ noun [as modifier] Chemistry of or denoting a radical derived from an aromatic hydrocarbon by removal of a hydrogen atom: *aryl groups*.
– ORIGIN early 20th cent.: from AROMATIC + -YL.

arytenoid /ˌarɪˈtiːnɔɪd/ (also **arytenoid cartilage**) ▶ noun Anatomy either of a pair of cartilages at the back of the larynx, used in the production of different kinds of voice quality (for example, creaky voice).
– ORIGIN early 18th cent.: from modern Latin *arytaenoides*, from Greek *arutainoeidēs*, from *arutaina* 'funnel'.

AS ▶ abbreviation Anglo-Saxon.

As ▶ symbol the chemical element arsenic.

as[1] /az, əz/ ▶ adverb used in comparisons to refer to the extent or degree of something: *go as fast as you can* | *it tasted like grape juice but not as sweet*. ■ used to emphasize an amount: ***as many as** twenty-two rare species may be at risk*.
▶ conjunction **1** used to indicate that something happens during the time when something else is taking place: *Frank watched him as he ambled through the crowd* | *as she grew older, she kept more to herself*.
2 used to indicate by comparison the way that something happens or is done: *they can do as they wish* | *she kissed him goodbye, **as usual***. ■ used to add or interject a comment relating to the statement of a fact: *as you can see, I didn't go after all*.
3 because; since: *I must stop now as I have to go out*.
4 even though: *sweet as he is, he doesn't pay his bills* | *try as he might, he failed to pull it off*.
▶ preposition **1** used to refer to the function or character that someone or something has: *it came as a shock* | *she got a job as a cook*.
2 during the time of being (the thing specified): *he had often been ill as a child*.
– PHRASES **as against** compared or contrasted with: *the adult literacy rate for women is 44.5 percent, as against 67.8 percent for men*. **as and when** at the time when (used to refer to an uncertain future event): *they deal with an issue as and when it rears its head*. **as for** with regard to: *as for you, you'd better be quick*. **as from** (or **of**) chiefly Brit. used to indicate the time or date from which something starts: *as from 1 January, a free market will be created* | *I'm on the dole as of now*. **as if** (or **though**) as would be the case if: *she behaved as if he wasn't there*. **as if!** informal I very much doubt it: *You know how pools winners always say it won't change their lives? Yeah, as if!* **as (it) is** in the existing circumstances: *I've got enough on my plate as it is*. **as it were** in a way (used to be less precise): *areas which have been, as it were, pushed aside*. **as long as** see LONG[1]. **as much** see MUCH. **as per** see PER. **as such** see SUCH. **as to** with respect to; concerning: *decisions as to which patients receive treatment*. **as was** formerly: *Guangzhou (Canton as was) is 2000 km from Beijing*. **as well** see WELL[1]. **as yet** [usu. with negative] until now or a particular time in the past: *the damage is as yet undetermined*.
– ORIGIN Middle English: reduced form of Old English *alswā* 'similarly' (see ALSO).

> **USAGE** For a discussion of whether it is correct to say *he's not as shy **as I** rather than he's not as shy **as me** or I live in the same street **as she** rather than I live in the same street **as her*** see USAGE at PERSONAL PRONOUN.

as[2] /as/ ▶ noun (pl. **asses**) an ancient Roman copper coin.
– ORIGIN Latin, 'a unit'.

as- ▶ prefix variant spelling of AD- assimilated before *s* (as in *assemble, assess*).

ASA ▶ abbreviation ■ Advertising Standards Authority. ■ Amateur Swimming Association. ■ American Standards Association (especially in film-speed specification): *a 400 ASA film*.

asafoetida /ˌasəˈfiːtɪdə, -ˈfɛt-/ (US **asafetida**) ▶ noun **1** [mass noun] a fetid resinous gum obtained from the

roots of a herbaceous plant, used in herbal medicine and Indian cooking.
2 a Eurasian plant of the parsley family, from which asafoetida gum is obtained. ● *Ferula assa-foetida*, family Umbelliferae.
– ORIGIN late Middle English: from medieval Latin, from *asa* (from Persian *azā* 'mastic') + *foetida* (see FETID).

asana /ˈɑːsənə/ ▶ **noun** a posture adopted in performing hatha yoga.
– ORIGIN from Sanskrit *āsana*.

Asansol /ˌasənˈsəʊl/ an industrial city in NE India, in West Bengal, north-west of Kolkata (Calcutta); pop. 499,300 (est. 2009).

Asante variant spelling of ASHANTI[1], ASHANTI[2].

asap ▶ **abbreviation** as soon as possible.

ASB ▶ **abbreviation** Alternative Service Book.

asbestos /azˈbɛstɒs, as-, -təs/ ▶ **noun** [mass noun] a highly heat-resistant fibrous silicate mineral that can be woven into fabrics, and is used in brake linings and in fire-resistant and insulating materials. ■ fabric containing asbestos.

> The asbestos minerals include chrysotile (**white asbestos**) and several kinds of amphibole, notably amosite (**brown asbestos**) and crocidolite (**blue asbestos**). The danger to health caused by breathing in highly carcinogenic asbestos particles has led to more stringent control of its use.

– ORIGIN early 17th cent., via Latin from Greek *asbestos* 'unquenchable' (applied by Dioscurides to quicklime), from *a-* 'not' + *sbestos* (from *sbennumi* 'quench').

asbestosis /ˌazbɛˈstəʊsɪs, ˌas-/ ▶ **noun** [mass noun] a lung disease resulting from the inhalation of asbestos particles, marked by severe fibrosis and a high risk of mesothelioma (cancer of the pleura).

ASBO ▶ **abbreviation** Brit. antisocial behaviour order, a court order which can be obtained by local authorities in order to restrict the behaviour of a person likely to cause harm or distress to the public.

Ascalon /ˈaskələn/ ancient Greek name for ASHQELON.

ascariasis /ˌaskəˈrʌɪəsɪs/ ▶ **noun** [mass noun] Medicine infection of the intestine with ascarids (parasitic nematode worms).

ascarid /ˈaskərɪd/ (also **ascaris** /-rɪs/) ▶ **noun** Zoology a parasitic nematode worm of a family (Ascaridae) whose members typically live in the intestines of vertebrates.
– ORIGIN late 17th cent.: from modern Latin *Ascaridae* (plural), from Greek *askarides*, plural of *askaris* 'intestinal worm'.

ascend ▶ **verb 1** [with obj.] go up or climb: *she ascended the stairs* | [no obj.] *we had ascended 3,000 ft.* ■ climb to the summit of (a mountain or hill): *the first traveller to ascend the mountain.* ■ (of a fish or boat) move upstream along (a river).
2 [no obj.] rise or move up through the air: *the lift ascended from his sight.* ■ (of a road or flight of steps) slope or lead up: *the road **ascends to** the loch* | (as adj. **ascending**) *a gently ascending forest track.* ■ move up to a higher social or professional rank: *some executives **ascend to** top-level positions.* ■ (of a voice or sound) rise in pitch: *Carolyn's voice had ascended into high-pitched giggles.*
– PHRASES **ascend the throne** become king or queen.
– ORIGIN late Middle English: from Latin *ascendere*, from *ad-* 'to' + *scandere* 'to climb'.

ascendancy (also **ascendency**) ▶ **noun** [mass noun] occupation of a position of dominant power or influence: *the ascendancy of good over evil* | [in sing.] *the poor have a moral ascendancy over the rich.* ■ short for PROTESTANT ASCENDANCY.

ascendant (also **ascendent**) ▶ **adjective 1** rising in power or influence: *the newly ascendant liberal party.*
2 Astrology (of a planet, zodiacal degree, or sign) on or close to the intersection of the ecliptic with the eastern horizon.
▶ **noun** Astrology the point on the ecliptic at which it intersects the eastern horizon at a particular time, typically that of a person's birth.
– PHRASES **in the ascendant** rising in power or influence: *the reformers are in the ascendant.*
– ORIGIN late Middle English: via Old French from Latin *ascendent-* 'climbing up', from the verb *ascendere* (see ASCEND).

ascender ▶ **noun 1** a part of a letter that extends above the level of the top of an *x* (as in *b* and *f*). ■ a letter having an ascender.
2 Climbing a device which can be clipped to a rope to act as a foothold or handhold, or to keep something in position.

ascending colon ▶ **noun** Anatomy the first main part of the large intestine, which passes upwards from the caecum on the right side of the abdomen.

ascension ▶ **noun** [in sing.] the action of rising to an important position or a higher level: *his ascension to the presidency.* ■ (**Ascension**) the ascent of Christ into heaven on the fortieth day after the Resurrection.
– DERIVATIVES **ascensional** adjective.
– ORIGIN Middle English (referring to the ascent of Christ): via Old French from Latin *ascensio(n-)*, from the verb *ascendere* (see ASCEND).

Ascension Day ▶ **noun** the Thursday forty days after Easter, on which Christ's Ascension is celebrated in the Christian Church.

Ascension Island a small island in the South Atlantic, incorporated with St Helena, with which it is a dependency of the UK; pop. 1,100 (est. 2009).

Ascensiontide ▶ **noun** the period of ten days from Ascension Day to Whitsun Eve.

ascent ▶ **noun** [usu. in sing.] **1** a climb or walk to the summit of a mountain or hill: *the first ascent of the Matterhorn.* ■ an upward slope or path that one may walk or climb: *the ascent grew steeper.*
2 an instance of rising or moving up through the air: *the first balloon ascent was in 1783.* ■ a rise to a higher social or professional rank: *his **ascent to** power.*
– ORIGIN late 16th cent.: from ASCEND, on the pattern of the pair of *descend, descent*.

ascertain /ˌasəˈteɪn/ ▶ **verb** [with obj.] find (something) out for certain; make sure of: *an attempt to ascertain the cause of the accident* | [with clause] *management should **ascertain whether** adequate funding can be provided.*
– DERIVATIVES **ascertainable** adjective, **ascertainment** noun.
– ORIGIN late Middle English (in the sense 'assure, convince'): from Old French *acertener*, based on Latin *certus* 'settled, sure'.

ascesis /əˈsiːsɪs/ ▶ **noun** [mass noun] the practice of severe self-discipline, typically for religious reasons.
– ORIGIN late 19th cent.: from Greek *askēsis* 'training', from *askein* 'to exercise'.

ascetic /əˈsɛtɪk/ ▶ **adjective** characterized by severe self-discipline and abstention from all forms of indulgence, typically for religious reasons: *an ascetic life of prayer, fasting, and manual labour.*
▶ **noun** a person who follows an ascetic life.
– DERIVATIVES **ascetically** adverb.
– ORIGIN mid 17th cent.: from medieval Latin *asceticus* or Greek *askētikos*, from *askētēs* 'monk', from *askein* 'to exercise'.

asceticism /əˈsɛtɪsɪz(ə)m/ ▶ **noun** [mass noun] severe self-discipline and avoiding of all forms of indulgence, typically for religious reasons: *acts of physical asceticism.*

Ascham /ˈaskəm/, Roger (*c.*1515–68), English humanist scholar and writer, noted for his treatise on archery, *Toxophilus* (1545), and *The Scholemaster* (1570), a practical and influential tract on education.

aschelminth /ˈaʃhɛlmɪnθ, ˈask-/ ▶ **noun** (pl. **aschelminths** or **aschelminthes**) Zoology an invertebrate animal belonging to a group of phyla that are distinguished by the lack of a well-developed coelom and blood vessels. Most are minute worm-like animals, including the nematodes, rotifers, and water bears. ● Phylum Nematoda and about seven minor phyla, formerly placed in a phylum Aschelminthes.
– ORIGIN from modern Latin *Aschelminthes* (former phylum name), from Greek *askos* 'sac' + *helminth* 'worm' (from the former belief that animals of this group had a fluid-filled internal sac).

asci plural form of ASCUS.

ascidian /əˈsɪdɪən/ ▶ **noun** Zoology a sea squirt.
– ORIGIN mid 19th cent.: from modern Latin plural *Ascidia* (genus name), from Greek *askidion*, diminutive of *askos* 'wineskin'.

ASCII /ˈaski/ ▶ **abbreviation** Computing American Standard Code for Information Interchange, a set of digital codes representing letters, numerals, and other symbols, widely used as a standard format in the transfer of text between computers.

ascites /əˈsʌɪtiːz/ ▶ **noun** [mass noun] Medicine the accumulation of fluid in the peritoneal cavity, causing abdominal swelling.
– DERIVATIVES **ascitic** adjective.
– ORIGIN late Middle English: via late Latin from Greek *askitēs*, from *askos* 'wineskin'.

Asclepius /əˈskliːpɪəs/ Greek Mythology a hero and god of healing, son of Apollo.

ascomycete /ˌaskəˈmʌɪsiːt/ ▶ **noun** (pl. **ascomycetes** /-ˈmʌɪsiːts, -mʌɪˈsiːtiːz/) Botany a fungus whose spores develop within asci (cylindrical sacs). They include most moulds, mildews, and yeasts, the fungal component of most lichens, and a few large forms such as morels and truffles. Compare with BASIDIOMYCETE. ● Subdivision Ascomycotina (formerly class Ascomycetes): several classes.
– ORIGIN mid 19th cent.: from modern Latin *Ascomycetes* (former class name), from Greek *askos* 'sac' + *mukētes* 'fungi'.

ascorbate ▶ **noun** Chemistry a salt, ester, or the anion of ascorbic acid.

ascorbic acid /əˈskɔːbɪk/ ▶ **noun** [mass noun] a vitamin found particularly in citrus fruits and green vegetables. It is essential in maintaining healthy connective tissue, and is also thought to act as an antioxidant. Severe deficiency causes scurvy. Also called VITAMIN C. ● A lactone; chem. formula: $C_6H_8O_6$.
– ORIGIN 1930s: from A-[1] 'without' + medieval Latin *scorbutus* 'scurvy' + -IC.

Ascot a town in southern England, south-west of Windsor. Its racecourse is the site of an annual race meeting.

ascot (also **ascot tie**) ▶ **noun** a man's broad silk necktie.
– ORIGIN early 20th cent.: from the place name ASCOT, by association with formal dress at race meetings held there.

ascribe ▶ **verb** [with obj.] (**ascribe something to**) regard something as being due to (a cause): *he ascribed Jane's short temper to her upset stomach.* ■ regard a text, quotation, or work of art as being produced by or belonging to (a particular person or period): *a quotation ascribed to Thomas Cooper.* ■ regard a quality as belonging to: *tough-mindedness is a quality commonly ascribed to top bosses.*
– DERIVATIVES **ascribable** adjective.
– ORIGIN Middle English: from Latin *ascribere*, from *ad-* 'to' + *scribere* 'write'.

ascription ▶ **noun** [mass noun] the attribution of something to a cause: *the **ascription of** effect **to** cause.* ■ the attribution of a text, quotation, or work of art to a particular person or period: *her **ascription of** the text **to** Boccaccio* | *questions of authorial ascription.* ■ the action of regarding a quality as belonging to someone or something: *the **ascription of** special personal qualities **to** political leaders.* ■ [count noun] a preacher's words ascribing praise to God at the end of a sermon.
– ORIGIN late 16th cent.: from Latin *ascriptio(n-)*, from the verb *ascribere* (see ASCRIBE).

ascus /ˈaskəs/ ▶ **noun** (pl. **asci** /ˈaskʌɪ, -iː/) Botany a sac, typically cylindrical in shape, in which the spores of ascomycete fungi develop.
– ORIGIN mid 19th cent.: modern Latin, from Greek *askos* 'bag'.

ASDIC /ˈazdɪk/ ▶ **noun** [mass noun] chiefly Brit. an early form of sonar used to detect submarines.
– ORIGIN First World War: acronym from *Anti Submarine Detection Investigation Committee.*

-ase ▶ **suffix** Biochemistry forming names of enzymes: *amylase.*
– ORIGIN from *(diast)ase.*

ASEAN /ˈasɪən/ ▶ **abbreviation** Association of South-east Asian Nations.

aseismic /eɪˈsʌɪzmɪk/ ▶ **adjective** Geology not characterized by earthquake activity.

asepsis /eɪˈsɛpsɪs/ ▶ **noun** [mass noun] the absence of bacteria, viruses, and other microorganisms. ■ the exclusion of bacteria and other microorganisms, typically during surgery. Compare with ANTISEPSIS.

aseptic ▶ **adjective** free from contamination caused by harmful bacteria, viruses, or other microorganisms; surgically sterile or sterilized. ■ (of surgical practice) aiming at the complete exclusion of harmful micro-organisms.
– DERIVATIVES **aseptically** adverb.

asexual ▶ **adjective 1** without sexual feelings or associations: *she wore a grey frock, discreet and asexual.*
2 Biology (of reproduction) not involving the fusion of gametes. ■ without sex or sexual organs: *asexual parasites.*
▶ **noun** a person who has no sexual feelings or desires.
– DERIVATIVES **asexuality** noun, **asexually** adverb.

A

Asgard /ˈazgɑːd/ Scandinavian Mythology a region in the centre of the universe, inhabited by the gods.

ASH ▶ **abbreviation** (in the UK) Action on Smoking and Health.

ash¹ ▶ **noun 1** [mass noun] (also **ashes**) the powdery residue left after the burning of a substance: *cigarette ash | I turned over the ashes.* ■ (**ashes**) the remains of a human body after cremation or burning. ■ the mineral component of an organic substance, as assessed from the residue left after burning: *coal contains higher levels of ash than premium fuels.*
2 (**the Ashes**) a trophy for the winner of a series of Test matches in a cricket season between England and Australia. [from a mock obituary notice published in the *Sporting Times* (2 September 1882), with reference to the symbolical remains of English cricket being taken to Australia after a sensational victory by the Australians at the Oval.]
– PHRASES **turn to ashes in one's mouth** become bitterly disappointing or worthless. **rise** (or **emerge**) **from the ashes** be renewed after destruction. [see *rise like a phoenix from the ashes* (at **PHOENIX**).]
– DERIVATIVES **ashy** adjective.
– ORIGIN Old English *æsce, axe*, of Germanic origin; related to Dutch *as* and German *Asche*.

ash² ▶ **noun 1** (also **ash tree**) a tree with compound leaves, winged fruits, and hard pale timber, widely distributed throughout north temperate regions.
● Genus *Fraxinus*, family Oleaceae: many species, especially the **common** (or **European**) **ash** (*F. excelsior*).
■ used in names of trees unrelated to the ash but with similar leaves, e.g. **mountain ash**.
2 an Old English runic letter, ᚫ, a vowel intermediate between a and e. It is represented in the Roman alphabet by the symbol æ or Æ (see also **Æ**). [so named from the word of which it was the first letter.]
– ORIGIN Old English *æsc*, of Germanic origin; related to Dutch *es* and German *Esche*.

ashamed ▶ **adjective** [predic.] embarrassed or guilty because of something one has done or characteristics one has: *you should be ashamed of yourself* | [with clause] *she felt ashamed that she had hit him.* ■ [with infinitive] reluctant to do something through fear of embarrassment or humiliation: *I'm ashamed to say I followed him home | I am not ashamed to be seen with them.*
– DERIVATIVES **ashamedly** adverb.
– ORIGIN Old English *āscamod*, past participle of *āscamian* 'feel shame', from *ā-* (as an intensifier) + the verb **SHAME**.

Ashanti¹ /əˈʃanti/ (also **Asante**) a region of central Ghana. It was annexed by Britain in 1902, becoming part of the former British colony of the Gold Coast.

Ashanti² /əˈʃanti/ (also **Asante**) ▶ **noun** (pl. **same**) **1** a member of a people of south central Ghana.
2 [mass noun] the dialect of Akan spoken by the Ashanti.
▶ **adjective** relating to the Ashanti or their language.
– ORIGIN the name in Akan.

ash blonde (also **ash blond**) ▶ **adjective** (of a person's hair) very pale blonde.
▶ **noun** a woman with very pale blonde hair.

ashcan ▶ **noun** US a dustbin.

Ashcan School a group of American realist painters active from *c.*1908 until the First World War, who painted scenes from the slums of New York. The school grew out of the group called 'the Eight'.

Ashdod /ˈaʃdɒd/ a seaport on the Mediterranean coast of Israel, situated to the south of Tel Aviv; pop. 209,200 (est. 2008).

ashen¹ ▶ **adjective 1** (of a person's face) very pale with shock, fear, or illness: *Eleanor's ashen face.*
2 literary of or resembling ashes.

ashen² ▶ **adjective** archaic made of timber from the ash tree.

ashen-faced ▶ **adjective** very pale with shock, fear, or illness.

Asher /ˈaʃə/ (in the Bible) a Hebrew patriarch, son of Jacob and Zilpah (Gen. 30:12, 13). ■ the tribe of Israel traditionally descended from the Hebrew patriarch Asher.

ashet /ˈaʃɪt/ ▶ **noun** Scottish & N. English a large plate or dish.
– ORIGIN mid 16th cent.: from French *assiette*.

Ashgabat /ˈaʃgəbat/ (also **Ashkhabad**) the capital of the central Asian republic of Turkmenistan; pop. 744,000 (est. 2007). Former name (1919–27) **POLTORATSK**.

ashine ▶ **adjective** [predic.] literary shining: *eyes ashine in the darkness.*

Ashkelon variant spelling of **ASHQELON**.

Ashkenazi /ˌaʃkəˈnɑːzi/ ▶ **noun** (pl. **Ashkenazim** /-zɪm/) a Jew of central or eastern European descent. More than 80 per cent of Jews today are Ashkenazim; they preserve Palestinian rather than Babylonian Jewish traditions and some still use Yiddish. Compare with **SEPHARDI**.
– DERIVATIVES **Ashkenazic** adjective.
– ORIGIN from modern Hebrew, from *Ashkenaz*, grandson of Japheth, one of the sons of Noah (Gen. 10:3).

ash key ▶ **noun** Brit. the winged fruit of an ash tree, growing in clusters resembling bunches of keys.

Ashkhabad /ˌaʃkəˈbad/ variant spelling of **ASHGABAT**.

ashlar /ˈaʃlə/ ▶ **noun** [mass noun] masonry made of large square-cut stones, used as a facing on walls of brick or stone rubble.
– ORIGIN Middle English: from Old French *aisselier* from Latin *axilla*, diminutive of *axis* 'plank'.

ashlaring ▶ **noun** [mass noun] **1** ashlar masonry.
2 upright boarding fixed from the joists to the rafters of an attic to cut off the acute angle between the roof and the floor.

Ashmole, Elias (1617–92), English antiquary. His collection of rarities, presented to Oxford University in 1677, formed the nucleus of the Ashmolean Museum.

Ashmolean Museum /aʃˈməʊlɪən/ a museum of art and antiquities in Oxford. It opened in 1683 and was the first public institution of its kind in England.

Ashmore and Cartier Islands /ˈaʃmɔː, ˈkɑːtɪeɪ/ an external territory of Australia in the Indian Ocean, comprising the uninhabited Ashmore Reef and Cartier Islands.

Ashoka /əˈʃəʊkə/ variant spelling of **ASOKA**.

ashore ▶ **adverb** to or on the shore or land from the direction of the sea: *the seals come ashore to breed.* ■ on land as opposed to at sea: *we spent the day ashore.*

ash pan ▶ **noun** a tray fitted beneath a grate in which ashes can be collected and removed.

ashplant ▶ **noun** a sapling from an ash tree, typically used as a walking stick.

Ashqelon /ˈaʃkəlɒn/ (also **Ashkelon**) an ancient Mediterranean city, situated to the south of modern Tel Aviv, in Israel. Greek name **ASCALON**.

ashram /ˈaʃrəm/ ▶ **noun** (especially in South Asia) a hermitage, monastic community, or other place of religious retreat.
– ORIGIN from Sanskrit *āśrama* 'hermitage'.

ashrama /ˈaʃrəmə/ ▶ **noun** Hinduism any of the four stages of an ideal life, ascending from the status of pupil to the total renunciation of the world.
– ORIGIN from Sanskrit *āśrama*.

Ash Shariqah /ˌaʃ ʃɑːˈriːkə/ Arabic name for **SHARJAH**.

ashtanga /aʃˈtɑːŋə/ (also **astanga** /asˈtɑːŋə/) ▶ **noun** [mass noun] a type of yoga based on eight principles and consisting of a series of poses executed in swift succession, combined with deep, controlled breathing.
– ORIGIN from Hindi *aṣṭaṅ* or its source, Sanskrit *aṣṭaṅga* 'having eight parts', from *aṣṭán* 'eight'.

Ashton, Sir Frederick (William Mallandaine) (1904–88), British ballet dancer, choreographer, and director. As a choreographer he created new works as well as popular adaptations of classical ballets.

ashtray ▶ **noun** a small receptacle for tobacco ash and cigarette ends.

Ashur /ˈaʃʊə/ variant spelling of **ASSUR**.

Ashurbanipal /ˌaʃʊəˈbanɪpal, -ˈbanɪpɑːl/, king of Assyria *c.*668–627 BC, grandson of Sennacherib. A patron of the arts, he established a library of more than 20,000 clay tablets at Nineveh.

Ash Wednesday ▶ **noun** the first day of Lent in the Western Christian Church, marked by services of penitence.
– ORIGIN from the custom of marking the foreheads of penitents with ashes on that day.

ASI ▶ **abbreviation** airspeed indicator.

Asia /ˈeɪʃə, -ʒə/ the largest of the world's continents, constituting nearly one third of the land mass, lying entirely north of the equator except for some SE Asian islands. It is connected to Africa by the Isthmus of Suez, and borders Europe (part of the same land mass) along the Ural Mountains and across the Caspian Sea.

asiago /asɪˈɑːgəʊ/ ▶ **noun** [mass noun] a strong-flavoured cow's milk cheese made in northern Italy.
– ORIGIN named after *Asiago*, the plateau and town in northern Italy where the cheese was first made.

Asia Minor the western peninsula of Asia, which now constitutes the bulk of modern Turkey.

Asian /ˈeɪʃ(ə)n, -ʒ(ə)n/ ▶ **adjective** relating to Asia or its people, customs, or languages.
▶ **noun** a native of Asia or a person of Asian descent.
– DERIVATIVES **Asianness** noun.
– ORIGIN late Middle English: from Latin *Asianus*, from Greek *Asianos*, from *Asia* (see **ASIA**).

> **USAGE** In Britain **Asian** is generally used to refer to people who come from (or whose parents came from) India, Pakistan, or elsewhere in South Asia, while in North America it refers to people from China, Japan, and other countries of East Asia.

Asian American ▶ **noun** an American who is of Asian (chiefly East Asian) descent.
▶ **adjective** relating to Asian Americans.

Asian Development Bank a bank with forty-seven member countries (thirty-two are from the Asia–Pacific region) located in Manila. Its aim is to promote the economic and social progress of its developing member countries.

Asian elephant ▶ **noun** another term for **INDIAN ELEPHANT**.

Asian pear ▶ **noun** another term for **NASHI**.

Asia-Pacific (also **Asia-Pacific region**) ▶ **noun** a business region consisting of the whole of Asia as well as the countries of the Pacific Rim.

Asiatic /ˌeɪʃɪˈatɪk, ˌeɪzɪ-/ ▶ **adjective** relating to or deriving from Asia: *Asiatic coastal regions.*
▶ **noun** offensive an Asian person.
– ORIGIN via Latin *Asiaticus* from Greek *Asiatikos*, from *Asia* (see **ASIA**).

> **USAGE** The standard and accepted term when referring to individual people is **Asian** rather than **Asiatic**, which can be offensive. However, **Asiatic** is standard in scientific and technical use, for example in biological and anthropological classifications.

ASIC ▶ **abbreviation** Electronics application specific integrated circuit.

aside ▶ **adverb** to one side; out of the way: *he pushed his plate aside | they stood aside to let a car pass | she must put aside all her antagonistic feelings.* ■ in reserve; for future use: *she set aside some money for rent.* ■ used to indicate that one is dismissing a topic or changing to a new subject: ***joking aside**, I've certainly had my fill.*
▶ **noun** a remark or passage in a play that is intended to be heard by the audience but is supposed to be unheard by the other characters in the play. ■ an incidental remark, or one not intended to be heard by everyone present: *'Does that make him a murderer?' whispered Alice in an aside to Fred.*
– PHRASES **aside from** chiefly N. Amer. apart from. **set something aside 1** remove land from agricultural production for fallow or other use. **2** annul a legal decision or order. **take** (or **draw**) **someone aside** move someone away from a group of people in order to talk to them privately: *he took him aside and urged him to quit wasting his time and talent.*
– ORIGIN Middle English (originally *on side*): see **A²**, **SIDE**.

A-side ▶ **noun** the side of a pop single regarded as the main one.

Asimov /ˈazɪmɒf/, Isaac (1920–92), Russian-born American writer and scientist, particularly known for his works of science fiction and books on science for non-scientists. Notable science-fiction works: *I, Robot* (1950) and *Foundation* (trilogy, 1951–3).

asinine /ˈasɪnʌɪn/ ▶ **adjective** extremely stupid or foolish: *Lydia ignored his asinine remark.*
– DERIVATIVES **asininity** noun.
– ORIGIN late 15th cent.: from Latin *asininus*, from *asinus* 'ass'.

Asir Mountains /əˈsɪə/ a range of mountains in SW Saudi Arabia, running parallel to the Red Sea.

-asis (often **-iasis**) ▶ **suffix** forming the names of diseases: *onchocerciasis | psoriasis.*
– ORIGIN via Latin from Greek.

asity /ˈasɪti/ ▶ **noun** (pl. **asities**) a stocky perching bird related to the pittas, found only in Madagascar. ● Family Philepittidae: two genera, in particular *Philepitta* (two species).
– ORIGIN probably a local word.

ask ▶ **verb 1** [reporting verb] say something in order to obtain an answer or some information: [with obj. and clause] ***I asked her what she meant*** | [with obj.] *people are always asking questions* | [with direct speech] *'How much further?' I asked* | [no obj.] *the old man **asked about** her job.* ■ [no obj.] (**ask around**) talk to different people in order to find out something: *there are fine meals to be had if you ask around.* ■ [no obj.] (**ask after** or Scottish **for**) Brit. enquire about the health or well-being of: *if I see him I'll tell him you were asking after him.*
2 [with obj.] say to (someone) that one wants them to do or give something: *Mary **asked** her father **for** money* | [with obj. and infinitive] ***I asked him to call the manager*** | [no obj.] ***don't be afraid to ask for advice.*** ■ [with clause] say that one wants permission to do something: *she **asked if** she could move in* | [with infinitive] *he asked to see the officer involved* | [with obj.] *you should have asked my permission first.* ■ [no obj.] (**ask for**) say that one wants to speak to: *when I arrived I asked for Katrina.* ■ say that one wants (a specified amount) as a price for selling something: *he was **asking** £250 **for** the guitar.* ■ expect or demand (something) of someone: *it's asking a lot, but could you look through Billy's things?*
3 [with obj.] invite (someone) to one's home or a function: *it's about time we **asked** Pam **to dinner*** | *she **asked** him **round for** a drink.* ■ (**ask someone along**) invite someone to join one on a group outing. ■ (**ask someone out**) invite someone out on a date.
▶ **noun** [in sing.] **1** US the price at which an item, especially a financial security, is offered for sale: [as modifier] *ask prices for bonds.*
2 [with adj.] informal a demand or situation that requires a specified degree of effort or commitment: *it is **a big ask** for him to go and play 90 minutes* | *it was a tough ask, but they delivered.*
– PHRASES **be asking for trouble** (or **it**) informal behave in a way that is likely to result in difficulty for oneself. **don't ask me!** informal used to indicate that one has no idea of the answer to a question. **for the asking** used to indicate that someone can easily have something if they want it: *the job was his for the asking.* **I ask you!** informal an exclamation of shock or disapproval intended to elicit agreement from one's listener: *ringing me up on Christmas Day, I ask you!* **if you ask me** informal used to emphasize that a statement is one's personal opinion: *if you ask me, it's just an excuse for laziness.*
– DERIVATIVES **asker** noun.
– ORIGIN Old English *āscian, āhsian, āxian*, of West Germanic origin.

> **WORD TRENDS** Should sports commentators be reviled or celebrated for their contribution to our language? In the excitement of the match, both creativity and clichés abound, such as the conversion of **ask** from a verb to a noun. The usage, which originated in Australia, is a favourite of sports pundits, usually in combination with emphasizing adjectives like *big, massive, hard*, and *tough*: *it was always going to be a hard ask against a class side* | *beating Millwall in any cup competition is a massive ask.* It has now spread into politics, business, and everyday speech: *the children are expected to stay focused for about two hours, which is a big ask.* **Miss** undergoes a similar verb-to-noun conversion at the hands of some soccer managers and commentators: *he's been playing well and he'll be a big miss* means that the injured player will be missed a great deal.

askance /əˈskans, əˈskɑːns/ (also **askant** /-ˈskant, -ˈskɑːnt/) ▶ **adverb** with an attitude or look of suspicion or disapproval: *the reformers **looked askance at** the mystical tradition* | *a waiter **looked askance at** his jeans.*
– ORIGIN late 15th cent.: of unknown origin.

askari /əˈskɑːri/ ▶ **noun** (pl. **same** or **askaris**) **1** (in East Africa) a soldier or police officer.
2 (**Askari**) S. African historical a member of the ANC who changed sides and joined the apartheid government's police force.
– ORIGIN late 19th cent.: from Arabic *ʿaskarī* 'soldier'.

askew /əˈskjuː/ ▶ **adverb & adjective** not in a straight or level position: [as predic. adj.] *her hat was slightly askew.* ■ wrong; awry: [as adv.] *the plan went sadly askew.*
– ORIGIN mid 16th cent.: from **A-²** 'on' + **SKEW**.

Askey /ˈaski/, Arthur (Bowden) (1900–82), English comedian and actor. He was particularly famous for his radio show, *Band Waggon* (1938–9), and also appeared in a number of films.

asking price ▶ **noun** the price at which something is offered for sale.

ASL ▶ **abbreviation** American Sign Language.

aslant ▶ **adverb** at an angle or in a sloping direction: *some of the paintings hung aslant.*
▶ **preposition** across (something) at an angle.

asleep ▶ **adjective & adverb** in or into a state of sleep: [as adj.] *she had been asleep for over three hours* | [as adv.] *he soon **fell asleep**.* ■ not attentive or alert; inactive: [as adj.] *the competition was not asleep.* ■ (of a limb) having no feeling; numb: [as adj.] *his legs were asleep.* ■ literary used euphemistically to indicate that someone is dead.
– PHRASES **asleep at the wheel** (or N. Amer. **switch**) informal not attentive or alert.

ASLEF /ˈazlɛf/ ▶ **abbreviation** (in the UK) Associated Society of Locomotive Engineers and Firemen.

AS level ▶ **noun** (in the UK except Scotland) an examination or pass at advanced subsidiary level, representing the first component of an A level qualification.

aslope ▶ **adjective & adverb** archaic or literary in a sloping position: [as adj.] *the steps are aslope and broken* | [as adv.] *against the mast he leans aslope.*
– ORIGIN late Middle English: origin uncertain; this form appears earlier than **SLOPE**.

ASM ▶ **abbreviation** ■ air-to-surface missile. ■ assistant stage manager.

Asmara /asˈmɑːrə/ (also **Asmera** /-ˈmɛːrə/) the capital of Eritrea; pop. 601,000 (est. 2007).

asocial ▶ **adjective** avoiding social interaction; inconsiderate of or hostile to others: *a tendency to asocial behaviour.*

Asoka /əˈsəʊkə/ (also **Ashoka** /əˈʃəʊkə/) (died *c.*232 BC), emperor of India *c.*269–232 BC. He converted to Buddhism and established it as the state religion.

Asoka Chakra /ˈtʃʌkrə/ the wheel on the Indian flag, designed after a wheel on a column set up by the Emperor Asoka.

Asoka pillar a pillar with four lions on the capital, built by the Emperor Asoka at Sarnath in Uttar Pradesh to mark the spot where the Buddha publicly preached his first sermon, and adopted as a symbol by the government of India.

ASP ▶ **abbreviation** application service provider, a company providing Internet access to software applications that would otherwise have to be installed on individual computers.

asp /asp/ ▶ **noun 1** (also **asp viper**) a small southern European viper with an upturned snout. ● *Vipera aspis*, family Viperidae.
■ another term for **EGYPTIAN COBRA**.
2 a large predatory Eurasian freshwater fish of the carp family. ● *Aspius aspius*, family Cyprinidae.
– ORIGIN Middle English: from Latin *aspis*, from Greek.

asparagine /əˈsparədʒiːn/ ▶ **noun** [mass noun] Biochemistry a hydrophilic amino acid which is a constituent of most proteins. ● An amide of aspartic acid; chem. formula: $CONH_2CH_2CH(NH_2)COOH$.
– ORIGIN early 19th cent.: from **ASPARAGUS** (which contains it) + **-INE⁴**.

asparagus /əˈsparəgəs/ ▶ **noun** a tall plant of the lily family with fine feathery foliage, cultivated for its edible shoots. ● *Asparagus officinalis*, family Liliaceae.
■ [mass noun] the tender young shoots of the asparagus plant, eaten as a vegetable.
– ORIGIN mid 16th cent.: via Latin from Greek *asparagos*.

asparagus fern ▶ **noun** a decorative indoor or greenhouse plant with feathery foliage, which is related to the edible asparagus. ● Genus *Asparagus*, family Liliaceae: several species.

asparagus pea ▶ **noun** a pea plant which has edible cylindrical pods with four longitudinal wavy flanges. ● *Tetragonolobus* (or *Lotus*) *purpurea*, family Leguminosae.

aspartame /əˈspɑːteɪm/ ▶ **noun** [mass noun] a very sweet substance used as an artificial sweetener, chiefly in low-calorie products. It is a derivative of aspartic acid and phenylalanine.

aspartate /əˈspɑːteɪt/ ▶ **noun** a salt or ester of aspartic acid.

aspartic acid /əˈspɑːtɪk/ ▶ **noun** [mass noun] Biochemistry an acidic amino acid which is a constituent of most proteins, and also occurs in sugar cane. It is important in the metabolism of nitrogen in animals, and also acts as a neurotransmitter. ● Chem. formula: $COOHCH_2CH(NH_2)COOH$.
– ORIGIN mid 19th cent.: *aspartic* from French *aspartique*, formed arbitrarily from Latin *asparagus* (see **ASPARAGUS**).

aspect ▶ **noun 1** a particular part or feature of something: *personal effectiveness in all aspects of life* | *the financial aspect can be overstressed.* ■ a particular way in which something may be considered: *from every aspect theirs was a changing world.* ■ a particular appearance or quality: *the air of desertion lent the place a sinister aspect* | [mass noun] *a man of decidedly foreign aspect.*
2 [usu. in sing.] the positioning of a building or other structure in a particular direction: *a greenhouse with a southern aspect.* ■ the side of a building facing a particular direction: *the front aspect of the hotel was unremarkable.*
3 [mass noun] Grammar a category or form which expresses the way in which time is denoted by a verb.

> There are three aspects in English, the progressive or continuous aspect (expressing duration, typically using the auxiliary verb *be* with a form in *-ing*, as in *I was reading a book*), the perfect or perfective (expressing completed action, typically using the auxiliary verb *have* with a past participle, as in *I have read the book*), and unmarked aspect (as in *he reads books*).

4 Astrology any of a number of particular angular relationships between one celestial body or point on the ecliptic and another: *the sun in Aries formed an adverse aspect with Uranus in Capricorn.*
▶ **verb** [with obj.] Astrology (of a planet) form an aspect with (another celestial body).
– DERIVATIVES **aspectual** adjective.
– ORIGIN late Middle English (denoting the action or a way of looking): from Latin *aspectus*, from *aspicere* 'look at', from *ad-* 'to, at' + *specere* 'to look'.

aspect ratio ▶ **noun 1** the ratio of the width to the height of the image on a television screen.
2 Aeronautics the ratio of the span to the mean chord of an aerofoil.

Aspen a ski resort in south central Colorado; pop. 5,902 (est. 2008).

aspen ▶ **noun** a poplar tree with small rounded long-stalked leaves that tremble in the breeze. ● Genus *Populus*, family Salicaceae: several species, in particular the European *P. tremula* and the North American **quaking aspen** (*P. tremuloides*).
– ORIGIN late Middle English: from dialect *asp* (in the same sense) + **-EN²**, forming an adjective later used as a noun (late 16th cent.).

Asperger's syndrome /ˈaspəːdʒə(r)z/ ▶ **noun** [mass noun] Psychiatry a rare and relatively mild autistic disorder characterized by awkwardness in social interaction, pedantry in speech, and preoccupation with very narrow interests.
– ORIGIN named after Hans Asperger (1906–80), the Austrian psychiatrist who described the condition in 1944.

asperges /əˈspəːdʒiːz/ ▶ **noun** [mass noun] Christian Church the rite of sprinkling holy water at the beginning of the Mass, still used occasionally in Catholic churches. ■ [count noun] another term for **ASPERGILLUM**.
– ORIGIN late 16th cent.: the first word of the Latin text of Psalms 50(51):7 (literally 'thou shalt purge', but translated in the Authorized Version as 'purge me'), recited before mass during the sprinkling of holy water.

aspergillosis /ˌaspədʒɪˈləʊsɪs/ ▶ **noun** [mass noun] a condition in which certain fungi infect the tissues, most commonly the lungs. ● The fungi are blackish moulds of the genus *Aspergillus*, subdivision Deuteromycotina.
– ORIGIN late 19th cent.: from modern Latin *Aspergillus*, from **ASPERGILLUM**, + **-OSIS**.

aspergillum /ˌaspəˈdʒɪləm/ ▶ **noun** (pl. **aspergilla** or **aspergillums**) an implement for sprinkling holy water.
– ORIGIN mid 17th cent.: from Latin.

asperity /əˈspɛrɪti/ ▶ **noun** (pl. **asperities**) [mass noun] harshness of tone or manner: *he pointed this out with some asperity.* ■ (**asperities**) harsh qualities or conditions: *the asperities of a harsh and divided society.*
– ORIGIN Middle English (in the sense 'hardship, rigour'): from Old French *asperite*, or Latin *asperitas*, from *asper* 'rough'.

aspermia /eɪˈspəːmɪə/ ▶ **noun** [mass noun] Medicine failure to produce semen, or absence of sperms from the semen.

asperse /əˈspəːs/ ▶ **verb** [with obj.] literary attack or criticize the reputation or integrity of: *he aspersed the place and its inhabitants.*

A

– ORIGIN late 15th cent. (in the sense 'spatter with liquid'): from Latin *aspers-* 'sprinkled', from the verb *aspergere*, from *ad-* 'to' + *spargere* 'sprinkle'.

aspersion /əˈspəːʃ(ə)n/ ▶ **noun** (usu. **aspersions**) an attack on the reputation or integrity of someone or something: *I don't think anyone is **casting aspersions on** you.*
– ORIGIN late Middle English (denoting the sprinkling of water, especially at baptism): from Latin *aspersio(n-)*, from *aspergere* (see **ASPERSE**).

asphalt /ˈasfalt, -əlt/ ▶ **noun** [mass noun] a mixture of dark bituminous pitch with sand or gravel, used for surfacing roads, flooring, roofing, etc. ■ the pitch used in asphalt, sometimes found in natural deposits but usually made by the distillation of crude oil.
▶ **verb** [with obj.] surface with asphalt.
– DERIVATIVES **asphaltic** adjective.
– ORIGIN late Middle English: from French *asphalte*, based on late Latin *asphalton, asphaltum*, from Greek *asphalton*.

aspherical ▶ **adjective** (especially of an optical lens) not spherical.
– DERIVATIVES **aspheric** adjective, **aspherically** adverb.

asphodel /ˈasfədɛl/ ▶ **noun 1** a Eurasian plant of the lily family, typically having long slender leaves and flowers borne on a spike. ● Genera *Asphodelus* and *Asphodeline*, family Liliaceae. See also **BOG ASPHODEL**.
2 literary an everlasting flower said to grow in the Elysian fields.
– ORIGIN late Middle English: via Latin from Greek *asphodelos*; compare with **DAFFODIL**.

asphyxia /əsˈfɪksɪə/ ▶ **noun** [mass noun] a condition arising when the body is deprived of oxygen, causing unconsciousness or death; suffocation.
– DERIVATIVES **asphyxial** adjective, **asphyxiant** adjective & noun.
– ORIGIN early 18th cent. (in the sense 'stopping of the pulse'): modern Latin, from Greek *asphuxia*, from *a-* 'without' + *sphuxis* 'pulse'.

asphyxiate ▶ **verb** [with obj.] kill (someone) by depriving them of air: *they were asphyxiated by the carbon monoxide fumes.* ■ [no obj.] die by being deprived of air: *they slowly asphyxiated.*
– DERIVATIVES **asphyxiation** noun.

aspic ▶ **noun** [mass noun] a savoury jelly made with meat stock, set in a mould and used to contain pieces of meat, seafood, or eggs: *chicken in aspic* | figurative *a world preserved in aspic, far removed from mass unemployment.*
– ORIGIN late 18th cent.: from French, literally 'asp', from the colours of the jelly as compared with those of the snake.

aspidistra /ˌaspɪˈdɪstrə/ ▶ **noun** a bulbous plant of the lily family with broad tapering leaves, native to eastern Asia and widely grown as a houseplant. ● Genus *Aspidistra*, family Liliaceae.
– ORIGIN early 19th cent.: modern Latin, from Greek *aspis, aspid-* 'shield' (because of the shape of the stigma), on the pattern of *Tupistra*, a related genus.

aspirant /əˈspʌɪər(ə)nt, ˈasp(ɪ)r-/ ▶ **adjective** [attrib.] having ambitions to achieve something, typically to follow a particular career: *an aspirant politician.*
▶ **noun** a person who has ambitions to achieve something: *an **aspirant to** the throne.*
– ORIGIN mid 18th cent. (as a noun): from Latin *aspirant-* 'aspiring', from the verb *aspirare* (see **ASPIRE**).

aspirate ▶ **verb** /ˈaspəreɪt/ [with obj.] **1** (often as adj. **aspirated**) Phonetics pronounce (a sound) with an exhalation of breath: *the aspirated allophone of p occurs in 'pie'.* ■ [no obj.] pronounce the sound of *h* at the beginning of a word.
2 Medicine breathe (something) in; inhale: *some drowning victims don't aspirate any water.* ■ draw (fluid) by suction from a vessel or cavity.
3 (usu. as adj. **aspirated**) provide (an internal-combustion engine) with air: *the superchargers produce twice the power of standard aspirated engines.* See also **NORMALLY ASPIRATED**.
▶ **noun** /ˈasp(ə)rət/ **1** Phonetics an aspirated consonant. ■ a sound of *h*.
2 [mass noun] Medicine matter that has been drawn from the body by suction.
▶ **adjective** /ˈasp(ə)rət/ Phonetics (of a sound) pronounced with an exhalation of breath; aspirated.
– ORIGIN mid 16th cent. (as an adjective): from Latin *aspiratus* 'breathed', past participle of *aspirare* (see **ASPIRE**).

aspiration ▶ **noun 1** (usu. **aspirations**) a hope or ambition of achieving something: *the needs and aspirations of the people* | [mass noun] *the yawning gulf between aspiration and reality.*
2 [mass noun] Medicine the action or process of drawing breath. ■ the action of drawing fluid by suction from a vessel or cavity.
3 [mass noun] Phonetics the action of pronouncing a sound with an exhalation of breath.
– ORIGIN late Middle English (in sense 3): from Latin *aspiratio(n-)*, from the verb *aspirare* (see **ASPIRE**).

aspirational ▶ **adjective** having or characterized by aspirations to achieve social prestige and material success: *young, aspirational, and independent women.*
– DERIVATIVES **aspirationally** adverb.

aspirator ▶ **noun** Medicine an instrument or apparatus for aspirating fluid from a vessel or cavity.

aspire ▶ **verb** [no obj.] **1** direct one's hopes or ambitions towards achieving something: *we never thought that we might **aspire to** those heights* | [with infinitive] *other people will aspire to be like you.*
2 literary rise high; tower.
– ORIGIN late Middle English: from French *aspirer* or Latin *aspirare*, from *ad-* 'to' + *spirare* 'breathe'.

aspirin ▶ **noun** (pl. **same** or **aspirins**) [mass noun] a synthetic compound used medicinally to relieve mild or chronic pain and to reduce fever and inflammation, usually taken in tablet form. ● Alternative name: **acetylsalicylic acid**; chem. formula: $C_6H_4(OCOCH_3)COOH$. ■ (in general use) a tablet of any mild painkilling drug.
– ORIGIN late 19th cent.: from German, from *acetylierte Spirsäure* 'acetylated salicylic acid' (the element *Spir-* being from the plant genus name *Spiraea*).

aspiring ▶ **adjective** [attrib.] directing one's hopes or ambitions towards becoming a specified type of person: *an aspiring artist.*

asportation ▶ **noun** [mass noun] English Law, rare the detachment, movement, or carrying away of property, formerly an essential component of the crime of larceny.
– ORIGIN late 15th cent.: from Latin *asportatio(n-)*, from *asportare* 'carry away'.

asprawl ▶ **adverb & adjective** sprawling: [as predic. adj.] *she lay, legs and arms asprawl.*

asp viper ▶ **noun** see **ASP** (sense 1).

asquint ▶ **adverb & adjective** with a glance to one side or from the corner of the eyes: [as adv.] *a woman **looked asquint at** me.*
– ORIGIN Middle English: perhaps from **A-**[2] 'on' + a Low German or Dutch word related to modern Dutch *schuinte* 'slant'.

Asquith /ˈaskwɪθ/, Herbert Henry, 1st Earl of Oxford and Asquith (1852–1928), British Liberal statesman, Prime Minister 1908–16.

ass[1] /as/ ▶ **noun 1** a hoofed mammal of the horse family, which is typically smaller than a horse and has longer ears and a braying call. ● Genus *Equus*, family Equidae: *E. africanus* of Africa, which is the ancestor of the domestic ass or donkey, and *E. hemionus* of Asia. ■ (in general use) a donkey.
2 Brit. informal a foolish or stupid person: *that ass of a young man.*
– PHRASES **make an ass of oneself** informal behave in a way that makes one look foolish or stupid.
– ORIGIN Old English *assa*, from a Celtic word related to Welsh *asyn*, Breton *azen*, based on Latin *asinus*.

ass[2] /ɑːs, as/ ▶ **noun** N. Amer. vulgar slang a person's buttocks or anus. ■ [mass noun] women regarded as a source of sexual gratification. ■ oneself (used in phrases for emphasis).
– PHRASES **bust one's ass** try very hard to do something. **chew (someone's) ass** reprimand (someone) severely. **drag** (or **tear** or **haul**) **ass** hurry or move fast. **get your ass in** (or **into**) **gear** hurry. **not give a rat's ass** not care at all about something. **put** (or **have**) **someone's ass in a sling** get someone in trouble. **whip** (or **bust**) **someone's ass** beat someone in a fight or contest.
– DERIVATIVES **assed** adjective [in combination] *fat-assed guys.*
– ORIGIN variant of **ARSE**.

-ass ▶ **combining form** N. Amer. informal used in derogatory terms as an intensifier: *smart-ass.*

Assad /ˈasad/, Hafiz al- (1928–2000), Syrian Baath statesman, President 1971–2000. He strengthened Syria's oil-based economy and suppressed political opposition such as the uprising of Muslim extremists (1979–82).

assagai ▶ **noun & verb** variant spelling of **ASSEGAI**.

assai /aˈsʌɪ/ ▶ **adverb** [usu. postpositive] [as submodifier] Music (in directions) very: *allegro assai.*
– ORIGIN Italian, 'very much'.

assail /əˈseɪl/ ▶ **verb** [with obj.] make a concerted or violent attack on: *the Scots army assailed Edward's army from the rear.* ■ (of an unpleasant feeling or physical sensation) come upon (someone) suddenly and strongly: *she was assailed by doubts and regrets.* ■ criticize strongly.
– DERIVATIVES **assailable** adjective.
– ORIGIN Middle English: from Old French *asaill-*, stressed stem of *asalir*, from medieval Latin *assalire*, from Latin *assilire*, from *ad-* 'to' + *salire* 'to leap'; compare with **ASSAULT**.

assailant ▶ **noun** a person who physically attacks another.

Assam /aˈsam/ a state in NE India; capital, Dispur. Most of the state lies in the valley of the Brahmaputra River; it is noted for the production of tea.

Assamese /ˌasəˈmiːz/ ▶ **noun** (pl. **same**) **1** a native or inhabitant of Assam.
2 [mass noun] the Indic language which is the official language of Assam, related to Bengali and spoken by around 23 million people, roughly half in Assam and half in Bangladesh.
▶ **adjective** relating to Assam, its people, or their language.

assart /əˈsɑːt/ Brit. historical ▶ **noun** a piece of land converted from forest to arable use. ■ [mass noun] the action of converting forest to arable use.
▶ **verb** [with obj.] convert (forest) to arable use.
– ORIGIN late Middle English (as a noun): from Old French *essarter*, from medieval Latin *ex(s)artare*, based on *ex* 'out' + *sar(r)ire* 'to weed'. The verb dates from the early 16th cent.

assassin /əˈsasɪn/ ▶ **noun 1** a person who murders an important person for political or religious reasons.
2 (**Assassin**) a member of the Nizari branch of Ismaili Muslims at the time of the Crusades, when the newly established sect ruled part of northern Persia (1094–1256). They were renowned as militant fanatics, and were popularly reputed to use hashish before going on murder missions.
– ORIGIN mid 16th cent.: from French, or from medieval Latin *assassinus*, from Arabic *ḥašīšī* 'hashish-eater'.

assassinate ▶ **verb** [with obj.] murder (an important person) for political or religious reasons.
– ORIGIN early 17th cent.: from medieval Latin *assassinat-* 'killed', from the verb *assassinare*, from *assassinus* (see **ASSASSIN**).

assassination ▶ **noun** [mass noun] the action of assassinating someone: *the assassination of President Kennedy* | [as modifier] *a failed assassination attempt.*

assassin bug ▶ **noun** a long-legged predatory or bloodsucking bug which occurs chiefly in the tropics and feeds mainly on other arthropods. Some of those that bite humans can transmit microorganisms such as that causing Chagas' disease. ● Family Reduviidae, suborder Heteroptera: numerous species.

assault ▶ **verb** [with obj.] make a physical attack on: *he pleaded guilty to assaulting a police officer* | *she was sexually assaulted as a child.* ■ carry out a military attack or raid on (an enemy position). ■ bombard with something undesirable or unpleasant: *thunder assaulted the ears.*
▶ **noun 1** a physical attack: *his imprisonment for an **assault on** the film director* | *a sexual assault.* ■ Law an act that threatens physical harm to a person, whether or not actual harm is done: *he admitted an assault and two thefts* | [mass noun] *he appeared in court charged with assault.* ■ a military attack or raid on an enemy position: *troops began an **assault on** the city.* ■ a strong verbal attack: *an articulate **assault on** all forms of prejudice.*
2 a concerted attempt to do something demanding: *a winter **assault on** Mt. Everest.*
– DERIVATIVES **assaulter** noun.
– ORIGIN Middle English: from Old French *asaut* (noun), *assauter* (verb), based on Latin *ad-* 'to' + *saltare*, frequentative of *salire* 'to leap'. Compare with **ASSAIL**.

assault and battery ▶ **noun** [mass noun] Law the action of threatening a person together with the action of making physical contact with them.

assault course ▶ **noun** Brit. a course through which the participants must run, negotiating obstacles to be climbed, crawled under, crossed on suspended ropes, etc., as used for training soldiers.

assaultive ▶ **adjective** tending or likely to commit an assault: *they found that assaultive men had abusive parents.* ■ aggressive or forcefully assertive.

assault rifle ▶ noun a lightweight rifle developed from the sub-machine gun, which may be set to fire automatically or semi-automatically.

assay /əˈseɪ, ˈaseɪ/ ▶ noun [mass noun] the testing of a metal or ore to determine its ingredients and quality: *submission of plate for assay.* ■ [count noun] a procedure for measuring the biochemical or immunological activity of a sample.
▶ verb [with obj.] **1** determine the content or quality of (a metal or ore). ■ determine the biochemical or immunological activity of (a sample). ■ examine (something) in order to assess its nature: *stepping inside, I quickly assayed the clientele.*
2 archaic attempt: *I assayed a little joke of mine on him.*
– DERIVATIVES **assayer** noun.
– ORIGIN Middle English (in the general sense 'testing, or a test of, the merit of someone or something'): from Old French *assai* (noun), *assaier* (verb), variant of *essai* 'trial', *essayer* 'to try' (see ESSAY).

assay office ▶ noun an establishment for the assaying of ores and metals. ■ Brit. an institution authorized to award hallmarks to articles made from precious metals. There are currently four in Britain, at London, Birmingham, Sheffield, and Edinburgh.

ass-backwards N. Amer. informal ▶ adverb in a manner contrary to what is usual, expected, or logical: *I never did like to do anything simple when I could do it ass-backwards.*
▶ adjective contrary to what is usual, expected, or logical.

assegai /ˈasəɡʌɪ/ (also **assagai**) ▶ noun (pl. **assegais**) **1** a slender, iron-tipped, hardwood spear used chiefly by southern African peoples.
2 (also **assegai wood**) a South African tree of the dogwood family, which yields hard timber. ● *Curtisia dentata*, family Cornaceae.
▶ verb (**assegais**, **assegaing**, **assegaied**) [with obj.] wound or kill with an assegai.
– ORIGIN early 17th cent.: from obsolete French *azagaie* or Portuguese *azagaia*, from Arabic *az-zaḡāyah*, from *az*, *al* 'the' + Berber *zaḡāyah* 'spear'.

assemblage ▶ noun a collection or gathering of things or people: *a loose assemblage of diverse groups.* ■ a machine or object made of pieces fitted together: *some vast assemblage of gears and cogs.* ■ a work of art made by grouping together found or unrelated objects. ■ [mass noun] the action of gathering or fitting things together.

assemble ▶ verb **1** [no obj.] (of people) gather together in one place for a common purpose: *a crowd had assembled outside the gates.* ■ [with obj.] cause (people or things) to gather together for a common purpose: *he assembled the surviving members of the group for a tour.* ■ (usu. as noun **assembling**) Entomology (of male moths) gather for mating in response to a pheromone released by a female.
2 [with obj.] fit together the separate component parts of (a machine or other object): *my new machine is being assembled and my old one dismantled.*
3 [with obj.] Computing translate (a program) from a symbolic language into machine code.
– ORIGIN Middle English: from Old French *asembler*, based on Latin *ad-* 'to' + *simul* 'together'.

assemblé /ˌasɒ̃ˈbleɪ/ ▶ noun (pl. pronunc. **same**) Ballet a leap in which the feet are brought together before landing.

assembler ▶ noun **1** a person who assembles a machine or its parts.
2 Computing a program for converting instructions written in low-level symbolic code into machine code. ■ another term for ASSEMBLY LANGUAGE.

assembly ▶ noun (pl. **assemblies**) **1** a group of people gathered together in one place for a common purpose: *an assembly of dockers and labourers.* ■ a group of people elected to make laws or decisions for a particular country or region.
2 [mass noun] the action of gathering together as a group for a common purpose: *a decree guaranteeing freedom of assembly.* ■ the regular gathering of the teachers and pupils of a school at the start or end of the day: *he was told off for talking in assembly.* ■ (usu. **the assembly**) chiefly historical a signal for troops to assemble, given by drum or bugle.
3 [mass noun] [often as modifier] the action of fitting together the component parts of a machine or other object: *a car assembly plant.* ■ [count noun] a unit consisting of components that have been fitted together: *the tail assembly of the aircraft.*
4 [mass noun] [usu. as modifier] Computing the conversion of instructions in low-level code to machine code.
– ORIGIN Middle English: from Old French *asemblee*, feminine past participle of *asembler* (see ASSEMBLE).

assembly language ▶ noun Computing a low-level symbolic code converted by an assembler.

assembly line ▶ noun a series of workers and machines in a factory by which a succession of identical items is progressively assembled.

assemblyman (or **assemblywoman**) ▶ noun (pl. **assemblymen** or **assemblywomen**) chiefly US a person who is a member of a legislative assembly.

assembly room ▶ noun chiefly Brit. a public room or hall in which meetings or social functions are held.

assembly shop ▶ noun a place where a machine or its components are assembled.

assent /əˈsɛnt/ ▶ noun [mass noun] the expression of approval or agreement: *a loud murmur of assent | he nodded assent.* ■ official agreement or sanction: *the act was given the Royal Assent.*
▶ verb [no obj.] (often **assent to**) express approval or agreement: *the Prime Minister assented to the change* | [with direct speech] *'Guest house, then,' Frank assented cheerfully.*
– ORIGIN Middle English: from Old French *as(s)enter* (verb), *as(s)ente* (noun), based on Latin *assentire*, from *ad-* 'towards' + *sentire* 'feel, think'.

assert ▶ verb [reporting verb] state a fact or belief confidently and forcefully: [with clause] *the company asserts that the cuts will not affect development* | [with obj.] *he asserted his innocence.* ■ [with obj.] cause others to recognize (one's authority or a right) by confident and forceful behaviour: *the good librarian is able to assert authority when required.* ■ (**assert oneself**) behave or speak in a confident and forceful manner: *it was time to assert himself.*
– DERIVATIVES **asserter** (also **assertor**) noun.
– ORIGIN early 17th cent.: from Latin *asserere* 'claim, affirm', from *ad-* 'to' + *serere* 'to join'.

assertion ▶ noun a confident and forceful statement of fact or belief: [with clause] *his assertion that his father had deserted the family.* ■ [mass noun] the action of asserting something: *the assertion of his legal rights.*
– ORIGIN late Middle English: from Latin *assertio(n-)*, from the verb *asserere* (see ASSERT).

assertive ▶ adjective having or showing a confident and forceful personality: *the job may call for assertive behaviour.*
– DERIVATIVES **assertively** adverb, **assertiveness** noun.

asses plural form of AS^2, ASS^1, ASS^2.

asses' bridge ▶ noun English term for PONS ASINORUM.

assess ▶ verb [with obj.] evaluate or estimate the nature, ability, or quality of: *the committee must assess the relative importance of the issues* | [with clause] *it is difficult to assess whether this is a new trend.* ■ calculate or estimate the price or value of: *the damage was assessed at £5 billion.* ■ set the value of a tax, fine, etc., for (a person or property) at a specified level: *all empty properties will be assessed at 50 per cent.*
– DERIVATIVES **assessable** adjective, **assessor** noun.
– ORIGIN late Middle English: from Old French *assesser*, based on Latin *assidere* 'sit by' (in medieval Latin 'levy tax'), from *ad-* 'to, at' + *sedere* 'sit'. Compare with ASSIZE.

assessment ▶ noun [mass noun] the action of assessing someone or something: *the assessment of educational needs | assessments of market value.*

asset ▶ noun a useful or valuable thing or person: *quick reflexes were his chief assets | the school is an asset to the community.* ■ (usu. **assets**) an item of property owned by a person or company, regarded as having value and available to meet debts, commitments, or legacies: *growth in net assets.*
– ORIGIN mid 16th cent. (in the plural in the sense 'sufficient estate to allow discharge of a will'): from an Anglo-Norman French legal term, from Old French *asez* 'enough', based on Latin *ad* 'to' + *satis* 'enough'.

asset-backed ▶ adjective denoting securities having as collateral the return on a series of mortgages, credit agreements, or other forms of lending.

asset-stripping ▶ noun [mass noun] the practice of taking over a company in financial difficulties and selling each of its assets separately at a profit without regard for the company's future.
– DERIVATIVES **asset-stripper** noun.

asseveration /əˌsɛvəˈreɪʃ(ə)n/ ▶ noun [mass noun] the solemn or emphatic declaration or statement of something: *I fear that you offer only unsupported asseveration* | [count noun] *the dogmatic outlook marks many of his asseverations.*
– DERIVATIVES **asseverate** verb.
– ORIGIN mid 16th cent.: from Latin *asseveratio(n-)*, from the verb *asseverare*, from *ad-* 'to' + *severus* 'serious'.

asshat /ˈashat/ ▶ noun N. Amer. vulgar slang a stupid person.

asshole ▶ noun vulgar slang US spelling of ARSEHOLE.

assibilate /əˈsɪbɪleɪt/ ▶ verb [with obj.] Phonetics pronounce (a sound) as a sibilant or affricate ending in a sibilant (e.g. sound *t* as *ts*).
– DERIVATIVES **assibilation** noun.
– ORIGIN mid 19th cent.: from Latin *assibilat-* 'hissed at', from the verb *assibilare*, from *ad-* 'to' + *sibilare* 'to hiss'.

assiduity /ˌasɪˈdjuːɪti/ ▶ noun (pl. **assiduities**) [mass noun] constant or close attention to what one is doing: *the assiduity with which he could wear down his opponents.* ■ (**assiduities**) archaic or literary constant attentions to someone.
– ORIGIN late Middle English: from Latin *assiduitas*, from *assiduus* 'occupied with' (see ASSIDUOUS).

assiduous /əˈsɪdjʊəs/ ▶ adjective showing great care and perseverance: *she was **assiduous in** pointing out every feature.*
– DERIVATIVES **assiduously** adverb, **assiduousness** noun.
– ORIGIN mid 16th cent.: from Latin *assiduus*, from *assidere* 'be engaged in doing' (see ASSESS), + -OUS.

assign ▶ verb [with obj.] **1** allocate (a job or duty): *Congress had **assigned** the task **to** the agency* | [with two objs] *his leader assigned him this mission.* ■ appoint (someone) to a job, task, or organization: *she has been **assigned to** a new job.*
2 designate or set (something) aside for a specific purpose: *managers happily **assign** large sums of money **to** travel budgets.* ■ (**assign something to**) attribute something as belonging to: *it is difficult to decide whether to assign the victory to Godwin.*
3 transfer (legal rights or liabilities).
▶ noun Law another term for ASSIGNEE (sense 1).
– DERIVATIVES **assignable** adjective, **assigner** (also **assignor**) noun.
– ORIGIN Middle English: from Old French *asigner*, *assiner*, from Latin *assignare*, from *ad-* 'to' + *signare* 'to sign'.

assignation ▶ noun **1** an appointment to meet someone in secret, typically one made by lovers: *his **assignation with** an older woman.*
2 [mass noun] the allocation or attribution of someone or something as belonging to something.
– ORIGIN late Middle English (in the senses 'command, appointment to office, or allotment of revenue'): via Old French from Latin *assignatio(n-)*, from the verb *assignare* (see ASSIGN).

assignee ▶ noun chiefly Law **1** a person to whom a right or liability is legally transferred.
2 a person appointed to act for another.
– ORIGIN Middle English: from Old French *assigne*, past participle of *assigner* 'allot' (see ASSIGN).

assignment ▶ noun **1** a task or piece of work allocated to someone as part of a job or course of study: *a homework assignment.* ■ [mass noun] the allocation of a job or task to someone: *the effective assignment of tasks.*
2 [mass noun] the allocation of someone or something as belonging to a particular group or category: *the **assignment** of individuals **to** particular social positions.*
3 an act of making a legal transfer of a right or liability: *an assignment of leasehold property.* ■ a document effecting a legal transfer of a right or liability.
– ORIGIN late Middle English: from Old French *assignement*, from medieval Latin *assignamentum*, from Latin *assignare* 'allot' (see ASSIGN).

assimilate ▶ verb [with obj.] **1** take in and understand fully (information or ideas): *Marie tried to assimilate the week's events.* ■ absorb and integrate (people, ideas, or culture) into a wider society or culture: *pop trends are **assimilated into** the mainstream with alarming speed.*
2 (of the body or any biological system) absorb and digest (food or nutrients).
3 regard as similar; liken: *philosophers had **assimilated** thought **to** perception.* ■ [no obj.] become similar: *the Churches **assimilated to** a certain cultural norm.* ■ Phonetics make (a sound) more like another in the same or next word.
– DERIVATIVES **assimilable** adjective, **assimilation** noun, **assimilative** adjective, **assimilator** noun, **assimilatory** adjective.

A

– ORIGIN late Middle English: from Latin *assimilat-* 'absorbed, incorporated', from the verb *assimilare*, from *ad-* 'to' + *similis* 'like'.

assimilationist ▶ noun a person who advocates or participates in racial or cultural integration.

Assisi[1] /əˈsiːsi/ a town in the region of Umbria in central Italy; pop. 27,507 (2008). It is famous as the birthplace of St Francis, whose tomb is located there.

Assisi[2] see CLARE OF ASSISI, ST.

Assisi[3] see FRANCIS OF ASSISI, ST.

assist ▶ verb [with obj.] help (someone), typically by doing a share of the work: *a senior academic would assist him in his work* | [no obj.] *their presence would* ***assist in*** *keeping the peace.* ■ help by providing money or information: *they were assisting police with their inquiries* | [no obj.] *funds to* ***assist with*** *capital investment.* ■ [no obj.] be present as a helper: *two midwives who* ***assisted at*** *a water birth.*
▶ noun chiefly N. Amer. an act of giving help, typically by providing money: *the budget must have an assist from tax policies.* ■ (in sport) an act of touching the ball in a play in which a teammate scores or an opposing batter is put out: *Elliot had 10 points and five assists.*
– DERIVATIVES **assister** noun, **assistive** adjective.
– ORIGIN late Middle English: from Old French *assister*, from Latin *assistere* 'take one's stand by', from *ad-* 'to, at' + *sistere* 'take one's stand'.

assistance ▶ noun [mass noun] the action of helping someone by sharing work: *the work was completed* ***with the assistance of*** *carpenters.* ■ the provision of money, resources, or information to help someone: *schemes offering financial* ***assistance to*** *employers* | *she will be glad to give advice and assistance.*
– PHRASES **be of assistance** be of practical use or help: *the guide will* ***be of assistance to*** *development groups.* **come to someone's assistance** act to help someone.
– ORIGIN late Middle English: from Old French, or from medieval Latin *assistentia*, from Latin *assistere* (see ASSIST).

assistant ▶ noun a person who ranks below a senior person: *the managing director and his assistant* | [as modifier] *an assistant manager.* ■ [with adj. or noun modifier] a person who helps in particular work: *a care assistant.*
– ORIGIN late Middle English: from Old French, or from medieval Latin *assistent-* 'taking one's stand beside', from the verb *assistere* (see ASSIST).

assistant professor ▶ noun N. Amer. a university teacher ranking immediately below an associate professor.

assistantship ▶ noun N. Amer. a paid academic appointment made to a graduate student that involves part-time teaching or research.

assisted area ▶ noun (in the UK) a region receiving government grants or loans for industrial development.

assisted place ▶ noun (in the UK) a place in an independent school for a pupil whose fees are wholly or partially subsidized by the state.

assisted suicide ▶ noun [mass noun] the suicide of a patient suffering from an incurable disease, effected by the taking of lethal drugs provided by a doctor for this purpose.

assize /əˈsʌɪz/ ▶ noun (usu. **assizes**) historical a court which formerly sat at intervals in each county of England and Wales to administer the civil and criminal law. In 1972 the civil jurisdiction of assizes was transferred to the High Court, and the criminal jurisdiction to the Crown Court.
– ORIGIN Middle English: from Old French *assise*, feminine past participle of *asseeir* 'sit, settle, assess', from Latin *assidere* (see ASSESS).

ass-kicking ▶ adjective N. Amer. vulgar slang forceful or aggressive.

ass-kissing ▶ noun [mass noun] N. Amer. vulgar slang obsequious behaviour in order to gain favour.

ass-licking ▶ noun vulgar slang US spelling of ARSE-LICKING.

assload ▶ noun N. Amer. vulgar slang a large number or amount of something.

Assoc. ▶ abbreviation (as part of a title) Association.

associate ▶ verb /əˈsəʊʃɪeɪt, -sɪeɪt/ [with obj.] (often **associate someone/thing with**) connect (someone or something) with something else in one's mind: *I associated wealth with freedom.* ■ connect (something) with something else because they occur together or one produces the other: *the environmental problems associated with nuclear waste.* ■ (**be associated with**) be involved with. ■ (**associate oneself with**) allow oneself to be connected with or seen to be supportive of: *I cannot associate myself with some of the language used.* ■ [no obj.] meet or have dealings with someone regarded with disapproval: *he began to* ***associate with*** *the Mafia.*
▶ noun /əˈsəʊʃɪət, -sɪət/ **1** a partner or companion in business or at work: *a close associate of the Minister.*
2 a person with limited or subordinate membership of an organization.
3 chiefly Psychology a concept connected with another.
▶ adjective /əˈsəʊʃɪət, -sɪət/ [attrib.] connected with an organization or business: *an associate company.* ■ having shared function or membership but with a lesser status: *the associate director of the academy.*
– DERIVATIVES **associability** noun, **associable** adjective, **associateship** noun, **associator** noun.
– ORIGIN late Middle English (as a verb in the sense 'join with in a common purpose'; as an adjective in the sense 'allied'): from Latin *associat-* 'joined', from the verb *associare*, from *ad-* 'to' + *socius* 'sharing, allied'.

associated ▶ adjective (of a person or thing) connected with something else: *two associated events.* ■ (of a company) connected or amalgamated with another company or companies. ■ Chemistry (of liquids) in which the molecules are held together by hydrogen bonding or other weak interaction.

Associated Press (abbrev.: **AP**) an international news agency based in New York City.

associate professor ▶ noun N. Amer. an academic ranking immediately below full professor.

association ▶ noun **1** (often in names) a group of people organized for a joint purpose: *the National Association of Probation Officers.* ■ Ecology a stable plant community including a characteristic group of dominant plant species.
2 a connection or cooperative link between people or organizations: *he developed a close* ***association with*** *the university* | [mass noun] *the programme was promoted* ***in association with*** *the Department of Music.* ■ [mass noun] the process or state of becoming a subordinate member of an organization: [as modifier] *an association agreement between Bulgaria and the EU.* ■ Chemistry the linking of molecules through hydrogen bonding or other interaction short of full bond formation.
3 (usu. **associations**) a mental connection between things: *the word bureaucracy has unpleasant associations.* ■ [mass noun] the action of making a mental connection: *there's nothing new in the association of fasting with spirituality.*
4 [mass noun] the state of occurring with something else; co-occurrence: *cases of cancer found* ***in association with*** *colitis.*
– DERIVATIVES **associational** adjective.
– ORIGIN mid 16th cent. (in the sense 'uniting in a common purpose'): from medieval Latin *associatio(n-)*, from Latin *associare* 'to unite, ally' (see ASSOCIATE).

association area ▶ noun Anatomy a region of the cortex of the brain which connects sensory and motor areas, and which is thought to be concerned with higher mental activities.

Association football ▶ noun [mass noun] Brit. more formal term for SOCCER.

associationism ▶ noun [mass noun] a theory in philosophy or psychology which regards the simple association or co-occurrence of ideas or sensations as the primary basis of meaning, thought, or learning.
– DERIVATIVES **associationist** noun & adjective.

Association of Southeast Asian Nations (abbrev.: **ASEAN**) a regional organization intended to promote economic cooperation and now comprising the countries of Indonesia, Malaysia, the Philippines, Singapore, Thailand, Vietnam, and Brunei.

associative ▶ adjective **1** of or involving the association of things: *making associative links.* ■ Computing of or denoting computer storage in which items are identified by content rather than by address.
2 Mathematics involving the condition that a group of quantities connected by operators gives the same result whatever their grouping, i.e. in whichever order the operations are performed, as long as the order of the quantities remains the same, e.g. $(a \times b) \times c = a \times (b \times c)$.

assonance /ˈas(ə)nəns/ ▶ noun [mass noun] resemblance of sound between syllables of nearby words, arising particularly from the rhyming of two or more stressed vowels, but not consonants (e.g. *sonnet, porridge*), but also from the use of identical consonants with different vowels (e.g. *killed, cold, culled*).
– DERIVATIVES **assonant** adjective,.
– ORIGIN early 18th cent.: from French, from Latin *assonare* 'respond to', from *ad-* 'to' + *sonare* (from *sonus* 'sound').

assort ▶ verb **1** [no obj.] Genetics (of genes or characteristics) become distributed among cells or progeny.
2 [with obj.] archaic place in a group; classify: *he would assort it with the fabulous dogs as a monstrous invention.*
– ORIGIN late 15th cent.: from Old French *assorter*, from *a-* (from Latin *ad* 'to, at') + *sorte* 'sort, kind'.

assortative ▶ adjective denoting or involving the preferential mating of animals or marriage between people with similar characteristics.

assorted ▶ adjective [attrib.] of various sorts put together; miscellaneous: *bowls in assorted colours.*

assortment ▶ noun a miscellaneous collection of things or people: *the room was filled with* ***an assortment of*** *clothes.*

ASSR ▶ abbreviation historical Autonomous Soviet Socialist Republic.

Asst ▶ abbreviation Assistant.

assuage /əˈsweɪdʒ/ ▶ verb [with obj.] make (an unpleasant feeling) less intense: *the letter assuaged the fears of most members.* ■ satisfy (an appetite or desire): *an opportunity occurred to assuage her desire for knowledge.*
– DERIVATIVES **assuagement** noun.
– ORIGIN Middle English: from Old French *assouagier*, *asouagier*, based on Latin *ad-* 'to' (expressing change) + *suavis* 'sweet'.

As Sulaymaniyah /as/ full name of SULAYMANIYAH.

assume ▶ verb [with obj.] **1** suppose to be the case, without proof: *topics which assume detailed knowledge of local events* | [with clause] *it is reasonable to assume that such changes have significant social effects* | [with obj. and infinitive] *they were assumed to be foreign.*
2 take or begin to have (power or responsibility): *he assumed full responsibility for all organizational work.* ■ seize (power or control).
3 begin to have (a specified quality, appearance, or extent): *militant activity had assumed epidemic proportions.* ■ take on or adopt (a manner or identity), sometimes falsely: *Oliver assumed an expression of penitence* | (as adj. **assumed**) *a man living under an assumed name.*
– DERIVATIVES **assumable** adjective, **assumedly** adverb.
– ORIGIN late Middle English: from Latin *assumere*, from *ad-* 'towards' + *sumere* 'take'.

assuming ▶ conjunction used for the purpose of argument to indicate a premise on which a statement can be based: ***assuming that*** *the treaty is ratified, what is its relevance?*
▶ adjective archaic arrogant or presumptuous.

assumption ▶ noun **1** a thing that is accepted as true or as certain to happen, without proof: *they made certain assumptions about the market* | [with clause] *we're working on the assumption that the time of death was after midnight.*
2 [mass noun] the action of taking on power or responsibility.
3 (**Assumption**) the reception of the Virgin Mary bodily into heaven. This was formally declared a doctrine of the Roman Catholic Church in 1950. ■ the feast in honour of the Assumption, celebrated on 15 August.
4 [mass noun] archaic arrogance or presumption.
– ORIGIN Middle English (in sense 3): from Old French *asompsion* or Latin *assumptio(n-)*, from the verb *assumere* (see ASSUME).

assumptive ▶ adjective **1** rare of the nature of an assumption.
2 archaic arrogant or presumptuous.
– ORIGIN mid 16th cent. (in the sense 'taken, adopted'): from Latin *assumptivus*, from the verb *assumere* (see ASSUME).

Assur /ˈaʃʊə/ (also **Asur** or **Ashur**) an ancient city-state of Mesopotamia, situated on the River Tigris to the south of modern Mosul. It was the traditional capital of the Assyrian empires.

assurance ▶ noun **1** a positive declaration intended to give confidence; a promise: [with clause] ***he gave an assurance that*** *work would begin on Monday.*
2 [mass noun] confidence or certainty in one's own abilities: *she drove with assurance.* ■ certainty about something: *assurance of faith depends on our trust in God.*

3 [mass noun] chiefly Brit. insurance, specifically life insurance.
– ORIGIN late Middle English (in sense 2): from Old French, from *assurer* 'assure'.

> **USAGE** In the context of life insurance, a technical distinction is made between **assurance** and **insurance**. **Assurance** is used of policies under whose terms a payment is guaranteed, either after a fixed term or on the death of the insured person; **insurance** is the general term, and is used in particular of policies under whose terms a payment would be made only in certain circumstances (e.g. accident or death within a limited period).

assure ▶ **verb 1** [reporting verb] tell someone something positively to dispel any doubts: [with obj. and clause] *Tony assured me that there was a supermarket in the village* | [with obj. and direct speech] *'I quite understand,' Mrs Lewis assured her* | [with obj.] *they* **assured** *him* **of** *their full confidence.* ■ (**assure oneself**) make sure of something: *she assured herself that he was asleep.*
2 [with obj.] make (something) certain to happen: *victory was now assured* | [with clause] *their influence assured that the report would be tough.* ■ (**be assured of**) be certain to get: *you would be assured of a welcome.*
3 chiefly Brit. cover (a life) by assurance. ■ secure the future payment of (an amount) with insurance.
– DERIVATIVES **assurer** noun.
– ORIGIN late Middle English: from Old French *assurer*, based on Latin *ad-* 'to' (expressing change) + *securus* (see **SECURE**).

assured ▶ **adjective 1** confident: *an extremely assured performance.*
2 [attrib.] protected against discontinuance or change: *an assured tenancy.*
– DERIVATIVES **assuredly** adverb [sentence adverb] *if they lose their hold, they will assuredly drown.*

Assyria /əˈsɪrɪə/ an ancient country in what is now northern Iraq. From the early part of the 2nd millennium BC Assyria was the centre of a succession of empires; it was at its peak in the 8th and late 7th centuries BC, when its rule stretched from the Persian Gulf to Egypt. It fell in 612 BC to a coalition of Medes and Babylonians.

Assyrian ▶ **noun 1** an inhabitant of ancient Assyria.
2 [mass noun] the language of ancient Assyria, a dialect of Akkadian.
3 [mass noun] a dialect of Aramaic still spoken by a group of people of mainly Christian faith living in the mountains of Syria, northern Iraq, and surrounding regions.
▶ **adjective 1** relating to ancient Assyria or its language.
2 relating to or denoting modern Assyrian or its speakers.

Assyriology /əˌsɪrɪˈɒlədʒi/ ▶ **noun** [mass noun] the study of the language, history, and antiquities of ancient Assyria.
– DERIVATIVES **Assyriologist** noun.

AST ▶ **abbreviation** Atlantic Standard Time (see **ATLANTIC TIME**).

astable /əˈsteɪb(ə)l, eɪ-/ ▶ **adjective** chiefly Electronics relating to a system or electric circuit which oscillates spontaneously between unstable states.

Astaire /əˈstɛː/, Fred (1899–1987), American dancer, singer, and actor; born *Frederick Austerlitz*. He is famous for starring in a number of film musicals, including *Top Hat* (1935), in a successful partnership with Ginger Rogers.

Astana /əˈstɑːnə/ a city in Kazakhstan, the capital since 1997; pop. 550,400 (est. 2006). Former name **AKMOLA**.

astanga ▶ **noun** variant spelling of **ASHTANGA**.

Astarte /əˈstɑːti/ a Phoenician goddess of fertility and sexual love who corresponds to the Babylonian and Assyrian goddess Ishtar and who became identified with the Egyptian Isis, the Greek Aphrodite, and others.

astatic /əˈstatɪk/ ▶ **adjective** Physics (of a system or instrument) consisting of or employing a combination of magnets suspended in a uniform magnetic field on a single wire or thread in such a way that no torque is present.
– ORIGIN early 19th cent.: from Greek *astatos* 'unstable' + **-IC**.

astatine /ˈastətiːn/ ▶ **noun** [mass noun] the chemical element of atomic number 85, a radioactive member of the halogen group. Astatine was first produced by bombarding bismuth with alpha particles, and it occurs in traces in nature as a decay product. (Symbol: **At**)
– ORIGIN 1940s: from Greek *astatos* 'unstable' + **-INE**[4].

aster /ˈastə/ ▶ **noun** a plant of a large genus that includes the Michaelmas daisy, typically having purple or pink rayed flowers. ● Genus *Aster*, family Compositae: numerous species. See also **CHINA ASTER**.
– ORIGIN early 17th cent. (in the sense 'a star'): via Latin from Greek *astēr* 'star'.

-aster ▶ **suffix** forming nouns: **1** denoting poor quality: *criticaster* | *poetaster*.
2 Botany denoting incomplete resemblance: *oleaster*.
– ORIGIN from Latin.

asterisk /ˈastərɪsk/ ▶ **noun** a symbol (*) used in text as a pointer to an annotation or footnote.
▶ **verb** [with obj.] mark (a word or piece of text) with an asterisk: (as adj. **asterisked**) *asterisked entries.*
– ORIGIN late Middle English: via late Latin from Greek *asteriskos* 'small star', diminutive of *astēr*.

> **USAGE** Asterisk is pronounced with an *-isk* sound at the end, to match the spelling, and not as though it were spelled **-ix**. **Asterix** is a character in a cartoon strip.

asterism /ˈastərɪz(ə)m/ ▶ **noun 1** Astronomy a prominent pattern or group of stars that is smaller than a constellation.
2 a group of three asterisks (⁂) drawing attention to a piece of text.
– ORIGIN late 16th cent.: from Greek *asterismos*, from *astēr* 'star'.

astern ▶ **adverb** behind or towards the rear of a ship or aircraft: *the engine rooms lay astern.*
– ORIGIN late Middle English: from **A-**[2] (expressing position or direction) + **STERN**[2].

asteroid /ˈastərɔɪd/ ▶ **noun 1** a small rocky body orbiting the sun. Large numbers of these, ranging enormously in size, are found between the orbits of Mars and Jupiter, though some have more eccentric orbits.
2 Zoology an echinoderm of the class Asteroidea, which comprises the starfishes.
▶ **adjective** Zoology relating to or denoting echinoderms of the class Asteroidea.
– DERIVATIVES **asteroidal** adjective.
– ORIGIN early 19th cent.: from Greek *asteroeidēs* 'starlike', from *astēr* 'star'.

Asteroidea /ˌastəˈrɔɪdɪə/ ▶ **plural noun** Zoology a class of echinoderms that comprises the starfishes.
– ORIGIN modern Latin (plural), from Greek *asteroeidēs* 'starlike', from *astēr* 'star'.

asthenia /əsˈθiːnɪə/ ▶ **noun** [mass noun] Medicine abnormal physical weakness or lack of energy.
– DERIVATIVES **asthenic** adjective.
– ORIGIN late 18th cent.: modern Latin, from Greek *astheneia*, from *asthenēs* 'weak'.

asthenosphere /əsˈθɛnəsfɪə/ ▶ **noun** Geology the upper layer of the earth's mantle, below the lithosphere, in which there is relatively low resistance to plastic flow and convection is thought to occur.
– DERIVATIVES **asthenospheric** adjective.
– ORIGIN early 20th cent.: from Greek *asthenēs* 'weak' + **SPHERE**.

asthma /ˈasmə/ ▶ **noun** [mass noun] a respiratory condition marked by attacks of spasm in the bronchi of the lungs, causing difficulty in breathing. It is usually connected to allergic reaction or other forms of hypersensitivity.
– ORIGIN late Middle English: from medieval Latin *asma*, from Greek *asthma*, from *azein* 'breathe hard'.

asthmatic ▶ **adjective** relating to or suffering from asthma.
▶ **noun** a person who suffers from asthma.
– DERIVATIVES **asthmatically** adverb.
– ORIGIN early 16th cent.: via Latin from Greek *asthmatikos*, from *asthma* (see **ASTHMA**).

Asti /ˈasti/ ▶ **noun** [mass noun] **1** a white wine from the Italian province of Asti and neighbouring parts of Piedmont.
2 a light sparkling wine from the Asti region.

astigmatism /əˈstɪgmətɪz(ə)m/ ▶ **noun** [mass noun] a defect in the eye or in a lens caused by a deviation from spherical curvature, which results in distorted images, as light rays are prevented from meeting at a common focus.
– DERIVATIVES **astigmatic** /astɪgˈmatɪk/ adjective.
– ORIGIN mid 19th cent.: from **A-**[1] 'without' + Greek *stigma* 'point' + **-ISM**.

astilbe /əˈstɪlbi/ ▶ **noun** an Old World plant of the saxifrage family, with plumes of tiny white, pink, or red flowers. ● Genus *Astilbe*, family Saxifragaceae.
– ORIGIN modern Latin, from Greek *a-* 'not' + *stilbē*, feminine of *stilbos* 'glittering' (because the individual flowers are small and inconspicuous).

astir ▶ **adjective** [predic.] in a state of excited movement: *the streets are all astir.* ■ awake and out of bed: *he woke before anyone was astir.*
– ORIGIN late 18th cent.: from **A-**[2] 'on' + the noun **STIR**[1].

Asti Spumante /ˌasti sp(j)uːˈmanteɪ, -ti/ ▶ **noun** another term for **ASTI** (sense 2).

astonish ▶ **verb** [with obj.] surprise or impress (someone) greatly: *you never fail to astonish me* | [with obj. and clause] *it astonished her that he was so anxious.*
– ORIGIN early 16th cent. (as *astonished*, in the sense 'stunned, bewildered, dismayed'): from obsolete *astone* 'stun, stupefy', from Old French *estoner*, based on Latin *ex-* 'out' + *tonare* 'to thunder'.

astonished ▶ **adjective** greatly surprised or impressed; amazed: *he was* **astonished at** *the change in him* | *we were astonished to hear of this decision.*

astonishing ▶ **adjective** extremely surprising or impressive; amazing: *an astonishing achievement* | *I find it astonishing that they ever thought it could work.*
– DERIVATIVES **astonishingly** adverb [as submodifier] *an astonishingly successful programme.*

astonishment ▶ **noun** [mass noun] great surprise: *she looked at him* **in astonishment**.

Astor /ˈastə/, Nancy Witcher Langhorne, Viscountess (1879–1964), American-born British Conservative politician. She became the first woman to sit in the House of Commons when she succeeded her husband as MP for Plymouth in 1919.

astound ▶ **verb** [with obj.] shock or greatly surprise: *her bluntness astounded him.*
– ORIGIN Middle English (as an adjective in the sense 'stunned'): from *astoned*, past participle of obsolete *astone* (see **ASTONISH**).

astounding ▶ **adjective** surprisingly impressive or notable: *the summit offers astounding views.*
– DERIVATIVES **astoundingly** adverb [as submodifier] *an astoundingly good performance.*

astraddle ▶ **preposition** with the legs stretched widely on each side of: *policemen sitting astraddle motorcycles.*
▶ **adjective & adverb** with the legs stretched widely on each side: [as predic. adj.] *with her legs astraddle* | [as adv.] *the guys got me astraddle of the wheel.*

Astraea /əˈstriːə/ Astronomy asteroid 5, discovered in 1845 (diameter 125 km).
– ORIGIN from the name of a Roman goddess associated with justice.

astragal /ˈastrəg(ə)l/ ▶ **noun 1** a moulding or wooden strip of semicircular cross section. ■ Architecture a narrow semicircular moulding round the top or bottom of a column.
2 a bar separating panes of glass in cabinetmaking.
– ORIGIN mid 17th cent.: from **ASTRAGALUS**, partly via French *astragale*.

astragalus /əˈstrag(ə)ləs/ ▶ **noun** (pl. **astragali** /-lʌɪ/) **1** chiefly Zoology another term for **TALUS**[1] (ankle bone). ■ (**astragali**) historical small bones used as dice.
2 a plant of a genus that includes milk vetch. ● Genus *Astragalus*, family Leguminosae.
– ORIGIN mid 16th cent.: via Latin from Greek *astragalos* 'ankle bone, moulding', also the name of a plant.

Astrakhan /ˌastrəˈkɑːn/ a city in southern Russia, on the delta of the River Volga; pop. 503,100 (est. 2008).

astrakhan /ˌastrəˈkan/ ▶ **noun** [mass noun] the dark curly fleece of young karakul lambs from central Asia. ■ a fabric imitating astrakhan.
– ORIGIN mid 18th cent.: named after the city of **ASTRAKHAN**, from which the fleeces were exported.

astral /ˈastr(ə)l/ ▶ **adjective** [attrib.] relating to or resembling the stars: *astral navigation.* ■ relating to a supposed non-physical realm of existence to which various psychic and paranormal phenomena are ascribed, and in which the physical human body is said to have a counterpart: *spiritual beings from the astral plane.*
– ORIGIN early 17th cent.: from late Latin *astralis*, from *astrum* 'star'.

astrantia /əˈstrantɪə/ ▶ **noun** a plant of the parsley family with small compact starlike heads of tiny flowers surrounded by prominent bracts, native to Europe and western Asia. ● Genus *Astrantia*, family Umbelliferae: several species, in particular *A. major*, which is often grown in gardens.
– ORIGIN modern Latin, perhaps from Greek *astēr* 'star'.

astray ▶ **adverb 1** away from the correct path or direction: *we went astray but a man redirected us.*

A

2 into error or morally questionable behaviour: *he was led astray by boozy colleagues.*
– PHRASES **go astray** (of an object) become lost or mislaid: *the money had gone astray.*
– ORIGIN Middle English (in the sense 'distant from the correct path'): from an Anglo-Norman French variant of Old French *estraie*, past participle of *estraier*, based on Latin *extra* 'out of bounds' + *vagari* 'wander'.

astride ▸ **preposition & adverb 1** with a leg on each side of: [as prep.] ***he was sitting astride the bike*** | [as adv.] *he sat on the chair astride.* ■ [as adv.] (of a person's legs) apart: *he stood, legs astride.*
2 [as prep.] extending across: *the port **stands astride** an international route.*

astringent /əˈstrɪn(d)ʒ(ə)nt/ ▸ **adjective 1** causing the contraction of skin cells and other body tissues: *an astringent skin lotion.*
2 sharp or severe in manner or style: *her astringent words had their effect.* ■ (of taste or smell) sharp or bitter.
▸ **noun** an astringent lotion applied to the skin to reduce bleeding from minor abrasions or as a cosmetic to make the skin less oily.
– DERIVATIVES **astringency** noun, **astringently** adverb.
– ORIGIN mid 16th cent.: from French, from Latin *astringent-* 'pulling tight', from the verb *astringere*, from *ad-* 'towards' + *stringere* 'bind, pull tight'.

astro- /ˈastrəʊ/ ▸ **combining form** relating to the stars or celestial objects: *astrodome* | *astrophotography.* ■ relating to outer space: *astrochemistry.*
– ORIGIN from Greek *astron* 'star'.

astro-archaeology ▸ **noun** another term for ARCHAEOASTRONOMY.

astrobiology ▸ **noun** [mass noun] the branch of biology concerned with the study of life on earth and in space.
– DERIVATIVES **astrobiological** adjective, **astrobiologist** noun.

astrobleme /ˈastrəʊbliːm/ ▸ **noun** Geology an eroded remnant of a large crater made by the impact of a meteorite or comet.
– ORIGIN 1960s: from Greek *astron* 'star' + *blēma* 'wound'.

astrochemistry ▸ **noun** [mass noun] the study of molecules and ions occurring in stars and interstellar space.
– DERIVATIVES **astrochemical** adjective, **astrochemist** noun.

astrocompass ▸ **noun** an instrument designed to indicate direction with respect to the stars.

astrocyte /ˈastrə(ʊ)sʌɪt/ ▸ **noun** Anatomy a star-shaped glial cell of the central nervous system.
– DERIVATIVES **astrocytic** adjective.

astrodome ▸ **noun 1** chiefly US an enclosed stadium with a domed roof.
2 a domed window in an aircraft for astronomical observations.

astrogation /ˌastrə(ʊ)ˈɡeɪʃ(ə)n/ ▸ **noun** [mass noun] (in science fiction) navigation in outer space.
– DERIVATIVES **astrogator** noun.
– ORIGIN 1930s: blend of ASTRO- and NAVIGATION.

astroid /ˈastrɔɪd/ ▸ **noun** Mathematics a hypocycloid with four cusps (like a square with concave sides).

astrolabe /ˈastrəleɪb/ ▸ **noun** chiefly historical an instrument used to make astronomical measurements, typically of the altitudes of celestial bodies, and in navigation for calculating latitude, before the development of the sextant.
– ORIGIN late Middle English: from Old French *astrelabe*, from medieval Latin *astrolabium*, from Greek *astrolabon*, neuter of *astrolabos* 'star-taking'.

astrology ▸ **noun** [mass noun] the study of the movements and relative positions of celestial bodies interpreted as having an influence on human affairs and the natural world.

> Ancient observers of the heavens developed elaborate systems of explanation based on the movements of the sun, moon, and planets through the constellations of the zodiac, for predicting events and for casting horoscopes. By 1700 astrology had lost intellectual credibility in the West, but continued to have popular appeal. Modern astrology is based on that of the Greeks, but other systems are extant, e.g. that of China.

– DERIVATIVES **astrologer** noun, **astrological** adjective, **astrologically** adverb, **astrologist** noun.
– ORIGIN late Middle English: from Old French *astrologie*, from Latin *astrologia*, from Greek, from *astron* 'star'.

astrometric binary ▸ **noun** Astronomy a binary star system in which one companion is invisible, but is known to be present from its effect on measurements relating to the other.

astrometry ▸ **noun** [mass noun] the measurement of the positions, motions, and magnitudes of stars.
– DERIVATIVES **astrometric** adjective.

astronaut ▸ **noun** a person who is trained to travel in a spacecraft.
– DERIVATIVES **astronautical** adjective.
– ORIGIN 1920s: from ASTRO-, on the pattern of *aeronaut* and *aquanaut*.

astronautics ▸ **plural noun** [treated as sing.] the science and technology of space travel and exploration.

astronomer ▸ **noun** an expert in or student of astronomy.

astronomical ▸ **adjective 1** relating to astronomy.
2 informal (of an amount) extremely large: *he wanted an astronomical fee.*
– DERIVATIVES **astronomic** adjective (sense 2), **astronomically** adverb.
– ORIGIN mid 16th cent.: via Latin from Greek *astronomikos*, from *astronomia* (see ASTRONOMY).

astronomical unit (abbrev.: **AU**) ▸ **noun** Astronomy a unit of measurement equal to 149.6 million kilometres, the mean distance from the centre of the earth to the centre of the sun.

astronomical year ▸ **noun** see YEAR (sense 1).

astronomy ▸ **noun** [mass noun] the branch of science which deals with celestial objects, space, and the physical universe as a whole.

> In ancient times, observation of the sun, moon, stars, and planets formed the basis of timekeeping and navigation. Astronomy was greatly furthered by the invention of the telescope, but modern observations are made in all parts of the spectrum, including X-ray and radio frequencies, using terrestrial and orbiting instruments and space probes.

– ORIGIN Middle English (also denoting astrology): from Old French *astronomie*, from Latin *astronomia*, from Greek, from *astronomos* (adjective) 'star-arranging'.

astrophotography ▸ **noun** [mass noun] the use of photography in astronomy.
– DERIVATIVES **astrophotographer** noun, **astrophotographic** adjective.

astrophysics ▸ **plural noun** [treated as sing.] the branch of astronomy concerned with the physical nature of stars and other celestial bodies, and the application of the laws and theories of physics to the interpretation of astronomical observations.
– DERIVATIVES **astrophysical** adjective, **astrophysicist** noun.

AstroTurf ▸ **noun** [mass noun] trademark an artificial grass surface, used for sports fields.
– ORIGIN 1960s: from ASTRODOME (sense 1) (where it was first used) + TURF.

astroturfing ▸ **noun** [mass noun] the deceptive practice of presenting an orchestrated marketing or public relations campaign in the guise of unsolicited comments from members of the public.
– ORIGIN 1990s: from ASTROTURF, the idea being that such a campaign is an artificial version of a *grassroots* campaign (see GRASS ROOTS).

Asturias /aˈstʊərɪəs/ an autonomous region and former principality of NW Spain; capital, Oviedo.
– DERIVATIVES **Asturian** noun & adjective.

astute ▸ **adjective** having or showing an ability to accurately assess situations or people and turn this to one's advantage: *an astute businessman.*
– DERIVATIVES **astutely** adverb, **astuteness** noun.
– ORIGIN early 17th cent.: from obsolete French *astut* or Latin *astutus*, from *astus* 'craft'.

astylar /əˈstʌɪlə/ ▸ **adjective** Architecture (of a classical building) lacking columns or pilasters.
– ORIGIN mid 19th cent.: from A-[1] 'without' + Greek *stulos* 'column' + -AR[1].

Asunción /əˌsʊnsɪˈɒn/, Spanish /asunˈsjəɔn, -ˈθjəɔn/ the capital and chief port of Paraguay; pop. 519,100 (est. 2007).

asunder ▸ **adverb** archaic or literary apart: *those whom God hath joined together let no man put asunder.*
– ORIGIN Old English *on sundran* 'in or into a separate place'; compare with SUNDER.

Asur /ˈaʃʊə/ variant spelling of ASSUR.

asura /ˈʌsʊrə/ ▸ **noun** a member of a class of divine beings in the Vedic period, which in Indian mythology tend to be evil and in Zoroastrianism are benevolent. Compare with DEVA.

ASV ▸ **abbreviation** American Standard Version (of the Bible).

Aswan /asˈwɑːn/ a city on the Nile in southern Egypt, 16 km (10 miles) north of Lake Nasser; pop. 266,000 (est. 2006). Two dams across the Nile have been built nearby. The controlled release of water from Lake Nasser behind the High Dam produces the greater part of Egypt's electricity.

aswarm ▸ **adjective** [predic.] crowded or full: *the streets **were aswarm with** vendors.*

aswim ▸ **adjective** [predic.] swimming: *sardines aswim in oil.*

aswirl ▸ **adjective & adverb** covered or surrounded with something swirling; swirling: [as adv.] *she shook her head, sending the streamers aswirl.*

asylee /əsʌɪˈliː/ ▸ **noun** a person who is seeking or has been granted political asylum.

asylum ▸ **noun 1** [mass noun] (also **political asylum**) the protection granted by a state to someone who has left their native country as a political refugee: *people seeking asylum in Britain* | [as modifier] *an asylum seeker.* ■ shelter or protection from danger.
2 dated an institution for the care of people who are mentally ill.
– ORIGIN late Middle English (in the sense 'place of refuge', especially for criminals): via Latin from Greek *asulon* 'refuge', from *asulos* 'inviolable', from *a-* 'without' + *sulon* 'right of seizure'. Current senses date from the 18th cent.

asymmetrical ▸ **adjective** having parts which fail to correspond to one another in shape, size, or arrangement; lacking symmetry: *the church has an asymmetrical plan with an aisle only on one side.* ■ having parts or aspects which are not equal or equivalent: *the asymmetrical relationship between a landlord and a tenant.*
– DERIVATIVES **asymmetric** adjective, **asymmetrically** adverb.

asymmetrical warfare ▸ **noun** [mass noun] warfare involving surprise attacks by small, simply armed groups on a nation armed with modern high-tech weaponry.

asymmetric bars ▸ **plural noun** a pair of bars of different heights used in women's gymnastics.

asymmetry /eɪˈsɪmɪtri/ ▸ **noun** (pl. **asymmetries**) [mass noun] lack of equality or equivalence between parts or aspects of something; lack of symmetry.
– ORIGIN mid 17th cent.: from Greek *asummetria*, from *a-* 'without' + *summetria* (see SYMMETRY).

asymptomatic ▸ **adjective** Medicine (of a condition or a person) producing or showing no symptoms.

asymptote /ˈasɪm(p)təʊt/ ▸ **noun** a straight line that continually approaches a given curve but does not meet it at any finite distance.
– DERIVATIVES **asymptotic** /ˌasɪm(p)ˈtɒtɪk/ adjective, **asymptotically** adverb.
– ORIGIN mid 17th cent.: from modern Latin *asymptota (linea)* '(line) not meeting', from Greek *asumptōtos* 'not falling together', from *a-* 'not' + *sun* 'together' + *ptōtos* 'apt to fall' (from *piptein* 'to fall').

asynchronous ▸ **adjective 1** not existing or occurring at the same time.
2 Computing & Telecommunications controlling the timing of operations by the use of pulses sent when the previous operation is completed rather than at regular intervals.
3 (of a machine or motor) not working in time with the alternations of current.
4 Astronomy (of a satellite) revolving round the parent planet at a different rate from that at which the planet rotates.
– DERIVATIVES **asynchronously** adverb, **asynchrony** noun.

asyndeton /əˈsɪndɪt(ə)n/ ▸ **noun** (pl. **asyndeta** /-tə/) [mass noun] the omission or absence of a conjunction between parts of a sentence, as in *I came, I saw, I conquered.*
– DERIVATIVES **asyndetic** /asɪnˈdɛtɪk/ adjective.
– ORIGIN mid 16th cent.: modern Latin, from Greek *asundeton*, neuter of *asundetos* 'unconnected', from *a-* 'not' + *sundetos* 'bound together'.

asystole /eɪˈsɪstəli/ ▸ **noun** [mass noun] Medicine a condition in which the heart ceases to beat.
– DERIVATIVES **asystolic** /eɪsɪsˈtɒlɪk/ adjective.

At ▸ **symbol** the chemical element astatine.

at¹ ▸ **preposition 1** expressing location or arrival in a particular place or position: *they live at Conway House | they stopped at a small trattoria.* ■ used in speech to indicate the sign @ in email addresses, separating the address holder's name from their location.
2 expressing the time when an event takes place: *the children go to bed at nine o'clock | his death came at a time when the movement was split.* ■ (followed by a noun without a determiner) denoting a particular period of time: *the sea is cooler at night.* ■ (followed by a noun without a determiner) denoting the time spent by someone attending an educational institution or workplace: *it was at university that he first began to perform.*
3 denoting a particular point or level on a scale: *prices start at £18,500 | driving at 50 mph.* ■ referring to someone's age: *at fourteen he began to work as a postman.*
4 expressing a particular state or condition: *his ready smile put her at ease | they were at a disadvantage.* ■ expressing a relationship between an individual and a skill: *boxing was the only sport I was any good at | she was getting much better at hiding her reactions.*
5 expressing the object of a look, thought, action, or plan: *I looked at my watch | Leslie pointed at him | policies aimed at reducing taxation.* ■ expressing an incomplete or attempted action, typically involving repeated movements: *she clutched at the thin gown | he hit at her face with the gun.*
6 expressing the means by which something is done: *holding a prison officer at knifepoint* | figurative *her pride had taken a beating at his hands.*
– PHRASES **at all** see ALL. **at first** see FIRST. **at it** engaged in some activity, typically a reprehensible one: *the council is at it again, wanting to turn another green patch into a carpark.* **at last** see LAST¹. **at least** see LEAST. **at most** see MOST. **at once** see ONCE. **at that** in addition; furthermore: *it was not fog but smoke, and very thick at that.* **where it's at** informal the focus of fashion or style: *building your own palace is where it's at.* **where someone is at** informal someone's true or fundamental nature or character: *I think we've got enough information to have an idea of where he's at.*
– ORIGIN Old English *æt*, of Germanic origin; related to Old Frisian *et* and Old Norse *at*, from an Indo-European root shared by Latin *ad* 'to'.

at² /ɑːt, at/ ▸ **noun** a monetary unit of Laos, equal to one hundredth of a kip.
– ORIGIN Thai.

at- ▸ **prefix** variant spelling of AD- assimilated before *t* (as in *attend, attenuate*).

Atabrine /ˈatɪbriːn/ ▸ **noun** variant spelling of ATEBRIN.

Atacama Desert /ˌatəˈkɑːmə/ an arid region of western Chile, extending roughly 965 km (600 miles) southwards from the Peruvian border.

atactic /əˈtaktɪk/ ▸ **adjective** Chemistry (of a polymer or polymer structure) in which the repeating units have no regular stereochemical configuration.
– ORIGIN mid 19th cent.: from Greek *ataktos*, from *a-* 'not' + *taktos* 'arranged' + -IC.

Atalanta /ˌatəˈlantə/ Greek Mythology a huntress who would marry only someone who could beat her in a foot race. She was beaten when a suitor threw down three golden apples which she stopped to pick up.

ataman /ˈatəman/ ▸ **noun** (pl. **atamans**) a Cossack leader.
– ORIGIN mid 19th cent.: from Russian.

atap ▸ **noun** variant spelling of ATTAP.

ataraxy /ˈatəraksi/ (also **ataraxia** /ˌatəˈraksɪə/) ▸ **noun** [mass noun] literary a state of serene calmness.
– DERIVATIVES **ataraxic** adjective.
– ORIGIN early 17th cent.: from French *ataraxie*, from Greek *ataraxia* 'impassiveness', from *a-* 'not' + *tarassein* 'disturb'.

Atatürk /ˈatətəːk/, Kemal (1881–1938), Turkish general and statesman, President 1923–38; also called **Kemal Pasha**. He was elected the first President of the Turkish republic, taking the name of Atatürk ('father of the Turks') in 1934. He abolished the caliphate and introduced other policies designed to make Turkey a modern secular state.

atavistic /ˌatəˈvɪstɪk/ ▸ **adjective** relating to or characterized by reversion to something ancient or ancestral: *atavistic fears and instincts.*
– DERIVATIVES **atavism** noun, **atavistically** adverb.
– ORIGIN late 19th cent.: based on Latin *atavus* 'forefather' + the adjectival suffix *-istic*.

ataxia /əˈtaksɪə/ (also **ataxy** /-si/) ▸ **noun** [mass noun] Medicine the loss of full control of bodily movements.
– DERIVATIVES **ataxic** adjective.
– ORIGIN late 19th cent.: modern Latin, from Greek, from *a-* 'without' + *taxis* 'order'. The original sense was 'irregularity, disorder', later (in medical use) denoting irregularity of function or symptoms.

ATB ▸ **abbreviation** all-terrain bike.

at-bat Baseball ▸ **noun** a player's turn at batting, as officially recorded: *he had three singles in four at-bats.*
▸ **adverb** (**at bat**) batting.

ATC ▸ **abbreviation** ■ air traffic control or air traffic controller. ■ (in Britain) Air Training Corps.

ATE ▸ **abbreviation** automated test equipment.

ate past of EAT.

-ate¹ ▸ **suffix** forming nouns: **1** denoting status or office: *doctorate | episcopate.* ■ denoting a state or function: *curate | mandate.*
2 denoting a group: *electorate.*
3 Chemistry denoting a salt or ester, especially of an acid with a corresponding name ending in *-ic*: *chlorate | nitrate.*
4 denoting a product of a chemical process: *condensate | filtrate.*
– ORIGIN from Old French *-at* or Latin *-atus, -ata, -atum.*

-ate² ▸ **suffix 1** forming adjectives and nouns such as *associate, duplicate, separate.*
2 forming adjectives from Latin: *caudate.*
– ORIGIN from Latin *-atus, -ata, -atum.*

-ate³ ▸ **suffix** forming verbs such as *fascinate, hyphenate.*
– ORIGIN from **-ATE²**; originally forms were based on existing past participial adjectives ending in *-atus*, but were later extended to any Latin verb ending in *-are* and to French verbs ending in *-er*.

A-team ▸ **noun** a group of elite soldiers or the top advisers or other staff in an organization.
– ORIGIN 1970s: from sports terminology in which an organization's A-team is its best team.

Atebrin /ˈatɪbrɪn/ (US **Atabrine**) ▸ **noun** trademark for QUINACRINE.
– ORIGIN 1930s: of unknown origin.

atelectasis /ˌatɪˈlɛktəsɪs/ ▸ **noun** [mass noun] Medicine partial collapse or incomplete inflation of the lung.
– ORIGIN mid 19th cent.: from Greek *atelēs* 'imperfect' + *ektasis* 'extension'.

atelier /əˈtɛlɪeɪ/ ▸ **noun** a workshop or studio, especially one used by an artist or designer.
– ORIGIN late 17th cent.: from French, from Old French *astelle* 'splinter of wood', from Latin *astula*.

a tempo /ɑː ˈtɛmpəʊ/ ▸ **adverb & adjective** Music (especially as a direction) in the previous tempo.
– ORIGIN Italian, literally 'in time'.

atemporal /eɪˈtɛmp(ə)r(ə)l/ ▸ **adjective** existing or considered without relation to time.
– DERIVATIVES **atemporality** noun.

Aten /ˈɑːt(ə)n/ (also **Aton**) Egyptian Mythology the sun or solar disc, the deity of a strong monotheistic cult, particularly during the reign of Akhenaten.

atenolol /əˈtɛnəlɒl/ ▸ **noun** [mass noun] Medicine a beta blocker used mainly to treat angina and high blood pressure.
– ORIGIN 1970s: perhaps from *a(ngina)* + *ten(sion)* + *(propran)olol*, a related compound.

ATF ▸ **abbreviation** (in the US) (Federal Bureau of) Alcohol, Tobacco, and Firearms.

Athabaskan /ˌaθəˈbask(ə)n/ (also **Athapaskan**) ▸ **adjective** denoting or relating to a family of North American Indian languages, including a southern group of which the most important are Navajo and Apache, and a northern group in Alaska and the Canadian North-West, many of which are now rare or extinct.
▸ **noun 1** [mass noun] the Athabaskan family of languages, sometimes classified in the Na-Dene phylum.
2 a speaker of any of the Athabaskan languages.
– ORIGIN from *Athabasca*, the name of a lake in western Canada, from Cree *Athap-askaw* 'grass and reeds here and there', + -AN.

athame /əˈθeɪmi, əˈθɑːmeɪ/ ▸ **noun** a black-handled, double-edged ritual knife used in modern witchcraft.
– ORIGIN 1930s: of unknown origin.

Athanasian Creed /ˌaθəˈneɪʃ(ə)n/ a summary of Christian doctrine formerly attributed to St Athanasius, but probably dating from the 5th century.

Athanasius, St /ˌaθəˈneɪʃəs/ (*c.*296–373), Greek theologian and upholder of Christian orthodoxy against Arianism. Feast day, 2 May.

athanor /ˈaθənɔː/ ▸ **noun** historical a type of furnace used by alchemists, able to maintain a steady heat for long periods.
– ORIGIN late 15th cent.: from Arabic *at-tannūr*, from *al-* 'the' + *tannūr* 'baker's oven'.

Atharva Veda /əˌtəːvə ˈveɪdə, ˈviːdə/ Hinduism a collection of hymns and ritual utterances in early Sanskrit, added at a later stage to the existing Veda material.
– ORIGIN from Sanskrit *Atharvan* (the name of Brahma's eldest son, said to be the author of the collection) + *veda* '(sacred) knowledge'.

atheism /ˈeɪθɪɪz(ə)m/ ▸ **noun** [mass noun] disbelief in the existence of God or gods.
– ORIGIN late 16th cent.: from French *athéisme*, from Greek *atheos*, from *a-* 'without' + *theos* 'god'.

atheist ▸ **noun** a person who does not believe in the existence of God or gods: *he is a committed atheist.*
– DERIVATIVES **atheistic** adjective, **atheistical** adjective.

atheling /ˈaθ(ə)lɪŋ/ ▸ **noun** historical a prince or lord in Anglo-Saxon England.
– ORIGIN Old English *ætheling*, of West Germanic origin, from a base meaning 'race, family'.

Athelstan /ˈaθəlstən/ (895–939), king of England 925–39. Athelstan came to the thrones of Wessex and Mercia in 924 before effectively becoming the first king of all England.

athematic /ˌaθɪˈmatɪk, eɪ-/ ▸ **adjective 1** Music (of a composition) not based on the use of themes.
2 Grammar (of a verb form) having a suffix attached to the stem without a connecting (thematic) vowel.

Athenaeum /ˌaθɪˈniːəm/ (US also **Atheneum**) ▸ **noun** used in the names of libraries or institutions for literary or scientific study: *the Boston Athenaeum.* ■ used in the titles of periodicals concerned with literature, science, and art. ■ (**the Athenaeum**) a London club founded in 1824, originally for men of distinction in literature, art, and learning.
– ORIGIN mid 18th cent.: via Latin from Greek *Athēnaion*, denoting the temple of the goddess Athene in ancient Athens (which was used for teaching).

Athene /əˈθiːni/ (also **Athena**) Greek Mythology the patron goddess of Athens, typically allegorized into a personification of wisdom. Also called PALLAS. Roman equivalent MINERVA.

Athenian empire see DELIAN LEAGUE.

Athens /ˈaθɪnz/ the capital of Greece; pop. 745,500 (est. 2009). Greek name ATHÍNAI.

> A flourishing city-state of ancient Greece, Athens was an important cultural centre in the 5th century BC. It came under Roman rule in 146 BC and fell to the Goths in AD 267. After its capture by the Turks in 1456 Athens declined to the status of a village, until chosen as the capital of a newly independent Greece in 1834.

– DERIVATIVES **Athenian** adjective & noun.

atherogenic /ˌaθərə(ʊ)ˈdʒɛnɪk/ ▸ **adjective** Physiology tending to promote the formation of fatty deposits in the arteries.
– DERIVATIVES **atherogenesis** noun.
– ORIGIN 1950s: from ATHEROMA + -GENIC.

atheroma /ˌaθəˈrəʊmə/ ▸ **noun** [mass noun] Medicine degeneration of the walls of the arteries caused by accumulated fatty deposits and scar tissue, and leading to restriction of the circulation and a risk of thrombosis. See also ATHEROSCLEROSIS. ■ the fatty material which forms deposits in the arteries.
– DERIVATIVES **atheromatous** adjective.
– ORIGIN late 16th cent.: via Latin from Greek *athērōma*, from *athērē, atharē* 'groats'.

atherosclerosis /ˌaθərəʊsklɪəˈrəʊsɪs, -sklə-/ ▸ **noun** [mass noun] Medicine a disease of the arteries characterized by the deposition of fatty material on their inner walls. See also ATHEROMA.
– DERIVATIVES **atherosclerotic** adjective.
– ORIGIN early 20th cent.: coined in German from Greek *athērē* 'groats' + *sklērōsis* 'hardening' (see SCLEROSIS).

athetosis /ˌaθɪˈtəʊsɪs/ ▸ **noun** [mass noun] Medicine a condition in which abnormal muscle contraction causes involuntary writhing movements. It affects some people with cerebral palsy, impairing speech and use of the hands.
– DERIVATIVES **athetoid** adjective, **athetotic** adjective.
– ORIGIN late 19th cent.: from Greek *athetos* 'without position' + -OSIS.

A

Athínai /aˈθiːne/ Greek name for **Athens**.

athirst ▸ adjective [predic.] archaic thirsty. ■ very eager to get something: *she was athirst for news.*
– ORIGIN Old English *ofthyrst*, shortened from *ofthyrsted*, past participle of *ofthyrstan* 'be thirsty'.

athlete ▸ noun a person who is proficient in sports and other forms of physical exercise. ■ Brit. a person who takes part in competitive track and field events (athletics).
– ORIGIN late Middle English: from Latin *athleta*, from Greek *athlētēs*, from *athlein* 'compete for a prize', from *athlon* 'prize'.

athlete's foot ▸ noun [mass noun] a fungal infection affecting mainly the skin between the toes. It is a form of ringworm.

athletic ▸ adjective **1** physically strong, fit, and active: *big, muscular, athletic boys.*
2 [attrib.] Brit. relating to athletes or athletics: *athletic events | an athletic club.*
– DERIVATIVES **athletically** adverb, **athleticism** noun.
– ORIGIN mid 17th cent.: from French *athlétique* or Latin *athleticus*, from Greek *athlētikos*, from *athlētēs* (see **athlete**).

athletics ▸ plural noun [usu. treated as sing.] Brit. the sport of competing in track and field events, including running races and various competitions in jumping and throwing. ■ N. Amer. physical sports and games of any kind.

athletic support (also **athletic supporter**) ▸ noun another term for **jockstrap**.

at-home ▸ noun a party in a person's home. ■ dated a period when a person has announced that they will receive visitors in their home.

-athon ▸ suffix forming nouns denoting an action or activity which is carried on for a very long time or on a very large scale, typically to raise funds for charity: *talkathon | walkathon.*
– ORIGIN on the pattern of *(mar)athon.*

Athos, Mount /ˈaθɒs, ˈeɪθ-/ a narrow, mountainous peninsula in NE Greece, projecting into the Aegean Sea. It is inhabited by monks of the Orthodox Church, who forbid women and even female animals to set foot on the peninsula.
– DERIVATIVES **Athonite** /ˈaθəˌnʌɪt/ adjective & noun.

athwart /əˈθwɔːt/ ▸ preposition **1** from side to side of; across: *a counter was placed athwart the entrance.*
2 in opposition to; counter to: *these statistics* **run** *sharply* **athwart** *conventional presumptions.*
▸ adverb **1** across from side to side; transversely: *one table running athwart was all the room would hold.*
2 so as to be perverse or contradictory: *our words* **ran athwart** *and we ended up at cross purposes.*
– ORIGIN late Middle English: from **a-²** 'on' + **thwart**.

-atic ▸ suffix forming adjectives and nouns such as *aquatic, idiomatic.*
– ORIGIN from French *-atique* or Latin *-aticus*, sometimes based on Greek *-atikos*.

atilt ▸ adverb tilted and nearly falling.
– ORIGIN mid 16th cent.: from **a-²** + **tilt**.

-ation ▸ suffix (forming nouns) denoting an action or an instance of it: *exploration | hesitation.* ■ denoting a result or product of action: *plantation.*
– ORIGIN from French *-ation* or Latin *-ation-*.

Ativan /ˈatɪvan/ ▸ noun trademark for **lorazepam**.

-ative ▸ suffix (forming adjectives) denoting a characteristic or propensity: *pejorative | talkative.*
– ORIGIN from French *-atif, -ative* or Latin *-ativus* (from past participial stems ending in *-at*).

Atkins diet ▸ noun (trademark in the US) a high-protein, high-fat diet in which carbohydrates are severely restricted.
– ORIGIN 1970s: named after the American cardiologist Robert C. Atkins (1930–2003).

Atkinson, Sir Harry (Albert) (1831–92), British-born New Zealand statesman, Prime Minister 1876–7, 1883–4, and 1887–91.

Atlanta the state capital of Georgia in the US; pop. 537,958 (est. 2008).
– DERIVATIVES **Atlantan** noun & adjective.

atlantes plural form of **atlas** (sense 3).

Atlantic ▸ adjective **1** of or adjoining the Atlantic Ocean: *the Atlantic coast of Europe.*
2 Geology relating to or denoting the third climatic stage of the postglacial period in northern Europe, between the Boreal and Sub-Boreal stages (about 7,500 to 5,000 years ago), marked by a moist oceanic climate.
▸ noun **(the Atlantic) 1** short for **Atlantic Ocean**.
2 Geology the Atlantic climatic stage.
– ORIGIN late Middle English: via Latin from Greek *Atlantikos*, from *Atlas, Atlant-* (see **atlas**). The term originally referred to Mount Atlas in Libya, hence to the sea near the west African coast, later extended to the whole ocean.

Atlantic, Battle of the a succession of sea operations during the Second World War in which Axis naval and air forces attempted to destroy ships carrying supplies from North America to the UK.

Atlantic Charter a declaration of eight common principles in international relations drawn up by Churchill and Roosevelt in August 1941, which provided the ideological basis for the United Nations organization.

Atlanticism /ətˈlantɪˌsɪz(ə)m/ ▸ noun [mass noun] belief in or support for a close relationship between western Europe and the US, or particularly for NATO.
– DERIVATIVES **Atlanticist** noun & adjective.

Atlantic Ocean the ocean lying between Europe and Africa to the east and North and South America to the west. It is divided by the equator into the North Atlantic and the South Atlantic oceans.

Atlantic Provinces the Canadian provinces of Newfoundland, Labrador, and the Maritime Provinces.

Atlantic seal ▸ noun another term for **grey seal**.

Atlantic time the standard time in a zone including the easternmost parts of mainland Canada, Puerto Rico, and the Virgin Islands, specifically: ● **(Atlantic Standard Time** abbrev.: **AST)** standard time based on the mean solar time at longitude 60° W, four hours behind GMT. ● **(Atlantic Daylight Time** abbrev.: **ADT)** Atlantic time during daylight saving, three hours behind GMT.

Atlantis a legendary island, beautiful and prosperous, which was overwhelmed by the sea.
– DERIVATIVES **Atlantean** adjective & noun.

Atlas Greek Mythology one of the Titans, who was punished for his part in their revolt against Zeus by being made to support the heavens. He became identified with the Atlas Mountains.
– DERIVATIVES **Atlantean** adjective.

atlas ▸ noun **1** a book of maps or charts: *I looked in the atlas to see where Naples was | a road atlas.*
2 (also **atlas vertebra**) Anatomy the topmost vertebra of the backbone, articulating with the occipital bone of the skull.
3 (pl. **atlantes** /atˈlantiːz/) Architecture a stone carving of a male figure, used as a column to support the entablature of a Greek or Greek-style building.
– ORIGIN late 16th cent. (originally denoting a person who supported a great burden): via Latin from Greek **Atlas**, the Titan of Greek mythology who supported the heavens and whose picture appeared at the front of early atlases.

atlas moth ▸ noun a very large boldly marked silk moth which occurs in both the Old and New World tropics. ● Genus *Attacus*, family Saturniidae: several species, in particular *A. atlas* of Asia, which is the largest moth in the world.

Atlas Mountains a range of mountains in North Africa extending from Morocco to Tunisia in a series of chains.

ATM ▸ abbreviation ■ Telecommunications asynchronous transfer mode. ■ automated teller machine.

atman /ˈɑːtmən/ ▸ noun [mass noun] Hinduism the spiritual life principle of the universe, especially when regarded as immanent in the individual's real self. ■ [count noun] a person's soul.
– ORIGIN from Sanskrit *ātman*, literally 'essence, breath'.

atmosphere ▸ noun [usu. in sing.] **1** the envelope of gases surrounding the earth or another planet: *part of the sun's energy is absorbed by the earth's atmosphere.* ■ the air in any particular place: *these beetles breed best in a damp atmosphere.* ■ (abbrev.: **atm**) Physics a unit of pressure equal to mean atmospheric pressure at sea level, 101,325 pascals.
2 the pervading tone or mood of a place, situation, or creative work: *the hotel has won commendations for its friendly, welcoming atmosphere.* ■ [mass noun] a pleasurable and interesting mood: *a superb restaurant, full of atmosphere.*
– ORIGIN mid 17th cent.: from modern Latin *atmosphaera*, from Greek *atmos* 'vapour' + *sphaira* 'ball, globe'.

atmospheric ▸ adjective **1** relating to the atmosphere of the earth: *atmospheric pollution.*
2 creating a distinctive mood, typically of romance or nostalgia: *atmospheric lighting.*
– DERIVATIVES **atmospherical** adjective (archaic), **atmospherically** adverb.

atmospheric pressure ▸ noun [mass noun] the pressure exerted by the weight of the atmosphere, which at sea level has a mean value of 101,325 pascals (roughly 14.6959 pounds per square inch).

atmospherics ▸ plural noun **1** electrical disturbances in the atmosphere due to lightning and other phenomena, especially as they interfere with telecommunications.
2 effects intended to create a particular atmosphere or mood, especially in music: *a smoky jazz sound with spooky atmospherics.*

ATOL /ˈatɒl/ ▸ abbreviation (in the UK) Air Travel Organizer's Licence.

atoll /ˈatɒl, əˈtɒl/ ▸ noun a ring-shaped reef, island, or chain of islands formed of coral.
– ORIGIN early 17th cent.: from Maldivian *atolu*.

atom ▸ noun **1** the smallest particle of a chemical element that can exist. ■ (usu. **the atom**) atomic particles as a source of nuclear energy: *the power of the atom.* ■ [usu. with negative] an extremely small amount of something: *I shall not have one atom of strength left.*

> Atoms consist of a tiny, dense, positively charged nucleus made of neutrons and protons, surrounded by a cloud of negatively charged electrons, roughly 10^{-8} cm in diameter. Each chemical element consists of atoms with a characteristic number of protons. Atoms are held together in molecules by the sharing of electrons.

2 [usu. as modifier] Canadian a level of amateur sport, typically involving children aged between nine and eleven: *eight atom hockey teams.*
– ORIGIN late 15th cent.: from Old French *atome*, via Latin from Greek *atomos* 'indivisible', based on *a-* 'not' + *temnein* 'to cut'.

atom bomb (also **atomic bomb**) ▸ noun a bomb which derives its destructive power from the rapid release of nuclear energy by fission of heavy atomic nuclei, causing damage through heat, blast, and radioactivity.

> Such a bomb contains a critical mass of a material such as uranium-235 or plutonium-239, which when detonated by a conventional explosive charge is capable of maintaining a nuclear chain reaction, releasing large amounts of energy almost instantaneously.

atomic ▸ adjective relating to an atom or atoms. ■ Chemistry (of a substance) consisting of uncombined atoms rather than molecules. ■ of or forming a single irreducible unit or component in a larger system: *a society made up of atomic individuals pursuing private interests.* ■ relating to or using the energy released in nuclear fission or fusion: *the atomic age required a new way of political thinking | atomic weapons.*
– DERIVATIVES **atomically** adverb.
– ORIGIN late 17th cent.: from modern Latin *atomicus*, from *atomus* 'indivisible' (see **atom**).

atomic clock ▸ noun an extremely accurate type of clock which is regulated by the vibrations of an atomic or molecular system such as caesium or ammonia.

atomic energy ▸ noun another term for **nuclear energy**.

atomicity ▸ noun **1** Chemistry the number of atoms in the molecules of an element.
2 [mass noun] the state or fact of being composed of indivisible units.

atomic mass ▸ noun the mass of an atom of a chemical element expressed in atomic mass units. It is approximately equivalent to the number of protons and neutrons in the atom (the mass number) or to the average number allowing for the relative abundances of different isotopes.

atomic mass unit (abbrev.: **amu**) ▸ noun a unit of mass used to express atomic and molecular weights, equal to one twelfth of the mass of an atom of carbon-12.

atomic number ▸ noun Chemistry the number of protons in the nucleus of an atom, which is characteristic of a chemical element and determines its place in the periodic table. (Symbol: **Z**)

atomic physics ▸ plural noun [treated as sing.] the branch of physics concerned with the structure of the atom and the characteristics of subatomic particles.

atomic pile ▸ noun see **pile¹** (sense 4 of the noun).

atomic power ▸ **noun** another term for **NUCLEAR POWER**.

atomic spectrum ▸ **noun** the spectrum of frequencies of electromagnetic radiation emitted or absorbed during transitions of electrons between energy levels within an atom. Each element has a characteristic spectrum by which it can be recognized.

atomic theory ▸ **noun** [mass noun] the theory that all matter is made up of tiny indivisible particles (atoms). According to modern interpretations of the theory, the atoms of each element are effectively identical, but differ from those of other elements, and unite to form compounds in fixed proportions.

atomic volume ▸ **noun** Chemistry the volume occupied by one gram-atom of an element under standard conditions.

atomic weight ▸ **noun** Chemistry another term for **RELATIVE ATOMIC MASS**.

atomism ▸ **noun** [mass noun] chiefly Philosophy a theoretical approach that regards something as interpretable through analysis into distinct, separable, and independent elementary components. The opposite of **HOLISM**.
– DERIVATIVES **atomist** noun, **atomistic** adjective.

atomize (also **atomise**) ▸ **verb** [with obj.] convert (a substance) into very fine particles or droplets. ■ reduce to atoms. ■ break up into small units: *by disrupting our ties with our neighbours, crime atomizes society*.
– DERIVATIVES **atomization** noun.

atomizer (also **atomiser**) ▸ **noun** a device for emitting water, perfume, or other liquids as a fine spray.

atom smasher ▸ **noun** informal term for **PARTICLE ACCELERATOR**.

atomy /ˈatəmi/ ▸ **noun** (pl. **atomies**) archaic a skeleton or emaciated body.
– ORIGIN late 16th cent.: from **ANATOMY**, taken as *an atomy*.

Aton variant spelling of **ATEN**.

atonal /eɪˈtəʊn(ə)l, ə-/ ▸ **adjective** Music not written in any key or mode.
– DERIVATIVES **atonalism** noun, **atonalist** noun, **atonality** noun.

atone ▸ **verb** [no obj.] make amends or reparation: *a human sacrifice to* ***atone for*** *the sin*.
– ORIGIN Middle English (originally in the sense 'make or become united or reconciled', rare before the 16th cent.): from *at one* in early use; later by back-formation from **ATONEMENT**.

atonement ▸ **noun** [mass noun] the action of making amends for a wrong or injury: *he submitted his resignation as an act of atonement*. ■ (in religious contexts) reparation or expiation for sin: *an annual ceremony of confession and* ***atonement for*** *sin*. ■ (**the Atonement**) Christian Theology the reconciliation of God and mankind through Jesus Christ.
– ORIGIN early 16th cent. (denoting unity or reconciliation, especially between God and man): from *at one* + **-MENT**, influenced by medieval Latin *adunamentum* 'unity', and earlier *onement* from an obsolete verb *one* 'to unite'.

atonic /əˈtɒnɪk/ ▸ **adjective 1** Linguistics (of a syllable) without accent or stress.
2 Physiology lacking muscular tone.
– DERIVATIVES **atony** /ˈatəni/ noun.

atop literary ▸ **preposition** on the top of: *the weathervane is perched atop the Great Tower*.
▸ **adverb** on the top: *the air-raid siren* ***atop of*** *the County Courthouse*.

atopic /eɪˈtɒpɪk/ ▸ **adjective** denoting a form of allergy in which a hypersensitivity reaction such as eczema or asthma may occur in a part of the body not in contact with the allergen.
– DERIVATIVES **atopy** noun.
– ORIGIN early 20th cent.: from Greek *atopia* 'unusualness', from *atopos* 'unusual', from *a-* 'without' + *topos* 'place'.

-ator ▸ **suffix** forming agent nouns such as *agitator*. ■ used in names of implements, machines, etc.: *escalator*.
– ORIGIN from Latin, or sometimes representing French *-ateur*.

-atory ▸ **suffix** (forming adjectives) relating to or involving an action: *explanatory* | *predatory*.
– ORIGIN from Latin *-atorius*.

A to Z (also **A–Z**) ▸ **noun** an alphabetically arranged handbook; a complete guide to a subject: *an A to Z of tools* | [as modifier] *an A–Z guide*. ■ a book containing lists and maps of city streets: *having consulted the A–Z of Greater London, I knew how to get there*.

ATP ▸ **abbreviation** ■ Biochemistry adenosine triphosphate. ■ Brit. automatic train protection, a system for automatically stopping a train if its driver does not observe signal warnings or speed restrictions.

atrabilious /ˌatrəˈbɪlɪəs/ ▸ **adjective** literary melancholy or irritable: *an atrabilious old man*.
– ORIGIN mid 17th cent. (in the sense 'affected by black bile', one of the four supposed cardinal humours of the body, believed to cause melancholy): from Latin *atra bilis* 'black bile', translation of Greek *melankholia* 'melancholy', + **-IOUS**.

atraumatic ▸ **adjective** (of a medical or surgical procedure) causing minimal tissue injury.

atrazine /ˈatrəziːn/ ▸ **noun** [mass noun] a synthetic compound derived from triazine, used as an agricultural herbicide.
– ORIGIN 1960s: blend of **AMINO** and **TRIAZINE**.

atremble ▸ **adjective** [predic.] literary trembling.

atresia /əˈtriːʃə, -zɪə/ ▸ **noun** [mass noun] **1** Medicine absence or abnormal narrowing of an opening or passage in the body.
2 Physiology the degeneration of those ovarian follicles which do not ovulate during the menstrual cycle.
– ORIGIN early 19th cent.: from **A-**[1] 'without' + Greek *trēsis* 'perforation' + **-IA**[1].

Atreus /ˈeɪtrɪəs/ Greek Mythology the son of Pelops and father of Agamemnon and Menelaus. He quarrelled with his brother Thyestes and invited him to a banquet at which he served up the flesh of Thyestes' own children.

atrioventricular /ˌeɪtrɪə(ʊ)vɛnˈtrɪkjʊlə/ ▸ **adjective** Anatomy & Physiology relating to the atrial and ventricular chambers of the heart, or the connection or coordination between them.

atrium /ˈeɪtrɪəm/ ▸ **noun** (pl. **atria** /ˈeɪtrɪə/ or **atriums**) **1** Architecture an open-roofed entrance hall or central court in an ancient Roman house. ■ a central hall in a modern building, typically rising through several stories and having a glazed roof. ■ the forecourt of a large church built on the basilican plan.
2 Anatomy each of the two upper cavities of the heart from which blood is passed to the ventricles. The right atrium receives deoxygenated blood from the veins of the body, the left atrium oxygenated blood from the pulmonary vein. Also called **AURICLE**.
– DERIVATIVES **atrial** adjective.
– ORIGIN late 16th cent.: from Latin.

atrocious ▸ **adjective** horrifyingly wicked: *atrocious cruelties*. ■ of a very poor quality; extremely bad or unpleasant: *he attempted an atrocious imitation of my English accent* | *atrocious weather*.
– DERIVATIVES **atrociously** adverb, **atrociousness** noun.
– ORIGIN mid 17th cent.: from Latin *atrox, atroc-* 'cruel' + **-IOUS**.

atrocity ▸ **noun** (pl. **atrocities**) an extremely wicked or cruel act, typically one involving physical violence or injury: *a textbook which detailed war atrocities*. ■ humorous a highly unpleasant or distasteful object: *atrocities in cheap red nylon*.
– ORIGIN mid 16th cent. (in the sense 'cruelty'): from French *atrocité* or Latin *atrocitas*, from *atrox, atroc-* 'cruel'.

atrophy /ˈatrəfi/ ▸ **verb** (**atrophies**, **atrophying**, **atrophied**) [no obj.] **1** (of body tissue or an organ) waste away, especially as a result of the degeneration of cells, or become vestigial during evolution: *the calf muscles will atrophy* | (as adj. **atrophied**) *in some beetles, the hindwings are atrophied*.
2 gradually decline in effectiveness or vigour due to underuse or neglect: *the imagination can atrophy from lack of use*.
▸ **noun** [mass noun] the process of atrophying or state of having atrophied: *gastric atrophy* | *extensive TV viewing may lead to atrophy of children's imaginations*.
– DERIVATIVES **atrophic** adjective.
– ORIGIN late 16th cent.: from French *atrophier* (verb), *atrophie* (noun), from late Latin *atrophia*, from Greek, 'lack of food', from *a-* 'without' + *trophē* 'food'.

atropine /ˈatrəpiːn, -ɪn/ ▸ **noun** [mass noun] Chemistry a poisonous compound found in deadly nightshade and related plants. It is used in medicine as a muscle relaxant, e.g. in dilating the pupil of the eye. ● An alkaloid; chem. formula: $C_{17}N_{23}NO_3$.
– ORIGIN mid 19th cent.: modern Latin *Atropa belladonna* 'deadly nightshade', from **ATROPOS** + **-INE**[4].

Atropos /ˈatrəpɒs/ Greek Mythology one of the three Fates.
– ORIGIN Greek, literally 'inflexible'.

at sign ▸ **noun** the symbol @.

attaboy ▸ **exclamation** an informal expression of encouragement or admiration to a man or boy.
– ORIGIN early 20th cent.: probably representing a casual pronunciation of *that's the boy*.

attacca /əˈtakə/ ▸ **verb** [in imperative] a musical instruction used to indicate that the next section should follow without a pause.
– ORIGIN Italian, literally 'attack'.

attach ▸ **verb** [with obj.] **1** join or fasten (something) to something else: ***attach*** *your safety line* ***to*** *the bridge*. ■ add or fasten (a related document) to another, or to an email: *I attach a copy of the memo for your information*. ■ include (a condition) as part of an agreement: *the Commission can attach appropriate conditions to the operation of the agreement*. ■ (**attach oneself to**) accompany (a person or group) without being invited. ■ appoint (someone) for special or temporary duties: *I was* ***attached to*** *another working group*.
2 (**attach something to**) attribute importance or value to: *he doesn't attach too much importance to fixed ideas*. ■ [no obj.] (**attach to**) (of importance or value) be attributed to: *a good deal of prominence attaches to the central union federations*.
3 Law, archaic seize (a person or property) by legal authority: *the Earl Marshal attached Gloucester for high treason*.
– DERIVATIVES **attachable** adjective.
– ORIGIN Middle English (in the sense 'seize by legal authority'): from Old French *atachier* or *estachier* 'fasten, fix', based on an element of Germanic origin related to **STAKE**[1]; compare with **ATTACK**.

attaché /əˈtaʃeɪ/ ▸ **noun 1** a person on the staff of an ambassador having a specialized area of responsibility: *naval and air attachés*.
2 N. Amer. short for **ATTACHÉ CASE**.
– ORIGIN early 19th cent.: from French, literally 'attached', past participle of *attacher*.

attaché case ▸ **noun** a small, flat, rigid, rectangular case used for carrying documents.

attached ▸ **adjective 1** joined, fastened, or connected to something: *please complete the attached form* | *a ground floor bedroom with a toilet attached*.
2 full of affection or fondness: *during the journey Mark became increasingly* ***attached to*** *Tara*.
3 (**attached to**) appointed to (an organization) for special or temporary duties: *he was attached to Military Intelligence*. ■ (of an organization) affiliated to (a larger organization): *a science policy agency attached to the Council of Ministers*.

attachment ▸ **noun 1** an extra part or extension that is or may be attached to something to perform a particular function: *the processor comes complete with a blender attachment*. ■ a computer file appended to an email.
2 [mass noun] affection, fondness, or sympathy for someone or something: *she felt a sentimental* ***attachment to*** *the place creep over her*. ■ [count noun] an affectionate relationship: *he formed an attachment with a young widow*.
3 Brit. temporary secondment to an organization: *the students are placed* ***on attachment*** *to schools for one day a week*.
4 [mass noun] the action of attaching something: *the case has a loop for attachment to your waist belt*. ■ legal seizure of property.
– PHRASES **attachment of earnings** English Law payment of debts by direct deduction from the debtor's earnings, under a court order.
– ORIGIN late Middle English (in the sense 'arrest for contempt of court'): from Old French *attachement*, from *atachier* 'fasten, fix' (see **ATTACH**).

attachment parenting ▸ **noun** [mass noun] an approach to raising infants that aims to promote a close relationship between the baby and its parents by methods such as feeding on demand and letting the baby sleep with its parents.

attack ▸ **verb** [with obj.] **1** take aggressive military action against (a place or enemy forces) with weapons or armed force: *in February the Germans attacked Verdun* | [no obj.] *the terrorists did not attack again until March*. ■ act against (someone or something) aggressively in an attempt to injure or kill: *a doctor was attacked by two youths*. ■ (of a disease, chemical, or insect) act harmfully on: *HIV is thought to attack certain cells in the brain*.

A

2 criticize or oppose fiercely and publicly: *he attacked the government's defence policy.*
3 begin to deal with (a problem or task) in a determined and vigorous way: *a plan of action to attack unemployment.*
4 [no obj.] (in sport) make a forceful attempt to score a goal or point or otherwise gain an advantage against an opposing team or player: *Crystal Palace attacked swiftly down the left* | (as adj. **attacking**) *Leeds showed some good attacking play.* ■ [with obj.] Chess move into or be in a position to capture (an opponent's piece or pawn).
▶ **noun 1** an aggressive and violent act against a person or place: *he was killed in an **attack on** a checkpoint* | *three classrooms were gutted in the arson attack* | *the north-western suburbs came **under attack** in the latest fighting.* ■ [mass noun] destructive action by a disease, chemical, or insect: *the tissue is open to attack by fungus.* ■ a determined attempt to tackle a problem or task: *an **attack on** inflation.* ■ [mass noun] forceful and decisive style in performing music or another art: *the sheer attack of Hendrix's playing.*
2 an instance of fierce public criticism or opposition: *he launched a stinging **attack on** the Prime Minister.*
3 a sudden short bout of an illness or stress: *an attack of nausea* | *an asthma attack.*
4 (in sport) an aggressive attempt to score a goal or point or otherwise gain an advantage. ■ Brit. the players in a team who are in the position of trying to score a goal or win points: *Baxter was recalled to the attack.* ■ Chess a threat to capture an opponent's piece or pawn.
– ORIGIN early 17th cent.: from French *attaque* (noun), *attaquer* (verb), from Italian *attacco* 'an attack', *attaccare* 'join battle', based on an element of Germanic origin (see ATTACH).

attack dog ▶ **noun** a dog trained to attack on command and kept for this purpose. ■ a person who is very aggressive in their defence or support of someone or something: *he was accused of being an all-purpose attack dog for the government.*

attacker ▶ **noun 1** a person or animal that attacks someone or something.
2 (in sport) a player whose task is to attack the other side's goal in the attempt to score; a forward.

attagirl ▶ **exclamation** an informal expression of encouragement or admiration to a woman or girl.
– ORIGIN 1920s: on the pattern of *attaboy*.

attain ▶ **verb** [with obj.] succeed in achieving (something that one has worked for): *clarify your objectives and ways of attaining them* | *he attained the rank of Brigadier.* ■ reach (a specified age, size, or amount): *dolphins can attain speeds in water which man cannot yet emulate.*
– ORIGIN Middle English (in the senses 'bring to justice' and 'reach a state'): from Old French *ateindre*, from Latin *attingere*, from *ad-* 'at, to' + *tangere* 'to touch'.

attainable ▶ **adjective** able to be attained; achievable: *yields in excess of 6 % are easily attainable* | *an attainable target.*
– DERIVATIVES **attainability** noun.

attainder /əˈteɪndə/ ▶ **noun** historical the forfeiture of land and civil rights suffered as a consequence of a sentence of death for treason or felony.
– PHRASES **act** (or **bill**) **of attainder** an item of legislation inflicting attainder without judicial process.
– ORIGIN late Middle English: from Anglo-Norman French, variant (used as a noun) of Old French *ateindre* in the sense 'convict, bring to justice' (see ATTAIN).

attainment ▶ **noun** [mass noun] the action or fact of achieving a goal towards which one has worked: *the attainment of corporate aims.* ■ [count noun] (often **attainments**) a thing achieved, especially a skill or educational achievement: *he spoke of the low educational attainments of his workforce.*

attaint ▶ **verb** [with obj.] **1** historical subject (someone) to attainder.
2 archaic affect or infect with disease or corruption.
– ORIGIN Middle English (in the sense 'touch, reach, attain'): from obsolete *attaint* (adjective), from Old French *ataint, ateint*, past participle of *ateindre* 'bring to justice' (see ATTAIN); influenced in meaning by TAINT.

Attalid /ˈatəlɪd/ ▶ **noun** a member of a Hellenistic dynasty named after Attalus I (reigned 241–197 BC), which flourished in the 3rd and 2nd centuries BC.
▶ **adjective** relating to this dynasty.

attap /ˈatəp/ (also **atap**) ▶ **noun** [mass noun] thatch made in SE Asia from palm fronds.
– ORIGIN early 19th cent.: from Malay *atap* 'roof, thatch'.

attar /ˈatə/ (also **otto**) ▶ **noun** a fragrant essential oil, typically made from rose petals.
– ORIGIN late 17th cent.: via Persian from Arabic *ʿiṭr* 'perfume, essence'.

attempt ▶ **verb** [with obj.] make an effort to achieve or complete (something difficult): *she attempted a comeback in 2001* | [with infinitive] *troops shot civilians who attempted to flee.* ■ try to climb to the top of (a mountain): *the expedition was the first to attempt Everest.* ■ archaic try to take (a life): *he would not have attempted the life of a friend.*
▶ **noun** an effort to achieve or complete a difficult task or action: [with infinitive] *an attempt to halt the bombings.* ■ an effort to surpass a record or conquer a mountain: *an **attempt on** the unclimbed north-east ridge.* ■ a bid to kill someone: *Karakozov made an **attempt on** the Tsar's life.* ■ a thing produced as a result of trying to make or achieve something: *she picked her first **attempt at** a letter out of the wastebasket.*
– ORIGIN late Middle English: from Old French *attempter*, from Latin *attemptare*, from *ad-* 'to' + *temptare* 'to tempt'.

Attenborough[1] /ˈat(ə)nb(ə)rə/, Sir David (Frederick) (b.1926), English naturalist and broadcaster, brother of Richard Attenborough. He is known for films of animals in their natural habitats, including *Life on Earth* (1979), *The Trials of Life* (1990), and *The Life of Mammals* (2002).

Attenborough[2] /ˈat(ə)nb(ə)rə/, Richard (Samuel), Baron Attenborough of Richmond-upon-Thames (b.1923), English film actor, producer, and director; brother of David Attenborough. Notable films directed: *Oh! What a Lovely War* (1969), *Gandhi* (1982), and *Shadowlands* (1993).

attend ▶ **verb** [with obj.] **1** be present at (an event, meeting, or function): *the whole sales force attended the conference* | [no obj.] *her family were not invited to attend.* ■ go regularly to (a school, church, or clinic): *all children are required to attend school.*
2 [no obj.] (**attend to**) deal with: *he muttered that he had business to attend to.* ■ give practical help and care to; look after: *the severely wounded had two medics to attend to their wounds* | [with obj.] *each of the beds in the intensive-care unit is attended by a nurse.* ■ pay attention to: *Alice hadn't attended to a word of his sermon.*
3 escort and wait on (a member of royalty or other important person): *Her Royal Highness was attended by Mrs Jane Stevens.*
4 occur with or as a result of: *people feared that the switch to a peacetime economy would be attended by a severe slump.*
– DERIVATIVES **attender** noun.
– ORIGIN Middle English (in the sense 'apply one's mind or energies to'): from Old French *atendre*, from Latin *attendere*, from *ad-* 'to' + *tendere* 'stretch'.

attendance ▶ **noun** [mass noun] the action or state of going regularly to or being present at a place or event: *my **attendance at** church was very patchy.* ■ [count noun] the number of people present at a particular place or event: *she is being blamed for the museum's low attendances.*
– PHRASES **in attendance 1** present at a function or a place: *some 200 were in attendance at the fourteenth reunion.* **2** accompanying a member of royalty or other important person as an assistant or servant.
– ORIGIN late Middle English: from Old French, from *atendre* 'give one's attention to' (see ATTEND).

attendance allowance ▶ **noun** [mass noun] (in the UK) a state benefit paid to disabled people who need constant care at home.

attendance centre ▶ **noun** (in the UK) a place to which young offenders are ordered by a court to report regularly for a set period, as a minor penalty.

attendant ▶ **noun 1** a person employed to provide a service to the public in a particular place: *a cloakroom attendant.* ■ an assistant to an important person; a servant or courtier.
2 a person who is present on a particular occasion: *he had become a regular attendant at chapel.*
▶ **adjective 1** occurring with or as a result of: *the sea and its attendant attractions.*
2 (of a person) accompanying another as a companion or assistant: *a child in a pram with attendant nursemaid.*
– ORIGIN late Middle English (as an adjective): from Old French, from *atendre* 'give one's attention to' (see ATTEND).

attendee ▶ **noun** a person who attends a conference or other gathering.

attention ▶ **noun** [mass noun] **1** notice taken of someone or something; the regarding of someone or something as interesting or important: *he **drew attention to** three spelling mistakes.* ■ the mental faculty of considering or taking notice of someone or something: *he **turned his attention to** the educational system.*
2 the action of dealing with or taking special care of someone or something: *her business needed her attention* | *he was found guilty of failing to give a patient adequate medical attention.* ■ (**attentions**) things done to express interest in or please someone: *she felt flattered by his attentions.*
3 Military a position assumed by a soldier, standing very straight with the feet together and the arms straight down the sides of the body: *Saunders **stood** stolidly **to attention.*** ■ [as exclamation] an order to assume a straight standing position.
– PHRASES **pay attention** take notice of someone or something: *students used to know how to pay attention, even when the lecture was boring* | *if you **pay attention to** one thing, you have to ignore something else.*
– DERIVATIVES **attentional** adjective.
– ORIGIN late Middle English: from Latin *attentio(n-)*, from the verb *attendere* (see ATTEND).

attention deficit disorder (N. Amer. also **attention deficit hyperactivity disorder**) ▶ **noun** any of a range of behavioural disorders occurring primarily in children, including such symptoms as poor concentration, hyperactivity, and learning difficulties.

attention span ▶ **noun** the length of time for which a person is able to concentrate on a particular activity or subject.

attentive ▶ **adjective** paying close attention to something: *never before had she had such an attentive audience* | *ministers should be more **attentive to** the interests of taxpayers.* ■ assiduously attending to the comfort or wishes of others; very polite or courteous: *the hotel has a pleasant atmosphere and attentive service.*
– DERIVATIVES **attentively** adverb, **attentiveness** noun.
– ORIGIN late Middle English: from Old French *attentif, -ive*, from *atendre* 'give one's attention to' (see ATTEND).

attenuate ▶ **verb** /əˈtɛnjʊeɪt/ [with obj.] **1** reduce the force, effect, or value of: *her intolerance was attenuated by an unexpected liberalism.* ■ reduce the amplitude of (a signal, electric current, or other oscillation). ■ reduce the virulence of (a pathogenic organism or vaccine): *researchers hoped that the substance would attenuate the course of the disease.*
2 reduce in thickness; make thin.
▶ **adjective** /əˈtɛnjʊət/ rare reduced in force, effect, or physical thickness.
– DERIVATIVES **attenuation** noun.
– ORIGIN mid 16th cent.: from Latin *attenuat-* 'made slender', from the verb *attenuare*, from *ad-* 'to' + *tenuare* 'make thin' (from *tenuis* 'thin').

attenuated ▶ **adjective 1** (especially of a person) extremely thin: *she was a drooping, attenuated figure.*
2 (of a pathogenic organism or vaccine) reduced in virulence: *attenuated strains of rabies virus.*

attenuator ▶ **noun** a device consisting of an arrangement of resistors which reduces the strength of a radio or audio signal.

attest /əˈtɛst/ ▶ **verb 1** [with obj.] provide or serve as clear evidence of: *his status is attested by his becoming an alderman* | [no obj.] *his numerous drawings of babies **attest to** his fascination with them.* ■ [no obj.] declare that something exists or is the case: *I can **attest to** his tremendous energy* | [with clause] *the deceased's solicitor attested that he had been about to institute divorce proceedings.* ■ witness or certify formally.
2 [no obj.] historical enrol as ready for military service. ■ [with obj.] recruit (someone) for military service by putting them on oath to serve if called upon.
– DERIVATIVES **attestation** noun.
– ORIGIN early 16th cent.: from French *attester*, from Latin *attestari*, from *ad-* 'to' + *testari* 'to witness' (from *testis* 'a witness').

Attic /ˈatɪk/ ▶ **adjective** relating to ancient Athens or Attica, or the dialect of Greek spoken there.
▶ **noun** [mass noun] the dialect of Greek used by the ancient Athenians. It was the chief literary form of classical Greek.
– ORIGIN late 16th cent.: via Latin from Greek *Attikos*.

attic ▸ **noun** a space or room inside or partly inside the roof of a building.
– ORIGIN late 17th cent. (as an architectural term designating a small order (column and entablature) above a taller one): from French *attique*, from Latin *Atticus* 'relating to Athens or Attica'.

Attica /ˈatɪkə/ a triangular promontory of eastern Greece. With the islands in the Saronic Gulf it forms a department of Greece, of which Athens is the capital.

Atticism /ˈatɪsɪz(ə)m/ ▸ **noun** a word or form characteristic of Attic Greek, regarded as having particular literary elegance.
– ORIGIN late 16th cent.: from Greek *Attikismos*, from *Attikos* (see ATTIC).

Attila /əˈtɪlə/ (406–53), king of the Huns 434–53. He ravaged vast areas between the Rhine and the Caspian Sea before being defeated by the joint forces of the Roman army and the Visigoths at Châlons in 451.

Attila Line the boundary separating Greek and Turkish-occupied Cyprus, named after the Attila Plan, a secret Turkish plan of 1964 to partition the country. Also called SAHIN LINE.

attire formal or literary ▸ **noun** [mass noun] clothes, especially fine or formal ones: *the usually sober attire of British security service personnel.*
▸ **verb** (**be attired**) be dressed in clothes of a specified kind: *Lady Agatha was attired in an elaborate evening gown* | (as adj., with submodifier **attired**) *stylishly attired teenagers in stonewashed jeans.*
– ORIGIN Middle English: from Old French *atirier*, *atirer* 'equip', from *a tire* 'in order', of unknown origin.

Attis /ˈatɪs/ Anatolian Mythology the youthful consort of Cybele. His death and resurrection were associated with the spring festival.

attitude ▸ **noun 1** a settled way of thinking or feeling about something: *he was questioned on his* ***attitude to*** *South Africa* | *being competitive is* ***an attitude of mind.*** ■ a position of the body indicating a particular mental state: *the boy was standing in an* ***attitude of*** *despair.* ■ Ballet a position in which one leg is lifted behind with the knee bent at right angles and turned out, and the corresponding arm is raised above the head, the other extended to the side.
2 [mass noun] informal, chiefly N. Amer. truculent or uncooperative behaviour: *I asked the waiter for a clean fork and all I got was attitude.* ■ individuality and self-confidence: *she snapped her fingers* ***with attitude.***
3 the orientation of an aircraft or spacecraft, relative to the direction of travel.
– DERIVATIVES **attitudinal** adjective.
– ORIGIN late 17th cent. (denoting the placing or posture of a figure in art): from French, from Italian *attitudine* 'fitness, posture', from late Latin *aptitudo*, from *aptus* 'fit'.

attitudinize /ˌatɪˈtjuːdɪnʌɪz/ (also **attitudinise**) ▸ **verb** [no obj.] adopt or express a particular attitude or attitudes, typically just for effect.
– DERIVATIVES **attitudinizer** noun.
– ORIGIN late 16th cent.: from Italian *attitudine* (see ATTITUDE) + -IZE.

Attlee /ˈatli/, Clement Richard, 1st Earl Attlee (1883–1967), British Labour statesman, Prime Minister 1945–51. His term saw the creation of the modern welfare state and the nationalization of major industries.

attn ▸ **abbreviation** (on an envelope or at the top of a letter or fax) attention (i.e. for the attention of): *attn: Harold Carter.*

atto- /ˈatəʊ/ ▸ **combining form** (used in units of measurement) denoting a factor of 10^{-18}: *attowatt.*
– ORIGIN from Danish or Norwegian *atten* 'eighteen'.

attorn /əˈtəːn/ ▸ **verb** [no obj.] Law formally make or acknowledge a transfer of something. ■ [with obj.] archaic transfer (something) to someone else.
– PHRASES **attorn tenant** Law formally make or acknowledge a transfer of tenancy.
– ORIGIN Middle English (in the senses 'turn, change, transform'): from Old French *atorner* 'appoint, assign', from *a-* (from Latin *ad* 'to, at') + *torner* 'to turn'. The spelling with *o*, rather than *u* or *ou*, as might have been expected in English, is due to the late Anglo-Norman French form *attorner*, adopted in legal use.

attorney /əˈtəːni/ ▸ **noun** (pl. **attorneys**) a person, typically a lawyer, appointed to act for another in business or legal matters. Compare with BARRISTER, SOLICITOR. ■ chiefly US a qualified lawyer. ■ South African term for SOLICITOR.
– ORIGIN Middle English: from Old French *atorne*, past participle of *atorner* 'assign', from *a* 'towards' + *torner* 'to turn'.

attorney general ▸ **noun** (pl. **attorneys general**) the principal legal officer who represents the Crown or a state in legal proceedings and gives legal advice to the government. ■ (**Attorney General**) the head of the US Department of Justice.

attract ▸ **verb** [with obj.] cause to come to a place or participate in a venture by offering something of interest or advantage: *a campaign to attract more visitors to Shetland* | *he hoped this strategy would attract foreign investment by multinationals.* ■ evoke (a specified reaction): *I did not want to attract attention* | *his criticism of the government attracted widespread support.* ■ cause (someone) to have a liking for or interest in something: *I was* ***attracted to*** *the idea of working for a ballet company.* ■ (**be attracted to**) have a sexual or romantic interest in: *despite all her denials, she was still violently attracted to him.* ■ exert a force on (an object) which is directed towards the source of the force: *the negatively charged ions attract particles of dust.*
– DERIVATIVES **attractor** noun.
– ORIGIN late Middle English: from Latin *attract-* 'drawn near', from the verb *attrahere*, from *ad-* 'to' + *trahere* 'draw'.

attractant ▸ **noun** a substance which attracts: *a sex attractant given off by female moths to attract a mate.*

attraction ▸ **noun** [mass noun] the action or power of evoking interest in or liking for someone or something: *the timeless attraction of a good tune* | *she has very romantic ideas about sexual attraction.* ■ [count noun] a quality or feature that evokes interest, liking, or desire: *this reform has many* ***attractions for*** *those on the left.* ■ [count noun] a place which draws visitors by providing something of interest or pleasure: *the church is the town's main tourist attraction.* ■ Physics a force under the influence of which objects tend to move towards each other. ■ Grammar the influence exerted by one word on another which causes it to change to an incorrect form, e.g. *the wages of sin is* (for *are*) *death.*
– ORIGIN late Middle English (denoting the action of a poultice in drawing matter from the tissues): from Latin *attractio(n-)*, from the verb *attrahere* (see ATTRACT).

attractive ▸ **adjective** pleasing or appealing to the senses: *an attractive village* | *foliage can be as attractive as flowers.* ■ (of a person) appealing to look at; sexually alluring: *a stunningly attractive, charismatic man.* ■ having qualities or features which arouse interest: *the site is close to other prestige schemes which should make it* ***attractive to*** *developers.* ■ relating to attraction between physical objects.
– DERIVATIVES **attractively** adverb, **attractiveness** noun.
– ORIGIN late Middle English (in the sense 'absorbent'): from French *attractif, -ive*, from late Latin *attractivus*, from the verb *attrahere* (see ATTRACT).

attribute ▸ **verb** /əˈtrɪbjuːt/ [with obj.] (**attribute something to**) regard something as being caused by: *he attributed the firm's success to the efforts of the managing director* | *his resignation was attributed to stress.* ■ ascribe a work or remark to (a particular author, artist, or speaker): *the building was attributed to Inigo Jones.* ■ regard a quality or feature as characteristic of or possessed by: *ancient peoples attributed magic properties to certain stones.*
▸ **noun** /ˈatrɪbjuːt/ **1** a quality or feature regarded as a characteristic or inherent part of someone or something: *flexibility and mobility are the key attributes of Britain's army.* ■ a material object recognized as symbolic of a person, especially a conventional object used in art to identify a saint or mythical figure.
2 Computing a piece of information which determines the properties of a field or tag in a database or a string of characters in a display.
3 Grammar an attributive adjective or noun.
4 Statistics a real property which a statistical analysis is attempting to describe.
– DERIVATIVES **attributable** /əˈtrɪbjʊtəb(ə)l/ adjective, **attribution** noun, **attributional** adjective.
– ORIGIN late 15th cent.: the noun from Old French *attribut*; the verb from Latin *attribut-* 'allotted': both from the verb *attribuere*, from *ad-* 'to' + *tribuere* 'assign'.

attribution theory ▸ **noun** [mass noun] Psychology a theory which supposes that people attempt to understand the behaviour of others by attributing feelings, beliefs, and intentions to them.

attributive /əˈtrɪbjʊtɪv/ ▸ **adjective** Grammar (of an adjective or other modifier) preceding the word that it modifies and expressing an attribute, as *old* in *the old dog* (but not in *the dog is old*) and *expiry* in *expiry date.* Contrasted with PREDICATIVE.
– DERIVATIVES **attributively** adverb.
– ORIGIN mid 18th cent. (as a noun in the sense 'a word expressing an attribute'): from French *attributif, -ive*, from *attribut* 'an attribute', from Latin *attribuere* 'add to' (see ATTRIBUTE).

attrit /əˈtrɪt/ ▸ **verb** (**attrits, attriting, attrited**) [with obj.] US informal wear down (an opponent or enemy) by sustained action: *his defense was designed to attrit us.*
– ORIGIN 1950s: back-formation from ATTRITION.

attrition /əˈtrɪʃ(ə)n/ ▸ **noun** [mass noun] **1** the process of reducing something's strength or effectiveness through sustained attack or pressure: *the council is trying to wear down the opposition by attrition* | *the squadron suffered severe attrition of its bombers.* ■ chiefly N. Amer. & Austral./NZ the gradual reduction of a workforce by employees leaving and not being replaced rather than by redundancy. ■ wearing away by friction; abrasion: *the skull shows attrition of the edges of the teeth.*
2 (in scholastic theology) sorrow for sin, falling short of contrition.
– DERIVATIVES **attritional** adjective.
– ORIGIN late Middle English (in sense 2): from late Latin *attritio(n-)*, from *atterere* 'to rub'.

attune ▸ **verb** [with obj.] make receptive or aware: *a society more* ***attuned to*** *consumerism than ideology* | (as adj. **attuned**) *the Department is very attuned politically.* ■ accustom or acclimatize: *students are not* ***attuned to*** *making decisions.* ■ make harmonious: *the interests of East and West are now closely attuned.*
– DERIVATIVES **attunement** noun.
– ORIGIN late 16th cent.: from AT- + TUNE.

Atty ▸ **abbreviation** Attorney.

ATV ▸ **abbreviation** ■ N. Amer. all-terrain vehicle. ■ historical (in the UK) Associated Television, an independent television company founded in 1956 and replaced in 1981 by Central Television.

Atwood, Margaret (Eleanor) (b.1939), Canadian novelist, poet, critic, and short-story writer. Notable novels: *The Edible Woman* (1969), *Cat's Eye* (1989), *The Blind Assassin* (Booker Prize, 2000).

atypical ▸ **adjective** not representative of a type, group, or class: *a sample of people who are rather* ***atypical of*** *the target audience* | *there were somewhat atypical results in May and November.*
– DERIVATIVES **atypically** adverb.

AU ▸ **abbreviation** ■ African Union. ■ angstrom unit(s). ■ (also **a.u.**) astronomical unit(s).

Au ▸ **symbol** the chemical element gold.
– ORIGIN from Latin *aurum.*

aubade /əʊˈbɑːd/ ▸ **noun** a poem or piece of music appropriate to the dawn or early morning.
– ORIGIN late 17th cent.: from French, from Spanish *albada*, from *alba* 'dawn'.

auberge /əʊˈbɛːʒ/, French /obɛʀʒ/ ▸ **noun** an inn in a French-speaking country.
– ORIGIN French, from Provençal *alberga* 'lodging'.

aubergine /ˈəʊbəʒiːn/ ▸ **noun** chiefly Brit. **1** the purple egg-shaped fruit of a tropical Old World plant, which is eaten as a vegetable. Also called EGGPLANT. ■ [mass noun] a dark purple colour like the skin of an aubergine.
2 the large plant of the nightshade family which bears aubergines. ● *Solanum melongena*, family Solanaceae.
– ORIGIN late 18th cent.: from French, from Catalan *albergínia*, from Arabic *al-bāḏinjān* (based on Persian *bādingān*, from Sanskrit *vātiṃgaṇa*).

aubretia /ɔːˈbriːʃə/ (also **aubrietia**) ▸ **noun** a dwarf evergreen Eurasian trailing plant with dense masses of foliage and purple, pink, or white flowers, widely cultivated in rock gardens. ● *Aubrieta deltoidea*, family Cruciferae.
– ORIGIN early 19th cent.: modern Latin, named after Claude *Aubriet* (1668–1743), French botanist.

> **USAGE** Aubretia is named after a French botanist called Claude *Aubriet*, and the original spelling was **aubrieta**, which is the plant's genus name. In non-technical use, however, the forms **aubretia** and **aubrietia** are now more usual.

Aubrey /ˈɔːbri/, John (1626–97), English antiquarian and author. He is chiefly remembered for *Brief Lives*, a collection of biographies of eminent people.

auburn /ˈɔːbən, ˈɔːbəːn/ ▸ **adjective** (of hair) of a reddish-brown colour.

▸ noun [mass noun] a reddish-brown colour.
– ORIGIN late Middle English: from Old French *auborne, alborne*, from Latin *alburnus* 'whitish', from *albus* 'white'. The original sense was 'yellowish white', but the word became associated with *brown* because in the 16th and 17th centuries it was often written *abrune* or *abroun*.

Aubusson /'əubjusɒn, -sɒ̃/ ▸ noun a fine tapestry or carpet made at Aubusson, a town in central France, especially one from the late 18th century.

AUC ▸ abbreviation used to indicate a date reckoned from 753 BC, the year of the foundation of Rome: *765 auc.*
– ORIGIN from Latin *ab urbe condita* 'from the foundation of the city', also *anno urbis conditae* 'in the year of the foundation of the city'.

Auckland /'ɔːklənd/ the largest city and chief seaport of New Zealand, in the North Island; pop. 404,658 (2006). It was the site of the first Parliament of New Zealand in 1854, remaining the capital until 1865.

au courant /ˌəʊ kʊ'rɒ̃/ ▸ adjective aware of what is going on; well informed: *they were **au courant with** the literary scene.* ■ fashionable: *frocks with au courant details like ruching and asymmetrical hemlines.*
– ORIGIN mid 18th cent.: from French, literally 'in the (regular) course'.

auction /'ɔːkʃ(ə)n/ ▸ noun **1** a public sale in which goods or property are sold to the highest bidder: *the books are expected to fetch a six-figure sum at tomorrow's auction.* ■ [mass noun] the action or process of selling something to the highest bidder: *the Ferrari sold **at auction** for £10 million.*
2 Bridge the part of the play in which players bid to decide the contract in which the hand shall be played.
▸ verb [with obj.] sell or offer for sale at an auction: *the painting was auctioned at Christie's.*
– ORIGIN late 16th cent.: from Latin *auctio(n-)* 'increase, auction', from the verb *augere* 'to increase'.

auction bridge ▸ noun [mass noun] an obsolete form of the card game bridge, in which all tricks won counted towards the game whether bid or not.

auctioneer ▸ noun a person who conducts auctions by accepting bids and declaring goods sold.
– DERIVATIVES **auctioneering** noun.

auction house ▸ noun a company that runs auctions.

auction room (also **auction rooms**) ▸ noun a building in which auctions are held.

aucuba /'ɔːkjʊbə/ ▸ noun a hardy East Asian evergreen shrub of the dogwood family, resembling a laurel. ● Genus *Aucuba*, family Cornaceae: several species, in particular the Japanese laurel (*A. japonica*).
– ORIGIN modern Latin, from Japanese *aokiba*.

audacious /ɔː'deɪʃəs/ ▸ adjective **1** showing a willingness to take surprisingly bold risks: *a series of audacious takeovers.*
2 showing an impudent lack of respect: *he made an audacious remark.*
– DERIVATIVES **audaciously** adverb, **audaciousness** noun.
– ORIGIN mid 16th cent.: from Latin *audax, audac-* 'bold' (from *audere* 'dare') + **-IOUS**.

audacity /ɔː'dasɪti/ ▸ noun [mass noun] **1** a willingness to take bold risks: *he whistled at the sheer audacity of the plan.*
2 rude or disrespectful behaviour; impudence: *she **had the audacity to** suggest I'd been carrying on with him.*
– ORIGIN late Middle English: from medieval Latin *audacitas*, from *audax, audac-* 'bold' (see **AUDACIOUS**).

Auden /'ɔːd(ə)n/, W. H. (1907–73), British-born poet, resident in America from 1939; full name *Wystan Hugh Auden. Look, Stranger!* (1936) and *Spain* (1937, on the Civil War) secured his position as a leading left-wing poet. He was awarded the Pulitzer Prize for *The Age of Anxiety* (1947).

Audh /'ʌwəd/ variant spelling of **OUDH**.

audial /'ɔːdɪəl/ ▸ adjective relating to or perceived through the sense of hearing.
– ORIGIN late 20th cent.: formed irregularly from Latin *audire* 'hear' (compare with **AUDILE**), on the pattern of *visual.*

audible ▸ adjective able to be heard: *some ultrasound is audible to dogs.*
▸ noun American Football a change of playing tactics called by the quarterback at the line of scrimmage.
– DERIVATIVES **audibility** noun, **audibly** adverb.
– ORIGIN late 15th cent.: from late Latin *audibilis*, from *audire* 'hear'.

audience ▸ noun **1** the assembled spectators or listeners at a public event such as a play, film, concert, or meeting: *he asked for questions from members of the audience.* ■ the people who watch or listen to a television or radio programme: *the programme attracted an audience of almost twenty million.* ■ the readership of a newspaper, magazine, or book: *the newspaper has a sophisticated audience.* ■ the people giving attention to something: *the report deserves consideration by a much wider audience.*
2 a formal interview with a person in authority: *he demanded an audience with the Pope.*
3 [mass noun] archaic formal hearing.
– ORIGIN late Middle English: from Old French, from Latin *audientia*, from *audire* 'hear'.

audile /'ɔːdʌɪl/ ▸ adjective another term for **AUDITORY**.
– ORIGIN late 19th cent.: formed irregularly from Latin *audire* 'hear', on the pattern of *tactile.*

audio ▸ noun [mass noun] [usu. as modifier] sound, especially when recorded, transmitted, or reproduced: *audio equipment | the machine can retrieve and play audio from a CD-ROM.*
– ORIGIN 1930s: independent usage of **AUDIO-**.

audio- ▸ combining form relating to hearing or sound: *audiometer | audiovisual.*
– ORIGIN from Latin *audire* 'hear'.

Audio-Animatronics ▸ plural noun trademark for **ANIMATRONICS**.
– DERIVATIVES **Audio-Animatronic** adjective.

audiobook ▸ noun a recording on CD or cassette of a reading of a book, typically a novel.

audio cassette ▸ noun a cassette of audio tape.

audio frequency ▸ noun a frequency of oscillation capable of being perceived by the human ear, generally between 20 and 20,000 Hz.

audiogram ▸ noun a graphic record produced by audiometry.

audio guide ▸ noun a handheld device which provides recorded information for visitors touring a museum, gallery, or other place of interest.

audiology /ˌɔːdɪ'ɒlədʒi/ ▸ noun [mass noun] the branch of science and medicine concerned with the sense of hearing.
– DERIVATIVES **audiological** adjective, **audiologist** noun.

audiometry /ˌɔːdɪ'ɒmɪtri/ ▸ noun [mass noun] measurement of the range and sensitivity of a person's sense of hearing.
– DERIVATIVES **audiometer** noun, **audiometric** adjective.

audiophile ▸ noun informal a hi-fi enthusiast.

audio tape ▸ noun [mass noun] magnetic tape on which sound can be recorded. ■ [count noun] a length of this, typically in the form of a cassette.
▸ verb (**audiotape**) [with obj.] record (sound) on tape: *each interview was audiotaped and transcribed.*

audio typist ▸ noun a typist who transcribes letters or other documents from recorded dictation.

audiovisual ▸ adjective using both sight and sound, typically in the form of slides or video and recorded speech or music: *learners can be encouraged to use audiovisual aids.*

audit ▸ noun an official inspection of an organization's accounts, typically by an independent body. ■ a systematic review or assessment of something: *a complete audit of flora and fauna at the site.*
▸ verb (**audits, auditing, audited**) [with obj.] **1** conduct an official financial inspection of (a company or its accounts): *unlimited companies must also have their accounts audited.* ■ conduct a systematic review of: *a method of auditing obstetric and neonatal care.*
2 N. Amer. attend (a class) informally, without working for credit.
– DERIVATIVES **auditability** noun, **auditable** adjective.
– ORIGIN late Middle English: from Latin *auditus* 'hearing', from *audire* 'hear', in medieval Latin *auditus (compoti)* 'audit (of an account)', an audit originally being presented orally.

Audit Commission (in the UK) an independent body that monitors public spending, especially that by local government, on behalf of the government.

audition /ɔː'dɪʃ(ə)n/ ▸ noun **1** an interview for a role or job as a singer, actor, dancer, or musician, consisting of a practical demonstration of the candidate's suitability and skill.
2 [mass noun] archaic the power of hearing or listening.
▸ verb [no obj.] perform an audition: *I auditioned and was lucky enough to get the part.* ■ [with obj.] assess the suitability of (someone) for a role by means of an audition: *she was auditioning people for her new series.*
– DERIVATIVES **auditionee** noun.
– ORIGIN late 16th cent. (in the sense 'power of hearing or listening'): from Latin *auditio(n-)*, from *audire* 'hear'. Sense 1 of the noun dates from the late 19th cent.

auditive ▸ adjective another term for **AUDITORY**.

auditor ▸ noun **1** a person who conducts an audit.
2 a listener: *so low was Deems's voice that his auditors had to give it close attention.* ■ N. Amer. a person who attends a class informally without working for credit.
– DERIVATIVES **auditorial** adjective.
– ORIGIN Middle English: from Old French *auditeur*, from Latin *auditor*, from *audire* 'to hear'.

auditorium ▸ noun (pl. **auditoriums** or **auditoria**)
1 the part of a theatre, concert hall, or other public building in which the audience sits.
2 chiefly N. Amer. a large building or hall used for public gatherings, typically concerts or sports events.
– ORIGIN early 17th cent. (originally in the general sense 'a place for hearing'): from Latin, neuter of *auditorius* 'relating to hearing' (see **AUDITORY**).

auditory ▸ adjective relating to the sense of hearing: *the auditory nerves | teaching methods use both visual and auditory stimulation.*
– ORIGIN late 16th cent.: from Latin *auditorius*, from *audire* 'hear'.

Audubon /'ɔːdəb(ə)n/, John James (1785–1851), American naturalist and artist. He is noted for *The Birds of America* (1827–38).

au fait /əʊ 'feɪ/, French /o fɛ(t)/ ▸ adjective (**au fait with**) having a good or detailed knowledge of: *you should **be au fait with** the company and its products.*
– ORIGIN mid 18th cent.: from French, literally 'to the fact, to the point'.

au fond /əʊ 'fɒ̃/, French /o fɔ̃/ ▸ adverb in essence.
– ORIGIN French.

Aug. ▸ abbreviation August.

Augean /ɔː'dʒiːən/ ▸ adjective relating to Augeas: *the Augean stables.* ■ (of a task or problem) requiring so much effort to complete or solve as to seem impossible: *there are Augean amounts of debris to clear.*

Augeas /ɔː'dʒiːəs/ Greek Mythology a legendary king whose vast stables had never been cleaned. Hercules cleaned them in a day by diverting the River Alpheus to flow through them.

auger /'ɔːɡə/ ▸ noun **1** a tool resembling a large corkscrew, for boring holes in wood. ■ a similar larger tool for boring holes in the ground.
2 (also **auger shell**) a marine mollusc of warm seas with a slender tapering spiral shell. ● *Terebra* and other genera, family Terebridae, class Gastropoda.
– ORIGIN Old English *nafogār*, from *nafu* (see **NAVE**[2]) + *gār* 'piercer'. The *n* was lost by wrong division of *a nauger*; compare with **ADDER**[1] and **APRON**.

> **USAGE** See **USAGE** at **AUGUR**.

Auger effect /'əʊʒeɪ/ ▸ noun Physics an effect whereby an atom which has been ionized by removal of an electron from an inner shell loses energy by emitting an electron from an outer shell.
– ORIGIN 1930s: named after Pierre V. *Auger* (1899–1993), French physicist.

aught[1] /ɔːt/ (also **ought**) ▸ pronoun archaic anything at all: *know you aught of this fellow, young sir?*
– ORIGIN Old English *āwiht* (see **AYE**[2], **WIGHT**).

aught[2] ▸ noun variant spelling of **OUGHT**[2].

augite /'ɔːdʒʌɪt/ ▸ noun [mass noun] a dark green or black aluminosilicate mineral of the pyroxene group. It occurs in many igneous rocks, including basalt, gabbro, and dolerite.
– ORIGIN early 19th cent.: from Latin *augites*, denoting a precious stone (probably turquoise), from Greek *augitēs*, from *augē* 'lustre'.

augment ▸ verb /ɔːɡ'mɛnt/ [with obj.] make (something) greater by adding to it; increase: *her secretarial work helped to augment her husband's income.*
▸ noun /'ɔːɡm(ə)nt/ Linguistics a vowel prefixed to past tenses of verbs in Greek and certain other Indo-European languages.
– ORIGIN late Middle English: from Old French *augmenter* (verb), *augment* (noun), or late Latin *augmentare*, from Latin *augere* 'to increase'.

augmentation ▸ noun [mass noun] the action or process of making or becoming greater in size or amount. ■ Music the lengthening of the time values of notes in a melodic part. ■ [count noun] Heraldry an addi-

tion to a coat of arms granted as a mark of special honour.
– ORIGIN late Middle English: from late Latin *augmentatio(n-)*, from the verb *augmentare* (see AUGMENT).

augmentative ▶ adjective Linguistics (of an affix or derived word) reinforcing the idea of the original word, especially by meaning 'a large one of its kind', as with the Italian suffix *-one* in *borrone* 'ravine', compared with *borro* 'ditch'.
– ORIGIN late Middle English (in the sense 'having a tendency to increase'): from Old French *augmentatif, -ive* or medieval Latin *augmentativus*, from the verb *augmentare* (see AUGMENT).

augmented ▶ adjective **1** having been made greater in size or value: *augmented pensions for those retiring at 65.*
2 Music denoting or containing an interval which is one semitone greater than the corresponding major or perfect interval: *augmented fourths.*

augmented reality ▶ noun [mass noun] a technology that superimposes a computer-generated image on a user's view of the real world, thus providing a composite view.

Augrabies Falls /ə'grɑːbiːz/ a series of waterfalls on the Orange River in the province of Northern Cape, South Africa.

au gratin /əʊ 'gratã/, French /o ɡʀatɛ̃/ ▶ adjective [postpositive] sprinkled with breadcrumbs or grated cheese and browned: *lentil and mushroom au gratin.*
– ORIGIN French, literally 'by grating', from the verb *gratter* 'to grate'.

Augsburg /'aʊgzbəːg/, German /'aʊksbʊrk/ a city in southern Germany, in Bavaria; pop. 262,500 (est. 2006).

Augsburg Confession a statement of the Lutheran position, drawn up mainly by Melanchthon and approved by Luther before being presented to the Emperor Charles V at Augsburg on 25 June 1530.

augur /'ɔːgə/ ▶ verb [no obj.] (**augur well/badly/ill**) (of an event or circumstance) portend a good or bad outcome: *the end of the cold war seemed to augur well.*
▶ noun historical (in ancient Rome) a religious official who observed natural signs, especially the behaviour of birds, interpreting these as an indication of divine approval or disapproval of a proposed action.
– DERIVATIVES **augural** /'ɔːgjʊ(ə)r(ə)l/ adjective (archaic).
– ORIGIN late Middle English (as a noun): from Latin, 'diviner'.

> **USAGE** The spellings **augur** (a verb meaning 'portend a good or bad outcome', as in *this augurs well*) and **auger** (a type of tool used for boring) are sometimes confused, but the two words are quite different in both their present meaning and their origins.

augury /'ɔːgjʊri/ ▶ noun (pl. **auguries**) a sign of what will happen in the future; an omen: *they heard the sound as an augury of death.* ■ [mass noun] the interpretation of omens.
– ORIGIN late Middle English (in the sense 'divination'): from Old French *augurie* or Latin *augurium* 'interpretation of omens', from *augur* (see AUGUR).

August ▶ noun the eighth month of the year, in the northern hemisphere usually considered the last month of summer: *the sultry haze of late August | the wettest August in six years.*
– ORIGIN Old English, from Latin *augustus* 'consecrated, venerable'; named after AUGUSTUS, the first Roman emperor.

august /ɔː'gʌst/ ▶ adjective respected and impressive: *she was in august company.*
– DERIVATIVES **augustly** adverb, **augustness** noun.
– ORIGIN mid 17th cent.: from French *auguste* or Latin *augustus* 'consecrated, venerable'.

Augusta /ɔː'gʌstə/ **1** a resort in eastern Georgia in the US; pop. (with Richmond) 199,486 (est. 2008).
2 the state capital of Maine; pop. 18,282 (est. 2008).

Augustan /ɔː'gʌst(ə)n/ ▶ adjective connected with or occurring during the reign of the Roman emperor Augustus. ■ relating to or denoting Latin literature of the reign of Augustus, including the works of Virgil, Horace, Ovid, and Livy. ■ relating to or denoting 17th- and 18th-century English literature of a style considered refined and classical, including the works of Pope, Addison, and Swift.
▶ noun a writer of the (Latin or English) Augustan period or style.
– ORIGIN from Latin *Augustanus* 'relating to Augustus' (see AUGUSTUS).

Augustine /ɔː'gʌstɪn/ ▶ noun an Augustinian friar.
– ORIGIN late Middle English: from Old French *augustin*, from Latin *Augustinus* 'Augustine' (see AUGUSTINIAN).

Augustine, St[1] /ɔː'gʌstɪn/ (died *c.*604), Italian churchman; known as **St Augustine of Canterbury**. Sent from Rome by Pope Gregory the Great to refound the Church in England in 597, he founded a monastery at Canterbury and became its first archbishop. Feast day, 26 May.

Augustine, St[2] /ɔː'gʌstɪn/ (354–430), Doctor of the Church; known as **St Augustine of Hippo**. He became bishop of Hippo in North Africa in 396. His writings, such as *Confessions* and the *City of God*, dominated subsequent Western theology. Feast day, 28 August.

Augustinian /,ɔːgə'stɪnɪən/ ▶ adjective **1** relating to St Augustine of Hippo or his doctrines.
2 relating to a religious order observing a rule derived from St Augustine's writings.
▶ noun **1** a member of an Augustinian order.
2 an adherent of the doctrines of St Augustine.

Augustus /ɔː'gʌstəs/ (63 BC–AD 14), the first Roman emperor; born *Gaius Octavius*; also called (until 27 BC) **Octavian**. He was adopted by the will of his great-uncle Julius Caesar and gained supreme power by his defeat of Antony in 31 BC. In 27 BC he was given the title Augustus ('venerable') and became in effect the first Roman emperor.

auk /ɔːk/ ▶ noun a short-winged diving seabird found in northern oceans, typically with a black head and back and white underparts. ● Family Alcidae (the **auk family**), which comprises the guillemots, razorbills, puffins, and their relatives.
– ORIGIN late 17th cent.: from Old Norse *álka* 'razorbill'.

auklet /'ɔːklɪt/ ▶ noun a small, stubby auk (seabird) found in the North Pacific, typically with grey underparts. ● *Aethia* and three other genera, family Alcidae: several species.

auld /ɔːld, ɑːld/ ▶ adjective Scottish form of OLD.
– PHRASES **auld Reekie** informal a name for Edinburgh. [literally 'old Smoky', from REEK (sense 2 of the noun).]
– ORIGIN Old English *ald*, Anglian form of OLD.

auld lang syne /,ɔːld laŋ 'sʌɪn/ ▶ noun [mass noun] times long past.
– PHRASES **for auld lang syne** for old times' sake.
– ORIGIN late 18th cent.: Scots (see AULD, LANG SYNE). The phrase was popularized as the title and refrain of a song by Robert Burns (1788).

aumbry /'ɔːmbri/ (also **ambry**) ▶ noun (pl. **aumbries**) a small recess or cupboard in the wall of a church. ■ historical a small cupboard.
– ORIGIN Middle English: from Old French *armarie*, from Latin *armarium* 'closet, chest', from *arma* 'utensils'.

au naturel /,əʊ natjʊ'rɛl/, French /o natyʀɛl/ ▶ adjective & adverb with no elaborate treatment, dressing, or preparation: [as adj.] *the cheese is delicious whether au naturel or seasoned.* ■ humorous naked: [as adv.] *the remote beach where we'd been camping au naturel.*
– ORIGIN French, literally 'in the natural (state)'.

Aung San /,aʊŋ 'san/ (1914–47), Burmese nationalist leader. As leader of the Council of Ministers he negotiated a promise of self government from the British shortly before his assassination.

Aung San Suu Kyi /aʊŋ ,san suː 'tʃiː/ (b.1945), Burmese political leader, daughter of Aung San and leader of the National League for Democracy (NLD) since 1988. She was held under house arrest from 1989 to 1995, and the ruling military government refused to recognize her party's victory in the 1990 elections. Since 2000 she has frequently been detained again. Nobel Peace Prize (1991).

aunt ▶ noun the sister of one's father or mother or the wife of one's uncle. ■ informal an unrelated adult female friend, especially of a child.
– ORIGIN Middle English: from Old French *ante*, from Latin *amita*.

auntie (also **aunty**) ▶ noun (pl. **aunties**) informal term for AUNT. ■ (**Auntie**) Brit. informal the BBC.

Aunt Sally ▶ noun (pl. **Aunt Sallies**) [mass noun] a game played in some parts of Britain in which players throw sticks or balls at a wooden dummy. ■ [count noun] a dummy used in this game. ■ [count noun] a person or thing set up as an easy target for criticism.

au pair /əʊ 'pɛː/ ▶ noun a young foreign person, typically a woman, who helps with housework or childcare in exchange for food, a room, and some pocket money.
– ORIGIN late 19th cent.: from French, literally 'on equal terms'. The phrase was originally adjectival, describing an arrangement between two parties paid for by the exchange of mutual services; the noun usage dates from the 1960s.

aura /'ɔːrə/ ▶ noun (pl. **auras** or **aurae** /-riː/) **1** the distinctive atmosphere or quality that seems to surround and be generated by a person, thing, or place: *the ceremony retains an aura of mystery.*
2 (in spiritualism and some forms of alternative medicine) a supposed emanation surrounding the body of a living creature and regarded as an essential part of the individual. ■ any invisible emanation, especially an odour.
3 Medicine a warning sensation experienced before an attack of epilepsy or migraine.
– ORIGIN late Middle English (originally denoting a gentle breeze): via Latin from Greek, 'breeze, breath'. Current senses date from the 18th cent.

aural /'ɔːr(ə)l/ ▶ adjective relating to the ear or the sense of hearing: *information held in written, aural, or visual form | aural anatomy.*
– DERIVATIVES **aurally** adverb.
– ORIGIN mid 19th cent.: from Latin *auris* 'ear' + -AL.

> **USAGE** The words **aural** and **oral** have the same pronunciation in standard English, which is sometimes a source of confusion. A distinctive pronunciation for **aural** has been proposed, with the first syllable rhyming with *cow*, but it has not become standard.

Aurangzeb /'ɔːraŋzɛb, 'aʊərəŋ-/ (1618–1707), Mogul emperor of Hindustan 1658–1707, who increased the Mogul empire to its greatest extent.

aurar plural form of EYRIR.

aureate /'ɔːrɪət/ ▶ adjective made of or having the colour of gold. ■ (of language) highly ornamented or elaborate.
– ORIGIN late Middle English: from late Latin *aureatus*, from Latin *aureus* 'golden', from *aurum* 'gold'.

Aurelian /ɔː'riːlɪən/ (*c.*215–75), Roman emperor 270–5; Latin name *Lucius Domitius Aurelianus*. Originally a common soldier, he rose through the ranks and was elected emperor by the army.

Aurelius /ɔː'riːlɪəs/, Marcus (121–80), Roman emperor 161–80; full name *Caesar Marcus Aurelius Antoninus Augustus*. He was occupied for much of his reign with wars against invading Germanic tribes. His *Meditations*, a collection of aphorisms and reflections, are evidence of his philosophical nature.

aureole /'ɔːrɪəʊl/ (also **aureola** /ɔː'rɪələ/) ▶ noun **1** a circle of light or brightness surrounding something, especially as depicted in art around the head or body of a person represented as holy. ■ a corona around the sun or moon.
2 another term for AREOLA.
3 Geology the zone of metamorphosed rock surrounding an igneous intrusion.
– ORIGIN Middle English: from Old French *aureole*, from Latin *aureola (corona)* 'golden (crown)', feminine of *aureolus* (diminutive of *aureus*, from *aurum* 'gold').

aureus /'ɔːrɪəs/ ▶ noun (pl. **aurei**) a Roman coin of the late republic and empire, worth 25 silver denarii.
– ORIGIN Latin, noun use of *aureus* 'golden', from *aurum* 'gold'.

au revoir /,əʊ rə'vwɑː/, French /o ʀəvwaʀ/ ▶ exclamation goodbye until we meet again.
– ORIGIN late 17th cent.: from French, literally 'to the seeing again'.

auric[1] /'ɔːrɪk/ ▶ adjective relating to the aura supposedly surrounding a living creature.

auric[2] /'ɔːrɪk/ ▶ adjective Chemistry of gold with a valency of three; of gold(III).
– ORIGIN early 19th cent.: from Latin *aurum* 'gold' + -IC.

auricle /'ɔːrɪk(ə)l/ ▶ noun Anatomy & Biology **1** a structure resembling an ear or ear lobe. ■ the external part or pinna of the ear.
2 another term for ATRIUM (of the heart). ■ a small muscular flap on the surface of each atrium of the heart.
– ORIGIN late Middle English: from Latin *auricula* 'external part of the ear', diminutive of *auris* 'ear'.

auricula /ɔː'rɪkjʊlə/ ▶ noun an Alpine primula from which a wide range of flowering cultivars have been developed. It has leaves that supposedly resemble bears' ears. Also called BEAR'S EAR. ● *Primula auricula*, family Primulaceae.
– ORIGIN mid 17th cent.: from Latin, diminutive of *auris* 'ear'.

A

auricular /ɔːˈrɪkjʊlə/ ▸ **adjective 1** relating to the ear or hearing.
2 relating to or shaped like an auricle.
– ORIGIN late Middle English: from late Latin *auricularis*, from *auricula*, diminutive of *auris* 'ear'.

auriculate /ɔːˈrɪkjʊlət/ ▸ **adjective** chiefly Botany & Zoology having one or more structures shaped like an ear or ear lobe.
– ORIGIN early 18th cent.: from Latin *auricula* 'external part of the ear' (diminutive of *auris* 'ear') + **-ATE**[2].

auriculotherapy /ɔːˌrɪkjələʊˈθɛrəpi/ ▸ **noun** [mass noun] a form of acupuncture applied to points on the ear in order to treat other parts of the body.
– ORIGIN 1970s: from Latin *auricula* 'external part of the ear' + **-O-** + **THERAPY**.

auriferous /ɔːˈrɪf(ə)rəs/ ▸ **adjective** (of rocks or minerals) containing gold.
– ORIGIN mid 17th cent.: from Latin *aurifer* 'gold-bearing' (from *aurum* 'gold') + **-OUS**.

Auriga /ɔːˈrʌɪɡə/ Astronomy a large northern constellation (the Charioteer), said to represent a man holding a whip.
– ORIGIN Latin.

Aurignacian /ˌɔːrɪˈnjeɪʃ(ə)n, ˌɔːrɪɡˈneɪ-/ ▸ **adjective** Archaeology relating to or denoting the early stages of the Upper Palaeolithic culture in Europe and the Near East. It is dated in most places to about 34,000–29,000 years ago, and is associated with Cro-Magnon Man. ■ (as noun **the Aurignacian**) the Aurignacian culture or period.
– ORIGIN early 20th cent.: from French *Aurignacien*, from *Aurignac* in SW France, where objects from this culture were found.

auriscope /ˈɔːrɪskəʊp/ (also **auroscope** /ˈɔːrəskəʊp/) ▸ **noun** another term for **OTOSCOPE**.
– ORIGIN mid 19th cent.: from Latin *auris* 'ear' + **-SCOPE**.

aurochs /ˈɔːrɒks, ˈaʊ-/ ▸ **noun** (pl. **same**) a large wild Eurasian ox that was the ancestor of domestic cattle. It was probably exterminated in Britain in the Bronze Age, and the last one was killed in Poland in 1627. Also called **URUS**. ● *Bos primigenius*, family Bovidae.
– ORIGIN late 18th cent.: from German, early variant of *Auerochs*, from Old High German *ūrohso*, from *ūr* (form also found in Old English, of unknown origin) + *ohso* 'ox'.

Aurora /ɔːˈrɔːrə/ Roman Mythology goddess of the dawn. Greek equivalent **Eos**.

aurora /ɔːˈrɔːrə/ ▸ **noun** (pl. **auroras** or **aurorae** /-riː/) **1** a natural electrical phenomenon characterized by the appearance of streamers of reddish or greenish light in the sky, especially near the northern or southern magnetic pole. The effect is caused by the interaction of charged particles from the sun with atoms in the upper atmosphere. In northern and southern regions it is respectively called **aurora borealis** or **Northern Lights** and **aurora australis** or **Southern Lights**. [*borealis* from Latin, 'northern', based on Greek *Boreas*, the god of the north wind; *australis* from Latin, 'southern', from *Auster* 'the south, the south wind'.]
2 literary the dawn.
– DERIVATIVES **auroral** adjective.
– ORIGIN late Middle English (originally in sense 2): from Latin, 'dawn, goddess of the dawn'. Sense 1 dates from the early 18th cent.

AUS ▸ **abbreviation** Australia (international vehicle registration).

Auschwitz /ˈaʊʃvɪts/ a Nazi concentration camp in the Second World War, near the town of Oświęcim (Auschwitz) in Poland.

auscultation /ˌɔːsk(ə)lˈteɪʃ(ə)n/ ▸ **noun** [mass noun] the action of listening to sounds from the heart, lungs, or other organs, typically with a stethoscope, as a part of medical diagnosis.
– DERIVATIVES **auscultate** verb, **auscultatory** /ɔːˈskʌltət(ə)ri/ **adjective**.
– ORIGIN mid 17th cent.: from Latin *auscultatio(n-)*, from *auscultare* 'listen to'.

Auslese /ˈaʊsleɪzə/ ▸ **noun** [mass noun] a white wine of German origin or style made from selected bunches of grapes picked later than the general harvest.
– ORIGIN from German, from *aus* 'out' + *Lese* 'picking, vintage'.

auspice /ˈɔːspɪs/ ▸ **noun** archaic a divine or prophetic token.
– PHRASES **under the auspices of** with the help, support, or protection of: *the course is run under the auspices of the Anglican Church*.
– ORIGIN mid 16th cent. (originally denoting the observation of bird flight in divination): from French, or from Latin *auspicium*, from *auspex* 'observer of birds', from *avis* 'bird' + *specere* 'to look'.

auspicious /ɔːˈspɪʃəs/ ▸ **adjective** conducive to success; favourable: *it was not the most auspicious moment to hold an election*. ■ giving or being a sign of future success: *they said it was an auspicious moon—it was rising*. ■ archaic characterized by success; prosperous.
– DERIVATIVES **auspiciously** adverb, **auspiciousness** noun.
– ORIGIN late 16th cent.: from **AUSPICE** + **-OUS**.

Aussie /ˈɒzi, ˈɒsi/ (also **Ozzie**) ▸ **noun & adjective** informal term for **AUSTRALIA** or **AUSTRALIAN**.

Austen /ˈɒstɪn, ˈɔː-/, Jane (1775–1817), English novelist. Her major novels are *Sense and Sensibility* (1811), *Pride and Prejudice* (1813), *Mansfield Park* (1814), *Emma* (1815), *Northanger Abbey* (1818), and *Persuasion* (1818). They are notable for skilful characterization, dry wit, and penetrating social observation.

austenite /ˈɒstɪnʌɪt, ˈɔː-/ ▸ **noun** [mass noun] Metallurgy a solid solution of carbon in a non-magnetic form of iron stable at high temperatures. It is a constituent of some forms of steel.
– DERIVATIVES **austenitic** adjective.
– ORIGIN early 20th cent.: from the name of Sir William Roberts-*Austen* (1843–1902), English metallurgist, + **-ITE**[1].

austere /ɒˈstɪə, ɔː-/ ▸ **adjective** (**austerer**, **austerest**) severe or strict in manner or attitude: *he was an austere man, with a rigidly puritanical outlook*. ■ (of living conditions or a way of life) having no comforts or luxuries: *conditions in the prison could hardly be more austere*. ■ having a plain and unadorned appearance: *the cathedral is impressive in its austere simplicity*.
– DERIVATIVES **austerely** adverb.
– ORIGIN Middle English: via Old French from Latin *austerus*, from Greek *austēros* 'severe'.

austerity ▸ **noun** (pl. **austerities**) [mass noun] **1** sternness or severity of manner or attitude: *he was noted for his austerity and his authoritarianism*. ■ plainness and simplicity in appearance: *the room was decorated with a restraint bordering on austerity*. ■ [count noun] (usu. **austerities**) a feature of an austere way of life: *his uncle's austerities had undermined his health*.
2 difficult economic conditions created by government measures to reduce public expenditure: *the country was subjected to acute economic austerity* | [count noun] (**austerities**) *the austerities of post-war London*.
– ORIGIN late Middle English: from French *austérité*, from Latin *austeritas*, from *austerus* 'severe' (see **AUSTERE**).

Austerlitz, Battle of /ˈaʊstəlɪts, ˈɔːstə-/ a battle in 1805 near the town of Austerlitz (now in the Czech Republic), in which Napoleon defeated the Austrians and Russians.

Austin[1] /ˈɒstɪn, ˈɔː-/ the state capital of Texas; pop. 757,688 (est. 2008). First settled in 1835, it was named in 1839 after Stephen F. Austin, son of Moses Austin, leader of the first Texas colony.

Austin[2] /ˈɒstɪn, ˈɔː-/, Herbert, 1st Baron Austin of Longbridge (1866–1941), British motor manufacturer. Among the cars produced by his factory the Austin Seven ('Baby Austin') was particularly popular. His company merged with Morris Motors in 1952 to form the British Motor Corporation.

Austin[3] /ˈɒstɪn, ˈɔː-/, John (1790–1859), English jurist. His work is significant for its strict delimitation of the sphere of law and its distinction from that of morality.

Austin[4] /ˈɒstɪn, ˈɔː-/, J. L. (1911–60), English philosopher; full name *John Langshaw Austin*. A careful exponent of linguistic philosophy, he pioneered the theory of speech acts, pointing out that utterances can be used to perform actions as well as to convey information.

Austin Friars ▸ **plural noun** another name for Augustinian Friars.

austral /ˈɒstr(ə)l, ˈɔː-/ ▸ **adjective** technical relating to the southern hemisphere. ■ (**Austral**) of Australia or Australasia.
– ORIGIN late 15th cent.: from Latin *australis*, from *Auster* 'the south, the south wind'.

Australasia /ˌɒstrəˈleɪʒə, -ʃə/ the region consisting of Australia, New Zealand, New Guinea, and the neighbouring islands of the Pacific.
– DERIVATIVES **Australasian** adjective & noun.

Australia an island country and continent of the southern hemisphere, in the SW Pacific, a member state of the Commonwealth; pop. 21,262,600 (est. 2009); official language, English; capital, Canberra.

> Inhabited by Aboriginal peoples since prehistoric times, Australia was explored by the Dutch from 1606; British colonization began in 1788, as did the transportation of convicts (discontinued in 1868). Australia was declared a Commonwealth in 1901, when the six colonies (New South Wales, Victoria, Queensland, South Australia, Western Australia, and the offshore island of Tasmania) federated as sovereign states; Northern Territory achieved similar status in 1978.

Australia Day ▸ **noun** a national public holiday in Australia, commemorating the founding on 26 January 1788 of the colony of New South Wales.

Australian ▸ **noun** a native or inhabitant of Australia, or a person of Australian descent.
▸ **adjective** relating to Australia. ■ Zoology relating to or denoting a zoogeographical region comprising Australasia together with Indonesia east of Wallace's line, in which monotremes and marsupials dominate the fauna. Compare with **NOTOGAEA**. ■ Botany relating to or denoting a phytogeographical kingdom comprising only Australia and Tasmania.
– DERIVATIVES **Australianism** noun.
– ORIGIN from French *australien*, from Latin *australis* in the phrase *Terra Australis* 'the southern land', the name of the supposed southern continent.

Australian Antarctic Territory an area of Antarctica administered by Australia, lying between longitudes 142° east and 136° east.

Australian Capital Territory a federal territory in New South Wales, Australia, consisting of two enclaves ceded by New South Wales, one in 1911 to contain Canberra, the other in 1915 containing Jervis Bay; the latter became the Jervis Bay Territory in 1988.

Australian crawl ▸ **noun** chiefly Austral. another term for **CRAWL** (sense 2 of the noun).

Australian flatworm ▸ **noun** an orange or yellow terrestrial flatworm up to 8 cm in length, accidentally introduced from Australia to Britain where it is destroying earthworm populations. ● *Coenoplana alba*, order Tricladida, class Turbellaria.

Australian Labor Party (abbrev.: **ALP**) Australia's oldest political party, founded in 1891. The party is moderate left-of-centre; it has provided three recent Australian Prime Ministers, Gough Whitlam, Bob Hawke, and Paul Keating.

Australian Rules (also **Australian Rules football**) ▸ **noun** [mass noun] a form of football played on an oval ground with an oval ball by teams of eighteen players.

> The game dates from 1858. Players may run with the ball if they touch it to the ground every fifteen metres, and may pass it in any direction by punching. There are both inner and outer goalposts: a behind (between the outer posts) scores one point and a goal (between the inner posts) scores six.

Australian salute ▸ **noun** Austral. humorous a wave of the hand to brush flies off the face.

Australian terrier ▸ **noun** a wire-haired terrier of a breed originating in Australia.

Austral Islands another name for **TUBUAI ISLANDS**.

australite /ˈɒstrəlʌɪt/ ▸ **noun** Geology a tektite from the strewn field in Australia.

Australoid /ˈɒstrəlɔɪd/ ▸ **adjective** relating to the broad division of humankind represented by Australian Aboriginal peoples.
▸ **noun** a person belonging to this division of humankind.

> **USAGE** The term **Australoid** belongs to a set of terms introduced by 19th-century anthropologists attempting to categorize human races. Such terms are associated with outdated notions of racial types, and so are now potentially offensive and best avoided. See **USAGE** at **MONGOLOID**.

Australopithecus /ˌɒstrələʊˈpɪθɪkəs/ ▸ **noun** a fossil bipedal primate with both apelike and human characteristics, found in Pliocene and Lower Pleistocene deposits (*c*.4 million to 1 million years old) in Africa. ● Genus *Australopithecus*, family Hominidae: several species, including the lightly built *A. africanus*, which is thought to be the immediate ancestor of the human genus *Homo*.
– DERIVATIVES **australopithecine** /-ɪsiːn/ **noun & adjective**.

– ORIGIN modern Latin, from Latin *australis* 'southern' (see **AUSTRAL**) + Greek *pithēkos* 'ape'.

Australorp /ˈɒstrəlɔːp/ ▶ **noun** a black Orpington chicken of an Australian breed.
– ORIGIN early 20th cent.: blend of **AUSTRALIAN** and **ORPINGTON**.

Austria a republic in central Europe; pop. 8,210,300 (est. 2009); official language, German; capital, Vienna. German name **ÖSTERREICH**.

> Austria was dominated from the early Middle Ages by the Habsburg family, and became the centre of a massive central European empire which lasted until 1918. The country was incorporated within the Nazi Reich in 1938 and after the Second World War was occupied by the Allies, regaining its sovereignty in 1955. A referendum in 1994 approved Austria's entry into the European Union.

– DERIVATIVES **Austrian** adjective & noun.

Austria–Hungary (also **Austro-Hungarian Empire**) the dual monarchy established in 1867 by the Austrian emperor Franz Josef, according to which Austria and Hungary became autonomous states under a common sovereign.

Austrian blind ▶ **noun** a blind made from ruched fabric, which extends about a third of the way down a window.

Austrian Succession, War of the a group of several related conflicts (1740–8), involving most of the states of Europe, that were triggered by the death of the Emperor Charles VI and the accession of his daughter Maria Theresa in 1740 to the Austrian throne. See also **PRAGMATIC SANCTION**.

Austro-¹ /ˈɒstrəʊ/ ▶ **combining form** Austrian; Austrian and ...: *Austro-Hungarian*.

Austro-² /ˈɒstrəʊ/ ▶ **combining form** Australian; Australian and ...: *Austro-Malayan*. ■ southern: *Austro-Asiatic*.

Austro-Asiatic ▶ **adjective** relating to or denoting a phylum or superfamily of languages spoken in SE Asia, consisting of the Mon-Khmer family, the Munda family, and one or two other isolated languages.
▶ **noun** [mass noun] this phylum of languages.

Austronesian /ˌɒstrə(ʊ)ˈniːʒən, -zɪən/ ▶ **adjective** relating to or denoting a family of languages spoken in an area extending from Madagascar in the west to the Pacific islands in the east. Also called **MALAYO-POLYNESIAN**.
▶ **noun** [mass noun] this family of languages.

> Austronesian languages are spoken by about 140 million people, of whom all but 1 million speak a language of the Indonesian group, which includes Indonesian, Javanese, Tagalog, and Malagasy. The other groups are Micronesian, Melanesian, and Polynesian, scattered across the islands of the South Pacific.

– ORIGIN from German *austronesisch*, based on Latin *australis* 'southern' (see **AUSTRAL**) + Greek *nēsos* 'island'.

AUT ▶ **abbreviation** (in the UK) Association of University Teachers.

aut- ▶ **prefix** variant spelling of **AUTO-¹** shortened before a vowel (as in *autoxidation*).

autarch /ˈɔːtɑːk/ ▶ **noun** a ruler who has absolute power.
– ORIGIN early 19th cent.: from Greek *autarkhos*, from *autos* 'self' + *arkhos* 'leader'.

autarchy /ˈɔːtɑːki/ ▶ **noun** (pl. **autarchies**) **1** another term for **AUTOCRACY**.
2 variant spelling of **AUTARKY**.
– DERIVATIVES **autarchic** adjective.

autarky (also **autarchy**) ▶ **noun** [mass noun] economic independence or self-sufficiency. ■ [count noun] a country, state, or society which is economically independent.
– DERIVATIVES **autarkic** adjective.
– ORIGIN early 17th cent.: from Greek *autarkeia*, from *autarkēs* 'self-sufficiency', from *autos* 'self' + *arkein* 'suffice'.

autecology /ˌɔːtɪˈkɒlədʒi/ ▶ **noun** [mass noun] Biology the ecological study of a particular species. Contrasted with **SYNECOLOGY**.
– DERIVATIVES **autecological** adjective.

auteur /əʊˈtəː, ɔː-/ ▶ **noun** a film director who influences their films so much that they rank as their author.
– DERIVATIVES **auteurism** noun, **auteurist** adjective.
– ORIGIN 1960s: from French, literally 'author'.

authentic ▶ **adjective 1** of undisputed origin and not a copy; genuine: *the letter is now accepted as an authentic document*. ■ made or done in the traditional or original way, or in a way that faithfully resembles an original: *the restaurant serves authentic Italian meals | every detail of the film was totally authentic*. ■ based on facts; accurate or reliable: *an authentic depiction of the situation*. ■ (in existentialist philosophy) relating to or denoting an emotionally appropriate, significant, purposive, and responsible mode of human life.
2 Music (of a church mode) containing notes between the final (the principal note) and the note an octave higher. Compare with **PLAGAL**.
– DERIVATIVES **authentically** adverb [as submodifier] *the food is authentically Cajun*.
– ORIGIN late Middle English: via Old French from late Latin *authenticus*, from Greek *authentikos* 'principal, genuine'.

authenticate ▶ **verb** [with obj.] prove or show (something) to be true, genuine, or valid: *they were invited to authenticate artefacts from the Italian Renaissance*. ■ [no obj.] Computing (of a user or process) have one's identity verified.
– DERIVATIVES **authentication** /-ˈkeɪʃ(ə)n/ noun, **authenticator** noun.
– ORIGIN early 17th cent.: from medieval Latin *authenticat-* 'established as valid', from the verb *authenticare*, from late Latin *authenticus* 'genuine' (see **AUTHENTIC**).

authenticity /ɔːθenˈtɪsɪti/ ▶ **noun** [mass noun] the quality of being authentic: *the paper should have established the authenticity of the documents before publishing them*.

authigenic /ˌɔːθɪˈdʒenɪk/ ▶ **adjective** Geology (of minerals and other materials) formed in their present position. Often contrasted with **ALLOGENIC**.
– ORIGIN late 19th cent.: from Greek *authigenēs* 'born on the spot' + **-IC**.

author ▶ **noun** a writer of a book, article, or document: *he is the author of several books on the subject*. ■ someone who writes books as a profession. ■ the writings of such a person: *I had to read authors I disliked*. ■ an originator of a plan or idea: *the authors of the peace plan*.
▶ **verb** [with obj.] be the author of (a book or piece of writing): *she has authored several articles on wildlife*. ■ be the originator of: *the concept has been authored largely by insurance companies*.
– DERIVATIVES **authorial** /ɔːˈθɔːrɪəl/ adjective, **authorship** noun.
– ORIGIN Middle English (in the sense 'a person who invents or causes something'): from Old French *autor*, from Latin *auctor*, from *augere* 'increase, originate, promote'. The spelling with *th* arose in the 15th cent., and perhaps became established under the influence of *authentic*.

authoress ▶ **noun** a female author.

authoring ▶ **noun** [mass noun] Computing the creation of programs and databases for computer applications such as computer-assisted learning or multimedia products: [as modifier] *an authoring system*.

authoritarian /ɔːˌθɒrɪˈtɛːrɪən/ ▶ **adjective** favouring or enforcing strict obedience to authority at the expense of personal freedom: *the transition from an authoritarian to a democratic regime*. ■ showing a lack of concern for the wishes or opinions of others; dictatorial: *he had an authoritarian and at times belligerent manner*.
▶ **noun** an authoritarian person.
– DERIVATIVES **authoritarianism** noun.

authoritative /ɔːˈθɒrɪtətɪv, -ˌteɪtɪv/ ▶ **adjective 1** able to be trusted as being accurate or true; reliable: *clear, authoritative information and advice | an authoritative source*. ■ (of a text) considered to be the best of its kind and unlikely to be improved upon: *this is likely to become the authoritative study of the subject*.
2 commanding and self-confident; likely to be respected and obeyed: *his voice was calm and authoritative*. ■ proceeding from an official source and requiring compliance or obedience: *authoritative directives*.
– DERIVATIVES **authoritatively** adverb, **authoritativeness** noun.

authority ▶ **noun** (pl. **authorities**) **1** [mass noun] the power or right to give orders, make decisions, and enforce obedience: *he had absolute authority over his subordinates | a rebellion against those in authority*. ■ [often with infinitive] the right to act in a specified way, delegated from one person or organization to another: *military forces have the legal authority to arrest drug traffickers*. ■ official permission; sanction: *the money was spent without parliamentary authority*.
2 (often **authorities**) a person or organization having political or administrative power and control: *health authorities issued a worldwide alert*.
3 [mass noun] the power to influence others, especially because of one's commanding manner or one's recognized knowledge about something: *he has the natural authority of one who is used to being obeyed*. ■ the confidence resulting from personal expertise: *he hit the ball with authority*. ■ [count noun] a person with extensive or specialized knowledge about a subject; an expert: *he was an authority on the stock market*. ■ [count noun] a book or other source able to supply reliable information or evidence.
– PHRASES **have something on good authority** have ascertained something from a reliable source.
– ORIGIN Middle English: from Old French *autorite*, from Latin *auctoritas*, from *auctor* 'originator, promoter' (see **AUTHOR**).

authority figure ▶ **noun** a person who has or represents authority: *these techniques can help parents re-establish their role as authority figures*.

authorization (also **authorisation**) ▶ **noun** [mass noun] the action of authorizing: *the raising of revenue and the authorization of spending*. ■ [count noun] a document giving official permission.

authorize (also **authorise**) ▶ **verb** [with obj.] give official permission for or approval to (an undertaking or agent): *the government authorized further aircraft production* | [with obj. and infinitive] *the troops were authorized to use force*.
– ORIGIN late Middle English: from Old French *autoriser*, from medieval Latin *auctorizare*, from *auctor* 'originator, promoter' (see **AUTHOR**).

authorized ▶ **adjective** having official permission or approval: *an authorized dealer | authorized access to the computer*.

Authorized Version ▶ **noun** chiefly Brit. an English translation of the Bible made in 1611 at the order of James I and still widely used, though never formally 'authorized'. Also called **KING JAMES BIBLE**.

autism /ˈɔːtɪz(ə)m/ ▶ **noun** [mass noun] a mental condition, present from early childhood, characterized by great difficulty in communicating and forming relationships with other people and in using language and abstract concepts. ■ a mental condition in which fantasy dominates over reality, as a symptom of schizophrenia and other disorders.
– DERIVATIVES **autist** noun.
– ORIGIN early 20th cent.: from Greek *autos* 'self' + **-ISM**.

autistic /ɔːˈtɪstɪk/ ▶ **adjective** relating to or affected by autism.
▶ **noun** an autistic person.

autistic spectrum disorder ▶ **noun** [mass noun] any condition in which the subject displays autistic characteristics.

auto¹ ▶ **noun** (pl. **autos**) [usu. as modifier] informal, chiefly N. Amer. a car: *the auto industry*.
– ORIGIN late 19th cent.: abbreviation of **AUTOMOBILE**.

auto² ▶ **adjective & noun** short for **AUTOMATIC**.

auto-¹ (usu. **aut-** before a vowel) ▶ **combining form** self: *auto-analysis*. ■ one's own: *autograph*. ■ by oneself or spontaneous: *autoxidation*. ■ by itself or automatic: *autofocusing*.
– ORIGIN from Greek *autos* 'self'.

auto-² ▶ **combining form** relating to cars: *autocross*.
– ORIGIN abbreviation of **AUTOMOBILE**.

autoantibody ▶ **noun** (pl. **autoantibodies**) Physiology an antibody produced by an organism in response to a constituent of its own tissues.

autobahn /ˈɔːtə(ʊ)bɑːn/, German /ˈaʊtəbaːn/ ▶ **noun** a German, Austrian, or Swiss motorway.
– ORIGIN 1930s: from German, from *Auto* 'motor car' + *Bahn* 'path, road'.

autobiographical ▶ **adjective** (of a written work) dealing with the writer's own life: *an autobiographical account | the book is partly autobiographical*.
– DERIVATIVES **autobiographic** adjective, **autobiographically** adverb.

autobiography ▶ **noun** (pl. **autobiographies**) an account of a person's life written by that person. ■ [mass noun] such writing as a literary genre.
– DERIVATIVES **autobiographer** noun.

autocar ▶ **noun** archaic a motor vehicle.

autocatalysis ▶ **noun** [mass noun] Chemistry catalysis of a reaction by one of its products.
– DERIVATIVES **autocatalytic** adjective.

A

autocephalous /ˌɔːtə(ʊ)ˈsɛf(ə)ləs, -ˈkɛf-/ ▶ adjective (of an Eastern Christian Church) appointing its own head, not subject to the authority of an external patriarch or archbishop.
– ORIGIN mid 19th cent.: from Greek *autokephalos* (from *autos* 'self' + *kephalē* 'head') + **-OUS**.

autochanger (also **autochange**) ▶ noun a mechanism for the automatic substitution of one CD or record for another during use.

autochrome ▶ noun [mass noun] [usu. as modifier] an early form of colour photography using plates coated with dyed starch grains, patented by the Lumière brothers in 1904. ■ [count noun] a colour photograph made by this process.

autochthon /ɔːˈtɒkθ(ə)n, -θəʊn/ ▶ noun (pl. **autochthons** or **autochthones** /-θəniːz/) an original or indigenous inhabitant of a place; an aborigine.
– ORIGIN late 16th cent.: from Greek, literally 'sprung from the earth', from *autos* 'self' + *khthōn* 'earth, soil'.

autochthonous /ɔːˈtɒkθənəs/ ▶ adjective (of an inhabitant of a place) indigenous rather than descended from migrants or colonists. ■ Geology (of a deposit or formation) formed in its present position. Often contrasted with **ALLOCHTHONOUS**.

autoclave /ˈɔːtə(ʊ)kleɪv/ ▶ noun a strong heated container used for chemical reactions and other processes using high pressures and temperatures, e.g. steam sterilization.
▶ verb [with obj.] heat (something) in an autoclave.
– ORIGIN late 19th cent.: from French, from *auto-* 'self' + Latin *clavus* 'nail' or *clavis* 'key' (so named because it is self-fastening).

autocomplete ▶ noun Computing a software function that completes words or strings without the user needing to type them in full.

autocorrelation ▶ noun [mass noun] Mathematics & Statistics correlation between the elements of a series and others from the same series separated from them by a given interval. ■ [count noun] a calculation of such correlation.

autocracy /ɔːˈtɒkrəsi/ ▶ noun (pl. **autocracies**) [mass noun] a system of government by one person with absolute power. ■ [count noun] a state or society governed by one person with absolute power. ■ domineering rule or control: *a boss who shifts between autocracy and consultation*.
– ORIGIN mid 17th cent. (in the sense 'autonomy'): from Greek *autokrateia*, from *autokratēs* (see **AUTOCRAT**).

autocrat ▶ noun a ruler who has absolute power. ■ an imperious person who insists on complete obedience from others.
– ORIGIN early 19th cent.: from French *autocrate*, from Greek *autokratēs*, from *autos* 'self' + *kratos* 'power'.

autocratic ▶ adjective relating to a ruler who has absolute power: *the constitutional reforms threatened his autocratic power*. ■ taking no account of other people's wishes or opinions; domineering: *a man with a reputation for an autocratic management style*.
– DERIVATIVES **autocratically** adverb.

autocrine /ˈɔːtə(ʊ)krʌɪn/ ▶ adjective Biochemistry denoting or relating to a cell-produced substance that has an effect on the cell by which it is secreted.
– ORIGIN 1980s: from **AUTO-**[1] + Greek *krinein* 'to separate'.

autocross ▶ noun [mass noun] Brit. a form of motor racing in which cars are driven singly or in heats over a course including rough terrain or unmade roads. Compare with **RALLYCROSS**. ■ N. Amer. a form of competition in which cars are driven around an obstacle course, typically marked out by cones on an empty car park.
– ORIGIN 1960s: blend of **AUTOMOBILE** and **CROSS-COUNTRY**.

autocue ▶ noun trademark, Brit. a device which projects an enlarged image of a script on to a clear glass screen in front of a person speaking on television or in public, so enabling the speaker to read their speech while appearing to be looking at the viewers or audience.

auto-da-fé /ˌɔːtəʊdɑːˈfeɪ/ ▶ noun (pl. **autos-da-fé** /ˌɔːtəʊz-/) the burning of a heretic by the Spanish Inquisition. ■ a sentence of such a kind.
– ORIGIN early 18th cent.: from Portuguese, literally 'act of the faith'.

autodial ▶ verb (**autodials**, **autodialling**, **autodialled**; US **autodials**, **autodialing**, **autodialed**) [no obj.] Computing (of a modem) automatically dial a telephone number or establish a connection with a computer.
– DERIVATIVES **autodialler** noun.

autodidact /ˈɔːtəʊdɪdakt/ ▶ noun a self-taught person.
– DERIVATIVES **autodidactic** adjective.
– ORIGIN mid 18th cent.: from Greek *autodidaktos* 'self-taught', from *autos* 'self' + *didaskein* 'teach'.

auto-erotic ▶ adjective relating to sexual excitement generated by stimulating or fantasizing about one's own body.
– DERIVATIVES **auto-eroticism** noun.

auto-exposure ▶ noun a device which sets the exposure automatically on a camera. ■ [mass noun] the facility to set exposure automatically.

autofill ▶ noun Computing a software function that completes data in browser forms without the user needing to type it in full.

autofocus ▶ noun a device focusing a camera or other piece of equipment automatically. ■ [mass noun] the facility for automatic focusing.
– DERIVATIVES **autofocusing** noun.

autogamy /ɔːˈtɒgəmi/ ▶ noun Biology self-fertilization, especially the self pollination of a flower. Compare with **ALLOGAMY**.
– DERIVATIVES **autogamous** adjective.
– ORIGIN late 19th cent.: from **AUTO-**[1] 'self' + Greek *-gamia* (from *gamos* 'marriage').

autogenic /ˌɔːtə(ʊ)ˈdʒɛnɪk/ ▶ adjective technical self-generated: *autogenic succession*.

autogenic training ▶ noun [mass noun] a form of relaxation therapy involving auto-suggestion.

autogenous /ɔːˈtɒdʒɪnəs/ ▶ adjective arising from within or from a thing itself. ■ (of welding) done either without a filler or with a filler of the same metal as the pieces being welded.

autogiro (also **autogyro**) ▶ noun (pl. **autogiros**) a form of aircraft with freely rotating horizontal blades and a propeller. It differs from a helicopter in that the blades are not powered but rotate in the slipstream, propulsion being by a conventional mounted engine.
– ORIGIN 1920s: from Spanish, from *auto-* 'self' + *giro* 'gyration'.

autograft ▶ noun a graft of tissue from one point to another of the same individual's body.

autograph ▶ noun **1** a signature, especially that of a celebrity written as a memento for an admirer: *fans surged around the car asking for autographs*.
2 a manuscript or musical score in an author's or musician's own handwriting. ■ [mass noun] a person's handwriting.
▶ verb [with obj.] write one's signature on (something); sign: *the whole team autographed a shirt for him* | (as adj. **autographed**) *an autographed photo*.
▶ adjective written in the author's own handwriting: *an autograph manuscript*. ■ (of a painting or sculpture) done by the artist, not by a copier.
– DERIVATIVES **autographic** adjective.
– ORIGIN early 17th cent.: from French *autographe* or late Latin *autographum*, from Greek *autographon*, neuter of *autographos* 'written with one's own hand', from *autos* 'self' + *graphos* 'written'.

autography ▶ noun [mass noun] **1** writing done with one's own hand.
2 the facsimile reproduction of writing or illustration.
3 [count noun] an autobiography.

autoharp ▶ noun a kind of zither fitted with a series of sprung and padded bars which allow the playing of chords by damping selected strings.

autohypnosis ▶ noun [mass noun] induction of a hypnotic state in oneself; self-hypnosis.
– DERIVATIVES **autohypnotic** adjective.

autoimmune ▶ adjective Medicine relating to disease caused by antibodies or lymphocytes produced against substances naturally present in the body: *the infection triggers an autoimmune response*.
– DERIVATIVES **autoimmunity** noun.

autointoxication ▶ noun [mass noun] Medicine poisoning by a toxin formed within the body itself.

autologous /ɔːˈtɒləgəs/ ▶ adjective (of cells or tissues) obtained from the same individual.

autolysis /ɔːˈtɒlɪsɪs/ ▶ noun [mass noun] Biology the destruction of cells or tissues by their own enzymes, especially those released by lysosomes.
– DERIVATIVES **autolytic** adjective.

automagically /ɔːtəˈmadʒɪkli/ ▶ adverb informal (especially in relation to the operation of a computer process) automatically and in a way that seems ingenious, inexplicable, or magical: *just type in the name of what you want to listen to, and it automagically appears on your computer*.
– ORIGIN 1940s: blend of **AUTOMATICALLY** and **MAGICALLY**.

automaker ▶ noun N. Amer. a company which manufactures cars.

automat ▶ noun US historical a cafeteria in which food and drink were obtained from slot machines.
– ORIGIN late 17th cent. (denoting an automaton): from German, from French *automate*, from Latin *automaton* (see **AUTOMATON**). The current sense dates from the early 20th cent.

automate ▶ verb [with obj.] convert (a process or facility) to be operated by largely automatic equipment: *industry is investing in automating production* | (as adj. **automated**) *a fully automated process*.
– ORIGIN 1950s: back-formation from **AUTOMATION**.

automated teller machine ▶ noun a machine that automatically provides cash and performs other banking services on insertion of a special card by the account holder.

automatic ▶ adjective **1** (of a device or process) working by itself with little or no direct human control: *an automatic kettle that switches itself off when it boils* | *calibration is fully automatic*. ■ (of a firearm) self-loading and able to fire continuously until the ammunition is exhausted or the pressure on the trigger is released. ■ (of a motor vehicle or its transmission) using gears that change by themselves according to speed and acceleration.
2 done or occurring spontaneously, without conscious thought or attention: *automatic physical functions such as breathing* | *'Nice to meet you,' he said, with automatic politeness*. ■ done or occurring as a matter of course and without debate: *he is the automatic choice for the senior team*. ■ (especially of a legal sanction) given or imposed as a necessary and inevitable result of a fixed rule or particular set of circumstances: *he received an automatic one-match suspension*.
▶ noun **1** a gun that continues firing until the ammunition is exhausted or the pressure on the trigger is released.
2 a vehicle with automatic transmission.
– DERIVATIVES **automatically** adverb, **automaticity** noun.
– ORIGIN mid 18th cent.: from Greek *automatos* 'acting of itself' (see **AUTOMATON**) + **-IC**.

automatic gain control ▶ noun [mass noun] Electronics a feature of certain amplifier circuits which gives a constant output over a wide range of input levels.

automatic pilot ▶ noun a device for keeping an aircraft on a set course without the intervention of the pilot.
– PHRASES **on automatic pilot** out of routine or habit, without concentration or conscious thought: *I leapt out of bed and dressed on automatic pilot*.

automatic translation ▶ noun another term for **MACHINE TRANSLATION**.

automatic writing ▶ noun [mass noun] writing said to be produced by a spiritual, occult, or subconscious agency rather than by the conscious intention of the writer.

automation ▶ noun [mass noun] the use or introduction of automatic equipment in a manufacturing or other process or facility.
– ORIGIN 1940s (originally US): irregular formation from **AUTOMATIC** + **-ATION**.

automatism /ɔːˈtɒmətɪz(ə)m/ ▶ noun [mass noun] Psychiatry the performance of actions without conscious thought or intention. ■ [count noun] an action performed unconsciously or involuntarily. ■ Art the avoidance of conscious intention in producing works of art, especially by using mechanical techniques or subconscious associations.
– ORIGIN mid 19th cent.: from French *automatisme*, from *automate* 'automaton', from Greek *automatos* 'acting of itself' (see **AUTOMATON**).

automatize /ɔːˈtɒmətʌɪz/ (also **automatise**) ▶ verb [with obj.] (usu. as adj. **automatized**) make automatic or habitual: *the need to refresh automatized forms of literature*.
– DERIVATIVES **automatization** noun.

automaton /ɔːˈtɒmət(ə)n/ ▶ noun (pl. **automata** /-tə/ or **automatons**) a moving mechanical device made in imitation of a human being. ■ a machine which performs a range of functions according to a predetermined set of coded instructions.
– ORIGIN early 17th cent.: via Latin from Greek, neuter of *automatos* 'acting of itself', from *autos* 'self'.

A

automobile ▶ noun chiefly N. Amer. a car.
– ORIGIN late 19th cent.: from French, from *auto-* 'self' + *mobile* 'mobile'.

automotive /ˌɔːtəˈməʊtɪv/ ▶ adjective relating to or concerned with motor vehicles.

autonomic /ˌɔːtəˈnɒmɪk/ ▶ adjective chiefly Physiology involuntary or unconscious; relating to the autonomic nervous system.
– ORIGIN mid 19th cent. (in the sense 'self-governing'): from AUTONOMY + -IC.

autonomic nervous system ▶ noun the part of the nervous system responsible for control of the bodily functions not consciously directed, such as breathing, the heartbeat, and digestive processes.

autonomous ▶ adjective (of a country or region) having the freedom to govern itself or control its own affairs: *the federation included sixteen autonomous republics.* ■ having the freedom to act independently: *school governors are legally autonomous.* ■ (in Kantian moral philosophy) acting in accordance with one's moral duty rather than one's desires. Compare with HETERONOMOUS.
– DERIVATIVES **autonomously** adverb.
– ORIGIN early 19th cent.: from Greek *autonomos* 'having its own laws' + -OUS.

autonomy /ɔːˈtɒnəmi/ ▶ noun (pl. **autonomies**) [mass noun] the right or condition of self-government: *between the First and Second World Wars, Canada gained greater autonomy from Britain.* ■ [count noun] a self-governing country or region. ■ freedom from external control or influence; independence. ■ (in Kantian moral philosophy) the capacity of an agent to act in accordance with objective morality rather than under the influence of desires.
– DERIVATIVES **autonomist** noun & adjective.
– ORIGIN early 17th cent.: from Greek *autonomia*, from *autonomos* 'having its own laws', from *autos* 'self' + *nomos* 'law'.

autopilot ▶ noun short for AUTOMATIC PILOT.

autopista /ˌɔːtə(ʊ)ˈpiːstə/, Spanish /autəʊˈpista/ ▶ noun a motorway in a Spanish-speaking country.
– ORIGIN 1950s: from Spanish, from *auto* 'automobile' + *pista* 'track'.

autopsy /ˈɔːtɒpsi, ɔːˈtɒpsi/ ▶ noun (pl. **autopsies**) a post-mortem examination to discover the cause of death or the extent of disease.
▶ verb (**autopsies, autopsying, autopsied**) [with obj.] perform an autopsy on (a body or organ).
– ORIGIN mid 17th cent. (in the sense 'personal observation'): from French *autopsie* or modern Latin *autopsia*, from Greek, from *autoptēs* 'eyewitness', from *autos* 'self' + *optos* 'seen'.

autoradiogram /ˌɔːtəʊˈreɪdɪə(ʊ)gram/ ▶ noun another term for AUTORADIOGRAPH.

autoradiograph ▶ noun a photograph of an object produced by radiation from radioactive material in the object.
▶ verb [with obj.] make an autoradiograph of.
– DERIVATIVES **autoradiographic** adjective, **autoradiography** noun.

autorickshaw ▶ noun (in South Asia) a motorized, three-wheeled rickshaw for public hire.

autorotation ▶ noun [mass noun] rotation of an object caused by the flow of moving air or water around the shape of the object (e.g. a winged seed). ■ autorotation in the rotor blades of a helicopter that is descending without engine power.
– DERIVATIVES **autorotate** verb.

autoroute ▶ noun a French motorway.
– ORIGIN 1960s: from French, from *auto(mobile)* 'car' + *route* 'route'.

autosave Computing ▶ noun a software facility which automatically saves a user's work at regular intervals.
▶ verb [with obj.] save (work) automatically using the autosave facility.

autoshaping ▶ noun [mass noun] Psychology conditioning in which the conditioned response has not been reinforced by reward or punishment, but is a modified instinctive response to certain stimuli.

autosome /ˈɔːtəsəʊm/ ▶ noun Biology any chromosome that is not a sex chromosome.
– DERIVATIVES **autosomal** adjective.

autostrada /ˈɔːtə(ʊ)ˌstrɑːdə/, Italian /autəʊˈstrada/ ▶ noun (pl. **autostradas** or **autostrade** /-deɪ/, Italian /-de/) an Italian motorway.
– ORIGIN 1920s: from Italian, from *auto* 'automobile' + *strada* 'road'.

autosuggestion ▶ noun [mass noun] the hypnotic or subconscious adoption of an idea which one has originated oneself.

autotelic /ˌɔːtə(ʊ)ˈtɛlɪk/ ▶ adjective formal (of an activity or a creative work) having an end or purpose in itself.
– ORIGIN early 20th cent.: from AUTO-[1] 'self' + Greek *telos* 'end' + -IC.

autotomy /ɔːˈtɒtəmi/ ▶ noun [mass noun] Zoology the casting off of a part of the body (e.g. the tail of a lizard) by an animal under threat.

autotoxin ▶ noun a substance produced by an organism which is toxic to itself.
– DERIVATIVES **autotoxic** adjective.

autotransformer ▶ noun an electrical transformer which has a single winding of which part is common to both primary and secondary circuits.

autotransplantation ▶ noun [mass noun] transplantation of tissue from one site to another in the same individual.
– DERIVATIVES **autotransplant** noun, **autotransplanted** adjective.

autotroph /ˈɔːtə(ʊ)trəʊf, -trɒf/ ▶ noun Biology an organism that is able to form nutritional organic substances from simple inorganic substances such as carbon dioxide. Compare with HETEROTROPH.
– DERIVATIVES **autotrophic** adjective, **autotrophy** noun.

autotune ▶ noun a device or facility for tuning something automatically.

autotype ▶ noun 1 a facsimile.
2 [mass noun] a photographic printing process for monochrome reproduction.

autoworker ▶ noun chiefly N. Amer. a worker in the motor vehicle manufacturing industry.

autoxidation /ˌɔːtɒksɪˈdeɪʃ(ə)n/ ▶ noun [mass noun] Chemistry spontaneous oxidation of a substance at ambient temperatures in the presence of oxygen.
– DERIVATIVES **autoxidize** (also **autoxidise**) verb.

autumn ▶ noun chiefly Brit. the season after summer and before winter, in the northern hemisphere from September to November and in the southern hemisphere from March to May: *the countryside is ablaze with colour in autumn* | figurative *he was in the autumn of his life.* ■ Astronomy the period from the autumn equinox to the winter solstice.
– ORIGIN late Middle English: from Old French *autompne*, or later directly from Latin *autumnus*.

autumnal ▶ adjective of, characteristic of, or occurring in autumn: *rich autumnal colours.*
– ORIGIN late 16th cent.: from Latin *autumnalis*, from *autumnus* 'autumn'.

autumn crocus ▶ noun a crocus-like Eurasian plant of the lily family, cultivated for its autumn-blooming flowers. ● Genus *Colchicum*, family Liliaceae: several species, in particular meadow saffron.

autumn equinox (also **autumnal equinox**) ▶ noun the equinox in autumn, on about 22 September in the northern hemisphere and 20 March in the southern hemisphere. ■ Astronomy the equinox in September.

autunite /ˈɔːtʌnʌɪt/ ▶ noun [mass noun] a yellow mineral occurring as square crystals which fluoresce in ultraviolet light. It is a hydrated phosphate of calcium and uranium.
– ORIGIN mid 19th cent.: from *Autun*, the name of a town in eastern France, + -ITE[1].

Auvergne /əʊˈvɛːn/, French /ovɛʀɲ/ a region of south central France and a province of the Roman Empire. The region is mountainous and contains the extinct volcanic cones known as the Puys.
– ORIGIN from Latin *Arverni*, the name of a Celtic tribe who lived there in Roman times.

auxiliary /ɔːgˈzɪlɪəri, ɒg-/ ▶ adjective providing supplementary or additional help and support: *auxiliary airport staff* | *the ship has an auxiliary power source.* ■ (of troops) engaged in the service of a nation at war but not part of the regular army. ■ (of a sailing vessel) equipped with a supplementary engine: *an auxiliary schooner.*
▶ noun (pl. **auxiliaries**) an auxiliary person or thing: *a nursing auxiliary* | *there are two main fuel tanks and two auxiliaries.* ■ N. Amer. a group of volunteers giving supplementary support to an organization or institution: *members of the Volunteer Fire Department's women's auxiliary.* ■ Grammar an auxiliary verb. ■ a naval vessel with a supporting role, not armed for combat.
– ORIGIN late Middle English: from Latin *auxiliarius*, from *auxilium* 'help'.

auxiliary verb ▶ noun Grammar a verb used in forming the tenses, moods, and voices of other verbs. The primary auxiliary verbs in English are *be, do,* and *have*; the modal auxiliaries are *can, could, may, might, must, shall, should, will,* and *would.*

auxin /ˈɔːksɪn/ ▶ noun [mass noun] a plant hormone which causes the elongation of cells in shoots and is involved in regulating plant growth. See also INDOLEACETIC ACID.
– ORIGIN 1930s: coined in German from Greek *auxein* 'to increase' + -IN[1].

auxotroph /ˈɔːksətrəʊf, -trɒf/ ▶ noun Biology a mutant organism (especially a bacterium or fungus) that requires a particular additional nutrient which the normal strain does not.
– DERIVATIVES **auxotrophic** adjective.
– ORIGIN 1950s: from Latin *auxilium* 'help' + Greek *trophos* 'feeder'.

AV ▶ abbreviation ■ audiovisual (teaching aids). ■ Authorized Version.

Av ▶ noun variant spelling of AB[1].

avadavat /ˈavədəvat/ (also **amadavat**) ▶ noun a small South Asian waxbill that is widely kept as a cage bird. The male has red or green plumage and a red bill. Also called MUNIA. ● Genus *Amandava*, family Estrildidae: the **red avadavat** (*A. amandava*) and the **green avadavat** (*A. formosa*).
– ORIGIN late 17th cent.: named after the city of AHMADABAD in India, where the birds were sold.

avail ▶ verb 1 (**avail oneself of**) formal use or take advantage of (an opportunity or available resource): *my daughter did not avail herself of my advice.*
2 [with obj.] literary help or benefit: *no amount of struggle availed Charles.*
▶ noun (usu. in phrase **of/to no avail**) use or benefit: *he begged her to reconsider, but to no avail.*
– PHRASES **avail someone nothing** archaic (of an action) be of no help at all to someone.
– ORIGIN Middle English: from obsolete *vail* 'be of use or value' (apparently on the pattern of pairs such as *amount, mount*), from Old French *valoir*, from Latin *valere* 'be strong, be of value'.

available ▶ adjective able to be used or obtained; at someone's disposal: *refreshments will be available all afternoon* | *community health services* **available to** *Londoners.* ■ (of a person) not otherwise occupied; free to do something: *the nurse is only available at certain times* | *the minister was not available for comment.*
– DERIVATIVES **availability** noun.
– ORIGIN late Middle English (in the senses 'effectual, serviceable' and 'legally valid'): from AVAIL + -ABLE. The sense 'at someone's disposal' dates from the early 19th cent.

avalanche /ˈavəlɑːnʃ/ ▶ noun 1 a mass of snow, ice, and rocks falling rapidly down a mountainside. ■ a large mass of mud or other material moving rapidly downhill: *an avalanche of mud.*
2 a sudden arrival or occurrence of something in overwhelming quantities: *we have had an avalanche of applications for the post.*
3 Physics a cumulative process in which a fast-moving ion or electron generates further ions and electrons by collision.
▶ verb [no obj.] 1 (of a mass of snow, ice, etc.) descend rapidly down a mountainside. ■ [with obj.] engulf or carry off by an avalanche: *the climbers were avalanched down the south face of the mountain.*
2 Physics undergo a rapid increase in conductivity due to an avalanche process.
– ORIGIN late 18th cent.: from French, alteration of the Alpine dialect word *lavanche* (of unknown origin), influenced by *avaler* 'descend'; compare with Italian *valanga*.

Avalon /ˈavəlɒn/ (in Arthurian legend) the place to which Arthur was conveyed after death.

avant- /ˈavɒ̃/ ▶ combining form (especially with reference to popular music) original or innovative; avant-garde: *even in avant-rock, a song's words are usually its focus.*

avant-garde /ˌavɒ̃ˈgɑːd/ ▶ noun (usu. **the avant-garde**) new and experimental ideas and methods in art, music, or literature: *he has been called a promoter of the avant-garde.* ■ a group of artists, musicians, or writers working with new and experimental ideas and methods: *works by artists of the Russian avant-garde.*

A

▸ **adjective** favouring or introducing new and experimental ideas and methods: *a controversial avant-garde composer.*
– DERIVATIVES **avant-gardism** noun, **avant-gardist** noun.
– ORIGIN late Middle English (denoting the vanguard of an army): from French, literally 'vanguard'. Current senses date from the early 20th cent.

Avar /ə'vɑː/ ▸ **noun 1** a member of a nomadic equestrian people from central Asia who built up a large kingdom in SE Europe from the 6th century but were conquered by Charlemagne (791–9).
2 a member of a pastoral people of Dagestan in Russia, of uncertain relationship to the ancient Avars.
3 [mass noun] the North Caucasian language of the modern Avars.
▸ **adjective** relating to the Avars or their language.
– ORIGIN the name in Avar.

avarice ▸ **noun** [mass noun] extreme greed for wealth or material gain.
– ORIGIN Middle English: from Old French, from Latin *avaritia*, from *avarus* 'greedy'.

avaricious ▸ **adjective** having or showing an extreme greed for wealth or material gain: *an avaricious, manipulative woman.*
– DERIVATIVES **avariciously** adverb, **avariciousness** noun.
– ORIGIN late Middle English: from Old French *avaricieux*, based on Latin *avarus* 'greedy'.

avascular /ə'vaskjʊlə, eɪ-/ ▸ **adjective** Medicine characterized by or associated with a lack of blood vessels.

avast /ə'vɑːst/ ▸ **exclamation** Nautical stop; cease: *a sailor is expected to keep hauling until the mate hollers 'Avast!'.*
– ORIGIN early 17th cent.: from Dutch *hou'vast, houd vast* 'hold fast!'.

avatar /'avətɑː/ ▸ **noun 1** chiefly Hinduism a manifestation of a deity or released soul in bodily form on earth; an incarnate divine teacher. ■ an incarnation, embodiment, or manifestation of a person or idea: *he chose John Stuart Mill as the avatar of the liberal view.*
2 Computing an icon or figure representing a particular person in computer games, Internet forums, etc.
– ORIGIN from Sanskrit *avatāra* 'descent', from *ava* 'down' + *tar-* 'to cross'.

avaunt /ə'vɔːnt/ ▸ **exclamation** archaic go away: *avaunt, you worm-faced fellows of the night!*
– ORIGIN late Middle English: from an Anglo-Norman French variant of Old French *avant*, from Latin *ab* 'from' + *ante* 'before'.

ave /'ɑːveɪ/ ▸ **exclamation** literary used to express good wishes on meeting or parting.
▸ **noun 1** (**Ave**) short for AVE MARIA.
2 literary a shout of welcome or farewell.
– ORIGIN Middle English: from Latin, 'fare well!', singular imperative of *avere*.

Ave. ▸ **abbreviation** Avenue.

Avebury /'eɪvb(ə)ri/ a village in Wiltshire, site of one of Britain's major henge monuments of the late Neolithic period. The monument consists of a bank and ditch containing the largest known stone circle, with two smaller circles within it.

Ave Maria /ˌɑːveɪ mə'riːə/ ▸ **noun** a prayer to the Virgin Mary used in Catholic worship. The first line is adapted from Luke 1:28. Also called HAIL MARY.
– ORIGIN the opening words in Latin, literally 'hail, Mary!'.

avenge ▸ **verb** [with obj.] inflict harm in return for (an injury or wrong done to oneself or another): *he vowed in silent fervour to avenge their murders.* ■ inflict harm in return for an injury or wrong on behalf of (oneself or another): *we must avenge our dead | they **avenged** themselves **on** the interlopers.*
– DERIVATIVES **avenger** noun.
– ORIGIN late Middle English: from Old French *avengier*, from *a-* (from Latin *ad* 'to') + *vengier*, from Latin *vindicare* 'vindicate'.

avens /'eɪv(ə)nz/ ▸ **noun** a plant of the rose family, typically having serrated, divided leaves and seeds bearing small hooks. ● Genus *Geum*, family Rosaceae: several species, including the widespread **water avens** (*G. rivale*), with drooping pinkish flowers, and **wood avens** or herb bennet.
– ORIGIN Middle English: from Old French *avence* (medieval Latin *avencia*), of unknown origin.

aventurine /ə'vɛntʃərɪn/ ▸ **noun** [mass noun] **1** brownish glass containing sparkling particles of copper or gold: [as modifier] *aventurine glass.*
2 a translucent mineral containing small reflective particles, especially quartz containing mica or iron compounds, or feldspar containing haematite.
– ORIGIN early 18th cent.: from French, from Italian *avventurino*, from *avventura* 'chance' (because of its accidental discovery).

avenue ▸ **noun 1** a broad road in a town or city, typically having trees at regular intervals along its sides: *tree-lined avenues surround the hotel* | [in names] *Shaftesbury Avenue.* ■ [in names] N. Amer. a thoroughfare running at right angles to the streets in a city laid out on a grid pattern: *7th Avenue.* ■ Brit. a tree-lined approach to a country house or similar building: *an avenue of limes.*
2 a way of approaching a problem or making progress towards something: *three possible avenues of research suggested themselves.*
– ORIGIN early 17th cent. (in sense 2): from French, feminine past participle of *avenir* 'arrive, approach', from Latin *advenire*, from *ad-* 'towards' + *venire* 'come'.

aver /ə'vəː/ ▸ **verb** (**avers**, **averring**, **averred**) [reporting verb] formal state or assert to be the case: [with clause] *he averred that he was innocent of the allegations* | [with direct speech] *'I don't have to do anything—it's his problem,' Rory averred.* ■ [with obj.] Law allege as a fact in support of a plea.
– ORIGIN late Middle English (in the sense 'declare or confirm to be true'): from Old French *averer*, based on Latin *ad* 'to' (implying 'cause to be') + *verus* 'true'.

average ▸ **noun 1** the result obtained by adding several amounts together and then dividing this total by the number of amounts; the mean: *the proportion of over-60s is above the EU average of 19 per cent.* ■ an amount, standard, level, or rate regarded as usual or ordinary: *underground water reserves are **below average** | they take about thirty minutes **on average**.*
2 [mass noun] the apportionment of financial liability resulting from loss of or damage to a ship or its cargo. ■ reduction in the amount payable under an insurance policy, e.g. in respect of partial loss.
▸ **adjective** constituting the result obtained by adding together several amounts and then dividing this total by the number of amounts: *the average temperature in May was 4°C below normal.* ■ of the usual or ordinary amount, standard, level, or rate: *a woman of average height.* ■ having qualities that are seen as typical of a particular person, group, or thing: *the average lad likes a good night out.* ■ mediocre; not very good: *a very average director making very average movies.*
▸ **verb** [with obj.] amount to or achieve as an average rate or amount over a period of time; mean: *annual inflation averaged 2.4 per cent.* ■ calculate or estimate the average of: *the women earned only £35 weekly when their seasonal earnings were **averaged out**.* ■ [no obj.] (**average out**) result in an even distribution; even out: *it is reasonable to hope that the results will average out.* ■ [no obj.] (**average out at/to**) result in an average figure of: *the cost should average out at about £6 per page.*
– DERIVATIVES **averagely** adverb, **averageness** noun.
– ORIGIN late 15th cent.: from French *avarie* 'damage to ship or cargo', earlier 'customs duty', from Italian *avaria*, from Arabic *'awār* 'damage to goods'; the suffix *-age* is on the pattern of *damage*. Originally denoting a duty payable by the owner of goods to be shipped, the term later denoted the financial liability from goods lost or damaged at sea, and specifically the equitable apportionment of this between the owners of the vessel and of the cargo (late 16th cent.); this gave rise to the general sense of calculating the mean (mid 18th cent.).

avermectin /ˌeɪvə'mɛktɪn/ ▸ **noun** any of a group of compounds with strong anthelmintic properties, isolated from a strain of bacteria. Chemically, they are macrocyclic lactones with a disaccharide ring attached.
– ORIGIN 1970s: from modern Latin (*Streptomyces*) *averm(itilis)*, the name of the source actinomycete, + *ect-* (of unknown origin) + -IN[1].

averment /ə'vəːm(ə)nt/ ▸ **noun** formal an affirmation or allegation. ■ Law a formal statement by a party in a case of a fact or circumstance which the party offers to prove or substantiate.
– ORIGIN late Middle English: from Old French *averrement, averement*, from *averer* 'declare true' (see AVER).

Avernus /ə'vəːnəs/ a lake near Naples in Italy, which fills the crater of an extinct volcano. It was described by Virgil and other Latin writers as the entrance to the underworld.

Averroës /ə'vɛrəʊiːz/ (*c.*1126–98), Spanish-born Islamic philosopher, judge, and physician; Arabic name *ibn-Rushd*. His highly influential commentaries on Aristotle sought to reconcile Aristotle with Plato and the Greek philosophical tradition with the Arabic.

averse ▸ **adjective** [predic.] [usu. with negative] having a strong dislike of or opposition to something: *as a former CIA director, he is **not averse to** secrecy* | [in combination] *the bank's approach has been risk-averse.*
– ORIGIN late 16th cent.: from Latin *aversus* 'turned away from', past participle of *avertere* (see AVERT).

> **USAGE** 1 On the confusion of **averse** and **adverse**, see **USAGE** at **ADVERSE**
> 2 Traditionally, and according to Dr Johnson, **averse** *from* is preferred to **averse** *to*. The latter is condemned on etymological grounds (the Latin root translates as 'turn *from*'). However, **averse to** is entirely consistent with ordinary usage in modern English (on the analogy of *hostile to, disinclined to*, etc.) and is part of normal standard English.

aversion ▸ **noun** a strong dislike or disinclination: *they made plain their **aversion to** the use of force.* ■ someone or something that arouses such feelings.
– DERIVATIVES **aversive** adjective.
– ORIGIN late 16th cent. (originally denoting the action of turning away or averting one's eyes): from Latin *aversio(n-)*, from *avertere* 'turn away from' (see AVERT).

aversion therapy ▸ **noun** [mass noun] a type of behaviour therapy designed to make patients give up an undesirable habit by causing them to associate it with an unpleasant effect.

avert ▸ **verb** [with obj.] **1** turn away (one's eyes or thoughts): *she averted her eyes while we made stilted conversation.*
2 prevent or ward off (an undesirable occurrence): *talks failed to avert a rail strike.*
– DERIVATIVES **avertable** adjective.
– ORIGIN late Middle English (in the sense 'divert or deter someone from a place or a course of action'): from Latin *avertere*, from *ab-* 'from' + *vertere* 'to turn'; reinforced by Old French *avertir*.

Aves /'eɪviːz, 'ɑːveɪz/ ▸ **plural noun** Zoology a class of vertebrates which comprises the birds.
– ORIGIN Latin, plural of *avis* 'bird'.

Avesta /ə'vɛstə/ ▸ **noun** the sacred texts of Zoroastrianism, compiled in the 4th century.
– ORIGIN Persian.

Avestan /ə'vɛst(ə)n/ ▸ **adjective** relating to the Avesta or to the ancient Iranian language in which it is written, closely related to Vedic Sanskrit.
▸ **noun** [mass noun] the Avestan language.

avgas /'avgas/ ▸ **noun** [mass noun] aircraft fuel.
– ORIGIN 1940s: from *av(iation)* + GAS.

avian /'eɪvɪən/ ▸ **adjective** relating to birds: *avian tuberculosis.*
▸ **noun** a bird.
– ORIGIN late 19th cent.: from Latin *avis* 'bird' + -AN.

avian flu ▸ **noun** formal term for BIRD FLU.

aviary /'eɪvɪəri/ ▸ **noun** (pl. **aviaries**) a large cage, building, or enclosure for keeping birds in.
– ORIGIN late 16th cent.: from Latin *aviarium*, from *avis* 'bird'.

aviate /'eɪvɪeɪt/ ▸ **verb** pilot or fly in an aircraft: [with obj.] *an aircraft that can be aviated without effort* | [no obj.] *there are fewer opportunities to aviate in winter.*
– ORIGIN late 19th cent.: back-formation from AVIATION.

aviation ▸ **noun** [mass noun] the flying or operating of aircraft: [as modifier] *the aviation industry.*
– ORIGIN mid 19th cent.: from French, formed irregularly from Latin *avis* 'bird'.

aviator ▸ **noun** dated a pilot.

aviatrix /ˌeɪvɪ'eɪtrɪks/ ▸ **noun** (pl. **aviatrices** /-trɪsiːz/) dated a female pilot.

Avicenna /ˌavɪ'sɛnə/ (980–1037), Persian-born Islamic philosopher and physician; Arabic name *ibn-Sina*. His philosophical system, drawing on Aristotle but in many ways closer to Neoplatonism, was the major influence on the development of scholasticism. His *Canon of Medicine* was a standard medieval medical text.

avicularium /əˌvɪkjʊ'lɛːrɪəm/ ▸ **noun** (pl. **avicularia** /-rɪə/) Zoology (in some bryozoans) any of a number of modified zooids that take the form of a pair of snapping jaws resembling a bird's head, serving to prevent other organisms from settling on the colony. Compare with VIBRACULUM.

– ORIGIN mid 19th cent.: modern Latin, from *avicula*, diminutive of *avis* 'bird'.

aviculture /ˈeɪvɪˌkʌltʃə/ ▶ **noun** [mass noun] the breeding and rearing of birds.
– DERIVATIVES **avicultural** adjective, **aviculturalist** noun, **aviculturist** noun.
– ORIGIN late 19th cent.: from Latin *avis* 'bird' + CULTURE.

avid /ˈavɪd/ ▶ **adjective** having or showing a keen interest in or enthusiasm for something: *an avid reader of science fiction.* ■ (**avid for**) having an eager desire for: *she was avid for information about the murder inquiry.*
– DERIVATIVES **avidly** adverb.
– ORIGIN mid 18th cent.: from French *avide* or Latin *avidus*, from *avere* 'crave'.

avidin /ˈavɪdɪn/ ▶ **noun** [mass noun] Biochemistry a protein found in raw egg white, which combines with biotin and hinders its absorption.
– ORIGIN 1940s: from AVID + -IN[1].

avidity ▶ **noun** [mass noun] **1** keen interest or enthusiasm.
2 Biochemistry the overall strength of binding between an antibody and an antigen.
– ORIGIN late Middle English: from French *avidité* or Latin *aviditas*, from *avidus* 'eager, greedy'.

avifauna /ˈeɪvɪfɔːnə/ ▶ **noun** [mass noun] Zoology the birds of a particular region, habitat, or geological period.
– DERIVATIVES **avifaunal** adjective.
– ORIGIN late 19th cent.: from Latin *avis* 'bird' + FAUNA.

Avignon /ˈavɪnjɒ̃/, French /avijɔ̃/ a city on the Rhône in SE France; pop. 94,787 (2006). From 1309 until 1377 it was the residence of the popes during their exile from Rome, and was papal property until the French Revolution.

Ávila, Teresa of see TERESA OF ÁVILA, ST.

avionics /ˌeɪvɪˈɒnɪks/ ▶ **plural noun** [usu. treated as sing.] electronics as applied to aviation. ■ [usu. treated as pl.] electronic equipment fitted in an aircraft.
– ORIGIN 1940s: blend of AVIATION and ELECTRONICS.

avirulent /eɪˈvɪrjʊl(ə)nt, a-/ ▶ **adjective** (of a microorganism) not virulent.

avitaminosis /eɪˌvɪtəmɪˈnəʊsɪs, -ˌvʌɪt-/ ▶ **noun** (pl. **avitaminoses** /-siːz/) Medicine a condition resulting from a deficiency of a particular vitamin.

avizandum /ˌavɪˈzandəm/ ▶ **noun** [mass noun] Scots Law time taken for further consideration of a judgement.
– ORIGIN early 17th cent.: from medieval Latin, literally 'consideration', gerund of *avizare* 'consider, advise', from *ad-* 'to' + *visere*, frequentative of *videre* 'to see'.

avo /ˈɑːvəʊ/ ▶ **noun** (pl. **avos**) a monetary unit of Macao, equal to one hundredth of a pataca.
– ORIGIN Portuguese.

avocado /ˌavəˈkɑːdəʊ/ ▶ **noun** (pl. **avocados**) **1** (Brit. also **avocado pear**) a pear-shaped fruit with a rough leathery skin and smooth, oily edible flesh. Also called ALLIGATOR PEAR. ■ [mass noun] a light green colour like that of the flesh of avocados.
2 the tropical evergreen tree which bears the avocado fruit, native to Central America and widely cultivated elsewhere. ● *Persea americana*, family Lauraceae.
– ORIGIN mid 17th cent.: from Spanish, alteration (influenced by *avocado* 'advocate') of *aguacate*, from Nahuatl *ahuacatl*.

avocation /ˌavəˈkeɪʃ(ə)n/ ▶ **noun** formal a hobby or minor occupation.
– DERIVATIVES **avocational** adjective.
– ORIGIN mid 17th cent.: from Latin *avocatio(n-)*, from *avocare* 'call away', from *ab-* 'from' + *vocare* 'to call'.

avocet /ˈavəsɛt/ ▶ **noun** a long-legged wading bird with a slender upturned bill and strikingly patterned plumage. ● Genus *Recurvirostra*, family Recurvirostridae: four species, in particular *R. avosetta* of Eurasia, which has black-and-white plumage.
– ORIGIN late 17th cent.: from French *avocette*, from Italian *avosetta*.

Avogadro /ˌavəˈgɑːdrəʊ/, Amedeo (1776–1856), Italian chemist and physicist. His law, formulated in 1811, was used to derive both molecular weights and a system of atomic weights.

Avogadro's constant (also **Avogadro's number**) ▶ **noun** Chemistry the number of atoms or molecules in one mole of a substance, equal to 6.023×10^{23}.

Avogadro's law (also **Avogadro's hypothesis**) ▶ **noun** Chemistry a law stating that equal volumes of gases at the same temperature and pressure contain equal numbers of molecules.

avoid ▶ **verb** [with obj.] **1** keep away from or stop oneself from doing (something): *avoid excessive exposure to the sun* | *Gerard avoided meeting his eye.* ■ contrive not to meet (someone): *boys queued up to take Gloria out, but avoided Deirdre.* ■ not go to or through (a place): *this route avoids downtown Boston.* ■ prevent from happening: *book early to avoid disappointment.*
2 Law repudiate, nullify, or render void (a decree or contract).
PHRASES **avoid someone/thing like the plague** try hard to avoid someone or something: *a place that Robyn normally avoided like the plague.*
– DERIVATIVES **avoidance** noun, **avoider** noun.
– ORIGIN late Middle English: from Old French *evuider* 'clear out, get rid of', from *vuide* 'empty' (see VOID).

avoidable ▶ **adjective** able to be avoided or prevented: *the accident was entirely avoidable* | *avoidable costs.*
– DERIVATIVES **avoidably** adverb.

avoidance relationship ▶ **noun** a familial relationship that is forbidden according to rules operating in some traditional societies. In Australian Aboriginal society, for example, mothers-in-law and sons-in-law may not meet face to face or speak directly with one another.

avoidant ▶ **adjective** Psychology relating to or denoting a type of personality or behaviour characterized by the avoidance of intimacy or social interaction.

avoirdupois /ˌavwɑːdjʊˈpwɑː, ˌavədəˈpɔɪz/ ▶ **noun** a system of weights based on a pound of 16 ounces or 7,000 grains, widely used in English-speaking countries: [as modifier] *avoirdupois weights* | [postpositive] *a pound avoirdupois.* Compare with TROY. ■ humorous weight; heaviness: *she was putting on the avoirdupois like nobody's business.*
– ORIGIN Middle English (denoting merchandise sold by weight): from Old French *aveir de peis* 'goods of weight', from *aveir* 'to have' (infinitive used as a noun, from Latin *habere*) + *peis* 'weight' (see POISE[1]).

Avon 1 a river of central England which rises near the Leicestershire–Northamptonshire border and flows 154 km (96 miles) south-west through Stratford to the River Severn.
2 a river of SW England which rises near the Gloucestershire–Wiltshire border and flows 121 km (75 miles) through Bath and Bristol to the River Severn.
3 a former county of SW England, formed in 1974 from parts of north Somerset and Gloucestershire and replaced in 1996 by unitary councils of North Somerset, Bristol, South Gloucestershire, and Bath and NE Somerset.

avouch ▶ **verb** [with obj.] archaic affirm or assert.
– ORIGIN late 15th cent.: from Old French *avochier*, from Latin *advocare* 'summon in defence', from *ad-* 'to' + *vocare* 'to call'.

avow ▶ **verb** [reporting verb] assert or confess openly: [with clause] *he avowed that he had voted Labour in every election* | [with obj.] *he avowed his change of faith.*
– DERIVATIVES **avowal** noun.
– ORIGIN Middle English (in the senses 'acknowledge, approve' and 'vouch for'): from Old French *avouer* 'acknowledge', from Latin *advocare* 'summon in defence' (see AVOUCH).

avowed ▶ **adjective** [attrib.] that has been asserted, admitted, or stated publicly: *an avowed atheist* | *they came to power with the avowed aim of promoting religious toleration.*
– DERIVATIVES **avowedly** adverb.

avulsion /əˈvʌlʃ(ə)n/ ▶ **noun** [mass noun] chiefly Medicine the action of pulling or tearing away. ■ Law the sudden separation of land from one property and its attachment to another, especially by flooding or a change in the course of a river. Compare with ALLUVION.
– DERIVATIVES **avulse** verb.
– ORIGIN early 17th cent.: from Latin *avulsio(n-)*, from the verb *avellere*, from *ab-* 'from' + *vallere* 'pluck'.

avuncular /əˈvʌŋkjʊlə/ ▶ **adjective 1** kind and friendly towards a younger or less experienced person: *he was avuncular, reassuring, and trustworthy.*
2 Anthropology relating to the relationship between men and the children of their siblings.
– ORIGIN mid 19th cent.: from Latin *avunculus* 'maternal uncle', diminutive of *avus* 'grandfather'.

avunculate /əˈvʌŋkjʊlət/ ▶ **noun** (**the avunculate**) Anthropology the special relationship in some societies between a man and his sister's son.
– ORIGIN early 20th cent.: from Latin *avunculus* 'maternal uncle' + -ATE[2].

aw ▶ **exclamation** chiefly N. Amer. & Scottish used to express mild protest, entreaty, commiseration, or disapproval: *aw, come on, Andy.*
– ORIGIN natural exclamation: first recorded in American English in the mid 19th cent.

AWACS /ˈeɪwaks/ ▶ **abbreviation** airborne warning and control system, an airborne radar system for detecting enemy aircraft and directing friendly forces.

Awadh /ˈʌwəd/ variant spelling of OUDH.

await ▶ **verb** [with obj.] wait for (an event): *we await the proposals with impatience* | *remand prisoners awaiting trial* | (as adj., with submodifier **awaited**) *an eagerly awaited debut.* ■ (of an event or circumstance) be in store for (someone): *many dangers await them.*
– ORIGIN Middle English: from Anglo-Norman French *awaitier*, from *a-* (from Latin *ad* 'to, at') + *waitier* 'to wait'.

awake ▶ **verb** (past **awoke** ; past participle **awoken**) [no obj.] stop sleeping; wake from sleep: *she awoke to find the streets covered in snow.* ■ [with obj.] cause (someone) to wake from sleep: *my screams awoke my parents.* ■ regain consciousness: *I awoke none the worse for the operation.* ■ (**awake to**) become aware of; come to a realization of: *the authorities finally awoke to the extent of the problem.* ■ make or become active again: [with obj.] *there were echoes and scents which awoke some memory in me.*
▶ **adjective** [predic.] not asleep: *the noise might keep you awake at night.* ■ (**awake to**) aware of: *too few are awake to the dangers.*
– ORIGIN Old English *āwæcnan*, *āwacian*, both used in the sense 'come out of sleep' (see A-[2], WAKE[1]).

awaken ▶ **verb** [with obj.] rouse from sleep; cause to stop sleeping: *Anna was awakened by the telephone.* ■ [no obj.] stop sleeping: *he sighed but did not awaken.* ■ rouse (a feeling): *different images can awaken new emotions within us.* ■ (**awaken someone to**) make someone aware of (something) for the first time: *the film helped to awaken many to the horrors of apartheid.*
– ORIGIN Old English *onwæcnan*, from *on* 'on' + WAKEN.

awakening ▶ **noun 1** formal an act of waking from sleep.
2 an act or moment of becoming suddenly aware of something: *the war came as* ***a rude awakening to*** *the hardships of life.* ■ the beginning or rousing of something: *her sexual awakening* | *the awakening of vigorous political debate.*
▶ **adjective** coming into existence or awareness: *his awakening desire* | *an awakening conscience.*

award ▶ **verb** [with two objs] give or order the giving of (something) as an official payment, compensation, or prize to (someone): *he was awarded the Military Cross* | *a 3.5 per cent pay rise was awarded to staff.* ■ grant or assign (a contract or commission) to (a person or organization).
▶ **noun** a prize or other mark of recognition given in honour of an achievement: *the company's annual award for high-quality service.* ■ an amount of money given as an official payment, compensation, or grant: *a 1.5 per cent pay award.* ■ [mass noun] the action of giving a payment, compensation, or prize: *the award of an honorary doctorate* | [count noun] *an award of damages.*
– DERIVATIVES **awardee** noun, **awarder** noun.
– ORIGIN late Middle English (in the sense 'issue a judicial decision', also denoting the decision itself): from Anglo-Norman French *awarder*, variant of Old French *esguarder* 'consider, ordain', from *es-* (from Latin *ex* 'thoroughly') + *guarder* 'watch (over)', based on a word of Germanic origin related to WARD; compare with GUARD.

award-winning ▶ **adjective** having won a prize in recognition of quality: *award-winning food.*

aware ▶ **adjective** [predic.] having knowledge or perception of a situation or fact: *most people are* ***aware of*** *the dangers of sunbathing* | [with clause] *he was aware that a problem existed.* ■ [with adv. or in combination] concerned and well informed about a particular situation or development: *everyone needs to become more* ***environmentally aware***.
– ORIGIN Old English *gewær*, of West Germanic origin; related to German *gewahr*, also to WARE[3].

awareness ▶ **noun** [mass noun] knowledge or perception of a situation or fact: *we need to raise public awareness of the issue.* ■ concern about and well-informed interest in a particular situation or development: *a growing environmental awareness.*

awash ▶ **adjective** [predic.] covered or flooded with water, especially seawater or rain: *the boat rolled violently, her decks awash.* ■ containing large numbers or amounts of someone or something: *the city was awash with journalists.* ■ level with the surface of water so that it just washes over: *a rock awash outside the reef entrance.*

away ▶ **adverb 1** to or at a distance from a particular place or person: *she landed badly, and crawled away* | *they walked* ***away from*** *the vicarage in silence* | *we'll only be away for four nights.* ■ at a specified distance: *when he was ten or twelve feet away he stopped* | *we have had patients* ***from as far away as*** *Wales.* ■ at a specified future distance in time: *the wedding is only weeks away.* ■ towards a lower level; downwards: *in front of them the land fell away to the river.* ■ (with reference to sports fixtures) at the opponents' ground.
2 into an appropriate place for storage or safekeeping: *he put away the pistol.*
3 into non-existence: *Marie felt her distress ebbing away.*
4 constantly, persistently, or continuously: *there was Morrissey crooning away.*
▶ **adjective** (of a sporting contest) played at the opponents' ground: *tomorrow night's away game at Leicester.*
▶ **noun** an away match or win.
– PHRASES **away with** see **WITH**.
– ORIGIN Old English *onweg, aweg* 'on one's way' (see **A-²**, **WAY**).

awayday ▶ **noun** Brit. a day's leave or a day trip. ■ a day on which employees meet at a venue away from the workplace to plan strategy or to discuss a particular issue.
– ORIGIN 1970s: first denoting a type of money-saving return rail ticket.

awe ▶ **noun** [mass noun] a feeling of reverential respect mixed with fear or wonder: *they gazed in awe at the small mountain of diamonds* | *the sight filled me with awe.* ■ archaic capacity to inspire awe: *is it any wonder that Christmas Eve has lost its awe?*
▶ **verb** [with obj.] inspire with awe: *they were both awed by the vastness of the forest.*
– PHRASES **be** (or **stand**) **in awe of** feel awe for: *his staff members are in awe of him.*
– ORIGIN Old English *ege* 'terror, dread, awe', replaced in Middle English by forms related to Old Norse *agi*.

aweary ▶ **adjective** literary form of **WEARY**: *I am well aweary of it now.*

awed ▶ **adjective** filled with awe or wonder: *he spoke in a hushed, awed whisper* | *I watched her in awed silence.*

aweigh ▶ **adjective** [predic.] Nautical (of an anchor) raised just clear of the seabed.
– ORIGIN early 17th cent.: from **A-²** 'on' + **WEIGH¹**.

awe-inspiring ▶ **adjective** arousing awe through being impressive or formidable: *Michelangelo's awe-inspiring masterpiece.*
– DERIVATIVES **awe-inspiringly** adverb.

awesome ▶ **adjective** extremely impressive or daunting; inspiring awe: *the awesome power of the atomic bomb.* ■ informal extremely good; excellent: *the band is truly awesome!*
– DERIVATIVES **awesomely** adverb, **awesomeness** noun.
– ORIGIN late 16th cent. (in the sense 'filled with awe'): from **AWE** + **-SOME¹**.

awestruck (also **awestricken**) ▶ **adjective** filled with or revealing awe: *people were awestruck by the pictures sent back to earth.*

awful ▶ **adjective 1** very bad or unpleasant: *the place smelled awful* | *I look awful in a swimsuit* | *an awful speech.* ■ extremely shocking; horrific: *awful, bloody images.* ■ (of a person) very unwell or troubled: *I felt awful for being so angry with him* | *you look awful—you should go and lie down.*
2 [attrib.] used to emphasize the extent of something, especially something unpleasant or negative: *I've made an awful fool of myself.*
3 archaic inspiring reverential wonder or fear.
▶ **adverb** [as submodifier] informal, chiefly N. Amer. awfully; very: *we're an awful long way from the motorway.*
– PHRASES **an awful lot** a very large amount; a great deal: *we've had an awful lot of letters.*
– DERIVATIVES **awfulness** noun.
– ORIGIN Old English (see **AWE**, **-FUL**).

awfully ▶ **adverb 1** [as submodifier] informal very: *I'm awfully sorry to bother you so late* | *an awfully nice man.* ■ very much: *thanks awfully for the tea, Mr Oakley.*
2 very badly or unpleasantly: *we played awfully.*

awhile ▶ **adverb** for a short time: *stand here awhile.*
– ORIGIN Old English *āne hwīle* '(for) a while'.

> **USAGE** The single word **awhile** is an adverb meaning 'for a short time', and should not be confused with the noun use of **a while**, 'a period of time': *stand here* ***awhile***, but *we stood there* ***for a while***.

awhirl ▶ **adjective** [predic.] in a whirl; whirling: *her mind was awhirl with images.*

awkward ▶ **adjective 1** causing difficulty; hard to do or deal with: *some awkward questions* | *the wheelbarrow can be awkward to manoeuvre.* ■ deliberately unreasonable or uncooperative: *you're being damned awkward!*
2 causing or feeling uneasy embarrassment or inconvenience: *he had put her in a very awkward position* | *she felt awkward alone with him.*
3 not smooth or graceful; ungainly: *Luther's awkward movements impeded his progress.* ■ uncomfortable or abnormal: *make sure the baby isn't sleeping in an awkward position.*
– DERIVATIVES **awkwardly** adverb.
– ORIGIN late Middle English (in the sense 'the wrong way round, upside down'): from dialect *awk* 'backwards, perverse, clumsy' (from Old Norse *afugr* 'turned the wrong way') + **-WARD**.

awkwardness ▶ **noun** [mass noun] the quality of being awkward: *there was a moment of awkwardness* | *the awkwardness of youth.*

awl /ɔːl/ ▶ **noun** a small pointed tool used for piercing holes, especially in leather.
– ORIGIN Old English *æl*, of Germanic origin; related to German *Ahle*.

awn /ɔːn/ ▶ **noun** Botany a stiff bristle, especially one of those growing from the ear or flower of barley, rye, and many grasses.
– DERIVATIVES **awned** adjective.
– ORIGIN Old English, from Old Norse *ǫgn*; related to Swedish *agn*, Danish *avn*.

awning ▶ **noun** a sheet of canvas or other material stretched on a frame and used to keep the sun or rain off a shop window, doorway, or ship's deck.
– ORIGIN early 17th cent. (originally in nautical use): of unknown origin.

awoke past of **AWAKE**.

awoken past participle of **AWAKE**.

AWOL /ˈeɪwɒl/ ▶ **adjective** [usu. predic.] Military absent from where one should be but without intent to desert: *the men have* ***gone AWOL*** | humorous *now the parrot* ***has gone AWOL.***
– ORIGIN 1920s: acronym from *absent without (official) leave.*

awry /əˈrʌɪ/ ▶ **adverb & adjective** away from the usual or expected course; amiss: [as adv.] *many youthful romances* ***go awry*** | [as predic. adj.] *I got the impression that something was awry.* ■ out of the normal or correct position; askew: [as predic. adj.] *he was hatless, his silver hair awry.*
– ORIGIN late Middle English: from **A-²** 'on' + **WRY**.

AWS ▶ **abbreviation** Brit. automatic warning system, a system of providing train drivers with audible indications regarding signals and where necessary applying brakes automatically.

aw-shucks ▶ **adjective** N. Amer. informal self-deprecating and shy: *he's filled with aw-shucks niceness.*
– ORIGIN late 20th cent.: from **AW** + *shucks* (see **SHUCK**).

ax (also **aks**) ▶ **verb** dialect and West Indian form of **ASK**: *I'm axing plenty question.*

axe (US also **ax**) ▶ **noun 1** a tool used for chopping wood, typically of iron with a steel edge and wooden handle. ■ a measure intended to reduce costs drastically, especially one involving redundancies: *thirty staff are* ***facing the axe*** *at the Royal Infirmary.*
2 informal a musical instrument used in popular music or jazz, especially a guitar or (originally) a saxophone.
▶ **verb** [with obj.] **1** end, cancel, or dismiss suddenly and ruthlessly: *the company is axing 125 jobs* | *2,500 staff were axed as part of a rationalization programme.* ■ reduce (costs or services) drastically: *the Chancellor warned the cabinet to axe public spending.*
2 cut or strike with an axe, especially violently or destructively.
– PHRASES **have an axe to grind** have a private reason for doing or being involved in something.
– ORIGIN Old English *æx*, of Germanic origin; related to Dutch *aaks* and German *Axt*.

axe kick ▶ **noun** a type of kick used in tae kwon do and other martial arts, in which the opponent's head is struck with the heel of the foot.

axel /ˈaks(ə)l/ ▶ **noun** a jump in skating from the forward outside edge of one skate to the backward outside edge of the other, with one (or more) and a half turns in the air.
– ORIGIN 1930s: named after *Axel* R. Paulsen (1885–1938), Norwegian skater.

axeman (US also **axman**) ▶ **noun** (pl. **axemen**) **1** a man who works, fights, or commits violent attacks with an axe: *a mad axeman.* ■ informal a man who cuts costs drastically or ruthlessly.
2 informal a male rock or jazz guitarist.

axenic /eɪˈzɛnɪk/ ▶ **adjective** chiefly Botany relating to or denoting a culture that is free from living organisms other than the species required.
– DERIVATIVES **axenically** adverb.
– ORIGIN 1940s: from *a-* 'not' + Greek *xenikos* 'alien, strange' + **-IC**.

axes plural form of **AXIS¹**.

axial /ˈaksɪəl/ ▶ **adjective** relating to or forming an axis: *the main axial road.* ■ around an axis: *the axial rotation rate of the Earth.*
– DERIVATIVES **axially** adverb.

axil /ˈaksɪl/ ▶ **noun** Botany the upper angle between a leaf stalk or branch and the stem or trunk from which it is growing.
– ORIGIN late 18th cent.: from Latin *axilla* 'armpit' (see **AXILLA**).

axilla /akˈsɪlə/ ▶ **noun** (pl. **axillae** /-liː/) **1** Anatomy an armpit, or the corresponding part in a bird or other animal.
2 Botany an axil.
– ORIGIN early 17th cent.: from Latin, diminutive of *ala* 'wing'.

axillary /akˈsɪləri/ ▶ **adjective 1** Anatomy relating to the armpit or a corresponding part: *enlargement of the axillary lymph nodes.*
2 Botany in or growing from an axil: *axillary buds.* Often contrasted with **TERMINAL**.
▶ **noun** (also **axillary feather**) Ornithology feathers growing from the axilla.

axiom /ˈaksɪəm/ ▶ **noun** a statement or proposition which is regarded as being established, accepted, or self-evidently true: *the axiom that sport builds character.* ■ chiefly Mathematics a statement or proposition on which an abstractly defined structure is based.
– ORIGIN late 15th cent.: from French *axiome* or Latin *axioma*, from Greek *axiōma* 'what is thought fitting', from *axios* 'worthy'.

axiomatic /ˌaksɪəˈmatɪk/ ▶ **adjective** self-evident or unquestionable: *it is axiomatic that dividends have to be financed.* ■ chiefly Mathematics relating to or containing axioms.
– DERIVATIVES **axiomatically** adverb.
– ORIGIN late 18th cent.: from Greek *axiōmatikos*, from *axiōma* 'what is thought fitting' (see **AXIOM**).

axiomatize /ˌaksɪˈɒmətʌɪz/ (also **axiomatise**) ▶ **verb** [with obj.] express (a theory) as a set of axioms: *the attempts that are made to axiomatize linguistics.*

axion /ˈaksɪɒn/ ▶ **noun** Physics a hypothetical subatomic particle postulated to account for the rarity of processes which break charge–parity symmetry.
– ORIGIN 1970s: from **AXIAL** + **-ON**.

axis¹ /ˈaksɪs/ ▶ **noun** (pl. **axes** /-siːz/) **1** an imaginary line about which a body rotates: *the Earth revolves on its axis once every 24 hours.* ■ Geometry an imaginary straight line passing through the centre of a symmetrical solid, about which a plane figure can be conceived as rotating to generate the solid. ■ an imaginary line which divides something into equal or roughly equal halves, especially in the direction of its greatest length.
2 Mathematics a fixed reference line for the measurement of coordinates.
3 a straight central part in a structure to which other parts are connected. ■ Botany the central column of an inflorescence or other growth. ■ Zoology the skull and backbone of a vertebrate animal.
4 Anatomy the second cervical vertebra, below the atlas at the top of the backbone.
5 an agreement or alliance between two or more countries that forms a centre for an eventual larger grouping of nations: *the Anglo-American axis.* ■ (**the Axis**) the alliance of Germany and Italy formed before and during the Second World War, later extended to include Japan and other countries: [as modifier] *the Axis Powers.*
– ORIGIN late Middle English: from Latin, 'axle, pivot'.

axis² /ˈaksɪs/ (also **axis deer**) ▶ **noun** (pl. **same**) another term for **CHITAL**.

– ORIGIN early 17th cent.: from Latin, the name of an Indian animal mentioned by Pliny.

axisymmetric /ˌaksɪsɪˈmɛtrɪk/ ▶ **adjective** Geometry symmetrical about an axis.

axle /ˈaks(ə)l/ ▶ **noun** a rod or spindle (either fixed or rotating) passing through the centre of a wheel or group of wheels.
– ORIGIN Middle English (originally *axle-tree*): from Old Norse *ǫxultré*.

axle box ▶ **noun** (on a railway vehicle) a metal enclosure within which the end of an axle revolves.

axman ▶ **noun** US spelling of **AXEMAN**.

Axminster /ˈaksmɪnstə/ (also **Axminster carpet**) ▶ **noun** a kind of machine-woven patterned carpet with a cut pile.
– ORIGIN early 19th cent.: named after the town of *Axminster* in southern England, noted since the 18th cent. for the production of carpets.

axolotl /ˈaksəlɒt(ə)l/ ▶ **noun** a Mexican salamander which in natural conditions retains its aquatic newt-like larval form throughout life but is able to breed.
● *Ambystoma mexicanum*, family Ambystomatidae.
– ORIGIN late 18th cent.: from Nahuatl, from *atl* 'water' + *xolotl* 'servant'.

axon /ˈaksɒn/ ▶ **noun** the long thread-like part of a nerve cell along which impulses are conducted from the cell body to other cells. Compare with **DENDRITE**.
– DERIVATIVES **axonal** adjective.
– ORIGIN mid 19th cent. (denoting the body axis): from Greek *axōn* 'axis'.

axoneme /ˈaksə(ʊ)niːm/ ▶ **noun** Biology the central strand of a cilium or flagellum. It is composed of an array of microtubules, typically in nine pairs around two single central ones.
– DERIVATIVES **axonemal** adjective.
– ORIGIN early 20th cent.: from Greek *axōn* 'axis' + *nēma* 'thread'.

axonometric /ˌaks(ə)nə(ʊ)ˈmɛtrɪk/ ▶ **adjective** using or denoting an orthographic projection of an object, such as a building, on a plane inclined to each of the three principal axes of the object; three-dimensional but without perspective.

axoplasm /ˈaksə(ʊ)plaz(ə)m/ ▶ **noun** [mass noun] Biology the cytoplasm of a nerve axon.
– DERIVATIVES **axoplasmic** adjective.

Axum variant spelling of **AKSUM**.

ay ▶ **exclamation & noun** variant spelling of **AYE**[1].

Ayacucho /ˌʌɪəˈkuːtʃəʊ/ a city in the Andes of south central Peru; pop. 151,000 (est. 2009).

ayah /ˈʌɪə/ ▶ **noun** a nursemaid or nanny employed by Europeans in India or another former British territory.
– ORIGIN Anglo-Indian, from Portuguese *aia* 'nurse', feminine of *aio* 'tutor'.

ayahuasca /ˌʌɪəˈwaskə/ ▶ **noun** a tropical vine of the Amazon region, noted for its hallucinogenic properties. ● Genus *Banisteriopsis*, family Malpighiaceae: several species.
■ [mass noun] a hallucinogenic drink prepared from the bark of ayahuasca.
– ORIGIN from South American Spanish, from Quechua *ayawáskha*, from *aya* 'corpse' + *waskha* 'rope'.

ayatollah /ˌʌɪəˈtɒlə/ ▶ **noun** a high-ranking religious leader among Shiite Muslims, especially in Iran.
– ORIGIN 1950s: from Persian, from Arabic *'āyatu-llāh*, literally 'token of God'.

Ayatollah Khomeini see **KHOMEINI**.

Ayckbourn /ˈeɪkbɔːn/, Sir Alan (b.1939), English dramatist. He is known chiefly for comedies dealing with suburban and middle-class life, such as *Relatively Speaking* (1967) and *Absurd Person Singular* (1973).

aye[1] /ʌɪ/ (also **ay**) ▶ **exclamation** archaic or dialect said to express assent; yes: *aye, you're right there.* ■ (**aye aye**) Nautical a response accepting an order: *aye aye, captain.* ■ (in voting) I assent: *all in favour say aye.*
▶ **noun** an affirmative answer, especially in voting.
– PHRASES **the ayes have it** the affirmative votes are in the majority.
– ORIGIN late 16th cent.: probably from *I*, first person personal pronoun, expressing assent.

aye[2] /eɪ, ʌɪ/ ▶ **adverb** archaic or Scottish always or still: *I've aye fancied seeing Edinburgh.*
– PHRASES **for aye** forever.
– ORIGIN Middle English: from Old Norse *ei, ey*; related to Latin *aevum* 'age' and Greek *aie(i)* 'ever', *aiōn* 'aeon'.

aye-aye /ˈʌɪʌɪ/ ▶ **noun** a rare nocturnal Madagascan primate related to the lemurs. It has rodent-like incisor teeth and an elongated twig-like finger on each hand with which it prises insects from bark.
● *Daubentonia madagascariensis*, the only member of the family Daubentoniidae.
– ORIGIN late 18th cent.: from French, from Malagasy *aiay*.

Ayer /ɛː/, Sir A. J. (1910–89), English philosopher; full name *Alfred Jules Ayer*. Involved with the Vienna Circle in the 1930s, he was an important proponent of logical positivism. Notable work: *Language, Truth, and Logic* (1936).

Ayers Rock /ɛːz/ a red rock mass in Northern Territory, Australia, south-west of Alice Springs. The largest monolith in the world, it is 348 m (1,143 ft) high and about 9 km (6 miles) in circumference. Official name **ULURU**.
– ORIGIN named after Sir Henry *Ayers*, Premier of South Australia in 1872–3.

Ayesha /ɑːˈ(j)iːʃə/ the youngest wife of Muhammad.

Áyios Nikólaos /ˌajiɔs niˈkɔlaɔs/ Greek name for **AGHIOS NIKOLAOS**.

Aylesbury[1] /ˈeɪlzb(ə)ri/ a town in south central England, the county town of Buckinghamshire; pop. 69,300 (est. 2008).

Aylesbury[2] /ˈeɪlzb(ə)ri/ (also **Aylesbury duck**) ▶ **noun** (pl. **Aylesburys**) a domestic duck of a breed with white plumage.

Aymara /ˈʌɪmərɑː/ ▶ **noun** (pl. **same** or **Aymaras**) **1** a member of an American Indian people inhabiting the high plateau region of Bolivia and Peru near Lake Titicaca.
2 [mass noun] the language of the Aymara, with over 2 million speakers. It may be related to Quechua.
▶ **adjective** relating to the Aymara or their language.
– ORIGIN Bolivian Spanish.

Ayr /ɛː/ a port in SW Scotland, on the Firth of Clyde, the administrative centre of South Ayrshire council area; pop. 45,900 (est. 2009).

Ayrshire[1] /ˈɛːʃɪə, -ʃə/ a former county of SW Scotland, on the Firth of Clyde, now divided into the council areas of **North Ayrshire**, **East Ayrshire**, and **South Ayrshire**.

Ayrshire[2] /ˈɛːʃə/ ▶ **noun** an animal of a mainly white breed of dairy cattle.

Ayurveda /ˌɑːjʊəˈveɪdə, -ˈviːdə/ ▶ **noun** [mass noun] the traditional Hindu system of medicine (incorporated in Atharva Veda, the last of the four Vedas), which is based on the idea of balance in bodily systems and uses diet, herbal treatment, and yogic breathing.
– DERIVATIVES **Ayurvedic** adjective.
– ORIGIN from Sanskrit *āyus* 'life' + *veda* '(sacred) knowledge'.

AZ ▶ **abbreviation** Arizona (in official postal use).

Azad Kashmir /ˌɑːzad kaʃˈmɪə/ an autonomous state in NE Pakistan, formerly part of Kashmir; administrative centre, Muzzafarabad. It was established in 1949 after Kashmir was split as a result of the partition of India.
– ORIGIN from Urdu, literally 'Free Kashmir'.

azalea /əˈzeɪlɪə/ ▶ **noun** a deciduous flowering shrub with clusters of brightly coloured, sometimes fragrant flowers. Azaleas are typically smaller than other rhododendrons and there are numerous cultivars. ● Genus *Rhododendron*, family Ericaceae.
– ORIGIN mid 18th cent.: modern Latin, from Greek, feminine of *azaleos* 'dry', because the shrub flourishes in dry soil.

azan /əˈzɑːn/ (also **adhan**) ▶ **noun** the Muslim call to ritual prayer made by a muezzin from the minaret of a mosque (or now often played from a recording).
– ORIGIN mid 19th cent.: from Arabic *'aḏān* 'announcement'.

Azande /aˈzandi/ ▶ **noun & adjective** see **ZANDE**.

Azania /əˈzeɪnɪə/ an alternative name for South Africa, proposed in the time of apartheid by some supporters of majority rule for the country.
– DERIVATIVES **Azanian** noun & adjective.
– ORIGIN Greek (taken from classical geography), probably based on Arabic *Zanj*, denoting a black African.

azarole /ˈazərəʊl/ ▶ **noun** **1** an edible Mediterranean fruit which resembles a tiny apple and is used for making preserves.
2 the small hawthorn-like tree bearing azaroles.
● *Crataegus azarolus*, family Rosaceae.
– ORIGIN mid 17th cent.: from French *azerole*, from Spanish *azarolla*.

azeotrope /ˈeɪzɪətrəʊp, əˈziːə-/ ▶ **noun** Chemistry a mixture of two liquids which has a constant boiling point and composition throughout distillation.
– DERIVATIVES **azeotropic** /-ˈtrəʊpɪk, -ˈtrɒpɪk/ adjective.
– ORIGIN early 20th cent.: from **A-**[1] 'without' + Greek *zein* 'to boil' + *tropos* 'turning'.

Azerbaijan /ˌazəbʌɪˈdʒɑːn/ a country in the Caucasus of SW Asia, on the western shore of the Caspian Sea; pop. 8,238,700 (est. 2009); languages, Azerbaijani (official), Russian; capital, Baku.

> Historically, the name Azerbaijan referred to a larger region which formed part of Persia. The northern part of this was ceded to Russia in the early 19th century, the southern part remaining a region of NW Iran. Russian Azerbaijan was absorbed into the Soviet Union in 1922, gaining independence on the break-up of the USSR in 1991.

Azerbaijani ▶ **adjective** relating to Azerbaijan or its people or their language.
▶ **noun** (pl. **Azerbaijanis**) **1** a native or inhabitant of Azerbaijan, or a person of Azerbaijani descent.
2 [mass noun] the Turkic language spoken by over 14 million people in Azerbaijan and adjacent regions.

Azeri /əˈzɛːri/ ▶ **noun** (pl. **Azeris**) **1** a member of a Turkic people forming the majority population of Azerbaijan, and also living in Armenia and northern Iran.
2 [mass noun] the Azerbaijani language.
▶ **adjective** relating to the Azeris or their language.
– ORIGIN from Turkish *azerî*.

azide /ˈeɪzʌɪd/ ▶ **noun** Chemistry a compound containing the anion N_3^- or the group $-N_3$.
– ORIGIN early 20th cent.: from **AZO-** + **-IDE**.

azidothymidine /ˌeɪzɪdəʊˈθʌɪmɪdiːn, eɪˌzʌɪdəʊ-/ ▶ **noun** former name for the drug **ZIDOVUDINE**.

Azikiwe /ˌɑːzɪˈkiːweɪ/, (Benjamin) Nnamdi (1904–96), Nigerian statesman, the first Governor General of an independent Nigeria 1960–3 and its first President 1963–6.

Azilian /əˈzɪlɪən/ ▶ **adjective** Archaeology relating to or denoting an early Mesolithic culture in Europe, succeeding the Magdalenian and dated to about 11,500–9,500 years ago. It is characterized by flat bone harpoons, painted pebbles, and microliths.
■ (as noun **the Azilian**) the Azilian culture or period.
– ORIGIN late 19th cent.: named after *Mas d'Azil* in the French Pyrenees, where objects from this culture were found.

azimuth /ˈazɪməθ/ ▶ **noun** the direction of a celestial object from the observer, expressed as the angular distance from the north or south point of the horizon to the point at which a vertical circle passing through the object intersects the horizon. ■ the horizontal angle or direction of a compass bearing.
– DERIVATIVES **azimuthal** /-ˈmjuːθ(ə)l/ adjective.
– ORIGIN late Middle English (denoting the arc of a celestial circle from the zenith to the horizon): from Old French *azimut*, from Arabic *as-samt*, from *al* 'the' + *samt* 'way, direction'.

azimuthal projection /ˌazɪˈmjuːθ(ə)l/ ▶ **noun** a map projection in which a region of the earth is projected on to a plane tangential to the surface, usually at a pole or the equator.

azine /ˈeɪziːn/ ▶ **noun** Chemistry a cyclic organic compound having a ring including one or (usually) more nitrogen atoms.
– ORIGIN late 19th cent.: from **AZO-** + **-INE**[4].

azo- /ˈeɪzəʊ/ ▶ **prefix** Chemistry containing two adjacent nitrogen atoms between carbon atoms: *azobenzene*.
– ORIGIN from obsolete *azote* 'nitrogen', from French, from Greek *a-* 'without' + *zōē* 'life'.

azobenzene /ˌeɪzəʊˈbɛnziːn/ ▶ **noun** [mass noun] Chemistry a synthetic crystalline organic compound used chiefly in dye manufacture. ● Chem. formula: $(C_6H_5)N{=}N(C_6H_5)$.

azo dye ▶ **noun** Chemistry any of a large class of synthetic dyes whose molecules contain two adjacent nitrogen atoms between carbon atoms.

azoic /eɪˈzəʊɪk/ ▶ **adjective** having no trace of life or organic remains. ■ (**the Azoic**) Geology another term for **ARCHAEAN**.
– ORIGIN mid 19th cent.: from Greek *azōos* 'without life' + **-IC**.

azonal /eɪˈzəʊn(ə)l/ ▶ **adjective** (especially of soils) having no zonal organization or structure.

azoospermia /ˌeɪzəʊəˈspəːmɪə, əˈzəʊ-/ ▶ **noun** [mass noun] Medicine absence of motile (and hence viable) sperm in the semen.

A

– DERIVATIVES **azoospermic** adjective.

Azores /əˈzɔːz/ a group of volcanic islands in the Atlantic Ocean, west of Portugal, in Portuguese possession but partially autonomous; pop. 244,780 (2007); capital, Ponta Delgada.

azoturia /ˌazə(ʊ)ˈtjʊərɪə/ ▶ **noun** [mass noun] Medicine abnormal excess of nitrogen compounds in the urine. ■ Veterinary Medicine a condition that can affect horses exercised after a period of stabling, causing painful stiffness in the hindquarters and back, and dark urine containing products of muscle cell destruction. Also called **TYING-UP**.
– ORIGIN mid 19th cent.: from obsolete *azote* 'nitrogen' + **-URIA**.

Azov, Sea of /ˈazɒf/ an inland sea of southern Russia and Ukraine, separated from the Black Sea by the Crimea and linked to it by a narrow strait.

Azrael /ˈazreɪl/ (in Jewish and Islamic Mythology) the angel who severs the soul from the body at death.

AZT ▶ **abbreviation** trademark azidothymidine.

Aztec /ˈaztɛk/ ▶ **noun 1** a member of the American Indian people dominant in Mexico before the Spanish conquest of the 16th century.
2 [mass noun] the extinct language of the Aztecs, a Uto-Aztecan language from which modern Nahuatl is descended.
▶ **adjective** relating to or denoting the Aztecs or their language.
– ORIGIN from French *Aztèque* or Spanish *Azteca*, from Nahuatl *aztecatl* 'person of Aztlan', their legendary place of origin.

azulejo /ˌazjʊˈleɪhəʊ/ ▶ **noun** (pl. **azulejos**) a kind of glazed coloured tile traditionally used in Spanish and Portuguese buildings.
– ORIGIN from Spanish, from *azul* 'blue'.

azure /ˈaʒə, -ʒj(ʊ)ə, ˈeɪ-/ ▶ **adjective** bright blue in colour like a cloudless sky. ■ Heraldry blue: [postpositive] *a saltire azure*.
▶ **noun 1** [mass noun] a bright blue colour. ■ literary the clear sky.
2 a small butterfly which is typically blue or purplish. ● *Celastrina* and other genera, family Lycaenidae.
– ORIGIN Middle English (denoting a blue dye): from Old French *asur, azur*, from medieval Latin *azzurum, azolum*, from Arabic *al* 'the' + *lāzaward* (from Persian *lāžward* 'lapis lazuli').

azurite /ˈaʒʊrʌɪt, -ʒj(ʊ)ə-, ˈeɪ-/ ▶ **noun** [mass noun] a blue mineral consisting of basic copper carbonate. It occurs as blue prisms or crystal masses, typically with malachite.
– ORIGIN early 19th cent.: from **AZURE** + **-ITE**[1].

azygos vein /ˈazɪgəs/ ▶ **noun** Anatomy a large vein on the right side at the back of the thorax, draining into the superior vena cava.
– ORIGIN mid 17th cent.: *azygos* from Greek *azugos*, from *a-* 'without' + *zugon* 'yoke', the vein not being one of a pair.

azygous /ˈazɪgəs/ ▶ **adjective** Anatomy & Biology (of an organic structure) single; not existing in pairs.
– ORIGIN mid 19th cent.: from Greek *azugos* 'unyoked' (compare with **AZYGOS VEIN**) + **-OUS**.

az-Zarqa variant form of **ZARQA**.

Bb

B[1] (also **b**) ▸ **noun** (pl. **Bs** or **B's**) **1** the second letter of the alphabet. ■ denoting the second in a set of items, categories, sizes, etc. ■ the second highest class of academic mark. ■ (in the UK) denoting a secondary road: *the B4248* | *B-roads*. ■ denoting the second-highest-earning socio-economic category for marketing purposes, including intermediate management and professional personnel. ■ (**b**) Chess denoting the second file from the left, as viewed from White's side of the board. ■ (usu. **b**) the second fixed constant to appear in an algebraic equation. ■ Geology denoting a soil horizon of intermediate depth, typically the subsoil. ■ the human blood type (in the ABO system) containing the B antigen and lacking the A. ■ (with numeral) denoting a series of international standard paper sizes each twice the area of the next, as *B0, B1, B2, B3, B4*, etc., B4 being 250 × 353 mm.
2 (usu. **B**) Music the seventh note of the diatonic scale of C major. ■ a key based on a scale with B as its keynote.
– PHRASES **plan B** an alternative strategy.

B[2] ▸ **abbreviation** ■ Belgium (international vehicle registration). ■ bishop (used in recording moves in chess): *Be5*. ■ black (used in describing grades of pencil lead): *2B pencils*. ■ bomber (in designations of US aircraft types): *a B-52*.
▸ **symbol** ■ the chemical element boron. ■ Physics magnetic flux density.

b ▸ **abbreviation** ■ Physics barn(s). ■ (**b.**) born (used to indicate a date of birth): *George Lloyd (b.1913)*. ■ Cricket (on scorecards) bowled by: *AC Hudson b Prasad 146*. ■ Cricket (on scorecards) bye(s).

BA ▸ **abbreviation** ■ Bachelor of Arts: *David Brown, BA*. ■ British Airways. ■ British Association (for the Advancement of Science). ■ Buenos Aires.

Ba ▸ **symbol** the chemical element barium.

ba /bɑː/ ▸ **noun** in ancient Egypt, the supposed soul of a person or god, which survived after death but had to be sustained with offerings of food. It was typically represented as a human-headed bird. See also **KA**.

baa ▸ **verb** (**baas, baaing, baaed**) [no obj.] (of a sheep or lamb) bleat.
▸ **noun** the cry of a sheep or lamb.
– ORIGIN early 16th cent.: imitative.

Baader–Meinhof Group /ˌbɑːdəˈmʌɪnhɒf/ another name for **RED ARMY FACTION**.

Baal /bɑːl/ (also **Bel**) a male fertility god whose cult was widespread in ancient Phoenician and Canaanite lands.
– ORIGIN from Hebrew *baʿal* 'lord'.

Baalbek /ˈbɑːlbɛk/ a town in eastern Lebanon, site of the ancient city of Heliopolis.

baap /bɑːp/ ▸ **noun** Indian a father.
– ORIGIN from Hindi *bāp*.

baas /bɑːs/ ▸ **noun** S. African, often offensive a supervisor or employer, especially a white man in charge of coloured or black people.
– ORIGIN Dutch, 'master'; compare with **BOSS**[1].

baasie /ˈbɑːsi/ ▸ **noun** S. African, often offensive a form of address to a young white male.
– ORIGIN Afrikaans (from earlier Dutch *baasje*), literally 'little master'.

Baath Party /bɑːθ/ (also **Ba'ath Party**) a pan-Arab socialist party founded in Syria in 1943. Different factions of the Baath Party hold power in Syria and formerly held power in Iraq.
– DERIVATIVES **Baathism noun**, **Baathist adjective & noun**.
– ORIGIN *Baath*, from Arabic *baʿt* 'resurrection, renaissance'.

baba[1] /ˈbɑːbɑː/ (also **rum baba**) ▸ **noun** a small, rich sponge cake, typically soaked in rum-flavoured syrup.
– ORIGIN via French from Polish, literally 'married peasant woman'.

baba[2] /ˈbɑːbɑː/ ▸ **noun** Indian informal **1** father (often as a proper name or as a familiar form of address). ■ a respectful form of address for an older man. ■ (often **Baba**) a holy man.
2 a child, especially a male one.
– ORIGIN from Hindi *bābā*.

baba ganoush /ˌbɑːbə gaˈnuːʃ/ (also **baba ghanouj** /gaˈnuːʒ/) ▸ **noun** [mass noun] a thick sauce or spread made from puréed aubergines and sesame seeds, typical of eastern Mediterranean cuisine.
– ORIGIN from Egyptian Arabic, from Arabic *bābā*, literally 'father' + *ghannūj*, perhaps a personal name.

babalaas /ˈbabəlas, -lɑːs/ S. African ▸ **noun** [mass noun] the after-effects of drinking an excess of alcohol.
▸ **adjective** hung-over.
– ORIGIN Afrikaans, from Zulu *ibhabhalazi*.

babassu /ˌbabəˈsuː/ (also **babaçu**) ▸ **noun** a Brazilian palm that yields an edible oil which is sometimes used in cosmetics. ● Genus *Orbignya*, family Palmae.
– ORIGIN 1920s: from Brazilian Portuguese *babaçu*, from Tupi *ybá* 'fruit' + *guasu* 'large'.

Babbage /ˈbabɪdʒ/, Charles (1791–1871), English mathematician, inventor, and pioneer of machine computing. He designed a mechanical computer with Ada Lovelace but was unable to complete it in his lifetime.

Babbitt[1] /ˈbabɪt/, Milton (Byron) (b.1916), American composer and mathematician. His compositions developed from the twelve note system of Schoenberg and Webern.

Babbitt[2] /ˈbabɪt/ ▸ **noun** dated, chiefly N. Amer. a materialistic, complacent, and conformist businessman.
– DERIVATIVES **Babbittry noun**.
– ORIGIN from the name George *Babbitt*, the protagonist of the novel *Babbitt* (1922) by Sinclair Lewis.

babbitt metal /ˈbabɪt/ ▸ **noun** [mass noun] a soft alloy of tin, antimony, copper, and usually lead, used to line bearings.
– ORIGIN late 19th cent.: named after Isaac *Babbitt* (1799–1862), the American inventor of the lining.

babble ▸ **verb** [no obj.] **1** talk rapidly and continuously in a foolish, excited, or incomprehensible way: *they babbled on about their holiday*. ■ [reporting verb] utter something rapidly and incoherently: [with direct speech] *'Thank goodness you're all right,' she babbled*. ■ reveal something secret or confidential by talking carelessly: *he babbled to another convict while he was in jail*.
2 (usu. as adj. **babbling**) (of a stream) make the continuous murmuring sound of water flowing over stones: *a gently babbling brook*.
▸ **noun 1** [in sing.] the confused sound of a group of people talking simultaneously: *a babble of protest*. ■ foolish, excited, or confused talk: *her soft voice stopped his babble*. ■ [mass noun] background disturbance caused by interference from conversations on other telephone lines.
2 the continuous murmuring sound of water flowing over stones in a stream: *the babble of a brook*.
– ORIGIN Middle English: from Middle Low German *babbelen*, or an independent English formation, as a frequentative based on the repeated syllable *ba*, typical of a child's early speech.

-babble ▸ **combining form** [mass noun] informal forming nouns denoting confusing or pretentious jargon, especially that characteristic of a particular field or group: *psychobabble* | *technobabble*.

babbler ▸ **noun 1** a thrush-like Old World songbird with a long tail, short rounded wings, and a loud, discordant or musical voice. ● Family Timaliidae (the **babbler family**): numerous genera.
2 a person who babbles.

babby ▸ **noun** (pl. **babbies**) dialect form of **BABY**.

babe ▸ **noun 1** literary a baby: *a babe in arms, less than twelve months old*.
2 informal an affectionate form of address for a lover.
3 informal a sexually attractive young woman.
– ORIGIN late Middle English: probably imitative of an infant's first attempts at speech. Compare with **BABY**.

babel /ˈbeɪb(ə)l/ ▸ **noun** [in sing.] a confused noise made by a number of voices: *the babel of voices on the road*. ■ a confused situation.
– ORIGIN early 16th cent.: from *Babel* (see **TOWER OF BABEL**), where, according to the biblical story, God made the builders all speak different languages.

Babel, Tower of see **TOWER OF BABEL**.

babelicious /ˌbeɪbˈlɪʃəs/ ▸ **adjective** N. Amer. informal (of a woman) very sexually attractive.
– ORIGIN 1992: coined in the film *Wayne's World*.

babesiosis /bəˌbiːzɪˈəʊsɪs/ (also **babesiasis** /ˌbɑːbɪˈzʌɪəsɪs/) ▸ **noun** [mass noun] a disease of cattle and other livestock, transmitted by the bite of ticks. It affects the red blood cells and causes the passing of red or blackish urine. Also called **PIROPLASMOSIS**, **REDWATER**, or **MURRAIN**. ● The disease is caused by protozoans of the genus *Babesia*, phylum Sporozoa.
– ORIGIN early 20th cent.: from modern Latin *Babesia*, from the name Victor *Babès* (1854–1926), Romanian bacteriologist.

Babi /ˈbɑːbi/ ▸ **noun** an adherent of Babism.

babiche /bəˈbiːʃ/ ▸ **noun** [mass noun] raw hide, typically formed into strips, as used by North American Indians for making fastenings and animal snares.
– ORIGIN early 19th cent.: from Canadian French, from Micmac *a:papi:č*.

babirusa /ˌbɑːbɪˈruːsə/ ▸ **noun** a forest-dwelling wild pig with several upturned horn-like tusks, native to Malaysia. ● *Babyrousa babyrussa*, family Suidae.
– ORIGIN late 17th cent.: from Malay, from *babi* 'hog' + *rusa* 'deer'.

Babism /ˈbɑːbɪz(ə)m/ ▸ **noun** [mass noun] a religion founded in 1844 by the Persian Mirza Ali Muhammad of Shiraz (1819–50) (popularly known as 'the Bab'), who taught that a new prophet would follow Muhammad. See also **BAHA'I**.
– ORIGIN mid 19th cent.: via Persian from Arabic *bāb* 'intermediary', literally 'gate' (taken as a name by the founder) + **-ISM**.

B

baboon ▶ **noun** a large Old World ground-dwelling monkey with a long doglike snout and large teeth. ● Genera *Papio* and *Mandrillus*, family Cercopithecidae: several species, including the drill and mandrill.
■ an ugly or uncouth person.
– ORIGIN Middle English (denoting a grotesque figure used in architecture): from Old French *babuin* or medieval Latin *babewynus*, perhaps from Old French *baboue* 'muzzle, grimace'.

baboon spider ▶ **noun** a large, hairy burrowing spider found in Africa. ● *Ceratogyrus*, *Harpactira*, and other genera, family Theraphosidae, suborder Mygalomorphae.

babouche /bəˈbuːʃ/ ▶ **noun** a heelless slipper, typically in oriental style.
– ORIGIN late 17th cent.: from French, from Arabic *bābūj*, Persian *pāpūš*, literally 'foot covering'.

Babruisk /bəˈbruːɪsk/ (also **Babruysk**) a river port in central Belarus, on the Byarezina River south-east of Minsk; pop. 219,000 (est. 2009). Russian name **Bobruisk** or **Bobruysk**.

babu /ˈbɑːbuː/ ▶ **noun** (pl. **babus**) Indian a respectful title or form of address for a man, especially an educated one. ■ an office worker.
– ORIGIN from Hindi *bābū*, literally 'father'.

babul /bəˈbuːl/ ▶ **noun** (in South Asia) a tropical acacia introduced from Africa, used as a source of fuel, gum arabic, and (formerly) tannin. ● *Acacia nilotica*, family Leguminosae.
– ORIGIN early 19th cent.: from Hindi *babūl*.

Babur /ˈbɑːbʊə/ (1483–1530), first Mogul emperor of India 1526–30, descendant of Tamerlane; born *Zahir ad-Din Muhammad*. He invaded India *c.*1525 and conquered the territory from the Oxus to Patna.

babushka /bəˈbʊʃkə, ˈbabʊʃˌkə/ ▶ **noun** (in Russia) an old woman or grandmother. ■ N. Amer. a headscarf tied under the chin, typical of those traditionally worn by Russian women.
– ORIGIN Russian, 'grandmother'.

Babuyan Islands /ˌbɑːbʊˈjɑːn/ a group of twenty-four volcanic islands lying to the north of the island of Luzon in the northern Philippines.

baby ▶ **noun** (pl. **babies**) **1** a very young child: *his wife's just had a baby* | [as modifier] *a baby girl*. ■ a very young animal. ■ the youngest member of a family or group. ■ a timid or childish person: *'Don't be such a baby!' she said witheringly*. ■ (**one's baby**) informal one's particular responsibility or concern.
2 informal a lover or spouse (often as a form of address): *my baby left me for another guy*. ■ a thing regarded with affection or familiarity: *this baby can reach speeds of 120 mph*.
▶ **adjective** [attrib.] comparatively small or immature of its kind: *a baby version of the Oxford Movement*. ■ (of vegetables) picked before reaching their usual size: *baby carrots*.
▶ **verb** (**babies**, **babying**, **babied**) [with obj.] treat (someone) as a baby; pamper or be overprotective towards.
– PHRASES **throw the baby out with the bathwater** discard something valuable along with other things that are undesirable.
– DERIVATIVES **babyhood** noun.
– ORIGIN late Middle English: probably imitative of an infant's first attempts at speech.

baby blue ▶ **noun 1** [mass noun] a pale shade of blue. ■ (**baby blues**) informal blue eyes.
2 (**baby blues**) informal postnatal depression.

baby boom ▶ **noun** informal a temporary marked increase in the birth rate, especially the one following the Second World War.
– DERIVATIVES **baby boomer** noun.

baby bouncer ▶ **noun** Brit. a harness suspended by elastic or a spring, into which a baby is put, with its feet within reach of the floor, to exercise its legs.

baby buggy ▶ **noun** Brit. trademark a light pushchair with a soft seat that allows the chair to be collapsed inwards.

baby bust ▶ **noun** informal, chiefly N. Amer. a temporary marked decrease in the birth rate.
– DERIVATIVES **baby buster** noun.

baby carriage ▶ **noun** N. Amer. a pram.

baby corn ▶ **noun** [mass noun] individual cobs of maize which have been harvested when very small and immature, eaten as a vegetable.

baby-doll ▶ **adjective** denoting a style of women's clothing resembling that traditionally worn by a doll or young child, especially short, high-waisted, short-sleeved dresses.

baby face ▶ **noun** a smooth round face like a baby's.

baby-faced ▶ **adjective** having a youthful or innocent face: *baby-faced tough guys*.

baby fat ▶ **noun** [mass noun] fat on the body of a baby or child that disappears as it grows up. ■ the extra body fat that a woman may develop during pregnancy.

baby grand ▶ **noun** the smallest size of grand piano, about 1.5 metres long.

Babygro ▶ **noun** (pl. **Babygros**) Brit. trademark an all-in-one stretch garment for babies.
– ORIGIN 1950s (originally US): from **baby** + **grow**.

babyish ▶ **adjective** derogatory typical of or suitable for a baby; childish: *he pursed his mouth into a babyish pout*.
– DERIVATIVES **babyishly** adverb, **babyishness** noun.

Babylon[1] /ˈbabɪlɒn/ an ancient city in Mesopotamia, the capital of Babylonia in the 2nd millennium BC. The city (of which only ruins now remain) lay on the Euphrates and was noted by classical writers for its luxury, its fortifications, and its legendary Hanging Gardens.
– ORIGIN Greek *Babulōn* (from Hebrew *bāḇel*), also the name of the mystical city of the Apocalypse. Compare with **babel**.

Babylon[2] /ˈbabɪlɒn/ ▶ **noun** [mass noun] black English (chiefly among Rastafarians) a contemptuous or dismissive term for aspects of white culture seen as degenerate or oppressive, especially the police.
– ORIGIN 1940s: by association with **Babylon[1]**.

Babylonia /ˌbabɪˈləʊnɪə/ an ancient region of Mesopotamia, formed when the kingdoms of Akkad in the north and Sumer in the south combined in the first half of the 2nd millennium BC.

Babylonian /ˌbabɪˈləʊnɪən/ ▶ **noun 1** an inhabitant of Babylon or Babylonia.
2 [mass noun] the dialect of Akkadian spoken in ancient Babylon.
▶ **adjective** relating to Babylon or Babylonia.

Babylonian Captivity the captivity of the Israelites in Babylon, lasting from their deportation by Nebuchadnezzar in 586 BC until their release by Cyrus the Great in 539 BC.

babymother (or **babyfather**) ▶ **noun** black English the mother (or father) of one or more of one's children.

baby oil ▶ **noun** [mass noun] a mineral oil used to soften the skin.

baby's breath ▶ **noun** a herbaceous plant of delicate appearance which bears tiny scented pink or white flowers. ● *Gypsophila paniculata*, family Caryophyllaceae.

babysit ▶ **verb** (**babysits**, **babysitting**; past and past participle **babysat**) [no obj.] look after a child or children while the parents are out: *I babysit for my neighbour sometimes* | [with obj.] *she was babysitting Sophie*.
– DERIVATIVES **babysitter** noun, **babysitting** noun.

baby stay ▶ **noun** Sailing an additional forestay sometimes used on offshore racing yachts.

baby step ▶ **noun** a tentative act or measure which is the first stage in a long or challenging process: *the country is just taking its first baby steps towards the future*.

baby talk ▶ **noun** [mass noun] childish talk used by or to young children.

baby tooth ▶ **noun** another term for **milk tooth**.

baby walker ▶ **noun** Brit. a wheeled frame in which a baby is suspended in a harness and can move itself about a room with its feet.

bacalao /ˌbakəˈlaʊ/ ▶ **noun** [mass noun] codfish, typically dried or salted, as used in Spanish and Latin American cookery.
– ORIGIN Spanish.

Bacall /bəˈkɔːl/, Lauren (b.1924), American actress. She co-starred with her husband, Humphrey Bogart, in a number of successful thrillers, including *The Big Sleep* (1946) and *Key Largo* (1948).

baccalaureate /ˌbakəˈlɔːrɪət/ ▶ **noun 1** an examination intended to qualify successful candidates for higher education. See also **International Baccalaureate**.
2 a university bachelor's degree.
3 US a religious service held at some educational institutions before commencement, including a farewell sermon to the graduating students.
– ORIGIN mid 17th cent. (in sense 2): from French *baccalauréat* or medieval Latin *baccalaureatus*, from *baccalaureus* 'bachelor'. The earlier form *baccalarius* was altered by wordplay to conform with *bacca lauri* 'laurel berry', because of the laurels awarded to scholars. Sense 1 dates from 1970.

baccarat /ˈbakərɑː/ ▶ **noun** [mass noun] a gambling card game in which players hold two- or three-card hands, the winning hand being that giving the highest remainder when its face value is divided by ten.
– ORIGIN mid 19th cent.: from French *baccara*, of unknown origin.

Bacchae /ˈbakiː/ the priestesses or female devotees of the Greek god Bacchus.

bacchanal /ˈbakən(ə)l, -nal/ chiefly literary ▶ **noun 1** a wild and drunken celebration.
2 a priest, worshipper, or follower of Bacchus.
▶ **adjective** another term for **bacchanalian**.
– ORIGIN mid 16th cent.: from Latin *bacchanalis*, from the name of the god **Bacchus**.

Bacchanalia /ˌbakəˈneɪlɪə/ ▶ **plural noun** [also treated as sing.] **1** the Roman festival of Bacchus.
2 (**bacchanalia**) drunken celebrations.
– ORIGIN late 16th cent.: from Latin *bacchanalia*, neuter plural of the adjective *bacchanalis* (see **bacchanal**).

bacchanalian /ˌbakəˈneɪlɪən/ ▶ **adjective** characterized by or given to drunken revelry: *a bacchanalian orgy*.

bacchant /ˈbakənt/ ▶ **noun** (pl. **bacchants** or **bacchantes** /bəˈkantiːz/; fem. **bacchante** /bəˈkant, bəˈkanti/) a priest, priestess, or follower of Bacchus.
– ORIGIN late 16th cent.: from French *bacchante*, from Latin *bacchari* 'celebrate the feast of Bacchus'.

Bacchus /ˈbakəs/ Greek Mythology another name for **Dionysus**.
– DERIVATIVES **Bacchic** adjective.
– ORIGIN Latin, from Greek *Bakkhos*.

baccy ▶ **noun** Brit. informal term for **tobacco**.

Bach /bɑːx/, Johann Sebastian (1685–1750), German composer.

> An exceptional and prolific baroque composer, he produced works ranging from violin concertos, suites, and the six *Brandenburg Concertos* (1720–1) to clavier works and sacred cantatas. Large-scale choral works include *The Passion according to St John* (1723), *The Passion according to St Matthew* (1729), and the *Mass in B minor* (1733–8). He had twenty children: **Carl Philipp Emanuel Bach** (1714–88) wrote church music, keyboard sonatas, and a celebrated treatise on clavier playing, and **Johann Christian Bach** (1735–82) became music master to the British royal family and composed thirteen operas.

bach[1] /bax/ ▶ **noun** Welsh used as a term of endearment, often after a personal name: *Thomas bach, you are looking tired*.
– ORIGIN Welsh, literally 'little'.

bach[2] /batʃ/ informal ▶ **verb** [no obj.] N. Amer. & Austral./NZ (especially of a man) live alone and do one's own cooking and housekeeping: *Baldy bached in a hut down the road a bit*.
▶ **noun** NZ a small holiday house.
– ORIGIN late 19th cent. (as a verb): abbreviation of **bachelor**.

Bacharach /ˈbakərak/, Burt (b.1929), American writer of popular songs. His songs, many of which were written with lyricist Hal David (b.1921), include 'Walk On By' (1961), 'Alfie' (1966), and 'Raindrops Keep Falling on my Head' (1969).

bachata /baˈtʃata/ ▶ **noun** [mass noun] a style of romantic music originating in the Dominican Republic. ■ [count noun] a bachata song.
– ORIGIN Caribbean Spanish, literally 'a party, good time'.

bachcha /ˈbʌtʃəː/ ▶ **noun** Indian informal a young person.
– ORIGIN from Hindi *baccā* 'child'.

bachelor ▶ **noun 1** a man who is not and has never been married: *one of the country's most eligible bachelors*. ■ Zoology a male bird or mammal prevented from breeding by a dominant male.
2 a person who holds a first degree from a university or other academic institution (only in titles or set expressions): *a Bachelor of Arts*.
3 Canadian a bachelor apartment.
4 historical a young knight serving under another's banner. See also **knight bachelor**. [said to be from French *bas chevalier*, literally 'low knight' (i.e. knight of a low order).]
– DERIVATIVES **bachelorhood** noun.
– ORIGIN Middle English: from Old French *bacheler*; of uncertain origin.

bachelor apartment ▶ **noun** N. Amer. an apartment consisting of a single large main room; a studio flat.

bachelorette ▶ **noun** N. Amer. **1** a young unmarried woman.
2 a very small bachelor apartment.

bachelor girl ▶ **noun** an independent, unmarried young woman.

bachelor party (or **bachelorette party**) ▸ **noun** N. Amer. a party given for a man (or woman) about to get married, typically attended by men (or women) only.

bachelor's buttons ▸ **plural noun** [treated as sing. or pl.] any of a number of ornamental plants which bear small, button-like, double flowers, in particular: ● a white flower of the daisy family (*Achillea ptarmica*, family Compositae). ● a yellow buttercup (*Ranunculus acris*, family Ranunculaceae).

Bach flower remedies /batʃ/ (also **Bach remedies**) ▸ **plural noun** preparations of the flowers of various plants used in a system of complementary medicine intended to relieve ill health by influencing underlying emotional states.
– ORIGIN 1970s: named after Edward *Bach* (1886–1936), British physician.

bacilliform /bəˈsɪlɪfɔːm/ ▸ **adjective** chiefly Biology rod-shaped.

bacillus /bəˈsɪləs/ ▸ **noun** (pl. **bacilli** /-lʌɪ, -liː/) a rod-shaped bacterium. ■ a disease-causing bacterium.
– DERIVATIVES **bacillary** adjective.
– ORIGIN late 19th cent.: from late Latin, diminutive of Latin *baculus* 'stick'.

back ▸ **noun 1** the rear surface of the human body from the shoulders to the hips: *he lay on his back* | [as modifier] *back pain.* ■ the corresponding upper surface of an animal's body. ■ the spine of a person or animal. ■ the main structure of a ship's hull or an aircraft's fuselage. ■ the part of a garment that covers a person's back. ■ a person's back regarded as carrying a load or bearing an imposition: *the Press are **on my back**.*
2 the side or part of something that is away from the spectator or from the direction in which it moves or faces; the rear: *at the back of the hotel is a secluded garden* | *a rubber dinghy with an engine at the back.* ■ the position directly behind someone or something: *she unbuttoned her dress from the back.* ■ the side or part of an object that is not normally seen or used: *write on the back of a postcard.* ■ the part of a chair against which the sitter's back rests.
3 a player in a team game who plays in a defensive position behind the forwards.
4 (**the Backs**) the grounds of Cambridge colleges which back on to the River Cam.
▸ **adverb 1** in the opposite direction from the one that one is facing or travelling towards: *he moved back a pace* | *she walked away without looking back.* ■ expressing movement of the body into a reclining position: *he leaned back in his chair* | *sit back and relax.* ■ at a distance away: *keep back from the roadside.* ■ (**back of**) N. Amer. informal behind: *he knew that other people were back of him.* ■ N. Amer. informal losing by a specified margin: *the team was five points back.*
2 so as to return to an earlier or normal position or condition: *she put the book back on the shelf* | *he drove to Glasgow and back in a day* | *things were back to normal.* ■ at a place previously left or mentioned: *the folks back home are counting on him.* ■ fashionable again: *sideburns are back.*
3 in or into the past: *he made his fortune back in 1955.*
4 in return: *they wrote back to me.*
▸ **verb 1** [with obj.] give financial, material, or moral support to: *he had a newspaper empire backing him* | *his mother **backed** him **up** on everything.* ■ supplement in order to strengthen: *firefighters, **backed up** by helicopters and planes, fought to bring the flames under control.* ■ bet money on (a person or animal) winning a race or contest: *he backed the horse at 33–1.*
2 [with obj.] cover the back of (an article) in order to support, protect, or decorate it: *a mirror backed with tortoiseshell.*
3 [no obj., with adverbial of direction] walk or drive backwards: *she tried to back away* | figurative *the government **backed away from** the plan* | [with obj.] *he backed the Mercedes into the yard.* ■ [no obj.] (of the wind) change direction anticlockwise around the points of the compass: *the wind had backed to the north-west.* The opposite of **VEER**[1]. ■ [with obj.] Sailing put (a sail) aback in order to slow the vessel down or assist in turning through the wind.
4 [no obj.] (**back on /on to**) (of a building or other structure) have its back facing or adjacent to: *his garage wall backs on to the neighbouring property.* ■ [with obj.] lie behind or at the back of: *the promenade is backed by lots of cafes.* ■ put a piece of music on the less important side of (a vinyl recording): *the new single is backed with a track from the LP.*
5 (in popular music) provide musical accompaniment to (a singer or musician): *on his new album he is backed by an American group.*
▸ **adjective** [attrib.] **1** of or at the back of something: *the back garden* | *the back pocket of his jeans.* ■ in a remote or subsidiary position: *back roads.*
2 from or relating to the past: *she was owed back pay.*
3 directed towards the rear or in a reversed course: *a back header.*
4 Phonetics (of a sound) articulated at the back of the mouth.
– PHRASES **at someone's back** in pursuit or support of someone. **back and forth** to and fro. **back in the day** in the past; some time ago: *back in the day, he'd had one of the greatest minds I'd ever come across.* **one's back is turned** one's attention is elsewhere: *he kissed her quickly, when the landlady's back was turned.* **the back of beyond** a very remote or inaccessible place. **back o'Bourke** Austral. informal the outback. [from the name of a town in north-west New South Wales.] **the back of one's mind** used to express that something is in one's mind but is not consciously thought of or remembered: *she had a little nagging worry at the back of her mind.* **back someone into a corner** force someone into a difficult situation: *I was backed into a corner – there was no way out.* **back to front** Brit. with the back at the front and the front at the back: *the exhausts had been fitted back to front.* **back water** reverse the action of a boat's oars to slow down or stop. **back the wrong horse** make a wrong or inappropriate choice. **behind someone's back** without a person's knowledge and in an unfair way: *Carla made fun of him behind his back.* **get** (or **put**) **someone's back up** make someone annoyed or angry. **in back** N. Amer. at the back of something, especially a building: *my dad demolished a shed **in back of** his barn.* **know something like the back of one's hand** be entirely familiar with a place or route. **on one's back** in bed recovering from an injury or illness. **put one's back into** approach (a task) with vigour. **turn one's back on** ignore (someone) by turning away from them. ■ reject or abandon (a person or thing that one was previously involved with). **with one's back to** (or **up against**) **the wall** in a desperate situation.
– PHRASAL VERBS **back down** withdraw a claim or assertion in the face of opposition: *party leaders backed down and rescinded the resolution.* **back off** draw back from action or confrontation: *they **backed off from** fundamental reform of the system.* ■ N. Amer. back down. **back out** withdraw from a commitment: *if he **backs out of** the deal they'll sue him.* **back up 1** (of vehicles) form into a queue due to congestion. **2** (of running water) accumulate behind an obstruction. **back something up 1** Computing make a spare copy of data or a disk. **2** cause vehicles to form into a queue due to congestion: *the traffic was backed up a mile in each direction.*
– DERIVATIVES **backmost** adjective.
– ORIGIN Old English *bæc*, of Germanic origin; related to Middle Dutch and Old Norse *bak*. The adverb use dates from late Middle English and is a shortening of **ABACK**.

backache ▸ **noun** [mass noun] prolonged pain in one's back: *a cure for backache.*

back alley ▸ **noun** a narrow passage behind or between buildings. ■ [as modifier] secret and illegal: *a back-alley abortion.*

back-arc ▸ **adjective** Geology relating to or denoting the area behind an island arc.

backbar ▸ **noun** chiefly US a structure behind a bar counter, with shelves for holding bottles, other supplies, and equipment.

backbeat ▸ **noun** Music a strong accent on one of the normally unaccented beats of the bar, used especially in jazz and popular music.

backbencher ▸ **noun** (in the UK) a Member of Parliament who does not hold office in the government or opposition and who sits behind the front benches in the House of Commons.
– DERIVATIVES **backbench** adjective.

backbiting ▸ **noun** [mass noun] malicious talk about someone who is not present.
– DERIVATIVES **backbite** verb, **backbiter** noun.

backblocks ▸ **plural noun** (**the backblocks**) Austral./NZ land in the remote and sparsely inhabited interior: [as modifier] *backblocks roads.*

backboard ▸ **noun** a board placed at or forming the back of something, such as a piece of electronic equipment. ■ a board used to support or straighten a person's back, especially after an accident. ■ Basketball an upright board behind the basket, off which the ball may rebound.

back boiler ▸ **noun** Brit. a boiler supplying hot water or heating that is built in behind a fireplace or is an integral part of a gas fire.

backbone ▸ **noun 1** the series of vertebrae extending from the skull to the pelvis; the spine. ■ US the spine of a book. ■ Biochemistry the main chain of a polymeric molecule.
2 the chief support of a system or organization: *these firms are the backbone of our industrial sector.* ■ [mass noun] strength of character: *he has enough backbone to see us through this difficulty.*
3 Computing & Telecommunications a high-speed, high-capacity digital connection which forms the axis of a local or wide area network.

back-breaking ▸ **adjective** (of manual labour) physically demanding: *a day's back-breaking work.*

back-burner ▸ **verb** [with obj.] US postpone consideration of or action on: *a planned test of the new ale has been back-burnered.*
– PHRASES **on the back burner** see **BURNER**.

backcast ▸ **noun** a backward swing of a fishing line preparatory to casting.
▸ **verb** (past and past participle **backcast**) [no obj.] make a backcast.

back catalogue ▸ **noun** all the works previously produced by a recording artist or record company: *the owner of the Elvis Presley back catalogue.*

backchannel ▸ **noun 1** a secondary or covert route for the passage of information: *we used him as a diplomatic backchannel.*
2 Psychology a sound or gesture made to give continuity to a conversation by a person who is listening to another.

backchat ▸ **noun** [mass noun] Brit. informal rude or cheeky remarks made in reply to someone in authority.

backcloth ▸ **noun** Brit. another term for **BACKDROP**.

backcomb ▸ **verb** [with obj.] chiefly Brit. comb (the hair) from the ends of the strands towards the scalp to make it look thicker.

backcountry ▸ **noun** (**the backcountry**) chiefly N. Amer. sparsely inhabited rural areas.

backcourt ▸ **noun 1** (in tennis, basketball, and other games) the part of each side of the court nearest the back wall or back boundary line.
2 the defensive players in a basketball team.
3 (especially in Glasgow) a courtyard behind a house or tenement.

backcrawl ▸ **noun** another term for **BACKSTROKE**.

backcross Genetics ▸ **verb** [with obj.] cross (a hybrid) with one of its parents or an organism with the same genetic characteristics as one of the parents.
▸ **noun** an instance or result of backcrossing.

backdate ▸ **verb** [with obj.] Brit. make (something, especially a pay increase) retrospectively valid: *the 4 per cent increase was backdated to June.* ■ put an earlier date to (a document) than the actual one.

back door ▸ **noun** the rear door of a building. ■ [as modifier] achieved by using indirect or dishonest means: *a back-door tax increase.* ■ a feature or defect of a computer system that allows surreptitious unauthorized access to data.
– PHRASES **by** (or **through**) **the back door** using indirect or dishonest means to achieve an objective.

backdown ▸ **noun** an act of backing down.

backdraught (US **backdraft**) ▸ **noun 1** a current of air or water that flows backwards down a chimney, pipe, etc.
2 a phenomenon in which a fire that has consumed all available oxygen suddenly explodes when more oxygen is made available, typically because a door or window has been opened.

backdrop ▸ **noun** a painted cloth hung at the back of a theatre stage as part of the scenery. ■ the setting or background for a scene, event, or situation: *the conference took place **against a backdrop of** increasing diplomatic activity.*
▸ **verb** (**backdrops, backdropping, backdropped**) [with obj.] lie behind or beyond; serve as a background to: *the rolling hills that backdropped our camp.*

back end ▸ **noun** the end of something which is furthest from the front or the working end: *the back end of the car swung round.* ■ informal the rump or buttocks. ■ the latter part of a period of time: *the book takes us up to the back end of last year.*
▸ **adjective** [attrib.] **1** relating to the end of a project, process, or investment: *many annuities have back-end surrender charges.*

2 Computing denoting a subordinate processor or program, not directly accessed by the user, which performs a specialized function on behalf of a main processor or software system.

B

backer ▸ noun a person, institution, or country that supports someone or something, especially financially: *a struggle to find a new financial backer.* ▪ a person that bets on a horse.

back-fanged ▸ adjective Zoology (of a snake such as a boomslang) having the rear one or two pairs of teeth modified as fangs, with grooves to conduct the venom. Compare with FRONT-FANGED.

backfield ▸ noun [mass noun] American Football the area of play behind the line of scrimmage. ▪ the players (quarterback and running backs) positioned in this area.

backfill ▸ verb [with obj.] refill (an excavated hole) with the material dug out of it.
▸ noun [mass noun] material used for backfilling.

backfire ▸ verb /bakˈfʌɪə/ [no obj.] **1** (of a vehicle or its engine) undergo a mistimed explosion in the cylinder or exhaust.
2 (of a plan or action) have an opposite and undesirable effect to what was intended: *overzealous publicity* ***backfired on*** *her.*
▸ noun /ˈbakfʌɪə/ **1** a mistimed explosion in the cylinder or exhaust of a vehicle or engine.
2 N. Amer. a fire started deliberately to stop the progress of an approaching fire by creating a burned area in its path.

backfist ▸ noun (in martial arts) a punch made with the back of the fist.

backflip ▸ noun a backward somersault done in the air with the arms and legs stretched out straight.

back focus ▸ noun Photography the distance between the back of a lens and the image of an object at infinity.

back-formation ▸ noun a word that is formed from an existing word which looks as though it is a derivative, typically by removal of a suffix (e.g. *edit* from *editor*). ▪ [mass noun] the process by which such words are formed.

backgammon ▸ noun [mass noun] a board game in which two players move their pieces around twenty-four triangular points according to the throw of dice, the winner being the first to remove all their pieces from the board. ▪ [count noun] the most complete form of win in this game.
– ORIGIN mid 17th cent.: from BACK + GAMMON².

background ▸ noun **1** the part of a picture, scene, or design that forms a setting for the main figures or objects, or appears furthest from the viewer: *the house stands against a background of sheltering trees* | *the word is written in white on a red background.* ▪ a less important or conspicuous position or function: *after that evening, she remained* ***in the background.*** ▪ Computing used in reference to tasks or processes that do not need input from the user: *programs can be left running* ***in the background.*** ▪ Physics low-intensity radiation from radioisotopes present in the natural environment. ▪ unwanted signals, such as noise in the reception or recording of sound.
2 the circumstances or situation prevailing at a particular time or underlying a particular event: *the political and economic background* | [as modifier] *background information.* ▪ a person's education, experience, and social circumstances: *she has a background in nursing* | *her voice suggested a tenacious, working-class background.*
▸ verb [with obj.] **1** form a background to: *windswept land backgrounded by the Rockies.*
2 provide with background: *the embassy backgrounded American reporters.*

backgrounder ▸ noun N. Amer. an official briefing or handout giving background information.

background music ▸ noun [mass noun] music intended as an unobtrusive accompaniment to an activity or to provide atmosphere in a film.

background radiation ▸ noun [mass noun] Astronomy the uniform microwave radiation remaining from the Big Bang.

backhand ▸ noun (in tennis and other racket sports) a stroke played with the back of the hand facing in the direction of the stroke, with the arm across the body: [as modifier] *a backhand volley.*
▸ verb [with obj.] strike with a backhanded blow or stroke: *in a flash, he backhanded Ace across the jaw.*

backhanded ▸ adjective **1** made with the back of the hand facing in the direction of movement: *a backhanded pass.*
2 having a meaning that is expressed indirectly or ambiguously: *coming from me, teasing is a backhanded compliment.*

backhander ▸ noun **1** a blow made with the back of the hand: *shut up, or I'll give you a backhander.* ▪ a backhand stroke or shot in a game.
2 Brit. informal a secret and illegal payment; a bribe: *a fortune had been paid in backhanders to local officials.*

back-heel ▸ verb [with obj.] kick (something) backwards with the heel: *Johnson back-heeled the ball.*

backhoe (Brit. also **backhoe loader**) ▸ noun a mechanical excavator which draws towards itself a bucket attached to a hinged boom.

backing ▸ noun [mass noun] **1** help or support: *the foreign secretary won the backing of opposition parties.* ▪ a layer of material that forms, protects, or strengthens the back of something. ▪ (especially in popular music) the musical or vocal accompaniment to the main singer or soloist: *the trio provided backing* | [as modifier] *a backing group.*
2 Phonetics the movement of the place of formation of a sound towards the back of the mouth.

backing store ▸ noun Computing a device for secondary storage of data that typically has greater capacity than the primary store but is slower to access.

backing track ▸ noun a recorded musical accompaniment, especially one for a soloist to play or sing along with.

back issue ▸ noun a past issue of a journal or magazine.

backland ▸ noun [mass noun] **1** (also **backlands**) another term for BACKCOUNTRY.
2 land behind an area which is built on or otherwise developed.

backlash ▸ noun **1** [in sing.] a strong negative reaction by a large number of people, especially to a social or political development: *a public* ***backlash against*** *racism.*
2 [mass noun] recoil arising between parts of a mechanism. ▪ degree of play between parts of a mechanism.

backless ▸ adjective (of a woman's garment) cut low at the back: *a backless lycra dress.*

backlift ▸ noun (in sport) a backward movement of the bat or leg before playing a stroke or kicking the ball.

backlight ▸ noun [mass noun] illumination from behind.
▸ verb (past **backlit**; past participle **backlit** or **backlighted**) [with obj.] illuminate from behind.
– DERIVATIVES **backlighting** noun.

backline ▸ noun **1** a line marking the back of something, especially the area of play in a game. ▪ Rugby the players lined out across the field behind a scrum or line-out.
2 the amplifiers used by a popular music group for guitars and other instruments, typically placed across the back of the stage.

backlist ▸ noun a publisher's list of books published before the current season and still in print.

backload ▸ noun a load transported on the return journey of a delivery truck.
▸ verb **1** [no obj.] transport a load on a return journey.
2 [with obj.] place more charges at the later stages of (a financial agreement) than at the earlier stages.

backlog ▸ noun an accumulation of uncompleted work or matters needing to be dealt with: *the company took on extra staff to clear the backlog of work.*

backlot ▸ noun an outdoor area in a film studio where large exterior sets are made and some outside scenes are filmed.

backmarker ▸ noun Brit. a competitor who is among the last in a race.

back number ▸ noun Brit. an issue of a periodical earlier than the current one. ▪ informal a person or thing seen as outdated or past their prime.

back office ▸ noun an office or centre in which the administrative work of a business is carried out, as opposed to its dealings with customers.

back order ▸ noun a retailer's order for a product which is temporarily out of stock with the supplier: *the phone I wanted was* ***on back order.***
▸ verb (**back-order**) [with obj.] place an order for (a product) which is temporarily out of stock.

backpack ▸ noun a rucksack. ▪ a piece of equipment carried on a person's back.
▸ verb [no obj.] (usu. as noun **backpacking**) travel or hike carrying one's belongings in a rucksack: *a week's backpacking in the Pyrenees.*
– DERIVATIVES **backpacker** noun.

back pass ▸ noun Soccer a deliberate pass to one's own goalkeeper (who is not allowed to pick up the ball if the pass was kicked).

back passage ▸ noun Brit., euphemistic the rectum.

back-pedal ▸ verb [no obj.] **1** reverse one's previous action or opinion: *Boyd quickly back-pedalled when asked to explain her suggestion.* ▪ move hastily backwards: *Cook forced the goalkeeper to back-pedal and push a shot over the bar.*
2 move the pedals of a bicycle backwards (formerly to brake).

backplane ▸ noun a board to which the main circuit boards of a computer may be connected, and which provides connections between them.

backplate ▸ noun a plate placed at or forming the back of something.

back-projection ▸ noun [mass noun] the projection of a picture on to the back of a translucent screen for viewing or for use as a background in filming. ▪ [count noun] an image projected in this way.
– DERIVATIVES **back-project** verb.

backrest ▸ noun a support for a person's back when they are seated.

back room ▸ noun a place where secret, administrative, or supporting work is done: *this would lead to weak government, and deals in back rooms* | [as modifier] *the back-room staff.*

back row ▸ noun [treated as sing. or pl.] Rugby the forwards who are in the third row in a scrum.
– DERIVATIVES **back-rower** noun.

backscatter ▸ noun [mass noun] Physics deflection of radiation or particles through an angle of 180°. ▪ radiation or particles that have been deflected in this way. ▪ Photography light from a flashgun or other light source that is deflected directly into a lens.
▸ verb [with obj.] Physics deflect (radiation or particles) through an angle of 180°.

backscratcher ▸ noun an implement for scratching one's back.

backscratching ▸ noun [mass noun] the reciprocal provision of help or support, typically in an underhand or illicit manner.

back seat ▸ noun a seat at the back of a vehicle.
– PHRASES **take a back seat** take or be given a less important position or role: *in future he would take a back seat in politics.*

back-seat driver ▸ noun informal a passenger in a car who gives the driver unwanted advice.
– DERIVATIVES **back-seat driving** noun.

backsheesh ▸ noun variant spelling of BAKSHEESH.

backshift ▸ noun [mass noun] Grammar the changing of a present tense in direct speech to a past tense in reported speech (or a past tense to pluperfect).

backside ▸ noun **1** informal a person's buttocks.
2 chiefly N. Amer. the reverse or rear side of something: *the backside of the hill.*
▸ adjective (of a manoeuvre in surfing and other board sports) done clockwise for a regular rider and anticlockwise for a goofy rider.

backsight ▸ noun **1** the sight of a rifle or other weapon that is nearer the eye of the person aiming.
2 Surveying a sight or reading taken backwards or towards the point of starting.

back slang ▸ noun [mass noun] slang in which words are spoken as though they were spelled backwards (e.g. *redraw* for *warder*).

backslapping ▸ noun [mass noun] the action of slapping a person's back in congratulation or encouragement. ▪ the action of congratulating someone in a hearty or effusive way: *the awards are about industry politics and backslapping.*
▸ adjective vigorously hearty: *those cheerful, backslapping journalists.*
– DERIVATIVES **backslapper** noun.

backslash ▸ noun a backward-sloping diagonal line (\), used in some computer commands.

backslide ▸ verb (past **backslid**; past participle **backslid** or archaic **backslidden**) [no obj.] relapse into bad ways or error: *there are many things that can cause slimmers to backslide* | (as noun **backsliding**) *there would be no backsliding from the government's sound policies.*
– DERIVATIVES **backslider** noun.

backspace ▶ noun **1** a key on a typewriter or computer keyboard used to cause the carriage or cursor to move backwards.
2 a device on a video recorder or camcorder which produces a slight backward run between shots to eliminate disturbance caused by the interruption of the scanning process.
▶ verb [no obj.] move a typewriter carriage or computer cursor backwards.

backspin ▶ noun [mass noun] a backward spin given to a moving ball, causing it to stop more quickly or rebound at a steeper angle on hitting a surface.

backsplash ▶ noun North American term for SPLASHBACK.

back-stabbing ▶ noun [mass noun] the action of criticizing someone in a treacherous manner while feigning friendship: *the media world of back-stabbing, scheming, and downright malice.*
– DERIVATIVES **back-stabber** noun.

backstage ▶ adverb in or to the area behind the stage in a theatre, especially the wings or dressing rooms: *I went backstage after the show* | [as modifier] *a backstage tour of the opera house.* ■ in secret: *we planned our strategies backstage.*

backstairs ▶ plural noun stairs at the back or side of a building. ■ [as modifier] underhand; clandestine: *I won't make backstairs deals with politicians.*

backstamp ▶ noun a mark stamped on the back of a plate or a letter.

backstay ▶ noun a stay on a sailing ship leading downwards and aft from the top or upper part of a mast.

backstitch ▶ noun [mass noun] a method of sewing with overlapping stitches.
▶ verb [with obj.] sew using backstitch.

backstop ▶ noun a thing placed at the rear of something as a barrier or support. ■ Baseball a high fence or similar structure behind the home plate area. ■ Baseball a catcher. ■ an emergency precaution or last resort: *the human operator has to act as the ultimate backstop when things go badly wrong.*
▶ verb [with obj.] Baseball act as backstop for. ■ Ice Hockey act as goaltender for. ■ support or reinforce: *the founding banks were backstopping the loans.*

backstory ▶ noun (pl. **backstories**) a history or background created for a fictional character in a film or television programme: *a brief prologue detailing our hero's backstory.*

back straight ▶ noun Brit. the part of a racecourse that is furthest from the grandstand and parallel to the home straight.

backstreet ▶ noun a minor street away from the main roads. ■ [as modifier] acting or done secretly and typically illegally: *backstreet abortions.*

backstretch ▶ noun N. Amer. another term for BACK STRAIGHT. ■ the area adjacent to a racecourse where the horses are stabled and stable employees have temporary living accommodation.

backstroke ▶ noun **1** a swimming stroke performed on the back with the arms lifted alternately out of the water in a backward circular motion and the legs extended and kicking.
2 Bell-ringing a pull of the tail end of the rope from its highest position so as to swing the bell through a full circle. Compare with HANDSTROKE.
– DERIVATIVES **backstroker** noun (sense 1).

backswept ▶ adjective swept, slanted, or sloped backwards: *his backswept hair.*

backswimmer ▶ noun another term for WATER BOATMAN (sense 1).

backswing ▶ noun a backward swing, especially of an arm or of a golf club when about to hit a ball.

backsword ▶ noun a sword with only one cutting edge.

back talk ▶ noun North American term for BACKCHAT.

back-to-back ▶ adjective **1** Brit. (of houses) built in a continuous terrace backing on to another terrace, with a party wall or a narrow alley between.
2 consecutive: *his back-to-back victories in the Hungarian and Belgian Grands Prix.*
▶ noun Brit. a house in a back-to-back terrace.
▶ adverb (**back to back**) **1** (of two people) facing in opposite directions with their backs touching.
2 consecutively; in succession: *the games were played back to back.*

back-to-nature ▶ adjective [attrib.] advocating or relating to reversion to a simpler way of life: *a back-to-nature lifestyle.*

backtrack ▶ verb **1** [no obj.] retrace one's steps: *Marilyn backtracked and went down into the basement.* ■ reverse one's previous position or opinion: *the unions have had to* **backtrack on** *their demands.*
2 [with obj.] US pursue, trace, or monitor: *he was able to backtrack the buck to a ridge nearby.*

backup ▶ noun **1** [mass noun] help or support: *no police backup could be expected.* ■ someone or something that can be called upon if necessary; a reserve: *I've got a security force as backup* | [as modifier] *a backup generator.*
2 [mass noun] Computing the procedure for making copies of data in case the original is lost or damaged. ■ [count noun] a copy made in such a way.
3 N. Amer. an accumulation of something caused by a blockage, as in traffic or water.

backup light ▶ noun North American term for REVERSING LIGHT.

backveld /ˈbakfɛlt/ ▶ noun (**the backveld**) S. African remote country districts, especially when considered to be unsophisticated or conservative.
– ORIGIN partial translation of Afrikaans *agterveld*, literally 'back countryside'.

backward ▶ adjective **1** directed behind or to the rear: *she left the room without a backward glance.* ■ reverting to an inferior state; retrograde: *the decision was a backward step.*
2 having made less progress than is normal or expected: *a backward agricultural country.* ■ (of a person) having learning difficulties.
3 [with negative] (**backward in**) lacking the confidence to do (something): *he was not backward in displaying his talents.*
4 Cricket (of a fielding position) behind an imaginary line passing through the stumps at the batsman's end at right angles to the wicket.
▶ adverb another word for BACKWARDS.
– DERIVATIVES **backwardly** adverb, **backwardness** noun.
– ORIGIN Middle English: from earlier *abackward*, from ABACK.

> **USAGE** In most adverbial uses **backward** and **backwards** are interchangeable: *the car rolled slowly* **backward** and *the car rolled slowly* **backwards** are both equally acceptable. In North American English **backward** tends to be preferred to **backwards**, while in British English it is the other way round. As an adjective, on the other hand, the standard form is **backward** rather than **backwards**: uses such as *a* **backwards** *glance* (as opposed to *a* **backward** *glance*) are unusual.

backwardation ▶ noun [mass noun] Stock Exchange, Brit. a situation in which the spot or cash price of a commodity is higher than the forward price. Often contrasted with CONTANGO. ■ a situation in which the offer price for stock is lower than the bid. ■ historical a percentage paid by a person selling stock for the right of delaying its delivery.

backward classes ▶ plural noun Indian the members of a caste or community who are recommended for special help in education and employment.

backward-looking ▶ adjective opposing progress and innovation; reactionary.

backwards (also **backward**) ▶ adverb **1** (of a movement) in the direction of one's back: *Penny glanced backwards* | *he took a step backwards.*
2 (of an object's motion) back towards the starting point: *the tape rolled backwards.*
3 in reverse of the usual direction or order: *count backwards from twenty to ten.* ■ towards the past: *the songs look backwards to long-ago battles.* ■ towards or into a worse state: *a step backwards for the economy.*
– PHRASES **backwards and forwards** in both directions alternately; to and fro. **bend** (or **fall** or **lean**) **over backwards** informal make every effort to achieve something, especially to be fair or helpful: *we have bent over backwards to ensure a fair trial for the defendants.* **know something backwards** be entirely familiar with something.

backwards-compatible (also **backward-compatible**) ▶ adjective (of computer hardware or software) able to be used with an older piece of hardware or software without special adaptation or modification.
– DERIVATIVES **backwards compatibility** noun.

backwash ▶ noun [mass noun] the motion of receding waves. ■ a backward current created by an object moving through water or air. ■ the unpleasant after-effects of an event: *the backwash of the Cuban missile crisis.*
▶ verb [with obj.] clean (a filter) by reversing the flow of fluid through it.

backwater ▶ noun a part of a river not reached by the current, where the water is stagnant. ■ an isolated or peaceful place. ■ a place or situation in which no development or progress is taking place: *the country remained an economic backwater.*

backwind Sailing ▶ verb [with obj.] (of a sail or vessel) deflect a flow of air into the back of (another sail or vessel).
▶ noun a flow of air deflected into the back of a sail.

backwoods ▶ plural noun [often as modifier] chiefly N. Amer. remote uncleared forest land: *backwoods homesteads.* ■ a remote or sparsely inhabited region, especially one considered backward.

backwoodsman ▶ noun (pl. **backwoodsmen**) chiefly N. Amer. an inhabitant of backwoods, especially one regarded as uncouth or backward. ■ Brit. informal a peer who very rarely attends the House of Lords.

backyard ▶ noun Brit. a yard at the back of a house or other building. ■ N. Amer. a back garden. ■ informal the area close to where one lives, regarded with proprietorial concern: *children must be made aware of environmental issues* ***in their own backyard.***

Bacolod /bɑːˈkəʊlɒd/ a city on the NW coast of the island of Negros in the central Philippines; pop. 499,500 (est. 2007). It is the chief city of the island and a major port.

Bacon[1], Francis, Baron Verulam and Viscount St Albans (1561–1626), English statesman and philosopher. As a scientist he advocated the inductive method, his views were instrumental in the founding of the Royal Society in 1660. Notable works: *The Advancement of Learning* (1605) and *Novum Organum* (1620).

Bacon[2], Francis (1909–92), Irish painter. His work chiefly depicts human figures in grotesquely distorted postures, set in confined interior spaces.

Bacon[3], Roger (*c.*1214–94), English philosopher, scientist, and Franciscan friar. Most notable for his work in the field of optics, he emphasized the need for an empirical approach to scientific study.

bacon ▶ noun [mass noun] cured meat from the back or sides of a pig.
– PHRASES **bring home the bacon** informal **1** supply material support: *I have to go to work because it brings home the bacon.* **2** achieve success.
– ORIGIN Middle English: from Old French, from a Germanic word meaning 'ham, flitch'; related to BACK.

bacon-and-eggs ▶ noun Austral. another term for EGGS AND BACON.

baconer ▶ noun a pig fit for being made into bacon and ham, typically heavier than both a porker and a cutter.

Baconian /beɪˈkəʊnɪən/ ▶ adjective relating to Sir Francis Bacon or his inductive method of reasoning and philosophy. ■ relating to or denoting the theory that Bacon wrote the plays attributed to Shakespeare.
▶ noun an adherent of Bacon's philosophical system. ■ a supporter of the theory that Bacon wrote the plays attributed to Shakespeare.

bacteraemia /ˌbaktəˈriːmɪə/ (US **bacteremia**) ▶ noun [mass noun] Medicine the presence of bacteria in the blood.
– DERIVATIVES **bacteraemic** adjective.
– ORIGIN late 19th cent.: from BACTERIUM + -AEMIA.

bacteria plural form of BACTERIUM.

bactericide /bakˈtɪərɪsʌɪd/ ▶ noun a substance which kills bacteria.
– DERIVATIVES **bactericidal** adjective.

bacterio- /bakˈtɪərɪəʊ/ ▶ combining form representing BACTERIUM.

bacteriocin /bakˈtɪərɪə(ʊ)sɪn/ ▶ noun Biology a protein produced by bacteria of one strain and active against those of a closely related strain.
– ORIGIN 1950s: from French *bactériocine*, from Greek *baktērion* 'small cane' + a shortened form of COLICIN.

bacteriological ▶ adjective relating to bacteriology or bacteria. ■ relating to or denoting germ warfare.
– DERIVATIVES **bacteriologic** adjective, **bacteriologically** adverb.

bacteriology ▶ noun [mass noun] the study of bacteria.
– DERIVATIVES **bacteriologist** noun.

bacteriolysis /bakˌtɪərɪˈɒlɪsɪs/ ▶ noun [mass noun] Biology the rupture of bacterial cells, especially by an antibody.
– DERIVATIVES **bacteriolytic** adjective.

bacteriophage /bakˈtɪərɪə(ʊ)feɪdʒ, -fɑːʒ/ ▶ noun Biology a virus which parasitizes a bacterium by infecting it and reproducing inside it. Bacteriophages are much used in genetic research.
– ORIGIN 1920s: from BACTERIUM + Greek *phagein* 'eat'.

B

bacteriostat /bak'tɪərɪə(ʊ)stat/ ▶ **noun** a substance that prevents the multiplying of bacteria without destroying them.
– DERIVATIVES **bacteriostasis** noun, **bacteriostatic** adjective.
– ORIGIN early 20th cent.: from BACTERIUM + Greek *statos* 'standing'.

bacterium /bak'tɪərɪəm/ ▶ **noun** (pl. **bacteria** /-rɪə/) a member of a large group of unicellular microorganisms which have cell walls but lack organelles and an organized nucleus, including some which can cause disease.

> Bacteria are widely distributed in soil, water, and air, and on or in the tissues of plants and animals. Formerly included in the plant kingdom, they are now classified separately (as prokaryotes). They play a vital role in global ecology, as the chemical changes they bring about include those of organic decay and nitrogen fixation. Much modern biochemical knowledge has been gained from the study of bacteria, as they grow easily and reproduce rapidly in laboratory cultures.

– DERIVATIVES **bacterial** adjective, **bacterially** adverb.
– ORIGIN mid 19th cent.: modern Latin, from Greek *baktērion*, diminutive of *baktēria* 'staff, cane' (because the first ones to be discovered were rod-shaped). Compare with BACILLUS.

> **USAGE** Bacteria is the plural form (derived from Latin) of **bacterium.** Like any other plural it should be used with the plural form of the verb: *the **bacteria** causing salmonella **are** killed by thorough cooking*, **not** *the **bacteria** causing salmonella **is** killed by thorough cooking*. However, the unfamiliarity of the form means that **bacteria** is sometimes mistakenly treated as a singular form, as in the example above.

bacteriuria /bak,tɪərɪ'jʊərɪə/ ▶ **noun** [mass noun] Medicine the presence of bacteria in the urine.

Bactria /'baktrɪə/ an ancient country in central Asia, corresponding to the northern part of modern Afghanistan. It was the seat of a powerful Indo-Greek kingdom in the 3rd and 2nd centuries BC.
– DERIVATIVES **Bactrian** adjective & noun.

Bactrian camel ▶ **noun** the two-humped camel, which has been domesticated but is still found wild in central Asia. • *Camelus ferus* (including the domesticated *C. bactrianus*), family Camelidae.

baculovirus /'bakjʊlə(ʊ),vʌɪrəs/ ▶ **noun** Biology a member of a family of DNA viruses infecting only invertebrate animals. Some have a very specific insect host, and may be used in biological pest control.
– ORIGIN 1980s: from Latin *baculum* 'rod, stick' + VIRUS.

baculum /'bakjʊləm/ ▶ **noun** (pl. **bacula** /-lə/) another term for OS PENIS.
– ORIGIN 1930s: modern Latin.

bad ▶ **adjective** (**worse, worst**) **1** of poor quality or a low standard: *a bad diet | bad eyesight.* ▪ not able to do a particular thing well: *I'm so* **bad at** *names | a bad listener.* ▪ [attrib.] not appropriate in a particular situation: *morning was a bad time to ask Andy about anything.*
2 not such as to be hoped for or desired; unpleasant or unwelcome: *bad news | it was the worst day of his life | bad luck.* ▪ (of something causing pain, danger, or other unwelcome consequences) severe or serious: *bad headaches | a bad crash.* ▪ unfavourable; adverse: *bad reviews.* ▪ (**bad for**) having a harmful effect on: *soap was bad for his face.*
3 lacking or failing to conform to moral virtue: *the bad guys | bad behaviour.* ▪ (of language) using words generally considered offensive.
4 (of a part of the body) injured, diseased, or painful: *a bad back.* ▪ [as complement] (of a person) unwell: *I feel bad.*
5 (of food) decayed; putrid: *everything in the fridge went bad.* ▪ (of the atmosphere) polluted; unhealthy: *bad air.*
6 [as complement] regretful, guilty, or ashamed about something: *working mothers who feel bad about leaving their child.*
7 worthless; not valid: *he ran up 87 bad cheques.*
8 (**badder, baddest**) informal, chiefly N. Amer. good; excellent: *they want the baddest, best-looking Corvette there is.*
▶ **adverb** N. Amer. informal badly: *he beat her up real bad.*
– PHRASES **a bad penny always turns up** see PENNY. **a bad workman always blames his tools** see WORKMAN. **come to a bad end** see END. **from bad to worse** into an even worse state. **in a bad way** ill or in trouble. **my bad** N. Amer. informal used to acknowledge responsibility for a mistake: *Sorry I lost your CD. It's my bad.* **not** (or **not so**) **bad** informal fairly good: *she discovered he wasn't so bad after all.* **to the bad 1** to ruin. **2** in deficit: *he was £80 to the bad.* **too bad** informal used to indicate that something is regrettable but is now beyond retrieval: *too bad, but that's the way it is.*
– DERIVATIVES **baddish** adjective, **badness** noun.
– ORIGIN Middle English: perhaps from Old English *bǣddel* 'hermaphrodite, womanish man'.

badam /bʌ'dɑːm/ ▶ **noun** Indian term for ALMOND.
– ORIGIN from Hindi *badām.*

badass N. Amer. informal ▶ **adjective 1** tough or aggressive: *a badass demeanour.*
2 formidable; excellent: *this was one badass camera.*
▶ **noun** an aggressive or uncooperative person.

bad blood ▶ **noun** [mass noun] ill feeling: *there has always been bad blood between these families.*

bad boy ▶ **noun** informal **1** a man who does not conform to approved standards of behaviour, especially in a particular sphere of activity: *the bad boy of British fashion.*
2 chiefly US something extremely impressive or effective: *we went 142 mph in that bad boy.*

bad break ▶ **noun** informal a piece of bad luck.

bad breath ▶ **noun** [mass noun] unpleasant-smelling breath; halitosis.

bad debt ▶ **noun** a debt that cannot be recovered.

baddeleyite /'bad(ə)lɪʌɪt/ ▶ **noun** [mass noun] a mineral consisting largely of zirconium dioxide, ranging from colourless to yellow, brown, or black.
– ORIGIN late 19th cent.: named after Joseph Baddeley, English traveller, + -ITE[1].

badderlocks /'badəlɒks/ (also **dabberlocks**) ▶ **plural noun** chiefly Scottish an edible seaweed with a long greenish frond and prominent midrib, occurring in northern Europe. • *Alaria esculenta*, class Phaeophyceae.
– ORIGIN late 18th cent.: perhaps from *Balderlocks*, based on the name of the god BALDER.

baddy (also **baddie**) ▶ **noun** (pl. **baddies**) informal a villain or criminal in a book, film, etc.

bade /beɪd, bad/ past of BID[2].

Baden /'bɑːd(ə)n/ a spa town in Austria, south of Vienna; pop. 25,255 (2006). It was a royal summer retreat and fashionable resort in the 19th century.

Baden-Baden /,bɑːd(ə)n'bɑːd(ə)n/ a spa town in the Black Forest; pop. 54,900 (est. 2007). It was a fashionable resort in the 19th century.

Baden-Powell /,beɪd(ə)n'pəʊəl/, Robert (Stephenson Smyth), 1st Baron Baden-Powell of Gilwell (1857–1941), English soldier and founder of the Boy Scout movement. He became a national hero after his successful defence of Mafeking (1899–1900) in the Boer War.

Baden-Württemberg /,bɑːd(ə)n'vʊətəm,bəːg/, German /,baːdn'vʏrtəmbɛrk/ a state of western Germany; capital, Stuttgart.

Bader /'bɑːdə/, Sir Douglas (Robert Steuart) (1910–82), British airman. Despite having lost both legs in a flying accident in 1931, he saw action as a fighter pilot during the Battle of Britain (1940–1). After the war he was noted for his work on behalf of disabled people.

bad faith ▶ **noun** [mass noun] **1** intent to deceive: *the Republicans accused the Democrats of negotiating* **in bad faith**.
2 (in existentialist philosophy) refusal to confront facts or choices.

bad form ▶ **noun** [mass noun] an offence against current social conventions: *it was considered bad form to talk about money.*

badge ▶ **noun** a small piece of metal, plastic, or cloth bearing a design or words, typically worn to identify a person or to indicate membership of an organization or support for a cause. ▪ a distinguishing object or emblem: *the car's front badge is much loved by thieves.* ▪ a feature or sign which reveals a particular quality: *philanthropy was regarded as a badge of social esteem.*
▶ **verb** [with obj.] mark with a badge or other distinguishing emblem.
– ORIGIN late Middle English: of unknown origin.

badge engineering ▶ **noun** [mass noun] the practice of marketing a motor vehicle under two or more brand names or badges.

badger ▶ **noun** a heavily built omnivorous nocturnal mammal of the weasel family, typically having a grey and black coat. • Several genera and species in the family Mustelidae, in particular the Eurasian *Meles meles*, which has a white head with two black stripes, and the North American *Taxidea taxus*, with a white stripe on the head.
▶ **verb** [with obj.] repeatedly and annoyingly ask (someone) to do something: *journalists badgered him about the deals | Tom had finally* **badgered** *her* **into** *going.*
– ORIGIN early 16th cent.: perhaps from BADGE, with reference to its distinctive head markings. The verb sense (late 18th cent.) originates from the sport of badger-baiting.

badger-baiting ▶ **noun** [mass noun] a sport in which dogs draw a badger from its sett and kill it, illegal in the UK since 1830.

Badger State informal name for WISCONSIN[1].

bad hair day ▶ **noun** informal a day on which everything seems to go wrong, characterized as a day on which one's hair is particularly unmanageable.

badinage /'badɪnɑːʒ/ ▶ **noun** [mass noun] humorous or witty conversation: *he developed a nice line in badinage with the Labour leader.*
– ORIGIN mid 17th cent.: from French, from *badiner* 'to joke', from *badin* 'fool', based on Provençal *badar* 'gape'.

badlands ▶ **plural noun** extensive tracts of heavily eroded, uncultivable land with little vegetation.
▪ (**Badlands**) a barren plateau region of the western US, mainly in North and South Dakota and Nebraska.
– ORIGIN mid 19th cent. (originally US): translation of French *mauvaises terres.*

badly ▶ **adverb** (**worse, worst**) **1** in an unsatisfactory, inadequate, or unsuccessful way: *England have played badly this year | the war was going badly.* ▪ in a critical or unfavourable way: *try not to think badly of me.* ▪ in an unacceptable or unpleasant way: *she realized she was behaving rather badly.*
2 used to emphasize the seriousness of an unpleasant event or action: *the building was badly damaged by fire.* ▪ very much or intensely: *I wanted a baby so badly.*
3 in a guilty or regretful way: *I felt badly about my unfriendliness.*
– PHRASES **badly off** at a disadvantage, especially by being poor.

bad manners ▶ **plural noun** lack of polite or well-bred social behaviour: *it's bad manners to talk with your mouth full.*
– DERIVATIVES **bad-mannered** adjective.

badmash /bʌd'mɑːʃ/ ▶ **noun** Indian a dishonest or unprincipled man.
– ORIGIN from Urdu, from Persian *bad* 'evil' + Arabic *ma'āš* 'means of livelihood'.

bad-minded ▶ **adjective** W. Indian malicious, unsympathetic, or cynical.

badminton ▶ **noun** [mass noun] a game with rackets in which a shuttlecock is hit back and forth across a net.
– ORIGIN named after *Badminton* in SW England, country seat of the Duke of Beaufort.

bad-mouth ▶ **verb** [with obj.] informal criticize (someone) behind their back: *no one wants to hire an individual who bad-mouths a prior employer.*

Badon Hill, Battle of /'beɪd(ə)n/ an ancient British battle in which, according to one theory, the forces of King Arthur successfully defended themselves against the Saxons in AD 516. Another source implies that the battle was fought *c.*500 but does not connect it with King Arthur.

bad-tempered ▶ **adjective** easily annoyed or made angry: *seldom has there been a more naughty and bad-tempered child.* ▪ characterized by anger: *a bad-tempered match.*
– DERIVATIVES **bad-temperedly** adverb.

BAe ▶ **abbreviation** historical British Aerospace (now **BAE Systems**).

Baedeker /'beɪdɪkə/, German /'bɛːdəkɐ/, Karl (1801–59), German publisher. He is remembered chiefly for the series of guidebooks to which he gave his name and which are still published today.

Baer /bɛː/, German /bɛːɐ/, Karl Ernest von (1792–1876), German biologist. He discovered that ova were particles within the ovarian follicles, and formulated the principle that in the developing embryo general characteristics appear before special ones. His studies were used by Darwin in the theory of evolution.

Baez /'bʌɪɛz/, Joan (b.1941), American folk singer. She is best known for her performances at civil rights demonstrations in the early 1960s.

Baffin, William (*c.*1584–1622), English navigator and explorer, the pilot of several expeditions in search of the North-West Passage 1612–16.

Baffin Bay an extension of the North Atlantic between Baffin Island and Greenland, linked to the

Arctic Ocean by three passages. It is largely ice-bound in winter.

Baffin Island a large island in the Canadian Arctic, situated at the mouth of Hudson Bay. It is separated from Greenland by Baffin Bay.

baffle ▸ verb [with obj.] **1** totally bewilder or perplex: *an unexplained occurrence that baffled everyone.*
2 restrain or regulate (a fluid, sound, etc.).
▸ noun a device used to restrain the flow of a fluid, gas, etc. or to prevent the spreading of sound or light in a particular direction.
– DERIVATIVES **bafflement** noun.
– ORIGIN late 16th cent. (in the sense 'cheat, deceive'): perhaps related to French *bafouer* 'ridicule' or obsolete French *beffer* 'mock, deceive'.

bafflegab /ˈbaf(ə)lgab/ ▸ noun [mass noun] N. Amer. informal incomprehensible or pretentious verbiage, especially bureaucratic jargon.

baffler ▸ noun another term for **BAFFLE**.

baffling ▸ adjective impossible to understand; perplexing: *the crime is a baffling mystery for the police.*
– DERIVATIVES **bafflingly** adverb [as submodifier] *his team selection has been bafflingly erratic.*

BAFTA /ˈbaftə/ ▸ abbreviation ■ British Academy of Film and Television Arts. ■ [as noun] an award made by this institution.

bafta /ˈbɑːftə/ (also **baft**) ▸ noun [mass noun] coarse fabric, typically of cotton.
– ORIGIN late 16th cent.: from Urdu, from Persian *bāft* 'textile', *bāfta* 'woven'.

bag ▸ noun **1** a flexible container with an opening at the top, used for carrying things: *brown paper bags.* ■ the amount held by such a container: *a* **bag** *of sugar.* ■ a woman's handbag. ■ a piece of luggage: *she began to unpack her bags.*
2 (**bags**) loose folds of skin under a person's eyes.
3 (**bags**) Brit. dated loose-fitting trousers.
4 (**bags of**) informal, chiefly Brit. plenty of: *I had bags of energy.*
5 informal a woman, especially an older one, perceived as unpleasant or unattractive: *an interfering* **old bag**.
6 (**one's bag**) informal one's particular interest or taste: *ask the manager about mild curries, if that's your bag.*
7 the amount of game shot by a hunter.
8 (in southern Africa) a unit of measurement, used especially of grain, equal to 70 kg (formerly 200 lb).
9 Baseball a base.
▸ verb (**bags, bagging, bagged**) [with obj.] **1** put (something) in a bag: *customers bagged their own groceries.*
2 succeed in killing or catching (an animal): *Mike bagged nineteen cod.* ■ succeed in securing (something): *we've bagged three awards for excellence | get there early to bag a seat in the front row.*
3 [no obj.] (of clothes, especially trousers) form loose bulges due to wear: *these trousers never bag at the knee.*
4 N. Amer. informal abandon or give up on: *she ought to just bag this marriage and get on with her life.*
5 (often as noun **bagging**) Austral./NZ informal criticize: *it's a pretty suspect outfit, deserving of the consistent bagging it gets from customers.*
6 N. Amer. informal fit (a patient) with an oxygen mask or other respiratory aid.
– PHRASES **bag and baggage** with all one's belongings: *he threw her out bag and baggage.* **a bag of bones** informal an emaciated person or animal. **a bag** (or **bundle**) **of nerves** see **NERVE**. **a bag of tricks** informal a set of ingenious plans, techniques, or resources. **bags** (or **bags I**) Brit. informal a child's expression used to make a claim to something: *bags I his jacket.* **in the bag** informal **1** (of something desirable) as good as secured: *the election is in the bag.* **2** N. Amer. drunk.
– DERIVATIVES **bagful** noun (pl. **bagfuls**), **bagger** noun.
– ORIGIN Middle English: perhaps from Old Norse *baggi*.

Baganda /bəˈgandə/ ▸ plural noun (sing. **Muganda**) an African people of the kingdom of Buganda, now forming part of Uganda.
– ORIGIN a local name; compare with Kiswahili *Waganda*.

bagasse /bəˈgas/ ▸ noun [mass noun] the dry pulpy residue left after the extraction of juice from sugar cane.
– ORIGIN early 19th cent.: from French, from Spanish *bagazo* 'pulp'.

bagatelle /ˌbagəˈtɛl/ ▸ noun **1** [mass noun] a game in which small balls are hit and then allowed to roll down a sloping board on which there are holes, each numbered with the score achieved if a ball goes into it, with pins acting as obstructions.
2 a thing regarded as too unimportant or easy to be worth much consideration: *dealing with these boats was* **a mere bagatelle** *for the world's oldest yacht club.*
3 a short, light piece of music, especially one for the piano.
– ORIGIN mid 17th cent. (in sense 2): from French, from Italian *bagatella*, perhaps from *baga* 'baggage' or from a diminutive of Latin *baca* 'berry'. Sense 1 dates from the early 19th cent.

Bagehot /ˈbadʒət/, Walter (1826–77), English economist and journalist. He became editor of the *Economist* in 1860, a post which he held until his death. Notable works: *The English Constitution* (1867), *Lombard Street* (1873).

bagel /ˈbeɪg(ə)l/ ▸ noun a dense bread roll in the shape of a ring, characteristic of Jewish baking.
– ORIGIN early 20th cent. (as *beigel*): from Yiddish *beygel*.

baggage ▸ noun [mass noun] **1** suitcases and bags containing personal belongings packed for travelling; luggage. ■ the portable equipment of an army.
2 past experiences or long-held attitudes perceived as burdensome encumbrances: *the emotional baggage I'm hauling around.*
3 [count noun] dated a cheeky or disagreeable girl or woman.
– ORIGIN late Middle English: from Old French *bagage* (from *baguer* 'tie up'), or *bagues* 'bundles'; perhaps related to **BAG**.

baggage reclaim (US **baggage claim**) ▸ noun the area in an airport where arriving passengers collect luggage that has been transported in the hold of the aircraft.

Baggie ▸ noun (pl. **Baggies**) N. Amer. trademark a plastic bag typically used for storing food.

baggy ▸ adjective (**baggier, baggiest**) (of clothing) loose and hanging in folds: *baggy trousers.* ■ (of eyes) with folds of puffy skin below them.
▸ noun (**baggies**) informal loose, wide-legged trousers or shorts.
– DERIVATIVES **baggily** adverb, **bagginess** noun.

bagh /bɑːg/ ▸ noun [usu. in place names] Indian a large garden or orchard: *Roshanara Bagh.*
– ORIGIN via Hindi from Persian *bāg*.

Baghdad /bagˈdad/ the capital of Iraq, on the River Tigris; pop. 6,194,800 (est. 2009). A thriving city under the Abbasid caliphs in the 8th and 9th centuries, it was taken by the Ottoman sultan Suleiman in 1534 and remained under Ottoman rule until the First World War. In 1920 it became the capital of the newly created state of Iraq.

bag lady ▸ noun informal a homeless woman who carries her possessions around in shopping bags.

bagless ▸ adjective (of a vacuum cleaner) designed to operate without a replaceable bag.

bag lunch ▸ noun variant of **BROWN-BAG LUNCH**.

bagman ▸ noun (pl. **bagmen**) **1** US & Austral./NZ informal an agent who collects or distributes the proceeds of illicit activities.
2 Canadian a political fundraiser.
3 Brit. informal, dated a travelling salesman.

bagnio /ˈbɑːnjəʊ, ˈbanjəʊ/ ▸ noun (pl. **bagnios**) **1** archaic a brothel.
2 historical (in East Asia) a prison.
– ORIGIN late 16th cent. (in sense 2): from Italian *bagno*, from Latin *balneum* 'bath'.

Bagot /ˈbagət/ ▸ noun a goat of a horned white breed with a black head, neck, and shoulders.

bagpipe ▸ noun (also **bagpipes**) a musical instrument with reed pipes that are sounded by the pressure of wind emitted from a bag squeezed by the player's arm. Bagpipes are associated especially with Scotland, but are also used in folk music in Ireland, Northumberland, and France, and in varying forms across Europe and western Asia.
– DERIVATIVES **bagpiper** noun.

bagsy /ˈbagzi/ ▸ verb (**bagsies, bagsying, bagsied**) [with obj.] informal succeed in securing (something) for oneself: *I'd managed to bagsy the front seat.*
– ORIGIN 1950s: representing a pronunciation of *bags I*.

ba gua /bɑː ˈgwɑː/ (also **pa kua**) ▸ noun a Chinese religious motif incorporating the eight trigrams of the *I Ching*, arranged octagonally around a symbol denoting the balance of yin and yang, or around a mirror. ■ (in feng shui) this motif regarded as a pattern determining the significance and auspicious qualities of spatial relationships. ■ [mass noun] a Chinese martial art in which movements are focused on a circle and the defence of eight points around it.
– ORIGIN from Chinese *bā* 'eight' + *guà* 'divinatory symbols'.

baguette /baˈgɛt/ ▸ noun **1** a long, narrow French loaf.
2 [often as modifier] a gem, especially a diamond, cut in a long rectangular shape: *a baguette diamond.*
3 Architecture a small moulding, semicircular in section.
4 a slim, rectangular handbag with a short strap.
– ORIGIN early 18th cent. (in sense 3): from French, from Italian *bacchetto*, diminutive of *bacchio*, from Latin *baculum* 'staff'. Sense 1 and sense 2 date from the 20th cent.

bagworm ▸ noun a drab moth, the caterpillar and flightless female of which live in a portable protective case constructed out of plant debris. ● Family Psychidae: many genera.

bah ▸ exclamation an expression of contempt or disagreement: *You think it was an accident? Bah!*
– ORIGIN early 19th cent.: probably from French.

bahada /bəˈhɑːdə/ ▸ noun variant spelling of **BAJADA**.

bahadur /ˌbɑːhəˈdʊə/ ▸ noun Indian a great man. ■ an honorific title, originally given to officers in British India: *Bahadur Shah.*
– ORIGIN from Urdu and Persian *bahādur*, from Mongolian.

Baha'i /bɑːˈhɑːi/ (also **Bahai**) ▸ noun (pl. **Baha'is**) [mass noun] a monotheistic religion founded in the 19th century as a development of Babism, emphasizing the essential oneness of humankind and of all religions and seeking world peace. The Baha'i faith was founded by the Persian Baha'ullah (1817–92) and his son Abdul Baha (1844–1921). ■ [count noun] an adherent of the Baha'i faith.
– DERIVATIVES **Baha'ism** /bɑːˈhɑːɪz(ə)m/ noun.
– ORIGIN Persian, from Arabic *bahā'* 'splendour'.

Bahamas a country consisting of an archipelago off the SE coast of Florida, part of the West Indies; pop. 307,600 (est. 2009); languages, English (official), Creole; capital, Nassau.

> It was there that Columbus made his first landfall in the New World (12 October 1492). The islands were a British colony from the 18th century until they gained independence within the Commonwealth in 1973.

– DERIVATIVES **Bahamian** /bəˈheɪmɪən/ adjective & noun.

Bahasa Indonesia /bəˈhɑːsə/ ▸ noun [mass noun] the official language of Indonesia. See **INDONESIAN**.
– ORIGIN from Malay *bahasa* 'language'.

Bahasa Malaysia /bəˈhɑːsə/ ▸ noun [mass noun] the official language of Malaysia. See **MALAY**.

Bahawalpur /bəˈhɑːwəlˌpʊə/ a city of central Pakistan, in Punjab province; pop. 530,400 (est. 2009). It was formerly the capital of a princely state established by the nawabs of Bahawalpur.

Bahia /bɑːˈiːə/ **1** a state of eastern Brazil, on the Atlantic coast; capital, Salvador.
2 former name for **SALVADOR**.

Bahía Blanca /bɑːˌiːə ˈblaŋkə/ a port in Argentina serving the southern part of the country; pop. 315,700 (est. 2008)

bahookie /bəˈhʊki/ ▸ noun Scottish informal a person's buttocks.
– ORIGIN 1930s: probably a blend of **BEHIND** and **HOUGH**, + **-IE**.

Bahrain /bɑːˈreɪn/ a sheikhdom consisting of a group of islands in the Persian Gulf; pop. 728,700 (est. 2009); official language, Arabic; capital, Manama.

> Ruled by the Portuguese in the 16th century and the Persians in the 17th century, the islands became a British protectorate in 1861 and gained independence in 1971. Bahrain's economy is dependent on the refining and export of oil.

– DERIVATIVES **Bahraini** adjective & noun.

baht /bɑːt/ ▸ noun (pl. **same**) the basic monetary unit of Thailand, equal to 100 satangs.
– ORIGIN from Thai *bāt*.

bahu /ˈbɑːhuː/ ▸ noun Indian a daughter-in-law.
– ORIGIN Hindi *bahū* 'daughter-in-law, wife', from Sanskrit *vadhū, vadhukā*.

Bahutu plural form of **HUTU**.

bai /bʌɪ/ ▸ noun (pl. **bais**) Indian **1** [often as name] a polite form of address for a woman.
2 a maid.
– ORIGIN Marathi, 'lady', possibly from Turkish *baaji*.

B

Baikal, Lake /bʌɪˈkɑːl/ (also **Baykal**) a large lake in southern Siberia, the largest freshwater lake in Europe and Asia and, with a depth of 1,743 m (5,714 ft), the deepest lake in the world.

Baikonur /ˌbʌɪkəˈnʊə/ (also **Baykonur**) a mining town in central Kazakhstan. The world's first satellite (1957) and the first manned space flight (1961) were launched from the former Soviet space centre nearby.

bail[1] ▸ noun [mass noun] the temporary release of an accused person awaiting trial, sometimes on condition that a sum of money is lodged to guarantee their appearance in court: *he has been released* ***on bail****.* ■ money paid by or for such a person as security.
▸ verb [with obj.] release or secure the release of (a prisoner) on payment of bail: *nine were bailed on drugs charges* | [with obj. and infinitive] *he was bailed to appear at Durham Crown Court.*
– PHRASES **go bail** (or **stand bail**) act as surety for an accused person. **jump bail** informal fail to appear for trial after being released on bail. **post bail** pay a sum of money as bail.
– DERIVATIVES **bailable** adjective.
– ORIGIN Middle English: from Old French, literally 'custody, jurisdiction', from *bailler* 'take charge of', from Latin *bajulare* 'bear a burden'.

bail[2] ▸ noun 1 (usu. **bails**) Cricket either of the two crosspieces bridging the stumps, which the bowler and fielders try to dislodge with the ball to get the batsman out.
2 a bar which holds something in place, in particular: ■ a bar on a typewriter or computer printer which holds the paper steady. ■ Climbing a bar on a crampon which fits into a groove in the sole of a boot. ■ a bar separating horses in an open stable. ■ Austral./NZ a movable framework for securing the head of a cow during milking.
▸ verb [with obj.] Austral./NZ 1 (usu. **bail up**) confront (someone) with the intention of robbing them: *they bailed up Mr Dyason and demanded his money.* ■ detain (someone) in conversation, especially against their will.
2 secure (a cow) during milking.
– ORIGIN Middle English (denoting the outer wall of a castle): from Old French *baile* 'palisade, enclosure', *baillier* 'enclose', perhaps from Latin *baculum* 'rod, stick'.

bail[3] (Brit. also **bale**) ▸ verb 1 [with obj.] scoop water out of (a ship or boat): *the first priority is to* ***bail out*** *the boat with buckets.* ■ scoop (water) out of a ship or boat.
2 [no obj.] (**bail on**) N. Amer. informal let (someone) down: *he looks a little like the other guy that bailed on me.*
– PHRASAL VERBS **bail out** make an emergency parachute descent from an aircraft. ■ withdraw from an obligation or commitment: *she felt ready to* ***bail out of*** *the corporate rat race.* **bail someone/thing out** rescue someone or something from a difficulty: *the state will not bail out loss-making enterprises.*
– DERIVATIVES **bailer** noun.
– ORIGIN early 17th cent.: from obsolete *bail* 'bucket', from French *baille*, based on Latin *bajulus* 'carrier'.

baile /ˈbʌɪleɪ/ ▸ noun (in the south-western US and parts of Central and South America) a gathering for dancing.
– ORIGIN Spanish, 'dance, dancing'.

Baile Átha Cliath /ˌblʲaː ˈkʲlʲiə/ Irish name for **Dublin**.

bailee /beɪˈliː/ ▸ noun Law a person or party to whom goods are delivered for a purpose, such as custody or repair, without transfer of ownership.

Bailey[1] a shipping forecast area in the NE Atlantic north of Rockall and south-west of the Faroes.

Bailey[2], David (b.1938), English photographer. He was a prominent figure of 1960s pop culture.

bailey ▸ noun (pl. **baileys**) the outer wall of a castle. ■ a court enclosed by a bailey.
– ORIGIN Middle English: probably from Old French *baile* 'palisade, enclosure' (see **bail[2]**).

Bailey bridge ▸ noun a temporary bridge of lattice steel designed for rapid assembly from prefabricated standard parts, used especially in military operations.
– ORIGIN Second World War: named after Sir D. *Bailey* (1901–85), the English engineer who designed it.

bailie /ˈbeɪli/ ▸ noun (pl. **bailies**) chiefly historical a municipal officer and magistrate in Scotland.
– ORIGIN Middle English (originally used interchangeably with **bailiff**): from Old French *bailli*.

bailiff /ˈbeɪlɪf/ ▸ noun 1 a sheriff's officer who executes writs and processes and carries out distraints and arrests. ■ the agent of a landlord.
2 N. Amer. an official in a court of law who keeps order, looks after prisoners, etc.
3 Brit. historical the sovereign's representative in a district, especially the chief officer of a hundred. ■ the first civil officer in the Channel Islands.
– ORIGIN Middle English: from Old French *baillif*, inflected form of *bailli* (see **bailie**), based on Latin *bajulus* 'carrier, manager'.

bailiwick /ˈbeɪlɪwɪk/ ▸ noun (**one's bailiwick**) 1 one's sphere of operations or area of interest: *after the war, the Middle East remained his bailiwick.*
2 Law the district or jurisdiction of a bailie or bailiff.
– ORIGIN late Middle English: from **bailie** + **wick[2]**.

bailment ▸ noun Law an act of delivering goods to a bailee for a particular purpose, without transfer of ownership.

bailor /beɪˈlɔː/ ▸ noun Law a person or party that entrusts goods to a bailee.

bailout ▸ noun informal an act of giving financial assistance to a failing business or economy to save it from collapse.

Baily's beads Astronomy a string of bright points seen at the edge of the darkened moon at the beginning or end of totality in an eclipse of the sun, caused by the unevenness of the lunar topography.
– ORIGIN mid 19th cent.: named after Francis *Baily* (1774–1844), English astronomer.

bain-marie /ˌbanməˈriː/ ▸ noun (pl. **bains-marie** or **bain-maries** pronunc. **same**) a pan of hot water in which a cooking container is placed for slow cooking.
– ORIGIN early 18th cent.: French, translation of medieval Latin *balneum Mariae* 'bath of Maria', translating Greek *kaminos Marias* 'furnace of Maria', said to be a Jewish alchemist.

Bairam /bʌɪˈrɑːm/ ▸ noun either of two annual Muslim festivals, **Greater Bairam** and **Lesser Bairam** (see **Eid**).
– ORIGIN from Turkish *baïram* (earlier form of *bayram*), from Persian *bazrām*.

Baird /bɛːd/, John Logie (1888–1946), Scottish pioneer of television. He made the first transatlantic transmission and demonstration of colour television in 1928 using a mechanical system which was soon superseded by an electronic system.

bairn /bɛːn/ ▸ noun chiefly Scottish & N. English a child.
– ORIGIN Old English *bearn*, of Germanic origin; related to the verb **bear[1]**.

Baisakhi /bʌɪˈsɑːkhi/ ▸ noun a Sikh festival held annually to commemorate the founding of the khalsa by Gobind Singh in 1699.
– ORIGIN from Sanskrit *Vaiśākha*, denoting a month of the Hindu lunar year corresponding to April–May, regarded in some areas as the start of the new year.

bait ▸ noun 1 [mass noun] food placed on a hook or in a net, trap, or fishing area to entice fish or other animals as prey. ■ something intended to entice someone to do something: *many potential buyers are reluctant to* ***take the bait****.*
2 variant spelling of **bate[1]**.
▸ verb [with obj.] 1 deliberately annoy or taunt (someone): *the other boys revelled in baiting him about his love of literature.* ■ cause dogs to attack (a trapped or restrained animal).
2 put bait on (a hook) or in (a trap, net, or fishing area) to entice fish or animals: *I used a hook baited with fat.*
– PHRASES **fish or cut bait** N. Amer. informal stop vacillating and decide to act on or disengage from something. **rise to the bait** react to a provocation or temptation exactly as intended.
– DERIVATIVES **baiter** noun.
– ORIGIN Middle English: from Old Norse *beit* 'pasture, food', *beita* 'to hunt or chase'.

bait-and-switch ▸ noun [mass noun] the action (generally illegal) of advertising goods which are an apparent bargain, with the intention of substituting inferior or more expensive goods.

baitcasting ▸ noun [mass noun] fishing by throwing a bait or lure into the water on the end of a line using a rod and reel.
– DERIVATIVES **baitcaster** noun.

baiza /ˈbʌɪzɑː/ ▸ noun (pl. **same** or **baizas**) a monetary unit of Oman, equal to one thousandth of a rial.
– ORIGIN Arabic.

baize /beɪz/ ▸ noun [mass noun] a coarse felt-like woollen material that is typically green, used for covering billiard and card tables and for aprons.
– ORIGIN late 16th cent.: from French *baies*, feminine plural of *bai* 'chestnut-coloured' (see **bay[4]**), treated as a singular noun. The name is presumably from the original colour of the cloth, although several colours are recorded.

Baja California /ˈbɑːhɑː/ a mountainous peninsula in NW Mexico, which extends southwards from the border with California and separates the Gulf of California from the Pacific Ocean. It consists of two states of Mexico: **Baja California** (capital, Mexicali) and **Baja California Sur** (capital, La Paz). Also called **Lower California**.

bajada /bəˈhɑːdə/ ▸ noun a broad slope of alluvial material at the foot of an escarpment.
– ORIGIN mid 19th cent.: from Spanish, 'descent, slope'.

Bajan /ˈbeɪdʒ(ə)n/ ▸ adjective & noun informal term for **Barbadian** (see **Barbados**).

bajra /ˈbɑːdʒrɑː/ ▸ noun [mass noun] (in South Asia) pearl millet or similar grain.
– ORIGIN from Hindi *bājrā*, *bājrī*.

baju /ˈbɑːdʒuː/ ▸ noun a short, loose jacket worn in Malaysia.
– ORIGIN Malay.

Baka /ˈbaka/ ▸ noun (pl. **same**) 1 a member of a nomadic Pygmy people inhabiting the rainforests of south-eastern Cameroon and northern Gabon.
2 [mass noun] the Bantu language of the Baka.
– ORIGIN perhaps from Lingala *Ba-aka* 'Pygmies'.

bake ▸ verb [with obj.] 1 cook (food) by dry heat without direct exposure to a flame, typically in an oven: *they bake their own bread and cakes.* ■ [no obj.] (of food) be cooked in such a way: *the bread was baking on hot stones.*
2 (of the sun or other agency) subject (something) to dry heat, especially so as to harden it. ■ [no obj.] informal be or become extremely hot in prolonged sun or hot weather: *the city was baking in a heatwave.*
▸ noun [with modifier] a dish consisting of a mixture of ingredients cooked in an oven: *a vegetable bake.* ■ [with modifier] N. Amer. a social gathering at which baked food of a specified kind is eaten: *lobster bakes.*
– ORIGIN Old English *bacan*, of Germanic origin; related to Dutch *bakken* and German *backen*.

bakeapple ▸ noun Canadian the fruit of the cloudberry.

baked ▸ adjective 1 (of food) cooked by dry heat in an oven: *baked apples.*
2 N. Amer. informal intoxicated by drink or drugs, especially cannabis: *I just want to* ***get baked*** *and watch a movie.*

baked Alaska ▸ noun [mass noun] a dessert of sponge cake and ice cream in a meringue covering, cooked in a hot oven for a very short time.

baked beans ▸ plural noun baked haricot beans, typically cooked in tomato sauce and tinned.

baked potato ▸ noun a potato baked in its skin.

bakehouse ▸ noun dated a building or area in which bread is made.

Bakelite /ˈbeɪk(ə)lʌɪt/ ▸ noun [mass noun] trademark an early form of brittle plastic, typically dark brown, made from formaldehyde and phenol, used chiefly for electrical equipment.
– ORIGIN early 20th cent.: named after Leo H. *Baekeland* (1863–1944), the Belgian-born American chemist who invented it, + **-ite[1]**.

bake-off ▸ noun N. Amer. a contest in which cooks prepare baked goods such as bread and cakes for judging. ■ informal a contest between companies to win a contract.

Baker[1], Dame Janet (Abbott) (b.1933), English operatic mezzo-soprano.

Baker[2], Josephine (1906–75), American dancer. She was a star of the Folies-Bergère in the 1930s, famed for her exotic dancing and risqué clothing.

baker ▸ noun a person whose trade is making and selling bread and cakes. ■ [often with modifier] an oven for a particular purpose: *a waffle baker.*
– PHRASES **baker's dozen** a group of thirteen. [from the former bakers' custom of adding an extra loaf to a dozen sold to a retailer, this constituting the latter's profit.]

bakery ▸ noun (pl. **bakeries**) a place where bread and cakes are made or sold. ■ [mass noun] baked goods such as bread and cakes.

bakeshop ▸ noun North American term for **bakery**.

bakeware ▸ noun [mass noun] tins, trays, and other items used during baking.

Bakewell tart ▸ noun Brit. a baked open pie consisting of a pastry case lined with jam and filled with almond sponge cake.
– ORIGIN named after the town of *Bakewell* in Derbyshire.

baking powder ▸ noun [mass noun] a mixture of sodium bicarbonate and cream of tartar, used instead of yeast in baking.

baking soda ▸ noun [mass noun] sodium bicarbonate used in cooking, for cleaning, or in toothpaste.

Bakker, Robert T. (b.1945), American palaeontologist. He proposed the controversial idea that dinosaurs were active and warm-blooded.

bakkie /ˈbaki, ˈbʌki/ ▸ noun (pl. **bakkies**) S. African **1** a light truck or pickup truck.
2 a small basin or other container.
– ORIGIN Afrikaans, from *bak* 'container' + the diminutive suffix *-ie*.

baklava /ˈbakləvə, bəˈklɑːvə/ ▸ noun [mass noun] a dessert originating in the Middle East made of filo pastry filled with chopped nuts and soaked in honey.
– ORIGIN Turkish.

baksheesh /bakˈʃiːʃ/ (also **backsheesh**) ▸ noun [mass noun] (in parts of Asia) a small sum of money given as alms, a tip, or a bribe.
– ORIGIN based on Persian *bakšiš*, from *bakšīdan* 'give'.

Bakst /bakst/, Léon (1866–1924), Russian painter and designer; born *Lev Samuilovich Rozenberg*. He was a member of the Diaghilev circle and the Ballets Russes, for which he designed exotic, richly coloured sets and costumes.

Baku /baˈkuː/ the capital of Azerbaijan, on the Caspian Sea; pop. 1,917,000 (est. 2008). It is an industrial port and a centre of the oil industry.

Bakunin /baˈkuːnɪn/, Mikhail (Aleksandrovich) (1814–76), Russian anarchist. He took part in the revolutions of 1848, and participated in the First International until his expulsion in 1872.

balaclava /ˌbaləˈklɑːvə/ (also **balaclava helmet**) ▸ noun chiefly Brit. a close-fitting garment covering the whole head and neck except for parts of the face, typically made of wool.
– ORIGIN late 19th cent. (worn originally by soldiers on active service in the Crimean War): named after the port of *Balaclava* in the Crimea (see **BALACLAVA, BATTLE OF**).

Balaclava, Battle of /ˌbaləˈklɑːvə/ a battle of the Crimean War, fought between Russia and an alliance of British, French, and Turkish forces in and around the small port of Balaclava (now Balaklava) in the southern Crimea in 1854. The battle ended inconclusively; it is chiefly remembered as the scene of the Charge of the Light Brigade.

balafon /ˈbaləfɒn/ ▸ noun a large xylophone with hollow gourds as resonators, used in West African music.
– ORIGIN via French from Manding *bala* 'xylophone' + *fo* 'to play'.

balalaika /ˌbaləˈlʌɪkə/ ▸ noun a Russian musical instrument like a guitar with a triangular body and typically three strings.
– ORIGIN late 18th cent.: from Russian, of Tartar origin.

balance ▸ noun **1** [mass noun] an even distribution of weight enabling someone or something to remain upright and steady: *she **lost her balance** and fell.* ■ Sailing the ability of a boat to stay on course without adjustment of the rudder.
2 [mass noun] a situation in which different elements are equal or in the correct proportions: *the obligations of political balance in broadcasting* | [in sing.] *try to **keep a balance between** work and relaxation.* ■ mental or emotional stability: *the way to some kind of peace and personal balance.* ■ the relative volume of various sources of sound: *the balance of the voices is good.* ■ Art harmony of design and proportion.
3 an apparatus for weighing, especially one with a central pivot, beam, and two scales. ■ (**the Balance**) the zodiacal sign or constellation Libra.
4 a counteracting weight or force. ■ (also **balance wheel**) the regulating device in a clock or watch.
5 [mass noun] a predominating amount; a preponderance: ***the balance of** opinion was that work was more important than leisure.*
6 a figure representing the difference between credits and debits in an account; the amount of money held in an account: *he accumulated a healthy balance with the savings bank.* ■ the difference between an amount due and an amount paid: *the holiday balance must be paid by 8 weeks before departure.*
▸ verb [with obj.] **1** put (something) in a steady position so that it does not fall: *a mug that she balanced on her knee.* ■ [no obj.] remain in a steady position without falling: *Richard balanced on the ball of one foot.*
2 offset or compare the value of (one thing) with another: *the cost of obtaining such information needs to be **balanced against** its benefits.* ■ counteract or equal the effect or importance of: *he balanced his radical remarks with more familiar declarations.* ■ establish equal or appropriate proportions of elements in: *policies that help women balance work and family life.*
3 compare debits and credits in (an account) so as to ensure that they are equal: *the law requires the council to **balance its books** each year.* ■ [no obj.] (of an account) have credits and debits equal.
– PHRASES **balance of payments** the difference in total value between payments into and out of a country over a period. **balance of power 1** a situation in which states of the world have roughly equal power. **2** the power held by a small group when larger groups are of equal strength. **balance of trade** the difference in value between a country's imports and exports. **in the balance** in an uncertain or critical state: *his survival **hung in the balance** for days.* **on balance** when all factors are taken into consideration: *on balance, he was pleased with how things had gone.* **strike a balance** choose a moderate course. **throw** (or **catch**) **someone off balance** make someone unsteady and in danger of falling. ■ surprise someone by doing something unexpected.
– DERIVATIVES **balancer** noun.
– ORIGIN Middle English (in sense 3 of the noun): from Old French *balance* (noun), *balancer* (verb), based on late Latin *(libra) bilanx* '(balance) having two scale pans', from *bi-* 'twice, having two' + *lanx* 'scale pan'.

balanced ▸ adjective keeping or showing a balance; in good proportions: *she assembled a balanced team.* ■ taking everything into account; fairly judged or presented: *accurate and balanced information.* ■ (especially of food) having different elements in the correct proportions: *a healthy, balanced diet.* ■ (of a person or state of mind) having no emotion too strong or too weak; stable: *a balanced personality.* ■ (of an electric circuit or signal) being symmetrical with respect to a reference point, usually earth.

balance sheet ▸ noun a statement of the assets, liabilities, and capital of a business or other organization at a particular point in time, detailing the balance of income and expenditure over the preceding period.

balance wheel ▸ noun the regulating device in a watch or clock.

Balanchine /ˈbalənʃiːn, -tʃiːn/, George (1904–83), Russian-born American ballet dancer and choreographer; born *Georgi Melitonovich Balanchivadze*. He was chief choreographer of Diaghilev's Ballets Russes during the 1920s, and in 1934 he co-founded the company which later became the New York City Ballet.

balancing act ▸ noun an action or activity that requires a delicate balance between different situations or requirements.

balander /bəˈlandə/ (also **balanda**) ▸ noun derogatory (in Australian Aboriginal English) a white man.
– ORIGIN mid 19th cent.: from Makasarese *balanda*, from Malay *belanda* (alteration of **HOLLANDER** in the sense 'Dutchman').

balanitis /ˌbaləˈnʌɪtɪs/ ▸ noun [mass noun] Medicine inflammation of the glans penis.
– ORIGIN mid 19th cent.: from Greek *balanos* 'glans penis' (literally 'acorn') + **-ITIS**.

balas ruby /ˈbaləs/ ▸ noun a ruby of a delicate rose-red variety.
– ORIGIN late Middle English: from Old French *balais*, from Arabic *balakš*, from Persian *Badakšān*, a district of Afghanistan where it is found.

balata /ˈbalətə, bəˈlɑːtə/ ▸ noun a tropical American tree which bears edible fruit and produces latex.
● Several species in the family Sapotaceae, in particular *Manilkara bidentata*.
■ [mass noun] the dried sap of this tree, used as a substitute for rubber.
– ORIGIN early 17th cent.: from Carib *balatá*.

Balaton, Lake /ˌbɒləˈtɒn/ a large, shallow lake in west central Hungary, situated in a resort and wine-producing region to the south of the Bakony mountains.

Balboa /balˈbəʊə/, Vasco Núñez de (1475–1519), Spanish explorer. In 1513 he reached the western coast of the isthmus of Darien (Panama), thereby becoming the first European to see the eastern shores of the Pacific Ocean.

balboa /balˈbəʊə/ ▸ noun the basic monetary unit of Panama, equal to 100 centésimos.
– ORIGIN named after Vasco Núñez de **BALBOA**.

balbriggan /balˈbrɪg(ə)n/ ▸ noun [mass noun] a knitted cotton fabric, used for stockings and underwear.
– ORIGIN late 19th cent.: named after the town of *Balbriggan* in Ireland, where it was originally made.

Balcon /ˈbɔːlk(ə)n/, Sir Michael (1896–1977), English film producer associated chiefly with Ealing Studios. He produced such famous comedies as *Kind Hearts and Coronets* and *Whisky Galore* (both 1949).

balcony ▸ noun (pl. **balconies**) **1** a platform enclosed by a wall or balustrade on the outside of a building, with access from an upper-floor window or door.
2 (**the balcony**) the highest tier of seats in a theatre, above the dress or upper circle. ■ the upstairs seats in a cinema. ■ N. Amer. the dress circle in a theatre.
– DERIVATIVES **balconied** adjective.
– ORIGIN early 17th cent.: from Italian *balcone*, probably ultimately of Germanic origin.

bald /bɔːld/ ▸ adjective **1** having a scalp wholly or partly lacking hair: *he was starting to **go bald**.* ■ (of an animal) not covered by the usual fur, hair, or feathers: *hedgehogs are born bald.* ■ (of a plant or an area of land) not covered by the usual leaves, bark, or vegetation. ■ (of a tyre) having the tread worn away.
2 without any extra detail or explanation; plain or blunt: *the bald statement in the preceding paragraph requires amplification.*
– PHRASES **(as) bald as a coot** completely bald.
– DERIVATIVES **baldish** adjective, **baldly** adverb (sense 2), **baldness** noun.
– ORIGIN Middle English: probably from a base meaning 'white patch', whence the archaic sense 'marked or streaked with white'. Compare with Welsh *ceffyl bal*, denoting a horse with a white mark on its face.

baldachin /ˈbɔːldəkɪn, ˈbɔːld-/ (also **baldaquin** /ˈbɔːldəkɪn/ or **baldacchino** /ˌbaldəˈkiːnəʊ/) ▸ noun a ceremonial canopy of stone, metal, or fabric over an altar, throne, or doorway.
– ORIGIN late 16th cent. (denoting a rich brocade of silk and gold thread): from Italian *baldacchino*, from *Baldacco* 'Baghdad', place of origin of the brocade.

bald cypress ▸ noun another term for **SWAMP CYPRESS**.

bald eagle ▸ noun a white-headed North American eagle that includes fish among its prey. It is the national bird of the US but is now common only in Alaska. ● *Haliaetus leucocephalus*, family Accipitridae.

Balder /ˈbɔːldə/ Scandinavian Mythology a son of Odin and god of the summer sun. He was invulnerable to all things except mistletoe, with which the god Loki, by a trick, induced the blind god Hödur to kill him.

balderdash /ˈbɔːldədaʃ/ ▸ noun [mass noun] senseless talk or writing; nonsense.
– ORIGIN late 16th cent. (denoting a frothy liquid; later, an unappetizing mixture of drinks): of unknown origin.

bald-faced ▸ adjective N. Amer. another term for **BAREFACED**.

baldhead ▸ noun (among Rastafarians) a person who is not a Rastafarian.

baldie ▸ noun & adjective variant spelling of **BALDY**.

balding /ˈbɔːldɪŋ/ ▸ adjective in the process of losing one's hair: *a balding middle-aged man stepped into the room.*

baldpate ▸ noun the American wigeon (in allusion to its white-crowned head).

baldric /ˈbɔːldrɪk/ ▸ noun historical a belt for a sword or other piece of equipment, worn over one shoulder and reaching down to the opposite hip.
– ORIGIN Middle English *baudry*, from Old French *baudre*, of unknown ultimate origin.

Baldwin[1] /ˈbɔːldwɪn/, James (Arthur) (1924–87), American novelist and black civil rights activist. Notable works: *Go Tell it on the Mountain* (1953) and *Giovanni's Room* (1956).

Baldwin[2] /ˈbɔːldwɪn/, Stanley, 1st Earl Baldwin of Bewdley (1867–1947), British Conservative statesman, Prime Minister 1923–4, 1924–9, and 1935–7. Despite the German occupation of the Rhineland and the outbreak of the Spanish Civil War (both 1936), Baldwin opposed demands for rearmament, believing that the public would not support it.

B

baldy (also **baldie**) ▸ **noun** (pl. **baldies**) informal, derogatory a bald-headed person.
▸ **adjective** chiefly Scottish & Irish bald.

bale[1] ▸ **noun** a large wrapped or bound bundle of paper, hay, or cotton. ■ the quantity in a bale as a measure, specifically (in the US) 500 lb of cotton.
▸ **verb** [with obj.] make up into bales: *the straw is left on the field to be baled later.*
– ORIGIN Middle English: probably from Middle Dutch, from Old French; ultimately of Germanic origin and related to **BALL**[1].

bale[2] ▸ **noun** [mass noun] archaic evil considered as a destructive force. ■ evil suffered; physical or mental torment.
– ORIGIN Old English *balu, bealu*, of Germanic origin.

bale[3] ▸ **verb** Brit. variant spelling of **BAIL**[3].

Bâle /bal/ French name for **BASLE**.

Balearic /ˌbalɪˈarɪk, bəˈlɪərɪk/ ▸ **adjective** relating to the Balearic Islands: *the Balearic government.* ■ relating to or denoting a style of synthesized dance music that developed in Ibiza: *the Balearic beat.*
– ORIGIN from Latin *Balearis* + **-IC**.

Balearic Islands (also **the Balearics**) a group of Mediterranean islands off the east coast of Spain, forming an autonomous region of that country, with four large islands (Majorca, Minorca, Ibiza, Formentera) and seven smaller ones; capital, Palma (on Majorca).

baleen /bəˈliːn/ ▸ **noun** [mass noun] whalebone.
– ORIGIN Middle English (also denoting a whale): from Old French *baleine*, from Latin *balaena* 'whale'.

baleen whale ▸ **noun** a whale that has plates of whalebone in the mouth for straining plankton from the water. Baleen whales include the rorqual, humpback, right whale, and grey whale. Also called **WHALEBONE WHALE**. ● Suborder Mysticeti, order Cetacea: three families and ten species.

balefire ▸ **noun** US a large open-air fire.
– ORIGIN Old English (recorded in poetry), from obsolete *bale* 'great fire' + **FIRE**.

baleful ▸ **adjective** threatening harm; menacing: *Bill shot a baleful glance in her direction.* ■ having a harmful or destructive effect: *the baleful influence of Rasputin.*
– DERIVATIVES **balefully** adverb.

Balenciaga /baˌlɛnsɪˈɑːɡə/, Spanish /balenˈθjaɣa, -ˈsjaɣa/, Cristóbal (1895–1972), Spanish couturier. In the 1950s he contributed to the move away from the tight-waisted New Look originated by Christian Dior to a looser, semi-fitted style.

baler ▸ **noun** a machine for making up material such as paper, hay, or cotton into bales.

Balfour /ˈbalfə/, Arthur James, 1st Earl of Balfour (1848–1930), British Conservative statesman, Prime Minister 1902–5. In 1917, in his capacity as Foreign Secretary, Balfour issued the declaration in favour of a Jewish national home in Palestine that came to be known as the Balfour Declaration.

Bali /ˈbɑːli/ a mountainous island of Indonesia, to the east of Java; chief city, Denpasar; pop. 3,470,700 (est. 2009).

Balinese /ˌbɑːlɪˈniːz/ ▸ **adjective** relating to Bali or its people or language.
▸ **noun** (pl. **same**) **1** a native or inhabitant of Bali.
2 [mass noun] the Indonesian language of Bali, with around 4 million speakers.

balk ▸ **verb & noun** chiefly N. Amer. variant spelling of **BAULK**.

Balkanize /ˈbɔːlkənʌɪz, ˈbɒl-/ (also **Balkanise**) ▸ **verb** [with obj.] divide (a region or body) into smaller mutually hostile states or groups.
– DERIVATIVES **Balkanization** /-ˈzeɪʃ(ə)n/ **noun**.
– ORIGIN 1920s: from *Balkan* Peninsula (where this was done in the late 19th and early 20th cent.) + **-IZE**.

Balkans /ˈbɔːlkənz/ **1** (also **Balkan Mountains**) a range of mountains stretching eastwards across Bulgaria from the Serbian frontier to the Black Sea. The highest peak is Botev Peak (2,375 m; 7,793 ft).
2 the countries occupying the part of SE Europe lying south of the Danube and Sava Rivers, forming a peninsula bounded by the Adriatic and Ionian Seas in the west, the Aegean and Black Seas in the east, and the Mediterranean in the south.
– DERIVATIVES **Balkan** adjective.

Balkan Wars two wars of 1912–13 that were fought over the last European territories of the Ottoman Empire.

In 1912 Bulgaria, Serbia, Greece, and Montenegro forced Turkey to give up Albania and Macedonia, leaving the area around Constantinople (Istanbul) as the only Ottoman territory in Europe. The following year Bulgaria disputed with Serbia, Greece, and Romania for possession of Macedonia, which was partitioned between Greece and Serbia.

Balkhash, Lake variant spelling of **BALQASH, LAKE**.

Balkis /ˈbɔːlkɪs, ˈbɒl-/ the name of the queen of Sheba in Arabic literature.

balky /ˈbɔːlki, ˈbɔːki/ (Brit. also **baulky**) ▸ **adjective** (**balkier, balkiest; baulkier, baulkiest**) chiefly US awkward; uncooperative.

Ball[1], John (d.1381), English rebel. Ball was a priest who preached an egalitarian social message. He was excommunicated and imprisoned for heresy, and following the Peasants' Revolt was hanged as a traitor.

Ball[2], Lucille (1911–89), American comedienne, known in particular for the popular television series *I Love Lucy* (1951–5).

ball[1] ▸ **noun 1** a solid or hollow spherical or egg-shaped object that is kicked, thrown, or hit in a game: *a cricket ball.* ■ a spherical object or mass of material: ***a ball of wool** | he crushed the card into a ball.* ■ historical a solid spherical non-explosive projectile for a cannon. ■ [mass noun] a game played with a ball: *he comes across a group of kids playing ball.* ■ [mass noun] N. Amer. baseball: *young men would graduate from college and enter pro ball.*
2 a single throw, kick, or hit of the ball in a game, in particular: ■ Cricket a delivery of the ball by the bowler to the batsman. ■ Baseball a pitch delivered outside the strike zone which the batter does not attempt to hit. ■ Soccer a pass of the ball in a specified direction or manner: *Whelan sent a long ball to Goddard.*
▸ **verb** [with obj.] **1** squeeze or form (something) into a rounded shape: *Robert **balled up** his napkin and threw it on to his plate.* ■ clench (one's fist) tightly. ■ [no obj.] form a round shape: *the fishing nets eventually **ball up** and sink.* ■ wrap the root ball of (a tree or shrub) in hessian to protect it during transportation.
2 N. Amer. vulgar slang have sexual intercourse with (someone).
3 [no obj.] Brit. (of a flower) fail to open properly, decaying in the half-open bud.
– PHRASES **the ball is in your court** it is up to you to make the next move. **a ball of fire** a person who is full of energy and enthusiasm. **the ball of the foot** the rounded protuberant part of the foot at the base of the big toe. **the ball of the thumb** the rounded protuberant part of the hand at the base of the thumb. **have a lot** (or **not much**) **on the ball** US have a lot of (or not much) ability. **keep the ball rolling** maintain the momentum of an activity. **keep one's eye on** (or **take one's eye off**) **the ball** keep (or fail to keep) one's attention focused on the matter in hand. **on the ball** aware of and quick to respond to new ideas and methods. **play ball** informal work willingly with others; cooperate: *if his solicitors won't play ball, there's nothing we can do.* **start** (or **get** or **set**) **the ball rolling** cause something to start happening. **the whole ball of wax** N. Amer. informal everything.
– ORIGIN Middle English: from Old Norse *bǫllr*, of Germanic origin.

ball[2] ▸ **noun** a formal social gathering for dancing.
– PHRASES **have a ball** informal enjoy oneself greatly.
– ORIGIN early 17th cent.: from French *bal* 'a dance', from late Latin *ballare* 'to dance'; related to Greek *ballizein* 'to dance' (also *ballein* 'to throw').

-ball ▸ **combining form** N. Amer. informal used in various derogatory terms as an intensifier: *sleazeball | goofball.*

ballad ▸ **noun 1** a poem or song narrating a story in short stanzas. Traditional ballads are typically of unknown authorship, having been passed on orally from one generation to the next.
2 a slow sentimental or romantic song.
– DERIVATIVES **balladist** noun.
– ORIGIN late 15th cent. (denoting a light, simple song): from Old French *balade*, from Provençal *balada* 'dance, song to dance to', from *balar* 'to dance', from late Latin *ballare* (see **BALL**[2]). The sense 'narrative poem' dates from the mid 18th cent.

ballade /baˈlɑːd/ ▸ **noun 1** a poem consisting of one or more triplets of stanzas with a repeated refrain and an envoi.
2 a piece of music in romantic style with dramatic elements, typically for piano.
– ORIGIN late Middle English: earlier spelling and pronunciation of **BALLAD**.

balladeer /ˌbaləˈdɪə/ ▸ **noun** a singer or composer of ballads.

ballad opera ▸ **noun** a theatrical entertainment popular in early 18th-century England, taking the form of a satirical play interspersed with traditional or operatic songs. The best-known example is John Gay's *The Beggar's Opera* (1728).

balladry ▸ **noun** [mass noun] ballads collectively. ■ the art of writing or performing ballads.

ball and chain ▸ **noun** a heavy metal ball secured by a chain to the leg of a prisoner to prevent escape. ■ used to convey the idea that someone or something is a crippling encumbrance: *the ball and chain of debt.*

ball-and-socket joint ▸ **noun** a natural or manufactured joint or coupling, such as the hip joint, in which a partially spherical end lies in a socket, allowing multidirectional movement and rotation.

Ballantyne /ˈbalənt ʌɪn/, R. M. (1825–94), Scottish author; full name *Robert Michael Ballantyne*. He wrote acclaimed adventure stories such as *The Coral Island* (1857).

ballan wrasse /ˈbalən/ ▸ **noun** a large European wrasse (fish) of rocky shores and reefs, popular as an angling fish. ● *Labrus bergylta*, family Labridae.
– ORIGIN mid 18th cent.: *ballan* from Irish *ballán*, from *ball* 'spot'.

Ballarat /ˈbalərat/ a mining and sheep-farming centre in Victoria, Australia; pop. 91,787 (2008). It is the site of the discovery in 1851 of the largest gold reserves in Australia.

Ballard, J. G. (1930–2009), British novelist and short-story writer; full name *James Graham Ballard*. He is known for dystopian science fiction such as his first novel, *The Drowned World* (1962), and *Crash* (1973).

ballast /ˈbaləst/ ▸ **noun** [mass noun] **1** heavy material, such as gravel, sand, or iron, placed in the bilge of a ship to ensure its stability. ■ a similar substance carried in an airship or on a hot-air balloon to stabilize it and jettisoned when greater altitude is required. ■ something providing stability or substance: *the film is an entertaining comedy with some serious ideas thrown in for ballast.*
2 gravel or coarse stone used to form the bed of a railway track or the substratum of a road. ■ a mixture of coarse and fine aggregate for making concrete.
3 [count noun] a passive component used in an electric circuit to moderate changes in current.
▸ **verb** [with obj.] **1** give stability to (a ship) by putting a heavy substance in its bilge.
2 form (the bed of a railway line or the substratum of a road) with gravel or coarse stone.
– PHRASES **in ballast** (of a ship) laden only with ballast.
– ORIGIN mid 16th cent.: probably of Low German or Scandinavian origin.

ball bearing ▸ **noun** a bearing in which the parts are separated by a ring of small freely rotating metal balls which reduce friction. ■ a ball used in such a bearing.

ballboy ▸ **noun** a boy who retrieves balls that go out of play during a game such as tennis or baseball.

ball-breaker (also **ball-buster**) ▸ **noun** informal a sexually demanding woman who destroys men's self-confidence.
– DERIVATIVES **ball-breaking** adjective.

ball carrier ▸ **noun** American Football a player in possession of the ball and attempting to advance it.

ball clay ▸ **noun** [mass noun] a fine-textured clay used in the manufacture of ceramics.

ballcock ▸ **noun** a valve which is linked by a hinged arm to a ball floating on top of a liquid and opens or closes a tap automatically according to the height of the ball, especially in the cistern of a flushing toilet.

baller ▸ **noun 1** chiefly US a player of a ball game, especially basketball.
2 a person or device that makes or forms something into balls: *a melon baller.*

ballerina ▸ **noun** a female ballet dancer.
– ORIGIN late 18th cent.: from Italian, feminine of *ballerino* 'dancing master', from *ballare* 'to dance', from late Latin.

Ballesteros /ˌbaləˈstɛːrɒs/, Spanish /bajesˈteɾos/, Sevvy (b.1957), Spanish golfer; full name *Severiano Ballesteros*. In 1979 he became the youngest player in the 20th century to win the British Open; the following year he was the youngest-ever winner of the US Masters.

ballet ▸ **noun** [mass noun] an artistic dance form performed to music, using precise and highly formalized set steps and gestures. Classical ballet, which originated in Renaissance Italy and established its present form during the 19th century, is characterized by light, graceful movements and the use of pointe shoes with reinforced toes. ■ [count noun] a creative work of this form or the music written for it. ■ [treated as sing. or pl.] a group of dancers who regularly perform ballets: *the Bolshoi Ballet*.
– ORIGIN mid 17th cent.: from French, from Italian *balletto*, diminutive of *ballo* 'a dance', from late Latin *ballare* 'to dance' (see BALL²).

ballet dancer ▸ **noun** a person who dances in ballets.

balletic /bəˈlɛtɪk/ ▸ **adjective** relating to or characteristic of ballet: *a graceful, balletic movement*.
– DERIVATIVES **balletically** adverb.

ballet master ▸ **noun** a person employed by a ballet company to teach and rehearse dancers.

balletomane /ˈbalɪtəʊˌmeɪn/ ▸ **noun** a ballet enthusiast.
– DERIVATIVES **balletomania** noun.

ballet shoe (also **ballet pump**) ▸ **noun** a light, round-toed shoe with very flat heels for women or girls, resembling the type worn by ballet dancers.

Ballets Russes /ˌbaleɪ ˈruːs/, French /bale ʀus/ a ballet company formed in Paris in 1909 by Sergei Diaghilev.

> The company commissioned music from the composers Stravinsky, Satie, and Rimsky-Korsakov, while Picasso and Jean Cocteau designed sets. The company's choreographers and dancers included Michel Fokine, Anna Pavlova, Vaslav Nijinsky, and George Balanchine. It was responsible for reviving ballet as an art form in western Europe.

ball float ▸ **noun** the spherical float attached to a hinged arm in the ballcock of a water cistern.

ball game ▸ **noun** a game played with a ball. ■ N. Amer. a baseball match.
– PHRASES **a different** (or **whole new**) **ball game** informal a situation that is completely different from a previous one: *making the film was a whole new ball game for her*.

ballgirl ▸ **noun** a girl who retrieves balls that go out of play during a game such as tennis or baseball.

ballgown ▸ **noun** a woman's elaborate full-length dress suitable for wearing to balls and similar social gatherings.

ballhawk ▸ **noun** N. Amer. informal a player who is good at getting possession of or catching the ball.
– DERIVATIVES **ballhawking** noun.

ballista /bəˈlɪstə/ ▸ **noun** (pl. **ballistae** /-stiː/ or **ballistas**) a catapult used in ancient warfare for hurling large stones.
– ORIGIN early 16th cent.: from Latin, based on Greek *ballein* 'to throw'.

ballistic /bəˈlɪstɪk/ ▸ **adjective 1** relating to projectiles or their flight.
2 moving under the force of gravity only.
– PHRASES **go ballistic** informal fly into a rage.
– DERIVATIVES **ballistically** adverb.
– ORIGIN late 18th cent.: from BALLISTA + -IC.

ballistic missile ▸ **noun** a missile with a high, arching trajectory, which is initially powered and guided but falls under gravity on to its target.

Ballistic Missile Defense Organization name given to STRATEGIC DEFENSE INITIATIVE after 1993.

ballistics ▸ **plural noun** [treated as sing.] the science of projectiles and firearms. ■ the scientific study of the effects of being fired on a bullet, cartridge, or gun.

ball lightning ▸ **noun** [mass noun] a rare and little known kind of lightning having the form of a moving globe of light several centimetres across which persists for periods of up to a minute.

ballock ▸ **verb** variant spelling of BOLLOCK.

ballocking ▸ **noun** variant spelling of BOLLOCKING.

ballocks ▸ **noun** variant spelling of BOLLOCKS.

ballon /ˈbalɔ̃/ ▸ **noun** [mass noun] (in dancing) the ability to appear effortlessly suspended while performing movements during a jump.
– ORIGIN French, from Italian *ballone*, from *balla* 'ball'.

balloon ▸ **noun 1** a small coloured rubber bag which is inflated with air and then sealed at the neck, used as a child's toy or a decoration.
2 (also **hot-air balloon**) a large bag filled with hot air or gas to make it rise in the air, typically one carrying a basket for passengers: *he set his sights on crossing the Pacific **by balloon***.
3 a rounded outline in which the words or thoughts of characters in a comic strip or cartoon are written.
4 (also **balloon glass**) a large rounded drinking glass, used especially for brandy.
5 Scottish informal a stupid person.
▸ **verb** [no obj.] **1** swell out in a spherical shape: *the trousers **ballooned out** below his waist*. ■ (of an amount of money spent or owed) increase rapidly: *the company's debt has ballooned in the last five years*. ■ (of a person) increase rapidly in weight: *I ate out of boredom and I just **ballooned up***.
2 Brit. (with reference to a ball) lob or be lobbed high in the air: *the ball ballooned into the air*.
3 travel by hot-air balloon: *he is famous for ballooning across oceans*.
– PHRASES **when the balloon goes up** Brit. informal when the action or trouble starts. [probably with allusion to the release of a balloon to mark the start of an event.]
– ORIGIN late 16th cent. (originally denoting a game played with a large inflated leather ball): from French *ballon* or Italian *ballone* 'large ball'.

balloon angioplasty ▸ **noun** [mass noun] Medicine surgical widening of a blocked or narrowed blood vessel, especially a coronary artery, by means of a balloon catheter.

balloon catheter ▸ **noun** Medicine a type of catheter incorporating a small balloon which may be introduced into a canal, duct, or blood vessel and then inflated in order to clear an obstruction or dilate a narrowed region.

balloonfish ▸ **noun** (pl. **same** or **balloonfishes**) a tropical porcupine fish which lives in shallow water and can inflate itself when threatened. ● *Diodon holocanthus*, family Diodontidae.

ballooning ▸ **noun** [mass noun] the sport or pastime of flying in a balloon.
– DERIVATIVES **balloonist** noun.

balloon payment ▸ **noun** a repayment of the outstanding principal sum made at the end of a loan period, interest only having been paid hitherto.

balloon tyre ▸ **noun** a large tyre containing air at low pressure for travel on soft or uneven surfaces.
– DERIVATIVES **balloon-tyred** adjective.

balloon vine ▸ **noun** a tropical American vine with inflated balloon-like pods. ● *Cardiospermum halicacabum*, family Sapiondaceae.

balloon whisk ▸ **noun** a hand whisk made of loops of wire.

ballot ▸ **noun** a system of voting secretly and in writing on a particular issue: *a strike ballot* | [mass noun] *the commissioners were elected by ballot*. ■ (**the ballot**) the total number of votes cast in such a process: *he won 54 per cent of the ballot*. ■ the piece of paper used to record a person's vote. ■ a lottery held to decide the allocation of tickets, shares, or other things among a number of applicants.
▸ **verb** (**ballots, balloting, balloted**) [with obj.] (of an organization) ask (members) to vote secretly on an issue: *the union is preparing to ballot its members on industrial action*. ■ [no obj.] cast one's vote on an issue: [with infinitive] *ambulance crews balloted unanimously to reject the deal*. ■ decide the allocation of (something) to applicants by drawing lots.
– ORIGIN mid 16th cent. (originally denoting a small coloured ball placed in a container to register a vote): from Italian *ballotta*, diminutive of *balla* (see BALL¹).

ballot box ▸ **noun** a sealed box into which voters put completed ballot papers. ■ (**the ballot box**) democratic principles and methods: *the proper remedy was the ballot box and not the court*.

ballotin /ˈbalətɪn/ ▸ **noun** a deep decorative cardboard box, slightly larger at the top and with broad flaps, in which chocolates are sold.
– ORIGIN French, from *ballot* 'a small package of goods'.

ballotine /ˈbalətiːn/ ▸ **noun** a piece of roasted meat which has first been boned, stuffed, and folded or rolled into an egg-like shape.
– ORIGIN mid 19th cent.: French, ultimately from *balle* 'a package of goods'.

ballot paper ▸ **noun** Brit. a slip of paper used to register a vote.

ballpark ▸ **noun 1** N. Amer. a baseball ground.
2 informal an area or range within which an amount or estimate is likely to be correct: *we can make a pretty good guess that this figure's in the ballpark*. ■ [as modifier] informal (of a price or cost) approximate: *the ballpark figure is $400–500*.

ballplayer ▸ **noun** N. Amer. a baseball player.

ballpoint (also **ballpoint pen**) ▸ **noun** a pen with a tiny ball as its writing point, especially one using stiffer ink than a rollerball.

ballroom ▸ **noun** a large room for formal dancing.

ballroom dancing ▸ **noun** [mass noun] formal social dancing in couples, popular as a recreation and also as a competitive activity. The ballroom dance repertoire includes dances developed from old European folk dances such as the waltz and minuet, Latin American dances such as the tango, rumba, and cha-cha, and dances of 20th-century origin such as the foxtrot and quickstep.

balls vulgar slang ▸ **plural noun 1** testicles.
2 [mass noun] courage or nerve.
3 [mass noun] Brit. nonsense; rubbish (often said to express strong disagreement).
▸ **verb** [with obj.] (**balls something up**) Brit. bungle something.
– PHRASES **have someone/thing by the balls** have complete control over someone or something: *they've got us by the balls, and they know it*.

balls-aching ▸ **adjective** vulgar slang causing annoyance, revulsion, or boredom.
– DERIVATIVES **balls-ache** noun, **balls-achingly** adverb.

balls-out ▸ **adjective & adverb** vulgar slang without moderation or restraint.

balls-up ▸ **noun** Brit. vulgar slang a bungled or badly carried out task or action; a mess.

ballsy ▸ **adjective** (**ballsier, ballsiest**) informal determined and courageous: *she was a cool, ballsy woman*.
– DERIVATIVES **ballsiness** noun.

ball-tampering ▸ **noun** [mass noun] Cricket unlawful alteration of the surface or seam of a ball on the field, to affect its motion when bowled.

ball-tearer ▸ **noun** Austral. informal something outstanding of its kind.

ball valve ▸ **noun** a one-way valve that is opened and closed by pressure on a ball which fits into a cup-shaped opening. ■ Brit. another term for BALLCOCK.

bally /ˈbali/ ▸ **adjective & adverb** Brit. old-fashioned euphemism for BLOODY².

ballyhoo informal ▸ **noun** [mass noun] extravagant publicity or fuss: *after all the ballyhoo, the film was a flop*.
▸ **verb** (**ballyhoos, ballyhooing, ballyhooed**) [with obj.] chiefly N. Amer. praise or publicize extravagantly.
– ORIGIN late 19th cent.: American coinage of unknown origin.

Ballymena /ˌbalɪˈmiːnə/ a town in Northern Ireland, to the north of Lough Neagh, capital of a district of the same name; pop. 29,400 (est. 2009).

ballyrag ▸ **verb** variant spelling of BULLYRAG.

balm /bɑːm/ ▸ **noun 1** a fragrant cream or liquid used to heal or soothe the skin. ■ something that has a soothing or restorative effect: *the murmur of the water can provide balm for troubled spirits*.
2 a tree which yields a fragrant resinous substance, especially one used in medicine. ● Species in several families, in particular those of the genus *Commiphora* (family Burseraceae).
■ [mass noun] resinous substance from such a tree.
3 (also **lemon** or **sweet balm**) [mass noun] a bushy herb of the mint family, with leaves smelling and tasting of lemon. ● *Melissa officinalis*, family Labiatae.
■ used in names of other aromatic herbs of the mint family, e.g. **bee balm**.
– ORIGIN Middle English (in the sense 'preparation for embalming, fragrant resinous substance'): from Old French *basme*, from Latin *balsamum* (see BALSAM).

balmacaan /balməˈkɑːn/ ▸ **noun** a loose-fitting overcoat with a small rounded collar, typically having raglan sleeves.
– ORIGIN early 20th cent.: named after *Balmacaan*, an estate near Inverness in Scotland.

bal masqué /ˌbal maˈskeɪ/, French /bal maske/ ▸ **noun** (pl. **bals masqués** pronunc. **same**) a masked ball.
– ORIGIN French.

Balmer series /ˈbɑːmə/ Physics a series of lines in the visible and ultraviolet spectrum of atomic hydrogen, between 656 and 365 nanometres.
– ORIGIN from the name of the Swiss physicist J. J. *Balmer* (1825–98).

B

balm of Gilead /ˈɡɪlɪad/ ▶ **noun 1** [mass noun] a fragrant medicinal resin obtained from certain trees.
2 a tree that yields such a resin, in particular: ● an Arabian tree traditionally of importance in medicine and perfumery (*Commiphora gileadensis*, family Burseraceae). ● either of two poplars with sticky aromatic buds (*Populus × gileadensis* (or *candicans*)) and the balsam poplar, family Salicaceae). ● the balsam fir.
– ORIGIN early 16th cent.: *balm* from a translation in Coverdale's Bible (Gen. 37:25), rendered 'resin' in the Vulgate; *Gilead* from the assumption that this resin is the substance mentioned in the Bible as coming from Gilead.

balmoral /balˈmɒr(ə)l/ ▶ **noun 1** a round brimless hat with a cockade or ribbons attached, worn by certain Scottish regiments.
2 a heavy laced leather walking boot.
– ORIGIN mid 19th cent. (in sense 2): named after **BALMORAL CASTLE** in Scotland.

Balmoral Castle a holiday residence of the British royal family, on the River Dee in Scotland.

bal musette /ˌbal mjuːˈzɛt/, French /bal myzɛt/ ▶ **noun** (pl. **bals musettes** pronunc. **same**) (in France) a dance hall with an accordion band.
– ORIGIN French, originally denoting dancing outdoors to bagpipe accompaniment.

balmy /ˈbɑːmi/ ▶ **adjective** (**balmier**, **balmiest**)
1 characterized by pleasantly warm weather: *the balmy days of late summer*.
2 N. Amer. or dated variant spelling of **BARMY**.
– DERIVATIVES **balmily** adverb, **balminess** noun.

balmyard ▶ **noun** (in the West Indies) a place where the rituals of Pocomania or obeah are practised.
– ORIGIN from **BALM** in the sense 'healing influence', possibly influenced by an African word.

balneology /ˌbalnɪˈɒlədʒi/ ▶ **noun** [mass noun] the study of medicinal springs and the therapeutic effects of bathing in them. ■ another term for **BALNEOTHERAPY**.
– DERIVATIVES **balneological** adjective.
– ORIGIN mid 19th cent.: from Latin *balneum* 'bath' + **-LOGY**.

balneotherapy /ˌbalnɪə(ʊ)ˈθɛrəpi/ ▶ **noun** [mass noun] the treatment of disease by bathing in mineral springs.
– ORIGIN late 19th cent.: from Latin *balneum* 'bath' + **THERAPY**.

baloney /bəˈləʊni/ ▶ **noun** informal **1** [mass noun] foolish or deceptive talk; nonsense: *I don't buy it—it's all a load of baloney*.
2 North American term for **BOLOGNA**.
– ORIGIN 1920s: sense 1 said to be a corruption of **BOLOGNA**.

Balqash, Lake /balˈkɑːʃ/ (also **Balkhash**) a shallow salt lake in Kazakhstan.

balsa /ˈbɔːlsə, ˈbɒlsə/ ▶ **noun** [mass noun] **1** (also **balsa wood**) very lightweight timber used chiefly for making models and rafts.
2 the fast-growing tropical American tree from which this timber is obtained. ● *Ochroma lagopus* (or *pyramidale*), family Bombacaceae.
– ORIGIN early 17th cent. (denoting a kind of South American raft or fishing boat): from Spanish, 'raft'.

balsam /ˈbɔːlsəm, ˈbɒl-/ ▶ **noun 1** [mass noun] an aromatic resinous substance, such as balm, exuded by various trees and shrubs and used as a base for certain fragrances and medical preparations. ■ [count noun] a tree or shrub which yields balsam.
2 a herbaceous plant cultivated for its helmeted pink or purple flowers. ● Genus *Impatiens*, family Balsaminaceae: several species.
– DERIVATIVES **balsamic** /-ˈsamɪk/ adjective.
– ORIGIN Old English, via Latin from Greek *balsamon*.

balsam fir ▶ **noun** a North American fir tree which yields Canada balsam. ● *Abies balsamea*, family Pinaceae.

balsamic vinegar ▶ **noun** [mass noun] dark, sweet Italian vinegar that has been matured in wooden barrels.

balsam poplar ▶ **noun** a North American poplar tree which yields balsam. ● *Populus balsamifera*, family Salicaceae.

bals masqués plural form of **BAL MASQUÉ**.

bals musettes plural form of **BAL MUSETTE**.

Balt /bɔːlt, bɒlt/ ▶ **noun 1** a speaker of a Baltic language; a Lithuanian or Latvian.
2 a native or inhabitant of one of the Baltic States of Lithuania, Latvia, and Estonia. ■ historical a German-speaking inhabitant of any of these states.
– ORIGIN late 19th cent.: from late Latin *Balthae* 'dwellers near the Baltic Sea'.

Balthasar /ˈbalθəzɑː/ the name of one of the three Magi.

balthazar /balˈθazə/ ▶ **noun** a very large wine bottle, equivalent in capacity to sixteen regular bottles.
– ORIGIN 1930s: from *Balthazar*, the name of the king of Babylon, who 'made a great feast ... and drank wine before a thousand' (Dan. 5:1).

Balti /ˈbalti/ ▶ **noun 1** a native or inhabitant of Baltistan.
2 [mass noun] the Tibetan language of the Baltis, with around 400,000 speakers.
▶ **adjective** relating to the Baltis or their language.
– ORIGIN the name in Ladakhi dialect.

balti /ˈbɔːlti, ˈbalti/ ▶ **noun** (pl. **baltis**) [mass noun] a type of spicy Pakistani cuisine in which the food is cooked in a small two-handled pan known as a karahi. ■ [count noun] a meal prepared in this way.
– ORIGIN of uncertain origin: perhaps from **BALTI**.

Baltic /ˈbɔːltɪk, ˈbɒlt-/ ▶ **adjective 1** relating to the Baltic Sea or the region surrounding it.
2 denoting or relating to a branch of the Indo-European family of languages consisting of Lithuanian, Latvian, and Old Prussian.
▶ **noun 1** (**the Baltic**) the Baltic Sea or the Baltic States.
2 [mass noun] the Baltic languages collectively.
– ORIGIN late 16th cent.: from medieval Latin *Balticus*, from late Latin *Balthae* 'dwellers near the Baltic Sea'.

Baltic Exchange an association of companies, based in London, whose members are engaged in numerous international trading activities, especially the chartering of vessels to carry cargo.
– ORIGIN from the name *Virginia and Baltic*, one of many coffee houses where shipowners and merchants met in London in the 18th cent., the coffee house being so named by association with areas of much of the trade.

Baltic Sea an almost landlocked sea of northern Europe, between Sweden, Finland, Russia, Poland, Germany, and Denmark. It is linked with the North Sea by the Kattegat strait and the Øresund channel.

Baltic States 1 the independent republics of Estonia, Latvia, and Lithuania.
2 the ten members of the Council of Baltic States established in 1992: Denmark, Estonia, Finland, Germany, Latvia, Lithuania, Norway, Poland, Russia, and Sweden.

Baltimore /ˈbɔːltɪmɔː, ˈbɒl-/ a seaport in north Maryland; pop. 636,919 (est. 2008).
– DERIVATIVES **Baltimorean** /bɔːltɪˈmɔːrɪən, bɒl-/ **noun & adjective**.
– ORIGIN named after George Calvert, the first Baron *Baltimore* (*c.*1580–1632), who in 1632 obtained a grant of land for the colony later to become Maryland.

Baltistan /ˌbɔːltɪˈstɑːn, ˌbɒl-, -ˈstan/ a region of the Karakoram range of the Himalayas, to the south of K2. Also called **LITTLE TIBET**.

Baluchi /bəˈluːtʃi/ ▶ **noun** (pl. **same** or **Baluchis**) **1** a native or inhabitant of Baluchistan.
2 [mass noun] the language of the Iranian group spoken by over 5 million people in and around Baluchistan.
▶ **adjective** relating to the Baluchi or their language.
– ORIGIN from Persian *Balūč(ī)*.

Baluchistan /bəˌluːtʃɪˈstɑːn, -ˈstan/ **1** a mountainous region of western Asia, which includes part of SE Iran, SW Afghanistan, and western Pakistan.
2 a province of western Pakistan; capital, Quetta.

balun /ˈbalʌn/ ▶ **noun** a type of electrical transformer used to connect an unbalanced circuit to a balanced one.
– ORIGIN from *bal(ance to) un(balance transformer)*.

Balunda plural form of **LUNDA**.

baluster /ˈbaləstə/ ▶ **noun** a short decorative pillar forming part of a series supporting a rail or coping.
– ORIGIN early 17th cent.: from French *balustre*, from Italian *balaustro*, from *balaust(r)a* 'wild pomegranate flower' (via Latin from Greek *balaustion*), so named because part of the pillar resembles the curving calyx tube of the flower.

balustrade /ˌbaləˈstreɪd/ ▶ **noun** a railing supported by balusters, especially one forming an ornamental parapet to a balcony, bridge, or terrace.
– DERIVATIVES **balustraded** adjective.
– ORIGIN mid 17th cent.: from French, from *balustre* (see **BALUSTER**).

Balzac /ˈbalzak/, Honoré de (1799–1850), French novelist. He is chiefly remembered for his series of ninety-one interconnected novels and stories known collectively as *La Comédie humaine*, which includes *Eugénie Grandet* (1833) and *Le Père Goriot* (1835).
– DERIVATIVES **Balzacian** /balˈzakɪən/ **adjective**.

bam ▶ **exclamation** used to imitate the sound of a hard blow or to convey something happening abruptly: *he'll have to make a dash for it, and when he does, bam, he's dead*.
– ORIGIN 1920s: imitative.

bama /ˈbamə/ (also **pama**) ▶ **noun** Austral. an Aborigine, especially one from northern Queensland.

Bamako /ˈbaməkəʊ/ the capital of Mali, in the south of the country, on the River Niger; pop. 1,728,400 (est. 2009).

Bambara /bamˈbɑːrə/ ▶ **noun** (pl. **same** or **Bambaras**)
1 a member of a West African people living chiefly in Mali.
2 [mass noun] the language of the Bambara, belonging to the Mande group. It has about 1.5 million speakers.
▶ **adjective** relating to the Bambara or their language.

bambino /bamˈbiːnəʊ/ ▶ **noun** (pl. **bambini** /-ni/ or **bambinos**) a baby or young child. ■ an image of the infant Jesus.
– ORIGIN early 18th cent.: Italian, diminutive of *bambo* 'silly'.

bamboo ▶ **noun** [mass noun] a giant woody grass which is grown chiefly in the tropics. ● *Bambusa* and other genera, family Gramineae.
■ the hollow jointed stem of this plant, used as a cane or to make furniture and implements.
– ORIGIN late 16th cent.: from Dutch *bamboes*, based on Malay *mambu*.

bamboo rat ▶ **noun** a large nocturnal burrowing rat that feeds chiefly on the roots of bamboo and other plants, found in the forests of SE Asia. ● Genus *Rhyzomys*, family Muridae: several species.

bamboo shoot ▶ **noun** a young shoot of bamboo, eaten as a vegetable.

bamboozle /bamˈbuːz(ə)l/ ▶ **verb** [with obj.] informal cheat or fool: *he bamboozled Canada's largest banks in a massive counterfeit scam*.
– DERIVATIVES **bamboozler** noun.
– ORIGIN early 18th cent.: of unknown origin.

Bamian /ˌbamɪˈɑːn/ a city in central Afghanistan; pop. 10,400 (est. 2006). Nearby are the remains of two colossal statues of Buddha, destroyed by the Taliban in 2001, and the ruins of the city of Ghulghuleh, which was destroyed by Genghis Khan *c.*1221.

bammy (also **bammie**) ▶ **noun** (in the West Indies) a flat roll or pancake made from cassava flour.
– ORIGIN probably from a West African language.

ban[1] /ban/ ▶ **verb** (**bans**, **banning**, **banned**) [with obj.] officially or legally prohibit (something): *parking is banned around the harbour in summer*. ■ officially prevent (someone) from doing something: *her son was banned for life from the Centre*.
▶ **noun 1** an official or legal prohibition: *a proposed **ban on** cigarette advertising | a three-year driving ban*.
■ an official exclusion of a person from an organization, country, or activity: *a **ban on** dangerous jet-ski riders*. ■ historical a sentence of outlawry.
2 archaic a curse.
– DERIVATIVES **bannable** adjective.
– ORIGIN Old English *bannan* 'summon by a public proclamation', of Germanic origin, reinforced by Old Norse *banna* 'curse, prohibit'; the noun is partly from Old French *ban* 'proclamation, summons, banishment'.

ban[2] /bɑːn/ ▶ **noun** (pl. **bani** /ˈbɑːni/) a monetary unit of Romania, equal to one hundredth of a leu.
– ORIGIN Romanian.

Banaba /bəˈnabə/ an island in the western Pacific, just south of the equator to the west of the Gilbert Islands. Formerly within the Gilbert and Ellice Islands, the island has been part of Kiribati since 1979. Also called **OCEAN ISLAND**.

banal /bəˈnɑːl, -ˈnal/ ▶ **adjective** so lacking in originality as to be obvious and boring: *songs with banal, repeated words*.
– DERIVATIVES **banally** adverb.
– ORIGIN mid 18th cent. (originally relating to feudal service in the sense 'compulsory', hence 'common to all'): from French, from *ban* 'a proclamation or call to arms'; ultimately of Germanic origin and related to **BAN**[1].

banality /bəˈnalɪti/ ▶ **noun** (pl. **banalities**) [mass noun] the fact or condition of being banal; unoriginality: *there is an essential banality to the story he tells*.

banana ▶ **noun 1** a long curved fruit which grows in clusters and has soft pulpy flesh and yellow skin when ripe.
2 (also **banana plant** or **banana tree**) the tropical and subtropical palm-like plant which bears bananas, having very large leaves but lacking a woody trunk. ● Genus *Musa*, family Musaceae: several species, in particular *M. sapientum*.
– PHRASES **go** (or **be**) **bananas** informal become (or be) mad or extremely silly. ■ become extremely angry or excited: *she went bananas when I said I was going to leave the job.* **top** (or **second**) **banana** informal the most (or second most) important person in an organization.
– ORIGIN late 16th cent.: via Portuguese or Spanish from Mande.

banana belt ▶ **noun** N. Amer. informal a region with a comparatively warm climate.

Banana bender ▶ **noun** Austral. informal a person from Queensland.

Bananaland ▶ **noun** Austral. informal Queensland.
– DERIVATIVES **Bananalander** noun.

banana plug ▶ **noun** Electronics, informal a single-pole connector with a curved strip of metal forming a spring along its tip.

bananaquit /bəˈnɑːnəkwɪt/ ▶ **noun** a small songbird with a curved bill, typically with a white stripe over the eye, a sooty grey back, and yellow underparts. It is common in the Caribbean and Central and South America. ● *Coereba flaveola*, the only member of the family Coerebidae; sometimes placed in the family Parulidae.
– ORIGIN see QUIT[2].

banana republic ▶ **noun** derogatory a small state that is politically unstable as a result of the domination of its economy by a single export controlled by foreign capital.

banana skin ▶ **noun** ■ Brit. informal used to refer to a cause of difficulty or embarrassment: *the minister was appointed to spot political banana skins.*

banana split ▶ **noun** a sweet dish made with bananas cut down the middle and filled with ice cream, sauce, and nuts.

banausic /bəˈnɔːsɪk/ ▶ **adjective** formal not operating on an elevated level; mundane. ■ relating to technical work.
– ORIGIN mid 19th cent.: from Greek *banausikos* 'of or for artisans'.

Banbury cake ▶ **noun** Brit. a flat pastry with a spicy currant filling.
– ORIGIN late 16th cent.: named after the town of *Banbury* in central England, where it was originally made.

bancassurance /ˈbaŋkəˌʃɔːrəns/ (also **bankassurance**) ▶ **noun** [mass noun] Brit. the selling of life assurance and other insurance products and services by banking institutions.
– DERIVATIVES **bancassurer** noun.

banco /ˈbaŋkəʊ/ ▶ **exclamation** (in baccarat, chemin de fer, and similar games) an indication of a player's willingness to meet the banker's whole stake single-handed.
– ORIGIN late 18th cent.: via French from Italian.

band[1] ▶ **noun 1** a flat, thin strip or loop of material, used as a fastener, for reinforcement, or as decoration. ■ a plain ring for the finger, especially a gold wedding ring. ■ Ornithology, N. Amer. a ring of metal placed round a bird's leg to identify it. ■ a belt or strap transmitting motion between two wheels or pulleys. ■ (**bands**) a collar with two hanging strips, worn by certain lawyers, clerics, and academics as part of their formal dress.
2 a stripe, line, or elongated area of a different colour, texture, or composition from its surroundings: *a long, narrow band of cloud.* ■ a narrow stratum of rock or coal.
3 a range of values or a specified category within a series (used especially in financial contexts): *your home was placed in one of eight valuation bands.* ■ a range of frequencies or wavelengths in a spectrum: *channels in the UHF band.* ■ any of several groups into which school pupils of the same age are divided on the basis of broadly similar ability: *the top band of pupils.*
4 archaic a thing that restrains, binds, or unites: *must I fall, and die in bands?*
▶ **verb** [with obj.] **1** provide or fit (an object) with something in the form of a strip or ring, for reinforcement or decoration: *doors are banded with iron to make them stronger.* ■ Ornithology, N. Amer. put a band on (a bird) for identification.
2 mark (something) with a stripe or stripes of a different colour: *the bird's bill is banded across the middle with black* | (as adj. **banded**) *banded agate.*
3 Brit. allocate to a range or category (used especially in financial contexts): *single adults in a property banded above D will pay more.* ■ group (school pupils) into classes or sets for teaching purposes.
– ORIGIN late Old English (in sense 4 of the noun), from Old Norse, reinforced in late Middle English by Old French *bande*, of Germanic origin; related to BIND.

band[2] ▶ **noun 1** a group of people who have a common interest or purpose or who share a common feature: *a band of eminent British researchers.* ■ Anthropology a subgroup of a tribe.
2 a small group of musicians and vocalists who play pop, jazz, or rock music. ■ a group of musicians who play brass, wind, or percussion instruments: *a military band.*
3 N. Amer. a herd or flock: *moving* **bands of** *caribou.*
▶ **verb** [no obj.] (of people or organizations) form a group to achieve a mutual objective: *local people* **banded together** *to fight the company.*
– ORIGIN late Middle English: from Old French *bande*, of Germanic origin; related to BANNER.

Banda /ˈbandə/, Hastings Kamuzu (1906–97), Malawian statesman, Prime Minister 1964–94 and the first President of the Republic of Malawi 1966–94. Banda was defeated in Malawi's first multiparty elections in 1994; the following year he was acquitted on charges of murdering four political opponents.

bandage ▶ **noun** a strip of woven material used to bind up a wound or to protect an injured part of the body: *her leg was swathed in bandages* | [mass noun] *a strip of bandage.*
▶ **verb** [with obj.] bind (a wound or a part of the body) with a protective strip of material: *bandage the foot so that the ankle is supported.*
– DERIVATIVES **bandaging** noun.
– ORIGIN late 16th cent.: from French, from *bande* (see BAND[1]).

Band-Aid ▶ **noun** trademark, chiefly N. Amer. a piece of sticking plaster of a type having a gauze pad. ■ (also **band-aid**) [often as modifier] a temporary solution, especially an unsatisfactory one: *a band-aid solution to a much deeper problem.*

bandana /banˈdanə/ (also **bandanna**) ▶ **noun** a large coloured handkerchief, typically with white spots, worn tied around the head or neck.
– ORIGIN mid 18th cent.: probably via Portuguese from Hindi.

Bandaranaike /ˌbandərəˈnʌɪkə/, Sirimavo Ratwatte Dias (1916–2000), Sinhalese stateswoman, Prime Minister of Sri Lanka 1960–5, 1970–7, and 1994–2000. The world's first woman Prime Minister, she succeeded her husband, S. W. R. D. Bandaranaike, after his assassination.

Bandar Lampung /ˌbandə ˈlampʊŋ/ a city at the southern tip of Sumatra, in Indonesia; pop. 916,600 (est. 2009). It was created in the 1980s as a result of the amalgamation of the city of Tanjungkarang and the nearby port of Telukbetung.

Bandar Seri Begawan /ˌbandə ˌsɛri bəˈɡɑːwən/ the capital of Brunei; pop. 32,300 (est. 2008).

Banda Sea /ˈbandə/ a sea in eastern Indonesia, between the central and south Molucca Islands.

B & B ▶ **abbreviation** bed and breakfast.

bandbox ▶ **noun** a circular cardboard box for carrying hats. ■ dated used in comparisons to convey the smartness and neatness of someone's appearance: *I'd go out looking fresh* **out of a bandbox**.
– ORIGIN mid 17th cent.: from BAND[1] + BOX[1], the box being used originally for neckbands.

bandeau /ˈbandəʊ/ ▶ **noun** (pl. **bandeaux** /-dəʊz/) **1** a narrow band worn round the head to hold the hair in position.
2 [usu. as modifier] a woman's strapless top formed from a band of fabric fitting around the bust: *a bandeau bikini top.*
– ORIGIN early 18th cent.: from French, from Old French *bandel*, diminutive of *bande* (see BAND[1]).

banded anteater ▶ **noun** another term for NUMBAT.

bander ▶ **noun** N. Amer. a bird ringer.

banderilla /ˌbandəˈriːjə, -ˈrɪljə/ ▶ **noun** a decorated dart thrust into a bull's neck or shoulders during a bullfight.
– ORIGIN Spanish, diminutive of *bandera* 'banner'.

banderillero /ˌbandərɪlˈjɛːrəʊ, -riːˈjɛːrəʊ/ ▶ **noun** (pl. **banderilleros**) a bullfighter who uses banderillas.
– ORIGIN Spanish.

banderole /ˈbandərəʊl/ (also **banderol**) ▶ **noun** a long, narrow flag with a cleft end, flown at a masthead. ■ historical an ornamental streamer on a knight's lance. ■ a ribbon-like stone scroll bearing an inscription. ■ a rectangular banner carried at the funerals of public figures and placed over the tomb.
– ORIGIN mid 16th cent.: from French, from Italian *banderuola*, diminutive of *bandiera* 'banner'.

bandersnatch /ˈbandəsnatʃ/ ▶ **noun** a fierce mythical creature immune to bribery and capable of moving very fast.
– ORIGIN 1871: coined by Lewis Carroll in *Through the Looking Glass*; probably a portmanteau word.

bandfish ▶ **noun** (pl. **same** or **bandfishes**) **1** an elongated marine fish with dorsal and often anal fins that extend the length of the body. ● Family Cepolidae: several genera and species.
2 a large edible freshwater fish that has a long trunk-like snout and lacks dorsal, pelvic, and tail fins, native to tropical South America. ● *Rhamphichthys rostratus*, family Rhamphichthyidae.

bandh /bʌnd/ ▶ **noun** Indian a general strike.
– ORIGIN via Hindi from Sanskrit *bandh* 'to stop'.

bandicoot /ˈbandɪkuːt/ ▶ **noun** a mainly insectivorous marsupial native to Australia and New Guinea. ● Family Peramelidae: several genera and species.
■ Indian a bandicoot rat.
– ORIGIN late 18th cent.: from Telugu *pandikokku*, literally 'pig-rat'.

bandicoot rat ▶ **noun** an Asian rat that is a destructive pest in many places. ● Genera *Bandicota* and *Nesokia*, family Muridae: four species, in particular the large *B. indica*.

banding ▶ **noun** [mass noun] the presence or formation of stripes of contrasting colour: *the yellow and black banding of bees and wasps.* ■ Biochemistry the pattern of regions on a chromosome made visible by staining.

bandit ▶ **noun** (pl. **bandits** or **banditti** /banˈdiːti/) a robber or outlaw belonging to a gang and typically operating in an isolated or lawless area. ■ military slang an enemy aircraft.
– DERIVATIVES **banditry** noun.
– ORIGIN late 16th cent.: from Italian *bandito*, 'banned', past participle of *bandire* 'to ban'.

bandito /banˈdiːtəʊ/ (also **bandido**) ▶ **noun** (pl. **banditos**) N. Amer. a Mexican bandit, especially as represented in films and popular culture.

Bandjarmasin variant spelling of BANJARMASIN.

bandleader ▶ **noun** a player at the head of a musical band.

bandmaster ▶ **noun** the conductor of a musical band, especially a brass or military one.

bandmate ▶ **noun** a fellow musician or singer in a band.

bandobast ▶ **noun** variant spelling of BUNDOBUST.

Band of Hope a British organization promoting total abstinence from alcohol.

bandog ▶ **noun** a fighting dog bred for its strength and ferocity by crossing aggressive breeds.
– ORIGIN Middle English (originally denoting a dog kept on a chain or 'band'): from BAND[1] + DOG.

bandolier /ˌbandəˈlɪə/ (also **bandoleer**) ▶ **noun** a shoulder belt with loops or pockets for cartridges.
– ORIGIN late 16th cent.: from French *bandoulière*; perhaps from Spanish *bandolera* (from *banda* 'sash'), or from Catalan *bandolera* (from *bandoler* 'bandit').

bandoneon /banˈdəʊnɪən/ ▶ **noun** a type of square concertina, especially popular in Argentina.
– ORIGIN via Spanish from German *Bandonion*, named after Heinrich *Band*, the 19th-cent. German musician who invented it, + *-on-* (as in *Harmonika* 'harmonica') + *-ion* (as in *Akkordion* 'accordion').

bandora /banˈdɔːrə/ (also **bandore** /banˈdɔː/) ▶ **noun** a kind of bass lute with a scallop-shaped body and metal strings, typical of English consorts of the late 16th and 17th centuries.
– ORIGIN mid 16th cent.: origin uncertain; compare with Dutch *bandoor*, Spanish *bandurria*, also with BANJO; probably based on Greek *pandoura* 'three-stringed lute'.

bandpass ▶ **adjective** (of a filter) transmitting only a set range of frequencies.
▶ **noun** the range of frequencies which are transmitted through such a filter.

bandsaw ▶ **noun** a saw consisting of an endless moving steel belt with a serrated edge.

B

bandshell ▶ noun chiefly N. Amer. a bandstand in the form of a large concave shell with special acoustic properties.

bandsman ▶ noun (pl. **bandsmen**) a player in a musical band, especially a military or brass one.

bandstand ▶ noun a covered outdoor platform for a band to play on, typically in a park.

bandulu /ban'du:lu:/ ▶ noun [mass noun] W. Indian crime or fraudulent dealings: [as modifier] *bandulu business*.

Bandung /'bandʊŋ/ a city in Indonesia; pop. 1,601,800 (est. 2009). Founded by the Dutch in 1810, it was the capital of the former Dutch East Indies.

bandura /ban'du:rə/ ▶ noun a Ukrainian stringed instrument resembling a large asymmetrical lute with many strings, held vertically and plucked like a zither.
– ORIGIN Ukrainian; compare with **BANDORA**.

bandwagon ▶ noun **1** (especially formerly) a wagon used for carrying a band in a parade or procession.
2 an activity or cause that has suddenly become fashionable or popular: *companies sought to strengthen their share prices by* ***jumping on the dot-com bandwagon*** | *they would not* ***climb aboard the bandwagon*** *of every fashionable social issue*.

bandwidth ▶ noun Electronics a range of frequencies within a given band, in particular that used for transmitting a signal. ■ the transmission capacity of a computer network or other telecommunication system.

bandy[1] ▶ adjective (**bandier**, **bandiest**) (of a person's legs) curved outwards so that the knees are wide apart. ■ having legs that are curved in such a way.
– ORIGIN late 17th cent.: perhaps from obsolete *bandy* 'curved stick used in hockey'.

bandy[2] ▶ verb (**bandies**, **bandying**, **bandied**) [with obj.] (usu. **be bandied about/around**) pass on or discuss (an idea or rumour) in a casual or uninformed way: *£40,000 is the figure that has been bandied about*.
– PHRASES **bandy words** argue pointlessly or rudely: *I'm not going to* ***bandy words with*** *you*.
– ORIGIN late 16th cent. (in the sense 'pass a ball to and fro'): perhaps from French *bander* 'take sides at tennis', from *bande* 'band, crowd' (see **BAND**[2]).

bandy[3] ▶ noun [mass noun] a form of hockey played on a field or on ice with a ball and large curved sticks. ■ [count noun] (pl. **bandies**) the curved stick used in this sport.
– ORIGIN late 17th cent.: perhaps from **BANDY**[2].

bandy-bandy ▶ noun (pl. **bandy-bandys**) a small mildly venomous nocturnal snake marked with distinctive black-and-white bands, native to Australia.
● *Vermicella annulata*, family Elapidae.
– ORIGIN 1920s: from Kattah (an Aboriginal language) *bandi bandi*.

bane ▶ noun [usu. in sing.] **1** a cause of great distress or annoyance: *the telephone was* ***the bane of my life***.
2 archaic something, especially poison, which causes death.
– DERIVATIVES **baneful** adjective (archaic).
– ORIGIN Old English *bana* 'thing causing death, poison', of Germanic origin.

baneberry ▶ noun (pl. **baneberries**) a plant of the buttercup family, which bears fluffy spikes of creamy-white flowers followed by shiny berries, found in north temperate regions. ● Genus *Actaea*, family Ranunculaceae, especially the common Eurasian *A. spicata* (also called **HERB CHRISTOPHER**), with black berries.
■ the bitter, often poisonous, berry of the baneberry.
– ORIGIN mid 18th cent.: from **BANE** in the sense 'poison' + **BERRY**.

Banffshire /'bamfʃɪə, -ʃə/ a former county of NE Scotland which became a part of Grampian region in 1975 and Aberdeenshire in 1996.

bang[1] ▶ noun **1** a sudden loud, sharp noise: *the door slammed with a bang*. ■ a sharp blow causing such a noise: *I went to answer a bang on the front door*. ■ a sudden painful blow: *a nasty bang on the head*.
2 (**bangs**) N. Amer. a fringe of hair cut straight across the forehead. [from a use of the adverb *bang* to mean 'abruptly'.]
3 vulgar slang an act of sexual intercourse.
4 Computing, chiefly N. Amer. the character '!'.
▶ verb [with obj.] **1** strike or put down (something) forcefully and noisily: *he began to bang the table with his fist* | *Sarah* ***banged*** *the phone* ***down*** | [no obj.] *someone was* ***banging on*** *the door*. ■ [with obj. and adverbial] cause (something) to strike something else unexpectedly and sharply: *I banged my head on the low beams* | [no obj.] *she banged into some shelves in the darkness*. ■ [no obj.] make a sudden loud noise, typically repeatedly: *the shutter was banging in the wind*. ■ (with reference to something such as a door) open or close noisily: [with obj. and complement] *he* ***banged*** *the kitchen* ***door shut behind him***. ■ [no obj., with adverbial of direction] (of a person) move around or do something noisily: *she was banging around the kitchen*.
2 N. Amer. cut (hair) in a fringe.
3 vulgar slang (of a man) have sexual intercourse with (a woman).
▶ adverb informal, chiefly Brit. exactly: *the train arrived bang on time*. ■ completely: *bring your wardrobe bang up to date*.
▶ exclamation **1** used to convey the sound of a sudden loud noise: *party poppers* ***went bang***.
2 used to convey the suddenness of an action: *the minute something becomes obsolete, bang, it's gone*.
– PHRASES **bang for one's** (or **the**) **buck** US informal value for money. **bang goes ——** Brit. used to express the sudden collapse of a plan or hope: *my first thought when I heard the news was 'Bang goes my knighthood!'*. **bang on** Brit. informal exactly right: *the programme is bang on about the fashion world*. **bang** (or **knock**) **people's heads together** see **HEAD**. **get a bang out of** N. Amer. informal derive excitement or pleasure from: *some people get a bang out of reading that stuff*. **with a bang 1** abruptly: *the remark brought me down to earth with a bang*. **2** successfully or impressively: *the occasion* ***went with a bang***.
– PHRASAL VERBS **bang away at** informal do something in a persistent or dogged way: *he was banging away at his novel*. **bang on about** Brit. informal talk at tedious length about (something): *the government banged on about competition and the free market*. **bang something out** informal **1** play music noisily, enthusiastically, and unskilfully. **2** produce something hurriedly or in great quantities: *they weren't banging out ads in my day the way they are now*. **bang someone/thing up** Brit. informal imprison someone: *they've been banged up for something they didn't do*. ■ N. Amer. informal damage or injure someone or something.
– ORIGIN mid 16th cent.: imitative, perhaps of Scandinavian origin; compare with Old Norse *bang* 'hammering'.

bang[2] /baŋ/ ▶ noun variant spelling of **BHANG**.

Bangalore /,baŋgə'lɔː/ a city in south central India, capital of the state of Karnataka; pop. 5,310,300 (est. 2009).

Bangalore torpedo ▶ noun a tube containing explosive used by infantry for blowing up wire entanglements or other barriers.

bangarang /'baŋəraŋ/ ▶ noun W. Indian an uproar or disturbance.
– ORIGIN probably imitative, but perhaps influenced by Portuguese *banguelê* 'riot, disorder'.

banger ▶ noun Brit. informal **1** a sausage.
2 an old car in poor condition: *they've only got an old banger*.
3 a loud explosive firework.

banging ▶ adjective Brit. informal (of dance music) having a loud relentless beat. ■ excellent: *a bangin' night out*.

Bangkok /baŋ'kɒk/ the capital and chief port of Thailand, on the Chao Phraya waterway, 40 km (25 miles) upstream from its outlet into the Gulf of Thailand; pop. 5,705,100 (est. 2007). Thai name **KRUNG THEP**.

Bangla /'bʌŋlə:/ ▶ noun [mass noun] the Bengali language.
▶ adjective **1** Bangladeshi.
2 Bengali.
– ORIGIN from Bengali *bāṅglā*.

Bangladesh /,baŋglə'dɛʃ/ a country of South Asia, in the Ganges delta; pop. 156,050,900 (est. 2009); official language, Bengali; capital, Dhaka.

> Formerly part of British India, the region became (as East Pakistan) one of the two geographical units of Pakistan. After civil war the independent republic of Bangladesh was proclaimed in 1971; it became a Commonwealth state in 1972.

– DERIVATIVES **Bangladeshi** adjective & noun.

bangle ▶ noun a rigid ornamental band worn round the arm or occasionally the ankle.
– ORIGIN late 18th cent.: from Hindi *baṅglī* 'glass bracelet'.

bangtail ▶ noun a horse's tail that has been cut straight across just below the level of the hocks.

bangtail muster ▶ noun Austral. a count of cattle on a station, involving cutting across the tufts at the tail ends as each is counted.
– ORIGIN late 19th cent.: *bang* in the sense 'cut (the tail of an animal) straight across'; compare with **BANG**[1] (sense 2 of the verb).

Bangui /'baŋgi:/ the capital of the Central African Republic; pop. 672,000 (est. 2007).

bang-up ▶ adjective N. Amer. informal excellent: *for a novice, he has done a bang-up job*.

bani plural form of **BAN**[2].

bania /'bʌnɪə/ ▶ noun (in India) a trader or merchant.
– ORIGIN from Hindi *baniyā*, from Sanskrit *vāṇija*.

banian ▶ noun variant spelling of **BANYAN**.

banish ▶ verb [with obj.] send (someone) away from a country or place as an official punishment: *a number of people were banished to Siberia for political crimes*. ■ get rid of (something unwanted): *all thoughts of romance were* ***banished from*** *her head*.
– DERIVATIVES **banishment** noun.
– ORIGIN late Middle English: from Old French *baniss-*, lengthened stem of *banir*; ultimately of Germanic origin and related to **BAN**[1].

banister /'banɪstə/ (also **bannister**) ▶ noun (also **banisters**) the structure formed by the uprights and handrail at the side of a staircase. ■ a single upright at the side of a staircase: *I stuck my head between the banisters*.
– ORIGIN mid 17th cent.: from earlier *barrister*, alteration of **BALUSTER**.

Banja Luka /,banjə 'lu:kə/ a town in northern Bosnia and Herzegovina; pop. 164,200 (est. 2008).

Banjarmasin /,bandʒə'mɑːsɪn/ (also **Bandjarmasin**) a deep-water port and capital of the province of Kalimantan in Indonesia, on the island of Borneo; pop. 576,400 (est. 2009).

banjax /'bandʒaks/ ▶ verb [with obj.] (usu. as adj. **banjaxed**) informal ruin, incapacitate, or break: *the kettle's banjaxed*.
– ORIGIN 1930s: originally Anglo-Irish, of unknown origin.

banjo ▶ noun (pl. **banjos** or **banjoes**) a stringed instrument of the guitar family, with a round open-backed soundbox of parchment stretched over a metal hoop. ■ an object resembling this in shape: [as modifier] *a banjo clock*.
– DERIVATIVES **banjoist** noun.
– ORIGIN mid 18th cent.: originally a black American alteration of *bandore* (see **BANDORA**).

Banjul /ban'dʒu:l/ the capital of Gambia; pop. 34,828 (2003). Former name (until 1973) **BATHURST**.

bank[1] ▶ noun **1** the land alongside or sloping down to a river or lake: *willows lined the bank of the stream*.
2 a long, high mass or mound of a particular substance: *a grassy bank* | *a bank of snow*. ■ an elevation in the seabed or a riverbed; a mudbank or sandbank. ■ a transverse slope given to a road, railway, or sports track to enable vehicles or runners to maintain speed round a curve. ■ [mass noun] the sideways tilt of an aircraft when turning in flight: *a rather steep angle of bank*.
3 a set of similar things, especially electrical or electronic devices, grouped together in rows: *the DJ had big banks of lights and speakers on either side of his console*. ■ a tier of oars.
4 the cushion of a pool table.
▶ verb [with obj.] **1** heap (a substance) into a mass or mound: *the rain* ***banked*** *the soil* ***up*** *behind the gate* | *snow was banked in humps at the roadside*. ■ [no obj.] form into a mass or mound: *purple clouds* ***banked up*** *over the hills*. ■ heap up (a fire) with tightly packed fuel so that it burns slowly: *she* ***banked up*** *the fire*. ■ edge or surround with a ridge or row of something: *steps banked with pots of chrysanthemums*.
2 (with reference to an aircraft or vehicle) tilt or cause to tilt sideways in making a turn: [no obj.] *the plane banked as if to return to the airport* | [with obj.] *I banked the aircraft steeply and turned*.
3 build (a road, railway, or sports track) higher at the outer edge of a bend to facilitate fast cornering.
4 (often as noun **banking**) Brit. (of a locomotive) provide additional power for (a train) in ascending an incline.
5 (of an angler) succeed in landing (a fish): *it was the biggest rainbow trout that had ever been banked*.
6 N. Amer. (in pool) play (a ball) so that it rebounds off a surface such as a cushion.
– ORIGIN Middle English: from Old Norse *bakki*, of Germanic origin; related to **BENCH**. The senses 'set of things in rows' and 'tier of oars' are from French *banc*, of the same ultimate origin.

bank[2] ▶ noun a financial establishment that uses money deposited by customers for investment, pays

it out when required, makes loans at interest, and exchanges currency: [as modifier] *a bank account.* ■ a stock of something available for use when required: *a blood bank* | figurative *Britain has a bank of highly exportable skills.* ■ a site or receptacle where something may be deposited for recycling: *a paper bank.* ■ (**the bank**) the store of money or tokens held by the banker in some gambling or board games. ■ the person holding this store; the banker.
▸ **verb** [with obj.] deposit (money or valuables) in a bank. ■ [no obj.] have an account at a particular bank: *the family has* ***banked with*** *Coutts for generations.* ■ informal win or earn (a sum of money): *he banked £100,000 for a hole-in-one.* ■ store (something, especially blood, tissue, or sperm) for future use.
– PHRASES **break the bank** (in gambling) win more money than is held by the bank. ■ [usu. with negative] informal cost more than one can afford: *at £30, the shirts won't break the bank.*
– PHRASAL VERBS **bank on** rely on confidently: *the prime minister cannot bank on their support.*
– ORIGIN late 15th cent. (originally denoting a money dealer's table): from French *banque* or Italian *banca*, from medieval Latin *banca*, *bancus*, of Germanic origin; related to **BANK**[1] and **BENCH**.

bankable ▸ **adjective** (especially in the entertainment industry) certain to bring profit and success: *he needed some bankable names to star in the film.*
– DERIVATIVES **bankability** /-ə'bɪlɪti/ **noun**.

bank account ▸ **noun** an arrangement made with a bank whereby one may deposit and withdraw money and in some cases be paid interest.

bankassurance ▸ **noun** variant spelling of **BANCASSURANCE**.

bank balance ▸ **noun** the amount of money held in a bank account at a given moment.

bank barn ▸ **noun** chiefly N. Amer. a barn built on a slope.

bank bill ▸ **noun 1** Brit. a bill of exchange drawn by one bank on another.
2 US another term for **BANKNOTE**.

bank book ▸ **noun** another term for **PASSBOOK**.

bank card ▸ **noun** a debit card or cash card.

bank draft ▸ **noun** a cheque drawn by a bank on its own funds.

banker[1] ▸ **noun 1** a person who manages or owns a bank or group of banks. ■ the person running the table, controlling play, or acting as dealer in some gambling or board games.
2 Brit. a supposedly certain bet: *the horse should be a banker for him in the Members' race.* ■ a result forecast identically (while other forecasts differ) in several football-pool entries on one coupon.

banker[2] ▸ **noun 1** a boat employed in cod fishing off Newfoundland. ■ a Newfoundland fisherman.
2 Austral./NZ informal a river flooded to the top of its banks.
3 an additional locomotive used to assist a train in ascending an incline.
4 a bench at which a stonemason works.

banker's card ▸ **noun** Brit. another term for **CHEQUE CARD**.

banker's draft ▸ **noun** another term for **BANK DRAFT**.

banker's hours ▸ **plural noun** N. Amer. short working hours (in reference to the typical opening hours of a bank).

banker's order ▸ **noun** Brit. a standing order to a bank to make specified payments from one's account to a particular recipient.

Bank for International Settlements a bank founded in 1930 to promote the cooperation of central banks and to provide facilities for international financial operations. It is located at Basle in Switzerland.

Bankhead, Tallulah (1903–68), American actress, noted for her uninhibited public persona. Her most successful film appearance was in Alfred Hitchcock's *Lifeboat* (1944).

bank holiday ▸ **noun** Brit. a day on which banks are officially closed, kept as a public holiday.

Ban Ki-moon /ˌban kiː'muːn/ (b.1944), South Korean diplomat, Secretary General of the United Nations since 2007.

banking[1] ▸ **noun** [mass noun] the business conducted or services offered by a bank: *with this account, you are entitled to free banking.*

banking[2] ▸ **noun** an embankment or artificial bank.

bank manager ▸ **noun** a person in charge of a local branch of a bank.

banknote ▸ **noun** a piece of paper money, constituting a central bank's promissory note to pay a stated sum to the bearer on demand.

Bank of England the central bank of England and Wales, which issues legal tender, manages the national debt, administers exchange rate policy, and since 1997 sets interest rates. Founded in 1694, it was nationalized in 1946.

bank rate ▸ **noun** another term for **BASE RATE** or **DISCOUNT RATE**.

bankroll ▸ **noun** N. Amer. a roll of banknotes. ■ financial resources.
▸ **verb** [with obj.] informal support (a person, organization, or project) financially: *the project is bankrolled by wealthy expatriates.*

bankrupt ▸ **adjective 1** (of a person or organization) declared in law as unable to pay their debts: *his father* ***went bankrupt*** *and the family had to sell their home.* ■ impoverished or depleted: *a bankrupt country with no natural resources.*
2 completely lacking in a particular good quality: *their cause is morally bankrupt.*
▸ **noun** a person judged by a court to be insolvent, whose property is taken and disposed of for the benefit of their creditors.
▸ **verb** [with obj.] reduce (a person or organization) to bankruptcy: *the strike nearly bankrupted the union.*
– ORIGIN mid 16th cent.: from Italian *banca rotta* 'broken bench', from *banca* (see **BANK**[2]) and *rompere* 'to break'. The change in the ending was due to association with Latin *rupt-* 'broken'.

bankruptcy ▸ **noun** (pl. **bankruptcies**) [mass noun]
1 the state of being bankrupt: *many companies were facing bankruptcy* | [count noun] *a 7% increase in bankruptcies.*
2 the state of being completely lacking in a particular good quality: *the intellectual bankruptcy of the corporate media.*

bankruptcy order ▸ **noun** English Law an order of the court declaring a person bankrupt and placing their affairs under the control of a receiver or trustee. Compare with **RECEIVING ORDER**.

Banks[1], Gordon (b.1937), English footballer. An outstanding goalkeeper, he played in the 1966 and 1970 World Cups. In 1972 a serious eye injury sustained in a car crash effectively ended his playing career.

Banks[2], Sir Joseph (1743–1820), English botanist. He accompanied Captain James Cook on his first voyage to the Pacific, and helped to establish the Royal Botanic Gardens at Kew.

banksia /'baŋksɪə/ ▸ **noun** an evergreen Australian shrub which typically has narrow leathery leaves and spikes of bottlebrush-like flowers. ● Genus *Banksia*, family Proteaceae.
– ORIGIN modern Latin, named after Sir Joseph *Banks* (see **BANKS**[2]).

banksia rose ▸ **noun** a small-flowered climbing rose native to China. ● *Rosa banksiae*, family Rosaceae.

bank statement ▸ **noun** a printed record of the balance in a bank account and the amounts that have been paid into it and withdrawn from it, issued periodically to the holder of the account.

bank swallow ▸ **noun** N. Amer. see **SAND MARTIN**.

bank vole ▸ **noun** a common reddish-brown Eurasian vole that lives in woodland and scrub. ● *Clethrionomys glareolus*, family Muridae.

banner ▸ **noun 1** a long strip of cloth bearing a slogan or design, carried in a demonstration or procession or hung in a public place. ■ historical a flag on a pole used as the standard of a monarch, knight, or army. ■ used in reference to support for a belief or principle: *the government is flying the free trade banner.*
2 a heading or advertisement appearing on a web page in the form of a bar, column, or box: [as modifier] *a banner ad.*
▸ **adjective** [attrib.] N. Amer. excellent; outstanding: *the company was having a banner year.*
– PHRASES **under the banner of** as part of a specified group: *the party is running under the banner of the Left-Wing Alliance.* ■ claiming to support a specified cause or principle: *campaigns fought under the banner of multiculturalism.*
– DERIVATIVES **bannered** **adjective**.
– ORIGIN Middle English: from Old French *baniere*, ultimately of Germanic origin and related to **BAND**[2].

banneret /'banərɪt/ ▸ **noun** historical **1** a knight who commanded his own troops in battle under his own banner.
2 a knighthood given on the battlefield for courage.
– ORIGIN Middle English: from Old French *baneret*, literally 'bannered', from *baniere* 'banner'.

banner headline ▸ **noun** a large newspaper headline, especially one across the top of the front page.

Bannister, Sir Roger (Gilbert) (b.1929), British middle-distance runner and neurologist. In May 1954 he became the first man to run a mile in under 4 minutes, with a time of 3 minutes 59.4 seconds.

bannister ▸ **noun** variant spelling of **BANISTER**.

bannock /'banək/ ▸ **noun** a round, flat loaf, typically unleavened, associated with Scotland and northern England.
– ORIGIN Old English *bannuc*, of Celtic origin; related to Welsh *ban*, Breton *bannac'h*, *banne*, and Cornish *banna* 'a drop'.

Bannockburn, Battle of /'banəkbəːn/ a battle which took place near Stirling in central Scotland in 1314, in which the English army of Edward II, advancing to break the siege of Stirling Castle, was defeated by the Scots under Robert the Bruce.

banns ▸ **plural noun** a notice read out on three successive Sundays in a parish church, announcing an intended marriage and giving the opportunity for objections.
– PHRASES **forbid the banns** archaic raise an objection to an intended marriage.
– ORIGIN Middle English: plural of **BAN**[1].

banoffi pie /bə'nɒfi/ (also **banoffee pie**) ▸ **noun** a pie or tart made with toffee, bananas, and cream.
– ORIGIN 1970s: *banoffi* from a blend of **BANANA** and **TOFFEE**.

banquet /'baŋkwɪt/ ▸ **noun** an elaborate and formal evening meal for many people: *a state banquet at Buckingham Palace.* ■ an elaborate meal with several courses; a feast: *a lavish five-course banquet* | figurative *a veritable banquet of seasonal events.*
▸ **verb** (**banquets**, **banqueting**, **banqueted**) [with obj.] (usu. as noun **banqueting**) entertain with a banquet: [as modifier] *a banqueting hall.*
– DERIVATIVES **banqueter** **noun**.
– ORIGIN late 15th cent.: from French, diminutive of *banc* 'bench' (see **BANK**[1]).

banquette /baŋ'kɛt/ ▸ **noun 1** an upholstered bench along a wall, especially in a restaurant or bar.
2 a raised step behind a rampart.
– ORIGIN early 17th cent. (in sense 2): from French, from Italian *banchetta*, diminutive of *banca* 'bench' (see **BANK**[2]). Sense 1 dates from the mid 19th cent.

banshee /ban'ʃiː, 'banʃiː/ ▸ **noun** (in Irish legend) a female spirit whose wailing warns of a death in a house: *the little girl dropped her ice cream and began to howl like a banshee* | [as modifier] *a horrible banshee wail.*
– ORIGIN late 17th cent.: from Irish *bean sídhe*, from Old Irish *ben síde* 'woman of the fairies'.

bansuri /ban'sʊəri/ ▸ **noun** a bamboo transverse flute of northern India.

bantam ▸ **noun** a chicken of a small breed, the cock of which is noted for its aggression. ■ [usu. as modifier] Canadian a level of amateur sport typically involving children aged between 13 and 15: *bantam hockey.* ■ short for **BANTAMWEIGHT**.
– ORIGIN mid 18th cent.: apparently named after the province of *Bantam* in Java, although the fowl is not native there.

bantamweight ▸ **noun** [mass noun] a weight in boxing and other sports intermediate between flyweight and featherweight. In the amateur boxing scale it ranges from 51 to 54 kg. ■ [count noun] a boxer or other competitor of this weight.

banteng /'bantɛŋ/ ▸ **noun** a SE Asian forest ox that resembles the domestic cow. It has been domesticated in Bali. ● *Bos javanicus*, family Bovidae.
– ORIGIN early 19th cent.: from Malay.

banter ▸ **noun** [mass noun] the playful and friendly exchange of teasing remarks: *there was much good-natured banter.*
▸ **verb** [no obj.] exchange remarks in a good-humoured teasing way: *the men* ***bantered with*** *the waitresses* | (as adj. **bantering**) *a bantering tone.*
– DERIVATIVES **banterer** **noun**.
– ORIGIN late 17th cent.: of unknown origin.

Banting, Sir Frederick Grant (1891–1941), Canadian physiologist and surgeon. With the assistance of C. H. Best, Banting discovered insulin in 1921–2, using it to treat the previously incurable and fatal disease diabetes. Nobel Prize for Physiology or Medicine (1923, shared with J. J. R. Macleod).

bantling ▸ **noun** archaic a young child.

B

– ORIGIN late 16th cent.: from BAND[1] + -LING, or a corruption of German *bänkling* 'bastard'.

Bantu /banˈtuː, ˈbantuː/ ▶ noun (pl. **same** or **Bantus**) **1** a member of an extensive group of indigenous peoples of central and southern Africa.
2 [mass noun] the group of Niger–Congo languages spoken by these peoples, including Swahili, Xhosa, and Zulu.
▶ **adjective** relating to these peoples or their languages.
– ORIGIN plural (in certain Bantu languages) of *-ntu* 'person'.

> **USAGE** The word **Bantu** became a strongly offensive term under the old apartheid regime in South Africa, especially when used to refer to a single individual. In standard current use in South Africa the term **black** or **African** is used as a collective or non-specific term for African peoples. The term **Bantu** has, however, continued to be accepted as a neutral 'scientific' term outside South Africa used to refer to the group of languages and their speakers collectively.

Bantu education ▶ noun [mass noun] historical, derogatory (in South Africa under apartheid) the official system of education for black South Africans.

Bantustan /ˌbantuːˈstɑːn, -ˈstan/ ▶ noun S. African historical, derogatory a partially self-governing area set aside during the period of apartheid for a particular indigenous African people; a so-called homeland.
– ORIGIN from BANTU + *-stan*, on the pattern of words such as *Hindustan*.

banyan /ˈbanjən/ (also **banian**) ▶ noun **1** (also **banyan tree**) an Indian fig tree, the branches of which produce wide-ranging aerial roots which later become accessory trunks. • *Ficus benghalensis*, family Moraceae.
2 a loose flannel undergarment worn in India.
– ORIGIN late 16th cent.: from Portuguese, from Gujarati *vāṇiyo* 'man of the trading caste', from Sanskrit. Originally denoting a Hindu merchant, the term was applied, by Europeans in the mid 17th cent., to a tree under which such traders had built a pagoda.

banzai /banˈzʌɪ/ ▶ exclamation **1** a Japanese battle cry.
2 a form of greeting used to the Japanese emperor.
▶ **adjective** (especially of troops) attacking fiercely and recklessly: *a banzai charge*. ■ informal behaving wildly; berserk.
– ORIGIN Japanese, literally 'ten thousand years (of life to you)'.

baobab /ˈbeɪə(ʊ)bab/ ▶ noun a short tree with a very thick trunk and large edible fruit, living to a great age. • Genus *Adansonia*, family Bombacaceae: several species, in particular the African *A. digitata* and the Australian *A. gregorii*.
– ORIGIN mid 17th cent.: probably from an African language; first recorded in Latin (1592), in a treatise on the plants of Egypt by the Italian botanist Prosper Alpinus.

BAOR ▶ abbreviation British Army of the Rhine.

Baotou /baʊˈtəʊ/ an industrial city in Inner Mongolia, northern China, on the Yellow River; pop. 1,194,600 (est. 2006).

bap ▶ noun Brit. **1** a large, round, flattish bread roll, typically with a spongy texture and floury top.
2 (**baps**) informal a woman's breasts.
– ORIGIN late 16th cent.: of unknown origin.

baptism ▶ noun [mass noun] the Christian religious rite of sprinkling water on to a person's forehead or of immersing them in water, symbolizing purification or regeneration and admission to the Christian Church. In many denominations, baptism is performed on young children and is accompanied by name-giving. ■ [count noun] a ceremony or occasion at which baptism takes place. ■ a person's initiation into a particular activity or role, typically one perceived as difficult: *this event constituted his baptism as a politician*.
– PHRASES **baptism of fire** a difficult introduction to a new job or activity. [from the original sense of 'a soldier's first battle'.]
– DERIVATIVES **baptismal** adjective.
– ORIGIN Middle English: from Old French *baptesme*, via ecclesiastical Latin from ecclesiastical Greek *baptismos* 'ceremonial washing', from *baptizein* 'immerse, baptize'.

baptismal name ▶ noun a personal name given at baptism.

baptist ▶ noun **1** (**Baptist**) a member of a Protestant Christian denomination advocating baptism only of adult believers by total immersion. Baptists form one of the largest Protestant bodies and are found throughout the world and especially in the US.
2 a person who baptizes someone.
– ORIGIN Middle English (in sense 2): from Old French *baptiste*, via ecclesiastical Latin from ecclesiastical Greek *baptistēs*, from *baptizein* 'immerse, baptize'.

baptistery (also **baptistry**) ▶ noun (pl. **baptisteries** or **baptistries**) the part of a church used for baptism. ■ historical a building next to a church, used for baptism. ■ (in a Baptist chapel) a sunken receptacle used for baptism by total immersion.
– ORIGIN Middle English: from Old French *baptistere*, via ecclesiastical Latin from ecclesiastical Greek *baptistērion*, from *baptizein* 'immerse, baptize'.

baptize (also **baptise**) ▶ verb [with obj. and often with complement] administer baptism to (someone); christen: *he was baptized Joshua*. ■ admit (someone) into a specified Church by baptism: *Mark had been baptized a Catholic*. ■ give a name or nickname to: *the media have baptized the murderer 'The Babysitter'*.
– ORIGIN Middle English: via Old French from ecclesiastical Latin *baptizare*, from Greek *baptizein* 'immerse, baptize'.

bapu /ˈbʌpuː/ (also **bappu**) ▶ noun Indian a father (often as a form of address).
– ORIGIN from Gujarati.

bar[1] ▶ noun **1** a long rigid piece of wood, metal, or similar material, typically used as an obstruction, fastening, or weapon. ■ an amount of food or another substance formed into a narrow block: *a **bar of** chocolate*. ■ a band of colour or light: *bars of sunlight shafting through the windows*. ■ Brit. the heating element of an electric fire. ■ (**the bar**) the crossbar of a goal. ■ Brit. a metal strip below the clasp of a medal, awarded as an additional distinction. ■ a sandbank or shoal at the mouth of a harbour or an estuary. ■ Heraldry a charge in the form of a narrow horizontal stripe across the shield.
2 a counter in a pub, restaurant, or cafe across which drinks or refreshments are served. ■ a room in a pub, restaurant, or hotel in which alcohol is served. ■ an establishment where alcohol and sometimes other refreshments are served. ■ [with modifier] a small shop, stall, or area in a department store that serves refreshments or provides a specified service: *a sandwich bar*.
3 a barrier or restriction to an action or advance: *political differences are not necessarily **a bar to** a good relationship*. ■ Law a plea suspending an action or claim in a lawsuit.
4 Music any of the short sections or measures, typically of equal time value, into which a piece of music is divided, shown on a score by vertical lines across the stave.
5 (**the bar**) a partition in a court room, now usually notional, beyond which most people may not pass and at which an accused person stands: *the prisoner **at the bar***. ■ Brit. a rail marking the end of each chamber in the Houses of Parliament.
6 (**the Bar**) the profession of barrister. ■ Brit. barristers collectively. ■ N. Amer. lawyers collectively. ■ a particular court of law.
▶ **verb** (**bars, barring, barred**) [with obj.] **1** fasten (something, especially a door or window) with a bar or bars: *she bolted and barred the door*. ■ prevent or prohibit (someone) from doing something or from going somewhere: *journalists had been **barred from** covering the elections*. ■ forbid someone from undertaking (an activity): *the job she loved had been **barred to** her*. ■ exclude (something) from consideration: *nothing is barred in the crime novel*. ■ Law prevent or delay (an action) by objection.
2 mark (something) with bars or stripes: *his face was barred with light*.
▶ **preposition** chiefly Brit. except for: *his kids were all gone now, bar one*. ■ Horse Racing, Brit. except the horses indicated (used when stating the odds).
– PHRASES **bar none** with no exceptions: *the greatest living American poet bar none*. **be called** (or **go**) **to the Bar** Brit. be admitted as a barrister. **be called within the Bar** Brit. be appointed a Queen's Counsel. **behind bars** in prison. **lower** (or **raise**) **the bar** lower (or raise) the standards which need to be met in order to qualify for something: *the restaurant raised the bar for contemporary Scottish cuisine in the capital* .
– DERIVATIVES **barred** adjective [in combination] *a five-barred gate*.
– ORIGIN Middle English: from Old French *barre* (noun), *barrer* (verb), of unknown origin.

bar[2] ▶ noun a unit of pressure equivalent to a hundred thousand newtons per square metre or approximately one atmosphere.
– ORIGIN early 20th cent.: from Greek *baros* 'weight'.

Bar. ▶ abbreviation Baruch (Apocrypha) (in biblical references).

bara brith /ˌbarə ˈbriːθ/ ▶ noun [mass noun] a traditional Welsh tea bread, typically made with raisins, currants, and candied peel.
– ORIGIN Welsh, literally 'speckled bread'.

Barak /baˈrak/, Ehud (b.1942), Israeli Labour statesman, Prime Minister 1999–2001.

barasingha /ˌbarəˈsɪŋgə/ ▶ noun (pl. **same**) another term for SWAMP DEER.
– ORIGIN mid 19th cent.: from Hindi *bārahsiṅghā*, literally 'twelve-tined'.

barathea /ˌbarəˈθɪə/ ▶ noun [mass noun] a fine woollen cloth, sometimes mixed with silk or cotton, used chiefly for coats and suits.
– ORIGIN mid 19th cent.: of unknown origin.

baraza /bəˈrɑːzə/ ▶ noun (in East Africa) a public meeting place.
– ORIGIN Kiswahili.

barb[1] ▶ noun **1** a sharp projection near the end of an arrow, fish hook, or similar object, which is angled away from the main point so as to make extraction difficult. ■ a cluster of spikes on barbed wire. ■ a deliberately hurtful remark: *his barb hurt more than she cared to admit*.
2 a beard-like filament at the mouth of some fish, such as barbel and catfish. ■ each of the fine hair-like filaments growing from the shaft of a feather, forming the vane.
3 a freshwater fish with barbels around the mouth, popular in aquaria. • *Barbus* and other genera, family Cyprinidae: numerous species.
– DERIVATIVES **barbless** adjective.
– ORIGIN Middle English (denoting a piece of linen worn over or under the chin by nuns): from Old French *barbe*, from Latin *barba* 'beard'.

barb[2] ▶ noun a small horse of a hardy breed originally from North Africa.
– ORIGIN mid 17th cent.: from French *barbe*, from Italian *barbero* 'of Barbary'.

Barbados /bɑːˈbeɪdɒs/ the most easterly of the Caribbean islands, one of the Windward Islands group; pop. 284,600 (est. 2009); official language, English; capital, Bridgetown. Barbados became a British colony in the 1630s and remained British until 1966, when it gained independence as a Commonwealth state.
– DERIVATIVES **Barbadian** adjective & noun.

barbarian ▶ noun (in ancient times) a member of a people not belonging to one of the great civilizations (Greek, Roman, Christian). ■ an uncultured or brutish person.
▶ **adjective** relating to ancient barbarians: *barbarian invasions*. ■ uncultured; brutish.
– ORIGIN Middle English (as an adjective used in a derogatory way to denote a person with different speech and customs): from Old French *barbarien*, from *barbare*, or from Latin *barbarus* (see BARBAROUS).

barbaric ▶ adjective **1** savagely cruel: *he carried out barbaric acts in the name of war*.
2 primitive; unsophisticated: *the barbaric splendour he found in civilizations since destroyed*. ■ uncivilized and uncultured.
– DERIVATIVES **barbarically** adverb.
– ORIGIN late Middle English (as a noun in the sense 'a barbarian'): from Old French *barbarique*, or via Latin from Greek *barbarikos*, from *barbaros* 'foreign' (especially with reference to speech).

barbarism ▶ noun [mass noun] **1** absence of culture and civilization: *the collapse of civilization and the return to barbarism*. ■ [count noun] a word or expression which is badly formed according to traditional philological rules, e.g. a word formed from elements of different languages, such as *breathalyser* (English and Greek) or *television* (Greek and Latin).
2 extreme cruelty or brutality: *she called the execution an act of barbarism*.
– ORIGIN late Middle English: from Old French *barbarisme*, via Latin from Greek *barbarismos*, from *barbarizein* 'speak like a foreigner', from *barbaros* 'foreign'.

barbarity ▶ noun (pl. **barbarities**) [mass noun]
1 extreme cruelty or brutality: *the barbarity displayed by the terrorists* | [count noun] *the barbarities of war*.
2 absence of culture and civilization: *beyond the Empire lay barbarity*.

barbarize (also **barbarise**) ▶ verb [with obj.] (usu. as adj. **barbarizing**) cause to become savage or

uncultured: *the barbarizing effect of four decades of rock 'n' roll.*
– DERIVATIVES **barbarization** noun.
– ORIGIN late Middle English (in the sense 'speak using barbarisms'): from late Latin *barbarizare*, from Greek *barbarizein* 'speak like a foreigner'.

Barbarossa[1] /ˌbɑːbəˈrɒsə/ see **FREDERICK I**.

Barbarossa[2] /ˌbɑːbəˈrɒsə/, (*c.*1483–1546), Barbary pirate; born *Khair ad-Din*. He was notorious for his successes against Christian vessels in the eastern Mediterranean.

barbarous ▶ **adjective 1** extremely brutal: *many early child-rearing practices were barbarous by modern standards.*
2 primitive and uncivilized: *a remote and barbarous country.* ■ (of language) coarse and unrefined.
– DERIVATIVES **barbarously** adverb, **barbarousness** noun.
– ORIGIN late Middle English (in sense 2): via Latin from Greek *barbaros* 'foreign' + **-OUS**.

Barbary /ˈbɑːbəri/ (also **Barbary States**) a former name for the Saracen countries of North and NW Africa, together with Moorish Spain. Compare with **MAGHRIB**.
– ORIGIN based on Arabic *barbar* (see **BERBER**).

Barbary ape ▶ **noun** a tailless macaque monkey that is native to NW Africa and also found on the Rock of Gibraltar. ● *Macaca sylvana*, family Cercopithecidae.

Barbary Coast a former name for the Mediterranean coast of North Africa from Morocco to Egypt.

Barbary sheep ▶ **noun** a short-coated sheep with a long neck ruff, found in the high deserts of northern Africa. Also called **AOUDAD**. ● *Ammotragus lervia*, family Bovidae.

Barbary States another name for **BARBARY**.

barbastelle /ˌbɑːbəˈstɛl, ˈbɑːbəstɛl/ ▶ **noun** an Old World bat with broad ears that meet over the head. ● Genus *Barbastella*, family Vespertilionidae: two species.
– ORIGIN late 18th cent.: from French, from Italian *barbastello*.

barbecue ▶ **noun** a meal or gathering at which meat, fish, or other food is cooked out of doors on a rack over an open fire or on a special appliance. ■ a rack or appliance used for the preparation of food at a barbecue. ■ [mass noun] N. Amer. food cooked on a barbecue.
▶ **verb** (**barbecues**, **barbecuing**, **barbecued**) [with obj.] cook (food) on a barbecue.
– ORIGIN mid 17th cent.: from Spanish *barbacoa*, perhaps from Arawak *barbacoa* 'wooden frame on posts'. The original sense was 'wooden framework for sleeping on, or for storing meat or fish to be dried'.

> **USAGE** **Barbecue** is often misspelled as *barbeque*. This form arises understandably from the word's pronunciation and from the informal abbreviations *BBQ* and *Bar-B-Q*. Although almost a quarter of citations in the Oxford English Corpus are for the *-que* spelling, it is not accepted in standard English.

barbecue sauce ▶ **noun** a highly seasoned sauce containing vinegar, spices, and usually chillies.

barbed ▶ **adjective** having a barb or barbs: *barbed arrows.* ■ (of a remark or joke) deliberately hurtful: *a fair degree of barbed wit.*

barbed wire ▶ **noun** [mass noun] wire with clusters of short, sharp spikes set at short intervals along it, used to make fences or in warfare as an obstruction.

barbel /ˈbɑːb(ə)l/ ▶ **noun 1** a fleshy filament growing from the mouth or snout of a fish.
2 a large European freshwater fish of the carp family, which has barbels hanging from the mouth. ● *Barbus barbus*, family Cyprinidae.
3 [with modifier] an African marine or freshwater fish with barbels round the mouth. ● Species in several families, including *Tachysurus feliceps* (family Aniidae), of southern African coasts and estuaries.
– ORIGIN late Middle English (in sense 2): via Old French from late Latin *barbellus*, diminutive of *barbus* 'barbel', from *barba* 'beard'.

barbell /ˈbɑːbɛl/ ▶ **noun** a long metal bar to which discs of varying weights are attached at each end, used for weightlifting.
– ORIGIN late 19th cent.: from **BAR**[1] + **BELL**[1].

Barber, Samuel (1910–81), American composer. He developed a style based on romanticism allied to classical forms; his music includes operas and orchestral and chamber music.

barber ▶ **noun** a person who cuts men's hair and shaves or trims beards as an occupation.
▶ **verb** [with obj.] cut or trim (a man's hair).
– ORIGIN Middle English: via Anglo-Norman French from Old French *barbe* (see **BARB**[1]).

barberry ▶ **noun** (pl. **barberries**) a spiny shrub which typically has yellow flowers and red berries, frequently grown for ornamental hedging. ● Genus *Berberis*, family Berberidaceae: many species.
– ORIGIN late Middle English: from Old French *berberis* (see **BERBERIS**). The change in the ending was due to association with **BERRY**.

barbershop ▶ **noun 1** chiefly N. Amer. a shop where a barber works.
2 [mass noun] [often as modifier] a popular style of close harmony singing, typically for four male voices. [from the custom in the 16th and 17th centuries of passing time in a barber's shop by harmonizing to a lute or guitar provided to entertain customers waiting their turn.]

barber's itch (also **barber's rash**) ▶ **noun** [mass noun] ringworm of the face or neck communicated by unsterilized shaving apparatus.

barber's pole ▶ **noun** a pole painted with spiralling red and white stripes and hung outside barbers' shops as a business sign.

Barberton daisy /ˈbɑːbət(ə)n/ ▶ **noun** South African term for **TRANSVAAL DAISY**.
– ORIGIN from the name of a town in the Transvaal.

barbet /ˈbɑːbɪt/ ▶ **noun** a large-headed, brightly coloured fruit-eating bird that has a stout bill with tufts of bristles at the base. Barbets are found on all continents, especially in the tropics. ● Family Capitonidae: numerous genera and species.
– ORIGIN late 16th cent. (denoting a poodle): from French, from *barbe* 'beard' (see **BARB**[1]). The current sense dates from the early 19th cent.

barbette /bɑːˈbɛt/ ▶ **noun** a fixed armoured housing at the base of a gun turret on a warship or armoured vehicle. ■ historical a platform on which a gun was placed to fire over a parapet.
– ORIGIN late 18th cent.: from French, diminutive of *barbe* 'beard' (see **BARB**[1]).

barbican /ˈbɑːbɪk(ə)n/ ▶ **noun** the outer defence of a castle or walled city, especially a double tower above a gate or drawbridge.
– ORIGIN Middle English: from Old French *barbacane*; probably based on Arabic.

barbie ▶ **noun** (pl. **barbies**) informal, chiefly Austral./NZ a barbecue.
– ORIGIN 1970s: abbreviation.

Barbie doll ▶ **noun** trademark a doll representing a conventionally attractive young woman. ■ informal a young woman who is glossily attractive but apparently characterless or unintelligent.
– ORIGIN 1950s: *Barbie*, diminutive of the given name *Barbara*.

bar billiards ▶ **noun** Brit. a form of billiards played on a small table, typically in a public bar, in which balls are struck into holes guarded by pegs.

Barbirolli /ˌbɑːbɪˈrɒli/, Sir John (Giovanni Battista) (1899–1970), English conductor, of Franco-Italian descent, conductor of the Hallé Orchestra from 1943.

barbital /ˈbɑːbɪt(ə)l/ ▶ **noun** North American term for **BARBITONE**.
– ORIGIN early 20th cent.: from **BARBITURIC ACID**, on the pattern of *veronal* (an alternative name).

barbitone /ˈbɑːbɪtəʊn/ ▶ **noun** [mass noun] a long-acting sedative and sleep-inducing drug of the barbiturate type. ● Chem. formula: $C_6H_{12}O_3N_2$.
– ORIGIN early 20th cent.: from **BARBITURIC ACID** + **-ONE**.

barbiturate /bɑːˈbɪtjʊrət, -reɪt/ ▶ **noun** any of a class of sedative and sleep-inducing drugs derived from barbituric acid. ■ Chemistry a salt or ester of barbituric acid.

barbituric acid /ˌbɑːbɪˈtjʊərɪk, -ˈtʃʊərɪk/ ▶ **noun** [mass noun] Chemistry a synthetic organic acid from which the barbiturates are derived. ● A cyclic derivative of urea and malonic acid; chem. formula: $C_4H_4O_3N_2$.
– ORIGIN mid 19th cent.: from French *barbiturique*, from German *Barbitursäure*, from the given name *Barbara* + *Säure* 'acid'.

Barbizon School a mid 19th-century school of French landscape painters who reacted against classical conventions and based their art on direct study of nature. Led by Théodore Rousseau, the group included Charles Daubigny and Jean-François Millet.
– ORIGIN named after *Barbizon*, a small village in the forest of Fontainebleau, near Paris, where Rousseau and others worked.

barbola /bɑːˈbəʊlə/ (also **barbola work**) ▶ **noun** [mass noun] the craft of making small models of fruit or flowers from a plastic paste.
– ORIGIN 1920s: an arbitrary formation from **BARBOTINE**.

barbotine /ˈbɑːbətiːn/ ▶ **noun** [mass noun] slip (liquid clay) used to decorate pottery.
– ORIGIN mid 19th cent.: from French.

Barbour[1] /ˈbɑːbə/, John (*c.*1320–95), Scottish poet and prelate. The only poem ascribed to him with certainty is *The Bruce*, a verse chronicle relating the deeds of Robert the Bruce.

Barbour[2] /ˈbɑːbə/ (also **Barbour jacket**) ▶ **noun** trademark a type of green waxed outdoor jacket.
– ORIGIN named after John *Barbour* (died 1918), a draper in NE England who sold waterproof clothing.

Barbuda see **ANTIGUA AND BARBUDA**.
– DERIVATIVES **Barbudan** adjective & noun.

barbule /ˈbɑːbjuːl/ ▶ **noun** a minute filament projecting from the barb of a feather.
– ORIGIN mid 19th cent.: from Latin *barbula*, diminutive of *barba* 'beard'.

barbwire ▶ **noun** [mass noun] N. Amer. barbed wire.

BarcaLounger /ˈbɑːkəˌlaʊndʒə/ ▶ **noun** US trademark a type of deeply padded reclining chair.
– ORIGIN 1970s: from the name of Edward J. *Barcolo*, who acquired the original licence to manufacture the chairs, and **LOUNGER**.

barcarole /ˈbɑːkərəʊl, ˌbɑːkəˈrəʊl/ (also **barcarolle** /-rɒl, -ˈrɒl/) ▶ **noun** a song traditionally sung by Venetian gondoliers. ■ a musical composition in the style of a barcarole.
– ORIGIN late 18th cent.: from French *barcarolle*, from Venetian Italian *barcarola* 'boatman's song', from *barca* 'boat'.

Barcelona /ˌbɑːsəˈləʊnə/, Spanish /barθeˈlaona, barse-/ a city on the coast of NE Spain, capital of Catalonia; pop. 1,615,908 (est. 2008).

barchan /ˈbɑːk(ə)n/ ▶ **noun** a crescent-shaped shifting sand dune, as found in the deserts of Turkestan.
– ORIGIN late 19th cent.: from Turkic *barkhan*.

bar chart (also chiefly N. Amer. **bar graph**) ▶ **noun** a diagram in which the numerical values of variables are represented by the height or length of lines or rectangles of equal width.

Bar-Cochba /bɑːˈkɒkbə/ Jewish rebel leader; known as **Simeon** in Jewish sources. He led the rebellion against the Romans in AD 132, and was accepted by some of his Jewish contemporaries as the Messiah.

barcode ▶ **noun** a machine-readable code in the form of numbers and a pattern of parallel lines of varying widths, printed on a commodity and used especially for stock control.
▶ **verb** [with obj.] mark with a barcode: *all the merchandise is barcoded and scanned.*

Barcoo /bɑːˈkuː/ ▶ **adjective** Austral. informal relating to the remote inland area of Australia: *Barcoo sickness.*
– ORIGIN late 19th cent.: from the name of a river (and the surrounding country) in western Queensland.

Barcoo rot ▶ **noun** [mass noun] Austral. informal scurvy.

bard[1] ▶ **noun** archaic or literary a poet, traditionally one reciting epics and associated with a particular oral tradition. ■ (**the Bard** or **the Bard of Avon**) Shakespeare. ■ (**Bard**) the winner of a prize for Welsh verse at an Eisteddfod.
– DERIVATIVES **bardic** adjective.
– ORIGIN Middle English: from Scottish Gaelic *bàrd*, Irish *bard*, Welsh *bardd*, of Celtic origin. In Scotland in the 16th cent. it was a derogatory term for an itinerant musician, but was later romanticized by Sir Walter Scott.

bard[2] ▶ **noun** a rasher of fat bacon placed on meat or game before roasting.
▶ **verb** [with obj.] cover (meat or game) with rashers of fat bacon.
– ORIGIN early 18th cent.: from French *barde*, a transferred sense of *barde* 'armour for the breast and flanks of a warhorse', based on Arabic *barda'a* 'saddlecloth, padded saddle'.

bardie /ˈbɑːdi/ (also **bardee** or **bardy**) ▶ **noun** (pl. **bardies**) Austral. the edible larva or pupa of certain insects, in particular: ● a longhorn beetle that bores within stems (*Bardistus cibarius*, family Cerambycidae). ● a moth that develops underground on roots (family Hepialidae, especially *Trictena argentata*).
– ORIGIN mid 19th cent.: from Nyungar (and other Aboriginal languages) *bardi*.

bardo /ˈbɑːdəʊ/ ▸ **noun** [mass noun] (in Tibetan Buddhism) a state of existence between death and rebirth, varying in length according to a person's conduct in life and manner of, or age at, death.
– ORIGIN Tibetan *bár-do*, from *bar* 'interval' + *do* 'two'.

bardolatry /bɑːˈdɒlətri/ ▸ **noun** [mass noun] humorous excessive admiration of Shakespeare.
– DERIVATIVES **bardolater** (or **bardolator**) **noun**.

Bardolino /ˌbɑːdəˈliːnəʊ/ ▸ **noun** [mass noun] a red wine from the Veneto region of Italy.
– ORIGIN Italian.

Bardot /bɑːˈdəʊ/, French /baʀdo/, Brigitte (b.1934), French actress; born *Camille Javal*. The film *And God Created Woman* (1956) established her reputation as an international sex symbol.

bardy ▸ **noun** (pl. **bardies**) variant spelling of **BARDIE**.

bare ▸ **adjective 1** (of a person or part of the body) not clothed or covered: *he was bare from the waist up* | *she padded in bare feet towards the door*. ■ without the appropriate, usual, or natural covering: *leaf fall had left the trees bare* | *bare floorboards*. ■ without the appropriate or usual contents: *a bare cell with just a mattress*. ■ (**bare of**) devoid of; without.
2 without addition; basic and simple: *he outlined the bare essentials of the story*. ■ [attrib.] only just sufficient: *the bare minimum of furniture*. ■ [attrib.] surprisingly small in number or amount: *all you need to get started with this program is a bare 10K bytes of memory*.
▸ **verb** [with obj.] uncover (a part of the body or other thing) and expose it to view: *he bared his chest to show his scar*.
– PHRASES **bare all** take off all of one's clothes and display oneself to others. **the bare bones** the basic facts about something, without any detail: *the bare bones of the plot*. ■ the very lowest level of resources necessary: *his squad is already* ***down to the bare bones*** *and has now been hit by a flu bug*. **bare one's soul** reveal one's innermost secrets and feelings to someone. **bare one's teeth** show one's teeth, typically when angry. **with one's bare hands** without using tools or weapons.
– DERIVATIVES **bareness** **noun**.
– ORIGIN Old English *bær* (noun), *barian* (verb), of Germanic origin; related to Dutch *baar*.

bareback ▸ **adjective & adverb** on an unsaddled horse or donkey: [as adj.] *a bareback circus rider* | [as adv.] *she's riding bareback*.

barebacking ▸ **noun** [mass noun] vulgar slang the practice of having anal intercourse without a condom.

bareboat ▸ **adjective** relating to or denoting a boat or ship hired without a crew: *bareboat charters*.

Barebones Parliament the nickname of Cromwell's Parliament of 1653, from one of its members, Praise-God Barbon, an Anabaptist leather seller of Fleet Street. It replaced the Rump Parliament, but was itself dissolved within a few months.

barefaced ▸ **adjective 1** shameless and undisguised: *a barefaced lie*.
2 having an uncovered face.

barefoot (also **barefooted**) ▸ **adjective & adverb** wearing nothing on the feet: [as adv.] *I won't walk barefoot*.

barefoot doctor ▸ **noun** a paramedical worker with basic medical training working in a rural district in China.

barège /bəˈreɪʒ/ ▸ **noun** [mass noun] a light, silky dress fabric resembling gauze, typically made from wool.
– ORIGIN French, named after the village of *Barèges* in SW France, where it was originally made.

barehanded ▸ **adjective & adverb** with nothing in or covering one's hands. ■ carrying no weapons.

bareheaded ▸ **adjective & adverb** without a covering for one's head.

Bareilly /bəˈreɪli/ an industrial city in northern India, in Uttar Pradesh; pop. 825,100 (est. 2009).

bare-knuckle (also **bare-knuckled**) ▸ **adjective** (of a boxer or boxing match) without gloves. ■ informal with no scruples or reservations: *an apostle of bare-knuckle capitalism*.

barely ▸ **adverb 1** only just; almost not: *she nodded, barely able to speak* | [as submodifier] *a barely perceptible pause*. ■ only a very short time before: *they had barely sat down before forty policemen swarmed in*.
2 in a simple and sparse way: *their barely furnished house*.
3 archaic openly; explicitly.

Barenboim /ˈbarənbɔɪm/, Daniel (b.1942), Israeli pianist and conductor, musical director of the Orchestre de Paris 1975–88 and of the Chicago Symphony Orchestra 1991–2006. In 1967 he married the cellist Jacqueline du Pré.

Barents /ˈbarənts/, Willem (d.1597), Dutch explorer. The leader of several expeditions in search of the North-East Passage to Asia, Barents discovered Spitsbergen and reached Novaya Zemlya, off the coast of which he died.

Barents Sea a part of the Arctic Ocean to the north of Norway and Russia, bounded to the west by Svalbard, to the north by Franz Josef Land, and to the east by Novaya Zemlya.

barf informal, chiefly N. Amer. ▸ **verb** [no obj.] vomit.
▸ **noun** an attack of vomiting. ■ [mass noun] vomited food.
– ORIGIN 1960s (originally US): of unknown origin.

barfi /ˈbʌrfiː/ ▸ **noun** variant spelling of **BURFI**.

barfly /ˈbɑːflʌɪ/ ▸ **noun** (pl. **barflies**) informal a person who spends much of their time drinking in bars.

barfly jumping ▸ **noun** [mass noun] the sport of jumping at and sticking to a Velcro-covered wall while wearing a Velcro suit.

bargain ▸ **noun 1** an agreement between two or more people or groups as to what each will do for the other: *bargains between political parties supporting the government*.
2 a thing bought or offered for sale much more cheaply than is usual or expected: *the table was a real bargain* | [as modifier] *a bargain price of 99p*.
▸ **verb** [no obj.] **1** negotiate the terms and conditions of a transaction: *he* ***bargained with*** *the local council to rent the stadium*. ■ [with obj.] (**bargain something away**) part with something after negotiation but get little or nothing in return.
2 (**bargain for/on**) be prepared for; expect: *I got more information than I'd bargained for* | *he didn't bargain on this storm*.
– PHRASES **drive a hard bargain** be uncompromising in making a deal. **into** (N. Amer. **in**) **the bargain** in addition to what has already been mentioned or was expected: *I am now tired and extremely hungry—with a headache into the bargain*. **keep one's side of the bargain** carry out the promises one has made as part of an agreement.
– DERIVATIVES **bargainer** **noun**.
– ORIGIN Middle English: from Old French *bargaine* (noun), *bargaignier* (verb); probably of Germanic origin and related to German *borgen* 'borrow'.

bargain basement ▸ **noun** a store or part of a store where goods are sold cheaply: [as modifier] *bargain-basement prices*.

bargaining chip (Brit. also **bargaining counter**) ▸ **noun** a potential concession or other factor which can be used to advantage in negotiations.

bargainous /ˈbɑːgɪnəs/ ▸ **adjective** Brit. informal costing less than is usual or than might be expected; cheap or relatively cheap: *the best and most bargainous sunglasses around*.

barge ▸ **noun** a long flat-bottomed boat for carrying freight on canals and rivers, either under its own power or towed by another. ■ a long ornamental boat used for pleasure or ceremony. ■ a boat used by the chief officers of a warship.
▸ **verb 1** [no obj., with adverbial of direction] move forcefully or roughly: *we can't just* ***barge into*** *a private garden*. ■ (**barge in**) intrude or interrupt rudely or awkwardly: *sorry to* ***barge in on*** *your cosy evening*. ■ [with obj.] (chiefly in a sporting context) run into and collide with (someone), typically intentionally.
2 [with obj.] convey (freight) by barge.
– ORIGIN Middle English (denoting a small seagoing vessel): from Old French, perhaps based on Greek *baris* 'Egyptian boat'.

bargeboard ▸ **noun** a board, typically an ornamental one, fixed to the gable end of a roof to hide the ends of the roof timbers.
– ORIGIN mid 19th cent.: from mid 16th-cent. *barge-* (used in architectural terms relating to the gable of a building), perhaps from medieval Latin *bargus* 'gallows'.

bargee /bɑːˈdʒiː/ ▸ **noun** chiefly Brit. a person in charge of or working on a barge.

Bargello /bɑːˈdʒɛləʊ/ ▸ **noun** [mass noun] a kind of embroidery worked on canvas in stitch patterns suggestive of flames.
– ORIGIN named after *Bargello* Palace, in Florence, Italy.

bargepole ▸ **noun** a long pole used to propel a barge and fend off obstacles.
– PHRASES **would not touch someone/thing with a bargepole** informal used to express a refusal to have anything to do with someone or something.

bar graph ▸ **noun** chiefly N. Amer. another term for **BAR CHART**.

bar-hop ▸ **verb** (**bar-hops**, **bar-hopping**, **bar-hopped**) [no obj.] (usu. as noun **bar-hopping**) visit several bars in succession, having a drink in each.
– DERIVATIVES **bar-hopper** **noun**.

Bari /ˈbɑːri/ an industrial seaport on the Adriatic coast of SE Italy, capital of Apulia region; pop. 320,677 (2008).

barilla /bəˈrɪlə/ ▸ **noun** [mass noun] an impure alkali formerly made from the ashes of burnt plants, especially saltworts.
– ORIGIN early 17th cent.: from Spanish *barrilla*, diminutive of *barra* 'bar'.

Barisal /ˈbʌrɪsʌl/ a river port in southern Bangladesh, on the Ganges delta; pop. 210,374 (est. 2008).

barista /bəˈrɪstə/ ▸ **noun** a person who serves in a coffee bar.
– ORIGIN 1980s: Italian, 'barman'.

barite /ˈbarʌɪt, ˈbɛː-/ ▸ **noun** variant spelling of **BARYTE**.

baritone ▸ **noun 1** an adult male singing voice between tenor and bass. ■ a singer with a baritone voice. ■ a part written for a baritone voice.
2 [usu. as modifier] an instrument that is second lowest in pitch in its family: *a baritone sax*. ■ a brass instrument similar to a euphonium, sounding in B flat and used in brass bands.
– DERIVATIVES **baritonal** /bariˈtəʊn(ə)l/ **adjective**, **baritonist** **noun**.
– ORIGIN early 17th cent.: from Italian *baritono*, from Greek *barutonos*, from *barus* 'heavy' + *tonos* (see **TONE**).

barium /ˈbɛːrɪəm/ ▸ **noun** [mass noun] the chemical element of atomic number 56, a soft white reactive metal of the alkaline earth group. (Symbol: **Ba**) ■ a mixture of barium sulphate and water, opaque to X-rays, which is swallowed to permit radiological examination of the stomach or intestines: [as modifier] *a barium meal*.

> Barium compounds are used in water purification, the glass industry, and pigments, and as an ingredient of signal flares and fireworks, to which they give a bright yellowish-green colour. Barium oxide is a component of high-temperature superconductors.

– ORIGIN early 19th cent.: from **BARYTA** + **-IUM**.

bark[1] ▸ **noun** the sharp explosive cry of a dog, fox, or seal. ■ a sound resembling a bark, typically one made by someone laughing or coughing: *a short bark of laughter*.
▸ **verb 1** [no obj.] (of a dog, fox, or seal) give a bark. ■ (of a person) make a sound resembling a bark: *she barked with laughter*.
2 [with obj.] utter (a command or question) abruptly or aggressively: *he began* ***barking out*** *his orders* | [with direct speech] *'Nobody is allowed up here,' he barked*. ■ [no obj.] US call out in order to sell or advertise something.
– PHRASES **one's bark is worse than one's bite** one is not as ferocious as one appears or sounds. **be barking up the wrong tree** informal be pursuing a mistaken or misguided line of thought or course of action.
– ORIGIN Old English *beorc* (noun), *beorcan* (verb), of Germanic origin; possibly related to **BREAK**[1].

bark[2] ▸ **noun** [mass noun] the tough protective outer sheath of the trunk, branches, and twigs of a tree or woody shrub.
▸ **verb** [with obj.] **1** chiefly Brit. strip the bark from (a tree or piece of wood). ■ scrape the skin off (one's shin) by accidentally hitting it against something hard.
2 technical tan or dye (leather or other materials) using the tannins found in bark.
– DERIVATIVES **barked** **adjective**.
– ORIGIN Middle English: from Old Norse *bǫrkr*; perhaps related to **BIRCH**.

bark[3] ▸ **noun** archaic or literary a ship or boat.
– ORIGIN late Middle English: variant of **BARQUE**.

bark beetle ▸ **noun** a small wood-boring beetle that tunnels under the bark of trees, which may die if heavily infested. ● Family Scolytidae: many genera and species, including the **elm bark beetle** (*Scolytus scolytus*), which is responsible for the spread of the fungus which causes Dutch elm disease.

barkcloth ▸ **noun** [mass noun] cloth made from the inner bark of the paper mulberry or similar tree.

barkeeper (US also **barkeep**) ▸ **noun** chiefly N. Amer. a person who owns or serves drinks in a bar.

barkentine ▸ noun US spelling of BARQUENTINE.

barker ▸ noun informal a tout at an auction, sideshow, etc., who calls out to passers-by to attract custom.
– ORIGIN late Middle English: from BARK[1] + -ER[1]. The original sense was 'a person or animal that barks; a noisy protestor', hence the current sense (late 17th cent.).

barking ▸ adjective Brit. informal completely mad or demented: *we are all a bit barking* | [as submodifier] *has she gone completely* ***barking mad?***

barking deer ▸ noun another term for MUNTJAC.

Barkly Tableland a plateau region lying to the north-east of Tennant Creek in Northern Territory, Australia.
– ORIGIN named after Sir Henry *Barkly*, governor of Victoria 1856–63.

barley ▸ noun [mass noun] a hardy cereal with coarse bristles extending from the ears, cultivated especially for use in brewing and stockfeed. ● Genus *Hordeum*, family Gramineae.
■ the grain of barley.
– ORIGIN Old English *bærlic* (adjective), from *bære*, *bere* 'barley' + *-lic* (see -LY[1]).

barleycorn ▸ noun a grain of barley. ■ a former unit of measurement (about a third of an inch) based on the length of a grain of barley.

barleymow ▸ noun archaic a stack of barley.

barley sugar ▸ noun [mass noun] an amber-coloured sweet made of boiled sugar, traditionally shaped as a twisted stick.

barley water ▸ noun [mass noun] Brit. a drink made from water and a boiled barley mixture, usually flavoured with orange or lemon.

barley wine ▸ noun [mass noun] a strong English ale.

bar line ▸ noun Music a vertical line used in a musical score to mark a division between bars.

barm ▸ noun **1** [mass noun] the froth on fermenting malt liquor. ■ archaic or dialect yeast or leaven.
2 short for BARM CAKE.
– ORIGIN Old English *beorma*, of West Germanic origin.

barmaid ▸ noun **1** Brit. a woman serving behind the bar of a pub or hotel.
2 N. Amer. a waitress who serves drinks in a bar.

barman ▸ noun (pl. **barmen**) chiefly Brit. a man serving behind the bar of a pub or hotel.

barmbrack (also **barnbrack**) ▸ noun [mass noun] a kind of soft, spicy bread containing dried fruit, originating in Ireland where it is traditionally eaten at Halloween.
– ORIGIN from Irish *bairin breac* 'speckled cake'.

barm cake ▸ noun N. English a soft, flattish bread roll.

Barmecide /ˈbɑːmɪsʌɪd/ ▸ adjective rare illusory or imaginary and therefore disappointing.
– ORIGIN early 18th cent. (as a noun): from Arabic *Barmakī*, the name of a prince in the *Arabian Nights' Entertainments*, who gave a beggar a feast consisting of ornate but empty dishes.

bar mitzvah /bɑː ˈmɪtsvə/ ▸ noun the initiation ceremony of a Jewish boy who has reached the age of 13 and is regarded as ready to observe religious precepts and eligible to take part in public worship. ■ the boy undergoing this ceremony.
▸ verb [with obj.] administer the bar mitzvah ceremony to (a boy).
– ORIGIN from Hebrew *bar miṣwāh*, literally 'son of the commandment'.

barmy ▸ adjective (**barmier**, **barmiest**) Brit. informal extremely foolish: *this is a barmy decision.* ■ mad; crazy: *I thought I was going barmy at first.*
– DERIVATIVES **barmily** adverb, **barminess** noun.
– ORIGIN late 15th cent. (in the sense 'frothy'): from BARM + -Y[1].

barn[1] ▸ noun a large farm building used for storing grain, hay, or straw or for housing livestock. ■ N. Amer. a large shed used for storing road or railway vehicles. ■ a large and uninviting building: *a great* ***barn of a pub.***
– ORIGIN Old English *bern*, *berern*, from *bere* 'barley' + *ern*, *ærn* 'house'.

barn[2] (abbrev.: **b**) ▸ noun Physics a unit of area, 10^{-28} square metres, used especially in particle physics.
– ORIGIN 1940s: apparently from the phrase *as big as a barn door.*

Barnabas, St /ˈbɑːnəbəs/ (died *c.*61), a Cypriot Levite and Apostle. He accompanied St Paul on the first missionary journey to Cyprus and Asia Minor. The traditional founder of the Cypriot Church, he is said to have been martyred in Cyprus. Feast day, 11 June.

barnacle /ˈbɑːnək(ə)l/ ▸ noun a marine crustacean with an external shell, which attaches itself permanently to a surface and feeds by filtering particles from the water using its modified feathery legs. ● Class Cirripedia. See ACORN BARNACLE, GOOSE BARNACLE.
– DERIVATIVES **barnacled** adjective.
– ORIGIN late 16th cent.: from medieval Latin *bernaca*, of unknown origin. In Middle English the term denoted the barnacle goose, whose breeding grounds were long unknown and which was believed to hatch from the shell of the crustacean to which it gave its name.

barnacle goose ▸ noun a goose with a white face and black neck, breeding in the arctic tundra of Greenland, Spitsbergen, and Novaya Zemlya. ● *Branta leucopsis*, family Anatidae.
– ORIGIN mid 18th cent.: see BARNACLE.

Barnard /ˈbɑːnɑːd/, Christiaan Neethling (1922–2001), South African surgeon. He pioneered human heart transplantation, performing the first operation of this kind in December 1967.

Barnardo /bəˈnɑːdəʊ/, Thomas John (1845–1905), Irish-born doctor and philanthropist. He founded the East End Mission for destitute children in 1867, the first of many such homes. Now known as Dr Barnardo's Homes, they cater chiefly for those with physical and mental disabilities.

Barnard's star Astronomy a red dwarf in the constellation Ophiuchus. It has a large proper motion and is one of the closest stars to the sun.
– ORIGIN named after Edward E. *Barnard* (1857–1923), the American astronomer who discovered it in 1916.

Barnaul /ˌbɑːnəˈuːl/ the capital of Altai territory in Russia on the River Ob; pop. 597,200 (est. 2008).

barnbrack ▸ noun variant spelling of BARMBRACK.

barn burner ▸ noun N. Amer. informal a very exciting or dramatic event, especially a sports contest.

barn dance ▸ noun **1** an informal social gathering for country dancing.
2 a dance for a number of couples moving round a circle, typically involving changes of partner.

barn door ▸ noun **1** the large door of a barn. ■ used to refer to a large and easy target: *on the shooting range he* ***could not hit a barn door.***
2 a hinged metal flap fitted to a spotlight to control the direction and intensity of its beam.

barnet /ˈbɑːnɪt/ ▸ noun Brit. informal a person's hair.
– ORIGIN mid 19th cent.: from rhyming slang *barnet fair*, the name of a famous horse fair held at *Barnet*, Herts.

barney ▸ noun (pl. **barneys**) Brit. informal a quarrel, especially a noisy one.
– ORIGIN mid 19th cent.: of unknown origin.

barn owl ▸ noun an owl with a heart-shaped face, black eyes, and relatively long, slender legs, typically nesting in farm buildings or in holes in trees. Also called SCREECH OWL. ● Genus *Tyto*, family Tytonidae: three species, especially *T. alba*, which is found throughout the world and (in western Europe) has a white face and underparts.

Barnsley a town in South Yorkshire, northern England; pop. 70,100 (est. 2009).

barnstorm ▸ verb [no obj.] chiefly N. Amer. tour rural districts giving theatrical performances, originally often in barns. ■ make a rapid tour of an area as part of a political campaign. ■ travel around giving exhibitions of flying and performing aeronautical stunts.
– DERIVATIVES **barnstormer** noun.

barnstorming ▸ adjective (of a performance or performer) flamboyantly energetic and successful: *his barnstorming oratory has been sorely missed.*

barn swallow ▸ noun see SWALLOW[2].

Barnum /ˈbɑːnəm/, P. T. (1810–91), American showman; full name *Phineas Taylor Barnum*. He billed his circus, opened in 1871, as 'The Greatest Show on Earth'; ten years later he founded the Barnum and Bailey circus with his former rival Anthony Bailey (1847–1906).

Barnum effect ▸ noun Psychology the tendency to accept as true types of information such as character assessments or horoscopes, even when the information is so vague as to be worthless.
– ORIGIN named after P. T. BARNUM; the word *Barnum* was in use from the mid 19th cent. as a noun in the sense 'nonsense, humbug'.

barnyard ▸ noun chiefly N. Amer. the area of open ground around a barn; a farmyard.

baro- /ˈbarəʊ/ ▸ combining form relating to pressure: *barotrauma* | *barotitis.*
– ORIGIN from Greek *baros* 'weight'.

Baroda /bəˈrəʊdə/ a former princely state of western India, now part of Gujarat. ■ former name (until 1976) for VADODARA.

barograph ▸ noun a barometer that records its readings on a moving chart.
– ORIGIN mid 19th cent.: from Greek *baros* 'weight' + -GRAPH.

Barolo /bəˈrəʊləʊ/, Italian /baˈrɔːlo/ ▸ noun [mass noun] a full-bodied red Italian wine from Barolo, a region of Piedmont.

barometer ▸ noun an instrument measuring atmospheric pressure, used especially in forecasting the weather and determining altitude. ■ something which reflects changes in circumstances or opinions: *furniture is a barometer of changing tastes.*
– DERIVATIVES **barometric** adjective, **barometrical** adjective, **barometry** noun.
– ORIGIN mid 17th cent.: from Greek *baros* 'weight' + -METER.

baron ▸ noun **1** a member of the lowest order of the British nobility. Baron is not used as a form of address, barons usually being referred to as 'Lord'. ■ a similar member of a foreign nobility. ■ historical a person who held lands or property from the sovereign or a powerful overlord.
2 [with modifier] an important or powerful person in a specified business or industry: *a press baron.*
– ORIGIN Middle English: from Old French, from medieval Latin *baro*, *baron-* 'man, warrior', probably of Germanic origin.

baronage ▸ noun **1** [treated as sing. or pl.] barons or nobles collectively.
2 an annotated list of barons or peers.

baroness ▸ noun the wife or widow of a baron. Baroness is not used as a form of address, baronesses usually being referred to as 'Lady'. ■ a woman holding the rank of baron either as a life peerage or as a hereditary rank.

baronet /ˈbar(ə)nɪt/ ▸ noun a member of the lowest hereditary titled British order, with the status of a commoner but able to use the prefix 'Sir'.
– ORIGIN late Middle English: from Anglo-Latin *baronettus*, from Latin *baro*, *baron-* 'man, warrior'. The term originally denoted a gentleman, not a nobleman, summoned by the king to attend parliament; the current order was instituted in the early 17th cent.

baronetage ▸ noun **1** [treated as sing. or pl.] baronets collectively.
2 an annotated list of baronets.

baronetcy ▸ noun (pl. **baronetcies**) the rank of a baronet.

baronial ▸ adjective **1** relating to a baron or barons.
2 in the turreted style characteristic of Scottish country houses.

baron of beef ▸ noun Brit. a joint of beef consisting of two sirloins joined at the backbone.

barony ▸ noun (pl. **baronies**) **1** the rank and estates of a baron.
2 historical (in Ireland) a division of a county.
3 historical (in Scotland) a large manor or estate.

baroque /bəˈrɒk, -ˈrəʊk/ ▸ adjective relating to or denoting a style of European architecture, music, and art of the 17th and 18th centuries that followed Mannerism and is characterized by ornate detail. In architecture the period is exemplified by the palace of Versailles and by the work of Wren in England. Major composers include Vivaldi, Bach, and Handel; Caravaggio and Rubens are important baroque artists. ■ highly ornate and extravagant in style.
▸ noun [mass noun] the baroque style or period.
– ORIGIN mid 18th cent.: from French (originally designating a pearl of irregular shape), from Portuguese *barroco*, Spanish *barrueco*, or Italian *barocco*; of unknown ultimate origin.

baroreceptor ▸ noun Zoology a receptor sensitive to changes in pressure.

barotitis /ˌbarə(ʊ)ˈtʌɪtɪs/ ▸ noun [mass noun] Medicine discomfort and inflammation in the ear caused by the changes of pressure occurring during air travel.

barotrauma ▸ noun [mass noun] Medicine injury caused by a change in air pressure, affecting typically the ear or the lung.

B

barouche /bə'ruːʃ/ ▸ **noun** historical a four-wheeled horse-drawn carriage with a collapsible hood over the rear half, a seat in front for the driver, and seats facing each other for the passengers.
– ORIGIN early 19th cent.: from German dialect *Barutsche*, from Italian *baroccio*, based on Latin *birotus* 'two-wheeled', from *bi-* 'having two' + *rota* 'wheel'.

barque /bɑːk/ ▸ **noun** a sailing ship, typically with three masts, in which the foremast and mainmast are square-rigged and the mizzenmast is rigged fore and aft. ■ literary a boat.
– ORIGIN Middle English: from Old French, probably from Provençal *barca*, from late Latin *barca* 'ship's boat'.

barquentine /'bɑːk(ə)ntiːn/ (US **barkentine**) ▸ **noun** a sailing ship similar to a barque but with only the foremast square-rigged and the remaining masts rigged fore and aft.
– ORIGIN late 17th cent.: from **BARQUE**, on the pattern of *brigantine*.

Barquisimeto /ˌbɑːkɪsɪ'meɪtəʊ/ a city in NW Venezuela; pop. 1,018,900 (est. 2009).

Barra /'barə/ a small island towards the southern end of the Outer Hebrides, to the south of South Uist, from which it is separated by the Sound of Barra.

barrack¹ ▸ **verb** [with obj.] provide (soldiers) with accommodation in a building or set of buildings.
– ORIGIN early 18th cent.: from **BARRACKS**.

barrack² ▸ **verb 1** [with obj.] Brit. jeer loudly at (someone performing or speaking in public) in order to express disapproval or to distract them: *opponents barracked him when he addressed the opening parliamentary session.*
2 [no obj.] (**barrack for**) Austral./NZ give support and encouragement to: *I take it you'll be barracking for Labour tonight?*
– ORIGIN late 19th cent.: probably from Northern Irish dialect.

barrack-room lawyer ▸ **noun** Brit. a person who likes to give authoritative-sounding opinions on subjects in which they are not qualified, especially legal matters.

barracks (also **barrack**) ▸ **plural noun** [often treated as sing.] a large building or group of buildings used to house soldiers: *the troops were ordered back to barracks.*
– ORIGIN late 17th cent.: *barrack* from French *baraque*, from Italian *baracca* or Spanish *barraca* 'soldier's tent', of unknown origin.

barrack square ▸ **noun** Brit. a drill ground near a barracks.

barracoon /ˌbarə'kuːn/ ▸ **noun** historical an enclosure in which black slaves were confined for a limited period.
– ORIGIN mid 19th cent.: from Spanish *barracón*, from *barraca* 'soldier's tent' (see **BARRACKS**).

barracouta /ˌbarə'kuːtə/ ▸ **noun** (pl. **same** or **barracoutas**) a long, slender fish of southern oceans, highly valued as food. Also called **SNOEK** in South Africa. ● *Thyrsites atun*, family Gempylidae.
– ORIGIN mid 19th cent.: alteration of **BARRACUDA**.

barracuda /ˌbarə'kuːdə/ ▸ **noun** (pl. **same** or **barracudas**) a large predatory tropical marine fish with a slender body and large jaws and teeth. ● Family Sphyraenidae and genus *Sphyraena*: several species, in particular *S. barracuda*.
– ORIGIN late 17th cent.: of unknown origin.

barracudina /ˌbarəkuː'diːnə/ ▸ **noun** a slender-bodied predatory fish with a long head, found in open oceans. ● Family Paralepididae: numerous species, including *Paralepis atlantica*.
– ORIGIN from American Spanish, diminutive of *barracuda* (see **BARRACUDA**), which it resembles.

barrage /'barɑːʒ/ ▸ **noun 1** a concentrated artillery bombardment over a wide area. ■ an overwhelming number of questions, criticisms, or complaints delivered simultaneously or in rapid succession: ***a barrage of questions.***
2 an artificial barrier across a river or estuary to prevent flooding, aid irrigation or navigation, or to generate electricity by tidal power.
▸ **verb** [with obj.] bombard (someone) with questions, criticisms, or complaints: *his doctor was barraged with unsolicited advice.*
– ORIGIN mid 19th cent. (in sense 2 of the noun): from French, from *barrer* 'to bar', of unknown origin.

barrage balloon ▸ **noun** a large balloon anchored to the ground by cables and typically with netting suspended from it, serving as an obstacle to low-flying enemy aircraft.

barramundi /ˌbarə'mʌndi/ ▸ **noun** (pl. **same** or **barramundis**) any of a number of large, chiefly freshwater fishes of Australia and SE Asia: ● a fish that migrates between the sea and rivers and is valued as a food fish (*Lates calcarifer*, family Centropomidae). ● a mouthbrooder (genus *Scleropages*, family Osteoglossidae), in particular *S. leichardti*.
– ORIGIN late 19th cent.: probably from an Aboriginal language of Queensland.

barranca /bə'raŋkə/ (also **barranco**) ▸ **noun** (pl. **barrancas** or **barrancos**) chiefly US a narrow, winding river gorge.
– ORIGIN late 17th cent.: from Spanish.

Barranquilla /ˌbaraŋ'kiːjə/ the chief port of Colombia; pop. 1,112,889 (2005). Founded in 1629, the city lies at the mouth of the Magdalena River, near the Caribbean Sea.

barratry /'barətri/ ▸ **noun** [mass noun] **1** archaic fraud or gross negligence of a ship's master or crew at the expense of its owners or users.
2 Law vexatious litigation or incitement to it (abolished as an offence in Britain in 1967).
3 historical trade in the sale of Church or state appointments.
– DERIVATIVES **barrator** noun, **barratrous** adjective.
– ORIGIN late Middle English (in sense 3): from Old French *baraterie*, from *barater* 'deceive', based on Greek *prattein* 'do, perform, manage' (sometimes dishonestly); perhaps influenced by Old Norse *barátta* 'contest'.

Barrault /ba'rəʊ/, French /baʀo/, Jean-Louis (1910–94), French actor and director. He directed a number of films, and appeared in *Les Enfants du Paradis* (1945).

Barr body ▸ **noun** Physiology a small, densely staining structure in the cell nuclei of females, consisting of a condensed, inactive X chromosome. It is regarded as diagnostic of genetic femaleness.
– ORIGIN 1960s: named after the Canadian anatomist M. L. *Barr* (1908–95).

barre /bɑː/ ▸ **noun 1** a horizontal bar at waist level on which ballet dancers rest a hand for support during certain exercises.
2 [as modifier] denoting a chord played using the barré method.
– ORIGIN French.

barré /'bareɪ/ ▸ **noun** Music a method of playing a chord on the guitar or a similar instrument in which one finger is laid across all the strings at a particular fret.
– ORIGIN late 19th cent.: French, literally 'barred', past participle of *barrer*.

barrel ▸ **noun 1** a cylindrical container bulging out in the middle, traditionally made of wooden staves with metal hoops round them. ■ a barrel together with its contents: ***a barrel of beer.*** ■ a measure of capacity used for oil and beer, usually equal to 36 imperial gallons for beer and 35 imperial gallons or 42 US gallons (roughly 159 litres) for oil.
2 a cylindrical tube forming part of an object such as a gun or a pen: *a gun barrel.*
3 the belly and loins of a four-legged animal such as a horse.
▸ **verb** (**barrels, barrelling, barrelled**; N. Amer. **barrels, barreling, barreled**) **1** [no obj., with adverbial of direction] informal, chiefly N. Amer. drive or move in a way that is so fast as to almost be out of control: *they shot him and then barreled away in the truck.*
2 [with obj.] put into a barrel or barrels.
– PHRASES **a barrel of laughs** [with negative] informal a source of amusement or pleasure: *life is not exactly a barrel of laughs at the moment.* **over a barrel** informal in a helpless position; at someone's mercy. **with both barrels** informal with unrestrained force or emotion.
– ORIGIN Middle English: from Old French *baril*, from medieval Latin *barriclus* 'small cask'.

barrel-chested ▸ **adjective** having a large rounded chest.

barrel distortion ▸ **noun** [mass noun] a type of defect in optical or electronic images in which vertical or horizontal straight lines appear as convex curves.

barrelfish ▸ **noun** (pl. **same** or **barrelfishes**) a fish which lives in the deep waters of the Atlantic when adult, and on the surface, typically among flotsam, when young. ● *Schedophilus medusophagus* and *Hyperoglyphe perciforma*, family Centrolophidae.

barrelhead ▸ **noun** the flat top of a barrel.
– PHRASES **on the barrelhead** North American term for **ON THE NAIL** (see **NAIL**).

barrelhouse ▸ **noun 1** N. Amer. a cheap or disreputable bar.
2 [mass noun, usu. as modifier] an unrestrained and unsophisticated style of jazz music.
– ORIGIN late 19th cent.: so named because of the rows of barrels along the walls of such a bar.

barrel organ ▸ **noun** a small pipe organ played by turning a handle, which rotates a cylinder studded with pegs that open the valves to produce a preset tune, formerly much used by street musicians.

barrel roll ▸ **noun** an aerobatic manoeuvre in which an aircraft follows a single turn of a spiral while rolling once about its longitudinal axis.

barrel vault ▸ **noun** Architecture a vault forming a half cylinder.
– DERIVATIVES **barrel-vaulted** adjective.

barren ▸ **adjective 1** (of land) too poor to produce much or any vegetation. ■ (of a tree or plant) not producing fruit or seed. ■ archaic (of a woman) infertile. ■ (of a female animal) not pregnant or unable to become so.
2 showing no results or achievements; unproductive: *he scored yesterday to end his barren spell.*
3 (of a place or building) bleak and lifeless. ■ empty of meaning or value. ■ (**barren of**) devoid of: *the room was barren of furniture.*
▸ **noun** (usu. **barrens**) chiefly N. Amer. a barren tract or tracts of land: *the Newfoundland barrens.*
– DERIVATIVES **barrenly** adverb, **barrenness** noun.
– ORIGIN Middle English: from Old French *barhaine*, of unknown origin.

barrenwort ▸ **noun** an Old World plant with cup-shaped spurred flowers, cultivated for its colourful foliage. It was formerly thought to cause infertility. ● Genus *Epimedium*, family Berberidaceae.

Barrett, Elizabeth, see **BROWNING¹**.

barrette /ba'rɛt/ ▸ **noun** a hairslide.
– ORIGIN early 20th cent.: from French, diminutive of *barre* 'bar'.

barricade /ˌbarɪ'keɪd/ ▸ **noun** an improvised barrier erected across a street or other thoroughfare to prevent or delay the movement of opposing forces.
▸ **verb** [with obj.] block or defend with a barricade: *they barricaded the building and occupied it all night.* ■ shut (someone) into a place by blocking all the entrances: *detainees who* ***barricaded themselves into*** *their dormitory.*
– PHRASES **man** (or **go to**) **the barricades** strongly protest against or defend something.
– ORIGIN late 16th cent.: from French, from *barrique* 'cask', from Spanish *barrica*; related to **BARREL** (barrels often being used to build barricades).

Barrie, Sir J. M. (1860–1937), Scottish dramatist and novelist; full name *James Matthew Barrie*. Barrie's most famous play is *Peter Pan* (1904), a fantasy for children about a boy who did not grow up.

barrier ▸ **noun** a fence or other obstacle that prevents movement or access. ■ Brit. a gate at a car park or railway station that controls access by being raised or lowered. ■ a circumstance or obstacle that keeps people or things apart or prevents communication or progress: *a language barrier | the cultural* ***barriers to*** *economic growth.*
– ORIGIN late Middle English (denoting a palisade or fortification defending an entrance): from Old French *barriere*, of unknown origin; related to **BARRE**.

barrier cream ▸ **noun** Brit. a cream used to protect the skin from damage or infection.

barrier method ▸ **noun** a method of contraception using a device or preparation which prevents live sperm from reaching an ovum.

barrier reef ▸ **noun** a coral reef close and running parallel to the shore but separated from it by a channel of deep water.

barring ▸ **preposition** except for; if not for: *barring accidents, we should win.*
– ORIGIN late 15th cent.: from the verb **BAR¹** + **-ING²**.

barrio /'barɪəʊ/ ▸ **noun** (pl. **barrios**) a district of a town in Spain and Spanish-speaking countries. ■ (in the US) the Spanish-speaking quarter of a town or city, especially one with a high poverty level.
– ORIGIN Spanish, perhaps from Arabic.

barrique /bə'riːk/, French /baʀik/ ▸ **noun** a wine barrel, especially a small one made of new oak in which Bordeaux and other wines are aged.
– ORIGIN late 18th cent.: French.

barrister (also **barrister-at-law**) ▸ **noun** chiefly Brit. a person called to the bar and entitled to practise as an advocate, particularly in the higher courts. Compare with **ATTORNEY, SOLICITOR**.

– ORIGIN late Middle English: from the noun **BAR**[1], perhaps on the pattern of *minister*.

barroom ▸ noun chiefly N. Amer. a room where alcoholic drinks are served over a counter.

barrow[1] ▸ noun Brit. a two-wheeled handcart used especially by street vendors. ■ a wheelbarrow.
– ORIGIN Old English *bearwe* 'stretcher, bier', of Germanic origin; related to **BEAR**[1].

barrow[2] ▸ noun Archaeology an ancient burial mound.
– ORIGIN Old English *beorg*, of Germanic origin; related to Dutch *berg*, German *Berg* 'hill, mountain'.

barrow boy ▸ noun Brit. a boy or man who sells wares from a barrow in the street.

Barry, Sir Charles (1795–1860), English architect, designer of the Houses of Parliament.

barry /'bɑːri/ ▸ adjective Heraldry divided into typically four, six, or eight equal horizontal bars of alternating tinctures.
– ORIGIN late 15th cent.: from French *barré* 'barred, striped', past participle of *barrer*.

Barrymore an American family of film and stage actors, notably **Lionel** (1878–1954), his sister **Ethel** (1879–1959), and their brother **John** (1882–1942).

Barsac /'bɑːsak/, French /barsak/ ▸ noun [mass noun] a sweet white wine from the district of Barsac, a department of the Gironde in France.

bar sinister ▸ noun popular and erroneous term for **BEND SINISTER**.

bar stool ▸ noun a tall stool for customers at a bar to sit on.

Bart[1], Lionel (1930–99), English composer and lyricist. His musicals include *Oliver!* (1960).

Bart[2] ▸ abbreviation Baronet.

bar tack ▸ noun a stitch made to strengthen a potential weak spot in a garment or other sewn item.
– DERIVATIVES **bar-tacked** adjective.

bartender ▸ noun a person serving drinks at a bar.
– DERIVATIVES **bartend** verb, **bartending** noun.

barter ▸ verb [with obj.] exchange (goods or services) for other goods or services without using money: *he often **bartered** a meal **for** drawings* | [no obj.] *they were able to buy or **barter for** most of what they needed.*
▸ noun [mass noun] the action or system of bartering.
■ goods or services used in bartering: *I took a supply of coffee and cigarettes to use as barter.*
– DERIVATIVES **barterer** noun.
– ORIGIN late Middle English: probably from Old French *barater* 'deceive' (see **BARRATRY**).

Barth /bɑːt, bɑːθ/, Karl (1886–1968), Swiss Protestant theologian. His seminal work *Epistle to the Romans* (1919) established a neo-orthodox or theocentric approach to contemporary religious thought which remains influential on Protestant theology.
– DERIVATIVES **Barthian** /'bɑːtɪən/ adjective.

Barthes /bɑːt/, French /baʀt/, Roland (1915–80), French writer and critic. Barthes was a leading exponent of structuralism and semiology in literary criticism, while later works were influential in the development of deconstruction and post-structuralism.

Bartholdi /bɑː'tɒldi, -'θɒldi/, French /baʀtɔldi/, (Frédéric) Auguste (1834–1904), French sculptor, known especially for the Statue of Liberty, which was presented to the US in 1886.

bartholinitis /,bɑːtəlɪ'nʌɪtɪs/ ▸ noun [mass noun] Medicine inflammation of Bartholin's gland, typically accompanied by cysts or abscesses.

Bartholin's gland /'bɑːtəlɪnz/ ▸ noun Anatomy either of a pair of glands lying near the entrance of the vagina, which secrete a fluid that lubricates the vulva.
– ORIGIN early 18th cent.: named by Caspar *Bartholin* (1655–1738), Danish anatomist, as a tribute to his father.

Bartholomew, St /bɑː'θɒlə,mjuː/ an Apostle. He is said to have been flayed alive in Armenia, and is hence regarded as the patron saint of tanners. Feast day, 24 August.

bartizan /,bɑːtɪ'zan/ ▸ noun Architecture a battlemented parapet or an overhanging corner turret at the top of a castle or church tower.
– ORIGIN early 19th cent.: from 17th-cent. *bertisene*, Scots variant of *bratticing* 'temporary breastwork or parapet', from **BRATTICE**; revived and reinterpreted by Sir Walter Scott.

Bartlett pear /'bɑːtlɪt/ ▸ noun a dessert pear of a juicy early-ripening variety.
– ORIGIN from the name of Enoch *Bartlett* (1779–1860), a US merchant who first distributed the pear.

Bartók /'bɑːtɒk/, Béla (1881–1945), Hungarian composer. His work owes much to Hungarian folk music and includes six string quartets, three piano concertos, and the *Concerto for Orchestra* (1943).

Bartolommeo /,bɑːtɒlə'meɪəʊ/, Italian /,bartəoləom'mɛəɔ/, Fra (*c.*1472–1517), Italian painter; born *Baccio della Porta*. He was a Dominican friar and worked chiefly in Florence, where he was impressed and influenced by the work of Raphael.

Barton, Sir Edmund (1849–1920), Australian statesman and jurist, first Prime Minister of Australia 1901–3.

barton ▸ noun archaic a farmyard.
– ORIGIN Old English *bere-tūn*, from *bere* 'barley' + *tūn* 'enclosed piece of land, homestead, village'.

bar tracery ▸ noun [mass noun] Architecture tracery with strips of stone across an aperture.

bartsia /'bɑːtsɪə/ ▸ noun a herbaceous plant of the figwort family, some kinds being partly parasitic on the roots of other plants, especially grasses. ● *Bartsia* and related genera, family Scrophulariaceae: several species.
– ORIGIN modern Latin, named after Johann *Bartsch* (1709–38), Prussian botanist.

Baruch /'bɑːrʊk/ a book of the Apocrypha, attributed in the text to Baruch, the scribe of Jeremiah (Jer. 36).

barwing ▸ noun an Asian bird of the babbler family, with barred feathers on the wings and tail. ● Genus *Actinodura*, family Timaliidae: several species.

barycentric /,barɪ'sɛntrɪk/ ▸ adjective relating to the centre of gravity.
– DERIVATIVES **barycentre** noun.
– ORIGIN late 19th cent.: from Greek *barus* 'heavy' + **-CENTRIC**.

baryon /'barɪɒn/ ▸ noun Physics a subatomic particle, such as a nucleon or hyperon, that has a mass equal to or greater than that of a proton.
– DERIVATIVES **baryonic** adjective.
– ORIGIN 1950s: from Greek *barus* 'heavy' + **-ON**.

Baryshnikov /bə'riːʃnɪ,kɒf/, Mikhail (Nikolaevich) (b.1948), American ballet dancer, born in Latvia of Russian parents. In 1974 he defected to the West while touring with the Kirov Ballet.

baryta /bə'rʌɪtə/ ▸ noun [mass noun] Chemistry barium hydroxide. ● Chem. formula: $Ba(OH)_2$.
– ORIGIN early 19th cent.: from **BARYTE**, on the pattern of words such as *soda*.

baryte /'barʌɪt, 'bɛː-/ (also **barytes** /bə'rʌɪtiːz/, **barite**) ▸ noun a mineral consisting of barium sulphate, typically occurring as colourless prismatic crystals or thin white flakes.
– ORIGIN late 18th cent. (as *barytes*): from Greek *barus* 'heavy' + endings based on Greek *-ites*.

baryton /'barɪtɒn/ ▸ noun an obsolete stringed instrument similar to a bass viol, with additional sympathetic strings, used mainly in 18th-century Germany and Austria.
– ORIGIN variant of **BARITONE**.

bas /bʌs/ ▸ exclamation Indian stop; enough: *Bas! Stop pestering me!*
– ORIGIN from Hindi, from Persian.

basal /'beɪs(ə)l/ ▸ adjective chiefly technical forming or belonging to a bottom layer or base.

basal cell carcinoma ▸ noun technical term for **RODENT ULCER**.

basal ganglia ▸ plural noun Anatomy a group of structures linked to the thalamus in the base of the brain and involved in coordination of movement.

basal metabolic rate ▸ noun the rate at which the body uses energy while at rest to maintain vital functions such as breathing and keeping warm.
– DERIVATIVES **basal metabolism** noun.

basalt /'basɔːlt, -(ə)lt/ ▸ noun [mass noun] a dark fine-grained volcanic rock that sometimes displays a columnar structure, typically composed largely of plagioclase with pyroxene and olivine. ■ a kind of black stoneware developed by Josiah Wedgwood.
– DERIVATIVES **basaltic** /bə'sɔːltɪk/ adjective.
– ORIGIN early 17th cent. (in the Latin form): from Latin *basaltes* (variant of *basanites*), from Greek *basanitēs*, from *basanos* 'touchstone'.

basanite /'basənʌɪt/ ▸ noun [mass noun] a dark grey or black basaltic rock consisting of plagioclase, augite, olivine, and a feldspathoid.
– ORIGIN late 18th cent.: from Latin *basanites* (see **BASALT**) + **-ITE**[1].

bascinet ▸ noun variant spelling of **BASINET**.

bascule /'baskjuːl/ (also **bascule bridge**) ▸ noun a type of bridge with a section which can be raised and lowered using counterweights. ■ a movable section of road forming part of a bascule bridge.
– ORIGIN late 19th cent.: earlier denoting a lever apparatus of which one end is raised while the other is lowered, from French (earlier *bacule*), 'see-saw', from *battre* 'to bump' + *cul* 'buttocks'.

base[1] ▸ noun **1** the lowest part or edge of something, especially the part on which it rests or is supported: *she sat down at the base of a tree.* ■ Architecture the part of a column between the shaft and pedestal or pavement. ■ Botany & Zoology the end at which a part or organ is attached to the trunk or main part. ■ Geometry a line or surface on which a figure is regarded as standing: *the base of the triangle.* ■ Surveying a known line used as a geometrical base for trigonometry. ■ Heraldry the lowest part of a shield.
2 a conceptual structure or entity on which something draws or depends: *the town's economic base collapsed.* ■ a foundation or starting point for further work: *she uses existing data as the base for the study.* ■ [with modifier] a group of people regarded as supporting an organization, for example by buying its products: *a customer base.*
3 a place used as a centre of operations by the armed forces or others; a headquarters: *he headed back to base.* ■ the main place where a person works or stays: *she makes the studio her base* | *your hotel is a good base from which to explore.*
4 a main or important element or ingredient to which other things are added: *soaps with a vegetable oil base.* ■ [mass noun] a substance into which a pigment is mixed to form paint, such as water, oil, or powdered aluminium hydroxide.
5 Chemistry a substance capable of reacting with an acid to form a salt and water, or (more broadly) of accepting or neutralizing hydrogen ions. Compare with **ACID** and **ALKALI**. ■ Biochemistry a purine or pyrimidine group in a nucleotide or nucleic acid.
6 Electronics the middle part of a bipolar transistor, separating the emitter from the collector.
7 Linguistics the root or stem of a word or a derivative. ■ the uninflected form of a verb.
8 Mathematics a number used as the basis of a numeration scale. ■ a number in terms of which other numbers are expressed as logarithms.
9 Baseball each of the four stations that must be reached in turn to score a run.
▸ verb [with obj.] **1** (**base something on**) use (something specified) as the foundation or starting point for something: *the film is based on a novel by Pat Conroy* | *entitlement will be based on income.*
2 situate at a specified place as the centre of operations: *the Science Policy Review Unit is based at the University of Sussex* | (as adj., in combination **-based**) *a London-based band.*
– PHRASES **get to first base** [usu. with negative] informal, chiefly N. Amer. achieve the first step towards one's objective. **off base** informal mistaken. **touch base** informal briefly make or renew contact with someone.
– ORIGIN Middle English: from Old French, from Latin *basis* 'base, pedestal', from Greek.

base[2] ▸ adjective **1** without moral principles; ignoble: *the electorate's baser instincts of greed and selfishness.*
2 archaic denoting or befitting a person of low social class.
3 (of coins or other articles) not made of precious metal.
– DERIVATIVES **basely** adverb.
ORIGIN late Middle English: from Old French *bas*, from medieval Latin *bassus* 'short' (found in classical Latin as a cognomen). Early senses included 'low, short' and 'of inferior quality'; from the latter arose a sense 'low in the social scale', and hence (mid 16th cent.) 'reprehensibly cowardly, selfish, or mean'.

baseball ▸ noun [mass noun] a ball game played between two teams of nine on a diamond-shaped circuit of four bases. It is played chiefly as a warm-weather sport in the US and Canada. ■ [count noun] the hard ball used in baseball.

baseball cap ▸ noun a cotton cap of a kind originally worn by baseball players, with a large peak and an adjustable strap at the back.

baseboard ▸ noun North American term for **SKIRTING**.

baseborn ▸ adjective archaic of low birth or origin. ■ illegitimate.

base camp ▸ noun a camp from which mountaineering expeditions set out or from which a particular activity can be carried out.

B

B

base dressing ▸ noun an application of manure or fertilizer to the earth, which is then ploughed or dug in.

basehead ▸ noun US informal a habitual user of free-base or crack.
– ORIGIN 1980s: from a shortened form of FREEBASE + -HEAD².

base hit ▸ noun Baseball a fair ball hit such that the batter can advance safely to a base without an error by the team in the field.

base hospital ▸ noun **1** a military hospital situated at some distance from the area of active operations during a war.
2 Austral./NZ a hospital serving a large rural area.

base jump (also **BASE jump**) ▸ noun a parachute jump from a fixed point, typically a high building or promontory, rather than an aircraft.
▸ verb (**base-jump**) [no obj.] perform a base jump.
– DERIVATIVES **base jumper** noun, **base jumping** noun.
– ORIGIN 1980s: *base* from *b*uilding, *a*ntenna-tower, *s*pan, *e*arth (denoting the types of structure used).

Basel /ˈbaːzl/ German name for BASLE.

baseless ▸ adjective **1** without foundation in fact: *baseless allegations*.
2 Architecture (of a column) not having a base between the shaft and pedestal.
– DERIVATIVES **baselessly** adverb, **baselessness** noun.

baseline ▸ noun **1** a minimum or starting point used for comparisons.
2 (in tennis, volleyball, and other games) the line marking each end of a court.
3 Baseball the line between bases which a runner must stay close to when running.
4 Printing the imaginary straight line through the feet of most letters in a line of type.

baseload ▸ noun the permanent minimum load that a power supply system is required to deliver.

baseman ▸ noun (pl. **basemen**) Baseball a fielder designated to cover either first, second, or third base.

basement ▸ noun the floor of a building which is partly or entirely below ground level. ■ Geology the oldest formation of rocks underlying a particular area.
– ORIGIN mid 18th cent.: probably from archaic Dutch *basement* 'foundation', perhaps from Italian *basamento* 'column base'.

basement membrane ▸ noun Anatomy a thin, delicate membrane of protein fibres and mucopolysaccharides separating an epithelium from underlying tissue.

base metal ▸ noun a common metal that is not considered precious, such as copper, tin, or zinc.

baseness ▸ noun [mass noun] lack of moral principles; bad character: *the baseness of human nature*.

basenji /bəˈsɛndʒi/ ▸ noun (pl. **basenjis**) a smallish hunting dog of a central African breed, which growls and yelps but does not bark.
– ORIGIN 1930s: a local word.

base pair ▸ noun Biochemistry a pair of complementary bases in a double-stranded nucleic acid molecule, consisting of a purine in one strand linked by hydrogen bonds to a pyrimidine in the other. Cytosine always pairs with guanine, and adenine with thymine (in DNA) or uracil (in RNA).

baseplate ▸ noun a sheet of metal forming the bottom of an object.

base rate ▸ noun (in the UK) the interest rate set by the Bank of England for lending to other banks, used as the benchmark for interest rates generally.

bases plural form of BASE¹ and BASIS.

base station ▸ noun **1** a relay located at the centre of any of the cells of a cellular telephone system.
2 a short-range transceiver which connects a cordless phone, computer, or other wireless device to a central hub and allows connection to a network.

base unit ▸ noun a fundamental unit that is defined arbitrarily and not by combinations of other units. The base units of the SI system are the metre, kilogram, second, ampere, kelvin, mole, and candela.

bash informal ▸ verb [with obj.] strike hard and violently: *she bashed him with the book* | [no obj.] *people bashed on the doors*. ■ (**bash something in**) damage or break something by striking it violently. ■ [no obj.] (**bash into**) collide with: *the other vehicle bashed into the back of them*. ■ fiercely criticize or oppose: *the dispute will be used as an excuse to bash the unions*.
▸ noun **1** a heavy blow: *a bash on the head*.
2 a party or social event: *a birthday bash*.
3 [in sing.] Brit. an attempt: *have a bash at this quiz*.
– PHRASAL VERBS **bash something out** produce something rapidly without preparation or attention to detail: *I didn't just want to bash out songs*. **bash on** (or **away**) Brit. continue despite difficulties: *nothing much we can do, except bash on*.
– DERIVATIVES **basher** noun.
– ORIGIN mid 17th cent. (as a verb): imitative, perhaps a blend of BANG¹ and SMASH, DASH, etc.

basha /ˈbaʃə/ ▸ noun an improvised shelter for one or a few soldiers.
– ORIGIN 1920s (originally denoting a bamboo hut with a thatched roof): Assamese.

bashert /baˈʃəːt/ ▸ noun (in Jewish use) a person's soulmate, especially when considered as an ideal or predestined marriage partner.
– ORIGIN Yiddish, 'fate, destiny'.

bashful ▸ adjective reluctant to draw attention to oneself; shy.
– DERIVATIVES **bashfully** adverb, **bashfulness** noun.
– ORIGIN late 15th cent.: from obsolete *bash* 'make or become abashed' (from ABASH) + -FUL.

bashing ▸ noun [mass noun] [usu. in combination] informal violent physical assault: *nine incidents of gay-bashing were reported to the police*. ■ fierce criticism or opposition: *union-bashing*.

Bashkir /baʃˈkɪə/ ▸ noun **1** a member of a Muslim people living in the southern Urals.
2 [mass noun] the Turkic language of the Bashkirs, with about 1 million speakers.
▸ adjective relating to the Bashkirs or their language.
– ORIGIN via Russian from Turkic *Başkurt*.

Bashkiria /baʃˈkɪərɪə/ an autonomous republic in central Russia, west of the Urals; pop. 4,042,900 (est. 2009); capital, Ufa. Also called **Bashkir Autonomous Republic**.

bashment /ˈbaʃmənt/ ▸ noun **1** W. Indian a large party or dance.
2 an uptempo style of popular music derived from dancehall and ragga.

basho /ˈbaʃəʊ/ ▸ noun (pl. **same** or **bashos**) a sumo wrestling tournament.
– ORIGIN Japanese, from *ba* 'place, occasion' + *shō* 'place, locality'.

BASIC ▸ noun [mass noun] a simple high-level computer programming language that uses familiar English words, designed for beginners and formerly used widely.
– ORIGIN 1960s: acronym from *Beginners' All-purpose Symbolic Instruction Code*.

basic ▸ adjective **1** forming an essential foundation or starting point; fundamental: *certain basic rules must be obeyed* | *the laying down of arms is* **basic to** *the agreement*. ■ offering or constituting the minimum required without elaboration or luxury: *the food was good, if a bit basic*. ■ common to or required by everyone; primary and ineradicable or inalienable: *basic human rights*.
2 Chemistry having the properties of a base, or containing a base; having a pH above 7. Often contrasted with ACIDIC and ALKALINE. ■ Geology (of rock, especially lava) relatively poor in silica. ■ Metallurgy relating to or denoting steel-making processes involving lime-rich refractories and slags.
▸ noun (**basics**) informal the essential facts or principles of a subject or skill: *I learnt the basics of programming on a course* | *teachers are going* **back to basics** *to encourage pupils to learn English*. ■ essential food and other supplies: *people are facing a shortage of basics like flour*.
– ORIGIN mid 19th cent.: from BASE¹ + -IC.

basically ▸ adverb [often as submodifier] in the most essential respects; fundamentally: *we started from a basically simple idea*. ■ [sentence adverb] used to indicate that a statement summarizes the most important aspects, or gives a roughly accurate account, of a more complex situation: *I basically played the same thing every night*.

Basic English ▸ noun [mass noun] a simplified form of English limited to 850 selected words, intended for international communication.

basicity /beɪˈsɪsɪti/ ▸ noun [mass noun] Chemistry the number of hydrogen atoms replaceable by a base in a particular acid.

basic oxygen process ▸ noun a steel-making process in which a jet of oxygen is delivered by a lance on to a molten mixture of pig iron and scrap steel in a retort lined with a basic refractory. Excess carbon is burnt away, producing enough heat to keep the iron molten, and the oxidized impurities are removed as gases or slag.

basic pay ▸ noun [mass noun] a standard rate of pay before additional payments such as allowances and bonuses.

basic slag ▸ noun [mass noun] slag formed as a by-product of basic steel-making processes. It is generally rich in lime and sometimes also in phosphates, and can be used as fertilizer.

basic wage ▸ noun the amount a person earns before additional payments such as overtime. ■ Austral./NZ another term for MINIMUM WAGE.

basidiomycete /bəˌsɪdɪəˈmʌɪsiːt/ ▸ noun (pl. **basidiomycetes** /-ˈmʌɪsiːts, -mʌɪˈsiːtiːz/) Botany a fungus whose spores develop in basidia. They include the majority of familiar mushrooms and toadstools. Compare with ASCOMYCETE. ● Subdivision Basidiomycotina (formerly class Basidiomycetes): several classes.
– ORIGIN late 19th cent.: anglicized singular of modern Latin *Basidiomycetes*, from *basidium* (see BASIDIUM) + Greek *mukētes* 'fungi'.

basidium /bəˈsɪdɪəm/ ▸ noun (pl. **basidia** /-dɪə/) a microscopic club-shaped spore-bearing structure produced by certain fungi.
– ORIGIN mid 19th cent.: modern Latin, from Greek *basidion*, diminutive of *basis* (see BASIS).

Basie /ˈbeɪsi/, Count (1904–84), American jazz pianist, organist, and bandleader; born *William Basie*. In 1935 he formed a big band, known as the Count Basie Orchestra, which became one of the most successful bands of the swing era.

basil /ˈbaz(ə)l, -zɪl/ ▸ noun [mass noun] **1** an aromatic plant of the mint family, native to tropical Asia. The leaves are used as a culinary herb, especially in Mediterranean dishes. ● Genus *Ocimum*, family Labiatae: several species, in particular the annual **sweet basil** (*O. basilicum*).
2 (also **wild basil**) a European plant which grows in hedges and scrub. ● *Clinopodium vulgare*, family Labiatae.
– ORIGIN late Middle English: from Old French *basile*, via medieval Latin from Greek *basilikon*, neuter of *basilikos* 'royal' (see BASILICA).

Basil, St (*c.*330–79), Doctor of the Church, bishop of Caesarea; known as **St Basil the Great**. Brother of St Gregory of Nyssa, he staunchly opposed Arianism and put forward a monastic rule which is still the basis of monasticism in the Eastern Church. Feast day, 14 June.

basilar /ˈbasɪlə/ ▸ adjective of or situated at the base of something, especially of the skull, or of the organ of Corti in the ear.
– ORIGIN mid 16th cent.: from modern Latin *basilaris*, formed irregularly from Latin *basis* (see BASIS).

Basildon /ˈbazɪldən/ a town in SE Essex; pop. 100,600 (est. 2009). It was developed as a new town from 1949.

basilect /ˈbasɪlɛkt, ˈbeɪsɪ-/ ▸ noun Linguistics a less prestigious dialect or variety of a particular language. Often contrasted with ACROLECT.
– DERIVATIVES **basilectal** /-ˈlɛkt(ə)l/ adjective.
– ORIGIN 1960s: from BASIS + *-lect* as in DIALECT.

Basilian /bəˈzɪlɪən/ ▸ adjective relating to St Basil the Great, or the order of monks and nuns following his monastic rule.
▸ noun a Basilian monk or nun.

basilica /bəˈsɪlɪkə, -ˈzɪl-/ ▸ noun a large oblong hall or building with double colonnades and a semicircular apse, used in ancient Rome as a law court or for public assemblies. ■ a similar building used as a Christian church. ■ the name given to certain churches granted special privileges by the Pope.
– DERIVATIVES **basilican** adjective.
– ORIGIN mid 16th cent.: from Latin, literally 'royal palace', from Greek *basilikē*, feminine of *basilikos* 'royal', from *basileus* 'king'.

Basilicata /bəˌsɪlɪˈkaːtə/ a region of southern Italy, lying between the 'heel' of Apulia and the 'toe' of Calabria; capital, Potenza.

basilisk /ˈbazɪlɪsk/ ▸ noun **1** a mythical reptile with a lethal gaze or breath, hatched by a serpent from a cock's egg. ■ Heraldry another term for COCKATRICE.
2 a long, slender, and mainly bright green lizard found in Central America, the male of which has a crest running from the head to the tail. It can swim well, and is able to run on its hind legs across the surface of water. ● *Basiliscus plumifrons*, family Iguanidae.
– ORIGIN late Middle English: via Latin from Greek *basiliskos* 'little king, serpent', from *basileus* 'king'.

basin ▸ **noun 1** chiefly Brit. a bowl for washing, typically attached to a wall and having taps connected to a water supply; a washbasin.
2 a wide open container used for preparing food or for holding liquid.
3 a circular or oval valley or natural depression on the earth's surface, especially one containing water: *the loch is cupped in a shallow basin among low hills.* ■ the tract of country drained by a river and its tributaries, or which drains into a lake or sea: *the Amazon basin.* ■ an enclosed area of water where boats can be moored. ■ Geology a circumscribed rock formation where the strata dip towards the centre.
– DERIVATIVES **basinful** noun (pl. **basinfuls**).
– ORIGIN Middle English: from Old French *bacin*, from medieval Latin *bacinus*, from *bacca* 'water container', perhaps of Gaulish origin.

basinet /ˈbasɪnɪt/ (also **bascinet**) ▸ **noun** historical a light, close-fitting steel helmet, typically having a visor.
– ORIGIN Middle English: from Old French *bacinet* 'little basin'.

basipetal /beɪˈsɪpɪt(ə)l/ ▸ **adjective** Botany (of growth or development) downwards towards the base or point of attachment. The opposite of **ACROPETAL**. ■ (of the movement of dissolved substances) inwards from the shoot and root apices.
– DERIVATIVES **basipetally** adverb.
– ORIGIN mid 19th cent.: from **BASIS** + Latin *petere* 'seek' + **-AL**.

basis ▸ **noun** (pl. **bases** /-siːz/) the underlying support or foundation for an idea, argument, or process: *trust is the only basis for a good working relationship.* ■ [with adj.] the system or principles according to which an activity or process is carried on: *she needed coaching **on a regular basis**.* ■ the justification for or reasoning behind something: ***on the basis of** these statistics important decisions are made.*
– ORIGIN late 16th cent. (denoting a base or pedestal): via Latin from Greek, 'stepping'. Compare with **BASE**¹.

basis point ▸ **noun** Finance one hundredth of one percentage point (used chiefly in expressing differences of interest rates).

bask ▸ **verb** [no obj.] lie exposed to warmth and light, typically from the sun, for relaxation and pleasure. ■ (**bask in**) revel in and make the most of (something pleasing): *he went on basking in the glory of his first book.*
– ORIGIN late Middle English (originally in the sense 'bathe'): perhaps related to Old Norse *batha* 'bathe'.

basket ▸ **noun 1** a container used to hold or carry things, typically made from interwoven strips of cane or wire. ■ a structure suspended from a hot-air balloon for carrying the crew, equipment, and ballast. ■ Finance a group or range of currencies or investments: *a basket of ten currencies.*
2 Basketball a net fixed on a hoop used as the goal. ■ a goal scored.
3 Brit. informal euphemism for **BASTARD** (sense 2 of the noun).
– DERIVATIVES **basketful** noun (pl. **basketfuls**).
– ORIGIN Middle English: from Old French *basket*, of unknown ultimate origin.

basketball ▸ **noun** [mass noun] a game played between two teams of five players in which goals are scored by throwing a ball through a netted hoop fixed at each end of the court. ■ [count noun] the inflated ball used in basketball.

basket case ▸ **noun** informal a person or thing regarded as useless or unable to cope.
– ORIGIN early 20th cent.: originally US slang denoting a soldier who had lost all four limbs, thus unable to move independently.

basket hilt ▸ **noun** a sword hilt with a guard resembling basketwork.

basketmaker ▸ **noun** a person who makes baskets.
– DERIVATIVES **basketmaking** noun.

Basket Maker ▸ **noun** a member of a culture of the south-western US, forming the early stages of the Anasazi culture, from the 1st century BC until *c.*700 AD. The name comes from the basketry and other woven fragments found in early cave sites.

basketry ▸ **noun** [mass noun] the craft of basket-making. ■ baskets collectively.

basket weave ▸ **noun** [mass noun] a style of weave or a pattern resembling basketwork.

basketwork ▸ **noun** [mass noun] material woven in the style of a basket. ■ the craft of making basketwork.

basking shark ▸ **noun** a large shark which feeds exclusively on plankton and typically swims slowly close to the surface, found chiefly in the open ocean. ● *Cetorhinus maximus*, the only member of the family Cetorhinidae.

Basle /bɑːl, ˈbɑːz(ə)l/ a commercial and industrial city on the Rhine in NW Switzerland; pop. 163,521 (2007). French name **Bâle**, German name **Basel**.

basmati /basˈmɑːti, -z-/ (also **basmati rice**) ▸ **noun** [mass noun] a kind of long-grain Indian rice with a delicate fragrance.
– ORIGIN from Hindi *bāsmatī*, literally 'fragrant'.

basophil /ˈbeɪsə(ʊ)fɪl/ ▸ **noun** Physiology a basophilic white blood cell.

basophilic /ˌbeɪsə(ʊ)ˈfɪlɪk/ ▸ **adjective** Physiology (of a cell or its contents) readily stained with basic dyes.

Basotho /bəˈsuːtuː/ ▸ **plural noun** (sing. **Mosotho**) the South Sotho people collectively, living chiefly in Lesotho.
– ORIGIN the name in Sesotho.

Basque /bask, bɑːsk/ ▸ **noun 1** a member of a people living in the Basque Country of France and Spain. Culturally one of the most distinct groups in Europe, the Basques were largely independent until the 19th century. The Basque separatist movement ETA is carrying on an armed struggle against the Spanish government.
2 [mass noun] the language of the Basques, which is not known to be related to any other language. It has about 1 million speakers.
▸ **adjective** relating to the Basques or their language.
– ORIGIN from French, from Latin *Vasco*; compare with **GASCON**.

basque /bask, bɑːsk/ ▸ **noun** a close-fitting bodice extending from the shoulders to the waist and typically with a short continuation below waist level.
– ORIGIN mid 19th cent.: from **BASQUE**, referring to Basque dress.

Basque Country a region of the western Pyrenees in both France and Spain, the homeland of the Basque people. French name **PAYS BASQUE**.

Basque Provinces an autonomous region of northern Spain, on the Bay of Biscay; capital, Vitoria.

Basra /ˈbazrə/ an oil port of Iraq, on the Shatt al-Arab waterway; pop. 870,000 (est. 2007).

bas-relief /ˈbasrɪˌliːf, ˈbɑː(s)-/ ▸ **noun** [mass noun] another term for **LOW RELIEF** (see **RELIEF** (sense 4)).
– ORIGIN early 17th cent. (as *basse relieve*): from Italian *basso-rilievo* 'low relief', later altered to the French form.

bass¹ /beɪs/ ▸ **noun 1** the lowest adult male singing voice. ■ a singer with such a voice. ■ a part written for such a voice.
2 [as modifier] denoting the member of a family of instruments that is the lowest in pitch: *a bass clarinet.* ■ a bass guitar or double bass.
3 [mass noun] the low-frequency output of a radio or audio system, corresponding to the bass in music.
– DERIVATIVES **bassy** adjective (**bassier**, **bassiest**).
– ORIGIN late Middle English: alteration of **BASE**², influenced by **BASSO**.

bass² /bas/ ▸ **noun** (pl. **same** or **basses**) **1** the common European freshwater perch.
2 any of a number of fish similar to or related to this, in particular: ● a mainly marine fish found in temperate waters (family Percichthyidae or Moronidae, including *Dicentrarchus labrax* of European waters and genus *Morone* of North America). ● an American freshwater fish of the sunfish family, popular with anglers (genera *Ambloplites* and *Micropterus*, family Centrarchidae). ● a sea bass.
– ORIGIN late Middle English: alteration of dialect *barse*, of Germanic origin; related to Dutch *baars* and German *Barsch*.

bass³ /bas/ ▸ **noun** another term for **BAST**.
– ORIGIN late 17th cent.: alteration.

bass-ackwards ▸ **adverb & adjective** N. Amer. informal variant of **ASS-BACKWARDS**.

bass clef ▸ **noun** Music a clef placing F below middle C on the second-highest line of the stave.

bass drum ▸ **noun** a large drum of indefinite low pitch.

Bassein /baˈseɪn/ a port on the Irrawaddy delta in SW Burma (Myanmar); pop. 215,600 (est. 2004).

Basse-Normandie /basˈnɔːməndi/, French /basnɔʀmɑ̃di/ a region of NW France, on the coast of the English Channel, including the Cherbourg peninsula and the city of Caen.

basset (also **basset hound**) ▸ **noun** a sturdy hunting dog of a breed with a long body, short legs, and long drooping ears.
– ORIGIN early 17th cent.: from French, diminutive of *bas* 'low', from medieval Latin *bassus* 'short'.

Basseterre /basˈtɛː/ the capital of St Kitts and Nevis in the Leeward Islands, on the island of St Kitts; pop. 13,000 (est. 2007).

Basse-Terre /basˈtɛː/ the main island of Guadeloupe in the Caribbean.

basset horn ▸ **noun** an alto clarinet in F, typically with a bent mouthpiece and upturned bell.
– ORIGIN mid 19th cent.: from German, translation of French *cor de bassette*, from Italian *corno di bassetto*, from *corno* 'horn' + *di* 'of' + *bassetto* (diminutive of *basso* 'low', from Latin *bassus* 'short').

bassinet /ˌbasɪˈnɛt/ ▸ **noun** a child's wicker cradle.
– ORIGIN mid 19th cent.: from French, diminutive of *bassin* 'basin'; compare with **BASINET**.

bassist /ˈbeɪsɪst/ ▸ **noun** a person who plays a double bass or bass guitar.

basslet /ˈbaslɪt/ ▸ **noun** a small, brightly coloured fish related to the sea basses. ● Genera *Gramma* and *Lipogramma*, family Grammidae: several species.

bassline /ˈbeɪslʌɪn/ ▸ **noun** the lowest part or sequence of notes in a piece of music.

basso /ˈbasəʊ/ ▸ **noun** (pl. **bassos** or **bassi** /-si/) a bass voice or vocal part.
– ORIGIN early 18th cent.: Italian, 'low', from Latin *bassus* 'short, low'.

basso continuo ▸ **noun** see **CONTINUO**.

bassoon ▸ **noun** a bass woodwind instrument of the oboe family, with a double-backed tube over four feet long, played with a double reed.
– DERIVATIVES **bassoonist** noun.
– ORIGIN early 18th cent.: from French *basson*, from Italian *bassone*, from *basso* 'low', from Latin *bassus* 'short, low'.

basso profundo /prəˈfʌndəʊ/ ▸ **noun** (pl. **bassos profundos** or **bassi profundi** /-di/) a bass singer with an exceptionally low range.
– ORIGIN mid 19th cent.: Italian, from *basso* 'low' + *profondo* 'deep'.

basso-relievo /ˌbasəʊrɪˈliːvəʊ/ ▸ **noun** (pl. **basso-relievos**) another term for **LOW RELIEF** (see **RELIEF** (sense 4)).
– ORIGIN mid 17th cent.: from Italian *basso-rilievo*.

Bass Strait /bas/ a channel separating Tasmania from the mainland of Australia.
– ORIGIN named after the English explorer George *Bass* (1771–1803), who discovered the strait.

bass viol ▸ **noun** a bass instrument of the viol family; a viola da gamba. ■ N. Amer. a double bass.

basswood /ˈbaswʊd/ ▸ **noun** a North American lime tree with large leaves, commonly planted as a street tree in the US. ● *Tilia americana*, family Tiliaceae.
– ORIGIN late 17th cent.: from **BASS**³ + **WOOD**.

bast /bast/ ▸ **noun** (also **bast fibre**) [mass noun] fibrous material from a plant, in particular the inner bark of a tree such as the lime, used as fibre in matting, cord, etc. ■ Botany the phloem or vascular tissue of a plant.
– ORIGIN Old English *bæst*; related to Dutch *bast*, German *Bast*; of unknown origin.

bastard /ˈbɑːstəd, ˈbast-/ ▸ **noun 1** archaic or derogatory a person born of parents not married to each other.
2 informal an unpleasant or despicable person. ■ [with adj.] Brit. a person of a specified kind: *he was a lucky bastard.* ■ Brit. a difficult or awkward undertaking, situation, or device: *it's been **a bastard of a week**.*
▸ **adjective** [attrib.] **1** archaic or derogatory born of parents not married to each other; illegitimate.
2 (of a thing) no longer in its pure or original form; debased: *a bastard Darwinism.* ■ (of a handwriting script or typeface) showing a mixture of different styles.
– DERIVATIVES **bastardy** noun (sense 1 of the noun).
– ORIGIN Middle English: via Old French from medieval Latin *bastardus*, probably from *bastum* 'packsaddle'; compare with Old French *fils de bast*, 'packsaddle son' (i.e. the son of a mule driver who uses a packsaddle for a pillow and is gone by morning).

USAGE In the past the word **bastard** was the standard term in both legal and non-legal use for 'an illegitimate child'. Today, however, it has little importance as a legal term and is retained in this older sense only as a term of abuse.

B

bastardize (also **bastardise**) ▸ verb [with obj.] **1** (often as adj. **bastardized**) corrupt or debase (a language, art form, etc.), typically by adding new elements: *a strange, bastardized form of French.* **2** archaic declare (someone) illegitimate.
– DERIVATIVES **bastardization** noun.

bastard-trench ▸ verb [with obj.] Horticulture dig (ground) by digging over the lower soil with the topsoil temporarily removed.

bastard wing ▸ noun a group of small quill feathers on the first digit of a bird's wing.

baste¹ ▸ verb [with obj.] pour fat or juices over (meat) during cooking in order to keep it moist.
– DERIVATIVES **baster** noun.
– ORIGIN late 15th cent.: of unknown origin.

baste² ▸ verb [with obj.] Needlework tack with long, loose stitches in preparation for sewing.
– ORIGIN late Middle English: from Old French *bastir* 'sew lightly', ultimately of Germanic origin and related to BAST.

baste³ ▸ verb [with obj.] informal, dated beat (someone) soundly; thrash.
– ORIGIN mid 16th cent.: perhaps a figurative use of BASTE¹.

Bastet /ˈbastɛt/ Egyptian Mythology a goddess usually shown as a woman with the head of a cat, wearing one gold earring. See also SEKHMET.

Bastia /ˈbastjə/ the chief port of Corsica; pop. 43,315 (2007).

bastide /baˈstiːd/ ▸ noun (in southern France) a country house. ▪ historical a fortified village or town in France.
– ORIGIN early 16th cent.: via Old French from Provençal *bastida*.

Bastille /baˈstiːl/ a fortress in Paris built in the 14th century and used in the 17th–18th centuries as a state prison. Its storming by the mob on 14 July 1789 marked the start of the French Revolution.
– ORIGIN via Old French from Provençal *bastida*, from *bastir* 'build'.

bastinado /ˌbastɪˈneɪdəʊ, -ˈnɑːdəʊ/ ▸ noun [mass noun] a form of punishment or torture that involved caning the soles of someone's feet.
▸ verb (**bastinadoes**, **bastinadoing**, **bastinadoed**) [with obj.] punish or torture (someone) in such a way.
– ORIGIN late 16th cent. (denoting a blow with a stick): from Spanish *bastonada*, from *bastón* 'stick, cudgel', from late Latin *bastum* 'stick'.

bastion /ˈbastɪən/ ▸ noun **1** a projecting part of a fortification built at an angle to the line of a wall, so as to allow defensive fire in several directions. ▪ a natural rock formation resembling such a fortification. **2** an institution, place, or person strongly maintaining particular principles, attitudes, or activities: *cricket's **last bastion of** discrimination.*
– ORIGIN mid 16th cent.: from French, from Italian *bastione*, from *bastire* 'build'.

bastnaesite /ˈbastneɪˌsʌɪt/ ▸ noun [mass noun] a yellow to brown mineral consisting of a fluoride and carbonate of cerium and other rare earth metals.
– ORIGIN late 19th cent.: from *Bastnäs*, the name of a district in Västmanland, Sweden, + -ITE¹.

basuco /bəˈsuːkəʊ/ ▸ noun [mass noun] impure or low-grade cocaine, especially when mixed with coca paste and tobacco and cannabis.
– ORIGIN 1980s: from Colombian Spanish; perhaps related to Spanish *bazucar* 'shake violently'.

Basutoland /bəˈsuːtəʊland/ former name (until 1966) for LESOTHO.

bat¹ ▸ noun an implement with a handle and a solid surface, typically of wood, used for hitting the ball in games such as cricket, baseball, and table tennis. ▪ a turn at playing with a bat. ▪ a person batting, especially in cricket; a batsman. ▪ each of a pair of objects resembling table tennis bats, used by a person on the ground to guide a taxiing aircraft. ▪ a slab on which pottery is formed, dried, or fired.
▸ verb (**bats**, **batting**, **batted**) [no obj.] **1** (of a sports team or player) take the role of hitting rather than throwing the ball. ▪ (**bat for** (or **go to bat for**)) informal, chiefly N. Amer. defend the interests of; support: *she turned out to have the law batting for her.* **2** [with obj. and adverbial of direction] hit at (someone or something) with the flat of one's hand: *he batted the flies away.*
– PHRASES **bat a thousand** US. informal be very successful; achieve perfection: *with tortellini in brodo, I batted a thousand—both kids had seconds.* **off one's own bat** Brit. at one's own instigation; spontaneously. **right off the bat** N. Amer. at the very beginning; straight away.
– PHRASAL VERBS **bat around** (or **about**) informal, chiefly N. Amer. travel widely, frequently, or casually: *I'm always batting around between England and America.* **bat something around** (or **about**) informal discuss an idea or proposal casually or idly: *we bat around a wide variety of issues.*
– ORIGIN late Old English *batt* 'club, stick, staff', perhaps partly from Old French *batte*, from *battre* 'to strike'.

bat² ▸ noun **1** a mainly nocturnal mammal capable of sustained flight, with membranous wings that extend between the fingers and limbs. ● Order Chiroptera: many families and numerous species. The large tropical fruit bats (suborder Megachiroptera) generally have good eyesight and feed mainly on fruit; the numerous smaller bats (suborder Microchiroptera) are mouse-like in appearance, mainly insectivorous, and use ultrasonic echolocation. **2** (usu. **old bat**) informal a woman regarded as unattractive or unpleasant. [from *bat*, a slang term for 'prostitute', or from BATTLEAXE.]
– PHRASES **have bats in the** (or **one's**) **belfry** informal be eccentric or mad. **like a bat out of hell** informal very fast and wildly.
– ORIGIN late 16th cent.: alteration, perhaps by association with medieval Latin *batta*, *blacta*, of Middle English *bakke*, of Scandinavian origin.

bat³ ▸ verb (**bats**, **batting**, **batted**) [with obj.] flutter (one's eyelashes), typically in a flirtatious manner: *she batted her long dark eyelashes at him.*
– PHRASES **not bat** (or **without batting**) **an eyelid** (or N. Amer. **eye** or **eyelash**) informal show (or showing) no surprise or concern: *she paid the bill without batting an eyelid.*
– ORIGIN late 19th cent. (originally US): from dialect and US *bat* 'to wink, blink', variant of obsolete *bate* 'to flutter'.

Bata /ˈbɑːtə/ a seaport in Equatorial Guinea; pop. 70,000 (est. 2009).

Batak /ˈbatək/ ▸ noun (pl. **same** or **Bataks**) **1** a member of a people of the northern part of Sumatra. **2** [mass noun] the Indonesian language of the Batak, with about 6 million speakers.
▸ adjective relating to the Batak or their language.
– ORIGIN the name in Batak.

Batan Islands /bəˈtɑːn/ the most northerly islands of the Philippines.

batata /bəˈtɑːtə/ ▸ noun [mass noun] (in the southern Caribbean) sweet potato.
– ORIGIN via Spanish from Taino.

Batavia /bəˈteɪvɪə/ former name (until 1949) for JAKARTA.

Batavian ▸ noun a member of the ancient Germanic people who inhabited the island of Betuwe between the Rhine and the Waal (now part of the Netherlands).
▸ adjective **1** relating to the Batavians. **2** historical or archaic relating to the people of the Netherlands. ▪ relating to Jakarta in Indonesia (formerly the Dutch East Indies).
– ORIGIN from Latin *Batavia* (from *Batavi* 'the people of Betuwe') + -AN.

Batavian lettuce ▸ noun another term for BATAVIAN ENDIVE (see ENDIVE).

batch ▸ noun a quantity or consignment of goods produced at one time. ▪ informal a number of things or people regarded as a group or set: ***a batch of** loyalists and sceptics.* ▪ Computing a group of records processed as a single unit, usually without input from a user.
▸ verb [with obj.] arrange (things) in sets or groups.
– ORIGIN late 15th cent. (in the senses 'process of baking', 'quantity produced at one baking'): based on an Old English word related to *bacan* (see BAKE). Current senses date from the early 18th cent.

batch file ▸ noun a computer file containing a list of instructions to be carried out in turn.

batchmate ▸ noun Indian a classmate.

batch processing ▸ noun [mass noun] the performing of an industrial process on material in batches of a limited quantity or number. ▪ Computing the processing of previously collected jobs in a single batch.

Batdambang variant spelling of BATTAMBANG.

bate¹ (also **bait**) ▸ noun [in sing.] Brit. informal, dated an angry mood: *he got into a stinking bate.*
– ORIGIN mid 19th cent.: from the verb BAIT 'torment', expressing the notion 'state of a baited person'.

bate² ▸ verb [no obj.] Falconry (of a hawk) beat the wings in agitation and flutter off the perch.
– ORIGIN late Middle English: from Old French *batre* 'to beat' (see also BATTER¹).

bat-eared fox ▸ noun a small fox found in southern and East Africa, with very large ears that are used to locate insect prey. ● *Otocyon megalotis*, family Canidae.

bateau /ˈbatəʊ/ ▸ noun (pl. **bateaux** /-əʊz/) a light flat-bottomed riverboat used in Canada.
– ORIGIN early 18th cent.: French, 'boat'.

bateau-mouche /ˌbatəʊ ˈmuːʃ/, French /batəo muʃ/ ▸ noun (pl. **bateaux-mouches** pronunc. **same**) a pleasure boat that takes sightseers on the Seine in Paris.
– ORIGIN French, literally 'fly boat', because of the boat's mobility.

bated ▸ adjective (in phrase **with bated breath**) in great suspense; very anxiously or excitedly: *he waited for a reply to his offer with bated breath.*
– ORIGIN late 16th cent.: from the past participle of obsolete *bate* 'restrain', from ABATE.

> **USAGE** The spelling **baited breath** instead of **bated breath** is a common mistake. Almost a third of citations for this idiom in the Oxford English Corpus are for the incorrect spelling.

bateleur /ˈbat(ə)ləː/ (also **bateleur eagle**) ▸ noun a short-tailed African eagle with mainly black plumage and a bare red face. ● *Terathopius ecaudatus*, family Accipitridae.
– ORIGIN mid 19th cent.: from French, literally 'acrobat, juggler' (with reference to the side-to-side tilting motion of the bird in flight).

Bateman, H. M. (1887–1970), Australian-born British cartoonist; full name *Henry Mayo Bateman*. He is known for the series of cartoons entitled 'The Man Who ...', which illustrated social gaffes based on snobbery.

Bates, H. E. (1905–74), English novelist and short-story writer; full name *Herbert Ernest Bates*. He is noted for novels such as *The Darling Buds of May* (1958).

Batesian mimicry /ˈbeɪtsɪən/ ▸ noun [mass noun] Zoology mimicry in which an edible animal is protected by its resemblance to one avoided by predators. Compare with MÜLLERIAN MIMICRY.
– ORIGIN late 19th cent.: named after Henry W. *Bates* (1825–92), the English naturalist who first described it.

Bates method ▸ noun [mass noun] a technique intended to improve eyesight using eye exercises rather than lenses or surgery.
– ORIGIN 1920s: named after William H. *Bates* (1860–1931), American ophthalmologist.

Bateson, William (1861–1926), English geneticist. He coined the term *genetics* in its current sense and publicized the work of Mendel.

batfish ▸ noun (pl. **same** or **batfishes**) **1** a fish of tropical and temperate seas with a flattened body that is round or almost triangular when viewed from above. ● Family Ogcocephalidae: several genera and species. **2** a deep-bodied, laterally compressed marine fish of the Indo-Pacific region, resembling an angelfish. ● Genus *Platax*, family Ephippidae: several species.

bat fly ▸ noun a bloodsucking fly of spider-like appearance, parasitic on bats and bearing live young. ● Family Nycteribiidae: *Nycteribia* and other genera.

Bath a spa town in SW England; pop. 81,600 (est. 2009). The town was founded by the Romans, who called it Aquae Sulis, and was a fashionable spa in the 18th and early 19th centuries.
– DERIVATIVES **Bathonian** adjective & noun.

bath¹ /bɑːθ/ ▸ noun (pl. **baths**) a large container for water, used for immersing and washing the body. ▪ an act or process of immersing and washing one's body in the water held by a bath: *she **took a** long, hot **bath**.* ▪ (usu. **baths**) Brit. a building containing a public swimming pool or washing facilities. ▪ chiefly N. Amer. a bathroom. ▪ [with modifier] a container holding a liquid in which something is immersed, typically when undergoing a process such as film developing.
▸ verb [with obj.] Brit. wash (someone) while immersing them in a bath: *how to bath a baby.* ▪ [no obj.] wash oneself while immersed in a bath: *there was no hot water to bath in.*
– PHRASES **an early bath** Brit. informal used in reference to the sending off of a sports player during a match: *the referee awarded a penalty and ordered an early bath for Thomas.* **take a bath** informal suffer a heavy financial loss.
– ORIGIN Old English *bæth*, of Germanic origin; related to Dutch *bad* and German *Bad*.

bath² /baθ/ ▸ **noun** an ancient Hebrew liquid measure equivalent to about 40 litres or 9 gallons.
– ORIGIN from Hebrew *bat*.

Bath, Order of the see ORDER OF THE BATH.

Bath bun ▸ **noun** Brit. a round yeast bun containing currants and topped with icing or sugar.
– ORIGIN named after the city of BATH, where it was originally made.

bath chair ▸ **noun** dated a kind of wheelchair for invalids, typically with a hood.
– ORIGIN early 19th cent.: named after the city of BATH, which attracted many invalids because of the supposed curative powers of its hot springs.

bath cube ▸ **noun** Brit. a cube of perfumed bath salts which is dissolved in bathwater.

bathe ▸ **verb** [no obj.] **1** wash by immersing one's body in water. ■ [with obj.] soak or wipe gently with liquid to clean or soothe: *she bathed and bandaged my knee.* ■ [with obj.] N. Amer. wash (someone) in a bath: *they bathed the baby.*
2 chiefly Brit. swim or spend time in the sea or a lake, river, or pool for pleasure.
3 [with obj.] suffuse or envelop in something: *the park lay bathed in sunshine.*
▸ **noun** [in sing.] Brit. an act or spell of swimming or spending time in the water: *a bathe in the cold North Sea.*
– ORIGIN Old English *bathian*, of Germanic origin; related to Dutch and German *baden*.

bather ▸ **noun 1** Brit. a person swimming or spending time in the water.
2 (**bathers**) Austral. informal a swimming costume.

bathetic /bəˈθɛtɪk/ ▸ **adjective** producing an unintentional effect of anticlimax: *the movie manages to be poignant without becoming bathetic.*

bathhouse ▸ **noun** a building containing baths for communal use.

bathing machine ▸ **noun** historical a wheeled hut drawn to the edge of the sea, used for changing in and bathing from.

bathing suit (Brit. also **bathing costume**) ▸ **noun** chiefly N. Amer. a swimming costume.

bath mat ▸ **noun** a mat for a person to stand on after getting out of a bath.

bathochromic /ˌbaθə(ʊ)ˈkrəʊmɪk/ ▸ **adjective** Chemistry relating to or denoting a shift of the absorption spectrum of a compound towards longer wavelengths.
– ORIGIN late 19th cent.: from Greek *bathos* 'depth' + *khrōma* 'colour' + -IC.

batholith /ˈbaθəlɪθ/ ▸ **noun** Geology a very large igneous intrusion extending to an unknown depth in the earth's crust.
– ORIGIN early 20th cent.: coined in German from Greek *bathos* 'depth' + -LITH.

bathos /ˈbeɪθɒs/ ▸ **noun** [mass noun] (especially in a literary work) an effect of anticlimax created by an unintentional lapse in mood from the sublime to the trivial or ridiculous.
– ORIGIN mid 17th cent. (first recorded in the Greek sense): from Greek, literally 'depth'. The current sense was introduced by Alexander Pope in the early 18th cent.

bathrobe ▸ **noun** a dressing gown, especially one made of towelling.

bathroom ▸ **noun** a room containing a bath and usually also a washbasin and a toilet. ■ N. Amer. a room containing a toilet: *I have to go to the bathroom.*

bathroom break ▸ **noun** informal a break in a meeting or other organized gathering to allow those in attendance to go to the toilet.

bath salts ▸ **plural noun** a crystalline substance that is dissolved in bathwater to soften or perfume it.

Bathsheba /baθˈʃiːbə, ˈbaθʃɪbə/ (in the Bible) the mother of Solomon. She was originally wife of Uriah the Hittite, and later one of the wives of David.

bath sponge ▸ **noun** a marine sponge of warm waters, the fibrous skeleton of which is used as a sponge for washing. ● Genera *Spongia* and *Hippospongia*, family Spongiidae.

Bath stone ▸ **noun** [mass noun] a type of oolitic limestone found especially near Bath in SW England, grey to yellowish in colour and used in building and sculpture.

bathtub ▸ **noun** chiefly N. Amer. a bath.

Bathurst /ˈbaθəːst/ former name (until 1973) for BANJUL.

bathwater ▸ **noun** the water in a bath.

bathy- /ˈbaθi/ ▸ **combining form** relating to depth: *bathymetry* | *bathysphere.*
– ORIGIN from Greek *bathus* 'deep'.

bathyal /ˈbaθɪəl/ ▸ **adjective** relating to the zone of the sea between the continental shelf and the abyssal zone.

bathymeter /bəˈθɪmɪtə/ ▸ **noun** an instrument used to measure the depth of water in seas or lakes.
– DERIVATIVES **bathymetric** adjective, **bathymetry** noun.

bathypelagic /ˌbaθɪpɪˈladʒɪk/ ▸ **adjective** Biology (of fish and other organisms) inhabiting the deep sea where the environment is dark and cold, between about 1000 and 3000 metres (approximately 3300 and 9800 ft) down.

bathyscaphe /ˈbaθɪskaf/ ▸ **noun** chiefly historical a manned submersible vessel of a kind used by the French deep-sea explorer Auguste Piccard (1884–1962).
– ORIGIN 1940s: coined in French by its inventor, Auguste Piccard, from Greek *bathus* 'deep' + *skaphos* 'ship'.

bathysphere ▸ **noun** a manned spherical chamber for deep-sea observation, lowered by cable from a ship.

batik /ˈbatɪk, bəˈtiːk/ ▸ **noun** [mass noun] a method (originally used in Java) of producing coloured designs on textiles by dyeing them, having first applied wax to the parts to be left undyed. ■ cloth treated in this way.
– ORIGIN late 19th cent.: from Javanese, literally 'painted'.

Batista /baˈtiːstə/, Fulgencio (1901–73), Cuban soldier and statesman, President 1940–4 and 1952–9; full name *Fulgencio Batista y Zaldívar.* Despite support from the US his second government was overthrown by Fidel Castro.

batiste /bəˈtiːst/ ▸ **noun** [mass noun] a fine, light linen or cotton fabric resembling cambric.
– ORIGIN early 19th cent.: from French (earlier *batiche*); probably related to *battre* 'to beat'.

Batman a US cartoon, TV, and film character, by day the millionaire socialite Bruce Wayne but at night a cloaked and masked figure fighting crime in Gotham City.

batman ▸ **noun** (pl. **batmen**) dated (in the British armed forces) an officer's personal servant.
– ORIGIN mid 18th cent. (originally denoting an orderly in charge of the *bat horse* 'packhorse' which carried the officer's baggage): from Old French *bat* (from medieval Latin *bastum* 'packsaddle') + MAN.

bat mitzvah /bɑːt ˈmɪtsvə/ ▸ **noun** a religious initiation ceremony for a Jewish girl aged twelve years and one day, regarded as the age of religious maturity. ■ the girl undergoing such a ceremony.
– ORIGIN from Hebrew *baṯ miṣwāh* 'daughter of commandment', suggested by BAR MITZVAH.

baton ▸ **noun** a short stick or something resembling one, in particular: ■ a thin stick used by a conductor to direct an orchestra or choir. ■ Athletics a short stick or tube passed from runner to runner in a relay race. ■ a long stick carried and twirled by a drum major. ■ a police officer's truncheon. ■ a staff of office or authority, especially one carried by a field marshal. ■ Heraldry a narrow bend truncated at each end. ■ a short bar replacing some figures on the dial of a clock or watch. ■ (**batons**) one of the suits in some tarot packs, corresponding to wands in others.
– PHRASES **pass (on) the baton** hand over a particular duty or responsibility. **take up** (or **pick up**) **the baton** accept a particular duty or responsibility.
– ORIGIN early 16th cent. (denoting a staff or cudgel): from French *bâton*, earlier *baston*, from late Latin *bastum* 'stick'.

Baton Rouge /ˌbat(ə)n ˈruːʒ/ the state capital of Louisiana; pop. 223,689 (est. 2008).
– ORIGIN French, literally 'red stick', with reference to a post placed as a boundary marker for the settlement.

baton round ▸ **noun** Brit. a large rubber or plastic projectile shot from a special gun and used especially in riot control.

Batrachia /bəˈtreɪkɪə/ ▸ **plural noun** Zoology another term for ANURA.
– ORIGIN modern Latin (plural), from Greek *batrakhos* 'frog'.

batrachian /bəˈtreɪkɪən/ ▸ **noun & adjective** Zoology another term for ANURAN.

bats ▸ **adjective** [predic.] informal, dated (of a person) mad.
– ORIGIN early 20th cent.: from the phrase *have bats in the belfry* (see BAT²).

batshit ▸ **adjective** N. Amer. vulgar slang completely mad or crazy.

batsman ▸ **noun** (pl. **batsmen**) a player, especially in cricket, who is batting or whose chief skill is in batting.
– DERIVATIVES **batsmanship** noun.

Batswana plural form of TSWANA.

batt /bat/ ▸ **noun** a piece of felted material used for lining or insulating items such as quilts and sleeping bags. ■ a piece of fibreglass used to insulate buildings.
– ORIGIN late Middle English (in the general sense 'lump, piece'): of unknown origin.

battalion /bəˈtalɪən/ ▸ **noun** a large body of troops ready for battle, especially an infantry unit forming part of a brigade. ■ a large organized group of people pursuing a common aim.
– ORIGIN late 16th cent.: from French *bataillon*, from Italian *battaglione*, from *battaglia* 'battle', from Latin (see BATTLE).

Battambang /ˈbatəmbaŋ/ (also **Batdambang**) the capital of a province of the same name in western Cambodia; pop. 182,600 (est. 2009).

battels /ˈbat(ə)lz/ ▸ **plural noun** (at Oxford University) a college account for food and accommodation expenses.
– ORIGIN late 16th cent.: perhaps from dialect *battle* 'nourish', from the earlier adjective *battle* 'nutritious'; probably related to BATTEN².

battement /ˈbat(ə)mɒ̃/ ▸ **noun** [with modifier] Ballet a movement in which one leg is moved outward from the body and in again. See also GRAND BATTEMENT, PETIT BATTEMENT.
– ORIGIN French, literally 'beating'.

Batten, Jean (1909–82), New Zealand aviator. She was the first woman to fly from England to Australia and back (1934–5), and in 1936 she made the first direct solo flight from England to New Zealand.

batten¹ ▸ **noun** a long flat strip of squared timber or metal used to hold something in place or as a fastening against a wall. ■ a strip of wood or metal for securing a tarpaulin over a ship's hatchway. ■ a strip of wood or plastic used to stiffen and hold the leech of a sail out from the mast.
▸ **verb** [with obj.] strengthen or fasten (something) with battens: *Stephen was **battening down** the shutters.*
– PHRASES **batten down the hatches** Nautical secure a ship's tarpaulins. ■ prepare for a difficulty or crisis.
– ORIGIN late 15th cent.: from Old French *batant*, present participle (used as a noun) of *batre* 'to beat', from Latin *battuere*.

batten² ▸ **verb** [no obj.] (**batten on**) thrive or prosper at the expense of: *multinational monopolies batten on the working classes.*
– ORIGIN late 16th cent. (in the sense 'improve in condition, grow fat'): from Old Norse *batna* 'get better', related to BETTER¹.

Battenberg (also **Battenberg cake**) ▸ **noun** chiefly Brit. an oblong sponge cake covered with marzipan, with a square cross section quartered with two colours of sponge.
– ORIGIN named after the town of *Battenberg* in Germany.

battening ▸ **noun** [mass noun] a structure formed with battens.

batter¹ ▸ **verb** [with obj.] strike repeatedly with hard blows: *a prisoner was **battered to death** with a table leg.* ■ (often as noun **battering**) subject (one's spouse, partner, or child) to repeated violence and assault: *outrage at wife-battering and child abuse.* ■ censure, criticize, or defeat severely or thoroughly.
– DERIVATIVES **batterer** noun.
– ORIGIN Middle English: from Old French *batre* 'to beat' (from Latin *battuere*) + -ER⁴.

batter² ▸ **noun 1** [mass noun] a semi-liquid mixture of flour, egg, and milk or water, used for making pancakes or for coating food before frying. ■ N. Amer. a mixture of ingredients for a cake.
2 Printing a damaged area of metal type or a printing block.
– ORIGIN late Middle English: from Old French *bateure* 'the action of beating', from *batre* 'to beat'.

batter³ ▸ **noun** (in various sports, especially baseball) a player who is batting.

batter⁴ ▸ **noun** a gradual backwards slope in a wall or similar structure.
▸ **verb** [no obj.] (of a wall) have a receding slope.

B

– ORIGIN mid 16th cent. (as a verb): of unknown origin.

battered[1] ▸ adjective (of food) coated in batter and deep-fried until crisp.

battered[2] ▸ adjective injured by repeated blows or punishment: *he finished the day battered and bruised.* ▪ having suffered repeated violence from a spouse, partner, or parent: *battered babies.* ▪ (of a thing) damaged by age and repeated use: *a pair of battered black boots.*

batterie /ˌbat(ə)ˈriː/ ▸ noun [mass noun] Ballet the action of beating the feet or calves together during a leap.
– ORIGIN French, literally 'beating'.

batterie de cuisine /batəˌriː də kwɪˈziːn/ ▸ noun the apparatus or set of utensils for serving or preparing a meal.
– ORIGIN French, 'set of equipment for the kitchen'. The sense of 'set' developed from the original meaning of 'collection of artillery equipment (for 'beating' the enemy)'; see also BATTERY.

battering ram ▸ noun a heavy beam, originally with an end in the form of a carved ram's head, formerly used in breaching fortifications. ▪ a heavy object swung or rammed against a door to break it down.

battery ▸ noun (pl. **batteries**) **1** a container consisting of one or more cells, in which chemical energy is converted into electricity and used as a source of power: *a camera battery* | [as modifier] *battery power.*
2 a fortified emplacement for heavy guns. ▪ an artillery subunit of guns, men, and vehicles.
3 a set of similar units of equipment, typically when connected together. ▪ an extensive series, sequence, or range of things: *children are given a battery of tests.*
4 [usu. as modifier] chiefly Brit. a series of small cages for the intensive rearing of farm animals, especially calves and poultry: *battery farming* | *battery hens.*
5 [mass noun] Law the infliction of unlawful personal violence on another person, even where the contact does no physical harm. See also ASSAULT AND BATTERY.
6 (**the battery**) Baseball the pitcher and the catcher.
– ORIGIN Middle English: from Old French *baterie*, from *battre* 'to strike', from Latin *battuere*. The original sense was 'metal articles wrought by hammering', later 'a number of pieces of artillery used together', whence 'a number of Leyden jars connected up so as to discharge simultaneously' (mid 18th cent.), giving rise to sense 1.

Batticaloa /ˌbatɪkəˈləʊə/ a city on the east coast of Sri Lanka; pop. 88,459 (2007).

batting[1] ▸ noun [mass noun] the action of hitting with or using a bat, especially in cricket or baseball. ▪ a cricket team's batsmen collectively.

batting[2] ▸ noun [mass noun] cotton wadding prepared in sheets for use in quilts.

batting average ▸ noun the average score of a batsman or batter, in cricket a batsman's runs scored per completed innings, and in baseball a batter's safe hits per official times at bat.

batting order ▸ noun the order in which batsmen or batters in cricket or baseball take their turn to bat.

battle ▸ noun a sustained fight between large organized armed forces: *the battle lasted for several hours* | [in names] *the Battle of Waterloo* | [mass noun] *he died in battle.* ▪ a lengthy and difficult conflict or struggle: *the battle against ageing.*
▸ verb [no obj.] struggle tenaciously to achieve or resist something: *he has been battling against the illness.* ▪ [with obj.] engage in a fight or struggle against: *firefighters battled a 9,800-acre brush fire.*
– PHRASES **battle it out** fight or compete to a definite conclusion. **battle royal** (pl. **battles royal**) a fiercely contested fight or dispute. **battle stations** chiefly US the positions taken by military personnel in preparation for battle (often used as a command or signal to prepare for battle). **half the battle** an important step towards achieving something: *he never gives in, and that's half the battle.*
– ORIGIN Middle English: from Old French *bataille* (noun), *bataillier* (verb), based on late Latin *battualia* 'military or gladiatorial exercises', from Latin *battuere* 'to beat'.

battleaxe (US also **battleax**) ▸ noun **1** a large broad-bladed axe used in ancient warfare.
2 informal a formidably aggressive older woman.

Battleborn State informal name for NEVADA.

battlebus ▸ noun Brit. informal a bus or coach used as a mobile operational centre during an election campaign.

battlecruiser ▸ noun historical a large warship of a type built in the early 20th century, carrying similar armament to a battleship but faster and more lightly armoured.

battle cry ▸ noun a word or phrase shouted by soldiers going into battle to express solidarity and intimidate the enemy. ▪ a slogan expressing the ideals of people engaged in a campaign.

battledore /ˈbat(ə)ldɔː/ ▸ noun historical **1** (also **battledore and shuttlecock**) [mass noun] a game played with a shuttlecock and rackets, a forerunner of badminton. ▪ [count noun] the small racket used in this game.
2 a wooden paddle-shaped implement formerly used in washing clothes for beating and stirring.
– ORIGIN late Middle English (in sense 2): perhaps from Provençal *batedor* 'beater', from *batre* 'to beat'.

battledress ▸ noun [mass noun] combat dress, particularly as worn by British soldiers during the Second World War.

battle fatigue ▸ noun another term for COMBAT FATIGUE.

battlefield (also **battleground**) ▸ noun the piece of ground on which a battle is or was fought. ▪ a place or situation of strife or conflict: *an ideological battlefield.*

battlefront ▸ noun the place where opposing armies engage in combat.

battle group ▸ noun a military force created to fight together, typically consisting of several different types of troops.

battlement ▸ noun (usu. **battlements**) a parapet at the top of a wall, especially of a fort or castle, that has regularly spaced squared openings for shooting through. ▪ a section of roof enclosed by battlements.
– DERIVATIVES **battlemented** adjective.
– ORIGIN late Middle English: from Old French *bataillier* 'fortify with movable defence turrets', possibly related to BATTLE.

Battle of Aboukir Bay, Battle of Bannockburn, etc. see ABOUKIR BAY, BATTLE OF; BANNOCKBURN, BATTLE OF, etc.

battler ▸ noun a person who battles or fights. ▪ chiefly Austral./NZ a person who refuses to admit defeat in the face of difficulty.

battleship ▸ noun a heavy warship of a type built chiefly in the late 19th and early 20th centuries, with extensive armour protection and large-calibre guns.
– ORIGIN late 18th cent.: shortening of *line-of-battle ship*, originally with reference to the largest wooden warships.

battue /baˈt(j)uː/ ▸ noun [mass noun] the driving of game towards hunters by beaters. ▪ [count noun] a shooting party arranged so that beaters can drive the game towards the hunters.
– ORIGIN early 19th cent.: from French, feminine past participle of *battre* 'to beat', from Latin *battuere*.

batty[1] ▸ adjective (**battier, battiest**) informal, chiefly Brit. mad; insane: *you'll drive me batty!*
– DERIVATIVES **battily** adverb, **battiness** noun.
– ORIGIN early 20th cent.: from BAT[2] + -Y[1]. Compare with BATS.

batty[2] ▸ noun W. Indian informal a person's bottom.
– ORIGIN 1930s: representing a pronunciation of BOTTY.

batty boy (also **batty man**) ▸ noun W. Indian informal, derogatory a homosexual man.

Batwa ▸ noun plural form of TWA.

batwing ▸ adjective [attrib.] (of a sleeve) having a deep armhole and a tight cuff. ▪ (of a garment) having such sleeves.

bauble /ˈbɔːb(ə)l/ ▸ noun **1** a small, showy trinket or decoration, especially (Brit.) a light, brightly coloured sphere hung on a Christmas tree. ▪ something of no importance or worth.
2 historical a baton formerly used as an emblem by jesters.
– ORIGIN Middle English: from Old French *baubel* 'child's toy', of unknown origin.

Baucis /ˈbɔːsɪs, ˈbaʊkɪs/ Greek Mythology the wife of Philemon.

baud /bɔːd/ ▸ noun (pl. **same** or **bauds**) chiefly Computing a unit used to express the speed of transmission of electronic signals, corresponding to one information unit or event per second. ▪ a unit of data transmission speed for a modem of one bit per second (in fact there is usually more than one bit per event).
– ORIGIN 1930s: coined in French from the name of Jean M. E. *Baudot* (1845–1903), French engineer who invented a telegraph printing system.

Baudelaire /ˈbəʊd(ə)lɛː/, French /bodlɛʀ/, Charles (Pierre) (1821–67), French poet and critic. He is largely known for *Les Fleurs du mal* (1857), a series of 101 lyrics that explore his isolation and melancholy and the attraction of evil and the macabre.
– DERIVATIVES **Baudelairean** /ˌbəʊd(ə)ˈlɛːrɪən/ adjective & noun.

Baudrillard /ˈbəʊdrɪjɑː/, French /bodʀijaʀ/, Jean (1929–2007), French sociologist and cultural critic, associated with postmodernism.

bauera /ˈbaʊərə/ ▸ noun a small evergreen shrub with pink or purple flowers, native to temperate regions of Australia. • Genus *Bauera*, family Cunoniaceae.
– ORIGIN modern Latin, named after the brothers Franz (1758–1840) and Ferdinand (1760–1826) *Bauer*, Austrian botanical draughtsmen.

Bauhaus /ˈbaʊhaʊs/ a school of applied arts established by Walter Gropius in Weimar in 1919 and noted for its refined functionalist approach to architecture and industrial design.
– ORIGIN German, 'house of architecture', from *Bau* 'building' + *Haus* 'house'.

baulk /bɔːlk, bɔːk/ (chiefly US also **balk**) ▸ verb [no obj.] hesitate or be unwilling to accept an idea or undertaking: *he **baulked at** such a drastic solution.* ▪ [with obj.] thwart or hinder (a plan or person): *he raised every objection he could to baulk this plan.* ▪ [with obj.] (**baulk someone of**) prevent a person or animal from having (something): *a tiger baulked of its prey.* ▪ [with obj.] archaic miss or refuse (a chance or invitation). ▪ (with reference to a horse) refuse or cause to refuse to go on.
▸ noun **1** a roughly squared timber beam.
2 the area on a billiard table between the baulk line and the bottom cushion, within which in some circumstances a ball is protected from a direct stroke.
3 Baseball an unlawful action made by a pitcher that may deceive a base runner.
4 a ridge left unploughed between furrows.
– ORIGIN late Old English *balc*, from Old Norse *bálkr* 'partition'. The original use was 'unploughed ridge', later 'land left unploughed by mistake', hence 'blunder, omission', giving rise to the verb use 'miss (a chance)'. A late Middle English sense 'obstacle' gave rise to the verb senses 'hesitate' and 'hinder'.

baulk line ▸ noun a transverse line marked on a billiard table, extending the diameter of the D to the sides of the table.

baulky ▸ adjective British spelling of BALKY.

bauxite /ˈbɔːksʌɪt/ ▸ noun [mass noun] an amorphous clayey rock that is the chief commercial ore of aluminium. It consists largely of hydrated alumina with variable proportions of iron oxides.
– DERIVATIVES **bauxitic** adjective.
– ORIGIN mid 19th cent.: from French, from *Les Baux* (the name of a village near Arles in SE France, near which it was first found) + -ITE[1].

bavardage /ˌbavɑːˈdɑːʒ/, French /bavaʀdaʒ/ ▸ noun [mass noun] idle gossip.
– ORIGIN French, from *bavarder* 'to chatter', from *bavard* 'talkative', from *bave* 'drivel'.

Bavaria /bəˈvɛːrɪə/ a state of southern Germany, formerly an independent kingdom; capital, Munich. German name BAYERN.
– DERIVATIVES **Bavarian** noun & adjective.

bavarois /ˌbavəˈwɑː/ (also **bavaroise** /ˌbavəˈwɑːz/) ▸ noun a dessert containing gelatin and whipped cream, served cold.
– ORIGIN French, literally 'Bavarian'.

bawbee /ˈbɔːbiː/ ▸ noun Scottish a coin of low value. ▪ a former silver coin worth three (later six) Scottish pennies.
– ORIGIN mid 16th cent.: from the name of the laird of Sille*bawby*, mint master under James V.

bawd /bɔːd/ ▸ noun archaic a woman in charge of a brothel.
– ORIGIN late Middle English: shortened from obsolete *bawdstrot*, from Old French *baudestroyt* 'procuress', from *baude* 'shameless'.

bawdry ▸ noun [mass noun] obscenity in speech or writing.

bawdy ▸ adjective (**bawdier, bawdiest**) dealing with sexual matters in a comical way; humorously indecent.
▸ noun [mass noun] humorously indecent talk or writing.
– DERIVATIVES **bawdily** adverb, **bawdiness** noun.
– ORIGIN early 16th cent.: from BAWD + -Y[1].

bawdy house ▶ noun archaic a brothel.

bawl ▶ verb **1** [reporting verb] shout or call out noisily and unrestrainedly: [with direct speech] *'Move!' bawled the drill corporal* | [with obj.] *we began to bawl out the words of the carol.*
2 [no obj.] weep or cry noisily: (as adj. **bawling**) *bawling babies.*
▶ noun a loud, unrestrained shout.
– PHRASAL VERBS **bawl someone out** informal reprimand someone angrily: *tales of how she bawled out employees.*
– ORIGIN late Middle English (in the sense '(of an animal) howl, bark'): imitative; possibly related to medieval Latin *baulare* 'to bark' or Icelandic *baula* 'to low'.

bawley /ˈbɔːli/ ▶ noun (pl. **bawleys**) a fishing smack of a kind formerly used on the coasts of Essex and Kent.
– ORIGIN late 19th cent.: of unknown origin.

bawn /bɔːn/ ▶ noun **1** Irish historical a fortified enclosure around a castle.
2 Irish & Canadian a meadow.
3 Canadian a flat expanse of rocks on a beach, on which fish are spread to dry.
– ORIGIN from Irish.

Bax, Sir Arnold (Edward Trevor) (1883–1953), English composer, noted for tone poems such as *Tintagel* (1917).

bay¹ ▶ noun a broad inlet of the sea where the land curves inwards: *a boat trip round the bay* | [in place names] *Sandy Bay* | *the Bay of Biscay.* ■ an indentation or recess in a range of hills or mountains.
– ORIGIN late Middle English: from Old French *baie*, from Old Spanish *bahia*, of unknown origin.

bay² (also **bay tree**, **bay laurel**, or **sweet bay**) ▶ noun an evergreen Mediterranean shrub with deep green leaves and purple berries. Its aromatic leaves are used in cookery and were formerly used to make triumphal crowns for victors. ● *Laurus nobilis*, family Lauraceae.
– ORIGIN late Middle English (denoting the laurel berry): from Old French *baie*, from Latin *baca* 'berry'.

bay³ ▶ noun **1** a space created by a window line projecting outwards from a wall. ■ a section of wall between two buttresses or columns, especially in the nave of a church.
2 [with modifier] a compartment with a specified function in a vehicle, aircraft, or ship: *a bomb bay.* ■ an area specially allocated or marked off: *a loading bay.* ■ (also **bay platform**) Brit. a short terminal platform at a railway station also having through lines.
– ORIGIN late Middle English: from Old French *baie*, from *baer* 'to gape', from medieval Latin *batare*, of unknown origin.

bay⁴ ▶ adjective (of a horse) brown with black points.
▶ noun a bay horse.
– ORIGIN Middle English: from Old French *bai*, from Latin *badius*.

bay⁵ ▶ verb [no obj.] (of a dog, especially a large one) bark or howl loudly. ■ (of a group of people) shout loudly, typically to demand something: *the crowd bayed for an encore.* ■ [with obj.] archaic bay at: *a pack of wolves baying the moon.*
▶ noun [in sing.] the sound of baying.
– PHRASES **at bay** forced to face or confront one's attackers or pursuers; cornered. **bay for blood** demand punishment or retribution. **bring someone/thing to bay** trap or corner a person or animal being hunted or chased: *the Athenians were brought to bay between the streams.* **hold** (or **keep**) **someone/thing at bay** prevent someone or something from approaching or having an effect.
– ORIGIN Middle English (as a noun): from Old French *(a)bai* (noun), *(a)baiier* (verb) 'to bark', of imitative origin.

baya /ˈbʌɪə/ (also **baya weaver**) ▶ noun a weaver bird that typically has a brown back, yellow cap, and black face, common throughout the Indian subcontinent and in SE Asia. ● *Ploceus philippinus*, family Ploceidae.
– ORIGIN from Hindi.

bayadère /ˌbʌɪəˈdɛː/ ▶ noun a Hindu dancing girl, especially one at a southern Indian temple.
– ORIGIN from French, from Portuguese *bailadeira*, from *bailar* 'to dance' (related to medieval Latin *ballare* 'to dance').

Bayard /ˈbeɪɑːd/, French /bajaʀ/, Pierre du Terrail, Chevalier de (1473–1524), French soldier. He became known as the knight 'sans peur et sans reproche' (fearless and above reproach).

bayberry ▶ noun (pl. **bayberries**) a North American shrub with aromatic leathery leaves and waxy berries. Also called WAX MYRTLE. ● Genus *Myrica*, family Myricaceae: several species.
– ORIGIN late 17th cent.: from BAY² + BERRY.

Bayern /ˈbaɪɐn/ German name for BAVARIA.

Bayes' theorem ▶ noun Statistics a theorem describing how the conditional probability of each of a set of possible causes for a given observed outcome can be computed from knowledge of the probability of each cause and the conditional probability of the outcome of each cause.
– DERIVATIVES **Bayesian** adjective.
– ORIGIN mid 19th cent.: named after Thomas *Bayes* (1702–61), English mathematician.

Bayeux Tapestry /bʌɪˈjəː/ an embroidered cloth, about 70 metres (230 feet) long, illustrating events leading up to the Norman Conquest and made between 1066 and 1077 for the bishop of Bayeux in Normandy.

Baykal, Lake variant spelling of BAIKAL, LAKE.

Baykonur variant spelling of BAIKONUR.

bay laurel ▶ noun another term for BAY².

bay leaf ▶ noun the aromatic dried leaf of the bay tree, used in cooking.

Baylis, Lilian Mary (1874–1937), English theatre manager, noted for her management of the Old Vic and for her initiative in reopening the old Sadler's Wells Theatre in 1931.

Bay of Bengal, Bay of Fundy, etc. see BENGAL, BAY OF; FUNDY, BAY OF, etc.

bayonet ▶ noun **1** a sword-like stabbing blade which may be fixed to the muzzle of a rifle for use in hand-to-hand fighting.
2 [as modifier] denoting a fitting for a light bulb, camera lens, etc. which is engaged by being pushed into a socket and then twisted to lock it in place.
▶ verb (**bayonets**, **bayoneting**, **bayoneted**) [with obj.] stab (someone) with a bayonet.
– ORIGIN late 17th cent. (denoting a kind of short dagger): from French *baïonnette*, from *Bayonne*, the name of a town in SW France, where they were first made.

bayou /ˈbʌɪuː/ ▶ noun (pl. **bayous**) (in the southern US) a marshy outlet of a lake or river.
– ORIGIN mid 18th cent.: from Louisiana French, from Choctaw *bayuk*.

bay platform ▶ noun see BAY³.

Bayreuth /bʌɪˈrɔɪt/ a town in Bavaria where Wagner is buried and where festivals of his operas are held regularly.

bay rum ▶ noun [mass noun] a perfume, chiefly for the hair, distilled originally from rum and bayberry leaves.

bayside ▶ noun the land alongside the shore of a bay: [as modifier] *a bayside hotel.*

Bay State informal name for MASSACHUSETTS.

bay tree ▶ noun another term for BAY².

bay window ▶ noun a window built to project outwards from an outside wall.

baza /ˈbɑːzə/ ▶ noun an Asian or Australasian hawk with a crest. ● Genus *Aviceda*, family Accipitridae: three species.
– ORIGIN modern Latin, via Hindi from Arabic *bāz*, denoting a goshawk.

bazaar /bəˈzɑː/ ▶ noun a market in a Middle Eastern country. ■ a fundraising sale of goods. ■ dated a large shop selling miscellaneous goods.
– ORIGIN late 16th cent.: from Italian *bazarro*, from Turkish, from Persian *bāzār* 'market'.

bazillion /bəˈzɪljən/ ▶ cardinal number informal, chiefly N. Amer. a very large number: *you were going a bazillion miles per hour!*
– ORIGIN 1980s: probably a blend of BILLION and GAZILLION.

bazoo /bəˈzuː/ ▶ noun (pl. **bazoos**) US informal **1** a person's mouth.
2 a person's bottom.
– ORIGIN late 19th cent.: of unknown origin; compare with Dutch *bazuin* 'trombone, trumpet'.

bazooka ▶ noun **1** a short-range tubular rocket launcher used against tanks.
2 a kazoo shaped like a trumpet.
– ORIGIN 1930s (in sense 2; originally US): apparently from US slang BAZOO in the original sense 'kazoo'.

bazoom ▶ noun (usu. **bazooms**) informal, chiefly N. Amer. a woman's breast.
– ORIGIN 1950s: probably an alteration of BOSOM.

BB ▶ symbol ■ Brit. double-black (used in describing grades of pencil lead). ■ N. Amer. a standard size of lead pellet used in air rifles.

b-ball ▶ noun [mass noun] N. Amer. informal basketball.
– ORIGIN 1980s: contraction.

BBC ▶ abbreviation British Broadcasting Corporation.

BBC English ▶ noun [mass noun] a form of standard spoken English associated with BBC announcers.

bbl. ▶ abbreviation barrels (especially of oil).

b-boy ▶ noun informal, chiefly US a young man involved with hip-hop culture.
– ORIGIN 1980s: *b*-probably from the noun BEAT or from BREAKDANCING.

BBQ ▶ abbreviation informal barbecue.

BBS ▶ abbreviation Computing bulletin board system.

BC ▶ abbreviation ■ before Christ (used to indicate that a date is before the Christian era). ■ British Columbia (in official postal use).

> **USAGE** BC is normally written in small capitals and placed **after** the numerals, as in *72 BC* (**not** *BC 72*). Compare with **AD**.

bcc (also **b.c.c.**) ▶ abbreviation blind carbon copy (used as an indication that a duplicate has been or should be sent to another person without the knowledge of the main recipient). Compare with **cc**.

BCD ▶ abbreviation binary coded decimal.

BCE ▶ abbreviation before the Common Era (used of dates before the Christian era, especially by non-Christians).

B-cell ▶ noun Physiology another term for B-LYMPHOCYTE.

BCF ▶ abbreviation ■ bromochlorodifluoromethane, a substance formerly used in fire extinguishers. ■ British Cycling Federation.

BCG ▶ abbreviation Bacillus Calmette–Guérin, an anti-tuberculosis vaccine developed by the French bacteriologists Albert Calmette (1863–1933) and Camille Guérin (1872–1961).

BD ▶ abbreviation ■ Bachelor of Divinity. ■ Bangladesh (international vehicle registration).

BDD ▶ abbreviation body dysmorphic disorder.

Bde ▶ abbreviation Brigade.

bdellium /ˈdɛlɪəm/ ▶ noun [mass noun] a fragrant resin produced by a number of trees related to myrrh, used in perfumes.
– ORIGIN late Middle English: via Latin from Greek *bdellion*, of Semitic origin.

Bdr ▶ abbreviation Brit. Bombardier.

BDS ▶ abbreviation Bachelor of Dental Surgery.

BE ▶ abbreviation ■ Bachelor of Education. ■ Bachelor of Engineering. ■ bill of exchange.

Be ▶ symbol the chemical element beryllium.

be ▶ verb (sing. present **am**; **are**; **is**; pl. present **are**; 1st and 3rd sing. past **was**; 2nd sing. past and pl. past **were**; present subjunctive **be**; past subjunctive **were**; present participle **being**; past participle **been**) **1** (usu. **there is/are**) exist: *there are no easy answers* | *there once was a man* | *there must be something wrong* | *I think, therefore I am.* ■ be present: *there were no curtains around the showers* | *are there any castles in this area?*
2 [with adverbial] occur; take place: *the exhibition will be in November* | *the opening event is on October 16* | *that was before the war.* ■ occupy a position in space: *Salvation Street was on his left* | *she was not at the window.* ■ stay in the same place or condition: *he's a tough customer—**let him be**.* ■ attend: *I'm at school doing A levels.* ■ come; go; visit: *he's from Missouri* | *I have just been to Thailand* | *the doctor's been twice today.*
3 [as copular verb] having the state, quality, identity, nature, role, etc., specified: *Amy was 91* | *the floor was uneven* | *I want to be a teacher* | *father was not well* | *it will be Christmas soon* | *'Be careful,' Mr Carter said.* ■ cost: *the tickets were £25.* ■ amount to: *one and one is two.* ■ represent: *let A be a square matrix of order n.* ■ signify: *we were everything to each other.* ■ consist of; constitute: *the monastery was several three-storey buildings.*
4 informal say: *last time I saw her she was all 'You need to quit smoking!'.*
▶ auxiliary verb **1** used with a present participle to form continuous tenses: *they are coming* | *he had been reading* | *she will be waiting.*
2 used with a past participle to form the passive voice: *it was done* | *it is said* | *his book will be published.*

B

3 [with infinitive] used to indicate something that is due or destined to happen: *construction is to begin next summer* | *his mum was never to see him win.* ■ used to express obligation or necessity: *you are to follow these orders* | *they said I was to remain on board.* ■ used to express possibility: *these snakes are* ***to be*** *found in North America* | *she was nowhere* ***to be*** *seen.* ■ used to hypothesize about something that might happen: ***if I were*** *to lose* | ***if I was*** *to tell you, you'd think I was mad.*
4 archaic used with the past participle of intransitive verbs to form perfect tenses: *I am returned.*
– PHRASES **as/that was** as someone or something was previously called: *former Sex Pistol John Lydon (Rotten, as was).* **the be-all and end-all** informal a feature of an activity or a way of life that is of greater importance than any other. **be at** informal be doing or trying to do: *what are you at there?* **be away** dialect leave or set out at once: *I'm away to my work.* **be off** [often in imperative] go away; leave: ***be off with you!*** **be oneself** act naturally, according to one's character and instincts. **been** (or **been and gone**) **and——** Brit. informal used to express surprise or annoyance at someone's actions: *they've been and carted Mum off to hospital.* **been there, done that** see THERE. **be that as it may** see MAY[1]. **be there for** be available to support or comfort (someone) while they are experiencing difficulties. **not be oneself** not feel in one's usual physical or mental state. **-to-be** [in combination] of the future: *my bride-to-be.*
– ORIGIN Old English *bēon*, an irregular and defective verb, whose full conjugation derives from several originally distinct verbs. The forms *am* and *is* are from an Indo-European root shared by Latin *sum* and *est*. The forms *was* and *were* are from an Indo-European root meaning 'remain'. The forms *be* and *been* are from an Indo-European root shared by Latin *fui* 'I was', *fio* 'I become', and Greek *phuein* 'bring forth, cause to grow'. The origin of *are* is uncertain.

USAGE For a discussion of whether it is correct to say *that must* **be he** *at the door and* **it is I** *rather than that must* **be him** *at the door and* **it is me**, see **USAGE** at **PERSONAL PRONOUN.**

be- ▸ **prefix** forming verbs: **1** all over; all round: *bespatter.* ■ thoroughly; excessively: *bewilder.*
2 (added to intransitive verbs) expressing transitive action: *bemoan.*
3 (added to adjectives and nouns) expressing transitive action: *befool* | *befriend.*
4 (added to nouns) affect with: *befog.* ■ (added to adjectives) cause to be: *befoul.*
5 (forming adjectives ending in *-ed*) having; covered with: *bejewelled.*
– ORIGIN Old English, weak form of *bī* 'by'.

BEA ▸ **abbreviation** historical British European Airways.

beach ▸ **noun** a pebbly or sandy shore, especially by the sea between high- and low-water marks: *fabulous sandy beaches.*
▸ **verb** [with obj.] run or haul up (a boat or ship) on to a beach: *at the water's edge a rowing boat was beached.* ■ (of an angler) land (a fish) on a beach. ■ (also **be beached**) [no obj.] (of a whale or similar animal) become stranded out of the water: *we don't know what causes whales to beach.* ■ leave (someone) at a loss: *competitive procurement seems to have beached several firms.*
– ORIGIN mid 16th cent. (denoting shingle on the seashore): perhaps related to Old English *bæce*, *bece* 'brook' (an element that survives in place names such as Wis*bech* and Sand*bach*), assuming an intermediate sense 'pebbly river valley'.

beach ball ▸ **noun** a large inflatable ball used for playing games on the beach.

beach buggy ▸ **noun** a low wide-wheeled motor vehicle for recreational driving on sand.

beach bum ▸ **noun** informal a person who spends time idly on or around a beach.

beachcomber ▸ **noun 1** a vagrant who makes a living by searching beaches for articles of value and selling them.
2 a long wave rolling in from the sea.

beached ▸ **adjective** hauled up or stranded on a beach: *a beached whale* | *beached fishing boats.*

beachfront ▸ **noun** chiefly N. Amer. another term for SEAFRONT.

beachhead ▸ **noun** a defended position on a beach taken from the enemy by landing forces, from which an attack can be launched.
– ORIGIN Second World War (originally US): formed on the pattern of *bridgehead.*

Beach-la-mar /ˌbiːtʃləˈmɑː/ ▸ **noun** variant spelling of BISLAMA.

beach plum ▸ **noun** a maritime shrub related to the plum, found on the east coast of North America.
● *Prunus maritima*, family Rosaceae.
■ the edible fruit of the beach plum.

beachside ▸ **noun** the area adjacent to a beach: [as modifier] *fine beachside hotels.*

beach volleyball ▸ **noun** [mass noun] a form of volleyball played on sand by teams of two players.

beachwear ▸ **noun** [mass noun] clothing suitable for wearing on the beach, though not necessarily for swimming in.

beacon ▸ **noun** a fire or light set up in a high or prominent position as a warning, signal, or celebration. ■ [often in place names] Brit. a hill suitable for a beacon: *Ivinghoe Beacon.* ■ a light or other visible object serving as a signal, warning, or guide at sea, on an airfield, etc. ■ a radio transmitter whose signal helps to fix the position of a ship, aircraft, or spacecraft.
– ORIGIN Old English *bēacn* 'sign, portent, ensign', of West Germanic origin; related to BECKON.

beaconfish ▸ **noun** (pl. **same** or **beaconfishes**) a popular aquarium characin from tropical South America, with a red and gold spot near the base of the tail fin and another near the eye. ● *Hemigrammus ocellifer*, family Characidae.

bead ▸ **noun 1** a small piece of glass, stone, or similar material that is threaded with others to make a necklace or rosary or sewn on to fabric.
2 a drop of a liquid on a surface: ***beads of*** *sweat.*
3 a small knob forming the foresight of a gun.
4 the reinforced inner edge of a pneumatic tyre that grips the rim of the wheel.
5 an ornamental plaster moulding resembling a string of beads or having a semicircular cross section.
▸ **verb** [with obj.] **1** (often as adj. **beaded**) decorate or cover with beads: *a beaded evening bag.*
2 cover (a surface) with drops of moisture: *his face* ***was beaded with*** *perspiration.*
– PHRASES **draw** (or **get**) **a bead on** chiefly N. Amer. take aim at with a gun. ■ fully understand or make sense of: *it's hard to draw a bead on the stock market these days.* **tell one's beads** use the beads of a rosary in counting prayers.
– ORIGIN Old English *gebed* 'prayer', of Germanic origin; related to Dutch *bede* and German *Gebet*, also to BID[2]. Current senses derive from the use of a rosary, each bead representing a prayer.

beaded lizard ▸ **noun** a venomous lizard with a stout body, short limbs, a large blunt head, and bead-like scales, occurring from the south-western US to Guatemala. ● Family Helodermatidae and genus *Heloderma*: the **Mexican beaded lizard** (*H. horridum*) and the Gila monster.

beading ▸ **noun** [mass noun] **1** decoration or ornamental moulding resembling a string of beads or having a semicircular cross section.
2 the bead of a tyre.

beadle ▸ **noun** Brit. a ceremonial officer of a church, college, or similar institution. ■ Scottish a church officer attending on the minister. ■ historical a minor parish officer dealing with petty offenders.
– ORIGIN Old English *bydel* 'a person who makes a proclamation', gradually superseded in Middle English by forms from Old French *bedel*, ultimately of Germanic origin; related to German *Büttel*, also to BID[1]. Compare with BEDEL.

beadlet anemone ▸ **noun** a common European coastal sea anemone which is typically rust-red with several rings of tentacles around the mouth. ● *Actinia equina*, order Actiniaria.

beadsman ▸ **noun** (pl. **beadsmen**) historical a pensioner provided for by a benefactor in return for prayers, especially one living in an almshouse.

beadwork ▸ **noun** [mass noun] decorative work made of beads.

beady ▸ **adjective** (**beadier**, **beadiest**) (of a person's eyes) small, round, and gleaming. ■ bright and keenly observant: *I shall certainly keep a beady eye on this development* | *a beady-eyed observer.*
– DERIVATIVES **beadily** adverb, **beadiness** noun.

beagle ▸ **noun** a small hound of a breed with a short coat, used for hunting hares.
▸ **verb** [no obj.] (usu. as noun **beagling**) hunt with beagles.
– DERIVATIVES **beagler** noun.
– ORIGIN late 15th cent.: perhaps from Old French *beegueule* 'open-mouthed', from *beer* 'open wide' + *gueule* 'throat'.

Beagle Channel a channel through the islands of Tierra del Fuego at the southern tip of South America.
– ORIGIN named after HMS *Beagle*, the ship of Charles Darwin's voyage of 1831–6.

beak[1] ▸ **noun** a bird's horny projecting jaws; a bill. ■ the similar horny projecting jaw of other animals, for example a turtle or squid. ■ informal a person's nose: *she can't wait to stick her beak in.* ■ a projection at the prow of an ancient warship, typically shaped to resemble the head of a bird or other animal, used to pierce the hulls of enemy ships.
– DERIVATIVES **beaked** adjective [in combination] *a yellow-beaked alpine chough*, **beak-like** adjective.
– ORIGIN Middle English: from Old French *bec*, from Latin *beccus*, of Celtic origin.

beak[2] ▸ **noun** Brit. informal a magistrate or a schoolmaster.
– ORIGIN late 18th cent.: probably from criminals' slang.

beaked whale ▸ **noun** a medium-sized whale with elongated jaws that form a beak, typically showing marked differences in size and body form between the sexes. ● Family Ziphiidae: four genera and several species, including the bottlenose whales.

beaker ▸ **noun** Brit. a tall drinking container, typically made of plastic, with straight sides and no handle. ■ a lipped cylindrical glass container for laboratory use. ■ archaic or literary a large drinking container with a wide mouth. ■ Archaeology a waisted pot characteristic of graves of the Beaker folk.
– ORIGIN Middle English (in the sense 'large drinking container'): from Old Norse *bikarr*, perhaps based on Greek *bikos* 'drinking bowl'.

Beaker folk ▸ **plural noun** Archaeology a late Neolithic and early Bronze Age European people (*c.*2700–1700 BC), named after distinctive waisted pots (**Beaker ware**) that were associated with their burials and appear to have been used for alcoholic drinks. It is now thought that the Beaker folk were not a separate race, but that the use of such pots spread as a result of migration, trade, and fashion.

beaky ▸ **adjective** informal (of a person's nose) resembling a bird's beak; hooked.

bealach /ˈbɛlax/ ▸ **noun** Scottish a narrow mountain pass.
– ORIGIN late 18th cent.: Gaelic, from Middle Irish *belach* 'a pass, road'.

beam ▸ **noun 1** a long, sturdy piece of squared timber or metal used to support the roof or floor of a building. ■ a narrow, raised horizontal piece of squared timber on which a gymnast balances while performing exercises. ■ a horizontal piece of squared timber or metal supporting the deck and joining the sides of a ship. ■ Nautical the direction of an object visible from the port or starboard side of a ship when it is perpendicular to the centre line of the vessel: *there was land in sight* ***on the port beam.*** ■ a ship's breadth at its widest point: *a cutter with a beam of 16 feet.* ■ informal the width of a person's hips: *notice how* ***broad in the beam*** *she's getting?* ■ the main stem of a stag's antler. ■ the crossbar of a balance. ■ an oscillating shaft which transmits the vertical piston movement of a beam engine to the crank or pump. ■ the shank of an anchor. ■ historical the main timber of a horse-drawn plough.
2 a ray or shaft of light: ***a beam of light*** *flashed in front of her* | *the torch beam dimmed perceptibly.* ■ a directional flow of particles or radiation: *beams of electrons.* ■ a series of radio or radar signals emitted as a navigational guide for ships or aircraft.
3 a radiant or good-natured look or smile: *a beam of satisfaction.*
▸ **verb 1** [with obj. and adverbial of direction] transmit (a radio signal or broadcast) in a specified direction: *the satellite beamed back radio signals to scientists on Earth.* ■ [with obj.] (**beam someone up/down**) (in science fiction) transport someone instantaneously to or from a spaceship. [phrase from the American television series *Star Trek.*]
2 [no obj., with adverbial of direction] (of a light or light source) shine brightly: *the sun's rays beamed down.*
3 [no obj.] smile radiantly: *she beamed with pleasure.* ■ [with obj.] express (an emotion) with a radiant smile: *the instructress beamed her approval.*
– PHRASES **a beam in one's eye** a fault that is greater in oneself than in the person one is finding fault with. [with biblical allusion to Matt. 7:3.] **off** (or **way off**) **beam** informal on the wrong track; mistaken. **on her** (or **its**) **beam ends** (of a ship) heeled over on its side; almost capsized. **on one's beam ends** near the end of one's resources; desperate.

– ORIGIN Old English *bēam* 'tree, beam', of West Germanic origin; related to Dutch *boom* and German *Baum*.

beam compass (also **beam compasses**) ▸ noun a drawing compass consisting of a horizontal rod or beam connected by sliding sockets to two vertical legs, used for drawing large circles.

beam engine ▸ noun a stationary steam engine with a large oscillating beam that transmits the vertical movement of the pistons to a crank or pump.

beamer ▸ noun Cricket a ball bowled directly at a batsman's head or upper body without bouncing (regarded as unsporting).

beaming ▸ adjective smiling broadly; grinning: *his beaming face told its own story | a beaming smile.*

beam sea ▸ noun Nautical a sea which is rolling against a ship's side approximately at right angles.

beam splitter ▸ noun a device for dividing a beam of light or other electromagnetic radiation into two or more separate beams.

beamy ▸ adjective (**beamier**, **beamiest**) (of a ship) broad-beamed.

bean ▸ noun **1** an edible seed, typically kidney-shaped, growing in long pods on certain leguminous plants. ■ the hard seed of coffee, cocoa, and certain other plants.
2 a leguminous plant that bears beans in pods. ● *Phaseolus* and other genera, family Leguminosae: numerous species, including the **runner bean** (*P. coccineus*), **French bean** (*P. vulgaris*), and **broad bean** (*Vicia faba*).
3 (N. Amer. also **beans**) [with negative] informal a very small amount or nothing at all of something (used emphatically): *there is not a single bean of substance in the report.* ■ used in reference to money: *he didn't have a bean.*
4 informal, dated a person's head, especially when regarded as a source of common sense.
▸ verb [with obj.] informal, chiefly N. Amer. hit (someone) on the head: *she picked up a rock and beaned him on the forehead.*
– PHRASES **full of beans** informal lively; in high spirits. **know how many beans make five** Brit. informal be sensible and intelligent. **old bean** Brit. informal, dated a friendly form of address to a man.
– ORIGIN Old English *bēan*, of Germanic origin; related to Dutch *boon* and German *Bohne*.

beanbag ▸ noun **1** a small bag filled with dried beans and used in children's games.
2 a large cushion filled with polystyrene beads and used as a seat.

bean counter ▸ noun informal a person, typically an accountant or bureaucrat, perceived as placing excessive emphasis on controlling expenditure and budgets.

bean curd ▸ noun another term for TOFU.

beaner ▸ noun N. Amer. informal, derogatory a Mexican or person of Mexican descent.

beanery ▸ noun (pl. **beaneries**) N. Amer. informal a cheap restaurant.

beanfeast ▸ noun Brit. informal a celebratory party with plentiful food and drink.
– ORIGIN early 19th cent.: from BEAN + FEAST. The term originally denoted an annual dinner given to employees by their employers, where beans and bacon were regarded as an indispensable dish.

bean goose ▸ noun a grey goose with orange-yellow bill and legs, breeding in the arctic tundra of Lapland and Siberia and overwintering in parts of Europe and Asia. ● *Anser fabalis*, family Anatidae.

beanie ▸ noun (pl. **beanies**) a small close-fitting hat worn on the back of the head.
– ORIGIN 1940s (originally US): perhaps from BEAN (in the sense 'head') + -IE.

beano ▸ noun (pl. **beanos**) Brit. informal a party.
– ORIGIN late 19th cent.: abbreviation of BEANFEAST.

beanpole ▸ noun a stick for supporting bean plants. ■ informal a tall, thin person.

bean sprouts ▸ plural noun the sprouting seeds of certain beans, especially mung beans, used chiefly in oriental cookery.

beanstalk ▸ noun the stem of a bean plant, proverbially fast-growing and tall.

bear[1] ▸ verb (past **bore**; past participle **borne**) [with obj.]
1 (of a person) carry: *he was bearing a tray of brimming glasses | the warriors bore lances tipped with iron.* ■ (of a vehicle or boat) convey (passengers or cargo): *steamboats bear the traveller out of Kerrerra Sound.* ■ have or display as a visible mark or feature: *many of the papers bore his flamboyant signature.* ■ be called by (a name or title): *he bore the surname Tiller.* ■ (**bear oneself**) carry or conduct oneself in a specified manner: *she bore herself with dignity.*
2 support; carry the weight of: *walls which cannot bear a stone vault.* ■ take responsibility for: *no one likes to **bear the responsibility for** such decisions | the expert's fee shall be borne by the tenant.* ■ be able to accept or stand up to: *it is doubtful whether either of these distinctions would **bear scrutiny**.*
3 endure (an ordeal or difficulty): *she bore the pain stoically.* ■ [with modal and negative] manage to tolerate (a situation or experience): *she **could hardly bear** his sarcasm* | [with infinitive] *I cannot bear to see you hurt.* ■ (**cannot bear someone/thing**) strongly dislike: *I can't bear caviar.*
4 give birth to (a child): *she bore sixteen daughters* | [with two objs] *his wife had borne him a son.* ■ (of a tree or plant) produce (fruit or flowers).
5 [no obj., with adverbial of direction] turn and proceed in a specified direction: *bear left and follow the old drove road.*
– PHRASES **bear the brunt of** see BRUNT. **bear the burden of** suffer the consequences of. **bear fruit** yield positive results. **bear a hand** archaic help in a task or enterprise. **bear in mind** remember and take into account: [with clause] *you need to bear in mind that the figures vary from place to place.* **bear someone malice** (or **ill will**) [with negative] wish someone harm. **bear a relation** (or **relationship**) **to** [with negative] be logically consistent with: *the map didn't seem to bear any relation to the roads.* **bear a resemblance** (or **similarity**) **to** resemble. **bear witness** (or **testimony**) **to** testify to: *little is left to bear witness to the past greatness of the city.* ■ state or show one's belief in: *people bearing witness to Jesus.* **be borne in on** (or **upon**) come to be realized by: *the folly of her action was borne in on her.* **bring pressure to bear on** attempt to coerce. **bring to bear 1** muster and use to effect: *she had reservations about how much influence she could bring to bear.* **2** aim (a weapon): *he brought his rifle to bear on a distant target.* **not bear thinking about** be too terrible to contemplate.
– PHRASAL VERBS **bear away** another way of saying BEAR OFF. **bear down** (of a woman in labour) exert downwards pressure in order to push the baby out. **bear down on** move directly towards someone or something in a purposeful or intimidating manner. ■ take strict measures to deal with: *a commitment to bear down on inflation.* **bear off** Sailing change course away from the wind. **bear on** be relevant to (something): *two kinds of theories which bear on literary studies.* ■ [with adverbial] be a burden on: *the extension of VAT to domestic fuel will **bear hard** on the low-paid.* **bear something out** support or confirm something: *this assumption is not borne out by any evidence.* **bear up** remain cheerful in the face of adversity: *she's bearing up remarkably well.* **bear with** be patient or tolerant with.
– ORIGIN Old English *beran*, of Germanic origin; from an Indo-European root shared by Sanskrit *bharati*, Greek *pherein*, and Latin *ferre*.

> **USAGE** Until the 18th century **borne** and **born** were simply variant forms of the past participle of **bear**, used interchangeably with no distinction in meaning. By around 1775, however, the present distinction in use had become established. At that time **borne** became the standard past participle used in all the senses listed in this dictionary entry, e.g. *she has **borne** you another son, the findings have been **borne** out*, and so on. **Born** became restricted to just one very common use, which remains the case today: in the passive, without **by**, as the standard, neutral way to refer to birth: *she was **born** in 1965, he was **born** lucky*, or *I was **born** and bred in Gloucester.*

bear[2] ▸ noun **1** a large, heavy mammal which walks on the soles of its feet, having thick fur and a very short tail. Bears are related to the dog family but have an omnivorous diet. ● Family Ursidae: several genera and species.
■ a teddy bear. ■ informal a rough, bad-mannered, or uncouth person. ■ a large, heavy, cumbersome man. ■ (**the Bear**) informal a nickname for Russia.
2 Stock Exchange a person who sells shares hoping to buy them back later at a lower price. Often contrasted with BULL[1]. [said to be from a proverb warning against 'selling the bear's skin before one has caught the bear'.]
– PHRASES **like a bear with a sore head** Brit. informal (of a person) very irritable. **loaded for bear** N. Amer. informal fully prepared for any eventuality, especially a confrontation or challenge.
– ORIGIN Old English *bera*, of West Germanic origin; related to Dutch *beer* and German *Bär*.

bearable ▸ adjective able to be endured.
– DERIVATIVES **bearability** noun, **bearably** adverb.

bear-baiting ▸ noun [mass noun] historical a form of entertainment which involved setting dogs to attack a captive bear.

bearberry ▸ noun (pl. **bearberries**) a creeping dwarf shrub of the heather family, with pinkish flowers and bright red berries. ● Genus *Arctostaphylos*, family Ericaceae: several species.

bearcat ▸ noun a bear-like climbing mammal, especially the red panda.

beard ▸ noun **1** a growth of hair on the chin and lower cheeks of a man's face. ■ a tuft of hair on the chin of certain mammals, for example a lion or goat. ■ a tuft of hairs or bristles on certain plants, especially the awn of a grass.
2 US informal a person who carries out a transaction, typically a bet, for someone else in order to conceal the other's identity.
3 N. Amer. informal a woman who accompanies a homosexual man as an escort to a social occasion, in order to help conceal his homosexuality.
▸ verb [with obj.] boldly confront or challenge (someone formidable).
– PHRASES **beard the lion in his den** (or **lair**) confront or challenge someone on their own ground.
– DERIVATIVES **beardless** adjective.
– ORIGIN Old English, of West Germanic origin; related to Dutch *baard* and German *Bart*.

bearded ▸ adjective having a growth of hair on one's cheeks and chin: *beside me sat a pair of bearded men* | [in combination] *a grey-bearded man.* ■ (of an animal) having a tuft of hair on its chin: *a bearded seal.* ■ (of a plant) having a tuft of hair or bristles: *bearded irises.*

bearded collie ▸ noun a dog of a shaggy breed of collie with long hair on the face.

bearded dragon (also **bearded lizard**) ▸ noun a semi-arboreal Australian lizard with spiny scales and a large throat pouch bearing sharp spines. ● Genus *Pogona* (or *Amphibolurus*), family Agamidae; several species.

bearded tit ▸ noun a small long-tailed Eurasian songbird of the parrotbill family, the male of which has dark markings resembling a moustache, frequenting reed beds. Also called REEDLING. ● *Panurus biarmicus*, family Panuridae (or Paradoxornithidae); formerly placed in the tit family.

bearded vulture ▸ noun another term for LAMMERGEIER.

beardfish ▸ noun (pl. **same** or **beardfishes**) a small bottom-dwelling marine fish of deep water, with a long pair of fleshy barbels beneath the chin. ● Family Polymixiidae and genus *Polymixia*: several species, in particular *P. lowei*.

beardie ▸ noun (pl. **beardies**) Brit. informal **1** a bearded man, especially one regarded as lacking in style.
2 a bearded collie.

Beardmore Glacier a glacier in Antarctica, flowing from the Queen Maud Mountains to the Ross Ice Shelf, at the southern edge of the Ross Sea.
– ORIGIN named after William *Beardmore* (1856–1936), an English shipbuilder who supported Antarctic exploration.

Beardsley, Aubrey (Vincent) (1872–98), English artist and illustrator, associated with art nouveau and the Aesthetic movement. He is known for his original and controversial illustrations, such as those for Oscar Wilde's *Salome* (1894).

bearer ▸ noun **1** a person or thing that carries or holds something: [in combination] *a flag-bearer* | figurative *I'm sorry to be the bearer of bad tidings.* ■ a carrier of equipment on an expedition. ■ Indian a domestic servant or other menial worker. ■ Indian a waiter. ■ a person who carries the coffin at a funeral.
2 a person who presents a cheque or other order to pay money: *promissory notes payable to the bearer.* ■ [as modifier] payable to the possessor: *bearer bonds.*

bear garden (also **bear pit**) ▸ noun a scene of uproar and confusion.
– ORIGIN late 16th cent.: *bear* from BEAR[2]. The original sense was 'a place set apart for bear-baiting'; bear gardens were often used for other rough sports, hence the figurative meaning.

beargrass ▸ noun a North American plant with long, coarse, grass-like leaves, in particular: ● a wild yucca (genus *Yucca*, family Agavaceae). ● a cultivated ornamental plant, the leaves of which were formerly used by American Indians to make watertight baskets (*Xerophyllum tenax*, family Liliaceae).

B

bear hug ▸ noun a rough, tight embrace.

bearing ▸ noun **1** a person's way of standing or moving: *a man of precise military bearing.* ■ the way a person behaves or conducts themselves: *she has the bearing of a First Lady.*
2 [mass noun] relation; relevance: *the case has no direct **bearing on** the issues being considered.*
3 [mass noun] the ability to tolerate something bad or to be tolerated: *school was bad enough, but now it's past bearing.*
4 (often **bearings**) a part of a machine that allows one part to rotate or move in contact with another part with as little friction as possible.
5 the direction or position of something, or the direction of movement, relative to a fixed point. It is usually measured in degrees, typically with magnetic north as zero. ■ (**one's bearings**) awareness of one's position relative to one's surroundings: *he flashed the torch around, trying to get his bearings.*
6 Heraldry a device or charge: *armorial bearings.*

bearing rein ▸ noun a fixed rein which causes the horse to raise its head and arch its neck.

bearish ▸ adjective **1** resembling or likened to a bear, typically in being rough, surly, or clumsy.
2 Stock Exchange characterized by or associated with falling share prices.
– DERIVATIVES **bearishly** adverb, **bearishness** noun.

bear market ▸ noun Stock Exchange a market in which share prices are falling, encouraging selling.

Béarnaise sauce /ˌbeɪəˈneɪz/ ▸ noun [mass noun] a rich sauce thickened with egg yolks and flavoured with tarragon.
– ORIGIN *Béarnaise*, feminine of French *béarnais* 'of *Béarn*', a region of SW France.

bear pit ▸ noun another term for BEAR GARDEN.

bear's breech ▸ noun a Mediterranean plant with large deep-cut leaves and tall spikes of purple-veined white flowers. ● *Acanthus mollis*, family Acanthaceae.

bear's ear ▸ noun another term for AURICULA.

bear's foot ▸ noun a hellebore, which has leaves that are said to resemble a bear's foot.

bearskin ▸ noun the pelt of a bear, especially when used as a rug or wrap. ■ a tall cap of black fur worn ceremonially by certain troops, such as the Guards in the British army.

Beas /beɪˈɑːs, biːˈɑːs/ a river of northern India which rises in the Himalayas and flows through Himachal Pradesh to join the Sutlej River in Punjab. It is one of the five rivers that gave Punjab its name.

beast ▸ noun an animal, especially a large or dangerous four-footed one: *a wild beast.* ■ (usu. **beasts**) a domestic animal, especially a bovine farm animal. ■ archaic or humorous an animal as opposed to a human. ■ an inhumanly cruel, violent, or depraved person. ■ informal an objectionable or unpleasant person or thing: *a scheming, manipulative little beast.* ■ (**the beast**) a person's brutish or untamed characteristics: ***the beast in you** is rearing its ugly head.* ■ [with adj.] informal a thing possessing a specified quality: *that much-maligned beast, the rave record.*
– ORIGIN Middle English: from Old French *beste*, based on Latin *bestia*.

beastie ▸ noun (pl. **beasties**) Scottish or humorous an insect or other small animal. ■ [with adj.] informal a vehicle or device of a specified kind: *these little beasties only have three wheels.*

beasting ▸ noun [mass noun] Brit. informal (especially in the armed forces) the process of subjecting a new recruit to harsh treatment in order to instil discipline.

beastly ▸ adjective (**beastlier**, **beastliest**) **1** Brit. informal very unpleasant: *this beastly war.* ■ unkind; malicious: *don't be beastly to him.*
2 archaic cruel and unrestrained: *beastly immorality.*
▸ adverb [as submodifier] Brit. informal, dated to an extreme and unpleasant degree: *a beastly dull wedding party.*
– DERIVATIVES **beastliness** noun.

beast of burden ▸ noun an animal, such as a mule or donkey, that is used for carrying loads.

beast of prey ▸ noun an animal, especially a mammal, that kills and eats other animals.

beat ▸ verb (past **beat**; past participle **beaten**) [with obj.]
1 strike (a person or an animal) repeatedly and violently so as to hurt or injure them, typically with an implement such as a club or whip: *aristocratic women were often beaten by their husbands | the victims were **beaten to death** with baseball bats.* ■ strike (an object) repeatedly so as to make a noise: *he beat the table with his hand.* ■ [no obj.] (of an instrument) make a rhythmical sound through being struck: *drums were beating in the distance.* ■ strike (a carpet, blanket, etc.) repeatedly in order to remove dust. ■ flatten or shape (metal) by striking it repeatedly with a hammer: *pure gold can be **beaten out** to form very thin sheets.* ■ (**beat something against/on**) strike something against (something): *she beat her fists against the wood.* ■ [no obj.] strike repeatedly at or on something: *Sidney **beat on** the door with the flat of his hand | Emmie began to **beat at** the flames.* ■ move across (an area of land) repeatedly striking at the ground cover in order to raise game birds for shooting.
2 defeat (someone) in a game or other competitive situation: *she beat him easily at chess | Juventus were beaten 2–1.* ■ overcome (a problem or disease): *the battle to beat car crime | he beat heroin addiction in 1992.* ■ do or be better than (a record or score): *he beat his own world record.* ■ informal be better than: ***you can't beat** the taste of fresh raspberries.* ■ informal baffle: ***it beats me how** you manage to work in this heat.*
3 succeed in getting somewhere ahead of (someone): *the defender beat him to the ball.* ■ take action to avoid (difficulty or inconvenience): *they set off early to beat the traffic.*
4 [no obj.] (of the heart) pulsate: *her heart beat faster with panic.*
5 (of a bird) move (the wings) up and down. ■ [no obj.] (of a bird) fly making rhythmic wing movements: *an owl beat low over the salt marsh.*
6 stir (cooking ingredients) vigorously to make a smooth or frothy mixture.
7 (**beat it**) informal leave: [in imperative] *now beat it, will you!*
8 [no obj., with adverbial of direction] Sailing sail into the wind, following a zigzag course with repeated tacking: *we beat southwards all that first day.*
▸ noun **1** a main accent or rhythmic unit in music or poetry: *the glissando begins on the second beat.* ■ a strong rhythm in popular music: *the music changed to a funky disco beat.* ■ [in sing.] a regular, rhythmic sound or movement: *the beat of the wipers became almost hypnotic.* ■ the sound made when something, especially a musical instrument, is struck: *he heard a regular drum beat.* ■ a pulsation of the heart. ■ a periodic variation of sound or amplitude due to the combination of two sounds, electrical signals, or other vibrations having similar but not identical frequencies.
2 the movement of a bird's wings.
3 an area allocated to a police officer and patrolled on foot: *his beat was in North London | public clamour for more policemen **on the beat**.* ■ a spell of duty allocated to a police officer: *his beat ended at 6 a.m.* ■ an area regularly frequented by someone. ■ informal a person's area of interest: *his beat is construction, property, and hotels.* ■ a stretch of water fished by an angler.
4 a brief pause or moment of hesitation: *she waited for a beat of three seconds.* [from the use of a stage direction referring to such a pause.]
5 informal short for BEATNIK.
▸ adjective **1** [predic.] informal completely exhausted: *I'm beat—I need an hour or so to rest.*
2 [attrib.] relating to the beat generation or its philosophy: *beat poet Allen Ginsberg.*
– PHRASES **beat about the bush** discuss a matter without coming to the point. **beat someone at their own game** see GAME[1]. **beat the bounds** historical mark parish boundaries by walking round them and striking certain points with rods. **beat one's breast** see BREAST. **beat the bushes** N. Amer. informal search thoroughly: *I was out **beating the bushes for** investors to split the risk.* **beat the clock** perform a task quickly or within a fixed time limit. **beat the drum for** see DRUM[1]. **be beaten at the post** be defeated at the last moment. **beat the pants off** informal prove to be vastly superior to. **beat a path to someone's door** (of a large number of people) hasten to make contact with someone regarded as interesting or inspiring. **beat a (hasty) retreat** withdraw quickly in order to avoid something unpleasant. **beat the system** succeed in finding a means of getting round rules, regulations, or other means of control. **beat time** indicate or follow a musical tempo with a baton or other means. **beat someone to it** succeed in doing something or getting somewhere before someone else. **if you can't beat them, join them** humorous if you are unable to outdo rivals in some endeavour, you might as well cooperate with them and thereby possibly gain an advantage. **to beat all ——s** infinitely better than all the things of the specified type: *a PC screen saver to beat all screen savers.* **to beat the band** N. Amer. informal in such a way as to surpass all competition: *they were talking to beat the band.*
– PHRASAL VERBS **beat someone back** force (someone trying to do something) to retreat: *I was beaten back by the flames.* **beat down** (of the sun) radiate intense heat and brightness. ■ (of rain) fall hard and continuously. **beat something down** quell defence or resistance. ■ fight to suppress a feeling or emotion. **beat someone down** force someone to reduce the price of something. **beat off** vulgar slang (of a man) masturbate. **beat someone/thing off** succeed in resisting an attacker or an attack. ■ win against a challenge or rival. **beat something out 1** produce a loud, rhythmic sound by striking something: *he beat out a rhythm on the drums.* **2** extinguish flames by striking at them with a suitable object. **beat someone up** assault and injure someone by hitting, kicking, or punching them repeatedly. ■ (**beat oneself up**) informal reproach or criticize oneself excessively. **beat up on someone** North American way of saying BEAT SOMEONE UP.
– DERIVATIVES **beatable** adjective.
– ORIGIN Old English *bēatan*, of Germanic origin.

beatbox ▸ noun informal **1** a drum machine.
2 a radio or radio cassette player used to play loud music, especially rap.
▸ verb [no obj.] imitate the sounds of a drum machine with the voice.
– DERIVATIVES **beatboxer** noun, **beatboxing** noun.

beaten past participle of BEAT. ▸ adjective **1** having been defeated: *last year's beaten finalist.* ■ exhausted and dejected: *he sat feeling old and beaten.*
2 having been beaten or struck: *he trudged home like a beaten cur.*
3 (of food) stirred vigorously to a uniform consistency: *beaten egg.* ■ (of metal) shaped by hammering, typically so as to give the surface a dimpled texture. ■ (of precious metal) hammered to form thin foil for ornamental use.
4 (of a path) well trodden; much used.
– PHRASES **off the beaten track** in or into an isolated place.

beater ▸ noun **1** a person who hits someone or something, in particular: ■ a person employed to raise game birds for shooting by striking at the ground cover. ■ [in combination] a person who habitually hits someone: *a wife-beater.*
2 an implement or machine used for beating.
3 [in combination] informal a means of defeating or preventing something: *a recession-beater.*
4 N. Amer. informal an old or dilapidated vehicle.

beat frequency ▸ noun Physics the number of beats per second, equal to the difference in the frequencies of two interacting tones or oscillations.

beat generation ▸ noun a movement of young people in the 1950s and early 1960s who rejected conventional society, valuing free self-expression and favouring modern jazz. Among writers associated with the movement were Jack Kerouac and Allen Ginsberg.

beatific /biːəˈtɪfɪk/ ▸ adjective **1** feeling or expressing blissful happiness: *a beatific smile.*
2 Christian Theology imparting holy bliss.
– DERIVATIVES **beatifically** adverb.
– ORIGIN mid 17th cent.: from French *béatifique* or Latin *beatificus*, from *beatus* 'blessed'.

beatification /bɪˌatɪfɪˈkeɪʃ(ə)n/ ▸ noun [mass noun] (in the Roman Catholic Church) declaration by the Pope that a dead person is in a state of bliss, constituting a first step towards canonization and permitting public veneration.
– ORIGIN early 16th cent. (in the sense 'action of making blessed'): from Old French, or from ecclesiastical Latin *beatificatio(n-)*, from *beatificare* 'make blessed', from Latin *beatus* 'blessed'.

beatify /bɪˈatɪfʌɪ/ ▸ verb (**beatifies**, **beatifying**, **beatified**) [with obj.] (in the Roman Catholic Church) announce the beatification of.
– ORIGIN mid 16th cent. (in the sense 'make blessed or supremely happy'): from Old French *beatifier* or ecclesiastical Latin *beatificare*, from Latin *beatus* 'blessed'.

beating ▸ noun **1** a punishment or assault in which the victim is hit repeatedly: *if he got dirt on his clothes he'd get a beating | [mass noun] torture methods included beating.*
2 [mass noun] pulsation or throbbing, typically of the heart.
3 a defeat in a competitive situation.

– PHRASES **take a beating** informal suffer damage or hurt: *her pride had taken a beating at his hands.* **take some** (or **a lot of**) **beating** informal be difficult to surpass or defeat.

beatitude /bɪˈatɪtjuːd/ ▶ **noun** [mass noun] supreme blessedness. ■ (**the Beatitudes**) the blessings listed by Jesus in the Sermon on the Mount (Matt. 5:3–11). ■ (**His/Your Beatitude**) a title given to patriarchs in the Orthodox Church.
– ORIGIN late Middle English: from Old French *beatitude* or Latin *beatitudo*, from *beatus* 'blessed'.

Beatles a pop and rock group from Liverpool consisting of George Harrison, John Lennon, Paul McCartney, and Ringo Starr. Remembered for the quality and stylistic diversity of their songs (mostly written by Lennon and McCartney), they achieved success with their first single 'Love Me Do' (1962) and went on to produce albums such as *Sergeant Pepper's Lonely Hearts Club Band* (1967). ■ (as modifier **Beatle**) characteristic of the Beatles: *a Beatle jacket.*

beatnik ▶ **noun** a young person in the 1950s and early 1960s belonging to a subculture associated with the beat generation.
– ORIGIN 1950s: from **BEAT** + *-nik* on the pattern of *sputnik*, perhaps influenced by US use of Yiddish *-nik*, denoting someone or something who acts in a particular way.

Beaton, Sir Cecil (Walter Hardy) (1904–80), English photographer famous for his fashion features and portraits of celebrities, particularly the British royal family. He later diversified into costume and set design, winning two Oscars for the film *My Fair Lady* (1964).

Beatty /ˈbiːti/, David, 1st Earl Beatty of the North Sea and of Brooksby (1871–1936), British admiral. During the First World War he played a major role in the Battle of Jutland and was Commander-in-Chief of the Grand Fleet from 1916.

beat-up ▶ **adjective** informal worn out by overuse; in a state of disrepair.

beau /bəʊ/ ▶ **noun** (pl. **beaux** or **beaus** /bəʊz, bəʊ/) dated **1** a boyfriend or male admirer.
2 a rich, fashionable young man; a dandy.
– ORIGIN late 17th cent. (in sense 2): from French, literally 'handsome', from Latin *bellus*.

Beaubourg Centre /ˈbəʊbɔːɡ/, French /bobuʀ/ another name for **POMPIDOU CENTRE**.

Beau Brummell see **BRUMMELL**.

Beaufort scale /ˈbəʊfət/ ▶ **noun** a scale of wind speed based on a visual estimation of the wind's effects, ranging from force 0 (less than 1 knot or 1 kph, 'calm') to force 12 (64 knots or 118 kph and above, 'hurricane').
– ORIGIN mid 19th cent.: named after Sir Francis *Beaufort* (1774–1857), the English admiral and naval hydrographer who devised it.

Beaufort Sea a part of the Arctic Ocean lying to the north of Alaska and Canada.
– ORIGIN named after the English admiral Sir Francis *Beaufort* (see **BEAUFORT SCALE**).

beau geste /bəʊ ˈʒɛst/, French /bo ʒɛst/ ▶ **noun** (pl. **beaux gestes** pronunc. **same**) a noble and generous act.
– ORIGIN French, literally 'splendid gesture'.

beau idéal /ˌbəʊ iːdeɪˈal/, French /bo ideal/ ▶ **noun** a person or thing representing the highest possible standard of excellence in a particular respect.
– ORIGIN French, literally 'ideal beauty'.

Beaujolais /ˈbəʊʒəleɪ/, French /boʒɔlɛ/ ▶ **noun** [mass noun] a light red or (less commonly) white burgundy wine produced in the Beaujolais district of SE France.

Beaujolais Nouveau /ˌbəʊʒəleɪ nuːˈvəʊ/, French /boʒɔlɛ nuvo/ ▶ **noun** [mass noun] a Beaujolais wine sold in the first year of a vintage.
– ORIGIN from **BEAUJOLAIS** + French *nouveau* 'new'.

Beaumarchais /ˈbəʊmɑːˌʃeɪ/, French /bomaʀʃɛ/, Pierre Augustin Caron de (1732–99), French dramatist. He is chiefly remembered for his comedies *The Barber of Seville* (1775) and *The Marriage of Figaro* (1784), which inspired operas by Rossini and Mozart.

beau monde /bəʊ ˈmɒnd/, French /bo mɔ̃d/ ▶ **noun** (**the beau monde**) fashionable society.
– ORIGIN French, literally 'fine world'.

Beaumont /ˈbəʊmɒnt/, Francis (1584–1616), English dramatist. He collaborated with John Fletcher on *Philaster* (1609), *The Maid's Tragedy* (1610–11), and many other plays. *The Knight of the Burning Pestle* (*c.*1607) is attributed to Beaumont alone.

Beau Nash see **NASH**[4].

Beaune /bəʊn/ ▶ **noun** [mass noun] a red burgundy wine from the region around Beaune in eastern France.

beau sabreur /ˌbəʊ saˈbrəː/, French /bo sabʀœʀ/ ▶ **noun** (pl. **beaux sabreurs** pronunc. **same**) a dashing adventurer.
– ORIGIN French, 'handsome swordsman', originally a sobriquet of Joachim Murat (1767–1815), French cavalry officer and brother-in-law of Napoleon.

beaut /bjuːt/ informal ▶ **noun** a particularly fine example of something: *the idea was a beaut.* ■ a beautiful person.
▶ **adjective** Austral./NZ very good or beautiful: *a beaut view.*

beauteous ▶ **adjective** literary beautiful.
– ORIGIN late Middle English: from **BEAUTY**, on the pattern of *bounteous* and *plenteous*.

beautician ▶ **noun** a person whose job is to give people beauty treatment.

beautiful ▶ **adjective** pleasing the senses or mind aesthetically: *beautiful poetry* | *a beautiful young woman.* ■ of a very high standard; excellent: *she spoke in beautiful English.*
– PHRASES **the beautiful game** Brit. soccer. **the beautiful people 1** fashionable, glamorous, and privileged people. **2** (in the 1960s) hippies. **the body beautiful** an ideal of physical beauty: *there is an array of products for producing the body beautiful.*
– DERIVATIVES **beautifully** adverb.

beautify ▶ **verb** (**beautifies, beautifying, beautified**) [with obj.] improve the appearance of.
– DERIVATIVES **beautification** noun, **beautifier** noun.

beauty ▶ **noun** (pl. **beauties**) **1** [mass noun] a combination of qualities, such as shape, colour, or form, that pleases the aesthetic senses, especially the sight: *I was struck by her beauty* | *an area of outstanding natural beauty.* ■ a combination of qualities that pleases the intellect. ■ [as modifier] denoting something intended to make someone more attractive: *beauty treatment.*
2 a beautiful or pleasing thing or person, in particular: ■ a beautiful woman: *a blonde beauty.* ■ an excellent example of something: *the fish was a beauty, around 14 pounds.* ■ (**the beauties of**) the pleasing or attractive features of (something): *the beauties of the English countryside.* ■ [in sing.] the best aspect or advantage of something: ***the beauty of** keeping cats is that they don't tie you down.*
▶ **adjective** Austral./NZ informal good; excellent (used as a general term of approval).
– PHRASES **beauty is in the eye of the beholder** proverb that which one person finds beautiful or admirable may not appeal to another. **beauty is only skin-deep** proverb a pleasing appearance is not a guide to character.
– ORIGIN Middle English: from Old French *beaute*, based on Latin *bellus* 'beautiful, fine'.

beauty contest ▶ **noun** a contest in which the winner is the woman judged the most beautiful. ■ informal a contest between rival institutions which depends heavily on presentation.

beauty mark ▶ **noun** North American term for **BEAUTY SPOT** (sense 2).

beauty pageant ▶ **noun** see **PAGEANT**.

beauty queen ▶ **noun** a woman judged most beautiful in a beauty contest.

beauty salon (also **beauty parlour**) ▶ **noun** an establishment in which hairdressing, make-up, and similar cosmetic treatments are carried out professionally.

beauty sleep ▶ **noun** [mass noun] humorous sleep considered to be sufficient to keep one looking young and beautiful.

beauty spot ▶ **noun 1** Brit. a place known for its beautiful scenery.
2 a small natural or artificial mark such as a mole on a woman's face, considered to enhance her attractiveness.

Beauvoir, Simone de, see **DE BEAUVOIR**.

beaux plural form of **BEAU**.

beaux arts /bəʊz ˈɑː/, French /boz aʀ/ ▶ **plural noun 1** fine arts.
2 (usu. **Beaux Arts**) [as modifier] relating to the classical decorative style maintained by the École des Beaux-Arts in Paris in the 19th century.
– ORIGIN French.

beaux esprits plural form of **BEL ESPRIT**.

beaux yeux /bəʊz ˈjəː/, French /boz jø/ ▶ **plural noun** literary beautiful eyes. ■ favourable regard.
– ORIGIN French.

beaver[1] ▶ **noun** (pl. **same** or **beavers**) **1** a large semiaquatic broad-tailed rodent native to North America and northern Eurasia. It is noted for its habit of gnawing through trees to fell them in order to make dams. ● Family Castoridae and genus *Castor*: the North American *C. canadensis* and the Eurasian *C. fiber*.
■ [mass noun] the soft light brown fur of the beaver. ■ (also **beaver hat**) chiefly historical a hat made of felted beaver fur. ■ (also **beaver cloth**) [mass noun] a heavy woollen cloth resembling felted beaver fur. ■ a very hard-working person.
2 (**Beaver**) a boy aged about 6 or 7 who is an affiliated member of the Scout Association.
▶ **verb** [no obj.] (usu. **beaver away**) informal work hard: *Bridget beavered away to keep things running smoothly.*
– ORIGIN Old English *beofor, befor*, of Germanic origin; related to Dutch *bever* and German *Biber*, from an Indo-European root meaning 'brown'.

beaver[2] ▶ **noun** the lower part of the face guard of a helmet in a suit of armour. The term is also used to refer to the upper part or visor, or to a single movable guard.
– ORIGIN late 15th cent.: from Old French *baviere* 'bib', from *baver* 'slaver'.

beaver[3] ▶ **noun 1** vulgar slang, chiefly N. Amer. a woman's genitals or pubic area. ■ a woman regarded in sexual terms.
2 Brit. informal, dated a bearded man.
– ORIGIN early 20th cent.: of unknown origin.

beaverboard ▶ **noun** [mass noun] chiefly N. Amer. a kind of fibreboard used in building.

Beaverbrook, Max Aitken, 1st Baron (1879–1964), Canadian-born British Conservative politician and newspaper proprietor; full name *William Maxwell Aitken*. He bought the *Daily Express* in 1916 and increased its circulation to record levels. Beaverbrook was also Minister of Aircraft Production in Churchill's cabinet (1940).

beaver lamb ▶ **noun** [mass noun] lambskin made to look like beaver fur.

Beaver State informal name for **OREGON**.

bebop /ˈbiːbɒp/ ▶ **noun** [mass noun] a type of jazz originating in the 1940s and characterized by complex harmony and rhythms. It is associated particularly with Charlie Parker, Thelonious Monk, and Dizzy Gillespie.
– DERIVATIVES **bebopper** noun.
– ORIGIN 1940s (originally US): imitative of the typical rhythm of this music.

becalm ▶ **verb** [with obj.] leave (a sailing ship) unable to move through lack of wind: *both boats hung on before the whole fleet was becalmed south of Rampholme.*

becalmed ▶ **adjective** unable to move through lack of wind: (of a sailing ship) *his ship was becalmed for nine days* | figurative *a place becalmed in its past.*

became past participle of **BECOME**.

becard /ˈbɛkəd, bəˈkɑːd/ ▶ **noun** a small bird of the tyrant flycatcher family with a large head and strong bill, found mainly in Central and South America. ● Genus *Pachyramphus*, family Tyrannidae: several species.
– ORIGIN mid 19th cent.: from French *bécarde*, from *bec* 'beak'.

because ▶ **conjunction** for the reason that; since: *we did it because we felt it our duty* | ***just because** I'm inexperienced doesn't mean that I lack perception.*
– PHRASES **because of** on account of; by reason of: *they moved here because of the baby.*
– ORIGIN Middle English: from the phrase *by cause*, influenced by Old French *par cause de* 'by reason of'.

USAGE **1** When **because** follows a negative construction the meaning can be ambiguous. In the sentence *he did not go **because** he was ill*, for example, it is not clear whether it means either 'the reason he did not go was that he was ill' or 'being ill wasn't the reason for him going; there was another reason'. Some usage guides recommend using a comma when the first interpretation is intended (*he did not go, because he was ill*) and no comma where the second interpretation is intended, but it is probably wiser to avoid using **because** after a negative altogether.
2 As with other conjunctions such as **but** and **and**, it is still widely held that it is incorrect to begin a sentence with **because**. It has, however, long been used in this way in both written and spoken English (typically for rhetorical effect), and is quite acceptable.
3 On the construction **the reason … is because**, see **USAGE** at **REASON**.

béchamel /ˈbeɪʃəmɛl/ (also **béchamel sauce**) ▶ **noun** [mass noun] a rich white sauce made with milk infused with herbs and other flavourings.
– ORIGIN named after the Marquis Louis de *Béchamel* (died 1703), steward to Louis XIV of France, who is said to have invented a similar sauce.

bêche-de-mer /ˌbɛʃdəˈmɛː/ ▶ **noun** (pl. **same** or **bêches-de-mer** pronunc. **same**) **1** a large sea cucumber which is eaten as a delicacy in China and Japan. Also called **TREPANG**.
2 [mass noun] (**Bêche-de-mer**) another term for **BISLAMA**.
– ORIGIN late 18th cent.: pseudo-French, alteration of Portuguese *bicho do mar*, literally 'sea worm'.

Bechstein /ˈbɛkstʌɪn, ˈbɛx-/ ▶ **noun** a piano made by the German piano-builder Friedrich Wilhelm Carl Bechstein (1826–1900) or by the firm which he founded in 1856.

Bechuanaland /ˌbɛtʃʊˈɑːnəland/ former name (until 1966) for **BOTSWANA**.

beck[1] ▶ **noun** N. English a stream.
– ORIGIN Middle English: from Old Norse *bekkr*, of Germanic origin; related to Dutch *beek* and German *Bach*. Used as the common term for a brook in northern areas, *beck* often refers, in literature, to a brook with a stony bed or following a rugged course, typical of such areas.

beck[2] ▶ **noun** literary a gesture requesting attention, such as a nod or wave.
– PHRASES **at someone's beck and call** always having to be ready to obey someone's orders immediately.
– ORIGIN Middle English: from archaic *beck*, abbreviated form of **BECKON**.

Beckenbauer /ˈbɛk(ə)nˌbaʊə/, German /ˈbɛknˌbaʊɐ/, Franz (b.1945), German footballer. A defender, he captained Germany when they won the World Cup in 1974. He was manager of the national team that won the World Cup again in 1990.

Becker /ˈbɛkə/, German /ˈbɛkɐ/, Boris (b.1967), German tennis player. In 1985 he became the youngest man and first unseeded player to win the men's singles championship at Wimbledon. He won it again in 1986 and 1989.

becket /ˈbɛkɪt/ ▶ **noun** a loop of rope or similar device for securing loose items on a ship.
– ORIGIN early 18th cent.: of unknown origin.

Becket, St Thomas à /ˈbɛkɪt/ (*c.*1118–70), English prelate and statesman, Archbishop of Canterbury 1162–70. He began openly to oppose Henry II, who uttered words in anger which led four knights to assassinate Becket in his cathedral. Henry was obliged to do public penance at Becket's tomb, which became a major centre of pilgrimage until its destruction under Henry VIII (1538). Feast day, 29 December.

Beckett /ˈbɛkɪt/, Samuel (Barclay) (1906–89), Irish dramatist, novelist, and poet. He is best known for his plays, especially *Waiting for Godot* (1952), a seminal work in the Theatre of the Absurd. Nobel Prize for Literature (1969).

Beckford, William (1759–1844), English writer and collector. As an author he is remembered for the oriental romance *Vathek* (1786, originally written in French).

Beckham, David (Robert Joseph) (b.1975), English footballer. A midfielder for Manchester United, Real Madrid, LA Galaxy, and Milan, he was England captain from 2001 to 2006.

beckon ▶ **verb** [no obj.] make a gesture with the hand, arm, or head to encourage or instruct someone to approach or follow: *Miranda* ***beckoned to*** *Adam.* ■ [with obj. and adverbial of direction] summon (someone) in this way: *he beckoned Cameron over* | [with obj. and infinitive] *he beckoned Duncan to follow.* ■ appear attractive or inviting: *the going is tough and soft options beckon.*
– ORIGIN Old English *bīecnan*, *bēcnan*, of West Germanic origin; related to **BEACON**.

becloud ▶ **verb** [with obj.] literary make obscure or muddled: *confusion beclouds the issue.*

become ▶ **verb** (**becomes**, **becoming**; past **became**; past participle **become**) **1** [no obj., with complement] begin to be: *she became angry and sulky all day* | *it is becoming clear that we are in a new situation.* ■ grow to be; develop into: *the child will become an adult.* ■ (of a person) qualify or be accepted as: *she wanted to become a doctor.* ■ (**become of**) (in questions) happen to: *what would become of her now?*
2 [with obj.] (of clothing) look good on or suit (someone): *mourning regalia became her.* ■ be appropriate to (someone): *minor celebrity status did not become Potter.*
– ORIGIN Old English *becuman* 'come to a place, come (to be or do something)' (see **BE-**, **COME**), of Germanic origin; related to Dutch *bekomen* and German *bekommen* 'get, receive'.

becoming ▶ **adjective** (of clothing) looking good on someone: *what a becoming dress!* ■ suitable or appropriate: *do not talk too much to your cousins, it's not becoming.*
– DERIVATIVES **becomingly** adverb, **becomingness** noun.

Becquerel /ˈbɛkərɛl/, French /bɛkʀɛl/, Antoine-Henri (1852–1908), French physicist. With Marie and Pierre Curie he discovered the natural radioactivity in uranium salts. Nobel Prize for Physics (1903, shared with the Curies).

becquerel /ˈbɛkərɛl/ (abbrev.: **Bq**) ▶ **noun** Physics the SI unit of radioactivity, corresponding to one disintegration per second.
– ORIGIN late 19th cent.: named after A. H. **BECQUEREL**.

BEd ▶ **abbreviation** Bachelor of Education.

bed ▶ **noun 1** a piece of furniture for sleep or rest, typically a framework with a mattress: *a large double bed* | *she was* ***in bed*** *by nine.* ■ a bed and associated facilities comprising a place for a patient in a hospital: *the unit has 20 geriatric beds.* ■ a bedroom: [in combination] *a three-bed detached house.* ■ a place or article used by a person or animal for sleep or rest: *a bed of straw.* ■ informal used with reference to a bed as the typical place for sexual activity: *he's incredibly good* ***in bed****.*
2 an area of ground, typically in a garden, where flowers and plants are grown: *a bed of tulips.*
3 a flat base or foundation on which something rests or is supported, in particular: ■ the foundation of a road or railway. ■ chiefly N. Amer. the open part of a truck, wagon, or cart, where goods are carried. ■ the flat surface beneath the baize of a billiard table.
4 a stratum or layer of rock: *a bed of clay.* ■ a layer of food on which other foods are served: *the salad is served on a bed of raw spinach.*
5 the bottom of the sea or a lake or river. ■ [with modifier] a place on the seabed where shellfish, especially oysters or mussels, breed or are bred: *an oyster bed.*
▶ **verb** (**beds**, **bedding**, **bedded**) [with obj.] **1** provide with sleeping accommodation: *the children were bedded in the attic.* ■ [no obj.] (**bed down**) settle down to sleep or rest for the night in an improvised place: *you can bed down in the shed.* ■ (**bed someone/thing down**) settle a person or animal down to sleep or rest for the night. ■ informal have sexual intercourse with.
2 transfer (a plant) from a pot or seed tray to a garden plot: *I* ***bedded out*** *some houseplants.*
3 fix firmly; embed: *the posts should be firmly bedded in concrete.* ■ lay or arrange (something, especially stone) in a layer. ■ [no obj.] (**bed in**) settle down and become established: *a period of calm will allow the changes to bed in.*
– PHRASES **bed and board** Brit. lodging and food, typically forming part of someone's wages. **bed of nails** a board with nails pointing out of it, as lain on by fakirs and ascetics. ■ a problematic or uncomfortable situation. **a bed of roses** [usu. with negative] used in reference to a situation or activity that is comfortable or easy: *farming is no bed of roses.* **be brought to bed** archaic give birth to a child: *she was* ***brought to bed of*** *a daughter.* **get out of bed on the wrong side** (or US **get up on the wrong side of the bed**) start the day in a bad mood, which continues all day long. **in bed with** informal having sexual intercourse with. ■ in undesirably close association with: *he was in bed with the Mob.* **keep one's bed** archaic stay in bed because of illness. **one has made one's bed and must lie in** (or **on**) **it** one must accept the consequences of one's actions. **put someone to bed** prepare someone, typically a child, for rest in bed: *Clare put her to bed and gave her a mug of cocoa.* **put something to bed** informal make a newspaper or book ready for press. ■ deal with conclusively: *I hope that puts to bed all the nonsense* | *the university debate needs putting to bed.* **take to one's bed** stay in bed because of illness.
– ORIGIN Old English *bed*, *bedd* (noun), *beddian* (verb), of Germanic origin; related to Dutch *bed* and German *Bett*.

bedabble /bɪˈdab(ə)l/ ▶ **verb** [with obj.] archaic stain or splash with dirty liquid or blood.

bedad /bɪˈdad/ ▶ **exclamation** Irish used to express surprise or for emphasis.
– ORIGIN early 18th cent.: alteration of *by God*; compare with **BEGAD** and **GAD**[2].

bed and breakfast ▶ **noun** sleeping accommodation for a night and a meal in the morning, provided in guest houses and hotels. ■ a guest house.
▶ **verb** (**bed-and-breakfast**) [with obj.] Stock Exchange, Brit. sell (shares) and buy them back by agreement the next day.

bedaub ▶ **verb** [with obj.] literary smear or daub with a sticky substance.

bedazzle ▶ **verb** [with obj.] greatly impress (someone) with outstanding ability: *bedazzled by him, they offered him a post in Paris.* ■ make (someone) unable to think clearly.
– DERIVATIVES **bedazzlement** noun.

bed-blocking ▶ **noun** [mass noun] Brit. the long-term occupation of hospital beds, chiefly by elderly people, due to a shortage of suitable care elsewhere.
– DERIVATIVES **bed-blocker** noun.

bedbug ▶ **noun** a bloodsucking bug which is a parasite of birds and mammals. ● Family Cimicidae, suborder Heteroptera: *Cimex* and other genera, and many species, in particular *C. lectularius*, which comes out to feed on humans at night.

bedchamber ▶ **noun** archaic a bedroom.

bedclothes ▶ **plural noun** coverings for a bed, such as sheets and blankets.

bedcover ▶ **noun** Brit. **1** a bedspread.
2 (**bedcovers**) bedclothes.

beddable /ˈbɛdəb(ə)l/ ▶ **adjective** informal sexually attractive or available.

bedded ▶ **adjective 1** [in combination] (of a place) having a specified number or type of beds: *a twin-bedded room.*
2 Geology (of rock) deposited in layers of strata: *thinly bedded carbonate mudstones.*

bedder ▶ **noun 1** a plant suitable for use as a bedding plant.
2 Brit. informal a servant employed to clean rooms in Cambridge colleges.
3 [in combination] Brit. informal a house or flat with a specified number of bedrooms: *a studio or one-bedder.*

bedding ▶ **noun** [mass noun] **1** bedclothes. ■ straw or similar material for animals to sleep on.
2 a base or bottom layer: [as modifier] *a bedding course of sand.*
3 a display of bedding plants.
4 Geology the stratification or layering of rocks: [as modifier] *bedding planes.*

bedding plant ▶ **noun** a plant set into a garden bed or container when it is about to bloom, typically an annual used for display and discarded at the end of the season.

Bede, St /biːd/ (*c.*673–735), English monk, theologian, and historian; known as **the Venerable Bede**. Bede wrote *The Ecclesiastical History of the English People* (completed in 731), a primary source for early English history. Feast day, 27 May.

bedeck ▶ **verb** [with obj.] decorate: *he led us into a room bedecked with tinsel.*

bedeguar /ˈbɛdɪɡɑː/ (also **bedeguar gall**) ▶ **noun** a reddish moss-like growth on rose bushes, forming in response to the developing larvae of a gall wasp. Also called **ROBIN'S PINCUSHION**. ● The wasp is *Diplolepis rosae*, family Cynipidae.
– ORIGIN late Middle English: from French *bédégar*, from Persian *bād-āwar*, literally 'wind-brought'.

bedel /ˈbiːd(ə)l, bɪˈdɛl/ (also **bedell**) ▶ **noun** Brit. (in some British universities) an official with largely ceremonial duties.
– ORIGIN late Middle English: archaic spelling of **BEADLE**.

bedevil ▶ **verb** (**bedevils**, **bedevilling**, **bedevilled**; US **bedevils**, **bedeviling**, **bedeviled**) [with obj.] (of something bad) cause great and continual trouble to: *projects like this are bedevilled by a shortage of cash.* ■ (of a person) torment or harass: *he bedevilled them with petty practical jokes.*
– DERIVATIVES **bedevilment** noun.

bedew /bɪˈdjuː/ ▶ **verb** [with obj.] literary cover or sprinkle with drops of water or other liquid.

bedfellow ▶ **noun** a person who shares a bed with another. ■ a person or thing allied or closely connected with another: *big business and politics were inseparable bedfellows.*

Bedford a town in south central England, on the River Ouse, the county town of Bedfordshire; pop. 83,400 (est. 2009).

Bedford cord ▸ noun [mass noun] a tough woven fabric with prominent ridges, similar to corduroy.
– ORIGIN late 19th cent.: named after the town of BEDFORD.

Bedfordshire a county of south central England; county town, Bedford.

bedhead ▸ noun Brit. an upright board or panel fixed at the head of a bed.

bed-hop ▸ verb [no obj.] informal engage in successive casual sexual affairs.
– DERIVATIVES **bed-hopper** noun.

bedight /bɪˈdʌɪt/ ▸ adjective archaic adorned: *a Christmas pudding bedight with holly*.
– ORIGIN late Middle English: past participle of archaic *bedight* 'equip, array' (see BE-, DIGHT).

bedim ▸ verb (**bedims, bedimming, bedimmed**) [with obj.] literary cause to become dim.

bedizen /bɪˈdʌɪz(ə)n, -ˈdɪz-/ ▸ verb [with obj.] literary dress up or decorate gaudily: *a uniform bedizened with resplendent medals*.
– ORIGIN mid 17th cent.: from BE- (as an intensifier) + obsolete *dizen* 'deck out', probably of Dutch origin.

bedjacket ▸ noun a jacket worn for extra warmth when sitting up in bed.

bed joint ▸ noun a horizontal layer of mortar underneath a layer of masonry.

bedlam /ˈbɛdləm/ ▸ noun **1** [mass noun] a scene of uproar and confusion: *there was bedlam in the courtroom*.
2 archaic an asylum.
– ORIGIN late Middle English: early form of BETHLEHEM, referring to the hospital of St Mary of Bethlehem in London, used as an asylum for the insane.

bed linen ▸ noun [mass noun] sheets, pillowcases, and duvet covers.

Bedlington terrier /ˈbɛdlɪŋt(ə)n/ ▸ noun a terrier of a breed with a narrow head, long legs, and curly grey hair.
– ORIGIN mid 19th cent.: named after the village of *Bedlington* in northern England, where the breed originated.

bedload ▸ noun [mass noun] Geology the sediment transported by a river in the form of particles too heavy to be in suspension.

bedmaker ▸ noun Brit. a person employed to clean and tidy students' rooms in a college, especially at Cambridge.

bedmate ▸ noun a person, especially a sexual partner, with whom one shares a bed.

Bedouin /ˈbɛdʊɪn/ (also **Beduin**) ▸ noun (pl. **same**) a nomadic Arab of the desert.
▸ adjective relating to the Bedouin.
– ORIGIN from Old French *beduin*, based on Arabic *badawī*, (plural) *badawīn* 'dwellers in the desert', from *badw* 'desert'.

bedpan ▸ noun a receptacle used by a bedridden patient for urine and faeces.

bedplate ▸ noun a metal plate forming the base of a machine.

bedpost ▸ noun any of the four upright supports of a bedstead.
– PHRASES **between you and me and the bedpost** (or **the gatepost** or **the wall**) informal in strict confidence.

bedraggled ▸ adjective dishevelled: *we got there, tired and bedraggled*.
– ORIGIN early 18th cent.: from BE- 'thoroughly' + DRAGGLE + -ED^2.

bed rest ▸ noun [mass noun] confinement of an invalid to bed as part of treatment.

bedridden ▸ adjective confined to bed by sickness or old age.
– ORIGIN Middle English: formed irregularly from archaic *bedrid* 'bedridden person', from the base of the verb RIDE.

bedrock ▸ noun [mass noun] solid rock underlying loose deposits such as soil or alluvium. ■ the fundamental principles on which something is based: *honesty is the bedrock of a good relationship*.

bedroll ▸ noun chiefly N. Amer. a sleeping bag or other bedding rolled into a bundle.

bedroom ▸ noun **1** a room for sleeping in: [in combination] *a two-bedroom flat*. ■ [as modifier] relating to sexual relations: *bedroom secrets*.
2 [as modifier] N. Amer. denoting a small town or suburb whose residents commute to a nearby city: *a bedroom community*.
– DERIVATIVES **bedroomed** adjective [in combination] *a three-bedroomed house*.

Beds. ▸ abbreviation Bedfordshire.

bedside ▸ noun the space beside a bed (used especially with reference to an invalid's bed): *he was summoned to the bedside of a dying man* | [as modifier] *a bedside lamp*.
– PHRASES **bedside manner** a doctor's approach or attitude to a patient.

bedsit (also **bedsitter** or **bed-sitting room**) ▸ noun Brit. a one-roomed unit of accommodation typically consisting of combined bedroom and sitting room with cooking facilities.

bedskirt ▸ noun N. Amer. a valance for a bed.

bedsock ▸ noun chiefly Brit. each of a pair of thick socks worn for extra warmth in bed.

bedsore ▸ noun a sore developed by an invalid because of pressure caused by lying in bed in one position. Also called DECUBITUS ULCER.

bedspread ▸ noun a decorative cloth used to cover a bed when it is not in use.

bedstead ▸ noun the framework of a bed on which the mattress and bedclothes are placed.

bedstraw ▸ noun a herbaceous plant with small white or yellow flowers and whorls of slender leaves, formerly used for stuffing mattresses. ● Genus *Galium*, family Rubiaceae: several species.

bedtime ▸ noun [in sing.] the usual time when someone goes to bed: *it was well past her bedtime* | *a bedtime story*.

Bedu /ˈbɛduː/ ▸ noun & adjective another term for BEDOUIN.

Beduin ▸ noun & adjective variant spelling of BEDOUIN.

bed-warmer ▸ noun a device for warming a bed, typically a metal pan filled with warm coals.

bed-wetting ▸ noun [mass noun] involuntary urination during the night.
– DERIVATIVES **bed-wetter** noun.

bee ▸ noun **1** (also **honeybee** or **hive bee**) a stinging winged insect which collects nectar and pollen, produces wax and honey, and lives in large communities. ● Four species in the genus *Apis*, family Apidae, in particular the widespread *A. mellifera*.
2 an insect of a large group to which the honeybee belongs, including many solitary as well as social kinds. ● Superfamily Apoidea, order Hymenoptera: several families, often now placed in the single family Apidae.
3 [with modifier] a meeting for communal work or amusement: *a sewing bee*.
– PHRASES **the bee's knees** informal an outstandingly good person or thing. [first used to denote something small and insignificant, transferred to the opposite sense in US slang.] **have a bee in one's bonnet** informal be preoccupied or obsessed with something.
– ORIGIN Old English *bēo*, of Germanic origin; related to Dutch *bij* and German dialect *Beie*.

Beeb Brit. informal name for the BBC.

bee balm ▸ noun another term for SWEET BERGAMOT (see BERGAMOT^1).

bee beetle ▸ noun a hairy yellowish chafer with broad black stripes, which flies by day and is typically seen on flowers. ● Genus *Trichius*, family Scarabaeidae: several species, in particular *T. fasciatus*.

bee bread ▸ noun [mass noun] honey or pollen used as food by bees.

beech ▸ noun (also **beech tree**) a large tree with smooth grey bark, glossy leaves, and hard, pale fine-grained timber. ● Genera *Fagus* (of the northern temperate zone) and *Notofagus* (the **southern beeches**, of Australasia and South America), family Fagaceae: many species.
■ (also **beechwood**) [mass noun] the hard, pale fine-grained timber of the beech.
– ORIGIN Old English *bēce*, of Germanic origin; related to Latin *fagus* 'beech', Greek *phagos* 'edible oak'.

Beecham, Sir Thomas (1879–1961), English conductor and impresario, founder of the London Philharmonic (1932) and the Royal Philharmonic (1947). He did much to stimulate interest in new or neglected composers such as Sibelius, Delius, and Richard Strauss.

Beecher, Henry Ward (1813–87), American Congregationalist clergyman, orator, and writer. He became famous as an orator attacking political corruption and slavery.

beech fern ▸ noun a fern with triangular, deeply lobed fronds, found in moist woodland habitats and beside streams in Eurasia and North America.
● Genus *Phegopteris*, family Thelypteridaceae.

Beeching, Richard, Baron (1913–85), English businessman and engineer. As Chairman of the British Railways Board (1963–5) he was responsible for the closure of a substantial proportion of the British rail network.

beech marten ▸ noun another term for STONE MARTEN.

beechmast ▸ noun [mass noun] the angular brown nuts of the beech tree, pairs of which are enclosed in a prickly case.
– ORIGIN late 16th cent.: from BEECH + MAST^2.

beechnut ▸ noun the small angular brown fruit of the beech tree, pairs of which are enclosed in a prickly case.

bee dance ▸ noun another term for WAGGLE DANCE.

beedi ▸ noun (pl. **beedis**) variant spelling of BIDI.

bee-eater ▸ noun a brightly coloured insectivorous bird with a large head and a long downcurved bill, typically having long central tail feathers. ● Family Meropidae: three genera, in particular *Merops*, and including the **European bee-eater** (*M. apiaster*).

beef ▸ noun **1** [mass noun] the flesh of a cow, bull, or ox, used as food. ■ [count noun] (pl. **beeves** /biːvz/ or US also **beefs**) Farming a cow, bull, or ox fattened for its meat.
2 [mass noun] informal flesh with well-developed muscle: *he needs a little more beef on his bones*. ■ strength or power: *he was brought in to give the team more beef*. ■ the substance of a matter: *it's more a sketch than a policy—where's the beef?*
3 (pl. **beefs**) informal a complaint or grievance: *he has a beef with education: it doesn't teach the basics of investing*.
4 US informal a criminal charge: *getting caught with pot in the sixties was a narco beef*.
▸ verb informal [no obj.] complain: *he was* ***beefing about*** *how the recession was killing the business*.
– PHRASAL VERBS **beef something up** give more substance or strength to something: *cost-cutting measures are planned to beef up performance*.
– ORIGIN Middle English: from Old French *boef*, from Latin *bos, bov-* 'ox'.

beefalo ▸ noun (pl. **same** or **beefaloes**) a hybrid animal of a cross between cattle and buffalo.
– ORIGIN 1970s: blend of BEEF and BUFFALO.

beefburger ▸ noun Brit. a flat round cake of minced beef, fried or grilled and typically eaten in a bun.

beefcake ▸ noun [mass noun] informal attractive men with well developed muscles.

beefeater ▸ noun a Yeoman Warder or Yeoman of the Guard in the Tower of London.
– ORIGIN early 17th cent. (originally a derogatory term for a well-fed servant): the current sense dates from the late 17th cent.

bee fly ▸ noun a squat, hairy bee-like fly that hovers to feed from flowers using its long tongue. Its larvae typically parasitize other insects, especially bees and wasps. ● Family Bombyliidae: many genera.

beefsteak ▸ noun a thick slice of lean beef, typically from the rump and eaten grilled or fried.

beefsteak fungus ▸ noun a reddish-brown bracket fungus which resembles raw beef and is sometimes considered edible, found in Eurasia and North America. ● *Fistulina hepatica*, family Fistulinaceae, class Hymenomycetes.

beef tea ▸ noun [mass noun] Brit. a drink made from stewed extract of beef, used as nourishment for invalids.

beef tomato (chiefly N. Amer. also **beefsteak tomato**) ▸ noun a tomato of an exceptionally large and firm variety.

beef Wellington ▸ noun [mass noun] a dish consisting of beef coated in pâté and wrapped in puff pastry.

beefwood ▸ noun a tropical hardwood tree with close-grained red timber. ● Species in several families, in particular *Casuarina equisetifolia* (family Casuarinaceae), of Australia and SE Asia.

beefy ▸ adjective (**beefier, beefiest**) **1** informal muscular or robust: *he shrugged his beefy shoulders*. ■ large and impressively powerful.
2 tasting like beef.
– DERIVATIVES **beefily** adverb, **beefiness** noun.

bee hawkmoth ▸ noun a small day-flying hawkmoth with partly transparent wings, resembling a bumblebee and hovering at flowers to feed. ● Genus *Hemaris*, family Sphingidae: several species.

B

beehive ▸ noun **1** a box-like or dome-shaped structure in which bees are kept. ■ [usu. as modifier] something having the domed shape of a traditional beehive: *a beehive hut*. ■ (**the Beehive**) another term for PRAESEPE.
2 a woman's domed and lacquered hairstyle popular in the 1960s.
– DERIVATIVES **beehived** adjective (sense 2).

Beehive State informal name for UTAH.

beekeeping ▸ noun [mass noun] the occupation of owning and breeding bees for their honey.
– DERIVATIVES **beekeeper** noun.

beeline ▸ noun a straight line between two places.
– PHRASES **make a beeline for** hurry directly to.
– ORIGIN early 19th cent.: with reference to the straight line supposedly taken instinctively by a bee when returning to the hive.

bee louse ▸ noun a minute fly which is a parasite of honeybees, the larvae feeding on wax and stored pollen. ● *Braula coeca*, family Braulidae.

Beelzebub /bɪˈɛlzɪbʌb/ a name for the Devil.
– ORIGIN from late Latin *Beëlzebub*, translating Hebrew *baʿal zĕbūb* 'lord of flies', the name of a Philistine god (2 Kings 1:2), and Greek *Beelzeboul* 'the Devil' (Matt. 12:24).

Beemer /ˈbiːmə/ (also **Beamer**) ▸ noun informal a car or motorcycle manufactured by the company BMW.
– ORIGIN 1980s (originally US): representing a pronunciation of the first two letters of *BMW* (*Bayerische Motoren Werke AG*) + -ER[1].

been past participle of BE.

bee orchid ▸ noun a European orchid with a flower that resembles a bee. ● *Ophrys apifera* and related species, family Orchidaceae.

beep ▸ noun a short, high-pitched sound emitted by electronic equipment or a vehicle horn.
▸ verb [no obj.] (of a horn or electronic device) produce a beep. ■ [with obj.] chiefly N. Amer. summon (someone) by means of a pager.
– ORIGIN 1920s: imitative.

beeper ▸ noun a device that emits short, high-pitched sounds as a signal.

beer ▸ noun [mass noun] an alcoholic drink made from yeast-fermented malt flavoured with hops: *a pint of beer* | [count noun] *he ordered a beer*.
– PHRASES **beer and skittles** [often with negative] Brit. amusement or enjoyment: *life isn't all beer and skittles*.
– ORIGIN Old English *bēor*, of West Germanic origin, based on monastic Latin *biber* 'a drink', from Latin *bibere* 'to drink'; related to Dutch *bier* and German *Bier*.

beer belly (also **beer gut**) ▸ noun informal a man's fat stomach caused by excessive consumption of beer.
– DERIVATIVES **beer-bellied** adjective.

Beerbohm /ˈbɪəbəʊm/, Max (1872–1956), English caricaturist, essayist, and critic; full name *Sir Henry Maximilian Beerbohm*. A central figure of the Aesthetic Movement, he is remembered chiefly for his novel, *Zuleika Dobson* (1911).

beer cellar ▸ noun **1** an underground room for storing beer.
2 a basement bar where beer is served.

Beerenauslese /ˈbɛːrən,aʊslɛːzə/ ▸ noun [mass noun] a white wine of German origin or style made from selected individual grapes picked later than the general harvest.
– ORIGIN German, from *Beeren* 'berries' + *aus* 'out' + *lese* 'picking'.

beer engine ▸ noun Brit. a machine that draws up beer from a barrel in a cellar.

beer garden ▸ noun a garden, typically one attached to a pub, where beer is served.

beer goggles ▸ plural noun informal used to refer to the supposed influence of alcohol on one's visual perception, whereby one is sexually attracted to people who would not otherwise be appealing.

beer gut ▸ noun another term for BEER BELLY.

beer hall ▸ noun a large room or building where beer is served. ■ (in black townships in South Africa) a state-run establishment selling beer.

beerhouse ▸ noun Brit. historical a public house licensed to sell beer but not spirits.

beer mat ▸ noun Brit. a small cardboard table mat for resting glasses on in a bar or pub.

beer money ▸ noun [mass noun] informal a small amount of money allowed or earned.
– ORIGIN early 19th cent.: from an allowance of money formerly made to servants instead of beer.

beer parlour ▸ noun Canadian a room in a hotel or tavern where beer is served.

Beersheba /,bɪəˈʃiːbə/ a town in southern Israel on the northern edge of the Negev desert; pop. 187,200 (est. 2008).

beer-swilling ▸ adjective drinking a large quantity of beer. ■ boorish or rowdy: *some beer-swilling yobs went on the rampage in Cranfield*.

beery ▸ adjective (**beerier**, **beeriest**) informal **1** influenced by the drinking of beer in large amounts: *many beery pledges were made*.
2 smelling or tasting of beer: *stale beery breath*.
– DERIVATIVES **beerily** adverb.

beestings ▸ plural noun [treated as sing.] the first milk produced by a cow or goat after giving birth.
– ORIGIN Old English *bӯsting*, of West Germanic origin; related to Dutch *biest* and German *Biest(milch)*.

bee-stung ▸ adjective informal (of a woman's lips) full, red, and pouting.

beeswax ▸ noun [mass noun] **1** the wax secreted by bees to make honeycombs and used to make wood polishes and candles.
2 N. Amer. informal a person's concern or business: *that's none of your beeswax*.
▸ verb [with obj.] (often as adj. **beeswaxed**) polish (furniture) with beeswax.

beeswing /ˈbiːzwɪŋ/ ▸ noun [mass noun] a filmy crust on old port.

beet ▸ noun a herbaceous plant widely cultivated as a source of food for humans and livestock, and for processing into sugar. Some varieties are grown for their leaves and some for their swollen nutritious root. ● *Beta vulgaris*, family Chenopodiaceae: several subspecies. ■ North American term for BEETROOT.
– ORIGIN Old English *bēte*, of West Germanic origin, from Latin *beta*, perhaps of Celtic origin; related to Dutch *beet* and German *Bete*.

Beethoven /ˈbeɪt,(h)əʊv(ə)n/, Ludwig van (1770–1827), German composer.

> Despite increasing deafness Beethoven was responsible for a prodigious output: nine symphonies, thirty-two piano sonatas, sixteen string quartets, the opera *Fidelio* (1814), and the Mass in D (the *Missa Solemnis*, 1823). In his Ninth Symphony (1824) he broke with precedent in the finale by introducing voices to sing Schiller's *Ode to Joy*. He is often seen as bridging the classical and romantic movements.

– DERIVATIVES **Beethovenian** /,beɪt(h)əʊˈviːnɪən/ adjective.

beetle[1] ▸ noun **1** an insect of a large order distinguished by having forewings that are typically modified into hard wing cases (elytra), which cover and protect the hindwings and abdomen. ● Order Coleoptera: see COLEOPTERA.
2 [mass noun] Brit. a dice game in which a picture of a beetle is drawn or assembled.
▸ verb [no obj., with adverbial of direction] informal make one's way hurriedly: *the tourist beetled off*.
– ORIGIN Old English *bitula*, *bitela* 'biter', from the base of *bītan* 'to bite'.

beetle[2] ▸ noun **1** a very heavy mallet, typically with a wooden head, used for ramming, crushing, etc.
2 a machine used for heightening the lustre of cloth by pressure from rollers.
▸ verb [with obj.] **1** ram or crush with a beetle.
2 finish (cloth) with a beetle.
– ORIGIN Old English *bētel*, of Germanic origin; related to BEAT.

beetle[3] ▸ verb [no obj.] (usu. as adj. **beetling**) (of a rock or a person's eyebrows) project or overhang.
▸ adjective [attrib.] (of a person's eyebrows) shaggy and projecting: *thick beetle brows*.
– DERIVATIVES **beetle-browed** adjective.
– ORIGIN mid 16th cent. (as an adjective): back-formation from *beetle-browed*, first recorded in Middle English. The verb was apparently used as a nonce word by Shakespeare and was later adopted by other writers.

beetle-crusher ▸ noun Brit. humorous a large boot, shoe, or foot.

beetling /ˈbiːtlɪŋ/ ▸ adjective [attrib.] (of a rock or a person's eyebrows) projecting or overhanging: *piercing eyes glittered beneath a great beetling brow*.

Beeton, Mrs Isabella Mary (1836–65), English writer on cookery, famous for her bestselling *Book of Cookery and Household Management* (1861).

beetroot ▸ noun chiefly Brit. **1** the edible dark-red spherical root of a kind of beet, eaten as a vegetable.
2 the variety of beet which produces this root. ● *Beta vulgaris* subsp. *vulgaris*, family Chenopodiaceae.

beeves plural form of BEEF (sense 1 of the noun).

beezer ▸ adjective Brit. informal, dated excellent: *a beezer time was had by all*.
– ORIGIN 1950s: from the earlier noun *beezer*, denoting something large or impressive, of unknown origin.

BEF ▸ abbreviation British Expeditionary Force.

befall ▸ verb (past **befell**; past participle **befallen**) [with obj.] literary (especially of something bad) happen to (someone): *a tragedy befell his daughter* | [no obj.] *she was to blame for anything that befell*.
– ORIGIN Old English *befeallan* 'to fall' (early use being chiefly figurative); related to German *befallen*.

befit ▸ verb (**befits**, **befitting**, **befitted**) [with obj.] be appropriate for; suit: *as befits a Quaker, he was a humane man*.

befitting ▸ adjective appropriate to the occasion: *a country which can run the prestigious tournament in a befitting manner*.
– DERIVATIVES **befittingly** adverb.

befog ▸ verb (**befogs**, **befogging**, **befogged**) [with obj.] make confused: *her brain was befogged with lack of sleep*.

befogged ▸ adjective incapable of clear thought; confused: *a thought swam through my befogged mind*.

befool ▸ verb [with obj.] archaic make a fool of.

before ▸ preposition, conjunction, & adverb **1** during the period of time preceding (a particular event or time): [as prep.] *she had to rest before dinner* | *the day before yesterday* | [as conjunction] *they lived rough for four days before they were arrested* | [as adv.] *his playing days had ended six years before* | *it's never happened to me before*.
2 in front of: [as prep.] *Matilda stood before her, panting* | [as adv.] archaic *trotting through the city with guards running before and behind*. ■ [prep.] in front of and required to answer to (a court of law, tribunal, or other authority): *he could be taken before a magistrate for punishment*.
3 in preference to; rather than: [as prep.] *a woman who placed duty before all else* | [as conjunction] *they would die before they would cooperate with each other*.
– ORIGIN Old English *beforan* (see BY, FORE), of Germanic origin; related to German *bevor*.

beforehand ▸ adverb before an action or event; in advance: *rooms must be booked beforehand*.
– PHRASES **be beforehand with** archaic anticipate or forestall.
– ORIGIN Middle English (originally as two words): from BEFORE + HAND; probably influenced by Old French *avant main*.

befoul ▸ verb [with obj.] make dirty; pollute: *the dangers of letting industry befoul the environment*.

befriend ▸ verb [with obj.] act as or become a friend to (someone), especially when they are in need of help or support: *he makes a point of befriending newcomers to Parliament*.

befuddle ▸ verb [with obj.] (usu. as adj. **befuddled**) cause to become unable to think clearly: *even in my befuddled state I could see that they meant trouble*.
– DERIVATIVES **befuddlement** noun.

befurred ▸ adjective dressed in or covered with furs.

beg ▸ verb (**begs**, **begging**, **begged**) **1** [reporting verb] ask someone earnestly or humbly for something: [with obj.] *he begged his fellow passengers for help* | [with obj. and infinitive] *she begged me to say nothing to her father* | [no obj.] *I must beg of you not to act impulsively*. ■ [with obj.] ask for (something) earnestly or humbly: *he begged their forgiveness*. ■ [with obj.] ask formally for (permission to do something): *I will now beg leave to make some observations* | [no obj., with infinitive] *I beg to second the motion*.
2 [no obj.] ask for food or money as charity: *they had to beg for food*. ■ [with obj.] acquire (something) from someone in this way: *a piece of bread which I begged from a farmer*. ■ (of a dog) sit up with the front paws raised expectantly in the hope of a reward.
– PHRASES **beg the question 1** (of a fact or action) raise a point that has not been dealt with; invite an obvious question. **2** assume the truth of an argument or proposition to be proved, without arguing it. **beg to differ** see DIFFER. **beg yours** Austral./NZ I beg your pardon. **go begging** (of an article) be available because unwanted by others. ■ (of an opportunity) fail to be taken.

– PHRASAL VERBS **beg off** withdraw from an undertaking: *I'd planned to take Christy to dinner, but I was in a mood, and I begged off.*
– ORIGIN Middle English: probably from Old English *bedecian*, of Germanic origin; related to **BID²**.

> **USAGE** The original meaning of the phrase **beg the question** belongs to the field of logic and is a translation of Latin *petitio principii*, literally meaning 'laying claim to a principle', i.e. assuming something that ought to be proved first, as in the following sentence: *by devoting such a large part of the budget for the fight against drug addiction to education, we are* ***begging the question*** *of its significance in the battle against drugs.* To some traditionalists this is still the only correct meaning. However, over the last 100 years or so another, more general use has arisen: 'invite an obvious question', as in *some definitions of mental illness* ***beg the question*** *of what constitutes normal behaviour.* This is by far the commonest use today and is the usual one in modern standard English.

begad /bɪˈgad/ ▸ **exclamation** archaic or Irish used to express surprise or for emphasis.
– ORIGIN late 16th cent.: altered form; compare with **BEDAD** and **GAD²**.

began past of **BEGIN**.

begat archaic past of **BEGET**.

beget ▸ **verb** (**begets**, **begetting**; past **begot**; past participle **begotten**) [with obj.] literary **1** (especially of a man) bring (a child) into existence by the process of reproduction: *they hoped that the King might beget an heir by his new queen.*
2 cause; bring about: *killings beget more killings.*
– DERIVATIVES **begetter** noun.
– ORIGIN Old English *begietan* 'get, obtain by effort' (see **BE-**, **GET**).

beggar ▸ **noun 1** a person, typically a homeless one, who lives by asking for money or food.
2 [with adj.] informal a person of a specified type, especially one to be envied or pitied: *poor little beggars.*
▸ **verb** [with obj.] reduce (someone) to poverty: *why should I beggar myself for you?*
– PHRASES **beggar belief** (or **description**) be too extraordinary to be believed or described. **beggars can't be choosers** proverb people with no other options must be content with what is offered. **set a beggar on horseback and he'll ride to the Devil** proverb someone unaccustomed to power or luxury will abuse or be corrupted by it.
– ORIGIN Middle English: from **BEG** + **-AR³**.

beggarly ▸ **adjective 1** pitifully or deplorably meagre or bad: *the stipend in 1522 was a beggarly 26 shillings.*
2 poverty-stricken; very poor.
– DERIVATIVES **beggarliness** noun.

beggar-my-neighbour ▸ **noun** [mass noun] a card game for two players in which the object is to acquire one's opponent's cards. Players alternately turn cards up and if an honour is revealed, the other player must find an honour within a specified number of turns or else forfeit the cards already played.
▸ **adjective** [attrib.] (especially of national policy) self-aggrandizing at the expense of competitors.

beggar's purse ▸ **noun** N. Amer. an appetizer consisting of a crêpe stuffed with a savoury filling, typically caviar and crème fraiche.

beggary ▸ **noun** [mass noun] a state of extreme poverty.

begging bowl ▸ **noun** a bowl held out by a beggar for food or donations. ▪ used in reference to an earnest appeal for financial help: *they went to the government with a begging bowl to seek cash to finance the scheme.*

begging letter ▸ **noun** a letter asking for a gift or a charitable donation.

Begin /ˈbeɪgɪn, ˈbɛgɪn/, Menachem (1913–92), Israeli statesman, Prime Minister 1977–83. His hard line on Arab–Israeli relations softened in a series of meetings with President Sadat of Egypt, which led to a peace treaty between the countries. Nobel Peace Prize (1978, shared with Sadat).

begin ▸ **verb** (**begins**, **beginning**; past **began**; past participle **begun**) **1** [with obj.] perform or undergo the first part of (an action or activity): *Peter had just begun a life sentence for murder* | [with infinitive or present participle] *it was beginning to snow* | [no obj.] *she* ***began by rewriting the syllabus.*** ▪ [no obj.] come into being or have its starting point at a certain time or place: *a new era had begun* | *the cycleway* ***begins at*** *Livingston village.* ▪ [no obj.] (of a person) hold a specified role before holding any other: *he* ***began as*** *a drummer.* ▪ [no obj.] (**begin with**) have as a first element: *words beginning with a vowel.* ▪ [no obj.] (**begin on/upon**) set to work at: *Picasso began on a great canvas.* ▪ [with direct speech] start speaking by saying: *'Mr Smith,' he began.* ▪ [no obj.] (**begin at**) (of an article) cost at least (a specified amount): *rooms begin at £139.*
2 [no obj., with infinitive] [with negative] informal not have any chance or likelihood of doing a specified thing: *I can't begin to tell you how much I hate that commercial.*
– PHRASES **to begin with** at first. ▪ used to introduce the first of several points.
– ORIGIN Old English *beginnan*, of Germanic origin; related to Dutch and German *beginnen*.

beginner ▸ **noun** a person just starting to learn a skill or take part in an activity.
– PHRASES **beginner's luck** good luck supposedly experienced by a beginner at a particular activity.

beginning ▸ **noun** the point in time or space at which something begins: *he left at the beginning of February* | *they had reached the beginning of the wood.* ▪ the first part or earliest stage of something: *the ending of one relationship and the beginning of another* | *she had the beginnings of a headache.* ▪ (**beginnings**) the background or origins of a person or organization: *he had risen from humble beginnings to great wealth.*
– PHRASES **the beginning of the end** the first sign of the failure or end of something.

begob /bɪˈgɒb/ ▸ **exclamation** Irish expressing amazement or emphasis.
– ORIGIN late 19th cent.: alteration of *by God!*; compare with **BEGAD**.

begone ▸ **exclamation** literary go away (as an expression of annoyance): *begone from my sight!*

begonia /bɪˈgəʊnɪə/ ▸ **noun** a herbaceous plant of warm climates, the flowers of which have brightly coloured sepals but no petals. Numerous cultivars are grown for their flowers or striking foliage.
• Genus *Begonia*, family Begoniaceae.
– ORIGIN modern Latin, named after Michel *Bégon* (1638–1710), the French amateur botanist who discovered the plant on the island of Santo Domingo and introduced it to Europe.

begorra /bɪˈgɒrə/ ▸ **exclamation** an exclamation of surprise traditionally attributed to the Irish.
– ORIGIN mid 19th cent.: alteration of *by God.*

begot past of **BEGET**.

begotten past participle of **BEGET**.

beg-pardon ▸ **noun** Austral./NZ informal an apology.

begrime ▸ **verb** [with obj.] (often as adj. **begrimed**) blacken with ingrained dirt.

begrudge ▸ **verb 1** [with two objs] envy (someone) the possession or enjoyment of (something): *she begrudged Martin his affluence.*
2 [with obj.] give reluctantly or resentfully: *nobody begrudges a single penny spent on health* | (as adj. **begrudging**) *begrudging admiration from a rival.*
– DERIVATIVES **begrudger** noun (chiefly Irish), **begrudgingly** adverb.

begrudgery ▸ **noun** [mass noun] chiefly Irish a bedgrudging attitude; envy: *their success should not be a matter of begrudgery.*

beguile ▸ **verb** [with obj.] **1** charm or enchant (someone), often in a deceptive way: *he beguiled the voters with his good looks.* ▪ trick (someone) into doing something: *they were* ***beguiled into*** *signing a peace treaty.*
2 literary help (time) pass pleasantly: *to beguile some of the time they went to the cinema.*
– DERIVATIVES **beguilement** noun, **beguiler** noun.
– ORIGIN Middle English (in the sense 'deceive, deprive of by fraud'): from **BE-** 'thoroughly' + obsolete *guile* 'to deceive' (see **GUILE**).

beguiling ▸ **adjective** charming or enchanting, often in a deceptive way: *a beguiling mixture of English, French and Italian.*
– DERIVATIVES **beguilingly** adverb [as submodifier] *the idea is beguilingly simple.*

beguine /beɪˈgiːn/ ▸ **noun** a popular dance of Caribbean origin, similar to the foxtrot.
– ORIGIN 1930s: from West Indian French, from French *béguin* 'infatuation'.

begum /ˈbeɪgəm/ ▸ **noun** Indian a Muslim woman of high rank. ▪ (**Begum**) the title of a married Muslim woman, equivalent to Mrs.
– ORIGIN from Urdu *begam*, from eastern Turkish *bigim* 'princess', feminine of *big* 'prince'.

begun past participle of **BEGIN**.

behalf ▸ **noun** (in phrase **on** (US also **in**) **behalf of** or **on someone's/something's behalf**) **1** in the interests of a person, group, or principle: *he campaigned on behalf of the wrongly convicted four.*
2 as a representative of: *he had to attend the funeral on Mama's behalf.*
3 on the part of; done by: *this wasn't simply a philanthropic gesture on his behalf.*
– ORIGIN Middle English: from a mixture of the earlier phrases *on his halve* and *bihalve him*, both meaning 'on his side' (see **BY**, **HALF**).

B

Behan /ˈbiːən/, Brendan (Francis) (1923–64), Irish dramatist and poet. A committed supporter of Irish nationalism, he is noted for the novel *Borstal Boy* (1958), which describes his punishment for involvement in terrorist activities, and the play *The Quare Fellow* (1956).

behave ▸ **verb** [no obj.] **1** [with adverbial] act or conduct oneself in a specified way, especially towards others: *he always behaved like a gentleman* | *it is not acceptable for a student to* ***behave*** *like that* ***towards*** *a teacher.* ▪ (of a machine or natural phenomenon) work or function in a specified way: *each car behaves differently.*
2 [often in imperative] (also **behave oneself**) conduct oneself in accordance with the accepted norms of a society or group: *'Just behave, Tom,' he said* | *they were expected to behave themselves.*
– ORIGIN late Middle English: from **BE-** 'thoroughly' + **HAVE** in the sense 'have or bear (oneself) in a particular way'.

behaved ▸ **adjective** [in combination or with submodifier] conducting oneself in a specified way: *a well-behaved child* | *some of the boys had been badly behaved.*

behaviour (US **behavior**) ▸ **noun** [mass noun] the way in which one acts or conducts oneself, especially towards others: *he will vouch for her good behaviour* | *his insulting* ***behaviour towards*** *me.* ▪ the way in which an animal or person behaves in response to a particular situation or stimulus: *the feeding behaviour of predators.* ▪ the way in which a machine or natural phenomenon works or functions: *the erratic behaviour of the old car.*
– PHRASES **be on one's best behaviour** behave well in a social situation or when being observed.
– ORIGIN late Middle English: from **BEHAVE**, on the pattern of *demeanour*, and influenced by obsolete *haviour* from **HAVE**.

behavioural (US **behavioral**) ▸ **adjective** involving, relating to, or emphasizing behaviour: *closely related species have similar behavioural patterns* | *a behavioural approach to children's language.*
– DERIVATIVES **behaviourally** adverb.

behaviouralism (US **behavioralism**) ▸ **noun** [mass noun] the methods and principles of the scientific study of animal (and human) behaviour. ▪ advocacy of or adherence to a behavioural approach to social phenomena.
– DERIVATIVES **behaviouralist** noun & adjective.

behavioural science ▸ **noun** [mass noun] the scientific study of human and animal behaviour.

behaviourism (US **behaviorism**) ▸ **noun** [mass noun] Psychology the theory that human and animal behaviour can be explained in terms of conditioning, without appeal to thoughts or feelings, and that psychological disorders are best treated by altering behaviour patterns.
– DERIVATIVES **behaviourist** noun & adjective, **behaviouristic** adjective.

behaviour therapy ▸ **noun** [mass noun] the treatment of neurotic symptoms by training the patient's reactions to stimuli.

behead ▸ **verb** cut off the head of (someone), especially as a form of execution.
– ORIGIN Old English *behēafdian*; from **BE-** 'off' (expressing removal) + *hēafod* (see **HEAD**).

beheld past and past participle of **BEHOLD**.

behemoth /bɪˈhiːmɒθ, ˈbiːhɪˌməʊθ/ ▸ **noun** a huge or monstrous creature. ▪ something enormous, especially a large and powerful organization.
– ORIGIN late Middle English: from Hebrew *bĕhēmōṯ*, intensive plural of *bĕhēmāh* 'beast'.

behest /bɪˈhɛst/ ▸ **noun** literary a person's orders or command: *they had assembled* ***at his behest.***
– ORIGIN Old English *behǣs* 'a vow', from a Germanic base meaning 'bid'; related to **HIGHT**.

behind ▸ **preposition 1** at or to the far side of (something), typically so as to be hidden by it: *the recording machinery was kept behind screens* | *the sun came out from behind a cloud.* ▪ underlying (something) but not apparent to the observer: *the agony behind his decision to retire.*
2 following or further back than (another member of a moving group): *we were stuck behind a slow-moving*

B

tractor. ■ at the back of (someone), after they have passed through a door: *she ran out of the room, slamming the door behind her.*
3 in support of or giving guidance to (someone else): *whatever you decide to do, I'll be behind you | the power behind the throne.* ■ controlling or responsible for (an event or plan): *the chances were that he was behind the death of the girl | the meticulous organization behind the coup.*
4 after the departure or death of (someone): *he left behind him a manuscript which was subsequently published.*
5 less advanced than (someone or something) in achievement or development: *the government admitted it is ten years behind the West in PC technology.*
6 having a lower score than (another competitor): *Woosnam moved to ten under par, five shots behind Fred Couples.*
▸ **adverb 1** at or to the far side of something: *Campbell grabbed him from behind.*
2 in a particular place after leaving or after others have moved on: *don't leave me behind.*
3 further back than other members of a moving group: *Ben led the way, with Joe a short distance behind.*
4 (in a contest or match) having a score lower than that of the opposing team: *England were still 382 runs behind.*
5 late in accomplishing a task: *I'm getting **behind with** my work.* ■ in arrears: *she was **behind with** her rent.*
▸ **noun 1** informal a person's buttocks: *she slid inelegantly down a few steps on her behind.*
2 Australian Rules a kick that sends the ball over a behind line, or a touch that sends it between the inner posts, scoring one point.
– ORIGIN Old English *behindan, bihindan*, from *bi* 'by' + *hindan* 'from behind'.

behindhand ▸ **adjective** [predic.] late or slow in doing something: *the Yoruba have not been **behindhand in** economic activity.* ■ archaic unaware of recent events: *you are miserably behindhand—Mr Cole gave me a hint of it six weeks ago.*
– ORIGIN mid 16th cent.: from BEHIND + HAND, on the pattern of *beforehand*.

behind line ▸ **noun** Australian Rules the line between an inner and outer goalpost.

Behn /beɪn, bɛn/, Aphra (1640–89), English novelist and dramatist, regarded as the first professional woman writer in England. Notable works: *The Rover* (comic play, 1678) and *Oroonoko, or the History of the Royal Slave* (novel, 1688).

behold ▸ **verb** (past and past participle **beheld**) [with obj.] [often in imperative] archaic or literary see or observe (someone or something, especially of remarkable or impressive nature): *behold your lord and prince! | the botanical gardens were a wonder **to behold**.*
– DERIVATIVES **beholder** noun.
– ORIGIN Old English *bihaldan*, from *bi-* 'thoroughly' + *haldan* 'to hold'. Parallel Germanic words have the sense 'maintain, retain'; the notion of 'looking' is found only in English.

beholden ▸ **adjective** [predic.] owing thanks or having a duty to someone in return for help or a service: *I don't like to be **beholden to** anybody.*
– ORIGIN late Middle English: archaic past participle of BEHOLD, in the otherwise unrecorded sense 'bound'.

behoof /bɪˈhuːf/ ▸ **noun** [mass noun] archaic benefit or advantage: *to make laws **for the behoof of** the colony.*
– ORIGIN Old English *behōf*, of West Germanic origin; related to Dutch *behoef* and German *Behuf*, also to HEAVE.

behove /bɪˈhəʊv/ (US **behoove** /-ˈhuːv/) ▸ **verb** [with obj.] (**it behoves someone to do something**) formal it is a duty or responsibility for someone to do something: *it behoves the House to assure itself that there is no conceivable alternative.* ■ [with negative] it is appropriate or suitable; it befits: ***it ill behoves** Opposition Members to decry the sale of arms to friendly countries.*
– ORIGIN Old English *behōfian*, from *behōf* (see BEHOOF).

Behrens /ˈbɛːr(ə)nz/, Peter (1868–1940), German architect and designer. He trained Walter Gropius and Le Corbusier.

Beiderbecke /ˈbʌɪdəbɛk/, Bix (1903–31), American jazz musician and composer; born *Leon Bismarck Beiderbecke*. A self-taught cornetist and pianist, he was one of a handful of white musicians who profoundly influenced the development of jazz.

beige ▸ **noun** [mass noun] a pale sandy fawn colour: *tones of beige and green* | [as modifier] *a beige raincoat.*
– ORIGIN mid 19th cent. (denoting a usually undyed and unbleached woollen fabric of this colour): from French, of unknown ultimate origin.

beignet /ˈbɛnjeɪ/ ▸ **noun** chiefly N. Amer. **1** a fritter.
2 a square of fried dough eaten hot sprinkled with icing sugar.
– ORIGIN French, from archaic *buyne* 'hump, bump'.

Beijing /beɪˈdʒɪŋ/ (also **Peking**) the capital of China, in the north-east of the country; pop. 8,580,400 (est. 2006). Beijing became the country's capital in 1421, at the start of the Ming period, and survived as the capital of the Republic of China after the revolution of 1912.

being ▸ **noun 1** [mass noun] existence: *the railway **brought** many towns **into being** | the single market **came into being** in 1993.* ■ being alive; living: *holism promotes a unified way of being.*
2 [in sing.] the nature or essence of a person: *sometimes one aspect of our being has been developed at the expense of the others.*
3 a real or imaginary living creature or entity, especially an intelligent one: *alien beings | a rational being.*

Beira /ˈbʌɪrə/ a port on the coast of Mozambique, capital of Sofala province; pop. 436,240 (2007).

beira /ˈbeɪrə/ (also **beira antelope**) ▸ **noun** a rare antelope found in Somalia and Ethiopia. ● *Dorcatragus megalotis*, family Bovidae.
– ORIGIN a local name.

Beirut /beɪˈruːt/ the capital and chief port of Lebanon; pop. 2,006,500 (est. 2009). The city was badly damaged during the Lebanese civil war of 1975–89.

beisa /ˈbeɪzə/ (also **beisa oryx**) ▸ **noun** a gemsbok of a race that is native to the Horn of Africa. ● *Oryx gazella beisa*, family Bovidae.
– ORIGIN mid 19th cent.: from Amharic.

Beit Din ▸ **noun** variant form of BETH DIN.

Beja /ˈbɛdʒə/ ▸ **noun** (pl. **same**) **1** a member of a nomadic people living between the Nile and the Red Sea.
2 [mass noun] the Cushitic language of the Beja, with about 1 million speakers.
▸ **adjective** relating to the Beja or their language.

bejabers /bɪˈdʒeɪbəz/ (also **bejabbers** /-ˈdʒabəz/) ▸ **exclamation** another way of saying BEJESUS.
– ORIGIN early 19th cent.: alteration of *by Jesus*.

Béjart /beɪˈʒɑː/, French /beʒaʀ/, Maurice (1927–2007), French choreographer; born *Maurice Jean Berger*. He is chiefly identified with The Ballet of the 20th Century, the company which he founded in Brussels in 1959. His choreography is noted for its fusion of classic and modern dance.

bejesus /bɪˈdʒiːzəs/ (also **bejeezus**) ▸ **exclamation** Irish informal used to express surprise or for emphasis.
– PHRASES **beat the bejesus out of** hit (someone) very hard or for a long time. **scare the bejesus out of** frighten (someone) very much.

bejewelled (US **bejeweled**) ▸ **adjective** adorned with jewels.

Bekaa /bɪˈkɑː/ (also **el-Beqa'a**) a fertile valley in central Lebanon between the Lebanon and Anti-Lebanon Mountains.

Bel /bɛl/ another name for BAAL.

bel ▸ **noun** a unit used in the comparison of power levels in electrical communication or of intensities of sound, corresponding to an intensity ratio of 10 to 1. See also DECIBEL.
– ORIGIN 1920s: from the name of A. G. *Bell* (see BELL[1]).

belabour (US **belabor**) ▸ **verb** [with obj.] **1** attack (someone) physically or verbally: *Bernard was belabouring Jed with his fists.*
2 argue or discuss (a subject) in excessive detail: *there is no need to belabour the point.*
– ORIGIN late Middle English: from BE- + the verb LABOUR.

Bel and the Dragon a book of the Apocrypha containing additional stories of Daniel, concerned mainly with his refusal to worship Bel and his slaying of a dragon.

Belarus /ˌbɛləˈruːs/ a country in eastern Europe; pop. 9,648,500 (est. 2009); official language, Belorussian; capital, Minsk. Formerly called BELORUSSIA, WHITE RUSSIA.

> Successively part of the grand duchy of Lithuania, Poland, and the Russian empire, the country became a republic of the Soviet Union in 1921. Belarus gained independence as a member of the Commonwealth of Independent States in 1991 but in 1996 signed a treaty with Russia that established a Community of Sovereign Republics.

– DERIVATIVES **Belarusian** noun & adjective.

belated ▸ **adjective** coming or happening later than should have been the case: *a belated apology.*
– DERIVATIVES **belatedly** adverb, **belatedness** noun.
– ORIGIN early 17th cent. (in the sense 'overtaken by darkness'): past participle of obsolete *belate* 'delay' (see BE-, LATE).

Belau /bəˈlaʊ/ variant spelling of PALAU.

belay /ˈbiːleɪ, bɪˈleɪ/ ▸ **verb** [with obj.] **1** fix (a running rope) round a cleat, rock, pin, or other object, to secure it. ■ secure (a rock climber) in this way: *he belayed his partner across the ice.*
2 [usu. in imperative] Nautical slang stop; desist from: *'Belay that, mister. Man your post.'*
▸ **noun 1** an act of belaying.
2 a spike of rock or other object used for belaying.
– DERIVATIVES **belayer** noun.
– ORIGIN mid 16th cent. (originally in nautical use): from BE- + LAY[1], on the pattern of Dutch *beleggen*.

belaying pin ▸ **noun** a fixed pin used on board ship and in rock climbing to secure a rope which is fastened around it.

bel canto /bɛl ˈkantəʊ/ ▸ **noun** [mass noun] a lyrical style of operatic singing using a full, rich, broad tone and smooth phrasing.
– ORIGIN late 19th cent.: Italian, literally 'fine song'.

belch ▸ **verb 1** [no obj.] emit wind noisily from the stomach through the mouth.
2 [with obj.] (especially of a chimney) send out large amounts of (smoke or flames): *a factory chimney **belches out** smoke.* ■ [no obj.] (**belch from**) (of smoke or flames) pour out from (a chimney or other opening): *flames belch from the wreckage.*
▸ **noun** an act of belching.
– ORIGIN Old English *belcettan*, probably imitative.

beldam /ˈbɛldəm/ (also **beldame**) ▸ **noun** archaic an old woman. ■ a malicious or loathsome old woman.
– ORIGIN late Middle English (originally in the sense 'grandmother'): from Old French *bel* 'beautiful' + DAM[2].

beleaguer ▸ **verb** [with obj.] (usu. as adj. **beleaguered**) lay siege to: *he led a relief force to the aid of the beleaguered city.* ■ put in a very difficult situation: *the board is supporting the beleaguered director.*
– ORIGIN late 16th cent.: from Dutch *belegeren* 'camp round', from *be-* '(all) about' + *leger* 'a camp'.

Belém /bɛˈlɛm/ a city and port of northern Brazil, at the mouth of the Amazon, capital of the state of Pará; pop. 1,408,847 (2007). It is the country's chief commercial centre.

belemnite /ˈbɛləmnʌɪt/ ▸ **noun** an extinct cephalopod mollusc with a bullet-shaped internal shell that is typically found as a fossil in marine deposits of the Jurassic and Cretaceous periods. ● Order Belemnoidea, class Cephalopoda: many genera.
– ORIGIN early 17th cent.: from modern Latin *belemnites*, based on Greek *belemnon* 'dart'.

bel esprit /ˌbɛl ɛˈspriː/, French /bɛl ɛspʀi/ ▸ **noun** (pl. **beaux esprits** /ˌbəʊz ɛˈspriː/, French /bəʊz ɛspʀi/) archaic a witty person.
– ORIGIN French, literally 'fine mind'.

Belfast /ˈbɛlfɑːst/ the capital and chief port of Northern Ireland; pop. 260,700 (est. 2009). The city suffered damage and population decline from the early 1970s as a result of sectarian violence by the IRA and Loyalist paramilitary groups.

Belfast sink ▸ **noun** a type of deep rectangular kitchen sink, traditionally made of glazed white porcelain.

belfry ▸ **noun** (pl. **belfries**) the part of a bell tower or steeple in which bells are housed. ■ a bell tower or steeple housing bells.
– ORIGIN Middle English *berfrey*, from Old French *berfrei*, later *belfrei*, of West Germanic origin. The change in the first syllable was due to association with BELL[1].

Belgae /ˈbɛldʒiː, ˈbɛlgʌɪ/ ▸ **plural noun** an ancient Celtic people inhabiting Gaul north of the Seine and Marne Rivers.
– ORIGIN from Latin.

Belgaum /ˈbɛlgaʊm/ an industrial city in western India, in the state of Karnataka; pop. 458,200 (est. 2009).

Belgian ▶ adjective relating to Belgium.
▶ noun a native or inhabitant of Belgium, or a person of Belgian descent.

Belgian Blue ▶ noun a heavily muscled animal of a breed of cattle kept for its meat.

Belgian Congo former name (1908–60) for the Democratic Republic of the Congo (see **CONGO, DEMOCRATIC REPUBLIC OF THE**).

Belgian endive ▶ noun another term for **ENDIVE** (sense 2).

Belgian hare ▶ noun a rabbit of a dark red long-eared domestic breed.

Belgian sheepdog ▶ noun a dog of a medium-sized breed, similar in appearance to an Alsatian.

Belgian waffle ▶ noun N. Amer. a waffle with large, deep indentations.

Belgic /ˈbɛldʒɪk/ ▶ adjective relating to the Belgae.

Belgium a low-lying country in western Europe on the south shore of the North Sea and English Channel; pop. 10,414,300 (est. 2009); official languages, Flemish and French; capital, Brussels. Flemish name **België** /ˈbɛlxiːə/, French name **Belgique** /bɛlʒik/.

> Belgium became independent from the Netherlands after a nationalist revolt in 1830. Occupied and devastated during both world wars, Belgium formed the Benelux Customs Union with the Netherlands and Luxembourg in 1948 and became a founder member of the EEC. Flemish is spoken mainly in the north of the country, and French and Walloon in the south.

– ORIGIN Latin, from **BELGAE**.

Belgorod /ˈbɛlgərɒd/ an industrial city in southern Russia, on the Donets River close to the border with Ukraine; pop. 353,000 (est. 2008).

Belgrade /bɛlˈgreɪd/ the capital of Serbia and formerly of Yugoslavia, situated on the River Danube; pop. 1,119,000 (est. 2008). Serbian name **BEOGRAD**.

Belial /ˈbiːlɪəl/ a name for the Devil.
– ORIGIN from Hebrew *bĕliyya'al* 'worthlessness'.

belie ▶ verb (**belies, belying, belied**) [with obj.] **1** (of an appearance) fail to give a true impression of (something): *his lively, alert manner belied his years.*
2 fail to fulfil or justify (a claim or expectation): *the quality of the music seems to belie the criticism.*
– ORIGIN Old English *belēogan* 'deceive by lying', from **BE-** 'about' + *lēogan* 'to lie'. Current senses date from the 17th cent.

belief ▶ noun **1** an acceptance that something exists or is true, especially one without proof: *his* ***belief in*** *extraterrestrial life* | [with clause] *a belief that climate can be modified beneficially.* ■ something one accepts as true or real; a firmly held opinion: *we're prepared to fight for our beliefs* | [mass noun] *contrary to popular belief existing safety regulations were adequate.* ■ a religious conviction: *Christian beliefs* | [mass noun] *the medieval system of fervent religious belief.*
2 (**belief in**) trust, faith, or confidence in (someone or something): *a belief in democratic politics.*
– PHRASES **be of the belief that** hold the opinion that; think: *I am firmly of the belief that we need to improve our product.* **beyond belief** astonishingly great, good, or bad; incredible: *riches beyond belief.* **in the belief that** thinking or believing that: *he took the property in the belief that he had consent.* **to the best of my belief** in my genuine opinion; as far as I know.
– ORIGIN Middle English: alteration of Old English *gelēafa*; compare with **BELIEVE**.

believable ▶ adjective able to be believed; credible: *she felt that Dawn's story was not quite believable.* ■ (of a fictional character or situation) convincing or realistic.
– DERIVATIVES **believability** noun, **believably** adverb.

believe ▶ verb [with obj.] **1** accept that (something) is true, especially without proof: *the superintendent believed Lancaster's story* | [with clause] *some 23 per cent believe that smoking keeps down weight.* ■ accept the statement of (someone) as true: *he didn't believe her.* ■ [no obj.] have religious faith. ■ (**believe something of**) feel sure that (someone) is capable of doing something: *I wouldn't have believed it of Lavinia—what an extraordinary woman!*
2 [with clause] hold (something) as an opinion; think: *I believe we've already met* | (**believe someone/thing to be**) *four men were believed to be trapped.*
– PHRASES **believe it or not** used to concede that a statement is surprising: *believe it or not, I was considered quite bright in those days.* **believe me** (or **believe you me**) used to emphasize the truth of a statement: *believe me, it is well worth the effort.* **be unable to** (or **be hardly able to**) **believe one's luck** be amazed by how lucky one is on a particular occasion. **be unable to believe one's eyes** (or **ears**) be amazed by what one sees or hears. **don't you believe it!** used to express disbelief in the truth of a statement. **would you believe** (**it**)**?** used to express amazement about something: *they're still arguing, would you believe it?*
– PHRASAL VERBS **believe in 1** have faith in the truth or existence of: *those who believe in God.* **2** be of the opinion that (something) is right or acceptable: *I don't believe in censorship of the arts.* **3** have confidence in (a person or a course of action): *he had finally begun to believe in her.*
– ORIGIN late Old English *belȳfan, belēfan*, alteration of *gelēfan*, of Germanic origin; related to Dutch *geloven* and German *glauben*, also to **LIEF**.

believer ▶ noun **1** a person who believes in the truth or existence of something: [with clause] *a firm believer that party politics has no place in local government.* ■ a person who believes that a specified thing is right, effective, or acceptable: *I'm a great* ***believer in*** *community policing.*
2 an adherent of a particular religion; someone with religious faith.

Belisha beacon /bəˈliːʃə/ ▶ noun (in the UK) an orange ball containing a flashing light, mounted on a striped post on the pavement at each end of a zebra crossing.
– ORIGIN 1930s: named after Leslie Hore-*Belisha* (1893–1957), British politician, Minister of Transport when the beacons were introduced.

belittle ▶ verb [with obj.] dismiss (someone or something) as unimportant: *she belittled Amy's riding skills whenever she could* | (as adj. **belittling**) *his cruel, belittling remarks.*
– DERIVATIVES **belittlement** noun, **belittler** noun.

Belitung /bɪˈliːtʊŋ/ an Indonesian island in the Java Sea, between Borneo and Sumatra. Former name **BILLITON**.

Belize /bɛˈliːz/ a country on the Caribbean coast of Central America; pop. 307,900 (est. 2009); languages, English (official), Creole, Spanish; capital, Belmopan. Former name (until 1973) **BRITISH HONDURAS**.

> Proclaimed as a British Crown Colony in 1862, Belize became an independent Commonwealth state in 1981. Guatemala, which bounds it on the west and south, has always claimed the territory on the basis of old Spanish treaties, although in 1992 it agreed to recognize the existence of Belize.

– DERIVATIVES **Belizean** (also **Belizian**) adjective & noun.
– ORIGIN named after a river with a Mayan name meaning 'muddy water'.

Belize City the principal seaport and former capital (until 1970) of Belize; pop. 65,200 (est. 2008).

Bell[1], Alexander Graham (1847–1922), Scottish-born American scientist. He invented a method for transmitting speech electrically and gave the first public demonstration of the telephone in 1876; he founded the Bell Telephone Company the following year.

Bell[2], Currer, Ellis, and Acton, the pseudonyms used by Charlotte, Emily, and Anne Brontë.

Bell[3], Gertrude (Margaret Lowthian) (1868–1926), English archaeologist, traveller, and supporter of Arab independence.

Bell[4], Vanessa (1879–1961), English painter and designer; born *Vanessa Stephen.* Together with her sister Virginia Woolf she was a prominent member of the Bloomsbury Group.

bell[1] ▶ noun **1** a hollow metal object, typically in the shape of a deep inverted cup widening at the lip, that sounds a clear musical note when struck, especially by means of a clapper inside. ■ a device that includes or sounds like a bell, used to give a signal or warning: *a bicycle bell.* ■ (**the bell**) (in boxing and other sports) a bell rung to mark the start or end of a round: *they were dragged off each other at the final bell.*
2 a bell-shaped object or part, in particular: ■ the end of a trumpet. ■ the corolla of a bell-shaped flower.
3 (**bells**) a musical instrument consisting of a set of metal tubes of different lengths, suspended in a frame and played by being struck with a hammer. Also called **TUBULAR BELLS**.
4 Nautical (preceded by a numeral) the time as indicated every half hour of a watch by the striking of the ship's bell one to eight times: *at five bells in the forenoon of June 11.*
▶ verb **1** [with obj.] provide with a bell or bells: (as adj. **belled**) *animals in gaudy belled harnesses.*
2 [no obj.] make a ringing sound likened to that of a bell: *the organ was belling away.* ■ [with obj.] Brit. informal telephone (someone).
3 [no obj.] spread outwards like the lip of a bell: *her shirt belled out behind.*
– PHRASES **bell the cat** take the danger of a shared enterprise upon oneself. [an allusion to a fable in which the mice (or rats) suggest hanging a bell around the cat's neck to have warning of its approach.] **bells and whistles** informal attractive additional features or trimmings. [an allusion to the various bells and whistles of old fairground organs.] **be saved by the bell** (in boxing and other sports) be saved from being counted out by the ringing of the bell at the end of a round. ■ escape from a difficult situation narrowly or by an unexpected intervention. (**as**) **clear** (or **sound**) **as a bell** perfectly clear (or sound). **give someone a bell** Brit. informal telephone someone. **ring a bell** informal sound vaguely familiar: *the name rings a bell.* **with bells on** N. Amer. informal enthusiastically: *everybody's waiting for you with bells on.*
– ORIGIN Old English *belle*, of Germanic origin; related to Dutch *bel*, and perhaps to **BELL**[2].

bell[2] ▶ noun the cry of a stag or buck at rutting time.
▶ verb [no obj.] (of a stag or buck) make this cry.
– ORIGIN Old English *bellan* 'to bellow', of Germanic origin; related to German *bellen* 'to bark, bray', and perhaps also to **BELL**[1].

belladonna /ˌbɛləˈdɒnə/ ▶ noun deadly nightshade. ■ [mass noun] a drug prepared from the leaves and root of deadly nightshade, containing atropine.
– ORIGIN mid 18th cent.: from modern Latin, from Italian *bella donna* 'fair lady', perhaps from the use of its juice to add brilliance to the eyes by dilating the pupils.

belladonna lily ▶ noun a South African amaryllis.

bellbird ▶ noun **1** a tropical American bird of the cotinga family, with a loud explosive call. ● Genus *Procnias*, family Cotingidae: four species.
2 any of a number of Australasian songbirds with a ringing call. ● (**New Zealand bellbird**) a New Zealand honeyeater (*Anthornis melanura*, family Meliphagidae). ● (**crested bellbird**) an Australian whistler (*Oreoica gutturalis*, family Pachycephalidae). ● the bell miner. See **MINER**[2].

bell-bottoms ▶ plural noun trousers with a marked flare below the knee: (as modifier **bell-bottom**) *bell-bottom trousers.*
– DERIVATIVES **bell-bottomed** adjective.

bellboy ▶ noun chiefly N. Amer. an attendant in a hotel who performs services such as carrying guests' luggage.

bell buoy ▶ noun a buoy equipped with a bell rung by the motion of the sea, warning shipping of shallow waters.

bell captain ▶ noun N. Amer. the supervisor of a group of bellboys.

bell crank (also **bell-crank lever**) ▶ noun a lever with two arms which have a common fulcrum at their junction.

bell curve ▶ noun Mathematics a graph of a normal (Gaussian) distribution, with a large rounded peak tapering away at each end.

belle /bɛl/ ▶ noun a beautiful girl or woman, especially the most beautiful at a particular event: *the belle of the ball.*
– ORIGIN early 17th cent.: from French, feminine of *beau*, from Latin *bella*, feminine of *bellus* 'beautiful'.

belle époque /ˌbɛl eɪˈpɒk/, French /bɛl epɔk/ ▶ noun the period of settled and comfortable life preceding the First World War: [as modifier] *a romantic, belle-époque replica of a Paris bistro.*
– ORIGIN French, 'fine period'.

Bellerophon /bɪˈlɛrəf(ə)n/ Greek Mythology a hero who slew the monster Chimera with the help of the winged horse Pegasus.

belles-lettres /bɛlˈlɛtr(ə)/, French /bɛllɛtʀ/ ▶ plural noun [also treated as sing.] essays, particularly on literary and artistic criticism, written and read primarily for their aesthetic effect.
– DERIVATIVES **belletrism** /bɛlˈlɛtrɪz(ə)m/ noun, **belletrist** noun, **belletristic** adjective.
– ORIGIN mid 17th cent.: from French, literally 'fine letters'.

bellflower ▶ noun a plant with bell-shaped flowers that are typically blue, purple, or white, many kinds being cultivated as ornamentals. ● Genus *Campanula*,

B

family Campanulaceae (the **bellflower family**): many species, including the Eurasian **clustered bellflower** (*C. glomerata*) and the harebell.

bell glass ▸ noun a bell-shaped glass cover used, especially formerly, as a cloche.

B

bell heather ▸ noun a common European heather with relatively large purplish-red flowers. ● *Erica cinerea*, family Ericaceae.

bellhop ▸ noun N. Amer. another term for **BELLBOY**.

bellicose /ˈbɛlɪkəʊs/ ▸ adjective demonstrating aggression and willingness to fight: *a mood of bellicose jingoism.*
– DERIVATIVES **bellicosity** /-ˈkɒsɪti/ noun.
– ORIGIN late Middle English: from Latin *bellicosus*, from *bellicus* 'warlike', from *bellum* 'war'.

belligerence /bəˈlɪdʒ(ə)r(ə)ns/ (also **belligerency**) ▸ noun [mass noun] aggressive or warlike behaviour.

belligerent ▸ adjective hostile and aggressive: *the mood at the meeting was belligerent.* ■ engaged in a war or conflict, as recognized by international law.
▸ noun a nation or person engaged in war or conflict, as recognized by international law.
– DERIVATIVES **belligerently** adverb.
– ORIGIN late 16th cent.: from Latin *belligerant-* 'waging war', from the verb *belligerare*, from *bellum* 'war'.

Bellingshausen Sea /ˈbɛlɪŋzˌhaʊz(ə)n/ a part of the SE Pacific off the coast of Antarctica, bounded to the east and south by the Antarctic Peninsula and Ellsworth Land.
– ORIGIN named after the Russian explorer Fabian Gottlieb von *Bellingshausen* (1778–1852), who in 1819–21 became the first to circumnavigate Antarctica.

Bellini[1] /bɛˈliːni/, a family of Italian painters in Venice, **Jacopo** (*c.*1400–70) and his sons **Gentile** (*c.*1429–1507) and **Giovanni** (*c.*1430–1516).

Bellini[2] /bɛˈliːni/, Vincenzo (1801–35), Italian composer. Notable operas: *La Sonnambula* (1831), *Norma* (1831), and *I Puritani* (1835).

Bellini[3] /bəˈliːni/ ▸ noun (pl. **Bellinis**) a cocktail consisting of peach juice mixed with champagne.
– ORIGIN from the name of the Venetian painter Giovanni **BELLINI**[1]: the cocktail is said to have been invented in Venice during a major exhibition of the artist's work in 1948.

bell jar ▸ noun a bell-shaped glass cover used in a laboratory, typically for enclosing samples.

bell magpie ▸ noun see **CURRAWONG** and **MAGPIE** (sense 2).

bellman ▸ noun (pl. **bellmen**) historical a town crier.

bell metal ▸ noun [mass noun] an alloy of copper and tin for making bells, with a higher tin content than in bronze.

Belloc /ˈbɛlɒk/, (Joseph) Hilaire (Pierre René) (1870–1953), French-born British writer, historian, and poet remembered chiefly for *Cautionary Tales* (1907).

Bellow, Saul (1915–2005), Canadian-born American novelist, of Russian-Jewish descent. Notable works: *The Adventures of Augie March* (1953) and *Herzog* (1964). Nobel Prize for Literature (1976).

bellow ▸ verb [no obj.] (of a person or animal) emit a deep loud roar, typically in pain or anger: *he bellowed in agony.* ■ [reporting verb] shout something with a deep loud roar: [with obj.] *he **bellowed out** the order* | [with direct speech] *'Not sausage and mash again!' he bellowed.* ■ [with obj.] sing (a song) loudly and tunelessly: *a dozen large men were bellowing 'Jerusalem'.*
▸ noun a deep roaring shout or sound: *a bellow of rage.*
– ORIGIN Middle English: perhaps from late Old English *bylgan*.

bellows ▸ plural noun [also treated as sing.] **1** (also **a pair of bellows**) a device with an air bag that emits a stream of air when squeezed together with two handles, used for blowing air into a fire. ■ a similar device used in a harmonium or small organ.
2 an object or device with concertinaed sides to allow it to expand and contract, such as a tube joining a lens to a camera body.
– ORIGIN Middle English: probably from Old English *belga*, plural of *belig* (see **BELLY**), used as a shortened form of earlier *blǣstbelig* 'blowing bag'.

bell pepper ▸ noun North American term for **SWEET PEPPER**.

bell pull ▸ noun a cord or handle which rings a bell when pulled, typically used to summon someone from another room.

bell push ▸ noun Brit. a button that operates an electric bell when pushed.

bell-ringing ▸ noun [mass noun] the activity or pastime of ringing church bells or handbells.
– DERIVATIVES **bell-ringer** noun.

Bell's palsy ▸ noun [mass noun] paralysis of the facial nerve causing muscular weakness in one side of the face.
– ORIGIN mid 19th cent.: named after Sir Charles *Bell* (1774–1842), the Scottish anatomist who first described it.

bell tent ▸ noun a cone-shaped tent supported by a central pole.

bellwether ▸ noun the leading sheep of a flock, with a bell on its neck. ■ something that leads or indicates a trend: *Basildon is now the bellwether of Britain's voting behaviour.*

belly ▸ noun (pl. **bellies**) **1** the front part of the human trunk below the ribs, containing the stomach and bowels. ■ the stomach, especially as representing the body's need for food: *they'll fight all the better on empty bellies.* ■ the underside of a bird or other animal. ■ (also **belly pork**) [mass noun] a cut of pork from the underside between the legs. ■ a pig's belly as food, especially as a traded commodity.
2 the rounded underside of a ship or aircraft. ■ the top surface of an instrument of the violin family, over which the strings are placed.
▸ verb (**bellies**, **bellying**, **bellied**) **1** swell or cause to swell: [no obj.] *as she leaned forward her pullover **bellied out*** | [with obj.] *the wind **bellied** the sail **out**.*
2 [no obj.] (**belly up to**) N. Amer. informal move or sit close to (a bar or table).
– PHRASES **go belly up** informal go bankrupt.
– DERIVATIVES **bellied** adjective [in combination] *fat-bellied men.*
– ORIGIN Old English *belig* 'bag', of Germanic origin, from a base meaning 'swell, be inflated'.

bellyache informal ▸ noun a stomach pain.
▸ verb [no obj.] complain noisily or persistently: *Heads of Department **bellyaching about** lack of resources.*
– DERIVATIVES **bellyacher** noun.

bellyband ▸ noun a band placed round a horse's belly to harness it to the shafts of a cart.

belly button ▸ noun informal a person's navel.

belly dance ▸ noun a dance originating in the Middle East, typically performed by a woman and involving undulating movements of the belly and rapid gyration of the hips.
– DERIVATIVES **belly dancer** noun, **belly dancing** noun.

bellyflop informal ▸ noun a dive into water, landing flat on one's front.
▸ verb (**bellyflops**, **bellyflopping**, **bellyflopped**) [no obj.] perform a bellyflop. ■ (of an aircraft) perform an emergency landing without lowering the undercarriage.

bellyful ▸ noun (pl. **bellyfuls**) a quantity of food sufficient to fill one's stomach; a sustaining meal.
– PHRASES **have a** (or **one's**) **bellyful** informal become intolerant of someone or something after lengthy or repeated contact: *he had had his bellyful of hospitals.*

belly landing ▸ noun a crash-landing of an aircraft on the underside of the fuselage, without lowering the undercarriage.

belly laugh ▸ noun a loud unrestrained laugh.

belly pork ▸ noun see **BELLY**.

Belmopan /ˌbɛlməʊˈpan/ the capital of Belize; pop. 18,100 (est. 2008).

Belo Horizonte /ˌbɛl ɒrɪˈzɒnteɪ, -ti/ a city in eastern Brazil, capital of the state of Minas Gerais; pop. 2,412,937 (2007).

belong ▸ verb [no obj.] **1** (**belong to**) be the property of: *the vehicle did not belong to him.* ■ be due to: *most of the credit belongs to Paul.* ■ (of a contest or period of time) be dominated by: *the race belonged completely to Fogarty.*
2 (**belong to**) be a member of (a particular group or organization): *he belonged to the local cricket club.* ■ [usu. with adverbial of place] (of a person) have an affinity for a specified place or situation: *she is a stranger, and doesn't belong here* | *you and me, we belong together* | (as noun **belonging**) *we feel a real sense of belonging.* ■ have the right personal or social qualities to be a member of a particular group: *young people are generally very anxious to belong.*
3 [with adverbial of place] (of a thing) be rightly placed in a specified position: *he put the rifle back in the locker where it belonged* | *such statements do not belong in a modern student textbook.* ■ be rightly assigned to a specified category: *these compounds **belong to** a class of chemical mediators called kairomones.*
– DERIVATIVES **belongingness** noun.
– ORIGIN Middle English: from **BE-** (as an intensifier) + the archaic verb *long* 'belong', based on Old English *gelang* 'at hand, together with'.

belongings ▸ plural noun a person's movable possessions.

Belorussia /ˌbɛlə(ʊ)ˈrʌʃə/ (also **Byelorussia**) former name for **BELARUS**.
– ORIGIN Russian *Belorossiya*, from *belyĭ* 'white' + *Rossiya* 'Russia'.

Belorussian (also **Byelorussian**) ▸ adjective relating to Belarus, its people, or its language.
▸ noun **1** a native of Belarus, or a person of Belorussian descent.
2 [mass noun] the Eastern Slavic language of Belarus, with about 9 million speakers.

Belostok /bʲilaˈstɔk/ Russian name for **BIAŁYSTOK**.

beloved ▸ adjective dearly loved: *his beloved son.* ■ (**beloved by/of**) very popular with (a specified set of people): *the stark council estates beloved of town planners in the 1960s.*
▸ noun a much loved person: *he watched his beloved from afar.*
– ORIGIN late Middle English: past participle of obsolete *belove* 'be pleasing', later 'love'.

below ▸ preposition **1** at a lower level or layer than: *just below the pocket was a stain* | *the blistered skin below his collar.* ■ lower in grade or rank than: *the aristocracy rank below the monarchy* | *they rated the company's financial soundness below its competitor's.* ■ lower than (a specified amount or standard): *pupils of below average ability* | *below freezing* | *below 50 mph.*
2 extending underneath: *the tunnel below the crags* | *cables running below the floorboards.*
▸ adverb at a lower level or layer: *he jumped from the window into the moat below.* ■ (in printed text) mentioned further down on the same page, or further on in the text: *our nutritionist is pictured below right.* ■ Nautical below deck: *I'll **go below** and fix us a drink.*
– PHRASES **below (the) ground** beneath the surface of the ground. **below stairs** Brit. dated in the basement of a house as occupied by servants.
– ORIGIN late Middle English (as an adverb): from **BE-** 'by' + the adjective **LOW**[1]. Not common until the 16th cent., the word developed a prepositional use and was frequent in Shakespeare.

below decks (also **below deck**) ▸ adjective & adverb in or into the space below the main deck of a ship.
▸ plural noun (**belowdecks**) the space below the main deck of a ship.

Bel Paese /ˌbɛl pɑːˈeɪzeɪ, -zi/ ▸ noun [mass noun] trademark a rich, white, mild, creamy cheese of a kind originally made in Italy.
– ORIGIN Italian, literally 'fair country'.

Belsen /ˈbɛls(ə)n/ a Nazi concentration camp in the Second World War, near the village of Belsen in NW Germany.

Belshazzar /bɛlˈʃazə/ (6th century BC), viceroy and son of the last king of Babylon. The Bible (Daniel 5) tells how his death in the sack of the city was foretold by a mysterious hand which wrote on the palace wall at a banquet.

belt ▸ noun **1** a strip of leather or other material worn, typically round the waist, to support or hold in clothes or to carry weapons. ■ short for **SEAT BELT**. ■ a belt worn as a sign of rank or achievement: *he was awarded the victor's belt.* ■ a belt of a specified colour, marking the attainment of a particular level in judo, karate, or similar sports: [as modifier] *brown-belt level.* ■ a person who has reached such a level: *Shaun became a brown belt in judo.* ■ (**the belt**) the punishment of being struck with a belt.
2 a strip of material used in various technical applications, in particular: ■ a continuous band of material used in machinery for transferring motion from one wheel to another. ■ a conveyor belt. ■ a flexible strip carrying machine-gun cartridges.
3 a strip or encircling area that is different in nature or composition from its surroundings: *the asteroid belt* | *a belt of trees.*
4 informal a heavy blow: *she administered a good belt with her stick.*
▸ verb **1** [with obj. and adverbial] fasten with a belt: *she belted her raincoat firmly.* ■ [no obj., with adverbial] be fastened with a belt: *the jacket belts at the waist.* ■ [with obj.] secure or attach with a belt: *he was securely belted into the passenger seat.*

2 [with obj.] beat or strike (someone), especially with a belt as a punishment: *I was belted and sent to my room.* ■ hit (something) hard: *he belted the ball downfield.*
3 [no obj., with adverbial of direction] informal rush or dash in a specified direction: *he belted out of the side door.* ■ (of rain) fall hard: *the rain **belted down** on the tin roof.*
– PHRASES **below the belt** disregarding the rules; unfair. [from the notion of an unfair and illegal blow in boxing.] **belt and braces** Brit. (of a policy or action) providing double security, by using two means to the same end. [from the literal *belt* and *braces* for holding up a pair of loose trousers.] **tighten one's belt** cut one's expenditure; live more frugally. **under one's belt 1** safely or satisfactorily achieved, experienced, or acquired: *he now has almost a year as minister under his belt.* **2** (of food or drink) consumed: *Gus already had a large brandy under his belt.*
– PHRASAL VERBS **belt something out** sing or play a song loudly and forcefully. **belt up** Brit. informal **1** [usu. in imperative] be quiet. **2** put on a seat belt.
– DERIVATIVES **belted** adjective (sense 1 of the noun).
– ORIGIN Old English, of Germanic origin, from Latin *balteus* 'girdle'.

Beltane /ˈbɛlteɪn/ ▸ noun an ancient Celtic festival celebrated on May Day.
– ORIGIN late Middle English: from Scottish Gaelic *bealltainn.*

belt drive ▸ noun a mechanism in which power is transmitted by the movement of a continuous flexible belt.

belted galloway ▸ noun an animal belonging to a variety of the galloway breed of cattle. See GALLOWAY.

belted sandfish ▸ noun see SANDFISH (sense 2).

belter ▸ noun informal **1** an exceptional or outstanding example of something: *Owen made the goal with a belter of a pass.*
2 a loud, forceful singer or song.

belting ▸ noun **1** [mass noun] belts collectively, or material for belts.
2 a beating, especially with a belt as a punishment.
▸ adjective informal outstanding: *they've come up with some belting songs.*

beltman ▸ noun (pl. **beltmen**) Austral./NZ the member of a surf life-saving team who swims out, wearing a belt with a line attached for safety, to give assistance to bathers or surfers in difficulties.

belt sander ▸ noun a sander that uses a moving abrasive belt to smooth surfaces.

beltway ▸ noun US a ring road. ■ (**Beltway**) [often as modifier] Washington DC, especially as representing the perceived insularity of the US government: *conventional Beltway wisdom.* [transferred use by association with the ring road encircling Washington.]

beluga /bəˈluːɡə/ ▸ noun (pl. **same** or **belugas**) **1** a small white toothed whale related to the narwhal, living in herds mainly in Arctic coastal waters. Also called WHITE WHALE. ● *Delphinapterus leucas*, family Monodontidae.
2 a very large sturgeon occurring in the inland seas and associated rivers of central Eurasia. ● *Huso huso*, family Acipenseridae.
■ (also **beluga caviar**) [mass noun] caviar obtained from this fish.
– ORIGIN late 16th cent. (in sense 2): from Russian *belukha* (sense 1), *beluga* (sense 2), both from *belyĭ* 'white'.

belvedere /ˈbɛlvɪdɪə/ ▸ noun a summer house or open-sided gallery, typically at rooftop level, commanding a fine view.
– ORIGIN late 16th cent.: from Italian, literally 'fair sight', from *bel* 'beautiful' + *vedere* 'to see'.

belying present participle of BELIE.

BEM ▸ abbreviation British Empire Medal, an award for public service (discontinued in 1993).

bema /ˈbiːmə/ ▸ noun (pl. **bemas** or **bemata** /ˈbiːmətə/) the altar part or sanctuary in ancient and Orthodox churches. ■ (usu. **bimah**) the podium or platform in a synagogue from which the Torah and Prophets are read. ■ historical the platform from which orators spoke in ancient Athens.
– ORIGIN late 17th cent.: from Greek *bēma* 'step, raised place'.

Bemba /ˈbɛmbə/ ▸ noun (pl. **same**) **1** a member of an African people of Zambia.
2 [mass noun] the Bantu language of the Bemba, with nearly 2 million speakers.
▸ adjective relating to the Bemba or their language.
– ORIGIN Bemba.

bemire /bɪˈmʌɪə/ ▸ verb [with obj.] archaic cover or stain with mud. ■ (**be bemired**) be stuck in mud.
– ORIGIN mid 16th cent.: from BE- (expressing transitivity) + MIRE.

bemoan ▸ verb [with obj.] express discontent or sorrow over (something): *it was no use bemoaning her lot.*
– ORIGIN Old English *bemǣnan* 'complain, lament'. The change in the second syllable (16th cent.) was due to association with MOAN, to which it is related.

bemuse ▸ verb [with obj.] (usu. as adj. **bemused**) puzzle, confuse, or bewilder: *her bemused expression* | *he was bemused by what was happening.*
– DERIVATIVES **bemusedly** adverb.
– ORIGIN mid 18th cent.: from BE- (as an intensifier) + MUSE².

bemusement ▸ noun [mass noun] the fact or condition of being bemused; puzzlement: *we turned to each other in utter bemusement.*

ben¹ ▸ noun Scottish (especially in place names) a high mountain or mountain peak: *Ben Nevis.*
– ORIGIN late 18th cent.: from Scottish Gaelic and Irish *beann.*

ben² ▸ noun Scottish the inner room in a two-roomed cottage. See also BUT².
– ORIGIN late 18th cent.: dialect variant of Middle English *binne* 'within' (adverb), from Old English *binnan* (related to Dutch and German *binnen*).

Benares /bɪˈnɑːrɪz/ former name for VARANASI.

Benbecula /bɛnˈbɛkjʊlə/ a small island in the Outer Hebrides, situated between North and South Uist and linked to them by causeways.

Ben Bella /bɛn ˈbɛlə/, (Muhammad) Ahmed (b.1916), Algerian statesman, Prime Minister 1962–3 and President 1963–5. The first President of an independent Algeria, he was overthrown in a military coup.

bench ▸ noun **1** a long seat for several people, typically made of wood or stone.
2 a long work table in a workshop or laboratory.
3 a judge's seat in a law court. ■ (**the bench**) the office of judge or magistrate: *his appointment to the civil bench.* ■ a judge or magistrate presiding over a particular case.
4 Brit. a long seat in Parliament for politicians of a specified party: *the Conservative benches.* ■ the politicians occupying such a seat: *the pledge that was given by the Opposition benches yesterday.*
5 (**the bench**) a seat at the side of a sports field for coaches, substitutes, and players not taking part in a game.
6 a flat ledge in masonry or on sloping ground.
▸ verb [with obj.] **1** exhibit (a dog) at a show: *Affenpinschers and Afghans were benched side by side.* [from the practice of exhibiting dogs on benches.]
2 N. Amer. withdraw (a sports player) from play: *the coach benched quarterback Cunningham in favour of McMahon.*
3 short for BENCH-PRESS.
– PHRASES **on the bench 1** appointed as or in the capacity of a judge or magistrate: *he retired after twenty-five years on the bench.* **2** acting as one of the possible substitutes in a sports match.
– ORIGIN Old English *benc*, of Germanic origin; related to Dutch *bank* and German *Bank*, also to BANK¹.

bencher ▸ noun Law (in the UK) a senior member of any of the Inns of Court.

benchmark ▸ noun **1** a standard or point of reference against which things may be compared: *the pay settlement will set a **benchmark for** other employers and workers.* ■ a problem designed to evaluate the performance of a computer system.
2 a surveyor's mark cut in a wall, pillar, or building and used as a reference point in measuring altitudes.
▸ verb [with obj.] evaluate (something) by comparison with a standard: *we are **benchmarking** our performance **against** external criteria.* ■ [no obj., with adverbial] give particular results during a benchmark test: *the device should benchmark at between 100 and 150 MHz.*

benchmark test ▸ noun a test using a benchmark to evaluate a computer system's performance.

bench press ▸ noun a bodybuilding and weightlifting exercise in which a lifter lies on a bench with the feet on the floor and raises a weight with both arms.
▸ verb (**bench-press**) [with obj.] raise (a weight) in a bench press.

bench seat ▸ noun a seat across the whole width of a car.

bench table ▸ noun a low stone seat on the inside of a wall or round the base of a pillar in a church, cloister, or other religious building.

bench test chiefly Computing ▸ noun a test carried out on a machine, a component, or software before it is released for use, to ensure that it works properly.
▸ verb (**bench-test**) [with obj.] run a bench test on.

benchwarmer ▸ noun N. Amer. informal a sports player who does not get selected to play; a substitute.

benchwork ▸ noun [mass noun] work carried out at a bench in a laboratory or workshop.

bend¹ ▸ verb (past and past participle **bent**) **1** [with obj.] shape or force (something straight) into a curve or angle: *the wire has to be bent back tightly.* ■ [no obj.] (of something straight) be shaped or forced into a curve or angle: *poppies bending in the wind.* ■ [no obj., usu. with adverbial of direction] (of a road, river, or path) deviate from a straight line in a specified direction: *the road bent left and then right.*
2 [no obj.] (of a person) incline the body downwards from the vertical: *she **bent down** and yanked out the flex* | *I **bent over** my plate.* ■ [with obj.] move (a jointed part of the body) to an angled position: *extend your left leg and bend your right.*
3 force or be forced to submit: [with obj.] *they want to **bend** me **to** their will* | [no obj.] *a refusal to **bend to** mob rule.* ■ [with obj.] interpret or modify (a rule) to suit someone: *we cannot bend the rules, even for Darren.*
4 [with obj.] direct (one's attention or energies) to a task: *Eric **bent** all his efforts **to** persuading them to donate some blankets* | [no obj.] *she **bent** once more **to** the task of diverting her guests.*
5 [with obj.] Nautical attach (a sail or cable) by means of a knot: *sailors were **bending** sails **to** the spars.*
▸ noun **1** a curve in a road, river, path, or racing circuit.
2 a curved or angled part of something: *make a bend in the wire.*
3 a kind of knot used to join two ropes together, or to tie a rope to another object, e.g. a carrick bend.
4 (**the bends**) decompression sickness, especially in divers.
– PHRASES **bend someone's ear** informal talk to someone, especially at length or to ask a favour. **bend one's elbow** N. Amer. drink alcohol. **bend one's** (or **the**) **knee** submit: *a country no longer willing to **bend its knee to** foreign powers.* **bend over backwards** see BACKWARDS. **on bended knee** (or **knees**) kneeling, especially when pleading or showing great respect. **round** (or US **around**) **the bend** informal mad: *I'd **go round the bend** looking after kids all day.*
– DERIVATIVES **bendable** adjective.
– ORIGIN Old English *bendan* 'put in bonds, tension a bow by means of a string', of Germanic origin; related to BAND¹.

bend² ▸ noun Heraldry an ordinary in the form of a broad diagonal stripe from top left (dexter chief) to bottom right (sinister base) of a shield or part of one.
– ORIGIN late Middle English: from Anglo-Norman French *bande*, Old French *bende* 'flat strip'.

bender ▸ noun **1** an object or person that bends something: *a metal bender.*
2 informal a wild drinking spree.
3 Brit. informal, derogatory a male homosexual.
4 Brit. a shelter made by covering a framework of bent branches with canvas or tarpaulin.
– ORIGIN late 15th cent. (denoting instruments such as pliers, for bending things): from BEND¹ + -ER¹.

Bendigo /ˈbɛndɪɡəʊ/ a former gold-mining town in the state of Victoria, Australia; pop. 100,054 (2008).

bendlet ▸ noun Heraldry a bend of half the normal width, usually borne in groups of two or three.
– ORIGIN late 16th cent.: probably from the earlier heraldic term *bendel* 'little bend' (Old French diminutive of *bende* 'band') + -ET¹.

bend sinister ▸ noun Heraldry a broad diagonal stripe from top right to bottom left of a shield (a supposed sign of bastardy).

bendy ▸ adjective (**bendier**, **bendiest**) **1** Brit. capable of bending; soft and flexible.
2 (especially of a road) having many bends.
– DERIVATIVES **bendiness** noun.

bendy bus ▸ noun Brit. informal a single-decker bus consisting of two rigid vehicles linked together by a flexible section.

beneath ▸ preposition **1** extending or directly underneath: *a 2.5-mile tunnel beneath the Alps.* ■ underneath so as to be hidden, covered, or protected: *the ancient city has lain hidden beneath the sea for 2,000 years.*
2 at a lower level or layer than: *beneath this floor there's a cellar* | *her eyes had dark shadows beneath*

B

B

them. ▪ lower in grade or rank than: *he was relegated to the rank beneath theirs.* ▪ considered of lower status or worth than: *she's in love with a man who is rather beneath her.* ▪ hidden behind (an appearance): *beneath the gloss of success was a tragic private life.*
▸ **adverb 1** extending or directly underneath something: *a house built on stilts to allow air to circulate beneath.*
2 at a lower level or layer: *upper layers can be removed to reveal internal parts beneath.* ▪ hidden behind an appearance: *the smile revealed the evil beneath.*
– ORIGIN Old English *binithan, bineothan*, from *bi* (see BY) + *nithan, neothan* 'below', of Germanic origin; related to NETHER.

benedicite /ˌbɛnɪˈdʌɪsɪti/ ▸ **noun** a blessing, especially a grace said at table in religious communities. ▪ **(the Benedicite)** the canticle used in the Anglican service of matins beginning 'O all ye works of the Lord, bless ye the Lord', the text being taken from the Apocrypha.
– ORIGIN Latin, 'bless ye!', plural imperative from *benedicere* 'wish well'; the first word of the canticle in Latin.

Benedict, St /ˈbɛnɪdɪkt/ (*c.*480–*c.*550), Italian hermit. He established a monastery at Monte Cassino and his *Regula Monachorum* (known as the Rule of St Benedict) formed the basis of Western monasticism. Feast day, 11 July (formerly 21 March).

Benedict XVI /ˈbɛnɪdɪkt/ (b.1927), German cleric, pope since 2005; born *Joseph Alois Ratzinger*.

Benedictine /ˌbɛnɪˈdɪktɪn/ ▸ **noun 1** a monk or nun of a Christian religious order following the rule of St Benedict and established *c.*540.
2 [mass noun] trademark a liqueur based on brandy, originally made by Benedictine monks in France.
▸ **adjective** relating to St Benedict or the Benedictines.
– ORIGIN from French *bénédictine* or modern Latin *benedictinus*, from the name *Benedictus* (see BENEDICT, ST).

benediction ▸ **noun** [mass noun] the utterance of a blessing, especially at the end of a religious service. ▪ **(Benediction)** (in the Roman Catholic Church) a service in which the congregation is blessed with the sacrament. ▪ [count noun] a prayer asking for divine blessing. ▪ the state of being blessed.
– ORIGIN late Middle English: via Old French from Latin *benedictio(n-)*, from *benedicere* 'wish well, bless', from *bene* 'well' + *dicere* 'say'.

benedictory ▸ **adjective** archaic relating to the giving of a blessing.
– ORIGIN late 18th cent.: from Latin *benedictorius*, from *benedicere* 'wish well' (see BENEDICTION).

Benedict's solution (also **Benedict's reagent**) ▸ **noun** [mass noun] a chemical solution that changes colour in the presence of glucose and other reducing sugars, used in clinical urine tests for diabetes. It is a mixture of sodium or potassium citrate, sodium carbonate, and copper sulphate.
– ORIGIN named after Stanley R. *Benedict* (1884–1936), American chemist.

Benedictus /ˌbɛnɪˈdɪktəs/ ▸ **noun** Christian Church **1** an invocation beginning *Benedictus qui venit in nomine Domini* (Blessed is he who comes in the name of the Lord) forming a set part of the Mass.
2 a canticle beginning *Benedictus Dominus Deus* (Blessed be the Lord God) from Luke 1:68–79.
– ORIGIN Latin, 'blessed', past participle of *benedicere* 'wish well'.

benefaction /ˌbɛnɪˈfakʃ(ə)n/ ▸ **noun** formal a donation or gift.
– ORIGIN mid 17th cent.: from late Latin *benefactio(n-)*, from *bene facere* 'do good (to)', from *bene* 'well' + *facere* 'do'.

benefactive /ˌbɛnɪˈfaktɪv/ Grammar ▸ **adjective** denoting a semantic case or construction that expresses the person or thing that benefits from the action of the verb, for example *for you* in *I bought this for you*.
▸ **noun** the benefactive case, or a word or expression in it.
– ORIGIN 1940s: from Latin *benefactus* 'capable of giving' + -IVE.

benefactor ▸ **noun** a person who gives money or other help to a person or cause.
– ORIGIN late Middle English: from Latin, from *bene facere* 'do good (to)' (see BENEFACTION).

benefactress ▸ **noun** a female benefactor.

benefic /bɪˈnɛfɪk/ ▸ **adjective** archaic beneficent or kindly. ▪ Astrology relating to or denoting the planets Jupiter and Venus, traditionally considered to have a favourable influence.
– ORIGIN early 17th cent.: from Latin *beneficus*, from *bene facere* 'do good (to)'.

benefice /ˈbɛnɪfɪs/ ▸ **noun** a permanent Church appointment, typically that of a rector or vicar, for which property and income are provided in respect of pastoral duties.
– DERIVATIVES **beneficed** adjective.
– ORIGIN Middle English: via Old French from Latin *beneficium* 'favour, support', from *bene* 'well' + *facere* 'do'.

beneficent /bɪˈnɛfɪs(ə)nt/ ▸ **adjective** (of a person) generous or doing good. ▪ resulting in good: *a beneficent democracy*.
– DERIVATIVES **beneficence** noun, **beneficently** adverb.
– ORIGIN early 17th cent.: from Latin *beneficent-* (stem of *beneficentior*, comparative of *beneficus* 'favourable, generous'), from *bene facere* 'do good (to)'.

beneficial ▸ **adjective 1** resulting in good; favourable or advantageous: *the beneficial effect on the economy* | *the process was **beneficial to** both supplier and customer*.
2 Law relating to rights to the use or benefit of property, other than legal title.
– DERIVATIVES **beneficially** adverb.
– ORIGIN late Middle English: from late Latin *beneficialis*, from *beneficium* (see BENEFICE).

beneficiary ▸ **noun** (pl. **beneficiaries**) a person who derives advantage from something, especially a trust, will, or life insurance policy.
– ORIGIN early 17th cent.: from Latin *beneficiarius*, from *beneficium* (see BENEFICE).

beneficiate /ˌbɛnɪˈfɪʃɪeɪt/ ▸ **verb** [with obj.] treat (a raw material) to improve its properties.
– DERIVATIVES **beneficiation** noun.
– ORIGIN late 19th cent.: from Spanish *beneficiar* (from *beneficio* 'benefit') + -ATE[3].

benefit ▸ **noun 1** an advantage or profit gained from something: *enjoy the benefits of being a member* | [mass noun] *the changes are **of benefit to** commerce*.
2 a payment made by the state or an insurance scheme to someone entitled to receive it: *part-time jobs supplemented by means-tested benefits* | [mass noun] *families **on benefit***.
3 an event such as a concert or game, intended to raise money for a particular player or charity.
▸ **verb** (**benefits**, **benefiting** or **benefitting**, **benefited** or **benefitted**) [no obj.] receive an advantage; profit: *areas that would **benefit from** regeneration*. ▪ [with obj.] bring advantage to: *the bill will benefit Britain*.
– PHRASES **benefit of clergy 1** historical exemption of the English clergy and nuns from the jurisdiction of the ordinary civil courts, granted in the Middle Ages but abolished in 1827. **2** ecclesiastical sanction: *they lived together **without benefit of clergy***. **the benefit of the doubt** a concession that a person or fact must be regarded as correct or justified, if the contrary has not been proven: *I'll **give you the benefit of the doubt** as to whether it was deliberate or not*. **for the benefit of** in order to help or be useful to: *a venue run for the benefit of the community*. ▪ in order to interest or impress (someone): *it was all an act put on for his benefit*.
– ORIGIN late Middle English (originally denoting a kind deed or something well done): from Old French *bienfet*, from Latin *benefactum* 'good deed', from *bene facere* 'do good (to)'.

benefit society ▸ **noun** another term for FRIENDLY SOCIETY.

benefit tourist ▸ **noun** Brit. informal a person who travels to or within Britain in order to live off social security payments while untruthfully claiming to be seeking work.
– DERIVATIVES **benefit tourism** noun.

Benelux /ˈbɛnɪlʌks/ a collective name for Belgium, the Netherlands, and Luxembourg, especially with reference to their economic union.
– ORIGIN 1947: acronym from *Be*lgium, *Ne*therlands, and *Lux*embourg.

Beneš /ˈbɛnɛʃ/, Edvard (1884–1948), Czechoslovak statesman, Prime Minister 1921–2, President 1935–8 and 1945–8. During the Second World War he served in London as head of the Czechoslovakian government in exile. In 1945 he regained the presidency but resigned after the 1948 communist coup.

benevolence ▸ **noun** [mass noun] the quality of being well meaning; kindness.

benevolent ▸ **adjective** well meaning and kindly. ▪ [attrib.] (of an organization) serving a charitable rather than a profit-making purpose: *a benevolent fund*.
– DERIVATIVES **benevolently** adverb.
– ORIGIN late Middle English: from Old French *benivolent*, from Latin *bene volent-* 'well wishing', from *bene* 'well' + *velle* 'to wish'.

BEng ▸ **abbreviation** Bachelor of Engineering.

benga /ˈbɛŋgə/ ▸ **noun** [mass noun] a style of African popular music originating in Kenya, characterized by a fusion of traditional Kenyan music and a lively arrangement of guitars, bass, and vocals.
– ORIGIN 1980s: from Luo.

Bengal /bɛŋˈgɔːl/ a region in South Asia, containing the Ganges and Brahmaputra River deltas. In 1947 the province was divided into West Bengal, which has remained a state of India, and East Bengal, now Bangladesh.

Bengal, Bay of a part of the Indian Ocean lying between India to the west and Burma (Myanmar) and Thailand to the east.

Bengali /bɛŋˈgɔːli/ ▸ **noun** (pl. **Bengalis**) **1** a native of Bengal.
2 [mass noun] the Indic language of Bangladesh and West Bengal, spoken by some 200 million people. It is written in a script similar to the Devanagari script.
▸ **adjective** relating to Bengal, its people, or their language.
– ORIGIN from Hindi *baṅgālī*.

bengaline /ˈbɛŋgəliːn/ ▸ **noun** [mass noun] a strong ribbed fabric made of a mixture of silk and either cotton or wool.
– ORIGIN late 19th cent.: from French, so named because of a similarity with archaic *Bengals* denoting fabrics, usually silks, imported from Bengal.

Bengal light ▸ **noun** a kind of firework giving off a blue flame and used for lighting or signalling.

Benghazi /bɛŋˈgɑːzi/ a Mediterranean port in NE Libya; pop. 670,800 (est. 2006). It was the joint capital (with Tripoli) from 1951 to 1972.

Benguela /bɛŋˈgwɛlə, -ˈgɛlə/ a port and railway terminal in Angola, on the Atlantic coast; pop. 115,900 (est. 2004). Copper is brought here from Zambia and the Democratic Republic of the Congo (Zaire).

Benguela Current a cold ocean current which flows from Antarctica northwards along the west coast of southern Africa as far as Angola.

Ben-Gurion /bɛnˈgʊərɪən/, David (1886–1973), Israeli statesman, Prime Minister 1948–53 and 1955–63, Israel's first Prime Minister and Minister of Defence.

benighted ▸ **adjective 1** in a state of pitiful or contemptible intellectual or moral ignorance: *they saw themselves as bringers of culture to poor benighted peoples*.
2 overtaken by darkness: *a storm developed and we were forced to wait benighted near the summit*.
– DERIVATIVES **benightedness** noun.
– ORIGIN late 16th cent. (in sense 2): past participle of archaic *benight* 'cover in the darkness of night, obscure' (see BE-, NIGHT).

benign ▸ **adjective 1** gentle and kind: *his benign but firm manner*. ▪ (of a climate or environment) mild and favourable.
2 Medicine (of a disease) not harmful in effect. ▪ (of a tumour) not malignant.
– DERIVATIVES **benignity** noun, **benignly** adverb.
– ORIGIN Middle English: from Old French *benigne*, from Latin *benignus*, probably from *bene* 'well' + *-genus* '-born'. Compare with GENTLE[1].

benignant /bɪˈnɪgnənt/ ▸ **adjective 1** kindly and benevolent: *an old man with a benignant expression*.
2 Medicine a less common term for BENIGN.
3 archaic having a good effect; beneficial: *the benignant touch of love and beauty*.
– DERIVATIVES **benignancy** noun, **benignantly** adverb.
– ORIGIN late 18th cent.: from BENIGN, or Latin *benignus*, on the pattern of *malignant*.

benign neglect ▸ **noun** [mass noun] non-interference that is intended to benefit someone or something more than continual attention would.

Benin /bɛˈniːn/ a country of West Africa, immediately west of Nigeria; pop. 8,791,800 (est. 2009); languages, French (official), West African languages; capital, Porto Novo. The country was conquered by the French in 1893 and became part of French West

Africa. In 1960 it became fully independent. Former name (until 1975) **DAHOMEY**.
– DERIVATIVES **Beninese** /ˌbɛnɪˈniːz/ **adjective & noun**.
– ORIGIN name adopted in 1975, formerly used of an African kingdom powerful in the 14th–17th cents.

Benin, Bight of a wide bay on the coast of Africa north of the Gulf of Guinea, bordered by Togo, Benin, and SW Nigeria. Lagos is its chief port.

Benioff zone /ˈbɛnɪɒf/ ▶ **noun** Geology an inclined zone in which many deep earthquakes occur, situated beneath a destructive plate boundary where oceanic crust is being subducted.
– ORIGIN 1960s: named after Victor H. *Benioff* (1899–1968), American seismologist.

benison /ˈbɛnɪz(ə)n, -s-/ ▶ **noun** literary a blessing: *the rewards and benisons of marriage.*
– ORIGIN Middle English: from Old French *beneiçun*, from Latin *benedictio* (see **BENEDICTION**).

Benjamin (in the Bible) a Hebrew patriarch, the youngest and favourite son of Jacob (Gen. 35:18, 42, etc.). ■ the smallest tribe of Israel, traditionally descended from him.

benne /ˈbɛni/ ▶ **noun** US term for **SESAME**.
– ORIGIN mid 18th cent.: from Malay *bene*.

Bennett¹, Alan (b.1934), English dramatist and actor. Notable works: *Beyond the Fringe* (1960), *Forty Years On* (1969), and *Talking Heads* (1987).

Bennett², (Enoch) Arnold (1867–1931), English novelist, dramatist, and critic. His fame rests on the novels and stories set in the Potteries ('the Five Towns') of his youth, notably *Anna of the Five Towns* (1902), *The Old Wives' Tale* (1908), and the *Clayhanger* series (1902–8).

Bennett³, Sir Richard Rodney (b.1936), English composer, whose works include film scores, operas, concertos, and chamber pieces.

Ben Nevis /bɛn ˈnɛvɪs/ a mountain in western Scotland. Rising to 1,343 m (4,406 ft), it is the highest mountain in the British Isles.

Benny, Jack (1894–1974), American comedian and actor; born *Benjamin Kubelsky*. Working notably on radio and then television, he was renowned for his timing, delivery, and mordant, self-effacing humour.

benny¹ ▶ **noun** (pl. **bennies**) informal, chiefly US a tablet of Benzedrine.

benny² ▶ **noun** (pl. **bennies**) US informal a benefit attached to employment; a perk.

benomyl /ˈbɛnəmɪl/ ▶ **noun** [mass noun] a systemic fungicide used on fruit and vegetable crops, derived from imidazole.
– ORIGIN 1960s: from *ben(z)o-* + *m(eth)yl*.

Benoni /bəˈnəʊni/ a city in South Africa, in the province of Gauteng, east of Johannesburg; pop. 654,500 (est. 2009). It is a gold-mining centre.

bent¹ past and past participle of **BEND¹**. ▶ **adjective**
1 sharply curved or having an angle: *a piece of bent wire.*
2 Brit. informal dishonest; corrupt: *a bent cop.*
3 Brit. informal, derogatory homosexual.
4 (**bent on**) determined to do or have: *a missionary bent on saving souls* | *a mob bent on violence.*
▶ **noun** a natural talent or inclination: *a man of a religious bent* | *she had no natural* **bent for** *literature.*
– PHRASES **bent out of shape** N. Amer. informal angry or agitated.

bent² ▶ **noun 1** (also **bent grass**) a stiff grass which is used for lawns and is a component of pasture and hay grasses. ● *Agrostis* and other genera, family Gramineae: several species, including **common bent** (*A. capillaris* (or *tenuis*)).
■ the stiff flowering stalk of a grass.
2 archaic or dialect a heath or unenclosed pasture.
– ORIGIN Middle English: from Old English *beonet* (recorded in place names), of West Germanic origin; related to German *Binse*.

Bentham /ˈbɛnθəm/, Jeremy (1748–1832), English philosopher and jurist, the first major proponent of utilitarianism. Notable works: *Introduction to the Principles of Morals and Legislation* (1789).
– DERIVATIVES **Benthamism noun, Benthamite noun & adjective.**

benthos /ˈbɛnθɒs/ ▶ **noun** [mass noun] Ecology the flora and fauna found on the bottom, or in the bottom sediments, of a sea or lake.
– DERIVATIVES **benthic adjective.**
– ORIGIN late 19th cent.: from Greek, 'depth of the sea'.

Bentley, Edmund Clerihew (1875–1956), English journalist and novelist, inventor of the comic verse form, the clerihew.

bento /ˈbɛntəʊ/ ▶ **noun** (pl. **bentos**) a lacquered or decorated wooden Japanese lunch box. ■ a Japanese-style packed lunch, consisting of such items as rice, vegetables, and sashimi.
– ORIGIN Japanese.

bentonite /ˈbɛntənʌɪt/ ▶ **noun** [mass noun] a kind of absorbent clay formed by breakdown of volcanic ash, used especially as a filler.
– ORIGIN late 19th cent.: from the name of Fort *Benton* in Montana, US, where it is found, + **-ITE¹**.

ben trovato /ˌbɛn trə(ʊ)ˈvɑːtəʊ/ ▶ **adjective** (of an anecdote) invented but plausible.
– ORIGIN Italian, literally 'well found'.

bentwood ▶ **noun** [mass noun] wood that is artificially shaped for use in making furniture.

Benue-Congo /ˈbɛnweɪ/ ▶ **noun** [mass noun] a major branch of the Niger–Congo family of languages, spoken mainly in Nigeria and including Efik and Fula.
▶ **adjective** relating to or denoting this group of languages.
– ORIGIN from the names of rivers.

benumb ▶ **verb** [with obj.] (often as adj. **benumbed**) deprive of physical or emotional feeling: *a hoarse shout cut through his benumbed senses.*
– ORIGIN late 15th cent.: from obsolete *benome*, past participle of *benim* 'deprive', from **BE-** (expressing removal) + Old English *niman* 'take'.

Benxi /bɛnˈʃiː/ a city in NE China, in the province of Liaoning; pop. 846,700 (est. 2006).

Benz /bɛnz/, German /bɛnts/, Karl Friedrich (1844–1929), German engineer and motor manufacturer. In 1885 he built the first vehicle to be driven by an internal-combustion engine.

benzaldehyde /bɛnˈzaldɪhʌɪd/ ▶ **noun** [mass noun] Chemistry a colourless liquid aldehyde with the odour of bitter almonds, used in the manufacture of dyes and perfumes. ● Chem. formula: C_6H_5CHO.

Benzedrine /ˈbɛnzɪdriːn/ ▶ **noun** trademark for **AMPHETAMINE**.
– ORIGIN 1930s: from **BENZOIC ACID** and **EPHEDRINE**.

benzene /ˈbɛnziːn/ ▶ **noun** [mass noun] a colourless volatile liquid hydrocarbon present in coal tar and petroleum, and used in chemical synthesis. Its use as a solvent has been reduced because of its carcinogenic properties. ● Chem. formula: C_6H_6.
– ORIGIN mid 19th cent.: from **BENZOIC ACID** + **-ENE**.

benzene ring ▶ **noun** Chemistry the hexagonal unsaturated ring of six carbon atoms present in benzene and many other aromatic molecules.

benzenoid /ˈbɛnzɪnɔɪd/ ▶ **adjective** Chemistry having the six-membered ring structure or aromatic properties of benzene.

benzine /ˈbɛnziːn/ (also **benzin** /-zɪn/) ▶ **noun** [mass noun] a mixture of liquid hydrocarbons obtained from petroleum.
– ORIGIN mid 19th cent. (denoting benzene): from **BENZOIN** + **-INE⁴**.

benzoate /ˈbɛnzəʊeɪt/ ▶ **noun** Chemistry a salt or ester of benzoic acid.

benzocaine /ˈbɛnzə(ʊ)keɪn/ ▶ **noun** [mass noun] Medicine a synthetic crystalline compound which is used as a local anaesthetic. ● Alternative name: **ethyl para-aminobenzoate**; chem. formula $NH_2C_6H_4COOC_2H_5$.
– ORIGIN 1920s: from **BENZOIC ACID** + *-caine* (from **COCAINE**).

benzodiazepine /ˌbɛnzəʊdʌɪˈeɪzɪpiːn, -ˈazəpiːn/ ▶ **noun** Medicine any of a class of heterocyclic organic compounds used as tranquillizers, such as Librium and Valium.
– ORIGIN 1930s: from **BENZENE** + **DI-¹** + **AZO-** + **EPI-** + **-INE⁴**.

benzoic acid /bɛnˈzəʊɪk/ ▶ **noun** [mass noun] Chemistry a white crystalline substance present in benzoin and other plant resins, used as a food preservative. ● Chem. formula: C_6H_5COOH.

benzoin /ˈbɛnzəʊɪn/ ▶ **noun** [mass noun] **1** (also **gum benzoin**) a fragrant gum resin obtained from a tropical East Asian tree, used in medicines, perfumes, and incense. Also called **GUM BENJAMIN**. ● This is obtained from several species of the genus *Styrax* (family Styracaceae), in particular *S. benzoin*.
2 Chemistry a white crystalline aromatic ketone present in this resin. ● Chem. formula: $C_6H_5CHOHCOC_6H_5$.
– ORIGIN mid 16th cent.: from French *benjoin*, based on Arabic *lubānjāwī* 'incense of Java'.

benzol /ˈbɛnzɒl/ (also **benzole** /-zəʊl/) ▶ **noun** [mass noun] crude benzene used as a fuel.
– ORIGIN mid 19th cent.: from **BENZOIC ACID** + **-OL**.

benzopyrene /ˌbɛnzə(ʊ)ˈpʌɪriːn/ ▶ **noun** [mass noun] Chemistry a compound which is the major carcinogen present in cigarette smoke, and also occurs in coal tar. ● A polycyclic aromatic hydrocarbon; chem. formula: $C_{20}H_{12}$.

benzoquinone /ˌbɛnzə(ʊ)ˈkwɪnəʊn/ ▶ **noun** [mass noun] Chemistry a yellow crystalline compound related to benzene but having two hydrogen atoms replaced by oxygen. ● Chem. formula: $C_6H_4O_2$; there are two isomers, with the oxygen atoms on opposite (**1,4-benzoquinone**) or adjacent (**1,2-benzoquinone**) carbon atoms.

benzoyl /ˈbɛnzəʊʌɪl, -zəʊl/ ▶ **noun** [as modifier] Chemistry of or denoting the acyl radical $-C(O)C_6H_5$, derived from benzoic acid: *benzoyl peroxide.*

benzyl /ˈbɛnzʌɪl, -zɪl/ ▶ **noun** [as modifier] Chemistry of or denoting the radical $-CH_2C_6H_5$, derived from toluene: *benzyl benzoate.*

Beograd /bɛˈɔgrad/ Serbian name for **BELGRADE**.

Beowulf /ˈbeɪəwʊlf/ an Old English epic poem celebrating the legendary Scandinavian hero Beowulf.

Generally dated to the 8th century, the poem was the first major poem in a European vernacular language and is the only complete Germanic epic that survives. It describes Beowulf's killing of the water monster Grendel and its mother and his death in combat with a dragon, and includes both pagan and Christian elements.

bequeath /bɪˈkwiːð/ ▶ **verb** [with obj.] leave (property) to a person or other beneficiary by a will: *he bequeathed his art collection to the town.* ■ pass (something) on or leave (something) to someone else: *he ditched the unpopular policies bequeathed to him.*
– DERIVATIVES **bequeathal noun, bequeather noun.**
– ORIGIN Old English *becwethan*, from **BE-** 'about' (expressing transitivity) + *cwethan* 'say' (see **QUOTH**).

bequest ▶ **noun** a legacy: *a bequest of over £300,000.* ■ [mass noun] the action of bequeathing something: *a painting acquired by bequest.*
– ORIGIN Middle English: from **BE-** 'about' + Old English *cwis* 'speech', influenced by **BEQUEATH**.

berate ▶ **verb** [with obj.] scold or criticize (someone) angrily: *she berated herself for being fickle.*
– ORIGIN mid 16th cent.: from **BE-** 'thoroughly' + **RATE²**.

Berber /ˈbəːbə/ ▶ **noun 1** a member of the indigenous people of North Africa, among whom are the nomadic Tuareg.
2 [mass noun] the Afro-Asiatic language of these peoples, spoken by about 11 million people. There are several different dialects; some of them, e.g. Tamashek, are regarded by some scholars as separate languages.
▶ **adjective** relating to the Berber peoples or their language.
– ORIGIN from Arabic *barbar*, from Greek *barbaros* 'foreigner' (see **BARBARIAN**).

Berbera /ˈbəːbərə/ a port on the north coast of Somalia; pop. 72,300 (est. 2009).

berberine /ˈbəːbəriːn/ ▶ **noun** [mass noun] Chemistry a bitter yellow compound of the alkaloid class, obtained from barberry and other plants.
– ORIGIN early 19th cent.: from **BERBERIS** + **-INE⁴**.

berberis /ˈbəːbərɪs/ ▶ **noun** a plant of a genus that comprises the barberries. ● Genus *Berberis*, family Berberidaceae.
– ORIGIN modern Latin and Old French, from medieval Latin *barbaris*.

berceuse /bɛːˈsəːz/ ▶ **noun** (pl. **berceuses** pronunc. **same**) a lullaby.
– ORIGIN French, from *bercer* 'to rock'.

Berchtesgaden /ˈbɛːxtəsˌgɑːd(ə)n/, German /ˈbɛrçtəsˌgaːdn/ a town in southern Germany, in the Bavarian Alps close to the border with Austria; pop. 8,200 (est. 2006). Hitler had a fortified retreat there.

bereave ▶ **verb** (**be bereaved**) be deprived of a close relation or friend through their death: *she had recently been bereaved* | (as adj. **bereaved**) *bereaved families* | (as noun **the bereaved**) *those who counsel the bereaved.*
– ORIGIN Old English *berēafian* (see **BE-**, **REAVE**). The original sense was 'deprive of' in general.

bereavement ▶ **noun** [mass noun] the action or condition of being bereaved: *there is no right way to experience bereavement* | [count noun] *the family suffered a sad bereavement.*

B

bereft ▶ adjective **1** (**bereft of**) deprived of or lacking (something): *her room was stark and bereft of colour.* **2** (of a person) sad and lonely, especially through someone's death or departure: *his death in 1990 left her bereft.*
– ORIGIN late 16th cent.: archaic past participle of BEREAVE.

Berenice /ˌbɛrɪˈnʌɪsi/ (3rd century BC), Egyptian queen, wife of Ptolemy III.

beret /ˈbɛreɪ, -ri/ ▶ noun a round flattish cap of felt or cloth.
– ORIGIN early 19th cent.: from French *béret* 'Basque cap', from Old Provençal *berret*, based on late Latin *birrus* 'hooded cape'. Compare with BIRETTA.

Berg /bɛːg/, Alban (Maria Johannes) (1885–1935), Austrian composer, a leading exponent of twelve-note composition. Notable works: the operas *Wozzeck* (1914–21) and *Lulu* (1928–35) and his violin concerto (1935).

berg[1] /bəːg/ ▶ noun short for ICEBERG.

berg[2] /bəːg/ ▶ noun S. African a mountain or hill. ■ (**the Berg**) the Drakensberg mountain range.
– ORIGIN Dutch.

bergamot[1] /ˈbəːgəmɒt/ ▶ noun **1** [mass noun] an oily substance extracted from the rind of a dwarf variety of Seville orange, used in cosmetics and as flavouring in Earl Grey tea.
2 (also **bergamot orange**) the tree which bears a variety of Seville orange from which bergamot is extracted. ● *Citrus aurantium* subsp. *bergamia*, family Rutaceae.
3 an aromatic North American herb of the mint family. ● Genus *Monarda*, family Labiatae: several species, in particular **sweet bergamot** (*M. didyma*) (also called BEE BALM, OSWEGO TEA), grown for its bright flowers.
– ORIGIN late 17th cent. (in sense 2): named after the city and province of *Bergamo* in northern Italy.

bergamot[2] /ˈbəːgəmɒt/ ▶ noun a dessert pear of a rich and sweet variety.
– ORIGIN early 17th cent.: from French *bergamotte*, from Italian *bergamotta*, from Turkish *begarmudu* 'prince's pear', from *beg* 'prince' + *armud* 'pear' + the possessive suffix *-u*.

Bergen 1 /ˈbɛːg(ə)n/ a seaport in SW Norway; pop. 220,418 (2007). It is a centre of the fishing and North Sea oil industries.
2 /ˈbɛrxə(n)/ Flemish name for MONS.

bergen /ˈbəːg(ə)n/ ▶ noun Brit. a type of rucksack supported by a frame, used by the military.
– ORIGIN 1920s: manufacturer's name.

bergenia /bəˈgiːnɪə/ ▶ noun an evergreen Asian plant with large, thick leaves and typically pink, red, or purple flowers. ● Genus *Bergenia*, family Saxifragaceae.
– ORIGIN modern Latin, named after Karl A. von *Bergen* (1704–60), German botanist and physician.

Bergerac[1] /ˈbɛːʒərak/ a wine-producing region in the Dordogne valley in SW France. ■ a town on the Dordogne River; pop. 28,760 (2006).

Bergerac[2] see CYRANO DE BERGERAC.

bergère /bɛːˈʒɛː/ ▶ noun a long-seated upholstered armchair fashionable in the 18th century.
– ORIGIN mid 18th cent.: from French, literally 'shepherdess'.

bergie /ˈbəːgi/ ▶ noun (pl. **bergies**) S. African informal a vagrant.
– ORIGIN from Dutch *berg* 'mountain' + the informal suffix -IE.

Bergman[1] /ˈbəːgmən/, (Ernst) Ingmar (1918–2007), Swedish film and theatre director. He used haunting imagery and symbolism often derived from Jungian dream analysis. Notable films: *Smiles of a Summer Night* (1955), *The Seventh Seal* (1956), and *Hour of the Wolf* (1968).

Bergman[2] /ˈbəːgmən/, Ingrid (1915–82), Swedish actress. Although her film career was long, she is probably best known for her romantic role opposite Humphrey Bogart in *Casablanca* (1942). Other notable films: *Notorious* (1946) and *Anastasia* (1956).

bergschrund /ˈbəːgʃrʊnd/ ▶ noun a crevasse at the junction of a glacier or snowfield with a steep upper slope.
– ORIGIN mid 19th cent.: from German, from *Berg* 'mountain' + *Schrund* 'crevice'.

Bergson /ˈbəːgs(ə)n/, French /bɛrksɔn/, Henri (Louis) (1859–1941), French philosopher. Dividing the world into life (or consciousness) and matter, he rejected Darwinian evolution and argued that life possesses an inherent creative impulse (*élan vital*) which creates new forms as life seeks to impose itself on matter. Nobel Prize for Literature (1927).
– DERIVATIVES **Bergsonian** adjective.

berg wind ▶ noun S. African a hot dry northerly wind blowing from the interior to coastal districts.

Beria /ˈbɛrɪə/, Lavrenti (Pavlovich) (1899–1953), Soviet politician and head of the secret police 1938–53. He was involved in the elimination or deportation of Stalin's opponents, but after Stalin's death he was arrested and executed.

beribboned ▶ adjective decorated with many ribbons.

beriberi /ˌbɛrɪˈbɛri/ ▶ noun [mass noun] a disease causing inflammation of the nerves and heart failure, ascribed to a deficiency of vitamin B_1.
– ORIGIN early 18th cent.: from Sinhalese, from *beri* 'weakness'.

Bering /ˈbɛːrɪŋ/, Vitus (Jonassen) (1681–1741), Danish navigator and explorer. He led several Russian expeditions aimed at discovering whether Asia and North America were connected by land.

Beringia /bɛˈrɪndʒɪə/ the area comprising the Bering Strait and adjacent parts of Siberia and Alaska (used especially in connection with the migration of animals across the former Bering land bridge).
– DERIVATIVES **Beringian** adjective.

Bering Sea an arm of the North Pacific lying between NE Siberia and Alaska, bounded to the south by the Aleutian Islands. It is linked to the Arctic Ocean by the Bering Strait. Both the sea and the strait are named after Vitus Bering.

Bering Strait a narrow sea passage which separates the eastern tip of Siberia from Alaska and links the Arctic Ocean with the Bering Sea, about 85 km (53 miles) wide at its narrowest point. During the Ice Age, as a result of a drop in sea levels, the **Bering land bridge** formed between the two continents, allowing the migration of animals and dispersal of plants in both directions.

Berio /ˈbɛrɪəʊ/, Luciano (1925–2003), Italian composer, an experimentalist who adopted serial, aleatory, and electronic techniques. Notable works: *Circles* (1960), *Sequenza* series (1958–75), and *Un Re in Ascolto* (opera, 1984).

berk /bəːk/ (also **burk** or **burke**) ▶ noun Brit. informal a stupid person.
– ORIGIN 1930s: abbreviation of *Berkeley* or *Berkshire Hunt*, rhyming slang for 'cunt'.

Berkeley[1] /ˈbəːkli/ a city in western California, on San Francisco Bay, site of a campus of the University of California; pop. 101,371 (est. 2008).

Berkeley[2] /ˈbəːkli/, Busby (1895–1976), American choreographer and film director; born *William Berkeley Enos*. He is remembered for spectacular and dazzling sequences in which huge casts of rhythmically moving dancers formed kaleidoscopic patterns on the screen. Notable films: the *Gold Diggers* series (1922–37) and *Babes in Arms* (1939).

Berkeley[3] /ˈbɑːkli/, George (1685–1753), Irish philosopher and bishop. He argued that material objects exist solely by being perceived, so there are only minds and mental events. Since God perceives everything all the time, objects have a continuous existence in the mind of God. Notable works: *A Treatise Concerning the Principles of Human Knowledge* (1710).

Berkeley[4] /ˈbɑːkli/, Sir Lennox (Randall Francis) (1903–89), English composer of four operas, four symphonies, music for ballet and film, and sacred choral music.

berkelium /bəːˈkiːlɪəm, ˈbəːklɪəm/ ▶ noun [mass noun] the chemical element of atomic number 97, a radioactive metal of the actinide series. Berkelium does not occur naturally and was first made by bombarding americium with helium ions. (Symbol: **Bk**)
– ORIGIN 1949: from BERKELEY[1] (where it was first made) + -IUM.

Berks. ▶ abbreviation Berkshire.

Berkshire /ˈbɑːkʃɪə, -ʃə/ a county of southern England, west of London, divided in 1998 into six unitary authorities.

Berlin[1] /bəːˈlɪn/ the capital of Germany; pop. 3,404,000 (est. 2006).

At the end of the Second World War the city was occupied by the Allies and divided into two parts: **West Berlin**, comprising the American, British, and French sectors, later a state of the Federal Republic of Germany despite forming an enclave within the German Democratic Republic; and **East Berlin**, the sector of the city occupied by the Soviet Union and later capital of the German Democratic Republic. Between 1961 and 1989 the Berlin Wall separated the two parts, which were reunited in 1990; occupation formally ended in 1994.

Berlin[2] /bəːˈlɪn/, Irving (1888–1989), Russian-born American songwriter; born *Israel Baline*. Notable works: the songs 'God Bless America' (1939) and 'White Christmas' (1942) and the score for *Annie Get Your Gun* (stage, 1946; film, 1950).

Berlin[3] /bəːˈlɪn/, Sir Isaiah (1909–97), Latvian-born British philosopher who concerned himself with the history of ideas. Notable works: *Karl Marx* (1939), *Four Essays on Liberty* (1959), and *Vico and Herder* (1976).

Berlin airlift an operation by British and American aircraft to airlift food and supplies to Berlin in 1948–9, while Russian forces blockaded the city to isolate it from the West and terminate the joint Allied military government of the city. After the blockade was lifted the city was formally divided into East and West Berlin.

Berliner ▶ noun **1** a native or citizen of Berlin.
2 a doughnut with jam filling and vanilla icing.
– ORIGIN German.

Berlin Wall a fortified and heavily guarded wall built in 1961 by the communist authorities on the boundary between East and West Berlin, chiefly to curb the flow of East Germans to the West. It was opened in November 1989 after the collapse of the communist regime in East Germany and subsequently dismantled.

Berlin work ▶ noun [mass noun] worsted embroidery on canvas.

Berlioz /ˈbɛːlɪəʊz/, French /bɛrljoz/, Hector (1803–69), French composer; full name *Louis-Hector Berlioz*. He wrote for large orchestras and choirs and employed dramatic, descriptive orchestral effects. Notable works: *Les Troyens* (opera, 1856–9), *Symphonie fantastique* (1830), and *La Damnation de Faust* (cantata, 1846).

Berlusconi /ˌbɛːlʊˈskəʊni/, Silvio (b.1936), Italian media entrepreneur and politician, Prime Minister of Italy briefly in 1994 and since 2001.

berm /bəːm/ ▶ noun a flat strip of land, raised bank, or terrace bordering a river or canal. ■ a path or grass strip beside a road. ■ an artificial ridge or embankment, such as one built as a defence against tanks. ■ a narrow space between a ditch and the base of a parapet.
– ORIGIN early 18th cent. (denoting a narrow space): from French *berme*, from Dutch *berm*.

Bermuda /bəˈmjuːdə/ (also **the Bermudas**) a group of about 150 small islands off the coast of North Carolina; pop. 67,800 (est. 2009); official language, English; capital, Hamilton. It is a British overseas territory with full internal self-government.
– DERIVATIVES **Bermudan** adjective & noun, **Bermudian** adjective & noun.
– ORIGIN named after a Spanish sailor, Juan *Bermúdez*, who sighted the islands early in the 16th cent.

Bermuda grass ▶ noun [mass noun] a creeping grass common in warmer parts of the world, used for lawns and pasture. ● *Cynodon dactylon*, family Gramineae.

Bermuda rig ▶ noun a fore-and-aft yachting rig with a tall tapering mainsail.

Bermuda shorts (also **Bermudas**) ▶ plural noun casual knee-length shorts.

Bermuda Triangle an area of the western Atlantic Ocean where a large number of ships and aircraft are said to have mysteriously disappeared.

Bern variant spelling of BERNE.

Bernadette, St /ˌbəːnəˈdɛt/ (1844–79), French peasant girl; born *Marie Bernarde Soubirous*. Her visions of the Virgin Mary in Lourdes in 1858 led to the town's establishment as a centre of pilgrimage. Bernadette later became a nun and was canonized in 1933. Feast day, 18 February.

Bernadotte[1] /ˌbəːnəˈdɒt/, Folke, Count (1895–1948), Swedish statesman. As vice-president of the Swedish Red Cross he arranged the exchange of prisoners of war and in 1945 conveyed a German offer of capitulation to the Allies.

Bernadotte[2] /ˌbəːnəˈdɒt/, French /bɛrnadɔt/, Jean Baptiste Jules (1763–1844), French soldier, king of Sweden (as Charles XIV) 1818–44. One of Napoleon's marshals, he was adopted by Charles XIII of Sweden in 1810 and later became king, thus founding Sweden's present royal house.

Bernard /bəːˈnɑː/, French /bɛrnar/, Claude (1813–78), French physiologist. Bernard showed the role of the pancreas in digestion, the method of regulation of body temperature, and the function of nerves supplying the internal organs.

Bernard, St /ˈbəːnəd/ (*c.*996–*c.*1081), French monk who founded two hospices for travellers in the Alps. The St Bernard passes, where the hospices were situated, and St Bernard dogs are named after him. Feast day, 28 May.

Bernard of Clairvaux, St /kleːˈvəʊ/, French /klɛʀvo/ (1090–1153), French theologian and abbot. He was the first abbot of Clairvaux and his monastery became one of the chief centres of the Cistercian order. Feast day, 20 August.

Berne /bəːn, bɛːn/, French /bɛʀn/, German /bɛrn/ (also **Bern**) the capital of Switzerland since 1848; pop. 122,658 (2007). ■ a canton of Switzerland.
– DERIVATIVES **Bernese** adjective & noun.

Berne Convention an international copyright agreement originally drawn up in 1886.

Berners-Lee /ˌbəːnəzˈliː/, Sir Tim (b.1955), English computer engineer. He proposed the World Wide Web in 1989 and designed its first software.

Bernhardt /ˈbəːnhɑːt/, French /bɛʀnaʀ/, Sarah (1844–1923), French actress; born *Henriette Rosine Bernard*. She was best known for her portrayal of Marguerite in *La Dame aux Camélias* and Cordelia in *King Lear*.

Bernini /bɛːˈniːni/, Italian /berˈnini/, Gian Lorenzo (1598–1680), Italian baroque sculptor, painter, and architect. His work includes the great canopy over the altar and the colonnade round the piazza at St Peter's, Rome.

Bernoulli /bəːˈnuːi/ the name of a Swiss family that produced many eminent mathematicians and scientists: ■ **Jakob** (1654–1705); also known as *Jacques* or *James Bernoulli*. He made discoveries in calculus and contributed to geometry and the theory of probabilities. ■ **Johann** (1667–1748), the brother of Jakob, who contributed to differential and integral calculus; also known as *Jean* or *John Bernoulli*. ■ **Daniel** (1700–82), son of Johann. His greatest contributions were to hydrodynamics and mathematical physics.

Bernstein /ˈbəːnstiːn, -stʌɪn/, Leonard (1918–90), American composer, conductor, and pianist. Notable works: *Candide* (operetta, 1954–6), *West Side Story* (musical, 1957), *Chichester Psalms* (1965), and film music for *On the Waterfront* (1954).

Berra /ˈbɛrə/, Yogi (b.1925), American baseball player; born *Lawrence Peter Berra*. He was especially famous as a catcher with the New York Yankees.

Berry[1] a former province of central France; chief town, Bourges.

Berry[2], Chuck (b.1931), American rock-and-roll singer, guitarist, and songwriter; born *Charles Edward Berry*. One of the first great rock-and-roll stars, he is known for songs such as 'Johnny B Goode' and 'Sweet Little Sixteen' (both 1958).

berry ▸ noun (pl. **berries**) **1** a small roundish juicy fruit without a stone: *juniper berries*. ■ Botany any fruit that has its seeds enclosed in a fleshy pulp, for example a banana or tomato.
2 any of various kernels or seeds, such as the coffee bean.
3 a fish egg or roe of a lobster or similar creature.
▸ verb [no obj.] (usu. as noun **berrying**) gather berries.
– DERIVATIVES **berried** adjective [often in combination] *red-berried elder trees*.
– ORIGIN Old English *berie*, of Germanic origin; related to Dutch *bes* and German *Beere*.

berserk /bəˈzəːk, -s-/ ▸ adjective out of control with anger or excitement; wild or frenzied: *a man went **berserk** with an arsenal of guns*.
– ORIGIN early 19th cent. (originally as a noun denoting an ancient Norse warrior who fought with wild or uncontrolled ferocity): from Old Norse *berserkr* (noun), probably from *birn-*, *bjorn* (see **BEAR**[2]) + *serkr* 'coat', but also possibly from *berr* 'bare' (i.e. without armour).

berserker ▸ noun an ancient Norse warrior who fought with wild or uncontrolled ferocity.

berth ▸ noun **1** a ship's allotted place at a wharf or dock.
2 a fixed bunk on a ship, train, or other means of transport.
3 informal (often in a sporting context) a position in an organization or event: *he looked at home in an unfamiliar right-back berth*.
▸ verb [with obj.] **1** moor (a ship) in its allotted place. ■ [no obj.] (of a ship) dock.
2 (of a passenger ship) provide a sleeping place for (someone).
– PHRASES **give someone/thing a wide berth** steer a ship well clear of something while passing it. ■ stay away from someone or something.
– ORIGIN early 17th cent. (in the sense 'adequate sea room'): probably from a nautical use of **BEAR**[1] + **-TH**[2].

bertha ▸ noun chiefly historical a deep collar, typically made of lace, attached to the top of a dress that has a low neckline.
– ORIGIN mid 19th cent.: from the given name *Bertha*.

berthing ▸ noun [mass noun] accommodation for ships in berths: *there were more than 12 miles of berthing*.

Bertolucci /ˌbɛːtəˈluːtʃi/, Italian /bertoˈluttʃi/, Bernardo (b.1940), Italian film director. Notable works: *The Spider's Stratagem* (1970), *Last Tango in Paris* (1972), and *The Last Emperor* (1988).

Berwickshire /ˈbɛrɪkʃɪə, -ʃə/ a former county of SE Scotland, on the border with England. It became a part of Borders region (now Scottish Borders) in 1975.

Berwick-upon-Tweed /ˌbɛrɪkəpɒnˈtwiːd/ a town at the mouth of the River Tweed in NE England, close to the Scottish border; pop. 13,000 (est. 2009). Having been held alternately by England and Scotland, it was ceded by Scotland to England in 1482.

beryl /ˈbɛrɪl/ ▸ noun [mass noun] a transparent pale green, blue, or yellow mineral consisting of a silicate of beryllium and aluminium, sometimes used as a gemstone.
– ORIGIN Middle English: from Old French *beril*, via Latin from Greek *bērullos*.

berylliosis /bəˌrɪlɪˈəʊsɪs/ ▸ noun [mass noun] Medicine poisoning by beryllium or beryllium compounds, especially by inhalation causing fibrosis of the lungs.

beryllium /bəˈrɪlɪəm/ ▸ noun [mass noun] the chemical element of atomic number 4, a hard grey metal. (Symbol: **Be**)

> Beryllium is the lightest of the alkaline earth metals, and its chief source is the mineral beryl. It is used in the manufacture of light corrosion-resistant alloys and in windows in X-ray equipment.

Berzelius /bəːˈziːlɪəs/, Jöns Jakob (1779–1848), Swedish analytical chemist. He determined the atomic weights of many elements and discovered cerium, selenium, and thorium.

Bes /bɛs/ Egyptian Mythology a grotesque god depicted as having short legs, an obese body, and an almost bestial face, who dispelled evil spirits.

Besançon /ˈbɛz(ə)nsɒn/, French /bəzɑ̃sɔ̃/ the capital of Franche-Comté in NE France; pop. 121,012 (2006).

Besant /ˈbɛz(ə)nt, bɪˈzant/, Annie (1847–1933), English theosophist, writer, and politician, president of the Theosophical Society. She settled in Madras (Chennai), where she worked for Indian self-government.

beseech ▸ verb (past and past participle **besought** or **beseeched**) [reporting verb] literary ask someone urgently and fervently to do or give something: [with obj. and infinitive] *they beseeched him to stay* | [with obj. and direct speech] *'You have got to believe me,' Violet beseeched him* | [with obj.] *they earnestly beseeched his forgiveness*.
– DERIVATIVES **beseechingly** adverb.
– ORIGIN Middle English: from **BE-** (as an intensifier) + Old English *sēcan* (see **SEEK**).

beset ▸ verb (**besetting**; past and past participle **beset**) [with obj.] **1** (of a problem or difficulty) trouble (someone or something) persistently: *the social problems that beset the UK* | *she was **beset with** self-doubt*. ■ surround and harass: *I was beset by clouds of flies*.
2 (**be beset with**) archaic be covered or studded with: *springy grass all beset with tiny jewel-like flowers*.
– PHRASES **besetting sin** a fault to which a person or institution is especially prone.
– ORIGIN Old English *besettan*, from **BE-** 'about' + *settan* (see **SET**[1]).

beside ▸ preposition **1** at the side of; next to: *he sat beside me in the front seat* | *the table beside the bed*. ■ compared with: *beside Paula she always felt clumsy*.
2 in addition to; apart from: *he commissioned work from other artists beside Minton*.
– PHRASES **beside oneself** overcome with worry, grief, or anger; distraught: *she was **beside herself** with rage*. **beside the point** see **POINT**.
– ORIGIN Old English *be sīdan* (adverb) 'by the side' (see **BY**, **SIDE**).

> **USAGE** Some people say that **beside** should not be used to mean 'apart from' and that **besides** should be used instead (*he commissioned work from other artists besides Minton* rather than *he commissioned work from other artists **beside** Minton*). Although there is little logical basis for such a view, and in standard English both **beside** and **besides** are used for this sense, it is worth being aware of the potential ambiguity in the use of **beside**: ***beside** the cold meat, there are platters of trout and salmon* means either 'the cold meat is next to the trout and salmon' or 'apart from the cold meat, there are also trout and salmon'.

B

besides ▸ preposition in addition to; apart from: *I have no other family besides my parents* | *besides being a player, he was my friend*.
▸ adverb in addition; as well: *I'm capable of doing the work, and a lot more besides*. ■ [sentence adverb] used to introduce an additional idea or explanation: *I had no time to warn you. Besides, I wasn't sure*.

besiege ▸ verb [with obj.] surround (a place) with armed forces in order to capture it or force its surrender: *the king marched north to besiege Berwick* | (as adj. **besieged**) *the besieged city*. ■ surround and harass: *she spent the whole day besieged by newsmen*. ■ (**be besieged**) be inundated by large numbers of requests or complaints: *the television station was **besieged with** calls*.
– DERIVATIVES **besieger** noun.
– ORIGIN Middle English: alteration (by change of prefix) of *assiege*, from Old French *asegier*.

besmear ▸ verb [with obj.] literary smear or cover with a greasy or sticky substance.
– ORIGIN Old English *bismierwan* (see **BE-**, **SMEAR**).

besmirch /bɪˈsməːtʃ/ ▸ verb [with obj.] **1** damage (someone's reputation): *he had besmirched the good name of his family*.
2 literary make (something) dirty or discoloured: *the ground was **besmirched with** blood*.

besom /ˈbiːz(ə)m, ˈbɪz-/ ▸ noun **1** a broom made of twigs tied round a stick.
2 Scottish & N. English derogatory a woman or girl.
– ORIGIN Old English *besema*, of West Germanic origin; related to Dutch *bezem* and German *Besen*.

besotted /bɪˈsɒtɪd/ ▸ adjective **1** strongly infatuated: *he became **besotted with** a local barmaid*.
2 archaic intoxicated; drunk.
– ORIGIN late 16th cent.: past participle of *besot* 'make foolishly affectionate', from **BE-** 'cause to be' + **SOT**.

besought past and past participle of **BESEECH**.

bespangle ▸ verb [with obj.] literary cover or adorn with something that glitters or sparkles.

bespatter ▸ verb [with obj.] splash drops of a liquid substance all over (an object): *his elegant shoes and trousers were **bespattered with** mud*.

bespeak ▸ verb (past **bespoke**; past participle **bespoken**) [with obj.] **1** be evidence of; indicate: *the attractive tree-lined road bespoke money*.
2 order or reserve (something) in advance: *the defendant's insurers took steps to bespeak his medical records*.
3 archaic speak to.
– ORIGIN Old English *bisprecan* 'speak up, speak out' (see **BE-**, **SPEAK**), later 'discuss, decide on', hence 'order' (sense 2, late 16th cent.).

bespectacled ▸ adjective wearing glasses.

bespoke ▸ adjective Brit. (of goods, especially clothing) made to order: *a bespoke suit*. ■ (of a trader) making such goods: *bespoke tailors*. ■ (of a computer program) written or adapted for a specific user or purpose.

bespoken past participle of **BESPEAK**.

besprinkle ▸ verb [with obj.] literary sprinkle all over with small drops or amounts of a substance.

Bessarabia /ˌbɛsəˈreɪbɪə/ a region in eastern Europe between the Dniester and Prut Rivers, from 1918 to 1940 part of Romania. The major part of the region now falls in Moldova, the remainder in Ukraine.
– DERIVATIVES **Bessarabian** adjective & noun.

Bessel /ˈbɛs(ə)l/, Friedrich Wilhelm (1784–1846), German astronomer and mathematician. He determined the positions of some 75,000 stars, obtained accurate measurements of stellar distances, and following a study of the orbit of Uranus, predicted the existence of an eighth planet.

Bessemer /ˈbɛsəmə/, Sir Henry (1813–98), English engineer and inventor. By 1860 he had developed the Bessemer process, the first successful method of making steel in quantity at low cost.

Bessemer process ▸ noun a steel-making process, now largely superseded, in which carbon, silicon, and other impurities are removed from molten pig iron

B

by oxidation in a blast of air in a special tilting retort (a **Bessemer converter**).

Best[1], Charles Herbert (1899–1978), American-born Canadian physiologist who assisted F. G. Banting in research leading to the discovery of insulin in 1922.

Best[2], George (1946–2005), Northern Irish footballer. A winger for Manchester United, he was named European Footballer of the Year in 1968.

best ▸ adjective of the most excellent or desirable type or quality: *the best midfielder in the country | how to obtain the best results from your machine | her best black suit.* ▪ most enjoyable: *some of the best times of my life.* ▪ most appropriate, advantageous, or well advised: *do whatever you think best | it's best if we both go.*
▸ adverb to the highest degree; most (used with verbs suggesting a desirable action or state or a successful outcome): *they named the pictures they liked best | you knew him best | well-drained soil suits this plant best.* ▪ to the highest standard: *the best-dressed man in Britain | the things we do best.* ▪ most appropriately or usefully: *pruning is best done in spring | jokes are best avoided in essays.*
▸ noun (**the best**) that which is the most excellent, outstanding, or desirable: *buy the best you can afford | Sarah always had to be the best at everything | this film represents the best of mainstream popular cinema.* ▪ the finest aspect of a person or thing: *he **brought out the best in** people.* ▪ (**one's best**) the highest standard or level that someone or something can reach: *this is jazz **at its best** | try to look your best.* ▪ (**one's best**) one's smartest or most formal clothes: *she dressed in her best.* ▪ (in sport) a record performance: *a lifetime best of 12.0 seconds | a personal best.* ▪ written at the end of a letter to wish a person well: *See you soon, best, Michael.*
▸ verb [with obj.] informal outwit or get the better of (someone): *she refused to allow herself to be bested.*
– PHRASES **all the best** said or written to wish a person well on ending a letter or parting. **as best one can** (or **may**) as effectively as possible under the circumstances: *I went about my job as best I could.* **at best** taking the most optimistic view: *what signs there are of recovery are patchy at best.* **at the best of times** even in the most favourable circumstances: *his memory is poor at the best of times.* **best of breed** the animal in a show judged to be the best representative of its breed. ▪ any item or product considered to be the best of its kind: *their technology is still considered best of breed and demand for their products is still growing.* **one's best friend** one's closest friend: *Michael was Frank's best friend | he's **best friends with** Eddie.* **the best-laid plans of mice and men gang aft agley** proverb even the most careful planning doesn't necessarily ensure success. [see GANG[2].] **be the best of friends** be very close friends: *she's really nice and we're the best of friends.* **the best of three** (or **five** etc.) victory achieved by winning the majority of a specified odd number of games. **the best part of** most of: *the tedious ceremony took the best part of a day.* **best wishes** an expression of hope for someone's future happiness or welfare, often written at the end of a letter. **one's best years** the most vigorous and productive period of one's life; one's prime. **do** (or **try**) **one's best** do all one can: *Ruth **did her best to** reassure her.* **be for** (or **all for**) **the best** be desirable in the end, although not at first seeming so. **get the best of** overcome (someone): *his drinking got the best of him and he was fired.* **give someone/thing best** Brit. dated admit the superiority of someone or something. **had best do something** find it most sensible or well advised to do the thing mentioned: *I'd best be going.* **make the best of** derive what limited advantage one can from (something unsatisfactory): *you'll just have to make the best of the situation.* ▪ use (resources) as well as possible: *he tried to make the best of his talents.* **make the best of a bad job** Brit. do something as well as one can under difficult circumstances. **six of the best** Brit., chiefly historical or humorous a caning as a punishment, traditionally with six strokes of the cane. **to the best of one's ability** (or **knowledge**) as far as one can do (or know): *the text is free of errors, to the best of my knowledge.* **with the best of them** as well or as much as anyone: *he'll be out there dancing with the best of them.*
– ORIGIN Old English *betest* (adjective), *betost, betst* (adverb), of Germanic origin; related to Dutch and German *best*, also to BETTER[1].

best ball ▸ noun Golf the better score at a hole of two or more players competing as a team: [as modifier] *a best-ball match.*

best boy ▸ noun the assistant to the chief electrician of a film crew.

best buy ▸ noun an item or product which gives the best value for money out of all its competitors.

best end ▸ noun [mass noun] Brit. the rib end of a neck of lamb or other meat.

bestial /ˈbɛstɪəl/ ▸ adjective of or like an animal or animals: *Darwin's revelations about our bestial beginnings.* ▪ savagely cruel and depraved: *bestial and barbaric acts.*
– DERIVATIVES **bestialize** (also **bestialise**) verb, **bestially** adverb.
– ORIGIN late Middle English: via Old French from late Latin *bestialis*, from Latin *bestia* 'beast'.

bestiality ▸ noun [mass noun] **1** savagely cruel or depraved behaviour.
2 sexual intercourse between a person and an animal.

bestiary /ˈbɛstɪəri/ ▸ noun (pl. **bestiaries**) a descriptive or anecdotal treatise on various kinds of animal, especially a medieval work with a moralizing tone.
– ORIGIN mid 19th cent.: from medieval Latin *bestiarium*, from Latin *bestia* 'beast'.

bestir ▸ verb (**bestirs, bestirring, bestirred**) (**bestir oneself**) make a physical or mental effort; exert or rouse oneself: *they rarely bestir themselves except in the most pressing of circumstances.*

best known ▸ adjective most famous: *Lennon was best known for his music | his best-known book.*

best man ▸ noun a male friend or relative chosen by a bridegroom to assist him at his wedding.

best-of ▸ noun informal a list or collection comprising the best examples of something, especially songs by a particular band or artist: *yet another Frank Sinatra best-of* | [as modifier] *a best-of CD.*

bestow ▸ verb [with obj.] confer or present (an honour, right, or gift): *the office was **bestowed on** him by the monarch of this realm.* ▪ archaic put (something) in a specified place: *stooping to bestow the presents into eager hands.*
– DERIVATIVES **bestowal** noun.
– ORIGIN Middle English (in the sense 'use for, devote to'): from BE- (as an intensifier) + Old English *stōw* 'place'.

best practice ▸ noun [mass noun] commercial or professional procedures that are accepted or prescribed as being correct or most effective.

bestrew ▸ verb (past participle **bestrewed** or **bestrewn**) [with obj.] literary cover or partly cover (a surface) with scattered objects: *the court was all **bestrewn with** herbs.* ▪ (of objects) lie scattered over (a surface): *to sweep away the sand and rubbish which bestrewed the floor.*
– ORIGIN Old English *bestrēowian* (see BE-, STREW).

bestride ▸ verb (past **bestrode**; past participle **bestridden**) **1** [with obj.] stand astride over; straddle: *he bestrode me, defending my prone body* | figurative *creatures that bestride the dividing line between amphibians and reptiles.* ▪ sit astride on: *he bestrode his horse with the easy grace of a born horseman.*
2 dominate: *he bestrides Alberta politics today.*
– PHRASES **bestride something like a colossus** see COLOSSUS.
– ORIGIN Old English *bestrīdan* (see BE-, STRIDE).

bestseller ▸ noun a book or other product that sells in very large numbers.

bestselling ▸ adjective selling in greater quantities than others of its kind: *a bestselling novel | he is also a bestselling author.*

besuited ▸ adjective (of a man) wearing a suit: *a quiet, besuited bank manager.*

bet ▸ verb (**bets, betting**; past and past participle **bet** or **betted**) **1** [no obj.] risk a sum of money or valued item against someone else's on the basis of the outcome of an unpredictable event such as a race or game: *he **bet on** baseball games* | [with clause] *I would be prepared to bet that he wanted to leave* | [with obj.] *most people would bet their life savings **on** the prospect.* ▪ [with obj. and clause] risk a sum of money against (someone) on the outcome or likelihood of a future event: [with two objs] *I bet you £15 you won't chat her up.*
2 [with clause] informal used to express certainty: ***I bet** this place is really spooky late at night | he'll be surprised to see me, **I'll bet**.*
▸ noun an act of betting a sum of money: *she had a **bet on** the Derby | **for a bet** he once rode 200 miles in nine hours.* ▪ a sum of money staked: *the bookies are taking bets on his possible successor.* ▪ [with adj.] informal a candidate or option offering a specified likelihood of success: *City looked **a good bet** for victory | your **best bet** is to call the official liquidators.* ▪ (**one's bet**) informal one's opinion about a future event: *my bet is that Arsenal won't win anything.*
– PHRASES **all bets are off** informal the outcome of a situation is unpredictable. **bet the farm** N. Amer. informal risk everything that one owns on a bet, investment, or enterprise: *this isn't a great time to bet the farm on the Internet.* **don't** (or **I wouldn't**) **bet on it** informal used to express doubt about something: *he may be a suitable companion—but don't bet on it.* **want to bet?** informal used to express strong disagreement with a confident assertion: *'You can't be with me every moment.' 'Want to bet?'* **you bet** informal you may be sure; certainly: *'Would you like this piece of pie?' 'You bet!'*
– ORIGIN late 16th cent.: perhaps a shortening of the obsolete noun *abet* 'abetment'.

beta /ˈbiːtə/ ▸ noun the second letter of the Greek alphabet (Β, β), transliterated as 'b'. ▪ [as modifier] denoting the second of a series of items, categories, forms of a chemical compound, etc.: *beta carotene | beta blocker.* ▪ Brit. a second-class mark given for a piece of work or an examination paper. ▪ informal short for BETA TEST. ▪ (**Beta**) [followed by Latin genitive] Astronomy the second (typically second-brightest) star in a constellation: *Beta Virginis.* ▪ [as modifier] relating to beta decay or beta particles: *beta emitters.* ▪ (also **beta coefficient**) a measure of the movement in price of a security relative to the stock market as a whole, used to indicate possible risk.
– ORIGIN via Latin from Greek.

beta blocker ▸ noun any of a class of drugs which prevent the stimulation of the adrenergic receptors responsible for increased cardiac action, used to control heart rhythm, treat angina, and reduce high blood pressure.

Betacam /ˈbiːtəkam/ ▸ noun [mass noun] trademark a high-quality format for video cameras and recorders. ▪ [count noun] a camera using this format.

beta-carotene ▸ noun see CAROTENE.

beta decay ▸ noun [mass noun] radioactive decay in which an electron is emitted.

betaine /ˈbiːtəiːn/ ▸ noun [mass noun] Chemistry a crystalline compound with basic properties found in many plant juices. • Chem. formula: $(CH_3)_3N^+{-}CH_2CO_2^-$.
▪ [count noun] any zwitterionic compound of the type represented by this.
– ORIGIN mid 19th cent.: formed irregularly from Latin *beta* 'beet' (because originally isolated from sugar beet) + -INE[4].

betake ▸ verb (past **betook**; past participle **betaken**) [with obj.] (**betake oneself to**) literary go to: *I shall betake myself to my lodgings.*

Betamax /ˈbiːtəmaks/ ▸ noun [mass noun] trademark a format for video recorders, now largely obsolete.
– ORIGIN 1970s: from Japanese *beta* 'all over' + *-max* from MAXIMUM.

beta particle (also **beta ray**) ▸ noun Physics a fast-moving electron emitted by radioactive decay of substances (originally regarded as rays).

beta rhythm ▸ noun [mass noun] Physiology the normal electrical activity of the brain when conscious and alert, consisting of oscillations (**beta waves**) with a frequency of 18 to 25 hertz.

beta test ▸ noun a trial of machinery, software or other products in the final stages of development, carried out by a party unconnected with the development process.
▸ verb (**beta-test**) [with obj.] subject (a product) to a beta test.

betatron /ˈbiːtətrɒn/ ▸ noun Physics an apparatus for accelerating electrons in a circular path by magnetic induction.
– ORIGIN 1940s: from BETA + -TRON.

betcha ▸ verb a non-standard contraction of 'bet you', used in representing informal speech.

betel /ˈbiːt(ə)l/ ▸ noun [mass noun] **1** the leaf of an Asian evergreen climbing plant, which in the East is chewed as a mild stimulant.
2 the plant, related to pepper, from which these leaves are taken. • *Piper betle*, family Piperaceae.
– ORIGIN mid 16th cent.: via Portuguese from Malayalam *veṟṟila*.

Betelgeuse /ˈbiːt(ə)l,dʒəːz/ (also **Betelgeux**) Astronomy the tenth-brightest star in the sky, in the constellation Orion. It is a red supergiant, and variations in its brightness are associated with pulsations in its outer envelope.

– ORIGIN French, alteration of Arabic *yad al-jauzā* 'hand of the giant' (the giant being Orion).

betel nut ▸ noun another term for **ARECA NUT**.
– ORIGIN Portuguese *betel*.

bête noire /beɪt ˈnwɑː, bɛt/, French /bɛt nwaʀ/ ▸ noun (pl. **bêtes noires** pronunc. **same**) a person or thing that one particularly dislikes.
– ORIGIN French, literally 'black beast'.

Beth Din /beɪt ˈdiːn/ (also **Beit Din**) ▸ noun a Jewish court of law composed of three rabbinic judges, responsible for matters of Jewish religious law and the settlement of civil disputes between Jews.
– ORIGIN from Hebrew *bēṯ dīn*, literally 'house of judgement'.

bethink ▸ verb (past and past participle **bethought**) (**bethink oneself**) formal or archaic come to think: *he **bethought himself of** the verse from the Book of Proverbs*.
– ORIGIN Old English *bithencan* (see **BE-**, **THINK**).

Bethlehem /ˈbɛθlɪhɛm/ a small town 8 km (5 miles) south of Jerusalem, in the West Bank; pop. 43,100 (est. 2009). It was the native city of King David and is the reputed birthplace of Jesus.

betide ▸ verb [no obj.] literary happen: *I waited with beating heart, not knowing what would betide.* ■ [with obj.] happen to (someone): *she was trembling with fear lest worse might betide her.*
– PHRASES **woe betide** see **WOE**.
– ORIGIN Middle English: from **BE-** (as an intensifier) + obsolete *tide* 'befall', from Old English *tīdan* 'happen', from *tīd* (see **TIDE**).

betimes ▸ adverb **1** archaic before the usual or expected time; early: *next morning I was up betimes.*
2 chiefly N. Amer. sometimes; on occasion.
– ORIGIN Middle English: from obsolete *betime* (see **BY**, **TIME**).

bêtise /beɪˈtiːz, bɛˈtiːz/, French /betiz/ ▸ noun a foolish or ill-timed remark or action.
– ORIGIN French, 'stupidity', from *bête* 'foolish'.

Betjeman /ˈbɛtʃəmən/, Sir John (1906–84), English poet, noted for his self-deprecating, witty, and gently satirical poems. He was appointed Poet Laureate in 1972.

betoken ▸ verb [with obj.] literary be a sign of: *she wondered if his cold, level gaze betokened indifference or anger.* ■ be a warning or indication of (a future event): *the falling comet betokened the true end of Merlin's powers.*
– ORIGIN Old English *betācnian*, from **BE-** (as an intensifier) + *tācnian* 'signify', of Germanic origin; related to **TOKEN**.

betony /ˈbɛtəni/ ▸ noun (pl. **betonies**) a Eurasian plant of the mint family, which bears spikes of showy purple flowers. ● *Stachys officinalis*, family Labiatae.
■ used in names of plants that resemble the betony, e.g. **water betony**.
– ORIGIN Middle English: from Old French *betoine*, based on Latin *betonica*, perhaps from the name of an Iberian tribe.

betook past of **BETAKE**.

betray ▸ verb [with obj.] **1** expose (one's country, a group, or a person) to danger by treacherously giving information to an enemy: *a double agent who **betrayed** some 400 British and French agents **to** the Germans.* ■ treacherously reveal (information): *many of those employed by diplomats betrayed secrets.* ■ be gravely disloyal to: *the men who have betrayed British people's trust.*
2 unintentionally reveal; be evidence of: *she drew a deep breath that betrayed her indignation.*
– DERIVATIVES **betrayer** noun.
– ORIGIN Middle English: from **BE-** 'thoroughly' + obsolete *tray* 'betray', from Old French *trair*, based on Latin *tradere* 'hand over'.

betrayal ▸ noun [mass noun] the action of betraying one's country, a group, or a person; treachery: *the betrayal by the French of their own refugees* | [count noun] *these developments represented a betrayal of democracy.*

betroth /bɪˈtrəʊð, -θ/ ▸ verb [with obj.] dated formally engage (someone) to be married: *in no time I shall be **betrothed to** Isabel.*
– ORIGIN Middle English *betreuthe*: from **BE-** (expressing transitivity) + **TRUTH**. The change in the second syllable was due to association with **TROTH**.

betrothal ▸ noun [mass noun] dated formal engagement to be married; engagement.

betrothed ▸ noun (**one's betrothed**) the person to whom one is engaged: *how long have you known your betrothed?*

better[1] ▸ adjective **1** more desirable, satisfactory, or effective: *we're hoping for better weather tomorrow* | *the new facilities were far better* | *I'm **better at** doing sums than Alice.* [comparative of the adjective **GOOD**.] ■ more appropriate, advantageous, or well advised: *there couldn't be a better time to take up this job* | *it might be better to borrow the money.*
2 [predic. or as complement] partly or fully recovered from illness, injury, or mental stress: *his leg was getting better.* [comparative of the adjective **WELL**[1].]
▸ adverb more excellently or effectively: *Jonathon could do better if he tried* | *sound travels better in water than in air* | *instruments are generally better made these days.* ■ to a greater degree; more (used in connection with success or with desirable actions or conditions): *I liked it better when we lived in the country* | *well-fed people are better able to fight off infection.* ■ more suitably, appropriately, or usefully: *the money could be better spent on more urgent cases.*
▸ noun **1** [mass noun] the better one; that which is better: *the Natural History Museum book is by far the better of the two* | *you've a right to expect better than that* | *a change **for the better**.*
2 (**one's betters**) chiefly dated or humorous one's superiors in social class or ability: *educating the young to respect their **elders and betters**.*
▸ verb [with obj.] improve on or surpass (an existing or previous level or achievement): *his account can hardly be bettered* | *bettering his previous time by ten minutes.* ■ make (something) better; improve: *his ideas for bettering the lot of the millhands.* ■ (**better oneself**) achieve a higher social position or status: *the residents are mostly Londoners who have bettered themselves.* ■ overcome or defeat (someone): *she had almost bettered him at archery.*
– PHRASES **the —— the better** used to emphasize the importance or desirability of the thing specified: *the sooner we're off the better.* **better the devil you know than the devil you don't know** proverb it's wiser to deal with an undesirable but familiar situation than to risk a change that might lead to an even worse situation. **better off** in a more desirable or advantageous position, especially in financial terms: *the proposals would make her about £400 a year better off.* **the better part of** almost all of; most of: *it is the better part of a mile.* **better safe than sorry** proverb it's wiser to be cautious and careful than to be hasty or rash and so do something you may later regret. **better than** N. Amer. more than: *he'd lived there for better than twenty years.* **the better to ——** so as to —— better: *he leaned closer the better to hear her.* **for better or (for) worse** whether the outcome is good or bad. **get the better of** gain an advantage over or defeat (someone) by superior strength or ability: *no one has ever got the better of her yet.* ■ (of a feeling or urge) be too strong to conceal or resist: *curiosity got the better of her.* **go one better** narrowly surpass a previous effort or achievement: *I want to go one better this time and score.* ■ narrowly outdo (another person). **had better do something** would find it wiser to do something; ought to do something: *you had better be careful.* **have the better of** be more successful in (a contest): *Attlee had the better of these exchanges.* **no** (or **little**) **better than** just (or almost) the same as (something bad); merely: *viceroys who were often no better than bandits.* **no better than one should** (or **ought to**) **be** regarded as sexually promiscuous or of doubtful moral character.
– ORIGIN Old English *betera* (adjective), of Germanic origin; related to Dutch *beter* and German *besser*, also to **BEST**.

> **USAGE** In the verb phrase **had better do something** the word **had** acts like an auxiliary verb, and in informal spoken contexts it is often dropped, as in *you **better** not come tonight*. In writing, the **had** may be contracted to **'d** but should not be dropped altogether.

better[2] ▸ noun variant spelling of **BETTOR**.

better half ▸ noun informal a person's wife, husband, or partner.

betterment ▸ noun [mass noun] the improvement of something: *they believed that what they were doing was vital for the betterment of society.* ■ Law the enhanced value of real property arising from local improvements.

Betterton, Thomas (1635–1710), English actor. A leading actor of the Restoration period, he also adapted the plays of John Webster, Molière, and Beaumont and Fletcher for his own productions.

betting ▸ noun [mass noun] the action of gambling money on the outcome of a race, game, or other unpredictable event. ■ the odds offered by bookmakers for such events: *Atlantic Way headed the betting at 2-1.*
– PHRASES **the betting is** informal it is likely: *the betting is that the company will slash the dividend.* **in** (or **out of**) **the betting** likely (or unlikely) to be among the winners of a horse race and given appropriate odds. **what's the betting?** Brit. informal used to express a belief that something is likely: *what's the betting he's up to no good?*

betting shop (also **betting office**) ▸ noun Brit. an establishment licensed to handle bets on races and other events.

betting slip ▸ noun a slip of paper on which a bet is entered.

bettong /ˈbɛtɒŋ/ ▸ noun a short-nosed rat-kangaroo found in Australia. ● Family Potoroidae: two genera, in particular *Bettongia*, and several species. See also **BOODIE**, **WOYLIE**.
– ORIGIN early 19th cent.: from Dharuk.

bettor (also **better**) ▸ noun chiefly US a person who bets, especially on a regular basis.

between ▸ preposition **1** at, into, or across the space separating (two objects or regions): *the border between Mexico and the United States* | *the dog crawled between us and lay down at our feet* | *those who travel by train between London and Paris.*
2 in the period separating (two points in time): *they snack between meals* | *the long, cold nights between autumn and spring.*
3 in the interval separating (two points on a scale): *a man aged between 18 and 30* | *between 25 and 40 per cent off children's clothes.*
4 indicating a connection or relationship involving two or more parties: *links between science and industry* | *negotiations between the two companies are continuing.* ■ with reference to a collision or conflict: *a collision in mid-air between two light aircraft* | *the 14th- and 15th-century wars between England and France.* ■ with reference to a contrast or failure to correspond: *the difference between income and expenditure.* ■ with reference to a choice or differentiation involving two or more things being considered together: *you have to choose between two or three different options.*
5 by combining the resources or actions of (two or more people or other entities): *we have created something between us* | *oxygen and nitrogen between them account for 99 per cent of air.* ■ shared by (two or more people or things): *they had drunk between them a bottle of Chianti.*
▸ adverb **1** in or along the space separating two objects or regions: *layers of paper with tar **in between*** | *from Leipzig to Dresden, with the gentle Elbe flowing between.*
2 in the period separating two points in time: *sets of exercises with no rest **in between**.*
– PHRASES **between ourselves** (or **you and me**) in confidence: *just between you and me, he's a bit boring.* (**in**) **between times** (or **whiles**) in the intervals between other actions.
– ORIGIN Old English *betwēonum*, from *be* 'by' + a Germanic word related to **TWO**.

> **USAGE** In standard English it is correct to say **between you and me** and wrong to say **between you and I**. Why is this? A preposition such as **between** should be followed by object pronouns such as **me, him, her**, and **us** rather than subject pronouns such as **I, he, she**, and **we**. Thus it is right to say **between us** or **between him and her** and it is clearly wrong to say **between we** or **between he and she**. The mistake **between you and I** arises from a confusion between what follows a preposition and what ordinarily comes at the beginning of a sentence. Many people know that it is wrong to say ***John and me** went to the shops* and that the right wording is ***John and I** went to the shops* – after all, no adult would say ***me** went to the shops*. Some people assume that 'and me' should in all cases be replaced by 'and I', and so in trying to avoid one kind of error create another one.

betwixt ▸ preposition & adverb archaic term for **BETWEEN**.
– PHRASES **betwixt and between** informal neither one thing nor the other.
– ORIGIN Old English *betwēox*, from *be* 'by' + a Germanic word related to **TWO**.

beurré /ˈbjʊəri/ ▸ noun a class of pear of a mellow variety.
– ORIGIN early 18th cent.: French, literally 'buttered, buttery'.

B

B

beurre blanc /bəː ˈblɒ̃/, French /bœr blɑ̃/ ▸ **noun** [mass noun] a creamy sauce made with butter, onions, and vinegar or lemon juice, usually served with seafood dishes.
– ORIGIN French, literally 'white butter'.

beurre manié /bəː ˈmanjeɪ/, French /bœr manje/ ▸ **noun** [mass noun] a mixture of flour and butter used for thickening sauces or soups.
– ORIGIN French, literally 'worked butter'.

Beuthen /ˈbɔytn/ German name for **BYTOM**.

Beuys /bɔɪs/, Joseph (1921–86), German artist. One of the most influential figures of the avant-garde movement in Europe in the 1970s and 1980s, his work consisted of 'assemblages' of various articles of rubbish. In 1979 he co-founded the German Green Party.

BeV ▸ **abbreviation** another term for **GEV**.
– ORIGIN 1940s: from *b*illion (10^9) *e*lectron*v*olts.

Bevan /ˈbɛv(ə)n/, Nye (1897–1960), British Labour politician; full name *Aneurin Bevan*. MP for Ebbw Vale 1929–60, his most notable contribution was the creation of the National Health Service (1948) during his time as Minister of Health 1945–51.

bevatron /ˈbɛvətrɒn/ ▸ **noun** a synchrotron used to accelerate protons to energies in the billion electron-volt range.
– ORIGIN 1940s: from **BEV** + **-TRON**.

bevel /ˈbɛv(ə)l/ ▸ **noun** a slope from the horizontal or vertical in carpentry and stonework; a sloping surface or edge. ■ (also **bevel square**) a tool for marking angles in carpentry and stonework.
▸ **verb** (**bevels**, **bevelling**, **bevelled**; US **bevels**, **beveling**, **beveled**) [with obj.] (often as adj. **bevelled**) reduce (a square edge on an object) to a sloping edge: *a bevelled mirror*.
– ORIGIN late 16th cent. (as an adjective in the sense 'oblique'): from an Old French diminutive of *baif* 'open-mouthed', from *baer* 'to gape' (see **BAY**[3]).

bevel gear ▸ **noun** a gear working another gear at an angle to it by means of bevel wheels.

bevel wheel ▸ **noun** a toothed wheel whose working face is oblique to the axis.

beverage /ˈbɛv(ə)rɪdʒ/ ▸ **noun** (chiefly in commercial use) a drink other than water.
– ORIGIN Middle English: from Old French *bevrage*, based on Latin *bibere* 'to drink'.

Beveridge /ˈbɛvərɪdʒ/, William Henry, 1st Baron (1879–1963), British economist and social reformer, born in India. He was chairman of the committee which prepared the Beveridge Report, which formed the basis of much of the social legislation on which the welfare state in the UK is founded.

Beverly Hills a largely residential city in California, on the NW side of the Los Angeles conurbation; pop. 34,445 (est. 2008). It is famous as the home of many film stars.

Bevin /ˈbɛvɪn/, Ernest (1881–1951), British Labour statesman and trade unionist. He was one of the founders of the Transport and General Workers' Union and a leading organizer of the General Strike (1926).

Bevin boy ▸ **noun** (during the Second World War), a young man of age for National Service selected by lot to work as a miner.
– ORIGIN named after Ernest **BEVIN**.

bevvied /ˈbɛvɪd/ ▸ **adjective** Brit. informal having consumed a lot of alcohol; drunk.

bevvy /ˈbɛvi/ ▸ **noun** (pl. **bevvies**) Brit. informal an alcoholic drink.
– ORIGIN late 19th cent.: abbreviation of **BEVERAGE**.

bevy /ˈbɛvi/ ▸ **noun** (pl. **bevies**) a large group of people or things of a particular kind: *he was surrounded by a bevy of beautiful girls*.
– ORIGIN late Middle English: of unknown origin.

bewail ▸ **verb** [with obj.] express great regret, sadness, or disappointment about (something): *men will bewail the loss of earlier freedoms*.

beware ▸ **verb** [no obj.] [in imperative or infinitive] be cautious and alert to risks or dangers: *shoppers were warned to **beware of** cut-price fakes* | *Beware! Dangerous submerged rocks ahead* | [with obj.] *we should beware the incompetence of legislators*.
– ORIGIN Middle English: from the phrase *be ware* (see **BE-**, **WARE**[3]).

bewdy ▸ **noun & adjective** non-standard Australian spelling of **BEAUTY**.

bewhiskered ▸ **adjective** having hair or whiskers growing on the face.

Bewick /ˈbjuːɪk/, Thomas (1753–1828), English artist and wood engraver, noted especially for the animal studies in such books as *A History of British Birds* (1797, 1804).

Bewick's swan ▸ **noun** a bird of the Eurasian race of the tundra swan, breeding in Arctic regions of Russia and overwintering in northern Europe and central Asia. ● *Cygnus columbianus bewickii*, family Anatidae.

bewigged ▸ **adjective** wearing a wig.

bewilder ▸ **verb** [with obj.] cause (someone) to become perplexed and confused: *she was bewildered by his sudden change of mood*.
– DERIVATIVES **bewilderment** noun.
– ORIGIN late 17th cent.: from **BE-** 'thoroughly' + obsolete *wilder* 'lead or go astray', of unknown origin.

bewildered ▸ **adjective** confused and indecisive; puzzled: *he saw the bewildered look on my face*.
– DERIVATIVES **bewilderedly** adverb.

bewildering ▸ **adjective** confusing or perplexing: *there is a bewildering array of holidays to choose from*.
– DERIVATIVES **bewilderingly** adverb [as submodifier] *the regulations are bewilderingly complex*.

bewitch ▸ **verb** [with obj.] cast a spell over (someone): *a handsome prince who had been bewitched by a sorceress*. ■ enchant and delight (someone): *they both were bewitched by the golden luminosity of Italy* | (as adj. **bewitching**) *she was certainly a bewitching woman*.
– DERIVATIVES **bewitchingly** adverb, **bewitchment** noun.
– ORIGIN Middle English: from **BE-** 'thoroughly' + **WITCH**.

bey /beɪ/ ▸ **noun** (pl. **beys**) historical the governor of a district or province in the Ottoman Empire. ■ formerly used in Turkey and Egypt as a courtesy title.
– ORIGIN Turkish, modern form of *beg* 'prince, governor'.

beyond ▸ **preposition & adverb 1** at or to the further side of: [as prep.] *he pointed to a spot beyond the concealing trees* | [as adv.] *from south of Dortmund as far as Essen **and beyond***. ■ [prep.] outside the physical limits or range of: *the hook which held the chandelier was beyond her reach*. ■ more extensive or extreme than; further-reaching than: [as prep.] *what these children go through is **far beyond** what most adults endure in a lifetime* | *the authority of the inspectors goes beyond ordinary police powers* | [as adv.] *pushing the laws to their limits **and beyond***.
2 happening or continuing after (a specified time, stage, or event): [as prep.] *training beyond the age of 14* | [as adv.] *music going on into the night **and beyond***.
3 having progressed or achieved more than (a specified stage or level): [as prep.] *we need to get beyond square one* | *his failure to rise beyond the rank of Undersecretary*. ■ above or greater than (a specified amount): [as prep.] *raising its stake beyond 15%* | [as adv.] *he could count up to a hundred thousand million now, **and beyond***.
4 [prep.] to or in a degree or condition where a specified action is impossible: *the landscape has changed beyond recognition* | *their integrity is beyond question*. ■ too much for (someone) to achieve or understand: *the questions were well beyond the average adult*.
5 [prep.] [with negative] apart from; except: *beyond telling us that she was well educated, he has nothing to say about her* | *there was little vegetation beyond brushgrowth*.
▸ **noun** (**the beyond**) the unknown, especially in references to life after death: *messages from the beyond*.
– PHRASES **the back of beyond** see **BACK**.
– ORIGIN Old English *begeondan*, from *be* 'by' + *geondan* of Germanic origin (related to **YON** and **YONDER**).

bezant /ˈbɛz(ə)nt/ ▸ **noun 1** historical a gold or silver coin originally minted at Byzantium.
2 Heraldry a roundel or (i.e. a solid gold circle).
– ORIGIN Middle English: from Old French *besant*, from Latin *Byzantius* 'Byzantine'. Sense 2 dates from the late 15th cent.

bezel /ˈbɛz(ə)l/ ▸ **noun** a grooved ring holding the cover of a watch face or other instrument in position. ■ a groove holding the crystal of a watch or the stone of a gem in its setting.
– ORIGIN late 16th cent.: from Old French, of unknown origin.

bezique /bɪˈziːk/ ▸ **noun** [mass noun] a trick-taking card game for two, played with a double pack of 64 cards, including the seven to ace only in each suit. ■ the holding of the queen of spades and the jack of diamonds in bezique.
– ORIGIN mid 19th cent.: from French *bésigue*, perhaps from Persian *bāzīgar* 'juggler' or *bāzī* 'game'.

bezoar /ˈbiːzɔː, ˈbɛzəʊɑː/ ▸ **noun 1** a small stony concretion which may form in the stomachs of certain animals, especially ruminants, and which was once used as an antidote for various ailments.
2 a wild goat with flat scimitar-shaped horns, found from Greece to Pakistan. The ancestor of the domestic goat, it was the best-known source of bezoars. ● *Capra aegagrus*, family Bovidae.
– ORIGIN late 15th cent. (in the general sense 'stone or concretion'): from French *bezoard*, based on Arabic *bāzahr*, *bādizahr*, from Persian *pādzahr* 'antidote'.

BF (also **bf**) ▸ **noun** (pl. **BFs**) informal a person's boyfriend: *I've been dating my BF since January*. ■ a person's best friend: *Lottie is my absolute BF*.

b.f. ▸ **abbreviation** ■ Brit. informal bloody fool. ■ (in bookkeeping) brought forward.

BFF ▸ **noun** (pl. **BFFs**) informal a person's best friend: *my BFF's boyfriend is cheating on her*.
– ORIGIN 1996: from the initial letters of *best friend forever*.

BFI ▸ **abbreviation** British Film Institute.

B-film ▸ **noun** another term for **B-MOVIE**.

BFN ▸ **abbreviation** informal bye for now: *will post more when I have some more time, BFN*.

BFPO ▸ **abbreviation** British Forces Post Office (or British Field Post Office, when in a combat zone).

BG ▸ **abbreviation** Bulgaria (international vehicle registration).

BGH ▸ **abbreviation** bovine growth hormone.

BH ▸ **abbreviation** Belize (international vehicle registration).
– ORIGIN from *British Honduras*.

Bh ▸ **symbol** the chemical element bohrium.

bhadralok /ˈbʌdrəlɒk/ (also **bhadralog**) ▸ **noun** [mass noun] Indian prosperous, well-educated people, typically Bengalis, regarded as members of a social class: [as modifier] *Kolkata's bhadralok circles*. ■ [count noun] a member of this class.
– ORIGIN from Hindi *bhadralog*, Bengali *bhadralok*, from Sanskrit *bhadrá* 'worthy, respectable' + *loká* 'folk, people'.

Bhagavadgita /ˌbʌɡəvədˈɡiːtə/ Hinduism a poem composed between the 2nd century BC and the 2nd century AD and incorporated into the Mahabharata. Presented as a dialogue between the Kshatriya prince Arjuna and his divine charioteer Krishna, it stresses the importance of doing one's duty and of faith in God. Also called **GITA**.

Bhagwan /bʌɡˈwɑːn/ ▸ **noun** Indian God. ■ a guru or revered person (often used as a proper name or form of address).
– ORIGIN from Hindi *bhagwān*, from Sanskrit *bhagavān*, from the root *bhaj* 'to honour, adore'.

bhai /bʌɪ/ ▸ **noun** Indian a brother. ■ a friendly form of address for a man. ■ (as suffix **-bhai**) added to proper names to form an affectionate form of address to an older person: *Abdulbhai*.
– ORIGIN from Hindi *bhāī*, based on Sanskrit *bhrātṛ* 'brother'.

bhajan /ˈbʌdʒ(ə)n/ ▸ **noun** Hinduism a devotional song.
– ORIGIN from Sanskrit *bhajana*, from *bhaj* 'to honour, adore'.

bhaji /ˈbɑːdʒi/ ▸ **noun** (pl. **bhajis** or **bhajia** /ˈbɑːdʒɪə/) (in Indian cuisine) a small flat cake or ball of vegetables, fried in batter. ■ an Indian dish of fried vegetables.
– ORIGIN from Hindi *bhājī* 'fried vegetables'.

bhakti /ˈbʌkti/ ▸ **noun** [mass noun] Hinduism devotional worship directed to one supreme deity, usually Vishnu (especially in his incarnations as Rama and Krishna) or Shiva, by whose grace salvation may be attained by all regardless of sex, caste, or class. It is followed by the majority of Hindus today.
– ORIGIN Sanskrit.

bhang /baŋ/ (also **bang**) ▸ **noun** [mass noun] the leaves and flower tops of cannabis, used as a narcotic.
– ORIGIN from Hindi *bhāṅg*.

bhangra /ˈbɑːŋɡrə/ ▸ **noun** [mass noun] a type of popular music combining Punjabi folk traditions with Western pop music.
– ORIGIN 1960s (denoting a traditional folk dance): from Punjabi *bhāṅgṛā*.

bharal /ˈbʌr(ə)l/ ▸ **noun** a Himalayan wild sheep with a bluish coat and backward-curving horns. Also called **BLUE SHEEP**. ● *Pseudois nayaur*, family Bovidae.
– ORIGIN mid 19th cent.: from Hindi.

Bharat /ˈbʌrət/ Hindi name for **INDIA**.

Bharatanatyam /ˌbʌrʌtəˈnɑːtjʌm/ ▸ **noun** [mass noun] a classical dance form of southern India.
– ORIGIN from Sanskrit *bharatanāṭya*, literally 'the dance of Bharata', from *Bharata*, reputed to be the author of the *Nāṭyaśāstra*, a manual of dramatic art.

bhasha /ˈbɑːʃə/ ▸ **noun** [mass noun] Indian language.
– ORIGIN from Hindi *bhāṣā*.

bhava /ˈbɑːvə/ ▸ **noun** [mass noun] (in Indian dance and other performing arts) the emotion or mood conveyed by a performer.
– ORIGIN Hindi *bhāv* 'emotion, feeling', from Sanskrit *bhāvā* 'manner of acting, behaviour'.

bhavan /ˈbɑːvʌn/ ▸ **noun** [often in place names] Indian a building used for a special purpose, such as meetings or concerts.
– ORIGIN Hindi.

Bhavnagar /bʌvˈnʌgə/ an industrial port in NW India, in Gujarat, on the Gulf of Cambay; pop. 600,600 (est. 2009). It was the capital of a former Rajput princely state of the same name.

BHC ▸ **abbreviation** benzene hexachloride.

bhelpuri /ˈbeɪlˌpuːri/ ▸ **noun** [mass noun] an Indian dish of puffed rice, onions, spices, and hot chutney.
– ORIGIN from Hindi *bhel* 'mixture' + *pūrī* 'deep-fried bread'.

bhikkhu /ˈbɪkuː/ (also **bhikku**) ▸ **noun** a Buddhist monk or devotee.
– ORIGIN Pali, from Sanskrit *bhikṣú* 'beg'.

Bhil /biːl/ (also **Bheel**) ▸ **noun** a member of an indigenous people of central India.
▸ **adjective** relating to the Bhils.
– ORIGIN from Hindi *Bhīl*, from Sanskrit *Bhilla*.

Bhili /ˈbiːliː/ ▸ **noun** [mass noun] the Indic language of the Bhils.

bhindi /ˈbɪndiː/ ▸ **noun** Indian term for OKRA.
– ORIGIN from Hindi *bhiṇḍī*.

Bhisho /ˈbiːʃəʊ/ a town in southern South Africa, the capital of the province of Eastern Cape, situated near the coast to the north-east of Port Elizabeth; pop. 147,600 (est. 2009). Former name BISHO.

Bhojpuri /ˌbəʊdʒˈpʊəri/ ▸ **noun** [mass noun] one of the Bihari group of languages, spoken by some 20 million people in western Bihar and eastern Uttar Pradesh.

bhoona ▸ **noun** variant spelling of BHUNA.

Bhopal /bəʊˈpɑːl/ a city in central India, the capital of the state of Madhya Pradesh; pop. 1,752,200 (est. 2009). In December 1984 leakage of poisonous gas from an American-owned pesticide factory in the city caused the death of about 2,500 people.

bhp ▸ **abbreviation** brake horsepower.

Bhubaneswar /ˌbʊbəˈneɪʃwə/ a city in eastern India, capital of the state of Orissa; pop. 904,200 (est. 2009).

bhuna /ˈbuːnə/ (also **bhoona**) ▸ **noun** [mass noun] a medium-hot dry curry originating in Bengal, prepared typically by frying meat with spices at a high temperature: *lamb bhuna*.
– ORIGIN from Bengali, Urdu *bhunnā* 'to be fried', ultimately from Sanskrit *bhrajj* 'fry, parch, roast'.

Bhutan /buːˈtɑːn/ a small independent kingdom on the south-eastern slopes of the Himalayas, a protectorate of the Republic of India; pop. 691,100 (est. 2009); languages, Dzongkha (official), Nepali; capital, Thimphu.
– DERIVATIVES **Bhutanese** /ˌbuːtəˈniːz/ **adjective & noun.**

Bhutto[1] /ˈbuːtəʊ/, Benazir (1953–2007), Pakistani stateswoman, Prime Minister 1988–90 and 1993–6, daughter of Zulfikar Ali Bhutto. She was the first woman Prime Minister of a Muslim country. Defeated in elections in 1997, she was later charged with corruption offences and banned from public office; the conviction was subsequently overturned. She was assassinated after returning to Pakistan to campaign for re-election.

Bhutto[2] /ˈbuːtəʊ/, Zulfikar Ali (1928–79), Pakistani statesman, President 1971–3 and Prime Minister 1973–7. He was ousted by a military coup and executed for conspiring to murder a political rival.

Bi ▸ **symbol** the chemical element bismuth.

bi /bʌɪ/ ▸ **abbreviation** informal bisexual.

bi- /bʌɪ/ ▸ **combining form** two; having two: *bicoloured* | *biathlon*. See also BIN-. ■ occurring twice in every one or once in every two: *bicentennial*. ■ lasting for two: *biennial*. ■ doubly; in two ways: *biconcave*. ■ Chemistry (in names of compounds) containing two atoms or groups of a specified kind: *biphenyl*. ■ Chemistry denoting an acid salt: *bicarbonate*. ■ Botany & Zoology (of division and subdivision) twice over: *bipinnate*.
– ORIGIN from Latin, 'doubly, having two'; related to Greek *di-* 'two'.

> **USAGE** The meaning of **bimonthly** (and other similar words such as **biweekly** and **biyearly**) is ambiguous. Such words can either mean 'occurring or produced twice a month' or 'occurring or produced every two months'. The only way to avoid this ambiguity is to use alternative expressions like *every two months* and *twice a month*. **Biannual** and **biennial** are also confusing: **biannual** means 'occurring twice a year' and **biennial** means 'occurring every two years'.

Biafra /bɪˈafrə/ a state proclaimed in 1967, when part of eastern Nigeria, inhabited chiefly by the Igbo people, sought independence from the rest of the country. In the ensuing civil war the new state's troops were overwhelmed by numerically superior forces, and by 1970 it had ceased to exist.
– DERIVATIVES **Biafran adjective & noun.**

bialy /bɪˈɑːli/ ▸ **noun** (pl. **bialys**) US a flat bread roll topped with chopped onions.
– ORIGIN Yiddish, from BIAŁYSTOK, where such bread was originally made.

Białystok /bɪˈalɪstɒk/ an industrial city in NE Poland, close to the border with Belarus; pop. 294,817 (2007). Russian name BELOSTOK.

bi-amping ▸ **noun** [mass noun] informal the use of two amplifiers for high- and low-frequency ranges in an audio circuit.

biannual ▸ **adjective** occurring twice a year: *the biannual meeting of the planning committee*. Compare with BIENNIAL.
– DERIVATIVES **biannually adverb.**

> **USAGE** See USAGE at BIENNIAL and BI-.

Biarritz /ˌbɪəˈrɪts/, French /bjaʀits/ a seaside resort in SW France, on the Bay of Biscay; pop. 27,398 (2006).

bias ▸ **noun 1** [mass noun] inclination or prejudice for or against one person or group, especially in a way considered to be unfair: *there was evidence of* ***bias against*** *black applicants* | *the* ***bias towards*** *younger people in recruitment*. ■ a concentration on or interest in one particular area or subject: *his work showed a discernible* ***bias towards*** *philosophy*. ■ a systematic distortion of a statistical result due to a factor not allowed for in its derivation.
2 a direction diagonal to the weave of a fabric: *a turquoise silk dress* ***cut on the bias***.
3 Bowls the irregular shape given to one side of a bowl. ■ the oblique course that such a shape causes a bowl to run.
4 Electronics a steady voltage, magnetic field, or other factor applied to a system or device to cause it to operate over a predetermined range.
▸ **verb** (**biases, biasing, biased**) [with obj.] **1** cause to feel or show inclination or prejudice for or against someone or something: *readers said the paper was* ***biased towards*** *the Conservatives* | *editors were* ***biased against*** *authors from provincial universities*.
2 Electronics give a bias to.
– ORIGIN mid 16th cent. (in the sense 'oblique line'; also as an adjective meaning 'oblique'): from French *biais*, from Provençal, perhaps based on Greek *epikarsios* 'oblique'.

bias binding ▸ **noun** [mass noun] a narrow strip of fabric cut obliquely and used to bind edges or for decoration.

bias-cut ▸ **adjective** (of a garment or fabric) cut obliquely or diagonally across the grain.

biased ▸ **adjective** unfairly prejudiced for or against someone or something: *we will not tolerate this biased media coverage*.

bias-ply ▸ **adjective** North American term for CROSS-PLY.

biathlon ▸ **noun** a Nordic skiing event in which the competitors combine cross-country skiing and rifle shooting.
– DERIVATIVES **biathlete noun.**
– ORIGIN 1950s: from BI- 'two' + Greek *athlon* 'contest', on the pattern of *pentathlon*.

biaxial ▸ **adjective** having or relating to two axes. ■ (of crystals) having two optic axes, as in the orthorhombic, monoclinic, and triclinic systems.
– DERIVATIVES **biaxially adverb.**

bib[1] ▸ **noun 1** a piece of cloth or plastic fastened round a child's neck to keep its clothes clean while eating. ■ a loose-fitting sleeveless garment worn on the upper body for identification, especially by competitors and officials at sporting events. ■ the part above the waist of the front of an apron or pair of dungarees. ■ a patch of colour on the throat of a bird or other animal.
2 a common European inshore fish of the cod family. Also called POUT[2] or POUTING. ● *Trisopterus luscus*, family Gadidae.
– PHRASES **one's best bib and tucker** informal one's smartest clothes. **stick** (or **poke**) **one's bib in** Austral. informal interfere.
– ORIGIN late 16th cent.: probably from BIB[2].

bib[2] ▸ **verb** (**bibs, bibbing, bibbed**) [with obj.] archaic drink (something alcoholic).
– ORIGIN late Middle English: probably from Latin *bibere* 'to drink'.

bibber ▸ **noun** [in combination] a person who regularly drinks a specified drink: *a winebibber*.

bibb lettuce ▸ **noun** N. Amer. a butterhead lettuce of a variety that has crisp dark green leaves.
– ORIGIN late 19th cent.: named after Jack Bibb (1789–1884), the American horticulturalist who developed it.

bibcock ▸ **noun** a tap with a bent nozzle fixed at the end of a pipe.
– ORIGIN late 18th cent.: perhaps from BIB[1] and COCK[1].

bibelot /ˈbɪbələʊ/ ▸ **noun** a small, decorative ornament or trinket.
– ORIGIN late 19th cent.: from French, fanciful formation based on *bel* 'beautiful'.

bibi /ˈbiːbiː/ ▸ **noun** (pl. **bibis**) Indian a man's wife. ■ dated a man's non-European girlfriend.
– ORIGIN from Urdu *bībī*, from Persian.

Bible ▸ **noun** (**the Bible**) the Christian scriptures, consisting of the Old and New Testaments. ■ (**the Bible**) the Jewish scriptures, consisting of the Torah or Law, the Prophets, and the Hagiographa or Writings. ■ (also **bible**) a copy of the Christian or Jewish scriptures. ■ a particular edition or translation of the Bible: *the New English Bible*. ■ (**bible**) informal a book regarded as authoritative in a particular sphere: *a brand-new edition of this filmgoers' bible*.
– ORIGIN Middle English: via Old French from ecclesiastical Latin *biblia*, from Greek *(ta) biblia* '(the) books', from *biblion* 'book', originally a diminutive of *biblos* 'papyrus, scroll', of Semitic origin.

Bible-basher (also **Bible-thumper**) ▸ **noun** informal a person who expounds or follows the teachings of the Bible in an aggressively evangelical way.
– DERIVATIVES **Bible-bashing** (also **Bible-thumping**) **adjective & noun.**

Bible Belt ▸ **noun** (**the Bible Belt**) those areas of the southern and middle western United States and western Canada where Protestant fundamentalism is widely practised.

biblical ▸ **adjective** relating to or contained in the Bible: *the biblical account of creation* | *biblical times*. ■ resembling the language or style of the Bible: *there is a biblical cadence in the last words he utters*. ■ very great; on a very large scale: *we need rainfall of* ***biblical proportions*** *to bring us back to normal*.
– DERIVATIVES **biblically adverb.**

biblicist /ˈbɪblɪsɪst/ ▸ **noun** a person who interprets the Bible literally.
– ORIGIN mid 19th cent.: from BIBLICAL + -IST.

biblio- /ˈbɪblɪəʊ/ ▸ **combining form** relating to a book or books: *bibliomania* | *bibliophile*.
– ORIGIN from Greek *biblion* 'book'.

bibliography /ˌbɪblɪˈɒgrəfi/ ▸ **noun** (pl. **bibliographies**) a list of the books referred to in a scholarly work, typically printed as an appendix. ■ a list of the books of a specific author or publisher, or on a specific subject. ■ [mass noun] the history or systematic description of books, their authorship, printing, publication, editions, etc.
– DERIVATIVES **bibliographer noun, bibliographic** /-əˈgrafɪk/ **adjective, bibliographical** /-əˈgrafɪk(ə)l/ **adjective, bibliographically** /-əˈgrafɪk(ə)li/ **adverb.**
– ORIGIN early 19th cent.: from French *bibliographie* or modern Latin *bibliographia*, from Greek *biblion* 'book' + *-graphia* 'writing'.

bibliomancy /ˈbɪblɪə(ʊ)mansi/ ▸ **noun** [mass noun] the practice of foretelling the future by interpreting a randomly chosen passage from a book, especially the Bible.

bibliomania ▸ **noun** [mass noun] passionate enthusiasm for collecting and possessing books.
– DERIVATIVES **bibliomaniac noun & adjective.**

bibliometrics ▶ **plural noun** [treated as sing.] statistical analysis of books, articles, or other publications.
– DERIVATIVES **bibliometric** adjective.

bibliophile ▶ **noun** a person who collects or has a great love of books.
– DERIVATIVES **bibliophilic** adjective, **bibliophily** /-ˈbɪfɪli/ noun.
– ORIGIN early 19th cent.: from French, from Greek *biblion* 'book' + *philos* 'loving'.

bibliopole /ˈbɪblɪə(ʊ)pəʊl/ ▶ **noun** archaic a person who buys and sells books, especially rare ones.
– ORIGIN late 18th cent.: via Latin from Greek *bibliopōlēs*, from *biblion* 'book' + *pōlēs* 'seller'.

Bibliothèque nationale /ˌbɪblɪəʊˌtɛk ˌnasjəˈnɑːl/, French /bibljɔtɛk nasjɔnal/ the French national library in Paris, which receives a copy of every book and periodical etc. published in France.

bibliotherapy ▶ **noun** [mass noun] the use of books as therapy in the treatment of mental or psychological disorders.

bib overalls ▶ **plural noun** N. Amer. dungarees.

bib tap ▶ **noun** another term for **BIBCOCK**.

bibulous /ˈbɪbjʊləs/ ▶ **adjective** formal excessively fond of drinking alcohol.
– DERIVATIVES **bibulously** adverb, **bibulousness** noun.
– ORIGIN late 17th cent. (in the sense 'absorbent'): from Latin *bibulus* 'freely or readily drinking' (from *bibere* 'to drink') + **-OUS**.

bicameral /bʌɪˈkam(ə)r(ə)l/ ▶ **adjective** (of a legislative body) having two chambers.
– DERIVATIVES **bicameralism** noun.
– ORIGIN mid 19th cent.: from **BI-** 'two' + Latin *camera* 'chamber' + **-AL**.

bicarb ▶ **noun** [mass noun] informal sodium bicarbonate.

bicarbonate /bʌɪˈkɑːbənɪt, -nət/ ▶ **noun 1** Chemistry a salt containing the anion HCO_3^-.
2 (also **bicarbonate of soda**) [mass noun] sodium bicarbonate.

bice /bʌɪs/ ▶ **noun** [mass noun] a medium blue or blue-green pigment made from basic copper carbonate.
– ORIGIN Middle English (originally in the sense 'dark or brownish grey'): from Old French *bis* 'dark grey', of unknown ultimate origin.

bicentenary /ˌbʌɪsɛnˈtiːnəri, -ˈtɛn-/ ▶ **noun** (pl. **bicentenaries**) the two-hundredth anniversary of a significant event.
▶ **adjective** relating to a two-hundredth anniversary: *the huge bicentenary celebrations*.

bicentennial ▶ **noun & adjective** another term for **BICENTENARY**.

bicephalous /bʌɪˈsɛf(ə)ləs, -ˈkɛf-/ ▶ **adjective** having two heads.
– ORIGIN early 19th cent.: from **BI-** 'two' + Greek *kephalē* 'head' + **-OUS**.

biceps /ˈbʌɪsɛps/ ▶ **noun** (pl. **same**) any of several muscles having two points of attachment at one end, in particular: ■ (also **biceps brachii** /ˈbreɪkɪʌɪ/) a large muscle in the upper arm which turns the hand to face palm uppermost and flexes the arm and forearm. ■ (also **biceps femoris** /fɪˈmɔːrɪs/ or **leg biceps**) Anatomy a muscle in the back of the thigh which helps to flex the leg.
– ORIGIN mid 17th cent.: from Latin, literally 'two-headed', from *bi-* 'two' + *-ceps* (from *caput* 'head').

bichir /ˈbɪʃɪə/ ▶ **noun** an elongated African freshwater fish with an armour of hard shiny scales and a series of separate fins along its back. ● Genus *Polypterus*, family Polypteridae: several species, including *P. senegalus*.
– ORIGIN 1960s: via French from dialect Arabic *abu shīr*.

bichon frise /biːʃ(ə)n ˈfriːz/ ▶ **noun** (pl. **bichons frise** or **bichon frises**) a small dog of a breed with a fine, curly white coat.
– ORIGIN from French *barbichon* 'little water spaniel' + *frisé* 'curly-haired'.

bicker ▶ **verb** [no obj.] **1** argue about petty and trivial matters: *couples who **bicker over** who gets what from the divorce*.
2 literary (of water) flow or fall with a gentle repetitive noise; patter. ■ (of a flame or light) flash, gleam, or flicker.
– ORIGIN Middle English: of unknown origin.

bicky (also **bikky**) ▶ **noun** (pl. **bickies**) informal a biscuit.
– PHRASES **big bikkies** Austral./NZ informal a large sum of money: *just showing up is worth big bickies*.
– ORIGIN 1930s: diminutive of **BISCUIT**.

bicoastal /bʌɪˈkəʊst(ə)l/ ▶ **adjective** US living on, taking place in, or involving both the Atlantic and Pacific coasts of the US: *a bicoastal businessman*.

Bicol ▶ **noun & adjective** variant spelling of **BIKOL**.

bicolour ▶ **adjective** having two colours: *a male bicolour damselfish*.
▶ **noun** a bicolour flower or breed.
– DERIVATIVES **bicoloured** adjective & noun.

biconcave ▶ **adjective** concave on both sides.

biconvex ▶ **adjective** convex on both sides.

bicultural ▶ **adjective** having or combining the cultural attitudes and customs of two nations, peoples, or ethnic groups.
– DERIVATIVES **biculturalism** noun.

bicuspid ▶ **adjective** having two cusps or points.
▶ **noun** a tooth with two cusps, especially a human premolar tooth.
– ORIGIN mid 19th cent.: from **BI-** 'two' + Latin *cuspis*, *cuspid-* 'sharp point'.

bicuspid valve ▶ **noun** Anatomy another term for **MITRAL VALVE**.

bicycle ▶ **noun** a vehicle consisting of two wheels held in a frame one behind the other, propelled by pedals and steered with handlebars attached to the front wheel.
▶ **verb** [no obj., with adverbial of direction] ride a bicycle: *they spent the holidays bicycling around the beautiful Devonshire countryside*.
– DERIVATIVES **bicyclist** noun.
– ORIGIN mid 19th cent.: from **BI-** 'two' + Greek *kuklos* 'wheel'.

bicycle chain ▶ **noun** a chain that transmits the driving power from the pedals of a bicycle to its rear wheel.

bicycle clip ▶ **noun** each of a pair of metal clips worn by a cyclist round their ankles to prevent their trouser legs from becoming entangled with the bicycle chain.

bicycle pump ▶ **noun** a portable pump for inflating bicycle tyres.

bicycle rickshaw ▶ **noun** another term for **CYCLE RICKSHAW**.

bicyclic /bʌɪˈsʌɪklɪk, -ˈsɪk-/ ▶ **adjective** Chemistry having two fused rings of atoms in its molecule.

bid[1] ▶ **verb** (**bids**, **bidding**; past and past participle **bid**)
1 [with obj.] offer (a certain price) for something, especially at an auction: *a consortium of dealers bid a world record price for a snuff box* | [no obj.] *guests will **bid for** pieces of fine jewellery*. ■ [no obj.] (**bid for**) (of a contractor) offer to do (work) for a stated price; tender for: *nineteen companies have indicated their intention to bid for the contract*. ■ Bridge make a statement during the auction undertaking to make (a certain number of tricks with a stated suit as trumps) if the bid is successful and one becomes the declarer: *North bids four hearts*.
2 [no obj.] make an effort or attempt to achieve: [with infinitive] *she's now bidding to become a top female model* | *the two forwards are **bidding for** places in the England side*.
▶ **noun 1** an offer of a price, especially at an auction: *at the fur tables, several buyers make bids for the pelts*. ■ an offer to buy the shares of a company in order to gain control of it: *a takeover bid*. ■ an offer to do work or supply goods at a stated price; a tender. ■ Bridge an undertaking by a player in the auction to make a stated number of tricks with a stated suit as trumps.
2 an attempt or effort to achieve something: *he **made a bid for** power in 1984* | [with infinitive] *an investigation would be carried out **in a bid to** establish what had happened*.
– DERIVATIVES **bidder** noun.
– ORIGIN Old English *bēodan* 'to offer, command', of Germanic origin; related to Dutch *bieden* and German *bieten*.

bid[2] ▶ **verb** (**bids**, **bidding**; past **bid** or **bade**; past participle **bid**) [with obj.] **1** utter (a greeting or farewell) to: *James bade a tearful farewell to his parents*.
2 archaic or literary command or order (someone) to do something: *I did as he bade me*. ■ invite (someone) to do something: *he bade his companions enter*.
– PHRASES **bid fair to** archaic or literary seem likely to: *the girl bade fair to be pretty*.
– ORIGIN Old English *biddan* 'ask', of Germanic origin; related to German *bitten*.

bidarka /bʌɪˈdɑːkə/ ▶ **noun** a canoe covered with animal skins, used by the Inuit of Alaska and adjacent regions.
– ORIGIN early 19th cent.: from Russian *baĭdarka*, diminutive of *baĭdara* 'an umiak'.

biddable ▶ **adjective 1** meekly ready to accept and follow instructions.
2 Bridge strong enough to justify a bid.
– DERIVATIVES **biddability** /-ˈbɪlɪti/ noun.

bidden archaic or literary past participle of **BID**[2].

bidding ▶ **noun** [mass noun] **1** the offering of particular prices for something, especially at an auction. ■ the offers made in such a situation: *the bidding rose to £280,000*. ■ (in bridge and whist) the action of stating before play how many tricks one intends to make.
2 the ordering or requesting of someone to do something: *women came running **at his bidding*** | *Balfour refused to **do their bidding***.

bidding paddle ▶ **noun** a paddle-shaped baton, typically marked with an identifying number, used to signal bids at auctions.

bidding prayer ▶ **noun** (in church use) a prayer in the form of an invitation by a minister or leader to the congregation to pray about something.

biddy ▶ **noun** (pl. **biddies**) informal a woman, especially an elderly one, regarded as annoying or interfering: *the old biddies were muttering in his direction*.
– ORIGIN early 17th cent. (originally denoting a chicken): of unknown origin; probably influenced by the use of *biddy* denoting an Irish maidservant, from *Biddy*, pet form of the given name *Bridget*.

bide ▶ **verb** [no obj., with adverbial of place] archaic or dialect remain or stay somewhere: *how long must I bide here to wait for the answer?*
– PHRASES **bide one's time** wait quietly for a good opportunity to do something: *she patiently bided her time before making an escape bid*.
– ORIGIN Old English *bīdan*, of Germanic origin.

bidet /ˈbiːdeɪ/ ▶ **noun** a low oval basin used for washing one's genital and anal area.
– ORIGIN mid 17th cent. (in the sense 'horse'): from French, literally 'pony', from *bider* 'to trot', of unknown origin.

bidi /ˈbiːdiː/ (also **beedi** or **biri**) ▶ **noun** (pl. **bidis**) (in South Asia) a type of cheap cigarette made of unprocessed tobacco wrapped in leaves.
– ORIGIN from Hindi *bīḍī* 'betel plug, cigar', from Sanskrit *vīṭikā*.

bidirectional ▶ **adjective** functioning in two directions.

bidonville /ˈbɪd(ə)nvɪl/ ▶ **noun** a shanty town built of oil drums or other metal containers, especially on the outskirts of a North African city.
– ORIGIN 1950s: from French, from *bidon* 'container for liquids' + *ville* 'town'.

bid price ▶ **noun** the price at which a market-maker or dealer is prepared to buy securities or other assets. Compare with **OFFER PRICE**.

bidri /ˈbɪdri/ ▶ **noun** [mass noun] an alloy of copper, lead, tin, and zinc, used as a ground for inlaying with gold and silver.
– ORIGIN late 18th cent.: from Urdu *bidrī*, from *Bidar*, the name of a town in India.

Biedermeier /ˈbiːdəˌmʌɪə/ ▶ **adjective** denoting or relating to a style of furniture and interior decoration current in Germany in the period 1815–48, characterized by restraint, conventionality, and utilitarianism.
– ORIGIN from the name of Gottlieb *Biedermaier*, a fictitious German provincial schoolmaster and poet created by L. Eichrodt (1854).

Bielefeld /ˈbiːləˌfɛlt/ an industrial city in North Rhine-Westphalia in western Germany; pop. 325,800 (est. 2006).

biennale /ˌbiːɛˈnɑːleɪ, -li/ ▶ **noun** a large art exhibition or music festival, especially one held biennially.
– ORIGIN 1930s (used originally as the name of an international art exhibition held in Venice): from Italian, literally 'biennial'.

biennial /bʌɪˈɛnɪəl/ ▶ **adjective 1** taking place every other year: *the first of a series of biennial exhibitions*. Compare with **BIANNUAL**.
2 (of a plant) taking two years to grow from seed to fruition and die. Compare with **ANNUAL**, **PERENNIAL**.
▶ **noun 1** a biennial plant.
2 an event celebrated or taking place every two years.
– DERIVATIVES **biennially** adverb.
– ORIGIN early 17th cent.: from Latin *biennis* (from *bi-* 'twice' + *annus* 'year') + **-AL**.

> **USAGE** **Biennial** and **biannual** are often confused. **Biennial** means 'occurring every two years' (*the biennial Ryder Cup tournament*), while **biannual** means 'twice a year' (*the solstice is a biannual event*). See also **USAGE** at **BI-**.

biennium /bʌɪˈɛnɪəm/ ▶ **noun** (pl. **biennia** /-nɪə/ or **bienniums**) (usu. **the biennium**) a specified period of two years: *the budget for the next biennium.*
– ORIGIN early 20th cent.: from Latin, from *bi-* 'twice' + *annus* 'year'.

bien pensant /ˌbjã pɒ̃ˈsɒ̃/, French /bjɛ̃ pɑ̃sɑ̃/ ▶ **adjective** conventional or orthodox in attitude.
▶ **noun** (**bien-pensant**) a conventional or orthodox person.
– ORIGIN French, from *bien* 'well' + *pensant*, present participle of *penser* 'think'.

bier /bɪə/ ▶ **noun** a movable frame on which a coffin or a corpse is placed before burial or cremation or on which they are carried to the grave.
– ORIGIN Old English *bēr*, of Germanic origin; related to German *Bahre*, also to **BEAR**[1].

Bierce /bɪəs/, Ambrose (Gwinnett) (1842–*c.*1914), American writer, best known for his sardonic short stories and *The Devil's Dictionary* (1911). In 1913 he travelled to Mexico and mysteriously disappeared.

biface /ˈbʌɪfeɪs/ ▶ **noun** Archaeology a type of prehistoric stone implement flaked on both faces.

bifacial ▶ **adjective** having two faces, in particular: ■ Botany (of a leaf) having upper and lower surfaces that are structurally different. ■ Archaeology (of a flint or other artefact) worked on both faces.

biff informal ▶ **verb** [with obj.] strike (someone) roughly or sharply with the fist: *he biffed me on the nose.*
▶ **noun** a sharp blow with the fist.
– ORIGIN mid 19th cent. (originally US): symbolic of a short sharp movement.

biffin ▶ **noun** an English cooking apple of a dark red variety.
– ORIGIN late 18th cent.: representing a dialect pronunciation of *beefing*, from **BEEF** + **-ING**[1], with reference to the colour.

biffo ▶ **noun** [mass noun] Austral. informal physical or verbal conflict: *he got a red card for a bit of biffo in the box with the keeper.*

bifid /ˈbʌɪfɪd/ ▶ **adjective** Botany & Zoology (of a part of a plant or animal) divided by a deep cleft or notch into two parts: *a bifid leaf* | *the gut is bifid.*
– ORIGIN mid 17th cent.: from Latin *bifidus*, from *bi-* 'doubly' + *fidus* (from *findere* 'to split').

bifilar /bʌɪˈfʌɪlə/ ▶ **adjective** consisting of or involving two threads or wires.
– ORIGIN mid 19th cent.: from **BI-** 'two' + *filum* 'thread' + **-AR**[1].

bifocal ▶ **adjective** denoting a lens having two parts each with a different focal length, one for distant vision and one for near vision.
▶ **noun** (**bifocals**) a pair of glasses with bifocal lenses.

bifold ▶ **adjective** double or twofold.

bifter ▶ **noun** Brit. informal a cigarette or a cannabis cigarette.
– ORIGIN 1980s: of unknown origin.

BIFU ▶ **abbreviation** (in the UK) Banking, Insurance, and Finance Union.

bifurcate ▶ **verb** /ˈbʌɪfəkeɪt/ divide into two branches or forks: [no obj.] *just below Cairo the river bifurcates* | [with obj.] *the trail was bifurcated by a mountain stream.*
▶ **adjective** /bʌɪˈfəːkət/ divided into two branches or forks: *a bifurcate tree.*
– ORIGIN early 17th cent.: from medieval Latin *bifurcat-* 'divided into two forks', from the verb *bifurcare*, from Latin *bifurcus* 'two-forked', from *bi-* 'having two' + *furca* 'a fork'.

bifurcation ▶ **noun** [mass noun] the division of something into two branches or parts. ■ [count noun] either of two branches into which something divides.

big ▶ **adjective** (**bigger**, **biggest**) **1** of considerable size or extent: *her big hazel eyes* | *big buildings* | *big staff cuts.* ■ [attrib.] larger than other items of the same kind: *my big toe.* ■ grown-up: *I'm a big girl now.* ■ [attrib.] elder: *my big sister.* ■ informal on an ambitiously large scale: *a small company with big plans.* ■ [attrib.] informal doing a specified action very often or on a very large scale: *a big eater* | *a big gambler.* ■ informal showing great enthusiasm: *a big tennis fan.* ■ informal very popular or successful: *African bands which are big in Britain.*
2 of considerable importance or seriousness: *it's a big decision* | *his biggest problem is money* | *he made a big mistake.* ■ informal holding an important position or playing an influential role: *as a senior in college, he was a big man on campus.*
3 [predic.] informal, often ironic generous: *'I'm inclined to take pity on you.' 'That's big of you!'.*
▶ **verb** [with obj.] (**big something up**) Brit. informal praise or recommend something highly: *the record's been on the streets a while now, but it's certainly still worth bigging up.*
▶ **noun** (**the bigs**) N. Amer. informal the major league in a professional sport.
– PHRASES **be big with child** archaic be in a late stage of pregnancy. **the Big Board** US informal the New York Stock Exchange. **big cheese** informal an important person. [1920s: *cheese*, probably via Urdu from Persian *čīz* 'thing': the phrase *the cheese* was used earlier to mean 'first-rate' (i.e. *the* thing).] **Big Chief** (also **Big Daddy**) informal a person in authority; the head of an organization or enterprise. **the big idea** chiefly ironic a clever or important intention or scheme: *the government's big idea was to make public services competitive.* **the big lie** a gross distortion or misrepresentation of the facts, especially when used as a propaganda device by a politician or official body. **big money** (chiefly N. Amer. also **big bucks**) informal large amounts of money. **big name** (or **big noise**) informal a person who is famous in a particular sphere: *he's a big name in athletics.* **the big screen** informal the cinema. **big shot** informal an important or influential person. **the big stick** informal the use or threat of force or power: *the authorities used quiet persuasion instead of the big stick.* **the Big Three** (or **Four** etc.) informal the three, four, etc., most important or powerful figures in a particular field: *increased competition between the Big Three cider-makers.* **come** (or **go**) **over big** informal have a great effect; be a success: *the story went over big with the children.* **give someone the big E** Brit. informal reject someone. [*E* from *elbow*.] **in a big way** informal to a great extent or high degree: *he contributed to the film in a big way.* **make it big** informal become very successful or famous. **talk big** informal talk confidently or boastfully. **think big** informal be ambitious. **too big for one's boots** (or dated **breeches**) informal conceited.
– DERIVATIVES **biggish** adjective, **bigness** noun.
– ORIGIN Middle English (in the sense 'strong, mighty'): of unknown origin.

big air ▶ **noun** a high jump in sports such as skateboarding, snowboarding, and BMX.

bigamy ▶ **noun** [mass noun] the offence of marrying someone while already married to another person.
DERIVATIVES **bigamist** noun, **bigamous** adjective.
– ORIGIN Middle English: from Old French *bigamie*, from *bigame* 'bigamous', from late Latin *bigamus*, from *bi-* 'twice' + Greek *-gamos* 'married'.

Big Apple informal a name for New York City.

big band ▶ **noun** a large group of musicians playing jazz or dance music: [as modifier] *the big-band sound.*

Big Bang ▶ **noun 1** Astronomy the explosion of dense matter which according to current cosmological theories marked the origin of the universe.

> A fireball of radiation at extremely high temperature and density, but occupying a tiny volume, is believed to have formed. This expanded and cooled, extremely fast at first, but more slowly as subatomic particles condensed into matter which later accumulated to form galaxies and stars. The galaxies are currently still retreating from one another. What was left of the original radiation continued to cool and has been detected as a uniform background of weak microwave radiation.

2 (in the UK) the introduction in 1986 of major changes in trading on the Stock Exchange, principally involving widening of membership, relaxation of rules for brokers, and computerization.

Big Ben the great clock tower of the Houses of Parliament in London and its bell.

big box ▶ **noun** N. Amer. informal a very large store which sells goods at discount prices, especially one specializing in a particular type of merchandise.

Big Brother ▶ **noun** informal a person or organization exercising total control over people's lives.
– ORIGIN 1950s: from the name of the head of state in George Orwell's *Nineteen Eighty-Four* (1949).

big bud ▶ **noun** [mass noun] a disease of blackcurrant bushes in which the buds become swollen due to the presence of gall mites. ● The mite is *Cecidophyopsis ribis*, family Eriophyidae.

big business ▶ **noun** [mass noun] large-scale or important financial or commercial activity: *the children's toy market is big business now.*

big cat ▶ **noun** any of the large members of the cat family, including the lion, tiger, leopard, jaguar, snow leopard, clouded leopard, cheetah, and puma. ● *Panthera* and other genera, family Felidae.

big crunch ▶ **noun** Astronomy a contraction of the universe to a state of extremely high density and temperature (a hypothetical opposite of the big bang).

big dipper ▶ **noun 1** Brit. a roller coaster.
2 (**the Big Dipper**) North American term for **PLOUGH** (sense 2 of the noun).

Big Easy informal a name for New Orleans.

big end ▶ **noun** (in a piston engine) the larger end of the connecting rod, encircling the crankpin.

bigeneric /ˌbʌɪdʒɪˈnɛrɪk/ ▶ **adjective** Botany relating to or denoting a hybrid between two genera.

bigeye ▶ **noun 1** (also **bigeye tuna**) a large migratory tuna which is found in warm seas and is very important to the fishing industry. ● *Thunnus obesus*, family Scombridae.
2 a reddish fish with large eyes which lives in moderately deep waters of the tropical Atlantic and the western Indian Ocean. Also called **CATALUFA**. ● *Priacanthus arenatus*, family Priacanthidae.

Bigfoot ▶ **noun** (pl. **Bigfeet**) a large, hairy apelike creature resembling a yeti, supposedly found in NW America. See also **SASQUATCH**.
– ORIGIN from the size of its footprints.

big game ▶ **noun** [mass noun] large animals hunted for sport.

biggie ▶ **noun** (pl. **biggies**) informal a big, important, or successful person or thing: *composers including most of the biggies like Brahms, Wagner, Mendelssohn.*

big government ▶ **noun** [mass noun] chiefly N. Amer. government perceived as excessively interventionist and intruding into all aspects of the lives of its citizens.

bigha /ˈbiːɡə/ ▶ **noun** (in South Asia) a measure of land area varying locally from $^{1}/_{3}$ to 1 acre ($^{1}/_{8}$ to $^{2}/_{5}$ hectare).
– ORIGIN from Hindi *bīghā*.

big hair ▶ **noun** [mass noun] informal a bouffant hairstyle, especially one that has been teased, permed, or sprayed to create volume.

big-head ▶ **noun** informal a conceited or arrogant person.

big-headed ▶ **noun** informal conceited or arrogant: *I'm trying not to get too big-headed.*
– DERIVATIVES **big-headedness** noun.

big-hearted ▶ **adjective** (of a person or action) kind and generous.

big hitter ▶ **noun** another term for **HEAVY HITTER**.

bighorn (also **bighorn sheep**) ▶ **noun** (pl. **same** or **bighorns**) a stocky brown wild sheep with large horns, found in North America and NE Asia. ● Genus *Ovis*, family Bovidae: two species, in particular the **American bighorn** *O. canadensis* (also called **MOUNTAIN SHEEP**), found chiefly in the Rocky Mountains.

big house ▶ **noun** (usu. **the big house**) **1** the largest house in a village or area, typically inhabited by a family of high social standing.
2 US informal a prison.

bight /bʌɪt/ ▶ **noun 1** a curve or recess in a coastline, river, or other geographical feature.
2 a loop of rope.
– ORIGIN Old English *byht* 'a bend or angle', of Germanic origin; related to **BOW**[2].

big league ▶ **noun** a group of teams in a professional sport, especially baseball, competing for a championship at the highest level. ■ (**the big league**) informal a very successful or important group: *the film brought him into the movie world's big league.*
– DERIVATIVES **big leaguer** noun.

big media ▶ **noun** [treated as sing. or pl.] the main means of mass communication, i.e. television, radio, and the press, as opposed to blogs or other personal websites.

big mouth ▶ **noun** informal an indiscreet or boastful person.
– DERIVATIVES **big-mouthed** adjective.

big-note ▶ **verb** [with obj.] (**big-note oneself**) Austral./NZ informal boastfully exaggerate one's own wealth or importance: *he's continually trying to big-note himself.*

bigot /ˈbɪɡət/ ▶ **noun** a person who is bigoted.
– ORIGIN late 16th cent. (denoting a superstitious religious hypocrite): from French, of unknown origin.

bigoted ▶ **adjective** having or revealing an obstinate belief in the superiority of one's own opinions and

a prejudiced intolerance of the opinions of others: *a bigoted group of reactionaries | a bigoted article*.
– DERIVATIVES **bigotedly** adverb.

bigotry ▶ noun [mass noun] intolerance towards those who hold different opinions from oneself: *the report reveals racism and right-wing bigotry*.
– ORIGIN late 17th cent.: from **BIGOT**, reinforced by French *bigoterie*.

big science ▶ noun [mass noun] informal scientific research that is expensive and involves large teams of scientists.

big tent ▶ noun used in reference to a political party's policy of permitting or encouraging a broad spectrum of views among its members: [as modifier] *we're running a big-tent campaign*.

big-ticket ▶ adjective [attrib.] N. Amer. informal constituting a major expense: *big-ticket items such as cars, houses, and expensive vacations*.

big time informal ▶ noun (**the big time**) the highest or most successful level in a career, especially in entertainment: *a bit-part actor who finally made the big time in Hollywood*.
▶ adverb on a large scale; to a great extent: *this time they've messed up big time*.
– DERIVATIVES **big-timer** noun.

big top ▶ noun the main tent in a circus.

big tree ▶ noun North American term for **GIANT REDWOOD** (see **REDWOOD**).

biguanide /bʌɪˈɡwɑːnʌɪd/ ▶ noun [mass noun] Chemistry a crystalline compound with basic properties, made by condensation of two guanidine molecules. ● Chem. formula: $NH(C(NH)(NH_2))_2$.

big wheel ▶ noun **1** Brit. a Ferris wheel.
2 North American term for **BIGWIG**.

bigwig ▶ noun informal an important person, especially in a particular sphere: *government bigwigs*.
– ORIGIN early 18th cent.: so named from the large wigs formerly worn by distinguished men.

BIH ▶ abbreviation Bosnia and Herzegovina.
– ORIGIN from Bosnian *Bosna i Hercegovina*.

Bihar /bɪˈhɑː/ a state in NE India; capital, Patna.

Bihari /bɪˈhɑːri/ ▶ noun **1** a native or inhabitant of Bihar.
2 [mass noun] a group of three closely related Indic languages (Bhojpuri, Maithili, and Magahi) spoken principally in Bihar.
▶ adjective relating to Bihar, its peoples, or their languages.
– ORIGIN from Hindi *Bihārī*.

bijection /bʌɪˈdʒɛkʃ(ə)n/ ▶ noun Mathematics a mapping that is both one-to-one (an injection) and onto (a surjection), i.e. a function which relates each member of a set *S* (the domain) to a separate and distinct member of another set *T* (the range), where each member in *T* also has a corresponding member in *S*.
– DERIVATIVES **bijective** adjective.

bijou /ˈbiːʒuː/ ▶ adjective chiefly Brit. (especially of a house or flat) small and elegant.
▶ noun (pl. **bijoux** pronunc. **same**) archaic a jewel or trinket.
– ORIGIN French, from Breton *bizou* 'finger ring', from *biz* 'finger'.

bijouterie /biːˈʒuːt(ə)ri/, French /biʒutʀi/ ▶ noun [mass noun] jewellery or trinkets.
– ORIGIN French, from **BIJOU**.

bike informal ▶ noun a bicycle or motorcycle.
▶ verb [no obj., with adverbial of direction] ride a bicycle or motorcycle: *Danny bikes to the park and back every day*. ■ [with obj.] Brit. cause (a letter or package) to be delivered by bicycle or motorcycle: *I'll get them to bike the scripts over*.
– PHRASES **get off one's bike** Austral./NZ informal become annoyed. **on your bike!** Brit. informal go away (used as an expression of annoyance).
– ORIGIN late 19th cent.: abbreviation.

biker ▶ noun informal a motorcyclist, especially one who is a member of a gang. ■ a cyclist.

bikeway ▶ noun chiefly N. Amer. a path or lane for the use of bicycles.

bikie ▶ noun (pl. **bikies**) Austral./NZ informal a member of a gang of motorcyclists.

Bikini an atoll in the Marshall Islands, in the western Pacific, used by the US between 1946 and 1958 as a site for testing nuclear weapons.

bikini ▶ noun (pl. **bikinis**) a two-piece swimming costume for women.
– ORIGIN 1940s: named after **BIKINI**, where an atom bomb was exploded in 1946 (because of the supposed 'explosive' effect created by the garment).

bikini briefs ▶ plural noun scanty briefs worn by women as underwear.

bikini line ▶ noun the area of skin around the edge of the bottom half of a bikini (used especially with reference to the cosmetic removal of the pubic hair in this area).

bikini wax ▶ noun a cosmetic treatment in which unwanted pubic hair is removed from the bikini line by applying hot wax and then peeling off the wax and hair together.

bikky ▶ noun (pl. **bikkies**) variant spelling of **BICKY**.

Biko /ˈbiːkəʊ/, Steve (1946–77), South African radical leader; full name *Stephen Bantu Biko*. He was banned from political activity in 1973; after his death in police custody he became a symbol of heroic resistance to apartheid.

Bikol /bɪˈkɒl/ (also **Bicol**) ▶ noun (pl. **same** or **Bikols**) **1** a member of an indigenous people of SE Luzon in the Philippines.
2 [mass noun] the Austronesian language of the Bikol, with over 3 million speakers.
▶ adjective relating to the Bikol or their language.

Bikram yoga /ˈbɪkram/ ▶ noun [mass noun] trademark a type of hatha yoga characterized by a set series of postures and breathing exercises, performed in a room heated to a very high temperature.
– ORIGIN 1980s: named after the Indian yoga teacher *Bikram* Choudhury (b. 1946), who developed it.

bilabial ▶ adjective Phonetics (of a speech sound) formed by closure or near closure of the lips, e.g. *p*, *b*, *m*, *w*.
▶ noun a consonant sound made in such a way.

bilal /bɪˈlɑːl/ ▶ noun (in Malaysia) a muezzin.
– ORIGIN Malay, from Arabic *Bilal*, the first name of an Abyssinian slave appointed as the first muezzin following Muhammad's pilgrimage to Mecca in 629.

bilateral ▶ adjective **1** having or relating to two sides; affecting both sides: *bilateral hearing*.
2 involving two parties, especially countries: *the bilateral agreements with Japan*.
– DERIVATIVES **bilaterally** adverb.

bilateral symmetry ▶ noun [mass noun] the property of being divisible into symmetrical halves on either side of a unique plane.

bilayer ▶ noun Biochemistry a film two molecules thick (formed e.g. by lipids), in which each molecule is arranged with its hydrophobic end directed inwards towards the opposite side of the film and its hydrophilic end directed outwards.

Bilbao /bɪlˈbaʊ, -ˈbeɪəʊ/, Spanish /bilˈβaəo/ a seaport and industrial city in northern Spain; pop. 353,340 (2008).

bilberry ▶ noun (pl. **bilberries**) a hardy dwarf shrub with red drooping flowers and dark blue edible berries, growing on heathland and mountains in northern Eurasia. ● Genus *Vaccinium*, family Ericaceae: several species, in particular *V. myrtillus*.
■ the small blue edible berry of this plant.
– ORIGIN late 16th cent.: probably of Scandinavian origin; compare with Danish *bøllebær*.

bilbo ▶ noun (pl. **bilbos** or **bilboes**) a sword used in former times, noted for the temper and elasticity of its blade.
– ORIGIN mid 16th cent.: from *Bilboa*, an earlier English form of the name **BILBAO**, noted for the manufacture of fine blades.

bilboes ▶ plural noun an iron bar with sliding shackles, formerly used for confining a prisoner's ankles.
– ORIGIN mid 16th cent.: of unknown origin.

bilby /ˈbɪlbi/ ▶ noun (pl. **bilbies**) another term for **RABBIT-EARED BANDICOOT**.
– ORIGIN late 19th cent.: probably from an Aboriginal language.

Bildungsroman /ˈbɪldʊŋzrəʊˌmɑːn/ ▶ noun a novel dealing with one person's formative years or spiritual education.
– ORIGIN German, from *Bildung* 'education' + *Roman* 'a novel'.

bile ▶ noun [mass noun] **1** a bitter greenish-brown alkaline fluid which aids digestion and is secreted by the liver and stored in the gall bladder.
2 anger, bitterness, or irritability: *his response was full of bile and hatred*.
– ORIGIN mid 16th cent.: from French, from Latin *bilis*.

bile duct ▶ noun the duct which conveys bile from the liver and the gall bladder to the duodenum.

bi-level ▶ adjective having or functioning on two levels; arranged on two planes: *a bi-level ventilation system*. ■ N. Amer. denoting a style of two-storey house in which the lower storey is partially sunk below ground level, and the main entrance is between the two storeys. ■ denoting a railway carriage with seats on two levels.
▶ noun N. Amer. a bi-level house.

bilge ▶ noun **1** the area on the outer surface of a ship's hull where the bottom curves to meet the vertical sides. ■ (**bilges**) the lowest internal portion of the hull. ■ (also **bilge water**) [mass noun] dirty water that collects inside the bilges.
2 [mass noun] informal nonsense; rubbish: *romantic bilge dreamed up by journalists*.
▶ verb [with obj.] archaic break a hole in the bilge of (a ship).
– ORIGIN late 15th cent.: probably a variant of **BULGE**.

bilge keel ▶ noun each of a pair of plates or timbers fastened under the sides of the hull of a ship to provide lateral resistance to the water, prevent rolling, and support its weight in dry dock.

bilharzia /bɪlˈhɑːtsɪə/ ▶ noun [mass noun] a chronic disease, endemic in parts of Africa and South America, caused by infestation with blood flukes (schistosomes). Also called **BILHARZIASIS** or **SCHISTOSOMIASIS**. ■ a blood fluke (schistosome).
– ORIGIN mid 19th cent.: modern Latin, former name of the genus *Schistosoma*, named after T. *Bilharz* (1825–62), the German physician who discovered the parasite.

bilharziasis /ˌbɪlhɑːˈtsʌɪəsɪs/ ▶ noun Medicine another term for **BILHARZIA** (the disease).

biliary /ˈbɪlɪəri/ ▶ adjective Medicine relating to bile or the bile duct.
– ORIGIN mid 18th cent.: from French *biliaire*, from *bile* 'bile'.

bilinear ▶ adjective Mathematics **1** rare relating to or contained by two straight lines.
2 relating to or denoting a function of two variables that is linear and homogeneous in both independently.

bilingual ▶ adjective speaking two languages fluently: *a bilingual secretary*. ■ (of a text or an activity) written or conducted in two languages: *bilingual dictionaries | bilingual education*. ■ (of a country, city, or other community) using two languages, especially officially.
▶ noun a person fluent in two languages.
– DERIVATIVES **bilingualism** noun, **bilingually** adverb.
– ORIGIN mid 19th cent.: from Latin *bilinguis*, from *bi-* 'having two' + *lingua* 'tongue' + **-AL**.

bilious ▶ adjective **1** affected by or associated with nausea or vomiting: *a bilious attack*. ■ (of a colour) lurid or sickly: *a bilious yellow hue*.
2 spiteful; bad-tempered: *his bilious temperament*.
3 Physiology relating to bile.
– DERIVATIVES **biliously** adverb, **biliousness** noun.
– ORIGIN mid 16th cent. (in the sense 'biliary'): from Latin *biliosus*, from *bilis* 'bile'.

bilirubin /ˌbɪlɪˈruːbɪn/ ▶ noun [mass noun] Biochemistry an orange-yellow pigment formed in the liver by the breakdown of haemoglobin and excreted in bile.
– ORIGIN late 19th cent.: coined in German from Latin *bilis* 'bile' + *ruber* 'red' + **-IN**[1].

biliverdin /ˌbɪlɪˈvəːdɪn/ ▶ noun [mass noun] Biochemistry a green pigment excreted in bile. It is an oxidized derivative of bilirubin.
– ORIGIN mid 19th cent.: from Latin *bilis* 'bile' + French *vert* 'green' + **-IN**[1].

bilk informal ▶ verb [with obj.] **1** obtain or withhold money from (someone) unfairly or by deceit; cheat or defraud: *government waste has **bilked** the taxpayer **of** billions of dollars*. ■ obtain (money) fraudulently: *some businesses bilk thousands of dollars from unsuspecting elderly consumers*.
2 archaic evade; elude.
– DERIVATIVES **bilker** noun.
– ORIGIN mid 17th cent. (originally used in cribbage meaning 'spoil one's opponent's score'): perhaps a variant of **BAULK**.

Bill ▶ noun (**the Bill** or **the Old Bill**) [treated as sing. or pl.] Brit. informal the police.
– ORIGIN 1960s: pet form of the given name *William*.

bill[1] ▶ noun **1** a printed or written statement of the money owed for goods or services: *the bill for their meal came to £17*.

2 a draft of a proposed law presented to parliament for discussion: *a debate over the civil rights bill.*
3 a programme of entertainment at a theatre or cinema: *she was **top of the bill** at America's leading vaudeville house.*
4 N. Amer. a banknote: *a ten-dollar bill.*
5 a poster or handbill.
▸ **verb** [with obj.] **1** list (a person or event) in a programme: *they were billed to appear but did not show up.* ■ (**bill someone/thing as**) describe or advertise someone or something in a particular way: *he was billed as 'the new Sean Connery'.*
2 send a bill to (someone): *we shall be billing them for the damage caused* | [with two objs] *he had been billed £3,000 for his licence.* ■ charge (a sum of money): *we billed £400,000.*
– PHRASES **fit** (or **fill**) **the bill** be suitable for a particular purpose.
– DERIVATIVES **billable adjective**.
– ORIGIN Middle English (denoting a written list or catalogue): from Anglo-Norman French *bille*, probably based on medieval Latin *bulla* 'seal, sealed document' (see also **BULL**[2]).

bill[2] ▸ **noun 1** the beak of a bird, especially when it is slender, flattened, or weak, or belongs to a web-footed bird or a bird of the pigeon family. ■ the muzzle of a platypus. ■ N. Amer. the peak of a cap.
2 the point of an anchor fluke.
3 [in place names] a narrow promontory: *Portland Bill.*
▸ **verb** [no obj.] (of birds, especially doves) stroke bill with bill during courtship.
– PHRASES **bill and coo** informal behave or talk in a very loving or sentimental way.
– DERIVATIVES **billed adjective** [usu. in combination] *the red-billed weaver bird.*
– ORIGIN Old English *bile*, of unknown origin.

bill[3] ▸ **noun** a medieval weapon like a halberd with a hook instead of a blade.
– ORIGIN Old English *bil*, of West Germanic origin; related to German *Bille* 'axe'.

billabong ▸ **noun** Austral. a branch of a river forming a backwater or stagnant pool, made by water flowing from the main stream during a flood.
– ORIGIN mid 19th cent.: from Wiradhuri *bilabang* 'channel that is dry except after rain'.

billboard ▸ **noun** a large outdoor board for displaying advertisements; a hoarding.

billet[1] ▸ **noun** a place, especially a civilian's house, where soldiers are lodged temporarily. ■ informal a place to stop or stay: *the young people's stay at each of their billets was short.*
▸ **verb** (**billets**, **billeting**, **billeted**) [with obj. and adverbial of place] lodge (soldiers) in a particular place, especially a civilian's house: *most of the army was billeted within the town.* ■ assign temporary accommodation to: *the American team was billeted at Uxbridge.*
– ORIGIN late Middle English (originally denoting a short written document): from Anglo-Norman French *billette*, diminutive of *bille* (see **BILL**[1]). The verb is recorded in the late 16th cent., and the noun sense, 'a written order requiring a householder to lodge the bearer, usually a soldier', from the mid 17th cent.; hence the current meaning.

billet[2] ▸ **noun 1** a thick piece of wood. ■ a small bar of metal for further processing.
2 Architecture each of a series of short cylindrical pieces inserted at intervals in Norman decorative mouldings.
3 Heraldry a rectangle placed vertically as a charge.
– ORIGIN late Middle English: from Old French *billette* and *billot*, diminutives of *bille* 'tree trunk', from medieval Latin *billa*, *billus* 'branch, trunk', probably of Celtic origin.

billet-doux /ˌbɪleɪˈduː/ ▸ **noun** (pl. **billets-doux** /-ˈduːz/) dated or humorous a love letter.
– ORIGIN late 17th cent.: French, literally 'sweet note'.

billfish ▸ **noun** (pl. **same** or **billfishes**) a large, fast-swimming fish of open seas, with a streamlined body and a long pointed spear-like snout. It occurs on the surface in warmer waters and is a popular sporting fish. ● Family Istiophoridae: three genera and several species, including the marlins, sailfish, and spearfish.

billfold ▸ **noun** N. Amer. a wallet.

billhook ▸ **noun** a tool having a sickle-shaped blade with a sharp inner edge, used for pruning or lopping branches or other vegetation.

billiards /ˈbɪljədz/ ▸ **plural noun** [usu. treated as sing.] a game for two people, played on a billiard table, in which three balls are struck with cues into pockets round the edge of the table: (as modifier **billiard**) *a billiard ball.*
– ORIGIN late 16th cent.: from French *billard*, denoting both the game and the cue, diminutive of *bille* (see **BILLET**[2]).

billiard table ▸ **noun** a smooth rectangular cloth-covered table used for billiards, snooker, and some forms of pool, with six pockets at the corners and sides into which the balls can be struck.

billing ▸ **noun** [mass noun] **1** the fact of being advertised or described in a particular way: *they can justify their billing as Premier League favourites* | *he shared **top billing** with his wife.*
2 the process of preparing or sending invoices: *faster, more accurate order fulfilment and billing.* ■ (usu. **billings**) the total amount of business conducted in a given time, especially that of an advertising agency: *the account was worth about $2 million a year in billings.*

Billingsgate a London fish market dating from the 16th century. In 1982 the market moved to the Isle of Dogs in the East End.

Billings method ▸ **noun** a system for finding the time of ovulation by examining cervical mucus. It can be used as a form of birth control by avoiding sexual intercourse at that time.
– ORIGIN 1960s: named after Drs John and Evelyn *Billings*, who devised the method.

billion ▸ **cardinal number** (pl. **billions** or (with numeral or quantifying word) **same**) the number equivalent to the product of a thousand and a million; 1,000,000,000 or 10^9: *a world population of nearly 5 billion* | *half a billion dollars.* ■ (**billions**) informal a very large number or amount of something: *our immune systems are killing billions of germs right now.* ■ a billion pounds or dollars: *the problem persists despite the billions spent on it.* ■ dated, Brit. a million million (1,000,000,000,000 or 10^{12}).
– DERIVATIVES **billionth ordinal number**.
– ORIGIN late 17th cent.: from French, from *million*, by substitution of the prefix *bi-* 'two' for the initial letters.

billionaire ▸ **noun** a person possessing assets worth at least a billion pounds or dollars.
– ORIGIN mid 19th cent.: from **BILLION**, on the pattern of *millionaire*.

Billiton /bɪˈliːtɒn/ former name of **BELITUNG**.

bill of costs ▸ **noun** Brit. a solicitor's account of charges and expenses incurred while carrying out a client's business.

bill of exchange ▸ **noun** a written order to a person requiring them to make a specified payment to the signatory or to a named payee; a promissory note.

bill of fare ▸ **noun** dated a menu.

bill of goods ▸ **noun** N. Amer. a consignment of merchandise.
– PHRASES **sell someone a bill of goods** deceive someone, especially by persuading them to accept something untrue or undesirable.

bill of health ▸ **noun** a certificate relating to the incidence of infectious disease on a ship or in the port from which it has sailed.
– PHRASES **a clean bill of health** a declaration or confirmation that someone is healthy or that something is in good condition.

bill of indictment ▸ **noun** historical or N. Amer. a written accusation as presented to a grand jury.

bill of lading ▸ **noun** a detailed list of a ship's cargo in the form of a receipt given by the master of the ship to the person consigning the goods.

bill of quantities ▸ **noun** a detailed statement of work, prices, dimensions, and other details, for the erection of a building by contract.

Bill of Rights ▸ **noun** Law a statement of the rights of a class of people, in particular: ■ the English constitutional settlement of 1689, confirming the deposition of James II and the accession of William and Mary, guaranteeing the Protestant succession, and laying down the principles of parliamentary supremacy. ■ the first ten amendments to the Constitution of the US, ratified in 1791.

bill of sale ▸ **noun** a certificate of transfer of personal property, used especially where something is transferred as security for a debt.

billon /ˈbɪlən/ ▸ **noun** [mass noun] an alloy formerly used for coinage, containing gold or silver with a predominating amount of copper or other base metal.
– ORIGIN early 18th cent.: from French, literally 'bronze or copper money', in Old French 'ingot', from *bille* (see **BILLET**[2]).

billow ▸ **noun** a large undulating mass of something, typically cloud, smoke, or steam. ■ archaic a large sea wave.
▸ **verb** [no obj., with adverbial of direction] (of fabric) fill with air and swell outwards: *her dress **billowed out** around her.* ■ (of smoke, cloud, or steam) move or flow outward with an undulating motion: *smoke was billowing from the chimney-mouth* | (as adj. **billowing**) *all I could see was thick, billowing smoke.*
– DERIVATIVES **billowy adjective**.
– ORIGIN mid 16th cent.: from Old Norse *bylgja*.

billposter (also **billsticker**) ▸ **noun** a person who pastes up advertisements on hoardings.
– DERIVATIVES **billposting noun**.

billy[1] (also **billycan**) ▸ **noun** (pl. **billies**) Brit. a tin or enamel cooking pot with a lid and a wire handle, for use when camping.
– ORIGIN mid 19th cent.: perhaps from Aboriginal *billa* 'water'.

billy[2] ▸ **noun** (pl. **billies**) **1** short for **BILLY GOAT**.
2 (also **billy club**) N. Amer. a truncheon.
– ORIGIN mid 19th cent.: from *Billy*, pet form of the given name *William*.

billycart ▸ **noun** Austral. a go-kart.
– ORIGIN 1920s (in the sense 'a small handcart'): perhaps from **BILLY**[2]: formerly such carts were sometimes pulled by a goat.

billycock ▸ **noun** historical a kind of bowler hat.
– ORIGIN mid 19th cent.: said to be from the name of William *Coke*, nephew of Thomas William Coke, Earl of Leicester (1752–1842).

billy goat ▸ **noun** a male goat.

billy-o ▸ **noun** (in phrase **like billy-o**) Brit. informal very much, hard, or strongly: *I had to run like billy-o.*
– ORIGIN late 19th cent.: of unknown origin.

Billy the Kid see **BONNEY**.

bilobed (also **bilobate**) ▸ **adjective** having or consisting of two lobes.

bilocation ▸ **noun** [mass noun] the supposed phenomenon of being in two places simultaneously.

biltong /ˈbɪltɒŋ, ˈbəl-/ ▸ **noun** [mass noun] chiefly S. African lean meat which is salted and dried in strips.
– ORIGIN Afrikaans, from Dutch *bil* 'buttock' + *tong* 'tongue'.

BIM ▸ **abbreviation** British Institute of Management.

Bim /bɪm/ ▸ **noun** informal a native or inhabitant of Barbados.
– ORIGIN mid 19th cent.: of unknown origin.

bim ▸ **noun** US informal short for **BIMBO**.

bimah ▸ **noun** see **BEMA**.

bimanual ▸ **adjective** performed with both hands.
– DERIVATIVES **bimanually adverb**.

bimbo ▸ **noun** (pl. **bimbos**) informal, derogatory an attractive but unintelligent or frivolous young woman.
– DERIVATIVES **bimbette noun**.
– ORIGIN early 20th cent. (originally in the sense 'fellow, chap'): from Italian, literally 'little child'.

bi-media ▸ **adjective** involving or working in two of the mass communication media, especially radio and television: *a bi-media journalist.*

bimetallic ▸ **adjective 1** made of two metals.
2 historical relating to bimetallism.
– ORIGIN late 19th cent.: from French *bimétallique*, from *bi-* 'two' + *métallique* 'metallic'.

bimetallic strip ▸ **noun** a temperature-sensitive electrical contact used in some thermostats, consisting of two bands of different metals joined lengthwise. When heated, the metals expand at different rates, causing the strip to bend.

bimetallism /bʌɪˈmɛt(ə)lɪz(ə)m/ ▸ **noun** [mass noun] historical a system of allowing the unrestricted currency of two metals (e.g. gold and silver) as legal tender at a fixed ratio to each other.
– DERIVATIVES **bimetallist noun**.

bimillenary /ˌbʌɪmɪˈlɛnəri, -ˈliːn-, bʌɪˈmɪlənəri/ ▸ **adjective** [attrib.] relating to a period of two thousand years or a two-thousandth anniversary.
▸ **noun** (pl. **bimillenaries**) a period of two thousand years or a two-thousandth anniversary.

bimodal ▸ **adjective** having or involving two modes, in particular (of a statistical distribution) having two maxima.

bimolecular ▸ **adjective** Chemistry consisting of or involving two molecules.

bimonthly ▸ **adjective** occurring or produced twice a month or every two months: *a bimonthly newsletter.*
▸ **adverb** twice a month or every two months.

▶ noun (pl. **bimonthlies**) a periodical produced twice a month or every two months.

bin Brit. ▶ noun **1** a receptacle in which to deposit rubbish. ■ [with modifier] a capacious receptacle for storing a specified substance: *a compost bin.* ■ a partitioned stand for storing bottles of wine.
2 Statistics each of a series of ranges of numerical value into which data are sorted in statistical analysis.
▶ verb (**bins, binning, binned**) [with obj.] **1** informal throw (something) away by putting it in a bin: *piles of junk that should have been binned years ago.* ■ discard or reject: *the whole idea had to be binned.* ■ (**bin someone off**) Brit. informal end a relationship with someone: *she was a bit weird so I binned her off.*
2 store (something, especially wine) in a bin.
3 Statistics group together (data) in bins.
– ORIGIN Old English *bin(n), binne*, of Celtic origin; related to Welsh *ben* 'cart'. The original meaning was 'receptacle' in a general sense; also 'a receptacle for provender in a stable' and 'container for grain, bread, or other foodstuffs'. The sense 'receptacle for rubbish' dates from the mid 19th cent.

bin- ▶ prefix variant form of **BI-** before a vowel (as in *binaural*).

binary /ˈbʌɪnəri/ ▶ adjective **1** relating to, composed of, or involving two things.
2 relating to, using, or denoting a system of numerical notation that has 2 rather than 10 as a base.
▶ noun (pl. **binaries**) **1** [mass noun] the binary system of notation.
2 something having two parts. ■ a binary star.
– ORIGIN late Middle English (in the sense 'duality, a pair'): from late Latin *binarius*, from *bini* 'two together'.

binary code ▶ noun [mass noun] Electronics a coding system using the binary digits 0 and 1 to represent a letter, digit, or other character in a computer or other electronic device.

binary coded decimal (abbrev.: **BCD**) ▶ noun [mass noun] Electronics a system for coding a number in which each digit of a decimal number is represented individually by its binary equivalent. ■ [count noun] a number represented in this way.

binary digit ▶ noun one of two digits (0 or 1) in a binary system of notation.

binary star ▶ noun Astronomy a system of two stars in which one star revolves round the other or both revolve round a common centre.

binary system ▶ noun **1** a system in which information can be expressed by combinations of the digits 0 and 1.
2 a system consisting of two parts: *the binary system of state and public schools.* ■ Astronomy a star system containing two stars orbiting around each other.

binary tree ▶ noun Computing a data structure in which a record is linked to two successor records, usually referred to as the left branch when greater and the right when less than the previous record.

binational ▶ adjective concerning or consisting of two nations.

binaural /bɪˈnɔːr(ə)l, bʌɪ-/ ▶ adjective relating to or involving both ears: *human hearing is binaural.* ■ relating to sound recorded using two microphones and usually transmitted separately to the two ears of the listener.

bin bag ▶ noun Brit. a large, strong plastic bag used as a container for household rubbish.

bind ▶ verb (past and past participle **bound**) [with obj.]
1 tie or fasten (something) tightly together: *logs **bound together** with ropes | they bound her hands and feet.* ■ restrain (someone) by tying their hands and feet: *the raider then bound and gagged Mr Glenn.* ■ wrap (something) tightly: *her hair was **bound up** in a towel.* ■ bandage (a wound): *Shelley cleaned the wound and **bound** it **up** with a clean dressing.* ■ (**be bound with**) (of an object) be encircled by something, typically metal bands, so as to have greater strength: *an ancient oak chest bound with brass braces.*
2 stick together or cause to stick together in a single mass: [with obj.] *mix the flour with the coconut and enough egg white to bind them.* ■ cause (painting pigments) to form a smooth medium by mixing them with oil. ■ hold by chemical bonding. ■ [no obj.] (**bind to**) combine with (a substance) through chemical bonding.
3 cause (people) to feel united: *the comradeship that had **bound** such a disparate bunch of lads **together**.* ■ (**bind someone to**) cause someone to feel strongly attached to (a person or place): *touches like that had bound men to him for life.*
4 impose a legal or contractual obligation on: *a party who signs a document will normally be bound by its terms.* ■ indenture (someone) as an apprentice. ■ (**bind oneself**) formal make a contractual or enforceable undertaking: *the government cannot bind itself as to the form of subsequent legislation.* ■ (of a court of law) require (someone) to fulfil an obligation, typically by paying a sum of money as surety: *he was bound over to keep the peace by magistrates.* ■ (**be bound by**) be hampered or constrained by: *Sarah did not want to be bound by a rigid timetable.*
5 fix together and enclose (the pages of a book) in a cover: *a small, fat volume, bound in red morocco.*
6 trim (the edge of a piece of material) with a decorative strip: *a frill with the edges **bound in** a contrasting colour.*
7 Logic (of a quantifier) be applied to (a given variable) so that the variable falls within its scope. For example, in an expression of the form 'For every *x*, if *x* is a dog, *x* is an animal', the universal quantifier is binding the variable *x*.
8 Linguistics (of a rule or set of grammatical conditions) determine the relationship between (coreferential noun phrases).
9 (of a food or medicine) make (someone) constipated.
▶ noun **1** informal a nuisance: *I know being disturbed on Christmas Day is a bind.* ■ a problematical situation: *he is in a political bind over the abortion issue.*
2 formal a statutory constraint: *the moral bind of the law.*
3 Music another term for **TIE**.
4 another term for **BINE**.
– PHRASES **bind someone hand and foot** see **HAND**.
– PHRASAL VERBS **bind off** N. Amer. cast off in knitting.
– ORIGIN Old English *bindan*, of Germanic origin; related to Dutch and German *binden*, from an Indo-European root shared by Sanskrit *bandh*.

bindaas /ˈbɪndɑːs/ ▶ adjective Indian informal carefree, fashionable, and independent-minded: *Bollywood's most bindaas babe.*
– ORIGIN Gujarati *bin-dās*, literally 'without servitude', from Sanskrit *vinā* + *dāsya*.

binder ▶ noun **1** a cover for holding magazines or loose sheets of paper together.
2 a substance used to make other substances or materials stick or mix together.
3 a reaping machine that binds grain into sheaves.
4 a bookbinder.

binder twine ▶ noun [mass noun] (in farming) strong cord made from plastic or natural fibre, used in a baling machine to tie hay and straw bales.

bindery ▶ noun (pl. **binderies**) a workshop or factory in which books are bound.

bindi /ˈbɪndiː/ ▶ noun (pl. **bindis**) a decorative mark worn in the middle of the forehead by Indian women, especially Hindus.
– ORIGIN from Hindi *bindī*.

bindi-eye /ˈbɪndɪʌɪ/ ▶ noun a small perennial Australian plant of the daisy family, with a bur-like fruit.
● *Calotis cuneifolia*, family Compositae.
– ORIGIN early 20th cent.: perhaps from an Aboriginal language.

binding ▶ noun **1** a strong covering holding the pages of a book together.
2 [mass noun] fabric cut or woven in a strip, used for binding the edges of a piece of material.
3 (also **ski binding**) Skiing a mechanical device fixed to a ski to grip a ski boot, especially either of a pair used for downhill skiing which hold the toe and heel of the boot and release it automatically in a fall.
4 [mass noun] (in Chomskyan linguistics) the relationship between a referentially dependent noun (such as a reflexive) and the independent noun phrase which determines its reference.
▶ adjective (of an agreement or promise) involving an obligation that cannot be broken: *business agreements are intended to be legally binding.*

binding energy ▶ noun [mass noun] Physics the energy that holds a nucleus together. This is equal to the mass defect of the nucleus.

binding post ▶ noun Electronics a connector consisting of a threaded screw to which bare wires are attached and held in place by a nut.

binding site ▶ noun Biochemistry a location on a macromolecule or cellular structure at which chemical interaction with a specific active substance takes place.

bindlestiff /ˈbɪnd(ə)lstɪf/ ▶ noun US informal a tramp.
– ORIGIN early 20th cent.: probably from an alteration of **BUNDLE** + **STIFF** (in the sense 'useless person').

bindweed /ˈbʌɪndwiːd/ ▶ noun [mass noun] a twining plant with trumpet-shaped flowers, several kinds of which are invasive weeds. ● Genera *Convolvulus* and *Calystegia*, family Convolvulaceae: several species, in particular the **hedge** (or **larger**) **bindweed** (*Calystegia sepium*).
■ used in names of similar twining plants, e.g. **black bindweed**.

bine /bʌɪn/ ▶ noun a long, flexible stem of a climbing plant, especially the hop.
– ORIGIN early 19th cent.: originally a dialect form of **BIND**.

bin-end ▶ noun Brit. one of the last bottles from a bin of wine, usually sold at a reduced price.

Binet /ˈbiːneɪ/, Alfred (1857–1911), French psychologist. He devised a mental age scale which described performance in relation to the average performance of students of the same physical age, and with the psychiatrist **Théodore Simon** (1873–1961) pioneered a system of intelligence tests.

bing[1] ▶ noun chiefly Scottish a heap, especially of metallic ore or of waste from a mine.
– ORIGIN early 16th cent.: from Old Norse *bingr* 'heap'.

bing[2] ▶ exclamation indicating a sudden action or event: *then, bing, the lights went on.*
– ORIGIN late 19th cent.: (originally dialect in the sense 'sudden bang'): imitative.

binge informal ▶ noun a period of excessive indulgence in an activity, especially drinking alcohol or eating: *he **went on a binge** and was in no shape to drive.*
▶ verb (**binges, bingeing** or **binging, binged**) [no obj.] indulge in an activity, especially eating, to excess: *she **binged on** ice cream.*
– DERIVATIVES **binger** noun.
– ORIGIN mid 19th cent.: from English dialect *binge* 'to soak a wooden vessel'.

binge drinking ▶ noun [mass noun] the consumption of an excessive amount of alcohol in a short period of time: *teenagers as young as 16 admit to binge drinking.*
– DERIVATIVES **binge-drink** verb, **binge drinker** noun.

binge eating ▶ noun [mass noun] the consumption of large quantities of food in a short period of time, typically as part of an eating disorder.
– DERIVATIVES **binge eater** noun.

bingle /ˈbɪŋg(ə)l/ ▶ noun Austral. informal a collision.
– ORIGIN 1940s: diminutive of dialect *bing* 'thump, blow' (compare **BING**[2]).

bingo ▶ noun a game in which players mark off numbers on cards as the numbers are drawn randomly by a caller, the winner being the first person to mark off all their numbers.
▶ exclamation **1** a call by someone who wins a game of bingo.
2 used to express satisfaction at a sudden positive event or outcome: *Just swipe the pen over a bar code and bingo! The recorder's programmed itself.*
– ORIGIN 1920s (as exclamation): of unknown origin.

bingo wings ▶ plural noun Brit. informal folds of loose flesh or skin hanging from the undersides of a woman's upper arms.
– ORIGIN 1990s: from an association with the game of **BINGO**, in which the loose flesh may be visible when a winner calls out and raises their card.

bin liner ▶ noun Brit. a plastic bag used for lining a rubbish bin.

binman ▶ noun (pl. **binmen**) Brit. informal a dustman.

binnacle /ˈbɪnək(ə)l/ ▶ noun a built-in housing for a ship's compass.
– ORIGIN late 15th cent. (as *bittacle*): from Spanish *bitácula, bitácora* or Portuguese *bitacola*, from Latin *habitaculum* 'dwelling place', from *habitare* 'inhabit'. The change to *binnacle* occurred in the mid 18th cent.

binocs ▶ plural noun informal short for **BINOCULARS**.

binocular /bɪˈnɒkjʊlə/ ▶ adjective adapted for or using both eyes: *a binocular microscope.*
– DERIVATIVES **binocularly** adverb.
– ORIGIN early 18th cent. (in the sense 'having two eyes'): from Latin *bini* 'two together' + *oculus* 'eye', on the pattern of *ocular*.

binoculars (also **a pair of binoculars**) ▶ plural noun an optical instrument with a lens for each eye, used for viewing distant objects.
– ORIGIN late 19th cent.: plural of **BINOCULAR**.

binocular vision ▶ noun [mass noun] vision using two eyes with overlapping fields of view, allowing good perception of depth.

binomial /bʌɪˈnəʊmɪəl/ ▶ noun **1** Mathematics an algebraic expression of the sum or the difference of two terms.
2 a two-part name, especially the Latin name of a species of living organism (consisting of the genus followed by the specific epithet).
3 Grammar a noun phrase with two heads joined by a conjunction, in which the order is relatively fixed (as in *knife and fork*).
▶ adjective **1** Mathematics consisting of two terms. ■ relating to a binomial or to the binomial theorem.
2 having or using two names (used especially of the Latin name of a species of living organism).
– ORIGIN mid 16th cent.: from French *binôme* or modern Latin *binomium* (from *bi-* 'having two' + Greek *nomos* 'part, portion') + -AL.

binomial distribution ▶ noun Statistics a frequency distribution of the possible number of successful outcomes in a given number of trials in each of which there is the same probability of success.

binomial nomenclature ▶ noun [mass noun] Biology the system of nomenclature in which two terms are used to denote a species of living organism, the first one indicating the genus and the second the specific epithet.

binomial theorem ▶ noun a formula for finding any power of a binomial without multiplying at length.

binominal ▶ adjective another term for BINOMIAL (sense 2 of the adjective).
– ORIGIN late 19th cent.: from Latin *binominis*, from *bi-* 'having two' + *nomen, nomin-* 'name' + -AL.

bins ▶ plural noun informal short for BINOCULARS.

bint ▶ noun Brit. informal, derogatory a girl or woman.
– ORIGIN mid 19th cent.: from Arabic, literally 'daughter, girl'.

binturong /ˈbɪntjʊrɒŋ/ ▶ noun a tree-dwelling Asian civet with a coarse blackish coat and a muscular prehensile tail. ● *Arctictis binturong*, family Viverridae.
– ORIGIN early 19th cent.: from Malay.

binucleate /bʌɪˈnjuːklɪət/ ▶ adjective Biology (of a cell) having two nuclei.

bio ▶ noun (pl. **bios**) informal a biography.
– ORIGIN 1960s: abbreviation.

bio- /ˈbʌɪəʊ/ ▶ combining form relating to life: *biosynthesis*. ■ biological; relating to biology: *biohazard*. ■ of living beings: *biogenesis*. ■ relating to or involving the use of toxic biological or biochemical substances as weapons of war: *bioterrorism*.
– ORIGIN from Greek *bios* '(course of) human life'. The sense is extended in modern scientific usage to mean 'organic life'.

bioaccumulate ▶ verb [no obj.] (of a substance) become concentrated inside the bodies of living things.
– DERIVATIVES **bioaccumulation** noun.

bioacoustics ▶ plural noun [treated as sing.] the branch of acoustics concerned with sounds produced by or affecting living organisms, especially as relating to communication.

bioactive ▶ adjective (of a substance) having a biological effect.
– DERIVATIVES **bioactivity** noun.

bioassay /ˌbʌɪəʊəˈseɪ/ ▶ noun [mass noun] measurement of the concentration or potency of a substance by its effect on living cells or tissues.

bioavailability ▶ noun [mass noun] Physiology the proportion of a drug or other substance which enters the circulation when introduced into the body and so is able to have an active effect.
– DERIVATIVES **bioavailable** adjective.

biocenosis ▶ noun US spelling of BIOCOENOSIS.

biocentrism ▶ noun [mass noun] the view or belief that the rights and needs of humans are not more important than those of other living things.
– DERIVATIVES **biocentric** adjective.

biochemical ▶ adjective relating to the chemical processes and substances which occur within living organisms.
▶ noun a biochemical substance.
– DERIVATIVES **biochemically** adverb.

biochemistry ▶ noun [mass noun] the branch of science concerned with the chemical and physico-chemical processes and substances which occur within living organisms. ■ processes and substances of this kind: *abnormal brain biochemistry*.
– DERIVATIVES **biochemist** noun.

biochip ▶ noun a microchip designed or intended to function in a biological environment, especially inside a living organism. ■ a logical device analogous to the silicon chip, whose components are formed from biological molecules or structures.

biocide ▶ noun **1** a poisonous substance, especially a pesticide.
2 [mass noun] the destruction of life.
– DERIVATIVES **biocidal** adjective.

biocircuit ▶ noun an integrated circuit incorporating biological molecules or structures.

bioclast /ˈbʌɪə(ʊ)klast/ ▶ noun Geology a fragment of a shell or fossil forming part of a sedimentary rock.
– DERIVATIVES **bioclastic** adjective.

bioclimatic ▶ adjective Ecology relating to the interrelation of climate and the activities and distribution of living organisms.

biocoenosis /ˌbʌɪə(ʊ)sɪˈnəʊsɪs/ (US **biocenosis**) ▶ noun (pl. **biocoenoses** /-siːz/) Ecology an association of different organisms forming a closely integrated community.
– ORIGIN late 19th cent.: modern Latin, from BIO- 'life' + Greek *koinōsis* 'sharing' (from *koinos* 'common').

biocompatible ▶ adjective (especially of material used in surgical implants) not harmful or toxic to living tissue.
– DERIVATIVES **biocompatibility** noun.

biocomputer ▶ noun a (hypothetical) computer based on circuits and components formed from biological molecules or structures. ■ the brain regarded as a computer.
– DERIVATIVES **biocomputing** noun.

biocontrol ▶ noun short for BIOLOGICAL CONTROL.

bioconversion ▶ noun [mass noun] the conversion of one chemical compound, or one form of energy, into another by living organisms.

biodata ▶ plural noun [treated as sing. or pl.] biographical details. ■ [treated as sing.] Indian a curriculum vitae.

biodegradable ▶ adjective (of a substance or object) capable of being decomposed by bacteria or other living organisms and thereby avoiding pollution.
– DERIVATIVES **biodegradability** noun.

biodegrade ▶ verb [no obj.] (of a substance or object) be decomposed by bacteria or other living organisms.
– DERIVATIVES **biodegradation** noun.

biodiesel ▶ noun [mass noun] a biofuel intended as a substitute for diesel.

biodiverse ▶ adjective (of a habitat or region) having a high level of biodiversity: *Australia is one of the most biodiverse regions on earth*.

biodiversity ▶ noun [mass noun] the variety of plant and animal life in the world or in a particular habitat, a high level of which is usually considered to be important and desirable.

biodynamics ▶ plural noun [treated as sing.] **1** the study of physical motion or dynamics in living systems.
2 a method of organic farming that incorporates certain astrological and spiritual principles and practices.
– DERIVATIVES **biodynamic** adjective.

bioelectric ▶ adjective relating to electricity or electrical phenomena produced within living organisms.
– DERIVATIVES **bioelectrical** adjective.

bioelectronics ▶ plural noun [treated as sing.] the branch of science concerned with the application of biological materials and processes in electronics, and the use of electronic devices in living systems.

bioenergetics ▶ plural noun [treated as sing.] **1** the study of the transformation of energy in living organisms.
2 a system of holistic therapy in which massage and other physical therapies are used in conjunction with psychotherapy.
– DERIVATIVES **bioenergetic** adjective.

bioenergy ▶ noun [mass noun] renewable energy produced by living organisms.

bioengineering ▶ noun [mass noun] **1** another term for GENETIC ENGINEERING.
2 the use of artificial tissues, organs, or organ components to replace damaged or absent body parts.
3 the use in engineering or industry of organisms or biological processes.
– DERIVATIVES **bioengineer** noun & verb.

bioethanol ▶ noun [mass noun] ethanol produced from plants such as sugar cane or maize, used as an alternative to petrol.

bioethics ▶ plural noun [treated as sing.] the ethics of medical and biological research.
– DERIVATIVES **bioethical** adjective, **bioethicist** noun.

biofeedback ▶ noun [mass noun] the use of electronic monitoring of a normally automatic bodily function in order to train someone to acquire voluntary control of that function.

biofilm ▶ noun a thin but robust layer of mucilage adhering to a solid surface and containing a community of bacteria and other microorganisms.

bioflavonoid ▶ noun any of a group of compounds occurring mainly in citrus fruits and blackcurrants, formerly regarded as vitamins.

biofouling ▶ noun [mass noun] the fouling of underwater pipes and other surfaces by organisms such as barnacles and algae.

biofuel ▶ noun a fuel derived immediately from living matter.

biog ▶ noun informal a biography.

biogas ▶ noun [mass noun] gaseous fuel, especially methane, produced by the fermentation of organic matter.

biogenesis /ˌbʌɪə(ʊ)ˈdʒɛnɪsɪs/ ▶ noun [mass noun] the synthesis of substances by living organisms. ■ historical the hypothesis that living matter arises only from other living matter.
– DERIVATIVES **biogenetic** adjective.

biogenic /ˌbʌɪə(ʊ)ˈdʒɛnɪk/ ▶ adjective produced or brought about by living organisms.

biogeochemical ▶ adjective relating to or denoting the cycle in which chemical elements and simple substances are transferred between living systems and the environment.
– DERIVATIVES **biogeochemist** noun, **biogeochemistry** noun.

biogeography ▶ noun [mass noun] the branch of biology that deals with the geographical distribution of plants and animals.
– DERIVATIVES **biogeographer** noun, **biogeographic** adjective, **biogeographical** adjective, **biogeographically** adverb.

biographee ▶ noun a person who is the subject of a biography.

biographical ▶ adjective (of data or a written work) dealing with a particular person's life: *biographical information* | *biographical books on the Beatles*.
– DERIVATIVES **biographic** adjective, **biographically** adverb.

biography ▶ noun (pl. **biographies**) an account of someone's life written by someone else. ■ [mass noun] writing of such a type as a literary genre.
– DERIVATIVES **biographer** noun.
– ORIGIN late 17th cent.: from French *biographie* or modern Latin *biographia*, from medieval Greek, from *bios* 'life' + *-graphia* 'writing'.

biohazard ▶ noun a risk to human health or the environment arising from biological work, especially with microorganisms.

bioindicator ▶ noun an organism used as an indicator of the quality of an ecosystem, especially in terms of pollution.

bioinformatics ▶ plural noun [treated as sing.] the science of collecting and analysing complex biological data such as genetic codes.
– DERIVATIVES **bioinformatic** adjective.

Bioko /bɪˈəʊkəʊ/ an island of Equatorial Guinea, in the eastern part of the Gulf of Guinea. Its chief town is Malabo, the capital of Equatorial Guinea. Former names FERNANDO PÓO and MACIAS NGUEMA.

biolistics ▶ plural noun [treated as sing.] a technique in genetic engineering in which tiny metal pellets coated with DNA are propelled into living cells at high velocities.
– DERIVATIVES **biolistic** adjective.
– ORIGIN late 20th cent.: apparently from BIO- and BALLISTICS.

biological ▶ adjective **1** relating to biology or living organisms. ■ (of a detergent or other cleaning product) containing enzymes to assist the process of cleaning. ■ relating to or involving the use of microorganisms or toxins of biological origin as weapons of war.
2 (of a parent or child) related by blood; natural: *his biological mother*.
– DERIVATIVES **biologic** adjective, **biologically** adverb.

biological clock ▶ noun an innate mechanism that controls the physiological activities of an organism which change on a daily, seasonal, yearly, or other regular cycle.

B

biological control ▸ noun [mass noun] the control of a pest by the introduction of a natural enemy or predator.

biologism /bʌɪˈɒlədʒɪz(ə)m/ ▸ noun [mass noun] the interpretation of human life from a strictly biological point of view.
– DERIVATIVES **biologistic** adjective.

biology ▸ noun [mass noun] the study of living organisms, divided into many specialized fields that cover their morphology, physiology, anatomy, behaviour, origin, and distribution. ■ the plants and animals of a particular area: *the biology of the Chesapeake Bay.* ■ the physiology, behaviour, and other qualities of a particular organism or class of organisms: *human biology.*
– DERIVATIVES **biologist** noun.
– ORIGIN early 19th cent.: coined in German, via French from Greek *bios* 'life' + **-LOGY**.

bioluminescence ▸ noun [mass noun] the biochemical emission of light by living organisms such as glow-worms and deep-sea fish. ■ the light emitted in such a way.
– DERIVATIVES **bioluminescent** adjective.

biomagnetism ▸ noun [mass noun] the interaction of living organisms with magnetic fields.

biomarker ▸ noun a naturally occurring molecule, gene, or characteristic by which a particular pathological or physiological process, disease, etc. can be identified.

biomass ▸ noun [mass noun] **1** the total quantity or weight of organisms in a given area or volume. **2** organic matter used as a fuel, especially in a power station for the generation of electricity.

biomaterial ▸ noun [mass noun] a biological or synthetic substance which can be introduced into body tissue as part of an implanted medical device or used to replace an organ, bodily function, etc.

biomathematics ▸ plural noun [treated as sing.] the science of the application of mathematics to biology.

biome /ˈbʌɪəʊm/ ▸ noun Ecology a large naturally occurring community of flora and fauna occupying a major habitat, e.g. forest or tundra.
– ORIGIN early 20th cent.: from **BIO-** 'life' + **-OME**.

biomechanics ▸ plural noun [treated as sing.] the study of the mechanical laws relating to the movement or structure of living organisms.
– DERIVATIVES **biomechanical** adjective, **biomechanically** adverb, **biomechanist** noun.

biomedical ▸ adjective relating to both biology and medicine.
– DERIVATIVES **biomedicine** noun.

biometeorology ▸ noun [mass noun] the study of the relationship between living organisms and weather.

biometric signature ▸ noun the unique pattern of a bodily feature such as the retina, iris, or voice, encoded on an identity card and used for recognition and identification purposes.

biometry /bʌɪˈɒmɪtri/ (also **biometrics** /bʌɪə(ʊ)ˈmɛtrɪks/) ▸ noun [mass noun] the application of statistical analysis to biological data.
– DERIVATIVES **biometric** adjective, **biometrical** adjective, **biometrician** noun.

biomimetic ▸ adjective Biochemistry relating to or denoting synthetic methods which mimic biochemical processes.

biomimicry ▸ noun [mass noun] the design and production of materials, structures, and systems that are modelled on biological entities and processes.

biomolecule ▸ noun a molecule that is involved in the maintenance and metabolic processes of living organisms.

biomorph ▸ noun a decorative form or object based on or resembling a living organism. ■ a graphical representation of an organism generated on a computer, used to model evolution.
– DERIVATIVES **biomorphic** adjective.

bionic ▸ adjective having artificial body parts, especially electromechanical ones. ■ informal having ordinary human powers increased by or as if by the aid of such devices: *working out in gyms in an attempt to become bionic men.* ■ relating to bionics.
– DERIVATIVES **bionically** adverb.
– ORIGIN 1960s: from **BIO-** 'human', on the pattern of *electronic*.

bionics ▸ plural noun [treated as sing.] the study of mechanical systems that function like living organisms or parts of living organisms.

bionomics /ˌbʌɪə(ʊ)ˈnɒmɪks/ ▸ plural noun [treated as sing.] the study of the mode of life of organisms in their natural habitat and their adaptations to their surroundings; ecology.
– DERIVATIVES **bionomic** adjective.
– ORIGIN late 19th cent.: from **BIO-** 'life', on the pattern of *economics*.

biopharmaceutical ▸ noun a biological macromolecule or cellular component, such as a blood product, used as a pharmaceutical.

biopharmaceutics ▸ plural noun [treated as sing.] the study of the chemical and physical properties of drugs and the biological effects they produce.

biophilia ▸ noun [mass noun] (according to a theory of the biologist E. O. Wilson) an innate and genetically determined affinity of human beings with the natural world.

biophysics ▸ plural noun [treated as sing.] the science of the application of the laws of physics to biological phenomena.
– DERIVATIVES **biophysical** adjective, **biophysicist** noun.

biopic /ˈbʌɪəʊpɪk/ ▸ noun informal a biographical film.

biopiracy /ˌbʌɪəʊˈpʌɪrəsi/ ▸ noun [mass noun] the practice of commercially exploiting naturally occurring biochemical or genetic material, especially by obtaining patents that restrict its future use, while failing to pay fair compensation to the community from which it originates.

bioplastic ▸ noun [mass noun] a type of biodegradable plastic derived from biological substances rather than petroleum.

biopolymer ▸ noun a polymeric substance occurring in living organisms, e.g. a protein, cellulose, or DNA.

bioprospecting ▸ noun [mass noun] the search for plant and animal species from which medicinal drugs and other commercially valuable compounds can be obtained.
– DERIVATIVES **bioprospector** noun.
– ORIGIN 1990s: from *bio(diversity) prospecting*.

biopsy /ˈbʌɪɒpsi/ ▸ noun (pl. **biopsies**) an examination of tissue removed from a living body to discover the presence, cause, or extent of a disease.
▸ verb (**biopsies**, **biopsying**, **biopsied**) [with obj.] conduct a biopsy on (tissue removed from a living body): *the lesions may be malignant and should be biopsied.*
– ORIGIN late 19th cent.: coined in French from Greek *bios* 'life' + *opsis* 'sight', on the pattern of *necropsy*.

biopsychology ▸ noun [mass noun] the branch of psychology concerned with its biological and physiological aspects.
– DERIVATIVES **biopsychological** adjective.

bioreactor ▸ noun an apparatus in which a biological reaction or process is carried out, especially on an industrial scale.

bioregion ▸ noun a region defined by characteristics of the natural environment rather than by man-made divisions.
– DERIVATIVES **bioregional** adjective.

bioregionalism ▸ noun [mass noun] advocacy of the belief that human activity should be largely constrained by ecological or geographical boundaries rather than political ones.
– DERIVATIVES **bioregionalist** noun.

bioremediation /ˌbʌɪə(ʊ)rɪˌmiːdiˈeɪʃ(ə)n/ ▸ noun [mass noun] the use of either naturally occurring or deliberately introduced microorganisms to consume and break down environmental pollutants, in order to clean a polluted site.

biorhythm ▸ noun a recurring cycle in the physiology or functioning of an organism, such as the daily cycle of sleeping and waking. ■ a cyclic pattern of physical, emotional, or mental activity believed to occur in a person's life: *I found that the music suited my biorhythms.*
– DERIVATIVES **biorhythmic** adjective.

BIOS /ˈbʌɪɒs/ ▸ noun Computing a set of computer instructions in firmware which control input and output operations.
– ORIGIN acronym from *Basic Input-Output System*.

biosafety ▸ noun another term for **BIOSECURITY**.

bioscience ▸ noun any of the life sciences.
– DERIVATIVES **bioscientist** noun.

bioscope ▸ noun dated, chiefly S. African a cinema or film.

biosecurity ▸ noun [mass noun] procedures or measures designed to protect the population against harmful biological or biochemical substances.

biosensor ▸ noun a device which uses a living organism or biological molecules, especially enzymes or antibodies, to detect the presence of chemicals.

biosignature ▸ noun another term for **BIOMARKER**.

biosocial ▸ adjective relating to the interaction of biological and social factors.

biosolids ▸ plural noun organic matter recycled from sewage, especially for use in agriculture.

biosphere ▸ noun **1** the regions of the surface and atmosphere of the earth or another planet occupied by living organisms. **2** an artificial structure enclosing a self-contained ecosystem or ecosystems.
– DERIVATIVES **biospheric** adjective.
– ORIGIN late 19th cent.: coined in German from Greek *bios* 'life' + *sphaira* (see **SPHERE**).

biostatistics ▸ plural noun [treated as sing.] the branch of statistics that deals with data relating to living organisms.
– DERIVATIVES **biostatistical** adjective, **biostatistician** noun.

biostratigraphy /ˌbʌɪə(ʊ)strəˈtɪɡrəfi/ ▸ noun [mass noun] the branch of stratigraphy concerned with fossils and their use in dating rock formations.
– DERIVATIVES **biostratigrapher** noun, **biostratigraphic** adjective, **biostratigraphical** adjective, **biostratigraphically** adverb.

biosurgery ▸ noun [mass noun] the medical use of maggots to clean infected wounds, especially in cases where an infection is resistant to conventional antibiotic treatment.

biosynthesis ▸ noun [mass noun] the production of complex molecules within living organisms or cells.
– DERIVATIVES **biosynthetic** adjective.

biosystematics ▸ plural noun [treated as sing.] taxonomy based on the study of the genetic evolution of plant and animal populations.
– DERIVATIVES **biosystematist** noun.

biota /bʌɪˈəʊtə/ ▸ noun [mass noun] Ecology the animal and plant life of a particular region, habitat, or geological period: *the biota of the river.*
– ORIGIN early 20th cent.: modern Latin, from Greek *biotē* 'life'.

biotech ▸ noun short for **BIOTECHNOLOGY**.

biotechnology ▸ noun [mass noun] the exploitation of biological processes for industrial and other purposes, especially the genetic manipulation of microorganisms for the production of antibiotics, hormones, etc.
– DERIVATIVES **biotechnological** adjective, **biotechnologist** noun.

biotecture /ˈbʌɪəʊˌtɛktʃə/ ▸ noun [mass noun] the use of living plants as an integral part of the design of buildings.
– ORIGIN 1980s: from **BIO-** 'of living organisms' + a shortened form of **ARCHITECTURE**.

bioterrorism ▸ noun [mass noun] the use of infectious agents or other harmful biological or biochemical substances as weapons of terrorism.
– DERIVATIVES **bioterrorist** noun.

biotherapy ▸ noun [mass noun] the use of living organisms in the treatment of disease.

biotic /bʌɪˈɒtɪk/ ▸ adjective relating to or resulting from living organisms: *biotic interactions.*
– ORIGIN mid 19th cent.: from French *biotique*, or via late Latin from Greek *biōtikos*, from *bios* 'life'.

biotin /ˈbʌɪətɪn/ ▸ noun [mass noun] Biochemistry a vitamin of the B complex, found in egg yolk, liver, and yeast. It is involved in the synthesis of fatty acids and glucose. Also called **VITAMIN H**, especially in North America.
– ORIGIN 1930s: coined in German from Greek *bios* 'life' + **-IN**[1].

biotite /ˈbʌɪətʌɪt/ ▸ noun [mass noun] a black, dark brown, or greenish black micaceous mineral, occurring as a constituent of many igneous and metamorphic rocks.
– ORIGIN mid 19th cent.: named after J.-B. *Biot* (1774–1862), French mineralogist.

biotope /ˈbʌɪətəʊp/ ▸ noun Ecology the region of a habitat associated with a particular ecological community.
– ORIGIN 1920s: from German *Biotop*, based on Greek *topos* 'place'.

biotransformation ▸ noun [mass noun] the alteration of a substance, typically a drug, within the body.

bioturbation /ˌbʌɪəʊtəːˈbeɪʃ(ə)n/ ▸ **noun** [mass noun] Geology the disturbance of sedimentary deposits by living organisms.
– DERIVATIVES **bioturbated** adjective.
– ORIGIN 1960s: from **BIO-** + Latin *turbatio(n-)*, from *turbare* 'disturb'.

biotype ▸ **noun** a group of organisms having an identical genetic constitution.

biowarfare ▸ **noun** [mass noun] biological warfare.

bioweapon ▸ **noun** a harmful biological agent used as a weapon of war.

bipartisan /ˌbʌɪpɑːtɪˈzan/ ▸ **adjective** of or involving the agreement or cooperation of two political parties that usually oppose each other's policies: *the reforms received considerable bipartisan approval.*
– DERIVATIVES **bipartisanship** noun.

bipartite /bʌɪˈpɑːtʌɪt/ ▸ **adjective 1** involving or made by two separate parties: *a bipartite agreement.*
2 consisting of two parts: *a bipartite uterus.*
– ORIGIN late Middle English (in the sense 'divided into two parts'): from Latin *bipartitus*, past participle of *bipartire*, from *bi-* 'two' + *partire* 'to part'.

biped /ˈbʌɪpɛd/ ▸ **noun** an animal that uses two legs for walking.
▸ **adjective** using two legs for walking.
– ORIGIN mid 17th cent. (earlier (early 17th cent.) as *bipedal*): from Latin *bipes*, *biped-* (from *bi-* 'having two' + *pes*, *ped-* 'foot').

bipedal /bʌɪˈpiːd(ə)l/ ▸ **adjective** Zoology (of an animal) using only two legs for walking.
– DERIVATIVES **bipedalism** noun, **bipedality** /ˌbʌɪpiːˈdalɪti/ noun.

biphasic /bʌɪˈfeɪzɪk/ ▸ **adjective** technical having two phases.

biphenyl /bʌɪˈfiːnʌɪl, bʌɪˈfɛnɪl/ ▸ **noun** Chemistry an organic compound containing two phenyl groups bonded together, e.g. the PCBs.

bipinnate /bʌɪˈpɪneɪt/ ▸ **adjective** Botany (of a pinnate leaf) having leaflets that are further subdivided in a pinnate arrangement.

biplane ▸ **noun** an early type of aircraft with two pairs of wings, one above the other.

bipod /ˈbʌɪpɒd/ ▸ **noun** a two-legged stand or support.

bipolar ▸ **adjective 1** having or relating to two poles or extremities: *a sharply bipolar division of affluent and underclass.* ■ relating to or occurring in both North and South polar regions: *bipolar species.*
2 (of psychiatric illness) characterized by both manic and depressive episodes, or manic ones only. ■ (of a person) suffering from bipolar disorder.
3 (of a nerve cell) having two axons, one either side of the cell body.
4 Electronics (of a transistor or other device) using both positive and negative charge carriers.
– DERIVATIVES **bipolarity** noun.

bipolar disorder (also **bipolar affective disorder**) ▸ **noun** [mass noun] a mental condition marked by alternating periods of elation and depression.

> **USAGE** The terms **bipolar disorder** or **bipolar affective disorder** are increasingly being used in place of **manic depression**. See **USAGE** at **MANIC DEPRESSION**.

bippy /ˈbɪpi/ ▸ **noun** (pl. **bippies**) US informal a person's buttocks.
– ORIGIN 1960s: popularized by the US television programme *Rowan & Martin's Laugh-In*, where it was used as a nonsense word with an air of innuendo but intentionally vague meaning: of unknown origin.

biracial ▸ **adjective** concerning or containing members of two racial groups.

biramous /bʌɪˈreɪməs/ ▸ **adjective** Zoology (especially of crustacean limbs and antennae) dividing to form two branches.
– ORIGIN late 19th cent.: from **BI-** 'two' + **RAMUS** + **-OUS**.

birch ▸ **noun 1** (also **birch tree**) a slender hardy tree which has thin peeling bark and bears catkins. Birch trees grow chiefly in northern temperate regions and yield hard, pale, fine-grained timber. ● Genus *Betula*, family Betulaceae: many species, including the **silver birch** (*B. pendula*) of Europe.
2 (**the birch**) chiefly historical a formal punishment in which a person is flogged with a bundle of birch twigs.
▸ **verb** [with obj.] chiefly historical beat (someone) with a bundle of birch twigs as a formal punishment.
– DERIVATIVES **birchen** adjective (archaic).
– ORIGIN Old English *bierce*, *birce*, of Germanic origin; related to German *Birke*.

birchbark ▸ **noun** [mass noun] the impervious bark of the North American paper birch, formerly used by American Indians to make canoes and other items.

Bircher /ˈbəːtʃə/ ▸ **noun** a member or supporter of the John Birch Society, an extreme right-wing and anti-communist American organization founded in 1958.
– ORIGIN from the name of John *Birch*, a USAF officer and 'first casualty of the Cold War', killed by Chinese communists in 1945.

bird ▸ **noun 1** a warm-blooded egg-laying vertebrate animal distinguished by the possession of feathers, wings, a beak, and typically by being able to fly. ● Class Aves; birds probably evolved in the Jurassic period from small dinosaurs that may already have been warm-blooded. ■ informal, chiefly N. Amer. an aircraft, spacecraft, or satellite.
2 informal a person of a specified kind or character: *she's a sharp old bird.*
3 Brit. informal a young woman or a man's girlfriend.
– PHRASES **the bird has flown** the person one is looking for has escaped or left. **a bird in the hand is worth two in the bush** proverb it's better to be content with what you have than to risk losing everything by seeking to get more. **the birds and the bees** informal basic facts about sex and reproduction, as told to a child. **birds of a feather flock together** proverb people of the same sort or with the same tastes and interests will be found together. **do (one's) bird** Brit. informal serve a prison sentence. [*bird* from rhyming slang *birdlime* 'time'.] **flip someone the bird** (or **flip the bird**) US informal stick one's middle finger up at someone as a sign of contempt or anger. **(strictly) for the birds** informal not worthy of consideration. **get the bird** Brit. informal be booed or jeered at. **give someone the bird** Brit. informal boo or jeer at someone. ■ N. Amer. another way of saying **FLIP SOMEONE THE BIRD**. **have a bird** N. Amer. informal be very shocked or agitated. **a little bird told me** humorous used to indicate that the speaker knows something but chooses to keep the identity of their informant secret: *a little bird told me it was your birthday.*
– DERIVATIVES **bird-like** adjective.
– ORIGIN Old English *brid* 'chick, fledgling', of unknown origin.

bird banding ▸ **noun** North American term for **BIRD RINGING**.
– DERIVATIVES **bird bander** noun.

birdbath ▸ **noun** a small basin placed in a garden and filled with water for birds to bathe in.

birdbrain ▸ **noun** informal a silly or stupid person.
– DERIVATIVES **birdbrained** adjective.

birdcage ▸ **noun** a cage for pet birds, typically made of wire or cane.

bird call ▸ **noun** the characteristic cry of a bird.

bird cherry ▸ **noun** a small wild cherry tree or shrub, with bitter black fruit that is eaten by birds. ● *Prunus padus*, family Rosaceae.

bird dog N. Amer. ▸ **noun 1** a gun dog trained to retrieve birds.
2 informal a talent scout.
▸ **verb** (**bird-dog**) [with obj.] informal search out or pursue with dogged determination: *reporters bird-dogged the candidates for several weeks.*

bird-eating spider (also **bird spider**) ▸ **noun** another term for **TARANTULA** (sense 1).

birder ▸ **noun** chiefly N. Amer. a birdwatcher.

bird fancier's lung ▸ **noun** [mass noun] a respiratory disease caused by inhaling dust consisting of feathers, droppings, and other organic matter from birds.

bird flu ▸ **noun** [mass noun] a severe, often fatal, type of influenza that affects birds, especially poultry, and that can also be transmitted to humans.

birdhouse ▸ **noun** North American term for **NEST BOX**.

birdie ▸ **noun** (pl. **birdies**) **1** informal a child's term for a bird.
2 Golf a score of one stroke under par at a hole.
▸ **verb** (**birdies, birdying, birdied**) [with obj.] Golf play (a hole) with a score of one stroke under par: *Drummond birdied the 16th and 17th for a 73.*
– ORIGIN late 18th cent.: diminutive of **BIRD**; the golf term from US slang *bird*, denoting any first-rate thing.

birding ▸ **noun** [mass noun] chiefly N. Amer. the observation of birds in their natural habitats as a hobby.

birdlime ▸ **noun** [mass noun] a sticky substance spread on to twigs to trap small birds.

bird of paradise ▸ **noun 1** (pl. **birds of paradise**) a tropical Australasian bird, the male of which is noted for the beauty and brilliance of its plumage and its spectacular courtship display. Most kinds are found in New Guinea. ● Family Paradisaeidae: numerous genera.
2 (also **bird of paradise flower**) a southern African plant related to the banana, which bears a showy irregular flower with a long projecting tongue. ● Genus *Strelitzia*, family Strelitziaceae: several species, in particular *S. regina*, with orange and dark blue flowers.

B

bird of passage ▸ **noun 1** a person who passes through a place without staying for long.
2 dated a migratory bird.

bird of prey ▸ **noun** a bird that feeds on animal flesh, distinguished by a hooked bill and sharp talons; a raptor. ● Orders Falconiformes (the diurnal birds of prey) and Strigiformes (the owls).

bird pepper ▸ **noun** a tropical American capsicum pepper which is thought to be the ancestor of both sweet and chilli peppers. ● *Capsicum annuum* var. *glabriusculum* (or *C. frutescens* var. *typicum*), family Solanaceae. ■ the small, red, very hot fruit of this plant. ■ a variety of small hot pepper grown in Asia or Africa.

bird ringing ▸ **noun** [mass noun] the practice of catching birds, marking them with an identifying band around the leg, and then releasing them.
– DERIVATIVES **bird ringer** noun.

birdseed ▸ **noun** [mass noun] a blend of different seeds for feeding to birds.

Birdseye, Clarence (1886–1956), American businessman and inventor. He developed a process of rapid freezing of foods in small packages suitable for retail, creating a revolution in eating habits.

bird's-eye ▸ **noun 1** [usu. as modifier] any of a number of plants with small flowers that have contrasting petals and centres, in particular: ● (also **bird's-eye primrose**) a primrose with yellow-centred purple flowers (*Primula farinosa*, family Primulaceae). ● (also **bird's-eye speedwell**) North American term for **GERMANDER SPEEDWELL**.
2 (also **bird's-eye chilli** or **bird's-eye pepper**) a small, very hot chilli pepper.
3 a small geometric pattern woven with a dot in the centre, typically used in suiting and lining fabrics.

bird's-eye maple ▸ **noun** [mass noun] the timber of an American maple which contains eye-like markings, used in decorative woodwork.

bird's-eye view ▸ **noun** a general view from above.

bird's-foot ▸ **noun** (pl. **bird's-foots**) a European plant of the pea family, which bears pods shaped like the foot of a bird. ● *Ornithopus perpusillus*, family Leguminosae.

bird's-foot trefoil ▸ **noun** a small plant of the pea family which has three-lobed leaves, yellow flowers streaked with red, and triple pods that resemble the feet of a bird. Also called **EGGS AND BACON** or **TOM THUMB**. ● *Lotus corniculatus*, family Leguminosae.

birdshot ▸ **noun** [mass noun] the smallest size of shot for sporting rifles or other guns.

bird's-nest ▸ **noun 1** a brownish or yellowish saprophytic flowering plant of the wintergreen family, with scale-like leaves. ● Two species in the family Monotropaceae (or Pyrolaceae): the **yellow bird's-nest** (*Monotropa hypopitys*) of north temperate regions, and the **giant bird's-nest** (*Pterospora andromeda*) of North America.
2 (also **bird's-nest fungus**) a Eurasian and North American fungus with a small bowl-shaped fruiting body that opens to reveal egg-shaped organs containing the spores. ● Family Nidulariaceae, class Gasteromycetes, including the **common bird's-nest** (*Crucibulum laeve*).

bird's-nesting ▸ **noun** [mass noun] the action or practice of hunting for birds' nests in order to take the eggs.

bird's-nest orchid ▸ **noun** a European woodland orchid which lacks chlorophyll, the whole plant being yellowish brown. Its nest-like mass of thick roots absorbs nutrients from a soil-dwelling fungus. ● *Neottia nidus-avis*, family Orchidaceae.

bird's nest soup ▸ **noun** [mass noun] a soup made in Chinese cookery from the dried gelatinous coating of the nests of swifts and other birds.

birdsong ▸ **noun** [mass noun] the musical vocalizations of a bird or birds, typically uttered by a male songbird in characteristic bursts or phrases for territorial purposes.

bird strike ▸ **noun** a collision between a bird and an aircraft.

bird table ▸ **noun** Brit. a small platform or table in a garden on which food for birds is placed.

birdwatching ▸ **noun** [mass noun] the practice of observing birds in their natural environment as a hobby.
– DERIVATIVES **birdwatcher** noun.

B

birdwing (also **bird-winged butterfly**) ▸ noun a very large boldly marked butterfly occurring in the tropical parts of Australasia. ● Genus *Ornithoptera*, family Papilionidae: several species, including **Queen Alexandra's birdwing** (*O. alexandrae*), which is the world's largest butterfly.

birefringent /ˌbʌɪrɪˈfrɪn(d)ʒ(ə)nt/ ▸ adjective Physics having two different refractive indices.
– DERIVATIVES **birefringence** noun.

bireme /ˈbʌɪriːm/ ▸ noun an ancient warship with two files of oarsmen on each side.
– ORIGIN late 16th cent.: from Latin *biremis*, from *bi-* 'having two' + *remus* 'oar'.

biretta /bɪˈrɛtə/ ▸ noun a square cap with three flat projections on top, worn by Roman Catholic clergymen.
– ORIGIN late 16th cent.: from Italian *berretta* or Spanish *birreta*, based on late Latin *birrus* 'hooded cape'. Compare with BERET.

Birgitta, St /ˌbɪəˈgɪtə/ variant spelling of BRIDGET, ST².

biri ▸ noun (pl. **biris**) variant spelling of BIDI.

biriani ▸ noun variant spelling of BIRYANI.

Birkenhead /ˌbəːkənˈhɛd/ a town in NW England on the Wirral Peninsula, across the River Mersey from Liverpool; pop. 79,700 (est. 2009).

Birkenstock ▸ noun trademark a type of shoe or sandal with a contoured cork-filled sole and a thick leather upper.
– ORIGIN 1970s: from the name of the manufacturer.

birl /bəːl/ Scottish ▸ verb spin; whirl: [no obj.] *my dad would have birled in his grave at the very idea.*
▸ noun a spin or whirl.
– ORIGIN early 18th cent.: imitative.

birlinn /ˈbəːlɪn, ˈbɪə-/ ▸ noun a large rowing boat or barge of a kind formerly used in the Western Islands of Scotland.
– ORIGIN late 16th cent.: Scottish Gaelic.

Birman /ˈbəːmən/ ▸ noun a cat of a long-haired breed, typically with a cream body, dark head, tail, and legs, and white paws.
– ORIGIN variant of BURMAN.

Birmingham 1 an industrial city in west central England; pop. 945,700 (est. 2009).
2 an industrial city in north central Alabama; pop. 228,798 (est. 2008).

biro /ˈbʌɪrəʊ/ ▸ noun (pl. **biros**) Brit. trademark a kind of ballpoint pen.
– ORIGIN 1940s: named after László József *Bíró* (1899–1985), Hungarian inventor of the ballpoint.

birr /bəː/ ▸ noun the basic monetary unit of Ethiopia, equal to 100 cents.
– ORIGIN from Amharic.

birth ▸ noun [mass noun] the emergence of a baby or other young from the body of its mother; the start of life as a physically separate being: *he was blind from birth* | [count noun] *despite a difficult birth he's fit and healthy.* ■ the beginning or coming into existence of something: *the birth of Socialist Realism.* ■ a person's origin, descent, or ancestry: *the mother is English by birth* | *he is of noble birth.*
▸ verb [with obj.] chiefly N. Amer. give birth to (a baby or other young): *she birthed five children within ten years.*
– PHRASES **give birth** bear a child or young: *she gave birth to a son.*
– ORIGIN Middle English: from Old Norse *byrth*; related to BEAR¹.

birth certificate ▸ noun an official document issued to record a person's birth and identify them by name, place, date of birth, and parentage.

birth control ▸ noun [mass noun] the practice of preventing unwanted pregnancies, especially by use of contraception.

birthdate ▸ noun the date on which a person was born.

birthday ▸ noun the anniversary of the day on which a person was born. ■ the day of a person's birth: *he shares a birthday with Rod Stewart.* ■ the anniversary of something's origin or foundation: *the seventy-fifth birthday of the Institute.*
– PHRASES **in one's birthday suit** humorous naked.

Birthday Honours ▸ plural noun (in Britain) the titles and decorations awarded on a sovereign's official birthday: [as modifier] *the Birthday Honours list.*

birthing ▸ noun [mass noun] the action or process of giving birth.

birthing pool ▸ noun a large bath in which a woman may give birth.

birthmark ▸ noun an unusual, typically permanent, mark on someone's body which is there from birth.

birth mother ▸ noun a woman who has given birth to a child, as opposed to an adoptive mother.

birth parent ▸ noun a biological as opposed to an adoptive parent.

birthplace ▸ noun the place where a person was born. ■ the place where something started or originated: *Florence was the birthplace of the Renaissance.*

birth rate ▸ noun the number of live births per thousand of population per year.

birthright ▸ noun a particular right of possession or privilege a person has from birth, especially as an eldest son. ■ a natural or moral right, possessed by everyone: *she saw a liberal education as the birthright of every child.*

birth sign ▸ noun Astrology the zodiacal sign through which the sun is passing when a person is born.

birthstone ▸ noun a gemstone popularly associated with the month or astrological sign of a person's birth.

birthweight ▸ noun [mass noun] the weight of a baby at birth.

birthwort ▸ noun a climbing or herbaceous plant which typically has heart-shaped leaves and deep-throated, pipe-shaped flowers. It was formerly used as an aid to childbirth and to induce abortion. ● Genus *Aristolochia*, family Aristolochiaceae.

Birtwistle /ˈbəːtˌwɪs(ə)l/, Sir Harrison (Paul) (b.1934), English composer and clarinettist. His early work was influenced by Stravinsky; later compositions are more experimental.

biryani /ˌbɪrɪˈɑːni/ (also **biriani**) ▸ noun [mass noun] an Indian dish made with highly seasoned rice and meat, fish, or vegetables.
– ORIGIN Urdu, from Persian *biryānī*, from *biriyān* 'fried, grilled'.

BIS ▸ abbreviation Bank for International Settlements.

bis /bis/ ▸ adverb Music (as a direction) again.
– ORIGIN via French and Italian from Latin, literally 'twice'.

bis- /bɪs/ ▸ combining form Chemistry used to form the names of compounds containing two groups identically substituted or coordinated: *bis(2-aminoethyl) ether.*

Biscay, Bay of /ˈbɪskeɪ/ a part of the North Atlantic between the north coast of Spain and the west coast of France, noted for its strong currents and storms. The shipping forecast area **Biscay** extends approximately as far west as the longitude of Gijón in Spain.

biscotti /bɪˈskɒti/ ▸ plural noun small rectangular biscuits containing nuts, made originally in Italy.
– ORIGIN Italian.

biscuit ▸ noun 1 Brit. a small baked unleavened cake, typically crisp, flat, and sweet: *a chocolate biscuit.* ■ N. Amer. a small, soft round cake like a scone.
2 [mass noun] porcelain or other pottery which has been fired but not glazed.
3 [mass noun] a light brown colour.
4 Carpentry a small flat piece of wood used to join two larger pieces of wood together, fitting into slots in each.
– PHRASES **take the biscuit** (or chiefly N. Amer. **cake**) informal be the most remarkable or foolish of its kind.
– DERIVATIVES **biscuity** adjective.
– ORIGIN Middle English: from Old French *bescuit*, based on Latin *bis* 'twice' + *coctus*, past participle of *coquere* 'to cook' (so named because originally biscuits were cooked in a twofold process: first baked and then dried out in a slow oven so that they would keep).

biscuit barrel ▸ noun Brit. a small barrel-shaped container for biscuits.

biscuit beetle ▸ noun a small beetle related to the furniture beetle, with larvae that feed on dried foodstuffs and stored products such as biscuits, pasta, and seeds. Also called DRUGSTORE BEETLE. ● *Stegobium paniceum*, family Anobiidae.

biscuit firing (also **biscuit fire**) ▸ noun [mass noun] the first firing of pottery, which permanently hardens the clay.

biscuit jointer ▸ noun a tool used to cut slots into pieces of wood so that they can be joined using a biscuit (see BISCUIT (sense 4)).

bisect ▸ verb [with obj.] divide into two parts: *a landscape of ploughland bisected by long straight roads.* ■ Geometry divide (a line, angle, or shape) into two exactly equal parts.
– DERIVATIVES **bisection** noun, **bisector** noun.
– ORIGIN mid 17th cent.: from BI- 'two' + Latin *sect-* (from *secare* 'to cut').

biserial ▸ adjective Botany & Zoology arranged in or consisting of two series or rows.

bisexual ▸ adjective 1 sexually attracted to both men and women.
2 Biology having characteristics of both sexes.
▸ noun a person who is sexually attracted to both men and women.
– DERIVATIVES **bisexuality** noun.

bish ▸ noun Brit. informal, dated a mistake or blunder.
– ORIGIN 1930s: of unknown origin.

Bishkek /bɪʃˈkɛk/ the capital of Kyrgyzstan; pop. 837,000 (est. 2007). Former names PISHPEK, FRUNZE.

Bisho former name for BHISHO.

Bishop, Elizabeth (1911–79), American poet. She was awarded the Pulitzer Prize for her first two collections, *North and South* (1946) and *A Cold Spring* (1955).

bishop ▸ noun 1 a senior member of the Christian clergy, usually in charge of a diocese and empowered to confer holy orders.
2 (also **bishop bird**) an African weaver bird, the male of which has red, orange, yellow, or black plumage. ● Genus *Euplectes*, family Ploceidae: several species, including the **red bishop** (*E. orix*), which has scarlet plumage with a black face and underparts.
3 a chess piece, typically with its top shaped like a mitre, that can move in any direction along a diagonal on which it stands. Each player starts the game with two bishops, one moving on white squares and the other on black.
4 [mass noun] mulled and spiced wine.
– ORIGIN Old English *biscop*, *bisceop*, based on Greek *episkopos* 'overseer', from *epi* 'above' + *-skopos* '-looking'.

bishopric /ˈbɪʃəprɪk/ ▸ noun the office or rank of a bishop. ■ a district under a bishop's control; a diocese.
– ORIGIN Old English *bisceoprīce*, from *bisceop* (see BISHOP) + *rīce* 'realm'.

bishop suffragan ▸ noun see SUFFRAGAN.

Bislama /ˈbɪʃləˌmɑː/ (also **Beach-la-mar** or **Bêche-de-mer**) ▸ noun [mass noun] an English-based pidgin language used as the national language of Vanuatu, where it shares official status with English and French.
– ORIGIN alteration of Portuguese *bicho do mar* 'sea cucumber' (traded as a commodity, the word later being applied to the language of trade).

Bismarck¹ /ˈbɪzmɑːk/ the state capital of North Dakota; pop. 60,389 (est. 2008). A terminus of the Northern Pacific Railway, it took the name of the German Chancellor in order to attract German capital for railroad-building.

Bismarck² /ˈbɪzmɑːk/, German /ˈbɪsmark/, Otto Eduard Leopold von, Prince of Bismarck, Duke of Lauenburg (1815–98), Prussian minister and German statesman, Chancellor of the German Empire 1871–90; known as the **Iron Chancellor**. He was the driving force behind the unification of Germany, orchestrating wars with Denmark (1864), Austria (1866), and France (1870–1) in order to achieve this end.
– DERIVATIVES **Bismarckian** adjective.

Bismarck Sea an arm of the Pacific Ocean north-east of New Guinea and north of New Britain.

bismillah /bɪsˈmɪlə/ ▸ exclamation in the name of God (an invocation used by Muslims at the beginning of an undertaking).
– ORIGIN from Arabic *bi-smi-llāh*, the first word of the Koran.

bismuth /ˈbɪzməθ/ ▸ noun [mass noun] the chemical element of atomic number 83, a brittle reddish-tinged grey metal. (Symbol: **Bi**) ■ a compound of this element used medicinally.
– ORIGIN mid 17th cent.: from modern Latin *bisemutum*, Latinization of German *Wismut*, of unknown origin.

bison /ˈbʌɪs(ə)n/ ▸ noun (pl. **same**) a humpbacked shaggy-haired wild ox native to North America and Europe. ● Genus *Bison*, family Bovidae: *B. bison* of North American prairies (also called BUFFALO), and *B. bonasus* of European forests (also called WISENT), now found only in Poland. These are sometimes regarded as a single species.
– ORIGIN late Middle English: from Latin, ultimately of Germanic origin and related to WISENT.

bisphenol A /ˈbɪsfiːnɒl/ ▸ noun [mass noun] Chemistry a synthetic organic compound used in the manufacture of epoxy resins and other polymers. • A bicyclic phenol; chem. formula: $C(CH_3)_2(C_6H_4OH)_2$.

bisque¹ /bɪsk, biːsk/ ▶ **noun** [mass noun] a rich shellfish soup, typically made from lobster.
– ORIGIN French, 'crayfish soup'.

bisque² /bɪsk/ ▶ **noun** an extra turn or stroke allowed to a weaker player in croquet.
– ORIGIN mid 17th cent. (originally a term in real tennis): from French, of unknown ultimate origin.

bisque³ /bɪsk/ ▶ **noun** another term for BISCUIT (sense 2).

Bissagos Islands /bɪˈsɑːgəs/ a group of islands off the coast of Guinea-Bissau, West Africa.

Bissau /bɪˈsaʊ/ the capital of Guinea-Bissau; pop. 330,000 (est. 2007).

bistable ▶ **noun** an electronic circuit which has two stable states.
▶ **adjective** (of a system) having two stable states.

bistort /ˈbɪstɔːt/ ▶ **noun** a Eurasian herbaceous plant with a spike of flesh-coloured flowers and a twisted root. • Genus *Polygonum*, family Polygonaceae: several species, in particular *P. bistorta*.
– ORIGIN early 16th cent.: from French *bistorte* or medieval Latin *bistorta*, from *bis* 'twice' + *torta* (feminine past participle of *torquere* 'to twist').

bistoury /ˈbɪstʊri/ ▶ **noun** (pl. **bistouries**) a surgical knife with a long, narrow, straight or curved blade.
– ORIGIN mid 18th cent.: from French *bistouri*, originally *bistorie* 'dagger', of unknown origin.

bistre /ˈbɪstə/ (US also **bister**) ▶ **noun** [mass noun] a brownish-yellow pigment made from the soot of burnt wood. ■ the colour of this pigment.
– ORIGIN early 18th cent.: from French, of unknown origin.

bistro /ˈbiːstrəʊ, ˈbɪs-/ ▶ **noun** (pl. **bistros**) a small, inexpensive restaurant.
– ORIGIN 1920s: French; perhaps related to *bistouille*, a northern colloquial term meaning 'bad alcohol', perhaps from Russian *bystro* 'rapidly'.

bisulphate (US **bisulfate**) ▶ **noun** Chemistry a salt of the anion HSO_4^-.

bit¹ ▶ **noun 1** a small piece, part, or quantity of something: *give the duck* ***a bit of*** *bread* | *he read* ***bits of*** *his work to me.* ■ **(a bit)** a short time or distance: *I fell asleep for a bit* | *can you move over a bit?* ■ **(a bit)** a fairly large amount: *working in a foreign country took* ***quite a bit of*** *getting used to.*
2 [with adj.] informal a set of actions or ideas associated with a specific group or activity: *Miranda could go off and do her theatrical bit.*
3 informal a girl or young woman: *he went and married some young bit half his age.*
4 (bits) Brit. informal a person's genitals.
5 N. Amer. informal a unit of $12\frac{1}{2}$ cents (used only in even multiples).
– PHRASES **a bit** somewhat; to some extent: *he came back looking a bit annoyed.* **bit by bit** gradually: *bit by bit the truth started to emerge.* **a bit of a ——** used to suggest that something is not severe or extreme, or is the case only to a limited extent: *I have had a bit of an accident* | *he's a bit of a womanizer.* ■ used to denote a young person or one of slight build: *you're just a bit of a girl yourself.* **a bit of all right** Brit. informal a pleasing person or thing, especially a woman regarded in sexual terms. **bit of fluff** (or **skirt** or **stuff**) Brit. informal a woman regarded in sexual terms. **bit of rough** see ROUGH. **bit on the side** Brit. informal **1** a person with whom one is unfaithful to one's partner. **2** money earned outside one's normal job. **bits and pieces** (or Brit. **bobs**) an assortment of small items. **do one's bit** informal make a useful contribution to an effort or cause: *I was persuaded to do my bit for the environment.* **in bits** Brit. informal very upset or emotionally affected. **not a bit** not at all: *I'm not a bit tired.* **not a bit of it** Brit. not at all: *Am I being unduly cynical? Not a bit of it.* **to bits 1** into pieces: *both cars were smashed to bits.* **2** informal very much; to a great degree: *Vicky was thrilled to bits* | *I just love him to bits.*
– ORIGIN Old English *bita* 'bite, mouthful', of Germanic origin; related to German *Bissen*, also to BITE.

bit² past of BITE.

bit³ ▶ **noun 1** a mouthpiece, typically made of metal, which is attached to a bridle and used to control a horse.
2 a tool or piece for boring or drilling: *a drill bit.* ■ the cutting or gripping part of a plane, pincers, or other tool. ■ the part of a key that engages with the lock lever. ■ the copper head of a soldering iron.
▶ **verb** [with obj.] put a bit into the mouth of (a horse).
– PHRASES **get** (or **take** or **have**) **the bit between** (or N. Amer. **in**) **one's teeth** begin to tackle a problem or task in a determined or independent way. **off the bit** (or **bridle**) (of a horse) ridden on a loose rein to allow it to gallop freely. **on the bit** (or **bridle**) (of a horse) ridden with a light but firm contact on the mouth.
– DERIVATIVES **bitted** adjective [in combination] *a double-bitted axe.*
– ORIGIN Old English *bite* 'biting, a bite', of Germanic origin; related to Dutch *beet* and German *Biss*, also to BITE.

bit⁴ ▶ **noun** Computing a unit of information expressed as either a 0 or 1 in binary notation.
– ORIGIN 1940s: blend of BINARY and DIGIT.

bitch ▶ **noun 1** a female dog, wolf, fox, or otter.
2 informal a spiteful or unpleasant woman. ■ black slang a woman (used in a non-derogatory sense). ■ a person who is completely subservient to another.
3 (a bitch) informal a difficult or unpleasant situation or thing: *working the night shift is a bitch.*
4 informal a complaint: *my big bitch is that there's nothing new here.*
▶ **verb** [no obj.] informal make spitefully critical comments: *everybody was* ***bitching about*** *their colleagues.*
– ORIGIN Old English *bicce*, of Germanic origin.

bitchery ▶ **noun** [mass noun] informal malicious or spiteful behaviour.

bitching (also **bitchen**) US informal ▶ **adjective** excellent: *a bitching new album.*
▶ **adverb** [as submodifier] extremely: *it's bitchin' hot, ain't it?*

bitch-slap ▶ **verb** [with obj.] US informal deliver a stinging blow to (someone), typically in order to humiliate them: *I would have bitch-slapped him for talking that way.*
– ORIGIN 1990s: originally black English, referring to a woman hitting or haranguing her male partner.

bitchy ▶ **adjective** (**bitchier**, **bitchiest**) informal malicious or spitefully critical: *bitchy remarks.*
– DERIVATIVES **bitchily** adverb, **bitchiness** noun.

bite ▶ **verb** (past **bit**; past participle **bitten**) [with obj.] **1** use the teeth to cut into (something): *the woman's arm was* ***bitten off*** *by an alligator* | [no obj.] *Rosa* ***bit into*** *a cream cake.* ■ use the teeth in order to inflict injury on: *she had bitten, scratched, and kicked her assailant.* ■ (of a snake, insect, or spider) wound with fangs, pincers, or a sting: *while on holiday she was bitten by an adder.* ■ [no obj.] (of an acid) corrode a surface: *chemicals have* ***bitten deep into*** *the stone.* ■ [no obj.] (of a fish) take the bait or lure on the end of a fishing line into the mouth. ■ [no obj.] informal be persuaded to accept a deal or offer: *a hundred or so retailers should bite.* ■ informal annoy or worry: *what's biting you today?*
2 [no obj.] (of a tool, tyre, boot, etc.) grip or take hold on a surface: *once on the slab, my boots failed to bite.* ■ (of an object) press into a part of the body, causing pain: *the handcuffs* ***bit into*** *his wrists.* ■ cause emotional pain: *Cheryl's betrayal had* ***bitten deep.*** ■ (of a policy or situation) take effect, with unpleasant consequences: *the cuts in art education were starting to bite.* ■ N. Amer. informal be very bad, unpleasant, or unfortunate.
▶ **noun 1** an act of biting something in order to eat it: *Stephen ate a hot dog in three big bites.* ■ a wound inflicted by an animal's or a person's teeth: *Percy's dog had given her a nasty bite.* ■ a wound inflicted by a snake, insect, or spider: *my legs were covered in mosquito bites.* ■ an instance of bait being taken by a fish: *by four o'clock he still hadn't had a single bite.* ■ Dentistry the bringing together of the teeth in occlusion.
2 a piece cut off by biting: *Robyn took a large bite out of her sandwich.* ■ informal a quick snack: *I plan to stop off in the village and have* ***a bite to eat.*** ■ a small morsel of prepared food, intended to constitute one mouthful: *bacon bites with cheese.* ■ a short piece of information.
3 a sharp or pungent flavour: *a fresh, lemony bite.* ■ [mass noun] incisiveness or cogency of style: *the tale has added bite if its characters appear to be real.* ■ a feeling of cold in the air or wind: *by early October there's a bite in the air.*
– PHRASES **someone's bark is worse than their bite** said of someone whose fierce and intimidating manner does not reflect their nature. **be bitten by the —— bug** develop a passionate interest in a specified activity: *Joe was badly bitten by the showbiz bug at the age of four.* **bite the big one** N. Amer. informal die. **bite the bullet** decide to do something difficult or unpleasant that one has been putting off or hesitating over. [from the old custom of giving wounded soldiers a bullet to bite on when undergoing surgery without anaesthetic.] **bite the dust** informal be killed. ■ fail or come to an end: *she hoped the new course would not bite the dust for lack of funding.* **bite the hand that feeds one** deliberately hurt or offend a benefactor. **bite someone's head off** see HEAD. **bite one's lip** dig one's front teeth into one's lip in embarrassment, grief, or annoyance, or to prevent oneself from saying something. **bite one's nails** chew at one's nails as a nervous habit. **bite off more than one can chew** take on a commitment one cannot fulfil. **the biter bitten** (or **bit**) used to indicate that someone is being treated in the same way that they have treated others, typically badly. **bite one's tongue** make a desperate effort to avoid saying something: *I had to bite my tongue and accept his explanation.* **once bitten, twice shy** proverb an unpleasant experience induces caution. **put the bite on** N. Amer. & Austral./NZ informal borrow or extort money from. [1930s (originally US): *bite*, from the slang sense 'deception'.] **take a bite out of** informal reduce by a significant amount: *commissions that can take a bite out of your retirement funds.*
– PHRASAL VERBS **bite something back** refrain with difficulty from saying something, making a sound, or expressing an emotion: *Melissa bit back a scathing comment.*
– DERIVATIVES **biter** noun.
– ORIGIN Old English *bītan*, of Germanic origin; related to Dutch *bijten* and German *beissen*.

biternate /bʌɪˈtəːneɪt/ ▶ **adjective** Botany (especially of a ternate leaf) having leaflets or other parts that are further subdivided in a ternate arrangement.

bite-sized (also **bite-size**) ▶ **adjective** (of a piece of food) small enough to be eaten in one mouthful: *cut the potatoes into bite-sized pieces.* ■ informal very small or short: *a series of bite-sized essays.*

Bithynia /bɪˈθɪnɪə/ the ancient name for the region of NW Asia Minor west of ancient Paphlagonia, bordering the Black Sea and the Sea of Marmara.

biting ▶ **adjective 1** (of insects and certain other animals) able to wound the skin with a sting or fangs.
2 (of wind or cold) so cold as to be painful: *he leant forward to protect himself against the biting wind.* ■ (of wit or criticism) harsh or cruel: *his biting satire on corruption and power.*
– DERIVATIVES **bitingly** adverb.

biting midge ▶ **noun** a minute fly which typically occurs in large swarms. The female has piercing mouthparts and feeds on the blood of a variety of animals, including humans. • Family Ceratopogonidae: numerous genera and species, including the common European *Culicoides obsoletus*.

bitmap Computing ▶ **noun** a representation in which each item corresponds to one or more bits of information, especially the information used to control the display of a computer screen.
▶ **verb** (**bitmaps**, **bitmapping**, **bitmapped**) [with obj.] represent (an item) as a bitmap.

bitonal /bʌɪˈtəʊn(ə)l/ ▶ **adjective** (of music) having parts in two different keys sounding together.
– DERIVATIVES **bitonality** noun.

bit part ▶ **noun** a small acting role in a play or a film.

bit rate ▶ **noun** Electronics the number of bits per second that can be transmitted along a digital network.

Bitrex /ˈbɪtrɛks/ ▶ **noun** [mass noun] trademark a bitter-tasting synthetic organic compound added to cleaning fluids or other products to make them unpalatable.
– ORIGIN 1960s: an invented name.

bitser ▶ **noun** variant spelling of BITZER.

bitstream /ˈbɪtstriːm/ ▶ **noun** Electronics a stream of data in binary form. ■ **(Bitstream)** trademark a system of digital-to-analogue signal conversion used in some audio CD players, in which the signal from the CD is digitally processed to give a signal at a higher frequency before being converted to an analogue signal.

bitten past participle of BITE.

bitter ▶ **adjective 1** having a sharp, pungent taste or smell; not sweet: *raw berries have an intensely bitter flavour.* ■ (of chocolate) dark and unsweetened.
2 feeling or showing anger, hurt, or resentment because of bad experiences or a sense of unjust treatment: *I don't feel jealous or bitter* | *she wept bitter tears of self-reproach.* ■ (of a conflict, argument, or opponent) full of anger and acrimony: *a bitter five-year legal battle.*
3 painful or unpleasant to accept or contemplate: *today's decision has come as a bitter blow* | *she knew from bitter experience how treacherous such feelings could be.*

B

4 (of wind or weather) intensely cold: *a bitter February night*.
▶ noun 1 [mass noun] Brit. beer that is strongly flavoured with hops and has a bitter taste.
2 (**bitters**) [treated as sing.] alcohol flavoured with bitter plant extracts, used as an additive in cocktails or as a medicinal substance to promote appetite or digestion.
– PHRASES **to the bitter end** used to indicate that one will continue doing something until it is finished, no matter what: *the workers would fight to the bitter end*. [perhaps associated with a nautical word *bitter* denoting the last part of a cable inboard of the BITTS, perhaps influenced by the biblical phrase 'her end is bitter as wormwood' (Prov. 5:4).]
– DERIVATIVES **bitterly** adverb.
– ORIGIN Old English *biter*, of Germanic origin; related to Dutch and German *bitter*, and probably to BITE.

bitter aloes ▶ noun see ALOE.

bitter apple ▶ noun another term for COLOCYNTH.

bittercress ▶ noun a plant with small white flowers, which grows widely as a temperate weed, especially in damp soils. ● Genus *Cardamine*, family Cruciferae: several species.

bitter-ender ▶ noun informal a person who holds out until the end, no matter what. ■ (in southern African history) a Boer who refused to surrender towards the end of the Second Boer War.

bitter greens ▶ plural noun N. Amer. mixed green leaves of a variety of salad vegetables with a bitter taste, such as endives, chicory, or spinach.

bitter lemon ▶ noun [mass noun] Brit. a carbonated semi-sweet soft drink flavoured with lemons.

bitterling ▶ noun a small brightly coloured freshwater fish of central Europe. The eggs are deposited inside a mussel, in which they are fertilized and the young eventually hatch. ● *Rhodeus amarus*, family Cyprinidae.
– ORIGIN late 19th cent.: from German *Bitterling*, from *bitter* 'bitter' (translating Latin *amarus*) + -LING.

bittern[1] /ˈbɪtən/ ▶ noun a large marshbird of the heron family, which is typically smaller than a heron, with brown streaked plumage. The larger kinds are noted for the deep booming call of the male in the breeding season. ● Genera *Botaurus* and *Ixobrychus*, family Ardeidae: several species, especially the **Eurasian bittern** (*B. stellaris*) and the **American bittern** (*B. lentiginosus*).
– ORIGIN late Middle English *bitore*, from Old French *butor*, based on Latin *butio* 'bittern' + *taurus* 'bull' (because of its call). The *-n* was added in the 16th cent., perhaps by association with *hern*, obsolete variant of HERON.

bittern[2] /ˈbɪt(ə)n/ (also **bitterns**) ▶ noun [mass noun] a concentrated solution of various salts remaining after the crystallization of salt from seawater.
– ORIGIN late 17th cent.: probably from the adjective BITTER.

bitterness ▶ noun 1 sharpness of taste; lack of sweetness: *the lime juice imparts a slight bitterness*.
2 anger and disappointment at being treated unfairly; resentment: *he expressed bitterness over his dismissal without notice*.

bitter orange ▶ noun another term for SEVILLE ORANGE.

bitter pit ▶ noun [mass noun] a disease of apples caused by calcium deficiency, characterized by sunken brown spots.

bittersweet ▶ adjective 1 (of food or drink) sweet with a bitter aftertaste.
2 arousing pleasure tinged with sadness or pain: *bittersweet memories of his time in London*.
▶ noun 1 another term for WOODY NIGHTSHADE (see NIGHTSHADE).
2 a vine-like American climbing plant which bears clusters of bright orange pods. ● Genus *Celastrus*, family Celastraceae: several species.
3 (also **bittersweet shell**) a widely distributed bivalve mollusc which has a pale rounded shell that is typically marked with wavy lines. ● Genus *Glycymeris*, family Glycymeridae.

bittersweet chocolate ▶ noun North American term for PLAIN CHOCOLATE.

BitTorrent ▶ noun Computing, trademark a peer-to-peer file transfer protocol for sharing large amounts of data over the Internet, in which each part of a file downloaded by a user is transferred to other users.
– ORIGIN early 21st cent.: blend of BIT[4] and TORRENT.

bitts ▶ plural noun a pair of posts on the deck of a ship for fastening mooring lines or cables.
– ORIGIN Middle English: probably of Low German origin.

bitty informal ▶ adjective (**bittier**, **bittiest**) 1 chiefly Brit. made up of small parts that seem unrelated: *the text is rather bitty*.
2 [usu. in combination] N. Amer. tiny: *a **little-bitty** girl*.
– DERIVATIVES **bittiness** noun.

bitumen /ˈbɪtjʊmən/ ▶ noun [mass noun] a black viscous mixture of hydrocarbons obtained naturally or as a residue from petroleum distillation. It is used for road surfacing and roofing. ■ Austral. informal a tarred road surface: *a kilometre and a half of bitumen*.
– ORIGIN late Middle English (denoting naturally occurring asphalt used as mortar): from Latin.

bituminous /bɪˈtjuːmɪnəs/ ▶ adjective of, containing, or of the nature of bitumen.
– ORIGIN mid 16th cent.: from French *bitumineux*, from Latin *bituminosus*.

bituminous coal ▶ noun [mass noun] black coal having a relatively high volatile content and burning with a characteristically bright smoky flame.

bitwise ▶ adjective Computing denoting an operator in a programming language which manipulates the individual bits in a byte or word.

bitzer /ˈbɪtsə/ (also **bitser**) ▶ noun Austral./NZ informal a contraption made from previously unrelated parts. ■ a mongrel dog.
– ORIGIN 1920s: abbreviation of the phrase *bits and pieces*.

bivalence /bʌɪˈveɪl(ə)ns/ ▶ noun [mass noun] Logic the existence of only two states or truth values (e.g. true and false).

bivalent ▶ adjective 1 /ˈbɪv(ə)l(ə)nt/ Biology (of homologous chromosomes) associated in pairs.
2 /bʌɪˈveɪl(ə)nt/ Chemistry another term for DIVALENT.
▶ noun /ˈbɪv(ə)l(ə)nt/ Biology a pair of homologous chromosomes.
– ORIGIN mid 19th cent.: from BI- 'two' + Latin *valent-* 'being strong' (from the verb *valere*).

bivalve ▶ noun an aquatic mollusc which has a compressed body enclosed within a hinged shell, such as oysters, mussels, and scallops. Also called PELECYPOD or LAMELLIBRANCH. ● Class Bivalvia (formerly Pelecypoda or Lamellibranchia).
▶ adjective (also **bivalved**) 1 (of a mollusc or other aquatic invertebrate) having a hinged double shell.
2 Botany having two valves.

bivariate /bʌɪˈvɛːrɪət/ ▶ adjective Statistics involving or depending on two variates.

bivouac /ˈbɪvʊak, ˈbɪvwak/ ▶ noun a temporary camp without tents or cover, used especially by soldiers or mountaineers.
▶ verb (**bivouacs**, **bivouacking**, **bivouacked**) [no obj.] stay in a bivouac: *we bivouacked on the north side of the town*.
– ORIGIN early 18th cent. (denoting a night watch by the whole army): from French, probably from Swiss German *Bîwacht* 'additional guard at night', apparently denoting a citizens' patrol supporting the ordinary town watch.

bivvy informal ▶ noun (pl. **bivvies**) a small tent or temporary shelter.
▶ verb (**bivvies**, **bivvying**, **bivvied**) [no obj.] stay in a small tent or temporary shelter.
– ORIGIN early 20th cent.: abbreviation of BIVOUAC.

biweekly ▶ adjective & adverb appearing or taking place every two weeks or twice a week: [as adj.] *a biweekly bulletin*.
▶ noun (pl. **biweeklies**) a periodical that appears every two weeks or twice a week.

bi-wiring ▶ noun [mass noun] the use of two wires between an amplifier and a loudspeaker to operate the low- and high-frequency speaker circuits separately.

biyearly ▶ adjective & adverb appearing or taking place every two years or twice a year.

biz ▶ noun informal a business, especially one connected with entertainment: *the music biz*.
– ORIGIN mid 19th cent. (originally US): abbreviation.

bizarre /bɪˈzɑː/ ▶ adjective very strange or unusual: *a bizarre situation* | *his behaviour became more and more bizarre*.
– DERIVATIVES **bizarrely** adverb [sentence adverb] *bizarrely, he doesn't like desserts*, **bizarreness** noun.
– ORIGIN mid 17th cent.: from French, from Italian *bizzarro* 'angry', of unknown origin.

bizarrerie /bɪˈzɑːrəri/ ▶ noun (pl. **bizarreries**) a thing considered extremely strange and unusual, especially in an amusing way.
– ORIGIN mid 18th cent.: from French, from BIZARRE.

bizarro /bɪˈzɑːrəʊ/ ▶ adjective informal, chiefly N. Amer. bizarre.

Bizerta /bɪˈzəːtə/ (also **Bizerte**) a seaport on the northern coast of Tunisia; pop. 114,400 (est. 2004).

Bizet /ˈbiːzeɪ/, Georges (1838–75), French composer; born *Alexandre César Léopold Bizet*. He is best known for the opera *Carmen* (1875).

bizzy ▶ noun (pl. **bizzies**) variant spelling of BUSY.

Bjerknes /ˈbjəːknəs/, Vilhelm Frimann Koren (1862–1951), Norwegian geophysicist and meteorologist. He developed a theory of physical hydrodynamics for atmospheric and oceanic circulation, and mathematical models for weather prediction. His son **Jacob** (1897–1975) built on his father's work, and through his development of a model for the structure and behaviour of cyclones (he introduced the term *front* to meteorology) became a major contributor to theoretical meteorology and practical weather forecasting.

Bk ▶ symbol the chemical element berkelium.

bk ▶ abbreviation book.

BL ▶ abbreviation ■ (in Scotland and Ireland) Bachelor of Law. ■ bill of lading. ■ historical British Leyland. ■ British Library.

bl ▶ abbreviation barrel.

blab ▶ verb (**blabs**, **blabbing**, **blabbed**) [no obj.] informal reveal secrets by indiscreet talk: *she blabbed to the press* | [with obj.] *there's no need to blab the whole story*. ■ talk foolishly or mindlessly: *they **blab on** about responsibility*.
– ORIGIN Middle English (as a noun): probably of Germanic origin; ultimately imitative.

blabber informal ▶ verb [no obj.] talk foolishly, indiscreetly, or excessively: *she **blabbered on and on**.*
▶ noun a person who blabbers. ■ [mass noun] foolish, indiscreet, or excessive talk: *the obsequious blabber of her servants*.

blabbermouth ▶ noun informal a person who talks excessively or indiscreetly.

Black, Joseph (1728–99), Scottish chemist. He was important in developing accurate techniques for following chemical reactions by weighing reactants and products, and formulated the concepts of latent heat and thermal capacity.

black ▶ adjective 1 of the very darkest colour due to the absence of or complete absorption of light; the opposite of white: *black smoke* | *her long black hair*. ■ (of the sky or night) completely dark due to the sun, moon, or stars not being visible: *the sky was moonless and black*. ■ (of a plant or animal) dark in colour as distinguished from a lighter variety: *Japanese black pine*. ■ (of coffee or tea) served without milk. ■ of or denoting the suits spades and clubs in a pack of cards. ■ (of a ski run) of the highest level of difficulty, as indicated by black markers positioned along it.
2 (also **Black**) belonging to or denoting any human group having dark-coloured skin, especially of African or Australian Aboriginal ancestry. ■ relating to black people: *black culture*.
3 characterized by tragic or disastrous events; causing despair or pessimism: *five thousand men were killed on the blackest day of the war* | *the future looks black*. ■ (of a person's state of mind) full of gloom or misery; very depressed: *Jean had disappeared and Mary was in a black mood*. ■ (of humour) presenting tragic or harrowing situations in comic terms. ■ full of anger or hatred: *Rory shot her a black look*. ■ archaic very evil or wicked: *my soul is steeped in the blackest sin*.
4 denoting a covert military procedure: *clearance for black operations came from the highest political level*.
5 Brit. dated (of goods or work) not to be handled or undertaken by trade union members, especially so as to express support for an industrial dispute elsewhere: *the union declared the ship black*.
▶ noun 1 [mass noun] black colour or pigment: *a tray decorated in black and green*. ■ black clothes or material, typically worn as a sign of mourning: *only one or two of the mourners were in black*. ■ darkness, especially of night or an overcast sky: *the only thing visible in the black was the light of the torch*. ■ (**Black**) the player of the black pieces in chess or draughts. ■ [count noun] a black thing, in particular the black ball in snooker.

2 (also **Black**) a member of a dark-skinned people, especially one of African or Australian Aboriginal ancestry.
3 Brit. informal blackcurrant cordial: *a rum and black.*
▸ **verb** [with obj.] **1** make (something) black, especially with polish: *the steps of the house were neatly blacked.* ■ make (one's face and other visible parts) black with polish or make-up so as not to be seen at night or to play the role of a black person in a play or film: *white extras **blacking up** their faces to play Ethiopians.*
2 Brit. dated refuse to handle (goods), undertake (work), or have dealings with (a person or business) as a way of taking industrial action: *the printers blacked firms trying to employ women.*
– PHRASES **black someone's eye** hit someone in the eye so as to cause bruising. **in the black** not owing any money; solvent. **in someone's black books** informal in disfavour with someone. **look on the black side** informal view a situation from a pessimistic angle. **men in black** informal anonymous dark-clothed men who supposedly visit people who have reported an encounter with a UFO or an alien in order to prevent them publicizing it. **the new black** a colour that is currently so popular that it rivals the traditional status of black as the most reliably fashionable colour: *brown is the new black this season.* ■ something which is suddenly extremely popular or fashionable: *retro sci-fi is the new black.* **not as black as one is painted** informal not as bad as one is said to be.
– PHRASAL VERBS **black out** undergo a sudden and temporary loss of consciousness. **black something out 1** extinguish all lights or completely cover windows, especially for protection against an air attack. ■ subject a place to an electricity failure: *Chicago was blacked out yesterday after a freak flood.* **2** obscure something completely so that it cannot be read or seen: *the number plate had been blacked out with masking tape.* ■ (of a television company) decide not to broadcast a disputed or controversial programme.
– DERIVATIVES **blackish** adjective, **blackly** adverb, **blackness** noun.
– ORIGIN Old English *blæc*, of Germanic origin.

> **USAGE Black** has been used to refer to African peoples and their descendants since at least the late 14th century. Although the word has been in continuous use ever since, other terms have enjoyed prominence too: in the US **coloured** was the term adopted in preference by emancipated slaves following the American Civil War, and **coloured** was itself superseded in the US in the early 20th century by **Negro** as the term preferred by prominent black American campaigners such as Booker T. Washington. In Britain, on the other hand, **coloured** was the most widely used and accepted term in the 1950s and early 1960s. With the civil rights and Black Power movements of the 1960s, **black** was adopted by Americans of African origin to signify a sense of racial pride, and it remains the most widely used and generally accepted term in Britain today. In the US **African American** replaced **black** in many contexts during the 1980s, but both are now generally acceptable.

black Africa the area of Africa, generally south of the Sahara, where black people predominate.

blackamoor /ˈblakəmɔː, -mʊə/ ▸ **noun** archaic a black African or a very dark-skinned person.
– ORIGIN early 16th cent.: from BLACK + MOOR.

black and blue ▸ **adjective** covered in livid bruises.

black and tan ▸ **noun 1** a terrier of a breed with a black back and tan markings on face, flanks, and legs.
2 [mass noun] Brit. a drink composed of stout and bitter.

Black and Tans an armed force recruited by the British government to fight Sinn Fein in Ireland in 1920–1. Their harsh methods caused an outcry in Britain and America.
– ORIGIN so named because of the mixture of military khaki and black constabulary colours of their uniform.

black and white ▸ **adjective 1** (of a photograph, film, television programme, etc.) in black, white, shades of grey, and no other colour: *old black-and-white movies.*
2 (of a situation or debate) involving clearly defined opposing principles or issues: *it was all grey areas; no black-and-white certainties.*
▸ **noun** US informal a police car.
– PHRASES **in black and white 1** in writing or print: *she had abandoned all hope of getting her contract down in black and white.* **2** in terms of clearly defined opposing principles or issues: *children think in black and white, good and bad.*

black ant ▸ **noun** a small ant which is black in colour and is typically found in and around houses. ● Several species in the family Formicidae.

black art ▸ **noun** (often **the black arts**) another term for BLACK MAGIC. ■ humorous a technique or practice considered mysterious and sinister: *the black art of political news management.*

blackball ▸ **verb** [with obj.] reject (a candidate applying to become a member of a private club), typically by means of a secret ballot.
– ORIGIN late 18th cent.: from the practice of registering an adverse vote by placing a black ball in a ballot box.

black ban ▸ **noun** Austral. a mass refusal to supply or purchase goods or services in an attempt to force a particular decision or action.

black bass ▸ **noun** a North American freshwater fish of the sunfish family, which is a popular sporting and food fish. ● Genus *Micropterus*, family Centrarchidae: several species, in particular the **largemouth bass** (*M. salmoides*) and the **smallmouth bass** (*M. dolomieui*).

black bean ▸ **noun 1** either of two cultivated varieties of bean plant having small black seeds: ● a variety of soy bean, used fermented in oriental cooking. ● a Mexican variety of the French bean.
■ the dried seed of the black bean plants, used as a vegetable.
2 either of two Australian plants of the pea family: ● a liana with blackish flowers (*Kennedia nigricans*, family Leguminosae). ● another term for MORETON BAY CHESTNUT.

black bear ▸ **noun** a medium-sized forest-dwelling bear with blackish fur and a paler face, found in North America and eastern Asia. ● Two species, family Ursidae: the **American black bear** (*Ursus americanus*), with a wide range of coat colour, and the smaller **Asian black bear** (*Selenarctos thibetanus*).

black beetle ▸ **noun** Brit. informal the common cockroach.

black belt ▸ **noun** a black belt worn by an expert in judo, karate, and other martial arts. ■ a person qualified to wear a black belt.

BlackBerry ▸ **noun** trademark a handheld wireless device that provides Internet access and email, telephone, and text-messaging facilities.

blackberry ▸ **noun** (pl. **blackberries**) **1** an edible soft fruit consisting of a cluster of soft purple-black drupelets.
2 the prickly climbing shrub of the rose family which bears blackberries. Also called BRAMBLE. ● *Rubus fruticosus*, family Rosaceae (sometimes treated as an aggregate of many species).
▸ **verb** (**blackberries**, **blackberrying**, **blackberried**) [no obj.] (usu. as noun **blackberrying**) gather blackberries in the wild.

black bile ▸ **noun** [mass noun] (in medieval science and medicine) one of the four bodily humours, believed to be associated with a melancholy temperament. Also called MELANCHOLY.
– ORIGIN late 18th cent.: translation of Greek *melankholia* (see MELANCHOLY). Compare with ATRABILIOUS.

black bindweed ▸ **noun** [mass noun] a twining European weed related to the docks, with heart shaped leaves and small white flowers. ● *Fallopia convolvulus*, family Polygonaceae.

blackbird ▸ **noun 1** an Old World thrush with mainly black plumage. ● Genus *Turdus*, family Turdidae: four species, in particular *T. merula*, the male of which has all-black plumage and a yellow bill.
2 (also **American blackbird**) a New World songbird with a strong pointed bill. The male has black plumage that is iridescent or has patches of red or yellow. ● Family Icteridae (the **American blackbird family**): several genera and species, including the abundant **red-winged blackbird** (*Agelaius phoeniceus*).
3 historical a black or Polynesian captive on a slave ship.

blackboard ▸ **noun** a large board with a smooth dark surface attached to a wall or supported on an easel and used by teachers in schools for writing on with chalk.

black body ▸ **noun** Physics a hypothetical perfect absorber and radiator of energy, with no reflecting power.

black book ▸ **noun** a book containing a list of secret contacts, or of the names of people liable to be punished: *he lists his sexual conquests in his little black book.*

black bottom ▸ **noun** a popular American dance of the 1920s.

black box ▸ **noun** a flight recorder in an aircraft. ■ informal a complex piece of equipment with contents which are mysterious to the user.

blackboy ▸ **noun** an Australian tree or erect shrub with long, stiff grass-like leaves. Flowering in some species is stimulated by fire. Also called GRASS TREE. ● Genus *Xanthorrhoea*, family Xanthorrhoeaceae: several species, including a tree (*X. preissii*) with a thick dark trunk and a palm-like crown of leaves, and a shrub (*X. australis*) with a short buried trunk and leaves on the surface of the ground.

black bread ▸ **noun** [mass noun] a coarse dark-coloured type of rye bread.

black bryony ▸ **noun** a climbing European hedgerow plant with broad glossy leaves, poisonous red berries, and black tubers. ● *Tamus communis*, the only European member of the yam family (Dioscoreaceae).

blackbuck ▸ **noun** a small Indian gazelle, the horned male of which has a black back and white underbelly, the female being hornless. Also called SASIN. ● *Antilope cervicapra*, family Bovidae.

black bun ▸ **noun** [mass noun] rich fruit cake in a pastry case, traditionally eaten in Scotland at New Year.

Blackburn an industrial town in Lancashire, NW England; pop. 104,100 (est. 2009).

blackbutt ▸ **noun** a tall straight-trunked Australian eucalyptus tree, typically with fire-charred fibrous bark on the lower trunk and with pale brown timber. ● *Eucalyptus pilularis*, family Myrtaceae.
– ORIGIN early 19th cent.: from BLACK + BUTT[3] in the sense 'tree trunk'.

black butter ▸ **noun** [mass noun] a sauce made by heating butter until it is brown and, typically, adding vinegar.

blackcap ▸ **noun 1** a mainly European warbler with a black cap in the male and a reddish-brown one in the female. ● *Sylvia atricapilla*, family Sylviidae.
2 N. Amer. the black-capped chickadee. ● *Parus atricapillus*, family Paridae.

Black Carib ▸ **noun** [mass noun] a language derived from Island Carib with borrowings from Spanish, English, and French, spoken in isolated parts of Central America by descendants of people transported from the Lesser Antilles.

black caucus ▸ **noun** US a political caucus composed of black people interested in advancing the concerns of blacks.

blackcock ▸ **noun** (pl. **same**) the male of the black grouse.

black consciousness ▸ **noun** [mass noun] awareness of one's identity as a black person.

Black Country a district of the English Midlands with much heavy industry.

blackcurrant ▸ **noun 1** a small round edible black berry which grows in loose hanging clusters.
2 the widely cultivated shrub which bears blackcurrants. ● *Ribes nigrum*, family Grossulariaceae.

Black Death the great epidemic of a disease thought to be bubonic plague, that killed a large proportion of the population of Europe in the mid 14th century. It originated in central Asia and China and spread rapidly through Europe, carried by the fleas of black rats, reaching England in 1348 and killing between one third and one half of the population in a matter of months.
– ORIGIN a modern term (compare with earlier *the (great) pestilence, great death, the plague*), said to have been introduced into English history by Mrs Markham (pseudonym of Mrs Penrose) in 1823, and into medical literature by a translation of German *der Schwarze Tod* (1833).

black diamond ▸ **noun 1** informal a lump of coal.
2 a dark, opaque form of diamond. Also called CARBONADO.
3 [usu. as modifier] N. Amer. a difficult ski slope: *a steep, black-diamond run.*

black dog ▸ **noun** a metaphorical representation of melancholy or depression.
– ORIGIN late 18th cent. (earlier as a name used during Queen Anne's reign for a bad shilling). Winston Churchill used the expression when alluding to his periodic bouts of depression.

black durgon /ˈdəːɡ(ə)n/ ▸ **noun** a black triggerfish that occurs worldwide in tropical seas. ● *Melichthys niger*, family Balistidae.

B

– ORIGIN mid 20th cent.: *durgon* perhaps from English dialect *durgan* or *durgen* 'undersized person or animal'.

black economy ▶ noun Brit. the part of a country's economic activity which is unrecorded and untaxed by its government.

blacken ▶ verb make or become black or dark, especially as a result of burning, decay, or bruising: [with obj.] *stone blackened by the soot of ages* | (as adj. **blackened**) *she smiled at Mary, revealing blackened teeth* | [no obj.] *he set light to the paper, watching the end blacken as it burned.* ■ [with obj.] dye or colour (the face or hair) black for camouflage or cosmetic effect. ■ [with obj.] damage or destroy (someone's reputation) by speaking badly of them: *she won't thank you for blackening her husband's name.*

black English ▶ noun [mass noun] any of various forms of English spoken by black people, especially as an urban dialect in the US.

black eye ▶ noun an area of bruised skin around the eye resulting from a blow.

black-eyed bean (also **black-eye bean**, US **black-eyed pea**) ▶ noun a creamy-white edible bean which has a black mark at the point where it was attached to the pod. ● This bean is obtained from *Vigna sinensis*, family Leguminosae.

black-eyed Susan ▶ noun any of a number of plants having flowers with yellowish petals and a dark centre: ● a slender tropical climber popular as an indoor or greenhouse plant (*Thunbergia alata*, family Acanthaceae). ● a rudbeckia grown in gardens (*Rudbeckia hirta* and its hybrids, family Compositae).

blackface ▶ noun **1** a sheep of a breed with a black face.
2 [mass noun] make-up used by a non-black performer playing a black role.

blackfellow ▶ noun Austral. offensive an Aboriginal.

black-figure ▶ noun [usu. as modifier] a type of ancient Greek pottery, originating in Corinth in the 7th century BC, in which figures are painted in black, details being added by incising through to the red clay background: *a black-figure amphora*. Compare with **RED-FIGURE**.

blackfish ▶ noun (pl. **same** or **blackfishes**) **1** any of a number of dark-coloured fish: ● an open-ocean fish related to the perches (genera *Centrolophus* and *Schedophilus*, family Centrolophidae), in particular the large and widespread *C. niger*. ● (**Alaska blackfish**) a small fish occurring along the Arctic coasts of Alaska and Siberia, noted for its ability to withstand freezing (*Dallia pectoralis*, family Umbridae). ● (**river blackfish**) a large fish of Australian rivers (*Gadopsis marmoratus*, family Gadopsidae). ● another term for **LUDERICK** ● another term for **GALJOEN** ● a salmon just after spawning.
2 another term for **PILOT WHALE**.

black flag ▶ noun **1** historical a pirate's ensign, typically thought to feature a white skull and crossbones on a black background.
2 historical a black flag hoisted outside a prison to announce an execution.
3 Motor Racing a black flag used to signal to a driver that he must stop at the pits as a punishment for a misdemeanour.

blackfly ▶ noun (pl. **same** or **blackflies**) **1** a black or dark green aphid which is a common pest of crops and gardens. ● Several species in the family Aphididae, in particular *Aphis fabae*.
2 (also **black fly**) a small black fly, the female of which sucks blood and can transmit a number of serious human and animal diseases. ● Family Simuliidae: *Simulium* and other genera.

Blackfoot ▶ noun (pl. **same** or **Blackfeet**) **1** a member of a confederacy of North American Indian peoples of the north-western plains. The Blackfoot confederacy was made up of three closely related tribes: the Blackfoot proper or Siksika, the Bloods, and the Peigan.
2 [mass noun] the Algonquian language of the Blackfoot, with about 6,000 speakers.
▶ adjective relating to the Blackfoot or their language.

Black Forest a hilly wooded region of SW Germany, lying to the east of the Rhine valley. German name **SCHWARZWALD**.

Black Forest gateau (N. Amer. **Black Forest cake**) ▶ noun a chocolate sponge having layers of morello cherries or cherry jam and whipped cream and topped with chocolate icing.

Black Friar ▶ noun a Dominican friar.
– ORIGIN early 16th cent.: so named because of the colour of the order's habit.

black frost ▶ noun [mass noun] frost which does not have a white surface.

black gold ▶ noun [mass noun] N. Amer. informal oil.

black grouse ▶ noun (pl. **same**) a large Eurasian grouse, the male of which has glossy blue-black plumage and a lyre-shaped tail. The males display in communal leks. ● *Tetrao tetrix*, family Tetraonidae (or Phasianidae); the male is called a **blackcock** and the female a **greyhen**.

blackguard /ˈblaɡɑːd, -ɡəd/ dated ▶ noun a man who behaves in a dishonourable or contemptible way.
▶ verb [with obj.] abuse or disparage (someone) scurrilously.
– DERIVATIVES **blackguardly** adjective.
– ORIGIN early 16th cent. (originally as two words): from **BLACK** + **GUARD**. The term originally denoted a body of attendants or servants, especially the menials who had charge of kitchen utensils, but the exact significance of the epithet 'black' is uncertain. The sense 'scoundrel, villain' dates from the mid 18th cent., and was formerly considered highly offensive.

black guillemot ▶ noun a seabird of the auk family with black summer plumage and large white wing patches, breeding on the coasts of the Arctic and North Atlantic. ● *Cepphus grylle*, family Alcidae.

Black Hamburg ▶ noun see **HAMBURG²**.

blackhead ▶ noun **1** a plug of sebum in a hair follicle, darkened by oxidation.
2 [mass noun] an infectious disease of turkeys producing discoloration of the head, caused by a protozoon.

Black Hills a range of mountains in east Wyoming and west South Dakota. The highest point is Harney Peak (2,207 m, 7,242 ft); the range also includes the sculptured granite face of Mount Rushmore.

black hole ▶ noun Astronomy a region of space having a gravitational field so intense that no matter or radiation can escape. ■ informal a place where money or lost items apparently disappear without trace.

> Black holes are probably formed when a massive star exhausts its nuclear fuel and collapses under its own gravity. If the star is massive enough no known force can counteract the increasing gravity, and it will collapse to a point of infinite density. Before this stage is reached, within a certain radius (the event horizon) light itself becomes trapped and the object becomes invisible.

Black Hole of Calcutta a dungeon 6 metres (20 feet) square in Fort William, Calcutta (now Kolkata), where perhaps as many as 146 English prisoners were confined overnight following the capture of the city by the nawab of Bengal in 1756. Only twenty-three of them were still alive the next morning.

black house ▶ noun a traditional single-storeyed Scottish house built of turf or mortarless stone, typically lacking a chimney and roofed with turf or thatch.

black ice ▶ noun [mass noun] a transparent coating of ice, especially on a road surface.

black information ▶ noun [mass noun] information held by banks, credit agencies, or other financial institutions about people who are considered bad credit risks.

blacking ▶ noun [mass noun] black paste or polish, especially that used on shoes.

blackjack ▶ noun **1** [mass noun] chiefly N. Amer. a gambling card game in which players try to acquire cards with a face value totalling 21 and no more. Also called **PONTOON¹**, **VINGT-ET-UN**.
2 a widely distributed weed related to the bur-marigold, with barbed black seeds. [perhaps from sense 3, drawing a comparison between the shape of the seeds and a bludgeon.] ● *Bidens pilosa*, family Compositae.
3 N. Amer. a flexible lead-filled truncheon.
4 historical a pirates' black ensign.
5 historical a tar-coated leather container used to hold beer.

Black Jew ▶ noun another term for **FALASHA**.

black kite ▶ noun a bird of prey with dark plumage and a slightly forked tail, feeding mainly by scavenging and found throughout much of the Old World. ● *Milvus migrans*, family Accipitridae.

black knight ▶ noun Stock Exchange a person or company making an unwelcome takeover bid for another company.
– ORIGIN by association with **WHITE KNIGHT**.

blacklead ▶ noun another term for **GRAPHITE**.
▶ verb [with obj.] polish (metal, especially cast iron) with graphite.

blackleg ▶ noun **1** Brit. derogatory a person who continues working when fellow workers are on strike.
2 [mass noun] an acute infectious bacterial disease of cattle and sheep, causing necrosis in one or more legs. ● The bacterium is *Clostridium chauvoei*.
3 [mass noun] any of a number of plant diseases in which part of the stem blackens and decays, in particular: ● a fungal disease of cabbages and related plants (caused by *Leptosphaeria*, *Pleospora*, and other genera). ● a bacterial disease of potatoes (caused by *Erwinia carotovora* subsp. *atroseptica*).
▶ verb (**blacklegs**, **blacklegging**, **blacklegged**) [no obj.] Brit. derogatory continue working when one's fellow workers are on strike.

black letter ▶ noun [mass noun] an early ornate, bold style of type.

black light ▶ noun [mass noun] ultraviolet or infrared radiation, invisible to the eye.

blacklist ▶ noun a list of people or groups regarded as unacceptable or untrustworthy and often marked down for punishment or exclusion.
▶ verb [with obj.] put (a person or group) on a blacklist.

black lung ▶ noun [mass noun] chiefly N. Amer. pneumoconiosis caused by inhalation of coal dust.

black magic ▶ noun [mass noun] magic involving the supposed invocation of evil spirits for evil purposes.

blackmail ▶ noun [mass noun] the action, treated as a criminal offence, of demanding money from someone in return for not revealing compromising information which one has about them. ■ money demanded in this way: *we do not pay blackmail.* ■ the use of threats or the manipulation of someone's feelings to force them to do something: *some people use emotional blackmail.*
▶ verb [with obj.] demand money from (someone) in return for not revealing compromising information about them. ■ force (someone) to do something by using threats or manipulating their feelings: ***he had blackmailed her into sailing with him.***
– DERIVATIVES **blackmailer** noun.
– ORIGIN mid 16th cent. (denoting protection money levied by Scottish chiefs): from **BLACK** + obsolete *mail* 'tribute, rent', from Old Norse *mál* 'speech, agreement'.

black mamba ▶ noun a highly venomous slender olive-brown to dark grey snake that moves with great speed and agility. Native to eastern and southern Africa, it is the largest poisonous snake on the continent. ● *Dendroaspis polylepis*, family Elapidae.

Black Maria /blak məˈrʌɪə/ ▶ noun **1** informal a police vehicle for transporting prisoners.
2 [mass noun] a card game in which players try to avoid winning tricks containing the queen of spades or any hearts. ■ a name for the queen of spades in this game.
– ORIGIN mid 19th cent. (originally US): said to be named after a black woman, *Maria Lee*, who kept a boarding house in Boston and helped police in escorting drunk and disorderly customers to jail.

black mark ▶ noun Brit. informal a note or record of a person's misdemeanour or discreditable action: *a black mark went down against his name for turning down the job.*

black market ▶ noun an illegal traffic or trade in officially controlled or scarce commodities: *the men planned to sell the meat* ***on the black market*** | [as modifier] *black market currency trading.*
DERIVATIVES **black marketeer** noun, **black-marketeering** noun.

black mass ▶ noun a travesty of the Roman Catholic Mass in worship of the Devil.

black metal ▶ noun [mass noun] a type of heavy metal music having lyrics which deal with the Devil and the supernatural.

Black Monday ▶ noun **1** Monday 19 October 1987, when massive falls in the value of stocks on Wall Street triggered similar falls in markets around the world.
2 archaic Easter Monday.

black money ▶ noun [mass noun] income illegally obtained or not declared for tax purposes.

Black Monk ▶ noun a Benedictine monk.
– ORIGIN Middle English: so named because of the colour of the order's habit.

Blackmore, R. D. (1825–1900), English novelist and poet; full name *Richard Doddridge Blackmore*. He is known for his romantic novel *Lorna Doone* (1869), set on 17th-century Exmoor.

black Muslim ▸ **noun** a member of the **Nation of Islam**.

black nationalism ▸ **noun** [mass noun] the advocacy of the national civil rights of black people, especially in the US.

blackout ▸ **noun 1** a period when all lights must be turned out or covered to prevent them being seen by the enemy during an air raid. ■ (usu. **blackouts**) Brit. dark curtains put up in windows to cover lights during an air raid. ■ a failure of an electrical power supply: *due to a power blackout their hotel was in total darkness.* ■ a moment in the theatre when the lights on stage are suddenly dimmed. ■ a suppression of information, especially one imposed on the media by government: *there is a total information blackout on minority interests.*
2 a temporary loss of consciousness.

Black Panther ▸ **noun** a member of a militant political organization set up in the US in 1966 to fight for black rights.

black panther ▸ **noun** a leopard that has black fur rather than the typical spotted coat.

black pepper ▸ **noun** [mass noun] the dried black berries of the pepper, harvested while still unripe and used either whole or ground as a spice and condiment.

blackpoll /ˈblakpəʊl/ (also **blackpoll warbler**) ▸ **noun** a North American warbler with a black cap, white cheeks, and white underparts streaked with black. ● *Dendroica striata*, family Parulidae.

Blackpool a seaside resort in Lancashire, NW England; pop. 142,600 (est. 2009).

black poplar ▸ **noun** a Eurasian poplar with a blackish-brown trunk and arching lower branches. ● *Populus nigra*, family Salicaceae.

black powder ▸ **noun** [mass noun] gunpowder.

Black Power ▸ **noun** [mass noun] a movement in support of rights and political power for black people, especially prominent in the US in the 1960s and 1970s.

Black Prince (1330–76), eldest son of Edward III of England; name given to *Edward, Prince of Wales and Duke of Cornwall*. He was responsible for the English victory at Poitiers in 1356. He predeceased his father, but his son became king as Richard II.

black pudding ▸ **noun** Brit. a black sausage containing pork, dried pig's blood, and suet.

black rat ▸ **noun** a rat with dark fur, large ears, and a long tail. It is found throughout the world, being particularly common in the tropics, and is the chief host of the plague-transmitting flea. Also called **ship rat, house rat**, or **roof rat**. ● *Rattus rattus*, family Muridae.

black rhinoceros ▸ **noun** a two-horned rhinoceros with a prehensile upper lip, found in Africa south of the Sahara. ● *Diceros bicornis*, family Rhinocerotidae.

Black Rod (in full **Gentleman Usher of the Black Rod**) ▸ **noun** (in the UK) the chief usher of the Lord Chamberlain's department of the royal household, who is also usher to the House of Lords.
– ORIGIN mid 17th cent.: so named because of the black wand carried as a symbol of office.

black rot ▸ **noun** [mass noun] any of a number of fungal or bacterial diseases of plants, fruits, and vegetables, producing blackening, rotting, and shrivelling.

black salsify ▸ **noun** another term for **scorzonera**.

Black Sea a tideless almost landlocked sea bounded by Ukraine, Russia, Georgia, Turkey, Bulgaria, and Romania, connected to the Mediterranean through the Bosporus and the Sea of Marmara.

black sheep ▸ **noun** informal a member of a family or group who is regarded as a disgrace to it.
– ORIGIN late 18th cent.: from the proverb *there is a black sheep in every flock.*

blackshirt ▸ **noun** a member of a Fascist organization, in particular: ■ (in Italy) a member of a paramilitary group founded by Mussolini. ■ (in Nazi Germany) a member of the SS. ■ (in the UK) a supporter of Oswald Mosley's British Union of Fascists.
– ORIGIN 1920s: so named because of the colour of the Italian Fascist uniform.

blacksmith ▸ **noun** a person who makes and repairs things in iron by hand. ■ a farrier.

black smoker ▸ **noun** Geology a geothermal vent on the seabed which ejects superheated water containing much suspended matter, typically black sulphide minerals.

black spot ▸ **noun 1** Brit. a place or area marked by a particular trouble or concern: *an unemployment black spot | an accident black spot.*
2 [mass noun] a fungal or bacterial disease of plants, especially roses, producing black blotches on the leaves. ● **Rose black spot** is caused by the fungus *Diplocarpon rosae*, subdivision Ascomycotina.

Blackstone, Sir William (1723–80), English jurist. His major work was the *Commentaries on the Laws of England* (1765–9), an exposition of English law.

Black Stone the sacred reddish-black stone built into the outside wall of the Kaaba and ritually touched by Muslim pilgrims.

black stump ▸ **noun** Austral. informal a notional place in the outback imagined as being the last outpost of civilization: *he was born not in the capital city, but somewhere out **beyond the black stump**.*
– ORIGIN early 20th cent.: *black* in the sense 'fire-blackened'.

black swan ▸ **noun** a mainly black swan with white flight feathers which is common in Australia and Tasmania and has been introduced elsewhere. ● *Cygnus atratus*, family Anatidae.
■ archaic something extremely rare: *husbands without faults, if such black swans there be.* [proverbial, from Juvenal's *Satires*.]

black-tailed deer ▸ **noun** another term for **mule deer**.

black tea ▸ **noun** [mass noun] **1** tea served without milk.
2 tea of the most usual type, that is fully fermented before drying. Compare with **green tea**.

blackthorn ▸ **noun** a thorny Eurasian shrub which bears white flowers before the leaves appear, followed by astringent blue-black fruits (sloes). Also called **sloe**. ● *Prunus spinosa*, family Rosaceae.
■ a walking stick or cudgel made from a stem of the blackthorn shrub.

blackthorn winter ▸ **noun** Brit. a spell of cold weather at the time in early spring when the blackthorn flowers.

black tie ▸ **noun** a black bow tie worn with a dinner jacket. ■ [mass noun] formal evening dress: *the audience wears black tie* | [as modifier] *evening meals were black-tie affairs.*

blacktop chiefly N. Amer. ▸ **noun** [mass noun] asphalt, tarmacadam, or other black material used for surfacing roads. ■ [count noun] a road or area surfaced with blacktop.
▸ **verb** (**blacktops, blacktopping, blacktopped**) [with obj.] surface (a road or area) with blacktop: *41 km had been blacktopped to date.*

black tracker ▸ **noun** Austral. an Aborigine employed to help find people lost or hiding in the bush.

black velvet ▸ **noun** [mass noun] a drink consisting of a mixture of stout and champagne.

black vulture ▸ **noun 1** a very large Old World vulture with blackish-brown plumage, now rare in Europe. Also called **cinereous vulture**. ● *Aygypius monachus*, family Accipitridae.
2 a New World vulture with black plumage and a bare black head. ● *Coragyps atratus*, family Cathartidae.

blackwall tyre ▸ **noun** a tyre with black side walls.

Black Watch the Royal Highland Regiment.
– ORIGIN in the early 18th cent. the term *Watch* was given to certain companies of irregular troops in the Highlands; *Black Watch* referred to some of these companies raised *c.*1729–30, distinguished by their dark-coloured tartan.

black water ▸ **noun** [mass noun] technical waste water and sewage from toilets. Compare with **grey water**.

blackwater fever ▸ **noun** [mass noun] a severe form of malaria in which blood cells are rapidly destroyed, resulting in dark urine.

black widow ▸ **noun** a highly venomous American spider which has a black body with red markings. ● *Latrodectus mactans*, family Theridiidae; subspecies also occur on other continents (see **katipo, redback, button spider**).

blackwood ▸ **noun** a tropical hardwood tree of the pea family, which produces high-quality dark timber. ● *Dalbergia* and other genera, family Leguminosae: several species.

blackwork ▸ **noun** [mass noun] a type of embroidery done in black thread on white cloth, popular especially in Tudor times.

bladder ▸ **noun 1** a muscular membranous sac in the abdomen which receives urine from the kidneys and stores it for excretion.
2 an inflated or hollow flexible bag or chamber.
– ORIGIN Old English *blǣdre*, of Germanic origin; related to Dutch *blaar* and German *Blatter*, also to **blow**[1].

bladder campion ▸ **noun** a white-flowered Eurasian campion with a swollen bladder-like calyx behind the deeply cut petals. ● *Silene vulgaris*, family Caryophyllaceae.

bladdered ▸ **adjective** Brit. informal extremely drunk.

bladder fern ▸ **noun** a small, delicate fern with rounded spore cases, growing on rocks and walls in both Eurasia and North America. ● Genus *Cystopteris*, family Woodsiaceae: several species.

bladdernut ▸ **noun** a shrub or small tree of northern temperate regions, which bears white flowers and inflated seed capsules. ● Genus *Staphylea*, family Staphyleaceae: several species.

bladder senna ▸ **noun** a Mediterranean shrub of the pea family, which bears yellow flowers followed by inflated reddish pods. ● *Colutea arborescens*, family Leguminosae.

bladder worm ▸ **noun** an immature form of a tapeworm, which lives in the flesh of the secondary host. Further development is suspended until it is eaten by the primary host.

bladderwort ▸ **noun** an aquatic plant of north temperate regions, with small air-filled bladders which keep the plant afloat and trap tiny animals that provide additional nutrients. ● Genus *Utricularia*, family Lentibulariaceae.

bladderwrack ▸ **noun** [mass noun] a common brown shoreline seaweed which has tough strap-like fronds containing air bladders that give buoyancy. ● *Fucus vesiculosus*, class Phaeophyceae.

blade ▸ **noun 1** the flat cutting edge of a knife, saw, or other tool or weapon. ■ literary a sword. ■ (**blades**) Austral./NZ hand shears used in sheep shearing. ■ Archaeology a long, narrow flake.
2 the flat, wide section of an implement or device such as an oar or a propeller. ■ a thin, flat metal runner on an ice skate. ■ (also **blade bone**) a shoulder bone in a joint of meat, or the joint itself. ■ the flat part of the tongue behind the tip.
3 a long, narrow leaf of grass or another similar plant: ***a blade of grass***. ■ Botany the broad, thin part of a leaf apart from the stalk.
4 informal, dated a dashing or energetic young man.
▸ **verb** [no obj.] US informal skate using Rollerblades.
– DERIVATIVES **bladed adjective** [in combination] *double-bladed paddles*, **blader noun**.
– ORIGIN Old English *blæd* 'leaf of a plant' (also in sense 2 of the noun), of Germanic origin; related to Dutch *blad* and German *Blatt*.

blaeberry /ˈbleɪb(ə)ri, -bɛri/ ▸ **noun** (pl. **blaeberries**) Scottish and northern English term for **bilberry**.
– ORIGIN Middle English: from Scots and northern English dialect *blae* 'blackish-blue' (from Old Norse *blár*, related to **blue**[1]) + **berry**.

blag Brit. informal ▸ **noun 1** a violent robbery or raid.
2 an act of using clever talk or lying to obtain something: *blags and scams on the allowance scheme.*
▸ **verb** (**blags, blagging, blagged**) [with obj.] **1** steal (something) in a violent robbery or raid: *I could lie in wait and blag her fur coat.*
2 obtain (something) by clever talk or lying: *they blagged two free tickets to France.*
– DERIVATIVES **blagger noun**.
– ORIGIN late 19th cent.: sense 1 of the noun of unknown origin; sense 2 of the noun perhaps from French *blaguer* 'tell lies'.

blague /blɑːɡ/ ▸ **noun** rare a joke or piece of nonsense.
– ORIGIN French.

blagueur /blaˈɡəː/, French /blagœʀ/ ▸ **noun** rare a person who talks nonsense.
– ORIGIN French, from **blague**.

blah informal ▸ **noun 1** (also **blah-blah**) [mass noun] used to refer to something which is boring or without meaningful content: *talking all kinds of blah to him.* ■ used to substitute for actual words in contexts where these are felt to be too tedious or lengthy to give in full: *he said nations great and small could come together to blah blah blah.*
2 (**the blahs**) N. Amer. depression: *a case of the blahs.*
▸ **adjective** N. Amer. dull or unexciting.
– ORIGIN early 20th cent. (originally US): imitative.

blain /bleɪn/ ▸ **noun** rare an inflamed swelling or sore on the skin.

B

– ORIGIN Old English *blegen*, of West Germanic origin; related to Dutch *blein*.

Blair, Tony (b.1953), British Labour statesman, Prime Minister 1997–2007; full name *Anthony Charles Lynton Blair*. He was elected leader of the Labour Party in 1994. His landslide victory in the election of 1997 gave his party its biggest-ever majority and made him the youngest Prime Minister since Lord Liverpool in 1812.
– DERIVATIVES **Blairism** noun, **Blairite** noun & adjective.

Blake[1], Sir Peter (b.1932), English painter, prominent in the pop art movement in the late 1950s and early 1960s. He is best known for the cover design for the Beatles album *Sergeant Pepper's Lonely Hearts Club Band* (1967).

Blake[2], William (1757–1827), English artist and poet. Blake's poems mark the beginning of romanticism and a rejection of the Age of Enlightenment. His watercolours and engravings, like his writings, were only fully appreciated after his death. Notable collections of poems: *Songs of Innocence* (1789) and *Songs of Experience* (1794).
– DERIVATIVES **Blakeian** adjective.

Blakey ▶ noun (pl. **Blakeys**) Brit. a protective metal plate fitted to the sole of a shoe or boot.
– ORIGIN late 19th cent.: named after the manufacturers, E. *Blakey* and Sons, of Leeds.

blame ▶ verb [with obj.] feel or declare that (someone or something) is responsible for a fault or wrong: *the inquiry **blamed** the train driver **for** the accident*. ▪ (**blame something on**) assign the responsibility for a bad or unfortunate situation or phenomenon to (someone or something): *they blame youth crime on unemployment*.
▶ noun [mass noun] responsibility for a fault or wrong: *his players had to **take the blame for** the defeat | they are trying to **put the blame on** us*.
– PHRASES **be to blame** be responsible for a fault or wrong: *he **was to blame for** their deaths*. **I don't** (or **can't**) **blame you** (or **her** etc.) used to indicate that one agrees that the action or attitude taken was reasonable: *he was becoming impatient and I couldn't blame him*. **have only oneself to blame** be solely responsible for a bad or unwelcome state of affairs.
– DERIVATIVES **blameable** (US also **blamable**) adjective, **blameful** adjective.
– ORIGIN Middle English: from Old French *blamer*, *blasmer* (verb), from a popular Latin variant of ecclesiastical Latin *blasphemare* 'reproach, revile, blaspheme', from Greek *blasphēmein* (see BLASPHEME).

blame game ▶ noun informal a situation in which one party blames others for something bad or unfortunate rather than attempting to seek a solution.
– DERIVATIVES **blame-gaming** noun.

blameless ▶ adjective innocent of wrongdoing: *he led a blameless life*.
– DERIVATIVES **blamelessly** adverb, **blamelessness** noun.

blamestorming ▶ noun [mass noun] group discussion regarding the assigning of responsibility for a failure or mistake.
– ORIGIN 1990s: on the pattern of *brainstorming*.

blameworthy ▶ adjective responsible for wrongdoing and deserving of censure or blame.
– DERIVATIVES **blameworthiness** noun.

blanc /blɒ̃/ ▶ adjective (of wine) white.
– ORIGIN French.

blanch /blɑːn(t)ʃ/ ▶ verb [with obj.] **1** make white or pale by extracting colour: *the cold light blanched her face*. ▪ whiten (a plant) by depriving it of light.
2 [no obj.] flinch or grow pale from shock, fear, or a similar emotion: *he visibly **blanched at** this reminder of mortality*.
3 prepare (vegetables) for freezing or further cooking by immersing briefly in boiling water. ▪ (often as adj. **blanched**) peel (almonds) by scalding them.
– ORIGIN Middle English: from Old French *blanchir*, from *blanc* 'white', ultimately of Germanic origin.

Blanchard /ˈblɑ̃ʃɑː/, French /blɑ̃ʃaʀ/, Jean Pierre François (1753–1809), French balloonist. He made the first crossing of the English Channel by air, flying by balloon, on 7 January 1785.

blancmange /bləˈmɒnʒ, -ˈmɑːnʒ/ ▶ noun Brit. a sweet opaque gelatinous dessert made with flavoured cornflour and milk.
– ORIGIN late Middle English *blancmanger*: from Old French *blanc mangier*, from *blanc* 'white' + *mangier* 'eat' (used as a noun to mean 'food'). The shortened form without *-er* arose in the 18th cent.

blanco /ˈblaŋkəʊ/ Brit. ▶ noun [mass noun] a white substance used for whitening belts and other items of military equipment.
▶ verb (**blancoes**, **blancoing**, **blancoed**) [with obj.] whiten (equipment) with blanco.
– ORIGIN late 19th cent.: from French *blanc* 'white', ultimately of Germanic origin.

bland ▶ adjective lacking strong features or characteristics and therefore uninteresting: *bland, mass-produced pop music*. ▪ (of food or drink) unseasoned, mild-tasting, or insipid. ▪ showing no strong emotion: *his expression was bland and unreadable*.
– DERIVATIVES **blandly** adverb, **blandness** noun.
– ORIGIN late Middle English (in the sense 'gentle in manner'): from Latin *blandus* 'soft, smooth'.

blandish /ˈblandɪʃ/ ▶ verb [with obj.] archaic coax (someone) with kind words or flattery.
– ORIGIN Middle English: from Old French *blandiss-*, lengthened stem of *blandir*, from Latin *blandiri*, from *blandus* 'soft, smooth'.

blandishment ▶ noun (often **blandishments**) a flattering or pleasing statement or action used as a means of gently persuading someone to do something.

blank ▶ adjective **1** (of a surface or background) unrelieved by decorative or other features; bare, empty, or plain: *a blank wall | the screen went blank*. ▪ not written or printed on: *a blank sheet of paper*. ▪ (of a document) with spaces left for a signature or details: *blank tax-return forms*. ▪ (of a tape) with nothing recorded on it: *blank cassettes*.
2 showing a lack of comprehension or reaction: *we were met by blank looks*. ▪ temporarily having no knowledge or understanding: *her mind went blank*. ▪ lacking incident or result: *those blank moments aboard airplanes*.
3 [attrib.] complete; absolute (used emphatically with negative force): *he was met with a blank refusal to discuss the issue*.
4 used euphemistically in place of an adjective regarded as obscene, profane, or abusive: *show the miserable blank-blank Englishman how to fight this war*.
▶ noun **1** a space left to be filled in a document: *leave blanks to type in the appropriate names*. ▪ a document with blank spaces to be filled.
2 (also **blank cartridge**) a cartridge containing gunpowder but no bullet, used for training or as a signal.
3 an empty space or period of time, especially in terms of a lack of knowledge or understanding: *my mind was a total blank*.
4 an object which has no mark or design on it, in particular: ▪ a roughly cut metal or wooden block intended for further shaping or finishing. ▪ a domino with one or both halves blank. ▪ a plain metal disc from which a coin is made by stamping a design on it.
5 a dash written instead of a word or letter, especially instead of an obscenity or profanity. ▪ used euphemistically in place of a noun regarded as obscene, profane, or abusive.
▶ verb [with obj.] **1** make (something) blank or empty: *electronic countermeasures **blanked out** the radar signals*. ▪ [no obj.] become blank or empty: *the picture **blanked out***. ▪ cut (a metal blank).
2 N. Amer. defeat (a sports team) without allowing them to score: *Baltimore blanked Toronto in a 7–0 victory*.
3 Brit. informal deliberately ignore (someone): *I just blanked them and walked out*.
– PHRASES **be firing blanks** humorous (of a man) be infertile. **draw a blank** elicit no successful response; fail: *the search drew a blank*.
– DERIVATIVES **blankly** adverb, **blankness** noun.
– ORIGIN Middle English (in the sense 'white, colourless'): from Old French *blanc* 'white', ultimately of Germanic origin.

blank call ▶ noun Indian an anonymous telephone call, or one that is made to threaten, annoy, or harass its recipient.

blank cheque ▶ noun a signed cheque with the amount left for the payee to fill in. ▪ an unlimited freedom of action: *the elections did not hand the president a blank cheque to carry on as before*.

blanket ▶ noun **1** a large piece of woollen or similar material used as a covering on a bed or elsewhere for warmth. ▪ a thick covering mass or layer: *a dense grey **blanket of** cloud*.
2 Printing a rubber surface used for transferring the image in ink from the plate to the paper in offset printing.
▶ adjective [attrib.] covering all cases or instances; total and inclusive: *a blanket ban on tobacco advertising*.
▶ verb (**blankets**, **blanketing**, **blanketed**) [with obj.] **1** cover completely with a thick layer of something: *the countryside **was blanketed in** snow*. ▪ stifle or keep quiet (sound): *the double glazing blankets the noise a bit*.
2 Sailing take wind from the sails of (another craft) by passing to windward.
– PHRASES **born on the wrong side of the blanket** dated illegitimate.
– ORIGIN Middle English (denoting undyed woollen cloth): via Old Northern French from Old French *blanc* 'white', ultimately of Germanic origin.

blanket bath ▶ noun Brit. an all-over wash given to a person confined to bed.

blanket bog ▶ noun [mass noun] an extensive flat peat bog formed in cool regions of high rainfall or humidity.

blanket coat ▶ noun N. Amer. a coat made from a blanket or from blanket-like material.

blanket finish ▶ noun a very close finish in a race.

blanketing ▶ noun [mass noun] material used for making blankets.

blanket roll ▶ noun N. Amer. a soldier's blanket and kit made into a roll for use on active service.

blanket stitch ▶ noun [mass noun] a buttonhole stitch used on the edges of a blanket or other material too thick to be hemmed.

blanket weed ▶ noun [mass noun] a common green freshwater alga which forms long unbranched filaments, sometimes becoming a problem in over-enriched water and garden ponds. ● Genus *Spirogyra*, division Chlorophyta (or phylum Chlorophyta, kingdom Protista).

blankety (also **blankety-blank**) ▶ adjective & noun informal used euphemistically to replace a word considered obscene or taboo: [as adj.] *it's time to ditch the blankety-blank tax code*.

blanking plate ▶ noun a plate that covers an opening in a device or a wall to protect it from moisture or dust.

blank verse ▶ noun [mass noun] verse without rhyme, especially that which uses iambic pentameters.

blanquette /blɒ̃ˈkɛt/ ▶ noun a dish consisting of white meat in a white sauce.
– ORIGIN French, based on *blanc* 'white'.

Blantyre /blanˈtʌɪə/ the chief commercial and industrial city of Malawi; pop. 661,444 (2008).

blare ▶ verb make or cause to make a loud, harsh sound: [no obj.] *the ambulance arrived outside, siren blaring* | [with obj.] *the wireless was **blaring out** organ music*.
▶ noun [in sing.] a loud, harsh sound: *a blare of trumpets*.
– ORIGIN late Middle English (in the sense 'roar, bellow'): from Middle Dutch *blaren*, *bleren*, or Low German *blaren*, of imitative origin. Current senses date from the late 18th cent.

blarney ▶ noun [mass noun] talk which aims to charm, flatter, or persuade (often considered typical of Irish people): *it took all my Irish blarney to keep us out of court*. ▪ amusing and harmless nonsense: *this story is perhaps just a bit of blarney*.
– ORIGIN late 18th cent.: named after *Blarney*, a castle near Cork in Ireland, where there is a stone said to give the gift of persuasive speech to anyone who kisses it.

blasé /ˈblɑːzeɪ/ ▶ adjective unimpressed with or indifferent to something because one has experienced or seen it so often before: *she was becoming quite blasé about the dangers*.
– ORIGIN early 19th cent.: French, past participle of *blaser* 'cloy', probably ultimately of Germanic origin.

blaspheme /blasˈfiːm/ ▶ verb [no obj.] speak irreverently about God or sacred things: *he has **blasphemed against** the Holy Spirit*.
– DERIVATIVES **blasphemer** noun.
– ORIGIN Middle English: via Old French from ecclesiastical Latin *blasphemare* 'reproach, revile, blaspheme', from Greek *blasphēmein*, from *blasphēmos* 'evil-speaking'. Compare with BLAME.

blasphemous /ˈblasfəməs/ ▶ adjective sacrilegious against God or sacred things; profane: *blasphemous and heretical talk*.
– DERIVATIVES **blasphemously** adverb.
– ORIGIN late Middle English: via ecclesiastical Latin from Greek *blasphēmos* 'evil-speaking' + **-ous**.

blasphemy ▶ noun (pl. **blasphemies**) [mass noun] the action or offence of speaking sacrilegiously about

God or sacred things; profane talk: *he was detained on charges of blasphemy* | [count noun] *he was screaming incomprehensible blasphemies.*
– ORIGIN Middle English: from Old French, via ecclesiastical Latin from Greek *blasphēmia* 'slander, blasphemy'.

blast /blɑːst/ ▸ **noun 1** a destructive wave of highly compressed air spreading outwards from an explosion: *they were thrown backwards by the blast.* ■ an explosion or explosive firing: *a bomb blast* | *a shotgun blast.* ■ a forceful attack or assault: *United's four-goal blast.*
2 a strong gust of wind or air: *the icy blast hit them.* ■ a strong current of air used in smelting.
3 a single loud note of a horn, whistle, or similar: *a blast of the ship's siren.*
4 informal a severe reprimand: *I braced myself for the inevitable blast.*
5 N. Amer. informal an enjoyable experience or lively party: *it could turn out to be a real blast.*
▸ **verb** [with obj.] **1** blow up or break apart (something solid) with explosives: *the school was blasted by an explosion.* ■ produce (damage) by means of an explosion: *the force of the collision* ***blasted out*** *a tremendous crater.* ■ [with obj. and adverbial of direction] force or throw (something) in a specified direction by impact or explosion: *the car was blasted thirty feet into the sky.* ■ shoot with a gun: *Fowler was blasted with an air rifle.* ■ [no obj., with adverbial of direction] move very quickly and loudly in a specified direction: *four low-flying jets blasted down the glen.*
2 produce or cause to produce loud continuous music or other noise: [no obj.] *music blasted out at full volume* | [with obj.] *an impatient motorist blasted his horn.*
3 kick or strike (a ball) hard: *the striker blasted the free kick into the net.*
4 informal criticize fiercely: *the school was blasted by government inspectors.*
5 literary (of a wind or other natural force) wither, shrivel, or blight (a plant): *corn blasted before it be grown up.* ■ strike with divine anger (used to express annoyance or dislike): *damn and blast this awful place!* ■ destroy or ruin: *your reputation is blasted already in the village.*
▸ **exclamation** informal, chiefly Brit. expressing annoyance: *'Blast! The car won't start!'.*
– PHRASES **a blast from the past** informal something powerfully nostalgic: *the soundtrack is a real blast from the past.* **(at) full blast** at maximum power or intensity: *the heat is on full blast.*
– PHRASAL VERBS **blast off** (of a rocket or spacecraft) take off from a launching site.
– DERIVATIVES **blaster** noun.
– ORIGIN Old English *blǣst*, of Germanic origin; related to BLAZE³.

-blast ▸ **combining form** Biology denoting an embryonic cell: *erythroblast.* Compare with -CYTE. ■ denoting a germ layer of an embryo: *epiblast.*
– ORIGIN from Greek *blastos* 'germ, sprout'.

blast chiller ▸ **noun** a machine used in commercial kitchens to cool food rapidly by circulating very cold air over it.

blasted ▸ **adjective 1** [attrib.] informal used to express annoyance: *make your own blasted coffee!*
2 [attrib.] literary withered or blighted; laid waste: *a blasted heath* | *an area of blasted trees.*
3 [predic.] informal drunk: *I got really blasted.*

blast furnace ▸ **noun** a smelting furnace in the form of a tower into which a blast of hot compressed air can be introduced from below. Such furnaces are used chiefly to make iron from a mixture of iron ore, coke, and limestone.

blasting gelatin ▸ **noun** see GELATIN.

blasto- /ˈblastəʊ/ ▸ **combining form** relating to germination: *blastoderm.*
– ORIGIN from Greek *blastos* 'germ, sprout'.

blastocyst ▸ **noun** Embryology a mammalian blastula in which some differentiation of cells has occurred.

blastoderm ▸ **noun** Embryology a blastula having the form of a disc of cells on top of the yolk.

blast-off ▸ **noun** [mass noun] the launching of a rocket or spacecraft.

blastomere /ˈblastə(ʊ)mɪə/ ▸ **noun** Embryology a cell formed by cleavage of a fertilized ovum.

blastomycosis /ˌblastə(ʊ)mʌɪˈkəʊsɪs/ ▸ **noun** [mass noun] Medicine a disease caused by infection with parasitic fungi affecting the skin or the internal organs.
● The fungi belong to the genus *Blastomyces*, subdivision Deuteromycotina.

blastula /ˈblastjʊlə/ ▸ **noun** (pl. **blastulae** /-liː/ or US **blastulas**) Embryology an animal embryo at the early stage of development when it is a hollow ball of cells.
– ORIGIN late 19th cent.: modern Latin, from Greek *blastos* 'sprout'.

blat informal, chiefly N. Amer. ▸ **verb** (**blats, blatting, blatted**) [no obj.] **1** make a bleating sound.
2 [no obj., with adverbial of direction] travel quickly: *blatting down the motorway.*
▸ **noun** a bleat or similar noise: *the blat of Jack's horn.*
– ORIGIN mid 19th cent.: imitative.

blatant /ˈbleɪt(ə)nt/ ▸ **adjective** (of bad behaviour) done openly and unashamedly: *blatant lies.* ■ completely lacking in subtlety; very obvious: *she forced herself to resist his blatant charm.*
– DERIVATIVES **blatancy** noun, **blatantly** adverb.
– ORIGIN late 16th cent.: perhaps an alteration of Scots *blatand* 'bleating'. It was first used by Spenser as an epithet for a thousand-tongued monster produced by Cerberus and Chimaera, a symbol of calumny, which he called the *blatant beast.* It was subsequently used to mean 'clamorous, offensive to the ear', first of people (mid 17th cent.), later of things (late 18th cent.); the sense 'unashamedly conspicuous' arose in the late 19th cent.

blather /ˈblaðə/ (also **blither** or chiefly Scottish **blether**) ▸ **verb** [no obj.] talk long-windedly without making very much sense: *she began* ***blathering on about*** *spirituality and life after death* | (as noun **blathering**) *now stop your blathering and get back to work.*
▸ **noun** [mass noun] long-winded talk with no real substance.
– ORIGIN late Middle English (as a verb; originally Scots and northern English dialect): from Old Norse *blathra* 'talk nonsense', from *blathr* 'nonsense'.

blatherskite /ˈblaðəskʌɪt/ (also **bletherskate**) ▸ **noun** chiefly N. Amer. a person who talks at great length without making much sense. ■ [mass noun] foolish talk; nonsense.
– ORIGIN mid 17th cent.: from BLATHER + *skite*, a Scots derogatory term adopted into American colloquial speech during the War of Independence from the Scottish song *Maggie Lauder*, by F. Semphill, which was popular with American troops.

blatter ▸ **verb** [no obj., with adverbial] informal move with a clatter: *the pickup blattered down the road.* ■ strike repeatedly and noisily: *I blattered away at the old typewriter.*
– ORIGIN early 18th cent.: originally Scots, of imitative origin.

Blaue Reiter /ˌblaʊə ˈrʌɪtə/ a group of German expressionist painters formed in 1911, based in Munich. The group included Wassily Kandinsky, Jean Arp, and Paul Klee.
– ORIGIN German, literally 'blue rider', the title of a painting by Kandinsky.

Blavatsky /bləˈvatski/, Helena (Petrovna) (1831–91), Russian spiritualist, born in Ukraine; born *Helena Petrovna Hahn*; known as **Madame Blavatsky**. In 1875 she co-founded the Theosophical Society in New York.

blaxploitation /ˌblaksplɔɪˈteɪʃ(ə)n/ ▸ **noun** [mass noun] the exploitation of black people, especially with regard to stereotyped roles in films.
– ORIGIN 1970s: blend of *blacks* (see BLACK) and EXPLOITATION.

blaze¹ ▸ **noun 1** a very large or fiercely burning fire: *twenty firemen fought the blaze.* ■ [in sing.] a very bright display of light or colour: *the gardens in summer are* ***a blaze of*** *colour.* ■ [in sing.] a conspicuous display or outburst of something: *their relationship broke up* ***in a blaze of*** *publicity.*
2 (**blazes**) informal used in various expressions of anger, bewilderment, or surprise as a euphemism for 'hell': *'Go to blazes!' he shouted* | *what the blazes are you all talking about?* [with reference to the flames associated with hell.]
▸ **verb** [no obj.] **1** burn fiercely or brightly: *the fire blazed merrily.* ■ (**blaze up**) burst into flame. ■ shine brightly or powerfully: *the sun* ***blazed down*** | figurative *Barbara's eyes were* ***blazing with*** *anger.*
2 fire a gun repeatedly or indiscriminately: *they stormed with main entrance with guns blazing.*
3 informal achieve something in an impressive manner: *she blazed to a gold medal in the 200-metre sprint.* ■ [with obj.] hit (a ball) with impressive strength: *he blazed a drive into the rough.*
4 informal smoke cannabis.
– PHRASES **like blazes** informal very fast or forcefully: *I ran like blazes homewards.* [see sense 2 of the noun.] **with all guns blazing** informal with great but reckless determination and energy.
– ORIGIN Old English *blæse* 'torch, bright fire', of Germanic origin; related ultimately to BLAZE².

blaze² ▸ **noun 1** a white spot or stripe on the face of a mammal or bird. ■ a broad white stripe running the length of a horse's face.
2 a mark made on a tree by cutting the bark so as to mark a route.
▸ **verb** (**blaze a trail**) **1** set an example by being the first to do something; pioneer: *small firms would set the pace, blazing a trail for others to follow.*
2 mark out a path or route.
– ORIGIN mid 17th cent.: ultimately of Germanic origin; related to German *Blässe* 'blaze' and *blass* 'pale', also to BLAZE¹, and probably to BLEMISH.

blaze³ ▸ **verb** [with obj.] present or proclaim (news) in a prominent, typically sensational, manner.
– ORIGIN late Middle English (in the sense 'blow out on a trumpet'): from Middle Low German or Middle Dutch *blāzen* 'to blow'; related to BLOW¹.

blazer ▸ **noun** a coloured jacket worn by schoolchildren or sports players as part of a uniform. ■ a plain jacket not forming part of a suit but considered appropriate for formal wear.
– ORIGIN late 19th cent.: from BLAZE¹ + -ER¹. The original general sense was 'a thing that blazes or shines' (mid 17th cent.), giving rise to the term for a brightly coloured sporting jacket.

blazing ▸ **adjective** very hot: *the delicious cool of marble corridors after the blazing heat outside.* ■ (of an argument) very heated: *she had a blazing row with Eddie and stormed out.*
– DERIVATIVES **blazingly** adverb.

blazing star ▸ **noun** any of a number of North American plants, some of which are cultivated for their flowers, in particular: ● a plant of the daisy family with tall spikes of purple or white flowers (genus *Liatris*, family Compositae). ● a plant of the lily family bearing spikes of white flowers (*Chamaelirium luteum*, family Liliaceae). Also called DEVIL'S BIT, UNICORN ROOT.

blazon /ˈbleɪz(ə)n/ ▸ **verb** [with obj.] **1** [with adverbial of place] display prominently or vividly: *they saw their company name blazoned all over the media.* ■ report (news), especially in a sensational manner: *accounts of their ordeal were blazoned to the entire nation.*
2 Heraldry describe or depict (armorial bearings) in a correct heraldic manner. ■ inscribe or paint (an object) with arms or a name.
▸ **noun** Heraldry a correct description of armorial bearings. ■ archaic a coat of arms.
– ORIGIN Middle English (denoting a shield, later one bearing a heraldic device): from Old French *blason* 'shield', of unknown origin. The sense of the verb has been influenced by BLAZE³.

blazonry ▸ **noun** [mass noun] Heraldry the art of describing or painting heraldic devices or armorial bearings. ■ [treated as pl.] devices or bearings of this type.

bleach ▸ **verb** [with obj.] **1** cause (a material such as cloth, paper, or hair) to become white or much lighter by a chemical process or by exposure to sunlight: *a new formula to bleach and brighten clothing* | (as adj. **bleached**) *permed and bleached hair.* ■ deprive of vitality or substance: *his contributions to the album are* ***bleached of*** *personality.*
2 clean or sterilize (a drain, sink, etc.) with bleach.
▸ **noun** [mass noun] a chemical (typically a solution of sodium hypochlorite or hydrogen peroxide) used to make materials whiter or for sterilizing drains, sinks, etc.
– ORIGIN Old English *blǣcan* (verb), *blǣce* (noun), from *blǣc* 'pale', of Germanic origin; related to BLEAK¹.

bleacher ▸ **noun 1** a person or thing that bleaches.
2 (usu. **bleachers**) N. Amer. a cheap bench seat at a sports ground, typically in an outdoor uncovered stand.

bleacherite ▸ **noun** N. Amer. a person sitting in the bleachers.

bleaching powder ▸ **noun** [mass noun] a powder containing calcium hypochlorite, used chiefly to remove colour from materials.

bleak¹ ▸ **adjective** (of an area of land) lacking vegetation and exposed to the elements: *a bleak and barren moor.* ■ (of a building or room) charmless and inhospitable; dreary: *he looked round the bleak little room in despair.* ■ (of the weather) cold and miserable: *a bleak midwinter's day.* ■ (of a situation) not hopeful or encouraging; unlikely to have a favourable outcome: *he paints a bleak picture of a company that has*

B

lost its way | *the future looks bleak.* ■ (of a person's expression) cold and forbidding: *his mouth was set and his eyes were bleak.*
– DERIVATIVES **bleakly** adverb, **bleakness** noun.
– ORIGIN Old English *blāc* 'shining, white', or in later use from synonymous Old Norse *bleikr*; ultimately of Germanic origin and related to BLEACH.

bleak² ▶ noun a small silvery shoaling fish of the carp family, found in Eurasian rivers. ● Genera *Alburnus* and *Chalcalburnus*, family Cyprinidae: several species, in particular *A. alburnus*.
– ORIGIN late 15th cent.: from Old Norse *bleikja*.

blear archaic ▶ adjective dim, dull, or filmy: *a medicine to lay to sore and blear eyes.*
▶ verb [with obj.] make dim; blur: *he bleared his eyes with books.*
– ORIGIN Middle English (as a verb): probably related to Middle High German *blerre* 'blurred vision' and Low German *blarroged* 'bleary-eyed'.

bleary ▶ adjective (**blearier**, **bleariest**) (of the eyes) looking or feeling dull and unfocused from sleep or tiredness: *Boris opened a bleary eye* | *bleary-eyed business travellers.*
– DERIVATIVES **blearily** adverb, **bleariness** noun.

bleat ▶ verb [no obj.] (of a sheep, goat, or calf) make a characteristic weak, wavering cry: *the lamb was bleating weakly* | (as noun **bleating**) *the plaintive bleating of sheep.* ■ [reporting verb] speak or complain in a weak, querulous, or foolish way: *it's no good just* **bleating on** *about the rising tide of crime.*
▶ noun the weak, wavering cry made by a sheep, goat, or calf: *the distant bleat of sheep.* ■ a person's weak or plaintive cry: *his despairing bleat touched her heart.* ■ informal a complaint: *they're hoping that I'll bow to their idiotic arrangements without a bleat.*
– DERIVATIVES **bleater** noun.
– ORIGIN Old English *blǣtan*, of imitative origin.

bleb ▶ noun a small blister on the skin. ■ a small bubble in glass or in a fluid. ■ Biology a rounded outgrowth on the surface of a cell.
– ORIGIN early 17th cent.: variant of BLOB.

bleed ▶ verb (past and past participle **bled**) **1** [no obj.] lose blood from the body as a result of injury or illness: *the cut was bleeding steadily* | *some casualties were left to* **bleed to death** | (as noun **bleeding**) *the bleeding has stopped now.*
2 [with obj.] draw blood from (someone), especially as a former method of treatment in medicine. ■ informal drain (someone) of money or resources: *his policy of attempting to bleed British unions of funds.*
3 [with obj.] allow (fluid or gas) to escape from a closed system through a valve. ■ release fluid or gas from (a system) in this way: *air can be got rid of by bleeding the radiator at the vent.*
4 [no obj.] (of a liquid substance such as dye or colour) seep into an adjacent colour or area: *I worked loosely with the oils, allowing colours to bleed into one another.* ■ Printing (with reference to an illustration or design) print or be printed so that it runs off the page after trimming: *the picture bleeds on three sides.*
▶ noun **1** an instance of bleeding: *a lot of blood was lost from the placental bleed.*
2 [mass noun] the escape of fluid or gas from a closed system through a valve.
3 Printing an instance of printing an illustration or design so as to leave no margin after the page has been trimmed: *the picture has an unfortunate bleed.* ■ [mass noun] the seeping of a dye or colour into an adjacent colour or area: *colour bleed is apparent on brighter hues.*
– PHRASES **bleed someone dry** (or **white**) drain someone of all their money or resources. **my heart bleeds** (**for you**) used ironically to imply that the person referred to does not deserve the sympathetic response they are seeking: *'I flew out here feeling tired and overworked.' 'My heart bleeds for you!' she replied.*
– ORIGIN Old English *blēdan*, of Germanic origin; related to BLOOD.

bleeder ▶ noun **1** [with adj.] Brit. informal a person regarded with contempt or pity: *the poor bleeder split his head open.*
2 informal a person who bleeds easily, especially a haemophiliac.
3 Baseball a ground ball hit that barely passes between two infielders.

bleeding ▶ adjective [attrib.] Brit. informal used for emphasis, or to express annoyance: *the watch was a bleeding copy* | [as submodifier] *she looks so bleeding bored all day.*

bleeding edge ▶ noun the very forefront of technological development.
– ORIGIN 1980s: on the pattern of LEADING EDGE, CUTTING EDGE.

bleeding heart ▶ noun **1** informal, derogatory a person considered to be excessively soft-hearted or liberal: [as modifier] *bleeding-heart environmentalists.*
2 any of a number of plants which have red, or partly red, heart-shaped flowers, in particular: ● a popular herbaceous garden plant related to Dutchman's breeches (genus *Dicentra*, family Fumariaceae, in particular *D. cucullaria*). ● a tropical twining shrub with cream and red flowers, widely cultivated under glass (*Clerodendrum thomsoniae*, family Verbenaceae).
3 (also **bleeding heart dove**) a dove with an oval red patch on the breast, found on islands around the Philippines. ● Genus *Gallicolumba*, family Columbidae: several species.

bleep ▶ noun a short high-pitched sound made by an electronic device as a signal or to attract attention. ■ a sound of this type used in broadcasting as a substitute for a censored word or phrase. ■ Brit. another term for BLEEPER.
▶ verb [no obj.] (of an electronic device) make a short high-pitched sound or sounds as a signal or to attract attention: *the screen flickered for a few moments and bleeped.* ■ [with obj.] Brit. summon (someone) with a bleeper: *I'll get Jan to bleep you if I need transport.* ■ [with obj.] substitute a bleep or bleeps for (a censored word or phrase): *I may have to bleep a few words in his testimony.*
– ORIGIN 1950s: imitative.

bleeper ▶ noun Brit. a small portable electronic device which emits a series of high-pitched sounds when someone wants to contact the wearer.

blemish ▶ noun a small mark or flaw which spoils the appearance of something: *the girl's hands were without a blemish.* ■ a moral defect or fault: *the offences were an uncharacteristic blemish on an otherwise clean record* | [mass noun] *local government is not without blemish.*
▶ verb [with obj.] (often as adj. **blemished**) spoil the appearance or quality of (something): *my main problem was a blemished skin* | *his reign as world champion has been blemished by controversy.*
– ORIGIN late Middle English (as a verb): from Old French *ble(s)miss-*, lengthened stem of *ble(s)mir* 'make pale, injure'; probably of Germanic origin.

blench¹ /blɛn(t)ʃ/ ▶ verb [no obj.] make a sudden flinching movement out of fear or pain: *he blenched and struggled to regain his composure.*
– ORIGIN Old English *blencan* 'deceive', of Germanic origin; later influenced by BLINK.

blench² /blɛn(t)ʃ/ ▶ verb chiefly dialect variant spelling of BLANCH.

blend ▶ verb [with obj.] mix (a substance) with another substance so that they combine together: **blend** *the cornflour* **with** *a tablespoon of water* | *add the grated cheese and blend well.* ■ (often as adj. **blended**) mix (different types of the same substance, such as tea, coffee, spirits, etc.) together so as to make a product of the desired quality: *a blended whisky.* ■ put or combine (abstract things) together: *I blend basic information for the novice with some scientific gardening for the more experienced* | (as noun **blending**) *a blending of romanticism with a more detached modernism.* ■ [no obj.] form a harmonious combination: *costumes, music, and lighting all* **blend together** *beautifully.* ■ (**blend in**/**into**) be an unobtrusive or harmonious part of a greater whole by being similar in appearance or behaviour: *she would have to employ a permanent bodyguard in the house, someone who would blend in.*
▶ noun a mixture of different substances or other things: *the chutney is a blend of bananas, raisins, and ginger* | *Ontario offers a cultural blend you'll find nowhere else on earth.* ■ a mixture of different types of the same substance. ■ a word made up of parts of two other words and combining their meanings, for example *motel* from *motor* and *hotel*.
– ORIGIN Middle English: probably of Scandinavian origin and related to Old Norse *blanda* 'to mix'.

blende /blɛnd/ ▶ noun another term for SPHALERITE.
– ORIGIN late 17th cent.: from German, from *blenden* 'deceive' (so named because it often resembles galena, but is deceptive in that it yields no lead).

blended family ▶ noun chiefly N. Amer. a family consisting of a couple, the children they have had together, and their children from previous relationships.

blender ▶ noun a person or thing that mixes things together, in particular an electric mixing machine used in food preparation for liquidizing, chopping, or puréeing.

Blenheim¹ /ˈblɛnɪm/ **1** a battle in 1704 in Bavaria, near the village of Blindheim, in which the English, under the Duke of Marlborough, defeated the French and the Bavarians.
2 (also **Blenheim Palace**) the Duke of Marlborough's seat at Woodstock near Oxford, a stately home designed by Vanbrugh (1705). The house and its estate were given to the first Duke of Marlborough in honour of his victory at Blenheim.

Blenheim² /ˈblɛnɪm/ ▶ noun a dog of a small red and white breed of spaniel.
– ORIGIN mid 19th cent.: from the name of *Blenheim* palace (see BLENHEIM¹).

Blenheim Orange ▶ noun an English dessert apple of a golden or orange-red variety which ripens late in the season.
– ORIGIN so named because it was discovered growing by the boundary wall of the Blenheim estate (see BLENHEIM¹) in the 18th cent.

blenny ▶ noun (pl. **blennies**) a small spiny-finned marine fish with scaleless skin and a blunt head, typically living in shallow inshore or intertidal waters. ● Family Blenniidae: several genera, in particular *Blennius*. ■ used in names of other small fishes that resemble or are related to the true blennies, e.g. **eel blenny**.
– ORIGIN mid 18th cent.: from Latin *blennius*, from Greek *blennos* 'mucus' (because of its mucous coating).

blent literary past and past participle of BLEND.

bleomycin /ˌbliːəʊˈmʌɪsɪn/ ▶ noun [mass noun] Medicine an antibiotic used to treat Hodgkin's disease and other cancers. ● The drug is obtained from the bacterium *Streptomyces verticillus*.
– ORIGIN 1960s: an arbitrary alteration of earlier *phleomycin*, the name of a related antibiotic.

blepharitis /ˌblɛfəˈrʌɪtɪs/ ▶ noun [mass noun] Medicine inflammation of the eyelid.
– ORIGIN mid 19th cent.: from Greek *blepharon* 'eyelid' + -ITIS.

blepharoplasty /ˈblɛf(ə)rə(ʊ)ˌplasti/ ▶ noun [mass noun] Medicine surgical repair or reconstruction of an eyelid.
– ORIGIN mid 19th cent.: from Greek *blepharon* 'eyelid' + -PLASTY.

blepharospasm /ˈblɛf(ə)rəʊˌspaz(ə)m/ ▶ noun [mass noun] involuntary tight closure of the eyelids.
– ORIGIN late 19th cent.: from Greek *blepharon* 'eyelid' + SPASM.

Blériot /ˈblɛrɪəʊ/, French /bleʀjo/, Louis (1872–1936), French aviation pioneer. On 25 July 1909 he became the first to fly the English Channel (Calais to Dover), in a monoplane of his own design.

blesbok /ˈblɛsbɒk/ ▶ noun an antelope with a mainly reddish-brown coat and white face, found in southwestern South Africa. It belongs to the same species as the bontebok. ● *Damaliscus dorcas phillipsi*, family Bovidae.
– ORIGIN early 19th cent.: from Afrikaans, from Dutch *bles* 'blaze' (because of the white mark on its forehead) + *bok* 'buck'.

bless ▶ verb [with obj.] pronounce words in a religious rite in order to confer or invoke divine favour upon; ask God to look favourably on: *he blessed the dying man and anointed him.* ■ (especially in Christian church services) call (God) holy; praise (God). ■ (**bless someone with**) (of God or some notional higher power) endow someone with (a particular cherished thing or attribute): *we have been blessed with a baby boy* | *a beautiful city blessed with huge sandy beaches.* ■ express or feel gratitude to; thank: *she silently blessed the premonition which had made her pack her best dress.* ■ (**bless oneself**) make the sign of the cross. ■ used in expressions of surprise, endearment, gratitude, etc.: *bless my soul, Alan, what are you doing?* | *Nurse Jones, bless her, had made a pot of tea* | *she even bought me a little present—bless!*
– PHRASES **bless you!** said to a person who has just sneezed. [from the phrase *(may) God bless you.*] **not have a penny to bless oneself with** dated be completely impoverished. [alluding to the cross on an old silver penny or to the practice of crossing a person's palm with silver for luck.]
– ORIGIN Old English *blēdsian*, *blētsian*, based on *blōd* 'blood' (i.e. originally perhaps 'mark or consecrate with blood'). The meaning was influenced by its being used to translate Latin *benedicere* 'to praise, worship', and later by association with BLISS.

blessed /ˈblɛsɪd, blɛst/ ▶ **adjective 1** made holy; consecrated: *the Blessed Sacrament.* ■ a title preceding the name of a dead person considered to have led a holy life, especially a person formally beatified by the Roman Catholic Church: *the Convent of the Blessed Agnes.* ■ endowed with divine favour and protection: *blessed are the meek.* ■ [as plural noun] (**the Blessed**) those who live with God in heaven.
2 informal used in mild expressions of annoyance or exasperation: *he'll want to go and see his blessed allotment.*
– DERIVATIVES **blessedly** adverb.

blessedness /ˈblɛsɪdnɪs/ ▶ **noun** [mass noun] the state of being blessed with divine favour.

Blessed Sacrament ▶ **noun** see SACRAMENT.

Blessed Virgin Mary, a title given to Mary, the mother of Jesus (see MARY[1]).

blessing ▶ **noun** God's favour and protection: *may God continue to give us his blessing.* ■ a prayer asking for divine favour and protection: *a priest gave a blessing as the ship was launched.* ■ grace said before or after a meal. ■ a beneficial thing for which one is grateful: *great intelligence can be a curse as well as a blessing | it's a blessing we're alive.* ■ a person's sanction or support: *he gave the plan his blessing even before it was announced.*
– PHRASES **a blessing in disguise** an apparent misfortune that eventually has good results.

blest ▶ **adjective** archaic or literary term for BLESSED.

blether /ˈblɛðə/ ▶ **noun** chiefly Scottish variant spelling of BLATHER.

bletherskate /ˈblɛðəskeɪt/ ▶ **noun** variant spelling of BLATHERSKITE.

blew past of BLOW[1] and BLOW[3].

blewit /ˈbluːɪt/ (also **blewits**) ▶ **noun** an edible European mushroom with a pale buff or lilac cap and a lilac stem. ● Genus *Lepista*, family Tricholomataceae, class Hymenomycetes: several species, including **common blewit** (*L. saeva*) and **wood blewit** (*L. nuda*).
– ORIGIN early 19th cent.: probably from BLUE[1].

Bligh /blʌɪ/, William (1754–1817), British naval officer, captain of HMS *Bounty*. In 1789 part of his crew, led by the first mate Fletcher Christian, mutinied and Bligh was set adrift in an open boat, arriving safely at Timor, nearly 6,400 km (4,000 miles) away, a few weeks later.

blight ▶ **noun** [mass noun] **1** a plant disease, typically one caused by fungi such as mildews, rusts, and smuts: *the vines suffered blight and disease | potato blight.*
2 [in sing.] a thing that spoils or damages something: *her remorse could be **a blight on** that happiness.* ■ the degeneration of a landscape or urban area as a result of neglect: *the city's high-rise social housing had become synonymous with urban blight.*
▶ **verb 1** [with obj.] infect (plants) with blight.
2 spoil, harm, or destroy: *the scandal blighted the careers of several leading politicians.* ■ (usu. as adj. **blighted**) subject (an urban area) to neglect: *plans to establish enterprise zones in blighted areas.*
– ORIGIN mid 16th cent. (denoting inflammation of the skin): of unknown origin.

blighter ▶ **noun** [with adj.] Brit. informal a person who is regarded with contempt, irritation, or pity: *you little blighter!*
– ORIGIN early 19th cent.: from BLIGHT + -ER[1].

Blighty ▶ **noun** Brit. an informal term for Britain or England, used by soldiers of the First and Second World Wars. ■ military slang a wound suffered by a soldier in the First World War which was sufficiently serious to merit being shipped home to Britain: *he had copped a Blighty and was on his way home.*
– ORIGIN first used by soldiers in the Indian army; Anglo-Indian alteration of Urdu *bilāyatī, wilāyatī* 'foreign, European', from Arabic *wilāyat, wilāya* 'dominion, district'.

blimey (also **cor blimey**) ▶ **exclamation** Brit. informal used to express surprise, excitement, or alarm.
– ORIGIN late 19th cent.: altered form of *(God) blind (or blame) me!*

blimp ▶ **noun** informal **1** (also **Colonel Blimp**) Brit. a pompous, reactionary type of person: *you'll still find Colonel Blimps at local party level.*
2 a small airship or barrage balloon. ■ N. Amer. a fat person: *I could work out four hours a day and still end up a blimp.*
3 a soundproof cover for a cine camera.
– DERIVATIVES **blimpish** adjective.
– ORIGIN First World War (in sense 2): of uncertain origin. Sense 1 derives from the character invented by cartoonist David Low, used in anti-German or anti-government drawings before and during the Second World War.

blin /blɪn/ singular form of BLINI.

blind ▶ **adjective 1** unable to see because of injury, disease, or a congenital condition: *a blind man with a stick | he was blind in one eye* | (as plural noun **the blind**) *guide dogs for the blind.* ■ (of an action, especially a test or experiment) done without being able to see or without having relevant information: *a blind tasting of eight wines.* ■ Aeronautics (of flying) using instruments only: *blind landings during foggy conditions.*
2 lacking perception, awareness, or judgement: *a blind acceptance of the status quo | she was **blind to** the realities of her position.* ■ not controlled by reason: *they left in blind panic.* ■ not governed by purpose: *a world of blind chance.*
3 concealed or closed, in particular: ■ (of a corner or bend in a road) impossible to see round: *two trucks collided on a blind curve in the road.* ■ (of a door or window) walled up. ■ closed at one end: *a blind pipe.*
4 [with negative] Brit. informal not the slightest (used in emphatic expressions): *this declaration is not a blind bit of good to the workers.*
5 (of a plant) without buds, eyes, or terminal flowers.
▶ **verb** [with obj.] **1** cause (someone) to be unable to see, permanently or temporarily: *the injury temporarily blinded him | her eyes were blinded with scalding tears.*
2 deprive (someone) of understanding, judgement, or perception: *he was blinded by his faith | somehow Clare and I were **blinded to** the truth.* ■ (**blind someone with**) confuse or overawe someone with (something they do not understand): *they try to **blind you with science**.*
3 [no obj., with adverbial of direction] Brit. informal, dated move very fast and dangerously: *I could see the bombs blinding along above the roof tops.*
▶ **noun 1** a screen for a window, especially one on a roller or made of slats: *she pulled down the blinds.* ■ Brit. an awning over a shop window.
2 [in sing.] something designed to conceal one's real intentions: *he phoned again from his own home: that was just a blind for his wife.* ■ N. Amer. a camouflaged shelter used for observing or hunting wildlife: *a duck blind.*
3 Brit. informal, dated a heavy drinking bout: *he's off on a blind again.*
▶ **adverb** without being able to see clearly: *he was the first pilot in history to fly blind | wines were tasted blind.* ■ without having all the relevant information; unprepared: *he was going into the interview blind.* ■ (of a stake in poker or brag) put up by a player before the cards dealt are seen.
– PHRASES **bake something blind** bake a pastry or flan case without a filling. **(as) blind as a bat** informal having very bad eyesight. **blind drunk** informal extremely drunk. **there's none so blind as those who will not see** proverb there's no point trying to reason with someone who does not want to listen to reason. **turn a blind eye** pretend not to notice. [said to be in allusion to Nelson, who lifted a telescope to his blind eye at the Battle of Copenhagen (1801), thus not seeing the signal to 'discontinue the action'.] **when the blind lead the blind, both shall fall into a ditch** proverb those people without knowledge or experience should not try to guide or advise others in a similar position: *I didn't know anything about fighting and neither did my students—it was the blind leading the blind.*
– DERIVATIVES **blindness** noun.
– ORIGIN Old English, of Germanic origin; related to Dutch and German *blind*.

blind alley ▶ **noun** an alley or road that is closed at one end; a cul-de-sac. ■ a course of action leading nowhere: *many technologies that show early promise lead up blind alleys.*

blind coal ▶ **noun** [mass noun] chiefly Scottish anthracite.

blind date ▶ **noun** a social engagement with a person one has not previously met, arranged with a view to the development of a romantic or sexual relationship.

blinder ▶ **noun 1** Brit. informal an excellent performance in a game or race: *Marinello **played a blinder** in his first game.*
2 (**blinders**) N. Amer. blinkers on a horse's bridle.

blindfold ▶ **noun** a piece of cloth tied round the head to cover someone's eyes.
▶ **verb** [with obj.] deprive (someone) of sight by tying a blindfold round their head.
▶ **adverb & adjective** Brit. with a blindfold covering the eyes: [as adv.] *the reporter was driven blindfold to meet the gangster.* ■ (of a game of chess) conducted without sight of board and pieces. ■ [as adv.] used to convey that something is done with great ease and confidence: *he missed putts that he would normally hole blindfold.*
– ORIGIN mid 16th cent.: alteration, by association with FOLD[1], of *blindfeld*, past participle of obsolete *blindfell* 'strike blind, blindfold', from Old English *geblindfellan* (see BLIND, FELL[2]).

B

blind gut ▶ **noun** the caecum.

blinding ▶ **adjective 1** (of light) very bright and likely to dazzle or cause temporary blindness: *the sunlight outside was blinding* | figurative ***a blinding flash** of inspiration.* ■ temporarily obstructing the vision: *blinding rain.* ■ (especially of pain) very intense: *I've got a blinding headache.*
2 Brit. informal (of an action) remarkably skilful and exciting: *he denied Norwich victory with two blinding saves.*
▶ **noun** [mass noun] the process of covering a newly made road with grit to fill cracks. ■ the grit used in such a process. ■ a thin bed of concrete laid down over an area before the main mass of concrete is put in place.
– DERIVATIVES **blindingly** adverb [as submodifier] *the reason was blindingly obvious.*

blindly ▶ **adverb 1** without being able to see; unseeingly: *she began groping blindly in the dark.*
2 without understanding or using one's judgement; unthinkingly: *don't blindly accept dogma as justification.*

blind man's buff (US also **blind man's bluff**) ▶ **noun** a game in which a blindfold player tries to catch others while being pushed about by them.
– ORIGIN early 17th cent.: from *buff* 'a blow', from Old French *bufe* (see BUFFET[2]).

blind pig ▶ **noun** another term for BLIND TIGER.

blind side ▶ **noun** [in sing.] a direction in which a person has a poor view of approaching traffic or danger. ■ Rugby the side of the scrum opposite that on which the main line of the opponents' backs is ranged.
▶ **verb** (**blindside**) [with obj.] N. Amer. hit or attack (someone) on their blind side. ■ make (someone) unable to perceive the truth of a situation.

blindsight ▶ **noun** [mass noun] Medicine the ability to respond to visual stimuli without consciously perceiving them, a condition which can occur after certain types of brain damage.

blind snake ▶ **noun** a small burrowing insectivorous snake which lacks a distinct head and has very small inefficient eyes. Also called WORM SNAKE. ● Infraorder Scolecophidia: three families, in particular Typhlopidae, and several genera.

blind spot ▶ **noun 1** Anatomy the point of entry of the optic nerve on the retina, insensitive to light.
2 an area where a person's view is obstructed. ■ an area in which a person lacks understanding or impartiality: *Ed had a blind spot where these ethical issues were concerned.*
3 Telecommunications a point within the normal range of a transmitter where there is unusually weak reception.

blind stamping (also **blind tooling**) ▶ **noun** [mass noun] the impressing of text or a design on a book cover without the use of colour or gold leaf.

blind stitch ▶ **noun** [mass noun] a sewing stitch producing stitches visible on one side only.
▶ **verb** (**blind-stitch**) [with obj.] sew (something) using blind stitches.

blind tiger (also **blind pig**) ▶ **noun** N. Amer. informal an illegal bar.
– ORIGIN mid 19th cent.: probably so named to evade prohibition laws, the bars being disguised as exhibition halls for the display of natural curiosities.

blind trust ▶ **noun** chiefly N. Amer. a trust independently administering the private business interests of a person in public office to prevent conflict of interest.

blindworm ▶ **noun** another term for SLOW-WORM.

bling /blɪŋ/ (also **bling-bling**) informal ▶ **noun** [mass noun] expensive, ostentatious clothing and jewellery: *look at the bling he's already wearing on his left arm.*
▶ **adjective** denoting expensive, ostentatious clothing or jewellery, or the style or materialistic attitudes associated with them: *the bling lifestyle of diamond rings, flashy cars, and champagne.*
– ORIGIN 1990s: perhaps imitative of light reflecting off jewellery, or of jewellery clashing together.

blini /ˈblɪni, ˈbliːni/ (also **bliny** or **blinis**) ▶ **plural noun** (sing. **blin**) pancakes made from buckwheat flour and served with sour cream.
– ORIGIN Russian (plural).

blink ▸ verb [no obj.] **1** shut and open the eyes quickly: *I blinked in astonishment* | [with obj.] *he blinked his eyes nervously* | *she* ***blinked away*** *her tears.* ■ [with obj.] (**blink something back**) try to control or prevent tears by blinking. ■ [usu. with negative] (**blink at**) react to (something) with surprise or disapproval: *he doesn't blink at the unsavoury aspects of his subject.* ■ back down from a confrontation: *the government blinked only after losing 46 of the first 48 hearings.*
2 (of a light) flash on and off in a regular or intermittent way: *the car's right-hand indicator was blinking.*
▸ noun **1** an act of shutting and opening the eyes very quickly: *he was observing her every blink.* ■ a moment's hesitation: *Feargal would have given her all this without a blink.*
2 a momentary gleam of light.
– PHRASES **in the blink of an eye** (or **in a blink**) very quickly. **not blink an eye** show no reaction. **on the blink** informal (of a machine) not working properly; out of order: *the computer's on the blink.*
– ORIGIN Middle English: from *blenk*, Scots variant of BLENCH[1], reinforced by Middle Dutch *blinken* 'to shine'. Early senses included 'deceive', 'flinch' (compare with BLENCH[1]), and also 'open the eyes after sleep': hence sense 1 of the verb (mid 16th cent.).

blinker ▸ noun **1** (**blinkers**) chiefly Brit. a pair of small leather screens attached to a horse's bridle to prevent it seeing sideways and behind and being startled. ■ something which prevents someone from gaining a full understanding of a situation: *we are having a fresh look at ourselves without blinkers.*
2 (usu. **blinkers**) a vehicle indicator or other device that gives out an intermittent light.
▸ verb [with obj.] put blinkers on (a horse). ■ cause (someone) to have a narrow or limited outlook on a situation.

blinkered ▸ adjective (of a horse) wearing blinkers. ■ having or showing a narrow or limited outlook: *a blinkered attitude.*

blinking ▸ adjective [attrib.] Brit. informal used to express annoyance: *computers can be a blinking nuisance to operators* | [as submodifier] *I'll sign off however I blinking well like.*

blinks (also **water blinks**) ▸ plural noun [usu. treated as sing.] a small fleshy plant with tiny white flowers, which grows in damp and wet habitats in temperate regions. The leaves are sometimes eaten in salads.
● *Montia fontana*, family Portulacaceae.
– ORIGIN late 17th cent.: from BLINK in the sense 'momentary gleam of light' (referring to the small flowers).

blintze /blɪn(t)s/ ▸ noun a thin rolled pancake filled with cheese or fruit and then fried or baked.
– ORIGIN from Yiddish *blintse*, from Russian *blinets* 'little pancake'; compare with BLINI.

bliny ▸ plural noun variant spelling of BLINI.

blip ▸ noun **1** an unexpected, minor, and typically temporary deviation from a general trend: *the Chancellor dismissed rising inflation as a blip.*
2 a very short high-pitched sound made by an electronic device. ■ a small flashing point of light on a radar screen representing an object.
▸ verb (**blips**, **blipping**, **blipped**) **1** [no obj.] (of an electronic device) make a very short high-pitched sound or succession of sounds.
2 [with obj.] open (the throttle of a motor vehicle) momentarily.
– ORIGIN late 19th cent. (denoting a sudden rap or tap): imitative; the noun sense 'unexpected deviation' dates from the 1970s.

Bliss, Sir Arthur (Edward Drummond) (1891–1975), English composer. He moved from the influence of Stravinsky, in works such as *A Colour Symphony* (1922), to a rich style closer to Elgar, as in his choral symphony *Morning Heroes* (1930).

bliss ▸ noun [mass noun] perfect happiness; great joy: *she gave a sigh of bliss.* ■ a state of spiritual blessedness, typically that reached after death.
▸ verb (**bliss out** or **be blissed out**) informal reach a state of perfect happiness, oblivious of everything else: *Josh is just blissed out, always smiling* | [as adj.] *blissed-out hippies.*
– ORIGIN Old English *blīths*, *bliss*, of Germanic origin; related to BLITHE.

blissful ▸ adjective extremely happy; full of joy: *a blissful couple holding a baby.* ■ providing perfect happiness or great joy: *the blissful caress of cool cotton sheets.*
– PHRASES **blissful ignorance** complete unawareness of something important or unpleasant.
– DERIVATIVES **blissfully** adverb [as submodifier] *she was blissfully happy*, **blissfulness** noun.

blister ▸ noun **1** a small bubble on the skin filled with serum and caused by friction, burning, or other damage. ■ a similar swelling, filled with air or fluid, on the surface of a plant, heated metal, painted wood, etc. ■ Medicine, chiefly historical a preparation applied to the skin to form a blister.
2 Brit. informal, dated an annoying person: *the child is a disgusting little blister.*
▸ verb [no obj.] form blisters on the skin or other surface: *the surface of the door began to blister* | (as adj. **blistered**) *he had blistered feet.* ■ [with obj.] cause blisters to form on the surface of: *a caustic liquid which blisters the skin.*
– ORIGIN Middle English: perhaps from Old French *blestre* 'swelling, pimple'.

blister beetle ▸ noun a beetle that, when alarmed, secretes a substance that causes blisters. The larvae are typically parasites of other insects. ● *Lytta* and other genera, family Meloidae: several species.

blister copper ▸ noun [mass noun] partly purified copper with a blistered surface formed during smelting.

blister gas ▸ noun [mass noun] poison gas which causes blisters and intense irritation to the skin.

blistering ▸ adjective (of heat) intense: *the blistering heat of the desert.* ■ (of criticism) expressed with great vehemence: *a blistering attack on the government's transport policy.* ■ extremely fast, forceful, or impressive: *Burke set a blistering pace.*
– DERIVATIVES **blisteringly** adverb.

blister pack ▸ noun another term for BUBBLE PACK.

blithe ▸ adjective showing a casual and cheerful indifference considered to be callous or improper: *a blithe disregard for the rules of the road.* ■ literary happy or carefree: *a blithe seaside comedy.*
– DERIVATIVES **blithely** adverb, **blitheness** noun, **blithesome** /-s(ə)m/ adjective (literary).
– ORIGIN Old English *blīthe*, of Germanic origin; related to Dutch *blijde*, also to BLISS.

blither /ˈblɪðə/ ▸ verb & noun variant spelling of BLATHER.

blithering ▸ adjective [attrib.] informal complete; utter (used to express annoyance or contempt): *a blithering idiot.*
– ORIGIN late 19th cent.: from BLITHER + -ING[2].

BLitt ▸ abbreviation Bachelor of Letters.
– ORIGIN from Latin *Baccalaureus Litterarum*.

blitz ▸ noun **1** an intensive or sudden military attack. ■ (**the Blitz**) the German air raids on Britain in 1940–1.
2 informal a sudden concerted effort to deal with something: *Katrina and I had* ***a blitz on*** *the cleaning.* ■ American Football a play in which one or more defensive backs charge the quarterback of the opposing team.
3 another term for LIGHTNING CHESS.
▸ verb [with obj.] **1** attack or seriously damage (a place) in a blitz: *news came that Rotterdam had been blitzed* | figurative *she blitzed her own world record in the 400m freestyle.*
2 process (food) in an electric mixing machine: *add the eggs and blitz the mixture until it becomes granular.*
3 American Football charge (the opposing team's quarterback) in a blitz.
– PHRASES **Blitz spirit** (also **the spirit of the Blitz**) Brit. stoicism and determination in a difficult or dangerous situation, especially as displayed by a group of people: *he urged the British public to show their Blitz spirit in the face of the recession.*
– ORIGIN 1930s: abbreviation of BLITZKRIEG.

blitzed ▸ adjective N. Amer. informal intoxicated by drink or drugs.

blitzkrieg /ˈblɪtskriːg/ ▸ noun an intense military campaign intended to bring about a swift victory.
– ORIGIN Second World War: from German, literally 'lightning war'.

Blixen, Karen (Christentze), Baroness Blixen-Finecke (1885–1962), Danish novelist and short-story writer; born *Karen Dinesen*; also known by the pseudonym of **Isak Dinesen**. She is best known for *Seven Gothic Tales* (1934) and her autobiography *Out of Africa* (1937), which she wrote after living in Kenya from 1914 to 1931.

blizzard ▸ noun a severe snowstorm with high winds. ■ a large or overwhelming number of things arriving suddenly: ***a blizzard of*** *forms.*
– ORIGIN early 19th cent. (originally US, denoting a violent blow): of unknown origin.

BL Lac object ▸ noun Astronomy a type of remote elliptical galaxy with a very compact starlike nucleus, remarkable for its considerable short-term variations in brightness and radio emissions.
– ORIGIN *BL Lac*, short for *BL Lacertae*, the designation of the first such object discovered (originally thought to be a variable star).

bloat[1] ▸ verb make or become swollen with fluid or gas: [with obj.] *the fungus has bloated their abdomens* | (as noun **bloating**) *she suffered from abdominal bloating.*
▸ noun [mass noun] a disease of livestock characterized by an accumulation of gas in the stomach.
– ORIGIN late 17th cent.: from obsolete *bloat* 'swollen, soft', perhaps from Old Norse *blautr* 'soft, flabby'.

bloat[2] ▸ verb [with obj.] cure (a herring) by salting and smoking it lightly.
– ORIGIN late 16th cent.: related to the adjective *bloat* used in the compound *bloat herring* 'bloater' from the late 16th to mid 17th cent.; of obscure origin.

bloated ▸ adjective swollen with fluid or gas: *he had a bloated, unshaven face.* ■ excessive in size or amount: *the company trimmed its bloated labour force.* ■ (of a person) excessively wealthy and pampered: *the bloated captains of industry.*

bloater ▸ noun a herring cured by salting and light smoking.

bloatware ▸ noun [mass noun] Computing, informal software whose usefulness is reduced because of the excessive disk space and memory it requires.

blob ▸ noun a drop of a thick liquid or viscous substance: ***blobs of*** *paint.* ■ a spot of colour: *the town is much more than a brown blob on the map.* ■ an indeterminate roundish mass or shape: *a big pink blob of a face was at the window.* ■ informal a score of 0 in a game.
▸ verb (**blobs**, **blobbing**, **blobbed**) [with obj.] put small drops of thick liquid or spots of colour on: *her nose was blobbed with paint.*
– DERIVATIVES **blobby** adjective (**blobbier**, **blobbiest**).
– ORIGIN late Middle English (denoting a bubble): perhaps symbolic of a drop of liquid; compare with BLOTCH, BLUBBER[1], and PLOP.

bloc ▸ noun a group of countries or political parties with common interests who have formed an alliance: *the Soviet bloc* | *a parliamentary bloc.*
– ORIGIN early 20th cent.: from French, literally 'block'.

block ▸ noun **1** a large solid piece of hard material, especially rock, stone, or wood, typically with flat surfaces on each side: *a block of marble.* ■ a sturdy flat-topped piece of wood used as a work surface: *a chopping block.* ■ a packaged rectangular portion of butter, ice cream, chocolate, etc.: *a family* ***block of*** *ice cream.* ■ chiefly Brit. a set of sheets of paper glued along one edge, used for drawing or writing on: *a sketching block.* ■ (usu. **blocks**) a starting block: *Jackson jetted out of his blocks.* ■ Printing a piece of wood or metal engraved for printing on paper or fabric. ■ (also **cylinder block** or **engine block**) a large metal moulding containing the cylinders of an internal-combustion engine. ■ a head-shaped mould for shaping hats or wigs.
2 Brit. a large single building subdivided into separate rooms, flats, or offices: *a block of flats.* ■ a building or part of a complex used for a particular purpose: *a shower block.* ■ a group of buildings bounded by four streets: *she went for a run round the block.* ■ N. Amer. any urban or suburban area bounded by four streets: *ours was the ugliest house on the block.* ■ N. Amer. the length of one side of a block, especially as a measure of distance: *he lives a few blocks away from the museum.*
3 a large quantity or allocation of things regarded as a unit: ***a block of*** *shares* | *final examinations will be taken* ***in a block*** *at the end of the course* | [as modifier] *a block booking.* ■ Computing a large piece of text processed as a unit.
4 an obstacle to the normal progress or functioning of something: *substantial demands for time off may constitute* ***a block to*** *career advancement* | *an emotional block.* ■ an act of blocking someone or something: *Marshall's shot drew a fine block from the goalkeeper.* ■ a chock for stopping the motion of a wheel. ■ (also **blockhole**) Cricket the spot on which a batsman rests the end of the bat while waiting to receive a ball.
5 a flat area of something, especially a solid area of colour: *cover the eyelid with a neutral* ***block of*** *colour.* ■ Austral./NZ historical an area of land, in particular a

tract offered to an individual settler by a government. ■ Austral. an urban or suburban building plot. **6** a pulley or system of pulleys mounted in a case.
▸ **verb** [with obj.] **1** make the movement or flow in (a passage, pipe, road, etc.) difficult or impossible: ***block up*** *the holes with sticky tape | the narrow roads were blocked by cars* | (as adj. **blocked**) *a blocked nose.* ■ put an obstacle in the way of (something proposed or attempted): *he stood up, blocking her escape | the government tried to block an agreement on farm subsidies.* ■ prevent access to or the use of (email or a website or mobile phone): *some companies use these IMEI numbers to block stolen phones.* ■ restrict the use or conversion of (currency or any other asset). ■ American Football impede the progress of (a tackler) with one's body. ■ (in martial arts or soccer) stop (a blow or ball) from finding its mark: *Knight did well to block Soloman's shot.* ■ Cricket stop (a ball) with the bat defensively. ■ Bridge play in such a way that opponents are prevented from establishing (a long suit). **2** impress text or a design on (a book cover). **3** shape or reshape (a hat) on a mould.
– PHRASES **have been around the block (a few times)** N. Amer. informal (of a person) have a lot of experience. **the new kid on the block** informal a newcomer to a particular place or sphere of activity. **on the (auction) block** for sale at auction: *the original first manuscript for Ravel's Bolero goes on the block today.* **put (or lay) one's head (or neck) on the block** informal put one's standing or reputation at risk by proceeding with a particular course of action. [with reference to an executioner's block.]
– PHRASAL VERBS **block something in 1** paint something with solid areas of colour. ■ add something in a unit: *it's a good idea to block in regular periods of exercise.* ■ mark something out roughly. **2** park one's car in such a way as to prevent another car from moving away: *he blocked in Vera's Mini.* **block something out 1** stop something such as light or noise from reaching somewhere: *you're blocking out my sun.* ■ exclude something unpleasant from one's thoughts or memory. **2** mark or sketch something out roughly.
– DERIVATIVES **blocky** adjective (**blockier**, **blockiest**).
– ORIGIN Middle English (denoting a log or tree stump): from Old French *bloc* (noun), *bloquer* (verb), from Middle Dutch *blok*, of unknown ultimate origin.

blockade ▸ **noun** an act or means of sealing off a place to prevent goods or people from entering or leaving: *they voted to* ***lift the blockade*** *of major railway junctions.* ■ an obstruction of a physiological or mental function, especially of a biochemical receptor.
▸ **verb** [with obj.] seal off (a place) to prevent goods or people from entering or leaving.
– PHRASES **run a blockade** (of a ship) manage to enter or leave a blockaded port.
– DERIVATIVES **blockader** noun.
– ORIGIN late 17th cent.: from BLOCK + -ADE[1], probably influenced by *ambuscade*.

blockade runner ▸ **noun** a ship which manages to enter or leave a blockaded port. ■ the owner, master, or one of the crew of such a ship.

blockage ▸ **noun** an obstruction which makes movement or flow difficult or impossible: *a blockage in the pipes* | [mass noun] *the pumps are prone to blockage.*

block and tackle ▸ **noun** a lifting mechanism consisting of ropes, a pulley block, and a hook.

blockboard ▸ **noun** [mass noun] Brit. a building material consisting of a core of wooden strips between two layers of plywood.

blockbuster ▸ **noun** informal a thing of great power or size, in particular a film, book, or other product that is a great commercial success: [as modifier] *a blockbuster film.*
– ORIGIN 1940s (denoting a huge aerial bomb capable of destroying a whole block of streets): from BLOCK + BUSTER.

blockbusting informal ▸ **adjective** very successful commercially: *his blockbusting novel.*
▸ **noun** [mass noun] N. Amer. the practice of persuading owners to sell property cheaply because of the fear of people of another race or class moving into the neighbourhood, and then profiting by reselling at a higher price.

block capitals ▸ **plural noun** plain capital letters.

block diagram ▸ **noun** a diagram showing in schematic form the general arrangement of the parts or components of a complex system or process, such as an industrial apparatus or an electronic circuit.

blocker ▸ **noun 1** a substance which prevents or inhibits a given physiological function. **2** Cricket a habitually defensive batsman. ■ American Football a player whose task it is to block for the ball carrier.

block grant ▸ **noun** a grant from central government which a local authority can allocate to a wide range of services.

blockhead ▸ **noun** informal a very stupid person.
– DERIVATIVES **blockheaded** adjective.

block heater ▸ **noun 1** Brit. a storage heater. **2** N. Amer. a device for heating the engine block of a vehicle.

blockhole ▸ **noun** see BLOCK (sense 4 of the noun).

blockhouse ▸ **noun** a reinforced concrete shelter used as an observation point. ■ historical a one-storeyed timber building with loopholes, used as a fort. ■ US a house made of squared logs.

blocking ▸ **noun** [mass noun] **1** the action of blocking or obstructing someone or something, in particular: ■ Psychiatry the sudden halting of the flow of thought or speech, as a symptom of schizophrenia or other mental disorder. ■ failure to recall or consider an unpleasant memory or train of thought. **2** the grouping or treatment of things (e.g. shades of colour) in blocks. ■ the physical arrangement of actors on a stage or film set.

blockish ▸ **adjective 1** big, bulky, or crude in form or appearance: *his blockish architecture is ugly if functional.* **2** unintelligent.

block letters ▸ **plural noun** plain capital letters; block capitals.

block mountain ▸ **noun** Geology a mountain formed by natural faults in the earth's crust.

block party ▸ **noun** N. Amer. a party for all the residents of a block or neighbourhood, usually held outdoors.

block plane ▸ **noun** a carpenter's plane with a blade set at an acute angle, used especially for planing across the end grain of wood.

block release ▸ **noun** [mass noun] Brit. a system of allowing employees the whole of a stated period off work in order to undertake an educational course.

blockship ▸ **noun** a ship which is moored or grounded in a channel in order to block it, for purposes of war or to provide shelter.

block system ▸ **noun** a system of railway signalling which divides the track into sections and allows no train to enter a section that is not completely clear.

block vote ▸ **noun** Brit. a vote proportional in power to the number of people a delegate represents, used particularly at a trade-union conference.

blockwork ▸ **noun** [mass noun] blocks of concrete, cement, or similar material in a wall or other structure.

Bloemfontein /ˈbluːmfɒnˌteɪn, ˈblʊm-/ the capital of Free State province and judicial capital of South Africa; pop. 583,300 (est. 2009).

blog ▸ **noun** a personal website or web page on which an individual records opinions, links to other sites, etc. on a regular basis.
▸ **verb** (**blogs, blogging, blogged**) [no obj.] add new material to or regularly update a blog: *it's about a week since I last blogged.*
– DERIVATIVES **blogger** noun.
– ORIGIN 1990s: abbreviation of WEBLOG.

blogosphere /ˈblɒɡəsfɪə/ ▸ **noun** (**the blogosphere**) informal personal websites and blogs collectively.

blogroll ▸ **noun** informal (on a blog) a list of hyperlinks to other blogs or websites.

bloke ▸ **noun** Brit. informal a man: *he's a nice bloke.*
– ORIGIN mid 19th cent.: from Shelta.

blokeish (also **blokish**) ▸ **adjective** Brit. informal indulging in or relating to stereotypically male behaviour and interests.
– DERIVATIVES **blokeishness** noun.

blokey ▸ **adjective** another term for BLOKEISH.

blonde ▸ **adjective** (also **blond**) (chiefly of hair) fair or pale yellow: *her long blonde hair | I had my hair dyed blonde.* ■ having hair of a fair or pale yellow colour: *a tall blonde woman.* ■ having fair hair and a light complexion (especially when regarded as a racial characteristic).
▸ **noun** a woman with blonde hair. ■ [mass noun] the colour of blonde hair.
– DERIVATIVES **blondish** adjective, **blondness** noun.
– ORIGIN late 17th cent. (earlier as *blond*): from French, feminine of *blond*, from medieval Latin *blundus* 'yellow', perhaps from Germanic.

> **USAGE** The alternative spellings **blonde** and **blond** correspond to the feminine and masculine forms in French, but in English the distinction is not always made, as English does not have such distinctions of grammatical gender. Thus, ***blond*** *woman* or ***blonde*** *woman*, ***blond*** *man* or ***blonde*** *man* are all used. The word is more commonly used of women, though, and in the noun the spelling is typically **blonde**. In American usage the usual spelling is **blond** for both adjective and noun.

blonde moment ▸ **noun** humorous an instance of being silly or scatterbrained.
– ORIGIN 1990s: from the stereotypical perception of blonde-haired women as unintelligent.

Blondin /ˈblɒndɪn/, French /blɔ̃dɛ̃/, Charles (1824–97), French acrobat; born *Jean-François Gravelet*. He is famous for walking across a tightrope suspended over Niagara Falls on several occasions.

Blood /blʌd/ ▸ **noun** (pl. **same** or **Bloods**) a member of a North American Indian people belonging to the Blackfoot Confederacy.

blood ▸ **noun** [mass noun] **1** the red liquid that circulates in the arteries and veins of humans and other vertebrate animals, carrying oxygen to and carbon dioxide from the tissues of the body: *drops of blood.* ■ an internal bodily fluid which performs a similar function in invertebrates. ■ (**bloods**) blood samples or tests: *his bloods were normal*.

> Blood consists of a mildly alkaline aqueous fluid (plasma) containing red cells (erythrocytes), white cells (leucocytes), and platelets; it is red when oxygenated and purple when deoxygenated. Red blood cells carry the protein haemoglobin, which gives blood its colour and can combine with oxygen, thus enabling the blood to carry oxygen from the lungs to the tissues. White blood cells protect the body against the invasion of foreign agents (e.g. bacteria). Platelets and other factors present in plasma are concerned in the clotting of blood, preventing haemorrhage. In medieval science and medicine, blood was regarded as one of the four bodily humours, believed to be associated with a confident and optimistic temperament.

2 violence involving bloodshed: *a commando operation full of blood and danger.* **3** fiery or passionate temperament: *a ritual that fires up his blood.* **4** [with modifier] family background; descent or lineage: *she must have Irish blood in her.* ■ [count noun] a person of specified descent: *a mixed blood.* ■ [count noun] US informal a fellow black person. **5** [count noun] dated a fashionable and dashing young man: *a group of* ***young bloods***.
▸ **verb** [with obj.] chiefly Brit. **1** initiate (someone) in a particular activity: *clubs are too slow to blood young players.* **2** Hunting smear the face of (a novice) with the blood of the kill. ■ give (a hound) a first taste of blood.
– PHRASES **be like getting blood out of (or from) a stone** (N. Amer. also **turnip**) be extremely difficult (said in reference to obtaining something from someone): *getting a story out of her is like getting blood out of a stone!* **blood and guts** informal violence and bloodshed, especially in fiction. **blood and thunder** informal unrestrained and violent action or behaviour. **blood is thicker than water** proverb family relationships and loyalties are the strongest and most important ones. **one's blood is up** one is in a fighting mood. **blood, sweat, and tears** extremely hard work; unstinting effort. **blood will tell** proverb family characteristics cannot be concealed. **first blood 1** the first shedding of blood, especially in a boxing match or formerly in duelling with swords. **2** the first point or advantage gained in a contest: *King drew* ***first blood*** *when he took the opening set.* **give blood** allow blood to be removed medically from one's body in order to be stored for use in transfusions. **have blood on one's hands** be responsible for someone's death. **in one's blood** ingrained in or fundamental to one's character: *racing is in his blood.* **make someone's blood boil** informal infuriate someone. **make someone's blood run cold** horrify someone. **new (or fresh) blood** new members admitted to a group, especially as an invigorating force. **of the blood (royal)** literary royal. **out for (someone's) blood** set on getting revenge. **taste blood** achieve an early success that stimulates further efforts: *the speculators have tasted blood and could force a devaluation of the currency.* **young blood** a younger member or members of a group, especially as an invigorating force.

B

– ORIGIN Old English *blōd*, of Germanic origin; related to German *Blut* and Dutch *bloed*.

blood bank ▶ noun a place where supplies of blood or plasma for transfusion are stored.

bloodbath ▶ noun an event or situation in which many people are killed in an extremely violent way.

blood boosting ▶ noun another term for BLOOD DOPING.

blood-borne ▶ adjective (of a disease, bacterium, virus, etc.) carried by the blood.

blood–brain barrier ▶ noun Anatomy a semipermeable membrane separating the blood from the cerebrospinal fluid, and constituting a barrier to the passage of cells, particles, and large molecules.

blood brother ▶ noun a man who has sworn to treat another man as a brother, typically by a ceremonial mingling of blood.

blood cell ▶ noun any of the kinds of cell normally found circulating in the blood.

blood count ▶ noun a determination of the number of corpuscles in a specific volume of blood. ■ the number found in such a procedure: *a low blood count*.

blood-curdling ▶ adjective causing or expressing terror or horror: *a blood-curdling scream*.

blood donor ▶ noun a person who gives blood for transfusion.

blood doping ▶ noun [mass noun] the injection of oxygenated blood into an athlete before an event in an (illegal) attempt to enhance athletic performance.

blooded ▶ adjective 1 [usu. in combination] having blood or a temperament of a specified kind: *thin-blooded*.
2 chiefly N. Amer. (of horses or cattle) of good pedigree: *a blooded stallion*.

blood feud ▶ noun a lengthy conflict between families involving a cycle of retaliatory killings.

bloodfin ▶ noun a small South American freshwater fish that is silvery yellow with bright red fins, popular in aquaria. ● *Aphyocharax rubripinnis*, family Characidae.

blood fluke ▶ noun another term for SCHISTOSOME.

blood group ▶ noun any of the various types of human blood whose antigen characteristics determine compatibility in transfusion. The best-known blood groups are those of the ABO system.

blood heat ▶ noun [mass noun] the normal body temperature of a healthy human being, about 37 °C or 98.4 °F.

blood horse ▶ noun dated a thoroughbred horse.

bloodhound ▶ noun a large hound of a breed with a very keen sense of smell, used in tracking.

blood knot ▶ noun a type of knot used by anglers to join two fishing lines.

bloodless ▶ adjective 1 (of a revolution or conflict) without violence or killing: *a bloodless coup*.
2 (of the skin) drained of colour: *his bloodless lips*. ■ (of a person) cold or ruthless. ■ lacking in vitality; feeble: *a bloodless chorus*.
– DERIVATIVES **bloodlessly** adverb, **bloodlessness** noun.

bloodletting ▶ noun [mass noun] 1 chiefly historical the surgical removal of some of a patient's blood for therapeutic purposes.
2 the violent killing and wounding of people during a war or conflict: *gang members have halted their internecine bloodletting*. ■ bitter division and quarrelling within an organization.

bloodline ▶ noun an animal's set of ancestors or pedigree, especially with reference to the desirable characteristics bred into it. ■ a set of ancestors or line of descent of an important person.

bloodlust ▶ noun [mass noun] uncontrollable desire to kill or maim others.

blood meal ▶ noun [mass noun] dried blood used for feeding animals and as a fertilizer.

blood money ▶ noun [mass noun] 1 money paid in compensation to the family of someone who has been killed.
2 money paid to a hired killer.

blood orange ▶ noun an orange of a variety with red or red-streaked flesh.

blood poisoning ▶ noun [mass noun] the presence of microorganisms or their toxins in the blood, causing a diseased state; septicaemia.

blood pressure ▶ noun [mass noun] the pressure of the blood in the circulatory system, often measured for diagnosis since it is closely related to the force and rate of the heartbeat and the diameter and elasticity of the arterial walls.

blood pudding (also chiefly N. Amer. **blood sausage**) ▶ noun [mass noun] black pudding.

blood red ▶ noun [mass noun] a deep red: [as modifier] *a blood-red lipstick*.

blood relation (also **blood relative**) ▶ noun a person who is related to another by birth rather than by marriage.

bloodroot ▶ noun 1 a North American plant of the poppy family, which has white flowers and fleshy underground rhizomes which exude red sap when cut. ● *Sanguinaria canadensis*, family Papaveraceae.
2 a lily-like Australian plant with a red rhizome which is roasted and eaten by some Aborigines. ● *Haemodorum coccineum*, family Haemodoraceae.

blood sausage ▶ noun chiefly N. Amer. another term for BLOOD PUDDING.

bloodshed ▶ noun [mass noun] the killing or wounding of people, typically on a large scale during a conflict.

bloodshot ▶ adjective (of the eyes) inflamed or tinged with blood, typically as a result of tiredness.

blood sport ▶ noun (usu. **blood sports**) a sport involving the hunting, wounding, or killing of animals.

bloodstain ▶ noun a mark or discoloration on fabric or a surface caused by blood.

bloodstained ▶ adjective marked or covered with blood.

bloodstock ▶ noun [treated as sing. or pl.] thoroughbred horses considered collectively.

bloodstone ▶ noun [mass noun] a green gemstone that is spotted or streaked with red, consisting of a variety of chalcedony.

bloodstream ▶ noun [in sing.] the blood circulating through the body of a person or animal.

bloodsucker ▶ noun 1 an animal or insect that sucks blood, especially a leech or a mosquito.
2 a long-tailed arboreal Asian lizard which carries its head in a raised position. The head and shoulders of the male become bright red when it is excited. ● *Calotes versicolor*, family Agamidae.
3 informal a person who extorts money or otherwise lives off other people.
– DERIVATIVES **bloodsucking** adjective.

blood sugar ▶ noun [mass noun] the concentration of glucose in the blood.

blood test ▶ noun a scientific examination of a sample of blood, typically for the diagnosis of illness or for the detection and measurement of drugs or other substances.

bloodthirsty ▶ adjective (**bloodthirstier**, **bloodthirstiest**) having or showing a desire to kill and maim: *a bloodthirsty dictator*. ■ (of a story or film) containing or depicting much violence.
– DERIVATIVES **bloodthirstily** adverb, **bloodthirstiness** noun.

blood transfusion ▶ noun an injection of a volume of blood, previously taken from a healthy person, into a patient.

blood vessel ▶ noun a tubular structure carrying blood through the tissues and organs; a vein, artery, or capillary.

bloodwood ▶ noun any of a number of hardwood trees with deep red timber, in particular: ● an Australian gum tree (genus *Eucalyptus*, family Myrtaceae, in particular *E. gummifera*). ● a tree of the Old World tropics (genus *Pterocarpus*, family Leguminosae), including kiaat.

bloodworm ▶ noun 1 the bright red aquatic larva of a non-biting midge, the blood of which contains haemoglobin that allows it to live in poorly oxygenated water. ● Genus *Chironomus*, family Chironomidae.
2 another term for TUBIFEX.

bloody[1] ▶ adjective (**bloodier**, **bloodiest**) 1 covered, smeared, or running with blood: *his bloody hands*. ■ composed of or resembling blood: *a bloody discharge*.
2 involving or characterized by bloodshed or cruelty: *a bloody coup* | *the bloody tyrannies of Europe*.
▶ verb (**bloodies**, **bloodying**, **bloodied**) [with obj.] cover or stain with blood.
– PHRASES **bloody** (or **bloodied**) **but unbowed** proud of what one has achieved despite having suffered great difficulties or losses.
– DERIVATIVES **bloodily** adverb, **bloodiness** noun.
– ORIGIN Old English *blōdig* (see BLOOD, -Y[1]).

bloody[2] ▶ adjective (**bloodier**, **bloodiest**) informal, chiefly Brit. 1 [attrib.] used to express anger, annoyance, or shock, or simply for emphasis: *you took your bloody time* | [as exclamation] *bloody Hell!—what was that?* | [as submodifier] *it's bloody cold outside*.
2 dated unpleasant or perverse: *don't be too bloody to poor Nigel*.
– ORIGIN mid 17th cent.: from BLOODY[1]. The use of *bloody* to add emphasis to an expression is of uncertain origin, but is thought to have a connection with the 'bloods' (aristocratic rowdies) of the late 17th and early 18th centuries; hence the phrase *bloody drunk* (= as drunk as a blood) meant 'very drunk indeed'. After the mid 18th cent. until quite recently *bloody* used as a swear word was regarded as unprintable, probably from the mistaken belief that it implied a blasphemous reference to the blood of Christ, or that the word was an alteration of 'by Our Lady'; hence a widespread caution in using the term even in phrases, such as *bloody battle*, merely referring to bloodshed.

Bloody Assizes the trials of the supporters of the Duke of Monmouth after their defeat at the Battle of Sedgemoor, held in SW England in 1685. The government's representative, Judge Jeffreys, sentenced several hundred rebels to death and about 1,000 others to transportation to America as plantation slaves.

bloody hand ▶ noun Heraldry another term for RED HAND.

Bloody Mary[1] the nickname of Mary I of England (see MARY[2]).

Bloody Mary[2] ▶ noun (pl. **Bloody Marys**) a drink consisting of vodka and tomato juice.

bloody-minded ▶ adjective Brit. informal deliberately uncooperative.
– DERIVATIVES **bloody-mindedly** adverb, **bloody-mindedness** noun.

Bloody Sunday 1 (in Northern Ireland) 30 January 1972, when British troops shot dead thirteen marchers in Londonderry who were protesting against the government's policy of internment.
2 (in Britain) 13 November 1887, when police violently broke up a socialist demonstration in Trafalgar Square, London, against the British government's Irish policy.
3 (in Russia) 9 January 1905 (22 January in the New Style calendar), when troops attacked and killed hundreds of unarmed workers who had gathered in St Petersburg to present a petition to the tsar.

blooey /'blu:i/ (also **blooie**) US informal ▶ adverb & adjective awry; amiss: [as adv.] *the ignition switch went blooey*.
– ORIGIN 1920s: of unknown origin.

bloom[1] ▶ noun 1 a flower, especially one cultivated for its beauty: *an exotic bloom*. ■ [mass noun] the state or period of flowering: *the apple trees were* ***in bloom***. ■ [mass noun] the state or period of greatest beauty, freshness, or vigour: *a young girl, still in the bloom of youth*. ■ [in sing.] a youthful or healthy glow in a person's complexion: *her face had lost its usual bloom*. ■ [mass noun] a full, bright sound in a recording: *the remastering has lost some of the bloom of the strings*.
2 a delicate powdery surface deposit on certain fresh fruits, leaves, or stems. ■ [mass noun] a greyish-white appearance on chocolate caused by cocoa butter rising to the surface. ■ short for ALGAL BLOOM.
▶ verb 1 [no obj.] produce flowers; be in flower: *a chalk pit where cowslips bloomed*. ■ come into or be in full beauty or health; flourish: *the children had bloomed in the soft Devonshire air*. ■ (of fire, colour, or light) become radiant and glowing: *colour bloomed in her cheeks*.
2 [with obj.] technical coat (a lens) with a special surface layer so as to reduce reflection from its surface.
– PHRASES **the bloom is off the rose** N. Amer. the thing in question is no longer new, fresh, or exciting.
– ORIGIN Middle English: from Old Norse *blóm* 'flower, blossom', *blómi* 'prosperity', *blómar* 'flowers'.

bloom[2] ▶ noun a mass of iron, steel, or other metal hammered or rolled into a thick bar for further working. ■ historical an unworked mass of puddled iron.
▶ verb [with obj.] (usu. as noun **blooming**) make (metal) into such a mass.
– ORIGIN Old English *blōma*, of unknown origin.

bloomer[1] ▶ noun Brit. informal, dated a serious or stupid mistake.
– ORIGIN late 19th cent.: equivalent to *blooming error*.

bloomer[2] ▶ noun Brit. a large loaf with diagonal slashes on a rounded top.
– ORIGIN 1930s: of unknown origin.

B

bloomer³ ▸ **noun** [usu. in combination] a plant that produces flowers at a specified time: *fragrant night-bloomers such as nicotiana.* ▪ [with adj.] a person who matures or flourishes at a specified time: *he was a late bloomer.*

bloomers ▸ **plural noun** women's loose-fitting knee-length knickers, considered old-fashioned. ▪ historical women's and girls' loose-fitting trousers, gathered at the knee or, originally, the ankle.
– ORIGIN mid 19th cent.: named after Mrs Amelia J. *Bloomer* (1818–94), an American social reformer who advocated a similar garment.

bloomery ▸ **noun** (pl. **bloomeries**) historical a forge or mill producing blooms of wrought iron.

Bloomfield, Leonard (1887–1949), American linguist, one of the founders of American structural linguistics.

blooming ▸ **adjective** [attrib.] Brit. informal used to express annoyance or for emphasis: *of all the blooming cheek!* | [as submodifier] *a blooming good read.*

Bloomsbury an area of central London noted for its large squares and gardens and for its associations with the Bloomsbury Group. The British Museum is located there. ▪ [as modifier] associated with or similar to the Bloomsbury Group: *a Bloomsbury artist.*

Bloomsbury Group a group of writers, artists, and philosophers living in or associated with Bloomsbury in the early 20th century. Members of the group, which included Virginia Woolf, Lytton Strachey, Vanessa Bell, Duncan Grant, and Roger Fry, were known for their unconventional lifestyles and attitudes and were a powerful force in the growth of modernism.

bloop N. Amer. informal ▸ **verb 1** [no obj.] (of an electronic device) emit a short low-pitched noise: *a fruit machine blooping in the corner.*
2 [no obj.] make a mistake: *the company admitted it had blooped.*
3 [with obj.] Baseball hit (a ball) weakly or make (a hit) that lands just beyond the reach of the infielders.
▸ **noun 1** a short low-pitched noise emitted by an electronic device.
2 a mistake: *a typical beginner's bloop.*
3 Baseball another term for **BLOOPER** (sense 2).
– DERIVATIVES **bloopy adjective.**
– ORIGIN 1920s: imitative.

blooper ▸ **noun** informal, chiefly N. Amer. **1** an embarrassing error.
2 Baseball a weakly hit fly ball landing just beyond the reach of the infielders.
– ORIGIN 1926 (originally US, denoting a radio which caused others to *bloop*, i.e. emit a loud howling noise): from imitative **BLOOP** + **-ER¹**.

blooter /ˈbluːtə/ ▸ **verb** [with obj.] Scottish hit or kick (something) hard and wildly: *he blootered the ball over the bar.*
– ORIGIN 1980s: earlier senses include 'blunder' and 'talk foolishly', but ultimately of unknown origin.

blossom ▸ **noun** a flower or a mass of flowers, especially on a tree or bush: *tiny white blossoms* | [mass noun] *the slopes were ablaze with almond blossom.* ▪ [mass noun] the state or period of flowering: *fruit trees in blossom.*
▸ **verb** [no obj.] (of a tree or bush) produce flowers or masses of flowers: *a garden in which roses blossom* | (as adj. **blossoming**) *blossoming magnolia.* ▪ mature or develop in a promising or healthy way: *their friendship blossomed into romance* | (as noun **blossoming**) *the blossoming of experimental theatre.*
– DERIVATIVES **blossomy adjective.**
– ORIGIN Old English *blōstm, blōstma* (noun), *blōstmian* (verb), of Germanic origin; related to Dutch *bloesem*, also to **BLOOM¹**.

blot ▸ **noun 1** a dark mark or stain made by ink, paint, dirt, etc.: *an ink blot.* ▪ a shameful act or quality that damages an otherwise good character or reputation: *the only blot on an otherwise clean campaign.* ▪ a thing that mars the appearance of something: *wind power turbines are a blot on the landscape.*
2 Biochemistry a procedure in which proteins or nucleic acids separated on a gel are transferred directly to an immobilizing medium for identification.
▸ **verb (blots, blotting, blotted)** [with obj.] **1** dry (a wet surface or substance) using an absorbent material: *Henry blotted the page.*
2 mark or stain (something): (as adj. **blotted**) *the writing was messy and blotted.* ▪ damage the good character or reputation of: *the turmoil blotted his memory of the school.*
3 (**blot something out**) cover writing or pictures with ink or paint so that they cannot be seen. ▪ obscure a view: *a dust shield blotting out the sun.* ▪ obliterate or disregard something painful in one's memory or existence: *the concentration necessary to her job blotted out all the feelings.*
4 Biochemistry transfer by means of a blot.
– PHRASES **blot one's copybook** Brit. tarnish one's good reputation.
– ORIGIN late Middle English: probably of Scandinavian origin and related to Old Norse *blettr.*

blotch ▸ **noun** a large irregular patch or unsightly mark on the skin or another surface: *red blotches on her face.*
▸ **verb** [with obj.] cover with blotches.
– DERIVATIVES **blotchiness noun.**
– ORIGIN early 17th cent. (as a verb): partly an alteration of obsolete *plotch* in the same sense (of unknown origin), influenced by **BLOT**; partly a blend of **BLOT** and **BOTCH**.

blotchy ▸ **adjective** (**blotchier, blotchiest**) covered with blotches; patchy: *discoloration or blotchy skin on the legs.*

blotter ▸ **noun 1** a sheet or pad of blotting paper in a frame, kept on a desk.
2 N. Amer. a temporary recording book, especially a police charge sheet.

blotting paper ▸ **noun** [mass noun] absorbent paper used for soaking up excess ink when writing.

blotto ▸ **adjective** [predic.] informal extremely drunk.
– ORIGIN early 20th cent.: from **BLOT** + **-O**.

blouse ▸ **noun** a woman's upper garment resembling a shirt, typically with a collar, buttons, and sleeves. ▪ a loose linen or cotton garment formerly worn by peasants and manual workers, typically belted at the waist. ▪ a type of jacket worn as part of military uniform.
▸ **verb** [with obj. and adverbial] make (a garment) hang in loose folds: *I bloused my trousers over my boots.*
– PHRASES **big girl's blouse** Brit. informal a weak, cowardly, or oversensitive man.
– ORIGIN early 19th cent. (denoting a belted loose garment worn by peasants): from French, of unknown origin.

blouson /ˈbluːzɒn/ ▸ **noun** a short loose-fitting jacket, typically bloused and finishing at the waist.
– ORIGIN early 20th cent.: from French, diminutive of **BLOUSE**.

bloviate /ˈbləʊvɪeɪt/ ▸ **verb** [no obj.] US informal talk at length, especially in an inflated or empty way.
– DERIVATIVES **bloviation noun, bloviator noun.**
– ORIGIN mid 19th cent.: perhaps from **BLOW¹**.

Blow, John (*c.*1649–1708), English composer and organist. The organist of Westminster Abbey 1668–79 and 1695–1708, he wrote much church music and taught Henry Purcell. His masque *Venus and Adonis* (*c.*1682) was a forerunner of English opera.

blow¹ ▸ **verb** (past **blew**; past participle **blown**) **1** [no obj.] (of wind) move creating an air current: *a cold breeze was blowing in off the sea.* ▪ [with obj. and adverbial of direction] (of wind) cause (something) to move; propel: *a gust of wind blew a cloud of smoke into his face* | *the spire was blown down during a gale.* ▪ [no obj., with adverbial of direction] be carried, driven, or moved by the wind or an air current: *it was so windy that the tent nearly blew away* | *cotton curtains blowing in the breeze.* ▪ N. Amer. informal leave: *I'd better blow.*
2 [no obj.] (of a person) expel air through pursed lips: *Willie took a deep breath, and blew* | *he blew on his tea to cool it.* ▪ [with obj.] use one's breath to propel (something): *he blew cigar smoke in her face.* ▪ breathe hard; pant: *Uncle Albert was soon puffing and blowing.* ▪ (as adj. **blown**) out of breath; panting: *an exhausted, blown horse.* ▪ [with obj.] force air through the mouth into (an instrument) in order to make a sound: *the umpire blew his whistle.* ▪ (of an instrument) make a sound when air is forced into it: *police whistles blew.* ▪ [with obj.] sound (the horn of a vehicle). ▪ informal play jazz or rock music in an unrestrained style. ▪ [with obj.] force air through a tube into (molten glass) in order to create an artefact. ▪ [with obj.] remove the contents of (an egg) by forcing air through it. ▪ (of a whale) eject air and vapour through the blowhole.
3 [with obj. and adverbial of direction] (of an explosion or explosive device) displace violently or send flying: *the blast had blown the windows out of the van.* ▪ [no obj.] (of a vehicle tyre) burst suddenly while the vehicle is in motion. ▪ burst or cause to burst due to pressure or overheating: [no obj.] *the engines sounded as if their exhausts had blown.* ▪ (with reference to an electric circuit) burn out through overloading: [no obj.] *the fuse had blown* | [with obj.] *the floodlights blew a fuse.*
4 [with obj.] informal spend recklessly: *they blew £100,000 in just eighteen months.*
5 [with obj.] informal completely bungle (an opportunity): *he'd been given a second chance and he'd **blown it*** | *they blew a 4–2 lead.* ▪ expose (a stratagem): *a man whose cover was blown.*
6 (past participle **blowed**) [with obj.] Brit. informal damn: [as imperative] *'Well, **blow me**', he said, 'I never knew that.'* | [with clause] ***I'm blowed if** I want to see him again.*
7 [with obj.] vulgar slang perform fellatio on (a man).
8 [with obj.] (of flies) lay eggs in or on (something).
▸ **noun 1** [in sing.] a strong wind: *we're in for a bit of a blow.* ▪ an act of getting some fresh air: *I'll go down to the sea and get a blow before supper.*
2 an act of blowing an instrument: *a number of blows on the whistle.* ▪ informal a spell of playing jazz or rock music. ▪ an act of blowing one's nose: *give your nose a good blow.* ▪ (in steel-making) an act of sending an air or oxygen blast through molten metal in a converter.
3 [mass noun] informal cannabis.
– PHRASES **be blown off course** (of a project) be disrupted by some circumstance. **be blown out of the water** be shown to lack all credibility. **blow away the cobwebs** refresh oneself when feeling weary, especially by having some fresh air. **blow someone's brains out** informal kill someone with a shot in the head. **blow chunks** N. Amer. informal vomit. **blow a fuse** (or **gasket**) informal lose one's temper. **blow hot and cold** alternate inconsistently between two moods, attitudes, or courses of action. **blow someone a kiss** kiss the tips of one's fingers then blow across them towards someone as a gesture of affection. **blow someone's mind** informal impress or otherwise affect someone very strongly: *the sound of a twelve-string guitar just blew my mind.* **blow one's nose** clear one's nose of mucus by blowing through it into a handkerchief. **blow off steam** see **LET OFF STEAM** at **STEAM**. **blow something to bits** (or **pieces** or **smithereens**) use bombs or other explosives to destroy something, typically a building, completely: *the commandos blew the base to smithereens.* **blow one's top** (or chiefly N. Amer. **lid** or **stack**) informal lose one's temper. **blow up in one's face** (of an action, project, or situation) go drastically wrong with damaging effects to oneself. **blow with the wind** be incapable of maintaining a consistent course of action.
– PHRASAL VERBS **blow someone away** informal **1** kill someone using a firearm. **2** impress someone greatly: *I'm blown away by his new poem.* **blow in** informal arrive casually and unannounced. **blow off** informal break wind noisily. **blow someone off** N. Amer. informal fail to keep an appointment with someone. ▪ end a romantic or sexual relationship with someone. **blow something off** N. Amer. informal ignore or make light of something. ▪ fail to attend something: *Ivy blew off class.* **blow out 1** be extinguished by an air current: *the candles blew out.* **2** (of a tyre) puncture while the vehicle is in motion. **3** (of an oil or gas well) emit gas suddenly and forcefully. **4** (**blow itself out**) (of a storm) finally lose its force. **blow someone out** N. Amer. informal defeat someone convincingly. **blow something out 1** use one's breath to extinguish a flame: *he blew out the candle.* **2** puff out one's cheeks. **3** N. Amer. informal render a part of the body useless: *he blew out his knee playing basketball.* **blow over** (of trouble) fade away without serious consequences. **blow up 1** explode. ▪ lose one's temper: *Mum had blown up at Dad with more than her usual vehemence.* **2** (of a wind or storm) begin to develop. ▪ (of a scandal or dispute) emerge or become public. **3** inflate: *my stomach had started to blow up.* **blow someone up** informal, dated reprimand someone severely: *she got blown up by her boss for being late.* **blow something up 1** cause something to explode. **2** inflate something: *a small pump for blowing up balloons.* ▪ exaggerate the importance of something: *it was a domestic tiff which had been blown up out of all proportion.* **3** enlarge a photograph or text.
– ORIGIN Old English *blāwan*, of Germanic origin; related to German *blähen* 'blow up, swell', from an Indo-European root shared by Latin *flare* 'blow'.

blow² ▸ **noun** a powerful stroke with a hand, weapon, or hard object: *he received a blow to the skull.* ▪ a sudden shock or disappointment: *the news came as a crushing blow to the cast.*
– PHRASES **at one blow** by a single stroke; in one operation: *the letter had destroyed his certainty at one blow.* **blow-by-blow** (of a description of an event) giving all the details in the order in which they

B

occurred: *a blow-by-blow account of how England lost to Portugal*. **come to blows** start fighting after a disagreement. **soften** (or **cushion**) **the blow** make it easier to cope with a difficult change or upsetting news: *monetary compensation was offered to soften the blow*. **strike a blow for** (or **against**) act in support of (or opposition to): *a chance to strike a blow for freedom*.
– ORIGIN late Middle English: of unknown origin.

blow[3] archaic or literary ▶ **verb** (past **blew**; past participle **blown**) [no obj.] produce flowers or be in flower: *I know a bank where the wild thyme blows*.
▶ **noun** [mass noun] the state or period of flowering: *stocks in fragrant blow*.
– ORIGIN Old English *blōwan*, of Germanic origin; related to Dutch *bloeien* and German *blühen*, also to **BLOOM**[1] and **BLOSSOM**.

blowback ▶ **noun 1** a process in which gases expand or travel in a direction opposite to the usual one, especially through escape of pressure or delayed combustion.
2 chiefly US the unintended adverse results of a political action or situation: *this is the blowback from all those aggressive public health campaigns*.

blowdown ▶ **noun** [mass noun] **1** N. Amer. trees that have been blown down by the wind. ■ the blowing down of a tree or trees.
2 the removal of solids or liquids from a container or pipe using pressure.

blow-dry ▶ **verb** [with obj.] dry and style (hair) with a handheld dryer.
▶ **noun** [in sing.] an act of blow-drying the hair.
– DERIVATIVES **blow-dryer** (also **blow-drier**) **noun**.

blower ▶ **noun 1** a person or thing that blows, especially a mechanical device for creating a current of air used to dry or heat something.
2 Brit. informal a telephone.

blowfish ▶ **noun** (pl. **same** or **blowfishes**) any of a number of fishes that are able to inflate their bodies when alarmed, such as a globefish.

blowfly ▶ **noun** (pl. **blowflies**) a large and typically metallic blue or green fly which lays its eggs on meat and carcasses. ● Family Calliphoridae: numerous species, including the bluebottle.

blowgun ▶ **noun** another term for **BLOWPIPE**.

blowhard ▶ **noun** N. Amer. informal a boastful or pompous person.

blowhole ▶ **noun 1** the nostril of a whale or dolphin on the top of its head.
2 a hole in ice through which a sea mammal breathes or a person fishes. ■ a vent for air or smoke in a tunnel or other structure.

blowie ▶ **noun** (pl. **blowies**) Austral./NZ informal a blowfly.

blow-in ▶ **noun** Austral. informal a newcomer or recent arrival.

blow job ▶ **noun** vulgar slang an act of fellatio.

blowlamp ▶ **noun** British term for **BLOWTORCH**.

blown[1] past participle of **BLOW**[1]. ▶ **adjective** informal (of a vehicle or its engine) provided with a turbocharger.

blown[2] past participle of **BLOW**[3].

blowout ▶ **noun 1** an occasion when a tyre on a vehicle bursts or an electric fuse melts. ■ an uprush of oil or gas from a well. ■ N. Amer. informal an outburst of anger or an argument.
2 informal a large or lavish meal or social gathering.
3 N. Amer. informal an easy victory in a sporting contest or election.
4 a hollow eroded by the wind.

blowpipe ▶ **noun 1** a primitive weapon consisting of a long tube through which an arrow or dart is propelled by force of the breath.
2 a long tube by means of which molten glass is blown into the required shape. ■ a tube used to intensify the heat of a flame by blowing air or other gas through it at high pressure.

blowsy /ˈblaʊzi/ (also **blowzy**) ▶ **adjective** (**blowsier**, **blowsiest**; **blowzier**, **blowziest**) (of a woman) coarse, untidy, and red-faced.
– ORIGIN early 17th cent.: from obsolete *blowze* 'beggar's female companion', of unknown origin.

blowtorch ▶ **noun** a portable device producing a hot flame which can be directed on to a surface, typically to burn off paint.

blow-up ▶ **noun 1** an enlargement of a photograph.
2 informal an outburst of anger.
▶ **adjective** [attrib.] inflatable: *a blow-up pillow*.

blowy ▶ **adjective** (**blowier**, **blowiest**) windy or windswept: *a blowy day*.

BLT ▶ **noun** informal, chiefly N. Amer. a sandwich filled with bacon, lettuce, and tomato.

blub ▶ **verb** (**blubs**, **blubbing**, **blubbed**) [no obj.] informal cry noisily and uncontrollably; sob.
– ORIGIN early 19th cent.: abbreviation of **BLUBBER**[2].

blubber[1] ▶ **noun** [mass noun] the fat of sea mammals, especially whales and seals. ■ informal, derogatory excessive human fat.
▶ **adjective** archaic (of a person's lips) swollen or protruding. [alteration of obsolete *blabber* 'swollen'.]
– DERIVATIVES **blubbery** **adjective**.
– ORIGIN late Middle English (denoting the foaming of the sea, also a bubble on water): perhaps symbolic; compare with **BLOB** and **BLOTCH**.

blubber[2] ▶ **verb** [no obj.] informal cry noisily and uncontrollably; sob: *he was blubbering like a child* | [with direct speech] *'I don't like him,' blubbered Jonathan*.
– ORIGIN late Middle English: probably symbolic; compare with **BLOB** and **BLUBBER**[1].

bluchers /ˈbluːkəz/ ▶ **plural noun** historical strong leather half-boots or high shoes.
– ORIGIN mid 19th cent.: named after G. L. von *Blücher* (1742–1819), Prussian general.

bludge Austral./NZ informal ▶ **verb** [no obj.] shirk responsibility and live off the efforts of others: *they were sick of bludging on the public*. ■ [with obj.] cadge or scrounge: *the girls bludged smokes*.
▶ **noun** an easy job or assignment.
– ORIGIN late 19th cent.: back-formation from **BLUDGER**.

bludgeon /ˈblʌdʒ(ə)n/ ▶ **noun** a thick stick with a heavy end, used as a weapon.
▶ **verb** [with obj.] beat (someone) repeatedly with a bludgeon or other heavy object. ■ force or bully (someone) to do something: *she was determined not to be* ***bludgeoned into submission***. ■ (**bludgeon one's way**) make one's way by brute force.
– ORIGIN mid 18th cent.: of unknown origin.

bludger ▶ **noun** Austral./NZ informal a scrounger. ■ an idle or lazy person.
– ORIGIN mid 19th cent. (originally British slang denoting a pimp, specifically one who robbed his prostitute's clients): abbreviation of *bludgeoner*, from **BLUDGEON**.

blue[1] ▶ **adjective** (**bluer**, **bluest**) **1** of a colour intermediate between green and violet, as of the sky or sea on a sunny day: *the clear blue sky* | *blue jeans* | *deep blue eyes*. ■ (of a person's skin) having turned blue as a result of cold or breathing difficulties: *Ashley went blue and I panicked*. ■ (of a bird or other animal) having blue markings: *a blue jay*. ■ (of a cat, fox, or rabbit) having fur of a smoky grey colour: *the blue fox*. ■ (of a ski run) of the second-lowest level of difficulty, as indicated by coloured markers positioned along it. ■ Physics denoting one of three colours of quark.
2 informal (of a person or mood) melancholy, sad, or depressed: *he's feeling blue*.
3 informal (of a film, joke, or story) having sexual or pornographic content: *a blue movie*.
4 Brit. informal politically conservative: *the successful blue candidate*.
▶ **noun 1** [mass noun] blue colour or pigment: *she was dressed* ***in blue*** | *the dark blue of his eyes* | [count noun] *armchairs in pastel blues and greens*. ■ blue clothes or material: *Susan wore blue*.
2 a blue thing, in particular: ■ the blue ball in snooker. ■ (**the blue**) literary the sky or sea, or the unknown: *far out upon the blue were many sails*. ■ another term for **BLUING**.
3 [usu. with modifier] a small butterfly, the male of which is predominantly blue while the female is typically brown. ● Numerous genera in the family Lycaenidae.
4 Brit. a person who has represented Cambridge University (a **Cambridge blue**) or Oxford University (an **Oxford blue**) at a particular sport in a match between the two universities: *a flyweight boxing blue*. ■ a distinction awarded to such a person: *Adrian's brother won a rugby blue in December*.
5 Austral./NZ informal an argument or fight. [1940s: perhaps by association with phrases such as *make the air blue*, alluding to swearing.]
6 Austral./NZ informal a mistake.
7 Austral./NZ informal a nickname for a red-headed person. [1930s: of unknown origin.]
8 Brit. informal a supporter of the Conservative Party.
▶ **verb** (**blues**, **bluing** or **blueing**, **blued**) **1** make or become blue. ■ [with obj.] heat (metal) so as to give it a greyish-blue finish.
2 [with obj.] chiefly historical wash (white clothes) with bluing.
– PHRASES **blue on blue** Military denoting or relating to an attack made by one's own side that accidentally harms one's own forces: *blue-on-blue incidents*. [from the use of blue to indicate friendly forces in military exercises.] **do something until** (or **till**) **one is blue in the face** informal put all one's efforts into doing something to no avail: *she could talk to him until she was blue in the face, but he was just not hearing*. **once in a blue moon** informal very rarely. [because a 'blue moon' is a phenomenon that occurs only very rarely.] **out of the blue** (or **out of a clear blue sky**) informal without warning; unexpectedly: *she phoned me out of the blue*. [with reference to a 'blue' (i.e. clear) sky, from which nothing unusual is expected.] **talk a blue streak** N. Amer. informal speak continuously and at great length.
– DERIVATIVES **blueness** **noun**.
– ORIGIN Middle English: from Old French *bleu*, ultimately of Germanic origin and related to Old English *blǣwen* 'blue' and Old Norse *blár* 'dark blue' (see also **BLAEBERRY**).

blue[2] ▶ **verb** (**blues**, **bluing** or **blueing**, **blued**) Brit. informal, dated squander or recklessly spend (money).
– ORIGIN mid 19th cent.: perhaps a variant of **BLOW**[1].

blue baby ▶ **noun** a baby with a blue complexion from lack of oxygen in the blood due to a congenital defect of the heart or major blood vessels.

blueback ▶ **noun** chiefly N. Amer. a bird or fish, especially a trout or a sockeye salmon, having a bluish back.

Bluebeard a character in a tale by Charles Perrault, who killed several wives in turn for disobeying his order to avoid a locked room, which contained the bodies of his previous wives. Local tradition in Brittany identifies him with Gilles de Rais (*c*.1400–40), a perpetrator of atrocities, although he had only one wife (who left him). ■ (as noun **a Bluebeard**) a man who murders his wives.

blue beat ▶ **noun** another term for **SKA**.

bluebell ▶ **noun 1** a European woodland plant of the lily family, which produces clusters of blue bell-shaped flowers in spring. ● *Hyacinthoides* (or *Endymion*) *nonscripta*, family Liliaceae.
2 any of a number of other plants with blue bell-shaped flowers, in particular: ● Scottish term for **HAREBELL**. ● a North American plant of the borage family (genus *Mertensia*, family Boraginaceae). ● an Australian and South African plant of the bellflower family (genus *Wahlenbergia*, family Campanulaceae).

blueberry ▶ **noun** (pl. **blueberries**) **1** a small sweet blue-black edible berry which grows in clusters on North American shrubs related to the bilberry.
2 one of the dwarf shrubs that produces blueberries, some kinds being cultivated for their fruit or as ornamentals. ● Genus *Vaccinium*, family Ericaceae: several species.

bluebill ▶ **noun 1** a large African waxbill with a stout metallic blue bill and red and black plumage. ● Genus *Spermophaga*, Estrildidae: three species.
2 any of a number of ducks with blue bills: ● N. Amer. the scaup duck. ● Austral. the blue-billed duck (*Oxyura australis*).

bluebird ▶ **noun** an American songbird of the thrush family, the male of which has a blue head, back, and wings. ● Genus *Sialia*, family Turdidae: three species.

blue-black ▶ **adjective** black with a tinge of blue.

blue blood ▶ **noun** [mass noun] noble birth. ■ [count noun] a person of noble birth.
– DERIVATIVES **blue-blooded** **adjective**.

blue bonnet ▶ **noun** a pale grey-brown Australian parrot with a deep blue face and variously coloured wings, tail, and belly. ● *Psephotus* (or *Northiella*) *haematogaster*, family Psittacidae.

Blue Book ▶ **noun** (in the UK) a report bound in a blue cover and issued by Parliament or the Privy Council. ■ (in the US) an official book listing government officials. ■ (usu. **blue book**) an authoritative handbook.

bluebottle ▶ **noun 1** a common blowfly with a metallic blue body, the female of which often comes into houses searching for a suitable food source on which to lay her eggs. ● *Calliphora vomitoria*, family Calliphoridae.
2 Austral. & S. African the Portuguese man-of-war. [so named because of its blue balloon-like float.]
3 Brit. the wild cornflower.
4 Brit. informal, dated a police officer.

blue box ▶ **noun 1** chiefly US an electronic device used to access long-distance telephone lines illegally.
2 Canadian a blue plastic box for the collection of recyclable household materials.

blue channel ▸ noun (at a customs area in an airport or port) the passage which should be taken by arriving passengers who have only travelled within the European Union.

blue cheese ▸ noun [mass noun] cheese containing veins of blue mould, such as Stilton and Danish Blue.

blue-chip ▸ adjective [attrib.] denoting companies or their shares considered to be a reliable investment, though less secure than gilt-edged stock. ■ of the highest quality: *blue-chip art*.
– ORIGIN early 20th cent. (originally US): from the *blue chip* used in gambling games, which usually has a high value.

blue chipper ▸ noun N. Amer. informal a highly valued person, especially a sports player.

blue coat ▸ noun **1** historical a soldier in a blue uniform.
2 (**Blue Coat**) Brit. a student at a charity school with a blue uniform.

blue-collar ▸ adjective chiefly N. Amer. relating to manual work or workers, particularly in industry: *a blue-collar neighbourhood*.

blue corn ▸ noun [mass noun] N. Amer. a variety of maize with bluish grains.

blue crab ▸ noun a large edible swimming crab of the Atlantic coast of North America. ● *Callinectes sapidus*, family Portunidae.

blue crane ▸ noun a large South African crane with blue-grey plumage, the national bird of South Africa. Also called **STANLEY CRANE**. ● *Anthropoides paradisea*, family Gruidae.

blue ensign ▸ noun a blue flag with the Union Jack in the top corner next to the flagstaff, flown chiefly by British naval auxiliary vessels.

blue-eyed boy ▸ noun Brit. informal, chiefly derogatory a person highly regarded by someone and treated with special favour.

blue-eyed grass ▸ noun a North American plant of the iris family, cultivated for its blue flowers. ● Genus *Sisyrinchium*, family Iridaceae: several species.

blue-eyed Mary ▸ noun a low-growing southern European plant of the borage family, which bears bright blue flowers and spreads by means of runners. ● *Omphalodes verna*, family Boraginaceae.

Blue-faced Leicester ▸ noun see **LEICESTER**[3] (sense 3).

Bluefields a port on the Mosquito Coast of Nicaragua, situated on an inlet of the Caribbean Sea; pop. 45,547 (2006).

bluefin (also **bluefin tuna**) ▸ noun the commonest large tuna, which occurs worldwide in warm seas. It is probably the largest bony fish, and is very important as a food and game fish. Also called **TUNNY**. ● *Thunnus thynnus*, family Scombridae.

bluefish ▸ noun (pl. **same** or **bluefishes**) a predatory blue-coloured marine fish, which inhabits tropical and temperate waters and is popular as a game fish. ● *Pomatomus saltatrix*, the only member of the family Pomatomidae.

blue flag ▸ noun **1** a European award for beaches, based on cleanliness and safety.
2 Motor Racing a blue flag used to indicate to a driver that there is another driver trying to lap him.

blue flyer ▸ noun Austral. a female red kangaroo.
– ORIGIN mid 19th cent.: *blue*, by association with the informal nickname for red-headed people (see **BLUE**[1] (sense 7 of the noun)).

blue funk ▸ noun see **FUNK**[1].

bluegill /ˈbluːɡɪl/ ▸ noun an edible North American freshwater fish of the sunfish family, with a deep body and bluish cheeks and gill covers. ● *Lepomis macrochirus*, family Centrarchidae.

bluegrass ▸ noun [mass noun] **1** (also **Kentucky bluegrass**) a bluish-green grass which was introduced into North America from northern Europe, widely grown (especially in Kentucky and Virginia) for fodder. ● Genus *Poa*, family Gramineae: several species, in particular the common Eurasian meadow grass.
2 a kind of country music characterized by virtuoso playing of banjos and guitars and high-pitched, close-harmony vocals.

Bluegrass State informal name for **KENTUCKY**.

blue-green algae ▸ plural noun another term for **CYANOBACTERIA** (see **CYANOBACTERIA**).

blue ground ▸ noun another term for **KIMBERLITE**.

bluegum ▸ noun a eucalyptus tree with blue-green aromatic leaves and smooth bark. ● Genus *Eucalyptus*, family Myrtaceae: several species, in particular *E. regnans*.

blue hare ▸ noun another term for **MOUNTAIN HARE**.

bluehead ▸ noun a small wrasse (fish) of the tropical East Atlantic, the large males of which have a blue head and green body with vertical stripes, and the females and smaller males are predominantly yellowish. ● *Thalassoma bifasciatum*, family Labridae.

blue heeler ▸ noun Austral./NZ a cattle dog with a dark speckled body.
– ORIGIN early 20th cent.: *blue* from the characteristic blue (or red) flecked coat of the breed.

blue helmet ▸ noun a member of a UN peacekeeping force.

blue ice ▸ noun [mass noun] ice of a vivid blue colour, formed when a large body of water freezes suddenly.

blueing ▸ noun variant spelling of **BLUING**.

blueish ▸ adjective variant spelling of **BLUISH**.

bluejacket ▸ noun informal a sailor in the navy.

blue jay ▸ noun a common North American jay with a blue crest, back, wings, and tail. ● *Cyanocitta cristata*, family Corvidae.
■ another term for **ROLLER**[1] (sense 4).

blue jet ▸ noun a very faint short-lived cone of deep blue light sometimes observed in the upper atmosphere above an intense thunderstorm.

Blue John ▸ noun [mass noun] a blue or purple banded variety of fluorite found in Derbyshire.

blue law ▸ noun N. Amer. a law prohibiting certain activities, such as shopping, on a Sunday. ■ (in colonial New England) a strict puritanical law, particularly one preventing entertainment or leisure activities on a Sunday.

blue line ▸ noun Ice Hockey either of the two lines running across the ice between the centre line and the goal line.

blue metal ▸ noun [mass noun] Brit. broken blue stone used for road-making.

blue mould ▸ noun a bluish fungus which grows on food, some kinds of which are used to produce blue cheeses or antibiotics such as penicillin. ● *Penicillium* and other genera, subdivision Deuteromycotina.

Blue Mountains 1 a section of the Great Dividing Range in New South Wales, Australia.
2 a range of mountains in eastern Jamaica.
3 a range of mountains running from central Oregon to SE Washington State in the US.

Blue Nile one of the two principal headwaters of the Nile. Rising from Lake Tana in NW Ethiopia, it flows some 1,600 km (1,000 miles) southwards then northwestwards into Sudan, where it meets the White Nile at Khartoum.

bluenose ▸ noun informal **1** US a priggish or puritanical person.
2 (**Bluenose**) Canadian a person from Nova Scotia.
– DERIVATIVES **bluenosed** adjective (sense 1).

blue note ▸ noun Music a minor interval where a major would be expected, used especially in jazz.

blue-pencil ▸ verb [with obj.] censor or make cuts in (a manuscript, film, or other work).

Blue Peter ▸ noun a blue flag with a white square in the centre, raised by a ship about to leave port.

blue plate ▸ adjective [attrib.] N. Amer. (of a restaurant meal) consisting of a full main course ordered as a single menu item.
ORIGIN with reference to the original blue plates divided into compartments, on which fixed-price restaurant meals were served.

blue pointer ▸ noun another term for **MAKO**[1].

blueprint ▸ noun a design plan or other technical drawing. ■ something which acts as a plan, model, or template for others: *the scheme was **a blueprint for** future development programmes*.
▸ verb [with obj.] N. Amer. draw up (a plan or model): (as adj. **blueprinted**) *a neatly blueprinted scheme*.
– ORIGIN late 19th cent.: from the original process in which prints were composed of white lines on a blue ground or of blue lines on a white ground.

blue riband ▸ noun **1** (N. Amer. also **blue ribbon**) a ribbon of blue silk given to the winner of a competition or as a mark of great distinction. ■ a badge worn by members of the Order of the Garter.
2 (**Blue Riband** or **Ribbon**) a trophy for the ship making the fastest eastward sea crossing of the Atlantic Ocean on a regular commercial voyage.
▸ adjective (**blue-ribbon**) [attrib.] N. Amer. **1** of the highest quality; first-class.
2 (of a jury or committee) specially selected.

Blue Ridge Mountains a range of the Appalachian Mountains in the eastern US, stretching from southern Pennsylvania to northern Georgia. Mount Mitchell is the highest peak, rising to a height of 2,037 m (6,684 ft).

blue rinse ▸ noun a preparation used as a rinse on grey or white hair so as to give it a temporary blue tint. ■ (also **blue-rinsed**) [as modifier] informal, derogatory relating to conservative elderly women: *the blue-rinse brigade*.

blue roan ▸ adjective denoting an animal's coat consisting of black-and-white hairs evenly mixed, giving it a blue-grey hue.
▸ noun an animal with such a coat.

blue rock ▸ noun (in pigeon-fancying) a pigeon showing the coloration of the wild rock dove.

blues ▸ plural noun **1** (often **the blues**) [treated as sing. or pl.] melancholic music of black American folk origin, typically in a twelve-bar sequence. It developed in the rural southern US towards the end of the 19th century, finding a wider audience in the 1940s, as blacks migrated to the cities. This urban blues gave rise to rhythm and blues and rock and roll. ■ [treated as sing.] a piece of such music: *a blues in C*.
2 (**the blues**) informal feelings of melancholy, sadness, or depression: *she's got the blues*.
– DERIVATIVES **bluesy** adjective (**bluesier**, **bluesiest**) (sense 1).
– ORIGIN mid 18th cent. (in sense 2): elliptically from *blue devils* 'depression or delirium tremens'.

Blues and Royals ▸ plural noun Brit. a regiment of the Household Cavalry.
– ORIGIN formed from the amalgamation (1969) of the Royal Horse Guards (also known as the *Blues*) and the *Royal* Dragoons.

blueschist /ˈbluːʃɪst/ ▸ noun [mass noun] a metamorphic rock with a blue colour, formed under conditions of high pressure and low temperature.

blue screen (also **green screen**) ▸ noun [often as modifier] (in film and video techniques such as chromakey) a blue (or green) background in front of which moving subjects are filmed and which allows a separately filmed background to be added to the final image: *a blue-screen effect*.

blue shark ▸ noun a long, slender shark with an indigo-blue back and white underparts, found typically in the open sea. ● *Prionace glauca*, family Carcharhinidae.

blue sheep ▸ noun another term for **BHARAL**.

blue shift ▸ noun [mass noun] Astronomy the displacement of the spectrum to shorter wavelengths in the light coming from distant celestial objects moving towards the observer. Compare with **RED SHIFT**.

blue-sky (also **blue-skies**) ▸ adjective [attrib.] informal creative or visionary and unconstrained by practicalities: *blue-sky thinking*.

bluesman ▸ noun (pl. **bluesmen**) a male performer of blues music: *archive footage of legendary bluesmen like Howlin' Wolf*.

blue state ▸ noun a US state that predominantly votes for or supports the Democratic Party. Compare with **RED STATE**.
– ORIGIN from the typical colour used to represent the Democratic Party on maps during elections.

bluestocking ▸ noun often derogatory an intellectual or literary woman: *an uptight bluestocking who likes to dress as a man and write feminist philosophy* | [as modifier] *bluestocking women*.
– ORIGIN late 17th cent.: originally used to describe a man wearing blue worsted (instead of formal black silk) stockings; extended to mean 'in informal dress'. Later the term denoted a person who attended the literary assemblies held (*c.*1750) by three London society ladies, where some of the men favoured less formal dress. The women who attended became known as *blue-stocking ladies* or *blue-stockingers*.

bluestone ▸ noun [mass noun] any of various bluish or grey building stones. ■ [count noun] any of the smaller stones made of dolerite found in the inner part of Stonehenge.

bluet /ˈbluːɪt/ ▸ noun a low-growing evergreen North American plant with milky-blue flowers. ● *Hedyotis* (or *Houstonia*) *caerulea*, family Rubiaceae.
– ORIGIN early 18th cent.: from French, diminutive of *bleu* 'blue'.

B

bluethroat ▸ noun a songbird resembling the robin, found in northern Eurasia and Alaska. The male has a blue throat with a red or white spot in the centre. • *Luscinia svecicus*, family Turdidae.

blue tit ▸ noun a small tit (songbird) with a blue cap, greenish-blue back, and yellow underparts, widespread in Eurasia and NW Africa. • *Parus caeruleus*, family Paridae.

bluetongue ▸ noun [mass noun] an insect-borne viral disease of sheep (transmissible with less serious effects to cattle and goats), characterized by fever, lameness, and a blue, swollen mouth and tongue.

Bluetooth ▸ noun [mass noun] trademark a standard for the short-range wireless interconnection of mobile phones, computers, and other electronic devices.
– ORIGIN 1990s: said to be named after King Harald *Bluetooth* (910–85), credited with uniting Denmark and Norway, as Bluetooth technology unifies the telecommunications and computing industries.

blue vinny /ˈvɪni/ (also **blue vinney**) ▸ noun [mass noun] a blue-mould skimmed-milk cheese from Dorset.
– ORIGIN mid 16th cent.: *vinny* from Old English *fyniğ* 'mouldy, musty'.

blue vitriol ▸ noun [mass noun] archaic crystalline copper sulphate.

blue water ▸ noun open sea: [as modifier] *blue-water navigation*.

blue whale ▸ noun a mottled bluish-grey rorqual which is the largest living animal and reaches lengths of up to 27 m (90 ft). • *Balaenoptera musculus*, family Balaenopteridae.

bluey ▸ adjective [often in combination] almost or partly blue: *bluey-green foliage*.
▸ noun (pl. **blueys**) Austral./NZ informal, dated **1** a bundle of possessions carried by a bushman. [because the outer covering was generally a blue blanket.]
2 a nickname for a red-headed person.

bluff[1] ▸ noun an attempt to deceive someone into believing that one can or is going to do something: *the offer was denounced as a bluff* | [mass noun] *his game of bluff*.
▸ verb [no obj.] try to deceive someone as to one's abilities or intentions: *he's been bluffing all along* | *they **bluffed their way** past the sentries* | [with obj.] *the object is to **bluff** your opponent **into** submission*.
■ (**bluff it out**) survive a difficult situation by maintaining a pretence.
– PHRASES **call someone's bluff 1** challenge someone to carry out a stated intention, in the expectation of being able to expose it as a pretence. **2** (in poker or brag) make an opponent show their hand in order to reveal that its value is weaker than their heavy betting suggests.
– DERIVATIVES **bluffer** noun.
– ORIGIN late 17th cent. (originally in the sense 'blindfold, hoodwink'): from Dutch *bluffen* 'brag', or *bluf* 'bragging'. The current sense (originally US, mid 19th cent.) originally referred to bluffing in the game of poker.

bluff[2] ▸ adjective direct in speech or behaviour but in a good-natured way: *a big, bluff, hearty man*.
– DERIVATIVES **bluffly** adverb, **bluffness** noun.
– ORIGIN early 18th cent. (in the sense 'surly, abrupt in manner'): figurative use of **BLUFF**[3]. The current positive connotation dates from the early 19th cent.

bluff[3] ▸ noun **1** a steep cliff, bank, or promontory.
2 Canadian a grove or clump of trees.
▸ adjective (of a cliff or a ship's bows) having a vertical or steep broad front.
– ORIGIN early 17th cent. (as an adjective, originally in nautical use): of unknown origin.

bluing (also **blueing**) ▸ noun [mass noun] **1** chiefly historical blue powder used to preserve the whiteness of laundry.
2 a greyish-blue finish on metal produced by heating.

bluish (also **blueish**) ▸ adjective having a blue tinge; slightly blue.

Blum /bluːm/, Léon (1872–1950), French statesman, Prime Minister 1936–7, 1938, 1946–7. As France's first socialist and Jewish Prime Minister, Blum introduced significant labour reforms.

Blumenbach /ˈbluːmənbɑːx/, Johann Friedrich (1752–1840), German physiologist and anatomist. He is regarded as the founder of physical anthropology, though his approach has since been much modified. He classified modern humans into five broad categories (Caucasian, Mongoloid, Malayan, Ethiopian, and American) based mainly on cranial measurements.

Blunden, Edmund (Charles) (1896–1974), English poet and critic. His poetry reveals his love of the English countryside, while his prose work *Undertones of War* (1928) deals with his experiences in the First World War.

blunder ▸ noun a stupid or careless mistake.
▸ verb [no obj.] make a stupid or careless mistake; act or speak clumsily: *he knew he'd blundered* | (as adj. **blundering**) *one's first blundering attempts*. ■ [no obj., with adverbial of direction] move clumsily or as if unable to see: *we were blundering around in the darkness*.
– DERIVATIVES **blunderer** noun, **blunderingly** adverb.
– ORIGIN Middle English: probably of Scandinavian origin and related to **BLIND**.

blunderbuss ▸ noun **1** historical a short large-bored gun firing balls or slugs.
2 an action or way of doing something regarded as lacking in subtlety and precision: *economists resort too quickly to the blunderbuss of regulation*.
– ORIGIN mid 17th cent.: alteration (by association with **BLUNDER**) of Dutch *donderbus*, literally 'thunder gun'.

blunge /blʌn(d)ʒ/ ▸ verb [with obj.] mix (clay or other materials) with water in a revolving apparatus, for use in ceramics.
– DERIVATIVES **blunger** noun.
– ORIGIN early 19th cent.: blend of **BLEND** and **PLUNGE**.

Blunt, Anthony (Frederick) (1907–83), British art historian, Foreign Office official, and Soviet spy. He confessed in 1965 that he had been a Soviet agent since the 1930s and had facilitated the escape of Guy Burgess and Donald Maclean. When these facts were made public in 1979 he was stripped of his knighthood.

blunt ▸ adjective **1** (of a cutting implement) not having a sharp edge or point: *a blunt knife*. ■ having a flat or rounded end: *the blunt tip of the leaf*.
2 (of a person or remark) uncompromisingly forthright: *a blunt statement of fact*.
▸ verb make or become less sharp: [with obj.] *wood can blunt your axe* | [no obj.] *the edge may blunt very rapidly*. ■ [with obj.] weaken or reduce the force of (something): *their determination had been blunted*.
▸ noun black slang a hollowed-out cigar filled with cannabis.
– DERIVATIVES **bluntly** adverb, **bluntness** noun.
– ORIGIN Middle English (in the sense 'dull, insensitive'): perhaps of Scandinavian origin and related to Old Norse *blunda* 'shut the eyes'.

blunt instrument ▸ noun a heavy object without a sharp edge or point, used as a weapon. ■ an imprecise or heavy-handed way of doing something: *as a promotional method direct mail is a blunt instrument*.

blur ▸ verb (**blurs, blurring, blurred**) make or become unclear or less distinct: [with obj.] *tears blurred her vision* | *his novels blur the boundaries between criticism and fiction* | [no obj.] *in front of him the page blurred*.
▸ noun a thing that cannot be seen or heard clearly: *the pale blur of her face* | *the words were a blur*.
■ something remembered or perceived indistinctly, typically because it happened very fast: *the day before was a blur*.
– DERIVATIVES **blurry** adjective (**blurrier, blurriest**).
– ORIGIN mid 16th cent. (in the sense 'smear that partially obscures something'): perhaps related to **BLEAR**.

Blu-ray ▸ noun [mass noun] a format of DVD designed for the storage of high-definition video and data.
– ORIGIN early 21st cent.: from *blu*, a respelling of **BLUE**[1] (from the colour of the laser used to read and write this type of DVD), + **RAY**[1].

blurb ▸ noun a short description of a book, film, or other product written for promotional purposes.
▸ verb [with obj.] informal, chiefly N. Amer. write or contribute a blurb for (a book, film, or other product).
– ORIGIN early 20th cent.: coined by Gelett Burgess (died 1951), American humorist.

blurred ▸ adjective unable to see or be seen clearly: *blurred vision* | *the camera caught only two blurred images*. ■ not clear or distinct; hazy: *the blurred distinctions between childhood and adulthood*.

blurt ▸ verb [with obj.] say (something) suddenly and without careful consideration: *she **blurted out** the truth* | [with direct speech] *'It wasn't my idea,' Gordon blurted*.
– ORIGIN late 16th cent.: probably imitative.

blush ▸ verb **1** [no obj.] show shyness, embarrassment, or shame by becoming red in the face: *she blushed at the unexpected compliment* | [with complement] *Kate felt herself blushing scarlet*. ■ feel embarrassed or ashamed: [with infinitive] *he blushed to think of how he'd paraded himself*.
2 (often as adj. **blushing**) literary be or become pink or pale red: *the trees are loaded with blushing blossoms*.
▸ noun **1** a reddening of the face as a sign of shyness, embarrassment, or shame: *he had brought a faint blush to her cheeks*.
2 a pink or pale red tinge: *the roses were white with a lovely pink blush*.
3 [mass noun] [often as modifier] a wine with a slight pink tint made in the manner of white wine but from red grape varieties: *blush Zinfandel*.
4 [mass noun] N. Amer. another term for **BLUSHER** (sense 1).
– PHRASES **at first blush** at the first glimpse or impression. **spare** (or **save**) **someone's blushes** refrain from causing someone embarrassment.
– DERIVATIVES **blushingly** adverb.
– ORIGIN Old English *blyscan*; related to modern Dutch *blozen*.

blusher ▸ noun **1** [mass noun] chiefly Brit. a cosmetic of a powder or cream consistency used to give a warm colour to the cheeks.
2 a toadstool with a buff cap bearing fluffy white spots and with white flesh that turns pink when bruised or cut, found in woodland in Eurasia and North America. • *Amanita rubescens*, family Amanitaceae, class Hymenomycetes.

bluster ▸ verb [no obj.] **1** talk in a loud, aggressive, or indignant way with little effect: *you threaten and bluster, but won't carry it through* | [with direct speech] *'I don't care what he says,' I blustered*.
2 (of a storm, wind, or rain) blow or beat fiercely and noisily: *a winter gale **blustered against** the sides of the house* | (as adj. **blustering**) *the blustering wind*.
▸ noun [mass noun] loud, aggressive, or indignant talk with little effect: *their threats contained a measure of bluster*.
– DERIVATIVES **blusterer** noun.
– ORIGIN late Middle English: ultimately imitative.

blustery ▸ adjective (of weather) characterized by strong winds: *a gusty, blustery day*. ■ (of a wind) blowing in strong gusts.

Blu-tack Brit. ▸ noun [mass noun] trademark a blue sticky material used to attach paper to walls.
▸ verb [with obj.] attach (something) using Blu-tack.

B-lymphocyte ▸ noun Physiology a lymphocyte not processed by the thymus gland, and responsible for producing antibodies. Also called **B-CELL**. Compare with **T-LYMPHOCYTE**.
– ORIGIN *B* for **BURSA**, referring to the organ in birds where it was first identified.

Blyton, Enid (1897–1968), English writer of children's fiction. Her best-known creation for young children is the character Noddy, who first appeared in 1949; her books for older children include the series of *Famous Five* and *Secret Seven* adventure stories.

BM ▸ abbreviation ■ Bachelor of Medicine. ■ British Museum.

BMA ▸ abbreviation British Medical Association.

BMI ▸ abbreviation body mass index.

B-movie ▸ noun a low-budget film of inferior quality made for use as a supporting feature in a cinema programme: [as modifier] *a B-movie actress*.

BMR ▸ abbreviation basal metabolic rate.

BMus ▸ abbreviation Bachelor of Music.

BMX ▸ noun [mass noun] [usu. as modifier] the organized racing of robust bicycles on a dirt-track or cross-country course: *BMX riders*.
– ORIGIN 1970s: from the initial letters of *bicycle motocross*, with *X* standing for *cross*.

Bn ▸ abbreviation ■ Baron. ■ Battalion.

bn ▸ abbreviation billion.

B'nai B'rith /bəˌneɪ bəˈriːθ, ˈbrɪθ/ a Jewish organization founded in New York in 1843, which pursues educational, humanitarian, and cultural activities and attempts to safeguard the rights and interests of Jews around the world.
– ORIGIN Hebrew, literally 'sons of the covenant'.

BNP ▸ abbreviation British National Party.

BO ▸ abbreviation informal body odour.

bo[1] ▸ exclamation another term for **BOO**[1].
– ORIGIN late Middle English: imitative.

bo[2] ▸ noun US informal used as a friendly form of address.
– ORIGIN early 19th cent.: perhaps an abbreviated form of **BOY**.

boa /ˈbəʊə/ ▸ noun **1** a constrictor snake which bears live young and may reach great size, native

to America, Africa, Asia, and some Pacific islands. ● Family Boidae, several genera and numerous species.
■ (in general use) any snake which is a constrictor.
2 a long, thin stole of feathers or fur worn around a woman's neck, typically as part of evening dress.
– ORIGIN late Middle English: from Latin (mentioned in the writings of Pliny), of unknown ultimate origin.

boab /ˈbəʊab/ ▸ **noun** Austral. another term for BAOBAB.

BOAC ▸ **abbreviation** historical British Overseas Airways Corporation.

boa constrictor ▸ **noun** a large snake, typically with bold markings, that kills by coiling around its prey and asphyxiating it, native to tropical America. ● *Boa constrictor*, family Boidae.

Boadicea /ˌbəʊdɪˈsiːə/ another name for BOUDICCA.

boak /ˈbəʊk/ ▸ **verb** variant spelling of BOKE.

boar ▸ **noun** (pl. **same** or **boars**) **1** (also **wild boar**) a tusked Eurasian wild pig from which domestic pigs are descended, exterminated in Britain in the 17th century. ● *Sus scrofa*, family Suidae.
■ [mass noun] the flesh of the wild boar as food.
2 an uncastrated domestic male pig.
3 the full-grown male of certain other animals, especially a badger, guinea pig, or hedgehog.
– ORIGIN Old English *bār*, of West Germanic origin; related to Dutch *beer* and German *Bär*.

board ▸ **noun 1** a long, thin, flat piece of wood or other hard material, used for floors or other building purposes: *loose boards creaked as I walked on them* | [mass noun] *sections of board*. ■ (**the boards**) informal the stage of a theatre. ■ (**the board**) Austral./NZ the part of the floor of a shearing shed where the shearers work. [late 19th cent.: originally boards running alongside the pens.]
2 a thin, flat piece of wood or other stiff material used for various purposes, in particular: ■ a vertical surface on which to write or pin notices. ■ a horizontal surface on which to cut things, play games, or perform other activities. ■ a flat insulating sheet used as a mounting for an electronic circuit: *a graphics board*. ■ the piece of equipment on which a person stands in surfing, skateboarding, snowboarding, and certain other sports. ■ (**boards**) pieces of thick stiff card used for book covers. ■ (**boards**) the structure, typically of wood surmounted with panels of glass, surrounding an ice-hockey rink. ■ (**boards**) Basketball informal term for BACKBOARD.
3 [treated as sing. or pl.] a group of people constituted as the decision-making body of an organization: *he sits on the board of directors* | [as modifier] *a board meeting*.
4 [mass noun] the provision of regular meals when one stays somewhere, in return for payment or services: *board and lodging*. ■ [count noun] archaic a table set for a meal.
5 Sailing a distance covered by a vessel in a single tack.
▸ **verb 1** [with obj.] get on or into (a ship, aircraft, or other vehicle): *we boarded the plane for Oslo* | [no obj.] *they would not be able to board without a ticket*. ■ (**be boarding**) (of an aircraft) be ready for passengers to get on: *Flight 172 to Istanbul is now boarding*.
2 [no obj.] live and receive regular meals in a house in return for payment or services: *the cousins boarded for a while with Ruby*. ■ (of a pupil) live in school during term time. ■ [with obj.] provide (a person or animal) with regular meals and somewhere to live in return for payment: *dogs may have to be boarded at kennels*.
3 [with obj.] (**board something up/over**) cover or seal a window or building with pieces of wood: *the shop was still boarded up*.
4 [no obj.] ride on a snowboard.
– PHRASES **go by the board** (of something planned or previously upheld) be abandoned, rejected, or ignored: *my education just went by the board*. [earlier in nautical use meaning 'fall overboard', used of a mast falling past the *board*, i.e. the side of the ship.] **on board** on or in a ship, aircraft, or other vehicle. ■ informal on to a team as a member: *the need to bring on board a young manager*. ■ informal (of a jockey) riding. **take something on board** informal fully consider or assimilate a new idea or situation: *we've got to take accusations of sexism on board*. **tread** (or **walk**) **the boards** informal appear on stage as an actor.
– ORIGIN Old English *bord*, of Germanic origin; related to Dutch *boord* and German *Bort*; reinforced in Middle English by Old French *bort* 'edge, ship's side' and Old Norse *borth* 'board, table'.

boarded ▸ **adjective** (of a floor, roof, or other structure) built with pieces of wood. ■ (of a window or building) covered or sealed with pieces of wood.

boarder ▸ **noun 1** a person who receives regular meals when staying somewhere, in return for payment or services. ■ a pupil who lives in school during term time.
2 a person who forces their way on to a ship in an attack.
3 a person who takes part in a sport using a board, such as surfing or snowboarding.

board foot ▸ **noun** (pl. **board feet**) a unit of volume for timber equal to 144 cu. inches.

board game ▸ **noun** a game that involves the movement of counters or other objects round a board.

boarding ▸ **noun** [mass noun] **1** long, flat, thin pieces of wood used to build or cover something.
2 the arrangement according to which pupils live in school during term time.
3 the action of getting on or into a ship, aircraft, or other vehicle.
4 Ice Hockey the illegal action of body-checking an opponent violently into the boards from behind.

boarding house ▸ **noun** a private house providing food and lodging for paying guests.

boarding kennel ▸ **noun** Brit. a place in which dogs are kept and looked after, especially while their owners are on holiday.

boarding pass (also **boarding card**) ▸ **noun** a pass for boarding an aircraft, given to passengers when checking in.

boarding school ▸ **noun** a school which provides accommodation and meals for the pupils during term time.

Board of Green Cloth ▸ **noun** full form of GREEN CLOTH.

Board of Trade ▸ **noun 1** North American term for CHAMBER OF COMMERCE. ■ (in full **Chicago Board of Trade**) the Chicago futures exchange.
2 a now nominal British government department within the Department of Trade and Industry concerned with commerce and industry.

boardroom ▸ **noun** a room in which a board of directors of a company or other organization meets regularly. ■ the directors of a company or organization considered collectively.

boardsailing ▸ **noun** another term for WINDSURFING.
– DERIVATIVES **boardsailor** noun.

board school ▸ **noun** historical an elementary school under the management of a School Board, established in Britain by the Education Act of 1870.

board shorts ▸ **plural noun** long shorts of a kind originally worn by surfers.

boardslide ▸ **noun** (in skateboarding and snowboarding) a manoeuvre in which the board slides along a rail, ledge, edge of a ramp, etc. on the flat part of its underside between the trucks.

boardwalk ▸ **noun** a wooden walkway across sand or marshy ground. ■ N. Amer. a promenade along a beach or waterfront, typically made of wood.

boarfish ▸ **noun** (pl. **same** or **boarfishes**) any of a number of deep-bodied fishes with a protruding snout, a small mouth, small toothed scales, and a spiny dorsal fin: ● a temperate marine fish occurring around southern Africa, the North Pacific, and Australasia (*Pentaceros richardsoni* and others in the family Pentacerotidae). ● a marine fish of the NE Atlantic (family Caproidae, in particular *Capros aper*).

boart ▸ **noun** variant spelling of BORT.

boast[1] ▸ **verb 1** [reporting verb] talk with excessive pride and self-satisfaction about one's achievements, possessions, or abilities: [no obj.] *she boasted about her many conquests* | [with clause] *he boasted that he had taken part in the crime* | [with direct speech] *Ted used to boast 'I manage ten people.'*
2 [with obj.] (of a person, place, or thing) possess (a feature that is a source of pride): *the hotel boasts high standards of comfort*.
▸ **noun** an act of talking with excessive pride and self-satisfaction: *I said I would win and it wasn't an idle boast*.
– DERIVATIVES **boaster** noun, **boastingly** adverb.
– ORIGIN Middle English (as a noun): of unknown origin.

boast[2] ▸ **noun** (in squash) a stroke in which the ball is made to hit one of the side walls before hitting the front wall.
– ORIGIN late 19th cent.: perhaps from French *bosse* denoting a rounded projection in the wall of a court for real tennis.

boastful ▸ **adjective** showing excessive pride and self-satisfaction in one's achievements, possessions, or abilities.
– DERIVATIVES **boastfully** adverb, **boastfulness** noun.

boat ▸ **noun** a small vessel for travelling over water, propelled by oars, sails, or an engine: *a fishing boat* | [as modifier] *a boat trip*. ■ a vessel of any size, especially a large one.
▸ **verb** [no obj.] travel in a boat for pleasure: *they boated through fjords*. ■ [with obj. and adverbial of direction] transport (someone or something) in a boat: *they boated the timber down the lake*. ■ [with obj.] (of an angler) draw (a hooked fish) into a boat.
– PHRASES **be in the same boat** informal be in the same difficult circumstances as others. **off the boat** informal, often offensive recently arrived from a foreign country, and by implication naive or an outsider: *what are you, fresh off the boat?* **push the boat out** Brit. informal be lavish in one's spending or celebrations. **rock the boat** informal say or do something to disturb an existing situation and upset people.
– DERIVATIVES **boatful** noun (pl. **boatfuls**).
– ORIGIN Old English *bāt*, of Germanic origin.

boatbill ▸ **noun 1** (also **boat-billed heron**) a small Central and South American heron with a broad flattened bill and a prominent black crest. ● *Cochlearius cochlearius*, family Ardeidae.
2 a flycatcher that has a very broad flattened bill with a hooked tip, found mainly in New Guinea. Also called FLATBILL FLYCATCHER. ● Genus *Machaerirhynchus*, family Monarchidae: two species.

boatbuilding ▸ **noun** [mass noun] the occupation or industry of building boats.
– DERIVATIVES **boatbuilder** noun.

boat deck ▸ **noun** the deck from which a ship's lifeboats are launched.

boatel /bəʊˈtɛl/ (also **botel**) ▸ **noun 1** a waterside hotel with facilities for mooring boats.
2 a ship moored at a wharf and used as a hotel.
– ORIGIN 1950s (originally US): blend of BOAT and HOTEL.

boater ▸ **noun 1** a flat-topped hardened straw hat with a brim. [so named because originally worn while boating.]
2 a person who uses or travels in a boat for pleasure.

boathook ▸ **noun** a long pole with a hook and a spike at one end, used for fending off or pulling a boat.

boathouse ▸ **noun** a shed at the edge of a river or lake used for housing boats.

boatie ▸ **noun** (pl. **boaties**) informal, chiefly Austral./NZ a boating enthusiast.

boating ▸ **noun** [mass noun] rowing or sailing in boats as a sport or form of recreation.

boatload ▸ **noun** an amount of cargo or number of passengers which will fill a ship or boat: ***a boatload of** coal*. ■ informal a large amount: *the Telecommunications Reform Act created **a boatload of** new regulations*.

boatman ▸ **noun** (pl. **boatmen**) a person who hires out boats or provides transport by boat.

boat neck ▸ **noun** a type of wide neckline on a garment that sits just below the collarbone.

boat people ▸ **plural noun** refugees who have left a country by sea, in particular the Vietnamese people who fled in small boats to Hong Kong, Australia, and elsewhere after the conquest of South Vietnam by North Vietnam in 1975.

boat race ▸ **noun 1** a race between rowing crews. ■ (**the Boat Race**) the annual boat race between Oxford and Cambridge. First rowed at Henley in 1829, it has been held over its present course, from Putney to Mortlake (6.8 km, 4.25 miles), since 1845.
2 Brit. rhyming slang a person's face.

boat shell ▸ **noun** North American term for SLIPPER LIMPET.

boatswain /ˈbəʊs(ə)n/ (also **bo'sun** or **bosun**) ▸ **noun** a ship's officer in charge of equipment and the crew.
– ORIGIN late Old English *bātswegen* (see BOAT, SWAIN).

boatswain's chair ▸ **noun** a seat suspended from ropes, used for work on the body or masts of a ship or the face of a building.

boat train ▸ **noun** a train scheduled to connect with the arrival or departure of a boat.

boatyard ▸ **noun** an enclosed area of land where boats are built or stored.

Boa Vista /ˌbəʊə ˈvɪstə/ a town in northern Brazil, capital of the state of Roraima; pop. 249,853 (2007).

B

B

Bob ▶ noun (in phrase **Bob's your uncle**) Brit. informal used to express the ease with which a task can be achieved: *fill in the form, and Bob's your uncle.*
– ORIGIN 1930s: pet form of the given name *Robert*.

bob¹ ▶ verb (**bobs**, **bobbing**, **bobbed**) [no obj., with adverbial of direction] make a quick, short movement up and down: *I could see his head bobbing about | the boat bobbed up and down.* ■ [with obj.] cause (something) to make such a movement: *she bobbed her head.* ■ [no obj., with adverbial of direction] make a sudden move so as to appear or disappear: *a lady bobbed up from beneath the counter.* ■ [no obj.] make a brief curtsy.
▶ noun a quick, short movement up and down: *she could only manage a slight bob of her head.* ■ a brief curtsy.
– PHRASES **bob and weave** make rapid bodily movements up and down and from side to side, for example as an evasive tactic by a boxer. **bob for apples** try to catch floating or hanging apples with one's mouth alone, as a game.
– ORIGIN late Middle English: of unknown origin.

bob² ▶ noun **1** a style in which the hair is cut short and evenly all round so that it hangs above the shoulders. **2** a weight on a pendulum, plumb line, or kite-tail. **3** a bobsleigh. **4** a short line at or towards the end of a stanza.
▶ verb (**bobs**, **bobbing**, **bobbed**) **1** [with obj.] (usu. as adj. **bobbed**) cut (someone's hair) in a bob. **2** [no obj.] ride on a bobsleigh.
– ORIGIN late Middle English (denoting a bunch or cluster): of unknown origin.

bob³ ▶ noun (pl. **same**) Brit. informal a shilling. ■ used with reference to a moderately large but unspecified amount of money: *those vases are worth a few bob.*
– ORIGIN late 18th cent.: of unknown origin.

bob⁴ ▶ noun a change of order in bell-ringing. ■ used in names of change-ringing methods: *plain bob.*
– ORIGIN late 17th cent.: perhaps connected with BOB¹ in the sense 'sudden movement up and down'.

boba /ˈbəʊbə/ ▶ noun another term for BUBBLE TEA.
– ORIGIN early 21st cent.: origin unknown.

bobber ▶ noun **1** a person who rides on a bobsleigh. **2** a float used in angling.

bobbin ▶ noun **1** a cylinder or cone holding thread, yarn, or wire, used especially in weaving and machine sewing. ■ a spool or reel. **2** a small bar attached to a string used for raising a door latch.
– ORIGIN mid 16th cent.: from French *bobine*, of unknown origin.

bobbinet /ˈbɒbɪnɛt/ ▶ noun [mass noun] machine-made cotton net (imitating bobbin lace).

bobbin lace ▶ noun [mass noun] lace made by hand with thread wound on bobbins.

bobble¹ ▶ noun a small ball made of strands of wool used as a decoration on a hat or on furnishings. ■ (**bobbles**) small plastic balls attached to a circular piece of elastic, used for fastening girls' hair.
– DERIVATIVES **bobbly** adjective.
– ORIGIN 1920s: diminutive of BOB².

bobble² /ˈbɒb(ə)l/ informal ▶ verb **1** [no obj.] move with a feeble or irregular bouncing motion: *some of those goals have bobbled in off the post.* **2** [with obj.] N. Amer. mishandle (a ball): *Andy bobbled the ball, so his throw home was too late.*
▶ noun **1** a feeble or irregular bouncing motion. **2** N. Amer. a mishandling of a ball.
– ORIGIN early 19th cent.: frequentative of BOB¹.

bobby ▶ noun (pl. **bobbies**) Brit. informal a police officer.
– ORIGIN mid 19th cent.: pet form of *Robert*, given name of Sir Robert PEEL.

bobby calf ▶ noun an unweaned calf slaughtered for veal.
– ORIGIN 1920s: perhaps from BOB², *bobby calf* being one of a number of collocations where *bobby* has the sense 'small, short'. Compare with the dialect term *staggering bob* for a very young calf or its meat, recorded from the late 18th cent., perhaps from the pet form of *Robert*.

bobby-dazzler ▶ noun Brit. informal, dated a person or thing considered remarkable or excellent.
– ORIGIN mid 19th cent. (originally northern English dialect): related to DAZZLE; the origin of the first element is unknown.

bobby pin ▶ noun N. Amer. & Austral./NZ a kind of sprung hairpin or small clip.
▶ verb (**bobby-pin**) [with obj.] fix (hair) in place with a bobby pin.
– ORIGIN 1930s: from BOB² (because bobby pins were originally used with bobbed hair) + -Y².

bobby socks (also **bobby sox**) ▶ plural noun N. Amer. short socks reaching just above the ankle, as worn by teenage girls in the 1940s and 1950s.
– ORIGIN compare with BOB² in the sense 'cut short'.

bobby-soxer ▶ noun N. Amer. informal, dated a teenage girl.

bobcat ▶ noun a small North American lynx with a barred and spotted coat and a short tail. ● *Felis rufus*, family Felidae.
– ORIGIN late 19th cent.: from BOB² (with reference to its short tail) + CAT¹.

Bobo /ˈbəʊbəʊ/ ▶ noun (pl. **Bobos**) informal a person having both the values of the counterculture of the 1960s and the materialism of the 1980s; a bourgeois Bohemian.
– ORIGIN 1990s: abbreviation.

bobolink /ˈbɒbəlɪŋk/ ▶ noun a North American songbird of the American blackbird family, with a finch-like bill. The male has black, buff, and white plumage. ● *Dolichonyx oryzivorus*, family Icteridae.
– ORIGIN late 18th cent. (originally *Bob o'Lincoln*, *Bob Lincoln*): imitative of its call.

bobotie /bəˈbuːti, -ˈbʊəti/ ▶ noun [mass noun] a South African dish of curried minced meat baked with a rich savoury custard.
– ORIGIN Afrikaans, probably of Malay or Javanese origin.

Bobruisk /baˈbrujsk/ (also **Bobruysk**) Russian name for BABRUISK.

bobskate ▶ noun Canadian an adjustable skate for a child, consisting of two sections of double runners.

bobsled ▶ noun North American term for BOBSLEIGH.
– DERIVATIVES **bobsledding** noun.

bobsleigh ▶ noun Brit. a mechanically steered and braked sledge, typically for two or four people, used for racing down an ice-covered run.
– DERIVATIVES **bobsleighing** noun.
– ORIGIN mid 19th cent. (originally US, denoting a sleigh made of two short sleighs coupled together and used for hauling logs): from BOB² in the sense 'short' + SLEIGH.

bobstay ▶ noun a rope used to hold down the bowsprit of a ship and keep it steady.
– ORIGIN mid 18th cent.: probably from BOB¹ + STAY².

bobsy-die /ˌbɒbzɪˈdʌɪ/ ▶ noun [mass noun] dialect & NZ a great deal of fuss or trouble: *she'll kick up bobsy-die later.*
– ORIGIN early 19th cent.: contraction of earlier *Bob's-a-dying*.

bobtail ▶ noun a docked tail of a horse or dog.
– ORIGIN mid 16th cent.: probably from BOB² + TAIL¹. It was originally recorded as a humorous term for a kind of broad-headed arrow, probably because it looked as though it had been cut short.

bob weight ▶ noun a component used as a counterweight to a moving part in a machine.

bobwhite (also **bobwhite quail**) ▶ noun a New World quail with mottled reddish-brown plumage, and typically a pale throat and eyestripe. ● Genus *Colinus*, family Phasianidae: two species, in particular the **northern bobwhite** (*C. virginianus*).
– ORIGIN early 19th cent.: imitative of its call.

bocage /bəˈkɑːʒ/ ▶ noun [mass noun] **1** (in France) pastureland divided into small hedged fields interspersed with groves of trees. **2** the modelling of leaves, flowers, and plants in clay, especially for porcelain figurines.
– ORIGIN late 16th cent.: from French, from Old French *boscage* (see BOSCAGE).

Boccaccio /bəˈkatʃɪəʊ/, Giovanni (1313–75), Italian writer, poet, and humanist. He is most famous for the *Decameron* (1348–58), a collection of a hundred tales told by ten young people who have moved to the country to escape the Black Death.

bocce /ˈbɒtʃeɪ, ˈbɒtʃi/ (also **boccia** /ˈbɒtʃə/) ▶ noun [mass noun] an Italian game similar to bowls but played on a shorter, narrower green.
– ORIGIN Italian, 'bowls', plural of *boccia* 'ball'.

Boccherini /ˌbɒkəˈriːni/, Luigi (1743–1805), Italian composer and cellist, known chiefly for his cello concertos and sonatas.

bocconcini /ˌbɒkɒnˈtʃiːni/ ▶ plural noun small balls of mozzarella cheese.
– ORIGIN Italian.

Boche /bɒʃ/ informal, dated ▶ noun a German, especially a soldier. ■ (**the Boche**) Germans, especially German soldiers, considered collectively.
▶ adjective German.
– ORIGIN French soldiers' slang, originally in the sense 'rascal', later used in the First World War meaning 'German'.

Bochum /ˈbəʊxʊm/, German /ˈboːxʊm/ an industrial city in the Ruhr valley, North Rhine-Westphalia, Germany; pop. 383,700 (est. 2006).

bock ▶ noun [mass noun] a strong, dark German beer.
– ORIGIN mid 19th cent.: via French from an abbreviation of German *Eimbockbier* 'beer from *Einbeck*', a town in Lower Saxony, Germany.

bockety /ˈbɒkɪti/ ▶ adjective Irish unsteady; wobbly: *the bockety wheelchair trundled off down the street.*
– ORIGIN late 19th cent.: from Irish *bacach* 'lame'.

BOD ▶ abbreviation biochemical oxygen demand.

bod ▶ noun informal a body: *a line-up of stunning bods.* ■ chiefly Brit. a person: *some clever bod wrote a song about them.*

bodach /ˈbəʊdaːx/ ▶ noun Scottish & Irish **1** a man, especially a peasant or an old man. **2** a ghost; a spectre.
– ORIGIN early 19th cent. (earlier as *buddough*): from Scottish Gaelic.

bodacious /bəʊˈdeɪʃəs/ ▶ adjective N. Amer. informal excellent, admirable, or attractive: *bodacious babes.* ■ US audacious in a way considered admirable.
– ORIGIN mid 19th cent.: perhaps a variant of SW dialect *boldacious*, blend of BOLD and AUDACIOUS.

bode ▶ verb [no obj.] (**bode well/ill**) be a portent of a particular outcome: *their argument did not bode well for the future* | [with obj.] *the 12 per cent interest rate bodes dark days ahead for retailers.*
– ORIGIN Old English *bodian* 'proclaim, foretell', from *boda* 'messenger', of Germanic origin; related to German *Bote*, also to BID¹.

bodega /bəˈdeɪɡə/ ▶ noun a cellar or shop selling wine and food, especially in a Spanish-speaking country or area.
– ORIGIN mid 19th cent.: from Spanish, via Latin from Greek *apothēkē* 'storehouse'. Compare with BOUTIQUE.

Bodensee /ˈboːdn̩ˌzeː/ German name for Lake Constance (see CONSTANCE, LAKE).

bodge ▶ verb [with obj.] Brit. informal make or repair (something) badly or clumsily: *the door was bodged together from old planks.*
– ORIGIN mid 16th cent.: alteration of BOTCH.

bodger informal ▶ noun Brit. a person who makes or repairs something badly or clumsily.
▶ adjective Austral. another term for BODGIE.

bodgie Austral./NZ informal ▶ noun (pl. **bodgies**) a youth, especially of the 1950s, analogous to the British Teddy boy.
▶ adjective (also **bodgy**) worthless or inferior; false: *a bodgie second-hand car with bodgie number plates.*
– ORIGIN probably from BODGER, a term said to have arisen as a result of the post-war black market trade in cloth in Sydney: when inferior cloth was passed off as American-made, it was called *bodgie*, extended to denote any young man who adopted an American accent and manner.

Bodhgaya /ˌbɒdɡəˈjɑː, ˌbəʊd-/ (also **Bodh Gaya**, **Buddh Gaya**) a village in the state of Bihar, NE India, where the Buddha attained enlightenment.

bodhisattva /ˌbɒdɪˈsɑːtvə/ ▶ noun (in Mahayana Buddhism) a person who is able to reach nirvana but delays doing so through compassion for suffering beings.
– ORIGIN Sanskrit, 'a person whose essence is perfect knowledge', from *bodhi* 'perfect knowledge' (from *budh-* 'know perfectly') + *sattva* 'being, essence'.

bodhi tree ▶ noun variant spelling of BO TREE.

bodhrán /ˈbaʊrɑːn, baʊˈrɑːn/ ▶ noun a shallow one-sided Irish drum typically played using a short stick with knobbed ends.
– ORIGIN Irish.

bodice ▶ noun the part of a woman's dress (excluding the sleeves) which is above the waist. ■ a woman's sleeveless undergarment, often laced at the front.
– ORIGIN mid 16th cent. (originally *bodies*): plural of BODY, retaining the original pronunciation. The term probably first denoted an undergarment, then known as a *pair of bodice*, although this sense is not recorded until the early 17th cent.

bodice-ripper ▶ noun informal or humorous a sexually explicit romantic novel or film with a historical setting.
– DERIVATIVES **bodice-ripping** adjective.

bodiless ▸ adjective lacking a body: *a bodiless head.* ▪ having no material form or being; incorporeal: *a sinister, bodiless voice.*

bodily ▸ adjective [attrib.] of or concerning the body: *children learn to control their bodily functions.* ▪ material or actual as opposed to spiritual or incorporeal: *God is not present in bodily form.*
▸ adverb **1** by moving a person's or one's own body with force: *he hauled her bodily from the van.*
2 in one mass; as a whole.

bodkin ▸ noun **1** a thick, blunt needle with a large eye, used for drawing tape or cord through a hem. ▪ historical a long pin used for fastening up the hair.
2 Printing a pointed tool used for removing pieces of metal type for correction.
3 archaic a dagger.
– ORIGIN Middle English: perhaps of Celtic origin and related to Irish *bod*, Welsh *bidog*, Scottish Gaelic *biodag* 'dagger'.

Bodleian Library /'bɒdlɪən/ the library of Oxford University, one of six copyright libraries in the UK.

Bodley, Sir Thomas (1545–1613), English scholar and diplomat. He refounded and greatly enlarged the Oxford University library, which was renamed the Bodleian in 1604. ▪ an informal name for the Bodleian Library.

Bodoni /bə'dəʊni/, Giambattista (1740–1813), Italian printer. He designed a typeface characterized by extreme contrast between uprights and diagonals, which is named after him.

Bodrum /'bɒdrəm/ a resort town on the Aegean coast of western Turkey, site of the ancient city of Halicarnassus.

body ▸ noun (pl. **bodies**) **1** the physical structure, including the bones, flesh, and organs, of a person or an animal: *it's important to keep your body in good condition.* ▪ the trunk apart from the head and the limbs: *the blow almost severed his head from his body.* ▪ a corpse: *they found his body washed up on the beach.* ▪ [mass noun] the physical and mortal aspect of a person as opposed to the soul or spirit: *we're together in body and spirit.* ▪ informal a person's body regarded as an object of sexual desire: *he was just after her body.* ▪ informal, dated a person of a specified type: *a motherly body.*
2 (**the body of**) the main or central part of something, especially a building or text: *the main body of the house was built in 1625.* ▪ the main section of a motor vehicle or aircraft: *the body of the aircraft was filled with smoke.*
3 a large amount or collection of something: *a rich **body of** Canadian folklore | large **bodies of** seawater.*
4 an organized group of people with a common purpose or function: *a regulatory body | international bodies of experts.*
5 [often with adj.] technical a material object: *the path taken by the falling body.*
6 [mass noun] a full or substantial quality of flavour in wine. ▪ fullness or thickness of a person's hair: *restructuring formulations help to add body.*
7 Brit. a woman's close-fitting stretch garment for the upper body, fastening at the crotch.
8 (in pottery) a clay used for making the main part of ceramic ware, as distinct from a glaze.
▸ verb (**bodies, bodying, bodied**) [with obj.] **1** (**body something forth**) formal give material form to something abstract: *he bodied forth the traditional Prussian remedy for all ills.*
2 build the bodywork of (a motor vehicle).
– PHRASES **body and soul** involving every aspect of a person; completely: *the company owned them body and soul.* **in a body** all together; as a group: *they departed in a body.* **keep body and soul together** stay alive, especially in difficult circumstances. **over my dead body** informal used to emphasize that one completely opposes something: *she moves into our home over my dead body.*
– DERIVATIVES **bodied** adjective [in combination] *a wide-bodied jet.*
– ORIGIN Old English *bodig*, of unknown origin.

body armour ▸ noun [mass noun] clothing worn by army and police personnel to protect against gunfire.

body art ▸ noun [mass noun] **1** tattoos or jewellery ornamenting the body and regarded as art. ▪ the practice of decorating the body by means of tattooing, piercing, etc.
2 an artistic genre, originating in the 1970s, in which the actual body of the artist or model is integral to the work.

body bag ▸ noun a bag used for carrying a corpse from a battlefield or the scene of an accident or crime.

body blow ▸ noun a heavy punch to the body. ▪ something that causes problems or severe disappointment; a setback: *a tax on books would be a body blow for education.*

bodyboard ▸ noun a short, light type of surfboard ridden in a prone position.
– DERIVATIVES **bodyboarder** noun, **bodyboarding** noun.

bodybuilder ▸ noun **1** a person who strengthens and enlarges the muscles of their body through strenuous exercise.
2 a person or company that builds the bodies of vehicles.
– DERIVATIVES **bodybuilding** noun.

body-centred ▸ adjective denoting a crystal structure in which there is an atom at each vertex and at the centre of the unit cell.

body check ▸ noun (especially in ice hockey) an attempt to obstruct a player by bumping into them, typically with the shoulder or hip.
▸ verb (**body-check**) [with obj.] obstruct (a player) in such a way.

body clock ▸ noun a person's or animal's biological clock.

body colour ▸ noun [mass noun] opaque pigment used in painting, especially gouache.

body-con ▸ adjective relating to or denoting a very tight-fitting style of clothing: *fab though the body-con trend is, I can't give up on smocks just yet.*
– ORIGIN 1990s: shortening of *body-conscious*.

body corporate ▸ noun formal term for CORPORATION.

body double ▸ noun a stand-in for a film actor used during stunt or nude scenes.

body dysmorphic disorder ▸ noun [mass noun] a psychological disorder in which a person becomes obsessed with imaginary defects in their appearance.

body English ▸ noun [mass noun] N. Amer. **1** follow-through movement after throwing or hitting a ball.
2 another term for BODY LANGUAGE.

bodyguard ▸ noun a person or group of people employed to escort and protect an important or famous person.

body language ▸ noun [mass noun] the conscious and unconscious movements and postures by which attitudes and feelings are communicated: *his intent was clearly expressed in his body language.*

bodyline ▸ noun [mass noun] Cricket, historical persistent short-pitched fast bowling on the leg side, threatening the batsman's body, especially as employed by England in the Ashes series in Australia in 1932–3.

body louse ▸ noun a louse which infests the human body and is especially prevalent where hygiene is poor. It is able to transmit several diseases through its bite, including typhus. ● *Pediculus humanus humanus*, family Pediculidae, order Anoplura. See also HEAD LOUSE.

body man ▸ noun N. Amer. informal a political leader's personal aide or assistant.

body mass index (abbrev.: **BMI**) ▸ noun (pl. **body mass indices**) an approximate measure of whether someone is over- or underweight, calculated by dividing their weight in kilograms by the square of their height in metres.

body odour ▸ noun [mass noun] the unpleasant smell of a person's unwashed body.

body piercing ▸ noun [mass noun] the piercing of holes in parts of the body other than the ear lobes in order to insert rings or other decorative objects.

body politic ▸ noun (usu. **the body politic**) the people of a nation, state, or society considered collectively as an organized group of citizens.

body-popping ▸ noun [mass noun] a kind of street dancing characterized by jerky robotic movements of the joints.

body press ▸ noun Wrestling a move in which a wrestler uses their body weight to pin an opponent to the floor.

body scrub ▸ noun an exfoliating cosmetic preparation applied to the body to cleanse the skin. ▪ a type of beauty treatment in which the skin is cleansed and exfoliated.

body search ▸ noun a search of a person's body and clothing for illicit weapons, drugs, or other articles, conducted typically by customs officials or the police.

bodyshell ▸ noun the metal frame of a motor or railway vehicle, to which the metal panels are attached.

body shop ▸ noun chiefly N. Amer. a garage where repairs to the bodywork of vehicles are carried out.

bodyside ▸ noun the side of the body of a vehicle.

body slam ▸ noun Wrestling a move (illegal in some codes) in which the opponent's body is lifted and then thrown hard on to the floor.

bodysnatcher ▸ noun historical a person who illicitly disinterred corpses for dissection, for which there was no legal provision until 1832.
– DERIVATIVES **bodysnatching** noun.

body stocking ▸ noun a woman's one-piece undergarment which covers the torso and legs.

bodysuit ▸ noun a close-fitting one-piece stretch garment for women, worn typically for sporting activities.

bodysurf ▸ verb [no obj.] (often as noun **bodysurfing**) float on the crest of incoming waves without using a board.
– DERIVATIVES **bodysurfer** noun.

body swerve ▸ noun an abrupt swerving movement of the whole body, used as a tactic to avoid contact or collision.

body text ▸ noun (usu. **the body text**) the main part of a printed text, excluding items such as headings and footnotes.

body warmer ▸ noun a sleeveless quilted or padded jacket worn as an outdoor garment.

body wave ▸ noun a soft, light permanent wave designed to give the hair fullness.

bodywork ▸ noun [mass noun] **1** the metal outer shell of a vehicle.
2 therapies and techniques in complementary medicine which involve touching or manipulating the body.
– DERIVATIVES **bodyworker** noun (sense 2).

body wrap ▸ noun a type of beauty treatment intended to result in a reduction in body measurements, involving the application of skin-cleansing ingredients to the body, which is then wrapped in hot bandages.

Boeing /'bəʊɪŋ/, William Edward (1881–1956), US industrialist. In 1927 he founded United Aircraft and Transport, which in 1934 was divided into Boeing Aircraft, United Aircraft, and United Airlines.

Boeotia /bɪ'əʊʃə/ a department of central Greece, to the north of the Gulf of Corinth, and a region of ancient Greece of which the chief city was Thebes.
– DERIVATIVES **Boeotian** adjective & noun.

Boer /bɔː, 'bəʊə, bʊə/ chiefly historical ▸ noun **1** a member of the Dutch and Huguenot population which settled in southern Africa in the late 17th century. The Boers' present-day descendants are the Afrikaners.
2 (**boer**) S. African an Afrikaner farmer.
3 (**boer**) S. African informal (under apartheid) a member of the police, prison service, or security forces.
▸ adjective relating to the Boers.
– ORIGIN from Dutch *boer* 'farmer'.

boerboel /'bʊəbʊl/ (also **boerbull**) ▸ noun S. African a large cross-breed dog bred from the mastiff and indigenous African dogs.
– ORIGIN 1960s: Afrikaans, from *boer* (commonly applied to indigenous plants and animals) + *boel*, from Dutch *bul* (as in *bulhond* 'mastiff').

boeremusiek /'bʊərə,mjuːsɪk/ ▸ noun [mass noun] S. African traditional Afrikaner music, often for dancing.
– ORIGIN Afrikaans, from *boere* 'Afrikaner' + *musiek* 'music'.

boerewors /'buːrə,vɔːs, 'bʊ-/ ▸ noun [mass noun] S. African a type of traditional sausage, typically containing coarsely ground beef and pork seasoned with spices.
– ORIGIN Afrikaans, from *boere* 'Afrikaner or farmer's' + *wors* 'sausage'.

boer goat ▸ noun a goat of a hardy breed, originally from South Africa.
– ORIGIN from Afrikaans *boer* 'farmer' + GOAT.

boerie /'bʊri/ ▸ noun S. African informal another term for BOEREWORS.

Boer Wars two wars fought by Great Britain in southern Africa between 1880 and 1902.

The first war (1880–1) began with the revolt of the Boer settlers in Transvaal against British rule and ended with the establishment of an independent Boer Republic under British suzerainty. The second (1899–1902) was caused by the Boer refusal to grant equal rights to recent British immigrants and by the imperialist ambitions of Cecil Rhodes. The British eventually won through superior numbers and the employment of concentration camps to control the countryside.

B

Boethius /bəʊ'iːθɪəs/, Anicius Manlius Severinus (*c.*480–524), Roman statesman and philosopher, best known for *The Consolation of Philosophy*, which he wrote while in prison on a charge of treason.

boeuf bourguignon /ˌbəːf 'bɔːgɪnjɒ̃/ ▶ **noun** [mass noun] a dish consisting of beef stewed in red wine.
– ORIGIN French, literally 'Burgundy beef'.

boff[1] N. Amer. informal ▶ **verb** [with obj.] **1** have sexual intercourse with (someone).
2 hit (someone).
▶ **noun 1** an act of sexual intercourse.
2 a blow or punch.
– ORIGIN 1920s (in the sense 'a blow or punch'): imitative.

boff[2] ▶ **noun** short for BOFFIN.

boffin ▶ **noun** Brit. informal a person engaged in scientific or technical research: *the boffins at the Telecommunications Research Establishment.* ■ a person with knowledge or a skill considered to be complex or arcane: *a computer boffin.*
– DERIVATIVES **boffiny** adjective.
– ORIGIN Second World War: of unknown origin.

boffo N. Amer. informal ▶ **adjective 1** (of a theatrical production or film, or a review of one) very successful or wholeheartedly commendatory: *a boffo box office certainty.*
2 (of a laugh) deep and unrestrained. ■ boisterously funny.
▶ **noun** (pl. **boffos**) a success.
– ORIGIN 1940s: from US *boff* 'roaring success' + **-o**.

boffola /bɒ'fəʊlə/ N. Amer. informal ▶ **noun** a joke or a line in a script intended to get a laugh.
▶ **adjective** (of a laugh) hearty and unrestrained.
– ORIGIN 1940s: extension of slang *boff* 'hearty laugh'.

Bofors gun /'bəʊfəz/ ▶ **noun** a type of light anti-aircraft gun.
– ORIGIN 1930s: named after *Bofors* in Sweden, where it was first manufactured.

bog ▶ **noun 1** an area of wet muddy ground that is too soft to support a heavy body: *a peat bog* | figurative *a bog of legal complications* | [mass noun] *the island is a wilderness of bog and loch.* ■ Ecology wetland with acid peaty soil, typically dominated by peat moss. Compare with FEN[1].
2 (**the bog**) Brit. informal the toilet.
▶ **verb** (**bogs**, **bogging**, **bogged**) **1** (**be/get bogged down**) be or become stuck in mud or wet ground: *the family Rover became bogged down on the beach road.* ■ be prevented from making progress in a task or activity: *you must not* **get bogged down in** *detail.*
2 [no obj.] (**bog off**) Brit. informal go away.
3 [no obj.] (**bog in**) Austral./NZ start a task enthusiastically: *if he saw a trucker in difficulty, he would just bog in and give a hand.* [early 20th cent.: *bog* probably in the sense 'sink, immerse (oneself)'.]
– ORIGIN Middle English: from Irish or Scottish Gaelic *bogach*, from *bog* 'soft'.

bogan[1] /'bəʊg(ə)n/ ▶ **noun** Austral./NZ informal **1** a boringly conventional or old-fashioned person.
2 an uncouth or uncultured person.
– ORIGIN of unknown origin.

bogan[2] /'bəʊg(ə)n/ ▶ **noun** Canadian a side stream.
– ORIGIN Algonquian.

Bogarde /'bəʊgɑːd/, Sir Dirk (1921–99), British actor and writer, of Dutch descent; born *Derek Niven van den Bogaerde*. He became famous in the 'Doctor' series of comedy films, and played more serious roles in films such as *The Servant* (1963) and *Death in Venice* (1971).

Bogart /'bəʊgɑːt/, Humphrey (DeForest) (1899–1957), American actor. His many films include *Casablanca* (1942), *The Big Sleep* (1946, in which he played opposite his fourth wife Lauren Bacall), and *The African Queen* (1951, for which he won an Oscar).

bogart /'bəʊgɑːt/ ▶ **verb** [with obj.] informal, chiefly US selfishly appropriate or keep (something, especially a cannabis cigarette): *don't bogart that joint, my friend.*
– ORIGIN 1960s: from Humphrey BOGART, who often smoked in films.

bog arum ▶ **noun** a plant of the arum family, with heart-shaped leaves, a white spathe, and a green spadix. It grows in swamps and boggy ground in north temperate regions. Also called CALLA or WATER CALLA. ● *Calla palustris*, family Araceae.

bog asphodel ▶ **noun** a yellow-flowered European marsh plant of the lily family. ● *Narthecium ossifragum*, family Liliaceae.

bogbean ▶ **noun** a plant of bogs and shallow water which has creeping rhizomes, bean-like three-lobed leaves, and hairy white or pinkish flowers. Also called BUCKBEAN. ● *Menyanthes trifoliata*, family Menyanthaceae.

bog cotton ▶ **noun** another term for COTTON GRASS.

bogey[1] Golf ▶ **noun** (pl. **bogeys**) a score of one stroke over par at a hole. ■ old-fashioned term for PAR[1] (sense 1 of the noun).
▶ **verb** (**bogeys**, **bogeying**, **bogeyed**) [with obj.] play (a hole) in one stroke over par.
– ORIGIN late 19th cent.: perhaps from *Bogey*, denoting the Devil (see BOGEY[2]), regarded as an imaginary player.

bogey[2] (also **bogy**) ▶ **noun** (pl. **bogeys**) **1** an evil or mischievous spirit. ■ a person or thing that causes fear or alarm: *the bogey of recession.* ■ US military slang an enemy aircraft.
2 Brit. informal a piece of nasal mucus.
– ORIGIN mid 19th cent. (as a proper name applied to the Devil): of unknown origin; probably related to BOGLE.

bogey[3] ▶ **noun** Austral. informal an act of swimming or bathing.
– ORIGIN mid 19th cent.: from Dharuk *bu-gi* 'to swim'.

bogeyman (also **bogyman**) ▶ **noun** (pl. **bogeymen**) an imaginary evil spirit, used to frighten children. ■ a person or thing that is widely regarded as an object of fear: *nuclear power is the environmentalists' bogeyman.*

bog garden ▶ **noun** a piece of land laid out and irrigated to grow plants which prefer a damp habitat.

boggart /'bɒgət/ ▶ **noun** Scottish & N. English an evil or mischievous spirit.
– ORIGIN late 16th cent.: related to obsolete *bog* 'bugbear', BOGGLE, and BOGLE.

boggle ▶ **verb** [no obj.] informal (of a person or their mind) be astonished or baffled when trying to imagine something: ***the mind boggles*** *at the spectacle.* ■ [with obj.] cause (a person or their mind) to be astonished: *the inflated salary of a star boggles the mind.* ■ (**boggle at**) (of a person) hesitate to do or accept: *you never boggle at plain speaking.*
– ORIGIN late 16th cent.: probably of dialect origin and related to BOGLE and BOGEY[2].

boggy ▶ **adjective** (**boggier**, **boggiest**) too wet and muddy to be easily walked on; marshy: *the shrub grows naturally in boggy ground.*
– DERIVATIVES **bogginess** noun.

bogie /'bəʊgi/ ▶ **noun** (pl. **bogies**) chiefly Brit. an undercarriage with four or six wheels pivoted beneath the end of a railway vehicle. ■ Indian a railway carriage. ■ chiefly N. English a low truck on four small wheels; a trolley.
– ORIGIN early 19th cent. (originally in northern English dialect use): of unknown origin.

bog iron (also **bog iron ore**) ▶ **noun** [mass noun] an impure porous form of limonite deposited in bogs.

bogland ▶ **noun** [mass noun] marshy land.

bogle /'bəʊg(ə)l/ ▶ **noun** a phantom or goblin. ■ Scottish & N. English a scarecrow.
– ORIGIN early 16th cent.: of unknown origin; probably related to BOGEY[2].

bogman ▶ **noun** (pl. **bogmen**) Irish derogatory a person from a rural area.

bog moss ▶ **noun** another term for PEAT MOSS (sense 1).

bog myrtle ▶ **noun** a deciduous shrub of boggy places, with short upright catkins and aromatic grey-green leaves with insecticidal properties. Also called SWEET GALE. ● *Myrica gale*, family Myricaceae.

bog oak ▶ **noun** an ancient oak tree which has been preserved in peat, with hard black wood.

BOGOF /'bɒgɒf/ ▶ **abbreviation** buy one, get one free.

Bogomil /'bəʊgəmɪl, 'bɒg-/ ▶ **noun** historical a member of a heretical medieval Balkan sect professing a modified form of Manichaeism.
– DERIVATIVES **Bogomilism** noun.
– ORIGIN mid 19th cent.: from medieval Greek *Bogomilos*, from *Bogomil*, literally 'beloved of God', the name of the person who first disseminated the heresy, from Old Church Slavonic.

bogong /'bəʊgɒŋ/ (also **bogong moth**) ▶ **noun** a large brown moth of southern Australia, formerly eaten by Aborigines. ● *Agrotis infusa*, family Noctuidae.
– ORIGIN mid 19th cent.: from Ngayawung (an Aboriginal language).

Bogotá /ˌbɒgə'tɑː/ the capital of Colombia, situated in the eastern Andes at about 2,610 m (8,560 ft); pop. 6,778,691 (2005). It was founded by the Spanish in 1538 on the site of a pre-Columbian centre of the Chibcha culture. Official name SANTA FÉ DE BOGOTÁ.

bog rosemary ▶ **noun** a pink-flowered evergreen dwarf shrub, which grows in boggy soils in north temperate regions. Also called ANDROMEDA. ● Genus *Andromeda*, family Ericaceae: two species, in particular the common *A. polifolia*.

bog spavin ▶ **noun** a soft swelling of the joint capsule of the hock of horses, which most commonly occurs in young, fast-growing horses.

bog-standard ▶ **adjective** Brit. informal, derogatory ordinary or basic: *a bog-standard PC.*

bogtrotter ▶ **noun** informal, offensive an Irish person.

bogus /'bəʊgəs/ ▶ **adjective** not genuine or true (used in a disapproving manner when deception has been attempted): *a bogus insurance claim.*
– DERIVATIVES **bogusly** adverb, **bogusness** noun.
– ORIGIN late 18th cent. (originally US, denoting a machine for making counterfeit money): of unknown origin.

bogy ▶ **noun** (pl. **bogies**) variant spelling of BOGEY[2].

bogyman ▶ **noun** variant spelling of BOGEYMAN.

Bo Hai /bəʊ 'hʌɪ/ (also **Po Hai**) a large inlet of the Yellow Sea, on the coast of eastern China. Also called CHIHLI, GULF OF.

bohea /bəʊ'hiː/ ▶ **noun** [mass noun] a black China tea that comes from the last crop of the season and is usually regarded as of low quality.
– ORIGIN early 18th cent.: named after the *Bu-yi* (*Wuyi*) hills in China, from where black tea first came to Britain.

Bohemia /bəʊ'hiːmɪə/ a region forming the western part of the Czech Republic. Formerly a Slavic kingdom, it became a province of the newly formed Czechoslovakia by the Treaty of Versailles in 1919.

Bohemian ▶ **noun 1** a native or inhabitant of Bohemia.
2 (also **bohemian**) a socially unconventional person, especially one who is involved in the arts. [mid 19th cent.: from French *bohémien* 'Gypsy' (because Gypsies were thought to come from Bohemia, or because they perhaps entered the West through Bohemia).]
▶ **adjective 1** relating to Bohemia or its people.
2 (also **bohemian**) socially unconventional: *she revelled in the Bohemian life of Montparnasse.*
– DERIVATIVES **Bohemianism** noun (sense 2 of the noun).

boho /'bəʊhəʊ/ ▶ **noun** (pl. **bohos**) informal term for BOHEMIAN (sense 2 of the noun).
▶ **adjective** informal term for BOHEMIAN (sense 2 of the adjective).

Bohol /bəʊ'hɒl/ an island lying to the north of Mindanao in the central Philippines; pop. 1,384,800 (est. 2009); chief town, Tagbilaran.

Bohr /bɔː/, Niels Hendrik David (1885–1962), Danish physicist and pioneer in quantum physics. Bohr's theory of the structure of the atom incorporated quantum theory for the first time, and is the basis for present-day quantum-mechanical models. Bohr helped to develop the atom bomb in Britain and then in the US. Nobel Prize for Physics (1922). His son, **Aage Niels Bohr** (b.1922), shared the 1975 prize for his studies of the physics of the atomic nucleus.

bohrium /'bɔːrɪəm/ ▶ **noun** [mass noun] the chemical element of atomic number 107, a very unstable element made by high-energy atomic collisions. (Symbol: **Bh**)

bohunk /'bəʊhʌŋk/ ▶ **noun** N. Amer. informal, derogatory an immigrant from central or SE Europe.
– ORIGIN early 20th cent.: apparently from BOHEMIAN + *-hunk*, alteration of HUNGARIAN.

boil[1] ▶ **verb 1** (with reference to a liquid) reach or cause to reach the temperature at which it bubbles and turns to vapour: [with obj.] *we asked people to boil their drinking water* | [no obj.] *he waited for the water to boil.* ■ (with reference to a kettle, pan, or other container) heat or be heated until the liquid inside reaches such a temperature: [with obj.] *she boiled the kettle and took down a couple of mugs* | [no obj.] *the kettle boiled and he filled the teapot.*
2 [with obj.] subject (something) to the heat of boiling liquid, in particular: ■ (with reference to food) cook or be cooked by immersing in boiling water or stock: [with obj.] *boil the potatoes until well done* | (as adj. **boiled**) *two boiled eggs* | [no obj.] *make the sauce while*

the lobsters are boiling. ■ wash or sterilize (clothes) in water of a very high temperature.
3 [no obj.] (of the sea or clouds) be turbulent and stormy: *a huge cliff with the black sea boiling below.* ■ (of a person or strong emotion) be stirred up: *he was boiling with rage.*
▶ **noun 1** [in sing.] the temperature at which a liquid bubbles and turns to vapour: *bring the sauce* ***to the boil*** *and simmer for 10 minutes.* ■ the process of heating a liquid to such a temperature: *the kettle's* ***on the boil.*** ■ Brit. a state of great activity or excitement: *he has* ***gone off the boil*** *since opening the campaign.*
2 Fishing a sudden rise of a fish at a fly.
– PHRASES **keep the pot boiling** maintain the brisk momentum of something: *a home win over Sheffield kept the pot boiling.*
– PHRASAL VERBS **boil down to** amount to; be essentially a matter of: *everything boiled down to cash in the end.* **boil something down** reduce the volume of a liquid by boiling. **boil over** (of a liquid) flow over the sides of the container in boiling. ■ (of a situation or strong emotion) reach a state of such intensity that it can no longer be controlled or contained: *one woman's anger boiled over.*
– ORIGIN Middle English: from Old French *boillir*, from Latin *bullire* 'to bubble', from *bulla* 'bubble'.

boil[2] ▶ **noun** an inflamed pus-filled swelling on the skin, caused typically by the infection of a hair follicle.
– ORIGIN Old English *bȳle, bȳl*, of West Germanic origin; related to Dutch *buil* and German *Beule*.

Boileau /ˈbwʌləʊ/, French /bwalo/, Nicholas (1636–1711), French critic and poet; full name *Nicholas Boileau-Despréaux*. Boileau is considered particularly important as one of the founders of French literary criticism. His didactic poem *Art poétique* (1674) defined principles of composition and criticism.

boiled shirt ▶ **noun** dated a dress shirt with a starched front.

boiled sweet ▶ **noun** Brit. a hard sweet made of boiled sugar.

boiler ▶ **noun 1** a fuel-burning apparatus or container for heating water, in particular: ■ a household device providing a hot-water supply or serving a central heating system. ■ a tank for generating steam under pressure in a steam engine. ■ dated a metal tub for washing or sterilizing clothes at a very high temperature.
2 Brit. informal a chicken suitable for cooking only by boiling.
3 Brit. informal an unattractive or unpleasant woman.

boilermaker ▶ **noun 1** a worker who makes metal boilers for generating steam. ■ a metalworker in heavy industry.
2 N. Amer. a shot of whisky followed immediately by a glass of beer as a chaser.

boilerplate ▶ **noun 1** [mass noun] rolled steel plates for making boilers.
2 (**boilerplates**) Climbing smooth, overlapping, and undercut slabs of rock.
3 [mass noun] N. Amer. clichéd or predictable ideas or writing: *they exposed the truth behind the patriotic boilerplate.* ■ standardized pieces of text for use as clauses in contracts or as part of a computer program.

boiler room ▶ **noun 1** a room in a building or a compartment in a ship containing a boiler and related heating equipment.
2 a room or office in which many operators engage in high-pressure telephone sales, especially of risky or worthless investments: [as modifier] *a boiler-room operation.*

boiler suit ▶ **noun** Brit. a one-piece suit worn as overalls for heavy manual work.

boilie /ˈbɔɪli/ ▶ **noun** (pl. **boilies**) a type of flavoured fishing bait, spherical in shape with a hard outer layer, used chiefly to catch carp.

boiling ▶ **adjective** at or near boiling point: *boiling water.* ■ informal extremely hot: *Saturday is forecast to be boiling and sunny* | [as submodifier] *I felt boiling hot.*
▶ **noun** [mass noun] boiling point: *reheat the sauce to just below boiling.*

boiling point ▶ **noun** the temperature at which a liquid boils and turns to vapour. ■ the point at which anger or excitement breaks out into violent expression: *emotions had reached boiling point and could spill over into violence.*

boiling-water reactor (abbrev.: **BWR**) ▶ **noun** a nuclear reactor in which the fuel is uranium oxide clad in zircaloy and the coolant and moderator is water, which is boiled to produce steam for driving turbines.

boilover ▶ **noun** Austral./NZ informal a surprise result, especially the defeat of a favourite in a sporting event.

boing /bɔɪŋ/ ▶ **exclamation** representing a reverberating sound, especially the noise made by the release of a compressed spring.
▶ **noun** a reverberating sound.
▶ **verb** [no obj.] make a reverberating sound.
– ORIGIN 1950s: imitative.

boink ▶ **verb & noun** N. Amer. variant spelling of **BONK**.

Boise /ˈbɔɪsi/ the state capital of Idaho; pop. 205,314 (est. 2008).

boisterous ▶ **adjective** noisy, energetic, and cheerful: *a group of boisterous lads.* ■ (of weather or water) wild or stormy: *the boisterous wind was lulled.*
– DERIVATIVES **boisterously** adverb, **boisterousness** noun.
– ORIGIN late Middle English (in the sense 'rough, stiff'): variant of earlier *boistuous* 'rustic, coarse, boisterous', of unknown origin.

boîte /bwʌt/ ▶ **noun** (pl. pronunc. **same**) a small restaurant or nightclub.
– ORIGIN French, literally 'box'.

Bokassa /bəˈkasə/, Jean Bédel (1921–96), African statesman and military leader, President 1972–6 of the Central African Republic, self-styled emperor 1976–9.

bok choy /bɒk ˈtʃɔɪ/ ▶ **noun** US spelling of **PAK CHOI**.

boke /bəʊk/ (also **boak**) ▶ **verb** [no obj.] Scottish vomit.
▶ **noun** a vomiting fit.
– ORIGIN Middle English *bolke*; related to **BELCH**.

Bokhara /bəˈkɑːrə/ variant spelling of **BUKHARA**.

bokken /ˈbɒk(ə)n/ ▶ **noun** a wooden sword used as a practice weapon in kendo.
– ORIGIN Japanese.

bokmakierie /ˌbɒkməˈkɪəri/ (also **bokmakierie shrike**) ▶ **noun** (pl. **bokmakieries**) a bush shrike with conspicuous yellow underparts and a black band across the breast, common in southern Africa. ● *Telophorus* (or *Malaconotus*) *zeylonus*, family Laniidae.
– ORIGIN mid 19th cent.: from Afrikaans, imitative of its call.

Bokmål /ˈbuːkmɔːl/ ▶ **noun** [mass noun] one of two standard forms of the Norwegian language, a modified form of Danish. See **NORWEGIAN**.
– ORIGIN from Norwegian *bok* 'book' + *mål* 'language'.

bolas /ˈbəʊləs/ ▶ **noun** [treated as sing. or pl.] (especially in South America) a missile consisting of a number of balls connected by strong cord, which when thrown entangles the limbs of the quarry.
– ORIGIN early 19th cent.: from Spanish and Portuguese, plural of *bola* 'ball'.

bold ▶ **adjective 1** (of a person, action, or idea) showing a willingness to take risks; confident and courageous: *a bold attempt to solve the crisis* | *no journalist was bold enough to take on the Prime Minister.* ■ dated (of a person or their manner) so confident as to be impudent or presumptuous: *she tossed him a bold look.* ■ Irish (especially of a child) naughty; badly behaved: *I slapped him when he was bold.*
2 (of a colour, design, or shape) having a strong, vivid, or clear appearance: *a coat with bold polka dots.* ■ of a kind of typeface having dark, heavy strokes, used especially for emphasis.
▶ **noun** [mass noun] a bold typeface or letter: *Shadow cabinet members listed* ***in bold.***
– PHRASES **be** (or **make**) **so bold** (**as to do something**) formal dare to do something that might be considered audacious (used when politely asking a question or making a suggestion): *what would he be calling for, if I might make so bold* as to ask? (**as**) **bold as brass** confident to the point of impudence.
– DERIVATIVES **boldly** adverb, **boldness** noun.
– ORIGIN Old English *bald*, of Germanic origin; related to Dutch *boud* and to German *bald* 'soon'.

boldface ▶ **noun** [mass noun] a kind of typeface with dark, heavy strokes.
▶ **adjective** printed in boldface type.

boldfaced ▶ **adjective 1** printed in boldface type.
2 flagrant or audacious: *boldfaced lies.*

boldo /ˈbɒldəʊ/ ▶ **noun** (pl. **boldos**) an evergreen Chilean tree from which are obtained an edible fruit, a dye, and a medicinal leaf infusion. ● *Peumus boldus*, family Monimiaceae.
■ [mass noun] a medicinal preparation of the leaves of the boldo tree, used as a tonic and digestive aid.
– ORIGIN early 18th cent.: via American Spanish from Araucanian *voldo*.

bole[1] ▶ **noun** the trunk of a tree.
– ORIGIN Middle English: from Old Norse *bolr*; perhaps related to **BAULK**.

bole[2] ▶ **noun** [mass noun] a fine, smooth, reddish clay containing iron oxide, used especially as a ground for oil painting and gilding.
– ORIGIN Middle English: from late Latin *bolus* 'rounded mass' (see **BOLUS**).

bolection /bəˈlɛkʃ(ə)n/ ▶ **noun** [usu. as modifier] Architecture a decorative moulding above or around a panel or other architectural feature.
– ORIGIN mid 17th cent.: of unknown origin.

bolero /bəˈlɛːrəʊ/ ▶ **noun** (pl. **boleros**) **1** a Spanish dance in simple triple time. ■ a piece of music for or in the time of this dance.
2 (also **bolero jacket**) a woman's short open jacket.
– ORIGIN late 18th cent.: from Spanish.

boletus /bəˈliːtəs/ (also **bolete**) ▶ **noun** (pl. **boletuses**) a toadstool with pores rather than gills on the underside of the cap, typically having a thick stem. ● Genus *Boletus*, family Boletaceae, class Hymenomycetes.
– ORIGIN from Latin, from Greek *bōlitēs*, perhaps from *bōlos* 'lump'.

Boleyn /bəˈlɪn/, Anne (1507–36), second wife of Henry VIII and mother of Elizabeth I. Henry divorced Catherine of Aragon in order to marry Anne (1533), but she fell from favour when she failed to provide him with a male heir and was eventually executed on the grounds of alleged infidelities.

Bolger /ˈbɒldʒə/, James (Brendan) (b.1935), New Zealand National Party statesman, Prime Minister 1990–7.

bolide /ˈbəʊlʌɪd/ ▶ **noun** a large meteor which explodes in the atmosphere.
– ORIGIN early 19th cent.: from French, from Latin *bolis, bolid-*, from Greek *bolis* 'missile'.

Bolingbroke /ˈbɒlɪŋbrʊk/ the surname of Henry IV of England (see **HENRY[1]**).

bolivar /ˌbɒlɪˈvɑː, bɒˈliːvɑː/, Spanish /boˈliβar/ ▶ **noun** the basic monetary unit of Venezuela, equal to 100 centimos.
– ORIGIN named after Simón **BOLÍVAR**.

Bolívar /bɒˈliːvɑː/, Spanish /boˈliβar/, Simón (1783–1830), Venezuelan patriot and statesman; known as **the Liberator**. He succeeded in driving the Spanish from Venezuela, Colombia, Peru, and Ecuador. Upper Peru was named Bolivia in his honour.

Bolivia /bəˈlɪvɪə/, Spanish /boˈliβja/ a landlocked country in South America; pop. 9,775,200 (est. 2009); languages, Spanish (official), Aymara, and Quechua; capital, La Paz; legal capital and seat of the judiciary, Sucre.

Bolivia's chief topographical feature is the altiplano, the high central plateau between the eastern and western chains of the Andes. Following Pizarro's defeat of the Incas the country became part of Spain's American empire. It was freed from Spanish rule in 1825, but has suffered continually from political instability.

– DERIVATIVES **Bolivian** adjective & noun.
– ORIGIN named after Simón **BOLÍVAR**.

boliviano /bəˌlɪvɪˈɑːnəʊ/, Spanish /boliˈβjano/ ▶ **noun** (pl. **bolivianos**) the basic monetary unit of Bolivia (1863–1962 and since 1987), equal to 100 centavos or cents.
– ORIGIN Spanish, literally 'Bolivian', from **BOLIVIA**.

boll /bəʊl/ ▶ **noun** the rounded seed capsule of plants such as cotton or flax.
– ORIGIN Middle English (originally denoting a bubble): from Middle Dutch *bolle* 'rounded object'; related to **BOWL[1]**.

Böll /bəːl/, German /bœl/, Heinrich (Theodor) (1917–85), German novelist and short-story writer. His years in the German army (1938–44) provided the material for his earliest novel, *Adam, Where Art Thou?* (1951). His later work, such as *The Lost Honour of Katharina Blum* (1974), is frequently critical of post-war German society. Nobel Prize for Literature (1972).

bollard /ˈbɒlɑːd, -ləd/ ▶ **noun 1** Brit. a short post used to prevent traffic from entering an area.
2 a short, thick post on the deck of a ship or a quayside, to which a ship's rope may be secured.
– ORIGIN Middle English (in sense 2): perhaps from Old Norse *bolr* (see **BOLE[1]**) + **-ARD**.

bollito misto /bɒˌliːtəʊ ˈmɪstəʊ/ ▸ **noun** (pl. **bolliti misti** /bɒˌliːti ˈmɪsti/) an Italian dish of mixed meats, such as chicken, veal, and sausage, boiled with vegetables in broth.
– ORIGIN Italian, literally 'boiled mixed (meat)'.

bollix vulgar slang ▸ **verb** [with obj.] (usu. **bollix something up**) bungle (a task).
▸ **noun 1** [treated as pl.] variant spelling of **BOLLOCKS**.
2 [treated as sing.] Irish a foolish or contemptible man.

bollock /ˈbɒlək/ (also **ballock**) ▸ **verb** [with obj.] Brit. vulgar slang reprimand (someone) severely.

bollocking (also **ballocking**) ▸ **noun** Brit. vulgar slang a severe reprimand.

bollocks (also **ballocks**) ▸ **plural noun** Brit. vulgar slang **1** the testicles.
2 [treated as sing.] nonsense; rubbish (used to express contempt or disagreement, or as an exclamation of annoyance).
– ORIGIN mid 18th cent.: plural of *bollock*, variant of earlier *ballock*, of Germanic origin; related to **BALL**[1].

bollocky ▸ **adjective** Austral. informal naked.

boll weevil ▸ **noun** a small weevil which feeds on the fibres of the cotton boll and is a major pest of the American cotton crop. ● *Anthonomus grandis*, family Curculionidae.

bollworm ▸ **noun** a moth caterpillar which attacks the cotton boll, in particular: ● (**pink bollworm**) a small moth caterpillar which is a serious pest of the North American cotton crop (*Pectinophora gossypiella*, family Gelechiidae). ● (also **cotton bollworm**) another term for **CORN EARWORM**.

Bollywood ▸ **noun** a name for the Indian popular film industry, based in Mumbai (Bombay).
– ORIGIN 1970s: blend of **BOMBAY** and **HOLLYWOOD**.

bolo /ˈbəʊləʊ/ ▸ **noun** (pl. **bolos**) a large single-edged knife used in the Philippines.
– ORIGIN Spanish.

Bologna /bəˈləʊnjə, -ˈlɒnjə/, Italian /baoˈlɔɲɲa/ a city in northern Italy, capital of Emilia-Romagna region; pop. 374,944 (2008). Its university, which dates from the 11th century, is the oldest in Europe.

bologna /bəˈləʊnjə, bəˈlɒnjə/ (also **bologna sausage**) ▸ **noun** N. Amer. a large smoked sausage made of bacon, veal, pork suet, and other meats.

bolometer /bəˈlɒmɪtə/ ▸ **noun** a sensitive electrical instrument for measuring radiant energy.
– DERIVATIVES **bolometric** adjective.
– ORIGIN late 19th cent.: from Greek *bolē* 'ray of light' + **-METER**.

boloney ▸ **noun** variant spelling of **BALONEY**.

bolo tie ▸ **noun** N. Amer. a type of tie consisting of a cord worn around the neck with a large ornamental fastening at the throat.

Bolshevik /ˈbɒlʃɪvɪk/ ▸ **noun** historical a member of the majority faction of the Russian Social Democratic Party, which seized power in the October Revolution of 1917. ■ chiefly derogatory (in general use) a person with politically subversive or radical views; a revolutionary.
▸ **adjective** relating to or characteristic of Bolsheviks or Bolshevism.
– DERIVATIVES **Bolshevism** noun, **Bolshevist** noun.
– ORIGIN Russian, from *bol'she* 'greater' (with reference to the greater faction).

bolshie (also **bolshy**) Brit. informal ▸ **adjective** (of a person or attitude) deliberately combative or uncooperative: *policemen with bolshie attitudes*.
▸ **noun** (**Bolshie**) (pl. **Bolshies**) dated a Bolshevik or socialist.
– DERIVATIVES **bolshiness** noun.

Bolshoi Ballet /ˈbɒlʃɔɪ/ a Moscow ballet company. Since 1825 it has been based at the Bolshoi Theatre, where it staged the first production of Tchaikovsky's *Swan Lake* (1877).

bolster[1] /ˈbəʊlstə/ ▸ **noun 1** a long, thick pillow that is placed under other pillows for support.
2 a part on a vehicle or tool providing structural support or reducing friction. ■ Building a short timber cap over a post designed to increase the bearing of the beams it supports.
▸ **verb** [with obj.] **1** support or strengthen: *the fall in interest rates is starting to bolster confidence*.
2 provide (a seat) with padded support: (as adj. **bolstered**) *I snuggled down into the heavily bolstered seat*.
– DERIVATIVES **bolsterer** noun.
– ORIGIN Old English, of Germanic origin; related to Dutch *bolster* and German *Polster*.

bolster[2] /ˈbəʊlstə/ ▸ **noun** a heavy chisel used for cutting bricks.
– ORIGIN early 20th cent.: of unknown origin.

Bolt[1], Robert (Oxton) (1924–95), English writer best known for the play *A Man for All Seasons* (1960) and the screenplays for *Lawrence of Arabia* (1962) and *Dr Zhivago* (1965).

Bolt[2], Usain (St Leo) (b.1986), Jamaican athlete. At the 2008 Olympic Games in Beijing he won gold medals in the 100 metre and 200 metre races, setting a new world record time for each. He also won a gold, and set a new world record, as part of the Jamaican 4×100 metre relay team.

bolt[1] ▸ **noun 1** a large metal pin, in particular: ■ a bar that slides into a socket to fasten a door or window. ■ a long pin with a head that screws into a nut, used to fasten things together. ■ the sliding piece of the breech mechanism of a rifle. ■ Climbing a long pin that is driven into a rock face so that a rope can be attached to it.
2 a short, heavy arrow shot from a crossbow.
3 a jagged white flash of lightning.
▸ **verb** [with obj.] fasten with a bolt, in particular: ■ fasten (a door or window) with a bar that slides into a socket. ■ [with obj. and adverbial of place] fasten (something) to something else with a long pin that screws into a nut: *the lid was bolted down* | figurative *new benefits have been bolted on to the social security system*.
– PHRASES **a bolt from** (or **out of**) **the blue** a sudden and unexpected event: *the job came like a bolt from the blue*. [with reference to the unlikelihood of a thunderbolt coming from a clear blue sky.] **bolt upright** with the back very straight. **have shot one's bolt** informal have done all that is in one's power.
– ORIGIN Old English, 'arrow', of unknown origin; related to Dutch *bout* and German *Bolzen* 'arrow, bolt for a door'.

bolt[2] ▸ **verb 1** [no obj.] (of a horse or other animal) run away suddenly, typically from fear: *the horses shied and bolted*. ■ [no obj., with adverbial of direction] (of a person) move or run away suddenly in an attempt to escape: *they bolted down the stairs*. ■ [with obj.] (in hunting) cause (a rabbit or fox) to run from its burrow or hole. ■ (of a plant) grow quickly upwards and stop flowering as seeds develop: *the lettuces have bolted*.
2 [with obj.] eat (food) quickly: *there's no need to bolt your food*.
– PHRASES **make a bolt for** try to escape by moving suddenly towards (something): *Ellie made a bolt for the door*.
– ORIGIN Middle English: from **BOLT**[1], expressing the sense 'fly like an arrow'.

bolt[3] ▸ **noun 1** a roll of fabric, originally as a measure: *the room was stacked with **bolts** of cloth*.
2 a folded edge of a piece of paper that is trimmed off to allow it to be opened, as on a section of a book.
– ORIGIN Middle English: transferred use of **BOLT**[1].

bolt[4] (also **boult**) ▸ **verb** [with obj.] archaic pass (flour, powder, or other material) through a sieve.
– ORIGIN Middle English: from Old French *bulter*, of unknown ultimate origin. The change in the first syllable was due to association with **BOLT**[1].

bolt-action ▸ **adjective** (of a gun) having a breech which is opened by turning a bolt and sliding it back.

bolter ▸ **noun** a person or animal that bolts or runs away. ■ Austral./NZ an outsider in a sporting event or other competition. ■ Austral. historical an escaped convict or absconder.

bolt-hole ▸ **noun 1** a place where a person can escape and hide: *he thought of Antwerp as a possible bolt-hole*.
2 chiefly Brit. a hole or burrow by which a rabbit or other wild animal can escape.

bolting ▸ **noun** [mass noun] Climbing the action of driving long metal pins into a rock face so that ropes can be attached to them.

Bolton a town in NW England, near Manchester; pop. 135,200 (est. 2009).

bolt-on ▸ **adjective** (of an extra part of a machine) able to be fastened on with a bolt or catch. ■ denoting something that has been or can be added to an existing object or arrangement: *there's no obligation to buy any type of bolt-on insurance product with a personal loan*.
▸ **noun** a bolt-on part of a machine.

Boltzmann /ˈbɒltsman/, Ludwig (1844–1906), Austrian physicist, who made contributions to the kinetic theory of gases, statistical mechanics, and thermodynamics.

Boltzmann distribution another term for **MAXWELL–BOLTZMANN DISTRIBUTION**.

Boltzmann's constant ▸ **noun** Chemistry the ratio of the gas constant to Avogadro's constant, equal to 1.381×10^{-23} joules per kelvin. (Symbol: **k**)

bolus /ˈbəʊləs/ ▸ **noun** (pl. **boluses**) **1** a small rounded mass of a substance, especially of chewed food at the moment of swallowing.
2 a type of large pill used in veterinary medicine. ■ Medicine a single dose of a drug or other medicinal preparation given all at once.
– ORIGIN mid 16th cent. (denoting a large pill): via late Latin from Greek *bōlos* 'clod'.

Bolzano /bɒlˈtsɑːnəʊ/ a city in NE Italy, capital of the Bolzano-Bozen province; pop. 99,200 (est. 2009).

boma /ˈbəʊmə/ ▸ **noun** (in eastern and southern Africa) an enclosure, especially for animals.
– ORIGIN Kiswahili.

bomb ▸ **noun 1** a container filled with explosive or incendiary material, designed to explode on impact or when detonated by a timing, proximity, or remote-control device. ■ (**the bomb**) nuclear weapons considered collectively as agents of mass destruction: *she joined the fight against the bomb*.
2 a thing resembling a bomb in shape, in particular: ■ (also **volcanic bomb**) a lump of lava thrown out by a volcano. ■ a pear-shaped weight used to anchor a fishing line to the bottom.
3 (**a bomb**) Brit. informal a large sum of money: *that silk must have cost a bomb*.
4 informal a film, play, or other event that fails badly: *that bomb of an old movie*.
5 (**the** (or **da**) **bomb**) US informal an outstandingly good person or thing: *the site would really be da bomb if its content were updated more frequently*.
6 a long forward pass or hit in a ball game: *a two-run bomb*.
7 informal a cannabis cigarette.
▸ **verb 1** [with obj.] attack (a place or object) with a bomb or bombs: *they bombed the city at dawn*. ■ (**bomb someone out**) make someone homeless by destroying their home with bombs.
2 [no obj., with adverbial of direction] Brit. informal move very quickly: *we were bombing down the motorway at breakneck speed*.
3 [no obj.] informal (of a film, play, or other event) fail badly: *it just became another big-budget film that bombed*.
– PHRASES **go down a bomb** Brit. informal be very well received: *those gigs we did went down a bomb*. **go like a bomb** Brit. informal **1** be very successful: *the party went like a bomb*. **2** (of a vehicle or person) move very fast. **look like a bomb's hit it** informal (of a place) be extremely messy or untidy in appearance: *the room looked like a bomb had hit it*.
– DERIVATIVES **bomblet** noun.
– ORIGIN late 17th cent.: from French *bombe*, from Italian *bomba*, probably from Latin *bombus* 'booming, humming', from Greek *bombos*, of imitative origin.

bombard ▸ **verb** /bɒmˈbɑːd/ [with obj.] attack (a place or person) continuously with bombs, shells, or other missiles: *the city was bombarded by federal forces*. ■ subject (someone) to a continuous flow of questions, criticisms, or information: *they will be **bombarded with** complaints*. ■ Physics direct a stream of high-speed particles at (a substance).
▸ **noun** /ˈbɒmbɑːd/ historical a cannon of the earliest type, which fired a stone ball or large shot.
– ORIGIN late Middle English (as a noun denoting an early form of cannon, also a shawm) from Old French *bombarde*, probably based on Latin *bombus* 'booming, humming' (see **BOMB**). The verb (late 16th cent.) is from French *bombarder*.

bombarde /ˈbɒmbɑːd/ ▸ **noun 1** a shawm (wind instrument) of alto pitch, used in medieval bands and in Breton folk music.
2 a powerful bass reed organ stop.
– ORIGIN late Middle English: from Old French, denoting a shawm (see **BOMBARD**).

bombardier /ˌbɒmbəˈdɪə/ ▸ **noun 1** a rank of non-commissioned officer in certain artillery regiments, equivalent to corporal.
2 a member of a bomber crew in the US air force responsible for aiming and releasing bombs.
– ORIGIN mid 16th cent. (denoting a soldier in charge of a *bombard*, an early form of cannon): from French, from Old French *bombarde* 'cannon' (see **BOMBARD**).

bombardier beetle ▶ **noun** a ground beetle that discharges a puff of irritant vapour from its anus with an audible pop when alarmed. ● Several species in the family Carabidae, in particular the European *Brachinus crepitans*.

bombardment /bɒmˈbɑːdm(ə)nt/ ▶ **noun** a continuous attack with bombs, shells, or other missiles: *an aerial bombardment will precede the attack*. ■ a continuous flow of questions, criticisms, or information: *a steady bombardment of emails and phone calls*.

bombardon /ˈbɒmbɑːd(ə)n/ ▶ **noun** a bass tuba.
– ORIGIN mid 19th cent.: from Italian *bombardone*, from *bombardo* 'cannon'. Compare with **BOMBARDE**.

bombast /ˈbɒmbast/ ▶ **noun** [mass noun] high-sounding language with little meaning, used to impress people.
– ORIGIN mid 16th cent. (denoting raw cotton or cotton wool used as padding, later used figuratively): from Old French *bombace*, from medieval Latin *bombax*, *bombac-*, alteration of *bombyx* 'silkworm' (see **BOMBAZINE**).

bombastic ▶ **adjective** high-sounding but with little meaning; inflated: *bombastic rhetoric* | *bombastic music that drowned out what anyone was saying*.
– DERIVATIVES **bombastically** adverb.

Bombay former name (until 1995) for **MUMBAI**.

Bombay duck ▶ **noun** [mass noun] the bummalo (fish), especially when dried and eaten as an accompaniment to curries.
– ORIGIN mid 19th cent.: alteration of **BUMMALO** by association with **BOMBAY** (Mumbai) in India, from which bummalo were exported; the reason for the use of the term *duck* is unknown.

Bombay mix ▶ **noun** [mass noun] an Indian-style spiced snack consisting of lentils, peanuts, and deep-fried strands of gram flour (sev).

bombazine /ˈbɒmbəziːn/ ▶ **noun** [mass noun] a twilled dress fabric of worsted and silk or cotton, especially a black kind formerly used for mourning clothes.
– ORIGIN mid 16th cent. (denoting raw cotton): from French *bombasin*, from medieval Latin *bombacinum*, from *bombycinum*, neuter of *bombycinus* 'silken', based on Greek *bombux* 'silkworm'.

bomb bay ▶ **noun** a compartment in the fuselage of an aircraft in which bombs are held and from which they may be dropped.

bomb calorimeter ▶ **noun** a thick-walled steel container used to determine the energy contained in a substance by measuring the heat generated during its combustion.

bomb disposal ▶ **noun** [mass noun] the defusing or removal and detonation of unexploded and delayed-action bombs.

bombe /bɒmb/ ▶ **noun** a frozen dome-shaped dessert. ■ a dome-shaped mould in which a bombe is made.
– ORIGIN French, literally 'bomb'.

bombé /ˈbɒ̃beɪ/, French /bɔ̃be/ ▶ **adjective** (of furniture) rounded.
– ORIGIN early 20th cent.: French, literally 'swollen out'.

bombed ▶ **adjective 1** (of an area or building) subjected to bombing.
2 informal intoxicated by drink or drugs.

bombed-out ▶ **adjective** (of a building or city) destroyed by bombing: *a bombed-out factory*. ■ (of a person) driven out of a place by bombing: *bombed-out families*.

bomber ▶ **noun 1** an aircraft designed to carry and drop bombs.
2 a person who plants, detonates, or throws bombs, especially as a terrorist.
3 informal a large cigarette containing cannabis.
4 a bomber jacket.

bomber jacket ▶ **noun** a short jacket tightly gathered at the waist and cuffs by elasticated bands and typically having a zip front.

bombinate /ˈbɒmbɪneɪt/ ▶ **verb** [no obj.] literary buzz; hum.
– ORIGIN late 19th cent.: from medieval Latin *bombinat-* 'buzzed', from the verb *bombinare*, from Latin *bombus* 'humming' (see **BOMBARD**).

bombing ▶ **noun** an act or instance of dropping or detonating a bomb somewhere: *a series of terrorist bombings*.

bombora /bɒmˈbɔːrə/ ▶ **noun** Austral. a wave which forms over a submerged offshore reef or rock, sometimes breaking heavily and producing a dangerous stretch of broken water. ■ a submerged offshore reef or rock.
– ORIGIN 1930s: from an Aboriginal word, perhaps Dharuk *bumbora*.

bombproof ▶ **adjective** strong enough to resist the effects of blast from a bomb.

bombshell ▶ **noun 1** an unexpected and surprising event, especially an unpleasant one: *the news came as a bombshell*.
2 informal a very attractive woman: *a twenty-year-old blonde bombshell*.
3 dated an artillery shell.

bombsight ▶ **noun** a mechanical or electronic device used in an aircraft for aiming bombs.

bomb site ▶ **noun** an area in a town or city where the buildings have been destroyed by bombs.

bomb squad ▶ **noun** a division of a police force appointed to investigate the planting and detonation of terrorist bombs.

Bon /bɒn/ (also **O-Bon**) ▶ **noun** a Japanese Buddhist festival held annually in August to honour the dead. Also called **FESTIVAL OF THE DEAD** and **LANTERN FESTIVAL**.
– ORIGIN from Japanese.

Bon, Cape a peninsula of NE Tunisia, extending into the Mediterranean Sea.

bona fide /ˌbəʊnə ˈfʌɪdi/ ▶ **adjective** genuine; real: *she was a bona fide expert*.
▶ **adverb** chiefly Law without intention to deceive: *the court will assume that they have acted bona fide*.
– ORIGIN Latin, literally 'with good faith', ablative singular of **BONA FIDES**.

bona fides /ˌbəʊnə ˈfʌɪdiːz/ ▶ **noun** [mass noun] a person's honesty and sincerity of intention: *he went to great lengths to establish his liberal bona fides*. ■ [treated as pl.] informal documentary evidence showing that a person is what they claim to be; credentials.
– ORIGIN Latin, literally 'good faith'.

Bonaire /bɒˈnɛː/ one of the two principal islands of the Netherlands Antilles (the other is Curaçao); chief town, Kralendijk; pop. 12,877 (2009).

bonanza /bəˈnanzə/ ▶ **noun** a situation which creates a sudden increase in wealth, good fortune, or profits: *a natural gas bonanza for Britain* | [as modifier] *a bonanza year for the computer industry*. ■ a large amount of something desirable: *the festive feature-film bonanza*.
– ORIGIN early 19th cent. (originally US, especially with reference to success when mining): from Spanish, literally 'fair weather, prosperity', from Latin *bonus* 'good'.

Bonaparte /ˈbəʊnəpɑːt/, French /bɔnapaʀt/ (Italian **Buonaparte**) a Corsican family including the three French rulers named Napoleon.
– DERIVATIVES **Bonapartism** noun, **Bonapartist** noun & adjective.

bon appétit /ˌbɒn apɛˈtiː/, French /bɔn apeti/ ▶ **exclamation** used as a salutation to a person about to eat.
– ORIGIN French, literally 'good appetite'.

bona vacantia /ˌbəʊnə vəˈkantɪə/ ▶ **noun** [mass noun] Law (in the UK) goods without an apparent owner, such as treasure trove or the estate of a person dying intestate and without heirs, to which the Crown may have right.
– ORIGIN Latin, 'ownerless goods'.

Bonaventura, St /ˌbɒnəvɛnˈtjʊərə/ (1221–74), Franciscan theologian; born *Giovanni di Fidanza*; known as **the Seraphic Doctor**. He wrote the official biography of St Francis and had a lasting influence as a spiritual writer. Feast day, 15 (formerly 14) July.

bonbon ▶ **noun** a piece of confectionery; a sweet.
– ORIGIN late 18th cent.: from French, reduplication of *bon* 'good', from Latin *bonus*.

bonbonnière /ˌbɒnbɒnˈjɛː/ ▶ **noun** a small ornamental box or lidded jar for confectionery.
– ORIGIN French.

bonce ▶ **noun** Brit. informal a person's head.
– ORIGIN mid 19th cent. (denoting a large marble): of unknown origin.

Bond[1], Edward (b.1934), English dramatist. Many of his plays are marked by scenes of violence and cruelty. Notable works: *Saved* (1965) and *Lear* (1971).

Bond[2], James, a British secret agent in the spy novels of Ian Fleming, known also by his code name 007.

bond /bɒnd/ ▶ **noun 1** a thing used to tie something or to fasten things together: *she brushed back a curl which had strayed from its bonds*. ■ (**bonds**) ropes, chains, or other restraints used to hold someone prisoner. ■ a force or feeling that unites people; a shared emotion or interest: *there was a bond of understanding between them*.
2 an agreement with legal force, in particular: ■ Law a deed by which a person is committed to make payment to another. ■ South African term for **MORTGAGE**. ■ a certificate issued by a government or a public company promising to repay borrowed money at a fixed rate of interest at a specified time. ■ an insurance policy held by a company, which protects against losses resulting from circumstances such as bankruptcy. ■ US a sum of money paid as bail.
3 (also **chemical bond**) a strong force of attraction holding atoms together in a molecule or crystal, resulting from the sharing or transfer of electrons.
4 [with modifier] Building a pattern in which bricks are laid in order to ensure the strength of the resulting structure.
▶ **verb 1** join or be joined securely to something else, especially by means of an adhesive substance, heat, or pressure: [with obj.] *press the material to* **bond** *the layers together* | [no obj.] *this material will* **bond** *well to stainless steel rods* | (as adj. **bonding**) *a bonding agent*. ■ [no obj.] establish a relationship or link with someone based on shared feelings, interests, or experiences: *the failure to properly* **bond with** *their children* | (as noun modifier **bonding**) *the film has some great male bonding scenes*.
2 join or be joined by a chemical bond.
3 [with obj.] (usu. as adj. **bonding**) lay (bricks) in an overlapping pattern so as to form a strong structure: *a bonding course*.
4 (usu. as noun **bonding**) place (dutiable goods) in bond.
– PHRASES **in bond** (of dutiable goods) stored in a bonded warehouse until the importer pays the duty owing.
– ORIGIN Middle English: variant of **BAND**[1].

bondage ▶ **noun** [mass noun] **1** the state of being a slave: *the deliverance of the Israelites from Egypt's bondage* | figurative *the bondage of drug addiction*.
2 sexual practice that involves the tying up or restraining of one partner.
– ORIGIN Middle English: from Anglo-Latin *bondagium*, from Middle English *bond* 'serf' (earlier 'peasant, householder'), from Old Norse *bóndi* 'tiller of the soil', based on *búa* 'dwell'; influenced in sense by **BOND**.

bondager ▶ **noun** historical a person who performed services as a condition of feudal tenure. ■ (in southern Scotland and NE England) a female outworker supplied to a proprietor by a tenant.

bonded ▶ **adjective 1** (of a thing or things) joined securely to another or each other, especially by an adhesive, heat process, or pressure. ■ emotionally or psychologically linked: *a strongly bonded group of females*.
2 held by a chemical bond: *bonded atoms*.
3 (of a person or company) bound by a legal agreement, in particular: ■ (of a travel agent or tour operator) holding an insurance policy which protects travellers' holidays and money should the company go bankrupt. ■ (of a worker or workforce) obliged to work for a particular employer, typically in a condition close to slavery.
4 (of dutiable goods) placed in bond.

bonded warehouse ▶ **noun** a customs-controlled warehouse for the retention of imported goods until the duty owed is paid.

bondholder ▶ **noun** a person owning a bond or bonds issued by a government or a public company.

Bondi /ˈbɒndʌɪ/ a coastal resort in New South Wales, Australia, a suburb of Sydney. It is noted for its popular beach.

bond paper ▶ **noun** [mass noun] high-quality writing paper.

bondsman ▶ **noun** (pl. **bondsmen**) **1** a person who stands surety for a bond.
2 archaic a slave. [mid 18th cent.: variant of Middle English *bondman*, from obsolete *bond* 'serf' (see also **BONDAGE**).]

Bône /bəʊn/ former name for **ANNABA**.

bone ▶ **noun 1** any of the pieces of hard whitish tissue making up the skeleton in humans and other vertebrates: *his injuries included many broken bones* | *a shoulder bone*. ■ (**one's bones**) one's body: *he hauled his tired bones upright*. ■ (**bones**) a corpse or skeleton. ■ a bone of an animal with meat on it fed to a dog.

B

The substance of bones is formed by specialized cells (osteoblasts) which secrete around themselves a material containing calcium salts (which provide hardness and strength in compression) and collagen fibres (which provide tensile strength).

2 [mass noun] the calcified material of which bones consist: *an earring of bone.* ■ a substance similar to bone, such as ivory or whalebone. ■ (often **bones**) a thing made or formerly made of bone, such as a strip of stiffening for a foundation garment. ■ (usu. **bones**) (in southern Africa) one of a set of carved dice or bones used by traditional healers in divination.
3 (**bones**) the basic or essential framework of something: *you need to put some flesh on the bones of your idea.*
▸ **verb 1** [with obj.] remove the bones from (meat or fish) before cooking, serving, or selling.
2 [no obj.] (**bone up on**) informal study (a subject) intensively, typically in preparation for something: *she boned up on languages she had learned long ago.*
3 [with obj.] US vulgar slang (of a man) have sexual intercourse with (someone).
– PHRASES **bone of contention** a subject or issue over which there is continuing disagreement: *the examination system has long been a serious bone of contention.* **close to** (or **near**) **the bone** (of a remark) penetrating and accurate to the point of causing discomfort. ■ (of a joke or story) likely to cause offence because near the limit of decency. **cut** (or **pare**) **something to the bone** reduce something to the bare minimum: *costs will have to be cut to the bone.* **have a bone to pick with someone** informal have reason to disagree or be annoyed with someone. **in one's bones** felt, understood, or believed very deeply or instinctively. **make no bones about** have no hesitation in stating or dealing with (something), however unpleasant or awkward it is: *he makes no bones about his feelings towards the militants.* **make old bones** [with negative] reach an advanced age: *he knew he would never make old bones.* **not have a —— bone in one's body** have not the slightest trace of the specified quality: *she hasn't got a sympathetic bone in her body.* **off** (or **on**) **the bone** (of meat or fish) having had the bone or bones removed (or left in) before being cooked, served, or sold. **point the bone at** Austral. (of an Aborigine) cast a spell on (someone) so as to cause their sickness or death. ■ openly accuse or blame someone. [from an Australian Aboriginal ritual, in which a bone is pointed at a victim.] **to the bone** (of a wound) so deep as to expose a person's bone: *his thigh had been axed open to the bone* | figurative *his contempt cut her to the bone.* **to one's bones** (or **to the bone**) used to emphasize the essential nature of a specified quality: *he's a cop to the bone.* **what's bred in the bone will come out in the flesh** (or **blood**) proverb a person's behaviour or characteristics are determined by their heredity. **work one's fingers to the bone** work very hard.
– ORIGIN Old English *bān*, of Germanic origin; related to Dutch *been* and German *Bein*.

bone ash ▸ **noun** [mass noun] the mineral residue of calcined bones.

bone china ▸ **noun** [mass noun] white porcelain containing bone ash, made in Britain since about 1800.

boned ▸ **adjective 1** (of meat or fish) having had the bones removed before being sold, cooked, or served.
2 [in combination] (of a person) having bones of the specified type: *she was fine-boned and boyishly slim.*
3 (of a garment) stiffened with strips of plastic or whalebone to give shape to the wearer's figure or the garment.

bone dry ▸ **adjective** completely or extremely dry.

bonefish ▸ **noun** (pl. **same** or **bonefishes**) a silvery game fish of warm coastal waters. Also called LADYFISH. ● Family Albulidae and genus *Albula*: several species, in particular *A. vulpes*.

bonehead ▸ **noun** informal a stupid person.
– DERIVATIVES **boneheaded** adjective.

bone idle (also **bone lazy**) ▸ **adjective** Brit. extremely idle or lazy.
– ORIGIN early 19th cent.: expressing *idle through to the bone.*

boneless ▸ **adjective** (of meat or fish) having had the bones removed before being sold, cooked, or served. ■ lacking physical or mental strength: *I think her Harry's a boneless little drip.*
– DERIVATIVES **bonelessly** adverb.

bone marrow ▸ **noun** see MARROW[1] (sense 3).

bonemeal ▸ **noun** [mass noun] crushed or ground bones used as a fertilizer.

boner ▸ **noun 1** N. Amer. informal a stupid mistake.
2 N. Amer. vulgar slang an erection of the penis.
3 NZ a low-grade farm animal, with meat only suitable for use in sausages or other processed products.
– PHRASES **pull a boner** N. Amer. informal make a stupid mistake.
– ORIGIN early 20th cent.: from BONE or (in sense 1) from BONEHEAD, + -ER[1].

boneset ▸ **noun** a North American plant of the daisy family, which bears clusters of small white flowers and is used in herbal medicine. ● *Eupatorium perfoliatum*, family Compositae.
■ Brit. the common comfrey, the ground-up root of which was formerly used as a 'plaster' to set broken bones.

bonesetter ▸ **noun** historical a person, usually not formally qualified, who set broken or dislocated bones.

boneshaker ▸ **noun** Brit. informal an old vehicle with poor suspension: *a boneshaker of a van.* ■ an early type of bicycle without rubber tyres.

bone spavin ▸ **noun** osteoarthritis of the hock in horses, which may cause swelling and lameness.

bone-tired (also **bone-weary**) ▸ **adjective** extremely tired.

boneyard ▸ **noun** informal a cemetery.

bonfire ▸ **noun** a large open-air fire used for burning rubbish or as part of a celebration.
– ORIGIN late Middle English: from BONE + FIRE. The term originally denoted a large open-air fire on which bones were burnt (sometimes as part of a celebration), also one for burning heretics or proscribed literature. Dr Johnson accepted the mistaken idea that the word came from French *bon* 'good'.

Bonfire Night ▸ **noun** (in the UK) 5 November, on which fireworks are displayed and figures representing Guy Fawkes burnt in memory of the Gunpowder Plot.

bong[1] ▸ **noun** a low-pitched sound, as of a bell.
▸ **verb** [no obj.] emit such a sound.
– ORIGIN 1920s (originally US): imitative.

bong[2] ▸ **noun** a water pipe used for smoking cannabis or other drugs.
– ORIGIN 1970s: from Thai *baung*, literally 'cylindrical wooden tube'.

bong[3] ▸ **noun** Climbing a large piton.
– ORIGIN 1960s: probably imitative.

bongo[1] /ˈbɒŋɡəʊ/ ▸ **noun** (pl. **bongos**) each of a joined pair of small deep-bodied drums, typically held between the knees and played with the fingers.
– ORIGIN 1920s: from Latin American Spanish *bongó*.

bongo[2] /ˈbɒŋɡəʊ/ ▸ **noun** (pl. **same** or **bongos**) a forest antelope that has a chestnut coat with narrow white vertical stripes, native to central Africa. ● *Tragelaphus euryceros*, family Bovidae.
– ORIGIN mid 19th cent.: from Kikongo.

bonham /ˈbɒnəm/ ▸ **noun** Irish a piglet.
– ORIGIN late 19th cent.: dialect variant of Irish *banbh* 'pig'.

Bonhoeffer /ˈbɒnhəːfə/, German /ˈbɔnhøfɐ/, Dietrich (1906–45), German Lutheran theologian and pastor. He was an active opponent of Nazism and was involved in the German resistance movement. Arrested in 1943, he was sent to Buchenwald concentration camp and later executed.

bonhomie /ˈbɒnəmiː, ˌbɒnəˈmiː/ ▸ **noun** [mass noun] cheerful friendliness; geniality: *he exuded good humour and bonhomie.*
– DERIVATIVES **bonhomous** adjective.
– ORIGIN late 18th cent.: from French, from *bonhomme* 'good fellow'.

boniato /ˌbɒnɪˈɑːtəʊ/ ▸ **noun** (pl. **boniatos**) a variety of sweet potato with white flesh.
– ORIGIN Spanish.

Boniface, St /ˈbɒnɪfeɪs/ (680–754), Anglo-Saxon missionary; born *Wynfrith*; known as **the Apostle of Germany**. He was sent to Frisia and Germany to spread the Christian faith and was appointed Primate of Germany in 732; he was martyred in Frisia. Feast day, 5 June.

Bonington /ˈbɒnɪŋtən/, Chris (b.1934), English mountaineer; full name *Christian John Storey Bonington*. He made the first British ascent of the north face of the Eiger in 1962 and led expeditions to Mount Everest in 1975 and 1985 (when he reached the summit).

bonito /bəˈniːtəʊ/ ▸ **noun** (pl. **bonitos**) a small tuna with dark oblique stripes on the back, important as a food and game fish. ● *Sarda* and related genera, family Scombridae: several species.
■ another term for SKIPJACK (sense 1).
– ORIGIN late 16th cent.: from Spanish.

bonk (also N. Amer. **boink**) informal ▸ **verb 1** [with obj.] hit (someone or something): *he bonked his head on the plane's low bulkhead.*
2 [no obj.] Brit. have sexual intercourse.
3 [no obj.] (of a cyclist or runner) reach a point of exhaustion that makes it impossible to go further.
▸ **noun 1** an act or the sound of hitting someone or something: *give it a bonk with a hammer.*
2 Brit. an act of sexual intercourse.
3 (**the bonk**) a level of exhaustion that makes a cyclist or runner unable to go further.
– ORIGIN 1930s: imitative.

bonkbuster ▸ **noun** Brit. informal a type of popular novel characterized by frequent explicit sexual encounters.
– ORIGIN 1980s: from BONK, on the pattern of *blockbuster.*

bonkers ▸ **adjective** [predic.] informal mad; crazy: *you're stark raving bonkers!*
– ORIGIN 1940s: of unknown origin.

bon mot /bɒn ˈməʊ/ ▸ **noun** (pl. **bon mots** or **bons mots** pronunc. **same** or /-məʊz/) a witty remark.
– ORIGIN mid 18th cent.: French, literally 'good word'.

Bonn a city in the state of North Rhine-Westphalia in Germany; pop. 314,300 (est. 2006). From 1949 until the reunification of Germany in 1990 Bonn was the capital of the Federal Republic of Germany.

Bonnard /ˈbɒnɑː/, French /bɔnaʀ/, Pierre (1867–1947), French painter and graphic artist, a member of the Nabi Group. Notable for their rich, glowing colours, his works continue and develop the Impressionist tradition; they mostly depict domestic interior scenes, nudes, and landscapes.

bonne /bɒn/ ▸ **noun** dated a nursemaid or housemaid, typically a French one.
– ORIGIN late 18th cent.: from French, feminine of *bon* 'good'.

bonne bouche /bɒn ˈbuːʃ/, French /bɔn buʃ/ ▸ **noun** (pl. **bonne bouches** or **bonnes bouches** pronunc. **same**) an appetizing item of food, especially something sweet eaten at the end of a meal.
– ORIGIN French, literally 'a good taste in the mouth', from *bonne*, feminine of *bon* 'good', and *bouche* 'mouth'.

bonne femme /bɒn ˈfam/ ▸ **adjective** [postpositive] (of fish dishes, stews, and soups) cooked in a simple way: *sole bonne femme.*
– ORIGIN French, from the phrase *à la bonne femme* 'in the manner of a good housewife'.

bonnet ▸ **noun 1** a woman's or child's hat tied under the chin and with a brim framing the face. ■ a soft, round brimless hat like a beret, as worn by men and boys in Scotland. ■ Heraldry the velvet cap within a coronet. ■ (also **war bonnet**) the ceremonial feathered headdress of an American Indian.
2 Brit. the hinged metal canopy covering the engine of a motor vehicle.
3 a cowl on a chimney.
4 Sailing, historical an additional canvas laced to the foot of a sail to catch more wind.
– DERIVATIVES **bonneted** adjective.
– ORIGIN late Middle English (denoting a soft brimless hat for men): from Old French *bonet*, from medieval Latin *abonnis* 'headgear'. Sense 1 dates from the late 15th cent.

bonnethead (also **bonnethead shark**) ▸ **noun** a small hammerhead shark with a relatively narrow rounded head, found in American waters. Also called SHOVELHEAD. ● *Sphyrna tiburo*, family Sphyrnidae.

bonnet macaque (also **bonnet monkey**) ▸ **noun** a South Indian macaque with a bonnet-like tuft of hair on the head. ● *Macaca radiata*, family Cercopithecidae.

bonnetmouth ▸ **noun** a small, slender shoaling fish with an extensible mouth and a long spiny dorsal fin, occurring in the tropical western Atlantic. ● *Inermia vittata*, family Emmelichthyidae.

Bonney, William H. (1859–81), American outlaw; born *Henry McCarty*; known as **Billy the Kid**. A notorious robber and murderer, he was captured by Sheriff Pat Garrett in 1880, and was shot by Garrett after he escaped.

Bonnie Prince Charlie see STUART[1].

bonny (also **bonnie**) ▸ **adjective** (**bonnier**, **bonniest**) chiefly Scottish & N. English attractive or beautiful: *a*

bonny lass. ■ (of a baby) plump and healthy-looking. ■ sizeable (usually expressing approval): *it's worth a thousand pounds, a bonny sum.*
– DERIVATIVES **bonnily** adverb.
– ORIGIN late 15th cent.: perhaps related to Old French *bon* 'good'.

bonny clabber ▶ noun another term for CLABBER.
– ORIGIN early 17th cent.: from Irish *bainne clabair*, denoting thick milk for churning.

bonobo /ˈbɒnəbəʊ/ ▶ noun (pl. **bonobos**) a chimpanzee with a black face and black hair, found in the rainforests of the Democratic Republic of the Congo (Zaire). It is believed to be the closest living relative of humans. Also called PYGMY CHIMPANZEE. ● *Pan paniscus*, family Pongidae.
– ORIGIN 1950s: a local word.

bonsai /ˈbɒnsʌɪ/ ▶ noun [mass noun] the art of growing ornamental, artificially dwarfed varieties of trees and shrubs in pots. ■ [count noun] (pl. **same**) (also **bonsai tree**) an ornamental tree or shrub grown in such a way.
– ORIGIN 1950s: from Japanese, from *bon* 'tray' + *sai* 'planting'.

bonsella /bɒnˈsɛlə/ (also **bonsela**) ▶ noun S. African a tip or bonus.
– ORIGIN from Zulu *bansela* 'express thanks with a gift', or from *umbanselo* 'small gift'.

bonspiel /ˈbɒnspiːl/ ▶ noun a curling match.
– ORIGIN mid 16th cent. (originally Scots): probably of Low German origin.

bontebok /ˈbɒntəbɒk/ ▶ noun (pl. **same** or **bonteboks**) an antelope with a mainly reddish-brown coat and white face, found in eastern South Africa. It belongs to the same species as the blesbok. ● *Damaliscus dorcas dorcas*, family Bovidae.
– ORIGIN late 18th cent.: from Afrikaans, from Dutch *bont* 'pied' + *bok* 'buck'.

bonus ▶ noun a sum of money added to a person's wages as a reward for good performance: *big Christmas bonuses.* ■ Brit. an extra dividend or issue paid to the shareholders of a company. ■ Brit. a distribution of profits to holders of an insurance policy. ■ an extra and unexpected advantage: *good weather is an added bonus but the real appeal is the landscape.*
– ORIGIN late 18th cent. (probably originally Stock Exchange slang): from Latin *bonus* (masculine) 'good', used in place of *bonum* (neuter) 'good, good thing'.

bonus issue ▶ noun Brit. an issue of additional shares to shareholders instead of a dividend, in proportion to the shares already held.

bon vivant /bɒ̃ viːˈvɒ̃/, French /bɔ̃ vivɑ̃/ ▶ noun (pl. **bon vivants** or **bons vivants** pronunc. **same**) a person who devotes themselves to a sociable and luxurious lifestyle.
– ORIGIN late 17th cent.: from French, literally 'person living well', from *bon* 'good' and *vivre* 'to live'.

bon viveur /bɒ̃ viːˈvəː/ ▶ noun (pl. **bon viveurs** or **bons viveurs** pronunc. **same**) another term for BON VIVANT.
– ORIGIN mid 19th cent.: pseudo-French, from French *bon* 'good' and *viveur* 'a living person', on the pattern of *bon vivant*.

bon voyage /ˌbɒn vɔɪˈjɑːʒ/, French /bɔn vwajaʒ/ ▶ exclamation used to express good wishes to someone about to set off on a journey.
– ORIGIN late 17th cent.: French, literally 'good journey'.

bonxie /ˈbɒŋksi/ ▶ noun (pl. **bonxies**) Scottish the great skua (seabird).
– ORIGIN late 18th cent.: from Norwegian *bunksi*, from *bunke* 'dumpy body'.

bony ▶ adjective (**bonier**, **boniest**) of or like bone: *the bony plates that protect turtles and tortoises.* ■ (of a fish eaten as food) having many bones. ■ (of a person or part of the body) so thin that the bones can be seen: *he held up his bony fingers.*
– DERIVATIVES **boniness** noun.

bony fish ▶ noun a fish of a large class distinguished by a skeleton of bone, and comprising the majority of modern fishes. Compare with CARTILAGINOUS FISH. ● Class Osteichthyes: two or three subclasses.

bony labyrinth ▶ noun see LABYRINTH.

bonze /bɒnz/ ▶ noun a Japanese or Chinese Buddhist religious teacher.
– ORIGIN late 16th cent.: probably from Japanese *bonzō, bonsō* 'priest'.

bonzer (also **bonza**) ▶ adjective Austral./NZ informal excellent; first-rate.
– ORIGIN early 20th cent.: perhaps an alteration of BONANZA.

boo[1] ▶ exclamation **1** said suddenly to surprise someone who is unaware of one's presence. [probably an alteration of earlier *bo*, used in the same way since late Middle English.]
2 said to show disapproval or contempt: *'There's only one bar.' 'Boo!'.*
▶ noun an utterance of 'boo' to show disapproval of a speaker or performer: *the audience greeted this comment with boos and hisses.*
▶ verb (**boos**, **booing**, **booed**) say 'boo' to show disapproval of a speaker or performer: [no obj.] *they booed and hissed when he stepped on stage* | [with obj.] *the team were booed off the pitch.*
– PHRASES **wouldn't say boo to a goose** (or US **not say boo**) used to emphasize that someone is very timid.
– ORIGIN early 19th cent. (in sense 2 of the exclamation): imitative of the lowing of oxen.

boo[2] ▶ noun US informal a person's boyfriend or girlfriend.
– ORIGIN 1980s: origin uncertain; probably an alteration of French *beau* 'boyfriend, male admirer'.

booay /ˈbuːʌɪ/ (also **booai** or **boohai**) ▶ noun (**the booay**) NZ remote rural districts.
– PHRASES **up the booay** completely wrong or astray.
– ORIGIN perhaps from the place name *Puhoi* in North Auckland, New Zealand.

boob[1] informal ▶ noun **1** Brit. an embarrassing mistake.
2 N. Amer. a foolish or stupid person.
▶ verb [no obj.] Brit. make an embarrassing mistake.
– ORIGIN early 20th cent.: abbreviation of BOOBY[1].

boob[2] ▶ noun (usu. **boobs**) informal a woman's breast.
– ORIGIN 1950s (originally US): abbreviation of BOOBY[2], from dialect *bubby*, of uncertain origin; perhaps related to German dialect *Bübbi* 'teat'.

booboisie /ˌbuːbwɑːˈziː/ ▶ noun [mass noun] US informal stupid people regarded as a social class.
– ORIGIN 1920s: from BOOB[1], humorous formation on the pattern of *bourgeoisie*.

boo-boo ▶ noun (pl. **boo-boos**) informal a mistake. ■ N. Amer. a minor injury.
– ORIGIN 1950s (originally US): reduplication of BOOB[1].

boobook /ˈbuːbʊk/ ▶ noun a small Australasian owl which has a characteristic double hoot reminiscent of the call of the European cuckoo. Also called MOPOKE or MOREPORK. ● Genus *Ninox*, family Strigidae: two species, especially the common *N. novaeseelandiae*.
– ORIGIN early 19th cent.: imitative of its call.

boob tube ▶ noun informal **1** Brit. a woman's tight-fitting strapless top made of stretchy material.
2 (usu. **the boob tube**) N. Amer. television or a television set: *librarians are scrambling for ways to compete with the boob tube.*

booby[1] ▶ noun (pl. **boobies**) **1** a stupid person.
2 a large tropical seabird of the gannet family, with brown, black, or white plumage and brightly coloured feet. ● Genus *Sula*, family Sulidae: several species.
– ORIGIN early 17th cent.: probably from Spanish *bobo* (in both senses), from Latin *balbus* 'stammering'.

booby[2] ▶ noun (pl. **boobies**) informal a woman's breast.
– ORIGIN 1930s: alteration of dialect *bubby* (see BOOB[2]).

booby hatch ▶ noun N. Amer. informal a psychiatric hospital.

booby prize ▶ noun a prize given as a joke to the person who is last in a race or competition.

booby trap ▶ noun **1** an apparently harmless object containing a concealed explosive device designed to detonate when someone touches it.
2 a trap intended as a practical joke, especially one involving an object placed on top of a door ajar ready to fall on a person passing through.
▶ verb (**booby-trap**) [with obj.] place a booby trap in or on (an object or area): (as adj. **booby-trapped**) *a booby-trapped parcel.*

boodie /ˈbuːdi/ ▶ noun a burrowing rat-kangaroo found only on islands off Western Australia. ● *Bettongia lesueur*, family Potoroidae. Also called **burrowing bettong**.
– ORIGIN mid 19th cent.: from Nyungar *burdi*.

boodle ▶ noun [mass noun] informal money, especially that gained or spent illegally or improperly.
– ORIGIN early 17th cent. (denoting a pack or crowd): from Dutch *boedel, boel* 'possessions, disorderly mass'. Compare with CABOODLE.

boofhead ▶ noun Austral. informal a fool.
– ORIGIN 1940s: probably from *bufflehead* 'simpleton', based on obsolete *buffle* 'buffalo'.

boogaloo /ˌbuːɡəˈluː/ US ▶ noun a dance to rock-and-roll music performed with swivelling and shuffling movements of the body, originally popular in the 1960s.
– ORIGIN 1960s: perhaps an alteration of BOOGIE-WOOGIE.

booger /ˈbʊɡə, ˈbuːɡə/ ▶ noun N. Amer. informal a piece of nasal mucus.
– ORIGIN late 19th cent.: perhaps an alteration of BUGGER or BOGEY[2].

boogie ▶ noun (also **boogie-woogie**) (pl. **boogies**) [mass noun] a style of blues played on the piano with a strong, fast beat. ■ [count noun] informal a dance to pop or rock music.
▶ verb (**boogies**, **boogieing**, **boogied**) [no obj.] informal dance to pop or rock music: *Pat went off to boogie to a steel band.* ■ [no obj., with adverbial of direction] N. Amer. move or leave somewhere fast: *I think we'd better* **boogie on** *out of here.*
– ORIGIN early 20th cent. (originally US in the sense 'party'): of unknown origin.

boogie board ▶ noun a short, light type of surfboard ridden in a prone position.

boohai ▶ noun variant spelling of BOOAY.

boohoo ▶ exclamation used to represent the sound of someone crying noisily.
▶ verb (**boohoos**, **boohooing**, **boohooed**) [no obj.] cry noisily.
– ORIGIN mid 19th cent.: imitative.

boojum /ˈbuːdʒəm/ ▶ noun an imaginary dangerous animal.
– ORIGIN 1876: nonsense word coined by Lewis Carroll in *The Hunting of the Snark*.

book ▶ noun **1** a written or printed work consisting of pages glued or sewn together along one side and bound in covers: *a book of selected poems.* ■ a literary composition that is published or intended for publication as such a work: *I'm writing a book.* ■ a main division of a literary work or of the Bible: *the Book of Genesis.* ■ (also **book of words**) the libretto of a musical or opera, or the script of a play. ■ (**one's books**) used to refer to studying: *he was so deep in his books he would forget to eat.* ■ informal a magazine. ■ an imaginary record or list (often used to emphasize the comprehensiveness of someone's actions or experience): *she felt every emotion in the book of love.*
2 [with modifier] a bound set of blank sheets for writing in: *an accounts book.* ■ (**books**) a set of records or accounts: *a bid to* **balance the books**. ■ a bookmaker's record of bets accepted and money paid out. ■ Soccer the notebook in which a referee writes the names of players who are cautioned for foul play.
3 a set of tickets, stamps, matches, samples of cloth, etc., bound together: *a pattern book.*
4 (**the book**) the first six tricks taken by the declarer in a hand of bridge, after which further tricks count towards fulfilling the contract.
▶ verb [with obj.] **1** reserve (accommodation, a place, etc.); buy (a ticket) in advance: *I have booked a table at the Swan* | [no obj.] *book early to avoid disappointment.* ■ reserve accommodation for (someone): *his secretary had* **booked him into** *the Howard Hotel* | [with two objs] *book me a single room at my usual hotel.* ■ [no obj.] (**book in/into**) register one's arrival at a hotel. ■ engage (a performer or guest) for an event. ■ (**be booked up**) have all places reserved; be full.
2 make an official note of the personal details of (a person who has broken a law or rule): *the cop booked me and took me down to the station.* ■ Soccer (of a referee) note down the name of (a player) who is cautioned for foul play.
– PHRASES **bring someone to book** chiefly Brit. officially punish someone or call them to account for their behaviour. **by the book** strictly according to the rules: *a cop who doesn't exactly* **play it by the book**. **close the books** make no further entries at the end of an accounting period; cease trading. **in someone's bad** (or **good**) **books** in disfavour (or favour) with someone. **in my book** in my opinion: *that counts as a lie in my book.* **make** (or **open**) **a book** (US **make book**) take bets and pay out winnings on the outcome of a race or other contest or event. **on the books** contained in a list of members, employees, or clients. **People of the Book** Jews and Christians as regarded by Muslims. **suit one's book** Brit. be convenient to one. **take a leaf out of someone's book** imitate or emulate someone in a particular way. **throw the book at** informal charge or punish (someone) as severely as possible. **you can't judge a book by its cover** proverb outward appearances

B

are not a reliable indication of the true character of someone or something.
– ORIGIN Old English *bōc* (originally also 'a document or charter'), *bōcian* 'to grant by charter', of Germanic origin; related to Dutch *boek* and German *Buch*, and probably to **BEECH** (on which runes were carved).

bookable ▶ adjective **1** able to be reserved: *tickets are bookable in advance.*
2 Soccer (of an offence) serious enough for the offending player to be cautioned by the referee.

bookbinder ▶ noun a person who binds books as a profession.
– DERIVATIVES **bookbinding** noun.

bookcase ▶ noun an open cabinet containing shelves on which to keep books.

book club ▶ noun a society which sells its members selected books, typically at reduced prices.

bookend ▶ noun a support placed at the end of a row of books to keep them upright, typically forming one of a pair.
▶ verb [with obj.] informal be positioned at the end or on either side of (something): *the narrative is bookended by a pair of incisive essays.*

booker ▶ noun a person employed to engage performers for a theatre or similar.

Booker Prize a literary prize awarded annually for a novel published by a British, Irish, or Commonwealth citizen during the previous year, formerly sponsored by Booker plc and since 2002 by Man Group plc. Full name **Man Booker Prize**.

book group ▶ noun a group of people who meet regularly to discuss books that all members of the group have read.

book hand ▶ noun [mass noun] a formal style of handwriting as used by professional copiers of books before the invention of printing.

bookie ▶ noun (pl. **bookies**) informal a bookmaker.

booking ▶ noun **1** an act of reserving accommodation, a ticket, etc. in advance: *the hotel does not handle group bookings* | [mass noun] *early booking is essential.*
2 Soccer an instance of a player being cautioned by the referee for foul play.

booking clerk ▶ noun Brit. an official selling tickets, especially at a railway station.

booking hall ▶ noun Brit. a room or area at a railway station in which tickets are sold.

booking office ▶ noun chiefly Brit. a place where tickets are sold, especially at a railway station or theatre.

bookish ▶ adjective (of a person or way of life) devoted to reading and studying. ■ (of language or writing) literary in style or allusion.
– DERIVATIVES **bookishly** adverb, **bookishness** noun.

bookkeeping ▶ noun [mass noun] the activity or occupation of keeping records of the financial affairs of a business.
– DERIVATIVES **bookkeeper** noun.

bookland ▶ noun [mass noun] Brit. historical an area of common land granted by charter to a private owner before the Norman conquest.
– ORIGIN Old English, from *bóc* 'charter' + **LAND**. The term was applied eventually to all land that was not *folcland*, i.e. land subject to traditional communal obligations.

book learning ▶ noun [mass noun] knowledge gained from books or study rather than personal experience.

booklet ▶ noun a small, thin book with paper covers, typically giving information on a particular subject.

booklouse ▶ noun (pl. **booklice**) a minute insect that typically has reduced or absent wings, frequently found in buildings where it may cause damage to books and paper. ● Liposcelidae and related families in the order Psocoptera: many species, in particular the common *Liposcelis bostrychophilus*.

book lung ▶ noun Zoology (in a spider or other arachnid) each of a pair of respiratory organs composed of many fine lamellae. They are situated in the abdomen and have openings on the underside.

bookmaker ▶ noun a person whose job is to take bets (especially on horse races), calculate odds, and pay out winnings; the manager of a betting shop.
– DERIVATIVES **bookmaking** noun.

bookman ▶ noun (pl. **bookmen**) archaic a literary man.

bookmark ▶ noun a strip of leather, card, or other material, used to mark one's place in a book. ■ a record of the address of a website, file, or other data made to enable quick access in future.
▶ verb [with obj.] record the address of (a website, file, etc.) to enable quick access in future: *fans will want to bookmark this site.*

bookmobile ▶ noun N. Amer. a mobile library.
– ORIGIN 1930s: from **BOOK**, on the pattern of *automobile*.

Book of Changes ▶ noun English name for **I CHING**.

Book of Common Prayer ▶ noun the official service book of the Church of England, compiled by Thomas Cranmer and others, first issued in 1549, and largely unchanged since the revision of 1662.

book of hours ▶ noun a book of prayers appointed for particular canonical hours or times of day, used by Roman Catholics for private devotions and popular especially in the Middle Ages, when they were often richly illuminated.

Book of Proverbs see **PROVERBS**.

Book of the Dead ▶ noun **1** a collection of ancient Egyptian religious and magical texts, selections from which were often written on or placed in tombs.
2 (in full **Tibetan Book of the Dead**) a Tibetan Buddhist text recited during funerary rites, describing the passage from death to rebirth.

book of words ▶ noun see **BOOK** (sense 1 of the noun).

bookplate ▶ noun a decorative label stuck in the front of a book, bearing the name of the book's owner.

bookrest ▶ noun Brit. an adjustable support for an open book on a table.

bookseller ▶ noun a person who sells books, especially as the owner or manager of a bookshop.
– DERIVATIVES **bookselling** noun.

bookshelf ▶ noun (pl. **bookshelves**) a shelf on which books can be stored.

bookshop (US also **bookstore**) ▶ noun a shop where books are sold.

Books of the Maccabees ▶ plural noun see **MACCABEES**.

bookstall ▶ noun chiefly Brit. a stand where books and sometimes newspapers are sold, especially out of doors or at a railway station.

book token ▶ noun Brit. a voucher which can be exchanged for books costing up to a specified amount.

book value ▶ noun the value of a security or asset as entered in a firm's books. Often contrasted with **MARKET VALUE**.

bookwork ▶ noun [mass noun] **1** the activity of keeping records of accounts.
2 the studying of textbooks, as opposed to practical work.

bookworm ▶ noun **1** informal a person who enjoys reading.
2 (especially formerly) the larva of a wood-boring beetle which feeds on the paper and glue in books.

Boole, George (1815–64), English mathematician responsible for Boolean algebra. The study of mathematical or symbolic logic developed mainly from his ideas.

Boolean /ˈbuːlɪən/ ▶ adjective denoting a system of algebraic notation used to represent logical propositions by means of the binary digits 0 (false) and 1 (true), especially in computing and electronics.
▶ noun Computing a binary variable with these possible values.

boom¹ ▶ noun a loud, deep, resonant sound: *the deep boom of the bass drum.* ■ the characteristic resonant cry of the bittern.
▶ verb [no obj.] make a loud, deep, resonant sound: *thunder boomed in the sky.* ■ [with direct speech] say in a loud, deep, resonant voice: *'Stop right there,' boomed the Headmaster.* ■ (of a bittern) utter its characteristic resonant cry.
– PHRASES **boom boom** Brit. informal an exclamation made after delivering the punchline of a joke. [popularized by the fox puppet Basil Brush, a character in a British television comedy show.]
– DERIVATIVES **boominess** noun, **boomy** adjective (**boomier**, **boomiest**).
– ORIGIN late Middle English (as a verb): ultimately imitative; perhaps from Dutch *bommen* 'to hum, buzz'.

boom² ▶ noun a period of great prosperity or rapid economic growth: *the London property boom* | [mass noun] *the eras of boom and bust.*
▶ verb [no obj.] experience a period of great prosperity or rapid economic growth: *business is booming.*
– DERIVATIVES **boomlet** noun, **boomy** adjective (**boomier**, **boomiest**).
– ORIGIN late 19th cent. (originally US): probably from **BOOM¹**.

boom³ ▶ noun **1** a pivoted spar to which the foot of a vessel's sail is attached, allowing the angle of the sail to be changed.
2 [often as modifier] a movable arm over a television or film set, carrying a microphone or camera: *a boom mike.*
3 a floating beam used to contain oil spills or to form a barrier across the mouth of a harbour or river.
– ORIGIN mid 16th cent. (in the general sense 'beam, pole'): from Dutch, 'beam, tree, pole'; related to **BEAM**.

boom box ▶ noun informal a large portable radio and cassette player capable of powerful sound.

boomer ▶ noun informal **1** something large or notable of its kind, in particular: ■ Austral. a large male kangaroo. ■ a large wave.
2 N. Amer. short for **BABY BOOMER** (see **BABY BOOM**).
3 US a nuclear submarine with ballistic missiles.
– ORIGIN early 19th cent.: probably from the verb **BOOM¹** + **-ER¹**.

boomerang ▶ noun a curved flat piece of wood that can be thrown so that it will return to the thrower, traditionally used by Australian Aborigines as a hunting weapon.
▶ verb [no obj.] (of a plan or action) recoil on the originator: *misleading consumers about quality will eventually boomerang on a car-maker.*
– ORIGIN early 19th cent.: from Dharuk.

booming ▶ adjective **1** having a period of great prosperity or rapid economic growth: *the booming economy of the 1920s.*
2 (of a sound or voice) loud, deep, and resonant.
3 struck with great force: *a booming kick from the touchline.*

boomslang ▶ noun a large, highly venomous southern African tree snake, the male of which is bright green and the female dull olive brown. ● *Dispholidus typus*, family Colubridae.
– ORIGIN late 18th cent.: from Afrikaans, from Dutch *boom* 'tree' + *slang* 'snake'.

boom vang ▶ noun see **VANG**.

boon ▶ noun **1** [usu. in sing.] a thing that is helpful or beneficial: *the route will be a boon to many travellers.*
2 archaic a favour or request.
– ORIGIN Middle English (originally in the sense 'request for a favour'): from Old Norse *bón*.

boon companion ▶ noun a close friend with whom one enjoys spending time.
– ORIGIN mid 16th cent.: *boon* from Old French *bon*, from Latin *bonus* 'good'. The early literal sense was 'good fellow', originally denoting a drinking companion.

boondocks /ˈbuːndɒks/ ▶ plural noun N. Amer. informal rough or isolated country: *this place is out in the boondocks, you'll never get here by bus.*
– ORIGIN 1940s: *boondock* from Tagalog *bundok* 'mountain'.

boondoggle /ˈbuːndɒɡ(ə)l/ N. Amer. informal ▶ noun an unnecessary, wasteful, or fraudulent project.
▶ verb [no obj.] waste money or time on such projects.
– ORIGIN 1930s: of unknown origin.

Boone, Daniel (*c*.1734–1820), American pioneer. Boone made trips west from Pennsylvania into the unexplored area of Kentucky, organizing settlements and successfully defending them against hostile American Indians.

boong /bʊŋ/ ▶ noun Austral. offensive an Aborigine.
– ORIGIN 1920s: origin uncertain.

boonies /ˈbuːnɪz/ ▶ plural noun short for **BOONDOCKS**.

boor /bɔː, bʊə/ ▶ noun a rough and bad-mannered person.
– ORIGIN mid 16th cent. (in the sense 'peasant'): from Low German *būr* or Dutch *boer* 'farmer'.

boorish ▶ adjective rough and bad-mannered; coarse: *boorish behaviour.*
– DERIVATIVES **boorishly** adverb, **boorishness** noun.

boost ▶ verb [with obj.] **1** help or encourage (something) to increase or improve: *a range of measures to boost tourism.* ■ amplify (an electrical signal).
2 N. Amer. push from below.
3 N. Amer. informal steal (something): *he'd had his wallet boosted in a bar.*
▶ noun **1** a source of help or encouragement leading to increase or improvement: *the cut in interest rates will give a further boost to the economy.* ■ an increase or improvement: *a boost in exports.*

2 N. Amer. a push from below.
– ORIGIN early 19th cent. (originally US, in sense 2 of the verb): of unknown origin.

booster ▶ noun 1 a device for increasing electrical voltage or signal strength.
2 the first stage of a rocket or spacecraft, used to give initial acceleration and then jettisoned.
3 Medicine a dose of a vaccine that increases or renews the effect of an earlier one.
4 [in combination] a source of help or encouragement: *job fairs are a great morale booster.* ■ N. Amer. a keen promoter of a person, organization, or cause.
5 N. Amer. informal a shoplifter.

boosterism ▶ noun [mass noun] chiefly N. Amer. the keen promotion of a person, organization, or cause.
– DERIVATIVES **boosterish** adjective.

booster seat (also **booster cushion**) ▶ noun an extra seat or cushion placed on an existing seat for a small child to sit on.

boot[1] ▶ noun 1 a sturdy item of footwear covering the foot and ankle, and sometimes also the lower leg: *a pair of walking boots.* ■ a covering to protect the lower part of a horse's leg. ■ historical an instrument of torture encasing and crushing the foot. ■ US short for DENVER BOOT.
2 informal a hard kick: *he got a boot in the stomach.*
3 Brit. an enclosed space at the back of a car for carrying luggage or other goods.
4 (also **boot-up**) [usu. as modifier] the process of starting a computer and putting it into a state of readiness for operation: *a boot disk.*
▶ verb [with obj.] 1 [with obj. and adverbial of direction] kick (something) hard in a specified direction: *he ended up booting the ball into the stand.* ■ (**boot someone off**) informal force someone to leave a vehicle unceremoniously: *a guard booted two children off a train.* ■ (**boot someone out**) informal force someone to leave a place or job unceremoniously: *she had been booted out of school.*
2 start (a computer) and put it into a state of readiness for operation: *the menu will be ready as soon as you boot up your computer* | [no obj.] *the system won't boot from the original drive.* [from BOOTSTRAP (sense 2 of the noun).]
3 US place a wheel clamp on (an illegally parked car).
– PHRASES **the boot** (or N. Amer. **shoe**) **is on the other foot** the situation, in particular the holding of advantage, has reversed. **boots and all** Austral./NZ informal with no holds barred; wholeheartedly: *Canberra's cabbies go in boots and all for a fair deal.* **die with one's boots on** die in battle or while actively occupied. **get the boot** informal be dismissed from one's job. **give someone the boot** informal dismiss someone from their job. **old boot** informal an ugly or disliked old woman. **put the boot in** (or **into someone**) Brit. informal kick someone hard when they are on the ground. ■ treat someone vulnerable in a cruel way. **with one's heart in one's boots** in a state of great depression or trepidation. **you (can) bet your boots** informal used to express absolute certainty: *you can bet your boots that the patrol has raised the alarm.*
– DERIVATIVES **booted** adjective (sense 1 of the noun, sense 3 of the noun).
– ORIGIN Middle English: from Old Norse *bóti* or its source, Old French *bote*, of unknown ultimate origin.

boot[2] ▶ noun (in phrase **to boot**) as well; in addition: *she was a woman of uninspiring appearance and a dreadful bore to boot.*
– ORIGIN Old English *bōt* 'advantage, remedy', of Germanic origin; related to Dutch *boete* and German *Busse* 'penance, fine', also to BETTER[1] and BEST.

bootable ▶ adjective (of a disk) containing the software required to boot a computer.

bootblack ▶ noun chiefly historical a person employed to polish boots and shoes.

bootboy ▶ noun 1 informal a rowdy or violent youth typically having close-cropped hair and wearing heavy boots.
2 historical a boy employed to clean boots and shoes.

boot camp ▶ noun chiefly N. Amer. a military training camp for new recruits, with very harsh discipline. ■ a prison for young offenders, run on military lines.

boot-cut ▶ adjective (of jeans or other trousers) flared very slightly below the knee, so as to be worn comfortably over boots.

bootee /buːˈtiː/ (also **bootie**) ▶ noun 1 a baby's soft woollen shoe.
2 a woman's short boot.
3 a protective shoe or lining for a shoe.

Boötes /bəʊˈəʊtiːz/ Astronomy a northern constellation (the Herdsman), said to represent a man holding the leash of two dogs (Canes Venatici) while driving a bear (Ursa Major). It contains the bright star Arcturus.
– ORIGIN Greek.

boot-faced ▶ adjective Brit. informal having a grim or scowling expression: *a boot-faced police sergeant.*

Booth, William (1829–1912), English religious leader, founder and first general of the Salvation Army. A Methodist revivalist preacher, in 1865 he established a mission in the East End of London which later became the Salvation Army.

booth /buːð, buːθ/ ▶ noun 1 a small temporary tent or structure at a market, fair, or exhibition, used for selling goods, providing information, or staging shows.
2 an enclosed compartment that allows privacy, for example when telephoning, voting, or sitting in a restaurant.
– ORIGIN Middle English (in the sense 'temporary dwelling or shelter'): from Old Norse *buth*, based on *búa* 'dwell'.

booth capturing ▶ noun [mass noun] chiefly Indian a method of fraudulently interfering with the process of an election whereby members of a party occupy a polling booth, excluding and voting in place of those people who are registered to vote there.

Boothia, Gulf of /ˈbuːθɪə/ a gulf in the Canadian Arctic, between the Boothia Peninsula and Baffin Island, in the Northwest Territories.
– ORIGIN named in honour of Sir Felix *Booth* (1775–1850), patron of the expedition to the Arctic (1829–33) led by Sir John Ross.

Boothia Peninsula a peninsula of northern Canada, in the Northwest Territories, situated between Victoria Island and Baffin Island.

bootie ▶ noun (pl. **booties**) variant spelling of BOOTEE.

bootjack ▶ noun a device for holding a boot by the heel to ease the withdrawal of one's foot.

bootlace ▶ noun a cord or leather strip for lacing boots.

bootlace fungus ▶ noun another term for HONEY FUNGUS.

bootlace tie ▶ noun Brit. a narrow necktie, popular in the 1950s.

bootleg ▶ adjective (of alcoholic drink or a recording) made, distributed, or sold illegally: *bootleg cassettes.*
▶ verb (**bootlegs**, **bootlegging**, **bootlegged**) [with obj.] make, distribute, or sell (alcoholic drink or a recording) illegally: (as noun **bootlegging**) *bootlegging is rife in America.*
▶ noun an illegal musical recording, especially one made at a concert.
– DERIVATIVES **bootlegger** noun.
– ORIGIN late 19th cent.: from the smugglers' practice of concealing bottles in their boots.

bootless ▶ adjective archaic (of a task or undertaking) ineffectual; useless: *remonstrating with him seems ever to have been a bootless task.*
– ORIGIN Old English *bōtlēas* 'not able to be compensated for by payment' (see BOOT[2], -LESS).

bootlicker ▶ noun informal an obsequious or servile person.
– DERIVATIVES **bootlicking** noun & adjective.

bootmaker ▶ noun a maker of boots and shoes.

boots ▶ noun Brit. dated a person employed in a hotel to clean boots and shoes, carry luggage, and perform other menial tasks.

boot-scooting ▶ noun informal term for LINE DANCING.

bootstrap ▶ noun 1 a loop at the back of a boot, used to pull it on.
2 Computing a technique of loading a program into a computer by means of a few initial instructions which enable the introduction of the rest of the program from an input device.
3 [usu. as modifier] the technique of starting with existing resources to create something more complex and effective: *we see the creative act as a bootstrap process.*
▶ verb [with obj.] 1 Computing fuller form of BOOT[1] (sense 2 of the verb).
2 start up (an Internet-based business or other enterprise) with minimal financial resources. ■ get (oneself or something) into or out of a situation using existing resources: *the company is bootstrapping itself out of a marred financial past.*
– PHRASES **pull** (or **drag**) **oneself up by one's** (**own**) **bootstraps** improve one's position by one's own efforts.
– DERIVATIVES **bootstrapping** noun.

boot top ▶ noun the part of the hull of a ship just above the waterline, typically marked by a line of contrasting colour.

boot-up ▶ noun see BOOT[1] (sense 4 of the noun).

booty[1] ▶ noun [mass noun] valuable stolen goods, especially those seized in war. ■ informal something gained or won.
– ORIGIN late Middle English (originally denoting plunder acquired in common): from Middle Low German *būte*, *buite* 'exchange, distribution', of uncertain origin.

booty[2] ▶ noun (pl. **booties**) N. Amer. informal a person's bottom.
– PHRASES **shake one's booty** dance energetically.
– ORIGIN 1920s: probably an alteration of BOTTY.

booty call ▶ noun US informal a sexual invitation or rendezvous.
– ORIGIN 1990s: from BOOTY[2] and CALL.

bootylicious /ˌbuːtɪˈlɪʃəs/ ▶ adjective US informal (of a woman) sexually attractive.
– ORIGIN 1990s: from BOOTY[2], on the pattern of *delicious*.

boo word ▶ noun informal a word or expression denoting something that is regarded with disapproval or dislike: *positivism has become something of a boo word among many social scientists.*

booze informal ▶ noun [mass noun] alcoholic drink: *I wonder where he's hidden his booze.*
▶ verb [no obj.] drink alcohol, especially in large quantities.
– ORIGIN Middle English *bouse*, from Middle Dutch *būsen* 'drink to excess'. The spelling *booze* dates from the 18th cent.

booze cruise ▶ noun Brit. informal an excursion to Europe by ferry, the aim of which is to bring back cheap or tax-free alcohol.

boozer ▶ noun informal a person who drinks large quantities of alcohol. ■ Brit. a pub or bar.

booze-up ▶ noun Brit. informal a heavy drinking session.

boozy ▶ adjective (**boozier**, **booziest**) informal characterized by drinking large quantities of alcohol: *a boozy lunch.*
– DERIVATIVES **boozily** adverb, **booziness** noun.

bop[1] informal ▶ noun 1 Brit. a dance to pop music. ■ an organized social occasion with such dancing.
2 short for BEBOP.
▶ verb (**bops**, **bopping**, **bopped**) [no obj.] dance to pop music: *everyone was bopping until the small hours.* ■ move or travel energetically: *entrepreneurial types bopping around Italy.*
– DERIVATIVES **bopper** noun.
– ORIGIN 1940s: shortening of BEBOP.

bop[2] informal ▶ verb (**bops**, **bopping**, **bopped**) [with obj.] hit or punch quickly: *Rex bopped him on the head.*
▶ noun a quick blow or punch.
– ORIGIN 1930s (originally US): imitative.

bo-peep ▶ noun Austral./NZ informal a quick look.
– ORIGIN early 16th cent. (originally denoting a game of hiding and reappearing): from *bo*, an exclamation intended to startle someone (compare with BOO[1]) + the verb PEEP[1]. The current sense dates from the 1940s.

Bophuthatswana /ˌbə(ʊ)puːtətˈswɑːnə/ a former homeland established in South Africa for the Tswana people, now part of North West and Mpumalanga.

bora[1] /ˈbɔːrə/ ▶ noun a strong, cold, dry NE wind blowing in the upper Adriatic.
– ORIGIN mid 19th cent.: dialect variant of Italian *borea*, from Latin *boreas* 'north wind' (see BOREAL).

bora[2] /ˈbɔːrə/ ▶ noun an Australian Aboriginal rite in which boys are initiated into manhood.
– ORIGIN mid 19th cent.: from Kamilaroi *buuru*.

Bora-Bora /ˌbɔːrəˈbɔːrə/ an island of the Society Islands group in French Polynesia.

boracic /bəˈrasɪk/ ▶ adjective 1 consisting of or containing boric acid, especially as an antiseptic.
2 Brit. informal having no money. [from *boracic lint*, rhyming slang for 'skint'.]
– ORIGIN late 18th cent.: from medieval Latin *borax*, *borac-* (see BORAX) + -IC.

borage /ˈbɒrɪdʒ/ ▶ noun a European herbaceous plant with bright blue flowers and hairy leaves, which is attractive to bees. ● *Borago officinalis*, family Boraginaceae (the **borage family**). This family includes many plants that typically have blue or purple flowers, including forget-me-not, comfrey, bugloss, and alkanet.

– ORIGIN Middle English: from Old French *bourrache*, from medieval Latin *borrago*, perhaps from Arabic *'abū ḥuraš* 'father of roughness' (referring to the leaves).

B

boraginaceous /ˌbɒrɪdʒɪ'neɪʃəs/ ▸ **adjective** Botany relating to or denoting plants of the borage family (Boraginaceae).

borane /'bɔːreɪn/ ▸ **noun** Chemistry any of a series of unstable binary compounds of boron and hydrogen, analogous to the alkanes. The simplest example is diborane, B_2H_6.
– ORIGIN early 20th cent.: from **BORON** + **-ANE**[2].

Borås /bʊ'rɔːs/ an industrial city in SW Sweden; pop. 101,487 (2008).

borate /'bɔːreɪt/ ▸ **noun** Chemistry a salt in which the anion contains both boron and oxygen, as in borax.

borax /'bɔːraks/ ▸ **noun** [mass noun] a white compound which occurs as a mineral in some alkaline salt deposits and is used in making glass and ceramics, as a metallurgical flux, and as an antiseptic. ● A hydrated sodium borate; chem. formula: $Na_2B_4O_7 10H_2O$.
– ORIGIN late Middle English: from medieval Latin, from Arabic *būraq*, from Pahlavi *būrak*.

Borazon /'bɔːrəzɒn/ ▸ **noun** [mass noun] trademark an industrial abrasive consisting of boron nitride.
– ORIGIN 1950s: from **BORON**, with the insertion of **AZO-**.

borborygmus /ˌbɔːbə'rɪgməs/ ▸ **noun** (pl. **borborygmi** /-mʌɪ/) technical a rumbling or gurgling noise made by the movement of fluid and gas in the intestines.
– ORIGIN early 18th cent.: modern Latin, from Greek *borborugmos*.

Bordeaux[1] /bɔː'dəʊ/, French /bɔRdo/ a port of SW France on the River Garonne, capital of Aquitaine; pop. 235,878 (2006). It is a centre of the wine trade.

Bordeaux[2] /bɔː'dəʊ/ ▸ **noun** (pl. **same** /-'dəʊz/) [mass noun] a red, white, or rosé wine from the district of Bordeaux.

Bordeaux mixture ▸ **noun** [mass noun] a fungicide for vines, fruit trees, and other plants, composed of equal quantities of copper sulphate and calcium oxide in water.
– ORIGIN late 19th cent.: first used in the vineyards of the Bordeaux region.

bordelaise /ˌbɔːdə'leɪz/ ▸ **adjective** denoting or served with a sauce of red wine and onions: *bordelaise sauce* | [postpositive] *lobster bordelaise*.
– ORIGIN French, from (*à la*) *bordelaise* 'Bordeaux-style'.

bordello /bɔː'dɛləʊ/ ▸ **noun** (pl. **bordellos**) chiefly N. Amer. a brothel.
– ORIGIN late 16th cent. (gradually replacing Middle English *bordel*): from Italian, probably from Old French *bordel*, diminutive of *borde* 'small farm, cottage', ultimately of Germanic origin.

Border, Allan (Robert) (b.1955), Australian cricketer. A batsman and occasional spin bowler, he made 156 Test match appearances (93 as captain) and scored 11,174 runs (all three figures being world records).

border ▸ **noun 1** a line separating two countries, administrative divisions, or other areas: *Panama's western border with Costa Rica* | [as modifier] *border controls*. ■ a district near such a line: *a refugee camp **on the border***. ■ (**the Border**) the boundary and adjoining districts between Northern Ireland and the Republic of Ireland. ■ (**the Border** or **the Borders**) the boundary and adjoining districts between Scotland and England.
2 the edge or boundary of something, or the part near it: *the northern border of their distribution area* | figurative *the unknown regions at the borders of physics and electronics*.
3 a decorative strip around the edge of something. ■ a strip of ground along the edge of a lawn or path for planting flowers or shrubs.
▸ **verb 1** [with obj.] form an edge along or beside (something): *a pool bordered by palm trees*. ■ provide (something) with a decorative edge: *the walls were bordered with carved scrolls and cornices*.
2 (of a country or area) be adjacent to (another country or area): *regions bordering Azerbaijan* | [no obj.] *the states **bordering on** the Black Sea*.
3 [no obj.] (**border on**) come close to or be developing into (an extreme condition): *Sam arrived in a state of excitement bordering on hysteria*.
– DERIVATIVES **borderless** adjective.
– ORIGIN late Middle English: from Old French *bordeure*; ultimately of Germanic origin and related to **BOARD**.

Border collie ▸ **noun** a common working sheepdog, typically with a black-and-white coat, of a medium-sized breed originating near the border between England and Scotland.

borderer ▸ **noun** (chiefly in historical contexts) a person living near the border between two countries, especially that between Scotland and England.

borderland ▸ **noun** (usu. **borderlands**) a district near the line separating two countries or areas. ■ an area of overlap between two things: *the murky borderland between history and myth*.

Border Leicester ▸ **noun** see **LEICESTER**[3] (sense 2).

borderline ▸ **noun** a boundary separating two countries or areas. ■ a division between two distinct or opposite things: *the borderline between ritual and custom*.
▸ **adjective** only just acceptable in quality or as belonging to a category: *references may be requested in borderline cases*.

Border terrier ▸ **noun** a small terrier of a breed with rough hair, originating in the Cheviot Hills.

bordure /'bɔːdjʊə/ ▸ **noun** Heraldry a broad border used as a charge in a coat of arms, often as a mark of difference.
– ORIGIN late Middle English: variant of **BORDER**.

bore[1] ▸ **verb 1** [with obj.] make (a hole) in something with a tool or by digging: *bore a hole in the wall to pass the cable through* | [no obj.] *the drill can bore through rock* | figurative *his eyes bored into hers*. ■ hollow out (a gun barrel or other tube): *an 1100 cc road bike **bored out** to 1168 cc*.
2 [no obj.] (of an athlete or racehorse) push another competitor out of the way.
▸ **noun 1** the hollow part inside a gun barrel or other tube. ■ [often in combination] the diameter of a bore; the calibre: *a small-bore rifle*. ■ [in combination] a gun of a specified bore: *he shot a guard in the leg with a twelve-bore*.
2 short for **BOREHOLE**.
– ORIGIN Old English *borian* (verb), of Germanic origin; related to German *bohren*.

bore[2] ▸ **noun** a person whose talk or behaviour is dull and uninteresting: *he can be a crashing bore*. ■ [in sing.] a tedious or annoying situation or activity: *it's such a bore cooking when one's alone*.
▸ **verb** [with obj.] cause (someone) to feel weary and uninterested by dull talk or behaviour: *she is too polite to bore us with anecdotes* | [with obj. and complement] *timid women quickly bore her silly*.
– PHRASES **bore someone to death** (or **to tears**) make someone feel extremely bored: *he would bore everyone to death with tales about his wonderful daughter*.
– ORIGIN mid 18th cent. (as a verb): of unknown origin.

bore[3] ▸ **noun** a steep-fronted wave caused by the meeting of two tides or by the constriction of a tide rushing up a narrow estuary.
– ORIGIN early 17th cent.: perhaps from Old Norse *bára* 'wave'; the term was used in the general sense 'billow, wave' in Middle English.

bore[4] past of **BEAR**[1].

boreal /'bɔːrɪəl/ ▸ **adjective 1** Ecology relating to or characteristic of the climatic zone south of the Arctic, especially the cold temperate region dominated by taiga and forests of birch, poplar, and conifers: *northern boreal forest*. ■ (**Boreal**) Botany relating to or denoting a phytogeographical kingdom comprising the arctic and temperate regions of Eurasia and North America.
2 (**Boreal**) Geology relating to or denoting the second climatic stage of the postglacial period in northern Europe, between the Preboreal and Atlantic stages (about 9,000 to 7,500 years ago), marked by a warm, dry climate.
– ORIGIN late Middle English: from late Latin *borealis*, from Latin *Boreas*, denoting the god of the north wind, from Greek.

bored[1] ▸ **adjective** feeling weary and impatient because one is unoccupied or lacks interest in one's current activity: *she got **bored with** staring out of the window* | *they hung around all day, **bored stiff*** | *bored teenagers*.
– DERIVATIVES **boredly** /'bɔːdli/ **adverb**.

> **USAGE** The traditional constructions for **bored** are **bored by** or **bored with**. The construction **bored of** emerged more recently, and is extremely common, especially in informal language. Although it is perfectly logical by analogy with constructions such as **tired of**, it is not fully accepted in standard English.

bored[2] ▸ **adjective** [in combination] (of a gun) having a specified bore: *large-bored guns*.

bore da /'bɒrɛ ˌdɑː/ ▸ **exclamation** Welsh good morning!
– ORIGIN Welsh, from *bore* 'morning' + *da* 'good'.

boredom ▸ **noun** [mass noun] the state of feeling bored: *I'll die of boredom if I live that long*.

boreen /bɔː'riːn/ ▸ **noun** Irish a narrow country road.
– ORIGIN mid 19th cent.: from Irish *bóithrín*, diminutive of *bóthar* 'road'.

borehole ▸ **noun** a deep, narrow hole made in the ground, especially to locate water or oil.

borek /bʊ'rɛk/ ▸ **noun** (pl. **same** or **boreks**) (in Turkish and Middle Eastern cookery) a pie of filo pastry filled with cheese, spinach, or minced meat.
– ORIGIN Turkish *börek*.

borer ▸ **noun 1** a worm, mollusc, insect, or insect larva which bores into wood, other plant material, or rock.
2 a tool for boring.

borescope ▸ **noun** an instrument used to inspect the inside of a structure through a small hole.

Borg, Björn (Rune) (b.1956), Swedish tennis player. He won five consecutive men's singles titles at Wimbledon (1976–80), beating the record of three consecutive wins held by Fred Perry.

borgata /bɔː'gɑːtə/ ▸ **noun** (pl. **borgatas** or **borgate**) US an organized branch of the Mafia.
– ORIGIN 1960s: Italian, 'district, village'.

Borges /'bɔːxɛs/, Jorge Luis (1899–1986), Argentinian poet, short-story writer, and essayist. The volume of short stories *A Universal History of Infamy* (1935, revised 1954) is regarded as a founding work of magic realism.
– DERIVATIVES **Borgesian** adjective.

Borgia[1] /'bɔːʒə/, Italian /'bɔrdʒa/, Cesare (*c.*1476–1507), Italian statesman, cardinal, and general. The illegitimate son of Cardinal Rodrigo Borgia (later Pope Alexander VI) and brother of Lucrezia Borgia, he was captain general of the papal army from 1499, and became master of a large portion of central Italy.

Borgia[2] /'bɔːʒə/, Italian /'bɔrdʒa/, Lucrezia (1480–1519), Italian noblewoman, sister of Cesare Borgia. She married three times, according to the political alliances useful to her family; after her third marriage in 1501 she established herself as a patron of the arts.

boric /'bɔːrɪk/ ▸ **adjective** Chemistry of boron: *boric oxide*.

boric acid ▸ **noun** Chemistry a weakly acid crystalline compound derived from borax, used as a mild antiseptic and in the manufacture of heat-resistant glass and enamels. See also **BORACIC**. ● Chem. formula: $B(OH)_3$.

boride /'bɔːrʌɪd/ ▸ **noun** a binary compound of boron with a metallic element.

boring ▸ **adjective** not interesting; tedious: *I've got a boring job in an office*.
– DERIVATIVES **boringly** adverb [as submodifier] *my boringly respectable uncle*, **boringness** noun.

Boris Godunov /'bɒrɪs/ see **GODUNOV**.

bork ▸ **verb** [with obj.] US informal obstruct (someone, especially a candidate for public office) by systematically defaming or vilifying them.
– ORIGIN 1980s: from the name of Robert *Bork* (born 1927), an American judge whose nomination to the Supreme Court (1987) was rejected following unfavourable publicity for his allegedly extreme views.

Borlaug /'bɔːlɔːg/, Norman Ernest (1914–2009), American scientist, a central figure in the green revolution. He worked for many years on the improvement of wheat crops and the adaptation of new strains of wheat to parts of the world where it had not previously been grown. Nobel Peace Prize (1970).

borlotti bean /bɔː'lɒti/ ▸ **noun** a type of kidney bean with a pink speckled skin that turns brown when cooked.
– ORIGIN Italian *borlotti*, plural of *borlotto* 'kidney bean'.

Bormann /'bɔːmən/, German /'bɔɔːɐman/, Martin (1900–*c.*1945), German Nazi politician. Considered to be Hitler's closest collaborator, he disappeared at the end of the Second World War; his skeleton, exhumed in Berlin, was identified in 1973.

Born /bɔːn/, German /bɔrn/, Max (1882–1970), German theoretical physicist, a founder of quantum mechanics. Nobel Prize for Physics (1954).

born ▸ **adjective** existing as a result of birth: *she was born in Aberdeen* | *I was **born with** a sense of curiosity* | *a newly born baby*. ■ [in combination] having a spe-

B

cific nationality: *a German-born philosopher*. ■ [attrib.] having a natural ability to do a particular job: *he's a born engineer*. ■ [predic., with infinitive] perfectly suited or trained to do a particular job: *men born to rule*. ■ (of an organization, movement, or idea) brought into existence: *on 1 January 1992, the new company was born*. ■ (**born of**) existing as a result of (a particular situation or feeling): *his work is born of despair*.
– PHRASES **born and bred** by birth and upbringing, especially with reference to someone considered a typical product of a place: *he was a Cambridge man born and bred*. **born on the wrong side of the blanket** see BLANKET. **be born with a silver spoon in one's mouth** see SILVER. **in all one's born days** used to express surprise at something one has not encountered before: *in all my born days I've never seen the like of it*. **not know one is born** Brit. used to convey that someone has an easy life without realizing how easy it is. **there's one** (or **a sucker**) **born every minute** informal there are many gullible people. **I** (or **he**, **she**, etc.) **wasn't born yesterday** used to indicate that one (or another person) is not foolish or gullible.
– ORIGIN Old English *boren*, past participle of *beran* 'to bear' (see BEAR[1]).

USAGE On the difference between born and borne, see USAGE at BEAR[1].

born-again ▶ **adjective** relating to or denoting a person who has converted to a personal faith in Christ (with reference to John 3:3): *a born-again Christian*. ■ newly converted to and very enthusiastic about an idea or cause: *born-again environmentalists*.
▶ **noun** chiefly N. Amer. a born-again Christian.

borne past participle of BEAR[1]. ▶ **adjective** [in combination] carried or transported by the thing specified: *waterborne bacteria*.

Borneo /'bɔːnɪəʊ/ a large island of the Malay Archipelago, comprising Kalimantan (a region of Indonesia), Sabah and Sarawak (states of Malaysia), and Brunei.
– DERIVATIVES **Bornean adjective & noun.**

Bornholm /'bɔːnhəʊm/ a Danish island in the Baltic Sea, south-east of Sweden.

Bornholm disease ▶ **noun** [mass noun] a viral infection with fever and pain in the muscles of the ribs.
– ORIGIN 1930s: named after the island of BORNHOLM, where it was first described.

bornite /'bɔːnʌɪt/ ▶ **noun** [mass noun] a brittle reddish-brown crystalline mineral with an iridescent purple tarnish, consisting of a sulphide of copper and iron.
– ORIGIN early 19th cent.: from the name of Ignatius von *Born* (1742–91), Austrian mineralogist, + -ITE[1].

boro- /'bɔːrəʊ/ ▶ **combining form** Chemistry representing BORON.

Borobudur /ˌbɒrəʊbʊ'dʊə/ a Buddhist monument in central Java, built *c.*800.

Borodin /'bɒrədɪn/, Aleksandr (Porfirevich) (1833–87), Russian composer. He is best known for the epic opera *Prince Igor* (completed after his death by Rimsky-Korsakov and Glazunov).

Borodino, Battle of /ˌbɒrə'diːnəʊ/ a battle in 1812 at Borodino, a village about 110 km (70 miles) west of Moscow, at which Napoleon's forces defeated the Russian army.

boron /'bɔːrɒn/ ▶ **noun** [mass noun] the chemical element of atomic number 5, a non-metallic solid. (Symbol: **B**)

Boron is usually prepared as an amorphous brown powder, but when very pure it forms hard, shiny, black crystals with semiconducting properties. The element has some specialized uses, such as in alloy steels and in nuclear control rods.

– ORIGIN early 19th cent.: from BORAX, on the pattern of *carbon* (which it resembles in some respects).

boronia /bə'rəʊnɪə/ ▶ **noun** a sweet-scented Australian shrub which is cultivated for its perfume and for the cut-flower trade. ● Genus *Boronia*, family Rutaceae.
– ORIGIN modern Latin, named after Francesco *Borone* (1769–94), Italian botanist.

borosilicate /ˌbɔːrəʊ'sɪlɪkeɪt/ ▶ **noun** [usu. as modifier] a low-melting glass made from a mixture of silica and boric oxide (B_2O_3).

borough /'bʌrə/ ▶ **noun** a town or district which is an administrative unit, in particular: ■ Brit. a town (as distinct from a city) with a corporation and privileges granted by a royal charter. ■ Brit. historical a town sending representatives to Parliament. ■ an administrative division of London. ■ a municipal corporation in certain US states. ■ each of five divisions of New York City. ■ (in Alaska) a district corresponding to a county elsewhere in the US.
– ORIGIN Old English *burg*, *burh* 'fortress, citadel', later 'fortified town', of Germanic origin; related to Dutch *burg* and German *Burg*. Compare with BURGH.

Borromini /ˌbɒrə'miːni/, Francesco (1599–1667), Italian architect, a leading figure of the Italian baroque.

Borrow, George (Henry) (1803–81), English writer. His travels with Gypsies provided material for the picaresque narrative *Lavengro* (1851) and its sequel *The Romany Rye* (1857).

borrow ▶ **verb** [with obj.] **1** take and use (something belonging to someone else) with the intention of returning it: *he had* ***borrowed*** *a car* ***from*** *one of his colleagues*. ■ take and use (money) from a person or bank under an agreement to pay it back later. ■ take and use (a book) from a library for a fixed period of time. ■ take (a word or idea) from another language, person, or source and use it in one's own language or work: *the term is* ***borrowed from*** *Greek*.
2 Golf allow (a certain distance) when playing a shot to compensate for sideways motion of the ball due to a slope or other irregularity.
▶ **noun** Golf a slope or other irregularity on a golf course which must be compensated for when playing a shot.
– PHRASES **be (living) on borrowed time** used to convey that someone has survived against expectations, with the implication that they will not do so for much longer. **borrow trouble** N. Amer. take needless action that may have detrimental effects.
– DERIVATIVES **borrower noun.**
– ORIGIN Old English *borgian* 'borrow against security', of Germanic origin; related to Dutch and German *borgen*.

borrowing ▶ **noun** [mass noun] the action of borrowing something: *a curb on government borrowing* | [count noun] *the group had total borrowings of $570 million*. ■ [count noun] a word or idea taken from another language, person, or source and used in one's own language or work: *the majority of designs were borrowings from the continent*.

borrow pit ▶ **noun** a pit resulting from the excavation of material for use in embankments.

Borsalino /ˌbɔːsə'liːnəʊ/ ▶ **noun** (pl. **Borsalinos**) trademark a man's wide-brimmed felt hat.
– ORIGIN early 20th cent.: from the name of the manufacturer.

borscht /bɔːʃt/ (also **borsch** /bɔːʃ/) ▶ **noun** [mass noun] a Russian or Polish soup made with beetroot and usually served with sour cream.
– ORIGIN Russian *borshch*.

Borscht Belt /bɔːʃt/ ▶ **noun** N. Amer. humorous a resort area in the Catskill Mountains frequented chiefly by Jewish people of eastern European origin.

borstal /'bɔːst(ə)l/ ▶ **noun** Brit. historical a custodial institution for young offenders.
– ORIGIN early 20th cent.: named after the village of *Borstal* in southern England, where the first of these was established.

bort /bɔːt/ (also **boart**) ▶ **noun** [mass noun] small, granular, opaque diamonds, used as an abrasive in cutting tools.
– ORIGIN early 17th cent.: from Dutch *boort*.

borzoi /'bɔːzɔɪ/ ▶ **noun** (pl. **borzois**) a large Russian wolfhound of a breed with a narrow head and silky, typically white, coat.
– ORIGIN late 19th cent.: from Russian *borzoĭ* (adjective), *borzaya* (noun), from *borzyĭ* 'swift'.

boscage /'bɒskɪdʒ/ (also **boskage**) ▶ **noun** [mass noun] a mass of trees or shrubs.
– ORIGIN late Middle English: from Old French; ultimately of Germanic origin and related to BUSH[1]. Compare with BOCAGE.

Bosch /bɒʃ/, Hieronymus (*c.*1450–1516), Dutch painter. Bosch's highly detailed works are typically crowded with half-human, half-animal creatures and grotesque demons in settings symbolic of sin and folly. His individual style prefigures that of the surrealists.

Bose /bəʊs/, Satyendra Nath (1894–1974), Indian physicist. With Einstein he described fundamental particles which later came to be known as *bosons*.

bosh ▶ **noun** [mass noun] informal nonsense; rubbish: *that's a load of bosh*.
– ORIGIN mid 19th cent.: from Turkish *boş* 'empty, worthless'.

bosie /'bəʊzi/ (also **bosey**) ▶ **noun** Cricket Australian term for GOOGLY.
– ORIGIN early 20th cent.: from the name of Bernard J. T. *Bosanquet* (1877–1936), English all-round cricketer, + -IE.

boskage ▶ **noun** variant spelling of BOSCAGE.

bosky /'bɒski/ ▶ **adjective** literary covered by trees or bushes; wooded: *a slow-moving river meandering between bosky banks*.
– ORIGIN late 16th cent.: from Middle English *bosk*, variant of BUSH[1].

Bosman /'bɒzmən/ ▶ **noun** [usu. as modifier] used with reference to a European Court ruling which obliges professional football or other sports clubs to allow players over the age of 25 to move freely between clubs once their contracts have expired.
– ORIGIN 1990s: named after Jean-Marc *Bosman*, a Belgian footballer who brought a legal case which resulted in the ruling.

Bosnia /'bɒznɪə/ short for BOSNIA AND HERZEGOVINA. ■ a region in the Balkans forming the larger, northern part of Bosnia and Herzegovina.
– DERIVATIVES **Bosniak** (also **Bosniac**) **adjective & noun.**

Bosnia and Herzegovina (also **Bosnia-Herzegovina**) a country in the Balkans, formerly a constituent republic of Yugoslavia; pop. 4,613,400 (est. 2009); capital, Sarajevo.

Bosnia and Herzegovina were conquered by the Turks in 1463. The province of Bosnia and Herzegovina was annexed by Austria in 1908, an event which contributed towards the outbreak of the First World War. In 1918 it became part of the Kingdom of Serbs, Croats, and Slovenes, which changed its name to Yugoslavia in 1929. In 1992 Bosnia and Herzegovina followed Slovenia and Croatia in declaring independence, but ethnic conflict among Muslims, Serbs, and Croats quickly reduced the republic to a state of civil war. An accord signed in December 1995 formally brought the conflict to an end.

Bosnian /'bɒznɪən/ ▶ **noun 1** a native or inhabitant of the Balkan country Bosnia and Herzegovina.
2 [mass noun] the Slavic language of the Bosnians.
▶ **adjective** relating to Bosnia and Herzegovina, its people, or their language.

bosom ▶ **noun** a woman's chest or breasts: *her ample bosom* | [mass noun] *the dress offered a fair display of bosom*. ■ a part of a dress covering the chest. ■ literary the space between a person's clothing and their chest used for carrying things: *he carried a letter* ***in his bosom***. ■ literary a person's loving care and protection: *Bruno went home each night* ***to the bosom of*** *his family*. ■ used to refer to the chest as the seat of emotions: *quivering dread was settling in her bosom*.
▶ **adjective** [attrib.] (of a friend) very close or intimate: *the two girls had become bosom friends*.
– DERIVATIVES **bosomed adjective** [in combination] *her small-bosomed physique*.
– ORIGIN Old English *bōsm*, of West Germanic origin; related to Dutch *boezem* and German *Busen*.

bosomy ▶ **adjective** having large breasts.

boson /'bəʊzɒn/ ▶ **noun** Physics a subatomic particle, such as a photon, which has zero or integral spin and follows the statistical description given by S. N. Bose and Einstein.
– ORIGIN 1940s: named after S. N. BOSE + -ON.

Bosporus /'bɒspərəs/ (also **Bosphorus** /'bɒsfə-/) a strait connecting the Black Sea with the Sea of Marmara, and separating Europe from the Anatolian peninsula of western Asia. Istanbul is located at its south end.

BOSS ▶ **abbreviation** Bureau of State Security.

boss[1] informal ▶ **noun** a person who is in charge of a worker or organization: *her boss offered her promotion* | *union bosses*. ■ a person in control of a group or situation: *does he see you as a partner, or is he already the boss?* ■ [often as modifier] (in computer gaming) a particularly tough enemy, usually appearing at the end of a section or level: *the boss characters provide more than enough challenge*.
▶ **verb** [with obj.] give (someone) orders in a domineering manner: *you're always* ***bossing*** *us* ***about***.
▶ **adjective** N. Amer. excellent; outstanding: *she's a real boss chick*.
– PHRASES **be one's own boss** be self-employed. **show someone who's boss** make it clear that it is oneself who is in charge: *now it's time to show her who's boss*.
– ORIGIN early 19th cent. (originally US): from Dutch *baas* 'master'.

boss[2] ▶ **noun 1** a stud on the centre of a shield. ■ Architecture an ornamental carving covering the

point where the ribs in a vault or ceiling cross. ■ the central part of a propeller.
2 Geology a large mass of igneous rock protruding through other strata.
– ORIGIN Middle English: from Old French *boce*, of unknown origin.

B

boss[3] ▶ **noun** US informal a cow.
– ORIGIN early 19th cent.: of unknown origin.

bossa nova /ˌbɒsə ˈnəʊvə/ ▶ **noun** a style of Brazilian music derived from samba but placing more emphasis on melody and less on percussion. ■ a dance to this music.
– ORIGIN 1960s: from Portuguese, from *bossa* 'tendency' and *nova* (feminine of *novo*) 'new'.

boss-cocky ▶ **noun** (pl. **boss-cockies**) Austral./NZ informal a farmer who employs labour. ■ a person in authority.

boss-eyed ▶ **adjective** Brit. informal cross-eyed or squinting.
– ORIGIN mid 19th cent.: compare with dialect *boss* 'miss, bungle', of unknown origin.

bossism ▶ **noun** [mass noun] US a situation whereby a political party is controlled by party managers.

bossy[1] ▶ **adjective** (**bossier**, **bossiest**) informal fond of giving people orders; domineering.
– DERIVATIVES **bossily** adverb, **bossiness** noun.

bossy[2] ▶ **noun** (pl. **bossies**) US informal a cow or calf.
– ORIGIN mid 19th cent. of unknown origin.

bossyboots ▶ **noun** Brit. informal a domineering person.

bosthoon /ˈbɒstuːn/ (also **bostoon**) ▶ **noun** Irish an uncouth or ignorant man or boy.
– ORIGIN mid 19th cent.: from Irish *bastún*.

bosting /ˈbɒstɪŋ/ (also **bostin** /ˈbɒstɪn/) ▶ **adjective** dialect very good; excellent: *we had a bosting time*.
– ORIGIN 1970s: probably a dialect pronunciation of *bursting* or *busting*.

Boston[1] the state capital of Massachusetts; pop. 609,023 (est. 2008). It was founded *c.*1630 and named after Boston in Lincolnshire.
– DERIVATIVES **Bostonian** noun & adjective.

Boston[2] ▶ **noun** [mass noun] **1** a card game resembling solo whist.
2 a variation of the waltz or of the two-step.

Boston baked beans ▶ **plural noun** an American dish of baked beans with salt pork and molasses.

Boston crab ▶ **noun** Wrestling a hold in which a wrestler sits astride a prone opponent and pulls upwards on the opponent's legs.

Boston ivy ▶ **noun** a Virginia creeper with three-lobed leaves, which is cultivated for its foliage.
● *Parthenocissus tricuspidata*, family Vitaceae.

Boston Tea Party a violent demonstration in 1773 by American colonists prior to the War of American Independence. Colonists boarded vessels in Boston harbour and threw the cargoes of tea into the water in protest at the imposition of a tax on tea by the British Parliament, in which the colonists had no representation.

Boston terrier ▶ **noun** a small smooth-coated terrier of a breed originating in Massachusetts from a crossing of a bulldog and terrier.

bosun /ˈbəʊs(ə)n/ (also **bo'sun**) ▶ **noun** variant spelling of BOATSWAIN.

Boswell, James (1740–95), Scottish author, companion and biographer of Samuel Johnson. He is known for *Journal of a Tour to the Hebrides* (1785) and *The Life of Samuel Johnson* (1791).
– DERIVATIVES **Boswellian** adjective.

Bosworth Field /ˈbɒzwəθ/ (also **Battle of Bosworth**) a battle of the Wars of the Roses fought in 1485 near Market Bosworth in Leicestershire. Henry Tudor defeated and killed the Yorkist king Richard III, enabling him to take the throne as Henry VII.

bot[1] ▶ **noun** **1** the larva of the botfly, which is an internal parasite of horses. ■ (**sheep bot**) the sheep nostril fly. See NOSTRIL FLY.
2 Austral./NZ informal a person who persistently borrows or cadges from others.
– ORIGIN early 16th cent.: probably of Low German origin.

bot[2] ▶ **noun** (chiefly in science fiction) a robot.
■ Computing an autonomous program on a network (especially the Internet) which can interact with systems or users, especially one designed to behave like a player in some computer games.
– ORIGIN 1960s: shortening of ROBOT.

bot. ▶ **abbreviation** ■ (with reference to journal titles) botanic; botanical; botany. ■ bottle. ■ bought.

botanical ▶ **adjective** relating to botany: *botanical specimens*.
▶ **noun** (usu. **botanicals**) a substance obtained from a plant and used typically in medicinal or cosmetic products.
– DERIVATIVES **botanic** adjective, **botanically** adverb.

botanic garden (also **botanical garden**) ▶ **noun** an establishment where plants are grown for scientific study and display to the public.

botanize (also **botanise**) ▶ **verb** [no obj.] (usu. as noun **botanizing**) study plants, especially in their natural habitat.
– ORIGIN mid 18th cent.: from modern Latin *botanizare*, from Greek *botanizein* 'gather plants', from *botanē* 'plant'.

Botany /ˈbɒt(ə)ni/ (also **Botany wool**) ▶ **noun** [mass noun] merino wool, especially from Australia.
– ORIGIN late 19th cent.: named after BOTANY BAY, from where the wool originally came.

botany /ˈbɒt(ə)ni/ ▶ **noun** [mass noun] the scientific study of the physiology, structure, genetics, ecology, distribution, classification, and economic importance of plants. ■ the plant life of a particular region, habitat, or geological period: *the botany of North America*.
– DERIVATIVES **botanist** noun.
– ORIGIN late 17th cent.: from earlier *botanic* (from French *botanique*, based on Greek *botanikos*, from *botanē* 'plant') + -Y³.

Botany Bay an inlet of the Tasman Sea in New South Wales, Australia, just south of Sydney. It was the site of Captain James Cook's landing in 1770 and of an early British penal settlement.
– ORIGIN named by Cook after the large variety of plants collected there by his companion, Sir Joseph Banks.

botch ▶ **verb** [with obj.] informal carry out (a task) badly or carelessly: *he was accused of botching the job* | (as adj. **botched**) *a botched attempt to kill them*.
▶ **noun** (also **botch-up**) informal a bungled task: *I've probably **made a botch of** things*.
– DERIVATIVES **botcher** noun.
– ORIGIN late Middle English (in the sense 'repair' but originally not implying clumsiness): of unknown origin.

botel ▶ **noun** variant spelling of BOATEL.

botfly /ˈbɒtflʌɪ/ ▶ **noun** (pl. **botflies**) a stout hairy-bodied fly whose larvae are internal parasites of mammals, in particular: ● a fly whose larvae (bots) develop within the guts of horses (*Gasterophilus* and other genera, family Gasterophilidae). ● chiefly N. Amer. a fly of the warble fly family (Oestridae).

both ▶ **predeterminer, determiner, & pronoun** used for emphasis to refer to two people or things, regarded and identified together: [as predeterminer] *both his parents indulged him* | [as determiner] *she held on with both hands* | *cars parked on both sides of the road* | [as pronoun] *a picture of **both of** us together* | *he looked at them both*.
▶ **adverb** used before the first of two alternatives to emphasize that the statement being made applies to each (the other alternative being introduced by 'and'): *the film has won favour with both young and old* | *studies of zebra finches, both in the wild and in captivity*.
– PHRASES **have it both ways** benefit from two incompatible ways of thinking or behaving: *countries cannot have it both ways: the cost of a cleaner environment may sometimes be fewer jobs*.
– ORIGIN Middle English: from Old Norse *báthir*.

> **USAGE** When **both** is used in constructions with **and**, the structures following 'both' and 'and' should be symmetrical. Thus, *studies of zebra finches, both **in the wild** and **in captivity*** is better than, for example, *studies of zebra finches, both **in the wild** and **captivity***. In the second example, the symmetry of 'in the wild' and 'in captivity' has been lost. Other examples: *her article is detrimental both **to understanding** and **to peace*** (not *her article is detrimental to both **understanding** and **to peace***).

Botha[1] /ˈbəʊtə/, Louis (1862–1919), South African soldier and statesman, first Prime Minister of the Union of South Africa 1910–19.

Botha[2] /ˈbəʊtə/, P. W. (1916–2006), South African statesman, Prime Minister 1978–84, State President 1984–9; full name *Pieter Willem Botha*. An authoritarian leader, he continued to enforce apartheid but in response to pressure introduced limited reforms; his resistance to more radical change ultimately led to his fall from power.

Botham /ˈbəʊθəm/, Sir Ian (Terence) (b.1955), English all-round cricketer. In 1978 he became the first player to score 100 runs and take eight wickets in a single Test match; in 1982 he also achieved the record of 3,000 runs and 250 wickets in Test matches overall.

bother ▶ **verb** **1** [no obj., with negative] take the trouble to do something: *scientists rarely **bother with** such niceties* | [with infinitive] *the driver didn't bother to ask why*.
2 [with obj.] (of a circumstance or event) worry, disturb, or upset (someone): *secrecy is an issue which bothers journalists* | [with obj. and clause] *it **bothered me that** I hadn't done anything*. ■ [no obj.] [usu. with negative] feel concern about or interest in: *don't **bother about** me—I'll find my own way home* | *he wasn't to **bother himself with** day-to-day things* | (as adj. **bothered**) *I'm not particularly **bothered about** how I look*. ■ cause trouble or annoyance to (someone) by interrupting or otherwise inconveniencing them: *I'm sorry to bother you at this time of night*.
▶ **noun** [mass noun] effort, trouble, or difficulty: *he saved me the bother of having to come up with a speech* | *it may seem like too much bother to cook just for yourself*. ■ (**a bother**) a person or thing that causes annoyance or difficulty: *I hope she hasn't been a bother*.
▶ **exclamation** Brit. used to express mild irritation or impatience: *'Bother!' she muttered*.
– PHRASES **can't be bothered (to do something)** be unwilling to make the effort needed to do something. **hot and bothered** in a state of anxiety or physical discomfort, especially as a result of being pressured: *others struggle with bags and briefcases, looking hot and bothered*.
– ORIGIN late 17th cent. (as a noun in the dialect sense 'noise, chatter'): of Anglo-Irish origin; probably related to Irish *bodhaire* 'noise', *bodhraim* 'deafen, annoy'. The verb (originally dialect) meant 'confuse with noise' in the early 18th cent.

botheration informal ▶ **noun** [mass noun] effort, worry, or difficulty; bother.
▶ **exclamation** dated used to express mild irritation or annoyance.

bothersome ▶ **adjective** annoying; troublesome: *most childhood stomach aches, though bothersome, aren't serious*.

Bothnia, Gulf of /ˈbɒθnɪə/ a northern arm of the Baltic Sea, between Sweden and Finland.

both ways ▶ **adverb & adjective** another term for EACH-WAY: [as adv.] *put me down for a fiver both ways*.

Bothwell /ˈbɒθwɛl/, James Hepburn, 4th Earl of (*c.*1536–78), Scottish nobleman and third husband of Mary, Queen of Scots. He was implicated in the murder of Mary's previous husband, Lord Darnley (1567), a crime for which he was tried but acquitted; he married Mary later the same year.

bothy /ˈbɒθi/ (also **bothie**) ▶ **noun** (pl. **bothies**) (in Scotland) a small hut or cottage, especially one for housing farm labourers or for use as a mountain refuge.
– ORIGIN late 18th cent.: obscurely related to Irish and Scottish Gaelic *both*, *bothan*, and perhaps to BOOTH.

botnet ▶ **noun** a network of private computers infected with malicious software and controlled as a group without the owners' knowledge, e.g. to send spam.
– ORIGIN early 21st cent.: blend of BOT² and NETWORK.

boto /ˈbəʊtəʊ/ (also **boutu**) ▶ **noun** (pl. **botos**) a pink and grey river dolphin found in the Amazon and Orinoco River systems. Also called AMAZON DOLPHIN.
● *Inia geoffrensis*, family Platanistidae.

Botox /ˈbəʊtɒks/ ▶ **noun** [mass noun] trademark a drug prepared from botulin, used medically to treat certain muscular conditions and cosmetically to remove wrinkles by temporarily paralysing facial muscles.
– DERIVATIVES **Botoxed** adjective.
– ORIGIN 1990s: from BOTULINUM TOXIN.

bo tree /bəʊ/ (also **bodhi tree**) ▶ **noun** a fig tree native to India and SE Asia, regarded as sacred by Buddhists. Also called PEEPUL or PIPAL. ● *Ficus religiosa*, family Moraceae.
– ORIGIN mid 19th cent.: representing Sinhalese *bōgaha* 'tree of knowledge' (Buddha's enlightenment having occurred beneath such a tree), from *bō* (from Sanskrit *budh* 'understand thoroughly') + *gaha* 'tree'.

botryoidal /ˌbɒtrɪˈɔɪd(ə)l/ ▶ **adjective** (chiefly of minerals) having a shape reminiscent of a cluster of grapes.
– ORIGIN late 18th cent.: from Greek *botruoeidēs* (from *botrus* 'bunch of grapes') + -AL.

botrytis /bəˈtrʌɪtɪs/ ▶ noun [mass noun] a greyish powdery mould which causes a number of plant diseases and is deliberately cultivated (as noble rot) on the grapes used for certain wines. ● Genus *Botrytis*, subdivision Deuteromycotina (or Ascomycotina), in particular the grey mould *B. cinerea*.
– ORIGIN modern Latin, from Greek *botrus* 'cluster of grapes'.

Botswana /bɒˈtswɑːnə/ a landlocked country in southern Africa; pop. 1,990,900 (est. 2009); official languages, Setswana and English; capital, Gaborone.

> Inhabited by Sotho people and, in the Kalahari Desert, San (Bushmen), the area was made the British Protectorate of Bechuanaland in 1885. It became an independent republic within the Commonwealth in 1966, adopting the name Botswana.

– DERIVATIVES **Botswanan** adjective & noun.

bott ▶ abbreviation bottle.

bottarga /bəˈtɑːɡə/ ▶ noun [mass noun] salted and dried tuna or grey mullet roe.
– ORIGIN Italian, from Arabic *buṭarkhah*, from Coptic *outarakhon*.

botte /bɒt/ ▶ noun Fencing an attack or thrust.
– ORIGIN French.

Botticelli /ˌbɒtɪˈtʃɛli/, Sandro (1445–1510), Italian painter, born *Alessandro di Mariano Filipepi*. He worked in Renaissance Florence under the patronage of the Medicis. Botticelli is best known for his mythological works such as *Primavera* (*c.*1478) and *The Birth of Venus* (*c.*1480).

bottle ▶ noun **1** a glass or plastic container with a narrow neck, used for storing drinks or other liquids. ■ the contents of such a container: *she managed to get through **a bottle of** wine.* ■ (**the bottle**) informal used in reference to the heavy drinking of alcohol: *more women are **taking to the bottle**.* ■ a bottle fitted with a teat for giving milk or other drinks to babies and very young children. ■ a large metal cylinder holding liquefied gas.
2 [mass noun] Brit. informal the courage or confidence needed to do something difficult or dangerous: *I **lost my bottle** completely and ran.*
▶ verb **1** [with obj.] place (drinks or other liquid) in bottles for storage: *the wine was bottled in 1997.* ■ Brit. place (fruit or vegetables) in glass jars with other ingredients in order to preserve them. ■ (usu. as adj. **bottled**) store (gas) in a container in liquefied form.
2 [with obj.] informal throw a glass bottle at (someone): *he was bottled offstage at a club.*
– PHRASES **bottle and glass** Brit. rhyming slang arse. **hit the bottle** informal start to drink alcohol heavily. **in bottle** (of wine) having been aged for a specified number of years in its bottle: *the wine can be drunk after eight years in bottle.*
– PHRASAL VERBS **bottle out** Brit. informal lose one's nerve and decide not to do something: *the Minister has **bottled out of** real reforms.* **bottle something up** repress or conceal feelings over time: *his anger and frustration had been bottled up for years.* **bottle someone/thing up** keep someone or something trapped or contained: *he had to stay bottled up in New York.*
– ORIGIN late Middle English: from Old French *boteille*, from medieval Latin *butticula*, diminutive of late Latin *buttis* 'cask, wineskin' (see BUTT[4]).

bottle age ▶ noun [mass noun] time spent by a wine maturing in its bottle.

bottle bank ▶ noun Brit. a place where used glass bottles may be deposited for recycling.

bottle blonde (also **bottle blond**) derogatory
▶ adjective (of a woman's hair) of a shade of blonde that looks as if it has been artificially lightened or bleached.
▶ noun a woman with dyed or bleached blonde hair.

bottlebrush ▶ noun **1** a cylindrical brush for cleaning inside bottles.
2 an Australian shrub or small tree with spikes of scarlet or yellow flowers which resemble bottlebrushes. ● Genus *Callistemon*, family Myrtaceae.
■ any of a number of plants bearing similar flowers.

bottle-feed ▶ verb [with obj.] feed (a baby) with milk from a feeding bottle.

bottle green ▶ noun [mass noun] dark green: [as modifier] *a bottle-green uniform.*

bottleneck ▶ noun **1** the neck or mouth of a bottle.
2 a narrow section of road or a junction that impedes traffic flow. ■ a situation that causes delay in a process or system.
3 a device shaped like the neck of a bottle that is worn on a guitarist's finger and used to produce sliding effects on the strings. ■ (also **bottleneck guitar**) [mass noun] the style of playing that uses a bottleneck.

bottlenose dolphin (also **bottle-nosed dolphin**) ▶ noun a stout-bodied dolphin with a distinct short beak, found in tropical and temperate coastal waters. ● *Tursiops truncatus*, family Delphinidae.

bottlenose whale (also **bottle-nosed whale**) ▶ noun a beaked whale of variable colour, with a bulbous forehead. ● Genus *Hyperoodon*, family Ziphiidae: two species.

bottle party ▶ noun Brit. a party to which guests bring bottles of drink.

bottler ▶ noun **1** a person or company that bottles drinks.
2 Brit. informal a person with little mental strength or resilience: *he turned out to be one of the biggest bottlers in boxing.*
3 Austral./NZ informal an admirable person or thing: *he's getting married to a real little bottler.*

bottlescrew ▶ noun British term for TURNBUCKLE.

bottle store (also **bottle shop**) ▶ noun chiefly Austral./NZ & S. African another term for OFF-LICENCE.

bottle tree ▶ noun either of two Australian trees with swollen bottle-shaped trunks containing water: ● the Australian baobab of the Kimberley region (*Adansonia gregorii*, family Bombacaceae). ● a relative of the flame tree occurring in Queensland (*Brachychiton rupestre*, family Sterculiaceae).

bottom ▶ noun (usu. **the bottom**) **1** the lowest point or part of something: *the bottom of the page* | *she paused at the bottom of the stairs.* ■ the ground under a sea, river, or lake: *the liner plunged to the bottom of the sea.* ■ the lowest surface on the inside of a container: *place the fruit on the bottom of the dish.* ■ chiefly Brit. the furthest part or point of something: *the shed at the bottom of the garden.* ■ the lowest position in a competition or ranking: *he started at the bottom and now has his own business.* ■ (also **bottoms**) the lower half of a specified two-piece garment: *a pair of pyjama bottoms.* ■ (**bottoms**) another term for BOTTOMLAND. ■ the keel or hull of a ship.
2 chiefly Brit. a person's buttocks: *Toby pinched her bottom.*
3 [mass noun] Physics one of six flavours of quark.
4 [mass noun] archaic stamina or strength of character.
5 archaic a ship, especially a cargo carrier.
▶ adjective in the lowest position: *the books on the bottom shelf.* ■ (of a place) in the furthest position away in a downhill direction: *the bottom field.* ■ in the lowest or last position in a competition or ranking: *I was put in the bottom class* | *they **came bottom** with 17 points.*
▶ verb **1** [no obj.] (of a ship) reach or touch the ground under the sea: *nuclear submarines cannot bottom.* ■ [with obj.] Austral./NZ excavate (a hole or mine) to the level of a mineral-bearing stratum. ■ [no obj.] Austral./NZ find gold or other minerals while mining: *he's **bottomed on** opal there.* ■ [with obj.] archaic find the extent or real nature of.
2 [no obj.] (usu. **bottom out**) (of a situation) reach the lowest point before stabilizing or improving: *encouraging signs suggested the recession was bottoming out.*
– PHRASES **at bottom** fundamentally: *at bottom, science is exploration.* **be at the bottom of** be the basic cause or origin of (something). **the bottom falls** (or **drops**) **out** used to refer to the sudden collapse or failure of something: *the bottom fell out of the market for classic cars.* **bottoms up!** informal used to express friendly feelings towards one's companions before drinking. **from the bottom of one's heart** see HEART. **from the bottom up** starting at the lower end or beginning of a hierarchy or process and proceeding to the top: *we began to study history from the bottom up.* **get to the bottom of** find an explanation for (a mystery). **knock the bottom out of** cause (something) to collapse or fail suddenly. **you (can) bet your bottom dollar** informal used to state one's conviction that a particular thing is going to happen: *you can bet your bottom dollar it'll end in tears.*
– DERIVATIVES **bottomed** adjective [in combination] *a glass-bottomed boat* | *bare-bottomed toddlers,* **bottommost** adjective.
– ORIGIN Old English *botm*, of Germanic origin; related to Dutch *bodem* 'bottom, ground' and German *Boden* 'ground, earth'.

bottom drawer ▶ noun Brit. dated household linen stored by a woman in preparation for her marriage.

bottom-dwelling ▶ adjective (of an aquatic organism) living on or near the bed of the sea, a lake, or other body of water.
– DERIVATIVES **bottom-dweller** noun.

bottom feeder ▶ noun **1** any marine creature that lives on the seabed and feeds by scavenging.
2 N. Amer. informal a member of a group of very low social status who survives by any means possible.

bottom fermentation ▶ noun [mass noun] the process by which lager-type beers are fermented, proceeding for a relatively long period at low temperature with the yeast falling to the bottom.

bottomland ▶ noun [mass noun] N. Amer. low-lying land, typically by a river.

bottomless ▶ adjective without a bottom. ■ very deep: *the cold dark sea in whose bottomless depths monsters swam.* ■ (of a supply of money or other resources) inexhaustible: *I don't have **a bottomless pit** of money.*

bottom line ▶ noun [usu. in sing.] informal the final total of an account or balance sheet: *the rise in turnover failed to add to the company's bottom line.* ■ the fundamental and most important factor: *the bottom line is I'm still married to Denny.*

bottomry ▶ noun [mass noun] dated a system of merchant insurance in which a ship is used as security against a loan to finance a voyage, the lender losing their money if the ship sinks.
– ORIGIN late 16th cent.: from BOTTOM (in the sense 'ship') + -RY, influenced by Dutch *bodemerij*.

bottom-up ▶ adjective proceeding from the bottom or beginning of a hierarchy or process upwards; non-hierarchical: *bottom-up decisions.*

botty ▶ noun (pl. **botties**) Brit. a child's word for a person's bottom.

botulin /ˈbɒtjʊlɪn/ ▶ noun [mass noun] the bacterial toxin involved in botulism.

botulinum toxin /ˌbɒtjʊˈlʌɪnəm/ (also **botulinus toxin**) ▶ noun another term for BOTULIN.

botulism /ˈbɒtjʊlɪz(ə)m/ ▶ noun [mass noun] food poisoning caused by a bacterium growing on improperly sterilized tinned meats and other preserved foods. ● The bacterium is *Clostridium botulinum*.
– ORIGIN late 19th cent.: from German *Botulismus*, originally 'sausage poisoning', from Latin *botulus* 'sausage'.

boubou /ˈbuːbuː/ (also **boubou shrike**) ▶ noun **1** an African bush shrike (songbird) with the upper parts mainly blackish in colour. It is noted for the duet of bell-like calls produced by the male and female together. Compare with BRUBRU. ● Genus *Laniarius*, family Laniidae: several species.
2 a long, colourful, loose-fitting garment worn by both sexes in parts of Africa. [French, from Malinke *bubu*.]

bouchée /ˈbuːʃeɪ/ ▶ noun a small pastry with a sweet or savoury filling.
– ORIGIN mid 19th cent.: French, literally 'mouthful', from *bouche* 'mouth'.

Boucher /ˈbuːʃeɪ/, French /buʃe/, François (1703–70), French painter and decorative artist, one of the foremost artists of the rococo style in France. Notable paintings: *The Rising of the Sun* (1753) and *Summer Pastoral* (1749).

bouclé /ˈbuːkleɪ/ ▶ noun [mass noun] [often as modifier] yarn with a looped or curled ply, or fabric woven from this yarn: *a bouclé sweater.*
– ORIGIN late 19th cent.: French, literally 'buckled, curled'.

Boudicca /ˈbuːdɪkə, bəʊˈdɪkə/ (d. AD 62), a queen of the Britons, ruler of the Iceni tribe in eastern England; also known as **Boadicea**. Boudicca led her forces in revolt against the Romans and sacked Colchester, St Albans, and London before being defeated by the Roman governor Suetonius Paulinus.

boudin /ˈbuːdã/ ▶ noun **1** (pl. pronunc. **same**) a French type of black pudding.
2 (**boudins** /ˈbuːdɪnz, ˈbuːdãz/) Geology a series of elongated parallel sections formed by the fracturing of a sedimentary rock stratum during folding.
– ORIGIN French.

boudoir /ˈbuːdwɑː/ ▶ noun chiefly historical or humorous a woman's bedroom or small private room.
– ORIGIN late 18th cent.: French, literally 'sulking-place', from *bouder* 'pout, sulk'.

bouffant /ˈbuːfɒ̃/ ▶ adjective (of a person's hair) styled so as to stand out from the head in a rounded shape.

B

B

▸ **noun** a bouffant hairstyle.
– ORIGIN early 19th cent.: from French, literally 'swelling', present participle of *bouffer*.

Bougainville[1] /ˈbuːɡənvɪl/ a volcanic island in the South Pacific, forming a province of Papua New Guinea. It is the largest of the islands in the Solomon Islands archipelago.
– ORIGIN named after Louis de *Bougainville* (see **BOUGAINVILLE**[2]), who visited it in 1768.

Bougainville[2] /ˈbuːɡənvɪl/, French /buɡɛ̃vil/, Louis Antoine de (1729–1811), French explorer. Bougainville led the first French circumnavigation of the globe 1766–9, visiting many of the islands of the South Pacific and compiling an invaluable scientific record of his findings.

bougainvillea /ˌbuːɡ(ə)nˈvɪlɪə/ (also **bougainvillaea**) ▸ **noun** an ornamental shrubby climbing plant that is widely cultivated in the tropics. The insignificant flowers are surrounded by large, brightly coloured papery bracts which persist on the plant for a long time. ● Genus *Bougainvillea*, family Nyctaginaceae.
– ORIGIN named after Louis de *Bougainville* (see **BOUGAINVILLE**[2]).

bough /baʊ/ ▸ **noun** a main branch of a tree: *apple boughs laden with blossom.*
– ORIGIN Old English *bōg*, *bōh* 'bough or shoulder', of Germanic origin; related to Dutch *boeg* 'shoulders or ship's bow', German *Bug* 'ship's bow' and 'horse's hock or shoulder', also to **BOW**[3].

bought past and past participle of **BUY**.

boughten /ˈbɔːt(ə)n/ ▸ **adjective** dialect, chiefly N. Amer. bought rather than home-made: *her first store-boughten doll.*
– ORIGIN late 18th cent.: dialect variant of **BOUGHT**.

bougie /ˈbuːʒiː/ ▸ **noun** (pl. **bougies**) Medicine a thin, flexible surgical instrument for exploring or dilating a passage of the body.
– ORIGIN mid 18th cent.: from French, literally 'wax candle', from Arabic *Bijāya*, an Algerian town which traded in wax.

bouillabaisse /ˈbuːjəˌbeɪs/ ▸ **noun** [mass noun] a rich, spicy stew or soup made with various kinds of fish, originally from Provence.
– ORIGIN French, from modern Provençal *bouiabaisso*.

bouilli /ˈbuːji/ ▸ **noun** [mass noun] stewed or boiled meat.
– ORIGIN French, 'boiled'.

bouillon /ˈbuːjɒ̃/ ▸ **noun** [mass noun] thin soup or stock made by stewing meat, fish, or vegetables in water.
– ORIGIN French, literally 'liquid in which something has boiled', from *bouillir* 'to boil'.

boulder ▸ **noun** a large rock, typically one that has been worn smooth by erosion.
– DERIVATIVES **bouldery** adjective.
– ORIGIN late Middle English: shortened from earlier *boulderstone*, of Scandinavian origin.

boulder clay ▸ **noun** [mass noun] clay containing many large stones and boulders, formed by deposition from melting glaciers and ice sheets.

bouldering ▸ **noun** [mass noun] Climbing climbing on large boulders, either for practice or as a sport in its own right.

boule[1] /buːl/ ▸ **noun** (pl. **boules** pronunc. **same**) a metal ball used in the French game of **boules**, a form of bowls played on rough ground.
– ORIGIN 1920s (originally denoting a form of roulette): French, literally 'bowl'.

boule[2] /ˈbuːliː/ ▸ **noun** a legislative body of ancient or modern Greece.
– ORIGIN from Greek *boulē* 'senate'.

boulevard /ˈbuːləvɑːd/ ▸ **noun** a wide street in a town or city, typically one lined with trees: [in names] *Sunset Boulevard.*
– ORIGIN mid 18th cent.: French, 'a rampart' (later 'a promenade on the site of one'), from German *Bollwerk* (see **BULWARK**).

boulevardier /ˌbuːləvɑːˈdjeɪ/ ▸ **noun** a wealthy, fashionable socialite.
– ORIGIN late 19th cent.: from French, originally in the sense 'person who frequents boulevards'.

Boulez /ˈbuːlɛz/, Pierre (b.1925), French composer and conductor. His works explore and develop serialism and aleatory music, making use of both traditional and electronic instruments.

boulle /buːl/ (also **buhl**) ▸ **noun** [mass noun] brass, tortoiseshell, or other material cut to make a pattern and used for inlaying furniture: [as modifier] *boulle cabinets.*
– ORIGIN early 19th cent.: from French *boule*, from the name of André Charles *Boulle* (1642–1732), French cabinetmaker. The variant *buhl* is apparently a modern Germanized spelling.

Boulogne /bʊˈlɔɪn/, French /bulɔɲ/ a ferry port and fishing town in northern France; pop. 45,036 (2006). Full name **Boulogne-sur-Mer** /-sjʊəˈmɛː/, French /-syʀmɛʀ/.

Boult /bəʊlt/, Sir Adrian (Cedric) (1889–1983), English conductor. Noted especially for his championship of English composers, he was music director of the BBC 1930–49 and principal conductor of the London Philharmonic Orchestra 1950–7.

boult ▸ **verb** variant spelling of **BOLT**[4].

Boulting /ˈbəʊltɪŋ/, John (1913–85) and Roy (1913–2001), English film producers and directors. Twin brothers, they shared responsibilities as producer and director on films such as *Brighton Rock* (1947) and *I'm All Right Jack* (1959).

Boulton /ˈbəʊlt(ə)n/, Matthew (1728–1809), English engineer and manufacturer. With his partner James Watt he pioneered the manufacture of steam engines, which they began to produce in 1774.

bounce ▸ **verb 1** [no obj., usu. with adverbial of direction] (with reference to an object, especially a ball) move quickly up, back, or away from a surface after hitting it: *the ball bounced away and he chased it* | [with obj.] *he was bouncing the ball against the wall.* ■ (of light, sound, or an electronic signal) come into contact with an object or surface and be reflected back: *short sound waves **bounce off** even small objects.* ■ (also **bounce back**) (of an email) be returned to its sender after failing to reach its destination: *I tried to email him, but the message bounced.* ■ **(bounce back)** recover well after a setback or problem: *the savings rate has already started to bounce back and is sure to rise further.* ■ [with obj.] W. Indian come into sudden forceful contact with; collide with: *people cross the road as slowly as possible, as if daring the cars to bounce them.*
2 [no obj., usu. with adverbial of direction] jump repeatedly up and down, typically on something springy: *Emma was happily bouncing up and down on the mattress.* ■ move up and down repeatedly: *the gangplank bounced under his confident step.* ■ [with obj.] cause (a child) to move lightly up and down on one's knee as a game. ■ [with adverbial of direction] (of a vehicle) move jerkily along a bumpy surface: *the car bounced down the narrow track.* ■ [with adverbial of direction] move in a particular direction in an energetic, happy, or enthusiastic manner: *Linda bounced in through the open front door.*
3 [no obj.] informal (of a cheque) be returned by a bank when there are insufficient funds in an account to meet it: *a further two cheques of £160 also bounced.* ■ [with obj.] (of a bank) return a cheque in such circumstances.
4 [with obj.] informal eject (a troublemaker) forcibly from a nightclub or similar establishment. ■ chiefly N. Amer. dismiss (someone) from a job: *those who put in a dismal performance will be **bounced from** the tour.*
5 [with obj.] Brit. informal pressurize (someone) into doing something, typically by presenting them with a fait accompli: *the government should beware being **bounced into** any ill-considered foreign gamble.*
▸ **noun 1** a rebound of a ball or other object: *the wicket was causing the occasional erratic bounce.* ■ [mass noun] the ability of a surface to make a ball rebound in a specified way: *a pitch of low bounce.* ■ W. Indian a collision.
2 an act of jumping or of moving up and down jerkily: *every bounce of the truck brought them into fresh contact.* ■ [mass noun] exuberant self-confidence: *the bounce was now back in Jenny's step.* ■ [mass noun] health and body in a person's hair: *use conditioner to help hair regain its bounce.*
– PHRASES **be bouncing off the walls** N. Amer. informal be full of nervous excitement or agitation. **bounce an idea off** informal share an idea with (someone) in order to refine it. **on the bounce** as something rebounds: *he caught the ball on the bounce.* ■ informal in quick succession: *it's nice to get four victories on the bounce.*
– ORIGIN Middle English *bunsen* 'beat, thump', perhaps imitative, or from Low German *bunsen* 'beat', Dutch *bons* 'a thump'.

bouncebackability /ˌbaʊnsbakəˈbɪlɪti/ ▸ **noun** [mass noun] informal (especially in sport) the capacity to recover quickly from a setback: *promotion-chasing sides need to show the requisite bouncebackability after defeat.*

bounce flash ▸ **noun** a device for giving reflected photographic flashlight.

bouncer ▸ **noun 1** a person employed by a nightclub or similar establishment to prevent troublemakers and other unwanted people entering or to eject them from the premises.
2 Cricket a ball bowled fast and short so as to rise high after pitching.

bouncing ▸ **adjective 1** (of a baby) vigorous and healthy: *Lisa gave birth to a bouncing baby boy.*
2 lively and confident: *by the next day she was her usual bouncing, energetic self.*

bouncing Bet ▸ **noun** another term for **SOAPWORT**.

bouncy ▸ **adjective** (**bouncier**, **bounciest**) bouncing or causing things to bounce: *bouncy floorboards* | *a bouncy ball.* ■ (of a person) confident and lively: *she was still the girl he remembered, bouncy and full of life.* ■ (of music) having a pleasingly jaunty rhythm: *bouncy 1960s tunes.*
– DERIVATIVES **bouncily** adverb, **bounciness** noun.

bouncy castle ▸ **noun** Brit. a large inflatable structure, typically in the form of a stylized castle or other building, on which children can jump and play.

bound[1] ▸ **verb** [no obj., with adverbial of direction] walk or run with leaping strides: *Louis came **bounding down** the stairs* | figurative *shares **bounded ahead** in early dealing.* ■ (of an object) rebound from a surface: *bullets **bounded off** the veranda.*
▸ **noun** a leaping movement towards or over something: *I went up the steps in two effortless bounds.*
– ORIGIN early 16th cent. (as a noun): from French *bond* (noun), *bondir* (verb) 'resound', later 'rebound', from late Latin *bombitare*, from Latin *bombus* 'humming'.

bound[2] ▸ **noun** (often **bounds**) a territorial limit; a boundary: *the ancient bounds of the forest.* ■ a limitation or restriction on feeling or action: *it is not **beyond the bounds of possibility** that the issue could arise again* | *enthusiasm to join the union **knew no bounds**.* ■ technical a limiting value.
▸ **verb** [with obj.] form the boundary of; enclose: *the ground was bounded by a main road on one side and a meadow on the other.* ■ place within certain limits; restrict: *freedom of action is bounded by law.*
– PHRASES **in bounds** inside the part of a sports field or court in which play is conducted. **out of bounds 1** outside the part of a sports field or court in which play is conducted. **2** outside the limits of where one is permitted to be: *his kitchen was **out of bounds** to me at mealtimes.* ■ beyond what is acceptable: *Paul felt that this conversation was getting out of bounds.*
– ORIGIN Middle English (in the senses 'landmark' and 'borderland'): from Old French *bodne*, from medieval Latin *bodina*, earlier *butina*, of unknown ultimate origin.

bound[3] ▸ **adjective** going or ready to go towards a specified place: *an express train **bound for** Edinburgh* | [in combination] *the three moon-bound astronauts.* ■ destined or very likely to have a specified experience: *they were **bound for** disaster.*
– ORIGIN Middle English *boun* (in the sense 'ready, dressed'), from Old Norse *búinn*, past participle of *búa* 'get ready'; the final *-d* is euphonic, or influenced by **BOUND**[4].

bound[4] past and past participle of **BIND**. ▸ **adjective 1** [in combination] restricted or confined to a specified place: *his job kept him city-bound.* ■ prevented from operating normally by the specified conditions: *blizzard-bound Boston.*
2 [with infinitive] certain to be or to do or have something: *there is bound to be a change of plan.* ■ obliged by law, circumstances, or duty to do something: *I'm bound to do what I can to help Sam* | *I'm **bound to say** that I have some doubts.*
3 [in combination] (of a book) having a specified binding: *fine leather-bound books.*
4 (of a grammatical element) occurring only in combination with another form. ■ in Chomskyan linguistics, (of a reflexive, reciprocal, or other linguistic unit) dependent for its reference on another noun phrase in the same sentence.
– PHRASES **bound up in** focusing on to the exclusion of all else: *she was too bound up in her own misery to care that other people were hurt.* **bound up with** (or **in**) closely connected with or related to: *democracy is bound up with a measure of economic and social equality.* **I'll be bound** Brit. used to emphasize that one is sure of something: *she's hatching more little plots, I'll be bound!*

boundary ▸ **noun** (pl. **boundaries**) **1** a line which marks the limits of an area; a dividing line: *a county boundary* | *the river marks the boundary between the two regions* | [as modifier] *a boundary wall.* ■ (often

boundaries) a limit of something abstract, especially a subject or sphere of activity: *a community without class or political boundaries.*
2 Cricket a hit crossing the limits of the field, scoring four or six runs.
– ORIGIN early 17th cent.: variant of dialect *bounder*, from **BOUND²** + **-ER¹**, perhaps on the pattern of *limitary*.

boundary condition ▶ noun Mathematics a condition that is required to be satisfied at all or part of the boundary of a region in which a set of differential conditions is to be solved.

boundary layer ▶ noun a layer of more or less stationary fluid (such as water or air) immediately surrounding an immersed moving object.

boundary rider ▶ noun Austral./NZ a person employed to maintain the outer fences of a cattle or sheep station.

boundary umpire ▶ noun Australian Rules an umpire on the boundary line who signals when the ball is out and throws it back in to restart play.

boundary value ▶ noun Mathematics a value specified by a boundary condition.

bounden /ˈbaʊnd(ə)n/ archaic past participle of **BIND**.
– PHRASES **a** (or **one's**) **bounden duty** a responsibility regarded by oneself or others as obligatory: *his bounden duty to respond to the call for help.*

bounder ▶ noun Brit. informal, dated a dishonourable man: *he is nothing but a fortune-seeking bounder.*

boundless ▶ adjective unlimited or immense: *enthusiasts who devote boundless energy to their hobby.*
– DERIVATIVES **boundlessly** adverb, **boundlessness** noun.

bounteous ▶ adjective archaic generously given or giving; bountiful: *the earth yields a bounteous harvest.*
– DERIVATIVES **bounteously** adverb, **bounteousness** noun.
– ORIGIN late Middle English: from Old French *bontif, -ive* 'benevolent' (from *bonte* 'bounty'), on the pattern of *plenteous*.

bountiful ▶ adjective large in quantity; abundant: *the ocean provided a bountiful supply of fresh food.* ■ giving generously: *this bountiful God has thought of everything.*
– DERIVATIVES **bountifully** adverb.
– ORIGIN early 16th cent.: from **BOUNTY** + **-FUL**.

Bounty a ship of the British navy on which in 1789 part of the crew, led by Fletcher Christian, mutinied against their commander, William Bligh, and set him adrift in an open boat with eighteen companions.

bounty ▶ noun (pl. **bounties**) **1** a sum paid for killing or capturing a person or animal: *there was an increased* **bounty on his head**.
2 historical a sum paid by the state to encourage trade. ■ a sum paid by the state to army or navy recruits on enlistment.
3 literary something given or occurring in generous amounts: *the bounties of nature.* ■ [mass noun] generosity: *for millennia the people along the Nile have depended entirely on its bounty.*
– ORIGIN Middle English (denoting goodness or generosity): from Old French *bonte* 'goodness', from Latin *bonitas*, from *bonus* 'good'. The sense 'monetary reward' dates from the early 18th cent.

bounty hunter ▶ noun a person who pursues a criminal for whom a reward is offered.

bouquet /bʊˈkeɪ, bəʊˈkeɪ, ˈbʊkeɪ/ ▶ noun **1** an attractively arranged bunch of flowers, especially one presented as a gift or carried at a ceremony. ■ an expression of approval; a compliment: *we will happily publish the bouquets and brickbats.*
2 the characteristic scent of a wine or perfume: *the aperitif has a faint bouquet of almonds.*
– ORIGIN early 18th cent.: from French (earlier 'clump of trees'), from a dialect variant of Old French *bos* 'wood'. Sense 2 dates from the mid 19th cent.

bouquet garni /bʊˌkeɪ ˈɡɑːni, bəʊˈkeɪ, ˈbʊkeɪ/ ▶ noun (pl. **bouquets garnis** pronunc. **same**) a bunch of herbs, typically encased in a muslin bag, used for flavouring a stew or soup.
– ORIGIN French, literally 'garnished bouquet'.

Bourbaki /ˌbʊəˈbɑːki/, Nicolas, a pseudonym of a group of mathematicians, mainly French, attempting to give a complete account of the foundations of pure mathematics. Their first publication was in 1939.
– ORIGIN the group was named, humorously, after a defeated French general of the Franco-Prussian War (1870–1).

Bourbon¹ /ˈbʊəb(ə)n, ˈbɔːbɒn/ the surname of a branch of the royal family of France. The Bourbons ruled France from 1589, when Henry IV succeeded to the throne, until the monarchy was overthrown in 1848, and reached the peak of their power under Louis XIV in the late 17th century. Members of this family have also been kings of Spain (1700–1931 and since 1975).

Bourbon² /ˈbʊəb(ə)n/ ▶ noun **1** Brit. a chocolate-flavoured biscuit with a chocolate-cream filling.
2 US a reactionary.
3 (also **Bourbon rose**) a rose of a variety which flowers over a long period and has a rich scent. It arose as a natural hybrid on the island of Réunion (formerly Île de Bourbon) and was introduced into Europe in the early 19th century. ● *Rosa* × *borboniana*, a hybrid of *Rosa chinensis* and *R. damascena*, family Rosaceae.
– ORIGIN mid 19th cent. (in sense 2): from **BOURBON¹**. Sense 1 dates from the 1930s.

bourbon /ˈbəːb(ə)n, ˈbʊə-/ ▶ noun [mass noun] a kind of American whisky distilled from maize and rye.
– ORIGIN mid 19th cent.: named after *Bourbon* County, Kentucky, where it was first made.

Bourbonnais /ˌbʊəbɒˈneɪ/ a former duchy and province of central France; chief town, Moulins. It forms part of the Auvergne and Centre regions.

bourdon /ˈbʊəd(ə)n/ ▶ noun a low-pitched stop in an organ or harmonium, typically a stopped diapason of 16-foot pitch.
– ORIGIN Middle English (in the sense 'drone of a bagpipe'): from Old French, 'drone', of imitative origin.

Bourdon gauge /ˈbʊədɒn/ ▶ noun a pressure gauge employing a coiled metallic tube which tends to straighten out when pressure is exerted within it.
– ORIGIN mid 19th cent.: named after Eugène *Bourdon* (1808–84), French hydraulic engineer.

bourgeois /ˈbʊəʒwɑː/ ▶ adjective belonging to or characteristic of the middle class, typically with reference to its perceived materialistic values or conventional attitudes: *a rich, bored, bourgeois family | these views will shock the bourgeois critics.* ■ (in Marxist contexts) upholding the interests of capitalism; not communist: *bourgeois society took for granted the sanctity of property.*
▶ noun (pl. **same**) a bourgeois person.
– ORIGIN mid 16th cent.: from French, from late Latin *burgus* 'castle' (in medieval Latin 'fortified town'), ultimately of Germanic origin and related to **BOROUGH**. Compare with **BURGESS**.

bourgeoise /ˈbʊəʒwɑːz/ ▶ adjective belonging to or characteristic of female members of the bourgeoisie.
▶ noun a female member of the bourgeoisie.
– ORIGIN late 18th cent.: French, feminine of *bourgeois* 'citizen' (see **BOURGEOIS**).

bourgeoisie /ˌbʊəʒwɑːˈziː/ ▶ noun [treated as sing. or pl.] the middle class, typically with reference to its perceived materialistic values or conventional attitudes. ■ (in Marxist contexts) the capitalist class who own most of society's wealth and means of production.
– ORIGIN early 18th cent.: French, from **BOURGEOIS**.

Bourgogne /burɡɔɲ/ French name for **BURGUNDY**.

Bourguiba /ˌbʊəˈɡiːbə/, Habib ibn Ali (1903–2000), Tunisian nationalist and statesman, the first President of independent Tunisia 1957–87.

Bourke-White /bəːk/, Margaret (1906–71), American photojournalist. During the Second World War she was the first female photographer to be attached to the US armed forces, at the end of the war accompanying the Allied forces when they entered the concentration camps.

bourn¹ /bɔːn, bʊən/ ▶ noun dialect a small stream, especially one that flows intermittently or seasonally.
– ORIGIN Middle English: southern English variant of **BURN²**.

bourn² /bɔːn, bʊən/ (also **bourne**) ▶ noun literary a limit or boundary. ■ a goal or destination.
– ORIGIN early 16th cent. (denoting a boundary of a field): from French *borne*, from Old French *bodne* (see **BOUND²**).

Bournemouth /ˈbɔːnməθ/ a resort town on the south coast of England, in Dorset; pop. 159,500 (est. 2009).

bourrée /ˈbʊəreɪ/ ▶ noun a lively French dance like a gavotte. ■ Ballet a series of very fast little steps, with the feet close together, usually performed on the tips of the toes and giving the impression that the dancer is gliding over the floor.
▶ verb [no obj.] perform a bourrée.
– ORIGIN late 17th cent.: French, literally 'faggot of twigs' (the dance being performed around a fire made with such twigs).

bourse /bʊəs/ ▶ noun a stock market in a non-English-speaking country, especially France. Compare with **BURSE**. ■ (**the Bourse**) the Paris stock exchange.
– ORIGIN mid 16th cent. (as *burse*, the usual form until the mid 19th cent.): from French, literally 'purse', via medieval Latin from Greek *bursa* 'leather'.

Boursin /ˈbʊəsã/, French /bursɛ̃/ ▶ noun [mass noun] trademark a kind of soft cheese from France.
– ORIGIN French.

boustrophedon /ˌbaʊstrəˈfiːd(ə)n, ˌbuː-/ ▶ adjective & adverb (of written words) from right to left and from left to right in alternate lines.
– ORIGIN early 17th cent.: from Greek, literally 'as an ox turns in ploughing', from *bous* 'ox' + *-strophos* 'turning'.

bout /baʊt/ ▶ noun **1** a short period of intense activity of a specified kind: *occasional bouts of strenuous exercise | a drinking bout.* ■ an attack of illness or strong emotion: *a severe bout of flu.* ■ a wrestling or boxing match.
2 a curve in the side of a violin, guitar, or other musical instrument.
– ORIGIN mid 16th cent. (denoting a curve or circuit, hence later a 'turn' of activity): from dialect *bought* 'bend, loop'; probably of Low German origin.

boutade /buːˈtɑːd/ ▶ noun formal a sudden outburst or outbreak.
– ORIGIN early 17th cent.: French, from *bouter* 'to thrust'.

boutique /buːˈtiːk/ ▶ noun **1** a small shop selling fashionable clothes or accessories.
2 a business serving a sophisticated or specialized clientele: [as modifier] *California's boutique wineries.*
– ORIGIN mid 18th cent.: from French, 'small shop', via Latin from Greek *apothēkē* 'storehouse'. Compare with **BODEGA**.

boutique hotel ▶ noun a stylish small hotel, typically one situated in a fashionable urban location.

bouton /ˈbuːtɒn/ ▶ noun Anatomy an enlarged part of a nerve fibre or cell, especially an axon, where it forms a synapse with another nerve.
– ORIGIN 1930s: from French, literally 'button'.

boutonnière /ˌbuːtɒnˈjɛː/ ▶ noun a spray of flowers worn in a buttonhole.
– ORIGIN late 19th cent.: French, 'buttonhole', from *bouton* 'button'.

Boutros-Ghali /ˌbuːtrɒsˈɡɑːli/, Boutros (b.1922), Egyptian diplomat and politician, Secretary General of the United Nations 1992–7.

boutu ▶ noun another term for **BOTO**.

Bouvet Island /ˈbuːveɪ/ an uninhabited Norwegian island in the South Atlantic.
– ORIGIN named after the French navigator François Lozier-*Bouvet* (1705–86), who visited it in 1739.

bouvier /ˈbuːvɪeɪ/ ▶ noun a large, powerful dog of a rough-coated breed originating in Belgium.
– ORIGIN French, literally 'cowherd'.

bouzouki /bʊˈzuːki/ ▶ noun (pl. **bouzoukis**) a long-necked Greek form of mandolin.
– ORIGIN 1950s: from modern Greek *mpouzouki*, possibly related to Turkish *bozuk* 'spoilt' (with reference to roughly made instruments).

bovid /ˈbəʊvɪd/ ▶ noun Zoology a mammal of the cattle family (Bovidae).
– ORIGIN late 19th cent.: from modern Latin *Bovidae* (plural), from *bos, bov-* 'ox'.

bovine /ˈbəʊvʌɪn/ ▶ adjective relating to or affecting cattle: *bovine tuberculosis | bovine tissue.* ■ (of a person or their manner) sluggish or stupid: *a look of bovine contentment came into her face.*
▶ noun an animal of the cattle group, which also includes buffaloes and bison.
– DERIVATIVES **bovinely** adverb.
– ORIGIN early 19th cent.: from late Latin *bovinus*, from Latin *bos, bov-* 'ox'.

bovine somatotrophin /ˌsəʊmətə(ʊ)ˈtrəʊfɪn/ ▶ noun [mass noun] a growth hormone occurring naturally in cows that is added to cattle feed to increase milk production.

bovine spongiform encephalopathy ▶ noun see **BSE**.

Bovril ▶ noun [mass noun] trademark a concentrated essence of beef diluted with hot water to make a drink.
– ORIGIN late 19th cent.: from Latin *bos, bov-* 'ox', the second element perhaps from *vril*, an imaginary

B

form of energy described in E. Bulwer-Lytton's novel *The Coming Race* (1871).

bovver ▶ noun [mass noun] [usu. as modifier] Brit. informal hooliganism or violent disorder, especially as caused by gangs of skinheads: *a bovver boy*.
– ORIGIN 1960s: representing a cockney pronunciation of BOTHER.

bovver boots ▶ noun Brit. informal heavy laced boots extending to the mid-calf, typically worn by skinheads.

Bow /bəʊ/, Clara (1905–65), American actress. One of the most popular stars and sex symbols of the 1920s, she was known as the 'It Girl'.

bow¹ /bəʊ/ ▶ noun **1** a knot tied with two loops and two loose ends, used especially for tying shoelaces and decorative ribbons: *a girl with long hair tied back in a bow*. ■ a decorative ribbon tied in a bow.
2 a weapon for shooting arrows, typically made of a curved piece of wood joined at both ends by a taut string.
3 a long, partially curved rod with horsehair stretched along its length, used for playing the violin and other stringed instruments. ■ a single passage of such a rod over the strings.
4 a curved stroke forming part of a letter (e.g. *b*, *p*).
5 a metal ring forming the handle of a key or pair of scissors. ■ N. Amer. a side piece or lens frame of a pair of glasses.
▶ verb [with obj.] play (a stringed instrument or music) using a bow.
– PHRASES **have** (or **add**) **another string to one's bow** Brit. have a further resource that one can make use of. **have many strings to one's bow** Brit. have a wide range of resources that one can make use of.
– ORIGIN Old English *boga* 'bend, bow, arch', of Germanic origin; related to Dutch *boog* and German *Bogen*, also to BOW².

bow² /baʊ/ ▶ verb [no obj.] **1** bend the head or upper part of the body as a sign of respect, greeting, or shame: *he turned and **bowed to** his father* | [with obj.] *she knelt and bowed her head* | *councillors stood **with heads bowed***.
2 bend with age or under pressure: *the roof trusses bowed as the wind fought to rip the roof free* | [with obj.] *the creepers were **bowed down with** flowers*. ■ submit to pressure or demands: *the government has **bowed to** pressure from farmers to increase compensation*.
3 chiefly N. Amer. (of a new film or product) be premiered or launched: *the trailer bowed in theaters nationwide on December 23*.
▶ noun an act of bending the head or upper body as a sign of respect or greeting: *the man gave a little bow*.
– PHRASES **bow and scrape** behave in an obsequious way to someone in authority. **make one's bow** make one's first formal appearance in a particular role: *the midfielder only made his England bow nine months ago*. **take a bow** acknowledge applause after a performance by bowing.
– PHRASAL VERBS **bow out** withdraw or retire from an activity or role: *many artists are forced to **bow out** of the profession at a relatively early age*.
– ORIGIN Old English *būgan* 'bend, stoop', of Germanic origin; related to German *biegen*, also to BOW¹.

bow³ /baʊ/ (also **bows**) ▶ noun the front end of a ship: *water sprayed high over her bows*.
– PHRASES **on the bow** Nautical within 45° of the point directly ahead. **a (warning) shot across the bows** a statement or gesture intended to frighten someone into changing their course of action: *supporters are firing a warning shot across the President's bows*.
– ORIGIN late Middle English: from Low German *boog*, Dutch *boeg*, 'shoulder or ship's bow'; related to BOUGH.

bow compass (also **bow compasses**) ▶ noun a compass with jointed legs.

bowdlerize /ˈbaʊdlərʌɪz/ (also **bowdlerise**) ▶ verb [with obj.] remove material that is considered improper or offensive from (a text or account), especially with the result that the text becomes weaker or less effective: (as adj. **bowdlerized**) *a bowdlerized version of the story*.
– DERIVATIVES **bowdlerization** noun.
– ORIGIN mid 19th cent.: from the name of Dr Thomas *Bowdler* (1754–1825), who published an expurgated edition of Shakespeare in 1818, + -IZE.

bowel /ˈbaʊəl/ ▶ noun (often **bowels**) the part of the alimentary canal below the stomach; the intestine. ■ (**the bowels of**) the deepest inner parts or areas of (something): *the mineshaft descended deep into the bowels of the earth*.
– ORIGIN Middle English: from Old French *bouel*, from Latin *botellus*, diminutive of *botulus* 'sausage'.

bowel movement ▶ noun an act of defecation. ■ the faeces discharged in an act of defecation.

Bowen /ˈbəʊɪn/, Elizabeth (Dorothea Cole) (1899–1973), British novelist and short-story writer, born in Ireland. Notable novels: *The Death of the Heart* (1938) and *The Heat of the Day* (1949).

bower¹ /ˈbaʊə/ ▶ noun a pleasant shady place under trees or climbing plants in a garden or wood. ■ literary a summer house or country cottage. ■ literary a woman's private room or bedroom.
▶ verb [with obj.] literary shade or enclose (a place or person): (as adj. **bowered**) *the bowered pathways into the tangle of vines*.
– ORIGIN Old English *būr* 'dwelling, inner room', of Germanic origin; related to German *Bauer* 'birdcage'.

bower² /ˈbaʊə/ (also **bower anchor**) ▶ noun each of two anchors carried at a ship's bow, formerly distinguished as the **best bower** (starboard) or **small bower** (port).
– ORIGIN late 15th cent.: from BOW³ + -ER¹.

bowerbird ▶ noun a strong-billed Australasian bird, noted for the male's habit of constructing an elaborate run or bower adorned with feathers, shells, and other objects to attract the female for courtship.
● Family Ptilonorhynchidae: several genera and species.

Bowery /ˈbaʊəri/ a street and district in New York City associated with drunks and vagrants.
– ORIGIN mid 17th cent.: built on the site of governor Peter Stuyvesant's *bowery* 'farm', from Dutch *bouwerij*; the district became noted for its cheap lodging houses and saloons.

bowfin /ˈbəʊfɪn/ ▶ noun a predatory American freshwater fish with a large blunt head and a long dorsal fin. It is able to survive for long periods out of water.
● *Amia calva*, the only living member of the family Amiidae.
– ORIGIN late 19th cent.: from BOW¹ + FIN.

bow-fronted ▶ adjective (of furniture) having a convexly curved front.
– DERIVATIVES **bow front** noun & adjective.

bowhead /ˈbəʊhɛd/ (also **bowhead whale**) ▶ noun an Arctic right whale with black skin, feeding by skimming the surface for plankton. Also called GREENLAND RIGHT WHALE. ● *Balaena mysticetus*, family Balaenidae.
– ORIGIN late 19th cent.: from BOW¹ + HEAD.

bowhunting ▶ noun [mass noun] N. Amer. the practice of hunting animals with a bow rather than a gun.
– DERIVATIVES **bowhunter** noun.

Bowie¹ /ˈbəʊi/, David (b.1947), English rock singer, songwriter, and actor; born *David Robert Jones*. He is known for his theatrical performances and for his adoption of a number of different stage personae. Notable albums: *Ziggy Stardust* (1972) and *Heroes* (1977).

Bowie² /ˈbəʊi/, Jim (1799–1836), American frontiersman; full name *James Bowie*. He shared command of the garrison that resisted the Mexican attack on the Alamo, where he died.

bowie /ˈbəʊi/ (also **bowie knife**) ▶ noun (pl. **bowies**) a long knife with a blade that is double-edged at the point.
– ORIGIN mid 19th cent.: named after J. *Bowie* (see BOWIE²).

bowknot ▶ noun a double-looped ornamental knot in a ribbon, tie, or other fastening.

bowl¹ ▶ noun **1** a round, deep dish or basin used for food or liquid: *a mixing bowl* | *a sugar bowl*. ■ the contents of a bowl: *they ate huge **bowls of** steaming spaghetti*. ■ [usu. in names] a decorative round dish awarded as a prize in a competition: *the McGeorge Rose Bowl*. ■ a rounded, concave part of an object: *a toilet bowl* | *the bowl of a spoon*. ■ Geography a natural basin.
2 [in names] chiefly US a stadium for sporting or musical events: *the Hollywood Bowl*. ■ an American football game played after the regular season between leading teams.
– DERIVATIVES **bowlful** noun (pl. **bowlfuls**).
– ORIGIN Old English *bolle*, *bolla*, of Germanic origin; related to Dutch *bol* 'round object', also to BOLL.

bowl² ▶ noun **1** a wooden or hard rubber ball, slightly asymmetrical so that it runs on a curved course, used in the game of bowls. ■ a large ball with indentations for gripping, used in tenpin bowling. ■ a wooden ball or disc used in playing skittles.
2 a spell or turn of bowling in cricket.
▶ verb **1** [with obj. and adverbial of direction] roll (a ball or other round object) along the ground: *she snatched her hat off and bowled it ahead of her*.
2 [with obj.] Cricket (of a bowler) propel (the ball) with a straight arm towards the batsman, typically in such a way that the ball bounces once: *Lillee bowled another bouncer* | [no obj.] *Sobers bowled to Willis*. ■ (also **bowl someone out**) dismiss (a batsman) by knocking down the wicket with the ball which one has bowled: *Stewart **was bowled for** 33*. ■ (**bowl a side out**) get an entire team out: *they **bowled** Lancashire **out for** 143*.
3 [no obj., with adverbial of direction] Brit. move rapidly and smoothly in a specified direction: *they bowled along the country roads*.
– PHRASAL VERBS **bowl someone over** knock someone down. ■ informal greatly impress someone by one's good qualities, looks, or achievements: *when he met Angela he was just bowled over by her*.
– ORIGIN late Middle English (in the general sense 'ball'): from Old French *boule*, from Latin *bulla* 'bubble'.

bow legs ▶ plural noun legs that curve outwards at the knee; bandy legs.
– DERIVATIVES **bow-legged** adjective.

bowler¹ ▶ noun **1** Cricket a member of the fielding side who bowls or is bowling.
2 a player at bowls, tenpin bowling, or skittles.

bowler² (also **bowler hat**) ▶ noun chiefly Brit. a man's hard felt hat with a round dome-shaped crown.
– ORIGIN mid 19th cent.: named after William *Bowler*, the English hatter who designed it in 1850.

Bowles /bəʊlz/, Paul (Frederick) (1910–99), American writer and composer. His novels, which include *The Sheltering Sky* (1949) and *The Spider's House* (1966), typically concern westerners in the Arab world.

bowline /ˈbəʊlɪn/ ▶ noun **1** a rope attaching the weather side of a square sail to a ship's bow.
2 a simple knot for forming a non-slipping loop at the end of a rope.
– ORIGIN Middle English: from Middle Low German *bōline*, Middle Dutch *boechlijne*, from *boeg* 'ship's bow' + *lijne* 'line'.

bowling ▶ noun [mass noun] **1** the game of bowls as a sport or recreation. ■ the game of tenpin bowling. ■ the game of skittles.
2 Cricket the action of a bowler in sending down balls towards the batsman's wicket: *fast bowling*. ■ the bowlers in a team: *on paper their bowling looks weak*.

bowling alley ▶ noun a long, narrow track along which balls are rolled in the games of skittles or tenpin bowling. ■ a building containing such tracks.

bowling average ▶ noun Cricket the number of runs conceded by a bowler per wicket taken.

bowling crease ▶ noun Cricket the line from behind which a bowler delivers the ball.

bowling green ▶ noun an area of closely mown grass on which the game of bowls is played.

bowling rink ▶ noun see RINK.

bowls /bəʊlz/ ▶ plural noun [treated as sing.] a game played with heavy bowls, the object of which is to propel one's bowl so that it comes to rest as close as possible to a previously bowled small ball (the jack). Bowls is played chiefly out of doors (though indoor bowls is also popular) on a closely trimmed lawn called a green. ■ Brit. tenpin bowling or skittles.

bowman¹ /ˈbəʊmən/ ▶ noun (pl. **bowmen**) an archer.

bowman² /ˈbaʊmən/ ▶ noun (pl. **bowmen**) the rower who sits nearest the bow of a boat, especially a racing boat.

bow saw /ˈbəʊsɔː/ ▶ noun a saw with a narrow blade stretched like a bowstring on a light frame.

bowser /ˈbaʊzə/ ▶ noun trademark a tanker used for fuelling aircraft and other vehicles or for supplying water. ■ Austral./NZ a petrol pump.
– ORIGIN 1920s: from the name of a company of oil storage engineers.

bowshot /ˈbəʊʃɒt/ ▶ noun [in sing.] the distance to which a bow can send an arrow: *the two armies camped almost **within bowshot of** each other*.

bowsie /ˈbaʊzi:/ ▶ noun (pl. **bowsies**) Irish a low-class or unruly person.
– ORIGIN of unknown origin.

bowsprit /ˈbəʊsprɪt/ ▶ noun a spar running out from a ship's bow, to which the forestays are fastened.

– ORIGIN Middle English: from Middle Low German *bōgsprēt*, Middle Dutch *boechspriet*, from *boech* 'bow' + *spriet* 'sprit'.

Bow Street Runner /ˈbəʊ/ ▶ noun the popular name for a London policeman during the first half of the 19th century.
– ORIGIN named after *Bow Street* in London, site of the chief metropolitan magistrates' court.

bowstring /ˈbəʊstrɪŋ/ ▶ noun the string of an archer's bow, traditionally made of three strands of hemp.
▶ verb (past and past participle **bowstrung**) [with obj.] historical strangle with a bowstring (a former Turkish method of execution).

bow tie ▶ noun a necktie in the form of a bow or a knot with two loops.

bow wave ▶ noun a wave or system of waves set up at the bows of a moving ship.

bow window ▶ noun a curved bay window.

bow-wow ▶ exclamation /baʊˈwaʊ/ an imitation of a dog's bark.
▶ noun /ˈbaʊwaʊ/ a child's word for a dog.

bowyang /ˈbəʊjaŋ/ ▶ noun Austral./NZ dated a band or strap worn round the trouser leg below the knee.
– ORIGIN late 19th cent.: from British dialect *bow-yanks*, *bow yankees* 'leather leggings', of unknown origin.

bowyer /ˈbəʊjə/ ▶ noun a person who makes or sells archers' bows.

box[1] ▶ noun **1** a container with a flat base and sides, typically square or rectangular and having a lid: *a cigarette box | a hat box.* ■ the contents of a box: *she ate a whole box of chocolates that night.* ■ **(the box)** informal, chiefly Brit. television or a television set: *we sat around watching the box.* ■ informal a coffin: *I always thought I'd be in a box when I finally left here.* ■ vulgar slang, chiefly N. Amer. a woman's vagina.
2 an area or space enclosed within straight lines, in particular: ■ an area on a page that is to be filled in or that contains separate printed matter: *tick the box on the coupon.* ■ an area on a computer screen for user input or displaying information. ■ Brit. a box junction. ■ **(the box)** Soccer the penalty area. ■ **(the box)** Baseball the area occupied by the batter.
3 a separate section or enclosed area reserved for a group of people in a theatre or sports ground, or for witnesses or the jury in a law court: *the royal box.* ■ historical a coachman's seat. ■ Brit. a small country house for use when shooting or fishing.
4 a protective casing for a piece of a mechanism. ■ informal short for GEARBOX. ■ Brit. a light shield for protecting a man's genitals in sport, especially in cricket.
5 a facility at a newspaper office for receiving replies to an advertisement: *write to me care of Box 112.* ■ a facility at a post office whereby letters are kept until called for by the addressee.
▶ verb [with obj.] **1** (often as adj. **boxed**) put in or provide with a box: *the books are sold as a boxed set | Muriel **boxed up** all Christopher's clothes.* ■ enclose (a piece of text) within printed lines: *boxed sections in magazines.* ■ **(box someone in)** restrict the ability of (a person or vehicle) to move freely: *a van had double-parked alongside her car and totally boxed her in.*
2 **(box sheep up)** Austral./NZ mix up different flocks.
– PHRASES **be a box of birds** NZ informal be fine or happy. **box of tricks** informal an ingenious gadget: *all those magical effects were produced by this little box of tricks here.* **out of the box** Austral./NZ informal unusually good: *the novel is nothing out of the box.* [by association with the phrase *look fresh out of a bandbox* 'look very smart' (see BANDBOX).] **out of one's box** Brit. informal intoxicated with alcohol or drugs. **think outside the box** informal think in an original or creative way.
– DERIVATIVES **boxful** noun (pl. **boxfuls**), **box-like** adjective.
– ORIGIN late Old English, probably from late Latin *buxis*, from Latin *pyxis* 'boxwood box', from Greek *puxos* (see BOX[3]).

box[2] ▶ verb [no obj.] fight an opponent using one's fists; compete in the sport of boxing: *he boxed for England |* [with obj.] *he had to box Benn for the title.*
▶ noun [in sing.] a slap with the hand on the side of a person's head: *she gave him **a box on the ear**.*
– PHRASES **box clever** Brit. informal act so as to outwit someone: *she had to box clever, let Adam think she had accepted what he said.* **box someone's ears** slap someone on the side of the head, especially as a punishment.
– ORIGIN late Middle English (in the general sense 'a blow'): of unknown origin.

box[3] ▶ noun **1** (also **box tree**) a slow-growing European evergreen shrub or small tree with small glossy dark green leaves. It is widely used in hedging and for topiary, and yields hard, heavy timber. ● *Buxus sempervirens*, family Buxaceae.
2 any of a number of trees which have similar timber or foliage, in particular: ● several Australian eucalyptus trees (genus *Eucalyptus*, family Myrtaceae). ● the tropical American **Venezuelan** (or **West Indian**) **box** (*Casearia praecox*, family Flacourtiaceae), the timber of which has now largely replaced that of the European box.
– ORIGIN Old English, via Latin from Greek *puxos*.

box[4] ▶ verb (in phrase **box the compass**) chiefly Nautical
1 recite the compass points in correct order.
2 make a complete change of direction.
– ORIGIN mid 18th cent.: perhaps from Spanish *bojar* 'sail round', from Middle Low German *bōgen* 'bend', from the base of BOW[1].

Box and Cox ▶ noun [often as modifier] Brit. used to refer to an arrangement whereby people make use of the same accommodation or facilities at different times, according to a strict arrangement: *a Box and Cox arrangement.*
– ORIGIN the title of a play (1847) by J. M. Morton, in which two characters, John *Box* and James *Cox*, unknowingly become tenants of the same room.

box-and-whisker plot ▶ noun another term for BOX PLOT.

box beam ▶ noun another term for BOX GIRDER.

boxboard ▶ noun [mass noun] a type of stiff cardboard used to make boxes.

box camera ▶ noun a simple box-shaped hand camera.

box canyon ▶ noun N. Amer. a narrow canyon with a flat bottom and vertical walls.

boxcar ▶ noun N. Amer. an enclosed railway freight wagon, typically with sliding doors on the sides.

boxed set ▶ noun another term for BOX SET.

box elder ▶ noun an American maple with leaves that resemble those of the elder and green or purplish twigs. ● *Acer negundo*, family Aceraceae.

Boxer ▶ noun a member of a fiercely nationalistic Chinese secret society which flourished in the 19th century. In 1899 the society led a Chinese uprising against Western domination which was eventually crushed by a combined European force, aided by Japan and the US.
– ORIGIN from BOXER, translating Chinese *yì hé quán*, literally 'righteous harmony fists'.

boxer ▶ noun **1** a person who takes part in boxing, especially for sport.
2 a medium-sized dog of a breed with a smooth brown coat and pug-like face.

boxercise ▶ noun [mass noun] trademark a form of exercise based on boxing training and using boxing equipment.
– ORIGIN 1980s: blend of BOXER and EXERCISE.

boxer shorts (also **boxers**) ▶ plural noun men's loose underpants similar in shape to the shorts worn by boxers.

boxfish ▶ noun (pl. **same** or **boxfishes**) a tropical marine fish that has a shell of bony plates enclosing the body, from which spines project. Also called TRUNKFISH. ● Family Ostraciontidae: numerous species.

box girder ▶ noun a hollow girder square in cross section.

Boxgrove man ▶ noun a fossil hominid of the Middle Pleistocene period, whose fragmentary remains were found at Boxgrove near Chichester, SE England, in 1993 and 1995. Dated (controversially) to about 500,000 years ago, it is one of the earliest known humans in Europe. ● *Homo heidelbergensis* (or *H. erectus*), family Hominidae.

boxing ▶ noun the sport or practice of fighting with the fists, especially with padded gloves in a roped square ring according to prescribed rules (the Queensberry Rules).

Boxing Day ▶ noun Brit. a public holiday celebrated on the first day (strictly, the first weekday) after Christmas Day.
– ORIGIN mid 19th cent.: from the custom of giving tradespeople a Christmas box on this day.

boxing glove ▶ noun a heavily padded mitten worn in boxing.

boxing weight ▶ noun each of a series of fixed weight ranges at which boxers are matched.

box jelly ▶ noun a jellyfish with a box-shaped swimming bell, living in warm seas. See also SEA WASP. ● Class Cubozoa (formerly order Cubomedusae).

box junction ▶ noun Brit. a road area at a junction marked with a yellow grid, which a vehicle should enter only if its exit from it is clear.

box kite ▶ noun a tailless kite in the form of a long box open at each end.

box number ▶ noun a number identifying a private advertisement in a newspaper and functioning as an address for replies.

box office ▶ noun a place at a theatre, cinema, etc. where tickets are bought or reserved. ■ used to refer to the commercial success of a film, play, or actor in terms of the audience size or takings that they command: [as modifier] *the movie was a huge box office hit.*

boxout ▶ noun a piece of text written to accompany a larger text and printed in a separate area of the page.

box pew ▶ noun an old-fashioned church pew enclosed by wooden partitions.

box pleat ▶ noun a pleat consisting of two parallel creases facing opposite directions and forming a raised band.

box plot (also **box-and-whisker plot**) ▶ noun Statistics a simple way of representing statistical data on a plot in which a rectangle is drawn to represent the second and third quartiles, usually with a vertical line inside to indicate the median value. The lower and upper quartiles are shown as horizontal lines either side of the rectangle.

box room ▶ noun Brit. a very small room used for storage or as a bedroom.

box score ▶ noun N. Amer. the tabulated results of a baseball game or other sporting event, with statistics given for each player's performance.

box seat ▶ noun **1** a seat in a box in a theatre or sports stadium.
2 historical a coachman's seat.
– PHRASES **in the box seat** Austral./NZ informal in an advantageous position.

box set (also **boxed set**) ▶ noun a set of related items, typically books or recordings, packaged together in a box and sold as a unit.

box-shifter ▶ noun informal a retail company which aims to maximize sales with little regard for quality or customer care.

box spanner ▶ noun Brit. a cylindrical spanner with a hexagonal end fitting over the head of a nut.

box spring ▶ noun each of a set of vertical springs housed in a frame in a mattress or upholstered chair base.

boxthorn ▶ noun a thorny shrub of warm-temperate regions, which bears red berries. Some kinds are used for hedging. ● Genus *Lycium*, family Solanaceae: several species (see also TEA TREE (sense 2)).

box turtle ▶ noun a land-living turtle which has a lower shell with hinged lobes that can be drawn up tightly to enclose the animal. It is native to North America and Mexico and is commonly kept as a pet in the US. ● Genus *Terrapene*, family Emydidae: several species.

boxty /ˈbɒksti/ (also **boxty bread**) ▶ noun [mass noun] a type of bread made using grated raw potatoes and flour, originally in Ireland.
– ORIGIN from Irish *bacstaí*.

boxy ▶ adjective (**boxier**, **boxiest**) squarish in shape: *a boxy jacket.* ■ (of a room or space) cramped. ■ (of recorded sound) restricted in tone.

boy ▶ noun **1** a male child or youth. ■ a person's son: *she put her little boy to bed.* ■ [with modifier] a male child or young man who does a specified job: *a delivery boy.*
2 [usu. with adj.] a man, especially a young or relatively young one: *I was the new boy at the office.* ■ **(boys)** informal men who mix socially or who belong to a particular group, team, or profession: *he wants to stay one of the boys | our boys have finished bombing.* ■ dated a friendly form of address from one man to another, especially from an older man to a young man: *my dear boy, don't say another word!* ■ dated, offensive (often used as a form of address) a black male servant or worker. ■ a form of address to a male dog: *down boy!*
▶ exclamation informal used to express strong feelings, especially of excitement or admiration: *oh boy, that's wonderful!*
– PHRASES **boys in blue** informal policemen; the police. **boys will be boys** used to express the view that

B

mischievous or childish behaviour is typical of boys or young men and should not cause surprise when it occurs. **the big boys** the most powerful and successful men or organizations. **that's my boy** (or **girl**)! used as an expression of encouragement or admiration: *Papa beamed, "That's my boy!".*
– DERIVATIVES **boyhood** noun.
– ORIGIN Middle English (denoting a male servant): of unknown origin.

boyar /'bɔɪɑː(r), bəʊ'jɑː/ ▸ **noun** historical a member of the old aristocracy in Russia, next in rank to a prince.
– ORIGIN late 16th cent.: from Russian *boyarin* 'grandee'.

boy band (or **girl band**) ▸ **noun** a pop group composed of attractive young men (or young women), whose music and image are designed to appeal primarily to a young teenage audience.

Boyce, William (1711–79), English composer and organist. His compositions include songs, overtures, and eight symphonies; one of his most famous songs is 'Hearts of Oak'. He is also noted for his *Cathedral Music* (1760–73).

Boycott, Geoffrey (b.1940), English cricketer. He was an opening batsman for England, and was captain of Yorkshire 1971–5.

boycott ▸ **verb** [with obj.] withdraw from commercial or social relations with (a country, organization, or person) as a punishment or protest. ▪ refuse to buy or handle (goods) as a punishment or protest. ▪ refuse to cooperate with or participate in (a policy or event).
▸ **noun** a punitive ban on relations with other bodies, cooperation with a policy, or the handling of goods.
– ORIGIN from the name of Captain Charles C. *Boycott* (1832–97), an Irish land agent so treated in 1880, in an attempt instigated by the Irish Land League to get rents reduced.

Boyd, Arthur (Merric Bloomfield) (1920–99), Australian painter, potter, etcher, and ceramic artist. He was famous for large ceramic sculptures and for pictures inspired by his travels among Aborigines.

boyfriend ▸ **noun 1** a person's regular male companion with whom they have a romantic or sexual relationship.
2 [as modifier] denoting an item of clothing for a woman or girl that is designed to be loose-fitting or slightly oversized: *a boyfriend cardigan.*

boyish ▸ **adjective** of, like, or characteristic of a male child or young man: *his boyish charm | she looked boyish and defiant.*
– DERIVATIVES **boyishly** adverb, **boyishness** noun.

Boyle, Robert (1627–91), Irish-born scientist. Boyle put forward a view of matter based on particles which was a precursor of the modern theory of chemical elements and a cornerstone of his mechanical philosophy, which became very influential. He is best known for his experiments with the air pump, which led to the law named after him.

Boyle's law ▸ **noun** Chemistry a law stating that the pressure of a given mass of an ideal gas is inversely proportional to its volume at a constant temperature.

boylya /'bɔɪljə/ ▸ **noun** Austral. an Aborigine thought to have spiritual and magical powers.
– ORIGIN from Nyungar *bolya*.

Boyne, Battle of the /bɔɪn/ a battle fought near the River Boyne in Ireland in 1690, in which the Protestant army of William of Orange, the newly crowned William III, defeated the Catholic army (including troops from both France and Ireland) led by the recently deposed James II. The battle is celebrated annually (on 12 July) in Northern Ireland as a victory for the Protestant cause.

boyo ▸ **noun** (pl. **boyos**) Welsh & Irish informal a boy or man (used chiefly as a form of address).

boy racer ▸ **noun** Brit. informal a youth or young man fond of driving very fast and aggressively in high-powered cars.

Boys' Brigade the oldest of the national organizations for boys in Britain, founded in 1883 with the aim of promoting 'Christian manliness', discipline, and self-respect. Companies are now also found in the US and in Commonwealth countries; each is connected with a church.

Boy Scout ▸ **noun** North American or old-fashioned term for **scout**[1] (sense 3 of the noun).

boysenberry /'bɔɪz(ə)n,b(ə)ri, -,bɛri/ ▸ **noun** (pl. **boysenberries**) **1** a large red edible blackberry-like fruit.
2 the shrubby plant that bears the boysenberry, which is a hybrid of several kinds of bramble. • *Rubus loganobaccus*, family Rosaceae.
– ORIGIN 1930s: named after Robert *Boysen* (died 1950), the American horticulturalist who developed it.

boy toy ▸ **noun** informal a young woman considered sexually attractive to men.
– ORIGIN 1980s: inversion of **toy boy**.

boy wonder ▸ **noun** informal an exceptionally talented young man or boy.

Boz /bɒz/ the pseudonym used by Charles Dickens in his *Pickwick Papers* and contributions to the *Morning Chronicle*.

bozo /'bəʊzəʊ/ ▸ **noun** (pl. **bozos**) informal, chiefly N. Amer. a stupid or insignificant man.
– ORIGIN 1920s: of unknown origin.

BP ▸ **abbreviation** ▪ before the present (era): *18,000 years BP.* ▪ blood pressure. ▪ British Petroleum, a large multinational oil company. ▪ (indicating listing in the) British Pharmacopoeia.

Bp ▸ **abbreviation** Bishop.

bp ▸ **abbreviation** ▪ Biochemistry base pair(s), as a unit of length in nucleic acid chains. ▪ Finance basis point(s). ▪ (**b.p.**) boiling point.

BPC ▸ **abbreviation** British Pharmaceutical Codex.

BPH ▸ **abbreviation** Medicine benign prostatic hyperplasia (or hypertrophy), an enlargement of the prostate gland common in elderly men.

BPhil ▸ **abbreviation** Bachelor of Philosophy.

bpi ▸ **abbreviation** Computing bits per inch, used to indicate the density of data that can be stored on magnetic tape or similar media.

B-picture ▸ **noun** another term for **B-movie**.

bpm ▸ **abbreviation** beats per minute: *a pulse rate of 40 bpm.*

BPO ▸ **abbreviation** business process outsourcing.

BPR ▸ **abbreviation** business process re-engineering.

bps ▸ **abbreviation** Computing bits per second.

Bq ▸ **abbreviation** becquerel.

BR ▸ **abbreviation** ▪ N. Amer. bedroom or bedrooms. ▪ Brazil (international vehicle registration). ▪ (in the UK) British Rail or (formerly) British Railways.

Br ▸ **symbol** the chemical element bromine.

Br. ▸ **abbreviation** ▪ (with reference to journal titles) British. ▪ (with reference to religious orders) Brother.

bra ▸ **noun** an undergarment worn by women to support the breasts.
– DERIVATIVES **braless** adjective.
– ORIGIN 1930s: abbreviation of **brassiere**.

braai /'brʌɪ/ S. African ▸ **noun** (pl. **braais**) short for **braaivleis**. ▪ a structure on which a fire can be made for the outdoor grilling of meat.
▸ **verb** (**braais**, **braaiing** or **braaing**, **braaied**) [with obj.] grill (meat) over an open fire.
– ORIGIN Afrikaans.

braaivleis /'brʌɪ,fleɪs/ ▸ **noun** S. African a picnic or barbecue where meat is grilled over an open fire. ▪ [mass noun] meat cooked in this way.
– ORIGIN Afrikaans, 'grilled meat', from *braai* 'to grill' + *vleis* 'meat'.

braata /'brɑːtə/ ▸ **noun** W. Indian a small amount added to a purchase in a market to encourage the customer to return.
– ORIGIN probably from Spanish *barata* 'bargain'.

Brabant /brə'bant/ a former duchy in western Europe, lying between the Meuse and Scheldt Rivers. Its capital was Brussels. It is now divided into two provinces in two countries: North Brabant in the Netherlands, of which the capital is 's-Hertogenbosch; and Brabant in Belgium, of which the capital remains Brussels.

Brabham /'brabəm/, Sir Jack (b.1926), Australian motor-racing driver; full name *John Arthur Brabham*. He won the Formula One world championship three times (1959, 1960, 1966).

brace ▸ **noun 1** a device fitted to something, in particular a weak or injured part of the body, to give support: *a neck brace.* ▪ a strengthening piece of iron or timber used in building or carpentry. ▪ (also **braces**) a wire device fitted in the mouth to straighten the teeth. ▪ (also **brace and bit**) a drilling tool with a crank handle and a socket to hold a bit. ▪ a rope attached to the yard of a ship for trimming the sail.
2 (**braces**) Brit. a pair of straps that pass over the shoulders and fasten to the top of trousers at the front and back to hold them up.
3 (pl. **same**) a pair of something, typically of birds or mammals killed in hunting: *thirty* ***brace of*** *grouse.*
4 Printing either of the two marks { and }, used either to indicate that two or more items on one side have the same relationship as each other to the single item to which the other side points, or in pairs to show that words between them are connected. ▪ Music a similar mark connecting staves to be performed at the same time.
▸ **verb** [with obj.] make (a structure) stronger or firmer with wood, iron, or other forms of support: *the posts were braced by lengths of timber.* ▪ press (one's body or part of one's body) firmly against something in order to stay balanced: *she* ***braced*** *her feet* ***against*** *a projecting shelf | he stood with legs braced.* ▪ prepare (someone) for something difficult or unpleasant: *both stations are* ***bracing themselves for*** *job losses.*
– PHRASAL VERBS **brace up** be strong or courageous: *she was about to tell him to brace up.*
– ORIGIN Middle English (as a verb meaning 'clasp, fasten tightly'): from Old French *bracier* 'embrace', from *brace* 'two arms', from Latin *bracchia*, plural of *bracchium* 'arm', from Greek *brakhiōn*.

bracelet ▸ **noun** an ornamental band, hoop, or chain worn on the wrist or arm. ▪ (**bracelets**) informal handcuffs.
– ORIGIN late Middle English: from Old French, from *bras* 'arm', from Latin *bracchium*.

bracelet sleeve ▸ **noun** a sleeve on a woman's garment that reaches to just above the wrist.

bracer[1] ▸ **noun** informal an alcoholic drink intended to prepare one for something difficult or unpleasant.

bracer[2] ▸ **noun 1** a type of wrist guard used in archery and other sports.
2 historical a portion of a suit of armour covering the arm.
– ORIGIN late Middle English: from Old French *braciere*, from *bras* 'arm' (see **bracelet**).

bracero /brə'sɪərəʊ, brə'sɛːrəʊ/ ▸ **noun** (pl. **braceros**) a Mexican labourer allowed into the United States for a limited time as a seasonal agricultural worker.
– ORIGIN 1970s: Spanish, literally 'labourer', from *brazo* 'arm'.

brachial /'breɪkɪəl/ ▸ **adjective** Anatomy relating to the arm or an arm-like structure: *the brachial artery.* ▪ Zoology denoting the upper valve of a brachiopod's shell.
– ORIGIN late Middle English: from Latin *brachialis*, from *brac(c)hium* 'arm'.

brachiate ▸ **verb** /'brakɪeɪt/ [no obj.] (of certain apes) move by using the arms to swing from branch to branch.
▸ **adjective** /'brakɪət, 'breɪkɪət/ Biology **1** branched, especially having widely spread paired branches on alternate sides.
2 having arms.
– DERIVATIVES **brachiation** noun, **brachiator** noun.
– ORIGIN mid 18th cent. (originally in the sense 'having paired branches'): from Latin *brachium* 'arm' + **-ate**[2].

brachiopod /'brakɪə(ʊ)pɒd/ ▸ **noun** Zoology a marine invertebrate of the phylum Brachiopoda, which comprises the lamp shells.

Brachiopoda /,brakɪə'pəʊdə/ ▸ **plural noun** Zoology a phylum of marine invertebrates that comprises the lamp shells.
– ORIGIN modern Latin (plural), from Greek *brakhiōn* 'arm' + *pous, pod-* 'foot'.

brachiosaurus /,brakɪə(ʊ)'sɔːrəs/ ▸ **noun** a huge herbivorous dinosaur of the late Jurassic to mid Cretaceous periods, with forelegs much longer than the hind legs. • Genus *Brachiosaurus*, infraorder Sauropoda, order Saurischia.
– ORIGIN modern Latin, from Greek *brakhiōn* 'arm' + *sauros* 'lizard'.

brachistochrone /brə'kɪstəkrəʊn/ ▸ **noun** Mathematics a curve between two points along which a body can move under gravity in a shorter time than for any other curve.
– ORIGIN late 18th cent.: from Greek *brakhistos* 'shortest' + *khronos* 'time'.

brachy- /'braki/ ▸ **combining form** short: *brachycephalic.*
– ORIGIN from Greek *brakhus* 'short'.

brachycephalic /,brakɪsɪ'falɪk, -kɛ'falɪk/ ▸ **adjective** Anatomy having a relatively broad, short skull

(typically with the breadth at least 80 per cent of the length). Often contrasted with **DOLICHOCEPHALIC**.
– DERIVATIVES **brachycephaly** noun.

brachytherapy /ˌbrakɪˈθɛrəpi/ ▸ **noun** the treatment of cancer, especially prostate cancer, by the insertion of radioactive implants directly into the tissue.

bracing ▸ **adjective 1** fresh and invigorating: *the bracing sea air*.
2 (of a support) serving to brace a structure: *bracing struts*.
– DERIVATIVES **bracingly** adverb (sense 1).

brack ▸ **noun** Irish a cake or bun containing dried fruit.
– ORIGIN shortening of **BARMBRACK**.

bracken ▸ **noun** [mass noun] a tall fern with coarse lobed fronds, which occurs worldwide and can cover large areas. ● *Pteridium aquilinum*, family Dennstaedtiaceae (or Hypolepidaceae).
■ informal any large coarse fern resembling bracken.
– ORIGIN Middle English: of Scandinavian origin; related to Danish *bregne*, Swedish *bräken*.

bracket ▸ **noun 1** each of a pair of marks ( ) [ ] { } ⟨ ⟩ used to enclose words or figures so as to separate them from the context: *symbols are given in brackets*.
2 [with adj. or noun modifier] a category of people or things that are similar or fall between specified limits: *those in a high income bracket*.
3 a right-angled support attached to a wall for holding a shelf, lamp, or other object.
4 (**the bracket**) Brit. informal, dated a person's nose or jaw.
5 Military the distance between two artillery shots fired either side of the target to establish range.
▸ **verb** (**brackets, bracketing, bracketed**) [with obj.]
1 enclose (words or figures) in brackets: (as adj. **bracketed**) *the relevant data is included as bracketed points*. ■ Mathematics enclose (a complex expression) in brackets to denote that the whole of the expression rather than just a part of it has a particular relation, such as multiplication or division, to another expression.
2 place (one or more people or things) in the same category or group: *he is sometimes bracketed with the 'new wave' of film directors*.
3 hold or attach (something) by means of a right-angled support: *pipes should be bracketed*.
4 Military establish the range of (a target) by firing two preliminary shots, one short of the target and the other beyond it. ■ Photography establish (the correct exposure) by taking several pictures with slightly more or less exposure.
– ORIGIN late 16th cent.: from French *braguette* or Spanish *bragueta* 'codpiece, bracket, corbel', from Provençal *braga*, from Latin *braca*, (plural) *bracae* 'breeches'.

bracket fungus ▸ **noun** a fungus which forms shelf-like projections on the trunks of living or dead trees, sending hyphae into the wood and sometimes causing the death of the tree or decay of the timber.
● Several families in the order Aphyllophorales, class Hymenomycetes.

brackish ▸ **adjective** (of water) slightly salty, as in river estuaries. ■ (of fish or other organisms) living in or requiring brackish water.
– DERIVATIVES **brackishness** noun.
– ORIGIN mid 16th cent.: from obsolete *brack* 'salty', from Middle Low German, Middle Dutch *brac*.

braconid /ˈbrakənɪd/ ▸ **noun** Entomology a small parasitic wasp of a family (Braconidae) which is related to the ichneumons. Unlike the latter, braconids lay numerous eggs in a single host.
– ORIGIN late 19th cent.: from modern Latin *Braconidae* (plural), formed irregularly from Greek *brakhus* 'short'.

bract ▸ **noun** Botany a modified leaf or scale, typically small, with a flower or flower cluster in its axil. Bracts are sometimes larger and more brightly coloured than the true flower, as in poinsettia.
– ORIGIN late 18th cent.: from Latin *bractea* 'thin plate of metal'.

bracteate /ˈbraktɪət, -tɪeɪt/ ▸ **adjective** Botany having or bearing bracts.
▸ **noun** Archaeology an ornament or plate of thinly beaten precious metal, typically a thin gold disc.
– ORIGIN early 19th cent.: from Latin *bracteatus*, from *bractea* (see **BRACT**).

brad ▸ **noun** a nail of rectangular cross section with a flat tip and a small, typically asymmetrical head.
– ORIGIN late Middle English: from Old Norse *broddr* 'spike'.

bradawl /ˈbradɔːl/ ▸ **noun** a tool for boring holes, resembling a small, sharpened screwdriver.
– ORIGIN early 19th cent.: from **BRAD** + **AWL**.

Bradbury, Ray (b.1920), American writer of science fiction; full name *Raymond Douglas Bradbury*. Notable works: *The Martian Chronicles* (short story collection, 1950) and *Fahrenheit 451* (novel, 1951).

Bradenham ham /ˈbrad(ə)nəm/ ▸ **noun** [mass noun] trademark a dark sweet-cured ham.

Bradford an industrial city in West Yorkshire, northern England; pop. 280,400 (est. 2009).

Bradley, James (1693–1762), English astronomer. Bradley was appointed Astronomer Royal in 1742. He discovered the aberration of light and also observed the oscillation of the earth's axis (*nutation*). His star catalogue was published posthumously.

Bradman, Sir Don (1908–2001), Australian cricketer; full name *Sir Donald George Bradman*. Bradman holds the record for the highest Australian Test score against England (334 in 1930), and his Test match batting average of 99.94 is well above that of any other cricketer of any era.

bradoon /brəˈduːn/ ▸ **noun** variant spelling of **BRIDOON**.

Bradshaw ▸ **noun** a timetable of all passenger trains in Britain, issued 1839–1961.
– ORIGIN named after its first publisher, George *Bradshaw* (1801–53), printer and engraver.

bradycardia /ˌbradɪˈkɑːdɪə/ ▸ **noun** [mass noun] Medicine abnormally slow heart action.
– ORIGIN late 19th cent.: from Greek *bradus* 'slow' + *kardia* 'heart'.

bradykinin /ˌbradɪˈkʌɪnɪn/ ▸ **noun** [mass noun] Biochemistry a compound released in the blood in some circumstances which causes contraction of smooth muscle and dilation of blood vessels. It is a peptide with nine amino-acid residues.
– ORIGIN 1940s: from Greek *bradus* 'slow' + *kinēsis* 'motion' + **-IN**[1].

brae /breɪ/ ▸ **noun** Scottish a steep bank or hillside.
– ORIGIN Middle English: from Old Norse *brá* 'eyelash'. Compare with **BROW**[1], in which a similar sense development occurred.

Braeburn /ˈbreɪbəːn/ ▸ **noun** a dessert apple of a variety with crisp flesh, first grown in New Zealand.
– ORIGIN 1950s: from *Braeburn* Orchards, where it was first grown commercially.

brag ▸ **verb** (**brags, bragging, bragged**) [reporting verb] say something in a boastful manner: [with clause] *he bragged that he was sure of victory* | [no obj.] *they were **bragging about** how easy it had been*.
▸ **noun 1** [mass noun] a gambling card game which is a simplified form of poker.
2 a boastful statement.
▸ **adjective** [attrib.] US informal excellent; first-rate.
– DERIVATIVES **bragger** noun, **bragging** noun & adjective, **braggingly** adverb.
– ORIGIN Middle English (as an adjective in the sense 'boastful'): of unknown origin (French *braguer* is recorded only later).

Braga /ˈbrɑːgə/ a city in northern Portugal, capital of a mountainous district of the same name; pop. 175,063 (2007).

Braganza[1] /brəˈganzə/ a city in NE Portugal, capital of a mountainous district of the same name; pop 34,489 (2007). It was the original seat of the Braganza dynasty. Portuguese name **Bragança** /brəˈɣɐ̃sə/.

Braganza[2] /brəˈganzə/ the dynasty that ruled Portugal from 1640 until the end of the monarchy in 1910 and Brazil (on its independence from Portugal) from 1822 until the formation of the republic in 1889.

Bragg, Sir William Henry (1862–1942), English physicist, a founder of solid-state physics. He collaborated with his son, **Sir (William) Lawrence Bragg** (1890–1971), in developing the technique of X-ray diffraction for determining the atomic structure of crystals; for this they shared the 1915 Nobel Prize for Physics.

braggadocio /ˌbragəˈdəʊtʃɪəʊ/ ▸ **noun** [mass noun] boastful or arrogant behaviour.
– ORIGIN late 16th cent. (denoting a boaster): from *Braggadocchio*, the name of a braggart in Spenser's *The Faerie Queene*, from **BRAG** or **BRAGGART** + the Italian suffix *-occio*, denoting something large of its kind.

braggart /ˈbragət, -ɑːt/ ▸ **noun** a person who boasts about their achievements or possessions.
– ORIGIN late 16th cent.: from French *bragard*, from *braguer* 'to brag'.

bragging rights ▸ **plural noun** informal a temporary position of ascendancy in a closely contested rivalry: *he walked off with a guaranteed $25,000 and bragging rights for at least a year*.

Brahe /ˈbrɑːhi, ˈbrɑːə/, Tycho (1546–1601), Danish astronomer. He built an observatory equipped with precision instruments, but despite demonstrating that comets follow sun-centred paths he adhered to a geocentric view of the planets.

Brahma /ˈbrɑːmə/ **1** the creator god in Hinduism, who forms a triad with Vishnu and Shiva. Brahma was an important god of late Vedic religion, but has been little worshipped since the 5th century AD.
2 another term for **BRAHMAN** (sense 2).
– ORIGIN from Sanskrit *brahman*.

brahma /ˈbrɑːmə/ ▸ **noun** short for **BRAHMAPUTRA**.

Brahman /ˈbrɑːmən/ ▸ **noun** (pl. **Brahmans**) **1** (also **Brahmin**) a member of the highest Hindu caste, originally that of the priesthood.
2 [mass noun] the ultimate reality underlying all phenomena in the Hindu scriptures.
3 US spelling of **BRAHMIN** (sense 3).
– DERIVATIVES **Brahmanic** /-ˈmanɪk/ adjective, **Brahmanical** /-ˈmanɪk(ə)l/ adjective.
– ORIGIN from Sanskrit *brāhmaṇa* (sense 1), *brahman* (sense 2).

Brahmana /ˈbrɑːmənə/ ▸ **noun** (in Hinduism) any of the lengthy commentaries on the Vedas, composed in Sanskrit *c.*900–700 BC and containing expository material relating to Vedic sacrificial ritual.

Brahmanism /ˈbrɑːməˌnɪz(ə)m/ (also **Brahminism**) ▸ **noun** [mass noun] the complex sacrificial religion that emerged in post-Vedic India (*c.*900 BC) under the influence of the dominant priesthood (Brahmans), an early stage in the development of Hinduism.

Brahmaputra /ˌbrɑːməˈpuːtrə/ a river of southern Asia, rising in the Himalayas and flowing 2,900 km (1,800 miles) through Tibet, NE India, and Bangladesh, to join the Ganges at its delta on the Bay of Bengal.

brahmaputra /ˌbrɑːməˈpuːtrə/ ▸ **noun** a chicken of a large Asian breed.
– ORIGIN mid 19th cent.: named after the **BRAHMAPUTRA**, where it originated.

Brahmin /ˈbrɑːmɪn/ ▸ **noun 1** variant spelling of **BRAHMAN** (sense 1).
2 US a socially or culturally superior person, especially one from New England.
3 (also **Brahminy bull** or US **Brahman**) an ox of a humped breed originally domesticated in India, which is tolerant of heat and drought and is now kept widely in tropical and warm temperate countries. Also called **ZEBU**. ● *Bos indicus*, family Bovidae; now usually included under the name *B. taurus* with other domestic cattle.
– DERIVATIVES **Brahminical** adjective (sense 1, sense 2).

Brahms /brɑːmz/, Johannes (1833–97), German composer and pianist. He eschewed programme music and opera and concentrated on traditional forms. He composed four symphonies, four concertos, chamber and piano music, choral works including the *German Requiem* (1857–68), and nearly 200 songs.
– DERIVATIVES **Brahmsian** adjective.

Brahms and Liszt ▸ **adjective** [predic.] Brit. informal drunk.
– ORIGIN 1930s: rhyming slang for 'pissed'.

Brahui /brəˈhuːi/ ▸ **noun** (pl. **same**) **1** a member of a pastoral people of western Pakistan.
2 [mass noun] the language of the Brahui, a Dravidian language isolated for several thousand years from other members of the family. It has nearly 2 million speakers.
▸ **adjective** relating to the Brahui or their language.
– ORIGIN from Brahui.

braid ▸ **noun 1** [mass noun] threads of silk, cotton, or other material woven into a decorative band for edging or trimming garments: *a coat trimmed with gold braid* | [count noun] *fancy braids*.
2 chiefly N. Amer. a length of hair made up of three or more interlaced strands: *her hair curled neatly in blonde braids*. ■ a length made up of three or more interlaced strands of any flexible material: *a flexible copper braid*.
▸ **verb** [with obj.] **1** interlace three or more strands of (hair or other flexible material) to form a length: *their long hair was tightly braided*.
2 (often as adj. **braided**) edge or trim (a garment) with braid: *braided red trousers*.
3 (usu. as adj. **braided**) (of a river or stream) flow into shallow interconnected channels divided by deposited earth or alluvium.

– ORIGIN Old English *bregdan* 'make a sudden movement', also 'interweave', of Germanic origin; related to Dutch *breien* (verb).

braiding ▶ **noun** [mass noun] decorative braid or braided work: *curtains heavy with gold braiding.*

brail Sailing ▶ **noun** (**brails**) small ropes that are led from the leech of a fore-and-aft sail to pulleys on the mast for temporarily furling it.
▶ **verb** [with obj.] (**brail a sail up**) furl a sail by hauling on brails.
– ORIGIN late Middle English: from Old French *braiel*, from medieval Latin *bracale* 'girdle', from *braca* 'breeches'.

Brăila /brəˈiːlə/ an industrial city and port on the Danube, in eastern Romania; pop. 216,814 (2006).

Braille[1] /breɪl/, French /bʀaj/, Louis (1809–52), French educationist. Blind from the age of 3, by the age of 15 he had developed his own system of raised-point reading and writing, which was officially adopted two years after his death.

Braille[2] /breɪl/ ▶ **noun** [mass noun] a form of written language for blind people, in which characters are represented by patterns of raised dots that are felt with the fingertips.
▶ **verb** (**Brailles, Brailling, Brailled**) [with obj.] print or transcribe in Braille.

brain ▶ **noun 1** an organ of soft nervous tissue contained in the skull of vertebrates, functioning as the coordinating centre of sensation and intellectual and nervous activity. ■ (**brains**) the substance of an animal's brain used as food. ■ informal an electronic device with functions comparable to those of the human brain.

> The human brain consists of three main parts. (i) The forebrain, greatly developed into the cerebrum, consists of two hemispheres joined by a bridge of nerve fibres, and is responsible for the exercise of thought and control of speech. (ii) The midbrain, the upper part of the tapering brainstem, contains cells concerned in eye movements. (iii) The hindbrain, the lower part of the brainstem, contains cells responsible for breathing and for regulating heart action, the flow of digestive juices, and other unconscious actions and processes. The cerebellum, which lies behind the brain stem, plays an important role in the execution of highly skilled movements.

2 intellectual capacity: *I didn't have enough brains for the sciences* | [mass noun] *success requires brain as well as brawn.* ■ (**the brains**) informal a clever person who supplies the ideas and plans for a group of people: *Tom was the brains of the outfit.* ■ a person's mind: *a tiny alarm bell began to ring in her brain.*
▶ **verb** [with obj.] informal hit (someone) hard on the head with an object: *she brained me with a rolling pin.*
– PHRASES **have (got) something on the brain** informal be obsessed with something: *John has cars on the brain.*
– ORIGIN Old English *brægen*, of West Germanic origin; related to Dutch *brein.*

brainbox ▶ **noun** Brit. informal a very clever person.

braincase ▶ **noun** the cranium.

brain cell ▶ **noun** a cell in the tissue of the brain. ■ informal used to refer to someone's intellectual capabilities: *I couldn't get my brain cells around the questions never mind the answers.*

brainchild ▶ **noun** (pl. **brainchildren**) informal an idea or invention which is considered to be a particular person's creation: *the statue is the brainchild of a local landscape artist.*

brain coral ▶ **noun** a compact coral with a convoluted surface resembling that of the brain. ● *Diploria* and other genera, order Scleractinia.

brain damage ▶ **noun** [mass noun] injury to the brain that impairs its functions, especially permanently.
– DERIVATIVES **brain-damaged** adjective.

brain-dead ▶ **adjective** having suffered brain death: *brain-dead patients.* ■ informal extremely stupid: *the brain-dead politics of the past.*

brain death ▶ **noun** [mass noun] irreversible brain damage causing the end of independent respiration, regarded as indicative of death.

brain drain ▶ **noun** [in sing.] informal the emigration of highly trained or qualified people from a particular country.

Braine, John (Gerard) (1922–86), English novelist, famous for his first novel, *Room at the Top* (1957), whose opportunistic hero was hailed as a representative example of an 'angry young man'.

brained ▶ **adjective** [in combination] having a brain of a certain size or kind: *large-brained mammals.* ■ derogatory having an intellectual capacity of a certain quality or kind: *half-brained twits.*

brain fever ▶ **noun** [mass noun] dated inflammation of the brain.

brainfever bird ▶ **noun** the common hawk cuckoo of India and Sri Lanka, which has a monotonous and maddeningly persistent call. ● *Cuculus varius*, family Cuculidae.

brain fungus ▶ **noun 1** (also **yellow brain fungus**) a soft yellow gelatinous fungus with a lobed and folded surface, living on dead wood in both Eurasia and North America. ● *Tremella mesenterica*, family Tremellaceae, class Hymenomycetes.
2 another term for CAULIFLOWER FUNGUS.

brainiac ▶ **noun** N. Amer. informal an exceptionally intelligent person.
– ORIGIN 1950s: from the name of a supremely intelligent alien character in the *Superman* comic strip, from a blend of BRAIN and MANIAC.

brainless ▶ **adjective** stupid; very foolish: *a brainless bimbo.*
– DERIVATIVES **brainlessly** adverb, **brainlessness** noun.

brainpan ▶ **noun** informal, chiefly N. Amer. a person's skull.

brainpower ▶ **noun** [mass noun] mental ability; intelligence.

brainstem ▶ **noun** Anatomy the central trunk of the mammalian brain, consisting of the medulla oblongata, pons, and midbrain, and continuing downwards to form the spinal cord.

brainstorm ▶ **noun 1** Brit. informal a moment in which one is suddenly unable to think clearly or act sensibly.
2 a spontaneous group discussion to produce ideas and ways of solving problems. ■ N. Amer. informal a sudden clever idea.
▶ **verb** [no obj.] hold a group discussion to produce ideas: (as noun modifier **brainstorming**) *a brainstorming session.*

brains trust ▶ **noun 1** Brit. a group of experts who give impromptu answers to questions in front of an audience or on the radio.
2 (usu. **brain trust**) N. Amer. a group of experts appointed to advise a government or politician.

brain-teaser (also **brain-twister**) ▶ **noun** informal a problem or puzzle, typically one designed to be solved for amusement.
– DERIVATIVES **brain-teasing** adjective.

brainwash ▶ **verb** [with obj.] pressurize (someone) into adopting radically different beliefs by using systematic and often forcible means: *people are brainwashed into believing family life is the best* | (as noun **brainwashing**) *victims of brainwashing.*

brainwave ▶ **noun 1** (usu. **brainwaves**) an electrical impulse in the brain.
2 [usu. in sing.] informal a sudden clever idea.

brainwork ▶ **noun** [mass noun] mental activity; thought.

brainy ▶ **adjective** (**brainier, brainiest**) having or showing intelligence: *a brainy discussion* | *she was brainy, except for maths.*
– DERIVATIVES **braininess** noun.

braise ▶ **verb** [with obj.] fry (food) lightly and then stew it slowly in a closed container: (as adj. **braised**) *braised veal.*
– ORIGIN mid 18th cent.: from French *braiser*, from *braise* 'live coals' (in which the container was formerly placed).

brak /brak/ ▶ **adjective** S. African (of water or soil) brackish or alkaline.
– ORIGIN Afrikaans, from Dutch.

brake[1] ▶ **noun 1** a device for slowing or stopping a moving vehicle, typically by applying pressure to the wheels: *he slammed on his brakes* | [as modifier] *a brake pedal.* ■ a thing that slows or hinders a process: *constrained resources will act as a brake on research.*
2 another term for BRAKE VAN.
▶ **verb** [no obj.] make a moving vehicle slow down or stop by using a brake: *she had to brake hard to avoid a milk float* | (as noun modifier **braking**) *an anti-lock braking system.*
– ORIGIN late 18th cent.: of unknown origin.

brake[2] ▶ **noun** historical an open horse-drawn carriage with four wheels.
– ORIGIN mid 19th cent.: variant of BREAK[2].

brake[3] ▶ **noun** a toothed instrument used for crushing flax and hemp. ■ (also **brake harrow**) a heavy machine formerly used in agriculture for breaking up large lumps of earth.
– ORIGIN late Middle English: possibly related to Middle Low German *brake* and Dutch *braak*, and perhaps also to BREAK[1].

brake[4] ▶ **noun** archaic or literary a thicket. See also FERN-BRAKE.
– ORIGIN Old English *bracu* (first recorded in the plural in *fearnbraca* 'thickets of fern'), related to Middle Low German *brake* 'branch, stump'.

brake[5] (also **brake fern**) ▶ **noun** a coarse fern of warm and tropical countries, frequently having the fronds divided into long linear segments. ● Genus *Pteris*, family Pteridaceae.
■ archaic term for BRACKEN.
– ORIGIN Middle English: perhaps an abbreviation of BRACKEN (interpreted as plural).

brake[6] archaic past of BREAK[1].

brake block ▶ **noun** a block of hard material pressed against the rim of a wheel to slow it down by friction, especially on a bicycle.

brake caliper ▶ **noun** see CALIPER (sense 1).

brake disc ▶ **noun** the disc attached to the wheel in a disc brake.

brake drum ▶ **noun** a broad, very short cylinder attached to a wheel, against which the brake shoes press in a drum brake.

brake fluid ▶ **noun** [mass noun] fluid used in a hydraulic brake system.

brake harrow ▶ **noun** see BRAKE[3].

brake horsepower (abbrev.: **b.h.p.**) ▶ **noun** (pl. **same**) an imperial unit of power, equal to one horsepower but used only as a measure of the power available at the shaft of an engine. ■ the available power of an engine, assessed by measuring the force needed to brake it.

brake light ▶ **noun** a red light at the back of a vehicle that is automatically illuminated when the brakes are applied.

brake lining ▶ **noun** a layer of hard material attached to a brake shoe or brake pad to increase friction against the drum or disc.

brakeman ▶ **noun** (pl. **brakemen**) **1** (Brit. also **brakesman**) chiefly N. Amer. a railway worker responsible for a train's brakes or for other duties such as those of a guard.
2 a person in charge of brakes, especially in a bobsleigh.

brake pad ▶ **noun** a thin block, typically one of a pair, which presses on to the disc in a disc brake.

brake shoe ▶ **noun** a long curved block, typically one of a pair, which presses on to the drum in a drum brake.

brake van ▶ **noun** Brit. a railway carriage or wagon from which the train's brakes can be controlled by the guard.

Bramah /ˈbrɑːmə/, Joseph (1748–1814), English inventor. One of the most influential engineers of the Industrial Revolution, Bramah is best known for his hydraulic press, used for heavy forging.

Bramante /brəˈmanteɪ/, Donato (di Angelo) (1444–1514), Italian architect. As architect to Pope Julius II he drew up the first plan for the new St Peter's (begun in 1506), instigating the concept of a huge central dome.

bramble ▶ **noun** a prickly scrambling shrub of the rose family, especially a blackberry. ■ Brit. the fruit of the blackberry.
▶ **verb** [no obj.] (usu. as noun **brambling**) Brit. gather blackberries.
– DERIVATIVES **brambly** adjective.
– ORIGIN Old English *bræmbel, brǣmel*, of Germanic origin; related to BROOM.

bramble shark ▶ **noun** a heavy-bodied, dull-coloured shark of the tropical Atlantic, with numerous thornlike spines on the back. ● *Echinorhinus brucus*, family Echinorhinidae.

brambling /ˈbramblɪŋ/ ▶ **noun** a northern Eurasian finch with a white rump, related to the chaffinch. The male has a black head and orange breast in summer. ● *Fringilla montifringilla*, family Fringillidae.
– ORIGIN mid 16th cent.: perhaps from or related to the obsolete German synonym *Brämling*, related to BRAMBLE, or a variant of BRANDLING (because both are streaked).

Bramley (also **Bramley's seedling**) ▶ **noun** (pl. **Bramleys**) an English cooking apple of a large green variety with firm flesh.

– ORIGIN early 20th cent.: named after Matthew *Bramley*, the English butcher in whose garden it is said to have first grown *c.*1850.

bran ▶ **noun** [mass noun] pieces of grain husk separated from flour after milling.
– ORIGIN Middle English: from Old French, of unknown origin.

branch ▶ **noun** a part of a tree which grows out from the trunk or from a bough. ■ a lateral extension or subdivision extending from the main part of a river, road, railway, etc. ■ a division or office of a large business or organization, operating locally or having a particular function: *he went to work at our Birmingham branch*. ■ a conceptual subdivision of a family, subject, group of languages, etc.: *a branch of mathematics called graph theory*.
▶ **verb** [no obj.] **1** (of a road or path) divide into one or more subdivisions: *follow this track south until it branches into two*. ■ (**branch off**) diverge from the main route or part: *the road branched off at the market town*. ■ (**branch out**) extend or expand one's activities or interests in a new direction: *the company is branching out into Europe*.
2 (of a tree or plant) bear or send out branches.
– DERIVATIVES **branched** adjective, **branchlet** noun, **branch-like** adjective, **branchy** adjective.
– ORIGIN Middle English: from Old French *branche*, from late Latin *branca* 'paw'.

branchia /ˈbraŋkɪə/ ▶ **noun** (pl. **branchiae** /-kɪiː/) the gills of fish and some invertebrate animals.
– DERIVATIVES **branchial** adjective.
– ORIGIN late 17th cent.: from Latin *branchia*, (plural) *branchiae*, from Greek *brankhia* (plural).

branchiopod /ˈbraŋkɪə(ʊ)pɒd/ ▶ **noun** Zoology a small aquatic crustacean of the class Branchiopoda, such as a water flea or fairy shrimp.

Branchiopoda /ˌbraŋkɪəˈpəʊdə/ ▶ **plural noun** Zoology a class of small aquatic crustaceans that includes water fleas and fairy shrimps, which are distinguished by having gills upon the feet.
– ORIGIN modern Latin (plural), from Greek *brankhia* 'gills' + *pous, pod-* 'foot'.

branch line ▶ **noun** a secondary railway line running from a main line to a terminus.

Brancusi /braŋˈkuːzi/, Constantin (1876–1957), Romanian sculptor, who spent much of his working life in France. His sculpture represents an attempt to move away from a representational art and to capture the essence of forms by reducing them to their ultimate, almost abstract, simplicity.

brand ▶ **noun 1** a type of product manufactured by a particular company under a particular name: *a new brand of soap powder*. ■ a brand name: *the firm will market computer software under its own brand*. ■ a particular identity or image regarded as an asset: *you can still invent your own career, be your own brand*. ■ a particular type or kind of something: *they entertained millions with their inimitable brand of comedy*.
2 an identifying mark burned on livestock or (especially in former times) criminals or slaves with a branding iron. ■ archaic a branding iron. ■ a habit or quality that causes someone public shame or disgrace: *the brand of Paula's dipsomania*.
3 a piece of burning or smouldering wood: *he took two burning brands from the fire*.
4 literary a sword.
▶ **verb** [with obj.] **1** mark with a branding iron. ■ mark out as having a particular bad or shameful quality: *anyone who says anything bad about the country is branded as a traitor* | [with obj. and complement] *she was branded a liar*.
2 assign a brand name to: (as adj. **branded**) *cut-price branded goods*. ■ (as noun **branding**) the promotion of a particular product or company by means of advertising and distinctive design.
– DERIVATIVES **brander** noun.
– ORIGIN Old English *brand* 'burning' (also in sense 3 of the noun), of Germanic origin; related to German *Brand*, also to BURN[1]. The verb sense 'mark with a hot iron' dates from late Middle English, giving rise to the noun sense 'a mark of ownership made by branding' (mid 17th cent.), whence sense 1 of the noun (early 19th cent.).

WORD TRENDS Once upon a time most people rarely thought about **brands**, although they may have favoured a particular make of soap powder, cigarettes, or baked beans. Now a **brand** is primarily something to *build, promote, sell, create*, or *develop*, according to the Oxford English Corpus. Marketing and advertising are so pervasive that organizations, public figures, and even ordinary people may be considered as **brands**: *the first soccer club to promote its brand in Asia* | *the Beckham brand implies certain values* | *by developing a strong personal brand, you'll create a life that's more successful and fulfilling*.

brandade /brɒ̃ˈdɑːd/ ▶ **noun** [mass noun] a Provençal dish consisting of salt cod mixed into a purée with olive oil and milk.
– ORIGIN French, from modern Provençal *brandado*, literally 'something that has been shaken'.

brand awareness ▶ **noun** [mass noun] the extent to which consumers are familiar with the qualities or image of a particular brand of goods or services.

Brandenburg /ˈbrandənˌbəːɡ/, German /ˈbrandn̩ˌbʊrk/ a state of NE Germany; capital, Potsdam. The modern state corresponds to the western part of the former Prussian electorate, of which the eastern part was ceded to Poland after the Second World War.

Brandenburg Gate one of the city gates of Berlin (built 1788–91), the only one that survives. After the construction of the Berlin Wall in 1961 it stood in East Berlin, a conspicuous symbol of a divided city. It was reopened in December 1989.

brand equity ▶ **noun** [mass noun] the commercial value that derives from consumer perception of the brand name of a particular product or service, rather than from the product or service itself.

brand extension ▶ **noun** an instance of using an established brand name or trademark on new products, so as to increase sales.

branding iron ▶ **noun** a metal implement which is heated and used to brand livestock (or, in former times, criminals or slaves).

brandish ▶ **verb** [with obj.] wave or flourish (something, especially a weapon) as a threat or in anger or excitement: *a man leaped out brandishing a knife*.
– DERIVATIVES **brandisher** noun.
– ORIGIN Middle English: from Old French *brandiss-*, lengthened stem of *brandir*; ultimately of Germanic origin and related to BRAND.

brand leader ▶ **noun** the bestselling or most highly regarded product or brand of its type.

brandling ▶ **noun** a red earthworm with rings of a brighter colour, typically found in manure, and used as bait by anglers and in composting kitchen waste.
● *Eisenia fetida*, family Lumbricidae.
– ORIGIN mid 17th cent.: from BRAND + -LING.

brand loyalty ▶ **noun** [mass noun] the tendency of some consumers to continue buying the same brand of goods rather than competing brands.

brand name ▶ **noun** a name given by the maker to a product or range of products, especially a trademark.

brand new ▶ **adjective** completely new: *Graham's uniform was brand new* | *a brand-new Oxford dictionary*.
– ORIGIN late 16th cent.: from BRAND + NEW, with the idea 'straight from the fire'.

Brando, Marlon (1924–2004), American actor. An exponent of method acting, he first attracted critical acclaim in the stage production of *A Streetcar Named Desire* (1947); he starred in the film version four years later. Other notable films: *On the Waterfront* (1954, for which he won an Oscar) and *The Godfather* (1972).

Brands Hatch a motor-racing circuit near Farningham in Kent.

Brandt[1] /brant/, Bill (1904–83), German-born British photographer; full name *Hermann Wilhelm Brandt*. He is best known for his almost abstract treatment of the nude, as in *Perspectives of Nudes* (1961).

Brandt[2] /brant/, Willy (1913–92), German statesman, Chancellor of West Germany 1969–74; born *Karl Herbert Frahm*. He achieved international recognition for his policy of détente and the opening of relations with the countries of the Eastern bloc (Ostpolitik). Nobel Peace Prize (1971).

Brand X ▶ **noun** a name used for an unidentified brand contrasted unfavourably with a product of the same type which is being promoted.

brandy ▶ **noun** (pl. **brandies**) [mass noun] a strong alcoholic spirit distilled from wine or fermented fruit juice.
– ORIGIN mid 17th cent.: from earlier *brandwine*, *brandewine*, from Dutch *brandewijn*, from *branden* 'burn, distil' + *wijn* 'wine'.

brandy-bottle ▶ **noun** the common yellow water lily, the flowers of which produce an alcoholic smell which is attractive to beetles.

brandy butter ▶ **noun** [mass noun] Brit. a stiff mixture of brandy, butter, and sugar, served with hot desserts.

brandy snap ▶ **noun** Brit. a crisp rolled gingerbread wafer, usually filled with cream.

brane ▶ **noun** Physics an extended object analogous to the strings of string theory but having any number of dimensions rather than one dimension.
– ORIGIN 1980s: short for MEMBRANE.

branks /braŋks/ ▶ **plural noun** historical an instrument of punishment for a scolding woman, consisting of an iron framework for the head and a sharp metal gag for restraining the tongue.
– ORIGIN mid 16th cent.: origin uncertain; compare with German *Pranger* 'a pillory or bit for a horse' and Dutch *prang* 'a fetter'; also with late Middle English *barnacle(s)*, denoting a powerful bit for restraining a horse.

branle /ˈbran(ə)l/ ▶ **noun** a 16th-century court dance of French origin.
– ORIGIN late 16th cent.: from French, from *branler* 'shake'.

brannigan /ˈbranɪɡ(ə)n/ (also **branigan**) ▶ **noun** N. Amer. informal a brawl or violent argument.
– ORIGIN late 19th cent.: of unknown origin; perhaps from the surname *Brannigan*.

Branson, Sir Richard (b.1950), English businessman. He made his name with the company Virgin Records, which he set up in 1969. He later influenced the opening up of air routes with Virgin Atlantic Airways, established in 1984.

brant ▶ **noun** North American term for BRENT GOOSE.

bran tub ▶ **noun** Brit. a lucky dip in which the hidden items are buried in bran.

Braque /brak/, French /bʀak/, Georges (1882–1963), French painter. His collages, which introduced commercial lettering and fragmented objects into pictures to contrast the real with the 'illusory' painted image, were the first stage in the development of synthetic cubism.

brash[1] ▶ **adjective** self-assertive in a rude, noisy, or overbearing way: *he was brash, cocky, and arrogant*. ■ having an ostentatious or tasteless appearance: *the cafe was a brash new building*.
– DERIVATIVES **brashly** adverb, **brashness** noun.
– ORIGIN early 19th cent. (originally dialect); perhaps a form of RASH[1].

brash[2] ▶ **noun** [mass noun] **1** loose broken rock or ice.
2 clippings from hedges, shrubs, or other plants.
– ORIGIN late 18th cent.: of unknown origin.

Brasil /braˈziw/ Portuguese name for BRAZIL[1].

Brasilia /brəˈzɪlɪə/ the capital, since 1960, of Brazil; pop. 2,455,903 (2007). Designed by Lúcio Costa in 1956, the city was located in the centre of the country with the intention of drawing people away from the crowded coastal areas.

Braşov /braˈʃɒv/ a city in Romania; pop. 281,375 (2006). It belonged to Hungary until after the First World War, and was ceded to Romania in 1920. Hungarian name BRASSÓ; German name KRONSTADT.

brass ▶ **noun 1** [mass noun] a yellow alloy of copper and zinc: [as modifier] *a brass plate on the door*. ■ [count noun] a decorative object made of brass: *shining brasses stood on the mantelpiece*. ■ (also **horse brass**) [count noun] Brit. a round flat brass ornament for the harness of a draught horse. ■ [count noun] a memorial, typically a medieval one, consisting of a flat piece of inscribed brass, laid in the floor or set into the wall of a church. ■ [count noun] a brass block or die used for stamping a design on a book binding.
2 Music brass wind instruments (including trumpet, horn, and trombone) forming a band or a section of an orchestra: *the brass were consistently too loud*.
3 (also **top brass**) informal people in authority or of high military rank.
4 Brit. informal money: *they wanted to spend their newly acquired brass*.
– PHRASES **brassed off** Brit. informal exasperated. **a brass farthing** [with negative] informal any money or assets at all: *she hasn't got two brass farthings to rub together*. **brass monkey** Brit. informal used in phrases to refer to extremely cold weather: *it's brass monkey weather tonight* | *it was cold enough to freeze the balls off a brass monkey*. [often said to be from a type of brass rack or 'monkey' once used to stack cannonballs on ships, and from which the balls might be ejected as a result of the metal contracting in very cold weather; this explanation has not been proved.] **brass neck** informal cheek or effrontery: *I didn't think that his mother would* ***have the brass neck to*** *come round here*. **the brass ring** N. Amer. informal success or

B

reward. [with reference to the reward of a free ride given on a merry-go-round to the person hooking a brass ring suspended over the horses.] **get down to brass tacks** informal start to consider the basic facts or practical details.
– ORIGIN Old English *bræs*, of unknown origin.

brassard /ˈbrasɑːd/ ▶ **noun 1** a band worn on the sleeve, typically with a uniform.
2 historical a piece of armour for the upper arm.
– ORIGIN late 16th cent.: from French, from *bras* 'arm'.

brass band ▶ **noun** a group of musicians playing brass instruments and sometimes also percussion.

brasserie /ˈbrasəri/ ▶ **noun** (pl. **brasseries**) a restaurant in France or in a French style.
– ORIGIN mid 19th cent.: French, originally 'brewery', from *brasser* 'to brew'.

Brassey /ˈbrasi/, Thomas (1805–70), English engineer and railway contractor. He built more than 10,000 km (6,500 miles) of railways in Europe, India, South America, and Australia.

brass hat ▶ **noun** Brit. informal a high-ranking officer in the armed forces.
– ORIGIN late 19th cent.: so named because of the gilt insignia on the caps of such officers.

brassica /ˈbrasɪkə/ ▶ **noun** a plant of a genus that includes cabbage, swede, rape, and mustard. ● Genus *Brassica*, family Cruciferae.
– ORIGIN modern Latin, from Latin, literally 'cabbage'.

brassie /ˈbrasi, ˈbrɑːsi/ (also **brassy**) ▶ **noun** (pl. **brassies**) Golf, informal a number two wood.
– ORIGIN late 19th cent.: so named because the wood was originally shod with brass.

brassiere /ˈbrazɪə, ˈbrazɪɛː/ ▶ **noun** full form of **BRA**.
– ORIGIN early 20th cent.: from French *brassière*, literally 'bodice, child's vest'.

Brassó /ˈbrɔʃʃoː/ Hungarian name for **BRAŞOV**.

brass rubbing ▶ **noun** [mass noun] the action of rubbing heelball or chalk over paper laid on an engraved brass to reproduce its design. ■ [count noun] an image created by brass rubbing.

brassware ▶ **noun** [mass noun] utensils or other objects made of brass.

brassy[1] ▶ **adjective** (**brassier**, **brassiest**) resembling brass in colour. ■ sounding like a brass musical instrument; harsh and loud. ■ (of a person, typically a woman) tastelessly showy or loud in appearance or manner: *her brassy, audacious exterior*.
– DERIVATIVES **brassily** adverb, **brassiness** noun.

brassy[2] ▶ **noun** variant spelling of **BRASSIE**.

brat ▶ **noun** derogatory or humorous a badly behaved child.
– DERIVATIVES **brattish** adjective, **brattishness** noun, **bratty** adjective (**brattier**, **brattiest**).
– ORIGIN mid 16th cent.: perhaps an abbreviation of synonymous Scots *bratchet*, from Old French *brachet* 'hound, bitch'; or perhaps from dialect *brat* 'rough garment, rag', based on Old Irish *bratt* 'cloak'.

Bratislava /ˌbratɪˈslɑːvə/ the capital of Slovakia, a port on the Danube; pop. 426,927 (2007). From 1526 to 1784 it was the capital of Hungary. German name **PRESSBURG**; Hungarian name **POZSONY**.

brat pack ▶ **noun** informal a rowdy and ostentatious group of young celebrities, especially film stars.
– DERIVATIVES **brat packer** noun.
– ORIGIN 1980s: after **RAT PACK**[1].

brattice /ˈbratɪs/ ▶ **noun** a partition or shaft lining in a coal mine, typically made of wood or heavy cloth.
– ORIGIN Middle English (denoting a temporary wooden gallery for use in a siege): from Old French *bretesche*, from medieval Latin *britisca*, from Old English *brittisc* 'British'. The current sense dates from the mid 19th cent.

brattle dialect ▶ **noun** a sharp rattling sound: *a distant brattle of thunder*.
▶ **verb** make or cause to make a rattling sound.
– ORIGIN early 16th cent.: probably imitative, from a blend of **BREAK**[1] and **RATTLE**.

bratwurst /ˈbratvəːst/ ▶ **noun** [mass noun] a type of fine German pork sausage that is generally fried or grilled.
– ORIGIN German, from *Brat* 'a spit' + *Wurst* 'sausage'.

Braun[1] /braʊn/, Eva (1910–45), German mistress of Adolf Hitler. Braun and Hitler are thought to have married during the fall of Berlin, shortly before committing suicide together in the air-raid shelter of his Berlin headquarters.

Braun[2] /braʊn/, Karl Ferdinand (1850–1918), German physicist. Braun invented the coupled system of radio transmission and the Braun tube (forerunner of the cathode ray tube), in which a beam of electrons could be deflected. Nobel Prize for Physics (1909).

Braun[3] /braʊn/, Wernher Magnus Maximilian von (1912–77), German-born American rocket engineer. Braun led development on the V-2 rockets used by Germany in the Second World War. After the war he moved to the US, where he pioneered the work which resulted in the US space programme.

Braunschweig /ˈbraʊnˌʃvaɪk/ German name for **BRUNSWICK**.

bravado ▶ **noun** [mass noun] a bold manner or a show of boldness intended to impress or intimidate.
– ORIGIN late 16th cent.: from Spanish *bravada*, from *bravo* 'bold' (see **BRAVE**, **-ADO**).

brave ▶ **adjective** ready to face and endure danger or pain; showing courage: *she was very brave about the whole thing* | (as plural noun **the brave**) *it was a time to remember the brave*. ■ literary fine or splendid in appearance: *his medals made a brave show*.
▶ **noun** dated an American Indian warrior. ■ a young man who shows courage or fighting spirit.
▶ **verb** [with obj.] endure or face (unpleasant conditions or behaviour) without showing fear: *he pulled on his coat ready to brave the elements*.
– PHRASES **brave new world** used to refer, often ironically, to a new and hopeful period in history resulting from major changes in society: ***the brave new world of the health care market***. [title of a satirical novel by Aldous Huxley (1932), after Shakespeare's *The Tempest* (V. i. 183).] **put a brave face on something** see **FACE**.
– DERIVATIVES **bravely** adverb, **braveness** noun.
– ORIGIN late 15th cent.: from French, from Italian *bravo* 'bold' or Spanish *bravo* 'courageous, untamed, savage', based on Latin *barbarus* (see **BARBAROUS**).

bravery ▶ **noun** [mass noun] courageous behaviour or character.
– ORIGIN mid 16th cent. (in the sense 'bravado'): from French *braverie* or Italian *braveria* 'boldness', based on Latin *barbarus* (see **BARBAROUS**).

bravo[1] /brɑːˈvəʊ, ˈbrɑːvəʊ/ ▶ **exclamation** used to express approval when a performer or other person has done something well: *bravo, you're improving!*
▶ **noun** (pl. **bravos**) **1** a cry of bravo: *bravos rang out*.
2 a code word representing the letter B, used in radio communication.
– ORIGIN mid 18th cent.: from French, from Italian, literally 'bold' (see **BRAVE**).

bravo[2] /ˈbrɑːvəʊ/ ▶ **noun** (pl. **bravos** or **bravoes**) a thug or hired assassin.
– ORIGIN late 16th cent.: from Italian, from *bravo* 'bold (one)' (see **BRAVE**).

bravura /brəˈv(j)ʊərə/ ▶ **noun** [mass noun] great technical skill and brilliance shown in a performance or activity: *the recital ended with a blazing display of bravura* | [as modifier] *a bravura performance*. ■ the display of great daring: *the show of bravura hid a guilty timidity*.
– ORIGIN mid 18th cent.: from Italian, from *bravo* 'bold'.

braw /brɔː/ ▶ **adjective** Scottish fine, good, or pleasing: *it was a braw day*.
– DERIVATIVES **brawly** adverb.
– ORIGIN late 16th cent.: variant of **BRAVE**.

brawl ▶ **noun** a rough or noisy fight or quarrel.
▶ **verb** [no obj.] fight or quarrel in a rough or noisy way: *he ended up **brawling with** a lout outside his house*. ■ literary (of a stream) flow noisily.
– DERIVATIVES **brawler** noun.
– ORIGIN late Middle English: perhaps ultimately imitative and related to **BRAY**[1].

brawn ▶ **noun** [mass noun] **1** physical strength in contrast to intelligence: *commando work required as much brain as brawn*.
2 Brit. meat from a pig's or calf's head that is cooked and pressed in a pot with jelly.
– ORIGIN Middle English: from Old French *braon* 'fleshy part of the leg', of Germanic origin; related to German *Braten* 'roast meat'.

brawny ▶ **adjective** (**brawnier**, **brawniest**) physically strong; muscular.
– DERIVATIVES **brawniness** noun.

Braxton Hicks contractions /ˌbrakstən ˈhɪks/ ▶ **plural noun** Medicine intermittent weak contractions of the uterus occurring during pregnancy.
– ORIGIN early 20th cent.: named after John *Braxton Hicks* (1823–97), English gynaecologist.

braxy /ˈbraksi/ ▶ **noun** [mass noun] a fatal bacterial infection of young sheep, occurring chiefly in upland areas in winter. ● The bacterium is *Clostridium septicum*.
– ORIGIN late 18th cent.: perhaps from obsolete *brack* 'break, flaw', from Germanic base of **BREAK**[1].

bray[1] ▶ **noun** the loud, harsh cry of a donkey or mule. ■ a sound, voice, or laugh resembling a bray.
▶ **verb** [no obj.] (of a donkey or mule) utter a bray. ■ (of a person) speak or laugh loudly and harshly: *he brayed with laughter* | [with direct speech] *'Leave!' brayed a voice behind her*.
– ORIGIN Middle English: from Old French *brait* 'a shriek', *braire* 'to cry' (the original senses in English), perhaps ultimately of Celtic origin.

bray[2] ▶ **verb** [with obj.] archaic pound or crush (something) to small pieces, typically with a pestle and mortar.
– ORIGIN late Middle English: from Old French *breier*, of Germanic origin; related to **BREAK**[1].

Bray, Vicar of the protagonist of an 18th-century song who kept his benefice from Charles II's reign to George I's by changing his beliefs to suit the times. The song is apparently based on an anecdote about an unidentified vicar of Bray, Berkshire, in Thomas Fuller's *Worthies of England* (1662).

braze ▶ **verb** [with obj.] (often as adj. **brazed**) form, fix, or join by soldering with an alloy of copper and zinc at high temperature.
▶ **noun** a brazed joint.
– ORIGIN late 17th cent.: from French *braser* 'solder', ultimately of Germanic origin.

brazen ▶ **adjective 1** bold and without shame: *he went about his illegal business with a brazen assurance* | *a brazen hussy*.
2 literary or archaic made of brass. ■ harsh in sound: *the music's brazen chords*.
▶ **verb** [with obj.] (**brazen something out**) endure an embarrassing or difficult situation by behaving with apparent confidence and lack of shame: *there was nothing to do but brazen it out*.
– DERIVATIVES **brazenly** adverb, **brazenness** /ˈbreɪz(ə)nnɪs/ noun.
– ORIGIN Old English *bræsen* 'made of brass', from *bræs* 'brass', of unknown ultimate origin.

brazier[1] /ˈbreɪzɪə, -ʒə/ ▶ **noun 1** a portable heater consisting of a pan or stand for holding lighted coals.
2 N. Amer. a barbecue.
– ORIGIN late 17th cent.: from French *brasier*, from *braise* 'hot coals'.

brazier[2] /ˈbreɪzjə, -ʒə/ ▶ **noun** a worker in brass.
– ORIGIN Middle English: probably from **BRASS** + **-IER**, on the pattern of *glass* and *glazier*.

Brazil[1] the largest country in South America; pop. 198,739,300 (est. 2009); official language, Portuguese; capital, Brasilia. Portuguese name **BRASIL**.

> Brazil is the fifth-largest country in the world. Previously inhabited largely by Tupi and Guarani peoples, Brazil was colonized by the Portuguese, who imported large numbers of slaves from West Africa to work on sugar plantations. The country was proclaimed an independent empire in 1822, becoming a republic after the overthrow of the monarchy in 1889.

Brazil[2] ▶ **noun 1** (also **Brazil nut**) a large three-sided nut with an edible kernel, several of which develop inside a large woody capsule borne by a South American forest tree. ● The tree is *Bertholletia excelsa*, family Lecythidaceae.
2 (also **Brazil wood**) [mass noun] hard red timber from which dye may be obtained. ● The timber is obtained from several tropical trees of the genus *Caesalpinia*, family Leguminosae.
– ORIGIN Middle English (in sense 2): from medieval Latin *brasilium*. The South American country *Brazil* (see **BRAZIL**[1]) takes its name from the wood.

Brazilian ▶ **noun 1** a native or inhabitant of Brazil.
2 a style of waxing a woman's pubic hair in which almost all the hair is removed, with only a very small central strip remaining.
▶ **adjective** relating to Brazil.

Brazzaville /ˈbrazəvɪl/ the capital of Congo, a major port; pop. 1,357,392 (est. 2009). It was founded in 1880 by the French explorer Savorgnan de Brazza (1852–1905) and was capital of French Equatorial Africa from 1910 to 1958.

BRB ▶ **abbreviation** informal be right back: *I'm takin' a juice break, BRB.*

breach ▶ **noun 1** an act of breaking or failing to observe a law, agreement, or code of conduct: *a breach of confidence* | [mass noun] *I sued for breach of*

contract. ■ a break in relations: *a widening* ***breach*** *between government and Church.*
2 a gap in a wall, barrier, or defence, especially one made by an attacking army.
▸ **verb** [with obj.] **1** make a gap in and break through (a wall, barrier, or defence): *the river breached its bank.* ■ break or fail to observe (a law, agreement, or code of conduct).
2 [no obj.] (of a whale) rise and break through the surface of the water.
– PHRASES **breach of the peace** Brit. public disturbance, or an act considered likely to cause one. **breach of promise** the action of breaking a sworn assurance to do something, formerly especially to marry someone. **step into the breach** replace someone who is suddenly unable to do a job or task.
– ORIGIN Middle English: from Old French *breche*, ultimately of Germanic origin; related to BREAK[1].

bread ▸ **noun** [mass noun] **1** food made of flour, water, and yeast mixed together and baked: *a loaf of bread* | [as modifier] *a bread roll* | [count noun] *Italian breads.* ■ the bread or wafer used in the Eucharist: *altar bread.* ■ the food that one needs in order to live: *his day job puts bread on the table.*
2 informal money: *I hate doing this, but I need the bread.*
– PHRASES **be the best** (or **greatest**) **thing since sliced bread** informal be very good: *they think that she is the greatest thing since sliced bread.* **bread and circuses** entertainment or political policies used to keep the mass of people happy and docile. [translating Latin *panem et circenses* (Juvenal's *Satires*, x.80).] **bread and water** a frugal diet that is eaten in poverty, chosen in abstinence, or given as a punishment. **bread and wine** the consecrated elements used in the celebration of the Eucharist; the sacrament of the Eucharist. **the bread of life** a source of spiritual nourishment. **break bread** celebrate the Eucharist. ■ dated share a meal with someone. **one cannot live by bread alone** people have spiritual as well as physical needs. [with biblical allusion to Deut. 8:3, Matt. 4:4.] **cast one's bread upon the waters** do good without expecting gratitude or reward. [with biblical allusion to Eccles. 11:1.] **one's daily bread** the money or food that one needs in order to live: *she earned her daily bread by working long hours.* **know which side one's bread is buttered (on)** informal know where one's advantage lies. **take the bread out of** (or **from**) **people's mouths** deprive people of their livings by competition or unfair working practices. **want one's bread buttered on both sides** informal want more than is practicable or than is reasonable to expect.
– ORIGIN Old English *brēad*, of Germanic origin; related to Dutch *brood* and German *Brot*.

bread and butter ▸ **noun** [mass noun] a person's livelihood or main source of income: *their bread and butter is reporting local events* | [as modifier] *bread-and-butter occupations.* ■ used in reference to something everyday or ordinary: *the bread and butter of non-League soccer.*

bread-and-butter letter ▸ **noun** a letter expressing thanks for hospitality.

bread-and-butter pudding ▸ **noun** [mass noun] a dessert consisting of slices of bread and butter layered with dried fruit and sugar and baked with a mixture of milk and egg.

breadbasket ▸ **noun 1** a part of a region that produces cereals for the rest of it.
2 informal a person's stomach, considered as the target for a blow.

bread bin ▸ **noun** Brit. a container for keeping bread in.

breadboard ▸ **noun 1** a board for cutting bread on.
2 a board for making an experimental model of an electric circuit.
▸ **verb** [with obj.] make (an experimental electric circuit).

breadcrumb ▸ **noun** (usu. **breadcrumbs**) a small fragment of bread.
– DERIVATIVES **breadcrumbed** adjective.

breaded ▸ **adjective** (of food) coated with breadcrumbs and then fried: *breaded scampi.*

breadfruit ▸ **noun 1** the large round starchy fruit of a tropical tree, which is used as a vegetable and sometimes to make a substitute for flour.
2 (also **breadfruit tree**) the large evergreen tree which bears breadfruit, which is widely cultivated on the islands of the Pacific and the Caribbean. ● *Artocarpus altilis*, family Moraceae.
3 South African term for BREAD TREE.

breadhead ▸ **noun** informal a person who is motivated by, or obsessed with, making money.

bread-kind ▸ **noun** [mass noun] W. Indian food with a consistency resembling bread, such as yams or sweet potatoes.

breadline ▸ **noun 1** (**the breadline**) Brit. the poorest condition in which it is acceptable to live: *they are not well off, but they are not* ***on the breadline.***
2 N. Amer. a queue of people waiting to receive free food.

bread pudding ▸ **noun** [mass noun] a rich, heavy cake or pudding made from pieces of bread soaked in milk and baked with eggs, sugar, dried fruit, and spices, eaten hot or cold.

bread sauce ▸ **noun** [mass noun] sauce made with milk and breadcrumbs, typically eaten with roast chicken or turkey.

breadstick ▸ **noun** a long, thin, crisp piece of baked dough.

breadth ▸ **noun** [mass noun] the distance or measurement from side to side of something; width: *the boat measured 27 feet* ***in breadth*** | [in sing.] *the bank reaches a maximum breadth of about 100 km.* ■ wide range or extent: *she has the advantage of breadth of experience* | *the minister is not noted for his breadth of vision.* ■ [count noun] dated a piece of cloth of standard or full width.
ORIGIN early 16th cent.: from obsolete *brede* in the same (related to BROAD) + -TH[2], on the pattern of *length*.

breadthways (also **breadthwise**) ▸ **adverb** in a direction parallel with a thing's width.

bread tree (also **bread palm**) ▸ **noun** a cycad native to tropical and southern Africa, which yields an edible sago-like starch. ● Genus *Encephalartos*, family Zamiaceae.

breadwinner ▸ **noun** a person who earns money to support their family, typically the sole one.
– DERIVATIVES **breadwinning** noun & adjective.

break[1] ▸ **verb** (past **broke**; past participle **broken**) **1** separate into pieces as a result of a blow, shock, or strain: [no obj.] *the rope broke with a loud snap* | [with obj.] *windows in the street were broken by the blast.* ■ sustain an injury involving the fracture of a bone or bones in a part of the body: [with obj.] *she had broken her leg in two places* | [no obj.] *what if his leg had broken?* ■ [with obj.] cause a cut or graze in (the skin): *the bite had scarcely broken the skin.* ■ make or become inoperative: [no obj.] *the machine has broken and they can't fix it until next week* | [with obj.] *he's broken the video.* ■ [no obj.] (of the amniotic fluid surrounding a fetus) be discharged when the sac is ruptured in the first stages of labour: *she realized her waters had broken.* ■ [with obj.] informal open (a safe) forcibly. ■ [with obj.] use (a banknote) to pay for something and receive change out of the transaction: *she had to break a tenner.* ■ [no obj.] (of two boxers or wrestlers) come out of a clinch, especially at the referee's command. ■ [no obj.] make the first stroke at the beginning of a game of billiards, pool, or snooker. ■ [with obj.] unfurl (a flag or sail). ■ [with obj.] succeed in deciphering (a code). ■ [with obj.] disprove (an alibi).
2 [with obj.] interrupt (a continuity, sequence, or course): *the new government broke the pattern of growth* | *his concentration was broken by a sound.* ■ put an end to (a silence) by speaking or making contact. ■ chiefly Brit. make a pause in (a journey). ■ [no obj.] stop proceedings in order to have a pause or vacation: *at mid-morning they* ***broke for*** *coffee.* ■ lessen the impact of (a fall). ■ disconnect or interrupt (an electric circuit). ■ stop oneself being subject to (a habit): *try to break the habit of adding salt at the table.* ■ surpass (a record): *the film broke box office records in the US.*
3 [with obj.] fail to observe (a law, regulation, or agreement): *the council says it will prosecute traders who break the law* | *a legally binding contract which can only be broken by mutual consent.* ■ fail to continue with (a self-imposed discipline): *diets started without preparation are broken all the time.*
4 [with obj.] crush the emotional strength, spirit, or resistance of: *the idea was to better the prisoners, not to break them.* ■ [no obj.] (of a person's emotional strength or control) give way: *her self-control finally broke.* ■ destroy the power of (a movement or organization). ■ destroy the effectiveness of (a strike), typically by moving in other people to replace the striking workers.
5 [no obj.] undergo a change or enter a new state, in particular: ■ (of the weather) change suddenly, especially after a fine spell: *the weather broke and thunder rumbled through a leaden sky.* ■ (of a storm) begin violently. ■ (of dawn or a day) begin as the sun rises: *dawn was just breaking.* ■ (of clouds) move apart and begin to disperse. ■ (of waves) curl over and dissolve into foam: *the Caribbean sea was breaking gently on the shore.* ■ (of a person's voice) falter and change tone, due to emotion: *her voice broke as she relived the experience.* ■ (of a boy's voice) change in tone and register at puberty. ■ Phonetics (of a vowel) develop into a diphthong, under the influence of an adjacent sound. ■ (of prices on the stock exchange) fall sharply.
6 [no obj.] (of news or a scandal) suddenly become public: *since the news broke I've received thousands of wonderful letters.* ■ [with obj.] (**break something to**) make bad news known to (someone).
7 [no obj., with adverbial] (chiefly of an attacking player or team, or of a military force) make a rush or dash in a particular direction: *Mitchell won possession and broke quickly, allowing Hughes to score.* ■ (of a bowled cricket ball) change direction on bouncing, due to spin. ■ Sport (of the ball) rebound unpredictably: *the ball broke to Craig but his shot rebounded from the post.*
▸ **noun 1** an interruption of continuity or uniformity: *the magazine has been published without a break since 1950.* ■ an act of separating oneself from a pre-existing state of affairs: ***a break with*** *the past.* ■ a change in the weather. ■ [with modifier] a change of line, paragraph, or page: *dotted lines on the screen show page breaks.* ■ a change of tone in a person's voice due to emotion. ■ an interruption in an electric circuit. ■ (also **break of serve** or **service break**) Tennis the winning of a game against an opponent's serve.
2 a pause in work or during an activity or event: *I need a* ***break from*** *mental activity* | *those returning to work after a career break* | *a coffee break.* ■ Brit. an interval during the school day: *the bell went for break.* ■ a short holiday: *a weekend break in the Cotswolds.* ■ a short solo or instrumental passage in jazz or popular music. ■ (**breaks**) dance music featuring breakbeats.
3 a gap or opening: *the track bends left through a break in the hedge* | *he stopped to wait for a break in the traffic.*
4 an instance of breaking something, or the point where something is broken: *he was stretchered off with a break to the leg.*
5 a rush or dash in a particular direction, especially by an attacking player or team: *Norwich scored on a rare break with 11 minutes left.* ■ informal an escape, typically from prison. ■ Cricket a change in the direction of a bowled ball on bouncing.
6 informal an opportunity or chance, especially one leading to professional success: *his big break came when a critic gave him a rave review.*
7 Snooker & Billiards a consecutive series of successful shots, scoring a specified number of points: *a break of 83 put him in front for the first time.* ■ a player's turn to make the opening shot of a game.
8 a bud or shoot sprouting from a stem.
– PHRASES **break one's back** put great effort into achieving something. **break the back of** accomplish the main or hardest part of (a task): *we've broken the back of the problem.* ■ overwhelm or defeat: *I thought we really had broken the back of inflation.* **break the bank** see BANK[2]. **break bread** see BREAD. **break camp** see CAMP[1]. **break cover** (of game being hunted) emerge into the open. **break even** reach a point in a business venture when the profits are equal to the costs. **break someone's heart** see HEART. **break the ice** see ICE. **break in two** break into two parts. **break a leg!** theatrical slang good luck! **break the mould** see MOULD[1]. **break of day** dawn. **break something open** open something forcibly. **break rank** see RANK[1]. **break (someone's) serve** (or **service**) win a game in a tennis match against an opponent's service. **break ship** Nautical fail to rejoin one's ship after absence on leave. **break step** see STEP. **break wind** release gas from the anus. **a clean break** a complete separation from a situation or relationship: *Dan decided it was best to* ***make a clean break with*** *the past.* **give someone a break** [usu. in imperative] informal stop putting pressure on someone about something. ■ (**give me a break**) used to express contemptuous disagreement or disbelief about what has been said: *He's seven times as quick and he's only 20 years old—give me a break!* **make a break for** make a sudden dash in the direction of, especially in a bid to escape: *he made a break for the door.* **that's** (or **them's**) **the breaks** N. Amer. informal that's the way things turn out (used to express resigned acceptance of a situation).
– PHRASAL VERBS **break away** escape from someone's hold. ■ escape from the control of a person, group, or practice: *an attempt to* ***break away from*** *the elitism that has dominated the book trade.* ■ (of

B

a competitor in a race) move into the lead. **break down 1** (of a machine or motor vehicle) suddenly cease to function: *his van broke down.* ■ (of a relationship, agreement, or process) cease to continue; collapse: *pay negotiations with management broke down.* ■ lose control of one's emotions when in a state of distress: *the old woman broke down in tears.* ■ (of a person's health or emotional control) fail or collapse. **2** undergo chemical decomposition: *waste products which* ***break down into*** *low-level toxic materials.* **break something down 1** demolish a door or other barrier: *they had to get the police to break the door down* | figurative *class barriers can be broken down by educational reform.* **2** separate something into a number of parts: *each tutorial is broken down into more manageable units.* ■ analyse information: *bar graphs show how the information can be broken down.* ■ convert a substance into simpler compounds by chemical action: *almost every natural substance can be broken down by bacteria.* **break free** another way of saying **BREAK AWAY**. **break in 1** force entry to a building. **2** [with direct speech] interject: *'I don't want to interfere,' Mrs Hendry broke in* | *the doctor's voice* ***broke in on*** *her thoughts.* **break someone in 1** familiarize someone with a new job or situation: *there was no time to break in a new foreign minister.* **2** (**break a horse in**) accustom a horse to a saddle and bridle, and to being ridden. **break something in** wear something, typically a pair of new shoes, until it becomes supple and comfortable. **break into 1** enter or open (a place, vehicle, or container) forcibly, especially for the purposes of theft: *two raiders broke into his home* | *a friend of mine had his car broken into.* ■ succeed in winning a share of (a market or a position in a profession): *foreign companies have largely failed to break into the domestic-equity business.* ■ interrupt (a conversation). **2** suddenly or unexpectedly burst forth into (laughter or song). **3** change one's pace to (a faster one): *Greg broke into a sprint.* **break off 1** become severed: *the fuselage had broken off just behind the pilot's seat.* **2** abruptly stop talking: *she broke off, stifling a sob.* **break something off 1** remove something from a larger unit or whole: *Tucker broke off a piece of bread.* **2** abruptly end or discontinue something: *Britain threatened to break off diplomatic relations.* **break out 1** (of war, fighting, or similarly undesirable things) start suddenly: *forest fires have broken out across Indonesia.* ■ (of a physical discomfort) suddenly manifest itself: *prickles of sweat had broken out along her backbone.* **2** escape: *a prisoner* ***broke out of*** *his cell.* **break out in** be suddenly affected by an unpleasant sensation or condition: *she had broken out in a rash.* **break something out** informal open and start using something: *it was time to break out the champagne.* **break through** make or force a way through (a barrier): *demonstrators attempted to break through the police lines* | *the sun might break through in a few spots.* ■ achieve success in a particular area: *so many talented players are struggling to break through.* **break up** disintegrate or disperse: *the grey clouds had begun to break up.* ■ (of a gathering or collective) disband; end. ■ chiefly Brit. end the school term: *we broke up for the summer.* ■ (of a couple in a relationship) part company. ■ (of a radio or telephone signal) be interrupted by interference. ■ chiefly N. Amer. start laughing uncontrollably: *the whole cast broke up.* ■ chiefly N. Amer. become emotionally upset. **break someone up** chiefly N. Amer. cause someone to become extremely upset. **break something up** cause something to separate into several pieces, parts, or sections: *break up the chocolate and place it in a bowl* | *he intends to break the company up into strategic business units.* ■ cut something up for scrap metal: *she was towed to Bo'Ness and broken up.* ■ disperse or put an end to a gathering: *police broke up a demonstration in the capital.* ■ cause a relationship to dissolve: *I'm not going to let you break up my marriage.* **break with** quarrel or cease relations with (someone): *he had broken with his family long before.* ■ act in a way that is not in accordance with (a custom or tradition).
– ORIGIN Old English *brecan* (verb), of Germanic origin; related to Dutch *breken* and German *brechen*, from an Indo-European root shared by Latin *frangere* 'to break'.

break^{2} ▶ **noun 1** former term for **BREAKING CART**. **2** historical another term for **BRAKE^{2}**.
– ORIGIN mid 19th cent.: perhaps from 16th-cent. *brake* 'cage', later 'framework', of unknown origin.

breakable ▶ **adjective** capable of breaking or being broken easily: *breakable ornaments* | *an encrypted password isn't easily breakable.*
▶ **plural noun** (**breakables**) things which are fragile and easily broken.

breakage ▶ **noun** [mass noun] the action of breaking something, or the fact of being broken: *some breakage of bone has occurred* | [count noun] *there had been three breakages in the overhead wires.*

breakaway ▶ **noun 1** a divergence or radical change from something established or long-standing: *rock was a* ***breakaway from*** *pop.* ■ a secession of a number of people from an organization, resulting in the establishment of a new organization: [as modifier] *a breakaway group.*
2 a sudden attack or forward movement, especially in a race or a soccer game. ■ Rugby each of the two flank forwards on the outsides of the second row of a scrum formation. ■ Austral./NZ a stampede of animals, typically at the sight or smell of water.

breakbeat ▶ **noun** a sample of a syncopated drum beat, usually repeated to form a rhythm used as a basis for dance music, hip hop, etc. ■ [mass noun] dance music featuring breakbeats.

breakbone fever ▶ **noun** another term for **DENGUE**.

break-bulk ▶ **adjective** denoting a system of transporting cargo as separate pieces rather than in containers.

break crop ▶ **noun** a crop grown between fields of cereals to ensure a varied planting pattern.

breakdancing ▶ **noun** [mass noun] an energetic and acrobatic style of street dancing, developed by US black people.
– DERIVATIVES **breakdance** verb & noun, **breakdancer** noun.

breakdown ▶ **noun 1** a mechanical failure.
2 a failure of a relationship or system: *a* ***breakdown in*** *military discipline* | *a communications breakdown* | [mass noun] *some of these women will have experienced marital breakdown.* ■ a sudden collapse in someone's mental health.
3 the chemical or physical decomposition of something: *the breakdown of ammonia to nitrites.* ■ an explanatory analysis, especially of statistics: *a detailed cost breakdown.*

breaker ▶ **noun 1** a heavy sea wave that breaks into white foam on the shore.
2 a person or thing that breaks something: [in combination] *a rule-breaker.* ■ chiefly Brit. a person who breaks up disused machinery.
3 a person who interrupts a conversation on a Citizens' Band radio channel, indicating that they wish to transmit a message. ■ any CB radio user.

break-even ▶ **noun** the point or state at which a person or company breaks even.

break-fall ▶ **noun** (in martial arts) a controlled fall in which most of the impact is absorbed by the arms or legs.

breakfast ▶ **noun** a meal eaten in the morning, the first of the day: *a breakfast of bacon and eggs* | [mass noun] *I don't eat breakfast.*
▶ **verb** [no obj.] eat breakfast: *she* ***breakfasted on*** *fried bread and bacon.*
– PHRASES **have** (or **eat**) **someone for breakfast** informal deal with or defeat someone with contemptuous ease.
– DERIVATIVES **breakfaster** noun.
– ORIGIN late Middle English: from the verb **BREAK^{1}** + **FAST^{2}**.

breakfast television ▶ **noun** [mass noun] television programmes broadcast early in the morning.

break feeding ▶ **noun** [mass noun] NZ a system of controlling the feeding of grazing animals by dividing their paddock with movable electric fences.

breakfront ▶ **noun** a piece of furniture having the line of its front broken by a curve or angle: [as modifier] *a breakfront bookcase.*

break-in ▶ **noun** an illegal forced entry of a building or vehicle, typically to steal something.

breaking and entering ▶ **noun** [mass noun] (in North American, and formerly also British, legal use) the crime of entering a building by force so as to commit burglary.

breaking cart ▶ **noun** a two-wheeled, low, open carriage with a skeleton body, used for breaking in young horses.

breaking point ▶ **noun** the moment of greatest strain at which someone or something gives way: *the refugee crisis* ***reached breaking point*** | *her nerves were stretched* ***to breaking point.***

breakneck ▶ **adjective** dangerously or extremely fast: *he drove at breakneck speed.*

break-off ▶ **noun** an instance of breaking something off or of discontinuing something: *the break-off of the talks was temporary.*

breakout ▶ **noun 1** a forcible escape, especially from prison. ■ (in soccer and other sports) a sudden attack by a team that has been defending.
2 an outbreak: *a breakout of hostilities.*
3 [mass noun] the deformation or splintering of wood, stone, or other material being drilled or planed.
▶ **adjective** N. Amer. informal **1** suddenly and extremely popular or successful: *a breakout movie.*
2 denoting a group which breaks away from a larger gathering for discussion.

break point ▶ **noun 1** a place or time at which an interruption or change is made. ■ (usu. **breakpoint**) Computing a place in a computer program where the sequence of instructions is interrupted, especially by another program or operator intervention.
2 Tennis the state of a game when the player or side receiving service needs only one more point to win the game: *he hit a winner to reach break point.*

Breakspear, Nicholas, see **ADRIAN IV**.

breakthrough ▶ **noun** a sudden, dramatic, and important discovery or development: *a major breakthrough in the fight against AIDS.*

breakthrough bleeding ▶ **noun** [mass noun] bleeding from the uterus occurring between menstrual periods, a side effect of some oral contraceptives.

break-up ▶ **noun** the separation or breaking up of something into several pieces or sections: *the break-up of the Ottoman Empire.* ■ the end of a relationship: *a marriage break-up.*

breakwater ▶ **noun** a barrier built out into the sea to protect a coast or harbour from the force of waves.

breakwind ▶ **noun** Austral./NZ a windbreak.

bream^{1} ▶ **noun** (pl. **same**) a greenish-bronze deep-bodied freshwater fish native to Europe. ● *Abramis brama*, family Cyprinidae.
■ used in names of other fishes resembling or related to this, e.g. **sea bream**, **Ray's bream**.
– ORIGIN late Middle English: from Old French *bresme*, of Germanic origin; related to German *Brachsen*, *Brassen*.

bream^{2} ▶ **verb** [with obj.] Nautical, archaic clear (a ship or its bottom) of weeds, shells, or other accumulated matter by burning and scraping it.
– ORIGIN late 15th cent.: probably of Low German origin and related to **BROOM**.

breast ▶ **noun 1** either of the two soft, protruding organs on the upper front of a woman's body which secrete milk after childbirth.
2 a person's chest, especially when regarded as the seat of the emotions: *wild feelings of frustration were rising up in his breast* | *her heart was hammering in her breast.* ■ the corresponding part of a bird or mammal: [as modifier] *the breast feathers of the doves.* ■ a joint of meat or portion of poultry cut from such a part: *Lisa popped a breast of chicken into the microwave.* ■ the part of a garment that covers the chest: [as modifier] *a breast pocket.*
▶ **verb** [with obj.] face and move forwards against or through (something): *I watched him breast the wave.* ■ reach the top of (a hill).
– PHRASES **beat one's breast** make an exaggerated show of sorrow, despair, or regret.
– DERIVATIVES **breasted** adjective [in combination] *a bare breasted woman* | *a crimson-breasted bird.*
– ORIGIN Old English *brēost*, of Germanic origin; related to Dutch *borst* and German *Brust*.

breastbone ▶ **noun** a thin, flat bone running down the centre of the chest, to which the ribs are attached. Also called **STERNUM**.

breast collar ▶ **noun** a thick chest strap which forms part of a horse's harness, often used instead of an ordinary collar on horses pulling lightweight or show vehicles.

breast drill ▶ **noun** a drill on which pressure is brought to bear by the operator's chest.

breastfeed ▶ **verb** (past and past participle **breastfed**) [with obj.] (of a woman) feed (a baby) with milk from the breast: *she breastfed her first child* | [no obj.] *sometimes it is not possible to breastfeed.* ■ [no obj.] (of a baby) feed from the breast.

breast implant ▶ **noun** a prosthesis consisting of a gel-like or fluid material in a flexible sac, implanted behind or in place of a female breast in reconstructive or cosmetic surgery.

breastpin ▸ noun archaic a small brooch or badge worn on the chest, typically to fasten a garment.

breastplate ▸ noun **1** a piece of armour covering the chest.
2 a set of straps attached to the front of a saddle, which pass across the horse's chest and prevent the saddle slipping backward.

breast pump ▸ noun a device for drawing milk from a woman's breasts by suction.

breast shell ▸ noun a shallow plastic receptacle that fits over the nipple of a lactating woman to catch any milk that flows.

breaststroke ▸ noun a swimming stroke in which the arms are pushed forwards and then swept back in a circular movement, while the legs are tucked in towards the body and then kicked out in a corresponding movement.
– DERIVATIVES **breaststroker** noun.

breastsummer ▸ noun Architecture a beam across a broad opening, sustaining a superstructure.
– ORIGIN early 17th cent.: from **BREAST** and **SUMMER**[2].

breastwork ▸ noun a low temporary defence or parapet.

breath ▸ noun [mass noun] the air taken into or expelled from the lungs: *I was gasping for breath* | *his breath smelled of garlic.* ■ an inhalation or exhalation of air from the lungs: *she drew in a quick breath.* ■ [mass noun] archaic the power of breathing; life. ■ [in sing.] a slight movement of air: *the weather was balmy, not a* ***breath of*** *wind.* ■ [in sing.] a sign, hint, or suggestion: *he avoided the slightest breath of scandal.*
– PHRASES **before one can** (or **has time to**) **draw breath** before one can do anything. **a breath of fresh air** informal a refreshing change: *Mike, my present husband, was a breath of fresh air.* **the breath of life** a thing that someone needs or depends on: *politics has been the breath of life to her for 50 years.* **catch one's breath 1** cease breathing momentarily in surprise or fear. **2** rest after exercise to restore normal breathing. **don't hold your breath** informal used to indicate that something is unlikely to happen: *next thing you know I'll be knitting baby clothes—but don't hold your breath!* **draw breath** breathe in. **get one's breath** (**back**) Brit. begin to breathe normally again after exercise or exertion. **hold one's breath** cease breathing temporarily. ■ be in a state of suspense or anticipation: *France held its breath while the Senate chose its new president.* **in the same** (or **next**) **breath** in the same statement: *she admitted it but said in the same breath that it was of no consequence.* **the** (or **one's**) **last breath** the last moment of one's life: *she would fight to the last breath to preserve her good name.* **out of breath** gasping for air, typically after exercise. **take breath** pause to recover free and easy breathing: *she had great need of a moment of silence to take breath.* **take someone's breath away** astonish or inspire someone with awed respect or delight. **under one's breath** in a very quiet voice; almost inaudibly: *he swore violently under his breath.* **waste one's breath** talk or give advice without effect: *I've far better things to do than waste my breath arguing.*
– ORIGIN Old English *brǣth* 'smell, scent', of Germanic origin; related to **BROOD**.

breathable ▸ adjective (of the air) fit or pleasant to breathe. ■ (of clothes or material) admitting air to the skin and allowing sweat to evaporate.
– DERIVATIVES **breathability** noun.

breathalyse (US **breathalyze**) ▸ verb [with obj.] (of the police) use a breathalyser to test how much alcohol (a driver) has consumed.

breathalyser (US trademark **Breathalyzer**) ▸ noun a device used by police for measuring the amount of alcohol in a driver's breath.
– ORIGIN 1960s: blend of **BREATH** and **ANALYSE**, + **-ER**[1].

breatharian /brɛθ'ɛːrɪən/ ▸ noun a person who believes that it is possible, through meditation, to reach a level of consciousness where one can obtain all the nutrients one needs from the air or sunlight.

breathe ▸ verb [no obj.] take air into the lungs and then expel it, especially as a regular physiological process: *she was breathing deeply* | ***breathe in*** *through your nose* | *he* ***breathed out*** *heavily* | [with obj.] *we are polluting the air we breathe.* ■ be alive; remain living: *at least I'm still breathing.* ■ literary (of wind) blow softly. ■ [with direct speech] say something with quiet intensity: *'We're together at last,' she breathed.* ■ (of an animal or plant) respire or exchange gases: *plants breathe through their roots.* ■ [with obj.] give an impression of (something): *the whole room breathed an air of hygienic efficiency.* ■ (of wine) be exposed to fresh air: *letting a wine breathe allows oxygen to enter.* ■ (of material or soil) admit or emit air or moisture: *let your lawn breathe by putting air into the soil.* ■ [with obj.] allow (a horse) to rest after exertion.
– PHRASES **breathe** (**freely**) **again** relax after being frightened or tense about something: *she wouldn't breathe freely again until she was airborne.* **breathe down someone's neck** follow closely behind someone. ■ constantly check up on someone. **breathe one's last** die. **breathe** (**new**) **life into** fill with enthusiasm and energy; reinvigorate: *the Prime Minister would breathe new life into his party.* **breathe a sigh of relief** exhale noisily as a sign of relief: *they breathed a great sigh of relief after the election was won.* **not breathe a word** remain silent about something secret.
– ORIGIN Middle English (in the sense 'exhale, steam'): from **BREATH**.

breather ▸ noun **1** a person or animal that breathes in a particular way: *a heavy breather.*
2 informal a brief pause for rest: *let's* ***take a breather.***
3 a vent or valve to release pressure or to allow air to move freely around something.

breathing ▸ noun **1** [mass noun] the process of taking air into and expelling it from the lungs: *his breathing was shallow.*
2 a sign in Greek (ʽ or ʼ) indicating the presence of an aspirate (**rough breathing**) or the absence of an aspirate (**smooth breathing**) at the beginning of a word.

breathing space ▸ noun an opportunity to pause, relax, or decide what to do next.

breathless ▸ adjective **1** gasping for breath, typically due to exertion: *the climb left me breathless.* ■ feeling or causing great excitement or other strong feelings: *she was breathless with shock.*
2 (of the air) not stirred by any wind or breeze; stiflingly still: *the warm breathless air.*
– DERIVATIVES **breathlessly** adverb, **breathlessness** noun.

breathtaking ▸ adjective astonishing or awe-inspiring in quality, so as to take one's breath away: *the scene was one of breathtaking beauty.*
– DERIVATIVES **breathtakingly** adverb.

breath test ▸ noun a test in which a driver is made to blow into a breathalyser to check whether they have drunk more than the legally permitted amount.
▸ verb (**breath-test**) [with obj.] give (someone) a breath test.

breathy /'brɛθi/ ▸ adjective (**breathier**, **breathiest**) producing or causing an audible sound of breathing, typically as a result of physical exertion or strong feelings: *a breathy laugh.*
– DERIVATIVES **breathily** adverb, **breathiness** noun.

breccia /'brɛtʃə, -tʃɪə/ ▸ noun [mass noun] Geology rock consisting of angular fragments of stones cemented by finer calcareous material.
– DERIVATIVES **brecciate** verb, **brecciation** noun.
– ORIGIN late 18th cent.: from Italian, literally 'gravel', ultimately of Germanic origin and related to **BREAK**[1].

Brecht /brɛxt/, German /brɛçt/, (Eugen) Bertolt (Friedrich) (1898–1956), German dramatist, producer, and poet. His interest in combining music and drama led to collaboration with Kurt Weill, for example in *The Threepenny Opera* (1928), an adaptation of John Gay's *The Beggar's Opera*. Brecht's later drama, written in exile after Hitler's rise to power, uses techniques of theatrical alienation and includes *Mother Courage* (1941) and *The Caucasian Chalk Circle* (1948).
– DERIVATIVES **Brechtian** adjective.

Breconshire /'brɛkənˌʃɪə, -ʃə/ (also **Brecknockshire** /'brɛknɒk-/) a former county of south central Wales. It was divided between Powys and Gwent in 1974.

bred past and past participle of **BREED**. ▸ adjective [usu. in combination] (of a person or animal) reared in a specified environment or way: *the bareness of the scene intimidated the city-bred Elizabeth.*

Breda /'breɪdə/ a manufacturing town in the SW Netherlands; pop. 170,960 (2008). It is noted for the Compromise of Breda of 1566, a protest against Spanish rule over the Netherlands; the 1660 manifesto of Charles II (who lived there in exile), stating his terms for accepting the throne of Britain; and the Treaty of Breda, which ended the Anglo-Dutch war of 1665–7.

bredie /'briːdi, 'brɪədi/ ▸ noun a traditional southern African dish consisting of a stew of meat (typically mutton) and vegetables.
– ORIGIN Afrikaans, perhaps from Portuguese *bredo*, denoting several species of *Amaranthus*, sometimes cooked as a vegetable.

breech ▸ noun **1** the part of a cannon behind the bore. ■ the back part of a rifle or gun barrel.
2 archaic a person's buttocks.
▸ verb [with obj.] archaic dress (a boy) in breeches after he has been in petticoats since birth.
– ORIGIN Old English *brēc* (plural of *brōc*, of Germanic origin; related to Dutch *broek*), interpreted as a singular form. The original sense was 'garment covering the loins and thighs' (compare with **BREECHES**), hence 'the buttocks' (sense 2 of the noun, mid 16th cent.), later 'the hind part' of anything.

breech birth (also **breech delivery**) ▸ noun a delivery of a baby which is so positioned in the womb that the buttocks or feet are delivered first.

breechblock ▸ noun a metal block which closes the aperture at the back part of a rifle or gun barrel.

breechclout ▸ noun North American term for **LOINCLOTH**.

breeches /'brɪtʃɪz, briːtʃɪz/ ▸ plural noun short trousers fastened just below the knee, now chiefly worn for riding or as part of ceremonial dress. ■ informal trousers.
– ORIGIN Middle English: plural of **BREECH**.

Breeches Bible ▸ noun the Geneva Bible of 1560, so named because the word *breeches* is used in Gen. 3:7 for the garments made by Adam and Eve.

breeches buoy ▸ noun a lifebuoy with canvas breeches attached which, when suspended from a rope, can be used to hold and transfer a passenger to safety from a ship.

breeching ▸ noun [mass noun] **1** a strong leather strap passing round the hindquarters of a horse harnessed to a vehicle and enabling the horse to push backwards.
2 historical a thick rope used to secure the carriages of cannon on a ship and to absorb the force of the recoil.
3 the hair or wool on the hindquarters of an animal.

breech-loader ▸ noun a gun designed to have ammunition inserted at the breech rather than through the muzzle.
– DERIVATIVES **breech-loading** adjective.

breed ▸ verb (past and past participle **bred**) [no obj.] (of animals) mate and then produce offspring: *toads are said to return to the pond of their birth to breed.* ■ [with obj.] cause (an animal) to produce offspring, especially in a controlled and organized way: *bitches may not be* ***bred from*** *more than once a year.* ■ [with obj.] develop (a variety of animal or plant) for a particular purpose or quality: *these horses are* ***bred for*** *this sport.* ■ [with obj.] rear and train (someone) to behave in a particular way: *Theodora had been beautifully bred.* ■ [with obj.] produce or lead to (something) over a period of time: *success had bred a certain arrogance.* ■ [with obj.] Physics create (fissile material) by nuclear reaction.
▸ noun a stock of animals or plants within a species having a distinctive appearance and typically having been developed by deliberate selection. ■ a sort or kind of person or thing: *a new breed of entrepreneurs was brought into being.*
– PHRASES **a breed apart** a kind of person that is very different from the norm: *health-service staff are a breed apart with their dedication to duty.* **a dying breed** a kind of person that is slowly disappearing: *the country's dying breed of elder statesmen.* **what's bred in the bone will come out in the flesh** (or **blood**) see **BONE**.
– ORIGIN Old English *brēdan* 'produce (offspring), bear (a child)', of Germanic origin; related to German *brüten*, also to **BROOD**.

breeder ▸ noun a person who breeds animals or plants: *a dog breeder.* ■ an animal that breeds at a particular time or in a particular way: *emperor penguins are winter breeders.* ■ informal, derogatory (among homosexuals) a heterosexual person.

breeder reactor ▸ noun a nuclear reactor which creates fissile material (typically plutonium-239 by irradiation of uranium-238) at a faster rate than it uses another fissile material (typically uranium-235) as fuel.

breeding ▸ noun [mass noun] **1** the mating and production of offspring by animals: *the flooding of the rivers is a trigger for breeding to start.*
2 the good manners regarded as characteristic of the aristocracy and conferred by heredity: *a girl of good breeding.*

B

breeding ground ▶ noun an area where birds, fish, or other animals habitually breed. ■ a place or situation that favours the development or occurrence of something: *the situation is a breeding ground for political unrest.*

breeks ▶ plural noun chiefly Scottish & N. English another term for **BREECHES**.

breeze[1] ▶ noun 1 a gentle wind. ■ [with modifier] a wind of force 2 to 6 on the Beaufort scale (4–27 knots or 7–50 kph).
2 informal a thing that is easy to do or accomplish: *travelling through London was a breeze.*
▶ verb [no obj., with adverbial of direction] informal come or go in a casual or light-hearted manner: *Roger breezed into her office.* ■ [no obj.] (**breeze through**) deal with something with apparently casual ease: *Milan had breezed through their first defence of the European Cup.*
– ORIGIN mid 16th cent.: probably from Old Spanish and Portuguese *briza* 'NE wind' (the original sense in English).

breeze[2] ▶ noun [mass noun] small cinders mixed with sand and cement to make breeze blocks.
– ORIGIN late 16th cent.: from French *braise*, (earlier) *brese* 'live coals'.

breeze block ▶ noun Brit. a lightweight building brick made from small cinders mixed with sand and cement.

breezeway ▶ noun N. Amer. a roofed outdoor passage, as between a house and a garage.

breezy ▶ adjective (**breezier**, **breeziest**) 1 pleasantly windy: *it was a bright, breezy day.*
2 appearing relaxed, informal, and cheerily brisk: *the text is written in a breezy matter-of-fact manner.*
– DERIVATIVES **breezily** adverb, **breeziness** noun.

Bregenz /'breɪgənts/, German /'bre:gɛnts/ a city in western Austria, on the eastern shores of Lake Constance; pop. 27,035 (2006). It is the capital of the state of Vorarlberg.

brekkie (also **brekky**) ▶ noun [mass noun] informal breakfast.

Brel /brɛl/, French /bʀɛl/, Jacques (1929–78), Belgian singer and composer. He gained a reputation in Paris as an original songwriter whose satirical wit was balanced by his idealism and hope.

Bremen /'breɪmən/ a state of NW Germany. Divided into two parts, which centre on the city of Bremen and the port of Bremerhaven, it is surrounded by the state of Lower Saxony. ■ its capital, an industrial city linked by the River Weser to the port of Bremerhaven and the North Sea; pop. 547,900 (est. 2006).

bremsstrahlung /'brɛmz,ʃtrɑ:lʊŋ/ ▶ noun [mass noun] Physics electromagnetic radiation produced by the acceleration or especially the deceleration of a charged particle after passing through the electric and magnetic fields of a nucleus.
– ORIGIN 1940s: from German, from *bremsen* 'to brake' + *Strahlung* 'radiation'.

Bren (also **Bren gun**) ▶ noun a lightweight quick-firing machine gun used by the Allied forces in the Second World War.
– ORIGIN 1930s: blend of *Brno* (a town in the Czech Republic where it was originally made) and *Enfield* in England (site of the Royal Small Arms Factory where it was later made).

Brendan, St (*c.*486–*c.*575), Irish abbot. The legend of the 'Navigation of St Brendan' (*c.*1050), describing his voyage with a band of monks to a promised land (possibly Orkney or the Hebrides), was widely popular in the Middle Ages. Feast day, 16 May.

Brenner Pass /'brɛnə/ an Alpine pass at the border between Austria and Italy, on the route between Innsbruck and Bolzano, at an altitude of 1,371 m (4,450 ft).

brent goose ▶ noun a small goose with a mainly black head and neck, breeding in the arctic tundra of Eurasia and Canada. ● *Branta bernicla*, family Anatidae.
– ORIGIN late Middle English: of unknown origin.

bresaola /brɛ'saʊlə/ ▶ noun [mass noun] an Italian dish of raw beef cured by salting and air-drying, typically served in slices with an olive oil, lemon juice, and pepper dressing.
– ORIGIN Italian, from *bresada*, past participle of *brasare* 'braise'.

Brescia /'brɛʃə/ an industrial city in Lombardy, in northern Italy; pop. 190,844 (2008).

Breslau /'brɛslaʊ/ German name for **WROCŁAW**.

Bresson /'brɛsɔ̃/, French /bʀɛsɔ̃/, Robert (1907–99), French film director. His most notable films, most of which feature unknown actors, include *Diary of a Country Priest* (1951) and *The Trial of Joan of Arc* (1962).

Brest /brɛst/, French /bʀɛst/ 1 a port and naval base on the Atlantic coast of Brittany, in NW France; pop. 148,316 (2006).
2 a river port and industrial city in Belarus, situated close to the border with Poland; pop. 318,000 (est. 2009). The peace treaty between Germany and Russia was signed there in March 1918. Former name (until 1921) **Brest-Litovsk**. Polish name **BRZEŚĆ NAD BUGIEM**.

Bretagne /bʀə'taɲ/ French name for **BRITTANY**.

brethren archaic plural of **BROTHER**. ▶ plural noun fellow Christians or members of a male religious order. See also **BROTHER** (sense 2 of the noun). ■ ironic or humorous people belonging to a particular group: *our brethren in the popular national press.*

Breton[1] /'brɛt(ə)n/ ▶ noun 1 a native of Brittany.
2 [mass noun] the Celtic language of Brittany, derived from Cornish. It has around 500,000 speakers.
▶ adjective relating to Brittany or its people or language.
– ORIGIN from Old French, 'Briton'.

Breton[2] /'brɛt(ə)n/, French /bʀətɔ̃/, André (1896–1966), French poet, essayist, and critic. First involved with Dadaism, Breton later launched the surrealist movement, outlining the movement's philosophy in his manifesto of 1924. His creative writing is characterized by surrealist techniques such as 'automatic' writing.

Breughel variant spelling of **BRUEGEL**.

breve ▶ noun 1 Music a note, rarely used in modern music, having the time value of two semibreves, and represented as a semibreve with two short bars either side, or as a square.
2 a written or printed mark (˘) indicating a short or unstressed vowel.
3 historical an authoritative letter from a pope or monarch.
– ORIGIN Middle English: variant of **BRIEF**. In the musical sense, the term was originally used in a series where a *long* was of greater time value than a *breve*.

brevet /'brɛvɪt/ ▶ noun [often as modifier] a former type of military commission conferred especially for outstanding service, by which an officer was promoted to a higher rank without the corresponding pay: *a brevet lieutenant.*
▶ verb (**brevets**, **breveting** or **brevetting**, **breveted** or **brevetted**) [with obj.] confer a brevet rank on.
– ORIGIN late Middle English (denoting an official letter, especially a papal indulgence): from Old French *brievet* 'little letter', diminutive of *bref*.

breviary /'bri:vɪəri/ ▶ noun (pl. **breviaries**) a book containing the service for each day, to be recited by those in orders in the Roman Catholic Church.
– ORIGIN late Middle English (also denoting an abridged version of the Psalms): from Latin *breviarium* 'summary, abridgement', from *breviare* 'abridge', from *brevis* 'short, brief'.

brevity /'brɛvɪti/ ▶ noun [mass noun] concise and exact use of words in writing or speech. ■ shortness of time: *the brevity of human life.*
– PHRASES **brevity is the soul of wit** proverb the essence of a witty statement lies in its concise wording and delivery. [from Shakespeare's *Hamlet* (II. ii. 90).]
– ORIGIN late 15th cent.: from Old French *brievete*, from Latin *brevitas*, from *brevis* 'brief'.

brew ▶ verb [with obj.] 1 make (beer) by soaking, boiling, and fermentation.
2 make (tea or coffee) by mixing it with hot water: *I've just brewed some coffee.* ■ (**brew up**) Brit. informal make tea.
3 [no obj.] (of an unwelcome event or situation) begin to develop: *there was more trouble brewing as the miners went on strike | a storm was brewing.*
▶ noun 1 a kind of beer. ■ informal a glass or can of beer.
2 a cup or mug of tea or coffee.
3 a mixture of events, people, or things which interact to form a more potent whole: *a dangerous brew of political turmoil and violent conflict.*
– DERIVATIVES **brewer** noun.
– ORIGIN Old English *brēowan* (verb), of Germanic origin; related to Dutch *brouwen* and German *brauen*.

brewer's yeast ▶ noun [mass noun] a yeast which is used in the brewing of top-fermenting beer and is also eaten as a source of vitamin B. ● *Saccharomyces cerevisiae*, subdivision Ascomycotina.

brewery ▶ noun (pl. **breweries**) a place where beer is made commercially.
– ORIGIN mid 17th cent.: from **BREW**, probably on the pattern of Dutch *brouwerij*.

brewhouse ▶ noun a brewery.

brewmaster ▶ noun a person who supervises the brewing process in a brewery.

brewpub ▶ noun chiefly US an establishment, typically one including a restaurant, selling beer brewed on the premises.

brewski ▶ noun (pl. **brewskis** or **brewskies**) N. Amer. informal a beer.
– ORIGIN 1980s: from **BREW** + a fanciful ending, perhaps after the common Slavonic surname suffix *-ski*.

brew-up ▶ noun Brit. informal a session of making tea.

breyani /brɪ'ɑ:ni/ ▶ noun South African spelling of **BIRYANI**.

Brezhnev /'brɛʒnɛf/, Leonid (Ilich) (1906–82), Soviet statesman, General Secretary of the Communist Party of the USSR 1966–82 and President 1977–82. His period in power was marked by intensified persecution of dissidents at home and by attempted détente followed by renewed Cold War in 1968; he was largely responsible for the invasion of Czechoslovakia (1968).

Briansk variant spelling of **BRYANSK**.

briar[1] (also **brier**) ▶ noun any of a number of prickly scrambling shrubs, especially a wild rose. ● Genus *Rosa*, family Rosaceae: several species, including the Eurasian **sweet briar** (*R. rubiginosa*).
– DERIVATIVES **briary** adjective.
– ORIGIN Old English *brǣr*, *brēr*, of unknown origin.

briar[2] (also **brier**) ▶ noun 1 (also **briar pipe**) a tobacco pipe made from woody nodules borne at ground level by a large woody plant of the heather family.
2 the tree heath, which bears these nodules.
– ORIGIN mid 19th cent.: from French *bruyère* 'heath, heather', from medieval Latin *brucus*.

bribe ▶ verb [with obj.] dishonestly persuade (someone) to act in one's favour by a gift of money or other inducement: *they attempted to **bribe** opponents **into** losing* | [with obj. and infinitive] *they had bribed an official to sell them a certificate.*
▶ noun a sum of money or other inducement offered or given to bribe someone.
– DERIVATIVES **bribable** adjective, **briber** noun.
– ORIGIN late Middle English: from Old French *briber*, *brimber* 'beg', of unknown origin. The original sense was 'rob, extort', hence (as a noun) 'theft, stolen goods', also 'money extorted or demanded for favours', later 'offer money as an inducement' (early 16th cent.).

bribery ▶ noun [mass noun] the giving or offering of a bribe: *his opponent had been guilty of bribery and corruption* | [as modifier] *a bribery scandal.*

BRIC ▶ abbreviation Brazil, Russia, India, and China (regarded in terms of their fast-growing economies).

bric-a-brac ▶ noun [mass noun] miscellaneous objects and ornaments of little value.
– ORIGIN mid 19th cent.: from French, from obsolete *à bric et à brac* 'at random'.

brick ▶ noun 1 a small rectangular block typically made of fired or sun-dried clay, used in building. ■ [mass noun] bricks collectively as a building material: *this mill was built of brick* | [as modifier] *a large brick building.* ■ a small, rectangular object: ***a brick of** ice cream.* ■ Brit. a child's toy building block.
2 Brit. informal, dated a generous, helpful, and reliable person: *'You are really a brick, Vi,' Gloria said.*
▶ verb 1 [with obj. and usu. with adverbial] block or enclose with a wall of bricks: *the doors have been **bricked up**.*
2 (**be bricking oneself**) Brit. vulgar slang be extremely worried or nervous.
– PHRASES **a brick short of a load** see **SHORT**. **bricks and mortar** buildings, typically housing: *untold acres are being buried under bricks and mortar.* ■ a house considered in terms of its value as an investment. ■ [as modifier] used to denote a business that operates conventionally rather than (or as well as) over the Internet: *the bricks-and-mortar banks.* **brick by brick** a little bit at a time: *he built IBM brick by brick from an agglomeration of small enterprises.* **come up against** (or **hit**) **a brick wall** face an insuperable problem or obstacle while trying to do something. **like a ton of bricks** informal with crushing weight, force, or authority: *the FA came down on him like a ton of bricks.* **you can't make bricks without**

straw proverb nothing can be made or accomplished without proper or adequate material or information. [with biblical allusion to Exod. 5; 'without straw' meant 'without having straw provided' (i.e. the Israelites were required to gather the straw for themselves). A misinterpretation has led to the current sense.]
– ORIGIN late Middle English: from Middle Low German, Middle Dutch *bricke, brike*; probably reinforced by Old French *brique*; of unknown ultimate origin.

brickbat ▶ noun a piece of brick used as a missile. ■ a critical remark or comment: *the plaudits were beginning to outnumber the brickbats.*

brick-built ▶ adjective (of a building or structure) made of bricks.

brickfield ▶ noun an area of ground where bricks are made.

brickie ▶ noun (pl. **brickies**) Brit. informal a bricklayer.

bricklayer ▶ noun a person whose job is to build walls, houses, and other structures with bricks.
– DERIVATIVES **bricklaying** noun.

brick red ▶ noun [mass noun] a deep brownish red: [as modifier] *he had a brick-red face.*

brickwork ▶ noun 1 [mass noun] the bricks in a wall, house, or other structure in terms of their type or layout: *the patterned brickwork of the gables.*
2 (**brickworks**) [treated as sing.] Brit. a factory where bricks are made.

brickyard ▶ noun a place where bricks are made.

bricolage /ˌbrɪkəˈlɑːʒ/ ▶ noun (pl. **same** or **bricolages**) [mass noun] (in art or literature) construction or creation from a diverse range of available things. ■ [count noun] something constructed or created from a diverse range of things.
– ORIGIN French.

bricoleur /ˌbrɪkəˈləː/ ▶ noun a person who engages in bricolage.
– ORIGIN French, literally 'handyman'.

bridal ▶ adjective of or concerning a bride or a newly married couple: *her white bridal gown* | *the bridal party came out into the church porch.*
– ORIGIN late Middle English: from Old English *brȳd-ealu* 'wedding feast', from *brȳd* 'bride' + *ealu* 'ale-drinking'. Since the late 16th cent., the word has been associated with adjectives ending in **-AL**.

bridal suite ▶ noun a suite of rooms in a hotel for the use of a newly married couple.

bride ▶ noun a woman on her wedding day or just before and after the event.
– ORIGIN Old English *brȳd*, of Germanic origin; related to Dutch *bruid* and German *Braut*.

Bride, St /ˈbriːdə, brʌɪd/ see **BRIDGET, ST**[1].

bridegroom ▶ noun a man on his wedding day or just before and after the event.
– ORIGIN Old English *brȳdguma*, from *brȳd* 'bride' + *guma* 'man'. The change in the second syllable was due to association with **GROOM**.

bride price ▶ noun a sum of money or quantity of goods given to a bride's family by that of the groom in some tribal societies.

bridesmaid ▶ noun 1 a girl or woman, usually one of several, who accompanies a bride on her wedding day.
2 informal a person who never attains a desire or goal. [from the saying 'always the bridesmaid and never the bride']
– ORIGIN late 18th cent.: alteration of earlier *bridemaid*.

bridewell ▶ noun archaic a prison or reform school for petty offenders.
– ORIGIN mid 16th cent.: named after *St Bride's Well* in the City of London, near which such a building stood.

bridge[1] ▶ noun 1 a structure carrying a road, path, railway, etc. across a river, road, or other obstacle: *a bridge across the River Thames* | *a railway bridge.* ■ something intended to reconcile or connect two seemingly incompatible things: *a committee which was formed to create a* **bridge between** *rival party groups.*
2 the elevated, enclosed platform on a ship from which the captain and officers direct operations.
3 the upper bony part of a person's nose: *he pushed his spectacles further up the bridge of his nose.* ■ the central part of a pair of glasses, fitting over the bridge of the nose.
4 a partial denture supported by natural teeth on either side.
5 Music the part of a stringed instrument over which the strings are stretched.
6 Music a bridge passage or middle eight.
7 the support for the tip of a billiard cue formed by the hand. ■ a long stick with a frame at the end which is used to support a cue for a difficult shot.
8 an electric circuit with two branches across which a detector or load is connected, used to measure resistance or other property by equalizing the potential across the two ends of a detector, or to rectify an alternating voltage or current.
▶ verb [with obj.] be or make a bridge over (something): *a covered walkway bridged the gardens* | *earlier attempts to bridge St George's Channel had failed.* ■ make (a difference between two groups) smaller or less significant: *new initiatives were needed to bridge the great abyss of class.*
– PHRASES **a bridge too far** a step or act that is regarded as being too drastic to take: *having Botox would be a bridge too far.* ■ something that is very difficult to achieve: *that second goal proved a bridge too far.* **build bridges** promote friendly relations between groups: *the challenge for all politicians now is to* **build bridges** *between communities.* **cross that bridge when one comes to it** deal with a problem when and if it arises.
– DERIVATIVES **bridgeable** adjective.
– ORIGIN Old English *brycg* (noun), of Germanic origin; related to Dutch *brug* and German *Brücke*.

bridge[2] ▶ noun [mass noun] a card game related to whist, played by two partnerships of two players who at the beginning of each hand bid for the right to name the trump suit, the highest bid also representing a contract to make a specified number of tricks with a specified suit as trumps.
– ORIGIN late 19th cent.: of unknown origin.

bridge-and-tunnel ▶ adjective US informal (of a person) living in the suburbs and perceived as unsophisticated: *a bridge-and-tunnel guy from Queens.*
– ORIGIN 1980s: with reference to the routes used for commuting into New York.

bridge-building ▶ noun [mass noun] the promotion of friendly relations between groups.
– DERIVATIVES **bridge-builder** noun.

bridgehead ▶ noun a strong position secured by an army inside enemy territory from which to advance or attack.

bridge loan ▶ noun North American term for **BRIDGING LOAN**.

bridge of boats ▶ noun a bridge formed by mooring boats side by side across a river.

Bridge of Sighs a 16th-century enclosed bridge in Venice between the Doges' Palace and the state prison, originally crossed by prisoners on their way to torture or execution.

bridge passage ▶ noun a transitional section in a musical composition leading to a new section or theme.

bridge roll ▶ noun Brit. a small, soft bread roll with a long, thin shape.

Bridges, Robert (Seymour) (1844–1930), English poet and literary critic. His long philosophical poem *The Testament of Beauty* (1929), written in the Victorian tradition, was instantly popular. He was Poet Laureate 1913–30.

Bridget, St[1] (also **Bride** or **Brigid**) (6th century), Irish abbess; also known as **St Bridget of Ireland**. She was venerated in Ireland as a virgin saint and noted in miracle stories for her compassion; her cult soon spread over most of western Europe. Feast day, 1 February.

Bridget, St[2] (also **Birgitta**) (*c.*1303–73), Swedish nun and visionary; also known as **St Bridget of Sweden**. She experienced her first vision of the Virgin Mary at the age of 7. Feast day, 23 July.

Bridgetown the capital of Barbados, a port on the south coast; pop. 116,000 (est. 2007).

bridgework ▶ noun [mass noun] 1 dental bridges collectively.
2 Building the component parts of a bridge. ■ the construction of bridges.

bridging /ˈbrɪdʒɪŋ/ ▶ noun [mass noun] Climbing a method of climbing a wide chimney by using the left hand and foot on one side wall and the right hand and foot on the other.

bridging loan ▶ noun Brit. a sum of money lent by a bank to cover an interval between two transactions, typically the buying of one house and the selling of another.

bridie ▶ noun (pl. **bridies**) Scottish a meat pasty.
– ORIGIN perhaps from obsolete *bride's pie*.

bridle ▶ noun the headgear used to control a horse, consisting of buckled straps to which a bit and reins are attached. ■ a line, rope, or device that is used to restrain or control the action or movement of something. ■ Nautical a mooring cable.
▶ verb 1 [with obj.] put a bridle on (a horse). ■ bring (something) under control; curb: *the fact that he was their servant bridled his tongue.*
2 [no obj.] show one's resentment or anger, especially by throwing up one's head and drawing in one's chin: *she* **bridled at** *his tone.*
– PHRASES **off** (or **on**) **the bridle** see **BIT**[3].
– ORIGIN Old English *bridel* (noun), *bridlian* (verb), of Germanic origin; related to Dutch *breidel* (noun). Sense 2 of the verb use is from the action of a horse when reined in.

bridleway (also **bridle path**) ▶ noun Brit. a path or track along which horse riders have right of way.

bridoon /brɪˈduːn/ (also **bradoon**) ▶ noun a snaffle bit which is frequently used in conjunction with a curb bit in a double bridle.
– ORIGIN mid 18th cent.: from French *bridon*, from *bride* 'bridle', of Germanic origin.

Brie /briː/ ▶ noun [mass noun] a kind of soft, mild, creamy cheese with a firm white skin.
– ORIGIN named after *Brie* in northern France, where it was originally made.

brief ▶ adjective 1 of short duration; not lasting for long: *the president made a brief working visit to Moscow.* ■ concise in expression; using few words: *introductions were brief and polite* | *be brief and don't talk for longer than is necessary.*
2 (of a piece of clothing) not covering much of the body; scanty: *Alison sported a pair of extremely brief black shorts.*
▶ noun 1 Brit. a set of instructions given to a person about a job or task: *his brief is to turn round the county's fortunes.*
2 Law, Brit. a summary of the facts and legal points in a case given to a barrister to argue in court. ■ a piece of work for a barrister. ■ Brit. informal a solicitor or barrister: *it was only his brief's eloquence that had saved him from prison.* ■ US a written statement of the facts and legal points supporting one side of a case, for presentation to a court.
3 a letter from the Pope to a person or community on a matter of discipline.
▶ verb [with obj.] 1 instruct or inform (someone) thoroughly, especially in preparation for a task: *she briefed him on last week's decisions.*
2 Brit. instruct (a barrister) by brief.
– PHRASES **hold a brief for** Brit. be retained as counsel for. **hold no brief for** Brit. not support or argue in favour of: *I hold no brief for dishonest policemen.* **in brief** in a few words; in short: *he is, in brief, the embodiment of evil* | *the news in brief.*
– DERIVATIVES **briefer** noun, **briefness** noun.
– ORIGIN Middle English: from Old French *brief*, from Latin *brevis* 'short'. The noun is via late Latin *breve* 'note, dispatch', hence 'an official letter'.

briefcase ▶ noun a leather or plastic rectangular container with a handle for carrying books and documents.

briefing ▶ noun a meeting for giving information or instructions: *a media briefing in the House of Commons.* ■ [mass noun] the action of informing or instructing someone: *today's briefing of Nato allies.*

briefless ▶ adjective Law, Brit. (of a barrister) having no clients.

briefly ▶ adverb for a short time; fleetingly: *he worked briefly as a lawyer.* ■ using few words; concisely: *as I briefly mentioned earlier* | [sentence adverb] *briefly, the plot is as follows ....*

briefs ▶ plural noun short, close-fitting underpants or knickers.

brier[1] ▶ noun variant spelling of **BRIAR**[1].

brier[2] ▶ noun variant spelling of **BRIAR**[2].

brig[1] ▶ noun 1 a two-masted square-rigged ship, typically having an additional lower fore-and-aft sail on the gaff and a boom to the mainmast.
2 informal a prison, especially on a warship.
– ORIGIN early 18th cent.: abbreviation of **BRIGANTINE** (the original sense).

brig[2] ▶ noun Scottish & N. English a bridge.
– ORIGIN from Old Norse *bryggja*.

Brig. ▶ abbreviation Brigadier.

B

brigade ▶ **noun** a subdivision of an army, typically consisting of a small number of infantry battalions and/or other units and forming part of a division: *he commanded a brigade of 3,000 men.* ■ an organization with a military or quasi-military structure: *a volunteer ambulance brigade.* ■ informal, often derogatory a group of people with a characteristic in common: *the anti-smoking brigade.*
▶ **verb** [with obj.] rare form into a brigade.
– ORIGIN mid 17th cent.: from French, from Italian *brigata* 'company', from *brigare* 'contend', from *briga* 'strife'.

brigade major ▶ **noun** Military the principal staff officer to the brigadier in command at the headquarters of a brigade.

brigadier ▶ **noun** a rank of officer in the British army, above colonel and below major general.
– ORIGIN late 17th cent.: from French (see BRIGADE, -IER).

brigadier general ▶ **noun** a rank of officer in the US army, air force, and marine corps, above colonel and below major general.

brigalow /ˈbrɪɡələʊ/ ▶ **noun** an Australian acacia tree. ● Genus *Acacia*, family Leguminosae: several species, in particular *A. harpophylla*, with silver leaves and dark furrowed bark.
– ORIGIN mid 19th cent.: from an Aboriginal word, perhaps Kamilaroi *burigal*.

brigand /ˈbrɪɡ(ə)nd/ ▶ **noun** a member of a gang that ambushes and robs people in forests and mountains.
– DERIVATIVES **brigandage** noun, **brigandry** noun.
– ORIGIN late Middle English (also denoting an irregular foot soldier): from Old French, from Italian *brigante*, literally '(person) contending', from *brigare* 'contend' (see BRIGADE).

brigandine /ˈbrɪɡ(ə)ndiːn/ ▶ **noun** historical a coat of mail, typically one made of iron rings or plates attached to canvas or other fabric.
– ORIGIN late Middle English: from Old French, from *brigand* (see BRIGAND).

brigantine /ˈbrɪɡ(ə)ntiːn/ ▶ **noun** a two-masted sailing ship with a square-rigged foremast and a mainmast rigged fore and aft.
– ORIGIN early 16th cent. (denoting a small vessel used by pirates): from Old French, from Italian *brigantino*, from *brigante* (see BRIGAND).

Briggs, Henry (1561–1630), English mathematician. He was renowned for his work on logarithms, in which he introduced the decimal base, made the thousands of calculations necessary for the tables, and popularized their use. Briggs also devised a standard method used for long division.

Bright, John (1811–89), English Liberal politician and reformer. A noted orator, Bright was the leader, along with Richard Cobden, of the campaign to repeal the Corn Laws. He was also a vociferous opponent of the Crimean War (1854) and was closely identified with the 1867 Reform Act.

bright ▶ **adjective 1** giving out or reflecting much light; shining: *the sun was dazzlingly bright* | *her bright, dark eyes.* ■ full of light: *the rooms are bright and spacious.* ■ (of a period of time) having sunny, cloudless weather: *the long, bright days of June.* ■ (of colour) vivid and bold: *the bright green leaves.* ■ having a vivid colour: *a bright tie.*
2 intelligent and quick-witted: *she was amiable, but not very bright* | *a bright idea.*
3 cheerful and lively: *at breakfast she would be persistently bright and chirpy* | *she gave a bright smile.* ■ (of someone's future) likely to be successful and happy: *these young people have a bright future ahead of them.*
4 (of sound) clear, vibrant, and typically high-pitched: *her voice is fresh and bright.*
▶ **adverb** chiefly literary brightly: *a full moon shining bright.*
▶ **noun** (**brights**) **1** bold and vivid colours: *a choice of colours from pastels through to brights.*
2 N. Amer. headlights switched to full beam: *he turned the brights on and we drove along the dirt road.*
– PHRASES **bright and early** very early in the morning. (**as**) **bright as a button** Brit. informal intelligently alert and lively. **bright lights** the glamour and excitement of city life: *they hankered for the bright lights of the capital.* **look on the bright side** be optimistic or cheerful in spite of difficulties.
– DERIVATIVES **brightish** adjective, **brightly** adverb, **brightness** noun.
– ORIGIN Old English *beorht*, of Germanic origin.

brighten ▶ **verb** make or become more light: [no obj.] *most of the country should brighten up later* | [with obj.] *the fire began to blaze fiercely, brightening the room.* ■ [with obj.] make (something) more attractively colourful: *daffodils **brighten up** many gardens and parks.* ■ make or become happier and more cheerful: [no obj.] *Sarah **brightened up** considerably as she thought of Emily's words* | [with obj.] *she seems to brighten his life.*
– ORIGIN Old English (*ge*)*beorhtnian*.

bright-eyed ▶ **adjective** having shining eyes. ■ alert and lively: *bright-eyed young lawyers.*
– PHRASES **bright-eyed and bushy-tailed** informal alert and lively. [from the conventional description of a squirrel.]

Brighton a resort on the south coast of England, in East Sussex; pop. 127,700 (est. 2009). It was patronized by the Prince of Wales (later George IV) from *c.*1780 to 1827, and is noted for its Regency architecture. It became a city (with Hove) in 2000.

Bright's disease ▶ **noun** [mass noun] a disease involving chronic inflammation of the kidneys.
– ORIGIN mid 19th cent.: named after Richard *Bright*, (1789–1858), the English physician who established its nature.

bright spark ▶ **noun** Brit. informal, often ironic a clever or witty person.

brightwork ▶ **noun** [mass noun] polished metalwork on ships or other vehicles.

bright young thing ▶ **noun** an enthusiastic, ambitious, and self-consciously fashionable young person, a term originally applied in the 1920s to a member of a young fashionable set noted for exuberant and outrageous behaviour.

Brigid, St /ˈbrɪdʒɪd/ see BRIDGET, ST[1].

brill[1] ▶ **noun** a European flatfish that resembles a turbot. ● *Scophthalmus rhombus*, family Scophthalmidae (or Bothidae).
– ORIGIN late 15th cent.: of unknown origin.

brill[2] ▶ **adjective** Brit. informal excellent; marvellous: *a brill new series* | [as exclamation] *'She says I can spend half-term with you.' 'Hey, brill!'*
– ORIGIN 1980s: abbreviation of BRILLIANT.

brilliance (also **brilliancy**) ▶ **noun** [mass noun]
1 intense brightness of light: *the nights were dark, lit only by the brilliance of Aegean stars.* ■ vividness of colour.
2 exceptional talent or intelligence: *he's played the stock market with great brilliance.*

brilliant ▶ **adjective 1** (of light or colour) very bright: *brilliant sunshine illuminated the scene.*
2 exceptionally clever or talented: *he was quite brilliant and was promoted almost at once* | *the germ of a brilliant idea hit her.* ■ outstanding; impressive: *his brilliant career at Harvard.*
3 Brit. informal excellent; marvellous: *we had a brilliant time* | [as exclamation] *'Brilliant!' he declared excitedly.*
▶ **noun** a diamond of brilliant cut.
– DERIVATIVES **brilliantly** adverb.
– ORIGIN late 17th cent.: from French *brillant* 'shining', present participle of *briller*, from Italian *brillare*, probably from Latin *beryllus* (see BERYL).

brilliant cut ▶ **noun** a circular cut for diamonds and other gemstones in the form of two many-faceted pyramids joined at their bases, the upper one truncated near its apex.

brilliantine ▶ **noun** [mass noun] **1** dated scented oil used on men's hair to make it look glossy.
2 US shiny dress fabric made from cotton and mohair or cotton and worsted.
– DERIVATIVES **brilliantined** adjective (sense 1).
– ORIGIN late 19th cent.: from French *brillantine*, from *brillant* 'shining' (see BRILLIANT).

Brillo pad ▶ **noun** trademark a pad made of steel wool impregnated with soap, used for scouring pans. ■ [as modifier] informal denoting wiry or tightly curled hair: *teachers hated my Brillo-pad hairstyle.*

brim ▶ **noun 1** the projecting edge around the bottom of a hat: *a soft hat with a turned-up brim.*
2 the upper edge or lip of a cup, bowl, or other container: *he filled her glass **to the brim**.*
▶ **verb** (**brims, brimming, brimmed**) [no obj.] (often as adj. **brimming**) be full to the point of overflowing: *a brimming cup.* ■ fill something so completely that it almost overflows: *large tears brimmed in her eyes.* ■ be full of a particular quality, feeling, etc.: *he is **brimming with** ideas.*
– DERIVATIVES **brimless** adjective, **brimmed** adjective [in combination] *a wide-brimmed hat.*
– ORIGIN Middle English (denoting the edge of the sea or other body of water): perhaps related to German *Bräme* 'trimming'.

brimful ▶ **adjective** [predic.] filled with something to the point of overflowing: *a jug **brimful of** custard.*

brimstone /ˈbrɪmst(ə)n, -stəʊn/ ▶ **noun 1** [mass noun] archaic sulphur.
2 a bright yellow butterfly or moth: ● (also **brimstone butterfly**) a European butterfly of the white family, the male of which is yellow and the female greenish-white (*Gonepteryx rhamni*, family Pieridae). ● (also **brimstone moth**) a small yellow European moth (*Opisthograptis luteolata*, family Geometridae).
– ORIGIN late Old English *brynstān*, probably from *bryne* 'burning' + *stān* 'stone'.

brindle ▶ **noun** [mass noun] a brownish or tawny colour of animal fur, with streaks of other colour. ■ [count noun] an animal with such a coat.
▶ **adjective** (also **brindled**) (especially of a domestic animal) brownish or tawny with streaks of other colour: *a brindle pup.*
– ORIGIN late 17th cent.: back-formation from *brindled*, alteration of Middle English *brinded*, probably of Scandinavian origin.

Brindley /ˈbrɪndli/, James (1716–72), pioneering English canal-builder. He designed some 600 km (375 miles) of waterway with a minimum of locks, cuttings, or tunnels, connecting most of the major rivers of England.

brine ▶ **noun** [mass noun] water strongly impregnated with salt: *the olives have been stored in brine.* ■ seawater. ■ [count noun] technical a strong solution of a salt or salts.
▶ **verb** [with obj.] (often as adj. **brined**) soak or preserve in salty water: *brined anchovies.*
– ORIGIN Old English *brine*, of unknown origin.

brine shrimp ▶ **noun** a small fairy shrimp which lives in brine pools and salt lakes and is used as food for aquarium fish. ● *Artemia salina*, class Branchiopoda.

bring ▶ **verb** (past and past participle **brought**) [with obj.]
1 take or go with (someone or something) to a place: *she brought Luke home from hospital* | [with two objs] *Liz brought her a glass of water.* ■ cause (someone or something) to come to a place: *what brings you here?* | *a felony case brought before a jury* | figurative *his inner confidence has **brought** him **through** his ordeal.* ■ (**bring someone in**) involve (someone) in a particular activity: *he has brought in a consultancy company.* ■ cause someone to receive (an amount of money) as income or profit: *two important Chippendale lots brought £10,000 each* | [with two objs] *five more novels brought him £150,000.* ■ cause (someone or something) to move in a particular direction: *he brought his hands out of his pockets* | *heavy rain **brought down** the ceiling.* ■ cause (something): *the bad weather brought famine.*
2 cause (someone or something) to be in a particular state or condition: *an economic policy that would have **brought** the country **to** bankruptcy* | *I'll give you an aspirin to **bring down** your temperature.*
3 initiate (legal action) against someone: *riot and conspiracy charges should be **brought against** them.*
4 [usu. with negative] (**bring oneself to do something**) force oneself to do something unpleasant: *she could not bring herself to mention it.*
– PHRASES **bring home the bacon** see BACON. **bring something home to** see HOME. **bring the house down** make an audience laugh or applaud very enthusiastically. **bring it on** informal used to express confidence in meeting a challenge. **bring something to bear** exert influence or pressure so as to achieve a particular result: *he was released after pressure had been brought to bear by the aid agencies.* **bring someone to book** see BOOK. **bring something to light** see LIGHT[1]. **bring someone/thing to mind** cause one to remember or think of someone or something: *all that marble brought to mind a mausoleum.* **bring something to pass** chiefly literary cause something to happen. **bring something to the table** (or **party**) contribute something of value to a discussion, project, etc. **what brings you here?** for what reason have you come here?: *so what brings you here at this time of night?*
– PHRASAL VERBS **bring something about 1** cause something to happen. **2** cause a ship to head in a different direction. **bring something back** reintroduce something: *bringing back capital punishment would solve nothing.* ■ cause something to return: *the smell of the tiny church brought back every memory of my childhood.* **bring someone down** cause someone to lose power: *the vote will not bring down the government.* ■ cause someone to fall over, especially by tackling them during a football or rugby match. ■ make someone unhappy. **bring someone/thing**

down cause someone or something to fall over by shooting them. **bring something forth** archaic give birth to something. **bring something forward** **1** move a meeting or event to an earlier date or time. **2** (often as adj. **brought forward**) (in book-keeping) transfer a total sum from the bottom of one page to the top of the next. **3** propose a plan or idea for consideration. **bring something in 1** introduce a new law or product: *Congress brought in reforms to prevent abuse of presidential power.* **2** (of a jury) give a decision in court: *the jury brought in a unanimous verdict.* **bring someone off 1** rescue someone from a ship in difficulties. **2** vulgar slang give someone or oneself an orgasm. **bring something off** achieve something successfully: *a good omelette is very hard to bring off.* **bring someone on** encourage someone who is learning something to develop or improve. **bring something on 1** cause something, typically something unpleasant, to occur: *ulcers are not brought on by a rich diet.* ■ (**bring something on/ upon**) be responsible for something unpleasant that happens to (oneself or someone else): *he's brought it upon himself—he's not a victim.* **2** (of the weather) promote the growth of crops. **bring someone out 1** encourage someone to feel more confident: *she needs friends to* ***bring her out of herself.*** **2** Brit. cause someone to go on strike. **bring something out 1** produce and launch a new product or publication: *the band are bringing out a video.* **2** make something more evident; emphasize something: *the shawl brings out the colour of your eyes.* **bring someone round** (or US **around**) **1** (also **bring someone to**) restore someone to consciousness. **2** persuade someone to agree to something. **bring something to** cause a boat to stop, especially by turning into the wind. **bring up** (chiefly of a ship) come to a stop. **bring someone up** look after a child until it is an adult. ■ (**be brought up**) be taught as a child to adopt particular behaviour or attitudes: *he had been brought up to believe that marriage was forever.* **bring something up 1** vomit something. **2** raise a matter for discussion or consideration: *she tried repeatedly to bring up the subject of money.*
– DERIVATIVES **bringer** noun.
– ORIGIN Old English *bringan*, of Germanic origin; related to Dutch *brengen* and German *bringen*.

bring and buy (also **bring-and-buy sale**) ▸ **noun** Brit. a charity sale at which people bring items for sale and buy those brought by others.

brinjal /ˈbrɪndʒɔːl, -dʒɒl/ ▸ **noun** Indian & S. African an aubergine.
– ORIGIN based on Portuguese *berinjela*, from Arabic *al-bāḏinjān* (see **AUBERGINE**).

Brink, André (b.1935), South African novelist, short-story writer, and dramatist. He gained international recognition with his novel *Looking on Darkness* (1973), which became the first novel in Afrikaans to be banned by the South African government. Other notable novels: *A Dry White Season* (1979) and *A Chain of Voices* (1982).

brink ▸ **noun** the extreme edge of land before a steep slope or a body or water: ***the brink of*** *the cliffs.* ■ a point at which something, typically something unwelcome, is about to happen; the verge: *the country was* ***on the brink of*** *a constitutional crisis.*
– ORIGIN Middle English: of Scandinavian origin.

brinkmanship /ˈbrɪŋkmənʃɪp/ (US also **brinksmanship**) ▸ **noun** [mass noun] the art or practice of pursuing a dangerous policy to the limits of safety before stopping, especially in politics.

brinny ▸ **noun** (pl. **brinnies**) Austral. a stone, typically one thrown as a missile.
– ORIGIN 1940s: probably from an Aboriginal language.

briny /ˈbrʌɪni/ ▸ **adjective** (**brinier**, **briniest**) of salty water or the sea; salty: *the briny tang of the scallops.*
▸ **noun** (**the briny**) Brit. informal the sea.

brio /ˈbriːəʊ/ ▸ **noun** [mass noun] vigour or vivacity of style or performance: *she told her story with some brio.* See also **CON BRIO**.
– ORIGIN mid 18th cent.: from Italian.

brioche /briːˈɒʃ, ˈbriːɒʃ/ ▸ **noun** a light sweet yeast bread typically in the form of a small round roll.
– ORIGIN French, from Norman French *brier*, synonym of *broyer*, literally 'split up into very small pieces by pressure'.

briquette /brɪˈkɛt/ (also **briquet**) ▸ **noun** a block of compressed coal dust or peat used as fuel.
– ORIGIN late 19th cent.: from French, diminutive of *brique* 'brick'.

bris /brɪs/ ▸ **noun** the ceremony in which a Jewish baby boy is circumcised.
– ORIGIN Hebrew *bĕrîṯ*, short for *bĕrîṯ milah* 'covenant of circumcision'.

Brisbane[1] /ˈbrɪzbən/ the capital of Queensland, Australia; pop. 1,945,639 (est. 2008). It was founded in 1824 as a penal colony.
– ORIGIN named after Sir Thomas *Brisbane* (see **BRISBANE**[2]).

Brisbane[2] /ˈbrɪzbən/, Sir Thomas Makdougall (1773–1860), Scottish soldier and astronomer. In 1790 he joined the army, becoming major general in 1813. He was governor of New South Wales (1821–5) and became an acclaimed astronomer.

brisé /ˈbriːzeɪ/ ▸ **noun** Ballet a jump in which the dancer sweeps one leg into the air to the side while jumping off the other, brings both legs together in the air and beats them before landing.
▸ **adjective** (of a fan) consisting entirely of pierced sticks of ivory, horn, or tortoiseshell.
– ORIGIN French, literally 'broken'.

brisk ▸ **adjective** active and energetic: *a good brisk walk* | *business appeared to be brisk.* ■ showing a wish to deal with things quickly; slightly brusque: *she adopted a brisk, businesslike tone.* ■ (of wind or the weather) cold but pleasantly invigorating.
▸ **verb** [with obj.] (**brisk something up**) quicken something: *Mary brisked up her pace.*
– DERIVATIVES **brisken** verb, **briskly** adverb, **briskness** noun.
– ORIGIN late 16th cent.: probably from French *brusque* (see **BRUSQUE**).

brisket ▸ **noun** [mass noun] meat cut from the breast of an animal, typically a cow.
– ORIGIN Middle English: perhaps from Old Norse *brjósk* 'cartilage, gristle'.

brisling /ˈbrɪslɪŋ, ˈbrɪz-/ ▸ **noun** (pl. **same** or **brislings**) a sprat, typically one seasoned and smoked in Norway and sold in a can.
– ORIGIN early 20th cent.: from Norwegian and Danish.

bristle /ˈbrɪs(ə)l/ ▸ **noun** (usu. **bristles**) a short, stiff hair on an animal's skin or a man's face. ■ a stiff animal hair, or a man-made substitute, used to make a brush: *a toothbrush with nylon bristles* | [mass noun] *the heads are made with natural bristle.*
▸ **verb** [no obj.] **1** (of hair or fur) stand upright away from the skin, typically as a sign of anger or fear: *the hair on the back of his neck bristled.* ■ (of an animal) react in such a way that its hair or fur stands on end: *the cat bristled in annoyance.* ■ (of a person) react angrily or defensively: *she* ***bristled at*** *his rudeness.* **2** (**bristle with**) be covered with or abundant in: *the roof bristled with antennae.*
– ORIGIN Middle English: from Old English *byrst* (of Germanic origin, related to German *Borste*) + **-LE**[1].

bristlebird ▸ **noun** an Australian songbird with mainly brown plumage, a long cocked tail, a fringe of bristles around the bill, and secretive habits. ● Genus *Dasyornis*, family Acanthizidae (or Maluridae): two or three species.

bristlecone pine ▸ **noun** a very long-lived shrubby pine of western North America. It has been used in dendrochronology to check radiocarbon dating. ● *Pinus longaeva*, family Pinaceae.

bristle fern ▸ **noun** a mainly tropical filmy fern with hair-like bristles protruding from the spore-containing bodies. ● Genus *Trichomanes*, family Hymenophyllaceae.

bristletail ▸ **noun** a small primitive wingless insect which has bristles at the end of the abdomen. ● Orders Thysanura (the **true bristletails**, with three bristles, including the silverfish) and Diplura (the **two-pronged bristletails**), subclass Apterygota.

bristle worm ▸ **noun** a marine annelid worm which has a segmented body with numerous bristles on the fleshy lobes of each segment. Also called **POLYCHAETE**. ● Class Polychaeta: numerous species, including ragworms, lugworms, fan worms, and their relatives.

bristling ▸ **adjective 1** (especially of hair) short, stiff, and spiky. **2** aggressively brisk or tense: *he fills the screen with a restless, bristling energy.*

bristly ▸ **adjective** (of hair or foliage) having a stiff and prickly texture. ■ covered with short, stiff hairs: *he rubbed his bristly chin.*

Bristol /ˈbrɪst(ə)l/ a city in SW England; pop. 374,000 (est. 2009). Situated on the River Avon about 10 km (6 miles) from the Bristol Channel, it has been a leading port since the 12th century.

Bristol board ▸ **noun** [mass noun] a type of stiff, smooth cardboard used as a drawing surface or for cutting and shaping.

Bristol Channel a wide inlet of the Atlantic between South Wales and the south-western peninsula of England, narrowing into the estuary of the River Severn.

Bristol fashion ▸ **adjective** [predic.] Brit. informal, dated in good order; neat and clean: *it gave him pleasure to keep things* ***shipshape and Bristol fashion.***
– ORIGIN mid 19th cent.: originally in nautical use, referring to the commercial prosperity brought to Bristol by its shipping.

bristols ▸ **plural noun** Brit. informal a woman's breasts.
– ORIGIN 1960s: from rhyming slang *Bristol Cities* 'titties'.

Brit informal ▸ **noun** a British person.
▸ **adjective** British.
– ORIGIN early 20th cent.: abbreviation.

Britain the island containing England, Wales, and Scotland. The name is broadly synonymous with Great Britain, but the longer form is more usual for the political unit. See also **GREAT BRITAIN**, **UNITED KINGDOM**.
– ORIGIN Old English *Breoton*, from Latin *Brittones* 'Britons', superseded in Middle English by forms from Old French *Bretaigne* (from Latin *Brit(t)annia*). It became a largely historical term until revived in the mid 16th cent., as the possible union of England and Scotland became a subject of political concern.

Britain, Battle of a series of air battles fought over Britain during August–October 1940, in which the RAF successfully resisted raids by the numerically superior German air force. This led Hitler to abandon plans to invade Britain, although the Germans continued to bomb British cities by night for several months afterwards.

Britannia /brɪˈtanjə/ the personification of Britain, usually depicted as a helmeted woman with shield and trident. The figure appeared on Roman coins and was revived with the name Britannia on the coinage of Charles II.
– ORIGIN the Latin name for **BRITAIN**.

Britannia metal ▸ **noun** [mass noun] a silvery alloy consisting of tin with about 5–15 per cent antimony and usually some copper, lead, or zinc.

Britannia silver ▸ **noun** [mass noun] hallmarked silver that is at least 95.8 per cent pure.

Britannic /brɪˈtanɪk/ ▸ **adjective** dated (chiefly in names or titles) of Britain or the British Empire: *he answered His Britannic Majesty's call to arms.*
– ORIGIN mid 17th cent.: from Latin *Britannicus*, from *Britannia* (see **BRITANNIA**).

britches /ˈbrɪtʃɪz/ ▸ **plural noun** another form of **BREECHES**, representing a pronunciation.

Briticism /ˈbrɪtɪsɪz(ə)m/ (also **Britishism** /-ʃɪz(ə)m/) ▸ **noun** an idiom used in Britain but not in other English-speaking countries.
– ORIGIN mid 19th cent.: from **BRITISH**, on the pattern of words such as *Gallicism*.

British ▸ **adjective 1** relating to Great Britain or the United Kingdom, or to its people or language. **2** of the British Commonwealth or (formerly) the British Empire.
▸ **noun** (as plural noun **the British**) the British people.
– DERIVATIVES **Britishness** noun.
– ORIGIN Old English *Brettisc* 'relating to the ancient Britons', from *Bret* 'Briton', from Latin *Britto*, or its Celtic equivalent.

British Academy an institution founded in 1901 for the promotion of historical, philosophical, and philological studies.

British Antarctic Territory that part of Antarctica claimed by Britain. Designated in 1962 from territory that was formerly part of the Falkland Islands Dependencies, it includes some 388,500 sq. km (150,058 sq. miles) of the continent of Antarctica as well as the South Orkney Islands and South Shetland Islands in the South Atlantic.

British Broadcasting Corporation (abbrev.: **BBC**) a public corporation for radio and television broadcasting in Britain.

> The BBC was established in 1927 by royal charter and held a monopoly until the introduction of the first commercial TV station in 1954. It is financed by the sale of television viewing licences rather than by revenue from advertising and has an obligation to remain impartial in its reporting.

B

British Columbia a province on the west coast of Canada; pop. 4,113,487 (2006); capital, Victoria. Formed in 1866 by the union of Vancouver Island (a former British colony) and the mainland area, then called New Caledonia, the province includes the Queen Charlotte Islands.
– DERIVATIVES **British Columbian** adjective & noun.

British Council an organization established in 1934 with the aims of promoting a wider knowledge of Britain and the English language abroad, and of developing closer cultural relations with other countries.

British Empire a former empire consisting of Great Britain and its possessions, dominions, and dependencies.

> Colonization of North America and domination of India began in the 17th century. A series of small colonies, mostly in the West Indies, were gained during the late 17th–early 19th centuries, and Australia, New Zealand, various parts of the Far East, and large areas of Africa were added in the 19th century. Self-government was granted to Canada, Australia, New Zealand, and South Africa in the mid 19th century, and most of the remaining colonies have gained independence since the end of the Second World War.

British Empire, Order of the see **ORDER OF THE BRITISH EMPIRE**.

British English ▸ **noun** [mass noun] English as used in Great Britain, as distinct from that used elsewhere.

Britisher ▸ **noun** informal (in North America and old-fashioned British English) a native or inhabitant of Britain.

British Expeditionary Force a British force made available by the army reform of 1908 for service overseas. Such forces were sent to France in 1914 and 1939.

British Guiana see **GUYANA**.

British Honduras former name (until 1973) for **BELIZE**.

British India that part of the Indian subcontinent administered by the British from 1765, when the East India Company acquired control over Bengal, until 1947, when India became independent and Pakistan was created. By 1850 British India was coterminous with India's boundaries in the west and north and by 1885 it included Burma in the east. The period of British rule was known as the Raj.

British Indian Ocean Territory a British overseas territory in the Indian Ocean, comprising the Chagos Archipelago and (until 1976) parts of the Seychelles. Ceded to Britain by France in 1814, the islands became a dependency in 1965. There are no permanent inhabitants, but British and US naval personnel occupy the island of Diego Garcia.

British Isles a group of islands lying off the coast of NW Europe, from which they are separated by the North Sea and the English Channel. They include Britain, Ireland, the Isle of Man, the Hebrides, the Orkney Islands, the Shetland Islands, the Scilly Isles, and the Channel Islands.

Britishism ▸ **noun** variant spelling of **BRITICISM**.

British Legion short for **ROYAL BRITISH LEGION**.

British Library the national library of Britain, containing the former library departments of the British Museum. The principal copyright library, it was established separately from the British Museum in 1972, and moved to a new headquarters in 1998.

British Lion ▸ **noun** see **LION**.

British Museum a national museum of antiquities in London. Established with public funds in 1753, it includes among its holdings the Magna Carta, the Elgin Marbles, and the Rosetta Stone.

British National Party (abbrev.: **BNP**) an extreme right-wing political party in Britain supporting racial discrimination and strongly opposing immigration. The party arose in the 1980s as a breakaway group from the National Front.

British overseas territory ▸ **noun** a territory that is under the sovereignty of the UK but does not form part of the UK itself, represented by a governor.

British Sign Language ▸ **noun** [mass noun] a form of sign language developed in the UK for the use of deaf people, the fourth most widely used indigenous language in Britain.

British Somaliland /səˈmɑːlɪˌland/ a former British protectorate established on the Somali coast of East Africa in 1884. In 1960 it united with former Italian territory to form the independent republic of Somalia.

British Standard ▸ **noun** the specification of recommended procedure, quality of output, terminology, and other details, in a particular field, drawn up and published by the British Standards Institution.

British Summer Time (abbrev.: **BST**) time as advanced one hour ahead of Greenwich Mean Time for daylight saving in the UK between March and October.

British thermal unit ▸ **noun** the amount of heat needed to raise 1 lb of water at maximum density through one degree Fahrenheit, equivalent to 1.055×10^3 joules.

British Union of Fascists an extreme right-wing British political party founded by Sir Oswald Mosley in 1932. It promoted strongly anti-Semitic views and its supporters were known as blackshirts. The party was effectively destroyed by the Public Order Act of 1936.

British Virgin Islands see **VIRGIN ISLANDS**.

British warm ▸ **noun** a short, thick military overcoat or duffel coat.

Briton ▸ **noun 1** a native or inhabitant of Great Britain, or a person of British descent.
2 a Celtic inhabitant of southern Britain before and during Roman times.
– ORIGIN from Old French *Breton*, from Latin *Britto*, *Britton-*, or its Celtic equivalent.

Britpop ▸ **noun** [mass noun] British pop music of the mid 1990s that was typically influenced by the Beatles and other British groups of the 1960s and perceived as a reaction against American grunge music.

Brittany /ˈbrɪtəni/ a region and former duchy of NW France, forming a peninsula between the Bay of Biscay and the English Channel. It was occupied in the 5th and 6th centuries by Britons fleeing the Saxons, and was incorporated into France in 1532. French name **BRETAGNE**.

Britten /ˈbrɪt(ə)n/, (Edward) Benjamin, Lord Britten of Aldeburgh (1913–76), English composer, pianist, and conductor. He founded the Aldeburgh festival with Peter Pears in 1948, and in 1976 became the first composer to be made a life peer. Notable operas: *Peter Grimes* (1945), *A Midsummer Night's Dream* (1960), and *Death in Venice* (1973).

brittle ▸ **adjective** hard but liable to break easily: *her bones became fragile and brittle.* ■ (of a person's voice) unpleasantly hard and sharp and showing signs of instability or nervousness: *a brittle laugh.* ■ appearing decisive or cheerful but unstable or nervous within.
▸ **noun** [mass noun] a brittle sweet made from nuts and set melted sugar: *peanut brittle.*
– DERIVATIVES **brittlely** (or **brittly**) adverb, **brittleness** noun.
– ORIGIN late Middle English, ultimately of Germanic origin and related to Old English *brēotan* 'break up'.

brittle bone disease ▸ **noun** [mass noun] Medicine another term for **OSTEOGENESIS IMPERFECTA** or **OSTEOPOROSIS**.

brittle fracture ▸ **noun** [mass noun] fracture of a metal or other material occurring without appreciable prior plastic deformation.

brittlestar ▸ **noun** a marine animal related to starfishes, with long, thin, flexible arms radiating from a small central disk. ● Class Ophiuroidea: *Ophiura* and other genera.

Brittonic /brɪˈtɒnɪk/ ▸ **adjective & noun** variant of **BRYTHONIC**.
– ORIGIN from Latin *Britto*, *Britton-* 'Briton' + **-IC**.

britzka /ˈbrɪtskə/ (also **britzska**) ▸ **noun** historical an open carriage with a folding hood and space for people to recline.
– ORIGIN early 19th cent.: from Polish *bryczka*.

BRN ▸ **abbreviation** Bahrain (international vehicle registration).

Brno /ˈbəː(r)nəʊ/ an industrial city in the Czech Republic; pop. 366,812 (est. 2007). It is the capital of Moravia.

bro /brəʊ/ ▸ **noun** informal short for **BROTHER**: *his baby bro.* ■ (**Bro.**) Brother (used before a first name when referring in writing to a member of a religious order of men): *Bro. Felix.* ■ chiefly N. Amer. a friendly greeting or form of address: *'Yo bro!'*

broach[1] ▸ **verb** [with obj.] **1** raise (a difficult subject) for discussion: *he broached the subject he had been avoiding all evening.*
2 pierce (a cask) to draw out liquid. ■ open and start using the contents of (a bottle or other container).
3 [no obj.] (of a fish or sea mammal) rise through the water and break the surface: *the salmon broach, then fall to slap the water.*
– ORIGIN Middle English: from Old French *brochier*, based on Latin *brocchus*, *broccus* 'projecting'. The earliest recorded sense was 'prick with spurs', generally 'pierce', which gave rise (late Middle English) to sense 2. Sense 1, a figurative use of this, dates from the late 16th cent.

broach[2] Nautical ▸ **verb** [no obj.] (of a ship) veer and pitch forward, presenting a side to the wind and waves and losing steerage control.
▸ **noun** a sudden and unwelcome veering of a ship that causes it to broach.
– ORIGIN early 18th cent.: of unknown origin.

broach spire ▸ **noun** an octagonal church spire rising from a square tower without a parapet.

broad ▸ **adjective 1** having a distance larger than usual from side to side; wide: *a broad staircase.* ■ (after a measurement) giving the distance from side to side: *the valley is three miles long and half a mile broad.* ■ large in area: *a broad expanse of paddy fields.*
2 covering a large number and wide scope of subjects: *the company has a broad range of experience.* ■ having a wide range of meanings or applications; loosely defined: *our range of programmes comprises three broad categories.* ■ including many people of many kinds: *the polls registered broad support for Labour.*
3 general; without detail: *a broad outline of the legal framework for pension schemes.* ■ (of a hint) clear and unambiguous; not subtle. ■ (of a phonetic transcription) showing only meaningful distinctions in sound and ignoring minor details.
4 somewhat coarse and indecent: *the broad humour has been toned down.*
5 (of a regional accent) very noticeable and strong: *the words had a distinct tang of broad Lancashire.*
▸ **noun** N. Amer. informal a woman.
– PHRASES **broad in the beam** informal (of a person) fat around the hips. **in broad daylight** during daylight hours, and surprising for this reason: *the kidnap took place in broad daylight.*
– DERIVATIVES **broadness** noun.
– ORIGIN Old English *brād*, of Germanic origin; related to Dutch *breed* and German *breit*.

broadacre ▸ **adjective** Austral. (of farming practices or equipment) used in or suitable for large-scale production.

broadband ▸ **noun** [mass noun] a high-capacity transmission technique using a wide range of frequencies, which enables a large number of messages to be communicated simultaneously: *it's important to have a firewall if you have broadband* | [as modifier] *broadband networks.*

broad bean ▸ **noun 1** a large flat edible green bean which is usually eaten without the pod. Also called **FAVA BEAN** in North America.
2 the plant which yields broad beans. ● *Vicia faba*, family Leguminosae.

broadbill ▸ **noun 1** a small, colourful bird of the Old World tropics, with a stocky body, a large head, and a flattened bill with a wide gape. ● Family Eurylaimidae: several genera.
2 chiefly N. Amer. a bird with a broad bill, especially a duck such as the shoveler or the scaup.

broad-brush ▸ **adjective** lacking in detail and finesse: *a broad-brush measure of inflation.*

broadcast ▸ **verb** (past and past participle **broadcast**) [with obj.] **1** transmit (a programme or some information) by radio or television: *the announcement was broadcast live* | (as noun **broadcasting**) *the state monopoly on broadcasting.* ■ [no obj.] take part in a radio or television transmission: *they regularly **broadcast on** Radio 2.* ■ tell (something) to many people: *we don't want to broadcast our unhappiness to the world.*
2 scatter (seeds) by hand or machine rather than placing in drills or rows.
▸ **noun** a radio or television programme or transmission.
▸ **adjective** relating to radio or television programmes: *a broadcast journalist.*
▸ **adverb** by scattering: *green manures can be sown broadcast or in rows.*
– DERIVATIVES **broadcaster** noun.
– ORIGIN mid 18th cent. (in the sense 'sown by scattering'): from **BROAD** + the past participle of **CAST**[1]. Senses relating to radio and television date from the early 20th cent.

Broad Church ▶ noun a tradition or group within the Anglican Church favouring a liberal interpretation of doctrine. ■ a group or doctrine which allows for and caters to a wide range of opinions and people.

broadcloth ▶ noun [mass noun] clothing fabric of fine twilled wool or worsted, or plain-woven cotton.
– ORIGIN late Middle English: originally denoting cloth made 72 inches wide, as opposed to 'strait' cloth, 36 inches wide. The term now implies quality rather than width.

broaden ▶ verb [no obj.] become larger in distance from side to side; widen: *her smile broadened | the river slowed and **broadened out** slightly.* ■ expand to encompass more people or things: *her interests broadened as she grew up* | [with obj.] *he has to broaden Labour's appeal to the whole community.*
– PHRASES **broaden one's horizons** expand one's range of interests, activities, and knowledge: *they want to broaden their horizons with a change of scenery and culture.*

broad gauge ▶ noun a railway gauge which is wider than the standard gauge of 4 ft 8½ in (1.435 m).

broad jump ▶ noun North American term for LONG JUMP.

broadleaf ▶ adjective another term for BROADLEAVED.
▶ noun a tree or plant with wide flat leaves.

broadleaved ▶ adjective (of a tree or plant) having relatively wide flat leaves rather than needles; non-coniferous. ■ (of a wood or woodland) consisting of broadleaved trees.

broadloom ▶ noun [mass noun] carpet woven in wide widths: *wall-to-wall broadloom.*
– DERIVATIVES **broadloomed** adjective.

broadly ▶ adverb **1** [sentence adverb] in general and without considering minor details: *the climate is broadly similar in the two regions | **broadly speaking**, the risks are as follows.*
2 widely and openly: *he was grinning broadly.*

broad-minded ▶ adjective tolerant or liberal in one's views and reactions; not easily offended: *a broad-minded approach to religion.*
– DERIVATIVES **broad-mindedly** adverb, **broad-mindedness** noun.

broad money ▶ noun [mass noun] Economics money in any form including bank or other deposits as well as notes and coins.

Broadmoor /ˈbrɔːdmɔː, -mʊə/ a special hospital near Reading in southern England for the secure holding of patients regarded as both mentally ill and potentially dangerous. It was established in 1863.

broad pennant (also **broad pendant**) ▶ noun a short swallow-tailed pennant distinguishing the commodore's ship in a squadron.

broad reach Sailing ▶ noun a point of sailing in which the wind blows over a boat's quarter, between the beam and the stern: ***on a broad reach** they are magnificent craft.*
▶ verb (**broad-reach**) [no obj.] sail with the wind in this position.

Broads (often **the Norfolk Broads**) a network of shallow freshwater lakes, traversed by slow-moving rivers, in Norfolk and Suffolk. They were formed by the gradual natural flooding of medieval peat diggings.

broadscale ▶ adjective on a broad scale; extensive.

broadsheet ▶ noun a large piece of paper printed with information on one side only. ■ (also **broadsheet newspaper**) a newspaper with a large format, regarded as more serious and less sensationalist than tabloids.

broadside ▶ noun **1** a fierce verbal attack: *he launched a **broadside against** the economic reforms.*
2 historical a firing of all the guns from one side of a warship. ■ the set of guns which can fire on each side of a warship. ■ the side of a ship above the water between the bow and quarter.
3 a sheet of paper printed on one side only, forming one large page: *a broadside of Lee's farewell address.*
▶ adverb with the side turned in a particular direction: *the yacht was drifting **broadside to** the wind.* ■ on the side: *her car was hit broadside by another vehicle.*
▶ verb [with obj.] N. Amer. collide with the side of (a vehicle): *I had to skid my bike sideways to avoid broadsiding her.*
– PHRASES **broadside on** sideways on.

broad-spectrum ▶ adjective denoting antibiotics, pesticides, etc. effective against a large variety of organisms.

broadsword ▶ noun a sword with a wide blade, used for cutting rather than thrusting.

broadtail ▶ noun a karakul sheep. ■ [mass noun] the fleece or wool from a karakul lamb.

Broadway a street traversing the length of Manhattan, New York. It is famous for its theatres, and its name has become synonymous with show business.

broadway ▶ noun [usu. in names] a large open or main road: *Fulham Broadway.*

broast ▶ verb [with obj.] N. Amer. cook (food) by a combination of broiling and roasting: [as adjective] (**broasted**) *broasted chicken.*
– ORIGIN 1980s: blend of BROIL¹ and ROAST.

Brobdingnagian /ˌbrɒbdɪŋˈnaɡɪən/ ▶ adjective huge; gigantic: *a beam engine of Brobdingnagian proportions.*
▶ noun a giant.
– ORIGIN early 18th cent.: from *Brobdingnag*, the name given by Swift (in *Gulliver's Travels*) to a land where everything is of huge size, + -IAN.

brocade ▶ noun [mass noun] a rich fabric woven with a raised pattern, typically with gold or silver thread: [as modifier] *a heavy brocade curtain.*
▶ verb [with obj.] (usu. as adj. **brocaded**) weave (something) in such a way: *a heavily brocaded blanket.*
– ORIGIN late 16th cent.: from Spanish and Portuguese *brocado* (influenced by French *brocart*), from Italian *broccato*, from *brocco* 'twisted thread'.

Broca's area /ˈbrəʊkəz/ ▶ noun Anatomy a region of the brain concerned with the production of speech, located in the cortex of the dominant frontal lobe. Damage in this area causes **Broca's aphasia**, characterized by hesitant and fragmented speech with little grammatical structure.
– ORIGIN late 19th cent.: named after Paul *Broca* (1824–80), French surgeon.

broccoli /ˈbrɒkəli/ ▶ noun [mass noun] a cultivated variety of cabbage which bears heads of green or purplish flower buds that are eaten as a vegetable.
● There are several kinds of broccoli, in particular those in the 'Italica' group, including **sprouting broccoli**, which bears small loose clusters of heads on several shoots, and the bright green dense-headed variety which is also called CALABRESE.
– ORIGIN mid 17th cent.: from Italian, plural of *broccolo* 'cabbage sprout, head', diminutive of *brocco* 'shoot', based on Latin *brocchus, broccus* 'projecting'.

broch /brɒk, brɒx/ ▶ noun a prehistoric circular stone tower in north Scotland and adjacent islands.
– ORIGIN late 15th cent.: alteration of BURGH (the original sense). The current sense dates from the mid 17th cent.

brochette /brɒˈʃɛt/ ▶ noun a skewer or spit on which chunks of meat or fish are barbecued, grilled, or roasted: *beef and lamb **en brochette**.* ■ a dish of meat or fish chunks cooked in such a way.
– ORIGIN French, diminutive of *broche* 'skewer'.

brochure /ˈbrəʊʃə, brɒˈʃʊə/ ▶ noun a small book or magazine containing pictures and information about a product or service: *a holiday brochure.*
– ORIGIN mid 18th cent.: from French, literally 'something stitched', from *brocher* 'to stitch' (see BROACH¹).

brochureware ▶ noun [mass noun] websites or web pages produced by converting a company's printed marketing or advertising material into an Internet format.

brock ▶ noun Brit. a name for a badger.
– ORIGIN Old English *brocc, broc*, of Celtic origin; related to Welsh and Cornish *broch*, Irish and Scottish Gaelic *broc*, and Breton *broc'h*.

Brocken /ˈbrɒk(ə)n/ the highest of the Harz Mountains in north central Germany, rising to 1,143 m (3,747 ft). It is noted for the phenomenon of the Brocken spectre and for witches' revels which reputedly took place there on Walpurgis night.

Brocken spectre ▶ noun a magnified shadow of an observer, typically surrounded by rainbow-like bands, thrown on to a bank of cloud in high mountain areas when the sun is low.
– ORIGIN early 19th cent.: named after BROCKEN, where the phenomenon was first reported.

brocket (also **brocket deer**) ▶ noun a small deer with short straight antlers, found in Central and South America. ● Genus *Mazama*, family Cervidae: four species.
– ORIGIN late Middle English (denoting any red deer stag in its second year, with straight antlers): from Anglo-Norman French *broquet*, diminutive of *broque*, variant of *broche* (see BROOCH). The current sense dates from the mid 19th cent.

broderie anglaise /ˌbrəʊd(ə)rɪ ˈɒɡleɪz/ ▶ noun [mass noun] open embroidery, typically in floral patterns, on fine white cotton or linen.
– ORIGIN mid 19th cent.: French, literally 'English embroidery'.

Brodsky /ˈbrɒdski/, Joseph (1940–96), Russian-born American poet; born *Iosif Aleksandrovich Brodsky*. He wrote both in Russian and in English, and was most famous for his collection *The End of a Beautiful Era* (1977). Nobel Prize for Literature (1987).

brogan /ˈbrəʊɡ(ə)n/ ▶ noun a coarse stout leather shoe reaching to the ankle.
– ORIGIN mid 19th cent.: from Irish *brógán*, Scottish Gaelic *brógan*, literally 'small brogue'.

brogue¹ ▶ noun a strong outdoor shoe with ornamental perforated patterns in the leather. ■ a rough shoe of untanned leather, formerly worn in parts of Ireland and the Scottish Highlands.
– ORIGIN late 16th cent.: from Scottish Gaelic and Irish *bróg*, from Old Norse *brók* (related to BREECH).

brogue² ▶ noun a marked accent, especially Irish or Scottish, when speaking English.
– ORIGIN early 18th cent.: perhaps allusively from BROGUE¹, referring to the rough footwear of Irish peasants.

broil¹ ▶ verb [with obj.] N. Amer. cook (meat or fish) by exposure to direct heat. ■ [no obj.] become very hot, especially from the sun: *the countryside lay broiling in the sun.*
– ORIGIN late Middle English (also in the sense 'burn, char'): from Old French *bruler* 'to burn', of unknown origin.

broil² ▶ noun archaic a quarrel or commotion.
– ORIGIN early 16th cent.: from obsolete *broil* 'to muddle'. Compare with EMBROIL.

broiler ▶ noun **1** (also **broiler chicken**) a young chicken suitable for roasting, grilling, or barbecuing.
2 N. Amer. a gridiron, grill, or special part of a stove for cooking meat or fish by exposure to direct heat.

broiling ▶ adjective N. Amer. extremely hot; scorching: *the women toil in the broiling sun.*

broke past (and archaic past participle) of BREAK¹.
▶ adjective [predic.] informal having completely run out of money: *he went broke owing two million pounds.*
– PHRASES **go for broke** informal risk everything in an all-out effort. **if it ain't broke, don't fix it** informal if something is reasonably successful or effective, there is no need to change or replace it.

broken past participle of BREAK¹. ▶ adjective **1** having been broken: *he had a broken arm.* ■ (of a relationship) ended, typically through infidelity: *a broken marriage.*
2 (of a person) having given up all hope; despairing: *he went to his grave a broken man.*
3 having breaks or gaps in continuity: *a broken white line across the road.* ■ (of a language) spoken falteringly and with many mistakes, as by a foreigner: *a young man talking in broken Italian.*
4 having an uneven and rough surface: *he pressed onwards over the broken ground.*
– DERIVATIVES **brokenly** adverb, **brokenness** /ˈbrəʊk(ə)nnɪs/ noun.

broken chord ▶ noun [usu. as modifier] Music a chord in which the notes are played successively.

broken colour ▶ noun [mass noun] a colour mixed or juxtaposed closely with another.

broken-down ▶ adjective worn out and dilapidated by age, use, or ill-treatment: *a broken-down shack.* ■ (of a machine or vehicle) not functioning, due to mechanical failure. ■ (of a horse) with serious damage to the legs, in particular the tendons, caused by excessive strain.

broken-field ▶ adjective American Football relating to or occurring in the area beyond the line of scrimmage where defenders are relatively scattered: *a broken-field run.* ■ informal (of a movement) with starts, stops, and changes of direction, in the manner of a broken-field ball carrier: *a broken-field chase.*

broken-hearted ▶ adjective overwhelmed by grief or disappointment.
– DERIVATIVES **broken-heartedness** noun.

Broken Hill 1 a town in New South Wales, Australia; pop. 20,001 (2008). It is a centre of lead, silver, and zinc mining.
2 former name (1904–65) for KABWE.

broken home ▶ noun a family in which the parents are divorced or separated.

broken wind ▶ noun [mass noun] another term for COPD in horses.

– DERIVATIVES **broken-winded** adjective.

broker ▶ noun a person who buys and sells goods or assets for others. Compare with BROKER-DEALER.
▶ verb [with obj.] arrange or negotiate (an agreement): *fighting continued despite attempts to broker a ceasefire.*
– ORIGIN Middle English (denoting a retailer or pedlar): from Anglo-Norman French *brocour*, of unknown ultimate origin.

> **USAGE** The term **broker** was officially replaced in the UK Stock Exchange by **broker-dealer** in 1986, broker-dealers being entitled to act both as agents and principals in share dealings.

brokerage ▶ noun [mass noun] the business of acting as a broker. ■ [mass noun] a fee or commission charged by a broker: *a revenue of £1,400 less a sales brokerage of £12.50.* ■ [count noun] a company that buys or sells goods or assets for clients.

broker-dealer ▶ noun (in the UK) a person combining the former functions of a broker and jobber on the Stock Exchange.

> **USAGE** Now the official term on the UK Stock Exchange, replacing **broker** in 1986.

broking ▶ noun [mass noun] Brit. the business or service of buying and selling goods or assets for others: [as modifier] *a broking house.*

brolga /ˈbrɒlgə/ ▶ noun a large grey Australian crane which has an elaborate courtship display that involves leaping, wing-flapping, and trumpeting.
● *Grus rubicundus*, family Gruidae.
– ORIGIN late 19th cent.: from Kamilaroi *burralga* (also found in other Aboriginal languages).

brolly ▶ noun (pl. **brollies**) Brit. informal an umbrella.

brom- /ˈbrəʊm/ ▶ combining form variant spelling of BROMO- shortened before a vowel (as in *bromide*).

bromance /brə(ʊ)ˈmans/ ▶ noun informal a close but non-sexual relationship between two men.
– ORIGIN early 21st cent.: blend of BROTHER and ROMANCE.

bromate /ˈbrəʊmeɪt/ ▶ noun Chemistry a salt or ester of bromic acid.

Bromberg /ˈbrɒmbɛrk/ German name for BYDGOSZCZ.

brome /brəʊm/ ▶ noun [mass noun] an oat-like grass which is sometimes grown for fodder or ornamental purposes. ● Genus *Bromus*, family Gramineae.
– ORIGIN mid 18th cent.: from modern Latin *Bromus*, from Greek *bromos* 'oat'.

bromeliad /brəˈmiːlɪad/ ▶ noun a plant of tropical and subtropical America, typically having short stems with rosettes of stiff, spiny leaves. Some kinds are epiphytic and many are cultivated as pot plants.
● Family Bromeliaceae: *Bromelia* and other genera, and numerous species, including the pineapple and Spanish moss.
– ORIGIN mid 19th cent.: from modern Latin *Bromelia* (named by Linnaeus after Olaf *Bromel* (1639–1705), Swedish botanist) + -AD[1].

bromic acid /ˈbrəʊmɪk/ ▶ noun [mass noun] Chemistry a strongly oxidizing acid known only in aqueous solutions. ● Chem. formula: $HBrO_3$.

bromide /ˈbrəʊmʌɪd/ ▶ noun **1** Chemistry a compound of bromine with another element or group, especially a salt containing the anion Br^- or an organic compound with bromine bonded to an alkyl radical.
2 a trite statement that is intended to soothe or placate: *feel-good bromides create the illusion of problem-solving.* ■ dated a sedative preparation containing potassium bromide.
3 a reproduction or piece of typesetting on bromide paper.
– DERIVATIVES **bromidic** adjective (sense 2).

bromide paper ▶ noun [mass noun] photographic printing paper coated with silver bromide emulsion.

bromine /ˈbrəʊmiːn/ ▶ noun [mass noun] the chemical element of atomic number 35, a dark red fuming toxic liquid with a choking, irritating smell. It is a member of the halogen group and occurs chiefly in the form of salts in seawater and brines. (Symbol: **Br**)
– ORIGIN early 19th cent.: from French *brome*, from Greek *brōmos* 'a stink', + -INE[4].

bromo- /ˈbrəʊməʊ/ (usu. **brom-** before a vowel) ▶ combining form Chemistry representing BROMINE.

bromocriptine /ˌbrəʊməʊˈkrɪptiːn/ ▶ noun [mass noun] Medicine a drug used in the treatment of parkinsonism, galactorrhoea, and other conditions. It is a synthetic analogue of the ergot alkaloids and stimulates the dopaminergic receptors of the brain, inhibiting the release of prolactin.
– ORIGIN 1970s: from BROMO- + *ergocryptine* (an ergot alkaloid, from ERGOT + Greek *kruptos* 'hidden') + -INE[4].

Brompton cocktail /ˈbrɒmpt(ə)n/ ▶ noun a powerful painkiller and sedative consisting of vodka or other liquor laced with morphine and sometimes also cocaine.
– ORIGIN late 20th cent.: said to be from the name of *Brompton* Hospital, London, where the mixture was invented for cancer patients.

bronc /brɒŋk/ ▶ noun N. Amer. informal short for BRONCO.

bronchi plural form of BRONCHUS.

bronchial /ˈbrɒŋkɪəl/ ▶ adjective relating to the bronchi or bronchioles: *bronchial pneumonia.*

bronchial tree ▶ noun the branching system of bronchi and bronchioles, conducting air from the windpipe into the lungs.

bronchiectasis /ˌbrɒŋkɪˈɛktəsɪs/ ▶ noun [mass noun] Medicine abnormal widening of the bronchi or their branches, causing a risk of infection.
– ORIGIN late 19th cent.: from Greek *bronkhia* (denoting the branches of the main bronchi) + *ektasis* 'dilatation'.

bronchiole /ˈbrɒŋkɪəʊl/ ▶ noun Anatomy any of the minute branches into which a bronchus divides.
– DERIVATIVES **bronchiolar** adjective.
– ORIGIN mid 19th cent.: from modern Latin *bronchiolus, bronchiolum*, diminutives of late Latin *bronchia*, denoting the branches of the main bronchi.

bronchiolitis /ˌbrɒŋkɪəˈlʌɪtɪs/ ▶ noun [mass noun] Medicine inflammation of the bronchioles.

bronchitis ▶ noun [mass noun] inflammation of the mucous membrane in the bronchial tubes. It typically causes bronchospasm and coughing.
– DERIVATIVES **bronchitic** adjective & noun.

broncho- /ˈbrɒŋkəʊ/ ▶ combining form relating to the bronchi: *bronchopneumonia.*
– ORIGIN from Greek *bronkho-*, from *bronkhos* 'windpipe'.

bronchocele /ˈbrɒŋkə(ʊ)siːl/ ▶ noun a goitre.
– ORIGIN mid 17th cent.: from Greek *bronkhokēlē*.

bronchodilator /ˌbrɒŋkə(ʊ)dʌɪˈleɪtə/ ▶ noun Medicine a drug that causes widening of the bronchi, for example any of those taken by inhalation for the alleviation of asthma.
– DERIVATIVES **bronchodilation** noun.

bronchogenic /ˌbrɒŋkə(ʊ)ˈdʒɛnɪk/ ▶ adjective of bronchial origin.

bronchopneumonia /ˌbrɒŋkə(ʊ)njuːˈməʊnɪə/ ▶ noun [mass noun] inflammation of the lungs, arising in the bronchi or bronchioles.

bronchoscope ▶ noun a fibre-optic cable that is passed into the windpipe in order to view the bronchi.
– DERIVATIVES **bronchoscopy** noun.

bronchospasm ▶ noun [mass noun] Medicine spasm of bronchial smooth muscle, producing narrowing of the bronchi.

bronchus /ˈbrɒŋkəs/ ▶ noun (pl. **bronchi** /-kʌɪ/) any of the major air passages of the lungs which diverge from the windpipe.
– ORIGIN late 17th cent.: from late Latin, from Greek *bronkhos* 'windpipe'.

bronco ▶ noun (pl. **broncos**) a wild or half-tamed horse of the western US.
– ORIGIN mid 19th cent.: from Spanish, literally 'rough, rude'.

broncobuster ▶ noun informal a cowboy who breaks in wild or half-tamed horses.

Brontë the name of three English novelists:
■ **Charlotte** (1816–55), author of *Jane Eyre* (1847), *Shirley* (1849), and *Villette* (1853). ■ **Emily** (1818–48), author of *Wuthering Heights* (1847); also a poet.
■ **Anne** (1820–49), author of *Agnes Grey* (1845) and *The Tenant of Wildfell Hall* (1847).

> The three sisters (with their brother **Branwell**, 1817–48) grew up in the Yorkshire village of Haworth, and had limited experience of the outside world. Their works were published under the pseudonyms Currer, Ellis, and Acton Bell.

brontosaurus /ˌbrɒntəˈsɔːrəs/ (also **brontosaur** /ˈbrɒntəsɔː/) ▶ noun former term for APATOSAURUS.
– ORIGIN modern Latin (former genus name), from Greek *brontē* 'thunder' + *sauros* 'lizard'.

brontothere /ˈbrɒntəʊθɪə/ ▶ noun a large ungulate mammal of the Eocene epoch with a horn-like bony growth on the nose. ● Family Brontotheriidae, order Perissodactyla.
– ORIGIN modern Latin, from Greek *brontē* 'thunder' + *thērion* 'wild beast'.

Bronx /brɒŋks/ (**the Bronx**) a borough in the northeast of New York City.
– ORIGIN named after Jonas *Bronck*, a Dutch settler who purchased land there in 1641.

Bronx cheer ▶ noun N. Amer. informal a sound of derision or contempt made by blowing through closed lips with the tongue between them.
– ORIGIN 1920s: named after the BRONX in New York.

bronze ▶ noun [mass noun] a yellowish-brown alloy of copper with up to one-third tin. ■ [count noun] a sculpture or other object made of bronze. ■ [count noun] short for BRONZE MEDAL. ■ a yellowish-brown colour: *rich, gleaming shades of bronze.*
▶ verb [with obj.] **1** make (a person or part of the body) suntanned: *Alison was bronzed by outdoor life.*
2 give (something) a surface of bronze or something resembling bronze: *the doors were bronzed with sculpted reliefs.*
– DERIVATIVES **bronzy** adjective.
– ORIGIN mid 17th cent. (as a verb): from French *bronze* (noun), *bronzer* (verb), from Italian *bronzo*, probably from Persian *birinj* 'brass'.

Bronze Age a prehistoric period that followed the Stone Age and preceded the Iron Age, when weapons and tools were made of bronze rather than stone. See also COPPER AGE.

> The Bronze Age began in the Near East and SE Europe in the late 4th and early 3rd millennium BC. It is associated with the first European civilizations, the beginnings of urban life in China, and the final stages of some Meso-American civilizations, but did not appear in Africa and Australasia at all.

bronzed ▶ adjective attractively and evenly suntanned; tanned: *bronzed and powerful arms.*

bronze medal ▶ noun a medal made of or coloured bronze, customarily awarded for third place in a race or competition.

bronzer ▶ noun a cosmetic liquid or powder applied to the skin to give it colour or shine, typically to give the appearance of a suntan.

bronzewing (also **bronze-winged pigeon**) ▶ noun an Australian pigeon with a metallic bronze band on the wing. ● Genus *Phaps*, family Columbidae: three species.

Bronzino /brɒnˈziːnəʊ/, Agnolo (1503–72), Italian mannerist painter; born *Agnolo di Cosimo*. He spent most of his career in Florence as court painter to Cosimo de' Medici. Notable works: *Venus, Cupid, Folly, and Time* (*c.*1546).

broo /bruː/ ▶ noun (in phrase **on the broo**) Scottish informal claiming unemployment benefit.
– ORIGIN 1930s: alteration of BUREAU.

brooch ▶ noun an ornament fastened to clothing with a hinged pin and catch.
– ORIGIN Middle English: variant of *broach*, a noun originally meaning 'skewer, bodkin', from Old French *broche* 'spit for roasting', based on Latin *brocchus, broccus* 'projecting'. Compare with BROACH[1].

brood ▶ noun **1** a family of birds or other young animals produced at one hatching or birth: *a brood of chicks.* ■ informal a large family of children: *she was brought up as part of a brood of eight.*
2 [mass noun] bee or wasp larvae.
▶ verb **1** [no obj.] think deeply about something that makes one unhappy, angry, or worried: *she had brooded over the subject a thousand times.*
2 [with obj.] (of a bird) sit on (eggs) to hatch them.
■ (of a fish, frog, or invertebrate) hold (developing eggs) within the body.
▶ adjective [attrib.] (of an animal) kept to be used for breeding: *a brood mare.*
– ORIGIN Old English *brōd*, of Germanic origin; related to Dutch **broed** and German *Brut*, also to BREED. The verb was originally used with an object, i.e. 'to nurse (feelings) in the mind' (late 16th cent.), a figurative use of the idea of a hen nursing chicks under her wings.

brooder ▶ noun **1** a heated house for chicks or piglets.
2 a person who broods about something.

brooding ▶ adjective engaged in or showing deep thought about something that makes one sad, angry, or worried: *he stared with brooding eyes.* ■ appearing darkly menacing: *the brooding moorland.*
– DERIVATIVES **broodingly** adverb.

brood pouch ▶ noun a pouch in certain fish, frogs, and invertebrates in which the eggs are protected before hatching.

broody ▶ adjective (**broodier**, **broodiest**) **1** (of a hen) inclined to incubate eggs. ■ informal (of a woman) having a strong desire to have a baby.
2 engaging in or arising from deep thought: *his broody concern for the future*.
– DERIVATIVES **broodily** adverb, **broodiness** noun.

Brook, Peter (Stephen Paul) (b.1925), English theatre director. As co-director of the Royal Shakespeare Company he earned critical acclaim with *King Lear* (1963) and *A Midsummer Night's Dream* (1970).

brook¹ ▶ noun a small stream.
– DERIVATIVES **brooklet** noun.
– ORIGIN Old English *brōc*, of unknown origin; related to Dutch *broek* and German *Bruch* 'marsh'.

brook² ▶ verb [with obj.] [with negative] formal tolerate or allow (something, typically dissent or opposition): *Jenny would brook no criticism of Matthew*.
– ORIGIN Old English *brūcan* 'use, possess', of Germanic origin; related to Dutch *bruiken* and German *brauchen*. The current sense dates from the mid 16th cent., a figurative use of an earlier sense 'digest, stomach'.

Brooke, Rupert (Chawner) (1887–1915), English poet. He is most famous for his wartime poetry *1914 and Other Poems* (1915). He died while on naval service in the Mediterranean.

Brooklands a motor-racing circuit near Weybridge in Surrey, England, opened in 1907. During the Second World War the course was converted for aircraft manufacture.

brooklime ▶ noun [mass noun] a Eurasian speedwell with smooth fleshy leaves and deep blue flowers on long stalks. It grows in wet areas, where the stems take root or float in the water. ● *Veronica beccabunga*, family Scrophulariaceae.
– ORIGIN Middle English *broklemok*, from **BROOK¹** + *hleomoce*, the name of the plant in Old English.

Brooklyn a borough of New York City, at the south-western corner of Long Island. The Brooklyn Bridge (1869–83) links Long Island with lower Manhattan.

Brooklynese ▶ noun [mass noun] an uncultivated form of New York speech associated especially with the borough of Brooklyn.

Brooklynite ▶ noun a native or inhabitant of the borough of Brooklyn, in New York City.

Brookner /ˈbrʊknə/, Anita (b.1928), English novelist and art historian. She won the Booker Prize for *Hotel du Lac* (1984).

Brooks¹, Cleanth (1906–94), American teacher and critic. A leading proponent of the New Criticism movement, he edited *The Southern Review* (1935–1942) and taught at Yale University (1947–75). Notable works: *Modern Poetry and Tradition* (1939).

Brooks², Mel (b.1927), American film director and comic actor; born *Melvin Kaminsky*. His debut *The Producers* (1967) was followed by films including the spoof western *Blazing Saddles* (1974).

brookweed ▶ noun [mass noun] a small white-flowered European plant which grows in wet ground, typically near the sea. ● *Samolus valerandi*, family Primulaceae.

broom ▶ noun **1** a long-handled brush of bristles or twigs, used for sweeping. ■ an implement for sweeping the ice in the game of curling.
2 a flowering shrub with long, thin green stems and small or few leaves, cultivated for its profusion of flowers. ● *Cytisus*, *Genista*, and related genera, family Leguminosae: many species and cultivars.
– PHRASES **a new broom sweeps clean** proverb people newly appointed to positions of responsibility tend to make far-reaching changes.
– ORIGIN Old English *brōm* (in sense 2), of Germanic origin; related to Dutch *braam*, also to **BRAMBLE**.

broomball ▶ noun [mass noun] a game similar to ice hockey in which players run rather than skate and use rubber brooms or broom handles to push a ball into the goal.

broomie ▶ noun (pl. **broomies**) Austral./NZ informal a person who sweeps the floor in a shearing shed.

broomrape ▶ noun a parasitic plant which bears tubular flowers on a leafless brown stem. It is attached by its tubers to the roots of the host plant. ● Genus *Orobanche*, family Orobanchaceae.
– ORIGIN late 16th cent.: from **BROOM** + Latin *rapum* 'tuber'.

broomstick ▶ noun a brush with twigs at one end and a long handle, on which, in children's literature, witches are said to fly.

Bros /brɒs/ ▶ plural noun brothers (in names of companies): *Moss Bros the tailors*.

brose /brəʊz/ ▶ noun chiefly Scottish a kind of porridge made with oatmeal or dried peas and boiling water or milk.
– ORIGIN mid 17th cent.: originally a Scots form of Middle English *brewis* 'broth', from Old French *brouez*; ultimately of Germanic origin and related to **BROTH**.

broth ▶ noun [mass noun] **1** soup consisting of meat or vegetables cooked in stock, sometimes thickened with barley or other cereals: *mutton broth*. ■ meat or fish stock.
2 Microbiology a liquid medium containing proteins and other nutrients for the culture of bacteria. ■ a liquid mixture for the preservation of tissue.
– PHRASES **a broth of a boy** Irish used approvingly to refer to a very lively boy or young man.
– ORIGIN Old English, of Germanic origin; related to **BREW**.

brothel ▶ noun a house where men visit prostitutes.
– ORIGIN mid 16th cent. (originally *brothel-house*): from late Middle English *brothel* 'worthless man, prostitute', related to Old English *brēothan* 'degenerate, deteriorate'.

brothel creepers ▶ plural noun informal soft-soled suede shoes.

brother ▶ noun **1** a man or boy in relation to other sons and daughters of his parents. ■ a male associate or fellow member of an organization: *the time is coming, brothers, for us to act*. ■ (also **brotha** or **brutha**) N. Amer. informal a black man (often used as a term of address by other black people). ■ a thing which resembles or is connected to another thing: *the machine is almost identical to its larger brother*.
2 (pl. also **brethren**) Christian Church a (male) fellow Christian. ■ a member of a religious order of men: *a Benedictine brother*. ■ a member of a fundamentalist Protestant denomination: *the Plymouth Brethren*.
▶ exclamation chiefly N. Amer. used to express annoyance or surprise.
– PHRASES **be one's brother's keeper** be responsible for the behaviour of a relative, friend, or associate: *we are, it seems, at last becoming a world in which each of us is our brother's keeper*. **brothers in arms** soldiers fighting together on the same side.
– ORIGIN Old English *brōthor*, of Germanic origin; related to Dutch *broeder* and German *Bruder*, from an Indo-European root shared by Latin *frater*.

brother-german ▶ noun (pl. **brothers-german**) archaic a brother sharing both parents, as opposed to a half-brother or stepbrother.

brotherhood ▶ noun **1** [mass noun] the relationship between brothers. ■ the feeling of kinship with and closeness to a group of people or all people: *a gesture of solidarity and brotherhood*.
2 an association or community of people linked by a common interest, religion, or trade: *a religious brotherhood*. ■ N. Amer. a trade union.
– ORIGIN Middle English: probably from obsolete *brotherred* (based on Old English *-rǣden* 'condition, state'; compare with **KINDRED**). The change of suffix was due to association with words ending in **-HOOD** and **-HEAD¹**.

brother-in-law ▶ noun (pl. **brothers-in-law**) the brother of one's wife or husband. ■ the husband of one's sister or sister-in-law.

brotherly ▶ adjective typical of how brothers behave towards each other; fraternal: *he and I had such a brotherly bond*. ■ showing affection and concern; affectionate: *you could feel the warmth and the brotherly kindness*.
– DERIVATIVES **brotherliness** noun.

brotherly love ▶ noun [mass noun] Christian Church feelings of humanity and compassion towards one's fellow humans.

brougham /ˈbruː(ə)m/ ▶ noun historical a horse-drawn carriage with a roof, four wheels, and an open driver's seat in front. ■ a car with an open driver's seat.
– ORIGIN mid 19th cent.: named after Lord *Brougham* (1778–1868), who designed the carriage.

brought past and past participle of **BRING**.

brouhaha /ˈbruːhɑːhɑː/ ▶ noun a noisy and overexcited reaction or response to something: *the brouhaha over those infamous commercials* | [mass noun] *all that election brouhaha*.
– ORIGIN late 19th cent.: from French, probably imitative.

Brouwer /ˈbraʊə/, Adriaen (*c*.1605–38), Flemish painter. His most typical works represent peasant scenes in taverns.

brow¹ ▶ noun **1** a person's forehead: *he wiped his brow*.
2 (usu. **brows**) an eyebrow: *his brows lifted in surprise*.
3 the summit of a hill or pass: *the cottages were built on the brow of a hill*.
– DERIVATIVES **browed** adjective [in combination] *furrow-browed*.
– ORIGIN Old English *brū* 'eyelash, eyebrow', of Germanic origin. Current senses arose in Middle English; compare with **BRAE**.

brow² ▶ noun a gangway from a ship to the shore. ■ a hinged part of a ferry or landing craft forming a landing platform.
– ORIGIN mid 19th cent.: probably from Norwegian *bru*, from Old Norse *brú* 'bridge'.

browbeat ▶ verb (past **browbeat**; past participle **browbeaten**) [with obj.] intimidate (someone), typically into doing something, with stern or abusive words: *a witness is being browbeaten under cross-examination*.
– DERIVATIVES **browbeater** noun.

Brown¹, Sir Arthur Whitten (1886–1948), Scottish aviator. He made the first transatlantic flight in 1919 with Sir John William Alcock.

Brown², Ford Madox (1821–93), English painter. His early work was inspired by the Pre-Raphaelites, and in 1861 he became a founder member of William Morris's company, designing stained glass and furniture.

Brown³, Gordon (James) (b.1951), British Labour statesman, Prime Minister 2007–10.
– DERIVATIVES **Brownite** noun & adjective.

Brown⁴, James (1928–2006), American soul and funk singer and songwriter. In the 1960s he played a leading role in the development of funk with songs such as 'Papa's Got a Brand New Bag' (1965) and 'Sex Machine' (1970).

Brown⁵, John (1800–59), American abolitionist. In 1859 he was executed after raiding a government arsenal at Harpers Ferry in Virginia, intending to arm black slaves and start a revolt. He became a hero of the abolitionists in the Civil War.

Brown⁶, Lancelot (1716–83), English landscape gardener; known as **Capability Brown**. He evolved an English style of natural-looking landscape parks. Notable examples of his work are at Blenheim Palace, Chatsworth House in Derbyshire, and Kew Gardens.

brown ▶ adjective of a colour produced by mixing red, yellow, and blue, as of dark wood or rich soil: *an old brown coat* | *she had warm brown eyes*. ■ dark-skinned or suntanned: *his face was brown from the sun*. ■ South African term for **COLOURED** (sense 2 of the adjective). ■ (of bread) made from unsifted or unbleached flour.
▶ noun **1** [mass noun] brown colour or pigment: *the brown of his eyes* | *a pair of boots **in brown*** | [count noun] *the print is rich with velvety browns*. ■ brown clothes or material: *a woman all in brown*.
2 a brown thing, in particular the brown ball in snooker.
3 [with modifier] a satyrid butterfly, which typically has brown wings with small eyespots. ● Subfamily Satyrinae, family Nymphalidae: many genera and species.
4 South African term for **COLOURED** (sense 1 of the noun).
▶ verb make or become brown, typically by cooking: [with obj.] *a skillet in which food has been browned* | [no obj.] *grill the pizza until the cheese has browned*.
– PHRASES **(as) brown as a berry** (of a person) very suntanned. **in a brown study** see **STUDY**.
– PHRASAL VERBS **be browned off** Brit. informal be irritated or depressed: *they're getting browned off with the overtime*.
– DERIVATIVES **brownish** adjective, **brownness** noun, **browny** adjective.
– ORIGIN Old English *brūn*, of Germanic origin; related to Dutch *bruin* and German *braun*.

brown ale ▶ noun [mass noun] Brit. dark, mild beer sold in bottles.

brown algae ▶ plural noun a large group of algae that are typically olive brown or greenish in colour, including many seaweeds. They contain xanthophyll in addition to chlorophyll. ● Class Phaeophyceae, division Heterokontophyta (also phylum Heterokonta, kingdom Protista); formerly division Phaeophyta.

brown-bag lunch ▶ noun (also **bag lunch**) N. Amer. a packed lunch carried to work, school, etc.

▸ verb (**brown-bag it**) N. Amer. take a packed lunch to work, school, etc.

brown bear ▸ noun a large bear with a coat colour ranging from cream to black, occurring chiefly in forests in Eurasia and North America. It is widely persecuted, and was exterminated in Britain, probably before the 10th century. Compare with GRIZZLY BEAR. ● *Ursus arctos*, family Ursidae.

brown belt ▸ noun a belt of a brown colour marking a level of proficiency below that of a black belt in judo, karate, or other martial arts. ■ a person qualified to wear a brown belt.

Brown Betty ▸ noun **1** N. Amer. a baked pudding made with apples or other fruit and breadcrumbs.
2 Brit. a large brown earthenware teapot.

brown coal ▸ noun another term for LIGNITE.

brown dwarf ▸ noun Astronomy a celestial object intermediate in size between a giant planet and a small star, believed to emit mainly infrared radiation.

Browne, Sir Thomas (1605–82), English author and physician. He achieved prominence with *Religio Medici* (1642), a collection of opinions on a vast number of subjects connected with religion.

brown earth ▸ noun [mass noun] Soil Science a type of soil having a brown humus-rich surface layer.

brown fat ▸ noun [mass noun] a dark-coloured adipose tissue with many blood vessels, involved in the rapid production of heat in hibernating animals and human babies.

brownfield ▸ adjective Brit. denoting or relating to urban sites for potential building development that have had previous development on them. Compare with GREENFIELD.

brown goods ▸ plural noun television sets, audio equipment, and similar household appliances. Compare with GREY GOODS, WHITE GOODS.

brown hare ▸ noun a hare found commonly in much of Eurasia, though absent from Ireland. ● *Lepus europaeus* (or *capensis*), family Leporidae.

brown holland ▸ noun [mass noun] unbleached holland linen.

Brownian motion /ˈbraʊnɪən/ ▸ noun [mass noun] Physics the erratic random movement of microscopic particles in a fluid, as a result of continuous bombardment from molecules of the surrounding medium.
– ORIGIN late 19th cent.: named after Robert *Brown* (1773–1858), the Scottish botanist who first observed the motion.

Brownie ▸ noun (pl. **Brownies**) **1** (**the Brownies**) the junior branch of the Guide Association, for girls aged between about 7 and 10, wearing a brown uniform. ■ (Brit. also **Brownie Guide**) a member of the Brownies.
2 (**brownie**) a small square of rich chocolate cake, with nuts. ■ Austral./NZ a piece of sweet currant bread.
3 (**brownie**) a benevolent elf that supposedly haunts houses and does housework secretly. [diminutive of BROWN; a 'wee brown man' often appears in Scottish ballads and fairy tales.]
– PHRASES **brownie point** informal, humorous an imaginary award given to someone for an attempt to please: *his policy will win brownie points with voters*.

Brownie Guider ▸ noun the adult leader of a group of Brownies. See also BROWN OWL (sense 2).

Browning[1], Elizabeth Barrett (1806–61), English poet; born *Elizabeth Barrett*. She established her reputation with *Poems* (1844). In 1846 she eloped to Italy with Robert Browning.

Browning[2], Robert (1812–89), English poet. In 1842 he established his name with *Dramatic Lyrics*, containing 'The Pied Piper of Hamelin' and 'My Last Duchess'.

Browning[3] ▸ noun (also **Browning machine gun**) a type of water-cooled automatic machine gun. ■ (also **Browning automatic**) a type of automatic pistol.
– ORIGIN early 20th cent.: named after John M. *Browning* (1855–1926), American designer of the weapons.

browning ▸ noun [mass noun] **1** the process or result of making something brown, typically by cooking or burning.
2 Brit. darkened flour, typically with other additives, for colouring gravy.

brown-nose informal ▸ noun (also **brown-noser**) an extremely obsequious person.
▸ verb [with obj.] curry favour with (someone) by acting very obsequiously: *academics were brown-nosing the senior faculty* | [no obj.] *if I can't learn to brown-nose, at least I can keep my mouth shut*.

brown-out ▸ noun chiefly N. Amer. a partial blackout.

brown owl ▸ noun **1** another term for TAWNY OWL.
2 (**Brown Owl**) Brit. informal the adult leader of a group of Brownies, officially termed the Brownie Guider since 1968.

brown rat ▸ noun a rat found throughout the world, typically living in association with man and regarded as a pest. It is commonly kept as a laboratory animal and as a pet, and is also bred in the albino form. Also called COMMON RAT, NORWAY RAT. ● *Rattus norvegicus*, family Muridae.

brown rice ▸ noun [mass noun] unpolished rice with only the husk of the grain removed.

brown rot ▸ noun [mass noun] a fungal disease causing the rotting and browning of parts of plants, in particular: ● a disease producing discoloration and shrivelling of apples, pears, plums, and other fruit (caused by fungi of the genus *Sclerotinia*, subdivision Ascomycotina). ● a disease resulting in the softening and cracking of timber (caused by bracket fungi of the family Polyporaceae, class Hymenomycetes).

brown sauce ▸ noun [mass noun] **1** a savoury sauce made with fat and flour cooked to a brown colour.
2 a commercially prepared relish containing vinegar and spices.

Brownshirt ▸ noun historical a member of a Nazi militia founded by Hitler in Munich in 1921, with brown uniforms resembling those of Mussolini's Blackshirts. They aided Hitler's rise to power, but were eclipsed by the SS after the 'night of the long knives' in June 1934. Also called STORM TROOPS or STURMABTEILUNG.

brown snake ▸ noun **1** a fast-moving, aggressive venomous Australian snake, with a variety of colour forms. ● *Pseudonaja* and other genera, family Elapidae: several species, in particular *P. textilis*.
2 a small, secretive harmless North American snake that is typically brown in colour. ● *Storeria dekayi*, family Colubridae.

brownstone ▸ noun [mass noun] N. Amer. a kind of reddish-brown sandstone used for building. ■ [count noun] a building faced with such sandstone.

brown sugar ▸ noun [mass noun] unrefined or partially refined sugar.

browntop (also **browntop bent**) ▸ noun another term for the grass COMMON BENT (see BENT[2]).

brown trout ▸ noun (pl. **same**) the common trout of Europe, especially one of a non-migratory race having dark spotted skin and occurring in small rivers and pools. ● *Salmo trutta*, family Salmonidae, in particular *S. trutta fario*.

browse /braʊz/ ▸ verb [no obj.] **1** survey goods for sale in a leisurely and casual way: *he stopped to* ***browse around*** *a second-hand bookshop*. ■ scan through a text, website, or collection of data to gain an impression of the contents: *she* ***browsed through*** *the newspaper* | [with obj.] *I decided to spend the night browsing the Internet*.
2 (of an animal) feed on leaves, twigs, or other high-growing vegetation: *they reach upward to* ***browse on*** *bushes*.
▸ noun **1** [in sing.] an act of casual looking or reading: *a* ***browse through*** *the sports pages* | *I was just having a quick* ***browse around*** *the antique stalls*. ■ a book, magazine, or website to be casually looked through: *this book is a useful browse for a new worker in the field*.
2 [mass noun] vegetation, such as twigs and young shoots, eaten by animals.
– DERIVATIVES **browsable** adjective.
– ORIGIN late Middle English (in sense 2 of the verb): from Old French *broster*, from *brost* 'young shoot', probably of Germanic origin.

WORD TRENDS The move of **browse** from the existing sense of 'read or look at something in a leisurely way' into Internet use is a natural one. The metaphor of an animal feeding from vegetation here and there is an apt description of a person moving from link to link rather than searching specifically for a particular term. Almost all of the top collocates of **browse** in the Oxford English Corpus are now Internet-related, with *site*, *Web*, *Internet*, and *website* all appearing as objects far more frequently than *shelf*, *shop*, or *book*. **Browse** is typically qualified by adverbs such as *casually* and *idly*, although it can also imply more focused use of the Internet: *after about 45 minutes of intense web browsing I couldn't find answers to my questions*.

browser ▸ noun **1** a person who looks casually through publications or websites or at goods for sale.
2 a computer program with a graphical user interface for displaying HTML files, used to navigate the World Wide Web: *a Web browser*.
3 an animal which feeds mainly on high-growing vegetation.

brrr ▸ exclamation used to express someone's reaction to feeling cold: *Brrr! It's a freezing cold day*.

BRU ▸ abbreviation Brunei (international vehicle registration).

Brubeck /ˈbruːbɛk/, Dave (b.1920), American jazz pianist, composer, and bandleader; full name *David Warren Brubeck*. He formed the Dave Brubeck Quartet in 1951 and won international recognition with the album *Time Out*, which included 'Take Five' (1959).

brubru /ˈbruːbruː/ (also **brubru shrike**) ▸ noun a small tropical African shrike (bird) with striking black-and-white plumage and chestnut flanks. Compare with BOUBOU. ● *Nilaus afer*, family Laniidae.

Bruce[1], Robert the, see ROBERT I.

Bruce[2], James (1730–94), Scottish explorer. In 1770 he was the first European to discover the source of the Blue Nile, although his *Travels to Discover the Sources of the Nile* (1790), recounting his expedition, was dismissed by his contemporaries as fabrication.

Bruce[3], Lenny (1925–66), American comedian; born *Leonard Alfred Schneider*. He gained notoriety for flouting the bounds of respectability with his humour, and was imprisoned for obscenity in 1961. He died following an accidental drugs overdose.

brucellosis /ˌbruːsəˈləʊsɪs/ ▸ noun [mass noun] a bacterial disease typically affecting cattle and causing undulant fever in humans. ● This disease is caused by Gram-negative bacteria of the genus *Brucella*, in particular *B. abortus*.
– ORIGIN 1930s: from modern Latin *Brucella* + **-osis**: named after Sir David *Bruce* (1855–1931), the Scottish physician who identified the bacterium.

brucite /ˈbruːsʌɪt/ ▸ noun [mass noun] a white, grey, or greenish mineral typically occurring in the form of tabular crystals. It consists of hydrated magnesium hydroxide.
– ORIGIN early 19th cent.: named after Archibald *Bruce* (1777–1818), American mineralogist, + -ITE[1].

Bruckner /ˈbrʊknə/, Anton (1824–96), Austrian composer and organist. He wrote ten symphonies, four masses, and a *Te Deum* (1884).

Bruegel /ˈbrɔɪɡ(ə)l/ (also **Breughel** or **Brueghel**) the name of a family of Flemish artists: ■ **Pieter** (*c.*1525–69); known as **Pieter Bruegel the Elder**. He produced landscapes, religious allegories, and satires of peasant life. Notable works: *The Procession to Calvary* (1564). ■ **Pieter Bruegel the Younger** (1564–1638), son of Pieter Bruegel the Elder; known as **Hell Bruegel**. A very able copyist of his father's work, he is also noted for his paintings of devils. ■ **Jan** (1568–1623), son of Pieter Bruegel the Elder; known as **Velvet Bruegel**. He was a celebrated painter of flowers, landscapes, and mythological scenes.

Bruges /bruːʒ/ a city in NW Belgium, capital of the province of West Flanders; pop. 117,071 (2008). A centre of the Flemish textile trade until the 15th century, it is a well-preserved medieval city surrounded by canals. Flemish name **Brugge** /ˈbrʏxə/.

bruin /ˈbruːɪn/ ▸ noun a name for a bear, especially in children's fables.
– ORIGIN late 15th cent.: from Dutch *bruin* (see BROWN); used as a name for the bear in the 13th-cent. fable *Reynard the Fox*.

bruise ▸ noun an injury appearing as an area of discoloured skin on the body, caused by a blow or impact rupturing underlying blood vessels. ■ a mark indicating damage on a fruit, vegetable, or plant.
▸ verb [with obj.] **1** (often as adj. **bruised**) inflict a bruise on (someone or something): *a bruised knee*. ■ [no obj.] be susceptible to bruising: *potatoes bruise easily, so treat them with care*. ■ hurt (someone's feelings): *she tried to bolster her bruised pride*.
2 crush or pound (food): *the mix contains bruised oats*.
– ORIGIN Old English *brȳsan* 'crush or injure with a blow', reinforced in Middle English by Old French *bruisier* 'break'.

bruiser ▸ noun informal, derogatory a person who is tough and aggressive and enjoys a fight or argument. ■ a professional boxer.

bruising ▶ **adjective** causing a bruise or bruises: *his legs took the bruising blows.* ■ (of a competitive situation) conducted in an aggressive way and likely to be stressful: *a bruising cabinet battle over public spending.*
▶ **noun** [mass noun] bruises on the skin: *her arm showed signs of bruising.*
– DERIVATIVES **bruisingly** adverb.

bruit /bruːt/ ▶ **verb** [with obj. and adverbial] spread (a report or rumour) widely: *I didn't want to have our relationship **bruited about** the office.*
▶ **noun 1** archaic a report or rumour.
2 Medicine a sound, especially an abnormal one, heard through a stethoscope; a murmur.
– ORIGIN late Middle English (as a noun): from Old French *bruit* 'noise', from *bruire* 'to roar'.

Brum /brʌm/ Brit. an informal name for Birmingham.
– ORIGIN mid 19th cent.: abbreviation of **BRUMMAGEM**.

Brumaire /bruːˈmɛː/, French /bʀymɛʀ/ ▶ **noun** the second month of the French Republican calendar (1793–1805), originally running from 22 October to 20 November.
– ORIGIN French, from *brume* 'mist'.

brumby /ˈbrʌmbi/ ▶ **noun** (pl. **brumbies**) (in Australia) a wild or unbroken horse.
– ORIGIN late 19th cent.: of unknown origin.

brume /bruːm/ ▶ **noun** [mass noun] literary mist or fog: *the birds rise like brume.*
– ORIGIN early 18th cent.: from French, from Latin *bruma* 'winter'.

Brummagem /ˈbrʌmədʒ(ə)m/ ▶ **adjective** [attrib.]
1 informal relating to Birmingham or the dialect of English spoken there.
2 dated cheap, showy, or counterfeit: *a vile Brummagem substitute for the genuine article.*
– ORIGIN mid 17th cent.: dialect form of **BIRMINGHAM**, England; sense 2 is with reference to counterfeit coins and cheap plated goods once made there.

Brummell /ˈbrʌm(ə)l/, George Bryan (1778–1840), English dandy; known as **Beau Brummell**. He was the arbiter of British fashion for the first decade and a half of the 19th century, owing his social position to his friendship with the Prince Regent.

Brummie (also **Brummy**) informal ▶ **noun** (pl. **Brummies**) Brit. a native of the British city of Birmingham.
▶ **adjective 1** Brit. from or relating to Birmingham: *a Brummie accent.*
2 (**brummy**) Austral./NZ counterfeit, showy, or cheaply made: *brummy jewels.*
– ORIGIN 1940s: from **BRUM**.

brumous /ˈbruːməs/ ▶ **adjective** literary foggy and wintry.
– ORIGIN mid 19th cent.: from French *brumeux*, from late Latin *brumosus* (from *bruma* 'winter').

brunch ▶ **noun** a late morning meal eaten instead of breakfast and lunch.
– ORIGIN late 19th cent.: blend of **BREAKFAST** and **LUNCH**.

Brundtland /ˈbrʊntland/, Gro Harlem (b.1939), Norwegian Labour stateswoman, Prime Minister 1981, 1986–9, and 1990–6. She was Norway's first woman Prime Minister, and was director general of the World Health Organization 1998–2003.

Brunei /bruːˈnʌɪ/ a small, oil-rich sultanate on the NW coast of Borneo, pop. 388,200 (est. 2009); languages, Malay (official), English (official), Chinese; capital, Bandar Seri Begawan.

> In the 16th century Brunei dominated Borneo and parts of the Philippines, but its power declined as that of the Portuguese and Dutch grew, and in 1888 it was placed under British protection. It became a fully independent Commonwealth state in 1984.

– DERIVATIVES **Bruneian** /bruːˈnʌɪən/ **adjective & noun**.

Brunel¹ /brʊˈnɛl/, Isambard Kingdom (1806–59), English engineer, son of Sir Marc Isambard Brunel. He was chief engineer of the Great Western Railway. His achievements include designing the Clifton suspension bridge (1829–30), the first transatlantic steamship, the *Great Western* (1838), and the *Great Eastern* (1858), at the time the world's largest ship.

Brunel² /brʊˈnɛl/, Sir Marc Isambard (1769–1849), French-born English engineer, father of Isambard Kingdom Brunel. He introduced mass-production machinery to Portsmouth dockyard and designed other machines for woodworking, boot-making, knitting, and printing. He also worked to construct the first tunnel under the Thames (1825–43).

Brunelleschi /ˌbruːnəˈlɛski/, Filippo (1377–1446), Italian architect; born *Filippo di Ser Brunellesco*. He is especially noted for the dome of Florence cathedral (1420–61), which he raised without the use of temporary supports. He is often credited with the Renaissance 'discovery' of perspective.

brunette /bruːˈnɛt, brʊ-/ (US also **brunet**) ▶ **noun** a woman or girl with dark brown hair.
– ORIGIN mid 16th cent.: from French, feminine of *brunet*, diminutive of *brun* 'brown'.

brung dialect past and past participle of **BRING**.

Brunhild /ˈbruːnhɪlt/ Germanic Mythology in the Nibelungenlied, the wife of Gunther, who instigated the murder of Siegfried. In the Norse versions she is a Valkyrie whom Sigurd (the counterpart of Siegfried) wins by penetrating the wall of fire behind which she lies in an enchanted sleep.

Bruno /ˈbruːnəʊ/, Giordano (1548–1600), Italian philosopher. He was a follower of Hermes Trismegistus and a supporter of the heliocentric Copernican view of the solar system. Bruno was tried by the Inquisition for heresy and burned at the stake.

Bruno, St /ˈbruːnəʊ/ (*c.*1032–1101), German-born French churchman. In 1084 he founded the Carthusian order at La Grande Chartreuse near Grenoble. Feast day, 6 October.

brunoise /bruːnˈwɑːz/ ▶ **noun** a mixture of finely diced vegetables fried in butter and used to flavour soups and sauces.
– ORIGIN French, from *brun* 'brown'.

Brunswick /ˈbrʌnzwɪk/ a former duchy and state of Germany, mostly incorporated into Lower Saxony. German name **BRAUNSCHWEIG**. ■ the capital of this former duchy, an industrial city in Lower Saxony, Germany; pop. 245,500 (est. 2006).

Brunswick stew ▶ **noun** [mass noun] US a stew originally made with squirrel or rabbit, but now consisting of chicken and vegetables including onion and tomatoes.

brunt /brʌnt/ ▶ **noun** (**the brunt**) the worst part or chief impact of a specified action: *education will **bear the brunt of** the cuts.*
– ORIGIN late Middle English (denoting a blow or an attack, also the force or shock of something): of unknown origin.

bruschetta /brʊˈskɛtə/ ▶ **noun** [mass noun] toasted Italian bread drenched in olive oil and served typically with garlic or tomatoes.
– ORIGIN Italian, from *bruscare* 'to toast'.

brush¹ ▶ **noun 1** an implement with a handle and a block of bristles, hair, or wire, used especially for cleaning, applying a liquid or powder to a surface, or arranging the hair: *a shaving brush.* ■ an act of sweeping, applying, or arranging with a brush or with one's hand: *he gave the seat a brush.*
2 a light and fleeting touch: *the lightest brush of his lips against her cheek.* ■ a brief encounter with someone or something unpleasant or notable: ***a brush with death** | my first brush with fame.*
3 the bushy tail of a fox.
4 (usu. **brushes**) a drumstick with long wire bristles, used to make a soft hissing sound on drums or cymbals.
5 a piece of carbon or metal serving as an electrical contact with a moving part in a motor or alternator.
6 [mass noun] Austral./NZ informal girls or women regarded sexually: *'Beer first, brush later.'* [1940s: probably from *brush* in the sense 'animal's tail', by association with *tail* 'buttocks' (see **TAIL¹**).]
▶ **verb** [with obj.] **1** [with adverbial] remove (dust or dirt) by sweeping or scrubbing: *we'll be able to **brush** the mud **off** easily.* ■ use a brush or one's hand to remove dust or dirt from (something): *she **brushed down** her best coat.* ■ clean (one's teeth) with a brush. ■ arrange (one's hair) by running a brush through it. ■ apply a liquid to (a surface) with a brush: *brush the potatoes with oil.*
2 [no obj.] touch lightly and gently: *stems of grass **brush against** her legs | she **brushed past** him to leave the room.* ■ [with obj.] push (something) away with a quick movement of the hand: *she **brushed** a wisp of hair **away** from her face.*
– PHRASAL VERBS **brush someone/thing aside** dismiss someone or something curtly and confidently: *he brushed aside attacks on his policies.* **brush someone/thing off** dismiss someone or something in an abrupt way: *the judge brushed off his pleas for leniency.* **brush up on** (or **brush something up**) improve one's existing knowledge or skill in a particular area: *brush up on your telephone skills.*
– DERIVATIVES **brushless** adjective (chiefly technical), **brush-like** adjective.
– ORIGIN Middle English: noun from Old French *broisse*; verb partly from Old French *brosser* 'to sweep'.

brush² ▶ **noun** [mass noun] chiefly N. Amer. & Austral./NZ undergrowth, small trees, and shrubs. ■ land covered with such growth. ■ N. Amer. cut brushwood. ■ Austral./NZ dense forest.
– ORIGIN Middle English: from Old French *broce*, perhaps based on Latin *bruscum*, denoting an excrescence on a maple.

B

brushback (also **brushback pitch**) ▶ **noun** Baseball a pitch aimed close to the body so that the batter must step back to avoid it.

brush discharge ▶ **noun** a broad electrical discharge from a conductor occurring when the potential difference is high but not sufficient for a spark or arc.

brushed ▶ **adjective 1** (of fabric) having a soft raised nap: *brushed cotton.*
2 (of metal) finished with a non-reflective surface: *brushed aluminium.*

brush-off ▶ **noun** [in sing.] informal a rejection or dismissal of someone by treating them as unimportant: *he's given her **the brush-off**.*

brushstroke ▶ **noun** a mark made by a paintbrush drawn across a surface.

brushtail (also **brush-tailed possum**) ▶ **noun** a nocturnal and mainly tree-dwelling Australasian marsupial, which has a pointed muzzle and a furred tail with a naked tip. ● Genus *Trichosurus*, family Phalangeridae: three species, in particular the **common brushtail** (*T. vulpecula*), frequently found in suburban areas.

brush-turkey ▶ **noun** a large mound-building bird of the megapode family, resembling a turkey and found mainly in New Guinea. Also called **SCRUB-TURKEY**.
● Family Megapodiidae: several genera and species, including *Alectura lathami* of eastern Australia.

brush-up ▶ **noun** [usu. in sing.] Brit. an act of cleaning or smartening oneself or something up: *he must want **a wash and brush-up** after the long journey.* ■ [usu. as modifier] an act of improving existing knowledge or skill in a particular area: *a two-day brush-up course.*

brush wolf ▶ **noun** North American term for **COYOTE**.

brushwood ▶ **noun** [mass noun] undergrowth, twigs, and small branches.

brushwork ▶ **noun** [mass noun] the way in which a painter uses their brush, as evident in their paintings: *canvases characterized by lively, flowing brushwork.*

brushy ▶ **adjective 1** covered in or consisting of brushwood: *a brushy hillside.*
2 Art displaying bold use of the brush in painting: *brushy outlining of form.*

brusque /brʊsk, bruːsk/ ▶ **adjective** abrupt or offhand in speech or manner: *she could be brusque and impatient.*
– DERIVATIVES **brusquely** adverb, **brusqueness** noun.
– ORIGIN mid 17th cent.: from French, 'lively, fierce', from Italian *brusco* 'sour'.

Brussels¹ the capital of Belgium and of the Belgian province of Brabant; pop. 1,048,491 (2008). The headquarters of the European Commission is located there. Flemish name **Brussel** /ˈbrys(ə)l/. French name **Bruxelles** /bʀysɛl/.

Brussels² ▶ **plural noun** informal Brussels sprouts.

Brussels carpet ▶ **noun** a carpet with a heavy woollen pile and a strong linen back.

Brussels griffon ▶ **noun** see **GRIFFON** (sense 1).

Brussels lace ▶ **noun** [mass noun] an elaborate kind of lace, typically with a raised design, made using a needle or lace pillow.

Brussels sprout (also **Brussel sprout**) ▶ **noun** a vegetable consisting of the small compact bud of a variety of cabbage. ■ the plant which yields the Brussels sprout, bearing many such buds along a tall single stem.

brut /bruːt/, French /bʀy/ ▶ **adjective** (of sparkling wine) unsweetened; very dry.
– ORIGIN French, literally 'raw, rough'.

brutal ▶ **adjective** savagely violent: *a brutal murder.* ■ unpleasant or harsh: *the brutal morning light.* ■ direct and without attempting to disguise unpleasantness: *the brutal honesty of his observations.*
– DERIVATIVES **brutally** adverb.
– ORIGIN late 15th cent. (in the sense 'relating to the lower animals'): from Old French, or from medieval Latin *brutalis*, from *brutus* 'dull, stupid' (see **BRUTE**).

brutalism ▶ **noun 1** [mass noun] cruelty and savageness.

2 a stark style of functionalist architecture, especially of the 1950s and 1960s, characterized by the use of steel and concrete in massive blocks.
– DERIVATIVES **brutalist** noun & adjective.

B

brutality ▶ noun [mass noun] savage physical violence; great cruelty: *brutality against civilians*.

brutalize (also **brutalise**) ▶ verb [with obj.] make (someone) cruel, violent, or insensitive to the pain of others by repeated exposure to violence: *he had been brutalized in prison and become cynical* | (as adj. **brutalizing**) *the brutalizing effects of warfare*. ■ treat (someone) in a savage and violent way: *they brutalize and torture persons in their custody*.
– DERIVATIVES **brutalization** noun.

brute ▶ noun 1 a savagely violent man or animal: *he was a cold-blooded brute*. ■ informal a cruel or insensitive person: *what an unfeeling little brute you are*. ■ something awkward, difficult, or unpleasant: *a great **brute of a** machine*.
2 an animal as opposed to a human being.
▶ adjective [attrib.] unreasoning and animal-like: *a brute struggle for social superiority*. ■ merely physical: *we achieve little by brute force*. ■ fundamental, inescapable, and unpleasant: *the brute necessities of basic subsistence*.
– ORIGIN late Middle English (as an adjective): from Old French *brut(e)*, from Latin *brutus* 'dull, stupid'.

brutha ▶ noun see BROTHER (sense 1 of the noun).

brutish ▶ adjective resembling or characteristic of a brute: *he was coarse and brutish* | *brutish behaviour*.
– DERIVATIVES **brutishly** adverb, **brutishness** noun.

Bruton /ˈbruːt(ə)n/, John (Gerard) (b.1947), Irish Fine Gael statesman, Taoiseach (Prime Minister) 1994–7.

Brutus[1] a legendary Trojan hero, great-grandson of Aeneas and supposed ancestor of the British people. In medieval legend he was said to have brought a group of Trojans to England and founded Troynovant or New Troy (London).

Brutus[2], Lucius Junius, legendary founder of the Roman Republic. Traditionally he led a popular uprising, after the rape of Lucretia, against the king (his uncle) and drove him from Rome. He and the father of Lucretia were elected as the first consuls of the Republic (509 BC).

Brutus[3], Marcus Junius (85–42 BC), Roman senator. With Cassius he led the conspirators who assassinated Julius Caesar in 44. They were defeated by Caesar's supporters, Antony and Octavian, at the battle of Philippi in 42, after which Brutus committed suicide.

Bruxelles /bʀysɛl/ French name for BRUSSELS[1].

bruxism /ˈbrʌksɪz(ə)m/ ▶ noun [mass noun] involuntary habitual grinding of the teeth, typically during sleep.
– ORIGIN 1930s: from Greek *brukhein* 'gnash the teeth' + -ISM.

Bryansk /brɪˈansk/ (also **Briansk**) an industrial city in European Russia, south-west of Moscow, on the Desna River; pop. 413,900 (est. 2008).

Brylcreem /ˈbrɪlkriːm/ ▶ noun [mass noun] trademark a cream used on men's hair to give it a smooth, shiny appearance.
– DERIVATIVES **Brylcreemed** adjective.

bryology /brʌɪˈɒlədʒi/ ▶ noun [mass noun] the study of mosses and liverworts.
– DERIVATIVES **bryological** adjective, **bryologist** noun.
– ORIGIN mid 19th cent.: from Greek *bruon* 'moss' + -LOGY.

bryony /ˈbrʌɪəni/ (also **white bryony**) ▶ noun (pl. **bryonies**) a climbing Eurasian hedgerow plant with lobed hairy leaves, red berries, and spring-like tendrils. See also BLACK BRYONY. ● *Bryonia dioica*, the only British member of the gourd family (Cucurbitaceae).
– ORIGIN Old English, via Latin from Greek *bruōnia*.

Bryophyta /ˌbrʌɪə(ʊ)ˈfʌɪtə/ ▶ plural noun Botany a division of small flowerless green plants which comprises the mosses and liverworts. They lack true roots and reproduce by spores released from a stalked capsule. ● Division Bryophyta: classes Musci (mosses) and Hepaticae (liverworts).
– ORIGIN modern Latin (plural), from Greek *bruon* 'moss' + *phuta* 'plants'.

bryophyte /ˈbrʌɪə(ʊ)fʌɪt/ ▶ noun Botany a small flowerless green plant of the division Bryophyta, which comprises the mosses and liverworts.

Bryozoa /ˌbrʌɪəˈzəʊə/ ▶ plural noun Zoology a phylum of sedentary aquatic invertebrates that comprises the moss animals. Also called ECTOPROCTA, POLYZOA.
– ORIGIN modern Latin (plural), from Greek *bruon* 'moss' + *zōia* 'animals'.

bryozoan Zoology ▶ noun a sedentary aquatic invertebrate of the phylum Bryozoa, which comprises the moss animals.
▶ adjective relating to or denoting bryozoans.

Brythonic /brɪˈθɒnɪk/ (also **Brittonic**) ▶ adjective denoting or relating to the southern group of Celtic languages, consisting of Welsh, Cornish, and Breton. They were spoken in Britain before and during the Roman occupation, surviving as Welsh and Cornish after the Anglo-Saxon invasions, and being taken to Brittany by emigrants. Compare with GOIDELIC. Also called P-CELTIC.
▶ noun [mass noun] the Brythonic languages collectively.
– ORIGIN from Welsh *Brython* 'Britons' + -IC.

Brześć nad Bugiem /ˌbʒɛʃtʃ nad ˈbugjɛm/ Polish name for BREST (sense 2).

BS ▶ abbreviation ■ US Bachelor of Science. ■ Brit. Bachelor of Surgery. ■ Blessed Sacrament. ■ British Standard(s). ■ N. Amer. vulgar slang bullshit.

BSc ▶ abbreviation Bachelor of Science, a first degree in a science subject.

BSE ▶ abbreviation bovine spongiform encephalopathy, a disease of cattle which affects the central nervous system, causing agitation and staggering, and is usually fatal. It is believed to be caused by an agent such as a prion or a virino, and to be related to Creutzfeldt–Jakob disease in humans. Also (popularly) called MAD COW DISEASE.

BSI ▶ abbreviation British Standards Institution.

B-side ▶ noun the side of a pop single regarded as the less important one.

BSL ▶ abbreviation British Sign Language.

BST ▶ abbreviation ■ bovine somatotrophin. ■ historical British Standard Time, one hour ahead of GMT, in continuous use 1968–71. ■ British Summer Time.

BT ▶ abbreviation British Telecom.

Bt ▶ abbreviation Baronet.

B2B ▶ abbreviation business-to-business, denoting trade conducted via the Internet between businesses.

B2C ▶ abbreviation business-to-consumer, denoting trade conducted via the Internet between businesses and consumers.

Btu (also **BTU**) ▶ abbreviation British thermal unit(s).

BTW ▶ abbreviation informal by the way.

Bual /ˈbuːal/ ▶ noun [mass noun] a variety of wine grape grown chiefly in Madeira. ■ a Madeira wine of a medium-sweet type made from such grapes.
– ORIGIN from Portuguese *boal*.

BUAV ▶ abbreviation British Union for the Abolition of Vivisection.

bub ▶ noun N. Amer. informal an aggressive or rude way of addressing a boy or man: *hey, bub, I'm looking for someone*.
– ORIGIN mid 19th cent.: from earlier *bubby* (perhaps a child's form of BROTHER), or from German *Bube* 'boy'.

bubal /ˈbjuːb(ə)l/ ▶ noun a hartebeest, especially one of an extinct race that was formerly found in North Africa. ● *Alcelaphus buselaphus buselaphus*, family Bovidae.
– ORIGIN late 18th cent.: from French *bubale*, via Latin from Greek *boubalos* 'wild ox, antelope'.

bubba /ˈbʌbə/ ▶ noun N. Amer. informal 1 used as an affectionate form of address to a brother.
2 derogatory an uneducated conservative white male of the southern US.
– ORIGIN late 19th cent.: alteration of BROTHER.

bubbie ▶ noun US informal (in Jewish use) one's grandmother.
– ORIGIN from Yiddish *bube* 'grandmother'.

bubble ▶ noun 1 a thin sphere of liquid enclosing air or another gas. ■ an air- or gas-filled spherical cavity in a liquid or a solidified liquid such as glass.
2 used to refer to a situation or feeling that is unlikely to last: *many companies enjoyed rapid expansion before **the bubble burst*** | *a bubble of confidence*.
3 a transparent domed cover or enclosure: *piglets born into a sterile bubble*. ■ a place or position that is protected from danger or unpleasant reality: *they are not on tour packages seeing foreign ports from a bubble*.
4 (also **bubble shell**) a marine mollusc that typically has a thin scroll-like shell. ● Bullidae and other families, order Cephalaspidea, class Gastropoda.
▶ verb [no obj.] (of a liquid) contain rising bubbles of air or gas: *a pot of coffee bubbled away on the stove*. ■ (often as adj. **bubbling**) make a sound resembling this: *a bubbling fountain*. ■ (**bubble with/over with**) be filled with an irrepressible positive feeling: *Ellen was bubbling with enthusiasm*. ■ (**bubble up**) (of a feeling) become more intense and approach the point of being expressed: *the fury bubbling up inside her*.
– PHRASES **burst someone's bubble** shatter someone's illusions about something or destroy their sense of well-being. **on the bubble** N. Amer. informal (of a sports player or team) occupying the last qualifying position on a team or for a tournament, and liable to be replaced by another. [from *sit on the bubble*, with the implication that the bubble may burst.]
– ORIGIN Middle English: partly imitative, partly an alteration of BURBLE.

bubble and squeak ▶ noun [mass noun] Brit. cooked cabbage fried with cooked potatoes and often meat.
– ORIGIN late 18th cent.: from the sounds of the mixture cooking.

bubble bath ▶ noun [mass noun] liquid, crystals, or powder added to bathwater to make it foam and have a fragrant smell.

bubble canopy ▶ noun a transparent domed canopy on a fighter aircraft or bubble car.

bubble car ▶ noun a small car with a transparent domed canopy and typically three wheels.

bubble chamber ▶ noun Physics an apparatus designed to make the tracks of ionizing particles visible as a row of bubbles in a liquid.

bubblegum ▶ noun [mass noun] 1 chewing gum that can be blown into bubbles. ■ (also **bubblegum pink**) [mass noun] the bright pink colour that is typical of bubblegum.
2 [usu. as modifier] chiefly N. Amer. pop music that is catchy and repetitive and designed to appeal especially to teenagers: *rockers hate bubblegum pop*.

bubblehead ▶ noun informal a foolish or empty-headed person.

bubblejet printer ▶ noun a form of inkjet printer in which the ink is heated, producing bubbles which force droplets of ink on to the paper.

bubble pack ▶ noun a small package enclosing goods in transparent dome-shaped plastic on a flat cardboard backing. ■ another term for BUBBLE WRAP.

bubbler ▶ noun Austral. & US a drinking fountain.

bubble shell ▶ noun see BUBBLE (sense 4 of the noun).

bubble tea ▶ noun [mass noun] an East Asian drink of tea containing grains of tapioca and often blended with sweetener and flavourings, shaken to a froth and usually served cold with a straw.

bubble wrap ▶ noun [mass noun] (trademark in the US) plastic packaging material in sheets containing numerous small air cushions designed to protect fragile goods.

bubbly ▶ adjective (**bubblier**, **bubbliest**) 1 containing bubbles: *bake until the top is crisp and bubbly*.
2 (of a person) full of cheerful high spirits: *a bright and bubbly personality*.
▶ noun [mass noun] informal champagne.

bubinga /bjuːˈbɪŋgə/ ▶ noun [mass noun] reddish-brown timber used chiefly for inlay work and as a veneer.
● The timber is obtained from several tropical African trees of the genus *Guibourtia*, family Leguminosae.
– ORIGIN a local name.

bubo /ˈbjuːbəʊ/ ▶ noun (pl. **buboes**) a swollen inflamed lymph node in the armpit or groin.
– DERIVATIVES **bubonic** /bjuːˈbɒnɪk/ adjective.
– ORIGIN late Middle English: from Latin, from Greek *boubōn* 'groin or swelling in the groin'.

bubonic plague ▶ noun the commonest form of plague in humans, characterized by fever, delirium, and the formation of buboes.

> The plague bacterium, *Yersinia pestis*, is transmitted by rat fleas. Epidemics occurred in Europe throughout the Middle Ages (notably as the Black Death and the Great Plague of 1665–6); the disease is still endemic in parts of Asia.

bucatini /ˌbukəˈtiːni/ ▶ plural noun small hollow tubes of pasta.
– ORIGIN Italian.

buccal /ˈbʌk(ə)l/ ▶ adjective technical relating to the cheek: *the buccal side of the molars*. ■ relating to the mouth: *the buccal cavity*.
– ORIGIN early 19th cent.: from Latin *bucca* 'cheek' + -AL.

buccaneer /ˌbʌkəˈnɪə/ ▶ noun historical a pirate, originally one operating in the Caribbean. ■ a person who

acts in a recklessly adventurous and often unscrupulous way, especially in business.
– ORIGIN mid 17th cent. (originally denoting European hunters in the Caribbean): from French *boucanier*, from *boucan* 'a frame on which to cook or cure meat', from Tupi *mukem*.

buccaneering ▸ adjective (especially in a business context) high-risk and adventurous: *the buccaneering nature of the oil-transport industry*.

buccinator /ˈbʌksɪneɪtə/ ▸ noun Anatomy a flat, thin muscle in the wall of the cheek.
– ORIGIN late 17th cent.: from Latin, from *buccinare* 'blow a trumpet', from *buccina*, denoting a kind of trumpet.

Bucephalus /bjuːˈsɛfələs/ the favourite horse of Alexander the Great, who tamed the horse as a boy and took it with him on his campaigns until its death, after a battle, in 326 BC.

Buchan /ˈbʌk(ə)n/, John, 1st Baron Tweedsmuir (1875–1940), Scottish novelist. His adventure stories feature recurring heroes such as Richard Hannay. Notable works: *The Thirty-Nine Steps* (1915).

Buchanan /bjuːˈkanən/, James (1791–1868), American Democratic statesman, 15th President of the US 1857–61. His leanings towards the pro-slavery side in the developing dispute over slavery made the issue more fraught and he retired from politics in 1861.

Bucharest /ˌbuːkəˈrɛst/ the capital of Romania; pop. 1,931,236 (2006). It was founded in the 14th century on the trade route between Europe and Constantinople. Romanian name **BUCUREȘTI**.

Buchenwald /ˈbuːkənˌvald/, German /ˈbuːxn̩ˌvalt/ a Nazi concentration camp in the Second World War, near Weimar in eastern Germany.

buchu /ˈbʌkuː/ ▸ noun a heather-like South African shrub which is cultivated for its essential oil and as an ornamental. ● Genus *Agathosma* (or *Barosma*) and *Diosma*, family Rutaceae.
■ [mass noun] a diuretic drug made from the powdered leaves of the buchu.
– ORIGIN mid 18th cent.: from Khoikhoi.

buck[1] ▸ noun **1** the male of some horned animals, especially the fallow deer, roe deer, reindeer, and antelopes. ■ a male hare, rabbit, ferret, rat, or kangaroo. ■ S. African an antelope of either sex.
2 another term for **VAULTING HORSE**.
3 a vertical jump performed by a horse, with the head lowered, back arched, and back legs thrown out behind.
4 archaic a fashionable and spirited young man.
▸ verb **1** [no obj.] (of a horse) to perform a buck: *he's got to get his head down to buck* | [with obj.] *she* ***bucked*** *them off if they tried to get on her back*. ■ (of a vehicle) make sudden jerky movements.
2 [with obj.] oppose or resist (something oppressive or inevitable): *the shares bucked the market trend*.
3 (**buck someone** or **buck up**) informal make or become more cheerful: [with obj.] *Bella and Jim need me to buck them up* | [no obj.] *buck up, kid, it's not the end of the game*.
▸ adjective US military slang lowest of a particular rank: *a buck private*.
– PHRASES **buck up one's ideas** Brit. informal become more serious, energetic, and hard-working.
– ORIGIN Old English, partly from *buc* 'male deer' (of Germanic origin, related to Dutch *bok* and German *Bock*); reinforced by *bucca* 'male goat', of the same ultimate origin.

buck[2] ▸ noun N. Amer. & Austral./NZ informal a dollar: *a run-down hotel room for five bucks a night*. ■ S. African informal a rand. ■ Indian informal a rupee.
– PHRASES **big bucks** a lot of money. **a fast** (or **quick**) **buck** easily and quickly earned money: *itinerant traders out to make a fast buck*.
– ORIGIN mid 19th cent.: of unknown origin.

buck[3] ▸ noun an article placed as a reminder in front of a player whose turn it is to deal at poker.
– PHRASES **the buck stops here** (or **with someone**) informal the responsibility for something cannot or should not be passed to someone else. **pass the buck** informal shift the responsibility for something to someone else.
– ORIGIN mid 19th cent.: of unknown origin.

buck-and-wing ▸ noun US, chiefly historical a lively solo tap dance, performed typically in wooden-soled shoes.

buckaroo /ˌbʌkəˈruː/ ▸ noun N. Amer. dated a cowboy.
– ORIGIN early 19th cent.: alteration of **VAQUERO**.

buckbean ▸ noun another term for **BOGBEAN**.
– ORIGIN late 16th cent.: from Flemish *bocks boonen* 'goat's beans'.

buckboard ▸ noun N. Amer. an open horse-drawn carriage with four wheels and seating that is attached to a plank stretching between the front and rear axles.
– ORIGIN mid 19th cent.: from *buck* 'body of a cart' (perhaps a variant of obsolete *bouk* 'belly, body') + **BOARD**.

buckbrush ▸ noun [mass noun] N. Amer. coarse vegetation on which wild deer browse.

buckeen /bʌˈkiːn/ ▸ noun historical a poor but aspiring young man of the lower Anglo-Irish gentry.

bucket ▸ noun **1** a roughly cylindrical open container with a handle, made of metal or plastic and used to hold and carry liquids. ■ the contents of a bucket or the amount it can contain: *she emptied* ***a bucket of water*** *over them*. ■ (**buckets**) informal large quantities of something, especially liquid: *I wept buckets*. ■ a compartment on the outer edge of a waterwheel. ■ the scoop of a dredger or grain elevator. ■ a scoop attached to the front of a loader, digger, or tractor.
2 Computing a unit of data that can be transferred from a backing store in a single operation.
▸ verb (**buckets, bucketing, bucketed**) [no obj.] **1** (**it buckets down, it is bucketing down**, etc.) Brit. informal rain heavily.
2 [with adverbial of direction] informal (of a vehicle) move quickly and jerkily: *the car came bucketing out of a side road*.
– DERIVATIVES **bucketful** noun (pl. **bucketfuls**).
– ORIGIN Middle English: from Anglo-Norman French *buquet* 'tub, pail', perhaps from Old English *būc* 'belly, pitcher'.

bucket hat ▸ noun a simple soft cloth hat with a brim.

bucketload ▸ noun as much as can be held by a bucket. ■ informal a large amount or number.

bucket seat ▸ noun a seat in a car or aircraft with a rounded back to fit one person.

bucket shop ▸ noun informal, derogatory **1** an unauthorized office for speculating in stocks or currency using the funds of unwitting investors.
2 Brit. a travel agency that specializes in providing cheap air tickets.

bucketwheel ▸ noun a machine with a series of scoops or buckets on a rotating belt, used to excavate or move material.

buckeye ▸ noun **1** an American tree or shrub related to the horse chestnut, with showy red or white flowers. ● Genus *Aesculus*, family Hippocastanaceae: several species.
■ the nut of the buckeye.
2 (also **buckeye butterfly**) an orange and brown New World butterfly with conspicuous eyespots on the wings. ● *Junonia coenia*, subfamily Nymphalinae, family Nymphalidae.
3 (**Buckeye**) US informal a native of the state of Ohio.
4 (also **buckeye coupling**) a kind of automatic coupling for railway rolling stock. [named after the *Buckeye* Steel Castings Company, Columbus, Ohio.]

Buckeye State informal name for **OHIO**.

buck fever ▸ noun [mass noun] N. Amer. informal nervousness felt by novice hunters when they first sight game.

buckhorn ▸ noun a horn of a deer. ■ [mass noun] such horn, used for knife handles, small containers, and rifle sights.

buckhound ▸ noun a staghound of a small breed.

Buckingham Palace the London residence of the British sovereign since 1837, adjoining St James's Park, Westminster. It was built for the Duke of Buckingham in the early 18th century and bought by George III in 1761.

Buckinghamshire a county of central England; county town, Aylesbury.

buckjump Austral./NZ ▸ verb [no obj.] (of a horse) jump vertically with its head lowered, back arched, and legs drawn together in an attempt to unseat its rider.
▸ noun an act of buckjumping.
– DERIVATIVES **buckjumper** noun.

buckjumping ▸ noun [mass noun] Austral./NZ a rodeo event in which a rider attempts to stay in the saddle of a bucking horse for a period of eight seconds.

Buckland, William (1784–1856), English geologist. He helped to redefine geology, correlating deposits and associated fossils with former conditions, and developed the idea of an ice age. He was the first to describe and name a dinosaur (*Megalosaurus*), in 1824.

buckle ▸ noun a flat, typically rectangular frame with a hinged pin, used for joining the ends of a belt or strap. ■ a similarly shaped ornament on a shoe.
▸ verb **1** [with obj.] fasten or decorate with a buckle: *he buckled his belt*. ■ [no obj.] (**buckle up**) fasten one's seat belt in a car or aircraft.
2 [no obj.] bend and give way under pressure or strain: *the earth* ***buckled under*** *the titanic stress*. ■ [with obj.] bend (something) out of shape: *a lorry backed into the wall and buckled the gate*. ■ (of a person) suffer a psychological collapse as a result of stress: *a weaker person might have* ***buckled under*** *the strain*.
– PHRASAL VERBS **buckle down** tackle a task with determination: *they will* ***buckle down to*** *negotiations over the next few months*. **buckle to** dated make a determined effort.
– ORIGIN Middle English: from Old French *bocle*, from Latin *buccula* 'cheek strap of a helmet', from *bucca* 'cheek'. Sense 2 of the verb is from French *boucler* 'to bulge'.

buckler ▸ noun historical a small round shield held by a handle or worn on the forearm.
– ORIGIN Middle English: from Old French (*escu*) *bocler*, literally '(shield) with a boss', from *bocle* 'buckle, boss' (see **BUCKLE**).

buckler fern ▸ noun a European fern with deeply divided lobes and with stalks that are typically covered with brown scales. ● Several species in the genus *Dryopteris*, family Dryopteridaceae.

Buckley's ▸ noun (in phrase (**not**) **have Buckley's** (or **Buckley's chance**)) Austral./NZ informal have little or no chance of doing or achieving something: *the vehicle had* ***Buckley's chance*** *of stopping*.
– ORIGIN late 19th cent.: sometimes said to be from the name of William *Buckley* (died 1856), who, despite dire predictions as to his chances of survival, lived with the Aborigines for many years.

buckling ▸ noun a smoked herring.
– ORIGIN early 20th cent.: from German *Bückling* 'bloater'.

buckminsterfullerene /ˌbʌkmɪnstəˈfʊləriːn/ ▸ noun [mass noun] Chemistry a form of carbon having molecules of 60 atoms arranged in a polyhedron resembling a geodesic sphere. See also **FULLERENE**.
– ORIGIN 1980s: named after Richard *Buckminster Fuller* (see **FULLER**[1]).

buck naked ▸ adjective informal, chiefly N. Amer. completely naked.

bucko ▸ noun (pl. **buckoes** or **buckos**) informal a young man (often as a form of address): *I know you, my bucko, you're a troublemaker*.
– ORIGIN late 19th cent. (originally nautical slang): from **BUCK**[1] + **-O**.

buck-passing ▸ noun [mass noun] informal the practice of shifting the responsibility for something to someone else.

buckra /ˈbʌkrə/ ▸ noun (pl. **same** or **buckras**) US & W. Indian informal, chiefly derogatory a white person, especially a man.
– ORIGIN mid 18th cent.: from Ibibio and Efik (*m*)*bakara* 'European, master'.

buckram /ˈbʌkrəm/ ▸ noun [mass noun] coarse linen or other cloth stiffened with gum or paste, and used as interfacing and in bookbinding.
– PHRASES **men in buckram** archaic non-existent people. [with allusion to Shakespeare's *1 Henry IV* II. iv. 210–50.]
– ORIGIN Middle English (denoting a kind of fine linen or cotton cloth): from Old French *boquerant*, perhaps from **BUKHARA** in central Asia.

buck rarebit ▸ noun Brit. a dish of melted cheese on toast with a poached egg on top.

Bucks ▸ abbreviation Buckinghamshire.

Buck's Fizz ▸ noun [mass noun] Brit. champagne or sparkling white wine mixed with orange juice as a cocktail.
– ORIGIN 1930s: from the name of *Buck's Club*, in London, and **FIZZ**.

buckshee /bʌkˈʃiː, ˈbʌkʃiː/ ▸ adjective informal, chiefly Brit. free of charge: *a buckshee brandy*.
– ORIGIN First World War (originally soldiers' slang): alteration of **BAKSHEESH**.

buckshot ▸ noun [mass noun] coarse lead shot used in shotgun shells.

buckskin ▸ noun **1** the skin of a male deer. ■ [mass noun] greyish leather with a suede finish, traditionally made from buckskin but now often made from sheepskin: [as modifier] *a pair of buckskin moccasins*.
■ (**buckskins**) clothes or shoes made from such

leather. ■ [mass noun] thick, smooth cotton or woollen fabric.
2 N. Amer. a horse of a greyish-yellow colour.
– DERIVATIVES **buckskinned** adjective.

B

buckthorn ▶ **noun** a shrub or small tree which typically bears thorns and black berries. Some kinds yield dyes and others have been used medicinally. ● Genus *Rhamnus*, family Rhamnaceae: several species, including the **common buckthorn** (*R. cathartica*), with berries formerly used as a cathartic.
– ORIGIN late 16th cent.: from **BUCK**[1] in the sense 'deer' + **THORN**, translating modern Latin *spina cervina*.

buck tooth ▶ **noun** an upper tooth that projects over the lower lip.
– DERIVATIVES **buck-toothed** adjective.

buckwheat ▶ **noun** an Asian plant of the dock family, producing starchy seeds that are used for fodder and also milled into flour which is widely used in the US. ● *Fagopyrum esculentum*, family Polygonaceae.
– ORIGIN mid 16th cent.: from Middle Dutch *boecweite* 'beech wheat', its grains being shaped like beechmast.

buckyballs ▶ **plural noun** Chemistry, informal spherical molecules of a fullerene, especially buckminsterfullerene. Related cylindrical molecules are termed **buckytubes**.

bucolic /bjuːˈkɒlɪk/ ▶ **adjective** relating to the pleasant aspects of the countryside and country life: *the church is lovely for its bucolic setting.*
▶ **noun** (usu. **bucolics**) a pastoral poem.
– DERIVATIVES **bucolically** adverb.
– ORIGIN early 16th cent. (as a noun): via Latin from Greek *boukolikos*, from *boukolos* 'herdsman', from *bous* 'ox'.

Bucureşti /ˌbukuˈrɛʃtj/ Romanian name for **BUCHAREST**.

bud[1] ▶ **noun** a compact knob-like growth on a plant which develops into a leaf, flower, or shoot. ■ Biology an outgrowth from an organism, e.g. a yeast cell, that separates to form a new individual without sexual reproduction taking place. ■ [with modifier] Zoology a rudimentary leg or other appendage of an animal which has not yet grown, or never will grow, to full size.
▶ **verb** (**buds**, **budding**, **budded**) [no obj.] Biology (of a plant or animal) form a bud: *new blood vessels bud out from the vascular bed.* ■ [with obj.] graft a bud of (a plant) on to another plant.
– PHRASES **in bud** (of a plant) having newly formed buds.
– ORIGIN late Middle English: of unknown origin.

bud[2] ▶ **noun** N. Amer. informal a friendly form of address from one boy or man to another.
– ORIGIN mid 19th cent.: abbreviation of **BUDDY**.

Budapest /ˌb(j)uːdəˈpɛst/ the capital of Hungary; pop. 1,712,210 (2009). The city was formed in 1873 by the union of the hilly city of Buda on the right bank of the River Danube with the low-lying city of Pest on the left.

Buddha /ˈbʊdə/ (often **the Buddha**) a title given to the founder of Buddhism, Siddartha Gautama (*c.*563–*c.*483 BC). Born an Indian prince in what is now Nepal, he renounced wealth and family to become an ascetic, and after achieving enlightenment while meditating, taught all who came to learn from him. ■ (as noun **a Buddha**) Buddhism a person who has attained full enlightenment. ■ a statue or picture of the Buddha.
– ORIGIN Sanskrit, literally 'enlightened', past participle of *budh* 'know'.

Buddh Gaya /ˌbʊd gəˈjɑː/ variant spelling of **BODHGAYA**.

Buddhism /ˈbʊdɪz(ə)m/ ▶ **noun** [mass noun] a widespread Asian religion or philosophy, founded by Siddartha Gautama in NE India in the 5th century BC.

> Buddhism has no god, and gives a central role to the doctrine of karma. The 'four noble truths' of Buddhism state that all existence is suffering, that the cause of suffering is desire, that freedom from suffering is nirvana, and that this is attained through the 'eightfold path' of ethical conduct, wisdom, and mental discipline (including meditation). There are two major traditions, Theravada and Mahayana.

– DERIVATIVES **Buddhist** noun & adjective, **Buddhistic** adjective.

buddhu /ˈbʊduː/ ▶ **noun** Indian informal an idiot.
– ORIGIN from Hindi *buddhū*.

budding ▶ **adjective** (of a plant) having or developing buds: *a budding chrysanthemum.* ■ (of a body part) becoming larger as part of normal growth. ■ (of a person) beginning and showing signs of promise in a particular sphere: *budding young actors.* ■ beginning and showing promising signs of continuing: *their budding relationship.*

buddle ▶ **noun** a shallow inclined container in which ore is washed.
– ORIGIN mid 16th cent.: of unknown origin.

buddleia /ˈbʌdlɪə/ ▶ **noun** a widely cultivated shrub with clusters of fragrant lilac, white, or yellow flowers. ● Genus *Buddleia* (or *Buddleja*), family Loganiaceae: several species, especially the butterfly bush.
– ORIGIN modern Latin; named in honour of the English botanist Adam *Buddle* (died 1715), by Linnaeus, at the suggestion of Sir William Houston, who introduced the plant to Europe from South America.

buddy informal, chiefly N. Amer. ▶ **noun** (pl. **buddies**) a close friend. ■ a working companion with whom close cooperation is required. ■ a person who befriends and helps another with an incapacitating disease, typically AIDS. ■ used as a form of address to a man whose name is not known: *I'm working on it, buddy.*
▶ **verb** (**buddies**, **buddying**, **buddied**) [no obj.] become friendly and spend time with someone: *I decided to buddy up to them.*
– ORIGIN mid 19th cent. (originally US): perhaps an alteration of **BROTHER**, or a variant of **BUTTY**[2].

buddy-buddy ▶ **adjective** informal, chiefly derogatory very friendly: *he's buddy-buddy with the Ambassador.*

buddy system ▶ **noun** a cooperative arrangement whereby individuals are paired or teamed up and assume responsibility for one another's welfare or safety.

Budge, Don (1915–2000), American tennis player; born *John Donald Budge*. He was the first to win the four major singles championships—Australia, France, Britain, and the US—in one year (1938). In both 1937 and 1938 he won the Wimbledon singles, men's doubles, and mixed doubles.

budge ▶ **verb** [usu. with negative] make or cause to make the slightest movement: [no obj.] *the queue in the bank hasn't budged* | [with obj.] *I couldn't budge the door.* ■ [no obj.] (**budge up** or US **over**) informal make room for another person by moving: *budge up, boys, make room for your uncle.* ■ [usu. with modal] change an opinion: [no obj.] *he wouldn't budge on his decision.*
– ORIGIN late 16th cent.: from French *bouger* 'to stir', based on Latin *bullire* 'to boil'.

budgerigar ▶ **noun** a small gregarious Australian parakeet which is green with a yellow head in the wild. It is popular as a cage bird and has been bred in a variety of colours. ● *Melopsittacus undulatus*, family Psittacidae.
– ORIGIN mid 19th cent.: of Aboriginal origin, perhaps an alteration of Kamilaroi *gijirrigaa* (also in related languages).

budget ▶ **noun 1** an estimate of income and expenditure for a set period of time: *keep within the household budget.* ■ (**Budget**) an annual or other regular estimate of national revenue and expenditure put forward by a finance minister. ■ the amount of money needed or available for a purpose: *they have a limited budget.*
2 archaic a quantity of written or printed material.
▶ **verb** (**budgets**, **budgeting**, **budgeted**) [no obj.] allow or provide a particular amount of money in a budget: *the university is **budgeting for** a deficit.* ■ [with obj.] provide (a sum of money) for a particular purpose from a budget: *the council proposes to budget £100,000 to provide grants* | (as adj. **budgeted**) *a budgeted figure of £31,000.*
▶ **adjective** [attrib.] inexpensive: *a budget guitar.*
– PHRASES **on a budget** with a restricted amount of money: *we're travelling on a budget.*
– DERIVATIVES **budgetary** adjective.
– ORIGIN late Middle English: from Old French *bougette*, diminutive of *bouge* 'leather bag', from Latin *bulga* 'leather bag, knapsack', of Gaulish origin. Compare with **BULGE**. The word originally meant a pouch or wallet, and later its contents. In the mid 18th cent., the Chancellor of the Exchequer, in presenting his annual statement, was said 'to open the budget'. In the late 19th cent. the use of the term was extended from governmental to other finances.

budgie ▶ **noun** (pl. **budgies**) informal a budgerigar.

budo /ˈbuːdəʊ/ ▶ **noun** [mass noun] martial arts. ■ the code on which martial arts are all based.
– ORIGIN Japanese *budō*, from *bu* 'military' + *dō* 'way'.

budstick ▶ **noun** a small piece of plant stem with a bud, prepared for grafting on to another plant.

Budweis /ˈbʊtvaɪs/ German name for **ČESKÉ BUDĚJOVICE**.

budwood ▶ **noun** [mass noun] short lengths of young branches with buds prepared for grafting on to the rootstock of another plant.

budworm ▶ **noun** a moth caterpillar that is destructive to buds. See also **SPRUCE BUDWORM**.

Buenaventura /ˌbweɪnəvɛnˈtjʊərə/, Spanish /bwenaβenˈtura/ the chief Pacific port of Colombia; pop. 324,207 (est. 2005).

Buenos Aires /ˌbweɪnəs ˈʌɪriːz/, Spanish /bwenəɔs ˈajres/ the capital city and chief port of Argentina, on the River Plate; pop. 3,042,600 (est. 2008).

Buerger's disease /ˈbəːgəz/ ▶ **noun** [mass noun] inflammation and thrombosis in small and medium-sized blood vessels, typically in the legs and leading to gangrene. It has been associated with smoking.
– ORIGIN early 20th cent.: named after Leo *Buerger* (1879–1943), American surgeon.

buff[1] ▶ **noun** [mass noun] **1** a yellowish-beige colour: [as modifier] *a buff envelope.*
2 a stout dull yellow leather with a velvety surface.
3 [count noun] a stick, wheel, or pad used for polishing.
▶ **verb** [with obj.] polish (something): *he buffed the glass until it gleamed.* ■ give (leather) a velvety finish by removing the surface of the grain.
▶ **adjective** N. Amer. informal (of a person or their body) in good physical shape with well-developed muscles: *the driver was a buff blond named March.*
– PHRASES **in the buff** informal naked.
– ORIGIN mid 16th cent.: probably from French *buffle*, from Italian *bufalo*, from late Latin *bufalus* (see **BUFFALO**). The original sense in English was 'buffalo', later 'oxhide' or 'colour of oxhide'.

buff[2] ▶ **noun** [with modifier] informal a person who is enthusiastically interested in and very knowledgeable about a particular subject: *a computer buff.*
– ORIGIN early 20th cent.: from **BUFF**[1], originally applied to enthusiastic fire-watchers, because of the buff uniforms formerly worn by New York volunteer firemen.

Buffalo an industrial city in New York State; pop. 270,919 (est. 2008). Situated at the eastern end of Lake Erie, it is a major port of the St Lawrence Seaway.

buffalo ▶ **noun** (pl. **same** or **buffaloes**) **1** a heavily built wild ox with backward-curving horns, found mainly in the Old World tropics: ● four species native to South Asia (genus *Bubalus*, family Bovidae). See also **WATER BUFFALO**, **ANOA** ● a wild ox with large horns, native to Africa south of the Sahara (*Synceros caffer*, family Bovidae, the **African buffalo**), sometimes considered to be two species, the **Cape buffalo** and the **forest** (or **dwarf**) **buffalo**. ■ the North American bison.
2 (also **buffalo fish**) a large greyish-olive freshwater fish with thick lips, common in North America. ● Genus *Ictiobus*, family Catostomidae: several species.
▶ **verb** (**buffaloes**, **buffaloing**, **buffaloed**) [with obj.] N. Amer. informal overawe or intimidate (someone): *she didn't like being buffaloed.* ■ baffle (someone): *the problem has buffaloed the advertising staff.*
– ORIGIN mid 16th cent.: probably from Portuguese *bufalo*, from late Latin *bufalus*, from earlier *bubalus*, from Greek *boubalos* 'antelope, wild ox'.

Buffalo Bill (1846–1917), American showman; born *William Frederick Cody*. He gained his nickname for killing 4,280 buffalo in eight months to feed the Union Pacific Railroad workers, and subsequently devoted his life to his travelling Wild West Show.

buffalo gnat ▶ **noun** North American term for **BLACKFLY** (sense 2).

buffalo grass ▶ **noun** [mass noun] any of a number of grasses, in particular: ● a creeping grass of the North American plains (*Buchloe dactyloides*, family Gramineae). ● a North American grass (*Stenotaphrum secundatum*, family Gramineae), naturalized in Australia, New Zealand, and South Africa.

buffalo thorn ▶ **noun** a tropical African shrub or small tree with glossy leaves and thorns which grow in pairs, one of each pair being straight and the other curved. ● *Ziziphus mucronata*, family Rhamnaceae.

buffalo weaver ▶ **noun** a large thickset African weaver bird that is either all black or has a white head and red rump. ● Genera *Bubalornis* and *Dinemellia*, family Ploceidae: three species.

Buffalo wings (also **Buffalo chicken wings**) ▶ **plural noun** N. Amer. deep-fried chicken wings coated in a spicy sauce and served with blue cheese dressing.

buffed (also **buffed-out**) ▶ **adjective** another term for BUFF[1].

buffer[1] ▶ **noun 1** a person or thing that reduces a shock or that forms a barrier between incompatible or antagonistic people or things: *family and friends can provide a buffer against stress.* ■ (**buffers**) Brit. a pair of shock-absorbing pistons projecting from a cross-beam at the end of a railway track or on the front and rear of a railway vehicle.
2 (also **buffer solution**) Chemistry a solution which resists changes in pH when acid or alkali is added to it.
3 Computing a temporary memory area or queue used when creating or editing text, or when transferring data between devices or programs operating at different speeds.
▶ **verb** [with obj.] **1** lessen or moderate the impact of (something): *the massage helped to buffer the strain.*
2 treat with a chemical buffer.
– PHRASES **hit the buffers** Brit. come to a sudden unsuccessful end: *his world championship campaign looked as if it had hit the buffers.*
– ORIGIN mid 19th cent.: probably from obsolete *buff* (verb), imitative of the sound of a blow to a soft body.

buffer[2] ▶ **noun** Brit. informal an elderly man who is considered to be foolishly old-fashioned, unworldly, or incompetent: *a distinguished **old buffer**.*
– ORIGIN mid 18th cent.: probably from obsolete *buff* (see BUFFER[1]), or from dialect *buff* 'stutter, splutter' (possibly the same word). In late Middle English *buffer* had the sense 'stammerer'.

buffer state ▶ **noun** a small neutral country situated between two larger hostile countries and serving to prevent the outbreak of regional conflict.

buffer stock ▶ **noun** a reserve of a commodity that can be used to offset price fluctuations.

buffer zone ▶ **noun** a neutral area serving to separate hostile forces or nations. ■ an area of land designated for environmental protection.

buffet[1] /ˈbʊfeɪ, ˈbʌfeɪ/ ▶ **noun 1** a meal consisting of several dishes from which guests serve themselves: [as modifier] *a cold buffet lunch.*
2 a room or counter in a station, hotel, or other public building selling light meals or snacks. ■ (also **buffet car**) Brit. a railway carriage selling light meals or snacks.
3 also /ˈbʌfɪt/ North American term for SIDEBOARD (sense 1).
– ORIGIN early 18th cent. (denoting a sideboard): from French, from Old French *bufet* 'stool', of unknown origin.

buffet[2] /ˈbʌfɪt/ ▶ **verb** (**buffets, buffeting, buffeted**) [with obj.] (especially of wind or waves) strike repeatedly and violently; batter: *rough seas buffeted the coast* | [no obj.] *the wind was buffeting at their bodies.* ■ knock (someone) off course: *he was buffeted from side to side.* ■ (of difficulties) afflict (someone) over a long period: *they were buffeted by a major recession.*
▶ **noun 1** dated a blow or punch. ■ a shock or misfortune: *the daily buffets of urban civilization.*
2 [mass noun] Aeronautics another term for BUFFETING.
– ORIGIN Middle English: from Old French *buffeter* (verb), *buffet* (noun), diminutive of *bufe* 'a blow'.

buffet[3] /ˈbʌfɪt/ ▶ **noun** Scottish & N. English a low stool or hassock.
– ORIGIN late Middle English: from Old French *bufet*, of unknown origin.

buffeting ▶ **noun** [mass noun] **1** the action of buffeting someone or something: *the roofs have survived the buffeting of worse winds than this.*
2 Aeronautics irregular oscillation of part of an aircraft, caused by turbulence.

bufflehead /ˈbʌf(ə)lhɛd/ ▶ **noun** a small North American diving duck related to the goldeneye, with a large puffy head. The male has white plumage with a black back. ● *Bucephala albeola*, family Anatidae.
– ORIGIN mid 17th cent. (in the sense 'simpleton'): from obsolete *buffle* 'buffalo' + HEAD. The current sense (mid 18th cent.) may be an independent formation because of the duck's large square-shaped head.

buffo /ˈbʊfəʊ/ ▶ **noun** (pl. **buffos**) a comic actor in Italian opera.
▶ **adjective** of or typical of Italian comic opera: *a buffo character.*
– ORIGIN mid 18th cent.: Italian, 'puff of wind, buffoon', from *buffare* 'to puff', of imitative origin.

Buffon /ˈbuːfɒn/, French /byfɔ̃/, Georges-Louis Leclerc, Comte de (1707–88), French naturalist. A founder of palaeontology, he emphasized the unity of all living species, minimizing the apparent differences between animals and plants. He produced a compilation of the animal kingdom, the *Histoire Naturelle*, which had reached thirty-six volumes by the time of his death.

buffoon /bəˈfuːn/ ▶ **noun** a ridiculous but amusing person; a clown.
– DERIVATIVES **buffoonish** adjective.
– ORIGIN mid 16th cent.: from French *bouffon*, from Italian *buffone*, from medieval Latin *buffo* 'clown'. Originally recorded as a rare Scots word for a kind of pantomime dance, the term later (late 16th cent.) denoted a professional jester.

buffoonery ▶ **noun** (pl. **buffooneries**) [mass noun] behaviour that is ridiculous but amusing.

bug ▶ **noun 1** informal a harmful microorganism, typically a bacterium. ■ an illness caused by a microorganism: *he'd just recovered from a flu bug.* ■ [with modifier] an enthusiastic interest in something: *they caught the sailing **bug**.*
2 chiefly N. Amer. a small insect.
3 (also **true bug**) Entomology an insect of a large order distinguished by having mouthparts that are modified for piercing and sucking. ● Order Hemiptera: see HEMIPTERA.
4 a concealed miniature microphone, used for secret eavesdropping or recording.
5 an error in a computer program or system.
▶ **verb** (**bugs, bugging, bugged**) [with obj.] **1** conceal a miniature microphone in (a room or telephone) in order to eavesdrop on or record someone's conversations secretly: *the telephones in the presidential palace were bugged.* ■ record or eavesdrop on (a conversation) in this way.
2 informal annoy or bother (someone): *a persistent reporter was bugging me.*
– PHRASAL VERBS **bug off** N. Amer. informal go away. **bug out 1** leave quickly: *if you see enemy troops, bug out.* **2** N. Amer. informal bulge outwards: *men's eyes bug out when she walks past.*
– ORIGIN early 17th cent.: of unknown origin. Current verb senses date from the early 20th cent.

bugaboo /ˈbʌɡəbuː/ ▶ **noun** chiefly N. Amer. an object of fear or alarm; a bogey.
– ORIGIN mid 18th cent.: probably of Celtic origin and related to Welsh *bwci bo* 'bogey, the Devil', *bwci* 'hobgoblin' and Cornish *bucca*.

Buganda /b(j)uːˈɡandə/ a former kingdom of East Africa, on the north shore of Lake Victoria, now part of Uganda.

bugbane ▶ **noun** a tall plant of the buttercup family, with spikes of cream or yellow flowers and fern-like leaves, native to north temperate regions. ● Genus *Cimicifuga*, family Ranunculaceae: several species, in particular *C. foetida*.
– ORIGIN early 19th cent.: from BUG + BANE, with reference to the former use of the species *C. foetida* to drive away bedbugs.

bugbear ▶ **noun 1** a cause of obsessive fear, anxiety, or irritation.
2 archaic an imaginary being invoked to frighten children, typically a sort of hobgoblin supposed to devour them.
– ORIGIN late 16th cent.: probably from obsolete *bug* 'bogey' (of unknown origin) + BEAR[2].

bug-eyed ▶ **adjective** with bulging eyes: *a bug-eyed monster.*

bugger vulgar slang, chiefly Brit. ▶ **noun 1** [with adj.] used as a term of abuse, especially for a man. ■ used to refer to a person, typically a man, for whom one feels pity or respect. ■ an annoyingly awkward thing.
2 derogatory a person who commits buggery.
▶ **verb** [with obj.] **1** penetrate the anus of (someone) during sexual intercourse.
2 (often **bugger someone/thing about**) cause serious harm or trouble to. ■ [no obj.] (**bugger about/around**) act in a stupid or feckless way. ■ used to express an angrily dismissive attitude to (someone or something).
▶ **exclamation** (also **buggeration**) used to express annoyance or anger.
– PHRASES **bugger all** nothing. **bugger me** used to express surprise or amazement. **I'm buggered if ——** used to make the following clause negative. **not give a bugger** not care in the slightest. **play silly buggers** act in a foolish way.
– PHRASAL VERBS **bugger off** [usu. in imperative] go away.
– ORIGIN Middle English (originally denoting a heretic, specifically an Albigensian): from Middle Dutch, from Old French *bougre* 'heretic', from medieval Latin *Bulgarus* 'Bulgarian', particularly one belonging to the Orthodox Church and therefore regarded as a heretic by the Roman Church. The sense 'sodomite' (16th cent.) arose from an association of heresy with forbidden sexual practices; its use as a general insult dates from the early 18th cent.

B

buggered ▶ **adjective** [predic.] Brit. vulgar slang (of a person) extremely tired.

buggery ▶ **noun** [mass noun] **1** anal intercourse. In law the term also covers bestiality.
2 Brit. vulgar slang used in various expressions as an intensifier.
– ORIGIN Middle English (in the sense 'heresy'): from Middle Dutch *buggerie*, from Old French *bougrerie*, from *bougre* (see BUGGER).

Buggins' turn ▶ **noun** Brit. informal a system by which appointments or awards are made in rotation rather than by merit.
– ORIGIN early 20th cent.: from *Buggins*, used to represent a typical surname.

buggy[1] ▶ **noun** (pl. **buggies**) **1** a small motor vehicle, typically with an open top: *a golf buggy.*
2 short for BABY BUGGY.
3 historical a light horse-drawn vehicle for one or two people, with two or (in North America) four wheels.
– ORIGIN mid 18th cent.: of unknown origin.

buggy[2] ▶ **adjective** (**buggier, buggiest**) **1** infested with bugs.
2 (of a computer program or system) faulty in operation.
3 N. Amer. informal mad; insane.

bughouse informal ▶ **noun 1** N. Amer. a psychiatric hospital or asylum.
2 dated a seedy, run-down cinema.
▶ **adjective** N. Amer. crazy.

bugle[1] ▶ **noun** (also **bugle-horn**) a brass instrument like a small trumpet, typically without valves or keys and used for military signals.
▶ **verb** [no obj.] sound a bugle. ■ [with obj.] sound (a note or call) on a bugle: *he bugled a warning.*
– DERIVATIVES **bugler** noun.
– ORIGIN Middle English: via Old French from Latin *buculus*, diminutive of *bos* 'ox'. The early English sense was 'wild ox', hence the compound *bugle-horn*, denoting the horn of an ox used to give signals, originally in hunting.

bugle[2] ▶ **noun** [mass noun] a creeping Eurasian plant of the mint family, with blue flowers held on upright stems. ● Genus *Ajuga*, family Labiatae: several species, especially the common *A. reptans*.
– ORIGIN Middle English: from late Latin *bugula*.

bugle[3] ▶ **noun** an ornamental tube-shaped glass or plastic bead sewn on to clothing.
– ORIGIN late 16th cent.: of unknown origin.

bugleweed ▶ **noun** North American term for BUGLE[2].

bugloss /ˈbjuːɡlɒs/ ▶ **noun** a bristly plant of the borage family, with bright blue flowers. ● *Anchusa* and other genera, family Boraginaceae: several species, including the Eurasian *A. arvensis* and the widespread **viper's bugloss**.
– ORIGIN late Middle English: from Old French *buglosse* or Latin *buglossus*, from Greek *bouglōssos* 'ox-tongued', from *bous* 'ox' + *glōssa* 'tongue'.

buhl /buːl/ ▶ **noun** variant spelling of BOULLE.

build ▶ **verb** (past and past participle **built**) [with obj.]
1 construct (something) by putting parts or material together: *the ironworks were built in 1736.* ■ commission, finance, and oversee the building of (something): *the county council plans to build a bypass.* ■ (**build something in/into**) incorporate something and make it a permanent part of a structure, system, or situation: *engineers want to build in extra traction.* ■ Computing compile (a program, database, index, etc.).
2 make or become stronger or more intense: [with obj.] *we **built up** confidence in our abilities* | [no obj.] *the air of excited anticipation builds.* ■ establish and develop (a business or situation) over a period of time: *he'd **built up** the store from nothing.* ■ [no obj.] (**build on**) use as a basis for further development: *Britain should build on the talents of its workforce.*
▶ **noun 1** [mass noun] the proportions of a person's or animal's body: *she was of medium height and slim build* | [in sing.] *he had an ideal build for a sprinter.*
2 the style or form of construction of something, especially a vehicle.
3 Computing a compiled version of a program. ■ [mass noun] the process of compiling a program.
– PHRASES **build one's hopes up** become ever more hopeful or optimistic about something: *don't build your hopes up, Julia, you'll only get hurt.* **built on**

B

sand without reliable foundations or any real substance.
– ORIGIN Old English *byldan*, from *bold*, *botl* 'dwelling', of Germanic origin; related to BOWER[1].

builder ▶ **noun** [usu. in combination] a person who constructs something by putting parts or material together: *a boatbuilder.* ■ a person whose job is to construct or repair houses. ■ [usu. in combination] a person or thing that creates or develops a particular thing: *breaking the record was a real confidence-builder.*

builders' merchant ▶ **noun** a supplier of construction materials.

building ▶ **noun 1** a structure with a roof and walls, such as a house or factory.
2 [mass noun] the action or trade of constructing something: *the building of motorways* | [as modifier] *building materials.* ■ the creation or development of something over a period of time: *the building of democracy in Guatemala.*

building block ▶ **noun 1** a child's wooden or plastic toy brick.
2 a basic unit from which something is built up: *sounds are the building blocks of language.*

building line ▶ **noun** a limit beyond which a house must not extend into a street.

building site ▶ **noun** an area where a structure is being constructed or repaired.

building society ▶ **noun** Brit. a financial organization which pays interest on investments by its members and lends capital for the purchase or improvement of houses.

> Building societies originally developed as non-profit-making cooperative societies from friendly societies. Since 1986 changes in legislation have allowed them to offer banking and other facilities, and some have become public limited companies.

buildout ▶ **noun** [mass noun] N. Amer. the growth, development, or expansion of something: *the rapid buildout of digital technology.*

build-up ▶ **noun** [usu. in sing.] **1** a gradual accumulation or increase, typically of something negative that leads to a problem: *the build-up of carbon dioxide in the atmosphere.*
2 a period of excitement and preparation before a significant event: *the build-up to Christmas.*

built past and past participle of BUILD. ▶ **adjective** (of a person) having a specified physical size or build: *a slightly built woman.*

built-in ▶ **adjective** forming an integral part of a structure: *a worktop with a built-in cooker.* ■ (of a characteristic) inherent; innate: *the system has a built-in resistance to change.*

built-up ▶ **adjective 1** (of an area) densely covered by buildings.
2 increased in height by the addition of parts: *shoes with built-up heels.*

Bujumbura /ˌbuːdʒəmˈbʊərə/ the capital of Burundi, at the north-eastern end of Lake Tanganyika; pop. 429,000 (est. 2007). It was known as Usumbura until 1962.

Bukhara /bʊˈkɑːrə/ (also **Bukhoro** /buːˈkɔːrə/, **Bokhara**) a city in the central Asian republic of Uzbekistan; pop. 249,000 (est. 2009). It is one of the oldest trade centres in central Asia, and is noted for the production of karakul fleeces.

Bukharin /bʊˈkɑːrɪn/, Nikolai (Ivanovich) (1888–1938), Russian revolutionary activist and theorist. Editor of *Pravda* (1918–29) and *Izvestia* (1934–7), a member of the Politburo (1924–9), and chairman of Comintern from 1926, he was executed in one of Stalin's purges.

Bukovina /ˌbʊkə(ʊ)ˈviːnə/ a region of SE Europe in the Carpathians, divided between Romania and Ukraine. Formerly a province of Moldavia, it was ceded to Austria by the Turks in 1775. After the First World War it was made part of Romania, the northern part being incorporated into the Ukrainian SSR in the Second World War.

Bulawayo /ˌbʊləˈweɪəʊ/ an industrial city in western Zimbabwe; pop. 740,100 (est. 2009).

bulb ▶ **noun 1** a rounded underground storage organ present in some plants, notably those of the lily family, consisting of a short stem surrounded by fleshy scale leaves or leaf bases, lying dormant over winter. Compare with CORM, RHIZOME. ■ a plant grown from a bulb.
2 short for LIGHT BULB.
3 an expanded part of a glass tube such as that forming the reservoir of a thermometer. ■ a hollow flexible container with an opening through which the air can be expelled by squeezing, such as that used to fill a syringe. ■ a spheroidal dilated part at the end of an anatomical structure.
– ORIGIN late Middle English: via Latin from Greek *bolbos* 'onion, bulbous root'.

bulb fly ▶ **noun** a hoverfly that resembles a bumblebee, with larvae that are pests of daffodil bulbs.
● *Merodon equestris*, family Syrphidae.

bulbil /ˈbʌlbɪl/ ▶ **noun** Botany a small bulb-like structure, in particular one in the axil of a leaf, which may fall to form a new plant.
– ORIGIN mid 19th cent.: from modern Latin *bulbillus*, diminutive of *bulbus* 'onion, bulbous root'.

bulbous ▶ **adjective 1** fat, round, or bulging: *a bulbous nose.*
2 (of a plant) growing from a bulb.

bulbul /ˈbʊlbʊl/ ▶ **noun** a tropical African and Asian songbird, typically having a crest, drab plumage, and a melodious voice. ● Family Pycnonotidae: several genera and numerous species.
– ORIGIN mid 17th cent.: from Persian, of imitative origin.

Bulganin /bʊlˈgɑːnɪn/, Nikolai (Aleksandrovich) (1895–1975), Soviet statesman, Chairman of the Council of Ministers (Premier) 1955–8. He was Vice-Premier in the government of Georgi Malenkov in 1953, and in 1955 shared the premiership with Khrushchev.

Bulgar /ˈbʌlgɑː/ ▶ **noun** a member of a Slavic people who settled in what is now Bulgaria in the 7th century.
– ORIGIN from medieval Latin *Bulgarus*, from Old Church Slavonic *Blŭgarinŭ*.

bulgar /ˈbʌlgə/ (also **bulgur**, **bulgar wheat**) ▶ **noun** [mass noun] a cereal food made from whole wheat partially boiled then dried, eaten especially in Turkey.
– ORIGIN 1930s: from Turkish *bulgur* 'bruised grain'.

Bulgaria /bʌlˈgɛːrɪə/ a country in SE Europe on the western shores of the Black Sea; pop. 7,204,700 (est. 2009); official language, Bulgarian; capital, Sofia.

> Part of the Ottoman Empire from the 14th century, Bulgaria remained under Turkish rule until the late 19th century, becoming independent in 1908. Bulgaria fought on the German side in both world wars. A communist state was set up by the Soviets after the Second World War, and a multiparty democratic system was introduced in 1989. In 2007 Bulgaria joined the EU.

– ORIGIN named after the Bulgars (see **BULGAR**).

Bulgarian ▶ **adjective** relating to Bulgaria, its people, or their language.
▶ **noun 1** a native or inhabitant of Bulgaria, or a person of Bulgarian descent.
2 [mass noun] the Southern Slavic language spoken in Bulgaria.

bulge ▶ **noun 1** a rounded swelling which distorts an otherwise flat surface. ■ Military a piece of land which projects outwards from an otherwise regular line.
2 [in sing.] informal an unusual temporary increase in number or size: *a bulge in the birth rate.*
▶ **verb** [no obj.] swell or protrude to an incongruous extent: *the veins in his neck bulged* | (as adj. **bulging**) *he stared with bulging eyes.* ■ be full of and distended with: *a briefcase* ***bulging with*** *documents.*
– DERIVATIVES **bulgingly** adverb, **bulgy** adjective (**bulgier**, **bulgiest**).
– ORIGIN Middle English: from Old French *boulge*, from Latin *bulga* (see BUDGET). The original meaning was 'wallet or bag', later 'a ship's bilge' (early 17th cent.); other senses presumably derived from association with the shape of a full bag.

Bulge, Battle of the (in the Second World War) a German counteroffensive in the Ardennes aimed at preventing an Allied invasion of Germany, in late 1944–early 1945. The Germans drove a 'bulge' about 60 miles (110 km) deep in the front line, but were later forced to retreat.

bulgur ▶ **noun** variant spelling of BULGAR.

bulimarexia /bjʊˌlɪməˈrɛksɪə, bʊ-/ ▶ **noun** [mass noun] chiefly US another term for BULIMIA NERVOSA (see BULIMIA).
– ORIGIN 1970s: blend of BULIMIA and ANOREXIA.

bulimia /bjʊˈlɪmɪə, bʊ-/ (also **bulimia nervosa**) ▶ **noun** [mass noun] an emotional disorder characterized by a distorted body image and an obsessive desire to lose weight, in which bouts of extreme overeating are followed by fasting or self-induced vomiting or purging.
– DERIVATIVES **bulimic** adjective & noun.
– ORIGIN late Middle English (as *bolisme*, later *bulimy*): modern Latin, or from medieval Latin *bolismos*, from Greek *boulimia* 'ravenous hunger', from *bous* 'ox' + *limos* 'hunger'.

bulk ▶ **noun 1** [mass noun] the mass or size of something large: *residents jump up and down on their rubbish to reduce its bulk.* ■ large size or shape: *he moved quickly in spite of his bulk.* ■ [count noun] a large mass or shape. ■ [as modifier] large in quantity: *bulk orders of over 100 copies.* ■ roughage in food: *potatoes supply energy, essential protein, and bulk.* ■ cargo in an unpackaged mass such as grain or oil. ■ Printing the thickness of paper or a book.
2 (**the bulk of**) the greater part of something: *the bulk of the traffic had passed.*
▶ **verb** [with obj.] **1** treat (a product) so that its quantity appears greater than it is: *traders were* ***bulking up*** *their flour with chalk.* ■ [no obj.] (**bulk up**) build up flesh and muscle, typically in training for sporting events.
2 combine (shares or commodities for sale): *your shares will be bulked with others and sold at the best prices available.*
– PHRASES **bulk large** be or seem to be of great importance: *territorial questions bulked large in diplomatic relations.* **in bulk 1** (of goods) in large quantities and generally at a reduced price: *retail multiples buy in bulk.* **2** (of a cargo or commodity) not packaged; loose.
– ORIGIN Middle English: the senses 'cargo as a whole' and 'heap, large quantity' (the earliest recorded) are probably from Old Norse *búlki* 'cargo'; other senses arose perhaps by alteration of obsolete *bouk* 'belly, body'.

bulk buying ▶ **noun** [mass noun] the purchase of goods in large amounts, typically at a discount.
– DERIVATIVES **bulk-buy** verb.

bulk carrier (also **bulker**) ▶ **noun** a ship that carries non-liquid cargoes such as grain or ore in bulk.

bulkhead ▶ **noun** a dividing wall or barrier between separate compartments inside a ship, aircraft, or other vehicle.
– ORIGIN late 15th cent.: from Old Norse *bálkr* 'partition' + HEAD.

bulk mail ▶ **noun** [mass noun] N. Amer. a category of mail for sending out large numbers of identical items at a reduced rate.

bulk modulus ▶ **noun** Physics the relative change in the volume of a body produced by a unit compressive or tensile stress acting uniformly over its surface.

bulky ▶ **adjective** (**bulkier**, **bulkiest**) taking up much space; large and unwieldy: *a bulky carrier bag.* ■ (of a person) heavily built.
– DERIVATIVES **bulkily** adverb, **bulkiness** noun.

bull[1] ▶ **noun 1** an uncastrated male bovine animal: [as modifier] *bull calves.* ■ a large male animal, especially a whale or elephant. ■ (**the Bull**) the zodiacal sign or constellation Taurus.
2 Brit. a bullseye.
3 Stock Exchange a person who buys shares hoping to sell them at a higher price later. Often contrasted with BEAR[2].
▶ **verb 1** [with obj. and adverbial of direction] informal push or move powerfully or violently: *he bulled the motor cycle clear of the tunnel.*
2 [no obj.] (**be bulling**) (of a cow) behave in a manner characteristic of being on heat.
– PHRASES **like a bull at a gate** taking action hastily and without thought. **like a bull in a china shop** behaving recklessly and clumsily in a situation where one is likely to cause damage. **take the bull by the horns** deal decisively with a difficult or dangerous situation.
– ORIGIN late Old English *bula* (recorded in place names), from Old Norse *boli*. Compare with BULLOCK.

bull[2] ▶ **noun** a papal edict.
– ORIGIN Middle English: from Old French *bulle*, from Latin *bulla* 'bubble, rounded object' (in medieval Latin 'seal or sealed document').

bull[3] ▶ **noun** [mass noun] informal stupid or untrue talk or writing; nonsense: *much of what he says is sheer bull.*
– ORIGIN early 17th cent.: of unknown origin.

bulla /ˈbʊlə/ ▶ **noun** (pl. **bullae** /ˈbʊliː/) **1** Medicine a large blister containing serous fluid. ■ an abnormal air-filled cavity in the lung.
2 Anatomy a rounded prominence.
3 a round seal attached to a papal bull, typically one made of lead.

B

– ORIGIN Latin, literally 'bubble'.

bullace /ˈbʊlɪs/ ▸ **noun** a thorny shrub or small tree with small purple-black plum-like fruits. The damson is probably a cultivated form. ● *Prunus domestica* subsp. *insititia* (or *P. insititia*), family Rosaceae.
– ORIGIN Middle English: from Old French *buloce* 'sloe': of unknown origin.

bull ant ▸ **noun** another term for **BULLDOG ANT**.

bullate /ˈbʊleɪt/ ▸ **adjective** Botany covered with rounded swellings like blisters.
– ORIGIN mid 18th cent.: from Latin *bullatus*, from Latin *bulla* 'bubble'.

bull-baiting ▸ **noun** [mass noun] historical the practice of setting dogs to harass a bull, popular as an entertainment in medieval Europe.

bull bar ▸ **noun** a strong metal grille fitted to the front of a motor vehicle to protect it against impact damage.

bulldike ▸ **noun** variant spelling of **BULLDYKE**.

bulldog ▸ **noun 1** a dog of a sturdy smooth-haired breed with a large head and powerful protruding lower jaw, a flat wrinkled face, and a broad chest. ■ a person noted for courageous or stubborn tenacity: [as modifier] *the bulldog spirit*.
2 informal (at Oxford and Cambridge Universities) an official who assists the proctors, especially in disciplinary matters.
▸ **verb** (**bulldogs**, **bulldogging**, **bulldogged**) [with obj.] N. Amer. wrestle (a steer) to the ground by holding its horns and twisting its neck.
– DERIVATIVES **bulldogger** noun.

bulldog ant ▸ **noun** a large Australian ant with large jaws and a powerful sting. Also called **BULL ANT**. ● Genus *Myrmecia*, family Formicidae.

bulldog bat ▸ **noun** a fish-eating bat that has long legs and very large feet with sharp claws, native to Central and South America. Also called **FISHERMAN BAT**, **MASTIFF BAT**. ● *Noctilio leporinus*, family Noctilionidae.

bulldog bond ▸ **noun** a sterling bond issued on the UK market by a foreign borrower.

bulldog clip ▸ **noun** Brit. trademark a strong sprung metal device with two flat plates that close so as to hold papers together.

bulldoze ▸ **verb** [with obj.] clear (ground) or destroy (buildings, trees, etc.) with a bulldozer: *developers are bulldozing the site*. ■ use force insensitively when dealing with (someone or something): *she believes that to build status you need to bulldoze everyone else*.
– ORIGIN late 19th cent. (originally US in the sense 'intimidate'): from **BULL**[1] + *-doze*, alteration of the noun **DOSE**.

bulldozer ▸ **noun** a powerful track-laying tractor with caterpillar tracks and a broad curved upright blade at the front for clearing ground. ■ a person or group exercising irresistible force, especially in disposing of opposition: *the new Duke was a political bulldozer*.

bulldust ▸ **noun** [mass noun] Austral./NZ **1** coarse dust.
2 vulgar slang nonsense; rubbish.

bulldyke (also **bulldike**) ▸ **noun** informal, derogatory a lesbian of masculine appearance or manner.

bullet ▸ **noun 1** a metal projectile for firing from a rifle, revolver, or other small firearm, typically cylindrical and pointed, and sometimes containing an explosive. ■ used in similes to refer to someone or something that moves very fast: *the ball sped across the grass like a bullet*. ■ US (in sporting contexts) a very fast ball. ■ (**the bullet**) informal dismissal from employment: *your record's bad, but it's doubtful they'll give you the bullet*.
2 Printing a small symbol used to introduce each item in a list, for emphasis.
– ORIGIN early 16th cent. (denoting a cannonball): from French *boulet*, *boulette* 'small ball', diminutive of *boule*, from Latin *bulla* 'bubble'.

bulleted ▸ **adjective** (of items in a list) preceded by a printed bullet or bullet point.

bullet-headed ▸ **adjective** derogatory having a small, round head.
– DERIVATIVES **bullet head** noun.

bulletin ▸ **noun** a short official statement or broadcast summary of news. ■ a regular newsletter or report issued by an organization.
– ORIGIN mid 17th cent. (denoting an official warrant in some European countries): from French, from Italian *bullettino*, diminutive of *bulletta* 'passport', diminutive of *bulla* 'seal, bull'.

bulletin board ▸ **noun** N. Amer. a noticeboard. ■ an Internet site where users can post comments about a particular issue or topic and reply to other users' postings.

bullet point ▸ **noun** each of several items in a list, preceded by a printed bullet for emphasis. ■ a printed bullet.

bulletproof ▸ **adjective** designed to resist the penetration of bullets: *a bulletproof vest*.

bullet train ▸ **noun** informal a Japanese high-speed passenger train.

bull fiddle ▸ **noun** informal, chiefly US a double bass.

bullfight ▸ **noun** a public spectacle, especially in Spain, at which a bull is baited and killed.
– DERIVATIVES **bullfighter** noun.

bullfighting ▸ **noun** [mass noun] the sport of baiting and killing a bull as a public spectacle in an outdoor arena.

> Bullfighting is the national spectator sport of Spain, and is found also in Latin America. Typically, the bull is tormented by mounted picadors with lances and banderilleros who stick darts into its neck; the matador then baits it with a red cape and attempts to kill it with a sword thrust beneath the shoulder blade.

bullfinch ▸ **noun 1** a stocky Eurasian finch with a short, thick bill, typically having grey or pinkish plumage, dark wings, and a white rump. ● Genus *Pyrrhula*, family Fringillidae: several species, in particular the common *P. pyrrhula*, the male of which has a pink breast.
2 a Caribbean songbird of the bunting family, resembling the Old World bullfinch. ● Genera *Loxigilla* and *Melopyrrha*, family Emberizidae (subfamily Emberizinae): four species.

bullfrog ▸ **noun** a very large frog which has a deep booming croak and is often a predator of smaller vertebrates. ● Genera *Rana* and *Pyxicephalus*, family Ranidae: the **North American bullfrog** (*R. catesbiana*), the **Asian bullfrog** (*R. tigrina*), and the **African bullfrog** (*P. adspersus*).

bullhead ▸ **noun 1** a small mainly freshwater Eurasian fish of the sculpin family, with a broad flattened head and spiny fins. ● Genera *Cottus* and *Taurulus*, family Cottidae: three species.
2 (also **bullhead catfish**) an American freshwater catfish. ● Genus *Ictalurus*, family Ictaluridae: several species.

bullheaded ▸ **adjective** determined in an obstinate and unthinking way: *a bullheaded belief that she is right*.
– DERIVATIVES **bullheadedly** adverb, **bullheadedness** noun.

bullhorn ▸ **noun** N. Amer. a megaphone.

bull huss ▸ **noun** see **HUSS**.

bullion ▸ **noun** [mass noun] **1** gold or silver in bulk before coining, or valued by weight.
2 ornamental braid or fringing made with twists of gold or silver thread.
– ORIGIN Middle English: from Anglo-Norman French, in the sense 'a mint', variant of Old French *bouillon*, based on Latin *bullire* 'to boil'.

bullion knot ▸ **noun** a decorative stitch in embroidery made by winding the thread several times round the needle before sewing a backstitch.

bullish ▸ **adjective 1** aggressively confident and self-assertive.
2 Stock Exchange characterized by rising share prices: *the market was bullish*. ■ (of a dealer) inclined to buy because of an anticipated rise in prices. ■ confident or optimistic about something: *we are very bullish about our prospects*.
– DERIVATIVES **bullishly** adverb, **bullishness** noun.

bull kelp ▸ **noun** [mass noun] a very large brown seaweed found in Pacific and Antarctic waters, growing up to 50 m in length off the north-western coasts of North America. ● *Nereocystis* and other genera, class Phaeophyceae.

bull market ▸ **noun** Stock Exchange a market in which share prices are rising, encouraging buying.

bull mastiff ▸ **noun** a dog that is a cross-breed of bulldog and mastiff.

bull-necked ▸ **adjective** (of a man) having a thick, strong neck: *a beefy, bull-necked cop*.
– DERIVATIVES **bull neck** noun.

bull-nosed ▸ **adjective** having a rounded edge or end: *a bull-nosed chisel*.
– DERIVATIVES **bull nose** noun.

bullock ▸ **noun** a male domestic bovine animal that has been castrated and is raised for beef.
▸ **verb** [no obj.] Austral./NZ informal work long and hard: *people have dropped dead bullocking their guts out*.
– ORIGIN late Old English *bulluc*, diminutive of *bula* (see **BULL**[1]). The verb (late 19th cent.) is by association with a bullock's use as a draught animal.

bullock's heart ▸ **noun** the edible fruit of a tropical American custard apple. ● The tree is *Annona reticulata*, family Annonaceae.

bullocky ▸ **noun** (pl. **bullockies**) Austral./NZ informal, historical a bullock driver.

bullous /ˈbʊləs/ ▸ **adjective** Medicine characterized by blisters or bullae on the skin.

bullpen ▸ **noun** chiefly N. Amer. an enclosure for bulls. ■ an exercise area for baseball pitchers. ■ an open-plan office area. ■ a large cell in which prisoners are held before a court hearing.

bullring ▸ **noun** an arena where bullfights are held.

bullroarer ▸ **noun** Austral. a sacred object used in Aboriginal religious ceremonies, consisting of a piece of wood attached to a string, whirled round to produce a roaring noise.

Bull Run a small river in eastern Virginia, scene of two Confederate victories, in 1861 and 1862, during the American Civil War.

bullrush ▸ **noun** variant spelling of **BULRUSH**.

bull session ▸ **noun** N. Amer. an informal group discussion.
– ORIGIN 1920s: *bull* from **BULL**[3].

bullseye ▸ **noun 1** the centre of the target in sports such as archery, shooting, and darts. ■ a shot that hits the centre of such a target. ■ used to refer to something that achieves exactly the intended effect: *the silence told him he'd **scored a bullseye***.
2 a large, hard round peppermint sweet.
3 dated a thick disc of glass forming a small window in a ship or the glass of a lamp: [as modifier] *a bullseye lantern*. ■ a thick knob of glass at the centre of a blown glass sheet.

bullshit vulgar slang ▸ **noun** [mass noun] stupid or untrue talk or writing; nonsense.
▸ **verb** (**bullshits**, **bullshitting**, **bullshitted**) [with obj.] talk nonsense to (someone) in an attempt to deceive them.
– DERIVATIVES **bullshitter** noun.
– ORIGIN early 20th cent.: from **BULL**[3] + **SHIT**.

bullshot ▸ **noun** a cocktail made with vodka, beef bouillon, and Worcester sauce.

bull snake ▸ **noun** a gopher snake of a race found on the plains and prairies of North America. ● *Pituophis catenifer sayi*, family Colubridae.

bull terrier ▸ **noun** a short-haired dog of a breed that is a cross between a bulldog and a terrier.

bull trout ▸ **noun** a North American trout that resembles the Dolly Varden, found in cold rivers and lakes. ● *Salvelinus confluentus*, family Salmonidae. ■ Brit. a sea trout.

bullwhip N. Amer. ▸ **noun** a whip with a long heavy lash.
▸ **verb** (**bullwhips**, **bullwhipping**, **bullwhipped**) [with obj.] strike or thrash with a bullwhip.

bully[1] ▸ **noun** (pl. **bullies**) a person who uses strength or influence to harm or intimidate those who are weaker.
▸ **verb** (**bullies**, **bullying**, **bullied**) [with obj.] use superior strength or influence to intimidate (someone), typically to force them to do something: *a local man was bullied into helping them*.
– ORIGIN mid 16th cent.: probably from Middle Dutch *boele* 'lover'. Original use was as a term of endearment applied to either sex; it later became a familiar form of address to a male friend. The current sense dates from the late 17th cent.

bully[2] ▸ **adjective** informal, chiefly N. Amer. very good; excellent: *the statue really looked bully*.
– PHRASES **bully for you!** (or **him** etc.) often ironic used to express admiration or approval: *he got away—bully for him!*
– ORIGIN late 16th cent. (originally used of a person, meaning 'admirable, gallant, jolly'): from **BULLY**[1]. The current sense dates from the mid 19th cent.

bully[3] ▸ **noun** (pl. **bullies**) (also **bully off**) the start of play in field hockey, in which two opponents strike each other's sticks three times and then go for the ball.
▸ **verb** (**bullies**, **bullying**, **bullied**) [no obj.] start play in this way.
– ORIGIN late 19th cent. (originally denoting a scrum in Eton football): of unknown origin.

bully[4] (also **bully beef**) ▸ **noun** [mass noun] informal corned beef.
– ORIGIN mid 18th cent.: alteration of **BOUILLI**.

B

bully boy ▸ noun a tough, aggressive man: [as modifier] *bully-boy tactics.*

bully pulpit ▸ noun N. Amer. a public office or position of authority that provides its occupant with an opportunity to speak out on any issue: *he could use the presidency as a bully pulpit to bring out the best in civic life.*
– ORIGIN early 20th cent.: apparently originally used by President Theodore Roosevelt, explaining his personal view of the presidency.

bullyrag (also **ballyrag**) ▸ verb (**bullyrags, bullyragging, bullyragged**) [with obj.] N. Amer. informal treat (someone) in a scolding or intimidating way: *he would **bullyrag** them **around** but lick up to his superiors.*
– ORIGIN late 18th cent.: of unknown origin.

bulrush (also **bullrush**) ▸ noun **1** a tall reed-like water plant with strap-like leaves and a dark brown velvety cylindrical head of numerous tiny flowers. Also called REED MACE. ● Genus *Typha*, family Typhaceae: several species, in particular *T. latifolia.*
2 another term for CLUBRUSH.
3 (in biblical use) a papyrus plant.
– ORIGIN late Middle English: probably from BULL[1] in the sense 'large or coarse', as in words such as *bullfrog.*

bulwark /ˈbʊlwək/ ▸ noun **1** a defensive wall. ■ a person or thing that acts as a defence: *the security forces are a **bulwark against** the breakdown of society.*
2 (usu. **bulwarks**) an extension of a ship's sides above the level of the deck.
– ORIGIN late Middle English: from Middle Low German and Middle Dutch *bolwerk*; related to BOLE[1] and WORK.

Bulwer-Lytton /ˌbʊlwə ˈlɪt(ə)n/ see LYTTON.

bum[1] ▸ noun Brit. informal a person's buttocks or anus.
– PHRASES **bums on seats** the audience at a theatre, cinema, or other entertainment, viewed as a source of income.
– ORIGIN late Middle English: of unknown origin.

bum[2] informal ▸ noun N. Amer. **1** a vagrant. ■ a lazy or worthless person: *you ungrateful bum!*
2 [in combination] a person who devotes a great deal of time to a specified activity: *a ski bum.*
▸ verb (**bums, bumming, bummed**) **1** [no obj.] (usu. **bum around**) travel with no particular purpose: *he bummed around Florida for a few months.* ■ pass one's time idly: *students bumming around at university.*
2 [with obj.] get by asking or begging: *they tried to bum quarters off us.*
3 [with obj.] (usu. **be bummed out**) N. Amer. make (someone) feel upset or disappointed.
▸ adjective [attrib.] of poor quality; bad or wrong: *not one bum note was played.*
– PHRASES **give someone** (or **get**) **the bum's rush** chiefly N. Amer. forcibly eject someone (or be forcibly ejected) from a place or gathering. ■ abruptly dismiss someone (or be abruptly dismissed) for a poor idea or performance. **on the bum** N. Amer. travelling rough and with no fixed home; vagrant.
– ORIGIN mid 19th cent.: probably from BUMMER.

bumbag ▸ noun Brit. informal a small pouch on a belt, for money and other valuables, worn round the waist or hips.

bum-bailiff ▸ noun historical, derogatory a bailiff empowered to collect debts or arrest debtors for non-payment.
– ORIGIN early 17th cent.: from BUM[1], so named because of the association of an approach from behind.

bumbershoot /ˈbʌmbəʃuːt/ ▸ noun US Informal an umbrella.
– ORIGIN late 19th cent.: alteration of UMBRELLA + PARACHUTE.

bumble ▸ verb **1** [no obj., with adverbial of direction] move or act in an awkward or confused manner: *they bumbled around the house.*
2 [no obj.] speak in a confused or indistinct way. ■ [with adverbial] (of an insect) buzz or hum.
– DERIVATIVES **bumbler** noun.
– ORIGIN late Middle English (in the sense 'hum, drone'): from BOOM[1] + -LE[4].

bumblebee ▸ noun a large hairy social bee which flies with a loud hum, living in small colonies in holes underground. Also called HUMBLE-BEE. ● Genus *Bombus*, family Apidae: many species.

bumbling ▸ adjective acting in a confused or ineffectual way; incompetent: *he's a bumbling fool.*

bumboat ▸ noun a small vessel carrying provisions for sale to moored or anchored ships.
– ORIGIN late 17th cent.: from BUM[1] + BOAT. The term originally denoted a scavenger's boat removing ships' refuse, often also bringing produce for sale.

bumboy ▸ noun vulgar slang a young male homosexual, especially a prostitute.

bumf (also **bumph**) ▸ noun [mass noun] Brit. informal useless or tedious printed material. ■ dated toilet paper.
– ORIGIN late 19th cent.: abbreviation of slang *bum-fodder*, in the same sense.

bumfluff ▸ noun [mass noun] Brit. informal, derogatory the first beard growth of an adolescent.

bumiputra /ˌbuːmɪˈpuːtrə/ ▸ noun (pl. **same** or **bumiputras**) a Malaysian of indigenous Malay origin.
– ORIGIN Malay, literally 'son of the soil'.

bummalo /ˈbʌmələʊ/ ▸ noun (pl. **same**) a small elongated fish of southern Asian coasts which is dried and used as food. Also called BOMBAY DUCK. ● *Harpodon nehereus*, family Harpadontidae.
– ORIGIN late 17th cent.: perhaps from Marathi *bombīl.*

bummaree /ˌbʌməˈriː/ ▸ noun a self-employed licensed porter at Smithfield meat market in London.
– ORIGIN late 18th cent.: of unknown origin.

bummer ▸ noun informal **1** (**a bummer**) a disappointing or unpleasant situation or experience: *the team's relegation is a real bummer.*
2 N. Amer. a loafer or vagrant.
– ORIGIN mid 19th cent.: perhaps from German *Bummler*, from *bummeln* 'stroll, loaf about'.

bump ▸ noun **1** a light blow or a jolting collision: *a nasty bump on the head.* ■ (**the bumps**) Brit. informal (on a person's birthday) a custom by which the person is lifted by the arms and legs and let down on to the ground, once for each year of their age. ■ Rowing (in races where boats make a spaced start one behind another) the point at which a boat begins to overtake or touch the boat ahead, thereby defeating it. ■ Aeronautics a rising air current causing an irregularity in an aircraft's motion.
2 a protuberance on a level surface: *bumps in the road.* ■ a swelling on the skin, especially one caused by illness or injury. ■ dated a lump on a person's skull, formerly thought to indicate a particular mental faculty.
3 informal, chiefly US an increase: *there was a bump in the number of outbound flights.*
4 [mass noun] a loosely woven fleeced cotton fabric used in upholstery and as lining material.
▸ verb **1** [no obj.] knock or run into someone or something with a jolt: *I almost **bumped into** him* | [with obj.] *she bumped the girl with her hip.* ■ (**bump into**) meet by chance: *we might just bump into each other.* ■ [with obj.] hurt or damage (something) by striking it on something else: *she **bumped** her head **on** the sink.* ■ [with obj.] Rowing (in a race) gain a bump against.
2 [no obj., with adverbial of direction] move or travel with much jolting: *the car **bumped along** the rutted track.* ■ [with obj. and adverbial of direction] push (something) jerkily in a specified direction: *she had to bump the pushchair down the steps.*
3 [with obj.] refuse (a passenger) a reserved place on a flight because of deliberate overbooking by the airline. ■ N. Amer. displace from a job, especially in favour of someone else: *she was bumped for a youthful model.*
– PHRASES **a bump in the road** informal a problem or setback: *their relationship has hit another **bump in the road.*** **with a bump** suddenly and shockingly: *the scandal brought them **down to earth with a bump.***
– PHRASAL VERBS **bump someone off** informal murder someone. **bump something up** informal increase something: *the hotel may well bump up the bill.*
– ORIGIN mid 16th cent. (as a verb): imitative, perhaps of Scandinavian origin.

bumper ▸ noun **1** a horizontal bar fixed across the front or back of a motor vehicle to reduce damage in a collision.
2 Cricket, dated another term for BOUNCER (sense 2).
3 (also **bumper race**) Horse Racing a flat race for inexperienced horses which are intended for future racing in hurdles or steeplechases. [said to be from an earlier racing term *bumper* 'amateur rider'.]
4 archaic a generous glassful of an alcoholic drink, typically one drunk as a toast.
▸ adjective exceptionally large, fine, or successful: *a bumper crop.*
– PHRASES **bumper-to-bumper** very close together, as cars in a traffic jam. ■ (of an insurance policy) comprehensive; all-inclusive.

bumper car ▸ noun another term for DODGEM.

bumph ▸ noun variant spelling of BUMF.

bumpkin ▸ noun an unsophisticated or socially awkward person from the countryside: *she thought Tom a **bit of a country bumpkin.***
– DERIVATIVES **bumpkinish** adjective.
– ORIGIN late 16th cent.: perhaps from Dutch *boomken* 'little tree' or Middle Dutch *bommekijn* 'little barrel', used to denote a dumpy person.

bump-start ▸ noun & verb another term for PUSH-START.

bumptious ▸ adjective irritatingly self-assertive: *an impossibly bumptious and opinionated ass.*
– DERIVATIVES **bumptiously** adverb, **bumptiousness** noun.
– ORIGIN early 19th cent.: humorously from BUMP, on the pattern of *fractious.*

bumpy ▸ adjective (**bumpier, bumpiest**) (of a surface) uneven, with many patches raised above the rest: *the car jolted on the bumpy road.* ■ (of a journey or other movement) involving sudden jolts and jerks: *the bumpy flight brought on a bout of airsickness* | figurative *investors could be in for a bumpy ride.*
– DERIVATIVES **bumpily** adverb, **bumpiness** noun.

bum rap ▸ noun [in sing.] informal, chiefly N. Amer. a false charge, typically one leading to imprisonment. ■ an unfair judgement on someone or something: *the industry often gets a bum rap for being dishonest.*

bum-rush ▸ verb [with obj.] US informal suddenly force or barge one's way into: *fans bum-rushed record stores.*

bum steer ▸ noun N. Amer. informal a piece of false information or unhelpful guidance.
– ORIGIN 1920s: from BUM[2] + STEER[1] in the sense 'advice, guidance'.

bumsters ▸ plural noun trousers that are cut very low on the hips.

bum-sucking ▸ noun [mass noun] Brit. vulgar slang obsequious, servile behaviour.
– DERIVATIVES **bum-sucker** noun.

bun ▸ noun **1** a small cake, typically containing dried fruit. ■ a bread roll. ■ (in Scotland and Jamaica) a rich fruit cake or currant bread.
2 a hairstyle in which the hair is drawn back into a tight coil at the back of the head.
3 (**buns**) N. Amer. informal a person's buttocks.
– PHRASES **have a bun in the oven** informal be pregnant.
– ORIGIN late Middle English: of unknown origin.

Bunbury a seaport and resort to the south of Perth in Western Australia; pop. 32,841 (2008).

bunce ▸ noun [mass noun] Brit. informal money or profit gained by someone: *they can turn their hand to many jobs as long as there's a bit of bunce in it.*
– ORIGIN early 18th cent.: of unknown origin.

bunch ▸ noun **1** a number of things, typically of the same kind, growing or fastened together: ***a bunch of** grapes.* ■ informal a group of people. ■ informal, chiefly N. Amer. a large number or quantity; a lot: *the bluesy style that earned him **a bunch of** '70s hits.*
2 (**bunches**) Brit. a girl's hairstyle in which the hair is tied back into two clumps at the back or on either side of the head.
▸ verb [with obj.] collect or fasten into a compact group: *she bunched the needles together.* ■ form or cause to form tight folds: [no obj.] *the bedclothes had **bunched up** around his waist.* ■ [no obj.] form into a tight group or crowd: *he halted, forcing the rest of the field to **bunch up** behind him.* ■ [no obj.] (of muscles) flex or bulge.
– PHRASES **the best** (or **the pick**) **of the bunch** informal the best in a particular group. **bunch of fives** Brit. informal a fist or punch. **thanks a bunch** ironic, chiefly Brit. thank you very much.
– DERIVATIVES **bunchy** adjective (**bunchier, bunchiest**).
– ORIGIN late Middle English: of unknown origin.

bunchberry ▸ noun (pl. **bunchberries**) a low-growing plant of the dogwood family, which produces white flowers followed by red berries and bright red autumn foliage. It is native to North America, eastern Asia, and Greenland. ● *Cornus canadensis*, family Cornaceae.

bunchflower ▸ noun a North American plant of the lily family, with yellowish-green flowers. ● *Melanthium virginicum*, family Liliaceae.

bunch grass ▸ noun [mass noun] N. Amer. a grass that grows in clumps. ● *Schizachyrium* and other genera, family Gramineae: several species, especially *S. scoparium*, used for grazing and in erosion control, especially on the Great Plains.

bunco N. Amer. informal ▸ noun (pl. **buncos**) [usu. as modifier] a swindle or confidence trick: *a bunco artist*.
▸ verb (**buncoes**, **buncoing**, **buncoed**) [with obj.] dated swindle or cheat.
– ORIGIN late 19th cent.: perhaps from Spanish *banca*, the name of a card game.

buncombe ▸ noun variant spelling of **BUNKUM**.

bund ▸ noun an embankment or causeway. ■ a wall surrounding an industrial fuel tank.
– ORIGIN early 19th cent.: via Urdu from Persian.

Bundesbank /'bʊndəsˌbaŋk/ the central bank of Germany, established in 1875. Its headquarters are in Frankfurt.
– ORIGIN German, from *Bund* 'federation' + *Bank* 'bank'.

Bundesrat /'bʊndəzˌrɑːt/ the upper house of Parliament in Germany or Austria.
– ORIGIN German, from *Bund* 'federation' + *Rat* 'council'.

Bundestag /'bʊndəzˌtɑːg/ the lower house of Parliament in Germany.
– ORIGIN German, from *Bund* 'federation' + *tagen* 'confer'.

bundle ▸ noun a collection of things or quantity of material tied or wrapped up together: *a thick **bundle** of envelopes*. ■ a set of nerve, muscle, or other fibres running in parallel close together. ■ a set of software or hardware sold together. ■ (**a bundle**) informal a large amount of money: *the new printer cost a bundle*.
▸ verb **1** [with obj.] tie or roll up (a number of things) together as though into a parcel: *she quickly **bundled** up her clothes*. ■ (usu. **be bundled up**) dress (someone) in many warm clothes: *they were bundled up in thick sweaters*. ■ sell (items of hardware and software) as a package.
2 [with obj. and adverbial of direction] informal push, carry, or send forcibly, hastily, or unceremoniously: *he was bundled into a van*. ■ [no obj., with adverbial of direction] (of a group of people) move in a disorganized way: *they bundled out into the corridor*.
3 [no obj.] (usu. as noun **bundling**) sleep fully clothed with another person, as a former local custom during courtship.
– PHRASES **a bundle of fun** (or **laughs**) informal, often ironic an extremely amusing or entertaining person or thing: *you're a bundle of laughs this evening*. **a bundle of joy** informal a baby: *enjoy your little bundle of joy now because he is going to grow up fast*. **a bundle of nerves** see **A BAG OF NERVES** at **BAG**. **drop one's bundle** Austral./NZ informal panic; lose one's self-control. [from obsolete *bundle* 'swag'.] **go a bundle on** [usu. with negative] Brit. informal be very keen on: *I don't go a bundle on seeing a man and woman snogging*.
– DERIVATIVES **bundler** noun.
– ORIGIN Middle English: perhaps originally from Old English *byndelle* 'a binding', reinforced by Low German and Dutch *bundel* (to which *byndelle* is related).

bundobust /'bʌndəbʌst/ (also **bandobast** /'bandəbʌst, 'bʌndəbast/) ▸ noun [mass noun] Indian arrangements or organization: *why all these big crowds and strict police bundobust, he wondered*.
– ORIGIN Urdu, from Persian *band-o-bast* 'tying and binding'.

bundu /'bʊnduː/ ▸ noun (**the bundu**) (in South Africa and Zimbabwe) the wilds; a distant or wilderness region.
– ORIGIN probably from Shona *bundo* 'grasslands'.

bunfight ▸ noun Brit. informal, humorous **1** a tea party or other function, typically of a grand or official kind.
2 a heated argument or exchange.

bun foot ▸ noun (pl. **bun feet**) a foot in the shape of a flattened sphere, used for chairs, tables, or other furniture in the late 17th century.

bung[1] ▸ noun a stopper for closing a hole in a container.
▸ verb [with obj.] close with a stopper. ■ (**bung something up**) block something: *you let vegetable peelings bung the sink up*.
– ORIGIN late Middle English: from Middle Dutch *bonghe* (noun).

bung[2] Brit. informal ▸ verb [with obj. and adverbial of direction] put or throw (something) somewhere in a careless or casual way: *fill out the reply-paid card and bung it in the post*.
▸ noun a bribe.
– ORIGIN early 19th cent.: symbolic; the noun sense dates from the 1950s.

bung[3] Austral./NZ informal ▸ adjective **1** broken down, ruined, or useless.
2 dated dead.
– PHRASES **go bung 1** break down; fail or go bankrupt. **2** die.
– ORIGIN mid 19th cent. (originally Australian pidgin): from Yagara (an extinct Aboriginal language).

bungalow /'bʌŋgələʊ/ ▸ noun a low house having only one storey or, in some cases, upper rooms set in the roof, typically with dormer windows. ■ (in SE Asia) a large detached house with more than one storey.
– ORIGIN late 17th cent.: from Hindi *baṅglā* 'belonging to Bengal', from a type of cottage built for early European settlers in Bengal.

bungarotoxin /ˌbʌŋgərə(ʊ)'tɒksɪn/ ▸ noun [mass noun] Biochemistry a compound found in the venom of the krait (snake) which is a powerful neurotoxin.
– ORIGIN 1960s: from the modern Latin genus name *Bungarus* (perhaps from Sanskrit *bhaṅgura* 'bent') + **TOXIN**.

bungee /'bʌndʒi/ ▸ noun (also **bungee cord** or **bungee rope**) a long nylon-cased rubber band used for securing luggage and in the sport of bungee jumping.
▸ verb [no obj.] perform a bungee jump.
– ORIGIN 1930s (denoting an elasticated cord for launching a glider): of unknown origin.

bungee jumping ▸ noun [mass noun] the sport of leaping from a bridge, crane, or other high place while secured by a long nylon-cased rubber band around the ankles.
– DERIVATIVES **bungee jump** noun, **bungee jumper** noun.

bunghole ▸ noun an aperture through which a cask can be filled or emptied.

bungle ▸ verb [with obj.] carry out (a task) clumsily or incompetently: *she had bungled every attempt to help* | (as adj. **bungled**) *a bungled bank raid*. ■ [no obj.] (usu. as adj. **bungling**) make or be prone to making many mistakes: *the work of a bungling amateur*.
▸ noun a mistake or badly carried out action: *a government bungle over state pensions*.
– ORIGIN mid 16th cent.: of unknown origin; compare with **BUMBLE**.

bungler ▸ noun a person who habitually bungles things; an amateur: *the government is evidently a bunch of bunglers*.

bunion /'bʌnj(ə)n/ ▸ noun a painful swelling on the first joint of the big toe.
– ORIGIN early 18th cent.: ultimately from Old French *buignon*, from *buigne* 'bump on the head'.

bunk[1] ▸ noun a narrow shelf-like bed, typically one of two or more arranged one on top of the other.
▸ verb [no obj.] chiefly N. Amer. sleep in a bunk or improvised bed, typically in shared quarters: *they bunk together in the dormitory*.
– ORIGIN mid 18th cent.: of unknown origin; perhaps related to **BUNKER**.

bunk[2] ▸ verb [no obj.] (**bunk off**) Brit. informal abscond or play truant from school or work.
– PHRASES **do a bunk** informal make a hurried or furtive departure or escape.
– ORIGIN mid 19th cent.: of unknown origin.

bunk[3] ▸ noun [mass noun] informal nonsense: *anyone with a brain cell would never believe such bunk*.
– ORIGIN early 20th cent.: abbreviation of **BUNKUM**.

bunk bed ▸ noun a piece of furniture consisting of two beds, one above the other, that form a unit.

bunker ▸ noun **1** a large container or compartment for storing fuel: *a coal bunker*.
2 a reinforced underground shelter, typically for use in wartime.
3 a hollow filled with sand, used as an obstacle on a golf course.
▸ verb [with obj.] **1** fill the fuel containers of (a ship); refuel.
2 (**be bunkered**) Golf (of a player) have one's ball lodged in a bunker: *he was bunkered at the fifth hole*. ■ hit (the ball) into a bunker: *he bunkered his second shot*. ■ Brit. informal cause difficulties to; hinder the progress of: *he may find his new sporting pursuits bunkered by activities he hadn't planned on*.
3 [with obj.] take refuge in a bunker or other shelter: *his family had **bunkered down** inside their home* | *the former Governor has spent four days **bunkered down** at Government House*.
– ORIGIN mid 16th cent. (originally Scots, denoting a seat or bench): perhaps related to **BUNK**[1].

Bunker Hill the first pitched battle (1775) of the War of American Independence (actually fought on Breed's Hill near Boston, Massachusetts). Although the British won, the good performance of the untrained Americans gave considerable impetus to the Revolution.

B

bunkhouse ▸ noun a building offering basic sleeping accommodation for workers.

bunkum (also **buncombe**) ▸ noun [mass noun] informal, dated nonsense: *they talk a lot of bunkum about their products*.
– ORIGIN mid 19th cent. (originally *buncombe*): named after *Buncombe* County in North Carolina, mentioned in an inconsequential speech made by its congressman solely to please his constituents (*c.*1820).

bunk-up ▸ noun informal a helping push or pull up.

bunny ▸ noun (pl. **bunnies**) informal **1** a child's term for a rabbit. ■ (also **bunny girl**) a club hostess or waitress wearing a skimpy costume with ears and a tail suggestive of a rabbit. ■ [with adj.] a person of a specified type or in a specified mood: *Alex had missed his plane—he was **not a happy bunny***.
2 Austral. a victim or dupe.
– ORIGIN early 17th cent. (originally used as a term of endearment to a person, later as a pet name for a rabbit): from dialect *bun* 'squirrel, rabbit', also used as a term of endearment, of unknown origin. Sense 2 dates from the early 20th cent.

bunny boiler ▸ noun informal a woman who acts vengefully after having been spurned by her lover.
– ORIGIN with reference to the film *Fatal Attraction* (1987), in which a rejected woman boils her lover's pet rabbit.

bunny chow ▸ noun (in South Africa) a takeaway food consisting of a hollowed-out half loaf of bread filled with vegetable or meat curry.
– ORIGIN probably from Hindi *banyā*, from Gujerati *vaniya*, denoting one of a Hindu caste of merchants, + **CHOW** in the sense 'food'.

bunny-hop ▸ verb [no obj.] jump forward in a crouched position: *he bunny-hopped around the stage*. ■ [with obj.] move (a vehicle) forward jerkily.
▸ noun a jump in a crouched position. ■ a short jump or jerky forward movement made on a bicycle or by a vehicle.

bunny hugger ▸ noun informal, derogatory an animal lover; a conservationist.

bunny slope ▸ noun US term for **NURSERY SLOPE**.

Bunsen /'bʌns(ə)n/, German /'bʊnzn/, Robert Wilhelm Eberhard (1811–99), German chemist. With Gustav Kirchhoff he pioneered spectroscopy, detecting new elements (caesium and rubidium) and determining the composition of many substances and of the sun and stars. He designed numerous items of chemical apparatus, notably the Bunsen burner (1855).

Bunsen burner ▸ noun a small adjustable gas burner used in laboratories as a source of heat.

bunt[1] /bʌnt/ ▸ verb [with obj.] **1** Baseball (of a batter) gently tap (a pitched ball) without swinging in an attempt to make it more difficult to field: *he tried to bunt the ball down the first baseline* | [no obj.] *Phil bunted and got to first*. ■ (of a batter) help (a base runner) to progress to a further base by tapping a ball in such a way: *he bunted Davis to third*.
2 push or butt: *Gary bunted her with his head*.
▸ noun **1** Baseball an act or result of bunting a pitched ball.
2 an act of flying an aircraft in part of an outside loop.
– ORIGIN mid 18th cent.: probably related to the noun **BUTT**[1] (the original sense).

bunt[2] /bʌnt/ (also **wheat bunt**) ▸ noun [mass noun] a disease of wheat caused by a smut fungus, the spores of which give off a smell of rotten fish. Also called **STINKING SMUT**. ● The fungus is *Tilletia caries*, class Teliomycetes.
– ORIGIN early 17th cent. (denoting the puffball fungus): of unknown origin.

bunt[3] /bʌnt/ ▸ noun the baggy centre of a fishing net or a sail.
– ORIGIN late 16th cent.: of unknown origin.

buntal /'bʌnt(ə)l/ ▸ noun [mass noun] [often as modifier] the straw from a talipot palm used for making hats: *a buntal hat*.
– ORIGIN early 20th cent.: from Tagalog.

Bunter /'bʌntə/, Billy, a schoolboy character, noted for his fatness and gluttony, in stories by Frank Richards (pseudonym of Charles Hamilton, 1876–1961).

B

Bunting, Basil (1900–85), English poet and journalist. He was influenced by modernists including Ezra Pound and T. S. Eliot. He published his early work abroad, not really gaining recognition until *Briggflatts* (1966).

bunting[1] ▶ noun 1 an Old World seed-eating songbird related to the finches, typically having brown streaked plumage and a boldly marked head. ● Family Emberizidae, subfamily Emberizinae (the **bunting family** and **subfamily**): several genera, in particular *Emberiza*, and numerous species.
2 a small New World songbird of the cardinal subfamily, the male of which is mainly or partly bright blue in colour. ● Family Emberizidae, subfamily Cardinalinae: genera *Passerina* and *Cyanocompsa*, and several species.
– ORIGIN Middle English: of unknown origin.

bunting[2] ▶ noun [mass noun] flags and other colourful festive decorations. ■ a loosely woven fabric used for such decoration.
– ORIGIN early 18th cent.: of unknown origin.

bunting[3] (also **bunting bag**) ▶ noun N. Amer. a hooded sleeping bag for babies.
– ORIGIN 1920s: origin uncertain; perhaps from BUNTING[2].

buntline /ˈbʌntlʌɪn/ ▶ noun a line for restraining the loose centre of a sail while it is furled.

Buñuel /buːˈnwɛl/, Spanish /buˈɲwel/, Luis (1900–83), Spanish film director. Influenced by surrealism, he wrote and directed his first film, *Un Chien andalou* (1928), jointly with Salvador Dalí. Other notable films: *Belle de jour* (1967) and *The Discreet Charm of the Bourgeoisie* (1972).

bunya /ˈbʌnjə/ (also **bunya pine** or **bunya bunya** /ˈbʌnjəˌbʌnjə/) ▶ noun a tall coniferous Australian tree related to the monkey puzzle, bearing large cones containing edible seeds. ● *Araucaria bidwillii*, family Araucariaceae.
– ORIGIN mid 19th cent.: from Wiradhuri.

Bunyan /ˈbʌnjən/, John (1628–88), English writer. A Nonconformist, he was imprisoned twice for unlicensed preaching, during which time he wrote his spiritual autobiography *Grace Abounding* (1666) and began his major work *The Pilgrim's Progress* (1678–84).

bunyip /ˈbʌnjɪp/ ▶ noun Austral. 1 a mythical amphibious monster said to inhabit inland waterways.
2 [usu. as modifier] an impostor or pretender: *Australia's bunyip aristocracy*.
– ORIGIN from an Aboriginal word.

Buonaparte /bwɔnaˈparte/ Italian spelling of BONAPARTE.

Buonarroti /ˌbwɒnəˈrɒti/, Michelangelo, see MICHELANGELO.

buoy /bɔɪ/ ▶ noun an anchored float serving as a navigation mark, to show reefs or other hazards, or for mooring.
▶ verb [with obj.] 1 (often **be buoyed up**) keep (someone or something) afloat: *the creatures could swim, both buoyed up and cooled by the water*. ■ make (someone) cheerful and confident: *she was buoyed up by his praise*. ■ cause (a price) to rise to or remain at a high level: *shares were up 4p, buoyed by his cut-and-thrust management style*.
2 (usu. as adj. **buoyed**) mark with an anchored float: *a buoyed channel*.
– DERIVATIVES **buoyage** noun.
– ORIGIN Middle English: probably from Middle Dutch *boye, boeie*, from a Germanic base meaning 'signal'. The verb is from Spanish *boyar* 'to float', from *boya* 'buoy'.

buoyancy ▶ noun [mass noun] 1 the ability or tendency of something to float in water or other fluid. ■ the power of a liquid to keep something afloat.
2 a cheerful and optimistic attitude or disposition.
3 a high level of activity in an economy or stock market: *there is renewed buoyancy in the demand for steel*.

buoyancy aid ▶ noun a sleeveless jacket lined with buoyant material, worn for water sports.

buoyant ▶ adjective 1 able or tending to keep afloat or rise to the top of a liquid or gas. ■ (of a liquid or gas) able to keep something afloat.
2 cheerful and optimistic: *the conference ended with the party in a buoyant mood*.
3 (of an economy, business, or market) involving or engaged in much successful trade or activity: *car sales were buoyant*.
– DERIVATIVES **buoyantly** adverb.
– ORIGIN late 16th cent.: from French *bouyant* or Spanish *boyante*, present participle of *boyar* 'to float' (see BUOY).

BUPA /ˈbuːpə/ ▶ abbreviation (in the UK) British United Provident Association, a private health insurance organization.

bupkis /ˈbʌpkɪs/ ▶ noun [mass noun] US informal nothing at all: *you know bupkis about fundraising*.
– ORIGIN from Yiddish.

buppie ▶ noun (pl. **buppies**) informal a young urban black professional; a black yuppie.

bupropion /bjuːˈprəʊpɪən/ ▶ noun [mass noun] an antidepressant drug which is also given to relieve the symptoms of nicotine withdrawal. Also called ZYBAN (trademark). ● Chem. formula: $C_{13}H_{18}ClNO$.
– ORIGIN 1970s: from BUTANE + *propion* (see PROPIONIC ACID) + *-n* (perhaps from -ONE).

BUR ▶ abbreviation Burma (international vehicle registration).

bur ▶ noun see BURR (sense 2 of the noun, sense 3 of the noun, sense 5 of the noun, sense 6 of the noun).

burb ▶ noun (usu. **the burbs**) N. Amer. informal short for SUBURB: *the leafy burbs of Connecticut*.

Burbage /ˈbəːbɪdʒ/, Richard (c.1567–1619), English actor. He was the creator of most of Shakespeare's great tragic roles — Hamlet, Othello, Lear, and Richard III — and was also associated with the building of the Globe Theatre.

Burbank /ˈbəːbaŋk/ a city in southern California, on the north side of the Los Angeles conurbation; pop. 102,968 (est. 2008). It is a centre of the film and television industries.

Burberry /ˈbəːb(ə)ri/ ▶ noun (pl. **Burberries**) trademark a kind of lightweight belted raincoat, typically beige in colour, with a distinctive tartan lining.
– ORIGIN early 20th cent.: from *Burberrys Ltd*, the name of the manufacturer.

burble ▶ verb 1 [no obj.] make a continuous murmuring noise: *a stream burbled through the woods*. ■ speak continuously and at length in an unintelligible or confused way: *he* **burbled on** *about annuities* | [with obj.] *he was burbling inanities*.
2 (often as noun **burbling**) Aeronautics (of an airflow) break up into turbulence.
▶ noun [mass noun] continuous murmuring noise: *the steady burble of running water*. ■ rambling speech: *an hour of boring burble*.
– DERIVATIVES **burbler** noun.
– ORIGIN Middle English (in the sense 'to bubble'): imitative. Current senses date from the late 19th cent.

burbot /ˈbəːbət/ ▶ noun an elongated bottom-dwelling fish that is the only freshwater member of the cod family, occurring in Eurasia and North America but almost extinct in Britain. ● *Lota lota*, family Gadidae.
– ORIGIN Middle English: from Old French *borbete*, probably from *borbe* 'mud, slime'.

burden ▶ noun 1 a load, typically a heavy one. ■ a duty or misfortune that causes worry, hardship, or distress: [with modifier] *the tax burden on low-wage earners*. ■ the main responsibility for achieving a specified aim or task: *the burden of establishing that the authority had misused its powers rests upon the prosecution*. ■ a ship's carrying capacity; tonnage.
2 (**the burden**) the main theme or gist of a speech, book, or argument.
3 archaic the refrain or chorus of a song.
▶ verb [with obj.] load heavily. ■ cause (someone) worry, hardship, or distress: *they were not yet burdened with adult responsibility*.
– PHRASES **burden of proof** the obligation to prove one's assertion.
– ORIGIN Old English *byrthen*, of West Germanic origin; related to BEAR[1].

burdensome ▶ adjective difficult to carry out or fulfil; taxing: *the burdensome responsibilities of professional life*. ■ undesirably restrictive: *bureaucratically burdensome assessment procedures*.

burdock /ˈbəːdɒk/ ▶ noun a large herbaceous Old World plant of the daisy family. The hook-bearing flowers become woody burrs after fertilization and cling to animals' coats to aid seed dispersal. ● Genus *Arctium*, family Compositae: several species, including the large-leaved **great burdock** (*A. lappa*), which has edible roots and is used in herbal medicine.
– ORIGIN late 16th cent.: from BURR + DOCK[3].

bureau /ˈbjʊərəʊ/ ▶ noun (pl. **bureaux** or **bureaus**)
1 Brit. a writing desk with drawers and typically an angled top opening downwards to form a writing surface. ■ N. Amer. a chest of drawers.
2 an office or department for transacting particular business: *a news bureau* | *the London bureau of the Washington Post*. ■ a government department: *the intelligence bureau*.
– ORIGIN late 17th cent.: from French, originally 'baize' (cover used for writing desks), from Old French *burel*, probably from *bure* 'dark brown', based on Greek *purros* 'red'.

bureaucracy /ˌbjʊ(ə)ˈrɒkrəsi/ ▶ noun (pl. **bureaucracies**) [mass noun] 1 a system of government in which most of the important decisions are taken by state officials rather than by elected representatives. ■ [count noun] a state or organization governed or managed according to such a system. ■ [count noun] the officials in such a system, considered as a group or hierarchy.
2 excessively complicated administrative procedure: *the unnecessary bureaucracy in local government*.
– ORIGIN early 19th cent.: from French *bureaucratie*, from *bureau* (see BUREAU).

bureaucrat ▶ noun an official in a government department, in particular one perceived as being concerned with procedural correctness at the expense of people's needs.
– ORIGIN mid 19th cent.: from French *bureaucrate*, from *bureaucratie* (see BUREAUCRACY).

bureaucratic ▶ adjective relating to the business of running an organization, or government: *well-established bureaucratic procedures*. ■ overconcerned with procedure at the expense of efficiency or common sense: *the scheme is overly bureaucratic and complex*.
– DERIVATIVES **bureaucratically** adverb.

bureaucratize (also **bureaucratise**) ▶ verb [with obj.] (usu. as adj. **bureaucratized**) govern (a state or organization) by an excessively complicated administrative procedure: *impersonal and bureaucratized welfare systems*.
– DERIVATIVES **bureaucratization** noun.

bureau de change /ˌbjʊərəʊ də ˈʃɒ̃ʒ/, French /byʀo də ʃɑ̃ʒ/ ▶ noun (pl. **bureaux de change** pronunc. **same**) an establishment at which customers can exchange foreign money.
– ORIGIN 1950s: French, literally 'office of exchange'.

Bureau of State Security (abbrev.: **BOSS**) the former South African intelligence and security organization under apartheid.

burette /bjʊˈrɛt/ (US also **buret**) ▶ noun a graduated glass tube with a tap at one end, for delivering known volumes of a liquid, especially in titrations.
– ORIGIN mid 19th cent.: from French, from *buire* 'jug', of Germanic origin; related to German *Bauch* 'stomach'.

burfi /ˈbəːfiː/ (also **barfi**) ▶ noun [mass noun] an Indian sweet made from milk solids and sugar and typically flavoured with cardamom or nuts.
– ORIGIN Hindi, from Persian *barfī*, literally, 'icy, snowy', also denoting a kind of sweet decorated with silver leaf.

burg /bəːg/ ▶ noun 1 an ancient or medieval fortress or walled town.
2 N. Amer. informal a town or city.
– ORIGIN mid 18th cent.: from late Latin *burgus* (see BURGESS). Sense 2 is from German *Burg* 'castle, city'.

burgage /ˈbəːgɪdʒ/ ▶ noun [mass noun] historical (in England and Scotland) tenure of land in a town held in return for service or annual rent. ■ [count noun] a house or other property held by such tenure.
– ORIGIN late Middle English: from medieval Latin *burgagium*, from late Latin *burgus* 'fortified town'.

Burgas /bʊəˈgas/ an industrial port and resort in Bulgaria, on the Black Sea; pop. 188,861 (est. 2008).

burgee /bəːˈdʒiː/ ▶ noun a flag bearing the colours or emblem of a sailing club, typically triangular.
– ORIGIN mid 18th cent.: perhaps from French *bourgeois* (see BURGESS) in the sense 'owner, master'.

Burgenland /ˈbʊəgənˌland/, German /ˈbʊrgnˌlant/ a state of eastern Austria; capital, Eisenstadt.

burgeon /ˈbəːdʒ(ə)n/ ▶ verb [no obj.] (often as adj. **burgeoning**) begin to grow or increase rapidly; flourish: *manufacturers are keen to cash in on the burgeoning demand*.
– ORIGIN Middle English: from Old French *bourgeonner* 'put out buds', from *borjon* 'bud', based on late Latin *burra* 'wool'.

burger ▶ noun a flat round cake of minced beef that is fried or grilled and generally eaten in a bread roll.

■ [with modifier] a similarly shaped cake made of a specified ingredient: *a nut burger*.
– ORIGIN 1930s (originally US): abbreviation of **HAMBURGER**.

Burgess¹, Anthony (1917–93), English novelist and critic; pseudonym of *John Anthony Burgess Wilson*. One of his best-known novels is *A Clockwork Orange* (1962), a disturbing, futuristic vision of juvenile delinquency and violence. Other notable works: *Earthly Powers* (1980).

Burgess², Guy (Francis de Moncy) (1911–63), British Foreign Office official and spy. Acting as a Soviet agent from the 1930s, he worked for MI5 while ostensibly employed by the BBC. After the war he worked at the British Embassy in Washington, under Kim Philby; charged with espionage in 1951, he fled to the USSR with Donald Maclean.

burgess ▶ **noun 1** archaic an inhabitant of a town or borough with full rights of citizenship.
2 Brit. historical a Member of Parliament for a borough, corporate town, or university.
3 (in the US and also historically in the UK) a magistrate or member of the governing body of a town. ■ US historical a member of the assembly of colonial Maryland or Virginia.
– ORIGIN Middle English: from Anglo-Norman French *burgeis*, from late Latin *burgus* 'castle, fort' (in medieval Latin 'fortified town'); related to **BOROUGH**.

Burgess Shale a stratum of sedimentary rock exposed in the Rocky Mountains in British Columbia, Canada. The bed, dated to the Cambrian period (about 540 million years ago), is rich in well-preserved fossils of early marine invertebrates, many of which represent evolutionary lineages unknown in later times.
– ORIGIN named after the *Burgess* Pass, British Columbia, where the shale outcrops.

burgh /ˈbʌrə/ ▶ **noun** historical or Scottish a borough or chartered town.
– DERIVATIVES **burghal** /ˈbəːg(ə)l/ **adjective**.
– ORIGIN late Middle English: Scots form of **BOROUGH**.

burgher /ˈbəːgə/ ▶ **noun 1** archaic or humorous a citizen of a town or city, typically a member of the wealthy bourgeoisie.
2 historical (in southern Africa) an Afrikaans citizen of a Boer Republic. ■ (in southern Africa) a civilian member of a local militia unit.
3 (**Burgher**) a descendant of a Dutch or Portuguese colonist in Sri Lanka.
– ORIGIN Middle English: from **BURGH**, reinforced by Dutch *burger*, from *burg* 'castle' (see **BOROUGH**).

Burghley /ˈbəːli/, William Cecil, 1st Baron (1520–98), English statesman. Secretary of State to Queen Elizabeth I 1558–72 and Lord High Treasurer 1572–98, he was the queen's most trusted councillor and minister.

burghul /bəːˈguːl/ ▶ **noun** another term for **BULGAR**.
– ORIGIN Persian.

burglar ▶ **noun** a person who commits burglary.
– DERIVATIVES **burglarious** /-ˈglɛːrɪəs/ **adjective** (archaic).
– ORIGIN mid 16th cent.: from legal French *burgler* or Anglo-Latin *burgulator*, *burglator*; related to Old French *burgier* 'pillage'.

burglarize (also **burglarise**) ▶ **verb** North American term for **BURGLE**.

burglary ▶ **noun** (pl. **burglaries**) illegal entry of a building with intent to commit a crime, especially theft: [mass noun] *a two-year sentence for burglary* | [count noun] *a series of burglaries*.

> In English law before 1968, burglary was a crime under statute and in common law; since 1968 it has been a statutory crime only. See also **HOUSEBREAKING**.

– ORIGIN early 16th cent.: from legal French *burglarie*, from *burgler* (see **BURGLAR**).

burgle ▶ **verb** [with obj.] chiefly Brit. enter (a building) illegally with intent to commit a crime, especially theft: *our house in London has been burgled*.
– ORIGIN late 19th cent.: originally a humorous and colloquial back-formation from **BURGLAR**.

burgomaster /ˈbəːgə(ʊ)mɑːstə/ ▶ **noun** the mayor of a Dutch, Flemish, German, Austrian, or Swiss town.
– ORIGIN late 16th cent.: from Dutch *burgemeester*, from *burg* 'castle, citadel' (see **BOROUGH**) + *meester* 'master'. The change in the final element was due to association with **MASTER¹**.

burgonet /ˈbəːgənɛt/ ▶ **noun** historical a kind of visored helmet. ■ a light steel cap worn by pikemen.
– ORIGIN late 16th cent.: from French *bourguignotte*, perhaps a use of the feminine of *bourgignot* 'Burgundian', the ending being assimilated to **-ET¹**.

burgoo /bəːˈguː/ ▶ **noun** [mass noun] **1** N. Amer. a stew or thick soup, typically one served at an outdoor meal.
2 chiefly Nautical a thick porridge.
– ORIGIN from Arabic *burġul* (see **BURGHUL**).

Burgos /ˈbʊəgɒs/, Spanish /ˈburɣos/ a town in northern Spain; pop. 177,879 (est. 2008). It was the capital of Castile during the 11th century, and the official seat of Franco's Nationalist government (1936–9).

Burgoyne /bəːˈgɔɪn/, John (1722–92), English general and dramatist; known as **Gentleman Johnny**. He surrendered to the Americans at Saratoga (1777) in the War of American Independence.

burgrave /ˈbəːgreɪv/ ▶ **noun** historical the governor or hereditary ruler of a German town or castle.
– ORIGIN mid 16th cent.: from German *Burggraf*, from *Burg* 'castle' (see **BOROUGH**) + *Graf* 'count, noble'.

Burgundian /bəːˈgʌndɪən/ ▶ **noun** a native or inhabitant of Burgundy. ■ historical a member of a Germanic people that invaded Gaul from the east and established the kingdom of Burgundy in the 5th century AD.
▶ **adjective** relating to Burgundy or the Burgundians.

Burgundy /ˈbəːgəndi/ a region and former duchy of east central France, centred on Dijon. The region is noted for its wine. French name **BOURGOGNE**.

burgundy ▶ **noun** (pl. **burgundies**) [mass noun] a wine from Burgundy (usually taken to be red unless otherwise specified). ■ a deep red colour like that of burgundy wine.

burial ▶ **noun** [mass noun] the action or practice of burying a dead body: *his remains were shipped home for burial*. ■ [count noun] a ceremony at which someone's body is buried; a funeral. ■ [count noun] Archaeology a grave or the remains found in it.
– ORIGIN Old English *byrgels* 'place of burial, grave' (interpreted as plural in Middle English, hence the loss of the final *-s*), of Germanic origin; related to **BURY**.

burial ground ▶ **noun** an area of ground set aside for the burying of human bodies.

burin /ˈbjʊərɪn/ ▶ **noun** a handheld steel tool used for engraving in metal or wood. ■ Archaeology a flint tool with a chisel point.
– ORIGIN mid 17th cent.: from French; perhaps related to Old High German *bora* 'boring tool'.

burk ▶ **noun** variant spelling of **BERK**.

burka /ˈbəːkə, ˈbʊrkɑː/ (also **burkha**, **burqa**) ▶ **noun** a long, loose garment covering the whole body from head to feet, worn in public by women in many Muslim countries.
– ORIGIN from Urdu and Persian *burqa'*, from Arabic *burqu'*.

Burke¹, Edmund (1729–97), British man of letters and Whig politician. Burke wrote on the issues of political emancipation and moderation, notably with respect to Roman Catholics and the American colonies.

Burke², John (1787–1848), Irish genealogical and heraldic writer. He compiled *Burke's Peerage* (1826), the guide to peers and baronets.

Burke³, Robert O'Hara (1820–61), Irish explorer. He led a successful expedition from south to north across Australia in the company of William Wills and two others—the first white men to make this journey. On the return journey, however, Burke, Wills, and a third companion died of starvation.

Burke⁴, William (1792–1829), Irish murderer. He was a bodysnatcher operating in Edinburgh with his accomplice **William Hare**.

burke ▶ **noun** variant spelling of **BERK**.

burkha /ˈbəːkə/ ▶ **noun** variant spelling of **BURKA**.

Burkina Faso /bəːˌkiːnə ˈfasəʊ/ a landlocked country in western Africa, in the Sahel; pop. 15,746,200 (est. 2009); official language, French; capital, Ouagadougou. A French protectorate from 1898, it became an autonomous republic within the French Community in 1958 and a fully independent republic in 1960. Former name (until 1984) **UPPER VOLTA**.
– DERIVATIVES **Burkinan adjective & noun**.

Burkitt's lymphoma /ˈbəːkɪts/ ▶ **noun** [mass noun] Medicine cancer of the lymphatic system, caused by the Epstein–Barr virus, chiefly affecting children in central Africa.
– ORIGIN 1960s: named after Denis P. *Burkitt* (1911–93), the British surgeon who described it.

burl¹ /bəːl/ ▶ **noun** a slub or lump in wool or cloth. ■ N. Amer. a rounded knotty growth on a tree, used especially in handcrafted objects and veneers.
– ORIGIN late Middle English: from Old French *bourle* 'tuft of wool', diminutive of *bourre* 'coarse wool', from late Latin *burra* 'wool'.

burl² /bəːl/ ▶ **noun** Austral./NZ informal an attempt: *we'll give it a burl*.
– ORIGIN early 20th cent.: regional usage of **BIRL**.

burlap /ˈbəːlap/ ▶ **noun** [mass noun] chiefly N. Amer. coarse canvas woven from jute, hemp, or a similar fibre, used especially for sacking. ■ lighter material of a similar kind used in dressmaking and furnishing.
– ORIGIN late 17th cent.: of unknown origin.

burlesque /bəːˈlɛsk/ ▶ **noun 1** an absurd or comically exaggerated imitation of something, especially in a literary or dramatic work; a parody: *a novel which is a burlesque of the literary life* | [mass noun] *the argument descends into music-hall burlesque*.
2 a variety show, typically including striptease: [as modifier] *burlesque clubs*.
▶ **verb** (**burlesques**, **burlesquing**, **burlesqued**) [with obj.] parody or imitate in an absurd or comically exaggerated way: *a mock-heroic farce that burlesques the affectations of Restoration heroic drama*.
– DERIVATIVES **burlesquer noun**.
– ORIGIN mid 17th cent.: from French, from Italian *burlesco*, from *burla* 'mockery', of unknown origin.

burley /ˈbəːli/ (also **burley tobacco**) ▶ **noun** [mass noun] a tobacco of a light coloured variety which is grown mainly in Kentucky, USA.
– ORIGIN late 19th cent.: of unknown origin.

Burlington a city in southern Canada, on Lake Ontario south-west of Toronto; pop. 164,415 (est. 2006).

burly ▶ **adjective** (**burlier**, **burliest**) (of a person) large and strong; heavily built.
– DERIVATIVES **burliness noun**.
– ORIGIN Middle English (in the sense 'dignified, imposing'): probably from an unrecorded Old English word meaning 'stately, fit for the bower' (see **BOWER¹**, **-LY¹**).

Burma /ˈbəːmə/ a country in SE Asia, on the Bay of Bengal; pop. 48,137,700 (est. 2009); official language, Burmese; capital, Naypyidaw. Official name (since 1989) **UNION OF MYANMAR**.

> Annexed by the British during the 19th century, Burma was occupied by the Japanese from 1942 to 1945 and became an independent republic in 1948. In 1962 an army coup led by Ne Win overthrew the government and established an authoritarian state. The National League for Democracy (NLD) won the election held in May 1990, even though its leader Aung San Suu Kyi was under house arrest; however, the military regime did not relinquish power.

> **USAGE** The military authorities in Burma have promoted the name Myanmar as the official name for their state since 1989; Burma is often preferred by people who oppose the current government.

Burman ▶ **noun** (pl. **Burmans**) & **adjective** another term for **BURMESE** (sense 1 of the noun).

bur-marigold ▶ **noun** a plant of the daisy family, with inconspicuous yellow flowers and small barbed fruit which cling to passing animals. Several kinds are widespread weeds. ● Genus *Bidens*, family Compositae: several species, in particular *B. frondosa*.

Burma Road a route linking Lashio in Burma to Kunming in China, covering 1,154 km (717 miles). Completed in 1939, it was built by the Chinese in response to the Japanese occupation of the Chinese coast, to serve as a supply route to the interior.

Burmese ▶ **noun** (pl. **same**) **1** a member of the largest ethnic group of Burma (Myanmar) in SE Asia.
2 a native or inhabitant of Burma.
3 [mass noun] the official language of Burma, which is the first language of about 22 million people (75 per cent of the population). It is a tonal Sino-Tibetan language written in an alphabet derived from that of ancient Pali.
4 (also **Burmese cat**) a cat of a short-coated breed originating in Asia.
▶ **adjective** relating to Burma, its people, or their language.

burn¹ ▶ **verb** (past and past participle **burned** or chiefly Brit. **burnt**) **1** [no obj.] (of a fire) flame or glow while consuming a material such as coal or wood: *a fire burned and crackled cheerfully in the grate*. ■ (of a candle or other source of light) be alight: *a light was burning in the hall*. ■ be in flames: *by nightfall, the whole*

B

B

city was burning. ■ [with obj.] use (a type of fuel) as a source of heat or energy: *a diesel engine converted to burn natural gas.* ■ [with obj.] (of the body of a person or animal) convert (calories) to energy: *exercise does help to **burn up** calories.*
2 be or cause to be destroyed by fire: [no obj.] *he watched his restaurant **burn to the ground*** | [with obj.] *he burned all the letters.* ■ be or cause to be damaged, injured, or spoiled by heat or fire: [with obj.] *I **burned myself** on the stove* | [no obj.] *the toast's burning.* ■ [no obj.] (of the skin) become red and painful through exposure to the sun: *my skin tans easily but sometimes burns.* ■ [no obj.] feel hot or sore, typically as a result of illness or injury: *her forehead was burning and her throat ached.*
3 (**be burning with**) be entirely possessed by (a desire or an emotion): *Martha was burning with curiosity.*
4 [no obj., with adverbial of direction] informal drive very fast: *a despatch rider **burning up** the highways.*
5 [with obj.] produce (a CD or DVD) by copying from an original or master copy.
▸ **noun 1** an injury caused by exposure to heat or flame: *he was treated in hospital for **burns** to his hands.* ■ a mark left on something as a result of being burned: *the carpet was covered in cigarette burns.* ■ an injury caused by friction: *they found rope burns around her waist.* ■ a hot, painful sensation in the muscles experienced as a result of sustained vigorous exercise.
2 consumption of a type of fuel as an energy source: *natural gas produces the cleanest burn of the lot.* ■ a firing of a rocket engine in flight.
3 N. Amer. & Austral./NZ an act of clearing of vegetation by burning. ■ an area of land cleared in this way.
4 Brit. informal a cigarette.
– PHRASES **be burned at the stake** historical be executed by being tied to a stake and publicly burned alive, typically for alleged heresy or witchcraft. **burn one's bridges** (or Brit. **boats**) do something which makes it impossible to return to an earlier state. **burn the candle at both ends** go to bed late and get up early. **burn a hole in someone's pocket** (of money) tempt someone to spend it quickly and extravagantly. **burn the midnight oil** read or work late into the night. **burn** (N. Amer. also **lay**) **rubber** informal drive very quickly. **go for the burn** informal push one's body to extremes when doing physical exercise. **a slow burn** informal a state of slowly mounting anger or annoyance.
– PHRASAL VERBS **burn something down** (or **burn down**) (with reference to a building or structure) destroy or be destroyed completely by fire. **burn something into** brand or imprint (something) with an image by burning: *designs are burnt into the skin* | figurative *a childhood incident that was burnt into her memory.* **burn out 1** cease to function as a result of excessive heat or friction: *the clutch had burned out.* **2** ruin one's health or become completely exhausted through overwork: *social pressures that can cause career women to burn out* | (as adj. **burned out**) *a burned-out undercover cop.* **burn someone out** make someone homeless by destroying their home by fire: *he and his family had been **burned out** of their house.* **burn something out** completely destroy a building or vehicle by fire, so that only a shell remains. **burn someone up** N. Amer. informal make someone very angry.
– ORIGIN Old English *birnan* 'be on fire' and *bærnan* 'consume by fire', both from the same Germanic base; related to German *brennen*.

burn[2] ▸ **noun** Scottish & N. English a small stream.
– ORIGIN Old English *burna, burn(e)*, of Germanic origin; related to Dutch *bron* and German *Brunnen* 'well'.

Burne-Jones, Sir Edward (Coley) (1833–98), English painter and designer. His work, which included tapestry and stained-glass window designs, reflected his interest in medieval and literary themes and is typical of the later Pre-Raphaelite style.

burner ▸ **noun 1** a person or thing that burns: [in combination] *uphill walking is a great calorie-burner.* ■ a part of a cooker, lamp, etc. that emits a flame. ■ an apparatus in which a substance is heated. ■ N. Amer. the heating element of an electric cooker.
2 a device for producing a CD or DVD by copying from an original or master copy.
– PHRASES **on the back burner** informal having low priority: *he wants the matter to **be put on the back burner**.*

burnet /ˈbəːnɪt/ ▸ **noun 1** a herbaceous plant of the rose family, with globular pinkish flower heads and leaves composed of many small leaflets. ● Genus *Sanguisorba*, family Rosaceae: several species, including the edible **salad burnet** (*S. minor*), and the spiny shrub-like **thorny burnet** (*S. spinosum*) of the eastern Mediterranean.
2 a day-flying moth that typically has greenish-black wings with crimson markings. ● *Zygaena* and other genera, family Zygaenidae.
– ORIGIN Middle English (denoting a kind of dark brown woollen cloth): from Old French *brunete, burnete* (denoting brown cloth or a plant with brown flowers), diminutives of *brun* 'brown'.

burnet rose ▸ **noun** a small wild Eurasian rose with white flowers and leaves like those of salad burnet. ● *Rosa pimpinellifolia*, family Rosaceae.

burnet saxifrage ▸ **noun** a slender white-flowered European plant of the parsley family. ● *Pimpinella saxifraga*, family Umbelliferae.

Burnett /bəːˈnɛt/, Frances (Eliza) Hodgson (1849–1924), British-born American novelist. She is remembered chiefly for her novels for children, including *Little Lord Fauntleroy* (1886), *A Little Princess* (1905), and *The Secret Garden* (1911).

Burney, Fanny (1752–1840), English novelist; born *Frances Burney*. Notable works: *Evelina* (1778), *Cecilia* (1782), and *Letters and Diaries* (1846).

burn-in ▸ **noun 1** [mass noun] damage to a computer or television screen which occurs when a very bright image has been displayed for too long.
2 a continuous period of operation undergone by an electronic device in order to check for defects.

burning ▸ **adjective** on fire: *a burning building.* ■ very hot or bright: *the burning midday sun.* ■ very keenly or deeply felt; intense: *he had a burning ambition to climb to the upper reaches of management.* ■ of urgent interest and importance; exciting or calling for debate: *pension reform is still a burning issue* | *the burning question of independence.*
– DERIVATIVES **burningly** adverb.

burning bush ▸ **noun 1** any of a number of shrubs noted for their bright red autumn foliage, in particular the kochia or the smoke tree.
2 any of a number of shrubs or trees with bright red leaves or fruits. ● Several plants, in particular North American spindles of the genus *Euonymus* (family Celastraceae), e.g. the wahoo (*E. atropurpurea*).
3 another term for GAS PLANT.
– ORIGIN mid 19th cent.: with biblical allusion to Exod. 3:2.

burning ghat ▸ **noun** see GHAT (sense 1).

burning glass ▸ **noun** a lens for concentrating the sun's rays on an object so as to set fire to it.

burnish ▸ **verb** [with obj.] (usu. as adj. **burnished**) polish (something, especially metal) by rubbing: *highly burnished armour.* ■ enhance or improve: *a man who took advantage of any opportunity to burnish his image.*
▸ **noun** [in sing.] the shine on a highly polished surface.
– DERIVATIVES **burnisher** noun.
– ORIGIN Middle English: from Old French *burniss-*, lengthened stem of *burnir*, variant of *brunir* 'make brown', from *brun* 'brown'.

burnous /bəːˈnuːs/ (US also **burnoose**) ▸ **noun** a long, loose hooded cloak worn by Arabs.
– ORIGIN late 16th cent.: French, from Arabic *burnus*, from Greek *birros* 'cloak'.

burnout ▸ **noun** [mass noun] **1** the reduction of a fuel or substance to nothing through use or combustion.
2 the failure of an electrical device or component through overheating.
3 physical or mental collapse caused by overwork or stress: *high levels of professionalism which may result in burnout.*

burn rate ▸ **noun** the rate at which a new company spends its initial capital.

Burns[1], George (1896–1996), American comedian; born *Nathan Birnbaum*. Known for his comedy partnership with his wife Gracie Allen (1902–64), he won an Oscar for the film *The Sunshine Boys* (1975).

Burns[2], Robert (1759–96), Scottish poet, best known for poems such as 'The Jolly Beggars' (1786) and 'Tam o' Shanter' (1791), and for old Scottish songs which he collected, including 'Auld Lang Syne'. Burns Night celebrations are held in Scotland and elsewhere on his birthday, 25 January.

burnside ▸ **noun** (usu. **burnsides**) a moustache in combination with whiskers on the cheeks but no beard on the chin.
– ORIGIN late 19th cent.: named after General Ambrose *Burnside* (1824–81), American army officer.

burnt chiefly Brit. past and past participle of BURN[1].

burnt ochre ▸ **noun** [mass noun] a deep, opaque yellow-brown pigment made by calcining ochre. ■ the colour of this pigment.

burnt offering ▸ **noun 1** an offering burnt on an altar as a religious sacrifice.
2 humorous an overcooked or charred meal or item of food.

burnt sienna ▸ **noun** [mass noun] a deep reddish-brown pigment made by calcining raw sienna. ■ the colour of this pigment.

burnt umber ▸ **noun** [mass noun] a deep brown pigment made by calcining raw umber. ■ the colour of this pigment.

bur oak ▸ **noun** a North American oak with large fringed acorn cups and timber that was formerly important in shipbuilding. ● *Quercus macrocarpa*, family Fagaceae.

buroo /bəˈruː/ ▸ **noun** variant form of BROO.

burp informal ▸ **verb** [no obj.] noisily release air from the stomach through the mouth; belch. ■ [with obj.] make (a baby) belch after feeding, typically by patting its back.
▸ **noun** a noise made by air released from the stomach through the mouth; a belch.
– ORIGIN 1930s (originally US): imitative.

burpee /ˈbəːpiː/ ▸ **noun** a physical exercise consisting of a squat thrust made from and ending in a standing position.
– ORIGIN 1930s: named after Royal H. *Burpee*, American psychologist. The original usage was *Burpee test*, in which a series of burpees are executed in rapid succession, designed to measure agility and coordination.

burp gun ▸ **noun** US informal a lightweight sub-machine gun.

burqa ▸ **noun** variant spelling of BURKA.

Burr, Aaron (1756–1836), American Democratic Republican statesman. In 1804, while Vice-President, he killed his rival Alexander Hamilton in a duel. He then plotted to form an independent administration in Mexico and was tried for treason but acquitted.

burr ▸ **noun 1** a whirring sound, such as a telephone ringing tone or the sound of cogs turning. ■ a rough pronunciation of the letter *r*, especially with a uvular trill as in a Northumberland accent. ■ (loosely) a regional accent: *a soft Scottish burr.*
2 (also **bur**) a rough edge or ridge left on an object (especially of metal) by the action of a tool or machine.
3 (also **bur**) a small rotary cutting tool with a shaped end, used chiefly in woodworking and dentistry. ■ a small surgical drill for making holes in bone, especially in the skull.
4 [mass noun] a siliceous rock used for millstones. ■ [count noun] a whetstone.
5 (also **bur**) a prickly seed case or flower head that clings to clothing and animal fur. ■ [usu. as modifier] a plant that produces burrs, for example bur-reed.
6 (also **bur**) [as modifier] denoting wood containing knots or other growths which show a pattern of dense swirls in the grain when sawn, used for veneers and other decorative woodwork: *burr walnut.*
7 the coronet of a deer's antler.
▸ **verb 1** [no obj.] make a whirring sound. ■ speak with a regional accent, especially one in which the letter *r* is prominent.
2 [with obj.] form a rough edge on (metal).
– PHRASES **a burr under someone's saddle** N. Amer. informal a persistent source of irritation.
– ORIGIN Middle English (in sense 5 of the noun): probably of Scandinavian origin and related to Danish *burre* 'burr, burdock', Swedish *kard borre* 'burdock'.

burra /ˈbʌrə/ ▸ **adjective** [attrib.] Indian big or important: *the burra sahibs.*
– ORIGIN from Hindi *baṛā* 'great, greatest'.

Burra Din /ˌbʌrə ˈdɪn/ ▸ **noun** Indian Christmas.
– ORIGIN from Hindi *baṛā* 'great' and *din* 'day'.

burrawang /ˈbʌrəwaŋ/ (also **burrawong**) ▸ **noun** an Australian cycad with palm-like leaves and a sunken underground trunk. ● *Macrozamia spiralis*, family Zamiaceae.
■ the poisonous nut of the burrawang, which becomes edible after prolonged soaking.
– ORIGIN early 19th cent.: from Dharuk.

bur-reed ▸ **noun** an aquatic reed-like plant with rounded flower heads. Its oily seeds are an important source of winter food for wildfowl. ● Genus *Sparganium*, family Sparganiaceae.

burrfish ▸ **noun** (pl. **same** or **burrfishes**) a porcupine fish with spines that are permanently erected, occurring in tropical waters of the Atlantic and Pacific. ● Genus *Chilomycterus*, family Diodontidae: several species, including the common *C. schoepfi* of the western Atlantic.

burrito /bʊˈriːtəʊ/ ▸ **noun** (pl. **burritos**) a Mexican dish consisting of a tortilla rolled round a savoury filling, typically of minced beef or beans.
– ORIGIN Latin American Spanish, diminutive of Spanish *burro*, literally 'donkey' (see BURRO).

burro /ˈbʊrəʊ/ ▸ **noun** (pl. **burros**) chiefly US a small donkey used as a pack animal.
– ORIGIN early 19th cent.: from Spanish.

Burroughs[1] /ˈbʌrəʊz/, Edgar Rice (1875–1950), American novelist and writer of science fiction. He is chiefly remembered for his adventure stories about Tarzan, who first appeared in *Tarzan of the Apes* (1914).

Burroughs[2] /ˈbʌrəʊz/, William (Seward) (1914–97), American novelist. In the 1940s he became addicted to heroin, and his best-known writing, for example *Junkie* (1953) and *The Naked Lunch* (1959), deals with life as a drug addict in a unique, surreal style.

burrow ▸ **noun** a hole or tunnel dug by a small animal, especially a rabbit, as a dwelling.
▸ **verb** [no obj.] (of an animal) make a hole or tunnel, typically for use as a dwelling: *moles burrowing away underground* | (as adj. **burrowing**) *burrowing earthworms.* ■ [with adverbial of direction] dig into or through something solid: *worms that burrow through dead wood.* ■ [with adverbial of direction] hide underneath or press close to something: *the child* ***burrowed*** *deeper into the bed.* ■ make a thorough inquiry; investigate: *journalists are* ***burrowing into*** *the prime minister's business affairs.*
– DERIVATIVES **burrower** noun.
– ORIGIN Middle English: variant of BOROUGH.

Bursa /ˈbəːsə/ a city in NW Turkey, capital of a province of the same name; pop. 1,431,200 (est. 2007). It was the capital of the Ottoman Empire from 1326 to 1402.

bursa /ˈbəːsə/ ▸ **noun** (pl. **bursae** /-siː/ or **bursas**) Anatomy a fluid-filled sac or sac-like cavity, especially one countering friction at a joint.
– DERIVATIVES **bursal** adjective.
– ORIGIN early 19th cent.: from medieval Latin, 'bag, purse', from Greek *bursa* 'leather'.

bursa of Fabricius ▸ **noun** Zoology a glandular sac opening into the cloaca of a bird, producing B-cells.
– ORIGIN mid 19th cent. (in the Latin form *bursa Fabricii*): from BURSA and a Latinized form of the name of Girolama *Fabrici* (1533–1619), Italian anatomist.

bursar ▸ **noun** chiefly Brit. **1** a person who manages the financial affairs of a college or school.
2 Scottish a student who holds a bursary.
– ORIGIN late Middle English: from French *boursier* or (in sense 1) medieval Latin *bursarius*, from *bursa* 'bag, purse' (see BURSA).

bursary /ˈbəːsəri/ ▸ **noun** (pl. **bursaries**) Brit. **1** a grant, especially one awarded to someone to enable them to study at university or college.
2 the room of a bursar in a college or school.
– DERIVATIVES **bursarial** /-ˈsɛːrɪəl/ adjective.
– ORIGIN late 17th cent. (in sense 2): from medieval Latin *bursaria*, from *bursa* 'bag, purse' (see BURSA).

burse /bəːs/ ▸ **noun 1** a flat, square, fabric-covered case in which a folded corporal cloth is carried to and from an altar in church.
2 (**the Burse**) historical the Royal Exchange in Cornhill, London. Compare with BOURSE.
– ORIGIN late Middle English (in sense 'purse'): from French *bourse* or medieval Latin *bursa* (see BOURSE, BURSA).

bursitis /bəːˈsʌɪtɪs/ ▸ **noun** [mass noun] Medicine inflammation of a bursa, typically one in a shoulder joint.

burst ▸ **verb** (past and past participle **burst**) [no obj.] **1** break open or apart suddenly and violently, especially as a result of an impact or internal pressure: *one of the balloons burst* | *the dam burst after days of torrential rain.* ■ [with obj.] cause to break open or apart in this way: *he burst the balloon* | *the swollen river was expected to burst its banks.* ■ be so full as almost to break open: *the wardrobe was* ***bursting with*** *piles of clothes.* ■ feel a very strong or irrepressible emotion or impulse: *he was* ***bursting with*** *joy and excitement* | [with infinitive] *she was bursting to say something.*
2 issue suddenly and uncontrollably: *the words* ***burst from him*** *in an angry rush.* ■ open suddenly and forcibly: *a door burst open and a girl raced out.* ■ [with adverbial of direction] move suddenly and violently: *he burst into the room without knocking* | figurative *she burst on to the British art scene in 1985.*
3 suddenly begin doing or producing something: *Sophie* ***burst out laughing*** | *she* ***burst into tears*** | *the aircraft* ***burst into flames.***
4 [with obj.] separate (continuous stationery) into single sheets.
▸ **noun 1** an instance of breaking or splitting as a result of internal pressure or puncturing; an explosion: *the mortar bursts were further away than before.*
2 a sudden brief outbreak: *a burst of activity* | *bursts of laughter.* ■ a sudden issuing forth: *her breath was coming in short bursts.*
3 a period of continuous and intense effort: *he sailed 474 miles in one 24-hour burst.*
– PHRASES **burst someone's bubble** see BUBBLE.
– ORIGIN Old English *berstan*, of Germanic origin; related to Dutch *bersten, barsten*.

burster ▸ **noun 1** Astronomy a cosmic source of powerful short-lived bursts of X-rays or other radiation.
2 informal a violent gale.
3 a machine which separates continuous stationery into single sheets.

bursty ▸ **adjective** informal or technical occurring at intervals in short, sudden episodes. ■ relating to or denoting the transmission of data in short, separate bursts of signals.

burthen ▸ **noun** archaic form of BURDEN.
– DERIVATIVES **burthensome** adjective.

Burton[1], Richard (1925–84), Welsh actor; born *Richard Jenkins*. He often co-starred with Elizabeth Taylor (to whom he was twice married) in films such as *Who's Afraid of Virginia Woolf?* (1966).

Burton[2], Sir Richard (Francis) (1821–90), English explorer, anthropologist, and translator. He and John Hanning Speke were the first Europeans to see Lake Tanganyika (1858). He translated the *Arabian Nights* (1885–8), the *Kama Sutra* (1883), *The Perfumed Garden* (1886), and other works.

Burton[3], Robert (1577–1640), English churchman and scholar, author of *The Anatomy of Melancholy* (first published 1621).

burton[1] ▸ **noun** (in phrase **go for a burton**) Brit. informal meet with disaster; be ruined, destroyed, or killed.
– ORIGIN Second World War (originally RAF slang): perhaps referring to *Burton* ale, from Burton upon Trent.

burton[2] (also **burton-tackle**) ▸ **noun** historical a light two-block tackle for hoisting.
– ORIGIN early 18th cent.: alteration of Middle English *Breton tackle*, a nautical term in the same (see BRETON[1]).

Burton upon Trent a town in west central England, in Staffordshire; pop. 45,500 (est. 2009). The town is noted for its breweries.

Burundi /bʊˈrʊndi/ a central African country on the east side of Lake Tanganyika, to the south of Rwanda; pop. 9,511,300 (est. 2009); official languages, French and Kirundi; capital, Bujumbura.

> Inhabited mainly by Hutu and Tutsi peoples, the area formed part of German East Africa from the 1890s until the First World War, after which it was administered by Belgium. The country became an independent monarchy in 1962 and a republic in 1966. Multiparty elections in 1993 resulted in the country being led for the first time by a member of the Hutu majority rather than the traditionally dominant Tutsis; this led within months to large-scale ethnic violence.

– DERIVATIVES **Burundian** adjective & noun.

bury ▸ **verb** (**buries, burying, buried**) **1** [with obj.] put or hide underground: *he buried the box in the back garden* | (as adj. **buried**) *buried treasure.* ■ place (a dead body) in the earth or in a tomb, usually with funeral rites: *he was buried in St John's churchyard.* ■ lose (someone, especially a relative) through death: *a rich old lady who had buried two husbands.*
2 cover (someone or something) completely: *the countryside has been buried under layers of concrete* | *the sheep were buried beneath six-foot drifts of snow.* ■ hide (something) from sight: *she buried her face in her hands.* ■ hide or try to forget (a feeling or memory): *they had buried their feelings of embarrassment and fear.* ■ (**bury oneself**) involve oneself deeply in something to the exclusion of other concerns: *he* ***buried himself in*** *work.* ■ informal (of a football player) shoot (the ball) into the goal.
– PHRASES **bury one's head in the sand** ignore unpleasant realities.
– ORIGIN Old English *byrgan*, of West Germanic origin; related to the verb BORROW and to BOROUGH.

Buryat /ˈbʊəjat/ ▸ **noun 1** a member of a people living in southern Siberia, Mongolia, and northern China.
2 [mass noun] the language of the Buryat, related to Mongolian and having over 400,000 speakers.
▸ **adjective** relating to the Buryat or their language.

Buryatia /bʊəˈjɑːtɪə/ (also **Buryat Republic** /ˌbʊəˈjɑːt/) an autonomous republic in SE Russia, between Lake Baikal and the Mongolian border; pop. 951,000 (est. 2009); capital, Ulan-Ude.

burying beetle ▸ **noun** a black beetle, typically with broad orange bands on its wing cases, which buries small animal carcasses to provide a food store for its larvae. Also called SEXTON BEETLE. ● *Nicrophorus* and other genera, family Silphidae.

bus ▸ **noun** (pl. **buses**; US also **busses**) **1** a large motor vehicle carrying passengers by road, typically one serving the public on a fixed route and for a fare: [as modifier] *a bus service.* ■ informal, dated a car, aircraft, or other vehicle.
2 Computing a distinct set of conductors carrying data and control signals within a computer system, to which pieces of equipment may be connected in parallel.
▸ **verb** (**busses, bussing, bussed** or **buses, busing, bused**) **1** [with obj. and adverbial of direction] transport in a communal road vehicle: *staff were bussed in and out of the factory.* ■ [no obj., with adverbial of direction] travel by bus: *the priest bussed in from a neighbouring parish.* ■ N. Amer. transport (a child of one ethnic group) to a school where another group is predominant, in an attempt to promote racial integration.
2 [with obj.] N. Amer. remove (dirty plates and dishes) from a table in a restaurant or cafeteria. ■ remove dirty plates and dishes from (a table).
– DERIVATIVES **busser** noun (sense 2 of the verb).
– ORIGIN early 19th cent.: shortening of OMNIBUS.

busbar /ˈbʌsbɑː/ ▸ **noun** a system of electrical conductors in a generating or receiving station on which power is concentrated for distribution.

busboy /ˈbʌsbɔɪ/ ▸ **noun** N. Amer. a young man who clears tables in a restaurant or cafe.

Busby, Sir Matt (1909–94), Scottish-born footballer and football manager. As manager of Manchester United 1945–69 he led them to win five League Championships and the European Cup in 1968.

busby /ˈbʌzbi/ ▸ **noun** (pl. **busbies**) a tall fur hat with a coloured cloth flap hanging down on the right-hand side and in some cases a plume on the top, worn by soldiers of certain regiments of hussars and artillerymen. ■ popular term for BEARSKIN (the cap).
– ORIGIN mid 18th cent. (denoting a large bushy wig): of unknown origin.

Bush[1], George (Herbert Walker) (b.1924), American Republican statesman, 41st President of the US 1989–93. He negotiated further arms reductions with the Soviet Union and organized international action to expel the Iraqis from Kuwait in 1990.

Bush[2], George W(alker) (b.1946), American Republican statesman, 43rd President of the US 2001–2009. He is the son of George Bush. One of his first acts as President was to launch a 'War on Terror' against the Taliban regime in Afghanistan following the September 11 attacks on the World Trade Center and Pentagon; he also ordered the invasion of Iraq in March 2003, maintaining that Saddam Hussein was developing chemical, biological, and nuclear weapons.
– DERIVATIVES **Bushism** noun.

bush[1] ▸ **noun 1** a shrub or clump of shrubs with stems of moderate length: *a rose bush.* ■ historical a bunch of ivy as a vintner's sign.
2 (**the bush**) (especially in Australia and Africa) wild or uncultivated country: *they have to spend a night camping in the bush.* ■ [mass noun] the vegetation growing in such a district: *the lowland country was covered in thick bush.* ■ NZ indigenous rainforest. ■ [as modifier] chiefly S. African uncivilized or primitive: *bush justice.*
3 a luxuriant growth of thick hair or fur: *a childish face with a bush of bright hair.* ■ vulgar slang a woman's pubic hair.
▸ **verb** [no obj.] spread out into a thick clump: *her hair* ***bushed out*** *like a halo.*
– PHRASES **go bush** Austral./NZ leave one's usual surroundings; run wild. [early 20th cent: by association with the phrase *take to the bush*, originally said of escaped convicts.]
– ORIGIN Middle English: from Old French *bos, bosc*, variants of *bois* 'wood', reinforced by Old Norse

B

buski, of Germanic origin and related to Dutch *bos* and German *Busch*. The sense 'uncultivated country' is probably directly from Dutch *bos*.

bush[2] ▶ **noun** Brit. **1** a metal lining for a round hole, especially one in which an axle revolves. ■ a bearing for a revolving shaft.
2 a sleeve that protects an electric cable where it passes through a panel.
– ORIGIN late 15th cent.: from Middle Dutch *busse*.

bushbaby ▶ **noun** (pl. **bushbabies**) a small nocturnal tree-dwelling African primate with very large eyes. Also called GALAGO. ● Genus *Galago*, family Lorisidae, suborder Prosimii: several species.

bushbuck ▶ **noun** a small antelope with a reddish-brown coat with white markings, found in southern Africa. ● *Tragelaphus scriptus*, family Bovidae.
– ORIGIN mid 19th cent.: from BUSH[1] + BUCK[1], influenced by Dutch *bosbok*.

bushchat ▶ **noun** an Asian songbird related to the stonechat, the males of which generally have black (or grey) and white plumage. ● Genus *Saxicola*, family Turdidae: several species.

bushcraft ▶ **noun** [mass noun] skill at living in the bush.

bush cricket ▶ **noun** an insect related to the grasshoppers, with very long antennae and a mainly carnivorous diet. Many kinds live among shrubby vegetation, active and singing mainly at dusk and in the night. Formerly called LONG-HORNED GRASSHOPPER. ● Family Tettigoniidae: many genera.

bush dog ▶ **noun** a small stocky carnivorous mammal of the dog family, with short legs and small ears. It is native to the forests of Central and South America. ● *Speothus venaticus*, family Canidae.

bushed ▶ **adjective** informal **1** tired out; exhausted.
2 Austral./NZ lost in the bush. ■ flummoxed or bewildered.
3 Canadian psychologically disturbed on account of isolation.

bushel /ˈbʊʃ(ə)l/ (abbrev.: **bu.**) ▶ **noun 1** Brit. a measure of capacity equal to 8 gallons (equivalent to 36.4 litres), used for corn, fruit, liquids, etc.
2 US a measure of capacity equal to 64 US pints (equivalent to 35.2 litres), used for dry goods.
– PHRASES **hide one's light under a bushel** see HIDE[1].
– DERIVATIVES **bushelful** noun (pl. **bushelfuls**).
– ORIGIN Middle English: from Old French *boissel*, perhaps of Gaulish origin.

bush fallow ▶ **noun** [mass noun] a system of farming in which bushes and trees are cleared from virgin land, which is then allowed to lie fallow for a while before cultivation begins.

bush fire ▶ **noun** a fire in scrub or a forest, especially one that spreads rapidly.

bush-hen ▶ **noun** an Australasian rail (bird) with plain brown and grey plumage. ● *Amaurornis olivaceus*, family Rallidae. Alternative name: **rufous-tailed moorhen**.

bushido /ˈbuːʃɪdəʊ, bʊˈʃiːdəʊ/ ▶ **noun** [mass noun] the code of honour and morals developed by the Japanese samurai.
– ORIGIN Japanese, from *bushi* 'samurai' + *dō* 'way'.

bushie ▶ **noun** variant spelling of BUSHY[2].

bushing ▶ **noun** another term for BUSH[2].

bush jacket ▶ **noun** another term for SAFARI JACKET.

bushland ▶ **noun** [mass noun] Austral. wild or uncultivated country.

bush lawyer ▶ **noun** Austral./NZ informal a person claiming legal or other knowledge who is unqualified to do so.

bush league N. Amer. ▶ **noun** a minor league of a professional sport, especially baseball.
▶ **adjective** (**bush-league**) informal of mediocre quality; second-rate.
– DERIVATIVES **bush-leaguer** noun.

Bushman ▶ **noun** (pl. **Bushmen**) **1** a member of any of several aboriginal peoples of southern Africa, especially of the Kalahari Desert. Traditionally nomadic hunter-gatherers, many are now employed by farmers. Also called SAN.
2 older term for SAN (the languages of these people).
3 (**bushman**) a person who lives, works, or travels in the Australian bush.

bushmaster ▶ **noun** a pit viper which is the largest venomous snake in the New World, found in Central and South America. ● *Lachesis muta*, family Viperidae.
– ORIGIN early 19th cent.: perhaps from Dutch *bosmeester*, from *bos* 'bush' + *meester* 'master'.

bushmeat ▶ **noun** [mass noun] the meat of African wild animals as food.

bush medicine ▶ **noun** [mass noun] chiefly Austral. & W. Indian traditional folk medicine, typically prepared from herbs and other plants.

bush pig (also **African bush pig**) ▶ **noun** a wild pig that is native to the forests and savannahs of Africa and Madagascar. Also called RED RIVER HOG. ● *Potamochoerus porcus*, family Suidae.

bushranger ▶ **noun 1** US a person living far from civilization.
2 Austral./NZ historical an outlaw living in the bush.

bush tea ▶ **noun** a tea made from dried leaves and twigs of various shrubs, especially in tropical countries.

bush telegraph ▶ **noun** a rapid informal network by which information or gossip is spread.

bushtit ▶ **noun** a small American songbird of the long-tailed tit family, with mainly pale grey plumage and sometimes a black mask. ● *Psaltriparus minimus*, family Aegithalidae (formerly Paridae); formerly regarded as two species.

bushveld /ˈbʊʃfɛlt, -vɛlt/ ▶ **noun** (**the Bushveld**) a region in the hot dry north-east of South Africa and adjoining countries. ■ [mass noun] the type of vegetation of the Bushveld, dominated by low-growing thorn trees and bush.
– ORIGIN late 19th cent.: from BUSH[1] + VELD, influenced by Afrikaans *bosveld*.

bushwa /ˈbʊʃwɑː/ (also **bushwah**) ▶ **noun** [mass noun] N. Amer. informal rubbish, nonsense.
– ORIGIN 1920s: apparently a euphemism for BULLSHIT.

bushwalking ▶ **noun** [mass noun] chiefly Austral./NZ hiking or backpacking.
– DERIVATIVES **bushwalker** noun.

bushwhack ▶ **verb 1** [no obj.] (often as noun **bushwhacking**) N. Amer. & Austral./NZ live or travel in bush country. ■ [with adverbial of direction] cut or push one's way through dense vegetation: *he'd bushwhacked down the steep slopes*. ■ work clearing scrub and felling trees in bush country.
2 [no obj.] N. Amer. engage in guerrilla warfare. ■ [with obj.] surprise (someone) by attacking them from a hidden place; ambush.

bushwhacked ▶ **adjective** chiefly N. Amer. exhausted or worn out.

bushwhacker ▶ **noun 1** N. Amer. & Austral./NZ a person who clears land in bush country. ■ a person who lives or travels in bush country.
2 US a guerrilla fighter (originally in the American Civil War).

bushy[1] ▶ **adjective** (**bushier**, **bushiest**) **1** growing thickly: *a dense, bushy plant | his eyebrows were thick and bushy*.
2 covered with bush or bushes: *bushy desert areas*.
– DERIVATIVES **bushily** adverb, **bushiness** noun.

bushy[2] (also **bushie**) ▶ **noun** (pl. **bushies**) Austral./NZ informal a person who lives in the bush (as distinct from in a town), typically regarded as uncultured or unsophisticated.

busily ▶ **adverb** in a very active way: *he was busily engaged in other activities*. ■ while giving all one's attention to something: *he was busily writing away*.

business ▶ **noun** [mass noun] **1** a person's regular occupation, profession, or trade: *experts who typically conduct their business over the Internet*. ■ an activity that someone is engaged in: *what is your business here?* ■ a person's concern: *this is none of your business | the neighbours make it their business to know all about you*. ■ work that has to be done or matters that have to be attended to: *government business | let's get down to business*.
2 commercial activity: *firms who want to **do business** with Japan | the tea business* | [as modifier] *the business community*. ■ trade considered in terms of its volume or profitability: *how's business? | the banks are continuing to lose business*. ■ [count noun] a commercial house or firm: *a catering business*.
3 [in sing.] informal a situation or series of events, typically a scandalous or discreditable one: *maybe something positive will come out of the whole awful business*. ■ a difficult matter: *what a business!*
4 Theatre actions on stage other than dialogue.
5 (**the business**) Brit. informal a very enjoyable or popular person or thing: *this brandy is the business*.
– PHRASES **business as usual** an ongoing and unchanging state of affairs despite difficulties or disturbances: *apart from being under new management, it's business as usual in the department*. **do the business** Brit. informal do what is required or achieve the desired result: *Rogers has got to do the business, score a hat trick or something*. ■ vulgar slang have sexual intercourse. **have no business** have no right to do something: *he had no business tampering with social services*. **in business** operating, especially in commerce: *they will have to import from overseas to remain in business*. ■ informal able to begin operations: *if you'll contact the right people, I should think we're in business*. **in the business of** engaged in or prepared to engage in: *I am not in the business of making accusations*. **like nobody's business** informal, chiefly Brit. to an extraordinarily high degree or standard: *these weeds spread like nobody's business*. **mind one's own business** refrain from meddling in other people's affairs. **send someone about their business** dated tell someone to go away.
– ORIGIN Old English *bisignis* 'anxiety' (see BUSY, -NESS); the sense 'state of being busy' was used from Middle English down to the 18th cent., but is now differentiated as *busyness*. The use 'appointed task' dates from late Middle English, and from it all the other current senses have developed.

business card ▶ **noun** a small card printed with one's name, occupation, business address, etc.

business casual chiefly N. Amer. ▶ **noun** relating to or denoting a style of clothing that is less formal than traditional business wear, but is still intended to give a professional and businesslike impression.
▶ **noun** [mass noun] business casual clothing: *business casual has become the standard in many work environments*.

business cycle ▶ **noun** a cycle or series of cycles of economic expansion and contraction. Also called TRADE CYCLE.

business day ▶ **noun** chiefly N. Amer. another term for WORKING DAY.

business double ▶ **noun** Bridge a double made with the intention of increasing the penalty points scored by a partnership if they defeat their opponents' contract. Often contrasted with TAKE-OUT DOUBLE.

business end ▶ **noun** (**the business end**) informal the functional part of a tool or device: *he found himself facing the business end of six lethal-looking weapons*. ■ the essential or basic part of a process or operation: *the rigs are the business end of the oil industry*.

business hours ▶ **plural noun** another term for OFFICE HOURS.

businesslike ▶ **adjective** having or indicating an efficient, practical, and systematic approach to one's work or a task: *his brisk, businesslike tone*.

businessman (or **businesswoman**) ▶ **noun** (pl. **businessmen** or **businesswomen**) a person who works in commerce, especially at executive level.

business model ▶ **noun** a plan for the successful operation of a business, identifying sources of revenue, the intended customer base, products, and details of financing.

business park ▶ **noun** an area where company offices and light industrial premises are built.

business person ▶ **noun** a businessman or businesswoman.

business process re-engineering (also **business process redesign**) ▶ **noun** [mass noun] the process of restructuring a company's organization and methods, especially so as to exploit the capabilities of computers.

business studies ▶ **plural noun** [treated as sing.] the study of economics and management, especially as an educational topic.

busk[1] ▶ **verb** [no obj.] **1** play music in the street or other public place for voluntary donations: *the group began by busking on Philadelphia sidewalks* | (as noun **busking**) *years of busking had taught him how to hold a crowd*.
2 (**busk it**) informal improvise.
– DERIVATIVES **busker** noun.
– ORIGIN mid 17th cent.: from obsolete French *busquer* 'seek', from Italian *buscare* or Spanish *buscar*, of Germanic origin. Originally in nautical use in the sense 'cruise about, tack', the term later meant 'go about selling things', hence 'go about performing' (mid 19th cent.).

busk[2] ▶ **noun** historical a stay or stiffening strip for a corset.
– ORIGIN late 16th cent.: from French *busc*, from Italian *busco* 'splinter' (related to French *bûche* 'log'), of Germanic origin.

buskin ▶ **noun** chiefly historical a calf-high or knee-high boot of cloth or leather. ■ a thick-soled laced boot worn by an ancient Athenian tragic actor to gain

height. ■ (**the buskin**) the style or spirit of tragic drama.
– DERIVATIVES **buskined adjective**.
– ORIGIN early 16th cent. (designating a calf-length boot): probably from Old French *bouzequin*, variant of *brousequin*, from Middle Dutch *broseken*, of unknown ultimate origin.

bus lane ▸ noun a division of a road marked off with painted lines for use by buses.

busload ▸ noun a group of people travelling in a bus.

busman ▸ noun (pl. **busmen**) a driver of a bus.
– PHRASES **a busman's holiday** a holiday or form of recreation that involves doing the same thing that one does at work.

Buss, Frances Mary (1827–94), English educationist. She was in charge of the North London Collegiate School for Ladies (1850–94) and campaigned for higher education for women with her friend Dorothea Beale.

buss archaic or N. Amer. informal ▸ noun a kiss.
▸ verb [with obj.] kiss.
– ORIGIN late 16th cent.: alteration of late Middle English *bass* (noun and verb), probably from French *baiser*, from Latin *basiare*.

bus shelter ▸ noun a roofed structure for people to wait under at a bus stop.

bus station ▸ noun a place in a town where buses arrive and depart.

bus stop ▸ noun a place where a bus regularly stops, usually marked by a sign.

bust¹ ▸ noun **1** a woman's chest as measured around her breasts: *a 36-inch bust*. ■ a woman's breasts, especially considered in terms of their size: *a woman with big hips and a big bust*.
2 a sculpture of a person's head, shoulders, and chest.
– ORIGIN mid 17th cent. (denoting the upper part or torso of a large sculpture): from French *buste*, from Italian *busto*, from Latin *bustum* 'tomb, sepulchral monument'.

bust² informal ▸ verb (past and past participle **busted** or **bust**) [with obj.] **1** break, split, or burst: *they bust the tunnel wide open* | figurative *the film bust every box office record* | [no obj.] *the colour control had bust*. ■ [no obj.] (**bust up**) (of a group or couple) separate, typically after a quarrel. ■ violently disrupt: *men hired to **bust up** union rallies*. ■ N. Amer. strike violently: *Tamara bust him in the eye*. ■ [no obj.] (**bust out**) escape: *she **busted out of** prison*. ■ [no obj.] (in blackjack and similar card games) exceed the score of 21, so losing one's stake.
2 chiefly N. Amer. (of the police) raid or search (premises where illegal activity is suspected): *my flat got busted*. ■ arrest: *two roadies were **busted for** drugs*. ■ (**be**/**get busted**) be caught in the act of doing something wrong: *I sneaked up on them and told them they were busted*. ■ chiefly US reduce (a soldier) to a lower rank; demote: *he was **busted to** private*.
▸ noun **1** a period of economic difficulty or depression: *the boom was followed by the present bust*.
2 a raid or arrest by the police: *a drug bust*.
3 a worthless thing: *cynics remain convinced the political process is a bust*.
4 chiefly N. Amer. a violent blow: *a bust on the snout*.
▸ adjective **1** Brit. damaged or broken: *the vacuum cleaner's bust*.
2 bankrupt: *six of their sponsors have **gone bust***.
– ORIGIN mid 18th cent. (originally US, as a noun in the sense 'an act of bursting or splitting'): variant of BURST.

bustard /ˈbʌstəd/ ▸ noun a large, heavily built, swift-running bird, found in open country in the Old World. The males of most bustards have a spectacular courtship display. ● Family Otididae: several genera and species, including the **great bustard** (*Otis tarda*), which is the heaviest flying land bird.
– ORIGIN late 15th cent.: perhaps an Anglo-Norman French blend of Old French *bistarde* and *oustarde*, both from Latin *avis tarda* 'slow bird': the name is unexplained, as the bustards are fast runners.

bustard quail ▸ noun the barred button-quail. See BUTTON-QUAIL.

busted flush ▸ noun **1** (in poker) a hand containing four cards of the same suit and one of a different suit.
2 informal a promising person or thing that turns out to be unsuccessful: *her leadership is already a busted flush*.

bustee /ˈbʌstiː/ ▸ noun Indian a slum area or shanty town.
– ORIGIN from Hindi *bastī* 'dwelling'.

buster ▸ noun informal **1** chiefly N. Amer. used as a mildly disrespectful form of address to a man or boy: *like it or lump it, buster*.
2 [usu. in combination] a person or thing that stops or gets rid of a specified thing: *a crime-buster* | *the drug's reputation as a cold-buster*.
3 a notable or impressive person or thing. ■ a violent gale.

bustier /ˈbʌstɪeɪ, ˈbʊst-/ ▸ noun a close-fitting strapless top worn by women.
– ORIGIN 1970s: from French, from *buste* (see BUST¹).

bustle¹ ▸ verb [no obj., with adverbial of direction] move in an energetic and busy manner: *people clutching clipboards bustled about*. ■ [with obj. and adverbial of direction] cause to move hurriedly in a particular direction: *she bustled us into the kitchen*. ■ [no obj.] (of a place) be full of activity: *the streets **bustled with** people* | (as adj. **bustling**) *the bustling little town*.
▸ noun [mass noun] excited activity and movement: *all the noise and the traffic and the bustle*.
– ORIGIN late Middle English: perhaps a variant of obsolete *buskle*, frequentative of *busk* 'prepare', from Old Norse.

bustle² ▸ noun historical a pad or frame worn under a skirt and puffing it out behind.
– ORIGIN late 18th cent.: of unknown origin.

bustline ▸ noun the measurement round a woman's body at the bust: *these figure-enhancing bras will immediately increase your bustline*.

bust-up ▸ noun informal, chiefly Brit. a serious quarrel: *the diplomatic bust-up with Germany*. ■ a fight or brawl: *a touchline bust-up*.

busty ▸ adjective (**bustier**, **bustiest**) informal (of a woman) having large breasts: *a busty starlet*.
– DERIVATIVES **bustiness noun**.

busway ▸ noun a road or section of a road set apart exclusively for buses, typically one equipped with tracks or grooves for guiding them.

busy ▸ adjective (**busier**, **busiest**) **1** having a great deal to do: *he had been too busy to enjoy himself*. ■ occupied with or concentrating on a particular activity or object of attention: *the team members are busy raising money*. ■ (of a time or place) full of activity: *the busy city streets* | *I've had a busy day*. ■ chiefly N. Amer. (of a telephone line) engaged.
2 excessively detailed or decorated: *the lavish set designs are a little too busy*.
▸ verb (**busies**, **busying**, **busied**) (**busy oneself**) keep oneself occupied: *she **busied herself with** her new home*.
▸ noun (also **bizzy**) (pl. **busies** or **bizzies**) Brit. informal a police officer.
– PHRASES **get busy 1** begin work or tasks that need to be done: *this meeting is dismissed—let's get busy, people*. **2** informal have sexual intercourse.
– DERIVATIVES **busyness noun**.
– ORIGIN Old English *bisgian* (verb), *bisig* (noun); related to Dutch *bezig*, of unknown origin.

busy bee ▸ noun informal an industrious person.

busybody ▸ noun (pl. **busybodies**) a meddling or prying person.

busy Lizzie ▸ noun (pl. **busy Lizzies**) Brit. an East African plant with abundant red, pink, or white flowers. It is widely grown as a houseplant, and its many hybrids are grown as bedding plants. ● *Impatiens walleriana*, family Balsaminaceae.

busy signal ▸ noun North American term for ENGAGED TONE.

busywork ▸ noun [mass noun] chiefly N. Amer. work that keeps a person busy but has little value in itself.

but¹ ▸ conjunction **1** used to introduce a phrase or clause contrasting with what has already been mentioned: *he stumbled but didn't fall* | *this is one principle, but it is not the only one* | *the food is cheap but delicious* | *the problem is not that they are cutting down trees, but that they are doing it in a predatory way*.
2 [with negative or in questions] used to indicate the impossibility of anything other than what is being stated: *one **cannot but** sympathize* | *there was nothing they could do but swallow their pride* | *they had no alternative but to follow*.
3 used to introduce a response expressing a feeling such as surprise or anger: *but that's an incredible saving!* | *but why?*
4 used after an expression of apology for what one is about to say: *I'm sorry, but I can't pay you*.
5 [with negative] archaic without it being the case that: *it never rains but it pours*.
▸ preposition except; apart from; other than: *we were never anything but poor* | *supply currently exceeds demand in all but the most rural areas* | *the last but one*. ■ used with repetition of certain words to give emphasis: *nobody, but nobody, was going to stop her*.
▸ adverb **1** no more than; only: *he is but a shadow of his former self* | *choose from a colourful array of mango, starfruit, and raspberries, to name but a few*.
2 Austral./NZ & Scottish informal (used at the end of a sentence) though; however: *he was a nice bloke but*.
▸ noun an argument against something; an objection: ***no buts**—just get out of here* | *as with all these proposals, **ifs and buts** abound*.
– PHRASES **but for** except for: *I walked along Broadway, deserted but for the occasional cab*. ■ if it were not for: *the game could be over but for you*. **but that** archaic other than that; except that: *she would have screamed, but that her cry would have fetched her masters*. **but then** on the other hand; that being so: *it's a very hard match, but then they all are*.
– ORIGIN Old English *be-ūtan*, *būtan*, *būta* 'outside, without, except' (see BY, OUT).

> **USAGE** For advice about using **but** and other conjunctions to begin a sentence, see **USAGE** at **AND**.

but² ▸ noun Scottish an outer room, especially in a two-roomed cottage.
– PHRASES **but and ben** a two-roomed cottage; a humble home.
– ORIGIN early 18th cent.: from BUT¹ in the early sense 'outside', specifically 'into the outer part of a house'.

butadiene /ˌbjuːtəˈdʌɪiːn/ ▸ noun [mass noun] Chemistry a colourless gaseous hydrocarbon made by catalytic dehydrogenation of butane. It is used in the manufacture of synthetic rubber. ● Chem. formula: $CH_2{=}CHCH{=}CH_2$.
– ORIGIN early 20th cent.: from BUTANE + DI-¹ + -ENE.

butane /ˈbjuːteɪn/ ▸ noun [mass noun] Chemistry a flammable hydrocarbon gas of the alkane series, present in petroleum and natural gas. It is used in bottled form as a fuel. See also ISOBUTANE. ● Chem. formula: $CH_3CH_2CH_2CH_3$.
– ORIGIN late 19th cent.: from BUTYL + -ANE².

butanoic acid /ˌbjuːtəˈnəʊɪk/ ▸ noun systematic chemical name for BUTYRIC ACID.

butanol /ˈbjuːtənɒl/ ▸ noun [mass noun] Chemistry each of two isomeric liquid alcohols used as solvents; butyl alcohol. ● Chem. formula: $CH_3CH_2CH_2CH_2OH$ (**1-butanol**, **butan-1-ol**) and $CH_3CH_2CH(OH)CH_3$ (**2-butanol**, **butan-2-ol**).

butch informal ▸ adjective mannish or masculine in appearance or behaviour, often aggressively or ostentatiously so.
▸ noun a mannish lesbian, typically as contrasted with a more feminine partner. Compare with FEMME.
– DERIVATIVES **butchy adjective**.
– ORIGIN 1940s: perhaps an abbreviation of BUTCHER.

butcher ▸ noun **1** a person whose trade is cutting up and selling meat in a shop. ■ a person who slaughters and cuts up animals for food: [with modifier] *a pork butcher*. ■ a person who kills people indiscriminately or brutally.
2 N. Amer. informal a person selling refreshments, newspapers, etc. on a train or in a theatre.
▸ verb [with obj.] slaughter or cut up (an animal) for food. ■ kill (a person or people) indiscriminately or brutally: *they rounded up and butchered 250 people*. ■ ruin (something) deliberately or through incompetence: *the film was butchered by the studio that released it*.
– PHRASES **have** (or **take**) **a butcher's** Brit. informal have a look. [*butcher's* from *butcher's hook*, rhyming slang for a 'look'.]
– ORIGIN Middle English: from an Anglo-Norman French variant of Old French *bochier*, from *boc* 'he-goat', probably of the same ultimate origin as BUCK¹.

butcher-bird ▸ noun **1** a shrike (family Laniidae), which impales its prey on thorns.
2 a crow-like predatory Australasian songbird, with a heavy hook-tipped bill. Compare with MAGPIE (sense 2). ● Family Cracticidae: three genera, in particular *Cracticus*, and several species.
– ORIGIN mid 17th cent.: from its habit of impaling its prey on thorns.

butcher's block ▸ noun a sturdy wooden kitchen table with a square top on which food may be chopped. ■ (also **butcher block**) [mass noun] N. Amer. a material used to make kitchen worktops and tables, consisting of strips of wood glued together.

butcher's broom ▸ noun a low evergreen Eurasian shrub of the lily family, with flat shoots that give the appearance of stiff spine-tipped leaves. ● *Ruscus aculeatus*, family Liliaceae.

B

butcher's meat (also **butcher meat**) ▶ **noun** [mass noun] Brit. fresh uncured meat excluding game and poultry.

butchery ▶ **noun** (pl. **butcheries**) [mass noun] **1** the work of slaughtering animals and preparing them for sale as meat. ■ [count noun] Brit. a slaughterhouse. ■ [count noun] Brit. a butcher's shop.
2 the savage killing of large numbers of people.
– ORIGIN Middle English (denoting a slaughterhouse or meat market): from Old French *boucherie*, from *bouchier* 'butcher'.

Bute /bjuːt/, John Stuart, 3rd Earl of (1713–92), Scottish courtier and Tory statesman, Prime Minister 1762–3.

bute /bjuːt/ ▶ **noun** informal term for PHENYLBUTAZONE.

buteo /ˈbjuːtɪəʊ/ ▶ **noun** (pl. **buteos**) Ornithology, chiefly US a bird of prey of a group distinguished by broad wings that are used for soaring. ● *Buteo* and related genera, family Accipitridae; many species, including the buzzards and the American red-tailed and Harris' hawks.
– ORIGIN from Latin *buteo* 'buzzard, hawk'.

Buteyko /buːˈteɪkəʊ/ ▶ **noun** [as modifier] of or denoting a technique of controlled breathing claimed to alleviate asthma.
– ORIGIN 1990s: named after the Russian physiologist Konstantin *Buteyko* (born 1923), who devised the technique.

Buthelezi /ˌbuːtəˈleɪzi/, Dr Mangosuthu (Gatsha) (b.1928), South African politician. He became leader of the Inkatha movement in 1975, and was Minister of Home Affairs 1994–2004.

Butler[1], Reg (1913–81), English sculptor; born *Reginald Cotterell*. Working mainly in forged or cast metal, he won an international competition in 1953 for a monument (never built) to the Unknown Political Prisoner.

Butler[2], Samuel (1612–80), English poet, most notable for his three-part satirical poem *Hudibras* (1663–78).

Butler[3], Samuel (1835–1902), English novelist. He is noted for *Erewhon* (1872), *Erewhon Revisited* (1901), and the semi-autobiographical *The Way of All Flesh* (1903).

butler ▶ **noun** the chief manservant of a house.
– ORIGIN Middle English: from Old French *bouteillier* 'cup-bearer', from *bouteille* 'bottle'.

butler sink ▶ **noun** another term for BELFAST SINK.

butoh /ˈbuːtəʊ/ ▶ **noun** [mass noun] a style of Japanese modern dance featuring dancers covered in white body paint.
– ORIGIN Japanese, literally 'dance'.

butt[1] ▶ **verb** [with obj.] (of a person or animal) hit (someone or something) with the head or horns: *she butted him in the chest*. ■ strike (one's head) against something.
▶ **noun** a push or blow, especially one given with the head.
– PHRASES **butt heads** N. Amer. informal engage in conflict or be in strong disagreement.
– PHRASAL VERBS **butt in** interrupt or intrude on a conversation or activity: *sorry to butt in on you*. **butt out** N. Amer. informal stop interfering: *politicians should butt out of these cases*.
– ORIGIN Middle English: from Old French *boter*, of Germanic origin.

butt[2] ▶ **noun 1** the person or thing at which criticism or ridicule is directed: *his singing is the butt of dozens of jokes*.
2 (usu. **butts**) an archery or shooting target or range. ■ a mound on or in front of which a target is set up for archery or shooting. ■ a grouse-shooter's stand, screened by low turf or a stone wall.
– ORIGIN Middle English (in the archery sense): from Old French *but*, of unknown origin; perhaps influenced by French *butte* 'rising ground'.

butt[3] ▶ **noun 1** (also **butt end**) the thicker end of something, especially a tool or a weapon: *a rifle butt*. ■ the square end of a plank or plate meeting the end or side of another, as in the side of a ship. ■ the thicker or hind end of a hide used for leather.
2 (also **butt end**) the stub of a cigar or a cigarette.
3 informal, chiefly N. Amer. a person's buttocks or anus.
4 the trunk of a tree, especially the part just above the ground.
▶ **verb** [no obj.] adjoin or meet end to end: *the shop butted up against the row of houses*. ■ [with obj.] join (pieces of stone, timber, and other building materials) with the ends or sides flat against each other.
– ORIGIN late Middle English: the noun apparently related to Dutch *bot* 'stumpy', also to BUTTOCK; the verb partly from BUTT[2], reinforced by ABUT.

butt[4] ▶ **noun 1** a cask, typically used for wine, beer, or water: *a butt of malmsey*.
2 US a liquid measure equal to 126 US gallons (equivalent to 477.5 litres).
– ORIGIN late Middle English: from Old French *bot*, from late Latin *buttis*.

butte /bjuːt/ ▶ **noun** N. Amer. & technical an isolated hill with steep sides and a flat top (similar to but narrower than a mesa).
– ORIGIN mid 19th cent.: from French, 'mound', from Old French *but*, of unknown origin (compare with BUTT[2]).

butter ▶ **noun** [mass noun] a pale yellow edible fatty substance made by churning cream and used as a spread or in cooking.
▶ **verb** [with obj.] spread (something) with butter: *Lily buttered a slice of toast* | (as adj. **buttered**) *lavishly buttered bread*.
– PHRASES **look as if butter wouldn't melt in one's mouth** informal appear gentle or innocent while typically being the opposite.
– PHRASAL VERBS **butter someone up** informal flatter or otherwise ingratiate oneself with someone.
– ORIGIN Old English *butere*, of West Germanic origin; related to Dutch *boter* and German *Butter*, based on Latin *butyrum*, from Greek *bouturon*.

butter-and-eggs ▶ **noun** any of a number of plants having two shades of yellow in the flower, especially yellow toadflax.

butterball ▶ **noun** N. Amer. a plump bird, especially a turkey or bufflehead. ■ informal, derogatory a fat person.

butter bean ▶ **noun** Brit. a lima bean, especially one of a variety with large flat white seeds.

butterbur /ˈbʌtəbəː/ ▶ **noun** a Eurasian waterside plant of the daisy family, the rounded flower heads of which are produced before the leaves. The large, soft leaves were formerly used to wrap butter, and extracts are used medicinally as an anticonvulsant. ● Genus *Petasites*, family Compositae: several species, in particular the common *P. hybridus*.

buttercream ▶ **noun** [mass noun] a soft mixture of butter and icing sugar used as a filling or topping for a cake.

buttercup ▶ **noun** a herbaceous plant with bright yellow cup-shaped flowers, which is common in grassland and as a garden weed. All kinds are poisonous and generally avoided by livestock. ● Genus *Ranunculus*, family Ranunculaceae (the **buttercup family**). This large family also includes anemones, celandines, aconites, clematis, and hellebores, many of which have poisonous seeds.

buttercup squash ▶ **noun** a winter squash of a variety with dark green rind and orange flesh.

butterfat ▶ **noun** [mass noun] the natural fat contained in milk and dairy products.

Butterfield, William (1814–1900), English architect, an exponent of the Gothic revival. Notable designs: Keble College, Oxford (1867–83).

butterfingers ▶ **noun** (pl. **same**) informal a clumsy person, especially one who fails to hold a catch.
– DERIVATIVES **butterfingered** adjective.

butterfish ▶ **noun** (pl. **same** or **butterfishes**) any of a number of fishes with oily flesh or slippery skin: ● a deep-bodied edible fish of temperate and tropical seas (family Stromateidae), in particular *Peprilus triacanthus* of eastern North America. ● another term for GUNNEL[1]. ● an Australasian reef fish (family Odacidae), in particular the edible *Odax pullus* of New Zealand, which has green bones and feeds on kelp. ● a tropical freshwater or marine fish that is popular in aquaria (several families, including Scatophagidae).

butterfly ▶ **noun** (pl. **butterflies**) **1** a nectar-feeding insect with two pairs of large, typically brightly coloured wings that are covered with microscopic scales. Butterflies are distinguished from moths by having clubbed or dilated antennae, holding their wings erect when at rest, and being active by day. ● Superfamilies Papilionoidea and Hesperioidea, order Lepidoptera: several families. Formerly placed in a grouping known as the Rhopalocera.
■ [as modifier] having a two-lobed shape resembling the spread wings of a butterfly: *a butterfly clip*. ■ a showy or frivolous person: *a social butterfly*. ■ (**butterflies**) informal a fluttering and nauseous sensation felt in the stomach when one is nervous.
2 a stroke in swimming in which both arms are raised out of the water and lifted forwards together.
▶ **verb** (**butterflies**, **butterflying**, **butterflied**) [with obj.] split (a piece of meat or fish) almost in two and spread it out flat: (as adj. **butterflied**) *butterflied shrimp*.
– ORIGIN Old English, from BUTTER + FLY[2]; perhaps from the cream or yellow colour of common species, or from an old belief that the insects stole butter.

butterfly bush ▶ **noun** a Chinese buddleia that is cultivated in the West for its large spikes of fragrant purplish-lilac or white flowers, which are highly attractive to butterflies. ● *Buddleia davidii*, family Loganiaceae.

butterfly cake ▶ **noun** Brit. a small sponge cake with its top cut off and divided into two pieces, which are then fixed to the cake with buttercream at an angle to resemble a butterfly's wings.

butterfly effect ▶ **noun** (with reference to chaos theory) the phenomenon whereby a minute localized change in a complex system can have large effects elsewhere.
– ORIGIN 1980s: from the notion in chaos theory that a butterfly fluttering in Rio de Janeiro could change the weather in Chicago.

butterfly fish ▶ **noun 1** any of a number of brightly coloured or boldly marked fish of warm waters, in particular: ● a reef-dwelling fish that is popular in marine aquaria (*Chaetodon* and other genera, family Chaetodontidae). ● a predatory marine fish that bears long venomous spines (genus *Pterois*, family Scorpaenidae).
2 a West African freshwater fish with large pectoral fins used in leaping out of the water and long fin rays used as stilts. ● *Pantodon buchholzi*, the only member of the family Pantodontidae.

butterfly knife ▶ **noun** a long, broad knife used in pairs in some forms of kung fu.

butterfly net ▶ **noun** a fine-meshed bag supported on a frame at the end of a handle, used for catching butterflies.

butterfly nut ▶ **noun** another term for WING NUT (sense 1).

butterfly orchid ▶ **noun** a wild orchid with a flower that somewhat resembles a butterfly in shape, found in both Eurasia and North America. ● Genus *Platanthera*, family Orchidaceae: many species, including two widely distributed European species with fragrant greenish-white flowers, *P. chlorantha* and the smaller *P. bifolia*.

butterfly valve ▶ **noun** a valve consisting of a rotating circular plate or a pair of hinged semicircular plates, attached to a transverse spindle and mounted inside a pipe in order to regulate or prevent flow.

butterfly weed ▶ **noun** [mass noun] a North American milkweed with bright orange flowers which are attractive to butterflies. ● *Asclepias tuberosa*, family Asclepiadaceae.

butterhead lettuce ▶ **noun** a class of lettuce varieties having soft leaves that grow in a loose head and are said to have the flavour of butter.

butter icing ▶ **noun** another term for BUTTERCREAM.

buttermilk ▶ **noun** [mass noun] the slightly sour liquid left after butter has been churned, used in baking or consumed as a drink. ■ a pale yellow colour like that of buttermilk.

butter muslin ▶ **noun** [mass noun] Brit. loosely woven cotton cloth, formerly used for wrapping butter.

butternut ▶ **noun** a North American walnut tree which is cultivated as an ornamental and also for its quality timber. ● *Juglans cinerea*, family Juglandaceae. ■ the edible oily nut of the butternut.

butternut squash ▶ **noun** a popular winter squash of a pear-shaped variety with light yellowish brown rind and orange flesh.

butterscotch ▶ **noun** [mass noun] a brittle yellow-brown sweet made with butter and brown sugar. ■ a sauce or syrup flavoured with butterscotch.

butterwort /ˈbʌtəwəːt/ ▶ **noun** a carnivorous bog plant which has violet flowers borne above a rosette of greasy yellowish-green leaves that trap and digest small insects, found in both Eurasia and North America. ● Genus *Pinguicula*, family Lentibulariaceae: several species, in particular the **common butterwort** (*P. vulgaris*).
– ORIGIN late 16th cent.: named from the plant's supposed ability to keep cows in milk, and so maintain the supply of butter.

buttery[1] ▶ **adjective** containing or tasting like butter: *layers of flaky buttery pastry*. ■ covered with butter: *buttery fingers*.
– DERIVATIVES **butteriness** noun.

buttery² ▶ noun (pl. **butteries**) Brit. a room in a college where food is kept and sold to students.
– ORIGIN Middle English: from Anglo-Norman French *boterie* 'butt store', from Old French *bot* (see **BUTT⁴**).

butthead ▶ noun N. Amer. informal a stupid or stubborn person: *only a butthead would drive a car like that*.

buttie ▶ noun (pl. **butties**) variant spelling of **BUTTY¹**.

buttinsky ▶ noun N. Amer. informal an interfering person.
– ORIGIN early 20th cent.: from *butt in* (see **BUTT¹**) and *-ski*, formed in humorous imitation of the final element in many Russian names.

buttle ▶ verb [no obj.] humorous work as a butler: *there is no one today worth **buttling for***.
– ORIGIN mid 19th cent.: back-formation from **BUTLER**.

butt naked ▶ adjective informal completely naked.

buttock ▶ noun either of the two round fleshy parts of the human body that form the bottom.
– ORIGIN Old English *buttuc*, probably from the base of **BUTT³** + **-OCK**.

buttock line ▶ noun each of a series of longitudinal lines or curves marked on a plan of a ship to show its fore-and-aft sections at various distances from the centre line.

Button, Jenson (Alexander Lyons) (b.1980), English motor-racing driver. He won the Formula One world championship in 2009.

button ▶ noun **1** a small disc or knob sewn on to a garment, either to fasten it by being pushed through a slit made for the purpose or for decoration. ■ a small round object resembling a button: *chocolate buttons*. ■ Fencing a knob fitted to the point of a foil to make it harmless. ■ used in reference to things of little worth: *he will never give away anything that is worth a button*.
2 a small device on a piece of electrical or electronic equipment which is pressed to operate it.
3 chiefly N. Amer. a badge bearing a design or slogan and pinned to clothing.
▶ verb **1** [with obj.] fasten (clothing) with buttons: ***he buttoned up** his jacket*. ■ (**button someone into**) fasten the buttons of a garment being worn by someone: *he buttoned himself into the raincoat*. ■ [no obj.] (of a garment) be fastened with buttons: *a dress which buttoned down the front*.
2 (usu. in imperative **button it**) informal stop talking.
– PHRASES **button one's lip** informal stop or refrain from talking. **on the button** informal, chiefly US punctually: *we arrived at 5.20 on the button*. ■ exactly right: *the programme is right on the button every time*. **press the button** informal initiate an action or train of events (often used to refer to the ease with which a nuclear war might be started). **push** (or **press**) **someone's buttons** informal arouse or provoke a reaction in someone: *don't allow co-workers to push your buttons*.
– PHRASAL VERBS **button something up** informal complete or conclude something satisfactorily: *they've buttoned up the league title by opening up a seven points gap*. ■ (often as adj. **buttoned up**) repress or inhibit something: *it was repressive enough to keep public opinion buttoned up*.
– DERIVATIVES **buttoned** adjective [in combination] *a gold-buttoned blazer*, **buttonless** adjective.
– ORIGIN Middle English: from Old French *bouton*, of Germanic origin and related to **BUTT¹**.

button-back ▶ noun [as modifier] denoting a chair or sofa with a quilted back, the stitching being hidden by buttons: *a button-back antique chair*.

buttonball tree ▶ noun see **BUTTONWOOD** (sense 1).

buttonbush ▶ noun a low-growing North American shrub that grows in water, with small tubular flowers forming globular flower heads. ● *Cephalanthus occidentalis*, family Rubiaceae.

button chrysanthemum ▶ noun a variety of chrysanthemum with small spherical flowers.

button-down ▶ adjective (of a collar) having points which are buttoned to the garment. ■ (of a shirt) having such a collar. ■ (also **buttoned down**) N. Amer. informal (of a person) conservative or unimaginative.
▶ noun a shirt with a button-down collar.

button grass ▶ noun [mass noun] chiefly Austral. a grass or sedge with compact rounded flowering heads. ● a large tufted sedge (*Gymnoschoenus spaerocephalus*, family Cyperaceae). ● an annual grass (*Dactyloctenium radulans*, family Gramineae).

buttonhole ▶ noun a slit made in a garment to receive a button for fastening. ■ Brit. a flower or spray worn in a buttonhole on the lapel of a jacket.
▶ verb [with obj.] **1** informal attract the attention of and detain (someone) in conversation, typically against their will.
2 make buttonholes in (a garment).

buttonholer ▶ noun an attachment for a sewing machine used to make buttonholes.

buttonhole stitch ▶ noun [mass noun] a looped stitch used for edging buttonholes or pieces of material.

buttonhook ▶ noun **1** a small hook with a long handle for fastening tight buttons (often formerly on buttoned boots).
2 American Football a play in which a pass receiver runs straight downfield and then doubles back sharply towards the line of scrimmage.

button lift ▶ noun another term for **POMA**.

button man ▶ noun N. Amer. informal a hired killer.

button mushroom ▶ noun a young unopened mushroom.

button-quail ▶ noun a small quail-like Old World bird related to the rails, with only three toes. Also called **HEMIPODE**. ● Family Turnicidae and genus *Turnix*: several species, including the widespread **barred button-quail** (*T. suscitator*) of Asia (also called **BUSTARD QUAIL**).

Buttons ▶ noun Brit. informal a nickname for a liveried pageboy, now normally only in pantomimes.
– ORIGIN mid 19th cent.: from the rows of buttons on his jacket.

button spider ▶ noun a highly venomous African spider which is a close relative of the American black widow. ● A subspecies of *Latrodectus mactans*, family Theridiidae.

button-through ▶ adjective Brit. (of clothing) fastened with buttons from top to bottom.
▶ noun a dress that fastens in such a way.

buttonwood ▶ noun **1** (also **buttonwood tree**) N. Amer. an American plane tree. Also called **SYCAMORE** in North America. ● Genus *Platanus*, family Platanaceae: several species, in particular *P. occidentalis* (also called **BUTTONBALL TREE**), which is the largest deciduous tree in the US and is grown for ornament and timber.
2 either of two mangroves found mainly in tropical America, used in the production of tanbark and for charcoal. ● *Conocarpus erectus* (the button mangrove) and *Laguncularia racemosa*, family Combretaceae.

buttress /ˈbʌtrɪs/ ▶ noun **1** a structure of stone or brick built against a wall to strengthen or support it: *the cathedral's massive buttresses*. ■ a projecting portion of a hill or mountain.
2 a source of defence or support: *the political police were the main buttress of the regime*.
▶ verb [with obj.] **1** provide (a building or structure) with buttresses: (as adj. **buttressed**) *a buttressed wall*.
2 increase the strength of or justification for; reinforce: *authority was buttressed by religious belief*.
– ORIGIN Middle English: from Old French (*ars*) *bouterez* 'thrusting (arch)', from *boter* 'to strike or thrust' (see **BUTT¹**).

butt ugly ▶ adjective informal, chiefly N. Amer. (chiefly of a person) extremely unattractive.

butty¹ (also **buttie**) ▶ noun (pl. **butties**) informal, chiefly N. English a filled or open sandwich: *a bacon butty*.
– ORIGIN mid 19th cent.: from **BUTTER** + **-Y²**.

butty² ▶ noun (pl. **butties**) Brit. **1** informal (among miners) a friend or workmate.
2 historical a middleman negotiating between miners and the mine owner.
3 (also **butty boat**) an unpowered freight barge intended to be towed.
– ORIGIN late 18th cent.: probably from **BOOTY¹** in the phrase *play booty* 'join in sharing plunder'.

butut /ˈbuːtuːt/ ▶ noun (pl. **same** or **bututs**) a monetary unit of Gambia, equal to one hundredth of a dalasi.
– ORIGIN a local word.

butyl /ˈbjuːtʌɪl, -tɪl/ ▶ noun [as modifier] Chemistry of or denoting an alkyl radical $-C_4H_9$, derived from butane: *butyl acetate*. See also **ISOBUTYL**. ■ short for **BUTYL RUBBER**.
– ORIGIN mid 19th cent.: from **BUTYRIC ACID** + **-YL**.

butyl rubber ▶ noun [mass noun] a synthetic rubber made by polymerizing isobutylene and isoprene.

butyrate /ˈbjuːtɪreɪt/ ▶ noun Chemistry a salt or ester of butyric acid.

butyric acid /bjuːˈtɪrɪk/ ▶ noun [mass noun] Chemistry a colourless syrupy liquid organic acid found in rancid butter and in arnica oil. ● Alternative name: **butanoic acid**; chem. formula: C_3H_7COOH.
– ORIGIN mid 19th cent.: *butyric* from Latin *butyrum* (see **BUTTER**) + **-IC**.

buxom /ˈbʌks(ə)m/ ▶ adjective (of a woman) plump, with a full figure and large breasts: *a buxom blonde*.
– DERIVATIVES **buxomness** noun.
– ORIGIN Middle English: from the stem of Old English *būgan* 'to bend' (see **BOW²**) + **-SOME¹**. The original sense was 'compliant, obliging', later 'lively and good-tempered', influenced by the traditional association of plumpness and good health with an easy-going nature.

Buxtehude /ˈbʊkstəˌhuːdə/, Dietrich (*c*.1637–1707), Danish organist and composer. Working in Lübeck, he wrote mainly for the organ.

buy ▶ verb (**buys, buying**; past and past participle **bought**) [with obj.] **1** obtain in exchange for payment: *she bought six first-class stamps* | *he had been able to **buy up** hundreds of acres* | [with two objs] *he bought me a new frock* | [no obj.] *homeowners who **buy into** housing developments*. ■ (**buy someone out**) pay someone to give up an ownership, interest, or share. ■ (**buy oneself out**) obtain one's release from the armed services by payment. ■ (**buy something in**) withdraw something at auction because it fails to meet the reserve price. ■ procure the loyalty and support of (someone) by bribery: *here was a man who could not be bought* | *I'll **buy off** the investigators*. ■ [often with negative] be a means of obtaining (something) through exchange or payment: *money can't buy happiness*. ■ get by sacrifice or great effort: *greatness is **dearly bought***. ■ [no obj.] be a buyer for a store or firm.
2 informal accept the truth of: *I am not prepared to buy the claim that the ends justify the means* | [no obj.] *I hate to **buy into** stereotypes*.
▶ noun informal a purchase: *wine is rarely a good buy in duty-free shops*. ■ an act of purchasing something: *a drug buy*.
– PHRASES **buy the farm** N. Amer. informal die. **buy it** informal be killed. **buy time** delay an event temporarily so as to have longer to improve one's own position.
– ORIGIN Old English *bycgan*, of Germanic origin.

buy-back ▶ noun [mass noun] the buying back of goods by the original seller. ■ a form of borrowing in which shares or bonds are sold with an agreement to repurchase them at a later date.

buyer ▶ noun a person who makes a purchase. ■ a person employed to select and purchase stock or materials for a large retail or manufacturing business.
– PHRASES **buyer's** (or **buyers'**) **market** an economic situation in which goods or shares are plentiful and buyers can keep prices down.

buy-in ▶ noun **1** a purchase of shares by a broker after a seller has failed to deliver similar shares, the original seller being charged any difference in cost.
2 (also **management buy-in**) a purchase of shares in a company by managers who are not employed by it.
3 [mass noun] the buying back by a company of its own shares.
4 agreement with, or acceptance of, a policy or suggestion: *there should be a moral buy-in from everyone in the organization*.

buyout ▶ noun the purchase of a controlling share in a company, especially by its own managers (also **management buyout**).

buzz ▶ noun **1** a low, continuous humming or murmuring sound, made by or similar to that made by an insect: *the buzz of the bees* | *a buzz of conversation*. ■ the sound of a buzzer or telephone. ■ informal a telephone call: *I'll give you a buzz*.
2 an atmosphere of excitement and activity: *there is a real buzz about the place*. ■ informal a feeling of excitement or euphoria; a thrill: *I got such a buzz out of seeing the kids' faces*.
3 informal a rumour: *there's a strong buzz that he's in Scotland*.
▶ verb [no obj.] **1** make a low, continuous humming sound: *mosquitoes were buzzing all around us*. ■ signal to someone with a buzzer: *the intercom buzzed loudly* | [with obj.] *he buzzed the stewardesses every five minutes*. ■ [with obj.] informal telephone (someone).
2 [with adverbial of direction] move quickly or busily: *she buzzed along the M1 back into town*. ■ [with obj.] Aeronautics, informal fly very close to (another aircraft, the ground, etc.) at high speed: *helicopter gunships were sent to buzz the villages*.
3 (usu. **be buzzing with**) be full of excitement or activity: *Westminster is buzzing with anticipation* | *within an hour, every department was buzzing with the news*. ■ (of a person) be euphoric or very stimulated: *twenty-four hours later Marcus was still buzzing*.
4 [with obj.] Brit. informal throw (something) hard.

– PHRASAL VERBS **buzz off** [often in imperative] informal go away.
– ORIGIN late Middle English: imitative.

buzzard /ˈbʌzəd/ ▶ noun **1** a large hawklike bird of prey with broad wings and a rounded tail, often seen soaring in wide circles. ● Family Accipitridae: several genera, in particular *Buteo*, and including the common (**Eurasian**) **buzzard** (*B. buteo*).
2 N. Amer. a vulture, especially a turkey vulture.
– ORIGIN late Middle English: from Old French *busard*, based on Latin *buteo* 'falcon'.

buzz bomb ▶ noun informal term for FLYING BOMB.

buzz cut ▶ noun a very short haircut in which the hair is clipped close to the head with a razor.

buzzer ▶ noun an electrical device that makes a buzzing noise and is used for signalling.
– PHRASES **at the buzzer** N. Amer. at the end of a game or period of play.

buzzkill ▶ noun N. Amer. informal a person or thing that has a depressing or dispiriting effect: *if you think bad weather at the zoo sounds like a buzzkill, you're right.*

buzz saw ▶ noun North American term for CIRCULAR SAW.

buzzword (also **buzz phrase**) ▶ noun informal a technical word or phrase that has become fashionable, typically as a slogan.

buzzy ▶ adjective (**buzzier**, **buzziest**) informal (especially of a place or atmosphere) lively and exciting: *a buzzy bar with live music.*

BVDs ▶ plural noun N. Amer. trademark a type of boxer shorts.
– ORIGIN late 19th cent.: abbreviation from the name of the manufacturers; the mistaken full form in folk etymology is *babies' ventilated diapers.*

BVI ▶ abbreviation British Virgin Islands.

BVM ▶ abbreviation Blessed Virgin Mary.

b/w ▶ abbreviation black and white (used especially to describe printing, film, photographs, or television pictures).

bwana /ˈbwɑːnə/ ▶ noun (in East Africa) a boss or master (often used as a title or form of address): *he can't hear you, bwana.*
– ORIGIN Kiswahili.

BWR ▶ abbreviation boiling-water reactor.

by ▶ preposition **1** identifying the agent performing an action: ■ after a passive verb: *the door was opened by my cousin Annie | damage caused by fire.* ■ after a noun denoting an action: *a clear decision by the electorate | years of hard fund-raising work by local people.* ■ identifying the author of a text, idea, or work of art: *a book by Ernest Hemingway.*
2 [often with verbal noun] indicating the means of achieving something: *malaria can be controlled by attacking the parasite | they substantiate their opinions by the use of precise textual reference | they plan to provide further working capital* ***by means of*** *borrowing.* ■ indicating a term to which an interpretation is to be assigned: *what is meant by 'fair'?* ■ indicating a name according to which a person is known: *she mostly calls me by my last name.* ■ indicating the means of transport selected for a journey: *the cost of travelling by bus | I travelled to Folkestone by rail.* ■ indicating the other parent of someone's child or children: *Richard is his son by his third wife.* ■ indicating the sire of a pedigree animal, especially a horse: *a black filly by Goldfuerst.* ■ (followed by a noun without a determiner) in various phrases indicating how something happens: *I heard by chance that she has married again | Anderson, by contrast, rejects this view | she ate by candlelight.*
3 indicating the amount or size of a margin: *the shot missed her by miles | the raising of VAT by 2.5%.* ■ indicating a quantity or amount: *billing is by the minute | the drunken yobbos who turned up by the cartload.* ■ in phrases indicating something happening repeatedly or progressively, typically with repetition of a unit of time: *colours changing minute by minute | the risk becomes worse by the day.* ■ identifying a parameter: *a breakdown of employment figures by age and occupation.* ■ expressing multiplication, especially in dimensions: *a map measuring 400 by 600 mm | she multiplied it by 89.*
4 indicating a deadline or the end of a particular time period: *I've got to do this report by Monday | by now Kelly needed extensive physiotherapy.*
5 indicating location of a physical object beside a place or object: *remains were discovered by the roadside | the pram was by the dresser.* ■ past and beyond: *I drove by our house.*
6 indicating the period in which something happens: *this animal always hunts* ***by night.***
7 concerning; according to: *anything you do is all right by me | she had done her duty by him.*
8 used in mild oaths: *it was the least he could do, by God | I swear by Almighty God.*
▶ adverb so as to go past: *a car flashed by on the other side of the road | he let only a moment go by.*
▶ noun (pl. **byes**) variant spelling of BYE¹.
– PHRASES **by and by** before long; eventually. **by the by** (or **bye**) incidentally: *where's Hector, by the by?* **by and large** on the whole; everything considered: *mammals have, by and large, bigger brains than reptiles.* [originally in nautical use, describing the handling of a ship both to the wind and off it.] **by oneself 1** alone: *she lives in the apartment by herself.* **2** unaided: *the patient often learns to undress by himself.* **by way of** see WAY.
– ORIGIN Old English *bī, bi, be*, of Germanic origin; related to Dutch *bij* and German *bei*.

by- (also **bye-**) ▶ prefix subordinate; incidental; secondary: *by-election | by-product.*

Byatt /ˈbʌɪət/, Dame A. S. (b.1936), English novelist and literary critic; born *Antonia Susan Byatt*. Notable novels: *The Virgin in the Garden* (1978) and *Possession* (1990, Booker Prize).

Byblos /ˈbɪblɒs/ an ancient Mediterranean seaport, situated on the site of modern Jebeil, to the north of Beirut in Lebanon. It became a thriving Phoenician city in the 2nd millennium BC.

by-blow ▶ noun Brit. dated a man's illegitimate child.

by-catch ▶ noun the unwanted fish and other marine creatures trapped by commercial fishing nets during fishing for a different species.

Bydgoszcz /ˈbɪdgɒʃtʃ/ an industrial river port in north central Poland; pop. 362,397 (2007). 20,000 of its citizens were massacred by Nazis in September 1939. German name BROMBERG.

bye¹ ▶ noun **1** the transfer of a competitor directly to the next round of a competition in the absence of an assigned opponent.
2 Cricket a run scored from a ball that passes the batsman without being hit (recorded as an extra, not credited to the individual batsman).
3 Golf one or more holes remaining unplayed after a match has been decided.
– PHRASES **by the bye** variant spelling of BY THE BY (see BY).
– ORIGIN mid 16th cent. (denoting a side issue or incidental matter): from BY.

bye² ▶ exclamation informal short for GOODBYE.

bye- ▶ prefix variant spelling of BY-.

bye-bye ▶ exclamation informal way of saying GOODBYE.
– ORIGIN early 18th cent.: child's reduplication.

bye-byes ▶ noun [mass noun] a child's word for sleep.
– ORIGIN mid 19th cent.: from the sound *bye-bye*, long used as a refrain in lullabies.

by-election ▶ noun Brit. the election of an MP in a single constituency to fill a vacancy arising during a government's term of office.

byeline ▶ noun variant spelling of BYLINE (sense 2).

Byelorussia /ˌbjɛlə(ʊ)ˈrʊʃə/ variant spelling of BELORUSSIA.

Byelorussian /ˌbjɛlə(ʊ)ˈrʌʃ(ə)n/ ▶ adjective & noun variant spelling of BELORUSSIAN.

by-form ▶ noun a secondary form of a word: *historically, 'inquire' is a by-form of 'enquire'.*

bygone ▶ adjective belonging to an earlier time: *relics of a bygone age.*
▶ noun (usu. **bygones**) a thing dating from an earlier time.
– PHRASES **let bygones be bygones** forget past offences or causes of conflict and be reconciled.

by-law (also **bye-law**) ▶ noun **1** Brit. a regulation made by a local authority or corporation.
2 a rule made by a company or society to control the actions of its members.
– ORIGIN Middle English: probably from obsolete *byrlaw* 'local law or custom', from Old Norse *býjar*, genitive singular of *býr* 'town', but associated with BY.

byline ▶ noun **1** a line in a newspaper naming the writer of an article.
2 (also **byeline**) (chiefly in soccer) the part of the goal line to either side of the goal.

byname ▶ noun a nickname, especially one given to distinguish a person from others with the same given name.

BYO (also **BYOB**) ▶ abbreviation bring your own (bottle).

bypass ▶ noun **1** a road passing round a town or its centre to provide an alternative route for through traffic.
2 a secondary channel, pipe, or connection to allow a flow when the main one is closed or blocked.
3 an alternative passage made by surgery, typically to aid the circulation of blood. ■ a surgical operation to make such a passage.
▶ verb [with obj.] go past or round: *bypass the farm and continue to the road.* ■ provide (a town) with a route diverting traffic from its centre. ■ avoid or circumvent (an obstacle or problem): *a manager might bypass formal channels of communication.*

bypath ▶ noun an indirect route.

byplay ▶ noun [mass noun] secondary or subsidiary action or involvement in a play or film.

by-product ▶ noun an incidental or secondary product made in the manufacture or synthesis of something else: *zinc is a by-product of the glazing process.* ■ an unintended but inevitable secondary result: *he saw poverty as the by-product of colonial prosperity.*

Byrd¹, Richard (Evelyn) (1888–1957), American explorer, naval officer, and aviator. He claimed to have made the first aircraft flight over the North Pole (1926), although his actual course has been disputed. He was the first to fly over the South Pole (1929).

Byrd², William (1543–1623), English composer. He was joint organist of the Chapel Royal with Tallis and is famous for his Latin masses and his Anglican Great Service.

byre ▶ noun Brit. a cowshed.
– ORIGIN Old English *býre*; perhaps related to BOWER¹.

byroad ▶ noun a minor road.

Byron /ˈbʌɪərən/, George Gordon, 6th Baron (1788–1824), English poet. Byron's poetry exerted considerable influence on the romantic movement, particularly on the Continent. Having joined the fight for Greek independence, he died of malaria before seeing serious action. Notable works: *Childe Harold's Pilgrimage* (1812–18) and *Don Juan* (1819–24).

Byronic /bʌɪˈrɒnɪk/ ▶ adjective characteristic of Lord Byron or his poetry. ■ (of a man) alluringly dark, mysterious, and moody.

byssinosis /ˌbɪsɪˈnəʊsɪs/ ▶ noun [mass noun] a lung disease caused by prolonged inhalation of textile fibre dust.
– ORIGIN late 19th cent.: from Latin *byssinus* 'made of byssus' (from Greek *bussinos*) + -OSIS.

byssus /ˈbɪsəs/ ▶ noun (pl. **byssuses** or **byssi** /-sʌɪ/)
1 [mass noun] historical a fine textile fibre and fabric of flax.
2 Zoology a tuft of tough silky filaments by which mussels and some other bivalves adhere to rocks and other objects.
– DERIVATIVES **byssal** adjective.
– ORIGIN late Middle English: from Latin, from Greek *bussos*, of Semitic origin.

bystander ▶ noun a person who is present at an event or incident but does not take part.

byte /bʌɪt/ ▶ noun Computing a group of binary digits or bits (usually eight) operated on as a unit. ■ such a group as a unit of memory size.
– ORIGIN 1960s: an arbitrary formation based on BIT⁴ and BITE.

by-the-wind sailor ▶ noun a surface-dwelling colonial marine coelenterate of the Atlantic and Mediterranean. It has a disc-like float bearing a sail that is used to catch the wind. ● *Velella velella*, suborder Chondrophora, order Hydroida.

Bytom /ˈbɪtəm/ a city in southern Poland, north-west of Katowice; pop. 185,793 (2007). German name BEUTHEN.

bytownite /ˈbʌɪtaʊnʌɪt/ ▶ noun [mass noun] a mineral present in many basic igneous rocks, consisting of a calcic plagioclase feldspar.
– ORIGIN mid 19th cent.: from *Bytown*, the former name of Ottawa, Canada, + -ITE¹.

byway ▶ noun a road or track not following a main route; a minor road or path: *the* ***highways and byways*** *of Dorset.* ■ a little-known area of knowledge: *the arcane byways of the laws of privilege.*

byword ▶ noun a person or thing cited as a notable and outstanding example or embodiment of something: *his name became a **byword** for luxury.* ■ a word or expression summarizing a thing's characteristics or a person's principles: *'Small is beautiful' may be the byword for most couturiers.*

Byzantine /bɪˈzantʌɪn, bʌɪ-/ ▸ **adjective 1** relating to Byzantium, the Byzantine Empire, or the Eastern Orthodox Church. ■ of an ornate artistic and architectural style which developed in the Byzantine Empire and spread to Italy, Russia, and elsewhere. The art is typified by religious wall paintings and icons and the architecture by many-domed churches. **2** (of a system or situation) excessively complicated, and typically involving a great deal of administrative detail: *Byzantine insurance regulations.* ■ characterized by deviousness or underhand procedure: *he has the most Byzantine mind in politics.*
▸ **noun** a citizen of Byzantium or the Byzantine Empire.
– DERIVATIVES **Byzantinism** /bɪˈzantɪnɪz(ə)m, bʌɪ-/ **noun.**
– ORIGIN late 16th cent.: from Latin *Byzantinus*, from **Byzantium.**

Byzantine Empire the empire in SE Europe and Asia Minor formed from the eastern part of the Roman Empire.

> The Roman Empire was divided in AD 395 by the Emperor Theodosius between his sons; Constantinople (Byzantium) became the capital of the Eastern Empire in 476, with the fall of Rome. In 1054 theological and political differences between Constantinople and Rome led to the breach between Eastern and Western Christianity (see **Great Schism** (sense 1)). After about 1100 the empire gradually declined; the loss of Constantinople to the Ottoman Turks in 1453 was the end of the empire, although its rulers held Trebizond (Trabzon) until 1461.

Byzantinist /bɪˈzantɪst, bʌɪ-/ ▸ **noun** a historian or other scholar specializing in the study of the Byzantine Empire, its history, art, and culture.

Byzantium /bɪˈzantɪəm, bʌɪ-/ an ancient Greek city, founded in the 7th century BC, at the southern end of the Bosporus, site of the modern city of Istanbul. It was rebuilt by Constantine the Great in AD 324–30 as Constantinople.

BZP ▸ **abbreviation** benzylpiperazine, a drug which has stimulant and euphoric properties similar to those of amphetamine. ● Chem. formula: $C_{11}H_{16}N_2$.

B

C

Cc

C[1] (also **c**) ▸ **noun** (pl. **Cs** or **C's**) **1** the third letter of the alphabet. ■ denoting the third in a set of items, categories, sizes, etc. ■ the third-highest class of academic mark. ■ denoting an intermediate socio-economic category for marketing purposes, including the majority of white-collar (**C1**) and skilled blue-collar personnel (**C2**). ■ (**c**) Chess denoting the third file from the left of a chessboard, as viewed from White's side of the board. ■ (usu. **c**) the third fixed constant to appear in an algebraic expression, or a known constant. ■ denoting the lowest soil horizon, comprising parent materials.
2 a shape like that of a letter C: [in combination] *C-springs*.
3 (usu. **C**) Music the first note of the diatonic scale of C major, the major scale having no sharps or flats. ■ a key based on a scale with C as its keynote.
4 the Roman numeral for 100. [abbreviation of Latin *centum* 'hundred'.]
5 (**C**) [mass noun] a computer programming language originally developed for implementing the Unix operating system. [formerly known as *B*, abbreviation of *BCPL*.]

C[2] ▸ **abbreviation** ■ (**C.**) Cape: *C. Hatteras*. ■ Celsius or centigrade: *29°C*. ■ (in names of sports clubs) City: *Lincoln C*. ■ (**C.**) Brit. Command Paper (second series, 1870–99). ■ (in Britain) Conservative. ■ (**©**) copyright. ■ Physics coulomb(s). ■ Cuba (international vehicle registration).
▸ **symbol** ■ Physics capacitance. ■ the chemical element carbon.
– PHRASES **the Big C** informal cancer.

c ▸ **abbreviation** ■ Cricket (on scorecards) caught by: *ME Waugh c Lara b Walsh 19*. ■ cent(s). ■ [in combination] (in units of measurement) centi-: *centistokes* (*cS*). ■ (**c.**) century or centuries: *a watch case, 19th c*. ■ (often **c.**) (preceding a date or amount) circa; approximately: *Isabella was born c.1759*. ■ (of water) cold: *all bedrooms have h & c*. ■ colt.
▸ **symbol** Physics the speed of light in a vacuum: $E = mc^2$.

c/- ▸ **abbreviation** Austral./NZ care of.

C & W ▸ **abbreviation** country and western (music).

CA ▸ **abbreviation** ■ California (in official postal use). ■ Scottish & Canadian chartered accountant.

Ca ▸ **symbol** the chemical element calcium.

ca ▸ **abbreviation** (preceding a date or amount) circa.

CAA ▸ **abbreviation** (in the UK) Civil Aviation Authority.

Caaba variant spelling of KAABA.

caatinga /ˈkɑːtɪŋɡə/ ▸ **noun** [mass noun] (in Brazil) vegetation in semi-arid country consisting of thorny shrubs and stunted trees.
– ORIGIN via Portuguese from Tupi, from *caá* 'natural vegetation' + *tinga* 'white'.

CAB ▸ **abbreviation** ■ Citizens' Advice Bureau. ■ US Civil Aeronautics Board.

cab[1] ▸ **noun 1** (also **taxi cab**) a taxi. ■ historical a horse-drawn vehicle for public hire.
2 the driver's compartment in a lorry, bus, or train.
▸ **verb** (**cabs, cabbing, cabbed**) [no obj.] travel in a taxi: *Roger cabbed home*.
– ORIGIN early 19th cent.: abbreviation of CABRIOLET.

cab[2] ▸ **noun** informal a cabinet containing a speaker or speakers for a guitar amplifier.
– ORIGIN late 20th cent.: abbreviation.

cabal /kəˈbal/ ▸ **noun** a secret political clique or faction: *a cabal of dissidents*. ■ archaic a secret intrigue.
– ORIGIN late 16th cent. (denoting the Kabbalah): from French *cabale*, from medieval Latin *cabala* (see KABBALAH).

Cabala ▸ **noun** variant spelling of KABBALAH.

cabaletta /ˌkabəˈlɛtə/ ▸ **noun** (pl. **cabalettas** or **cabalette**) a simple aria with a repetitive rhythm. ■ the uniformly quick final section of an aria.
– ORIGIN mid 19th cent.: from Italian, variant of *coboletta* 'short stanza', diminutive of *cobola*, from Old Provençal *cobla*, from Latin *copula* 'connection'.

caballero /ˌkabəˈljɛːrəʊ/ ▸ **noun** (pl. **caballeros**) **1** a Spanish gentleman.
2 US (in the south-western states) a horseman.
– ORIGIN mid 19th cent.: Spanish, 'gentleman, horseman', based on Latin *caballus* 'horse'. Compare with CAVALIER, CHEVALIER.

cabana /kəˈbɑːnə/ ▸ **noun** N. Amer. a hut, cabin, or shelter at a beach or swimming pool.
– ORIGIN late 19th cent.: from Spanish *cabaña*, from late Latin *capana*, *cavana* 'cabin'.

cabaret /ˈkabəreɪ, ˌkabəˈreɪ/ ▸ **noun** [mass noun] entertainment held in a nightclub or restaurant while the audience eat or drink at tables: *she was seen recently in cabaret* | [as modifier] *a cabaret act* | [count noun] *the cabaret drew to a close*. ■ [count noun] a nightclub or restaurant where cabaret is performed.
– ORIGIN mid 17th cent. (denoting a French inn): from Old French, literally 'wooden structure', via Middle Dutch from Old Picard *camberet* 'little room'. Current senses date from the early 20th cent.

cabbage ▸ **noun 1** a cultivated plant eaten as a vegetable, having thick green or purple leaves surrounding a spherical heart or head of young leaves. ● *Brassica oleracea*, family Cruciferae (or Brassicaceae; the **cabbage family**). As well as the brassicas, the members of this family (known as crucifers) include the mustards and cresses together with many ornamentals (candytuft, alyssum, stocks, nasturtiums, wallflowers).
■ [mass noun] the leaves of cabbage, eaten as a vegetable.
2 Brit. offensive a person whose physical or mental activity is impaired or destroyed by injury or illness. ■ informal a person who leads a very dull life.
– DERIVATIVES **cabbagey** adjective.
– ORIGIN late Middle English: from Old French (Picard) *caboche* 'head', variant of Old French *caboce*, of unknown origin.

cabbage moth ▸ **noun** a brown moth whose caterpillars are pests of cabbages and related plants. ● *Mamestra brassicae*, family Noctuidae.

cabbage palm ▸ **noun** any of a number of palms or palm-like plants that resemble a cabbage in some way, in particular: ● a Caribbean palm with edible buds that resemble a cabbage (*Roystonea oleraceae*, family Palmae). ● an evergreen plant occurring in warm regions and grown elsewhere as a greenhouse or indoor plant (genus *Cordyline*, family Agavaceae).

cabbage roll ▸ **noun** N. Amer. a boiled cabbage leaf that is formed into a roll with a stuffing of rice and minced meat and then baked.

cabbage rose ▸ **noun** a kind of rose with a large, round, compact double flower.

cabbage tree ▸ **noun** any of a number of palm-like trees that resemble a cabbage in some way, in particular: ● a New Zealand tree grown for its sugary sap or for ornament (*Cordyline australis*, family Agavaceae). ● a cabbage palm.

cabbage white ▸ **noun** a mainly white butterfly that has caterpillars which are pests of cabbages and related plants. ● Genus *Pieris*, family Pieridae: several species, in particular the **small white** (*P. rapae*) and the **large white** (*P. brassicae*).

cabbageworm ▸ **noun** N. Amer. any caterpillar that is a pest of cabbages, especially that of the cabbage white butterfly.

Cabbala ▸ **noun** variant spelling of KABBALAH.

cabbalistic /kabəˈlɪstɪk/ ▸ **adjective** relating to or associated with mystical interpretation or esoteric doctrine.
– DERIVATIVES **cabbalism** noun, **cabbalist** noun.
– ORIGIN variant of *Kabbalistic*: see KABBALAH.

cabby (also **cabbie**) ▸ **noun** (pl. **cabbies**) informal a taxi driver.

caber /ˈkeɪbə/ ▸ **noun** a roughly trimmed tree trunk used in the Scottish Highland sport of **tossing the caber**. This involves holding the caber upright and running forward to toss it so that it lands on the opposite end.
– ORIGIN early 16th cent.: from Scottish Gaelic *cabar* 'pole'.

Cabernet /ˈkabəneɪ/ ▸ **noun** short for CABERNET FRANC or CABERNET SAUVIGNON.

Cabernet Franc /frɒ̃/ ▸ **noun** [mass noun] a variety of black wine grape grown chiefly in parts of the Loire Valley and NE Italy. ■ a red wine made from the Cabernet Franc grape.
– ORIGIN French.

Cabernet Sauvignon /ˈsəʊvɪnjɒ̃/ ▸ **noun** [mass noun] a variety of black wine grape from the Bordeaux area of France, now grown throughout the world. ■ a red wine made from the Cabernet Sauvignon grape.
– ORIGIN French.

cabezon /ˈkabɪzɒn/ ▸ **noun** a heavy-bodied fish with a broad tentacle above each eye and a green-brown body with white patches, found on the west coast of North America. ● *Scorpaenichthys marmoratus*, family Cottidae.
– ORIGIN Spanish.

cab-forward ▸ **adjective** denoting a design of car or truck in which the driver's or passenger compartment is placed so as to extend further forward than the standard position.

cabildo /kəˈbɪldəʊ/ ▸ **noun** (pl. **cabildos**) (in Spain and Spanish-speaking countries) a town council or local government council. ■ a town hall.
– ORIGIN Spanish, from late Latin *capitulum* 'chapter house'.

cabin ▸ **noun 1** a private room or compartment on a ship. ■ the area for passengers in an aircraft.
2 a small wooden shelter or house in a wild or remote area.
3 Indian a cubicle or individual work space within a larger office.
▸ **verb** (**cabins, cabining, cabined**) [with obj.] (often as adj. **cabined**) dated confine in a small place.
– ORIGIN Middle English: from Old French *cabane*, from Provençal *cabana*, from late Latin *capanna*, *cavanna*.

cabin boy ▸ **noun** chiefly historical a boy employed to wait on a ship's officers or passengers.

cabin class ▶ noun [mass noun] the intermediate class of accommodation on a passenger ship.

cabin crew ▶ noun [treated as sing. or pl.] the members of an aircraft crew who attend to passengers.

cabin cruiser ▶ noun a motor boat with living accommodation.

Cabinda /kəˈbɪndə/ an enclave of Angola at the mouth of the River Congo, separated from the rest of Angola by a wedge of the Democratic Republic of the Congo (Zaire). ■ the capital of Cabinda; pop. 287,000 (est. 2004).

cabinet ▶ noun **1** a cupboard with drawers or shelves for storing or displaying articles: *a cocktail cabinet.* ■ a wooden box or piece of furniture housing a radio, television set, or speaker.
2 (also **Cabinet**) (in the UK, Canada, and other Commonwealth countries) the committee of senior ministers responsible for controlling government policy: [as modifier] *a cabinet meeting.* ■ (in the US) a body of advisers to the President, composed of the heads of the executive departments of the government.
3 archaic a small private room.
– ORIGIN mid 16th cent.: from CABIN + -ET[1], influenced by French *cabinet.*

cabinetmaker ▶ noun a skilled joiner who makes furniture or similar high-quality woodwork.
– DERIVATIVES **cabinetmaking** noun.

cabinet minister ▶ noun a member of a parliamentary cabinet.

cabinet pudding ▶ noun [mass noun] Brit. a steamed suet pudding containing dried fruit.

cabinetry ▶ noun [mass noun] cabinets collectively.

cabin fever ▶ noun [mass noun] informal, chiefly N. Amer. lassitude, irritability, and similar symptoms resulting from long confinement or isolation indoors during the winter.

cable ▶ noun **1** a thick rope of wire or hemp used for construction, mooring ships, and towing vehicles. ■ the chain of a ship's anchor. ■ Nautical a length of 200 yards (182.9 m) or (in the US) 240 yards (219.4 m). ■ (also **cable moulding**) Architecture a moulding resembling twisted rope.
2 an insulated wire or wires having a protective casing and used for transmitting electricity or telecommunication signals: *an underground cable* | [mass noun] *transatlantic phone calls went by cable.* ■ a cablegram. ■ short for CABLE TELEVISION.
▶ verb [with obj.] **1** send a message to (someone) by cablegram: *he cabled her to cancel all arrangements.* ■ transmit (a message) by cablegram. ■ [no obj.] send a cablegram.
2 provide (an area) with power lines or with the equipment necessary for cable television.
3 Architecture decorate (a structure) with rope-shaped mouldings.
– ORIGIN Middle English: from an Anglo-Norman French variant of Old French *chable*, from late Latin *capulum* 'halter'.

cable car ▶ noun **1** a transport system, typically one travelling up and down a mountain, in which cabins are suspended on a continuous moving cable driven by a motor at one end of the route. ■ a cabin on a cable-car system.
2 a carriage on a cable railway.

cablegram ▶ noun historical a telegraph message sent by cable.

cable-knit ▶ adjective (of a garment) knitted using cable stitch: *a white cable-knit sweater.*

cable-laid ▶ adjective (of rope) made of three triple strands.

cable railway ▶ noun a railway along which carriages are drawn by a continuous cable.

cable release ▶ noun Photography a cable attached to the shutter release of a camera, allowing the photographer to open the shutter without touching or moving the camera.

cable-stayed bridge ▶ noun a bridge in which the weight of the deck is supported by a number of cables running directly to one or more towers.

cable stitch ▶ noun [mass noun] a combination of knitted stitches resembling twisted rope.

cable television ▶ noun [mass noun] a system in which television programmes are transmitted to the sets of subscribers by cable rather than by a broadcast signal.

cable tier ▶ noun historical a place in a ship for stowing a coiled cable.

cableway ▶ noun a transport system in which goods are carried suspended from a continuous moving cable.

cabman ▶ noun (pl. **cabmen**) historical the driver of a horse-drawn hackney carriage.

caboched ▶ adjective variant spelling of CABOSHED.

cabochon /ˈkabəʃɒn/ ▶ noun a gem that has been polished but not faceted.
– PHRASES **en cabochon** (of a gem) polished but not faceted.
– ORIGIN mid 16th cent.: from French, diminutive of *caboche* 'head'.

caboclo /kəˈbəʊkləʊ/ ▶ noun (pl. **caboclos**) (in Brazil) an American Indian. ■ a Brazilian of mixed white and Indian or Indian and black ancestry.
– ORIGIN Brazilian Portuguese, perhaps from Tupi *Kaa-boc* 'person having copper-coloured skin'.

caboodle (also **kaboodle**) ▶ noun (in phrase **the whole caboodle** or **the whole kit and caboodle**) informal the whole number or quantity of people or things in question.
– ORIGIN mid 19th cent. (originally US): perhaps from the phrase *kit and boodle*, in the same (see KIT[1], BOODLE).

caboose ▶ noun **1** N. Amer. a railway wagon with accommodation for the train crew, typically attached to the end of the train.
2 archaic a kitchen on a ship's deck.
– ORIGIN mid 18th cent.: from Dutch *kabuis, kombuis*, of unknown origin.

caboshed /kəˈbɒʃt/ (also **caboched** or **cabossed** /-ˈbɒst/) ▶ adjective [usu. postpositive] Heraldry (of the head of a stag, bull, etc.) shown full face with no neck visible.
– ORIGIN late 16th cent.: from French *caboché*, in the same sense.

Cabot /ˈkabət/ the name of two Italian explorers and navigators: ■ **John** (*c.*1450–*c.*1498); Italian name *Giovanni Caboto*. He sailed from Bristol in 1497 in search of Asia, but in fact landed on the mainland of North America, the first European to do so.
■ **Sebastian** (*c.*1475–1557), son of John. Sebastian accompanied his father on his voyage in 1497 and made further voyages after the latter's death, most notably to Brazil and the River Plate (1526).

cabotage /ˈkabətɑːʒ, -ɪdʒ/ ▶ noun [mass noun] the right to operate sea, air, or other transport services within a particular territory. ■ restriction of the operation of sea, air, or other transport services within or into a particular country to that country's own transport services.
– ORIGIN mid 19th cent. (in the sense 'coastal trade'): from French, from *caboter* 'sail along a coast', perhaps from Spanish *cabo* 'cape, headland'.

cabover ▶ noun N. Amer. a truck where the driver's cab is mounted directly above the engine.

cabrio /ˈkabrɪəʊ/ ▶ noun (pl. **cabrios**) short for CABRIOLET (sense 1).

cabriole /ˈkabrɪəʊl/ ▶ noun Ballet a jump in which one leg is extended into the air forwards or backwards, the other is brought up to meet it, and the dancer lands on the second foot.
– ORIGIN French, literally 'light leap', from *cabrioler* (earlier *caprioler*), from Italian *capriolare* 'to leap in the air' (see CAPRIOLE).

cabriole leg ▶ noun a kind of curved leg characteristic of Chippendale and Queen Anne furniture.
– ORIGIN late 18th cent.: so named from the resemblance to the front leg of a leaping animal (see CABRIOLE).

cabriolet /ˈkabrɪə(ʊ)leɪ/ ▶ noun **1** a car with a roof that folds down.
2 a light two-wheeled carriage with a hood, drawn by one horse.
– ORIGIN mid 18th cent.: from French, from *cabriole* 'goat's leap', from *cabrioler* 'to leap in the air' (see CABRIOLE); so named because of the carriage's motion.

caca /ˈkakə, ˈkɑːkɑː/ ▶ noun [mass noun] informal excrement.
– ORIGIN late 19th cent.: from CACK, or directly from Latin *cacare* 'defecate'.

ca'canny /kɑːˈkani/ ▶ noun [mass noun] Brit. dated the policy of deliberately limiting output at work.
– ORIGIN late 19th cent. (originally Scots in the sense 'proceed warily'): from *ca'* (variant of CALL (verb)) and CANNY.

cacao /kəˈkɑːəʊ, kəˈkeɪəʊ/ ▶ noun (pl. **cacaos**) **1** [mass noun] bean-like seeds from which cocoa, cocoa butter, and chocolate are made.
2 the small tropical American evergreen tree which bears cacao seeds, now cultivated mainly in West Africa. ● *Theobroma cacao*, family Sterculiaceae.
– ORIGIN mid 16th cent.: via Spanish from Nahuatl *cacaua.*

cacciatore /ˌkatʃəˈtɔːreɪ, -ri/ (also **cacciatora** /-rə/) ▶ adjective [postpositive] prepared in a spicy tomato sauce with mushrooms and herbs: *chicken cacciatore.*
– ORIGIN Italian, literally 'hunter' (because of the use of ingredients that a hunter might have to hand).

C

cachaca /kəˈʃuːkə/ ▶ noun [mass noun] a Brazilian white rum made from sugar cane.
– ORIGIN mid 19th cent.: Brazilian Portuguese, from Portuguese *cacaça* '(white) rum'.

cachalot /ˈkaʃəlɒt/ ▶ noun old-fashioned term for SPERM WHALE.
– ORIGIN mid 18th cent.: from French, from Spanish and Portuguese *cachalote*, from *cachola* 'big head'.

cache /kaʃ/ ▶ noun a collection of items of the same type stored in a hidden or inaccessible place: *an arms cache* | *a cache of gold coins.* ■ a hidden or inaccessible storage place for valuables, provisions, or ammunition. ■ (also **cache memory**) Computing an auxiliary memory from which high-speed retrieval is possible.
▶ verb (**caches, cacheing** or **caching, cached**) [with obj.] store away in hiding or for future use. ■ Computing store (data) in a cache memory. ■ Computing provide (hardware) with a cache memory.
– DERIVATIVES **cacheable** adjective, **cacheless** adjective.
– ORIGIN late 18th cent.: from French, from *cacher* 'to hide'.

cachectic /kəˈkɛktɪk/ ▶ adjective Medicine relating to or having the symptoms of cachexia.

cachepot /ˈkaʃpəʊ, ˈkaʃpɒt/ ▶ noun (pl. pronunc. **same**) an ornamental holder for a flowerpot.
– ORIGIN late 19th cent.: from French *cache-pot*, from *cacher* 'to hide' + *pot* 'pot'.

cache-sexe /ˈkaʃsɛks/ ▶ noun (pl. pronunc. **same**) a covering for the genitals, typically worn by erotic dancers or tribal peoples.
– ORIGIN 1920s: from French, from *cacher* 'to hide' and *sexe* 'genitals'.

cachet /ˈkaʃeɪ/ ▶ noun **1** [mass noun] the state of being respected or admired; prestige: *no other shipping company had quite the cachet of Cunard.*
2 a distinguishing mark or seal.
3 a flat capsule enclosing a dose of unpleasant-tasting medicine.
– ORIGIN early 17th cent.: from French, from *cacher* in the sense 'to press', based on Latin *coactare* 'constrain'.

cachexia /kəˈkɛksɪə/ ▶ noun [mass noun] Medicine weakness and wasting of the body due to severe chronic illness.
– ORIGIN mid 16th cent.: via late Latin from Greek *kakhexia*, from *kakos* 'bad' + *hexis* 'habit'.

cachinnate /ˈkakɪneɪt/ ▶ verb [no obj.] rare laugh loudly.
– DERIVATIVES **cachinnation** noun.
– ORIGIN early 19th cent.: from Latin *cachinnat-* 'laughed loudly', from the verb *cachinnare*, of imitative origin.

cachou /ˈkaʃuː, kəˈʃuː/ ▶ noun (pl. **cachous**) dated a pleasant-smelling lozenge sucked to mask bad breath.
– ORIGIN late 16th cent. (in the sense 'catechu'): from French, from Portuguese *cachu*, from Malay *kacu*. The current sense dates from the early 18th cent.

cachucha /kəˈtʃuːtʃə/ ▶ noun a lively Spanish solo dance in triple time, performed with castanet accompaniment.
– ORIGIN Spanish.

cacique /kəˈsiːk/ ▶ noun **1** (in Latin America or the Spanish-speaking Caribbean) a native chief. ■ (in Spain or Latin America) a local political boss.
2 a gregarious tropical American bird that has black plumage with patches of red or yellow. ● Genus *Cacicus*, family Icteridae: several species.
– ORIGIN mid 16th cent.: from Spanish or French, from Taino.

cack Brit. informal ▶ noun [mass noun] excrement; dung. ■ rubbish: *they talk such a load of cack.*
▶ verb [with obj.] defecate in (one's clothes).
– ORIGIN Old English (as *cac-* in *cachūs* 'privy'); the verb dates from late Middle English and is related to Middle Dutch *cacken*; based on Latin *cacare* 'defecate'.

cack-handed ▶ adjective Brit. informal **1** inept; clumsy: *a great song ruined by cack-handed production.*

2 derogatory left-handed.
– DERIVATIVES **cack-handedly** adverb, **cack-handedness** noun.
– ORIGIN mid 19th cent.: from CACK, in the sense 'excrement', + HAND + -ED[2].

cackle ▸ verb [no obj.] (of a bird, especially a hen or goose) give a raucous clucking cry: *the hen was cackling as if demented* | (as adj. **cackling**) *cackling, whooping cries*. ■ laugh in a loud, harsh way: *she cackled with laughter*. ■ informal talk at length without acting on what is said.
▸ noun the raucous clucking cry of a bird such as a hen or a goose. ■ a loud, harsh laugh: *her delighted cackle*.
– PHRASES **cut the cackle** [usu. in imperative] informal stop talking aimlessly and come to the point.
– ORIGIN Middle English: probably from Middle Low German *kākelen*, partly imitative, reinforced by *kāke* 'jaw, cheek'.

cacodemon /ˌkakə(ʊ)ˈdiːmən/ (also **cacodaemon**) ▸ noun rare a malevolent spirit or person.
– ORIGIN late 16th cent.: from Greek *kakodaimōn*, from *kakos* 'bad' + *daimōn* 'spirit'.

cacodyl /ˈkakə(ʊ)dʌɪl, -dɪl/ ▸ noun [mass noun] Chemistry a malodorous, toxic, spontaneously flammable liquid compound containing arsenic. ● Chem. formula: $((CH_3)_2As)_2$.
■ [as modifier] of or denoting the radical $-As(CH_3)_2$, derived from cacodyl.
– ORIGIN mid 19th cent.: from Greek *kakōdēs* 'stinking' (from *kakos* 'bad') + -YL.

cacodylate /ˌkakəʊˈdʌɪleɪt/ ▸ noun Chemistry a salt or ester of cacodylic acid.

cacodylic acid /ˈkakə(ʊ)dʌɪlɪk, -dɪlɪk/ ▸ noun [mass noun] Chemistry a toxic crystalline acid containing arsenic, used as a herbicide. ● Chem. formula: $(CH_3)_2AsO(OH)$.

cacoethes /ˌkakəʊˈiːθiːz/ ▸ noun [in sing.] rare an urge to do something inadvisable.
– ORIGIN mid 16th cent.: via Latin from Greek *kakoēthes* 'ill-disposed', from *kakos* 'bad' + *ēthos* 'disposition'.

cacography /kəˈkɒɡrəfi/ ▸ noun [mass noun] archaic bad handwriting or spelling.
– ORIGIN late 16th cent.: from Greek *kakos* 'bad', on the pattern of *orthography*.

cacology /kəˈkɒlədʒi/ ▸ noun [mass noun] archaic bad choice of words or poor pronunciation.
– ORIGIN late 18th cent.: via late Latin from Greek *kakologia* 'abusive language', from *kakos* 'bad'.

cacomistle /ˈkakə(ʊ)ˌmɪs(ə)l/ ▸ noun a nocturnal raccoon-like animal with a dark-ringed tail, found in North and Central America. ● Genus *Bassariscus*, family Procyonidae: two species. .
– ORIGIN mid 19th cent.: from Latin American Spanish *cacomixtle*, from Nahuatl *tlacomiztli*.

cacophonous /kəˈkɒf(ə)nəs/ ▸ adjective involving or producing a harsh, discordant mixture of sounds: *the cacophonous sound of slot machines*.

cacophony /kəˈkɒf(ə)ni/ ▸ noun (pl. **cacophonies**) a harsh discordant mixture of sounds: *a cacophony of deafening alarm bells*.
– ORIGIN mid 17th cent.: from French *cacophonie*, from Greek *kakophōnia*, from *kakophōnos* 'ill-sounding', from *kakos* 'bad' + *phōnē* 'sound'.

cactus ▸ noun (pl. **cacti** /-tʌɪ/ or **cactuses**) a succulent plant with a thick fleshy stem which typically bears spines, lacks leaves, and has brilliantly coloured flowers. Cacti are native to arid regions of the New World and are cultivated elsewhere, especially as pot plants. ● Family Cactaceae: numerous genera and species.
– DERIVATIVES **cactaceous** adjective.
– ORIGIN early 17th cent. (in the sense 'cardoon'): from Latin, from Greek *kaktos* 'cardoon'.

cactus dahlia ▸ noun a dahlia of a variety which has rolled petals, giving the flower a prickly appearance.

cacuminal /kəˈkjuːmɪn(ə)l/ ▸ adjective Phonetics another term for RETROFLEX.
– ORIGIN mid 19th cent.: from Latin *cacuminare* 'make pointed' (from *cacumen, cacumin-* 'top, summit') + -AL.

CAD ▸ abbreviation computer-aided design.

cad ▸ noun informal, dated a man who behaves dishonourably, especially towards a woman: *her adulterous cad of a husband*.
– DERIVATIVES **caddish** adjective, **caddishly** adverb, **caddishness** noun.
– ORIGIN late 18th cent. (denoting a passenger picked up by the driver of a horse-drawn coach for personal profit): abbreviation of CADDIE or CADET.

cadastral /kəˈdastr(ə)l/ ▸ adjective (of a map or survey) showing the extent, value, and ownership of land, especially for taxation.
– ORIGIN mid 19th cent.: from French, from *cadastre* 'register of property', from Provençal *cadastro*, from Italian *catastro* (earlier *catastico*), from late Greek *katastikhon* 'list, register', from *kata stikhon* 'line by line'.

cadaver /kəˈdɑːvə, -ˈdeɪ-/ ▸ noun Medicine or literary a corpse.
– DERIVATIVES **cadaveric** adjective.
– ORIGIN late Middle English: from Latin, from *cadere* 'to fall'.

cadaverous ▸ adjective very pale, thin, or bony: *he was gaunt and cadaverous*.
– DERIVATIVES **cadaverously** adverb, **cadaverousness** noun.
– ORIGIN late Middle English: from Latin *cadaverosus*, from *cadaver* 'corpse'.

Cadbury /ˈkadb(ə)ri/, George (1839–1922) and Richard (1835–99), English cocoa and chocolate manufacturers and social reformers. As committed Quakers, they were concerned with improving their employees' working and living conditions, and established a new factory and housing estate at Bournville.

CADCAM ▸ abbreviation computer-aided design, computer-aided manufacture.

caddie (also **caddy**) ▸ noun (pl. **caddies**) a person who carries a golfer's clubs and provides other assistance during a match.
▸ verb (**caddies, caddying, caddied**) [no obj.] work as a caddie.
– ORIGIN mid 17th cent. (originally Scots): from French CADET. The original term denoted a gentleman who joined the army without a commission, intending to learn the profession and follow a military career, later coming to mean 'odd-job man'. The current sense dates from the late 18th cent.

caddis /ˈkadɪs/ (also **caddis fly**) ▸ noun a small moth-like insect with an aquatic larva that typically builds a protective portable case of sticks, stones, and other particles. ● Order Trichoptera: several families.
– ORIGIN mid 17th cent.: of unknown origin.

caddis worm ▸ noun the soft-bodied aquatic larva of a caddis fly, used as fishing bait.

Caddoan /ˈkadəʊən/ ▸ adjective relating to or denoting a group of American Indian peoples formerly inhabiting the Midwest, or their languages, now all virtually extinct.
▸ noun 1 a member of any of the Caddoan peoples.
2 [mass noun] the family of languages spoken by the Caddoan peoples, which includes Pawnee and may be related to Siouan and Iroquoian.
– ORIGIN from Caddo (a language of the Caddoan family) *kaduhdacu*, denoting a band belonging to this group, + -AN.

caddy[1] ▸ noun (pl. **caddies**) [usu. with modifier] a small storage container, typically one with divisions: *a tool caddy*. ■ (also **tea caddy**) chiefly Brit. a small tin in which tea is kept for daily use.
– ORIGIN late 18th cent.: from earlier *catty*, denoting a unit of weight of $1^{1}/_{3}$ lb (0.61 kg), from Malay *kati*.

caddy[2] ▸ noun & verb variant spelling of CADDIE.

caddy spoon ▸ noun a spoon used to dispense tea from a tea caddy, having a wide, shallow bowl and a short handle.

Cade /keɪd/, Jack (d.1450), Irish rebel; full name *John Cade*. In 1450 he assumed the name of Mortimer and led the Kentish rebels against Henry VI. They occupied London for three days and executed the treasurer of England and the sheriff of Kent.

cadelle /kəˈdɛl/ ▸ noun a small dark beetle that is frequently found in food stores, where it scavenges and preys on other insects. ● *Tenebroides mauritanicus*, family Cleridae.
– ORIGIN mid 19th cent.: from French, based on Latin *catella, catellus* 'young (of an animal), little dog'.

cadence /ˈkeɪd(ə)ns/ ▸ noun 1 a modulation or inflection of the voice: *the measured cadences that he employed in the Senate*. ■ a rhythmical effect in written text: *the dry cadences of the essay*. ■ a fall in pitch of the voice at the end of a phrase or sentence. ■ [mass noun] rhythm: *the thumping cadence of the engines*.
2 a sequence of notes or chords comprising the close of a musical phrase: *the final cadences of the Prelude*.
– DERIVATIVES **cadenced** adjective.
– ORIGIN late Middle English (in the sense 'rhythm or metrical beat'): via Old French from Italian *cadenza*, based on Latin *cadere* 'to fall'.

cadency ▸ noun [mass noun] chiefly Heraldry the status of a younger branch of a family.
– ORIGIN early 17th cent. (in the sense 'rhythm or metrical beat'): based on Latin *cadent-* 'falling', from the verb *cadere*. The current sense is apparently by association with CADET.

cadential ▸ adjective relating to a cadenza or cadence.
– ORIGIN mid 19th cent.: from CADENCE, on the pattern of pairs such as *essence, essential*.

cadenza /kəˈdɛnzə/ ▸ noun a virtuoso solo passage inserted into a movement in a concerto or other musical work, typically near the end.
– PHRASES **have a cadenza** S. African informal be extremely agitated. [said to be from Danny Kaye's *The Little Fiddle*, a humorous recording made in the 1940s.]
– ORIGIN mid 18th cent.: from Italian (see CADENCE).

cadet ▸ noun 1 a young trainee in the armed services or police force: *an air cadet*. ■ a boy or girl of 13–18 who undergoes voluntary army, navy, or air force training together with adventure training. ■ Austral. a trainee or novice, especially a trainee journalist.
2 formal or archaic a younger son or daughter. ■ [usu. as modifier] a junior branch of a family: *a cadet branch of the family*.
– DERIVATIVES **cadetship** noun.
– ORIGIN early 17th cent. (in sense 2): from French, from Gascon dialect *capdet*, a diminutive based on Latin *caput* 'head'. The notion 'little head' or 'inferior head' gave rise to that of 'younger, junior'.

cadge ▸ verb [with obj.] Brit. informal ask for or obtain (something to which one is not strictly entitled): *he cadged fivers off old school friends*.
▸ noun Falconry a padded wooden frame on which hooded hawks are carried to the field. [apparently an alteration of CAGE, perhaps confused with the dialect verb *cadge* 'carry about'.]
– PHRASES **on the cadge** informal looking for an opportunity to obtain something without paying for it.
– DERIVATIVES **cadger** noun.
– ORIGIN early 17th cent. (in the dialect sense 'carry about'): back-formation from the noun *cadger*, which dates from the late 15th cent., denoting (in northern English and Scots) an itinerant dealer, whence the verb sense 'hawk, peddle', giving rise to the current verb senses from the early 19th cent.

cadi /ˈkɑːdi, ˈkeɪdi/ (also **kadi**) ▸ noun (pl. **cadis**) (in Islamic countries) a judge.
– ORIGIN late 16th cent.: from Arabic *qāḍī*, from *qaḍā* 'to judge'.

Cadillac /ˈkadɪlak/ ▸ noun 1 a large luxury car manufactured by the US Cadillac motor company.
2 something that is an outstanding example of its kind, especially in terms of luxury, quality, or size: *the aircraft is widely regarded as **the Cadillac of** commuter planes*.
– ORIGIN from the name of the French explorer Antoine de La Mothe *Cadillac* (1658–1730), who founded the city of Detroit, where the cars are manufactured.

Cadiz /kəˈdɪz/ a city and port on the coast of SW Spain; pop. 127,200 (2008). Spanish name **Cádiz** /ˈkaðiθ, ˈkaðis/.

Cadmean /kadˈmiːən/ ▸ adjective relating to Cadmus.

cadmium /ˈkadmɪəm/ ▸ noun [mass noun] the chemical element of atomic number 48, a silvery-white metal. (Symbol: **Cd**)

> Cadmium occurs naturally in zinc ores and is obtained as a by-product of zinc smelting. It is used as a component in alloys with a low melting point and as a corrosion-resistant coating on other metals.

– ORIGIN early 19th cent.: from Latin *cadmia* 'calamine', so named because it is found with calamine in zinc ore. Compare with CALAMINE.

cadmium cell ▸ noun a primary electric cell with a cathode of cadmium amalgam and an electrolyte of saturated cadmium sulphate solution, used in laboratories as a standard of electromotive force.

cadmium yellow ▸ noun [mass noun] a bright yellow pigment containing cadmium sulphide. Deeper versions are called **cadmium orange**; the addition of cadmium selenide gives **cadmium red**. ■ a bright yellow colour.

Cadmus /ˈkadməs/ Greek Mythology the brother of Europa and traditional founder of Thebes in Boeotia. He killed a dragon which guarded a spring, and when (on Athene's advice) he sowed the dragon's teeth a harvest of armed men came up; he disposed of the majority by setting them to fight one another, and the survivors formed the ancestors of the Theban nobility.

cadre /ˈkɑːdə, ˈkɑːdr(ə), ˈkadri/ ▶ **noun 1** a small group of people specially trained for a particular purpose or profession: *a cadre of professional managers.*
2 also /ˈkeɪdə/ a group of activists in a communist or other revolutionary organization. ■ a member of an activist group.
– ORIGIN mid 19th cent.: from French, from Italian *quadro*, from Latin *quadrus* 'square'.

caduceus /kəˈdjuːsɪəs/ ▶ **noun** (pl. **caducei** /-sɪʌɪ/) an ancient Greek or Roman herald's wand, typically one with two serpents twined round it, carried by the messenger god Hermes or Mercury.
– ORIGIN Latin, from Doric Greek *karukeion* from Greek *kērux* 'herald'.

caducity /kəˈdjuːsɪti/ ▶ **noun** [mass noun] archaic the infirmity of old age; senility. ■ literary frailty or transitory nature.
– ORIGIN mid 18th cent.: from French *caducité*, from *caduc*, from Latin *caducus* 'liable to fall', from *cadere* 'to fall'.

caducous /kəˈdjuːkəs/ ▶ **adjective** chiefly Botany (of an organ or part) easily detached and shed at an early stage.
– ORIGIN late 17th cent. (in the sense 'epileptic'): from Latin *caducus* 'liable to fall' (from *cadere* 'to fall') + **-OUS**.

CAE ▶ **abbreviation** computer-aided engineering.

caecilian /sɪˈsɪlɪən/ (also **coecilian**) ▶ **noun** Zoology a burrowing worm-like amphibian of a tropical order distinguished by poorly developed eyes and the lack of limbs. ● Order Gymnophiona (or Apoda): five families.
– ORIGIN from modern Latin *Caecilia* (genus name), from Latin *caecilia* 'slow-worm', + **-AN**.

caecum /ˈsiːkəm/ (US **cecum**) ▶ **noun** (pl. **caeca**) Anatomy a pouch connected to the junction of the small and large intestines.
– DERIVATIVES **caecal** adjective.
– ORIGIN late Middle English: from Latin (*intestinum*) *caecum* 'blind (gut)', translation of Greek *tuphlon enteron*.

Caedmon /ˈkadmən/ (7th century), Anglo-Saxon monk and poet, said to have been an illiterate herdsman inspired in a vision to compose poetry on biblical themes. The only authentic fragment of his work is a song in praise of the Creation, quoted by Bede.

Caelum /ˈsiːləm/ Astronomy a small and faint southern constellation (the Chisel), next to Eridanus.
– ORIGIN Latin.

Caen /kɑːn/, French /kɑ̃/ an industrial city and river port in Normandy in northern France, on the River Orne, capital of the region of Basse-Normandie; pop. 113,249 (2006).

Caerdydd /ˈkaɪrdɪð/ Welsh name for **CARDIFF**.

Caerfyrddin /kaɪrˈvɪrðin/ Welsh name for **CARMARTHEN**.

Caergybi /kaɪrˈgʌbi/ Welsh name for **HOLY ISLAND** (sense 2).

Caernarfon /kəˈnɑːv(ə)n/, Welsh /kaɪrˈnarvɒn/ (also **Caernarvon**) a town in NW Wales on the shore of the Menai Strait, the administrative centre of Gwynedd; pop. 10,000 (est. 2009).

Caernarfonshire (also **Caernarvonshire**) a former county of NW Wales, part of Gwynedd from 1974.

Caerns. ▶ **abbreviation** Caernarfonshire.

Caerphilly /keːˈfɪli, kɑː-, kə-/ ▶ **noun** [mass noun] a kind of mild white cheese, originally made in Caerphilly in Wales.

Caesar /ˈsiːzə/ ▶ **noun 1** a title of Roman emperors, especially those from Augustus to Hadrian. ■ an autocrat.
2 Medicine, Brit. informal a caesarean section.
PHRASES **Caesar's wife** a person who is required to be above suspicion. [with reference to Plutarch's *Caesar* (x. 6) 'I thought my wife ought not even to be under suspicion'.]
– ORIGIN Middle English: from Latin *Caesar*, family name of the Roman statesman **JULIUS CAESAR**.

Caesarea /ˌsiːzəˈrɪə/ an ancient port on the Mediterranean coast of Israel, one of the principal cities of Roman Palestine.

Caesarea Mazaca /ˈmazəkə/ former name for **KAYSERI**.

caesarean /sɪˈzɛːrɪən/ (also **caesarian**) ▶ **adjective 1** (US also **cesarean**) of or effected by caesarean section: *a caesarean delivery.*
2 (**Caesarean**) of or connected with Julius Caesar or the Caesars.
▶ **noun** a caesarean section: *I had to have a caesarean* | [mass noun] *two sons both born by caesarean.*
– ORIGIN early 16th cent. (as a noun denoting a supporter of an emperor or imperial system): from Latin *Caesareus* 'of Caesar' + **-AN**.

caesarean section ▶ **noun** a surgical operation for delivering a child by cutting through the wall of the mother's abdomen.
– ORIGIN early 17th cent.: *Caesarian* from the story that Julius Caesar was delivered by this method.

Caesarea Philippi /ˈfɪlɪpʌɪ, fɪˈlɪpʌɪ/ a city in ancient Palestine, on the site of the present-day village of Baniyas in the Golan Heights.

Caesar salad ▶ **noun** a salad consisting of cos lettuce and croutons served with a dressing of olive oil, lemon juice, raw egg, Worcester sauce, and seasoning.
– ORIGIN named after *Caesar* Cardini, the Mexican restaurateur who invented it in 1924.

caesium /ˈsiːzɪəm/ (US **cesium**) ▶ **noun** [mass noun] the chemical element of atomic number 55, a soft, silvery, extremely reactive metal. It belongs to the alkali metal group and occurs as a trace element in some rocks and minerals. (Symbol: **Cs**)
– ORIGIN mid 19th cent.: from Latin *caesius* 'greyish-blue' (because it has characteristic lines in the blue part of the spectrum).

caesium clock ▶ **noun** an atomic clock that uses the vibrations of caesium atoms as a time standard.

caesura /sɪˈzjʊərə/ ▶ **noun** (in Greek and Latin verse) a break between words within a metrical foot. ■ (in modern verse) a pause near the middle of a line.
– DERIVATIVES **caesural** adjective.
– ORIGIN mid 16th cent.: from Latin, from *caes-* 'cut, hewn', from the verb *caedere*.

CAF ▶ **abbreviation** N. Amer. cost and freight.

cafard /kaˈfɑː/ ▶ **noun** [mass noun] melancholia.
– ORIGIN from French.

cafe /ˈkafeɪ, ˈkafi/ (also **café**) ▶ **noun 1** a small restaurant selling light meals and drinks.
2 N. Amer. a bar or nightclub.
3 S. African a shop selling sweets, cigarettes, newspapers, etc. and staying open after normal hours.
– ORIGIN early 19th cent.: from French *café* 'coffee or coffee house'.

café Americano /ˌkafeɪ əmɛrɪˈkɑːnəʊ, ˌkafɪ/ ▶ **noun** see **AMERICANO**.

café au lait /ˌkafeɪ əʊ ˈleɪ, ˌkafɪ/ ▶ **noun** [mass noun] coffee with milk. ■ the light brown colour of coffee with milk.
– ORIGIN French.

cafe bar ▶ **noun** a cafe which also serves alcoholic drinks.

cafe curtain ▶ **noun** a curtain covering the lower half of a window.

café noir /ˌkafeɪ ˈnwɑː, ˌkafɪ/ ▶ **noun** [mass noun] black coffee.
– ORIGIN French.

cafe society ▶ **noun** [mass noun] the regular patrons of fashionable restaurants and nightclubs.

cafeteria ▶ **noun** a restaurant in which customers serve themselves from a counter and pay before eating. ■ [as modifier] N. Amer. denoting a system in which people may choose from a number of available options, especially one in which an employee may select a personal package of company benefits: *employers who offer cafeteria plans and other flexible programs.*
– ORIGIN mid 19th cent. (originally US): from Latin American Spanish *cafetería* 'coffee shop'.

cafetière /ˌkaf(ə)ˈtjɛː/ ▶ **noun** a coffee pot containing a plunger made of fine mesh with which the grounds are pushed to the bottom when the coffee is ready to be poured.
– ORIGIN mid 19th cent.: from French, from *café* 'coffee'.

caff ▶ **noun** Brit. informal a cafe.

caffeinated /ˈkafɪneɪtɪd/ ▶ **adjective** (of coffee or tea) containing the natural amount of caffeine, or with caffeine added.

caffeine /ˈkafiːn/ ▶ **noun** [mass noun] an alkaloid compound which is found especially in tea and coffee plants and is a stimulant of the central nervous system. ● chem. formula: $C_8H_{10}N_4O_2$.
– ORIGIN mid 19th cent.: from French *caféine*, from *café* 'coffee'.

CAFOD /ˈkafɒd/ ▶ **abbreviation** Catholic Fund for Overseas Development.

caftan ▶ **noun** variant spelling of **KAFTAN**.

Cagayan Islands /ˌkɑːgəˈjɑːn/ a group of seven small islands in the Sulu Sea in the western Philippines.

Cage, John (Milton) (1912–92), American composer, pianist, and writer. He was notable for his experimental approach, which included the use of aleatory music and periods of silence.

cage ▶ **noun** a structure of bars or wires in which birds or other animals are confined: *she kept a canary in a cage* | figurative *his cage of loneliness.* ■ a prison cell or camp. ■ an open framework forming the compartment in a lift. ■ a structure of crossing bars or wires designed to hold or support something. ■ Baseball a portable backstop situated behind the batter during batting practice.
▶ **verb** [with obj.] confine in a cage: *the parrot screamed, furious at being caged* | (as adj. **caged**) *a caged bird.* ■ informal put in prison.
– ORIGIN Middle English: via Old French from Latin *cavea*.

cage bird ▶ **noun** a bird of a kind customarily kept in a cage.

cage fungus ▶ **noun** a fetid-smelling fungus that forms a hollow latticed spherical structure, the inner surface of which bears the spores. ● Genus *Clathrus*, family Clathraceae, class Gasteromycetes.

cagey ▶ **adjective** (**cagier**, **cagiest**) informal reluctant to give information owing to caution or suspicion: *a spokesman was cagey about the arrangements his company had struck.*
– DERIVATIVES **cagily** adverb, **caginess** noun.
– ORIGIN early 20th cent. (originally US): of unknown origin.

Cagliari /kalˈɪɑːri, ˈkaljəri/ the capital of Sardinia, a port on the south coast; pop. 157,297 (2008).

Cagney /ˈkagni/, James (1899–1986), American actor. He is chiefly remembered for playing gangster roles in films such as *The Public Enemy* (1931), but he was also a skilled dancer and comedian who received an Oscar for his part in the musical *Yankee Doodle Dandy* (1942).

cagoule /kəˈguːl/ (also **kagoul**) ▶ **noun** Brit. a lightweight, hooded, thigh-length waterproof jacket.
– ORIGIN 1950s: from French, literally 'cowl'.

cahier /ˈkʌɪjeɪ/, French /kaje/ ▶ **noun** (pl. pronunc. **same**) an exercise book or notebook.
– ORIGIN mid 19th cent.: French; compare with **QUIRE**.

cahoots /kəˈhuːts/ ▶ **plural noun** (in phrase **in cahoots**) informal colluding or conspiring together secretly: *the area is dominated by guerrillas in cahoots with drug traffickers.*
– ORIGIN early 19th cent. (originally US): of unknown origin.

Cahora Bassa /kəˌhɔːrə ˈbasə/ a lake on the Zambezi River in western Mozambique. Its waters are impounded by a dam and massive hydroelectric complex.

cahow /kəˈhaʊ/ ▶ **noun** a large endangered Atlantic petrel which breeds in Bermuda. ● *Pterodroma cahow*, family Procellariidae.
– ORIGIN early 17th cent.: imitative of its call.

CAI ▶ **abbreviation** computer-assisted (or -aided) instruction.

caiman /ˈkeɪmən/ (also **cayman**) ▶ **noun** a semiaquatic reptile similar to the alligator but with a heavily armoured belly, native to tropical America. ● *Caiman* and other genera, family Alligatoridae: three species.
– ORIGIN late 16th cent.: from Spanish *caimán*, Portuguese *caimão*, from Carib *acayuman*.

Cain (in the Bible) the eldest son of Adam and Eve and murderer of his brother Abel.
– PHRASES **raise Cain** informal create trouble or a commotion.

Caine, Sir Michael (b.1933), English film actor; born *Maurice Micklewhite*. He has appeared in a wide variety of films, including *The Ipcress File* (1965) and *Hannah and Her Sisters* (1986, for which he won an Oscar).

Cainozoic /ˌkʌɪnəˈzəʊɪk/ ▶ **adjective** variant spelling of **CENOZOIC**.

caipirinha /ˌkʌɪpɪˈrɪnjə/ ▶ **noun** a Brazilian cocktail made with cachaca, lime or lemon juice, sugar, and crushed ice.
– ORIGIN Brazilian Portuguese, from *caipira* 'yokel'.

caique /kʌɪˈiːk, kɑː-/ ▶ **noun 1** a light rowing boat used on the Bosporus.
2 a small eastern Mediterranean sailing ship.
– ORIGIN early 17th cent.: from French *caïque*, from Italian *caicco*, from Turkish *kayık*.

C

C

cairn ▶ noun **1** a mound of rough stones built as a memorial or landmark, typically on a hilltop or skyline. ■ a prehistoric burial mound made of stones.
2 (also **cairn terrier**) a small terrier of a breed with short legs, a longish body, and a shaggy coat. [perhaps so named from being used to hunt among cairns.]
– ORIGIN late Middle English: from Scottish Gaelic *carn*.

cairngorm /ˈkɛːnɡɔːm/ ▶ noun another term for SMOKY QUARTZ.
– ORIGIN late 18th cent.: named after the CAIRNGORM MOUNTAINS.

Cairngorm Mountains (also **the Cairngorms**) a mountain range in northern Scotland.
– ORIGIN from Scottish Gaelic *carn gorm* 'blue cairn'.

Cairo /ˈkʌɪrəʊ/ the capital of Egypt, a port on the Nile near the head of its delta; pop. 6,758,600 (est. 2006). Arabic name AL-QAHIRA.
– DERIVATIVES **Cairene** /ˈkʌɪriːn/ adjective & noun.

caisson /ˈkeɪs(ə)n, kəˈsuːn/ ▶ noun **1** a large watertight chamber, open at the bottom, from which the water is kept out by air pressure and in which construction work may be carried out under water. ■ a floating vessel or watertight structure used as a gate across the entrance of a dry dock or basin.
2 historical a chest or wagon for holding or conveying ammunition.
– ORIGIN late 17th cent.: from French, literally 'large chest', from Italian *cassone*, the spelling having been altered in French by association with *caisse* 'case'.

caisson disease ▶ noun another term for DECOMPRESSION SICKNESS.

Caithness /keɪθˈnɛs/ a former county in the extreme north-east of Scotland. It became part of Highland region in 1975.

caitiff /ˈkeɪtɪf/ ▶ noun archaic a contemptible or cowardly person: [as modifier] *a caitiff knight*.
– ORIGIN Middle English (denoting a captive or prisoner): from Old French *caitif* 'captive', based on Latin *captivus* '(person) taken captive' (see CAPTIVE).

cajole /kəˈdʒəʊl/ ▶ verb [with obj.] persuade (someone) to do something by sustained coaxing or flattery: *he hoped to cajole her into selling him her house*.
– DERIVATIVES **cajolement** noun.
– ORIGIN mid 17th cent.: from French *cajoler*.

cajolery /kəˈdʒəʊl(ə)ri/ ▶ noun [mass noun] coaxing or flattery intended to persuade someone to do something: *she uses cajolery, deception, and manipulation to get what she wants*.

Cajun /ˈkeɪdʒ(ə)n/ ▶ noun a member of any of the largely self-contained communities in the bayou areas of southern Louisiana formed by descendants of French Canadians, speaking an archaic form of French.
▶ adjective relating to the Cajuns, especially with reference to their folk music or spicy cuisine.
– ORIGIN alteration of ACADIAN.

cajuput /ˈkadʒəpʌt/ (also **cajeput**) ▶ noun **1** (also **cajuput oil**) [mass noun] an aromatic medicinal oil obtained from a tree of the myrtle family.
2 a chiefly Australasian tree related to the bottlebrushes, with papery bark. Also called PAPERBARK.
● Genus *Melaleuca*, family Myrtaceae: *M. cajuputi*, which produces cajuput oil, and *M. quinquenervia*.
– ORIGIN late 18th cent.: from Malay *kayu putih*, literally 'white tree'.

cake ▶ noun **1** an item of soft sweet food made from a mixture of flour, fat, eggs, sugar, and other ingredients, baked and sometimes iced or decorated: *a fruit cake* | [as modifier] *a cake shop* | [mass noun] *a mouthful of cake*. ■ (**the cake**) Brit. the amount of money or assets available to be divided up or shared: *you have not received a fair slice of the education cake*.
2 an item of savoury food formed into a flat round shape, and typically baked or fried: *crab cakes*. ■ a flattish compact mass of something, especially soap: *a cake of soap*.
▶ verb [with obj.] (of a thick or sticky substance that hardens when dry) cover and become encrusted on (the surface of an object): *his clothes were caked in mud*. ■ [no obj.] (of a thick or sticky substance) dry or harden into a solid mass: *the blood under his nose was beginning to cake*.
– PHRASES **cakes and ale** dated lively enjoyment.
a piece of cake informal something easily achieved: *I never said that training him would be a piece of cake*.
sell like hot cakes Brit. informal be sold quickly and in large quantities. **take the cake** see TAKE THE BISCUIT at BISCUIT. **you can't have your cake and eat it (too)** proverb you can't enjoy both of two desirable but mutually exclusive alternatives.
– DERIVATIVES **cakey** adjective.
– ORIGIN Middle English (denoting a small flat bread roll): of Scandinavian origin; related to Swedish *kaka* and Danish *kage*.

cake flour ▶ noun North American term for PLAIN FLOUR.

cakehole ▶ noun Brit. informal a person's mouth.

cakewalk ▶ noun **1** informal an absurdly or surprisingly easy task: *winning the league won't be a cakewalk for them*.
2 a strutting dance popular at the end of the 19th century, developed from an American black contest in graceful walking which had a cake as a prize.
▶ verb [no obj.] **1** informal achieve or win something easily: *he cakewalked to a 5-1 triumph*.
2 walk or dance in the manner of a cakewalk.

CAL ▶ abbreviation computer-assisted (or -aided) learning.

Cal ▶ abbreviation large calorie(s).

cal ▶ abbreviation small calorie(s).

Cal. ▶ abbreviation California.

Calabar /ˈkaləbɑː/ a seaport in Nigeria; pop. 429,700 (est. 2005).

Calabar bean ▶ noun the poisonous seed of a tropical West African climbing plant, containing physostigmine and formerly used for tribal ordeals.
● The plant is *Physostigma venosum*, family Leguminosae.

calabash /ˈkaləbaʃ/ ▶ noun (also **calabash tree**) an evergreen tropical American tree which bears fruit in the form of large woody gourds. ● *Crescentia cujete*, family Bignoniaceae.
■ a gourd from the calabash tree. ■ a water container, tobacco pipe, or other object made from the dried shell of a calabash or a similar gourd.
– ORIGIN mid 17th cent.: from French *calebasse*, from Spanish *calabaza*, perhaps from Persian *ḵarbuz* 'melon'.

calabaza /ˌkaləˈbɑːzə/ ▶ noun West Indian and US term for CALABASH.

calaboose /ˌkaləˈbuːs/ ▶ noun US informal a prison.
– ORIGIN late 18th cent.: from black French *calabouse*, from Spanish *calabozo* 'dungeon'.

calabrese /ˈkaləbriːs, ˌkaləˈbriːs, -ˈbreɪsi/ ▶ noun see BROCCOLI.
– ORIGIN 1930s: from Italian, literally 'Calabrian'.

Calabria /kəˈlabrɪə/ a region of SW Italy, forming the 'toe' of the Italian peninsula; capital, Catanzaro.
– DERIVATIVES **Calabrian** adjective & noun.

caladium /kəˈleɪdɪəm/ ▶ noun (pl. **caladiums**) a tropical South American plant of the arum family, which is cultivated for its brilliantly coloured ornamental foliage. ● Genus *Caladium*, family Araceae.
– ORIGIN modern Latin, from Malay *keladi*.

Calah /ˈkeɪlə/ biblical name for NIMRUD.

Calais /ˈkaleɪ/, French /kalɛ/ a ferry port in northern France; pop. 75,790 (2006). Captured by Edward III in 1347 after a long siege, it remained an English possession until it was retaken by the French in 1558.

calamanco /ˌkaləˈmaŋkəʊ/ ▶ noun (pl. **calamancoes**) [mass noun] historical a glossy woollen cloth chequered on one side only.
– ORIGIN late 16th cent.: of unknown origin.

calamander /ˈkaləmandə/ (also **calamander wood**) ▶ noun another term for COROMANDEL.
– ORIGIN early 19th cent.: from Sinhalese *kaḷumadīriya*, perhaps from *Coromandel ebony* (see COROMANDEL), changed by association with Sinhalese *kaḷu* 'black'.

calamari /ˌkaləˈmɑːri/ (also **calamares** /ˌkaləˈmɑːreɪz/) ▶ plural noun squid served as food.
– ORIGIN Italian, plural of *calamaro*, from medieval Latin *calamarium* 'pen case', from Greek *kalamos* 'pen' (with reference to the squid's long tapering internal shell and its ink). The variant *calamares* is Spanish.

calamine /ˈkaləmʌɪn/ ▶ noun **1** [mass noun] a pink powder consisting of zinc carbonate and ferric oxide, used to make a soothing lotion or ointment.
2 dated smithsonite or a similar zinc ore.
– ORIGIN late Middle English: via Old French from medieval Latin *calamina*, alteration of Latin *cadmia* 'calamine', from Greek *kadmeia* (*gē*) 'Cadmean (earth)', from *Kadmos* 'Cadmus' (see CADMUS).

calamint /ˈkaləmɪnt/ ▶ noun an aromatic Eurasian herbaceous plant or shrub with blue or lilac flowers.
● Genus *Calamintha*, family Labiatae.
– ORIGIN Middle English: from Old French *calament*, from medieval Latin *calamentum*, from late Latin *calaminthe*, from Greek *kalaminthē*.

calamites /ˌkaləˈmʌɪtiːz/ ▶ noun (pl. **same**) a swamp plant with jointed stems that belonged to an extinct group related to the horsetails, growing to a height of 18 m (60 ft). ● *Calamites* and other genera, family Calamitaceae, class Sphenopsida.
– ORIGIN modern Latin, from CALAMUS.

calamitous ▶ adjective involving calamity; catastrophic or disastrous: *such calamitous events as fires, hurricanes, and floods*.
– DERIVATIVES **calamitously** adverb.

calamity ▶ noun (pl. **calamities**) an event causing great and often sudden damage or distress; a disaster: *emergency measures may be necessary in order to avert a calamity* | [mass noun] *the journey had led to calamity and ruin*.
– ORIGIN late Middle English (in the sense 'disaster and distress'): from Old French *calamite*, from Latin *calamitas*.

Calamity Jane (*c.*1852–1903), American frontierswoman, noted for her skill at shooting and riding; born *Martha Jane Cannary*.

calamondin /ˌkaləˈmʌndɪn/ (also **calamondin orange**) ▶ noun a small hybrid citrus plant which bears fragrant white flowers followed by small orange-yellow fruit, native to the Philippines and grown as a houseplant. ● × *Citrofortunella microcarpa* (formerly *Citrus mitis*), family Rutaceae.
– ORIGIN early 20th cent.: from Tagalog *kalamunding*.

calamus /ˈkaləməs/ ▶ noun (pl. **calami** /-mʌɪ/)
1 another term for SWEET FLAG. ■ (also **calamus root**) [mass noun] a preparation of the aromatic root of the sweet flag.
2 Zoology the hollow lower part of the shaft of a feather, which lacks barbs; a quill.
– ORIGIN late Middle English (denoting a reed or an aromatic plant mentioned in the Bible): from Latin, from Greek *kalamos*. Sense 1 dates from the mid 17th cent.

calando /kəˈlandəʊ/ ▶ adverb Music (especially as a direction) gradually decreasing in speed and volume.
– ORIGIN Italian, literally 'slackening'.

calandra /kəˈlandrə/ (also **calandra lark**) ▶ noun a large Eurasian lark with a stout bill and a black patch on each side of the neck. ● Genus *Melanocorypha*, family Alaudidae: two species.
– ORIGIN late 16th cent.: from Old French *calandre*, via medieval Latin from Greek *kalandros*.

calash /kəˈlaʃ/ ▶ noun another term for CALECHE.

calathea /ˌkaləˈθɪə/ ▶ noun a tropical American plant which typically has variegated leaves, grown as a greenhouse or indoor plant. ● Genus *Calathea*, family Marantaceae: many species, including the zebra plant.
– ORIGIN modern Latin, from Greek *kalathos* 'basket'.

calc- ▶ combining form (used chiefly in geological terms) of lime or calcium: *calcalkaline*.
– ORIGIN from German *Kalk* 'lime', with spelling influenced by Latin *calx* 'lime' (see CALX).

calcalkaline /kalˈkalkəlʌɪn/ ▶ adjective Geology (chiefly of rocks) relatively rich in both calcium and alkali metals.

calcaneus /kalˈkeɪnɪəs/ (also **calcaneum** /-nɪəm/) ▶ noun (pl. **calcanei** /-nɪʌɪ/ or **calcanea** /-nɪə/) Anatomy the large bone forming the heel. It articulates with the cuboid bone of the foot and the talus bone of the ankle, and the Achilles tendon is attached to it.
– DERIVATIVES **calcaneal** adjective.
– ORIGIN mid 18th cent.: from Latin.

calcareous /kalˈkɛːrɪəs/ ▶ adjective containing calcium carbonate; chalky. ■ Ecology (of vegetation) occurring on chalk or limestone.
– ORIGIN late 17th cent.: from Latin *calcarius* (from *calx*, *calc-* 'lime') + -EOUS.

calceolaria /ˌkalsɪəˈlɛːrɪə/ ▶ noun a South American plant which is cultivated for its brightly coloured slipper- or pouch-shaped flowers. Also called SLIPPER FLOWER. ● Genus *Calceolaria*, family Scrophulariaceae.
– ORIGIN late 18th cent.: modern Latin, from Latin *calceolus*, diminutive of *calceus* 'shoe'.

calces plural form of CALX.

calci- ▶ combining form relating to calcium or its compounds: *calcifuge*.
– ORIGIN from Latin *calx*, *calc-* 'lime'.

calcic /ˈkalsɪk/ ▶ adjective (chiefly of minerals) containing or relatively rich in calcium.

calcicole /ˈkalsɪkəʊl/ ▶ noun Botany a plant that grows best in calcareous soil (occurring chiefly on chalk and limestone).
– DERIVATIVES **calcicolous** adjective.
– ORIGIN late 19th cent.: from CALCI- + Latin *colere* 'inhabit'.

calciferol /kalˈsɪfərɒl/ ▶ noun [mass noun] Biochemistry one of the D vitamins, a sterol which is formed when its isomer ergosterol is exposed to ultraviolet light, and which is routinely added to dairy products. Also called ERGOCALCIFEROL, VITAMIN D_2.
– ORIGIN 1930s: from CALCIFEROUS + -OL.

calciferous /kalˈsɪf(ə)rəs/ ▶ adjective containing or producing calcium salts, especially calcium carbonate.

calcifuge /ˈkalsɪfjuːdʒ/ ▶ noun Botany a plant that is not suited to calcareous soil.

calcify /ˈkalsɪfʌɪ/ ▶ verb (**calcifies, calcifying, calcified**) [with obj.] (usu. as adj. **calcified**) harden by deposition of or conversion into calcium carbonate or some other insoluble calcium compounds: *calcified cartilage*.
– DERIVATIVES **calcific** adjective, **calcification** noun.

calcimine /ˈkalsɪmʌɪn/ ▶ noun & verb variant spelling of KALSOMINE.

calcine /ˈkalsʌɪn, -sɪn/ ▶ verb [with obj.] (usu. as adj. **calcined**) reduce, oxidize, or desiccate by roasting or exposing to strong heat: *calcined bone ash*.
– DERIVATIVES **calcination** noun.
– ORIGIN late Middle English: from medieval Latin *calcinare*, from late Latin *calcina* 'lime', from Latin *calx, calc-* 'lime' (see CALX).

calcite /ˈkalsʌɪt/ ▶ noun [mass noun] a white or colourless mineral consisting of calcium carbonate. It is a major constituent of sedimentary rocks such as limestone and is deposited in caves to form stalactites and stalagmites.
– DERIVATIVES **calcitic** adjective.
– ORIGIN mid 19th cent.: coined in German from Latin *calx, calc-* 'lime' (see CALX).

calcitonin /ˌkalsɪˈtəʊnɪn/ ▶ noun [mass noun] Biochemistry a hormone secreted by the thyroid that has the effect of lowering blood calcium.
– ORIGIN 1960s: from CALCI- + TONIC + -IN[1].

calcium ▶ noun [mass noun] the chemical element of atomic number 20, a soft grey metal. (Symbol: **Ca**)

> Calcium is one of the alkaline earth metals. Its compounds occur naturally in limestone, fluorite, gypsum, and other minerals. Many physiological processes involve calcium ions, and calcium salts are an essential constituent of bone, teeth, and shells.

– ORIGIN early 19th cent.: from Latin *calx, calc-* 'lime' (see CALX) + -IUM.

calcium antagonist ▶ noun a compound of a type that reduces the influx of calcium into the cells of cardiac and smooth muscle, reducing the strength of contractions. Drugs of this kind are used to treat angina and high blood pressure.

calcium carbonate ▶ noun [mass noun] a white insoluble solid occurring naturally as chalk, limestone, marble, and calcite, and forming mollusc shells and stony corals. ● Chem. formula: $CaCO_3$.

calcium hydroxide ▶ noun [mass noun] a soluble white crystalline solid commonly produced in the form of slaked lime. ● Chem. formula: $Ca(OH)_2$.

calcium oxide ▶ noun [mass noun] a white caustic alkaline solid, commonly produced in the form of quicklime. ● Chem. formula: CaO.

calcrete /ˈkalkriːt/ ▶ noun [mass noun] Geology a breccia or conglomerate cemented together by calcareous material, formed in soils in semi-arid conditions. Also called CALICHE.
– ORIGIN early 20th cent.: from CALC- + a shortened form of CONCRETE.

calculable ▶ adjective able to be measured or assessed.
– DERIVATIVES **calculability** noun, **calculably** adverb.

calculate ▶ verb [with obj.] **1** determine (the amount or number of something) mathematically: *the program can calculate the number of words that will fit in the space available* | [with clause] *local authorities have calculated that full training would cost around £5,000 per teacher*. ■ determine by reasoning, experience, or common sense; reckon or judge: *I was bright enough to calculate that she had been on vacation*. ■ [no obj.] (**calculate on**) include as an essential element in one's plans.
2 (usu. **be calculated to do something**) intend (an action) to have a particular effect: *his last words were calculated to wound her*.
3 [with clause] US dialect suppose or believe: *I calculate it's pretty difficult to git edication down there*.
– DERIVATIVES **calculative** adjective.
– ORIGIN late Middle English: from late Latin *calculat-* 'counted', from the verb *calculare*, from *calculus* 'a small pebble (as used on an abacus)'.

calculated ▶ adjective (of an action) done with full awareness of the likely consequences: *victims of vicious and calculated assaults*.
– DERIVATIVES **calculatedly** adverb.

calculating ▶ adjective acting in a scheming and ruthlessly determined way: *he was a coolly calculating, ruthless man*.
– DERIVATIVES **calculatingly** adverb.

calculation ▶ noun a mathematical determination of the amount or number of something: *finding ways of saving money involves complicated calculations* | [mass noun] *the calculation of depreciation*. ■ an assessment of the risks, possibilities, or effects of a situation or course of action: *decisions are shaped by political calculations*.
– ORIGIN late Middle English: via Old French from late Latin *calculatio(n-)*, from the verb *calculare* (see CALCULATE).

calculator ▶ noun something used for making mathematical calculations, in particular a small electronic device with a keyboard and a visual display.

calculus /ˈkalkjʊləs/ ▶ noun **1** (pl. **calculuses**) (also **infinitesimal calculus**) [mass noun] the branch of mathematics that deals with the finding and properties of derivatives and integrals of functions, by methods originally based on the summation of infinitesimal differences. The two main types are **differential calculus** and **integral calculus**.
2 (pl. **calculuses**) a particular method or system of calculation or reasoning.
3 (pl. **calculi** /-lʌɪ, -liː/) Medicine a hard mass formed by minerals within the body, especially in the kidney or gall bladder. ■ another term for TARTAR.
– ORIGIN mid 17th cent.: from Latin, literally 'small pebble (as used on an abacus)'.

Calcutta /kalˈkʌtə/ former name (until 2000) for KOLKATA.

caldarium /kalˈdɛːrɪəm/ ▶ noun (pl. **caldaria** /-rɪə/) a hot room in an ancient Roman bath.
– ORIGIN Latin.

Caldecott /ˈkɔːldɪkɒt/, Randolph (1846–86), English graphic artist and watercolour painter. He is best known for his illustrations for children's books.

caldera /kɒlˈdɛːrə, -ˈdɪərə/ ▶ noun a large volcanic crater, especially one formed by a major eruption leading to the collapse of the mouth of the volcano.
– ORIGIN late 17th cent.: from Spanish, from late Latin *caldaria* 'boiling pot'.

Calderón de la Barca /ˌkaldəˌrɒn deɪ la ˈbɑːkə/, Pedro (1600–81), Spanish dramatist and poet. He wrote some 120 plays, more than seventy of them religious dramas.

caldron ▶ noun chiefly US variant spelling of CAULDRON.

Caldwell /ˈkɔːldwɛl/, Erskine (Preston) (1903–87), American novelist and short-story writer. Caldwell reproduced the dialect of the poor whites in his realistic, earthy, and popular novels, such as *Tobacco Road* (1932).

caleche /kəˈlɛʃ/ (also **calash**) ▶ noun historical **1** a light low-wheeled carriage with a removable folding hood.
2 a woman's hooped silk hood.
– ORIGIN mid 17th cent.: from French *calèche*, via German from Polish *kolasa*, from *kolo* 'wheel'.

Caledonian /ˌkalɪˈdəʊnɪən/ ▶ adjective **1** (chiefly in names or geographical terms) relating to Scotland or the Scottish Highlands: *the Caledonian Railway*.
2 Geology relating to or denoting a mountain-forming period (orogeny) in NW Europe and Greenland during the Lower Palaeozoic era, especially the late Silurian.
▶ noun **1** chiefly humorous or literary a person from Scotland.
2 (**the Caledonian**) Geology the Caledonian orogeny.
– ORIGIN from *Caledonia*, the Latin name for northern Britain, + -AN.

Caledonian Canal a system of lochs and canals crossing Scotland from Inverness on the east coast to Fort William on the west.

calefacient /ˌkalɪˈfeɪʃ(ə)nt/ ▶ noun archaic a drug or other substance that gives a sensation of warmth.
– ORIGIN mid 17th cent.: from Latin *calefacient-* 'making warm', from the verb *calefacere*, from *calere* 'be warm' + *facere* 'make'.

calendar /ˈkalɪndə/ ▶ noun a chart or series of pages showing the days, weeks, and months of a particular year, or giving particular seasonal information. ■ a system by which the beginning, length, and subdivisions of the year are fixed. See also JULIAN CALENDAR and GREGORIAN CALENDAR. ■ a list of days or events of a specified kind: *the social calendar*. ■ N. Amer. a book in which to note daily appointments.
▶ verb [with obj.] enter (something) in a calendar or timetable.
– DERIVATIVES **calendric** /-ˈlɛndrɪk/ adjective, **calendrical** adjective.
– ORIGIN Middle English: from Old French *calendier*, from Latin *kalendarium* 'account book', from *kalendae* (see CALENDS).

C

calendarize (also **calendarise**) ▶ verb [with obj.] (usu. as adj. **calendarized**) schedule, allocate, or record (something) on a month-by-month basis: *a calendarized budget*.

calendar month ▶ noun see MONTH.

calendar year ▶ noun see YEAR (sense 2).

calender /ˈkalɪndə/ ▶ noun a machine in which cloth or paper is pressed by rollers to glaze or smooth it.
▶ verb [with obj.] press in a calender.
– ORIGIN late 15th cent. (as a verb): from French *calendre* (noun), *calendrer* (verb), of unknown origin.

calends /ˈkalɪndz/ (also **kalends**) ▶ plural noun the first day of the month in the ancient Roman calendar.
– ORIGIN Old English (denoting an appointed time): from Old French *calendes*, from Latin *kalendae*, *calendae* 'first day of the month' (when accounts were due and the order of days was proclaimed); related to Latin *calare* and Greek *kalein* 'call, proclaim'.

calendula /kəˈlɛndjʊlə/ ▶ noun a Mediterranean plant of a genus that includes the common or pot marigold. ● Genus *Calendula*, family Compositae.
– ORIGIN modern Latin, diminutive of *calendae* (see CALENDS); perhaps because it flowers for most of the year.

calenture /ˈkal(ə)ntjʊə/ ▶ noun [mass noun] feverish delirium formerly thought of as afflicting sailors in the tropics.
– ORIGIN late 16th cent.: from French, from Spanish *calentura* 'fever', from *calentar* 'be hot', based on Latin *calere* 'be warm'.

calf[1] ▶ noun (pl. **calves**) **1** a young bovine animal, especially a domestic cow or bull in its first year. ■ the young of some other large mammals, such as elephants, rhinoceroses, large deer and antelopes, and whales. ■ short for CALFSKIN.
2 a floating piece of ice detached from an iceberg.
– PHRASES **in** (or **with**) **calf** (of a cow) pregnant.
– DERIVATIVES **calf-like** adjective.
– ORIGIN Old English *cælf*, of Germanic origin; related to Dutch *kalf* and German *Kalb*.

calf[2] ▶ noun (pl. **calves**) the fleshy part at the back of a person's leg below the knee.
– ORIGIN Middle English: from Old Norse *kálfi*, of unknown origin.

calf love ▶ noun another term for PUPPY LOVE.

calfskin ▶ noun [mass noun] leather made from the hide or skin of a calf, used in bookbinding and shoemaking.

Calgary /ˈkalgəri/ a city in southern Alberta, SW Canada; pop. 988,193 (2006).

Cali /ˈkɑːli/ an industrial city in western Colombia, pop. 2,075,525 (2005).

calibrate /ˈkalɪbreɪt/ ▶ verb [with obj.] mark (a gauge or instrument) with a standard scale of readings. ■ correlate the readings of (an instrument) with those of a standard in order to check the instrument's accuracy. ■ adjust (experimental results) to take external factors into account or to allow comparison with other data. ■ carefully assess, set, or adjust (something abstract): *the regulators cannot properly calibrate the risks involved* | (as adj. **calibrated**) *their carefully calibrated economic policies*.
– DERIVATIVES **calibrator** noun.
– ORIGIN mid 19th cent.: from CALIBRE + -ATE[3].

calibration ▶ noun [mass noun] the action or process of calibrating something: *the measuring devices require calibration*. ■ [count noun] each of a set of graduations on an instrument.

C

calibre /ˈkalɪbə/ (US **caliber**) ▶ **noun 1** [mass noun] the quality of someone's character or the level of their ability: *they could ill afford to lose a man of his calibre.* ■ the standard reached by something: *educational facilities of a very high calibre.*
2 the internal diameter or bore of a gun barrel: [in combination] *a small-calibre revolver.* ■ the diameter of a bullet, shell, or rocket. ■ the diameter of a body of circular section, such as a tube, blood vessel, or fibre.
– ORIGIN mid 16th cent. (in the sense 'social standing or importance'): from French, from Italian *calibro*, perhaps from Arabic *ḳālib* 'mould', based on Greek *kalapous* 'shoemaker's last'.

caliche /kəˈliːtʃi/ ▶ **noun** [mass noun] a mineral deposit of gravel, sand, and nitrates, found in dry areas of America. ■ another term for **CALCRETE**.
– ORIGIN mid 19th cent.: from Latin American Spanish.

calico /ˈkalɪkəʊ/ ▶ **noun** (pl. **calicoes** or US also **calicos**) [mass noun] Brit. a type of cotton cloth, typically plain white or unbleached: [as modifier] *a calico dress.*
■ N. Amer. printed cotton fabric.
▶ **adjective** N. Amer. (of an animal, typically a cat) multi-coloured or piebald.
– ORIGIN mid 16th cent. (originally also *calicut*): alteration of **CALICUT**, where the fabric originated.

Calicut /ˈkalɪkʌt/ former name for **KOZHIKODE**.

Calif. ▶ **abbreviation** California.

California a state of the US, on the Pacific coast; pop. 36,756,666 (est. 2008); capital, Sacramento. Formerly part of Mexico, it was ceded to the US in 1847, and became the 31st state of the US in 1850.
– DERIVATIVES **Californian** adjective & noun.

California, Gulf of an arm of the Pacific Ocean separating the Baja California peninsula from mainland Mexico.

California Current a cold ocean current of the eastern Pacific that flows south along the west coast of North America.

California poppy (also **Californian poppy**) ▶ **noun** an annual poppy native to western North America, which is cultivated for its brilliant yellow or orange flowers. ● *Eschscholtzia californica*, family Papaveraceae.

californium /ˌkalɪˈfɔːnɪəm/ ▶ **noun** [mass noun] the chemical element of atomic number 98, a radioactive metal of the actinide series, first produced by bombarding curium with helium ions. (Symbol: **Cf**)
– ORIGIN 1950s: named after *California University* (where it was first made) + **-IUM**.

caliginous /kəˈlɪdʒɪnəs/ ▶ **adjective** literary dark, dim, or misty: *the caliginous sky.*
– ORIGIN mid 16th-cent.: from Latin *caliginosus* 'misty', from *caligo, caligin-* 'mistiness'.

Caligula /kəˈlɪgjʊlə/ (AD 12–41), Roman emperor 37–41; born *Gaius Julius Caesar Germanicus*. His reign was notorious for its tyrannical excesses.

caliper /ˈkalɪpə/ (also **calliper**) ▶ **noun 1** (**calipers**) an instrument for measuring external or internal dimensions, having two hinged legs resembling a pair of compasses and in-turned or out-turned points. ■ (also **caliper rule**) a measuring instrument having one linear component sliding along another, with two parallel jaws and a vernier scale. ■ (also **brake caliper**) a motor-vehicle or bicycle brake consisting of two or more hinged components.
2 (also **caliper splint**) Brit. a metal support for a person's leg.
– ORIGIN late 16th cent.: apparently an alteration of **CALIBRE**.

caliph /ˈkeɪlɪf, ˈka-/ ▶ **noun** historical the chief Muslim civil and religious ruler, regarded as the successor of Muhammad. The caliph ruled in Baghdad until 1258 and then in Egypt until the Ottoman conquest of 1517; the title was then held by the Ottoman sultans until it was abolished in 1924 by Atatürk.
– DERIVATIVES **caliphate** noun.
– ORIGIN late Middle English: from Old French *caliphe*, from Arabic *ḵalīfa* meaning 'deputy (of God)' (from the title *ḵalīfat Allāh*), or meaning 'successor (of Muhammad)' (from the title *ḵalīfat rasūl Allāh* 'of the Messenger of God'), from *ḵalafa* 'succeed'.

calisthenics ▶ **plural noun** US spelling of **CALLISTHENICS**.

calix ▶ **noun** variant spelling of **CALYX**.

calk ▶ **noun & verb** US spelling of **CAULK**.

call ▶ **verb 1** [with obj.] cry out to (someone) in order to summon them or attract their attention: *she heard Terry calling her* | [no obj.] *I distinctly heard you call.* ■ cry out (a word or words): *he heard an insistent voice calling his name* | *Meredith was already calling out a greeting.* ■ [no obj.] (of an animal, especially a bird) make its characteristic cry: *the mother bird was calling from the twig.* ■ shout out or chant (the steps and figures) to people performing a square dance or country dance. ■ telephone (a person or telephone number): *could I call you back?* ■ summon (an emergency service, taxi, etc.) by telephone: *if you are suspicious, call the police.* ■ bring (a witness) into court to give evidence. ■ [with obj. and infinitive] archaic inspire or urge (someone) to do something: *I am called to preach the Gospel.* ■ fix a date or time for (a meeting, strike, or election). ■ Bridge make (a particular bid) during the auction. ■ [no obj.] guess the outcome of tossing a coin: *'You call,' he said. 'Heads or tails?'* ■ predict the result of (a future event, especially an election or a vote): *in the Midlands the race remains **too close to call**.* ■ Cricket (of an umpire) no-ball (a bowler) for throwing. ■ Computing cause the execution of (a subroutine).
2 [with obj. and complement] give (an infant or animal) a specified name: *they called their daughter Hannah.*
■ (**be called**) have a specified name: *her companion was called Ethel* | *he has written a book called The Secret Life of Wombats.* ■ address or refer to (someone) by a specified name, title, etc.: *please call me Lucy.* ■ refer to or consider (someone or something) as being: *he's the only person I would call a friend.* ■ (of an umpire or other official in a game) pronounce (a ball, stroke, etc.) to be the thing specified: *the linesman called the ball wide.*
3 [no obj., with adverbial of place] chiefly Brit. (of a person) pay a brief visit: *I've got to call at the bank to get some cash* | *he had promised Celia he would **call in** at the clinic.* ■ (**call for**) stop to collect (someone) at the place where they are living or working: *I'll call for you around seven.* ■ (**call at**) (of a train or coach) stop at (a specified station or stations) on a particular route: *the 8.15 service to Paddington, calling at Reading.*
▶ **noun 1** a cry made as a summons or to attract someone's attention: *in response to the call, a figure appeared.* ■ [with modifier] a series of notes sounded on a brass instrument as a signal to do something: *a bugle call to rise at 8.30.* ■ a telephone communication or conversation: *I'll give you a call at around five.* ■ (**a call for**) an appeal or demand for: *the call for action was welcomed.* ■ a summons: *a messenger arrived bringing news of his call to the throne.* ■ [in sing., with infinitive] a vocation: *his call to be a disciple.*
■ [in sing.] a powerful force of attraction: *walkers can't resist the call of the Cairngorms.* ■ [usu. with negative] (**call for**) demand or need for (goods or services): *there is little call for antique furniture.* ■ a shout by an official in a game indicating that the ball has gone out of play or that a rule has been breached. ■ Bridge a bid, response, or double. ■ a direction in a square dance given by the caller. ■ a demand for payment of lent or unpaid capital. ■ Stock Exchange short for **CALL OPTION**.
2 the characteristic cry of a bird or other animal: *it is best distinguished by its call, a loud 'pwit'.*
3 a brief visit: *we **paid a call on** an elderly Spaniard.*
■ a visit or journey made in response to an emergency appeal for help: *the doctor was out on a call.*
– PHRASES **at call** another way of saying **ON CALL** (sense 2). **call attention to** cause people to notice: *he is seeking to call attention to himself by his crimes.* **call someone's bluff** see **BLUFF**[1]. **call collect** N. Amer. make a telephone call reversing the charges. **call something into** (or **in**) **question** cast doubt on something: *these findings call into question the legitimacy of the proceedings.* **call it a day** see **DAY**. **call someone names** see **NAME**. **call of nature** see **NATURE**. **call the shots** (or **tune**) take the initiative in deciding how something should be done. **call a spade a spade** see **SPADE**[1]. **call someone to account** see **ACCOUNT**. **call someone/thing to mind** cause one to think of someone or something, especially through similarity: *the still lifes call to mind certain of Cézanne's works.* ■ [with negative] remember someone or something: [with clause] *I cannot call to mind where I have seen you.* **call someone/thing to order** ask those present at a meeting to be silent so that business may proceed. **don't call us, we'll call you** informal used as a dismissive way of saying that someone has not been successful in an audition or job application. **good call** (or **bad call**) informal used to express approval (or criticism) of a person's decision or suggestion. [with reference to decisions made by referees or umpires.] **on call 1** (of a person) able to be contacted in order to provide a professional service if necessary, but not formally on duty. **2** (of money lent) repayable on demand. **to call one's own** used to describe something that one can genuinely feel belongs to one: *I had not an item to call my own.* **within call** near enough to be summoned by calling: *she moved into the guest room, within call of her father's room.*
– PHRASAL VERBS **call for 1** make necessary: *desperate times call for desperate measures.* **2** publicly ask for or demand: *the report calls for an audit of endangered species.* **call something forth** elicit a specified response: *few things call forth more compassion.* **call someone/thing down 1** cause or provoke someone or something to appear or occur: *nothing called down the wrath of Nemesis quicker.* **2** dated reprimand someone. **call someone in** enlist someone's aid or services. **call something in** require payment of a loan or promise of money. **call someone/thing off** order a person or dog to stop attacking someone. **call something off** cancel an event or agreement. **call on 1** pay a visit to (someone): *he's planning to call on Katherine today.* **2** (also **call upon**) have recourse to: *we are able to call on academic staff with a wide variety of expertise.* ■ [with infinitive] demand that (someone) do something: *he called on the government to hold a vote.* **call someone out 1** summon someone to deal with an emergency or to do repairs. **2** order or advise workers to strike. **3** archaic challenge someone to a duel. **call something over** dated read out a list of names to determine those present. **call someone up 1** informal, chiefly N. Amer. telephone someone. **2** summon someone to serve in the army. ■ select someone to play in a team: *he was called up for the international against Turkey.* **call something up** summon for use something that is stored or kept available: *icons which allow you to call up a graphic.* ■ evoke something: *the imaginative intensity with which he called up the Devon landscape.*
– ORIGIN late Old English *ceallian*, from Old Norse *kalla* 'summon loudly'.

calla /ˈkalə/ ▶ **noun** either of two plants of the arum family: ● (also **water calla**) another term for **BOG ARUM** ● (usu. **calla lily**) chiefly N. Amer. another term for **ARUM LILY**.
– ORIGIN early 19th cent.: modern Latin.

callable ▶ **adjective** Finance denoting a bond that can be paid off earlier than the maturity date.

Callaghan /ˈkaləhan/, (Leonard) James, Baron Callaghan of Cardiff (1912–2005), British Labour statesman, Prime Minister 1976–9.

callaloo /ˌkaləˈluː/ (also **callalou**) ▶ **noun 1** [mass noun] the spinach-like leaves of a tropical American plant, used in Caribbean cookery. ■ a soup or stew made with callaloo leaves.
2 the plant of the arum family from which callaloo leaves are obtained. ● Genus *Xanthosoma*, family Araceae.
– ORIGIN mid 18th cent.: from American Spanish *calalú*.

Callanetics /ˌkaləˈnɛtɪks/ ▶ **plural noun** [treated as sing. or pl.] trademark a system of physical exercises based on small repeated movements.
– ORIGIN 1980s: named after *Callan* Pinckney (born 1939), American deviser of the system, perhaps on the pattern of *athletics*.

Callao /kaˈjaʊ/ the principal seaport of Peru; pop. 415,900 (est. 2007).

Callas /ˈkaləs/, Maria (1923–77), American-born operatic soprano, of Greek parentage; born *Maria Cecilia Anna Kalageropoulos*. She was a coloratura soprano whose bel canto style of singing was especially suited to 19th-century Italian opera.

callback ▶ **noun 1** chiefly N. Amer. an invitation to return for a second audition or interview.
2 a telephone call made to return one that someone has received.
3 [mass noun] a security feature used by some computer systems accessed by telephone, in which a user must log on from a previously registered phone number, to which the system then places a return call.

call box ▶ **noun 1** Brit. a public telephone booth.
2 N. Amer. a telephone for emergency use.

call centre ▶ **noun** an office in which large numbers of telephone calls are handled, especially one providing the customer services functions of a large organization.

caller ▶ **noun 1** a person who pays a brief visit or makes a telephone call.
2 a person who calls out numbers in a game of bingo or directions in a dance. ■ Austral./NZ a racing or sports commentator.

caller ID ▶ **noun** [mass noun] a facility that identifies and displays the telephone numbers of incoming calls made to a particular line.

call girl ▶ **noun** a female prostitute who accepts appointments by telephone.

Callicrates /kəˈlɪkrətiːz/ (5th century BC), Greek architect. He was the leading architect in Periclean Athens, and with Ictinus designed the Parthenon (447–438 BC).

calligraph /ˈkalɪɡrɑːf/ ▶ **verb** [with obj.] write in calligraphic style.

calligraphy /kəˈlɪɡrəfi/ ▶ **noun** [mass noun] decorative handwriting or handwritten lettering. ■ the art of producing decorative handwriting or lettering with a pen or brush.
– DERIVATIVES **calligrapher** noun, **calligraphic** adjective, **calligraphist** noun.
– ORIGIN early 17th cent.: from Greek *kalligraphia*, from *kalligraphos* 'person who writes beautifully', from *kallos* 'beauty' + *graphein* 'write'.

Callimachus /kəˈlɪməkəs/ (*c*.305–*c*.240 BC), Greek poet and scholar. He is famed for his hymns and epigrams, and was head of the library at Alexandria.

call-in ▶ **noun** North American term for **PHONE-IN**.

calling ▶ **noun 1** [mass noun] the action or sound of calling.
2 a strong urge towards a particular way of life or career; a vocation: *those who have a special calling to minister to others' needs.* ■ a profession or occupation: *he considered engineering one of the highest possible callings.*

calling bell ▶ **noun** Indian a doorbell.

calling card ▶ **noun 1** a card bearing a person's name and address, sent or left in lieu of a formal social or business visit. ■ an action by which someone or something can be identified: *holistic, sustainable design is the calling card of the green architect.*
2 N. Amer. a phonecard or telephone charge card.

Calliope /kəˈlʌɪəpi/ Greek & Roman Mythology the Muse of epic poetry.
– ORIGIN from Greek *Kalliopē*, literally 'having a beautiful voice'.

calliope /kəˈlʌɪəpi/ ▶ **noun** an American keyboard instrument resembling an organ but with the notes produced by steam whistles, formerly used on showboats and in travelling fairs.
– ORIGIN mid 19th cent.: from the Greek name *Kalliopē* (see **CALLIOPE**).

calliper /ˈkalɪpə/ ▶ **noun** variant spelling of **CALIPER**.

callipygian /ˌkalɪˈpɪdʒɪən/ (also **callipygean**) ▶ **adjective** rare having well-shaped buttocks.
– DERIVATIVES **callipygous** /ˌkalɪˈpɪdʒəs, ˌkalɪˈpʌɪdʒəs/ adjective.
– ORIGIN late 18th cent.: from Greek *kallipūgos* (used to describe a famous statue of Venus), from *kallos* 'beauty' + *pūgē* 'buttocks', + **-IAN**.

callistemon /ˌkalɪˈstiːmən/ ▶ **noun** a plant of a genus that comprises the bottlebrushes. ● Genus *Callistemon*, family Myrtaceae.
– ORIGIN modern Latin, from Greek *kallos* 'beauty' + *stēmōn* 'thread or stamen'.

callisthenics /ˌkalɪsˈθɛnɪks/ (US **calisthenics**) ▶ **plural noun** [treated as sing. or pl.] gymnastic exercises to achieve bodily fitness and grace of movement.
– DERIVATIVES **callisthenic** adjective.
– ORIGIN early 19th cent.: from Greek *kallos* 'beauty' + *sthenos* 'strength' + **-ICS**.

Callisto /kəˈlɪstəʊ/ **1** Greek Mythology a nymph who was changed into a bear by Zeus. See also **URSA MAJOR**.
2 Astronomy one of the Galilean moons of Jupiter, the eighth-closest satellite to the planet, icy with a dark, cratered surface (diameter 4,800 km).

callitrichid /ˌkalɪˈtrʌɪkɪd/ ▶ **noun** Zoology a primate of a family (Callitrichidae or Callithricidae) that comprises the marmosets and tamarins.
– ORIGIN late 18th cent.: from modern Latin *Callitrichidae* (plural), from Greek *kallitrikhos* 'having beautiful hair'.

call letters ▶ **plural noun** N. Amer. a sequence of letters used by a television or radio station as an identifying code.

call money ▶ **noun** [mass noun] money loaned by a bank or other institution which is repayable on demand.

callop /ˈkaləp/ ▶ **noun** a deep-bodied edible gold and green freshwater fish found in Australia. Also called **GOLDEN PERCH**. ● *Plectroplites ambiguus*, family Serranidae.
– ORIGIN 1920s: perhaps from an Aboriginal language of southern Australia.

call option ▶ **noun** Stock Exchange an option to buy assets at an agreed price on or before a particular date.

callosity /kəˈlɒsɪti/ ▶ **noun** (pl. **callosities**) technical a thickened and hardened part of the skin; a callus.
– ORIGIN late Middle English: from French *callosité*, from Latin *callositas*, from *callosus* 'hard-skinned', from *callum*, *callus* 'hardened skin'.

callous ▶ **adjective** showing or having an insensitive and cruel disregard for others: *his callous comments about the murder made me shiver.*
▶ **noun** variant spelling of **CALLUS**.
– DERIVATIVES **callously** adverb, **callousness** noun.
– ORIGIN late Middle English (in the Latin sense): from Latin *callosus* 'hard-skinned'.

calloused (also **callused**) ▶ **adjective** (of a part of the body) having an area of hardened skin: *a calloused palm.*

call-out ▶ **noun 1** an instance of being summoned to deal with an emergency or do repairs: [as modifier] *a call-out charge.*
2 Printing a letter, word, number, or symbol identifying an illustration or a specific part of one. ■ a short piece of text set in larger type than the rest of the page and intended to attract attention.

call-over ▶ **noun** Brit. dated a roll-call at school.

callow ▶ **adjective** (of a young person) inexperienced and immature: *earnest and callow undergraduates.*
– DERIVATIVES **callowly** adverb, **callowness** noun.
– ORIGIN Old English *calu* 'bald', of West Germanic origin, probably from Latin *calvus* 'bald'. This was extended to mean 'unfledged', which led to the present sense 'immature'.

Calloway /ˈkaləweɪ/, Cab (1907–94), American jazz singer and bandleader; full name *Cabell Calloway*. He was famous for his style of scat singing, for his flamboyant appearance, and for songs such as 'Minnie the Moocher' (1931).

call sign (also **call signal**) ▶ **noun** a message, code, or tune that is broadcast by radio to identify the broadcaster or transmitter.

calluna /kəˈluːnə/ ▶ **noun** [mass noun] the common heather of Europe and Asia Minor.
– ORIGIN early 19th cent.: modern Latin, from Greek *kallunein* 'beautify, sweep clean' (from *kallos* 'beauty'). The notion of 'sweeping' is also seen in the noun **BROOM**, brooms being originally made of twigs of heather or broom.

call-up ▶ **noun** an instance of being summoned to serve in the armed forces or a sports team: [as modifier] *my call-up papers.*

callus /ˈkaləs/ (also **callous**) ▶ **noun** a thickened and hardened part of the skin or soft tissue, especially in an area that has been subjected to friction. ■ Medicine the bony healing tissue which forms around the ends of broken bone. ■ Botany a hard formation of tissue, especially new tissue formed over a wound.
– ORIGIN mid 16th cent.: from Latin *callus* (more commonly *callum*) 'hardened skin'.

callused ▶ **adjective** variant spelling of **CALLOUSED**.

call waiting ▶ **noun** [mass noun] a service whereby someone making a telephone call is notified of an incoming call on the line that they are already using, and is able to place the first call on hold while the second is answered.

calm ▶ **adjective 1** not showing or feeling nervousness, anger, or other strong emotions: *she had to **keep calm** at all costs | his voice was calm.* ■ (of a place) peaceful after violent activity: *the city was reported to be calm, but army patrols remained.*
2 (of the weather) pleasantly free from wind: *the night was clear and calm.* ■ (of the sea) not disturbed by large waves.
▶ **noun** [mass noun] **1** the absence of strong emotions; calm feelings: *his usual calm deserted him.* ■ the absence of violent activity in a place: *the elections proceeded in an atmosphere of relative calm* | [in sing.] *an edgy calm reigned in the capital.*
2 the absence of wind: *in the centre of the storm calm prevailed.* ■ still air represented by force 0 on the Beaufort scale (less than 1 knot or 1 kph). ■ [count noun] (often **calms**) an area of the sea without wind.
▶ **verb** [with obj.] make (someone) tranquil and quiet; soothe: *I took him inside and tried to **calm him down**.* ■ [no obj.] (**calm down**) (of a person) become tranquil and quiet.
– PHRASES **the calm before the storm** see **STORM**.
– DERIVATIVES **calmly** adverb, **calmness** noun.
– ORIGIN late Middle English: via one of the Romance languages from Greek *kauma* 'heat (of the day)'.

calmative /ˈkɑːmətɪv, ˈkal-/ ▶ **adjective** (of a drug) having a sedative effect.
▶ **noun** a calmative drug.

calmodulin /kalˈmɒdjʊlɪn/ ▶ **noun** [mass noun] Biochemistry a protein which binds calcium and is involved in regulating a variety of activities in cells.
– ORIGIN 1970s: from *cal(cium)* + *modul(ate)* + **-IN**[1].

calomel /ˈkaləmɛl/ ▶ **noun** [mass noun] mercurous chloride, a white powder formerly used as a purgative. ● Chem. formula: Hg_2Cl_2.
– ORIGIN late 17th cent.: modern Latin, perhaps from Greek *kalos* 'beautiful' + *melas* 'black' (perhaps because it was originally obtained from a black mixture of mercury and mercuric chloride).

Calor gas /ˈkalə/ ▶ **noun** [mass noun] Brit. trademark liquefied butane stored under pressure in portable containers, used domestically as a substitute for mains gas and in camping as a portable fuel.
– ORIGIN 1930s: *Calor* from Latin *calor* 'heat'.

caloric /kəˈlɒrɪk, ˈkalərɪk/ ▶ **adjective** chiefly N. Amer. or technical relating to heat; calorific: *a caloric value of 7 calories per gram.*
▶ **noun** [mass noun] a hypothetical fluid substance formerly thought to be responsible for the phenomena of heat.
– DERIVATIVES **calorically** adverb.
– ORIGIN late 18th cent. (as a noun): from French *calorique*, from Latin *calor* 'heat'.

calorie ▶ **noun** (pl. **calories**) either of two units of heat energy: ■ (also **small calorie**) (abbrev.: **cal**) the energy needed to raise the temperature of 1 gram of water through 1 °C (now usually defined as 4.1868 joules). ■ (also **large calorie**) (abbrev.: **Cal**) the energy needed to raise the temperature of 1 kilogram of water through 1 °C, equal to one thousand small calories and often used to measure the energy value of foods.
– ORIGIN mid 19th cent.: from French, from Latin *calor* 'heat' + French suffix *-ie* (see **-Y**[3]).

calorific ▶ **adjective** relating to the amount of energy contained in food or fuel: *she knew the calorific contents of every morsel.* ■ (of food or drink) containing many calories and so likely to be fattening: *there is fruit salad for those who can resist the more calorific concoctions.*
– DERIVATIVES **calorifically** adverb.
– ORIGIN late 17th cent.: from Latin *calorificus*, from *calor* 'heat'.

calorific value ▶ **noun** the energy contained in a fuel or food, determined by measuring the heat produced by the complete combustion of a specified quantity of it. This is now usually expressed in joules per kilogram.

calorimeter /ˌkaləˈrɪmɪtə/ ▶ **noun** an apparatus for measuring the amount of heat involved in a chemical reaction or other process.
– DERIVATIVES **calorimetric** adjective, **calorimetry** noun.
– ORIGIN late 18th cent.: from Latin *calor* 'heat' + **-METER**.

calotype /ˈkalətʌɪp/ (also **calotype process**) ▶ **noun** [mass noun] historical an early photographic process in which negatives were made using paper coated with silver iodide.
– ORIGIN mid 19th cent.: from Greek *kalos* 'beautiful' + **TYPE**.

calque /kalk/ Linguistics ▶ **noun** another term for **LOAN TRANSLATION**.
▶ **verb** (**be calqued on**) originate or function as a loan translation of.
– ORIGIN 1930s: from French, literally 'copy, tracing', from *calquer* 'to trace', via Italian from Latin *calcare* 'to tread'.

caltrop /ˈkaltrəp/ ▶ **noun 1** a spiked metal device thrown on the ground to impede wheeled vehicles or (formerly) cavalry horses.
2 a creeping plant with woody carpels that typically have hard spines and resemble military caltrops. ● Genus *Tribulus*, family Zygophyllaceae.
3 (also **water caltrop**) another term for **WATER CHESTNUT** (sense 3).
– ORIGIN Old English *calcatrippe*, denoting any plant which tended to catch the feet, from medieval Latin *calcatrippa*, from *calx* 'heel' or *calcare* 'to tread' + a word related to **TRAP**[1]. Sense 1 was probably adopted from French.

calumet /ˈkaljʊmɛt/ ▶ **noun** a North American Indian peace pipe.
– ORIGIN late 17th cent.: from French, from late Latin *calamellus* 'little reed', diminutive of Latin *calamus* (referring to the pipe's reed stem).

calumniate /kəˈlʌmnɪeɪt/ ▶ **verb** [with obj.] formal make false and defamatory statements about: *he has been*

C

C

calumniating the Crown and all the conservative decencies.
– DERIVATIVES **calumniation** noun, **calumniator** noun.
– ORIGIN mid 16th cent.: from Latin *calumniari*, from *calumnia* (see CALUMNY).

calumny /ˈkaləmni/ ▶ noun (pl. **calumnies**) [mass noun] the making of false and defamatory statements about someone in order to damage their reputation; slander. ■ [count noun] a false and slanderous statement: *a change in the law would prevent the press from publishing calumnies.*
▶ verb (**calumnies, calumnying, calumnied**) [with obj.] formal slander (someone).
– DERIVATIVES **calumnious** /kəˈlʌmnɪəs/ adjective.
– ORIGIN late Middle English: from Latin *calumnia*.

calutron /kəˈluːtrɒn/ ▶ noun a device that uses large electromagnets to separate uranium isotopes from uranium ore, developed in the 1940s to produce highly enriched weapons-grade uranium.
– ORIGIN from *Cal(ifornia) U(niversity) (cyclo)tron*.

Calvados /ˈkalvədɒs/ ▶ noun [mass noun] apple brandy, traditionally made in the Calvados region of Normandy.

Calvary /ˈkalv(ə)ri/ the hill outside Jerusalem on which Christ was crucified. ■ (as noun **a calvary**) a sculpture or picture representing the scene of the Crucifixion.
– ORIGIN from late Latin *calvaria* 'skull', translation of Greek *golgotha* 'place of a skull' (Matt. 27:33) (see GOLGOTHA).

calve ▶ verb **1** [no obj.] (of cows and certain other large animals) give birth to a calf. ■ [with obj.] (of a person) help (a cow) give birth to a calf.
2 [with obj.] (of an iceberg or glacier) split and shed (a smaller mass of ice). ■ [no obj.] (of a mass of ice) split off from an iceberg or glacier.
– ORIGIN Old English *calfian*, from *cælf* 'calf'.

calves plural form of CALF[1], CALF[2].

Calvin[1], John (1509–64), French Protestant theologian and reformer. On becoming a Protestant he fled to Switzerland, where he attempted to reorder society on reformed Christian principles and established the first Presbyterian government, in Geneva. His *Institutes of the Christian Religion* (1536) was the first systematic account of reformed Christian doctrine.

Calvin[2], Melvin (1911–97), American biochemist, who investigated photosynthesis and discovered the cycle of reactions (the **Calvin cycle**) which constitute the dark reaction. Nobel Prize for Chemistry (1961).

Calvinism ▶ noun [mass noun] the Protestant theological system of John Calvin and his successors, which develops Luther's doctrine of justification by faith alone into an emphasis on the grace of God and centres on the doctrine of predestination.
– DERIVATIVES **Calvinist** noun, **Calvinistic** adjective, **Calvinistical** adjective.

calx /kalks/ ▶ noun (pl. **calces** /ˈkalsiːz/) Chemistry, archaic a powdery metallic oxide formed when an ore or mineral has been heated.
– ORIGIN late Middle English: from Latin, 'lime', probably from Greek *khalix* 'pebble, limestone'.

Calypso /kəˈlɪpsəʊ/ Greek Mythology a nymph who kept Odysseus on her island, Ogygia, for seven years.
– ORIGIN Greek, literally 'she who conceals'.

calypso /kəˈlɪpsəʊ/ ▶ noun (pl. **calypsos**) [mass noun] a kind of West Indian (originally Trinidadian) music in syncopated African rhythm, typically with words improvised on a topical theme. ■ [count noun] a calypso song.
– DERIVATIVES **calypsonian** adjective & noun.
– ORIGIN 1930s: of unknown origin.

calyx /ˈkalɪks, ˈkeɪ-/ (also **calix**) ▶ noun (pl. **calyces** /-lɪsiːz/ or **calyxes**) **1** Botany the sepals of a flower, typically forming a whorl that encloses the petals and forms a protective layer around a flower in bud. Compare with COROLLA.
2 Zoology a cup-like cavity or structure, in particular: ■ a portion of the pelvis of a mammalian kidney. ■ the cavity in a calcareous coral skeleton that surrounds the polyp.
– ORIGIN late 17th cent.: from Latin, from Greek *kalux* 'case of a bud, husk', related to *kaluptein* 'to hide'.

calzone /kalˈtsəʊneɪ, -ni/ ▶ noun (pl. **calzoni** or **calzones**) a type of pizza that is folded in half before cooking to contain a filling.
– ORIGIN Italian dialect, probably a special use of *calzone* 'trouser leg', with reference to the shape of the pizza.

CAM ▶ abbreviation computer aided manufacturing.

cam ▶ noun **1** a projection on a rotating part in machinery, designed to make sliding contact with another part while rotating and impart reciprocal or variable motion to it. ■ a camshaft.
2 informal a camera.
– ORIGIN late 18th cent.: from Dutch *kam* 'comb', as in *kamrad* 'cogwheel'.

camaraderie /ˌkaməˈrɑːd(ə)ri, -riː/ ▶ noun [mass noun] mutual trust and friendship among people who spend a lot of time together: *the enforced camaraderie of office life.*
– ORIGIN mid 19th cent.: from French, from *camarade* 'comrade'.

Camargue /kəˈmɑːg/, French /kamaʀg/ (**the Camargue**) a region of the Rhône delta in SE France, characterized by numerous shallow salt lagoons. The region is known for its white horses and as a nature reserve.

camarilla /ˌkaməˈrɪl(j)ə/ ▶ noun derogatory a small group of people, especially a group of advisers to a ruler or politician, with a shared purpose: *a military camarilla that has lost any sense of political reality.*
– ORIGIN mid 19th cent.: from Spanish, diminutive of *camara* 'chamber'.

camas /kəˈmas/ (also **camass** or **quamash**) ▶ noun a North American plant of the lily family, cultivated for its starry blue or purple flowers. ● Genera *Camassia* and *Zigadenus*, family Liliaceae: several species.
– ORIGIN mid 19th cent.: from Chinook Jargon *kamass*, perhaps from Nootka.

Cambay, Gulf of /kamˈbeɪ/ (also **Gulf of Khambat**) an inlet of the Arabian Sea on the Gujarat coast of western India, north of Mumbai (Bombay).

camber /ˈkambə/ ▶ noun the slightly convex or arched shape of a road or other horizontal surface. ■ Brit. a tilt built into a road at a bend or curve, enabling vehicles to maintain speed. ■ the slight sideways inclination of the front wheels of a motor vehicle. ■ the extent of curvature of a section of an aerofoil.
– DERIVATIVES **cambered** adjective.
– ORIGIN late Middle English: from Old French *cambre*, dialect variant of *chambre* 'arched', from Latin *camurus* 'curved inwards'.

Camberwell beauty ▶ noun Brit. a migratory butterfly with deep purple yellow-bordered wings, which is a rare visitor to Britain. ● *Nymphalis antiopa*, subfamily Nymphalinae, family Nymphalidae.
– ORIGIN mid 19th cent.: named after *Camberwell* in London, then a village, where the first specimens were captured.

cambium /ˈkambɪəm/ ▶ noun (pl. **cambia** or **cambiums**) [mass noun] Botany a cellular plant tissue from which phloem, xylem, or cork grows by division, resulting (in woody plants) in secondary thickening.
– DERIVATIVES **cambial** adjective.
– ORIGIN late 16th cent. (denoting one of the alimentary humours once supposed to nourish the body): from medieval Latin, 'change, exchange'.

Cambodia /kamˈbəʊdɪə/ a country in SE Asia between Thailand and southern Vietnam; pop. 14,494,300 (est. 2009); official language, Khmer; capital, Phnom Penh. Also officially called the KHMER REPUBLIC and KAMPUCHEA.

> The country was made a French protectorate in 1863 and remained under French influence until it became fully independent in 1953. During the Vietnam War it was bombed and invaded by US forces, and then, following a civil war (1970–5), came under the control of the Khmer Rouge; more than 2 million Cambodians died before the regime was toppled by a Vietnamese invasion in 1979.

Cambodian ▶ noun **1** a native or inhabitant of Cambodia, or a person of Cambodian descent.
2 another term for KHMER (the language).
▶ adjective relating to Cambodia, its people, or their language.

cambozola /ˌkambəˈzəʊlə/ (also **cambazola**) ▶ noun [mass noun] trademark a type of German blue soft cheese with a rind like Camembert, produced using Gorgonzola blue mould.
– ORIGIN 1980s: an invented name, blend of CAMEMBERT and GORGONZOLA, with the insertion of *-bo-*.

Cambrelle /kamˈbrɛl/ ▶ noun [mass noun] trademark a synthetic fabric which absorbs perspiration, used as a lining material for climbing and walking boots.

Cambrian /ˈkambrɪən/ ▶ adjective **1** (chiefly in names or geographical terms) Welsh: *the Cambrian Railway.*
2 Geology relating to or denoting the first period in the Palaeozoic era, between the end of the Precambrian aeon and the beginning of the Ordovician period. ■ (as noun **the Cambrian**) the Cambrian period or the system of rocks deposited during it.

> The Cambrian lasted from about 570 to 510 million years ago and was a time of widespread seas. It is the earliest period in which fossils, notably trilobites, can be used in geological dating.

– ORIGIN mid 17th cent.: from Latin *Cambria* 'Wales', variant of *Cumbria*, from Welsh *Cymry* 'Welshman' or *Cymru* 'Wales'.

cambric /ˈkambrɪk, ˈkeɪm-/ ▶ noun [mass noun] a lightweight, closely woven white linen or cotton fabric.
– ORIGIN late Middle English: from *Kamerijk*, Flemish form of *Cambrai*, a town in northern France, where it was originally made. Compare with CHAMBRAY.

Cambridge 1 a city in eastern England, the county town of Cambridgeshire; pop. 116,900 (est. 2009). Cambridge University is located there.
2 a city in eastern Massachusetts, forming part of the conurbation of Boston; pop. 105,596 (est. 2008). Harvard University and the Massachusetts Institute of Technology are located there.

Cambridge blue ▶ noun Brit. **1** [mass noun] a pale blue colour.
2 a person who has represented Cambridge University at a particular sport in a match against Oxford University.

Cambridgeshire a county of eastern England; county town, Cambridge.

Cambridge University a university at Cambridge in England, founded in 1230. The university comprises a federation of thirty-one colleges.

Cambs. ▶ abbreviation Cambridgeshire.

Cambyses /kamˈbʌɪsiːz/ (d.522 BC), king of Persia 529–522 BC, son of Cyrus. He is chiefly remembered for his conquest of Egypt in 525 BC.

camcorder ▶ noun a portable combined video camera and video recorder.
– ORIGIN 1980s: blend of CAMERA[1] and RECORDER.

came[1] past tense of COME.

came[2] ▶ noun each of a number of strips forming a framework for enclosing a pane of glass, especially in a leaded window.
– ORIGIN late 16th cent.: of unknown origin.

camel ▶ noun **1** a large, long-necked ungulate mammal of arid country, with long slender legs, broad cushioned feet, and either one or two humps on the back. Camels can survive for long periods without food or drink, chiefly by using up the fat reserves in their humps. ● Genus *Camelus*, family Camelidae (the **camel family**): two species (see ARABIAN CAMEL, BACTRIAN CAMEL). The camel family also includes the llama and its relatives.
■ [mass noun] a fabric made from camel hair. ■ [mass noun] a yellowish-fawn colour like that of camel hair.
2 an apparatus for raising a sunken ship, consisting of one or more watertight chests to provide buoyancy.
– ORIGIN Old English, from Latin *camelus*, from Greek *kamēlos*, of Semitic origin.

camelback ▶ noun a back with a hump-shaped curve on a sofa or other piece of furniture: [as modifier] *a camelback sofa.*

camel cricket ▶ noun a humpbacked wingless insect related to the grasshoppers, typically living in caves or holes. Also called CAVE CRICKET. ● Family Raphidophoridae: several genera.

cameleer /ˌkaməˈlɪə/ ▶ noun a person who controls or rides a camel.

camel hair (also **camel's hair**) ▶ noun [mass noun] **1** a fabric made from the hair of a camel: [as modifier] *a camel-hair coat.*
2 [usu. as modifier] fine, soft hair from a squirrel's tail, used in artists' brushes.

camelid /kəˈmiːlɪd, ˈkaməlɪd/ ▶ noun Zoology a mammal of the camel family (Camelidae).
– ORIGIN late 20th cent.: from modern Latin *Camelidae* (plural), from Latin *camelus* 'camel', from Greek *kamēlos*.

camellia /kəˈmiːlɪə, -ˈmɛlɪə/ ▶ noun an evergreen East Asian shrub related to the tea plant, grown for its showy flowers and shiny leaves. ● Genus *Camellia*, family Theaceae: several species, in particular the **common camellia** (*C. japonica*).
– ORIGIN modern Latin, named by Linnaeus after Joseph *Kamel* (Latinized as *Camellus*), Moravian botanist (1661–1706), who described the flora of Luzon.

camelopard /ˈkamɪlə(ʊ)pɑːd, kəˈmɛləpɑːd/ ▶ **noun** archaic a giraffe.
– ORIGIN late Middle English: via Latin from Greek *kamēlopardalis*, from *kamēlos* 'camel' + *pardalis* (see PARD).

Camelopardalis /kə,mɛlə(ʊ)ˈpɑːd(ə)lɪs/ Astronomy a large but inconspicuous northern constellation (the Giraffe), between the Pole Star and Perseus.
– ORIGIN via Latin from Greek *kamēlopardalis* (see CAMELOPARD).

Camelot /ˈkamɪlɒt/ (in Arthurian legend) the place where King Arthur held his court. ■ (as noun **a Camelot**) a place associated with glittering romance and optimism.

camel spider ▶ **noun** another term for SUN SPIDER.

camel thorn ▶ **noun** either of two spiny leguminous shrubs occurring in arid country. ● *Alhagi camelorum* (of the Middle East) and *Acacia giraffae* (of southern Africa), family Leguminosae.

Camembert /ˈkaməmbɛː/ ▶ **noun** [mass noun] a kind of rich, soft, creamy cheese with a whitish rind, originally made near Camembert in Normandy.

cameo /ˈkamɪəʊ/ ▶ **noun** (pl. **cameos**) **1** a piece of jewellery, typically oval in shape, consisting of a portrait in profile carved in relief on a background of a different colour.
2 a short descriptive literary sketch which neatly encapsulates someone or something: *cameos of street life*. ■ a small character part in a play or film, played by a distinguished actor: [as modifier] *he played numerous cameo roles*.
– ORIGIN late Middle English: from Old French *camahieu*, *cama(h)u*; later influenced by Italian *cam(m)eo*, from medieval Latin *cammaeus*, related to the Old French word.

cameo glass ▶ **noun** [mass noun] decorative glass consisting of layers of different colours, the outermost being cut away to leave a design in relief.

camera[1] ▶ **noun** a device for recording visual images in the form of photographs, movie film, or video signals.
– PHRASES **on** (or **off**) **camera** while being filmed or televised (or not being filmed or televised).
– ORIGIN mid 19th cent.: from Latin (see CAMERA[2], CAMERA OBSCURA).

camera[2] ▶ **noun** [in names] a chamber or round building: *the Radcliffe Camera*.
– PHRASES **in camera** chiefly Law in private, in particular taking place in the private chambers of a judge, with the press and public excluded.
– ORIGIN late 17th cent. (denoting a council or legislative chamber in Italy or Spain): from Latin, 'vault, arched chamber', from Greek *kamara* 'object with an arched cover'.

camera lucida /,kam(ə)rə ˈluːsɪdə/ ▶ **noun** an instrument in which rays of light are reflected by a prism to produce an image on a sheet of paper, from which a drawing can be made.
– ORIGIN mid 18th cent.: from Latin, 'bright chamber', on the pattern of *camera obscura*.

cameraman (or **camerawoman**) ▶ **noun** (pl. **cameramen** or **camerawomen**) a person whose profession is operating a video, television, or film camera.

camera obscura /ɒbsˈkjʊərə/ ▶ **noun** a darkened box with a convex lens or aperture for projecting the image of an external object on to a screen inside, a forerunner of the modern camera. ■ a small round building with a rotating angled mirror at the apex of the roof, projecting an image of the landscape on to a horizontal surface inside.
– ORIGIN early 18th cent.: from Latin, 'dark chamber'.

camera phone ▶ **noun** a mobile phone incorporating a digital camera.

camera-ready ▶ **adjective** (of material to be printed) in the right form and of good enough quality to be reproduced photographically on to a printing plate.

camerawork ▶ **noun** [mass noun] the way in which cameras are used in a film or television programme.

Cameron[1], David (b.1966), British Conservative statesman, Prime Minister since 2010 (in coalition with the Liberal Democrats); full name *David William Donald Cameron*.

Cameron[2], James (b.1954), Canadian-born American film director. His films include *The Terminator* (1984) and *Titanic* (1997).

Cameron[3], Julia Margaret (1815–79), English photographer, credited with being the first to use soft-focus techniques. Her work often reflects the influence of contemporary painting, especially that of the Pre-Raphaelites.

Cameron Highlands a hill resort region in Pahang, Malaysia.
– ORIGIN named after the surveyor William *Cameron*, who mapped the area in 1885.

Cameroon /,kaməˈruːn/ a country on the west coast of Africa between Nigeria and Gabon; pop. 18,879,300 (est. 2009); languages, French (official), English (official), many local languages, pidgin; capital, Yaoundé. French name **Cameroun** /kamʀun/.

> The territory was a German protectorate from 1884 to 1916, after which it was administered by France and Britain, latterly under League of Nations (later United Nations) trusteeship. In 1960 the French part became an independent republic, to be joined in 1961 by part of the British Cameroon; the remainder became part of Nigeria. Cameroon became a member of the Commonwealth in 1995.

– DERIVATIVES **Cameroonian** adjective & noun.

cam follower ▶ **noun** the part of a machine in sliding or rolling contact with a rotating cam and given motion by it.

cami ▶ **noun** (pl. **camis**) informal a camisole.

camiknickers ▶ **plural noun** Brit. a woman's one-piece undergarment which combines camisole and French knickers.

Camisard /ˈkamɪsɑː, ,kamɪˈsɑː/, French /kamisaʀ/ ▶ **noun** a member of the French Protestant insurgents who rebelled against the persecution that followed the revocation of the Edict of Nantes.
– ORIGIN French, from Provençal *camisa*, from late Latin *camisia* 'shirt', because of the white shirts worn by the insurgents over their clothing for ease of recognition.

camisole /ˈkamɪsəʊl/ ▶ **noun** a woman's loose-fitting undergarment for the upper body, typically held up by shoulder straps.
– ORIGIN early 19th cent.: from French, either from Italian *camiciola*, diminutive of *camicia*, or from Spanish *camisola*, diminutive of *camisa*, both from late Latin *camisia* 'shirt or nightgown'.

camo /kaməʊ/ ▶ **noun** informal short for CAMOUFLAGE: [as modifier] *a camo jacket*.

Camões /kaˈmɔɪnʃ/ (also **Camoëns** /ˈkaməʊɛns/), Luis (Vaz) de (*c.*1524–80), Portuguese poet. His most famous work, *The Lusiads* (1572), describes Vasco da Gama's discovery of the sea route to India.

camogie /kəˈməʊgi/ ▶ **noun** [mass noun] an Irish game resembling hurling, played by women or girls.
– ORIGIN early 20th cent.: from Irish *caméog*.

camomile /ˈkaməmʌɪl/ (also chiefly N. Amer. **chamomile**) ▶ **noun** an aromatic European plant of the daisy family, with white and yellow daisy-like flowers. ● The perennial **sweet** (or **Roman**) **camomile** (*Chamaemelum nobile* (or *Anthemis nobilis*), family Compositae), traditionally used for lawns and herbal medicine, the annual **German camomile** (*Matricaria recutita*), used medicinally, and the yellow-flowered **dyer's camomile** (*Anthemis tinctoria*), used to produce a yellow-brown dye.
– ORIGIN Middle English: from Old French *camomille*, from late Latin *chamomilla*, from Greek *khamaimēlon* 'earth-apple' (because of the apple-like smell of its flowers).

camomile tea (also chiefly N. Amer. **chamomile tea**) ▶ **noun** [mass noun] an infusion of dried flowers of sweet camomile.

Camorra /kəˈmɒrə/ (**the Camorra**) a secret criminal society originating in Naples and Neapolitan emigrant communities in the 19th century. Some members later moved to the US and formed links with the Mafia.
– ORIGIN Italian, perhaps from Spanish *camorra* 'dispute, quarrel'.

camouflage /ˈkaməflɑːʒ/ ▶ **noun** [mass noun] the disguising of military personnel, equipment, and installations by painting or covering them to make them blend in with their surroundings: *on the trenches were pieces of turf which served for camouflage*. ■ clothing or materials used as camouflage: *figures dressed in army camouflage*. ■ the natural colouring or form of an animal which enables it to blend in with its surroundings: *the whiteness of polar bears provides camouflage*. ■ actions or devices intended to disguise or mislead: *much of my apparent indifference was merely protective camouflage*.
▶ **verb** [with obj.] hide or disguise the presence of (a person, animal, or object) by means of camouflage: *the caravan was camouflaged with netting and branches from trees*. ■ conceal the existence of (something undesirable): *grievances should be discussed, not camouflaged*.
– ORIGIN First World War: from French, from *camoufler* 'to disguise' (originally thieves' slang), from Italian *camuffare* 'disguise, deceive', perhaps by association with French *camouflet* 'whiff of smoke in the face'.

camp[1] ▶ **noun 1** a place with temporary accommodation of huts, tents, or other structures, typically used by soldiers, refugees, or travelling people. ■ a complex of buildings for holiday accommodation, with recreational facilities. ■ (also **summer camp**) N. Amer. a summer holiday programme for children, offering a range of activities. ■ [mass noun] temporary overnight lodging in tents: *we **pitched camp** at a fine spot*. ■ Archaeology, Brit. an enclosed or fortified prehistoric site, especially an Iron Age hill fort.
2 the supporters of a particular party or doctrine regarded collectively: *both the liberal and conservative camps were annoyed by his high-handed manner*.
3 S. African a fenced field or enclosed area for grazing. ■ Austral./NZ a place where livestock regularly congregate or where a mustered herd is assembled.
▶ **verb** [no obj.] **1** live for a time in a tent or caravan, especially while on holiday: *holiday parks in which you can camp or stay in a chalet* | (as noun **camping**) *camping attracts people of all ages*. ■ lodge temporarily, especially in an inappropriate or uncomfortable place: *we **camped out** for the night in a mission schoolroom*. ■ remain persistently in one place: *the press will be camping on your doorstep once they get on to this story*.
2 Austral./NZ (of livestock) assemble together for rest.
3 [with obj.] S. African divide (land) and enclose with fences.
– PHRASES **break camp** take down a tent or the tents of an encampment ready to leave.
– ORIGIN early 16th cent.: from French *camp*, *champ*, from Italian *campo*, from Latin *campus* 'level ground', specifically applied to the *Campus Martius* in Rome, used for games, athletic practice, and military drill.

camp[2] informal ▶ **adjective** (of a man or his manner) ostentatiously and extravagantly effeminate: *a heavily made-up and highly camp actor*. ■ deliberately exaggerated and theatrical in style: *the movie seems more camp than shocking or gruesome*.
▶ **noun** [mass noun] deliberately exaggerated and theatrical behaviour or style: *Hollywood camp*.
▶ **verb** [no obj.] (of a man) behave in an ostentatiously effeminate way: *he **camped it up** a bit for the cameras*.
– DERIVATIVES **campery** noun, **campness** noun.
– ORIGIN early 20th cent.: of unknown origin.

campaign ▶ **noun** a series of military operations intended to achieve a goal, confined to a particular area, or involving a specified type of fighting: *a desert campaign* | [mass noun] *the army set off **on campaign***. ■ an organized course of action to achieve a goal: *an election campaign* | *the **campaign for** a full inquiry into the regime*.
▶ **verb** [no obj.] work in an organized and active way towards a goal: *people who campaigned against child labour* | [with infinitive] *the services he had campaigned to protect*.
– PHRASES **on the campaign trail** engaged in a political campaign: *he has studiously avoided the subject on the campaign trail*.
– ORIGIN early 17th cent. (denoting a tract of open country): from French *campagne* 'open country', via Italian from late Latin *campania*, from *campus* 'level ground' (see CAMP[1]). The change in sense arose from an army's practice of 'taking the field' (i.e. moving from a fortress or town to open country) at the onset of summer.

campaigner ▶ **noun** a person who works in an organized and active way towards a goal: *human rights campaigners are furious at the government's decision*.

Campaign for Nuclear Disarmament (abbrev.: **CND**) a British organization which campaigns for the abolition of nuclear weapons worldwide and calls for unilateral disarmament.

Campania /kamˈpeɪnɪə, -ˈpanjə/ a region of southern Italy; capital, Naples.
– DERIVATIVES **Campanian** noun & adjective.

campanile /,kampəˈniːleɪ/ ▶ **noun** an Italian bell tower, especially a free-standing one.
– ORIGIN mid 17th cent.: from Italian, from *campana* 'bell'.

campanology /,kampəˈnɒlədʒi/ ▶ **noun** [mass noun] the art or practice of bell-ringing.

C

– DERIVATIVES **campanological** adjective, **campanologist** noun.
– ORIGIN mid 19th cent.: from modern Latin *campanologia*, from late Latin *campana* 'bell'.

campanula /kam'panjʊlə/ ▶ noun another term for BELLFLOWER.
– ORIGIN modern Latin, diminutive of late Latin *campana* 'bell'.

campanulate /kam'panjʊlət/ ▶ adjective Botany (of a flower) bell-shaped, like a campanula.

Campari /kam'pɑːri/ ▶ noun [mass noun] trademark a pinkish aperitif flavoured with bitters.
– ORIGIN named after the manufacturer.

camp bed ▶ noun Brit. a folding portable bed, typically made of canvas stretched over a metal frame.

Campbell[1] /'kamb(ə)l/, Sir Malcolm (1885–1948), English motor-racing driver. In 1935 he became the first man to exceed a land speed of 300 mph (483 kph). He also achieved a water-speed record of 141.74 mph (228 kph), in 1939. His son **Donald (Malcolm)** (1921–67) was also a motor-racing driver, and in 1964 achieved a speed of 276.33 mph (445 kph) on water and 403 mph (649 kph) on land. He was killed attempting to break his own water speed record.

Campbell[2] /'kamb(ə)l/, Mrs Patrick (1865–1940), English actress; born *Beatrice Stella Tanner*. George Bernard Shaw wrote the part of Eliza Doolittle in *Pygmalion* (1914) for her.

Campbell[3] /'kamb(ə)l/, Roy (1901–57), South African poet; full name *Ignatius Royston Dunnachie Campbell*. His long poem *Flowering Rifle* (1939) shows strong right-wing sympathies; he fought for Franco's side in the Spanish Civil War.

Campbell[4] /'kamb(ə)l/, Thomas (1777–1844), Scottish poet, chiefly remembered for his patriotic lyrics such as 'The Battle of Hohenlinden' and 'Ye Mariners of England'.

Campbell-Bannerman, Sir Henry (1836–1908), British Liberal statesman, Prime Minister 1905–8. His premiership saw the grant of self-government to the defeated Boer republics of Transvaal (1906) and the Orange River Colony (1907).

campcraft ▶ noun [mass noun] knowledge and skill required for an outdoor life lacking modern conveniences.

Camp David the country retreat of the President of the US, in the Appalachian Mountains in Maryland. President Carter hosted talks there between the leaders of Israel and Egypt which resulted in the Camp David agreements (1978) and the Egypt–Israel peace treaty of 1979.

campdrafting ▶ noun [mass noun] Australian an equestrian sport in which each rider in turn selects a bullock from a herd and drives it round a set course.

Campeche /kam'pɛtʃeɪ/ a state of SE Mexico, on the Yucatán Peninsula. ■ the capital of Campeche, a seaport on the Gulf of Mexico; pop. 238,850 (2005).

camper ▶ noun **1** a person who spends a holiday in a tent or holiday camp. ■ [with adj.] informal a person in a specified mood: *I understand that this is necessary, but I am not a happy camper.*
2 (also **camper van**) Brit. a large motor vehicle with living accommodation. ■ N. Amer. a caravan.

campesino /ˌkampə'siːnəʊ/ ▶ noun (pl. **campesinos** /-əʊz/) (in Spain and Spanish-speaking countries) a peasant farmer.
– ORIGIN Spanish.

campfire ▶ noun an open-air fire in a camp, used for cooking and as a focal point for social activity.

camp follower ▶ noun a civilian who works in or is attached to a military camp. ■ a person who is nominally attached to a group but does not make a substantial contribution to its activities: *cynical opportunists and camp followers.*

campground ▶ noun North American term for CAMPSITE.

camphor /'kamfə/ ▶ noun [mass noun] a white volatile crystalline substance with an aromatic smell and bitter taste, occurring in certain essential oils. ● A terpenoid ketone; chem. formula: $C_{10}H_{16}O$.
– DERIVATIVES **camphoric** /-'fɒrɪk/ adjective.
– ORIGIN Middle English: from Old French *camphore* or medieval Latin *camphora*, from Arabic *kāfūr*, via Malay from Sanskrit *karpūra*.

camphorate ▶ verb [with obj.] (usu. as adj. **camphorated**) impregnate or treat with camphor.

camphor tree ▶ noun an East Asian tree of the laurel family, the chief natural source of camphor. ● *Cinnamomum camphora*, family Lauraceae.

Campinas /kam'piːnəs/ a city in SE Brazil, northwest of São Paulo; pop. 1,039,297 (2007).

Campion /'kampɪən/, St Edmund (1540–81), English Jesuit priest and martyr. He was canonized in 1970. Feast day, 1 December.

campion /'kampɪən/ ▶ noun a plant of the pink family, typically having pink or white flowers with notched petals, found in both Eurasia and North America. ● Genera *Silene* and *Lychnis*, family Caryophyllaceae.
– ORIGIN mid 16th cent.: perhaps related to CHAMPION. The name was originally used for the rose campion, whose name in Latin (*Lychnis coronaria*) and Greek (*lukhnis stephanōmatikē*) means 'campion fit for a crown', and which was said in classical times to have been used for victors' garlands.

camp meeting ▶ noun N. Amer. a religious meeting held in the open air or in a tent.

campo /'kampəʊ/ ▶ noun (pl. **campos**) **1** (in South America, especially Brazil) a grass plain with occasional stunted trees.
2 a square in an Italian or Spanish town.
– ORIGIN from Spanish, Portuguese, and Italian *campo*, literally 'field'.

Campobasso /ˌkampəʊ'basəʊ/ a city in central Italy, capital of Molise region; pop. 51,218 (2008).

Campo Grande /ˌkampuː 'grandi/ a city in SW Brazil, capital of the state of Mato Grosso do Sul; pop. 724,524 (2007).

camporee /'kampəriː/ ▶ noun chiefly N. Amer. a local or regional camping event for Scouts.
– ORIGIN 1960s: blend of CAMP[1] and JAMBOREE.

campsite ▶ noun a place used for camping, especially one equipped for holidaymakers.

campus ▶ noun (pl. **campuses**) the grounds and buildings of a university or college: *for the first year I had a room on campus.* ■ N. Amer. the grounds of a school, hospital, or other institution.
– ORIGIN late 18th cent. (originally US): from Latin *campus* 'field' (see CAMP[1]).

campy ▶ adjective (**campier**, **campiest**) another word for CAMP[2].
– DERIVATIVES **campily** adverb, **campiness** noun.

campylobacter /'kampɪləʊˌbaktə, ˌkampɪləʊ'baktə/ ▶ noun a bacterium which may cause abortion in animals and food poisoning in humans. ● Genus *Campylobacter*: several species; curved or spiral Gram-negative bacteria.
– ORIGIN 1970s: modern Latin, from Greek *kampulos* 'bent' + BACTERIUM.

CAMRA /'kamrə/ ▶ abbreviation Brit. Campaign for Real Ale.

camshaft /'kamʃɑːft/ ▶ noun a shaft with one or more cams attached to it, especially one operating the valves in an internal-combustion engine.

Camulodunum /ˌkamjʊlə(ʊ)'d(j)uːnəm/ Roman name for COLCHESTER.

Camus /'kamuː/, French /kamy/, Albert (1913–60), French novelist, dramatist, and essayist, closely aligned with existentialism. Notable works: *The Outsider* (novel, 1942), *The Plague* (novel, 1947), and *The Rebel* (essay, 1951). Nobel Prize for Literature (1957).

camwood ▶ noun **1** [mass noun] the hard red timber of an African tree.
2 either of two trees of the pea family which yield camwood timber. ● *Baphia nitida* and (now usually) *Pterocarpus soyauxii* (the African padouk), family Leguminosae.
– ORIGIN late 17th cent.: probably from Temne *k'am* + WOOD.

can[1] ▶ modal verb (3rd sing. present **can**; past **could**) **1** be able to: *they can run fast | I could hear footsteps | he can't afford it.* ■ be able to through acquired knowledge or skill: *I can speak Italian.* ■ have the opportunity or possibility to: *there are many ways holidaymakers can take money abroad.* ■ [with negative or in questions] used to express doubt or surprise about the possibility of something's being the case: *he can't have finished | where can she have gone?* ■ used to indicate that something is typically the case: *antique clocks can seem out of place in modern homes | he could be very moody.*
2 be permitted to: *you can use the phone if you want to | nobody could legally drink on the premises.*
3 used to request someone to do something: *can you open the window? | can't you leave me alone?* ■ used to make a suggestion or offer: *we can have another drink if you like.*
– ORIGIN Old English *cunnan* 'know' (in Middle English 'know how to'), related to Dutch *kunnen* and German *können*; from an Indo-European root shared by Latin *gnoscere* 'know' and Greek *gignōskein* 'know'.

> **USAGE** Is there any difference between **may** and **can** when used to request or express permission, as in *may/can I ask you a few questions?* Many people feel that **can** should be reserved for expressions denoting capability, as in *can you swim?*, rather than for those relating to permission. **May** is, generally speaking, a politer and more formal way of asking for something, and is the better choice in more formal contexts.

can[2] ▶ noun **1** a cylindrical metal container: *a petrol can | a can of paint.* ■ a small steel or aluminium container in which food or drink is hermetically sealed for storage over long periods: *a beer can.* ■ the quantity of food or drink held by a can: *he drank two cans of lager.*
2 (**the can**) N. Amer. informal prison.
3 (**the can**) N. Amer. informal the toilet.
4 (**cans**) informal headphones.
▶ verb (**cans, canning, canned**) [with obj.] **1** preserve (food) in a can.
2 N. Amer. informal dismiss from a job. ■ reject as inadequate: *they canned the project.*
– PHRASES **can it** [in imperative] N. Amer. informal **1** stop talking; be quiet: *"Can it!" I growled.* **2** stop doing something: *I told him to can it, 'cause he was getting to be annoying.* **a can of worms** a complicated matter likely to prove awkward or embarrassing. **in the can** informal on tape or film and ready to be broadcast or released.
– DERIVATIVES **canner** noun.
– ORIGIN Old English *canne*, related to Dutch *kan* and German *Kanne*; either of Germanic origin or from late Latin *canna*.

Can. ▶ abbreviation Canada or Canadian.

Cana /'keɪnə/ an ancient small town in Galilee, where Christ is said to have performed his first miracle by changing water into wine during a marriage feast (John 2:1–11).

Canaan /'keɪnən/ the biblical name for the area of ancient Palestine west of the River Jordan, the Promised Land of the Israelites, who conquered and occupied it during the latter part of the 2nd millennium BC.
– DERIVATIVES **Canaanite** noun & adjective.
– ORIGIN early 17th cent.: via ecclesiastical Latin from ecclesiastical Greek *Khanaan*, from Hebrew *kĕnaʻan*.

Canada the second-largest country in the world, covering the entire northern half of North America with the exception of Alaska; pop. 33,487,200 (est. 2009); official languages, English and French; capital, Ottawa.

> Eastern Canada was colonized by the French in the 17th century, with the British emerging as the ruling colonial power in 1763 after the Seven Years War. Canada became a federation of provinces with dominion status in 1867, and the final step in attaining legal independence from the UK was taken with the signing of the Constitution Act of 1982; Canada remains a member of the Commonwealth. French-speakers are largely concentrated in Quebec, the focal point for the French-Canadian separatist movement.

– DERIVATIVES **Canadian** noun & adjective, **Canadianism** noun.

Canada balsam ▶ noun [mass noun] a yellowish resin obtained from the balsam fir and used for mounting preparations on microscope slides.

Canada goose ▶ noun a common North American goose with a black head and neck, a white chinstrap, and a loud trumpeting call. It has been introduced widely in Britain and elsewhere. ● *Branta canadensis*, family Anatidae.

Canada jay ▶ noun another term for GREY JAY.

Canada thistle ▶ noun N. Amer. the European creeping or field thistle, which has become naturalized as a serious weed in North America. ● *Cirsium arvense*, family Compositae.

Canadian football ▶ noun [mass noun] a form of football played in Canada, resembling American football, with twelve players a side.

Canadian French ▶ noun [mass noun] the form of the French language written and spoken by French Canadians.

Canadian Shield a large plateau which occupies over two fifths of the land area of Canada and is drained by rivers flowing into Hudson Bay. Also called **LAURENTIAN PLATEAU**.

Canadien /ˌkanaˈdjɑ̃/, French /kanadjɛ̃/ Canadian ▶ **noun** a French Canadian.
▶ **adjective** French Canadian.
– ORIGIN French.

canaille /kəˈnɑːi/, French /kanaj/ ▶ **noun** (**the canaille**) derogatory the common people; the masses: *the haughty contempt of a grandee sneering at the canaille.*
– ORIGIN French, from Italian *canaglia* 'pack of dogs', from *cane* 'dog'.

canal ▶ **noun 1** an artificial waterway constructed to allow the passage of boats or ships inland or to convey water for irrigation.
2 a tubular duct in a plant or animal, serving to convey or contain food, liquid, or air: *the ear canal.*
3 Astronomy any of a number of linear markings formerly reported as seen by telescope on the planet Mars.
– ORIGIN late Middle English: from Old French, alteration of *chanel* 'channel', from Latin *canalis* 'pipe, groove, channel', from *canna* 'cane'.

canal boat ▶ **noun** a long, narrow boat used on canals.

Canaletto /ˌkanəˈlɛtəʊ/ (1697–1768), Italian painter; born *Giovanni Antonio Canal*. He is famous for his paintings of Venetian festivals and scenery.

canalize /ˈkan(ə)lʌɪz/ (also **canalise**) ▶ **verb** [with obj.] **1** convert (a river) into a navigable canal.
2 convey (something) through a duct or channel.
– DERIVATIVES **canalization** noun.

Canal Zone see **PANAMA CANAL**.

canapé /ˈkanəpeɪ/ ▶ **noun 1** a small piece of bread or pastry with a savoury topping, served with drinks at receptions or formal parties.
2 a decorative French antique sofa.
– ORIGIN French, sense 1 being a figurative extension of the sense 'sofa' (as a 'couch' on which to place toppings). See also **CANOPY**.

canard /kəˈnɑːd, ˈkanɑːd/ ▶ **noun 1** an unfounded rumour or story: *the old canard that LA is a cultural wasteland.*
2 a small wing-like projection attached to an aircraft forward of the main wing to provide extra stability or control, sometimes replacing the tail.
– ORIGIN mid 19th cent.: from French, literally 'duck', also 'hoax', from Old French *caner* 'to quack'.

Canarese ▶ **noun & adjective** variant spelling of **KANARESE**.

Canaries Current a cold ocean current in the North Atlantic that flows south-westwards from Spain to meet equatorial waters near the Canary Islands.

canary ▶ **noun** (pl. **canaries**) **1** a mainly African finch with a melodious song, typically having yellowish-green plumage. One kind is popular as a cage bird and has been bred in a variety of colours, especially bright yellow. ● Genus *Serinus*, family Fringillidae: several species, especially the **island canary** (*S. canaria*), which is native to the Canary Islands, the Azores, and Madeira, and from which the domestic canary was developed.
2 (also **canary yellow**) [mass noun] a bright yellow colour resembling the plumage of a canary.
3 (also **canary wine**) [mass noun] historical a sweet wine from the Canary Islands, similar to Madeira.
– ORIGIN late 16th cent.: from French *canari*, from Spanish *canario* 'canary' or 'person from the Canary Islands' (see **CANARY ISLANDS**).

canary creeper ▶ **noun** a South American climbing plant related to the nasturtium. It has bright yellow flowers with deeply toothed petals, which give the appearance of a small bird in flight. ● *Tropaeolum peregrinum*, family Tropaeolaceae.

canary grass ▶ **noun** [mass noun] a tall grass of NW Africa and the Canary Islands, grown for its seeds which are fed to canaries and other caged finches. ● Genus *Phalaris*, family Gramineae: several species.

Canary Islands (also **the Canaries**) a group of islands in the Atlantic Ocean, off the NW coast of Africa, forming an autonomous region of Spain; capital, Las Palmas; pop. 2,098,593 (2009). The group includes the islands of Tenerife, Gomera, La Palma, Hierro, Gran Canaria, Fuerteventura, and Lanzarote.
– ORIGIN from French *Canarie*, via Spanish from Latin *Canaria* (*insula*) '(island) of dogs', from *canis* 'dog', one of the islands being noted in Roman times for large dogs.

canasta /kəˈnastə/ ▶ **noun** [mass noun] a card game resembling rummy, using two packs. It is usually played by two pairs of partners, and the aim is to collect sets (or melds) of cards. ■ [count noun] a meld of seven cards in canasta.
– ORIGIN 1940s: from Spanish (of Uruguayan origin), literally 'basket', based on Latin *canistrum* 'basket' (see **CANISTER**).

Canaveral, Cape /kəˈnavər(ə)l/ a cape on the east coast of Florida, known as Cape Kennedy from 1963 until 1973. It is the site of the John F. Kennedy Space Center, from which the Apollo space missions were launched.

Canberra /ˈkanbərə/ the capital of Australia and seat of the federal government, in Australian Capital Territory, an enclave of New South Wales; pop. 345,257 (2008).

cancan ▶ **noun** a lively, high-kicking stage dance originating in 19th-century Parisian music halls and performed by women in long skirts and petticoats.
– ORIGIN mid 19th cent.: from French, child's word for *canard* 'duck', from Old French *caner* 'to quack'.

cancel ▶ **verb** (**cancels**, **cancelling**, **cancelled**; US also **cancels**, **canceling**, **canceled**) [with obj.] **1** decide or announce that (a planned event) will not take place: *he was forced to cancel his visit.* ■ annul or revoke (a formal arrangement which is in effect): *his visa had been cancelled.* ■ abolish or make void (a financial obligation): *I intend to cancel your debt to me.* ■ mark, pierce, or tear (a ticket or stamp) to show that it has been used or invalidated: *cancelling stamps on registered mail.*
2 (usu. **cancel something out**) (of a factor or circumstance) neutralize or negate the force or effect of (another): *the electric fields may cancel each other out.* ■ Mathematics delete (an equal factor) from both sides of an equation or from the numerator and denominator of a fraction.
▶ **noun 1** a mark made on a postage stamp to show that it has been used.
2 Printing a new page or section inserted in a book to replace the original text, typically to correct an error.
– DERIVATIVES **canceller** noun.
– ORIGIN late Middle English (in the sense 'obliterate or delete writing by drawing or stamping lines across it'): from Old French *canceller*, from Latin *cancellare*, from *cancelli* 'crossbars'.

cancellation (US also **cancelation**) ▶ **noun** [mass noun] the action of cancelling something: *the project was threatened with cancellation by the government* | [count noun] *the show is sold out, but check for cancellations.* ■ [count noun] a crossing out of something written. ■ [count noun] a mark made on a postage stamp to show that it has been used.

cancellous /ˈkans(ə)ləs/ ▶ **adjective** Anatomy denoting bone tissue with a mesh-like structure containing many pores, typical of the interior of mature bones.
– ORIGIN mid 19th cent.: from Latin *cancelli* 'cross-bars' + **-OUS**.

Cancer 1 Astronomy a constellation (the Crab), said to represent a crab crushed under the foot of Hercules. It contains the globular star cluster of Praesepe or the Beehive.
2 Astrology the fourth sign of the zodiac, which the sun enters at the northern summer solstice (about 21 June). ■ (**a Cancer**) a person born when the sun is in the sign of Cancer.
– PHRASES **tropic of Cancer** see **TROPIC**[1].
– DERIVATIVES **Cancerian** /-ˈsɪərɪən, -ˈsɛːrɪən/ **noun & adjective** (sense 2).
– ORIGIN Latin.

cancer ▶ **noun** [mass noun] a disease caused by an uncontrolled division of abnormal cells in a part of the body: *he's got cancer* | *lung cancer.* ■ [count noun] a malignant growth or tumour resulting from an uncontrolled division of cells: *most skin cancers are curable.* ■ [count noun] an evil or destructive practice or phenomenon that is hard to contain or eradicate: *racism is a cancer sweeping across Europe.*
– DERIVATIVES **cancerous** adjective.
– ORIGIN Old English, from Latin, 'crab or creeping ulcer', translating Greek *karkinos*, said to have been applied to such tumours because the swollen veins around them resembled the limbs of a crab. **CANKER** was the usual form until the 17th cent. Compare with **CANCER**.

cancer stick ▶ **noun** informal, humorous a cigarette.

Cancún /kanˈkuːn/ a resort in SE Mexico, on the NE coast of the Yucatán Peninsula; pop. 526,701 (2005).

candela /kanˈdɛlə, -ˈdiːlə, ˈkandɪlə/ (abbrev.: **cd**) ▶ **noun** Physics the SI unit of luminous intensity. One candela is the luminous intensity, in a given direction, of a source that emits monochromatic radiation of frequency 540×10^{12} Hz and that has a radiant intensity in that direction of $^{1}/_{683}$ watt per steradian.
– ORIGIN 1950s: from Latin, 'candle'.

candelabra tree ▶ **noun** either of two trees with upward-curving boughs: ● a tropical African tree (genus *Euphorbia*, family Euphorbiaceae). ● a South American pine tree related to the monkey puzzle (*Araucaria angustifolia*, family Araucariaceae).

candelabrum /ˌkandɪˈlɑːbrəm, -ˈleɪ-/ (also **candelabra** /-brə/) ▶ **noun** (pl. **candelabra** or **candelabras**) a large branched candlestick or holder for several candles or lamps.
– ORIGIN early 19th cent.: from Latin, from *candela* (see **CANDLE**).

> **USAGE** Based on the Latin forms, the correct singular is **candelabrum** and the plural is **candelabra**. However, in practice **candelabra** is increasingly used as the singular form, with the plural as **candelabras**. In the Oxford English Corpus these forms are commoner than the traditional ones, and are coming to be regarded as part of standard English.

candid ▶ **adjective 1** truthful and straightforward; frank: *his responses were remarkably candid* | *a candid discussion.*
2 (of a photograph of a person) taken informally, especially without the subject's knowledge.
– DERIVATIVES **candidly** adverb, **candidness** noun.
– ORIGIN mid 17th cent. (in the Latin sense): from Latin *candidus* 'white'. Subsequent early senses were 'pure, innocent', 'unbiased', and 'free from malice', hence 'frank' (late 17th cent.). Compare with **CANDOUR**.

candida /ˈkandɪdə/ ▶ **noun** [mass noun] a yeast-like parasitic fungus that can sometimes cause thrush. ● Genus *Candida*, subdivision Deuteromycotina.
– ORIGIN modern Latin, feminine of Latin *candidus* 'white'.

candidate /ˈkandɪdeɪt, -dət/ ▶ **noun** a person who applies for a job or is nominated for election: *candidates applying for this position should be computer-literate* | *the Green Party candidate.* ■ Brit. a person taking an examination: *an A-level candidate.* ■ a person or thing regarded as suitable for or likely to receive a particular fate, treatment, or position: *she was the perfect* ***candidate for*** *a biography.*
– DERIVATIVES **candidacy** noun, **candidature** noun (Brit.).
– ORIGIN early 17th cent.: from Latin *candidatus* 'white-robed', also denoting a candidate for office (who traditionally wore a white toga), from *candidus* 'white'.

candidiasis /ˌkandɪˈdʌɪəsɪs/ ▶ **noun** [mass noun] infection with candida, especially as causing oral or vaginal thrush.

candiru /ˌkandɪˈruː/ ▶ **noun** a minute, slender catfish of the Amazon region, feeding by sucking blood from other fishes and sometimes entering the body orifices of mammals. It is notorious for its occasional habit of entering the urethra of human bathers. ● *Vandellia cirrhosa*, family Trichomycteridae.
– ORIGIN mid 19th cent.: via Portuguese from Tupi *candirú*.

candle ▶ **noun 1** a cylinder or block of wax or tallow with a central wick which is lit to produce light as it burns.
2 (also **international candle**) Physics a unit of luminous intensity, superseded by the candela.
▶ **verb** [with obj.] (of a poultry breeder) test (an egg) for freshness or fertility by holding it to the light.
– PHRASES **be able to hold a candle to** [with negative] informal be nearly as good as: *nobody in the final could hold a candle to her.* **the game's not worth the candle** the potential advantages to be gained from doing something do not justify the cost or trouble involved.
– DERIVATIVES **candler** noun.
– ORIGIN Old English *candel*, from Latin *candela*, from *candere* 'be white or glisten'.

candleberry ▶ **noun** (pl. **candleberries**) any of a number of trees or shrubs whose berries or seeds yield a wax or oil which can be used for making candles, in particular: ● a bayberry or related North American shrub. ● the candlenut.

candlefish ▶ **noun** (pl. **same** or **candlefishes**) a small edible marine fish with oily flesh, occurring on the west coast of North America. Also called **EULACHON**. ● *Thaleichthys pacificus*, family Osmeridae.
– ORIGIN so named because the Chinook Indians formerly burnt the oily bodies of these fish as candles.

C

candleholder ▶ noun a holder or support for a candle.

candlelight ▶ noun [mass noun] dim light provided by a candle or candles: *we dined by candlelight*.

candlelit ▶ adjective lit by a candle or candles: *a romantic candlelit dinner*.

Candlemas /ˈkand(ə)lmas, -məs/ ▶ noun a Christian festival held on 2 February to commemorate the purification of the Virgin Mary (after childbirth, according to Jewish law) and the presentation of Christ in the Temple. Candles were traditionally blessed at this festival.
– ORIGIN Old English *Candelmæsse* (see CANDLE, MASS).

candlenut ▶ noun an evergreen tree of the spurge family, with large seeds that yield an oil used for lighting and other purposes, native to SE Asia and the South Pacific islands. Also called CANDLEBERRY. ● *Aleurites moluccana*, family Euphorbiaceae.

candlepower ▶ noun [mass noun] illuminating power expressed in candelas or candles: [as modifier] *a 16-candlepower lamp*.

candlestick ▶ noun a support or holder for one or more candles, typically one that is tall and thin.

candlewick ▶ noun [mass noun] a thick, soft cotton fabric with a raised, tufted pattern: [as modifier] *a candlewick dressing gown*. ■ the yarn used to make candlewick.

can-do ▶ adjective informal having or showing a determination or willingness to take action and achieve results: *I like his can-do attitude*.

Candolle /kanˈdɒl/, French /kɑ̃dɔl/, Augustin Pyrame de (1778–1841), Swiss botanist. He introduced a new scheme of plant classification based on morphological characteristics, which prevailed for many years.

candomblé /ˌkandɒmˈbleɪ/ ▶ noun [mass noun] a Brazilian sect of the macumba cult.
– ORIGIN Brazilian Portuguese.

candour (US **candor**) ▶ noun [mass noun] the quality of being open and honest; frankness: *a man of refreshing candour*.
– ORIGIN late Middle English (in the Latin sense): from Latin *candor* 'whiteness'. The current sense dates from the mid 18th cent.; the development of the senses paralleled that of CANDID.

CANDU /ˈkanduː, kanˈduː/ (also **Candu**) ▶ noun a nuclear reactor of a Canadian design in which the fuel is unenriched uranium oxide clad in zircaloy and the coolant and moderator is heavy water.
– ORIGIN from *Can(ada)* + the initial letters of DEUTERIUM and URANIUM.

candy ▶ noun (pl. **candies**) (also **sugar candy**) [mass noun] N. Amer. sweets; confectionery: [as modifier] *a candy bar* | [count noun] *pink and yellow candies*. ■ chiefly Brit. sugar crystallized by repeated boiling and slow evaporation.
▶ verb (**candies**, **candying**, **candied**) [with obj.] (often as adj. **candied**) preserve (fruit) by coating and impregnating it with a sugar syrup: *candied fruit*.
– ORIGIN mid 17th cent. (as a verb): the noun use is from late Middle English *sugar-candy*, from French *sucre candi* 'crystallized sugar', from Arabic *sukkar* 'sugar' + *qandī* 'candied', based on Sanskrit *khaṇḍa* 'fragment'.

candy apple ▶ noun N. Amer. a toffee apple. ■ (also **candy-apple red**) [mass noun] a bright red colour.

candy-ass ▶ noun N. Amer. informal a timid, cowardly, or despicable person.
– DERIVATIVES **candy-assed** adjective.

candy cane ▶ noun N. Amer. a cylindrical stick of striped sweet rock with a curved end, resembling a walking stick.

candyfloss ▶ noun [mass noun] Brit. a mass of pink or white fluffy spun sugar wrapped round a stick. ■ something perceived as lacking in worth or substance: *their music is just aural candyfloss*.

candyman ▶ noun (pl. **candymen**) N. Amer. informal a person who sells illegal drugs.
– ORIGIN mid 19th cent.: from CANDY + MAN, an earlier sense denoting a ragman who gave toffee in exchange for goods.

candy-striped ▶ adjective (of material or a garment) patterned with alternating stripes of white and another colour, typically pink.
– DERIVATIVES **candy-stripe** adjective & noun.

candy-striper ▶ noun N. Amer. informal a female voluntary nurse in a hospital.
– ORIGIN so named because of the candy-striped uniforms of such nurses.

candytuft ▶ noun a European plant with small heads of white, pink, or purple flowers, grown as a garden or rockery plant. ● Genus *Iberis*, family Cruciferae.
– ORIGIN early 17th cent.: from *Candy* (obsolete form of *Candia*, former name of Crete) + TUFT.

cane ▶ noun **1** the hollow jointed stem of a tall grass, especially bamboo or sugar cane, or the stem of a slender palm such as rattan. ■ any plant that produces canes. ■ [mass noun] stems of bamboo, rattan, or wicker used as a material for making furniture or baskets: [as modifier] *a cane coffee table*. ■ short for SUGAR CANE. ■ a flexible woody stem of the raspberry plant or any of its relatives.
2 a length of cane or a slender stick, especially one used as a support for plants, a walking stick, or an instrument of punishment. ■ (**the cane**) a form of corporal punishment used in certain schools, involving beating with a cane: *wrong answers were rewarded by the cane*.
▶ verb [with obj.] **1** beat with a cane as a punishment. ■ Brit. informal defeat heavily or punish severely: *they have caned Essex and Durham in the Championship*.
2 Brit. informal take (drink or drugs) in large quantities: *the others were probably out caning it in some bar*.
– DERIVATIVES **caner** noun.
– ORIGIN late Middle English: from Old French, via Latin from Greek *kanna*, *kannē*, of Semitic origin.

canebrake ▶ noun N. Amer. a piece of ground covered with a dense growth of canes.

cane chair ▶ noun a chair with a seat made of woven cane strips.

caned ▶ adjective **1** (of furniture) made or repaired with cane: *armchairs with caned seats*.
2 Brit. informal intoxicated with drink or drugs.

cane rat ▶ noun a large rat-like African rodent found in wetlands south of the Sahara. It is often a pest of sugar plantations. ● Family Thryonomyidae and genus *Thryonomys*: two species.

cane sugar ▶ noun [mass noun] sugar obtained from sugar cane.

Canes Venatici /ˌkeɪniːz vɪˈnatɪsʌɪ/ Astronomy a small northern constellation (the Hunting Dogs), said to represent two dogs (Asterion and Chara) held on a leash by Boötes.
– ORIGIN Latin.

cane toad ▶ noun a large brown toad native to tropical America. It has been introduced elsewhere as a pest control agent but can become a serious pest itself, partly because animals eating it are killed by its toxins. Also called MARINE TOAD, GIANT TOAD. ● *Bufo marinus*, family Bufonidae.

cane trash ▶ noun see TRASH (sense 3 of the noun).

Canetti /kəˈnɛti/, Elias (1905–94), Bulgarian-born British writer. Notable works: *Auto-da-Fé* (1936) and *Crowds and Power* (1960). Nobel Prize for Literature (1981).

Canfield ▶ noun [mass noun] chiefly N. Amer. a form of the card game patience or solitaire.
– ORIGIN early 20th cent.: named after Richard A. *Canfield* (1855–1914), an American gambler.

canid /ˈkanɪd/ ▶ noun Zoology a mammal of the dog family (Canidae).
– ORIGIN late 19th cent.: from modern Latin *Canidae* (plural), from Latin *canis* 'dog'.

canine /ˈkeɪnʌɪn, ˈka-/ ▶ adjective relating to or resembling a dog or dogs: *canine behavioural problems*. ■ Zoology relating to animals of the dog family.
▶ noun **1** a dog. ■ Zoology an animal of the dog family.
2 (also **canine tooth**) a pointed tooth between the incisors and premolars of a mammal, often greatly enlarged in carnivores.
– ORIGIN late Middle English (in sense 2 of the noun): from French, from Latin *caninus*, from *canis* 'dog'.

caning ▶ noun a beating with a cane as a punishment. ■ Brit. informal a resounding defeat or severe reprimand: *the team suffered a caning at Blackburn*.

Canis Major /ˌkeɪnɪs ˈmeɪdʒə/ Astronomy a small constellation (the Great Dog), said to represent one of the dogs following Orion. It is just south of the celestial equator and contains the brightest star, Sirius.
– ORIGIN Latin.

Canis Minor /ˈmʌɪnə/ Astronomy a small constellation (the Little Dog), said to represent one of the dogs following Orion. It is close to the celestial equator and contains the bright star Procyon.
– ORIGIN Latin.

canister ▶ noun a round or cylindrical container used for storing such things as food, chemicals, or rolls of film. ■ [mass noun] historical small bullets packed in cases that fit the bore of a gun: *another deadly volley of canister*.
– ORIGIN late 15th cent. (denoting a basket): from Latin *canistrum*, from Greek *kanastron* 'wicker basket', from *kanna* 'cane, reed' (see CANE).

canker ▶ noun [mass noun] **1** a destructive fungal disease of apple and other trees that results in damage to the bark. ■ [count noun] an open lesion in plant tissue caused by infection or injury. ■ fungal rot in some fruits and vegetables, e.g. parsnips and tomatoes.
2 an ulcerous condition or disease of a human or animal, in particular: ■ (also **canker sore**) N. Amer. a small ulcer of the mouth or lips. ■ another term for THRUSH[2] (sense 2). ■ inflammation of the ear of a dog, cat, or rabbit, typically caused by a mite infestation.
3 a malign and corrupting influence that is difficult to eradicate: [in sing.] *racism remains a canker at the heart of the nation*.
▶ verb **1** [no obj.] (of woody plant tissue) become infected with canker.
2 (as adj. **cankered**) infected with a pervasive and corrupting bitterness: *he hated her with a cankered, shameful abhorrence*.
– DERIVATIVES **cankerous** adjective.
– ORIGIN Middle English (denoting a tumour): from Old French *chancre*, from Latin *cancer* 'crab' (see CANCER).

cankerworm ▶ noun the caterpillar of a North American moth that has wingless females. Cankerworms consume the buds and leaves of trees and can be a major pest. ● Several species in the family Geometridae.

cankle ▶ noun informal a woman's fat or swollen ankle whose flesh merges unattractively with that of the calf.
– ORIGIN early 21st cent.: blend of CALF[2] and ANKLE.

canna /ˈkanə/ (also **canna lily**) ▶ noun a lily-like tropical American plant with bright flowers and ornamental strap-like leaves. ● Genus *Canna*, family Cannaceae: several species.
– ORIGIN from modern Latin, from Latin *canna* 'cane, reed' (see CANE).

cannabinoid /ˈkanəbɪˌnɔɪd/ ▶ noun [mass noun] Chemistry any of a group of closely related compounds which include cannabinol and the active constituents of cannabis.

cannabinol /ˈkanəbɪˌnɒl, kəˈnab-/ ▶ noun [mass noun] Chemistry a crystalline compound whose derivatives, especially THC, are the active constituents of cannabis. ● A polycyclic phenol; chem. formula: $C_{21}H_{26}O_2$.
– ORIGIN late 19th cent.: from CANNABIS + -OL.

cannabis ▶ noun [mass noun] a tall plant with a stiff upright stem, divided serrated leaves, and glandular hairs. It is used to produce hemp fibre and as a psychotropic drug. Also called INDIAN HEMP, MARIJUANA. ● *Cannabis sativa*, family Cannabaceae (or Cannabidaceae): two subspecies (sometimes considered two species), *C. s. sativa*, which is chiefly used for hemp, and *C. s. indica*, from which the drug is usually obtained.
■ a dried preparation of the flowering tops or other parts of the cannabis plant, or a resinous extract of it (**cannabis resin**), used (generally illegally) as a psychotropic drug, chiefly in cigarettes.
– ORIGIN from Latin, from Greek *kannabis*.

canned ▶ adjective **1** (of food or drink) preserved or supplied in a sealed can: *canned beans*.
2 informal, often derogatory (of music, laughter, or applause) pre-recorded.
3 informal drunk.

cannel coal /ˈkan(ə)l/ ▶ noun [mass noun] a hard, compact kind of bituminous coal.
– ORIGIN mid 16th cent. (originally a northern English usage): of unknown origin.

cannellini bean /ˌkanəˈliːni/ ▶ noun a kidney-shaped bean of a medium-sized creamy-white variety.
– ORIGIN Italian *cannellini*, literally 'small tubes'.

cannelloni /ˌkanəˈləʊni/ ▶ plural noun rolls of pasta stuffed with a meat or vegetable mixture. ■ [mass noun] an Italian dish consisting of cannelloni cooked in a cheese sauce.
– ORIGIN Italian, literally 'large tubes', from *cannello* 'tube'.

cannelure /ˈkan(ə)ljʊə/ ▶ noun a groove round the cylindrical part of a bullet.
– ORIGIN mid 18th cent.: from French, from *canneler* 'provide with a channel', from *canne* 'reed, cane'.

cannery ▶ noun (pl. **canneries**) a factory where food is canned.

Cannes /kan/ a resort on the Mediterranean coast of France; pop. 71,526 (2006). An international film festival is held there annually.

cannibal ▸ **noun** a person who eats the flesh of other human beings: [as modifier] *cannibal tribes.* ■ an animal that feeds on flesh of its own species.
– DERIVATIVES **cannibalism** noun, **cannibalistic** adjective, **cannibalistically** adverb.
– ORIGIN mid 16th cent.: from Spanish *Canibales* (plural), variant (recorded by Columbus) of *Caribes*, the name of a West Indian people reputed to eat humans (see CARIB).

cannibalize (also **cannibalise**) ▸ **verb** [with obj.] **1** use (a machine) as a source of spare parts for another, similar machine. ■ (of a company) reduce the sales of (one of its products) by introducing another similar product.
2 (of an animal) eat (an animal of its own kind): *female spiders cannibalize courting males.*
– DERIVATIVES **cannibalization** noun.

Canning, George (1770–1827), British Tory statesman, Prime Minister 1827. After two periods as Foreign Secretary he succeeded Lord Liverpool as Prime Minister but died shortly afterwards.

cannoli /kaˈnəʊli/ ▸ **plural noun** N. Amer. a dessert consisting of small deep-fried pastry tubes with a creamy filling, typically of sweetened ricotta cheese.
– ORIGIN Italian, from *canna* 'reed'.

cannon ▸ **noun 1** (pl. usu. **same**) a large, heavy piece of artillery, typically mounted on wheels, formerly used in warfare. ■ a heavy automatic gun that fires shells from an aircraft or tank.
2 Billiards & Snooker, chiefly Brit. a stroke in which the cue ball strikes two balls successively. [early 19th cent.: alteration of CAROM.]
3 Engineering a heavy cylinder or hollow drum that is able to rotate independently on a shaft.
▸ **verb** [no obj., with adverbial of direction] chiefly Brit. **1** collide with something forcefully or at an angle: *the couple behind almost **cannoned into us** | his shot **cannoned off** the crossbar.*
2 Billiards & Snooker make a cannon shot.
– ORIGIN late Middle English: from French *canon*, from Italian *cannone* 'large tube', from *canna* 'cane, reed' (see CANE).

cannonade /ˌkanəˈneɪd/ ▸ **noun** a period of continuous heavy gunfire.
▸ **verb** [no obj.] (often as noun **cannonading**) discharge heavy guns continuously.
– ORIGIN mid 16th cent.: from French, from Italian *cannonata*, from *cannone* (see CANNON).

cannonball ▸ **noun 1** a round metal or stone projectile fired from a cannon.
2 (also **cannonball dive**) N. Amer. a jump into water feet first with the knees clasped to the chest.

cannon bone ▸ **noun** a long tube-shaped bone in the lower leg of a horse or other large quadruped, between the fetlock and the knee or hock.

cannoneer ▸ **noun** historical an artilleryman who positioned and fired a cannon.

cannon fodder ▸ **noun** [mass noun] soldiers regarded merely as material to be expended in war.

cannot ▸ **contraction** can not.

> **USAGE** Both the one-word form **cannot** and the two-word form **can not** are acceptable, but **cannot** is more common (in the Oxford English Corpus, three times as common). The two-word form is better only in a construction in which **not** is part of a set phrase, such as '**not only ... but (also)**': *Paul can not only sing well, he also paints brilliantly.*

cannula /ˈkanjʊlə/ ▸ **noun** (pl. **cannulae** /-liː/ or **cannulas**) Surgery a thin tube inserted into a vein or body cavity to administer medication, drain off fluid, or insert a surgical instrument.
– ORIGIN late 17th cent.: from Latin 'small reed', diminutive of *canna* (see CANE).

cannulate ▸ **verb** [with obj.] Surgery introduce a cannula or thin tube into (a vein or body cavity).
– DERIVATIVES **cannulation** noun.

canny ▸ **adjective** (**cannier**, **canniest**) **1** having or showing shrewdness and good judgement, especially in money or business matters: *canny investors will switch banks if they think they are getting a raw deal.*
2 N. English & Scottish pleasant; nice: *she's a canny lass.*
– DERIVATIVES **cannily** adverb, **canniness** noun.
– ORIGIN late 16th cent. (originally Scots): from CAN[1] (in the obsolete sense 'know') + -Y[1].

canoe ▸ **noun** a narrow keelless boat with pointed ends, propelled by using a paddle or paddles.
▸ **verb** (**canoes**, **canoeing**, **canoed**) [no obj., with adverbial of direction] travel in or paddle a canoe: *he had once canoed down the Nile.*
– DERIVATIVES **canoeing** noun, **canoeist** noun, **canoer** noun.
– ORIGIN mid 16th cent.: from Spanish *canoa*, from Arawak, from Carib *canaoua*.

canola /kəˈnəʊlə/ ▸ **noun** [mass noun] oilseed rape of a variety developed in Canada and grown in North America, which yields a valuable culinary oil.
– ORIGIN 1970s: from CANADA + *-ola* (based on Latin *oleum* 'oil').

canon[1] ▸ **noun 1** a general law, rule, principle, or criterion by which something is judged: *the appointment violated the canons of fair play and equal opportunity.* ■ a Church decree or law.
2 a collection or list of sacred books accepted as genuine: *the biblical canon.* ■ the works of a particular author or artist that are recognized as genuine: *the Shakespeare canon.* ■ the list of works considered to be permanently established as being of the highest quality: *Hopkins was firmly established in the canon of English poetry.*
3 (also **canon of the Mass**) (in the Roman Catholic Church) the part of the Mass containing the words of consecration.
4 Music a piece in which the same melody is begun in different parts successively, so that the imitations overlap.
– PHRASES **in canon** Music with different parts successively beginning the same melody.
– ORIGIN Old English: from Latin, from Greek *kanōn* 'rule', reinforced in Middle English by Old French *canon*.

canon[2] ▸ **noun** a member of the clergy who is on the staff of a cathedral, especially one who is a member of the chapter. ■ (also **canon regular** or **regular canon**) (in the Roman Catholic Church) a member of certain orders of clergy that live communally according to an ecclesiastical rule in the same way as monks.
– ORIGIN Middle English (in the sense 'canon regular'): from Old French *canonie*, from Latin *canonicus* 'according to rule' (see CANONIC). The other sense dates from the mid 16th cent.

canon cancrizans /ˈkaŋkrɪˌzanz/ ▸ **noun** Music a canon in which the theme or subject is repeated backwards in the second part. Also called CRAB CANON.
– ORIGIN late 19th cent.: from CANON[1] + medieval Latin *cancrizans* 'walking backwards' (from *cancer* 'crab').

canoness /ˈkanənɪs/ ▸ **noun** (in the Roman Catholic Church) a member of certain religious orders of women living communally according to an ecclesiastical rule in the same way as nuns.

canonic /kəˈnɒnɪk/ ▸ **adjective 1** Music in canon form.
2 another term for CANONICAL.
– ORIGIN Old English (as a noun): from Old French *canonique* or Latin *canonicus* 'canonical', from Greek *kanonikos*, from *kanon* 'rule' (see CANON[1]). The adjective dates from the late 15th cent.

canonical /kəˈnɒnɪk(ə)l/ ▸ **adjective 1** according to or ordered by canon law: *the canonical rites of the Roman Church.*
2 included in the list of sacred books officially accepted as genuine: *the canonical Gospels of the New Testament.* ■ accepted as being accurate and authoritative: *the canonical method of comparative linguistics.* ■ (of a writer or work) belonging to the literary canon: *canonical writers like Jane Austen.* ■ according to recognized rules or scientific laws: *canonical nucleotide sequences.*
3 relating to a cathedral chapter or a member of it.
▸ **plural noun** (**canonicals**) the prescribed official dress of the clergy: *Cardinal Bea in full canonicals.*
– DERIVATIVES **canonically** adverb.

canonical hours ▸ **plural noun 1** the times of daily Christian prayer appointed in the breviary, or the offices set for them (namely matins with lauds, prime, terce, sext, nones, vespers, and compline).
2 (in the Church of England) the time during which a marriage may lawfully be celebrated (usually between 8 a.m. and 6 p.m.).

canonicity ▸ **noun** [mass noun] the fact or status of being canonical: *established standards of canonicity.*

canonist ▸ **noun** an expert in canon law.
– DERIVATIVES **canonistic** adjective.

canonize (also **canonise**) ▸ **verb** [with obj.] **1** (in the Roman Catholic Church) officially declare (a dead person) to be a saint: *he was the last English saint to be canonized prior to the Reformation.*
2 sanction by Church authority.
– DERIVATIVES **canonization** noun.
– ORIGIN late Middle English: from late Latin *canonizare* 'admit as authoritative' (in medieval Latin 'admit to the list of recognized saints'), from Latin *canon* (see CANON[1]).

canon law ▸ **noun** [mass noun] ecclesiastical law, especially (in the Roman Catholic Church) that laid down by papal pronouncements.

canon regular ▸ **noun** see CANON[2].

canonry ▸ **noun** (pl. **canonries**) the office or benefice of a canon.

canoodle ▸ **verb** [no obj.] informal kiss and cuddle amorously: *she was caught **canoodling with** her boyfriend.*
– ORIGIN mid 19th cent. (originally US): of unknown origin.

can opener ▸ **noun** a tin opener.

Canopic jar /kəˈnəʊpɪk/ (also **Canopic vase**) ▸ **noun** a covered urn used in ancient Egyptian burials to hold the entrails and other visceral organs from an embalmed body.
– ORIGIN late 19th cent.: *Canopic* from Latin *Canopicus*, from *Canopus*, the name of a town in ancient Egypt.

Canopus /kəˈnəʊpəs/ Astronomy the second-brightest star in the sky, and the brightest in the constellation Carina. It is a supergiant, visible only to observers in the southern hemisphere.
– ORIGIN Latin, from Greek *Kanōpus*, the name of the pilot of the fleet of King Menelaus in the Trojan War.

canopy ▸ **noun** (pl. **canopies**) **1** an ornamental cloth covering hung or held up over something, especially a throne or bed: *a romantic four-poster bed complete with drapes and a canopy* | figurative *a full moon and a canopy of stars.* ■ Architecture a roof-like projection or shelter. ■ the transparent plastic or glass cover of an aircraft's cockpit. ■ the expanding, umbrella-like part of a parachute, made of silk or nylon.
2 [in sing.] the uppermost branches of the trees in a forest, forming a more or less continuous layer of foliage: *woolly monkeys spend hours every day sitting high in the canopy.*
▸ **verb** (**canopies**, **canopying**, **canopied**) [with obj.] (usu. as adj. **canopied**) cover or provide with a canopy.
– ORIGIN late Middle English: from medieval Latin *canopeum* 'ceremonial canopy', alteration of Latin *conopeum* 'mosquito net over a bed', from Greek *kōnōpeion* 'couch with mosquito curtains', from *kōnōps* 'mosquito'.

canorous /kəˈnɔːrəs/ ▸ **adjective** rare (of song or speech) melodious or resonant.
– ORIGIN mid 17th cent.: from Latin *canorus* (from *canere* 'sing') + -OUS.

Canova /kəˈnəʊvə/, Italian /kaˈnɔva/, Antonio (1757–1822), Italian sculptor, a leading exponent of neoclassicism. Notable works: *Cupid and Psyche* (1792) and *The Three Graces* (1813–16).

canst archaic second person singular present of CAN[1].

cant[1] /kant/ ▸ **noun** [mass noun] **1** hypocritical and sanctimonious talk, typically of a moral, religious, or political nature: *he had no time for the cant of the priests about sin.*
2 language specific to a particular group or profession and regarded with disparagement: *thieves' cant.* ■ [as modifier] denoting a phrase or catchword temporarily current or in fashion: *'herstories' rather than 'histories' as the cant phrase goes.*
▸ **verb** [no obj.] dated talk hypocritically and sanctimoniously about something: *if they'd stop canting about 'honest work' they might get somewhere.*
– ORIGIN early 16th cent.: probably from Latin *cantare* 'to sing' (see CHANT). The early meaning was 'musical sound, singing'; in the mid 17th cent. this gave rise to the senses 'whining manner of speaking' and 'form of words repeated mechanically in such a manner' (for example a beggar's plea), hence 'jargon' (of beggars and other such groups).

cant[2] /kant/ ▸ **verb** have or cause to have a slanting or oblique position; tilt: [with obj.] *he canted his head to look at the screen* | [no obj.] *mismatched slate roofs canted at all angles.* ■ [no obj.] (of a ship) swing round: *the ship canted to starboard.*
▸ **noun 1** [in sing.] a slope or tilt: *the outward cant of the curving walls.*
2 a wedge-shaped block of wood, especially one remaining after the better-quality pieces have been cut off.
– ORIGIN Middle English (denoting an edge or brink): from Middle Low German *kant*, *kante*, Middle Dutch *cant* 'point, side, edge', based on a Romance word related to medieval Latin *cantus* 'corner, side'.

C

Cant. ▶ abbreviation Canticles (the Song of Songs) (in biblical references).

can't ▶ contraction cannot.

Cantab /ˈkantab/ ▶ abbreviation of Cambridge University: *John Smith, MA (Cantab)*.
– ORIGIN from Latin *Cantabrigiensis*, from *Cantabrigia* 'Cambridge'.

cantabile /kanˈtɑːbɪleɪ/ ▶ adverb & adjective Music in a smooth singing style.
– ORIGIN Italian, literally 'singable'.

Cantabria /kanˈtabrɪə/ an autonomous region of northern Spain; capital, Santander.
– DERIVATIVES **Cantabrian** adjective & noun.

Cantabrigian /ˌkantəˈbrɪdʒɪən/ ▶ adjective relating to Cambridge (in England) or Cambridge University.
▶ noun a member of Cambridge University.
– ORIGIN mid 16th cent.: from Latin *Cantabrigia* (see CAMBRIDGE (sense 1) + -IAN).

cantal /ˈkantɑːl/ ▶ noun [mass noun] a hard, strong cheese made chiefly in the Auvergne.
– ORIGIN named after *Cantal*, a department of Auvergne, France.

cantaloupe /ˈkantəluːp/ (also **cantaloupe melon**) ▶ noun a small round melon of a variety with orange flesh and ribbed skin.
– ORIGIN late 18th cent.: from French *cantaloup*, from *Cantaluppi* near Rome, where it was first grown in Europe after being introduced from Armenia.

cantankerous ▶ adjective bad-tempered, argumentative, and uncooperative: *he can be a cantankerous old fossil at times*.
– DERIVATIVES **cantankerously** adverb, **cantankerousness** noun.
– ORIGIN mid 18th cent.: of unknown origin; perhaps a blend of Anglo-Irish *cant* 'auction' and *rancorous* (see RANCOUR).

cantata /kanˈtɑːtə/ ▶ noun a medium-length narrative piece of music for voices with instrumental accompaniment, typically with solos, chorus, and orchestra.
– ORIGIN early 18th cent.: from Italian *cantata (aria)* 'sung (air)', from *cantare* 'sing'.

cant dog ▶ noun another term for CANT HOOK.

canteen ▶ noun **1** chiefly Brit. a restaurant provided by an organization such as a college, factory, or company for its students or staff.
2 Brit. a specially designed case or box containing a set of cutlery.
3 a small water bottle, as used by soldiers or campers.
– ORIGIN mid 18th cent. (originally denoting a shop selling provisions or alcohol in a barracks or garrison town): from French *cantine*, from Italian *cantina* 'cellar'. A French use of *cantine* denoting a small compartmented case for carrying bottles of wine may have given rise to sense 2.

canteen culture ▶ noun [mass noun] informal (in the UK) a set of conservative and discriminatory attitudes said to exist within the police force.

canter ▶ noun [in sing.] a pace of a horse or other quadruped between a trot and a gallop, with not less than one foot on the ground at any time: *I rode away at a canter*. ■ a ride on a horse at a canter: *we came back from one of our canters*.
▶ verb [no obj., with adverbial of direction] (of a horse) move at a canter in a particular direction: *they cantered down into the village*.
– PHRASES **in** (or **at**) **a canter** Brit. without much effort; easily: *they retained their leadership of the Second Division at a canter*.
– ORIGIN early 18th cent. (as a verb): short for *Canterbury pace* or *Canterbury gallop*, from the supposed easy pace of medieval pilgrims to CANTERBURY.

Canterbury 1 a city in Kent, SE England, the seat of the Archbishop of Canterbury; pop. 41,900 (est. 2009). St Augustine established a church and monastery there in 597 and it became a place of medieval pilgrimage.
2 a region on the central east coast of the South Island, New Zealand.

canterbury ▶ noun (pl. **canterburies**) a low open-topped cabinet with partitions for holding music or books.
– ORIGIN early 19th cent.: named after CANTERBURY in Kent (from a belief that the Archbishop of Canterbury ordered such a piece to be made).

Canterbury, Archbishop of ▶ noun the archbishop of the southern province of the Church of England, who is Primate of All England and first peer of the realm, and plays a leading role in the worldwide Anglican Church.

Canterbury bell ▶ noun a tall, sturdy cultivated bellflower with large pale blue flowers. ● *Campanula medium*, family Campanulaceae.
– ORIGIN late 16th cent.: named after the bells on Canterbury pilgrims' horses (see CANTER).

cantharides /kanˈθarɪdiːz/ ▶ plural noun see SPANISH FLY.
– ORIGIN late Middle English: from Latin, plural of *cantharis*, from Greek *kantharis* 'Spanish fly'.

cantharus /ˈkanθ(ə)rəs/ ▶ noun (pl. **canthari**) (in ancient Greece and Rome) a large two-handled drinking cup.
– ORIGIN Latin, from Greek *kantharos*.

cant hook ▶ noun a hinged metal hook at the end of a long handle, used for gripping and rolling logs.

canthus /ˈkanθəs/ ▶ noun (pl. **canthi** /-θʌɪ/) the outer or inner corner of the eye, where the upper and lower lids meet.
– ORIGIN mid 17th cent.: from Latin, from Greek *kanthos*.

canticle /ˈkantɪk(ə)l/ ▶ noun **1** a hymn or chant, typically with a biblical text, forming a regular part of a church service.
2 (**Canticles** or **Canticle of Canticles**) another name for SONG OF SONGS (especially in the Vulgate Bible).
– ORIGIN Middle English: from Latin *canticulum* 'little song', diminutive of *canticum*, from *canere* 'sing'.

cantilena /ˌkantɪˈleɪnə, -ˈliːnə/ ▶ noun Music the part carrying the melody in a composition.
– ORIGIN mid 18th cent.: from Italian, from Latin, 'song'.

cantilever /ˈkantɪliːvə/ ▶ noun a long projecting beam or girder fixed at only one end, used in bridge construction. ■ a long bracket or beam projecting from a wall to support a balcony, cornice, etc.
▶ verb [with obj.] (usu. as adj. **cantilevered**) support by a cantilever or cantilevers: *a cantilevered deck*.
– ORIGIN mid 17th cent.: of unknown origin.

cantilever bridge ▶ noun a bridge in which each span is constructed from cantilevers built out sideways from piers.

cantina /kanˈtiːnə/ ▶ noun (especially in a Spanish-speaking country or the south-western US) a bar. ■ (in Italy) a wine shop.
– ORIGIN late 19th cent.: from Spanish and Italian.

canting arms ▶ plural noun Heraldry arms containing an allusion to the name of the bearer.
– ORIGIN early 17th cent.: *canting* from CANT¹, in the obsolete sense 'speak, say (in a particular way)'.

cantle /ˈkant(ə)l/ ▶ noun the raised curved part at the back of a horse's saddle.
– ORIGIN Middle English (in the sense 'a corner'): from Anglo-Norman French *cantel*, variant of Old French *chantel*, from medieval Latin *cantellus*, from *cantus* 'corner, side'.

canto /ˈkantəʊ/ ▶ noun (pl. **cantos**) one of the sections into which certain long poems are divided.
– ORIGIN late 16th cent.: from Italian, literally 'song', from Latin *cantus*.

Canton /kanˈtɒn/ another name for GUANGZHOU.

canton ▶ noun **1** /ˈkantɒn, kanˈtɒn/ a subdivision of a country established for political or administrative purposes. ■ a state of the Swiss Confederation.
2 /ˈkant(ə)n/ Heraldry a square charge smaller than a quarter and positioned in the upper (usually dexter) corner of a shield.
– DERIVATIVES **cantonal** /ˈkantən(ə)l, kanˈtəʊn(ə)l/ adjective.
– ORIGIN early 16th cent.: from Old French, literally 'corner', from Provençal, based on a Romance word related to medieval Latin *cantus* (see CANT²).

Cantonese ▶ adjective relating to Canton (Guangzhou), its inhabitants, or their dialect.
▶ noun (pl. **same**) **1** a native or inhabitant of Canton.
2 [mass noun] a form of Chinese spoken by over 54 million people, mainly in SE China (including Hong Kong). Also called YUE.

cantonment /kanˈtɒnm(ə)nt, -ˈtuːn-/ ▶ noun a military garrison or camp. ■ historical a permanent military station in British India.
– ORIGIN mid 18th cent.: from French *cantonnement*, from *cantonner* 'to quarter' (see CANTON).

Cantopop ▶ noun [mass noun] SE Asian a type of popular music combining Cantonese lyrics and Western disco music.
– ORIGIN 1990s: blend of CANTONESE and POP².

cantor /ˈkantɔː, -ə/ ▶ noun **1** an official who sings liturgical music and leads prayer in a synagogue.
2 (in formal Christian worship) a person who sings solo verses or passages to which the choir or congregation respond.
– ORIGIN mid 16th cent.: from Latin, 'singer', from *canere* 'sing'.

cantorial ▶ adjective relating to a cantor. ■ relating to or denoting the north side of the choir of a church, the side on which the cantor sits. The opposite of DECANAL.

cantoris /kanˈtɔːrɪs/ ▶ noun the section of a church or cathedral choir conventionally placed on the north side and taking the second or lower part in antiphonal singing. The opposite of DECANI.
– ORIGIN mid 17th cent.: from Latin, literally 'of the cantor' (see CANTOR).

cantrail /ˈkantreɪl/ ▶ noun Brit. a piece of metal or timber supporting the roof of a railway carriage.
– ORIGIN late 19th cent.: from CANT² + RAIL¹.

cantrip /ˈkantrɪp/ ▶ noun Scottish archaic a mischievous or playful act; a trick.
– ORIGIN late 16th cent. (also in the sense 'witch's trick'): of unknown origin.

cantus /ˈkantəs/ ▶ noun the highest voice in polyphonic choral music.
– ORIGIN late 16th cent.: from Latin.

cantus firmus /ˌkantəs ˈfəːməs/ ▶ noun (pl. **cantus firmi** /ˌkantuːs ˈfəːmʌɪ/) Music a melody used as the basis for a polyphonic composition.
– ORIGIN mid 19th cent.: from Latin, literally 'firm song'.

Canuck /kəˈnʌk/ ▶ noun informal a Canadian.
– ORIGIN apparently from CANADA.

Canute /kəˈnjuːt/ (also **Cnut** or **Knut**) (d.1035), Danish king of England 1017–35, Denmark 1018–35, and Norway 1028–35, son of Sweyn I. He is remembered for demonstrating to fawning courtiers his inability to stop the rising tide; this has become distorted in folklore to suggest that Canute really expected to turn back the tide.

canvas ▶ noun [mass noun] (pl. **canvases** or **canvasses**) a strong, coarse unbleached cloth made from hemp, flax, or a similar yarn, used to make items such as sails and tents and as a surface for oil painting.
■ [count noun] a piece of canvas prepared for use as the surface for an oil painting. ■ [count noun] an oil painting: *Turner's late canvases*. ■ (**the canvas**) the canvas-covered floor of a boxing or wrestling ring.
■ [count noun] either of a racing boat's tapering ends, originally covered with canvas.
▶ verb (**canvases, canvassing, canvassed**; US **canvases, canvasing, canvased**) [with obj.] cover with canvas: *the door had been canvassed over*.
– PHRASES **by a canvas** (in boat racing) by a very small margin. **under canvas 1** in a tent or tents: *the family will be living under canvas*. **2** with sails spread.
– ORIGIN late Middle English: from Old Northern French *canevas*, based on Latin *cannabis* 'hemp', from Greek.

canvasback ▶ noun a North American diving duck with a long, sloping black bill, related to the common pochard. ● *Aythya valisineria*, family Anatidae.
– ORIGIN late 16th cent.: so named because of the white back of the male.

canvass ▶ verb [with obj.] **1** solicit votes from (electors or members): *in each ward, two workers canvassed some 2,000 voters* | [no obj.] *he's **canvassing for** the Green Party*. ■ try to obtain (support): *they're canvassing support among shareholders*. ■ question (someone) in order to ascertain their opinion: *they promised to canvass all member clubs for their views*.
2 propose (an idea or plan) for discussion: *early retirement was canvassed as a solution to the problem of unemployment*. ■ discuss thoroughly: *the issues that were canvassed are still unresolved*.
▶ noun an act of canvassing: *a house-to-house canvass*.
– DERIVATIVES **canvasser** noun.
– ORIGIN early 16th cent. (in the sense 'toss in a canvas sheet' (as a sport or punishment)): from CANVAS. Later extended senses include 'criticize, discuss' (mid 16th cent.) and 'propose for discussion'; hence 'seek support for'.

canyon ▶ noun a deep gorge, typically one with a river flowing through it, as found in North America.
– ORIGIN mid 19th cent.: from Spanish *cañón* 'tube', based on Latin *canna* 'reed, cane'.

canyoning (also **canyoneering**) ▶ noun [mass noun] the sport of jumping into a fast-flowing mountain stream and allowing oneself to be carried downstream at high speed.

canzona /kanˈtsəʊnə, -z-/ ▶ noun an instrumental arrangement of a French or Flemish song, typical of 16th-century Italy.
– ORIGIN late 19th cent.: from Italian, from CANZONE.

canzone /kanˈtsəʊneɪ, -z-/ ▶ noun (pl. **canzoni** /-ni/) an Italian or Provençal song or ballad. ■ a type of lyric resembling a madrigal.
– ORIGIN late 16th cent.: from Italian, 'song', from Latin *cantio(n-)* 'singing', from *canere* 'sing'.

canzonetta /ˌkanzəˈnɛtə, ˌkantsəˈnɛtə/ ▶ noun (pl. **canzonettas** or **canzonette** /-ˈnɛteɪ/) a short, light vocal piece, especially in the Italian style of the 17th century.
– ORIGIN late 16th cent.: from Italian 'little song', diminutive of *canzone* (see CANZONE).

caoutchouc /ˈkaʊtʃʊk/ ▶ noun [mass noun] natural rubber that has not been vulcanized.
– ORIGIN late 18th cent.: from French, from obsolete Spanish *cauchuc*, from Quechua *kauchuk*.

CAP ▶ abbreviation Common Agricultural Policy.

cap[1] ▶ noun **1** a kind of soft, flat hat without a brim and typically with a peak. ■ [with adj. or noun modifier] a kind of soft, close-fitting head covering worn for a particular purpose: *a shower cap | a bathing cap*. ■ Brit. a cap awarded as a sign of membership of a particular sports team, especially a national team: *he has won three caps for Scotland*. ■ Brit. a player to whom a cap is awarded: *a former naval officer and rugby cap*. ■ an academic mortar board: *school-leavers in cap and gown*.
2 a protective lid or cover for an object such as a bottle, the point of a pen, or a camera lens. ■ an artificial protective covering for a tooth. ■ the top of a bird's head when distinctively coloured.
3 an upper limit imposed on spending or borrowing: *he raised the cap on local authority spending*.
4 (also **Dutch cap**) Brit. informal a contraceptive diaphragm.
5 the broad upper part of the fruiting body of most mushrooms and toadstools, at the top of a stem and bearing gills or pores.
6 short for PERCUSSION CAP.
▶ verb (**caps, capping, capped**) [with obj.] **1** put a lid or cover on: *he capped his pen*. ■ form a covering layer or topmost part of: (as adj., in combination **-capped**) *snow-capped mountains*. ■ put an artificial protective covering on (a tooth).
2 provide a fitting climax or conclusion to: *he capped a memorable season by becoming champion of champions*. ■ follow or reply to (a story, remark, or joke) by producing a better one.
3 Brit. place a limit or restriction on (prices, expenditure, or borrowing): *council budgets will be capped*.
4 (**be capped**) Brit. be chosen as a member of a particular sports team, especially a national one: *he was capped ten times by England*.
5 Scottish & NZ confer a university degree on.
– PHRASES **cap and bells** historical the insignia of the professional jester. **cap in hand** (N. Amer. **hat in hand**) Brit. humbly asking for a favour: *we have to go cap in hand begging for funds*. **cap of liberty** a conical cap given to Roman slaves when they were freed, used as a republican symbol in more recent times. **cap of maintenance** Brit. a cap or hat worn as a symbol of official dignity or carried in front of a sovereign on ceremonial occasions. **if the cap fits, wear it** (N. Amer. **if the shoe fits, wear it**) Brit. used as a way of suggesting that someone should accept a generalized remark or criticism as applying to themselves. **set one's cap at** (or US **for**) dated (of a woman) try to attract (a particular man) as a suitor. **to cap it all** as the final unfortunate incident in a long series: *she was on edge, her nerves taut, and to cap it all, she could feel the beginnings of a headache*.
– DERIVATIVES **capful** noun (pl. **capfuls**).
– ORIGIN Old English *cæppe* 'hood', from late Latin *cappa*, perhaps from Latin *caput* 'head'.

cap[2] ▶ noun Finance short for CAPITALIZATION: [as modifier] *mid-cap companies | small-cap stocks*.

cap. ▶ abbreviation ■ capacity. ■ capital (city). ■ capital letter.

capability ▶ noun (pl. **capabilities**) (often **capability of doing/to do something**) the power or ability to do something: *he had an intuitive capability of bringing the best out in people | the company's capability to increase productivity*. ■ (often **capabilities**) the extent of someone's or something's ability: *the job is beyond my capabilities*. ■ a facility on a computer for performing a specified task: *a graphics capability*. ■ forces or resources giving a country the ability to undertake a particular kind of military action: *their nuclear weapons capability*.

Capability Brown see BROWN[6].

capable ▶ adjective **1** (**capable of doing something**) having the ability, fitness, or quality necessary to do or achieve a specified thing: *I'm quite capable of taking care of myself | the aircraft is capable of flying 5,000 miles non-stop*. ■ open to or admitting of something: *the strange events are capable of rational explanation*.
2 able to achieve efficiently whatever one has to do; competent: *she looked enthusiastic and capable | a highly capable man*.
– DERIVATIVES **capably** adverb.
– ORIGIN mid 16th cent. (in the sense 'able to take in', physically or mentally): from French, from late Latin *capabilis*, from Latin *capere* 'take or hold'.

capacious ▶ adjective having a lot of space inside; roomy: *she rummaged in her capacious handbag*.
– DERIVATIVES **capaciously** adverb, **capaciousness** noun.
– ORIGIN early 17th cent.: from Latin *capax, capac-* 'capable' + -IOUS.

capacitance /kəˈpasɪt(ə)ns/ ▶ noun [mass noun] Physics the ability of a system to store an electric charge. ■ the ratio of the change in an electric charge in a system to the corresponding change in its electric potential. (Symbol: **C**)
– ORIGIN late 19th cent.: from CAPACITY + -ANCE.

capacitate ▶ verb [with obj.] formal or archaic make (someone) capable of a particular action or legally competent to act in a particular way. ■ (**be capacitated**) Physiology (of spermatozoa) undergo changes inside the female reproductive tract enabling them to penetrate and fertilize an ovum.
– DERIVATIVES **capacitation** noun.

capacitor /kəˈpasɪtə/ ▶ noun a device used to store an electric charge, consisting of one or more pairs of conductors separated by an insulator.

capacity ▶ noun (pl. **capacities**) **1** [in sing.] the maximum amount that something can contain: *the capacity of the freezer is 1.1 cubic feet | the stadium's seating capacity* | [mass noun] *the room was* ***filled to capacity***. ■ [as modifier] fully occupying the available area or space: *they played to a capacity crowd*. ■ the total cylinder volume that is swept by the pistons in an internal-combustion engine. ■ former term for CAPACITANCE.
2 the amount that something can produce: *the company aimed to double its electricity-generating capacity | when running* ***at full capacity***, *the factory will employ 450 people*.
3 the ability or power to do or understand something: *I was impressed by her* ***capacity for*** *hard work | their intellectual capacities*. ■ [in sing.] a person's legal competence: *cases where a patient's testamentary capacity is in doubt*.
4 [in sing.] a specified role or position: *I was engaged in a voluntary capacity | writing* ***in his capacity as*** *legal correspondent*.
– DERIVATIVES **capacitive** (also **capacitative**) adjective (chiefly Physics).
– ORIGIN late Middle English: from French *capacité*, from Latin *capacitas*, from *capax, capac-* 'that can contain', from *capere* 'take or hold'.

caparison /kəˈparɪs(ə)n/ ▶ noun an ornamental covering spread over a horse's saddle or harness.
▶ verb (**be caparisoned**) (of a horse) be decked out in rich decorative coverings.
– ORIGIN early 16th cent.: from obsolete French *caparasson*, from Spanish *caparazón* 'saddlecloth', from *capa* 'hood'.

cape[1] ▶ noun **1** a sleeveless cloak, typically a short one. ■ a part of a longer coat or cloak that falls loosely over the shoulders from the neckband.
2 N. Amer. the pelt from the head and neck of an animal, for preparation as a hunting trophy.
▶ verb [with obj.] (in bullfighting) taunt (the bull) by flourishing a cape.
– DERIVATIVES **caped** adjective.
– ORIGIN mid 16th cent.: from French, from Provençal *capa*, from late Latin *cappa* 'covering for the head'.

cape[2] ▶ noun a headland or promontory. ■ (**the Cape**) the Cape of Good Hope. ■ (**the Cape**) the former Cape Province of South Africa.
– ORIGIN late Middle English: from Old French *cap*, from Provençal, based on Latin *caput* 'head'.

Cape Agulhas, Cape Bon, etc. see AGULHAS, CAPE; BON, CAPE, etc.

Cape Barren goose ▶ noun a pale grey Australian goose with a short black bill that is almost covered by a waxy yellow cere. Also called CEREOPSIS GOOSE. ● *Cereopsis novaehollandiae*, family Anatidae.
– ORIGIN mid 19th cent.: named after *Cape Barren*, an island in the Bass Strait, Australia.

Cape Breton Island /ˈbrɛt(ə)n/ an island forming the north-eastern part of the province of Nova Scotia, Canada.

Cape Cod a sandy peninsula in SE Massachusetts, forming a wide curve enclosing Cape Cod Bay.

Cape Colony early name (1814–1910) for the former CAPE PROVINCE.

Cape coloured ▶ noun (pl. **same** or **Cape coloureds**) (in South Africa) a person of mixed ethnic descent resident in the province of Western Cape, speaking Afrikaans or English as their first language, and typically not a follower of Islam. Compare with CAPE MALAY.
▶ adjective relating to Cape coloured people.

Cape doctor ▶ noun S. African informal the strong prevailing SE wind in the province of Western Cape.

Cape Dutch ▶ noun [mass noun] historical the form of Dutch spoken by the early settlers at the Cape of Good Hope, which developed into Afrikaans.
▶ adjective **1** historical relating to the Cape Dutch language.
2 of or denoting a style of furniture or architecture used by early settlers in South Africa.

capeesh /kəˈpiːʃ/ ▶ exclamation informal, chiefly US do you understand?: *Upstairs is off limits. Capeesh?*
– ORIGIN 1940s: from Italian *capisce* third person singular present tense of *capire* 'understand'.

Cape gooseberry ▶ noun **1** a soft edible yellow berry enclosed in a husk that resembles a lantern in shape.
2 the tropical South American plant with heart-shaped leaves which bears the Cape gooseberry. ● *Physalis peruviana*, family Solanaceae.

Cape hen ▶ noun the white-chinned petrel of southern oceans, with mainly dark brown plumage. ● *Procellaria aequinoctialis*, family Procellariidae.

Cape hunting dog ▶ noun see HUNTING DOG.

Cape jasmine ▶ noun a fragrant Chinese gardenia, some kinds of which have flowers that are used to perfume tea. ● Genus *Gardenia*, family Rubiaceae: several species.

Čapek /ˈtʃapɛk/, Karel (1890–1938), Czech novelist and dramatist. He is known for *R.U.R.* (*Rossum's Universal Robots*) (1920), which introduced the word *robot* to the English language, and *The Insect Play* (1921), written with his brother **Josef** (1887–1945).

capelin /ˈkeɪplɪn, ˈkap-/ (also **caplin**) ▶ noun a small fish of the North Atlantic, resembling a smelt. It is abundant in coastal waters and provides a staple food for humans and many animals. ● *Mallotus villosus*, family Osmeridae.
– ORIGIN early 17th cent.: from French, from Provençal *capelan*, from medieval Latin *cappellanus* 'custodian' (see CHAPLAIN).

Capella /kəˈpɛlə/ Astronomy the sixth-brightest star in the sky, and the brightest in the constellation Auriga. It is a yellow giant.
– ORIGIN Latin, 'she-goat', diminutive of *caper* 'goat'.

capellini /ˌkapɛˈliːniː/ ▶ plural noun pasta in the form of very thin strands.
– ORIGIN 1950s: Italian, diminutive of *capello* 'hair'.

Cape Malay (also **Cape Muslim**) ▶ noun (in South Africa) a member of a predominantly Afrikaans-speaking and Muslim group resident mainly in the province of Western Cape. Compare with CAPE COLOURED.
▶ adjective relating to the Cape Malay people.

Cape marigold ▶ noun another term for AFRICAN DAISY.

Cape of Good Hope see GOOD HOPE, CAPE OF.

Cape pigeon (also **Cape petrel**) ▶ noun another term for PINTADO PETREL.

Cape primrose ▶ noun another term for STREPTOCARPUS.

Cape Province a former province of South Africa, containing the Cape of Good Hope. The area became a British colony in 1814; it was known as Cape Colony from then until 1910, when it joined the Union of South Africa. In 1994 it was divided into the provinces of Northern Cape, Western Cape, and Eastern Cape.

caper[1] ▶ verb [no obj., with adverbial of direction] skip or dance about in a lively or playful way: *children were capering about the room*.
▶ noun **1** a playful skipping movement: *she did a little caper or dance*.

2 informal an illicit or ridiculous activity or escapade: *I'm too old for this kind of caper.* ■ a light-hearted, far-fetched film, especially about crime: *a cop caper about intergalactic drug dealers.*
– PHRASES **cut a caper** make a playful skipping movement.
– DERIVATIVES **caperer** noun.
– ORIGIN late 16th cent.: abbreviation of CAPRIOLE.

caper[2] ▶ noun 1 (usu. **capers**) the cooked and pickled flower bud of a bramble-like southern European shrub, used to flavour food.
2 the shrub from which capers are taken. ● *Capparis spinosa*, family Capparidaceae.
– ORIGIN late Middle English: from French *câpres* or Latin *capparis*, from Greek *kapparis*; later interpreted as plural, hence the loss of the final *-s* in the 16th cent.

capercaillie /ˌkapəˈkeɪli/ (Scottish also **capercailzie** /-ˈkeɪlzi/) ▶ noun (pl. **capercaillies**) a large turkey-like Eurasian grouse of mature pine forests. ● Genus *Tetrao*, family Tetraonidae (or Phasianidae): two species, in particular *T. urogallus*, which has been re-established in the Scottish Highlands.
– ORIGIN mid 16th cent.: from Scottish Gaelic *capull coille*, literally 'horse of the wood'.

caper spurge ▶ noun an ornamental European spurge which has become naturalized in North America. It has poisonous seeds, but the buds can be used as a substitute for capers. ● *Euphorbia lathyris*, family Euphorbiaceae.

Cape sparrow ▶ noun a dark brown sparrow native to southern Africa. ● *Passer melanurus*, family Passeridae (or Ploceidae).

Capet /ˈkapɪt, kaˈpɛt/, French /kapɛ/, Hugh (938–96), king of France 987–96, founder of the Capetian dynasty.

Capetian /kəˈpiːʃ(ə)n/ ▶ adjective relating to or denoting the dynasty ruling France 987–1328.
▶ noun a member of the Capetian dynasty.

Cape Town the legislative capital of South Africa and administrative capital of the province of Western Cape; pop. 3,569,400 (est. 2009).
– DERIVATIVES **Capetonian** noun & adjective.

Cape Verde Islands /vəːd/ a country consisting of a group of islands in the Atlantic off the coast of Senegal, named after the most westerly cape of Africa; pop. 429,500 (est. 2009); languages, Portuguese (official), Creole; capital, Praia. Previously uninhabited, the islands were settled by the Portuguese from the 15th century. They remained a Portuguese colony until 1975, when an independent republic was established.
– DERIVATIVES **Cape Verdean** adjective & noun.

Cape Wrath see WRATH, CAPE.

Cape York see YORK, CAPE.

capias /ˈkeɪpɪəs, ˈkap-/ ▶ noun (pl. **capiases**) Law a writ ordering the arrest of a named person.
– ORIGIN late Middle English: from Latin *capias (ad respondendum)*, literally 'you are to seize (until reply is made)', from *capere* 'take'.

capillarity ▶ noun [mass noun] the tendency of a liquid in a capillary tube or absorbent material to rise or fall as a result of surface tension. Also called CAPILLARY ACTION.
– ORIGIN mid 19th cent.: from French *capillarité*, from Latin *capillaris* 'like a hair' (see CAPILLARY).

capillary /kəˈpɪləri/ ▶ noun (pl. **capillaries**) 1 Anatomy any of the fine branching blood vessels that form a network between the arterioles and venules.
2 (also **capillary tube**) a tube which has an internal diameter of hair-like thinness.
▶ adjective [attrib.] relating to capillaries or capillarity.
– ORIGIN mid 17th cent.: from Latin *capillaris*, from *capillus* 'hair', influenced by Old French *capillaire*.

capillary action ▶ noun another term for CAPILLARITY.

capillary joint ▶ noun a joint made between two pipes by putting their ends into a fitting that is only slightly larger than the pipes and filling the gap with molten solder.

capital[1] ▶ noun 1 (also **capital city** or **town**) the city or town that functions as the seat of government and administrative centre of a country or region: *Warsaw is the capital of Poland.* ■ [with modifier] a place associated more than any other with a specified activity or product: *the fashion capital of the world.*
2 [mass noun] wealth in the form of money or other assets owned by a person or organization or available for a purpose such as starting a company or investing: *rates of return on invested capital were high.*
■ the excess of a company's assets over its liabilities. ■ people who possess wealth and use it to control a society's economic activity, considered collectively: *a conflict of interest between capital and labour.* ■ [with modifier] a valuable resource of a particular kind: *there is insufficient investment in **human capital**.*
3 (also **capital letter**) a letter of the size and form used to begin sentences and names: *he wrote the name in capitals.*
▶ adjective 1 [attrib.] (of an offence or charge) liable to the death penalty: *murder is the only capital crime in the state.*
2 [attrib.] (of a letter of the alphabet) large in size and of the form used to begin sentences and names.
3 informal, dated excellent: *he's a really capital fellow.*
▶ exclamation Brit. informal, dated used to express approval, satisfaction, or delight: *That's splendid! Capital!*
– PHRASES **make capital out of** use to one's own advantage: *the opposition are seeking to make political capital out of the scandal.* **with a capital ——** used to give emphasis to the word in question: *she was ugly with a capital U.*
– DERIVATIVES **capitally** adverb.
– ORIGIN Middle English (as an adjective in the sense 'relating to the head or top', later 'standing at the head or beginning'): via Old French from Latin *capitalis*, from *caput* 'head'.

capital[2] ▶ noun Architecture the distinct, typically broader section at the head of a pillar or column.
– ORIGIN Middle English: from Old French *capitel*, from late Latin *capitellum* 'little head', diminutive of Latin *caput*.

capital adequacy ▶ noun [mass noun] the statutory minimum reserves of capital which a bank or other financial institution must have available.

capital gain ▶ noun (often **capital gains**) a profit from the sale of property or an investment.

capital gains tax (abbrev.: **CGT**) ▶ noun [mass noun] a tax levied on profit from the sale of property or an investment.

capital goods ▶ plural noun goods that are used in producing other goods, rather than being bought by consumers. Often contrasted with CONSUMER GOODS.

capital-intensive ▶ adjective (of a business or industrial process) requiring the investment of large sums of money.

capitalism ▶ noun [mass noun] an economic and political system in which a country's trade and industry are controlled by private owners for profit, rather than by the state.

capitalist ▶ noun a person who uses their wealth to invest in trade and industry for profit in accordance with the principles of capitalism.
▶ adjective supporting or based on the principles of capitalism: *capitalist countries* | *the global economy is essentially capitalist.*
– DERIVATIVES **capitalistic** adjective, **capitalistically** adverb.

capitalization (also **capitalisation**) ▶ noun 1 Finance the provision of capital for a company, or the conversion of income or assets into capital.
2 the action of writing or printing in capital letters or with an initial capital.

capitalize (also **capitalise**) ▶ verb 1 [no obj.] (**capitalize on**) take the chance to gain advantage from: *an attempt by the opposition to capitalize on the government's embarrassment.*
2 [with obj.] provide (a company) with capital: (as adj. **capitalized**) *a highly capitalized industry.*
3 [with obj.] realize (the present value of an income); convert into capital. ■ reckon (the value of an asset) by setting future benefits against the cost of maintenance: *a trader will want to capitalize repairs expenditure.*
4 [with obj.] write or print (a word or letter) in capital letters. ■ begin (a word) with a capital letter.

capital levy ▶ noun a tax by means of which the state appropriates a fixed proportion of private wealth.

capital market ▶ noun the part of a financial system concerned with raising capital by dealing in shares, bonds, and other long-term investments.

capital punishment ▶ noun [mass noun] the legally authorized killing of someone as punishment for a crime.

capital ship ▶ noun a large warship such as a battleship or aircraft carrier.

capital sum ▶ noun a lump sum of money payable to an insured person or paid as an initial fee or investment.

capital territory ▶ noun (in Australia, Nigeria, Pakistan, etc.) the territory containing the capital city of the country.

capital transfer tax (abbrev.: **CTT**) ▶ noun [mass noun] (in the UK) a tax levied on the transfer of capital by gift or bequest (replaced in 1986 by inheritance tax).

capitano /ˌkapɪˈtɑːnəʊ/ ▶ noun (pl. **capitanos**) (in Italy or among Italian-speakers) a captain or chief.
– ORIGIN Italian.

capitate /ˈkapɪteɪt/ ▶ adjective Botany & Zoology ending in a distinct compact head.
▶ noun (also **capitate bone**) Anatomy the largest of the carpal bones, situated at the base of the palm of the hand and articulating with the third metacarpal.
– ORIGIN mid 17th cent.: from Latin *capitatus*, from *caput, capit-*, 'head'.

capitation ▶ noun [mass noun] the payment of a fee or grant to a doctor, school, etc., the amount of which is determined by the number of patients, pupils, or customers that are served: [as modifier] *income from capitation fees.*
– ORIGIN early 17th cent. (denoting the counting of heads): from late Latin *capitatio* 'poll tax', from *caput* 'head'.

Capitol /ˈkapɪt(ə)l/ (usu. **the Capitol**) 1 the seat of the US Congress in Washington DC. ■ (**capitol**) US a building housing a legislative assembly: *the work is on display at the Utah state capitol.*
2 the temple of Jupiter on the Capitoline Hill in ancient Rome.
– ORIGIN from Old French *capitolie, capitoile*, later assimilated to Latin *Capitolium* (from *caput, capit-* 'head').

Capitol Hill the region around the Capitol in Washington DC (often as an allusive reference to the US Congress itself).

capitular /kəˈpɪtjʊlə/ ▶ adjective 1 relating to a cathedral chapter.
2 Anatomy & Biology relating to a capitulum.
– ORIGIN early 16th cent.: from late Latin *capitularis*, from Latin *capitulum* 'small head'.

capitulary /kəˈpɪtjʊləri/ ▶ noun (pl. **capitularies**) historical a royal command under the Merovingian dynasty.
– ORIGIN mid 17th cent.: from late Latin *capitularius*, from Latin *capitulum* in the sense 'section of a law'.

capitulate /kəˈpɪtjʊleɪt/ ▶ verb [no obj.] cease to resist an opponent or an unwelcome demand; yield: *the patriots had to **capitulate to** the enemy forces.*
– DERIVATIVES **capitulator** noun.
– ORIGIN mid 16th cent. (in the sense 'parley, draw up terms'): from French *capituler*, from medieval Latin *capitulare* 'draw up under headings', from Latin *capitulum*, diminutive of *caput* 'head'.

capitulation ▶ noun [mass noun] the action of ceasing to resist an opponent or demand: *she gave a sigh of capitulation* | [count noun] ***a capitulation to** wage demands.* ■ (**capitulations**) historical an agreement or set of conditions.

capitulum /kəˈpɪtjʊləm/ ▶ noun (pl. **capitula** /-lə/) Anatomy & Biology a compact head of a structure, in particular a dense flat cluster of small flowers or florets, as in plants of the daisy family.
– ORIGIN early 18th cent.: from Latin, diminutive of *caput* 'head'.

caplet ▶ noun trademark a coated oral medicinal tablet.
– ORIGIN 1930s: blend of CAPSULE and TABLET.

caplin ▶ noun variant spelling of CAPELIN.

cap'n /ˈkapn/ ▶ noun informal contraction of CAPTAIN, used in representing speech.

capo[1] /ˈkapəʊ/ (also **capo tasto**) ▶ noun (pl. **capos**) a clamp fastened across all the strings of a fretted musical instrument to raise their tuning by a chosen amount.
– ORIGIN late 19th cent.: from Italian *capo tasto*, literally 'head stop'.

capo[2] /ˈkapəʊ/ ▶ noun (pl. **capos**) chiefly N. Amer. the head of a crime syndicate, especially the Mafia, or a branch of one.
– ORIGIN 1950s: from Italian, from Latin *caput* 'head'.

Capo di Monte /ˌkapəʊ dɪ ˈmɒnteɪ, ˈmɒnti/ ▶ noun [mass noun] a type of porcelain first produced at the Capo di Monte palace near Naples in the mid 18th century, generally white with richly coloured rococo decoration.

capoeira /ˌkapuˈeɪrə/ ▶ noun [mass noun] a system of physical discipline and movement originating among

Brazilian slaves, treated as a martial art and dance form.
– ORIGIN Portuguese.

capon /ˈkeɪp(ə)n/ ▶ **noun** a castrated domestic cock fattened for eating.
– DERIVATIVES **caponize** (also **caponise**) verb.
– ORIGIN late Old English: from Old French, based on Latin *capo, capon-*.

caponata /ˌkapə(ʊ)ˈnɑːtə/ ▶ **noun** [mass noun] a dish of aubergines, olives, and onions seasoned with herbs, served as an appetizer.
– ORIGIN Italian.

Capone /kəˈpəʊn/, Al (1899–1947), American gangster, of Italian descent; full name *Alphonse Capone*. He dominated organized crime in Chicago in the 1920s and was indirectly responsible for many murders, including the St Valentine's Day Massacre.

caponier /ˌkapəˈnɪə/ ▶ **noun** a covered passage across a ditch round a fort.
– ORIGIN late 17th cent.: from Spanish *caponera*, literally 'capon enclosure'.

capot /kəˈpɒt/ ▶ **noun** (in piquet) the winning of all twelve tricks in the hand by one player, for which a bonus is awarded.
▶ **verb** (**capots, capotting, capotted**) [with obj.] score a capot against (one's opponent).
– ORIGIN mid 17th cent.: from French, perhaps from a dialect variant of *chapoter* 'castrate'.

capo tasto /ˌkapəʊ ˈtastəʊ/ ▶ **noun** (pl. **capo tastos**) another term for CAPO[1].

Capote /kəˈpəʊti/, Truman (1924–84), American writer; born *Truman Streckfus Persons*. Notable works: *Breakfast at Tiffany's* (1958) and *In Cold Blood* (1966), a meticulous recreation of a brutal multiple murder.

capote /kəˈpəʊt/ ▶ **noun** N. Amer. historical a long cloak or coat with a hood, worn especially as part of an army or company uniform.
– ORIGIN early 19th cent.: from French, diminutive of *cape* (see CAPE[1]).

Capp, Al (1909–79), American cartoonist; full name *Alfred Gerald Caplin*. He is best known for his comic strip 'Li'l Abner', which appeared in the *New York Mirror* from 1934 to 1977.

Cappadocia /ˌkapəˈdəʊʃə/ an ancient region of central Asia Minor, between Lake Tuz and the Euphrates, north of Cilicia. It was an important centre of early Christianity.
– DERIVATIVES **Cappadocian** adjective & noun.

cappelletti /ˌkapəˈlɛti/ ▶ **plural noun** small pieces of pasta folded and stuffed with meat or cheese.
– ORIGIN Italian, literally 'little hats'.

capper ▶ **noun** N. Amer. informal a more surprising, upsetting, or entertaining event or situation than all others that have gone before: *the capper was him accusing her of ripping off his car*.

cappuccino /ˌkapʊˈtʃiːnəʊ/ ▶ **noun** (pl. **cappuccinos**) a type of coffee made with milk that has been frothed up with pressurized steam.
– ORIGIN from Italian, literally 'Capuchin', because its colour resembles that of a Capuchin's habit.

Capra /ˈkaprə/, Frank (1897–1991), Italian-born American film director. He is known for comedies such as *It Happened One Night* (1934), *Arsenic and Old Lace* (1944), and *It's a Wonderful Life* (1946). He won six Oscars.

Capri /kəˈpriː/, Italian /ˈkapri/ an island off the west coast of Italy, south of Naples.

capriccio /kəˈprɪtʃɪəʊ/ ▶ **noun** (pl. **capriccios**) **1** a lively piece of music, typically one that is short and free in form.
2 a painting or other work of art representing a fantasy or a mixture of real and imaginary features.
– ORIGIN early 17th cent. (denoting a sudden change of mind): from Italian, literally 'head with the hair standing on end', hence 'horror', later 'a sudden start' (influenced by *capra* 'goat', associated with frisky movement), from *capo* 'head' + *riccio* 'hedgehog'.

capriccioso /kəˌprɪtʃɪˈəʊzəʊ, -səʊ/ ▶ **adverb & adjective** Music (especially as a direction) in a free and impulsive style.
– ORIGIN Italian, literally 'capricious', from CAPRICCIO.

caprice /kəˈpriːs/ ▶ **noun 1** a sudden and unaccountable change of mood or behaviour: *her caprices made his life impossible* | [mass noun] *a land where men were ruled by law and not by caprice*.
2 Music another term for CAPRICCIO.
– ORIGIN mid 17th cent.: from French, from Italian (see CAPRICCIO).

capricious /kəˈprɪʃəs/ ▶ **adjective** given to sudden and unaccountable changes of mood or behaviour: *a capricious and often brutal administration*. ■ changing according to no discernible rules; unpredictable: *a capricious climate*.
– DERIVATIVES **capriciously** adverb, **capriciousness** noun.
– ORIGIN early 17th cent.: from French *capricieux*, from Italian (see CAPRICCIOSO).

Capricorn /ˈkaprɪkɔːn/ Astrology the tenth sign of the zodiac (the Goat), which the sun enters at the northern winter solstice (about 21 December). ■ (**a Capricorn**) a person born when the sun is in the sign of Capricorn.
– PHRASES **tropic of Capricorn** see TROPIC[1].
– DERIVATIVES **Capricornian** noun & adjective.
– ORIGIN Old English, from Latin *capricornus*, from *caper, capr-* 'goat' + *cornu* 'horn', on the pattern of Greek *aigokerōs* 'goat-horned, Capricorn'.

Capricornus /ˈkaprɪkɔːnəs/ Astronomy a constellation (the Goat), said to represent a goat with a fish's tail.
– ORIGIN Latin (see CAPRICORN).

caprine /ˈkaprʌɪn/ ▶ **adjective** relating to or resembling goats.
– ORIGIN late Middle English: from Latin *caprinus*, from *caper, capr-* 'goat'.

capriole /ˈkaprɪəʊl/ ▶ **noun** a movement performed in classical riding, in which the horse leaps from the ground and kicks out with its hind legs. ■ a leap or caper in dancing, especially a cabriole.
– ORIGIN late 16th cent.: from obsolete French (now *cabriole*), from Italian *capriola* 'leap', from *capriolo* 'roebuck', from Latin *capreolus*, diminutive of *caper, capr-* 'goat'.

capri pants /kəˈpriː/ (also **capris**) ▶ **plural noun** close-fitting tapered trousers for women.
– ORIGIN 1950s (originally US): named after the island of CAPRI.

Caprivi Strip /kəˈpriːvi/ a narrow strip of Namibia which extends towards Zambia from the north-eastern corner of Namibia and reaches the Zambezi River.
– ORIGIN named after Leo Graf von *Caprivi*, German imperial Chancellor (1890–4) at the time when this region became part of the colony of German South West Africa.

caproate /ˈkaprəʊeɪt/ ▶ **noun** Chemistry a salt or ester of caproic acid.

cap rock ▶ **noun** [mass noun] a layer of hard impervious rock overlying and often sealing in a deposit of oil, gas, or coal.

caproic acid /kəˈprəʊɪk/ ▶ **noun** [mass noun] Chemistry a liquid fatty acid present in milk fat and coconut and palm oils. ● Alternative name: **hexanoic acid**; chem. formula: $CH_3(CH_2)_4COOH$.
– ORIGIN mid 19th cent.: *caproic* from Latin *caper, capr-* 'goat' (because of its smell) + -IC.

caprolactam /ˌkaprə(ʊ)ˈlaktam/ ▶ **noun** [mass noun] Chemistry a synthetic crystalline compound which is an intermediate in nylon manufacture. ● A lactam; chem. formula: $C_6H_{11}NO$.
– ORIGIN 1940s: from CAPROIC ACID + LACTAM.

caprylate /ˈkaprɪleɪt/ ▶ **noun** Chemistry a salt or ester of caprylic acid.

caprylic acid /kaˈprɪlɪk/ ▶ **noun** [mass noun] Chemistry a liquid fatty acid present in butter and other fats. ● Chem. formula: $CH_3(CH_2)_6COOH$.
– ORIGIN mid 19th cent.: from Latin *caper, capr-*, 'goat' + -YL + -IC.

caps ▶ **abbreviation** capital letters.

capsaicin /kapˈseɪɪsɪn/ ▶ **noun** [mass noun] Chemistry a compound that is responsible for the pungency of capsicums. ● A cyclic amide; chem. formula: $C_{18}H_{27}NO_3$.
– ORIGIN late 19th cent.: alteration of *capsicine*, the name of a substance formerly thought to have the same property.

Capsian /ˈkapsɪən/ ▶ **adjective** Archaeology relating to or denoting a Palaeolithic culture of North Africa and southern Europe, noted for its microliths and dated to *c.*8000–4500 BC. ■ (as noun **the Capsian**) the Capsian culture or period.
– ORIGIN early 20th cent.: from Latin *Capsa* (now *Gafsa* in Tunisia), where objects from this culture were found, + -IAN.

capsicum /ˈkapsɪkəm/ ▶ **noun** (pl. **capsicums**) a tropical American plant of the nightshade family with fruits (peppers) containing many seeds. Many cultivated kinds have been developed. ● Genus *Capsicum*, family Solanaceae: several species and varieties, in particular *C. annuum* var. *annuum*, the cultivated forms of which include the '*grossum*' group (sweet peppers) and the '*longum*' group (chilli peppers).
■ the fruit of any of the capsicum plants, varying in size, colour, and pungency.
– ORIGIN late 16th cent.: modern Latin, perhaps from Latin *capsa* (see CASE[2]).

capsid[1] ▶ **noun** another term for MIRID.
– ORIGIN late 19th cent.: from modern Latin *Capsidae* (plural), from *Capsus* (genus name).

C

capsid[2] ▶ **noun** Microbiology the protein coat or shell of a virus particle, surrounding the nucleic acid or nucleoprotein core.
– ORIGIN 1960s: coined in French from Latin *capsa* (see CASE[2]).

capsize ▶ **verb** [no obj.] (of a boat) be overturned in the water: *the craft capsized in heavy seas* | (as adj. **capsized**) *a capsized dinghy*. ■ [with obj.] cause (a boat) to overturn.
▶ **noun** [in sing.] an instance of capsizing.
– ORIGIN late 18th cent.: perhaps based on Spanish *capuzar* 'sink (a ship) by the head', from *cabo* 'head' + *chapuzar* 'to dive or duck'.

cap sleeve ▶ **noun** a sleeve extending only a short distance from the shoulder and tapering to nothing under the arm.
– DERIVATIVES **cap-sleeved** adjective.

capstan /ˈkapst(ə)n/ ▶ **noun** a broad revolving cylinder with a vertical axis used for winding a rope or cable, powered by a motor or pushed round by levers. ■ the motor-driven spindle on a tape recorder that makes the tape travel past the head at constant speed.
– ORIGIN late Middle English: from Provençal *cabestan*, from *cabestre* 'halter', from Latin *capistrum*, from *capere* 'seize'.

capstan lathe ▶ **noun** a lathe with a revolving tool holder that enables several tools to be permanently mounted on it.

capstone ▶ **noun** a stone fixed on top of something, typically a wall. ■ Archaeology a large flat stone forming a roof over the chamber of a megalithic tomb.

capsule /ˈkapsjuːl, -sjʊl/ ▶ **noun 1** a small case or container, especially a round or cylindrical one. ■ a small soluble case of gelatin containing a dose of medicine, swallowed whole. ■ short for SPACE CAPSULE.
2 Anatomy a tough sheath or membrane that encloses an organ or other structure in the body, such as a kidney or a synovial joint. ■ Biology a gelatinous layer forming the outer surface of some bacterial cells.
3 the foil or plastic covering the cork of a wine bottle.
4 Botany a dry fruit that releases its seeds by bursting open when ripe, such as a pea pod.
5 Botany the spore-producing structure of mosses and liverworts, typically borne on a stalk.
6 [as modifier] (of a piece of writing) shortened but retaining the essence of the original; condensed: *a capsule review of the movie*. ■ (of a collection of clothing) consisting of a relatively small set of key items: *a capsule wardrobe*.
– DERIVATIVES **capsular** adjective, **capsulate** adjective.
– ORIGIN late Middle English (in the general sense 'small container'): via French from Latin *capsula*, diminutive of *capsa* (see CASE[2]).

capsulize (also **capsulise**) ▶ **verb** [with obj.] put (information) in condensed form; summarize.

Capt. ▶ **abbreviation** Captain.

captain ▶ **noun 1** the person in command of a ship. ■ the pilot in command of a civil aircraft. ■ a rank of naval officer above commander and below commodore. ■ a rank of officer in the army and in the US and Canadian air forces, above lieutenant and below major.
2 the leader of a team, especially in sports. ■ a powerful or influential person in a particular field: *a captain of industry*. ■ Brit. a head boy or girl in a school. ■ N. Amer. a supervisor of waiters or bellboys.
3 (in the US) a police officer in charge of a precinct, ranking below a chief.
▶ **verb** [with obj.] be the captain of (a ship, aircraft, or sports team).
– DERIVATIVES **captaincy** noun.
– ORIGIN late Middle English (in the general sense 'chief or leader'): from Old French *capitain* (superseding earlier *chevetaigne* 'chieftain'), from late Latin *capitaneus* 'chief', from Latin *caput, capit-* 'head'.

Captain Cooker ▶ **noun** NZ a wild boar.
– ORIGIN late 19th cent.: named after Captain J. Cook (see COOK[1]), who brought domesticated pigs (from

which the wild boar is supposedly descended) to New Zealand.

captain general ▶ noun an honorary rank of senior officer in the British army, most commonly in an artillery regiment.

captain's chair ▶ noun a wooden chair with a back that curves round to form armrests.

captan /'kapt(ə)n/ ▶ noun [mass noun] a synthetic fungicide and insecticide derived from a mercaptan.

captcha /'kaptʃə/ (also **CAPTCHA**) ▶ noun a computer program or system intended to distinguish human from machine input, typically as a way of thwarting spam and automated extraction of data from websites.
– ORIGIN early 21st cent.: acronym from *Completely Automated Public Turing test to tell Computers and Humans Apart*.

caption ▶ noun a title or brief explanation accompanying an illustration, cartoon, or poster. ■ a piece of text appearing on a cinema or television screen as part of a film or broadcast. ■ Law the heading of a legal document.
▶ verb [with obj.] provide (an illustration) with a title or explanation: [with two objs] *the photograph was captioned 'Three little maids'*.
– ORIGIN late Middle English (in the sense 'seizing, capture'): from Latin *captio(n-)*, from *capere* 'take, seize'. Early senses 'arrest' and 'warrant for arrest' gave rise to 'statement of where, when, and by whose authority a warrant was issued' (late 17th cent.): this was usually appended to a legal document, hence the sense 'heading or accompanying wording' (late 18th cent.).

captious /'kapʃəs/ ▶ adjective formal tending to find fault or raise petty objections: *a captious teacher*.
– DERIVATIVES **captiously** adverb, **captiousness** noun.
– ORIGIN late Middle English (also in the sense 'intended to deceive someone'): from Old French *captieux* or Latin *captiosus*, from *captio(n-)* 'seizing', (figuratively) 'deceiving' (see CAPTION).

captivate ▶ verb [with obj.] attract and hold the interest and attention of; charm: *he was captivated by her beauty*.
– DERIVATIVES **captivation** noun.
– ORIGIN early 16th cent.: from late Latin *captivat-* 'taken captive', from the verb *captivare*, from *captivus* (see CAPTIVE).

captivating ▶ adjective capable of attracting and holding interest; charming: *a captivating smile*.
– DERIVATIVES **captivatingly** adverb.

captive ▶ noun a person who has been taken prisoner or an animal that has been confined.
▶ adjective **1** imprisoned or confined: *the farm was used to **hold** prisoners of war **captive** | a captive animal*. ■ [attrib.] having no freedom to choose alternatives or to avoid something: *advertisements at the cinema reach a captive audience*.
2 (of a facility or service) controlled by, and typically for the sole use of, an organization: *a captive power plant*.
– ORIGIN late Middle English: from Latin *captivus*, from *capere* 'seize, take'.

captive balloon ▶ noun a lighter-than-air balloon secured by a rope to the ground, used to carry radar equipment or for parachute jumps.

captivity ▶ noun (pl. **captivities**) [mass noun] the condition of being imprisoned or confined: *he was released after 865 days **in captivity** | the third month of their captivity passed*. ■ (**the Captivity**) short for BABYLONIAN CAPTIVITY.
– ORIGIN late Middle English: from Latin *captivitas*, from *captivus* 'taken captive' (see CAPTIVE).

captor ▶ noun a person that catches or confines another.
– ORIGIN mid 16th cent.: from Latin, from *capt-* 'seized, taken', from the verb *capere*.

capture ▶ verb [with obj.] **1** take into one's possession or control by force: *the island was captured by Australian forces in 1914*. ■ (in chess and other board games) make a move that secures the removal of (an opposing piece) from the board. ■ Astronomy (of a star, planet, or other celestial body) bring (a less massive body) permanently within its gravitational influence.
2 record accurately in words or pictures: *she did a series of sketches, trying to capture all his moods*.
3 cause (data) to be stored in a computer.
4 Physics absorb (an atomic or subatomic particle).
5 (of a stream) divert the upper course of (another stream) by encroaching on its catchment area.
▶ noun [mass noun] the action of capturing or of being captured: *the capture of the city | he was killed while resisting capture*. ■ [count noun] a person or thing that has been captured.
– PHRASES **capture someone's imagination** (or **attention**) fascinate someone: *the project has captured the imagination of the local public*.
– DERIVATIVES **capturer** noun.
– ORIGIN mid 16th cent. (as a noun): from French, from Latin *captura*, from *capt-* 'seized, taken', from the verb *capere*.

Capuchin /'kapʊtʃɪn/ ▶ noun **1** a friar belonging to a branch of the Franciscan order that observes a strict rule drawn up in 1529.
2 a cloak and hood formerly worn by women.
3 (**capuchin** or **capuchin monkey**) a South American monkey with a cap of hair on the head which has the appearance of a cowl. ● Genus *Cebus*, family Cebidae: four species.
4 (**capuchin**) a pigeon of a breed with head and neck feathers resembling a cowl.
– ORIGIN late 16th cent.: from obsolete French, earlier form of *capucin*, from Italian *cappuccino*, from *cappuccio* 'hood, cowl', from *cappa* (see CAPE[1]), the friars being so named because of their sharp-pointed hoods.

capybara /,kapɪ'bɑːrə/ ▶ noun (pl. **same** or **capybaras**) a South American mammal that resembles a giant long-legged guinea pig. It lives in groups near water and is the largest living rodent. ● *Hydrochaerus hydrochaeris*, the only member of the family Hydrochaeridae.
– ORIGIN early 17th cent.: from Spanish *capibara* or Portuguese *capivara*, from Tupi *capiuára*, from *capī* 'grass' + *uára* 'eater'.

car ▶ noun a road vehicle, typically with four wheels, powered by an internal-combustion engine and able to carry a small number of people: *we're going **by car** |* [as modifier] *a car crash*. ■ a railway carriage or (N. Amer.) wagon: *the first-class cars*. ■ the passenger compartment of a lift, cableway, or balloon. ■ literary a chariot.
– DERIVATIVES **carful** noun (pl. **carfuls**).
– ORIGIN late Middle English (in the general sense 'wheeled vehicle'): from Old Northern French *carre*, based on Latin *carrum*, *carrus*, of Celtic origin.

carabao /,karə'beɪəʊ/ ▶ noun (pl. **same** or **carabaos**) another term for WATER BUFFALO.
– ORIGIN early 20th cent.: from Spanish, from a local word in the Philippines.

carabid /'karəbɪd/ ▶ noun Entomology a fast-running beetle of a family (Carabidae) that comprises the predatory ground beetles.
– ORIGIN late 19th cent.: from modern Latin *Carabidae* (plural), from Latin *carabus*, denoting a kind of crab.

carabineer /,karəbɪ'nɪə/ (also **carabinier**) ▶ noun historical a cavalry soldier whose principal weapon was a carbine.
– ORIGIN mid 17th cent.: from French *carabinier*, from *carabine* (see CARBINE).

carabiner ▶ noun variant spelling of KARABINER.

carabinero /,karabɪ'nɛːrəʊ/ ▶ noun (pl. **carabineros** /-əʊz/) a Spanish or South American frontier guard or customs officer.
– ORIGIN Spanish, literally 'soldier armed with a carbine'.

carabiniere /,karəbɪ'njɛːri/ ▶ noun (pl. **carabinieri** pronunc. **same**) a member of the Italian paramilitary police.
– ORIGIN Italian, literally 'carabineer'.

caracal /'karəkal/ ▶ noun a long-legged lynx-like cat with black tufted ears and a uniform brown coat, native to Africa and western Asia. Also called AFRICAN LYNX. ● *Felis caracal*, family Felidae.
– ORIGIN mid 19th cent.: from French or Spanish, from Turkish *karakulak*, from *kara* 'black' + *kulak* 'ear' (because of its black ear tufts).

Caracalla /,karə'kalə/ (188–217), Roman emperor 211–17; born *Septimius Bassanius*; later called *Marcus Aurelius Severus Antoninus Augustus*. In 212 he granted Roman citizenship to all free inhabitants of the Roman Empire.

caracara /,karə'kɑːrə/ ▶ noun (pl. **same** or **caracaras**) a large New World bird of prey of the falcon family, with a bare face and a deep bill, feeding largely on carrion. ● Family Falconidae: four genera and several species.
– ORIGIN mid 19th cent.: from Spanish or Portuguese *caracará*, from Tupi-Guarani, imitating its cry.

Caracas /kə'rakəs/ the capital of Venezuela; pop. 2,097,400 (est. 2009).

caracole /'karəkəʊl/ ▶ noun a half turn to the right or left by a horse.
▶ verb [no obj., with adverbial of direction] (of a horse) perform a caracole.
– ORIGIN early 17th cent.: from French *caracole*, *caracol* 'snail's shell, spiral'.

Caractacus /kə'raktəkəs/ variant spelling of CARATACUS.

caracul ▶ noun variant spelling of KARAKUL.

carafe /kə'raf, -'rɑːf/ ▶ noun an open-topped glass flask used for serving wine or water in a restaurant.
– ORIGIN late 18th cent.: from French, from Italian *caraffa*, probably based on Arabic *ġarafa* 'draw water'.

caragana /,karə'gɑːnə/ ▶ noun a shrub or small tree of the pea family, which is native to central Asia and Siberia and is sometimes planted as an ornamental. ● Genus *Caragana*, family Leguminosae: several species.
– ORIGIN modern Latin, of Turkic origin.

Carajás /,karə'ʒɑːs/ a mining region in north Brazil, the site of one of the richest deposits of iron ore in the world.

caramba /kə'rambə/ ▶ exclamation informal, often humorous an expression of surprise or dismay.
– ORIGIN mid 19th cent.: from Spanish.

carambola /,kar(ə)m'bəʊlə/ ▶ noun **1** a golden-yellow juicy fruit with a star-shaped cross section. Also called STAR FRUIT.
2 the small tropical tree which bears carambolas. ● *Averrhoa carambola*, family Oxalidaceae.
– ORIGIN late 16th cent.: from Portuguese, probably from Marathi *karambal*.

caramel /'karəm(ə)l, -mɛl/ ▶ noun [mass noun] sugar or syrup heated until it turns brown, used as a flavouring or colouring for food or drink: *a gateau frosted with caramel |* [as modifier] *caramel ice cream*. ■ the light brown colour of caramel. ■ [count noun] a soft toffee made with sugar and butter that have been melted and further heated.
– ORIGIN early 18th cent.: from French, from Spanish *caramelo*.

caramelize (also **caramelise**) ▶ verb [no obj.] (of sugar or syrup) be converted into caramel. ■ [with obj.] (usu. as adj. **caramelized**) cook (food) with sugar so that it becomes coated with caramel.
– DERIVATIVES **caramelization** noun.

carangid /kə'randʒɪd/ ▶ noun Zoology a marine fish of the jack family (Carangidae), whose members typically have a sloping forehead and two dorsal fins.
– ORIGIN late 19th cent.: from modern Latin *Carangidae* (plural), from the genus name *Caranx*.

carapace /'karəpeɪs/ ▶ noun the hard upper shell of a tortoise, crustacean, or arachnid.
– ORIGIN mid 19th cent.: from French, from Spanish *carapacho*, of unknown origin.

carat /'karət/ ▶ noun **1** a unit of weight for precious stones and pearls, equivalent to 200 milligrams: *a half-carat diamond ring*.
2 (US also **karat**) a measure of the purity of gold, pure gold being 24 carats: *23-carat gold*.
– ORIGIN late Middle English (in sense 2): from French, from Italian *carato*, from Arabic *qīrāṭ* (a unit of weight), from Greek *keration* 'fruit of the carob' (also denoting a unit of weight), diminutive of *keras* 'horn', with reference to the elongated seed pod of the carob.

Caratacus /kə'ratəkəs/ (also **Caractacus**) (1st century AD), British chieftain, son of Cymbeline. He took part in the resistance to the Roman invasion of AD 43.

Caravaggio /,karə'vadʒɪəʊ/, Italian /kara'vaddʒəʊ/, Michelangelo Merisi da (*c.*1571–1610), Italian painter. An influential figure in the transition from late Mannerism to Baroque, he made use of naturalistic realism and dramatic light and shade.
– DERIVATIVES **Caravaggesque** /,karəva'dʒɛsk/ adjective.

caravan ▶ noun **1** Brit. a vehicle equipped for living in, typically towed by a car and used for holidays. ■ a covered horse-drawn wagon: *a Gypsy caravan*. ■ N. Amer. a covered lorry.
2 historical a group of people, especially traders or pilgrims, travelling together across a desert in Asia or North Africa. ■ any large group of people, typically with vehicles or animals, travelling together in single file: *a caravan of cars and trucks*.
– ORIGIN late 15th cent. (in sense 2): from French *caravane*, from Persian *kārwān*. The sense 'covered horse-drawn wagon' dates from the early 19th cent.

caravanette ▶ noun Brit. a motor vehicle with a rear compartment equipped for living in.

caravanning ▶ **noun** [mass noun] Brit. the activity of spending a holiday in a caravan.
– DERIVATIVES **caravanner** noun.

caravanserai /ˌkarəˈvansərʌɪ, -ri/ (US also **caravansary**) ▶ **noun** (pl. **caravanserais** or **caravansaries**) **1** historical an inn with a central courtyard for travellers in the desert regions of Asia or North Africa.
2 a group of people travelling together; a caravan.
– ORIGIN late 16th cent.: from Persian *kārwānsarāy*, from *kārwān* 'caravan' + *sarāy* 'palace'.

caravan site (also **caravan park**) ▶ **noun** Brit. an area where caravans may be parked and used for holidays or as permanent homes.

caravel /ˈkarəvɛl/ (also **carvel**) ▶ **noun** historical a small, fast Spanish or Portuguese sailing ship of the 15th–17th centuries.
– ORIGIN early 16th cent.: from French *caravelle*, from Portuguese *caravela*, diminutive of *caravo*, via Latin from Greek *karabos* 'horned beetle' or 'light ship'.

caraway /ˈkarəweɪ/ ▶ **noun** [mass noun] **1** (also **caraway seed**) the seeds of a plant of the parsley family, used for flavouring and as a source of oil.
2 the white-flowered Mediterranean plant which bears caraway seeds. ● *Carum carvi*, family Umbelliferae.
– ORIGIN Middle English: from medieval Latin *carui*, from Arabic *al-karāwiyā*, probably from Greek *karon* 'cumin'.

carb[1] ▶ **noun** short for CARBURETTOR.

carb[2] ▶ **noun** short for CARBOHYDRATE.

carbamate /ˈkɑːbəmeɪt/ ▶ **noun** Chemistry a salt or ester containing the anion NH_2COO^- or the group $-OOCNH_2$, derived from the hypothetical compound **carbamic acid**.
– ORIGIN mid 19th cent.: from *carbamic* (from CARBO- + AMIDE + -IC) + -ATE[1].

carbamazepine /ˌkɑːbəˈmeɪzɪpiːn/ ▶ **noun** [mass noun] Medicine a synthetic compound of the benzodiazepine class, used as an anticonvulsant and analgesic drug.
– ORIGIN 1960s: from CARBO- + AMIDE, on the pattern of *benzodiazepine*.

carbanion /kɑːˈbanʌɪən/ ▶ **noun** Chemistry an organic anion in which the negative charge is located on a carbon atom.

carbaryl /ˈkɑːbərʌɪl, -rɪl/ ▶ **noun** [mass noun] a synthetic insecticide used to protect crops and in the treatment of fleas and lice. ● Chem. formula: $C_{12}H_{11}NO_2$.
– ORIGIN mid 20th cent.: from CARBAMATE + -YL.

carbazole /ˌkɑːbəˈzəʊl/ ▶ **noun** [mass noun] Chemistry a colourless crystalline substance obtained from coal tar, used in dye production. ● Chem. formula: $C_{12}H_9N$.
– ORIGIN late 19th cent.: from CARBO- + AZO- + -OLE.

carbene /ˈkɑːbiːn/ ▶ **noun** Chemistry a highly reactive molecule containing a divalent carbon atom, examples of which occur as intermediates in some organic reactions.

carbide /ˈkɑːbʌɪd/ ▶ **noun** Chemistry a binary compound of carbon with an element of lower or comparable electronegativity. ■ [mass noun] calcium carbide (CaC_2), used to generate acetylene by reaction with water and formerly used in portable lamps: [as modifier] *a carbide lamp*.

carbine /ˈkɑːbʌɪn/ ▶ **noun** a light automatic rifle. ■ historical a short rifle or musket used by cavalry.
– ORIGIN early 17th cent.: from French *carabine*, from *carabin* 'mounted musketeer', of unknown origin.

carbo- ▶ **combining form** representing CARBON.

carbocation /ˌkɑːbə(ʊ)ˈkatʌɪən/ ▶ **noun** Chemistry another term for CARBONIUM ION.
– ORIGIN 1950s: from CARBO- + CATION.

carbohydrate ▶ **noun** any of a large group of organic compounds occurring in foods and living tissues and including sugars, starch, and cellulose. They contain hydrogen and oxygen in the same ratio as water (2:1) and typically can be broken down to release energy in the animal body.

carbolic ▶ **noun** [mass noun] **1** (also **carbolic acid**) phenol, especially when used as a disinfectant.
2 (also **carbolic soap**) disinfectant soap containing phenol.
– ORIGIN mid 19th cent.: from CARBO- + -OL + -IC.

carbo-load ▶ **verb** [no obj.] (of a sports player or an athlete) saturate the muscles with stored glycogen by exercising and dieting and then shortly before a competition eating a large amount of carbohydrates.

car bomb ▶ **noun** a bomb concealed in or under a parked car, used especially by terrorists.
▶ **verb** (**car-bomb**) [with obj.] attack with a car bomb.
– DERIVATIVES **car bomber** noun.

carbon ▶ **noun** **1** [mass noun] the chemical element of atomic number 6, a non-metal which has two main forms (diamond and graphite) and which also occurs in impure form in charcoal, soot, and coal. (Symbol: **C**) ■ [usu. as modifier] carbon fibre: *a bike with a carbon frame*. ■ [count noun] a rod of carbon in an arc lamp. ■ [count noun] a piece of carbon paper or a carbon copy.
2 carbon dioxide or other gaseous carbon compounds released into the atmosphere, associated with climate change: *the level of carbon in the atmosphere has been consistently rising* | [as modifier] *fossil fuel consumption and carbon emissions continued to rise*.

> Compounds of carbon (organic compounds) form the physical basis of all living organisms. Carbon atoms are able to link with each other and with other atoms to form chains and rings, and an infinite variety of carbon compounds exist.

– DERIVATIVES **carbonless** adjective.
– ORIGIN late 18th cent.: from French *carbone*, from Latin *carbo*, *carbon-* 'coal, charcoal'.

> **WORD TRENDS** No longer just a simple noun for a chemical element, **carbon** is now most commonly used as shorthand for carbon dioxide or other carbon compounds released into the atmosphere and associated with climate change. It was first used in this sense in 1977, in the phrase *carbon emissions*, which is still the second most common compound noun containing *carbon* in the Oxford English Corpus, after *carbon dioxide* itself. Other common compounds reflect concerns over the impact of humans on the environment, with *carbon tax*, *carbon footprint*, *carbon credit*, and *carbon trading* all frequently seen. Concern is also shifting from limiting the release of carbon to managing its levels in the atmosphere, as seen from the verbs regularly paired with the word—*store* is now twice as common as *release*, with *sequester*, *absorb*, and *capture* all close behind.

carbon-12 ▶ **noun** [mass noun] the commonest natural carbon isotope, of mass 12. It is the basis for the accepted scale of atomic mass units.

carbon-14 ▶ **noun** [mass noun] a long-lived naturally occurring radioactive carbon isotope of mass 14, used in carbon dating and as a tracer in biochemistry.

carbonaceous ▶ **adjective** (chiefly of rocks or sediments) consisting of or containing carbon or its compounds.

carbonado /ˌkɑːbəˈneɪdəʊ/ ▶ **noun** (pl. **carbonados**) a dark opaque diamond, used in abrasives and cutting tools. Also called BLACK DIAMOND.
– ORIGIN mid 19th cent.: from Portuguese.

carbonara /ˌkɑːbəˈnɑːrə/ ▶ **adjective** denoting a pasta sauce made with bacon or ham, egg, and cream: [postpositive] *spaghetti carbonara*.
– ORIGIN Italian, literally 'charcoal kiln', perhaps influenced by *carbonata*, a dish of charcoal-grilled salt pork.

carbonate /ˈkɑːbəneɪt/ ▶ **noun** a salt of the anion CO_3^{2-}, typically formed by reaction of carbon dioxide with bases.
▶ **verb** [with obj.] dissolve carbon dioxide in (a liquid). ■ Chemistry convert into a carbonate, typically by reaction with carbon dioxide.
– DERIVATIVES **carbonation** noun.

carbonated /ˈkɑːbəneɪtɪd/ ▶ **adjective** (of a soft drink) effervescent on account of containing dissolved carbon dioxide.

carbonatite /kɑːˈbɒnətʌɪt/ ▶ **noun** Geology a lava or other igneous rock composed chiefly of carbonates rather than silicates.

carbon black ▶ **noun** [mass noun] a fine carbon powder used as a pigment, made by burning hydrocarbons in insufficient air.

carbon capture and storage ▶ **noun** [mass noun] the process of trapping carbon dioxide produced by burning fossil fuels or other chemical or biological process and storing it in such a way that it is unable to affect the atmosphere.

carbon copy ▶ **noun** a copy of written or typed material made with carbon paper. ■ a person or thing identical or very similar to another: *the children were carbon copies of their father*.

carbon credit ▶ **noun** a permit which allows a country or organization to produce a certain amount of carbon emissions and which can be traded if the full allowance is not used.

carbon cycle ▶ **noun** **1** the series of processes by which carbon compounds are interconverted in the environment, involving the incorporation of carbon dioxide into living tissue by photosynthesis and its return to the atmosphere through respiration, the decay of dead organisms, and the burning of fossil fuels.
2 Astronomy the cycle of thermonuclear reactions believed to occur in stars, in which carbon nuclei are repeatedly formed and broken down in the conversion of hydrogen into helium.

carbon dating ▶ **noun** [mass noun] the determination of the age of an organic object from the relative proportions of the carbon isotopes carbon-12 and carbon-14 that it contains. The ratio between them changes as radioactive carbon-14 decays and is not replaced by exchange with the atmosphere.

carbon dioxide ▶ **noun** [mass noun] a colourless, odourless gas produced by burning carbon and organic compounds and by respiration. It is naturally present in air (about 0.03 per cent) and is absorbed by plants in photosynthesis. ● Chem. formula: CO_2.

carbon disulphide ▶ **noun** [mass noun] a colourless toxic flammable liquid used as a solvent, especially for rubber and sulphur. ● Chem. formula: CS_2.

carbon fibre ▶ **noun** [mass noun] a material consisting of thin, strong crystalline filaments of carbon, used as a strengthening material, especially in resins and ceramics: [as modifier] *a carbon-fibre brake disc*.

carbon fixation ▶ **noun** [mass noun] Biology the incorporation of carbon into organic compounds by living organisms, chiefly by photosynthesis in green plants.

carbon footprint ▶ **noun** the amount of carbon dioxide released into the atmosphere as a result of the activities of a particular individual, organization, or community.

carbonic /kɑːˈbɒnɪk/ ▶ **adjective** relating to carbon or its compounds, especially carbon dioxide.

carbonic acid ▶ **noun** [mass noun] a very weak acid formed in solution when carbon dioxide dissolves in water. ● Chem. formula: H_2CO_3.

carbonic acid gas ▶ **noun** archaic term for CARBON DIOXIDE.

carbonic anhydrase /anˈhʌɪdreɪz/ ▶ **noun** [mass noun] Biochemistry an enzyme which catalyses the conversion of dissolved bicarbonates into carbon dioxide.

Carboniferous /ˌkɑːbəˈnɪf(ə)rəs/ ▶ **adjective** Geology relating to or denoting the fifth period of the Palaeozoic era, between the Devonian and Permian periods. ■ [as noun] (**the Carboniferous**) the Carboniferous period or the system of rocks deposited during it.

> The Carboniferous lasted from about 363 to 290 million years ago. During this time the first reptiles and seed-bearing plants appeared, and there were extensive coral reefs and coal-forming swamp forests.

carbonium ion /kɑːˈbəʊnɪəm/ ▶ **noun** Chemistry an organic cation in which the positive charge is located on a carbon atom.
– ORIGIN early 20th cent.: *carbonium* from CARBO- 'carbon', on the pattern of *ammonium*.

carbonize (also **carbonise**) ▶ **verb** convert or be converted into carbon, typically by heating or burning or during fossilization: [with obj.] *the steak was carbonized on the outside*. ■ (usu. as adj. **carbonized**) coat with carbon.
– DERIVATIVES **carbonization** noun.

carbon monoxide ▶ **noun** [mass noun] a colourless, odourless toxic flammable gas formed by incomplete combustion of carbon. ● Chem. formula: CO.

carbonnade /ˌkɑːbəˈnɑːd, -ˈneɪd/ ▶ **noun** a rich beef stew made with onions and beer.
– ORIGIN mid 17th cent. (denoting a piece of meat or fish cooked on hot coals): from French, from Latin *carbo*, *-onis* 'coal, charcoal'.

carbon-neutral ▶ **adjective** making or resulting in no net release of carbon dioxide into the atmosphere, especially as a result of carbon offsetting.

carbon offsetting ▶ **noun** [mass noun] the counteracting of carbon dioxide emissions with an equivalent reduction of carbon dioxide in the atmosphere.

carbon paper ▶ **noun** [mass noun] thin paper coated with carbon or another pigmented substance, used for making a second impression of a document as it is being written or typed.

carbon sequestration ▶ **noun** [mass noun] a natural or artificial process by which carbon dioxide is removed from the atmosphere and held in solid or liquid form.

carbon sink ▶ **noun** Ecology a forest, ocean, or other natural environment viewed in terms of its ability to absorb carbon dioxide from the atmosphere.

C

carbon steel ▶ noun [mass noun] steel in which the main alloying element is carbon.

carbon tax ▶ noun a tax on fossil fuels, especially those used by motor vehicles, intended to reduce the emission of carbon dioxide.

carbon tetrachloride ▶ noun [mass noun] a colourless toxic volatile liquid used as a solvent, especially for fats and oils. ● Chem. formula: CCl_4.

carbon trading ▶ noun another term for EMISSIONS TRADING.

carbonyl /ˈkɑːbənʌɪl, -nɪl/ ▶ noun [as modifier] Chemistry of or denoting the divalent radical =C=O, present in such organic compounds as aldehydes, ketones, amides, and esters, and in organic acids as part of the carboxyl group: *carbonyl compounds*. ■ [count noun] a coordination compound in which one or more carbon monoxide molecules are bonded as neutral ligands to a central metal atom: *nickel carbonyl*.

carbonyl chloride ▶ noun another term for PHOSGENE.

car boot sale ▶ noun Brit. an outdoor sale at which people sell unwanted possessions, typically from the boots of their cars.

carborundum /ˌkɑːbəˈrʌndəm/ ▶ noun [mass noun] a very hard black solid consisting of silicon carbide, used as an abrasive.
– ORIGIN late 19th cent. (originally US, as a trademark): blend of CARBON and CORUNDUM.

carboxyhaemoglobin /kɑːˌbɒksɪˌhiːməˈɡləʊbɪn/ ▶ noun [mass noun] Biochemistry a compound formed in the blood by the binding of carbon monoxide to haemoglobin. It is stable and therefore cannot absorb or transport oxygen.

carboxyl /kɑːˈbɒksʌɪl, -sɪl/ (also **carboxy**) ▶ noun [as modifier] Chemistry of or denoting the acid radical −COOH, present in most organic acids: *the carboxyl group*.
– ORIGIN mid 19th cent.: from CARBO- + OX- 'oxygen' + -YL.

carboxylase /kɑːˈbɒksɪleɪz/ ▶ noun Biochemistry an enzyme which catalyses the addition of a carboxyl group to a specified substrate.

carboxylate /kɑːˈbɒksɪleɪt/ Chemistry ▶ noun a salt or ester of a carboxylic acid.
▶ verb [with obj.] add a carboxyl group to (a compound): (as adj. **carboxylated**) *carboxylated polysaccharides*.
– DERIVATIVES **carboxylation** noun.

carboxylic acid /ˌkɑːbɒkˈsɪlɪk/ ▶ noun Chemistry an organic acid containing a carboxyl group. The simplest examples are methanoic (or formic) acid and ethanoic (or acetic) acid.

carboy ▶ noun a large globular glass bottle with a narrow neck, typically protected by a frame and used for holding acids or other corrosive liquids.
– ORIGIN mid 18th cent.: from Persian *qarāba* 'large glass flagon'.

carbuncle /ˈkɑːbʌŋk(ə)l/ ▶ noun 1 a severe abscess or multiple boil in the skin, typically infected with staphylococcus bacteria.
2 a bright red gem, in particular a garnet cut en cabochon.
– DERIVATIVES **carbuncular** adjective.
– ORIGIN Middle English (in sense 2): from Old French *charbuncle*, from Latin *carbunculus* 'small coal', from *carbo* 'coal, charcoal'.

carburation /ˌkɑːbjʊˈreɪʃ(ə)n/ ▶ noun [mass noun] the process of mixing air with a fine spray of liquid hydrocarbon fuel, as in an internal-combustion engine.
– ORIGIN late 19th cent.: from archaic *carburet* 'combine or charge with a hydrocarbon' + -ATION.

carburetted (US **carbureted**) ▶ adjective (of a vehicle or engine) having fuel supplied through a carburettor, rather than an injector.
– ORIGIN early 19th cent.: from archaic *carburet* 'carbide' + -ED[2].

carburettor /kɑːbjʊˈrɛtə, -bə-/ (also US **carburetor**) ▶ noun a device in an internal-combustion engine for mixing air with a fine spray of liquid fuel.
– ORIGIN mid 19th cent.: from archaic *carburet* 'combine or charge with a hydrocarbon' + -OR[1].

carburize /ˈkɑːbjʊrʌɪz, -bə-/ (also **carburise**) ▶ verb [with obj.] add carbon to (iron or steel), in particular by heating in the presence of carbon to harden the surface.
– DERIVATIVES **carburization** noun.
– ORIGIN mid 19th cent.: from French *carbure* 'carbide' + -IZE.

carcajou /ˈkɑːkədʒuː, -əʒuː/ ▶ noun North American term for WOLVERINE.
– ORIGIN early 18th cent.: from Canadian French, apparently of Algonquian origin (compare with KINKAJOU).

carcass (Brit. also **carcase**) ▶ noun the dead body of an animal. ■ the trunk of an animal such as a cow, sheep, or pig, for cutting up as meat. ■ the remains of a cooked bird after all the edible parts have been removed. ■ humorous a person's body, living or dead: *my obsession will last while there's life in this old carcass*. ■ the structural framework of a building, ship, or piece of furniture. ■ the remains of something: *automotive carcasses stripped of radios, hubcaps and even body panels*.
– ORIGIN Middle English: from Anglo-Norman French *carcois*, variant of Old French *charcois*; in later use from French *carcasse*; of unknown ultimate origin.

carcass meat ▶ noun [mass noun] Brit. raw meat as distinct from corned or tinned meat.

Carcassonne /ˌkɑːkəˈsɒn/, French /karkasɔn/ a walled city in SW France; pop. 48,212 (2006).

carceral /ˈkɑːs(ə)r(ə)l/ ▶ adjective literary relating to a prison.
– ORIGIN late 16th cent.: from late Latin *carceralis*, from *carcer* 'prison'.

Carchemish /ˈkɑːkɪmɪʃ/ an ancient city on the upper Euphrates, north-east of Aleppo.

carcinogen /kɑːˈsɪnədʒ(ə)n/ ▶ noun a substance capable of causing cancer in living tissue.
– ORIGIN mid 19th cent.: from an abbreviation of CARCINOMA + -GEN.

carcinogenesis /ˌkɑːs(ɪ)nəˈdʒɛnɪsɪs/ ▶ noun [mass noun] the initiation of cancer formation.

carcinogenic /ˌkɑːs(ɪ)nəˈdʒɛnɪk/ ▶ adjective having the potential to cause cancer.
– DERIVATIVES **carcinogenicity** noun.

carcinoid /ˈkɑːsɪnɔɪd/ ▶ noun Medicine a tumour of a type occurring in the glands of the intestine (especially the appendix) or in the bronchi, and sometimes secreting hormones.
– ORIGIN late 19th cent.: from an abbreviation of CARCINOMA + -OID.

carcinoma /ˌkɑːsɪˈnəʊmə/ ▶ noun (pl. **carcinomas** or **carcinomata** /-mətə/) a cancer arising in the epithelial tissue of the skin or of the lining of the internal organs.
– DERIVATIVES **carcinomatous** adjective.
– ORIGIN early 18th cent.: via Latin from Greek *karkinōma*, from *karkinos* 'crab' (compare with CANCER).

carcinomatosis /ˌkɑːsɪnəʊməˈtəʊsɪs/ ▶ noun [mass noun] the widespread dissemination of carcinoma in the body.

car coat ▶ noun a short, square-cut style of coat designed to be worn when driving a car.

car crash ▶ noun informal a chaotic or disastrous situation that holds a ghoulish fascination for observers: *her life is turning into a car crash* | [as modifier] *a classic piece of car-crash television*.

card[1] ▶ noun 1 a piece of thick, stiff paper or thin pasteboard, in particular one used for writing or printing on: *some notes jotted down on a card* | [mass noun] *a piece of card*. ■ a card printed with a picture and used to send a message or greeting: *a birthday card*. ■ a card with a person's name and other details printed on it for purposes of identification, for example a business card.
2 a small rectangular piece of plastic containing personal data in a machine-readable form and used to obtain cash or credit or to pay for a telephone call, gain entry to a room or building, etc.
3 a playing card: *a pack of cards*. ■ (**cards**) a game played with playing cards.
4 Computing short for EXPANSION CARD.
5 (**cards**) Brit. informal documents relating to an employee, especially for tax and national insurance, held by the employer.
6 a programme of events at a race meeting. ■ a record of scores in a sporting event; a scorecard.
7 informal, dated a person regarded as odd or amusing: *He laughed: 'You're a card, you know'*.
▶ verb [with obj.] 1 write (something) on a card, especially for indexing.
2 informal (in golf and other sports) score (a certain number of points on a scorecard): *he carded 68 in the final round*.
3 N. Amer. check the identity card of (someone), in particular as evidence of legal drinking age.
4 (**be carded**) Canadian (of an amateur athlete) be in receipt of government funding to pursue training.
– PHRASES **a card up one's sleeve** a plan or asset that is kept secret until it is needed. **get one's cards** Brit. informal be dismissed from one's employment. **give someone their cards** Brit. informal dismiss someone from employment. **hold all the cards** be in a very strong or advantageous position. **on** (or N. Amer. **in**) **the cards** Brit. informal possible or likely: *our marriage has been on the cards from day one*. **play** (or **use**) **the —— card** exploit the specified issue or idea mentioned, especially for political advantage: *the government tried to play the nationalist card*. **play one's cards right** make the best use of one's assets and opportunities. **put** (or **lay**) **one's cards on the table** be completely open and honest in declaring one's resources, intentions, or attitude.
– ORIGIN late Middle English (in sense 3 of the noun): from Old French *carte*, from Latin *carta*, *charta*, from Greek *khartēs* 'papyrus leaf'.

card[2] ▶ verb [with obj.] comb and clean (raw wool, hemp fibres, or similar material) with a sharp-toothed instrument in order to disentangle the fibres before spinning.
▶ noun a toothed implement or machine for carding wool.
– DERIVATIVES **carder** noun.
– ORIGIN late Middle English: from Old French *carde*, from Provençal *carda*, from *cardar* 'tease, comb', based on Latin *carere* 'to card'.

Card. ▶ abbreviation Cardinal.

cardamom /ˈkɑːdəməm/ (also **cardamon**) ▶ noun [mass noun] 1 the aromatic seeds of a plant of the ginger family, used as a spice and also medicinally.
2 the SE Asian plant which bears cardamom seeds.
● *Elettaria cardamomum*, family Zingiberaceae.
– ORIGIN late Middle English: from Old French *cardamome* or Latin *cardamomum*, from Greek *kardamōmon*, from *kardamon* 'cress' + *amōmon*, the name of a kind of spice plant.

Cardamom Mountains a range of mountains in western Cambodia, rising to a height of 1,813 m (5,886 ft) at its highest point.

cardan joint /ˈkɑːd(ə)n/ ▶ noun Brit. another term for UNIVERSAL JOINT.
– ORIGIN early 20th cent.: named after Gerolamo *Cardano* (1501–76), Italian mathematician.

cardan shaft /ˈkɑːd(ə)n/ ▶ noun Brit. a shaft with a universal joint at one or both ends.

cardboard ▶ noun 1 [mass noun] pasteboard or stiff paper: [as modifier] *a cardboard box*.
2 [as modifier] (of a character in a literary work) lacking depth and realism; artificial: *with its superficial, cardboard characters, the novel was typical of her work*.

cardboard city ▶ noun an urban area where homeless people congregate under makeshift shelters made from cardboard boxes.

card-carrying ▶ adjective registered as a member of a political party or trade union. ■ often humorous confirmed in or dedicated to a specified pursuit or outlook: *a card-carrying pessimist*.

card game ▶ noun a game in which playing cards are used.

cardholder ▶ noun a person who has a credit card or debit card.

cardia /ˈkɑːdɪə/ ▶ noun Anatomy the upper opening of the stomach, where the oesophagus enters.
– ORIGIN late 18th cent.: from Greek *kardia*.

cardiac /ˈkɑːdɪak/ ▶ adjective 1 relating to the heart.
2 relating to the part of the stomach nearest the oesophagus.
▶ noun informal a heart attack.
– ORIGIN late Middle English (as a noun denoting heart disease): from French *cardiaque* or Latin *cardiacus*, from Greek *kardiakos*, from *kardia* 'heart or upper opening of the stomach'. The adjective dates from the early 17th cent.

cardiac arrest ▶ noun a sudden, sometimes temporary, cessation of the heart's functioning.

cardiac tamponade ▶ noun see TAMPONADE (sense 1).

Cardiff the capital of Wales, a seaport on the Bristol Channel; pop. 314,100 (est. 2009). Welsh name CAERDYDD.

cardigan ▶ noun a knitted jumper fastening down the front.
– ORIGIN mid 19th cent. (Crimean War): named after James Thomas Brudenel, 7th Earl of *Cardigan* (1797–1868), leader of the Charge of the Light Brigade, whose troops first wore such garments.

Cardiganshire a former county of SW Wales. It became part of Dyfed in 1974; the area became a county once more in 1996, as Ceredigion.

Cardin /ˈkɑːdã/, French /kaʀdɛ̃/, Pierre (b.1922), French couturier, the first designer of haute couture to show a collection of clothes for men as well as women.

cardinal ▸ **noun 1** a leading dignitary of the Roman Catholic Church. Cardinals are nominated by the Pope, and form the Sacred College which elects succeeding popes (now invariably from among their own number). ■ (also **cardinal red**) [mass noun] a deep scarlet colour like that of a cardinal's cassock.
2 a New World songbird of the bunting family, having a stout bill and typically a conspicuous crest. The male is partly or mostly red in colour. ● Family Emberizidae, subfamily Cardinalinae (the **cardinal grosbeak subfamily**): four genera and several species.
▸ **adjective** [attrib.] of the greatest importance; fundamental: *two cardinal points must be borne in mind.*
– DERIVATIVES **cardinalate** noun, **cardinally** adverb.
– ORIGIN Old English, from Latin *cardinalis*, from *cardo, cardin-* 'hinge'. Sense 1 of the noun has arisen through the notion of the important function of such priests as 'pivots' of church life.

cardinal beetle ▸ **noun** a mainly bright red beetle with feathery or comb-like antennae, which typically lives under loose bark. ● Family Pyrochroidae: several genera.

cardinal fish ▸ **noun** a small brightly coloured fish found in shallow tropical seas around reefs. The male often broods the eggs in his mouth. ● Family Apogonidae: several genera, in particular *Apogon*, and numerous species.

cardinal flower ▸ **noun** a tall scarlet-flowered lobelia found in North America. ● *Lobelia cardinalis*, family Campanulaceae.

cardinal humour ▸ **noun** see HUMOUR (sense 3 of the noun).

cardinality ▸ **noun** (pl. **cardinalities**) Mathematics the number of elements in a set or other grouping, as a property of that grouping.

cardinal number ▸ **noun** a number denoting quantity (one, two, three, etc.), as opposed to an ordinal number (first, second, third, etc.).

cardinal point ▸ **noun** each of the four main points of the compass (north, south, east, and west).

cardinal sin ▸ **noun** (in Christian tradition) any of the seven deadly sins. ■ chiefly humorous a serious error of judgement: *he committed the cardinal sin of criticizing his teammates.*

cardinal virtue ▸ **noun** each of the chief moral attributes of scholastic philosophy: justice, prudence, temperance, and fortitude. Compare with THEOLOGICAL VIRTUES.

cardinal vowel ▸ **noun** Phonetics each of a series of vowel sounds used as a standard reference point to assist in the description and classification of vowel sounds in any language.

card index ▸ **noun** a catalogue or similar collection of information in which each item is entered on a separate card and the cards are arranged in a particular order, typically alphabetical.
▸ **verb** (**card-index**) [with obj.] list on a card index.

carding wool ▸ **noun** [mass noun] short-stapled pieces of wool which result from the carding process, spun and woven to make standard-quality fabrics. Compare with COMBING WOOL.

cardio ▸ **noun** [mass noun] informal cardiovascular exercise.

cardio- /ˈkɑːdɪəʊ/ ▸ **combining form** relating to the heart: *cardiograph* | *cardiopulmonary.*
– ORIGIN from Greek *kardia* 'heart'.

cardiogram /ˈkɑːdɪə(ʊ)gram/ ▸ **noun** a record of muscle activity within the heart made by a cardiograph.

cardiograph /ˈkɑːdɪə(ʊ)grɑːf/ ▸ **noun** an instrument for recording heart muscle activity, such as an electrocardiograph.
– DERIVATIVES **cardiography** noun.

cardioid ▸ **noun** Mathematics a heart-shaped curve traced by a point on the circumference of a circle as it rolls around another identical circle. ■ (also **cardioid microphone**) a directional microphone with a heart-shaped pattern of sensitivity.
▸ **adjective** of the shape of a cardioid.
– ORIGIN mid 18th cent.: from Greek *kardioeidēs* 'heart-shaped', from *kardia* 'heart' + *eidos* 'form'.

cardiology ▸ **noun** [mass noun] the branch of medicine that deals with diseases and abnormalities of the heart.
– DERIVATIVES **cardiological** adjective, **cardiologist** noun.

cardiomegaly /ˌkɑːdɪəʊˈmɛgəli/ ▸ **noun** [mass noun] Medicine abnormal enlargement of the heart.
– ORIGIN 1960s: from CARDIO- + Greek *megas, megal-* 'great'.

cardiomyopathy /ˌkɑːdɪəʊmʌɪˈɒpəθi/ ▸ **noun** [mass noun] Medicine chronic disease of the heart muscle.

cardiopathy /kɑːdɪˈɒpəθi/ ▸ **noun** [mass noun] heart disease.

cardiopulmonary ▸ **adjective** Medicine relating to the heart and the lungs.

cardiorespiratory ▸ **adjective** Medicine relating to the action of both heart and lungs.

cardiothoracic ▸ **adjective** Medicine relating to the heart and chest or lungs.

cardiovascular ▸ **adjective** Medicine relating to the heart and blood vessels.

cardiovascular system ▸ **noun** another term for CIRCULATORY SYSTEM.

carditis /kɑːˈdʌɪtɪs/ ▸ **noun** [mass noun] Medicine inflammation of the heart.

card key ▸ **noun** another term for KEY CARD.

cardoon /kɑːˈduːn/ ▸ **noun** a tall thistle-like southern European plant related to the globe artichoke, with leaves and roots that may be used as vegetables. ● *Cynara cardunculus*, family Compositae.
– ORIGIN early 17th cent.: from French *cardon*, from *carde* 'edible part of an artichoke', from modern Provençal *cardo*, based on Latin *carduus, cardus* 'thistle, artichoke'.

cardphone ▸ **noun** Brit. a public telephone operated by a phonecard rather than coins.

card reader ▸ **noun 1** an electronic sensor that reads a magnetic strip or bar code on a credit card, membership card, etc.
2 an electronic device that reads and transfers data from various portable memory storage devices.

card sharp (also **card sharper**) ▸ **noun** a person who cheats at cards in order to win money.

card swipe ▸ **noun** an electronic reader through which a credit or charge card or cheque guarantee card is passed in order to record the information it bears: [as modifier] *a card swipe system.*

card table ▸ **noun** a table for playing cards on, typically having legs that fold flat for storage and a baize surface.

card vote ▸ **noun** Brit. another term for BLOCK VOTE.

cardy (also **cardie**) ▸ **noun** (pl. **cardies**) Brit. informal short for CARDIGAN.

care ▸ **noun** [mass noun] **1** the provision of what is necessary for the health, welfare, maintenance, and protection of someone or something: *the care of the elderly* | *the child is* **in the care of** *her grandparents* | *health care.* ■ Brit. protective custody or guardianship provided by a local authority for children whose parents are dead or unable to look after them properly: *she was taken* **into care** | *children* **in care**.
2 serious attention or consideration applied to doing something correctly or to avoid damage or risk: *he planned his departure with great care.* ■ [count noun] an object of concern or attention: *the cares of family life.* ■ [count noun] a feeling of or occasion for anxiety: *she was driving along without a care in the world.*
▸ **verb** [no obj.] **1** [often with negative] feel concern or interest; attach importance to something: *they don't* **care about** *human life* | [with clause] *I don't care what she says.* ■ feel affection or liking: *you* **care** *very deeply* **for** *him.* ■ (**care for/to do something**) like or be willing to do or have something: *would you care for some tea?*
2 (**care for**) look after and provide for the needs of: *he has numerous animals to care for.*
– PHRASES **care in the community** another term for COMMUNITY CARE. **care of** at the address of: *write to me care of Ann.* **I** (or **he**, **she**, etc.) **couldn't** (N. Amer. informal also **could**) **care less** informal used to express complete indifference: *he couldn't care less about football.* **for all you care** (or **he**, **she**, etc. **cares**) informal used to indicate that someone feels no interest or concern: *I could drown for all you care.* **have a care** [often in imperative] dated be cautious: *'Have a care!' she warned.* **take care 1** [often in imperative] be cautious; keep oneself safe: *take care if you're planning to go out tonight.* **2** [with infinitive] make sure of doing something: *he would take care to provide himself with an escape clause.* **take care of 1** keep (someone or something) safe and provided for: *I can take care of myself.* **2** deal with: *he has the equipment to take care of my problem.*
– ORIGIN Old English *caru* (noun), *carian* (verb), of Germanic origin; related to Old High German *chara* 'grief, lament', *charon* 'grieve', and Old Norse *kǫr* 'sickbed'.

careen /kəˈriːn/ ▸ **verb 1** [with obj.] turn (a ship) on its side for cleaning, caulking, or repair. ■ [no obj.] (of a ship) tilt; lean over: *a heavy flood tide caused my vessel to careen dizzily.*
2 [no obj., with adverbial of direction] chiefly N. Amer. move swiftly and in an uncontrolled way: *an electric golf cart careened around the corner.*
– ORIGIN late 16th cent. (as a noun denoting the position of a careened ship): from French *carène*, from Italian *carena*, from Latin *carina* 'a keel'. Sense 2 was influenced by the verb CAREER.

career ▸ **noun** an occupation undertaken for a significant period of a person's life and with opportunities for progress. ■ the time spent by a person in a career: *the end of a distinguished career in the Royal Navy.* ■ the progress through history of an institution, organization, etc.: *the court has had a* **chequered career**. ■ [as modifier] working permanently in or committed to a particular profession: *a career diplomat.* ■ [as modifier] (of a woman) interested in pursuing a profession rather than devoting all her time to childcare and housekeeping: *a career girl.*
▸ **verb** [no obj., with adverbial of direction] move swiftly and in an uncontrolled way: *the coach careered across the road and went through a hedge.*
– PHRASES **in full career** archaic at full speed.
– ORIGIN mid 16th cent. (denoting a road or racecourse): from French *carrière*, from Italian *carriera*, based on Latin *carrus* 'wheeled vehicle'.

careerist derogatory ▸ **adjective** concerned mainly with advancement in one's profession: *a careerist politician.*
▸ **noun** a careerist person.
– DERIVATIVES **careerism** noun.

career structure ▸ **noun** Brit. a recognized pattern of advancement within a job or profession.

carefree ▸ **adjective** free from anxiety or responsibility: *we were young and carefree* | *the carefree days of the holidays.*
– DERIVATIVES **carefreeness** noun.

careful ▸ **adjective 1** making sure of avoiding potential danger, mishap, or harm; cautious: *I begged him to be more careful* | *be careful not to lose her address.* ■ (**careful of/about**) anxious to protect (something) from harm or loss; solicitous: *he was very careful of his reputation.* ■ prudent in the use of something, especially money: *his mother had always been careful with money.*
2 done with or showing thought and attention: *a careful consideration of the facts.*
– DERIVATIVES **carefully** adverb, **carefulness** noun.
– ORIGIN Old English *carful* (see CARE, -FUL).

caregiver ▸ **noun** N. Amer. another term for CARER.
– DERIVATIVES **caregiving** noun & adjective.

care label ▸ **noun** a label giving instructions for the washing and care of a fabric or garment.

careless ▸ **adjective** not giving sufficient attention or thought to avoiding harm or errors: *she had been careless and had left the window unlocked* | *a careless error.* ■ (of an action or its result) showing or caused by a lack of attention: *he admitted careless driving* | *a careless error.* ■ (**careless of/about**) not concerned or worried about: *he was careless of his own safety.* ■ showing no interest or effort; casual: *she gave a careless shrug.*
– DERIVATIVES **carelessly** adverb.
– ORIGIN Old English *carlēas* 'free from care' (see CARE, -LESS).

carelessness ▸ **noun** [mass noun] failure to give sufficient attention to avoiding harm or errors; negligence: *most road accidents are caused by carelessness on the part of motorists.*

careline ▸ **noun** Brit. a telephone service provided by the manufacturers of a product to deal with queries and complaints from consumers.

care package ▸ **noun** N. Amer. a parcel of food, money, or luxury items sent to a loved one who is away from home for an extended period.
– ORIGIN 1940s: from *CARE*, an acronym from the initial letters of *Cooperative for American Remittances to Europe*, a relief organization which arranged aid packages after the Second World War.

carer ▸ **noun** Brit. a family member or paid helper who regularly looks after a child or a sick, elderly, or disabled person.

C

caress ▶ **verb** [with obj.] touch or stroke gently or lovingly: *she caressed the girl's forehead* | figurative *a gentle breeze caressed his skin* | (as adj. **caressing**) *his caressing touch.*
▶ **noun** a gentle or loving touch.
– DERIVATIVES **caressingly** adverb.
– ORIGIN mid 17th cent.: from French *caresser* (verb), *caresse* (noun), from Italian *carezza*, based on Latin *carus* 'dear'.

caret /ˈkarət/ ▶ **noun** a mark (^, ʎ) placed below the line to indicate a proposed insertion in a text.
– ORIGIN late 17th cent.: from Latin, 'is lacking'.

caretaker ▶ **noun 1** a person employed to look after a building. ■ [as modifier] holding power temporarily: *the club's caretaker manager.*
2 chiefly N. Amer. a person employed to look after people or animals.
– DERIVATIVES **caretake** verb.

care worker ▶ **noun** Brit. a person employed to support and supervise vulnerable, infirm, or disadvantaged people, or those under the care of the state.

careworn ▶ **adjective** tired and unhappy because of prolonged worry: *a careworn expression.*

carex /ˈkɛːrɛks/ ▶ **noun** (pl. **carices** /-rɪsiːz/) a sedge (grass-like plant) of a large genus found chiefly in temperate and cold regions. ● Genus *Carex*, family Cyperaceae.
– ORIGIN modern Latin, from Latin, 'sedge'.

Carey[1] /ˈkɛːri/, George (Leonard) (b.1935), English Anglican churchman, Archbishop of Canterbury 1991–2002.

Carey[2] /ˈkɛːri/, Peter (b.1943), Australian novelist. He has twice won the Booker Prize, for *Oscar and Lucinda* (1988) and *True History of the Kelly Gang* (2001).

carfare /ˈkɑːfɛː/ ▶ **noun** [mass noun] N. Amer. the fare for travel on a bus, underground train, or similar public transport.

cargo ▶ **noun** (pl. **cargoes** or **cargos**) [mass noun] goods carried on a ship, aircraft, or motor vehicle: *transportation of bulk cargo* | [count noun] *a cargo of oil.*
– ORIGIN mid 17th cent.: from Spanish *cargo, carga*, from late Latin *carricare, carcare* 'to load', from Latin *carrus* 'wheeled vehicle'.

cargo cult ▶ **noun** (in the Melanesian Islands) a system of belief based around the expected arrival of ancestral spirits in ships bringing cargoes of food and other goods.

cargo pants ▶ **plural noun** loose-fitting casual cotton trousers with large patch pockets halfway down each leg.

carhop ▶ **noun** N. Amer. informal, dated a waiter or waitress at a drive-in restaurant.

Caria /ˈkɛːrɪə/ an ancient region of SW Asia Minor, south of the Maeander River and north-west of Lycia.
– DERIVATIVES **Carian** adjective & noun.

cariad /ˈkarɪad/ ▶ **noun** Welsh darling; sweetheart: *how's it going, cariad?*
– ORIGIN Welsh, 'love'.

cariama /ˌkarɪˈɑːmə, s-/ ▶ **noun** variant spelling of **SERIEMA**.

Carib /ˈkarɪb/ ▶ **noun 1** a member of an indigenous South American people living mainly in coastal regions of French Guiana, Suriname, Guyana, and Venezuela.
2 [mass noun] the language of the Caribs, the only member of the Cariban family of languages still spoken by a substantial number of people (around 20,000). Also called **GALIBI**. ■ the Cariban family of languages.
3 (also **Island Carib**) [mass noun] an unrelated Arawakan language, now extinct, formerly spoken in the Lesser Antilles. See also **BLACK CARIB**.
▶ **adjective** relating to the Caribs or their language. ■ relating to Island Carib or Black Carib.
– ORIGIN from Spanish *caribe*, from Haitian Creole. Compare with **CANNIBAL**.

Cariban /ˈkarɪb(ə)n/ ▶ **noun** [mass noun] a family of South American languages scattered widely throughout Brazil, Suriname, Guyana, French Guiana, Venezuela, and Colombia. With the exception of Carib, they are all extinct or have few speakers.
▶ **adjective** relating to or denoting this family of languages.

Caribbean /ˌkarɪˈbiːən, kəˈrɪbɪən/ ▶ **noun** (**the Caribbean**) the region consisting of the Caribbean Sea, its islands (including the West Indies), and the surrounding coasts.
▶ **adjective** relating to the Caribbean.

> **USAGE** There are two possible pronunciations of the word **Caribbean**. The first, more common in British English, puts the stress on the **-be-**, while the second, found in the US and the Caribbean itself, stresses the **-rib-**.

Caribbean Community and Common Market (abbrev.: **CARICOM**) an organization established in 1973 to promote cooperation in economic affairs and social services and to coordinate foreign policy among its members, all of which are independent states of the Caribbean region.

Caribbean Sea the part of the Atlantic Ocean lying between the Antilles and the mainland of Central and South America.

caribou /ˈkarɪbuː/ ▶ **noun** (pl. **same**) North American term for **REINDEER**.
– ORIGIN mid 17th cent.: from Canadian French, from Micmac *γalipu*, literally 'snow-shoveller' (because the caribou scrapes away snow to feed on the vegetation underneath).

caricature /ˈkarɪkətjʊə, ˈkarɪkətʃʊə/ ▶ **noun** a picture, description, or imitation of a person in which certain striking characteristics are exaggerated in order to create a comic or grotesque effect. ■ a ludicrous or grotesque version of someone or something: *he looked a caricature of his normal self.*
▶ **verb** [with obj.] make or give a caricature of: *he was famous enough to be caricatured by Private Eye.*
– DERIVATIVES **caricatural** adjective, **caricaturist** noun.
– ORIGIN mid 18th cent.: from French, from Italian *caricatura*, from *caricare* 'load, exaggerate', from Latin *carricare* (see **CHARGE**).

CARICOM /ˈkarɪkɒm/ ▶ **abbreviation** Caribbean Community and Common Market.

caries /ˈkɛːriːz/ ▶ **noun** [mass noun] decay and crumbling of a tooth or bone.
– ORIGIN late 16th cent.: from Latin.

carillon /ˈkarɪljən, -lɒn, kəˈrɪljən/ ▶ **noun** a set of bells played using a keyboard or by an automatic mechanism similar to a piano roll. ■ a tune played on a carillon.
– DERIVATIVES **carillonneur** /ˌkarɪljəˈnəː, -ˈrɪlə-, kə-/ noun.
– ORIGIN late 18th cent.: from French, from Old French *quarregnon* 'peal of four bells', based on Latin *quattuor* 'four'.

Carina /kəˈrʌɪnə, -ˈriː-/ Astronomy a southern constellation (the Keel) partly in the Milky Way, originally part of Argo. It contains the second-brightest star in the sky, Canopus.
– ORIGIN Latin.

carina /kəˈrʌɪnə, -ˈriː-/ ▶ **noun** (pl. **carinae** /-niː/ or **carinas**) chiefly Biology a keel-shaped structure, in particular: ■ the ridge of a bird's breastbone, to which the main flight muscles are attached. ■ a cartilage situated at the point where the trachea (windpipe) divides into the two bronchi.
– DERIVATIVES **carinal** adjective.
– ORIGIN early 18th cent.: from Latin, 'keel'.

carinate /ˈkarɪneɪt, -ət/ ▶ **adjective** having a keel-like ridge. ■ (of a bird) having a deep ridge on the breastbone for the attachment of flight muscles. Contrasted with **RATITE**.
– DERIVATIVES **carinated** adjective, **carination** noun.
– ORIGIN late 18th cent.: from Latin *carinatus* 'having a keel', from *carina* 'keel'.

caring ▶ **adjective** displaying kindness and concern for others: *a caring and invaluable friend.*
▶ **noun** [mass noun] the work or practice of looking after those unable to care for themselves, especially on account of age or illness: [as modifier] *the caring professions.*
– DERIVATIVES **caringly** adverb.

caring profession ▶ **noun** a job that involves looking after other people, such as nursing, teaching, or social work.

Carinthia /kəˈrɪnθɪə/ an Alpine state of southern Austria; capital, Klagenfurt. German name **KÄRNTEN**.
– DERIVATIVES **Carinthian** noun & adjective.

Carioca /ˌkarɪˈəʊkə/ ▶ **noun 1** a native of Rio de Janeiro.
2 (**carioca**) a Brazilian dance resembling the samba.
– ORIGIN mid 19th cent.: from Portuguese, from Tupi *kari'oka* 'house of the white man'.

cariogenic /ˌkɛːrɪə(ʊ)ˈdʒɛnɪk, ˌka-/ ▶ **adjective** technical causing tooth decay.

cariole ▶ **noun** variant spelling of **CARRIOLE**.

carious /ˈkɛːrɪəs/ ▶ **adjective** (of bones or teeth) decayed.
– ORIGIN mid 16th cent.: from Latin *cariosus* (see **CARIES**).

caritas /ˈkarɪtɑːs/ ▶ **noun** [mass noun] Christian love of humankind; charity.
– ORIGIN mid 19th cent.: Latin.

carjacking ▶ **noun** [mass noun] the action of violently stealing an occupied car.
– DERIVATIVES **carjack** verb, **carjacker** noun.
– ORIGIN 1990s: blend of **CAR** and *hijacking* (see **HIJACK**).

cark (also **kark**) ▶ **verb** [no obj.] Austral. informal die: *he's always bragged about carking it before he hit twenty.*
– ORIGIN 1970s: probably imitative of the caw of a carrion crow.

carking ▶ **adjective** [attrib.] archaic causing distress or worry: *her carking doubts.*
– ORIGIN mid 16th cent.: present participle of Middle English *cark* 'worry, burden', from Old Northern French *carkier*, based on late Latin *carcare* (see **CHARGE**).

carl ▶ **noun** archaic a peasant or man of low birth. ■ Scottish a man; a fellow.
– ORIGIN Old English (denoting a peasant or villein): from Old Norse *karl* 'man, freeman', of Germanic origin; related to **CHURL**.

Carley float /ˈkɑːli/ ▶ **noun** a large emergency raft carried on board ship, consisting of a buoyant canvas ring with a wooden grid deck.
– ORIGIN early 20th cent.: named after Horace S. Carley (*fl.* 1900), American inventor.

carline[1] /ˈkɑːlɪn/ (also **carline thistle**) ▶ **noun** a thistle-like European plant with flower heads that bear shiny persistent straw-coloured bracts. ● Genus *Carlina*, family Compositae: several species.
– ORIGIN late 16th cent.: from French, from medieval Latin *carlina*, perhaps an alteration of *cardina* (from Latin *carduus* 'thistle'), by association with *Carolus Magnus* (see **CHARLEMAGNE**), to whom its medicinal properties were said to have been revealed.

carline[2] /ˈkɑːlɪn/ ▶ **noun** (usu. **carlines**) any of the pieces of squared timber fitted fore and aft between the deck beams of a wooden ship to support the deck planking.
– ORIGIN Middle English (in the sense '(old) woman, witch'): from Old Norse *karling*; the reason for nautical use of the word remains obscure.

Carlisle /kɑːˈlʌɪl/ a city in NW England, the county town of Cumbria; pop. 73,600 (est. 2009).

Carlism /ˈkɑːlɪz(ə)m/ ▶ **noun** [mass noun] historical a Spanish conservative political movement originating in support of Don Carlos, brother of Fernando VII (died 1833), who claimed the throne in place of Fernando's daughter Isabella. The movement supported the Catholic Church and opposed centralized government; it was revived in support of the Nationalist side during the Spanish Civil War.
– DERIVATIVES **Carlist** adjective & noun.

carload ▶ **noun** the number of people that can travel in a car: ***a carload of passengers.*** ■ N. Amer. the quantity of goods that can be carried in a railway freight car.

Carlovingian /ˌkɑːlə(ʊ)ˈvɪndʒɪən/ ▶ **adjective & noun** another term for **CAROLINGIAN**.
– ORIGIN from French *carlovingien*, from *Karl* 'Charles', on the pattern of *mérovingien* 'Merovingian'.

Carlow /ˈkɑːləʊ/ a county of the Republic of Ireland, in the province of Leinster.

Carlsbad plum /ˈkɑːlzbad/ ▶ **noun** a dessert plum of a blue-black variety, that is often crystallized.
– ORIGIN late 19th cent.: named after *Karlsbad* (now Karlovy Vary) in the Czech Republic.

Carlyle /kɑːˈlʌɪl/, Thomas (1795–1881), Scottish historian and political philosopher. He established his reputation as a historian with his *History of the French Revolution* (1837). Influenced by German romanticism, many of his works, including *Sartor Resartus* (1833–4), celebrate the force of the 'strong, just man' as against the degraded masses.

carmaker ▶ **noun** a company which manufactures cars.

carman ▶ **noun** (pl. **carmen**) dated a driver of a van or cart; a carrier.

Carmarthen /kəˈmɑːðən/ a town in SW Wales, the administrative centre of Carmarthenshire; pop. 16,000 (est. 2009). Welsh name **CAERFYRDDIN**.

Carmarthenshire a county of South Wales; administrative centre, Carmarthen. It was part of Dyfed between 1974 and 1996.

Carmel, Mount /ˈkɑːm(ə)l/ a group of mountains near the Mediterranean coast in NW Israel, sheltering the port of Haifa. In the Bible it is the scene of the defeat of the priests of Baal by the prophet Elijah (I Kings 18).

Carmelite /ˈkɑːmɪlʌɪt/ ▶ noun a friar or nun of a contemplative Catholic order founded at Mount Carmel during the Crusades and dedicated to Our Lady.
▶ adjective relating to the Carmelites.

Carmichael /kɑːˈmʌɪk(ə)l/, Hoagy (1899–1981), American jazz pianist, composer, and singer; born *Howard Hoagland Carmichael*. His best-known songs include 'Stardust' (1929), 'Two Sleepy People' (1938), and 'In the Cool, Cool, Cool of the Evening' (1951).

carminative /ˈkɑːmɪnətɪv, kɑːˈmɪnətɪv/ ▶ adjective (chiefly of a drug) relieving flatulence.
▶ noun a drug that relieves flatulence.
– ORIGIN late Middle English: from Old French *carminatif, -ive*, or medieval Latin *carminat-* 'healed (by incantation)', from the verb *carminare*, from Latin *carmen* (see CHARM).

carmine /ˈkɑːmʌɪn, -mɪn/ ▶ noun [mass noun] a vivid crimson colour: [as modifier] *carmine roses*. ■ a vivid crimson pigment made from cochineal.
– ORIGIN early 18th cent.: from French *carmin*, based on Arabic *qirmiz* (see KERMES). Compare with CRIMSON.

Carnaby Street /ˈkɑːnəbi/ a street in the West End of London. It became famous in the 1960s as a centre of the popular fashion industry.

Carnac /ˈkɑːnak/ the site in Brittany of nearly 3,000 megalithic stones dating from the Neolithic period.

carnage /ˈkɑːnɪdʒ/ ▶ noun [mass noun] the killing of a large number of people.
– ORIGIN early 17th cent.: from French, from Italian *carnaggio*, from medieval Latin *carnaticum*, from Latin *caro, carn-* 'flesh'.

carnal /ˈkɑːn(ə)l/ ▶ adjective relating to physical, especially sexual, needs and activities: *carnal desire*.
– DERIVATIVES **carnality** noun, **carnally** adverb.
– ORIGIN late Middle English: from Christian Latin *carnalis*, from *caro, carn-* 'flesh'.

carnal knowledge ▶ noun [mass noun] dated, chiefly Law sexual intercourse.

carnallite /ˈkɑːn(ə)lʌɪt/ ▶ noun [mass noun] a white or reddish mineral consisting of a hydrated chloride of potassium and magnesium.
– ORIGIN mid 19th cent.: named after Rudolf von *Carnall* (1804–74), German mining engineer, + -ITE[1].

Carnap /ˈkɑːnap/, Rudolf (1891–1970), German-born American philosopher, a founding member of the Vienna Circle. Notable works: *The Logical Structure of the World* (1928) and *The Logical Foundations of Probability* (1950).

carnassial /kɑːˈnasɪəl/ ▶ adjective Zoology denoting the large upper premolar and lower molar teeth of a carnivore, adapted for shearing flesh.
– ORIGIN mid 19th cent.: from French *carnassier* 'carnivorous', based on Latin *caro, carn-* 'flesh'.

Carnatic /kɑːˈnatɪk/ ▶ adjective of or denoting the main style of classical music in southern India, as distinct from the Hindustani music of the north.
– ORIGIN Anglicization of KARNATAKA in SW India.

carnation[1] ▶ noun a double-flowered cultivated variety of clove pink, with grey-green leaves and showy pink, white, or red flowers. ● *Dianthus caryophyllus*, family Caryophyllaceae: many cultivars.
– ORIGIN late 16th cent.: perhaps based on a misreading of Arabic *qaranful* 'clove or clove pink', from Greek *karyophyllon*. The early forms suggest confusion with CARNATION[2], with *incarnation*, and with *coronation*.

carnation[2] ▶ noun a rosy pink colour: [as modifier] *sage and carnation throw pillows*.
– ORIGIN early 16th cent.: from French *carnation* 'colour of one's flesh', based on Latin *carn-* 'flesh'.

carnauba /kɑːˈnɔːbə, -ˈnaʊbə/ ▶ noun a NE Brazilian fan palm, the leaves of which exude a yellowish wax. Also called WAX PALM. ● *Copernicia cerifera*, family Palmae. ■ (also **carnauba wax**) [mass noun] wax from the carnauba palm, used as a polish.
– ORIGIN mid 19th cent.: from Portuguese, from Tupi.

Carné /kɑːˈneɪ/, French /karne/, Marcel (1906–96), French film director. He gained his reputation for the films he made with the poet and scriptwriter **Jacques Prévert** (1900–77), notably *Le Jour se lève* (1939) and *Les Enfants du paradis* (1945).

Carnegie /kɑːˈneɪgi, ˈkɑːnəgi/, Andrew (1835–1919), Scottish-born American industrialist and philanthropist. He built up a fortune in the steel industry in the US, then retired from business in 1901 and devoted his wealth to charitable purposes, in particular libraries, education, and the arts.

carnelian /kɑːˈniːlɪən/ (also **cornelian**) ▶ noun [mass noun] a semi-precious stone consisting of a dull red or reddish-white variety of chalcedony (quartz). ■ a dull red colour.
– ORIGIN late Middle English: from Old French *corneline*; the prefix *car-* being suggested by Latin *caro, carn-* 'flesh'.

carnet /ˈkɑːneɪ/ ▶ noun 1 a book of tickets for use on public transport in some countries.
2 a customs permit allowing a motor vehicle to be taken across a frontier for a limited period.
– ORIGIN 1920s: from French, 'notebook'.

carnival ▶ noun 1 an annual festival, typically during the week before Lent in Roman Catholic countries, involving processions, music, dancing, and the use of masquerade: [as modifier] *a carnival parade*. ■ an exciting or riotous mixture of elements: *the film is a visual and aural carnival*.
2 N. Amer. a travelling funfair or circus.
– DERIVATIVES **carnivalesque** adjective.
– ORIGIN mid 16th cent.: from Italian *carnevale, carnovale*, from medieval Latin *carnelevamen, carnelevarium* 'Shrovetide', from Latin *caro, carn-* 'flesh' + *levare* 'put away'.

Carnivora /kɑːˈnɪvərə/ ▶ plural noun Zoology an order of mammals that comprises the cats, dogs, bears, hyenas, weasels, civets, raccoons, and mongooses. They are distinguished by having powerful jaws and teeth adapted for stabbing, tearing, and eating flesh.

carnivore /ˈkɑːnɪvɔː/ ▶ noun an animal that feeds on other animals. ■ Zoology a mammal of the order Carnivora. ■ informal a person who is not a vegetarian.
– ORIGIN mid 19th cent.: from French, from Latin *carnivorus* (see CARNIVOROUS).

carnivorous /kɑːˈnɪv(ə)rəs/ ▶ adjective (of an animal) feeding on other animals. ■ (of a plant) able to trap and digest small animals, especially insects.
– DERIVATIVES **carnivorously** adverb, **carnivorousness** noun, **carnivory** /kɑːˈnɪv(ə)ri/ noun.
– ORIGIN late 16th cent.: from Latin *carnivorus*, from *caro, carn-* 'flesh' + *-vorus* (see -VOROUS).

carnosaur /ˈkɑːnəsɔː/ ▶ noun a large bipedal carnivorous dinosaur, typically one with greatly reduced forelimbs. ● Infraorder Carnosauria, suborder Theropoda, order Saurischia; includes tyrannosaurus, allosaurus, and megalosaurus.
– ORIGIN 1930s: from modern Latin, from Latin *caro, carn-* 'flesh' + Greek *sauros* 'lizard'.

Carnot /ˈkɑːnəʊ/, French /karno/, Nicolas Léonard Sadi (1796–1832), French scientist. His work in analysing the efficiency of steam engines was posthumously recognized as being of crucial importance to the theory of thermodynamics.

carnotite /ˈkɑːnətʌɪt/ ▶ noun [mass noun] a lemon-yellow radioactive mineral consisting of hydrated vanadate of uranium, potassium, and other elements.
– ORIGIN late 19th cent.: named after Marie Adolphe *Carnot* (1839–1920), French inspector of mines, + -ITE[1].

carny (also **carney**) ▶ noun (pl. **carnies** or **carneys**) N. Amer. informal a carnival or funfair. ■ a person who works in a carnival or funfair.

carob /ˈkarəb/ ▶ noun 1 [mass noun] a brown floury powder extracted from the carob bean, used as a substitute for chocolate.
2 (also **carob tree**) a small evergreen Arabian tree which bears long brownish-purple edible pods. Also called LOCUST TREE. ● *Ceratonia siliqua*, family Leguminosae. ■ (also **carob bean**) the edible pod of the carob tree. Also called LOCUST BEAN.
– ORIGIN late Middle English (denoting the carob bean): from Old French *carobe*, from medieval Latin *carrubia*, from Arabic *karrūba*.

carol ▶ noun a religious folk song or popular hymn, particularly one associated with Christmas: *we sang carols by candlelight*.
▶ verb (**carols, carolling, carolled**; US **carols, caroling, caroled**) 1 [with obj.] sing or say (something) happily: [with direct speech] *'Goodbye,' he carolled*.
2 (as noun **carolling**) the activity of singing Christmas carols.
– DERIVATIVES **caroller** noun.
– ORIGIN Middle English: from Old French *carole* (noun), *caroler* (verb), of unknown origin.

Carolina duck /ˌkarəˈlʌɪnə/ ▶ noun another term for WOOD DUCK.

Carolina parakeet ▶ noun a small long-tailed parakeet with mainly green plumage and a yellow and orange head. It was formerly common in the eastern US but was exterminated by about 1920. ● *Conuropsis* (or *Aratinga*) *carolinensis*, family Psittacidae.

Caroline /ˈkarəlʌɪn/ ▶ adjective 1 (also **Carolean** /-ˈliːən/) relating to the reigns of Charles I and II of England: *a Caroline poet*.
2 another term for CAROLINGIAN.
– ORIGIN early 17th cent.: from medieval Latin *Carolus* 'Charles'.

Caroline Islands (also **the Carolines**) a group of islands in the western Pacific Ocean, north of the equator, divided between the Federated States of Micronesia and Palau.

Carolingian /ˌkarəˈlɪndʒɪən/ (also **Carlovingian**) ▶ adjective relating to the Frankish dynasty, founded by Charlemagne's father (Pepin III), that ruled in western Europe from 750 to 987. ■ denoting or relating to a style of minuscule script developed in France during the time of Charlemagne, on which modern lower-case letters are largely based.
▶ noun a member of the Carolingian dynasty.
– ORIGIN alteration of earlier CARLOVINGIAN, by association with medieval Latin *Carolus* 'Charles'.

Carolingian Renaissance a period during the reign of Charlemagne and his successors that was marked by achievements in art, architecture, learning, and music.

Carolinian /ˌkarəˈlʌɪnɪən/ ▶ noun a native or inhabitant of the US states of South or North Carolina.
▶ adjective 1 of or relating to South or North Carolina.
2 denoting a forest region extending from South Ontario to South Carolina.

carol-singing ▶ noun [mass noun] the singing of carols, especially by groups going from door to door at Christmas with the object of raising money.
– DERIVATIVES **carol-singer** noun.

carom /ˈkarəm/ chiefly N. Amer. ▶ noun a cannon in billiards or pool. ■ (also **carom billiards**) [mass noun] a game resembling billiards, played on a table without pockets and depending on cannons for scoring.
▶ verb [no obj.] make a carom; strike and rebound.
– ORIGIN late 18th cent.: abbreviation of *carambole*, from Spanish *carambola*, apparently from *bola* 'ball'.

carotene /ˈkarətiːn/ ▶ noun [mass noun] Chemistry an orange or red plant pigment found in carrots and many other plant structures. It is a terpenoid hydrocarbon with several isomers, of which one (**beta-carotene**) is important in the diet as a precursor of vitamin A.
– ORIGIN mid 19th cent.: coined in German from Latin *carota* (see CARROT).

carotenoid /kəˈrɒtɪnɔɪd/ ▶ noun Chemistry any of a class of mainly yellow, orange, or red fat-soluble pigments, including carotene, which give colour to plant parts such as ripe tomatoes and autumn leaves.

Carothers /kəˈrʌðəz/, Wallace Hume (1896–1937), American industrial chemist. He developed the first successful synthetic rubber, neoprene, and the synthetic fibre Nylon 6.6.

carotid /kəˈrɒtɪd/ ▶ adjective relating to or denoting the two main arteries which carry blood to the head and neck, and their two main branches.
▶ noun each of the carotid arteries.
– ORIGIN early 17th cent.: from French *carotide* or modern Latin *carotides*, from Greek *karōtides*, plural of *karōtis* 'drowsiness', from *karoun* 'stupefy' (because compression of these arteries was thought to cause stupor).

carouse /kəˈraʊz/ ▶ verb [no obj.] drink alcohol and enjoy oneself with others in a noisy, lively way: *they danced and caroused until the drink ran out* | (as noun **carousing**) *a night of carousing*.
▶ noun a noisy, lively drinking party.
– DERIVATIVES **carousal** noun, **carouser** noun.
– ORIGIN mid 16th cent.: originally as an adverb meaning 'right out, completely' in the phrase *drink carouse*, from German *gar aus trinken*; hence 'drink heavily, have a drinking bout'.

carousel /ˌkarəˈsɛl, -ˈzɛl/ ▶ noun 1 chiefly N. Amer. a merry-go-round at a fair.
2 a conveyor system at an airport from which arriving passengers collect their luggage.
3 historical a tournament in which groups of knights took part in demonstrations of equestrian skills.
– ORIGIN mid 17th cent.: from French *carrousel*, from Italian *carosello*.

C

carp[1] ▸ noun (pl. **same**) a deep-bodied freshwater fish, typically with barbels around the mouth. Carp are farmed for food in some parts of the world and are often kept in large ponds. ● Family Cyprinidae (the **carp family**): several genera and species. The family includes the majority of freshwater fishes in Eurasia, Africa, and North and Central America.
– ORIGIN late Middle English: from Old French *carpe*, from late Latin *carpa*.

carp[2] ▸ verb [no obj.] complain or find fault continually about trivial matters: *I don't want to carp about the way you did it.*
– DERIVATIVES **carper** noun.
– ORIGIN Middle English (in the sense 'talk, chatter'): from Old Norse *karpa* 'brag'; later influenced by Latin *carpere* 'pluck at, slander'.

Carpaccio /kɑːˈpatʃɪəʊ/, Italian /karˈpattʃo/, Vittore (*c.*1455–1525), Italian painter noted especially for his paintings of Venice.

carpaccio /kɑːˈpatʃɪəʊ/, Italian /karˈpattʃo/ ▸ noun [mass noun] an Italian hors d'oeuvre consisting of thin slices of raw beef or fish served with a sauce.
– ORIGIN Italian, named after Vittore CARPACCIO (from his use of red pigments, resembling raw meat).

carpal /ˈkɑːp(ə)l/ ▸ adjective relating to the bones forming the human carpus (wrist), or to their equivalent in an animal's forelimb.
▸ noun any of the carpal bones.

carpal tunnel syndrome ▸ noun [mass noun] a painful condition of the hand and fingers caused by compression of a major nerve where it passes over the carpal bones through a passage at the front of the wrist. It may be caused by continual repetitive movements or by fluid retention.

car park ▸ noun Brit. an area or building where cars or other vehicles may be left temporarily.

Carpathian Mountains /kɑːˈpeɪθɪən/ (also **the Carpathians**) a mountain system extending south-eastwards from southern Poland and Slovakia into Romania.

carpe diem /ˌkɑːpeɪ ˈdiːɛm, ˈdʌɪɛm/ ▸ exclamation used to urge someone to make the most of the present time and give little thought to the future.
– ORIGIN Latin, 'seize the day!', a quotation from Horace (*Odes* I.xi).

carpel /ˈkɑːp(ə)l/ ▸ noun Botany the female reproductive organ of a flower, consisting of an ovary, a stigma, and usually a style. It may occur singly or as one of a group.
– DERIVATIVES **carpellary** adjective.
– ORIGIN mid 19th cent.: from French *carpelle* or modern Latin *carpellum*, from Greek *karpos* 'fruit'.

Carpentaria, Gulf of /ˌkɑːpənˈtɛːrɪə/ a large bay on the north coast of Australia, between Arnhem Land and the Cape York Peninsula.

carpenter ▸ noun a person who makes and repairs wooden objects and structures.
▸ verb [with obj.] make by shaping wood: *the rails were carpentered very skilfully.*
– ORIGIN Middle English: from Anglo-Norman French, from Old French *carpentier*, *charpentier*, from late Latin *carpentarius* (*artifex*) 'carriage (maker)', from *carpentum* 'wagon', of Gaulish origin; related to CAR.

carpenter ant ▸ noun a large ant which burrows into wood to make a nest. ● Genus *Camponotus*, family Formicidae: numerous species.

carpenter bee ▸ noun a large solitary black bee with purplish wings, which nests in tunnels bored in dead wood or plant stems. ● Genus *Xylocopa*, family Apidae: several species.

carpenter trousers ▸ plural noun loose-fitting trousers with many pockets of various sizes and loops for tools at the tops or sides of the legs.

carpentry ▸ noun [mass noun] the activity or occupation of making or repairing things in wood. ■ the work made or done by a carpenter: *the superb carpentry of the timber roof.*
– ORIGIN late Middle English: from Anglo-Norman French *carpentrie*, Old French *charpenterie*, from *charpentier* (see CARPENTER).

carpet ▸ noun **1** a floor covering made from thick woven fabric: *the house has fitted carpets throughout* | [mass noun] *the floor was covered with carpet.* ■ a large rug, especially an oriental one: *priceless Persian carpets.* ■ a thick or soft expanse or layer of something: *carpets of wood anemones and bluebells.* ■ informal, chiefly US a type of artificial playing surface on a tennis court or sports field.
2 [with modifier] a slender moth marked with undulating bands of colour across the wings. ● Many species in the family Geometridae, including the **garden carpet** (*Xanthorhoe fluctuata*).
▸ verb (**carpets**, **carpeting**, **carpeted**) [with obj.] **1** cover with carpet: *the stairs were carpeted in a lovely shade of red.* ■ cover with a thick or soft expanse or layer of something: *the meadows are carpeted with flowers.*
2 Brit. informal reprimand severely: *the Chancellor of the Exchequer carpeted the bank bosses.*
– PHRASES **on the carpet** informal being severely reprimanded by someone in authority: *we've all been on the carpet for the chances we took.* [possibly from *carpet* in the sense 'table covering', referring to 'the carpet of the council table', before which one would be summoned for reprimand; or simply referring to the carpet in front of a superior's desk.] **sweep something under the carpet** conceal or ignore a problem or difficulty in the hope that it will be forgotten.
– ORIGIN Middle English (denoting a thick fabric used as a cover for a table or bed): from Old French *carpite* or medieval Latin *carpita*, from obsolete Italian *carpita* 'woollen counterpane', based on Latin *carpere* 'pluck, pull to pieces'.

carpet bag ▸ noun a travelling bag of a kind originally made of carpet-like material.
▸ verb (**carpet-bag**) [no obj.] informal act as a carpetbagger: (as adj. **carpet-bagging**) *he's the carpet-bagging king.*

carpetbagger ▸ noun informal, derogatory a political candidate who seeks election in an area where they have no local connections. ■ Brit. a person who becomes a member of a mutually owned building society or insurance company in order to gain financially in the event of the organization demutualizing.
– ORIGIN mid 19th cent.: originally applied to people from the northern states of the US who went to the South after the Civil War to profit from the Reconstruction.

carpet beetle ▸ noun a small beetle whose larva (the woolly bear) is destructive to carpets, fabrics, and other materials. ● Genus *Anthrenus*, family Dermestidae.

carpet-bomb ▸ verb [with obj.] (often as noun **carpet-bombing**) bomb (an area) intensively.

carpeting ▸ noun **1** [mass noun] carpets collectively: *offices with wall-to-wall carpeting.* ■ the fabric from which carpets are made.
2 [in sing.] Brit. informal a severe reprimand: *I was called to her office for a carpeting.*

carpet knight ▸ noun archaic a man who avoids hard work in favour of leisure activities or philandering.
– ORIGIN late 16th cent.: with reference to a knight's exploits being restricted to a carpeted boudoir, instead of to the field of battle.

carpet python (also **carpet snake**) ▸ noun a common large Australian climbing snake that is typically brightly patterned. ● *Morelia spilota*, family Pythonidae.

carpet shark ▸ noun a conspicuously marked small shallow-water shark with barbels around the nose or mouth, found in the Indo-Pacific region and the Red Sea. ● Family Orectolobidae: *Orectolobus* and other genera, and several species, including the wobbegong.

carpet shell ▸ noun a burrowing bivalve mollusc of temperate and warm seas, with concentric growth rings and irregular coloured markings. ● Genus *Venerupis*, family Veneriidae.

carpet slipper ▸ noun Brit. a soft slipper whose upper part is made of wool or thick cloth.

carpet snake ▸ noun another term for CARPET PYTHON.

carpet sweeper ▸ noun a manual household implement used for sweeping carpets, having a revolving brush or brushes and a receptacle for dust and dirt.

carphology /kɑːˈfɒlədʒi/ ▸ noun [mass noun] rare plucking at the bedclothes by a delirious patient.
– ORIGIN mid 19th cent.: from Greek *karphologia*, from *karphos* 'straw' + *legein* 'collect'.

car phone ▸ noun a cellular phone designed for use in a motor vehicle.

carping ▸ adjective difficult to please; critical: *she has silenced the carping critics with a successful debut tour.*

carpology /kɑːˈpɒlədʒi/ ▸ noun [mass noun] rare the study of fruits and seeds.
– DERIVATIVES **carpological** adjective.
– ORIGIN early 19th cent.: from Greek *karpos* 'fruit' + -LOGY.

carpool chiefly N. Amer. ▸ noun an arrangement between people to make a regular journey in a single vehicle, typically with each person taking turns to drive the others. ■ a group of people in a carpool.
▸ verb [no obj.] form or participate in a carpool.
– DERIVATIVES **carpooler** noun.

carpophore /ˈkɑːpə(ʊ)fɔː/ ▸ noun Botany (in a flower) an elongated axis that raises the stem of the pistil above the stamens. ■ (in a fungus) the stem of the fruiting body.
– ORIGIN late 19th cent.: from Greek *karpos* 'fruit' + -PHORE.

carport ▸ noun a shelter for a car consisting of a roof supported on posts, built beside a house.

carpus /ˈkɑːpəs/ ▸ noun (pl. **carpi** /-pʌɪ/) the group of small bones between the main part of the forelimb and the metacarpus in terrestrial vertebrates. The eight bones of the human carpus form the wrist and part of the hand, and are arranged in two rows.
– ORIGIN late Middle English: from modern Latin, from Greek *karpos* 'wrist'.

carr ▸ noun [mass noun] Brit. fen woodland or scrub that is typically dominated by alder or willow.
– ORIGIN Middle English: from Old Norse *kjarr* 'brushwood', in *kjarr-mýrr* 'marsh overgrown with brushwood'.

Carracci /kəˈratʃi/ the name of a family of Italian painters comprising the brothers **Annibale** (1560–1609) and **Agostino** (1557–1602) and their cousin **Ludovico** (1555–1619). Together they established a teaching academy at Bologna, while Annibale became famed for his frescoes on the ceiling of the Farnese Gallery in Rome and for his invention of the caricature.

carrack /ˈkarək/ ▸ noun a large merchant ship of a kind operating in European waters from the 14th to the 17th century.
– ORIGIN late Middle English: from Old French *caraque*; perhaps from Spanish *carraca*, from Arabic, perhaps from *qarāqir*, plural of *qurqūra*, a type of merchant ship.

carrageen /ˈkarəgiːn/ (also **carragheen** or **carrageen moss**) ▸ noun [mass noun] an edible red shoreline seaweed with flattened branching fronds, found in both Eurasia and North America. Also called IRISH MOSS. ● *Chondrus crispus*, division Rhodophyta.
– ORIGIN early 19th cent.: from Irish *carraigín*.

carrageenan /ˌkarəˈgiːnən/ ▸ noun [mass noun] a substance extracted from red and purple seaweeds, consisting of a mixture of polysaccharides. It is used as a thickening or emulsifying agent in food products.
– ORIGIN 1960s: from CARRAGEEN + -AN.

Carrara /kəˈrɑːrə/, Italian /karˈrara/ a town in Tuscany in west central Italy, famous for the white marble quarried there since Roman times; pop. 65,760 (2008).

carrel /ˈkar(ə)l/ ▸ noun a small cubicle with a desk for the use of a reader or student in a library. ■ historical a small enclosure or study in a cloister.
– ORIGIN late 16th cent.: apparently related to CAROL in the old sense 'ring'.

carriage ▸ noun **1** a means of conveyance, in particular: ■ Brit. any of the separate sections of a train that carry passengers: *the first-class carriages.* ■ a four-wheeled passenger vehicle pulled by two or more horses: *a horse-drawn carriage.* ■ a wheeled support for moving a heavy object such as a gun.
2 [mass noun] Brit. the conveying of goods or passengers from one place to another: *the carriage of bikes on public transport.*
3 a moving part of a machine that carries other parts into the required position: *a typewriter carriage.*
4 [in sing.] a person's bearing or deportment: *her carriage was graceful, her movements quick and deft.*
– ORIGIN late Middle English: from Old Northern French *cariage*, from *carier* (see CARRY).

carriage and pair ▸ noun a four-wheeled passenger carriage pulled by two horses.

carriage bolt ▸ noun North American term for COACH BOLT.

carriage clock ▸ noun Brit. a portable clock in a rectangular case with a handle on top.

carriage dog ▸ noun archaic term for DALMATIAN (sense 1 of the noun).
– ORIGIN early 19th cent.: because Dalmatians were formerly trained to run behind carriages as guard dogs.

carriage house ▸ noun N. Amer. a building for housing a carriage, typically one which has been converted into a dwelling.

carriage release ▸ noun a function or lever which enables the carriage on a manual or electric typewriter to move freely, instead of only in one direction when the keys are pressed.

carriage return (also **carriage return key**) ▶ noun another term for RETURN (sense 5 of the noun).

carriage trade ▶ noun [mass noun] N. Amer. the wealthy clientele of a business.
– ORIGIN with reference to people who formerly would have been wealthy enough to maintain a private carriage.

carriageway ▶ noun Brit. each of the two sides of a dual carriageway or motorway, each of which usually have two or more lanes. ■ the part of a road intended for vehicles rather than pedestrians.

carrick bend ▶ noun a kind of knot used to join ropes end to end, especially so that they can go round a capstan without jamming.
– ORIGIN early 19th cent.: from BEND[2]: *carrick* perhaps an alteration of CARRACK.

Carrick-on-Shannon the county town of Leitrim in the Republic of Ireland, on the River Shannon; pop. 3,163 (2006).

carrier ▶ noun **1** a person or thing that carries, holds, or conveys something: *water carriers.* ■ Brit. a carrier bag: *a plastic carrier.*
2 a person or company that undertakes the professional conveyance of goods or people: *the instruments can be sent by carrier.* ■ a vessel or vehicle for transporting goods in bulk. ■ an aircraft carrier. ■ a company that provides facilities for conveying telecommunications messages.
3 a person or animal that transmits a disease-causing organism to others, especially without suffering from it themselves: *the badger is a carrier of bovine tuberculosis.* ■ an individual that possesses a particular gene, especially as a single copy whose effect is masked by a dominant allele, so that the associated characteristic (such as a hereditary disease) is not displayed but may be passed to offspring.
4 a substance used to support or convey another substance such as a pigment, catalyst, or radioactive material. ■ Physics short for CHARGE CARRIER. ■ Biochemistry a molecule that transfers a specified molecule or ion within the body, especially across a cell membrane.

carrier bag ▶ noun Brit. a plastic or paper bag with handles, especially one supplied by a shop to carry goods purchased there.

carrier pigeon ▶ noun a pigeon trained to carry messages tied to its neck or leg.

carrier shell ▶ noun a mollusc of warm seas which camouflages itself by cementing shell fragments and pebbles to its shell. ● Family Xenophoridae, class Gastropoda: *Xenophora* and other genera.

carrier wave ▶ noun a high-frequency electromagnetic wave modulated in amplitude or frequency to convey a signal.

Carrington /ˈkarɪŋtən/, Dora (de Houghton) (1893–1932), English painter, a member of the Bloomsbury Group.

carriole /ˈkarɪəʊl/ (also **cariole**) ▶ noun **1** historical a small open horse-drawn carriage for one person. ■ a light covered cart.
2 (in Canada) a kind of sledge pulled by a horse or dogs.
– ORIGIN mid 18th cent.: from French, from Italian *carriuola*, diminutive of *carro*, from Latin *carrum* (see CAR).

carrion ▶ noun [mass noun] the decaying flesh of dead animals.
– ORIGIN Middle English: from Anglo-Norman French and Old Northern French *caroine, caroigne*, Old French *charoigne*, based on Latin *caro* 'flesh'.

carrion beetle ▶ noun a beetle that feeds on decaying animal and plant matter. ● Family Silphidae: many species, including the burying beetles.

carrion crow ▶ noun a medium-sized, typically all-black crow which is common throughout much of Eurasia. ● *Corvus corone*, family Corvidae. See also HOODED CROW.

carrion flower ▶ noun another term for STAPELIA.

Carroll, Lewis (1832–98), English writer; pseudonym of *Charles Lutwidge Dodgson.* He wrote the children's classics *Alice's Adventures in Wonderland* (1865) and *Through the Looking Glass* (1871), which were inspired by Alice Liddell, the young daughter of the dean at the Oxford college where Carroll was a mathematics lecturer.

carronade /ˌkarəˈneɪd/ ▶ noun historical a short large-calibre cannon, formerly in naval use.
– ORIGIN late 18th cent.: from *Carron*, near Falkirk in Scotland, where this kind of cannon was first made.

carrot ▶ noun **1** a tapering orange-coloured root eaten as a vegetable.
2 a cultivated plant of the parsley family with feathery leaves, which yields carrots. ● *Daucus carota*, family Umbelliferae: two subspecies and many varieties; wild forms lack the swollen root.
3 an offer of something enticing as a means of persuasion (often contrasted with the threat of something punitive or unwelcome): *carrots will promote cooperation over the environment far more effectively than sticks.* Compare with STICK[1] (sense 3). [with allusion to the proverbial encouragement of a donkey to move by enticing it with a carrot.]
4 (**carrots**) informal, chiefly derogatory a nickname for a red-haired person.
– ORIGIN late 15th cent.: from French *carotte*, from Latin *carota*, from Greek *karōton*.

carrot-and-stick ▶ adjective (of a method of persuasion or coercion) characterized by both the offer of reward and the threat of punishment: *a carrot-and-stick approach.*

carrot fly ▶ noun a small fly whose larvae are a widespread pest of carrots, burrowing into the roots. ● *Psila rosae*, family Psilidae.

carroty ▶ adjective (of a person's hair) orange-red in colour.

carry ▶ verb (**carries, carrying, carried**) [with obj.]
1 support and move (someone or something) from one place to another: *medics were carrying a wounded man on a stretcher.* ■ transport, conduct or transmit: *the train service carries 20,000 passengers daily | nerves carry visual information from the eyes.* ■ have on one's person: *he was killed for the money he was carrying* | figurative *she had carried the secret all her life.* ■ be infected with (a disease) and liable to transmit it to others: *ticks can carry a nasty disease which affects humans.*
2 support the weight of: *the bridge is capable of carrying even the heaviest loads.* ■ be pregnant with: *she was carrying twins.*
3 [no obj.] (of a sound, ball, missile, etc.) reach a specified point: *his voice carried clearly across the room | the ball* ***carried to*** *second slip.* ■ [with obj.] (of a gun or similar weapon) propel (a missile) to a specified distance. ■ [with obj.] take or develop (an idea or activity) to a specified point: *he carried the criticism much further.*
4 assume or accept (responsibility or blame): *they must carry management responsibility for the mess they have got the company into.* ■ be responsible for the effectiveness of: *they relied on dialogue to carry the plot.*
5 (**carry oneself**) stand and move in a specified way: *she carried herself straight and with assurance.*
6 have as a feature or consequence: *being a combat sport, karate* ***carries with it*** *the risk of injury | each bike carries a ten-year guarantee.* ■ (of a newspaper or a television or radio station) publish or broadcast: *the paper carried a detailed account of the current crisis.* ■ (of a shop) keep a regular stock of (goods for sale): *550 off-licences carry the basic range.* ■ be known or marked by: *the product does not carry the swallow symbol.*
7 approve (a proposed measure) by a majority of votes: *the resolution was carried by a two-to-one majority.* ■ persuade (others) to support one's policy: *he could not carry the cabinet.* ■ N. Amer. gain (a state or district) in an election.
8 transfer (a figure) to an adjacent column during an arithmetical operation (e.g. when a column of digit adds up to more than ten).
▶ noun (pl. **carries**) [usu. in sing.] **1** an act of carrying something from one place to another. ■ American Football an act of running or rushing with the ball. ■ [mass noun] N. Amer. the action of keeping a gun on one's person: *this pistol is the right choice for on-duty or off-duty carry.* ■ N. Amer. historical a place between navigable waters over which boats or supplies had to be carried. ■ the transfer of a figure into an adjacent column (or the equivalent part of a computer memory) during an arithmetical operation.
2 the range of a gun or similar weapon. ■ Golf the distance a ball travels before reaching the ground.
3 Finance the maintenance of an investment position in a securities market, especially with regard to the costs or profits accruing.
– PHRASES **carry all before one** overcome all opposition. **carry one's bat** Cricket (of an opening or high-order batsman) be not out at the end of a side's completed innings. **carry the can** Brit. informal take responsibility for a mistake or misdeed. **carry the day** be victorious or successful. **carry weight** be influential: *the report is expected to carry considerable* ***weight with*** *the administration.*
– PHRASAL VERBS **be/get carried away** lose self-control: *I got a bit carried away when describing his dreadful season.* **carry something away** Nautical lose a mast or other part of a ship through breakage. **carry something forward** transfer figures to a new page or account. ■ keep something to use or deal with at a later time: *we carried forward a reserve which allowed us to meet demands.* **carry someone/thing off** take someone or something away by force. ■ (of a medical condition) kill someone: *Parkinson's disease carried him off in September.* **carry something off** win a prize: *she failed to carry off the gold medal.* ■ succeed in doing something difficult: *he could not have carried it off without government help.* **carry on 1** continue an activity or task: *you can* ***carry on with*** *a sport as long as you feel comfortable | she carries on watching the telly.* ■ continue to move in the same direction: *I knew I was going the wrong way, but I just carried on.* **2** informal behave in a specified way: *they carry on in a very adult fashion.* ■ behave in an overemotional way. **3** informal be engaged in a love affair, typically one of which the speaker disapproves: *she was* ***carrying on with*** *young Adam.* **carry something on** engage in an activity: *he could not carry on a logical conversation.* **carry something out** perform a task: *we're carrying out a market-research survey.* **carry something over** retain something and apply or deal with it in a new context: *much of the wartime economic planning was carried over into the peace.* ■ postpone an event: *the match had to be carried over till Sunday.* ■ another way of saying CARRY SOMETHING FORWARD. **carry something through** bring a project to completion.
– ORIGIN late Middle English: from Anglo-Norman French and Old Northern French *carier*, based on Latin *carrus* 'wheeled vehicle'.

carryall ▶ noun **1** N. Amer. a large bag or case.
2 historical a light carriage. [early 18th cent.: apparently altered by folk etymology from French *carriole*, denoting a small covered carriage.] ■ US a large car or truck with seats facing each other along the sides.

carrycot ▶ noun Brit. a small portable bed for a baby.

carrying capacity ▶ noun [mass noun] the number or quantity of people or things which can be conveyed by a vehicle or container. ■ Ecology the number of people, animals, or crops which a region can support without environmental degradation.

carrying charge ▶ noun **1** Finance, chiefly N. Amer. an expense or effective cost arising from unproductive assets such as stored goods or unoccupied premises.
2 a sum payable for the conveyance of goods.

carrying trade ▶ noun the business of transporting commercial goods from one place to another by land, sea, or air.

carry-on ▶ noun [usu. in sing.] Brit. informal a display of excitement or fuss over an unimportant matter: *I never saw such a carry-on!* ■ (also **carryings-on**) questionable behaviour, typically involving sexual impropriety: *the sort of carry-on that goes on behind the chintz curtains of suburbia.*
▶ adjective (of a bag or suitcase) suitable for taking on to an aircraft as handheld luggage.

carry-out ▶ adjective & noun chiefly Scottish & US another term for TAKEAWAY.

carry-over ▶ noun [usu. in sing.] something transferred or resulting from a previous situation: *the slow trading was a carry-over from the big losses of last week.*

carse /kɑːs/ ▶ noun [mass noun] Scottish fertile lowland beside a river.
– ORIGIN Middle English: perhaps an alteration of *carrs*, plural of CARR.

carsick ▶ adjective affected with nausea caused by the motion of a car or other vehicle in which one is travelling.
– DERIVATIVES **carsickness** noun.

Carson, Rachel (Louise) (1907–64), American zoologist, a pioneer ecologist and popularizer of science. She is noted especially for *The Sea Around Us* (1951) and *Silent Spring* (1963), an attack on the indiscriminate use of pesticides.

Carson City the state capital of Nevada; pop. 54,867 (est. 2008).

cart ▶ noun a strong open vehicle with two or four wheels, typically used for carrying loads and pulled by a horse: *a horse and cart.* ■ a shallow open container on wheels that may be pulled or pushed by hand. ■ (also **shopping cart**) N. Amer. a supermarket trolley.

▸ **verb** [with obj.] **1** convey or put in a cart or similar vehicle: *the meat was pickled in salt and carted to El Paso.*
2 [with obj. and adverbial of direction] informal carry (a heavy or cumbersome object) somewhere with difficulty: *they carted the piano down three flights of stairs.* ■ remove or convey (someone) somewhere unceremoniously: *they were carted off to the nearest police station.* ■ Cricket hit (the ball) with a powerful stroke that sends it a long way.
– PHRASES **in the cart** Brit. informal in trouble or difficulty. **put the cart before the horse** reverse the proper order or procedure of something.
– DERIVATIVES **carter** noun, **cartful** noun (pl. **cartfuls**).
– ORIGIN Middle English: from Old Norse *kartr*, probably influenced by Anglo-Norman French and Old Northern French *carete*, diminutive of *carre* (see CAR).

cartage ▸ **noun** [mass noun] the conveyance of something in a cart or other vehicle.

Cartagena /ˌkɑːtəˈdʒiːnə/, Spanish /kartaˈxena/ **1** a port in SE Spain; pop. 210,376 (2008). Originally named Mastia, it was refounded as Carthago Nova (New Carthage) by Hasdrubal in *c.*225 BC, as a base for the Carthaginian conquest of Spain.
2 a port, resort, and oil-refining centre in NW Colombia, on the Caribbean Sea; pop. 885,400 (2005).

carte ▸ **noun** variant spelling of QUART (sense 2).

carte blanche /kɑːt ˈblɑːnʃ/ ▸ **noun 1** [mass noun] complete freedom to act as one wishes: *the architect given carte blanche to design the store.*
2 (in piquet) a hand containing no court cards as dealt.
– ORIGIN late 17th cent.: French, literally 'blank paper' (i.e. a blank sheet on which to write whatever one wishes, particularly one's own terms for an agreement).

carte de visite /ˌkɑːt də vɪˈziːt/ ▸ **noun** (pl. **cartes de visite** pronunc. **same**) historical a small photographic portrait of a person, mounted on a piece of card.
– ORIGIN mid 19th cent.: French, 'visiting card'.

cartel /kɑːˈtɛl/ ▸ **noun** an association of manufacturers or suppliers with the purpose of maintaining prices at a high level and restricting competition: *the Columbian drug cartels.*
– ORIGIN late 19th cent.: from German *Kartell*, from French *cartel*, from Italian *cartello*, diminutive of *carta*, from Latin *carta* (see CARD[1]). It was originally used to refer to the coalition of the Conservatives and National Liberal parties in Germany (1887), and hence any political combination; later to denote a trade agreement (early 20th cent.).

cartelize /kɑːˈtɛlʌɪz, ˈkɑːtəlʌɪz/ (also **cartelise**) ▸ **verb** [with obj.] (of manufacturers or suppliers) form a cartel in (an industry or trade).

Carter[1], Elliott (Cook) (b.1908), American composer. He is noted for his innovative approach to metre and his choice of sources as diverse as modern jazz and Renaissance madrigals.

Carter[2], Howard (1874–1939), English archaeologist. In 1922, while excavating in the Valley of the Kings at Thebes, he discovered the tomb of Tutankhamen.

Carter[3], Jimmy (b.1924), American Democratic statesman, 39th President of the US 1977–81; full name *James Earl Carter*. He hosted the talks which led to the Camp David agreements (1978) and was awarded the Nobel Peace Prize in 2002.

Cartesian /kɑːˈtiːzɪən, -ʒ(ə)n/ ▸ **adjective** relating to Descartes and his ideas.
▸ **noun** a follower of Descartes.
– DERIVATIVES **Cartesianism** noun.
– ORIGIN mid 17th cent.: from modern Latin *Cartesianus*, from *Cartesius*, Latinized form of the name of *Descartes*.

Cartesian coordinates ▸ **plural noun** numbers which indicate the location of a point relative to a fixed reference point (the origin), being its shortest (perpendicular) distances from two fixed axes (or three planes defined by three fixed axes) which intersect at right angles at the origin.

Carthage /ˈkɑːθɪdʒ/ an ancient city on the coast of North Africa near present-day Tunis. Founded by the Phoenicians *c.*814 BC, Carthage became a major force in the Mediterranean, and came into conflict with Rome in the Punic Wars. It was finally destroyed by the Romans in 146 BC.
– DERIVATIVES **Carthaginian** noun & adjective.

carthorse ▸ **noun** a large, strong horse suitable for heavy work.

Carthusian /kɑːˈθjuːzɪən/ ▸ **noun** a monk or nun of an austere contemplative order founded by St Bruno in 1084.
▸ **adjective** relating to the Carthusians.
– ORIGIN from medieval Latin *Carthusianus*, from *Cart(h)usia*, Latin name of *Chartreuse*, near Grenoble, where the order was founded.

Cartier /ˈkɑːtɪeɪ/, French /kartje/, Jacques (1491–1557), French explorer. The first to establish France's claim to North America, he made three voyages to Canada between 1534 and 1541.

Cartier-Bresson /ˌkɑːtɪeɪˈbrɛsɒ̃/, French /kaʀtjebʀɛsɔ̃/, Henri (1908–2004), French photographer and film director. He was noted for his collection of photographs *The Decisive Moment* (1952) and his documentary film about the Spanish Civil War, *Return to Life* (1937).

Cartier Islands see ASHMORE AND CARTIER ISLANDS.

cartilage /ˈkɑːt(ɪ)lɪdʒ/ ▸ **noun** [mass noun] firm, flexible connective tissue found in various forms in the larynx and respiratory tract, in structures such as the external ear, and in the articulating surfaces of joints. It is more widespread in the infant skeleton, being replaced by bone during growth. ■ [count noun] a particular structure made of cartilage.
– ORIGIN late Middle English: from French, from Latin *cartilago, cartilagin-*.

cartilaginous /ˌkɑːtɪˈladʒɪnəs/ ▸ **adjective** Anatomy made of cartilage. ■ Zoology (of a vertebrate animal) having a skeleton of cartilage.
– ORIGIN late Middle English: from Old French, or from Latin *cartilaginosus*, from *cartilago, cartilagin-* 'cartilage'.

cartilaginous fish ▸ **noun** a fish of a class distinguished by having a skeleton of cartilage rather than bone, including the sharks, rays, and chimaeras. Compare with BONY FISH. ● Class Chondrichthyes: subclasses Elasmobranchii (sharks and rays) and Hoplocephali (chimaeras).

cartload ▸ **noun** the amount held by a cart. ■ informal a large quantity or number of people or things: *drunken yobbos who turned up by the cartload.*

cartogram /ˈkɑːtəgram/ ▸ **noun** a map on which statistical information is shown in diagrammatic form.
– ORIGIN late 19th cent.: from French *cartogramme*, from *carte* 'map or card' + *-gramme* (from Greek *gramma* 'thing written').

cartography /kɑːˈtɒgrəfi/ ▸ **noun** [mass noun] the science or practice of drawing maps.
– DERIVATIVES **cartographer** noun, **cartographic** adjective, **cartographical** adjective, **cartographically** adverb.
– ORIGIN mid 19th cent.: from French *cartographie*, from *carte* 'map, card' (see CARD[1]) + *-graphie* (see -GRAPHY).

cartomancy /ˈkɑːtə(ʊ)ˌmansi/ ▸ **noun** [mass noun] fortune telling by interpreting a random selection of playing cards.
– DERIVATIVES **cartomancer** noun.
– ORIGIN late 19th cent.: from French *cartomancie*, from *carte* 'card' + *-mancie* (see -MANCY).

carton ▸ **noun** a small, light box or container in which drinks or foodstuffs are packaged. ■ N. Amer. a large container of goods.
– ORIGIN early 19th cent.: from French, from Italian *cartone* (see CARTOON).

cartonnage /ˈkɑːt(ə)nɪdʒ/ ▸ **noun** an ancient Egyptian mummy case made of tightly fitting layers of linen or papyrus glued together.
– ORIGIN mid 19th cent.: French.

cartoon ▸ **noun 1** a simple drawing showing the features of its subjects in a humorously exaggerated way, especially a satirical one in a newspaper or magazine. ■ (also **cartoon strip**) a narrative sequence of humorous drawings in a comic, magazine, or newspaper, usually with captions. ■ a simplified or exaggerated version or interpretation of something: [as modifier] *Dolores becomes a cartoon housewife, reading glossy magazines in a bathrobe.*
2 a film using animation techniques to photograph a sequence of drawings rather than real people or objects.
3 a full-size drawing made by an artist as a preliminary design for a painting or other work of art.
▸ **verb** [with obj.] make a drawing of (someone) in a simplified or exaggerated way. ■ (as noun **cartooning**) the activity or occupation of drawing cartoons.
– DERIVATIVES **cartoonish** adjective, **cartoonist** noun, **cartoony** adjective.
– ORIGIN late 16th cent. (in sense 3 of the noun): from Italian *cartone*, from *carta*, from Latin *carta, charta* (see CARD[1]). Sense 1 of the noun dates from the mid 19th cent.

cartophily /kɑːˈtɒfɪli/ ▸ **noun** [mass noun] the collecting of picture cards, such as postcards or cigarette cards, as a hobby.
– ORIGIN 1930s: from French *carte* or Italian *carta* 'card' + -PHILY.

cartouche /kɑːˈtuːʃ/ ▸ **noun 1** a carved tablet or drawing representing a scroll with rolled-up ends, used ornamentally or bearing an inscription. ■ a decorative architectural feature, such as a modillion or corbel, resembling a scroll.
2 an ornate frame around a design or inscription. ■ Archaeology an oval or oblong enclosing a group of Egyptian hieroglyphs, typically representing the name and title of a monarch.
– ORIGIN early 17th cent.: from French *cartouche* (masculine noun), earlier *cartoche*, from Italian *cartoccio*, from *carta*, from Latin *carta, charta* (see CARD[1]).

cartridge ▸ **noun** a container holding a spool of photographic film, a quantity of ink, etc., designed for insertion into a mechanism. ■ a casing containing a charge and a bullet or shot for small arms or an explosive charge for blasting. ■ a component carrying the stylus on the pickup head of a record player.
– ORIGIN late 16th cent.: from French *cartouche* (feminine noun), from Italian *cartoccio* (see CARTOUCHE).

cartridge belt ▸ **noun** a belt with pockets or loops for cartridges of ammunition.

cartridge paper ▸ **noun** [mass noun] Brit. thick, rough-textured paper used for drawing and for strong envelopes.
– ORIGIN mid 17th cent.: originally used to make cartridge cases.

cartwheel ▸ **noun 1** the wheel of a cart.
2 a circular sideways handspring with the arms and legs extended.
▸ **verb** [no obj., with adverbial of direction] perform a cartwheel or cartwheels: *he cartwheeled across the room.*

Cartwright, Edmund (1743–1823), English engineer, inventor of the power loom.

cartwright ▸ **noun** chiefly historical a person whose job is making carts.

caruncle /ˈkarəŋk(ə)l, kəˈrʌŋ-/ ▸ **noun 1** a wattle of a bird such as a turkeycock.
2 the red prominence at the inner corner of the eye.
3 Botany a coloured waxy or oily outgrowth from a seed near the micropyle, attractive to ants which aid the seed's dispersal.
– DERIVATIVES **caruncular** adjective.
– ORIGIN late 16th cent.: obsolete French, from Latin *caruncula*, from *caro, carn-* 'flesh'.

Caruso /kəˈruːzəʊ, -səʊ/, Italian /kaˈruso/, Enrico (1873–1921), Italian operatic tenor. He was the first major tenor to be recorded on gramophone records.

carve ▸ **verb** [with obj.] **1** cut (a hard material) in order to produce an object, design, or inscription: *the wood was carved with runes* | (as adj. **carved**) *bookcases of carved oak.* ■ produce (an object, inscription, or design) by cutting into a hard material: *the altar was carved from a block of solid jade* | *I carved my initials on the tree.*
2 cut (cooked meat) into slices for eating. ■ cut (a slice of meat) from a larger piece.
3 Skiing make (a turn) by tilting one's skis on to their edges and using one's weight to bend them so that they slide in an arc.
– PHRASES **be carved on tablets of stone** see STONE.
– PHRASAL VERBS **carve something out 1** take something from a larger whole, especially with difficulty: *the company hopes to carve out a greater share of the $20 bn market.* **2** establish or create something through painstaking effort: *he managed to carve out a successful photographic career for himself.* **carve someone up** informal **1** slash someone with a knife or other sharp object. **2** drive aggressively into the path of another driver while overtaking. **carve something up** divide something ruthlessly into separate areas or parts: *West Africa was carved up by the Europeans.*
– ORIGIN Old English *ceorfan* 'cut, carve', of West Germanic origin; related to Dutch *kerven*.

carvel /ˈkɑːv(ə)l/ ▸ **noun** variant spelling of CARAVEL.

carvel-built ▸ **adjective** (of a boat) having external planks which do not overlap. Compare with CLINKER-BUILT.

carven archaic past participle of CARVE.

carver ▶ noun **1** a person who carves a hard material professionally: *an ivory carver*.
2 a knife designed for slicing meat. ■ (**carvers**) a knife and fork for slicing meat.
3 a person who cuts and serves the meat at a meal. ■ Brit. the principal chair, with arms, in a set of dining chairs, intended for the person carving meat.

carvery ▶ noun (pl. **carveries**) Brit. a buffet or restaurant where cooked joints are displayed and carved as required in front of customers.

carve-up ▶ noun [in sing.] Brit. informal a ruthless division of something into separate areas or parts: *the carve-up of the brewing industry by vested interests*.

carving ▶ noun [mass noun] the action of carving. ■ [count noun] an object or design carved from a hard material as an artistic work.

carving knife ▶ noun a knife with a long blade used for carving cooked meat into slices.

car wash ▶ noun a building containing equipment for washing vehicles automatically.

caryatid /ˌkarɪˈatɪd/ ▶ noun (pl. **caryatides** /-diːz/ or **caryatids**) Architecture a stone carving of a draped female figure, used as a pillar to support the entablature of a Greek or Greek-style building.
– ORIGIN mid 16th cent.: via French and Italian from Latin *caryatides*, from Greek *karuatides*, plural of *karuatis* 'priestess of Artemis at Caryae', from *Karuai* (Caryae) in Laconia.

caryophyllaceous /ˌkarɪə(ʊ)fɪˈleɪʃəs/ ▶ adjective Botany relating to or denoting plants of the pink family (Caryophyllaceae).
– ORIGIN mid 19th cent.: from modern Latin *Caryophyllaceae* (plural), based on Greek *karuophullon* 'clove pink', + **-ous**.

caryopsis /ˌkarɪˈɒpsɪs/ ▶ noun (pl. **caryopses** /-siːz/) Botany a dry one-seeded fruit in which the ovary wall is united with the seed coat, typical of grasses and cereals.
– ORIGIN early 19th cent.: from modern Latin, from Greek *karuon* 'nut' + *opsis* 'appearance'.

casaba /kəˈsɑːbə/ ▶ noun N. Amer. a winter melon of a variety with a wrinkled yellow rind and sweet flesh. ■ (**casabas**) informal a woman's breasts.
– ORIGIN early 20th cent.: named after *Kasaba* (now Turgutlu) in Turkey, from which the melons were first exported.

Casablanca /ˌkasəˈblaŋkə/ the largest city of Morocco, a seaport on the Atlantic coast; pop. 2,949,805 (2004).

Casals /kəˈsalz/, Pablo (1876–1973), Spanish cellist, conductor, and composer. He was noted especially for his performances of Bach suites and the Dvořák Cello Concerto.

Casanova /ˌkasəˈnəʊvə, -z-/, Giovanni Jacopo (1725–98), Italian adventurer; full name *Giovanni Jacopo Casanova de Seingalt*. He is famous for his memoirs describing his sexual encounters and other exploits. ■ (as noun usu. **a Casanova**) a man notorious for seducing women.

casbah ▶ noun variant spelling of **KASBAH**.

cascabel /ˈkaskəb(ə)l/ ▶ noun a small red chilli pepper of a mild-flavoured variety.
– ORIGIN mid 17th cent.: from Spanish, from Catalan *cascavel*, from medieval Latin *cascabellus* 'little bell'.

cascade ▶ noun **1** a small waterfall, typically one of several that fall in stages down a steep rocky slope. ■ a mass of something that falls or hangs in copious quantities: *a cascade of pink bougainvillea*. ■ a large number or amount of something occurring at the same time: *a cascade of anti-war literature*.
2 a process whereby something, typically information or knowledge, is successively passed on. ■ a succession of devices or stages in a process, each of which triggers or initiates the next.
▶ verb **1** [no obj., with adverbial of direction] (of water) pour downwards rapidly and in large quantities: *water was* ***cascading down*** *the stairs*. ■ fall or hang in copious quantities: *blonde hair* ***cascaded down*** *her back*.
2 [with obj.] pass (something) on to a succession of others: *teachers who are able to cascade their experience effectively*.
3 [with obj.] arrange (a number of devices or objects) in a series or sequence.
– ORIGIN mid 17th cent.: from French, from Italian *cascata*, from *cascare* 'to fall', based on Latin *casus* (see **CASE¹**).

Cascade Range a range of volcanic mountains in western North America, extending from southern British Columbia through Washington and Oregon to northern California.

cascara /kasˈkɑːrə/ (also **cascara sagrada** /səˈgrɑːdə/) ▶ noun **1** [mass noun] a purgative made from the dried bark of an American buckthorn.
2 the tree from which cascara is obtained, native to western North America. ● *Rhamnus purshiana*, family Rhamnaceae.
– ORIGIN late 19th cent.: from Spanish *cáscara (sagrada)*, literally '(sacred) bark'.

case¹ ▶ noun **1** an instance of a particular situation; an example of something occurring: *a case of mistaken identity* | ***in many cases*** *farmers do have a deep feeling for their land*. ■ [usu. in sing.] the situation affecting or relating to a particular person or thing: *I'll make an exception* ***in your case***. ■ an incident or set of circumstances under official investigation by the police: *a murder case*.
2 an instance of a disease, injury, or problem: *200,000 cases of hepatitis B*. ■ a person or their particular problem requiring or receiving medical or welfare attention: *most breast cancer cases were older women* | *the local social services discussed Gemma's case*. ■ [with adj. or noun modifier] informal a person whose situation is regarded as pitiable or as having no chance of improvement: *Vicky was a very* ***sad case***. ■ informal, dated an amusing or eccentric person.
3 a legal action, especially one to be decided in a court of law: *a libel case* | *a former employee brought the case against the council*. ■ a set of facts or arguments supporting one side in a legal case: *the case for the defence*. ■ a set of facts or arguments supporting one side of a debate or controversy: *the* ***case against*** *tobacco advertising*. ■ (also **case stated**) an agreed summary of the facts relating to a legal case, drawn up for review or decision on a point of law by a higher court.
4 Grammar any of the forms of a noun, adjective, or pronoun that express the semantic relation of the word to other words in the sentence: *the accusative case*.
– PHRASES **as the case may be** according to the circumstances (used when referring to two or more alternatives): *the authorities will decide if they are satisfied or not satisfied, as the case may be*. **be the case** be so. **in any case** whatever happens or may have happened. ■ moreover: *he wasn't allowed out yet, and in any case he wasn't well enough*. (**just**) **in case 1** as a provision against something happening or being true: *we put on thick jumpers, in case it was cold*. **2** if it is true that: *in case you haven't figured it out, let me explain*. **in case of** in the event of (a particular situation): *instructions about what to do in case of fire*. **in no case** under no circumstances: *in no case is a specific funding target set*. **in that case** if that is or will be the situation: *'I'm free this evening.' 'In that case, why not have dinner with me?'* **it's a case of ——** used to introduce a summary of a particular situation, especially one that is unavoidable under the circumstances: *it's not a case of wanting to return to work but having to*. **on** (or **off**) **someone's case** informal continually (or no longer) criticizing or harassing someone: *teachers, you know,* ***get on your case***.
– ORIGIN Middle English: from Old French *cas*, from Latin *casus* 'fall', related to *cadere* 'to fall'; in sense 4 directly from Latin, translating Greek *ptôsis*, literally 'fall'.

case² ▶ noun **1** a container designed to hold or protect something: *a silver cigarette case*. ■ the outer protective covering of a natural or manufactured object: *a seed case*. ■ an item of luggage; a suitcase. ■ a box containing twelve bottles of wine or other drink, sold as a unit: *a case of champagne*.
2 each of the two forms, capital or minuscule, in which a letter of the alphabet may be written or printed. See also **UPPER CASE, LOWER CASE**. [from the use in printing to mean 'partitioned container for loose metal type'.]
▶ verb [with obj.] **1** surround in a material or substance: *the towers are of steel* ***cased in*** *granite*. ■ enclose in a protective container: (as adj. **cased**) *a cased pair of pistols*.
2 informal reconnoitre (a place) before carrying out a robbery: *I was* ***casing the joint***.
– ORIGIN late Middle English: from Old French *casse*, *chasse* (modern *caisse* 'trunk, chest', *châsse* 'reliquary, frame'), from Latin *capsa*, related to *capere* 'to hold'.

caseation /ˌkeɪsɪˈeɪʃ(ə)n/ ▶ noun [mass noun] Medicine a condition characteristic of tuberculosis, in which diseased tissue forms a firm, dry mass like cheese in appearance.
– ORIGIN mid 19th cent.: from medieval Latin *caseatio(n-)*, from Latin *caseus* 'cheese'.

casebook ▶ noun a written record of cases dealt with, especially one kept by a doctor or investigator. ■ a book containing extracts of important legal cases. ■ US a book containing a selection of source materials on a particular subject, used as a reference work or in teaching.

casebound ▶ adjective (of a book) hardback.

case conference ▶ noun a meeting of professionals such as teachers or social workers to discuss a particular case.

case-hardened ▶ adjective (of a material) having a hard surface. ■ (of iron or steel) having been given a hard surface by being carburized. ■ made callous or tough by experience: *a case-hardened politician*.
– DERIVATIVES **case-harden** verb.

case history ▶ noun a record of a person's background or medical history kept by a doctor or social worker.

casein /ˈkeɪsiːn, -sɪɪn/ ▶ noun [mass noun] the main protein present in milk and (in coagulated form) in cheese. It is used in processed foods and in adhesives, paints, and other industrial products.
– ORIGIN mid 19th cent.: from Latin *caseus* 'cheese' + **-IN¹**.

case knife ▶ noun archaic a type of dagger carried in a sheath.

case law ▶ noun [mass noun] the law as established by the outcome of former cases. Compare with **COMMON LAW, STATUTE LAW**.

caseload ▶ noun the number of cases with which a doctor, lawyer, or social worker is concerned at one time.

casemate /ˈkeɪsmeɪt/ ▶ noun **1** historical a small room in the wall of a fortress, with openings from which guns or missiles could be fired.
2 an armoured enclosure for guns on a warship.
– ORIGIN mid 16th cent.: from French, from Italian *casamatta*, perhaps from Greek *khasma*, *khasmat-* (see **CHASM**).

Casement, Sir Roger (David) (1864–1916), Irish diplomat and nationalist. In 1914 he sought German support for an Irish uprising, and was subsequently hanged by the British for treason.

casement ▶ noun a window or part of a window set on a vertical hinge so that it opens like a door. ■ literary a window of any kind. ■ the sash of a sash window.
– ORIGIN late Middle English (as an architectural term denoting a hollow moulding): from Anglo-Latin *cassimentum*, from *cassa*, from Latin *capsa* (see **CASE²**).

caseous /ˈkeɪsɪəs/ ▶ adjective Medicine characterized by caseation.
– ORIGIN mid 17th cent.: from Latin *caseus* 'cheese' + **-OUS**.

case-sensitive ▶ adjective (of a computer program or function) differentiating between capital and lower-case letters.

case-shot ▶ noun [mass noun] historical bullets or pieces of metal in an iron case fired from a cannon.

case stated ▶ noun see **CASE¹** (sense 3).

case study ▶ noun **1** a process or record of research into the development of a particular person, group, or situation over a period of time.
2 a particular instance of something used or analysed in order to illustrate a thesis or principle: *airline deregulation provides a case study of the effects of the internal market*.

casevac /ˈkazɪvak, ˈkaʒɪ-/ military slang ▶ noun [mass noun] evacuation of casualties by air.
▶ verb (**casevacs, casevacing, casevaced**) [with obj.] evacuate (a casualty) by air.
– ORIGIN 1950s: blend of **CASUALTY** and **EVACUATION**.

casework¹ ▶ noun [mass noun] social work directly concerned with individuals, especially that involving a study of a person's family history and personal circumstances.
– DERIVATIVES **caseworker** noun.

casework² ▶ noun [mass noun] the decorative outer case protecting the workings of a complex mechanism such as an organ or harpsichord.

Cash, Johnny (b.1932), American country music singer and songwriter. Notable songs: 'I Walk the Line' (1956) and 'A Boy Named Sue' (1969).

cash¹ ▶ noun [mass noun] money in coins or notes, as distinct from cheques, money orders, or credit: *the staff were paid in cash* | *a discount for cash*. ■ money in any form: *she was always short of cash*.

▶ **verb** [with obj.] **1** give or obtain notes or coins for (a cheque or money order): *the bank cashed her cheque.* **2** Bridge lead (a high card) so as to take the opportunity to win a trick.
– PHRASES **cash and carry** a system of wholesale trading whereby goods are paid for in full at the time of purchase and taken away by the purchaser. ■ a wholesale store operating the cash-and-carry system. **cash in one's chips** informal die. [with reference to gambling in a casino.] **cash in hand** Brit. payment for goods and services in cash rather than by cheque or other means, typically as a way of avoiding the payment of tax on the amount earned: [as modifier] *a cash-in-hand job.* **cash on delivery** the system of paying for goods when they are delivered.
– PHRASAL VERBS **cash in** informal take advantage of or exploit (a situation): *the breweries were cashing in on the rediscovered taste for real ales.* **cash something in** (or N. Amer. **cash out**) convert an insurance policy, savings account, or other investment into money: *hundreds of savers cashed in their investments.* **cash up** (or N. Amer. **cash out**) count and check takings at the end of a day's trading: *two staff were cashing up at one of the tills.*
– DERIVATIVES **cashable** adjective.
– ORIGIN late 16th cent. (denoting a box for money): from Old French *casse* or Italian *cassa* 'box', from Latin *capsa* (see CASE[2]).

cash[2] ▶ **noun** (pl. **same**) historical a coin of low value from China, southern India, or SE Asia.
– ORIGIN late 16th cent.: from Portuguese *caixa*, from Tamil *kāsu*, influenced by CASH[1].

cashback ▶ **noun** a form of incentive offered to buyers of certain products whereby they receive a cash refund after making their purchase. ■ a facility offered by some retailers whereby the customer may withdraw cash when making a debit card purchase.

cash bar ▶ **noun** a bar at a social function at which guests buy drinks rather than having them provided free.

cash book ▶ **noun** a book in which receipts and payments of money are recorded.

cash box ▶ **noun** a metal box with a lock for keeping cash in.

cash card ▶ **noun** Brit. a plastic card issued by a bank or building society which enables the holder to withdraw money from a cash machine.

cash cow ▶ **noun** informal a business, investment, or product that provides a steady income or profit.

cash crop ▶ **noun** a crop produced for its commercial value rather than for use by the grower.
– DERIVATIVES **cash cropping** noun.

cash desk ▶ **noun** Brit. a counter or compartment in a shop or restaurant where payments are made.

cashew /ˈkaʃuː, kəˈʃuː/ ▶ **noun 1** (also **cashew nut**) an edible kidney-shaped nut, rich in oil and protein, which is roasted and shelled before it can be eaten. Oil extracted from the shells is used as a lubricant, in the production of plastics, etc.
2 (also **cashew tree**) a bushy tropical American tree related to the mango, bearing cashew nuts singly at the tip of each swollen fruit. Also called ACAJOU. ● *Anacardium occidentale*, family Anacardiaceae.
– ORIGIN late 16th cent.: from Portuguese, from Tupi *acajú, cajú*.

cashew apple ▶ **noun** the swollen edible fruit of the cashew tree, from which the cashew nut hangs, sometimes used to make wine.

cash flow ▶ **noun** the total amount of money being transferred into and out of a business, especially as affecting liquidity.

cashier[1] ▶ **noun** a person handling payments and receipts in a shop, bank, or business.
– ORIGIN late 16th cent.: from Dutch *cassier* or French *caissier*, from *caisse* 'cash'.

cashier[2] ▶ **verb** [with obj.] dismiss (someone) from the armed forces in disgrace because of a serious misdemeanour. ■ informal suspend or dismiss from an office or position: *the team owner had been cashiered for consorting with a gambler.*
– ORIGIN late 16th cent. (in the sense 'dismiss or disband troops'): from Flemish *kasseren* 'disband (troops)' or 'revoke (a will)', from French *casser* 'revoke, dismiss', from Latin *quassare* (see QUASH).

cashless ▶ **adjective** characterized by the exchange of funds by cheque, debit or credit card, or electronic methods rather than the use of cash: *the age of the cashless society.*

cash machine (Brit. also **cash dispenser**, trademark **cashpoint**) ▶ **noun** another term for AUTOMATED TELLER MACHINE.

cashmere ▶ **noun** [mass noun] fine, soft wool, originally that from the Kashmir goat. ■ woollen material made from or resembling cashmere: [as modifier] *a cashmere jumper.*
– ORIGIN late 17th cent.: an early spelling of KASHMIR.

cash nexus ▶ **noun** the relationship constituted by monetary transactions.

cash ratio ▶ **noun** the ratio of the liquid assets of a company to its current liabilities. ■ the ratio of cash to deposits in a bank (for which minimum values are generally set officially).

cash register ▶ **noun** a machine used in shops that has a drawer for money and totals, displays, and records the amount of each sale.

cash-strapped ▶ **adjective** informal extremely short of money: *cash-strapped consumers have gone deeper into debt.*

casing ▶ **noun 1** a cover or shell that protects or encloses something: *a waterproof casing.*
2 the frame round a door or window.

casino ▶ **noun** (pl. **casinos**) a public room or building where gambling games are played.
– ORIGIN mid 18th cent.: from Italian, diminutive of *casa* 'house', from Latin *casa* 'cottage'.

casita /kəˈsiːtə/ ▶ **noun** N. Amer. a small house or other building, especially a wooden cabin.
– ORIGIN early 19th cent.: from Spanish, diminutive of *casa* 'house'.

cask ▶ **noun** a large barrel-like container used for storing liquids, typically alcoholic drinks. ■ the quantity of liquid held in a cask: ***a cask of cider.***
– ORIGIN early 16th cent.: from French *casque* or Spanish *casco* 'helmet'. The current senses appear only in English; from the late 16th to the late 18th centuries the word also denoted a helmet (compare with CASQUE).

cask beer ▶ **noun** [mass noun] draught beer brewed and stored in the traditional way, maturing naturally in the cask from which it is served. Compare with KEG BEER.

cask-conditioned ▶ **adjective** (of beer) undergoing a secondary fermentation in the cask and not filtered, pasteurized, or further processed before serving.

casket ▶ **noun** a small ornamental box or chest for holding jewels, letters, or other valued objects. ■ Brit. a small wooden box for cremated ashes. ■ chiefly N. Amer. a coffin.
– ORIGIN late Middle English: perhaps an Anglo-Norman French form of Old French *cassette*, diminutive of *casse* (see CASE[2]).

Casnewydd /kasˈnewɪð/ Welsh name for NEWPORT.

Caspar /ˈkaspə, -pɑː/ one of the three Magi.

Caspian Sea /ˈkaspɪən/ a large landlocked salt lake, bounded by Russia, Kazakhstan, Turkmenistan, Azerbaijan, and Iran. It is the world's largest body of inland water with an area of about 371,800 sq. km (143,550 sq. miles). Its surface lies 28 m (92 ft) below sea level.

casque /kɑːsk/ ▶ **noun 1** historical a helmet.
2 Zoology a helmet-like structure, such as that on the bill of a hornbill or the head of a cassowary.
– ORIGIN late 17th cent.: from French, from Spanish *casco*. Compare with CASK.

Cassandra /kəˈsandrə/ Greek Mythology a daughter of the Trojan king Priam. She was given the gift of prophecy by Apollo, but when she cheated him, he turned this into a curse by causing her prophecies, though true, to be disbelieved. ■ (as noun **a Cassandra**) a prophet of disaster, especially one who is disregarded.

cassareep /ˈkasəriːp/ ▶ **noun** [mass noun] W. Indian a thick brown syrup made by boiling down the juice of grated cassava with sugar and spices, used as a flavouring for pepper pot (see PEPPER POT (sense 2)).
– ORIGIN from Arawak *casiripe*.

cassata /kəˈsɑːtə/ ▶ **noun** [mass noun] Neapolitan ice cream containing candied or dried fruit and nuts.
– ORIGIN 1920s: Italian.

cassation /kəˈseɪʃ(ə)n/ ▶ **noun** Music an informal instrumental composition of the 18th century, similar to a divertimento and often performed outdoors.
– ORIGIN late 19th cent.: from German *Kassation* 'serenade', from Italian *cassazione*.

cassava /kəˈsɑːvə/ ▶ **noun 1** [mass noun] the starchy tuberous root of a tropical tree, used as food in tropical countries. ■ starch or flour obtained from cassava. Also called MANIOC.
2 the shrubby tree from which cassava is obtained, native to tropical America and cultivated throughout the tropics. ● Genus *Manihot*, family Euphorbiaceae: several species.
– ORIGIN mid 16th cent.: from Taino *casávi, cazábbi*, influenced by French *cassave*.

Cassegrain telescope /ˈkasɪgreɪn/ ▶ **noun** a reflecting telescope in which light reflected from a convex secondary mirror passes through a hole in the primary mirror.
– ORIGIN late 19th cent.: named after N. *Cassegrain* (1625–1712), the French astronomer who devised it.

casserole ▶ **noun** a kind of stew that is cooked slowly in an oven: *a chicken casserole.* ■ a large covered dish used for cooking casseroles.
▶ **verb** [with obj.] cook (food) slowly in a casserole.
– ORIGIN early 18th cent.: from French, diminutive of *casse* 'spoon-like container', from Old Provençal *casa*, from late Latin *cattia* 'ladle, pan', from Greek *kuathion*, diminutive of *kuathos* 'cup'.

cassette ▶ **noun** a sealed plastic unit containing a length of audio tape, videotape, film, etc. wound on a pair of spools, for insertion into a recorder, playback device, or other machine.
– ORIGIN late 18th cent.: from French, diminutive of *casse* (see CASE[2]).

cassette tape ▶ **noun** a cassette of audio tape or videotape.

cassia /ˈkasɪə/ ▶ **noun 1** a tree, shrub, or herbaceous plant of the pea family, native to warm climates. Cassias yield a variety of products, including fodder, timber, and medicinal drugs (such as senna), and many are cultivated as ornamentals. ● Genus *Cassia*, family Leguminosae: many species.
2 (also **cassia bark**) [mass noun] the aromatic bark of an East Asian tree, yielding an inferior kind of cinnamon which is sometimes used to adulterate true cinnamon. ● *Cinnamomum aromaticum*, family Lauraceae.
– ORIGIN Old English (in sense 2), from Latin, probably denoting the wild cinnamon, via Greek from Hebrew *qĕṣīʿāh*.

Cassini[1] /kaˈsiːni/, Giovanni Domenico (1625–1712), Italian-born French astronomer. He discovered the gap in the rings of Saturn known as Cassini's division.

Cassini[2] a spacecraft launched in 1997 to explore Saturn and Titan, which it reached in 2004. It consists of an orbiter and a probe (see HUYGENS[2]).

Cassiopeia /ˌkasɪə(ʊ)ˈpiːə/ **1** Greek Mythology the wife of Cepheus, king of Ethiopia, and mother of Andromeda.
2 Astronomy a constellation near the north celestial pole, recognizable by the conspicuous 'W' pattern of its brightest stars.

cassis[1] /kaˈsiːs, ˈkasɪs/ (also **crème de cassis**) ▶ **noun** [mass noun] a syrupy blackcurrant liqueur produced mainly in Burgundy.
– ORIGIN French, 'blackcurrant', apparently from Latin *cassia* (see CASSIA).

cassis[2] /kaˈsi/ ▶ **noun** [mass noun] a wine produced in the region of Cassis, a small town near Marseilles.

cassiterite /kəˈsɪtərʌɪt/ ▶ **noun** [mass noun] a reddish, brownish, or yellowish mineral consisting of tin dioxide. It is the main ore of tin.
– ORIGIN mid 19th cent.: from Greek *kassiteros* 'tin' + -ITE[1].

Cassius /ˈkasɪəs/, Gaius (d.42 BC), Roman general; full name *Gaius Cassius Longinus*. He was one of the leaders of the conspiracy in 44 BC to assassinate Julius Caesar.

cassock ▶ **noun** a full-length garment worn by certain Christian clergy, members of church choirs, and others having an office or role in a church.
– DERIVATIVES **cassocked** adjective.
– ORIGIN mid 16th cent.: from French *casaque* 'long coat', from Italian *casacca* 'riding coat', probably from Turkic *kazak* 'vagabond'. Compare with COSSACK.

cassone /kaˈsəʊne, -ni/ ▶ **noun** (pl. **cassones** /-nɪz/ or **cassoni** /-ni/) (in Italy) a large chest, especially one used to hold a bride's trousseau.
– ORIGIN late 19th cent.: Italian, 'large chest'.

cassoulet /ˈkasʊleɪ/ ▶ **noun** [mass noun] a French stew made with meat (typically pork, goose, and duck) and beans.
– ORIGIN French, diminutive of dialect *cassolo* 'stew pan', from Old Provençal *cassa* 'pan'; related to CASSEROLE.

cassowary /ˈkasəwəri, -wɛːri/ ▶ **noun** (pl. **cassowaries**) a very large flightless bird related to the emu, with a bare head and neck, a tall horny crest, and one or two coloured wattles. It is native mainly to the forests of New Guinea. ● Family Casuariidae and genus *Casuarius*: three species.
– ORIGIN early 17th cent.: from Malay *kesuari*.

cast¹ ▶ **verb** (past and past participle **cast**) [with obj.] **1** [usu. with adverbial of direction] chiefly literary throw (something) forcefully in a specified direction: *he cast the book down on to the chair angrily* | *the fishermen cast a large net around a school of tuna* | figurative *individuals who do not accept the norms are* ***cast out*** *from the group*. ■ throw the hooked and baited end of (a fishing line) out into the water. ■ let down (an anchor or sounding line).
2 [with adverbial of place] cause (light or shadow) to appear on a surface: *the moon cast a pale light over the cottages*. ■ [with adverbial of direction] direct (one's eyes or a look) at something: *she cast down her eyes* | [with two objs] *she cast him a desperate glance*. ■ cause (uncertainty or disparagement) to be associated with something: *journalists* ***cast doubt on*** *the government's version of events*.
3 [with adverbial of direction] discard: *he jumped in, casting* ***caution to the wind***. ■ shed (skin or horns) in the process of growth: *the antlers are cast each year*. ■ (of a horse) lose (a shoe).
4 shape (metal or other material) by pouring it into a mould while molten. ■ make (a moulded object) by casting metal: *a bell was cast for the church*. ■ arrange and present in a specified form or style: *he issued statements* ***cast in*** *tones of reason*.
5 register (a vote): *votes have been cast in 40 per cent of the seats*.
6 cause (a magic spell) to take effect: *the witch* ***cast a spell on*** *her to turn her into a beast* | figurative *the city* ***casts a spell on*** *the visitor*.
7 calculate and record details of (a horoscope).
8 [no obj., usu. with adverbial of direction] (in country dancing) change one's position by moving a certain number of places in a certain direction along the outside of the line in which one is dancing.
9 [no obj.] Hunting (of a dog) search in different directions for a lost scent: *the dog cast furiously for the vanished rabbit*. ■ [with obj.] let loose (hounds) on a scent.
10 immobilize (an animal, especially a cow) by using a rope to cause it to fall on its side.
▶ **noun 1** an object made by shaping molten metal or similar material in a mould: *bronze casts of the sculpture*. ■ (also **plaster cast**) a mould used to make an object by casting. ■ (also **plaster cast**) a bandage stiffened with plaster of Paris, moulded to the shape of a limb that is broken and used to support and protect it.
2 an act of throwing something forcefully: *he grabbed a spear for a third cast*. ■ Fishing a throw of a fishing line. ■ Brit. the leader of a fishing line.
3 [in sing.] [with adj. or noun modifier] the form or appearance of something, especially someone's features or complexion: *she had a somewhat masculine cast of countenance* | *the colours he wore emphasized the olive cast of his skin*. ■ the character of something: *this question is for minds of a more philosophical cast than mine*.
4 a slight squint: *he had a cast in one eye*.
5 short for WORM CAST.
6 a pellet regurgitated by a hawk or owl.
7 Hunting a wide search made by a hound or pack of hounds to find a trail. ■ Austral./NZ a wide sweep made by a sheepdog in mustering sheep.
– PHRASES **be cast in a —— mould** (of a person) be of the type specified: *he was cast in a cautious mould*. **cast one's bread upon the waters** see BREAD. **cast one's eyes over** have a quick appraising look at. **cast light on** see LIGHT¹. **cast lots** see LOT. **cast one's mind back** think back to a particular event or time: *he cast his mind back to the fatal evening*. **cast the** (or **one's**) **net** search for suitable options or candidates in a specified way: *Martin vowed he would cast the net far and wide in the search for the best person*.
– PHRASAL VERBS **cast about** (or **around** or **round**) search far and wide (physically or mentally): *he is restlessly casting about for novelties*. [from sense 9 of the verb.] **be cast away** be stranded after a shipwreck. **be cast down** feel depressed: *she was greatly cast down by abusive criticism of her novels*. **cast off** (or **cast something off**) **1** Knitting take the stitches off the needle by looping each over the next to finish the edge. **2** set a boat or ship free from her moorings: *the boatmen cast off and rowed downriver*. ■ (**cast off**) (of a boat or ship) be set free from her moorings. **3** let loose a hunting hound or hawk. **4** Printing estimate the space that will be taken in print by manuscript copy. **cast on** (or **cast something on**) Knitting make the first row of a specified number of loops on the needle.
– ORIGIN Middle English: from Old Norse *kasta* 'to cast or throw'.

cast² ▶ **noun** [treated as sing. or pl.] the actors taking part in a play, film, or other production: *he draws sensitive performances from his inexperienced cast*.
▶ **verb** (past and past participle **cast**) [with obj.] assign a part in a play or film to (an actor): *he was* ***cast as*** *a young knight in her lavish historical epic*. ■ allocate parts in (a play or film).
– ORIGIN mid 17th cent.: a special use of CAST¹ in sense 4 of the verb.

Castalia /kaˈsteɪlɪə/ a spring on Mount Parnassus, sacred in antiquity to Apollo and the Muses.
– DERIVATIVES **Castalian** adjective.

castanets ▶ **plural noun** small concave pieces of wood, ivory, or plastic, joined in pairs by a cord and clicked together by the fingers as a rhythmic accompaniment to Spanish dancing.
– ORIGIN early 17th cent.: from Spanish *castañeta*, diminutive of *castaña*, from Latin *castanea* 'chestnut'.

castaway ▶ **noun** a person who has been shipwrecked and stranded in an isolated place.

caste ▶ **noun** each of the hereditary classes of Hindu society, distinguished by relative degrees of ritual purity or pollution and of social status: *members of the lower castes* | [mass noun] *a man of high caste*. ■ [mass noun] the system of dividing society into castes. ■ any class or group of people who inherit exclusive privileges or are perceived as socially distinct: *those educated in private schools belong to a privileged caste*. ■ Entomology (in some social insects) a class of physically distinct individuals with a particular function in the society.

> There are four basic classes or varnas in Hindu society: Brahman (priest), Kshatriya (warrior), Vaisya (merchant or farmer), and Sudra (labourer). The lowest class, the scheduled caste (formerly known as untouchables), fall outside the varna system and have historically suffered extreme discrimination.

– PHRASES **lose caste** descend in the caste system, e.g. by taking employment regarded as of lower status. ■ come to be regarded with less respect; lose status.
– ORIGIN mid 16th cent. (in the general sense 'race, breed'): from Spanish and Portuguese *casta* 'lineage, race, breed', feminine of *casto* 'pure, unmixed', from Latin *castus* 'chaste'.

caste Hindu ▶ **noun** a Hindu who belongs to one of the four main castes.

casteism ▶ **noun** [mass noun] **1** adherence to a caste system.
2 prejudice or discrimination on the grounds of caste.
– DERIVATIVES **casteist** adjective.

Castel Gandolfo /ˌkastɛl ganˈdɒlfəʊ/ the summer residence of the pope, situated on the edge of Lake Albano near Rome.

castellan /ˈkastələn/ ▶ **noun** historical the governor of a castle.
– ORIGIN late Middle English: from Old Northern French *castelain*, from medieval Latin *castellanus*, from Latin *castellum* (see CASTLE).

castellated /ˈkastəleɪtɪd/ ▶ **adjective** having battlements: *a castellated gatehouse*. ■ (of a nut or other mechanical part) having grooves or slots on its upper face.
– ORIGIN late 17th cent.: from medieval Latin *castellatus*, from Latin *castellum* (see CASTLE).

castellations /ˌkastəˈleɪʃ(ə)nz/ ▶ **plural noun** defensive or decorative parapets with regularly spaced notches; battlements. ■ (**castellation**) [mass noun] the use or building of castellations.
– ORIGIN early 19th cent.: based on medieval Latin *castellare* 'to build castles', from *castellum* (see CASTLE).

Castell-Nedd /ˌkastelˈneð/ Welsh name for NEATH.

caste mark ▶ **noun** a symbol on the forehead denoting membership of a particular Hindu caste.

caster ▶ **noun 1** a person who casts something or a machine for casting something.
2 Fishing a fly pupa used as bait.
3 variant spelling of CASTOR¹.

caster sugar (also **castor sugar**) ▶ **noun** [mass noun] Brit. finely granulated white or pale golden sugar.
– ORIGIN mid 19th cent.: so named because it was suitable for use in a castor (see CASTOR¹ (sense 2)).

castigate /ˈkastɪgeɪt/ ▶ **verb** [with obj.] formal reprimand (someone) severely: *he was castigated for not setting a good example*.
– DERIVATIVES **castigation** noun, **castigator** noun, **castigatory** adjective.
– ORIGIN early 17th cent.: from Latin *castigare* 'reprove', from *castus* 'pure, chaste'.

Castile /kaˈstiːl/ a region of central Spain, on the central plateau of the Iberian peninsula, formerly an independent Spanish kingdom.
– ORIGIN from French *Castille*, from Spanish *Castilla*.

Castile soap ▶ **noun** [mass noun] fine, hard white or mottled soap made with olive oil and soda.

Castilian /kaˈstɪlɪən/ ▶ **noun 1** a native of Castile.
2 [mass noun] the language of Castile, being the standard spoken and literary Spanish.
▶ **adjective** relating to Castile, Castilians, or the Castilian form of Spanish.

Castilla-La Mancha /kaˌstiːjəlaˈmantʃə, -ljə-/ an autonomous region of central Spain; capital, Toledo.

Castilla-León /kaˌstiːjəleɪˈɒn, -ljə-/ an autonomous region of northern Spain; capital, Valladolid.

casting ▶ **noun** an object made by pouring molten metal or other material into a mould.

casting couch ▶ **noun** informal used in reference to the supposed practice whereby actresses are awarded parts in films or plays in return for granting sexual favours to the casting director: *she was no stranger to the casting couch*.

casting director ▶ **noun** the person responsible for assigning roles in a film or play.

casting vote ▶ **noun** an extra vote given by a chairperson to decide an issue when the votes on each side are equal.
– ORIGIN early 17th cent.: from an obsolete sense of *cast* 'turn the scale'.

cast iron ▶ **noun** [mass noun] **1** a hard, relatively brittle alloy of iron and carbon which can be readily cast in a mould and contains a higher proportion of carbon than steel (typically 2–4.3 per cent).
2 [as modifier] firm and unchangeable: *there are no cast-iron guarantees*.

castle ▶ **noun** a large building, typically of the medieval period, fortified against attack with thick walls, battlements, towers, and often a moat. ■ a magnificent and imposing old mansion: [in names] *Castle Howard*. ■ Chess, informal old-fashioned term for ROOK².
▶ **verb** [no obj.] (often as noun **castling**) Chess make a special move (no more than once in a game by each player) in which the king is transferred from its original square two squares along the back rank towards a rook on its corner square which is then transferred to the square passed over by the king. ■ [with obj.] move (the king) by castling.
– PHRASES **castles in the air** (or **in Spain**) visionary unattainable schemes; daydreams: *my father built castles in the air about owning a boat*.
– DERIVATIVES **castled** adjective (archaic).
– ORIGIN late Old English: from Anglo-Norman French and Old Northern French *castel*, from Latin *castellum*, diminutive of *castrum* 'fort'.

Castlebar /ˌkɑːs(ə)lˈbɑː/ the county town of Mayo, in the Republic of Ireland; pop. 10,655 (2006).

Castlereagh /ˈkɑːs(ə)lreɪ/, Robert Stewart, Viscount (1769–1822), British Tory statesman. He became Foreign Secretary in 1812 and represented Britain at the Congress of Vienna (1814–15).

cast net ▶ **noun** a fishing net that is thrown out and immediately drawn in again, rather than being set up and left.

cast-off Brit. ▶ **adjective** no longer wanted; abandoned or discarded: *a pile of cast-off clothes*.
▶ **noun** something, especially a garment, that is no longer wanted: *I'm not going out in her cast-offs!*

Castor /ˈkɑːstə/ **1** Greek Mythology the twin brother of Pollux. See DIOSCURI.
2 Astronomy the second-brightest star in the constellation Gemini, close to Pollux. It is a multiple star system, the three components visible in a moderate telescope being close binaries.

castor¹ /ˈkɑːstə/ (also **caster**) ▶ **noun 1** each of a set of small swivelling wheels fixed to the legs or base of a heavy piece of furniture so that it can be moved easily.
2 a small container with holes in the top, especially one used for sprinkling sugar or pepper.

C

– ORIGIN late 17th cent. (in sense 2): originally a variant of CASTER, in the general sense 'something that casts'.

castor[2] /ˈkɑːstə/ ▸ **noun** [mass noun] an oily reddish-brown substance secreted by beavers, used in medicine and perfumes.
– ORIGIN late Middle English (in the sense 'beaver'): from Old French or Latin, from Greek *kastōr*.

castor bean ▸ **noun** the seed of the castor oil plant, which contains a number of poisonous compounds, especially ricin, as well as castor oil. ■ N. Amer. the castor oil plant.

castor oil ▸ **noun** [mass noun] a pale yellow oil obtained from castor beans, used as a purgative, a lubricant, and in manufacturing oil-based products.
– ORIGIN mid 18th cent.: perhaps so named because it succeeded CASTOR[2] in medicinal use.

castor oil plant ▸ **noun** an African shrub with lobed serrated leaves, which yields the seeds from which castor oil is obtained and is widely naturalized in warm countries. ● *Ricinus communis*, family Euphorbiaceae.

castor sugar ▸ **noun** variant spelling of CASTER SUGAR.

castrate ▸ **verb** [with obj.] remove the testicles of (a male animal or man). ■ deprive of power, vitality, or vigour: *a restrictive classicism would have castrated England's literature.*
▸ **noun** a man or male animal whose testicles have been removed.
– DERIVATIVES **castration** noun, **castrator** noun.
– ORIGIN mid 16th cent. (earlier (Middle English) as *castration*): from Latin *castrare*.

castration complex ▸ **noun** Psychoanalysis (in Freudian theory) an unconscious anxiety arising during psychosexual development, represented in males as a fear that the penis will be removed by the father in response to sexual interest in the mother, and in females as a compulsion to demonstrate that they have an adequate symbolic equivalent to the penis, whose absence is blamed on the mother.

castrato /kaˈstrɑːtəʊ/ ▸ **noun** (pl. **castrati** /-ti/) historical a male singer castrated in boyhood so as to retain a soprano or alto voice. The practice of castration was banned in 1903.
– ORIGIN mid 18th cent.: from Italian, past participle of *castrare* (see CASTRATE).

Castries /kaˈstriːs/ the capital of the Caribbean island of St Lucia, a seaport on the NW coast; pop. 14,000 (est. 2007).

Castro /ˈkastrəʊ/, Fidel (b.1927), Cuban statesman, Prime Minister 1959–76 and President 1976–2008. After overthrowing President Batista he set up a communist regime which survived the abortive Bay of Pigs invasion, the Cuban Missile Crisis, and the collapse of the Soviet bloc. In 2008 he stood down in favour of his brother Raúl Castro.

casual /ˈkaʒjʊəl, -zj-/ ▸ **adjective 1** relaxed and unconcerned: *a casual attitude to life.* ■ made or done without much thought or premeditation: *a casual remark.* ■ done or acting in a desultory way: *to the casual observer, rugby looks something like football.* ■ done or acting without sufficient care or thoroughness: *the casual way in which victims were treated.*
2 not regular or permanent, in particular: ■ employed or established on a temporary or irregular basis: *a casual worker | casual jobs.* ■ (of a sexual relationship or encounter) occurring between people who are not established sexual partners.
3 [attrib.] happening by chance; accidental: *he pretended it was a casual meeting.*
4 without formality of style or manner, in particular (of clothing) suitable for everyday wear rather than formal occasions: *a casual short-sleeved shirt | an ideal coat for casual occasions.*
▸ **noun 1** a person who does something irregularly: *a number of casuals became regular customers.* ■ Brit. a worker employed on an irregular or temporary basis. ■ historical a person admitted to a workhouse for a short period.
2 (**casuals**) Brit. clothes or shoes suitable for everyday wear rather than formal occasions.
3 Brit. a youth belonging to a subculture characterized by the wearing of expensive casual clothing and frequently associated with football hooliganism.
– DERIVATIVES **casually** adverb, **casualness** noun.
– ORIGIN late Middle English (in sense 2 of the adjective, sense 3 of the adjective): from Old French *casuel* and Latin *casualis*, from *casus* 'fall' (compare with CASE[1]).

casual Friday ▸ **noun** Friday as a designated day of the week when organizations allow employees to dress more casually than on other weekdays.

casualization (also **casualisation**) ▸ **noun** [mass noun] the transformation of a workforce from one employed chiefly on permanent contracts to one engaged on a short-term temporary basis.
– DERIVATIVES **casualize** (also **casualise**) verb.

casualty ▸ **noun** (pl. **casualties**) a person killed or injured in a war or accident: *the shelling caused thousands of civilian casualties.* ■ a person or thing badly affected by an event or situation: *the building industry has been one of the casualties of the recession.* ■ Brit. the casualty department of a hospital: *he went to casualty to have a cut stitched.* ■ (chiefly in insurance) an accident or disaster.
– ORIGIN late Middle English (in the sense 'chance, a chance occurrence'): from medieval Latin *casualitas*, from *casualis* (see CASUAL), on the pattern of words such as *penalty*.

casualty department (also **casualty ward**) ▸ **noun** Brit. the department of a hospital providing immediate treatment for emergency cases.

casual ward ▸ **noun** historical a ward in a workhouse providing accommodation for those temporarily unable to support themselves.

casual water ▸ **noun** [mass noun] Golf water that has accumulated temporarily and does not constitute a recognized hazard of the course. A player may move a ball from casual water without penalty.

casuarina /ˌkasjʊəˈriːnə/ ▸ **noun** a tree with slender, jointed, drooping twigs which resemble horsetails and bear tiny scale-like leaves, native to Australia and SE Asia. Also called SHE-OAK. ● Genus *Casuarina*, family Casuarinaceae.
– ORIGIN from modern Latin *casuarius* 'cassowary' (from the resemblance of the branches to the bird's feathers).

casuist /ˈkazjʊɪst, -ʒj-/ ▸ **noun 1** a person who uses clever but unsound reasoning, especially in relation to moral questions; a sophist.
2 a person who resolves moral problems by the application of theoretical rules.
– DERIVATIVES **casuistic** adjective, **casuistical** adjective, **casuistically** adverb.
– ORIGIN early 17th cent.: from French *casuiste*, from Spanish *casuista*, from Latin *casus* (see CASE[1]).

casuistry ▸ **noun** [mass noun] **1** the use of clever but unsound reasoning, especially in relation to moral questions; sophistry.
2 the resolving of moral problems by the application of theoretical rules.

casus belli /ˌkeɪsəs ˈbɛlʌɪ, ˌkɑːsʊs ˈbɛli/ ▸ **noun** (pl. **same**) an act or situation that provokes or justifies a war.
– ORIGIN Latin, from *casus* (see CASE[1]) and *belli*, genitive of *bellum* 'war'.

CAT ▸ **abbreviation** ■ clear air turbulence. ■ computer-assisted (or -aided) testing. ■ Medicine computerized axial tomography.

cat[1] ▸ **noun 1** a small domesticated carnivorous mammal with soft fur, a short snout, and retractile claws. It is widely kept as a pet or for catching mice, and many breeds have been developed. ● *Felis catus*, family Felidae (the **cat family**); it was probably domesticated in ancient Egypt from the local race of wildcat. The cat family also includes the ocelot, serval, margay, lynx, and the big cats. ■ a wild animal of the cat family: *a marbled cat.* See also BIG CAT. ■ used in names of catlike animals of other families, e.g. **native cat**, **ring-tailed cat**. ■ informal a malicious or spiteful woman. ■ historical short for CAT-O'-NINE-TAILS.
2 informal, chiefly N. Amer. (especially among jazz enthusiasts) a man.
3 historical a short tapered stick used in the game of tipcat.
▸ **verb** (**cats**, **catting**, **catted**) [with obj.] Nautical raise (an anchor) from the surface of the water to the cathead.
– PHRASES **all cats are grey in the dark** (or US **at night all cats are gray**) proverb the qualities that distinguish people from one another are obscured in some circumstances, and if they can't be perceived they don't matter. **cat and mouse** a series of cunning manoeuvres designed to thwart an opponent: *he continues to play cat and mouse with the UN inspection teams.* **a cat may look at a king** proverb even a person of low status or importance has rights. **the cat's whiskers** (or chiefly N. Amer. **meow** or **pyjamas**) informal an excellent person or thing: *this car is the cat's whiskers.* **has the cat got your tongue?** said to someone who remains silent when they are expected to speak. **let the cat out of the bag** informal reveal a secret carelessly or by mistake. **like a cat on a hot tin roof** (Brit. also **on hot bricks**) informal very agitated or anxious. **like herding cats** informal used to refer to a difficult or impossible task, typically an attempt to organize a group of people: *controlling the members of this expedition is like herding cats.* **like the cat that got** (or **stole**) **the cream** informal self-satisfied, having achieved one's objective: *you sit in this office like the cat that got the cream and expect the world to revolve around you.* **look like something the cat brought in** informal look very dirty or dishevelled. **not have a cat in hell's chance** informal have no chance at all. **put** (or **set**) **the cat among the pigeons** Brit. say or do something that is likely to cause trouble or controversy. **see which way the cat jumps** informal see what direction events are taking before committing oneself. **when** (or **while**) **the cat's away, the mice will play** proverb people will naturally take advantage of the absence of someone in authority to do as they like. **who's she—the cat's mother?** see SHE.
– ORIGIN Old English *catt, catte*, of Germanic origin; related to Dutch *kat* and German *Katze*; reinforced in Middle English by forms from late Latin *cattus*.

cat[2] ▸ **noun** short for CATALYTIC CONVERTER.

cat[3] ▸ **noun** short for CATAMARAN.

cata- (also **cat-**) ▸ **prefix 1** down; downwards: *catadromous.*
2 wrongly; badly: *catachresis.*
3 completely: *cataclysm.*
4 against; alongside: *catapult.*
– ORIGIN from Greek *kata* 'down'.

catabolism /kəˈtabəlɪz(ə)m/ ▸ **noun** [mass noun] Biology the breakdown of complex molecules in living organisms to form simpler ones, together with the release of energy; destructive metabolism.
– DERIVATIVES **catabolic** /katəˈbɒlɪk/ **adjective**, **catabolize** /-ˌlʌɪz/ **verb**.
– ORIGIN late 19th cent.: from Greek *katabolē* 'throwing down', from *kata-* 'down' + *ballein* 'to throw'.

catabolite /kəˈtabəlʌɪt/ ▸ **noun** Biochemistry a product of catabolism.

catachresis /ˌkatəˈkriːsɪs/ ▸ **noun** (pl. **catachreses** /-siːz/) [mass noun] the use of a word in an incorrect way, for example the use of *mitigate* for *militate*.
– DERIVATIVES **catachrestic** /-ˈkriːstɪk, -ˈkrɛstɪk/ **adjective**.
– ORIGIN mid 16th cent.: from Latin, from Greek *katakhrēsis*, from *katakhrēsthai* 'misuse', from *kata-* 'down' (expressing the sense 'wrongly') + *khrēsthai* 'use'.

cataclasis /ˌkatəˈkleɪsɪs/ ▸ **noun** [mass noun] Geology the fracture and breaking up of rock by natural processes.
– DERIVATIVES **cataclastic** /-ˈklastɪk/ **adjective**.
– ORIGIN 1950s: from CATA- 'completely' + Greek *klasis* 'breaking'.

cataclysm /ˈkatəˌklɪz(ə)m/ ▸ **noun** a large-scale and violent event in the natural world. ■ a sudden violent political or social upheaval: *the cataclysm of the First World War.*
– ORIGIN early 17th cent. (originally denoting the biblical Flood described in Genesis): from French *cataclysme*, via Latin from Greek *kataklusmos* 'deluge', from *kata-* 'down' + *kluzein* 'to wash'.

cataclysmic ▸ **adjective** (of a natural event) large-scale and violent: *a cataclysmic earthquake.* ■ causing sudden and violent upheaval: *a novel about a cataclysmic world war.*
– DERIVATIVES **cataclysmically** adverb.

catacomb /ˈkatəkuːm, -kəʊm/ ▸ **noun** (usu. **catacombs**) an underground cemetery consisting of a subterranean gallery with recesses for tombs, as constructed by the ancient Romans.
– ORIGIN Old English, from late Latin *catacumbas*, the name of the subterranean cemetery of St Sebastian near Rome.

catadioptric /ˌkatədʌɪˈɒptrɪk/ ▸ **adjective** Optics denoting an optical system which involves both the reflecting and refracting of light, in order to reduce aberration.

catadromous /kəˈtadrəməs/ ▸ **adjective** Zoology (of a fish such as the eel) migrating down rivers to the sea to spawn. The opposite of ANADROMOUS.
– ORIGIN late 19th cent.: from CATA- 'down' + Greek *dromos* 'running', on the pattern of *anadromous*.

catafalque /ˈkatəfalk/ ▸ **noun** a decorated wooden framework supporting the coffin of a distinguished person during a funeral or while lying in state.
– ORIGIN mid 17th cent.: from French, from Italian *catafalco*, of unknown origin. Compare with SCAFFOLD.

Catalan /ˈkatəlan/ ▸ **noun 1** a native of Catalonia in Spain.
2 [mass noun] a Romance language closely related to Castilian Spanish and Provençal, widely spoken in Catalonia (where it has official status alongside Castilian Spanish) and in Andorra, the Balearic Islands, and parts of southern France. It has about 6 million speakers in all.
▸ **adjective** relating to Catalonia, its people, or its language.
– ORIGIN from French, from Spanish *catalán*, related to Catalan *català* 'Catalan', *Catalunya* 'Catalonia'.

catalase /ˈkatəleɪz/ ▸ **noun** [mass noun] Biochemistry an enzyme that catalyses the reduction of hydrogen peroxide.
– ORIGIN early 20th cent.: from CATALYSIS + -ASE.

catalectic /ˌkatəˈlɛktɪk/ ▸ **adjective** Prosody (of a metrical line of verse) lacking one syllable in the last foot.
– ORIGIN late 16th cent.: from late Latin *catalecticus*, from Greek *katalēktikos*, from *katalēgein* 'leave off'.

catalepsy /ˈkat(ə)lɛpsi/ ▸ **noun** [mass noun] a medical condition characterized by a trance or seizure with a loss of sensation and consciousness accompanied by rigidity of the body.
– DERIVATIVES **cataleptic** adjective & noun.
– ORIGIN late Middle English: from French *catalepsie* or late Latin *catalepsia*, from Greek *katalēpsis*, from *katalambanein* 'seize upon'.

catalogue (US **catalog**) ▸ **noun** a complete list of items, typically one in alphabetical or other systematic order, in particular: ■ a list of all the books or resources in a library. ■ a publication containing details of items for sale, especially one produced by a mail-order company. ■ a list of works of art in an exhibition or collection, with detailed comments and explanations. ■ US a list of courses offered by a university or college. ■ [in sing.] a series of unwelcome or unpleasant things: *his life was a catalogue of dismal failures*.
▸ **verb** (**catalogues, cataloguing, catalogued**; US also **catalogs, cataloging, cataloged**) [with obj.] make a systematic list of (items of the same type). ■ enter (an item) in a catalogue. ■ list (similar situations, qualities, or events) in succession: *the report catalogues dangerous work practices in the company*.
– DERIVATIVES **cataloguer** (US also **cataloger**) noun.
– ORIGIN late Middle English: via Old French from late Latin *catalogus*, from Greek *katalogos*, from *katalegein* 'pick out or enrol'.

catalogue raisonné /ˌreɪzɒˈneɪ/ ▸ **noun** (pl. **catalogues raisonnés** pronunc. **same**) a descriptive catalogue of works of art with explanations and scholarly comments.
– ORIGIN late 18th cent.: French, 'explained catalogue'.

Catalonia /ˌkatəˈləʊnɪə/ an autonomous region of NE Spain; capital, Barcelona. The region has a strong separatist tradition; the normal language for everyday purposes is Catalan, which has also won acceptance in recent years for various official purposes. Catalan name **Catalunya** /ˌkatəˈluːnjə/; Spanish name **Cataluña** /ˌkataˈluɲa/.
– DERIVATIVES **Catalonian** adjective & noun.

catalpa /kəˈtalpə/ ▸ **noun** a tree with large heart-shaped leaves, clusters of trumpet-shaped flowers, and slender bean-like seed pods, native to North America and eastern Asia and cultivated as an ornamental. ● Genus *Catalpa*, family Bignoniaceae: several species, in particular the Indian bean tree.
– ORIGIN from Creek.

catalufa /ˌkatəˈluːfə/ ▸ **noun** another term for BIGEYE (sense 2).
– ORIGIN from Spanish.

catalyse /ˈkat(ə)lʌɪz/ (US **catalyze**) ▸ **verb** [with obj.] cause or accelerate (a reaction) by acting as a catalyst. ■ cause (an action or process) to begin: *the introduction of the canal and the railway catalysed the city's industrial growth*.
– ORIGIN late 19th cent.: from CATALYSIS, on the pattern of *analyse*.

catalyser ▸ **noun** Brit. another term for CATALYTIC CONVERTER.

catalysis /kəˈtalɪsɪs/ ▸ **noun** [mass noun] the acceleration of a chemical reaction by a catalyst.
– ORIGIN mid 19th cent.: from modern Latin, from Greek *katalusis*, from *kataluein* 'dissolve', from *kata-* 'down' + *luein* 'loosen'.

catalyst ▸ **noun** a substance that increases the rate of a chemical reaction without itself undergoing any permanent chemical change. ■ a person or thing that precipitates an event: *the prime minister's speech acted as a catalyst for debate*.
– ORIGIN early 20th cent.: from CATALYSIS, on the pattern of *analyst*.

catalytic ▸ **adjective** relating to or involving the action of a catalyst.
– DERIVATIVES **catalytically** adverb.
– ORIGIN mid 19th cent.: from CATALYSIS, on the pattern of pairs such as *analysis, analytic*.

catalytic converter ▸ **noun** a device incorporated in the exhaust system of a motor vehicle, containing a catalyst for converting pollutant gases into less harmful ones.

catalyze ▸ **verb** US spelling of CATALYSE.

catamaran ▸ **noun** a yacht or other boat with twin hulls in parallel.
– ORIGIN early 17th cent.: from Tamil *kaṭṭumaram*, literally 'tied wood'.

catamite /ˈkatəmʌɪt/ ▸ **noun** archaic a boy kept for homosexual practices.
– ORIGIN late 16th cent.: from Latin *catamitus*, via Etruscan from Greek *Ganumēdēs* (see GANYMEDE).

catamount /ˈkatəmaʊnt/ (also **catamountain** /ˌkatəˈmaʊntɪn/) ▸ **noun** N. Amer. a puma. ■ archaic any medium-sized or large wild cat.
– ORIGIN late Middle English (as *catamountain*): from the phrase *cat of the mountain*.

Catania /kəˈtɑːnɪə, -ˈteɪnɪə/ a seaport situated at the foot of Mount Etna, on the east coast of Sicily; pop. 296,469 (2008).

cataphatic /ˌkatəˈfatɪk/ ▸ **adjective** Theology (of knowledge of God) obtained through defining God with positive statements. The opposite of APOPHATIC.
– ORIGIN mid 19th cent.: from Greek *kataphatikos* 'affirmative', from *kataphasis* 'affirmation', from *kata-* (as an intensifier) + *phanai* 'speak'.

cataphor /ˈkatəfə, -fɔː/ ▸ **noun** Grammar a word or phrase that refers to or stands for a later word or phrase (e.g. in *when they saw Ruth, the men looked slightly abashed, they* is used as a cataphor for *the men*).
– ORIGIN late 20th cent.: back-formation from CATAPHORA.

cataphora /kəˈtaf(ə)rə/ ▸ **noun** [mass noun] Grammar the use of a word or phrase that refers to or stands for a later word or phrase (e.g. the pronoun *he* in *he may be approaching 37, but Jeff has no plans to retire from the sport yet*). Compare with ANAPHORA.
– DERIVATIVES **cataphoric** /katəˈfɒrɪk/ adjective.
– ORIGIN 1970s: from CATA- on the pattern of *anaphora*.

cataphract /ˈkatəfrakt/ ▸ **noun** archaic a soldier in full armour.
– ORIGIN late 17th cent.: via Latin from Greek *kataphraktos* 'clothed in full armour'.

cataplasm /ˈkatəplaz(ə)m/ ▸ **noun** archaic a plaster or poultice.
– ORIGIN Middle English: from Old French *cataplasme* or late Latin *cataplasma*, from Greek *kataplasma*, from *kataplassein* 'plaster over'.

cataplexy /ˈkatəˌplɛksi/ ▸ **noun** [mass noun] a medical condition in which strong emotion or laughter causes a person to suffer sudden physical collapse though remaining conscious.
– DERIVATIVES **cataplectic** adjective.
– ORIGIN late 19th cent.: from Greek *kataplēxis* 'stupefaction', from *kataplessein*, from *kata-* 'down' + *plēssein* 'strike'.

catapult ▸ **noun 1** Brit. a forked stick with an elastic band fastened to the two prongs, used by children for shooting small stones.
2 historical a military machine worked by a lever and ropes for hurling large stones or other missiles.
3 a mechanical device for launching a glider or other aircraft, especially from the deck of a ship.
▸ **verb** [with obj. and adverbial of direction] hurl or launch (something) with or as if with a catapult: *the explosion catapulted the car 30 yards along the road* | figurative *their music catapulted them to the top of the charts*. ■ [no obj., with adverbial of direction] move suddenly or at great speed as though hurled by a catapult: *the horse catapulted away from the fence*.
– ORIGIN late 16th cent.: from French *catapulte* or Latin *catapulta*, from Greek *katapeltēs*, from *kata-* 'down' + *pallein* 'hurl'.

cataract /ˈkatərakt/ ▸ **noun 1** a large waterfall. ■ a sudden rush of water; a downpour: *the rain enveloped us in a deafening cataract*.
2 a medical condition in which the lens of the eye becomes progressively opaque, resulting in blurred vision: *she had cataracts in both eyes*.
– ORIGIN late Middle English: from Latin *cataracta* 'waterfall, floodgate', also 'portcullis' (medical sense 2 probably being a figurative use of this), from Greek *kataraktēs* 'down-rushing', from *katarassein*, from *kata-* 'down' + *arassein* 'strike, smash'.

catarrh /kəˈtɑː/ ▸ **noun** [mass noun] excessive discharge or build-up of mucus in the nose or throat, associated with inflammation of the mucous membrane.
– DERIVATIVES **catarrhal** adjective.
– ORIGIN early 16th cent.: from French *catarrhe*, from late Latin *catarrhus*, from Greek *katarrhous*, from *katarrhein* 'flow down', from *kata-* 'down' + *rhein* 'flow'.

catarrhine /ˈkatərʌɪn/ Zoology ▸ **adjective** relating to primates of a group that comprises the Old World monkeys, gibbons, great apes, and humans. They are distinguished by having nostrils that are close together and directed downwards, and do not have a prehensile tail. Compare with PLATYRRHINE.
▸ **noun** a catarrhine primate. ● Infraorder Catarrhini, order Primates: four families.
– ORIGIN mid 19th cent.: from CATA- 'down' + Greek *rhis, rhin-* 'nose'.

catastrophe /kəˈtastrəfi/ ▸ **noun 1** an event causing great and usually sudden damage or suffering; a disaster: *an environmental catastrophe* | [mass noun] *inaction will only bring us closer to catastrophe*. ■ something very unfortunate or unsuccessful: *the tax would be a catastrophe for the industry*.
2 the denouement of a drama, especially a classical tragedy.
– ORIGIN mid 16th cent. (in the sense 'denouement'): from Latin *catastropha*, from Greek *katastrophē* 'overturning, sudden turn', from *kata-* 'down' + *strophē* 'turning' (from *strephein* 'to turn').

catastrophe theory ▸ **noun** [mass noun] a branch of mathematics concerned with systems displaying abrupt discontinuous change.

catastrophic ▸ **adjective** involving or causing sudden great damage or suffering: *a catastrophic earthquake*. ■ extremely unfortunate or unsuccessful: *catastrophic mismanagement of the economy*. ■ involving a sudden and large-scale alteration in state: *the body undergoes catastrophic collapse towards the state of a black hole*. ■ relating to geological catastrophism.
– DERIVATIVES **catastrophically** adverb.

catastrophism ▸ **noun** [mass noun] Geology the theory that changes in the earth's crust during geological history have resulted chiefly from sudden violent and unusual events. Often contrasted with UNIFORMITARIANISM.
– DERIVATIVES **catastrophist** noun & adjective.

catastrophize ▸ **verb** [no obj.] view or present a situation as considerably worse than it actually is: *traumatic experiences can predispose people to catastrophize*.

catatonia /ˌkatəˈtəʊnɪə/ ▸ **noun** [mass noun] Psychiatry abnormality of movement and behaviour arising from a disturbed mental state (typically schizophrenia). It may involve repetitive or purposeless overactivity, or catalepsy, resistance to passive movement, and negativism. ■ informal a state of immobility and stupor.
– ORIGIN late 19th cent.: from CATA- 'badly' + Greek *tonos* 'tone or tension'.

catatonic ▸ **adjective** Psychiatry relating to or characterized by catatonia: *catatonic schizophrenia*. ■ informal of or in an immobile or unresponsive stupor.

Catawba /kəˈtɔːbə/ ▸ **noun** [mass noun] a North American variety of grape. ■ a white wine made from the Catawba grape.
– ORIGIN named after the River *Catawba* in North and South Carolina.

cat-bear ▸ **noun** another term for RED PANDA.

catbird ▸ **noun 1** a long-tailed American songbird of the mockingbird family, with mainly dark grey or black plumage and catlike mewing calls. ● Two genera and species, family Mimidae.
2 a thickset Australasian bird of the bowerbird family, having a loud call like a yowling cat. ● Genus *Ailuroedus* (and *Scenopoeetes*), family Ptilonorhynchidae: several species.
– PHRASES **in the catbird seat** N. Amer. informal in a superior or advantageous position. [said to be an allusion to a baseball player in the fortunate position of having no strikes and therefore three balls still to play (a reference made in James Thurber's short story *The Catbird Seat*).]

catboat ▸ **noun** a sailing boat with a single mast placed well forward and carrying only one sail.
– ORIGIN mid 19th cent.: perhaps from *cat* (denoting a type of merchant ship formerly used in the coal and timber trades in NE England) + BOAT.

C

cat burglar ▸ noun a thief who enters a building by climbing to an upper storey.

catcall ▸ noun a shrill whistle or shout of disapproval made at a public meeting or performance. ▪ a loud whistle or a comment of a sexual nature made by a man to a passing woman.
▸ verb [no obj.] make a catcall: *they were fired for catcalling at women.*
– ORIGIN mid 17th cent.: from CAT[1] + CALL, originally denoting a kind of whistle or squeaking instrument used to express disapproval at a theatre.

catch ▸ verb (past and past participle **caught**) [with obj.] **1** intercept and hold (something which has been thrown, propelled, or dropped): *she threw the bottle into the air and caught it again.* ▪ intercept the fall of (someone). ▪ seize or take hold of: *he* ***caught hold of*** *her arm as she tried to push past him.* ▪ [no obj.] (**catch at**) grasp or try to grasp: *his hands caught at her arms as she tried to turn away.* ▪ Cricket dismiss (a batsman) by catching the ball before it touches the ground.
2 capture (a person or animal that tries or would try to escape): *we hadn't caught a single rabbit.* ▪ succeed in reaching a person who is ahead of one. ▪ (**be caught in**) unexpectedly find oneself in (an unwelcome situation): *my sister was caught in a thunderstorm.* ▪ surprise (someone) in an incriminating situation or in the act of doing something wrong: *he was caught with bomb-making equipment in his home.* ▪ come upon (someone) unexpectedly: *unexpected snow* ***caught*** *us* ***by surprise.***
3 [no obj., with adverbial of place] (of an object) accidentally become entangled or trapped in something: *a button caught in her hair.* ▪ [with obj. and adverbial of place] have (a part of one's body or clothing) become entangled or trapped in something: *she caught her foot in the bedspread* | figurative *companies face increased risks of being caught in a downward spiral.* ▪ [with obj. and adverbial of place] fix or fasten in place: *her hair was caught up in a chignon.*
4 reach in time and board (a train, bus, or aircraft): *they caught the 12.15 from Oxford.* ▪ reach or be in a place in time to see (a person, performance, programme, etc.): *she was hurrying downstairs to catch the news.* ▪ N. Amer. informal attend or watch (a performance): *we'll get some burgers and catch a movie.*
5 engage (a person's interest or imagination). ▪ perceive fleetingly: *she* ***caught a glimpse of*** *herself in the mirror.* ▪ hear or understand (something said), especially with effort: *he bellowed something Jess couldn't catch.* ▪ succeed in evoking or representing: *the programme caught something of the flavour of Minoan culture.*
6 [with obj. and adverbial of place] strike (someone) on a part of the body: *Ben caught him on the chin with an uppercut.* ▪ accidentally strike (a part of one's body) against something: *she fell and caught her head on the corner of the hearth.*
7 contract (an illness) through infection or contagion.
8 [no obj.] become ignited and start burning: *the rafters have caught.* ▪ (of an engine) fire and start running.
▸ noun **1** an act of catching something, typically a ball. ▪ Cricket a chance or act of catching the ball to dismiss a batsman: *he took a brilliant catch at deep square leg.* ▪ an amount of fish caught: *the UK's North Sea haddock catch.*
2 [mass noun] a game in which a ball is thrown back and forth between two or more players.
3 a device for securing something such as a door, window, or box: *the window catch was rusty.*
4 a hidden problem or disadvantage in an apparently ideal situation: *there's a catch in it somewhere.*
5 [in sing.] informal a person considered desirable as a partner or spouse: *Giles is a good catch for any girl.*
6 [in sing.] an unevenness in a person's voice caused by emotion: *there was a catch in Anne's voice.*
7 Music a round, typically one with words arranged to produce a humorous effect.
– PHRASES **catch (a) cold** see COLD. **catch one's death (of cold)** see DEATH. **catch someone's eye 1** be noticed by someone. **2** attract someone's attention by making eye contact with them: *he caught Eva's eye and beckoned.* **catch fire** see FIRE. **catch it** (N. Amer. **catch hell**) Brit. informal be punished or told off. **catch the light** shine or glint in the light. **catch sight of** see SIGHT. **catch the sun 1** be in a sunny position. **2** Brit. become tanned or sunburned. **you wouldn't catch —— doing something** informal used to indicate that there is no possibility of the person mentioned doing what is specified: *you wouldn't catch me walking back to the house alone at night.*
– PHRASAL VERBS **catch on** informal **1** (of a practice or fashion) become popular. **2** understand what is meant or how to do something: *I caught on to what it was the guy was saying.* ▪ (**catch yourself on**) Irish become aware of something: *catch yourself on, Michael, people don't get arrested for no reason.* **catch someone out 1** detect that someone has done something wrong or made a mistake. ▪ put someone in a difficult situation for which they are unprepared: *you might get caught out by the weather.* **2** Cricket dismiss a batsman by catching the ball before it touches the ground. **catch up** succeed in reaching a person who is ahead of one: *he stopped and waited for Lily to catch up.* ▪ do tasks which one should have done earlier: *he normally used the afternoons to* ***catch up on*** *paperwork.* **catch up with 1** succeed in reaching a person who is ahead of one: *you go with Stasia and Katie, and I'll catch up with you.* **2** talk to (someone) whom one has not seen for some time in order to find out what they have been doing. **3** begin to have a damaging effect on: *the physical exertions began to catch up with Sue.* **catch someone up 1** Brit. succeed in reaching a person who is ahead of one. **2** (**be/get caught up in**) become involved in (something that one had not intended to become involved in): *he had no desire to be caught up in political activities.* **catch something up** pick something up hurriedly.
– DERIVATIVES **catchable** adjective.
– ORIGIN Middle English (also in the sense 'chase'): from Anglo-Norman French and Old Northern French *cachier*, variant of Old French *chacier*, based on Latin *captare* 'try to catch', from *capere* 'take'.

catch-all ▸ noun [usu. as modifier] a term or category that encompasses a variety of different elements: *the stigmatizing catch-all term 'schizophrenia'.*

catch-as-catch-can ▸ noun [mass noun] **1** archaic wrestling in which all holds are permitted.
2 [usu. as modifier] a situation of using whatever is available: *the catch-as-catch-can repair of fences.*

catch crop ▸ noun a crop grown in the space between two main crops or at a time when no main crops are being grown.

catcher ▸ noun a person or thing that catches something. ▪ Baseball a fielder positioned behind home plate to catch pitches not hit by the batter.

catchfly ▸ noun (pl. **catchflies**) a campion or similar plant of the pink family, with a sticky stem. ● *Silene*, *Lychnis*, and other genera, family Caryophyllaceae.

catching ▸ adjective [predic.] (of a disease) infectious: *chicken pox is catching until scabs form on all the blisters.* ▪ (of a person's emotion or mood) likely to spread to other people: *her enthusiasm is catching.*

catchlight ▸ noun a gleam of reflected light in the eye of a person in a photograph.

catchline ▸ noun Brit. ▪ an advertising slogan: *there was an advert for tea that had the catchline: 'Tea. Best Drink of the Day'.* ▪ Printing a short, eye-catching line of type, such as a running head.

catchment ▸ noun **1** [mass noun] the action of collecting water, especially the collection of rainfall over a natural drainage area.
2 a catchment area.

catchment area ▸ noun **1** the area from which a hospital's patients or school's pupils are drawn.
2 the area from which rainfall flows into a river, lake, or reservoir.

catchpenny ▸ adjective [attrib.] having a cheap superficial attractiveness designed to encourage quick sales: *the catchpenny world of commercial publishing.*

catchphrase ▸ noun a well-known sentence or phrase, especially one that is associated with a particular famous person.

catch points ▸ plural noun railway points positioned so as to derail any vehicle running in the wrong direction on a line, as a safety precaution.

catch-22 ▸ noun a dilemma or difficult circumstance from which there is no escape because of mutually conflicting or dependent conditions: [as modifier] *a catch-22 situation.*
– ORIGIN 1970s: title of a novel by Joseph Heller (1961), in which the main character feigns madness in order to avoid dangerous combat missions, but his desire to avoid them is taken to prove his sanity.

catchup /ˈkatʃʌp/ ▸ noun old-fashioned term for KETCHUP.

catch-up (also **catchup**) ▸ noun informal an act of catching someone up in a particular activity.
– PHRASES **play catch-up 1** fall behind continually with work or financial matters: *I'm always playing catch-up with my homework.* **2** N. Amer. try to equal a competitor in a sport or game.

catchweight ▸ noun [mass noun] [usu. as modifier] chiefly historical unrestricted weight in a wrestling match or other sporting contest: *a catchweight contest.*

catchword ▸ noun **1** a popular word or phrase encapsulating a particular concept: *'motivation' is a great catchword.*
2 a word printed or placed so as to attract attention. ▪ Printing, chiefly historical the first word of a page given at the foot of the previous one.

catchy ▸ adjective (**catchier**, **catchiest**) (of a tune or phrase) instantly appealing and memorable: *catchy pop melodies.*
– DERIVATIVES **catchily** adverb, **catchiness** noun.

cate /keɪt/ ▸ noun (usu. **cates**) archaic a choice food; a delicacy.
– ORIGIN late Middle English (in the sense 'selling, a bargain'): from obsolete *acate* 'purchasing, things purchased', from Old French *acat, achat*, from *acater, achater* 'buy', based on Latin *captare* 'seize', from *capere* 'take'.

catechesis /ˌkatɪˈkiːsɪs/ ▸ noun [mass noun] religious instruction given with a catechism in preparation for Christian baptism or confirmation. ▪ (in Roman Catholic use) religious instruction in general.
– ORIGIN mid 18th cent.: via ecclesiastical Latin from Greek *katēkhēsis* 'oral instruction'.

catechetical /ˌkatɪˈkɛtɪk(ə)l/ ▸ adjective relating to religious instruction given in preparation for Christian baptism or confirmation. ▪ relating to religious teaching by means of questions and answers.
– DERIVATIVES **catechetically** adverb.
– ORIGIN early 17th cent.: from ecclesiastical Greek *katēkhētikos*, from *katēkhētēs* 'catechist', from *katēkhein* 'instruct orally' (see CATECHIZE).

catechetics /ˌkatɪˈkɛtɪks/ ▸ plural noun [treated as sing.] the branch of theology that deals with the instruction given to Christians before baptism or confirmation. ▪ religious teaching in general, especially that given to children in the Roman Catholic Church.

catechin /ˈkatɪtʃɪn/ ▸ noun [mass noun] Chemistry a crystalline compound which is the major constituent of catechu. ● A phenol; chem. formula: $C_{15}H_{14}O_6$; several isomers.
– ORIGIN mid 19th cent.: from CATECHU + -IN[1].

catechism /ˈkatɪkɪz(ə)m/ ▸ noun a summary of the principles of Christian religion in the form of questions and answers, used for religious instruction. ▪ (in Roman Catholic use) religious instruction in general.
– DERIVATIVES **catechismal** adjective.
– ORIGIN early 16th cent.: from ecclesiastical Latin *catechismus*, from ecclesiastical Greek, from *katēkhizein* (see CATECHIZE).

catechist ▸ noun a teacher of the principles of Christian religion, especially one using a catechism.
– ORIGIN mid 16th cent.: via ecclesiastical Latin from ecclesiastical Greek *katēkhistēs*, from *katēkhein* 'instruct orally'.

catechize (also **catechise**) ▸ verb [with obj.] instruct (someone) in the principles of Christian religion by means of question and answer, typically by using a catechism.
– ORIGIN late Middle English: via late Latin from ecclesiastical Greek *katēkhizein*, from *katēkhein* 'instruct orally, make hear'.

catechol /ˈkatɪtʃɒl, -kɒl/ ▸ noun [mass noun] Chemistry a crystalline compound obtained by distilling catechu. ● Chem. formula: $C_6H_4(OH)_2$.
– ORIGIN late 19th cent.: from CATECHU + -OL.

catecholamine /ˌkatɪˈkəʊləmiːn/ ▸ noun Biochemistry any of a class of aromatic amines which includes a number of neurotransmitters such as adrenalin and dopamine.

catechu /ˈkatɪtʃuː/ ▸ noun [mass noun] a vegetable extract containing tannin, especially one (also called CUTCH) obtained from the heartwood of an Indian acacia tree, used for tanning and dyeing. ▪ another term for GAMBIER.
– ORIGIN late 17th cent.: modern Latin, from Malay *kacu*. Compare with CACHOU.

catechumen /ˌkatɪˈkjuːmɛn/ ▸ noun a person who is receiving instruction in preparation for Christian baptism or confirmation. ▪ a young Christian preparing for confirmation.
– ORIGIN late Middle English: via ecclesiastical Latin from Greek *katēkhoumenos* 'being instructed', present participle of *katēkhein* 'instruct orally' (see CATECHIZE).

categorical ▶ **adjective** unambiguously explicit and direct: *a categorical assurance.*
– DERIVATIVES **categoric** adjective, **categorically** adverb.
– ORIGIN late 16th cent.: from late Latin *categoricus* (from Greek *katēgorikos*, from *katēgoria* 'statement': see CATEGORY) + -AL.

categorical imperative ▶ **noun** Philosophy (in Kantian ethics) an unconditional moral obligation which is binding in all circumstances and is not dependent on a person's inclination or purpose.

categorize (also **categorise**) ▶ **verb** [with obj.] place in a particular class or group: ***silk is categorized as a*** *luxury import.*
– DERIVATIVES **categorization** noun.

category ▶ **noun** (pl. **categories**) **1** a class or division of people or things regarded as having particular shared characteristics: *the various categories of research.*
2 Philosophy each of a possibly exhaustive set of classes among which all things might be distributed. ■ each of the a priori conceptions applied by the mind to sense impressions.
– DERIVATIVES **categorial** adjective.
– ORIGIN late Middle English (in sense 2): from French *catégorie* or late Latin *categoria*, from Greek *katēgoria* 'statement, accusation', from *katēgoros* 'accuser'.

category killer ▶ **noun** a large store, typically one of a chain, which specializes in a particular type of discounted merchandise and becomes the dominant retailer in that category.

category mistake (also **category error**) ▶ **noun** Logic the error of assigning to something a quality or action which can only properly be assigned to things of another category, for example treating abstract concepts as though they had a physical location.

catena /kə'tiːnə/ ▶ **noun** (pl. **catenae** /-niː/ or **catenas**) technical a connected series or chain. ■ a connected series of texts written by early Christian theologians.
– ORIGIN mid 17th cent.: from Latin, 'chain', originally in *catena patrum* 'chain of the (Church) Fathers'.

catenaccio /ˌkatə'natʃɪəʊ/ ▶ **noun** [mass noun] Soccer a very defensive system of play, especially one employing a sweeper.
– ORIGIN 1970s: Italian, literally 'bolt', from *catena* 'chain' + the pejorative suffix *-accio*.

catenane /'katəneɪn/ ▶ **noun** Chemistry a molecule which consists of two or more connected rings like links in a chain.
– ORIGIN 1960s: from Latin *catena* 'chain' + -ANE[2].

catenary /kə'tiːnəri/ ▶ **noun** (pl. **catenaries**) a curve formed by a wire, rope, or chain hanging freely from two points that are not in the same vertical line: [as modifier] *a catenary wire.* ■ a wire, rope, or chain forming a catenary.
– ORIGIN mid 18th cent.: from Latin *catenarius* 'relating to a chain', from *catena* 'chain'.

catenated /'katɪneɪtɪd/ ▶ **adjective** technical connected in a chain or series: *catenated molecules.*
– DERIVATIVES **catenation** noun.
– ORIGIN late 19th cent.: past participle of the rare verb *catenate*, from Latin *catenat-* 'chained, fettered', from the verb *catenare*, from *catena* 'chain'.

catenative /kə'tɪnətɪv/ ▶ **adjective** Grammar denoting a verb that governs a non-finite form of another verb, for example *like* in *I like swimming.*
– ORIGIN late 20th cent.: from Latin *catena* 'chain' + -ATIVE.

catenoid /'katənɔɪd/ ▶ **noun** Geometry the surface generated by rotating a catenary about its horizontal axis.
– ORIGIN late 19th cent.: from Latin *catena* 'chain' + -OID.

cater ▶ **verb** [no obj.] **1** Brit. provide people with food and drink at a social event or other gathering: *my mother helped to cater for the party* | (as noun **catering**) *high standards of catering.* ■ [with obj.] N. Amer. provide food and drink for (an event): *he catered a lunch for 20 people.*
2 (**cater for/to**) provide with what is needed or required: *the school caters for children with learning difficulties.* ■ (**cater for**) take into account or make allowances for: *the scheme caters for interest rate fluctuations.* ■ (**cater to**) try to satisfy (a need or demand): *he catered to her every whim.*
– DERIVATIVES **caterer** noun.
– ORIGIN late 16th cent.: from obsolete *cater* 'caterer', from Old French *acateor* 'buyer', from *acater* 'buy' (see CATE).

cateran /'kat(ə)r(ə)n/ ▶ **noun** historical a warrior or raider from the Scottish Highlands.
– ORIGIN Middle English (originally in the plural or as a collective singular denoting the peasantry as fighters): from Scottish Gaelic *ceathairne* 'peasantry'.

cater-cornered /'keɪtəˌkɔːnəd/ (also **cater-corner, catty-cornered, kitty-corner**) ▶ **adverb & adjective** N. Amer. situated diagonally opposite someone or something: [as adj.] *a cater-cornered short cut.*
– ORIGIN mid 19th cent.: from dialect *cater* 'diagonally', from *cater* denoting the four on dice, from French *quatre* 'four', from Latin *quattuor*.

caterpillar ▶ **noun** **1** the larva of a butterfly or moth, which has a segmented body resembling a worm with three pairs of true legs and several pairs of leg-like appendages. ■ (in general use) any similar larva of various insects, especially sawflies.
2 (also **caterpillar track** or **tread**) trademark an articulated steel band passing round the wheels of a vehicle for travel on rough ground.
– ORIGIN late Middle English: perhaps from a variant of Old French *chatepelose*, literally 'hairy cat', influenced by obsolete *piller* 'ravager'. The association with 'cat' is found in other languages, e.g. Swiss German *Teufelskatz* (literally 'devil's cat'), Lombard *gatta* (literally 'cat'). Compare with French *chaton*, English CATKIN, which resembles a hairy caterpillar.

caters ▶ **noun** Bell-ringing a system of change-ringing using nine bells, with four pairs changing places each time.
– ORIGIN late 19th cent.: from French *quatre* 'four'.

caterwaul /'katəwɔːl/ ▶ **verb** [no obj.] (often as noun **caterwauling**) (of a cat) make a shrill howling or wailing noise.
▶ **noun** a shrill howling or wailing noise.
– ORIGIN late Middle English: from CAT[1] + imitative WAUL.

catfight ▶ **noun** informal a fight between women.
– DERIVATIVES **catfighting** noun.

catfish ▶ **noun** (pl. **same** or **catfishes**) **1** a freshwater or marine fish with whisker-like barbels round the mouth, typically bottom-dwelling. ● Order Siluriformes: many families, including the Eurasian family Siluridae (see WELS) and the Callichthyidae (which contains a number of species that are popular in aquaria, in particular the genus *Corydoras*).
2 another term for WOLF FISH.

cat flap ▶ **noun** a small hinged flap in an outer door, through which a cat may enter or leave a building.

catgut ▶ **noun** [mass noun] a material used for the strings of some musical instruments, made of the dried twisted intestines of sheep or horses (but not cats).
– ORIGIN late 16th cent.: the association with CAT[1] remains unexplained.

Cath. ▶ **abbreviation** ■ Cathedral. ■ Catholic.

Cathar /'kaθɑː/ ▶ **noun** a member of a heretical medieval Christian sect which professed a form of Manichaean dualism and sought to achieve great spiritual purity.
– DERIVATIVES **Catharism** noun, **Catharist** noun & adjective.
– ORIGIN mid 17th cent.: from medieval Latin *Cathari* (plural), from Greek *katharoi* 'the pure'.

catharsis /kə'θɑːsɪs/ ▶ **noun** (pl. **catharses** /-siːz/) [mass noun] **1** the process of releasing, and thereby providing relief from, strong or repressed emotions.
2 Medicine, rare purgation.
– ORIGIN early 19th cent. (in sense 2): from Greek *katharsis*, from *kathairein* 'cleanse', from *katharos* 'pure'. The notion of 'release' through drama (sense 1) derives from Aristotle's *Poetics*.

cathartic ▶ **adjective** **1** providing psychological relief through the open expression of strong emotions; causing catharsis: *crying is a cathartic release.*
2 Medicine purgative.
▶ **noun** Medicine a purgative drug.
– DERIVATIVES **cathartically** adverb.
– ORIGIN early 17th cent. (in medical use): via late Latin from Greek *kathartikos*, from *katharsis* 'cleansing' (see CATHARSIS).

Cathay /ka'θeɪ/ the name by which China was known to medieval Europe. Also called KHITAI.
– ORIGIN from medieval Latin *Cataya, Cathaya*, from Turkic *Khitāy*.

cathead ▶ **noun** a horizontal beam extending from each side of a ship's bow, used for raising and carrying an anchor.

cathectic /kə'θɛktɪk/ ▶ **adjective** Psychoanalysis relating to cathexis.
– ORIGIN 1920s: from Greek *kathektikos* 'capable of holding'.

cathedral ▶ **noun** the principal church of a diocese, with which the bishop is officially associated: [in names] *St Paul's Cathedral.*
– ORIGIN Middle English (as an adjective, the noun being short for *cathedral church* 'the church which contains the bishop's throne'): from late Latin *cathedralis*, from Latin *cathedra* 'seat', from Greek *kathedra*.

C

cathedral city ▶ **noun** a city in which there is a cathedral.

Cather /'kaðə/, Willa (Sibert) (1876–1974), American novelist and short-story writer. Her home state of Nebraska provides the setting for some of her best writing. Notable novels: *O Pioneers!* (1913) and *Death Comes for the Archbishop* (1927).

Catherine II (1729–96), empress of Russia, reigned 1762–96; known as **Catherine the Great**. She became empress after her husband, Peter III, was deposed; her attempted social and political reforms were impeded by the aristocracy. She formed alliances with Prussia and Austria, and made territorial advances at the expense of the Turks and Tartars.

Catherine, St (died *c*.307), early Christian martyr; known as **St Catherine of Alexandria**. According to tradition she opposed the persecution of Christians under the emperor Maxentius and refused to recant or to marry the emperor. She is said to have been tortured on a spiked wheel and then beheaded. Feast day, 25 November.

Catherine de' Medici (1519–89), queen of France, wife of Henry II. She ruled as regent (1560–74) during the minority reigns of her three sons, Francis II, Charles IX, and Henry III, and it was at her instigation that Huguenots were killed in the Massacre of St Bartholomew (1572).

Catherine of Aragon (1485–1536), first wife of Henry VIII, youngest daughter of Ferdinand and Isabella of Castile, mother of Mary I. Henry's wish to annul his marriage to Catherine (due to her failure to produce a male heir) led eventually to England's break with the Roman Catholic Church.

Catherine wheel ▶ **noun** Brit. a firework in the form of a flat coil which spins when fixed to something solid and lit.
– ORIGIN late 16th cent. (as a heraldic term for a spiked wheel): named after St *Catherine* (see CATHERINE, ST), with reference to her martyrdom.

catheter /'kaθɪtə/ ▶ **noun** Medicine a flexible tube inserted through a narrow opening into a body cavity, particularly the bladder, for removing fluid.
– ORIGIN early 17th cent.: from late Latin, from Greek *kathetēr*, from *kathienai* 'send or let down'.

catheterize (also **catheterise**) ▶ **verb** [with obj.] Medicine insert a catheter into (a body cavity).
– DERIVATIVES **catheterization** noun.

cathetometer /ˌkaθɪ'tɒmɪtə/ ▶ **noun** a telescope mounted on a graduated scale, used for accurate measurement of small vertical distances.
– ORIGIN mid 19th cent.: from Latin *cathetus* (from Greek *kathetos* 'perpendicular line', from *kathienai* 'send or let down') + -METER.

cathexis /kə'θɛksɪs/ ▶ **noun** [mass noun] Psychoanalysis the concentration of mental energy on one particular person, idea, or object (especially to an unhealthy degree).
– ORIGIN 1920s: from Greek *kathexis* 'retention', translating German *Libidobesetzung*, coined by Freud.

cathode /'kaθəʊd/ ▶ **noun** the negatively charged electrode by which electrons enter an electrical device. The opposite of ANODE. ■ the positively charged electrode of an electrical device, such as a primary cell, that supplies current.
– DERIVATIVES **cathodal** adjective, **cathodic** /kə'θɒdɪk/ adjective.
– ORIGIN mid 19th cent.: from Greek *kathodos* 'way down', from *kata-* 'down' + *hodos* 'way'.

cathode ray ▶ **noun** a beam of electrons emitted from the cathode of a high-vacuum tube.

cathode ray tube ▶ **noun** a high-vacuum tube in which cathode rays produce a luminous image on a fluorescent screen, used in televisions and computer terminals.

cathodic protection ▶ **noun** [mass noun] protection of a metal structure from corrosion under water by making it act as an electrical cathode.

cathodoluminescence /ˌkaθədə(ʊ)ˌluːmɪˈnɛs(ə)ns/ ▶ noun [mass noun] Physics luminescence excited by the impact of an electron beam.

catholic ▶ adjective **1** including a wide variety of things; all-embracing: *her tastes are pretty catholic.* **2** (**Catholic**) of the Roman Catholic faith. ■ of or including all Christians. ■ relating to the historic doctrine and practice of the Western Church.
▶ noun (**Catholic**) a member of the Roman Catholic Church.
– DERIVATIVES **catholicity** noun.
– ORIGIN late Middle English (in sense 2 of the adjective): from Old French *catholique* or late Latin *catholicus*, from Greek *katholikos* 'universal', from *kata* 'in respect of' + *holos* 'whole'.

Catholic Church ▶ noun short for ROMAN CATHOLIC CHURCH.

Catholic Emancipation the granting of full political and civil liberties to Roman Catholics in Britain and Ireland. This was effected by the Catholic Emancipation Act of 1829, which repealed restrictive laws, including that which barred Catholics from holding public office.

Catholicism /kəˈθɒlɪsɪz(ə)m/ ▶ noun [mass noun] the faith, practice, and church order of the Roman Catholic Church. ■ adherence to the forms of Christian doctrine and practice which are generally regarded as Catholic rather than Protestant or Eastern Orthodox.

Catholicize (also **Catholicise**) ▶ verb [with obj.] make Roman Catholic; convert to Catholicism.

Catholic League see HOLY LEAGUE.

Catholicos /kəˈθɒlɪkɒs/ ▶ noun (pl. **Catholicoses** /kəˌθɒlɪˈkəʊsiːz/ or **Catholicoi** /kəˈθɒlɪkɔɪ/) the Patriarch of the Armenian or the Nestorian Church.
– ORIGIN early 17th cent.: from medieval Greek *katholikos* 'universal' (see CATHOLIC).

cathouse ▶ noun N. Amer. informal a brothel.

cat ice ▶ noun [mass noun] thin ice from under which the water has receded.

Catiline /ˈkatɪlʌɪn/ (c.108–62 BC), Roman nobleman and conspirator; Latin name *Lucius Sergius Catilina*. In 63 BC he planned an uprising which was suppressed; his fellow conspirators were executed and he died in battle in Etruria.

cation /ˈkatʌɪən/ ▶ noun Chemistry a positively charged ion, i.e. one that would be attracted to the cathode in electrolysis. The opposite of ANION.
– DERIVATIVES **cationic** /katʌɪˈɒnɪk/ adjective.
– ORIGIN mid 19th cent.: from CATA- 'alongside' or from CATHODE, + ION.

catkin ▶ noun a downy, hanging flowering spike of trees such as willow and hazel, pollinated by the wind.
– ORIGIN late 16th cent.: from obsolete Dutch *katteken* 'kitten'.

cat ladder ▶ noun Brit. a ladder used for working on a sloping roof, with a hook at one end and pads to spread the load.

catlick ▶ noun Brit. informal a perfunctory wash.

catlike ▶ adjective resembling a cat in appearance, action, or character: *Marianne crossed the room with her usual catlike grace.*

catlinite /ˈkatlɪnʌɪt/ ▶ noun [mass noun] a red clay of the Upper Missouri region, the sacred pipestone of the American Indians.
– ORIGIN mid 19th cent.: from the name of George *Catlin* (1796–1872), American artist, + -ITE[1].

cat litter ▶ noun see LITTER (sense 3 of the noun).

catmint ▶ noun a plant of the mint family, with downy leaves, purple-spotted white flowers, and a pungent smell attractive to cats. Also called CATNIP. ● Genus *Nepeta*, family Labiatae: several species.

catnap ▶ noun a short sleep during the day.
▶ verb (**catnaps**, **catnapping**, **catnapped**) [no obj.] have a catnap.

catnip ▶ noun another term for CATMINT.
– ORIGIN late 18th cent. (originally US): from CAT[1] + *nip*, variant of dialect *nep, nept*, from medieval Latin *nepta*, from Latin *nepeta* 'catmint'.

Cato /ˈkeɪtəʊ/, Marcus Porcius (234–149 BC), Roman statesman, orator, and writer; known as **Cato the Elder** or **Cato the Censor**. As censor he initiated a vigorous programme of reform, and attempted to stem the growing influence of Greek culture.

cat-o'-nine-tails ▶ noun historical a rope whip with nine knotted cords, formerly used (especially at sea) to flog offenders.

catoptric /kaˈtɒptrɪk/ Physics ▶ adjective relating to a mirror, a reflector, or reflection.
▶ plural noun [treated as sing.] the branch of optics that deals with reflection.
– ORIGIN mid 16th cent.: from Greek *katoptrikos* 'reflecting', from *katoptron* 'mirror'.

CAT scan ▶ noun an X-ray image made using computerized axial tomography.
– DERIVATIVES **CAT scanner** noun.

cat's cradle ▶ noun [mass noun] a child's game in which a loop of string is put around and between the fingers and complex patterns are formed.

cat scratch fever (also **cat scratch disease**) ▶ noun [mass noun] an infectious disease occurring after a scratch by a cat's claw, a splinter, or a thorn.

cat's ear (also **cat's ears**) ▶ noun a plant which resembles the dandelion, with yellow flowers and rosettes of leaves. ● Genus *Hypochaeris*, family Compositae.

cat's eye ▶ noun **1** a semi-precious stone, especially chalcedony, with a band of bright lustre.
2 (**catseye**) Brit. trademark a reflective stud set into a road as one of a series to mark traffic lanes or the edge of the carriageway by reflecting light from headlights.

cat's foot ▶ noun a small white-flowered creeping plant of the daisy family, with soft white hairs on the flowering stems and undersides of the leaves. Also called MOUNTAIN EVERLASTING. ● *Antennaria dioica*, family Compositae.

cat shark ▶ noun a small bottom-dwelling shark that has catlike eyes and small dorsal fins set well back, inhabiting warmer waters. ● *Apristurus* and other genera, family Scyliorhinidae: several species.

Catskill Mountains /ˈkatskɪl/ (also **the Catskills**) a range of mountains in the state of New York, part of the Appalachian system.

cat's paw ▶ noun a person who is used by another to carry out an unpleasant or dangerous task.

cat's tail (also **cattail**) ▶ noun a plant with long, thin parts suggestive of cats' tails, in particular: ● the reed mace. ● (also **cat's-tail grass**) timothy grass.

catsuit ▶ noun a woman's close-fitting one-piece garment with trouser legs, covering the body from the neck to the feet.

catsup /ˈkatsəp/ ▶ noun US another term for KETCHUP.

cat's whisker ▶ noun a fine adjustable wire in a crystal radio receiver.

cattery ▶ noun (pl. **catteries**) Brit. a boarding or breeding establishment for cats.

cattish ▶ adjective another term for CATTY[1].
– DERIVATIVES **cattishly** adverb.

cattle ▶ plural noun **1** large ruminant animals with horns and cloven hoofs, domesticated for meat or milk, or as beasts of burden; cows and oxen. ● *Bos taurus* (including the zebu, *B. indicus*), family Bovidae; descended from the extinct aurochs.
2 animals of a group related to domestic cattle, including yak, bison, and buffaloes. ● Tribe Bovini, family Bovidae (the **cattle family**): four genera, in particular *Bos*. The cattle family also includes the sheep, goats, goat-antelopes, and antelopes.
– ORIGIN Middle English (also denoting personal property or wealth): from Anglo-Norman French *catel*, variant of Old French *chatel* (see CHATTEL).

cattle cake ▶ noun [mass noun] Brit. concentrated food for cattle in a compressed flat form.

cattle call ▶ noun N. Amer. informal an open audition for parts in a play or film.

cattle class ▶ noun [mass noun] humorous the cheapest class of seats on an aircraft.

cattle dog ▶ noun Austral./NZ a dog bred and trained to work cattle.

cattle duffing ▶ noun [mass noun] Austral. theft of cattle.
– DERIVATIVES **cattle duffer** noun.
– ORIGIN mid 19th cent.: *duffing* from DUFFER[2].

cattle egret ▶ noun a small white heron which feeds around grazing cattle and game herds. Native to southern Eurasia and Africa, it colonized North and South America and Australasia in the 20th century. ● *Bubulcus* (or *Ardeola*) *ibis*, family Ardeidae.

cattle grid (N. Amer. **cattle guard**) ▶ noun Brit. a metal grid covering a ditch, allowing vehicles and pedestrians to pass over but not cattle and other animals.

cattleman ▶ noun (pl. **cattlemen**) chiefly N. Amer. a person who tends or rears cattle.

cattle plague ▶ noun another term for RINDERPEST.

cattleya /ˈkatlɪə/ ▶ noun a tropical American orchid with brightly coloured showy flowers and thick leaves, typically growing as an epiphyte. ● Genus *Cattleya*, family Orchidaceae.
– ORIGIN early 19th cent.: modern Latin, named after William Cattley (died 1832), English patron of botany.

cat train ▶ noun N. Amer. a crawler tractor pulling a train of sleighs across snow or ice.
– ORIGIN *cat* from CATERPILLAR.

catty[1] ▶ adjective (**cattier**, **cattiest**) **1** deliberately hurtful in one's remarks; spiteful: *catty comments.*
2 relating to cats; catlike.
– DERIVATIVES **cattily** adverb, **cattiness** noun.

catty[2] ▶ noun S. African informal a catapult.

catty-cornered ▶ adjective another term for CATER-CORNERED.

Catullus /kəˈtʌləs/, Gaius Valerius (c.84–c.54 BC), Roman poet. He wrote on a range of subjects, but is best known for his love poems.

CATV ▶ abbreviation community antenna television (cable television).

catwalk ▶ noun **1** a platform extending into an auditorium, along which models walk to display clothes in fashion shows.
2 a narrow walkway or open bridge, especially in an industrial installation.

caubeen /kɔːˈbiːn/ ▶ noun an Irish beret, typically dark green in colour.
– ORIGIN early 19th cent.: Irish, literally 'old hat', from *cáibín* 'little cape', diminutive of *cába* 'cape'.

Caucasian /kɔːˈkeɪzɪən, -ʒ(ə)n/ ▶ adjective **1** relating to one of the traditional divisions of humankind, covering a broad group of peoples from Europe, western Asia, and parts of India and North Africa. [so named because the German physiologist Blumenbach believed that it originated in the Caucasus region of SE Europe.] ■ white-skinned; of European origin.
2 relating to the Caucasus.
3 relating to a group of languages spoken in the region of the Caucasus, of which thirty-eight are known, many not committed to writing. The most widely spoken is Georgian, of the small **South Caucasian** family, not related to the three **North Caucasian** families.
▶ noun a Caucasian person. ■ a white person; a person of European origin.

> **USAGE** In the racial classification as developed by Blumenbach and others in the 19th century, **Caucasian** (or **Caucasoid**) included peoples whose skin colour ranged from light (in northern Europe) to dark (in parts of North Africa and India). Although the classification is outdated and the categories are now not generally accepted as scientific (see USAGE at MONGOLOID), the term **Caucasian** has acquired a more restricted meaning. It is now used, especially in the US, as a synonym for 'white or of European origin', as in *the police are looking for a Caucasian male in his forties.*

Caucasoid /ˈkɔːkəsɔɪd/ ▶ adjective relating to the Caucasian division of humankind.

Caucasus /ˈkɔːkəsəs/ (also **Caucasia** /kɔːˈkeɪzɪə, -ˈkeɪʒə/) a mountainous region of SE Europe and SW Asia, lying between the Black Sea and the Caspian Sea, in Georgia, Armenia, Azerbaijan, and SE Russia.

Cauchy /ˈkəʊʃi/, French /koʃi/, Augustin Louis, Baron (1789–1857), French mathematician. He transformed the theory of complex functions by discovering his integral theorems, founded the modern theory of elasticity, and contributed substantially to the founding of group theory and analysis.

caucus /ˈkɔːkəs/ ▶ noun (pl. **caucuses**) **1** (in North America and New Zealand) a meeting of the members of a legislative body who are members of a particular political party, to select candidates or decide policy. ■ the members of a caucus.
2 a group of people with shared concerns within a political party or larger organization.
▶ verb (**caucuses**, **caucusing**, **caucused**) [no obj.] chiefly N. Amer. hold or form a caucus.
– ORIGIN mid 18th cent. (originally US): perhaps from Algonquian *cau'-cau'-as'u* 'adviser'.

caudal /ˈkɔːd(ə)l/ ▶ adjective of or like a tail. ■ at or near the tail or the posterior part of the body.
– DERIVATIVES **caudally** adverb.
– ORIGIN mid 17th cent.: from modern Latin *caudalis*, from Latin *cauda* 'tail'.

caudal fin ▶ noun Zoology another term for TAIL FIN.

Caudata /kɔːˈdeɪtə/ ▶ **plural noun** Zoology another term for **URODELA**.
– ORIGIN modern Latin (plural), from Latin *cauda* 'tail'.

caudate /ˈkɔːdeɪt/ ▶ **adjective 1** Anatomy relating to or denoting the caudate nucleus.
2 Zoology (of an animal) having a tail.
▶ **noun** short for **CAUDATE NUCLEUS**.
– ORIGIN early 17th cent.: from medieval Latin *caudatus*, from *cauda* 'tail'.

caudate nucleus ▶ **noun** Anatomy the upper of the two grey nuclei of the corpus striatum in the cerebrum of the brain.

caudex /ˈkɔːdɛks/ ▶ **noun** (pl. **caudices** /-dɪsiːz/) Botany the axis of a woody plant, especially a palm or tree fern, comprising the stem and root.
– ORIGIN late 18th cent.: from Latin, earlier form of **CODEX**.

caudillo /kaʊˈdiːjəʊ, -ˈdiːljəʊ/ ▶ **noun** (pl. **caudillos**) (in Spain and other Spanish-speaking countries) a military or political leader.
– ORIGIN Spanish, from late Latin *capitellum*, diminutive of Latin *caput* 'head'. The title *El Caudillo*, 'the leader', was assumed by General Franco of Spain in 1938.

caught past and past participle of **CATCH**.

caul /kɔːl/ ▶ **noun 1** the amniotic membrane enclosing a fetus. ■ part of the caul occasionally found on a child's head at birth, thought to bring good luck.
2 historical a woman's close-fitting indoor headdress or hairnet.
3 Anatomy the omentum.
– ORIGIN Middle English: perhaps from Old French *cale* 'head covering', but recorded earlier.

cauldron (also **caldron**) ▶ **noun 1** a large metal pot with a lid and handle, used for cooking over an open fire.
2 a situation characterized by instability and strong emotions: *a cauldron of repressed anger*.
– ORIGIN Middle English: from Anglo-Norman French *caudron*, based on Latin *caldarium*, *calidarium* 'cooking-pot', from *calidus* 'hot'.

cauliflower ▶ **noun** a cabbage of a variety which bears a large immature flower head of small creamy-white flower buds. ■ [mass noun] the flower head of the cauliflower eaten as a vegetable.
– ORIGIN late 16th cent.: from obsolete French *chou fleuri* 'flowered cabbage', probably from Italian *cavolfiore* or modern Latin *cauliflora*. The original English form *colieflorie* or *cole-flory* had its first element influenced by **COLE**; the second element was influenced by **FLOWER** during the 17th cent.

cauliflower cheese ▶ **noun** [mass noun] Brit. a savoury dish of cauliflower in a cheese sauce.

cauliflower ear ▶ **noun** a person's ear that has become thickened or deformed as a result of repeated blows, typically in boxing or rugby.

cauliflower fungus ▶ **noun** an edible fungus which forms a distinctive fruiting body with a yellowish lobed surface, growing on wood and other plant debris. Also called **BRAIN FUNGUS**. ● Genus *Sparassis* and family Sparassidaceae, class Hymenomycetes: several species.

caulk /kɔːk/ (US also **calk**) ▶ **noun** [mass noun] a waterproof filler and sealant, used in building work and repairs.
▶ **verb** [with obj.] seal (a gap or seam) with caulk. ■ make (a boat) watertight by stopping up any gaps in its hull.
– DERIVATIVES **caulker** noun.
– ORIGIN late Middle English (in the sense 'copulate', used of birds): from Old Northern French *cauquer*, *caukier*, variant of *cauchier* 'tread, press with force', from Latin *calcare* 'tread', from *calx*, *calc-* 'heel'.

causal ▶ **adjective** relating to or acting as a cause: *the causal factors associated with illness*. ■ Grammar & Logic expressing or indicating a cause: *a causal conjunction*.
– DERIVATIVES **causally** adverb.
– ORIGIN late Middle English (as a noun denoting a causal conjunction or particle): from late Latin *causalis*, from Latin *causa* 'cause'.

causalgia /kɔːˈzaldʒə/ ▶ **noun** [mass noun] severe burning pain in a limb caused by injury to a peripheral nerve.
– ORIGIN mid 19th cent.: from Greek *kausos* 'heat, fever' + **-ALGIA**.

causality ▶ **noun** [mass noun] **1** the relationship between cause and effect.
2 the principle that everything has a cause.
– ORIGIN late 15th cent.: from French *causalité* or medieval Latin *causalitas*, from Latin *causa* 'cause'.

causation ▶ **noun** [mass noun] the action of causing something: *the postulated role of nitrate in the causation of cancer*. ■ the relationship between cause and effect; causality.
– PHRASES **chain of causation** Law a linked series of events leading from cause to effect, typically in the assessment of liability for damages.
– ORIGIN late 15th cent.: from Latin *causatio(n-)* 'pretext' (in medieval Latin 'the action of causing'), from *causare* 'to cause'.

causative ▶ **adjective** acting as a cause: *a causative factor*. ■ Grammar expressing causation: *a causative verb*.
– DERIVATIVES **causatively** adverb.
– ORIGIN late Middle English: from Old French *causatif*, *-ive*, or late Latin *causativus*, from *causare* 'to cause'.

cause ▶ **noun 1** a person or thing that gives rise to an action, phenomenon, or condition: *the cause of the accident is not clear*. ■ [mass noun] reasonable grounds for doing, thinking, or feeling something: *Faye's condition had given no* ***cause for concern*** | [count noun] *class size is a cause for complaint in some schools*.
2 a principle, aim, or movement to which one is committed and which one is prepared to defend or advocate: *she devoted her whole adult life to the cause of deaf people* | *I'm raising money for good causes*.
3 a matter to be resolved in a court of law. ■ an individual's case offered at law.
▶ **verb** [with obj.] make (something, especially something bad) happen: *this disease can cause blindness* | [with two objs] *you could cause them problems*.
– PHRASES **cause and effect** the principle of causation. ■ the operation or relation of a cause and its effect. **cause of action** Law a fact or facts that enable a person to bring an action against another. **in the cause of** so as to support, promote, or defend something: *he gave his life in the cause of freedom*. **make common cause** unite in order to achieve a shared aim: *nationalist movements* ***made common cause*** *with the reformers*. **a rebel without a cause** a person who is dissatisfied with society but does not have a specific aim to fight for. [from the title of a US film, released in 1955.]
– DERIVATIVES **causeless** adjective, **causer** noun.
– ORIGIN Middle English: from Old French, from Latin *causa* (noun), *causare* (verb).

'cause ▶ **conjunction** informal short for **BECAUSE**.

cause célèbre /ˌkɔːz sɛˈlɛbr(ə)/, French /koz selɛbʀ/ ▶ **noun** (pl. **causes célèbres** pronunc. **same**) a controversial issue that attracts a great deal of public attention.
– ORIGIN mid 18th cent.: French, literally 'famous case'.

causerie /ˈkəʊzəri/, French /kozʀi/ ▶ **noun** (pl. **causeries** pronunc. **same**) an informal article or talk, typically on a literary subject.
– ORIGIN French, from *causer* 'to talk'.

causeway ▶ **noun** a raised road or track across low or wet ground.
– ORIGIN late Middle English: from **CAUSEY** + **WAY**.

causewayed camp ▶ **noun** Archaeology a type of Neolithic settlement in southern Britain, visible as an oval enclosure surrounded by concentric ditches that are crossed by several causeways.

causey /ˈkɔːzi, -si/ ▶ **noun** (pl. **causeys**) archaic or dialect term for **CAUSEWAY**.
– ORIGIN Middle English: from Anglo-Norman French *caucee*, based on Latin *calx* 'lime, limestone' (used for paving roads).

caustic /ˈkɔːstɪk, ˈkɒst-/ ▶ **adjective 1** able to burn or corrode organic tissue by chemical action: *a caustic cleaner*.
2 sarcastic in a scathing and bitter way: *the players were making caustic comments about the refereeing*.
3 Physics formed by the intersection of reflected or refracted parallel rays from a curved surface.
▶ **noun 1** a caustic substance.
2 Physics a caustic surface or curve.
– DERIVATIVES **caustically** adverb, **causticity** noun.
– ORIGIN late Middle English: via Latin from Greek *kaustikos*, from *kaustos* 'combustible', from *kaiein* 'to burn'.

caustic potash ▶ **noun** another term for **POTASSIUM HYDROXIDE**.

caustic soda ▶ **noun** another term for **SODIUM HYDROXIDE**.

cauterize /ˈkɔːtərʌɪz/ (also **cauterise**) ▶ **verb** [with obj.] burn the skin or flesh of (a wound) with a heated instrument or caustic substance in order to stop bleeding or to prevent infection.
– DERIVATIVES **cauterization** noun.
– ORIGIN late Middle English: from Old French *cauteriser*, from late Latin *cauterizare*, from Greek *kautēriazein*, from *kautērion* 'branding iron', from *kaiein* 'to burn'.

cautery /ˈkɔːt(ə)ri/ ▶ **noun** (pl. **cauteries**) an instrument or a caustic substance used for cauterizing. ■ [mass noun] the action of cauterizing something.
– ORIGIN late Middle English: via Latin from Greek *kautērion* 'branding iron' (see **CAUTERIZE**).

C

caution ▶ **noun 1** [mass noun] care taken to avoid danger or mistakes: *anyone receiving a suspect package should exercise extreme caution*. ■ [count noun] Brit. an official or legal warning given to someone who has committed a minor offence but has not been charged, to the effect that further action will be taken if they commit another such offence: *they let* ***him off with a caution***. ■ warning: *business advisers have sounded a note of caution*.
2 informal, dated an amusing or surprising person.
▶ **verb** [reporting verb] say something as a warning: [with clause] *the Chancellor cautioned that economic uncertainties remained* | [with direct speech] *'Be careful now,' he cautioned*. ■ [no obj.] (**caution against**) warn or advise against (doing something): *advisers have cautioned against tax increases*. ■ [with obj.] Brit. issue an official or legal warning to: *he* ***was cautioned for*** *possessing drugs*. ■ [with obj.] Brit. (of a police officer) advise (someone) of their legal rights when arresting them.
– PHRASES **err on the side of caution** take a comparatively safe course of action when presented with a choice. **throw caution to the wind** (or **winds**) act in a completely reckless manner. **under caution** having been told of one's legal rights when under arrest: *she made a statement under caution*.
– ORIGIN Middle English (denoting bail or a guarantee; now chiefly Scots and US): from Latin *cautio(n-)*, from *cavere* 'take heed'.

cautionary ▶ **adjective** serving as a warning: *a cautionary tale*.

caution money ▶ **noun** [mass noun] Brit. money deposited, especially by a college student, as security for good conduct.

cautious ▶ **adjective** (of a person) careful to avoid potential problems or dangers: *a cautious driver* | *firms have been unusually cautious about hiring new workers*. ■ (of an action) characterized by such an attitude: *the plan received a cautious welcome*.
– DERIVATIVES **cautiously** adverb, **cautiousness** noun.
– ORIGIN mid 17th cent.: from **CAUTION**, on the pattern of pairs such as *ambition*, *ambitious*.

Cauvery /ˈkɔːvəri/ (also **Kaveri**) a river in south India which rises in north Kerala and flows 765 km (475 miles) eastwards to the Bay of Bengal, south of Pondicherry. It is held sacred by Hindus.

cava /ˈkɑːvə/ ▶ **noun** [mass noun] a Spanish sparkling wine made in the same way as champagne.
– ORIGIN Spanish.

Cavafy /kəˈvɑːfi/, Constantine (Peter) (1863–1933), Greek poet; born *Konstantinos Petrou Kavafis*. His poems refer mainly to the Hellenistic and Graeco-Roman period of his native Alexandria.

cavalcade /ˌkav(ə)lˈkeɪd, ˈkav(ə)lkeɪd/ ▶ **noun** a formal procession of people walking, on horseback, or riding in vehicles.
– ORIGIN late 16th cent. (denoting a ride or raid on horseback): from French, from Italian *cavalcata*, from *cavalcare* 'to ride', based on Latin *caballus* 'horse'.

cavalier /ˌkavəˈlɪə/ ▶ **noun 1** (**Cavalier**) historical a supporter of King Charles I in the English Civil War.
2 archaic a courtly gentleman, especially one acting as a lady's escort. ■ a horseman, especially a cavalryman.
3 (also **Cavalier King Charles**) a small spaniel of a breed with a long snout.
▶ **adjective** showing a lack of proper concern; offhand: *Anne was irritated by his cavalier attitude*.
– DERIVATIVES **cavalierly** adverb.
– ORIGIN mid 16th cent.: from French, from Italian *cavaliere*, based on Latin *caballus* 'horse'. Compare with **CABALLERO** and **CHEVALIER**.

cavalry ▶ **noun** (pl. **cavalries**) [usu. treated as pl.] (in the past) soldiers who fought on horseback. ■ modern soldiers who fight in armoured vehicles.
– DERIVATIVES **cavalryman** noun (pl. **cavalrymen**).
– ORIGIN mid 16th cent.: from French *cavallerie*, from Italian *cavalleria*, from *cavallo* 'horse', from Latin *caballus*.

cavalry twill ▶ noun [mass noun] strong woollen twill used especially for making trousers.

Cavan /ˈkav(ə)n/ a county of the Republic of Ireland, part of the old province of Ulster. ■ the county town of Cavan; pop. 3,934 (2006).

cavaquinho /ˌkavəˈkiːnjəʊ/ ▶ noun (pl. **cavaquinhos**) a type of small, four-stringed guitar resembling a ukulele, popular in Brazil and Portugal.
– ORIGIN Portuguese.

C

cavatina /ˌkavəˈtiːnə/ ▶ noun (pl. **cavatine** /ˌkavəˈtiːneɪ/, **cavatinas**) Music a short operatic aria in simple style without repeated sections. ■ a similar piece of lyrical instrumental music.
– ORIGIN early 19th cent.: from Italian.

cave¹ /keɪv/ ▶ noun a natural underground chamber in a hillside or cliff.
▶ verb [no obj.] **1** Brit. explore caves as a sport.
2 US short for **CAVE IN** below.
– PHRASAL VERBS **cave in** (or **cave something in**) (with reference to a roof or similar structure) subside or collapse, or cause something to do this: *the tunnel walls caved in | storms caved the roof in.* ■ yield or submit under pressure: *the manager caved in to his demands.*
– DERIVATIVES **cave-like** adjective, **caver** noun.
– ORIGIN Middle English: from Old French, from Latin *cava*, from *cavus* 'hollow' (compare with **CAVERN**). The usage *cave in* may be from the synonymous dialect expression *calve in*, influenced by obsolete *cave* 'excavate, hollow out'.

cave² /ˈkeɪvi/ ▶ exclamation Brit. school slang, dated look out!
– PHRASES **keep cave** act as lookout.
– ORIGIN Latin, imperative of *cavere* 'beware'.

caveat /ˈkavɪat, ˈkeɪ-/ ▶ noun a warning or proviso of specific stipulations, conditions, or limitations. ■ Law a notice, especially in a probate, that certain actions may not be taken without informing the person who gave the notice.
– ORIGIN mid 16th cent.: from Latin, literally 'let a person beware'.

caveat emptor /ˈɛmptɔː/ ▶ noun the principle that the buyer alone is responsible for checking the quality and suitability of goods before a purchase is made.
– ORIGIN Latin, 'let the buyer beware'.

cave bear ▶ noun a large extinct bear of the Pleistocene epoch, whose remains are found commonly in caves throughout Europe. ● *Ursus spelaeus*, family Ursidae.

cave cricket ▶ noun another term for **CAMEL CRICKET**.

cave dweller ▶ noun a caveman or cavewoman.

cavefish ▶ noun (pl. **same** or **cavefishes**) a small colourless fish which lives only in limestone caves in North America. It has reduced or absent eyes, and the head and body are covered with papillae which are sensitive to vibration. ● Family Amblyopsidae: four genera, in particular *Amblyopsis* and *Typhlichthys*.

cave-in ▶ noun a collapse of a roof or underground structure. ■ an instance of yielding or submitting under pressure: *the government's cave-in to industry pressure.*

Cavell /ˈkav(ə)l/, Edith (Louisa) (1865–1915), English nurse. During the First World War she helped Allied soldiers to escape from occupied Belgium. She was subsequently executed by the Germans and became a heroine of the Allied cause.

caveman ▶ noun (pl. **cavemen**) a prehistoric man who lived in caves. ■ an uncivilized or violent man: [as modifier] *you can't change my mind by caveman tactics.*

Cavendish /ˈkav(ə)ndɪʃ/, Henry (1731–1810), English chemist and physicist. He identified hydrogen, studied carbon dioxide, and determined their densities relative to atmospheric air. He also established that water is a compound, and determined the density of the earth.

cavendish /ˈkav(ə)ndɪʃ/ ▶ noun [mass noun] tobacco softened, sweetened, and formed into cakes.
– ORIGIN mid 19th cent.: probably from the surname *Cavendish*.

cave painting ▶ noun a prehistoric picture on the interior of a cave, often depicting animals.

cavern /ˈkav(ə)n/ ▶ noun a large cave or chamber in a cave. ■ a large, dark place or space: *a dark cavern of a shop.*
– ORIGIN late Middle English: from Old French *caverne* or from Latin *caverna*, from *cavus* 'hollow'. Compare with **CAVE¹**.

cavernous ▶ adjective like a cavern in size, shape, or atmosphere: *a dismal cavernous hall.* ■ giving the impression of vast, dark depths: *his cavernous eyes.*
– DERIVATIVES **cavernously** adverb.
– ORIGIN late Middle English: from Old French *caverneux* or Latin *cavernosus* (from *caverna* 'cavern').

cavesson /ˈkavɪs(ə)n/ ▶ noun a type of heavy bridle which lacks a bit and has a thick noseband fitted with rings to which a rein may be attached. ■ a simple noseband on a horse's bridle.
– ORIGIN late 16th cent.: from French *caveçon*, Italian *cavezzone*, based on Latin *caput* 'head'.

cavewoman ▶ noun (pl. **cavewomen**) a prehistoric woman who lived in caves.

caviar /ˈkavɪɑː, ˌkavɪˈɑː/ (also **caviare**) ▶ noun [mass noun] the pickled roe of sturgeon or other large fish, eaten as a delicacy.
– PHRASES **caviar to the general** a good thing unappreciated by the ignorant.
– ORIGIN mid 16th cent.: from Italian *caviale* (earlier *caviaro*) or French *caviar*, probably from medieval Greek *khaviari*.

cavil /ˈkav(ə)l/ ▶ verb (**cavils, cavilling, cavilled**; US **cavils, caviling, caviled**) [no obj.] make petty or unnecessary objections: *they cavilled at the cost.*
▶ noun a petty or unnecessary objection.
– DERIVATIVES **caviller** noun.
– ORIGIN mid 16th cent.: from French *caviller*, from Latin *cavillari*, from *cavilla* 'mockery'.

caving ▶ noun [mass noun] Brit. the sport or pastime of exploring caves.

cavitation /ˌkavɪˈteɪʃ(ə)n/ ▶ noun [mass noun] Physics the formation of an empty space within a solid object or body. ■ the formation of bubbles in a liquid, typically by the movement of a propeller through it.

cavity ▶ noun (pl. **cavities**) an empty space within a solid object: *the abdominal cavity.* ■ a decayed part of a tooth.
– DERIVATIVES **cavitary** adjective.
– ORIGIN mid 16th cent.: from French *cavité* or late Latin *cavitas*, from Latin *cavus* 'hollow'.

cavity wall ▶ noun a wall formed from two thicknesses of brickwork or blockwork with a space between them.

cavolo nero /ˌkavələʊ ˈnɛːrəʊ/ ▶ noun [mass noun] a dark-leaved variety of kale used in Tuscan cookery.
– ORIGIN Italian, from *cavolo* 'cabbage' + *nero* 'black'.

cavort ▶ verb [no obj.] jump or dance around excitedly: *the players cavorted about the pitch.* ■ informal engage enthusiastically in sexual or disreputable pursuits: *he'd been cavorting with a hooker.*
– ORIGIN late 18th cent. (originally US): perhaps an alteration of **CURVET**.

Cavour /kəˈvʊə/, Camillo Benso, Conte di (1810–61), Italian statesman. A supporter of Italian unification under Victor Emmanuel II, he was Premier of Piedmont (1852–9; 1860–1), and in 1861 became the first Premier of a unified Italy.

cavy /ˈkeɪvi/ ▶ noun (pl. **cavies**) a South American rodent with a sturdy body and vestigial tail. ● Family Caviidae: five genera and several species, in particular the guinea pig.
– ORIGIN late 18th cent.: from modern Latin *cavia*, from Galibi *cabiai*.

caw ▶ noun the harsh cry of a rook, crow, or similar bird.
▶ verb [no obj.] utter a caw.
– ORIGIN late 16th cent.: imitative.

Cawley /ˈkɔːli/, Evonne (Fay) (b.1951), Australian tennis player; born *Evonne Fay Goolagong*. She won two Wimbledon singles titles (1971; 1980) and was three times Australian singles champion (1974–6).

Cawnpore /kɔːnˈpɔː/ former name for **KANPUR**.

Caxton, William (*c.*1422–91), the first English printer. He printed the first book in English in 1474 and went on to produce about eighty other texts, including editions of *Le Morte d'Arthur* and *Canterbury Tales*.

cay /keɪ, kiː/ ▶ noun a low bank or reef of coral, rock, or sand, especially one on the islands in Spanish America. Compare with **KEY²**.
– ORIGIN late 17th cent.: from Spanish *cayo* 'shoal, reef', from French *quai* 'quay'.

Cayenne /keɪˈɛn/ the capital and chief port of French Guiana; pop. 63,000 (est. 2007).

cayenne /keɪˈɛn/ (also **cayenne pepper**) ▶ noun [mass noun] a pungent hot-tasting red powder prepared from ground dried chilli peppers.
– ORIGIN early 18th cent.: from Tupi *kyynha, quiynha*, later associated with **CAYENNE**.

Cayley¹ /ˈkeɪli/, Arthur (1821–95), English mathematician and barrister. He wrote almost a thousand mathematical papers, including articles on determinants, group theory, and the algebra of matrices. The **Cayley numbers**, a generalization of complex numbers, are named after him.

Cayley² /ˈkeɪli/, Sir George (1773–1857), English engineer, the father of British aeronautics. He is best known for his understanding of the principles of flight and for building the first manned glider, which was flown in 1853. He was also a founder of the original Polytechnic Institution.

cayman ▶ noun variant spelling of **CAIMAN**.

Cayman Islands /ˈkeɪmən/ (also **the Caymans**) a group of three islands in the Caribbean Sea, south of Cuba; pop. 49,000 (est. 2009); official language, English; capital, George Town. The Cayman Islands are a British overseas territory.

Cayuga /ˈkeɪjuːgə, ˈkʌɪ-/ ▶ noun (pl. **same** or **Cayugas**) **1** a member of an American Indian people, one of the five of the original Iroquois confederacy, formerly inhabiting part of New York State.
2 [mass noun] the extinct Iroquoian language of the Cayuga.
▶ adjective relating to the Cayuga or their language.
– ORIGIN from an Iroquoian place name.

Cayuse /ˈkʌɪjuːs/ ▶ noun (pl. **same** or **Cayuses**) **1** a member of an American Indian people of Washington State and Oregon.
2 [mass noun] the extinct Penutian language of the Cayuse.
3 (**cayuse**) an American Indian pony.
▶ adjective relating to the Cayuse or their language.
– ORIGIN the name in Chinook Jargon.

CB ▶ abbreviation ■ Citizens' Band (radio frequencies). ■ (in the UK) Companion of the Order of the Bath.

CBC ▶ abbreviation Canadian Broadcasting Corporation.

CBE ▶ abbreviation (in the UK) Commander of the Order of the British Empire.

CBI ▶ abbreviation Confederation of British Industry.

CBS ▶ abbreviation (in the US) Columbia Broadcasting System.

CBT ▶ abbreviation cognitive behavioural therapy.

CC ▶ abbreviation ■ Brit. City Council. ■ Companion of the Order of Canada. ■ Brit. County Council. ■ Brit. County Councillor. ■ Cricket Club.

cc (also **c.c.**) ▶ abbreviation ■ carbon copy (used as an indication that a duplicate has been or should be sent to another person). ■ cubic centimetre(s).
▶ verb (**cc's, cc'ing, cc'd**) [with obj.] send a copy of an email to (a third party).

CCD ▶ abbreviation Electronics charge-coupled device, a high-speed semiconductor used chiefly in image detection.

CCJ ▶ abbreviation (in the UK) county court judgement, issued by a court after a person's failure to repay a debt and recorded in that person's credit history.

CCK ▶ abbreviation Biochemistry cholecystokinin.

CCS ▶ abbreviation carbon capture and storage.

CCTV ▶ abbreviation closed-circuit television.

CCU ▶ abbreviation critical care unit.

CD¹ ▶ noun (pl. **CDs**) a compact disc.

CD² ▶ abbreviation ■ civil defence. ■ corps diplomatique (diplomatic corps). [French.]

Cd ▶ symbol the chemical element cadmium.

cd ▶ abbreviation candela.

Cd. ▶ abbreviation (in the UK) Command Paper (third series, 1900–18).

CDC ▶ abbreviation ■ (in the US) Centers for Disease Control. ■ Commonwealth Development Corporation.

CDN ▶ abbreviation Canada (international vehicle registration).

cDNA ▶ abbreviation complementary DNA.

Cdr ▶ abbreviation (in the navy or air force) Commander.

CD-R ▶ noun a blank compact disc which can be recorded on once only.
– ORIGIN 1980s: abbreviation of *compact disc recordable*.

Cdre ▶ abbreviation Commodore.

CD-ROM ▶ noun a compact disc used as a read-only optical memory device for a computer system.

– ORIGIN 1980s: abbreviation of *compact disc read-only memory*.

CD-RW ▸ noun a blank compact disc that can be recorded, erased, and re-recorded many times.
– ORIGIN 1980s: abbreviation of *compact disc rewritable*.

CDT ▸ abbreviation ■ Central Daylight Time (see CENTRAL TIME). ■ craft, design, and technology (as a school subject in the UK).

CE ▸ abbreviation ■ Church of England. ■ civil engineer. ■ Common Era.

Ce ▸ symbol the chemical element cerium.

ceanothus /ˌsiːəˈnəʊθəs/ ▸ noun a North American shrub which is cultivated for its dense clusters of small, typically blue, flowers. ● Genus *Ceanothus*, family Rhamnaceae.
– ORIGIN modern Latin, from Greek *keanōthos*, denoting a kind of thistle.

Ceará /ˌseɪəˈrɑː/ a state in NE Brazil, on the Atlantic coast; capital, Fortaleza.

cease ▸ verb come or bring to an end: [no obj.] *the hostilities ceased and normal life was resumed* | [with infinitive] *on his retirement the job will cease to exist* | [with obj.] *they were asked to cease all military activity*.
– PHRASES **never cease to** (in hyperbolic use) do something very frequently: *her exploits never cease to amaze me*. **without cease** without stopping.
– ORIGIN Middle English: from Old French *cesser*, from Latin *cessare* 'stop', from *cedere* 'to yield'.

ceasefire ▸ noun a temporary suspension of fighting; a truce. ■ an order or signal to stop fighting.

ceaseless ▸ adjective constant and unending: *the fort was subjected to ceaseless bombardment*.
– DERIVATIVES **ceaselessly** adverb.

Ceauşescu /tʃaʊˈʃɛskuː/, Nicolae (1918–89), Romanian communist statesman, first President of the Socialist Republic of Romania 1974–89. His regime became increasingly totalitarian and corrupt; a popular uprising in December 1989 resulted in its downfall and in his execution.

cebid /ˈsiːbɪd/ ▸ noun Zoology a primate of a family (Cebidae) that includes most of the New World monkeys.
– ORIGIN late 19th cent.: from modern Latin *Cebidae* (plural), from the genus name *Cebus*.

Cebu /sɪˈbuː/ an island of the south central Philippines. ■ the chief city and port of Cebu; pop. 798,800 (est. 2007).

Cecil /ˈsɛs(ə)l, ˈsɪs-/, William, see BURGHLEY.

Cecilia, St /sɪˈsiːljə/ (2nd or 3rd century), Roman martyr. According to legend, she took a vow of celibacy but when forced to marry converted her husband to Christianity and both were martyred. She is the patron saint of church music. Feast day, 22 November.

cecropia /sɪˈkrəʊpɪə/ ▸ noun **1** a fast-growing tropical American tree which is typically among the first to colonize a cleared area. ● Genus *Cecropia*, family Cecropiaceae.
2 (also **cecropia moth**) a very large North American silk moth with boldly marked reddish-brown wings. ● *Platysamia* (or *Hyalophora*) *cecropia*, family Saturniidae.
– ORIGIN early 19th cent.: modern Latin, from the name *Cecrops*, a king of Attica.

cecum ▸ noun (pl. **ceca**) US spelling of CAECUM.

cedar ▸ noun any of a number of conifers which typically yield fragrant, durable timber, in particular: ● a large tree of the pine family (genus *Cedrus*, family Pinaceae), in particular the **cedar of Lebanon** (*C. libani*), with spreading branches, and the deodar. ● a tall slender North American or Asian tree (genus *Thuja*, family Cupressaceae), in particular the **western red cedar** (*T. plicata*).
– DERIVATIVES **cedarn** adjective (literary).
– ORIGIN Old English, from Old French *cedre* or Latin *cedrus*, from Greek *kedros*.

cede /siːd/ ▸ verb [with obj.] give up (power or territory): *in 1874, the islands were ceded to Britain*.
– ORIGIN early 16th cent.: from French *céder* or Latin *cedere* 'to yield'.

cedi /ˈsiːdi/ ▸ noun (pl. **same** or **cedis**) the basic monetary unit of Ghana, equal to 100 pesewas.
– ORIGIN of Ghanaian origin, perhaps an alteration of SHILLING.

cedilla /sɪˈdɪlə/ ▸ noun a mark (¸) written under the letter *c*, especially in French, to show that it is pronounced like an *s* rather than a *k* (e.g. *façade*). ■ a similar mark under *s* in Turkish and other oriental languages.
– ORIGIN late 16th cent.: from obsolete Spanish, earlier form of *zedilla*, diminutive of *zeda* (the letter Z), from Greek *zēta*.

Ceefax /ˈsiːfaks/ ▸ noun [mass noun] Brit. trademark a teletext service provided by the BBC.
– ORIGIN 1970s: representing the pronunciation of the initial syllables of *seeing* and *facsimile*.

ceiba /ˈsʌɪbə/ ▸ noun a very tall tropical American tree from which kapok is obtained, with lightweight yellowish or pinkish timber. Also called KAPOK. ● *Ceiba pentandra*, family Bombacaceae.
– ORIGIN via Spanish from Taino, literally 'giant tree'.

ceil /siːl/ ▸ verb [with obj.] archaic line or plaster the roof of (a building).
– ORIGIN late Middle English (in the sense 'line the interior of a room with plaster or panelling'): perhaps related to Latin *celare*, French *céler* 'conceal'.

ceilidh /ˈkeɪli/ (also Irish **ceili**) ▸ noun a social event with Scottish or Irish folk music and singing, traditional dancing, and storytelling.
– ORIGIN late 19th cent.: from Scottish Gaelic *ceilidh* and Irish *céilidhe* (earlier form of *céilí*), from Old Irish *céilide* 'visit, visiting', from *céile* 'companion'.

ceiling ▸ noun **1** the upper interior surface of a room or other similar compartment.
2 an upper limit set on prices, wages, or expenditure: *the government imposed a wage ceiling of 3 per cent*.
3 the maximum altitude that a particular aircraft can reach. ■ the altitude of the base of a cloud layer.
4 Nautical the inside planking of a ship's bottom and sides.
– DERIVATIVES **ceilinged** adjective [in combination] *high-ceilinged rooms*.
– ORIGIN Middle English (denoting the action of lining the interior of a room with plaster or panelling): from CEIL + -ING[1]. Sense 1 dates from the mid 16th cent.

ceiling rose ▸ noun a circular mounting on a ceiling, through which the wiring of an electric light passes.

cel /sɛl/ ▸ noun a transparent sheet of celluloid or similar film material, which can be drawn on and used in the production of cartoons.
– ORIGIN mid 20th cent.: abbreviation of CELLULOID.

celadon /ˈsɛlədɒn/ ▸ noun [mass noun] a willow-green colour. ■ a grey-green glaze used on pottery, especially that from China. ■ pottery made with celadon glaze.
– ORIGIN mid 18th cent.: from French *céladon*, a colour named after the hero in d'Urfé's pastoral romance *L'Astrée* (1607–27).

celandine /ˈsɛləndʌɪn/ (also **lesser celandine**) ▸ noun a common plant of the buttercup family which produces yellow flowers in the early spring. See also GREATER CELANDINE. ● *Ranunculus ficaria*, family Ranunculaceae.
– ORIGIN Middle English, from Old French *celidoine*, from medieval Latin *celidonia*, based on Greek *khelidōn* 'swallow' (the flowering of the plant being associated with the arrival of swallows).

-cele (also **-coele**) ▸ combining form Medicine denoting a swelling or hernia in a specified part: *meningocele*.
– ORIGIN from Greek *kēlē* 'tumour'.

celeb /sɪˈlɛb/ ▸ noun informal a celebrity: *a TV celeb*.
– ORIGIN early 20th cent. (originally US): abbreviation.

WORD TRENDS Has the culture of the **celeb** begun to decline? The Oxford English Corpus shows that use of **celebrity** has risen steadily since 2000, but that of the abbreviation **celeb** has dropped since 2006, suggesting that the public may be starting to tire of these *trashy*, *wannabe*, *Z-list* individuals (all words regularly found attached to **celeb** in the Corpus). Though it seems very much a product of the 21st century, with its glut of reality TV and promises of instant fame, the abbreviation of **celebrity** was first seen almost a hundred years ago. Since then **celeb** has taken on strong associations of a very particular type of fame and its attendant lifestyle, with celebs often famous simply for being famous, rather than for any particular skill or talent.

Celebes /ˈsɛlɪbiːz/ former name for SULAWESI.

Celebes Sea a part of the western Pacific between the Philippines and Sulawesi, bounded to the west by Borneo. It is linked to the Java Sea by the Makassar Strait.

Celebra /sɪˈlɛbrə/ ▸ noun [mass noun] trademark a synthetic drug used in the management of arthritic pain.
– ORIGIN 1990s: an invented word.

celebrant /ˈsɛlɪbr(ə)nt/ ▸ noun **1** a person who performs a rite, especially a priest at the Eucharist.
2 N. Amer. a person who celebrates something.
– ORIGIN mid 19th cent.: from French *célébrant* or Latin *celebrant-* 'celebrating', from the verb *celebrare* (see CELEBRATE).

celebrate ▸ verb [with obj.] **1** publicly acknowledge (a significant or happy day or event) with a social gathering or enjoyable activity: *they were celebrating their wedding anniversary at a swanky restaurant* | [no obj.] *she celebrated with a glass of champagne*. ■ reach (a birthday or anniversary).
2 perform (a religious ceremony), in particular officiate at (the Eucharist): *he celebrated holy communion*.
3 honour or praise publicly: *a film celebrating the actor's career*.
– DERIVATIVES **celebrator** noun, **celebratory** adjective.
– ORIGIN late Middle English (in sense 2): from Latin *celebrat-* 'celebrated', from the verb *celebrare*, from *celeber*, *celebr-* 'frequented or honoured'.

celebrated ▸ adjective greatly admired; renowned: *a celebrated mathematician*.

celebration ▸ noun [mass noun] the action of celebrating an important day or event: *the birth of his son was a cause for celebration*. ■ [count noun] a social gathering or enjoyable activity held to celebrate something: *a birthday celebration*.
– ORIGIN early 16th cent.: from Latin *celebratio(n-)*, from the verb *celebrare* (see CELEBRATE).

celebrity ▸ noun (pl. **celebrities**) a famous person, especially in entertainment or sport. ■ [mass noun] the state of being well known: *his prestige and celebrity grew*.
– ORIGIN late Middle English (in the sense 'solemn ceremony'): from Old French *celebrite* or Latin *celebritas*, from *celeber*, *celebr-* 'frequented or honoured'.

celebutante /sɪˈlɛbjuːtɑːnt/ ▸ noun a celebrity who is well known in fashionable society.
– ORIGIN 1930s: blend of CELEBRITY and DEBUTANTE.

celeriac /sɪˈlɛrɪak/ ▸ noun [mass noun] celery of a variety which forms a large swollen turnip-like root which can be eaten cooked or raw.
– ORIGIN mid 18th cent.: from CELERY + an arbitrary use of -AC.

celerity /sɪˈlɛrɪti/ ▸ noun [mass noun] archaic or literary swiftness of movement.
– ORIGIN late 15th cent.: from Old French *celerite*, from Latin *celeritas*, from *celer* 'swift'.

celery ▸ noun [mass noun] a cultivated plant of the parsley family, with closely packed succulent leaf stalks which are used as a salad or cooked vegetable. ● *Apium graveolens* var. *dulce*, family Umbelliferae.
– ORIGIN mid 17th cent.: from French *céleri*, from Italian dialect *selleri*, based on Greek *selinon* 'parsley'.

celery pine (also **celery-top pine**) ▸ noun a slow-growing evergreen tree with shoots that resemble celery leaves, growing from Borneo to New Zealand. ● Genus *Phyllocladus*, family Phyllocladaceae.

celery salt ▸ noun [mass noun] a mixture of salt and ground celery seed used for seasoning.

celesta /sɪˈlɛstə/ ▸ noun a small keyboard instrument in which felted hammers strike a row of steel plates suspended over wooden resonators, giving an ethereal bell-like sound.
– ORIGIN late 19th cent.: pseudo-Latin, based on French *céleste* 'heavenly'.

celeste /sɪˈlɛst/ ▸ noun **1** short for VOIX CELESTE.
2 another term for CELESTA.
– ORIGIN late 19th cent.: from French *céleste* 'heavenly', from Latin *caelestis*, from *caelum* 'heaven'.

celestial ▸ adjective [attrib.] positioned in or relating to the sky, or outer space as observed in astronomy: *a celestial body*. ■ belonging or relating to heaven: *the celestial city*. ■ supremely good: *the celestial beauty of music*.
– DERIVATIVES **celestially** adverb.
– ORIGIN late Middle English: via Old French from medieval Latin *caelestialis*, from Latin *caelestis*, from *caelum* 'heaven'.

celestial bamboo ▸ noun another term for NANDINA.

celestial equator ▸ noun the projection into space of the earth's equator; an imaginary circle equidistant from the celestial poles.

celestial globe ▸ noun a spherical representation of the sky showing the constellations.

celestial latitude ▸ noun Astronomy the angular distance of a point north or south of the ecliptic. Compare with DECLINATION (sense 1).

celestial longitude ▸ noun Astronomy the angular distance of a point east of the First Point of Aries,

C

measured along the ecliptic. Compare with RIGHT ASCENSION.

celestial mechanics ▶ plural noun [treated as sing.] the branch of theoretical astronomy that deals with the calculation of the motions of celestial objects such as planets.

celestial navigation ▶ noun [mass noun] the action of finding one's way by observing the sun, moon, and stars.

celestial pole ▶ noun Astronomy the point on the celestial sphere directly above either of the earth's geographic poles, around which the stars and planets appear to rotate during the course of the night.

celestial sphere ▶ noun an imaginary sphere of which the observer is the centre and on which all celestial objects are considered to lie.

celiac ▶ noun US spelling of COELIAC.

celibacy /ˈsɛlɪbəsi/ ▶ noun [mass noun] the state of abstaining from marriage and sexual relations: *a priest who had taken a vow of celibacy*.

celibate /ˈsɛlɪbət/ ▶ adjective abstaining from marriage and sexual relations, typically for religious reasons: *a celibate priest*. ■ having or involving no sexual relations: *a celibate lifestyle*.
▶ noun a person who abstains from marriage and sexual relations.
– ORIGIN early 19th cent. (earlier (mid 17th cent.) as *celibacy*): from French *célibat* or Latin *caelibatus* 'unmarried state' + -ATE[2].

Céline /seɪˈliːn/, Louis-Ferdinand (1894–1961), French novelist; pseudonym of *Louis-Ferdinand Destouches*. He is best known for his autobiographical novel, the satirical *Voyage au bout de la nuit* (1932).

cell ▶ noun **1** a small room in which a prisoner is locked up or in which a monk or nun sleeps. ■ historical a small monastery or nunnery dependent on a larger one.
2 Biology the smallest structural and functional unit of an organism, which is typically microscopic and consists of cytoplasm and a nucleus enclosed in a membrane. ■ an enclosed cavity in an organism. ■ a small compartment in a larger structure such as a honeycomb.
3 a small group forming a nucleus of political activity, typically a secret, subversive one: *terrorist cells*.
4 a device containing electrodes immersed in an electrolyte, used for generating current or for electrolysis. ■ a unit in a device for converting chemical or solar energy into electricity.
5 the local area covered by one of the short-range transmitters in a cellular telephone system. ■ N. Amer. a mobile phone.
– DERIVATIVES **celled** adjective [in combination] *a single-celled organism*, **cell-like** adjective.
– ORIGIN Old English, from Old French *celle* or Latin *cella* 'storeroom or chamber'.

cella /ˈkɛlə/ ▶ noun (pl. **cellae** /-liː/) the inner area of an ancient temple, especially one housing the hidden cult image in a Greek or Roman temple.
– ORIGIN Latin.

cellar ▶ noun a room below ground level in a house, often used for storing wine or coal. ■ a stock of wine.
▶ verb [with obj.] store (wine) in a cellar.
– ORIGIN Middle English (in the general sense 'storeroom'): from Old French *celier*, from late Latin *cellarium* 'storehouse', from Latin *cella* 'storeroom or chamber'.

cellarage ▶ noun [mass noun] cellars collectively. ■ money charged for the use of a cellar or storehouse.

cellarer /ˈsɛlərə/ ▶ noun the person in a monastery who is responsible for provisioning and catering. ■ a cellarman.

cellaret /ˌsɛləˈrɛt/ (US also **cellarette**) ▶ noun historical a cabinet or sideboard for keeping alcoholic drinks and glasses in a dining room.

cellarman ▶ noun (pl. **cellarmen**) Brit. a person in charge of a wine cellar.

cell block ▶ noun a large single building or part of a complex subdivided into separate prison cells.

cell division ▶ noun [mass noun] Biology the division of a cell into two daughter cells with the same genetic material.

Cellini /tʃɛˈliːni/, Benvenuto (1500–71), Italian goldsmith and sculptor, the most renowned goldsmith of his day.

cell line ▶ noun Biology a cell culture developed from a single cell and therefore consisting of cells with a uniform genetic make-up.

cellmate ▶ noun a person with whom one shares a cell.

cell-mediated ▶ adjective Physiology denoting the aspect of an immune response involving the action of white blood cells, rather than that of circulating antibodies. Often contrasted with HUMORAL.

cell membrane ▶ noun the semipermeable membrane surrounding the cytoplasm of a cell.

cello /ˈtʃɛləʊ/ ▶ noun (pl. **cellos**) a bass instrument of the violin family, held upright on the floor between the legs of the seated player.
– DERIVATIVES **cellist** noun.
– ORIGIN late 19th cent.: shortening of VIOLONCELLO.

cellophane /ˈsɛləfeɪn/ ▶ noun [mass noun] trademark a thin transparent wrapping material made from viscose.
– ORIGIN early 20th cent.: from CELLULOSE + *-phane*, from *diaphane*, a kind of semi-transparent woven silk (from medieval Latin *diaphanus* 'diaphanous').

cell phone ▶ noun chiefly N. Amer. a mobile phone.

cellular /ˈsɛljʊlə/ ▶ adjective **1** relating to or consisting of living cells: *cellular proliferation*.
2 denoting or relating to a mobile telephone system that uses a number of short-range radio stations to cover the area that it serves, the signal being automatically switched from one station to another as the user travels about.
3 (of a fabric item, such as a blanket or vest) knitted so as to form holes or hollows that trap air and provide extra insulation.
4 consisting of small compartments or rooms: *cellular accommodation*.
– DERIVATIVES **cellularity** noun.
– ORIGIN mid 18th cent.: from French *cellulaire*, from modern Latin *cellularis*, from *cellula* 'little chamber', diminutive of *cella*.

cellular automaton ▶ noun (pl. **cellular automata**) Computing each of a set of units in a mathematical model which have simple rules governing their replication and destruction, used to model complex systems composed of simple units such as living things or parallel processors.

cellular phone ▶ noun chiefly N. Amer. a mobile phone.

cellulase /ˈsɛljʊleɪz/ ▶ noun [mass noun] Biochemistry an enzyme that converts cellulose into glucose or a disaccharide.
– ORIGIN early 20th cent.: from CELLULOSE + -ASE.

cellulite /ˈsɛljʊlʌɪt/ ▶ noun [mass noun] persistent subcutaneous fat causing dimpling of the skin, especially on women's hips and thighs.
– ORIGIN 1960s: from French, from *cellule* 'small cell'.

cellulitis ▶ noun [mass noun] Medicine inflammation of subcutaneous connective tissue.

celluloid ▶ noun [mass noun] a transparent flammable plastic made in sheets from camphor and nitrocellulose, formerly used for cinematographic film. ■ the cinema as a genre: *having made the leap from theatre to celluloid, she can now make more money*.
– ORIGIN mid 19th cent.: from CELLULOSE + -OID.

cellulose /ˈsɛljʊləʊz, -s/ ▶ noun [mass noun] **1** an insoluble substance which is the main constituent of plant cell walls and of vegetable fibres such as cotton. It is a polysaccharide consisting of chains of glucose monomers.
2 paint or lacquer consisting principally of cellulose acetate or nitrate in solution.
– DERIVATIVES **cellulosic** adjective.
– ORIGIN mid 19th cent.: from French, from *cellule* 'small cell' + -OSE[2].

cellulose acetate ▶ noun [mass noun] a non-flammable thermoplastic polymer made by acetylating cellulose, used as the basis of artificial fibres and plastic.

cellulose nitrate ▶ noun another term for NITROCELLULOSE.

cellulose triacetate ▶ noun see TRIACETATE.

cell wall ▶ noun Biology a rigid layer of polysaccharides lying outside the plasma membrane of the cells of plants, fungi, and bacteria. In the algae and higher plants it consists mainly of cellulose.

celosia /sɪˈləʊsɪə, -ʃə/ ▶ noun a plant of a genus that includes cockscomb. ● Genus *Celosia*, family Amarantaceae.
– ORIGIN modern Latin, from Greek *kēlos* 'burnt or dry' (from the burnt appearance of the flowers in some species).

Celsius[1] /ˈsɛlsɪəs/, Anders (1701–44), Swedish astronomer, best known for his temperature scale.

Celsius[2] /ˈsɛlsɪəs/ (abbrev.: **C**) ▶ adjective [postpositive when used with a numeral] of or denoting a scale of temperature on which water freezes at 0° and boils at 100° under standard conditions.
▶ noun (also **Celsius scale**) the Celsius scale of temperature.

> **USAGE** Celsius rather than **centigrade** is the standard accepted term when giving temperatures: use *25° Celsius* rather than *25° centigrade*.

Celt /kɛlt, sɛlt/ ▶ noun a member of a group of peoples inhabiting much of Europe and Asia Minor in pre-Roman times. Their culture developed in the late Bronze Age around the upper Danube, and reached its height in the La Tène culture (5th to 1st centuries BC) before being overrun by the Romans and various Germanic peoples. ■ a native of any of the modern nations or regions in which Celtic languages are (or were until recently) spoken; a person of Irish, Highland Scottish, Manx, Welsh, or Cornish descent.
– ORIGIN from Latin *Celtae* (plural), from Greek *Keltoi*; in later use from French *Celte* 'Breton' (taken as representing the ancient Gauls).

celt /sɛlt/ ▶ noun Archaeology a prehistoric stone or metal implement with a bevelled cutting edge, probably used as a tool or weapon.
– ORIGIN early 18th cent.: from medieval Latin *celtis* 'chisel'.

Celtiberian /ˌkɛltɪˈbɪərɪən, -tʌɪ-, ˌsɛlt-/ ▶ noun another term for IBERIAN (sense 3 of the noun).

Celtic /ˈkɛltɪk, ˈs-/ ▶ adjective relating to the Celts or their languages, which constitute a branch of the Indo-European family and include Irish, Scottish Gaelic, Welsh, Breton, Manx, Cornish, and several extinct pre-Roman languages such as Gaulish.
▶ noun [mass noun] the Celtic language group. See also P-CELTIC, Q-CELTIC.
– DERIVATIVES **Celticism** /-sɪz(ə)m/ noun, **Celticist** noun.
– ORIGIN late 16th cent.: from Latin *Celticus* (from *Celtae* 'Celts'), or from French *Celtique* (from *Celte* 'Breton').

> **USAGE** Celt and Celtic can be pronounced either with an initial **k-** or **s-**, but in standard English the normal pronunciation is with a **k-**, except in the name of the Glaswegian football club.

Celtic Church the Christian Church in the British Isles from its foundation in the 2nd or 3rd century until its assimilation into the Roman Catholic Church (664 in England; 12th century in Wales, Scotland, and Ireland).

Celtic cross ▶ noun a Latin cross with a circle round the centre.

Celtic fringe ▶ noun the Highland Scots, Irish, Welsh, and Cornish in relation to the rest of Britain.

Celtic harp ▶ noun another term for CLARSACH.

Celtic Sea the part of the Atlantic Ocean between southern Ireland and SW England.

CE mark ▶ noun a symbol applied to products to indicate that they conform with relevant EU directives regarding health and safety or environmental protection.
– ORIGIN 1980s: *CE* from the initial letters of French *Conformité Européenne* 'European Conformity' or *Communauté Européenne* 'European Community'.

cembalo /ˈtʃɛmbələʊ/ ▶ noun (pl. **cembalos**) another term for HARPSICHORD.
– ORIGIN mid 19th cent.: from Italian, shortening of *clavicembalo*, from medieval Latin *clavicymbalum*, from Latin *clavis* 'key' + *cymbalum* 'cymbal'.

cement ▶ noun [mass noun] a powdery substance made by calcining lime and clay, mixed with water to form mortar or mixed with sand, gravel, and water to make concrete. ■ concrete. ■ a soft glue that hardens on setting. ■ a substance for filling cavities in teeth. ■ (also **cementum**) Anatomy a thin layer of bony material that fixes teeth to the jaw. ■ Geology the material which binds particles together in sedimentary rock.
▶ verb [with obj.] fix with cement. ■ settle or establish firmly: *the two firms are expected to cement an agreement soon*.
– ORIGIN Middle English: from Old French *ciment* (noun), *cimenter* (verb), from Latin *caementum* 'quarry stone', from *caedere* 'hew'.

cementation /ˌsiːmɛnˈteɪʃ(ə)n/ ▶ noun [mass noun] **1** the binding together of particles or other things by cement.
2 Metallurgy a process of altering a metal by heating it in contact with a powdered solid.

cementite /sɪˈmɛntʌɪt/ ▶ **noun** [mass noun] Metallurgy a hard, brittle iron carbide present in cast iron and most steels.

cementitious /ˌsiːmɛnˈtɪʃəs/ ▶ **adjective** of the nature of cement.

cement mixer ▶ **noun** a machine with a revolving drum used for mixing cement with sand, gravel, and water to make concrete.

cemetery ▶ **noun** (pl. **cemeteries**) a large burial ground, especially one not in a churchyard: *a military cemetery.*
– ORIGIN late Middle English: via late Latin from Greek *koimētērion* 'dormitory', from *koiman* 'put to sleep'.

cenacle /ˈsɛnək(ə)l/ ▶ **noun 1** formal a group of people such as a discussion group or literary clique.
2 the room in which the Last Supper was held.
– ORIGIN late Middle English: from Old French *cenacle*, from Latin *cenaculum*, from *cena* 'dinner'.

CEng ▶ **abbreviation** (in the UK) chartered engineer.

cenobite /ˈsiːnəbʌɪt/ (also **coenobite**) ▶ **noun** a member of a monastic community.
– DERIVATIVES **cenobitic** /-ˈbɪtɪk/ **adjective**.
– ORIGIN late Middle English: from Old French *cenobite* or ecclesiastical Latin *coenobita*, via late Latin from Greek *koinobion* 'convent', from *koinos* 'common' + *bios* 'life'.

cenotaph /ˈsɛnətɑːf, -taf/ ▶ **noun** a monument to someone buried elsewhere, especially one commemorating people who died in a war.
– ORIGIN early 17th cent.: from French *cénotaphe*, from late Latin *cenotaphium*, from Greek *kenos* 'empty' + *taphos* 'tomb'.

cenote /sɪˈnəʊteɪ/ ▶ **noun** a natural underground reservoir of water such as occurs in the limestone of Yucatán, Mexico.
– ORIGIN mid 19th cent.: from Yucatán Spanish, from Maya *tzonot*.

Cenozoic /ˌsiːnəˈzəʊɪk/ (also **Cainozoic**) ▶ **adjective** Geology relating to or denoting the most recent era, following the Mesozoic era and comprising the Tertiary and Quaternary periods. ■ (as noun **the Cenozoic**) the Cenozoic era, or the system of rocks deposited during it.

> The Cenozoic has lasted from about 65 million years ago to the present day. It has seen the rapid evolution and rise to dominance of mammals, birds, and flowering plants.

– ORIGIN mid 19th cent.: from Greek *kainos* 'new' + *zōion* 'animal' + **-IC**.

cense /sɛns/ ▶ **verb** [with obj.] archaic ritually perfume (something) with the odour of burning incense.
– ORIGIN late Middle English: from Old French *encenser*.

censer ▶ **noun** a container in which incense is burnt during a religious ceremony.
– ORIGIN Middle English: from Old French *censier*, from *encensier*, from *encens* (see **INCENSE¹**).

censor ▶ **noun 1** an official who examines books, films, news, etc. that are about to be published and suppresses any parts that are considered obscene, politically unacceptable, or a threat to security. ■ Psychoanalysis an aspect of the superego which is said to prevent certain ideas and memories from emerging into consciousness. [from a mistranslation of German *Zensur* 'censorship', coined by Freud.]
2 (in ancient Rome) either of two magistrates who held censuses and supervised public morals.
▶ **verb** [with obj.] examine (a book, film, etc.) officially and suppress unacceptable parts of it.
– DERIVATIVES **censorial** adjective, **censorship** noun.
– ORIGIN mid 16th cent. (in sense 2 of the noun): from Latin, from *censere* 'assess'.

> **USAGE** For an explanation of the difference between censor and censure, see **USAGE** at **CENSURE**.

censorious /sɛnˈsɔːrɪəs/ ▶ **adjective** severely critical of others: *censorious champions of morality.*
– DERIVATIVES **censoriously** adverb, **censoriousness** noun.
– ORIGIN mid 16th cent.: from Latin *censorius* (from *censor* 'magistrate') + **-IOUS**.

censure /ˈsɛnʃə/ ▶ **verb** [with obj.] express severe disapproval of (someone or something), especially in a formal statement.
▶ **noun** [mass noun] the formal expression of severe disapproval: *two MPs were singled out for censure* | [count noun] *despite episcopal censures, the practice continued.*
– DERIVATIVES **censurable** adjective.
– ORIGIN late Middle English (in the sense 'judicial sentence'): from Old French *censurer* (verb), *censure* (noun), from Latin *censura* 'judgement, assessment', from *censere* 'assess'.

> **USAGE** Censure and censor, although quite different in meaning, are frequently confused. Both words can function as verbs and nouns, but **censure** means 'express severe disapproval of' (*the country was censured for human rights abuses*) or 'the expression of severe disapproval', while **censor** means 'examine (a book, film, etc.) and suppress unacceptable parts of it' (*the letters she received were censored*) or 'an official who censors books, films, etc.'.

census ▶ **noun** (pl. **censuses**) an official count or survey, especially of a population: *a traffic census.*
– ORIGIN early 17th cent. (denoting a poll tax): from Latin, applied to the registration of citizens and property in ancient Rome, usually for taxation, from *censere* 'assess'. The current sense dates from the mid 18th cent.

cent ▶ **noun 1** a monetary unit in various countries, equal to one hundredth of a dollar, euro, or other decimal currency unit. ■ informal a small sum of money: *she saved every cent possible.* ■ [with negative] informal used for emphasis to denote no money at all: *he hadn't yet earned a cent.*
2 Music one hundredth of a semitone.
– ORIGIN late Middle English (in the sense 'a hundred'): from French *cent*, Italian *cento*, or Latin *centum* 'hundred'.

cent. ▶ **abbreviation** century.

centas /ˈsɛntas/ ▶ **noun** (pl. **same**) a monetary unit of Lithuania, equal to one hundredth of a litas.
– ORIGIN Lithuanian.

centaur /ˈsɛntɔː/ ▶ **noun** Greek Mythology a creature with the head, arms, and torso of a man and the body and legs of a horse.
– ORIGIN via Latin from Greek *kentauros*, the Greek name for a Thessalonian tribe of expert horsemen; of unknown ultimate origin.

centaurea /sɛnˈtɔːrɪə, ˌsɛntəˈriːə/ ▶ **noun** a plant of a Eurasian genus which includes the cornflower and knapweed. ● Genus *Centaurea*, family Compositae.
– ORIGIN modern Latin based on Greek *kentauros* 'centaur' (see **CENTAURY**).

Centaurus /sɛnˈtɔːrəs/ Astronomy a large southern constellation (the Centaur). It lies in the Milky Way and contains the stars Alpha and Proxima Centauri.
– ORIGIN Latin.

centaury /ˈsɛntɔːri/ ▶ **noun** (pl. **centauries**) a widely distributed herbaceous plant of the gentian family, typically having pink flowers. ● *Centaurium* and related genera, family Gentianaceae: many species.
– ORIGIN late Middle English: from late Latin *centaurea*, based on Greek *kentauros* 'centaur' (because its medicinal properties were said to have been discovered by the centaur Chiron).

centavo /sɛnˈtɑːvəʊ/ ▶ **noun** (pl. **centavos**) a monetary unit of Mexico, Brazil, and certain other countries (formerly including Portugal), equal to one hundredth of the basic unit.
– ORIGIN Spanish and Portuguese, from Latin *centum* 'a hundred'.

CENTCOM ▶ **abbreviation** Central Command.

centenarian /ˌsɛntɪˈnɛːrɪən/ ▶ **noun** a person who is a hundred or more years old.

centenary /sɛnˈtiːnəri, -ˈtɛn-/ Brit. ▶ **noun** (pl. **centenaries**) the hundredth anniversary of a significant event.
▶ **adjective** relating to a hundredth anniversary.
– ORIGIN early 17th cent. (denoting a century): from Latin *centenarius* 'containing a hundred', based on Latin *centum* 'a hundred'.

centennial /sɛnˈtɛnɪəl/ chiefly N. Amer. ▶ **adjective** relating to a hundredth anniversary.
▶ **noun** a hundredth anniversary.
– ORIGIN late 18th cent.: from Latin *centum* 'a hundred', on the pattern of *biennial*.

Centennial State informal name for **COLORADO**.

center ▶ **noun** US spelling of **CENTRE**.

centerboard ▶ **noun** US spelling of **CENTREBOARD**.

center field ▶ **noun** US spelling of **CENTRE FIELD**.

centerfold ▶ **noun** US spelling of **CENTREFOLD**.

centering ▶ **noun** US spelling of **CENTRING**.

centerpiece ▶ **noun** US spelling of **CENTREPIECE**.

centesimal /sɛnˈtɛsɪm(ə)l/ ▶ **adjective** relating to division into hundredths.
– DERIVATIVES **centesimally** adverb.
– ORIGIN early 19th cent.: from Latin *centesimus* 'hundredth', from *centum* 'a hundred'.

centesimo /tʃɛnˈtɛsɪməʊ/ ▶ **noun** (pl. **centesimos**) a former monetary unit of Italy, worth one hundredth of a lira (used only in calculations).
– ORIGIN Italian.

centésimo /sɛnˈtɛsɪməʊ/, Spanish /senˈtesimo, θen-/ ▶ **noun** (pl. **centésimos**) a monetary unit of Uruguay and Panama, equal to one hundredth of a peso in Uruguay, and one hundredth of a balboa in Panama.
– ORIGIN Spanish.

C

centi- ▶ **combining form** used commonly in units of measurement: **1** one hundredth: *centilitre*.
2 hundred: *centigrade* | *centipede*.
– ORIGIN from Latin *centum* 'hundred'.

centigrade ▶ **adjective** [postpositive when used with a numeral] another term for **CELSIUS²**.
▶ **noun** (also **centigrade scale**) the Celsius scale of temperature.
– ORIGIN early 19th cent.: from French, from Latin *centum* 'a hundred' + *gradus* 'step'.

> **USAGE** In giving temperatures, use **Celsius** rather than **centigrade** in all contexts.

centigram (abbrev.: **cg**) ▶ **noun** a metric unit of mass, equal to one hundredth of a gram.

centile /ˈsɛntʌɪl/ ▶ **noun** another term for **PERCENTILE**.

centilitre (US **centiliter**) (abbrev.: **cl**) ▶ **noun** a metric unit of capacity, equal to one hundredth of a litre.

centime /ˈsɒtiːm/, French /sɑ̃tim/ ▶ **noun** a monetary unit equal to one hundredth of a franc or some other decimal currency units (used in France, Belgium, and Luxembourg until the introduction of the euro in 2002).
– ORIGIN French, from Latin *centesimus* 'hundredth', from *centum* 'a hundred'.

centimetre (US **centimeter**) (abbrev.: **cm**) ▶ **noun** a metric unit of length, equal to one hundredth of a metre.

centimetre-gram-second system ▶ **noun** a system of measurement using the centimetre, the gram, and the second as basic units of length, mass, and time respectively.

centimo /ˈsɛntɪməʊ/, Spanish /ˈθentimo, ˈsen-/ ▶ **noun** (pl. **centimos**) a monetary unit of a number of Latin American countries (and formerly of Spain), equal to one hundredth of the basic unit.
– ORIGIN Spanish.

centimorgan /ˈsɛntɪˌmɔːg(ə)n/ (also **centiMorgan**) ▶ **noun** Genetics a map unit used to express the distance between two gene loci on a chromosome. A spacing of one centimorgan indicates a one per cent chance that two genes will be separated by crossing over.
– ORIGIN mid 20th cent.: from *centi-* (denoting a factor of one hundredth) + the name of T. H. *Morgan* (see **MORGAN²**).

centipede /ˈsɛntɪpiːd/ ▶ **noun** a predatory myriapod invertebrate with a flattened elongated body composed of many segments. Most segments bear a single pair of legs, the front pair being modified as poison fangs. ● Class Chilopoda: several orders.
– ORIGIN mid 17th cent.: from French *centipède* or Latin *centipeda*, from *centum* 'a hundred' + *pes, ped-* 'foot'.

cento /ˈsɛntəʊ/ ▶ **noun** (pl. **centos**) rare a literary work made up of quotations from other authors.
– ORIGIN early 17th cent.: Latin, 'patchwork garment', the original sense in English.

centra plural form of **CENTRUM**.

central ▶ **adjective 1** at the point or in the area that is in the middle of something: *the station has a central courtyard* | *central London.* ■ accessible from a variety of places: *coaches met at a central location.* ■ Phonetics (of a vowel) articulated in the centre of the mouth.
2 of the greatest importance; principal or essential: *his preoccupation with history is **central to** his work.* ■ [attrib.] having or denoting supreme power over a country or organization: *central government.*
▶ **noun** N. Amer. informal a place with a high concentration of a specified type of person or thing: *you're in workaholic central here.*
– DERIVATIVES **centrality** noun, **centrally** adverb.
– ORIGIN mid 17th cent.: from French, or from Latin *centralis*, from *centrum* (see **CENTRE**).

Central African Republic a country of central Africa; pop. 4,511,500 (est. 2009); languages, French (official), Sango; capital, Bangui. Formerly a French colony, it became a republic within the French

Community in 1958 and a fully independent state in 1960. Former name (until 1958) **Ubanghi Shari**.

Central America the southernmost part of North America, linking the continent to South America and consisting of the countries of Guatemala, Belize, Honduras, El Salvador, Nicaragua, Costa Rica, and Panama.
– DERIVATIVES **Central American** adjective & noun.

central bank ▶ noun a national bank that provides financial and banking services for its country's government and commercial banking system, as well as implementing the government's monetary policy and issuing currency.

central casting ▶ noun chiefly N. Amer. an agency or department that supplies actors for minor, usually stereotypical or generic film roles: *Lynch is a mild, methodical guy, a bureaucrat* ***from central casting***.
– ORIGIN 1920s: from the name of the US organization *Central Casting Corporation*.

Central Command (abbrev.: **CENTCOM**) a US military strike force consisting of units from the army, air force, and navy, established in 1979 (as the Rapid Deployment Force) to operate in the Middle East and North Africa.

Central Criminal Court official name for **Old Bailey**.

Central European Time (abbrev.: **CET**) the standard time based on the mean solar time at the meridian 15° E, used in central and western continental Europe. It is one hour ahead of GMT.

central heating ▶ noun [mass noun] a system for warming a building by heating water or air in one place and circulating it through pipes and radiators or vents.

Central Intelligence Agency (abbrev.: **CIA**) a federal agency in the US responsible for coordinating government intelligence activities. Established in 1947 and originally intended to operate only overseas, it has since also operated in the US.

centralism ▶ noun [mass noun] the control of disparate activities and organizations under a single authority.
– DERIVATIVES **centralist** noun & adjective.

centralize (also **centralise**) ▶ verb [with obj.] (often as adj. **centralized**) concentrate (control of an activity or organization) under a single authority: *a highly centralized country*. ■ bring (activities) together in one place.
– DERIVATIVES **centralization** noun.

central locking ▶ noun [mass noun] a locking system in a motor vehicle which enables the locks of all doors to be operated simultaneously.

central nervous system ▶ noun Anatomy the complex of nerve tissues that controls the activities of the body. In vertebrates it comprises the brain and spinal cord.

Central Park a large public park in the centre of Manhattan in New York City.

Central Powers the alliance of Germany, Austria-Hungary, Turkey, and Bulgaria during the First World War. ■ the alliance of Germany, Austria-Hungary, and Italy between 1882 and 1914.

central processing unit (also **central processor**) (abbrev.: **CPU**) ▶ noun Computing the part of a computer in which operations are controlled and executed.

central reservation ▶ noun Brit. the strip of land between the carriageways of a motorway or other major road.

central tendency ▶ noun Statistics the tendency for the values of a random variable to cluster round its mean, mode, or median.

Central time the standard time in a zone that includes the central states of the US and parts of central Canada, specifically: ● (**Central Standard Time** abbrev.: **CST**) standard time based on the mean solar time at longitude 90° W, six hours behind GMT. ● (**Central Daylight Time** abbrev.: **CDT**) Central time during daylight saving, five hours behind GMT.

Centre /ˈsɒ̃tr(ə)/, French /sɑ̃tʀ/ a region of central France, including the cities of Orleans, Tours, and Chartres.

centre (US **center**) ▶ noun **1** the point that is equally distant from every point on the circumference of a circle or sphere. ■ a point or part that is equally distant from all sides, ends, or surfaces of something: *the centre of the ceiling | the city centre*. ■ a political party or group whose opinions avoid extremes: [as modifier] *a new centre party*. ■ the middle player in a line or group in certain team games. ■ a kick, hit, or throw of the ball from the side to the middle of field in soccer, hockey, and other team games. ■ the filling in a chocolate: *truffles with liqueur centres*. ■ a pivot or axis of rotation. ■ a conical adjustable support for a workpiece in a lathe or similar machine.
2 the point from which an activity or process is directed, or on which it is focused: *the city was a* ***centre of*** *discontent | the managing director is at the* ***centre of*** *a row over policy*. ■ the most important place in the respect specified: *Geneva was then the centre of the banking world*.
3 a place or group of buildings where a specified activity is concentrated: *a conference centre*.
▶ verb **1** [no obj.] (**be centred in**) occur mainly in or around (a specified place): *the textile industry was centred in Lancashire and Yorkshire*. ■ (**centre around/on** or **centre something around/on**) have or cause to have (a specified concern or theme): *the case centres around the couple's adopted children* | [with obj.] *he is centring his discussion on an analysis of patterns of mortality*.
2 [with obj.] place in the middle: *to centre the needle, turn the knob*. ■ [no obj.] (in soccer, hockey, and other team games) kick, hit, or throw the ball from the side to the middle of the playing area. ■ [no obj.] chiefly N. Amer. play as the middle player of a line or group in certain team games.
– PHRASES **centre of attention** a person or thing that excites everyone's interest or concern. **centre of attraction 1** Physics the point to which bodies tend by gravity. **2** another term for **centre of attention**. **centre of buoyancy** Physics the centroid of the immersed part of a ship or other floating body. **centre of curvature** Mathematics the centre of a circle which passes through a curve at a given point and has the same tangent and curvature at that point. **centre of excellence** a place where the highest standards are maintained. **centre of flotation** the centre of gravity of a floating object. **centre of gravity** a point from which the weight of a body or system may be considered to act. In uniform gravity it is the same as the centre of mass. **centre of mass** a point representing the mean position of the matter in a body or system. **centre of pressure** Physics a point on a surface through which the resultant force due to pressure passes.
– DERIVATIVES **centremost** adjective.
– ORIGIN late Middle English: from Old French, or from Latin *centrum*, from Greek *kentron* 'sharp point, stationary point of a pair of compasses', related to *kentein* 'to prick'.

centre back ▶ noun Soccer a defender who plays in the middle of the field.

centre bit ▶ noun a drill bit with a central point and side cutters.

centreboard (US **centerboard**) ▶ noun a pivoted board that can be lowered through the keel of a sailing boat to reduce sideways movement.

centred (US **centered**) ▶ adjective **1** placed or situated in the centre.
2 [in combination] having a specified subject as the most important or focal element: *a child-centred school*.
3 [in combination] (of a chocolate) having a centre or filling of a specified type: *a soft-centred chocolate*.
4 chiefly US (of a person) well balanced and confident or serene.
– DERIVATIVES **centredness** noun.

centre field (US **center field**) ▶ noun Baseball the central part of the outfield.
– DERIVATIVES **centre fielder** noun.

centrefold (US **centerfold**) ▶ noun the two middle pages of a magazine, often taken up by a single illustration or feature. ■ an illustration on a centrefold, typically a picture of a naked or scantily clad model.

centre forward ▶ noun Soccer & Hockey an attacker who plays in the middle of the field.

centre half ▶ noun Soccer another term for **centre back**.

centre line ▶ noun a real or imaginary line through the centre of something, especially one following an axis of symmetry.

centrepiece (US **centerpiece**) ▶ noun an ornament or display placed in the middle of a dining table. ■ an item, issue, etc. intended to be a focus of attention: *a domestic programme with health care as the centrepiece*.

centre punch ▶ noun a tool consisting of a metal rod with a conical point for making an indentation, to allow a drill to make a hole at the same spot without slipping.

centre spread ▶ noun the two facing middle pages of a newspaper or magazine.

centre stage ▶ noun [in sing.] the centre of a stage. ■ the most prominent position: *finance is* ***taking centre stage*** *in debates on policy*.
▶ adverb at or towards the middle of a stage: *at the play's opening she stands centre stage*. ■ in or towards the most prominent position.

centrex ▶ noun [mass noun] a telephone service in which a group of phone lines can be joined by part of the local exchange acting as a private exchange.
– ORIGIN 1990s: blend of **central** and **exchange**.

centric ▶ adjective **1** in or at the centre; central: *centric and peripheral forces*.
2 Botany (of a diatom) radially symmetrical. Compare with **pennate**.
– DERIVATIVES **centrical** adjective, **centricity** /-ˈtrɪsɪti/ noun.
– ORIGIN late 16th cent.: from Greek *kentrikos*, from *kentron* 'sharp point' (see **centre**).

-centric ▶ combining form **1** having a specified centre: *geocentric*.
2 forming an opinion or evaluation originating from a specified viewpoint: *Eurocentric | ethnocentric*.
– DERIVATIVES **-centricity** combining form in corresponding nouns.
– ORIGIN from Greek *kentrikos*, on the pattern of words such as *(con)centric*.

centrifugal /ˌsɛntrɪˈfjuːg(ə)l, sɛnˈtrɪfjʊg(ə)l/ ▶ adjective Physics moving or tending to move away from a centre. The opposite of **centripetal**.
– DERIVATIVES **centrifugally** adverb.
– ORIGIN early 18th cent.: from modern Latin *centrifugus*, from Latin *centrum* (see **centre**) + *-fugus* 'fleeing' (from *fugere* 'flee').

centrifugal force ▶ noun Physics a force, arising from the body's inertia, which appears to act on a body moving in a circular path and is directed away from the centre around which the body is moving.

centrifugal pump ▶ noun a pump that uses an impeller to move water or other fluids.

centrifuge /ˈsɛntrɪfjuːdʒ/ ▶ noun a machine with a rapidly rotating container that applies centrifugal force to its contents, typically to separate fluids of different densities (e.g. cream from milk) or liquids from solids.
▶ verb [with obj.] subject to the action of a centrifuge.
– DERIVATIVES **centrifugation** /-fjʊˈgeɪʃ(ə)n/ noun.

centring (US **centering**) ▶ noun [mass noun] **1** the action or process of placing something in the middle of something else.
2 Architecture framing used to support an arch or dome while it is under construction.

centriole /ˈsɛntrɪəʊl/ ▶ noun Biology each of a pair of minute cylindrical organelles near the nucleus in animal cells, involved in the development of spindle fibres in cell division.
– ORIGIN late 19th cent.: from modern Latin *centriolum*, diminutive of *centrum* (see **centre**).

centripetal /ˌsɛntrɪˈpiːt(ə)l, sɛnˈtrɪpɪt(ə)l/ ▶ adjective Physics moving or tending to move towards a centre. The opposite of **centrifugal**.
– DERIVATIVES **centripetally** adverb.
– ORIGIN early 18th cent.: from modern Latin *centripetus*, from Latin *centrum* (see **centre**) + *-petus* 'seeking' (from *petere* 'seek').

centripetal force ▶ noun Physics a force which acts on a body moving in a circular path and is directed towards the centre around which the body is moving.

centrist ▶ adjective having moderate political views or policies.
▶ noun a person who holds moderate political views.
– DERIVATIVES **centrism** noun.
– ORIGIN late 19th cent.: from French *centriste*, from Latin *centrum* (see **centre**).

centroid ▶ noun Mathematics the centre of mass of a geometric object of uniform density.

centromere /ˈsɛntrə(ʊ)mɪə/ ▶ noun Biology the point on a chromosome by which it is attached to a spindle fibre during cell division.
– DERIVATIVES **centromeric** adjective.
– ORIGIN 1920s: from Latin *centrum* (see **centre**) + Greek *meros* 'part'.

centrosome /ˈsɛntrəsəʊm/ ▶ noun Biology an organelle near the nucleus of a cell which contains the centrioles (in animal cells) and from which the spindle fibres develop in cell division.
– ORIGIN late 19th cent.: from Latin *centrum* (see **centre**) + Greek *sōma* 'body'.

centrum /ˈsɛntrəm/ ▶ noun (pl. **centrums** or **centra** /-trə/) Anatomy the solid central part of a vertebra, to which the arches and processes are attached.

– ORIGIN mid 19th cent.: from Latin.

centuple /ˈsɛntjʊp(ə)l/ ▶ **verb** [with obj.] multiply by a hundred or by a very large amount: *they were centupling the national debt.*
– ORIGIN early 17th cent.: from French, or from ecclesiastical Latin *centuplus*, alteration of Latin *centuplex*, from Latin *centum* 'hundred'.

centurion /sɛnˈtjʊərɪən/ ▶ **noun** the commander of a century in the ancient Roman army.
– ORIGIN Middle English: from Latin *centurio(n-)*, from *centuria* (see **CENTURY**).

century ▶ **noun** (pl. **centuries**) **1** a period of one hundred years: *a century ago most people walked to work.* ■ a period of a hundred years reckoned from the traditional date of the birth of Christ: *the fifteenth century* | [as modifier] *a twentieth-century lifestyle.*
2 a score of a hundred in a sporting event, especially a batsman's score of a hundred runs in cricket.
3 a company in the ancient Roman army, originally of a hundred men. ■ an ancient Roman political division for voting.
– DERIVATIVES **centurial** adjective.
– ORIGIN late Middle English (in sense 3): from Latin *centuria*, from *centum* 'hundred'. Sense 1 dates from the early 17th cent.

> **USAGE** **1** Strictly speaking, centuries run from 01 to 100, meaning that the new century begins on the first day of the year 01 (i.e. 1 January 1901, 1 January 2001, etc.). In practice and in popular perception, however, the new century is held to begin when the significant digits in the date change, e.g. on 1 January 2000, when 1999 became 2000.
> **2** Since the 1st century ran from the year 1 to the year 100, the ordinal number (i.e. second, third, fourth, etc.) used to denote the century will always be one digit higher than the corresponding cardinal digit(s). Thus, 1066 is a date in the 11th century, 1542 is a date in the 16th century, and so on.

century plant ▶ **noun** a large stemless agave with long spiny leaves, which produces a very tall flowering stem after many years of growth and then dies. Also called **AMERICAN ALOE**. ● *Agave americana*, family Agavaceae.

CEO ▶ **abbreviation** chief executive officer.

cep /sɛp/ ▶ **noun** an edible European mushroom with a smooth brown cap, a stout white stalk, and pores rather than gills, growing in dry woodland and much sought after as a delicacy. Also called **PENNY BUN**. ● *Boletus edulis*, family Boletaceae, class Hymenomycetes.
– ORIGIN mid 19th cent.: from French *cèpe*, from Gascon *cep* 'tree trunk, mushroom', from Latin *cippus* 'stake'.

cephalic /sɪˈfalɪk, kɛ-/ ▶ **adjective** technical in or relating to the head.
– ORIGIN late Middle English: from Old French *cephalique*, from Latin *cephalicus*, from Greek *kephalikos*, from *kephalē* 'head'.

-cephalic ▶ **combining form** -headed (used most commonly in medical terms): *macrocephalic.*
– ORIGIN based on Greek *kephalē* 'head' + **-IC**.

cephalic index ▶ **noun** Anthropology a number expressing the ratio of the maximum breadth of a skull to its maximum length.

cephalin /ˈsɛf(ə)lɪn, ˈkɛf-/ ▶ **noun** [mass noun] Biochemistry any of a group of phospholipids present in cell membranes, especially in the brain.
– ORIGIN late 19th cent.: from Greek *kephalē* 'brain' + **-IN**[1].

cephalization /ˌsɛfəlʌɪˈzeɪʃ(ə)n, ˌkɛf-/ ▶ **noun** [mass noun] Zoology the concentration of sense organs, nervous control, etc., at the anterior end of the body, forming a head and brain, both during evolution and in the course of an embryo's development.

cephalo- /ˈsɛfələʊ, ˈkɛf-/ ▶ **combining form** relating to the head or skull: *cephalometry.*
– ORIGIN from Greek *kephalē* 'head'.

Cephalochordata /ˌsɛfələ(ʊ)kɔːˈdeɪtə, ˌkɛ-/ ▶ **plural noun** Zoology a small group of marine invertebrates that comprises the lancelets. ● Subphylum Cephalochordata, phylum Chordata.
– DERIVATIVES **cephalochordate** /ˌsɛfələ(ʊ)ˈkɔːdeɪt, ˌkɛ-/ noun & adjective.
– ORIGIN modern Latin (plural), from **CEPHALO-** 'head' + Greek *chorda* 'cord'.

cephalometry /ˌsɛfəˈlɒmɪtri, ˌkɛf-/ ▶ **noun** [mass noun] Medicine measurement and study of the proportions of the head and face, especially during development and growth.
– DERIVATIVES **cephalometric** adjective.

cephalon /ˈsɛfəlɒn, ˈkɛf-/ ▶ **noun** Zoology (in some arthropods, especially trilobites) the region of the head, composed of fused segments.
– ORIGIN late 19th cent.: from Greek *kephalē* 'head'.

Cephalonia /ˌkɛfəˈləʊnɪə/ a Greek island in the Ionian Sea; pop. 38,900 (est. 2006). Greek name **KEFALLINÍA**.

cephalopod /ˈsɛf(ə)lə(ʊ)pɒd, ˈkɛ-/ ▶ **noun** Zoology an active predatory mollusc of the large class Cephalopoda, such as an octopus or squid.

Cephalopoda /ˌsɛfələˈpəʊdə, ˌkɛ-/ ▶ **plural noun** Zoology a large class of active predatory molluscs comprising octopuses, squids, and cuttlefish. They have a distinct head with large eyes and a ring of tentacles around a beaked mouth, and are able to release a cloud of inky fluid to confuse predators.
– ORIGIN modern Latin (plural), from Greek *kephalē* 'head' + *pous, pod-* 'foot'.

cephalosporin /ˌsɛfələ(ʊ)ˈspɔːrɪn, ˌkɛ-/ ▶ **noun** any of a group of semi-synthetic broad-spectrum antibiotics resembling penicillin.
– ORIGIN 1950s: from modern Latin *Cephalosporium* (genus providing moulds for this) + **-IN**[1].

cephalothorax /ˌsɛf(ə)ləʊˈθɔːraks, ˌkɛf-/ ▶ **noun** Zoology the fused head and thorax of spiders and other chelicerate arthropods.

-cephalous ▶ **combining form** equivalent to **-CEPHALIC**.

cepheid /ˈsiːfɪɪd, ˈsɛ-/ (also **cepheid variable**) ▶ **noun** Astronomy a variable star having a regular cycle of brightness with a frequency related to its luminosity, so allowing estimation of its distance from the earth.
– ORIGIN early 20th cent.: from the name of the variable star *Delta Cephei*, which typifies this class of stars.

Cepheus /ˈsiːfɪəs/ Astronomy a constellation near the north celestial pole, with no very bright stars.
– ORIGIN from the name of a king of Ethiopia, the husband of Cassiopeia.

'cept ▶ **preposition, conjunction, & verb** non-standard contraction of **EXCEPT** used in representing speech: *everyone else had visitors—'cept for Captain.*

ceramic /sɪˈramɪk/ ▶ **adjective** made of clay and permanently hardened by heat: *a ceramic bowl.*
▶ **noun** (**ceramics**) pots and other articles made from clay hardened by heat. ■ [usu. treated as sing.] the art of making ceramic articles. ■ [mass noun] (**ceramic**) the material from which ceramics are made: *tableware in ceramic.* ■ [mass noun] (**ceramic**) any non-metallic solid which remains hard when heated.
– DERIVATIVES **ceramicist** noun.
– ORIGIN early 19th cent.: from Greek *keramikos*, from *keramos* 'pottery'.

ceramic hob ▶ **noun** an electric cooker hob made of ceramic, with heating elements fixed to its underside.

Ceram Sea /ˈseɪram/ (also **Seram Sea**) the part of the western Pacific Ocean at the centre of the Molucca Islands.

cerastes /sɪˈrastiːz/ ▶ **noun** a North African viper which has a spike over each eye. ● Genus *Cerastes*, family Viperidae: two species.
– ORIGIN late Middle English: from Latin, from Greek *kerastēs* 'horned', from *keras* 'horn'.

cerastium /sɪˈrastɪəm/ ▶ **noun** (pl. **cerastiums**) a plant of a genus that includes chickweed and snow-in-summer. ● Genus *Cerastium*, family Caryophyllaceae.
– ORIGIN modern Latin, from Greek *kerastēs* 'horned' (with reference to the shape of many seed capsules) + **-IUM**.

ceratite /ˈsɛrətʌɪt, ˈsɪər-/ ▶ **noun** an ammonoid fossil of an intermediate type found chiefly in the Permian and Triassic periods, typically with partly frilled and partly lobed suture lines. Compare with **AMMONITE** and **GONIATITE**. ● Typified by the genus *Ceratites*, order Ceratida.
– ORIGIN mid 19th cent.: from modern Latin *Ceratites* (from Greek *keras, kerat-* 'horn') + **-ITE**[1].

ceratobranchial /ˌsɛrətə(ʊ)ˈbraŋkɪəl, ˌkɛ-/ ▶ **noun** Zoology each of the paired ventral cartilaginous sections of the branchial arch in fishes.
– ORIGIN mid 19th cent.: from Greek *keras, kerat-* 'horn' + *branchial* (see **BRANCHIA**).

ceratopsian /ˌsɛrəˈtɒpsɪən, ˌkɛr-/ ▶ **noun** Palaeontology a gregarious quadrupedal herbivorous dinosaur of a group found in the Cretaceous period, including triceratops. ● Infraorder Ceratopsia, order Ornithischia.
– ORIGIN early 20th cent.: from modern Latin *Ceratopsia* (plural) (from Greek *keras, kerat-* 'horn' + *ops* 'face') + **-AN**.

Cerberus /ˈsəːbərəs/ Greek Mythology a monstrous watchdog with three (or in some accounts fifty) heads, which guarded the entrance to Hades.

cercaria /səːˈkɛːrɪə/ ▶ **noun** (pl. **cercariae** /-ɪiː/) Zoology a free-swimming larval stage in which a parasitic fluke passes from an intermediate host (typically a snail) to another intermediate host or to the final vertebrate host.
– ORIGIN mid 19th cent.: modern Latin, formed irregularly from Greek *kerkos* 'tail'.

cerclage /səːˈklɑːʒ/ ▶ **noun** [mass noun] Medicine the use of a ring or loop to bind together the ends of an obliquely fractured bone or encircle the opening of a malfunctioning cervix.
– ORIGIN early 20th cent.: from French, literally 'encirclement'.

cercopithecine /ˌsəːkə(ʊ)ˈpɪθɪsiːn/ ▶ **noun** Zoology an Old World monkey of a group that includes the macaques, mangabeys, baboons, and guenons. ● Subfamily Cercopithecinae, family Cercopithecidae.
– ORIGIN from modern Latin *Cercopithecinae* (plural), based on Greek *kerkopithēkos* 'long-tailed monkey', from *kerkos* 'tail' + *pithēkos* 'ape'.

cercopithecoid /ˌsəːkə(ʊ)ˈpɪθɪkɔɪd/ Zoology ▶ **noun** a primate of a group that comprises the Old World monkeys. ● Superfamily Cercopithecoidea and family Cercopithecidae.
▶ **adjective** relating to cercopithecoid monkeys.
– ORIGIN late 19th cent.: from modern Latin *Cercopithecoidea*, based on Greek *kerkopithēkos*, a long-tailed monkey (from *kerkos* 'tail' + *pithēkos* 'ape').

cercus /ˈsəːkəs/ ▶ **noun** (pl. **cerci** /-kʌɪ/) Zoology either of a pair of small appendages at the end of the abdomen of some insects and other arthropods.
– ORIGIN early 19th cent.: from modern Latin, from Greek *kerkos* 'tail'.

cere /sɪə/ ▶ **noun** Ornithology a waxy fleshy covering at the base of the upper beak in some birds.
– ORIGIN late 15th cent.: from Latin *cera* 'wax'.

cereal ▶ **noun** **1** a grain used for food, for example wheat, maize, or rye. ■ a grass producing edible grain that is grown as an agricultural crop: [as modifier] *cereal crops.*
2 [mass noun] a breakfast food made from roasted grain, typically eaten with milk: *a bowl of cereal.*
– ORIGIN early 19th cent. (as an adjective): from Latin *cerealis*, from **CERES**.

cereal bar ▶ **noun** a prepackaged food item similar in shape to a chocolate bar, made of cereal and, typically, fruit.

cerebellum /ˌsɛrɪˈbɛləm/ ▶ **noun** (pl. **cerebellums** or **cerebella**) Anatomy the part of the brain at the back of the skull in vertebrates, which coordinates and regulates muscular activity.
– DERIVATIVES **cerebellar** adjective.
– ORIGIN mid 16th cent.: from Latin, diminutive of **CEREBRUM**.

cerebral /ˈsɛrɪbr(ə)l, səˈriːbr(ə)l/ ▶ **adjective** **1** of the cerebrum of the brain: *a cerebral haemorrhage* | *the cerebral cortex.* ■ intellectual rather than emotional or physical: *she excelled in cerebral pursuits.*
2 Phonetics another term for **RETROFLEX**.
– DERIVATIVES **cerebrally** adverb.
– ORIGIN early 19th cent.: from Latin *cerebrum* 'brain' + **-AL**.

cerebral aqueduct ▶ **noun** another term for **AQUEDUCT OF SYLVIUS**.

cerebral dominance ▶ **noun** [mass noun] the normal tendency for one side of the brain to control particular functions, such as handedness and speech.

cerebral hemisphere ▶ **noun** see **HEMISPHERE**.

cerebral palsy ▶ **noun** [mass noun] a condition marked by impaired muscle coordination (spastic paralysis) and/or other disabilities, typically caused by damage to the brain before or at birth. See also **SPASTIC**.

cerebration /ˌsɛrɪˈbreɪʃ(ə)n/ ▶ **noun** [mass noun] technical or formal the working of the brain; thinking.
– DERIVATIVES **cerebrate** verb.

cerebro- ▶ **combining form** relating to the brain: *cerebrospinal.*
– ORIGIN from Latin *cerebrum* 'brain'.

cerebroside /ˈsɛrɪbrə(ʊ)sʌɪd/ ▶ **noun** Biochemistry any of a group of complex lipids present in the sheaths of nerve fibres.
– ORIGIN late 19th cent.: from Latin *cerebrum* 'brain' + **-OSE**[2] + **-IDE**.

cerebrospinal /ˌsɛrɪbrə(ʊ)ˈspʌɪn(ə)l/ ▶ **adjective** Anatomy relating to the brain and spine.

cerebrospinal fluid ▶ **noun** [mass noun] Anatomy clear watery fluid which fills the space between the arachnoid membrane and the pia mater.

cerebrovascular /ˌsɛrɪbrə(ʊ)ˈvaskjʊlə/ ▶ **adjective** Anatomy relating to the brain and its blood vessels.

cerebrum /ˈsɛrɪbrəm/ ▶ **noun** (pl. **cerebra** /-brə/) Anatomy the principal and most anterior part of the brain in vertebrates, located in the front area of the skull and consisting of two hemispheres, left and right, separated by a fissure. It is responsible for the integration of complex sensory and neural functions and the initiation and coordination of voluntary activity in the body.
– ORIGIN early 17th cent.: from Latin, 'brain'.

cerecloth /ˈsɪəklɒθ/ ▶ **noun** [mass noun] historical waxed cloth used for wrapping a corpse.
– ORIGIN late Middle English: from earlier *cered cloth*, from *cere* 'to wax', from Latin *cerare*, from *cera* 'wax'.

Ceredigion /ˌkɛrəˈdɪgɪən/ a county of western mid Wales; administrative centre, Aberaeron.

cerement /ˈsɪəm(ə)nt/ ▶ **noun** [mass noun] (also **cerements**) historical waxed cloth for wrapping a corpse.
– ORIGIN early 17th cent. (first used by Shakespeare in *Hamlet*, 1602): from *cere* (see CERECLOTH).

ceremonial ▶ **adjective 1** relating to or used for formal religious or public events: *a ceremonial occasion.*
2 (of a post or role) conferring or involving only nominal authority or power: *the largely ceremonial position of Lord Lieutenant of Kent.*
▶ **noun** [mass noun] the system of rules and procedures to be observed at a formal or religious occasion: *the procedure was conducted with all due ceremonial.*
■ [count noun] a rite or ceremony.
– DERIVATIVES **ceremonialism** noun, **ceremonialist** noun, **ceremonially** adverb.
– ORIGIN late Middle English: from late Latin *caerimonialis*, from Latin *caerimonia* 'religious worship' (see CEREMONY).

ceremonious ▶ **adjective** relating or appropriate to grand and formal occasions: *a Great Hall where ceremonious and public appearances were made.*
■ excessively polite; punctilious: *he accepted the gifts with ceremonious dignity.*
– DERIVATIVES **ceremoniously** adverb, **ceremoniousness** noun.
– ORIGIN mid 16th cent.: from French *cérémonieux* or late Latin *caerimoniosus*, from Latin *caerimonia* (see CEREMONY).

ceremony ▶ **noun** (pl. **ceremonies**) **1** a formal religious or public occasion, especially one celebrating a particular event, achievement, or anniversary.
■ an act or series of acts performed according to a traditional or prescribed form.
2 [mass noun] the ritual observances and procedures required or performed at grand and formal occasions: *the new Queen was proclaimed with due ceremony.* ■ formal polite behaviour: *he showed them to their table with great ceremony.*
– PHRASES **stand on ceremony** [usu. with negative] insist on the observance of formalities: *we don't stand on ceremony in this house.* **without ceremony** without preamble or politeness: *he was pushed without ceremony into the bathroom.*
– ORIGIN late Middle English: from Old French *ceremonie* or Latin *caerimonia* 'religious worship', (plural) 'ritual observances'.

Cerenkov, Pavel, see CHERENKOV.

Cerenkov radiation /tʃəˌrɛŋkɒf reɪdɪˈeɪʃ(ə)n/ (also **Cherenkov radiation**) ▶ **noun** [mass noun] Physics electromagnetic radiation emitted by particles moving in a medium at speeds faster than that of light in the same medium.

cereology /ˌsɪərɪˈɒlədʒɪ/ ▶ **noun** [mass noun] the study or investigation of crop circles.
– DERIVATIVES **cereologist** noun.
– ORIGIN 1990s: from CERES + -LOGY.

cereopsis goose /ˌsɛrɪˈɒpsɪs/ ▶ **noun** another term for CAPE BARREN GOOSE.
– ORIGIN late 19th cent.: from modern Latin *Cereopsis* (genus name), from Greek *kerinos* 'waxen' + *opsis* 'face' (because of its cere).

Ceres /ˈsɪəriːz/ **1** Roman Mythology the goddess of agriculture. Greek equivalent DEMETER.
2 Astronomy the first asteroid to be discovered, found by G. Piazzi of Palermo on 1 January 1801. It is also much the largest (diameter 913 km).

ceresin /ˈsɛrɪsɪn/ ▶ **noun** [mass noun] a hard whitish paraffin wax used with or instead of beeswax.
– ORIGIN late 19th cent.: from modern Latin *ceres* (from Latin *cera* 'wax') + -IN[1].

cereus /ˈsɪərɪəs/ ▶ **noun** see NIGHT-BLOOMING CEREUS.

cerise /səˈriːs, -z/ ▶ **noun** [mass noun] a light clear red colour: *a shade of vivid cerise.*
– ORIGIN mid 19th cent.: from French, literally 'cherry'.

cerium /ˈsɪərɪəm/ ▶ **noun** [mass noun] the chemical element of atomic number 58, a silvery-white metal. It is the most abundant of the lanthanide elements and is the main component of the alloy misch metal. (Symbol: **Ce**)
– ORIGIN early 19th cent.: named after the asteroid CERES, discovered shortly before.

cermet /ˈsəːmɛt/ ▶ **noun** any of a class of heat-resistant materials made of ceramic and sintered metal.
– ORIGIN 1950s: blend of CERAMIC and METAL.

CERN /səːn/ ▶ **abbreviation** European Organization for Nuclear Research.
– ORIGIN initial letters of French *Conseil Européen pour la Recherche Nucléaire*, its former title.

cero /ˈsɪərəʊ/ ▶ **noun** (pl. **same** or **ceros**) a large fish of the mackerel family, which is an important food fish in the tropical western Atlantic. ● *Scomberomorus regalis*, family Scombridae.
– ORIGIN late 19th cent.: from Spanish *sierra* 'saw or sawfish'.

cero- /ˈsɪərəʊ/ ▶ **combining form** relating to wax: *ceroplastic.*
– ORIGIN from Latin *cera* or Greek *kēros* 'wax'.

ceroc /sɪˈrɒk/ ▶ **noun** [mass noun] a type of modern social dance having elements of rock and roll, jive, and salsa.
– ORIGIN 1990s: invented word, apparently coined in English from French *ce* (as in *c'est* 'this is') + *roc* 'rock'.

cert ▶ **noun** Brit. informal an event regarded as inevitable: *of course Mum would cry, it was* ***a dead cert***. ■ a racehorse strongly tipped to win a race. ■ a person regarded as certain to do something: *the Scottish keeper was a cert to play.*
– ORIGIN late 19th cent.: abbreviation of CERTAINTY.

cert. ▶ **abbreviation** ■ certificate. ■ certified.

certain /ˈsəːt(ə)n, -tɪn/ ▶ **adjective 1** able to be firmly relied on to happen or be the case: *it's certain that more changes are in the offing | she looks certain to win an Oscar.* ■ having or showing complete conviction about something: *are you absolutely certain about this?*
2 [attrib.] specific but not explicitly named or stated: *he raised certain personal problems with me | the exercise was causing him a certain amount of pain.* ■ used when mentioning the name of someone not known to the reader or hearer: *a certain General Percy captured the town.*
▶ **pronoun** (**certain of**) some but not all: *certain of his works have been edited.*
– PHRASES **for certain** without any doubt: *I don't know for certain.* **make certain** [with clause] take action to ensure that something happens. ■ establish whether something is definitely the case: *he probably knew her, but it didn't do any harm to make certain.*
– ORIGIN Middle English: from Old French, based on Latin *certus* 'settled, sure'.

certainly ▶ **adverb** [sentence adverb] used to emphasize the speaker's belief that what is said is true: *the prestigious address certainly adds to the firm's appeal.* ■ used to indicate that a statement is made as a concession or contrasted with another: *our current revenues are certainly lower than anticipated.* ■ used to express complete agreement with something that has just been said.

certainty ▶ **noun** (pl. **certainties**) [mass noun] firm conviction that something is the case: *she knew with absolute certainty that they were dead.* ■ the quality of being reliably true: *there is a bewildering lack of certainty and clarity in the law.* ■ a general air of confidence: *a man exuding certainty.* ■ [count noun] a fact that is definitely true or an event that is definitely going to take place: *the passing of the act made a general election a certainty.* ■ [count noun] a person that is certain to do or win the specified thing: *he was expected to be a certainty for a gold medal.*
– PHRASES **for a certainty** beyond the possibility of doubt.
– ORIGIN Middle English: from Old French *certainete*, from *certain* (see CERTAIN).

CertEd ▶ **abbreviation** (in the UK) Certificate in Education.

certes /ˈsəːtɪz/ ▶ **adverb** archaic assuredly; I assure you.
– ORIGIN Middle English: from Old French, based on Latin *certus* 'settled, sure'.

certifiable ▶ **adjective 1** able or needing to be officially recorded: *encephalitis was a certifiable condition.*
2 officially recognized as needing treatment for mental disorder. ■ informal mad; crazy: *the world of fashion is almost entirely insane, the people who work in it mainly certifiable.*
– DERIVATIVES **certifiably** adverb.

certificate ▶ **noun** /səˈtɪfɪkət/ **1** an official document attesting a fact, in particular: ■ a document recording a person's birth, marriage, or death: *a birth certificate.* ■ a document confirming that someone has reached a certain level of achievement in a course of study or training. ■ a document attesting ownership of an item or the fulfilment of legal requirements: *a share certificate.*
2 an official classification awarded to a cinema film by a board of censors indicating its suitability for a particular age group: *an 18 certificate.*
▶ **verb** /səˈtɪfɪkeɪt/ [with obj.] Brit. provide with or attest in an official document.
– DERIVATIVES **certification** noun.
– ORIGIN late Middle English (in the sense 'certification, attestation'): from French *certificat* or medieval Latin *certificatum*, from *certificare* (see CERTIFY).

certificate of deposit ▶ **noun** a certificate issued by a bank to a person depositing money for a specified length of time at a specified rate of interest.

certified cheque ▶ **noun** a cheque which is guaranteed by a bank.

certified mail ▶ **noun** North American term for RECORDED DELIVERY.

certified public accountant ▶ **noun** US a member of an officially accredited professional body of accountants.

certify ▶ **verb** (**certifies, certifying, certified**) [with obj.] attest or confirm in a formal statement: *the profits for the year had been certified by the auditors* | [with clause] *the Law Society will certify that the sum charged is fair and reasonable.* ■ chiefly Brit. officially recognize as possessing certain qualifications or meeting certain standards: *scenes of violence had to be cut before the film could be certified* | (as adj. **certified**) *a certified accountant.* ■ officially declare insane.
– DERIVATIVES **certifier** noun.
– ORIGIN Middle English: from Old French *certifier*, from late Latin *certificare*, from Latin *certus* 'certain'.

certiorari /ˌsəːtɪə(ʊ)ˈrɑːri/ ▶ **noun** [mass noun] Law a writ or order by which a higher court reviews a case tried in a lower court: *an order of certiorari.*
– ORIGIN late Middle English: from Law Latin, 'to be informed', a phrase originally occurring at the start of the writ, from *certiorare* 'inform', from *certior*, comparative of *certus* 'certain'.

certitude /ˈsəːtɪtjuːd/ ▶ **noun** [mass noun] absolute certainty or conviction that something is the case: *the question may never be answered with certitude.*
■ [count noun] something that someone firmly believes is true: *the collapse of the old political certitudes in eastern Europe.*
– ORIGIN late Middle English: from late Latin *certitudo*, from *certus* 'certain'.

cerulean /sɪˈruːlɪən/ literary ▶ **adjective** deep blue in colour like a clear sky: *images of cerulean waters and golden sands.*
▶ **noun** [mass noun] a deep sky-blue colour.
– ORIGIN mid 17th cent.: from Latin *caeruleus* 'sky blue', from *caelum* 'sky'.

cerumen /sɪˈruːmən/ ▶ **noun** technical term for EARWAX.
– ORIGIN late 17th cent.: modern Latin, from Latin *cera* 'wax'.

ceruse /ˈsɪəruːs, sɪˈruːs/ ▶ **noun** archaic term for WHITE LEAD.
– ORIGIN late Middle English: via Old French from Latin *cerussa*, perhaps from Greek *kēros* 'wax'.

Cervantes /səːˈvantiːz/, Spanish /θerˈβantes, ser-/, Miguel de (1547–1616), Spanish novelist and dramatist; full name *Miguel de Cervantes Saavedra*. His most famous work is *Don Quixote* (1605–15), a satire on chivalric romances that greatly influenced the development of the novel.

cervelat /ˈsəːvəlɑː, -lat/ ▶ **noun** [mass noun] a kind of smoked pork sausage.
– ORIGIN early 17th cent.: from obsolete French, earlier form of *cervelas*, from Italian *cervellata*.

cervical /ˈsəːvɪk(ə)l, səːˈvʌɪk(ə)l/ ▶ **adjective 1** relating to the narrow neck-like passage forming the lower end of the womb: *cervical cancer.*
2 relating to the neck: *the fifth cervical vertebra.*

– ORIGIN late 17th cent.: from French, or from modern Latin *cervicalis*, from Latin *cervix*, *cervic-* 'neck'.

cervical screening ▶ noun [mass noun] Brit. the examination of cellular material from the neck of the womb for cancer.

cervical smear ▶ noun Brit. a specimen of cellular material from the neck of the womb spread on a microscope slide for examination for cancerous cells or precancerous changes.

cervicitis /ˌsəːvɪˈsʌɪtɪs/ ▶ noun [mass noun] Medicine inflammation of the neck of the womb.

cervid /ˈsəːvɪd/ ▶ noun Zoology a mammal of the deer family (Cervidae).
– ORIGIN late 19th cent.: from modern Latin *Cervidae* (plural), from Latin *cervus* 'deer'.

cervine /ˈsəːvʌɪn/ ▶ adjective rare relating to deer; deer-like.
– ORIGIN mid 19th cent.: from Latin *cervinus*, from *cervus* 'deer', + -INE[1].

cervix /ˈsəːvɪks/ ▶ noun (pl. **cervices** /-siːz/) **1** the narrow neck-like passage forming the lower end of the womb.
2 technical the neck.
– ORIGIN mid 18th cent.: Latin.

cesarean (also **cesarian**) ▶ adjective & noun US spelling of CAESAREAN.

Cesarewitch /sɪˈzarəwɪtʃ/ a horse race run annually over two miles at Newmarket, England.
– ORIGIN mid 19th cent.: from Russian *tsesarevich* 'heir to the throne', named in honour of the Russian Crown Prince (later Alexander II) who attended the inaugural race in 1839.

cesium ▶ noun US spelling of CAESIUM.

České Budějovice /ˌtʃeskeɪ ˈbuːdjɛjɒˌvɪtse/ a city in the south of the Czech Republic, on the River Vltava; pop. 94,925 (2007). It is noted for the production of lager. German name **BUDWEIS**.

cess[1] /sɛs/ (also **sess**) ▶ noun (in Scotland, Ireland, and India) a tax or levy.
– ORIGIN late 15th cent. (denoting the obligation placed on the Irish to supply the Lord Deputy's household and garrison with provisions at prices 'assessed' by the government): shortened from the obsolete noun *assess* 'assessment'.

cess[2] /sɛs/ ▶ noun (in phrase **bad cess to**) chiefly Irish a curse on: *bad cess to the day I joined that band!*
– ORIGIN mid 19th cent. (originally Anglo-Irish): perhaps from CESS[1].

cessation /sɛˈseɪʃ(ə)n/ ▶ noun [mass noun] the fact or process of ending or being brought to an end: *the cessation of hostilities* | [count noun] *a cessation of animal testing of cosmetics.*
– ORIGIN late Middle English: from Latin *cessatio(n-)*, from *cessare* 'cease'.

cesser /ˈsɛsə/ ▶ noun [mass noun] Law termination or cessation, especially of a period of tenure or legal liability.
– ORIGIN mid 16th cent.: from Old French *cesser* 'cease', used as a noun.

cession /ˈsɛʃ(ə)n/ ▶ noun [mass noun] the formal giving up of rights, property, or territory by a state: *the cession of twenty important towns.*
– ORIGIN late Middle English; from Latin *cessio(n-)*, from *cedere* 'cede'.

cesspit ▶ noun a pit for the disposal of liquid waste and sewage. ■ a disgusting or corrupt place: *the affair threatened to be a cesspit of scandal.*
– ORIGIN mid 19th cent.: from *cess* (the supposed base of CESSPOOL) + PIT[1].

cesspool ▶ noun an underground container for the temporary storage of liquid waste and sewage. ■ a disgusting or corrupt place.
– ORIGIN late 17th cent. (denoting a trap under a drain to catch solids): probably an alteration, influenced by POOL[1], of archaic *suspiral* 'vent, water pipe, settling tank', from Old French *souspirail* 'air hole', based on Latin *sub-* 'from below' + *spirare* 'breathe'.

c'est la vie /ˌseɪ laːˈviː/, French /sɛ la vi/ ▶ exclamation used to express acceptance or resignation in the face of a difficult or unpleasant situation: *if you get thwarted, c'est la vie.*
– ORIGIN French, literally 'that's life'.

Cestoda /sɛsˈtəʊdə/ (also **Cestoidea**) ▶ plural noun Zoology a class of parasitic flatworms that comprises the tapeworms.
– ORIGIN modern Latin (plural), from Latin *cestus*, from Greek *kestos*, literally 'stitched', used as a noun in the sense 'girdle'.

cestode /ˈsɛstəʊd/ ▶ noun Zoology a parasitic flatworm of the class Cestoda; a tapeworm.

cestui que trust /ˌsɛti: kiː ˈtrʌst/ ▶ noun Law the beneficiary of a trust.
– ORIGIN mid 16th cent.: from Law French, short for *cestui a que use le trust est créé*, 'the person for whose benefit anything is given in trust to another'.

CET ▶ abbreviation Central European Time.

Cetacea /sɪˈteɪʃə/ ▶ plural noun Zoology an order of marine mammals that comprises the whales, dolphins, and porpoises. These have a streamlined hairless body, no hindlimbs, a horizontal tail fin, and a blowhole on top of the head for breathing. See also **MYSTICETI**, **ODONTOCETI**.
– ORIGIN modern Latin (plural), from Latin *cetus*, from Greek *kētos* 'whale'.

cetacean ▶ noun a marine mammal of the order Cetacea; a whale, dolphin, or porpoise.
▶ adjective relating to or denoting cetaceans.

cetane /ˈsiːteɪn/ ▶ noun [mass noun] Chemistry a colourless liquid hydrocarbon of the alkane series, present in petroleum spirit. ● Chem. formula: $C_{16}H_{34}$.
– ORIGIN late 19th cent.: from Latin *cetus* 'whale', from Greek *kētos* (because related compounds were first derived from spermaceti) + -ANE[2].

cetane number ▶ noun a quantity indicating the ignition properties of diesel fuel relative to cetane as a standard.

ceteris paribus /ˌkeɪtərɪs ˈparɪbʊs, ˌsɛt-, ˌsiːt-/ ▶ adverb formal with other conditions remaining the same; other things being equal.
– ORIGIN early 17th cent.: modern Latin.

cetology /sɪˈtɒlədʒi/ ▶ noun [mass noun] the branch of zoology that deals with whales, dolphins, and porpoises.
– DERIVATIVES **cetologist** noun.
– ORIGIN mid 19th cent.: from Latin *cetus* 'whale' (see CETACEA) + -LOGY.

cetrimide /ˈsɛtrɪmʌɪd/ ▶ noun [mass noun] a synthetic detergent and antiseptic which is a quaternary ammonium compound derived from cetane.
– ORIGIN 1940s: from *cet(yl)trim(ethylammomium brom)ide*.

Cetshwayo /sɛˈtʃweɪəʊ/ (also **Cetewayo** /ˌsɛtɪˈweɪəʊ/) (*c.*1826–84), Zulu king. He became ruler of Zululand in 1873 and was involved in a series of battles with the Afrikaners and British; he was deposed as leader after the capture of his capital by the British in 1879.

Cetti's warbler /ˈtʃɛtɪz/ ▶ noun a chestnut-brown Eurasian warbler with a strikingly loud and abrupt song. ● *Cettia cetti*, family Sylviidae.
– ORIGIN late 19th cent.: named after Francesco *Cetti*, 18th-cent. Italian ornithologist.

Cetus /ˈsiːtəs/ Astronomy a large northern constellation (the Whale), said to represent the sea monster which threatened Andromeda. It contains the variable star Mira, but no other bright stars.
– ORIGIN Latin.

Ceuta /ˈseɪuːtə/, Spanish /ˈθeuta, ˈseuta/ a Spanish enclave on the coast of North Africa, in Morocco; pop. 77,389 (2008).

Cévennes /seɪˈvɛn/, French /sevɛn/ a mountain range on the south-eastern edge of the Massif Central in France.

ceviche /sɛˈviːtʃeɪ/ (also **seviche**) ▶ noun [mass noun] a South American dish of marinaded raw fish or seafood.
– ORIGIN South American Spanish.

Ceylon /sɪˈlɒn/ former name (until 1972) for **SRI LANKA**.

Ceylon moss ▶ noun [mass noun] a red seaweed of southern Asia, which is the main source of agar. ● *Gracilaria lichenoides*, division Rhodophyta.

Cézanne /seɪˈzan/, French /sezan/, Paul (1839–1906), French painter. He is closely identified with post-Impressionism and his later work had an important influence on cubism. Notable works: *Bathers* (sequence of paintings 1890–1905).

CF ▶ abbreviation ■ (in the UK) Chaplain to the Forces. ■ cystic fibrosis.

Cf ▶ symbol the chemical element californium.

cf. ▶ abbreviation compare with (used to refer a reader to another written work or another part of the same written work).
– ORIGIN from Latin *confer* 'compare'.

c.f. ▶ abbreviation carried forward (used to refer to figures transferred to a new page or account).

CFA (also **CFA franc**) ▶ noun the basic monetary unit of Cameroon, Congo, Gabon, and the Central African Republic, equal to 100 centimes.
– ORIGIN *CFA* from French *Communauté Financière Africaine* 'African Financial Community'.

CFC ▶ noun short for CHLOROFLUOROCARBON.

CFE ▶ abbreviation (in the UK) College of Further Education.

CFS ▶ abbreviation chronic fatigue syndrome.

CG ▶ abbreviation Democratic Republic of the Congo (international vehicle registration).

cg ▶ abbreviation centigram(s).

CGI ▶ abbreviation Computing ■ Common Gateway Interface, an interface standard by which World Wide Web servers may access external programs so that data is returned automatically in the form of a web page. ■ computer-generated imagery.

CGS ▶ abbreviation (in the UK) Chief of General Staff.

cgs ▶ abbreviation centimetre-gram-second.

CGT ▶ abbreviation capital gains tax.

CH ▶ abbreviation ■ (in the UK) Companion of Honour. ■ Switzerland (international vehicle registration). [from French *Confédération Helvétique* 'Swiss Confederation'.]

ch. ▶ abbreviation ■ chapter. ■ (of a horse) chestnut in colour. ■ church.

cha ▶ noun variant spelling of CHAR[3].

chaap /tʃaːp/ (also **chhaap**) ▶ noun Indian an official seal or stamp, used to approve or authenticate a permit or similar document.
– ORIGIN Hindi *chāp* 'stamp, brand'.

chaat /tʃaːt/ ▶ noun [mass noun] an Indian dish of boiled vegetables or raw fruit, with spices.
– ORIGIN from Hindi *cāṭ*.

chabazite /ˈkabəzʌɪt/ ▶ noun [mass noun] a colourless, pink, or yellow zeolite mineral, typically occurring as rhombohedral crystals.
– ORIGIN early 19th cent.: from French *chabazie*, from Greek *khabazie*, a misreading of *khalazie*, vocative form of *khalazios* 'hailstone' (from *khalaza* 'hail', because of its form and colour), + -ITE[1].

Chablis /ˈʃabliː/ ▶ noun [mass noun] a dry white burgundy wine from Chablis in eastern France.

Chabrol /ʃaˈbrɒl/, French /ʃabʀɔl/, Claude (b.1930), French film director, a member of the *nouvelle vague*. His films typically combine suspense with studies of personal relationships, and include *Les Biches* (1968).

chacha /ˈtʃʌtʃʌ/ ▶ noun Indian uncle (often used as a respectful form of address to a man around the same age as one's father).
– ORIGIN from Hindi *cācā*.

cha-cha /ˈtʃaːtʃaː/ (also **cha-cha-cha**) ▶ noun a ballroom dance with small steps and swaying hip movements, performed to a Latin American rhythm. ■ music for a cha-cha.
▶ verb (**cha-chas, cha-chaing** /-tʃaː(r)ɪŋ/, **cha-cha'd** or **cha-chaed** /-tʃaːd/) [no obj.] dance the cha-cha.
– ORIGIN 1950s: Latin American Spanish.

chachalaca /ˌtʃatʃəˈlakə/ ▶ noun a pheasant-like tree-dwelling bird of the guan family, found mainly in the forests of tropical America. ● Genus *Ortalis*, family Cracidae.
– ORIGIN late 19th cent.: via South American Spanish from Nahuatl, of imitative origin.

chacham /ˈxaːxəm/ ▶ noun variant spelling of **HAHAM**.

chack ▶ verb [no obj.] (of a bird) make a harsh call.
– ORIGIN early 16th cent.: imitative.

chacma baboon /ˈtʃakmə/ ▶ noun a dark grey baboon which lives on the savannah of southern Africa. ● *Papio ursinus*, family Cercopithecidae.
– ORIGIN mid 19th cent.: from Khoikhoi.

Chaco another name for **GRAN CHACO**.

chaconne /ʃəˈkɒn/ ▶ noun Music a composition in a series of varying sections in slow triple time. Compare with PASSACAGLIA. ■ a stately dance performed to a chaconne, popular in the 18th century. ■ a ballroom dance performed in Europe in the late 19th and early 20th centuries.
– ORIGIN late 17th cent.: from French, from Spanish *chacona*.

Chaco War /ˈtʃaːkəʊ/ a boundary dispute in 1932–5 between Bolivia and Paraguay, in which Paraguay eventually gained most of the disputed territory.

chacun à son goût /ˌʃakəːn a sɒn ˈguː/, French /ʃakœ̃ a sɔ̃ gu/ ▶ exclamation each to their own taste.
– ORIGIN French.

C

C

Chad /tʃad/ a landlocked country in northern central Africa; pop. 10,329,200 (est. 2009); official languages, French and Arabic; capital, N'Djamena.

> Much of the country lies in the Sahel and, in the north, the Sahara Desert. A French colony from 1913, Chad became autonomous within the French Community in 1958, and fully independent as a republic in 1960.

– DERIVATIVES **Chadian** adjective & noun.

chad /tʃad/ ▶ noun a piece of waste material removed from card or tape by punching.
– ORIGIN 1950s: of unknown origin.

Chad, Lake a shallow lake on the borders of Chad, Niger, and Nigeria in north central Africa. Its size varies seasonally from *c.*10,360 sq. km (4,000 sq. miles) to *c.*25,900 sq. km (10,000 sq. miles).

Chadic /ˈtʃadɪk/ ▶ noun [mass noun] a group of Afro-Asiatic languages spoken in the region of Lake Chad, of which the most important is Hausa.
▶ adjective relating to the Chadic languages.

chador /ˈtʃɑːdɔː, ˈtʃɑːdə, ˈtʃʌdə/ (also **chaddar** or **chuddar**) ▶ noun a large piece of cloth that is wrapped around the head and upper body leaving only the face exposed, worn especially by Muslim women.
– ORIGIN early 17th cent.: from Urdu *chādar, chaddar*, from Persian *čādar* 'sheet or veil'.

Chadwick /ˈtʃadwɪk/, Sir James (1891–1974), English physicist. He discovered the neutron, for which he received the 1935 Nobel Prize for Physics.

chaebol /ˈtʃeɪbɒl/ ▶ noun (pl. **same** or **chaebols**) (in South Korea) a large family-owned business conglomerate.
– ORIGIN 1980s: Korean, literally 'money clan'.

chaeta /ˈkiːtə/ ▶ noun (pl. **chaetae** /-tiː/) Zoology a stiff bristle made of chitin, especially in an annelid worm.
– ORIGIN mid 19th cent.: modern Latin, from Greek *khaitē* 'long hair'.

Chaetognatha /ˌkiːtəgˈnaθə, -ˈneɪθə/ ▶ plural noun Zoology a small phylum of marine invertebrates that comprises the arrow worms.
– DERIVATIVES **chaetognath** noun.
– ORIGIN modern Latin (plural), from Greek *khaitē* 'long hair' + *gnathos* 'jaw'.

chafe /tʃeɪf/ ▶ verb **1** (with reference to a part of the body) make or become sore by rubbing against something: [with obj.] *the collar chafed his neck* | [no obj.] *her arms chafed where the rope bit into them.* ■ [no obj.] (of an object) rub abrasively against another: *the grommet stops the cable chafing on the metal.*
2 [with obj.] rub (a part of the body) to restore warmth or sensation: *I chafed her feet and wrapped the blanket round her.*
3 become or make annoyed or impatient because of a restriction or inconvenience: [no obj.] *the bank chafed at the restrictions imposed upon it* | [with obj.] *it chafed him to be confined like this.*
▶ noun **1** [mass noun] wear or damage caused by rubbing: *to prevent chafe the ropes should lie flat.*
2 archaic a state of annoyance.
– PHRASES **chafe at the bit** see CHAMP AT THE BIT at CHAMP[1].
– ORIGIN late Middle English (in the sense 'make warm'): from Old French *chaufer* 'make hot', based on Latin *calefacere*, from *calere* 'be hot' + *facere* 'make'.

chafer /ˈtʃeɪfə/ ▶ noun a large flying beetle, the adult and larva of which can be very destructive to foliage and plant roots respectively. ● Several subfamilies of the family Scarabaeidae.
– ORIGIN Old English *ceafor, cefer*, of Germanic origin; related to Dutch *kever*.

chaff[1] /tʃɑːf, tʃaf/ ▶ noun [mass noun] **1** the husks of corn or other seed separated by winnowing or threshing. ■ chopped hay and straw used as fodder.
2 worthless things; rubbish: *he hopes to separate scientifically supported claims from pseudoscientific chaff.*
3 strips of metal foil released in the air to obstruct radar detection.
– PHRASES **separate** (or **sort**) **the wheat from the chaff** distinguish valuable people or things from worthless ones.
– ORIGIN Old English *cæf, ceaf*, probably from a Germanic base meaning 'gnaw'; related to Dutch *kaf*, also to CHAFER.

chaff[2] /tʃɑːf, tʃaf/ ▶ noun [mass noun] light-hearted joking; banter.
▶ verb [with obj.] tease.
– ORIGIN early 19th cent.: perhaps from CHAFE.

chaffer /ˈtʃafə/ ▶ verb [no obj.] haggle about the terms of an agreement or price of something.
▶ noun [mass noun] archaic haggling about the price of something.
– ORIGIN Middle English (in the sense 'trade or trading'): from Old English *cēap* 'a bargain' + *faru* 'journey'; probably influenced by Old Norse *kaupfǫr*.

chaffinch ▶ noun a Eurasian and North African finch, typically with a bluish top to the head and dark wings and tail. ● Genus *Fringilla*, family Fringillidae: two species, in particular the *F. coelebs*, which (in the male of the typical European form) has a pinkish face and breast.
– ORIGIN Old English *ceaffinc* 'chaff finch' (because it forages around barns, picking seeds out of the chaff).

chaffweed /ˈtʃafwiːd/ ▶ noun [mass noun] a tiny European pimpernel with pink or white flowers. ● *Anagallis minima*, family Primulaceae.
– ORIGIN mid 16th cent.: probably from the verb CHAFE + WEED.

chafing dish ▶ noun a cooking pot with an outer pan of hot water, used for keeping food warm. ■ a metal pan containing a spirit lamp or burning charcoal, used for cooking at table.
– ORIGIN late 15th cent.: from the original (now obsolete) sense of CHAFE 'become warm, warm up'.

Chagall /ʃaˈgal/, Marc (1887–1985), Russian-born French painter and graphic artist. His work was characterized by the use of rich emotive colour and dream imagery, and had a significant influence on surrealism.

Chagas' disease /ˈtʃɑːgəs/ ▶ noun [mass noun] a disease caused by a trypanosome transmitted by bloodsucking bugs, endemic in South and Central America and causing damage to the heart and central nervous system.
– ORIGIN early 20th cent.: named after Carlos *Chagas* (1879–1934), the Brazilian physician who first described it.

Chagos Archipelago /ˈtʃɑːgəs/ an island group in the Indian Ocean forming the British Indian Ocean Territory.

chagrin /ˈʃagrɪn, ʃəˈgrɪn/ ▶ noun [mass noun] annoyance or distress at having failed or been humiliated: *to my chagrin, he was nowhere to be seen.*
▶ verb (**be chagrined**) feel distressed or humiliated.
– ORIGIN mid 17th cent. (in the sense 'melancholy'): from French *chagrin* (noun), literally 'rough skin, shagreen', *chagriner* (verb), of unknown origin.

chai /tʃʌɪ/ ▶ noun [mass noun] Indian tea made by boiling tea leaves with milk, sugar, and sometimes spices.
– ORIGIN a term in various Indian languages.

Chain, Sir Ernst Boris (1906–79), German-born British biochemist. With Howard Florey he isolated and purified penicillin and in 1945 they shared a Nobel Prize with Alexander Fleming.

chain ▶ noun **1** a series of linked metal rings used for fastening or securing something, or for pulling loads: *he slid the bolts on the front door and put the safety chain across* | *the drug dealer is being kept in chains.* ■ a decorative chain worn round the neck as jewellery or as a badge of office. ■ a restrictive force or factor: *workers secured by the chains of the labour market.*
2 a sequence of items of the same type forming a line: *he kept the chain of buckets supplied with water.* ■ a series of connected elements: *the action would initiate a chain of events.* ■ a connected series of mountains: *a mountain chain.* ■ a group of hotels, restaurants, or shops owned by the same company. ■ a part of a molecule consisting of a number of atoms bonded together in a linear sequence. ■ a figure in a quadrille or similar dance, in which dancers meet and pass each other in a continuous sequence.
3 a jointed measuring line consisting of linked metal rods. ■ the length of such a measuring line (66 ft).
4 (**chains**) a structure of planks projecting horizontally from a sailing ship's sides abreast of the masts, used to widen the basis for the shrouds. [formed earlier of iron plates.]
▶ verb [with obj.] fasten or secure with a chain: *she chained her bicycle to the railings.* ■ confine with a chain: *he had been **chained up*** | figurative *as an actuary you will not be chained to a desk.*
– PHRASES **pull** (or **yank**) **someone's chain** informal tease someone by leading them to believe something untrue: *he's just pulling your chain.*
– ORIGIN Middle English: from Old French *chaine, chaeine*, from Latin *catena* 'a chain'.

chain armour ▶ noun another term for CHAIN MAIL.

chain bridge ▶ noun a suspension bridge held by chains rather than cables.

chain drive ▶ noun [mass noun] a mechanism in which power is transmitted from an engine to the wheels of a vehicle or a boat's propeller by means of a moving endless chain.
– DERIVATIVES **chain-driven** adjective.

chaîné /ˈʃɛneɪ/ ▶ noun (pl. **chaînés** pronunc. **same**) Ballet a sequence of fast turns from one foot to the other, executed in a straight line.
– ORIGIN French, literally 'linked'.

chain gang ▶ noun a group of convicts chained together while working outside the prison.

chain gear ▶ noun a gear transmitting motion by means of a moving endless chain, especially in a bicycle.

chain gun ▶ noun a machine gun that uses a motor-driven chain to power all moving parts.

chain harrow ▶ noun a harrow consisting of a net made of chains in a metal frame.

chain letter ▶ noun one of a sequence of letters, each recipient in the sequence being requested to send copies to a specific number of other people.

chain-link ▶ adjective [attrib.] made of wire in a diamond-shaped mesh: *a chain-link fence.*

chain mail ▶ noun [mass noun] historical flexible armour consisting of small metal rings linked together.

chain of command (also **command chain**) ▶ noun a system in a military or civil organization by which instructions are passed from one person to another.

chainplate ▶ noun a strong link or plate on the hull of a yacht or sailing ship, to which a shroud is secured.

chain reaction ▶ noun a chemical reaction or other process in which the products themselves promote or spread the reaction. ■ the self-sustaining fission reaction spread by neutrons which occurs in nuclear reactors and bombs. ■ a series of events, each caused by the previous one: *the wine provoked a chain reaction of memories.*

chainring ▶ noun a large cog carrying the chain on a bicycle, to which the pedals are attached.

chainsaw ▶ noun a mechanical power-driven cutting tool with teeth set on a chain which moves around the edge of a blade.

chain shot ▶ noun [mass noun] historical pairs of cannonballs or half balls joined by a chain, fired from cannons in sea battles in order to damage masts and rigging.

chain-smoke ▶ verb [no obj.] smoke continually, typically by lighting a cigarette from the stub of the last one smoked.
– DERIVATIVES **chain-smoker** noun.

chain stitch ▶ noun [mass noun] an embroidery or crochet stitch resembling a chain.

chain store ▶ noun one of a series of shops owned by one firm and selling the same goods.

chain wheel ▶ noun a wheel transmitting power by means of a chain fitted to its edges.

chair ▶ noun **1** a separate seat for one person, typically with a back and four legs. ■ (**the chair**) short for ELECTRIC CHAIR.
2 the person in charge of a meeting or of an organization (used as a neutral alternative to chairman or chairwoman): *she's the chair of a research committee.* ■ the post of a chairperson: *he was due to step down after a three-year stint in the chair.*
3 a professorship: *he held a chair in physics.*
4 chiefly Brit. a metal socket holding a rail in place on a railway sleeper.
▶ verb [with obj.] **1** act as chairperson of or preside over (an organization, meeting, or public event): *the debate was chaired by the Archbishop of York.*
2 Brit. carry (someone) aloft in a chair or in a sitting position to celebrate a victory.
– PHRASES **take the chair** act as chairperson.
– ORIGIN Middle English: from Old French *chaiere* (modern *chaire* 'bishop's throne, etc.', *chaise* 'chair'), from Latin *cathedra* 'seat', from Greek *kathedra*. Compare with CATHEDRAL.

chair car ▶ noun N. Amer. a railway carriage with adjustable seats in pairs either side of a central gangway.

chairlady ▶ noun (pl. **chairladies**) another term for CHAIRWOMAN.

chairlift ▶ noun **1** a series of chairs hung from a moving cable, used for carrying people up and down a mountain.
2 a device for carrying people in wheelchairs from one floor of a building to another.

chairman ▸ noun (pl. **chairmen**) **1** a person chosen to preside over a meeting. ■ the permanent or long-term president of a committee, company, or other organization. ■ (**Chairman**) (since 1949) the leading figure in the Chinese Communist Party.
2 historical a sedan-bearer.
– DERIVATIVES **chairmanship** noun.

> **USAGE** The word **chairman** found itself accused of sexism in the 1970s, with critics opposed to the way it combined the notion of power with a grammatical gender bias. Two neutral alternatives were proposed, **chair** (which was actually recorded in this sense in the 17th century) and the neologism **chairperson**. Both terms faced initial resistance, and although they have now become accepted in standard English, the Oxford English Corpus shows that they are still far less common than **chairman**.

chairperson ▸ noun (pl. **chairpersons**) a chairman or chairwoman (used as a neutral alternative).

chairwoman ▸ noun (pl. **chairwomen**) a female chairperson.

chaise /ʃeɪz/ ▸ noun **1** chiefly historical a horse-drawn carriage for one or two people, typically one with an open top and two wheels. ■ another term for POST-CHAISE.
2 US term for CHAISE LONGUE.
– ORIGIN mid 17th cent.: from French, variant of *chaire* (see CHAIR).

chaise longue /ˌʃeɪz ˈlɒŋ/ (N. Amer. also **chaise lounge**) ▸ noun (pl. **chaises longues** pronunc. **same**) a sofa with a backrest at only one end.
– ORIGIN early 19th cent.: French, literally 'long chair'.

> **USAGE** The unfamiliar-looking spelling of **chaise longue** ('long chair' in French) has led many people to interpret it as the more English **chaise lounge**. This is regarded as an error in British English but is a common and accepted variant in US English.

Chaka variant spelling of SHAKA.

chakka /ˈtʃʌkə/ ▸ noun Indian a wheel or tyre.
– ORIGIN from Hindi *cakkā*.

chakra /ˈtʃʌkrə/ ▸ noun (in Indian thought) each of seven centres of spiritual power in the human body.
– ORIGIN from Sanskrit *cakra* 'wheel or circle', from an Indo-European base meaning 'turn', shared by WHEEL.

chal[1] /tʃal/ ▸ noun a male Gypsy.
– ORIGIN mid 19th cent.: from Romany, literally 'person, fellow'.

chal[2] ▸ noun variant spelling of CHAWL.

chalaza /kəˈleɪzə/ ▸ noun (pl. **chalazae** /-ziː/) Zoology (in a bird's egg) each of two twisted membranous strips joining the yolk to the ends of the shell.
– DERIVATIVES **chalazal** adjective.
– ORIGIN early 18th cent.: modern Latin, from Greek *khalaza* 'small knot'.

Chalcedon /ˈkalsɪdɒn, kalˈsiːd(ə)n/ a former city on the Bosporus in Asia Minor, now part of Istanbul. Turkish name KADIKÖY.

Chalcedon, Council of the fourth ecumenical council of the Christian Church, held at Chalcedon in 451. It condemned the Monophysite position and affirmed the dual but united nature of Christ as god and man.
– DERIVATIVES **Chalcedonian** /ˌkalsɪˈdəʊnɪən/ noun & adjective.

chalcedony /kalˈsɛdəni/ ▸ noun (pl. **chalcedonies**) [mass noun] a microcrystalline type of quartz occurring in several different forms including onyx and agate.
– DERIVATIVES **chalcedonic** /ˌkalsɪˈdɒnɪk/ adjective.
– ORIGIN late Middle English: from Latin *calcedonius*, *chalcedonius* (often believed to mean 'stone of Chalcedon', but this is doubtful), from Greek *khalkēdōn*.

chalcid /ˈkalsɪd/ (also **chalcid wasp**) ▸ noun a minute metallic-coloured parasitic wasp of a large group whose members lay eggs inside the eggs of other insects. ● Superfamily Chalcidoidea, order Hymenoptera.
– ORIGIN late 19th cent.: from modern Latin *Chalcis* (genus name), from Greek *khalkos* 'copper, brass', + -ID[3].

Chalcis /ˈkalsɪs/ the chief town of the island of Euboea, on the coast opposite mainland Greece; pop. 51,000 (est. 2009). Greek name KHALKÍS.

Chalcolithic /ˌkalkə(ʊ)ˈlɪθɪk/ ▸ adjective Archaeology relating to or denoting a period in the 4th and 3rd millennia BC, chiefly in the Near East and SE Europe, during which some weapons and tools were made of copper. This period was still largely Neolithic in character. Also called ENEOLITHIC. ■ (as noun **the Chalcolithic**) the Chalcolithic period. Also called COPPER AGE.
– ORIGIN early 20th cent.: from Greek *khalkos* 'copper' + *lithos* 'stone' + -IC.

chalcopyrite /ˌkalkə(ʊ)ˈpʌɪrʌɪt/ ▸ noun [mass noun] a yellow crystalline mineral consisting of a sulphide of copper and iron. It is the principal ore of copper. Also called COPPER PYRITES.
– ORIGIN mid 19th cent.: from modern Latin *chalcopyrites*, from Greek *khalkos* 'copper' + *puritēs* (see PYRITES).

Chaldea /kalˈdiːə/ an ancient country in what is now southern Iraq, inhabited by the Chaldeans.
– ORIGIN from Greek *Khaldaia*, from Akkadian *Kaldû*, the name of a Babylonian tribal group.

Chaldean /kalˈdiːən/ ▸ noun **1** a member of an ancient people who lived in Chaldea *c.*800 BC and ruled Babylonia 625–539 BC. They were renowned as astronomers and astrologers.
2 [mass noun] the Semitic language of the ancient Chaldeans. ■ a language related to Aramaic and spoken in parts of Iraq.
3 a member of a Syrian Uniate (formerly Nestorian) Church based mainly in Iran and Iraq.
▸ adjective **1** relating to ancient Chaldea or its people or language.
2 relating to the East Syrian Uniate Church.

Chaldee /kalˈdiː, ˈkaldiː/ ▸ noun **1** [mass noun] the language of the ancient Chaldeans. ■ dated the Aramaic language as used in some books of the Old Testament.
2 a native of ancient Chaldea.
– ORIGIN from Latin *Chaldaei* 'Chaldeans', from Greek *Khaldaioi*, from *Khaldaia* (see CHALDEA).

chalet /ˈʃaleɪ/ ▸ noun a wooden house with overhanging eaves, typically found in the Swiss Alps. ■ Brit. a small cabin or house used by holidaymakers, forming a unit within a holiday complex.
– ORIGIN late 18th cent.: from Swiss French, diminutive of Old French *chasel* 'farmstead', based on Latin *casa* 'hut, cottage'.

chalice ▸ noun historical a large cup or goblet. ■ the wine cup used in the Christian Eucharist.
– ORIGIN Middle English: via Old French from Latin *calix*, *calic-* 'cup'.

chalicothere /ˈkalɪkəˌθɪə/ ▸ noun a large horse-like fossil mammal of the late Tertiary period, with stout claws on the toes rather than hoofs. ● Family Chalicotheriidae, order Perissodactyla: several genera.
– ORIGIN early 20th cent.: from modern Latin *Chalicotherium* (genus name), from Greek *khalix*, *khalik-* 'gravel' + *thērion* 'wild animal'.

chalk ▸ noun [mass noun] a white soft earthy limestone (calcium carbonate) formed from the skeletal remains of sea creatures. ■ a chalk-like substance (calcium sulphate), made into sticks used for writing or drawing on a blackboard. ■ [count noun] Geology a series of strata consisting mainly of chalk.
▸ verb [with obj.] **1** write or draw with chalk: *he chalked a message on the board*. ■ draw or write on (a surface) with chalk: *blackboards chalked with Japanese phrases*. ■ rub the tip of (a snooker cue) with chalk.
2 Brit. charge (drinks bought in a pub or bar) to a person's account: *he chalked the bill on to the Professor's private account*.
– PHRASES **as different as** (or **like**) **chalk and cheese** Brit. fundamentally different or incompatible. **by a long chalk** Brit. by far. **chalk and talk** Brit. teaching by traditional methods focusing on the blackboard and presentation by the teacher as opposed to more informal or interactive methods. **not by a long chalk** Brit. by no means; not at all: *they weren't beaten yet, not by a long chalk*. [with reference to the chalk used for marking up scores in competitive games.]
– PHRASAL VERBS **chalk something off** Brit. (in sport) disallow a goal for an infringement of the rules. **chalk something out** sketch or plan something: *we have already chalked out the strategy for conducting raids*. **chalk something up 1** achieve something noteworthy: *he has chalked up a box office success*. **2** ascribe something to a particular cause: *I chalked my sleeplessness **up to** nerves*.
– ORIGIN Old English *cealc* (also denoting lime), related to Dutch *kalk* and German *Kalk*, from Latin *calx* (see CALX).

chalkboard ▸ noun North American term for BLACKBOARD.

chalkface ▸ noun [in sing.] Brit. the day-to-day work of teaching in a school: *teachers at the chalkface*.

chalkhill blue ▸ noun a European blue butterfly of calcareous grassland, of which the male is silvery-blue with blackish markings and the female is brown. ● *Lysandra coridon*, family Lycaenidae.

chalk pit ▸ noun Brit. a quarry from which chalk is extracted.

chalk-stone ▸ noun Medicine, dated a chalky deposit of sodium urate formed in the hands and feet of sufferers from severe gout.

chalk-stripe ▸ adjective [attrib.] (of a garment or material) having a pattern of thin white stripes on a dark background: *a chalk-stripe suit*.
▸ noun (**chalk stripe**) a pattern of thin white stripes on a dark background.
– DERIVATIVES **chalk-striped** adjective.

chalk talk ▸ noun N. Amer. a talk or lecture in which the speaker uses a blackboard and chalk.

chalky ▸ adjective (**chalkier**, **chalkiest**) **1** consisting of or rich in chalk: *chalky soil*.
2 resembling chalk in texture or paleness of colour: *walls of chalky green*.
– DERIVATIVES **chalkiness** noun.

challah /ˈhɑːlə, xɑːˈlɑː/ ▸ noun (pl. **challahs** or **chalot**, **chaloth** /xɑːˈlɒt/) a plaited loaf of white leavened bread, traditionally baked to celebrate the Jewish sabbath.
– ORIGIN from Hebrew *ḥallah*.

challan /ˈtʃʌlən/ Indian ▸ noun an official form or document, such as a receipt, invoice, or summons.
▸ verb [with obj.] issue (someone) with an official notice of a traffic offence: *police challaned over 24 vehicle owners for violating the rules*.
– ORIGIN Hindi *chalān*.

challenge ▸ noun **1** a call to someone to participate in a competitive situation or fight to decide who is superior in terms of ability or strength. ■ a task or situation that tests someone's abilities: *the traverse of the ridge is a challenge for experienced climbers* | *he **took up the challenge** of organizing a sports afternoon*. ■ an attempt to win a contest or championship in a sport.
2 a call to prove or justify something: ***a challenge to** the legality of the banning order*. ■ a guard's call for a password or other proof of identity. ■ Law an objection regarding the eligibility or suitability of a jury member.
3 [mass noun] Medicine exposure of the immune system to pathogenic organisms or antigens: *recently vaccinated calves should be protected from challenge*.
▸ verb [with obj.] **1** dispute the truth or validity of: *it is possible to challenge the report's assumptions*. ■ Law object to (a jury member): *a certain number of jurors may be challenged*. ■ (of a guard) order (someone) to prove their identity.
2 invite (someone) to engage in a contest: *he challenged one of my men to a duel* | *organizations challenged the government in by-elections*. ■ enter into competition with or opposition against. ■ make a rival claim to or threaten someone's hold on (a position): *they were challenging his leadership*. ■ [with obj. and infinitive] invite (someone) to do or say something that one thinks will be difficult or impossible: *I challenge the Minister to deny these accusations*. ■ make demands on; prove testing to: *a new way of life that would challenge them*.
3 Medicine expose (the immune system) to pathogenic organisms or antigens.
– DERIVATIVES **challengeable** adjective, **challenger** noun.
– ORIGIN Middle English (in the senses 'accusation' and 'accuse'): from Old French *chalenge* (noun), *chalenger* (verb), from Latin *calumnia* 'calumny', *calumniari* 'calumniate'.

challenged ▸ adjective [with submodifier or in combination] used euphemistically to indicate that someone suffers disability in a specified respect: *my experience of being physically challenged*. ■ informal used to indicate that someone or something is lacking or deficient in a specified respect: *I didn't know he was so vertically challenged* | *today's attention-challenged teens*.

> **USAGE** The use with a preceding adverb (e.g. **physically challenged**), originally intended to give a more positive tone than terms such as **disabled** or **handicapped**, arose in the US in the 1980s and quickly spread to the UK and elsewhere. Despite the serious intention the term rapidly became stalled by uses whose intention was to make fun of the attempts at euphemism and whose tone was usually clearly ironic: examples include **cerebrally challenged**, **conversationally challenged**, and **follicularly challenged**. See also USAGE at DISABLED.

Challenger Deep the deepest part (11,034 m, 36,201 ft) of the Mariana Trench in the North Pacific, discovered by HMS *Challenger II* in 1948.

challenging ▶ **adjective** testing one's abilities; demanding: *challenging and rewarding employment* | *the current challenging economic environment*. ■ inviting competition; provocative: *there was a challenging glint in his eyes*.
– DERIVATIVES **challengingly** **adverb**.

> **WORD TRENDS** A fear of offending people has led to the replacement of many negative expressions with more positive alternatives, with the adjective **challenging** being a prime example. The Oxford English Corpus shows that it is used euphemistically for *difficult* or *trying* and applied to unpleasant situations (*a challenging period of slowing growth and rising unemployment*), troublesome individuals (*it's surprising how common it is for parents to encounter challenging behaviour with their teenagers*), and even avant-garde music (*the opera's challenging atonal score*). See also **ISSUE**.

challis /'ʃalɪs, 'ʃali/ ▶ **noun** [mass noun] a lightweight soft clothing fabric made from silk and worsted.
– ORIGIN mid 19th cent.: origin uncertain; perhaps from the surname *Challis*.

chalone /'kaləʊn, 'keɪ-/ ▶ **noun** Biochemistry a substance secreted like a hormone but having the effect of inhibiting a physiological process.
– ORIGIN early 20th cent.: from Greek *khalōn* 'slackening', present participle of *khalaein*, on the pattern of *hormone*.

chalumeau /'ʃalʊməʊ/ ▶ **noun** (pl. **chalumeaux** pronunc. **same**) a reed instrument of the early 18th century from which the clarinet was developed. ■ (also **chalumeau register**) the lowest octave of the clarinet's range.
– ORIGIN early 18th cent.: from French, from Latin *calamellus* 'little reed', diminutive of *calamus*.

chalupa /tʃə'luːpə/ ▶ **noun** (in Spain and Latin America) a small light boat or canoe. ■ a fried tortilla in the shape of a boat, with a spicy filling.
– ORIGIN late 19th cent.: Spanish, ultimately related to Dutch *sloep* 'sloop'.

chalybeate /kə'lɪbɪət/ ▶ **adjective** [attrib.] of or denoting natural mineral springs containing iron salts.
– ORIGIN mid 17th cent.: from modern Latin *chalybeatus*, from Latin *chalybs*, from Greek *khalups*, *khalub-* 'steel'.

Cham /tʃam/ ▶ **noun** (pl. **same** or **Chams**) **1** a member of an indigenous people of Vietnam and Cambodia, who formed an independent kingdom from the 2nd to 17th centuries AD.
2 [mass noun] the Austronesian language of the Cham, with about 230,000 speakers.
▶ **adjective** relating to the Cham, their culture, or their language.

Chamaeleon /kə'miːlɪən/ Astronomy a small and faint southern constellation (the Chameleon), close to the south celestial pole.
– ORIGIN from Greek.

chamaeleon ▶ **noun** variant spelling of **CHAMELEON**.

chamaephyte /'kamɪfʌɪt/ ▶ **noun** Botany a woody plant whose resting buds are on or near the ground.
– ORIGIN early 20th cent.: from Greek *khamai* 'on the ground' + **-PHYTE**.

chamber ▶ **noun 1** a large room used for formal or public events: *a council chamber*. ■ one of the houses of a parliament: *the upper chamber*. ■ (**chambers**) Law, Brit. rooms used by a barrister or barristers, especially in the Inns of Court. ■ Law a judge's office, where proceedings may be held if not required to be held in open court. ■ archaic a private room, especially a bedroom.
2 an enclosed space or cavity: *a burial chamber*. ■ a large underground cavern. ■ the part of a gun bore that contains the charge. ■ Biology a cavity in a plant, animal body, or organ.
3 [as modifier] Music of or for a small group of instruments: *a chamber concert*.
▶ **verb** [with obj.] place (a bullet) into the chamber of a gun.
– ORIGIN Middle English (in the sense 'private room'): from Old French *chambre*, from Latin *camera* 'vault, arched chamber', from Greek *kamara* 'object with an arched cover'.

chambered ▶ **adjective** (especially of a gun) having a chamber of a particular kind. ■ Archaeology (of a tomb) containing a burial chamber. ■ Biology (of a plant, animal body, or organ) having one or more body cavities: [in combination] *a four-chambered heart*.

Chamberlain[1] /'tʃeɪmbəlɪn/, (Arthur) Neville (1869–1940), British Conservative statesman, Prime Minister 1937–40, son of Joseph Chamberlain. He pursued a policy of appeasement with Germany, signing the Munich Agreement (1938), but was forced to abandon this policy following Hitler's invasion of Czechoslovakia in 1939.

Chamberlain[2] /'tʃeɪmbəlɪn/, Joseph (1836–1914), British Liberal statesman. He left the Liberal party in 1886 because of Gladstone's support of Irish Home Rule. The leader of the Liberal Unionists from 1891, he played a leading role in the handling of the Second Boer War.

Chamberlain[3] /'tʃeɪmbəlɪn/, Owen (1920–2006), American physicist. He investigated subatomic particles and in 1955 discovered the antiproton with **E. G. Segrè** (1905–89), for which they shared the 1959 Nobel Prize for Physics.

chamberlain /'tʃeɪmbəlɪn/ ▶ **noun** historical an officer who managed the household of a monarch or noble. ■ Brit. an officer who received revenue on behalf of a corporation or public body.
– DERIVATIVES **chamberlainship** **noun**.
– ORIGIN Middle English (denoting a servant in a bedchamber): via Old French from Old Saxon *kamera*, from Latin *camera* 'vault' (see **CHAMBER**).

chambermaid ▶ **noun** a woman who cleans bedrooms and bathrooms in a hotel.

chamber music ▶ **noun** [mass noun] instrumental music played by a small ensemble, with one player to a part, the most important form being the string quartet.

Chamber of Commerce ▶ **noun** a local association to promote and protect the interests of the business community in a particular place.

Chamber of Deputies ▶ **noun** the lower legislative assembly in some parliaments.

chamber of horrors ▶ **noun** a place of entertainment containing instruments or scenes of torture or execution.
– ORIGIN mid 19th cent.: from the name given to a room in Madame Tussaud's waxwork exhibition.

Chamber of Trade ▶ **noun** a national organization representing local Chambers of Commerce.

chamber orchestra ▶ **noun** a small orchestra.

chamber organ ▶ **noun** a movable pipe organ for playing in a small concert hall, chapel, or private house.

chamber pot ▶ **noun** a bowl kept in a bedroom and used as a toilet at night.

Chambers, Sir William (1723–96), Scottish architect. His neoclassical style is demonstrated in buildings such as Somerset House in London (1776).

Chambertin /'ʃɒ̃bəːtã/ ▶ **noun** [mass noun] a dry red burgundy wine of high quality from Gevrey Chambertin in eastern France.

Chambéry /'ʃɒ̃bəri/, French /ʃɑ̃beʀi/ a town in eastern France; pop. 59,188 (2006).

chambray /'ʃambreɪ/ ▶ **noun** [mass noun] a cloth with a white weft and a coloured warp.
– ORIGIN early 19th cent. (originally US): formed irregularly from *Cambrai*, the name of a town in northern France, where it was originally made. Compare with **CAMBRIC**.

chambré /'ʃɒmbreɪ, 'ʃɒ̃-/ ▶ **adjective** [predic.] (of red wine) at room temperature: *the French believe that Cabernet tastes best chambré*.
– ORIGIN 1950s: French, past participle of *chambrer* 'bring to room temperature', from *chambre* 'room' (see **CHAMBER**).

chamcha /'tʃʌmtʃə/ ▶ **noun** Indian informal an obsequious person.
– ORIGIN from Bengali and Hindi *chamra*, *cham*, literally 'skin, hide'. The extended sense may derive from the idea of an obsequious person staying very close to a superior.

chameleon /kə'miːlɪən/ (also **chamaeleon**) ▶ **noun** a small slow-moving Old World lizard with a prehensile tail, long extensible tongue, protruding eyes that rotate independently, and a highly developed ability to change colour. ● Family Chamaeleonidae: four genera, in particular *Chamaeleo*, and numerous species, including the **European chameleon** (*C. vulgaris*).
■ (also **American chameleon**) N. Amer. an anole (tree-dwelling lizard). ■ figurative a person who changes their opinions or behaviour according to the situation: *voters have misgivings about his performance as a political chameleon*.
– DERIVATIVES **chameleonic** **adjective**.
– ORIGIN Middle English: via Latin *chamaeleon* from Greek *khamaileōn*, from *khamai* 'on the ground' + *leōn* 'lion'.

chameli /tʃʌ'meɪli/ ▶ **noun** Indian term for **JASMINE**.
– ORIGIN from Hindi *camelī*.

chametz /hɑː'mɛts, 'xɑːmɛts/ (also **chometz**) ▶ **noun** [mass noun] Judaism leaven or food mixed with leaven, prohibited during Passover.
– ORIGIN mid 19th cent.: from Hebrew *ḥāmēṣ*.

chamfer /'tʃamfə/ Carpentry ▶ **verb** [with obj.] cut away (a right-angled edge or corner) to make a symmetrical sloping edge.
▶ **noun** a symmetrical sloping surface at an edge or corner.
– ORIGIN mid 16th cent. (in the sense 'flute or furrow'): back-formation from *chamfering*, from French *chamfrain*, from *chant* 'edge' (see **CANT**[2]) + *fraint* 'broken' (from Old French *fraindre* 'break', from Latin *frangere*).

chamise /(t)ʃə'miːz/ (also **chamiso** /tʃə'miːsəʊ/) ▶ **noun** (pl. **chamises** or **chamisos**) an evergreen shrub with small narrow leaves, common in the chaparral of California, US. ● *Adenostoma fasciculatum*, family Rosaceae.
– ORIGIN mid 19th cent.: from Mexican Spanish *chamiso*.

chamois ▶ **noun 1** /'ʃamwɑː/ (pl. **same** /-wɑːz/) an agile goat-antelope with short hooked horns, found in mountainous areas of Europe from Spain to the Caucasus. ● Genus *Rupicapra*, family Bovidae: two species.
2 /'ʃami, 'ʃamwɑː/ (pl. **same** /-mɪz, -wɑːz/) (also Brit. **chamois leather**) [mass noun] a type of soft pliable leather now made from sheepskin or lambskin.
■ [count noun] a piece of chamois leather, used for washing windows or cars.
– ORIGIN mid 16th cent.: from French, of unknown ultimate origin.

chamomile ▶ **noun** chiefly N. Amer. variant spelling of **CAMOMILE**.

Chamonix /'ʃamɒniː/, French /ʃamɔni/ a ski resort at the foot of Mont Blanc, in the Alps of eastern France; pop. 9,514 (2006). Full name **Chamonix-Mont-Blanc** /mɒn'blɒŋk/.

Chamorro /tʃə'mɒrəʊ/ ▶ **noun** (pl. **same** or **Chamorros**)
1 a member of the indigenous people of Guam.
2 [mass noun] the Austronesian language of the Chamorro, with about 73,000 speakers.

champ[1] ▶ **verb** [no obj.] **1** (of a horse) make a noisy biting or chewing action. ■ munch or chew enthusiastically or noisily: *he **champed on** his sandwich*.
2 fret impatiently: *he was already on the plane, champing to get off to Lagos*.
▶ **noun** [in sing.] a biting or chewing action.
– PHRASES **champ** (or **chomp** or **chafe**) **at the bit** be restlessly impatient to start doing something.
– ORIGIN late Middle English: probably imitative.

champ[2] ▶ **noun** informal a champion.
– ORIGIN mid 19th cent.: abbreviation.

Champagne /ʃam'peɪn/, French /ʃɑ̃paɲ/ a region and former province of NE France, which now corresponds to the Champagne-Ardenne administrative region. The region is noted for the white sparkling wine first produced there in about 1700.

champagne /ʃam'peɪn/ ▶ **noun** [mass noun] a white sparkling wine from Champagne. ■ a pale cream or straw colour.

Champagne-Ardenne a region of NE France, comprising part of the Ardennes forest and the wine-growing area of Champagne.

Champagne Charlie ▶ **noun** informal a man who lives a life of luxury and excess.
ORIGIN from the name of a popular song, first performed in 1868.

champagne socialist ▶ **noun** Brit. derogatory a person who espouses socialist ideals while enjoying a wealthy and luxurious lifestyle.
– DERIVATIVES **champagne socialism** **noun**.

champaign /'tʃampeɪn/ ▶ **noun** [mass noun] archaic open level countryside.
– ORIGIN late Middle English: from Old French *champagne*, from late Latin *campania*, based on Latin *campus* 'level ground'. Compare with **CAMPAIGN**.

champak /'tʃʌmpək, 'tʃam-/ (also **chempaka**) ▶ **noun** an Asian evergreen tree of the magnolia family, which bears fragrant orange flowers and is sacred to Hindus and Buddhists. ● *Michelia champaca*, family Magnoliaceae.
– ORIGIN from Sanskrit *campaka*.

champers ▶ **noun** [mass noun] Brit. informal champagne.

champerty /ˈtʃampəti/ ▶ **noun** [mass noun] Law an illegal agreement in which a person with no previous interest in a lawsuit finances it with a view to sharing the disputed property if the suit succeeds.
– DERIVATIVES **champertous** adjective.
– ORIGIN late Middle English: from Anglo-Norman French *champartie*, from Old French *champart* 'feudal lord's share of produce', from Latin *campus* 'field' + *pars* 'part'.

champignon /tʃamˈpɪnjən/ (also **fairy ring champignon**) ▶ **noun** a small edible mushroom with a light brown cap, growing in short grass in both Eurasia and North America and often forming fairy rings. • *Marasmius oreades*, family Tricholomataceae, class Hymenomycetes.
– ORIGIN late 16th cent.: from French, diminutive of Old French *champagne* 'open country' (see CHAMPAIGN).

champion ▶ **noun 1** a person who has surpassed all rivals in a sporting contest or other competition: [as modifier] *a champion hurdler*.
2 a person who vigorously supports or defends a person or cause: *he became the determined* ***champion of*** *a free press*. ■ historical a knight who fought in single combat on behalf of the monarch.
▶ **verb** [with obj.] vigorously support or defend the cause of: *he championed the rights of the working class and the poor*.
▶ **adjective** Brit. informal or dialect excellent: *'Thank ye, lad,' the farmer said. 'That's champion.'*
– ORIGIN Middle English (denoting a fighting man): from Old French, from medieval Latin *campio(n-)* 'fighter', from Latin *campus* (see CAMP[1]).

Champion of England ▶ **noun** (in the UK) a hereditary official who at coronations offers to defend the monarch's title to the throne.

championship ▶ **noun 1** a contest for the position of champion in a sport or game. ■ the position or title of the winner of a championship contest.
2 [mass noun] the vigorous support or defence of a person or cause: *Alan's championship of his estranged wife*.

Champlain /ʃamˈpleɪn/, French /ʃɑ̃plɛ̃/, Samuel de (1567–1635), French explorer and colonial statesman. He established a settlement at Quebec in 1608, developing alliances with the indigenous peoples, and was appointed Lieutenant Governor in 1612.

Champlain, Lake a lake in North America, situated to the east of the Adirondack Mountains.
– ORIGIN named after Samuel de CHAMPLAIN, who reached it in 1609.

champlevé /ˌʃam(p)ləˈveɪ, ʃɒ̃ˈləveɪ/ ▶ **noun** [mass noun] enamelwork in which hollows made in a metal surface are filled with coloured enamels.
– ORIGIN French, from *champ* 'field' + *levé* 'raised'.

Champollion /ʃɒ̃ˈpɒljɒ̃/, French /ʃɑ̃pɔljɔ̃/, Jean-François (1790–1832), French Egyptologist. A pioneer in the study of ancient Egypt, he is best known for his success in deciphering some of the hieroglyphic inscriptions on the Rosetta Stone in 1822.

Champs-Élysées /ˌʃɒ̃z eɪˈliːzeɪ/, French /ʃɑ̃z elize/ an avenue in Paris, leading from the Place de la Concorde to the Arc de Triomphe.

chana /ˈtʃʌnə/ (also **channa**) ▶ **noun** [mass noun] Indian chickpeas, especially when roasted and prepared as a snack.
– ORIGIN from Hindi *canā*.

chance ▶ **noun 1** a possibility of something happening: *there is a chance of winning the raffle* | [mass noun] *there is little chance of his finding a job*. ■ (**chances**) the probability of something desirable happening: *he played down his chances of becoming chairman*. ■ [in sing.] an opportunity to do or achieve something: *I gave her a chance to answer*.
2 [mass noun] the occurrence of events in the absence of any obvious intention or cause: *he met his brother* ***by chance***.
▶ **adjective** [attrib.] fortuitous; accidental: *a chance meeting*.
▶ **verb 1** [no obj., with infinitive] do something by accident or without intending to: *he was very effusive if they chanced to meet*. ■ (**chance upon/on/across**) find or see by accident: *he chanced upon an interesting advertisement*.
2 [with obj.] informal do (something) despite its being dangerous or of uncertain outcome: *they chanced a late holiday*.
– PHRASES **as chance would have it** as it happened. **by any chance** possibly (used in tentative enquiries or suggestions): *were you looking for me by any chance?* **chance one's arm** (or **luck**) Brit. informal undertake something although it may be dangerous or unsuccessful. **chance would be a fine thing** Brit. informal expressing a speaker's belief that something is desirable but the opportunity is unlikely to arise. **no chance** informal there is no possibility of that. **on the (off) chance** just in case. **stand a chance** have a prospect of success or survival: *his rivals don't stand a chance*. **take a chance** (or **chances**) behave in a way that leaves one vulnerable to danger or failure. ■ (**take a chance on**) put one's trust in (something or someone) knowing that it may not be safe or certain. **take one's chance** do something risky with the hope of success.
– ORIGIN Middle English: from Old French *cheance*, from *cheoir* 'fall, befall', based on Latin *cadere*.

chancel /ˈtʃɑːns(ə)l/ ▶ **noun** the part of a church near the altar, reserved for the clergy and choir, and typically separated from the nave by steps or a screen.
– ORIGIN Middle English: from Old French, from Latin *cancelli* 'crossbars'.

chancellery /ˈtʃɑːns(ə)l(ə)ri, -sləri/ ▶ **noun** (pl. **chancelleries**) **1** the position, office, or department of a chancellor. ■ the official residence of a chancellor.
2 US an office attached to an embassy or consulate.
– ORIGIN Middle English: from Old French *chancellerie*, from *chancelier* 'secretary' (see CHANCELLOR).

chancellor ▶ **noun** a senior state or legal official. ■ (**Chancellor**) short for CHANCELLOR OF THE EXCHEQUER. ■ (**Chancellor**) the head of the government in some European countries, such as Germany. ■ Brit. the honorary head of a university. ■ US the president or chief administrative officer of a university. ■ a bishop's law officer. ■ US the presiding judge of a chancery court. ■ (in the UK) an officer of an order of knighthood who seals commissions.
– DERIVATIVES **chancellorship** noun.
– ORIGIN late Old English from Old French *cancelier*, from late Latin *cancellarius* 'porter, secretary' (originally a court official stationed at the grating separating public from judges), from *cancelli* 'crossbars'.

Chancellor of the Duchy of Lancaster ▶ **noun** (in the UK) a member of the government legally representing the Crown as Duke of Lancaster, typically a cabinet minister employed on non-departmental work.

Chancellor of the Exchequer ▶ **noun** the chief finance minister of the United Kingdom, who prepares the nation's annual budgets.

chance-medley ▶ **noun** [mass noun] Law, rare the accidental killing of a person in a fight.
– ORIGIN late 15th cent.: from Anglo-Norman French *chance medlee*, literally 'mixed chance', from *chance* 'luck' + *medlee*, feminine past participle of *medler* 'to mix' (based on Latin *miscere*).

chancer ▶ **noun** Brit. informal a person who exploits any opportunity to further their own ends.

chancery ▶ **noun** (pl. **chanceries**) **1** (**Chancery** or **Chancery Division**) Law (in the UK) the Lord Chancellor's court, a division of the High Court of Justice. ■ US a court of law that decides legal cases based on the principle of equity. ■ historical the court of a bishop's chancellor.
2 chiefly Brit. an office attached to an embassy or consulate.
3 a public record office.
– ORIGIN late Middle English: contraction of CHANCELLERY.

Chan Chan /tʃan ˈtʃan/ the capital of the pre-Inca civilization of the Chimu. Its extensive adobe ruins are situated on the coast of north Peru.

Chan-chiang /tʃanˈtʃjaŋ/ variant of ZHANJIANG.

chancre /ˈʃaŋkə/ ▶ **noun** Medicine a painless ulcer, particularly one that develops on the genitals in venereal disease.
– ORIGIN late 16th cent.: from French, from Latin *cancer* 'creeping ulcer'.

chancroid /ˈʃaŋkrɔɪd/ ▶ **noun** [mass noun] a venereal infection causing ulceration of the lymph nodes in the groin. Also called SOFT SORE.

chancy ▶ **adjective** (**chancier**, **chanciest**) informal involving risks and uncertainty: *football coaching is a chancy business*.
– DERIVATIVES **chancily** adverb, **chanciness** noun.

chandelier /ˌʃandəˈlɪə/ ▶ **noun** a large, decorative hanging light with branches for several light bulbs or candles.
– ORIGIN mid 18th cent.: from French, from *chandelle* 'candle', from Latin *candela*, from *candere* 'be white, glisten'.

chandelle /ʃanˈdɛl/ ▶ **noun** a steep climbing turn executed in an aircraft to gain height while changing the direction of flight.
– ORIGIN mid 20th cent.: from French, literally 'candle'.

Chandigarh /ˌtʃʌndɪˈgɑː/ **1** a Union Territory of NW India, created in 1966.
2 a city in the territory of Chandigarh; pop. 1,033,700 (est. 2009). The present city was designed in 1950 by Le Corbusier as a new capital for the Punjab and is now the capital of the states of Punjab and Haryana.

Chandler /ˈtʃɑːndlə/, Raymond (Thornton) (1888–1959), American novelist. He is remembered as the creator of the private detective Philip Marlowe, who appeared in novels such as *The Big Sleep* (1939).

chandler /ˈtʃɑːndlə/ ▶ **noun 1** (also **ship chandler**) a dealer in supplies and equipment for ships and boats.
2 historical a dealer in household items such as oil, soap, paint, and groceries. ■ a person who makes and sells candles.
– ORIGIN Middle English (denoting a candle maker or candle seller): from Old French *chandelier*, from *chandelle* 'candle' (see CHANDELIER).

chandlery ▶ **noun** (pl. **chandleries**) the shop or business of a chandler. ■ [mass noun] goods sold by a chandler.

Chandragupta Maurya /ˌtʃʌndrəˌgʊptə ˈmaʊrɪə/ (*c*.325–297 BC), Indian emperor. He founded the Mauryan empire and annexed provinces deep into Afghanistan from Alexander's Greek successors.

Chandrasekhar /ˌtʃʌndrəˈsiːkə, -ˈseɪkə/, Subrahmanyan (1910–95), Indian-born American astronomer. He suggested how some stars could eventually collapse to form a dense white dwarf, provided that their mass does not exceed an upper limit (the **Chandrasekhar limit**).

Chanel /ʃəˈnɛl/, French /ʃanɛl/, Coco (1883–1971), French couturière; born *Gabrielle Bonheur Chanel*. Her simple but sophisticated garments were a radical departure from the stiff corseted styles of the day. She also diversified into perfumes, costume jewellery, and textiles.

Chaney /ˈtʃeɪni/, Lon (1883–1930), American actor; born *Alonso Chaney*. He played a wide variety of deformed villains and macabre characters in more than 150 films, including *The Hunchback of Notre Dame* (1923).

Changan /tʃaŋˈɑːn/ former name for XIAN.

Chang-chiakow /ˌtʃaŋtʃjɑːˈkaʊ/ variant of ZHANGJIAKOU.

Changchun /tʃaŋˈtʃʊn/ an industrial city in NE China, capital of Jilin province; pop. 2,455,900 (est. 2006).

change ▶ **verb 1** make or become different: [with obj.] *a proposal to change the law* | [no obj.] *a Virginia creeper just beginning to* ***change from*** *green* ***to*** *gold*. ■ [no obj., with complement] alter in terms of: *the ferns began to change shape*. ■ [no obj.] (of traffic lights) move from one colour of signal to another. ■ [no obj.] (of the moon) arrive at a fresh phase; become new.
2 [with obj.] take or use another instead of: *she decided to change her name*. ■ move from one to another: *she was a typist who changed jobs incessantly*. ■ [no obj.] move to a different train, bus, etc.: *we had to change at Rugby*. ■ give up or get rid of (something) in exchange for something else: *we* ***changed*** *the flagstones* ***for*** *quarry tiles*. ■ remove (something dirty or faulty) and replace it with another of the same kind: *he scarcely knew how to change a plug*. ■ put a clean nappy on (a baby or young child). ■ [no obj.] engage a different gear in a motor vehicle: *he changed into second*. ■ exchange (a sum of money) for the same sum in a different currency or denomination. ■ [no obj.] put different clothes on: *he changed for dinner*.
▶ **noun 1** an act or process through which something becomes different: *the* ***change from*** *a nomadic* ***to*** *an agricultural society* | [mass noun] *activities related to environmental change*. ■ the substitution of one thing for another: *we need a change of government*. ■ an alteration or modification: *a change came over Eddie's face*. ■ a new or refreshingly different experience: *couscous makes an interesting change from rice*. ■ [in sing.] a clean garment or garments as a replacement for something one is wearing: ***a change of*** *socks*. ■ (**the change** or **the change of life**) informal the menopause. ■ the moon's arrival at a fresh phase, typically at the new moon.
2 [mass noun] coins as opposed to banknotes: *a handful of loose change*. ■ money given in exchange for the same sum in larger units. ■ money returned to someone as the balance of the sum paid for something.
3 (usu. **changes**) an order in which a peal of bells can be rung.

C

4 (**Change** or **'Change**) historical a place where merchants met to do business.

– PHRASES **change address** move house or business premises. **change colour** blanch or flush. **change hands** (of a business or building) pass to a different owner. ■ (of money or a marketable commodity) pass to another person in the course of a business transaction. **a change is as good as a rest** proverb a change of work or occupation can be as restorative or refreshing as a period of relaxation. **change one's mind** adopt a different opinion or plan. **a change of air** a different climate, typically as a means of improving one's health. **a change of heart** a move to a different opinion or attitude. **change places** exchange places or roles: *under the bishop's plan, he and I were to change places.* **change sides** begin to support a different side in a war or dispute: *one of his supporters changed sides.* **change step** alter one's step so that the opposite leg is the one that marks time when marching. **change the subject** begin talking of something different, to avoid embarrassment or distress. **change one's tune** express a very different opinion or behave in a very different way. **for a change** contrary to how things usually happen or in order to introduce variety: *it's nice to be pampered for a change.* **get no change out of** Brit. informal fail to get information or a desired reaction from. **ring the changes** vary the ways of expressing or doing something. [with allusion to bell-ringing and the different orders in which a peal of bells may be rung.]

– PHRASAL VERBS **change down** Brit. engage a lower gear in a vehicle or on a bicycle. **change over 1** move from one system or situation to another: *arable farmers have to* ***change over to*** *dairy farming.* **2** swap roles or duties. **change up** Brit. engage a higher gear in a vehicle or on a bicycle.

– DERIVATIVES **changeful** adjective.

– ORIGIN Middle English: from Old French *change* (noun), *changer* (verb), from late Latin *cambiare*, from Latin *cambire* 'barter', probably of Celtic origin.

changeable ▶ adjective **1** liable to unpredictable variation: *the weather will be changeable with rain at times.*
2 able to be changed or exchanged: *cover the tables with changeable cloths.*

– DERIVATIVES **changeability** noun, **changeableness** noun, **changeably** adverb.

changeless ▶ adjective remaining the same: *changeless truths.*

– DERIVATIVES **changelessly** adverb, **changelessness** noun.

changeling ▶ noun a child believed to have been secretly substituted by fairies for the parents' real child in infancy.

change management ▶ noun [mass noun] **1** the management of change and development within a business or similar organization.
2 the controlled identification and implementation of required changes within a computer system.

changement de pieds /ˌʃɒ̃(d)ʒmɒ̃ də ˈpjeɪ/ (also **changement**) ▶ noun (pl. **changements de pieds** pronunc. **same**) Ballet a leap during which a dancer changes the position of the feet.

changeover ▶ noun a change from one system or situation to another.

change purse ▶ noun N. Amer. a purse used for carrying money.

changer ▶ noun a person or thing that changes something. ■ a device that holds several computer disks or CDs and is able to switch between them.

change-ringing ▶ noun [mass noun] the ringing of sets of church bells or handbells in a constantly varying order.

– DERIVATIVES **change-ringer** noun.

change-up ▶ noun Baseball an unexpectedly slow pitch designed to throw off the batter's timing.

Chang Jiang /tʃaŋ dʒaŋ/ another name for **YANGTZE**.

Changsha /tʃaŋˈʃɑː/ the capital of Hunan province in east central China; pop. 1,731,900 (est. 2006).

Chania /kɑːˈnjɑː/ a port on the north coast of Crete, capital of the island from 1841 to 1971; pop. 55,000 (est. 2002). Greek name **KHANIÁ**.

channa /ˈtʃʌnə/ ▶ noun variant spelling of **CHANA**.

channel ▶ noun **1** a length of water wider than a strait, joining two larger areas of water, especially two seas. ■ (**the Channel**) the English Channel. ■ a navigable passage in a stretch of water otherwise unsafe for vessels. ■ a hollow bed for a natural or artificial waterway.
2 a band of frequencies used in radio and television transmission, especially as used by a particular station. ■ a service or station using a channel of frequencies: *a new television channel.*
3 a method or system for communication or distribution: *they didn't apply through the proper channels | some companies have a variety of sales channels.*
4 an electric circuit which acts as a path for a signal. ■ Electronics the semiconductor region in a field-effect transistor that forms the main current path between the source and the drain.
5 Biology a tubular passage or duct for liquid.
▶ verb (**channels, channelling, channelled**; US **channels, channeling, channeled**) [with obj.] **1** direct towards a particular end or object: *the council is to channel public funds into training schemes.* ■ cause to pass along or through a specified route or medium: *many countries* ***channel*** *their aid* ***through*** *charities.* ■ (of a person) serve as a medium for (a spirit). ■ emulate or seem to be inspired by: *Meg Ryan plays Avery as if she's channelling Nicole Kidman.*
2 (usu. as adj. **channelled**) form channels or grooves in: *pottery with a distinctive channelled decoration.*

– DERIVATIVES **channeller** noun.

– ORIGIN Middle English: from Old French *chanel*, from Latin *canalis* 'pipe, groove, channel', from *canna* 'reed' (see **CANE**). Compare with **CANAL**.

> **WORD TRENDS** Mediums claim that they can **channel** the dead, allowing spirits to enter their bodies and communicate through them. This concept has been extended metaphorically to describe actors or musicians whose performances are strongly influenced by a predecessor, or just to comment on the style adopted by a noteworthy person. The path from the original psychic use can be clearly traced in some examples: *middle-aged white guys in acid-washed jeans think they can channel the ghost of Muddy Waters.* However, the sense is now commonly expressed without any reference to spirits or ghosts, with the object not necessarily being dead: *Griffiths, as Morris's wife, seems to be channelling the mid-80s Debra Winger.* The word can suggest a level of falseness or artifice in stealing someone else's ideas or image, and is often applied to politicians: *the presidential hopeful channelled his old idol, John F. Kennedy.*

channel cat (also **channel catfish**) ▶ noun a common North American freshwater catfish which has a pale blue to olive back with dark spots. ● *Ictalurus punctatus*, family Ictaluridae.

Channel Country an area of SW Queensland and NE South Australia, watered intermittently by natural channels, where rich grasslands produced by the summer rains provide grazing for cattle.

channel-hop ▶ verb [no obj.] informal **1** change frequently from one television channel to another, using a remote control device.
2 travel across the English Channel and back to Britain frequently or for only a brief trip.

– DERIVATIVES **channel-hopper** noun.

Channel Islands a group of islands in the English Channel off the NW coast of France, of which the largest are Jersey, Guernsey, and Alderney; pop. 200,000 (est. 2007). Formerly part of the dukedom of Normandy, they have owed allegiance to England since the Norman Conquest in 1066, and are now classed as a Crown dependency.

channelize (also **channelise**) ▶ verb chiefly N. Amer. another term for **CHANNEL** (sense 1 of the verb).

channel-surf ▶ verb informal another term for **CHANNEL-HOP** (sense 1).

– DERIVATIVES **channel-surfer** noun, **channel-surfing** noun.

Channel Tunnel a railway tunnel under the English Channel, linking the coasts of England and France, opened in 1994 and 49 km (31 miles) long.

chanson /ˈʃɒ̃sɒ̃/, French /ʃɑ̃sɔ̃/ ▶ noun a French song.

– ORIGIN French, from Latin *cantio(n-)* 'singing', from *canere* 'sing'.

chanson de geste /ˌʃɒ̃sɒ̃ də ˈʒɛst/, French /ʃɑ̃sɔ̃də ʒɛst/ ▶ noun (pl. **chansons de geste** pronunc. **same**) a medieval French historical verse romance.

– ORIGIN French, literally 'song of heroic deeds', from *chanson* 'song' (see **CHANSON**) and *geste* from Latin *gesta* 'actions, exploits', from *gerere* 'perform'.

chant ▶ noun **1** a repeated rhythmic phrase, typically one shouted or sung in unison by a crowd. ■ a repetitive song, typically an incantation or part of a ritual.
2 Music a short musical passage in two or more phrases used for singing unmetrical words; a psalm or canticle sung to such music. ■ [mass noun] the style of music consisting of such passages: *Gregorian chant.*
▶ verb [with obj.] say or shout repeatedly in a sing-song tone: *protesters were chanting slogans* | [no obj.] *everyone was singing and chanting.* ■ sing or intone (a psalm, canticle, or sacred text).

– ORIGIN late Middle English (in the sense 'sing'): from Old French *chanter* 'sing', from Latin *cantare*, frequentative of *canere* 'sing'.

chanter ▶ noun **1** a person who chants something.
2 Music the pipe of a bagpipe with finger holes, on which the melody is played.

– ORIGIN late Middle English: from Old French *chanteor*, from Latin *cantator*, from *cantare* (see **CHANT**).

chanterelle /ˈtʃɑːntərɛl, ˌtʃɑːntəˈrɛl/ ▶ noun an edible woodland mushroom with a yellow funnel-shaped cap, found in both Eurasia and North America. ● *Cantharellus cibarius*, family Cantharellaceae, class Hymenomycetes.

– ORIGIN late 18th cent.: from French, from modern Latin *cantharellus*, diminutive of *cantharus*, from Greek *kantharos*, denoting a kind of drinking container.

chanteuse /ʃɑːnˈtəːz/, French /ʃɑ̃tøz/ ▶ noun a female singer of popular songs.

– ORIGIN French, from *chanter* 'sing'.

chantey /ˈʃanti/ ▶ noun US spelling of **SHANTY**[2].

chanticleer /ˈtʃɑːntɪˌklɪə/ ▶ noun literary a name given to a domestic cock, especially in fairy tales.

– ORIGIN Middle English: from Old French *Chantecler*, the name of the cock in the fable *Reynard the Fox*, from *chanter* 'sing, crow' (see **CHANT**) + *cler* 'clear'.

Chantilly cream /ʃanˈtɪli/ ▶ noun [mass noun] sweetened or flavoured whipped cream.

– ORIGIN mid 19th cent.: named after *Chantilly*, a town near Paris, where it originated.

Chantilly lace ▶ noun [mass noun] a delicate kind of bobbin lace.

– ORIGIN mid 19th cent.: named after *Chantilly* (see **CHANTILLY CREAM**).

chanting goshawk ▶ noun a long-legged African hawk with pale grey upper parts, throat, and breast, noted for its prolonged musical fluting call. ● Genus *Melierax*, family Accipitridae: three species.

chantry /ˈtʃɑːntri/ ▶ noun (pl. **chantries**) an endowment for a priest or priests to celebrate masses for the founder's soul. ■ a chapel, altar, or other part of a church endowed for such a purpose.

– ORIGIN late Middle English: from Old French *chanterie*, from *chanter* 'to sing'.

chanty /ˈʃanti/ (also **chantey**) ▶ noun (pl. **chanties** or **chanteys**) archaic or N. Amer. variant spellings of **SHANTY**[2].

Chanukkah ▶ noun variant spelling of **HANUKKAH**.

Chanute /tʃəˈnuːt/, Octave (1832–1910), French-born American aviation pioneer. From 1898 he produced a number of gliders, including a biplane which made over 700 flights. He assisted the Wright brothers in making the world's first controlled powered flight.

chaology /keɪˈɒlədʒi/ ▶ noun [mass noun] Physics the study of chaotic systems.

– DERIVATIVES **chaologist** noun.

Chao Phraya /ˌtʃaʊ prəˈjɑː/ a major waterway of central Thailand, formed by the junction of the Ping and Nan Rivers.

chaos /ˈkeɪɒs/ ▶ noun [mass noun] complete disorder and confusion: *snow caused chaos in the region.* ■ Physics the property of a complex system whose behaviour is so unpredictable as to appear random, owing to great sensitivity to small changes in conditions. ■ the formless matter supposed to have existed before the creation of the universe. ■ (**Chaos**) Greek Mythology the first created being, from which came the primeval deities Gaia, Tartarus, Erebus, and Nyx.

– ORIGIN late 15th cent. (denoting a gaping void or chasm, later formless primordial matter): via French and Latin from Greek *khaos* 'vast chasm, void'.

chaos theory ▶ noun [mass noun] the branch of mathematics that deals with complex systems whose behaviour is highly sensitive to slight changes in conditions, so that small alterations can give rise to strikingly great consequences.

chaotic ▶ adjective in a state of complete confusion and disorder: *the political situation was chaotic.* ■ Physics relating to systems which exhibit chaos.

– DERIVATIVES **chaotically** adverb.

– ORIGIN early 18th cent.: from **CHAOS**, on the pattern of words such as *hypnotic*.

chaotic attractor ▶ noun Mathematics another term for **STRANGE ATTRACTOR**.

chap[1] ▸ **verb** (**chaps**, **chapping**, **chapped**) [no obj.] (of the skin) become cracked, rough, or sore, typically through exposure to cold weather: *his skin is very dry and chaps easily.* ■ [with obj.] (usu. as adj. **chapped**) (of the wind or cold) cause (skin) to crack or become sore: *chapped lips.*
▸ **noun** a cracked or sore patch on the skin.
– ORIGIN late Middle English: of unknown origin.

chap[2] ▸ **noun** Brit. informal a man or a boy. ■ dated a friendly form of address between men and boys: *best of luck, old chap.*
– ORIGIN late 16th cent. (denoting a buyer or customer): abbreviation of CHAPMAN. The current sense dates from the early 18th cent.

chap[3] ▸ **noun** (usu. **chaps**) the lower jaw or half of the cheek, especially that of a pig used as food.
– ORIGIN mid 16th cent.: of unknown origin. Compare with CHOPS.

chap. ▸ **abbreviation** chapter.

chaparajos /ˌʃapəˈreɪhəʊs, ˌtʃ-/ (also **chaparejos**) ▸ **plural noun** N. Amer. leather trousers without a seat, worn by a cowboy over ordinary trousers to protect the legs.
– ORIGIN mid 19th cent.: from Mexican Spanish *chaparreras*, from *chaparra* 'dwarf evergreen oak' (with reference to protection from thorny vegetation: see CHAPARRAL); probably influenced by Spanish *aparejo* 'equipment'.

chaparral /ˌʃapəˈral, ˌtʃ-/ ▸ **noun** [mass noun] N. Amer. vegetation consisting chiefly of tangled shrubs and thorny bushes.
– ORIGIN mid 19th cent.: from Spanish, from *chaparra* 'dwarf evergreen oak'.

chapatti /tʃəˈpɑːti, -ˈpati/ (also **chupatty**) ▸ **noun** (pl. **chapattis**) (in Indian cookery) a thin pancake of unleavened wholemeal bread cooked on a griddle.
– ORIGIN from Hindi *capātī*, from *capānā* 'flatten, roll out'.

chapbook ▸ **noun** historical a small pamphlet containing tales, ballads, or tracts, sold by pedlars. ■ N. Amer. a small paper-covered booklet, typically containing poems or fiction.
– ORIGIN early 19th cent.: from CHAPMAN + BOOK.

chape /tʃeɪp/ ▸ **noun 1** historical the metal point of a scabbard.
2 the metal pin of a buckle.
– ORIGIN Middle English (in the general sense 'plate of metal overlaying or trimming something'): from Old French, literally 'cape, hood', from late Latin *cappa* 'cap'.

chapeau /ˈʃapəʊ/ ▸ **noun** (pl. **chapeaux**) Heraldry a hat or cap, typically a red one with an ermine lining, on which the crests of some peers are borne.
– ORIGIN late 15th cent.: from French, from Latin *cappellum*, diminutive of *cappa* 'cap'.

chapeau-bras /ˌʃapəʊˈbrɑː/, French /ʃapobʀa/ ▸ **noun** (pl. **chapeaux-bras** pronunc. **same**) historical a man's three-cornered flat silk hat, typically carried under the arm.
– ORIGIN French, from *chapeau* 'hat' and *bras* 'arm'.

chapel ▸ **noun 1** a small building or room used for Christian worship in a school, prison, hospital, or large private house: *a service in the chapel.* ■ a part of a large church or cathedral with its own altar and dedication. ■ Brit. a place of worship for Nonconformist congregations: *she went to chapel twice on Sunday.* ■ a small building or room used for funeral services. ■ US a chapel of rest.
2 Brit. the members or branch of a print or newspaper trade union at a particular place of work.
▸ **adjective** Brit. informal belonging to or regularly attending a Nonconformist chapel: *staunch chapel folk.*
– ORIGIN Middle English: from Old French *chapele*, from medieval Latin *cappella*, diminutive of *cappa* 'cap or cape' (the first chapel being a sanctuary in which St Martin's cloak was preserved).

chapel of ease ▸ **noun** an Anglican chapel situated for the convenience of parishioners living a long distance from the parish church.

chapel of rest ▸ **noun** Brit. an undertaker's mortuary, where bodies are kept before a funeral.

chapel royal ▸ **noun** (pl. **chapels royal**) a chapel in a royal palace. ■ (**the Chapel Royal**) the body of clergy, singers, and musicians employed by the English monarch for religious services, now based at St James's Palace, London.

chapelry ▸ **noun** (pl. **chapelries**) a district served by an Anglican chapel.
– ORIGIN Middle English: from Old French *chapelerie*, medieval Latin *cappellaria*, from *cappella*, originally 'little cloak' (see CHAPEL).

chaperone /ˈʃapərəʊn/ (also **chaperon** /ˈʃapərɒn/) ▸ **noun** a person who accompanies and looks after another person or group of people. ■ dated an older woman responsible for the decorous behaviour of a young unmarried girl at social occasions.
▸ **verb** [with obj.] accompany and look after or supervise.
– DERIVATIVES **chaperonage** /ˈʃap(ə)r(ə)nɪdʒ/ **noun**.
– ORIGIN late Middle English (denoting a hood or cap, regarded as giving protection): from French, feminine of *chaperon* 'hood', diminutive of *chape* (see CHAPE). The current sense dates from the early 18th cent.

chaperonin /ˌʃapəˈrəʊnɪn/ ▸ **noun** Biochemistry a protein that aids the assembly and folding of other protein molecules in living cells.
– ORIGIN late 20th cent.: from CHAPERONE + -IN[1].

chap-fallen (also **chop-fallen**) ▸ **adjective** archaic with one's lower jaw hanging due to extreme exhaustion or dejection.
– ORIGIN late 16th cent.: from CHAP[3].

chaplain ▸ **noun** a member of the clergy attached to a private chapel, institution, ship, regiment, etc.
– DERIVATIVES **chaplaincy** **noun**.
– ORIGIN Middle English: from Old French *chapelain*, from medieval Latin *cappellanus*, originally denoting a custodian of the cloak of St Martin, from *cappella*, originally 'little cloak' (see CHAPEL).

chaplet /ˈtʃaplɪt/ ▸ **noun 1** a garland or circlet for a person's head.
2 a string of 55 beads (one third of the rosary number) for counting prayers, or as a necklace.
3 a metal support for the core of a hollow casting mould.
– DERIVATIVES **chapleted** **adjective**.
– ORIGIN late Middle English: from Old French *chapelet*, diminutive of *chapel* 'hat', based on late Latin *cappa* 'cap'.

Chaplin, Charlie (1889–1977), English film actor and director; full name *Sir Charles Spencer Chaplin*. He directed and starred in many short silent comedies, mostly playing a bowler-hatted tramp, a character which was his trademark for more than twenty-five years. Notable films: *The Kid* (1921).
– DERIVATIVES **Chaplinesque** **adjective**.

Chapman, George (*c.*1560–1634), English poet and dramatist. He is chiefly known for his translations of Homer; the complete *Iliad* and *Odyssey* were published in 1616.

chapman ▸ **noun** (pl. **chapmen**) archaic a pedlar.
– ORIGIN Old English *cēapman*, from *cēap* 'bargaining, trade' (see CHEAP) + MAN.

chappal /ˈtʃap(ə)l/ ▸ **noun** Indian a slipper.
– ORIGIN from Hindi *cappal*.

Chappaquiddick Island /ˌtʃapəˈkwɪdɪk/ a small island off the coast of Massachusetts, the scene of a car accident in 1969 involving Senator Edward Kennedy in which his assistant Mary Jo Kopechne drowned.

Chappell /ˈtʃap(ə)l/, Greg (b.1948), Australian cricketer; full name *Gregory Stephen Chappell*. Captain of Australia 1975–84, he was the first Australian to score more than 7,000 test-match runs.

chappie ▸ **noun** (pl. **chappies**) Brit. informal another term for CHAP[2].

chaprasi /tʃʌˈprɑːsi/ ▸ **noun** (pl. **chaprasis**) Indian a junior office worker who carries messages.
– ORIGIN from Hindi, from *caprās*, denoting a metal identity badge worn by messengers or orderlies.

chaps ▸ **plural noun** short for CHAPARAJOS.

chapstick ▸ **noun** N. Amer. trademark a small stick of a cosmetic substance used to prevent chapping of the lips.

chaptalization /ˌtʃaptəlʌɪˈzeɪʃ(ə)n/ (also **chaptalisation**) ▸ **noun** [mass noun] (in winemaking) the correction or improvement of must by the addition of calcium carbonate to neutralize acid, or of sugar to increase alcoholic strength.
– DERIVATIVES **chaptalize** (also **chaptalise**) **verb**.
– ORIGIN late 19th cent.: from the name of Jean A. Chaptal (1756–1832), the French chemist who invented the process, + *-ization* (see -IZE).

chapter ▸ **noun 1** a main division of a book, typically with a number or title. ■ an Act of Parliament numbered as part of a session's proceedings. ■ a section of a treaty.
2 a distinctive period in history or in a person's life: *the people are about to begin a new chapter in their history.* ■ a series or sequence: *the latest episode in a chapter of problems.*
3 the governing body of a religious community or knightly order.
4 chiefly N. Amer. a local branch of a society. ■ a local group of Hell's Angels.
– PHRASES **chapter and verse** an exact reference or authority: *she can give chapter and verse on current legislation.* **a chapter of accidents** Brit. a series of unfortunate events.
– ORIGIN Middle English: from Old French *chapitre*, from Latin *capitulum*, diminutive of *caput* 'head'.

Chapter 11 ▸ **noun** [mass noun] US protection from creditors given to a company in financial difficulties for a limited period to allow it to reorganize.
– ORIGIN with allusion to chapter 11 of the US bankruptcy code.

chapter house ▸ **noun** a building used for the meetings of the canons of a cathedral or other religious community. ■ US a place where a college fraternity or sorority meets.

char[1] /tʃɑː/ ▸ **verb** (**chars**, **charring**, **charred**) [with obj.] partially burn so as to blacken the surface: *a region charred by bush fires* | (as adj. **charred**) *charred remains.* ■ [no obj.] (of an object) become burned and discoloured in such a way: *the exposed surfaces of the beams may char in a fire.*
▸ **noun** [mass noun] material that has been charred.
– ORIGIN late 17th cent.: apparently a back-formation from CHARCOAL.

char[2] /tʃɑː/ Brit. informal ▸ **noun** a charwoman.
▸ **verb** (**chars**, **charring**, **charred**) [no obj.] work as a charwoman.

char[3] /tʃɑː/ (also **cha** /tʃɑː/ or **chai** /tʃʌɪ/) ▸ **noun** [mass noun] Brit. informal tea.
– ORIGIN late 16th cent. (as *cha*; rare before the early 20th cent.): from Chinese (Mandarin dialect) *chá*.

char[4] ▸ **noun** variant spelling of CHARR.

charabanc /ˈʃarəbaŋ/ ▸ **noun** Brit. an early form of bus, used typically for pleasure trips.
– ORIGIN early 19th cent.: from French *char-à-bancs* 'carriage with benches' (the original horse-drawn charabancs having rows of bench seats).

characin /ˈkarəsɪn/ ▸ **noun** a small and brightly coloured freshwater fish native to Africa and tropical America. ● Family Characidae: numerous species, including the piranhas and popular aquarium fishes such as the tetras.
– ORIGIN late 19th cent.: from modern Latin *Characinus* (genus name), from Greek *kharax*, literally 'pointed stake', denoting a kind of fish.

character ▸ **noun 1** the mental and moral qualities distinctive to an individual: *running away was not in keeping with her character.* ■ the distinctive nature of something: *gas lamps give the area its character.* ■ [mass noun] the quality of being individual in an interesting or unusual way: *the island is full of character.* ■ [mass noun] strength and originality in a person's nature: *she had character as well as beauty.* ■ a person's good reputation: *to what do I owe this attack on my character?* ■ dated a written statement of someone's good qualities; a testimonial.
2 a person in a novel, play, or film. ■ a part played by an actor. ■ [with adj.] a person seen in terms of a particular aspect of character: *he was a larger-than-life character* | *shady characters.* ■ informal an unusual or amusing person: *she's a right character with a will of her own.*
3 a printed or written letter or symbol. ■ Computing a symbol representing a letter or number.
4 chiefly Biology a characteristic, especially one that assists in the identification of a species.
▸ **verb** [with obj.] archaic inscribe or write (something). ■ describe: *you have well charactered him.*
– PHRASES **in** (or **out of**) **character** in keeping (or not in keeping) with someone's usual pattern of behaviour and motives.
– DERIVATIVES **characterful** **adjective**, **characterless** **adjective**.
– ORIGIN Middle English: from Old French *caractere*, via Latin from Greek *kharaktēr* 'a stamping tool'. From the early sense 'distinctive mark' arose 'token, feature, or trait' (early 16th cent.), and from this 'a description, especially of a person's qualities', giving rise to 'distinguishing qualities'.

character actor ▸ **noun** an actor who specializes in playing eccentric or unusual people rather than leading roles.

character assassination ▸ **noun** [mass noun] the malicious and unjustified harming of a person's good reputation.

character code ▶ **noun** Computing the binary code used to represent a letter or number.

character dance ▶ **noun** [mass noun] a style of ballet deriving inspiration from national or folk dances, or interpreting and representing a particular profession, mode of living, or personality.
– DERIVATIVES **character dancer** noun.

C

characteristic ▶ **adjective** typical of a particular person, place, or thing: *he began with a characteristic attack on extremism.*
▶ **noun 1** a feature or quality belonging typically to a person, place, or thing and serving to identify them: *certain defining characteristics of the school emerge from the study.*
2 Mathematics the whole number or integral part of a logarithm, which gives the order of magnitude of the original number.
– DERIVATIVES **characteristically** adverb.
– ORIGIN mid 17th cent.: from French *caractéristique* or medieval Latin *characteristicus*, from Greek *kharaktēristikos*, from *kharaktēr* 'a stamping tool'.

characteristic curve ▶ **noun** a graph showing the relationship between two variable but interdependent quantities.

characteristic function ▶ **noun** Mathematics a function whose result is unity for the members of a given set and zero for all non-members.

characteristic radiation ▶ **noun** [mass noun] radiation consisting of wavelengths which are peculiar to the element which emits them.

characterize (also **characterise**) ▶ **verb** [with obj.] **1** describe the distinctive nature or features of: *she characterized the period as the decade of revolution.* **2** (of a feature or quality) be typical or characteristic of: *the disease is characterized by weakening of the immune system.*
– DERIVATIVES **characterization** noun.
– ORIGIN late 16th cent. (in the sense 'engrave, inscribe'): from French *caractériser* or medieval Latin *characterizare*, from Greek *kharaktērizein*, from *kharaktēr* 'a stamping tool'.

character part ▶ **noun** a part played by a character actor.

character recognition ▶ **noun** [mass noun] the identification by electronic means of printed or written characters.

character string ▶ **noun** a linear sequence of characters stored in or processed by a computer.

character witness ▶ **noun** a person who attests to another's good reputation in a court of law.

charade /ʃəˈrɑːd/ ▶ **noun** an absurd pretence intended to create a pleasant or respectable appearance: *talk of unity was nothing more than a charade.* ■ (**charades**) a game in which players guess a word or phrase from a written or acted clue given for each syllable and for the whole item.
– ORIGIN late 18th cent.: from French, from modern Provençal *charrado* 'conversation', from *charra* 'chatter', perhaps of imitative origin.

charango /tʃəˈraŋgəʊ/ ▶ **noun** (pl. **charangos**) a small Andean guitar, traditionally made from an armadillo shell.
– ORIGIN 1920s: from South American Spanish.

charas /ˈtʃɑːrəs/ ▶ **noun** [mass noun] cannabis resin.
– ORIGIN from Hindi *caras*.

charbroil ▶ **verb** [with obj.] N. Amer. grill (food, especially meat) on a rack over charcoal.
– ORIGIN 1950s: blend of CHARCOAL and BROIL[1].

charcoal ▶ **noun** [mass noun] a porous black solid, consisting of an amorphous form of carbon, obtained as a residue when wood, bone, or other organic matter is heated in the absence of air. ■ briquettes of charcoal used for barbecuing: *lamb grilled on charcoal.* ■ charcoal used for drawing. ■ [count noun] a drawing made with charcoal. ■ a dark grey colour.
– ORIGIN late Middle English: probably related to COAL in the early sense 'charcoal'.

charcoal burner ▶ **noun 1** a person who makes charcoal.
2 a small stove using charcoal as fuel.

charcoal filter ▶ **noun** a filter containing charcoal to absorb impurities.

Charcot /ˈʃɑːkəʊ/, French /ʃaʀko/, Jean-Martin (1825–93), French neurologist, regarded as one of the founders of modern neurology. He established links between neurological conditions and particular lesions in the central nervous system. His work on hysteria was taken up by his pupil Sigmund Freud.

charcuterie /ʃɑːˈkuːt(ə)ri/ ▶ **noun** (pl. **charcuteries**) [mass noun] cold cooked meats. ■ [count noun] a shop selling cold meats.
– ORIGIN French, from obsolete *char* (earlier form of *chair*) 'flesh' + *cuite* 'cooked'.

chard /tʃɑːd/ ▶ **noun** (also **Swiss chard**) a beet of a variety with broad edible white leaf stalks and green blades.
– ORIGIN mid 17th cent.: from French *carde*, perhaps influenced by *chardon* 'thistle'.

Chardonnay /ˈʃɑːdəneɪ/ ▶ **noun** [mass noun] a variety of white wine grape used for making champagne and other wines. ■ a wine made from the Chardonnay grape.
– ORIGIN French.

charentais /ˈʃarənteɪ/ (also **charentais melon**) ▶ **noun** a melon of a small variety with a pale green rind and orange flesh.
– ORIGIN French, literally 'from the Charentes region'.

Charente /ʃaˈrɒnt/, French /ʃaʀɑ̃t/ a river of western France, which rises in the Massif Central and flows 360 km (225 miles) westwards to enter the Bay of Biscay at Rochefort.

charge ▶ **verb** [with obj.] **1** demand (an amount) as a price for a service rendered or goods supplied: *wedding planners may charge an hourly fee of up to £150* | [with two objs] *he charged me five dollars for the wine.* ■ (**charge something to**) record the cost of something as an amount payable by (someone) or on (an account): *they charge the calls to their credit-card accounts.*
2 formally accuse (someone) of something, especially an offence under law: *they were **charged with** assault.* ■ [with clause] make an accusation or assertion that: *opponents **charged that** below-cost pricing would reduce safety.* ■ Law formally accuse someone of (an offence).
3 entrust (someone) with a task as a duty or responsibility: *the committee was **charged with** reshaping the educational system.*
4 store electrical energy in (a battery or battery-operated device): *the shaver can be **charged up** and used while travelling.* ■ [no obj.] (of a battery or battery-operated device) receive and store electrical energy. ■ load or fill (a container, gun, etc.) to the full or proper extent. ■ fill or pervade with a quality or emotion: *the air was **charged with** menace.*
5 [no obj.] rush forward in attack: *the plan is to charge headlong at the enemy.* ■ [with obj.] rush aggressively towards (someone or something) in attack. ■ [with adverbial of direction] move quickly and forcefully: *Henry charged up the staircase.*
6 Heraldry place a heraldic bearing on: *a pennant argent, charged with a cross gules.*
▶ **noun 1** a price asked for goods or services: *our standard charge for a letter is £25.* ■ a financial liability or commitment.
2 an accusation, typically one formally made against a prisoner brought to trial: *he appeared in court **on a charge of** attempted murder.*
3 [mass noun] responsibility for the care or control of someone or something: *the people **in her charge** are pupils and not experimental subjects.* ■ [count noun] a person or thing entrusted to the care of someone: *the babysitter watched over her charges.* ■ [count noun] dated a responsibility or duty assigned to someone. ■ [count noun] an official instruction, especially one given by a judge to a jury regarding points of law.
4 the property of matter that is responsible for electrical phenomena, existing in a positive or negative form. ■ the quantity of matter responsible for electrical phenomena carried by a body. ■ [mass noun] energy stored chemically for conversion into electricity. ■ an act or period of storing electrical energy in a battery. ■ [in sing.] informal a thrill: *I get a **real charge out of** working hard.*
5 a quantity of explosive to be detonated in order to fire a gun or similar weapon.
6 a headlong rush forward, typically in attack: *a cavalry charge.*
7 Heraldry a device or bearing placed on a shield or crest.
– PHRASES **free of charge** without any payment due. **in charge** in control or with overall responsibility: *he was **in charge of** civil aviation matters.* **press charges** accuse someone formally of a crime so that they can be brought to trial. **take charge** assume control or responsibility: *the candidate must **take charge of** an actual flight.*
– DERIVATIVES **chargeable** adjective, **chargee** noun.
– ORIGIN Middle English (in the general senses 'to load' and 'a load'), from Old French *charger* (verb), *charge* (noun), from late Latin *carricare*, *carcare* 'to load', from Latin *carrus* 'wheeled vehicle'.

charge account ▶ **noun** N. Amer. an account to which goods and services may be charged on credit.

chargeback ▶ **noun** a demand by a credit-card provider for a retailer to make good the loss on a fraudulent or disputed transaction. ■ (in business use) an act or policy of allocating the cost of an organization's centrally located resources to the individuals or departments which use them.

charge-cap ▶ **verb** [with obj.] Brit. (of a government) subject (a local authority) to an upper limit on the charges it may levy on the public for services.

charge card ▶ **noun** a credit card for use with an account which must be paid in full when a statement is issued.

charge carrier ▶ **noun** a particle which carries an electric charge. ■ a mobile electron or hole by which electric charge passes through a semiconductor.

charge conjugation ▶ **noun** [mass noun] Physics replacement of a particle by its antiparticle.

charge-coupled device ▶ **noun** see **CCD**.

charged ▶ **adjective** having an electric charge. ■ filled with excitement, tension, or emotion: *the highly charged atmosphere created by the boycott.*

chargé d'affaires /ˌʃɑːʒeɪ daˈfɛː/, French /ʃaʀʒe dafɛʀ/ (also **chargé**) ▶ **noun** (pl. **chargés d'affaires** pronunc. **same**) an ambassador's deputy. ■ a state's diplomatic representative in a minor country.
– ORIGIN mid 18th cent.: French, '(a person) in charge of affairs'.

charge density ▶ **noun** [mass noun] Physics the electric charge per unit area of a surface, or per unit volume of a field or body.

chargehand ▶ **noun** Brit. a worker, ranking below a foreman, in charge of others on a particular job.

charge nurse ▶ **noun** Brit. a nurse in charge of a ward in a hospital.

Charge of the Light Brigade a British cavalry charge in 1854 during the Battle of Balaclava in the Crimean War. A misunderstanding between the commander of the Light Brigade and his superiors led to the British cavalry being destroyed. The charge was immortalized in verse by Alfred Tennyson.

charger[1] ▶ **noun 1** a horse ridden by a knight or cavalryman.
2 a device for charging a battery or battery-powered equipment.

charger[2] ▶ **noun** archaic a large flat dish.
– ORIGIN Middle English: from Anglo-Norman French *chargeour*, from *chargier* 'to load', from late Latin *carricare*, *carcare* 'to load' (see CHARGE).

charge sheet ▶ **noun** Brit. a record made in a police station of the charges against a person.

chargrill ▶ **verb** grill (food, typically meat or fish) quickly at a very high heat.
– ORIGIN late 20th cent.: on the pattern of *charbroil*.

chariot ▶ **noun 1** a two-wheeled vehicle drawn by horses, used in ancient racing and warfare.
2 historical a four-wheeled carriage with back seats and a coachman's seat.
3 literary a stately or triumphal carriage.
▶ **verb** [with obj.] literary convey in or as in a chariot.
– ORIGIN late Middle English: from Old French, augmentative of *char* 'cart', based on Latin *carrus* 'wheeled vehicle'.

charioteer ▶ **noun** a chariot driver. ■ (**the Charioteer**) the constellation Auriga.
– ORIGIN Middle English: from Old French *charieter*, from *chariot* 'large cart' (see CHARIOT). The sense in astronomy dates from the early 20th cent.

charism /ˈkarɪz(ə)m/ ▶ **noun** another term for CHARISMA (sense 2).

charisma /kəˈrɪzmə/ ▶ **noun 1** [mass noun] compelling attractiveness or charm that can inspire devotion in others: *he has tremendous charisma and stage presence.*
2 (pl. **charismata** /kəˈrɪzmətə/) a divinely conferred power or talent.
– ORIGIN mid 17th cent. (in sense 2): via ecclesiastical Latin from Greek *kharisma*, from *kharis* 'favour, grace'.

charismatic ▶ **adjective 1** exercising a compelling charm which inspires devotion in others: *he was a charismatic figure with great appeal to the public.*
2 relating to the charismatic movement in the Christian Church. ■ (of a power or talent) divinely conferred: *charismatic prophecy.*

▶ **noun** an adherent of the charismatic movement. ■ a person who claims divine inspiration.
– DERIVATIVES **charismatically** adverb.
– ORIGIN late 19th cent.: from Greek *kharisma, kharismat-* 'charisma', + **-IC**.

charismatic movement ▶ **noun** a fundamentalist movement within the Roman Catholic, Anglican, and other Christian Churches that emphasizes talents held to be conferred by the Holy Spirit, such as speaking in tongues and healing of the sick.

charitable ▶ **adjective 1** relating to the assistance of those in need: *he has spent £50,000 on charitable causes.* ■ (of an organization or activity) officially recognized as devoted to the assistance of those in need. ■ generous in giving to those in need.
2 apt to judge others leniently or favourably: *those who were less charitable called for his resignation.*
– DERIVATIVES **charitableness** noun, **charitably** adverb.
– ORIGIN Middle English (in the sense 'showing Christian love to God and man'): from Old French, from *charite* (see **CHARITY**).

charity ▶ **noun** (pl. **charities**) **1** an organization set up to provide help and raise money for those in need. ■ [mass noun] the body of organizations viewed collectively as the object of fund-raising or of donations: *the proceeds of the sale will go to charity.*
2 [mass noun] the voluntary giving of help, typically in the form of money, to those in need. ■ help or money given to those in need: *an unemployed teacher living on charity.*
3 [mass noun] kindness and tolerance in judging others: *she found it hard to look on her mother with much charity.* ■ archaic love of humankind, typically in a Christian context: *faith, hope, and charity.*
– PHRASES **charity begins at home** proverb a person's first responsibility is for the needs of their own family and friends.
– ORIGIN late Old English (in the sense 'Christian love of one's fellows'): from Old French *charite*, from Latin *caritas*, from *carus* 'dear'.

Charity Commission (in the UK) a board established to control charitable trusts.

charity school ▶ **noun** a school which is supported by charitable contributions.

charity shop ▶ **noun** Brit. a shop where second-hand goods are sold to raise money for a charity.

charivari /ˌʃɑːrɪˈvɑːri/ (chiefly US also **shivaree**) ▶ **noun** (pl. **charivaris**) chiefly historical a cacophonous mock serenade, typically performed by a group of people in derision of an unpopular person or in celebration of a marriage. ■ a series of discordant noises.
– ORIGIN mid 17th cent.: from French, of unknown origin.

charkha /ˈtʃəːkə/ (also **charka**) ▶ **noun** (in South Asia) a domestic spinning wheel used chiefly for cotton.
– ORIGIN from Urdu *charkā* 'spinning wheel', from Persian; related to Sanskrit *cakra* 'wheel'.

charlady ▶ **noun** (pl. **charladies**) Brit. a charwoman.

charlatan /ˈʃɑːlət(ə)n/ ▶ **noun** a person falsely claiming to have a special knowledge or skill.
– DERIVATIVES **charlatanism** noun, **charlatanry** noun.
– ORIGIN early 17th cent. (denoting an itinerant seller of supposed remedies): from French, from Italian *ciarlatano*, from *ciarlare* 'to babble'.

Charlemagne /ˈʃɑːləmeɪn/ (742–814), king of the Franks 768–814 and Holy Roman emperor (as Charles I) 800–14; Latin name *Carolus Magnus*; known as **Charles the Great**. As the first Holy Roman emperor Charlemagne promoted the arts and education, and his court became the cultural centre of the Carolingian Renaissance, the influence of which outlasted his empire.

Charleroi /ˈʃɑːlərwɑː/, French /ʃarlrwa/ an industrial city in SW Belgium; pop. 201,593 (2008).

Charles[1] the name of two kings of England, Scotland, and Ireland: ■ **Charles I** (1600–49), son of James I, reigned 1625–49. His reign was dominated by the deepening religious and constitutional crisis that resulted in the English Civil War 1642–9. After the battle of Naseby, Charles tried to regain power in alliance with the Scots, but his forces were defeated in 1648 and he was tried by a special Parliamentary court and beheaded. ■ **Charles II** (1630–85), son of Charles I, reigned 1660–85. Charles was restored to the throne after the collapse of Cromwell's regime and displayed considerable adroitness in handling the difficult constitutional situation, although continuing religious and political strife dogged his reign.

Charles[2] the name of four kings of Spain: ■ **Charles I** (1500–58), son of Philip I, reigned 1516–56, Holy Roman emperor (as Charles V) 1519–56. His reign was characterized by the struggle against Protestantism in Germany, rebellion in Castile, and war with France (1521–44). Exhausted by these struggles, Charles handed Naples, the Netherlands, and Spain over to his son Philip II and the imperial Crown to his brother Ferdinand, and retired to a monastery. ■ **Charles II** (1661–1700), reigned 1665–1700. He inherited a kingdom already in a decline which he was unable to halt. His choice of Philip of Anjou, grandson of Louis XIV of France, as his successor gave rise to the War of the Spanish Succession. ■ **Charles III** (1716–88), reigned 1759–88. He improved Spain's position as an international power through an increase in foreign trade, and brought Spain a brief cultural and economic revival. ■ **Charles IV** (1748–1819), reigned 1788–1808. During the Napoleonic Wars he suffered the loss of the Spanish fleet, destroyed along with that of France at Trafalgar in 1805. Following the French invasion of Spain in 1807, Charles was forced to abdicate.

Charles[3] the name of seven Holy Roman emperors: ■ **Charles I** see **CHARLEMAGNE**. ■ **Charles II** (823–877), reigned 875–877. ■ **Charles III** (839–888), reigned 881–887. ■ **Charles IV** (1316–1378), reigned 1355–1378. ■ **Charles V** Charles I of Spain (see **CHARLES**[2]). ■ **Charles VI** (1685–1740), reigned 1711–40. His claim to the Spanish throne instigated the War of the Spanish Succession, but he was ultimately unsuccessful. He drafted the Pragmatic Sanction in an attempt to ensure that his daughter succeeded to the Habsburg dominions; this triggered the War of the Austrian Succession after his death. ■ **Charles VII** (1697–1745), reigned 1742–45.

Charles[4], Ray (1930–2004), American pianist and singer; born *Ray Charles Robinson*. Totally blind from the age of 6, he drew on blues, jazz, and country music for songs such as 'What'd I Say' (1959) and 'Georgia On My Mind' (1960).

Charles VII (1403–61), king of France 1422–61. At the time of his accession much of northern France was under English occupation. After the intervention of Joan of Arc, however, the French experienced a dramatic military revival and the defeat of the English ended the Hundred Years War.

Charles XII (also **Karl XII**) (1682–1718), king of Sweden 1697–1718. In 1700 he embarked on the Great Northern War against Denmark, Poland-Saxony, and Russia. Initially successful, in 1709 he embarked on an expedition into Russia which ended in the destruction of his army and his internment.

Charles, Prince, Charles Philip Arthur George, Prince of Wales (b.1948), heir apparent to Elizabeth II. He married Lady Diana Spencer in 1981; the couple had two children, Prince William Arthur Philip Louis (b.1982) and Prince Henry Charles Albert David (known as Prince Harry, b.1984), and were divorced in 1996. In 2005 he married Mrs Camilla Parker Bowles (b.1947); she became HRH the Duchess of Cornwall.

Charles' law (also **Charles's law**) ▶ **noun** Chemistry a law stating that the volume of an ideal gas at constant pressure is directly proportional to the absolute temperature.
– ORIGIN late 19th cent.: named after Jacques A. C. Charles (1746–1823), the French physicist who first formulated it.

Charles Martel /mɑːˈtɛl/ (*c.*688–741), Frankish ruler of the eastern part of the Frankish kingdom from 715 and the whole kingdom from 719, grandfather of Charlemagne. His rule marked the beginning of Carolingian power.

Charles's Wain archaic the Plough in Ursa Major.
– ORIGIN Old English *Carles wægn* 'the wain of Carl (Charlemagne)', perhaps because the star Arcturus was associated with King Arthur, with whom Charlemagne was connected in legend.

Charleston[1] **1** the state capital of West Virginia; pop. 50,302 (est. 2008).
2 a city and port in South Carolina; pop. 111,978 (est. 2008). The bombardment in 1861 of Fort Sumter, in the harbour, by Confederate troops marked the beginning of the American Civil War.

Charleston[2] ▶ **noun** a lively dance of the 1920s which involved turning the knees inwards and kicking out the ankles.
▶ **verb** [no obj.] dance the Charleston.
– ORIGIN 1920s: named after **CHARLESTON**[1] in South Carolina, US.

charley horse ▶ **noun** [in sing.] N. Amer. informal a cramp or feeling of stiffness in an arm or leg.
– ORIGIN late 19th cent.: of unknown origin.

charlie ▶ **noun** (pl. **charlies**) **1** Brit. informal a fool.
2 (**charlies**) Brit. informal a woman's breasts.
3 [mass noun] informal cocaine.
4 a code word representing the letter C, used in radio communication.
5 US & Austral./NZ military slang a member of the Vietcong or the Vietcong collectively. [shortening of *Victor Charlie*, radio code for *VC*, representing *Vietcong*.]
– ORIGIN late 19th cent.: diminutive of the male given name *Charles*.

charlock /ˈtʃɑːlɒk/ ▶ **noun** [mass noun] a wild mustard with yellow flowers, which is a common weed of cornfields. ● *Sinapis arvensis*, family Cruciferae.
– ORIGIN Old English *cerlic, cyrlic*, of unknown origin.

Charlotte a commercial city and transportation centre in southern North Carolina; pop. 687,456 (est. 2008).

charlotte ▶ **noun** a pudding made of stewed fruit with a casing or covering of bread, sponge cake, biscuits, or breadcrumbs.
– ORIGIN French, from the female given name *Charlotte*.

Charlotte Amalie /əˈmɑːlɪə/ the capital of the Virgin Islands, on the island of St Thomas; pop. 10,100 (est. 2009).
– ORIGIN named after the wife of King Christian V of Denmark.

Charlotte Dundas /dʌnˈdas/ a paddle steamer launched in 1802 on the River Clyde, the first vessel to use steam propulsion commercially.

charlotte russe /ˈruːs/ ▶ **noun** a pudding consisting of custard enclosed in sponge cake or a casing of sponge fingers.
– ORIGIN French, literally 'Russian charlotte'.

Charlottetown the capital and chief port of Prince Edward Island, Canada; pop. 32,174 (2006).

Charlton[1] /ˈtʃɑːlt(ə)n/, Bobby (b.1937), English footballer, brother of Jack Charlton; full name *Sir Robert Charlton*. An outstanding Manchester United striker, he scored a record forty-nine goals for England and was a member of the side that won the World Cup in 1966.

Charlton[2], Jack (b.1935), English footballer and manager, brother of Bobby Charlton; full name *John Charlton*. A Leeds United defender, he was a member of the England side that won the World Cup in 1966. He later managed a number of teams including the Republic of Ireland national side (1986–95).

charm ▶ **noun 1** [mass noun] the power or quality of delighting, attracting, or fascinating others: *he was captivated by her youthful charm.* ■ [count noun] (usu. **charms**) an attractive or alluring characteristic or feature: *the hidden charms of the city.*
2 a small ornament worn on a necklace or bracelet.
3 an object, act, or saying believed to have magic power. ■ an object kept or worn to ward off evil and bring good luck: *a good luck charm.*
4 [mass noun] Physics one of six flavours of quark.
▶ **verb** [with obj.] **1** delight greatly: *the books have charmed children the world over.* ■ use one's ability to please and attract in order to influence (someone): *he **charmed** her **into** going out.*
2 control or achieve by or as if by magic: *a gesticulating figure endeavouring to charm a cobra* | [with adverbial] *she will charm your warts away.*
– PHRASES **turn on the charm** use one's ability to please in a calculated way so as to influence someone or to obtain something. **work like a charm** be completely successful or effective.
– ORIGIN Middle English (in the senses 'incantation or magic spell' and 'to use spells'): from Old French *charme* (noun), *charmer* (verb), from Latin *carmen* 'song, verse, incantation'.

charm bracelet ▶ **noun** a bracelet hung with small trinkets or ornaments.

charmed ▶ **adjective 1** (of a person's life or a period of this) unusually lucky or happy as though protected by magic: *I felt that I had a charmed life.*
2 Physics (of a particle) possessing the property charm.
▶ **exclamation** dated expressing polite pleasure at an introduction: *charmed, I'm sure.*

charmer ▶ **noun** a person with an attractive and engaging personality, typically one who uses this to impress or manipulate others.

charmeuse /ʃɑːˈməːz/ ▶ **noun** [mass noun] a soft, smooth silky dress fabric.

C

C

– ORIGIN early 20th cent.: from French, feminine of *charmeur* 'charmer', from *charmer* 'to charm'.

charming ▶ **adjective** very pleasant or attractive: *a charming country cottage.* ■ (of a person or their manner) very polite, friendly, and likeable: *he was a charming, affectionate colleague.*
▶ **exclamation** used as an ironic expression of displeasure or disapproval: *'I hate men.' 'Charming!' he said.*
– DERIVATIVES **charmingly** adverb.

charmless ▶ **adjective** unattractive or unpleasant: *a charmless sixties structure.*
– DERIVATIVES **charmlessly** adverb, **charmlessness** noun.

charm offensive ▶ **noun** a campaign of flattery, friendliness, and cajolement designed to achieve the support or agreement of others: *he launched a charm offensive against MPs who didn't support the government.*

charmonium /tʃɑːˈməʊnɪəm/ ▶ **noun** (pl. **charmonia**) Physics a combination of a charmed quark and antiquark.
– ORIGIN 1970s: from CHARM (sense 4 of the noun).

charm school ▶ **noun** dated or humorous an institution offering training in social graces such as etiquette: *not all of the bar staff appear to have benefited from a stint at charm school.*

charnel /ˈtʃɑːn(ə)l/ ▶ **noun** short for CHARNEL HOUSE.
▶ **adjective** associated with death: *I gagged on the charnel stench of the place.*
– ORIGIN late Middle English: from Old French, from medieval Latin *carnale*, neuter (used as a noun) of *carnalis* 'relating to flesh' (see CARNAL).

charnel house ▶ **noun** historical a building or vault in which corpses or bones are piled. ■ a place associated with violent death: *Europe in the immediate post-war period had become a charnel house.*

Charolais /ˈʃarə(ʊ)leɪ/ ▶ **noun** (pl. **same**) an animal of a breed of large white beef cattle.
– ORIGIN late 19th cent.: named after the *Monts du Charollais*, hills in eastern France where the breed originated.

Charon /ˈkɛːrən/ **1** Greek Mythology an old man who ferried the souls of the dead across the Rivers Styx and Acheron to Hades.
2 Astronomy the only satellite of Pluto, discovered in 1978, with a diameter (1,190 km) that is more than half that of Pluto.

Charophyta /ˈkɑːrə(ʊ)ˌfʌɪtə, ˈkarə(ʊ)-, ˈtʃarə(ʊ)-/ ▶ **plural noun** Botany a division of lower plants that includes the stoneworts, which are frequently treated as a class (Charophyceae) of the green algae.
– ORIGIN modern Latin (plural), former name of the family Characeae, from *Chara* (genus name) + *phuton* 'a plant'.

charophyte ▶ **noun** Botany a lower plant of the division Charophyta, such as a stonewort.

charpoy /ˈtʃɑːpɔɪ/ ▶ **noun** Indian a light bedstead.
– ORIGIN mid 17th cent.: from Urdu *cārpāī* 'four-legged', from Persian.

charr /tʃɑː/ (also **char**) ▶ **noun** (pl. **same**) a trout-like freshwater or marine fish of northern countries, valued as a food and game fish. ● Genus *Salvelinus*, family Salmonidae: several species, in particular the red-bellied **Arctic charr** (*S. alpinus*), which occurs in Arctic waters, and the North American **brook charr** or brook trout (*S. fontinalis*).
– ORIGIN mid 17th cent.: perhaps of Celtic origin.

charrette /ʃaˈrɛt/ (also **charette**) ▶ **noun** N. Amer. **1** a public meeting or workshop devoted to a concerted effort to solve a problem or plan the design of something.
2 a period of intense work, typically undertaken in order to meet a deadline.
– ORIGIN late Middle English (denoting a cart or wagon): from French *charrette*, literally 'cart'; current sense dates from the mid 20th cent., possibly with reference to the use of a cart in 19th-cent. Paris to collect architecture students' work on the day of an exhibition.

charro /ˈtʃɑːrəʊ/ ▶ **noun** (pl. **charros**) a traditionally dressed Mexican cowboy.
– ORIGIN Mexican Spanish, from Spanish, literally 'rustic'.

chart ▶ **noun** a sheet of information in the form of a table, graph, or diagram: *the doctor recorded her blood pressure on a chart.* ■ (usu. **the charts**) a weekly listing of the current bestselling pop records: *she topped the charts for eight weeks.* ■ a geographical map or plan, especially one used for navigation by sea or air. ■ (also **birth chart** or **natal chart**) Astrology a circular map showing the positions of the planets in the twelve houses at the time of someone's birth, from which astrologers are said to be able to deduce their character or potential.
▶ **verb 1** [with obj.] make a map of (an area): *Cook charted the coasts and waters of New Zealand.* ■ plot (a course) on a chart: *the pilot found his craft taking a route he had not charted.* ■ record the progress or development of: *the poems chart his descent into madness | a major series charting the history of country music.*
2 [no obj.] (of a record) sell enough copies to enter the music charts at a particular position: *the record will probably chart at about No. 74.*
– ORIGIN late 16th cent.: from French *charte*, from Latin *charta* 'paper, papyrus leaf' (see CARD¹).

chartbuster ▶ **noun** informal a popular singer or group that makes a bestselling recording. ■ a bestselling recording.

charter ▶ **noun 1** a written grant by the sovereign or legislative power of a country, by which a body such as a borough, company, or university is created or its rights and privileges defined. ■ a written constitution or description of an organization's functions. ■ [with modifier] (in the UK) a written statement of the rights of a specified group of people: *the standard set by the patient's charter.* ■ (**a charter for**) Brit. a policy or law regarded as enabling people to engage more easily in a specified undesirable activity: *he described the act as a charter for vandals.*
2 [mass noun] the hiring of an aircraft, ship, or motor vehicle for a special purpose: *a plane on charter to a multinational company.* ■ [count noun] a ship or vehicle that is hired. ■ [count noun] a trip made by a ship or vehicle under hire: *he liked to see the boat sparkling clean before each charter.*
▶ **verb** [with obj.] **1** (usu. as adj. **chartered**) grant a charter to (a city, university, or other body): *chartered corporations.*
2 hire (an aircraft, ship, or motor vehicle).
– ORIGIN Middle English: from Old French *chartre*, from Latin *chartula*, diminutive of *charta* 'paper' (see CARD¹).

chartered ▶ **adjective** [attrib.] **1** Brit. (of an accountant, engineer, librarian, etc.) qualified as a member of a professional body that has a royal charter.
2 (of an aircraft or ship) having been hired.

charterer ▶ **noun** a person or organization that charters a ship or aircraft.

charter flight ▶ **noun** a flight by an aircraft chartered for a specific journey, not part of an airline's regular schedule.

Charter Mark ▶ **noun** (in the UK) an award granted to institutions for exceptional public service under the terms of the Citizen's Charter.

charter member ▶ **noun** N. Amer. an original or founding member of a society or organization.

charter party ▶ **noun 1** a deed between a shipowner and a trader for the hire of a ship and the delivery of cargo.
2 a group of people using a hired aircraft or ship.
– ORIGIN late Middle English: from French *charte partie*, from medieval Latin *charta partita* 'divided charter', i.e. one written in duplicate on a single sheet, then divided in such a way that the two parts could be fitted together again as proof of authenticity.

charter school ▶ **noun 1** (in North America) a publicly funded independent school established by teachers, parents, or community groups under the terms of a charter with a local or national authority.
2 (**Charter School**) historical a school established by the Charter Society (founded for that purpose in 1733) to provide a Protestant education to poor Catholics in Ireland.

Chartism ▶ **noun** [mass noun] **1** a UK parliamentary reform movement of 1837–48, the principles of which were set out in a manifesto called *The People's Charter* and called for universal suffrage for men, equal electoral districts, voting by secret ballot, abolition of property qualifications for MPs, and annual general elections.
2 (**chartism**) the use of charts of financial data to predict future trends and to guide investment strategies.
– DERIVATIVES **Chartist** noun & adjective.

Chartres /ˈʃɑːtr(ə)/, French /ʃaʀtʀ/ a city in northern France; pop. 41,588 (2006). It is noted for its Gothic cathedral.

chartreuse /ʃɑːˈtrəːz/ ▶ **noun 1** [mass noun] a pale green or yellow liqueur made from brandy and aromatic herbs. ■ a pale yellow or green colour resembling the liqueur chartreuse.
2 a dish made in a mould using pieces of meat, game, vegetables, or (now most often) fruit in jelly.
– ORIGIN named after *La Grande Chartreuse*, the Carthusian monastery near Grenoble, where the liqueur (sense 1) was first made; sense 2 is an extended use.

chart-topping ▶ **adjective** informal (of a popular singer, group, or recording) having reached the top of the music charts.
– DERIVATIVES **chart-topper** noun.

charwoman ▶ **noun** (pl. **charwomen**) Brit. dated a woman employed as a cleaner in a house or office.
– ORIGIN late 16th cent.: from obsolete *char* or *chare* 'a turn of work, an odd job, chore' (obscurely related to CHORE) + WOMAN.

chary /ˈtʃɛːri/ ▶ **adjective** (**charier**, **chariest**) cautiously or suspiciously reluctant to do something: *she had been **chary of** telling the whole truth.*
– DERIVATIVES **charily** adverb.
– ORIGIN Old English *cearig* 'sorrowful, anxious', of West Germanic origin; related to CARE. The current sense arose in the mid 16th cent.

Charybdis /kəˈrɪbdɪs/ Greek Mythology a dangerous whirlpool in a narrow channel of the sea, opposite the cave of the sea monster Scylla.

Chas. ▶ **abbreviation** Charles.

chase¹ ▶ **verb** [with obj.] **1** pursue in order to catch or catch up with: *police chased the stolen car through the city* | [no obj.] *the dog **chased after** the stick.* ■ seek to attain: *the team are chasing their first home win this season.* ■ seek the company of (a member of the opposite sex) in an obvious way: *he spends all his free time chasing girls.*
2 [with obj. and adverbial of direction] drive or cause to go in a specified direction: *she chased him **out of** the house.* ■ [no obj., with adverbial of direction] rush in a specified direction: *he chased down the motorway.*
3 try to obtain (something owed or required): *the company employs people to **chase up** debts.* ■ try to make contact with (someone) in order to obtain something owed or required: *the council recently appointed its own team of bailiffs to chase non-payers.* ■ (**chase something up** (or US **down**)) make further investigation of an unresolved matter.
▶ **noun** an act of pursuing someone or something: *they captured the youths after a brief chase.* ■ short for STEEPLECHASE. ■ (**the chase**) hunting as a sport: *she was an ardent follower of the chase.* ■ [in place names] Brit. an area of unenclosed land formerly reserved for hunting: *Cannock Chase.* ■ archaic a hunted animal.
– PHRASES **chase the game** (in soccer) adopt attacking tactics, especially when losing, at the risk of being vulnerable to counter-attack. **chase shadows** pursue illusory targets: *I found that the three-day mission did little more than chase shadows.* **give chase** go in pursuit: *officers **gave chase to** one of the thieves.* **go and chase oneself** [in imperative] informal go away. **the thrill of the chase** see THRILL.
– ORIGIN Middle English: from Old French *chacier* (verb), *chace* (noun), based on Latin *captare* 'continue to take', from *capere* 'take'.

chase² ▶ **verb** [with obj.] (usu. as adj. **chased**) engrave (metal, or a design on metal): *a miniature container with a delicately chased floral design.*
– ORIGIN late Middle English: apparently from earlier *enchase*, from Old French *enchasser*.

chase³ ▶ **noun** (in letterpress printing) a metal frame for holding the composed type and blocks being printed at one time.
– ORIGIN late 16th cent.: from French *châsse*, from Latin *capsa* 'box' (see CASE²).

chase⁴ ▶ **noun 1** the part of a gun enclosing the bore.
2 a groove or furrow cut in the face of a wall or other surface to receive a pipe or wire.
– ORIGIN early 17th cent.: from French *chas* 'enclosed space', from Provençal *cas*, *caus*, from medieval Latin *capsum* 'thorax or nave of a church'.

chaser ▶ **noun 1** a person or thing that pursues someone or something: [in combination] *a woman-chaser.*
2 a horse for steeplechasing.
3 informal a strong alcoholic drink taken after a weaker one: *drinking pints of bitter with vodka chasers.*

Chasid /ˈxasɪd/ ▶ **noun** variant spelling of HASID.

Chasidism /ˈxasɪdɪz(ə)m/ ▶ **noun** variant spelling of HASIDISM.

chasm /ˈkaz(ə)m/ ▶ **noun** a deep fissure in the earth's surface. ■ a profound difference between people, viewpoints, feelings, etc.: *the chasm between rich and poor.*
– DERIVATIVES **chasmic** adjective (rare).

– ORIGIN late 16th cent. (denoting an opening up of the sea or land, as in an earthquake): from Latin *chasma*, from Greek *khasma* 'gaping hollow'.

chasse /ʃas/ ▸ **noun** a liqueur drunk after coffee.
– ORIGIN French, abbreviation of *chasse-café*, literally 'chase-coffee'.

chassé /ˈʃaseɪ/ ▸ **noun** a gliding step in dancing in which one foot displaces the other.
▸ **verb** (**chassés, chasséing, chasséd**) [no obj.] perform a chassé.
– ORIGIN French, literally 'chased'.

Chasselas /ˈʃas(ə)lɑː/ ▸ **noun** [mass noun] a variety of white grape, grown mainly in Europe and Chile for eating as a fruit or for making wine. ■ a wine made from the Chasselas grape.
– ORIGIN named after a village near Mâcon, France.

chasseur /ʃaˈsəː/, French /ʃasœʀ/ ▸ **noun** (pl. pronunc. **same**) historical a soldier equipped and trained for rapid movement, especially in the French army.
– ORIGIN mid 18th cent.: French, from *chasser* 'to chase or hunt'.

chasseur sauce ▸ **noun** [mass noun] a rich dark sauce with wine and mushrooms, typically served with poultry or game.
– ORIGIN from French *chasseur* 'huntsman', from *chasser* 'to chase or hunt'.

Chassid /ˈxasɪd/ ▸ **noun** variant spelling of **HASID**.

Chassidism /ˈxasɪˌdɪz(ə)m/ ▸ **noun** variant spelling of **HASIDISM**.

chassis /ˈʃasi, -iː/ ▸ **noun** (pl. **same** /-sɪz/) the base frame of a car, carriage, or other wheeled vehicle. ■ the outer structural framework of a piece of audio, radio, or computer equipment.
– ORIGIN early 20th cent.: from French *châssis* 'frame', based on Latin *capsa* 'box' (see **CASE²**).

chaste ▸ **adjective** abstaining from extramarital, or from all, sexual intercourse. ■ not having any sexual nature or intention: *a chaste, consoling embrace.* ■ without unnecessary ornamentation; simple or restrained: *chaste Classical symmetry.*
– DERIVATIVES **chastely** adverb, **chasteness** noun.
– ORIGIN Middle English: from Old French, from Latin *castus*.

chasten /ˈtʃeɪs(ə)n/ ▸ **verb** [with obj.] (of a reproof or misfortune) have a restraining or moderating effect on: *the director was somewhat chastened by his recent flops* | (as adj. **chastening**) *a chastening experience.* ■ archaic (especially of God) discipline; punish.
– DERIVATIVES **chastener** noun.
– ORIGIN early 16th cent.: from an obsolete verb *chaste*, from Old French *chastier*, from Latin *castigare* 'castigate', from *castus* 'morally pure, chaste'.

chaste tree ▸ **noun** a southern European shrub with blue or white flowers, grown as an ornamental. ● *Vitex agnus-castus*, family Verbenaceae.
– ORIGIN mid 16th cent.: so named because of its association with chastity in sacrifices to Ceres.

chastise ▸ **verb** [with obj.] rebuke or reprimand severely: *he chastised his colleagues for their laziness.* ■ dated punish, especially by beating.
– DERIVATIVES **chastisement** noun, **chastiser** noun.
– ORIGIN Middle English: apparently formed irregularly from the obsolete verb *chaste* (see **CHASTEN**).

chastity ▸ **noun** [mass noun] the state or practice of refraining from extramarital, or especially from all, sexual intercourse: *vows of chastity.*
– ORIGIN Middle English: from Old French *chastete*, from Latin *castitas*, from *castus* 'morally pure' (see **CHASTE**).

chastity belt ▸ **noun** historical a garment or device designed to prevent the woman wearing it from having sexual intercourse.

chasuble /ˈtʃazjʊb(ə)l/ ▸ **noun** an ornate sleeveless outer vestment worn by a Catholic or High Anglican priest when celebrating Mass.
– ORIGIN Middle English: from Old French *chesible*, later *chasuble*, from late Latin *casubla*, alteration of Latin *casula* 'hooded cloak or little cottage', diminutive of *casa* 'house'.

chat¹ ▸ **verb** (**chats, chatting, chatted**) [no obj.] talk in a friendly and informal way: *she chatted to her mother on the phone every day.* ■ exchange messages online in real time with one or more simultaneous users of a computer network: *I have chatted to a few women on the Net.*
▸ **noun** an informal conversation: *he dropped in for a chat* | [mass noun] *that's enough chat for tonight.* ■ the online exchange of messages in real time with one or more simultaneous users of a computer network: *online chat has been widely accepted by average Internet users.*
– PHRASAL VERBS **chat someone up** informal engage someone in flirtatious conversation: *the waiter attempted to chat her up.*
– ORIGIN Middle English: shortening of **CHATTER**.

> **WORD TRENDS** It seems that the Internet has taken over from the garden fence as the favourite place for a **chat**. The Oxford English Corpus shows that the most common collocates of both the noun and the verb are computer-related, such as *online, Internet,* and *Web*, with *chat room* now four times as common as *chat show*. Though webcams and microphones are widely available, most people still choose to conduct their online chatting via keyboard, meaning that the word has shifted from a completely verbal method of communication to one that encompasses typing. People who regularly chat together online may never actually hear each other's voices.

chat² ▸ **noun 1** [often in combination] a small Old World songbird of the thrush family, with black, white, and brown coloration and a harsh call. ● *Saxicola* and other genera, family Turdidae: numerous species. See also **BUSHCHAT, STONECHAT, WHINCHAT**.
2 [with modifier] any of a number of small songbirds with harsh calls: ● a New World warbler that typically has a yellow or pink breast (genera *Icteria* and *Granatellus*, family Parulidae). ● an Australian songbird related to the honeyeaters, the male of which is either mainly yellow or boldly marked (genera *Ephthianura* and *Ashbyia*, family Ephthianuridae).
– ORIGIN late 17th cent.: probably imitative of its call.

chateau /ˈʃatəʊ/ (also **château** /ˈʃatəʊ/, French /ʃɑto/) ▸ **noun** (pl. **chateaux** or **chateaus** pronunc. **same** or /-təʊz/) a large French country house or castle, often giving its name to wine made in its neighbourhood: [in names] *Château Margaux.*
– ORIGIN mid 18th cent.: French, from Old French *chastel* (see **CASTLE**).

Chateaubriand /ˌʃatəʊˈbriːɒ̃/, French /ʃatobʀijɑ̃/, François-René, Vicomte de (1768–1848), French writer and diplomat. He was an important figure in early French romanticism. Notable works: *Le Génie du Christianisme* (1802) and *Mémoires d'outre-tombe* (autobiography, 1849–50).

chateaubriand /ˌʃatəʊˈbriːɒ̃/ ▸ **noun** a thick fillet of beef steak.
– ORIGIN late 19th cent.: named after François-René, Vicomte de **CHATEAUBRIAND**, whose chef is said to have created the dish.

chatelain /ˈʃatəleɪn/ ▸ **noun** another term for **CASTELLAN**.
– ORIGIN late Middle English: from Old French *chastelain*, from medieval Latin *castellanus* 'castellan', from Latin *castellum* (see **CASTLE**).

chatelaine /ˈʃatəleɪn/ ▸ **noun** dated a woman in charge of a large house. ■ historical a set of short chains attached to a woman's belt, used for carrying keys or other items.
– ORIGIN mid 19th cent.: from French *châtelaine*, feminine of *châtelain* 'castellan', from medieval Latin *castellanus* (see **CHATELAIN**).

Chatham /ˈtʃatəm/, 1st Earl of, see **PITT**.

Chatham Islands a group of two islands, Pitt Island and Chatham Island, in the SW Pacific to the east of New Zealand.

chatline ▸ **noun** a telephone service which allows conversation among a number of separate callers.

chatoyant /ʃəˈtɔɪənt/ ▸ **adjective** (of a gem, especially when cut en cabochon) showing a band of bright lustre caused by reflection from inclusions in the stone.
– DERIVATIVES **chatoyance** noun, **chatoyancy** noun.
– ORIGIN late 18th cent.: French, present participle of *chatoyer* 'to shimmer'.

chat room ▸ **noun** an area on the Internet or other computer network where users can communicate, typically one dedicated to a particular topic.

chat show ▸ **noun** Brit. a television or radio programme in which celebrities are invited to talk informally about various topics.

chattel /ˈtʃat(ə)l/ ▸ **noun** (in general use) a personal possession. ■ Law an item of property other than freehold land, including tangible goods (**chattels personal**) and leasehold interests (**chattels real**). See also **GOODS AND CHATTELS**.
– ORIGIN Middle English: from Old French *chatel*, from medieval Latin *capitale*, from Latin *capitalis*, from *caput* 'head'. Compare with **CAPITAL¹** and **CATTLE**.

chattel mortgage ▸ **noun** N. Amer. a mortgage on a movable item of property.

chatter ▸ **verb** [no obj.] talk informally about unimportant matters: *she was chattering about her holiday.* ■ (of a bird, monkey, or machine) make a series of short, quick high-pitched sounds. ■ (of a person's teeth) click repeatedly together from cold or fear.
▸ **noun** [mass noun] informal talk: *he was full of inconsequential but amusing chatter.* ■ a series of short, quick high-pitched sounds: *the starlings' constant chatter.* ■ undesirable vibration in a mechanism: *the wipers should operate without chatter.*
– PHRASES **the chattering classes** Brit. derogatory intellectual or artistic people considered as a social group given to the expression of liberal opinions.
– DERIVATIVES **chattery** adjective.
– ORIGIN Middle English: imitative.

chatterbot ▸ **noun** a computer program designed to interact with people by simulating conversation.
– ORIGIN 1990s: blend of **CHATTER** and **ROBOT**.

chatterbox ▸ **noun** informal a person who likes to chatter.

chatterer ▸ **noun 1** a person who chatters at length. **2** informal any of a number of birds with chattering calls, especially a babbler, a waxwing, or a cotinga.

Chatterton, Thomas (1752–70), English poet, chiefly remembered for his fabricated poems professing to be those of a 15th-century monk. He committed suicide at the age of 17.

chatty ▸ **adjective** (**chattier, chattiest**) readily engaging in informal talk: *the driver was very chatty.* ■ (of a conversation, letter, etc.) informal and lively.
– DERIVATIVES **chattily** adverb, **chattiness** noun.

chat-up ▸ **noun** [often as modifier] Brit. informal an act of talking flirtatiously to someone: *a chat-up line.*

Chaucer /ˈtʃɔːsə/, Geoffrey (*c.*1342–1400), English poet. His most famous work, the *Canterbury Tales* (*c.*1387–1400), is a cycle of linked tales told by a group of pilgrims. His skills of characterization, humour, and versatility established him as the first great English poet. Other notable works: *Troilus and Criseyde* (1385).
– DERIVATIVES **Chaucerian** /tʃɔːˈsɪərɪən/ **adjective & noun.**

chaudhuri /ˈtʃaʊˌdʌri/ ▸ **noun** (pl. **chaudhuris**) Indian a government employee who supplies and is in charge of workers and materials for public works.
– ORIGIN from Hindi *caudharī*, literally 'holder of four', or from Sanskrit *cakradhārin*, denoting the bearer of a discus as a sign of authority.

chauffeur ▸ **noun** a person employed to drive a private or hired car.
▸ **verb** [with obj.] drive (a car or a passenger in a car), typically as part of one's job: *she insisted on being chauffeured around.*
– ORIGIN late 19th cent. (in the general sense 'motorist'): from French, literally 'stoker' (by association with steam engines), from *chauffer* 'to heat'.

chauffeuse /ʃəʊˈfəːz/ ▸ **noun** a female chauffeur.

Chauliac /ˈʃəʊlɪak/, French /ʃoljak/, Guy de (*c.*1300–68), French physician. His *Chirurgia Magna* (1363) was the first work to describe many surgical techniques.

chaulmoogra /tʃɔːlˈmuːɡrə/ ▸ **noun** a tropical Asian evergreen tree with narrow leathery leaves and oil-rich seeds. ● Genus *Hydnocarpus*, family Flacourtiaceae: several species, in particular *H. kurzii*, the main source of the oil. ■ (also **chaulmoogra oil**) [mass noun] oil obtained from the seeds of the chaulmoogra tree, used medically and as a preservative.
– ORIGIN early 19th cent.: from Bengali *cāul-mugrā*.

Chaumes /ʃəʊm/ ▸ **noun** [mass noun] a type of French cheese with an orange rind and a creamy flavour.
– ORIGIN French, possibly from *chaume* 'wheat stubble', in reference to the colours of the cheese and its rind.

chausses /ʃəʊs/ ▸ **plural noun** historical pantaloons or close-fitting coverings for the legs and feet, in particular those forming part of a knight's armour.
– ORIGIN late 15th cent.: French, literally 'clothing for the legs'.

chautauqua /tʃɔːˈtɔːkwə, ʃ-/ ▸ **noun** N. Amer. an institution that provided popular adult education courses and entertainment in the late 19th and early 20th centuries.
– ORIGIN late 19th cent.: named after *Chautauqua*, a county in New York State, where such an institution was first set up.

chauvinism /ˈʃəʊv(ɪ)nɪz(ə)m/ ▸ **noun** [mass noun] exaggerated or aggressive patriotism. ■ excessive or prejudiced support for one's own cause, group, or sex. See also **MALE CHAUVINISM**.

– ORIGIN late 19th cent.: named after Nicolas *Chauvin*, a Napoleonic veteran noted for his extreme patriotism, popularized as a character by the Cogniard brothers in *Cocarde Tricolore* (1831).

chauvinist /ˈʃəʊv(ɪ)nɪst/ ▸ **noun** a person displaying aggressive or exaggerated patriotism. ■ a person displaying excessive or prejudiced support for their own cause, group, or sex: *she wrote off all the local males as hopeless chauvinists.*
▸ **adjective** relating to or characteristic of a chauvinist: *a chauvinist rejection of foreign interference.*

C

chauvinistic /ʃəʊv(ɪ)ˈnɪstɪk/ ▸ **adjective** feeling or displaying aggressive or exaggerated patriotism. ■ displaying excessive or prejudiced support for their own cause, group, or sex.
– DERIVATIVES **chauvinistically** adverb.

chav ▸ **noun** Brit. informal, derogatory a young lower-class person typified by brash and loutish behaviour and the wearing of (real or imitation) designer clothes.
– DERIVATIVES **chavvy** adjective.
– ORIGIN 1990s: probably from Romany *chavo* 'boy, youth' or *chavvy* 'baby, child': sometimes said to have originated in *Chatham*, Kent, and to be a shortening of that name.

Chavín /tʃɑːˈviːn/ ▸ **noun** [usu. as modifier] Archaeology a civilization that flourished in Peru *c.*1000–200 BC, uniting a large part of the country's coastal region in a common culture.
– ORIGIN from the name of the town and temple complex of *Chavín* de Huantar in the northern highlands, where the civilization was centred.

chaw /tʃɔː/ informal, chiefly N. Amer. ▸ **noun** an act of chewing something, especially something not intended to be swallowed: *enjoying a good chaw.* ■ something chewed, especially a quid of tobacco: *a chaw of tobacco.*
▸ **verb** [with obj.] chew (something, especially tobacco).
– ORIGIN late Middle English (as a verb): variant of CHEW.

chawal /ˈtʃʌwəl, tʃɔːl/ ▸ **noun** [mass noun] rice, especially as part of a dish: *egg chawal.*
– ORIGIN from Hindi *cāval.*

chawl /tʃɔːl/ ▸ **noun** (in South Asia) a large building divided into many separate tenements, offering cheap, basic accommodation to labourers.
– ORIGIN from Marathi *cāḷ*, denoting a long narrow building.

chayote /ˈtʃeɪəʊti/ ▸ **noun** **1** a succulent green pear-shaped tropical fruit which resembles cucumber in flavour.
2 the tropical American vine which yields the chayote, also producing an edible yam-like tuberous root. ● *Sechium edule*, family Cucurbitaceae.
– ORIGIN late 19th cent.: from Spanish, from Nahuatl *chayotli.*

ChB ▸ **abbreviation** Bachelor of Surgery.
– ORIGIN from Latin *Chirurgiae Baccalaureus.*

CHD ▸ **abbreviation** coronary heart disease.

cheap ▸ **adjective** **1** low in price, especially in relation to similar items or services: *local buses were reliable and cheap.* ■ charging low prices: *a cheap restaurant.* ■ inexpensive because of inferior quality: *cheap, shoddy goods.*
2 of little worth because achieved in a discreditable way requiring little effort: *her moment of cheap triumph.* ■ deserving contempt: *a cheap trick.* ■ N. Amer. informal miserly: *she's too cheap to send me a postcard.*
▸ **adverb** at or for a low price: *a house that was going **cheap** because of the war.*
– PHRASES **cheap and cheerful** Brit. simple and inexpensive. **cheap and nasty** Brit. of low cost and bad quality: *the materials can seem a bit cheap and nasty.* **cheap at the price** (or humorous **at half the price**) Brit. well worth having, regardless of the cost. **on the cheap** informal at low cost.
– DERIVATIVES **cheapish** adjective, **cheaply** adverb, **cheapness** noun.
– ORIGIN late 15th cent.: from an obsolete phrase *good cheap* 'a good bargain', from Old English *cēap* 'bargaining, trade', based on Latin *caupo* 'small trader, innkeeper'.

cheapen ▸ **verb** [with obj.] reduce the price of: *the depreciation of the dollar would cheapen US exports.* ■ degrade: *the mass media cheapen the experience of art.*

cheapjack ▸ **noun** a seller of cheap inferior goods, typically a hawker at a fair or market.
▸ **adjective** chiefly N. Amer. of inferior quality.
– ORIGIN mid 19th cent.: from CHEAP + JACK[1].

cheapo (also **cheapie**) informal ▸ **adjective** [attrib.] inexpensive and of poor quality: *a cheapo version of the guitar.*
▸ **noun** (pl. **cheapos**) something that is inexpensive and of poor quality.

cheapskate ▸ **noun** informal a miserly person.
– ORIGIN late 19th cent. (originally US): from CHEAP + SKATE[3].

cheat ▸ **verb** **1** [no obj.] act dishonestly or unfairly in order to gain an advantage: *she always **cheats at** cards.* ■ [with obj.] gain an advantage over or deprive of something by using unfair or deceitful methods; defraud: *he had **cheated** her **out of** everything she had.* ■ informal be sexually unfaithful: *his wife was **cheating on** him.*
2 [with obj.] avoid (something undesirable) by luck or skill: *she cheated death in a spectacular crash.*
▸ **noun** a person who behaves dishonestly in order to gain an advantage. ■ an act of cheating; a fraud or deception. ■ [mass noun] a children's card game, the object of which is to get rid of one's cards while making declarations about them which may or may not be truthful.
– ORIGIN late Middle English: shortening of ESCHEAT (the original sense).

cheater ▸ **noun** chiefly N. Amer. **1** a person who acts dishonestly in order to gain an advantage.
2 (**cheaters**) informal a pair of glasses or sunglasses.

cheat grass ▸ **noun** [mass noun] chiefly N. Amer. a tough wild grass of open land, sometimes growing as a weed among cereal crops and in pasture. ● Genus *Bromus*, family Gramineae: several species.
– ORIGIN late 18th cent.: a local word for various wild plants, perhaps from their resemblance to the cereals among which they grew.

cheat sheet ▸ **noun** N. Amer. informal a piece of paper bearing written notes intended to aid one's memory, typically one used surreptitiously in an examination.

Cheboksary /ˌtʃɛbɒkˈsɑːri/ a city in west central Russia, on the River Volga, west of Kazan, capital of the autonomous republic of Chuvashia; pop. 441,600 (est. 2008).

Chechen /ˈtʃɛtʃɛn/ ▸ **noun** (pl. **same** or **Chechens**)
1 a member of the largely Muslim people inhabiting Chechnya.
2 [mass noun] the North Caucasian language of the Chechen people.
▸ **adjective** relating to the Chechen people or their language.
– ORIGIN from obsolete Russian *chechen* (earlier form of *chechenets*).

Chechnya /ˌtʃɛtʃˈnjɑː/ (also **Chechenia**) an autonomous republic in the Caucasus in SW Russia, on the border with Georgia; pop. 1,205,800 (est. 2009); capital, Grozny. The republic declared itself independent of Russia in 1991 and was invaded by Russian forces (1994). A peace treaty agreed the withdrawal of troops, but the Russians invaded again in 1999. Also called **Chechen Republic**.

check[1] ▸ **verb** [with obj.] **1** examine (something) in order to determine its accuracy, quality, or condition, or to detect the presence of something: *customs officers have the right to check all luggage* | [no obj.] *a simple blood test to **check for** anaemia.* ■ verify or establish to one's satisfaction: *phone us to check the availability of your chosen holiday* | [with clause] *she glanced over her shoulder to check that the door was shut.* ■ (**check something against**) verify the accuracy of something by comparing it with (something else): *keep your receipt to check against your statement.* ■ N. Amer. another way of saying CHECK SOMETHING OFF. ■ N. Amer. another way of saying CHECK SOMETHING IN. ■ [no obj.] agree or correspond when compared. ■ informal look at; take notice of: *check the remix.*
2 stop or slow the progress of (something, typically something undesirable): *efforts were made to check the disease.* ■ curb or control (one's feelings or reaction): *he learned to check his excitement.* ■ Ice Hockey hamper or neutralize (an opponent) with one's body or stick. ■ [no obj.] (**check against**) provide a means of preventing: *processes to check against deterioration in the quality of the data held.*
3 [with obj.] Chess move a piece or pawn to a square where it attacks (the opposing king).
4 [no obj.] (in poker) choose not to make a bet when called upon, allowing another player to do so instead.
5 [no obj.] (of a hound) pause to make sure of or regain a scent. ■ (of a trained hawk) abandon the intended quarry and fly after other prey.
▸ **noun** **1** an examination to test or ascertain accuracy, quality, or satisfactory condition: *a campaign calling for regular checks on gas appliances* | *a health check.*
2 a stopping or slowing of progress: *there was no check to the expansion of the market.* ■ a means of control or restraint: *a permanent check upon the growth or abuse of central authority.* ■ Ice Hockey an act of hampering or neutralizing an opponent with one's body or stick. ■ a temporary loss of the scent in hunting. ■ Falconry the movement made by a hawk when it abandons its intended quarry and pursues other prey.
3 Chess a move by which a piece or pawn directly attacks the opponent's king and by which the king may be checkmated.
4 N. Amer. the bill in a restaurant.
5 (also **baggage** or **luggage check**) a token of identification for left luggage.
6 a counter used as a stake in a gambling game.
7 (also **check mark**) North American term for TICK[1] (sense 1 of the noun).
8 a part of a piano which catches the hammer and prevents it retouching the strings.
9 a crack or flaw in timber.
▸ **exclamation** **1** informal, chiefly N. Amer. expressing assent or agreement.
2 used by a chess player to announce that the opponent's king has been placed in check.
– PHRASES **checks and balances** counterbalancing influences by which an organization or system is regulated, typically those ensuring that power in political institutions is not concentrated in the hands of particular individuals or groups. **in check 1** under control: *a way of keeping inflation in check.* **2** Chess (of a king) directly attacked by an opponent's piece or pawn; (of a player) having the king in this position. **keep a check on** monitor: *keep a regular check on your score.*
– PHRASAL VERBS **check in** (or **check someone in**) arrive and register at a hotel or airport: *you must check in at least one hour before take-off* | *they check in the passengers.* **check something in** have one's baggage weighed and put aside for consignment to the hold of an aircraft on which one is booked to travel. ■ register and leave baggage in a left-luggage department. **check into** register one's arrival at (a hotel). **check something off** N. Amer. tick or otherwise mark an item on a list to show that it has been dealt with. **check on 1** verify, ascertain, or monitor the state or condition of: *the doctor had come to check on his patient.* **2** another way of saying CHECK UP ON. **check out 1** settle one's hotel bill before leaving. ■ N. Amer. informal die. **2** prove to be true or correct. **check someone/thing out 1** establish the truth or inform oneself about someone or something: *they decided to go and check out a local restaurant.* ■ look at; take notice of: *do check out his website* | *check out the chick in the leopardskin top.* **2** (**check something out**) chiefly N. Amer. enter the price of goods in a supermarket into a cash machine. ■ register something as having been borrowed. **check through** inspect or examine thoroughly. **check up on** investigate in order to establish the truth about or accuracy of: *Don called me to check up on some facts.*
– DERIVATIVES **checkable** adjective.
– ORIGIN Middle English (originally as used in the game of chess): the noun and exclamation from Old French *eschec*, from medieval Latin *scaccus*, via Arabic from Persian *šāh* 'king'; the verb from Old French *eschequier* 'play chess, put in check'. The sense 'stop or control' arose from the use in chess, and led (in the late 17th cent.) to 'examine the accuracy of'.

check[2] ▸ **noun** a pattern of small squares: *a fine black-and-white check.* ■ a garment or fabric with a pattern of small squares: *on Wednesdays he wore the small check.*
▸ **adjective** [attrib.] having a checked pattern: *a blue check T-shirt.*
– ORIGIN late Middle English: probably from CHEQUER (sense 1 of the noun).

check[3] ▸ **noun** US spelling of CHEQUE.

checkbox ▸ **noun** Computing a small area on a computer screen which, when selected by the user, shows that a particular feature has been enabled.

checked ▸ **adjective** having a pattern of small squares: *a checked shirt.*

checker[1] ▸ **noun** **1** a person or thing that verifies or examines something: *a spelling and grammar checker.*
2 US a cashier in a supermarket.

checker[2] ▸ **noun & verb** US spelling of CHEQUER.

checkerberry ▸ **noun** (pl. **checkerberries**) a creeping evergreen North American shrub of the heather family, with spiny scented leaves and waxy white flowers. Also called WINTERGREEN. ● *Gaultheria procumbens*, family Ericaceae.

■ the edible red fruit of the checkerberry plant.
– ORIGIN late 18th cent.: from *checkers* or *chequers* 'berries of the service tree' (so named from their colour) + BERRY.

checkerboard ▶ noun US spelling of CHEQUERBOARD.

checkered ▶ adjective US spelling of CHEQUERED.

checkerspot ▶ noun a North American butterfly that resembles a fritillary, with pale markings on the wings that typically form a chequered pattern.
● *Euphydryas* and other genera, subfamily Melitaeinae, family Nymphalidae.

check-in ▶ noun [mass noun] [often as modifier] the action of registering one's presence, typically as a passenger at an airport: *the check-in counter*. ■ the point at which someone checks in.

checking account (Canadian **chequing account**) ▶ noun N. Amer. a current account at a bank.
– ORIGIN 1920s: from CHECK³.

checklist ▶ noun a list of items required, things to be done, or points to be considered, used as a reminder.

check mark ▶ noun N. Amer. another term for CHECK¹ (sense 7 of the noun).

checkmate ▶ noun [mass noun] Chess a position in which a player's king is directly attacked by an opponent's piece or pawn and has no possible move to escape the check. The attacking player thus wins the game. ■ [as exclamation] said by a player to announce that the opponent's king is in the position of checkmate. ■ a final defeat or deadlock: *if the rebel forces succeed in cutting off the road, they will have achieved checkmate*.
▶ verb [with obj.] Chess put into checkmate. ■ defeat or frustrate totally: *the vice president checkmated that strategy*.
– ORIGIN Middle English: from Old French *eschec mat*, from Arabic *šāh māta*, from Persian *šāh māt* 'the king is dead'.

checkout ▶ noun 1 a point at which goods are paid for in a supermarket or similar store.
2 [mass noun] the administrative procedure followed when a guest leaves a hotel at the end of their stay.

checkpoint ▶ noun a barrier or manned entrance, typically at a border, where security checks are carried out on travellers. ■ a place on the route in a long-distance race where the time for each competitor is recorded. ■ a location whose exact position can be verified visually or electronically, used by pilots to aid navigation.

check rein ▶ noun a bearing rein.

checkroom ▶ noun N. Amer. a cloakroom in a hotel or theatre. ■ an office for left luggage.

checksum ▶ noun a digit representing the sum of the correct digits in a piece of stored or transmitted digital data, against which later comparisons can be made to detect errors in the data.

check-up ▶ noun a thorough examination, especially a medical or dental one, to detect any problems.

check valve ▶ noun a valve that closes to prevent backward flow of liquid.

Cheddar ▶ noun [mass noun] a kind of firm smooth yellow cheese, originally made in Cheddar in SW England.

cheder /ˈxɛdə/ (also **heder**) ▶ noun (pl. **chedarim** /-ˈdɑːrɪm/, **cheders**) a school for Jewish children in which Hebrew and religious knowledge are taught.
– ORIGIN late 19th cent.: from Hebrew *ḥeder* 'room'.

cheechako /tʃiːˈtʃɑːkəʊ/ ▶ noun (pl. **cheechakos**) N. Amer. informal a person newly arrived in the mining districts of Alaska or NW Canada.
– ORIGIN late 19th cent.: Chinook Jargon, 'newcomer'.

chee-chee ▶ exclamation variant spelling of CHHI-CHHI.

cheek ▶ noun 1 either side of the face below the eye: *tears rolled down her cheeks*.
2 either of the buttocks.
3 either of two side pieces or parts arranged in lateral pairs in a structure.
4 [in sing.] talk or behaviour regarded as rude or lacking in respect: *he* **had the cheek** *to complain*.
▶ verb [with obj.] Brit. informal speak impertinently to: *Frankie always got away with cheeking his elders*.
– PHRASES **cheek by jowl** close together: *they lived cheek by jowl in a one-room flat*. [from a use of *jowl* in the sense 'cheek'; the phrase was originally *cheek by cheek*.] **cheek to cheek** (of two people dancing) with their heads close together in a romantic way. **turn the other cheek** refrain from retaliating when one has been attacked or insulted. [with biblical allusion to Matt. 5:39.]
– DERIVATIVES **cheeked** adjective [in combination] *rosy-cheeked*.
– ORIGIN Old English *cē(a)ce*, *cēoce* 'cheek, jaw', of West Germanic origin; related to Dutch *kaak*.

cheekbone ▶ noun the bone below the eye.

cheekpiece ▶ noun 1 a smooth block fitted to the stock of a rifle or shotgun and resting against the face when aiming from the shoulder.
2 either of the two straps of a horse's bridle joining the bit and the headpiece.
3 a bar on a horse's bit which lies outside the mouth.

cheeky ▶ adjective (**cheekier**, **cheekiest**) impudent or irreverent, typically in an amusing way: *a cheeky grin*.
– DERIVATIVES **cheekily** adverb, **cheekiness** noun.

cheep ▶ noun a short, high squeaky cry made by a young bird. ■ a short, high sound resembling the cry of a young bird: *an electronic cheep from the alarm*. ■ [in sing.] [with negative] [often as modifier] informal the slightest sound: *there has not been a cheep from anybody*.
▶ verb [no obj.] make a short, high squeaky sound.
– ORIGIN early 16th cent. (originally Scots): imitative (compare with PEEP²).

cheer ▶ verb 1 [no obj.] shout for joy or in praise or encouragement: *she cheered from the sidelines* | (as adj. **cheering**) *a cheering crowd*. ■ [with obj.] praise or encourage with shouts: *MPs rose to cheer the Chancellor* | *the cyclists were* **cheered on** *by the crowds*.
2 [with obj.] give comfort or support to: *he seemed greatly cheered by my arrival*. ■ (**cheer someone up** or **cheer up**) make or become less miserable: [with obj.] *I asked her out to lunch to cheer her up* | [no obj.] *he cheered up at the sight of the food*.
▶ noun 1 a shout of encouragement, praise, or joy: *a tremendous cheer from the audience*.
2 (also **good cheer**) [mass noun] cheerfulness, optimism, or confidence: *an attempt to inject a little cheer into this gloomy season*. ■ food and drink provided for a festive occasion: *they had partaken heartily of the Christmas cheer*.
– PHRASES **of good cheer** archaic cheerful; optimistic. **three cheers** three successive hurrahs shouted to express appreciation or congratulation: *three cheers for the winners!* **two cheers** qualified approval or mild enthusiasm. **what cheer?** archaic how are you?
– ORIGIN Middle English: from Old French *chiere* 'face', from late Latin *cara*, from Greek *kara* 'head'. The original sense was 'face', hence 'expression, mood', later specifically 'a good mood'.

cheerful ▶ adjective noticeably happy and optimistic: *how can she be so cheerful at six o'clock in the morning?* | *a cheerful voice*. ■ causing happiness by its nature or appearance: *cheerful news* | *the room was painted in cheerful colours*.
– DERIVATIVES **cheerfulness** noun.

cheerfully ▶ adverb in a cheerful way. ■ readily and willingly: *he cheerfully admits to being the wrong side of fifty*.

cheerio ▶ exclamation Brit. informal used as an expression of good wishes on parting; goodbye. ■ dated expressing good wishes before drinking.

cheerleader ▶ noun a member of a team of girls who perform organized cheering, chanting, and dancing in support of a sports team at matches in the US and elsewhere. ■ an enthusiastic and vocal supporter of someone or something: *he was a cheerleader for individual initiative*.
– DERIVATIVES **cheerleading** noun & adjective.

cheerless ▶ adjective gloomy; depressing: *the corridors were ill-lit and cheerless*.
– DERIVATIVES **cheerlessly** adverb, **cheerlessness** noun.

cheerly ▶ adverb archaic heartily (used as a cry of encouragement among sailors).

cheers ▶ exclamation informal 1 expressing good wishes before drinking.
2 Brit. expressing good wishes on parting or ending a conversation.
3 chiefly Brit. expressing gratitude or acknowledgement for something.

cheery ▶ adjective (**cheerier**, **cheeriest**) happy and optimistic: *a cheery smile*.
– DERIVATIVES **cheerily** adverb, **cheeriness** noun.

cheese¹ ▶ noun [mass noun] 1 a food made from the pressed curds of milk, firm and elastic or soft and semi-liquid in texture: *grated cheese* | [as modifier] *a cheese sandwich* | [count noun] *a cow's milk cheese*. ■ [count noun] a complete cake of cheese with its rind. ■ [with modifier] Brit. a conserve having the consistency of soft cheese: *lemon cheese*. ■ [count noun] a round, flat object resembling a cake of cheese, such as the heavy flat wooden disc used in skittles and other games.
2 informal the quality of being too obviously sentimental: *the conversations tend too far towards cheese*.
– PHRASES **hard cheese** Brit. informal used to express sympathy over a petty matter. **say cheese** said by a photographer to encourage the subject to smile.
– ORIGIN Old English *cēse*, *cȳse*, of West Germanic origin; related to Dutch *kaas* and German *Käse*; from Latin *caseus*.

cheese² ▶ verb [with obj.] (usu. **be cheesed off**) Brit. informal exasperate, frustrate, or bore (someone): *I got a bit cheesed off with the movie*.
– ORIGIN early 19th cent. (in the archaic phrase *cheese it*, used to urge someone to stop doing something): of unknown origin.

cheeseball N. Amer. informal ▶ adjective lacking taste, style, or originality: *I'll admit to watching some of those cheeseball daytime talk shows*.
▶ noun a person who lacks taste, style, or originality: *she's a walking cheeseball, but I love her anyway*.

cheeseboard ▶ noun Brit. a selection of cheeses served as a course of a meal. ■ a board on which cheese is served and cut.

cheeseburger ▶ noun a beefburger with a slice of cheese on it, served in a bread roll.

cheesecake ▶ noun 1 a kind of rich sweet tart made with cream and soft cheese on a biscuit base.
2 [mass noun] informal images portraying women in a manner which emphasizes idealized or stereotypical sexual attractiveness.

cheesecloth ▶ noun [mass noun] thin, loosely woven, unsized cotton cloth, used typically for light clothing and in preparing or protecting food.

cheese-cutter ▶ noun 1 an implement for cutting cheese, especially by means of a wire which can be pulled through the cheese.
2 (also **cheese-cutter cap**) informal a cap with a broad, squared peak.

cheese fly ▶ noun a small shiny black fly whose larvae infest cheese. Also called CHEESE-SKIPPER. ● *Piophila casei*, family Piophilidae.

cheese head ▶ noun Brit. a type of screw head with vertical sides and a slightly domed top.

cheesemaker ▶ noun a person who makes cheese.
– DERIVATIVES **cheesemaking** noun.

cheese mite ▶ noun a mite that infests cheese.
● Genus *Tyroglyphus*, order (or subclass) Acari.

cheesemonger ▶ noun Brit. a person who sells cheese, butter, and other dairy products.

cheese-paring ▶ adjective extremely careful or mean with money: *cheese-paring methods necessitated by desperate shortages*.
▶ noun [mass noun] meanness.

cheese plant ▶ noun see SWISS CHEESE PLANT.

cheese-skipper ▶ noun another term for CHEESE FLY.

cheesesteak ▶ noun US a long bread roll with a filling of thinly sliced sautéed beef, melted cheese, and sautéed onions.

cheese straw ▶ noun a thin strip of pastry, flavoured with cheese and eaten as a snack.

cheesewood ▶ noun a small tropical evergreen tree with white flowers and yellowish-orange fruit.
● Genus *Pittosporum*, family Pittosporaceae: several species, in particular the Australian *P. undulatum*, with fragrant flowers and hard yellowish timber used in making golf clubs, and the South African *P. viridifolium*.

cheesy ▶ adjective (**cheesier**, **cheesiest**) 1 like cheese in taste, smell, or consistency: *a pungent, cheesy sauce*.
2 informal cheap and of low quality: *cheesy motel rooms*. ■ hackneyed and obviously sentimental: *an album of cheesy pop hits*. ■ (of a smile) exaggerated and likely to be insincere: *a cheesy grin*.
– DERIVATIVES **cheesily** adverb, **cheesiness** noun.

cheetah /ˈtʃiːtə/ ▶ noun a large slender spotted cat found in Africa and parts of Asia. It is the fastest animal on land. ● *Acinonyx jubatus*, family Felidae.
– ORIGIN late 18th cent.: from Hindi *cītā*, perhaps from Sanskrit *citraka* 'leopard'.

Cheever /ˈtʃiːvə/, John (1912–82), American short-story writer and novelist. His stories frequently satirize affluent suburban New Englanders. Notable novels: *The Wapshot Chronicle* (1957).

chef ▶ noun a professional cook, typically the chief cook in a restaurant or hotel.
▶ verb (**chefs**, **cheffing**, **cheffed**) [no obj.] (usu. as noun **cheffing**) informal work as a chef.
– ORIGIN early 19th cent.: French, literally 'head'.

chef d'école /ˌʃɛf deɪˈkɒl/ ▶ **noun** (pl. **chefs d'école** pronunc. **same**) the initiator or leader of a school or style of music, painting, or literature.
– ORIGIN mid 19th cent.: French, 'head of school'.

chef-d'œuvre /ʃeɪ ˈdəːvr(ə)/ ▶ **noun** (pl. **chefs-d'œuvre** pronunc. **same**) a masterpiece.
– ORIGIN French, 'chief work'.

Chefoo /tʃiːˈfuː/ former name for **YANTAI**.

cheiro- ▶ **combining form** variant spelling of **CHIRO-**.

Cheka /ˈtʃɛkə/ an organization under the Soviet regime for the investigation of counter-revolutionary activities. It executed many real and alleged enemies of Lenin's regime from its formation in 1917 until 1922, when it was replaced by the OGPU.
– ORIGIN Russian, from *che*, *ka*, the initial letters of *Chrezvychaĭnaya komissiya* 'Extraordinary Commission (for combating Counter-revolution, Sabotage, and Speculation)'.

Chekhov /ˈtʃɛkɒf/, Anton (Pavlovich) (1860–1904), Russian dramatist and short-story writer. Chekhov's work, portraying upper-class life in pre-revolutionary Russia with a blend of naturalism and symbolism, had a considerable influence on 20th-century drama. Notable plays: *The Seagull* (1895), *Uncle Vanya* (1900), *The Three Sisters* (1901), and *The Cherry Orchard* (1904).
– DERIVATIVES **Chekhovian** /tʃɛˈkəʊvɪən/ **adjective**.

Chekiang /tʃɛˈkjaŋ/ variant of **ZHEJIANG**.

chela[1] /ˈkiːlə/ ▶ **noun** (pl. **chelae** /-liː/) Zoology a pincer-like claw, especially of a crab or other crustacean. Compare with **CHELICERA**.
– ORIGIN mid 17th cent.: modern Latin, from Latin *chele* or Greek *khēlē* 'claw'.

chela[2] /ˈtʃeɪlə/ ▶ **noun** a follower and pupil of a guru.
– ORIGIN from Hindi *celā*.

chelate /ˈkiːleɪt/ ▶ **noun** Chemistry a compound containing a ligand (typically organic) bonded to a central metal atom at two or more points.
▶ **adjective** Zoology (of an appendage) bearing chelae.
▶ **verb** [with obj.] Chemistry form a chelate with.
– DERIVATIVES **chelation** **noun**, **chelator** **noun**.

chelation therapy ▶ **noun** [mass noun] a therapy for mercury or lead poisoning that binds the toxins in the bloodstream by circulating a chelating solution. ■ a form of complementary therapy involving the intravenous infusion of substances intended to remove calcium from hardened arteries.

chelicera /kəˈlɪs(ə)rə/ ▶ **noun** (pl. **chelicerae** /-riː/) Zoology either of a pair of appendages in front of the mouth in arachnids and some other arthropods, usually modified as pincer-like claws. Compare with **CHELA**[1].
– DERIVATIVES **cheliceral** **adjective**.
– ORIGIN mid 19th cent.: modern Latin, from Greek *khēlē* 'claw' + *keras* 'horn'.

Chelicerata /kəˌlɪsəˈreɪtə/ ▶ **plural noun** Zoology a large group of arthropods that comprises the arachnids, sea spiders, and horseshoe crabs. They lack antennae, but possess a pair of chelicerae, a pair of pedipalps, and (typically) four pairs of legs. ● Subphylum Chelicerata, phylum Arthropoda.
– ORIGIN modern Latin (plural), from Greek *khēlē* 'claw' + *keras* 'horn'.

chelicerate /kəˈlɪsəreɪt, -(ə)rət/ Zoology ▶ **noun** an arthropod of the large group Chelicerata; an arachnid, sea spider, or horseshoe crab.
▶ **adjective** relating to or denoting chelicerates.

Chellean /ˈʃɛlɪən/ ▶ **adjective & noun** former term for **ABBEVILLIAN**.
– ORIGIN late 19th cent.: from French *Chelléen*, from *Chelles*, near Paris, where tools from this period were discovered.

Chelmsford /ˈtʃɛlmzfəd/ a cathedral city in SE England, the county town of Essex; pop. 107,800 (est. 2009).

Chelonia /kɪˈləʊnɪə/ ▶ **plural noun** Zoology former term for **TESTUDINES**.
– ORIGIN modern Latin (plural), from Greek *khelōnē* 'tortoise'.

chelonian /kɪˈləʊnɪən/ Zoology ▶ **noun** a reptile of the order Testudines (formerly Chelonia); a turtle, terrapin, or tortoise.
▶ **adjective** relating to or denoting chelonians.

Chelsea a residential district of London, on the north bank of the River Thames.

Chelsea boot ▶ **noun** an elastic-sided boot, typically with a high heel.

Chelsea bun ▶ **noun** Brit. a flat, spiral-shaped currant bun sprinkled with sugar.
– ORIGIN early 18th cent.: named after **CHELSEA**, where such buns were originally made.

Chelsea pensioner ▶ **noun** (in the UK) an inmate of the Chelsea Royal Hospital for old or disabled soldiers.

Chelsea tractor ▶ **noun** Brit. informal a large four-wheel drive vehicle used mainly in urban areas.

Chelsea ware ▶ **noun** [mass noun] a type of soft-paste porcelain made at Chelsea in the 18th century.

Cheltenham /ˈtʃɛlt(ə)nəm/ a town in western England, in Gloucestershire; pop. 104,300 (est. 2009). It became a fashionable spa town in the 19th century.

Chelyabinsk /tʃɪlˈjɑːbɪnsk/ an industrial city in southern Russia on the eastern slopes of the Ural Mountains; pop. 1,092,500 (est. 2008).

chemi- ▶ **combining form** representing **CHEMICAL**.

chemical ▶ **adjective** relating to chemistry, or the interactions of substances as studied in chemistry: *the chemical composition of the atmosphere*. ■ relating to chemicals: *chemical treatments for killing fungi*. ■ relating to or denoting the use of poison gas or other chemicals as weapons of war.
▶ **noun** a distinct compound or substance, especially one which has been artificially prepared or purified: *never mix disinfectant with other chemicals*. ■ an addictive drug: [as modifier] *chemical dependency*.
– DERIVATIVES **chemically** **adverb**.
– ORIGIN late 16th cent.: from French *chimique* or modern Latin *chimicus*, *chymicus*, from medieval Latin *alchymicus*, from *alchimia* (see **ALCHEMY**).

chemical bond ▶ **noun** see **BOND** (sense 3 of the noun).

chemical compound ▶ **noun** see **COMPOUND**[1].

chemical engineering ▶ **noun** [mass noun] the branch of engineering concerned with the design and operation of industrial chemical plants.
– DERIVATIVES **chemical engineer** **noun**.

chemical formula ▶ **noun** see **FORMULA** (sense 1).

chemical potential ▶ **noun** Chemistry a thermodynamic function expressing the ability of an uncharged atom or molecule in a chemical system to perform physical work.

chemical reaction ▶ **noun** a process that involves rearrangement of the molecular or ionic structure of a substance, as distinct from a change in physical form or a nuclear reaction.

chemical weathering ▶ **noun** [mass noun] the erosion or disintegration of rocks, building materials, etc., caused by chemical reactions (chiefly with water and substances dissolved in it) rather than by mechanical processes.

chemico- ▶ **combining form** representing **CHEMICAL**.

chemiluminescence ▶ **noun** [mass noun] the emission of light during a chemical reaction which does not produce significant quantities of heat.
– DERIVATIVES **chemiluminescent** **adjective**.

chemin de fer /ʃəˌmã də ˈfɛː/ ▶ **noun** [mass noun] a card game which is a variety of baccarat.
– ORIGIN late 19th cent.: French, literally 'railway'.

chemise /ʃəˈmiːz/ ▶ **noun** a dress hanging straight from the shoulders, popular in the 1920s. ■ a woman's loose-fitting undergarment or nightdress. ■ a priest's alb or surplice. ■ historical a smock.
– ORIGIN Middle English: from Old French, from late Latin *camisia* 'shirt or nightgown'.

chemisette /ˌʃɛmɪˈzɛt/ ▶ **noun** a woman's undergarment similar to a camisole.
– ORIGIN early 19th cent.: French, diminutive of *chemise*.

chemisorption /ˌkɛmɪˈsɔːpʃ(ə)n, -ˈzɔːp-/ ▶ **noun** [mass noun] Chemistry adsorption in which the adsorbed substance is held by chemical bonds.
– DERIVATIVES **chemisorbed** **adjective**.
– ORIGIN 1930s: from **CHEMI-** + a shortened form of **ADSORPTION** (see **ADSORB**).

chemist ▶ **noun** **1** Brit. a shop where medicinal drugs are dispensed and sold, and in which toiletries and other medical goods can be purchased. ■ a person authorized to dispense medicinal drugs.
2 a person engaged in chemical research or experiments.
– ORIGIN late Middle English (denoting an alchemist): from French *chimiste*, from modern Latin *chimista*, from *alchimista* 'alchemist', from *alchimia* (see **ALCHEMY**).

chemistry ▶ **noun** (pl. **chemistries**) [mass noun] **1** the branch of science concerned with the substances of which matter is composed, the investigation of their properties and reactions, and the use of such reactions to form new substances. ■ the chemical composition and properties of a substance or body.
2 the complex emotional or psychological interaction between people: *their affair was triggered by intense sexual chemistry*.

Chemnitz /ˈkɛmnɪts/ an industrial city in eastern Germany, on the Chemnitz River; pop. 245,700 (est. 2006). Former name (from 1953) **KARL-MARX-STADT**.

chemo /ˈkiːməʊ/ ▶ **noun** [mass noun] informal chemotherapy.

chemo- ▶ **combining form** representing **CHEMICAL**.

chemoattractant /ˌkiːməʊəˈtraktənt, ˌkɛm-/ ▶ **noun** Biology a substance which attracts motile cells of a particular type.

chemoautotroph /ˌkiːməʊˈɔːtətrəʊf, -trɒf, ˌkɛm-/ ▶ **noun** Biology an organism, typically a bacterium, which derives energy from the oxidation of inorganic compounds.
– DERIVATIVES **chemoautotrophic** /-ˈtrəʊfɪk, -ˈtrɒfɪk/ **adjective**,.

chemoprophylaxis /ˌkiːməʊprɒfɪˈlaksɪs, ˌkɛm-/ ▶ **noun** [mass noun] the use of drugs to prevent disease.
– DERIVATIVES **chemoprophylactic** **adjective**.

chemoreceptor /ˈkiːməʊrɪˌsɛptə, ˌkɛm-/ ▶ **noun** Physiology a sensory cell or organ responsive to chemical stimuli.
– DERIVATIVES **chemoreception** **noun**.

chemosensory /ˌkiːməʊˈsɛns(ə)ri/ ▶ **adjective** Physiology (of a sense organ or receptor) responsive to chemical stimuli. ■ of or relating to such organs or their action: *patients with chemosensory impairment*.

chemostat /ˈkiːmə(ʊ)stat, ˌkɛm-/ ▶ **noun** a system in which the chemical composition is kept at a controlled level, especially for the culture of microorganisms.

chemosynthesis /ˌkiːmə(ʊ)ˈsɪnθɪsɪs, ˌkɛm-/ ▶ **noun** [mass noun] Biology the synthesis of organic compounds by bacteria or other living organisms using energy derived from reactions involving inorganic chemicals, typically in the absence of sunlight. Compare with **PHOTOSYNTHESIS**.
– DERIVATIVES **chemosynthetic** **adjective**.

chemotaxis /ˌkiːmə(ʊ)ˈtaksɪs, ˌkɛm-/ ▶ **noun** [mass noun] Biology movement of a motile cell or organism, or part of one, in a direction corresponding to a gradient of increasing or decreasing concentration of a particular substance.
– DERIVATIVES **chemotactic** **adjective**.

chemotherapy /ˌkiːmə(ʊ)ˈθɛrəpi, ˌkɛm-/ ▶ **noun** [mass noun] the treatment of disease by the use of chemical substances, especially the treatment of cancer by cytotoxic and other drugs.
– DERIVATIVES **chemotherapist** **noun**.

chempaka /ˈtʃɛmpəkə/ ▶ **noun** variant spelling of **CHAMPAK**.

chemurgy /ˈkɛməːdʒi/ ▶ **noun** [mass noun] N. Amer. the chemical and industrial use of organic raw materials.
– ORIGIN 1930s: from **CHEMO-**, on the pattern of *metallurgy*.

Chenab /tʃɪˈnɑːb/ a river of northern India and Pakistan, which rises in the Himalayas and flows through Himachal Pradesh and Jammu and Kashmir, to join the Sutlej River in Punjab. It is one of the five rivers that gave Punjab its name.

chenar ▶ **noun** variant spelling of **CHINAR**.

Chen-chiang /tʃɛnˈtʃjaŋ/ variant of **ZHENJIANG**.

Chengchow /tʃɛŋˈtʃaʊ/ variant of **ZHENGZHOU**.

Chengdu /tʃɛŋˈduː/ the capital of Sichuan province in west central China; pop. 3,582,000 (est. 2006).

chenille /ʃəˈniːl/ ▶ **noun** [mass noun] a tufty, velvety cord or yarn, used for trimming furniture and made into carpets or clothing.
– ORIGIN mid 18th cent.: from French, literally 'hairy caterpillar', from Latin *canicula* 'small dog', diminutive of *canis*.

Chenin /ˈʃənã/ (also **Chenin blanc**) ▶ **noun** [mass noun] a variety of wine grape native to the Loire valley but widely cultivated elsewhere. ■ a white wine made from the Chenin grape.
– ORIGIN French, perhaps from the name of the manor of Mont-*Chenin*, Touraine.

Chennai /tʃɪnʌɪ/ a seaport on the east coast of India, capital of Tamil Nadu; pop. 4,590,300 (est. 2009). Former name (until 1995) **MADRAS**.

cheongsam /tʃɪɒŋˈsam, tʃɒŋ-/ ▶ **noun** a straight, close-fitting silk dress with a high neck and slit skirt, worn by Chinese and Indonesian women.

– ORIGIN Chinese (Cantonese dialect).

Cheops /ˈkiːɒps/ (*fl.* early 26th century BC), Egyptian pharaoh of the 4th dynasty; Egyptian name **Khufu**. He commissioned the building of the Great Pyramid at Giza.

cheque (US **check**) ▶ **noun** an order to a bank to pay a stated sum from the drawer's account, written on a specially printed form.
– ORIGIN early 18th cent. (originally denoting a counterfoil, or a form with a counterfoil): variant of CHECK[1], in the sense 'device for checking the amount of an item'.

chequebook ▶ **noun** a book of printed cheques ready for use.

chequebook journalism ▶ **noun** [mass noun] the practice of paying a large amount of money to acquire the exclusive right to publish a person's story in a newspaper.

chequer (US **checker**) ▶ **noun** **1** (**chequers**) a pattern of squares, typically alternately coloured: *a geometric shape bordered by chequers* | (as modifier **chequer**) *a chequer design*.
2 (**checkers**) [treated as sing.] N. Amer. the game of draughts. ■ (**checker**) a piece used in the game of draughts.
▶ **verb** [with obj.] divide into or mark with an arrangement of squares of different colour or character: *a great plain chequered with corn and green mosses*.
– ORIGIN Middle English: from EXCHEQUER. The original sense 'chessboard' gave rise to *chequered* meaning 'marked like a chessboard'; hence sense 1 of the noun (early 16th cent.).

chequerboard (US **checkerboard**) ▶ **noun** a board for playing checkers (draughts) and similar games, having a regular pattern of squares in alternating colours, typically black and white. ■ a pattern resembling such a board.

chequered (US **checkered**) ▶ **adjective** **1** having a pattern consisting of alternating squares of different colours.
2 marked by periods of varied fortune or discreditable incidents: *the chequered history of post-war Britain*.

chequered flag ▶ **noun** Motor Racing a flag with a black-and-white chequered pattern, displayed to drivers at the end of a race.
– PHRASES **take the chequered flag** finish first in a race.

Chequers a Tudor mansion in Buckinghamshire which serves as a country seat of the British Prime Minister in office.

Cher /ʃɛː/ a river of central France, which rises in the Massif Central, flowing 350 km (220 miles) northwards to meet the Loire near Tours.

Cherbourg /ˈʃəːbʊəɡ/, French /ʃɛʀbuʀ/ a seaport and naval base in Normandy, northern France; pop. 42,113 (2006).

Cheremis /ˈtʃɛrəmɪs/ ▶ **noun** former term for the Mari language (see MARI[2]).

Cherenkov /tʃɪˈrɛŋkɒf/ (also **Cerenkov**), Pavel (Alekseevich) (1904–90), Soviet physicist. He investigated the effects of high-energy particles and shared the 1958 Nobel Prize for Physics for discovering the cause of blue light (now called CERENKOV RADIATION) emitted by radioactive substances underwater.

Cherenkov radiation ▶ **noun** variant spelling of CERENKOV RADIATION.

Cherepovets /ˌtʃɛrɪpəˈvjɛts/ a city in NW Russia, on the Rybinsk reservoir; pop. 308,000 (est. 2008).

cherimoya /ˌtʃɛrɪˈmɔɪə/ (also **chirimoya**) ▶ **noun** **1** a kind of custard apple with scaly green skin and a flavour resembling that of pineapple.
2 the small tree which bears the cherimoya fruit, native to the Andes of Peru and Ecuador. ● *Annona cherimola*, family Annonaceae.
– ORIGIN mid 18th cent.: from Spanish, from Quechua, from *chiri* 'cold or refreshing' + *muya* 'circle'.

cherish ▶ **verb** [with obj.] protect and care for (someone) lovingly. ■ hold (something) dear: *I cherish the letters she wrote*. ■ keep (a hope or ambition) in one's mind: *he had long cherished a secret fantasy about his future*.
– ORIGIN Middle English (in the sense 'treat with affection'): from Old French *cheriss-*, lengthened stem of *cherir*, from *cher* 'dear', from Latin *carus*.

Cherkasy /tʃəˈkasi/ a port in central Ukraine, on the River Dnieper; pop. 288,600 (est. 2009). Russian name **Cherkassy**.

Cherkess /tʃəˈkɛs/ ▶ **noun** another term for CIRCASSIAN.

Cherkessk /tʃəˈkɛsk/ a city in the Caucasus in southern Russia, capital of the republic of Karachai-Cherkessia; pop 121,700 (est. 2002).

Chernenko /tʃəˈnjɛŋkəʊ/, Konstantin (Ustinovich) (1911–85), Soviet statesman, General Secretary of the Communist Party of the USSR and President 1984–5. He died after only thirteen months in office and was succeeded by Mikhail Gorbachev.

Chernihiv /tʃɛːˈniːhɪv/ a port in northern Ukraine, on the River Desna; pop. 297,800 (est. 2009). Russian name **Chernigov** /tʃəˈniːɡɒf/.

Chernivtsi /tʃəˈnɪvtsi/ a city in western Ukraine, in the foothills of the Carpathians, close to the border with Romania; pop. 249,500 (est. 2009). It was part of Romania between 1918 and 1940. Russian name **Chernovtsy** /ˌtʃɛrnəvˈtsi/.

Chernobyl /tʃəˈnɒbɪl, -ˈnəʊbɪl/ a town near Kiev in Ukraine where, in April 1986, an accident at a nuclear power station resulted in a serious escape of radioactive material.

Chernorechye /ˌtʃəːnəˈrɛtʃjə/ former name (until 1919) for DZERZHINSK.

chernozem /ˈtʃəːnəzɛm/ ▶ **noun** Soil Science a fertile black soil rich in humus and with a lighter lime-rich layer beneath, typically occurring in the temperate grasslands of the Russian steppes and North American prairies.
– ORIGIN mid 19th cent.: from Russian, from *chërnyĭ* 'black' + *zemlya* 'earth'.

Cherokee /ˌtʃɛrəˈkiː/ ▶ **noun** (pl. **same** or **Cherokees**) **1** a member of an American Indian people formerly inhabiting much of the southern US, now living on reservations in Oklahoma and North Carolina.
2 [mass noun] the Iroquoian language of the Cherokee, which has had its own script since 1820 and has about 11,000 speakers.
▶ **adjective** relating to the Cherokee or their language.
– ORIGIN from obsolete Cherokee *tsaraki*, earlier form of *tsaliki*.

Cherokee rose ▶ **noun** a climbing Chinese rose with fragrant white flowers, which has become naturalized in the southern US. ● *Rosa laevigata*, family Rosaceae.

cheroot /ʃəˈruːt/ ▶ **noun** a cigar with both ends open.
– ORIGIN late 17th cent.: from French *cheroute*, from Tamil *curuṭṭu* 'roll of tobacco'.

cherry ▶ **noun** (pl. **cherries**) **1** a small, soft round stone fruit that is typically bright or dark red.
2 (also **cherry tree**) the tree that bears the cherry. ● Genus *Prunus*, family Rosaceae: several species, the edible kinds being derived from the **sweet** (or **wild**) **cherry** (*P. avium*) and the **sour** (or **morello**) **cherry** (*P. cerasus*). ■ (also **cherrywood**) [mass noun] the wood of the cherry tree.
3 [mass noun] a bright deep red colour.
4 (**one's cherry**) informal one's virginity.
– PHRASES **a bite at the cherry** Brit. an attempt or opportunity to do something. **a bowl of cherries** [usu. with negative] a very pleasant or enjoyable situation or experience: *life isn't exactly a bowl of cherries*. **the cherry on the cake** (or **on top**) a desirable feature perceived as the finishing touch to something that is already very good: *the car is faster than a Ferrari, but the cherry on the cake is the price*.
– ORIGIN Middle English: from Old Northern French *cherise*, from medieval Latin *ceresia*, based on Greek *kerasos* 'cherry tree, cherry'. The final *-s* was lost because *cherise* was interpreted as plural (compare with CAPER[2] and PEA).

cherry brandy ▶ **noun** [mass noun] a sweet, dark red, cherry-flavoured liqueur made with brandy in which cherries have been steeped, or with crushed cherry stones.

cherry laurel ▶ **noun** an evergreen shrub or small tree with leathery leaves, white flowers, and cherry-like fruits, native to the Balkans and widely cultivated as the common 'laurel' of gardens. ● *Prunus laurocerasus*, family Rosaceae.

cherry-pick ▶ **verb** [with obj.] selectively choose (the most beneficial or profitable items, opportunities, etc.) from what is available: *the company should buy the whole airline and not just cherry-pick its best assets*.

cherry picker ▶ **noun** informal **1** a hydraulic crane with a railed platform at the end for raising and lowering people, for instance to work on overhead cables.
2 a person who cherry-picks.

cherry pie ▶ **noun** a garden heliotrope with fragrant blue flowers. ● Genus *Heliotropium*, family Boraginaceae: several species.

cherry plum ▶ **noun** a SW Asian shrub or small tree with white flowers and small red and yellow edible fruit. Also called MYROBALAN. ● *Prunus cerasifera*, family Rosaceae.
■ the fruit of the cherry plum tree.

cherry tomato ▶ **noun** a miniature tomato with a strong flavour.

Chersonese /ˈkəːsəniːz/ ancient name for the Gallipoli peninsula.
– ORIGIN from Latin *chersonesus*, from Greek *khersonēsos*, from *khersos* 'dry' + *nēsos* 'island'.

chert /tʃəːt/ ▶ **noun** [mass noun] a hard, dark, opaque rock composed of silica (chalcedony) with an amorphous or microscopically fine-grained texture. It occurs as nodules (flint) or, less often, in massive beds.
– DERIVATIVES **cherty** **adjective**.
– ORIGIN late 17th cent. (originally dialect): of unknown origin.

cherub ▶ **noun** (pl. **cherubim**) a winged angelic being described in biblical tradition as attending on God, represented in ancient Middle Eastern art as a lion or bull with eagles' wings and a human face and regarded in traditional Christian angelology as an angel of the second highest order of the ninefold celestial hierarchy. ■ (pl. **cherubim** or **cherubs**) a representation of a cherub in Western art, depicted as a chubby, healthy-looking child with wings. ■ (pl. **cherubs**) a beautiful or innocent-looking child.
– ORIGIN Old English *cherubin*, ultimately (via Latin and Greek) from Hebrew *kĕrūb*, plural *kĕrūbīm*. A rabbinic folk etymology, which explains the Hebrew singular form as representing Aramaic *kĕ-rabyā* 'like a child', led to the representation of the cherub as a child.

cherubic /tʃɪˈruːbɪk/ ▶ **adjective** having the innocence or plump prettiness of a young child: *a round, cherubic face*.
– DERIVATIVES **cherubically** **adverb**.

Cherubini /ˌkɛrʊˈbiːni/, (Maria) Luigi (Carlo Zenobio Salvatore) (1760–1842), Italian composer. He spent most of his composing career in Paris and is principally known for his church music and operas.

chervil /ˈtʃəːvɪl/ ▶ **noun** [mass noun] a Eurasian plant of the parsley family, with delicate fern-like leaves which are used as a culinary herb. ● *Anthriscus cerefolium*, family Umbelliferae.
– ORIGIN Old English, from Latin *chaerephylla*, from Greek *khairephullon*.

chervonets /ˌtʃəːvəʊˈnjɛts/ ▶ **noun** (pl. **chervontsy**) a pre-Revolutionary Russian gold coin, worth three roubles. ■ a currency note introduced by the Bolsheviks in 1922, worth ten roubles.
– ORIGIN Russian.

Ches. ▶ **abbreviation** Cheshire.

Chesapeake Bay /ˈtʃɛsəpiːk/ a large inlet of the North Atlantic on the US coast, extending 320 km (200 miles) northwards through the states of Virginia and Maryland.

chesed /ˈxɛsəd/ ▶ **noun** [mass noun] Judaism the attribute of grace, benevolence, or compassion, especially (in Kabbalism) as one of the sephiroth.
– ORIGIN Hebrew *ḥeseḏ* 'grace, loving-kindness'.

Cheshire[1] /ˈtʃɛʃɪə, -ʃə/ a county of west central England; county town, Chester.

Cheshire[2] /ˈtʃɛʃə/, (Geoffrey) Leonard (1917–92), British airman and philanthropist. A bomber pilot in the Second World War, he later founded the Cheshire Foundation Homes for disabled and incurably sick people.

Cheshire[3] /ˈtʃɛʃə/ ▶ **noun** [mass noun] a kind of firm crumbly cheese, originally made in Cheshire.

Cheshire cat ▶ **noun** a cat depicted with a broad fixed grin, as popularized through Lewis Carroll's *Alice's Adventures in Wonderland* (1865).
– PHRASES **grin like a Cheshire cat** have a broad fixed smile on one's face.
– ORIGIN late 18th cent.: of unknown origin, but it is said that *Cheshire* cheeses used to be marked with the face of a smiling cat.

Chesil Beach /ˈtʃɛz(ə)l/ (also **Chesil Bank**) a shingle beach in southern England, off the Dorset coast. It is over 25 km (17 miles) long and encloses a tidal lagoon.

chess ▶ **noun** [mass noun] a board game of strategic skill for two players, played on a chequered board on which each playing piece is moved according to precise rules. The object is to put the opponent's king under a direct attack from which escape is impossible (*checkmate*).

– ORIGIN Middle English: from Old French *esches*, plural of *eschec* 'a check' (see CHECK[1]).

chessboard ▸ noun a square board divided into sixty-four alternating dark and light squares (conventionally called 'black' and 'white'), used for playing chess or draughts (checkers).

chessman ▸ noun (pl. **chessmen**) a solid figure used as a chess piece.

chess set ▸ noun a chessboard and a set of chessmen.

chest ▸ noun **1** the front surface of a person's or animal's body between the neck and the stomach. ■ the whole of a person's upper trunk, especially as considered with reference to their respiratory health or to their size of clothes: *a bad chest* | *a 42-inch chest*.
2 a large strong box, typically made of wood and used for storage or transport. ■ a small cabinet for medicines, toiletries, etc.: *the medicine chest*. ■ Brit. the treasury or financial resources of some institutions: *the university chest*.
▸ verb [with obj. and adverbial of direction] Soccer propel (the ball) by means of one's chest.
– PHRASES **get something off one's chest** informal say something that one has wanted to say for a long time, resulting in a feeling of relief. **play** (or **keep**) **one's cards close to one's chest** (or N. Amer. **vest**) informal be extremely secretive and cautious about one's intentions.
– DERIVATIVES **chested** adjective [in combination] *a broad-chested athlete*.
– ORIGIN Old English *cest*, *cyst*, related to Dutch *kist* and German *Kiste*, based on Greek *kistē* 'box'.

Chester a city in NW England, the county town of Cheshire; pop. 80,600 (est. 2009).

Chesterfield a town in Derbyshire, north central England; pop. 71,100 (est. 2009).

chesterfield ▸ noun **1** a sofa with padded arms and back of the same height and curved outwards at the top. ■ Canadian any sofa.
2 a man's plain straight overcoat, typically with a velvet collar.
– ORIGIN mid 19th cent. (in sense 2): named after a 19th-cent. Earl of CHESTERFIELD.

Chesterton, G. K. (1874–1936), English essayist, novelist, and critic; full name *Gilbert Keith Chesterton*. His novels include *The Napoleon of Notting Hill* (1904) and a series of detective stories featuring Father Brown, a priest with a talent for crime detection.

Chester White ▸ noun a pig of a prolific white breed, developed in North America.
– ORIGIN named after *Chester* county, Pennsylvania.

chest freezer ▸ noun a freezer with a hinged lid rather than a door.

chestnut ▸ noun **1** (also **sweet chestnut**) a glossy hard brown edible nut which develops within a bristly case and which may be roasted and eaten. ■ [mass noun] a deep reddish-brown colour. ■ (also **chesnut**) a horse of a reddish-brown or yellowish-brown colour, with a brown mane and tail.
2 (also **chestnut tree**, **sweet chestnut**, or **Spanish chestnut**) the large European tree that produces the edible chestnut, with serrated leaves and heavy timber. ● *Castanea sativa*, family Fagaceae.
■ short for HORSE CHESTNUT.
3 a small horny patch on the inside of each of a horse's legs.
– PHRASES **an old chestnut** a joke, story, or subject that has become tedious and uninteresting through constant repetition. **pull someone's chestnuts out of the fire** succeed in a hazardous undertaking for someone else's benefit. [with reference to the fable of a monkey using a cat's paw to extract roasting chestnuts from a fire.]
– ORIGIN early 16th cent.: from Old English *chesten* (from Old French *chastaine*, via Latin from Greek *kastanea*) + NUT.

chestnut oak ▸ noun a North American oak which has leaves resembling those of the chestnut. ● Genus *Quercus*, family Fagaceae: several species.

chest of drawers ▸ noun a piece of furniture used for storage, consisting of an upright frame into which drawers are fitted.

chest voice ▸ noun [in sing.] the lowest register of the voice in singing or speaking.

chesty ▸ adjective (**chestier**, **chestiest**) informal **1** Brit. having a lot of catarrh in the lungs.
2 (of a woman) having large or prominent breasts.
3 N. Amer. conceited and arrogant.
– DERIVATIVES **chestily** adverb, **chestiness** noun.

Chesvan /ˈxɛsv(ə)n/ variant spelling of HESVAN.

Chetnik /ˈtʃɛtnɪk/ ▸ noun a member of a Slavic nationalist guerrilla force in the Balkans, especially during the Second World War.
– ORIGIN early 20th cent.: from Serbian *četnik*, from *četa* 'band, troop'.

chetrum /ˈtʃɛtru:m/ ▸ noun (pl. **same** or **chetrums**) a monetary unit of Bhutan, equal to one hundredth of a ngultrum.
– ORIGIN Dzongkha.

Chetumal /ˌtʃɛtʊˈmɑ:l/ a port in SE Mexico, on the Yucatán Peninsula at the border with Belize, capital of the state of Quintana Roo; pop. 136,825 (2005).

cheval glass /ʃəˈval/ (also **cheval mirror**) ▸ noun a tall mirror fitted at its middle to an upright frame so that it can be tilted.
– ORIGIN mid 19th cent.: *cheval* from French, in the sense 'frame'.

Chevalier /ʃəˈvalɪeɪ/, French /ʃ(ə)valje/, Maurice (1888–1972), French singer and actor. Notable films: *Innocents of Paris* (1929) and *Gigi* (1958).

chevalier /ˌʃɛvəˈlɪə/ ▸ noun historical a knight. ■ a member of certain orders of knighthood or of modern French orders such as the Legion of Honour. ■ (**Chevalier**) Brit. historical a title of the Old and Young Pretenders.
– ORIGIN late Middle English (denoting a horseman or mounted knight): from Old French, from medieval Latin *caballarius*, from Latin *caballus* 'horse'. Compare with CABALLERO and CAVALIER.

chevet /ʃəˈveɪ/ ▸ noun Architecture (in large churches) an apse with an ambulatory giving access behind the high altar to a series of chapels set in bays.
– ORIGIN early 19th cent.: from French, literally 'pillow', from Latin *capitium*, from *caput* 'head'.

Cheviot /ˈtʃɛvɪət, ˈtʃi:v-/ ▸ noun a large sheep of a breed with short thick wool. ■ (**cheviot**) [mass noun] the wool or tweed cloth obtained from the Cheviot sheep.

Cheviot Hills /ˈtʃɛvɪət, ˈtʃi:v-/ (also **the Cheviots**) a range of hills on the border between England and Scotland.

chèvre /ʃɛvr(ə)/ ▸ noun [mass noun] French cheese made with goat's milk.
– ORIGIN French, literally 'goat, she-goat', from Latin *capra*.

chevron ▸ noun a V-shaped line or stripe, especially one on the sleeve of a uniform indicating rank or length of service. ■ Heraldry an ordinary in the form of a broad inverted V-shape.
– ORIGIN late Middle English (in heraldic use): from Old French, based on Latin *caper* 'goat'; compare with Latin *capreoli* (diminutive of *caper*) used to mean 'pair of rafters'.

chevrotain /ˈʃɛvrəteɪn/ ▸ noun a small deer-like mammal with small tusks, typically nocturnal and found in the tropical rainforests of Africa and southern Asia. Also called MOUSE DEER. ● Family Tragulidae: genera *Tragulus* (three Asian species) and *Hyemoschus* (one African species).
– ORIGIN late 18th cent.: from French, diminutive of Old French *chevrot*, diminutive of *chèvre* 'goat'.

Chevy /ˈʃɛvi/ (also **Chevvy**) ▸ noun (pl. **Chevys** or **Chevvys**) informal a Chevrolet car.

chevy ▸ verb variant spelling of CHIVVY.

chew ▸ verb [with obj.] bite and work (food) in the mouth with the teeth, especially to make it easier to swallow: *he was chewing a mouthful of toast* | [no obj.] *he chewed for a moment, then swallowed*. ■ gnaw at (something) persistently: *he chewed his lip reflectively* | [no obj.] *she chewed at a fingernail*.
▸ noun a repeated biting or gnawing of something. ■ something that is meant for chewing: *a dog chew* | *a chew of tobacco*. ■ a chewy sweet.
– PHRASES **chew the cud** see CUD. **chew the fat** (or **rag**) informal chat in a leisurely and prolonged way.
– PHRASAL VERBS **chew someone out** N. Amer. informal reprimand someone severely: *he chewed me out for being late*. **chew something over** discuss or consider something at length: *executives met to chew over the company's future*. **chew something up** damage or destroy something as if by chewing: *the bikes were chewing up the paths*.
– DERIVATIVES **chewable** adjective, **chewer** noun [usu. in combination] *a tobacco-chewer*.
– ORIGIN Old English *cēowan*, of West Germanic origin; related to Dutch *kauwen* and German *kauen*.

chewing gum ▸ noun [mass noun] flavoured gum for chewing, typically made from chicle.

chew stick ▸ noun a Caribbean climbing plant of the buckthorn family, the twigs or bark of which are chewed to clean the teeth, for their flavour, or as a stimulant. ● *Gouania domingensis*, family Rhamnaceae.

chewy ▸ adjective (**chewier**, **chewiest**) (of food) needing to be chewed hard or for some time before being swallowed.
– DERIVATIVES **chewiness** noun.

Cheyenne[1] /ʃʌɪˈan, -ˈɛn/ the state capital of Wyoming; pop. 56,915 (est. 2008).

Cheyenne[2] /ʃʌɪˈan/ ▸ noun (pl. **same** or **Cheyennes**)
1 a member of an American Indian people formerly living between the Missouri and Arkansas Rivers but now on reservations in Montana and Oklahoma.
2 [mass noun] the Algonquian language of the Cheyenne, now almost extinct.
▸ adjective relating to the Cheyenne or their language.
– ORIGIN Canadian French, from Dakota *šahíyena*, from *šaia* 'speak incoherently', from *ša* 'red' + *ya* 'speak'.

Cheyne–Stokes breathing /tʃeɪn/ ▸ noun [mass noun] Medicine a cyclical pattern of breathing in which movement gradually decreases to a complete stop and then returns to normal. It occurs in various medical conditions, and at high altitudes.
– ORIGIN late 19th cent.: named after John *Cheyne* (1777–1836), Scottish physician, and William *Stokes* (1804–78), Irish physician.

chez /ʃeɪ/ ▸ preposition at the home of (used in conscious imitation of French): *I spent one summer chez Grandma*.
– ORIGIN mid 18th cent.: French, from Old French *chiese*, from Latin *casa* 'cottage'.

Chhattisgarh /ˌtʃatɪzˈgɑ:/ a state in central India, formed in 2000 from the SE part of Madhya Pradesh; capital, Raipur.

chhi-chhi /ˈtʃi:tʃi:/ (also **chee-chee**) ▸ exclamation Indian used to express disgust.
– ORIGIN perhaps from Hindi *chī-chī!* 'shame on you!' (literally 'dirt, excrement').

chi[1] /kʌɪ/ ▸ noun the twenty-second letter of the Greek alphabet (Χ, χ), transliterated as 'kh' or 'ch'. ■ (**Chi**) [followed by Latin genitive] Astronomy the twenty-second star in a constellation: *Chi Ophiuchi*.
– ORIGIN Greek.

chi[2] /ki:/ (also **qi** or **ki**) ▸ noun [mass noun] the circulating life force whose existence and properties are the basis of much Chinese philosophy and medicine.
– ORIGIN from Chinese *qì*, literally 'air, breath'.

Chiang Kai-shek /ˌtʃjaŋ kʌɪˈʃɛk/ (also **Jiang Jie Shi**) (1887–1975), Chinese statesman and general, President of China 1928–31 and 1943–9 and of Taiwan 1950–75. He tried to unite China by military means in the 1930s but was defeated by the communists after the end of the Second World War. Forced to abandon mainland China in 1949, he set up a separate Nationalist Chinese State in Taiwan.

Chiangmai /tʃjaŋˈmʌɪ/ a city in NW Thailand; pop. 148,800 (est. 2007).

Chianina /ˌkɪəˈni:nə/ ▸ noun an animal of a very large white breed of cattle, kept for its lean meat.
– ORIGIN from Italian.

Chianti /kɪˈanti/ ▸ noun (pl. **Chiantis**) [mass noun] a dry red Italian wine produced in Tuscany.
– ORIGIN named after the *Chianti* Mountains, Italy.

Chiapas /tʃɪˈɑ:pəs/ a state of southern Mexico, bordering Guatemala; capital, Tuxtla Gutiérrez.

chiaroscuro /kɪˌɑ:rəˈskʊərəʊ/ ▸ noun [mass noun] the treatment of light and shade in drawing and painting. ■ an effect of contrasted light and shadow: *the chiaroscuro of cobbled streets*.
– ORIGIN mid 17th cent.: from Italian, from *chiaro* 'clear, bright' (from Latin *clarus*) + *oscuro* 'dark, obscure' (from Latin *obscurus*).

chiasma /kʌɪˈazmə, kɪ-/ ▸ noun (pl. **chiasmata** /-tə/)
1 (also **optic chiasma**) Anatomy the X-shaped structure formed at the point below the brain where the two optic nerves cross over each other.
2 Biology a point at which paired chromosomes remain in contact during the first metaphase of meiosis, and at which crossing over and exchange of genetic material occur between the strands.
– ORIGIN mid 19th cent.: modern Latin, from Greek *chiasma* 'crosspiece, cross-shaped mark', from *khiazein* 'mark with the letter chi'.

chiasmus /kʌɪˈazməs, kɪ-/ ▸ noun a rhetorical or literary figure in which words, grammatical constructions, or concepts are repeated in reverse order.
– DERIVATIVES **chiastic** adjective.
– ORIGIN mid 17th cent. (in the sense 'crosswise arrangement'): modern Latin, from Greek *khiasmos*,

from *khiazein* 'mark with the letter chi', from *khi* 'chi'.

chiastolite /kʌɪˈastəlʌɪt, kɪ-/ ▶ **noun** [mass noun] a form of the mineral andalusite containing carbonaceous inclusions giving a cross-shaped appearance.
– ORIGIN early 19th cent.: from Greek *khiastos* 'arranged crosswise' + **-LITE**.

chib Scottish ▶ **noun** a knife used as a weapon.
▶ **verb** (**chibs, chibbing, chibbed**) [with obj.] stab (someone).
– ORIGIN perhaps a variant of **SHIV**.

Chiba /ˈtʃiːbə/ a city in Japan, on the island of Honshu, east of Tokyo; pop. 910,142 (2007).

Chibcha /ˈtʃɪbtʃə/ ▶ **noun** (pl. **same** or **Chibchas**) **1** a member of an American Indian people of Colombia whose ancient civilization was destroyed by Europeans.
2 [mass noun] the extinct Chibchan language of the Chibcha.
– ORIGIN American Spanish, from Chibcha *zipa* 'chief, hereditary leader'.

Chibchan /ˈtʃɪbtʃ(ə)n/ ▶ **noun** [mass noun] a language family of Colombia and Central America, most members of which are now extinct or nearly so.
▶ **adjective** relating to Chibchan.

chibouk /tʃɪˈbuːk/ ▶ **noun** a long Turkish tobacco pipe.
– ORIGIN early 19th cent.: French *chibouque*, from Turkish *çubuk*, literally 'tube'.

chic /ʃiːk/ ▶ **adjective** (**chicer, chicest**) elegantly and stylishly fashionable: *she looked every inch the chic Frenchwoman*.
▶ **noun** [mass noun] stylishness and elegance, typically of a specified kind: *the hotel's lobby and restaurant are the height of designer chic*.
– DERIVATIVES **chicly** adverb, **chicness** noun.
– ORIGIN mid 19th cent.: from French, probably from German *Schick* 'skill'.

Chicago a city in Illinois, on Lake Michigan; pop. 2,853,114 (est. 2008). Selected as a terminal for the new Illinois and Michigan canal, Chicago developed during the 19th century as a major grain market and food-processing centre.
– DERIVATIVES **Chicagoan** noun & adjective.

Chicago Board of Trade ▶ noun see **BOARD OF TRADE** (sense 1).

Chicana /tʃɪˈkaːnə, ʃɪ-, -ˈkeɪn-/ ▶ **noun** chiefly US a female North American of Mexican origin or descent. See also **CHICANO**.
– ORIGIN Mexican Spanish, alteration of Spanish *mejicana* (feminine) 'Mexican'.

chicane /ʃɪˈkeɪn/ ▶ **noun 1** a sharp double bend created to form an obstacle on a motor-racing track or a road.
2 dated (in card games) a hand without cards of one particular suit; a void.
3 [mass noun] archaic the use of deception; chicanery.
▶ **verb** [no obj.] archaic employ chicanery. ■ [with obj.] deceive (someone).
– ORIGIN late 17th cent. (in the senses 'chicanery' and 'use chicanery'): from French *chicane* (noun), *chicaner* (verb) 'quibble', of unknown origin.

chicanery ▶ **noun** [mass noun] the use of deception or subterfuge to achieve one's purpose: *storylines packed with political chicanery*.
– ORIGIN late 16th cent.: from French *chicanerie*, from *chicaner* 'to quibble' (see **CHICANE**).

Chicano /tʃɪˈkaːnəʊ, ʃɪ-, -ˈkeɪn-/ ▶ **noun** (pl. **Chicanos**) chiefly US a North American of Mexican origin or descent. See also **CHICANA**.
– ORIGIN Mexican Spanish, alteration of Spanish *mejicano* (masculine) 'Mexican'.

chicha /ˈtʃɪtʃə/ ▶ **noun** [mass noun] (in South and Central America) a kind of beer made typically from maize.
– ORIGIN American Spanish, from Kuna.

chicharron /ˌtʃiːtʃəˈrəʊn/ ▶ **noun** (pl. **chicharrones** /-əʊnɪz/) (in Mexican cooking) a piece of fried pork crackling.
– ORIGIN from American Spanish *chicharrón*.

Chichén Itzá /tʃɪˌtʃɛn ɪtˈsaː/ a site in northern Yucatán, Mexico, the centre of the Mayan empire after AD 918.

Chichester[1] /ˈtʃɪtʃɪstə/ a city in southern England, the county town of West Sussex; pop. 29,100 (est. 2009).

Chichester[2] /ˈtʃɪtʃɪstə/, Sir Francis (Charles) (1901–72), English yachtsman. In his yacht *Gipsy Moth IV* he was the first person to sail alone round the world with only one stop (1966–7).

Chichewa /tʃɪˈtʃeɪwə/ ▶ **noun** another term for **NYANJA** (the language).

chichi[1] /ˈʃiːʃiː/ ▶ **adjective** attempting stylish elegance but achieving only an over-elaborate pretentiousness: *the tiny chichi dining room*.
▶ **noun** [mass noun] pretentious and over-elaborate refinement: *a good restaurant without the chichi traditionally associated with French food*.
– ORIGIN early 20th cent. (in the sense 'showiness or pretentious object'): from French, of imitative origin.

chichi[2] /ˈtʃiːtʃiː/ ▶ **noun** US informal a woman's breast.
– ORIGIN late 20th cent.: military slang, of Japanese origin.

Chichimec /ˌtʃiːtʃɪˈmɛk/ ▶ **noun** (pl. **same** or **Chichimecs**) **1** a member of a group of American Indian peoples, including the Toltecs and the Aztecs, dominant in central Mexico from the 10th to the 16th centuries.
2 [mass noun] a Uto-Aztecan language of the Chichimec, with some 5,000 surviving speakers.
– ORIGIN Spanish, from Nahuatl.

chick[1] ▶ **noun 1** a young bird, especially one newly hatched. ■ a newly hatched young domestic fowl.
2 informal a young woman: *she's a great-looking chick*.
– PHRASES **neither chick nor child** N. Amer. or dialect no children at all.
– ORIGIN Middle English: abbreviation of **CHICKEN**.

chick[2] ▶ **noun** (in South Asia) a folding bamboo screen for a doorway.
– ORIGIN from Urdu *chik*, from Persian *čiğh*.

chickabiddy ▶ **noun** (pl. **chickabiddies**) informal an affectionate form of address for a small child or a loved one.
– ORIGIN late 18th cent.: from **CHICK**[1] + *-a-* (for ease of pronunciation) + **BIDDY**.

chickadee ▶ **noun** North American term for **TIT**[1].
– ORIGIN mid 19th cent.: imitative of its call.

chickaree ▶ **noun** a squirrel with red fur, found in the coniferous forests of North America. ● Genus *Tamiasciurus*, family Sciuridae: three species.
– ORIGIN early 19th cent.: imitative of its call.

Chickasaw /ˈtʃɪkəsɔː/ ▶ **noun** (pl. **same** or **Chickasaws**) **1** a member of an American Indian people formerly resident in Mississippi and Alabama, and now in Oklahoma.
2 [mass noun] the Muskogean language of the Chickasaw, now all but extinct.
▶ **adjective** relating to the Chickasaw or their language.
– ORIGIN the name in Chickasaw.

chicken ▶ **noun 1** a domestic fowl kept for its eggs or meat, especially a young one. ■ [mass noun] meat from a chicken: *roast chicken*.
2 [mass noun] informal a game in which the first person to lose their nerve and withdraw from a dangerous situation is the loser. ■ [count noun] a coward.
▶ **adjective** [predic.] informal cowardly: *I was too chicken to go to court*.
▶ **verb** [no obj.] (**chicken out**) informal withdraw from or fail in something through lack of nerve: *the referee chickened out of giving a penalty*.
– PHRASES **chicken-and-egg** denoting a situation in which each of two things appears to be necessary to the other. **don't count your chickens before they're hatched** see **COUNT**[1]. **like a headless chicken** informal in a panic-stricken and unthinking manner.
– ORIGIN Old English *cīcen, cȳcen*, of Germanic origin; related to Dutch *kieken* and German *Küchlein*, and probably also to **COCK**[1].

chicken à la king ▶ **noun** [mass noun] cooked breast of chicken in a cream sauce with mushrooms and peppers.
– ORIGIN said to be named after E. Clark *King*, proprietor of a New York hotel.

chicken cholera ▶ **noun** [mass noun] an infectious disease of fowls, a form of pasteurellosis.

chicken feed ▶ **noun** [mass noun] informal a ridiculously small sum of money.

chicken-fried steak ▶ **noun** US a thin piece of beef which is lightly battered and fried until crisp.

chicken hawk ▶ **noun 1** N. Amer. a hawk of a type that is reputed to prey on domestic fowl.
2 informal an older man who seeks younger men or boys as sexual partners.

chicken-hearted (also **chicken-livered**) ▶ **adjective** easily frightened; cowardly.

Chicken Little ▶ **noun** N. Amer. an alarmist or person who panics easily.
– ORIGIN 1990s: from the name of a character in a nursery story who repeatedly warns that the sky is falling down.

chickenpox ▶ **noun** [mass noun] an infectious disease causing a mild fever and a rash of itchy inflamed pimples which turn to blisters and then loose scabs. It is caused by the herpes zoster virus and mainly affects children. Also called **VARICELLA**.
– ORIGIN early 18th cent.: probably so named because of its mildness, as compared to smallpox.

chickenshit N. Amer. vulgar slang ▶ **adjective** worthless or contemptible (used as a general term of abuse). ■ cowardly.
▶ **noun** a worthless or contemptible person. ■ [mass noun] something worthless; rubbish.

chicken wire ▶ **noun** [mass noun] light wire netting with a hexagonal mesh.

chick flick ▶ **noun** informal, chiefly derogatory a film which appeals to young women.

chickling pea ▶ **noun** another term for **GRASS PEA**.
– ORIGIN mid 16th cent.: based on obsolete *chich* 'chickpea'.

chick lit ▶ **noun** [mass noun] informal, chiefly derogatory literature which appeals to young women.

chickpea ▶ **noun 1** a round yellowish edible seed, widely used as a pulse. Also called **GARBANZO**.
2 the Old World plant of the pea family which bears chickpeas. ● *Cicer arietinum*, family Leguminosae.
– ORIGIN early 18th cent. (earlier as *chiche-pease*): from late Middle English *chiche* (from Old French *chiche, cice*, from Latin *cicer* 'chickpea') + **PEASE**.

chickweed ▶ **noun** [mass noun] a small, widespread, white-flowered plant of the pink family, often growing as a garden weed, and sometimes eaten by poultry. ● *Stellaria* and other genera, family Caryophyllaceae: several species.

chicle /ˈtʃɪk(ə)l, -kli/ ▶ **noun** [mass noun] the milky latex of the sapodilla tree, formerly chewed by the Aztecs and now used to make chewing gum. ■ another term for **SAPODILLA**.
– ORIGIN via Latin American Spanish, from Nahuatl *tzictli*.

chicory /ˈtʃɪk(ə)ri/ ▶ **noun** (pl. **chicories**) **1** Brit. a blue-flowered Mediterranean plant of the daisy family, cultivated for its edible salad leaves and carrot-shaped root. ● *Cichorium intybus*, family Compositae.
■ [mass noun] the root of the chicory plant, which is roasted and ground for use as an additive to or substitute for coffee.
2 North American term for **ENDIVE**.
– ORIGIN late Middle English: from obsolete French *cicorée* (earlier form of *chicorée*) 'endive', via Latin from Greek *kikhorion*.

chide /tʃʌɪd/ ▶ **verb** (past **chided** or archaic **chid** /tʃɪd/; past participle **chided** or archaic **chidden** /ˈtʃɪd(ə)n/) [with obj.] scold or rebuke: *she chided him for not replying to her letters* | [with direct speech] *'Now, now,' he chided*.
– DERIVATIVES **chider** noun, **chiding** adjective, **chidingly** adverb.
– ORIGIN Old English *cīdan*, of unknown origin.

chief ▶ **noun 1** a leader or ruler of a people or clan: *the chief of the village* | [as title] *Chief Banawi*. ■ the head of an organization: *a union chief* | *the chief of police*. ■ an informal form of address to a man, especially one of superior rank or status: *it's quite simple, chief*.
2 Heraldry an ordinary consisting of a broad horizontal band across the top of the shield. ■ the upper third of the field.
▶ **adjective** most important: *the chief reason for the spending cuts* | *chief among her concerns is working alone at night*. ■ having or denoting the highest rank: *the chief economist of a leading bank*.
– PHRASES **chief cook and bottle-washer** informal a person who performs a variety of important but routine tasks. **in chief** Heraldry at the top; in the upper part. See also **-IN-CHIEF**. **too many chiefs and not enough Indians** used to describe a situation where there are too many people giving orders and not enough people to carry them out.
– DERIVATIVES **chiefdom** noun.
– ORIGIN Middle English: from Old French *chief, chef*, based on Latin *caput* 'head'.

chief constable ▶ **noun** Brit. the head of the police force of a county or other region.

chief inspector ▶ **noun** Brit. a police officer ranking above inspector and below superintendent.

chiefly ▶ **adverb** mainly: *he is remembered chiefly for his organ sonatas*. ■ for the most part; mostly: *an audience consisting chiefly of women between the ages of 18 and 54*.

chief of staff ▶ **noun** the senior staff officer of a service, command, or formation.

C

chief petty officer ▶ noun a rank of non-commissioned officer in a navy, above petty officer and below warrant officer or senior chief petty officer.

chief rabbi ▶ noun (in the UK and some other countries) the leading rabbi of a national Jewish community.

chieftain ▶ noun the leader of a people or clan. ■ informal a powerful member of an organization.
– DERIVATIVES **chieftaincy** /-si/ noun (pl. **chieftaincies**), **chieftainship** noun.
– ORIGIN Middle English and Old French *chevetaine*, from late Latin *capitaneus* (see CAPTAIN). The spelling was altered by association with CHIEF.

chief technician ▶ noun a rank of non-commissioned officer in the RAF, above sergeant and below flight sergeant.

chief warrant officer ▶ noun a rank in the US armed forces, above warrant officer and below the lowest-ranking commissioned officer.

chiffchaff ▶ noun a small Eurasian and North African migratory leaf warbler with drab plumage. ● Genus *Phylloscopus*, family Sylviidae: two species.
– ORIGIN late 18th cent.: imitative of its call.

chiffon ▶ noun **1** [mass noun] a light, transparent fabric typically made of silk or nylon: [as modifier] *a chiffon blouse.*
2 [as modifier] (of a cake or dessert) made with beaten egg to give a light consistency: *chiffon cake.*
– ORIGIN mid 18th cent. (originally plural, denoting trimmings on a woman's dress): from French, from *chiffe* 'rag'.

chiffonade /ˌʃɪfəˈnɑːd/ ▶ noun a preparation of shredded or finely cut leaf vegetables, used as a garnish for soup.
– ORIGIN French, from *chiffonner* 'to crumple'.

chiffonier /ˌʃɪfəˈnɪə/ ▶ noun **1** Brit. a low cupboard either used as a sideboard or with a raised bookshelf on top.
2 N. Amer. a tall chest of drawers.
– ORIGIN mid 18th cent.: from French *chiffonnier*, *chiffonnière*, literally 'ragpicker', also denoting a chest of drawers for odds and ends.

chifforobe /ˈʃɪfərəʊb/ ▶ noun US a piece of furniture with drawers on one side and hanging space on the other.
– ORIGIN early 20th cent.: blend of CHIFFONIER and WARDROBE.

Chifley /ˈtʃɪfli/, Joseph Benedict (1885–1951), Australian Labor statesman, Prime Minister 1945–9. He continued Labor's nationalization and welfare programme and initiated Australia's immigration policy.

chigger /ˈtʃɪɡə, ˈdʒ-/ (also **jigger**) ▶ noun **1** a tropical flea, the female of which burrows and lays eggs beneath the host's skin, causing painful sores. Also called CHIGOE, SAND FLEA. ● *Tunga penetrans*, family Tungidae.
2 N. Amer. a harvest mite.
– ORIGIN mid 18th cent.: variant of CHIGOE.

chignon /ˈʃiːnjɒ̃/ ▶ noun a knot or coil of hair arranged on the back of a woman's head.
– ORIGIN late 18th cent.: from French, originally 'nape of the neck', based on Latin *catena* 'chain'.

chigoe /ˈtʃɪɡəʊ/ ▶ noun another term for CHIGGER (sense 1).
– ORIGIN mid 17th cent.: from French *chique*, from a West African language.

Chihli, Gulf of /ˈtʃiːliː/ another name for **Bo Hai**.

Chihuahua /tʃɪˈwɑːwə/ a state of northern Mexico. ■ its capital, the principal city of north central Mexico; pop. 748,518 (2005).

chihuahua /tʃɪˈwɑːwə/ ▶ noun a very small dog of a smooth-haired large-eyed breed originating in Mexico.
– ORIGIN early 19th cent.: named after CHIHUAHUA.

chikan /ˈtʃɪk(ə)n/ ▶ noun [mass noun] (in South Asia) a type of hand embroidery using cutwork and shadow work.
– ORIGIN from Urdu, from Persian *čikan*.

chikungunya /ˌtʃɪk(ə)nˈɡʌnjə/ ▶ noun [mass noun] a viral disease resembling dengue, transmitted by mosquitoes and endemic in East Africa and parts of Asia.
– ORIGIN 1950s: a local word.

chilblain ▶ noun a painful, itching swelling on a hand or foot, caused by poor circulation in the skin when exposed to cold.
– ORIGIN mid 16th cent.: from CHILL + BLAIN.

child ▶ noun (pl. **children**) a young human being below the age of puberty or below the legal age of majority. ■ a son or daughter of any age. ■ an immature or irresponsible person. ■ a person who has little or no experience in a particular area: *he's a child in financial matters.* ■ (**children**) archaic the descendants of a family or people: *the children of Abraham.* ■ (**child of**) a person regarded as the product of (a specified influence or environment): *a child of the Sixties.*
– PHRASES **child's play** a task which is easily accomplished. **with child** archaic pregnant.
– DERIVATIVES **childless** adjective, **childlessness** noun.
– ORIGIN Old English *cild*, of Germanic origin. The Middle English plural *childer* or *childre* became *childeren* or *children* by association with plurals ending in *-en*, such as *brethren*.

child abuse ▶ noun [mass noun] physical maltreatment or sexual molestation of a child.

child allowance ▶ noun informal term for CHILD BENEFIT. ■ historical (in the UK) a tax allowance granted to parents of dependent children.

childbearing ▶ noun [mass noun] the process of giving birth to children: [as modifier] *women of childbearing age.*

childbed ▶ noun archaic term for CHILDBIRTH.

child benefit ▶ noun [mass noun] (in the UK) regular payment by the state to the parents of a child up to a certain age.

childbirth ▶ noun [mass noun] the process of giving birth to a child: *she died in childbirth.*

childcare ▶ noun [mass noun] the care of children, especially by a crèche, nursery, or childminder while parents are working.

child-centred ▶ adjective giving priority to the interests and needs of children: *child-centred teaching methods.*

Childe /tʃʌɪld/ ▶ noun [in names] archaic or literary a youth of noble birth: *Childe Harold.*
– ORIGIN late Old English, variant of CHILD.

Childermas /ˈtʃɪldəmas/ ▶ noun archaic the feast of the Holy Innocents, 28 December.
– ORIGIN Old English *cildramæsse*, from *cildra* 'of children', genitive plural of *cild* (see CHILD) + *mæsse* (see MASS).

Childers /ˈtʃɪldəz/, (Robert) Erskine (1870–1922), English-born Irish writer and political activist, shot for his involvement in the Irish civil war. Notable works: *The Riddle of the Sands* (novel, 1903). His son **Erskine Hamilton Childers** (1905–74) was President of Ireland 1973–4.

childhood ▶ noun [mass noun] the state or period of being a child: *he spent his childhood in Lewes* | [as modifier] *a childhood friend.*
– ORIGIN Old English *cildhād* (see CHILD, -HOOD).

childish ▶ adjective of, like, or appropriate to a child: *childish enthusiasm.* ■ silly and immature: *a childish outburst.*
– DERIVATIVES **childishly** adverb, **childishness** noun.

child labour ▶ noun [mass noun] the employment of children in an industry or business, especially when illegal or considered exploitative.

childlike ▶ adjective (of an adult) having the good qualities, such as innocence, associated with a child: *she speaks with a childlike directness.*

childminder ▶ noun Brit. a person who looks after children in their own home for payment.
– DERIVATIVES **childminding** noun.

childproof ▶ adjective designed to prevent children from injuring themselves or doing damage: *disinfectants that are fitted with childproof caps.*
▶ verb [with obj.] make inaccessible to children: *childproof those cabinets with safety latches.*

children plural form of CHILD.

children of Israel see ISRAEL[1] (sense 1).

Children's Crusade a crusade to the Holy Land in 1212 by tens of thousands of children, chiefly from France and Germany. Most never reached their destination, and were sold into slavery.

Child Support Agency (abbrev.: **CSA**) (in the UK) a government agency responsible for the assessment and collection of compulsory child maintenance payments from absent parents.

Chile /ˈtʃɪli/, Spanish /ˈtʃile/ a country occupying a long coastal strip down the southern half of the west of South America; pop. 16,601,700 (est. 2009); official language, Spanish; capital, Santiago.

> Most of Chile was part of the Inca empire and became part of Spanish Peru after Pizarro's conquest. Independence was achieved in 1818 with help from Argentina. After the overthrow of the Marxist democrat Salvador Allende in 1973, Chile was ruled by the right-wing military dictatorship of General Pinochet until a democratically elected President took office in 1990.

– DERIVATIVES **Chilean** adjective & noun.

chile ▶ noun US spelling of CHILLI.

Chile pine ▶ noun another term for MONKEY PUZZLE.

chile relleno /ˌtʃɪlɪ rɛˈljeməʊ/ ▶ noun (pl. **chiles rellenos**) (in Mexican cuisine) a stuffed chilli pepper, typically battered and deep-fried.
– ORIGIN Spanish, 'stuffed chilli'.

Chile saltpetre ▶ noun another term for SODIUM NITRATE, especially as a commercial product.

chili ▶ noun (pl. **chilies**) US spelling of CHILLI.

chiliad /ˈkɪlɪad/ ▶ noun rare a group of a thousand things. ■ a thousand years; a millennium.
– ORIGIN late Middle English: from late Latin *chilias*, *chiliad-* 'a thousand years', from Greek *khilias*, *khiliad-*, from *khilioi* 'thousand'.

chiliarch /ˈkɪlɪɑːk/ ▶ noun (in ancient Greece) a commander of a thousand men.
– ORIGIN late 16th cent.: via late Latin from Greek *khiliarkhēs*, from *khilioi* 'thousand'.

chiliast /ˈkɪlɪast/ ▶ noun another term for MILLENARIAN.
– DERIVATIVES **chiliasm** noun.
– ORIGIN late 16th cent.: via late Latin from Greek *khiliastēs*, from *khilias* 'a thousand years', from *khilioi* 'thousand'.

chiliastic /ˌkɪlɪˈastɪk/ ▶ adjective another term for MILLENARIAN.

chili dog ▶ noun N. Amer. a hot dog garnished with chilli con carne.

chill ▶ noun **1** an unpleasant feeling of coldness in the atmosphere, one's surroundings, or the body: *there was a chill in the air* | *heat exhaustion symptoms include nausea, chills, dizziness and dehydration.* ■ a feverish cold: *we had better return before you catch a chill.* ■ a coldness of manner: *the chill in relations between France and its former colony.* ■ a depressing influence: *his statements have **cast a chill over** this whole country.* ■ a sudden and powerful feeling of fear: *a chill ran down my spine.*
2 a metal mould, often cooled, designed to ensure rapid or even cooling of metal during casting.
▶ verb [with obj.] **1** make (someone) cold: *they were chilled by a sudden wind.* ■ cool (food or drink) in a refrigerator: (as adj. **chilled**) *chilled white wine.* ■ Metallurgy another term for CHILL-CAST.
2 horrify or frighten (someone): *the city was chilled by the violence* | (as adj. **chilling**) *a chilling account of the prisoners' fate.*
3 [no obj.] (usu. **chill out**) informal calm down and relax: *they like to get home, have a bath, and chill out.* ■ pass time idly with other people: *she always seems to be just chilling with friends.*
▶ adjective chilly: *the chill grey dawn* | figurative *the chill winds of public censure.*
– PHRASES **chill someone's blood** horrify or terrify someone. **take the chill off** warm slightly: *an electric heater took the chill off the house.*
– DERIVATIVES **chillingly** adverb, **chillness** noun, **chillsome** adjective (literary).
– ORIGIN Old English *cele*, *ciele* 'cold, coldness', of Germanic origin; related to COLD.

chillax /tʃɪˈlaks/ ▶ verb [no obj.] informal calm down and relax: *you can dance to your favourite tune, chillax, or have friends over.*
– ORIGIN early 21st cent.: blend of CHILL (sense 3 of the verb) and RELAX.

chill-cast ▶ verb [with obj.] Metallurgy rapidly solidify (cast iron or other metal) by contact with a cooled metal mould or other cold surface in order to produce a hard, dense surface.

chiller ▶ noun **1** a machine for cooling something, especially a cold cabinet or refrigerator for keeping stored food a few degrees above freezing point.
2 short for SPINE-CHILLER.

chill factor ▶ noun a quantity expressing the perceived lowering of the air temperature caused by the wind.

chilli /ˈtʃɪli/ (also **chilli pepper**, US **chile** or **chili**) ▶ noun (pl. **chillies**, US **chiles** or **chilies**) a small hot-tasting pod of a variety of capsicum, used in sauces, relishes, and spice powders. There are various forms with pods of differing size, colour, and strength of

flavour. ● *Capsicum annuum* var. *annuum*, 'longum' group (or var. *longum*).
■ short for **CHILLI POWDER**. ■ short for **CHILLI CON CARNE**.
– ORIGIN early 17th cent.: from Spanish *chile*, from Nahuatl *chilli*.

chilli con carne /kɒn ˈkɑːneɪ, -ni/ ▶ **noun** [mass noun] a stew of minced beef and beans flavoured with chillies or chilli powder.
– ORIGIN from Spanish *chile con carne*, literally 'chilli pepper with meat'.

chilli powder ▶ **noun** [mass noun] a hot-tasting mixture of ground dried red chillies and other spices.

chill-out ▶ **adjective** [attrib.] informal intended to induce or enhance a relaxed mood, in particular an area in a nightclub where quiet or ambient music is played.

chill pill ▶ **noun** informal a notional pill taken to make someone calm down or relax: *is Tom right to get so uptight, or should he just take a chill pill?*

chillum /ˈtʃɪləm/ ▶ **noun** (pl. **chillums**) a hookah. ■ a small pipe used for smoking cannabis.
– ORIGIN from Hindi *cilam*.

chilly ▶ **adjective** (**chillier**, **chilliest**) uncomfortably or unpleasantly cold: *a chilly February evening*. ■ (of a person) feeling cold. ■ unfriendly: *he got a chilly reception from Republican activists*.
– DERIVATIVES **chilliness** noun.

chillybin ▶ **noun** NZ a portable insulated container for keeping food and drink cool.
– ORIGIN from a proprietary name.

Chilopoda /ˌkʌɪləˈpəʊdə/ ▶ **plural noun** Zoology a class of myriapod arthropods which comprises the centipedes.
– ORIGIN modern Latin (plural), from Greek *kheilos* 'lip' + *pous, pod-* 'foot'.

Chilpancingo /ˌtʃɪlpanˈsɪŋɡəʊ/ a city in SW Mexico, capital of the state of Guerrero; pop. 166,796 (2005).

Chiltern Hills /ˈtʃɪlt(ə)n/ (also **the Chilterns**) a range of chalk hills in southern England, north of the River Thames and west of London.

Chiltern Hundreds (in the UK) a Crown manor, whose administration is a nominal office for which an MP applies as a way of resigning from the House of Commons. This is because stewardship of the district is legally an office of profit under the Crown, the holding of which disqualifies a person from being an MP.
– ORIGIN from **CHILTERN HILLS** and *Hundreds* (see the **HUNDRED** (noun)).

Chiluba /tʃɪˈluːbə/ ▶ **noun** another term for **LUBA** (the language).

chimaera ▶ **noun** variant spelling of **CHIMERA**.

Chimborazo /ˌtʃɪmbəˈrɑːzəʊ/ the highest peak of the Andes in Ecuador, rising to 6,310 m (20,487 ft).

chime[1] ▶ **noun** a bell or a metal bar or tube, tuned and used in a set to produce a melodious series of ringing sounds when struck. ■ a sound made by such an instrument: *the chimes of Big Ben*. ■ (**chimes**) a set of tuned bells used as a doorbell. ■ Bell-ringing a stroke of the clapper against one or both sides of a scarcely moving bell.
▶ **verb** [no obj.] **1** (of a bell or clock) make melodious ringing sounds, typically to indicate the time: [with complement] *the clock chimed eight*.
2 (**chime with** or **chime in with**) Brit. be in agreement with: *his poem chimes with our modern experience of loss*.
– PHRASAL VERBS **chime in** interject a remark: *'Yes, you do that,' Dave chimed in eagerly*.
– DERIVATIVES **chimer** noun.
– ORIGIN Middle English (in the senses 'cymbal' and 'ring out'): probably from Old English *cimbal* (see **CYMBAL**), later interpreted as *chime bell*.

chime[2] ▶ **noun** the projecting rim at the end of a cask.
– ORIGIN late Middle English: probably from an Old English word related to Dutch *kim* and German *Kimme*. Compare with **CHINE**[3].

chimenea /ˌtʃɪmɪˈneɪə, -ˈniːə/ ▶ **noun** a free-standing clay fireplace or oven which consists of a hollow bulbous body tapering to a short chimney-like smoke vent.
– ORIGIN 1990s: Spanish, 'chimney'.

chimera /kʌɪˈmɪərə, kɪ-/ (also **chimaera**) ▶ **noun** **1** (in Greek mythology) a fire-breathing female monster with a lion's head, a goat's body, and a serpent's tail. ■ any mythical animal formed from parts of various animals.
2 a thing which is hoped for but is illusory or impossible to achieve: *the economic sovereignty you claim to defend is a chimera*.
3 Biology an organism containing a mixture of genetically different tissues, formed by processes such as fusion of early embryos, grafting, or mutation. ■ a DNA molecule with sequences derived from two or more different organisms, formed by laboratory manipulation.
4 (**chimaera**) a cartilaginous marine fish with a long tail, an erect spine before the first dorsal fin, and typically a forward projection from the snout. ● Subclass Holocephali: three families, in particular Chimaeridae.
– DERIVATIVES **chimeric** /-ˈmɛrɪk/ **adjective**, **chimerical adjective**.
– ORIGIN late Middle English: via Latin from Greek *khimaira* 'she-goat or chimera'.

chimichanga /ˌtʃɪmɪˈtʃaŋɡə/ ▶ **noun** a tortilla rolled round a savoury filling and deep-fried.
– ORIGIN Mexican Spanish, literally 'trinket'.

chimney ▶ **noun** (pl. **chimneys**) **1** a vertical channel or pipe which conducts smoke and combustion gases up from a fire or furnace and typically through the roof of a building. ■ a chimney stack.
2 a glass tube protecting the flame of a lamp.
3 a very steep narrow cleft by which a rock face may be climbed.
– ORIGIN Middle English (denoting a fireplace or furnace): from Old French *cheminee* 'chimney, fireplace', from late Latin *caminata*, perhaps from *camera caminata* 'room with a fireplace', from Latin *caminus* 'forge, furnace', from Greek *kaminos* 'oven'.

chimney breast ▶ **noun** a part of an interior wall that projects to surround a chimney.

chimney corner ▶ **noun** a warm seat within an old-fashioned fireplace.

chimney piece ▶ **noun** Brit. a mantelpiece.

chimney pot ▶ **noun** an earthenware or metal pipe at the top of a chimney, narrowing the aperture and increasing the updraught.

chimney stack ▶ **noun** the part of a chimney that projects above a roof.

chimney sweep ▶ **noun** a person whose job is cleaning out the soot from chimneys.

chimney swift ▶ **noun** the common swift (bird) of the eastern part of North America, with mainly dark grey plumage. ● *Chaetura pelagica*, family Apodidae.

chimonanthus /ˌkʌɪmə(ʊ)ˈnanθəs/ ▶ **noun** a shrub of the Chinese genus *Chimonanthus* (family Calycanthaceae), especially the wintersweet.
– ORIGIN modern Latin, from Greek *kheimōn* 'winter' + *anthos* 'flower'.

chimp ▶ **noun** informal a chimpanzee.

chimpanzee ▶ **noun** a great ape with large ears, mainly black coloration, and lighter skin on the face, native to the forests of west and central Africa. Chimpanzees show advanced behaviour such as the making and using of tools. ● Genus *Pan*, family Pongidae: the **common chimpanzee** (*P. troglodytes*) and the bonobo.
– ORIGIN mid 18th cent.: from French *chimpanzé*, from Kikongo.

Chimu /tʃiːˈmuː/ ▶ **noun** (pl. **same** or **Chimus**) **1** a member of an indigenous people of Peru that developed the most important civilization before the Incas.
2 [mass noun] the extinct language of the Chimu.
▶ **adjective** relating to the Chimu or their language.
– ORIGIN from Spanish.

Chin[1] /tʃɪn/ ▶ **noun** (pl. **same** or **Chins**) **1** a member of a people of SW Burma (Myanmar) and neighbouring parts of India and Bangladesh.
2 [mass noun] the Tibeto-Burman language of the Chin, with about 800,000 speakers.
▶ **adjective** relating to the Chin or their language.
– ORIGIN from Burmese, 'hill man'.

Chin[2] /tʃɪn/ variant spelling of **JIN**.

chin ▶ **noun** the protruding part of the face below the mouth, formed by the apex of the lower jaw.
▶ **verb** [with obj.] **1** informal hit or punch (someone) on the chin.
2 draw one's body up so that one's chin is level with or above (a horizontal bar) with one's feet off the ground, as an exercise.
– PHRASES **keep one's chin up** informal remain cheerful in difficult circumstances. **take it on the chin** accept misfortune courageously or stoically.
– DERIVATIVES **chinned adjective** [in combination] *square-chinned*.
– ORIGIN Old English *cin, cinn*, of Germanic origin; related to Dutch *kin*, from an Indo-European root shared by Latin *gena* 'cheek' and Greek *genus* 'jaw'.

Ch'in variant spelling of **QIN**.

China a country in East Asia, the third largest and most populous in the world; pop. 1,338,613,000 (est. 2009); language, Chinese (of which Mandarin is the official form); capital, Beijing. Official name **PEOPLE'S REPUBLIC OF CHINA**.

> Chinese civilization stretches back until at least the 3rd millennium BC, the country being ruled by a series of dynasties until the Qing (or Manchu) dynasty was overthrown by Sun Yat-sen in 1911; China was proclaimed a republic the following year. After the Second World War the Kuomintang government of Chiang Kai-shek was overthrown by the communists under Mao Zedong, the People's Republic of China being declared in 1949. Market-oriented reforms were introduced in the last quarter of the twentieth century.

china ▶ **noun** **1** [mass noun] a fine white or translucent vitrified ceramic material: *a plate made of china* | [as modifier] *a china cup*. Also called **PORCELAIN**. ■ household tableware or other objects made from this or a similar material: *she had begun to remove the breakfast china*.
2 Brit. informal a friend. [from rhyming slang *china plate* 'mate'.]
– ORIGIN late 16th cent. (as an adjective): from Persian *chīnī* 'relating to China', where it was originally made.

China, Republic of official name for **TAIWAN**.

China aster ▶ **noun** a Chinese plant of the daisy family, which is cultivated for its bright showy flowers. ● *Callistephus chinensis*, family Compositae.

chinaberry (also **chinaberry tree**) ▶ **noun** (pl. **chinaberries**) a tall tree which bears fragrant lilac flowers and yellow berries, native to Asia and Australasia. ● *Melia azedarach*, family Meliaceae.
■ the fruit of the chinaberry, used to make insecticides and also rosary beads.

china blue ▶ **noun** [mass noun] a pale greyish blue.

china clay ▶ **noun** another term for **KAOLIN**.

chinagraph pencil ▶ **noun** Brit. a waxy pencil used to write on china, glass, or other hard surfaces.

Chinaman ▶ **noun** (pl. **Chinamen**) **1** chiefly archaic or derogatory a native of China.
2 Cricket a ball that spins from off to leg, bowled by a left-handed bowler to a right-handed batsman.

chinar /ˈtʃɪnɑː/ (also **chenar**) ▶ **noun** the oriental plane tree, found from SE Europe to northern Iran. ● *Platanus orientalis*, family Platanaceae.
– ORIGIN from Persian *chinār*.

China rose ▶ **noun** **1** a Chinese rose which was introduced into Europe in the 19th century. ● *Rosa chinensis*, family Rosaceae.
■ any of a number of garden rose varieties derived from crosses of this plant.
2 a tropical shrubby evergreen hibiscus, which is cultivated for its large showy flowers. ● *Hibiscus rosa-sinensis*, family Malvaceae.

China Sea the part of the Pacific Ocean off the coast of China, divided by the island of Taiwan into the **East China Sea** in the north and the **South China Sea** in the south.

china stone ▶ **noun** [mass noun] partly kaolinized granite containing plagioclase feldspar, which is ground and mixed with kaolin to make porcelain.

China syndrome ▶ **noun** [in sing.] a hypothetical sequence of events following the meltdown of a nuclear reactor, in which the core melts through its containment structure and deep into the earth.
– ORIGIN 1970s: from **CHINA** (as being on the opposite side of the earth from a reactor in the US).

China tea ▶ **noun** [mass noun] tea made from a small-leaved type of tea plant grown in China, typically flavoured by smoke curing or the addition of flower petals.

Chinatown ▶ **noun** a district of a large non-Chinese town or port in which the population is predominantly of Chinese origin.

china tree ▶ **noun** another term for **CHINABERRY**.

chinch /tʃɪn(t)ʃ/ (also **chinch bug**) ▶ **noun** a plant-eating ground bug that forms large swarms on grasses and rushes. ● Two species in the family Lygaeidae, suborder Heteroptera: the American *Blissus leucopterus* and the European *Ischnodemus sabuleti*.
– ORIGIN early 17th cent. (in the sense 'bedbug'): from Spanish *chinche*, from Latin *cimex, cimic-*.

chincherinchee /ˌtʃɪntʃərɪnˈtʃiː/ ▶ **noun** a white-flowered South African lily. ● *Ornithogalum thyrsoides*, family Liliaceae.

– ORIGIN early 20th cent.: imitative of the squeaky sound made by rubbing its stalks together.

chinchilla /tʃɪnˈtʃɪlə/ ▸ **noun 1** a small South American rodent with soft grey fur and a long bushy tail. ● Genus *Chinchilla*, family Chinchillidae: two species.
2 a cat or rabbit of a breed with silver-grey or grey fur.
3 [mass noun] the highly valued fur of the chinchilla, or of the chinchilla rabbit.
– ORIGIN early 17th cent.: from Spanish, from Aymara or Quechua.

chin-chin ▸ **exclamation** Brit. informal, dated used to express good wishes before drinking.
– ORIGIN late 18th cent.: representing a pronunciation of Chinese *qing qing*.

Chindit /ˈtʃɪndɪt/ ▸ **noun** a member of the Allied forces behind the Japanese lines in Burma in 1943–5.
– ORIGIN Second World War: from Burmese *chinthé*, a mythical creature.

Chindwin /tʃɪnˈdwɪn/ a river which rises in northern Burma (Myanmar) and flows southwards for 885 km (550 miles) to meet the Irrawaddy.

chine[1] /tʃʌɪn/ ▸ **noun 1** the backbone of an animal as it appears in a joint of meat. ■ a joint of meat containing all or part of this.
2 a mountain ridge.
▸ **verb** [with obj.] cut (meat) across or along the backbone.
– ORIGIN Middle English: from Old French *eschine*, based on a blend of Latin *spina* 'spine' and a Germanic word meaning 'narrow piece', related to **SHIN**.

chine[2] /tʃʌɪn/ ▸ **noun** (in the Isle of Wight or Dorset) a deep narrow ravine.
– ORIGIN Old English *cinu* 'cleft, chink', of Germanic origin; related to Dutch *keen*, also to **CHINK**[1].

chine[3] /tʃʌɪn/ ▸ **noun** the angle where the strakes of the bottom of a boat or ship meet the side.
– ORIGIN late Middle English: variant of **CHIME**[2] (the original sense).

Chinese ▸ **noun** (pl. **same**) **1** [mass noun] the language of China.
2 a native or inhabitant of China, or a person of Chinese descent. ■ Brit. informal a Chinese meal. ■ Brit. informal a Chinese restaurant.

> Chinese, a member of the Sino-Tibetan language family, is the world's most commonly spoken first language, with an estimated 1.2 billion native speakers worldwide. The script is logographic, using characters which originated as stylized pictographs but now also represent abstract concepts and the sounds of syllables. Though complex, it permits written communication between speakers of the many dialects, most of which are mutually incomprehensible in speech. For transliteration into the Roman alphabet, the Pinyin system is now usually used.

▸ **adjective** relating to China or its language, culture, or people. ■ belonging to the people forming the dominant ethnic group of China and also widely dispersed elsewhere. Also called **HAN**.

Chinese box ▸ **noun** each of a set of boxes graduated in size so as to fit inside each other.

Chinese burn ▸ **noun** informal an act of placing both hands on a person's arm and then twisting it to produce a burning sensation.

Chinese cabbage ▸ **noun** another term for **CHINESE LEAVES**.

Chinese chequers (US **Chinese checkers**) ▸ **plural noun** [usu. treated as sing.] a board game for two to six players who attempt to move marbles or counters from one corner to the opposite one on a star-shaped board.

Chinese fire drill ▸ **noun** N. Amer. informal, often offensive a state of disorder or confusion.

Chinese gooseberry ▸ **noun** former term for **KIWI FRUIT**.

Chinese lantern ▸ **noun 1** a collapsible paper lantern.
2 a Eurasian plant with white flowers and globular orange fruits enclosed in an orange-red papery calyx. ● *Physalis alkekengi*, family Solanaceae.

Chinese leaves (also **Chinese cabbage**) ▸ **plural noun** Brit. an oriental cabbage which does not form a firm heart. ● Genus *Brassica*, family Cruciferae: two species, **pak choi** (*B. chinensis*) and **pe tsai** (*B. pekinenis*), which resembles lettuce.

Chinese mitten crab ▸ **noun** see **MITTEN CRAB**.

Chinese puzzle ▸ **noun** an intricate puzzle consisting of many interlocking pieces.

Chinese red ▸ **noun** [mass noun] a vivid orange-red.

Chinese wall ▸ **noun** an insurmountable barrier, especially to the passage of information.
– ORIGIN early 20th cent.: with allusion to the **GREAT WALL OF CHINA**.

Chinese water chestnut ▸ **noun** another term for **WATER CHESTNUT** (sense 1).

Chinese water deer ▸ **noun** see **WATER DEER**.

Chinese whispers ▸ **plural noun** [treated as sing.] Brit. a game in which a message is distorted by being passed around in a whisper.

Chinese white ▸ **noun** [mass noun] white pigment consisting of zinc oxide.

ching ▸ **noun** an abrupt high-pitched ringing sound, typically one made by a cash register.
– ORIGIN imitative.

Ch'ing variant spelling of **QING**.

Chin Hills /tʃɪn/ a range of hills in western Burma (Myanmar), close to the borders with India and Bangladesh.

Chink ▸ **noun** informal, offensive a Chinese person.
– ORIGIN late 19th cent.: irregular formation from **CHINA**.

chink[1] ▸ **noun** a narrow opening, typically one that admits light: *a chink in the curtains*. ■ a narrow beam or patch of light admitted by such an opening: *I noticed a **chink of light** under the door*.
– PHRASES **a chink in someone's armour** a weak point in someone's character or arguments which makes them vulnerable to attack.
– ORIGIN mid 16th cent.: related to **CHINE**[2].

chink[2] ▸ **verb** make or cause to make a light, high-pitched ringing sound, as of glasses or coins striking together: [no obj.] *the chain joining the handcuffs chinked* | [with obj.] *they chinked glasses and kissed*.
▸ **noun** a high-pitched ringing sound: *the chink of glasses*.
– ORIGIN late 16th cent.: imitative.

chinkapin ▸ **noun** variant spelling of **CHINQUAPIN**.

chinkara /tʃɪŋˈkɑːrə/ ▸ **noun** (pl. **same**) (in South Asia) the Indian gazelle, which occurs from Iran to central India. ● *Gazella bennettii*, family Bovidae.
– ORIGIN mid 19th cent.: from Hindi *cikārā*, from Sanskrit *chikkāra*.

Chinkiang /tʃɪnˈkjaŋ/ variant of **ZHENJIANG**.

Chinky informal ▸ **noun** (pl. **Chinkies**) **1** offensive a Chinese person.
2 Brit. a Chinese restaurant or a Chinese meal.
▸ **adjective** offensive Chinese.

chinless ▸ **adjective** (of a person) lacking a well-defined chin. ■ informal lacking strength of character; ineffectual.

chinless wonder ▸ **noun** Brit. informal an ineffectual upper-class man.

chin music ▸ **noun** [mass noun] US informal idle chatter.

chino /ˈtʃiːnəʊ/ ▸ **noun** (pl. **chinos**) [mass noun] a cotton twill fabric, typically khaki-coloured. ■ (**chinos**) casual cotton trousers made from chino or a similar fabric.
– ORIGIN 1940s: from Latin American Spanish, literally 'toasted' (referring to the typical colour).

Chino- /ˈtʃʌɪnəʊ/ ▸ **combining form** equivalent to **SINO-**.

chinoiserie /ʃɪnˈwɑːzəri/ ▸ **noun** (pl. **chinoiseries**) [mass noun] a decorative style in Western art, furniture, and architecture, especially in the 18th century, characterized by the use of Chinese motifs and techniques. ■ objects or decorations in this style: *his apartment was filled with chinoiserie*.
– ORIGIN late 19th cent.: from French, from *chinois* 'Chinese'.

Chinook /tʃɪˈnuːk, -ˈnʊk, ʃɪ-/ ▸ **noun** (pl. **same** or **Chinooks**) **1** a member of an American Indian people originally inhabiting the region around the Columbia River in Oregon.
2 [mass noun] the extinct Penutian language of the Chinook.
▸ **adjective** relating to the Chinook or their language.
– ORIGIN from Salish *tsinúk*.

chinook /tʃɪˈnuːk, -nʊk, ʃɪ-/ ▸ **noun 1** (also **chinook wind**) a warm dry wind which blows down the east side of the Rocky Mountains at the end of winter.
2 (also **chinook salmon**) a large North Pacific salmon which is an important food fish. ● *Oncorhynchus tshawytscha*, family Salmonidae.
– ORIGIN mid 19th cent.: from attributive use of **CHINOOK**.

Chinook Jargon ▸ **noun** [mass noun] an extinct pidgin composed of elements from Chinook, Nootka, English, French, and other languages, formerly used in the Pacific North-West of North America.

chinquapin /ˈtʃɪŋkəpɪn/ (also **chinkapin**) ▸ **noun** a North American chestnut tree. ● Several species in the family Fagaceae, in particular *Castanea pumila*.
■ the edible nut of the chinquapin.
– ORIGIN early 17th cent.: from Virginia Algonquian.

chinstrap ▸ **noun** a strap attached to a hat, helmet, or other headgear, designed to hold it in place by fitting under the wearer's chin.

chintz ▸ **noun** [mass noun] printed multicoloured cotton fabric with a glazed finish, used for curtains and upholstery: [as modifier] *floral chintz curtains*.
– ORIGIN early 17th cent. (as *chints*, plural of *chint*, denoting a stained or painted calico cloth imported from India): from Hindi *chīṁt* 'spattering, stain'.

chintzy ▸ **adjective** (**chintzier**, **chintziest**) **1** Brit. of, like, or decorated with chintz: *a pretty, chintzy fabric*.
■ brightly colourful but gaudy and tasteless.
2 N. Amer. informal cheap and of poor quality. ■ miserly; mean: *a chintzy salary increase*.
– DERIVATIVES **chintziness** noun.

chin-up ▸ **noun** chiefly N. Amer. another term for **PULL-UP** (sense 1).

chinwag Brit. informal ▸ **noun** a chat.
▸ **verb** (**chinwags**, **chinwagging**, **chinwagged**) [no obj.] have a chat.

chionodoxa /ˌkʌɪənəˈdɒksə/ ▸ **noun** a bulbous Eurasian plant of the lily family, with early blooming blue flowers. Also called **GLORY-OF-THE-SNOW**. ● Genus *Chionodoxa*, family Liliaceae.
– ORIGIN modern Latin, from Greek *khiōn* 'snow' + *doxa* 'glory'.

Chios /ˈkʌɪɒs/ a Greek island in the Aegean Sea; pop. 53,100 (est. 2008). Greek name **KHIOS**.
– DERIVATIVES **Chian** noun & adjective.

chip ▸ **noun 1** a small piece of something removed in the course of chopping, cutting, or breaking a hard material such as wood or stone: *granite chips*. ■ a hole or mark left by the removal of such a piece.
■ [mass noun] Brit. wood or woody fibre split into thin strips and used for weaving hats or baskets.
2 Brit. a long rectangular piece of deep-fried potato.
■ (also **potato chip**) N. Amer. a potato crisp.
3 short for **MICROCHIP**.
4 a counter used in certain gambling games to represent money: *a poker chip*.
5 (in football, golf, and other sports) a short lofted kick or shot.
▸ **verb** (**chips**, **chipping**, **chipped**) [with obj.] **1** cut or break (a small piece) from a hard material: *we had to chip ice off the upper deck*. ■ [no obj.] (of a material or object) break at the edge or on the surface: *the paint had **chipped off** the gate*. ■ cut pieces off (a hard material) to shape it or break it up: *craftsmen chipped the blocks of flint to the required shape* | [no obj.] *she **chipped away at** the ground outside the door*.
■ Brit. cut (a potato) into strips.
2 (usu. as adj. **chipped**) Brit. cut (a potato) into chips.
3 (in football, golf, and other sports) kick or strike (a ball or shot) to produce a short lofted shot or pass: *he chipped a superb shot over the keeper*.
– PHRASES **a chip off the old block** informal someone who resembles their parent in character or appearance. **a chip on one's shoulder** informal a deeply ingrained grievance. **have had one's chips** Brit. informal be dead or defeated. **when the chips are down** informal when a very serious situation arises.
– PHRASAL VERBS **chip away at** gradually and relentlessly make something smaller or weaker: *rivals may chip away at one's profits by undercutting prices*. **chip in** (or **chip something in**) **1** contribute something as one's share of a joint activity, cost, etc.: *Rollie **chipped in with** nine saves and five wins* | *the council will chip in a further £30,000 a year*. **2** informal make an interjection: [with direct speech] *'He's right,' Gloria chipped in*.
– ORIGIN Middle English: related to Old English *forcippian* 'cut off'.

chip and PIN ▸ **noun** [mass noun] a way of paying for goods by debit or credit card whereby one enters one's personal identification number in an electronic device rather than signing a slip.

chipboard ▸ **noun** [mass noun] material made in rigid sheets from compressed wood chips and resin, often coated or veneered, used in furniture, buildings, etc.

Chipewyan /ˌtʃɪpəˈwʌɪən/ ▸ **noun** (pl. **same** or **Chipewyans**) **1** a member of a Dene people of NW Canada. Compare with **CHIPPEWA**.
2 [mass noun] the Athabaskan language of the Chipewyan, with about 8,000 speakers.

▶ **adjective** relating to the Chipewyan or their language.
– ORIGIN from Cree, literally '(wearing) pointed-skin (garments)'.

chip heater ▶ **noun** Austral./NZ a domestic water heater that burns wood chips.

chipmaker ▶ **noun** a company that manufactures microchips.

chipmunk ▶ **noun** a burrowing ground squirrel with cheek pouches and light and dark stripes running down the body, found in North America and northern Eurasia. ● Genus *Tamias*, family Sciuridae: many species.
– ORIGIN mid 19th cent.: from Ojibwa.

chipolata ▶ **noun** Brit. a small thin sausage.
– ORIGIN late 19th cent.: from French, from Italian *cipollata* 'a dish of onions', from *cipolla* 'onion'.

chipotle /tʃɪˈpəʊtleɪ/ ▶ **noun** a smoked hot chilli pepper used in Mexican cooking.
– ORIGIN Mexican Spanish, from Nahuatl.

Chippendale[1] /ˈtʃɪp(ə)ndeɪl/, Thomas (1718–79), English furniture-maker and designer. He produced furniture in a neoclassical vein, with elements of the French rococo, chinoiserie, and Gothic revival styles, and his book of furniture designs *The Gentleman and Cabinetmaker's Director* (1754) was highly influential.

Chippendale[2] /ˈtʃɪp(ə)ndeɪl/ ▶ **adjective** (of furniture) designed, made by, or in the style of Thomas Chippendale.

chipper[1] ▶ **adjective** informal cheerful and lively.
– ORIGIN mid 19th cent.: perhaps from northern English dialect *kipper* 'lively'.

chipper[2] ▶ **noun 1** a person or thing that turns something into chips. ■ a machine for chipping timber.
2 Irish informal a fish-and-chip shop.

Chippewa /ˈtʃɪpəwɔː, -wɑː/ ▶ **noun** (pl. **same**) chiefly N. Amer. another term for **OJIBWA**. Compare with **CHIPEWYAN**.
– ORIGIN alteration of **OJIBWA**.

chippie ▶ **noun** (pl. **chippies**) variant spelling of **CHIPPY**.

chipping ▶ **noun** Brit. a small fragment of stone, wood, or similar material.

chipping sparrow ▶ **noun** a common American songbird related to the buntings, with a chestnut crown and a white stripe over the eye. ● *Spizella passerina*, family Emberizidae (subfamily Emberizinae).
– ORIGIN early 19th cent.: *chipping* from US *chip* 'chirp', with reference to the bird's repetitive song.

chippy informal ▶ **noun** (also **chippie**) (pl. **chippies**)
1 Brit. a fish-and-chip shop.
2 Brit. a carpenter.
3 N. Amer. a promiscuous young woman, especially a prostitute.
▶ **adjective** touchy and irritable. ■ N. Amer. (of an ice-hockey game) rough and belligerent with numerous penalties.

chipset ▶ **noun** a collection of integrated circuits which are designed to function together as a unit, especially to perform a particular task within a computer system.

chip shot ▶ **noun** Golf a stroke at which the ball is or must be chipped into the air.

Chirac /ˈʃɪərak/, French /ʃiʀak/, Jacques (René) (b.1932), French statesman, Prime Minister 1974–6 and 1986–8 and President 1995–2007.

chiral /ˈkʌɪr(ə)l/ ▶ **adjective** Chemistry asymmetric in such a way that the structure and its mirror image are not superimposable.
– DERIVATIVES **chirality** noun.
– ORIGIN late 19th cent.: from Greek *kheir* 'hand' + **-AL**.

chi-rho ▶ **noun** a monogram of chi (X) and rho (P) as the first two letters of Greek *Khristos* Christ.

Chirico /ˈkɪrɪkəʊ/, Giorgio de (1888–1978), Greek-born Italian painter. His disconnected and unsettling dream images exerted a significant influence on surrealism.

chirimoya /ˌtʃɪrɪˈmɔɪə/ ▶ **noun** variant spelling of **CHERIMOYA**.

chiro- /ˈkʌɪrəʊ/ (also **cheiro-**) ▶ **combining form** of the hand or hands: *chiromancy*.
– ORIGIN from Greek *kheir* 'hand'.

chirography /kʌɪˈrɒɡrəfi/ ▶ **noun** [mass noun] handwriting, especially as distinct from typography.
– DERIVATIVES **chirographic** adjective.

chiromancy /ˈkʌɪrə(ʊ)mansi/ ▶ **noun** [mass noun] the prediction of a person's future from interpreting the lines on the palms of their hands; palmistry.

Chiron /ˈkʌɪərɒn/ **1** Greek Mythology a learned centaur who acted as teacher to Jason, Achilles, and many other heroes.
2 Astronomy asteroid 2060, discovered in 1977, which is unique in having an orbit lying mainly between the orbits of Saturn and Uranus. It is believed to have a diameter of 370 km.

chironomid /kʌɪˈrɒnəmɪd/ ▶ **noun** Entomology an insect of a family (Chironomidae) which comprises the non-biting midges.
– ORIGIN late 19th cent.: from modern Latin *Chironomidae* (plural), from the genus name *Chironomus*, from Greek *kheironomos* 'pantomime dancer'.

chiropody /kɪˈrɒpədi/ ▶ **noun** [mass noun] chiefly Brit. the treatment of the feet and their ailments.
– DERIVATIVES **chiropodist** noun.
– ORIGIN late 19th cent.: from **CHIRO-** 'hand' + Greek *pous, pod-* 'foot'.

chiropractic /ˌkʌɪrə(ʊ)ˈpraktɪk/ ▶ **noun** [mass noun] a system of complementary medicine based on the diagnosis and manipulative treatment of misalignments of the joints, especially those of the spinal column, which are believed to cause other disorders by affecting the nerves, muscles, and organs.
– DERIVATIVES **chiropractor** noun.
– ORIGIN late 19th cent.: from **CHIRO-** 'hand' + Greek *praktikos* 'practical', from *prattein* 'do'.

Chiroptera /kʌɪˈrɒpt(ə)rə/ ▶ **plural noun** Zoology an order of mammals that comprises the bats. See also **MEGACHIROPTERA**, **MICROCHIROPTERA**.
– ORIGIN modern Latin (plural), from **CHIRO-** 'hand' + Greek *pteron* 'wing'.

chiropteran Zoology ▶ **noun** a mammal of the order Chiroptera; a bat.
▶ **adjective** relating to or denoting chiropterans.

chirp ▶ **verb** [no obj.] **1** (of a small bird or an insect) make a short, sharp, high-pitched sound. ■ [with direct speech] (of a person) say something in a lively and cheerful way: *'Good morning!' chirped Alex.*
2 [with obj.] S. African speak to (someone) in a taunting way.
▶ **noun** a short, sharp, high-pitched sound.
– DERIVATIVES **chirper** noun.
– ORIGIN late Middle English: imitative.

chirpy ▶ **adjective** (**chirpier**, **chirpiest**) informal cheerful and lively.
– DERIVATIVES **chirpily** adverb, **chirpiness** noun.

chirr /tʃəː/ (also **churr**) ▶ **verb** [no obj.] (of an insect) make a prolonged low trilling sound.
▶ **noun** a low trilling sound.
– ORIGIN early 17th cent.: imitative.

chirrup ▶ **verb** (**chirrups**, **chirruping**, **chirruped**) [no obj.] (of a small bird) make repeated short, high-pitched sounds. ■ [with direct speech] (of a person) say something in a high-pitched voice: *'Yes, Miss Honey,' chirruped eighteen voices.*
▶ **noun** a short, high-pitched sound.
– DERIVATIVES **chirrupy** adjective.
– ORIGIN late 16th cent.: alteration of **CHIRP**, by trilling the *-r-*.

chiru /ˈtʃɪruː/ ▶ **noun** (pl. **same**) a sandy-coloured Tibetan gazelle with black horns. Also called **TIBETAN ANTELOPE**. ● *Pantholops hodgsoni*, family Bovidae.
– ORIGIN late 19th cent.: probably from Tibetan.

chisel /ˈtʃɪz(ə)l/ ▶ **noun** a long-bladed hand tool with a bevelled cutting edge and a handle which is struck with a hammer or mallet, used to cut or shape wood, stone, or metal.
▶ **verb** (**chisels**, **chiselling**, **chiselled**; US **chisels**, **chiseling**, **chiseled**) [with obj.] **1** cut or shape (something) with a chisel: *chisel a hole through the brickwork.*
2 informal, chiefly N. Amer. cheat or swindle (someone) out of something: *he's chiselled me out of my dues.*
– DERIVATIVES **chiseller** noun.
– ORIGIN late Middle English: from Old Northern French, based on Latin *cis-* (as in late Latin *cisorium*), variant of *caes-*, stem of *caedere* 'to cut'. Compare with **SCISSORS**.

chiselled ▶ **adjective** (of a man's facial features) strongly and clearly defined: *the chiselled features of a male model.*

Chişinău /ˌkɪʃɪˈnaʊ/ the capital of Moldova; pop. 630,300 (est. 2008). Russian name **KISHINYOV**.

chi-square test /kʌɪˈskwɛː test/ ▶ **noun** a statistical method assessing the goodness of fit between a set of observed values and those expected theoretically. (Symbol: χ^2)

chit[1] ▶ **noun** Brit. derogatory an impudent or arrogant young woman: *she is a mere chit of a girl.*
– ORIGIN late Middle English (denoting a whelp, cub, or kitten): perhaps related to dialect *chit* 'sprout'.

chit[2] ▶ **noun** a short official note, typically recording a sum owed.
– ORIGIN late 18th cent.: Anglo-Indian, from Hindi *ciṭṭhī* 'note, pass'.

chit[3] ▶ **verb** (**chits**, **chitting**, **chitted**) [with obj.] Brit. cause (a potato) to sprout by placing it in a cool light place.
– ORIGIN early 17th cent.: from dialect *chit* 'a shoot, sprout'.

chital /ˈtʃiːt(ə)l/ ▶ **noun** a deer having lyre-shaped antlers and a white-spotted fawn coat, native to India and Sri Lanka. ● *Cervus axis*, family Cervidae.
– ORIGIN late 19th cent.: from Hindi *cītal*, from Sanskrit *citrala* 'spotted', from *citra* 'spot, mark'.

chitarrone /ˌkɪtəˈrəʊneɪ, -ni/ ▶ **noun** a very large lute similar to a theorbo, used in Italy in the late 16th and early 17th centuries.
– ORIGIN Italian, literally 'large guitar'.

chit-chat informal ▶ **noun** [mass noun] inconsequential conversation.
▶ **verb** [no obj.] talk about trivial matters: *I can't stand around chit-chatting.*
– ORIGIN late 17th cent.: reduplication of **CHAT**[1].

chit fund ▶ **noun** (in South Asia) an institution which accepts savings at interest and lends money for house and other purchases.
– ORIGIN *chit* from **CHIT**[2].

chitin /ˈkʌɪtɪn/ ▶ **noun** [mass noun] Biochemistry a fibrous substance consisting of polysaccharides, which is the major constituent in the exoskeleton of arthropods and the cell walls of fungi.
– DERIVATIVES **chitinous** adjective.
– ORIGIN mid 19th cent.: from French *chitine*, formed irregularly from Greek *khitōn* (see **CHITON**).

chiton /ˈkʌɪtɒn, -t(ə)n/ ▶ **noun 1** a long woollen tunic worn in ancient Greece.
2 a marine mollusc that has an oval flattened body with a shell of overlapping plates. ● Class Polyplacophora.
– ORIGIN from Greek *khitōn* 'tunic'. Sense 2 is a modern Latin genus name.

Chittagong /ˈtʃɪtəɡɒŋ/ a seaport in SE Bangladesh, on the Bay of Bengal; pop. 2,579,107 (2008).

chitter ▶ **verb** [no obj.] **1** make a twittering or chattering sound.
2 Scottish & dialect shiver with cold: *they stand chittering at bus stops.*
– ORIGIN Middle English: imitative; compare with **CHATTER**.

chitterlings /ˈtʃɪtəlɪŋz/ ▶ **plural noun** the smaller intestines of a pig, cooked as food.
– ORIGIN Middle English: perhaps related to synonymous German *Kutteln*.

chitty ▶ **noun** (pl. **chitties**) Brit. informal term for **CHIT**[2].

chivalrous /ˈʃɪv(ə)lrəs/ ▶ **adjective** (of a man or his behaviour) courteous and gallant, especially towards women. ■ relating to the historical concept of chivalry.
– DERIVATIVES **chivalrously** adverb, **chivalrousness** noun.
– ORIGIN late Middle English (in the sense 'characteristic of a medieval knight'): from Old French *chevalerous*, from *chevalier* (see **CHEVALIER**).

chivalry /ˈʃɪv(ə)lri/ ▶ **noun** [mass noun] **1** the medieval knightly system with its religious, moral, and social code. ■ the combination of qualities expected of an ideal knight, namely courage, honour, courtesy, justice, and a readiness to help the weak. ■ courteous behaviour, especially that of a man towards women: *he still retained a sense of chivalry towards women.*
2 archaic knights, noblemen, and horsemen collectively.
– DERIVATIVES **chivalric** adjective.
– ORIGIN Middle English: from Old French *chevalerie*, from medieval Latin *caballerius*, for late Latin *caballarius* 'horseman' (see **CHEVALIER**).

chives ▶ **plural noun** a small Eurasian plant related to the onion, with purple-pink flowers and long tubular leaves which are used as a culinary herb: *freshly chopped chives* | [as modifier **chive**] *chive and garlic dressing.* ● *Allium schoenoprasum*, family Liliaceae (or Alliaceae).
– ORIGIN Middle English: from Old French, dialect variant of *cive*, from Latin *cepa* 'onion'.

chivvy (also **chivy**) ▶ **verb** (**chivvies**, **chivvying**, **chivvied**) [with obj.] chiefly Brit. tell (someone) repeatedly to do something: *an association which chivvies government into action.*

– ORIGIN late 18th cent.: probably from the ballad *Chevy Chase*, celebrating a skirmish (probably the battle of Otterburn, 1388) on the Scottish border. Originally a noun denoting a hunting cry, the term later meant 'a pursuit', hence the verb 'to chase, worry' (mid 19th cent.).

Chkalov /ˈtʃkɑːlɒf/ former name (1938–57) for **ORENBURG**.

Chladni figures /ˈkladni/ (also **Chladni patterns**) ▶ **plural noun** the patterns formed when a sand-covered surface is made to vibrate.
– ORIGIN early 19th cent.: named after Ernst *Chladni* (1756–1827), German physicist.

chlamydia /kləˈmɪdɪə/ ▶ **noun** (pl. **same** or **chlamydiae** /-dɪiː/) a very small parasitic bacterium which, like a virus, requires the biochemical mechanisms of another cell in order to reproduce. Bacteria of this type cause various diseases including trachoma, psittacosis, and non-specific urethritis. ● Genus *Chlamydia* and order Chlamydiales.
– DERIVATIVES **chlamydial** adjective.
– ORIGIN 1960s: modern Latin (plural), from Greek *khlamus*, *khlamud-* 'cloak'.

chlamydomonas /ˌklamɪdəˈməʊnəs/ ▶ **noun** (pl. **same**) Biology a common single-celled green alga which typically has two flagella for swimming, living in water and moist soil. ● Genus *Chlamydomonas*, division Chlorophyta (or phylum Chlorophyta, kingdom Protista).
– ORIGIN late 19th cent.: modern Latin, from Greek *khlamus*, *khlamud-* 'cloak' + *monas* (see **MONAD**).

chlamydospore /ˈklamɪdə(ʊ)spɔː/ ▶ **noun** Botany (in certain fungi) a thick-walled hyphal cell which functions like a spore.
– ORIGIN late 19th cent.: from Greek *khlamus*, *khlamud-* 'cloak' + **SPORE**.

chlamys /ˈklamɪs/ ▶ **noun** a short cloak worn by men in ancient Greece.
– ORIGIN late 17th cent.: from Greek *khlamus* 'cloak'.

chloasma /kləʊˈazmə/ ▶ **noun** [mass noun] a temporary condition, typically caused by hormonal changes, in which large brown patches form on the skin.
– ORIGIN mid 19th cent.: from Greek *khloazein* 'become green'.

chlor- ▶ **combining form** variant spelling of **CHLORO-** before a vowel (as in *chloracne*).

chloracne /klɔːˈrakni/ ▶ **noun** [mass noun] Medicine a skin disease resembling severe acne, caused by exposure to chlorinated chemicals.

chloral /ˈklɔːral/ ▶ **noun** [mass noun] Chemistry a colourless, viscous liquid made by chlorinating acetaldehyde. ● Chem. formula: CCl_3CHO.
■ short for **CHLORAL HYDRATE**.
– ORIGIN mid 19th cent.: from French, blend of *chlore* 'chlorine' and *alcool* 'alcohol'.

chloral hydrate ▶ **noun** [mass noun] Chemistry a colourless crystalline solid made from chloral and used as a sedative. ● Chem. formula: $CCl_3CH(OH)_2$.

chlorambucil /klɔːˈrambjʊsɪl/ ▶ **noun** [mass noun] Medicine a cytotoxic drug used in the treatment of cancer.
– ORIGIN 1950s: from *chlor(oethyl)am(inophenyl)-bu(tyric acid)*, the systematic name, + *-cil*.

chloramine /ˈklɔːrəmiːn/ ▶ **noun** Chemistry any of a group of antiseptics and disinfectants which are sulphonamide derivatives containing chlorine bonded to nitrogen.

chloramphenicol /ˌklɔːramˈfɛnɪkɒl/ ▶ **noun** [mass noun] Medicine an antibiotic used against serious infections such as typhoid fever.
– ORIGIN 1940s: from **CHLORO-** (representing **CHLORINE**) + *am(ide)* + **PHENO-** + *ni(tro-)* + *(gly)col*.

chlorate /ˈklɔːreɪt/ ▶ **noun** Chemistry a salt or ester of chloric acid.

chlordane /ˈklɔːdeɪn/ ▶ **noun** [mass noun] a synthetic viscous toxic compound used as an insecticide. ● A chlorinated derivative of indene; chem. formula: $C_{10}H_6Cl_8$.
– ORIGIN 1940s: from **CHLOR-** (representing **CHLORINE**) + *(in)dene* + **-ANE**[2].

chlordiazepoxide /ˌklɔːdʌɪazɪˈpɒksʌɪd/ ▶ **noun** [mass noun] Medicine a tranquillizer of the benzodiazepine group, used chiefly to treat anxiety and alcoholism. Also called **LIBRIUM** (trademark).
– ORIGIN 1960s: from **CHLOR-** + *diazo* + **EPOXIDE**.

chlorella /kləˈrɛlə/ ▶ **noun** [mass noun] Biology a common single-celled green alga of both terrestrial and aquatic habitats, responsible for turning stagnant water an opaque green. ● Genus *Chlorella*, division Chlorophyta (or phylum Chlorophyta, kingdom Protista).
– ORIGIN modern Latin, diminutive of Greek *khlōros* 'green'.

chlorhexidine /klɔːˈhɛksɪdiːn/ ▶ **noun** [mass noun] a synthetic compound used as a mild antiseptic. ● A biguanide derivative; chem. formula: $C_{22}H_{30}Cl_2N_{10}$.
– ORIGIN mid 20th cent.: from **CHLOR-** (representing **CHLORINE**) + *hex(ane)* + *-id(e)* + *(am)ine*.

chloric acid /ˈklɔːrɪk/ ▶ **noun** [mass noun] Chemistry a colourless liquid acid with strong oxidizing properties. ● Chem. formula: $HClO_3$.
– ORIGIN early 19th cent.: *chloric* from **CHLORINE** + **-IC**.

chloride /ˈklɔːrʌɪd/ ▶ **noun** Chemistry a compound of chlorine with another element or group, especially a salt of the anion Cl^- or an organic compound with chlorine bonded to an alkyl group.
– ORIGIN early 19th cent.: from **CHLORINE** + **-IDE**.

chlorinate /ˈklɔːrɪneɪt, ˈklɒ-/ ▶ **verb** [with obj.] (usu. as adj. **chlorinated**) impregnate or treat with chlorine: *chlorinated water*.
– DERIVATIVES **chlorination** noun, **chlorinator** noun.

chlorine /ˈklɔːriːn/ ▶ **noun** [mass noun] the chemical element of atomic number 17, a toxic, irritant, pale green gas. (Symbol: **Cl**)

> A member of the halogen group, chlorine occurs in nature mainly as sodium chloride in seawater and salt deposits. The gas was used as a poison gas in the First World War. Chlorine is added to water supplies as a disinfectant.

– ORIGIN early 19th cent.: named by Sir Humphrey Davy, from Greek *khlōros* 'green' + **-INE**[4].

chlorite[1] /ˈklɔːrʌɪt/ ▶ **noun** [mass noun] a dark green mineral consisting of a basic hydrated aluminosilicate of magnesium and iron. It occurs as a constituent of many rocks, typically forming flat crystals resembling mica.
– DERIVATIVES **chloritic** adjective.
– ORIGIN late 18th cent.: via Latin from Greek *khlōritis*, a green precious stone.

chlorite[2] /ˈklɔːrʌɪt/ ▶ **noun** Chemistry a salt of chlorous acid, containing the anion ClO_2^-.
– ORIGIN mid 19th cent.: from **CHLORINE** + **-ITE**[1].

chloritoid /ˈklɔːrɪtɔɪd/ ▶ **noun** [mass noun] a greenish-grey or black mineral resembling mica, consisting chiefly of a basic aluminosilicate of iron and found in metamorphosed clay sediments.

chloro- (usu. **chlor-** before a vowel) ▶ **combining form**
1 Biology & Mineralogy green.
2 Chemistry representing **CHLORINE**: *chloroquine*.
– ORIGIN from Greek *khlōros* 'green'.

chlorodyne /ˈklɔːrə(ʊ)dʌɪn, ˈklɒ-/ ▶ **noun** [mass noun] a preparation of chloroform and morphine formerly used to relieve pain.
– ORIGIN mid 19th cent.: blend of **CHLOROFORM** and **ANODYNE**.

chlorofluorocarbon /ˌklɔːrə(ʊ)ˌflʊərə(ʊ)ˈkɑːb(ə)n, -ˌflɔː-/ (abbr.: **CFC**) ▶ **noun** any of a class of compounds of carbon, hydrogen, chlorine, and fluorine, typically gases used in refrigerants and aerosol propellants. They are harmful to the ozone layer in the earth's atmosphere owing to the release of chlorine atoms on exposure to ultraviolet radiation.

chloroform ▶ **noun** [mass noun] a colourless, volatile, sweet-smelling liquid used as a solvent and formerly as a general anaesthetic. ● Chem. formula: $CHCl_3$.
▶ **verb** [with obj.] make (someone) unconscious with chloroform.
– ORIGIN mid 19th cent.: from **CHLORO-** (representing **CHLORINE**) + *form-* from **FORMIC ACID**.

chlorophyll /ˈklɔːrəfɪl, ˈklɒ-/ ▶ **noun** [mass noun] a green pigment, present in all green plants and in cyanobacteria, which is responsible for the absorption of light to provide energy for photosynthesis.
– DERIVATIVES **chlorophyllous** adjective.
– ORIGIN early 19th cent.: coined in French from Greek *khlōros* 'green' + *phullon* 'leaf'.

Chlorophyta /ˈklɔːrə(ʊ)ˌfʌɪtə, ˈklɒ-/ ▶ **plural noun** Botany a division of lower plants that comprises the green algae. They are frequently treated as a phylum of the kingdom Protista.
– ORIGIN modern Latin (plural), from Greek *khlōros* 'green' + *phuton* 'plant'.

chlorophyte ▶ **noun** Botany a lower plant of the division Chlorophyta, which comprises the green algae.

chloroplast /ˈklɔːrə(ʊ)plast, -plɑːst, ˈklɒ-/ ▶ **noun** Botany a plastid in green plant cells which contains chlorophyll and in which photosynthesis takes place.
– ORIGIN late 19th cent.: coined in German from Greek *khlōros* 'green' + *plastos* 'formed'.

chloroprene /ˈklɔːrə(ʊ)priːn, ˈklɒ-/ ▶ **noun** [mass noun] Chemistry a colourless liquid made from acetylene and hydrochloric acid and polymerized to form neoprene. ● Chem. formula: $CH_2{=}CClCH{=}CH_2$.
– ORIGIN 1930s: from **CHLORO-** + a shortened form of **ISOPRENE**.

chloroquine /ˈklɔːrə(ʊ)kwiːn, ˈklɒ-/ ▶ **noun** [mass noun] Medicine a synthetic drug related to quinoline, used against malaria.
– ORIGIN 1940s: from **CHLORO-** + *quin(olin)e*.

chlorosis /klɒˈrəʊsɪs/ ▶ **noun** [mass noun] (pl. **chloroses**)
1 Botany loss of the normal green coloration of leaves of plants, caused by iron deficiency in lime-rich soils, disease, or lack of light.
2 Medicine anaemia caused by iron deficiency, especially in adolescent girls, causing a pale, faintly greenish complexion.
– DERIVATIVES **chlorotic** adjective.

chlorothiazide /ˌklɔːrə(ʊ)ˈθʌɪəzʌɪd, ˈklɒ-/ ▶ **noun** [mass noun] Medicine a synthetic drug used to treat fluid retention and high blood pressure.

chlorous acid /ˈklɔːrəs/ ▶ **noun** [mass noun] Chemistry a weak acid with oxidizing properties, formed when chlorine dioxide dissolves in water. ● Chem. formula: $HClO_2$.

chlorpromazine /klɔːˈprəʊməzɪn, -ziːn/ ▶ **noun** [mass noun] Medicine a synthetic drug used as a tranquillizer, sedative, and anti-emetic.
– ORIGIN 1950s: from **CHLORO-** + *prom(eth)azine*.

chlortetracycline /ˌklɔːtɛtrəˈsʌɪkliːn/ ▶ **noun** [mass noun] Medicine an antibiotic of the tetracycline group, active against many bacterial and fungal infections.

ChM ▶ **abbreviation** Master of Surgery.
– ORIGIN from Latin *Chirurgiae Magister*.

choanocyte /ˈkəʊənə(ʊ)sʌɪt/ ▶ **noun** Zoology a flagellated cell with a collar of protoplasm at the base of the flagellum, numbers of which line the internal chambers of sponges.
– ORIGIN late 19th cent.: from Greek *khoanē* 'funnel' + **-CYTE**.

choc ▶ **noun** Brit. informal a chocolate.

chocaholic ▶ **noun** variant spelling of **CHOCOHOLIC**.

choccy ▶ **noun** (pl. **choccies**) [mass noun] informal chocolate. ■ [count noun] a chocolate sweet.

chocho /ˈtʃəʊtʃəʊ/ ▶ **noun** (pl. **chochos**) West Indian term for **CHOKO**.

choc ice ▶ **noun** Brit. a small bar of ice cream with a thin coating of chocolate.

chock ▶ **noun** a wedge or block placed against a wheel or rounded object, to prevent it from moving. ■ a support for a rounded structure, such as a cask or the hull of a boat.
▶ **verb** [with obj.] prevent the movement of (a wheel or vehicle) with a chock: *the front wheel will need to be chocked*. ■ support (a boat, cask, etc.) on chocks.
– ORIGIN Middle English: probably from an Old Northern French variant of Old French *çouche*, *çoche* 'block, log', of unknown ultimate origin.

chocka ▶ **adjective** Brit. short for **CHOCK-A-BLOCK**.

chock-a-block ▶ **adjective** [predic.] informal, chiefly Brit. crammed full of people or things: ***the manual is chock-a-block with information***.
– ORIGIN mid 19th cent. (originally in nautical use, with reference to tackle having the two blocks run close together): from *chock* (in **CHOCK-FULL**) and **BLOCK**.

chocker ▶ **adjective** [predic.] informal **1** Brit. tired of or disgusted with something: *I'm a little chocker with this place*.
2 (Austral. also **chockers**) Brit. full: ***the church was chocker with flowers***.
– ORIGIN Second World War (originally naval slang): from **CHOCK-A-BLOCK**.

chock-full ▶ **adjective** [predic.] informal filled to overflowing: *my case is chock-full of notes*.
– ORIGIN late Middle English: of unknown origin; later associated with **CHOCK**.

chockstone ▶ **noun** Climbing a stone that has become wedged in a vertical cleft.

chocoholic (also **chocaholic**) ▶ **noun** informal a person who is addicted to or very fond of chocolate.

chocolate ▶ **noun** [mass noun] a food in the form of a paste or solid block made from roasted and ground cacao seeds, typically sweetened and eaten as confectionery: *a bar of chocolate* | [as modifier] *a chocolate biscuit*. ■ [count noun] a sweet made of or covered with chocolate: *a box of chocolates*. ■ a drink made by mixing milk or water with chocolate. ■ a deep brown colour: *the former Great Western colours of chocolate and cream* | [as modifier] ***his chocolate brown eyes***.
– DERIVATIVES **chocolatey** (also **chocolaty**) adjective.
– ORIGIN early 17th cent. (in the sense 'a drink made with chocolate'): from French *chocolat* or Spanish

chocolate, from Nahuatl *chocolatl* 'food made from cacao seeds', influenced by unrelated *cacaua-atl* 'drink made from cacao'.

chocolate-box ▶ **adjective** Brit. (of a view or picture) pretty in a conventional or idealized way: *chocolate-box cottages lining narrow streets*.
– ORIGIN from the use of attractive images to decorate boxes of chocolates.

chocolate chip ▶ **noun** [usu. as modifier] a small piece of chocolate used in biscuits, cakes, and ice cream: *chocolate-chip cookies*.

chocolate spot ▶ **noun** [mass noun] a fungal disease affecting field and broad beans, characterized by dark brown spots on all parts of the plant. ● This is caused by the fungus *Botrytis fabae*, subdivision Deuteromycotina (or Ascomycotina).

chocolatier /ˌtʃɒkəˈlatɪə/, French /ʃɔkɔlatje/ ▶ **noun** (pl. pronunc. **same**) a maker or seller of chocolate.
– ORIGIN late 19th cent.: French.

Choctaw /ˈtʃɒktɔː/ ▶ **noun** (pl. **same** or **Choctaws**) **1** a member of an American Indian people now living mainly in Mississippi.
2 [mass noun] the Muskogean language of the Choctaw, closely related to Chickasaw and now almost extinct.
3 (in skating) a step from one edge of a skate to the other edge of the other skate in the opposite direction.
▶ **adjective** relating to the Choctaw or their language.
– ORIGIN from Choctaw *čahta*.

choice ▶ **noun** an act of choosing between two or more possibilities: *the* **choice between** *good and evil*. ■ [mass noun] the right or ability to choose: *I had to do it, I had no choice*. ■ a range of possibilities from which one or more may be chosen: *you can have a sofa made in a choice of forty fabrics*. ■ a thing or person which is chosen: *this disk drive is the perfect choice for your computer*.
▶ **adjective 1** (especially of food) of very good quality: *he picked some choice early plums*.
2 (of words or language) rude and abusive: *he had a few choice words at his command*.
– PHRASES **by choice** of one's own accord. **of choice** selected as one's favourite or the best: *champagne was his drink of choice*. **of one's choice** that one chooses or has chosen: *the college of her choice*.
– DERIVATIVES **choicely** adverb, **choiceness** noun.
– ORIGIN Middle English: from Old French *chois*, from *choisir* 'choose', of Germanic origin and related to CHOOSE.

choil /tʃɔɪl/ ▶ **noun** the end of a knife's cutting edge which is nearer to the handle.
– ORIGIN late 19th cent.: of unknown origin.

choir ▶ **noun** an organized group of singers, especially one that takes part in church services or performs in public. ■ the part of a cathedral or large church between the high altar and the nave, used by the choir and clergy. ■ a group of instruments of one family playing together: *a clarinet choir*.
– ORIGIN Middle English *quer, quere*, from Old French *quer*, from Latin *chorus* (see CHORUS). The spelling change in the 17th cent. was due to association with Latin *chorus* and modern French *choeur*.

choirboy (or **choirgirl**) ▶ **noun** a boy (or girl) who sings in a church or cathedral choir.

choirman ▶ **noun** (pl. **choirmen**) Brit. a man who sings in a church or cathedral choir.

choirmaster ▶ **noun** the conductor of a choir.

choir organ ▶ **noun** a separate division of many large organs, played using a third manual (keyboard), and typically having distinctively toned stops.

choir school ▶ **noun** a school which is attached to a cathedral or college and specializes in training choirboys and choirgirls.

choir stalls ▶ **plural noun** fixed seating in the choir of a church or chapel.

choi sum /tʃɔɪ ˈsʌm/ (also **choy sum**) ▶ **noun** a small Chinese cabbage of a variety with mild-tasting leaves and small edible yellow flowers. ● *Brassica rapa* var. *parachinensis*, family Cruciferae.
– ORIGIN Chinese (Cantonese dialect), literally 'vegetable heart'.

choisya /ˈtʃɔɪzɪə/ ▶ **noun** an evergreen Mexican shrub with sweet-scented white flowers, grown as an ornamental. ● *Choisya ternata*, family Rutaceae.
– ORIGIN named after Jacques D. *Choisy* (1799–1859), Swiss botanist.

choke[1] ▶ **verb 1** [no obj.] (of a person or animal) have severe difficulty in breathing because of a constricted or obstructed throat or a lack of air: *Willie choked on a mouthful of tea*. ■ [with obj.] prevent (a person or animal) from breathing in such a way. ■ [with obj.] prevent (a plant) from growing by depriving it of light, air, or nourishment: *the bracken will choke the wild gladiolus*. ■ [with obj.] prevent or inhibit the occurrence or development of: *higher rates of interest choke off investment demand*. ■ [no obj.] informal (in sports) fail to perform at a crucial point of a game or contest as a result of nervousness: *we were the only team not to choke when it came to the crunch*.
2 [with obj.] fill (a space) so as to make movement difficult or impossible: *the roads were choked with traffic*.
3 [with obj.] make (someone) speechless with a strong feeling or emotion: *he was choked with fury*. ■ (usu. **be choked up**) cause (someone) to feel tearful or extremely upset: *I was so choked up I started crying and couldn't sing any more* | [no obj.] *I just choked up reading it*. ■ suppress a strong emotion or the expression of such an emotion: *Liz was choking back her anger*.
4 [with obj.] enrich the fuel mixture in (a petrol engine) by reducing the intake of air.
▶ **noun 1** a valve in the carburettor of a petrol engine that is used to reduce the amount of air in the fuel mixture when the engine is started. ■ a knob which controls such a valve.
2 a narrowed part of a shotgun bore near the muzzle, serving to restrict the spread of the shot.
3 an inductance coil used to smooth the variations of an alternating current or to alter its phase.
4 an act or the sound of a person or animal having difficulty in breathing: *a little choke of laughter*.
– ORIGIN Middle English: from Old English *āceōcian* (verb), from *cēoce* (see CHEEK).

choke[2] ▶ **noun** the inedible mass of silky fibres at the centre of a globe artichoke.
– ORIGIN late 17th cent.: probably a confusion of the ending of *artichoke* with CHOKE[1].

chokeberry ▶ **noun** (pl. **chokeberries**) a North American shrub of the rose family, with white flowers and red autumn foliage, cultivated as an ornamental. ● Genus *Aronia*, family Rosaceae.
■ the bitter scarlet berry-like fruit of the chokeberry.

choke chain ▶ **noun** a chain formed into a loop by passing one end through a ring on the other, placed round a dog's neck to exert control by causing pressure on the windpipe when the dog pulls.

chokecherry ▶ **noun** a North American cherry with astringent fruit which is edible when cooked. ● *Prunus virginiana*, family Rosaceae.

choke-damp ▶ **noun** [mass noun] choking or suffocating gas, typically carbon dioxide, that is found in mines and other underground spaces.

chokehold ▶ **noun** a tight grip round a person's neck, used to restrain them by restricting their breathing: *the police have banned chokeholds* | figurative *the southern delegates had the convention in a chokehold*.

choke point ▶ **noun** N. Amer. a point of congestion or blockage: *the tunnel is a choke point at rush hour*.

choker ▶ **noun 1** a necklace or band of fabric that fits closely around the neck. ■ dated a clerical or other high collar.
2 N. Amer. a cable looped round a log to drag it.
3 informal an extremely upsetting experience: *saying our farewells—that was a bit of a choker*.
4 informal a sports player who fails to perform at a crucial point as a result of nervousness: *when I was playing on the tour, I was a choker*.

chokey (also **choky**) ▶ **noun** (pl. **chokeys** or **chokies**) [in sing.] Brit. informal, dated prison. ■ [mass noun] imprisonment: *three months' chokey*.
– ORIGIN early 17th cent. (in the sense 'customs or toll house'): Anglo-Indian, from Hindi *caukī*; influenced by CHOKE[1].

chokidar ▶ **noun** variant spelling of CHOWKIDAR.

choko /ˈtʃəʊkəʊ/ ▶ **noun** (pl. **chokos**) Austral./NZ the fruit of the chayote plant, eaten as a vegetable in the Caribbean, Australia, and New Zealand.
– ORIGIN mid 18th cent.: from Spanish *chocho*, from a Brazilian Indian word. The current spelling dates from the early 20th cent.

chokra /ˈtʃəʊkrə/ ▶ **noun** chiefly derogatory (in South Asia) a boy, especially one employed as a servant.
– ORIGIN from Hindi *chokrā*.

Chokwe /ˈtʃɒkweɪ/ ▶ **noun** (pl. **same**) **1** a member of a people living in the Democratic Republic of the Congo (Zaire) and northern Angola.
2 [mass noun] the Bantu language of the Chokwe, with over a million speakers.
▶ **adjective** relating to the Chokwe or their language.

choky[1] ▶ **adjective** having or causing difficulty in breathing: *the whole piazza was choky with tear gas*. ■ breathless with emotion: *'Nick,' she said, choky suddenly*.

choky[2] ▶ **noun** variant spelling of CHOKEY.

chola /ˈtʃəʊlə/ ▶ **noun** a female cholo.
– ORIGIN mid 19th cent.: American Spanish (see CHOLO).

cholangiography /ˌkɒlandʒɪˈɒgrəfi/ ▶ **noun** [mass noun] Medicine X-ray examination of the bile ducts, used to locate and identify an obstruction.
– DERIVATIVES **cholangiogram** noun.
– ORIGIN 1930s: coined in Spanish from Greek *kholē* 'bile' + *angeion* 'vessel' + *-graphia* (see -GRAPHY).

chole- /ˈkɒli/ (also **chol-** before a vowel) ▶ **combining form** Medicine & Chemistry relating to bile or the bile ducts: *cholesterol*.
– ORIGIN from Greek *kholē* 'gall, bile'.

cholecalciferol /ˌkɒlɪkalˈsɪf(ə)rɒl/ ▶ **noun** [mass noun] Biochemistry one of the D vitamins, a sterol essential for the deposition of calcium in bones and formed by the action of sunlight on dehydrocholesterol in the skin. Also called VITAMIN D_3.

cholecyst- /ˈkɒlɪsɪst/ ▶ **combining form** relating to the gall bladder: *cholecystectomy*.
– ORIGIN from modern Latin *cholecystis* 'gall bladder'.

cholecystectomy ▶ **noun** (pl. **cholecystectomies**) [mass noun] surgical removal of the gall bladder.

cholecystitis ▶ **noun** [mass noun] Medicine inflammation of the gall bladder.

cholecystography /ˌkɒlɪsɪˈstɒgrəfi/ ▶ **noun** [mass noun] Medicine X-ray examination of the gall bladder, used especially to detect the presence of gallstones.

cholecystokinin /ˌkɒlɪˌsɪstə(ʊ)ˈkʌɪnɪn/ ▶ **noun** [mass noun] Biochemistry a hormone which is secreted by cells in the duodenum and stimulates the release of bile into the intestine and the secretion of enzymes by the pancreas.

cholelithiasis /ˌkɒlɪlɪˈθʌɪəsɪs/ ▶ **noun** [mass noun] Medicine the formation of gallstones.

cholent /ˈtʃɒl(ə)nt, ˈʃɒ-/ ▶ **noun** [mass noun] a Jewish Sabbath dish of slowly baked meat and vegetables, prepared on a Friday and cooked overnight.
– ORIGIN from Yiddish *tsholnt*.

choler /ˈkɒlə/ ▶ **noun** [mass noun] (in medieval science and medicine) one of the four bodily humours, identified with bile and believed to be associated with a peevish or irascible temperament. Also called YELLOW BILE. ■ archaic anger or irascibility.
– ORIGIN late Middle English (also denoting diarrhoea): from Old French *colere* 'bile, anger', from Latin *cholera* 'diarrhoea' (from Greek *kholera*), which in late Latin acquired the senses 'bile or anger', from Greek *kholē* 'bile'.

cholera /ˈkɒlərə/ ▶ **noun** [mass noun] an infectious and often fatal bacterial disease of the small intestine, typically contracted from infected water supplies and causing severe vomiting and diarrhoea. ● The disease is caused by the bacterium *Vibrio cholerae*. See VIBRIO.
– ORIGIN late Middle English (originally denoting bile and later applied to various ailments involving vomiting and diarrhoea): from Latin (see CHOLER). The current sense dates from the early 19th cent.

choleraic /ˌkɒləˈreɪɪk/ ▶ **adjective** archaic infected with cholera.

choleric /ˈkɒlərɪk/ ▶ **adjective** bad-tempered or irritable. ■ (in medieval medicine) having choler as the predominant bodily humour.
– DERIVATIVES **cholerically** adverb.
– ORIGIN Middle English (in the sense 'bilious'): from Old French *cholerique*, via Latin from Greek *kholerikos*, from *kholera* (see CHOLER).

cholesterol /kəˈlɛstərɒl/ ▶ **noun** [mass noun] a compound of the sterol type found in most body tissues. Cholesterol and its derivatives are important constituents of cell membranes and precursors of other steroid compounds, but high concentrations in the blood are thought to promote atherosclerosis. ● Chem. formula: $C_{27}H_{45}OH$.
– ORIGIN late 19th cent.: from Greek *kholē* 'bile' + *stereos* 'stiff' + -OL.

choli /ˈtʃəʊli/ ▶ **noun** (pl. **cholis**) a short-sleeved bodice worn under a sari by Indian women.
– ORIGIN from Hindi *colī*.

choliamb /ˈkəʊlɪam(b)/ ▶ **noun** Prosody another term for SCAZON.
– DERIVATIVES **choliambic** /ˌkəʊlɪˈambɪk/ adjective.
– ORIGIN mid 19th cent.: via late Latin from Greek *khōliambos*, from *khōlos* 'lame' + *iambos* (see IAMBUS).

C

cholic acid /ˈkəʊlɪk, ˈkɒl-/ ▶ **noun** [mass noun] Biochemistry a compound produced by oxidation of cholesterol. It is a steroidal fatty acid and its salts are present in bile.
– ORIGIN mid 19th cent.: from Greek *kholikos*, from *kholē* 'bile'.

choline /ˈkəʊliːn, -lɪn/ ▶ **noun** [mass noun] Biochemistry a strongly basic compound important in the synthesis and transport of lipids in the body. ● Chem. formula: $HON(CH_3)_3CH_2CH_2OH$.
– ORIGIN mid 19th cent.: coined in German from Greek *kholē* 'bile'.

cholinergic /ˌkəʊlɪˈnəːdʒɪk/ ▶ **adjective** Physiology relating to or denoting nerve cells in which acetylcholine acts as a neurotransmitter. Contrasted with **ADRENERGIC**.
– ORIGIN 1930s: from **CHOLINE** + Greek *ergon* 'work' + **-IC**.

cholinesterase /ˌkəʊlɪˈnɛstəreɪz/ ▶ **noun** [mass noun] Biochemistry an enzyme, especially acetylcholinesterase, which hydrolyses esters of choline.

cholla /ˈtʃɔɪə/ ▶ **noun** a cactus with a cylindrical stem, native to Mexico and the south-western US. ● Genus *Opuntia*, family Cactaceae.
– ORIGIN mid 19th cent.: Mexican Spanish use of Spanish *cholla* 'skull, head', of unknown origin.

cholo /ˈtʃəʊləʊ/ ▶ **noun** (pl. **cholos**) a Latin American man with American Indian blood; a mestizo. ■ US derogatory a lower-class Mexican, especially in an urban area. ■ US a member of a Mexican street gang.
– ORIGIN mid 19th cent.: American Spanish, from *Cholollán* (now *Cholula*), in Mexico.

chometz /hɔːˈmɛts, ˈxɔːmɛts/ ▶ **noun** variant spelling of **CHAMETZ**.

Chomolungma variant form of **QOMOLUNGMA**.

chomp ▶ **verb** munch or chew noisily or vigorously: *she chomped on a roll*.
▶ **noun** [in sing.] a chewing noise or action.
– PHRASES **chomp at the bit** see **CHAMP AT THE BIT** at **CHAMP[1]**.
– ORIGIN mid 17th cent.: imitative.

Chomsky /ˈtʃɒmski/, (Avram) Noam (b.1928), American theoretical linguist, noted for expounding the theory of generative grammar. He also demonstrated that linguistic behaviour is innate, not learned, and that all languages share the same underlying grammatical base. Chomsky is known also for his opposition to American involvement in the Vietnam War and the Gulf War.
– DERIVATIVES **Chomskyan** (also **Chomskian**) **adjective**.

Chondrichthyes /kɒnˈdrɪkθɪiːz/ ▶ **plural noun** Zoology a class of fishes that includes those with a cartilaginous skeleton. Compare with **OSTEICHTHYES**.
– ORIGIN modern Latin, from Greek *khondros* 'cartilage' + *ikhthus* 'fish'.

chondrite /ˈkɒndrʌɪt/ ▶ **noun** a stony meteorite containing small mineral granules (chondrules).
– DERIVATIVES **chondritic adjective**.
– ORIGIN mid 19th cent.: from Greek *khondros* 'granule' + **-ITE[1]**.

chondro- /ˈkɒndrə(ʊ)/ ▶ **combining form** relating to cartilage: *chondrocyte*.
– ORIGIN from Greek *khondros* 'grain or cartilage'.

chondrocyte /ˈkɒndrə(ʊ)sʌɪt/ ▶ **noun** Biology a cell which has secreted the matrix of cartilage and become embedded in it.

chondroitin /kɒnˈdrəʊɪtɪn/ ▶ **noun** [mass noun] Biochemistry a mucopolysaccharide compound which is a major constituent of cartilage and other connective tissue.
– ORIGIN late 19th cent.: from **CHONDRO-** + **-ITE[1]** + **-IN[1]**.

chondrule /ˈkɒndruːl/ ▶ **noun** a spheroidal mineral grain present in large numbers in some stony meteorites.
– ORIGIN late 19th cent.: from **CHONDRITE** + **-ULE**.

Chongjin /tʃʌŋˈdʒɪn/ a port on the NE coast of North Korea; pop. 582,500 (est. 2005).

Chongqing /tʃʊŋˈtʃɪŋ/ (also **Chungking**) a city in Sichuan province in central China; pop. 4,776,000 (est. 2006). It was the capital of China from 1938 to 1946.

choo-choo (also **choo-choo train**) ▶ **noun** a child's word for a railway train or locomotive.
– ORIGIN early 20th cent. (originally US): imitative.

choof /tʃʊf/ ▶ **verb** [no obj., with adverbial of direction] Austral. informal go or move in a specified direction: *I used to drink beer at home with Dad before he choofed off*.
– ORIGIN 1940s: form of **CHUFF[1]**, used figuratively.

chook /tʃʊk/ (also **chookie**) ▶ **noun** Austral./NZ informal
1 a chicken or fowl.
2 derogatory an older woman.
– ORIGIN 1920s: probably from English dialect *chuck* 'chicken', of imitative origin.

choose ▶ **verb** (past **chose**; past participle **chosen**) [with obj.] pick out (someone or something) as being the best or most appropriate of two or more alternatives: *he chose a seat facing the door* | [no obj.] *there are many versions to* ***choose from***. ■ [no obj.] decide on a course of action: [with infinitive] *he chose to go* | *I'll stay as long as I choose*.
– PHRASES **cannot choose but do something** formal have no alternative to doing something. **there is little** (or **nothing**) **to choose between** there is little or no difference between.
– DERIVATIVES **chooser noun**.
– ORIGIN Old English *cēosan*, of Germanic origin; related to Dutch *kiezen*.

choosy ▶ **adjective** (**choosier, choosiest**) informal taking excessive care when making a choice: *she's become very choosy about food*.
– DERIVATIVES **choosily adverb, choosiness noun**.

chop[1] ▶ **verb** (**chops, chopping, chopped**) **1** [with obj.] cut (something) into pieces with repeated sharp blows of an axe or knife: *they* ***chopped up*** *the pulpit for firewood* | *finely chop 200g of skipjack tuna*. ■ (**chop something off**) remove something by cutting: *a paper guillotine chopped off all four fingers*. ■ cut through the base of (a tree or similar plant) with blows from an axe or other implement, in order to fell it: *the boy* ***chopped down*** *eight trees*. ■ strike (something) with a short heavy blow, as if cutting at something: *Benson chopped the ball onto the stumps*.
2 abolish or reduce the size of (something) in a way regarded as ruthless: *their training courses are to be chopped*.
▶ **noun 1** a downward cutting blow or movement, typically with the hand: *an effective chop to the back of the neck*.
2 a thick slice of meat, especially pork or lamb, adjacent to and often including a rib.
3 Austral./NZ informal a person's share of something.
4 [mass noun] N. Amer. crushed or ground grain used as animal feed.
5 [in sing.] the broken motion of water, owing to the action of the wind against the tide: *we started our run into a two-foot chop*.
– PHRASES **the chop** Brit. informal dismissal from employment: *hundreds more workers have been given the chop*. ■ cancellation or abolition: *all these projects are destined for the chop*. ■ the action of killing someone or the fact of being killed. **chop logic** argue in a tiresomely pedantic way; quibble. [mid 16th cent.: from a dialect use of *chop* meaning 'bandy words'.]
– ORIGIN late Middle English: variant of **CHAP[1]**.

chop[2] ▶ **verb** (**chops, chopping, chopped**) (in phrase **chop and change**) Brit. informal change one's opinions or behaviour repeatedly and abruptly.
– ORIGIN late Middle English (in the sense 'barter, exchange'): perhaps related to Old English *cēap* 'bargaining, trade'; compare with *chap-* in **CHAPMAN**.

chop[3] ▶ **noun** archaic a trademark; a brand of goods.
– PHRASES **not much chop** Austral./NZ informal unsatisfactory: *that veranda's not much chop in bad weather*.
– ORIGIN early 19th cent.: from Hindi *chāp* 'stamp, brand' (see **CHAAP**).

chop-chop ▶ **adverb & exclamation** quickly; quick: *'Two pints, chop-chop,' Jimmy called*.
– ORIGIN mid 19th cent.: pidgin English, based on Chinese dialect *kuài-kuài*. Compare with **CHOPSTICK**.

chop-fallen ▶ **adjective** variant spelling of **CHAP-FALLEN**.

chophouse ▶ **noun** a restaurant that specializes in steaks, chops, and similar fare.

Chopin[1] /ˈʃəʊpã/, Frédéric (François) (1810–49), Polish-born French composer and pianist; Polish name *Fryderyk Franciszek Szopen*. Writing almost exclusively for the piano, he composed numerous mazurkas and polonaises inspired by Polish folk music, as well as nocturnes, preludes, and two piano concertos (1829; 1830).

Chopin[2] /ˈʃəʊpan/, Kate (O'Flaherty) (1851–1904), American novelist and short-story writer. Notable works: *Bayou Folk* (1894), *A Night in Acidie* (1897), and *The Awakening* (1899).

chopper ▶ **noun 1** a short axe with a large blade. ■ a butcher's cleaver: *a meat chopper*. ■ a machine for chopping something: *a straw chopper*. ■ a device for regularly interrupting an electric current or a beam of light or particles. ■ (**choppers**) informal teeth.
2 informal a helicopter.
3 informal a type of motorcycle with high handlebars and the front-wheel fork extended forwards.
4 Brit. vulgar slang a man's penis.

chopping block ▶ **noun** a block for chopping wood or food. ■ historical an executioner's block.
– PHRASES **on the chopping block** likely to be abolished or drastically reduced.

chopping board ▶ **noun** Brit. a board on which vegetables and other types of food are chopped.

choppy ▶ **adjective** (**choppier, choppiest**) **1** (of a sea, lake, or river) having many small waves.
2 having a disjointed or jerky quality: *the choppy, electronic beat of hip hop*.
– DERIVATIVES **choppily adverb, choppiness noun**.
– ORIGIN early 17th cent. (in the sense 'full of chaps or clefts'): from **CHOP[1]** + **-Y[1]**.

chops ▶ **plural noun** informal **1** a person's or animal's mouth or jaws: *a smack in the chops*. ■ a person's cheeks: *his wobbling chops*.
2 the technical skill of a jazz or rock musician: *when I'm on tour my chops go down*.
– PHRASES **bust one's chops** N. Amer. informal exert oneself. **bust someone's chops** N. Amer. informal nag or criticize someone.
– ORIGIN late Middle English: variant of **CHAP[3]**.

chop shop ▶ **noun** N. Amer. informal a place where stolen vehicles are dismantled so that the parts can be sold or used to repair other stolen vehicles.

chopsocky /ˈtʃɒpsɒki/ ▶ **noun** [mass noun] [usu. as modifier] N. Amer. informal kung fu or a similar martial art, especially as depicted in violent action films: *chopsocky epics from Hong Kong*.
– ORIGIN 1970s: perhaps humorously suggested by **CHOP SUEY**.

chopstick ▶ **noun** (usu. **chopsticks**) each of a pair of small, thin, tapered sticks of wood, ivory, or plastic, held together in one hand and used as eating utensils especially by the Chinese and the Japanese.
– ORIGIN late 17th cent.: pidgin English, from *chop* 'quick' + **STICK[1]**, translating Chinese dialect *kuaizi*, literally 'nimble ones'. Compare with **CHOP-CHOP**.

chop suey /tʃɒpˈsuːi/ ▶ **noun** [mass noun] a Chinese-style dish of meat stewed and fried with bean sprouts, bamboo shoots, and onions, and served with rice.
– ORIGIN late 19th cent.: from Chinese (Cantonese dialect) *tsaâp suì* 'mixed bits'.

choral ▶ **adjective** composed for or sung by a choir or chorus: *a choral work*. ■ engaged in or concerned with singing: *a choral scholar*.
– DERIVATIVES **chorally adverb**.
– ORIGIN late 16th cent.: from medieval Latin *choralis*, from Latin *chorus* (see **CHORUS**).

chorale ▶ **noun 1** a musical composition consisting of or resembling a harmonized version of a simple, stately hymn tune. ■ a hymn tune of this kind.
2 US a choir or choral society.
– ORIGIN mid 19th cent.: from German *Choral(gesang)*, translating medieval Latin *cantus choralis*.

chord[1] ▶ **noun** a group of (typically three or more) notes sounded together, as a basis of harmony: *the triumphal opening chords* | *a G major chord*.
▶ **verb** [no obj.] (usu. as noun **chording**) play, sing, or arrange notes in chords.
– DERIVATIVES **chordal adjective**.
– ORIGIN Middle English *cord*, from **ACCORD**. The spelling change in the 18th cent. was due to confusion with **CHORD[2]**. The original sense was 'agreement, reconciliation', later 'a musical concord or harmonious sound'; the current sense dates from the mid 18th cent.

chord[2] ▶ **noun 1** Mathematics a straight line joining the ends of an arc.
2 Aeronautics the width of an aerofoil from leading to trailing edge.
3 Engineering each of the two principal members of a truss.
4 Anatomy variant spelling of **CORD**: *the spinal chord*.
5 literary a string on a harp or other instrument.
– PHRASES **strike** (or **touch**) **a chord** cause someone to feel sympathy, emotion, or enthusiasm: *the issue of food safety strikes a chord with almost everyone*. [with figurative reference to the emotions being the 'strings' of the mind visualized as a musical instrument.] **strike** (or **touch**) **the right chord** skilfully appeal to or arouse a particular emotion in others: *Dickens knew how to strike the right chord in the hearts of his readers*.
– ORIGIN mid 16th cent. (in the anatomical sense): a later spelling (influenced by Latin *chorda* 'rope') of **CORD**.

> **USAGE** In modern English there are two words spelled **chord**: the first is the musical term 'a group of notes sounded together', and the second is a technical term in mathematics, aeronautics, and engineering. **Cord** meaning 'string or rope made from twisted strands' is etymologically related to the second **chord** but is now regarded as a distinct word. The anatomical term generally uses the spelling **cord** (as in **spinal cord** and **vocal cord**), although **chord** is an acceptable variant.

Chordata /kɔːˈdeɪtə/ ▶ **plural noun** Zoology a large phylum of animals that includes the vertebrates together with the sea squirts and lancelets. They are distinguished by the possession of a notochord at some stage during their development.
– ORIGIN modern Latin (plural), from Latin *chorda* (see CHORD^{2}), on the pattern of words such as *Vertebrata*.

chordate /ˈkɔːdeɪt/ Zoology ▶ **noun** an animal of the large phylum Chordata, comprising the vertebrates together with the sea squirts and lancelets.
▶ **adjective** relating to or denoting chordates.

chordophone /ˈkɔːdəfəʊn/ ▶ **noun** Music, technical a stringed instrument.

chordotonal /ˌkɔːdə(ʊ)ˈtəʊn(ə)l/ ▶ **adjective** Entomology (in insects) denoting sense organs which are responsive to mechanical and sound vibrations.
– ORIGIN late 19th cent.: from CHORD^{2} + TONAL.

chore ▶ **noun** a routine task, especially a household one. ■ a tedious but necessary task: *he sees interviews as a chore.*
– ORIGIN mid 18th cent. (originally dialect and US): variant of obsolete *char* or *chare* (see CHARWOMAN).

chorea /kɒˈrɪə/ ▶ **noun** [mass noun] Medicine a neurological disorder characterized by jerky involuntary movements affecting especially the shoulders, hips, and face. See also HUNTINGTON'S DISEASE, SYDENHAM'S CHOREA.
– ORIGIN late 17th cent.: via Latin from Greek *khoreia* 'dancing in unison', from *khoros* 'chorus'.

choreograph /ˈkɒrɪəgrɑːf/ ▶ **verb** [with obj.] compose the sequence of steps and moves for (a ballet or other performance of dance). ■ plan and control (an event or operation): *the committee choreographs the movement of troops.*
– DERIVATIVES **choreographer** noun.
– ORIGIN 1940s: back-formation from CHOREOGRAPHY.

choreography /ˌkɒrɪˈɒgrəfi/ ▶ **noun** [mass noun] the sequence of steps and movements in dance or figure skating, especially in a ballet or other staged dance: *the rumbustious choreography reflects the themes of the original play.* ■ the art or practice of designing such sequences.
– DERIVATIVES **choreographic** adjective, **choreographically** adverb.
– ORIGIN late 18th cent. (in the sense 'written notation of dancing'): from Greek *khoreia* 'dancing in unison' (from *khoros* 'chorus') + -GRAPHY.

choreology /ˌkɒrɪˈɒlədʒi/ ▶ **noun** [mass noun] the notation of dance movement.
– DERIVATIVES **choreologist** noun.
– ORIGIN 1960s: from Greek *khoreia* 'dancing in unison' (from *khoros* 'chorus') + -LOGY.

choriambus /ˌkɒrɪˈambəs/ ▶ **noun** (pl. **choriambi** /-bʌɪ/) a metrical foot consisting of two short (or unstressed) syllables between two long (or stressed) ones.
– DERIVATIVES **choriambic** adjective.
– ORIGIN late 18th cent.: via late Latin from Greek *khoriambos*, from *khoreios* 'of the dance' + *iambos* (see IAMBUS).

choric /ˈkɒrɪk, ˈkɔːrɪk/ ▶ **adjective** belonging to, spoken by, or resembling a chorus in drama or recitation.
– ORIGIN mid 19th cent.: via late Latin from Greek *khorikos*, from *khoros* 'chorus'.

chorine /ˈkɔːriːn/ ▶ **noun** a chorus girl.
– ORIGIN 1920s (originally US): from CHORUS + -INE^{3}.

chorio- /ˈkɔːrɪəʊ/ ▶ **combining form** representing CHORION or CHOROID.

chorioallantoic /ˌkɔːrɪəʊˌalənˈtəʊɪk, ˌkɒrɪəʊ-/ ▶ **adjective** Embryology relating to or denoting fused chorionic and allantoic membranes around a fetus.

choriocarcinoma /ˌkɔːrɪə(ʊ)ˌkɑːsɪˈnəʊmə, ˈkɒrɪəʊ-/ ▶ **noun** (pl. **choriocarcinomas** or **choriocarcinomata** /-mətə/) Medicine a malignant tumour of the uterus which originates in the fetal chorion.

chorion /ˈkɔːrɪən/ ▶ **noun** Embryology the outermost membrane surrounding an embryo of a reptile, bird, or mammal. In mammals it contributes to the formation of the placenta.
– DERIVATIVES **chorionic** adjective.
– ORIGIN mid 16th cent.: from Greek *khorion*.

chorionic gonadotrophin /ˌkɒrɪˈɒnɪk/ ▶ **noun** [mass noun] a hormone secreted during pregnancy by the placenta which stimulates continued production of progesterone by the ovaries.

chorionic villus sampling ▶ **noun** [mass noun] Medicine a test made in early pregnancy to detect congenital abnormalities in the fetus, in which a tissue sample is taken from the villi of the chorion.

chorister ▶ **noun 1** a member of a choir, especially a choirboy or choirgirl.
2 US a person who leads the singing of a church choir or congregation.
– ORIGIN late Middle English *queristre*, from an Anglo-Norman French variant of Old French *cueriste*, from *quer* (see CHOIR). The change in the first syllable in the 16th cent. was due to association with obsolete *chorist* 'member of a choir or chorus', but the older form *quirister* long survived.

chorizo /tʃəˈriːzəʊ/, Spanish /tʃoˈriθo, -ˈriso/ ▶ **noun** (pl. **chorizos**) a spicy Spanish pork sausage.
– ORIGIN Spanish.

chorography /kɔːˈrɒgrəfi/ ▶ **noun** [mass noun] historical the systematic description and mapping of particular regions.
– DERIVATIVES **chorographer** noun, **chorographic** adjective.
– ORIGIN mid 16th cent.: via Latin from Greek *khōrographia*, from *khōra* or *khōros* 'region'.

choroid /ˈkɔːrɔɪd, ˈkɒr-/ ▶ **adjective** resembling the chorion, particularly in containing many blood vessels.
▶ **noun** (also **choroid coat**) the pigmented vascular layer of the eyeball between the retina and the sclera.
– DERIVATIVES **choroidal** adjective.
– ORIGIN mid 17th cent.: from Greek *khoroeidēs* (adjective), alteration of *khorioeidēs*, from *khorion* (see CHORION).

choroid plexus /ˈkɔːrɔɪd, ˈkɒr-/ ▶ **noun** (pl. **same** or **choroid plexuses**) a network of blood vessels in each ventricle of the brain, producing the cerebrospinal fluid.

choropleth map /ˈkɒrə(ʊ)plɛθ/ ▶ **noun** a map which uses differences in shading, colouring, or the placing of symbols within predefined areas to indicate the average values of a particular quantity in those areas. Compare with ISOPLETH.
– ORIGIN 1930s: *choropleth* from Greek *khōra* 'region' + *plēthos* 'multitude'.

chorten /ˈtʃɔːt(ə)n/ ▶ **noun** (chiefly in Tibet) a Buddhist shrine, typically a saint's tomb or a monument to the Buddha.
– ORIGIN Tibetan.

chortle ▶ **verb** [no obj.] laugh in a noisy, gleeful way: *he chortled at his own execrable pun.*
▶ **noun** a noisy, gleeful laugh: *Thomas gave a chortle.*
– ORIGIN 1871: coined by Lewis Carroll in *Through the Looking Glass*; probably a blend of CHUCKLE and SNORT.

chorus ▶ **noun** (pl. **choruses**) **1** a part of a song which is repeated after each verse. ■ a piece of choral music, especially one forming part of a larger work such as an opera.
2 a large organized group of singers, especially one which performs with an orchestra or opera company. ■ a group of singers or dancers performing together in a supporting role in a musical or opera.
3 a simultaneous utterance of something by many people: *a growing **chorus of** complaint* | *'Good morning,' we replied **in chorus**.*
4 (in ancient Greek tragedy) a group of performers who comment together on the main action. ■ a single character who speaks the prologue and other linking parts of the play, especially in Elizabethan drama. ■ a section of text spoken by the chorus in drama.
5 a device used with an amplified musical instrument to give the impression that more than one instrument is being played: [as modifier] *a chorus pedal.*
▶ **verb** (**choruses, chorusing, chorused**) [with obj.] (of a group of people) say the same thing at the same time: [with direct speech] *'Morning, Sister,' the nurses chorused.*
– ORIGIN mid 16th cent. (denoting a character speaking the prologue of a play): from Latin, from Greek *khoros*.

chorus girl ▶ **noun** a young woman who sings or dances in the chorus of a musical.

chose past of CHOOSE.

chosen past participle of CHOOSE. ▶ **adjective** having been selected as the best or most appropriate: *he is by no means a forerunner in his chosen field.*
– PHRASES **chosen few** a small group of people who enjoy special privileges or treatment, typically in a way thought to be unfair. **chosen people** the Jewish people considered (in Jewish and Christian tradition) as having been selected by God for a special relationship with him. ■ (in Christian use) those destined for salvation; believing Christians.

chota /ˈtʃəʊtə/ ▶ **adjective** Indian small or young. ■ lower in rank or importance.
– ORIGIN from Hindi *chotā*.

Chou /tʃəʊ/ variant spelling of ZHOU.

choucroute /ˈʃuːkruːt/ ▶ **noun** [mass noun] pickled cabbage; sauerkraut.
– ORIGIN French, from German dialect *Surkrut* 'sauerkraut', influenced by French *chou* 'cabbage'.

Chou En-lai /ˌtʃəʊ ɛnˈlʌɪ/ variant of ZHOU ENLAI.

chough /tʃʌf/ ▶ **noun 1** a black Eurasian and North African bird of the crow family, with a downcurved bill and broad, rounded wings, typically frequenting mountains and sea cliffs. ● Genus *Pyrrhocorax* (and *Pseudopodoces*), family Corvidae: three species, especially the (**red-billed**) **chough** (*P. pyrrhocorax*).
2 (also **white-winged chough**) a black and white Australian bird of the mud-nester family. ● *Corcorax melanorhamphos*, family Corcoracidae (or Grallinidae).
– ORIGIN Middle English (originally denoting the jackdaw): probably imitative.

choux pastry /ʃuː/ ▶ **noun** [mass noun] very light pastry made with egg, typically used for eclairs and profiteroles.
– ORIGIN late 19th cent.: from *choux* or *chou*, denoting a round cream-filled pastry (from French *chou* (plural *choux*) 'cabbage, rosette', from Latin *caulis*) + PASTRY.

chow /tʃaʊ/ ▶ **noun 1** [mass noun] informal food.
2 (also **chow chow**) a dog of a sturdy Chinese breed with a broad muzzle, a tail curled over the back, a bluish-black tongue, and typically a dense thick coat.
▶ **verb** N. Amer. informal eat: [no obj.] *he **chowed down** on lobster.*
– ORIGIN late 19th cent.: shortened from CHOW CHOW.

chow chow ▶ **noun 1** another term for CHOW (sense 2 of the noun).
2 [mass noun] a Chinese preserve of ginger, orange peel, and other ingredients, in syrup.
3 [mass noun] a mixed vegetable pickle.
– ORIGIN late 18th cent.: pidgin English, of unknown ultimate origin.

chowder ▶ **noun** [mass noun] a rich soup typically containing fish, clams, or corn with potatoes and onions: *clam chowder.*
– ORIGIN mid 18th cent.: perhaps from French *chaudière* 'stew pot', related to Old Northern French *caudron* (see CAULDRON).

chowderhead ▶ **noun** N. Amer. informal a stupid person.
– DERIVATIVES **chowderheaded** adjective.
– ORIGIN mid 19th cent.: probably a variant of early 17th-cent. *jolter-head* 'thickheaded person'.

chowhound ▶ **noun** US informal a very enthusiastic eater.
– ORIGIN early 20th cent.: (originally US military slang) from CHOW + HOUND.

chowk /tʃaʊk/ ▶ **noun** [usu. in names] (in South Asia) an open market area in a city at the junction of two roads: *Chandni Chowk.*
– ORIGIN from Hindi *cauk*.

chowki /ˈtʃɒki/ ▶ **noun** Indian **1** a police station or jail.
2 a low wooden seat or stool.
– ORIGIN from Hindi *caukī* (see CHOKEY).

chowkidar /ˈtʃɒkidɑː/ (also **chokidar** /ˈtʃɒkidɑː/) ▶ **noun** (in South Asia) a watchman or gatekeeper.
– ORIGIN from Urdu *caukīdār*, from *caukī* 'toll house' + *-dār* 'keeper'.

chow mein /tʃaʊ ˈmeɪn/ ▶ **noun** [mass noun] a Chinese-style dish of fried noodles with shredded meat or seafood and vegetables.
– ORIGIN late 19th cent.: from Chinese *chǎo miàn* 'stir-fried noodles'.

CHP ▶ **abbreviation** combined heat and power, a system in which steam produced in a power station as a by-product of electricity generation is used to heat nearby buildings.

Chr. ▶ **abbreviation** Chronicles (in biblical references).

chrestomathy /krɛˈstɒməθi/ ▶ **noun** (pl. **chrestomathies**) formal a selection of passages from an author or authors, designed to help in learning a language.

– ORIGIN mid 19th cent.: from Greek *khrēstomatheia*, from *khrēstos* 'useful' + *-matheia* 'learning'.

Chrétien /ˈkreɪtjã/, French /kretjɛ̃/, (Joseph-Jacques) Jean (b.1934), Canadian Liberal statesman, Prime Minister 1993–2003.

Chrétien de Troyes /ˌkreɪtjã də ˈtrwʌ/, French /kretjɛ̃ də trwa/ (12th century), French poet. His courtly romances on Arthurian themes include *Lancelot* (*c.*1177–81) and *Perceval* (1181–90, unfinished).

Chrimbo (also **Crimbo**) ▸ **noun** Brit. informal Christmas.
– ORIGIN 1920s: child's alteration.

chrism /ˈkrɪz(ə)m/ ▸ **noun** [mass noun] a mixture of oil and balsam, consecrated and used for anointing at baptism and in other rites of Catholic, Orthodox, and Anglican Churches.
– ORIGIN Old English, from medieval Latin *crisma*, ecclesiastical Latin *chrisma*, from Greek *khrisma* 'anointing', from *khriein* 'anoint'.

chrisom /ˈkrɪz(ə)m/ (also **chrisom-cloth**) ▸ **noun** historical a white robe put on a child at baptism, and used as its shroud if it died within the month.
– ORIGIN Middle English: alteration of **CHRISM**, representing a popular pronunciation with two syllables.

Chrissake /ˈkrʌɪseɪk/ (also **Chrissakes**) ▸ **noun** (in phrase **for Chrissake**) informal for Christ's sake (used as an exclamation of annoyance or exasperation): *for Chrissake, listen to me!*
– ORIGIN 1920s: representing a pronunciation.

Chrissie (also **Chrissy**) ▸ **noun** Brit. informal Christmas.

Christ ▸ **noun** the title, also treated as a name, given to Jesus.
▸ **exclamation** an oath used to express irritation, dismay, or surprise.
– PHRASES **before Christ** full form of **BC**.
– DERIVATIVES **Christhood** noun, **Christlike** adjective, **Christly** adjective.
– ORIGIN Old English *Crīst*, from Latin *Christus*, from Greek *Khristos*, noun use of an adjective meaning 'anointed', from *khriein* 'anoint', translating Hebrew *māšīaḥ* 'Messiah'.

Christadelphian /ˌkrɪstəˈdɛlfɪən/ ▸ **noun** a member of a Christian sect, founded in America in 1848, which claims to return to the beliefs and practices of the earliest disciples and holds that Christ will return in power to set up a worldwide theocracy beginning at Jerusalem.
▸ **adjective** of or adhering to the Christadelphian sect and its beliefs.
– ORIGIN from late Greek *Khristadelphos* 'in brotherhood with Christ' (from Greek *Khristos* 'Christ' + *adelphos* 'brother') + **-IAN**.

Christchurch a city on the South Island, New Zealand; pop. 348,435 (2006).

christen ▸ **verb** [with obj.] **1** give (a baby) a Christian name at baptism as a sign of admission to a Christian Church: [with obj. and complement] *their second daughter was christened Jeanette.* ■ give a name to (someone or something) which reflects a notable characteristic: [with obj. and complement] *we have christened our regular train home the ghost train.*
2 informal use for the first time.
– ORIGIN Old English *crīstnian* 'make Christian', from *crīsten* 'Christian', from Latin *Christianus*, from *Christus* 'Christ'.

Christendom ▸ **noun** [mass noun] dated the worldwide body or society of Christians. ■ the Christian world: *the greatest church in Christendom.*
– ORIGIN Old English *crīstendōm*, from *crīsten* (see **CHRISTEN**) + *-dōm* (see **-DOM**).

christening ▸ **noun** a Christian ceremony at which a baby is christened; a baptism.

Christer /ˈkrʌɪstə/ ▸ **noun** N. Amer. informal a sanctimonious or ostentatiously pious Christian.

Christian¹ /ˈkrɪstɪən, ˈkrɪstʃən/, Fletcher (*c.*1764–*c.*1793), English seaman and mutineer. As first mate under Captain Bligh on HMS *Bounty*, in April 1789 Christian seized the ship and cast Bligh and others adrift. In 1790 the mutineers settled on Pitcairn Island, where Christian was probably killed by Tahitians.

Christian² /ˈkrɪstɪən, -tʃ(ə)n/ ▸ **adjective** relating to or professing Christianity or its teachings: *the Christian Church.* ■ informal having qualities associated with Christians, especially those of decency, kindness, and fairness.
▸ **noun** a person who has received Christian baptism or is a believer in Christianity.
– DERIVATIVES **Christianization** (also **Christianisation**) noun, **Christianize** (also **Christianise**) verb, **Christianly** adverb.
– ORIGIN late Middle English: from Latin *Christianus*, from *Christus* 'Christ'.

Christian Aid a charity supported by most of the Christian Churches in the UK and operating chiefly in developing countries, where it works for disaster relief and supports development projects.

Christian Brothers a Roman Catholic lay teaching order founded in France in 1684.

Christian era ▸ **noun** (**the Christian era**) the period of time which begins with the traditional date of Christ's birth.

Christiania /ˌkrɪstɪˈɑːnɪə/ (also **Kristiania**) former name (1624–1924) for **OSLO**.

Christianity ▸ **noun** [mass noun] the religion based on the person and teachings of Jesus Christ, or its beliefs and practices. ■ Christian quality or character.

> Christianity is today the world's most widespread religion, with more than a billion members, mainly divided between the Roman Catholic, Protestant, and Eastern Orthodox Churches. It originated among the Jewish followers of Jesus of Nazareth, who believed that he was the promised Messiah (or 'Christ'), but the Christian Church soon became an independent organization, largely through the missionary efforts of St Paul. In 313 Constantine ended official persecution in the Roman Empire and in 380 Theodosius I recognized it as the state religion. Most Christians believe in one God in three Persons (the Father, the Son, and the Holy Spirit) and that Jesus is the Son of God who rose from the dead after being crucified; a Christian hopes to attain eternal life after death through faith in Jesus Christ and tries to live by his teachings as recorded in the New Testament.

– ORIGIN Middle English: from Old French *crestiente*, from *crestien* 'Christian', influenced by late Latin *christianitas*, from Latin *Christianus*, from *Christus* 'Christ'.

Christian name ▸ **noun** a first name, especially one given at baptism.

> **USAGE** In recognition of the fact that English-speaking societies have many religions and cultures, not just Christian ones, the term **Christian name** has largely given way, at least in official contexts, to alternative terms such as **given name**, **first name**, or **forename**.

Christian Science ▸ **noun** [mass noun] the beliefs and practices of the Church of Christ Scientist, a Christian sect founded by Mary Baker Eddy in 1879. Members hold that only God and the mind have ultimate reality, and that sin and illness are illusions which can be overcome by prayer and faith.
– DERIVATIVES **Christian Scientist** noun.

Christie¹, Dame Agatha (1890–1976), English writer of detective fiction. She wrote over seventy novels, many of which feature the Belgian sleuth Hercule Poirot or the resourceful Miss Marple. Notable works: *Murder on the Orient Express* (1934), *Death on the Nile* (1937), and *The Mousetrap* (play, 1952).

Christie² ▸ **noun** (pl. **Christies**) Skiing, dated a sudden turn in which the skis are kept parallel, used for changing direction fast or stopping short.
– ORIGIN 1920s (earlier as *Christiania*): named after **CHRISTIANIA** in Norway.

Christingle /ˈkrɪstɪŋg(ə)l/ ▸ **noun** a lighted candle symbolizing Christ as the light of the world, held by children at a special Advent service originating in the Moravian Church.
– ORIGIN 1950s: probably from German dialect *Christkindl* 'Christ child, Christmas gift'.

Christmas ▸ **noun** (pl. **Christmases**) the annual Christian festival celebrating Christ's birth, held on 25 December in the Western Church. ■ the period immediately before and after 25 December: *we had guests over Christmas.*
▸ **exclamation** informal expressing surprise, dismay, or despair.
– DERIVATIVES **Christmassy** adjective.
– ORIGIN Old English *Crīstes mæsse* (see **CHRIST**, **MASS**).

Christmas beetle ▸ **noun** any of a number of South African or Australian cicadas or beetles that are abundant or noticeable during the summer.

Christmas box ▸ **noun** Brit. a present given at Christmas to tradespeople and employees.

Christmas cactus ▸ **noun** a South American cactus with flattened segmented stems and red, pink, or white flowers, grown as a houseplant. ● *Schlumbergera bridgesii*, family Cactaceae.
– ORIGIN so named because it flowers at about the northern midwinter.

Christmas cake ▸ **noun** Brit. a rich fruit cake covered with marzipan and icing, eaten at Christmas.

Christmas card ▸ **noun** a greetings card sent at Christmas.

Christmas Day ▸ **noun** the day on which the festival of Christmas is celebrated, 25 December.

Christmas disease ▸ **noun** [mass noun] a form of haemophilia caused by deficiency of the blood-clotting factor IX rather than the more common factor VIII.
– ORIGIN 1950s: from the name of Stephen *Christmas*, the first patient examined in detail.

Christmas Eve the day or the evening before Christmas Day, 24 December.

Christmas flower ▸ **noun** S. African the hydrangea, which in South Africa blooms at Christmas.

Christmas Island 1 an island in the Indian Ocean 350 km (200 miles) south of Java, administered as an external territory of Australia since 1958; pop. 1,400 (est. 2009).
2 former name (until 1981) for **KIRITIMATI**.

Christmas pudding ▸ **noun** Brit. a rich boiled pudding eaten at Christmas, made with flour, suet, and dried fruit.

Christmas rose ▸ **noun 1** a small white-flowered winter-blooming hellebore, grown as a houseplant. ● *Helleborus niger*, family Ranunculaceae.
2 S. African another term for **CHRISTMAS FLOWER**.

Christmas stocking ▸ **noun** a long sock or similar receptacle hung up by children on Christmas Eve for Father Christmas to fill with presents.

Christmas tree ▸ **noun** an evergreen or artificial tree decorated with lights, tinsel, and other ornaments at Christmas.

Christo- ▸ **combining form** relating to Christ: *Christocentric.*
– ORIGIN from Latin *Christus* or Greek *Khristos* 'Christ'.

Christocentric ▸ **adjective** having Christ as its centre: *a thoroughly Christocentric theology.*

Christology ▸ **noun** [mass noun] the branch of Christian theology relating to the person, nature, and role of Christ.
– DERIVATIVES **Christological** adjective, **Christologically** adverb.

Christopher, St a legendary Christian martyr, adopted as the patron saint of travellers, since it is said that he once carried Jesus Christ as a child across a river.

christophine /ˈkrɪstəfiːn/ (also **christophene**) ▸ **noun** another term for **CHAYOTE** (sense 1).
– ORIGIN probably based on the French given name *Christophe*.

Christ's thorn ▸ **noun** a thorny shrub popularly supposed to have formed Christ's crown of thorns, in particular: ● either of two shrubs related to the buckthorn (*Paliurus spina-christi* and *Ziziphus spina-christi*, family Rhamnaceae). ● another term for **CROWN OF THORNS** (sense 2).

chroma /ˈkrəʊmə/ ▸ **noun** [mass noun] purity or intensity of colour.
– ORIGIN late 19th cent.: from Greek *khrōma* 'colour'.

chromaffin /krə(ʊ)ˈmafɪn/ ▸ **adjective** [attrib.] Physiology denoting granules or vesicles containing adrenalin and noradrenaline, and the secretory cells of the adrenal medulla in which they are found.
– ORIGIN early 20th cent.: from **CHROMO-¹** 'chromium' + Latin *affinis* 'akin' (because readily stained brown by chromates).

chromakey /ˈkrəʊməkiː/ ▸ **noun** [mass noun] a digital technique by which a block of a particular colour (often blue or green) in a film or video image can be replaced by another colour or image, enabling, for example, a weather forecaster to appear against a background of a computer-generated weather map.
▸ **verb** (**chromakeys**, **chromakeying**, **chromakeyed**) [with obj.] manipulate (an image) using this technique.

chromate /ˈkrəʊmeɪt/ ▸ **noun** Chemistry a salt in which the anion contains both chromium and oxygen, especially one of the anion CrO_4^{2-}.
– ORIGIN early 19th cent.: from **CHROMIC** + **-ATE¹**.

chromatic ▸ **adjective 1** Music relating to or using notes not belonging to the diatonic scale of the key in which a passage is written. ■ (of a scale) ascending or descending by semitones. ■ (of an instrument) able to play all the notes of the chromatic scale.
2 relating to or produced by colour.
– DERIVATIVES **chromatically** adverb, **chromaticism** noun.

– ORIGIN early 17th cent.: from French *chromatique* or Latin *chromaticus*, from Greek *khrōmatikos*, from *khrōma, khrōmat-* 'colour, chromatic scale'.

chromatic aberration ▶ **noun** [mass noun] Optics the effect produced by the refraction of different wavelengths of light through slightly different angles, resulting in a failure to focus.

chromaticity /ˌkrəʊməˈtɪsɪti/ ▶ **noun** [mass noun] the quality of colour, independent of brightness.

chromatid /ˈkrəʊmətɪd/ ▶ **noun** Biology each of the two thread-like strands into which a chromosome divides longitudinally during cell division. Each contains a double helix of DNA.
– ORIGIN early 20th cent.: from Greek *khrōma, khrōmat-* 'colour' + **-ID**[2].

chromatin /ˈkrəʊmətɪn/ ▶ **noun** [mass noun] Biology the material of which the chromosomes of organisms other than bacteria (i.e. eukaryotes) are composed, consisting of protein, RNA, and DNA.
– ORIGIN late 19th cent.: coined in German from Greek *khrōma, khrōmat-* 'colour'.

chromato- /ˈkrəʊmətəʊ/ (also **chromo-**) ▶ **combining form** colour; of or in colours: *chromatopsia*.
– ORIGIN from Greek *khrōma, khrōmat-* 'colour'.

chromatogram /krəˈ(ʊ)matəgram/ ▶ **noun** a visible record (such as a graph) showing the result of separating the components of a mixture by chromatography.

chromatograph ▶ **noun** an apparatus for performing chromatography. ■ another term for **CHROMATOGRAM**.

chromatography /ˌkrəʊməˈtɒgrəfi/ ▶ **noun** [mass noun] Chemistry a technique for the separation of a mixture by passing it in solution or suspension through a medium in which the components move at different rates.
– DERIVATIVES **chromatographic** adjective.
– ORIGIN 1930s: from German *Chromatographie* (see **CHROMATO-**, **-GRAPHY**), early separations being displayed as a number of coloured bands or spots.

chromatopsia /ˌkrəʊməˈtɒpsɪə/ ▶ **noun** [mass noun] Medicine abnormally coloured vision, a rare symptom with various causes.
– ORIGIN mid 19th cent.: from **CHROMATO-** 'colour' + Greek *-opsia* 'seeing'.

chrome ▶ **noun** [mass noun] chromium plate as a decorative or protective finish on motor-vehicle fittings and other objects: [as modifier] *a chrome bumper*. ■ [as modifier] denoting compounds or alloys of chromium: *chrome dyes*.
– ORIGIN early 19th cent.: from French, from Greek *khrōma* 'colour' (some chromium compounds having brilliant colours).

chrome alum ▶ **noun** [mass noun] a reddish-purple crystalline compound used in solution in photographic processing and as a mordant in dyeing.
● Chem. formula: $K_2SO_4Cr_2(SO_4)_3.24H_2O$.

chromed ▶ **adjective** chromium-plated.

chrome leather ▶ **noun** [mass noun] leather tanned with chromium salts.

chrome steel ▶ **noun** [mass noun] a hard fine-grained steel containing chromium, used for making tools.

chrome yellow ▶ **noun** [mass noun] a bright yellow pigment made from lead chromate.

chromic /ˈkrəʊmɪk/ ▶ **adjective** Chemistry of chromium with a higher valency, usually three. Compare with **CHROMOUS**.

chromic acid ▶ **noun** [mass noun] Chemistry a corrosive and strongly oxidizing acid existing only in solutions of chromium trioxide. ● Chem. formula: H_2CrO_4.

chromide ▶ **noun** a small deep bodied fish of India and Sri Lanka, found in brackish water. ● Genus *Etroplus*, family Cichlidae: the **orange chromide** (*E. maculatus*) and the **green chromide** (*E. suratensis*).
– ORIGIN 1930s: from modern Latin *Chromides* (former order name), formed irregularly from *Chromis* (genus name), from Latin *chromis* 'sea fish'.

chrominance /ˈkrəʊmɪnəns/ ▶ **noun** [mass noun] the colorimetric difference between a given colour in a television picture and a standard colour of equal luminance.
– ORIGIN 1950s: from Greek *khrōma* 'colour', on the pattern of *luminance*.

chromite /ˈkrəʊmʌɪt/ ▶ **noun** [mass noun] the principal ore of chromium, a brownish-black oxide of chromium and iron.
– ORIGIN mid 19th cent.: from **CHROME** or **CHROMIUM** + **-ITE**[1].

chromium ▶ **noun** [mass noun] the chemical element of atomic number 24, a hard white metal used in stainless steel and other alloys. (Symbol: **Cr**)
– ORIGIN early 19th cent.: from **CHROME** + **-IUM**.

chromium plate ▶ **noun** [mass noun] a decorative or protective coating of metallic chromium.
▶ **verb** (**chromium-plate**) [with obj.] electroplate (something) with chromium.

chromium steel ▶ **noun** another term for **CHROME STEEL**.

chromo /ˈkrəʊməʊ/ ▶ **noun** (pl. **chromos**) N. Amer. shortened form of **CHROMOLITHOGRAPH**.

chromo-[1] /ˈkrəʊməʊ/ ▶ **combining form** Chemistry representing **CHROMIUM**.

chromo-[2] /ˈkrəʊməʊ/ ▶ **combining form** variant spelling of **CHROMATO-**.

chromodynamics ▶ **plural noun** see **QUANTUM CHROMODYNAMICS**.

chromogen /ˈkrəʊmə(ʊ)dʒ(ə)n/ ▶ **noun** a substance which can be readily converted into a dye or other coloured compound.

chromogenic ▶ **adjective** **1** involving the production of colour or pigments.
2 Photography denoting a process of developing film which uses couplers to produce images of very high definition.

chromolithograph historical ▶ **noun** a coloured picture printed by lithography, especially in the late 19th and early 20th centuries.
▶ **verb** [with obj.] produce (a picture) by lithography.

chromoly /ˈkrəʊmɒli/ ▶ **noun** [mass noun] a form of steel containing chromium and molybdenum, used to make strong, lightweight components such as bicycle frames.
– ORIGIN 1980s: blend of **CHROMIUM** and **MOLYBDENUM**.

chromophore /ˈkrəʊməfɔː/ ▶ **noun** Chemistry an atom or group whose presence is responsible for the colour of a compound.
– DERIVATIVES **chromophoric** adjective.

chromoplast /ˈkrəʊməplast, -plɑːst/ ▶ **noun** Botany a coloured plastid other than a chloroplast, typically containing a yellow or orange pigment.
– ORIGIN late 19th cent.: from **CHROMO-**[2] 'colour' + Greek *plastos* 'formed'.

chromosome ▶ **noun** Biology a thread-like structure of nucleic acids and protein found in the nucleus of most living cells, carrying genetic information in the form of genes.

> Each chromosome consists of a DNA double helix bearing a linear sequence of genes, coiled and recoiled around aggregated proteins (histones). Their number varies from species to species: humans have 22 pairs plus the two sex chromosomes (two X chromosomes in females, one X and one Y in males). During cell division each DNA strand is duplicated, and the chromosomes condense to become visible as distinct pairs of chromatids joined at the centromere.

– DERIVATIVES **chromosomal** adjective.
– ORIGIN late 19th cent.: coined in German from Greek *khrōma* 'colour' + *sōma* 'body'.

chromosome map ▶ **noun** Genetics a diagram showing the relative positions of genes along the length of a chromosome.

chromosome number ▶ **noun** Genetics the characteristic number of chromosomes found in the cell nuclei of organisms of a particular species.

chromosphere ▶ **noun** Astronomy a reddish gaseous layer immediately above the photosphere of the sun or another star which, together with the corona, constitutes its outer atmosphere.
– DERIVATIVES **chromospheric** adjective.
– ORIGIN mid 19th cent.: from **CHROMO-**[2] 'colour' + **SPHERE**.

chromous ▶ **adjective** Chemistry of chromium with a valency of two. Compare with **CHROMIC**.

Chron. ▶ **abbreviation** Chronicles (in biblical references).

chronic ▶ **adjective** **1** (of an illness) persisting for a long time or constantly recurring: *chronic bronchitis*. Often contrasted with **ACUTE**. ■ (of a person) having such an illness: *a chronic asthmatic*. ■ (of a problem) long-lasting: *the school suffers from chronic overcrowding*. ■ (of a person) having a bad habit: *a chronic liar*.
2 Brit. informal of a very poor quality: *the film was absolutely chronic*.
– DERIVATIVES **chronically** adverb, **chronicity** noun.
– ORIGIN late Middle English: from French *chronique*, via Latin from Greek *khronikos* 'of time', from *khronos* 'time'.

chronic fatigue syndrome ▶ **noun** [mass noun] a medical condition of unknown cause, with fever, aching, and prolonged tiredness and depression, typically occurring after a viral infection.

chronicle ▶ **noun** a factual written account of important or historical events in the order of their occurrence. ■ a fictitious or factual work describing a series of events.
▶ **verb** [with obj.] record (a series of events) in a factual and detailed way: *his work chronicles 20th-century migration*.
– ORIGIN Middle English: from Anglo-Norman French *cronicle*, variant of Old French *cronique*, via Latin from Greek *khronika* 'annals', from *khronikos* (see **CHRONIC**).

chronicler ▶ **noun** a person who writes accounts of important or historical events: *a chronicler of 18th-century American life*.

Chronicles the name of two books of the Bible, recording the history of Israel and Judah until the return from Exile (536 BC).

chrono- /ˈkrɒnəʊ/ ▶ **combining form** relating to time: *chronometry*.
– ORIGIN from Greek *khronos* 'time'.

chronobiology ▶ **noun** [mass noun] the branch of biology concerned with cyclical physiological phenomena.
– DERIVATIVES **chronobiologist** noun.

chronograph ▶ **noun** an instrument for recording time with great accuracy. ■ a stopwatch.
– DERIVATIVES **chronographic** adjective.

chronological ▶ **adjective** (of a record of events) following the order in which they occurred: *the entries are in chronological order*. ■ calculated in terms of the passage of time: *medical decisions should be based on the individual's biological age, not chronological age*. ■ relating to the establishment of dates of past events: *the diary provided a chronological framework for the events*.
– DERIVATIVES **chronologically** adverb.

chronology /krəˈnɒlədʒi/ ▶ **noun** (pl. **chronologies**) [mass noun] the arrangement of events or dates in the order of their occurrence: *the novel abandons the conventions of normal chronology*. ■ [count noun] a list displaying such an arrangement. ■ the study of historical records to establish the dates of past events.
– DERIVATIVES **chronologist** noun.
– ORIGIN late 16th cent.: from modern Latin *chronologia*, from Greek *khronos* 'time' + *-logia* (see **-LOGY**).

chronometer /krəˈnɒmɪtə/ ▶ **noun** an instrument for measuring time accurately in spite of motion or variations in temperature, humidity, and air pressure.

chronometry ▶ **noun** [mass noun] the science of accurate time measurement.
– DERIVATIVES **chronometric** adjective, **chronometrical** adjective, **chronometrically** adverb.

chronostratigraphy /ˌkrɒnə(ʊ)strəˈtɪgrəfi/ ▶ **noun** [mass noun] the branch of geology concerned with establishing the absolute ages of strata.
– DERIVATIVES **chronostratigraphic** adjective.

chronotherapy /ˌkrɒnə(ʊ)ˈθɛrəpi/ ▶ **noun** [mass noun] the treatment of an illness or disorder by administering a drug at a time of day believed to be in harmony with the body's natural rhythms.

chrysalid /ˈkrɪs(ə)lɪd/ ▶ **noun** another term for **CHRYSALIS**.
– ORIGIN late 18th cent.: from Latin *chrysal(l)is, chrysal(l)id-* (see **CHRYSALIS**).

chrysalis /ˈkrɪs(ə)lɪs/ ▶ **noun** (pl. **chrysalises**) a quiescent insect pupa, especially of a butterfly or moth. ■ the hard outer case enclosing this. ■ a transitional state: *she emerged from the chrysalis of self-conscious adolescence*.
– ORIGIN early 17th cent.: from Latin *chrysal(l)is, chrysal(l)id-*, from Greek *khrusallis*, from *khrusos* 'gold' (because of the gold colour or metallic sheen of some pupae).

chrysanthemum /krɪˈsanθɪməm, -z-/ ▶ **noun** (pl. **chrysanthemums**) a plant of the daisy family with brightly coloured ornamental flowers, existing in many cultivated varieties. ● Genera *Chrysanthemum* or (most cultivated species) *Dendranthema*, family Compositae.
– ORIGIN mid 16th cent. (originally denoting the corn marigold): from Latin, from Greek *khrusanthemon*, from *khrusos* 'gold' + *anthemon* 'flower'.

chryselephantine /ˌkrɪselɪˈfantʌɪn/ ▶ **adjective** (of ancient Greek sculpture) overlaid with gold and ivory.
– ORIGIN early 19th cent.: from Greek *khruselephantinos*, from *khrusos* 'gold' + *elephas*, *elephant-* 'elephant' or 'ivory'.

chrysoberyl /ˌkrɪsə(ʊ)ˈbɛrɪl/ ▶ **noun** [mass noun] a greenish or yellowish-green oxide of beryllium and aluminium which occurs as tabular crystals, sometimes of gem quality.
– ORIGIN mid 17th cent.: from Latin *chrysoberyllus*, from Greek *khrusos* 'gold' + *bērullos* 'beryl'.

chrysocolla /ˌkrɪsə(ʊ)ˈkɒlə/ ▶ **noun** [mass noun] a greenish-blue mineral consisting of hydrated copper silicate, occurring as opaline crusts and masses.
– ORIGIN late 16th cent. (in the Greek sense): from Latin, from Greek *khrusokolla*, denoting a mineral used in ancient times for soldering gold.

chrysolite /ˈkrɪsəlʌɪt/ ▶ **noun** [mass noun] a yellowish-green or brownish variety of olivine, used as a gemstone.
– ORIGIN late Middle English: from Old French *crisolite*, from medieval Latin *crisolitus*, from Latin *chrysolithus*, based on Greek *khrusos* 'gold' + *lithos* 'stone'.

chrysomelid /ˌkrɪsə(ʊ)ˈmɛlɪd, -ˈmiːlɪd/ ▶ **noun** Entomology a beetle of a family (Chrysomelidae) that comprises the leaf beetles and their relatives.
– ORIGIN late 19th cent.: from modern Latin *Chrysomelidae* (plural), from *Chrysomela* (genus name), from Greek *khrusomēlon*, literally 'golden apple', influenced by *khrusomēlolonthion* 'little golden chafer'.

chrysoprase /ˈkrɪsə(ʊ)preɪz/ ▶ **noun** [mass noun] an apple-green gemstone consisting of a variety of chalcedony that contains nickel.
– ORIGIN Middle English (denoting a precious stone in the New Testament): from Old French *crisopace*, via Latin from Greek *khrusoprasos*, from *khrusos* 'gold' + *prason* 'leek'.

Chrysostom, St John /ˈkrɪsəstəm/ (*c.*347–407), Doctor of the Church, bishop of Constantinople. He attempted to reform the corrupt state of the court, clergy, and people; this offended many, including the Empress Eudoxia, who banished him in 403. His name means 'golden-mouthed' in Greek. Feast day, 27 January.

chrysotile /ˈkrɪsə(ʊ)tʌɪl/ ▶ **noun** [mass noun] a fibrous form of the mineral serpentine. Also called WHITE ASBESTOS.
– ORIGIN mid 19th cent.: from Greek *khrusos* 'gold' + *tilos* 'fibre'.

chthonic /ˈ(k)θɒnɪk/ (also **chthonian** /ˈ(k)θəʊnɪən/) ▶ **adjective** relating to or inhabiting the underworld: *a chthonic deity*.
– ORIGIN late 19th cent.: from Greek *khthōn* 'earth' + -IC.

chub ▶ **noun** (pl. **same** or **chubs**) a thick-bodied European river fish with a grey-green back and white underparts. ● *Leuciscus cephalus*, family Cyprinidae.
– ORIGIN late Middle English: of unknown origin.

Chubb ▶ **noun** trademark a lock with a device for fixing the bolt immovably to prevent it from being picked.
– ORIGIN mid 19th cent.: named after Charles *Chubb* (1773–1845), the London locksmith who invented it.

chubby ▶ **adjective** (**chubbier**, **chubbiest**) plump and rounded: *a pretty child with chubby cheeks*.
– DERIVATIVES **chubbily** adverb, **chubbiness** noun.
– ORIGIN early 17th cent. (in the sense 'short and thickset, like a chub'): from CHUB.

Chubu /ˈtʃuːbuː/ a mountainous region of Japan, on the island of Honshu; capital, Nagoya.

chuck[1] informal ▶ **verb** [with obj.] **1** throw (something) carelessly or casually: *someone chucked a brick through the window* | figurative *chucking money at the problem won't solve it*. ■ Cricket (of a bowler) deliver (a ball) with an unlawful action. ■ (often **chuck something away/out**) throw (something) away: *they make a living out of stuff people chuck away*.
2 end a relationship with (a partner): *Mary chucked him for another guy*. ■ give up (a job or activity): *Richard chucked in his course*. ■ (**chuck it**) dated stop doing something.
▶ **noun 1** a throw.
2 (**the chuck**) Brit. a dismissal or rejection.
– PHRASES **chuck it down** Brit. rain heavily.
– PHRASAL VERBS **chuck someone out** force someone to leave a building: *their landlord chucked them out last night*. **chuck up** vomit: *I nearly chucked up*.
– DERIVATIVES **chucker** noun.
– ORIGIN late 17th cent. (as a verb): from CHUCK[2].

chuck[2] ▶ **verb** [with obj.] touch (someone) playfully under the chin.
▶ **noun** a playful touch under the chin.
– ORIGIN early 17th cent. (as a noun): probably from Old French *chuquer*, later *choquer* 'to knock, bump', of unknown ultimate origin.

chuck[3] ▶ **noun 1** a device for holding a workpiece in a lathe or a tool in a drill, typically having three or four jaws that move radially in and out.
2 [mass noun] (also **chuck steak**) a cut of beef that extends from the neck to the ribs, typically used for stewing.
– ORIGIN late 17th cent., as a variant of CHOCK; see also CHUNK[1].

chuck[4] ▶ **noun** N. English informal used as a friendly form of address: *'Can I help you at all, chuck?'*.
– ORIGIN late 16th cent.: alteration of CHICK[1].

chucker-out ▶ **noun** informal a person employed to expel troublemakers from a place of entertainment.

chuckhole ▶ **noun** N. Amer. a hole or rut in a road or track.

chuck key ▶ **noun** a small metal device for tightening the chuck of a drill.

chuckle ▶ **verb** [no obj.] laugh quietly or inwardly: *I chuckled at the astonishment on her face*.
▶ **noun** a quiet or suppressed laugh.
– DERIVATIVES **chuckler** noun.
– ORIGIN late 16th cent. (in the sense 'laugh convulsively'): from *chuck* meaning 'to cluck' in late Middle English.

chucklehead ▶ **noun** informal a stupid person.
– DERIVATIVES **chuckleheaded** adjective.
– ORIGIN mid 18th cent.: from early 18th-cent. *chuckle* 'big and clumsy', probably related to CHUCK[3] (sense 2).

chucklesome ▶ **adjective** causing mild amusement; humorous: *the script is chucklesome rather than hilarious*.

chuck wagon ▶ **noun** N. Amer. a wagon with cooking facilities providing food on a ranch or by a roadside.
– ORIGIN late 19th cent.: *chuck*, in the informal sense 'food'.

chuckwalla /ˈtʃʌkwɒlə/ ▶ **noun** a large dark-bodied lizard, the male of which has a light yellow tail, native to the deserts of the south-western US and Mexico. ● *Sauromalus obesus*, family Iguanidae.
– ORIGIN late 19th cent.: from Mexican Spanish *chacahuala*, from American Indian.

chuddar ▶ **noun** variant spelling of CHADOR.

chuddies /ˈtʃʌdɪz/ ▶ **plural noun** informal (chiefly among British Asians) underpants.
– ORIGIN 1990s: Anglo-Indian, perhaps an alteration of CHURIDARS.

chuddy (also **chutty**) ▶ **noun** [mass noun] Austral./NZ informal or dialect chewing gum.
– ORIGIN 1940s: probably an alteration of *chewed*.

chufa /ˈtʃuːfə/ ▶ **noun** an Old World sedge which yields an edible tuber, cultivated in some marshy regions of Spain and Italy. Also called TIGER NUT. ● *Cyperus esculentus* var. *sativus*, family Cyperaceae.
■ [mass noun] the tuber of this plant, which may be roasted or made into flour or juice.
– ORIGIN mid 19th cent.: from Spanish.

chuff[1] ▶ **verb** [no obj., with adverbial of direction] (of a steam engine) move with a regular sharp puffing sound.
– ORIGIN early 20th cent.: imitative.

chuff[2] ▶ **noun** Brit. informal a person's buttocks or anus.
– ORIGIN 1940s: origin uncertain.

chuffed ▶ **adjective** [predic.] Brit. informal very pleased: *I'm dead chuffed to have won*.
– ORIGIN 1950s: from dialect *chuff* 'plump or pleased'.

chuffing ▶ **adjective** N. English informal used for emphasis or as a mild expletive: *the whole chuffing world's gone mad*.
– ORIGIN 1980s: perhaps related to CHUFF[2].

chug[1] ▶ **verb** (**chugs**, **chugging**, **chugged**) [no obj., with adverbial of direction] (of a vehicle or boat) move slowly making regular muffled explosive sounds, as of an engine running slowly: *a cabin cruiser was chugging down the river*. ■ [no obj.] make a series of such sounds: *he could hear the pipes chugging*.
▶ **noun** a muffled explosive sound or sounds: *the chug of a motor boat*.
– ORIGIN mid 19th cent. (as a noun): imitative.

chug[2] (also **chugalug**) N. Amer. informal ▶ **verb** (**chugs**, **chugging**, **chugged**) [with obj.] consume (a drink) in large gulps without pausing: *she chugged a glass of cola*.
▶ **noun** a large gulp of a drink: *Chris took a long chug of his beer*.
– ORIGIN 1950s: imitative.

chugger ▶ **noun** informal a person who approaches passers-by in the street asking for donations or subscriptions to a particular charity.
– ORIGIN blend of CHARITY and MUGGER[1].

Chugoku /tʃuːˈɡəʊkuː/ a region of Japan, on the island of Honshu; capital, Hiroshima.

chukar /ˈtʃʊkɑː/ (also **chukor** or **chukar partridge**) ▶ **noun** a Eurasian partridge similar to the red-legged partridge, but with a clucking call like a domestic hen. ● Genus *Alectoris*, family Phasianidae: two species.
– ORIGIN early 19th cent.: from Sanskrit *cakora*.

Chukchi /ˈtʃʊktʃiː/ ▶ **noun** (pl. **same** or **Chukchis**)
1 a member of an indigenous people of extreme NE Siberia.
2 [mass noun] the language of the Chukchi, which belongs to a small family also including Koryak.
▶ **adjective** relating to the Chukchi or their language.
– ORIGIN Russian (plural).

Chukchi Sea /ˈtʃʊktʃiː/ part of the Arctic Ocean lying between North America and Asia and to the north of the Bering Strait.

chukka /ˈtʃʌkə/ (US also **chukker**) ▶ **noun** each of a number of periods (typically six, of $7\frac{1}{2}$ minutes each) into which play in a game of polo is divided.
– ORIGIN late 19th cent.: from Hindi *cakkar*, from Sanskrit *cakra* 'circle or wheel'.

chum[1] informal ▶ **noun 1** a close friend.
2 used as a friendly or familiar form of address between men or boys: *it's your own fault, chum*.
▶ **verb** (**chums**, **chumming**, **chummed**) [no obj.] form a friendship with someone: *his sister chummed up with Sally*. ■ [with obj.] Scottish accompany (someone) somewhere: *I'll chum you down the road*.
– ORIGIN late 17th cent. (originally Oxford University slang, denoting a room-mate): probably short for *chamber-fellow*. Compare with COMRADE and CRONY.

chum[2] chiefly N. Amer. ▶ **noun** [mass noun] chopped fish and other material thrown overboard as angling bait.
■ refuse from fish, especially that remaining after oil has been expressed.
▶ **verb** (**chums**, **chumming**, **chummed**) [no obj.] fish using chum as bait.
– ORIGIN mid 19th cent.: of unknown origin.

chum[3] (also **chum salmon**) ▶ **noun** (pl. **same** or **chums**) a large North Pacific salmon that is commercially important as a food fish. ● *Oncorhynchus keta*, family Salmonidae.
– ORIGIN early 20th cent.: from Chinook Jargon *tzum (samun)*, literally 'spotted (salmon)'.

Chumash /ˈtʃuːmaʃ/ ▶ **noun** (pl. **same** or **Chumashes**)
1 a member of an American Indian people inhabiting coastal parts of southern California.
2 [mass noun] the extinct Hokan language of the Chumash.
▶ **adjective** relating to the Chumash or their language.

chumble ▶ **verb** [with obj.] dialect nibble; chew.
– ORIGIN early 19th cent.: probably imitative.

chummy ▶ **adjective** (**chummier**, **chummiest**) on friendly terms; friendly: *she's become rather chummy with Ted recently*.
– DERIVATIVES **chummily** adverb, **chumminess** noun.

chump ▶ **noun 1** informal a foolish or easily deceived person: *I was left feeling a bit of a chump*.
2 Brit. the thick end of something, especially a loin of lamb or mutton.
– PHRASES **off one's chump** Brit. informal mad.
– ORIGIN early 18th cent. (in the sense 'thick lump of wood'): probably a blend of CHUNK[1] and LUMP[1] or STUMP.

chump change ▶ **noun** [mass noun] N. Amer. informal a small or insignificant amount of money.
– ORIGIN 1960s: originally black English.

Chün /tʃuːn/ ▶ **noun** [mass noun] a type of thickly glazed, typically bluish or purplish grey stoneware originally made at Chün Chou in Honan province, China, during the Song dynasty.

chunder informal, chiefly Austral./NZ ▶ **verb** [no obj.] vomit.
▶ **noun** [mass noun] vomit.
– ORIGIN 1950s: probably from rhyming slang *Chunder Loo* 'spew', from the name of a cartoon character *Chunder Loo of Akim Foo*, who appeared in advertisements for Cobra boot polish in the Sydney *Bulletin* in the early 20th cent.

Chungking /tʃʊŋˈkɪŋ/ variant of CHONGQING.

Chung-shan /tʃʊŋˈʃan/ variant of ZHONGSHAN.

chunk[1] ▶ **noun** a thick, solid piece of something: *huge chunks of masonry littered the street*. ■ [in sing.] a significant amount of something: *she invested a chunk*

of her inheritance in the stock market. ■ Computing a section of information or data.
▶ **verb** [with obj.] **1** N. Amer. divide (something) into chunks: *chunk four pounds of pears.* ■ informal throw (something): *chunk a piece of wood on the fire, will you?*
2 (in psychology or linguistic analysis) group together (connected items or words) so that they can be stored or processed as single concepts. ■ Computing divide (data) into separate sections: *to prepare hypertext, information is chunked into small, manageable units.*
– ORIGIN late 17th cent.: apparently an alteration of CHUCK³.

chunk² ▶ **verb** [no obj.] chiefly N. Amer. move with or make a muffled, metallic sound: *the door chunked behind them.*
– ORIGIN late 19th cent.: imitative.

chunky ▶ **adjective** (**chunkier**, **chunkiest**) **1** bulky and thick: *a chunky bracelet.* ■ (of a person) short and sturdy.
2 (of food) containing chunks or thick pieces of something: *a chunky soup.*
– DERIVATIVES **chunkily** adverb, **chunkiness** noun.

Chunnel ▶ **noun** informal short for CHANNEL TUNNEL.
– ORIGIN 1920s (but rare before the 1950s): blend.

chunni /ˈtʃʊni/ ▶ **noun** (pl. **chunnis**) another term for DUPATTA.
– ORIGIN from Punjabi.

chunter ▶ **verb** [no obj.] Brit. informal **1** talk or grumble monotonously: *she chuntered on about her problems.*
2 [with adverbial of direction] move along slowly and noisily: *the car came chuntering up the track.*
– ORIGIN late 17th cent.: probably imitative.

chup /tʃʊp/ ▶ **exclamation** Indian be quiet!
– ORIGIN from Hindi *cuprao.*

chupacabra /tʃuːpəˈkabrə/ ▶ **noun** an animal said to exist in parts of Latin America, where it supposedly attacks animals, especially goats.
– ORIGIN Spanish, literally 'goatsucker', from *chupar* 'to suck' + *cabra* 'goat'.

chupatty ▶ **noun** (pl. **chupatties**) variant spelling of CHAPATTI.

chuppah /ˈxʊpə/ (also **chuppa**) ▶ **noun** (pl. **chuppot** /ˈxʊpəʊt/) a canopy beneath which Jewish marriage ceremonies are performed.
– ORIGIN late 19th cent.: from Hebrew *ḥuppāh* 'cover, canopy'.

Chuquisaca /ˌtʃuːkiːˈsɑːkə/ former name (1539–1840) for SUCRE¹.

church ▶ **noun** a building used for public Christian worship: *the church was largely rebuilt at the end of the 15th century* | *some people **go to church** every Sunday* | [in names] *St Luke's Church.* ■ (**Church**) a particular Christian organization with its own clergy, buildings, and distinctive doctrines: *the Church of England.* ■ (**the Church**) the hierarchy of clergy of such an organization: *Isobel would enter the Church as a deacon.* ■ [mass noun] institutionalized religion as a political or social force: *the separation of church and state.*
▶ **verb** [with obj.] archaic take (a woman who has recently given birth) to church for a service of thanksgiving.
– ORIGIN Old English *cir(i)ce, cyr(i)ce*, related to Dutch *kerk* and German *Kirche*, based on medieval Greek *kurikon*, from Greek *kuriakon (dōma)* 'Lord's (house)', from *kurios* 'master or lord'. Compare with KIRK.

Church Army a voluntary Anglican organization concerned with social welfare. It was founded in 1882 on the model of the Salvation Army, for evangelistic purposes.

Church Commissioners a body managing the finances of the Church of England.

Churches of Christ a number of Protestant denominations, chiefly in the US, originating in the Disciples of Christ but later separating over doctrinal issues.

churchgoer ▶ **noun** a person who goes to church regularly.
– DERIVATIVES **churchgoing** noun & adjective.

Churchill, Sir Winston (Leonard Spencer) (1874–1965), British Conservative statesman, Prime Minister 1940–5 and 1951–5.

> He served as Home Secretary (1910–11) under the Liberals and as First Lord of the Admiralty 1911–15, but lost this post after the unsuccessful Allied attack on the Turks in the Dardanelles. A consistent opponent of appeasement between the wars, he replaced Neville Chamberlain as Prime Minister of the coalition government in 1940 and led Britain throughout the war, forging and maintaining the alliance which defeated the Axis Powers. His writings include *The Second World War* (1948–53) and *A History of the English-Speaking Peoples* (1956–8); he won the Nobel Prize for Literature in 1953.

– DERIVATIVES **Churchillian** adjective.

churchman ▶ **noun** (pl. **churchmen**) a male member of the Christian clergy or of a Church.

Church Militant ▶ **noun** (**the Church Militant**) the whole body of living Christian believers, regarded as striving to combat evil on earth.
– ORIGIN mid 16th cent.: contrasted with the *Church Triumphant* in heaven.

Church of England the English branch of the Western Christian Church, which combines Catholic and Protestant traditions, rejects the Pope's authority, and has the monarch as its titular head. The English Church was part of the Catholic Church until the Reformation of the 16th century; after Henry VIII failed to obtain a divorce from Catherine of Aragon he repudiated papal supremacy, bringing the Church under the control of the Crown.

Church of Scotland the national (Presbyterian) Christian Church in Scotland. In 1560 John Knox reformed the established Church along Presbyterian lines, but there were repeated attempts by the Stuart monarchs to impose episcopalianism, and the Church of Scotland was not finally established as Presbyterian until 1690.

church planting ▶ **noun** [mass noun] the practice of establishing a core of Christian worshippers in a parish, with the intention that they should develop into a thriving congregation.

church school ▶ **noun** (in the UK) a school founded by or associated with the Church of England. ■ (in the US) a private school supported by a Church or parish.

Church Slavonic ▶ **noun** [mass noun] the liturgical language used in the Orthodox Church in Russia, Serbia, and some other countries.

Churchward /ˈtʃəːtʃwəd/, George Jackson (1857–1933), English railway engineer. The standard 4-6-0 locomotives that he built at the Swindon works of the Great Western Railway were the basis of many later designs.

churchwarden ▶ **noun** **1** either of the two elected lay representatives in an Anglican parish, formally responsible for movable church property and for keeping order in church. ■ US a church administrator.
2 Brit. a long-stemmed clay pipe.

churchwoman ▶ **noun** (pl. **churchwomen**) a female member of the Christian clergy or of a Church.

churchy ▶ **adjective** (**churchier**, **churchiest**) **1** (of a person) excessively pious and often narrow-minded.
2 resembling a church: *Gothic design looks too churchy.*
– DERIVATIVES **churchiness** noun.

churchyard ▶ **noun** an enclosed area surrounding a church, especially as used for burials.

churidars /ˈtʃʊrɪdɑːz/ (also **churidar**) ▶ **plural noun** tight trousers worn by people from South Asia, typically with a kameez or kurta.
– ORIGIN from Hindi *cūṛīdār* 'having a series of gathered rows' (i.e. at the bottom of the trouser legs, traditionally worn too long and tucked up).

churinga /tʃʌˈrɪŋɡə/ ▶ **noun** (pl. **same** or **churingas**) (among Australian Aborigines) a sacred object.
– ORIGIN late 19th cent.: from Arrernte, literally 'object from the dreaming'.

churl ▶ **noun** **1** a rude and mean-spirited person. ■ archaic a miser.
2 archaic a peasant.
– ORIGIN Old English *ceorl*, of West Germanic origin; related to Dutch *kerel* and German *Kerl* 'fellow', also to CARL.

churlish ▶ **adjective** rude in a mean-spirited and surly way: *it seems churlish to complain.*
– DERIVATIVES **churlishly** adverb, **churlishness** noun.
– ORIGIN Old English *cierlisc, ceorlisc* (see CHURL, -ISH¹).

churn ▶ **noun** **1** a machine for making butter by shaking milk or cream.
2 Brit. a large metal container for milk.
3 short for CHURN RATE.
▶ **verb** [with obj.] **1** shake (milk or cream) in a machine in order to produce butter: *the cream is ripened before it is churned.* ■ produce (butter) in such a way.
2 (with reference to liquid) move or cause to move about vigorously: [no obj.] *the seas churned* | figurative *her stomach was churning at the thought of the ordeal* | [with obj.] *in high winds most of the loch is **churned up**.* ■ break up the surface of (an area of ground): *the earth had been **churned up** where vehicles had passed through.*
3 (of a broker) encourage frequent turnover of (investments) in order to generate commission.
– PHRASAL VERBS **churn something out** produce something mechanically and in large quantities: *artists continued to churn out uninteresting works.*
– ORIGIN Old English *cyrin*, of Germanic origin; related to Middle Low German *kerne* and Old Norse *kirna.*

churn rate ▶ **noun** the annual percentage rate at which customers discontinue using a service, especially cable and satellite television.

churr ▶ **verb & noun** variant spelling of CHIRR.

churrascaria /tʃʊˌraskəˈrɪə/ ▶ **noun** a restaurant specializing in churrasco.
– ORIGIN South American Spanish.

churrasco /tʃʊˈraskəʊ/ ▶ **noun** [mass noun] a South American dish of steak barbecued over a wood or charcoal fire.
– ORIGIN South American Spanish, probably from Spanish dialect *churrascar* 'to burn', related to Spanish *soccarar* 'to scorch'.

Churrigueresque /ˌtʃʊərɪɡəˈrɛsk/ ▶ **adjective** Architecture relating to the lavishly ornamented late Spanish baroque style: *a Churrigueresque church.*
– ORIGIN mid 19th cent.: from the name José Benito de *Churriguera* (1665–1725), a Spanish architect who worked in this style.

churro /ˈtʃʌrəʊ/ ▶ **noun** (pl. **churros**) a sweet Spanish snack consisting of a strip of fried dough dusted with sugar or cinnamon.
– ORIGIN Spanish, of uncertain origin; perhaps related to *churro* 'coarse, rough'.

chute¹ (also **shoot**) ▶ **noun** a sloping channel or slide for conveying things to a lower level. ■ a water slide into a swimming pool.
– ORIGIN early 19th cent. (originally a North American usage): from French, 'fall' (of water or rocks), from Old French *cheoite*, feminine past participle of *cheoir* 'to fall', from Latin *cadere*; influenced by SHOOT.

chute² ▶ **noun** informal a parachute. ■ Sailing a spinnaker.
– ORIGIN 1920s: shortened form.

chutes and ladders ▶ **plural noun** US term for SNAKES AND LADDERS.

chutney ▶ **noun** (pl. **chutneys**) [mass noun] a spicy condiment of Indian origin, made of fruits or vegetables with vinegar, spices, and sugar.
– ORIGIN early 19th cent.: from Hindi *caṭnī.*

chutzpah /ˈxʊtspə, ˈhʊ-/ ▶ **noun** [mass noun] informal extreme self-confidence or audacity (usually used approvingly): *love him or hate him, you have to admire Cohen's chutzpah.*
– ORIGIN late 19th cent.: Yiddish, from Aramaic *ḥu ṣpā.*

Chuuk Islands /tʃʊk/ a group of fourteen volcanic islands and numerous atolls in the western Pacific, in the Caroline Islands group, forming part of the Federated States of Micronesia; pop. 53,300 (est. 2008). Former name TRUK ISLANDS.

Chuvash /ˈtʃuːvɑːʃ/ ▶ **noun** (pl. **same**) **1** a member of a people living mainly in Chuvashia.
2 [mass noun] the Turkic language of the Chuvash, with over a million speakers.
▶ **adjective** relating to the Chuvash or their language.

Chuvashia /tʃuːˈvɑːʃɪə/ an autonomous republic in European Russia, east of Nizhni Novgorod; pop. 1,278,600 (est. 2009); capital, Cheboksary.

chyle /kʌɪl/ ▶ **noun** [mass noun] Physiology a milky fluid containing fat droplets which drains from the lacteals of the small intestine into the lymphatic system during digestion.
– DERIVATIVES **chylous** adjective.
– ORIGIN late Middle English: from late Latin *chylus*, from Greek *khūlos* 'juice' (see CHYME).

chylomicron /ˌkʌɪlə(ʊ)ˈmʌɪkrɒn/ ▶ **noun** Physiology a droplet of fat present in the blood or lymph after absorption from the small intestine.
– ORIGIN 1920s: from *chylo-* (combining form of CHYLE) + MICRON.

chyme /kʌɪm/ ▶ **noun** [mass noun] Physiology the pulpy acidic fluid which passes from the stomach to the small intestine, consisting of gastric juices and partly digested food.
– ORIGIN late Middle English: from late Latin *chymus*, from Greek *khūmos* 'juice' (compare with CHYLE). The

Greek words *khūlos* and *khūmos* are from the same root and more or less identical in sense.

chymotrypsin /ˌkʌɪmə(ʊ)ˈtrɪpsɪn/ ▶ **noun** [mass noun] Biochemistry a digestive enzyme which breaks down proteins in the small intestine. It is secreted by the pancreas and converted into an active form by trypsin.
– ORIGIN 1930s: from *chymo-* (combining form of CHYME) + TRYPSIN.

chypre /ʃiːpr(ə)/ ▶ **noun** [mass noun] a heady perfume made from sandalwood.
– ORIGIN late 19th cent.: from French, literally 'Cyprus', perhaps where it was first made.

chyron /ˈkʌɪrɒn/ ▶ **noun** US trademark an electronically generated caption superimposed on a television or cinema screen.
– ORIGIN 1970s: origin uncertain.

CI ▶ **abbreviation** ■ Channel Islands. ■ Côte d'Ivoire (Ivory Coast) (international vehicle registration).

Ci ▶ **abbreviation** curie.

CIA ▶ **abbreviation** Central Intelligence Agency.

ciabatta /tʃəˈbɑːtə/ ▶ **noun** [mass noun] a flattish, open-textured Italian bread with a floury crust, made with olive oil.
– ORIGIN Italian, literally 'slipper' (from its shape).

ciao /tʃaʊ/ ▶ **exclamation** informal used as a greeting at meeting or parting.
– ORIGIN Italian, dialect alteration of *schiavo* '(I am your) slave', from medieval Latin *sclavus* 'slave'.

Cibber /ˈsɪbə/, Colley (1671–1757), English comic actor, dramatist, and theatre manager. After his much-ridiculed appointment as Poet Laureate in 1730 he wrote an *Apology for the Life of Mr Colley Cibber, Comedian* (1740).

ciborium /sɪˈbɔːrɪəm/ ▶ **noun** (pl. **ciboria** /-rɪə/) **1** a receptacle shaped like a shrine or a cup with an arched cover, used in the Christian Church to hold the Eucharist.
2 a canopy over an altar in a church, standing on four pillars.
– ORIGIN mid 16th cent.: via medieval Latin from Greek *kibōrion* 'seed vessel of the water lily or a cup made from it'. Sense 1 is probably influenced by Latin *cibus* 'food'.

cicada /sɪˈkɑːdə/ ▶ **noun** a large bug with long transparent wings, found chiefly in warm countries. The male cicada makes a loud, shrill droning noise after dark by vibrating two membranes on its abdomen.
● Family Cicadidae, suborder Homoptera: many genera.
– ORIGIN late Middle English: from Latin *cicada*, *cicala*.

cicatrix /ˈsɪkətrɪks/ (also **cicatrice** /ˈsɪkətrɪs/) ▶ **noun** (pl. **cicatrices** /-ˈtrʌɪsiːz/) the scar of a healed wound. ■ Botany a mark on a stem left after a leaf or other part has become detached.
– DERIVATIVES **cicatricial** /sɪkəˈtrɪʃ(ə)l/ **adjective**.
– ORIGIN late Middle English (as *cicatrice*): from Latin *cicatrix* or Old French *cicatrice*.

cicatrize /ˈsɪkətrʌɪz/ (also **cicatrise**) ▶ **verb** (with reference to a wound) heal by scar formation: [no obj.] *his wound had cicatrized*.
– DERIVATIVES **cicatrization** **noun**.
– ORIGIN late Middle English: from Old French *cicatriser*, from *cicatrice* 'scar' (see CICATRIX).

cicely /ˈsɪsɪli/ (also **sweet cicely**) ▶ **noun** (pl. **cicelies**) an aromatic white-flowered plant of the parsley family, with fern-like leaves. ● Genera *Myrrhis* and *Osmorhiza*, family Umbelliferae: several species, in particular the European *M. odorata*, grown as a culinary and medicinal herb.
– ORIGIN late 16th cent.: from Latin *seselis*, from Greek. The spelling change was due to association with the given name *Cicely*.

Cicero /ˈsɪsərəʊ/, Marcus Tullius (106–43 BC), Roman statesman, orator, and writer. As an orator and writer Cicero established a model for Latin prose; his surviving works include speeches, treatises on rhetoric, philosophical works, and letters. A supporter of Pompey against Julius Caesar, in the *Philippics* (43 BC) he attacked Mark Antony, who had him put to death.

cicerone /ˌtʃɪtʃəˈrəʊni, ˌsɪs-/ ▶ **noun** (pl. **ciceroni** pronunc. **same**) a guide who gives information about places of interest to sightseers.
– ORIGIN early 18th cent.: from Italian, from Latin *Cicero, Ciceron-* (see CICERO), apparently alluding humorously to his eloquence and learning.

Ciceronian /ˌsɪsəˈrəʊnɪən/ ▶ **adjective** characteristic of the work and thought of Cicero. ■ (of speech or writing) in an eloquent and rhythmic style similar to that of Cicero.

cichlid /ˈsɪklɪd/ ▶ **noun** Zoology a perch-like freshwater fish of a large tropical family (Cichlidae) which includes the angelfishes, discuses, mouthbrooders, and tilapia.
– ORIGIN late 19th cent.: from modern Latin *Cichlidae* (plural), from Greek *kikhlē*, denoting a kind of fish.

cicisbeo /ˌtʃɪtʃɪzˈbeɪəʊ/ ▶ **noun** (pl. **cicisbei** or **cicisbeos**) a married woman's male companion or lover.
– ORIGIN early 18th cent.: Italian, of unknown origin.

CID ▶ **abbreviation** (in the UK) Criminal Investigation Department.

Cid, El /ɛl ˈsɪd/, Spanish /el ˈθið, ˈsið/ (also **the Cid**), Count of Bivar (*c.*1043–99), Spanish soldier; born *Rodrigo Díaz de Vivar*. A champion of Christianity against the Moors, in 1094 he captured Valencia, which he went on to rule. He is immortalized in the Spanish *Poema del Cid* (12th century) and in Corneille's play *Le Cid* (1637).

-cide ▶ **combining form 1** denoting a person or substance that kills: *insecticide | regicide*.
2 denoting an act of killing: *suicide*.
– DERIVATIVES **-cidal** **combining form** in corresponding adjectives., **-cidally** **combining form** in corresponding adverbs.
– ORIGIN via French; sense 1 from Latin *-cida*; sense 2 from Latin *-cidium*, both from *caedere* 'kill'.

cider ▶ **noun** [mass noun] Brit. an alcoholic drink made from fermented apple juice. ■ (also **sweet cider**) N. Amer. an unfermented drink made by crushing fruit, typically apples.
– ORIGIN Middle English: from Old French *sidre*, via ecclesiastical Latin from ecclesiastical Greek *sikera*, from Hebrew *šēḵār* 'strong drink'.

cider gum ▶ **noun** a fast-growing, hardy Tasmanian eucalyptus, widely grown in northern Europe. ● *Eucalyptus gunnii*, family Myrtaceae.

cider press ▶ **noun** a press for crushing apples to make cider.

ci-devant /ˌsiːdəˈvɒ̃/, French /sidvɑ̃/ ▶ **adjective** [attrib.] from or in an earlier time; former: *her ci-devant pupil, now her lover*.
– ORIGIN French, 'heretofore'.

c.i.f. ▶ **abbreviation** cost, insurance, freight (as included in a price).

cig ▶ **noun** informal a cigarette or cigar.
– ORIGIN late 19th cent.: abbreviation.

cigar ▶ **noun** a cylinder of tobacco rolled in tobacco leaves for smoking.
– PHRASES **close but no cigar** N. Amer. informal (of an attempt) almost but not quite successful. [referring to a cigar received in congratulation.]
– ORIGIN early 18th cent.: from French *cigare*, or from Spanish *cigarro*, probably from Mayan *sik'ar* 'smoking'.

cigarette (US also **cigaret**) ▶ **noun** a thin cylinder of finely cut tobacco rolled in paper for smoking. ■ a similar cylinder containing a narcotic or herbal substance.
– ORIGIN mid 19th cent.: from French, diminutive of *cigare* (see CIGAR).

cigarette beetle ▶ **noun** a small reddish beetle that infests tobacco and other stored products. Also called TOBACCO BEETLE. ● *Lasioderma serricorne*, family Anobiidae.

cigarette card ▶ **noun** Brit. a small collectable card with a picture on it, formerly included in packets of cigarettes.

cigarette end ▶ **noun** Brit. the unsmoked remainder of a cigarette.

cigarette machine ▶ **noun** a slot machine that dispenses cigarettes.

cigarette pants ▶ **plural noun** women's trousers with straight, very narrow legs.

cigarette paper ▶ **noun** a piece of thin paper with a gummed edge for rolling tobacco in to make a cigarette.

cigarillo /ˌsɪɡəˈrɪləʊ/ ▶ **noun** (pl. **cigarillos**) a small cigar.
– ORIGIN mid 19th cent.: from Spanish, diminutive of *cigarro* (see CIGAR).

ciggy ▶ **noun** (pl. **ciggies**) informal a cigarette.
– ORIGIN 1960s: abbreviation.

ciguatera /ˌsɪɡwəˈtɛːrə/ ▶ **noun** [mass noun] poisoning by neurotoxins as a result of eating the flesh of tropical marine fish that carries a toxic dinoflagellate.
● This is caused by *Gambierdiscus toxicus*, division (or phylum) Dinophyta.
– ORIGIN mid 19th cent.: from American Spanish, from *cigua* 'sea snail'.

cilantro /sɪˈlantrəʊ/ ▶ **noun** [mass noun] N. Amer. coriander used as a seasoning or garnish.
– ORIGIN 1920s: from Spanish, from Latin *coliandrum* 'coriander'.

cilia plural form of CILIUM.

ciliary /ˈsɪlɪəri/ ▶ **adjective 1** Biology relating to or involving cilia.
2 Anatomy relating to the eyelashes or eyelids.

ciliary body ▶ **noun** Anatomy the part of the eye that connects the iris to the choroid. It consists of the **ciliary muscle** (which alters the curvature of the lens), a series of radial **ciliary process** (from which the lens is suspended by ligaments), and the **ciliary ring** (which adjoins the choroid).

ciliate /ˈsɪlɪeɪt/ ▶ **noun** Zoology a single-celled animal of a large and diverse phylum distinguished by the possession of cilia or ciliary structures. ● Phylum Ciliophora, kingdom Protista (formerly class Ciliata, phylum Protozoa).
▶ **adjective** Zoology (of an organism, cell, or surface) bearing cilia. ■ Botany (of a margin) having a fringe of hairs.
– DERIVATIVES **ciliated** **adjective**, **ciliation** **noun**.

cilice /ˈsɪlɪs/ ▶ **noun** a hair shirt. ■ a spiked garter or other device worn by penitents and ascetics.
– ORIGIN late 16th cent.: from French, from Latin *cilicium*, from Greek *kilikion*, from *Kilikia*, the Greek name for CILICIA in Asia Minor (because hair shirts were originally made of Cilician goats' hair).

Cilicia /sɪˈlɪʃə/ an ancient region on the coast of SE Asia Minor, corresponding to the present-day province of Adana, Turkey.
– DERIVATIVES **Cilician** **adjective & noun**.

Cilician Gates a mountain pass in the Taurus Mountains of southern Turkey, historically forming part of a route linking Anatolia with the Mediterranean coast.

cilium /ˈsɪlɪəm/ ▶ **noun** (usu. in pl. **cilia** /-lɪə/) **1** Biology a short microscopic hair-like vibrating structure found in large numbers on the surface of certain cells, either causing currents in the surrounding fluid, or, in some protozoans and other small organisms, providing propulsion.
2 Anatomy an eyelash.
– ORIGIN early 18th cent. (in the sense 'eyelash'): from Latin.

cill chiefly Building ▶ **noun** variant spelling of SILL.

cimbalom /ˈsɪmb(ə)l(ə)m/ ▶ **noun** a large Hungarian dulcimer (musical instrument).
– ORIGIN late 19th cent.: from Hungarian, from Italian *cembalo*, *cimbalo*, from Latin *cymbalum* (see CYMBAL).

cimetidine /sʌɪˈmɛtɪdiːn/ ▶ **noun** [mass noun] Medicine an antihistamine drug which is used to treat stomach acidity and peptic ulcers. It is a sulphur-containing derivative of imidazole.
– ORIGIN 1970s: from *ci-* (alteration of *cy-* in *cyano-*) + *met(hyl)* + -IDE + -INE[4].

Cimmerian /sɪˈmɪərɪən/ ▶ **noun 1** a member of an ancient nomadic people who overran Asia Minor in the 7th century BC.
2 Greek Mythology a member of a mythical people living in perpetual mist and darkness near the land of the dead.
▶ **adjective** relating to the Cimmerians.
– ORIGIN via Latin from Greek *Kimmerios* + -AN.

C.-in-C. ▶ **abbreviation** Commander-in-Chief.

cinch ▶ **noun 1** informal an extremely easy task: *the program was a cinch to use*. ■ chiefly N. Amer. a sure thing; a certainty: *he was a cinch to take a prize*.
2 chiefly N. Amer. a girth for a Western saddle or pack of a type used mainly in Mexico and the western US.
▶ **verb** [with obj.] chiefly N. Amer. **1** secure (a garment) with a belt. ■ fix (a saddle) securely by means of a girth.
2 informal make certain of: *his advice cinched her decision to accept the offer*.
– ORIGIN mid 19th cent. (in sense 2 of the noun): from Spanish *cincha* 'girth'.

cinchona /sɪŋˈkəʊnə/ ▶ **noun** an evergreen South American tree or shrub with fragrant flowers, cultivated for its bark. ● Genus *Cinchona*, family Rubiaceae: several species.
■ [mass noun] the dried bark of the cinchona, which is a source of quinine and other medicinal substances.

– ORIGIN mid 18th cent.: modern Latin, named after the Countess of *Chinchón* (died 1641), who was treated with a similar drug in South America.

cinchonine /ˈsɪŋkəniːn/ ▶ **noun** [mass noun] Chemistry a compound with antipyretic properties which occurs with quinine in cinchona bark. ● An alkaloid; chem. formula: $C_{19}H_{22}ON_2$.

Cincinnati /ˌsɪnsɪˈnati/ an industrial city in Ohio, on the Ohio River; pop. 333,336 (est. 2008).

cincture /ˈsɪŋktʃə/ ▶ **noun 1** literary a girdle or belt.
2 Architecture a ring at either end of a column shaft.
– ORIGIN late 16th cent. (in the sense 'encircling or enclosure'): from Latin *cinctura*, from *cinct-* 'encircled', from the verb *cingere*.

cinder ▶ **noun 1** a small piece of partly burnt coal or wood that has stopped giving off flames but still has combustible matter in it. ■ (**cinders**) ashes.
2 [mass noun] waste matter produced by smelting or refining ore; slag.
– PHRASES **burnt to a cinder** completely burnt.
– DERIVATIVES **cindery** adjective.
– ORIGIN Old English *sinder* 'slag', of Germanic origin; related to German *Sinter*. The similar but unconnected French *cendre* (from Latin *cinis* 'ashes') has influenced both the sense development and the spelling. Compare with SINTER.

cinder block ▶ **noun** North American term for BREEZE BLOCK.

cinder cone ▶ **noun** a cone formed round a volcanic vent by fragments of lava thrown out during eruptions.

Cinderella a girl in various traditional European fairy tales. In the version by Charles Perrault she is exploited as a servant by her family but enabled by a fairy godmother to attend a royal ball. She meets and captivates Prince Charming but has to flee at midnight, leaving the prince to identify her by the glass slipper which she leaves behind. ■ [as noun] a person or thing that is undeservedly neglected or ignored: *is research into breast cancer to remain the Cinderella of medicine?*
– ORIGIN from CINDER + the diminutive suffix *-ella*, on the pattern of French *Cendrillon*, from *cendre* 'cinders'.

cinder track ▶ **noun** a running track laid with fine cinders.

cine ▶ **adjective** Brit. cinematographic: *a cine camera*. ■ chiefly Indian relating to cinema: *a cine actor*.

cine- ▶ **combining form** representing CINEMATOGRAPHIC (see CINEMATOGRAPHY).

cineaste /ˈsɪnɪast/ (also **cineast**) ▶ **noun** a filmmaker. ■ a person who is fond of or knowledgeable about the cinema.
– ORIGIN 1920s: from French *cinéaste*, from *ciné* (from *cinéma*), on the pattern of *enthousiaste* 'enthusiast'.

cinema ▶ **noun** chiefly Brit. a theatre where films are shown for public entertainment. ■ [mass noun] the production of films as an art or industry: *one of the giants of British cinema*.
– ORIGIN early 20th cent.: from French *cinéma*, abbreviation of *cinématographe* (see CINEMATOGRAPH).

CinemaScope ▶ **noun** [mass noun] trademark a cinematographic process in which special lenses are used to compress a wide image into a standard frame and then expand it again during projection. It results in an image that is almost two and a half times as wide as it is high.

cinematheque /ˌsɪnɪməˈtɛk/ ▶ **noun 1** a film library or archive.
2 a small cinema.
– ORIGIN 1960s: from French *cinémathèque*, from *cinéma* 'cinema', on the pattern of *bibliothèque* 'library'.

cinematic ▶ **adjective** relating to the cinema: *cinematic output*. ■ having qualities characteristic of films: *the cinematic feel of their video*.
– DERIVATIVES **cinematically** adverb.

cinematograph /ˌsɪnɪˈmatəgrɑːf/ (also **kinematograph**) ▶ **noun** historical, chiefly Brit. an apparatus for showing motion-picture films.
– ORIGIN late 19th cent.: from French *cinématographe*, from Greek *kinēma*, *kinēmat-* 'movement', from *kinein* 'to move'.

cinematography /ˌsɪnɪməˈtɒgrəfi/ ▶ **noun** [mass noun] the art of photography and camerawork in film-making.
– DERIVATIVES **cinematographer** noun, **cinematographic** adjective, **cinematographically** adverb.

cinéma-vérité /ˌsɪnɪməˈvɛrɪteɪ/, French /sinemaveʀite/ ▶ **noun** [mass noun] a style of film-making characterized by realistic, typically documentary films which avoid artificiality and artistic effect and are generally made with simple equipment.
– ORIGIN French, literally 'cinema truth'.

cinephile ▶ **noun** a person who is fond of the cinema.
– DERIVATIVES **cinephilia** noun.

cineplex ▶ **noun** trademark, chiefly N. Amer. a cinema with several separate screens; a multiplex.
– ORIGIN 1970s: blend of CINEMA and COMPLEX.

cineraria /ˌsɪnəˈrɛːrɪə/ ▶ **noun** a plant of the daisy family with compact masses of bright flowers, cultivated as a winter-flowering pot plant. ● Genus *Pericallis* (formerly *Senecio* or *Cineraria*), family Compositae.
– ORIGIN modern Latin, feminine of Latin *cinerarius* 'of ashes', from *cinis*, *ciner-* 'ashes' (because of the ash-coloured down on the leaves).

cinerarium /ˌsɪnəˈrɛːrɪəm/ ▶ **noun** (pl. **cinerariums**) a place where a cinerary urn is kept.
– ORIGIN late 19th cent.: from late Latin, neuter (used as a noun) of *cinerarius* 'of ashes'.

cinerary urn /ˈsɪnərəri/ ▶ **noun** an urn for holding a person's ashes after cremation, especially as used by Classical and prehistoric cultures.
– ORIGIN mid 18th cent.: *cinerary* from Latin *cinerarius* 'of ashes'.

cinereous /sɪˈnɪərɪəs/ ▶ **adjective** (especially of hair or feathers) ash-grey.
– ORIGIN late Middle English: from Latin *cinereus* 'similar to ashes' (from *cinis*, *ciner-* 'ashes') + -OUS.

cinereous vulture ▶ **noun** another term for BLACK VULTURE (sense 1).

Cingalese /ˌsɪŋgəˈliːz/ ▶ **noun & adjective** archaic spelling of SINHALESE.
– ORIGIN late 16th cent.: from French *Cinghalais*, from Sanskrit *Siṃhala* 'Sri Lanka' + -ESE.

cingulum /ˈsɪŋgjʊləm/ ▶ **noun** (pl. **cingula** /-lə/) Anatomy **1** a curved bundle of nerve fibres in each hemisphere of the brain.
2 a ridge of enamel on the base or margin of the crown of a tooth.
– DERIVATIVES **cingulate** adjective.
– ORIGIN mid 19th cent.: from Latin, 'belt', from *cingere* 'gird'.

cinnabar /ˈsɪnəbɑː/ ▶ **noun 1** [mass noun] a bright red mineral consisting of mercury sulphide, sometimes used as a pigment. ■ the bright red colour of cinnabar.
2 (also **cinnabar moth**) a day-flying moth with black and red wings, whose black and yellow caterpillars feed on groundsel and ragwort. ● *Tyria jacobaeae*, family Arctiidae.
– ORIGIN Middle English: from Latin *cinnabaris*, from Greek *kinnabari*, of oriental origin.

cinnamon ▶ **noun 1** [mass noun] an aromatic spice made from the peeled, dried, and rolled bark of a SE Asian tree. ■ a yellowish-brown colour resembling that of cinnamon.
2 the tree which yields cinnamon. ● Genus *Cinnamomum*, family Lauraceae: several species.
– ORIGIN late Middle English: from Old French *cinnamome* (from Greek *kinnamōmon*), and Latin *cinnamon* (from Greek *kinnamon*), both from a Semitic language and perhaps based on Malay.

cinnamon bear ▶ **noun** a North American black bear of a variety with reddish-brown hair.

cinnamon fern ▶ **noun** a large North American fern with cinnamon-coloured fronds. ● *Osmunda cinnamomea*, family Osmundaceae.

cinnamon toast ▶ **noun** [mass noun] N. Amer. buttered toast spread with ground cinnamon and sugar.

cinquain /sɪŋˈkeɪn/ ▶ **noun** (in verse) a five-line stanza.
– ORIGIN late 19th cent.: French, from *cinq* 'five'.

cinque /sɪŋk/ (also **cinq**) ▶ **noun 1** the five on dice.
2 (**cinques**) Bell-ringing a system of change-ringing using eleven bells, with five pairs changing places each time.
– ORIGIN late Middle English: from Old French *cinc*, *cink*, from Latin *quinque* 'five'.

cinquecento /ˌtʃɪŋkwɪˈtʃɛntəʊ/ ▶ **noun** (**the cinquecento**) the 16th century as a period of Italian art, architecture, or literature, with a reversion to classical forms.
– ORIGIN Italian, literally '500' (shortened from *milcinquecento* '1500') used with reference to the years 1500–99.

cinquefoil /ˈsɪŋkfɔɪl/ ▶ **noun 1** a widely distributed herbaceous plant of the rose family, with compound leaves of five leaflets and five-petalled yellow flowers. ● Genus *Potentilla*, family Rosaceae.
2 Art an ornamental design of five lobes arranged in a circle, e.g. in architectural tracery or heraldry.
– ORIGIN Middle English: from Latin *quinquefolium*, from *quinque* 'five' + *folium* 'leaf'.

C

Cinque Ports /sɪŋk ˈpɔːts/ a group of medieval ports in Kent and East Sussex in SE England, which were formerly allowed trading privileges in exchange for providing the bulk of England's navy. The five original Cinque Ports were Hastings, Sandwich, Dover, Romney, and Hythe; later Rye and Winchelsea were added.
– ORIGIN from Old French *cink porz*, from Latin *quinque portus* 'five ports'.

Cintra variant spelling of SINTRA.

CIO ▶ **abbreviation** historical (in North America) Congress of Industrial Organizations.

cipher[1] /ˈsʌɪfə/ (also **cypher**) ▶ **noun 1** a secret or disguised way of writing; a code: *he wrote cryptic notes in a cipher* | [mass noun] *the information may be given in cipher*. ■ something written in a code. ■ a key to a code.
2 dated a zero; a figure 0. ■ a person of no importance, especially one who does the bidding of others and seems to have no will of their own.
3 a monogram.
▶ **verb 1** [with obj.] put (a message) into secret writing; encode.
2 [no obj.] archaic do arithmetic.
– ORIGIN late Middle English (in the senses 'symbol for zero' and 'Arabic numeral'): from Old French *cifre*, based on Arabic *ṣifr* 'zero'.

cipher[2] ▶ **noun** a continuous sounding of an organ pipe, caused by a mechanical defect.
▶ **verb** [no obj.] (of an organ pipe) sound continuously.
– ORIGIN late 18th cent.: perhaps from CIPHER[1].

cipolin /ˈsɪpəlɪn/ ▶ **noun** [mass noun] an Italian marble with veins of talc, mica, or quartz, showing alternating white and green streaks.
– ORIGIN late 18th cent.: from French, from Italian *cipollino*, from *cipolla* 'onion' (because its structure, having thin veins of other minerals, resembles onion skin).

circa /ˈsəːkə/ ▶ **preposition** (often preceding a date) approximately: *the church was built circa 1860*.
– ORIGIN mid 19th cent.: Latin.

circadian /səːˈkeɪdɪən/ ▶ **adjective** Physiology (of biological processes) recurring naturally on a twenty-four-hour cycle, even in the absence of light fluctuations: *a circadian rhythm*.
– ORIGIN 1950s: formed irregularly from Latin *circa* 'about' + *dies* 'day'.

Circassian /səːˈkasɪən/ ▶ **noun 1** a member of a group of mainly Sunni Muslim peoples of the NW Caucasus.
2 [mass noun] either of two North Caucasian languages of the Circassians, Adyghe and Kabardian. Also called CHERKESS.
▶ **adjective** relating to the Circassians or their language.
– ORIGIN from *Circassia*, Latinized form of Russian *Cherkes*, denoting a district in the northern Caucasus.

Circe /ˈsəːsi/ Greek Mythology an enchantress who lived on the island of Aeaea. When Odysseus visited the island his companions were changed into pigs by her potions, but he protected himself with the magic herb *moly* and forced her to restore his men to human form.
– ORIGIN via Latin from Greek *Kirkē*.

circinate /ˈsəːsɪnət, -eɪt/ ▶ **adjective 1** Botany denoting leaves or fronds that are rolled up with the tip in the centre, for example the young frond of a fern.
2 Medicine circular in appearance.
– ORIGIN early 19th cent.: from Latin *circinatus*, past participle of *circinare* 'make round', from *circinus* 'pair of compasses'.

Circinus /ˈsəːsɪnəs/ Astronomy a small and faint southern constellation (the Compasses), in the Milky Way next to Centaurus.
– ORIGIN Latin.

circle ▶ **noun 1** a round plane figure whose boundary (the circumference) consists of points equidistant from a fixed point (the centre). ■ something in the shape of a circle: *the lamp spread a circle of light* | *they all sat round in a circle*. ■ a dark circular mark below each eye caused by illness or tiredness. ■ Brit. a curved upper tier of seats in a theatre or cinema. ■ Hockey short for STRIKING CIRCLE.

C

2 a group of people with a shared profession, interests, or acquaintances: *she did not normally move in such exalted circles.*
▶ **verb** [with obj.] move all the way around (someone or something), especially more than once: *they were circling Athens airport* | (as adj. **circling**) *a circling helicopter* | [no obj.] *we circled round the island.* ■ [no obj.] (**circle back**) move in a wide loop back towards one's starting point: *he paced away from her, then circled back.* ■ form a ring around: *the abbey was circled by a huge wall.* ■ draw a line around: *circle the correct answers.*
– PHRASES **circle the wagons** N. Amer. informal unite in defence of a common interest. [with reference to the defensive position of a wagon train under attack.] **come** (or **turn**) **full circle** return to a past position or situation, especially in a way considered to be inevitable. [with reference to Shakespeare's *King Lear* v. iii. 165, 'The Wheele is come full circle': by association with the wheel represented in mythology and literature as turned by Fortune and symbolizing mutability.] **go** (or **run**) **round in circles** informal do something for a long time without achieving anything but purposeless repetition: *the discussion went round and round in circles.*
– ORIGIN Old English, from Old French *cercle*, from Latin *circulus* 'small ring', diminutive of *circus* 'ring'.

circle dance ▶ **noun** a country dance or folk dance in which dancers form a circle.

circlet ▶ **noun** a circular band, typically one made of precious metal, worn on the head as an ornament. ■ a small circular arrangement or object.
– ORIGIN late Middle English: from CIRCLE + -ET[1], perhaps reinforced by archaic French *cerclet.*

circlip /ˈsəːklɪp/ ▶ **noun** Brit. a metal ring sprung into a slot or groove in a bar to hold something in place.
– ORIGIN early 20th cent.: blend of CIRCLE or CIRCULAR and CLIP[1].

circs ▶ **plural noun** Brit. informal circumstances: *anyone would have done the same under the circs.*

circuit ▶ **noun 1** a roughly circular line, route, or movement that starts and finishes at the same place: *I ran a circuit of the village.* ■ Brit. a track used for motor racing, horse racing, or athletics.
2 an established itinerary of events or venues used for a particular activity, typically involving sport or public performance: *the alternative cabaret circuit.* ■ a series of athletic exercises performed consecutively in one training session: [as modifier] *circuit training.* ■ a regular journey made by a judge around a particular district to hear cases in court: [as modifier] *a circuit judge.* ■ a district administered or formerly administered by travelling judges. ■ a group of local Methodist Churches forming an administrative unit.
3 a complete and closed path around which a circulating electric current can flow. ■ a system of electrical conductors and components forming an electrical circuit.
▶ **verb** [with obj.] move all the way around (a place or thing).
– ORIGIN late Middle English: via Old French from Latin *circuitus*, from *circuire*, variant of *circumire* 'go round', from *circum* 'around' + *ire* 'go'.

circuit board ▶ **noun** a thin rigid board containing an electric circuit; a printed circuit.

circuit breaker ▶ **noun** an automatic device for stopping the flow of current in an electric circuit as a safety measure.

circuitous ▶ **adjective** (of a route or journey) longer than the most direct way: *the canal followed a circuitous route* | figurative *a circuitous line of reasoning.*
– DERIVATIVES **circuitously** adverb, **circuitousness** noun.
– ORIGIN mid 17th cent.: from medieval Latin *circuitosus*, from *circuitus* 'a way around' (see CIRCUIT).

circuit rider ▶ **noun** N. Amer. historical a clergyman who travelled on horseback from church to church, especially within a rural Methodist circuit.

circuitry ▶ **noun** (pl. **circuitries**) [mass noun] electric circuits collectively: *solid state circuitry.* ■ a circuit or system of circuits performing a particular function in an electronic device: *switching circuitry.*

circular ▶ **adjective 1** having the form of a circle: *the building features a circular atrium.* ■ (of a movement or journey) starting and finishing at the same place and often following roughly the circumference of an imaginary circle: *a circular walk.*
2 Logic (of an argument) already containing an assumption of what is to be proved, and therefore fallacious.
3 [attrib.] (of a letter or advertisement) for distribution to a large number of people.
▶ **noun** a letter or advertisement which is distributed to a large number of people.
– DERIVATIVES **circularity** noun, **circularly** adverb.
– ORIGIN late Middle English: from Old French *circulier*, from late Latin *circularis*, from Latin *circulus* 'small ring' (see CIRCLE).

circular breathing ▶ **noun** [mass noun] a technique of inhaling through the nose while blowing air through the lips from the cheeks, used to maintain constant exhalation especially by players of certain wind instruments.

circularize (also **circularise**) ▶ **verb** [with obj.] **1** distribute a large number of letters or leaflets to (a group of people) in order to advertise something or canvas opinion.
2 Biochemistry make (a stretch of DNA) into a circular loop.
– DERIVATIVES **circularization** noun.

circular polarization ▶ **noun** [mass noun] Physics polarization of an electromagnetic wave in which either the electric or the magnetic vector executes a circle perpendicular to the path of propagation with a frequency equal to that of the wave. It is frequently used in satellite communications.

circular saw ▶ **noun** a power saw with a rapidly rotating toothed disc.

circulate ▶ **verb 1** move continuously or freely through a closed system or area: [no obj.] *antibodies circulate in the bloodstream* | [with obj.] *the fan circulates hot air around the oven.* ■ [no obj.] move around a social function in order to talk to many different people.
2 pass from place to place or person to person: [no obj.] *rumours of his arrest circulated* | [with obj.] *they were circulating the list to conservation groups.* ■ [with obj.] send copies of a letter or leaflet to (a group of people): *tutors were circulated with the handout.*
– DERIVATIVES **circulator** noun.
– ORIGIN late 15th cent. (as an alchemical term meaning 'distil something in a closed container, allowing condensed vapour to return to the original liquid'): from Latin *circulat-* 'moved in a circular path', from the verb *circulare*, from *circulus* 'small ring' (see CIRCLE). Sense 1 dates from the mid 17th cent.

circulating library ▶ **noun** historical a small library with books lent for a small fee to subscribers.

circulating medium ▶ **noun** a commodity used in commercial exchange, especially coins or gold.

circulation ▶ **noun** [mass noun] **1** movement to and fro or around something, especially that of fluid in a closed system: *an extra pump for good water circulation.* ■ the continuous motion by which the blood travels through all parts of the body under the action of the heart.
2 the public availability or knowledge of something: *his music has achieved wide circulation.* ■ the movement, exchange, or availability of money in a country: *the new-look coins go into circulation today.* ■ [in sing.] the number of copies sold of a newspaper or magazine: *the magazine had a large circulation.*
– PHRASES **in** (or **out of**) **circulation** available (or unavailable) to the public: *there is a huge volume of video material in circulation.* ■ (of a person) seen (or not seen) in public: *Anne had made a good recovery and was back in circulation.*
– ORIGIN late Middle English (denoting continuous distillation of a liquid): from Latin *circulatio(n-)*, from the verb *circulare* (see CIRCULATE).

circulatory ▶ **adjective** relating to the circulation of blood or sap.

circulatory system ▶ **noun** the system that circulates blood and lymph through the body, consisting of the heart, blood vessels, blood, lymph, and the lymphatic vessels and glands. Also called CARDIOVASCULAR SYSTEM.

circum- /ˈsəːkəm/ ▶ **prefix** about; around (functioning within the word as an adverb as in *circumambulate*, or as a preposition as in *circumpolar*).
– ORIGIN from Latin *circum* 'round'.

circumambient /ˌsəːkəmˈambɪənt/ ▶ **adjective** literary or formal surrounding: *circumambient gases.*

circumambulate /ˌsəːkəmˈambjʊleɪt/ ▶ **verb** [with obj.] formal walk all the way round: *they used to circumambulate the perimeter wall.*
– DERIVATIVES **circumambulation** noun, **circumambulatory** adjective.

circumcircle ▶ **noun** Geometry a circle touching all the vertices of a triangle or polygon.

circumcise /ˈsəːkəmsʌɪz/ ▶ **verb** [with obj.] cut off the foreskin of (a young boy or man, especially a baby) as a religious rite, especially in Judaism and Islam, or as a medical treatment. ■ cut off the clitoris, and sometimes the labia, of (a girl or young woman) as a traditional practice among some peoples.
– DERIVATIVES **circumciser** noun.
– ORIGIN Middle English: from Old French *circonciser*, or from Latin *circumcis-* 'cut around', from the verb *circumcidere*, from *circum* 'around, about' + *caedere* 'to cut'.

circumcision ▶ **noun 1** [mass noun] the action or practice of circumcising a young boy or man. ■ (also **female circumcision**) (among some peoples) the traditional practice of cutting off the clitoris and sometimes the labia of girls or young women.
2 (**Circumcision**) (in church use) the feast of the Circumcision of Christ, 1 January.
– ORIGIN Middle English: from late Latin *circumcisio(n-)*, from the verb *circumcidere* (see CIRCUMCISE).

circumference /səˈkʌmf(ə)r(ə)ns/ ▶ **noun** the enclosing boundary of a curved geometric figure, especially a circle. ■ the distance around something: *babies who have small head circumferences* | [mass noun] *a rope two inches in circumference.*
– DERIVATIVES **circumferential** adjective, **circumferentially** adverb.
– ORIGIN late Middle English: from Old French *circonference*, from Latin *circumferentia*, from *circum* 'around, about' + *ferre* 'carry, bear'.

circumflex /ˈsəːkəmflɛks/ ▶ **noun** (also **circumflex accent**) a mark (^) placed over a vowel in some languages to indicate contraction, length, or a particular quality.
▶ **adjective** Anatomy bending round something else; curved: *circumflex coronary arteries.*
– ORIGIN late 16th cent.: from Latin *circumflexus* (from *circum* 'around, about' + *flectere* 'to bend'), translating Greek *perispōmenos* 'drawn around'.

circumfluent /səːˈkʌmflʊənt/ ▶ **adjective** rare flowing round; surrounding.
– DERIVATIVES **circumfluence** noun.
– ORIGIN late 16th cent.: from Latin *circumfluent-* 'flowing around', from the verb *circumfluere*, from *circum* 'around, about' + *fluere* 'to flow'.

circumfuse /ˌsəːkəmˈfjuːz/ ▶ **verb** [with obj.] archaic pour (a liquid) so as to cause it to surround something: *Earth with her nether Ocean circumfused.*
– ORIGIN late 16th cent.: from Latin *circumfus-* 'poured around', from the verb *circumfundere*, from *circum* 'around' + *fundere* 'pour'.

circumjacent /ˌsəːkəmˈdʒeɪs(ə)nt/ ▶ **adjective** archaic surrounding.
– ORIGIN late 15th cent.: from Latin *circumjacent-* 'lying round about, bordering upon', from the verb *circumjacere*, from *circum* 'around' + *jacere* 'to lie'.

circumlocution /ˌsəːkəmləˈkjuːʃ(ə)n/ ▶ **noun** [mass noun] the use of many words where fewer would do, especially in a deliberate attempt to be vague or evasive: *his admission came after years of circumlocution* | [count noun] *he used a number of poetic circumlocutions.*
– ORIGIN late Middle English: from Latin *circumlocutio(n-)* (translating Greek *periphrasis*), from *circum* 'around' + *locutio(n-)* from *loqui* 'speak'.

circumlocutory /ˌsəːkəmˈlɒkjʊt(ə)ri/ ▶ **adjective** using many words where fewer would do, especially in a deliberate attempt to be vague or evasive; long-winded: *he has a meandering, circumlocutory speaking style.*

circumlunar ▶ **adjective** moving or situated around the moon: *a circumlunar flight.*

circumnavigate ▶ **verb** [with obj.] sail all the way around (something, especially the world). ■ humorous go around or across (something): *he helped her to circumnavigate a frozen puddle.*
– DERIVATIVES **circumnavigation** noun, **circumnavigator** noun.

circumpolar /səːkəmˈpəʊlə/ ▶ **adjective** situated around or inhabiting one of the earth's poles: *circumpolar arctic areas.* ■ Astronomy (of a star or motion) above the horizon at all times in a given latitude: *the Plough is circumpolar from Britain.*

circumscribe ▶ **verb** [with obj.] **1** restrict (something) within limits: *the minister's powers are circumscribed both by tradition and the organization of local government.*
2 Geometry draw (a figure) round another, touching it at points but not cutting it. Compare with INSCRIBE.
– DERIVATIVES **circumscription** noun.

– ORIGIN late Middle English: from Latin *circumscribere*, from *circum* 'around' + *scribere* 'write'.

circumsolar /ˌsəːkəmˈsəʊlə/ ▶ **adjective** moving or situated around the sun.

circumspect ▶ **adjective** wary and unwilling to take risks: *the officials were very circumspect in their statements.*
– DERIVATIVES **circumspectly** adverb.
– ORIGIN late Middle English: from Latin *circumspectus*, from *circumspicere* 'look around', from *circum* 'around, about' + *specere* 'look'.

circumspection ▶ **noun** [mass noun] the quality of being wary and unwilling to take risks; prudence: *circumspection is required in the day-to-day exercise of administrative powers.*

circumstance ▶ **noun 1** (usu. **circumstances**) a fact or condition connected with or relevant to an event or action: *we wanted to marry but circumstances didn't permit.* ■ an event or fact that causes or helps to cause something to happen, typically something undesirable: *he was found dead but there were no suspicious circumstances* | [mass noun] *they were thrown together by circumstance.*
2 (**circumstances**) one's state of financial or material welfare: *the artists are living in reduced circumstances.*
3 archaic ceremony and public display: *pomp and circumstance.*
– PHRASES **under** (or **in**) **the circumstances** given the difficult nature of the situation: *she had every right to be cross under the circumstances.* **under** (or **in**) **no circumstances** never, whatever the situation is or might be.
– DERIVATIVES **circumstanced** adjective.
– ORIGIN Middle English: from Old French *circonstance* or Latin *circumstantia*, from *circumstare* 'encircle, encompass', from *circum* 'around' + *stare* 'stand'.

circumstantial ▶ **adjective 1** pointing indirectly towards someone's guilt but not conclusively proving it: *the prosecution will have to rely on circumstantial evidence.*
2 (of a description) containing full details: *the picture was so circumstantial that it began to be convincing.*
– DERIVATIVES **circumstantiality** noun, **circumstantially** adverb.
– ORIGIN late 16th cent.: from Latin *circumstantia* (see CIRCUMSTANCE) + -AL.

circumterrestrial ▶ **adjective** moving or situated around the earth: *circumterrestrial space.*

circumvallate /ˌsəːkəmˈvaleɪt/ ▶ **verb** [with obj.] literary surround with or as if with a rampart: *the walls were circumvallated with a ditch.*
▶ **adjective 1** literary surrounded or surrounding as if by a rampart: *circumvallate mountains.*
2 Anatomy denoting certain papillae near the back of the tongue, surrounded by taste receptors.
– ORIGIN mid 17th cent. (as an adjective): from Latin *circumvallat-* 'surrounded with a rampart', from the verb *circumvallare*, from *circum* 'around' + *vallare*, from *vallum* 'rampart'. The verb dates from the early 19th cent.

circumvent /səːkəmˈvɛnt/ ▶ **verb** [with obj.] **1** find a way around (an obstacle). ■ overcome (a problem or difficulty) in a clever and surreptitious way: *it was always possible to circumvent the regulations.*
2 archaic deceive; outwit.
– DERIVATIVES **circumvention** noun.
– ORIGIN late Middle English: from Latin *circumvent-* 'skirted around', from the verb *circumvenire*, from *circum* 'around' + *venire* 'come'.

circumvolution /ˌsəːkəmvəˈluːʃ(ə)n/ ▶ **noun** a winding movement, especially of one thing round another.
– ORIGIN late Middle English: from Latin *circumvolut-* 'rolled around', from the verb *circumvolvere*, from *circum* 'around' + *volvere* 'roll'.

circus ▶ **noun** (pl. **circuses**) **1** a travelling company of acrobats, clowns, and other entertainers which gives performances, typically in a large tent, in a series of different places. ■ informal a public scene of frenetic, noisy, or confused activity: *a media circus.*
2 (in ancient Rome) a rounded or oval arena lined with tiers of seats, used for equestrian and other sports and games.
3 [in place names] Brit. a rounded open space in a town where several streets converge: *Piccadilly Circus.*
– ORIGIN late Middle English (with reference to the arena of Roman antiquity): from Latin, 'ring or circus'. The sense 'travelling company of performers' dates from the late 18th cent.

ciré /ˈsiːreɪ/ ▶ **noun** [mass noun] a fabric with a smooth shiny surface obtained by waxing and heating.
– ORIGIN 1920s: French, literally 'waxed'.

Cirencester /ˈsʌɪrənˌsɛstə/ a town in Gloucestershire, in England; pop. 16,500 (est. 2009). It was a major town in Roman Britain, when it was known as Corinium Dobunorum.

cire perdue /ˌsɪə pəːˈdjuː/ ▶ **noun** [mass noun] a method of bronze casting using a clay core and a wax coating placed in a mould. The wax is melted in the mould and drained out, and bronze poured into the space left, producing a hollow bronze figure when the core is discarded. Also called LOST WAX.
– ORIGIN French, 'lost wax'.

cirl bunting /səːl/ ▶ **noun** an Old World bunting related to the yellowhammer, the male of which has a distinctive facial pattern and a black throat.
● *Emberiza cirlus*, family Emberizidae (subfamily Emberizinae).
– ORIGIN late 18th cent.: *cirl* from Italian *cirlo*, probably from *zirlare* 'whistle as a thrush'.

cirque /səːk/ ▶ **noun 1** Geology a half-open steep-sided hollow at the head of a valley or on a mountainside, formed by glacial erosion. Also called CORRIE or CWM.
2 literary a ring, circlet, or circle.
– ORIGIN late 17th cent. (in sense 2): from French, from Latin *circus*.

cirrhosis /sɪˈrəʊsɪs/ ▶ **noun** [mass noun] a chronic disease of the liver marked by degeneration of cells, inflammation, and fibrous thickening of tissue. It is typically a result of alcoholism or hepatitis.
– DERIVATIVES **cirrhotic** /sɪˈrɒtɪk/ adjective.
– ORIGIN early 19th cent.: modern Latin, from Greek *kirrhos* 'tawny' (because this is the colour of the liver in many cases).

cirriped (also **cirripede** /ˈsɪrɪpiːd/) ▶ **noun** Zoology a crustacean of the class Cirripedia; a barnacle.

Cirripedia /ˌsɪrɪˈpiːdɪə/ ▶ **plural noun** Zoology a class of crustaceans that comprises the barnacles.
– ORIGIN modern Latin (plural), from Latin *cirrus* 'a curl' (because of the form of the legs) + *pes, ped-* 'foot'.

cirrocumulus /ˌsɪrəʊˈkjuːmjʊləs/ ▶ **noun** [mass noun] cloud forming a broken layer of small fleecy clouds at high altitude (usually 5 to 13 km, 16,500 to 45,000 ft), typically with a rippled or granulated appearance (as in a mackerel sky).

cirrostratus /ˌsɪrəʊˈstrɑːtəs, -ˈstreɪtəs/ ▶ **noun** [mass noun] cloud forming a thin, more or less uniform semi-translucent layer at high altitude (usually 5 to 13 km, 16,500 to 45,000 ft).

cirrus /ˈsɪrəs/ ▶ **noun** (pl. **cirri** /-rʌɪ/) **1** [mass noun] cloud forming wispy filamentous tufted streaks or 'mare's tails' at high altitude (usually 5 to 13 km, 16,500 to 45,000 ft).
2 Zoology a slender tendril or hair-like filament, such as the appendage of a barnacle, the barbel of a fish, or the intromittent organ of an earthworm. ■ Botany a tendril.
– ORIGIN early 18th cent. (in the sense 'tendril'): from Latin, literally 'a curl'.

CIS ▶ **abbreviation** Commonwealth of Independent States.

cis /sɪs/ ▶ **adjective** Chemistry denoting or relating to a molecular structure in which two particular atoms or groups lie on the same side of a given plane in the molecule, in particular denoting an isomer in which substituents at opposite ends of a carbon–carbon double bond are on the same side of the bond: *the cis isomer of stilbene.* Compare with TRANS.
– ORIGIN independent usage of CIS-.

cis- ▶ **prefix 1** on this side of; on the side nearer to the speaker: *cisatlantic.* Often contrasted with TRANS- or ULTRA-. ■ historical on the side nearer to Rome: *cisalpine.* ■ (of time) closer to the present: *cis-Elizabethan.*
2 Chemistry (usu. *cis-*) denoting molecules with cis arrangements of substituents: *cis-1,2-dichloroethene.*
– ORIGIN from Latin *cis* 'on this side of'.

cisalpine /sɪsˈalpʌɪn/ ▶ **adjective** on the southern side of the Alps.

Cisalpine Gaul see GAUL[1].

cisatlantic /sɪsətˈlantɪk/ ▶ **adjective** on the same side of the Atlantic as the speaker.

cisco /ˈsɪskəʊ/ ▶ **noun** (pl. **ciscoes**) a freshwater whitefish of northern countries, most species of which are important food fishes. ● Genus *Coregonus*, family Salmonidae: several species.
– ORIGIN mid 19th cent.: of unknown origin.

Ciskei /sɪsˈkʌɪ/ a former homeland established in South Africa for the Xhosa people, now part of the province of Eastern Cape. See also HOMELAND.

cislunar /sɪsˈluːnə/ ▶ **adjective** between the earth and the moon: *the darkness of cislunar space.*

cisplatin /sɪsˈplatɪn/ ▶ **noun** [mass noun] Medicine a cytotoxic drug used in cancer chemotherapy. ● A coordination compound of platinum; chem. formula: $Pt(NH_3)_2Cl_2$.
– ORIGIN late 20th cent.: from CIS- (sense 2) + PLATINUM.

cispontine /sɪsˈpɒntʌɪn/ ▶ **adjective** archaic on the north side of the Thames bridges in London (originally the better-known side).
– ORIGIN mid 19th cent.: from CIS- + Latin *pons, pont-* 'bridge'.

cissing /ˈsɪsɪŋ/ ▶ **noun** [mass noun] (in decorating) failure of paint to adhere properly to a surface.
– ORIGIN late 19th cent.: of unknown origin.

cissus /ˈsɪsəs/ ▶ **noun** a woody climbing vine of a genus that includes the kangaroo vine. ● Genus *Cissus*, family Vitaceae.
– ORIGIN modern Latin: from Greek *kissos* 'ivy'.

cissy ▶ **noun & adjective** Brit. variant spelling of SISSY.

cist /sɪst/ (also **kist**) ▶ **noun 1** Archaeology an ancient coffin or burial chamber made from stone or a hollowed tree.
2 a box used in ancient Greece for sacred utensils.
– ORIGIN early 19th cent.: from Latin *cista*, from Greek *kistē* 'box'; sense 1 via Welsh.

Cistercian /sɪˈstəːʃ(ə)n/ ▶ **noun** a monk or nun of an order founded in 1098 as a stricter branch of the Benedictines. The monks are now divided into two observances, the strict observance, whose adherents are known popularly as Trappists, and the common observance, which has certain relaxations.
▶ **adjective** relating to the Cistercians: *a Cistercian abbey.*
– ORIGIN from French *cistercien*, from *Cistercium*, the Latin name of *Cîteaux* near Dijon in France, where the order was founded.

cistern ▶ **noun** a tank for storing water, especially one supplying taps or as part of a flushing toilet.
– ORIGIN Middle English: from Old French *cisterne*, from Latin *cisterna*, from *cista* 'box' (see CIST).

cisticola /sɪsˈtɪkələ, ˌsɪstɪˈkəʊlə/ ▶ **noun** a small Old World warbler with brownish streaked plumage, found mainly in Africa. ● Genus *Cisticola*, family Sylviidae: numerous species. See also FAN-TAILED WARBLER.
– ORIGIN modern Latin, from Greek *kistos* 'flowering shrub' + Latin *-col-* 'dwelling in' (from the verb *colere*).

cistron /ˈsɪstrɒn/ ▶ **noun** Biochemistry a section of a DNA or RNA molecule that codes for a specific polypeptide in protein synthesis.
– ORIGIN 1950s: from CIS- (sense 2) + TRANS- (because of the possibility of two genes being on the same or different chromosomes) + -ON.

cistus /ˈsɪstəs/ ▶ **noun** a southern European shrub with large white or red flowers, from which the resin ladanum may be extracted. Also called ROCK ROSE. ● Genus *Cistus*, family Cistaceae.
– ORIGIN modern Latin, from Greek *kistos*.

citadel /ˈsɪtəd(ə)l, -dɛl/ ▶ **noun 1** a fortress, typically one on high ground above a city.
2 a meeting hall of the Salvation Army.
– ORIGIN mid 16th cent.: from French *citadelle*, or from Italian *cittadella*, based on Latin *civitas* 'city' (see CITY).

citation /sʌɪˈteɪʃ(ə)n/ ▶ **noun 1** a quotation from or reference to a book, paper, or author, especially in a scholarly work: *the majority of the citations are to work published during the past twenty years.* ■ Law a reference to a previous case, used as guidance in the trying of comparable cases or in support of an argument.
2 a mention of a praiseworthy act in an official report, especially that of a member of the armed forces in wartime. ■ a note accompanying an award, describing the reasons for it: *a Nobel citation.*
3 N. Amer. a summons to appear in court: *a traffic citation.*
– ORIGIN Middle English (in sense 2): from Old French, from Latin *citatio(n-)*, from *citare* 'cite'.

cite /sʌɪt/ ▶ **verb** [with obj.] **1** refer to (a passage, book, or author) as evidence for or justification of an argument or statement, especially in a scholarly work. ■ mention as an example: *medics have been cited as a key example of a modern breed of technical expert.*
2 praise (someone, typically a member of the armed forces) in an official report for a courageous act.

C

C

3 summon (someone) to appear in court.
▸ noun US a citation.
– DERIVATIVES **citable** adjective.
– ORIGIN late Middle English (in sense 3 of the verb, originally with reference to a court of ecclesiastical law): from Old French *citer*, from Latin *citare*, from *ciere*, *cire* 'to call'.

CITES /'sʌɪtiːz/ ▸ abbreviation Convention on International Trade in Endangered Species.

cithara /'sɪθərə, 'kɪθ-/ (also **kithara** /'kɪθ-/) ▸ noun an ancient Greek and Roman stringed musical instrument similar to the lyre.
– ORIGIN late 18th cent.: Latin, from Greek *kithara*. Compare with CITTERN.

citified ▸ adjective chiefly derogatory characteristic of an urban environment: *we must look like citified dandies to them.*

citizen ▸ noun a legally recognized subject or national of a state or commonwealth, either native or naturalized: *a British citizen.* ■ an inhabitant of a particular town or city: *the good citizens of Edinburgh.*
– PHRASES **citizen of the world** a person who is at home in any country.
– ORIGIN Middle English: from Anglo-Norman French *citezein*, alteration (probably influenced by *deinzein* 'denizen') of Old French *citeain*, based on Latin *civitas* 'city' (see CITY).

citizen journalism ▸ noun [mass noun] the collection, dissemination, and analysis of news and information by the general public, especially by means of the Internet.
– DERIVATIVES **citizen journalist** noun.

citizenry ▸ noun [mass noun] the citizens of a place regarded collectively: *the legal obligations of the citizenry.*

Citizens' Advice Bureau ▸ noun (in the UK) an office at which the public can receive free advice and information on civil matters.

citizen's arrest ▸ noun an arrest by an ordinary person without a warrant, allowable in certain cases.

Citizens' Band (abbrev.: **CB**) ▸ noun [mass noun] a range of radio frequencies which are allocated for local communication by private individuals, especially by handheld or vehicle radio: [as modifier] *Citizens' Band radio.*

Citizen's Charter ▸ noun a document setting out the rights of citizens, especially a British government document of 1991 that guaranteed citizens the right of redress on occasions where a public service failed to meet certain standards.

citizenship ▸ noun [mass noun] the position or status of being a citizen of a particular country: *the refugees could be granted dual citizenship.*

Citlaltépetl /ˌsiːtlal'teɪpet(ə)l/ the highest peak in Mexico, in the east of the country, north of the city of Orizaba. It rises to a height of 5,699 m (18,503 ft) and is an extinct volcano. Spanish name PICO DE ORIZABA.
– ORIGIN Aztec, literally 'star mountain'.

citole /sɪ'təʊl/ ▸ noun a lute-like medieval stringed instrument, forerunner of the cittern.
– ORIGIN late Middle English: from Old French, based on Latin *cithara* (see CITTERN).

citral /'sɪtral/ ▸ noun [mass noun] Chemistry a fragrant liquid occurring in citrus and lemon grass oils and used in flavourings and perfumes. ● A terpene; chem. formula: $C_{10}H_{16}O$.

citrate /'sɪtreɪt/ ▸ noun Chemistry a salt or ester of citric acid.

citric ▸ adjective derived from or related to citrus fruit: *a citric flavour.*
– ORIGIN late 18th cent.: from Latin *citrus* 'citron tree' + -IC.

citric acid ▸ noun [mass noun] Chemistry a sharp-tasting crystalline acid present in the juice of lemons and other sour fruits. It is made commercially by the fermentation of sugar and used as a flavouring and setting agent. ● A tribasic acid; chem. formula: $C_6H_8O_7$.

citriculture /'sɪtrɪˌkʌltʃə/ ▸ noun [mass noun] the cultivation of citrus fruit trees.

citril /'sɪtrɪl/ (also **citril finch**) ▸ noun a small European and African finch related to the canary, with generally yellowish-green plumage. ● Genus *Serinus*, family Fringillidae: two species.
– ORIGIN late 17th cent.: apparently from Italian *citrinella*, diminutive of *citrina* 'citrine-coloured (bird)'.

citrine /'sɪtrɪn/ ▸ noun [mass noun] a glassy yellow variety of quartz. ■ a light greenish-yellow.
– ORIGIN late Middle English: from Old French *citrin* 'lemon-coloured', from medieval Latin *citrinus*, from Latin *citrus* 'citron tree'.

citron /'sɪtr(ə)n/ ▸ noun a shrubby Asian tree bearing fruits which resemble large lemons with less acid flesh and thick fragrant peel. ● *Citrus medica*, family Rutaceae; one of the ancestors of modern commercial citrus fruits.
■ the fruit of the citron tree.
– ORIGIN early 16th cent. (denoting the fruit): from French, from Latin *citrus* 'citron tree', on the pattern of *limon* 'lemon'.

citronella ▸ noun 1 (also **citronella oil**) [mass noun] a fragrant natural oil used as an insect repellent and in perfume and soap manufacture.
2 the South Asian grass from which citronella oil is obtained. ● *Cymbopogon nardus*, family Gramineae.
– ORIGIN mid 19th cent.: modern Latin, from CITRON + the diminutive suffix *-ella*.

citrus ▸ noun (pl. **citruses**) a tree of a genus that includes citron, lemon, lime, orange, and grapefruit. Native to Asia, citrus trees are cultivated in warm countries for their fruit. ● Genus *Citrus*, family Rutaceae.
■ (also **citrus fruit**) a fruit from a citrus tree: [as modifier] *citrus extracts.*
– DERIVATIVES **citrous** adjective, **citrusy** adjective.
– ORIGIN Latin, 'citron tree, thuja'.

cittern /'sɪt(ə)n/ ▸ noun a stringed instrument similar to a lute, with a flattened back and wire strings, used in 16th- and 17th-century Europe.
– ORIGIN mid 16th cent.: from Latin *cithara*, from Greek *kithara*, denoting a kind of harp. The spelling has been influenced by GITTERN.

city ▸ noun (pl. **cities**) 1 a large town: *one of Italy's most beautiful cities* | [as modifier] *the city centre.* ■ Brit. a town created a city by charter and usually containing a cathedral. ■ N. Amer. a municipal centre incorporated by the state or province. ■ [with modifier] informal a place or situation characterized by a specified attribute: *the staff were in turmoil—it was panic city.*
2 (**the City**) short for CITY OF LONDON. ■ the financial and commercial institutions located in the City of London: *the Budget got a stony reception from the City* | [as modifier] *a City analyst.*
– DERIVATIVES **cityward** adjective & adverb, **citywards** adverb.
– ORIGIN Middle English: from Old French *cite*, from Latin *civitas*, from *civis* 'citizen'. Originally denoting a town, and often used as a Latin equivalent to Old English *burh* 'borough', the term was later applied to the more important English boroughs. The connection between city and cathedral grew up under the Norman kings, as the episcopal sees (many had been established in villages) were removed to the chief borough of the diocese.

City and Guilds Institute (in the UK) an institute based in London which is responsible for courses and examinations in technical and craft subjects, generally at a lower level than university degrees.

City Company ▸ noun (in the UK) a corporation descended from an ancient trade guild of London.

city desk ▸ noun 1 Brit. the department of a newspaper dealing with business news.
2 N. Amer. the department of a newspaper dealing with local news.

city editor ▸ noun 1 Brit. a person dealing with financial news in a newspaper.
2 N. Amer. a person dealing with local news in a newspaper.

city father ▸ noun a person concerned with or experienced in the administration of a city: *the city fathers decided to build a museum.*

city gent ▸ noun Brit. informal a businessman working in the financial district of the City of London.

city hall ▸ noun the administrative building of a municipal government. ■ N. Amer. municipal offices or officers collectively: *they cultivated close ties with City Hall.*

city manager ▸ noun N. Amer. (in some cities) an official directing the administration of a city.

City of God Paradise, perceived as an ideal community in heaven. ■ the Christian Church. [from *The City of God* by St Augustine.]

City of London the part of London situated within the ancient boundaries and governed by the Lord Mayor and the Corporation.

city page ▸ noun (usu. **city pages**) Brit. the part of a newspaper or magazine that deals with the financial news.

city planning ▸ noun US term for TOWN PLANNING.

cityscape ▸ noun the visual appearance of a city or urban area; a city landscape. ■ a picture of a city.

city slicker ▸ noun informal, derogatory a person with the sophistication and values generally associated with urban dwellers.

city-state ▸ noun chiefly historical a city that with its surrounding territory forms an independent state.

City Technology College ▸ noun (in the UK) a type of secondary school set up through partnerships between the government and business to teach technology and science in inner-city areas.

citywide ▸ adjective & adverb extending throughout a city: [as adj.] *a citywide computer network* | [as adv.] *sales citywide reached a four-year high.*

Ciudad Bolívar /sjuːˌdad bɒ'liːvɑː/, Spanish /sju'ðað bəʊ'liβar, θju'ðað/ a city in SE Venezuela, on the Orinoco River; pop. 355,800 (est. 2009). Formerly called Angostura, its name was changed in 1846 to honour the country's liberator, Simón Bolívar.

Ciudad Trujillo /truː'hiːjəʊ, -'hiːljəʊ/ former name (1936–61) for SANTO DOMINGO.

Ciudad Victoria /vɪk'tɔːrɪə/, Spanish /βik'toərja/ a city in NE Mexico, capital of the state of Tamaulipas; pop. 278,455 (2005).

civet /'sɪvɪt/ ▸ noun (also **civet cat**) 1 a slender nocturnal carnivorous mammal with a barred and spotted coat and well-developed anal scent glands, native to Africa and Asia. ● Family Viverridae (the **civet family**): several genera and species. The civet family also includes the genets, linsang, and fossa, and formerly included the mongooses.
■ [mass noun] a strong musky perfume obtained from the secretions of the civet's scent glands.
2 US the ring-tailed cat or cacomistle.
– ORIGIN mid 16th cent.: from French *civette*, from Italian *zibetto*, from medieval Latin *zibethum*, from Arabic *zabād*, denoting the perfume.

civic ▸ adjective relating to a city or town, especially its administration; municipal: *a meeting of civic and business leaders.* ■ relating to the duties or activities of people in relation to their town, city, or local area: *he was active in the civic life of Swindon.*
– DERIVATIVES **civically** adverb.
– ORIGIN mid 16th cent.: from French *civique* or Latin *civicus*, from *civis* 'citizen'. The original use was in *civic garland*, *crown*, etc., translating Latin *corona civica*, denoting a garland of oak leaves and acorns given in ancient Rome to a person who saved a fellow citizen's life.

civic centre ▸ noun 1 Brit. the area in the centre of a town where municipal offices and other public buildings are situated.
2 N. Amer. a large public building or complex for meetings, sports, and entertainments.

civics ▸ plural noun [usu. treated as sing.] chiefly Brit. the study of the rights and duties of citizenship.

civil ▸ adjective 1 [attrib.] relating to ordinary citizens and their concerns, as distinct from military or ecclesiastical matters: *civil aviation.* ■ (of conflict) occurring between citizens of the same country: *civil strife.* ■ Law relating to private relations between members of a community; non-criminal: *a civil action* | *a civil court.* ■ Law relating to civil law.
2 courteous and polite: *they were comparatively civil to their daughter* | *they try to work out their differences in a civil manner.*
3 (of time) fixed by custom or law rather than being natural or astronomical: *civil twilight.*
– DERIVATIVES **civilly** adverb.
– ORIGIN late Middle English: via Old French from Latin *civilis*, from *civis* 'citizen'.

civil commotion ▸ noun English Law a riot or similar disturbance.

civil defence ▸ noun [mass noun] the organization and training of civilians to be prepared for attacks in wartime.

civil disobedience ▸ noun [mass noun] the refusal to comply with certain laws considered unjust, as a peaceful form of political protest.

civil engineer ▸ noun an engineer who designs and maintains roads, bridges, dams, and similar structures.
– DERIVATIVES **civil engineering** noun.

civilian ▸ noun a person not in the armed services or the police force.
▸ adjective relating to civilians: *civilian clothes.*
– ORIGIN late Middle English (denoting a practitioner of civil law): from Old French *civilien*, in the phrase

droit civilien 'civil law'. The current sense arose in the early 19th cent.

civilianize (also **civilianise**) ▶ verb [with obj.] make (something) non-military in character or function.
– DERIVATIVES **civilianization** noun.

civility ▶ noun (pl. **civilities**) [mass noun] formal politeness and courtesy in behaviour or speech: *I hope we can treat each other with civility and respect.* ■ (**civilities**) polite remarks used in formal conversation: *she was exchanging civilities with his mother.*
– ORIGIN late Middle English: from Old French *civilite*, from Latin *civilitas*, from *civilis* 'relating to citizens' (see CIVIL). In early use the term denoted the state of being a citizen and hence good citizenship or orderly behaviour. The sense 'politeness' arose in the mid 16th cent.

civilization (also **civilisation**) ▶ noun [mass noun] the stage of human social development and organization which is considered most advanced: *the Victorians equated the railways with progress and civilization.*
■ the process by which a society or place reaches this stage. ■ the society, culture, and way of life of a particular area: *the great books of Western civilization* | [count noun] *the early civilizations of Mesopotamia and Egypt.* ■ the comfort and convenience of modern life, regarded as available only in towns and cities: *in the UK nowhere is very far from civilization.*

civilize (also **civilise**) ▶ verb [with obj.] (usu. as adj. **civilized**) bring (a place or people) to a stage of social development considered to be more advanced: *a civilized society.* ■ (as adj. **civilized**) polite and good-mannered: *such an affront to civilized behaviour will no longer be tolerated.*
– DERIVATIVES **civilizer** noun.
– ORIGIN early 17th cent.: from French *civiliser*, from *civil* 'civil'.

civil law ▶ noun [mass noun] **1** the system of law concerned with private relations between members of a community rather than criminal, military, or religious affairs. Contrasted with CRIMINAL LAW.
2 the system of law predominant on the European continent, historically influenced by that of ancient Rome. Compare with COMMON LAW.

civil liberty ▶ noun [mass noun] the state of being subject only to laws established for the good of the community, especially with regard to freedom of action and speech. ■ (**civil liberties**) a person's rights to be subject only to laws established for the good of the community.
– DERIVATIVES **civil libertarian** noun.

Civil List ▶ noun (in the UK) a fixed annual allowance voted by Parliament to meet the official expenses incurred by the Queen in her role as head of state.

civil marriage ▶ noun a marriage solemnized as a civil contract without religious ceremony.

civil parish ▶ noun see PARISH.

civil partnership (also chiefly US **civil union**) ▶ noun (in some countries) a legally recognized union of a same-sex couple, with rights similar to those of marriage.

civil rights ▶ plural noun the rights of citizens to political and social freedom and equality.

civil servant ▶ noun a member of the civil service.

civil service ▶ noun the permanent professional branches of a state's administration, excluding military and judicial branches and elected politicians.
– ORIGIN late 18th cent.: originally applied to the part of the work of the British East India Company performed by staff who did not belong to the army or navy.

civil war ▶ noun a war between citizens of the same country.

civil wrong ▶ noun Law an infringement of a person's rights, especially a tort.

civil year ▶ noun see YEAR (sense 2).

civvy informal ▶ noun (pl. **civvies**) a civilian, as distinct from a member of the police force or armed services.
■ (**civvies**) civilian clothes, as opposed to uniform: *the Chief Constable came along in civvies.*
▶ adjective [attrib.] relating to civilians: *fliers who left the services for civvy airlines.*
– PHRASES **Civvy Street** Brit. informal civilian life: *ex-service people starting life on Civvy Street.*
– ORIGIN late 19th cent.: abbreviation.

CJ ▶ abbreviation Chief Justice.

CJD ▶ abbreviation Creutzfeldt–Jakob disease.

CL ▶ abbreviation ■ chemiluminescence. ■ Sri Lanka (international vehicle registration). [from *Ceylon*.]

Cl ▶ symbol the chemical element chlorine.

cl ▶ abbreviation centilitre: *70 cl bottles.*

clabber chiefly US ▶ noun [mass noun] milk that has naturally clotted on souring.
▶ verb curdle or cause to curdle.
– ORIGIN early 19th cent.: shortening of BONNY CLABBER.

clachan /ˈklax(ə)n/ ▶ noun (in Scotland or Northern Ireland) a small village or hamlet.
– ORIGIN late Middle English: from Scottish Gaelic and Irish *clachán*.

clack ▶ verb make a sharp sound or series of sounds as a result of a hard object striking another: [no obj.] *he heard the sound of her heels clacking across flagstones* | [with obj.] *he clacked the bones together.* ■ [no obj.] archaic chatter loudly: *he will sit clacking for hours.*
▶ noun a sharp sound or series of sounds: *the clack of her high heels.* ■ [mass noun] archaic loud chatter.
– DERIVATIVES **clacker** noun.
– ORIGIN Middle English: imitative.

Clackmannanshire /klakˈmanənʃɪə, -ʃə/ a council area and former county of central Scotland; administrative centre, Alloa.

Clactonian /klakˈtəʊnɪən/ ▶ adjective Archaeology relating to or denoting a Lower Palaeolithic culture represented by flint implements found at Clacton-on-Sea in SE England, dated to about 250,000–200,000 years ago. ■ (as noun **the Clactonian**) the Clactonian culture or period.

clad[1] archaic or literary past participle of CLOTHE.
▶ adjective **1** clothed: *they were clad in T-shirts and shorts* | [in combination] *leather-clad boys.*
2 covered with cladding: [in combination] *copper-clad boards.*

clad[2] ▶ verb (**clads**, **cladding**; past and past participle **cladded** or **clad**) [with obj.] encase (a structure) with a covering or coating.
– ORIGIN mid 16th cent. (in the sense 'clothe'): apparently from CLAD[1].

Claddagh ring /ˈkladə/ ▶ noun a ring in the form of two hands clasping a heart, traditionally given in Ireland as a token of love.
– ORIGIN from the name of a small fishing village on the edge of Galway city.

cladding ▶ noun [mass noun] a covering or coating on a structure or material: *timber cladding.*

clade /kleɪd/ ▶ noun Biology a group of organisms believed to comprise all the evolutionary descendants of a common ancestor.
– ORIGIN 1950s: from Greek *klados* 'branch'.

cladistics /kləˈdɪstɪks/ ▶ plural noun [treated as sing.] Biology a method of classification of animals and plants that aims to identify and take account of only those shared characteristics which can be deduced to have originated in the common ancestor of a group of species during evolution, not those arising by convergence.
– DERIVATIVES **cladism** /ˈkladɪz(ə)m/ noun, **cladistic** adjective.
– ORIGIN 1960s: from CLADE + -IST + -ICS.

clado- /ˈkleɪdəʊ, ˈkladəʊ/ ▶ combining form relating to a branch or branching: *cladogram.*
– ORIGIN from Greek *klados* 'branch or shoot'.

Cladocera /kləˈdɒs(ə)rə/ ▶ plural noun Zoology an order of minute branchiopod crustaceans which includes the water fleas. They typically have a transparent shell enclosing the trunk, and large antennae which are used for swimming.
– ORIGIN modern Latin (plural), from Greek *klados* 'branch or root' + *keras* 'horn' (because of the branched antennae).

cladoceran Zoology ▶ noun a minute branchiopod crustacean of the order Cladocera, which includes the water fleas.
▶ adjective relating to or denoting cladocerans.

cladode /ˈkleɪdəʊd/ ▶ noun Botany a flattened leaf-like stem.
– ORIGIN late 19th cent.: from Greek *kladōdēs* 'with many shoots', from *klados* 'shoot'.

cladogenesis /ˌkleɪdə(ʊ)ˈdʒɛnɪsɪs, ˈkladə(ʊ)-/ ▶ noun [mass noun] Biology the formation of a new group of organisms or higher taxon by evolutionary divergence from an ancestral form.
– DERIVATIVES **cladogenetic** adjective.

cladogram /ˈkleɪdə(ʊ)gram, ˈkladə(ʊ)-/ ▶ noun Biology a branching diagram showing the cladistic relationship between a number of species.

clafoutis /klaˈfuːti/ ▶ noun (pl. **same**) a type of flan made of fruit, typically cherries, baked in a sweet batter.
– ORIGIN French, from dialect *clafir* 'to stuff'.

claggy ▶ adjective Brit. dialect tending to form clots; sticky: *claggy mud.*
– ORIGIN late 16th cent.: perhaps of Scandinavian origin; compare with Danish *klag* 'sticky mud'.

claim ▶ verb **1** [reporting verb] state or assert that something is the case, typically without providing evidence or proof: [with clause] *the Prime Minister **claimed** that he was concerned about Third World debt* | [with direct speech] *'I'm entitled to be conceited,' he claimed* | [with obj.] *not every employee is eligible to claim unfair dismissal.* ■ [with obj.] assert that one has gained or achieved (something): *his supporters claimed victory in the presidential elections.*
2 [with obj.] formally request or demand; say that one owns or has earned (something): *if no one claims the items, they will become Crown property.* ■ [with obj.] make a demand for (money) under the terms of an insurance policy: [no obj.] *the premiums are reduced by fifty per cent if you don't **claim on** the policy.* ■ call for (someone's notice and thought): *a most unwelcome event **claimed his attention**.*
3 cause the loss of (someone's life).
▶ noun **1** an assertion that something is true: [with clause] *he was dogged by the **claim that** he had CIA links.*
■ (also **statement of claim**) a statement of the novel features in a patent.
2 a demand or request for something considered one's due: *the court had denied their **claims to** asylum.* ■ an application for compensation under the terms of an insurance policy. ■ a right or title to something: *they have first **claim on** the assets of the trust.* ■ a piece of land allotted to or taken by someone in order to be mined.
– PHRASES **claim to fame** a reason for being regarded as unusual or noteworthy: *the town's only claim to fame is that it is the birthplace of Elgar.*
– PHRASAL VERBS **claim something back** ask for money that one has paid to be returned in accordance with the law or one's rights: *you may be able to claim something back from the taxman.*
– DERIVATIVES **claimable** adjective.
– ORIGIN Middle English: from Old French *claime* (noun), *clamer* (verb), from Latin *clamare* 'call out'.

claimant ▶ noun a person making a claim, especially in a lawsuit or for a state benefit.

claimer ▶ noun Horse Racing **1** (N. Amer. also **claiming race**) a race in which every horse participating is for sale at a stipulated price related to the weight that the horse carries.
2 a jockey who claims a weight allowance in a race.

Clair /klɛː/, French /klɛʀ/, René (1898–1981), French film director; born *René Lucien Chomette*. His films typically contain elements of surrealism underpinned by satire; they include *Un Chapeau de paille d'Italie* (1927), *Sous les toits de Paris* (1930), and *Les Belles de nuit* (1952).

clairaudience /klɛːrˈɔːdɪəns/ ▶ noun [mass noun] the supposed faculty of perceiving, as if by hearing, what is inaudible.
– DERIVATIVES **clairaudient** adjective & noun.
– ORIGIN mid 19th cent.: from French *clair* 'clear' + AUDIENCE, on the pattern of *clairvoyance*.

clair de lune /ˌklɛːdəˈluːn/ ▶ noun [mass noun] a soft white or pale blue-grey colour. ■ a Chinese porcelain glaze of this colour.
ORIGIN late 19th cent.: French, literally 'moonlight'.

clairvoyance ▶ noun [mass noun] the supposed faculty of perceiving things or events in the future or beyond normal sensory contact.
– ORIGIN mid 19th cent.: from French, from *clair* 'clear' + *voir* 'to see'.

clairvoyant ▶ noun a person who claims to have a supernatural ability to perceive events in the future or beyond normal sensory contact.
▶ adjective having or exhibiting clairvoyance: *he didn't tell me about it and I'm not clairvoyant.*
– DERIVATIVES **clairvoyantly** adverb.
– ORIGIN late 17th cent. (in the sense 'clear-sighted, perceptive'): from French, from *clair* 'clear' + *voyant* 'seeing' (from *voir* 'to see'). The current sense dates from the mid 19th cent.

clam ▶ noun **1** a marine bivalve mollusc with shells of equal size. ● Subclass Heterodonta: several families and numerous species, including the edible North American **hardshell clam** (see QUAHOG) and **softshell clam**. See also GIANT CLAM.
■ informal any of a number of edible bivalve molluscs, e.g. a scallop.
2 US informal a dollar.

▸ verb (**clams, clamming, clammed**) [no obj.] **1** chiefly N. Amer. dig for or collect clams.
2 (**clam up**) informal abruptly stop talking.
– ORIGIN early 16th cent.: apparently from earlier *clam* 'a clamp', from Old English *clam, clamm* 'a bond or bondage', of Germanic origin; related to Dutch *klemme*, German *Klemme*, also to CLAMP[1].

C

clamant /ˈkleɪm(ə)nt, ˈklam-/ ▸ adjective urgently demanding attention: *the proper use of biotechnology has become a clamant question.*
– ORIGIN mid 17th cent.: from Latin *clamant-* 'crying out', from the verb *clamare*.

clambake ▸ noun N. Amer. a social gathering outdoors, especially for eating clams and other seafood.

clamber ▸ verb [no obj., with adverbial of direction] climb or move in an awkward and laborious way, typically using both hands and feet: *I clambered out of the trench.*
▸ noun an awkward and laborious climb or movement: *a clamber up the cliff path.*
– ORIGIN Middle English: probably from *clamb*, obsolete past tense of CLIMB.

clamdiggers ▸ plural noun close-fitting calf-length trousers for women.

clammy ▸ adjective (**clammier, clammiest**) unpleasantly damp and sticky or slimy to touch: *his skin felt cold and clammy.* ■ (of air or atmosphere) damp and unpleasant: *the clammy atmosphere of the cave.*
– DERIVATIVES **clammily** adverb, **clamminess** noun.
– ORIGIN late Middle English: from dialect *clam* 'to be sticky or adhere', of Germanic origin; related to CLAY.

clamorous ▸ adjective making a loud and confused noise: *a jostling, clamorous mob.* ■ expressing or characterized by vehement protests or demands: *the clamorous radical wing of the party.*
– DERIVATIVES **clamorously** adverb.

clamour (US **clamor**) ▸ noun [in sing.] a loud and confused noise, especially that of people shouting: *the questions rose to a clamour.* ■ a strongly expressed protest or demand from a large number of people: *the growing public* ***clamour for*** *more policemen on the beat.*
▸ verb [no obj.] (of a group of people) shout loudly and insistently: *the surging crowds* ***clamoured*** *for attention.* ■ make a vehement protest or demand: *scientists are* ***clamouring for*** *a ban on all chlorine substances.*
– ORIGIN late Middle English: via Old French from Latin *clamor*, from *clamare* 'cry out'.

clamp[1] ▸ noun **1** a brace, band, or clasp for strengthening or holding things together. ■ short for WHEEL CLAMP.
2 an electric circuit which serves to maintain the voltage limits of a signal at prescribed levels.
▸ verb **1** [with obj. and adverbial of place] fasten (something) in place with a clamp: *the sander is clamped on to the edge of a workbench.* ■ fasten (two things) firmly together: *the two frames are* ***clamped together***. ■ hold (something) tightly against another thing: *Maggie had to clamp a hand over her mouth to stop herself from laughing.* ■ [with obj.] immobilize (an unlawfully parked car) by fixing a wheel clamp to one of its wheels.
2 [with obj.] maintain the voltage limits of (an electrical signal) at prescribed values.
– PHRASAL VERBS **clamp down** suppress or prevent something in an oppressive or harsh manner: *the authorities have also* ***clamped down on*** *public demonstrations.*
– DERIVATIVES **clamper** noun.
– ORIGIN Middle English: probably of Dutch or Low German origin and related to CLAM.

clamp[2] ▸ noun Brit. **1** a heap of potatoes or other root vegetables stored under straw or earth.
2 a three-sided structure used to store silage.
– ORIGIN late 16th cent. (denoting a pile of bricks for firing): probably from Dutch *klamp* 'heap'; related to CLUMP.

clampdown ▸ noun informal a concerted or harsh attempt to suppress something: *a* ***clampdown on*** *crime.*

clamshell ▸ noun the shell of a clam, formed of two roughly equal valves with a hinge. ■ something, such as a mobile phone, with hinged parts that open and shut like a clamshell: [as modifier] *a clamshell cellular phone.*

clan ▸ noun a close-knit group of interrelated families, especially in the Scottish Highlands. ■ a large family: *the Watts clan is one of racing's oldest families.* ■ a group of people with a strong common interest: *New York's garrulous clan of artists.*
– DERIVATIVES **clanship** noun.
– ORIGIN late Middle English: from Scottish Gaelic *clann* 'offspring, family', from Old Irish *cland*, from Latin *planta* 'sprout'.

clandestine /klanˈdɛstɪn, ˈklandɛstɪn/ ▸ adjective kept secret or done secretively, especially because illicit: *she deserved better than these clandestine meetings.*
– DERIVATIVES **clandestinely** adverb, **clandestinity** noun.
– ORIGIN mid 16th cent.: from French *clandestin* or Latin *clandestinus*, from *clam* 'secretly'.

clang ▸ noun a loud, resonant metallic sound or series of sounds: *the steel door slammed shut with a clang.*
▸ verb make or cause to make a clang: [no obj.] *the bell of a fire engine clanged* | [with obj.] *the belfry still clangs its bell at 9 p.m.*
– ORIGIN late 16th cent.: imitative, influenced by Latin *clangere* 'resound'.

clanger ▸ noun Brit. informal an absurd or embarrassing blunder: *the minister had dropped a massive political clanger.*

clangour /ˈklaŋgə/ (US **clangor**) ▸ noun [in sing.] a continuous loud banging or ringing sound.
– DERIVATIVES **clangorous** adjective.
– ORIGIN late 16th cent.: from Latin *clangor*, from *clangere* 'resound'.

clank ▸ noun a loud, sharp sound or series of sounds, as is made by pieces of metal being struck together.
▸ verb make or cause to make a clank: [no obj.] *I could hear the chain clanking* | [with obj.] *he clanked his heavy ring of keys.*
– ORIGIN late Middle English (but rare before the mid 17th cent.): imitative.

clannish ▸ adjective chiefly derogatory (of a group or their activities) tending to exclude others outside the group.
– DERIVATIVES **clannishly** adverb, **clannishness** noun.

clansman (or **clanswoman**) ▸ noun (pl. **clansmen** or **clanswomen**) a member of a clan.

clap[1] ▸ verb (**claps, clapping, clapped**) [with obj.]
1 strike the palms of (one's hands) together repeatedly, typically in order to applaud someone or something: *Agnes clapped her hands in glee* | [no obj.] *the crowd was clapping and cheering.* ■ show approval of (a person or action) by clapping: *Louisa clapped his performance.* ■ (of a bird) flap (its wings) audibly.
2 slap (someone) encouragingly on the back or shoulder: *as they parted, he clapped Owen on the back.* ■ place (a hand) briefly against or over one's mouth or forehead as a gesture of dismay or regret: *he swore and clapped a hand to his forehead.*
▸ noun **1** an act of striking together the palms of the hands. ■ a friendly slap or pat on the back or shoulder.
2 an explosive sound, especially of thunder: *a clap of thunder echoed through the valley.*
– PHRASES **clap eyes on** see EYE. **clap hold of** informal grab someone or something roughly or abruptly. **clap someone in jail** (or **irons**) put someone in prison (or in chains).
– PHRASAL VERBS **clap something on** abruptly impose a restrictive or punitive measure: *most countries clapped on tariffs to protect their farmers.*
– ORIGIN Old English *clappan* 'throb, beat', of imitative origin. Sense 1 of the verb dates from late Middle English.

clap[2] ▸ noun [mass noun] (usu. **the clap**) informal a venereal disease, especially gonorrhoea.
– ORIGIN late 16th cent.: from Old French *clapoir* 'venereal bubo'.

clapboard /ˈklapbɔːd, ˈklabəd/ ▸ noun chiefly N. Amer. a long, thin, flat piece of wood with edges horizontally overlapping in series, used to cover the outer walls of buildings: [as modifier] *neat clapboard houses.* ■ informal a house with outer walls covered in clapboards.
– DERIVATIVES **clapboarded** adjective.
– ORIGIN early 16th cent. (denoting a piece of oak used for barrel staves or wainscot): partial translation of Low German *klappholt* 'barrel stave', from *klappen* 'to crack' + *holt* 'wood'.

clapped-out ▸ adjective Brit. informal worn out from age or heavy use and unable to work or operate: *a clapped-out old van.*

clapper ▸ noun the tongue or striker of a bell.
– PHRASES **like the clappers** Brit. informal very fast or very hard: *she ran off like the clappers.*

clapperboard ▸ noun a pair of hinged boards that are struck together at the beginning of filming to synchronize the starting of picture and sound machinery.

clapper bridge ▸ noun a simple bridge consisting of slabs of stone or planks laid across a series of rocks or piles of stones.

clapper rail ▸ noun a large greyish rail (bird) of American coastal marshes, which has a distinctive clattering rattle-like call. ● *Rallus longirostris*, family Rallidae.

Clapton, Eric (b.1945), English blues and rock guitarist, singer, and composer, known particularly for the song 'Layla' (1972) and for his group Cream (1966–8).

claptrap ▸ noun [mass noun] absurd or nonsensical talk or ideas: *such sentiments are just pious claptrap.*
– ORIGIN mid 18th cent. (denoting something designed to elicit applause): from CLAP[1] + TRAP[1].

claque /klak, klɑːk/ ▸ noun **1** a group of sycophantic followers: *the President was surrounded by a claque of scheming bureaucrats.*
2 a group of people hired to applaud (or heckle) a performer or public speaker.
– ORIGIN mid 19th cent.: French, from *claquer* 'to clap'. The practice of paying members of an audience for their support originated at the Paris opera.

claqueur /klaˈkəː, klɑː-/ ▸ noun a member of a claque.
– ORIGIN mid 19th cent.: French, from *claquer* 'to clap'.

clarabella /ˌklarəˈbɛlə/ ▸ noun an organ stop with the quality of a flute.
– ORIGIN mid 19th cent.: from the feminine forms of Latin *clarus* 'clear' and *bellus* 'pretty'.

Clare[1] a county of the Republic of Ireland, on the west coast in the province of Munster; county town, Ennis.

Clare[2], John (1793–1864), English poet, who wrote in celebration of the natural world. In 1837 he was certified insane and spent the rest of his life in an asylum. Notable works: *Poems Descriptive of Rural Life and Scenery* (1820) and *The Rural Muse* (1835).

clarence ▸ noun historical a closed horse-drawn carriage with four wheels, seating four inside and two outside next to the coachman.
– ORIGIN mid 19th cent.: named in honour of the Duke of *Clarence*, later William IV.

Clarenceux /ˈklar(ə)nsuː/ ▸ noun Heraldry (in the UK) the title given to the second King of Arms, with jurisdiction south of the Trent. See KING OF ARMS.
– ORIGIN Middle English: from Anglo-Norman French, named after the dukedom of *Clarence* created for the second son of Edward II, married to the heiress of *Clare* in Suffolk.

Clarendon /ˈklarənd(ə)n/, Edward Hyde, Earl of (1609–74), English statesman and historian, chief adviser to Charles II and Chancellor of Oxford University 1660–7. Notable works: *History of the Rebellion and Civil Wars in England* (published posthumously 1702–4).

Clare of Assisi, St (1194–1253), Italian saint and abbess. With St Francis she founded the order of Poor Ladies of San Damiano ('Poor Clares'), of which she was abbess. Feast day, 11 (formerly 12) August.

claret /ˈklarət/ ▸ noun [mass noun] a red wine from Bordeaux, or wine of a similar character made elsewhere. ■ a deep purplish-red colour. ■ archaic, informal blood.
– ORIGIN late Middle English (originally denoting a light red or yellowish wine, as distinct from a red or white): from Old French (*vin*) *claret* and medieval Latin *claratum* (*vinum*) 'clarified (wine)', from Latin *clarus* 'clear'.

clarification /ˌklarɪfɪˈkeɪʃ(ə)n/ ▸ noun [mass noun] the action of making a statement or situation less confused and more comprehensible: *please advise us if you require further clarification* | [count noun] *the remaining changes are small clarifications.*
– DERIVATIVES **clarificatory** adjective.

clarify /ˈklarɪfʌɪ/ ▸ verb (**clarifies, clarifying, clarified**) [with obj.] **1** make (a statement or situation) less confused and more comprehensible: *the report managed to clarify the government's position.*
2 (often as adj. **clarified**) melt (butter) in order to separate out the impurities.
– DERIVATIVES **clarifier** noun.
– ORIGIN Middle English (in the senses 'set forth clearly' and 'make pure and clean'): from Old French *clarifier*, from late Latin *clarificare*, from Latin *clarus* 'clear'.

clarinet ▸ noun a woodwind instrument with a single-reed mouthpiece, a cylindrical tube with a flared end, and holes stopped by keys. ■ an organ stop with a tone resembling that of a clarinet.

– DERIVATIVES **clarinettist** (US **clarinetist**) noun.
– ORIGIN mid 18th cent.: from French *clarinette*, diminutive of *clarine*, denoting a kind of bell; related to CLARION.

clarion /ˈklarɪən/ ▶ noun historical a shrill narrow-tubed war trumpet. ■ an organ stop with a quality resembling that of a clarion.
▶ adjective literary loud and clear: *clarion trumpeters*.
– PHRASES **clarion call** a strongly expressed demand or request for action: *he issued a clarion call to young people to join the Party*.
– ORIGIN Middle English: from medieval Latin *clario(n-)*, from Latin *clarus* 'clear'.

clarity ▶ noun [mass noun] the quality of being clear, in particular: ■ the quality of being coherent and intelligible: *for the sake of clarity, each of these strategies is dealt with separately*. ■ the quality of being easy to see or hear; sharpness of image or sound: *the clarity of the picture*. ■ the quality of being certain or definite: *it was clarity of purpose that he needed*. ■ the quality of transparency or purity: *the crystal clarity of water*.
– ORIGIN Middle English (in the sense 'glory, divine splendour'): from Latin *claritas*, from *clarus* 'clear'. The current sense dates from the early 17th cent.

Clark[1], Helen (b.1950), New Zealand Labour stateswoman, Prime Minister of New Zealand 1999–2008.

Clark[2], William (1770–1838), American explorer. With Meriwether Lewis, he commanded an expedition (1804–6) across the North American continent.

Clarke, Sir Arthur C. (1917–2008), English writer of science fiction; full name *Arthur Charles Clarke*. He co-wrote (with Stanley Kubrick) the screenplay for the film *2001: A Space Odyssey* (1968).

clarkia /ˈklɑːkɪə/ ▶ noun a North American plant with showy white, pink, or purple flowers, cultivated as a border plant in gardens. ● Genus *Clarkia*, family Onagraceae.
– ORIGIN modern Latin, named after William CLARK[1], who discovered it.

clarsach /ˈklɑːrsəx, ˈklɑːsək/ ▶ noun a small harp with wire strings, used in the folk and early music of Scotland and Ireland. Also called CELTIC HARP.
– ORIGIN late 15th cent.: from Scottish Gaelic, perhaps based on *clar* 'table, board'.

clart /klɑːt/ (also **clarts**) ▶ noun [mass noun] Scottish & N. English sticky mud; filth.
– DERIVATIVES **clarty** adjective.
– ORIGIN late 17th cent. (as a verb in the sense 'smear, plaster'): of unknown origin.

clary /ˈklɛːri/ ▶ noun [mass noun] an aromatic herbaceous plant of the mint family, some kinds of which are used as culinary and medicinal herbs. ● Genus *Salvia*, family Labiatae: several species.
– ORIGIN late Middle English: from obsolete French *clarie*, from medieval Latin *sclarea*.

clash ▶ noun **1** a violent confrontation: *there have been minor **clashes with** security forces*. ■ an incompatibility leading to disagreement: *a personality clash*. ■ Brit. a sports fixture (used chiefly in journalism): *the Euro 2000 **clash between** England and Germany*.
2 a mismatch of colours: *a clash of tweeds and a striped shirt*.
3 an inconvenient coincidence of the timing of events or activities: *it is hoped that clashes of dates will be avoided*.
4 a loud jarring sound, as of metal objects being struck together: *a clash of cymbals*.
▶ verb [no obj.] **1** meet and come into violent conflict: *protestors demanding self-rule **clashed with** police*. ■ have a forceful disagreement: *the prime minister **clashed with** other Commonwealth leaders*. ■ be incompatible or at odds: *his thriftiness **clashed with** Ross's largesse*. ■ Brit. (in reference to sports teams) play a match (used chiefly in journalism): *the two sides clashed in a goalless draw at Old Trafford in November*.
2 (of colours) appear discordant or ugly when placed close to each other: (as adj. **clashing**) *suits in clashing colours*.
3 inconveniently occur at the same time: *we play our home games when they do not **clash with** those of Liverpool or Everton*.
4 [with obj.] strike (cymbals) together, producing a loud discordant sound.
– ORIGIN early 16th cent.: imitative.

clasp ▶ verb [with obj.] **1** grasp (something) tightly with one's hand: *he clasped her arm*. ■ place (one's arms) around something so as to hold it tightly: *Kate's arms were **clasped around** her knees*. ■ hold (someone) tightly: *he clasped Joanne in his arms*.
2 archaic fasten (something) with a small brooch or similar device.
▶ noun **1** a device with interlocking parts used for fastening things together: *a gold bracelet with a turquoise clasp*. ■ a silver bar on a medal ribbon, inscribed with the name of the battle at which the wearer was present.
2 [in sing.] an embrace. ■ a grasp or handshake: *he took her hand in a firm clasp*.
– PHRASES **clasp hands** shake hands with fervour or affection. **clasp one's hands** press one's hands together with the fingers interlaced.
– ORIGIN Middle English: of unknown origin.

claspers ▶ plural noun Zoology a pair of appendages under the abdomen of a male shark or ray, or at the end of the abdomen of a male insect, used to hold the female during copulation.

clasp knife ▶ noun a knife with a blade that folds into the handle.

class ▶ noun **1** a set or category of things having some property or attribute in common and differentiated from others by kind, type, or quality: *it has good accommodation for a hotel of this class | a new class of heart drug*. ■ Biology a principal taxonomic grouping that ranks above order and below phylum or division, such as Mammalia or Insecta. ■ Brit. a division of candidates according to merit in a university examination.
2 [mass noun] a system of ordering society whereby people are divided into sets based on perceived social or economic status: *people who are socially disenfranchised by class* | [as modifier] *the class system*. ■ [count noun] a social division based on social or economic status: *the ruling class*. ■ (**the classes**) archaic the rich or educated. ■ informal impressive stylishness in appearance or behaviour: *she's got class—she looks like a princess*.
3 a group of students or pupils who are taught together. ■ an occasion when pupils meet with their teacher for instruction; a lesson: *I was late for a class*. ■ a course of instruction: *I took classes in Indian music*. ■ chiefly N. Amer. all of the college or school students of a particular year: ***the class of** 1999*.
▶ verb [with obj.] (often **be classed as**) assign or regard as belonging to a particular category: *conduct which is classed as criminal*.
▶ adjective [attrib.] informal showing stylish excellence: *he's a class player*.
– PHRASES **class A** (or **B** or **C**) **drug** an illegal narcotic drug classified as being of the most harmful and addictive (or a less harmful and addictive) kind, possession or sale of which incurs corresponding legal penalties. **class act** informal a person or thing displaying impressive and stylish excellence. **a class apart** much better than others of a similar kind: *his songs were definitely a class apart*. **in a class of its** (or **one's**) **own** unequalled, especially in excellence or performance: *British advertising is in a class of its own for inventiveness*.
– ORIGIN mid 16th cent. (in sense 3 of the noun): from Latin *classis* 'a division of the Roman people, a grade, or a class of pupils'.

class action ▶ noun Law, N. Amer. a lawsuit filed or defended by an individual acting on behalf of a group.

class consciousness ▶ noun [mass noun] awareness of one's place in a system of social class, especially (in Marxist terms) as it relates to the class struggle.
– DERIVATIVES **class-conscious** adjective.

classic ▶ adjective **1** judged over a period of time to be of the highest quality and outstanding of its kind: *a classic novel | a classic car*. ■ (of a garment or design) of a simple, elegant style not greatly subject to changes in fashion: *this classic navy blazer*.
2 very typical of its kind: *Hamlet is the classic example of a tragedy | I had all the classic symptoms of flu*.
▶ noun **1** a work of art of recognized and established value: *his books have become classics*. ■ a garment of a simple, elegant, and long-lasting style. ■ a thing which is memorable and a very good example of its kind: *he's hoping that tomorrow's game will be a classic*.
2 (**Classics**) a subject at school or university which involves the study of ancient Greek and Latin literature, philosophy, and history. ■ (**the classics**) the works of ancient Greek and Latin writers and philosophers. ■ dated a scholar of ancient Greek and Latin.
3 (**Classic**) a major sports tournament or competition, especially in golf or tennis. ■ (in the UK) each of the five main flat races of the horse-racing season.
– ORIGIN early 17th cent.: from French *classique* or Latin *classicus* 'belonging to a class or division', later 'of the highest class', from *classis* (see CLASS).

> **USAGE** Note that **classic** means 'typical, excellent as an example, timeless,' as in *John Ford directed many classic Westerns*, and **classical** means 'relating to Greek or Roman antiquity' (*the museum was built in the classical style*). Great art is considered **classic**, not **classical**, unless it is created in the forms of antiquity. **Classical music** is the exception to this rule, being formal music adhering to certain stylistic principles of the late 18th century.

C

classical ▶ adjective **1** relating to ancient Greek or Latin literature, art, or culture: *classical mythology | classical Latin*. ■ (of art or architecture) influenced by ancient Greek or Roman forms or principles.
2 representing an exemplary standard within a traditional and long-established form or style: *classical ballet*. ■ relating to the first significant period of an area of study: *classical mechanics*.
3 Physics relating to or based upon concepts and theories which preceded the theories of relativity and quantum mechanics; Newtonian: *classical physics*.
– DERIVATIVES **classicalism** noun, **classicality** noun, **classically** adverb [as submodifier] *the classically beautiful lines of her face*.
– ORIGIN late 16th cent. (in the sense 'outstanding of its kind'): from Latin *classicus* 'belonging to a class' (see CLASSIC) + -AL.

classical conditioning ▶ noun [mass noun] Psychology a learning process that occurs when two stimuli are repeatedly paired: a response which is at first elicited by the second stimulus is eventually elicited by the first stimulus alone.

classical music ▶ noun [mass noun] serious music following long-established principles rather than a folk, jazz, or popular tradition. ■ (more specifically) music written in the European tradition during a period lasting approximately from 1750 to 1830, when forms such as the symphony, concerto, and sonata were standardized.

classicism ▶ noun [mass noun] the following of ancient Greek or Roman principles and style in art and literature, generally associated with harmony, restraint, and adherence to recognized standards of form and craftsmanship, especially from the Renaissance to the 18th century. Often contrasted with ROMANTICISM. ■ the following of traditional and long-established theories or styles.

classicist ▶ noun **1** a person who studies Classics (ancient Greek and Latin).
2 a follower of classicism in the arts.

classicize (also **classicise**) ▶ verb [no obj.] (usu. as adj. **classicizing**) imitate a classical style: *the classicizing strains in Guercino's art*.

Classico /ˈklasɪkəʊ/ ▶ adjective [postpositive] (of Italian wine) produced in the region from which the type takes its name, and thus of a higher standard than a regional wine without the designation: *Chianti Classico*.
– ORIGIN Italian.

classification ▶ noun [mass noun] the action or process of classifying something: *the classification of disease according to symptoms*. ■ [count noun] a category into which something is put.

classified ▶ adjective **1** arranged in classes or categories: *a classified catalogue of books*. ■ [attrib.] (of newspaper or magazine advertisements) organized in categories according to what is being advertised. ■ Brit. (of a road) assigned to a category according to its importance within the overall system of road numbering.
2 (of information or documents) designated as officially secret and accessible only to authorized people: *classified information on nuclear experiments*.
▶ noun (**classifieds**) small advertisements placed in a newspaper and organized in categories.

classifier ▶ noun a person or thing that classifies something. ■ Linguistics an affix or word that indicates the semantic class to which a word belongs: *the English negative classifier 'un-'*.

classify ▶ verb (**classifies**, **classifying**, **classified**) [with obj.] **1** arrange (a group of people or things) in classes or categories according to shared qualities or characteristics: *mountain peaks are classified according to their shape*. ■ assign to a particular class or category: *elements are usually **classified as** metals or non-metals*.
2 designate (documents or information) as officially secret: *government officials classified 6.3 million documents in 1992*.

– DERIVATIVES **classifiable** adjective, **classificatory** adjective.
– ORIGIN late 18th cent.: back-formation from CLASSIFICATION, from French, from *classe* 'class', from Latin *classis* 'division'.

classifying ▶ adjective Grammar (of an adjective) describing the class that a head noun belongs to and characterized by not having a comparative or superlative (for example *American, mortal*). Contrasted with GRADABLE, QUALITATIVE.

class interval ▶ noun Statistics the size of each class into which a range of a variable is divided, as represented by the divisions of a histogram or bar chart.

classism ▶ noun [mass noun] prejudice against people belonging to a particular social class.
– DERIVATIVES **classist** adjective & noun.

classless ▶ adjective (of a society) not divided into social classes. ■ not showing obvious signs of belonging to a particular social class: *his voice was classless.*
– DERIVATIVES **classlessness** noun.

class list ▶ noun a list of the candidates who have taken an examination, showing the class or mark achieved by each.

classmate ▶ noun a fellow member of a class at school, college, or university.

classroom ▶ noun a room in which a class of pupils or students is taught.

class struggle (also **class war**) ▶ noun (in Marxist ideology) the conflict of interests between the workers and the ruling class in a capitalist society, regarded as inevitably violent.

classwork ▶ noun [mass noun] schoolwork that is done in class.

classy ▶ adjective (**classier**, **classiest**) informal stylish and sophisticated: *the hotel is classy but relaxed.*
– DERIVATIVES **classily** adverb, **classiness** noun.

clast /klast/ ▶ noun Geology a constituent fragment of a clastic rock.
– ORIGIN mid 20th cent.: back-formation from CLASTIC.

clastic ▶ adjective Geology denoting rocks composed of broken pieces of older rocks.
– ORIGIN late 19th cent.: from French *clastique*, from Greek *klastos* 'broken in pieces'.

clathrate /ˈklaθreɪt/ ▶ noun Chemistry a compound in which molecules of one component are physically trapped within the crystal structure of another.
– ORIGIN 1940s: from Latin *clathratus*, from *clathri* 'lattice bars', from Greek *klēthra*.

clatter ▶ noun [in sing.] a continuous rattling sound as of hard objects falling or striking each other: *the horse spun round with a clatter of hooves.*
▶ verb make or cause to make a continuous rattling sound: [no obj.] *her coffee cup clattered in the saucer* | [with obj.] *she clattered cups and saucers on to a tray.* ■ [no obj., with adverbial of direction] fall or move with a clatter: *they heard Sybil's shoes clattering up the stone steps* | *the knife clattered to the floor.* ■ [with obj.] Brit. informal (of a soccer player) foul (an opponent): *Bennett clattered Coleman ten yards out from goal* | [no obj.] *Thatcher* ***clattered into*** *Beckham.*
– ORIGIN Old English (as a verb), of imitative origin.

Claude Lorrain /ˌkləʊd ləˈreɪn/ (also **Lorraine**) (1600–82), French painter; born *Claude Gellée*. His classical landscapes are notable for their rendering of light and atmosphere. Notable works: *Ascanius and the Stag* (1682).

claudication /ˌklɔːdɪˈkeɪʃ(ə)n/ ▶ noun [mass noun] Medicine limping. ■ (also **intermittent claudication**) a condition in which cramping pain in the leg is induced by exercise, typically caused by obstruction of the arteries.
– ORIGIN late Middle English: from Latin *claudicatio(n-)*, from the verb *claudicare* 'to limp', from *claudus* 'lame'.

Claudius /ˈklɔːdɪəs/ (10 BC–AD 54), Roman emperor 41–54; full name *Tiberius Claudius Drusus Nero Germanicus*. His reign was noted for its restoration of order after Caligula's decadence and for its expansion of the Empire, in particular the invasion of Britain in AD 43. His fourth wife, Agrippina, is said to have poisoned him.

clause ▶ noun **1** a unit of grammatical organization next below the sentence in rank and in traditional grammar said to consist of a subject and predicate. See also MAIN CLAUSE, SUBORDINATE CLAUSE.
2 a particular and separate article, stipulation, or proviso in a treaty, bill, or contract.
– DERIVATIVES **clausal** adjective.
– ORIGIN Middle English: via Old French *clause*, based on Latin *claus-* 'shut, closed', from the verb *claudere*.

Clausewitz /ˈklaʊzəvɪts/, Karl von (1780–1831), Prussian general and military theorist. His study *On War* (1833) had a marked influence on strategic studies in the 19th and 20th centuries.

Clausius /ˈklaʊzɪəs/, Rudolf (1822–88), German physicist, one of the founders of modern thermodynamics. He was the first, in 1850, to formulate the second law of thermodynamics, developing the concept of a system's available thermal energy and coining the term *entropy* for it.

claustral /ˈklɔːstr(ə)l/ ▶ adjective **1** relating to a cloister or religious house: *claustral buildings.*
2 literary enveloping; confining: *this claustral heat.*
– ORIGIN late Middle English: from late Latin *claustralis*, from Latin *claustrum* 'lock, enclosed place' (see CLOISTER).

claustration /klɔːˈstreɪʃ(ə)n/ ▶ noun [mass noun] literary confinement, as if in a cloister.
– ORIGIN mid 19th cent.: from Latin *claustrum* 'lock, bolt' + -ATION.

claustrophobia /ˌklɔːstrəˈfəʊbɪə/ ▶ noun [mass noun] extreme or irrational fear of confined places.
– DERIVATIVES **claustrophobe** noun.
– ORIGIN late 19th cent.: modern Latin, from Latin *claustrum* 'lock, bolt' + -PHOBIA.

claustrophobic ▶ adjective (of a person) suffering from claustrophobia: *crowds always made him feel claustrophobic.* ■ (of a place or situation) inducing claustrophobia: *the claustrophobic interior of the cruiser.*
▶ noun a person who suffers from claustrophobia.
– DERIVATIVES **claustrophobically** adverb.

clavate /ˈkleɪveɪt/ ▶ adjective Botany & Zoology club-shaped; thicker at the apex than the base.
– ORIGIN mid 17th cent.: from modern Latin *clavatus*, from Latin *clava* 'club'.

clave archaic past of CLEAVE².

claves /kleɪvz, klɑːvz/ ▶ plural noun a pair of hardwood sticks used to make a hollow sound when struck together. ■ (**clave**) [mass noun] a syncopated rhythm typical of some Latin American music.
– ORIGIN 1920s: from Latin American Spanish, from Spanish *clave* 'keystone', from Latin *clavis* 'key'.

clavichord /ˈklavɪkɔːd/ ▶ noun a small rectangular keyboard instrument with a soft tone, used especially in private homes from the early 15th to early 19th centuries.
– ORIGIN late Middle English: from medieval Latin *clavichordium*, from Latin *clavis* 'key' + *chorda* 'string'.

clavicle /ˈklavɪk(ə)l/ ▶ noun technical term for COLLARBONE.
– DERIVATIVES **clavicular** /kləˈvɪkjʊlə/ adjective.
– ORIGIN early 17th cent.: from Latin *clavicula* 'small key', diminutive of *clavis* (because of its shape).

clavier /ˈklavɪə, kləˈvɪə/ ▶ noun Music a keyboard instrument.
– ORIGIN early 18th cent.: from German *Klavier*, from French *clavier*, from medieval Latin *claviarius* 'key-bearer', from Latin *clavis* 'key'.

claviform /ˈklavɪfɔːm/ ▶ adjective technical another term for CLAVATE.
– ORIGIN early 19th cent.: from Latin *clava* 'club' + -IFORM.

claw ▶ noun a curved pointed horny nail on each digit of the foot in birds, lizards, and some mammals. ■ either of a pair of small hooked appendages on an insect's foot. ■ the pincer of a crab, scorpion, or other arthropod. ■ a mechanical device resembling a claw, used for gripping or lifting.
▶ verb **1** [no obj.] scratch or tear something with the claws or the fingernails: *the kitten was* ***clawing at*** *Lowell's trouser leg* | [with obj.] *her hands clawed his shoulders.* ■ clutch at something with the hands: *his fingers* ***clawed at the air.*** ■ [with obj.] Scottish scratch (a part of one's body) gently so as to relieve itching.
2 [no obj.] Nautical (of a sailing ship) beat to windward: *the ability to* ***claw off*** *a lee shore.*
– PHRASES **get one's claws into** informal enter into a possessive relationship with: *she's already got her claws into the handyman.*
– PHRASAL VERBS **claw something back 1** Brit. regain a lost advantage or position laboriously and gradually: *a hostile majority were committed to clawing back power from the president.* **2** (of a government) recover money paid out in the form of an allowance or benefit, typically by taxation.
– DERIVATIVES **clawed** adjective, **clawless** adjective.
– ORIGIN Old English *clawu* (noun), *clawian* (verb), of West Germanic origin; related to Dutch *klauw* and German *Klaue*.

clawback ▶ noun Brit. an act of retrieving money already paid out, typically by taxation.

clawed frog ▶ noun a frog with a flattened body and claws on the hind toes. ● *Xenopus* and other genera, family Pipidae: several species. See also XENOPUS.

claw foot ▶ noun (pl. **claw feet**) **1** a foot on a piece of furniture, shaped to resemble a claw.
2 Medicine an excessively arched foot with an unnaturally high instep. ■ [mass noun] a disease causing such a distortion of the foot. Also called PES CAVUS.

claw hammer ▶ noun a hammer with one side of the head split and curved, used for extracting nails.

Clay, Cassius, see MUHAMMAD ALI².

clay ▶ noun **1** [mass noun] a stiff, sticky fine-grained earth that can be moulded when wet, and is dried and baked to make bricks, pottery, and ceramics. ■ technical sediment with particles smaller than silt, typically less than 0.002 mm. ■ a hardened clay surface for a tennis court: [as modifier] *a clay court.* ■ literary the substance of the human body: *this lifeless clay.*
2 a European moth with yellowish-brown wings. ● Several species in the family Noctuidae.
– DERIVATIVES **clayey** adjective, **clayish** adjective, **clay-like** adjective.
– ORIGIN Old English *clǣg*, of West Germanic origin; related to Dutch *klei*, also to CLEAVE² and CLIMB.

claymation ▶ noun [mass noun] (trademark in the US) a method of film animation using adjustable clay figures and stop-motion photography.
– ORIGIN 1980s: blend of CLAY and ANIMATION.

clay mineral ▶ noun any of a group of minerals which occur as colloidal crystals in clay. They are all hydrated aluminosilicates having layered crystal structures.

claymore ▶ noun **1** a broadsword formerly used by Scottish Highlanders, typically double-edged.
2 a type of anti-personnel mine.
– ORIGIN early 18th cent.: from Scottish Gaelic *claidheamh* 'sword' + *mór* 'great'.

claypan ▶ noun Austral. a shallow depression or hollow in the ground with an impermeable clay base which holds water after rain.

clay pigeon ▶ noun a saucer-shaped piece of baked clay or other material thrown up in the air from a trap as a target for shooting: [as modifier] *clay pigeon shooting.*

clay pipe ▶ noun a tobacco pipe made of hardened clay.

-cle ▶ suffix forming nouns such as *article, particle*, which were originally diminutives.
– ORIGIN via French from Latin *-culus, -cula, -culum.*

clean ▶ adjective **1** free from dirt, marks, or stains: *the room was spotlessly clean* | *keep the wound clean.* ■ having been washed since last worn or used: *a clean blouse.* ■ [attrib.] (of paper) not yet marked by writing or drawing: *he copied the advert on to a clean sheet of paper.* ■ (of a person) attentive to personal hygiene: *by nature he was clean and neat.* ■ free from pollutants or unpleasant substances: *we will create a cleaner, safer environment.* ■ free from or producing relatively little radioactive contamination.
2 morally uncontaminated; pure; innocent: *clean living.* ■ not sexually offensive or obscene: *it's all* ***good clean fun.*** ■ showing or having no record of offences or crimes: *a clean driving licence is essential for the job.* ■ played or done according to the rules: *we are not completely sure that the elections will be clean and fair.* ■ [predic.] informal not possessing or containing anything illegal, especially drugs or stolen goods: *I searched him and his luggage, and he was clean.* ■ [predic.] informal (of a person) not taking or having taken drugs or alcohol. ■ free from ceremonial defilement, according to Mosaic Law or other religious codes.
3 free from irregularities; having a smooth edge or surface: *a clean fracture of the leg.* ■ having a simple, well-defined, and pleasing shape: *the clean lines and pared-down planes of modernism.* ■ (of an action) smoothly and skilfully done: *he took a clean catch.*
4 (of a taste, sound, or smell) giving a clear and distinctive impression to the senses; sharp and fresh: *clean, fresh, natural flavours.*
▶ adverb **1** so as to be free from dirt, marks, or unwanted matter: *the room had been washed clean.*
2 informal used to emphasize the completeness of a reported action, condition, or experience: *he was knocked clean off his feet* | *I clean forgot her birthday.*

▸ **verb** [with obj.] make clean; remove dirt, marks, or stains from: *clean your teeth properly after meals* | *I cleaned up my room* | (as noun **cleaning**) *Anne will help with the cleaning.* ■ remove the innards of (fish or poultry) prior to cooking.
▸ **noun** [in sing.] an act of cleaning something: *he gave the room a clean.*
– PHRASES **(as) clean as a whistle** see WHISTLE. **clean and jerk** a weightlifting exercise in which a weight is raised above the head following an initial lift to shoulder level. **clean bill of health** see BILL OF HEALTH. **clean someone's clock** N. Amer. informal give someone a beating. ■ defeat or surpass someone decisively. **clean house** N. Amer. do housework. ■ eliminate corruption or inefficiency. **clean one's plate** eat up all the food put on one's plate. **a clean sheet** (or **slate**) an absence of existing restraints or commitments: *no government starts with a clean sheet.* ■ **(keep a clean sheet)** (in a football match) prevent the opposing side from scoring. **clean up one's act** informal begin to behave in a better way, especially by giving up alcohol, drugs, or illegal activities. **come clean** informal be completely honest; keep nothing hidden: *the Chancellor must come clean about his plans for increasing taxation.* **have clean hands** be uninvolved and blameless with regard to an immoral act: *no one involved in the conflict has clean hands.* **keep one's hands clean** not involve oneself in an immoral act. **keep one's nose clean** see NOSE. **make a clean breast of it** confess fully one's mistakes or wrongdoings. **make a clean sweep 1** remove all unwanted people or things ready to start afresh. **2** win all of a group of similar or related sporting competitions, events, or matches.
– PHRASAL VERBS **clean someone out** informal use up or take all someone's money: *they were cleaned out by the Englishman at the baccarat table.* **clean something out** thoroughly clean the inside of something: *my mom says I have to go and clean out the hamster's cage.* **clean up** informal make a substantial gain or profit. ■ win all the prizes available in a sporting competition. **clean something up** restore order or morality to: *the police chief was given the job of cleaning up a notorious district.*
– DERIVATIVES **cleanable** adjective, **cleanish** adjective, **cleanness** noun.
– ORIGIN Old English *clǣne*, of West Germanic origin; related to Dutch and German *klein* 'small'.

clean-cut ▸ **adjective** sharply outlined: *the normally clean-cut edge between sea and land has become blurred.* ■ (of a person, especially a man) appearing neat and respectable: *the part called for a clean-cut, conventional actor.*

cleaner ▸ **noun** a person or thing that cleans something, in particular: ■ a person employed to clean the interior of a building. ■ **(the cleaners)** a shop where clothes and fabrics are dry-cleaned: *my suit's at the cleaners.* ■ a device for cleaning, such as a vacuum cleaner. ■ a chemical substance used for cleaning: *an oven cleaner.*
– PHRASES **take someone to the cleaners** informal take all someone's money or possessions in a dishonest or unfair way. ■ inflict a crushing defeat on someone: *his team were taken to the cleaners by the Australians in the first Test.*

cleaner fish ▸ **noun** a small fish, especially a striped wrasse, that is permitted to remove parasites from the skin, gills, and mouth of larger fishes, to their mutual benefit. ● Genus *Labroides*, family Labridae: several species.

clean-limbed ▸ **adjective** (of a person) slim and well formed.

clean-living ▸ **adjective** not indulging in anything unhealthy or immoral.

cleanly ▸ **adverb** /ˈkliːnli/ **1** without difficulty or impediment; smoothly and efficiently: *he vaulted cleanly through the open window.*
2 in a way that produces no dirt, noxious gases, or other pollutants: *the engine burns very cleanly.*
▸ **adjective** /ˈklɛnli/ **(cleanlier, cleanliest)** archaic habitually clean and careful to avoid dirt.
– DERIVATIVES **cleanliness** noun.
– ORIGIN Old English *clǣnlīce* (adverb), *clǣnlīc* (adjective): see CLEAN, -LY[1], -LY[2].

clean room ▸ **noun** an environment free from dust and other contaminants, used chiefly for the manufacture of electronic components.

cleanse ▸ **verb** [with obj.] make (something, especially the skin) thoroughly clean: *this preparation will cleanse and tighten the skin* | (as adj. **cleansing**) *a cleansing cream.* ■ rid of something unpleasant or defiling: *the mission to **cleanse** America **of** subversives.* ■ free (someone) from sin or guilt. ■ archaic (in biblical translations) cure (a leper).
– ORIGIN Old English *clǣnsian* (verb), from *clǣne* (see CLEAN).

cleanser ▸ **noun** a substance that cleanses something, especially a cosmetic product for cleansing the skin.

clean-shaven ▸ **adjective** (of a man) without a beard or moustache.

cleansing department ▸ **noun** Brit. a department of local government that collects refuse or rubbish.

cleanskin ▸ **noun** another term for CLEARSKIN.

clean-up ▸ **noun 1** an act of cleaning a place: *an environmental clean-up.* ■ an act of putting an end to immorality or crime.
2 [usu. as modifier] Baseball the fourth position in a team's batting order, usually reserved for a strong batter whose hits are likely to enable any runner who is on base to score.

clear ▸ **adjective 1** easy to perceive, understand, or interpret: *clear and precise directions* | *her handwriting was clear* | *am I **making myself clear**?* ■ leaving no doubt; obvious or unambiguous: *it was **clear that** they were in a trap* | *a clear case of poisoning.* ■ having or feeling no doubt or confusion: *every pupil must be clear about what is expected.*
2 (of a substance) transparent; unclouded: *the clear glass of the French windows* | *a stream of clear water.* ■ free of cloud, mist, or rain: *the day was fine and clear.* ■ (of a person's skin) free from blemishes. ■ (of a colour) pure and intense: *clear blue delphiniums.* ■ archaic (of a fire) burning with little smoke: *a bright, clear flame.*
3 free of any obstructions or unwanted objects: *with a clear road ahead he shifted into high gear* | *I had a clear view in both directions.* ■ (of a period of time) free of any appointments or commitments: *the following Saturday, Mattie had a clear day.* ■ [predic.] (of a person) free of something undesirable or unpleasant: *after 18 months of treatment he was **clear of** TB.* ■ (of a person's mind) free of anything that impairs logical thought: *in the morning, with a clear head, she would tackle all her problems.* ■ (of a person's conscience) free of guilt.
4 (clear of) not touching; away from: *the lorry was wedged in the ditch, one wheel clear of the ground.*
5 [attrib.] complete; full: *you must give seven clear days' notice of the meeting.* ■ (of a sum of money) net: *a clear profit of £1,100.*
6 Phonetics denoting a palatalized form of the sound of the letter *l* (as in *leaf* in south-eastern English speech). Often contrasted with DARK.
▸ **adverb 1** so as to be out of the way of or away from: *he leapt **clear of** the car* | *stand clear, I'll start the plane up.* ■ so as not to be obstructed or cluttered: *the floor had been swept **clear of** litter.*
2 completely: *he had time to get clear away.* ■ **(clear to)** chiefly N. Amer. all the way to: *you could see clear to the bottom of the lagoon.*
▸ **verb 1** make or become clear, in particular: ■ [with obj.] remove an obstruction or unwanted item or items from: *the drive had been **cleared of** snow* | *Carolyn cleared the table and washed up.* ■ [with obj.] cause people to leave (a building or place): *the wardens shouted a warning and cleared the streets.* ■ [no obj.] gradually go away or disappear: *the fever clears in two to four weeks* | *the mist had **cleared away**.* ■ [no obj.] become free of cloud or rain: *we'll go out if the weather clears.* ■ [no obj.] (of a person's face or expression) assume a happier aspect following confusion or distress: *for a moment, Sam was confused; then his expression cleared.*
2 [with obj.] remove (an obstruction or unwanted item) from somewhere: *Karen cleared the dirty plates* | *park staff **cleared away** dead trees.* ■ (in soccer and other sports) send (the ball) away from the area near one's goal. ■ discharge (a debt).
3 [with obj.] get past or over (something) safely or without touching it: *the plane rose high enough to clear the trees* | *she cleared 1.50 metres in the high jump.*
4 [with obj.] officially show or declare (someone) to be innocent: *his sport's ruling body had **cleared** him **of** cheating.*
5 [with obj.] give official approval or authorization to: *I cleared him to return to his squadron.* ■ satisfy the necessary requirements to pass through (customs): *I can help her to clear customs quickly.* ■ (with reference to a cheque) pass through a clearing house so that the money goes into the payee's account: [no obj.] *there were more than sufficient funds in the account for both cheques to clear* | [with obj.] *the cheque could not be cleared until Monday.*
6 [with obj.] earn or gain (an amount of money) as a net profit: *I would hope to clear £50,000 profit from each match.*
– PHRASES **clear the air** make the air less humid. ■ defuse an angry or tense situation by frank discussion: *it's time a few things were said to clear the air.* **(as) clear as a bell** see BELL[1]. **(as) clear as day** very easy to see or understand. **(as) clear as mud** informal not at all easy to understand. **clear the decks** prepare for an event or course of action by dealing with anything that might hinder progress. **clear one's lines** Rugby & Soccer make a kick sending the ball well upfield from near one's own goal line. **clear the name of** show to be innocent: *the spokesman released a statement attempting to clear his client's name.* **clear the table** remove dishes and cutlery from a table after a meal: *afterwards, he cleared the table and washed up.* **clear one's throat** cough slightly so as to speak more clearly, attract attention, or to express hesitancy before saying something awkward. **clear the way** remove an obstacle or hindrance to allow progress: *the ruling could be enough to clear the way for impeachment proceedings* | [in imperative] *Stand back, there! Clear the way!* **in clear** not in code. **in the clear 1** no longer in danger or under suspicion: *the information put her in the clear.* **2** with nothing to hinder one in achieving something. **out of a clear sky** as a complete surprise: *his moods blew up suddenly out of a clear sky.*
– PHRASAL VERBS **clear off** (or **out**) [usu. in imperative] informal go away: *'Clear off!' he yelled.* **clear up 1** (of an illness or other medical condition) become cured: *all my health problems cleared up.* **2** (of the weather) become brighter. ■ (of rain) stop. **clear something up 1** (also **clear up**) tidy something up by removing rubbish or other unwanted items: *Thomas decided to clear up his cottage* | *he asked the youths to clear up their litter* | *I keep meaning to come down here and clear up.* **2** solve or explain something: *he wanted to clear up some misconceptions.* **3** cure an illness or other medical condition: *folk customs prescribed sage tea to clear up measles.*
– DERIVATIVES **clearable** adjective, **clearness** noun.
– ORIGIN Middle English: from Old French *cler*, from Latin *clarus*.

clearance ▸ **noun** [mass noun] **1** the action or process of clearing or of being dispersed: *cleaning of the machine should include clearance of blockages.* ■ the removal of buildings, people, or trees from land so as to free it for alternative uses: *slum clearance accelerated during the 1960s* | [count noun] *forest clearances.* ■ (also **house clearance**) the removal of contents from a house. ■ [count noun] (in soccer and other sports) a kick or hit that sends the ball away from one's goal. ■ [count noun] Snooker the potting of all the balls remaining on the table in a single break.
2 official authorization for something to proceed or take place: *the aircraft hadn't got diplomatic clearance to land in Mexico.* ■ (also **security clearance**) official permission for someone to have access to classified information: *these people don't have clearance.* ■ permission for an aircraft to take off or land at an airport: *he took off without air traffic clearance.* ■ the process of clearing cheques through a clearing house.
3 clear space allowed for a thing to move past or under another: *always give cyclists plenty of clearance.*

clearance sale ▸ **noun** a sale of goods at reduced prices to get rid of superfluous stock or because the shop is closing down.

clear-cut ▸ **adjective 1** sharply defined; easy to perceive or understand: *we now had a clear-cut objective.*
2 (of an area) from which every tree has been cut down and removed.
▸ **verb** (also **clear-fell**) [with obj.] cut down and remove every tree from (an area).

clearer ▸ **noun 1** Brit. a clearing bank.
2 a person or thing that clears away obstructions.

clear-eyed ▸ **adjective** having unclouded, bright eyes: *a handsome, clear-eyed young man.* ■ having a shrewd understanding and no illusions: *he was clear-eyed about the film industry.*

clear-headed ▸ **adjective** alert and thinking logically and coherently.
– DERIVATIVES **clear-headedness** noun.

clearing[1] ▸ **noun** an open space in a forest, especially one cleared for cultivation.

clearing[2] ▸ **noun** [mass noun] Brit. a system used by universities to fill the remaining available undergraduate places before the start of the academic year.

clearing bank ▸ **noun** Brit. a bank which is a member of a clearing house.

C

C

clearing house ▸ noun a bankers' establishment where cheques and bills from member banks are exchanged, so that only the balances need be paid in cash. ■ an agency or organization which collects and distributes something, especially information.

clearly ▸ adverb in a clear manner; with clarity: *her ability to write clearly* | [as submodifier] *on white paper, the seeds are clearly visible.* ■ [sentence adverb] without doubt; obviously: *clearly, things have changed in the last six weeks.*

clear-out ▸ noun chiefly Brit. a removal and disposal of unwanted items or material.

clear-sighted ▸ adjective thinking clearly and sensibly: *a clear-sighted sense of what is appropriate.*
– DERIVATIVES **clear-sightedness** noun.

clearskin (also **cleanskin**) ▸ noun Austral./NZ **1** an unbranded animal.
2 informal a person without a police record.

clearstory ▸ noun (pl. **clearstories**) US spelling of CLERESTORY.

clear-up ▸ noun **1** a removal and tidying away of rubbish or obstructions.
2 [mass noun] the solving of crimes by the police: [as modifier] *Welsh police had one of the most successful clear-up rates.*

clearway ▸ noun Brit. a main road other than a motorway on which vehicles are not normally permitted to stop.

clearwing (also **clearwing moth**) ▸ noun a day-flying moth which has narrow mainly transparent wings and mimics a wasp or bee in appearance.
● Family Sesiidae: several genera and many species, including the hornet moth.

cleat /kliːt/ ▸ noun **1** a T-shaped piece of metal or wood on a boat or ship, to which ropes are attached.
2 each of a number of projections on the sole of a shoe, designed to prevent the wearer losing their footing. ■ (**cleats**) N. Amer. athletic shoes with cleats on the soles. ■ a projecting wedge on a spar or other part of a ship, to prevent slipping. ■ a small wedge, especially one on a plough or scythe.
– DERIVATIVES **cleated** adjective.
– ORIGIN Middle English (in the sense 'wedge'): of West Germanic origin; related to Dutch *kloot* 'ball, sphere' and German *Kloss* 'clod, dumpling', also to CLOT and CLOUT.

cleavage ▸ noun **1** a sharp division; a split: *the old cleavage between the forces of the right and left.* ■ [mass noun] Biology cell division, especially of a fertilized egg cell. ■ [mass noun] the splitting of rocks or crystals in a preferred plane or direction.
2 the hollow between a woman's breasts when supported, especially as exposed by a low-cut garment.

cleave¹ ▸ verb (past **clove** or **cleft** or **cleaved**; past participle **cloven** or **cleft** or **cleaved**) [with obj.] split or sever (something), especially along a natural line or grain: *the large chopper his father used to cleave wood for the fire.* ■ split (a molecule) by breaking a particular chemical bond. ■ [no obj.] Biology (of a cell) divide. ■ make a way through (something) forcefully, as if by splitting it apart: *they watched a coot cleave the smooth water* | [no obj.] *an unstoppable warrior **clove through** their ranks.*
– DERIVATIVES **cleavable** adjective.
– ORIGIN Old English *clēofan*, of Germanic origin; related to Dutch *klieven* and German *klieben*.

cleave² ▸ verb [no obj.] (**cleave to**) literary stick fast to: *Rose's mouth was dry, her tongue cleaving to the roof of her mouth.* ■ adhere strongly to (a particular pursuit or belief): *part of why we cleave to sports is that excellence is so measurable.* ■ become very strongly involved with or emotionally attached to (someone): *it was his choice to cleave to the Brownings.*
– ORIGIN Old English *cleofian, clifian, clīfan*, of West Germanic origin; related to Dutch *kleven* and German *kleben*, also to CLAY and CLIMB.

cleaver ▸ noun a tool with a heavy, broad blade, used by butchers for chopping meat.

cleavers ▸ plural noun [treated as sing. or pl.] another term for GOOSEGRASS.
– ORIGIN Old English *clīfe*, related to CLEAVE².

Cleese /kliːz/, John (Marwood) (b.1939), English comic actor and writer, famous for *Monty Python's Flying Circus* (1969–74) and the situation comedy *Fawlty Towers* (1975, 1979).

clef ▸ noun Music any of several symbols placed at the left hand end of a stave, indicating the pitch of the notes written on it.
– ORIGIN late 16th cent.: from French, from Latin *clavis* 'key'.

cleft¹ past participle of CLEAVE¹. ▸ adjective split, divided, or partially divided into two: *a cleft chin.*
– PHRASES **be** (or **be caught**) **in a cleft stick** be in a situation in which any action one takes will have adverse consequences.

cleft² ▸ noun **1** a fissure or split, especially in rock or the ground. ■ a vertical indentation in the middle of a person's forehead or chin. ■ a deep division between two parts of the body.
2 (also **cleft sentence**) Grammar a sentence in which an element is emphasized by being put in a separate clause, with the use of an empty introductory word such as *it* or *that*, e.g. *it's money we want*; *it was today that I saw him*; *that was the King you were talking to.*
– ORIGIN Middle English *clift*: of Germanic origin; related to Dutch *kluft* and German *Kluft*, also to CLEAVE¹. The form of the word was altered in the 16th cent. by association with CLEFT¹.

cleft lip ▸ noun a congenital split in the upper lip on one or both sides of the centre, often associated with a cleft palate.

> **USAGE** Cleft lip is the standard accepted term and should be used instead of **harelip**, which can cause offence.

cleft palate ▸ noun a congenital split in the roof of the mouth.

cleg /klɛg/ ▸ noun Brit. another term for HORSEFLY.
– ORIGIN late Middle English: from Old Norse *kleggi*.

Cleisthenes /ˈklʌɪsθəniːz/ (*c.*570 BC–*c.*508 BC), Athenian statesman. His reforms consolidated the Athenian democratic process begun by Solon and influenced the policies of Pericles.

cleistogamy /klʌɪˈstɒgəmi/ ▸ noun [mass noun] Botany self-fertilization that occurs within a permanently closed flower.
– DERIVATIVES **cleistogamous** adjective.
– ORIGIN late 19th cent.: from Greek *kleistos* 'closed' + *-gamy* (from *gamos* 'marriage').

clematis /ˈklɛmətɪs, kləˈmeɪtɪs/ ▸ noun a climbing plant of the buttercup family which bears white, pink, or purple flowers and feathery seeds. Several kinds are cultivated as ornamentals. ● Genus *Clematis*, family Ranunculaceae.
– ORIGIN Latin (also denoting the periwinkle), from Greek *klēmatis*, from *klēma* 'vine branch'.

Clemenceau /ˈklɛmənsəʊ/, French /klɛmɑ̃so/, Georges (Eugène Benjamin) (1841–1929), French statesman, Prime Minister 1906–9 and 1917–20. At the Versailles peace talks he pushed hard for a punitive settlement with Germany.

clemency ▸ noun [mass noun] mercy; lenience: *an appeal for clemency.*
– ORIGIN late Middle English: from Latin *clementia*, from *clemens, clement-* 'clement'.

Clemens /ˈklɛmənz/, Samuel Langhorne, see TWAIN.

clement ▸ adjective **1** (of weather) mild.
2 (of a person or their actions) merciful.
– ORIGIN late Middle English (in sense 2): from Latin *clemens, clement-*.

Clement, St (1st century AD), pope (bishop of Rome) *c.*88–*c.*97, probably the third after St Peter; known as **St Clement of Rome**. Feast day, 23 November.

clementine /ˈklɛm(ə)ntʌɪn, -tiːn/ ▸ noun a tangerine of a deep orange-red North African variety which is grown around the Mediterranean and in South Africa.
– ORIGIN 1920s: from French *clémentine*, from the male given name *Clément*.

Clement of Alexandria, St (*c.*150–*c.*215), Greek theologian; Latin name *Titus Flavius Clemens*. His main contribution to theological scholarship was to relate the ideas of Greek philosophy to the Christian faith. Feast day, 5 December.

clenbuterol /klɛnˈbjuːtərɒl/ ▸ noun [mass noun] Medicine a synthetic drug used in the treatment of asthma and respiratory diseases and also in veterinary obstetrics. It also promotes the growth of muscle and has been used illegally by athletes to enhance performance.
– ORIGIN 1970s: from *c(h)l(oro-)* + *(ph)en(yl)* + *but(yl)* + *er* + -OL.

clench ▸ verb (with reference to the fingers or hand) close into a tight ball, especially as a manifestation of extreme anger: [with obj.] *she clenched her fists, struggling for control* | [no obj.] *Ian's right hand **clenched into a fist*** | (as adj. **clenched**) *he struck the wall with his clenched fist.* ■ (with reference to the teeth) press or be pressed tightly together, especially with anger or determination or so as to suppress a strong emotion: *he clenched his teeth, fighting waves of nausea.* ■ [with obj.] grasp (something) tightly and firmly: *he clenched the steering wheel so hard that the car wobbled.* ■ [no obj.] (of a muscular part of the body) tighten or contract sharply, especially with strong emotion: *Mark felt his stomach clench in alarm.*
▸ noun [in sing.] a contraction or tightening of part of the body: *she saw the anger rise, saw the clench of his fists.*
– ORIGIN Old English (in the sense of *clinch* 'fix securely'): of Germanic origin; related to CLING.

cleome /klɪˈəʊmi/ ▸ noun a plant of a chiefly tropical genus which includes the spider flower, noted for their long stamens. ● Genus *Cleome*, family Capparidaceae.
– ORIGIN modern Latin, from Greek, denoting a different plant.

Cleopatra /ˌkliːəˈpatrə/ (also **Cleopatra VII**) (69–30 BC), queen of Egypt 47–30 BC, the last Ptolemaic ruler. After a brief liaison with Julius Caesar she formed a political and romantic alliance with Mark Antony. Their ambitions ultimately brought them into conflict with Rome, and she and Antony were defeated at the battle of Actium in 31 BC. She is reputed to have committed suicide by allowing herself to be bitten by an asp.

cleopatra /ˌkliːəˈpatrə/ ▸ noun a European butterfly related to the brimstone, with wings that vary from pale cream to orange-yellow. ● *Gonepteryx cleopatra*, family Pieridae.

Cleopatra's Needles a pair of granite obelisks erected at Heliopolis by Tuthmosis III *c.*1475 BC. They were taken from Egypt in 1878, one being set up on the Thames Embankment in London and the other in Central Park, New York. They have no known historical connection with Cleopatra.

clepsydra /ˈklɛpsɪdrə/ ▸ noun (pl. **clepsydras** or **clepsydrae** /-driː/) an ancient time-measuring device worked by a flow of water.
– ORIGIN late Middle English: via Latin from Greek *klepsudra*, based on *kleptein* 'steal' + *hudōr* 'water'.

clerestory /ˈklɪəˌstɔːri/ (US also **clearstory**) ▸ noun (pl. **clerestories**) the upper part of the nave, choir, and transepts of a large church, containing a series of windows. ■ a series of similar windows in another large building. ■ a raised section of roof running down the centre of a railway carriage, with small windows or ventilators.
– ORIGIN late Middle English: from CLEAR + STOREY.

clerestory window ▸ noun each of a series of windows in a clerestory. ■ a window with no crosspiece dividing the light.

clergy /ˈkləːdʒi/ ▸ noun (pl. **clergies**) [usu. treated as pl.] the body of all people ordained for religious duties, especially in the Christian Church: *all marriages were to be solemnized by the clergy.*
– ORIGIN Middle English: from Old French, based on ecclesiastical Latin *clericus* 'clergyman' (see CLERIC).

clergyman (also **clergywoman**) ▸ noun (pl. **clergymen** or **clergywomen**) a male (or female) priest or minister of a Christian church.

cleric ▸ noun a priest or religious leader, especially a Christian or Muslim one.
– ORIGIN early 17th cent.: from ecclesiastical Latin *clericus* 'clergyman', from Greek *klērikos* 'belonging to the Christian clergy', from *klēros* 'lot, heritage' (Acts 1:26).

clerical ▸ adjective **1** concerned with or relating to work in an office, especially routine documentation and administrative tasks: *clerical duties.*
2 relating to the clergy: *he was still attired in his clerical outfit.*
– DERIVATIVES **clericalism** noun (sense 2), **clericalist** noun (sense 2), **clerically** adverb.
– ORIGIN late 15th cent. (in sense 2): from ecclesiastical Latin *clericalis*, from *clericus* 'clergyman' (see CLERIC).

clerical collar ▸ noun a stiff upright white collar which fastens at the back, worn by the clergy in some churches.

clerical error ▸ noun a mistake made in copying or writing out a document.

clerihew /ˈklɛrɪhjuː/ ▸ noun a short comic or nonsensical verse, typically in two rhyming couplets with lines of unequal length and referring to a famous person.
– ORIGIN 1920s: named after Edmund Clerihew BENTLEY, who invented it.

clerisy /ˈklɛrɪsi/ ▸ noun [usu. treated as pl.] learned or literary people regarded as a social group or class.
– ORIGIN early 19th cent.: apparently influenced by German *Klerisei*, based on Greek *klēros* 'heritage' (see CLERIC).

clerk /klɑːk/ ▶ **noun 1** a person employed in an office or bank to keep records, accounts, and undertake other routine administrative duties. ■ an official in charge of the records of a local council or court: *a clerk to the magistrates*. ■ a senior official in Parliament. ■ a lay officer of a cathedral, parish church, college chapel, etc.: *a chapter clerk*.
2 (also **desk clerk**) chiefly N. Amer. a receptionist in a hotel. ■ an assistant in a shop.
3 (also **clerk in holy orders**) formal a member of the clergy.
4 archaic a literate or scholarly person.
▶ **verb** [no obj.] chiefly N. Amer. work as a clerk.
– PHRASES **Clerk of the Closet** (in the UK) the sovereign's principal chaplain. **clerk of the course** an official who assists the judges in horse racing or motor racing. **clerk of (the) works** Brit. a person who oversees building work in progress.
– DERIVATIVES **clerkess noun** (chiefly Scottish), **clerkish adjective**, **clerkship noun**.
– ORIGIN Old English *cleric*, *clerc* (in the sense 'ordained minister, literate person'), from ecclesiastical Latin *clericus* 'clergyman' (see **CLERIC**); reinforced by Old French *clerc*, from the same source. Sense 1 of the noun dates from the early 16th cent.

clerkly ▶ **adjective** archaic **1** relating or appropriate to a clerk: *a list drawn up in a clerkly hand*.
2 scholarly; learned.

Clermont-Ferrand /ˌklɛːmɒ̃ fɛˈrɒ̃/, French /klɛʁmɔ̃ fɛʁɑ̃/ an industrial city in central France, capital of the Auvergne region, at the centre of the Massif Central; pop. 142,449 (2006).

Cleveland[1] /ˈkliːvlənd/ **1** a former county on the North Sea coast of NE England, formed in 1974 from parts of Durham and North Yorkshire and replaced in 1996 by the unitary councils of Middlesbrough, Hartlepool, Stockton-on-Tees, and Redcar and Cleveland.
2 a major port and industrial city in NE Ohio, situated on Lake Erie; pop. 433,748 (2008).

Cleveland[2] /ˈkliːvlənd/, (Stephen) Grover (1837–1908), American Democratic statesman, 22nd and 24th President of the US 1885–9 and 1893–7.

Cleveland bay ▶ **noun** a bay horse of a strong breed originating in the north of England, formerly popular as carriage horses.

clever ▶ **adjective** (**cleverer**, **cleverest**) **1** quick to understand, learn, and devise or apply ideas; intelligent: *she was an extremely clever and studious young woman* | *how **clever of** him to think of this!* ■ skilled at doing or achieving something; talented: *he was very **clever at** getting what he wanted* | *both Grandma and Mother were **clever with** their hands*. ■ showing skill and originality; ingenious: *a simple but clever idea for helping people learn computing* | *he taught the dog to perform some very clever tricks*. ■ [usu. with negative] informal sensible; well advised: *Joe had a feeling it wasn't too clever, leaving Dolly alone*.
2 [predic.] [with negative] Brit. informal healthy or well: *I was up and about by this time though still not too clever*.
– PHRASES **too clever by half** informal (of a person) annoyingly proud of their intelligence or skill, and liable to overreach themselves.
– DERIVATIVES **cleverly** adverb.
– ORIGIN Middle English (in the sense 'quick to catch hold', only recorded in this period): perhaps of Dutch or Low German origin, and related to **CLEAVE[2]**. In the late 16th cent. the term came to mean (probably through dialect use) 'manually skilful'; the sense 'possessing mental agility' dates from the early 18th cent.

clever-clever ▶ **adjective** derogatory excessively anxious to appear impressively clever or intelligent: *her silly little clever-clever theories of love and marriage*.

clever Dick (also **clever clogs**) ▶ **noun** Brit. informal a person who is irritatingly and ostentatiously knowledgeable or intelligent.

cleverness ▶ **noun** [mass noun] the quality of being clever; intelligence or shrewdness: *people marvelled at his cleverness* | *the cleverness of her strategy*.

clevis /ˈklɛvɪs/ ▶ **noun** a U-shaped or forked metal connector to which another part can be fastened by means of a bolt or pin passing through the ends of the connector.
– ORIGIN late 16th cent.: perhaps related to **CLEAVE[1]**.

clew /kluː/ ▶ **noun 1** the lower or after corner of a sail.
2 (**clews**) Nautical the cords by which a hammock is suspended.
3 archaic a ball of thread.
4 archaic variant of **CLUE**.
▶ **verb** [with obj.] (**clew a sail up** (or **down**)) Sailing raise (or lower) a square sail by the clews when furling (or unfurling).
– ORIGIN Old English *cliwen*, *cleowen* (denoting a rounded mass, also a ball of thread), of Germanic origin; related to Dutch *kluwen*. All senses are also recorded for the form **CLUE**.

clianthus /klʌɪˈanθəs, klɪ-/ ▶ **noun** an Australasian plant of the pea family, which bears drooping clusters of large scarlet flowers. Also called **GLORY PEA**.
● Genus *Clianthus*, family Leguminosae.
– ORIGIN modern Latin, apparently from Greek *kleos*, *klei-* 'glory' + *anthos* 'flower'.

cliché /ˈkliːʃeɪ/ (also **cliche**) ▶ **noun 1** a phrase or opinion that is overused and betrays a lack of original thought. ■ a very predictable or unoriginal thing or person.
2 Printing, chiefly Brit. a stereotype or electrotype.
– ORIGIN mid 19th cent.: French, past participle (used as a noun) of *clicher* 'to stereotype'.

clichéd (also **cliched**) ▶ **adjective** showing a lack of originality; based on frequently repeated phrases or opinions: *he has a horror of clichéd images of African-American life*.

click ▶ **noun** a short, sharp sound as of a switch being operated or of two hard objects coming smartly into contact: *she heard the click of the door*. ■ Phonetics a speech sound produced as a type of plosive by sudden withdrawal of the tongue from the soft palate, front teeth, or back teeth and hard palate, occurring in some southern African and other languages. ■ Computing an act of pressing a button on a mouse or similar device.
▶ **verb 1** make or cause to make a click: [no obj.] *the key clicked in the lock and the door opened* | *Martha clicked her tongue* | (as adj. **clicking**) *the clicking cameras outside the church*. ■ Computing press one of the buttons on a mouse to select a function or item on the screen: [no obj.] *you can **click on** an underlined word to jump to another section* | [with obj.] *click the left mouse button twice*. ■ (**click through**) Computing press one of the buttons on a mouse in order to follow a hyperlink to another file or web page :*click through to the website to buy the CD*.
2 [no obj.] informal become suddenly clear or understandable: *I wasn't used to such good treatment, then it clicked: we were wearing suits*. ■ quickly become friendly or intimate: *I couldn't help notice how pretty and intelligent she was and we just clicked* | *I didn't meet a woman who I really **clicked with** until I was 40*. ■ become successful or popular: *I don't think this issue has **clicked with** the voters*.
– PHRASES **click one's fingers** see **FINGER**. **click into place** become suddenly clear and understandable: *given this info, everything soon clicks into place*. **clicks and mortar** used to refer to a traditional business that has expanded its activities to operate also on the Internet.
– DERIVATIVES **clicky** adjective.
– ORIGIN late 16th cent. (as a verb): imitative.

clickable ▶ **adjective** Computing (of text or images) able to be clicked on with a mouse to produce a reaction.

click beetle ▶ **noun** a long, narrow beetle which can spring up with a click as a means of startling predators and escaping. Its larva is the wireworm. Also called **SKIPJACK**. ● Family Elateridae: numerous genera.

click-clack ▶ **noun** a repeated clicking sound as of shoe heels on a hard surface.
▶ **verb** [no obj., with adverbial of direction] move with such a sound: *a woman in high heels click-clacked past*.

clicker ▶ **noun** a device which clicks. ■ chiefly N. Amer. a remote control keypad.

clickstream ▶ **noun** Computing a series of mouse clicks made by a user while accessing the Internet, especially as monitored to assess a person's interests for marketing purposes.

click-through ▶ **noun** [mass noun] Computing the action or facility of following a hypertext link to a particular website, especially a commercial one: *the site allows click-through to the entire book* | [count noun] *these reports reveal which of the ads are receiving the most click-throughs* | [as modifier] *click-through banners*. ■ (also **click rate**, **click-through rate**) the proportion of visitors to a web page who follow a hypertext link to a particular site.

client ▶ **noun 1** a person or organization using the services of a lawyer or other professional person or company: *insurance tailor-made to a client's specific requirements*. ■ a person being dealt with by social or medical services: *a client referred for counselling*.
2 Computing (in a network) a desktop computer or workstation that is capable of obtaining information and applications from a server. ■ (also **client application** or **program**) a program that is capable of obtaining a service provided by another program.
3 (in ancient Rome) a plebeian under the protection of a patrician. ■ archaic a dependant; a hanger-on.
– DERIVATIVES **clientship** noun.
– ORIGIN late Middle English: from Latin *cliens*, *client-*, variant of *cluens* 'heeding', from *cluere* 'hear or obey'. The term originally denoted a person under the protection and patronage of another, hence a person 'protected' by a legal adviser (sense 1).

clientele /ˌkliːɒnˈtɛl/ ▶ **noun** [treated as sing. or pl.] clients collectively: *the solicitor's clientele*. ■ the customers of a shop, bar, or place of entertainment: *the dancers don't mix with the clientele*.
– ORIGIN mid 16th cent. (in the sense 'clientship, patronage'): via French from Latin *clientela* 'clientship', from *cliens*, *client-* (see **CLIENT**).

clientelism /ˌkliːɒnˈtɛlɪz(ə)m/ (also **clientism** /ˈklʌɪəntɪz(ə)m/) ▶ **noun** [mass noun] a social order which depends on relations of patronage.
– DERIVATIVES **clientelistic** adjective.
– ORIGIN 1970s: from Italian *clientelismo* 'patronage system'.

client-server ▶ **adjective** Computing denoting a computer system in which a central server provides data to a number of networked workstations.

Clifden nonpareil ▶ **noun** a large European moth of mostly subdued coloration, with a pale blue band on the underwing. ● *Catocala fraxini*, family Noctuidae.
– ORIGIN mid 18th cent.: from *Clifden* (now *Cliveden*), the name of a village in Buckinghamshire, England, and **NONPAREIL**.

cliff ▶ **noun** a steep rock face, especially at the edge of the sea: *a coast path along the top of rugged cliffs*.
– DERIVATIVES **cliff-like** adjective, **cliffy** adjective.
– ORIGIN Old English *clif*, of Germanic origin; related to Dutch *klif*.

cliffhanger ▶ **noun** a dramatic and exciting ending to an episode of a serial, leaving the audience in suspense and anxious not to miss the next episode. ■ a story or event with a strong element of suspense: *the match was a cliffhanger right up to the final whistle*.
– DERIVATIVES **cliffhanging** adjective.
– ORIGIN 1930s: from early film serials in which episodes ended with characters in desperate situations such as hanging off the edge of a cliff.

clifftop ▶ **noun** an area of land at the top of a cliff: *the windswept clifftops* | [as modifier] *clifftop paths*.

Clift, (Edward) Montgomery (1920–66), American actor. He received four Oscar nominations for films including *A Place in the Sun* (1951) and *From Here to Eternity* (1953).

climacteric /klʌɪˈmakt(ə)rɪk, ˌklʌɪmakˈtɛrɪk/ ▶ **noun 1** a critical period or event.
2 Medicine the period of life when fertility and sexual activity are in decline; (in women) menopause.
3 Botany the ripening period of certain fruits such as apples, involving increased metabolism and only possible while still on the tree.
▶ **adjective 1** having extreme and far-reaching implications or results; critical.
2 Medicine occurring at, characteristic of, or undergoing the climacteric; (in women) menopausal.
3 Botany (of a fruit) undergoing a climacteric.
– ORIGIN mid 16th cent. (in the sense 'constituting a critical period in life'): from French *climactérique* or via Latin from Greek *klimaktērikos*, from *klimaktēr* 'critical period', from *klimax* 'ladder, climax'.

climactic /klʌɪˈmaktɪk/ ▶ **adjective** acting as a culmination or resolution to a series of events; forming an exciting climax: *the film's climactic scenes*.
– DERIVATIVES **climactically** adverb.
– ORIGIN late 19th cent.: formed irregularly from **CLIMAX** + **-IC**, probably influenced by **CLIMACTERIC**.

> **USAGE** **Climactic** and **climatic** are very similar in spelling and are often confused. **Climactic** means 'forming a climax', as in *the film's climactic scene*, while **climatic** means 'relating to climate', as in *prevailing climatic conditions*.

climate ▶ **noun** the weather conditions prevailing in an area in general or over a long period: *our cold, wet climate* | [mass noun] *agricultural development is constrained by climate*. ■ a region with a particular climate: *he had grown up in a hot climate*. ■ the prevailing trend of public opinion or of another aspect of life: *the current economic climate*.

C

– ORIGIN late Middle English: from Old French *climat* or late Latin *clima*, *climat-*, from Greek *klima* 'slope, zone', from *klinein* 'to slope'. The term originally denoted a zone of the earth between two lines of latitude, then any region of the earth, and later, a region considered with reference to its atmospheric conditions. Compare with CLIME.

climate change ▶ noun [mass noun] the change in global climate patterns apparent from the mid to late 20th century onwards, attributed largely to the increased levels of atmospheric carbon dioxide produced by the use of fossil fuels.

WORD TRENDS In the early 2000s **global warming** was the buzzword of the environmentally minded, but it is apparently being overhauled by **climate change**. Although many people use the two terms interchangeably, there are important differences. **Global warming** describes a gradual heating up of the earth's atmosphere, whereas **climate change** can cover many other changes beyond an increase in temperature—such as alterations in precipitation patterns and sea level, and the increasing frequency of severe weather events. **Climate change** can also be seen as a less loaded and more politically neutral term, and is generally preferred by scientists, as many do not see rising temperature as the single most important effect of the changing climate. The Oxford English Corpus data from the year 2009 contains twice as many examples of **climate change** as of **global warming**.

climate control ▶ noun another term for AIR CONDITIONING.

climatic ▶ noun relating to climate: *under certain climatic conditions, desert locusts increase in number.*
– DERIVATIVES **climatical** adjective, **climatically** adverb.

USAGE See USAGE at CLIMACTIC.

climatology ▶ noun [mass noun] the scientific study of climate.
– DERIVATIVES **climatological** adjective, **climatologically** adverb, **climatologist** noun.

climax ▶ noun the most intense, exciting, or important point of something; the culmination: *she was nearing the climax of her speech | a thrilling climax to the game.* ■ an orgasm. ■ Ecology the final stage in a succession in a given environment, at which a plant community reaches a state of equilibrium. ■ Rhetoric a sequence of propositions or ideas in order of increasing importance, force, or effectiveness of expression.
▶ verb [no obj.] culminate in an exciting or impressive event; reach a climax: *the day **climaxed with** a gala concert.* ■ [with obj.] bring (something) to a climax: *three goals in the last two minutes climaxed a thrilling game.* ■ have an orgasm.
– ORIGIN mid 16th cent. (in rhetoric): from late Latin, from Greek *klimax* 'ladder, climax'. The sense 'culmination' arose in the late 18th cent.

climb ▶ verb 1 [with obj.] go or come up a (slope or staircase); ascend: *we began to climb the hill* | [no obj.] *the air became colder as they climbed higher | he **climbed up** the steps slowly.* ■ [no obj.] (of an aircraft or the sun) go upwards: *we decided to climb to 6,000 feet.* ■ [no obj.] (of a road or track) slope upwards: *the track climbed steeply up a narrow, twisting valley.* ■ (of a plant) grow up (a wall, tree, or trellis) by clinging with tendrils or by twining: *when ivy climbs a wall it infiltrates any crack* | [no obj.] *there were roses **climbing up** the walls.* ■ [no obj.] increase in scale, value, or power: *deer numbers have been climbing steadily | the stock market climbed 23.9 points.* ■ move to a higher position in (a chart or table): *the book climbed to number 18 on the New York Times bestseller list.*
2 [no obj., with adverbial of direction] move with effort, especially into or out of a confined space; clamber: *Howard started to climb out of the front seat.* ■ (**climb into**) put on (clothes): *he climbed into his suit.*
▶ noun an ascent, especially of a mountain or hill, by climbing: *this walk involves a long moorland climb* | figurative *how old will these graduates be before they begin a long climb out of debt?* ■ a mountain, hill, or slope that is climbed: *he was too full of alcohol to negotiate the climb safely.* ■ a recognized route up a mountain or cliff: *this may be the hardest rock climb in the world.* ■ an aircraft's flight upwards: *we levelled out from the climb at 600 feet* | [mass noun] *the rate of climb can be set by the pilot.* ■ a rise or increase in value, rank, or power: *an above-average climb in prices.*
– PHRASES **be climbing the walls** informal feel frustrated, helpless, and trapped: *his job soon had him climbing the walls.* **have a mountain to climb** be facing a very difficult task.
– PHRASAL VERBS **climb down** Brit. withdraw from a position taken up in argument or negotiation: *he was forced to climb down over the central package in the bill.*
– DERIVATIVES **climbable** adjective.
– ORIGIN Old English *climban*, of West Germanic origin; related to Dutch and German *klimmen*, also to CLAY and CLEAVE².

climbdown ▶ noun Brit. a withdrawal from a position taken up in argument or negotiation: *a humiliating climbdown by the government over economic policy.*

climber ▶ noun a person or animal that climbs: *leopards are great tree climbers.* ■ a mountaineer: *a rock climber.* ■ a climbing plant.

climbing ▶ noun [mass noun] the sport or activity of climbing mountains or cliffs.

climbing frame ▶ noun Brit. a structure of joined bars or logs for children to climb on.

climbing irons ▶ plural noun a set of spikes attached to boots for climbing trees or ice slopes.

climbing perch ▶ noun a small edible freshwater fish which is able to breathe air and move over land, native to Africa and Asia. ● Family Anabantidae: three genera and several species.

climbing wall ▶ noun a wall at a sports centre or in a gymnasium fitted with attachments to simulate a rock face for climbing practice.

climb-out ▶ noun the part of a flight of an aircraft after take-off and before it reaches a level altitude.

clime /klʌɪm/ ▶ noun (usu. **climes**) chiefly literary a region considered with reference to its climate: *long holidays in sunnier climes.*
– ORIGIN late Middle English: from late Latin *clima* 'zone' (see CLIMATE).

clinch ▶ verb [with obj.] 1 confirm or settle (a contract or bargain): *the Texan wanted to impress him to clinch a business deal.* ■ conclusively settle (an argument or debate): *these findings clinched the matter.* ■ confirm the winning or achievement of (a match, competition, or victory): *Johnson scored the goals which clinched victory.*
2 [no obj.] grapple at close quarters, especially (of boxers) so as to be too closely engaged for full-arm blows. ■ (of two people) embrace.
3 secure (a nail or rivet) by driving the point sideways when it has penetrated. ■ fasten (a rope or angling line) with a clinch knot.
▶ noun 1 a struggle or scuffle at close quarters. ■ an embrace, especially an amorous one: *we went into a passionate clinch on the sofa.*
2 (also **clinch knot**) a knot used to fasten ropes or angling lines, using a half hitch with the end seized back on its own part.
– ORIGIN late 16th cent. (in the senses 'something that grips' and 'fix securely'): variant of CLENCH.

clincher ▶ noun a fact, argument, or event that settles a matter conclusively: *Sixsmith scored the clincher after 81 minutes.*

Cline /klʌɪn/, Patsy (1932–63), American country singer; born *Virginia Petterson Hensley*. She had hits with songs such as 'Crazy' (1961) and 'Sweet Dreams of You' (1963) before dying in an air crash.

cline /klʌɪn/ ▶ noun a continuum with an infinite number of gradations from one extreme to the other: *a point along a cline of activity.* ■ Biology a gradation in one or more characteristics within a species or other taxon, especially between different populations.
– DERIVATIVES **clinal** adjective.
– ORIGIN 1930s: from Greek *klinein* 'to slope'.

cling ▶ verb (past and past participle **clung**) [no obj.] (**cling to/on to/on**) hold on tightly to: *she clung to Joe's arm | we sat on the sofa clinging on to one another* | figurative *she clung on to life for 16 days.* ■ adhere or stick firmly or closely to; be hard to part or remove from: *the smell of smoke clung to their clothes | the fabric clung to her smooth skin.* ■ remain very close to: *the fish cling to the line of the weed.* ■ remain persistently or stubbornly faithful to: *she clung resolutely to her convictions.* ■ be overly dependent on (someone) emotionally: *you are clinging to him for security.*
▶ noun (also **cling peach**) a clingstone peach.
– DERIVATIVES **clinger** noun.
– ORIGIN Old English *clingan* 'stick together', of Germanic origin; related to Middle Dutch *klingen* 'adhere', Middle High German *klingen* 'climb', also to CLENCH.

cling film ▶ noun [mass noun] Brit. a thin transparent plastic film that adheres to surfaces and to itself, used as a wrapping or covering for food.

clingfish ▶ noun (pl. **same** or **clingfishes**) a small fish occurring mainly in shallow or intertidal water, with a sucker for attachment to rocks and other surfaces. ● Family Gobiesocidae: several genera and species.

clinging ▶ adjective 1 (of a garment) fitting closely to the body and showing its shape: *she was wearing a clinging black dress.*
2 too dependent on someone emotionally: *she wasn't the clinging type.*

clingstone ▶ noun a peach or nectarine of a variety in which the flesh adheres to the stone. Contrasted with FREESTONE (sense 2).

clingy ▶ adjective (**clingier**, **clingiest**) 1 (of a garment) liable to cling; clinging: *a clingy top.*
2 (of a person) too emotionally dependent: *at about 18 months my son became very clingy.*
– DERIVATIVES **clinginess** noun.

clinic ▶ noun 1 a place or hospital department where outpatients are given medical treatment or advice, especially of a specialist nature: *an antenatal clinic.* ■ chiefly Brit. an occasion or time when medical treatment or advice is given: *we're now holding regular clinics.* ■ a gathering at a hospital bedside for the teaching of medicine or surgery.
2 a conference or short course on a particular subject: *a drum clinic.*
– ORIGIN mid 19th cent. (in the sense 'teaching of medicine at the bedside'): from French *clinique*, from Greek *klinikē (tekhnē)* 'bedside (art)', from *klinē* 'bed'.

clinical ▶ adjective 1 relating to the observation and treatment of actual patients rather than theoretical or laboratory studies: *clinical medicine | clinical drug trials.* ■ (of a disease or condition) causing observable and recognizable symptoms: *clinical depression.*
2 very efficient and without feeling; coldly detached: *nothing was left to chance—everything was clinical.* ■ (of a room or building) bare, functional, and clean.
– DERIVATIVES **clinically** adverb.
– ORIGIN late 18th cent.: from Greek *klinikē* 'bedside' (see CLINIC) + -AL.

clinical death ▶ noun [mass noun] death as judged by the medical observation of cessation of vital functions. It is typically identified with the cessation of heartbeat and respiration, though modern resuscitation methods and life-support systems have required the introduction of the alternative concept of brain death.

clinical psychology ▶ noun [mass noun] the branch of psychology concerned with the assessment and treatment of mental illness and behavioural problems.
– DERIVATIVES **clinical psychologist** noun.

clinical thermometer ▶ noun a small medical thermometer with a short but finely calibrated range, for taking a person's temperature.

clinician ▶ noun a doctor having direct contact with patients rather than being involved with theoretical or laboratory studies.

clink[1] ▶ noun a sharp ringing sound, such as that made by striking metal or glass: *the clink of ice in tall glasses.*
▶ verb make or cause to make a clink: [no obj.] *his ring clinked against the crystal* | [with obj.] *I heard Suzie clink a piece of crockery* | (as adj. **clinking**) *clinking chains.* ■ [with obj.] strike (one's glass) against another's to express friendly feelings before drinking: *she clinked her glass against mine.*
– ORIGIN Middle English (as a verb): probably from Middle Dutch *klinken*.

clink[2] ▶ noun [in sing.] informal prison: *some bloke he'd met in clink.*
– ORIGIN early 16th cent. (originally denoting a prison in Southwark, London): of unknown origin.

clinker[1] ▶ noun [mass noun] the stony residue from burnt coal or from a furnace. ■ (also **clinker brick**) [count noun] a brick with a vitrified surface.
– ORIGIN mid 17th cent.: from obsolete Dutch *klinckaerd* (earlier form of *klinker*), from *klinken* 'to clink'.

clinker[2] ▶ noun informal 1 N. Amer. something that is unsatisfactory, of poor quality, or a failure: *marketing couldn't save such clinkers as these films.*
2 Brit. dated something or someone excellent or outstanding: *she was a real clinker.*
– ORIGIN late 17th cent. (denoting a person or thing that clinks): from CLINK¹ + -ER¹. Sense 2 dates from the mid 19th cent., sense 1 from the 1930s.

clinker-built ▶ adjective (of a boat) having external planks which overlap downwards and are secured with clinched nails. Compare with CARVEL-BUILT.

– ORIGIN mid 18th cent.: *clinker* from *clink* (northern English variant of CLINCH).

clinometer /klʌɪˈnɒmɪtə, klɪ-/ ▸ noun Surveying an instrument used for measuring the angle or elevation of slopes.
– ORIGIN early 19th cent.: from Greek *klinein* 'to slope' + -METER.

clinopyroxene /ˌklʌɪnə(ʊ)pʌɪˈrɒksiːn/ ▸ noun [mass noun] a mineral of the pyroxene group crystallizing in the monoclinic system.
– ORIGIN early 20th cent.: from *clino-* in the sense 'monoclinic' + PYROXENE.

clint ▸ noun a block forming part of a natural limestone pavement, separated from others by fissures (grikes).
– ORIGIN Middle English: of Scandinavian origin; related to Danish *klint* 'cliff' and Swedish *klint* 'summit, cliff'.

Clinton, Bill (b.1946), American Democratic statesman, 42nd President of the US 1993–2001; full name *William Jefferson Clinton*. Re-elected in 1996, he was impeached in 1998 on charges of perjury and obstruction of justice, but was acquitted.
– DERIVATIVES **Clintonite** adjective & noun.

Clio /ˈklʌɪəʊ/ Greek & Roman Mythology the Muse of history.
– ORIGIN from Greek *kleiein* 'celebrate'.

cliometrics /ˌklʌɪə(ʊ)ˈmɛtrɪks/ ▸ plural noun [treated as sing.] a technique for the interpretation of economic history, based on the statistical analysis of large-scale numerical data from population censuses, parish registers, and similar sources.
– DERIVATIVES **cliometric** adjective, **cliometrician** noun.
– ORIGIN 1960s (originally US): from CLIO, on the pattern of words such as *econometrics*.

clip¹ ▸ noun **1** a flexible or spring-loaded device for holding an object or objects together or in place. ■ a piece of jewellery fastened by a clip. ■ a clip for holding banknotes.
2 a metal holder containing cartridges for an automatic firearm.
▸ verb (**clips, clipping, clipped**) [with adverbial of place] fasten or be fastened with a clip or clips: [with obj.] *she clipped on a pair of diamond earrings* | [no obj.] *the panels simply clip on to the framework.*
– ORIGIN Old English *clyppan* (verb), of West Germanic origin. The noun use dates from the late 15th cent.

clip² ▸ verb (**clips, clipping, clipped**) [with obj.] **1** cut short or trim (hair, vegetation, etc.) with shears or scissors: *I was clipping the hedge.* ■ trim or remove the hair or wool of (an animal). ■ (**clip something off**) cut off a thing or part of a thing with shears or scissors: *Philip clipped off another piece of wire* | figurative *she clipped nearly two seconds off the world record.* ■ cut (a section) from a newspaper or periodical: *a photograph clipped from a magazine.* ■ illicitly pare the edge of (a coin). ■ Brit. remove a small piece of (a bus or train ticket) to show that it has been used. ■ Computing process (an image) so as to remove the parts outside a certain area. ■ Electronics truncate the amplitude of (a signal) above or below predetermined levels.
2 Brit. strike smartly or with a glancing blow: *the car clipped the kerb* | *he'll clip your ear.*
3 informal, chiefly N. Amer. swindle or rob: *in all the years he ran the place, he was clipped only three times.*
4 [no obj., with adverbial of direction] informal, chiefly US move quickly: *we clip down the track.*
▸ noun **1** an act of clipping or trimming something: *I gave him a full clip.* ■ the quantity of wool clipped from a sheep or flock.
2 a short sequence taken from a film or broadcast: *clips from earlier shows* | *a film clip.*
3 Brit. informal a smart or glancing blow: *I'd give him a clip round the ear.*
4 [in sing.] informal a specified speed or rate of movement, especially when rapid: *we crossed the dance floor at an amazingly fast clip.*
– PHRASES **at a clip** US informal at a time; all at once: *I spent several days with him, eight hours at a clip.* **clip the wings of** trim the feathers of (a bird) so as to disable it from flight. ■ prevent (someone) from acting freely; check the aspirations of: *he finally clipped the wings of his high-flying chief of staff.*
– ORIGIN Middle English: from Old Norse *klippa*, probably imitative.

clip art ▸ noun [mass noun] simple pictures and symbols made available for computer users to add to their documents.

clipboard ▸ noun a small board with a spring clip at the top, used for holding papers and providing support for writing. ■ Computing a temporary storage area where material cut or copied from a file is kept for pasting into another file.

clip-clop ▸ noun [in sing.] the sound of a horse's hoofs beating on a hard surface.
▸ verb [no obj., with adverbial of direction] move with a clip clop: *the horses clip-clopped slowly along the street.*
– ORIGIN late 19th cent.: imitative.

clip joint ▸ noun informal a nightclub or bar that charges exorbitant prices.

clip-on ▸ adjective attached by a clip so as to be easy to fasten or remove: *a clip-on bow tie.*
▸ noun (**clip-ons**) things, especially sunglasses or earrings, that are attached by clips.

clipped ▸ adjective (of speech) having short, sharp vowel sounds and clear pronunciation: *his cold clipped tones.*

clipper ▸ noun **1** (also **clippers**) an instrument for cutting or trimming small pieces off things: *hedge clippers.*
2 (also **clipper ship**) a fast sailing ship, especially one of 19th-century design with concave bows and raked masts.
3 Electronics another term for LIMITER. ■ (also **clipper chip**) a microchip which inserts an identifying code into encrypted transmissions that allows them to be deciphered by a third party having access to a Government-held key.

clippie ▸ noun (pl. **clippies**) Brit. informal a bus conductress.

clipping ▸ noun (usu. **clippings**) a small piece trimmed from something: *hedge clippings and grass cuttings.* ■ an article cut from a newspaper or magazine.

clique /kliːk/ ▸ noun a small close-knit group of people who do not readily allow others to join them.
– DERIVATIVES **cliquey** adjective (**cliquier, cliquiest**), **cliquish** adjective, **cliquishness** noun.
– ORIGIN early 18th cent.: from French, from Old French *cliquer* 'make a noise'; the modern sense is related to CLAQUE.

CLit ▸ abbreviation (in the UK) Companion of Literature.

clit ▸ noun vulgar slang short for CLITORIS.

clitic /ˈklɪtɪk/ ▸ noun Grammar an unstressed word that normally occurs only in combination with another word, for example *'m* in *I'm*.
– ORIGIN 1940s: from *(en)clitic* and *(pro)clitic*.

clitoridectomy /ˌklɪt(ə)rɪˈdɛktəmi/ ▸ noun (pl. **clitoridectomies**) [mass noun] excision of the clitoris; female circumcision.

clitoris /ˈklɪt(ə)rɪs/ ▸ noun a small, sensitive, erectile part of the female genitals at the anterior end of the vulva.
– DERIVATIVES **clitoral** adjective.
– ORIGIN early 17th cent.: modern Latin, from Greek *kleitoris*.

clitter ▸ verb [no obj.] make a thin rattling sound.
– ORIGIN early 16th cent.: imitative.

Clive, Robert, 1st Baron Clive of Plassey (1725–74), British general and colonial administrator; known as **Clive of India**. In 1757 he recaptured Calcutta (now Kolkata), following the Black Hole incident, and gained control of Bengal. He served as governor of Bengal 1765–7, but was implicated in the East India company's corruption scandals and committed suicide.

clivia /ˈklʌɪvɪə/ ▸ noun a southern African plant of the lily family, with dark green strap-like leaves and trumpet-shaped orange, red, or yellow flowers. Also called KAFFIR LILY. ● Genus *Clivia*, family Liliaceae (or Amaryllidaceae).
– ORIGIN modern Latin, from *Clive*, the maiden name of Charlotte, Duchess of Northumberland (1787–1866).

Cllr ▸ abbreviation (in the UK) Councillor.

cloaca /kləʊˈeɪkə/ ▸ noun (pl. **cloacae** /-siː, -kiː/)
1 Zoology a common cavity at the end of the digestive tract for the release of both excretory and genital products in vertebrates (except most mammals) and certain invertebrates.
2 archaic a sewer.
– DERIVATIVES **cloacal** adjective.
– ORIGIN late 16th cent. (in the sense 'sewer'): from Latin, related to *cluere* 'cleanse'. The first sense dates from the mid 19th cent.

cloak ▸ noun **1** a sleeveless outdoor overgarment that hangs loosely from the shoulders. ■ something serving to hide or disguise something: *preparations had taken place under a cloak of secrecy.*
2 (**cloaks**) Brit. a cloakroom.
▸ verb [with obj.] dress in a cloak: *they sat cloaked and hooded.* ■ hide, cover, or disguise (something): *she cloaked her embarrassment by rushing into speech.*
– ORIGIN Middle English: from Old French *cloke*, dialect variant of *cloche* 'bell, cloak' (from its bell shape), from medieval Latin *clocca* 'bell'. Compare with CLOCK¹.

C

cloak-and-dagger ▸ adjective involving or characterized by mystery, intrigue, or espionage: *a cloak-and-dagger operation.*

cloakroom ▸ noun **1** a room in a public building where outdoor clothes or luggage may be left.
2 Brit. a room that contains a toilet or toilets.

clobber¹ ▸ noun [mass noun] Brit. informal clothing, personal belongings, or equipment: *I found all his clobber in the locker.*
– ORIGIN late 19th cent.: of unknown origin.

clobber² ▸ verb [with obj.] informal hit (someone) hard: *if he does that I'll clobber him!* ■ treat or deal with harshly: *the recession clobbered other parts of the business.* ■ defeat heavily.
– ORIGIN Second World War (apparently air force slang): of unknown origin.

clobber³ ▸ verb [with obj.] add enamelled decoration to (porcelain).
– ORIGIN late 19th cent.: of unknown origin.

clochard /ˈklɔʃɑː/, French /klɔʃaʀ/ ▸ noun (pl. **clochards** pronunc. **same**) (in France) a beggar; a vagrant.
– ORIGIN French, from *clocher* 'to limp'.

cloche /klɒʃ, kləʊʃ/ ▸ noun **1** a small translucent cover for protecting or forcing outdoor plants.
2 (also **cloche hat**) a woman's close-fitting bell-shaped hat.
– ORIGIN late 19th cent.: from French, literally 'bell' (see CLOAK).

clock¹ ▸ noun **1** a mechanical or electrical device for measuring time, indicating hours, minutes, and sometimes seconds by hands on a round dial or by displayed figures. ■ (**the clock**) time taken as a factor in an activity, especially in competitive sports: *this stage is played **against the clock**.* ■ informal a measuring device such as a speedometer, taximeter, or milometer: *a car with over 82,000 miles **on the clock**.* ■ Computing an electronic device used to initiate and synchronize internal operations.
2 Brit. a downy spherical seed head, especially that of a dandelion.
3 Brit. informal a person's face.
▸ verb [with obj.] **1** attain or register (a specified time, distance, or speed): *Thomas has **clocked up** forty years service* | [no obj.] *this is a generous CD, **clocking in** at more than 60 minutes.* ■ achieve (a victory): *he **clocked up** his first win of the year.* ■ record as attaining a specified time or rate: *the tower operators clocked a gust at 185 mph.*
2 Brit. informal notice or watch: *I noticed him clocking her in the mirror.*
3 informal, chiefly Brit. hit (someone), especially on the head: *someone clocked him for no good reason.*
4 Brit. informal wind back the milometer of (a car) illegally in order to make the vehicle appear to have travelled fewer miles than it really has.
– PHRASES **round** (or **around**) **the clock** all day and all night: *I've got a team working around the clock* | [as adj.] *round-the-clock surveillance.* **turn** (or **put**) **back the clock** return to the past or to a previous way of doing things. **watch the clock** another way of saying CLOCK-WATCH.
– PHRASAL VERBS **clock in** (or Brit. **on**) register one's arrival at work by means of an automatic recording clock: *staff should clock in on arrival.* **clock out** (or Brit. **off**) register one's departure from work by means of an automatic recording clock: *the night shift were clocking off.*
– ORIGIN late Middle English: from Middle Low German and Middle Dutch *klocke*, based on medieval Latin *clocca* 'bell'.

clock² ▸ noun an ornamental pattern woven or embroidered on the side of a stocking or sock near the ankle.
– ORIGIN mid 16th cent.: of unknown origin.

clocker ▸ noun informal **1** Brit. a person who illegally winds back the milometer of a car.
2 US a drug dealer, especially one who sells cocaine or crack.

clock golf ▸ noun [mass noun] a lawn game in which the players putt to a hole in the centre of a circle from successive points on its circumference.

clockmaker ▶ noun a person who makes and repairs clocks and watches.
– DERIVATIVES **clockmaking** noun.

clock radio ▶ noun a combined bedside radio and alarm clock, which can be set so that the radio will come on at the desired time.

clock speed ▶ noun the operating speed of a computer or its microprocessor, expressed in cycles per second (megahertz).

clock tower ▶ noun a tower, typically forming part of a church or civic building, with a large clock at the top.

clock-watch ▶ verb [no obj.] (often as noun **clock-watching**) (of an employee) be overly keen not to work more than one's allotted hours.
– DERIVATIVES **clock-watcher** noun.

clockwise ▶ adverb & adjective in a curve corresponding in direction to the movement of the hands of a clock: [as adv.] *turn the knob clockwise* | [as adj.] *a clockwise direction*.

clockwork ▶ noun [mass noun] a mechanism with a spring and toothed gearwheels, used to drive a mechanical clock, toy, or other device: *quartz watches are more accurate than those driven by clockwork*.
▶ adjective [attrib.] driven by clockwork: *a clockwork motor*. ■ very smooth and regular: *the clockwork precision of the galaxy*. ■ repetitive and predictable: *it was a clockwork existence for the children*.
– PHRASES **as regular as clockwork** very regularly; repeatedly and predictably. **like clockwork** very smoothly and easily: *the event ran like clockwork*. ■ with mechanical regularity: *these hens lay like clockwork*.

clod ▶ noun **1** a lump of earth or clay.
2 informal a stupid person.
3 [mass noun] Brit. a coarse cut of meat from the lower neck of an ox.
– ORIGIN late Middle English: variant of CLOT.

cloddish ▶ adjective foolish, awkward, or clumsy.
– DERIVATIVES **cloddishly** adverb, **cloddishness** noun.

clodhopper ▶ noun informal **1** a large, heavy shoe.
2 a foolish, awkward, or clumsy person.

clodhopping ▶ adjective informal foolish, awkward, or clumsy.

clodpole ▶ noun informal, dated a foolish, awkward, or clumsy person.

clog ▶ noun **1** a shoe with a thick wooden sole.
2 an encumbrance or impediment: *they found the tax to be an unacceptable clog on the market*.
▶ verb (**clogs, clogging, clogged**) block or become blocked with an accumulation of thick, wet matter: [with obj.] *the gutters were **clogged up** with leaves* | [no obj.] *too much fatty food makes your arteries **clog up*** | (as adj. **clogged**) *clogged drains*. ■ fill up or crowd (something) so as to obstruct passage: *tourists' cars clog the roads into Cornwall*.
– ORIGIN Middle English (in the sense 'block of wood to impede an animal's movement'): of unknown origin.

clog dance ▶ noun a dance performed in clogs with rhythmic beating of the feet, especially as a traditional dance in Ireland, Scotland, and the North of England.
– DERIVATIVES **clog dancer** noun, **clog dancing** noun.

clogger ▶ noun **1** a person or thing that clogs something: *pore-cloggers*.
2 Brit. informal a footballer who habitually fouls other players when tackling.
3 a person who makes clogs.

cloggy ▶ adjective (**cloggier, cloggiest**) thick and sticky: *cloggy mud*.

cloisonné /ˈklwɑːzɒneɪ, -ˈzɒneɪ/ ▶ noun [mass noun] decorative work in which enamel, glass, or gemstones are separated by strips of flattened wire placed edgeways on a metal backing.
– ORIGIN mid 19th cent.: French, literally 'partitioned', past participle of *cloisonner*, from *cloison* 'a partition or division'.

cloister /ˈklɔɪstə/ ▶ noun a covered walk in a convent, monastery, college, or cathedral, typically with a colonnade open to a quadrangle on one side. ■ a convent or monastery. ■ (**the cloister**) monastic life: *he was inclined more to the cloister than the sword*.
▶ verb [with obj.] seclude or shut up in a convent or monastery: *the monastery was where the Brothers would cloister themselves to meditate*.
– DERIVATIVES **cloistral** adjective.
– ORIGIN Middle English (in the sense 'place of religious seclusion'): from Old French *cloistre*, from Latin *claustrum*, *clostrum* 'lock, enclosed place', from *claudere*, 'to close'.

cloistered ▶ adjective **1** enclosed by or having a cloister: *a cloistered walkway*.
2 kept away from the outside world; sheltered: *a cloistered upbringing*.

clomiphene /ˈkləʊmɪfiːn/ ▶ noun [mass noun] Medicine a synthetic non-steroidal drug used to treat infertility in women by stimulating ovulation.
– ORIGIN 1970s: from *chlo(ro-)* + *(a)mi(ne)* + *phen(yl)*.

clomp ▶ verb [no obj., with adverbial of direction] walk with a heavy tread: *she clomped down the steps*.
▶ noun [in sing.] the sound of a heavy tread: *the clomp of booted feet*.
– ORIGIN early 19th cent.: imitative; compare with CLUMP.

clompy ▶ adjective variant spelling of CLUMPY (sense 1).

clone ▶ noun **1** Biology an organism or cell, or group of organisms or cells, produced asexually from one ancestor or stock, to which they are genetically identical. ■ a person or thing regarded as an exact copy of another: *guitarists who are labelled Hendrix clones*. ■ a computer designed to simulate exactly the operation of another, typically more expensive, model: *an IBM PC clone*.
2 informal (within gay culture) a homosexual man who adopts an exaggeratedly macho appearance and style of dress.
▶ verb [with obj.] propagate (an organism or cell) as a clone: *of the hundreds of new plants cloned the best ones are selected*. ■ make an identical copy of. ■ Biochemistry replicate (a fragment of DNA placed in an organism) so that there is sufficient to analyse or use in protein production. ■ illegally copy the security codes from (a mobile phone) to one or more others as a way of obtaining free calls.
– DERIVATIVES **clonal** adjective, **clonality** noun, **cloner** noun.
– ORIGIN early 20th cent.: from Greek *klōn* 'twig'.

clonk ▶ noun [in sing.] an abrupt, heavy sound of impact.
▶ verb **1** [no obj.] move with or make a clonk.
2 [with obj.] informal hit: *I'll clonk you on the head*.
– DERIVATIVES **clonky** adjective.
– ORIGIN mid 19th cent.: imitative.

Clonmel /klɒnˈmɛl/ the county town of Tipperary, in the Republic of Ireland; pop. 15,482 (2006).

clonus /ˈkləʊnəs/ ▶ noun [mass noun] Medicine muscular spasm involving repeated, often rhythmic, contractions.
– DERIVATIVES **clonic** adjective.
– ORIGIN early 19th cent.: from Greek *klonos* 'turmoil'.

clop ▶ noun [in sing.] a sound or series of sounds made by a horse's hoofs on a hard surface.
▶ verb (**clops, clopping, clopped**) [no obj., with adverbial of direction] (of a horse) move with a clop: *the animal clopped on at a steady pace*.
– ORIGIN mid 19th cent.: imitative.

cloqué /ˈkləʊkeɪ/ ▶ noun [mass noun] a fabric with an irregularly raised or embossed surface.
– ORIGIN French, literally 'blistered'. It was first recorded (1920s) in the anglicized form *cloky*; use of the French form dates from the 1950s.

close[1] /kləʊs/ ▶ adjective **1** only a short distance away or apart in space or time: *the hotel is **close to** the sea* | *her birthday and mine were **close together*** | *why don't we go straight to the shops, as we're so close?* ■ with very little or no space in between; dense: *cloth with a close weave* | *this work occupies over 1,300 pages of close print*. ■ narrowly enclosed: *animals in close confinement*. ■ (**close to**) very near to (being or doing something): *on a good day the climate in LA is close to perfection* | *she was close to tears*. ■ (with reference to a competitive situation) involving only a small margin between winner and loser: *the race will be a close contest* | *she finished a close second*.
2 [attrib.] denoting a family member who is part of a person's immediate family, typically a parent or sibling: *the family history of cancer in close relatives*. ■ on very affectionate or intimate terms: *they had always been very close, with no secrets at all*. ■ (of a connection or resemblance) strong: *the college has close links with many other institutions*.
3 (of observation, examination, etc.) done in a careful and thorough way: ***pay close attention to** what your body is telling you about yourself*. ■ carefully guarded: *his whereabouts are a close secret*. ■ not willing to give away money or information; secretive: *you're very close about your work, aren't you?*
4 uncomfortably humid or airless: *a close, hazy day* | *it was very close in the dressing room*.
5 Phonetics another term for HIGH (sense 7 of the adjective).
▶ adverb (often **close to**) very near to someone or something; with very little space between: *they stood close to the door* | *he was holding her close*.
▶ noun [often in names] Brit. a residential street without through access: *she lives at 12 Goodwood Close*. ■ the precinct surrounding a cathedral. ■ a playing field at certain traditional English public schools. ■ Scottish an entry from the street to a common stairway or to a court at the back of a building.
– PHRASES **at** (or **in**) **close quarters** very or uncomfortably close to someone or something: *he witnessed the atrocities of war at close quarters* | *housing shortages force people to live in close quarters*. **close by** very near; nearby: *her father lives quite close by*. **close shave** (also **close call**) informal a narrow escape from danger or disaster. **close to** (or **close on**) (of an amount) almost; very nearly: *he spent close to 30 years in jail*. **close to the bone** see BONE. **close to one's heart** see HEART. **close to home** see HOME. **close up** very near: *close up she was no less pretty*. **come close** almost achieve or do: *he came close to calling the Prime Minister a liar*. **run someone close** Brit. almost match the standards or level of achievement of someone else: *the Germans ran Argentina close in the 1986 World Cup final*. **too close for comfort** dangerously or uncomfortably near: *he sat on the edge of the bed, far too close for comfort* | figurative *an issue being discussed with a sufferer may be too close for comfort to the counsellor's personal experience*.
– DERIVATIVES **closely** adverb, **closeness** noun, **closish** adjective.
– ORIGIN Middle English: from Old French *clos* (as noun and adjective), from Latin *clausum* 'enclosure' and *clausus* 'closed', past participle of *claudere*.

close[2] /kləʊz/ ▶ verb **1** move so as to cover an opening: [no obj.] *she jumped on to the train just as the doors were closing* | [with obj.] *she closed the door quietly*. ■ [with obj.] block up (a hole or opening): *close the hole with a plug of cotton wool* | figurative *Stephen closed his ears to the sound*. ■ [with obj.] bring two parts of (something) together so as to block its opening or bring it into a folded state: *Loretta closed her mouth* | *Rex closed the book*. ■ [no obj.] (**close around/over**) come into contact with (something) so as to encircle and hold it: *my fist closed around the weapon*. ■ [with obj.] make (an electric circuit) continuous: *this will cause a relay to operate and close the circuit*.
2 bring or come to an end: [with obj.] *the members were thanked for attending and the meeting was closed* | [no obj.] *the concert closed with 'Silent Night'* | (as adj. **closing**) *the closing stages of the election campaign*. ■ [no obj.] finish speaking or writing: *we close with a point about truth* | (as adj. **closing**) *Nellie's closing words*. ■ [with obj.] bring (a business transaction) to a satisfactory conclusion: *right now we are trying to close the deal with our sponsors*.
3 [no obj.] (of a business, organization, or institution) cease to be in operation or accessible to the public, either permanently or at the end of a working day or other period of time: *the factory is to close with the loss of 150 jobs* | [with obj.] *a hoax call which closed the city's stations for 4 hours*. ■ [with obj.] remove all the funds from (a bank or building society account) and cease to use it. ■ [with obj.] Computing make (a file) inaccessible after use, so that it is securely stored until required again.
4 [no obj.] gradually get nearer to someone or something: *he tried to walk faster, but each time the man **closed up on** him again*.
▶ noun [in sing.] **1** the end of an event or of a period of time or activity: *the afternoon **drew to a close*** | *the seminar **was brought to a close** with a discussion of future trends*. ■ (**the close**) the end of a day's trading on a stock market: *by the close the Dow Jones average was down 13.52 points at 2,759.84*. ■ (**the close**) the end of a day's play in a cricket match. ■ Music the conclusion of a phrase; a cadence.
2 the shutting of something, especially a door: *the door jerked to a close behind them*.
– PHRASES **close the door on** (or **to**) see DOOR. **close one's eyes to** see EYE. **close one's mind to** see MIND. **close ranks** see RANK[1].
– PHRASAL VERBS **close down** (or **close something down**) cease or cause to cease business or operation, especially permanently: *the government promised to close down the nuclear plants within twenty years*. ■ (**close down**) Brit. (of a broadcasting station) end transmission until the next day. **close in** come nearer to someone being pursued: *the police were closing in on them*. ■ gradually surround, especially with the effect of hindering movement or vision: *the*

weather has now closed in so an attempt on the summit is unlikely. ■ (of days) get successively shorter with the approach of the winter solstice: *November was closing in.* **close something out** N. Amer. bring something to an end. **close up** (of a person's face) become blank and emotionless or hostile: *he didn't like her laughter and his face closed up angrily.* **close up 1** (also **close something up**) cease or cause to cease operation or being used: *the solicitor advised me to close the house up for the time being.* **2** (**close up**) (of an opening) grow smaller or become blocked by something: *she felt her throat close up.* **close with** come near, especially so as to engage with (an enemy force).
– DERIVATIVES **closable** adjective, **closer** noun.
– ORIGIN Middle English: from Old French *clos-*, stem of *clore*, from Latin *claudere* 'to shut'.

close-coupled ▶ adjective chiefly Brit. (of two parts of a structure) attached or fixed close together.

close-cropped ▶ adjective (of hair or grass) cut very short.

closed ▶ adjective **1** not open: *rooms with closed doors lined the hallway | he sat with his eyes closed.* ■ (of a society or system) not communicating with or influenced by others. ■ limited to certain people; not open or available to all: *the UN Security Council met in closed session.* ■ unwilling to accept new ideas: *you're facing the situation with a closed mind.*
2 (of a business) having ceased trading, especially for a short period: *he put the 'Closed' sign up on the door.*
3 Mathematics (of a set) having the property that the result of a specified operation on any element of the set is itself a member of the set. ■ (of a set) containing all its limit points. ■ Geometry (of a curve or figure) formed from a single unbroken line.
– PHRASES **behind closed doors** taking place secretly or without public knowledge. **closed book** a subject or person about which one knows nothing: *accounting has always been **a closed book to me**.*

closed caption ▶ noun one of a series of subtitles to a television programme, accessible through a decoder.
▶ verb (**closed-caption**) [with obj.] (usu. as noun **closed-captioning**) provide (a programme) with closed captions.

closed-circuit television (abbrev.: **CCTV**) ▶ noun [mass noun] a television system in which video signals are transmitted from one or more cameras by cable to a set of monitors, used especially for security purposes.

closed-end ▶ adjective having a predetermined and fixed extent: *a closed-end contract.* ■ N. Amer. denoting an investment trust or company that issues a fixed number of shares.

closed-in ▶ adjective oppressively enclosed or lacking in space: *her distress at being in closed-in places.*

close-down ▶ noun [in sing.] a cessation of work or business, especially on a permanent basis. ■ Brit. the end of broadcasting on television or radio until the next day.

closed season ▶ noun chiefly N. Amer. another term for CLOSE SEASON.

closed shop ▶ noun a place of work where all employees must belong to an agreed trade union. Compare with UNION SHOP. ■ an area of activity that is restricted to a particular small group: *it's a very closed shop, the pharmaceutical world.*

closed syllable ▶ noun a syllable ending in a consonant.

closed universe ▶ noun Astronomy the condition in which there is sufficient matter in the universe to halt the expansion driven by the Big Bang and cause eventual re-collapse.

close encounter ▶ noun a supposed encounter with a UFO or with aliens.
– PHRASES **close encounter of the first** (or **second** etc.) **kind** used to describe encounters involving increasing degrees of complexity and apparent exposure of the witness to aliens.

close-fisted ▶ adjective unwilling to spend money; mean.

close-fitting ▶ adjective (of a garment) fitting tightly and showing the contours of the body.

close-grained ▶ adjective having tightly packed fibres, crystals, or other structural elements.

close harmony ▶ noun [mass noun] Music harmony in which the notes of the chord are close together, typically in vocal music.

close-hauled ▶ adjective & adverb Sailing (of a ship) with the sails hauled aft to sail close to the wind.

close-in ▶ adjective only a short distance away: *a close-in shot.* ■ N. Amer. near to the centre of a town or city: *close-in parking.*

close-knit ▶ adjective bound together by strong relationships and common interests: *a close-knit community.*

close-mouthed (also **close-lipped**) ▶ adjective reticent; discreet.

closeout ▶ noun [usu. as modifier] US a sale of goods at reduced prices to get rid of superfluous stock.

close range ▶ noun a short distance between someone or something and a target: *Wilkinson scored **from close range** | they were shot **at close range** |* [as modifier] *a close-range shot.*

close reach ▶ noun Sailing a situation in sailing in which the wind blows from slightly in front of the beam: *we sailed **on a close reach** directly for Sharp's Island.*

close-run ▶ adjective won or lost by a very small margin: *the motion failed to obtain an absolute majority of 249 but it was **a close-run thing**.*

close season ▶ noun (also **closed season**) Brit. a period in the year when fishing or the killing of particular game is officially forbidden. ■ a part of the year when a particular sport is not played.

close-set ▶ adjective (of two or more things) having little space in between: *a large man with close-set eyes.*

close-stool ▶ noun historical a covered chamber pot enclosed in a wooden stool.

closet ▶ noun **1** chiefly N. Amer. a cupboard or wardrobe, especially one tall enough to walk into. ■ a small room, especially one used for storing things or for private study.
2 archaic a toilet.
3 (**the closet**) used to refer to a state of secrecy or concealment, especially about one's homosexuality: *lesbians who had **come out of the closet**.*
▶ adjective [attrib.] secret; covert: *a closet feminist.*
▶ verb (**closets**, **closeting**, **closeted**) [with obj.] shut (someone) away, especially in private conference or study: *he was closeted with the king | he returned home and closeted himself in his room.*
– ORIGIN late Middle English (denoting a private or small room): from Old French, diminutive of *clos* 'closed' (see CLOSE[1]).

closeted ▶ adjective keeping something secret, especially the fact of being homosexual.

closet play (also **closet drama**) ▶ noun a play to be read rather than acted.

close-up ▶ noun a photograph or film image taken at close range and showing the subject on a large scale: *a close-up of her face | they see themselves **in close-up**.* ■ an intimate and detailed description or study: [as modifier] *the book's close-up account of the violence.*

closing date ▶ noun the last date by which something must be submitted for consideration, especially a job application.

closing order ▶ noun English Law an order by a local authority prohibiting the use of premises for specified purposes.

closing price ▶ noun the price of a security at the end of the day's business in a financial market.

closing time ▶ noun the regular time at which a pub, shop, or other place closes to the public each day.

clostridium /klɒˈstrɪdɪəm/ ▶ noun (pl. **clostridia** /-dɪə/) Biology an anaerobic bacterium of a large genus that includes many pathogenic species, e.g. those causing tetanus, gas gangrene, botulism, and other forms of food poisoning. ● Genus *Clostridium*: typically rod-shaped and Gram-positive.
– DERIVATIVES **clostridial** adjective.
– ORIGIN modern Latin, based on Greek *klōstēr* 'spindle'.

closure ▶ noun [mass noun] **1** an act or process of closing something, especially an institution, thoroughfare, or frontier, or of being closed: *hospitals that face closure |* [count noun] *road closures.* ■ [count noun] a thing that closes or seals something, such as a cap or tie.
2 (in a legislative assembly) a procedure for ending a debate and taking a vote: [as modifier] *a closure motion.*
3 a sense of resolution or conclusion at the end of an artistic work: *he brings modernistic closure to his narrative.* a feeling that an emotional or traumatic experience has been resolved: *I am desperately trying to reach closure but I don't know how to do it without answers from him.*
▶ verb [with obj.] apply the closure to (a debate or speaker) in a legislative assembly.
– ORIGIN late Middle English: from Old French, from late Latin *clausura*, from *claus-* 'closed', from the verb *claudere*.

clot ▶ noun **1** a thick mass of coagulated liquid, especially blood, or of material stuck together: *a blood clot | a clot of dead leaves.*
2 Brit. informal a foolish or clumsy person: *Watch where you're going, you clot!*
▶ verb (**clots**, **clotting**, **clotted**) form or cause to form clots: [no obj.] *drugs that help blood to clot |* [with obj.] *a blood protein known as factor VIII clots blood.* ■ [with obj.] cover (something) with sticky matter: *its nostrils were clotted with blood.*
– ORIGIN Old English *clott, clot*, of Germanic origin; related to German *Klotz*.

clotbur /ˈklɒtbəː/ ▶ noun a herbaceous plant of the daisy family with burred fruits, native to tropical America but now found all over the world. ● Genus *Xanthium*, family Compositae: two or three species. ■ chiefly N. Amer. a burdock.
– ORIGIN mid 16th cent.: from dialect *clote* 'burdock' + BURR.

cloth ▶ noun (pl. **cloths**) **1** [mass noun] woven or felted fabric made from wool, cotton, or a similar fibre: *a broad piece of pleated cloth |* [as modifier] *a cloth bag.*
2 a piece of cloth for cleaning or covering something, e.g. a dishcloth or a tablecloth: *wipe clean with a damp cloth.*
3 (**the cloth**) the clergy; the clerical profession: *has he given up all ideas of the cloth?*
– ORIGIN Old English *clāth*, related to Dutch *kleed* and German *Kleid*, of unknown ultimate origin.

cloth cap ▶ noun Brit. a man's flat woollen cap with a peak. ■ [as modifier] relating to or associated with the working class: *Labour's traditional cloth-cap image.*

clothe ▶ verb (past and past participle **clothed** or archaic or literary **clad**) [with obj.] put clothes on (oneself or someone); dress: *Francesca was **clothed in** white | she took off her shoes and lay down **fully clothed** |* (as adj., with submodifier **clothed**) *a partially clothed body.* ■ provide (someone) with clothes: *they already had eight children to feed and clothe.* ■ (usu. **be clothed with**) endow with a particular quality: *it is clothed with an aura of respectability.*
– ORIGIN Old English (only recorded in the past participle *geclāded*), from *clāth* (see CLOTH).

cloth-eared ▶ adjective Brit. informal unable to hear or understand clearly.

clothes ▶ plural noun **1** items worn to cover the body: *he stripped off his clothes | baby clothes |* [as modifier] *a clothes shop.*
2 bedclothes.
– ORIGIN Old English *clāthas*, plural of *clāth* (see CLOTH).

clothes hanger ▶ noun a coat hanger.

clothes horse ▶ noun a frame on which washed clothes are hung to air indoors. ■ informal, often derogatory a person, typically a woman, who is excessively concerned with wearing fashionable clothes.

clothes line ▶ noun a rope or wire on which washed clothes are hung to dry.
▶ verb (**clothesline**) [with obj.] N. Amer. informal (chiefly in football and other sports) knock down (a runner) by placing one's outstretched arm in their path at neck level.

clothes moth ▶ noun a small, drab moth whose larvae feed on a range of animal fibres and can be destructive to clothing and other domestic textiles. ● Family Tineidae: several species.

clothes peg (N. Amer. also **clothespin**) ▶ noun Brit. a wooden or plastic clip for securing clothes to a clothes line.

clothier /ˈkləʊðɪə/ ▶ noun a person or company that makes or sells clothes or cloth.
– ORIGIN Middle English *clother*, from CLOTH. The change in the ending was due to association with -IER.

clothing ▶ noun [mass noun] clothes collectively: *bring warm clothing and waterproofs.*

Clotho /ˈkləʊθəʊ/ Greek Mythology one of the three Fates.
– ORIGIN Greek, literally 'she who spins'.

cloth of gold ▶ noun [mass noun] fabric made of silk or wool interwoven with gold threads.

clotted cream ▶ noun [mass noun] chiefly Brit. thick cream obtained by heating milk slowly and then allowing it to cool while the cream content rises to the top in coagulated lumps.

C

C

clotting factor ▶ **noun** Physiology any of a number of substances in blood plasma which are involved in the clotting process, such as factor VIII.

cloture /ˈkləʊtjʊə/ ▶ **noun & verb** US term for CLOSURE (sense 2 of the noun).
– ORIGIN late 19th cent.: from French *clôture*, from Old French *closure* (see CLOSURE).

clou /kluː/ ▶ **noun** the chief attraction, point of greatest interest, or central idea of a thing.
– ORIGIN French, literally 'nail'.

cloud ▶ **noun 1** a visible mass of condensed watery vapour floating in the atmosphere, typically high above the general level of the ground: *the sun had disappeared behind a cloud* | [mass noun] *the sky was almost free of cloud.* ■ an indistinct or billowing mass, especially of smoke or dust: ***a cloud of** dust.* ■ a large number of insects or birds moving together: ***clouds of** orange butterflies.* ■ an opaque patch within a transparent substance.
2 used to refer to a state or cause of gloom, suspicion, trouble, or worry: *the only cloud on the immediate horizon is raising a mortgage.*
▶ **verb 1** [no obj.] (of the sky) become overcast or gloomy: *the blue skies **clouded over** abruptly.*
2 make or become less clear or transparent: [with obj.] *blood pumped out, clouding the water* | [no obj.] *her eyes clouded with tears.* ■ [with obj.] make (a matter or mental process) unclear or uncertain: *don't allow your personal feelings to cloud your judgement.* ■ [with obj.] spoil (something): *the general election was clouded by violence.*
3 [no obj.] (of someone's face or eyes) show worry, sorrow, or anger: *his expression clouded over.* ■ [with obj.] (of such an emotion) show in (someone's face): *suspicion clouded her face.*
– PHRASES **every cloud has a silver lining** see SILVER. **on cloud nine** (or **seven**) extremely happy. [with reference to a ten-part classification of clouds in which 'nine' was next to the highest.] **under a cloud** under suspicion or discredited. **with one's head in the clouds** (of a person) out of touch with reality; daydreaming.
– DERIVATIVES **cloudless** adjective, **cloudlessly** adverb, **cloudlet** noun.
– ORIGIN Old English *clūd* 'mass of rock or earth'; probably related to CLOT. Sense 1 of the noun dates from Middle English.

cloud base ▶ **noun** [in sing.] the level or altitude of the lowest part of a general mass of clouds.

cloudberry ▶ **noun** (pl. **cloudberries**) a dwarf bramble with white flowers and edible orange fruit, which grows on the mountains and moorlands of northern Eurasia and northern North America.
● *Rubus chamaemorus*, family Rosaceae.
– ORIGIN late 16th cent.: apparently from the noun CLOUD in the obsolete sense 'hill' + BERRY.

cloudburst ▶ **noun** a sudden violent rainstorm.

cloud chamber ▶ **noun** Physics a device containing air or gas supersaturated with water vapour, used to detect charged particles, X-rays, and gamma rays by the condensation trails which they produce.

cloud computing ▶ **noun** [mass noun] the practice of using a network of remote servers hosted on the Internet to store, manage, and process data, rather than a local server or a personal computer.

cloud cover ▶ **noun** [in sing.] a mass of cloud covering all or most of the sky.

cloud cuckoo land ▶ **noun** [mass noun] a state of absurdly over-optimistic fantasy: *anyone who believes that the Bill will be effective is **living in cloud cuckoo land.***
– ORIGIN late 19th cent.: translation of Greek *Nephelokokkugia*, the name of the city built by the birds in Aristophanes' comedy *Birds*, from *nephelē* 'cloud' + *kokkux* 'cuckoo'.

clouded leopard ▶ **noun** a large spotted cat found in forests in SE Asia. ● *Neofelis nebulosa*, family Felidae.

clouded yellow ▶ **noun** a migratory Old World butterfly which has yellowish wings with black margins.
● Genus *Colias*, family Pieridae: several species, in particular *C. croceus*.

cloud hopping ▶ **noun** [mass noun] the flying of an aircraft from cloud to cloud for concealment.

cloudland ▶ **noun** literary an imaginary or utopian place.

cloudscape ▶ **noun** a large cloud formation considered in terms of its visual effect.
– ORIGIN mid 19th cent.: from CLOUD, on the pattern of words such as *landscape*.

cloud seeding ▶ **noun** [mass noun] the dropping of crystals into clouds to cause rain.

cloudy ▶ **adjective** (**cloudier**, **cloudiest**) **1** (of the sky or weather) covered with or characterized by clouds: *a very grey, cloudy day.*
2 (of a liquid) not transparent or clear: *the pond water is slightly cloudy.* ■ (of a person's eyes) misted with tears: *she stared at him, her eyes cloudy.* ■ uncertain; unclear: *the issue becomes more cloudy.*
– DERIVATIVES **cloudily** adverb, **cloudiness** noun.

Clough /klʌf/, Arthur Hugh (1819–61), English poet. He is especially remembered for longer poems such as *Amours de Voyage* (1858).

clough /klʌf/ ▶ **noun** N. English a steep valley or ravine.
– ORIGIN Old English *clōh* (recorded in place names), of Germanic origin; related to German dialect *Klinge*.

clout ▶ **noun 1** informal a heavy blow with the hand or a hard object: *a clout round the ear.*
2 [mass noun] informal influence or power, especially in politics or business: *I knew she carried a lot of clout.*
3 archaic a piece of cloth or article of clothing.
4 Archery a target twelve times the usual size, placed flat on the ground with a flag marking its centre and used in long-distance shooting.
5 short for CLOUT NAIL.
▶ **verb** [with obj.] **1** informal hit (someone or something) hard: *I clouted him round the head.*
2 archaic mend with a patch.
– PHRASES **ne'er cast a clout till May be out** proverb do not discard your winter clothes until the end of May. [*clout* in CLOUT (sense 3 of the noun).]
– ORIGIN Old English *clūt* (in the sense 'a patch or metal plate'); related to Dutch *kluit* 'lump, clod', also to CLEAT and CLOT. The shift of sense to 'heavy blow', which dates from late Middle English, is difficult to explain; possibly the change occurred first in the verb (from 'put a patch on' to 'hit hard').

clout nail ▶ **noun** a nail with a large flat head, used chiefly for securing roofing felt.

clove[1] ▶ **noun 1** the dried flower bud of a tropical tree, used as an aromatic spice. ■ (**oil of cloves**) [mass noun] aromatic analgesic oil extracted from cloves and used medicinally to relieve dental pain.
2 the Indonesian tree from which cloves are obtained. ● *Syzygium aromaticum* (also called *Eugenia caryophyllus*), family Myrtaceae.
3 (also **clove pink** or **clove gillyflower**) a clove-scented pink which is the original type from which the carnation and other double pinks have been bred. ● *Dianthus caryophyllus*, family Caryophyllaceae.
– ORIGIN Middle English: from Old French *clou de girofle*, literally 'nail of gillyflower' (from its shape), GILLYFLOWER being originally the name of the spice and later applied to the similarly scented pink.

clove[2] ▶ **noun** any of the small bulbs making up a compound bulb of garlic, shallot, etc.
– ORIGIN Old English *clufu*, of Germanic origin, corresponding to the first element of German *Knoblauch* (altered from Old High German *klovolouh*), and the base of CLEAVE[1].

clove[3] past of CLEAVE[1].

clove hitch ▶ **noun** a knot by which a rope is secured by passing it twice round a spar or another rope that it crosses at right angles in such a way that both ends pass under the loop of rope at the front.
– ORIGIN mid 18th cent.: *clove*, past tense of CLEAVE[1] (because the rope appears as separate parallel lines at the back of the knot).

cloven past participle of CLEAVE[1]. ▶ **adjective** split or divided in two.

cloven hoof (also **cloven foot**) ▶ **noun** the divided hoof or foot of ruminants such as cattle, sheep, goats, and deer. ■ a similar foot ascribed to a satyr, the god Pan, or to the Devil, sometimes used as a symbol or mark of the latter.
– DERIVATIVES **cloven-footed** adjective, **cloven-hoofed** adjective.

clove pink ▶ **noun** see CLOVE[1] (sense 3).

clover ▶ **noun** [mass noun] a herbaceous plant of the pea family, with dense globular flower heads and leaves which are typically three-lobed. It is an important fodder and rotational crop. ● Genus *Trifolium*, family Leguminosae: many species.
– PHRASES **in clover** in ease and luxury: *we'll be in clover down there, lying around in the sun and fishing on the lake.*
– ORIGIN Old English *clāfre*, of Germanic origin; related to Dutch *klaver* and German *Klee*.

cloverleaf ▶ **noun** a shape or pattern resembling a leaf of clover. ■ N. Amer. a junction of roads intersecting at different levels with connecting sections forming the pattern of a four-leaved clover.

Clovis[1] /ˈkləʊvɪs/ (465–511), king of the Franks 481–511. He extended Merovingian rule to Gaul and Germany, making Paris his capital. After his conversion to Christianity he championed orthodoxy against the Arian Visigoths, finally defeating them in the battle of Poitiers (507).

Clovis[2] /ˈkləʊvɪs/ ▶ **noun** [usu. as modifier] Archaeology a Palaeo-Indian culture of Central and North America, dated to about 11,500–11,000 years ago and earlier. The culture is distinguished by heavy leaf-shaped stone spearheads (**Clovis points**). Compare with FOLSOM.
– ORIGIN first found near *Clovis* in eastern New Mexico, US.

clown ▶ **noun 1** a comic entertainer, especially one in a circus, wearing a traditional costume and exaggerated make-up. ■ a playful, extrovert person: *Martin was always the class clown.* ■ a foolish or incompetent person: *we need a serious government, not a bunch of clowns.*
2 archaic an unsophisticated country person; a rustic.
▶ **verb** [no obj.] behave in a comical or playful way: *Harvey **clowned around** pretending to be a dog.*
– DERIVATIVES **clownish** adjective, **clownishly** adverb, **clownishness** noun.
– ORIGIN mid 16th cent. (in sense 2 of the noun): perhaps of Low German origin.

clownfish ▶ **noun** (pl. **same** or **clownfishes**) a small tropical marine fish with bold vertical stripes or other bright coloration. It lives in close association with anemones and is protected from their stings by mucus. Also called ANEMONE FISH. ● Genera *Amphiprion* and *Premnas*, family Pomacentridae: several species.

cloy ▶ **verb** [with obj.] (usu. as adj. **cloying**) disgust or sicken (someone) with an excess of sweetness, richness, or sentiment: *a romantic, rather cloying story* | [no obj.] *the first sip gives a malty taste that never cloys.*
– DERIVATIVES **cloyingly** adverb.
– ORIGIN late Middle English: shortening of obsolete *accloy* 'stop up, choke', from Old French *encloyer* 'drive a nail into', from medieval Latin *inclavare*, from *clavus* 'a nail'.

clozapine /ˈkləʊzəpiːn/ ▶ **noun** [mass noun] Medicine a sedative drug of the benzodiazepine group, used to treat schizophrenia.
– ORIGIN mid 20th cent.: from *c(h)lo(ro)-* + elements of BENZODIAZEPINE.

cloze test /kləʊz/ ▶ **noun** a procedure in which a subject is asked to supply words that have been removed from a passage as a test of their ability to comprehend text.
– ORIGIN 1950s: *cloze* representing a spoken abbreviation of CLOSURE.

club[1] ▶ **noun 1** [treated as sing. or pl.] an association dedicated to a particular interest or activity: *I belong to a photographic club* | [as modifier] *the club secretary.* ■ the premises of such an association. ■ an organization offering members social amenities, meals, and temporary residence: *we had dinner at his club.* ■ [usu. with modifier] a commercial organization offering members special benefits: *a shopping club.* ■ [with adj. or noun modifier] a group of people or nations having something in common: *the wild man of the movies refused to join the teetotal club.*
2 [treated as sing. or pl.] an organization constituted to play matches in a particular sport: *a football club.*
3 a nightclub playing fashionable dance music.
▶ **verb** (**clubs**, **clubbing**, **clubbed**) [no obj.] **1** (**club together**) Brit. combine with others so as to collect a sum of money for a particular purpose: *friends and colleagues **clubbed together** to buy him a present.*
2 informal go out to nightclubs: *she enjoys **going clubbing** in Oxford.*
– PHRASES **in the club** (or **the pudding club**) Brit. informal pregnant. **join the club** [in imperative] informal used as an observation that someone else is in a similar difficult situation to oneself: *if you're confused, join the club!*
– DERIVATIVES **clubber** noun informal (sense 2 of the verb).
– ORIGIN early 17th cent. (as a verb): formed obscurely from CLUB[2].

club[2] ▶ **noun 1** a heavy stick with a thick end, used as a weapon. ■ short for GOLF CLUB.
2 (**clubs**) one of the four suits in a conventional pack of playing cards, denoted by a black trefoil. ■ a card of such a suit.
▶ **verb** (**clubs**, **clubbing**, **clubbed**) [with obj.] beat (a person or animal) with a club or similar implement: *the islanders clubbed whales to death.*

– ORIGIN Middle English: from Old Norse *clubba*, variant of *klumba*; related to CLUMP.

clubbable ▸ adjective suitable for membership of a club because of one's sociability or popularity.
– DERIVATIVES **clubbability** noun.

clubby ▸ adjective (**clubbier**, **clubbiest**) informal friendly and sociable with fellow members of a group but not with outsiders.

club car ▸ noun N. Amer. a railway carriage equipped with a lounge and other amenities.

club class ▸ noun [mass noun] Brit. the intermediate class of seating on an aircraft, intended especially for business travellers.

club foot ▸ noun **1** a deformed foot which is twisted so that the sole cannot be placed flat on the ground. Also called TALIPES.
2 a woodland toadstool with a greyish-brown cap, pale yellow gills, and a stem with a swollen woolly base, found in both Eurasia and North America. ● *Clitocybe clavipes*, family Tricholomataceae, class Hymenomycetes.
– DERIVATIVES **club-footed** adjective.

clubhouse ▸ noun a building having a bar and other facilities for the members of a club.

clubland ▸ noun [mass noun] Brit. an area of a town or city with many nightclubs. ■ the world of nightclubs and nightclubbers.

clubman ▸ noun (pl. **clubmen**) a man who is a member of a gentleman's club.

clubmate ▸ noun a fellow member of a sports club.

clubmoss ▸ noun a low-growing flowerless plant that resembles a large moss, having branching stems with undivided leaves. ● Class Lycopsida, division Pteridophyta: three living families, in particular Lycopodiaceae and Selaginellaceae (the **lesser clubmosses**).

clubroot ▸ noun [mass noun] a fungal disease of cabbages, turnips, and related plants, in which the root becomes swollen and distorted by a single large gall or groups of smaller ones. ● The fungus is *Plasmodiophora brassicae*, subdivision Mastigomycotina.

clubrush ▸ noun a tall rush-like water plant of the sedge family. Also called BULRUSH. ● *Scirpus* and related genera, family Cyperaceae, in particular the common *S.* (or *Schoenoplectus*) *lacustris*, used for weaving.

club sandwich ▸ noun a sandwich consisting typically of chicken and bacon, tomato, lettuce, and dressing, with two layers of filling between three slices of bread.

club soda ▸ noun trademark North American term for SODA (sense 1).

cluck ▸ verb [no obj.] (of a hen) make a short, low sound. ■ (of a person) make such a sound with one's tongue to express concern or disapproval: *the bystanders shook their heads and clucked sympathetically* | [with obj.] *Carmichael clucked his tongue irritably*. ■ [no obj.] (**cluck over/around**) express fussy concern about: *Pauline became worried about her health and constantly clucked over her*.
▸ noun **1** the short, low sound made by a hen. ■ a similar sound made by a person to express concern or disapproval: *Loretta gave a cluck of impatience*.
2 N. Amer. informal a foolish person.
– ORIGIN late 15th cent.: imitative, corresponding to Danish *klukke*, Swedish *klucka*.

clucky ▸ adjective Austral./NZ informal (of a hen) sitting or ready to sit on eggs. ■ (of a woman) broody: *Mum's gone clucky*.

clue ▸ noun **1** a piece of evidence or information used in the detection of a crime: *police officers are still searching for clues*. ■ a fact or idea that serves to reveal something or solve a problem: *archaeological evidence can give clues about the past*.
2 a word or words giving an indication as to what is to be inserted in a particular space in a crossword.
▸ verb (**clues**, **clueing**, **clued**) [with obj.] (**clue someone in**) informal inform someone about a particular matter: *Stella had clued her in about Peter*.
– PHRASES **have a clue** [usu. with negative] informal know about something or about how to do something: *I didn't have a clue what was happening*.
– ORIGIN late Middle English: variant of CLEW. The original sense was 'a ball of thread'; hence one used to guide a person out of a labyrinth. Sense 1 of the noun dates from the early 17th cent.

clued-up (N. Amer. **clued-in**) ▸ adjective informal well informed about a particular subject.

clueful ▸ adjective informal having knowledge or understanding of something; well informed: *clueful helpline operators*.

clueless ▸ adjective having no knowledge, understanding, or ability: *you're clueless about how to deal with the world*.
– DERIVATIVES **cluelessly** adverb, **cluelessness** noun.

Cluj–Napoca /kluːʒˈnɑːpɒkə/ a city in west central Romania; pop. 305,620 (2006). The city was founded by 12th-century German-speaking colonists; by the 19th century it belonged to Hungary and was the cultural centre of Transylvania. The name was changed from Cluj in the mid 1970s to incorporate the name of a nearby ancient settlement. Hungarian name **Kolozsvár**; German name **Klausenburg**.

Clumber spaniel /ˈklʌmbə/ ▸ noun a spaniel of a slow, heavily built breed.
– ORIGIN mid 19th cent.: from the name of *Clumber Park*, Nottinghamshire.

clump ▸ noun **1** a small group of trees or plants growing closely together: ***a clump of** ferns*. ■ a small, compact group of people: *they sat on the wall in **clumps of** two and three*. ■ a compacted mass or lump of something: ***clumps of** earth*. ■ Physiology an agglutinated mass of blood cells or bacteria, especially as an indicator of the presence of an antibody to them.
2 another term for CLOMP.
▸ verb [no obj.] **1** form a clump or clumps: *the particles tend to **clump together***.
2 another term for CLOMP.
– ORIGIN Middle English (denoting a heap or lump): partly imitative, reinforced by Middle Low German *klumpe* and Middle Dutch *klompe*, related to CLUB[1].

clumpy ▸ adjective (**clumpier**, **clumpiest**) **1** (also **clompy**) (**clompier**, **clompiest**) Brit. (of shoes or boots) heavy and inelegant.
2 forming or showing a tendency to form clumps.

clumsy ▸ adjective (**clumsier**, **clumsiest**) awkward in movement or in handling things: *the cold made his fingers clumsy*. ■ done awkwardly or without skill: *a very clumsy attempt to park*. ■ difficult to handle or use; unwieldy: *clumsy devices | the legal procedure is far too clumsy*. ■ lacking social skills; tactless: *his choice of words was clumsy*.
– DERIVATIVES **clumsily** adverb, **clumsiness** noun.
– ORIGIN late 16th cent.: from obsolete *clumse* 'make or be numb', probably of Scandinavian origin and related to Swedish *klumsig*.

clunch ▸ noun [mass noun] Brit. soft limestone capable of being easily worked.
– ORIGIN early 19th cent.: perhaps from dialect *clunch* 'lumpy, thickset'.

clung past and past participle of CLING.

Cluniac /ˈkluːnɪak/ ▸ adjective relating to a reformed Benedictine monastic order founded at Cluny in eastern France in 910.
▸ noun a monk of the Cluniac order.

clunk ▸ noun **1** a dull sound such as that made by heavy metal objects striking together.
2 US informal a stupid or foolish person.
▸ verb [no obj.] move with or make such a sound: *the machinery clunked into life*.
– ORIGIN late 18th cent. (originally Scots, as a verb): imitative; compare with CLANK, CLINK[1], and CLONK.

clunker ▸ noun N. Amer. informal a dilapidated vehicle or machine. ■ a thing that is totally unsuccessful: *novel after novel and not a clunker among them*.

clunky ▸ adjective (**clunkier**, **clunkiest**) informal **1** solid, heavy, and old-fashioned: *even last year's laptops look clunky*. ■ (of shoes) clumpy: *clunky Dr Martens*.
2 making a clunking sound: *clunky conveyor belts*.

clupeoid /ˈkluːpɪɔɪd/ Zoology ▸ noun a marine fish of a group that includes the herring family together with the anchovies and related fish. ● Order Clupeiformes or suborder Clupeoidei.
▸ adjective relating to fish of this group.
– ORIGIN mid 19th cent.: from modern Latin *Clupeoidei* (plural), from Latin *clupea*, the name of a river fish.

cluster ▸ noun a group of similar things or people positioned or occurring closely together: ***clusters of** creamy-white flowers | they stood there in a frightened cluster*. ■ (also **consonant cluster**) Linguistics a group of consonants pronounced in immediate succession, as *str* in *strong*. ■ a natural subgroup of a population, used for statistical sampling or analysis. ■ Chemistry a group of atoms of the same element, typically a metal, bonded closely together in a molecule.
▸ verb [no obj.] form a cluster or clusters: *the children **clustered round** her skirts*. ■ Statistics (of data points) have similar numerical values: ***students tended to have marks clustering around** 70 per cent*.
– ORIGIN Old English *clyster*; probably related to CLOT.

cluster bean ▸ noun another term for GUAR.

cluster bomb ▸ noun a bomb which releases a number of projectiles on impact.

clustered ▸ adjective growing or situated in a group: *the spires and clustered roofs of the old town*. ■ Architecture (of pillars or columns) positioned close together, or arranged round or half-detached from a pier.

cluster fly ▸ noun a fly which enters buildings in large numbers while looking for a place to overwinter. ● *Pollenia rudis* (family Calliphoridae), and the smaller *Thaumatomyia notata* (family Chloropidae).

cluster headache ▸ noun a type of severe headache in which the pain is usually limited to one side of the head, tending to recur over a period of several weeks.

cluster pine ▸ noun another term for MARITIME PINE.

clutch[1] ▸ verb [with obj.] grasp (something) tightly: *he stood clutching a microphone* | figurative *Mrs Longhill clutched at the idea*.
▸ noun **1** a tight grasp: *she made a **clutch at** his body*. ■ (**someone's clutches**) a person's power or control, especially when regarded as inescapable: *Tom had fallen into Amanda's clutches*.
2 a mechanism for connecting and disconnecting an engine and the transmission system in a vehicle, or the working parts of any machine. ■ the pedal operating such a mechanism in a vehicle.
3 N. Amer. a clutch bag.
– PHRASES **clutch at straws** see STRAW.
– ORIGIN Middle English (in the sense 'bend, crook'): variant of obsolete *clitch* 'close the hand', from Old English *clyccan* 'crook, clench', of Germanic origin.

clutch[2] ▸ noun a group of eggs fertilized at the same time, laid in a single session and (in birds) incubated together. ■ a brood of chicks. ■ a small group of people or things: ***a clutch of** brightly painted holiday homes*.
– ORIGIN early 18th cent.: probably a southern variant of northern English dialect *cletch*, related to Middle English *cleck* 'to hatch', from Old Norse *klekja*.

clutch bag (N. Amer. **clutch**) ▸ noun a slim, flat handbag without handles or a strap.

Clutha /ˈkluːθə/ a gold-bearing river at the southern end of the South Island, New Zealand. It flows 338 km (213 miles) to the Pacific Ocean.

clutter ▸ verb [with obj.] cover or fill (something) with an untidy collection of things: *the room was **cluttered with** his bric-a-brac*.
▸ noun [mass noun] a collection of things lying about in an untidy state: *the attic is **full of clutter***. ■ [in sing.] an untidy state: *the room was **in a clutter** of smelly untidiness*.
– ORIGIN late Middle English: variant of dialect *clotter* 'to clot', influenced by CLUSTER and CLATTER.

Clwyd /ˈkluːɪd/ a former county of NE Wales, replaced in 1996 by Denbighshire and Flintshire.

Clyde a river in western central Scotland which flows 170 km (106 miles) from the Southern Uplands to the Firth of Clyde, formerly famous for the shipbuilding industries along its banks.

Clyde, Firth of the estuary of the River Clyde in western Scotland which separates southern Scotland to the east from the southern extremities of the Highlands to the north-west.

Clydesdale ▸ noun **1** a horse of a heavy, powerful breed, used for pulling heavy loads.
2 a dog of a small breed of terrier.
– ORIGIN from the name of the area around the River CLYDE in Scotland, where they were originally bred.

clypeus /ˈklɪpɪəs/ ▸ noun (pl. **clypei** /-pɪʌɪ/) Entomology a broad plate at the front of an insect's head.
– ORIGIN mid 19th cent.: from Latin, literally 'round shield'.

clyster /ˈklɪstə/ ▸ noun archaic term for ENEMA.
– ORIGIN late Middle English: from Old French *clystere* or Latin *clyster*, from Greek *klustēr* 'syringe', from *kluzein* 'wash out'.

Clytemnestra /ˌklʌɪtɪmˈnɛstrə/ Greek Mythology wife of Agamemnon. She conspired with her lover Aegisthus to murder Agamemnon on his return from the Trojan War, and was murdered in retribution by her son Orestes and her daughter Electra.

CM ▸ abbreviation ■ command module. ■ common metre. ■ Member of the Order of Canada.

Cm ▸ symbol the chemical element curium.

cm ▸ abbreviation centimetre(s).

Cm. ▸ abbreviation (in the UK) Command Paper (sixth series, 1986–).

C

CMC ▸ abbreviation computer-mediated communication, i.e. communication by means of email, instant messaging, social networking sites, etc.

Cmd. ▸ abbreviation (in the UK) Command Paper (fourth series, 1918–56).

Cmdr ▸ abbreviation Commander.

Cmdre ▸ abbreviation Commodore.

CMEA ▸ abbreviation Council for Mutual Economic Assistance.

CMG ▸ abbreviation (in the UK) Companion (of the Order) of St Michael and St George.

Cmnd. ▸ abbreviation (in the UK) Command Paper (fifth series, 1956–86).

c'mon ▸ contraction come on: *C'mon, it'll be fun!*

CMOS ▸ noun [often as modifier] Electronics a technology for making low power integrated circuits. ▪ a chip built using such technology.
– ORIGIN 1980s: from *Complementary Metal Oxide Semiconductor*.

CMV ▸ abbreviation cytomegalovirus.

CNAA ▸ abbreviation (formerly in the UK) Council for National Academic Awards.

CND ▸ abbreviation (in the UK) Campaign for Nuclear Disarmament.

cnemial crest /ˈ(k)niːmɪəl/ ▸ noun Zoology (in the legs of many mammals, birds, and dinosaurs) a ridge at the front of the head of the tibia or tibiotarsus to which the main extensor muscle of the thigh is attached.
– ORIGIN late 19th cent.: *cnemial*, from Greek *knēmē* 'tibia' + -AL.

CNG ▸ abbreviation compressed natural gas.

Cnidaria /(k)nʌɪˈdɛːrɪə/ ▸ plural noun Zoology a phylum of aquatic invertebrate animals that comprises the coelenterates.
– ORIGIN modern Latin (plural), from Greek *knidē* 'nettle'.

cnidarian Zoology ▸ noun an aquatic invertebrate animal of the phylum Cnidaria, which comprises the coelenterates.
▸ adjective relating to or denoting cnidarians.

CNN ▸ abbreviation Cable News Network.

cnr ▸ abbreviation corner.

CNS ▸ abbreviation central nervous system.

CN Tower a tower in Toronto, Canada, the tallest self-supporting man-made structure in the world when it was completed in 1976. It stands 553 m (1,815 ft) high including a 100 m (328 ft) communications mast.
– ORIGIN CN from Canadian National (Railways).

Cnut variant of CANUTE.

CO ▸ abbreviation ▪ Colombia (international vehicle registration). ▪ Colorado (in official postal use). ▪ Commanding Officer. ▪ conscientious objector.

Co ▸ symbol the chemical element cobalt.

Co. ▸ abbreviation ▪ company: *the Consett Iron Co.* ▪ county: *Co. Cork.*
– PHRASES **and Co.** /kəʊ/ ▪ used as part of the titles of businesses to designate the partner or partners not named. ▪ (also **and co.**) informal and the rest of them: *I waited for Mark and Co. to arrive.*

c/o ▸ abbreviation care of.

co- /kəʊ/ ▸ prefix **1** (forming nouns) joint; mutual; common: *co-driver* | *co-education*.
2 (forming adjectives) jointly; mutually: *coequal*.
3 (forming verbs) together with another or others: *co-produce*.
4 Mathematics of the complement of an angle: *cosine*. ▪ the complement of: *co-latitude*.
– ORIGIN from Latin, originally a form of COM-.

CoA ▸ abbreviation Biochemistry coenzyme A.

coacervate /kəʊˈasəveɪt/ ▸ noun Chemistry a colloid-rich viscous liquid phase which may separate from a colloidal solution on addition of a third component.
– ORIGIN early 20th cent.: back-formation from *coacervation*, based on Latin *cum* '(together) with' + *acervus* 'heap'.

coach¹ ▸ noun **1** Brit. a comfortably equipped single-decker bus used for longer journeys: [as modifier] *a coach trip*.
2 Brit. a railway carriage. ▪ N. Amer. (also **coach class**) the cheapest class of seating in an aircraft or train.
3 a closed horse-drawn carriage.
▸ verb [no obj., with adverbial of direction] travel by coach: *fly or coach to the shores of the Mediterranean.*
▸ adverb N. Amer. in economy class accommodation in an aircraft or train.
– PHRASES **drive a coach and horses through** Brit. make (something) ineffective: *he's driving a coach and horses through our environmental legislation.*
– ORIGIN mid 16th cent. (in sense 3 of the noun): from French *coche*, from Hungarian *kocsi (szekér)* '(wagon) from *Kocs*', a town in Hungary.

coach² ▸ noun an instructor or trainer in sport. ▪ a private tutor who gives extra teaching.
▸ verb [with obj.] train or instruct (a team or player): *he moved on to coach the England team.* ▪ give (someone) extra teaching: *she was coached for stardom by her mother.* ▪ teach (a subject or sport) as a coach: *he teaches history and coaches rugby.* ▪ give (someone) instructions as to what to do or say in a particular situation: *he had improperly coached a witness to testify more credibly.* ▪ give (someone) professional advice on how to attain their goals.
– ORIGIN early 18th cent. (as a verb): figuratively from COACH¹.

coach bolt ▸ noun Brit. a large bolt with a round head, used for fixing wooden panels to masonry or to one another.

coach-built ▸ adjective Brit. (of a vehicle) having specially or individually built bodywork.
– DERIVATIVES **coachbuilder** noun.

coach house ▸ noun a building in which a carriage is or was kept.

coaching inn ▸ noun historical an inn along a route followed by horse-drawn coaches, at which horses could be changed.

coachload ▸ noun Brit. a group of people travelling in a coach: *coachloads of tourists trudging round Oxford.*

coachman ▸ noun (pl. **coachmen**) a driver of a horse-drawn carriage.

coachroof ▸ noun a raised part of the cabin roof of a yacht.

coach station ▸ noun Brit. an area or building from or at which coaches leave or arrive on a regular basis.

coachwhip ▸ noun **1** (also **coachwhip snake**) a harmless fast-moving North American snake, whose scales form a pattern said to resemble a braided whip. ● *Masticophis flagellum*, family Colubridae.
2 (also **coachwhip bird**) Austral. the whipbird.

coachwood ▸ noun a slender tree of the rainforests of Australia and New Guinea, with close-grained timber that is used for cabinetmaking and veneers. ● *Ceratopetalum apetalum*, family Cunoniaceae.

coachwork ▸ noun [mass noun] the bodywork of a road or railway vehicle.

Coade stone /ˈkəʊd/ ▸ noun [mass noun] Brit. an artificial stone claimed to have greater resistance to frost and heat than natural stone, formerly much used for statues, decorative work, etc.
– ORIGIN from the name of the family whose company manufactured the stone.

coadjutor /kəʊˈadʒʊtə/ ▸ noun a bishop appointed to assist and often to succeed a diocesan bishop.
– ORIGIN late Middle English: via Old French from late Latin *coadjutor*, from *co-* (from Latin *cum* 'together with') + *adjutor* 'assistant' (from *adjuvare* 'to help').

coagulant /kəʊˈagjʊlənt/ ▸ noun a substance that causes blood or another liquid to coagulate.
– ORIGIN late 18th cent.: from Latin *coagulant-* 'curdling', from the verb *coagulare* (see COAGULATE).

coagulase /kəʊˈagjʊleɪz, -s/ ▸ noun [mass noun] Biochemistry a bacterial enzyme which brings about the coagulation of blood or plasma and is produced by disease-causing forms of staphylococcus.

coagulate /kəʊˈagjʊleɪt/ ▸ verb [no obj.] (of a fluid, especially blood) change to a solid or semi-solid state: *blood had coagulated round the edges of the gash.* ▪ [with obj.] cause (a fluid) to change to a solid or semi-solid state: *adrenalin coagulates the blood.*
– DERIVATIVES **coagulable** adjective, **coagulation** noun, **coagulative** adjective, **coagulator** noun.
– ORIGIN late Middle English: from Latin *coagulat-* 'curdled', from the verb *coagulare*, from *coagulum* 'rennet'.

coagulum /kəʊˈagjʊləm/ ▸ noun (pl. **coagula** /-lə/) a mass of coagulated matter.
– ORIGIN mid 16th cent. (denoting a coagulant): from Latin, literally 'rennet'.

Coahuila /ˌkəʊəˈwiːlə/ a state of northern Mexico, on the border with the US; capital, Saltillo.

coal ▸ noun [mass noun] a combustible black or dark brown rock consisting chiefly of carbonized plant matter, found mainly in underground seams and used as fuel. ▪ [count noun] Brit. a piece of coal. ▪ [count noun] a red-hot piece of coal or other material in a fire: *the glowing coals.*
▸ verb [with obj.] provide with a supply of coal: (as noun **coaling**) *the coaling and watering of the engine.* ▪ [no obj.] mine or extract coal: *we have now finished coaling at the site.*
– PHRASES **coals to Newcastle** something supplied to a place where it is already plentiful. **haul someone over the coals** Brit. reprimand someone severely.
– DERIVATIVES **coaly** adjective.
– ORIGIN Old English *col* (in the senses 'glowing ember' and 'charred remnant'), of Germanic origin; related to Dutch *kool* and German *Kohle*. The sense 'combustible mineral used as fuel' dates from Middle English.

coal-black ▸ adjective completely black: *a woman with coal-black eyes.*

coaler ▸ noun **1** a ship that transports coal.
2 a large mechanized structure for loading coal on to a ship, railway wagon, or steam locomotive.

coalesce /ˌkəʊəˈlɛs/ ▸ verb [no obj.] come together to form one mass or whole: *the puddles had coalesced into shallow streams.* ▪ [with obj.] combine (elements) in a mass or whole: *his idea served to coalesce all that happened into one connected whole.*
– DERIVATIVES **coalescence** noun, **coalescent** adjective.
– ORIGIN mid 16th cent.: from Latin *coalescere* 'grow together', from *co-* (from *cum* 'with') + *alescere* 'grow up' (from *alere* 'nourish').

coalface ▸ noun an exposed surface of coal in a mine.
– PHRASES **at the coalface** Brit. engaged in work at an active rather than a theoretical level in a particular field.

coalfield ▸ noun an extensive area containing a number of underground coal strata.

coal-fired ▸ adjective using coal as fuel: *a coal-fired power station.*

coalfish ▸ noun (pl. **same** or **coalfishes**) another term for SAITHE.

coal gas ▸ noun [mass noun] a mixture of gases (chiefly hydrogen, methane, and carbon monoxide) obtained by the destructive distillation of coal and formerly used for lighting and heating.

coal-hole ▸ noun Brit. a compartment or small cellar used for storing coal.

coalhouse ▸ noun a building used for storing coal.

coalition /ˌkəʊəˈlɪʃ(ə)n/ ▸ noun a temporary alliance for combined action, especially of political parties forming a government: *a coalition between Liberals and Conservatives* | [mass noun] *they had a taste of government in coalition with the Social Democrats.*
– DERIVATIVES **coalitionist** noun.
– ORIGIN early 17th cent. (in the sense 'fusion'): from medieval Latin *coalitio(n-)*, from the verb *coalescere* (see COALESCE). Usage in politics dates from the late 18th cent.

coalman ▸ noun (pl. **coalmen**) a man who delivers coal to people's houses.

coal measures ▸ plural noun Geology a series of strata of the Carboniferous period, including coal seams.

Coalport ▸ noun [mass noun] a kind of porcelain, frequently decorated with floral designs, produced at Coalport in Shropshire, England, from the late 18th century.

coal pot ▸ noun chiefly W. Indian a cooking device consisting of an iron grid over a raised iron bowl that holds burning charcoal.

Coalsack Astronomy a dark nebula of dust near the Southern Cross that gives the appearance of a gap in the stars of the Milky Way.

coal scuttle ▸ noun a metal container with a sloping lid used to carry coal for a domestic fire.

coal tar ▸ noun [mass noun] a thick black liquid produced by distilling bituminous coal, containing benzene, naphthalene, phenols, aniline, and many other organic chemicals.

coal tit (also **cole tit**) ▸ noun a small Eurasian and North African tit (songbird) with a grey back, black cap and throat, and white cheeks. ● *Parus ater*, family Paridae.

coaming /ˈkəʊmɪŋ/ (also **coamings**) ▸ **noun** a raised border round the cockpit or hatch of a yacht or other boat to keep out water.
– ORIGIN early 17th cent.: of unknown origin.

coaptation /ˌkəʊapˈteɪʃ(ə)n/ ▸ **noun** [mass noun] **1** the adaptation or adjustment of things or people to each other.
2 Medicine the drawing together of the separated tissue in a wound or fracture.
– ORIGIN mid 16th cent.: from late Latin *coaptatio(n-)*, from the verb *coaptare*, from *co-* (from Latin *cum* 'with, together') + *aptare* (from *aptus* 'apt').

coarctate /kəʊˈɑːkteɪt/ ▸ **adjective** chiefly Anatomy & Biology pressed close together; contracted; compressed.
– ORIGIN late Middle English: from Latin *coarctatus*, past participle of *coarctare* 'press or draw together'.

coarctation ▸ **noun** [mass noun] Medicine congenital narrowing of a short section of the aorta.
– ORIGIN late Middle English: from Latin *coarctatio(n-)*, from the verb *coarctare* (see COARCTATE).

coarse ▸ **adjective 1** rough or harsh in texture: *a coarse woollen cloth*. ■ consisting of large grains or particles: *coarse sand*. ■ (of grains or particles) large. ■ (of a person's features) not elegantly formed or proportioned. ■ (of food or drink) of inferior quality.
2 (of a person or their speech) rude or vulgar.
3 Brit. relating to the sport of angling for coarse fish: *coarse anglers*.
– ORIGIN late Middle English (in the sense 'ordinary or inferior'): origin uncertain; until the 17th cent. identical in spelling with COURSE, and possibly derived from the latter in the sense 'ordinary manner'.

coarse fish ▸ **noun** (pl. **same**) Brit. any freshwater fish other than salmon and trout. Compare with GAME FISH.

coarse-grained ▸ **adjective** coarse in texture or grain: *coarse-grained soil*. ■ coarse in manner or speech: *a coarse-grained man*. ■ rough rather than detailed or precise: *a very coarse-grained approximation of what is actually going on*.

coarsely ▸ **adverb 1** in a coarse manner: *Carter laughed coarsely*.
2 into large and irregularly shaped pieces: *chop the mushrooms coarsely | coarsely grated cheese*.

coarsen ▸ **verb 1** make or become rough: [with obj.] *her hands were coarsened by outside work* | [no obj.] *his facial features appeared to coarsen with age*.
2 make or become vulgar or unpleasant: [with obj.] *her experience has not coarsened her or made her cynical*.

coarseness /ˈkɔːsnəs/ ▸ **noun** [mass noun] **1** the quality of being rough or harsh: *the coarseness of her hair*. ■ the quality of being coarse in texture: *you can set the desired coarseness of your flour*.
2 rudeness; vulgarity: *he disliked the coarseness of the men around him*.

coarticulation /ˌkəʊɑːtɪkjʊˈleɪʃ(ə)n/ ▸ **noun** [mass noun] Phonetics the articulation of two or more speech sounds together, so that one influences the other.

coast ▸ **noun 1** the part of the land adjoining or near the sea: *the west coast of Africa | they sailed further up the coast*. ■ (**the Coast**) N. Amer. the Pacific coast of North America.
2 the easy movement of a vehicle without the use of power.
▸ **verb 1** [no obj.] (of a person or vehicle) move easily without using power: *they were coasting down a long hill*. ■ be successful without making much effort: *Colchester* ***coasted to victory***.
2 [no obj., with adverbial of direction] sail along the coast, especially in order to carry cargo: (as adj. **coasting**) *a coasting schooner*.
PHRASES **the coast is clear** there is no danger of being observed or caught.
– ORIGIN Middle English (in the sense 'side of the body'), from Old French *coste* (noun), *costeier* (verb), from Latin *costa* 'rib, flank, side'. Sense 1 of the noun arose from the phrase *coast of the sea* 'side of the sea'.

coastal ▸ **adjective** of or near a coast: *coastal erosion | coastal waters*.

coaster ▸ **noun 1** a small mat for a bottle or glass.
2 a ship used to carry cargo along the coast from port to port.
3 [with adj.] a person who inhabits a specified coast: *a West coaster*.
4 N. Amer. a toboggan.
5 short for ROLLER COASTER.

coastguard ▸ **noun** (**the coastguard**) an organization keeping watch on coastal waters in order to assist people or ships in danger and to prevent smuggling. ■ chiefly Brit. a member of the coastguard organization.

coastland ▸ **noun** [mass noun] (also **coastlands**) an expanse of land near the sea.

coastline ▸ **noun** [mass noun] the land along a coast: *the hotel has wonderful views of the rugged coastline*.

coast to coast ▸ **adjective & adverb** all the way across an island or continent: [as adv.] *the game was telecast coast to coast* | (as adj. **coast-to-coast**) *a coast-to-coast journey*.

coastwise ▸ **adjective & adverb** along or connected with the coast: [as adj.] *a small coastwise steamer* | [as adv.] *the cargo was ferried coastwise*.

coat ▸ **noun 1** an outer garment with sleeves, worn outdoors and typically extending below the hips: *a winter coat* | [as modifier] *his coat pocket*. ■ a protective outer garment worn indoors: *a laboratory coat*. ■ a man's jacket, especially as worn when hunting or by soldiers. ■ a woman's tailored jacket, worn with a skirt or dress.
2 an animal's covering of fur or hair.
3 an outer layer or covering. ■ a single application of paint or similar material on a surface: *apply a final top coat of varnish*. ■ a structure, especially a membrane, enclosing or lining an organ. ■ the skin or husk of a fruit or seed.
▸ **verb** [with obj.] provide with a layer or covering of something: *her right leg was* ***coated in*** *plaster | coat each part with a thin oil* | (as adj., in combination **-coated**) *plastic-coated wire*. ■ (of a substance) form a covering to: *a film of dust coated the floor*.
– ORIGIN Middle English: from Old French *cote*, of unknown ultimate origin.

coat armour ▸ **noun** [mass noun] heraldic arms.

coat check ▸ **noun** N. Amer. a cloakroom with an attendant.
– DERIVATIVES **coat-checker** noun.

coat dress ▸ **noun** a woman's tailored dress that resembles a coat.

coatee /kəʊˈtiː/ ▸ **noun** Brit. a woman's or infant's short coat.

coat hanger ▸ **noun** see HANGER[1] (sense 2).

coati /kəʊˈɑːti/ ▸ **noun** (pl. **coatis**) a raccoon-like animal found mainly in Central and South America, with a long flexible snout and a ringed tail. Also called COATIMUNDI. ● Genera *Nasua* and *Nasuella*, family Procyonidae: three or four species.
– ORIGIN early 17th cent.: from Spanish and Portuguese, from Tupi *kua'ti*, from *cua* 'belt' + *tim* 'nose'.

coatimundi /kəʊˌɑːtɪˈmʌndi/ ▸ **noun** (pl. **coatimundis**) another term for COATI.
– ORIGIN late 17th cent.: from Portuguese, from Tupi *kuatimu'ne*, from *kua'ti* (see COATI) + *mu'ne* 'snare or trick'. The *coatimundi* was originally thought to be a different species from the coati.

coating ▸ **noun 1** a thin layer or covering of something: *a coating of paint*.
2 [mass noun] material used for making coats.

coat of arms ▸ **noun** the distinctive heraldic bearings or shield of a person, family, corporation, or country.

coat of mail ▸ **noun** historical a jacket covered with or composed of metal rings or plates, serving as armour.

coatroom ▸ **noun** N. Amer. a cloakroom.

Coats Land a region of Antarctica, to the east of the Antarctic Peninsula.

coat stand (N. Amer. also **coatrack**) ▸ **noun** a stand with hooks on which to hang coats, hats, etc.

coat-tail ▸ **noun** (usu. **coat-tails**) each of the flaps formed by the back of a tailcoat.
– PHRASES **on someone's coat-tails** undeservedly benefiting from another's success: *he was elected on the coat-tails of his predecessor*.

co-author ▸ **noun** a joint author.
▸ **verb** [with obj.] be a joint author of (a book, paper, or report).

coax[1] /kəʊks/ ▸ **verb** [with obj.] persuade (someone) gradually or by flattery to do something: *the trainees were coaxed into doing boring work* | [with direct speech] *'Come on now,' I coaxed*. ■ (**coax something from/out of**) use such persuasion to obtain something from (someone): *we coaxed our fare money out of my father*. ■ [with obj. and adverbial] arrange (something) carefully into a particular shape or position: *her lovely hair had been coaxed into ringlets*.
– DERIVATIVES **coaxer** noun, **coaxingly** adverb.
– ORIGIN late 16th cent.: from obsolete *cokes* 'simpleton', of unknown origin. The original sense was 'fondle', hence 'persuade by caresses or flattery', the underlying sense being 'make a simpleton of'.

coax[2] /ˈkəʊaks/ informal ▸ **noun** [mass noun] coaxial cable.
▸ **adjective** coaxial.

coaxial /kəʊˈaksɪəl/ ▸ **adjective** having a common axis. ■ (of a cable or line) transmitting by means of two concentric conductors separated by an insulator.
– DERIVATIVES **coaxially** adverb.

C

COB ▸ **abbreviation** close of business: *you have until COB today to show us why you should not be disconnected*.

cob[1] ▸ **noun 1** Brit. a round loaf of bread.
2 (also **corncob**) the central cylindrical woody part of the maize ear to which the grains are attached.
3 (also **cobnut**) a hazelnut or filbert.
4 a powerfully built, short-legged horse.
5 a male swan.
6 Brit. a roundish lump of coal.
– ORIGIN late Middle English (denoting a strong man or leader): of unknown origin. The underlying general sense appears to be 'rounded, sturdy'.

cob[2] ▸ **noun** [mass noun] Brit. a mixture of compressed clay and straw used, especially in former times, for building walls.
– ORIGIN early 17th cent.: of unknown origin.

cob[3] ▸ **noun** (in phrase **have** or **get a cob on**) Brit. informal be or get annoyed.
– ORIGIN 1930s: of unknown origin.

cob[4] ▸ **noun** variant spelling of KOB[2].

cobalamin /kə(ʊ)ˈbaləmɪn/ ▸ **noun** Biochemistry any of a group of cobalt-containing substances including cyanocobalamin (vitamin B_{12}).
– ORIGIN 1950s: blend of COBALT and VITAMIN.

cobalt /ˈkəʊbɔːlt, -ɒlt/ ▸ **noun** [mass noun] the chemical element of atomic number 27, a hard silvery-white magnetic metal. (Symbol: **Co**) ■ cobalt blue: [as modifier] *a cobalt sky*.

> Cobalt is chiefly obtained as a by-product from nickel and copper ores. It is a transition metal similar in many respects to nickel and is mainly used as a component of magnetic alloys and those designed for use at high temperatures.

– DERIVATIVES **cobaltous** /kə(ʊ)ˈbɔːltəs, -ˈbɒlt-/ adjective.
– ORIGIN late 17th cent.: from German *Kobalt* 'imp, demon' (because the presence of cobalt-bearing ore made it more difficult to extract silver, and miners believed that it was harmful to the silver ore with which it occurred).

cobalt blue ▸ **noun** [mass noun] a deep blue pigment containing cobalt and aluminium oxides. ■ the deep blue colour of this pigment.

cobber ▸ **noun** Austral./NZ informal a companion or friend (often used as a form of address between men): *G'day cobbers!*
– ORIGIN late 19th cent.: perhaps related to English dialect *cob* 'take a liking to'.

Cobbett, William (1763–1835), English writer and political reformer. He started his political life as a Tory, but later became a radical and in 1802 founded the periodical *Cobbett's Political Register*. Notable works: *Rural Rides* (1830).

cobble[1] ▸ **noun** a small round stone used to cover road surfaces.
– ORIGIN late Middle English: from COB[1] + -LE[2].

cobble[2] ▸ **verb** [with obj.] **1** (**cobble something together**) roughly assemble or produce something from available parts or elements: *the film was imperfectly cobbled together from two separate stories*.
2 dated repair (shoes).
– ORIGIN late 15th cent.: back-formation from COBBLER.

cobbled ▸ **adjective** (of an area or roadway) paved with cobbles.

cobbler ▸ **noun 1** a person whose job is mending shoes.
2 [mass noun] an iced drink made with wine or sherry, sugar, and lemon.
3 chiefly N. Amer. a fruit pie with a rich, thick, cake-like crust.
4 (**cobblers**) Brit. informal a man's testicles. [from rhyming slang *cobbler's awls* 'balls'.] ■ nonsense: *I thought it was* ***a load of cobblers***.
5 Austral./NZ informal the last sheep to be shorn. [late 19th cent.: pun in allusion to the cobbler's last.]
– PHRASES **let the cobbler stick to his last** proverb people should only concern themselves with things they know something about. [translating Latin *ne sutor ultra crepidam*.]
– ORIGIN Middle English: of unknown origin.

cobblestone ▶ noun another term for COBBLE[1].

cobby ▶ adjective (of horses, dogs, and other animals) shortish and thickset; stocky.

Cobden /ˈkɒbd(ə)n/, Richard (1804–65), English political reformer, one of the leading spokesmen of the free-trade movement in Britain. From 1838, together with John Bright, he led the Anti-Corn-Law League in its successful campaign for the repeal of the Corn Laws (1846).

COBE /ˈkəʊbi/ a NASA satellite launched in 1989 to map the background microwave radiation in a search for evidence of the Big Bang.
– ORIGIN abbreviation of *Cosmic Background Explorer*.

co-belligerent ▶ noun any of two or more nations engaged in war as allies.
– DERIVATIVES **co-belligerence** noun.

cobia /ˈkəʊbɪə/ ▶ noun (pl. **same**) a large edible game fish that lives in open waters of the Atlantic, Indian, and West Pacific oceans. Also called SERGEANT FISH.
● *Rachycentron canadum*, family Rachycentridae.
– ORIGIN mid 19th cent.: of unknown origin.

coble /ˈkəʊb(ə)l/ ▶ noun a flat-bottomed fishing boat of a type used in Scotland and NE England.
– ORIGIN Old English, perhaps of Celtic origin and related to Welsh *ceubal* ‘ferry boat, skiff’.

cobnut ▶ noun see COB[1] (sense 3).

COBOL /ˈkəʊbɒl/ ▶ noun [mass noun] a computer programming language designed for use in commerce.
– ORIGIN 1960s: from *co(mmon) b(usiness) o(riented) l(anguage)*.

cobra /ˈkəʊbrə, ˈkɒbrə/ ▶ noun a highly venomous African or Asian snake that spreads the skin of its neck into a hood when disturbed. ● *Naja* and two other genera, family Elapidae: several species, in particular the **spectacled cobra**.
– ORIGIN mid 17th cent.: from Portuguese *cobra de capello*, literally ‘snake with hood’, based on Latin *colubra* ‘snake’.

co-branded ▶ adjective (of a product or service) marketed under or carrying two or more brand names.
– DERIVATIVES **co-branding** noun.

cobweb ▶ noun a spider's web, especially when old and dusty. ■ Zoology a tangled three-dimensional spider's web. ■ something resembling a cobweb in delicacy or intricacy: *the city fans south in a cobweb of canals*.
– PHRASES **blow** (or **clear**) **away the cobwebs** banish a state of lethargy; refresh oneself.
– DERIVATIVES **cobwebbed** adjective, **cobwebby** adjective.
– ORIGIN Middle English *coppeweb*, *copweb*, from obsolete *coppe* ‘spider’ + WEB.

coca /ˈkəʊkə/ ▶ noun a tropical American shrub grown for its leaves, which are the source of cocaine.
● *Erythroxylum coca*, family Erythroxylaceae.
■ [mass noun] the dried leaves of the coca shrub, which are mixed with lime and chewed as a stimulant by the indigenous people of western South America.
– ORIGIN late 16th cent.: from Spanish, from Aymara *kuka* or Quechua *koka*.

Coca-Cola ▶ noun [mass noun] trademark a carbonated non-alcoholic drink.
– ORIGIN late 19th cent.: from COCA and COLA.

cocaine /kə(ʊ)ˈkeɪn/ ▶ noun [mass noun] an addictive drug derived from coca or prepared synthetically, used as an illegal stimulant and sometimes medicinally as a local anaesthetic. ● Chem. formula: $C_{17}H_{21}NO_4$.
– ORIGIN mid 19th cent.: from COCA + -INE[4].

coccidia /kɒkˈsɪdɪə/ ▶ plural noun Biology parasitic protozoa of a group that includes those that cause diseases such as coccidiosis and toxoplasmosis. ● Suborder Eimeriorina, phylum Sporozoa.
– DERIVATIVES **coccidian** adjective & noun.
– ORIGIN mid 19th cent.: from modern Latin (former order name), from Greek *kokkis*, diminutive of *kokkos* ‘berry’.

coccidioidomycosis /kɒkˌsɪdɪˌɔɪdəʊmʌɪˈkəʊsɪs/ ▶ noun [mass noun] a serious fungal disease of the lungs and other tissues, endemic in the warmer, arid regions of America. ● The fungus is *Coccidioides immitis*, subdivision Deuteromycotina.
– ORIGIN 1930s: from modern Latin *Coccidioides* (part of the binomial of the fungus) + MYCOSIS.

coccidiosis /kɒkˌsɪdɪˈəʊsɪs/ ▶ noun [mass noun] a disease of birds and mammals that chiefly affects the intestines, caused by coccidia.
– ORIGIN late 19th cent.: from *coccidium* (singular of modern Latin *Coccidia*; see COCCIDIA) + -OSIS.

coccinellid /ˌkɒksɪˈnɛlɪd/ ▶ noun Entomology a beetle of a family (Coccinellidae) that includes the ladybirds.
– ORIGIN late 19th cent.: from modern Latin *Coccinellidae* (plural), from the genus name *Coccinella*, from Latin *coccineus* ‘scarlet’.

coccolith /ˈkɒkəlɪθ/ ▶ noun Biology a minute rounded calcareous platelet, numbers of which form the spherical shells of coccolithophores.
– ORIGIN mid 19th cent.: from Greek *kokkos* ‘grain or berry’ + *lithos* ‘stone’.

coccolithophore /ˌkɒkə(ʊ)ˈlɪθəfɔː/ ▶ noun Biology a single-celled marine flagellate that secretes a calcareous shell, forming an important constituent of the phytoplankton. ● Order Coccolithophorida, phylum Haptophyta.
– DERIVATIVES **coccolithophorid** noun & adjective.

coccus /ˈkɒkəs/ ▶ noun (pl. **cocci** /ˈkɒk(s)ʌɪ, ˈkɒk(s)iː/) Biology any spherical or roughly spherical bacterium.
– DERIVATIVES **coccal** adjective, **coccoid** adjective.
– ORIGIN mid 18th cent. (denoting a scale insect): modern Latin, from Greek *kokkos* ‘berry’. Compare with COCHINEAL.

coccyx /ˈkɒksɪks/ ▶ noun (pl. **coccyges** /-ɪdʒiːz/ or **coccyxes**) a small triangular bone at the base of the spinal column in humans and some apes, formed of fused vestigial vertebrae.
– DERIVATIVES **coccygeal** /kɒkˈsɪdʒɪəl/ adjective.
– ORIGIN late 16th cent.: via Latin from Greek *kokkux* ‘cuckoo’ (because the shape of the human bone resembles the cuckoo's bill).

Cochabamba /ˌkɒtʃəˈbambə/ a city in Bolivia, situated at the centre of a rich agricultural region; pop. 611,056 (2009).

co-chair ▶ noun a person who chairs a meeting jointly with another or others.
▶ verb [with obj.] chair (a meeting) in this way.

Cochin[1] /ˈkəʊtʃɪn, ˈkɒtʃɪn/ former name for KOCHI.

Cochin[2] /ˈkəʊtʃɪn, ˈkɒtʃɪn/ (also **Cochin China**) ▶ noun a chicken of an Asian breed with feathery legs.

Cochin-China /ˈkəʊtʃɪn, ˈkɒtʃɪn/ the former name for the southern region of what is now Vietnam. Part of French Indo-China from 1862, in 1946 it became a French overseas territory, then merged officially with Vietnam in 1949.

cochineal /ˌkɒtʃɪˈniːl, ˈkɒtʃɪniːl/ ▶ noun **1** [mass noun] a scarlet dye used for colouring food, made from the crushed dried bodies of a female scale insect. ■ a similar dye made from the oak kermes insect (see KERMES).
2 (**cochineal insect**) the scale insect that is used for cochineal, native to Mexico and formerly cultivated on cacti. ● *Dactylopius coccus*, family Dactylopiidae, suborder Homoptera.
– ORIGIN late 16th cent.: from French *cochenille* or Spanish *cochinilla*, from Latin *coccinus* ‘scarlet’, from Greek *kokkos* ‘berry’ (the insect bodies were mistaken for grains or berries). Compare with COCCUS, KERMES.

cochlea /ˈkɒklɪə/ ▶ noun (pl. **cochleae** /-klɪiː/) the spiral cavity of the inner ear containing the organ of Corti, which produces nerve impulses in response to sound vibrations.
– DERIVATIVES **cochlear** adjective.
– ORIGIN mid 16th cent. (used to denote spiral objects): from Latin, ‘snail shell or screw’, from Greek *kokhlias*. The current sense dates from the late 17th cent.

cochoa /ˈkəʊtʃəʊə, kəˈtʃəʊə/ ▶ noun an Asian thrush of evergreen forests, typically with predominantly purplish or green plumage and a pale blue crown.
● Genus *Cochoa*, family Turdidae: four species.
– ORIGIN modern Latin, from a Nepali name.

Cochran[1] /ˈkɒkrən/, Sir Charles Blake (1872–1951), English theatrical producer, noted for musical revues including Noël Coward's *Bitter Sweet* (1929) and *Cavalcade* (1931). He was also agent for Houdini.

Cochran[2] /ˈkɒkrən/, Eddie (1938–60), American rock-and-roll singer and songwriter; born *Edward Cochrane*. He was killed in a car crash during a British tour. Notable songs: ‘Summertime Blues’ (1958), ‘Three Steps to Heaven’ (1960).

cock[1] ▶ noun **1** Brit. a male bird, especially of a domestic fowl. ■ [in combination] used in names of birds, especially game birds, e.g. **watercock**. ■ Brit. a male lobster, crab, or salmon. ■ Brit. informal a friendly form of address among men: *please yourself, cock*.
2 vulgar slang a man's penis.
3 [mass noun] Brit. informal nonsense: *that's all a lot of cock*.
4 a firing lever in a gun which can be raised to be released by the trigger.
5 a stopcock.
▶ verb [with obj.] **1** tilt (something) in a particular direction: *she cocked her head slightly to one side*. ■ bend a (limb or joint) at an angle: *Madge threw herself into the armchair and cocked her legs over the side*. ■ (of a male dog) lift (a back leg) in order to urinate.
2 raise the cock of (a gun) in order to make it ready for firing.
3 (**cock something up**) Brit. informal ruin something as a result of incompetence or inefficiency: *the party cocked up the Euro-elections*.
– PHRASES **at full cock** (of a gun) with the cock lifted to the position at which the trigger will act. **cock one's ear** (of a dog) raise its ears to an erect position. ■ (of a person) listen attentively to or for something. **cock one's eye** glance in a quizzical or knowing manner with a raised eyebrow. **cock of the walk** someone who dominates others within a group. **cock a snook** see SNOOK[1].
– ORIGIN Old English *cocc*, from medieval Latin *coccus*; reinforced in Middle English by Old French *coq*.

cock[2] ▶ noun dated a small pile of hay, straw, or other material, with vertical sides and a rounded top.
▶ verb [with obj.] archaic pile (hay or other material) into such a shape.
– ORIGIN late Middle English: perhaps of Scandinavian origin and related to Norwegian *kok* ‘heap, lump’, Danish *kok* ‘haycock’, and Swedish *koka* ‘clod’.

cockabully /ˈkɒkəbʊli/ ▶ noun (pl. **cockabullies**) NZ a small blunt-nosed freshwater fish related to the sleepers. ● Genus *Gobiomorphus*, family Gobiidae (or Eleotridae).
– ORIGIN late 19th cent.: from Maori *kokopu*.

cockade /kɒˈkeɪd/ ▶ noun a rosette or knot of ribbons worn in a hat as a badge of office, or as part of a livery.
– DERIVATIVES **cockaded** adjective.
– ORIGIN mid 17th cent.: from French *cocarde*, originally in *bonnet à la coquarde*, from the feminine of obsolete *coquard* ‘saucy’.

cock-a-doodle-doo ▶ exclamation used to represent the sound made by a cock when it crows.

cock-a-hoop ▶ adjective extremely and obviously pleased, especially about an achievement.
– ORIGIN mid 17th cent.: from the phrase *set cock a hoop*, of unknown origin, apparently denoting the action of turning on the tap and allowing liquor to flow (prior to a drinking session).

cock-a-leekie ▶ noun [mass noun] a soup traditionally made in Scotland with chicken and leeks.
– ORIGIN mid 18th cent.: from COCK[1] and LEEK.

cockalorum /ˌkɒkəˈlɔːrəm/ ▶ noun (pl. **cockalorums**) informal, dated a self-important man.
– ORIGIN early 18th cent.: an arbitrary formation from COCK[1].

cockamamie /ˈkɒkəˌmeɪmi/ (also **cockamamy**) ▶ adjective N. Amer. informal ridiculous; implausible: *a cockamamie theory*.
– ORIGIN 1940s (originally denoting a design left by a transfer): probably an alteration of DECALCOMANIA.

cock and bull story ▶ noun informal an implausible story used as an explanation or excuse.

cockapoo /kɒkəˈpuː/ ▶ noun a dog that is a crossbreed of an American cocker spaniel and a miniature poodle.

cockatiel /ˌkɒkəˈtiːl/ ▶ noun a slender long-crested Australian parrot related to the cockatoos, with a mainly grey body, white shoulders, and a yellow and orange face. ● *Nymphicus hollandicus*, family Cacatuidae (or Psittacidae).
– ORIGIN late 19th cent.: from Dutch *kaketielje*, probably a diminutive of *kaketoe* ‘cockatoo’.

cockatoo /kɒkəˈtuː/ ▶ noun **1** a parrot with an erectile crest, found in Australia, eastern Indonesia, and neighbouring islands. ● Family Cacatuidae (or Psittacidae): several genera and numerous species.
2 Austral./NZ informal a small-scale farmer.
3 Austral./NZ informal a lookout posted by those engaged in illegal activity.
– ORIGIN mid 17th cent.: from Dutch *kaketoe*, from Malay *kakatua*, the spelling influenced by COCK[1]. Sense 2, sense 3 date from the 19th cent.

cockatrice /ˈkɒkətrʌɪs, -trɪs/ ▶ noun another term for BASILISK (sense 1). ■ Heraldry a mythical animal depicted as a two-legged dragon (or wyvern) with a cock's head.
– ORIGIN late Middle English: from Old French *cocatris*, from Latin *calcatrix* ‘tracker’ (from *calcare*

'to tread or track'), translating Greek *ikhneumōn* (see ICHNEUMON).

cockboat ▸ noun a small boat towed behind a larger vessel.
– ORIGIN late Middle English: from obsolete *cock* 'small boat' (from Old French *coque*, based on Latin *caudex*, *codex* 'block of wood') + BOAT.

cockchafer /ˈkɒkˌtʃeɪfə/ ▸ noun a large brown European beetle which flies at dusk and is a destructive plant pest, both as an adult and a larva. Also called MAY BUG. ● *Melolontha melolontha*, family Scarabaeidae.
– ORIGIN early 18th cent.: from COCK[1] (expressing size or vigour) + CHAFER.

Cockcroft, Sir John Douglas (1897–1967), English physicist. In 1932 he succeeded (with E. T. S. Walton) in splitting the atom, ushering in the whole field of nuclear and particle physics. Nobel Prize for Physics (1951, shared with Walton).

cockcrow ▸ noun literary dawn.

cocked hat ▸ noun a brimless triangular hat pointed at the front, back, and top. ■ historical a hat with a wide brim permanently turned up towards the crown, such as a tricorne.
– PHRASES **knock something into a cocked hat** utterly defeat or outdo something.

cocker (also **cocker spaniel**) ▸ noun a small spaniel of a breed with a silky coat.
– ORIGIN early 19th cent.: from COCK[1] + -ER[1] (the dog was bred to flush out game birds such as woodcock).

cockerel ▸ noun a young domestic cock.
– ORIGIN Middle English: diminutive of COCK[1].

Cockerell, Sir Christopher Sydney (1910–99), English engineer, the inventor of the hovercraft.

cockeyed ▸ adjective informal **1** crooked or askew; not level: *cockeyed camera angles*. ■ absurd; impractical: *do you expect us to believe a cockeyed story like that?*
2 (of a person or their eyes) having a squint.
– ORIGIN early 19th cent.: apparently from the verb COCK[1] and EYE.

cockfighting ▸ noun [mass noun] the sport (illegal in the UK and some other countries) of setting two cocks to fight each other.
– DERIVATIVES **cockfight** noun.

cockle[1] ▸ noun **1** an edible burrowing bivalve mollusc with a strong ribbed shell. ● Genus *Cardium*, family Cardiidae.
2 (also **cockleshell**) literary a small, shallow boat.
– PHRASES **warm the cockles of one's heart** give one a comforting feeling of contentment.
– ORIGIN Middle English: from Old French *coquille* 'shell', based on Greek *konkhulion*, from *konkhē* 'conch'.

cockle[2] ▸ verb [no obj.] (of paper) form wrinkles or puckers.
– ORIGIN mid 16th cent.: from French *coquiller* 'blister (bread in cooking)', from *coquille* 'shell' (see COCKLE[1]).

cocklebur ▸ noun a herbaceous plant of the daisy family with broad leaves and burred fruits, native to tropical America. ● Genus *Xanthium*, family Compositae: two or three species.
– ORIGIN mid 19th cent.: from COCKLE[2] + BURR.

cockling ▸ noun [mass noun] Brit. the activity or occupation of gathering cockles.
– DERIVATIVES **cockler** noun.

cockloft ▸ noun a small upper loft under the ridge of a roof.

cockney /ˈkɒkni/ ▸ noun (pl. **cockneys**) **1** a native of East London, traditionally one born within hearing of Bow Bells. ■ [mass noun] the dialect or accent typical of cockneys.
2 Austral. a young snapper fish (*Chrysophrys auratus*).
▸ adjective of or characteristic of cockneys or their dialect or accent: *cockney humour*.
– ORIGIN late Middle English (denoting a pampered child): origin uncertain; it is apparently not the same word as Middle English *cokeney* 'cock's egg', denoting a small misshapen egg (probably from COCK[1] + obsolete *ey* 'egg'). A later sense was 'a town-dweller regarded as affected or puny', from which the current sense arose in the early 17th cent.

cockneyism ▸ noun a feature or style of speech or idiom characteristic of cockneys.

cock-of-the-rock ▸ noun (pl. **cocks-of-the-rock**) a crested cotinga (bird) found in the tropical forests of South America. The male has brilliant orange or red plumage used in communal display. ● Genus *Rupicola*, family Cotingidae: two species.

cockpit ▸ noun **1** a compartment for the pilot, and sometimes also the crew, in an aircraft or spacecraft. ■ the driver's compartment in a racing car. ■ a space for the helmsman in some small yachts.
2 a place where cockfights are held. ■ a place where a battle or other conflict takes place.
– ORIGIN late 16th cent. (in sense 2): from COCK[1] + PIT[1]. Sense 1 dates from the early 20th cent. and derives from an early 18th-cent. nautical term denoting an area in the aft lower deck of a man-of-war where the wounded were taken, later coming to mean 'the pit' or well from which a yacht is steered'; hence the place housing the controls of other vehicles.

cockroach /ˈkɒkrəʊtʃ/ ▸ noun a beetle-like scavenging insect with long antennae and legs. Several tropical kinds have become established worldwide as household pests. ● Suborder Blattodea, order Dictyoptera: many genera and species, including the **common cockroach** (*Blatta orientalis*) and the **American cockroach** (*Periplaneta americana*).
– ORIGIN early 17th cent. (as *cacaroch*): from Spanish *cucaracha*. The spelling change was due to association with COCK[1] and ROACH[1].

cockscomb ▸ noun **1** the crest or comb of a domestic cock.
2 (also **coxcomb**) a tropical plant with a crest of tiny yellow, orange, or red flowers, grown as a pot plant. ● *Celosia cristata*, family Amaranthaceae.
3 a brightly coloured orchid of southern North America, related to the coralroots. Also called CORALROOT. ● Genus *Hexalectris*, family Orchidaceae.

cocksfoot ▸ noun (pl. **cocksfoots**) Brit. a pasture grass with broad leaves and green or purplish flowering spikes. ● *Dactylis glomerata*, family Gramineae.

cockshy /ˈkɒkʃʌɪ/ ▸ noun (pl. **cockshies**) Brit. dated a target for throwing sticks or stones at as a game. ■ an object of ridicule or criticism.
– ORIGIN from the original use of a replica of a cockerel as a target.

cocksman ▸ noun (pl. **cocksmen**) US vulgar slang a man who is reputed to be extremely virile or sexually accomplished.

cock sparrow ▸ noun dated a lively, quarrelsome person.

cockspur ▸ noun **1** the spur on the leg of a cock.
2 Austral. a European plant of the daisy family with yellow thistle-like flower heads that has become naturalized in Australia. ● *Centaurea melitensis*, family Compositae.

cockspur thorn ▸ noun a North American hawthorn which is grown for its rich orange autumn foliage. ● *Crataegus crus-galli*, family Rosaceae.

cocksucker ▸ noun vulgar slang, chiefly N. Amer. a contemptible person (used as a general term of abuse).
– DERIVATIVES **cocksucking** adjective.

cocksure ▸ adjective confident in an excessive or arrogant way.
– DERIVATIVES **cocksurely** adverb, **cocksureness** noun.
– ORIGIN early 16th cent.: from archaic *cock* (a euphemism for *God*) + SURE; later associated with COCK[1].

cocktail ▸ noun **1** an alcoholic drink consisting of a spirit or spirits mixed with other ingredients, such as fruit juice or cream: [as modifier] *a cocktail bar*. ■ a mixture of substances or factors, especially when dangerous or unpleasant: *he was killed by a cocktail of drink and drugs*.
2 a dish consisting of small pieces of food, typically served cold as an hors d'oeuvre: *a prawn cocktail*.
– ORIGIN early 17th cent.: from COCK[1] + TAIL[1]. The original use was as an adjective describing a creature with a tail like that of a cock, specifically a horse with a docked tail; hence (because hunters and coach-horses were generally docked) a racehorse which was not a thoroughbred, having a cock-tailed horse in its pedigree (early 19th cent.). Sense 1 (originally US, also early 19th cent.) is perhaps analogous, from the idea of an adulterated spirit.

cocktail dress ▸ noun a smart dress suitable for formal social occasions.

cocktail stick ▸ noun Brit. a small pointed stick on which olives, cherries, or similar items of food may be served.

cock-teaser /ˈkɒktiːzə/ (also **cock-tease**) ▸ noun vulgar slang a woman who leads a man to the mistaken belief that she is likely to have sexual intercourse with him.

cock-up ▸ noun Brit. informal something done badly or inefficiently: *we've made a total cock-up of it*.

cocky[1] ▸ adjective (**cockier**, **cockiest**) conceited or confident in a bold or cheeky way.
– DERIVATIVES **cockily** adverb, **cockiness** noun.
– ORIGIN mid 16th cent. (in the sense 'lecherous'): from COCK[1] + -Y[1].

cocky[2] ▸ noun (pl. **cockies**) Austral./NZ informal term for COCKATOO.

coco ▸ noun (pl. **cocos**) **1** [usu. as modifier] coconut: *a coco palm*.
2 [mass noun] W. Indian the root of the taro.
– ORIGIN mid 16th cent. (originally denoting the nut): from Spanish and Portuguese, literally 'grinning face' (because of the appearance of the base of the coconut).

cocoa ▸ noun [mass noun] a powder made from roasted and ground cacao seeds. ■ a hot drink made from cocoa powder mixed with milk or water.
– PHRASES **I should cocoa** (or **coco**) Brit. rhyming slang I should say so.
– ORIGIN early 18th cent. (denoting cacao seed): alteration of CACAO.

cocoa bean ▸ noun a cacao seed.

cocoa butter ▸ noun [mass noun] a fatty substance obtained from cocoa beans, used in the manufacture of confectionery and cosmetics.

cocoanut ▸ noun old-fashioned spelling of COCONUT.

cocobolo /ˌkəʊkə(ʊ)ˈbəʊləʊ/ ▸ noun (pl. **cocobolos**) a tropical American tree with hard reddish timber that is used to make cutlery handles. ● *Dalbergia retusa*, family Leguminosae.
– ORIGIN mid 19th cent.: via Spanish from Arawak *kukubuli*.

coco de mer /ˌkəʊkəʊdəˈmɛː/ ▸ noun a tall palm tree native to the Seychelles. Also called DOUBLE COCONUT. ● *Lodoicea maldivica*, family Palmae.
■ the immense nut of this palm tree, which is encased in a hard woody shell and is the largest known seed.
– ORIGIN early 19th cent.: from French *coco-de-mer*, literally 'coco from the sea' (because the tree was first known from nuts found floating in the sea).

coconut ▸ noun **1** the large oval brown seed of a tropical palm, consisting of a hard woody husk surrounded by fibre, lined with edible white flesh and containing a clear liquid. ■ [mass noun] the flesh of a coconut, often used as food.
2 (also **coconut palm** or **tree**) the tall palm tree that yields the coconut, which has become naturalized throughout the tropics. The tree is also a source of copra, coir, and other products. ● *Cocos nucifera*, family Palmae.

coconut butter ▸ noun [mass noun] a solid fat obtained from the flesh of the coconut, and used in the manufacture of soap, candles, ointment, etc.

coconut crab ▸ noun another term for ROBBER CRAB.
– ORIGIN so named because it climbs trees to reach coconuts.

coconut ice ▸ noun [mass noun] Brit. a sweet made from sugar and desiccated coconut.

coconut matting ▸ noun [mass noun] matting made of fibre from coconut husks.

coconut milk ▸ noun [mass noun] the watery white liquid found inside a coconut.

coconut palm ▸ noun see COCONUT (sense 2).

coconut shy ▸ noun Brit. a fairground sideshow where balls are thrown at coconuts in an attempt to knock them off stands.

cocoon /kəˈkuːn/ ▸ noun **1** a silky case spun by the larvae of many insects for protection as pupae.
■ something that envelops someone in a protective or comforting way: ***a cocoon of** bedclothes* | figurative ***a** warm **cocoon of** love*.
2 a covering that prevents the corrosion of metal equipment.
▸ verb [with obj.] **1** envelop in a protective or comforting way: *we felt cold even though we were **cocooned in** our sleeping bags* | figurative *we remain **cocooned in** our own little world of fantasies*. ■ [no obj.] N. Amer. retreat from the stressful conditions of public life into the cosy private world of the family: *Americans are spending more time cocooning at home*.
2 spray with a protective coating.
– DERIVATIVES **cocooner** noun.
– ORIGIN late 17th cent.: from French *cocon*, from medieval Provençal *coucoun* 'eggshell, cocoon', diminutive of *coca* 'shell'. The verb dates from the mid 19th cent.

Cocos Islands /ˈkəʊkəs/ a group of twenty-seven small coral islands in the Indian Ocean, administered as an external territory of Australia since 1955; pop. 600 (est. 2009). The islands were discovered in 1609

C

by Captain William Keeling of the East India Company. Also called **Keeling Islands**.

cocotte /kɒˈkɒt/ ▶ **noun 1** (usu. in phrase **en cocotte** /ɒ̃ kɒˈkɒt/) a small heatproof dish in which individual portions of food can be cooked and served. [early 20th cent.: from French *cocasse*, from Latin *cucuma* 'cooking container'.]
2 dated a fashionable prostitute. [mid 19th cent.: French, from a child's name for a hen.]

C

co-counselling ▶ **noun** [mass noun] a form of personal or psychological counselling in which two or more people alternate the roles of therapist and patient.

cocoyam /ˈkəʊkəʊjam/ ▶ **noun** (in West Africa) either of two plants of the arum family with edible corms, i.e. taro (also **old cocoyam**) and tannia (also **new cocoyam**).
– ORIGIN early 20th cent.: probably from **coco** (sense 2) + **yam**.

Cocteau /ˈkɒktəʊ/, Jean (1889–1963), French dramatist, novelist, and film director. His plays are noted for their striking blend of poetry, irony, and fantasy. Notable works: *La Machine infernale* (play, 1934), *La Belle et la bête* (film, 1946), and *Les Enfants terribles* (novel, 1929).

cocus wood /ˈkəʊkəs/ ▶ **noun** [mass noun] hard, heavy timber which blackens with age and is used for musical instruments. ● This timber is obtained from the Jamaican ebony (*Brya ebenus*, family Leguminosae).
– ORIGIN mid 17th cent.: *cocus*, of unknown origin.

COD ▶ **abbreviation** ■ cash on delivery. ■ N. Amer. collect on delivery.

cod¹ (also **codfish**) ▶ **noun** (pl. **same**) a large marine fish with a small barbel on the chin. ● Family Gadidae (the **cod family**): many genera and species, in particular the North Atlantic *Gadus morhua*, of great importance as a food fish. The cod family also includes the haddock, ling, pollack, whiting, and other food fishes.
■ used in names of similar or related fishes, e.g. **rock cod**, **tomcod**.
– ORIGIN Middle English: of unknown origin; one suggestion is that the word is the same as Old English *cod(d)* 'bag', because of the fish's appearance.

cod² Brit. informal ▶ **adjective** not authentic; fake: *a cod Mittel-European accent*.
▶ **noun 1** a joke or hoax.
2 Irish a foolish person: *he's making a cod of himself*.
▶ **verb** (**cods, codding, codded**) [with obj.] play a joke or trick on (someone): *he was definitely codding them*.
– ORIGIN late 17th cent. (denoting a person of a specified kind): of uncertain origin.

cod³ ▶ **noun** [mass noun] Brit. informal, dated nonsense.
– ORIGIN 1960s: abbreviation of **codswallop**.

coda /ˈkəʊdə/ ▶ **noun** Music the concluding passage of a piece or movement, typically forming an addition to the basic structure. ■ the concluding section of a dance, especially of a pas de deux or the finale of a ballet in which the dancers parade before the audience. ■ a concluding event, remark, or section: *his new novel is a kind of coda to his previous books*.
– ORIGIN mid 18th cent.: Italian, from Latin *cauda* 'tail'.

coddle ▶ **verb** [with obj.] **1** treat (someone) in an indulgent or overprotective way: *I was coddled and cosseted*.
2 cook (an egg) in water below boiling point.
– DERIVATIVES **coddler** noun.
– ORIGIN late 16th cent. (in the sense 'boil (fruit) gently'): origin uncertain; sense 1 is probably a dialect variant of obsolete *caudle* 'administer invalids' gruel', based on Latin *caldum* 'hot drink', from *calidus* 'warm'.

code ▶ **noun 1** a system of words, letters, figures, or symbols used to represent others, especially for the purposes of secrecy: *the Americans cracked their diplomatic code* | [mass noun] *messages written in code*. ■ a phrase or concept used to represent another in an indirect way: *researching 'the family' is usually a code for studying women*. ■ a series of letters, numbers, or symbols assigned to something for the purposes of classification or identification. ■ short for **dialling code**.
2 [mass noun] Computing program instructions: *assembly code*.
3 a systematic collection of laws or statutes: *a revision of the penal code*. ■ a set of conventions or moral principles governing behaviour in a particular sphere: *a strict dress code* | *a stern code of honour*.
▶ **verb** [with obj.] **1** convert (the words of a message) into a code so as to convey a secret meaning: *only Mitch knew how to read the message—even the name was coded*. ■ express the meaning of (a statement) in an indirect way: (as adj. **coded**) *journalists made coded allusions to his deficiencies*. ■ assign a code to (something) for purposes of classification or identification: *she coded the samples and sent them for dissection*.
2 write code for (a computer program).
3 [no obj.] (**code for**) Biochemistry be the genetic code for (an amino acid or protein): *genes that code for human growth hormone*. ■ be the genetic determiner of (a characteristic).
– PHRASES **bring something up to code** N. Amer. renovate or update an old building in line with the latest building regulations.
– DERIVATIVES **coder** noun.
– ORIGIN Middle English: via Old French from Latin *codex, codic-* (see **codex**). The term originally denoted a systematic collection of statutes made by Justinian or another of the later Roman emperors; compare with sense 3 of the noun (mid 18th cent.), the earliest modern sense.

codebreaker ▶ **noun** a person who solves a code or codes.
– DERIVATIVES **codebreaking** noun.

codec /ˈkəʊdɛk/ ▶ **noun** a device or program that compresses data to enable faster transmission and decompresses received data.
– ORIGIN 1960s: blend of *coder* (see **code**) and *decoder* (see **decode**).

codeine /ˈkəʊdiːn/ ▶ **noun** [mass noun] Medicine a sleep-inducing and analgesic drug derived from morphine.
● Chem. formula: $C_{18}H_{21}NO_3$.
– ORIGIN mid 19th cent.: from Greek *kōdeia* 'poppy head' + **-ine⁴**.

code name ▶ **noun** a word used for secrecy or convenience instead of the usual name.
– DERIVATIVES **code-named** adjective.

codependency ▶ **noun** [mass noun] excessive emotional or psychological reliance on a partner, typically one with an illness or addiction who requires support.
– DERIVATIVES **codependence** noun, **codependent** adjective & noun.

code-sharing ▶ **noun** [mass noun] agreement between two or more airlines to list certain flights in a reservation system under each other's names.
– DERIVATIVES **code-share** verb.

co-determination ▶ **noun** [mass noun] cooperation between management and workers in decision-making, especially by the representation of workers on management boards.

codex /ˈkəʊdɛks/ ▶ **noun** (pl. **codices** /ˈkəʊdɪsiːz, ˈkɒd-/ or **codexes**) **1** an ancient manuscript text in book form.
2 an official list of medicines, chemicals, etc.
– ORIGIN late 16th cent. (denoting a collection of statutes): from Latin, literally 'block of wood', later denoting a block split into leaves or tablets for writing on, hence a book.

codfish ▶ **noun** (pl. **same** or **codfishes**) another term for **cod¹**.

codger ▶ **noun** informal, derogatory an elderly man: ***old codgers*** *harping on about yesteryear*.
– ORIGIN mid 18th cent.: perhaps a variant of *cadger* (see **cadge**).

codices plural form of **codex**.

codicil /ˈkɒdɪsɪl, ˈkəʊ-/ ▶ **noun** an addition or supplement that explains, modifies, or revokes a will or part of one.
– ORIGIN late Middle English: from Latin *codicillus*, diminutive of *codex, codic-* (see **codex**).

codicology /ˌkəʊdɪˈkɒlədʒi/ ▶ **noun** [mass noun] the study of manuscripts and their interrelationships.
– DERIVATIVES **codicological** adjective.
– ORIGIN 1950s: from French *codicologie*, from Latin *codex, codic-* (see **codex**).

codify /ˈkəʊdɪfʌɪ/ ▶ **verb** (**codifies, codifying, codified**) [with obj.] arrange (laws or rules) into a systematic code. ■ arrange according to a plan or system: *this would codify existing intergovernmental cooperation on drugs*.
– DERIVATIVES **codification** noun, **codifier** noun.

coding ▶ **noun** [mass noun] **1** the process of assigning a code to something for classification or identification. ■ [count noun] a code assigned for such a purpose.
2 Biochemistry the process of coding genetically for an amino acid, protein, or characteristic.

codling¹ ▶ **noun** an immature cod.

codling² ▶ **noun** any of several varieties of cooking apple having a long tapering shape.
– ORIGIN late Middle English: from Anglo-Norman French *quer de lion* 'lionheart'.

codling moth ▶ **noun** a small greyish moth whose larvae feed on apples. ● *Cydia pomonella*, family Tortricidae.

cod liver oil ▶ **noun** [mass noun] oil pressed from the liver of cod, which is rich in vitamins D and A.

codology /kɒˈdɒlədʒi/ ▶ **noun** [mass noun] Irish informal foolish or untrue talk or writing; nonsense.

codomain /ˈkəʊdə(ʊ)meɪn/ ▶ **noun** Mathematics a set that includes all the possible values of a given function.

codon /ˈkəʊdɒn/ ▶ **noun** Biochemistry a sequence of three nucleotides which together form a unit of genetic code in a DNA or RNA molecule.
– ORIGIN 1960s: from **code** + **-on**.

codpiece ▶ **noun** a pouch attached to a man's breeches or close-fitting hose to cover the genitals, worn in the 15th and 16th centuries.
– ORIGIN from earlier *cod* 'scrotum' (from Old English *codd* 'bag, pod') + **piece**.

co-driver ▶ **noun** a person who shares the driving of a vehicle with another, especially in a race or rally.

codswallop ▶ **noun** [mass noun] Brit. informal nonsense.
– ORIGIN 1960s: perhaps named after Hiram *Codd*, who invented a bottle for fizzy drinks (1875); the derivation remains unconfirmed.

cod war ▶ **noun** informal any of several disputes between Britain and Iceland in the period 1958–76, concerning fishing rights in waters around Iceland.

Cody /ˈkəʊdi/, William Frederick, see **Buffalo Bill**.

Coe, Sebastian, Baron Coe of Ranmore (b.1956), British middle-distance runner and Conservative politician, an Olympic gold medal winner in the 1,500 metres in 1980 and 1984.

coecilian ▶ **noun** variant spelling of **caecilian**.

coed /ˈkəʊɛd, kəʊˈɛd/ informal ▶ **noun** N. Amer. dated a female student at a co-educational institution.
▶ **adjective** (of an institution or system) co-educational.

co-education ▶ **noun** [mass noun] the education of pupils of both sexes together.
– DERIVATIVES **co-educational** adjective.

coefficient /ˌkəʊɪˈfɪʃ(ə)nt/ ▶ **noun 1** Mathematics a numerical or constant quantity placed before and multiplying the variable in an algebraic expression (e.g. *4* in $4x^y$).
2 Physics a multiplier or factor that measures a particular property: *the drag coefficient*.
– ORIGIN mid 17th cent. (in the sense 'cooperating to produce a result'): from modern Latin *coefficient-*, from *com-* 'together' + *efficient-* 'accomplishing' (see **efficient**).

coelacanth /ˈsiːləkanθ/ ▶ **noun** a large bony marine fish with a three-lobed tail fin and fleshy pectoral fins. It was known only from fossils until one was found alive in 1938; since then others have been found near the Comoro Islands in the Indian Ocean and off Sulawesi, Indonesia. ● *Latimeria chalumnae*, family Latimeriidae (or Coelacanthidae), subclass Crossopterygii.
– ORIGIN mid 19th cent.: from modern Latin *Coelacanthus* (genus name), from Greek *koilos* 'hollow' + *akantha* 'spine' (its fins have hollow spines).

-coele ▶ **combining form** variant spelling of **-cele**.

coelenterate /siːˈlɛnt(ə)rət, -reɪt/ ▶ **noun** Zoology an aquatic invertebrate animal of a phylum that includes jellyfishes, corals, and sea anemones. They typically have a tube- or cup-shaped body with a single opening ringed with tentacles that bear stinging cells (nematocysts). Also called **cnidarian**.
● Phylum Cnidaria (formerly Coelenterata): four classes.
– ORIGIN late 19th cent.: from modern Latin *Coelenterata*, from Greek *koilos* 'hollow' + *enteron* 'intestine'.

coeliac /ˈsiːlɪak/ (US **celiac**) ▶ **adjective 1** Anatomy relating to the abdomen.
2 Medicine relating to or affected by coeliac disease.
▶ **noun** Medicine a person with coeliac disease.
– ORIGIN mid 17th cent.: from Latin *coeliacus*, from Greek *koiliakos*, from *koilia* 'belly'.

coeliac disease ▶ **noun** [mass noun] a disease in which the small intestine is hypersensitive to gluten, leading to difficulty in digesting food.

coelom /ˈsiːləm/ ▶ **noun** (pl. **coeloms** or **coelomata** /-ˈləʊmətə/) Zoology the principal body cavity in most animals, located between the intestinal canal and the body wall.
– DERIVATIVES **coelomate** adjective & noun, **coelomic** /sɪˈlɒmɪk/ adjective.
– ORIGIN late 19th cent.: from Greek *koilōma* 'cavity'.

coelostat /ˈsiːlə(ʊ)stat/ ▶ **noun** Astronomy an instrument with a rotating mirror that continuously reflects the

light from the same area of sky, used for monitoring the path of a celestial object.
– ORIGIN late 19th cent.: formed irregularly from Latin *caelum* 'sky' + -STAT.

coelurosaur /sɪˈljʊərəsɔː/ ▶ noun a small, slender bipedal carnivorous dinosaur with long forelimbs, believed to be an evolutionary ancestor of birds. ● Infraorder Coelurosauria, suborder Theropoda, order Saurischia: many genera.
– ORIGIN 1950s: from Greek *koilos* 'hollow' + *oura* 'tail' + *sauros* 'lizard'.

coenobite ▶ noun variant spelling of CENOBITE.

coenocyte /ˈsiːnəsʌɪt/ ▶ noun Botany a body of algal or fungal cytoplasm containing several nuclei, enclosed in a single membrane.
– DERIVATIVES **coenocytic** /-ˈsɪtɪk/ adjective.
– ORIGIN early 20th cent.: from Greek *koinos* 'common' + -CYTE.

coenzyme /ˈkəʊˌɛnzʌɪm/ ▶ noun Biochemistry a non-protein compound that is necessary for the functioning of an enzyme.

coenzyme A ▶ noun [mass noun] Biochemistry a coenzyme derived from pantothenic acid, important in respiration and other biochemical reactions.
– ORIGIN *A* from *acylation* (see ACYLATE).

coenzyme Q ▶ noun another term for UBIQUINONE.
– ORIGIN *Q* from QUINONE.

coequal ▶ adjective having the same rank or importance: *coequal partners*.
▶ noun a person or thing equal with another.
– DERIVATIVES **coequality** /kəʊɪˈkwɒlɪti/ noun.
– ORIGIN late Middle English: from Latin *coaequalis* 'of the same age', from *co-* 'jointly' + *aequalis* (see EQUAL).

coerce /kəʊˈəːs/ ▶ verb [with obj.] persuade (an unwilling person) to do something by using force or threats: *he was coerced into giving evidence*. ■ obtain (something) by such means: *their confessions were allegedly coerced by torture*.
– DERIVATIVES **coercible** adjective.
– ORIGIN late Middle English: from Latin *coercere* 'restrain', from *co-* 'together' + *arcere* 'restrain'.

coercion /kəʊˈəːʃ(ə)n/ ▶ noun [mass noun] the action or practice of persuading someone to do something by using force or threats: *it wasn't slavery because no coercion was used*.

coercive ▶ adjective relating to or using force or threats: *coercive measures*.
– DERIVATIVES **coercively** adverb, **coerciveness** noun.

coercive force ▶ noun Physics another term for COERCIVITY.

coercivity /ˌkəʊəˈsɪvɪti/ ▶ noun [mass noun] Physics the resistance of a magnetic material to changes in magnetization, equivalent to the field intensity necessary to demagnetize the fully magnetized material.

coeternal ▶ adjective existing with something else eternally: *creation is not **coeternal with** God*.

Coetzee /kʊtˈsɪə/, J. M. (b.1940), South African novelist; full name *John Maxwell Coetzee*. He won the Booker Prize with *Life and Times of Michael K* (1983) and *Disgrace* (1999), becoming the first author to win the prize twice, and in 2003 was awarded the Nobel Prize for Literature.

coeval /kəʊˈiːv(ə)l/ ▶ adjective having the same age or date of origin; contemporary: *these lavas were coeval with the volcanic activity*.
▶ noun a person of roughly the same age as oneself; a contemporary.
– DERIVATIVES **coevality** noun, **coevally** adverb.
– ORIGIN early 17th cent. (as a noun): from late Latin *coaevus*, from *co-* 'jointly' + Latin *aevum* 'age'.

co-evolution ▶ noun [mass noun] Biology the influence of closely associated species on each other in their evolution.
– DERIVATIVES **co-evolutionary** adjective, **co-evolve** verb.

coexist ▶ verb [no obj.] exist at the same time or in the same place: *dwarf mammoths may have survived in north-east Siberia to coexist with the Egyptian pharaohs*. ■ (of nations or peoples) exist in harmony despite different ideologies or interests: *the task of diplomacy was to help different states to coexist*.
– DERIVATIVES **coexistence** noun, **coexistent** adjective.
– ORIGIN mid 17th cent.: from late Latin *coexistere*, from *co-* 'together' + *existere* 'exist', from *ex-* 'out' + *sister* 'take a stand'.

coextensive ▶ adjective extending over the same area, extent, or time. ■ (of a term) denoting the same referent as another.

cofactor ▶ noun **1** a contributory cause of a disease.
2 Biochemistry a substance (other than the substrate) whose presence is essential for the activity of an enzyme.
3 Mathematics the quantity obtained from a determinant or a square matrix by removal of the row and column containing a specified element.

C of E ▶ abbreviation Church of England.

coffee ▶ noun [mass noun] **1** a hot drink made from the roasted and ground bean-like seeds of a tropical shrub: *a cup of coffee* | [as modifier] *a coffee pot*. ■ [count noun] a cup of coffee: *we went out for a coffee*. ■ coffee seeds roasted and ground, or a powder made from them: *a jar of instant coffee*. ■ a pale brown colour like that of milky coffee: ***coffee-coloured** skin*.
2 the shrub which yields coffee seeds, native to the Old World tropics. ● Genus *Coffea*, family Rubiaceae: several species.
– ORIGIN late 16th cent.: from Turkish *kahveh*, from Arabic *qahwa*, probably via Dutch *koffie*.

coffee bar ▶ noun a bar or cafe serving coffee and light refreshments.

coffee bean ▶ noun a bean-like seed of the coffee shrub.

coffee break ▶ noun a short break during the working day, during which people typically drink a cup of coffee or tea.

coffee cake ▶ noun N. Amer. a cake or sweet bread flavoured with cinnamon or topped or filled with cinnamon sugar, eaten usually with coffee.

coffee cup ▶ noun a cup, typically a small one, in which coffee is served.

coffee essence ▶ noun [mass noun] Brit. a concentrated extract of coffee, usually also containing chicory.

coffee house ▶ noun **1** a place serving coffee and other refreshments.
2 N. Amer. a place where coffee is served and people gather for poetry readings, music, and other informal entertainment.

coffee klatch (also **coffee klatsch** /ˈkɒfi klatʃ/) ▶ noun another term for KAFFEEKLATSCH.

coffee morning ▶ noun Brit. a morning social gathering at which coffee is served, typically one held in someone's house to raise money for charity.

coffee pot ▶ noun a tall covered pot with a spout, in which coffee is made or served.

coffee shop ▶ noun a small, informal restaurant, as found in a hotel or department store. ■ a cafe serving coffee and light refreshments.

coffee table ▶ noun a small, low table.

coffee-table book ▶ noun a large, expensive, lavishly illustrated book, intended especially for casual reading.

coffer ▶ noun **1** a strongbox or small chest for holding valuables. ■ (**coffers**) the funds or financial reserves of an organization: *there is not enough money in the coffers to finance the reforms*.
2 a decorative sunken panel in a ceiling.
– DERIVATIVES **coffered** adjective (sense 2).
– ORIGIN Middle English: from Old French *coffre* 'chest', via Latin from Greek *kophinos* 'basket'.

cofferdam ▶ noun a watertight enclosure pumped dry to permit construction work below the waterline, as when building bridges or repairing a ship.

cofferer ▶ noun historical one of the treasurers of the royal household.

coffin ▶ noun a long, narrow box, typically of wood, in which a dead body is buried or cremated. ■ informal an old and unsafe aircraft or ship.
▶ verb (**coffins, coffining, coffined**) [with obj.] put (a dead body) in a coffin.
– ORIGIN Middle English (in the general sense 'box, casket'): from Old French *cofin* 'little basket or case', from Latin *cophinus* (see COFFER).

coffin bone ▶ noun the terminal bone in a horse's hoof (the distal phalanx).

coffin nail ▶ noun informal a cigarette.

coffle /ˈkɒf(ə)l/ ▶ noun literary a line of animals or slaves fastened or driven along together.
– ORIGIN mid 18th cent.: from Arabic *qāfila* 'caravan'.

coffret /ˈkɒfrɪt/ ▶ noun a small box or container.
– ORIGIN late 15th cent.: from Old French, 'small chest', diminutive of *coffre* (see COFFER).

co-founder ▶ noun a joint founder.
– DERIVATIVES **co-found** verb.

cog¹ ▶ noun a wheel or bar with a series of projections on its edge, which transfers motion by engaging with projections on another wheel or bar. ■ each of such a series of projections.
– PHRASES **a cog in the** (or **a**) **machine** (or **wheel**) a small or insignificant member of a larger organization or system: *copywriters have been seen as just a cog in the big advertising machine*.
– DERIVATIVES **cogged** adjective.
– ORIGIN Middle English: probably of Scandinavian origin and related to Swedish *kugge* and Norwegian *kug*.

C

cog² ▶ noun a broadly built medieval ship with a rounded prow and stern.
– ORIGIN Middle English: related to Middle Dutch *kogge*, Old French *cogue*.

cog³ ▶ verb [with obj.] Irish informal copy (someone else's work) illicitly or without acknowledgement: *he's away cogging his homework from Aggie's wee girl*.
– ORIGIN mid 16th cent. (in senses 'practise tricks in throwing dice' and 'cheat'): of unknown origin.

cogency /ˈkəʊdʒ(ə)nsi/ ▶ noun [mass noun] the quality of being clear, logical, and convincing; lucidity: *the cogency of this argument*.

cogeneration ▶ noun [mass noun] the generation of electricity and useful heat jointly, especially the utilization of the steam left over from electricity generation for heating.

cogent /ˈkəʊdʒ(ə)nt/ ▶ adjective (of an argument or case) clear, logical, and convincing.
– DERIVATIVES **cogently** adverb.
– ORIGIN mid 17th cent.: from Latin *cogent-* 'compelling', from the verb *cogere*, from *co-* 'together' + *agere* 'drive'.

cogitable ▶ adjective rare able to be grasped by the mind; conceivable.
– ORIGIN late Middle English: from Latin *cogitabilis*, from the verb *cogitare* (see COGITATE).

cogitate /ˈkɒdʒɪteɪt/ ▶ verb [no obj.] formal think deeply about something; meditate or reflect: *he stroked his beard and retired to cogitate*.
– DERIVATIVES **cogitative** adjective, **cogitator** noun.
– ORIGIN late 16th cent.: from Latin *cogitat-* 'considered', from the verb *cogitare*, from *co-* 'together' + *agitare* 'turn over, consider'.

cogitation /kɒdʒɪˈteɪʃ(ə)n/ ▶ noun [mass noun] the action of thinking deeply about something; contemplation: *Sorry, did I interrupt your cogitation?*

cogito /ˈkəʊgɪtəʊ, -dʒɪ-/ ▶ noun (usu. **the cogito**) Philosophy the principle establishing the existence of a being from the fact of its thinking or awareness.
– ORIGIN Latin, 'I think', in Descartes's formula (1641) *cogito, ergo sum* 'I think therefore I am'.

cognac /ˈkɒnjak/ ▶ noun [mass noun] a high-quality brandy, strictly speaking that distilled in Cognac in western France.

cognate /ˈkɒgneɪt/ ▶ adjective **1** Linguistics (of a word) having the same linguistic derivation as another (e.g. English *father*, German *Vater*, Latin *pater*).
2 formal related; connected: *cognate subjects such as physics and chemistry*. ■ related to or descended from a common ancestor. Compare with AGNATE.
▶ noun **1** Linguistics a cognate word.
2 Law a blood relative, especially on the mother's side.
– ORIGIN early 17th cent.: from Latin *cognatus*, from *co-* 'together with' + *natus* 'born'.

cognate object ▶ noun Grammar a direct object that has the same linguistic derivation as the verb which governs it, as in 'sing a song'. ■ a direct object that makes explicit a semantic concept that is already present in the semantics of the verb which governs it, as in 'eat some food'.

cognition /kɒgˈnɪʃ(ə)n/ ▶ noun [mass noun] the mental action or process of acquiring knowledge and understanding through thought, experience, and the senses. ■ [count noun] a perception, sensation, idea, or intuition resulting from this.
– DERIVATIVES **cognitional** adjective.
– ORIGIN late Middle English: from Latin *cognitio*(-), from *cognoscere* 'get to know'.

cognitive /ˈkɒgnɪtɪv/ ▶ adjective relating to cognition.
– DERIVATIVES **cognitively** adverb.
– ORIGIN late 16th cent.: from medieval Latin *cognitivus*, from *cognit-* 'known', from the verb *cognoscere*.

cognitive behavioural therapy (also **cognitive therapy**) ▶ noun [mass noun] a type of psychotherapy in which negative patterns of thought about the self and the world are challenged in order to alter unwanted behaviour patterns or treat mood disorders such as depression.

cognitive dissonance ▶ **noun** [mass noun] Psychology the state of having inconsistent thoughts, beliefs, or attitudes, especially as relating to behavioural decisions and attitude change.

cognitive grammar ▶ **noun** [mass noun] a theory of grammar that seeks to characterize, in a psychologically realistic way, those structures and abilities that constitute a speaker's grasp of linguistic convention, and to relate them to other cognitive processes.

cognitive map ▶ **noun** a mental representation of one's physical environment.

cognitive science ▶ **noun** [mass noun] the study of thought, learning, and mental organization, which draws on aspects of psychology, linguistics, philosophy, and computer modelling.
– DERIVATIVES **cognitive scientist** noun.

cognitivist ▶ **noun** a person who believes or works in cognitive grammar.
▶ **adjective** relating to cognitive grammar.
– DERIVATIVES **cognitivism** noun.
– ORIGIN 1950s (in the sense 'believing that moral judgements are true or false statements about moral facts'): from **COGNITIVE** + **-IST**.

cognizable /ˈkɒ(g)nɪzəb(ə)l/ (also **cognisable**) ▶ **adjective 1** formal perceptible; clearly identifiable.
2 Law within the jurisdiction of a court.
– ORIGIN late 17th cent.: from **COGNIZANCE** + **-ABLE**.

cognizance /ˈkɒ(g)nɪz(ə)ns/ (also **cognisance**) ▶ **noun 1** [mass noun] formal knowledge or awareness: *the Renaissance cognizance of Greece was limited.* ■ Law the action of taking judicial notice.
2 Heraldry a distinctive emblem or badge formerly worn by retainers of a noble house.
– PHRASES **take cognizance of** formal attend to; take account of.
– ORIGIN Middle English *conisance*, from Old French *conoisance*, based on Latin *cognoscere* 'get to know'. The spelling with *g*, influenced by Latin, arose in the 15th cent. and gradually affected the pronunciation.

cognizant /ˈkɒ(g)nɪz(ə)nt/ (also **cognisant**) ▶ **adjective** formal having knowledge or awareness: *statesmen must be **cognizant of** the political boundaries within which they work.*
– ORIGIN early 19th cent.: probably directly from **COGNIZANCE**.

cognize /kɒgˈnʌɪz/ (also **cognise**) ▶ **verb** [with obj.] formal know or become aware of.
– ORIGIN early 19th cent.: from **COGNIZANCE**, on the pattern of words such as *recognize*.

cognomen /kɒgˈnəʊmən/ ▶ **noun** an extra personal name given to an ancient Roman citizen, functioning rather like a nickname and typically passed down from father to son. ■ a name; a nickname.
– ORIGIN Latin, from *co-* 'together with' + *gnomen*, *nomen* 'name'.

cognoscenti /ˌkɒgnəˈʃɛnti, ˌkɒnjəˈʃɛnti/ ▶ **plural noun** people who are especially well informed about a particular subject: *it's worth taking a tip from the fashion cognoscenti.*
– ORIGIN late 18th cent.: Italian, literally 'people who know', from Latin *cognoscent-* 'getting to know', from the verb *cognoscere*.

cog railway ▶ **noun** another term for **RACK RAILWAY**.

cogwheel ▶ **noun** another term for **COG**[1].

cohabit ▶ **verb** (**cohabits, cohabiting, cohabited**) [no obj.] **1** live together and have a sexual relationship without being married.
2 coexist: *animals that can **cohabit with** humans thrive.*
– DERIVATIVES **cohabitant** noun, **cohabitation** noun, **cohabitee** noun, **cohabiter** noun.
– ORIGIN mid 16th cent.: from Latin *cohabitare*, from *co-* 'together' + *habitare* 'dwell'.

Cohen /ˈkəʊən/, Leonard (b.1934), Canadian singer, songwriter, poet, and novelist. His works include the poetry collection *Let Us Compare Mythologies* (1956) and the album *The Songs of Leonard Cohen* (1968).

cohen ▶ **noun** variant spelling of **KOHEN**.

cohere /kə(ʊ)ˈhɪə/ ▶ **verb** [no obj.] **1** form a unified whole: *he made the series of fictions **cohere into** a convincing sequence.*
2 (of an argument or theory) be logically consistent: *this view does not **cohere with** their other beliefs.*
– ORIGIN mid 16th cent.: from Latin *cohaerere*, from *co-* 'together' + *haerere* 'to stick'.

coherence ▶ **noun** [mass noun] **1** the quality of being logical and consistent: *this raises further questions on the coherence of state policy.*
2 the quality of forming a unified whole: *the group began to lose coherence and the artists took separate directions.*
– DERIVATIVES **coherency** noun.

coherent ▶ **adjective 1** (of an argument, theory, or policy) logical and consistent: *they failed to develop a coherent economic strategy.* ■ (of a person) able to speak clearly and logically: *she was lucid and coherent and did not appear to be injured.*
2 forming a unified whole: *the arts could be systematized into one coherent body of knowledge.*
3 Physics (of waves) having a constant phase relationship.
– DERIVATIVES **coherently** adverb.
– ORIGIN mid 16th cent. (in the sense 'logically related to'): from Latin *cohaerent-* 'sticking together', from the verb *cohaerere* (see **COHERE**).

coherer /kə(ʊ)ˈhɪːrə/ ▶ **noun** an early form of radio detector consisting of a glass tube loosely filled with metal filings whose bulk electrical resistance decreased in the presence of radio waves.

cohesion /kə(ʊ)ˈhiːʒ(ə)n/ ▶ **noun** [mass noun] the action or fact of forming a united whole: *the work at present lacks cohesion.* ■ Physics the sticking together of particles of the same substance.
– ORIGIN mid 17th cent.: from Latin *cohaes-* 'cleaved together', from the verb *cohaerere* (see **COHERE**), on the pattern of *adhesion*.

cohesive ▶ **adjective** characterized by or causing cohesion.
– DERIVATIVES **cohesively** adverb, **cohesiveness** noun.

Cohn /kəʊn/, Ferdinand Julius (1828–98), German botanist, a founder of bacteriology and the first to devise a systematic classification of bacteria into genera and species.

coho /ˈkəʊhəʊ/ (also **coho salmon** or **cohoe**) ▶ **noun** (pl. **same**, **cohos**, or **cohoes**) a deep-bodied North Pacific salmon with small black spots. Also called **SILVER SALMON**. ● *Oncorhynchus kisutch*, family Salmonidae.
– ORIGIN mid 19th cent.: probably from Salish.

cohort /ˈkəʊhɔːt/ ▶ **noun 1** [treated as sing. or pl.] an ancient Roman military unit, comprising six centuries, equal to one tenth of a legion.
2 [treated as sing. or pl.] a group of people with a shared characteristic: ***a cohort of** civil servants patiently drafting legislation.* ■ a group of people with a common statistical characteristic: *the 1940–4 birth cohort of women.*
3 often derogatory a supporter or companion.
– ORIGIN late Middle English: from Old French *cohorte*, or from Latin *cohors*, *cohort-* 'yard, retinue'. Compare with **COURT**.

> **USAGE** The earliest sense of **cohort** is 'a unit of men within the Roman army'. In the mid 20th century a new sense developed in the US, meaning 'a companion or colleague', as in *young Jack arrived with three of his **cohorts***. Although this use is well established (it accounts for the majority of the citations for this word in the Oxford English Corpus), some people object to it on the grounds that **cohort** should only be used for groups of people, never for individuals.

cohosh /kəˈhɒʃ/ ▶ **noun** either of two medicinal plants native to North America: ● (also **black cohosh**) a plant of the buttercup family, with small white flowers (*Cimicifuga racemosa*, family Ranunculaceae). ● (also **blue cohosh**) a plant of the barberry family (*Caulophyllum thalictroides*, family Berberidaceae).
– ORIGIN late 18th cent.: from Eastern Abnaki.

co-host ▶ **noun** a person who hosts an event or broadcast with another or others.
▶ **verb** [with obj.] host (an event or broadcast) together with another or others.

cohune /kəˈhuːn/ ▶ **noun** a Central American palm whose nut is a valuable source of oil. ● *Orbignya cohune*, family Palmae.
– ORIGIN mid 18th cent.: from Miskito.

COI ▶ **abbreviation** (in the UK) Central Office of Information.

coif /kɔɪf/ ▶ **noun 1** a woman's close-fitting cap, now only worn under a veil by nuns. ■ historical a metal skullcap worn under armour.
2 also /kwɑːf/ informal, chiefly N. Amer. short for **COIFFURE**.
▶ **verb** /kwɑːf, kwɒf/ (**coifs, coiffing, coiffed**; US also **coifs, coifing, coifed**) [with obj.] style or arrange (someone's hair).
– ORIGIN Middle English: from Old French *coife* 'headdress', from late Latin *cofia* 'helmet'.

coiffeur /kwɑːˈfəː, kwɒ-/ ▶ **noun** a hairdresser.
– ORIGIN mid 19th cent.: French, from *coiffer* 'arrange the hair', in Old French 'cover with a coif' (see **COIF**).

coiffeuse /kwɑːˈfəːz, kwɒ-/ ▶ **noun** a female hairdresser.

coiffure /kwɑːˈfjʊə, kwɒ-/ ▶ **noun** a person's hairstyle.
– DERIVATIVES **coiffured** adjective.
– ORIGIN mid 17th cent.: French, from *coiffer* 'arrange the hair', in Old French 'cover with a coif' (see **COIF**).

coign /kɔɪn/ ▶ **noun** a projecting corner or angle of a wall.
– PHRASES **coign of vantage** a favourable position for observation or action. [from Shakespeare's *Macbeth* (I. iv. 7), popularized by Sir Walter Scott.]
– ORIGIN late Middle English: variant of **COIN**.

coil[1] ▶ **noun** a length of something wound in a joined sequence of concentric rings: *a coil of rope.* ■ a single ring in such a sequence: *the snake wrapped its coils around her.* ■ an intrauterine contraceptive device in the form of a coil. ■ an electrical device consisting of a coiled wire, for converting the level of a voltage, producing a magnetic field, or adding inductance to a circuit: *a relay coil.* ■ such a device used for transmitting high voltage to the spark plugs of an internal-combustion engine. ■ a slow-burning spiral made from the dried paste of pyrethrum powder, which produces a smoke that deters mosquitoes.
▶ **verb** [with obj.] arrange (something long and flexible) in a coil: *he began to **coil up** the heavy ropes | he coiled a lock of her hair **around** his finger.* ■ [no obj., with adverbial] move or twist into such a shape: *smoke coiled lazily towards the ceiling.*
– ORIGIN early 16th cent. (as a verb): from Old French *coillir*, from Latin *colligere* 'gather together' (see **COLLECT**[1]).

coil[2] ▶ **noun** archaic or dialect a confusion or turmoil.
– PHRASES **shuffle off this mortal coil** chiefly humorous die. [from Shakespeare's *Hamlet* (III. i. 67).]
– ORIGIN mid 16th cent.: of unknown origin.

Coimbatore /ˌkɔɪmbəˈtɔː/ a city in the state of Tamil Nadu, in southern India; pop. 1,008,300 (est. 2009).

Coimbra /kəʊˈɪmbrə, ˈkɔɪmbrə/ a university city in central Portugal; pop. 137,212 (2007).

coin ▶ **noun** a flat disc or piece of metal with an official stamp, used as money. ■ [mass noun] money in the form of coins: *large amounts of coin and precious metal.* ■ (**coins**) one of the suits in some tarot packs, corresponding to pentacles in others.
▶ **verb** [with obj.] **1** make (coins) by stamping metal. ■ make (metal) into coins. ■ Brit. informal earn a lot of (money) quickly and easily: *the company was **coining it in** at the rate of £90 a second.*
2 invent (a new word or phrase): *he coined the term 'desktop publishing'.*
– PHRASES **the other side of the coin** the opposite aspect of a matter. **pay someone back in their own coin** retaliate by similar behaviour. **to coin a phrase** said when introducing a new expression or a variation on a familiar one, or ironically to show one's awareness that one is using a hackneyed expression: *she was, to coin a phrase, swept off her feet.*
– ORIGIN Middle English: from Old French *coin* 'wedge, corner, die', *coigner* 'to mint', from Latin *cuneus* 'wedge'. The original sense was 'cornerstone', later 'angle or wedge' (senses now spelled **QUOIN**); in late Middle English the term denoted a die for stamping money, or a piece of money produced by such a die.

coinage ▶ **noun** [mass noun] **1** coins collectively: *the volume of coinage in circulation.* ■ the action or process of producing coins from metal. ■ [count noun] a system or type of coins in use: *decimal coinage.*
2 the invention of a new word or phrase: *the word is of Derrida's own coinage.* ■ [count noun] a newly invented word or phrase.
– ORIGIN late Middle English: from Old French *coigniage*, from *coignier* 'to mint' (see **COIN**).

coin box ▶ **noun** Brit. a public telephone operated by inserting coins.

coincide /ˌkəʊɪnˈsʌɪd/ ▶ **verb** [no obj.] **1** occur at the same time: *publication is timed to **coincide with** a major exhibition.* ■ be present at the same place and at the same time: *on Friday afternoons we generally coincided.* ■ correspond in position; meet: *the two long-distance walks briefly coincide here.*
2 correspond in nature; tally: *the interests of employers and employees do not always coincide.* ■ be in agreement: *the members of the College **coincide in** this opinion.*

– ORIGIN early 18th cent. (in the sense 'occupy the same space'): from medieval Latin *coincidere*, from *co-* 'together with' + *incidere* 'fall upon or into'.

coincidence ▶ noun **1** a remarkable concurrence of events or circumstances without apparent causal connection: *it was a coincidence that she was wearing a jersey like Laura's* | [mass noun] *they met* ***by coincidence.***
2 [mass noun] the fact of corresponding in nature or in time of occurrence: *the coincidence of interest between the mining companies and certain politicians.*
3 Physics the presence of ionizing particles or other objects in two or more detectors simultaneously, or of two or more signals simultaneously in a circuit.
– ORIGIN early 17th cent. (in the sense 'occupation of the same space'): from medieval Latin *coincidentia*, from *coincidere* 'coincide, agree' (see COINCIDE).

coincident ▶ adjective **1** occurring together in space or time: *the fall in the stock market was* ***coincident with*** *the slowdown in economic activity.*
2 in agreement or harmony: *the stake of defence attorneys is not always* ***coincident with*** *that of their clients.*
– DERIVATIVES **coincidently** adverb.
– ORIGIN mid 16th cent.: from medieval Latin *coincident-* 'coinciding', from the verb *coincidere* (see COINCIDE).

coincidental ▶ adjective **1** resulting from a coincidence; happening by chance: *any resemblance between their reports is purely coincidental.*
2 happening or existing at the same time: *it's convenient that his plan is* ***coincidental with*** *the group's closure.*
– DERIVATIVES **coincidentally** adverb [sentence adverb] *coincidentally, we had both left our jobs on the same day.*

coiner ▶ noun **1** historical a person who coins money, in particular a maker of counterfeit coins.
2 a person who invents a new word or phrase.

coin-op ▶ noun a machine which is operated by the insertion of coins.

Cointreau /ˈkwɒntrəʊ/ ▶ noun [mass noun] trademark a colourless orange-flavoured liqueur.
– ORIGIN named after the *Cointreau* family, liqueur producers based in Angers, France.

coir /ˈkɔɪə/ ▶ noun [mass noun] fibre from the outer husk of the coconut, used in potting compost and for making ropes and matting.
– ORIGIN late 16th cent.: from Malayalam *kayaṟu* 'cord, coir'.

coition /kəʊˈɪʃ(ə)n/ ▶ noun another term for COITUS.
– ORIGIN mid 16th cent. (in the sense 'meeting or uniting'): from Latin *coitio(n-)*, from the verb *coire*, from *co-* 'together' + *ire* 'go'.

coitus /ˈkəʊɪtəs/ ▶ noun [mass noun] formal sexual intercourse.
– DERIVATIVES **coital** adjective.
– ORIGIN mid 19th cent.: from Latin, from *coire* 'go together' (see COITION).

coitus interruptus /ˌɪntəˈrʌptəs/ ▶ noun [mass noun] sexual intercourse in which the penis is withdrawn before ejaculation.
– ORIGIN from COITUS + Latin *interruptus* 'interrupted'.

coitus reservatus /ˌrɛzəˈvɑːtəs/ ▶ noun [mass noun] the postponement or avoidance of ejaculation, to prolong sexual intercourse.
– ORIGIN from COITUS + Latin *reservatus* 'reserved, kept'.

cojones /kəˈhəʊneɪz/ ▶ plural noun **1** informal, chiefly N. Amer. a man's testicles.
2 courage; guts: *only he's got the cojones to go after the general direct.*
– ORIGIN Spanish.

Coke ▶ noun trademark short for COCA-COLA.

coke¹ ▶ noun [mass noun] a solid fuel made by heating coal in the absence of air so that the volatile components are driven off. ■ carbon residue left after the incomplete combustion of petrol or other fuels.
▶ verb [with obj.] (usu. as noun **coking**) convert (coal) into coke.
– ORIGIN late Middle English (in the sense 'charcoal'): of unknown origin. The current sense dates from the mid 17th cent.

coke² ▶ noun informal term for COCAINE.
– ORIGIN early 20th cent.: abbreviation.

Coke-bottle ▶ noun [as modifier] N. Amer. informal denoting very thick lenses for glasses, or glasses with such lenses.

coked ▶ adjective informal having taken a large amount of cocaine: *he was obviously drunk or* ***coked up.***

coking coal ▶ noun [mass noun] coal suitable for making into coke.

col ▶ noun **1** the lowest point of a ridge or saddle between two peaks, typically providing a pass from one side of a mountain range to another.
2 Meteorology a region of slightly elevated pressure between two anticyclones.
– ORIGIN mid 19th cent.: from French, literally 'neck', from Latin *collum*.

Col. ▶ abbreviation ■ Colonel. ■ the Epistle to the Colossians (in biblical references).

col. ▶ abbreviation column.

col- ▶ prefix variant spelling of COM- assimilated before *l* (as in *collocate*, *collude*).

cola ▶ noun **1** [mass noun] a brown carbonated drink that is flavoured with an extract of cola nuts, or with a similar flavouring.
2 (also **kola**) a small evergreen African tree which is cultivated in the tropics for its seeds (cola nuts). [from Temne *k'ola* 'cola nut'.] ● Genus *Cola*, family Sterculiaceae: several species.

colander /ˈkʌləndə, ˈkɒl-/ ▶ noun a perforated bowl used to strain off liquid from food after washing or cooking.
– ORIGIN Middle English: based on Latin *colare* 'to strain'.

cola nut (also **kola nut**) ▶ noun the seed of the cola tree, which contains caffeine and is chewed or made into a drink.

co-latitude ▶ noun Astronomy the difference between a given latitude and 90°.

Colbert /ˈkɒlbɛː/, French /kɔlbɛʀ/, Jean Baptiste (1619–83), French statesman, chief minister to Louis XIV 1665–83. He was responsible for reforming the country's finances and the navy, and for boosting industry and commerce.

colcannon /kɒlˈkanən/ ▶ noun [mass noun] an Irish and Scottish dish of cabbage and potatoes boiled and mashed together.
– ORIGIN late 18th cent.: from COLE; the origin of the second element is uncertain but it is said that cannonballs were used to mash such vegetables as spinach.

Colchester /ˈkəʊltʃɪstə/ a town in Essex, in England; pop. 101,700 (est. 2009). It was a prominent town in Roman Britain, when it was known as Camulodunum.

colchicine /ˈkɒltʃɪsiːn, ˈkɒlk-/ ▶ noun [mass noun] Chemistry a yellow compound present in the corms of colchicums, used to relieve pain in cases of gout. ● An alkaloid; chem. formula: $C_{22}H_{25}NO_6$.

colchicum /ˈkɒltʃɪkəm, ˈkɒlk-/ ▶ noun (pl. **colchicums**) a plant of a genus that includes the autumn crocuses. ● Genus *Colchicum*, family Liliaceae.
■ [mass noun] the dried corm or seed of meadow saffron, which has analgesic properties and is used medicinally.
– ORIGIN from Latin, from Greek *kolkhikon* 'of Colchis', alluding to the skills as a poisoner of the sorceress Medea of Colchis in classical mythology.

Colchis /ˈkɒlkɪs/ an ancient region south of the Caucasus mountains at the eastern end of the Black Sea. In classical mythology it was the goal of Jason's expedition for the Golden Fleece. Greek name **KOLKHIS**.

cold ▶ adjective **1** of or at a low or relatively low temperature, especially when compared with the human body: *a freezing cold day* | *it's cold outside* | *a sharp, cold wind.* ■ (of a person) feeling uncomfortably cold: *she was cold, and I put some more wood on the fire.* ■ (of food or drink) served or consumed without being heated or after cooling: *a cold drink* | *serve hot or cold.* ■ feeling or characterized by fear or horror: *a cold shiver of fear.* ■ [as complement] informal unconscious: *she was* ***out cold.*** ■ dead: *lying cold and stiff in a coffin.*
2 lacking affection or warmth of feeling; unemotional: *how cold and calculating he was* | *her cold black eyes.* ■ not affected by emotion; objective: *cold statistics.* ■ sexually unresponsive; frigid. ■ depressing or dispiriting; not suggestive of warmth: *a cold light streamed through the window.* ■ (of a colour) containing pale blue or grey.
3 (of the scent or trail of a hunted person or animal) no longer fresh and easy to follow: *the trail went cold.* ■ [predic.] (in children's games) far from finding or guessing what is sought.
4 [as complement] without preparation or rehearsal: *they went into the test cold.* ■ informal at one's mercy: *they had him cold.*
▶ noun **1** [mass noun] a low temperature; cold weather; a cold environment: *my teeth chattered with* ***the cold*** | *they nearly died of cold.*
2 a common infection in which the mucous membrane of the nose and throat becomes inflamed, typically causing running at the nose, sneezing, and a sore throat.
▶ adverb N. Amer. informal completely; entirely: *we stopped cold behind a turn in the staircase.*
– PHRASES **(as) cold as ice** (or **stone** or **the grave** etc.) very cold: *her hand was as cold as ice.* **catch a cold** (also **catch cold**) become infected with a cold. ■ encounter difficulties. **cold comfort** poor or inadequate consolation: *another drop in the inflation rate was cold comfort for the 2.74 million jobless.* **cold feet** loss of nerve or confidence: *after arranging to meet I got cold feet and phoned her saying I was busy.* **the cold shoulder** a show of intentional unfriendliness; rejection: *the new England manager* ***gave him the cold shoulder.*** **cold-shoulder someone** reject or be deliberately unfriendly to someone. **cold steel** weapons such as swords or knives collectively. **in cold blood** without feeling or mercy; ruthlessly: *the government forces killed them in cold blood.* **in the cold light of day** when one has had time to consider a situation objectively: *in the cold light of day it all seemed so ridiculous.* **out in the cold** ignored; neglected: *the talks* ***left*** *the French* ***out in the cold.*** **throw** (or **pour**) **cold water on** be discouraging or negative about.
– DERIVATIVES **coldish** adjective, **coldness** noun.
– ORIGIN Old English *cald*, of Germanic origin; related to Dutch *koud* and German *kalt*, also to Latin *gelu* 'frost'.

cold-blooded ▶ adjective **1** denoting animals whose body temperature varies with that of the environment (e.g. fish); poikilothermic.
2 without emotion or pity; deliberately cruel or callous: *a cold-blooded murder.*
– DERIVATIVES **cold-bloodedly** adverb, **cold-bloodedness** noun.

cold-call ▶ verb [with obj.] make an unsolicited visit or telephone call to (someone), in an attempt to sell goods or services.
▶ noun (**cold call**) an unsolicited call of this kind.
– DERIVATIVES **cold-caller** noun.

cold cash ▶ noun North American term for HARD CASH.

cold cathode ▶ noun Electronics a cathode that emits electrons without being heated.

cold chisel ▶ noun a chisel used for cutting metal.

cold-cock ▶ verb [with obj.] N. Amer. informal knock (someone) out, typically with a blow to the head.

cold cream ▶ noun [mass noun] a cosmetic preparation used for cleansing and softening the skin.

cold cuts ▶ plural noun chiefly N. Amer. slices of cold cooked meats.

cold dark matter ▶ noun see DARK MATTER.

cold deck ▶ noun **1** US informal a deck of cards which has been dishonestly arranged beforehand.
2 N. Amer. a pile of logs stored away from the immediate area where logging is taking place.

cold-drawn ▶ adjective (of metal) drawn out into a wire or bar while cold.

cold frame ▶ noun a frame with a glass top in which small plants are grown and protected without artificial heat.

cold front ▶ noun Meteorology the boundary of an advancing mass of cold air, in particular the trailing edge of the warm sector of a low-pressure system.

cold fusion ▶ noun [mass noun] nuclear fusion supposedly occurring at or close to room temperature.

cold-hearted ▶ adjective lacking affection or warmth; unfeeling.
– DERIVATIVES **cold-heartedly** adverb, **cold-heartedness** noun.

coldie ▶ noun (pl. **coldies**) Austral. informal a chilled can or bottle of beer.

Colditz /ˈkəʊldɪts, ˈkɒl-/ a medieval castle near Leipzig, used as a top-security camp for Allied prisoners in the Second World War.

cold light ▶ noun [mass noun] Physics light accompanied by little or no heat; luminescence.

coldly ▶ adverb without affection or warmth of feeling; unemotionally: *Doyle looked at her coldly* | [as submodifier] *a coldly contemptuous tone.*

C

cold-moulded ▶ adjective (of an object) moulded from a resin that hardens without being heated.

cold-rolled ▶ adjective Metallurgy (of metal) having been rolled into sheets while cold, resulting in a smooth, hard finish.
– DERIVATIVES **cold-rolling** noun.

cold-short ▶ adjective (of a metal) brittle in its cold state.
– ORIGIN early 17th cent.: from Swedish *kallskör*, from *kall* 'cold' + *skör* 'brittle', later associated with SHORT in the same sense.

cold sore ▶ noun an inflamed blister in or near the mouth, caused by infection with the herpes simplex virus.

cold start ▶ noun an act of starting an engine or other machine at the ambient temperature.
▶ verb (**cold-start**) [with obj.] start (an engine or machine) at the ambient temperature.

cold storage ▶ noun [mass noun] the keeping of something in a refrigerator or other cold place for preservation. ■ the temporary postponement of something: *the project went* ***into cold storage***.

cold store ▶ noun a large refrigerated room for preserving food at very low temperatures.

cold sweat ▶ noun a state of sweating induced by fear, anxiety, or illness: *the very thought of exams brought her out in a cold sweat*.

cold table ▶ noun Brit. a selection of dishes of cold food in a restaurant or at a formal meal.

cold turkey informal ▶ noun [mass noun] the abrupt and complete cessation of taking a drug to which one is addicted: *I had to* ***go cold turkey***. ■ the symptoms caused by this: *suddenly stopping the drug may result in cold turkey*.
▶ adverb chiefly N. Amer. in a sudden and abrupt manner: *I had to quit drinking cold turkey*.

cold war ▶ noun a state of political hostility between countries characterized by threats, propaganda, and other measures short of open warfare, in particular: (**the Cold War**) the state of hostility that existed between the Soviet bloc countries and the Western powers from 1945 to 1990.

cold warrior ▶ noun a person who promotes a cold war.

cold-weld ▶ verb [with obj.] join (a piece of metal) to another without the use of heat, by forcing them together so hard that the surface oxide films are disrupted and adhesion occurs.

cold-work ▶ verb [with obj.] shape (metal) while it is cold.
▶ noun (**cold work**) [mass noun] the shaping of metal while it is cold.

Cole, Nat King (1919–65), American singer and pianist; born *Nathaniel Adams Coles*. He became the first black man to have his own series both on radio (1948–9) and television (1956–7). Notable songs: 'Mona Lisa' (1950), 'Ramblin' Rose' (1962).

cole ▶ noun chiefly archaic a brassica, especially cabbage, kale, or rape.
– ORIGIN Old English *cāwel*, *caul*, related to Dutch *kool* and German *Kohl*, from Latin *caulis* 'stem, cabbage'; reinforced in Middle English by forms from Old Norse *kál*. Compare with KALE.

colectomy /kə(ʊ)ˈlɛktəmi/ ▶ noun (pl. **colectomies**) [mass noun] surgical removal of all or part of the colon.

colemanite /ˈkəʊlmənʌɪt/ ▶ noun [mass noun] a white crystalline mineral, typically occurring as glassy prisms, consisting of hydrated calcium borate.
– ORIGIN named after William T. *Coleman* (1824–93) + -ITE[1].

Coleman lantern (also **Coleman lamp**) ▶ noun N. Amer. trademark a type of bright gasoline lamp used by campers.

Coleoptera /ˌkɒlɪˈɒpt(ə)rə/ ▶ plural noun Entomology an order of insects that comprises the beetles (including weevils), forming the largest order of animals on the earth. ■ (**coleoptera**) insects of this order; beetles.
– ORIGIN modern Latin (plural), from Greek *koleopteros*, from *koleos* 'sheath' + *pteron* 'wing'.

coleopteran Entomology ▶ noun an insect of the order Coleoptera; a beetle.
▶ adjective relating to or denoting coleopterans.
– DERIVATIVES **coleopterous** adjective.

coleopterist /ˌkɒlɪˈɒptərɪst/ ▶ noun a person who studies or collects beetles.
– ORIGIN mid 19th cent.: from COLEOPTERA + -IST.

coleoptile /ˌkɒlɪˈɒptʌɪl/ ▶ noun Botany a sheath protecting a young shoot tip in a grass or cereal.
– ORIGIN mid 19th cent.: from Greek *koleon* 'sheath' + *ptilon* 'feather'.

coleorhiza /ˌkɒlɪə(ʊ)ˈrʌɪzə/ ▶ noun (pl. **coleorhizae** /-ˈrʌɪziː/) Botany a sheath protecting the root of a germinating grass or cereal grain.
– ORIGIN mid 19th cent.: from *koleos* 'sheath' + *rhiza* 'root'.

Coleraine /kəʊlˈreɪn/ a town in the north of Northern Ireland, on the River Bann in County Londonderry; pop. 24,300 (est. 2009).

Coleridge /ˈkəʊlərɪdʒ/, Samuel Taylor (1772–1834), English poet, critic, and philosopher. His *Lyrical Ballads* (1798), written with William Wordsworth, marked the start of English romanticism and included 'The Rime of the Ancient Mariner'. Other notable poems: 'Christabel' and 'Kubla Khan' (both 1816).

coleslaw ▶ noun [mass noun] a salad dish of shredded raw cabbage, carrots, and other vegetables mixed with mayonnaise.
– ORIGIN late 18th cent. (originally US): from Dutch *koolsla*, from *kool* 'cabbage' + *sla* (see SLAW).

cole tit ▶ noun variant spelling of COAL TIT.

Colette /kɒˈlɛt/ (1873–1954), French novelist; born *Sidonie Gabrielle Claudine*. Notable novels *Chéri* (1920) and *La Fin de Chéri* (1926).

coleus /ˈkəʊlɪəs/ ▶ noun a tropical SE Asian plant of the mint family with brightly coloured variegated leaves, popular as a houseplant. ● Genus *Solenostemon* (formerly *Coleus*), family Labiatae.
– ORIGIN modern Latin, from Greek *koleos* 'sheath' (because of the way the stamens are joined together, resembling a sheath).

colewort /ˈkəʊlwəːt/ ▶ noun archaic another term for COLE.

coley /ˈkəʊli/ ▶ noun (pl. **coleys**) another term for SAITHE.
– ORIGIN 1960s: perhaps from COALFISH.

colic ▶ noun [mass noun] severe pain in the abdomen caused by wind or obstruction in the intestines and suffered especially by babies.
– DERIVATIVES **colicky** adjective.
– ORIGIN late Middle English: from Old French *colique*, from late Latin *colicus*, from *colon* (see COLON[2]).

colicin /ˈkɒlɪsɪn/ ▶ noun Biology a bacteriocin produced by a coliform bacterium.
– ORIGIN 1940s: from French *colicine* (from *coli*, denoting a bacterium) + -IN[1].

colic root ▶ noun a North American plant of the lily family, with a rosette of leaves and a spike of small goblet-shaped white flowers, formerly used in the treatment of colic. ● *Aletris farinosa*, family Liliaceae.

coliform /ˈkɒlɪfɔːm/ ▶ adjective Biology belonging to a group of rod-shaped bacteria typified by *E. coli*.
– ORIGIN early 20th cent.: from modern Latin *coli* 'of the colon' + -IFORM.

Colima /kɒˈliːmə/ **1** a state of SW Mexico, on the Pacific coast.
2 the capital city of Colima; pop. 123,587 (2005).

colinearity /ˌkəʊlɪnɪˈarɪti/ ▶ noun [mass noun] Genetics the relationship between the linear sequence of nucleic acid bases in the DNA of the gene and the sequence of amino acids in the protein encoded by the DNA.

coliseum /ˌkɒlɪˈsiːəm/ (also **colosseum**) ▶ noun [in names] a large theatre, cinema, or stadium: *the London Coliseum*.
– ORIGIN late 19th cent.: from medieval Latin, alteration of Latin *colosseum* (see COLOSSEUM).

colitis /kəˈlʌɪtɪs/ ▶ noun [mass noun] Medicine inflammation of the lining of the colon.

Coll an island in the Inner Hebrides, to the west of the isle of Mull.

Coll. ▶ abbreviation ■ Collected or Collection (used in written references to published works or sources). ■ College.

collaborate /kəˈlabəreɪt/ ▶ verb [no obj.] **1** work jointly on an activity or project: *he* ***collaborated with*** *him on numerous hotel projects*.
2 cooperate traitorously with an enemy: *during the last war they* ***collaborated with*** *the Nazis*.
– ORIGIN late 19th cent.: from Latin *collaborat-* 'worked with', from the verb *collaborare*, from *col-* 'together' + *laborare* 'to work'.

collaboration ▶ noun [mass noun] **1** the action of working with someone to produce something: *he wrote a book* ***in collaboration with*** *his son*. ■ [count noun] something produced in this way: *his recent opera was a collaboration with Lessing*.
2 traitorous cooperation with an enemy: *he faces charges of collaboration*.
– DERIVATIVES **collaborationist** noun & adjective (sense 2).
– ORIGIN mid 19th cent.: from Latin *collaboratio(n-)*, from *collaborare* 'work together'.

collaborative ▶ adjective produced by or involving two or more parties working together: *collaborative research*.
– DERIVATIVES **collaboratively** adverb.

collaborator /kəˈlabəreɪtə/ ▶ noun **1** a person who works jointly on an activity or project; an associate: *his collaborator on the book*.
2 a person who cooperates traitorously with an enemy; a defector: *he was a collaborator during the occupation*.

collage /ˈkɒlɑːʒ, kəˈlɑːʒ/ ▶ noun [mass noun] a form of art in which various materials such as photographs and pieces of paper or fabric are arranged and stuck to a backing. ■ [count noun] a composition made in this way. ■ [count noun] a collection or combination of various things: *a collage of musical genres*.
– DERIVATIVES **collagist** noun.
– ORIGIN early 20th cent.: from French, literally 'gluing'.

collagen /ˈkɒlədʒ(ə)n/ ▶ noun [mass noun] Biochemistry the main structural protein found in animal connective tissue, yielding gelatin when boiled.
– ORIGIN mid 19th cent.: from French *collagène*, from Greek *kolla* 'glue' + French *-gène* (see -GEN).

collapsar /kəˈlapsɑː/ ▶ noun Astronomy an old star that has collapsed under its own gravity to form a white dwarf, neutron star, or black hole.
– ORIGIN late 20th cent.: from COLLAPSE, on the pattern of words such as *pulsar*.

collapse ▶ verb [no obj.] **1** (of a structure) suddenly fall down or give way: *the roof collapsed on top of me*. ■ [with obj.] cause (something) to fall down or give way: *it feels as if the slightest pressure would collapse it* | figurative *many people tend to collapse the distinction between the two concepts*. ■ (usu. as adj. **collapsed**) (of a lung or blood vessel) fall inwards and become flat and empty.
2 (of a person) fall down and become unconscious as a result of illness or injury: *he collapsed from loss of blood*. ■ sit or lie down as a result of exhaustion or amusement: *exhausted, he collapsed on the bed* | *the three of them* ***collapsed with laughter***.
3 fail suddenly and completely: *the talks collapsed last week over territorial issues*. ■ (of a price or currency) drop suddenly in value.
4 fold or be foldable into a small space: [no obj.] *some cots collapse down to fit into a holdall*. ■ [with obj.] compress a displayed part of (a spreadsheet or other electronic document): *tabulation programs can be used to collapse this list in various ways*.
▶ noun an instance of a structure falling down or giving way: *the collapse of a railway bridge* | [mass noun] *the church roof is in danger of collapse*. ■ a sudden failure of an institution or undertaking: *the collapse of a number of prominent banks*. ■ a physical or mental breakdown: *he suffered a collapse from overwork* | [mass noun] *she's lying there in a state of collapse*.
– ORIGIN early 17th cent. (as *collapsed*): from medical Latin *collapsus*, past participle of *collabi*, from *col-* 'together' + *labi* 'to slip'.

collapsible ▶ adjective (of an object) able to be folded into a small space: *a collapsible bed*.
– DERIVATIVES **collapsibility** noun.

collar ▶ noun **1** the part around the neck of a shirt, blouse, jacket or coat, either upright or turned over. ■ a band put around the neck of a domestic animal, used to restrain or control it. ■ a heavy rounded part of the harness worn by a draught animal, which rests at the base of its neck on the shoulders: *a shire horse leaning into its collar*.
2 a connecting band or pipe in machinery.
3 Brit. a piece of meat rolled up and tied. ■ a cut of bacon taken from the neck of a pig.
4 the part of a plant where the stem joins the roots.
▶ verb [with obj.] informal seize or apprehend (someone): *police collared the culprit*. ■ approach (someone) in order to talk to them: *he collared a departing guest for some last words*.
– DERIVATIVES **collared** adjective [in combination] *a fur-collared jacket*, **collarless** adjective.
– ORIGIN Middle English: from Old French *colier*, from Latin *collare* 'band for the neck, collar', from *collum* 'neck'.

collar beam ▸ noun a horizontal piece of squared timber connecting two rafters and forming with them an A-shaped roof truss.

collarbone ▸ noun either of the pair of bones joining the breastbone to the shoulder blades. Also called CLAVICLE.

collard /ˈkɒlɑːd/ (also **collards** or **collard greens**) ▸ noun dialect or N. Amer. a cabbage of a variety that does not develop a heart.
– ORIGIN mid 18th cent.: reduced form of *colewort*, in the same sense, from COLE + WORT.

collared dove ▸ noun an Old World dove related to the turtle dove, with buff, grey, or brown plumage and a narrow black band around the back of the neck. ● Genus *Streptopelia*, family Columbidae: several species, in particular the sandy grey *S. decaocto*.

collared lizard ▸ noun a lizard with a distinctive black and white collar, found in dry rocky areas in the southern US and Mexico. ● *Crotaphytus collaris*, family Iguanidae.

collar stud ▸ noun a stud used to fasten a detachable collar to a shirt.

collate /kəˈleɪt/ ▸ verb [with obj.] **1** collect and combine (texts, information, or data). ■ compare and analyse (two or more sources of information): *these accounts he **collated with** his own experience.* ■ Printing verify the number and order of (the sheets of a book).
2 appoint (a clergyman) to a benefice.
– DERIVATIVES **collator** noun
– ORIGIN mid 16th cent. (in the sense 'confer a benefice upon'): from Latin *collat-* 'brought together', from the verb *conferre* (see CONFER).

collateral /kəˈlat(ə)r(ə)l/ ▸ noun **1** [mass noun] something pledged as security for repayment of a loan, to be forfeited in the event of a default.
2 a person having the same ancestor as another but through a different line.
▸ adjective **1** additional but subordinate; secondary: *the collateral meanings of a word.* ■ euphemistic denoting inadvertent casualties and destruction in civilian areas in the course of military operations: *collateral damage to civilians | collateral casualties.*
2 descended from the same stock but by a different line: *a collateral descendant of Robert Burns.*
3 situated side by side; parallel: *collateral veins.*
– DERIVATIVES **collaterality** noun, **collaterally** adverb.
– ORIGIN late Middle English (as an adjective): from medieval Latin *collateralis*, from *col-* 'together with' + *lateralis* (from *latus, later-* 'side'). Sense 1 of the noun (originally US) is from the phrase *collateral security*, denoting something pledged in addition to the main obligation of a contract.

collateral contract ▸ noun Law a subsidiary contract which induces a person to enter into a main contract or which depends upon the main contract for its existence.

collateralize (also **collateralise**) ▸ verb [with obj.] provide something as collateral for (a loan).

collation /kəˈleɪʃ(ə)n/ ▸ noun **1** [mass noun] the action of collating something: *data management and collation.*
2 formal a light informal meal. ■ (in the Roman Catholic Church) a light meal allowed during a fast.
– ORIGIN Middle English: via Old French from Latin *collatio(n-)*, from *conferre* (see CONFER). Originally (in the plural) the term denoted John Cassian's *Collationes Patrum in Scetica Eremo Commorantium* 'Conferences of, or with, the Egyptian Hermits' (AD 415–20), from which a reading would be given in Benedictine communities prior to a light meal (see sense 2).

colleague ▸ noun a person with whom one works in a profession or business.
– ORIGIN early 16th cent.: from French *collègue*, from Latin *collega* 'partner in office', from *col-* 'together with' + *legare* 'depute'.

collect¹ /kəˈlɛkt/ ▸ verb [with obj.] **1** bring or gather together (a number of things): *he went round the office collecting old coffee cups.* ■ [no obj.] come together and form a group: *a small crowd collected at the back door.* ■ systematically seek and acquire (items of a particular kind) as a hobby: *I've started collecting stamps.* ■ accumulate over a period of time: *collect rainwater to use on the garden.*
2 call for and take away; fetch: *the children were collected from school.* ■ call for and obtain (payments) from a number of people: *he collected their rent each week.* ■ go somewhere and receive (something) as a right or award: *she came to Oxford to collect her honorary degree.* ■ ask for and receive (charitable donations): *they were collecting money for the war effort.*
3 (**collect oneself**) regain control of oneself, typically after a shock. ■ concentrate (one's thoughts).
4 archaic conclude; infer: [with clause] *by all best conjectures, I collect Thou art to be my fatal enemy.*
5 cause (a horse) to bring its hind legs further forward as it moves.
6 Austral./NZ informal collide with: *he lost control of the truck and collected two cats.*
▸ adverb & adjective N. Amer. (with reference to a telephone call) to be paid for by the person receiving it: [as adv.] *I called my mother collect.*
▸ noun Austral./NZ informal a winning bet.
– ORIGIN late Middle English: from Old French *collecter* or medieval Latin *collectare*, from Latin *collect-* 'gathered together', from the verb *colligere*, from *col-* 'together' + *legere* 'choose or collect'.

collect² /ˈkɒlɛkt, -lɪkt/ ▸ noun (in church use) a short prayer, especially one assigned to a particular day or season.
– ORIGIN Middle English: from Old French *collecte*, from Latin *collecta* 'gathering', feminine past participle of *colligere* 'gather together' (see COLLECT¹).

collectable /kəˈlɛktəb(ə)l/ (also **collectible**) ▸ adjective **1** (often **collectible**) (of an item) worth collecting; of interest to a collector.
2 able to be collected: *a hire car, collectable on your arrival.*
▸ noun (usu. **collectibles**) an item valued and sought by collectors.
– DERIVATIVES **collectability** /-ˈbɪlɪti/ noun.

collectanea /kɒlɛkˈtɑːnɪə, -ˈteɪn-/ ▸ plural noun [also treated as sing.] passages, remarks, and other pieces of text collected from various sources.
– ORIGIN mid 17th cent.: Latin, neuter plural of *collectaneus* 'gathered together'.

collected ▸ adjective **1** (of a person) calm and self-controlled: *outwardly they are cool, calm, and collected.*
2 [attrib.] (of individual works) brought together in one volume or edition: *the collected works of Shakespeare.* ■ (of a volume or edition) containing all the works of a particular person or category.
– DERIVATIVES **collectedly** adverb (sense 1).

collection ▸ noun **1** [mass noun] the action or process of collecting someone or something: *the collection of data | refuse collection | she left the envelope in the office **for collection**.* ■ [count noun] a regular removal of mail for dispatch or of refuse for disposal. ■ [count noun] an instance of collecting money in a church service or for a charity. ■ [count noun] a sum collected in this way.
2 a group of things or people: *a rambling collection of houses.* ■ a group of accumulated items of a particular kind: *a record collection.* ■ a book or recording containing various texts, poems, songs, etc.: *a collection of essays.* ■ a range of new clothes produced by a fashion house: *a preview of their autumn collection.*
3 (**collections**) Brit. college examinations held at the beginning or end of a term, especially at Oxford University.
– ORIGIN late Middle English: via Old French from Latin *collectio(n-)*, from *colligere* 'gather together' (see COLLECT¹).

collective ▸ adjective done by people acting as a group: *a collective protest.* ■ relating to or shared by all the members of a group: *ministers who share collective responsibility | a collective sigh of relief from parents.* ■ taken as a whole; aggregate: *the collective power of the workforce.*
▸ noun a cooperative enterprise. ■ a collective farm.
– DERIVATIVES **collectively** adverb, **collectiveness** noun, **collectivity** noun.
– ORIGIN late Middle English (in the sense 'representing many individuals'): from Old French *collectif*, *-ive* or Latin *collectivus*, from *collect-* 'gathered together', from the verb *colligere* (see COLLECT¹).

collective bargaining ▸ noun [mass noun] negotiation of wages and other conditions of employment by an organized body of employees.

collective farm ▸ noun a jointly operated amalgamation of several smallholdings, especially one owned by the state.

collective memory ▸ noun [mass noun] the memory of a group of people, passed from one generation to the next.

collective noun ▸ noun Grammar a count noun that denotes a group of individuals (e.g. *assembly, family, crew*).

> **USAGE** A **collective noun** can be used with either a singular verb (*my family **was** always hard-working*) or a plural verb (*his family **were** disappointed in him*). Generally speaking, in Britain it is more usual for collective nouns to be followed by a plural verb, while in the US the opposite is true. Notice that, if the verb is singular, any following pronouns must be too: *the government **is** prepared to act, but not until **it** knows the outcome of the latest talks* (not ... *until **they** know the outcome ...*).

C

collective ownership ▸ noun [mass noun] ownership of something, typically land or industrial assets, by all members of a group for the mutual benefit of all.

collective security ▸ noun [mass noun] the cooperation of several countries in an alliance to strengthen the security of each.

collective unconscious ▸ noun (in Jungian psychology) the part of the unconscious mind which is derived from ancestral memory and experience and is common to all humankind, as distinct from the individual's unconscious.

collectivism ▸ noun [mass noun] the practice or principle of giving a group priority over each individual in it. ■ the ownership of land and the means of production by the people or the state, as a political principle or system.
– DERIVATIVES **collectivist** adjective & noun, **collectivistic** adjective.

collectivize (also **collectivise**) ▸ verb [with obj.] (usu. as adj. **collectivized**) organize (an industry or activity) on the basis of public or state ownership: *collectivized agriculture.*
– DERIVATIVES **collectivization** noun.

collector /kəˈlɛktə/ ▸ noun **1** a person who collects things of a specified type, professionally or as a hobby: *an art collector.*
2 an official who is responsible for collecting money: *a tax collector.* ■ an official who collects tickets from bus or train passengers.
3 (in some South Asian countries) the chief administrative official of a district.
4 Electronics the region in a bipolar transistor that absorbs charge carriers.

collectorate /kəˈlɛktərət/ ▸ noun (in some South Asian countries) a district under the jurisdiction of a collector. See COLLECTOR (sense 3).

collector's item (also **collector's piece**) ▸ noun an object valued by collectors, because it is rare, beautiful, or has some special interest.

colleen /kɒˈliːn, ˈkɒliːn/ ▸ noun Irish a girl or young woman.
– ORIGIN early 19th cent.: from Irish *cailín*, diminutive of *caile* 'countrywoman'.

college ▸ noun **1** an educational institution or establishment, in particular: ■ one providing higher education or specialized professional or vocational training: *colleges of further education | I'm **at college**, studying graphic design.* ■ (in Britain) any of the independent institutions into which certain universities are separated, each having its own teaching staff, students, and buildings. ■ Brit. a private secondary school: [in names] *Eton College.* ■ US a university offering a limited curriculum or teaching only to a bachelor's degree. ■ the teaching staff and students of a college considered collectively: *the college was shocked by his death.*
2 an organized group of professional people with particular aims, duties, and privileges: [in names] *the Royal College of Physicians.*
– ORIGIN late Middle English: from Old French, from Latin *collegium* 'partnership', from *collega* 'partner in office', from *col-* 'together with' + *legare* 'depute'.

College of Arms (also **College of Heralds**) (in the UK) a corporation which officially records and grants armorial bearings. Formed in 1484, it comprises three Kings of Arms, six heralds, and four pursuivants. Also called HERALDS' COLLEGE.

College of Cardinals the body of cardinals of the Roman Catholic Church, founded in the 11th century and since 1179 responsible for the election of the Pope. Also called SACRED COLLEGE.

college of education ▸ noun an institution where schoolteachers are trained.

college pudding ▸ noun Brit. a small baked or steamed suet pudding with dried fruit.

collegia plural form of COLLEGIUM.

collegial /kəˈliːdʒɪəl, -dʒ(ə)l/ ▸ adjective **1** another term for COLLEGIATE (sense 1).
2 relating to or involving shared responsibility, as among a group of colleagues.

– DERIVATIVES **collegiality** noun.
– ORIGIN late Middle English: from Old French *collegial* or late Latin *collegialis*, from *collegium* 'partnership' (see COLLEGE).

collegian /kə'liːdʒɪən, -dʒ(ə)n/ ▶ **noun** a member of a college, especially within a university.
– ORIGIN late Middle English: from medieval Latin *collegianus*, from *collegium* 'partnership' (see COLLEGE).

collegiate /kə'liːdʒ(ɪ)ət/ ▶ **adjective 1** belonging or relating to a college or its students: *collegiate life*.
2 Brit. (of a university) composed of different colleges.
– DERIVATIVES **collegiately** adverb.
– ORIGIN late Middle English: from late Latin *collegiatus*, from *collegium* 'partnership' (see COLLEGE).

collegiate church ▶ **noun** a church endowed for a chapter of canons but without a bishop's see. ■ US & Scottish a church or group of churches established under two or more pastors.

collegiate Gothic ▶ **noun** [mass noun] N. Amer. a style of neo-Gothic architecture used for some US university buildings.

collegium /kə'liːdʒɪəm/ ▶ **noun** (pl. **collegia** /kə'liːdʒɪə, -dʒə/) **1** (in full **collegium musicum**) (pl. **collegia musica**) a society of amateur musicians, especially one attached to a German or US university.
2 historical an advisory or administrative board in Russia.
– ORIGIN late 19th cent.: from Latin, literally 'association'.

col legno /kɒl 'lɛnjəʊ/ ▶ **adverb** (of a passage of music for a bowed instrument) played by hitting the strings with the back of the bow.
– ORIGIN Italian, 'with the wood (of the bow)'.

Collembola /kə'lɛmbələ/ ▶ **plural noun** Entomology an order of insects that comprises the springtails. ■ (**collembola**) insects of this order; springtails.
– DERIVATIVES **collembolan** noun & adjective.
– ORIGIN modern Latin (plural), from Greek *kolla* 'glue' + *embolon* 'peg, stopper' (with reference to the sticky substance secreted by the ventral tube of the insects).

collenchyma /kə'lɛŋkɪmə/ ▶ **noun** [mass noun] Botany tissue strengthened by the thickening of cell walls, as in young shoots.
– ORIGIN mid 19th cent.: from Greek *kolla* 'glue' + *enkhuma* 'infusion'.

Colles fracture /'kɒlɪs/ ▶ **noun** Medicine a fracture of the radius in the wrist, with a characteristic backward displacement of the hand.
– ORIGIN late 19th cent.: named after Abraham *Colles* (1773–1843), Irish surgeon.

collet /'kɒlɪt/ ▶ **noun 1** a segmented band put round a shaft and tightened so as to grip it. ■ a small collar in a clock to which the inner end of a balance spring is attached.
2 a flange or socket for setting a gem in jewellery.
– ORIGIN late Middle English (denoting a piece of armour to protect the neck): from Old French, diminutive of *col* 'neck', from Latin *collum*.

colliculus /kə'lɪkjʊləs/ ▶ **noun** (pl. **colliculi** /-lʌɪ, -liː/) Anatomy any of a number of small swellings in the roof of the midbrain, involved in vision and hearing.
– DERIVATIVES **collicular** adjective.
– ORIGIN mid 19th cent.: from Latin, diminutive of *collis* 'hill'.

collide ▶ **verb** [no obj.] hit by accident when moving: *she* ***collided with*** *someone* | *two suburban trains collided*. ■ come into conflict or opposition: *in his work, politics and metaphysics collide*.
– ORIGIN early 17th cent. (in the sense 'cause to collide'): from Latin *collidere*, from *col-* 'together' + *laedere* 'to strike'.

collider ▶ **noun** Physics an accelerator in which two beams of particles are made to collide.

collie ▶ **noun** (pl. **collies**) a sheepdog of a breed originating in Scotland, having a long pointed nose and long thick hair.
– ORIGIN mid 17th cent.: perhaps from COAL (the breed originally being black).

collier /'kɒlɪə/ ▶ **noun** chiefly Brit. **1** a coal miner.
2 a ship carrying coal.
– ORIGIN Middle English: from COAL + -IER. The original sense was 'maker of charcoal', who usually brought it to market, hence 'person selling charcoal', later 'person selling coal', whence the current senses.

colliery ▶ **noun** (pl. **collieries**) chiefly Brit. a coal mine and the buildings and equipment associated with it.

colligate /'kɒlɪgeɪt/ ▶ **verb** Linguistics be or cause to be juxtaposed or grouped in a syntactic relation: [no obj.] *the two grammatical items are said to colligate*.
– DERIVATIVES **colligation** noun.
– ORIGIN mid 16th cent. (in the Latin sense): from Latin *colligat-* 'bound together', from the verb *colligare*, from *col-* 'together' + *ligare* 'bind'. The current sense dates from the 1960s.

colligative /kə'lɪgətɪv/ ▶ **adjective** Chemistry relating to the binding together of molecules.

collimate /'kɒlɪmeɪt/ ▶ **verb** [with obj.] make (rays of light or particles) accurately parallel: (as adj. **collimated**) *a collimated electron beam*. ■ accurately set the alignment of (an optical or other system).
– DERIVATIVES **collimation** noun.
– ORIGIN mid 19th cent.: from Latin *collimare*, an erroneous reading (in some editions of Cicero) of *collineare* 'align or aim', from *col-* 'together with' + *linea* 'line'.

collimator ▶ **noun** a device for producing a parallel beam of rays or radiation. ■ a small fixed telescope used for adjusting the line of sight of an astronomical telescope.

collinear /kə'lɪnɪə/ ▶ **adjective** Geometry (of points) lying in the same straight line.
– DERIVATIVES **collinearity** noun.

Collins[1], Michael (1890–1922), Irish nationalist leader and politician. A Member of Parliament for Sinn Fein, he was one of the negotiators of the Anglo-Irish Treaty of 1921. He commanded the Irish Free State forces in the civil war and became head of state but was assassinated ten days later.

Collins[2], (William) Wilkie (1824–89), English novelist, noted for his detective stories *The Woman in White* (1860) and *The Moonstone* (1868).

collision ▶ **noun 1** an instance of one moving object or person striking violently against another: *a midair collision between two aircraft* | [mass noun] *his car was* ***in collision with*** *a lorry*. ■ a conflict between opposing ideas, interests, or factions: *a collision of two diverse cultures and languages*.
2 Computing an instance of two or more records being assigned the same identifier or location in memory. ■ an instance of simultaneous transmission by more than one node of a network.
– PHRASES **on (a) collision course** adopting an approach that is certain to lead to conflict with another person or group: *nurses are on a collision course with the government*.
– DERIVATIVES **collisional** adjective.
– ORIGIN late Middle English: from late Latin *collisio(n-)*, from Latin *collidere* 'strike together' (see COLLIDE).

collocate ▶ **verb** /'kɒləkeɪt/ **1** [no obj.] Linguistics (of a word) be habitually juxtaposed with another with a frequency greater than chance: *'maiden' collocates with 'voyage'*.
2 [with obj.] rare place side by side or in a particular relation.
▶ **noun** /'kɒləkət/ Linguistics a word that is habitually juxtaposed with another with a frequency greater than chance: *collocates for the word 'mortgage' include 'lend' and 'property'*.
– ORIGIN early 16th cent. (in sense 2 of the verb): from Latin *collocat-* 'placed together', from the verb *collocare*, from *col-* 'together' + *locare* 'to place'. Sense 1 of the verb dates from the 1950s.

collocation ▶ **noun** [mass noun] **1** Linguistics the habitual juxtaposition of a particular word with another word or words with a frequency greater than chance: *the words have a similar range of collocation*. ■ [count noun] a pair or group of words that are juxtaposed in such a way: *'strong tea' and 'heavy drinker' are typical English collocations*.
2 the action of placing things side by side or in position: *the collocation of the two pieces*.
– ORIGIN late Middle English: from Latin *collocatio(n-)*, from *collocare* 'place together' (see COLLOCATE).

collocutor /'kɒlə,kjuːtə, kə'lɒkjʊtə/ ▶ **noun** rare a person who takes part in a conversation.
– ORIGIN mid 16th cent.: from late Latin, from *collocut-* 'conversed', from the verb *colloqui*.

collodion /kə'ləʊdɪən/ ▶ **noun** [mass noun] a syrupy solution of nitrocellulose in a mixture of alcohol and ether, used for coating things, chiefly in surgery.
– ORIGIN mid 19th cent.: from Greek *kollōdēs* 'gluelike', from *kolla* 'glue'.

collogue /kɒ'ləʊg/ ▶ **verb** (**collogues**, **colloguing**, **collogued**) [no obj.] archaic talk confidentially or conspiratorially.
– ORIGIN early 17th cent. (in the sense 'flatter, pretend to agree with or believe'): probably an alteration of obsolete *colleague* 'conspire', by association with Latin *colloqui* 'to converse'.

colloid /'kɒlɔɪd/ ▶ **noun** a homogeneous non-crystalline substance consisting of large molecules or ultramicroscopic particles of one substance dispersed through a second substance. Colloids include gels, sols, and emulsions; the particles do not settle, and cannot be separated out by ordinary filtering or centrifuging like those in a suspension. ■ [mass noun] Anatomy & Medicine a substance of gelatinous consistency.
▶ **adjective** relating to or characterized by a colloid or colloids.
– DERIVATIVES **colloidal** adjective.
– ORIGIN mid 19th cent.: from Greek *kolla* 'glue' + -OID.

collop /'kɒləp/ ▶ **noun** dialect & N. Amer. a slice of meat: *three collops of bacon*.
– ORIGIN late Middle English: of Scandinavian origin and related to Swedish *kalops* 'meat stew'.

colloquial /kə'ləʊkwɪəl/ ▶ **adjective** (of language) used in ordinary or familiar conversation; not formal or literary.
– DERIVATIVES **colloquially** adverb.
– ORIGIN mid 18th cent.: from Latin *colloquium* 'conversation' + -AL.

colloquialism ▶ **noun** a word or phrase that is not formal or literary and is used in ordinary or familiar conversation. ■ [mass noun] the use of such words or phrases.

colloquium /kə'ləʊkwɪəm/ ▶ **noun** (pl. **colloquiums** or **colloquia** /-kwɪə/) an academic conference or seminar.
– ORIGIN late 16th cent. (denoting a conversation): from Latin, from *colloqui* 'to converse', from *col-* 'together' + *loqui* 'to talk'.

colloquy /'kɒləkwi/ ▶ **noun** (pl. **colloquies**) **1** formal a conversation: *they broke off their colloquy at once* | [mass noun] *he found her in earnest colloquy with the postman*.
2 a gathering for discussion of theological questions.
– ORIGIN late Middle English: from Latin *colloquium* 'conversation'.

collotype /'kɒlətʌɪp/ ▶ **noun** [mass noun] Printing a process for making high-quality prints from a sheet of light-sensitive gelatin exposed photographically to the image without using a screen. ■ [count noun] a print made by such a process.
– ORIGIN late 19th cent.: from Greek *kolla* 'glue' + TYPE.

collude /kə'l(j)uːd/ ▶ **verb** [no obj.] come to a secret understanding; conspire: *the president accused his opponents of colluding with foreigners*.
– DERIVATIVES **colluder** noun.
– ORIGIN early 16th cent.: from Latin *colludere* 'have a secret agreement', from *col-* 'together' + *ludere* 'to play'.

collusion ▶ **noun** [mass noun] secret or illegal cooperation or conspiracy in order to deceive others: *the armed forces were working* ***in collusion with*** *drug traffickers*. ■ Law such cooperation or conspiracy between ostensible opponents in a lawsuit.
– DERIVATIVES **collusive** adjective, **collusively** adverb.
– ORIGIN late Middle English: from Latin *collusio(n-)*, from *colludere* 'have a secret agreement' (see COLLUDE).

colluvium /kə'l(j)uːvɪəm/ ▶ **noun** [mass noun] Geology material which accumulates at the foot of a steep slope.
– DERIVATIVES **colluvial** adjective.
– ORIGIN mid 20th cent.: from Latin *colluvies* 'confluence of matter', from *colluere* 'to rinse', from *col-* 'together' + *luere* 'to wash'.

collyrium /kə'lɪrɪəm/ ▶ **noun** (pl. **collyria** /-rɪə/)
1 archaic a medicated eyewash.
2 [mass noun] a kind of dark eyeshadow, used especially in Eastern countries.
– ORIGIN late Middle English: Latin, from Greek *kollurion* 'poultice', from *kollura* 'coarse bread roll'.

collywobbles ▶ **plural noun** informal, chiefly humorous stomach pain or queasiness: *an attack of collywobbles*. ■ intense anxiety or nervousness: *such organizations give him the collywobbles*.
– ORIGIN early 19th cent.: fanciful formation from COLIC and WOBBLE.

Colo. ▶ **abbreviation** Colorado.

colobine /'kɒləbʌɪn/ ▶ **noun** Zoology an Old World monkey of a mainly leaf-eating group that includes the colobus monkeys, langurs, and leaf monkeys.
● Subfamily Colobinae, family Cercopithicidae.

– ORIGIN 1950s: from modern Latin *Colobinae*, based on Greek *kolobos* 'cut short'.

coloboma /ˌkɒlə'bəʊmə/ ▶ **noun** [mass noun] Medicine a congenital malformation of the eye causing defects in the lens, iris, or retina.
– ORIGIN mid 19th cent.: modern Latin, from Greek *kolobōma* 'part removed in mutilation', from *kolobos* 'cut short'.

colobus /'kɒləbəs/ (also **colobus monkey**) ▶ **noun** (pl. **same**) a slender leaf-eating African monkey with silky fur, a long tail, and very small or absent thumbs. ● Genera *Colobus* and *Procolobus*, family Cercopithecidae: several species.
– ORIGIN modern Latin, from Greek *kolobos* 'cut short'.

co-locate ▶ **verb** (**be co-located**) share a location or facility with something else: *a United Kingdom battalion would* **be co-located with** *the home-base battalion.*

colocynth /'kɒləsɪnθ/ ▶ **noun** a tropical Old World climbing plant of the gourd family, which bears a pulpy fruit. Also called **BITTER APPLE**. ● *Citrullus colocynthis*, family Cucurbitaceae.
■ the fruit of the colocynth plant. ■ [mass noun] a bitter purgative drug obtained from this fruit.
– ORIGIN mid 16th cent.: via Latin from Greek *kolokunthis*.

Cologne /kə'ləʊn/ an industrial and university city in western Germany, in North Rhine-Westphalia; pop. 989,800 (est. 2006). Founded by the Romans and situated on the River Rhine, Cologne is notable for its medieval cathedral. German name **KÖLN**.

cologne /kə'ləʊn/ ▶ **noun** [mass noun] eau de cologne or similarly scented toilet water.
– ORIGIN early 19th cent.: named after **COLOGNE** in Germany.

Colombia /kə'lɒmbɪə/ a country in the extreme NW of South America, having a coastline on both the Atlantic and the Pacific Ocean; pop. 43,677,400 (est. 2009); official language, Spanish; capital, Bogotá.
Colombia was conquered by the Spanish in the early 16th century and achieved independence in the early 19th century.
– DERIVATIVES **Colombian** adjective & noun.

Colombo /kə'lʌmbəʊ/ the capital and chief port of Sri Lanka; pop. 672,700 (est. 2007).

colon[1] /'kəʊlən/ ▶ **noun** a punctuation mark (:) used to precede a list of items, a quotation, or an expansion or explanation. ■ this mark used to indicate a statement of proportion between two numbers: *10:1.* ■ this mark used to separate hours from minutes (and minutes from seconds) in a numerical statement of time: *4:30 p.m.* ■ this mark used to indicate the number of the chapter and verse respectively in biblical references: *Exodus 3:2.*
– ORIGIN mid 16th cent. (as a term in rhetoric denoting a section of a complex sentence, or a pause before it): via Latin from Greek *kōlon* 'limb, clause'.

colon[2] /'kəʊlən, -lɒn/ ▶ **noun** Anatomy the main part of the large intestine, which passes from the caecum to the rectum and absorbs water and electrolytes from food which has remained undigested.
– ORIGIN late Middle English: via Latin from Greek *kolon.*

Colón /kɒ'lɒn/ the chief port of Panama, at the Caribbean end of the Panama Canal; pop. 87,800 (est. 2009). It was founded in 1850 by the American William Aspinwall (1807–55), after whom it was originally named.

colón /kɒ'lɒn/ ▶ **noun** (pl. **colones** /-'lɒnɛz/) the basic monetary unit of Costa Rica and El Salvador, equal to 100 centimos in Costa Rica and 100 centavos in El Salvador.
– ORIGIN from Cristóbal *Colón*, the Spanish name of Christopher Columbus (see **COLUMBUS**[2]).

colonel /'kəːn(ə)l/ ▶ **noun** a rank of officer in the army and in the US air force, above a lieutenant colonel and below a brigadier or brigadier general. ■ informal short for **LIEUTENANT COLONEL**.
– DERIVATIVES **colonelcy** noun (pl. **colonelcies**).
– ORIGIN mid 16th cent.: from obsolete French *coronel* (earlier form of *colonel*), from Italian *colonnello* 'column of soldiers', from *colonna* 'column', from Latin *columna*. The form *coronel*, source of the modern pronunciation, was usual until the mid 17th cent.

Colonel Blimp ▶ **noun** another term for **BLIMP** (sense 1).

colonel-in-chief ▶ **noun** (pl. **colonels-in-chief**) a title given to the honorary head of a regiment in the British army.

colonial ▶ **adjective 1** relating to or characteristic of a colony or colonies: *British colonial rule | colonial expansion.* ■ denoting a predominantly neoclassical style of architecture characteristic of the period of the British colonies in America before independence, featuring a modification of the Queen Anne style.
2 (of animals or plants) living in colonies.
▶ **noun 1** a native or inhabitant of a colony.
2 a house built in colonial style.
– DERIVATIVES **colonially** adverb.

colonialism ▶ **noun** [mass noun] the policy or practice of acquiring full or partial political control over another country, occupying it with settlers, and exploiting it economically.
– DERIVATIVES **colonialist** noun & adjective.

colonic /kə'lɒnɪk/ ▶ **adjective** Anatomy relating to or affecting the colon.
▶ **noun** informal an act of colonic irrigation.

colonic irrigation ▶ **noun** [mass noun] the practice of injecting water via the anus to flush out the colon, used as a therapeutic treatment.

colonist ▶ **noun** a settler in or inhabitant of a colony.

colonize (also **colonise**) ▶ **verb** [with obj.] send settlers to (a place) and establish political control over it: *the Greeks colonized Sicily and southern Italy.* ■ settle among and establish control over (the indigenous people of an area). ■ appropriate (a place or domain) for one's own use: *a small town in a part of the Hudson Valley fast being colonized by weekenders.* ■ Ecology (of a plant or animal) establish itself in (an area).
– DERIVATIVES **colonization** noun, **colonizer** noun.

colonnade /ˌkɒlə'neɪd/ ▶ **noun** a row of evenly spaced columns supporting a roof, an entablature, or arches.
– DERIVATIVES **colonnaded** adjective.
– ORIGIN early 18th cent.: from French, from *colonne* 'column', from Latin *columna.*

colonoscope /kə'lɒnəskəʊp/ ▶ **noun** Medicine a flexible fibre-optic instrument inserted through the anus in order to examine the colon.
– DERIVATIVES **colonoscopy** noun (pl. **colonoscopies**).

colony ▶ **noun** (pl. **colonies**) **1** a country or area under the full or partial political control of another country and occupied by settlers from that country. ■ a group of people living in such a country or area, consisting of the original settlers and their descendants and successors. ■ (**the colonies**) all the foreign countries or areas formerly under British political control. ■ (**the colonies**) the thirteen areas on the east coast of North America that gained independence from Britain and founded the United States of America.
2 a group of people of one nationality or race living in a foreign place: *the British colony in New York.* ■ a place where a group of people with the same occupation or interest live together: *a nudist colony.*
3 Biology a community of animals or plants of one kind living close together or forming a physically connected structure: *a colony of seals.* ■ a group of fungi or bacteria grown from a single spore or cell on a culture medium.
– ORIGIN late Middle English (denoting a settlement formed mainly of retired soldiers, acting as a garrison in newly conquered territory in the Roman Empire): from Latin *colonia* 'settlement, farm', from *colonus* 'settler, farmer', from *colere* 'cultivate'.

colony-stimulating factor ▶ **noun** Biochemistry a substance secreted by bone marrow which promotes the growth and differentiation of stem cells into colonies of specific blood cells.

colophon /'kɒləf(ə)n/ ▶ **noun** a publisher's emblem or imprint, usually on the title page of a book.
■ historical a statement at the end of a book, typically with a printer's emblem, giving information about its authorship and printing.
– ORIGIN early 17th cent. (denoting a finishing touch): via late Latin from Greek *kolophōn* 'summit or finishing touch'.

colophony /kə'lɒfəni, 'kɒləˌfəʊni/ ▶ **noun** another term for **ROSIN**.
– ORIGIN Middle English: from Latin *colophonia* (*resina*) '(resin) from *Colophon*', a town in Lydia, Asia Minor.

color ▶ **noun & verb** US spelling of **COLOUR**.

Colorado /ˌkɒlə'rɑːdəʊ/ **1** a river which rises in the Rocky Mountains of northern Colorado and flows generally south-westwards for 2,333 km (1,468 miles) to the Gulf of California, passing through the Grand Canyon.
2 a state in the central US; pop. 4,939,456 (est. 2008); capital, Denver. Colorado extends from the Great Plains in the east to the Rocky Mountains in the west. Part of it was acquired by the Louisiana Purchase in 1803 and the rest ceded by Mexico in 1848. It became the 38th state in 1876.
– DERIVATIVES **Coloradan** noun & adjective.

Colorado beetle ▶ **noun** a yellow- and black-striped leaf beetle native to America, whose larvae are highly destructive to potato plants. ● *Leptinotarsa decemlineata*, family Chrysomelidae.
– ORIGIN late 19th cent.: named after the state of **COLORADO**.

C

coloration (also **colouration**) ▶ **noun 1** the appearance of something with regard to colour: *some bacterial structures take on a purple coloration.* ■ the natural colouring of animals or plants: *the red coloration of many maples.* ■ a scheme of applying colour in art.
2 the pervading character or tone of something: *the productions have taken on a political coloration.* ■ a variety of musical or vocal expression: *the subtle colorations of big-box speakers.*
– ORIGIN early 17th cent.: from late Latin *coloratio(n-)*, from *colorare* 'to colour'.

coloratura /ˌkɒlərə'tjʊərə/ ▶ **noun** [mass noun] elaborate ornamentation of a vocal melody, especially in operatic singing. ■ (also **coloratura soprano**) [count noun] a soprano skilled in coloratura singing.
– ORIGIN Italian, literally 'colouring', from Latin *colorare* 'to colour'.

colorectal /ˌkəʊləʊ'rɛkt(ə)l/ ▶ **adjective** relating to or affecting the colon and the rectum.

colorific /ˌkʌlə'rɪfɪk, ˌkɒl-/ (also **colourific**) ▶ **adjective** rare having much colour: *the colorific radiance of costume.*
– ORIGIN late 17th cent.: from French *colorifique* or modern Latin *colorificus*, from Latin *color* 'colour'.

colorimeter /ˌkʌlə'rɪmɪtə, ˌkɒl-/ ▶ **noun** an instrument for measuring the intensity of colour.
– DERIVATIVES **colorimetric** adjective, **colorimetry** noun.
– ORIGIN mid 19th cent.: from Latin *color* 'colour' + **-METER**.

colorize (Brit. also **colourize**) ▶ **verb** [with obj.] add colour to (a black-and-white film).
– DERIVATIVES **colorization** noun (trademark in the US), **colorizer** noun (trademark in the US).

colossal ▶ **adjective 1** extremely large or great: *a colossal amount of mail | a colossal mistake.* ■ Sculpture (of a statue) at least twice life size.
2 Architecture (of an order) having more than one storey of columns.
– DERIVATIVES **colossally** adverb.
– ORIGIN early 18th cent.: from French, from *colosse*, from Latin *colossus* (see **COLOSSUS**).

Colosseum /ˌkɒlə'siːəm/ ▶ **noun** the name since medieval times of the *Amphitheatrum Flavium*, a vast amphitheatre in Rome, begun *c.*75 AD.
– ORIGIN from Latin, neuter of *colosseus* 'gigantic', from *colossus* (see **COLOSSUS**).

colosseum ▶ **noun** variant spelling of **COLISEUM**.

Colossians, Epistle to the /kə'lɒʃ(ə)nz/ a book of the New Testament, an epistle of St Paul to the Church at Colossae in Phrygia.

colossus /kə'lɒsəs/ ▶ **noun** (pl. **colossi** /-sʌɪ/ or **colossuses**) a statue that is much bigger than life size.
■ a person or thing of enormous size, importance, or ability: *the Russian Empire was the colossus of European politics.*
– PHRASES **bestride something like a colossus** totally dominate a place or area of activity: *he bestrode French cinema like a colossus.*
– ORIGIN late Middle English: via Latin from Greek *kolossos* (applied by Herodotus to the statues of Egyptian temples).

Colossus of Rhodes a huge bronze statue of the sun god Helios, one of the Seven Wonders of the World. Built *c.*292–280 BC, it stood beside the harbour entrance at Rhodes for about fifty years.

colostomy /kə'lɒstəmi/ ▶ **noun** (pl. **colostomies**) a surgical operation in which the colon is shortened to remove a damaged part and the cut end diverted to an opening in the abdominal wall. ■ an opening so formed: [as modifier] *a colostomy bag.*
– ORIGIN late 19th cent.: from **COLON**[2] + Greek *stoma* 'mouth'.

colostrum /kə'lɒstrəm/ ▶ **noun** [mass noun] the first secretion from the mammary glands after giving birth, rich in antibodies.
– ORIGIN late 16th cent.: from Latin.

colour (US **color**) ▶ **noun 1** [mass noun] the property possessed by an object of producing different sensations

C

on the eye as a result of the way it reflects or emits light: *the lights flickered and changed colour.* ■ [count noun] one, or any mixture, of the constituents into which light can be separated in a spectrum or rainbow, sometimes including (loosely) black and white: *a rich brown colour* | *a range of bright colours.* ■ the use of all colours, not only black and white, in photography or television: *he has shot the whole film in colour* | [as modifier] *colour television.* ■ rosiness or redness of the face as an indication of health or of embarrassment, anger, etc.: *there was some colour back in his face* | *colour flooded her skin as she realized what he meant.* ■ a substance used to give something a particular colour: *lip colour.* ■ [count noun] Heraldry any of the major conventional colours used in coats of arms (gules, vert, sable, azure, purpure), especially as opposed to the metals, furs, and stains. ■ [count noun] Snooker any of the balls other than the white cue ball and the reds.
2 [mass noun] pigmentation of the skin, especially as an indication of someone's race: *discrimination on the basis of colour.* ■ [count noun] a group of people considered as being distinguished by skin pigmentation: *all colours and nationalities.*
3 [mass noun] vivid appearance resulting from the juxtaposition of many bright things: *for colour, plant groups of winter-flowering pansies.* ■ features that lend a particularly interesting quality to something: *a town full of colour and character.* ■ variety of musical tone or expression: *orchestral colour.*
4 (**colours**) an item or items of a particular colour worn to identify or distinguish an individual or a member of a group, in particular a jockey or a member of a sports team. ■ (also **school colours**) a badge, cap, or other item in the distinctive colours of a particular school, awarded to a pupil selected to represent the school in a sport. ■ chiefly Brit. the flag of a country, or of a regiment or ship.
5 a shade of meaning: *many events in her past had taken on a different colour.*
6 [mass noun] Physics a quantized property of quarks which can take three values (designated blue, green, and red) for each flavour.
▶ **verb 1** [with obj.] change the colour of (something) by painting, dyeing, or shading it: *he coloured her hair with a selection of blonde and brown shades.* ■ [no obj.] take on a different colour: *the foliage will not colour well if the soil is too rich.* ■ fill (a shape or outline) with colour: *he hated finger-painting and colouring in pictures.* ■ make vivid or picturesque: *he has coloured the dance with gestures from cabaret and vaudeville.*
2 [no obj.] (of a person or their skin) show embarrassment or shame by becoming red; blush: *she coloured slightly.* ■ [with obj.] cause (a person's skin) to change in colour: *rage coloured his pale complexion.* ■ [with obj.] (of an emotion) imbue (a person's voice) with a particular tone: *surprise coloured her voice.*
3 [with obj.] influence, especially in a negative way; distort: *the experiences had coloured her whole existence.* ■ misrepresent by distortion or exaggeration: *witnesses might colour evidence to make a story saleable.*
– PHRASES **lend** (or **give**) **colour to** make something seem true or probable: *this lent colour and credibility to his defence.* **show one's true colours** reveal one's real character or intentions, especially when these are disreputable or dishonourable. **under colour of** under the pretext of. **with flying colours** see FLYING.
– ORIGIN Middle English: from Old French *colour* (noun), *colourer* (verb), from Latin *color* (noun), *colorare* (verb).

colourable (US **colorable**) ▶ **adjective 1** capable of being coloured: *colourable illustrations.*
2 appearing to be correct or justified, but in fact not so: *a colourable legal claim.* ■ counterfeit.

colourant (US **colorant**) ▶ **noun** a dye, pigment, or other substance that colours something.

colouration ▶ **noun** variant spelling of COLORATION.

colour bar ▶ **noun** a social system in which black people are denied access to the same rights, opportunities, and facilities as white people.

colour-blind ▶ **adjective** unable to distinguish certain colours, or (rarely in humans) any colours at all. See PROTANOPIA.
– DERIVATIVES **colour blindness** noun.

colour code ▶ **noun** a system of marking things with different colours as a means of identification.
▶ **verb** (**colour-code**) [with obj.] mark (things) with different colours as a means of identification: *each unit is colour-coded for clarity.*

coloured (US **colored**) ▶ **adjective 1** having a colour or colours, especially as opposed to being black, white, or neutral: *brightly coloured birds are easier to see* | [in combination] *a peach-coloured sofa.* ■ imbued with an emotive or exaggerated quality: ***highly coloured** examples were used by both sides.*
2 (also **Coloured**) dated or offensive wholly or partly of non-white descent. ■ S. African used as an ethnic label for people of mixed ethnic origin, including Khoisan, African, Malay, Chinese, and white.
▶ **noun 1** (also **Coloured**) dated or offensive a person who is wholly or partly of non-white descent. ■ S. African a person of mixed descent usually speaking Afrikaans or English as their mother tongue.
2 (**coloureds**) clothes, sheets, etc. that are any colour but white.

> **USAGE** **Coloured** referring to skin colour is first recorded in the early 17th century and was adopted in the US by emancipated slaves as a term of racial pride after the end of the American Civil War. In Britain it was the accepted term until the 1960s, when it was superseded (as in the US) by **black**. The term **coloured** lost favour among black people during this period and is now widely regarded as offensive except in historical contexts.
> In South Africa the term **coloured** (also written **Coloured**) has a different history. It is used to refer to people of mixed-race parentage rather than, as elsewhere, to refer to African peoples and their descendants (i.e. as a synonym for **black**). Under apartheid it was imposed as an official racial designation. However, in modern use the term is not generally considered offensive or derogatory.

colour fast ▶ **adjective** dyed in colours that will not fade or be washed out.
– DERIVATIVES **colour fastness** noun.

colour-field painting ▶ **noun** [mass noun] a style of American abstract painting prominent from the late 1940s to the 1960s which features large expanses of unmodulated colour covering the greater part of the canvas. Barnett Newman and Mark Rothko were considered its chief exponents.

colour filter ▶ **noun** a photographic filter that absorbs light of certain colours.

colourful (US **colorful**) ▶ **adjective 1** having much or varied colour; bright: *a colourful array of fruit.*
2 full of interest; lively and exciting: *a controversial and colourful character* | *a colourful account.* ■ involving variously disreputable activities: *the financier had had a colourful career.* ■ (of language) vulgar or rude: *she made it clear, in colourful language, that she did not wish to talk to the police.*
– DERIVATIVES **colourfully** adverb, **colourfulness** noun.

colouring (US **coloring**) ▶ **noun** [mass noun] **1** the process of changing the colour of something by painting, dyeing, or shading it. ■ the filling in of a shape or outline with colour: [as modifier] *a colouring book.*
2 appearance with regard to colour: *the toad's colouring blended perfectly with its surroundings.* ■ the natural hues of a person's skin, hair, and eyes: *her fair colouring.* ■ the pervading character or tone of something: *her performance was strong on dramatic colouring.*
3 matter used to give a particular colour to something, especially food: *food colouring* | [count noun] *paint the eggs using edible food colourings.*

colourist (US **colorist**) ▶ **noun** an artist or designer who uses colour in a special or skilful way. ■ a person who tints black-and-white films. ■ a hairdresser who specializes in dyeing people's hair.

colouristic (US **coloristic**) ▶ **adjective** showing special use of colour: *his great colouristic wallpapers.* ■ having or showing a variety of musical or vocal expression: *the choir's colouristic resources.*
– DERIVATIVES **colouristically** adverb.

colourize (also **colourise**) ▶ **verb** Brit. variant spelling of COLORIZE.

colourless (US **colorless**) ▶ **adjective 1** (especially of a gas or liquid) without colour. ■ dull or pale in hue: *her colourless cheeks.*
2 lacking distinctive character or interest; dull: *the book is rather colourless, like its author.*
– DERIVATIVES **colourlessly** adverb, **colourlessness** noun.

colour phase ▶ **noun** a genetic or seasonal variation in the colour of the skin, pelt, or feathers of an animal.

colourpoint ▶ **noun** a cat of a long-haired breed having a pale coat with dark points, and blue eyes, developed by crossing Persian and Siamese cats.

colour reversal ▶ **noun** [mass noun] [usu. as modifier] Photography the process of producing a positive image directly from another positive: *colour reversal films.*

colour saturation ▶ **noun** see SATURATION.

colour scheme ▶ **noun** an arrangement or combination of colours, especially one used in interior decoration: *a brown or gold colour scheme.*
– DERIVATIVES **colour scheming** noun.

colour separation ▶ **noun** [mass noun] Photography & Printing the production of separate negative images of the same subject taken through green, red, and blue filters, which are combined to reproduce the full colour of the original. ■ [count noun] an image produced in this way.

colour sergeant ▶ **noun** a rank of non-commissioned officer in the Army and Royal Marines, above sergeant and below warrant officer.
– ORIGIN with reference to the sergeant's responsibility for carrying one of the regiment's colours in a guard of honour.

colour supplement ▶ **noun** Brit. a magazine printed in colour and issued with a newspaper, especially at weekends.

colour temperature ▶ **noun** Astronomy & Physics the temperature at which a black body would emit radiation of the same colour as a given object.

colour therapy ▶ **noun** [mass noun] a system of alternative medicine based on the use of colour, especially projected coloured light.

colour wash ▶ **noun** [mass noun] coloured distemper.
▶ **verb** (**colour-wash**) [with obj.] paint (something) with coloured distemper.

colourway (US **colorway**) ▶ **noun** any of a range of combinations of colours in which a style or design is available: *our sweater comes in two colourways.*

colour wheel ▶ **noun** a circle with different coloured sectors used to show the relationship between colours.

colporteur /ˈkɒlˌpɔːtə, ˌkɒlpɔːˈtəː/ ▶ **noun** a person who sells books, newspapers, and similar literature. ■ someone employed by a religious society to distribute bibles and other religious tracts.
– DERIVATIVES **colportage** /ˈkɒlˌpɔːtɪdʒ/ noun.
– ORIGIN late 18th cent.: French, from the verb *colporter*, probably an alteration of *comporter*, from Latin *comportare* 'carry with one'.

colposcope /ˈkɒlpəskəʊp/ ▶ **noun** a surgical instrument used to examine the vagina and the cervix of the womb.
– DERIVATIVES **colposcopy** /kɒlˈpɒskəpi/ noun.
– ORIGIN 1940s: from Greek *kolpos* 'womb' + -SCOPE.

Colt[1] /kəʊlt/, Samuel (1814–62), American inventor. He is remembered chiefly for the revolver named after him, which he patented in 1836.

Colt[2] /kəʊlt/ ▶ **noun** trademark a type of revolver.

colt /kəʊlt/ ▶ **noun** a young uncastrated male horse, in particular one less than four years old. ■ Brit. a member of a junior sports team: *England Colts.*
– ORIGIN Old English; perhaps related to Swedish *kult*, applied to boys or half-grown animals.

coltan /ˈkɒltan/ ▶ **noun** [mass noun] a dull metallic mineral which is a combination of columbite and tantalite and which is refined to produce tantalum.
– ORIGIN 1990s: from COLUMBITE + TANTALITE.

colter ▶ **noun** US spelling of COULTER.

coltish ▶ **adjective** energetic but awkward in one's movements or behaviour.
– DERIVATIVES **coltishly** adverb, **coltishness** noun.

Coltrane /kɒlˈtreɪn/, John (William) (1926–67), American jazz saxophonist. He was a leading figure in avant-garde jazz, bridging the gap between the harmonically dense jazz of the 1950s and the free jazz that evolved in the 1960s.

coltsfoot ▶ **noun** (pl. **coltsfoots**) a Eurasian plant of the daisy family, with yellow flowers which appear in the early spring before the large heart-shaped leaves. It is used in herbal medicine for the treatment of coughs and respiratory disorders. ● *Tussilago farfara*, family Compositae.
– ORIGIN mid 16th cent.: translating medieval Latin *pes pulli* 'foal's foot', with reference to the shape of the leaves.

colubrid /ˈkɒljʊbrɪd/ ▶ **noun** Zoology a snake of a very large family (Colubridae) which includes the majority of harmless species, such as grass snakes and garter snakes. The few venomous species have grooved fangs in the rear of the upper jaw.
– ORIGIN late 19th cent.: from modern Latin *Colubridae* (plural), from Latin *coluber* 'snake'.

colubrine /ˈkɒljʊbrʌɪn/ ▶ **adjective** relating to or resembling a snake.

– ORIGIN early 16th cent.: from Latin *colubrinus*, from *coluber* 'snake'.

colugo /kəˈluːgəʊ/ ▶ **noun** (pl. **colugos**) another term for FLYING LEMUR.
– ORIGIN late 18th cent.: of unknown origin.

Columba /kəˈlʌmbə/ Astronomy a small and faint southern constellation (the Dove), near Canis Major. It is sometimes said to represent the dove that Noah sent out from the Ark.
– ORIGIN Latin.

Columba, St /kəˈlʌmbə/ (*c.*521–97), Irish abbot and missionary. He established the monastery at Iona in *c.*563 and converted the Picts to Christianity. Feast day, 9 June.

columbarium /ˌkɒl(ə)mˈbɛːrɪəm/ ▶ **noun** (pl. **columbaria**) a room or building with niches for funeral urns to be stored.
– ORIGIN mid 18th cent.: from Latin, literally 'pigeon-house', from *columba* 'pigeon'.

Columbia /kəˈlʌmbɪə/ **1** a river in NW North America which rises in the Rocky Mountains of SE British Columbia, Canada, and flows 1,953 km (1,230 miles) generally southwards into the US, where it turns westwards to enter the Pacific south of Seattle.
2 the state capital of South Carolina; pop. 127,029 (est. 2008).

Columbia, District of see DISTRICT OF COLUMBIA.

Columbia University a university in New York City, one of the most prestigious in the US. It was founded in 1754.

Columbine /ˈkɒləmbʌɪn/ a character in Italian commedia dell'arte, the mistress of Harlequin.
– ORIGIN from French *Colombine*, from Italian *Colombina*, feminine of *colombino* 'dovelike', from *colombo* 'dove'.

columbine /ˈkɒləmbʌɪn/ ▶ **noun** an aquilegia which has long-spurred flowers that are typically purplish blue. ● Genus *Aquilegia*, family Ranunculaceae, especially *A. vulgaris* and its hybrids.
– ORIGIN late Middle English: from Old French *colombine*, from medieval Latin *colombina* (*herba*) 'dovelike (plant)', from Latin *columba* 'dove' (from the supposed resemblance of the flower to a cluster of five doves).

columbite /kəˈlʌmbʌɪt/ ▶ **noun** [mass noun] a black mineral, typically occurring as dense tabular crystals, consisting of an oxide of iron, manganese, niobium, and tantalum. It is the chief ore of niobium.
– ORIGIN early 19th cent.: from COLUMBIUM + -ITE[1].

columbium /kəˈlʌmbɪəm/ ▶ **noun** old-fashioned term for NIOBIUM.
– ORIGIN early 19th cent.: modern Latin, from *Columbia*, a poetic name for America from the name of Christopher *Columbus* (see COLUMBUS[2]).

Columbus[1] the state capital of Ohio; pop. 754,885 (est. 2008).

Columbus[2], Christopher (1451–1506), Italian-born Spanish explorer, credited as being the first European to reach the Americas; Spanish name *Cristóbal Colón*.

> Columbus persuaded the Spanish monarchs, Ferdinand and Isabella, to sponsor an expedition to sail across the Atlantic in search of Asia and to prove that the world was round. In 1492 he set sail with three small ships and reached the New World (in fact various Caribbean islands). He made three further voyages between 1493 and 1504, reaching the South American mainland in 1498.

Columbus Day ▶ **noun** (in the US) a legal holiday commemorating Christopher Columbus's first voyage to the Americas in 1492. It is observed by most states on the second Monday of October.

columella /ˌkɒljʊˈmɛlə/ ▶ **noun** (pl. **columellae** /-liː/)
1 Zoology an ossicle (small bone) of the middle ear of birds, reptiles, and amphibians. ■ Anatomy the pillar around which the cochlea spirals.
2 Zoology the axis of a spiral shell.
3 Botany the axis of the spore-producing body of some lower plants.
– DERIVATIVES **columellar** adjective.
– ORIGIN late 16th cent.: from Latin, 'small column'.

column ▶ **noun 1** an upright pillar, typically cylindrical, supporting an arch, entablature, or other structure or standing alone as a monument. ■ a similar vertical, roughly cylindrical thing: *a great column of smoke*. ■ an upright shaft for controlling a machine or vehicle: *a Spitfire control column*.
2 a vertical division of a page or text. ■ a vertical arrangement of figures or other information. ■ a regular section of a newspaper or magazine devoted to a particular subject or written by a particular person.
3 one or more lines of people or vehicles moving in the same direction: *a column of tanks moved north-west | we walked in a column*. ■ Military a narrow-fronted deep formation of troops in successive lines. ■ a military force or convoy of ships.
– DERIVATIVES **columnar** adjective, **columned** adjective [often in combination] *a four-columned portico*.
– ORIGIN late Middle English: partly from Old French *columpne*, reinforced by its source, Latin *columna* 'pillar'.

columnated /ˈkɒləmneɪtɪd/ ▶ **adjective** supported on or having columns: *a columnated church interior*.

column inch ▶ **noun** a one-inch length of a column in a newspaper or magazine.

columnist /ˈkɒləm(n)ɪst/ ▶ **noun** a journalist contributing regularly to a newspaper or magazine.

colure /kəˈljʊə/ ▶ **noun** Astronomy either of two great circles intersecting at right angles at the celestial poles and passing through the ecliptic at either the equinoxes or the solstices.
– ORIGIN late Middle English: from late Latin *coluri* (plural), from Greek *kolourai* (*grammai*) 'truncated (lines)', from *kolouros* 'truncated', so named because the lower part is permanently cut off from view.

coly /ˈkəʊli/ ▶ **noun** (pl. **colies**) another term for MOUSEBIRD.
– ORIGIN mid 19th cent.: from modern Latin *Colius*, from Greek *kolios*, denoting a type of woodpecker.

colza /ˈkɒlzə/ ▶ **noun** another term for RAPE[2].
– ORIGIN early 18th cent.: from Walloon French *kolza*, from Low German *kōlsāt*, Dutch *koolzaad*, from *kool* 'cole' + *zaad* 'seed'.

com- (also **co-**, **col-**, **con-**, or **cor-**) ▶ **prefix** with; together; jointly; altogether: *combine | command | collude*.
– ORIGIN from Latin *cum* 'with'.

coma[1] /ˈkəʊmə/ ▶ **noun** a prolonged state of deep unconsciousness, caused especially by severe injury or illness: *she went into a coma*. ■ humorous a state of extreme lethargy or sleepiness.
– ORIGIN mid 17th cent.: modern Latin, from Greek *kōma* 'deep sleep'; related to *koitē* 'bed' and *keisthai* 'lie down'.

coma[2] /ˈkəʊmə/ ▶ **noun** (pl. **comae** /-miː/) Astronomy a diffuse cloud of gas and dust surrounding the nucleus of a comet. ■ [mass noun] Optics aberration which causes the image of an off-axis point to be flared like a comet.
– ORIGIN early 17th cent. (in botanical sense 'tuft of hairs on seed'): via Latin from Greek *komē* 'hair of the head'.

Coma Berenices /ˌkəʊmə ˌbɛrɪˈnʌɪsiːz/ Astronomy a small inconspicuous northern constellation (Berenice's Hair), said to represent the tresses of Queen Berenice. It contains a large number of galaxies.
– ORIGIN Latin.

Comanche /kəˈmantʃi/ ▶ **noun** (pl. **same** or **Comanches**) **1** a member of an American Indian people of the south-western US. The Comanche were among the first to acquire horses (from the Spanish) and resisted white settlers fiercely.
2 [mass noun] the Uto-Aztecan language of the Comanche, now virtually extinct.
▶ **adjective** relating to the Comanche or their language.
– ORIGIN Spanish, from Comanche.

Comaneci /ˌkɒməˈnɛtʃ/, Nadia (b.1961), Romanian-born American gymnast. In 1976 she became the first Olympic competitor to be awarded the maximum score of 10.00.

comatose /ˈkəʊmətəʊs, -z/ ▶ **adjective** relating to or in a state of coma: *she had been comatose for seven months | a comatose patient*. ■ humorous extremely lethargic or sleepy.
– ORIGIN late 17th cent.: from Greek *kōma*, *kōmat-* 'deep sleep' + -OSE[1].

comb ▶ **noun 1** a strip of plastic, metal, or wood with a row of narrow teeth, used for untangling or arranging the hair. ■ [in sing.] an act of untangling or arranging the hair with comb: *she gave her hair a comb*. ■ a short curved type of comb, worn by women to hold the hair in place or as an adornment.
2 something resembling a comb in function or structure, in particular: ■ a device for separating and dressing textile fibres. ■ Austral./NZ the lower, fixed cutting piece of a sheep-shearing machine. ■ a row of brass points for collecting the electricity in an electrostatic generator.
3 the red fleshy crest on the head of a domestic fowl, especially a cock.
4 short for HONEYCOMB (sense 1 of the noun).
▶ **verb** [with obj.] **1** untangle or arrange (the hair) by drawing a comb through it: *she combed her hair and put some lipstick on* | (as adj., with submodifier **combed**) *neatly combed hair*. ■ (**comb something out**) remove something in the hair by drawing a comb through it: *she combed the burrs out of the dog's coat*.
2 prepare (wool, flax, or cotton) for manufacture with a comb. ■ (usu. as adj. **combed**) treat (a fabric) in such a way: *the socks are made of soft combed cotton*.
3 search carefully and systematically: *police combed the area for the murder weapon* | [no obj.] *his mother combed through the cardboard boxes*.
– DERIVATIVES **comb-like** adjective.
– ORIGIN Old English *camb*, of Germanic origin; related to Dutch *kam* and German *Kamm*.

combat ▶ **noun** [mass noun] fighting between armed forces: *five Hurricanes were shot down in combat* | [count noun] *pilots re-enacted the aerial combats of yesteryear* | [as modifier] *a combat zone*. ■ non-violent conflict or opposition: *electoral combat*.
▶ **verb** (**combats**, **combating** or **combatting**, **combated** or **combatted**) [with obj.] take action to reduce or prevent (something bad or undesirable): *an effort to combat drug trafficking*. ■ archaic engage in a fight with; oppose in battle.
– ORIGIN mid 16th cent. (originally denoting a fight between two people or parties): from French *combattre* (verb), from late Latin *combattere*, from *com-* 'together with' + *battere*, variant of Latin *batuere* 'to fight'.

combatant /ˈkɒmbət(ə)nt, ˈkʌm-/ ▶ **noun** a person or nation engaged in fighting during a war. ■ a person engaged in conflict or competition with another.
▶ **adjective** engaged in fighting during a war: *all the combatant armies went to war with machine guns*.
– ORIGIN late Middle English (as an adjective used in heraldry to describe two lions facing one another with raised forepaws): from Old French, present participle of *combatre* 'to fight' (see COMBAT).

combat dress ▶ **noun** [mass noun] uniform of a type intended to be worn by soldiers in actual combat.

combat fatigue ▶ **noun 1** more recent term for SHELL SHOCK.
2 (**combat fatigues**) combat dress.

combative /ˈkɒmbətɪv, ˈkʌm-/ ▶ **adjective** ready or eager to fight or argue: *he made some enemies with his combative style*.
– DERIVATIVES **combatively** adverb, **combativeness** noun.

combat jacket ▶ **noun** a jacket of a type worn by soldiers in combat, typically having a camouflage pattern.

combat trousers ▶ **plural noun** loose trousers with large patch pockets halfway down each leg, typically made of hard-wearing cotton.

comb-back ▶ **noun** a high-backed Windsor chair with a straight top rail: [as modifier] *a comb-back rocker*.

combe /kuːm/ (also **coomb** or **coombe**) ▶ **noun** Brit. a short valley or hollow on a hillside or coastline, especially in southern England. ■ Geology a dry valley in a limestone or chalk escarpment.
– ORIGIN Old English *cumb*, occurring in charters in the names of places in southern England, many of which survive; of Celtic origin, related to CWM.

comber[1] /ˈkəʊmə/ ▶ **noun 1** a long curling sea wave.
2 a person or machine that prepares cotton or wool for manufacture by separating and straightening the fibres.

comber[2] /ˈkɒmbə/ ▶ **noun** a small fish that gapes when dead, occurring in shallow waters from the western English Channel to the Mediterranean. Also called GAPER. ● *Serranus cabrilla*, family Serranidae.
– ORIGIN mid 18th cent.: of unknown origin.

combfish ▶ **noun** (pl. **same** or **combfishes**) a fish of the NE Pacific, with small rough scales and long spines in the comb-like dorsal fin. ● Family Zaniolepididae and genus *Zaniolepis*: several species.

combi ▶ **noun** a machine or appliance with two or more functions: [as modifier] *a combi oven*.
– ORIGIN 1960s: abbreviation of COMBINATION.

combination ▶ **noun 1** a joining or merging of different parts or qualities in which the component elements are individually distinct: *a magnificent combination of drama, dance, and music | the combination of recession and falling property values proved fatal to the business community | this colour*

C

combination is stunningly effective. ■ [mass noun] the state of being joined or merged in such a way: *these four factors work together **in combination**.* ■ a particular arrangement of different elements: *the canvases may be arranged in any number of combinations.* ■ (in sport) a coordinated and effective sequence of moves: *a good uppercut/hook combination.* ■ [as modifier] denoting an object or process that unites different uses, functions, or ingredients: *combination remedies contain painkiller, decongestant, and cough soother.* ■ [mass noun] Chemistry the joining of substances in a compound with new properties.
2 a sequence of numbers or letters used to open a combination lock.
3 Brit. a motorcycle with a sidecar attached.
4 (**combinations**) Brit. dated a single undergarment covering the body and legs.
5 Mathematics a selection of a given number of elements from a larger number without regard to their arrangement.
– DERIVATIVES **combinational** adjective, **combinative** adjective, **combinatorial** adjective (Mathematics), **combinatorially** adverb (Mathematics), **combinatory** adjective.
– ORIGIN late Middle English: from late Latin *combinatio(n-)*, from the verb *combinare* 'join two by two' (see COMBINE[1]).

combinational circuit ▸ noun Electronics a circuit whose output is dependent only on the state of its inputs. Compare with SEQUENTIAL CIRCUIT.

combination lock ▸ noun a lock that is opened by rotating a set of marked or numbered dials to show a specific sequence.

combination oven ▸ noun an oven operating by both conventional heating and microwaves.

combination skin ▸ noun [mass noun] a type of facial complexion characterized by an oily forehead, nose, and chin and relatively dry cheeks.

combination therapy ▸ noun [mass noun] treatment in which a patient is given two or more drugs (or other therapeutic agents) for a single disease.

combinatorics /ˌkɒmbɪnəˈtɒrɪks/ ▸ plural noun [treated as sing.] the branch of mathematics dealing with combinations of objects belonging to a finite set in accordance with certain constraints, such as those of graph theory.
– ORIGIN 1940s: from *combinatorial* (see COMBINATION), influenced by German *Kombinatorik*.

combine[1] ▸ verb /kəmˈbʌɪn/ **1** join or merge to form a single unit or substance: [with obj.] ***combine the flour with the margarine and salt*** | *a new product which combines the benefits of a hairspray and a gel* | [no obj., with infinitive] *high tides and winds combined to bring chaos to the east coast.* ■ [no obj.] Chemistry unite to form a compound: *oxygen and hydrogen do not combine at room temperatures* | *oxygen **combines with** haemoglobin.*
2 [no obj.] unite for a common purpose: [with infinitive] *groups of teachers combined to tackle a variety of problems.* ■ [with obj.] engage in simultaneously: *an ideal place to combine shopping and sightseeing.*
▸ noun /ˈkɒmbʌɪn/ a group of people or companies acting together for a commercial purpose: *one of the world's biggest food and personal products combines.*
– DERIVATIVES **combinable** adjective, **combiner** noun.
– ORIGIN late Middle English: from Old French *combiner* or late Latin *combinare* 'join two by two', from *com-* 'together' + Latin *bini* 'two together'.

combine[2] /ˈkɒmbʌɪn/ ▸ verb [with obj.] Brit. harvest (a crop) by means of a combine harvester.
▸ noun a combine harvester.

combined pill ▸ noun an oral contraceptive containing both an oestrogen and a progestogen.

combine harvester ▸ noun Brit. an agricultural machine that reaps, threshes, and cleans a cereal crop in one operation.

combings ▸ plural noun hairs removed as a result of combing.

combing wool ▸ noun [mass noun] long-stapled wool with straight, parallel fibres, suitable for combing and making into high-quality fabrics, in particular worsted. Compare with CARDING WOOL.

combining form ▸ noun Grammar a form of a word normally used in compounds in combination with another element to form a word (e.g. *Anglo-* 'English' in *Anglo-Irish*, *bio-* 'life' in *biology*, *-graphy* 'writing' in *biography*).

> **USAGE** In this dictionary, **combining form** is used to denote an element that contributes to the particular sense of words (as with **bio-** and **-graphy** in **biography**), as distinct from a prefix or suffix that adjusts the sense of or determines the function of words (as with **un-**, **-able**, and **-ation**).

comb jelly ▸ noun a marine animal with a jellyfish-like body bearing rows of fused cilia for propulsion. They are typically small planktonic animals and are noted for their luminescence. Also called CTENOPHORE.
● Phylum Ctenophora: two classes.

combo ▸ noun (pl. **combos**) informal **1** a small jazz, rock, or pop band.
2 chiefly N. Amer. a combination, typically of different foods: *a surf 'n' turf combo.*
3 a guitar amplifier with an integral speaker rather than a separate one.
– ORIGIN 1920s (originally US): abbreviation of COMBINATION + -O.

comb-over ▸ noun a strip of hair combed over a bald patch on a man's head in an attempt to conceal it.

combs /kɒmz/ ▸ plural noun Brit. informal, dated a single undergarment covering the body and legs.
– ORIGIN 1930s: abbreviation of *combination garments*.

combust /kəmˈbʌst/ ▸ verb [with obj.] consume or destroy by fire: *when fossil fuels are combusted, oxides are emitted into the atmosphere.* ■ [no obj.] be consumed or destroyed by fire.
– DERIVATIVES **combustor** noun.
– ORIGIN late 15th cent.: from obsolete *combust* 'burnt, calcined', from Latin *combustus*, past participle of *comburere* 'burn up'.

combustible /kəmˈbʌstɪb(ə)l/ ▸ adjective able to catch fire and burn easily: *a combustible gas.* ■ excitable; easily annoyed: *a volatile and combustible personality.*
▸ noun a combustible substance.
– DERIVATIVES **combustibility** noun.
– ORIGIN early 16th cent.: from Old French, from late Latin *combustibilis*, from Latin *combust-* 'burnt up', from the verb *comburere*.

combustion ▸ noun [mass noun] the process of burning something: *the combustion of fossil fuels* | [as modifier] *a large combustion plant.* ■ Chemistry rapid chemical combination of a substance with oxygen, involving the production of heat and light.
– DERIVATIVES **combustive** adjective.
– ORIGIN late Middle English: from late Latin *combustio(n-)*, from Latin *comburere* 'burn up'.

combustion chamber ▸ noun an enclosed space in which combustion takes place, especially in an engine or furnace.

come ▸ verb (past **came**; past participle **come**) **1** [no obj., usu. with adverbial of direction] move or travel towards or into a place thought of as near or familiar to the speaker: *Jess came into the kitchen* | *they came here as immigrants* | *he came rushing out.* ■ arrive at a specified place: *we walked along till we **came to** a stream* | *it was very late when she **came back*** | *my trunk hasn't come yet.* ■ (of a thing) reach or extend to a specified point: *women in slim dresses that came all the way to their shoes* | *the path comes straight down.* ■ (**be coming**) approach: *someone was coming* | *she heard the train coming.* ■ travel in order to be with a specified person, to do a specified thing, or to be present at an event: *the police came* | ***come and** live with me* | [with infinitive] *the electrician came to mend the cooker* | figurative *we have come a long way since Aristotle.* ■ [with present participle] join someone in participating in a specified activity or course of action: *do you want to come fishing tomorrow?* ■ (**come along/on**) make progress; develop: *he's coming along nicely* | *she asked them how their garden was coming on.* ■ (in imperative also **come, come!**) said to someone when correcting or reassuring someone: *Come, come, child, don't thank me.*
2 [no obj.] occur; happen; take place: *twilight had not yet come* | *his father waited for a phone call that never came* | *a chance like this doesn't **come along** every day.* ■ be heard, perceived, or experienced: *a voice came from the kitchen* | ***it came as** a great shock.* ■ [with adverbial] (of a quality) become apparent or noticeable through actions or performance: *as an actor your style and personality must **come through**.* ■ (**come across** or Brit. **over** or US **off**) (of a person) appear or sound in a specified way; give a specified impression: *he'd always **come across as** a decent sort.* ■ (of a thought or memory) enter one's mind: ***the basic idea came to me** while reading an article* | *a passage from a novel **came back to** Adam.*
3 [no obj., with complement] take or occupy a specified position in space, order, or priority: *prisons come well down the list of priorities* | *I make sure my kids come first.* ■ achieve a specified place in a race or contest: *she came second among sixty contestants.*
4 [no obj., with complement] pass into a specified state, especially one of separation or disunion: *his shirt had come undone.* ■ (**come to/into**) reach or be brought to a specified situation or result: *you will come to no harm* | *staff who come into contact with the public* | *the vehicle **came to rest** against a traffic signal.* ■ [with infinitive] eventually reach a certain condition or state of mind: *he had come to realize she was no puppet.*
5 [no obj., with adverbial] be sold, available, or found in a specified form: *the cars **come with** a variety of extras* | *the shirts **come in** three sizes.*
6 [no obj.] informal have an orgasm.
▸ preposition informal when a specified time is reached or event happens: *I don't think that they'll be far away from honours come the new season.*
▸ noun [mass noun] informal semen ejaculated at an orgasm.
– PHRASES **as —— as they come** used to describe someone or something that is a supreme example of the quality specified: *Smith is as tough as they come.* **come again?** informal used to ask someone to repeat or explain something they have said. **come and go** arrive and then depart again; move around freely. ■ exist or be present for a limited time; be transitory: *kings and queens may come and go, but the Crown goes on forever.* **come from behind** win after lagging. **come off it** [in imperative] informal said when vigorously expressing disbelief. **come right** informal have a good outcome; end well. **come the ——** informal play the part of; behave like: *don't come the innocent with me.* **come to nothing** have no significant or successful result in the end. **come to pass** chiefly literary happen; occur: *it came to pass that she had two sons.* **come to that** (or **if it comes to that**) Brit. informal in fact (said to introduce an additional point): *there isn't a clock on the mantelpiece—come to that, there isn't a mantelpiece!* **come to think of it** on reflection (said when an idea or point occurs to one while one is speaking). **come what may** no matter what happens. **have it coming** (**to one**) informal be due for retribution on account of something bad that one has done: *his uppity sister-in-law had it coming to her.* **how come?** informal said when asking how or why something happened or is the case: *how come you never married, Jimmy?* **to come** (following a noun) in the future: *films that would inspire generations to come* | *in years to come.* **where someone is coming from** informal someone's meaning, motivation, or personality.
– PHRASAL VERBS **come about 1** happen; take place: *the relative speed with which emancipation came about.* **2** (of a ship) change direction. **come across 1** meet or find by chance: *I came across these old photos recently.* **2** informal hand over or provide what is wanted: *she has **come across with** some details.* **come along** [in imperative] said when encouraging someone or telling them to hurry up. **come amid** (of an action or event) be accompanied by; happen at the same time as: *the cuts come amid increasing competition in Hong Kong.* **come around** see COME ROUND. **come at** launch oneself at (someone) to attack them. **come away** be left with a specified feeling, impression, or result after doing something: *she came away feeling upset.* **come back 1** (in sport) recover from a deficit: *the Mets **came back from** a 3–0 deficit.* **2** reply or respond to someone, especially vigorously: *he **came back at** Judy with a vengeance.* **come before** be dealt with by (a judge or court): *it is the most controversial issue to come before the Supreme Court.* **come between** interfere with or disturb the relationship of (two people): *I let my stupid pride come between us.* **come by 1** N. Amer. call casually and briefly as a visitor: *his friends came by* | *she came by the house.* **2** manage to acquire or obtain (something). **come down 1** (of a building or other structure) collapse or be demolished. ■ (of an aircraft) crash or crash-land. **2** be handed down by tradition or inheritance: *the name has **come down from** the last century.* **3** reach a decision or recommendation in favour of one side or another: *advisers and inspectors came down on our side.* **4** Brit. leave a university, especially Oxford or Cambridge, after finishing one's studies. **5** informal experience the lessening of an excited or euphoric feeling, especially one produced by a narcotic drug. **come down on** criticize or punish (someone) harshly: *she came down on me like a ton of bricks.* **come down to** (of a situation or outcome) be dependent on (a specified factor): *it came down to her word against Guy's.* **come down with** begin to suffer from (a specified illness): *I came down with influenza.* **come for 1** arrive to arrest or detain (someone). **2** launch oneself at (someone) to attack them: *he came for me with his fists.* **come forward** volunteer oneself for a task or

post or to give evidence about a crime. **come from** originate in; have as its source: *the word caviar comes from Italian*. ■ be the result of: *a dignity that comes from being in control*. ■ have as one's place of birth or residence: *I come from Sheffield*. ■ be descended from: *she comes from a family of Muslim scholars*. **come in 1** join or become involved in an enterprise: *that's where Jack comes in | I agreed to come in on the project*. ■ have a useful role or function: *this is where grammar comes in*. ■ [with complement] prove to have a specified good quality: *a car comes in handy for day trips from the city*. **2** [with complement] finish a race in a specified position: *the favourite came in first*. **3** (of money) be earned or received regularly. **4** [in imperative] begin speaking or make contact, especially in radio communication: *come in, London*. **5** (of a tide) rise; flow. **come in for** receive or be the object of (a reaction), typically a negative one: *he has come in for a lot of criticism*. **come into** suddenly receive (money or property), especially by inheriting it. **come of** result from: *no good will come of it*. ■ be descended from: *she came of Dorset stock*. **come off 1** (of an action) succeed; be accomplished. ■ fare in a specified way in a contest: *Geoffrey always came off worse in an argument*. **2** become detached or be detachable from something. ■ fall from a horse or cycle that one is riding. **3** stop taking or being addicted to (a drug or form of medication). **4** Brit. informal have an orgasm. **come on 1** (of a state or condition) start to arrive or happen: *she felt a mild case of the sniffles coming on* | [with infinitive] *it was coming on to rain*. **2** (also **come upon**) meet or find by chance. **3** [in imperative] said when encouraging someone to do something or to hurry up or when one feels that someone is wrong or foolish: *Come on! We must hurry!* **come on to** informal make sexual advances towards. **come out 1** (of a fact) emerge; become known: *it came out that the accused had illegally registered to vote*. ■ develop or happen as a result: *something good can come out of something that went wrong*. ■ (of a photograph) be produced satisfactorily or in a specified way: *I hope my photographs come out all right*. ■ (of the result of a calculation or measurement) emerge at a specified figure: *rough cider usually comes out at about eight per cent alcohol*. ■ (of patience or a similar card game) be played to a finish with all cards dealt with. **2** (of a book or other work) appear; be released or published. **3** declare oneself as being for or against something: *residents have come out against the proposals*. **4** [with complement] achieve a specified placing in an examination or contest: *he deservedly came out the winner on points*. ■ acquit oneself in a specified way: *surprisingly, it's Penn who comes out best*. **5** (of a stain) be removed or able to be removed. **6** Brit. go on strike. **7** informal openly declare that one is homosexual. [from the phrase *come out of the closet* (see CLOSET (sense 3 of the noun)).] **8** Brit. dated (of a young upper-class woman) make one's debut in society. **come out in** Brit. (of a person's skin) break out in (spots or a similar condition). **come out with** say (something) in a sudden, rude, or incautious way. **come over 1** (of a feeling or manner) begin to affect (someone): *a great weariness came over me*. ■ [with complement] informal (of a person) suddenly start to feel a specified way: *they come over all misty-eyed with nostalgia*. **2** change to another side or point of view. **come round** chiefly Brit. (chiefly US also **come around**) **1** recover consciousness: *I'd just come round from a drunken stupor*. **2** be converted to another person's opinion: *I came round to her point of view*. **3** (of a date or regular occurrence) recur; be imminent again: *Friday had come round so quickly*. **come through 1** succeed in surviving or dealing with (an illness or ordeal): *she's come through the operation very well*. **2** (of a message) be sent and received. ■ (of an official decree) be processed and notified. **come to 1** (also **come to oneself**) recover consciousness. **2** (of an expense) reach in total; amount to: *the bill came to £20,000*. **3** (of a ship) come to a stop. **come under 1** be classified as or among: *they all come under the general heading of opinion polls*. **2** be subject to (an influence or authority). ■ be subjected to (pressure or aggression): *his vehicle came under mortar fire*. **come up 1** (of an issue, situation, or problem) occur or present itself, especially unexpectedly. ■ (of a specified time or event) approach or draw near: *she's got exams coming up*. ■ (of a legal case) reach the time when it is scheduled to be dealt with. **2** become brighter in a specified way as a result of being polished or cleaned. **3** Brit. begin one's studies at a university, especially Oxford or Cambridge. **come up against** be faced with or opposed by: *I'd come up against this kind of problem before*. **come up with** produce (something), especially when pressured or challenged: *he keeps coming up with all kinds of lame excuses*. **come upon 1** attack (someone or something) by surprise. **2** see COME ON (sense 2).
– ORIGIN Old English *cuman*, of Germanic origin; related to Dutch *komen* and German *kommen*.

> **USAGE** The use of **come** followed by **and**, as in *come and see for yourself*, dates back to Old English, but is seen by some as incorrect or only suitable for informal English: for more details see **USAGE** at **AND**.

come-along ▸ **noun** N. Amer. informal a hand-operated winch.

comeback ▸ **noun 1** a return by a well-known person, especially an entertainer or sports player, to the activity in which they have formerly been successful: *the heavyweight champion is set to* ***make his comeback*** *in England* | [as modifier] *a comeback tour*. ■ a return to fashion of an item, activity, or style: *trouser suits are* ***making a comeback***.
2 informal a quick reply to a critical remark. ■ [mass noun] the opportunity to seek redress: *there's no comeback if he messes up your case*.
3 Austral./NZ a sheep bred from cross-bred and pure-bred parents for both wool and meat.

Comecon /ˈkɒmɪkɒn/ an economic association of east European countries founded in 1949 and analogous to the European Economic Community. With the collapse of communism in eastern Europe, the association was dissolved in 1991.
– ORIGIN contraction of COUNCIL FOR MUTUAL ECONOMIC ASSISTANCE.

comedian ▸ **noun** an entertainer on stage or television whose act is designed to make an audience laugh. ■ a comic actor or playwright. ■ often ironic a person who is or thinks themselves to be amusing or entertaining.
– ORIGIN late 16th cent. (denoting a comic playwright): from French *comédien*, from Old French *comedie* (see COMEDY). The sense 'entertainer' dates from the late 19th cent.

Comédie-Française /ˌkɒmɛdiːfrɒ̃ˈseɪz/, French /kɔmedi fʀɑ̃sɛz/ the French national theatre (used for both comedy and tragedy), in Paris, founded in 1680 by Louis XIV.

comedienne /kəˌmiːdɪˈɛn, -ˌmɛ-/ ▸ **noun** a female comedian.
– ORIGIN mid 19th cent.: from French *comédienne*, feminine of *comédien* (see COMEDIAN).

comedo /ˈkɒmɪdəʊ, kəˈmiːdəʊ/ ▸ **noun** (pl. **comedones** /-ˈdəʊniːz/) technical term for BLACKHEAD (sense 1).
– ORIGIN mid 19th cent.: from Latin, literally 'glutton', from *comedere* 'eat up', from *com-* 'altogether' + *edere* 'eat'. Used formerly as a name for parasitic worms, the term here alludes to the worm-like matter which can be squeezed from a blackhead.

comedogenic /ˌkɒmɪdə(ʊ)ˈdʒɛnɪk/ ▸ **adjective** tending to cause blackheads by blocking the pores of the skin.

comedown ▸ **noun** informal **1** a loss of status or importance: *Patrol duty? Bit of a* ***comedown for*** *a sergeant*.
2 a feeling of disappointment or depression. ■ a lessening of the sensations generated by a narcotic drug as its effects wear off.

comedy ▸ **noun** (pl. **comedies**) **1** [mass noun] professional entertainment consisting of jokes and sketches, intended to make an audience laugh. ■ [count noun] a film, play, or broadcast programme intended to make an audience laugh: [as modifier] *a comedy film*. ■ the style or genre of such types of entertainment. ■ the humorous or amusing aspects of something: *advertising people see the comedy in their work*.
2 a play characterized by its humorous or satirical tone and its depiction of amusing people or incidents, in which the characters ultimately triumph over adversity: *Shakespeare's comedies*. ■ the dramatic genre represented by such plays: *satiric comedy*. Compare with TRAGEDY (sense 2).
– DERIVATIVES **comedic** /kəˈmiːdɪk, -ˈmɛ-/ **adjective**.
– ORIGIN late Middle English (as a genre of drama, also denoting a narrative poem with a happy ending, as in Dante's *Divine Comedy*): from Old French *comedie*, via Latin from Greek *kōmōidia*, from *kōmōidos* 'comic poet', from *kōmos* 'revel' + *aoidos* 'singer'.

comedy of manners ▸ **noun** a play, novel, or film that gives a satirical portrayal of behaviour in a particular social group.

come-hither ▸ **adjective** informal (of a woman or her manner) playfully showing or expressing sexual interest; coquettish: *nymphs with come-hither looks*.

comely ▸ **adjective** (**comelier**, **comeliest**) archaic or humorous (typically of a woman) pleasant to look at; attractive. ■ agreeable; suitable.
– DERIVATIVES **comeliness** **noun**.
– ORIGIN Middle English: probably shortened from *becomely* 'fitting, becoming', from BECOME.

come-on ▸ **noun** informal a gesture or remark that is intended to attract someone sexually: *she was giving me the come-on*. ■ a marketing ploy, such as a free or cheap offer.

C

come-outer ▸ **noun** US, chiefly historical a person who dissociates themselves from an organization.

comer ▸ **noun 1** a person who arrives somewhere: *feeding every comer is still a sacred duty*.
2 [in sing.] N. Amer. informal a person or thing likely to succeed: *many in the party see tax relief as a comer*.

COMESA ▸ **abbreviation** Common Market for Eastern and Southern Africa.

comess /kɒˈmɛs/ ▸ **noun** W. Indian a confused or noisy situation.
– ORIGIN from French Creole *commece* 'confusion', from French *commerce* 'commerce'.

comestible /kəˈmɛstɪb(ə)l/ formal or humorous ▸ **noun** (usu. **comestibles**) an item of food: *a fridge groaning with comestibles*.
▸ **adjective** edible.
– ORIGIN late 15th cent.: from Old French, from medieval Latin *comestibilis*, from Latin *comest-* 'eaten up', from the verb *comedere*, from *com-* 'altogether' + *edere* 'eat'.

comet /ˈkɒmɪt/ ▸ **noun** a celestial object consisting of a nucleus of ice and dust and, when near the sun, a 'tail' of gas and dust particles pointing away from the sun.

> Originating in the remotest regions of the solar system, most comets follow regular eccentric orbits and appear in the inner solar system as periodic comets, some of which break up and can be the origin of annual meteor showers. They were formerly considered to be supernatural omens.

– DERIVATIVES **cometary** **adjective**.
– ORIGIN late Old English, from Latin *cometa*, from Greek *komētēs* 'long-haired (star)', from *komē* 'hair'; reinforced by Old French *comete*.

comeuppance ▸ **noun** [in sing.] informal a punishment or fate that someone deserves: *he got his comeuppance in the end*.

comfit /ˈkʌmfɪt/ ▸ **noun** dated a sweet consisting of a nut, seed, or other centre coated in sugar.
– ORIGIN Middle English: from Old French *confit*, from Latin *confectum* 'something prepared', neuter past participle of *conficere* 'put together' (see CONFECT).

comfort ▸ **noun** [mass noun] **1** a state of physical ease and freedom from pain or constraint: *there is room for four people to travel in comfort*. ■ (**comforts**) things that contribute to physical ease and well-being: *the low upholstered chair was one of the room's few comforts*. ■ prosperity and the pleasant lifestyle secured by it: *my father left us enough to live in comfort*.
2 consolation for grief or anxiety: *a few words of comfort | they should* ***take comfort*** *that help is available*. ■ [in sing.] a person or thing that gives consolation or alleviates a difficult situation: *his friendship was a great comfort*.
3 US dialect a warm quilt.
▸ **verb** [with obj.] make (someone) feel less unhappy; console: *her friend tried to comfort her*. ■ help (someone) feel at ease; reassure: *her strength comforted and protected me*.
– ORIGIN Middle English (as a noun, in the senses 'strengthening, support, consolation'; as a verb, in the senses 'strengthen, give support, console'): from Old French *confort* (noun), *conforter* (verb), from late Latin *confortare* 'strengthen', from *com-* (expressing intensive force) + Latin *fortis* 'strong'. The sense 'something producing physical ease' arose in the mid 17th cent.

comfortable ▸ **adjective 1** (especially of clothes or furnishings) providing physical ease and relaxation. ■ (of a person) physically relaxed and free from constraint: *he would not be comfortable in any other clothes*. ■ (of a hospital patient) not in pain or in danger. ■ free from stress or tension: *they appear very comfortable in each other's company | few of us are* ***comfortable with*** *confrontations*. ■ free from financial worry; having an adequate standard of living.
2 as large as is needed or wanted: *a comfortable income*. ■ with a wide margin: *a comfortable victory*.
▸ **noun** US dialect a warm quilt.

C

– DERIVATIVES **comfortableness** noun, **comfortably** adverb.
– ORIGIN Middle English (in the sense 'pleasant, pleasing'): from Anglo-Norman French *confortable*, from *conforter* 'to comfort' (see COMFORT).

comfort eating ▶ noun [mass noun] eating to make oneself feel happier, rather than to satisfy hunger.

comforter ▶ noun **1** a person or thing that provides consolation. ■ Brit. a baby's dummy.
2 dated a woollen scarf.
3 N. Amer. a warm quilt.
– ORIGIN late Middle English: from Old French *comforteor*, from *conforter* 'to comfort' (see COMFORT).

comfort food ▶ noun [mass noun] food that provides consolation or a feeling of well-being, typically having a high sugar or carbohydrate content and associated with childhood or home cooking.

comforting ▶ adjective giving consolation for grief or anxiety; soothing: *his comforting presence.*
– DERIVATIVES **comfortingly** adverb.

comfortless ▶ adjective **1** offering no means of relaxation and pleasure: *a comfortless prison.*
2 having or offering no consolation: *he had left her comfortless.*

comfort station ▶ noun N. Amer., euphemistic a public toilet.

comfort zone ▶ noun a situation where one feels safe or at ease: *the trip is an attempt to take the students out of their comfort zone.* ■ a settled method of working that requires little effort and yields only barely acceptable results: *if you stay within your comfort zone you will never improve.*

comfrey /ˈkʌmfri/ ▶ noun (pl. **comfreys**) a Eurasian plant of the borage family, which has large hairy leaves and clusters of purplish or white bell-shaped flowers. ● Genus *Symphytum*, family Boraginaceae: several species, in particular the **common comfrey** (*S. officinale*), which is used in herbal medicine (see BONESET).
– ORIGIN Middle English: from Anglo-Norman French *cumfirie*, based on Latin *conferva*, from *confervere* 'heal' (literally 'boil together', referring to the plant's medicinal use).

comfy ▶ adjective (**comfier**, **comfiest**) informal comfortable.
– DERIVATIVES **comfily** adverb, **comfiness** noun.
– ORIGIN early 19th cent.: abbreviation.

comic ▶ adjective causing or meant to cause laughter: *a comic monologue.* ■ relating to or in the style of comedy: *a comic actor | comic drama.*
▶ noun **1** a comedian.
2 a periodical containing comic strips, intended chiefly for children. ■ (**comics**) N. Amer. comic strips.
– ORIGIN late 16th cent.: via Latin from Greek *kōmikos*, from *kōmos* 'revel'.

comical ▶ adjective amusing, especially in a ludicrous or absurd way: *a series of comical misunderstandings.*
– DERIVATIVES **comicality** noun (archaic), **comically** adverb.
– ORIGIN late Middle English (in the sense 'relating to or in the style of comedy'): from Latin *comicus* (see COMIC) + -AL.

Comice /ˈkɒmɪs/ ▶ noun a large yellow dessert pear of a late-fruiting variety that is cultivated commercially.
– ORIGIN mid 19th cent.: from French, literally 'association, cooperative', referring to the *Comice Horticole* of Angers, France, where this variety was developed.

comic opera ▶ noun an opera that portrays humorous situations and characters, enhanced by much spoken dialogue.

comic relief ▶ noun [mass noun] humorous content in a dramatic or literary work intended to offset more serious episodes. ■ a character or characters providing this.

comic strip ▶ noun a sequence of drawings in boxes that tell an amusing story, typically printed in a newspaper or magazine.

coming ▶ adjective [attrib.] **1** due to happen or just beginning: *work is due to start in the coming year.*
2 likely to be important or successful in the future: *he was the coming man of French racing.*
▶ noun an arrival or approach: *the coming of a new age.*
– PHRASES **coming of age** the age or occasion when one formally becomes an adult: *time was when being offered a drink for the first time was a rite of passage, a coming of age.* **coming and going** (or **comings and goings**) busy, active movements of many people, especially in and out of a place. **not know if one is coming or going** informal be confused, especially as a result of being very busy.

Comino /kɒˈmiːnəʊ/ the smallest of the three main islands of Malta.

COMINT /ˈkɒmɪnt/ ▶ abbreviation communications intelligence.

Comintern /ˈkɒmɪntəːn/ the Third International, a communist organization (1919–43). See INTERNATIONAL (sense 2 of the noun).
– ORIGIN from Russian *Komintern*, blend of *kom(munisticheskiĭ)* 'communist' and *intern(atsional)* 'international'.

comital /ˈkɒmɪt(ə)l/ ▶ adjective chiefly historical relating to a count or earl.
– ORIGIN mid 19th cent.: from medieval Latin *comitalis*, from *comes, comit-* 'a count'.

comity /ˈkɒmɪti/ ▶ noun (pl. **comities**) formal **1** an association of nations for their mutual benefit. ■ (also **comity of nations**) [mass noun] the mutual recognition by nations of the laws and customs of others.
2 [mass noun] courtesy and considerate behaviour towards others.
– ORIGIN mid 16th cent. (in sense 2): from Latin *comitas*, from *comis* 'courteous'.

comm ▶ noun short for COMMUNICATION: [as modifier] *a comm link.* See also COMMS.

comma ▶ noun **1** a punctuation mark (,) indicating a pause between parts of a sentence or separating items in a list.
2 Music a minute interval or difference of pitch.
3 (also **comma butterfly**) a widespread butterfly that has orange and brown wings with ragged edges, and a white comma-shaped mark on the underside of the hindwing. ● *Polygonia c-album*, subfamily Nymphalinae, family Nymphalidae. .
– ORIGIN late 16th cent. (originally as a term in rhetoric denoting a group of words shorter than a colon; see COLON[1]): via Latin from Greek *komma* 'piece cut off, short clause', from *koptein* 'cut'.

command ▶ verb **1** [reporting verb] give an authoritative or peremptory order: [with obj. and infinitive] *a gruff voice commanded us to enter* | [with direct speech] *'Stop arguing!' he commanded* | [with clause] *he commanded that work should cease* | [with obj.] *my mother commands my presence.* ■ [with obj.] Military have authority over; be in charge of (a unit). ■ [with obj.] archaic control or restrain (oneself or one's feelings): *he commanded himself with an effort.*
2 [with obj.] dominate (a strategic position) from a superior height: *the fortress commands the shortest Channel crossing.*
3 [with obj.] be in a strong enough position to have or secure: *they command a majority in Parliament | he commanded considerable personal loyalty.*
▶ noun **1** an authoritative order: *he obeyed her commands without question.* ■ [mass noun] authority, especially over armed forces: *an officer* **took command** | *who's* **in command**? ■ [treated as sing. or pl.] Military a group of officers exercising control over a particular group or operation. ■ Military a body of troops or a district under the control of a particular officer.
2 [in sing.] the ability to use or control something: *he had a brilliant command of English.*
3 Computing an instruction or signal causing a computer to perform one of its basic functions.
– PHRASES **at someone's command** at someone's disposal to use or instruct: *I shall defend myself with all the eloquence at my command.* **word of command** Military an order for a movement in a drill. ■ a prearranged spoken signal for the start of an operation.
– ORIGIN Middle English: from Old French *comander* 'to command', from late Latin *commandare*, from *com-* (expressing intensive force) + *mandare* 'commit, command'. Compare with COMMEND.

command and control ▶ noun [mass noun] [usu. as modifier] chiefly Military the running of an armed force or other organization: *a command-and-control bunker.*

commandant /ˌkɒmənˈdant, ˈkɒmənˌdant, -dɑːnt/ ▶ noun an officer in charge of a particular force or institution: *the camp commandant.*
– ORIGIN late 17th cent.: from French *commandant*, or Italian or Spanish *commandante*, all from late Latin *commandare* 'to command' (see COMMAND).

command chain ▶ noun another term for CHAIN OF COMMAND.

command-driven ▶ adjective Computing (of a program or computer) operated by means of commands keyed in by the user or issued by another program or computer.

command economy ▶ noun another term for PLANNED ECONOMY.

commandeer /ˌkɒmənˈdɪə/ ▶ verb [with obj.] officially take possession or control of (something), especially for military purposes: *a nearby house had been commandeered by the army.* ■ take possession of (something) by force: *the truck was commandeered by a mob.* ■ [with obj. and infinitive] enlist (someone) to help in a task: *he commandeered the men to find a table.*
– ORIGIN early 19th cent.: from Afrikaans *kommandeer*, from Dutch *commanderen*, from French *commander* 'to command' (see COMMAND).

commander ▶ noun **1** a person in authority, especially over a body of troops or a military operation: *the commander of a paratroop regiment.* ■ a rank of naval officer, above lieutenant commander and below captain. ■ an officer in charge of a Metropolitan Police district in London.
2 a member of a higher class in some orders of knighthood. See also KNIGHT COMMANDER.
– DERIVATIVES **commandership** noun.
– ORIGIN Middle English: from Old French *comandeor*, from late Latin *commandare* (see COMMAND).

commander-in-chief ▶ noun (pl. **commanders-in-chief**) an officer in charge of all of the armed forces of a country, or a major subdivision of them. ■ a politician or head of state in supreme command of a country's armed forces.

Commander of the Faithful ▶ noun one of the titles of a caliph.

commanding ▶ adjective **1** (in military contexts) having a position of authority: *a commanding officer.* ■ indicating or expressing authority; imposing: *a man of commanding presence | her style is commanding.* ■ possessing or giving superior strength: *a commanding 13–6 lead.*
2 (of a place or position) dominating from above; giving a wide view of an area.
– DERIVATIVES **commandingly** adverb.

command language ▶ noun Computing a source language composed chiefly of a set of commands or operators, used especially for communicating with the operating system of a computer.

command line ▶ noun an interface for typing commands directly to a computer's operating system.

commandment ▶ noun a divine rule, especially one of the Ten Commandments. ■ humorous a rule to be observed as strictly as one of the Ten Commandments.
– ORIGIN Middle English: from Old French *comandement*, from *comander* 'to command' (see COMMAND).

command module ▶ noun the detachable control compartment of a manned spacecraft.

commando ▶ noun (pl. **commandos**) a soldier specially trained for carrying out raids. ■ a unit of commandos.
– PHRASES **go commando** informal wear no underpants.
– ORIGIN late 18th cent. (denoting a militia, originally consisting of Boers in South Africa): from Portuguese (earlier form of *comando*), from *commandar* 'to command', from late Latin *commandare* (see COMMAND).

commando knife ▶ noun a long, slender knife suitable for hand-to-hand combat.

Command Paper ▶ noun (in the UK) a document laid before Parliament by order of the Crown, though in practice by the government.

command performance (also **Royal Command Performance**) ▶ noun (in the UK) a presentation of a play, concert, film, or other show at the request of royalty, who usually attend.

command post ▶ noun the place from which a unit commander controls a military unit.

comme ci, comme ça /kɒm ˌsiː kɒm ˈsɑː/, French /kɔm si kɔm sa/ ▶ adverb & adjective used, especially in answer to a question, to convey that something is neither very good nor very bad.
– ORIGIN French, literally 'like this, like that'.

commedia dell'arte /kɒˈmeɪdɪə dɛlˈɑːteɪ/, Italian /kəomˈmɛdja delˈlarte/ ▶ noun [mass noun] an improvised kind of popular comedy in Italian theatres in the 16th–18th centuries, based on stock characters. Actors adapted their comic dialogue and action according to a few basic plots (commonly love intrigues) and to topical issues.
– ORIGIN Italian, 'comedy of art'.

comme il faut /ˌkɒm iːl ˈfəʊ/, French /kɔm il fo/ ▶ adjective correct in behaviour or etiquette.
– ORIGIN French, literally 'as is necessary'.

commemorate ▶ verb [with obj.] recall and show respect for (someone or something): *a wreath-laying*

ceremony to commemorate the war dead | a stone commemorating a boy who died at sea. ■ mark or celebrate (an event or person) by doing or producing something: *the victory was commemorated in songs.*
– ORIGIN late 16th cent.: from Latin *commemorat-* 'brought to remembrance', from the verb *commemorare*, from *com-* 'altogether' + *memorare* 'relate' (from *memor* 'mindful').

commemoration ▶ noun [mass noun] the action or fact of commemorating a dead person or past event: *local martyrs received public commemoration | the window was ordered by the duchess **in commemoration of** her son.* ■ [count noun] a ceremony or celebration in which a person or event is remembered.
– ORIGIN late Middle English: from Latin *commemoratio(n-)*, from the verb *commemorare* 'bring to remembrance' (see COMMEMORATE).

commemorative ▶ adjective acting as a memorial of an event or person.
▶ noun an object such as a stamp or coin made to mark an event or honour a person.

commence ▶ verb begin: [with obj.] *his design team commenced work* | [no obj.] *a public inquiry is due to commence on the 16th.*
– ORIGIN Middle English: from Old French *commencier, comencier*, based on Latin *com-* (expressing intensive force) + *initiare* 'begin'.

commencement ▶ noun **1** the beginning of something: *the commencement of the trial* | [mass noun] *the date of commencement.*
2 N. Amer. a ceremony in which degrees or diplomas are conferred on university or high-school students: [as modifier] *a commencement address.*
– ORIGIN Middle English: from Old French, from the verb *commencier* (see COMMENCE).

commend ▶ verb [with obj.] **1** praise formally or officially: *he was commended by the judge for his courageous actions.*
2 present as suitable for approval or acceptance; recommend: *I **commend** her **to** you without reservation.* ■ make (something) acceptable or pleasing: *the emphasis on peace will **commend itself to** all | most one-roomed flats have little to commend them.*
3 (**commend someone/thing to**) archaic or formal entrust someone or something to: *as they set out on their journey I commend them to your care.*
■ (**commend someone to**) pass on someone's good wishes to.
– PHRASES **highly commended** Brit. failing to win a prize but nevertheless considered meritorious.
– ORIGIN Middle English: from Latin *commendare*, from *com-* (expressing intensive force) + *mandare* 'commit, entrust'. Compare with COMMAND.

commendable ▶ adjective deserving praise: *he showed commendable restraint.*
– DERIVATIVES **commendably** adverb.
– ORIGIN late Middle English: via Old French from Latin *commendabilis*, from *commendare* (see COMMEND).

commendation ▶ noun [mass noun] formal or official praise: *the film deserved the highest commendation* | [count noun] *the book gives commendations for initiative.* ■ [count noun] an award given for very good performance: *the detectives received commendations for bravery.* ■ [count noun] a very good result in an examination or competition.
– ORIGIN Middle English: from Old French, from Latin *commendatio(n-)*, from *commendare* 'commit to the care of' (see COMMEND). Originally (in the plural) the term denoted a liturgical office ending with a prayer commending the souls of the dead to God.

Commendatore /kɒˌmɛndəˈtɔːreɪ/ ▶ noun (pl. **Commendatori** /-ri/) a knight of an Italian order of chivalry.
– ORIGIN Italian, from Latin *commendator*, based on *commendare* 'entrust'.

commendatory /kɒˈmɛndət(ə)ri/ ▶ adjective archaic serving to present something as suitable for approval or acceptance.
– ORIGIN mid 16th cent.: from late Latin *commendatorius*, from Latin *commendare* 'commit to the care of' (see COMMEND).

commensal /kəˈmɛns(ə)l/ Biology ▶ adjective relating to or exhibiting commensalism.
▶ noun a commensal organism, such as many bacteria.
– DERIVATIVES **commensality** /kɒmɛnˈsalɪti/ noun.
– ORIGIN late 19th cent.: from medieval Latin *commensalis*, from *com-* 'sharing' + *mensa* 'a table'.

commensalism ▶ noun [mass noun] Biology an association between two organisms in which one benefits and the other derives neither benefit nor harm.

commensurable /kəˈmɛnʃ(ə)rəb(ə)l, -sjə-/ ▶ adjective **1** measurable by the same standard: *the finite is not commensurable with the infinite.*
2 (**commensurable to**) rare proportionate to.
3 Mathematics (of numbers) in a ratio equal to a ratio of integers.
– DERIVATIVES **commensurability** noun, **commensurably** adverb.
– ORIGIN mid 16th cent.: from late Latin *commensurabilis*, from *com-* 'together' + *mensurabilis*, from *mensurare* 'to measure'.

commensurate /kəˈmɛnʃ(ə)rət, -sjə-/ ▶ adjective corresponding in size or degree; in proportion: *salary will be **commensurate with** age and experience | such heavy responsibility must receive commensurate reward.*
– DERIVATIVES **commensurately** adverb.
– ORIGIN mid 17th cent.: from late Latin *commensuratus*, from *com-* 'together' + *mensuratus*, past participle of *mensurare* 'to measure'.

comment ▶ noun a verbal or written remark expressing an opinion or reaction: *you asked for **comments on** the new proposals* | [mass noun] *the plans were sent to the council for comment.* ■ [mass noun] discussion, especially of a critical nature, of an issue or event: *the exhibition has aroused comment.* ■ an indirect expression of the views of the writer of a play, book, film, etc.: *she denies that the film is a comment on the perils of celebrity.* ■ an explanatory note in a book or other written text. ■ archaic a written explanation or commentary. ■ Computing a piece of text placed within a program to help other users to understand it, which the computer ignores when running the program.
▶ verb [reporting verb] express an opinion or reaction in speech or writing: [with clause] *teachers commented that children of all abilities would benefit* | [no obj.] *the company would not **comment on** the venture* | [with direct speech] *'She's an independent soul,' he commented.* ■ [with obj.] Computing place a piece of explanatory text within (a program) to assist other users. ■ [with obj.] Computing turn (part of a program) into a comment so that the computer ignores it when running the program: *you could try **commenting out** that line.*
– PHRASES **no comment** used in refusing to answer a question, especially in a sensitive situation.
– DERIVATIVES **commenter** noun.
– ORIGIN late Middle English (in the senses 'expository treatise' and 'explanatory note'): from Latin *commentum* 'contrivance' (in late Latin also 'interpretation'), neuter past participle of *comminisci* 'devise'.

commentariat /ˌkɒmənˈtɛːrɪət/ ▶ noun chiefly N. Amer. members of the news media considered as a class.
– ORIGIN late 20th cent.: blend of COMMENTARY and PROLETARIAT.

commentary ▶ noun (pl. **commentaries**) an expression of opinions or offering of explanations about an event or situation: *a biting social commentary about the divide between rich and poor* | [mass noun] *a narrative overlaid with commentary.* ■ a descriptive spoken account (especially on a broadcast) of an event or performance as it happens: *a live commentary on radio.* ■ a set of explanatory or critical notes on a text: *a commentary on the Old Testament.*
– ORIGIN late Middle English: from Latin *commentarius, commentarium* (adjective, used as a noun), from *commentari*, frequentative of *comminisci* 'devise'.

commentate ▶ verb [no obj.] Brit. report on an event as it occurs, especially for a news or sports broadcast; provide a commentary: *they **commentate on** live Monday matches.*
– ORIGIN mid 19th cent.: back-formation from COMMENTATOR.

commentator ▶ noun a person who comments on events or on a text. ■ a person who commentates on a sports match or other event.

commerce ▶ noun [mass noun] **1** the activity of buying and selling, especially on a large scale: *the changes in taxation are of benefit to commerce.*
2 dated social dealings between people.
3 archaic sexual intercourse.
– ORIGIN mid 16th cent. (in sense 2): from French, or from Latin *commercium* 'trade, trading', from *com-* 'together' + *mercium* (from *merx, merc-* 'merchandise').

commercial ▶ adjective **1** concerned with or engaged in commerce: *a commercial agreement.*
2 making or intended to make a profit: *commercial products.* ■ having profit rather than artistic or other value as a primary aim: *their work is too commercial.*
3 (of television or radio) funded by the revenue from broadcast advertisements.
4 (of chemicals) supplied in bulk and not of the highest purity.
▶ noun **1** a television or radio advertisement.
2 Brit. dated a travelling sales representative.
– DERIVATIVES **commerciality** noun, **commercially** adverb.

C

commercial art ▶ noun [mass noun] art used in advertising and selling.

commercial bank ▶ noun a bank that offers services to the general public and to companies.

commercial bill ▶ noun a bill of exchange issued by a commercial organization to raise money for short-term needs.

commercial break ▶ noun an interruption in the transmission of a broadcast programme, or an intermission between programmes, during which advertisements are broadcast.

commercialism ▶ noun [mass noun] emphasis on the maximizing of profit: *concern about state enterprise deficits prompted efforts for greater commercialism.* ■ derogatory concern with the making of profit at the expense of artistic or other value: *the cut-throat commercialism of the Paris art world.*

commercialize (also **commercialise**) ▶ verb [with obj.] manage or exploit (an organization, activity, etc.) in a way designed to make a profit: *the museum has been commercialized.*
– DERIVATIVES **commercialization** noun.

commercialized ▶ adjective designed principally for financial gain; profit-orientated: *Christmas is overly commercialized.*

commercial paper ▶ noun [mass noun] short-term unsecured promissory notes issued by companies.

commercial space ▶ noun see SPACE (sense 1 of the noun).

commercial traveller ▶ noun Brit. dated a travelling sales representative.

commercial vehicle ▶ noun a vehicle used for carrying goods or fare-paying passengers.

commère /ˈkɒmɛː/ ▶ noun Brit. a female compère.
– ORIGIN early 20th cent.: French, literally 'godmother', feminine of COMPÈRE.

commie informal, derogatory ▶ noun (pl. **commies**) a communist.
▶ adjective communist.
– ORIGIN 1940s: abbreviation.

commination /ˌkɒmɪˈneɪʃ(ə)n/ ▶ noun [mass noun] the action of threatening divine vengeance. ■ the recital of divine threats against sinners in the Anglican Liturgy for Ash Wednesday. ■ [count noun] the service that includes this.
– ORIGIN late Middle English: from Latin *comminatio(n-)*, from the verb *comminari*, from *com-* (expressing intensive force) + *minari* 'threaten'.

comminatory /ˈkɒmɪnəˌt(ə)ri/ ▶ adjective rare threatening, punitive, or vengeful.
– ORIGIN early 16th cent.: from medieval Latin *comminatorius*, from *comminat-* 'threatened', from the verb *comminari* (see COMMINATION).

commingle /kɒˈmɪŋg(ə)l/ ▶ verb literary mix; blend: [no obj.] *the part of the brain where the senses commingle* | [with obj.] *his humanitarian stance was **commingled with** a desire for survival*
– ORIGIN early 17th cent.: from COM- 'together' + MINGLE.

comminuted /ˈkɒmɪnjuːtɪd/ ▶ adjective technical reduced to minute particles or fragments. ■ Medicine (of a fracture) producing multiple bone splinters.
– ORIGIN early 17th cent.: past participle of *comminute*, from Latin *comminut-* 'broken into pieces', from the verb *comminuere*, from *com-* 'together' + *minuere* 'lessen'.

comminution /ˌkɒmɪˈnjuːʃ(ə)n/ ▶ noun [mass noun] technical the action of reducing a material, especially a mineral ore, to minute particles or fragments.

commis /ˈkɒmi/ (also **commis chef**) ▶ noun (pl. **same** /ˈkɒmi, ˈkɒmɪz/) a junior chef.
– ORIGIN 1930s: from French, 'deputy, clerk', past participle of *commettre* 'entrust', from Latin *committere* (see COMMIT).

commiserate /kəˈmɪzəreɪt/ ▶ verb [no obj.] express or feel sympathy or pity; sympathize: *she went over to **commiserate with** Rose on her unfortunate circumstances.* ■ [with obj.] archaic feel or express pity for (someone): *she did not exult in her rival's fall, but, on the contrary, commiserated her.*
– DERIVATIVES **commiserative** adjective.

– ORIGIN late 16th cent.: from Latin *commiserat-* 'commiserated', from the verb *commiserari*, from *com-* 'with' + *miserari* 'to lament' (from *miser* 'wretched').

commiseration /kəˌmɪzəˈreɪʃn/ ▶ **noun** [mass noun] sympathy and sorrow for the misfortunes of others; compassion: *the other actors offered him clumsy commiseration.* ■ (**commiserations**) expressions of sympathy and sorrow for another: *our commiserations to those who didn't win.*

C

commish /kəˈmɪʃ/ ▶ **noun** N. Amer. informal short for COMMISSIONER.

commissaire /ˌkɒmɪˈsɛː/, French /kɔmisɛʀ/ ▶ **noun** a senior police officer in France. ■ (in France) an official at a cycle race or other sporting event.
– ORIGIN French.

commissar /ˌkɒmɪˈsɑː/ ▶ **noun** an official of the Communist Party, especially in the former Soviet Union or present-day China, responsible for political education and organization. ■ a head of a government department in the former Soviet Union before 1946. ■ a strict or prescriptive figure of authority: *our academic commissars.*
– ORIGIN early 20th cent. (Russian Revolution): from Russian *komissar*, from French *commissaire*, from medieval Latin *commissarius* (see COMMISSARY).

commissariat /ˌkɒmɪˈsɛːrɪət/ ▶ **noun 1** chiefly Military a department for the supply of food and equipment.
2 a government department of the USSR before 1946.
– ORIGIN late 16th cent. (as a Scots legal term denoting the jurisdiction of a commissary, often spelled *commissariot*): from French *commissariat*, reinforced by medieval Latin *commissariatus*, both from medieval Latin *commissarius* 'person in charge', from Latin *committere* 'entrust'.

commissary /ˈkɒmɪs(ə)ri/ ▶ **noun** (pl. **commissaries**) **1** a deputy or delegate. ■ a representative or deputy of a bishop.
2 N. Amer. a restaurant or food store in a military base, prison, or other institution.
– ORIGIN late Middle English: from medieval Latin *commissarius* 'person in charge', from Latin *commiss-* 'joined, entrusted', from the verb *committere* (see COMMIT).

commission ▶ **noun 1** an instruction, command, or role given to a person or group: *one of his first commissions was to redesign the Great Exhibition building* | [with infinitive] *he received a commission to act as an informer.* ■ an order for something, especially a work of art, to be produced specially. ■ a work produced in response to such an order. ■ [mass noun] archaic the authority to perform a task or certain duties: *the divine Commission of Christ.*
2 a group of people entrusted by a government or other official body with authority to do something: *a commission was appointed to investigate allegations of police violence.*
3 a sum, typically a set percentage of the value involved, paid to an agent in a commercial transaction: *foreign banks may charge a commission* | *he sold cosmetics* ***on commission.***
4 a warrant conferring the rank of officer in an army, navy, or air force.
5 [mass noun] the action of committing a crime or offence.
▶ **verb** [with obj.] **1** order or authorize the production of (something): *the portrait was commissioned by his widow in 1792.* ■ [with obj. and infinitive] order or authorize (a person or organization) to do or produce something: *they commissioned an architect to manage the building project* | *he was commissioned to do a series of drawings.*
2 bring (something newly produced) into working condition: *we had a few hiccups getting the heating equipment commissioned* | *the aircraft carrier was commissioned in 1945.*
3 appoint (someone) to the rank of officer in an army, navy, or air force: *he was* ***commissioned into*** *the Royal Fusiliers* | (as adj. **commissioned**) *a commissioned officer.*
– PHRASES **in commission** in use or in service. **out of commission** not in service; not in working order. ■ (of a person) unable to work or function normally, especially through illness or injury.
– ORIGIN Middle English: via Old French from Latin *commissio(n-)*, from *committere* 'entrust' (see COMMIT).

commission agent ▶ **noun** Brit. a person who transacts business on commission, typically on behalf of a principal from another country.

commissionaire /kəˌmɪʃəˈnɛː/ ▶ **noun** Brit. a uniformed door attendant at a hotel, theatre, or other building.
– ORIGIN mid 17th cent.: from French, from medieval Latin *commissarius* 'person in charge', from Latin *committere* 'entrust' (see COMMIT).

commissioner ▶ **noun** a person appointed to a role on or by a commission. ■ a representative of the supreme authority in an area. ■ the head of the Metropolitan Police in London. ■ N. Amer. a person appointed to regulate a particular sport: *a baseball commissioner.*
– ORIGIN late Middle English: from medieval Latin *commissionarius*, from Latin *commissio* (see COMMISSION).

commissioner for oaths ▶ **noun** Brit. a solicitor authorized to administer an oath to a person making an affidavit.

commission of the peace ▶ **noun** Brit., chiefly historical the Justices of the Peace in a particular jurisdiction considered collectively.

commissure /ˈkɒmɪsjʊə/ ▶ **noun** Anatomy **1** the joint between two bones.
2 a band of nerve tissue connecting the hemispheres of the brain, the two sides of the spinal cord, etc.
3 the line where the upper and lower lips or eyelids meet.
– DERIVATIVES **commissural** /ˌkɒmɪˈsjʊər(ə)l/ **adjective.**
– ORIGIN late Middle English: from Latin *commissura* 'junction', from *committere* 'join' (see COMMIT).

commit ▶ **verb** (**commits, committing, committed**) [with obj.] **1** perpetrate or carry out (a mistake, crime, or immoral act): *he committed an uncharacteristic error.*
2 pledge or bind (a person or an organization) to a certain course or policy: *they were reluctant to* ***commit themselves to an opinion*** | [with obj. and infinitive] *the treaty commits each party to defend the other* | [no obj.] *try it out before you* ***commit to*** *a purchase.* ■ (**be committed to**) be dedicated to (something): *we are committed to the fundamental principles of democracy.* ■ pledge or set aside (resources) for future use: *manufacturers will have to* ***commit*** *substantial funds* ***to*** *developing new engines.* ■ (**commit oneself to**) resolve to remain in a long-term emotional relationship with (someone): *she didn't love him enough to commit herself to him* | [no obj.] *once I commit I tend to get scared.* ■ (**be committed to**) be in a long-term emotional relationship with (someone).
3 (**commit something to**) transfer something to (a state or place where it can be kept or preserved): *he composed a letter but didn't commit it to paper* | *she committed each tiny feature to memory.* ■ consign (someone) officially to prison, especially on remand: *he was* ***committed to*** *prison for contempt of court.* ■ send (a person or case) for trial in a higher court: *the magistrate decided to* ***commit*** *him* ***for trial.*** ■ send (someone) to be confined in a psychiatric hospital. ■ refer (a parliamentary or legislative bill) to a committee.
– DERIVATIVES **committable** **adjective**, **committer** **noun.**
– ORIGIN late Middle English: from Latin *committere* 'join, entrust' (in medieval Latin 'put into custody'), from *com-* 'with' + *mittere* 'put or send'.

commitment ▶ **noun 1** [mass noun] the state or quality of being dedicated to a cause, activity, etc.: *the company's* ***commitment to*** *quality* | *I could not fault my players for commitment.* ■ [count noun] a pledge or undertaking: *I cannot make such a commitment at the moment.*
2 an engagement or obligation that restricts freedom of action: *with so many business commitments time for recreation was limited.*

committal ▶ **noun** [mass noun] **1** the action of sending a person to prison or a psychiatric hospital: *his* ***committal to prison*** | [count noun] *the high level of committals* | [as modifier] *committal proceedings.*
2 the burial of a dead body.

committed ▶ **adjective 1** pledged or bound to a certain course or policy; dedicated: *a committed environmentalist.*
2 in or denoting a long-term emotional relationship: *a committed relationship* | *Esther has a committed boyfriend.*

committee ▶ **noun 1** /kəˈmɪti/ [treated as sing. or pl.] a group of people appointed for a specific function by a larger group and typically consisting of members of that group: *the housing committee* | [as modifier] *a committee meeting.* ■ (in the UK) a committee appointed by Parliament to consider the details of proposed legislation: *there was much scrutiny in committee.* ■ (**Committee of the whole House**) (in the UK) the whole House of Commons when sitting as a committee.
2 /ˌkɒmɪˈtiː/ Law a person entrusted with the charge of another person or another person's property. ■ chiefly US a person who has been judicially committed to the charge of another because of insanity or mental disability.
– ORIGIN late 15th cent. (in the general sense 'person to whom something has been entrusted'): from COMMIT + -EE.

committeeman (or **committeewoman**) ▶ **noun** (pl. **committeemen** or **committeewomen**) (in the US) a local political party leader.

Committee of Public Safety a French governing body set up in April 1793, during the Revolution. Under the influence of Robespierre it initiated the Terror but it was dissolved in 1795.

committee stage ▶ **noun** Brit. the third of five stages of a bill's progress through Parliament when it may be debated and amended.

commix /kɒˈmɪks/ ▶ **verb** [with obj.] archaic mix; mingle: *beat them till they be thoroughly commixed.*
– DERIVATIVES **commixture** **noun.**
– ORIGIN late Middle English (as the past participle *commixt*): from Latin *commixtus*, from *com-* 'together with' + *mixtus* 'mixed'.

commo ▶ **noun** [mass noun] US informal communication.

commode ▶ **noun 1** a piece of furniture containing a concealed chamber pot. ■ N. Amer. a toilet. ■ N. Amer. historical a movable washstand.
2 a chest of drawers or chiffonier of a decorative type popular in the 18th century.
– ORIGIN mid 18th cent. (in sense 2): from French, literally 'convenient, suitable', from Latin *commodus*. Sense 1 dates from the early 19th cent.

commodify /kəˈmɒdɪfʌɪ/ ▶ **verb** (**commodifies, commodifying, commodified**) [with obj.] turn into or treat as a mere commodity: (as adj. **commodified**) *art has become commodified.*
– DERIVATIVES **commodification** **noun.**
– ORIGIN 1980s: from COMMODITY + -FY.

commodious /kəˈməʊdɪəs/ ▶ **adjective 1** formal roomy and comfortable: *they moved to a more commodious dwelling.*
2 archaic convenient.
– DERIVATIVES **commodiously** **adverb**, **commodiousness** **noun.**
– ORIGIN late Middle English (in the sense 'beneficial, useful'): from French *commodieux* or medieval Latin *commodiosus*, based on Latin *commodus* 'convenient'.

commoditize (also **commoditise**) ▶ **verb** another term for COMMODIFY.
– DERIVATIVES **commoditization** **noun.**

commodity /kəˈmɒdɪti/ ▶ **noun** (pl. **commodities**) a raw material or primary agricultural product that can be bought and sold, such as copper or coffee. ■ a useful or valuable thing: *water is a precious commodity.*
– ORIGIN late Middle English: from Old French *commodite* or Latin *commoditas*, from *commodus* (see COMMODIOUS).

commodore /ˈkɒmədɔː/ ▶ **noun** a naval rank above captain and below rear admiral, generally given temporarily to an officer commanding a squadron or division of a fleet. ■ the president of a yacht club. ■ the senior captain of a shipping line.
– ORIGIN late 17th cent.: probably from Dutch *komandeur*, from French *commandeur* 'commander'.

common ▶ **adjective** (**commoner, commonest**) **1** occurring, found, or done often; prevalent: *salt and pepper are the two most common seasonings* | *it's* ***common for*** *a woman to be depressed after giving birth.* ■ (of an animal or plant) found or living in relatively large numbers; not rare. ■ denoting the most widespread or typical species of an animal or plant: *the common gull.* ■ ordinary; of ordinary qualities; without special rank or position: *the dwellings of common people* | *a common soldier.* ■ (of a quality) of a sort or level to be generally expected: *common decency.* ■ of the most familiar type: *the common or vernacular name.*
2 shared by, coming from, or done by two or more people, groups, or things: *the two republics' common border* | *problems* ***common to*** *both communities.* ■ belonging to or involving the whole of a community or the public at large: *common land.* ■ Mathematics belonging to two or more quantities.
3 Brit. showing a lack of taste and refinement supposedly typical of the lower classes; vulgar: *she's so common.*

4 Grammar (in Latin, Dutch, and certain other languages) of or denoting a gender of nouns that are conventionally regarded as masculine or feminine, contrasting with neuter. ■ (in English) denoting a noun that refers to individuals of either sex (e.g. *teacher*).
5 Prosody (of a syllable) able to be either short or long.
6 Law (of a crime) of lesser severity: *common assault*.
▶ noun **1** a piece of open land for public use.
2 Brit. informal common sense.
3 (in the Christian Church) a form of service used for each of a group of occasions.
4 (also **right of common**) English Law a person's right over another's land, e.g. for pasturage or mineral extraction.
– PHRASES **common currency 1** a system of money shared by two or more countries. **2** something shared by different groups: *a shared humanity is the common currency*. **the common good** the benefit or interests of all: *it is time our elected officials stood up for the common good*. **common ground** opinions or interests shared by each of two or more parties: *artists from different cultural backgrounds found common ground*. **common knowledge** something known by most people. **common or garden** Brit. informal of the usual or ordinary type: *a common or garden family saloon car*. **common property** a thing or things held jointly. ■ something known by most people. **common thread** a theme or characteristic found in various stories or situations: *a common thread through most of the stories is the support from the family*. **the common touch** the ability to get on with or appeal to ordinary people. **have something in common** have a specified amount or degree of shared interests or characteristics: *they had one thing in common, an obsession with rock and roll*. **in common** in joint use or possession; shared: *a sect that had wives in common*. ■ Law held or owned by two or more people each having undivided possession but with distinct, separately transferable interests. **in common with** in the same way as: *in common with other officers I had to undertake guard duties*. **out of the common** Brit. rarely occurring; unusual.
– DERIVATIVES **commonness** noun.
– ORIGIN Middle English: from Old French *comun* (adjective), from Latin *communis*.

commonable ▶ adjective Brit., chiefly historical (of land) allowed to be jointly used or owned. ■ (of an animal) allowed to be pastured on public land.
– ORIGIN early 17th cent.: from obsolete *common* 'to exercise right of common' + -ABLE.

commonage ▶ noun [mass noun] chiefly Brit. **1** the right of pasturing animals on common land. ■ land held in common.
2 the common people; the commonalty.

Common Agricultural Policy the system in the EU for establishing common prices for most agricultural products within the European Union, a single fund for price supports, and levies on imports.

commonality ▶ noun (pl. **commonalities**) **1** [mass noun] the state of sharing features or attributes: *the explanations show a high degree of commonality in their reasoning* | [in sing.] *a commonality of interest ensures cooperation*. ■ [count noun] a shared feature or attribute: *we discern the commonalities between these writers*.
2 (**the commonality**) another term for COMMONALTY.
– ORIGIN late Middle English (in sense 2): variant of COMMONALTY. Sense 1 dates from the mid 16th cent., but was rarely used before the 1950s.

commonalty /ˈkɒmən(ə)lti/ ▶ noun [treated as pl.] (**the commonalty**) chiefly historical people without special rank or position, usually viewed as an estate of the realm: *a petition by the earls, barons, and commonalty of the realm*.
– ORIGIN Middle English: from Old French *comunalte*, from medieval Latin *communalitas*, from Latin *communis* 'common, general' (see COMMON).

common carrier ▶ noun a person or company undertaking to transport any goods or passengers on regular routes at agreed rates. ■ N. Amer. a company providing public telecommunications facilities.

common chord ▶ noun Music a triad containing a root, a major or minor third, and a perfect fifth.

common cold ▶ noun (**the common cold**) another term for COLD (sense 2 of the noun).

common council ▶ noun a town or city council, now only in London and some parts of Canada and the US.

common denominator ▶ noun Mathematics a common multiple of the denominators of several fractions. See also LOWEST COMMON DENOMINATOR, LEAST COMMON DENOMINATOR. ■ a feature shared by all members of a group: *the common denominator in these companies is the awareness of the importance of quality*.

Common Entrance ▶ noun Brit. an examination taken, usually at 13, by pupils wishing to enter public schools.

commoner ▶ noun **1** one of the ordinary or common people, as opposed to the aristocracy or to royalty.
2 a person who has a right over another's land, e.g. for pasturage or mineral extraction.
3 (at some British universities) an undergraduate who does not have a scholarship.
– ORIGIN Middle English (denoting a citizen or burgess): from medieval Latin *communarius*, from *communa, communia* 'community', based on Latin *communis* (see COMMON).

Common Era ▶ noun (**the Common Era**) another term for CHRISTIAN ERA.

common gull ▶ noun a migratory gull with greenish-grey legs, found locally in northern and eastern Eurasia and NW North America. ● *Larus canus*, family Laridae.

commonhold ▶ noun [mass noun] Brit. a system of freehold tenure of a unit within a multi-occupancy building, but with shared responsibility for common services.

common jury ▶ noun Brit. historical a jury for which no qualification of property or social standing was required. Compare with SPECIAL JURY.

common law ▶ noun **1** [mass noun] the part of English law that is derived from custom and judicial precedent rather than statutes. Compare with CASE LAW, STATUTE LAW. ■ the body of English law as adopted and adapted by the different States of the US. Compare with CIVIL LAW.
2 [as modifier] denoting a partner in a marriage recognized in some jurisdictions (excluding the UK) as valid by common law, though not brought about by a civil or ecclesiastical ceremony: *a common-law husband*. ■ denoting a partner in a relationship in which a man and woman cohabit for a period long enough to suggest stability.

common logarithm ▶ noun a logarithm to the base 10.

commonly ▶ adverb very often; frequently: *a commonly used industrial chemical* | *shift workers commonly complain of not getting enough sleep*.

common market ▶ noun a group of countries imposing few or no duties on trade with one another and a common tariff on trade with other countries. ■ (**the Common Market**) a name for the European Economic Community or European Union, used especially in the 1960s and 1970s.

common metre ▶ noun [mass noun] a metrical pattern for hymns in which the stanzas have four lines containing eight and six syllables alternately.

common noun ▶ noun Grammar a noun denoting a class of objects or a concept as opposed to a particular individual. Often contrasted with PROPER NOUN.

commonplace ▶ adjective not unusual; ordinary: *unemployment was commonplace in his trade*. ■ not interesting or original; trite: *the usual commonplace remarks*.
▶ noun **1** a usual or ordinary thing: *bombing has become almost a commonplace of public life there*. ■ a trite saying or topic; a platitude: *it is a commonplace to talk of the young being alienated*.
2 a notable passage in a work copied into a commonplace book.
– DERIVATIVES **commonplaceness** noun.
– ORIGIN mid 16th cent. (originally *common place*): translation of Latin *locus communis*, rendering Greek *koinos topos* 'general theme'.

commonplace book ▶ noun a book into which notable extracts from other works are copied for personal use.

Common Pleas (in full **Court of Common Pleas**) Law, historical a court for hearing civil cases between subjects or citizens not involving Crown or state.

Common Prayer the Church of England liturgy, originally set forth in the *Book of Common Prayer* of Edward VI (1549) and revised in 1662.

common rat ▶ noun another term for BROWN RAT.

common room ▶ noun chiefly Brit. a room in a school or college for use of students or staff outside teaching hours.

commons ▶ plural noun **1** (**the Commons**) short for HOUSE OF COMMONS. ■ historical the common people regarded as a part of a political system, especially in Britain.
2 [treated as sing.] land or resources belonging to or affecting the whole of a community. ■ US a dining hall in a school or college.
3 archaic provisions shared in common; rations.
– PHRASES **short commons** archaic insufficient allocation of food: *a life of short commons*.
– ORIGIN Middle English: plural of COMMON.

common salt ▶ noun see SALT (sense 1 of the noun).

common seal[1] ▶ noun a seal with a mottled grey-brown coat and a concave profile, found along North Atlantic and North Pacific coasts. ● *Phoca vitulina*, family Phocidae.

common seal[2] ▶ noun an official seal of a corporate body.

common sense ▶ noun [mass noun] good sense and sound judgement in practical matters: *it is all a matter of common sense* | [as modifier] *a common-sense approach*.
– DERIVATIVES **commonsensical** adjective.

Common Serjeant ▶ noun (in the UK) a circuit judge of the Central Criminal Court with duties in the City of London.

common soldier ▶ noun see SOLDIER (sense 1 of the noun).

common stock ▶ plural noun (also **common stocks**) [mass noun] N. Amer. ordinary shares.

common time ▶ noun [mass noun] Music a rhythmic pattern in which there are two or four beats, especially four crotchets, in a bar.

commonweal /ˈkɒmənwiːl/ ▶ noun (**the commonweal**) archaic the welfare of the public.

commonwealth ▶ noun **1** an independent state or community, especially a democratic republic. ■ an aggregate or grouping of states or other bodies. ■ a community of shared interests in a non-political field: *the Christian commonwealth* | *the commonwealth of letters*. ■ a self-governing unit voluntarily grouped with the US, such as Puerto Rico. ■ a formal title of some of the states of the US, especially Kentucky, Massachusetts, Pennsylvania, and Virginia. ■ the title of the federated Australian states. ■ (**the Commonwealth**) the republican period of government in Britain between the execution of Charles I in 1649 and the Restoration of Charles II in 1660.
2 (**the Commonwealth**) (in full **the Commonwealth of Nations**) an international association consisting of the UK together with states that were previously part of the British Empire, and dependencies.
3 (**the commonwealth**) archaic the general good.
– ORIGIN late Middle English (originally as two words, denoting public welfare; compare with COMMONWEAL): from COMMON + WEALTH.

Commonwealth Day ▶ noun the second Monday in March, on which the British Commonwealth is celebrated. It was instituted to commemorate assistance given to Britain by the colonies during the Boer War (1899–1902). Formerly called EMPIRE DAY.

Commonwealth Games an amateur sports competition held every four years between member countries of the Commonwealth.

Commonwealth of Independent States (abbrev.: **CIS**) a confederation of independent states, formerly constituent republics of the Soviet Union, established in 1991. The member states are Armenia, Belarus, Kazakhstan, Kyrgyzstan, Moldova, Russia, Tajikistan, Turkmenistan, and Uzbekistan.

Common Worship ▶ noun a book containing the public liturgy of the Church of England, published in 2000 to replace the Alternative Service Book.

commotion ▶ noun a state of confused and noisy disturbance: *she was distracted by a commotion across the street* | [mass noun] *they set off firecrackers to make a lot of commotion*. ■ [mass noun] civil insurrection: *damage caused by civil commotion*.
– ORIGIN late Middle English: from Latin *commotio(n-)*, from *com-* 'altogether' + *motio* (see MOTION).

comms ▶ plural noun [usu. as modifier] communications: *comms software*.

communal /ˈkɒmjʊn(ə)l, kəˈmjuː-/ ▶ adjective
1 shared by all members of a community; for common use: *a communal bathroom and kitchen*. ■ involving the sharing of work and property:

communal living. ■ relating to or done by a community: *communal pride in impressive local buildings.*
2 (of conflict) between different communities, especially those having different religions or ethnic origins: *violent communal riots.*
– DERIVATIVES **communality** noun, **communally** adverb.
– ORIGIN early 19th cent. (in the sense 'relating to a commune, especially the Paris Commune'): from French, from late Latin *communalis*, from *communis* (see **COMMON**).

communalism ▶ noun [mass noun] **1** a principle of political organization based on federated communes. ■ the principle or practice of living together and sharing possessions and responsibilities.
2 allegiance to one's own ethnic group rather than to the wider society.
– DERIVATIVES **communalist** adjective & noun, **communalistic** adjective.

communalize (also **communalise**) ▶ verb [with obj.] rare organize (something) on the basis of shared ownership: *attempts to communalize farming.*
– DERIVATIVES **communalization** noun.

communard /ˈkɒmjʊnɑːd/ ▶ noun a member of a commune. ■ (**Communard**) historical a supporter of the Paris Commune.
– ORIGIN late 19th cent.: from French, from **COMMUNE**[1].

commune[1] /ˈkɒmjuːn/ ▶ noun **1** a group of people living together and sharing possessions and responsibilities. ■ a communal settlement in a communist country.
2 the smallest French territorial division for administrative purposes. ■ a similar division elsewhere.
3 (**the Commune**) the group which seized the municipal government of Paris in the French Revolution and played a leading part in the Reign of Terror until suppressed in 1794. ■ (also **the Paris Commune**) the municipal government organized on communalistic principles that was elected in Paris in 1871. It was soon brutally suppressed by government troops.
– ORIGIN late 17th cent. (in sense 2): from French, from medieval Latin *communia*, neuter plural of Latin *communis* (see **COMMON**).

commune[2] /kəˈmjuːn/ ▶ verb [no obj.] (**commune with**) share one's intimate thoughts or feelings with (someone), especially on a spiritual level: *the purpose of praying is to commune with God.* ■ feel in close spiritual contact with: *he spent an hour communing with nature on the bank of a stream.*
– ORIGIN Middle English: from Old French *comuner* 'to share', from *comun* (see **COMMON**).

communicable ▶ adjective able to be communicated to others: *the value of the product must be communicable to the potential consumers.* ■ (of a disease) able to be transmitted from one sufferer to another; contagious or infectious.
– DERIVATIVES **communicability** noun, **communicably** adverb.
– ORIGIN late Middle English (in the sense 'communicating, having communication'): from Old French, from late Latin *communicabilis*, from the verb *communicare* 'to share' (see **COMMUNICATE**).

communicant ▶ noun **1** a person who receives Holy Communion.
2 archaic a person who imparts information.
– ORIGIN mid 16th cent.: from Latin *communicant-* 'sharing', from the verb *communicare* (see **COMMUNICATE**).

communicate ▶ verb [no obj.] **1** share or exchange information, news, or ideas: *the prisoner was forbidden to **communicate with** his family.* ■ [with obj.] impart or pass on (information, news, or ideas): *he **communicated** his findings **to** the inspector.* ■ [with obj.] convey or transmit (an emotion or feeling) in a non-verbal way: *the ability of good teachers to communicate their own enthusiasm | his sudden fear **communicated itself**.* ■ succeed in conveying one's ideas or in evoking understanding in others: *a politician must have the ability to communicate.*
2 [with obj.] pass on (an infectious disease) to another person or animal. ■ transmit (heat or motion): *the heat is communicated through a small brass grating.*
3 (often as adj. **communicating**) (of two rooms) have a common connecting door: *he went into the communicating room to pick up the phone.*
4 receive Holy Communion.
– DERIVATIVES **communicator** noun, **communicatory** adjective.
– ORIGIN early 16th cent.: from Latin *communicat-* 'shared', from the verb *communicare*, from *communis* (see **COMMON**).

communication ▶ noun **1** [mass noun] the imparting or exchanging of information by speaking, writing, or using some other medium: *television is an effective means of communication | at the moment I am **in communication with** London.* ■ [count noun] a letter or message containing information or news. ■ the successful conveying or sharing of ideas and feelings: *there was a lack of **communication between** Pamela and her parents.* ■ social contact: *she gave him some hope of her return, or at least of their future communication.*
2 (**communications**) means of sending or receiving information, such as telephone lines or computers: *satellite communications* | [as modifier] *a communications network.* ■ [treated as sing.] the field of study concerned with the transmission of information.
3 (**communications**) means of travelling or of transporting goods, such as roads or railways: *a city providing excellent road and rail communications.*
– DERIVATIVES **communicational** adjective.
– ORIGIN late Middle English: from Old French *comunicacion*, from Latin *communicatio(n-)*, from the verb *communicare* 'to share' (see **COMMUNICATE**).

communication cord ▶ noun Brit. another term for **EMERGENCY CORD**.

communications satellite (also **communication satellite**) ▶ noun a satellite placed in orbit round the earth in order to relay television, radio, and telephone signals.

communication theory (also **communications theory**) ▶ noun [mass noun] the branch of knowledge dealing with the principles and methods by which information is conveyed.

communicative ▶ adjective willing, eager, or able to talk or impart information: *Lew was a very communicative chap.* ■ relating to the conveyance or exchange of information: *the communicative process in literary texts.*
– DERIVATIVES **communicatively** adverb.
– ORIGIN late Middle English: from late Latin *communicativus*, from *communicat-* 'shared', from the verb *communicare* (see **COMMUNICATE**).

communion ▶ noun **1** [mass noun] the sharing or exchanging of intimate thoughts and feelings, especially on a mental or spiritual level: *in this churchyard **communion with** the dead was almost palpable* | [in sing.] *for a moment there was a blessed **communion between** them.* ■ shared participation in a mental or spiritual experience: *the Coronation marked a high spot of national communion.*
2 (often **Communion** or **Holy Communion**) the service of Christian worship at which bread and wine are consecrated and shared. See **EUCHARIST**. ■ the consecrated bread and wine administered and received at Communion: *the priests gave him Holy Communion.*
3 a relationship of recognition and acceptance between Christian Churches or denominations, or between individual Christians or Christian communities and a Church: *the Eastern Churches are not **in communion with** Rome.* ■ [count noun] a group of Christian communities or Churches which recognize one another's ministries or that of a central authority. See also **ANGLICAN COMMUNION**.
– ORIGIN late Middle English: from Latin *communio(n-)*, from *communis* (see **COMMON**).

communion of saints ▶ noun a fellowship between Christians living and dead.

communiqué /kəˈmjuːnɪkeɪ/ (also **communique**) ▶ noun an official announcement or statement, especially one made to the media.
– ORIGIN mid 19th cent.: from French, past participle of *communiquer* 'communicate'.

communism ▶ noun [mass noun] a theory or system of social organization in which all property is owned by the community and each person contributes and receives according to their ability and needs. See also **MARXISM**.

> The most familiar form of communism is that established by the Bolsheviks after the Russian Revolution of 1917, and it has generally been understood in terms of the system practised by the former Soviet Union and its allies in eastern Europe, in China since 1949, and in some developing countries such as Cuba, Vietnam, and North Korea. In this form of communism it was held that the state would wither away after the overthrow of the capitalist system. In practice, however, the state grew to control all aspects of communist society. Communism in eastern Europe collapsed in the late 1980s and early 1990s against a background of failure to meet people's economic expectations, a shift to more democracy in political life, and increasing nationalism such as that which led to the break-up of the Soviet Union.

– ORIGIN mid 19th cent.: from French *communisme*, from *commun* (see **COMMON**).

Communism Peak former name (1962–98) for **ISMAIL SAMANI PEAK**.

communist ▶ noun a person who supports or believes in the principles of communism: *I was very left-wing but I was never a communist.*
▶ adjective adhering to or based on the principles of communism: *a French communist writer.*
– DERIVATIVES **communistic** adjective.

communitarianism ▶ noun [mass noun] a theory or system of social organization based on small self-governing communities. ■ an ideology which emphasizes the responsibility of the individual to the community and the social importance of the family unit.
– DERIVATIVES **communitarian** adjective & noun.
– ORIGIN mid 19th cent.: from **COMMUNITY** + **-ARIAN**, on the pattern of words such as *unitarian*.

community ▶ noun (pl. **communities**) **1** a group of people living in the same place or having a particular characteristic in common: *Montreal's Italian community | the gay community in London | the scientific community.* ■ a group of people living together and practising common ownership: *a community of nuns.* ■ a particular area or place considered together with its inhabitants: *a rural community | local communities.* ■ a body of nations or states unified by common interests: [in names] *the European Community.* ■ (**the community**) the people of a district or country considered collectively, especially in the context of social values and responsibilities; society: *preparing prisoners for life back in the community.* ■ [as modifier] denoting a worker or resource designed to serve the people of a particular area: *community health services.*
2 [mass noun] the condition of sharing or having certain attitudes and interests in common: *the sense of community that organized religion can provide.* ■ [in sing.] a similarity or identity: *the law presupposes a community of interest between an employer and employees.* ■ joint ownership or liability: *the community of goods.*
3 Ecology a group of interdependent plants or animals growing or living together in natural conditions or occupying a specified habitat: *communities of insectivorous birds.*
– PHRASES **the international community** the countries of the world considered collectively.
– ORIGIN late Middle English: from Old French *comunete*, reinforced by its source, Latin *communitas*, from *communis* (see **COMMON**).

community card ▶ noun (in some forms of poker) each of a number of cards dealt or turned face up for all active players to use.

community care (also **care in the community**) ▶ noun [mass noun] long-term care for people who are mentally ill, elderly, or disabled which is provided within the community rather than in hospitals or institutions, especially as implemented in the UK under the National Health Service and Community Care Act of 1990.

community centre ▶ noun a place where people from a particular neighbourhood can meet for social events, education classes, or recreational activities.

community charge ▶ noun [mass noun] (in the UK) a tax, introduced by the Conservative government in 1990 (1989 in Scotland), levied locally on every adult in a community. It was replaced in 1993 by the council tax. Informally called **POLL TAX**.

community chest ▶ noun a fund for charitable activities among the people in a particular area.

community college ▶ noun **1** chiefly N. Amer. a college providing further and higher education for people living in a particular area.
2 Brit. a secondary school whose educational and recreational facilities are available to adults in the local community.

community home ▶ noun Brit. a centre for housing young offenders and other young people in need of custodial care.

community hospital ▶ noun a non-specialized hospital serving a local area.

community medicine ▶ noun [mass noun] a branch of medicine dealing with health care issues affecting communities as a whole.

community of property ▶ noun [mass noun] (in South Africa) a marriage contract in which the possessions of the partners are merged in a joint estate and disposed of by means of a joint will.

community order ▶ noun English Law a non-custodial sentence which requires an offender to perform community service, observe a curfew, undergo treatment for drug or alcohol addiction, etc., instead of going to prison.

community policing ▶ noun [mass noun] the system of allocating police officers to particular areas so that they become familiar with the local inhabitants.

community sentence ▶ noun English Law a sentence whereby an offender is required to perform community service.

community service ▶ noun [mass noun] voluntary work intended to help people in a particular area. ■ English Law unpaid work, intended to be of social use, that an offender is required to do instead of going to prison: [as modifier] *a community-service order*.

community singing ▶ noun [mass noun] singing by a large crowd or group, especially of old popular songs or hymns.

community spirit ▶ noun [mass noun] a feeling of involvement in and concern for one's local community: *there has been a loss of community spirit*.

community worker ▶ noun a person who works among the people of a particular area to promote their welfare.

communize /ˈkɒmjʊnʌɪz/ (also **communise**) ▶ verb [with obj.] rare cause (a country or economic activity) to be organized on the principles of communism.
– DERIVATIVES **communization** noun.

commutable /kəˈmjuːtəb(ə)l/ ▶ adjective **1** (of a place or journey) allowing regular commuting to and from work: *commutable country homes*.
2 rare capable of being exchanged or converted.
– DERIVATIVES **commutability** noun.

commutate /ˈkɒmjʊteɪt/ ▶ verb [with obj.] regulate or reverse the direction of (an alternating electric current), especially to make it a direct current.
– ORIGIN late 19th cent.: from Latin *commutat-* 'changed altogether, exchanged, interchanged', from the verb *commutare* (see COMMUTE).

commutation ▶ noun [mass noun] **1** the action or process of commuting a judicial sentence. ■ the conversion of a legal obligation or entitlement into another form, e.g. the replacement of an annuity or series of payments by a single payment.
2 the process of commutating an electric current.
3 Mathematics the property of having a commutative relation.
– ORIGIN late Middle English (in the sense 'exchange, barter', later 'alteration'): from Latin *commutatio(n-)*, from *commutare* 'exchange, interchange' (see COMMUTE). Sense 1 dates from the late 16th cent.

commutative /kəˈmjuːtətɪv, ˈkɒmjʊˌtətɪv/ ▶ adjective **1** Mathematics involving the condition that a group of quantities connected by operators gives the same result whatever the order of the quantities involved, e.g. $a \times b = b \times a$.
2 rare relating to or involving substitution or exchange.
– ORIGIN mid 16th cent. (in the sense 'relating to transactions between people'): from French *commutatif, -ive* or medieval Latin *commutativus*, from *commutat-* 'exchanged', from the verb *commutare* (see COMMUTE).

commutator /ˈkɒmjʊˌteɪtə/ ▶ noun an attachment, connected with the armature of a motor or dynamo, through which electrical connection is made and which ensures the current flows as direct current. ■ a device for reversing the direction of flow of electric current.

commute ▶ verb **1** [no obj.] travel some distance between one's home and place of work on a regular basis: *he commuted from Corby to Kentish Town*.
2 [with obj.] reduce (a judicial sentence, especially a sentence of death) to another less severe one: *the governor commuted the sentence to fifteen years' imprisonment*. ■ (**commute something for/into**) change one kind of payment or obligation for (another): *tithes were commuted into an annual sum varying with the price of corn*. ■ replace (an annuity or other series of payments) with a single payment.
3 [no obj.] Mathematics (of two operations or quantities) have a commutative relation: *operators which do not commute with each other*.
▶ noun a regular journey of some distance to and from one's place of work.
– ORIGIN late Middle English (in the sense 'interchange (two things')): from Latin *commutare*, from *com-* 'altogether' + *mutare* 'to change'. Sense 1 of the verb originally meant to buy and use a *commutation ticket*, the US term for a season ticket (because the daily fare is commuted to a single payment).

commuter ▶ noun a person who travels some distance to work on a regular basis: *a fault on the line caused widespread delays for commuters*.

commuter belt ▶ noun Brit. the area surrounding a city from which a large number of people travel to work each day.

Como, Lake /ˈkəʊməʊ/ a lake in the foothills of the Alps in northern Italy.

Comodoro Rivadavia /ˌkɒməˌdɔːrəʊ ˌriːvəˈdɑːvɪə/, Spanish /kaomaoˌðaoraʊ riβaˈðaβja/ a port in Argentina situated on the Atlantic coast of Patagonia; pop. 142,800 (est. 2005).

co-morbid ▶ adjective Medicine relating to or denoting a medical condition that co-occurs with another.
– DERIVATIVES **co-morbidity** noun.

Comorin, Cape /ˈkɒmərɪn/ a cape at the southern tip of India, in the state of Tamil Nadu.

Comoros /ˈkɒmərəʊz/ a country consisting of a group of islands in the Indian Ocean north of Madagascar; pop. 752,400 (est. 2009); languages, French (official), Arabic (official), Comoran Swahili; capital, Moroni. The islands were first visited by the English at the end of the 16th century. At that time and for long afterwards Arab influence was dominant. In the mid 19th century they came under French protection, until in 1974 all but one of the four major islands voted for independence.
– DERIVATIVES **Comoran** adjective & noun.

comp informal ▶ noun short for: ■ Brit. a competition. ■ Brit. a comprehensive school. ■ a computer: *I have Windows XP installed on my comp*. ■ N. Amer. a complimentary ticket or voucher. ■ [mass noun] N. Amer. compensation. ■ Brit. a compositor. ■ a composition. ■ a compilation. ■ a musical accompaniment.
▶ verb **1** [no obj.] play music as an accompaniment, especially in jazz or blues.
2 [with obj.] N. Amer. give (something) away free, especially as part of a promotion: *the management did graciously comp our wine selection*.
3 [with obj.] short for COMPOSITE.
▶ adjective [attrib.] N. Amer. complimentary; free: *the average fan was unable to get comp press tickets*.

compact¹ ▶ adjective /kəmˈpakt/ **1** closely and neatly packed together; dense: *a compact cluster of houses*. ■ having all the necessary components or features neatly fitted into a small space: *this compact car has plenty of boot space*. ■ (of a person or animal) small, strong, and well proportioned. ■ (of speech or writing) concise in expression: *a compact summary of the play*.
2 (**compact of**) archaic composed or made up of: *towns compact of wooden houses*.
▶ verb /kəmˈpakt/ [with obj.] exert force on (something) so that it becomes more dense; compress: *the rubbish was taken to the depot to be compacted* | (as adj. **compacted**) *compacted earth*. ■ [no obj.] become compressed by the exertion of force: *the snow hardened and compacted*. ■ archaic form (something) by pressing its component parts firmly together: *the foundation of the walls, **compacted of** Granite and Lime*. ■ express in fewer words; condense: *the ideas are **compacted into** two sentences*.
▶ noun /ˈkɒmpakt/ **1** a small flat case containing face powder, a mirror, and a powder puff.
2 something that is a small and conveniently shaped example of its kind, in particular a compact camera.
3 Metallurgy a mass of powdered metal compacted together in preparation for sintering.
– DERIVATIVES **compaction** noun, **compactly** adverb, **compactness** noun, **compactor** noun.
– ORIGIN late Middle English: from Latin *compact-* 'closely put together, joined', from the verb *compingere*, from *com-* 'together' + *pangere* 'fasten'.

compact² /ˈkɒmpakt/ ▶ noun a formal agreement or contract between two or more parties.
▶ verb [with obj.] make or enter into (a formal agreement) with another party or parties: *the Democratic Party compacted an alliance with dissident groups*.
– ORIGIN late 16th cent.: from Latin *compactum*, past participle of *compacisci*, from *com-* 'with' + *pacisci* 'make a covenant'. Compare with PACT.

compact camera ▶ noun a small, simple 35 mm camera with automatic focusing and exposure.

compact car ▶ noun N. Amer. a medium-sized car.

compact disc (abbrev.: **CD**) ▶ noun a small plastic disc on which music or other digital information is stored in the form of a pattern of metal-coated pits from which it can be read using laser light reflected off the disc.

compadre /kɒmˈpɑːdreɪ/ ▶ noun (pl. **compadres**) informal, chiefly US a way of addressing or referring to a friend or companion.
– ORIGIN Spanish, literally 'godfather', hence 'benefactor, friend'. Compare with COMPÈRE and GOSSIP.

compand /kəmˈpand/ ▶ verb [with obj.] reduce the signal-to-noise ratio of (a signal) using a compander.
– ORIGIN 1950s: back-formation from COMPANDER.

compander (also **compandor**) ▶ noun a device that improves the signal-to-noise ratio of an electrical signal by compressing the range of amplitudes of the signal before transmission, and then expanding it on reproduction or reception.
– ORIGIN 1930s: blend of COMPRESSOR and EXPANDER (see EXPAND).

companion¹ ▶ noun **1** a person or animal with whom one spends a lot of time or with whom one travels: *his travelling companion* | figurative *fear became my constant companion*. ■ a person who shares the experiences of another, especially when these are unpleasant or unwelcome: *my **companions in misfortune***. ■ a person's long-term sexual partner outside marriage. ■ a person, usually a woman, employed to live with and assist another. ■ Astronomy a star, galaxy, or other celestial object that is close to or associated with another.
2 each of a pair of things intended to complement or match each other: [as modifier] *a companion volume*. ■ [usu. in names] a book that provides information about a particular subject: *the Oxford Companion to English Literature*. ■ Brit. dated a piece of equipment containing several objects used in a particular activity: *a traveller's companion*.
3 (**Companion**) a member of the lowest grade of certain orders of knighthood: *a Companion of the Order of Canada*.
▶ verb [with obj.] formal accompany: *he is companioned by a pageboy*.
– ORIGIN Middle English: from Old French *compaignon*, literally 'one who breaks bread with another', based on Latin *com-* 'together with' + *panis* 'bread'.

companion² ▶ noun a covering over the hatchway leading to a ship's companionway. ■ archaic a raised frame with windows on the quarterdeck of a ship to allow light into the decks below. ■ short for COMPANIONWAY.
– ORIGIN mid 18th cent.: from obsolete Dutch *kompanje* (earlier form of *kampanje*) 'quarterdeck', from Old French *compagne*, from Italian (*camera della*) *compagna* '(storeroom for) provisions'.

companionable ▶ adjective friendly and sociable: *a companionable young man*.
– DERIVATIVES **companionably** adverb.
– ORIGIN early 17th cent.: alteration of obsolete *companiable*, influenced by COMPANION¹.

companion animal ▶ noun a pet or other domestic animal.

companionate /kəmˈpanjənət/ ▶ adjective formal (of a marriage or relationship) between partners or spouses as equal companions.

companion-in-arms ▶ noun a fellow soldier.

companion ladder ▶ noun another term for COMPANIONWAY.

Companion of Honour (abbrev.: **CH**) ▶ noun (in the UK) a member of an order of knighthood founded in 1917.

Companion of Literature ▶ noun (in the UK) a holder of an honour awarded by the Royal Society of Literature and founded in 1961.

companion planting ▶ noun [mass noun] the close planting of different plants that enhance each other's growth or protect each other from pests.
– DERIVATIVES **companion plant** noun.

companion set ▶ noun Brit. a collection of fireside implements on a stand.

companionship ▶ noun [mass noun] a feeling of fellowship or friendship: *the love and companionship of a husband*.

companionway ▶ noun a set of steps leading from a ship's deck down to a cabin or lower deck.

company ▶ noun (pl. **companies**) **1** a commercial business: *a shipping company* | [in names] *the Ford Motor Company* | [as modifier] *a company director*.

C

2 [mass noun] the fact or condition of being with another or others, especially in a way that provides friendship and enjoyment: *I really enjoy his company.* ■ a person or people seen as a source of a specified kind of such friendship and enjoyment: *she is excellent company.* ■ the person or group of people whose society one is currently sharing: *he was silent among such distinguished company.* ■ a visiting person or group of people: *I'm expecting company.*
3 a number of individuals gathered together: *the Mayor addressed the assembled company.* ■ a body of soldiers, especially the smallest subdivision of an infantry battalion, typically commanded by a major or captain: *B Company of the Cheshire Regiment.* ■ a group of actors, singers, or dancers who perform together: *a national opera company.* ■ Brit. a group of Guides.
▸ verb (**companies, companying, companied**) [no obj.] (**company with**) literary associate with; keep company with: *these men which have companied with us all this time.* ■ [with obj.] archaic accompany (someone): *the fair dame, companied by Statius and myself.*
– PHRASES **and company** used after a person's name to denote those people usually associated with them. **be in good company** be in the same situation as someone important or respected. **in company** with another person or a group of people: *he feels at ease in company.* **in company with** together with: *the US dollar went through a bad patch in 1986, in company with the oil market.* **keep** (or archaic **bear**) **someone company** accompany or spend time with someone in order to prevent them feeling lonely or bored. ■ engage in the same activity as someone else in order to be sociable: *I'll have a drink myself, just to keep you company.* **keep company with** associate with habitually: *she began keeping company with a real-estate developer.*
– ORIGIN Middle English (in sense 2 of the noun, sense 3 of the noun): from Old French *compainie*; related to *compaignon* (see COMPANION[1]).

company car ▸ noun a car provided by a firm for the business and private use of an employee.

company officer ▸ noun an army officer serving within an infantry company.

company promoter ▸ noun see PROMOTER.

company sergeant major ▸ noun the highest-ranking non-commissioned officer of an infantry company.

comparable /ˈkɒmp(ə)rəb(ə)l/ ▸ adjective able to be likened to another; similar: *the situation in Holland is* ***comparable to*** *that in England.* ■ of equivalent quality; worthy of comparison: *nobody is* ***comparable*** *with this athlete.*
– DERIVATIVES **comparability** noun.
– ORIGIN late Middle English: from Old French, from Latin *comparabilis*, from the verb *comparare* (see COMPARE).

USAGE Although the correct pronunciation in standard English is with the stress on the first syllable rather than the second (**comparable**), an alternative pronunciation with the stress on the second syllable (**comparable**) is gaining in currency.

comparably /ˈkɒmp(ə)rəbli/ ▸ adverb in a similar way or to a similar degree: *a comparably priced CD player.*

comparatist /kəmˈparətɪst/ ▸ noun a person who carries out comparative study, especially of language or literature.

comparative /kəmˈparətɪv/ ▸ adjective 1 measured or judged by estimating the similarity or dissimilarity between one thing and another; relative: *he returned to the comparative comfort of his own home.*
2 involving the systematic observation of the similarities or dissimilarities between two or more branches of science or subjects of study: *comparative religion.*
3 Grammar (of an adjective or adverb) expressing a higher degree of a quality, but not the highest possible (e.g. *braver; more fiercely*). Contrasted with POSITIVE, SUPERLATIVE. ■ (of a clause) involving comparison (e.g. *he's not as good as he was*).
▸ noun Grammar a comparative adjective or adverb. ■ (**the comparative**) the middle degree of comparison.
– ORIGIN late Middle English (in sense 3 of the adjective): from Latin *comparativus*, from *comparare* 'to pair, match' (see COMPARE).

comparative advantage ▸ noun Economics the ability of an individual or group to carry out a particular economic activity (such as making a specific product) more efficiently than another activity.

comparative linguistics ▸ plural noun [treated as sing.] the study of similarities and differences between languages, in particular the comparison of related languages with a view to reconstructing forms in their lost parent languages.

comparatively ▸ adverb [as submodifier] to a moderate degree as compared to something else; relatively: *inflation was comparatively low.*

comparator /kəmˈparətə/ ▸ noun a device for comparing something measurable with a reference or standard. ■ an electronic circuit for comparing two electrical signals.
– ORIGIN late 19th cent.: from Latin *comparat-* 'paired, matched', from the verb *comparare* (see COMPARE), + -OR[1].

compare ▸ verb [with obj.] 1 estimate, measure, or note the similarity or dissimilarity between: *individual schools* ***compared*** *their facilities* ***with*** *those of others in the area* | *the survey compares prices in different countries* | *total attendance figures were 28,000,* ***compared to*** *40,000 at last year's event.* ■ (**compare something to**) point out or describe the resemblances with; liken to: *her novel was compared to the work of Daniel Defoe.* ■ (**compare something to**) draw an analogy between one thing and (another) for the purposes of explanation or clarification: *he compared the religions to different paths towards the peak of the same mountain.* ■ [no obj., with adverbial] have a specified relationship with another thing or person in terms of nature or quality: *salaries* ***compare*** *favourably* ***with*** *those of other professions.* ■ [no obj., usu. with negative] be of an equal or similar nature or quality: *the dried stuff just can't* ***compare with*** *the taste and aroma of fresh basil.*
2 Grammar form the comparative and superlative degrees of (an adjective or an adverb): *words of one syllable are usually compared by '-er' and '-est'.*
▸ noun (in phrase **beyond** or **without compare**) literary of a quality or nature surpassing all others of the same kind: *a diamond beyond compare.*
– PHRASES **compare notes** exchange ideas, opinions, or information about a particular subject.
– ORIGIN late Middle English: from Old French *comparer*, from Latin *comparare*, from *compar* 'like, equal', from *com-* 'with' + *par* 'equal'.

USAGE Is there any difference between **compare with** and **compare to**, and is one more correct than the other? There is a slight difference, in that it is usual to use **to** rather than **with** when describing the resemblance, by analogy, of two quite different things, as in *critics* ***compared*** *Ellington's music* ***to*** *the music of Beethoven and Brahms.* In the sense 'estimate the similarity or dissimilarity between', **with** is often preferred to **to**, as in *schools* ***compared*** *their facilities* ***with*** *those of others in the area.* However, in practice the distinction is not clear-cut and both **compare with** and **compare to** can be used in either context.

comparison ▸ noun 1 a consideration or estimate of the similarities or dissimilarities between two things or people: *they* ***drew a comparison between*** *Gandhi's teaching and that of other teachers* | [mass noun] *the two books invite comparison with one another.* ■ an analogy: *perhaps the best comparison is that of seasickness.* ■ [mass noun] the quality of being similar or equivalent: *when it comes to achievements this season,* ***there's no comparison between*** *Linfield and Bangor.*
2 [mass noun] Grammar the formation of the comparative and superlative forms of adjectives and adverbs.
– PHRASES **bear** (or **stand**) **comparison** be of sufficient quality to be likened favourably to someone or something of the same kind. **beyond comparison** surpassing all others of the same kind. **in** (or **by**) **comparison** when compared: *the Prime Minister's support staff is tiny* ***in comparison with*** *that of a US President.*
– ORIGIN Middle English: from Old French *comparesoun*, from Latin *comparatio(n-)*, from *comparare* 'to pair, match' (see COMPARE).

comparison shopping ▸ noun [mass noun] the practice of comparing the price of goods or services provided by different shops or companies before making a purchase.
– DERIVATIVES **comparison-shop** verb, **comparison shopper** noun.

compartment ▸ noun 1 a separate section or part of a structure or container: *there's some ice cream in the freezer compartment.* ■ a division of a railway carriage marked by partitions: *a first-class compartment.* ■ a division of a ship's hull: *the aft cargo compartment.* ■ an area in which something can be considered in isolation from other things: *religion and politics should be kept in different compartments.*
2 Heraldry a grassy mound or other support depicted below a shield.
▸ verb [with obj.] divide (something) into separate parts or sections: *the buildings are to be compartmented by fire walls.*
– DERIVATIVES **compartmentation** noun.
– ORIGIN mid 16th cent.: from French *compartiment*, from Italian *compartimento*, from *compartire*, from late Latin *compartiri* 'divide'.

compartmental ▸ adjective characterized by division into separate sections: *the compartmental interior of the church.*
– DERIVATIVES **compartmentally** adverb.

compartmentalize (also **compartmentalise**) ▸ verb [with obj.] divide into discrete sections or categories: *he had the ability to compartmentalize his life.*
– DERIVATIVES **compartmentalism** noun, **compartmentalization** noun.

compartment syndrome ▸ noun Medicine a condition resulting from increased pressure within a confined body space, especially of the leg or forearm.

compass ▸ noun 1 an instrument containing a magnetized pointer which shows the direction of magnetic north and bearings from it.
2 (also **compasses** or **a pair of compasses**) an instrument for drawing circles and arcs and measuring distances between points, consisting of two arms linked by a movable joint, one arm ending in a point and the other usually carrying a pencil or pen.
3 [in sing.] the range or scope of something: *the event had political repercussions which are* ***beyond the compass of*** *this book* | *goods and services which fall* ***within the compass of*** *the free market.* ■ the enclosing limits of an area: *this region had within its compass many types of agriculture.* ■ the range of notes that can be produced by a voice or a musical instrument: *the cellos were playing in a rather sombre part of their compass.*
▸ verb [with obj.] archaic 1 go round (something) in a circular course: *the ship wherein Magellan compassed the world.* ■ surround or hem in on all sides: *we were compassed round by a thick fog.*
2 contrive to accomplish (something): *he compassed his end only by the exercise of violence.*
– ORIGIN Middle English: from Old French *compas* (noun), *compasser* (verb), based on Latin *com-* 'together' + *passus* 'a step or pace'. Several senses ('measure', 'artifice', 'circumscribed area', and 'pair of compasses') which appeared in Middle English are also found in Old French, but their development and origin are uncertain. The transference of sense to the magnetic compass is held to have occurred in the related Italian word *compasso*, from the circular shape of the compass box.

compass card ▸ noun a circular rotating card showing the 32 principal bearings, forming the indicator of a magnetic compass.

compassion ▸ noun [mass noun] sympathetic pity and concern for the sufferings or misfortunes of others: *the victims should be treated with compassion.*
– ORIGIN Middle English: via Old French from ecclesiastical Latin *compassio(n-)*, from *compati* 'suffer with'.

compassionate ▸ adjective feeling or showing sympathy and concern for others.
– DERIVATIVES **compassionately** adverb.
– ORIGIN late 16th cent.: from COMPASSION + -ATE[2], influenced by archaic French *compassioné* 'feeling pity'.

compassionate leave ▸ noun [mass noun] Brit. a period of absence from work granted to someone as the result of particular personal circumstances, especially the death of a close relative.

compassion fatigue ▸ noun [mass noun] indifference to charitable appeals on behalf of suffering people, experienced as a result of the frequency or number of such appeals.

compass rose ▸ noun a graduated circle printed on a map or chart from which bearings can be taken.

compass saw ▸ noun a handsaw with a narrow blade for cutting curves.

compass window ▸ noun a bay window with a semicircular curve.

compatibility ▸ noun [mass noun] a state in which two things are able to exist or occur together without problems or conflict: *he argues for the compatibility of science and religion.* ■ a feeling of sympathy and friendship; like-mindedness: *they felt the bond of true* *compatibility*. ■ Computing the ability of one computer, piece of software, etc. to work with another.

compatible ▸ adjective (often **compatible with**) (of two things) able to exist or occur together without problems or conflict: *the careers structure here is not compatible with having a family*. ■ (of two people) able to have a harmonious relationship; well suited: *it's a pity we're not compatible*. ■ (of one thing) consistent with another: *the symptoms were compatible with gastritis or a peptic ulcer*. ■ Computing (of a computer, piece of software, etc.) able to be used with a specified piece of equipment or software without special adaptation or modification: *the printer is fully compatible with all leading software*.
▸ noun a computer that can use software designed for another make or type.
– DERIVATIVES **compatibly** adverb.
– ORIGIN late Middle English: from French, from medieval Latin *compatibilis*, from *compati* 'suffer with'.

compatriot /kəmˈpatrɪət, -ˈpeɪt-/ ▸ noun a fellow citizen or national of a country.
– ORIGIN late 16th cent.: from French *compatriote*, from late Latin *compatriota* (translating Greek *sumpatriōtēs*), from *com-* 'together with' + *patriota* (see **PATRIOT**).

compeer /kəmˈpɪə/ ▸ noun formal a person of equal rank, status, or ability. ■ archaic a companion or associate.
– ORIGIN late Middle English: from Old French *comper*, from *com-* 'with' + *per*, from Latin *par* 'equal' (compare with **PEER**[2]).

compel ▸ verb (**compels, compelling, compelled**) [with obj. and infinitive] force or oblige (someone) to do something: *a sense of duty compelled Harry to answer her questions*. ■ [with obj.] bring about (something) by the use of force or pressure: *they may compel a witness's attendance at court by issue of a summons* | *his striking appearance compelled attention*. ■ [with obj. and adverbial of direction] literary force to come or go in a particular direction: *by heav'n's high will compell'd from shore to shore*.
– ORIGIN late Middle English: from Latin *compellere*, from *com-* 'together' + *pellere* 'drive'.

compellable ▸ adjective Law (of a witness) able to be made to attend court or give evidence.

compelling ▸ adjective evoking interest, attention, or admiration in a powerfully irresistible way: *his eyes were strangely compelling* | *a compelling film*. ■ not able to be refuted; inspiring conviction: *there is compelling evidence that the recession is ending* | *a compelling argument*. ■ not able to be resisted; overwhelming: *the temptation to give up was compelling*.
– DERIVATIVES **compellingly** adverb.

compendious ▸ adjective formal containing or presenting the essential facts of something in a comprehensive but concise way: *a compendious study*.
– DERIVATIVES **compendiously** adverb, **compendiousness** noun.
– ORIGIN late Middle English: from Old French *compendieux*, from Latin *compendiosus* 'advantageous, brief', from *compendium* 'profit, saving, abbreviation'.

compendium ▸ noun (pl. **compendiums** or **compendia** /-dɪə/) a collection of concise but detailed information about a particular subject, especially in a book or other publication. ■ a collection or set of similar items. ■ a package of stationery for writing letters.
– ORIGIN late 16th cent.: from Latin, 'profit, saving' (literally 'what is weighed together'), from *compendere*, from *com-* 'together' + *pendere* 'weigh'.

compensable /kəmˈpɛnsəb(ə)l/ ▸ adjective (of a loss or hardship) for which compensation can be obtained.
– ORIGIN mid 17th cent.: French, from *compenser*, from Latin *compensare* 'weigh (something) against (another)'.

compensate ▸ verb **1** [with obj.] give (someone) something, typically money, in recognition of loss, suffering, or injury incurred; recompense: *payments were made to farmers to* **compensate** *them* **for** *cuts in subsidies*. ■ pay (someone) for work performed: *he will be richly compensated for his efforts*.
2 [no obj.] (**compensate for**) reduce or counteract (something unwelcome or unpleasant) by exerting an opposite force or effect: *the manager is hoping for victory to compensate for the team's dismal league campaign*. ■ act so as to neutralize or correct (a deficiency or abnormality in a physical property or effect): *the output voltage rises, compensating for the original fall*.
– DERIVATIVES **compensative** adjective, **compensator** noun.
– ORIGIN mid 17th cent. (in the sense 'counterbalance'): from Latin *compensat-* 'weighed against', from the verb *compensare*, from *com-* 'together' + *pensare* (frequentative of *pendere* 'weigh').

compensation ▸ noun [mass noun] **1** something, typically money, awarded to someone in recognition of loss, suffering, or injury: *he is seeking compensation for injuries suffered at work* | [as modifier] *a compensation claim*. ■ the action or process of making such an award: *the compensation of victims*. ■ something that counterbalances or makes up for an undesirable or unwelcome state of affairs: *the grey streets of London were small compensation for the loss of her beloved Africa* | [count noun] *getting older has some compensations*.
2 the process of concealing or offsetting a psychological difficulty by developing in another direction.
3 chiefly N. Amer. the money received by an employee from an employer as a salary or wages: *send your CV and current compensation to Executive Search Consultant*.
– DERIVATIVES **compensational** adjective.
– ORIGIN late Middle English: via Old French from Latin *compensatio(n-)*, from the verb *compensare* 'weigh against' (see **COMPENSATE**).

compensation pendulum ▸ noun Physics a pendulum constructed from metals with differing coefficients of expansion in order to neutralize the effects of temperature variation.

compensation water ▸ noun [mass noun] water supplied from a reservoir to a stream in time of drought.

compensatory ▸ adjective (of a payment) intended to recompense someone who has experienced loss, suffering, or injury: *$50 million in compensatory damages*. ■ reducing or offsetting the unpleasant or unwelcome effects of something: *the government is taking compensatory actions to keep the interest rate constant*.

compère /ˈkɒmpɛː/ Brit. ▸ noun a person who introduces the performers or contestants in a variety show.
▸ verb [with obj.] act as a compère for (a variety show).
– ORIGIN early 20th cent.: French, literally 'godfather', from medieval Latin *compater*, from *com-* 'together with' + Latin *pater* 'father'.

compete ▸ verb [no obj.] strive to gain or win something by defeating or establishing superiority over others: *universities are* **competing for** *applicants* | *he* **competed with** *a number of other candidates* | (as adj. **competing**) *competing political ideologies*. ■ [usu. with negative] be able to rival another or others: *no one* **can compete with** *his physical prowess*. ■ take part in a contest: *he competed in numerous track meets as a child*.
– ORIGIN early 17th cent.: from Latin *competere*, in its late sense 'strive or contend for (something)', from *com-* 'together' + *petere* 'aim at, seek'.

competence (also **competency**) ▸ noun **1** [mass noun] the ability to do something successfully or efficiently: *courses to improve the competence of staff* | *the players displayed varying degrees of competence*. ■ the legal authority of a court or other body to deal with a particular matter: *the court's competence has been accepted to cover these matters*. ■ (also **linguistic** or **language competence**) Linguistics a person's subconscious knowledge of the rules governing the formation of speech in their first language. Often contrasted with **PERFORMANCE**. ■ Biology & Medicine effective performance of the normal function.
2 dated an income large enough to live on, typically an unearned one: *he found himself with an ample competence and no obligations*.

competent ▸ adjective having the necessary ability, knowledge, or skill to do something successfully: *a highly competent surgeon* | [with infinitive] *make sure the firm is* **competent to** *carry out the work*. ■ (of a person) efficient and capable: *an infinitely competent mother of three*. ■ acceptable and satisfactory, though not outstanding: *she spoke quite competent French*. ■ (of a court or other body) accepted as having legal authority to deal with a particular matter: *the London Stock Exchange is the competent authority under the Financial Services Act*. ■ Biology & Medicine capable of performing the normal function effectively.
– DERIVATIVES **competently** adverb.
– ORIGIN late Middle English (in the sense 'suitable, adequate'): from Latin *competent-*, from the verb *competere* in its earlier sense 'be fit or proper' (see **COMPETE**).

competition ▸ noun [mass noun] the activity or condition of striving to gain or win something by defeating or establishing superiority over others: *there is fierce* **competition between** *banks* | *the* **competition for** *university places is greater than ever this year*. ■ [count noun] an event or contest in which people take part in order to establish superiority or supremacy in a particular area: *a beauty competition*. ■ [in sing.] the person or people over whom one is attempting to establish one's supremacy or superiority; the opposition: *I walked round to check out the competition*. ■ Ecology interaction between animal or plant species, or individual organisms, that are attempting to gain a share of a limited environmental resource.
– ORIGIN early 17th cent.: from late Latin *competitio(n-)* 'rivalry', from *competere* 'strive for' (see **COMPETE**).

competitive ▸ adjective **1** relating to or characterized by competition: *a competitive sport* | *the intensely competitive newspaper industry*. ■ having or displaying a strong desire to be more successful than others: *she had a competitive streak*.
2 as good as or better than others of a comparable nature: *a car industry competitive with any in the world*. ■ (of prices) low enough to compare well with those of rival traders: *we offer prompt service at competitive rates*.
– DERIVATIVES **competitively** adverb, **competitiveness** noun.
– ORIGIN early 19th cent.: from Latin *competit-* 'striven for', from the verb *competere* (see **COMPETE**), + **-IVE**.

competitive exclusion ▸ noun [mass noun] Ecology the inevitable elimination from a habitat of one of two different species with identical needs for resources.

competitor ▸ noun a person who takes part in a sporting contest. ■ an organization or country engaged in commercial or economic competition with others: *our main industrial competitors*.

compilation ▸ noun **1** [mass noun] the action or process of producing something, especially a list or book, by assembling information collected from other sources: *great care has been taken in the compilation of this guidebook*.
2 a thing, especially a book, record, or broadcast programme, that is put together by assembling previously separate items: *there are thirty-three stories in this compilation* | [as modifier] *a compilation album*.
– ORIGIN late Middle English: via Old French from Latin *compilatio(n-)*, from *compilare* 'to plunder' (see **COMPILE**).

compile ▸ verb [with obj.] **1** produce (a list or book) by assembling information collected from other sources: *the local authority must compile a list of the names and addresses of taxpayers*. ■ collect (information) in order to produce a list or book: *the figures were compiled from a survey of 2,000 schoolchildren*. ■ accumulate (a specified score): *the world champion compiled a break of 101*.
2 Computing convert (a program) into a machine-code or lower-level form in which the program can be executed.
– DERIVATIVES **compiler** noun.
– ORIGIN Middle English: from Old French *compiler* or its apparent source, Latin *compilare* 'plunder or plagiarize'.

comping ▸ noun [mass noun] **1** Brit. informal the practice of entering competitions, especially those promoting consumer products.
2 the action of playing a musical accompaniment, especially in jazz or blues.
3 the process of making composite images, especially electronically.
– DERIVATIVES **comper** noun (sense 1).

complacency (also **complacence**) ▸ noun [mass noun] a feeling of smug or uncritical satisfaction with oneself or one's achievements: *the figures are better, but there are no grounds for complacency*.
– ORIGIN mid 17th cent.: from medieval Latin *complacentia*, from Latin *complacere* 'to please'.

complacent /kəmˈpleɪs(ə)nt/ ▸ adjective showing smug or uncritical satisfaction with oneself or one's achievements: *you can't afford to be complacent about security*.
– DERIVATIVES **complacently** adverb.
– ORIGIN mid 17th cent. (in the sense 'pleasant'): from Latin *complacent-* 'pleasing', from the verb *complacere*.

USAGE Complacent and **complaisant** are two words which are similar in pronunciation and which both come from the Latin verb *complacere* 'to please', but in English they do not mean the same thing. **Complacent** is far commoner and means 'smug and self-satisfied'. **Complaisant**, on the other hand, means 'willing to please', as in *the local people proved* ***complaisant*** *and cordial.*

complain ▸ **verb 1** [reporting verb] express dissatisfaction or annoyance about something: [with clause] *local authorities complained that they lacked sufficient resources* | [with direct speech] *'You never listen to me,' Larry complained* | [no obj.] *we all complained bitterly about the food.* ■ [no obj.] (of a structure or mechanism) groan or creak under strain. ■ [no obj.] literary make a mournful sound: *let the warbling flute complain.*
2 [no obj.] (**complain of**) state that one is suffering from (a pain or other symptom of illness): *her husband began to complain of headaches.*
– DERIVATIVES **complainer** noun, **complainingly** adverb.
– ORIGIN late Middle English: from Old French *complaindre*, from medieval Latin *complangere* 'bewail', from Latin *com-* (expressing intensive force) + *plangere* 'to lament'.

complainant ▸ **noun** Law, Brit. a plaintiff in certain lawsuits.
– ORIGIN late Middle English: from French *complaignant*, present participle of *complaindre* 'to lament' (see COMPLAIN).

complaint ▸ **noun 1** a statement that something is unsatisfactory or unacceptable: *I intend to make an official complaint* | *there were* ***complaints that*** *the building was an eyesore.* ■ a reason for dissatisfaction: *I have no complaints about the hotel.* ■ [mass noun] the expression of dissatisfaction: *a letter of complaint* | *he hasn't any cause for complaint.* ■ Law the plaintiff's reasons for proceeding in a civil action.
2 an illness or medical condition, especially a relatively minor one: *she is receiving treatment for her skin complaint.*
– ORIGIN late Middle English: from Old French *complainte*, feminine past participle of *complaindre* 'to lament' (see COMPLAIN).

complaisant /kəm'pleɪz(ə)nt/ ▸ **adjective** willing to please others or to accept what they do or say without protest: *he went to join his apparently complaisant wife for Christmas.*
– DERIVATIVES **complaisance** noun.
– ORIGIN mid 17th cent.: French, from *complaire* 'acquiesce in order to please', from Latin *complacere* 'to please'.

USAGE Complaisant does not mean the same as complacent. See USAGE at COMPLACENT.

compleat ▸ **adjective & verb** archaic spelling of COMPLETE.

complected /kəm'plɛktɪd/ ▸ **adjective** [in combination] N. Amer. having a specified complexion: *the lighter-complected invaders from the north.*
– ORIGIN early 19th cent.: apparently from COMPLEXION.

complement ▸ **noun** /'kɒmplɪm(ə)nt/ **1** a thing that contributes extra features to something else in such a way as to improve or emphasize its quality: *local ales provide the perfect* ***complement to*** *fine food.*
2 [in sing.] a number or quantity of something, especially that required to make a group complete: *at the moment we have* ***a full complement of*** *staff.* ■ the number of people required to crew a ship: *almost half the ship's complement of 322 were wounded.* ■ Geometry the amount in degrees by which a given angle is less than 90°. ■ Mathematics the members of a set or class that are not members of a given subset.
3 Grammar one or more words, phrases, or clauses governed by a verb (or by a nominalization or a predicative adjective) that complete the meaning of the predicate. In generative grammar, all the constituents of a sentence that are governed by a verb form the complement. ■ (in systemic grammar) an adjective or noun that has the same reference as either the subject (as *mad* in *he is mad*) or the object (as *mad* in *he drove her mad* or *manager* in *they appointed him manager*).
4 [mass noun] Physiology a group of proteins present in blood plasma and tissue fluid which combine with an antigen–antibody complex to bring about the lysis of foreign cells.
▸ **verb** /'kɒmplɪmɛnt/ [with obj.] contribute extra features to (someone or something) in such a way as to improve or emphasize their qualities: *a classic blazer complements a look that's smart or casual.* ■ add to or make complete: *the proposals complement the incentives already available.*
– PHRASES **in her complement** Heraldry (of the moon) depicted as full.
– DERIVATIVES **complemental** adjective.
– ORIGIN late Middle English (in the sense 'completion'): from Latin *complementum*, from *complere* 'fill up' (see COMPLETE). Compare with COMPLIMENT.

USAGE **Complement** and **compliment** (together with related words such as **complementary** and **complimentary**) are frequently confused. They are pronounced in the same way but have quite different meanings: as a verb **complement** means 'add to something in a way that enhances or improves', as in *a classic blazer* ***complements*** *a look that's smart or casual*, while **compliment** means 'admire and praise someone for something', as in *he* ***complimented*** *her on her appearance.* **Complementary** means 'forming a complement or addition, completing,' as in *I purchased a suit with a complementary tie.* This is often confused with **complimentary**, for which one sense is 'given freely, as a courtesy': *honeymooners receive complimentary fruit and flowers.*

complementarity ▸ **noun** (pl. **complementarities**) [mass noun] a relationship or situation in which two or more different things improve or emphasize each other's qualities: *a culture based on the complementarity of men and women.* ■ Physics the concept that two contrasted theories, such as the wave and particle theories of light, may be able to explain a set of phenomena, although each separately only accounts for some aspects.

complementary ▸ **adjective 1** combining in such a way as to enhance or emphasize the qualities of each other or another: *they had different but complementary skills* | *the second TV network was* ***complementary to*** *the BBC.* ■ Biochemistry (of gene sequences, nucleotides, etc.) related by the rules of base pairing.
2 [attrib.] relating to complementary medicine: *complementary therapies such as aromatherapy.*
– DERIVATIVES **complementarily** adverb, **complementariness** noun.

complementary angle ▸ **noun** either of two angles whose sum is 90°.

complementary colour ▸ **noun** a colour that combined with a given colour makes white or black.

complementary distribution ▸ **noun** [mass noun] the occurrence of phenomena such as speech sounds in mutually exclusive contexts.

complementary DNA ▸ **noun** [mass noun] synthetic DNA in which the sequence of bases is complementary to that of a given example of DNA.

complementary function ▸ **noun** Mathematics the part of the general solution of a linear differential equation which is the general solution of the associated homogeneous equation obtained by substituting zero for the terms not containing the dependent variable.

complementary medicine ▸ **noun** [mass noun] Brit. any of a range of medical therapies that fall beyond the scope of conventional medicine but may be used alongside it in the treatment of disease and ill health. Examples include acupuncture and osteopathy. See also ALTERNATIVE MEDICINE.

complementation ▸ **noun 1** [mass noun] the action of complementing something.
2 Grammar all the clause constituents that are governed by a verb, nominalization, or adjective.
3 Genetics the phenomenon by which the effects of two different non-allelic mutations in a gene are partly or entirely cancelled out when they occur together.

complement fixation test ▸ **noun** Medicine a test for infection with a microorganism which involves measuring the amount of complement available in serum to bind with an antibody–antigen complex.

complementizer (also **complementiser**) ▸ **noun** Grammar a word or morpheme that marks an embedded clause as functioning as a complement, typically a subordinating conjunction or infinitival *to*.

complete ▸ **adjective 1** having all the necessary or appropriate parts: *a complete list of courses offered by the university* | *no woman's wardrobe is complete without this pretty top.* ■ entire; full: *I only managed one complete term at school* | *the complete works of Shakespeare.* ■ (**complete with**) having (something) as an additional part or feature: *the house* ***comes complete with*** *gas central heating and double glazing.* ■ [predic.] having run its full course; finished: *the restoration of the chapel is complete.*
2 [attrib.] (often used for emphasis) to the greatest extent or degree; total: *a complete ban on smoking* | *their marriage came as a complete surprise to me.* ■ (also **compleat**) chiefly humorous skilled at every aspect of a particular activity; consummate: *his range of skills made him the complete footballer.* [the spelling *compleat* is a revival of the 17th cent. use as in Walton's *The Compleat Angler*.]
▸ **verb** [with obj.] **1** finish making or doing: *he completed his PhD in 1993.* ■ [no obj.] Brit. conclude the sale of a property. ■ American Football (of a quarterback) successfully throw (a forward pass) to a receiver.
2 provide with the item or items necessary to make (something) full or entire: *complete your collection of Britain's brightest gardening magazine* | *quarry tiles and faded rugs complete the look.* ■ write the required information on (a form or questionnaire): *please complete the attached forms.*
– DERIVATIVES **completeness** noun.
– ORIGIN late Middle English: from Old French *complet* or Latin *completus*, past participle of *complere* 'fill up, finish, fulfil', from *com-* (expressing intensive force) + *plere* 'fill'.

USAGE On the question of the use of adjectives like **complete**, **equal**, and **unique** with submodifiers such as **very** or **more**, see USAGE at UNIQUE.

completely ▸ **adverb** totally; utterly: *the fire completely destroyed the building* | [as submodifier] *you must be completely mad!*

completion ▸ **noun** [mass noun] the action or process of completing or finishing something: *funds for the completion of the new building.* ■ the state of being finished: *work on the new golf course is nearing completion* | [as modifier] *the completion date is early next year.* ■ Brit. the final stage in the sale of a property, at which point it legally changes ownership: *the risk stays with the seller until completion.*
– ORIGIN late 15th cent.: from Latin *completio(n-)*, from *complere* 'fill up' (see COMPLETE).

completist ▸ **noun** an obsessive, typically indiscriminate, collector or fan of something.

completive ▸ **noun** Grammar a word or morpheme which adds a sense of completeness to a word or phrase (e.g. in the phrase *break up*, *up* is a completive).

complex ▸ **adjective 1** consisting of many different and connected parts: *a complex network of water channels.* ■ not easy to analyse or understand; complicated or intricate: *a complex personality* | *the situation is more complex than it appears.*
2 Mathematics denoting or involving numbers or quantities containing both a real and an imaginary part.
3 Chemistry denoting an ion or molecule in which one or more groups are linked to a metal atom by coordinate bonds.
▸ **noun 1** a group or system of different things that are linked in a close or complicated way; a network: *a complex of mountain roads.* ■ a group of similar buildings or facilities on the same site: *a leisure complex* | *a complex of hotels.*
2 Psychoanalysis a related group of repressed or partly repressed emotionally significant ideas which cause psychic conflict leading to abnormal mental states or behaviour. ■ informal a strong or disproportionate concern or anxiety about something: *there's no point having a* ***complex about*** *losing your hair.*
3 Chemistry an ion or molecule in which one or more groups are linked to a metal atom by coordinate bonds. ■ any loosely bonded species formed by the association of two molecules: *cross-linked protein–DNA complexes.*
▸ **verb** [with obj.] Chemistry make (an atom or compound) form a complex with another: *the DNA was* ***complexed with*** *the nuclear extract.*
– DERIVATIVES **complexation** noun (Chemistry), **complexly** adverb.
– ORIGIN mid 17th cent. (in the sense 'group of related elements'): from Latin *complexus*, past participle (used as a noun) of *complectere* 'embrace, comprise', later associated with *complexus* 'plaited'; the adjective is partly via French *complexe*.

complex conjugate ▸ **noun** Mathematics each of two complex numbers having their real parts identical and their imaginary parts of equal magnitude but opposite sign.

complexion ▸ **noun 1** the natural colour, texture, and appearance of a person's skin, especially of the face: *an attractive girl with a pale complexion.*
2 the general aspect or character of something: *the complexion of the game changed* | *successive governments of all complexions.*
– DERIVATIVES **complexioned** adjective [in combination] *they were both fair-complexioned.*
– ORIGIN Middle English: via Old French from Latin *complexio(n-)* 'combination' (in late Latin 'physical constitution'), from *complectere* 'embrace, comprise'. The term originally denoted physical constitution or

temperament determined by the combination of the four bodily humours, hence sense 1 (late 16th cent.) as a visible sign of this.

complexity ▶ **noun** (pl. **complexities**) [mass noun] the state or quality of being intricate or complicated: *an issue of great complexity*. ■ [count noun] (usu. **complexities**) a factor involved in a complicated process or situation: *the complexities of family life*.

complex sentence ▶ **noun** a sentence containing a subordinate clause or clauses.

compliance /kəmˈplʌɪəns/ ▶ **noun** [mass noun] **1** the action or fact of complying with a wish or command: *the ways in which the state maintains order and compliance*. ■ excessive acquiescence: *the appalling* ***compliance with*** *government views shown by the commission*. ■ the state or fact of according with or meeting rules or standards: *all imports of timber are* ***in compliance with*** *regulations* | [as modifier] *this paper estimates the compliance costs of such a policy change*.
2 Physics the property of a material of undergoing elastic deformation or (of a gas) change in volume when subjected to an applied force. It is equal to the reciprocal of stiffness. ■ Medicine the ability of an organ to distend in response to applied pressure.

compliance officer ▶ **noun** a person who is employed to ensure that a company does not contravene any statutes or regulations which apply to its activities.

compliant ▶ **adjective 1** disposed to agree with others or obey rules, especially to an excessive degree; acquiescent: *a compliant labour force*.
2 (often **compliant with**) meeting or in accordance with rules or standards: *food which is compliant with safety regulations*.
3 Physics & Medicine having the property of compliance.
– DERIVATIVES **compliantly** adverb.

complicate /ˈkɒmplɪkeɪt/ ▶ **verb** [with obj.] make more complicated: *increased choice will complicate matters for the consumer* | (as adj. **complicating**) *a complicating factor*. ■ Medicine introduce complications in (an existing condition): *smoking may complicate pregnancy* | (as adj. **complicating**) *patients with complicating biliary calculi*.
– ORIGIN early 17th cent. (in the sense 'combine, entangle, intertwine'): from Latin *complicat-* 'folded together', from the verb *complicare*, from *com-* 'together' + *plicare* 'to fold'.

complicated ▶ **adjective 1** consisting of many interconnecting parts or elements; intricate: *a complicated stereo system*. ■ involving many different and confusing aspects: *a long and complicated saga*.
2 Medicine involving complications: *complicated appendicitis*.
– DERIVATIVES **complicatedly** adverb.

complication ▶ **noun 1** a circumstance that complicates something; a difficulty: *there is a complication concerning ownership of the site*. ■ [mass noun] an involved or confused condition or state: *to add further complication, English-speakers use a different name*.
2 Medicine a secondary disease or condition aggravating an already existing one: *she developed complications after the surgery*.
– ORIGIN late Middle English: from late Latin *complicatio(n-)*, from Latin *complicare* 'fold together' (see COMPLICATE).

complicit /kəmˈplɪsɪt/ ▶ **adjective** involved with others in an activity that is unlawful or morally wrong: *the careers of those* ***complicit in*** *the cover-up were blighted*.
– ORIGIN 1940s: back-formation from COMPLICITY.

complicitous /kəmˈplɪsɪtəs/ ▶ **adjective** another term for COMPLICIT: *they were complicitous with Nazi authorities*.

complicity ▶ **noun** [mass noun] the fact or condition of being involved with others in an activity that is unlawful or morally wrong: *they were accused of* ***complicity in*** *the attempt to overthrow the government*.
– ORIGIN mid 17th cent.: from Middle English *complice* 'an associate', from Old French, from late Latin *complex, complic-* 'allied', from Latin *complicare* 'fold together' (see COMPLICATE). Compare with ACCOMPLICE.

compliment ▶ **noun** /ˈkɒmplɪm(ə)nt/ a polite expression of praise or admiration: *she paid me an enormous compliment*. ■ an act or circumstance that implies praise or respect: *it's* ***a compliment to*** *the bride to dress up on her special day*. ■ (**compliments**) congratulations or praise expressed to someone: *my compliments on your cooking*. ■ (**compliments**) formal greetings, especially when sent as a message: *carry my compliments to your kinsmen*.
▶ **verb** /ˈkɒmplɪmɛnt/ [with obj.] politely congratulate or praise (someone) for something: *he* ***complimented*** *Erika* ***on*** *her appearance*. ■ praise (something) politely: *the manager was heard to compliment the other team's good play*. ■ (**compliment someone with**) archaic present someone with (something) as a mark of courtesy: *Prince George expected to be complimented with a seat in the royal coach*.
– PHRASES **return the compliment** give a compliment in return for another. ■ retaliate or respond in kind. **with one's compliments** used to express the fact that what one is giving is free: *all drinks will be supplied with our compliments*.
– ORIGIN mid 17th cent.: from French *compliment* (noun), *complimenter* (verb), from Italian *complimento* 'fulfilment of the requirements of courtesy', from Latin *complementum* 'completion, fulfilment' (reflected in the earlier English spelling *complement*, gradually replaced by the French form between 1655 and 1715).

> **USAGE** **Compliment** (together with **complimentary**) is quite different in meaning from **complement** (and **complementary**). See USAGE at COMPLEMENT.

complimentary ▶ **adjective 1** expressing a compliment; praising or approving: *Jennie was very complimentary about Kath's riding* | *complimentary remarks*.
2 given or supplied free of charge: *a complimentary bottle of wine*.

compliments slip (also **compliment slip**) ▶ **noun** Brit. a small piece of paper on which a company's name, address, and logo are printed and which is sent out with goods or information, typically in place of a covering letter.

compline /ˈkɒmplɪn, -ʌɪn/ ▶ **noun** a service of evening prayers forming part of the Divine Office of the Western Christian Church, traditionally said (or chanted) before retiring for the night.
– ORIGIN Middle English: from Old French *complie*, feminine past participle of obsolete *complir* 'to complete', from Latin *complere* 'fill up' (see COMPLETE). The ending *-ine* was probably influenced by Old French *matines* 'matins'.

comply /kəmˈplʌɪ/ ▶ **verb** (**complies, complying, complied**) [no obj.] (often **comply with**) act in accordance with a wish or command: *we are unable to comply with your request*. ■ (of an article) meet specified standards: *all second-hand furniture must comply with the new regulations*.
– ORIGIN late 16th cent.: from Italian *complire*, Catalan *complir*, Spanish *cumplir*, from Latin *complere* 'fill up, fulfil' (see COMPLETE). The original sense was 'fulfil, accomplish', later 'fulfil the requirements of courtesy', hence 'to be agreeable, to oblige or obey'. Compare with COMPLIMENT.

compo[1] ▶ **noun** (pl. **compos**) [mass noun] **1** a material made up of a mixture of different substances.
2 (also **compo rations**) Brit. military rations consisting of a supply of tinned food designed to last a specified number of days and carried in a pack.
– ORIGIN early 19th cent.: abbreviation of COMPOSITE.

compo[2] ▶ **noun** [mass noun] Austral./NZ informal money paid to an employee as compensation for an industrial injury.
– ORIGIN 1940s: abbreviation of COMPENSATION.

component /kəmˈpəʊnənt/ ▶ **noun** a part or element of a larger whole, especially a part of a machine or vehicle. ■ each of two or more forces, velocities, or other vectors acting in different directions which are together equivalent to a given vector.
▶ **adjective** [attrib.] constituting part of a larger whole; constituent: *the component elements of the armed forces*.
– DERIVATIVES **componentize** (also **componentise**) verb.
– ORIGIN mid 17th cent.: from Latin *component-* 'putting together', from the verb *componere*, from *com-* 'together' + *ponere* 'put'. Compare with COMPOUND[1].

componential analysis /kɒmpəˌnɛnʃ(ə)l əˈnalɪsɪs/ ▶ **noun** [mass noun] Linguistics the analysis of the meaning of a word or other linguistic unit into discrete semantic components.

compony /kɒmˈpəʊni/ ▶ **adjective** [usu. postpositive] Heraldry divided into a single row of squares in alternating tinctures: *a bordure compony*.
– ORIGIN late 16th cent.: from French *compone*, from Old French *compondre*, from Latin *componere* 'put together'.

comport[1] /kəmˈpɔːt/ ▶ **verb 1** (**comport oneself**) formal conduct oneself; behave: *articulate students who comported themselves well in interviews*.
2 [no obj.] (**comport with**) archaic accord or agree with.
– ORIGIN late Middle English (in the sense 'tolerate'): from Latin *comportare*, from *com-* 'together' + *portare* 'carry, bear'.

comport[2] /ˈkɒmpɔːt/ ▶ **noun** another term for COMPOTE (sense 2).
– ORIGIN late 19th cent.: apparently an abbreviation of French *comportier*, variant of *compotier* 'dessert dish'.

comportment ▶ **noun** [mass noun] behaviour; bearing: *he displayed precisely the comportment expected of the rightful king*.
– ORIGIN late 16th cent.: from French *comportement*, from the verb *comporter*, from Latin *comportare* (see COMPORT[1]).

compose ▶ **verb** [with obj.] **1** write or create (a work of art, especially music or poetry): *he composed the First Violin Sonata four years earlier*. ■ phrase (a letter or piece of writing) with great care and thought: *the first sentence is so hard to compose*. ■ form (a whole) by ordering or arranging the parts, especially in an artistic way: *compose and draw a still life*.
2 (of elements) constitute or make up (a whole, or a specified part of it): *the National Congress* ***is composed of*** *ten senators* | *Christians compose 40 per cent of the state's population*.
3 calm or settle (oneself or one's features or thoughts): *she tried to* ***compose herself***. ■ archaic settle (a dispute): *the king, with some difficulty, composed this difference*.
4 prepare (a text) for printing by manually, mechanically, or electronically setting up the letters and other characters in the order to be printed.
– ORIGIN late Middle English (in the general sense 'put together, construct'): from Old French *composer*, from Latin *componere* (see COMPONENT), but influenced by Latin *compositus* 'composed' and Old French *poser* 'to place'.

> **USAGE** For an explanation of the differences between **compose** and **comprise**, see USAGE at COMPRISE.

composed ▶ **adjective** having one's feelings and expression under control; calm: *a very talented and composed young player*.
– DERIVATIVES **composedly** adverb.

composer ▶ **noun** a person who writes music, especially as a professional occupation.

composite /ˈkɒmpəzɪt/ ▶ **adjective 1** made up of several parts or elements: *this soup is one of those composite dishes which you gradually build up*. ■ (of a constructional material) made up of recognizable constituents: *modern composite materials*. ■ (of a railway carriage) having compartments of more than one class or function. ■ Mathematics (of an integer) being the product of two or more factors greater than unity; not prime.
2 (**Composite**) relating to or denoting a classical order of architecture consisting of elements of the Ionic and Corinthian orders.
3 usu. /ˈkɒmpəzʌɪt/ Botany relating to or denoting plants of the daisy family (Compositae).
▶ **noun 1** a thing made up of several parts or elements: *the English legal system is a composite of legislation and judicial precedent*. ■ a composite constructional material. ■ /ˈkɒmpəzʌɪt/ a motion for debate composed of two or more related resolutions.
2 usu. /ˈkɒmpəzʌɪt/ Botany a plant of the daisy family (Compositae).
3 (**Composite**) [mass noun] the Composite order of architecture.
▶ **verb** [with obj.] (usu. as noun **compositing**) combine (two or more images) to make a single picture: *photographic compositing by computer*.
– DERIVATIVES **compositely** adverb, **compositeness** noun.
– ORIGIN late Middle English (describing a number having more than one digit): via French from Latin *compositus*, past participle of *componere* 'put together'.

composition ▶ **noun 1** [mass noun] the nature of something's ingredients or constituents; the way in which a whole or mixture is made up: *the social composition of villages*. ■ the action of putting things together; formation or construction: *the composition of a new government was announced in November*. ■ [count noun] a thing composed of various elements: *a theory is a composition of interrelated facts*. ■ archaic mental constitution; character: *persons who have a touch of madness in their composition*. ■ [often as modifier] a compound artificial substance or material: *composition tiles*. ■ Mathematics the successive application of functions to a variable, the value of the first

function being the argument of the second, and so on: *composition of functions, when defined, is associative.* ■ Physics the process of finding the resultant of a number of forces.
2 a creative work, especially a poem or piece of music: *Chopin's most romantic compositions.* ■ [mass noun] the action or art of producing such a work: *the technical aspects of composition.* ■ an essay, especially one written by a school or college student. ■ the artistic arrangement of the parts of a picture: *none of the other photographs shared this particular composition.*
3 [mass noun] the preparation of text for printing by setting up characters or by establishing its style and appearance electronically.
4 a legal agreement to pay a sum in lieu of a larger debt or other obligation: *he had been released by deed on **making a composition with** the creditors.* ■ a sum paid in lieu of a larger debt.
– DERIVATIVES **compositional** adjective, **compositionally** adverb.
– ORIGIN late Middle English: via Old French from Latin *compositio(n-)*, from *componere* 'put together'.

compositor /kəmˈpɒzɪtə/ ▸ **noun** Printing a person who arranges type for printing or keys text into a composing machine.
– ORIGIN late Middle English (originally Scots, denoting an umpire or arbiter): from Anglo-Norman French *compositour*, from Latin *compositor*, from *composit-* 'put together', from the verb *componere* (see COMPOSITION).

compos mentis /ˌkɒmpɒs ˈmɛntɪs/ ▸ **adjective** [predic.] having full control of one's mind: *are you sure he was totally compos mentis?*
– ORIGIN early 17th cent.: Latin.

compossible ▸ **adjective** rare (of one thing) compatible or possible in conjunction with another.
– ORIGIN mid 17th cent.: from Old French, from medieval Latin *compossibilis*, from *com-* 'together with' + *possibilis* (see POSSIBLE).

compost ▸ **noun** [mass noun] decayed organic material used as a fertilizer for growing plants. ■ a mixture of compost or similar material with loam soil used as a growing medium.
▸ **verb** [with obj.] make (vegetable matter or manure) into compost. ■ treat (soil) with compost.
– DERIVATIVES **compostable** adjective, **composter** noun.
– ORIGIN late Middle English: from Old French *composte*, from Latin *composita, compositum* 'something put together', feminine and neuter past participle of *componere*.

compost heap (N. Amer. also **compost pile**) ▸ **noun** a pile of garden and organic kitchen refuse which decomposes to produce compost.

composure ▸ **noun** [mass noun] the state or feeling of being calm and in control of oneself: *she was struggling to regain her composure.*
– ORIGIN late 16th cent. (in the sense 'composing, composition'): from COMPOSE + -URE.

compote /ˈkɒmpəʊt, -ɒt/ ▸ **noun** **1** [mass noun] fruit preserved or cooked in syrup.
2 a bowl-shaped dessert dish with a stem.
– ORIGIN late 17th cent.: from French, from Old French *composte* 'mixture' (see COMPOST).

compound[1] ▸ **noun** /ˈkɒmpaʊnd/ a thing that is composed of two or more separate elements; a mixture: *the air smelled like a compound of diesel and petrol fumes.* ■ (also **chemical compound**) a substance formed from two or more elements chemically united in fixed proportions: *a compound of hydrogen and oxygen | lead compounds.* ■ a word made up of two or more existing words.
▸ **adjective** /ˈkɒmpaʊnd/ made up or consisting of several parts or elements: *a compound noun.* ■ (of interest) payable on both capital and the accumulated interest: *compound interest.* Compare with SIMPLE. ■ Biology (especially of a leaf, flower, or eye) consisting of two or more simple parts or individuals in combination.
▸ **verb** /kəmˈpaʊnd/ [with obj.] **1** make up (a composite whole); constitute: *a dialect **compounded of** Spanish and Dutch.* ■ mix or combine (ingredients or constituents): *the groundnuts were compounded into cattle food.* ■ reckon (interest) on previously accumulated interest: *the yield at which the interest is compounded.*
2 make (something bad) worse; intensify the negative aspects of: *prisoners' lack of contact with the outside world compounds their problems.*
3 Law forbear from prosecuting (a felony) in exchange for money or other consideration. ■ settle (a debt or other matter) in this way: *he compounded the case with the defendant for a cash payment.*
– DERIVATIVES **compoundable** adjective.
– ORIGIN late Middle English *compoune* (verb), from Old French *compoun-*, present tense stem of *compondre*, from Latin *componere* 'put together'. The final *-d* was added in the 16th cent. on the pattern of *expound* and *propound*. Sense 2 of the verb arose through a misinterpretation of the legal phrase *compound a felony*, which means 'refrain from prosecuting a felony in exchange for money or other consideration'. This led to the use of ***compound*** in legal contexts to mean 'make something bad worse', which then became accepted in general usage.

compound[2] /ˈkɒmpaʊnd/ ▸ **noun** an open area enclosed by a fence, for example around a factory or large house or within a prison. ■ S. African an area containing single-sex living quarters for migrant workers, especially miners. ■ another term for POUND[3].
– ORIGIN late 17th cent. (referring to such an area in SE Asia): from Portuguese *campon* or Dutch *kampoeng*, from Malay *kampong* 'enclosure, hamlet'; compare with KAMPONG.

compounder ▸ **noun** a person who mixes or combines ingredients in order to produce an animal feed, medicine, or other substance.

compound eye ▸ **noun** an eye consisting of an array of numerous small visual units, as found in insects and crustaceans. Contrasted with SIMPLE EYE.

compound fracture ▸ **noun** an injury in which a broken bone pierces the skin, causing a risk of infection.

compound interval ▸ **noun** Music an interval greater than an octave.

compound sentence ▸ **noun** a sentence with more than one subject or predicate.

compound time ▸ **noun** [mass noun] Music musical rhythm or metre in which each beat in a bar is subdivided into three smaller units, so having the value of a dotted note. Compare with SIMPLE TIME.

comprador /ˌkɒmprəˈdɔː/ (also **compradore**) ▸ **noun** a person who acts as an agent for foreign organizations engaged in investment, trade, or economic or political exploitation.
– ORIGIN early 17th cent. (denoting a local person employed in a European household in SE Asia or India to make small purchases and keep the household accounts): from Portuguese, 'buyer', from late Latin *comparator*, from Latin *comparare* 'to purchase', from *com-* 'with' + *parare* 'provide'.

comprehend /kɒmprɪˈhɛnd/ ▸ **verb** [with obj.] **1** [often with negative] grasp mentally; understand: *he couldn't comprehend her reasons for marrying Lovat* | [with clause] *I simply couldn't comprehend what had happened.*
2 formal include, comprise, or encompass: *a divine order comprehending all men.*
– ORIGIN Middle English: from Old French *comprehender*, or Latin *comprehendere*, from *com-* 'together' + *prehendere* 'grasp'.

comprehensible ▸ **adjective** able to be understood; intelligible: *clear and comprehensible English.*
– DERIVATIVES **comprehensibility** noun, **comprehensibly** adverb.
– ORIGIN late 15th cent.: from French *compréhensible* or Latin *comprehensibilis*, from *comprehens-* 'seized, comprised', from the verb *comprehendere* (see COMPREHEND).

comprehension ▸ **noun** [mass noun] **1** the ability to understand something: *some won't have the least comprehension of what I'm trying to do | the comprehension of spoken language.* ■ Brit. the setting of questions on a set text to test understanding, as a school exercise.
2 archaic inclusion. ■ historical the inclusion of Nonconformists within the Established Church of England (as proposed in the 17th to 19th centuries but not adopted).
– ORIGIN late Middle English: from French *compréhension* or Latin *comprehensio(n-)*, from the verb *comprehendere* 'seize, comprise' (see COMPREHEND).

comprehensive ▸ **adjective** **1** including or dealing with all or nearly all elements or aspects of something: *a comprehensive list of sources.* ■ of large content or scope; wide-ranging: *a comprehensive collection of photographs.* ■ (of a victory or defeat) achieved or suffered by a large margin: *a comprehensive victory for Swansea.* ■ (of motor-vehicle insurance) providing cover for most risks, including damage to the policyholder's own vehicle.
2 Brit. relating to or denoting a system of secondary education in which children of all abilities from a particular area are educated in one school: *a comprehensive school.*
3 archaic relating to understanding.
▸ **noun** Brit. a comprehensive school.
– DERIVATIVES **comprehensively** adverb, **comprehensiveness** noun.
– ORIGIN early 17th cent.: from French *compréhensif, -ive*, from late Latin *comprehensivus*, from the verb *comprehendere* 'grasp mentally'.

compresence ▸ **noun** [mass noun] chiefly Philosophy the simultaneous presence together of properties or experienced qualities.
– DERIVATIVES **compresent** adjective.

compress ▸ **verb** /kəmˈprɛs/ [with obj.] flatten by pressure; squeeze or press: *the skirt can be folded and **compressed into** a relatively small bag* | (as adj. **compressed**) *compressed gas.* ■ [no obj.] be squeezed or pressed together or into a smaller space: *her face **compressed into a frown**.* ■ (as adj. **compressed**) chiefly Biology having a narrow shape as if flattened, especially sideways: *most sea snakes have a compressed tail.* ■ squeeze or press (two things) together: *Viola compressed her lips together grimly.* ■ express in a shorter form; abridge: *in this chapter we **compress into** summary form the main findings.* ■ reduce the dynamic range of (a sound signal). ■ Computing alter the form of (data) to reduce the amount of storage necessary.
▸ **noun** /ˈkɒmprɛs/ a pad of lint or other absorbent material pressed on to part of the body to relieve inflammation or stop bleeding: *a cold compress.*
– DERIVATIVES **compressibility** /-ˈbɪlɪti/ noun, **compressible** /kəmˈprɛsɪb(ə)l/ adjective, **compressive** /kəmˈprɛsɪv/ adjective.
– ORIGIN late Middle English: from Old French *compresser* or late Latin *compressare*, frequentative of Latin *comprimere*, from *com-* 'together' + *premere* 'to press'; or directly from *compress-* 'pressed together', from the verb *comprimere*.

compressed air ▸ **noun** [mass noun] air that is at more than atmospheric pressure.

compression ▸ **noun** [mass noun] the action of compressing or being compressed. ■ the reduction in volume (causing an increase in pressure) of the fuel mixture in an internal-combustion engine before ignition.
– DERIVATIVES **compressional** adjective.
– ORIGIN late Middle English: via Old French from Latin *compressio(n-)*, from *comprimere* 'press together' (see COMPRESS).

compression joint ▸ **noun** a joint between two pipes made by tightening a threaded nut on to a metal ring, the compression thus caused creating the seal.

compression ratio ▸ **noun** the ratio of the maximum to minimum volume in the cylinder of an internal-combustion engine.

compressive strength ▸ **noun** the resistance of a material to breaking under compression. Compare with TENSILE STRENGTH.

compressor ▸ **noun** an instrument or device for compressing something. ■ a machine used to supply air or other gas at increased pressure, e.g. to power a gas turbine. ■ an electrical device which reduces the dynamic range of a sound signal.

comprise ▸ **verb** [with obj.] consist of; be made up of: *the country comprises twenty states.* ■ make up or constitute (a whole): *this single breed comprises 50 per cent of the Swiss cattle population* | (**be comprised of**) *documents are comprised of words.*
– ORIGIN late Middle English: from French, 'comprised', feminine past participle of *comprendre*, from Old French *comprehender* (see COMPREHEND).

> **USAGE** **1 Comprise** primarily means 'consist of', as in *the country **comprises** twenty states*. It can also mean 'constitute or make up a whole', as in *this single breed **comprises** 50 per cent of the Swiss cattle population*. When this sense is used in the passive (as in *the country **is comprised of** twenty states*), it is more or less synonymous with the first sense (*the country **comprises** twenty states*). This usage is part of standard English, but the construction **comprise of**, as in *the property **comprises of** bedroom, bathroom, and kitchen*, is regarded as incorrect.
> **2** On the differences between **comprise** and **include**, see USAGE at INCLUDE.

compromise ▸ **noun** **1** an agreement or settlement of a dispute that is reached by each side making concessions: *eventually they reached a compromise* | [mass

noun] *the secret of a happy marriage is compromise*. ■ an intermediate state between conflicting alternatives reached by mutual concession: *a **compromise between** the freedom of the individual and the need to ensure orderly government*.
2 [mass noun] the expedient acceptance of standards that are lower than is desirable: *sexism should be tackled without compromise*.
▶ **verb** [no obj.] **1** settle a dispute by mutual concession: *in the end we compromised and deferred the issue*.
2 expediently accept standards that are lower than is desirable: *we were not prepared to **compromise on** safety*. ■ [with obj.] weaken or harm by accepting standards that are lower than is desirable: *he won't accept any decisions which compromise his principles*. ■ [with obj.] bring into disrepute or danger by indiscreet, foolish, or reckless behaviour: *situations in which his troops could be compromised*.
– DERIVATIVES **compromiser** noun.
– ORIGIN late Middle English (denoting mutual consent to arbitration): from Old French *compromis*, from late Latin *compromissum* 'a consent to arbitration', neuter past participle of *compromittere*, from *com-* 'together' + *promittere* (see PROMISE).

compromising ▶ **adjective** (of information or a situation) revealing an embarrassing or incriminating secret about someone.

compte rendu /ˌkɔ̃t rɑ̃ˈdjuː/, French /kɔ̃t ʀɑ̃dy/ ▶ **noun** (pl. **comptes rendus** pronunc. **same**) a formal report or review. ■ (**Comptes Rendus**) the published proceedings of a French academy.
– ORIGIN early 19th cent.: French, literally 'account rendered'.

Compton[1], Arthur Holly (1892–1962), American physicist. He observed the Compton effect and thus demonstrated the dual particle and wave properties of electromagnetic radiation and matter, as predicted by quantum theory. Nobel Prize for Physics (1927).

Compton[2], Denis (Charles Scott) (1918–97), English cricketer and footballer. He played cricket for Middlesex and England, and football for Arsenal and England.

Compton-Burnett /ˌkɒmptənbəːˈnɛt, -ˈbəːnɪt/, Dame Ivy (1884–1969), English novelist. Notable novels: *Brothers and Sisters* (1929), *A Family and a Fortune* (1939), and *Manservant and Maidservant* (1947).

Compton effect ▶ **noun** Physics an increase in wavelength of X-rays or gamma rays that occurs when they are scattered.
– ORIGIN early 20th cent.: named after A. H. *Compton* (see COMPTON[1])

comptroller /kənˈtrəʊlə, kɒmp-/ ▶ **noun** a controller (used in the title of some financial officers).
– ORIGIN late 15th cent.: variant of CONTROLLER, by erroneous association with French *compte* 'calculation' or its source, late Latin *computus*.

compulsion ▶ **noun 1** [mass noun] the action or state of forcing or being forced to do something; constraint: *the payment was made **under compulsion***.
2 an irresistible urge to behave in a certain way: *he felt a compulsion to babble on about what had happened*.
– ORIGIN late Middle English: via Old French from late Latin *compulsio(n-)*, from *compellere* 'to drive, force' (see COMPEL).

compulsive ▶ **adjective 1** resulting from or relating to an irresistible urge: *compulsive eating*. ■ (of a person) acting as a result of an irresistible urge: *a compulsive liar*.
2 irresistibly interesting or exciting; compelling: *this play is compulsive viewing*.
– DERIVATIVES **compulsively** adverb, **compulsiveness** noun.
– ORIGIN late 16th cent. (in the sense 'compulsory'): from medieval Latin *compulsivus*, from *compuls-* 'driven, forced', from the verb *compellere* (see COMPEL). Sense 1 (originally a term in psychology) dates from the early 20th cent.

compulsory ▶ **adjective** required by law or a rule; obligatory: *compulsory military service | it was compulsory to attend mass*. ■ involving or exercising compulsion; coercive: *the abuse of compulsory powers*.
– DERIVATIVES **compulsorily** adverb.
– ORIGIN early 16th cent. (as a noun denoting a legal mandate which had to be obeyed): from medieval Latin *compulsorius*, from *compuls-* 'driven, forced', from the verb *compellere* (see COMPEL).

compulsory purchase ▶ **noun** [mass noun] Brit. the officially enforced purchase of privately owned land or property for public use: [as modifier] *the City Council has applied for a compulsory purchase order*.

compunction ▶ **noun** [mass noun] [usu. with negative] a feeling of guilt or moral scruple that prevents or follows the doing of something bad: *they used their tanks **without compunction***.
– DERIVATIVES **compunctious** adjective.
– ORIGIN Middle English: from Old French *componction*, from ecclesiastical Latin *compunctio(n-)*, from Latin *compungere* 'prick sharply', from *com-* (expressing intensive force) + *pungere* 'to prick'.

compurgation /ˌkɒmpəːˈɡeɪʃ(ə)n/ ▶ **noun** [mass noun] Law, historical acquittal from a charge or accusation obtained by statements of innocence given by witnesses under oath.
– ORIGIN mid 17th cent.: from medieval Latin *compurgatio(n-)*, from Latin *compurgare*, from *com-* (expressing intensive force) + *purgare* 'purify' (from *purus* 'pure').

compurgator /ˈkɒmpəːɡeɪtə/ ▶ **noun** Law, historical a sworn witness to the innocence or good character of an accused person.
– ORIGIN mid 16th cent.: medieval Latin, from Latin *com-* 'together with' + *purgator*, from *purgare* 'purify' (see COMPURGATION).

computation ▶ **noun 1** [mass noun] the action of mathematical calculation: *methods of computation* | [count noun] *statistical computations*.
2 the use of computers, especially as a subject of research or study.
– ORIGIN late Middle English: from Latin *computatio(n-)*, from the verb *computare* (see COMPUTE).

computational ▶ **adjective 1** using or relating to computers: *the computational analysis of English*.
2 relating to the process of mathematical calculation: *the exam only really tested computational ability*.
– DERIVATIVES **computationally** adverb.

computational linguistics ▶ **plural noun** [treated as sing.] the branch of linguistics in which the techniques of computer science are applied to the analysis and synthesis of language and speech.

compute ▶ **verb** [with obj.] reckon or calculate (a figure or amount): *the hire charge is computed on a daily basis*. ■ [no obj., with negative] informal seem reasonable; make sense: *the idea of a woman alone in a pub did not compute*. [from the phrase *does not compute*, once used as an error message in computing.]
– DERIVATIVES **computability** noun, **computable** adjective.
– ORIGIN early 17th cent.: from French *computer* or Latin *computare*, from *com-* 'together' + *putare* 'to settle (an account)'.

computer ▶ **noun** an electronic device which is capable of receiving information (data) in a particular form and of performing a sequence of operations in accordance with a predetermined but variable set of procedural instructions (program) to produce a result in the form of information or signals. ■ a person who makes calculations, especially with a calculating machine.

computer animation ▶ **noun** see ANIMATION.

computerate /kəmˈpjuːtərət/ ▶ **adjective** informal another term for COMPUTER-LITERATE.

computer conferencing ▶ **noun** [mass noun] the use of computer and telecommunications technology to hold discussions between people operating computers in separate locations.

computer dating ▶ **noun** [mass noun] the use of computer databases to identify potentially compatible partners for people.

computer game ▶ **noun** a game played using a computer, typically a video game.

computer graphics ▶ **plural noun** see GRAPHICS.

computerize (also **computerise**) ▶ **verb** [with obj.] (often as adj. **computerized**) convert (a system, device, etc.) to be operated by computer: *the advantages of computerized accounting*. ■ convert (information) to a form which is stored or processed by computer: *a computerized register of dogs*.
– DERIVATIVES **computerization** noun.

computer-literate ▶ **adjective** (of a person) having sufficient knowledge and skill to be able to use computers; familiar with the operation of computers.
– DERIVATIVES **computer literacy** noun.

computer science ▶ **noun** [mass noun] the study of the principles and use of computers.

computer virus ▶ **noun** see VIRUS.

computing ▶ **noun** [mass noun] the use or operation of computers: *developments in mathematics and computing* | [as modifier] *computing facilities*.

comrade ▶ **noun** (among men) a colleague or a fellow member of an organization. ■ (also **comrade-in-arms**) a fellow soldier or serviceman. ■ a fellow socialist or communist (often as a form of address). ■ (in South Africa) a young militant supporter of the African National Congress.
– DERIVATIVES **comradely** adjective.
– ORIGIN mid 16th cent. (originally also *camerade*): from French *camerade*, *camarade* (originally feminine), from Spanish *camarada* 'room-mate', from Latin *camera* 'chamber'. Compare with CHUM[1].

C

comradeship ▶ **noun** [mass noun] the company and friendship of others with common aims: *his greatest joy came from comradeship with others in the team*.

Comsat ▶ **noun** trademark a communications satellite.
– ORIGIN 1960s: blend.

Comte /kɒmt/, French /kɔ̃t/, Auguste (1798–1857), French philosopher, one of the founders of sociology. Comte's positivist philosophy attempted to define the laws of social evolution and to found a genuine social science that could be used for social reconstruction.

con[1] informal ▶ **verb** (**cons, conning, conned**) [with obj.] persuade (someone) to do or believe something by lying to them: *I **conned** him **into** giving me your home number | she was jailed for conning her aunt **out of** £500,000*.
▶ **noun** an instance of deceiving or tricking someone: *the Charter is a glossy public relations con*.
– ORIGIN late 19th cent. (originally US): abbreviation of CONFIDENCE, as in *confidence trick*.

con[2] ▶ **noun** a disadvantage of or argument against something: *borrowers have to weigh up **the pros and cons** of each mortgage offer*.
– ORIGIN late 16th cent.: from Latin *contra* 'against'.

con[3] ▶ **noun** informal a convict.
– ORIGIN late 19th cent.: abbreviation.

con[4] (US also **conn**) Nautical ▶ **verb** (**cons, conning, conned**) [with obj.] direct the steering of (a ship): *he hadn't conned anything bigger than a Boston whaler*.
▶ **noun** (**the con**) the action or post of conning a ship.
– ORIGIN early 17th cent.: apparently a weakened form of obsolete *cond* 'conduct, guide', from Old French *conduire*, from Latin *conducere* (see CONDUCE).

con[5] ▶ **verb** (**cons, conning, conned**) [with obj.] archaic study attentively or learn by heart (a piece of writing): *the girls conned their pages with a great show of industry*.
– ORIGIN Middle English *cunne*, *conne*, *con*, variants of CAN[1].

con[6] ▶ **noun** informal a convention, especially one for science fiction enthusiasts.
– ORIGIN 1970s: abbreviation.

Con. ▶ **abbreviation** Brit. ■ Conservative (denoting the political affiliation of a Member of Parliament). ■ constable (as part of a police officer's title).

con- ▶ **prefix** variant spelling of COM- assimilated before *c, d, f, g, j, n, q, s, t, v*, and sometimes before vowels (as in *concord, condescend, confide*, etc.).
– ORIGIN Latin variant of *com-*.

conacre /ˈkɒneɪkə/ ▶ **noun** [mass noun] (in Ireland) the letting by a tenant of small portions of land prepared for crops or grazing.
– ORIGIN early 19th cent.: from CORN[1] + ACRE.

Conakry /ˈkɒnəkri/ the capital and chief port of Guinea; pop. 1,484,000 (est. 2007).

con amore /ˌkɒn aˈmɔːreɪ/ ▶ **adverb** Music (especially as a direction) with tenderness.
– ORIGIN Italian, 'with love'.

Conan Doyle /ˈkəʊnən/ see DOYLE.

conation /kəˈneɪʃ(ə)n/ ▶ **noun** [mass noun] Philosophy & Psychology the mental faculty of purpose, desire, or will to perform an action; volition.
– ORIGIN early 17th cent. (denoting an attempt or endeavour): from Latin *conatio(n-)*, from *conari* 'to try'.

conative /ˈkɒnətɪv/ ▶ **adjective 1** Philosophy & Psychology of or involving conation.
2 Grammar denoting a word or structure that expresses attempted action as opposed to action itself, for example *at* in *he was kicking at the bicycle*.
– ORIGIN late 19th cent.: from Latin *conat-* 'endeavoured' (from the verb *conari*) + -IVE.

con brio /kɒn ˈbriːəʊ/ ▶ **adverb** Music (especially as a direction) with vigour.
– ORIGIN Italian.

concatenate /kənˈkatɪneɪt/ ▶ **verb** [with obj.] formal or technical link (things) together in a chain or series:

C

some words may be concatenated, such that certain sounds are omitted.
– ORIGIN late 15th cent. (as an adjective): from late Latin *concatenat-* 'linked together', from the verb *concatenare*, from *con-* 'together' + *catenare*, from *catena* 'chain'.

concatenation ▶ noun a series of interconnected things: *a concatenation of events which had finally led to the murder*. ■ [mass noun] the action of linking things together in a series, or the condition of being linked in such a way.

concave /ˈkɒnkeɪv/ ▶ adjective having an outline or surface that curves inwards like the interior of a circle or sphere. Compare with CONVEX (sense 1).
– DERIVATIVES **concavely** adverb.
– ORIGIN late Middle English: from Latin *concavus*, from *con-* 'together' + *cavus* 'hollow'.

concavity /kɒnˈkavɪti/ ▶ noun (pl. **concavities**) [mass noun] the state or quality of being concave. ■ [count noun] a concave surface or thing.

conceal ▶ verb [with obj.] not allow to be seen; hide: *a line of sand dunes concealed the distant sea*. ■ prevent (something) from being known; keep secret: *they were at great pains to **conceal** that information **from** the public*.
– ORIGIN Middle English: from Old French *conceler*, from Latin *concelare*, from *con-* 'completely' + *celare* 'hide'.

concealed ▶ adjective kept secret; hidden: *a concealed weapon | he spoke with barely concealed anger*.

concealer ▶ noun a flesh-toned cosmetic stick used to cover spots, blemishes, and dark under-eye circles.

concealment ▶ noun [mass noun] the action of hiding something or preventing it from being known: *the concealment of the weapons | the deliberate concealment of material facts*. ■ something that acts as a hiding place; cover: *he darted forwards from the concealment of the bushes*.

concede ▶ verb **1** [reporting verb] admit or agree that something is true after first denying or resisting it: [with clause] *I had to concede that I'd overreacted* | [with direct speech] *'All right then,' she conceded*. ■ [with obj.] admit (defeat) in a match or contest: *reluctantly, Ellen conceded defeat*. ■ [with obj.] admit defeat in (a match or contest): *they conceded the match to their opponents*.
2 [with obj.] surrender or yield (a possession, right, or privilege): *in 475 the emperor **conceded** the Auvergne **to** Euric*. ■ grant (a right, privilege, or demand): *their rights to redress of grievances were conceded once more*. ■ (in sport) fail to prevent an opponent scoring (a goal or point): *they have conceded only one goal in seven matches*. ■ allow (a lead or advantage) to slip: *he took an early lead which he never conceded*.
– ORIGIN late 15th cent.: from French *concéder* or Latin *concedere*, from *con-* 'completely' + *cedere* 'yield'.

conceit ▶ noun **1** [mass noun] excessive pride in oneself: *he was puffed up with conceit*.
2 an ingenious or fanciful comparison or metaphor: *the idea of the wind's singing is a prime romantic conceit*. ■ an artistic effect or device: *the director's brilliant conceit was to film this tale in black and white*. ■ a fanciful notion: *he is alarmed by the widespread conceit that he spent most of the 1980s drunk*.
– ORIGIN late Middle English (in the sense 'notion', also 'quaintly decorative article'): from CONCEIVE, on the pattern of pairs such as *deceive, deceit*.

conceited ▶ adjective excessively proud of oneself; vain: *Fred's so conceited he'd never believe anyone would refuse him*.
– DERIVATIVES **conceitedly** adverb, **conceitedness** noun.

conceivable ▶ adjective capable of being imagined or grasped mentally: *a mass uprising was entirely conceivable | in every conceivable way that action was entirely wrong | the body was photographed from every conceivable angle*.
– DERIVATIVES **conceivability** noun.

conceivably ▶ adverb [sentence adverb] it is conceivable or imaginable that: *it may conceivably cause liver disease*.

conceive ▶ verb [with obj.] **1** create (an embryo) by fertilizing an egg: *she was conceived when her father was 49*. ■ [no obj.] (of a woman) become pregnant: *five months ago Wendy conceived*.
2 form or devise (a plan or idea) in the mind: *the dam project was originally conceived in 1977* | (as adj., with submodifier **conceived**) *a brilliantly conceived and executed robbery*. ■ form a mental representation of; imagine: *without society an individual cannot be conceived as having rights* | [no obj.] *we could not **conceive of** such things happening to us*. ■ literary become affected by (a feeling): *I had conceived a passion for another*.
– ORIGIN Middle English: from Old French *concevoir*, from Latin *concipere*, from *com-* 'together' + *capere* 'take'.

concelebrate /kɒnˈsɛlɪbreɪt/ ▶ verb [with obj.] Christian Church officiate jointly at (a Mass): *the pro-nuncio will **concelebrate** Mass **with** bishops from Wales*.
– DERIVATIVES **concelebrant** noun, **concelebration** noun.
– ORIGIN late 19th cent.: from Latin *concelebrat-* 'celebrated together', from the verb *concelebrare*, from *con-* 'together' + *celebrare* (see CELEBRATE).

concentrate ▶ verb **1** [no obj.] focus all one's attention on a particular object or activity: *she couldn't **concentrate on** the film* | [with obj.] *a threatened tax rise **concentrates the mind wonderfully***. ■ (**concentrate on/upon**) do or deal with (one particular thing) above all others: *Luke wants to concentrate on his film career*.
2 [with obj.] gather (people or things) together in numbers or a mass: *the nation's wealth was **concentrated in** the hands of the governing elite*. ■ [no obj.] come together in this way: *troops were concentrating at the western front*.
3 [with obj.] increase the strength or proportion of (a substance or solution) by removing or reducing the other diluting agent or by selective accumulation of atoms or molecules.
▶ noun [mass noun] a substance made by removing or reducing the diluting agent; a concentrated form of something: *apple juice concentrate*.
– DERIVATIVES **concentrative** adjective, **concentrator** noun.
– ORIGIN mid 17th cent. (in the sense 'bring towards a centre'): Latinized form of CONCENTRE, or from French *concentrer* 'to concentrate'. Sense 1 of the verb dates from the early 20th cent.

concentrated ▶ adjective **1** wholly directed to one thing; intense: *a concentrated campaign*.
2 (of a substance or solution) present in a high proportion relative to other substances; having had water or other diluting agent removed or reduced: *pure concentrated fruit juice*.
– DERIVATIVES **concentratedly** adverb.

concentration ▶ noun **1** [mass noun] the action or power of focusing all one's attention: *she was frowning in concentration*. ■ (**concentration on/upon**) dealing with one particular thing above all others: *concentration on the needs of the young can mean that the elderly are forgotten*.
2 a close gathering of people or things: *the island has the greatest concentration of seabirds in the northwest*. ■ [mass noun] the action of gathering together closely: *the concentration of power in the hands of nobles*.
3 the relative amount of a particular substance contained within a solution or mixture or in a particular volume of space: *the gas can collect in dangerous concentrations*. ■ [mass noun] the action of strengthening a solution by the removal or reduction of the diluting agent or by the selective accumulation of atoms or molecules.

concentration camp ▶ noun a place in which large numbers of people, especially political prisoners or members of persecuted minorities, are deliberately imprisoned in a relatively small area with inadequate facilities, sometimes to provide forced labour or to await mass execution. The term is most strongly associated with the several hundred camps established by the Nazis in Germany and occupied Europe 1933–45, among the most infamous being Dachau, Belsen, and Auschwitz.

concentre (US **concenter**) ▶ verb [with obj.] concentrate (something) in a small space or area: *the property of this country is concentred in a very few hands*. ■ [no obj.] come together at a common centre: *here the produce of this extensive territory concentres*. ■ archaic bring (two or more things) towards a common centre: *a passion in which soul and body were concentred*.
– ORIGIN late 16th cent.: from French *concentrer*, from Latin *con-* 'together' + *centrum* 'centre'.

concentric ▶ adjective of or denoting circles, arcs, or other shapes which share the same centre, the larger often completely surrounding the smaller.
– DERIVATIVES **concentrically** adverb, **concentricity** noun.
– ORIGIN late Middle English: from Old French *concentrique* or medieval Latin *concentricus*, from *con-* 'together' + *centrum* 'centre'.

Concepción /kɒnˌsɛpsɪˈɒn/, Spanish /kaonsepˈsjaon, -θepˈθjaon/ an industrial city in south central Chile; pop. 220,000 (est. 2006).

concept ▶ noun an abstract idea: *structuralism is a difficult concept | the concept of justice*. ■ an idea or invention to help sell or publicize a commodity: *a new concept in corporate hospitality*. ■ [as modifier] (of a car or other vehicle) produced as an experimental model to test the viability of innovative design features: *a concept car for next month's Geneva motor show*. ■ Philosophy an idea or mental image which corresponds to some distinct entity or class of entities, or to its essential features, or determines the application of a term (especially a predicate), and thus plays a part in the use of reason or language.
– ORIGIN mid 16th cent. (in the sense 'thought, imagination'): from Latin *conceptum* 'something conceived', from Latin *concept-* 'conceived', from *concipere* (see CONCEIVE).

concept album ▶ noun a rock album featuring a cycle of songs expressing a particular theme or idea.

conception ▶ noun [mass noun] **1** the action of conceiving a child or of one being conceived: *an unfertilized egg before conception* | [count noun] *a rise in premarital conceptions*.
2 the forming or devising of a plan or idea: *the time between a product's conception and its launch*. ■ [count noun] the way in which something is perceived or regarded: *our conception of how language relates to reality*. ■ [count noun] an abstract idea; a concept: *the conception of a balance of power*. ■ [count noun] a plan or intention: *reconstructing Bach's original conceptions*. ■ ability to imagine; understanding: *the administration **had no conception of** women's problems*.
– DERIVATIVES **conceptional** adjective.
– ORIGIN Middle English: via Old French from Latin *conceptio(n-)*, from the verb *concipere* (see CONCEIVE).

conceptual ▶ adjective relating to or based on mental concepts: *philosophy deals with conceptual difficulties*.
– ORIGIN mid 17th cent.: from medieval Latin *conceptualis*, from Latin *concept-* 'conceived', from the verb *concipere* (see CONCEPT).

conceptual art ▶ noun [mass noun] art in which the idea or concept presented by the artist is considered more important than the finished product, if any such exists.

conceptualism ▶ noun [mass noun] Philosophy the theory that universals can be said to exist, but only as concepts in the mind.
– DERIVATIVES **conceptualist** noun.

conceptualize (also **conceptualise**) ▶ verb [with obj.] form a concept or idea of (something): *sex was conceptualized as an overpowering force in the individual*.
– DERIVATIVES **conceptualization** noun.

conceptually ▶ adverb in terms of a concept or abstract idea: [sentence adverb] *conceptually, this is a complex process | a conceptually simple task*.

conceptus /kənˈsɛptəs/ ▶ noun (pl. **conceptuses**) technical the embryo in the womb, especially during the early stages of pregnancy.
– ORIGIN mid 18th cent.: from Latin, 'conception, embryo', from *concept-* 'conceived', from the verb *concipere*.

concern ▶ verb [with obj.] **1** relate to; be about: *the story concerns a friend of mine | the report is mainly **concerned with** 1984 onwards*. ■ be relevant or important to; affect or involve: *she was prying into that which did not concern her | many thanks **to all concerned***. ■ (**concern oneself with**) interest or involve oneself in: *it is not necessary for us to concern ourselves with this point*. ■ (**be concerned in**) formal have a specific connection with or responsibility for: *those concerned in industry, academia, and government*. ■ (**be concerned with/to do something**) regard it as important to do something: *I was mainly concerned with making something that children could enjoy*.
2 make (someone) anxious or worried: *the roof of the barn concerns me because eventually it will fall in | **don't concern yourself**, old boy—my lips are sealed*.
▶ noun **1** [mass noun] anxiety; worry: *Carole gazed at her with concern*. ■ [count noun] a cause of anxiety or worry: *environmental concerns*.
2 a matter of interest or importance to someone: *housing is the concern of the Housing Executive* | [mass noun] *the prospect should be **of concern to** us all*.
3 a business: *the town's only travel agent was a small, debt-ridden concern*.
4 informal, dated a complicated or awkward object.

– PHRASES **as** (or **so**) **far as —— is concerned** as regards the interests or case of ——: *the measures are irrelevant as far as inflation is concerned.* **have no concern with** formal have nothing to do with: *drama seemed to have no concern with 'truth' at all.* **to whom it may concern** used at the beginning of a letter, notice, or testimonial when the identity of the reader or readers is unknown.
– ORIGIN late Middle English: from French *concerner* or late Latin *concernere* (in medieval Latin 'be relevant to'), from *con* (expressing intensive force) + *cernere* 'sift, discern'.

concerned ▶ **adjective** worried, troubled, or anxious: *the villagers are concerned about burglaries.*
– DERIVATIVES **concernedly** adverb.

concerning ▶ **preposition** on the subject of or in connection with; about: *further revelations concerning his role in the affair.*

concernment ▶ **noun** [mass noun] archaic importance: *matters of great public concernment.* ■ [count noun] a matter of interest or importance to someone; a concern: *if the captain has a family or any absorbing concernment of that sort.*

concert ▶ **noun** /'kɒnsət/ **1** a musical performance given in public, typically by several performers or of several compositions: *a pop concert* | [as modifier] *a concert pianist.* ■ [as modifier] relating to or denoting the performance of music written for opera, ballet, or theatre on its own without the accompanying dramatic action: *the concert version of the fourth interlude from the opera.*
2 [mass noun] formal agreement or harmony: *critics' inability to describe with any precision and concert the characteristics of literature.* ■ Law joint action, especially in the committing of a crime.
▶ **verb** /kən'sə:t/ [with obj.] formal arrange (something) by mutual agreement or coordination: *they started meeting regularly to concert their parliamentary tactics.*
– PHRASES **in concert 1** acting jointly: *we must take action in concert with our European partners.* **2** (of music or a performer) giving a public performance; live: *they saw Pink Floyd in concert.*
– ORIGIN late 16th cent. (in the sense 'unite'): from French *concerter*, from Italian *concertare* 'harmonize'. The noun use, dating from the early 17th cent. (in the sense 'a combination of voices or sounds'), is from French *concert*, from Italian *concerto*, from *concertare*.

concertante /ˌkɒntʃə'tanteɪ, -'tanti/ ▶ **adjective**
1 denoting a piece of music containing one or more solo parts, typically of less prominence than in a concerto. See also SINFONIA CONCERTANTE.
2 denoting prominent instrumental parts present throughout a piece of music, especially in baroque and early classical compositions.
– ORIGIN Italian, 'harmonizing', from *concertare* 'harmonize'.

concerted ▶ **adjective 1** [attrib.] jointly arranged or carried out; coordinated: *a concerted attempt to preserve religious unity.* ■ done with great effort or determination: *you must make a concerted effort to curb this.*
2 (of music) arranged in several parts of equal importance.
– DERIVATIVES **concertedly** adverb.

concertgoer ▶ **noun** a person who goes to concerts, especially on a regular basis.

concert grand ▶ **noun** the largest size of grand piano, up to 2.75 m long, used for concerts.

concert hall ▶ **noun** a large public building designed for the performance of concerts.

concertina /ˌkɒnsə'ti:nə/ ▶ **noun** a small musical instrument played by stretching and squeezing a central bellows between the hands to blow air over reeds, each note being sounded by a button. Compare with ACCORDION. ■ [as modifier] opening or closing in multiple folds: *concertina doors.*
▶ **verb** (**concertinas, concertinaing, concertinaed** or **concertina'd**) [with obj.] extend, compress, or collapse in folds like those of a concertina: *the car had concertinaed against the rear of the truck.*
– ORIGIN mid 19th cent.: from CONCERT + -INA.

concertino /ˌkɒntʃə'ti:nəʊ/ ▶ **noun** (pl. **concertinos**)
1 a simple or short concerto.
2 a solo instrument or solo instruments playing with an orchestra.
– ORIGIN late 18th cent.: Italian, diminutive of *concerto* (see CONCERTO).

concertize /'kɒnsətʌɪz/ ▶ **verb** [no obj.] N. Amer. give a concert or concerts.

concertmaster ▶ **noun** chiefly N. Amer. the leading first-violin player in some orchestras.

concerto /kən'tʃə:təʊ, -'tʃɛ:təʊ/ ▶ **noun** (pl. **concertos** or **concerti**) a musical composition for a solo instrument or instruments accompanied by an orchestra, especially one conceived on a relatively large scale.
– ORIGIN early 18th cent.: Italian, from *concertare* 'harmonize'.

concerto grosso /'grɒsəʊ/ ▶ **noun** (pl. **concerti grossi** /-si/) a musical composition for a group of solo instruments accompanied by an orchestra. The term is used mainly of baroque works.
– ORIGIN early 18th cent.: Italian, literally 'big concerto'.

concert overture ▶ **noun** a piece of music in the style of an overture but intended for independent performance.

concert party ▶ **noun 1** a group of performers giving variety concerts.
2 Stock Exchange a number of parties who separately invest in a company with the concealed intention of using their holdings as a single block.

concert performance ▶ **noun** Brit. a performance of a piece of music written for an opera, ballet, piece of theatre, religious service, etc., at a concert without the accompanying dramatic action or liturgy.

concert pianist ▶ **noun** a classical pianist who regularly performs as a soloist in concerts.

concert pitch ▶ **noun** [mass noun] Music an internationally agreed standard for the tuning of musical instruments, in which the note A above middle C has a frequency of 440 Hz. ■ a state of readiness, efficiency, and keenness: *slightly unnerved by the contretemps, I was not at concert pitch.*

concession ▶ **noun 1** a thing that is granted, especially in response to demands: *the government was unwilling to make any further concessions.* ■ [mass noun] the action of conceding or granting something: *this strict rule was relaxed by concession.* ■ (**a concession to**) a gesture made in recognition of a demand or prevailing standard: *her only concession to fashion was her ornate silver ring.*
2 a preferential allowance or rate given by an organization: *tax concessions.* ■ Brit. a reduction in the price of something for a certain category of person.
3 the right to use land or other property for a specified purpose, granted by a government, company, or other controlling body: *new logging concessions.* ■ a commercial operation set up by agreement within the premises of a larger concern. ■ the right, given by a company, to sell goods, especially in a particular place. ■ Canadian a piece of land into which surveyed land is divided.
– ORIGIN late Middle English: from Latin *concessio(n-)*, from the verb *concedere* (see CONCEDE).

concessionaire /kənˌsɛʃə'nɛ:/ (also **concessionnaire**) ▶ **noun** the holder of a concession or grant, especially for the use of land or commercial premises or for trading rights.
– ORIGIN mid 19th cent.: from French *concessionnaire*, from Latin *concessio* (see CONCESSION).

concessional ▶ **adjective** (of a rate or allowance) constituting a concession: *a concessional interest rate.*

concessionary ▶ **adjective** Brit. relating to or constituting a concession or reduced rate: *concessionary bus passes.*

concessive ▶ **adjective 1** characterized by or tending to concession: *we must look for a more concessive approach.*
2 Grammar (of a preposition or conjunction) introducing a phrase or clause denoting a circumstance which might be expected to preclude the action of the main clause, but does not (e.g. *in spite of, although*). ■ (of a phrase or clause) introduced by a concessive preposition or conjunction.

conch /kɒŋk, kɒn(t)ʃ/ ▶ **noun** (pl. **conchs** /kɒŋks/ or **conches** /'kɒntʃɪz/) **1** (also **conch shell**) a tropical marine mollusc with a robust spiral shell which may bear long projections and have a flared lip. ● *Strombus* and other genera, family Strombidae, class Gastropoda. ■ a shell of this kind blown like a trumpet to produce a hollow-sounding musical note, often depicted as played by Tritons.
2 Architecture the roof of a semicircular apse, shaped like half a dome.
3 another term for CONCHA.
– ORIGIN late Middle English: from Latin *concha* 'shellfish, shell', from Greek *konkhē* 'mussel, cockle, or shell-like cavity'.

concha /'kɒŋkə/ ▶ **noun** (pl. **conchae** /-ki:/) Anatomy & Zoology a part resembling a spiral shell, in particular: ■ the depression in the external ear leading to its central opening. ■ (also **nasal concha**) any of several thin, scroll-like (turbinate) bones in the sides of the nasal cavity.
– ORIGIN late 16th cent.: from Latin (see CONCH).

conchie /'kɒnʃi/ ▶ **noun** (pl. **conchies**) Brit. informal, derogatory a conscientious objector.
– ORIGIN First World War: abbreviation.

conchiglie /kɒn'ki:ljeɪ/ ▶ **plural noun** pasta in the form of small conch shells.
– ORIGIN Italian, plural of *conchiglia* 'conch shell'.

conchiolin /'kɒntʃɪə(ʊ)lɪn/ ▶ **noun** [mass noun] Zoology a tough, insoluble protein secreted by molluscs, forming the organic matrix of the shell within which calcium carbonate is deposited.
– ORIGIN late 19th cent.: from Latin *concha* 'shell' + the diminutive suffix *-iola* + -IN[1].

conchoid /'kɒŋkɔɪd/ ▶ **noun** Mathematics a plane quartic curve consisting of two separate branches either side of and asymptotic to a central straight line (the asymptote), such that if a line is drawn from a fixed point (the pole) to intersect both branches, the part of the line falling between the two branches is of constant length and is exactly bisected by the asymptote. ● Such curves are represented by the general equation $(x-a)^2(x^2+y^2)=b^2x^2$, where *a* is the distance between the pole and the asymptote, and *b* is the constant length. The branch on the same side of the asymptote as the pole typically has a cusp or loop.
– ORIGIN early 18th cent.: from CONCH + -OID.

conchoidal /kɒŋ'kɔɪd(ə)l/ ▶ **adjective** chiefly Mineralogy denoting a type of fracture in a solid (such as flint) which results in a smooth rounded surface resembling the shape of a scallop shell.

conchology /kɒŋ'kɒlədʒi/ ▶ **noun** [mass noun] the scientific study or collection of mollusc shells.
– DERIVATIVES **conchological** adjective, **conchologist** noun.
– ORIGIN late 18th cent.: from Greek *konkhē* 'shell' + -LOGY.

concierge /'kɒnsɪɛ:ʒ/ ▶ **noun 1** (especially in France) a resident caretaker of a block of flats or a small hotel.
2 a hotel employee whose job is to assist guests by booking tours, making theatre and restaurant reservations, etc.
– ORIGIN mid 16th cent. (denoting the warden of a house, castle, prison, or palace): French, probably based on Latin *conservus* 'fellow slave'.

conciliar /kən'sɪlɪə/ ▶ **adjective** relating to or proceeding from a council, especially an ecclesiastical one: *conciliar decrees.*
– ORIGIN late 17th cent.: from medieval Latin *consiliarius* 'counsellor', from Latin *concilium* (see COUNCIL).

conciliate /kən'sɪlɪeɪt/ ▶ **verb** [with obj.] **1** stop (someone) being angry or discontented; placate: *concessions were made to conciliate the peasantry.* ■ [no obj.] act as a mediator: *he sought to conciliate in the dispute.* ■ formal reconcile; make compatible: *all complaints about charges will be conciliated if possible.*
2 archaic gain (esteem or goodwill): *the arts which conciliate popularity.*
– ORIGIN mid 16th cent. (in sense 2): from Latin *conciliat-* 'combined, gained', from the verb *conciliare*, from *concilium* (see COUNCIL).

conciliation /kənˌsɪlɪ'eɪʃn/ ▶ **noun** [mass noun] the action of stopping someone being angry; placation: *he held his hands up in a gesture of conciliation.* ■ the action of mediating between two disputing people or groups: *many disputes are settled through conciliation by the official body.*

conciliator /kən'sɪlɪeɪtə(r)/ ▶ **noun** a person who acts as a mediator between two disputing people or groups: *he was seen as a conciliator, who would heal divisions in the party.*

conciliatory ▶ **adjective** intended or likely to placate or pacify: *a conciliatory approach.*

concinnity /kən'sɪnɪti/ ▶ **noun** [mass noun] rare the skilful and harmonious arrangement or fitting together of the different parts of something. ■ studied elegance of literary or artistic style.
– ORIGIN mid 16th cent.: from Latin *concinnitas*, from *concinnus* 'skilfully put together'.

concise ▶ **adjective** giving a lot of information clearly and in a few words; brief but comprehensive: *a concise account of the country's history.*

C

– DERIVATIVES **concisely** adverb, **conciseness** noun, **concision** noun.
– ORIGIN late 16th cent.: from French *concis* or Latin *concisus*, past participle of *concidere* 'cut up, cut down', from *con-* 'completely' + *caedere* 'to cut'.

conclave /ˈkɒŋkleɪv/ ▶ noun a private meeting. ■ (in the Roman Catholic Church) the assembly of cardinals for the election of a pope. ■ the meeting place for a conclave.
– ORIGIN late Middle English (denoting a private room): via French from Latin *conclave* 'lockable room', from *con-* 'with' + *clavis* 'key'.

conclude ▶ verb **1** bring or come to an end: [with obj.] *they conclude their study with these words* | [no obj.] *the talk concluded with slides.* ■ [with obj.] formally and finally settle or arrange (an agreement): *an attempt to conclude a ceasefire.*
2 [with clause] arrive at a judgement or opinion by reasoning: *the doctors concluded that Esther had suffered a stroke* | *what do you conclude from all this?* ■ [with direct speech] say in conclusion: *'It's a wicked old world,' she concluded.* ■ [with infinitive] US dated decide to do something: *we found some bread, which we concluded to eat.*
– PHRASES **conclude missives** Scots Law (of a buyer) sign a contract with the vendor of a property or piece of land to signify change of ownership.
– ORIGIN Middle English (in the sense 'convince'): from Latin *concludere*, from *con-* 'completely' + *claudere* 'to shut'.

conclusion ▶ noun **1** the end or finish of an event, process, or text: *the conclusion of World War Two.* ■ the summing-up of an argument or text. ■ [mass noun] the formal and final arrangement of an agreement: *the conclusion of a free-trade accord.*
2 a judgement or decision reached by reasoning: *each research group came to a similar conclusion.* ■ Logic a proposition that is reached from given premises.
– PHRASES **in conclusion** lastly; to sum up: *in conclusion, it is clear that the market is maturing.* **jump** (or **leap**) **to conclusions** make a hasty judgement before considering all the facts. **try conclusions with** formal engage in a trial of skill or argument with.
– ORIGIN late Middle English: from Latin *conclusio(n-)*, from the verb *concludere* (see CONCLUDE).

conclusive ▶ adjective (of evidence or argument) having or likely to have the effect of proving a case; decisive: *conclusive evidence* | *the findings were by no means conclusive.* ■ (of a victory) achieved easily or by a large margin.
– DERIVATIVES **conclusively** adverb, **conclusiveness** noun.
– ORIGIN late 16th cent. (in the sense 'summing up'): from late Latin *conclusivus*, from Latin *conclus-* 'closed up', from the verb *concludere* (see CONCLUSION).

concoct /kənˈkɒkt/ ▶ verb [with obj.] make (a dish or meal) by combining various ingredients: *she began to concoct a dinner likely to appeal to him.* ■ create or devise (a story or plan): *his cronies concocted a simple plan.*
– DERIVATIVES **concocter** (also **concoctor**) noun.
– ORIGIN mid 16th cent.: from Latin *concoct-*, literally 'cooked together', from *concoquere*. The original sense was 'refine metals or minerals by heating', later 'cook'.

concoction ▶ noun a mixture of various ingredients or elements: *the facade is a strange concoction of northern Mannerism and Italian Baroque.* ■ an elaborate story, especially a fabricated one: *her story is an improbable concoction.* ■ an elaborate or showy garment or hat.

concomitance /kənˈkɒmɪt(ə)ns/ (also **concomitancy**) ▶ noun [mass noun] the fact of existing or occurring together with something else. ■ Theology the doctrine that the body and blood of Christ are each present in both the bread and the wine of the Eucharist.
– ORIGIN mid 16th cent.: from medieval Latin *concomitantia*, from the verb *concomitari* 'accompany' (see CONCOMITANT).

concomitant /kənˈkɒmɪt(ə)nt/ formal ▶ adjective naturally accompanying or associated: *she loved travel, with all its concomitant worries* | *concomitant with his obsession with dirt was a desire for order.*
▶ noun a phenomenon that naturally accompanies or follows something: *he sought promotion without the necessary concomitant of hard work.*
– DERIVATIVES **concomitantly** adverb.
– ORIGIN early 17th cent.: from late Latin *concomitant-* 'accompanying', from *concomitari*, from *con-* 'together with' + *comitari*, from Latin *comes* 'companion'.

Concord[1] /ˈkɒŋkɔːd/ **1** the state capital of New Hampshire; pop. 42,255 (est. 2008).
2 a town in NE Massachusetts; pop. 17,450 (est. 2008). Battles there and at Lexington in April 1775 marked the start of the War of American Independence.

Concord[2] /ˈkɒŋkɔːd/ ▶ noun [mass noun] a variety of dessert grape developed at Concord, Massachusetts.

concord ▶ noun [mass noun] **1** formal agreement or harmony between people or groups: *a pact of peace and concord.* ■ [count noun] a treaty.
2 Grammar agreement between words in gender, number, case, person, or any other grammatical category which affects the forms of the words.
3 [count noun] Music a chord that is pleasing or satisfactory in itself.
– ORIGIN Middle English: from Old French *concorde*, from Latin *concordia*, from *concors* 'of one mind', from *con-* 'together' + *cor, cord-* 'heart'.

concordance /kənˈkɔːd(ə)ns/ ▶ noun **1** an alphabetical list of the words (especially the important ones) present in a text or texts, usually with citations of the passages concerned or with the context displayed on a computer screen: *a concordance to the Bible.*
2 [mass noun] formal agreement or consistency: *the concordance between the teams' research results.*
3 Medicine the inheritance by two related individuals (especially twins) of the same genetic characteristic, such as susceptibility to a disease.
▶ verb [with obj.] (often as adj. **concordanced**) make a concordance of: *the value of concordanced information.*
– ORIGIN late Middle English: from Old French, from medieval Latin *concordantia*, from *concordant-* 'being of one mind' (see CONCORDANT).

concordant ▶ adjective **1** in agreement; consistent: *the answers were roughly concordant.* ■ Music in harmony. ■ Geology corresponding in direction with the planes of adjacent or underlying strata.
2 Medicine (of twins) inheriting the same genetic characteristic.
– DERIVATIVES **concordantly** adverb.

concordat /kənˈkɔːdat/ ▶ noun an agreement or treaty, especially one between the Vatican and a secular government relating to matters of mutual interest.
– ORIGIN early 17th cent.: from French, or from Latin *concordatum* 'something agreed upon', neuter past participle of *concordare* 'be of one mind' (see CONCORD).

Concorde /ˈkɒŋkɔːd/ a supersonic airliner able to cruise at twice the speed of sound. Produced through Anglo-French cooperation, it made its maiden flight in 1969.

concours /ˈkɔ̃kuə/ (also **concours d'élégance** /ˌdeleɪˈgɒ̃s/) ▶ noun (pl. **same**) an exhibition or parade of vintage or classic motor vehicles in which prizes are awarded for those in the best or most original condition.
– ORIGIN French, 'contest (of elegance)'.

concourse ▶ noun **1** a large open area inside or in front of a public building: *a station concourse.*
2 formal a crowd or assembly of people: *a vast concourse of onlookers.* ■ [mass noun] the action of coming together or meeting: *the concourse of bodies.* ■ another term for CONCOURS.
– ORIGIN late Middle English (in sense 2): from Old French *concours*, from Latin *concursus*, from *concurs-* 'run together, met', from the verb *concurrere* (see CONCUR). Sense 1 (originally US) dates from the mid 19th cent.

concrescence /kənˈkrɛs(ə)ns/ ▶ noun [mass noun] Biology the coalescence or growing together of parts originally separate.
– DERIVATIVES **concrescent** adjective.
– ORIGIN early 17th cent. (in the senses 'growth by assimilation' and 'a concretion'): from CON- 'together' + *-crescence*, on the pattern of words such as *excrescence*. The current sense dates from the late 19th cent.

concrete ▶ adjective /ˈkɒŋkriːt/ existing in a material or physical form; not abstract: *concrete objects like stones.* ■ specific; definite: *I haven't got any concrete proof.* ■ (of a noun) denoting a material object as opposed to an abstract quality, state, or action.
▶ noun [mass noun] a building material made from a mixture of broken stone or gravel, sand, cement, and water, which can be spread or poured into moulds and forms a stone-like mass on hardening: *slabs of concrete* | [as modifier] *concrete blocks.*
▶ verb [with obj.] **1** /ˈkɒŋkriːt/ cover (an area) with concrete: *the precious English countryside may soon be concreted over.* ■ [with obj. and adverbial of place] fix in position with concrete: *the post is concreted into the ground.*
2 /kənˈkriːt/ archaic form (something) into a mass; solidify. ■ make real or concrete instead of abstract: *concreting God into actual form of man.*
– PHRASES **be set in concrete** (of a policy or idea) be fixed and unalterable: *I do not regard the constitution as set in concrete.*
– DERIVATIVES **concretely** adverb, **concreteness** noun.
– ORIGIN late Middle English (in the sense 'solidified'): from French *concret* or Latin *concretus*, past participle of *concrescere* 'grow together'. Early use was also as a grammatical term designating a quality belonging to a substance (usually expressed by an adjective such as *white* in *white paper*) as opposed to the quality itself (expressed by an abstract noun such as *whiteness*); later *concrete* came to be used to refer to nouns embodying attributes (e.g. *fool, hero*), as opposed to the attributes themselves (e.g. *foolishness, heroism*), and this is the basis of the modern use as the opposite of 'abstract'. The noun sense 'building material' dates from the mid 19th cent.

concrete jungle ▶ noun a city or urban area which has a high density of large, unattractive, modern buildings and is perceived as an unpleasant living environment.

concrete mixer ▶ noun a cement mixer.

concrete music ▶ noun another term for MUSIQUE CONCRÈTE.

concrete poetry ▶ noun [mass noun] poetry in which the meaning or effect is conveyed partly or wholly by visual means, using patterns of words or letters and other typographical devices.

concrete universal ▶ noun (in idealist philosophy) an abstraction which is manifest in a developing or organized set of instances, so having the qualities of both the universal and the particular.

concretion ▶ noun a hard solid mass formed by the local accumulation of matter, especially within the body or within a mass of sediment. ■ [mass noun] the formation of such a mass.
– DERIVATIVES **concretionary** adjective.
– ORIGIN mid 16th cent.: from Latin *concretio(n-)*, from *concrescere* 'grow together'.

concretize /ˈkɒŋkrɪtʌɪz/ (also **concretise**) ▶ verb [with obj.] make (an idea or concept) real; give specific or definite form to: *the theme park is an attempt to concretize our fantasies about America.*
– DERIVATIVES **concretization** noun.

concubinage /kɒnˈkjuːbɪnɪdʒ/ ▶ noun [mass noun] chiefly historical the practice of keeping a concubine, or the state of being a concubine.
– ORIGIN late Middle English: from French, from Old French *concubine* (see CONCUBINE).

concubine /ˈkɒŋkjʊbʌɪn/ ▶ noun chiefly historical (in polygamous societies) a woman who lives with a man but has lower status than his wife or wives. ■ archaic a mistress.
– DERIVATIVES **concubinary** /kənˈkjuːbɪn(ə)ri/ adjective.
– ORIGIN Middle English: from Old French, from Latin *concubina*, from *con-* 'with' + *cubare* 'to lie'.

concupiscence /kənˈkjuːpɪs(ə)ns/ ▶ noun [mass noun] formal strong sexual desire; lust.
– ORIGIN Middle English: via Old French from late Latin *concupiscentia*, from Latin *concupiscent-* 'beginning to desire', from the verb *concupiscere*, from *con-* (expressing intensive force) + *cupere* 'to desire'.

concupiscent ▶ adjective formal filled with sexual desire; lustful: *concupiscent dreams.*

concur ▶ verb (**concurs, concurring, concurred**) [no obj.] **1** be of the same opinion; agree: *the authors concurred with the majority* | [with direct speech] *'That's right,' the chairman concurred.* ■ (**concur with**) agree with (a decision or opinion): *we strongly concur with this recommendation.*
2 happen or occur at the same time; coincide: *in tests, cytogenetic determination has been found to concur with enzymatic determination.*
– ORIGIN late Middle English (also in the senses 'collide' and 'act in combination'): from Latin *concurrere* 'run together, assemble in crowds', from *con-* 'together with' + *currere* 'to run'.

concurrent ▶ adjective **1** existing, happening, or done at the same time: *there are three concurrent art fairs around the city.* ■ (of two or more prison sentences) to be served at the same time. ■ Mathematics (of three or more lines) meeting at or tending towards one point.

2 agreeing or consistent.
– DERIVATIVES **concurrence** noun, **concurrency** noun, **concurrently** adverb.
– ORIGIN late Middle English: from Latin *concurrent-* 'running together, meeting', from the verb *concurrere* (see CONCUR).

concuss /kən'kʌs/ ▶ verb [with obj.] (usu. as adj. **concussed**) hit the head of (a person or animal), causing them to become temporarily unconscious or confused: *Michael was a bit concussed.*
– DERIVATIVES **concussive** adjective.
– ORIGIN late 16th cent. (in the sense 'shake violently'): from Latin *concuss-* 'dashed together, violently shaken', from the verb *concutere*, from *con-* 'together' + *quatere* 'shake'.

concussion ▶ noun 1 [mass noun] temporary unconsciousness or confusion and other symptoms caused by a blow on the head.
2 a violent shock as from a heavy blow: *the ground shuddered with the concussion of the blast.*
– ORIGIN late Middle English: from Latin *concussio(n-)*, from the verb *concutere* 'dash together, shake' (see CONCUSS).

condemn ▶ verb [with obj.] 1 express complete disapproval of; censure: *most leaders roundly condemned the attack | the plan was condemned by campaigners.*
2 sentence (someone) to a particular punishment, especially death: *the rebels had been **condemned to death*** | (as adj. **condemned**) *the condemned men.* ■ (of circumstances) force (someone) to endure or accept something unpleasant: *the physical ailments that **condemned** him **to** a lonely childhood.* ■ prove or show to be guilty or unsatisfactory: *she could see in his eyes that her stumble had condemned her.*
3 officially declare (something) to be unfit for use: *the pool has been condemned as a health hazard.*
– DERIVATIVES **condemnable** adjective.
– ORIGIN Middle English (in sense 2): from Old French *condemner*, from Latin *condemnare*, from *con-* (expressing intensive force) + *damnare* 'inflict loss on' (see DAMN).

condemnation ▶ noun [mass noun] 1 the expression of very strong disapproval; censure: *there was strong international condemnation of the attack.*
2 the action of condemning someone to a punishment; sentencing.

condemnatory /ˌkɒndəm'neɪt(ə)ri/ ▶ adjective expressing strong disapproval; censorious: *condemnatory statements.*

condemned cell ▶ noun Brit. a prison cell in which a prisoner who has received a death sentence is kept.

condensate /'kɒnd(ə)nseɪt/ ▶ noun [mass noun] liquid collected by condensation. ■ [count noun] Chemistry a compound produced by a condensation reaction.

condensation ▶ noun [mass noun] 1 water which collects as droplets on a cold surface when humid air is in contact with it.
2 the conversion of a vapour or gas to a liquid. ■ (also **condensation reaction**) [count noun] Chemistry a reaction in which two molecules combine to form a larger molecule, producing a small molecule such as H_2O as a by-product. ■ Psychology the fusion of two or more images or ideas into a single composite or new image, as a primary process in unconscious thought exemplified in dreams.
3 [count noun] a concise version of something, especially a text: *a readable condensation of the recent literature.*
– ORIGIN early 17th cent.: from late Latin *condensatio(n-)*, from *condensare* 'press close together' (see CONDENSE).

condense ▶ verb 1 [with obj.] make (something) denser or more concentrated: *the morning play on Saturday was condensed into a half-hour package.* ■ express (written or spoken material) in fewer words; make concise: *he **condensed** the three plays **into** a three-hour drama.*
2 change or cause to change from a gas or vapour to a liquid: [no obj.] *the moisture vapour in the air **condenses into** droplets of water* | [with obj.] *the cold air was condensing his breath.*
– DERIVATIVES **condensable** adjective.
– ORIGIN late Middle English: from Old French *condenser* or Latin *condensare*, from *condensus* 'very thick', from *con-* 'completely' + *densus* 'dense'.

condensed ▶ adjective made denser or more concise; compressed or concentrated: *a condensed version of the report.* ■ (of a liquid) thickened by heating to reduce the water content; concentrated: *condensed soup.*

condensed milk ▶ noun [mass noun] milk that has been thickened by evaporation and sweetened, sold in tins.

condenser ▶ noun 1 an apparatus or container for condensing vapour.
2 a lens or system of lenses for collecting and directing light.
3 another term for CAPACITOR.

condescend ▶ verb [no obj.] show that one feels superior; be patronizing: *take care not to **condescend to** your reader.* ■ [with infinitive] do something in such a way as to emphasize that one clearly regards it as below one's dignity or level of importance: *he condescended to see me at my hotel.*
– ORIGIN Middle English (in the sense 'give way, defer'): from Old French *condescendre*, from ecclesiastical Latin *condescendere*, from *con-* 'together' + *descendere* 'descend'.

condescending ▶ adjective having or showing an attitude of patronizing superiority: *she thought the teachers were arrogant and condescending | a condescending smile.*
– DERIVATIVES **condescendingly** adverb.

condescension ▶ noun [mass noun] an attitude of patronizing superiority; disdain: *a tone of condescension | I'm treated with condescension.*

condign /kən'dʌɪn/ ▶ adjective formal (of punishment or retribution) appropriate to the crime or wrongdoing; fitting and deserved.
– DERIVATIVES **condignly** adverb.
– ORIGIN late Middle English (in the general sense 'worthy, appropriate'): from Old French *condigne*, from Latin *condignus*, from *con-* 'altogether' + *dignus* 'worthy'.

condiment ▶ noun a substance such as salt, mustard, or pickle that is used to add flavour to food.
– ORIGIN late Middle English: from Latin *condimentum*, from *condire* 'to pickle'.

condition ▶ noun 1 [mass noun] [usu. with adj.] the state of something with regard to its appearance, quality, or working order: *the wiring is in good condition* | [in sing.] *the bridge is in an extremely dangerous condition.* ■ a person's or animal's state of health or physical fitness: *the baby was in good condition at birth* | [in sing.] *she was in a serious condition.* ■ [count noun] [often with modifier] an illness or other medical problem: *a heart condition.* ■ [in sing.] the situation in life of a particular group: *the sorrows of the human condition.* ■ archaic social position: *those of humbler condition.*
2 (**conditions**) the circumstances or factors affecting the way in which people live or work, especially with regard to their well-being: *harsh working and living conditions.* ■ the factors or prevailing situation influencing the performance or outcome of a process: *present market conditions.* ■ the prevailing state of the weather, ground, or sea at a particular time, especially as it affects a sporting event: *the appalling conditions determined the style of play.*
3 a situation that must exist before something else is possible or permitted: *for a member to borrow money, three conditions have to be met | all personnel should comply with this policy as **a condition of** employment.*
▶ verb [with obj.] 1 have a significant influence on or determine (the manner or outcome of something): *national choices are conditioned by the international political economy.* ■ train or accustom to behave in a certain way or to accept certain circumstances: *our minds are heavily conditioned and circumscribed by habit* | [with obj. and infinitive] *they are beliefs which he has been conditioned to accept* | (as noun **conditioning**) *social conditioning.*
2 bring into the desired state for use: *a product for conditioning leather.* ■ (often as adj. **conditioned**) make (a person or animal) fit and healthy: *he was six feet two of perfectly conditioned muscle and bone.* ■ (often as adj. **conditioned**) bring (beer) to maturation after fermentation while the yeast is still present: [in combination] *cask-conditioned real ales.* ■ [no obj.] (of a beer) undergo such a process: *brews that are allowed to condition in the bottle.*
3 apply a conditioner to (the hair): *I condition my hair regularly.*
4 set prior requirements on (something) before it can occur or be done: *Congressmen have sought to limit and condition military and economic aid.*
– PHRASES **in** (or **out of**) **condition** in a fit (or unfit) physical state. **in no condition to do something** certainly not fit or well enough to do something: *you're in no condition to tackle the stairs.* **on condition that** with the stipulation that: *I got three years' probation, on condition that I stay at the hostel for a year.*
– ORIGIN Middle English: from Old French *condicion* (noun), *condicionner* (verb), from Latin *condicio(n-)* 'agreement', from *condicere* 'agree upon', from *con-* 'with' + *dicere* 'say'.

conditional ▶ adjective 1 subject to one or more conditions or requirements being met: *the consortium have made a conditional offer | Western aid was only granted conditional on further reform.*
2 Grammar (of a clause, phrase, conjunction, or verb form) expressing a condition.
▶ noun 1 Grammar & Philosophy a conditional clause or conjunction. ■ a sentence containing a conditional clause.
2 [mass noun] Grammar the conditional mood of a verb, for example *should* in *if I should die.*
– DERIVATIVES **conditionality** noun, **conditionally** adverb.

conditional discharge ▶ noun an order made by a criminal court whereby an offender will not be sentenced for an offence unless a further offence is committed within a stated period.

conditional probability ▶ noun Statistics the probability of an event (*A*), given that another (*B*) has already occurred.

conditional sale ▶ noun the sale of goods according to a contract under which ownership does not pass to the buyer until after a set time, usually after payment of the last instalment of the purchase price, although the buyer has possession and is committed to acquiring ownership.

condition code ▶ noun Computing a group of bits indicating the condition of something inside a computer, often used to decide which instructions the computer will subsequently execute.

conditioned response (also **conditioned reflex**) ▶ noun Psychology an automatic response established by training to an ordinarily neutral stimulus.

conditioner ▶ noun a substance or appliance used to improve the condition of something: *add a water conditioner to neutralize chlorine.* ■ a liquid applied to the hair after shampooing to improve its condition.

condo /'kɒndəʊ/ ▶ noun (pl. **condos**) N. Amer. informal short for CONDOMINIUM (sense 1): *a high-rise condo.*

condole /kən'dəʊl/ ▶ verb [no obj.] (**condole with**) express sympathy for (someone); grieve with: *the priest came to condole with Madeleine.*
– ORIGIN late 16th cent.: from Christian Latin *condolere*, from *con-* 'with' + *dolere* 'grieve, suffer'.

condolence ▶ noun (usu. **condolences**) an expression of sympathy, especially on the occasion of the death of a person's relative or close friend: *we offer our sincere condolences to his widow* | [mass noun] *letters of condolence.*
– ORIGIN early 17th cent.: from CONDOLE, influenced by French *condoléance*.

condom ▶ noun a thin rubber sheath worn on a man's penis during sexual intercourse as a contraceptive or as a protection against infection.
– ORIGIN early 18th cent.: of unknown origin; often said to be named after a physician who invented it, but no such person has been traced.

condominium /ˌkɒndə'mɪnɪəm/ ▶ noun (pl. **condominiums**) 1 N. Amer. a building or complex of buildings containing a number of individually owned apartments or houses. ■ each of the individual apartments or houses in a condominium. ■ [mass noun] the system of ownership by which condominiums operate, in which owners have full title to the individual apartment or house and an undivided interest in the shared parts of the property.
2 [mass noun] the joint control of a state's affairs by other states. ■ [count noun] a state so governed.
– ORIGIN early 18th cent.: modern Latin, from *con-* 'together with' + *dominium* 'right of ownership' (see DOMINION). Sense 1 dates from the 1960s.

condone /kən'dəʊn/ ▶ verb [with obj.] [often with negative] accept (behaviour that is considered morally wrong or offensive): *the college cannot condone any behaviour that involves illicit drugs.* ■ approve or sanction (something), especially with reluctance: *those arrested were released and the exhibition was officially condoned a few weeks later.*
– DERIVATIVES **condonation** /kɒndə'neɪʃ(ə)n/ noun, **condoner** noun.
– ORIGIN mid 19th cent.: from Latin *condonare* 'refrain from punishing', from *con-* 'altogether' + *donare* 'give'.

condor ▶ noun a very large New World vulture with a bare head and mainly black plumage, living in mountainous country and spending much time soaring on

massive outstretched wings. ● Two species in the family Cathartidae: the **Andean condor** (*Vultur gryphus*) of South America, and the **California** (or **Californian**) **condor** (*Gymnogyps californianus*), which is probably extinct in the wild.
– ORIGIN early 17th cent.: from Spanish *cóndor*, from Quechua *kuntur*.

condottiere /ˌkɒndɒˈtjɛːreɪ, -ri/ ▶ noun (pl. **condottieri** pronunc. **same**) historical a leader or member of a troop of mercenaries, especially in Italy.
– ORIGIN Italian, from *condotto* 'troop under contract', from *condotta* 'a contract', from *condurre* 'conduct', from Latin *conducere* (see CONDUCT).

conduce ▶ verb [no obj.] (**conduce to**) formal help to bring about (a particular situation or outcome): *nothing would conduce more to the unity of the nation.*
– ORIGIN late Middle English (in the sense 'lead or bring'): from Latin *conducere* 'bring together' (see CONDUCT).

conducive ▶ adjective (usu. **conducive to**) making a certain situation or outcome likely or possible: *the harsh lights and cameras were hardly conducive to a relaxed atmosphere.*
– ORIGIN mid 17th cent.: from CONDUCE, on the pattern of words such as *conductive*.

conduct ▶ noun /ˈkɒndʌkt/ [mass noun] **1** the manner in which a person behaves, especially in a particular place or situation: *they were arrested for disorderly conduct | a code of conduct for directors of listed companies.*
2 the manner in which an organization or activity is managed or directed: *the conduct of the elections.* ■ archaic the action of leading; guidance: *travelling through the world under the conduct of chance.*
▶ verb /kənˈdʌkt/ [with obj.] **1** organize and carry out: *in the second trial he conducted his own defence | surveys conducted among students.*
2 [with obj. and adverbial of direction] lead or guide (someone) to or around a particular place: *he conducted us through his personal gallery of the Civil War* | (as adj. **conducted**) *a conducted tour.*
3 Physics transmit (a form of energy such as heat or electricity) by conduction: *heat is conducted to the surface.*
4 direct the performance of (a piece of music or an orchestra, choir, etc.): *the concert is to be conducted by Sir Simon Rattle.*
5 (**conduct oneself**) behave in a specified way: *he conducted himself with the utmost propriety.*
– DERIVATIVES **conductibility** /kəndʌktɪˈbɪlɪti/ noun, **conductible** /kənˈdʌktɪb(ə)l/ adjective.
– ORIGIN Middle English: from Old French, from Latin *conduct-* 'brought together', from the verb *conducere*. The term originally denoted a provision for safe passage, surviving in SAFE CONDUCT; later the verb sense 'lead, guide' arose, hence 'manage' and 'management' (late Middle English), later 'management of oneself, behaviour' (mid 16th cent.). The original form of the word was *conduit*, which was preserved only in the sense 'channel' (see CONDUIT); in other uses the spelling was influenced by Latin.

conductance ▶ noun [mass noun] the degree to which an object conducts electricity, calculated as the ratio of the current which flows to the potential difference present. This is the reciprocal of the resistance, and is measured in siemens or mhos.

conduct disorder ▶ noun [mass noun] chiefly US a range of antisocial types of behaviour displayed in childhood or adolescence.

conduction ▶ noun [mass noun] the process by which heat or electricity is directly transmitted through the material of a substance when there is a difference of temperature or of electrical potential between adjoining regions, without movement of the material. ■ the process by which sound waves travel through a medium. ■ the transmission of impulses along nerves. ■ the conveying of fluid through a channel.
– ORIGIN mid 16th cent. (in the senses 'provision for safe passage' and 'leadership'): from Latin *conductio(n-)*, from the verb *conducere* (see CONDUCT).

conduction band ▶ noun Physics a delocalized band of energy levels in a crystalline solid which is partly filled with electrons. These electrons have great mobility and are responsible for electrical conductivity.

conductive ▶ adjective having the property of conducting something (especially heat or electricity): *a conductive material.* ■ relating to conduction.
– DERIVATIVES **conductively** adverb.

conductive education ▶ noun [mass noun] Brit. a system of training for people with motor disorders, especially children, which aims to reduce their dependence on artificial aids.

conductivity ▶ noun (pl. **conductivities**) [mass noun] (also **electrical conductivity**) the degree to which a specified material conducts electricity, calculated as the ratio of the current density in the material to the electric field which causes the flow of current. ■ (also **thermal conductivity**) the rate at which heat passes through a specified material, expressed as the amount of heat that flows per unit time through a unit area with a temperature gradient of one degree per unit distance.

conductor ▶ noun **1** a person who directs the performance of an orchestra or choir.
2 Brit. a person who collects fares and sells tickets on a bus. ■ N. Amer. a guard on a train.
3 Physics a material or device that conducts or transmits heat or electricity, especially when regarded in terms of its capacity to do this: *most polymers are poor conductors.* ■ short for LIGHTNING CONDUCTOR.
4 Brit. a person who is trained to provide conductive education.
– DERIVATIVES **conductorship** noun (sense 1).
– ORIGIN late Middle English (denoting a military leader): via Old French from Latin *conductor*, from *conducere* 'bring together' (see CONDUCT).

conductor rail ▶ noun a rail transmitting current to an electric train or other vehicle.

conductress ▶ noun a female conductor, especially in a bus or other passenger vehicle.

conductus /kənˈdʌktəs/ ▶ noun (pl. **conducti** /-tʌɪ/) a musical setting of a metrical Latin text, of the 12th or 13th century.
– ORIGIN from medieval Latin, from Latin *conducere* 'bring together' (see CONDUCT).

conduit /ˈkɒndjʊɪt, ˈkɒndɪt/ ▶ noun **1** a channel for conveying water or other fluid. ■ a person or organization that acts as a channel for the transmission of something: *as an actor you have to be a conduit for other people's words.*
2 a tube or trough for protecting electric wiring.
– ORIGIN Middle English: from Old French, from medieval Latin *conductus*, from Latin *conducere* 'bring together' (see CONDUCT).

condylarth /ˈkɒndɪlɑːθ/ ▶ noun a fossil herbivorous mammal of the early Tertiary period, ancestral to the ungulates. ● Order Condylarthra: several families.
– ORIGIN late 19th cent.: from modern Latin *Condylarthra* (plural), from Greek *kondulos* 'knuckle' + *arthron* 'joint'.

condyle /ˈkɒndɪl, -dʌɪl/ ▶ noun Anatomy a rounded protuberance at the end of some bones, forming an articulation with another bone.
– DERIVATIVES **condylar** adjective, **condyloid** adjective.
– ORIGIN mid 17th cent.: from French, from Latin *condylus*, from Greek *kondulos* 'knuckle'.

condyloma /ˌkɒndɪˈləʊmə/ ▶ noun (pl. **condylomas** or **condylomata** /-mətə/) Medicine a raised growth on the skin resembling a wart, typically in the genital region, caused by viral infection or syphilis and transmissible by contact.
– DERIVATIVES **condylomatous** adjective.
– ORIGIN late Middle English: via Latin from Greek *kondulōma* 'callous lump', from *kondulos* 'knuckle'.

cone ▶ noun **1** a solid or hollow object which tapers from a circular or roughly circular base to a point. ■ Mathematics a surface or solid figure generated by the straight lines which pass from a circle or other closed curve to a single point (the vertex) not in the same plane as the curve. ■ a conical mountain, especially one of volcanic origin. ■ (also **traffic cone**) a plastic cone-shaped object that is used to separate off or close sections of a road. ■ a coned-shaped wafer container in which ice cream is served. ■ (also **pyrometric cone**) a ceramic pyramid that melts at a known temperature and is used to indicate the temperature of a kiln.
2 the dry fruit of a conifer, typically tapering to a rounded end and formed of a tight array of overlapping scales on a central axis which separate to release the seeds. ■ a flower resembling a pine cone, especially that of the hop plant.
3 Anatomy one of two types of light-sensitive cell in the retina of the eye, responding mainly to bright light and responsible for sharpness of vision and colour perception. Compare with ROD (sense 5).
▶ verb [with obj.] (**cone something off**) Brit. separate off or mark a road with traffic cones: *part of the road has been coned off.*
– ORIGIN late Middle English (denoting an apex or vertex): from French *cône*, via Latin from Greek *kōnos*.

cone biopsy ▶ noun a surgical procedure in which a cone-shaped segment of tissue from the uterus is removed for examination.

coned ▶ adjective **1** conical in shape.
2 wound on a cone: *a coned yarn.*

coneflower ▶ noun a North American plant of the daisy family, which has flowers with cone-like centres. ● *Rudbeckia*, *Echinacea*, and other genera, family Compositae.

conehead ▶ noun a small bush cricket that is mostly active by day and sings for long periods without stopping. ● Genus *Conocephalus*, family Tettigoniidae.

cone shell ▶ noun a predatory mollusc of warm seas, with a conical, typically intricately patterned, shell. It captures prey by injecting venom, which can be lethal to humans, and the shells are popular with collectors. ● Genus *Conus*, family Conidae, class Gastropoda: numerous species.

Conestoga wagon /ˌkɒnɪˈstəʊɡə/ ▶ noun N. Amer. historical a large wagon used for long-distance travel.
– ORIGIN early 18th cent.: named after *Conestoga*, a town in Pennsylvania, US.

coney /ˈkəʊni/ (also **cony**) ▶ noun (pl. **coneys**) **1** Brit. & Heraldry a rabbit. ■ N. Amer. a pika. ■ (in biblical use) a hyrax.
2 a small grouper (fish) found on the coasts of the tropical western Atlantic, with variable coloration. ● *Epinephelus fulvus*, family Serranidae.
– ORIGIN Middle English: from Old French *conin*, from Latin *cuniculus*.

Coney Island a resort and amusement park on the Atlantic coast in Brooklyn, New York City, on the south shore of Long Island.

confab informal ▶ noun an informal private conversation or discussion. ■ N. Amer. a meeting or conference of members of a particular group.
▶ verb (**confabs**, **confabbing**, **confabbed**) [no obj.] engage in informal private conversation: *Peter was confabbing with a curly-haired guy.*
– ORIGIN early 18th cent.: abbreviation of *confabulation* (see CONFABULATE).

confabulate /kənˈfabjʊleɪt/ ▶ verb [no obj.] **1** formal engage in conversation; talk: *she could be heard on the telephone confabulating with someone.*
2 Psychiatry fabricate imaginary experiences as compensation for loss of memory.
– DERIVATIVES **confabulation** noun, **confabulatory** adjective.
– ORIGIN early 17th cent.: from Latin *confabulat-* 'chatted together', from the verb *confabulari*, from *con-* 'together' + *fabulari* (from *fabula* 'fable').

confect /kənˈfɛkt/ ▶ verb [with obj.] make (something elaborate or dainty) from various elements: *a trifle confected from angelica and piped cream.*
– ORIGIN late Middle English: from Latin *confect-* 'put together', from the verb *conficere*, from *con-* 'together' + *facere* 'make'.

confection ▶ noun **1** an elaborate sweet dish or delicacy: *a fruit confection.* ■ an elaborately constructed thing, especially a frivolous one: *his elaborate pop confections.* ■ an elaborate article of women's dress: *Therese was magnificent in a swirling confection of crimson.*
2 [mass noun] the action of mixing or compounding something: *the confection of a syllabub.*
– ORIGIN Middle English (in the general sense 'something made by mixing', especially a medicinal preparation): via Old French from Latin *confectio(n-)*, from *conficere* 'put together' (see CONFECT).

confectioner ▶ noun a person whose trade is making or selling confectionery.

confectioner's custard ▶ noun [mass noun] thick, sweet custard used as a filling for cakes and pastries.

confectioner's sugar ▶ noun US term for ICING SUGAR.

confectionery ▶ noun (pl. **confectioneries**) [mass noun] sweets and chocolates considered collectively.

confederacy ▶ noun (pl. **confederacies**) a league or alliance, especially of confederate states. ■ (**the Confederacy**) another term for CONFEDERATE STATES OF AMERICA. ■ a union of people or groups formed for an illicit purpose.

– ORIGIN late Middle English: from Old French *confederacie*, based on Latin *confoederare* 'join together in league' (see CONFEDERATION).

confederal ▶ **adjective** relating to or denoting a confederation.

– ORIGIN late 18th cent.: from CONFEDERATION, on the pattern of *federal*.

confederate ▶ **adjective** /kənˈfɛd(ə)rət/ [attrib.] joined by an agreement or treaty: *some local groups united to form confederate councils.* ■ (**Confederate**) relating to the Confederate States of America: *the Confederate flag.*

▶ **noun** /kənˈfɛd(ə)rət/ **1** a person one works with, especially in something secret or illegal; an accomplice. **2** (**Confederate**) a supporter of the Confederate States of America.

▶ **verb** /kənˈfɛdəreɪt/ [with obj.] (usu. as adj. **confederated**) bring (states or groups of people) into an alliance: *Switzerland is a model for the new confederated Europe.*

– ORIGIN late Middle English: from late (ecclesiastical) Latin *confoederatus*, from *con-* 'together' + *foederatus* (see FEDERATE).

Confederate States of America (also **the Confederacy**) the eleven Southern states (Alabama, Arkansas, Florida, Georgia, Louisiana, Mississippi, North Carolina, South Carolina, Tennessee, Texas, Virginia) which seceded from the United States in 1860–1, thus precipitating the American Civil War.

confederation ▶ **noun** an organization which consists of a number of parties or groups united in an alliance or league: *a confederation of trade unions.* ■ a more or less permanent union of states with some or most political power vested in a central authority. ■ [mass noun] the action of confederating or the state of being confederated: *a referendum on confederation.*

– ORIGIN late Middle English: from Old French *confederacion* or late Latin *confederatio(n-)*, from Latin *confoederare*, from *con-* 'together' + *foederare* 'join in league with' (from *foedus* 'league, treaty').

Confederation of British Industry (abbrev.: **CBI**) (in the UK) an organization to promote the prosperity of British business.

confer /kənˈfəː/ ▶ **verb** (**confers**, **conferring**, **conferred**) **1** [with obj.] grant (a title, degree, benefit, or right): *the Minister may have exceeded the powers **conferred on** him by Parliament.* **2** [no obj.] have discussions; exchange opinions: *the officials were **conferring with** allies.*

– DERIVATIVES **conferment** noun (sense 1), **conferral** noun (sense 1).

– ORIGIN late Middle English (in the general sense 'bring together', also in sense 2): from Latin *conferre*, from *con-* 'together' + *ferre* 'bring'.

conferee ▶ **noun 1** a person who attends a conference. **2** a person on whom something is conferred.

Conference ▶ **noun** a dessert pear of a firm-fleshed variety.

conference ▶ **noun 1** a formal meeting of people with a shared interest, typically one that takes place over several days: *an international conference on the environment | the Labour Party Conference.* ■ a formal meeting for discussion. ■ [usu. as modifier] a linking of several telephones or computers, so that each user may communicate with the others simultaneously: *a conference call.* **2** a commercial association for the regulation of an area of activity or the exchange of information. ■ an association of sports teams which play each other. ■ the governing body of some Christian Churches, especially Methodist Churches.

▶ **verb** [no obj.] (usu. as noun **conferencing**) take part in a conference or conference call: *video conferencing.*

– PHRASES **in conference** in a meeting.

– ORIGIN early 16th cent. (in the general sense 'conversation, talk'): from French *conférence* or medieval Latin *conferentia*, from Latin *conferre* 'bring together' (see CONFER).

Conference on Disarmament a committee with forty nations as members that seeks to negotiate multilateral disarmament.

confess ▶ **verb** [reporting verb] admit that one has committed a crime or done something wrong: [with clause] *he confessed that he had attacked the old man* | [no obj.] *he wants to **confess to** Caroline's murder* | [with direct speech] *'I damaged your car,' she confessed.* ■ acknowledge something reluctantly, typically because one feels slightly ashamed or embarrassed: [with clause] *I must confess that I half believed you* | [no obj.] *he **confessed to** a lifelong passion for food.* ■ [with obj.] declare (one's religious faith): *150 people confessed faith in Christ.* ■ declare one's sins formally to a priest: [with obj.] *I could not confess all my sins to the priest* | [no obj.] *he gave himself up after **confessing to** a priest.* ■ [with obj.] (of a priest) hear the confession of (someone) in such a way: *St Ambrose would weep bitter tears when confessing a sinner.*

– ORIGIN late Middle English: from Old French *confesser*, from Latin *confessus*, past participle of *confiteri* 'acknowledge', from *con-* (expressing intensive force) + *fateri* 'declare, avow'.

confessant ▶ **noun** a person who confesses to a priest; a penitent.

confessedly ▶ **adverb** by one's own admission: *many therapists have had clients who, confessedly or otherwise, have fallen in love with them.*

confession ▶ **noun 1** a formal statement admitting that one is guilty of a crime: *he signed a confession to both the murders* | [mass noun] *proof of this crime must be established by confession.* ■ an acknowledgement that one has done something about which one is ashamed or embarrassed: *by his own confession, he had strayed perilously close to alcoholism.* ■ a formal admission of one's sins with repentance and desire of absolution, especially privately to a priest as a religious duty: *she still had not been **to confession**.* See also SACRAMENT OF RECONCILIATION. **2** (also **confession of faith**) a statement setting out essential religious doctrine. ■ (also **Confession**) the religious body or Church sharing a confession of faith. ■ a statement of one's principles: *his words are a political confession of faith.*

– DERIVATIVES **confessionary** adjective.

– ORIGIN late Middle English: via Old French from Latin *confessio(n-)*, from *confiteri* 'acknowledge' (see CONFESS).

confessional ▶ **noun 1** an enclosed stall in a church divided by a screen or curtain in which a priest sits to hear confessions. **2** an acknowledgement that one has done something shameful or embarrassing; a confession.

▶ **adjective 1** (of speech or writing) in which a person reveals private thoughts or admits to past incidents, especially ones about which they feel ashamed or embarrassed: *the autobiography is remarkably confessional | his confessional outpourings.* ■ relating to religious confession: *the priest leaned forward in his best confessional manner.* **2** relating to confessions of faith or doctrinal systems: *the confessional approach to religious education.*

– ORIGIN late Middle English (as an adjective): the adjective from CONFESSION + -AL; the noun via French from Italian *confessionale*, from medieval Latin, neuter of *confessionalis*, from Latin *confessio(n-)*, from *confiteri* 'acknowledge' (see CONFESS).

– DERIVATIVES **confessionally** adverb.

confessor ▶ **noun 1** a priest who hears confessions and gives absolution and spiritual counsel. **2** a person who avows religious faith in the face of opposition, but does not suffer martyrdom. **3** a person who makes a confession.

– ORIGIN Old English (in sense 2): from Old French *confessour*, from ecclesiastical Latin *confessor*, from Latin *confess-* 'acknowledged' (see CONFESS).

confetti ▶ **noun** [mass noun] small pieces of coloured paper traditionally thrown over a bride and bridegroom by their wedding guests after the marriage ceremony has taken place.

– ORIGIN early 19th cent. (originally denoting the real or imitation sweets thrown during Italian carnivals): from Italian, literally 'sweets', from Latin *confectum* 'something prepared', neuter past participle of *conficere* 'put together' (see CONFECT).

confidant /ˈkɒnfɪdant, ˌkɒnfɪˈdant, -dɑːnt/ ▶ **noun** (fem. **confidante** pronunc. **same**) a person with whom one shares a secret or private matter, trusting them not to repeat it to others.

– ORIGIN mid 17th cent.: alteration of CONFIDENT (as a noun in the same sense in the early 17th cent.), probably to represent the pronunciation of French *confidente* 'having full trust'.

confide /kənˈfʌɪd/ ▶ **verb** [reporting verb] tell someone about a secret or private matter while trusting them not to repeat it to others: [with obj.] *he **confided** his fears **to** his mother* | [with clause] *he confided that stress had caused him to lose a stone in weight* | [with direct speech] *'I have been afraid,' she confided* | (as adj. **confiding**) *she was in a confiding mood.* ■ [no obj.] (**confide in**) trust (someone) enough to tell them of a secret or private matter: [with clause] *he confided in friends that he and his wife planned to separate.* ■ [with obj.] (**confide something to**) dated entrust something to (someone) in order for them to look after it: *the property of others confided to their care was unjustifiably risked.*

– DERIVATIVES **confidingly** adverb.

– ORIGIN late Middle English (in the sense 'place trust (in)'): from Latin *confidere* 'have full trust'. The sense 'impart as a secret' dates from the mid 18th cent.

C

confidence ▶ **noun** [mass noun] **1** the feeling or belief that one can have faith in or rely on someone or something: *we had every **confidence in** the staff | he had gained the young man's confidence.* ■ the state of feeling certain about the truth of something: *I can say with confidence that I have never before driven up this street.* ■ a feeling of self-assurance arising from an appreciation of one's own abilities or qualities: *she's brimming with confidence* | [in sing.] *he would walk up those steps with a confidence he didn't feel.* **2** the telling of private matters or secrets with mutual trust: *someone with whom you may raise your suspicions **in confidence**.* ■ [count noun] (often **confidences**) a secret or private matter told to someone under a condition of trust: *the girls exchanged confidences about their parents.*

– PHRASES **have every confidence in** feel that one can rely on or trust (someone): *we had every confidence in the staff.* **in someone's confidence** in a position of trust with someone. **take someone into one's confidence** tell someone one's secrets.

– ORIGIN late Middle English: from Latin *confidentia*, from *confidere* 'have full trust' (see CONFIDENT).

confidence interval ▶ **noun** Statistics a range of values so defined that there is a specified probability that the value of a parameter lies within it.

confidence level ▶ **noun** Statistics the probability that the value of a parameter falls within a specified range of values.

confidence man ▶ **noun** old-fashioned term for CONMAN.

confidence trick (N. Amer. **confidence game**) ▶ **noun** an act of cheating or tricking someone by gaining their trust and persuading them to believe something that is not true.

confidence trickster ▶ **noun** Brit. a person who sets out to defraud or deceive people by persuading them to believe something that is not true.

confident ▶ **adjective 1** feeling or showing confidence in oneself or one's abilities or qualities: *she was a confident, outgoing girl | people who are **confident in** their identity.* **2** feeling or showing certainty about something: *this time they're **confident of** a happy ending | I am not very **confident about** tonight's game.*

▶ **noun** archaic a confidant.

– DERIVATIVES **confidently** adverb.

– ORIGIN late 16th cent.: from French *confident(e)*, from Italian *confidente*, from Latin *confident-* 'having full trust', from the verb *confidere*, from *con-* (expressing intensive force) + *fidere* 'trust'.

confidential ▶ **adjective** intended to be kept secret: *confidential information.* ■ (of a person's tone of voice) indicating that what one says is private or secret: *he dropped his voice to a confidential whisper.* ■ [attrib.] entrusted with private or restricted information: *a confidential secretary.*

– DERIVATIVES **confidentiality** noun.

confidentially ▶ **adverb** in a way that is intended to be private or secret; privately: *all queries will be treated confidentially.*

configuration /kənˌfɪɡəˈreɪʃ(ə)n, -ɡjʊ-/ ▶ **noun 1** an arrangement of parts or elements in a particular form, figure, or combination: *the unrepeatable configuration of the stars at the moment of your birth | the broad configuration of the economy remains capitalist.* ■ Computing an arrangement or manner of interconnection of items of computer hardware or software. ■ Chemistry the fixed three-dimensional relationship of the atoms in a molecule, defined by the bonds between them. Compare with CONFORMATION. **2** Psychology another term for GESTALT.

– DERIVATIVES **configurational** adjective.

– ORIGIN mid 16th cent. (denoting the relative position of celestial objects): from late Latin *configuratio(n-)*, from Latin *configurare* 'shape after a pattern' (see CONFIGURE).

configure ▶ **verb** [with obj.] arrange or put together in a particular form or configuration: *two of the aircraft will be configured as VIP transports.* ■ Computing arrange or order (a computer system or an element of it) so as to fit it for a designated task: *the memory can be configured as a virtual drive.*

C

– DERIVATIVES **configurable** adjective.
– ORIGIN late Middle English (in the Latin sense): from Latin *configurare* 'shape after a pattern', from *con-* 'together' + *figurare* 'to shape' (from *figura* 'shape or figure').

confine ▶ verb /kənˈfʌɪn/ [with obj.] (**confine someone/thing to**) keep or restrict someone or something within certain limits of (space, scope, or time): *he does not confine his message to high politics* | *you've **confined yourself to** what you know.* ■ (**confine someone to/in**) restrain or forbid someone from leaving (a place): *the troops were confined to their barracks.* ■ (**be confined to**) (of a person) be unable to leave (one's bed, home, or a wheelchair) because of illness or disability: *he was confined to bed for four days with a bad dose of flu.* ■ (**be confined**) dated (of a woman) remain in bed for a period before, during, and after giving birth: *she was confined for nearly a month.*
▶ noun /ˈkɒnfʌɪn/ (**confines**) the borders or boundaries of a place, especially with regard to their restricting freedom of movement: *within **the confines of** the hall escape was difficult.* ■ the limits of something abstract, especially a sphere of activity: *the narrow confines of political life.*
– ORIGIN late Middle English (as a noun): from French *confins* (plural noun), from Latin *confinia*, from *confinis* 'bordering', from *con-* 'together' + *finis* 'end, limit' (plural *fines* 'territory'). The verb senses are from French *confiner*, based on Latin *confinis*.

confined ▶ adjective (of a space) restricted in area or volume; cramped: *her fear of confined spaces.*

confinement ▶ noun [mass noun] **1** the action of confining or state of being confined: *he was immediately released from his confinement.*
2 dated the condition of being in childbirth: *the pros and cons of home versus hospital confinement* | [count noun] *my grandmother's last six confinements.*

confirm ▶ verb [with obj.] **1** establish the truth or correctness of (something previously believed or suspected to be the case): *if these fears are confirmed, the outlook for the economy will be dire* | [with clause] *the report confirms that a diet rich in vitamin C can help to prevent cataracts.* ■ [reporting verb] state with assurance that a report or fact is true: [with clause] *he confirmed that the general was in the hands of the rebels* | [with direct speech] *'It is indeed proper coffee,' I confirmed.* ■ (**confirm someone in**) reinforce someone in (an opinion or feeling): *he fuelled his misogyny by cultivating women who confirmed him in this view.* ■ make (a provisional arrangement or appointment) definite: *Mr Baker's assistant telephoned to confirm his appointment with the chairman.* ■ make (a decision or an agreement) formally valid: *the organization has confirmed the appointment of Mr Collins as managing director.* ■ declare (someone) formally to be appointed to a particular post: *he was **confirmed as** the new EC peace envoy.*
2 administer the religious rite of confirmation to: *he had been baptized and confirmed.*
– DERIVATIVES **confirmative** adjective, **confirmatory** adjective.
– ORIGIN Middle English: from Old French *confermer*, from Latin *confirmare*, from *con-* 'together' + *firmare* 'strengthen' (from *firmus* 'firm').

confirmand /ˈkɒnfəmand/ ▶ noun a person who is to undergo the religious rite of confirmation.

confirmation ▶ noun [mass noun] **1** the action of confirming something or the state of being confirmed: *high unemployment figures were further confirmation that the economy was in recession.*
2 (in the Christian Church) the rite at which a baptized person, especially one baptized as an infant, affirms Christian belief and is admitted as a full member of the Church. ■ the Jewish ceremony of bar mitzvah or bat mitzvah.
– ORIGIN Middle English: via Old French from Latin *confirmatio(n-)*, from *confirmare* 'make firm, establish' (see CONFIRM).

confirmed ▶ adjective (of a person) firmly established in a particular habit, belief, or way of life and unlikely to change their ways: *a confirmed bachelor* | *a confirmed teetotaller.*

confiscate /ˈkɒnfɪskeɪt/ ▶ verb [with obj.] take or seize (someone's property) with authority: *the guards confiscated his camera* | (as adj. **confiscated**) *confiscated equipment.* ■ appropriate (something, especially land) to the public treasury as a penalty.
– DERIVATIVES **confiscator** noun, **confiscatory** adjective.
– ORIGIN mid 16th cent.: from Latin *confiscat-* 'put away in a chest, consigned to the public treasury', from the verb *confiscare*, based on *con-* 'together' + *fiscus* 'chest, treasury'.

confiscation /ˌkɒnfɪˈskeɪʃ(ə)n/ ▶ noun [mass noun] the action of taking or seizing someone's property with authority; seizure: *a court ordered the confiscation of her property.*

confit /ˈkɒnfi/ ▶ noun [mass noun] duck or other meat cooked very slowly in its own fat.
– ORIGIN French, 'conserved', from *confire* 'prepare'.

Confiteor /kɒnˈfɪtɪɔː/ ▶ noun a form of prayer confessing sins, used in the Roman Catholic Mass and some other sacraments.
– ORIGIN Latin, 'I confess', from the formula *Confiteor Deo Omnipotenti* 'I confess to Almighty God'.

conflab ▶ noun & verb informal another term for CONFAB.
– ORIGIN late 19th cent.: alteration.

conflagration /ˌkɒnfləˈɡreɪʃ(ə)n/ ▶ noun an extensive fire which destroys a great deal of land or property.
– ORIGIN late 15th cent. (denoting consumption by fire): from Latin *conflagratio(n-)*, from the verb *conflagrare*, from *con-* (expressing intensive force) + *flagrare* 'to blaze'.

conflate ▶ verb [with obj.] combine (two or more sets of information, texts, ideas, etc.) into one: *the urban crisis conflates a number of different economic, political, and social issues.*
– DERIVATIVES **conflation** noun.
– ORIGIN late Middle English (in the sense 'fuse or melt down metal'): from Latin *conflat-* 'kindled, fused', from the verb *conflare*, from *con-* 'together' + *flare* 'to blow'.

conflict ▶ noun /ˈkɒnflɪkt/ a serious disagreement or argument, typically a protracted one: *the eternal **conflict between** the sexes* | [mass noun] *doctors often **come into conflict with** politicians.* ■ a prolonged armed struggle: *regional conflicts.* ■ [mass noun] a state of mind in which a person experiences a clash of opposing feelings or needs: *bewildered by her own inner conflict, she could only stand there feeling vulnerable.* ■ a serious incompatibility between two or more opinions, principles, or interests: *there was **a conflict between** his business and domestic life.*
▶ verb /kənˈflɪkt/ [no obj.] be incompatible or at variance; clash: *parents' and children's interests sometimes conflict* | *the date for the match **conflicted with** a religious festival.* ■ (as adj. **conflicted**) N. Amer. having or showing confused and mutually inconsistent feelings: *he remains a little conflicted about Marlene.*
– DERIVATIVES **conflictual** adjective.
– ORIGIN late Middle English: from Latin *conflict-* 'struck together, fought', from the verb *confligere*, from *con-* 'together' + *fligere* 'to strike'; the noun is via Latin *conflictus* 'a contest'.

conflict diamond ▶ noun (in Africa) a rough diamond traded illicitly to finance an armed struggle.

conflicting /kənˈflɪktɪŋ/ ▶ adjective incompatible or at variance; contradictory: *there are conflicting accounts of what occurred.*

confluence /ˈkɒnflʊəns/ ▶ noun the junction of two rivers, especially rivers of approximately equal width. ■ an act or process of merging: *a major confluence of the world's financial markets.*
– ORIGIN late Middle English: from late Latin *confluentia*, from Latin *confluere* 'flow together' (see CONFLUENT).

confluent ▶ adjective flowing together or merging.
– ORIGIN late 15th cent.: from Latin *confluent-* 'flowing together', from *confluere*, from *con-* 'together' + *fluere* 'to flow'.

conflux /ˈkɒnflʌks/ ▶ noun another term for CONFLUENCE.
– ORIGIN early 17th cent.: from late Latin *confluxus*, from *con-* 'together' + *fluxus* (see FLUX).

confocal /kɒnˈfəʊk(ə)l/ ▶ adjective having a common focus or foci: *confocal ellipses.* ■ denoting or using a microscope whose imaging system only collects light from a small spot on the specimen, giving greater resolution.

conform ▶ verb [no obj.] comply with rules, standards, or laws: *the kitchen does not **conform to** hygiene regulations* | *the changes were introduced to **conform with** international classifications.* ■ (of a person) behave according to socially acceptable conventions or standards: *the pressure to conform.* ■ be similar in form or type; agree: *the countryside should **conform to** a certain idea of the picturesque.*
– ORIGIN Middle English (in the sense 'make (something) like another thing'): from Old French *conformer*, from Latin *conformare*, from *con-* 'together' + *formare* 'to form'.

conformable ▶ adjective (usu. **conformable to**) (of a person) disposed or accustomed to conform to what is acceptable. ■ similar in form or nature; consistent: *the human adoption of practices which are conformable to biological constraints.* ■ Geology (of strata in contact) deposited in a continuous sequence, and having the same direction of stratification.
– DERIVATIVES **conformability** noun, **conformably** adverb.
– ORIGIN late 15th cent. (in the sense 'compliant (to) or tractable'): from medieval Latin *conformabilis*, from Latin *conformare* 'to form, fashion' (see CONFORM).

conformal ▶ adjective (of a map or a mathematical mapping) preserving the correct angles between directions within small areas (though distorting distances).
– DERIVATIVES **conformally** adverb.
– ORIGIN mid 17th cent. (in the sense 'conformable'): from late Latin *conformalis*, from *con-* 'together' + *formalis* 'formal'. The current sense was coined in German.

conformance ▶ noun another term for CONFORMITY.

conformation ▶ noun the shape or structure of something, especially an animal. ■ Chemistry any of the spatial arrangements which the atoms in a molecule may adopt and freely convert between, especially by rotation about individual single bonds. Compare with CONFIGURATION.
– DERIVATIVES **conformational** adjective.
– ORIGIN early 16th cent. (in the sense 'conforming, adaptation'): from Latin *conformatio(n-)*, from *conformare* 'to shape, fashion' (see CONFORM).

conformer ▶ noun Chemistry a form of a compound having a particular molecular conformation.
– ORIGIN 1960s: blend of *conformational* (see CONFORMATION) and ISOMER.

conformist ▶ noun a person who conforms to accepted behaviour or established practices. ■ Brit. historical a person who conforms to the practices of the Church of England.
▶ adjective conforming to accepted behaviour or established practices; conventional: *the poet became more conformist in his later years.*
– DERIVATIVES **conformism** noun.

conformity ▶ noun [mass noun] compliance with standards, rules, or laws: ***conformity to** regulations* | *the goods were **in conformity with** the contract.* ■ behaviour in accordance with socially accepted conventions: *a word of praise or an encouraging smile provide rewards for **conformity to** social norms.* ■ Brit. historical compliance with the practices of the Church of England. ■ similarity in form or type; agreement in character: *these changes are intended to ensure **conformity between** all schemes.*
– ORIGIN late Middle English: from Old French *conformite* or late Latin *conformitas*, from *conformare* 'to form, fashion' (see CONFORM).

confound ▶ verb [with obj.] **1** cause surprise or confusion in (someone), especially by not according with their expectations: *the inflation figure confounded economic analysts.* ■ prove (a theory or expectation) wrong: *the rise in prices confounded expectations.* ■ defeat (a plan, aim, or hope): *we will confound these tactics by the pressure groups.* ■ archaic overthrow (an enemy).
2 mix up (something) with something else: *he was forever **confounding** managerialism **with** idealism.*
▶ exclamation dated used to express anger or annoyance: *oh **confound it**, where is the thing?*
– ORIGIN Middle English: from Old French *confondre*, from Latin *confundere* 'pour together, mix up'. Compare with CONFUSE.

confounded ▶ adjective [attrib.] informal, dated used for emphasis, especially to express anger or annoyance: *he was a confounded nuisance.*
– DERIVATIVES **confoundedly** adverb.

confraternity ▶ noun (pl. **confraternities**) a brotherhood, especially with a religious or charitable purpose.
– ORIGIN late Middle English: from Old French *confraternite*, from medieval Latin *confraternitas*, from *confrater* (see CONFRÈRE).

confrère /ˈkɒnfrɛː/ ▶ noun a fellow member of a profession: *Pooley's police confrères.*
– ORIGIN mid 18th cent.: French, from medieval Latin *confrater*, from *con-* 'together with' + *frater* 'brother'.

confront ▸ verb [with obj.] come face to face with (someone) with hostile or argumentative intent: *300 policemen confronted an equal number of union supporters.* ■ (of a problem or difficulty) present itself to (someone) so that action must be taken: *the new government was **confronted with** many profound difficulties.* ■ face up to and deal with (a problem or difficulty): *we knew we couldn't ignore the race issue and decided we'd confront it head on.* ■ compel (someone) to face or consider something, especially by way of accusation: *Merrill **confronted** him **with** her suspicions.* ■ appear or be placed in front of (someone) so as to unsettle or threaten them: *we were **confronted with** pictures of moving skeletons.*
– ORIGIN mid 16th cent.: from French *confronter*, from medieval Latin *confrontare*, from Latin *con-* 'with' + *frons, front-* 'face'.

confrontation ▸ noun a hostile or argumentative situation or meeting between opposing parties: *a **confrontation with** the legislature* | [mass noun] *four months of violent confrontation between government and opposition forces.* ■ a situation where two players or sides compete to win a sporting contest: *the race promised a classic confrontation between the two top runners in the world.*

confrontational ▸ adjective tending to deal with situations in an aggressive way; hostile or argumentative: *he distanced himself from the confrontational approach adopted by his predecessor.*
– DERIVATIVES **confrontationally** adverb.

Confucian /kən'fjuːʃ(ə)n/ ▸ adjective relating to Confucius or Confucianism.
▸ noun an adherent of Confucianism.

Confucianism /kən'fjuːʃənɪz(ə)m/ ▸ noun [mass noun] a system of philosophical and ethical teachings founded by Confucius and developed by Mencius.
– DERIVATIVES **Confucianist** noun & adjective.

Confucius /kən'fjuːʃəs/ (551–479 BC), Chinese philosopher; Latinized name of *Kongfuze* (*K'ung Fu-tzu*) 'Kong the master'. His ideas about the importance of practical moral values, collected by his disciples in the *Analects*, formed the basis of the philosophy of Confucianism.

confusable ▸ adjective able or liable to be confused with something else: *convocation was by 1327 no longer **confusable with** parliament.*
▸ noun a word or phrase that is easily confused with another in meaning or usage, such as *mitigate*, which is often confused with *militate*.
– DERIVATIVES **confusability** noun.

confuse ▸ verb [with obj.] make (someone) bewildered or perplexed: *past and present blurred together, confusing her still further.* ■ make (something) more complex or less easy to understand: *the points made by the authors confuse rather than clarify the issue.* ■ identify wrongly; mistake: *a lot of people **confuse** a stroke **with** a heart attack* | *purchasers might confuse the two products.*
– ORIGIN Middle English (in the sense 'rout, bring to ruin'): from Old French *confus*, from Latin *confusus*, past participle of *confundere* 'mingle together' (see CONFOUND). Originally all senses of the verb were passive, and therefore appeared only as the past participle *confused*; the active voice occurred rarely until the 19th cent. when it began to replace *confound*.

confused ▸ adjective **1** (of a person) unable to think clearly; bewildered: *she was utterly **confused about** what had happened.* ■ showing bewilderment: *a confused expression crossed her face.* ■ not in possession of all one's mental faculties, especially because of old age: *interviewing confused old people does take longer.*
2 lacking order and so difficult to understand: *the confused information supplied by authorities* | *reports about the incident were rather confused.* ■ lacking clear distinction of elements; jumbled: *the sound of a sort of confused hammering and shouting.*
– DERIVATIVES **confusedly** adverb.

confusing ▸ adjective bewildering or perplexing: *he found being in Egypt very confusing.*
– DERIVATIVES **confusingly** adverb.

confusion ▸ noun [mass noun] **1** uncertainty about what is happening, intended, or required: *there seems to be some **confusion about** which system does what* | *he cleared up the **confusion over** the party's policy.* ■ a situation of panic or disorder: *the guaranteed income bond market was **thrown into confusion**.* ■ [in sing.] a disorderly jumble: *all I can see is **a confusion of** brown cardboard boxes.*
2 the state of being bewildered or unclear in one's mind about something: *she looked about her **in confusion**.* ■ the mistaking of one person or thing for another: *there is some confusion between 'unlawful' and 'illegal'* | [count noun] *most of the errors are reasonable confusions between similar words.*
– ORIGIN Middle English: from Latin *confusio(n-)*, from the verb *confundere* 'mingle together' (see CONFUSE).

confute ▸ verb [with obj.] formal prove (a person or an assertion or accusation) to be wrong: *restorers who sought to confute this view were accused of ignorance.*
– DERIVATIVES **confutation** noun.
– ORIGIN early 16th cent.: from Latin *confutare* 'restrain, answer conclusively', from *con-* 'altogether' + the base of *refutare* 'refute'.

conga /'kɒŋgə/ ▸ noun **1** a Latin American dance of African origin, usually with several people in a single line, one behind the other.
2 (also **conga drum**) a tall, narrow, low-toned drum beaten with the hands.
▸ verb (**congas**, **congaing**, **congaed** or **conga'd**) [no obj.] perform the conga.
– ORIGIN 1930s: from Latin American Spanish, from Spanish, feminine of *congo* 'Congolese'.

congé /'kɒ̃ʒeɪ/ ▸ noun an unceremonious dismissal or rejection of someone.
– ORIGIN late Middle English (in the general sense 'permission to do something'): from Old French *congie*, from Latin *commeatus* 'leave of absence', from *commeare* 'go and come'. The word is now usually treated as equivalent to modern French.

congeal /kən'dʒiːl/ ▸ verb [no obj.] become semi-solid, especially on cooling: *the blood had **congealed into** blobs* | (as adj. **congealed**) *a lump of congealed moussaka.* ■ take shape or coalesce, especially to form a satisfying whole: *the ballet failed to congeal as a single oeuvre.*
– DERIVATIVES **congealment** noun (archaic).
– ORIGIN late Middle English: from Old French *congeler*, from Latin *congelare*, from *con-* 'together' + *gelare* 'freeze' (from *gelu* 'frost').

congee /'kɒndʒiː/ ▸ noun [mass noun] (in Chinese cookery) broth or porridge made from rice.
– ORIGIN from Tamil *kañci*.

congelation /ˌkɒndʒə'leɪʃ(ə)n/ ▸ noun [mass noun] the process of congealing or the state of being congealed: *the component of metals that causes their congelation.*
– ORIGIN late Middle English: from Latin *congelatio(n-)*, from the verb *congelare* 'freeze together' (see CONGEAL).

congener /'kɒndʒɪnə, kən'dʒiːnə/ ▸ noun **1** a thing or person of the same kind or category as another. ■ an animal or plant of the same genus as another: *these birds or their congeners may be found in East Africa.*
2 a minor chemical constituent, especially one which gives a distinctive character to a wine or spirit or is responsible for some of its physiological effects.
– ORIGIN mid 18th cent.: from Latin, from *con-* 'together with' + *genus, gener-* 'race, stock'.

congeneric /ˌkɒndʒɪ'nɛrɪk/ ▸ adjective (of an animal or plant species) belonging to the same genus: *this animal is **congeneric with** the later species.* ■ of a related nature or origin.
– DERIVATIVES **congenerous** /kən'dʒɛn(ə)rəs/ adjective.
– ORIGIN mid 17th cent.: from Latin *congener* (see CONGENER) + -IC.

congenial /kən'dʒiːnɪəl/ ▸ adjective (of a person) pleasing or liked on account of having qualities or interests that are similar to one's own: *his need for some congenial company.* ■ (of a thing) pleasant or agreeable because suited to one's taste or inclination: *he went back to a climate more **congenial to** his cold stony soul.*
– DERIVATIVES **congeniality** noun, **congenially** adverb.

congenital /kən'dʒɛnɪt(ə)l/ ▸ adjective (of a disease or physical abnormality) present from birth: *a congenital malformation of the heart.* ■ (of a person) having a particular trait from birth or by firmly established habit: *a congenital liar.*
– DERIVATIVES **congenitally** adverb.
– ORIGIN late 18th cent.: from Latin *congenitus*, from *con-* 'together' + *genitus* (past participle of *gignere* 'beget') + -AL.

conger /'kɒŋgə/ (also **conger eel**) ▸ noun a large edible predatory eel of shallow coastal waters.
● *Conger* and other genera, family Congridae: several species, in particular the European *C. conger* and the American *C. oceanica*.
– ORIGIN Middle English: from Old French *congre*, via Latin from Greek *gongros*.

congeries /kɒn'dʒɪəriːz, 'kɒndʒəriz/ ▸ noun (pl. **same**) a disorderly collection; a jumble: *a congeries of European states.*
– ORIGIN mid 16th cent.: from Latin *congeries* 'heap, pile', from *congerere* 'heap up'.

congested ▸ adjective **1** (of a road or place) so crowded with traffic or people as to hinder or prevent freedom of movement: *the congested streets of the West End* | *the road was **congested with** refugees.*
2 (of a part of the body) abnormally full of blood: *congested arteries.* ■ (of the respiratory tract) blocked with mucus so as to hinder breathing: *his nose was congested.*
– DERIVATIVES **congest** verb.
– ORIGIN late Middle English (as *congest* in the sense 'heap up, accumulate'): from Latin *congerere* 'heap up', from *con-* 'together' + *gerere* 'bring'.

congestion /kən'dʒɛstʃ(ə)n/ ▸ noun [mass noun] the state of being congested: *the new bridge should ease congestion in the area.*
– ORIGIN late Middle English: via Old French from Latin *congestio(n-)*, from *congere* 'heap up', from *con-* 'together' + *gerere* 'bring'.

congestion charge ▸ noun Brit. a charge made to drive into an area, typically a city centre, that suffers heavy traffic.
– DERIVATIVES **congestion-charging** noun.

congestive ▸ adjective Medicine involving or produced by congestion of a part of the body: *congestive heart failure.*
– ORIGIN mid 19th cent.: from *congest* (see CONGESTED) + -IVE.

conglomerate ▸ noun /kən'glɒm(ə)rət/ **1** a thing consisting of a number of different and distinct parts or items that are grouped together: *the Earth is a specialized conglomerate of organisms.* ■ a large corporation formed by the merging of separate and diverse firms: *a media conglomerate.*
2 [mass noun] Geology a coarse-grained sedimentary rock composed of rounded fragments embedded in a matrix of cementing material such as silica: *the sediments vary from coarse conglomerate to fine silt and clay.*
▸ adjective /kən'glɒm(ə)rət/ relating to a conglomerate, especially a large corporation: *conglomerate firms.*
▸ verb /kən'glɒməreɪt/ [no obj.] gather together into a compact mass: *atoms which conglomerate at the centre.* ■ form a conglomerate by merging diverse firms.
– ORIGIN late Middle English (as an adjective describing something gathered up into a rounded mass): from Latin *conglomeratus*, past participle of *conglomerare*, from *con-* 'together' + *glomus, glomer-* 'ball'. The geological sense dates from the early 19th cent.; the other noun senses are later.

conglomeration /kənˌglɒmə'reɪʃ(ə)n/ ▸ noun **1** a number of different things, parts or items that are grouped together; collection: *a loose conglomeration of pieces.*
2 [mass noun] the process of forming a conglomerate: *the practice of media conglomeration.*

Congo /'kɒŋgəʊ/ **1** a major river of central Africa, which rises as the Lualaba to the south of Kisangani in northern Democratic Republic of the Congo (Zaire) and flows 4,630 km (2,880 miles) in a great curve westwards, turning south-westwards to form the border with the Congo before emptying into the Atlantic. Also called ZAIRE RIVER.
2 an equatorial country in Africa, with a short Atlantic coastline; pop. 4,012,800 (est. 2009); languages, French (official), Kikongo, and other Bantu languages; capital, Brazzaville. Also called **the Congo**, **Republic of the Congo**, **Congo-Brazzaville**.

> The region was colonized in the 19th century by France, and as Middle Congo formed part of the larger territory of French Congo (later, French Equatorial Africa). The country became independent in 1960.

Congo, Democratic Republic of the a large equatorial country in central Africa with a short coastline on the Atlantic Ocean; pop. 68,692,500 (est. 2009); languages, French (official), Kongo, Lingala, Swahili, and others; capital, Kinshasa. Also called **Congo-Kinshasa**. Former name (1971–97) ZAIRE.

> The Democratic Republic of the Congo is a former Belgian colony, which was known as the Congo Free State (1885–1908) and the Belgian Congo (1908–60). Independence in 1960 was followed by civil war and UN intervention. General Mobutu seized control in a coup in 1965 and changed the name of the country from the Republic of the Congo to Zaire in 1971. The country experienced a huge influx of refugees following the violence in Rwanda in 1994, and

C

the first of three destructive civil wars broke out in 1996. Mobutu was overthrown in 1997 by Laurent Kabila, who changed the country's name to the Democratic Republic of the Congo.

Congolese /ˌkɒŋɡəˈliːz/ ▸ **adjective** relating to Congo or the Democratic Republic of the Congo (Zaire).
▸ **noun** (pl. **same**) **1** a native or inhabitant of Congo or the Democratic Republic of the Congo (Zaire).
2 [mass noun] any of the Bantu languages spoken in the Congo region, in particular Kikongo.
– ORIGIN from French *Congolais*.

Congo red ▸ **noun** [mass noun] a red-brown azo dye which becomes blue in acidic conditions, used as a chemical indicator and as a stain in histology.

congrats ▸ **plural noun** informal congratulations: [as exclamation] *congrats on your exams, Cal!*
– ORIGIN late 19th cent.: abbreviation.

congratulate ▸ **verb** [with obj.] give (someone) one's good wishes when something special or pleasant has happened to them: *he had taken the chance to **congratulate** him **on** his marriage.* ■ praise (someone) for an achievement: *the operators are to be **congratulated for** the service that they provide.* ■ (**congratulate oneself**) feel pride or satisfaction: *she **congratulated herself on** her powers of deduction.*
– DERIVATIVES **congratulator** noun, **congratulatory** adjective.
– ORIGIN mid 16th cent.: from Latin *congratulat-* 'congratulated', from the verb *congratulari*, from *con-* 'with' + *gratulari* 'show joy' (from *gratus* 'pleasing').

congratulation ▸ **noun** (**congratulations**) words expressing one's praise for an achievement or good wishes on a special occasion: *our congratulations to the winners* | [as exclamation] *congratulations on a job well done!* ■ [mass noun] the expression of such praise or good wishes: *he began pumping the hand of his son in congratulation.*
– ORIGIN late Middle English: from Latin *congratulatio(n-)*, from the verb *congratulari* (see **CONGRATULATE**).

congregant /ˈkɒŋɡrɪɡ(ə)nt/ ▸ **noun** a member of a congregation, especially that of a church or synagogue.
– ORIGIN late 19th cent.: from Latin *congregant-* 'collecting (into a flock), uniting', from the verb *congregare* (see **CONGREGATE**).

congregate ▸ **verb** [no obj.] gather into a crowd or mass: *some 4,000 demonstrators had congregated at a border point.*
– ORIGIN late Middle English: from Latin *congregat-* 'collected (into a flock), united', from the verb *congregare*, from *con-* 'together' + *gregare* (from *grex, greg-* 'a flock').

congregation ▸ **noun 1** a group of people assembled for religious worship. ■ a group of people regularly attending a particular place of worship: *he was a member of the Emmanuel Chapel congregation.*
2 a gathering or collection of people, animals, or things: *large congregations of birds may cause public harm.* ■ [mass noun] the action of gathering together in a crowd: *drought conditions lead to the congregation of animals around watering points.*
3 (often **Congregation**) (in the Roman Catholic Church) a permanent committee of the College of Cardinals: *the Congregation for the Doctrine of the Faith.* ■ Brit. (in some universities) a general assembly of resident senior members.
4 a group of people obeying a common religious rule but under less solemn vows than members of the older religious orders: *the sisters of the Congregation of Our Lady.* ■ a group of communities within a religious order sharing particular historical or regional links.
– ORIGIN late Middle English (in sense 2, sense 3, sense 4): from Latin *congregatio(n-)*, from *congregare* 'collect (into a flock)' (see **CONGREGATE**).

congregational ▸ **adjective 1** relating to a congregation: *congregational singing.*
2 (**Congregational**) of or adhering to Congregationalism: *the Congregational Church.*

Congregationalism ▸ **noun** [mass noun] a system of organization among Christian churches whereby individual local churches are largely self-governing.
– DERIVATIVES **Congregationalist** noun & adjective.

congress ▸ **noun 1** a formal meeting or series of meetings for discussion between delegates, especially those from a political party, trade union, or from within a particular sphere of activity: *an international congress of mathematicians.*
2 (**Congress**) a national legislative body, especially that of the US. The US Congress, which meets at the Capitol in Washington DC, was established by the Constitution of 1787 and is composed of the Senate and the House of Representatives.
3 (often in names) a political society or organization.
4 [mass noun] the action of coming together: *sexual congress.*
– DERIVATIVES **congressional** adjective, **congressionally** adverb.
– ORIGIN late Middle English (denoting an encounter during battle): from Latin *congressus*, from *congredi* 'meet', from *con-* 'together' + *gradi* 'walk'.

congressman (or **congresswoman**) ▸ **noun** (pl. **congressmen** or **congresswomen**) a member of the US Congress (also used as a form of address).

Congress of Industrial Organizations (abbrev.: **CIO**) a federation of North American trade unions, organized largely by industry rather than craft. In 1955 it merged with the American Federation of Labor to form the AFL-CIO.

Congreve /ˈkɒŋɡriːv/, William (1670–1729), English dramatist. A close associate of Swift, Pope, and Steele, he wrote plays such as *Love for Love* (1695) and *The Way of the World* (1700), which epitomize the wit and satire of Restoration comedy.

congruence /ˈkɒŋɡrʊəns/ ▸ **noun** [mass noun] agreement or harmony; compatibility: *the results show quite good **congruence with** recent studies.*
– DERIVATIVES **congruency** noun.

congruent /ˈkɒŋɡrʊənt/ ▸ **adjective 1** in agreement or harmony: *the rules may not be **congruent with** the requirements of the law* | *institutional and departmental objectives are very largely congruent.*
2 Geometry (of figures) identical in form; coinciding exactly when superimposed.
– DERIVATIVES **congruently** adverb.
– ORIGIN late Middle English: from Latin *congruent-* 'agreeing, meeting together', from the verb *congruere*, from *con-* 'together' + *ruere* 'fall or rush'.

congruous /ˈkɒŋɡrʊəs/ ▸ **adjective** in agreement or harmony: *this explanation is **congruous with** earlier observations.*
– DERIVATIVES **congruity** /kɒnˈɡruːɪti, kən-/ noun, **congruously** adverb.
– ORIGIN late 16th cent.: from Latin *congruus*, from *congruere* 'agree' (see **CONGRUENT**), + **-OUS**.

conic /ˈkɒnɪk/ Mathematics ▸ **adjective** of a cone.
▸ **noun** short for **CONIC SECTION**.
– ORIGIN late 16th cent.: from modern Latin *conicus*, from Greek *kōnikos*, from *kōnos* 'cone'.

conical ▸ **adjective** having the shape of a cone.
– DERIVATIVES **conically** adverb.

conical projection (also **conic projection**) ▸ **noun** a map projection in which an area of the earth is projected on to a cone, of which the vertex is usually above one of the poles.

conics ▸ **plural noun** [treated as sing.] the branch of mathematics concerned with conic sections.

conic section ▸ **noun** a figure formed by the intersection of a plane and a circular cone. Depending on the angle of the plane with respect to the cone, a conic section may be a circle, an ellipse, a parabola, or a hyperbola.

conidiophore /kəʊˈnɪdɪə(ʊ)fɔː/ ▸ **noun** Botany (in certain fungi) a conidium-bearing hypha or filament.
– ORIGIN late 19th cent.: from *conidio-* (combining form of **CONIDIUM**) + **-PHORE**.

conidium /kəʊˈnɪdɪəm/ ▸ **noun** (pl. **conidia** /-dɪə/) Botany a spore produced asexually by various fungi at the tip of a specialized hypha.
– ORIGIN late 19th cent.: modern Latin, from Greek *konis* 'dust' + the diminutive suffix *-idium*.

conifer /ˈkɒnɪfə, ˈkəʊn-/ ▸ **noun** a tree which bears cones and needle-like or scale-like leaves that are typically evergreen. Conifers are of major importance as the source of softwood, and also supply resins and turpentine. ● Order Coniferales, class Coniferopsida, subdivision Gymnospermae: several families, including the pines and firs (Pinaceae) and the cypresses (Cupressaceae).
– DERIVATIVES **coniferous** adjective.
– ORIGIN mid 19th cent.: from Latin, literally 'cone-bearing', from *conus* (see **CONE**).

coniform /ˈkəʊnɪfɔːm/ ▸ **adjective** rare having the shape of a cone.
– ORIGIN late 18th cent.: from Latin *conus* 'cone' + **-IFORM**.

coniine /ˈkəʊniːn/ ▸ **noun** [mass noun] Chemistry a volatile poisonous compound found in hemlock and other plants. It affects the motor nerves, causing paralysis and asphyxia. ● An alkaloid, 2-propylpiperidine; chem. formula: $C_8H_{17}N$.
– ORIGIN mid 19th cent.: from Latin *conium* (from Greek *kōneion* 'hemlock') + **-INE**[4].

conjectural ▸ **adjective** based on or involving conjecture: *the evidence was deemed too conjectural.*
– DERIVATIVES **conjecturally** adverb.
– ORIGIN mid 16th cent.: via French from Latin *conjecturalis*, from *conjectura* 'inference' (see **CONJECTURE**).

conjecture /kənˈdʒɛktʃə/ ▸ **noun** an opinion or conclusion formed on the basis of incomplete information: *conjectures about the newcomer were many and varied* | [mass noun] *a matter for conjecture.* ■ an unproven mathematical or scientific theorem. ■ [mass noun] (in textual criticism) the suggestion of a reading of a text not present in the original source.
▸ **verb** [reporting verb] form an opinion or supposition about (something) on the basis of incomplete information: [with clause] *many conjectured that she had a second husband in mind.* ■ (in textual criticism) propose (a reading).
– DERIVATIVES **conjecturable** adjective.
– ORIGIN late Middle English (in the senses 'to divine' and 'divination'): from Old French, or from Latin *conjectura*, from *conicere* 'put together in thought', from *con-* 'together' + *jacere* 'throw'.

conjoin ▸ **verb** [with obj.] formal join; combine: *an approach which conjoins theory and method.*
– ORIGIN late Middle English: from Old French *conjoindre*, from Latin *conjungere*, from *con-* 'together' + *jungere* 'to join'.

conjoined twins ▸ **plural noun** twins that are physically joined at birth, sometimes sharing organs, and sometimes separable by surgery (depending on the degree of fusion).

USAGE The term **conjoined twins** has supplanted **Siamese twins** in all contexts other than informal conversation.

conjoint ▸ **adjective** [attrib.] combining all or both people or things involved.
– DERIVATIVES **conjointly** adverb.
– ORIGIN Middle English: from Old French, past participle of *conjoindre* (see **CONJOIN**).

conjugal /ˈkɒndʒʊɡ(ə)l/ ▸ **adjective** relating to marriage or the relationship between husband and wife: *conjugal loyalty.*
– DERIVATIVES **conjugality** noun, **conjugally** adverb.
– ORIGIN early 16th cent.: from Latin *conjugalis*, from *conjux, conjug-* 'spouse', from *con-* 'together' + *jugum* 'a yoke'.

conjugal rights ▸ **plural noun** the rights, especially to sexual relations, regarded as exercisable in law by each partner in a marriage.

conjugate ▸ **verb** /ˈkɒndʒʊɡeɪt/ **1** [with obj.] Grammar give the different forms of (a verb in an inflected language such as Latin) as they vary according to voice, mood, tense, number, and person.
2 [no obj.] Biology (of bacteria or unicellular organisms) become temporarily united in order to exchange genetic material: *E. coli only conjugate when one of the cells possesses fertility genes.* ■ (of gametes) become fused.
3 [with obj.] Chemistry be combined with or joined to reversibly: *bilirubin is then conjugated by liver enzymes and excreted in the bile.*
▸ **adjective** /ˈkɒndʒʊɡət/ technical coupled, connected, or related, in particular: ■ Chemistry (of an acid or base) related to the corresponding base or acid by loss or gain of a proton. ■ Mathematics joined in a reciprocal relation, especially having the same real parts and equal magnitudes but opposite signs of imaginary parts. ■ Geometry (of angles) adding up to 360°; (of arcs) combining to form a complete circle. ■ Biology (of gametes) fused.
▸ **noun** /ˈkɒndʒʊɡət/ **1** chiefly Biochemistry a substance formed by the reversible combination of two or more others.
2 a mathematical value or entity having a reciprocal relation with another. See also **COMPLEX CONJUGATE**.
– DERIVATIVES **conjugacy** noun.
– ORIGIN late 15th cent. (as an adjective): from Latin *conjugat-* 'yoked together', from the verb *conjugare*, from *con-* 'together' + *jugum* 'yoke'.

conjugated ▸ **adjective 1** Chemistry relating to or denoting double or triple bonds in a molecule which are separated by a single bond, across which some sharing of electrons occurs.
2 chiefly Biochemistry (of a substance) reversibly combined with another: *conjugated bile salts.*

conjugate diameter ▶ **noun** Anatomy the distance between the front and rear of the pelvis.

conjugation ▶ **noun** [mass noun] **1** Grammar the variation of the form of a verb in an inflected language such as Latin, by which the voice, mood, tense, number, and person are identified. ■ [count noun] the class in which a verb is put according to the manner of this variation: *a past participle of the first conjugation.*
2 technical the formation or existence of a link between things, in particular: ■ Biology the temporary union of two bacteria or unicellular organisms for the exchange of genetic material. ■ Biology the fusion of two gametes, especially when they are of a similar size. ■ chiefly Biochemistry the combination of two substances: *toxic compounds eliminated from the body by conjugation with glutathione.* ■ Chemistry the sharing of electron density between nearby multiple bonds in a molecule. ■ Mathematics the solution of a problem by transforming it into an equivalent problem of a different form, solving this, and then reversing the transformation.
– DERIVATIVES **conjugational** adjective.
– ORIGIN late Middle English (in sense 1): from Latin *conjugatio(n-)*, from *conjugare* 'join together' (see CONJUGATE).

conjunct ▶ **adjective** /kən'dʒʌŋ(k)t/ joined together, combined, or associated. ■ Music relating to the movement of a melody between adjacent notes of the scale. ■ Astrology in conjunction with.
▶ **noun** /'kɒndʒʌŋ(k)t/ each of two or more things which are joined or associated. ■ Logic each of the terms of a conjunctive proposition. ■ Grammar an adverbial whose function is to join two sentences or other discourse units (e.g. *however, anyway, in the first place*).
– ORIGIN late Middle English: from Latin *conjunctus*, past participle of *conjungere* 'join together' (see CONJOIN).

conjunction ▶ **noun 1** Grammar a word used to connect clauses or sentences or to coordinate words in the same clause (e.g. *and, but, if*).
2 the action or an instance of two or more events or things occurring at the same point in time or space: *a conjunction of favourable political and economic circumstances | he postulated that the Americas were formed by the conjunction of floating islands.* ■ Astronomy & Astrology an alignment of two planets or other celestial objects so that they appear to be in the same, or nearly the same, place in the sky.
– PHRASES **in conjunction** together: *herbal medicine was used* ***in conjunction with*** *acupuncture and massage.*
– DERIVATIVES **conjunctional** adjective.
– ORIGIN late Middle English: via Old French from Latin *conjunctio(n-)*, from the verb *conjungere* (see CONJOIN).

conjunctiva /ˌkɒndʒʌŋ(k)'tʌɪvə, kən'dʒʌŋ(k)tɪvə/ ▶ **noun** (pl. **conjunctivae** /-iː/) Anatomy the mucous membrane that covers the front of the eye and lines the inside of the eyelids.
– DERIVATIVES **conjunctival** adjective.
– ORIGIN late Middle English: from medieval Latin *(membrana) conjunctiva* 'conjunctive (membrane)', from late Latin *conjunctivus*, from *conjungere* 'join together' (see CONJOIN).

conjunctive ▶ **adjective 1** relating to or forming a connection or combination of things: *the conjunctive tissue.* ■ involving the combination or co-occurrence of two or more conditions or properties.
2 Grammar of the nature of or relating to a conjunction.
▶ **noun** Grammar a word or expression acting as a conjunction.
– DERIVATIVES **conjunctively** adverb.
– ORIGIN late Middle English: from late Latin *conjunctivus*, from *conjungere* 'join together' (see CONJUNCT).

conjunctivitis /kənˌdʒʌŋ(k)tɪ'vʌɪtɪs/ ▶ **noun** [mass noun] Medicine inflammation of the conjunctiva of the eye.

conjuncture ▶ **noun** a combination of events: *the happy conjuncture of two facts.* ■ a state of affairs: *the wider political conjuncture.*
– ORIGIN early 17th cent.: from CONJUNCTION, by substitution of the suffix; influenced by obsolete French *conjuncture*, from Italian *congiuntura*, based on Latin *conjungere* 'join together' (see CONJOIN).

conjunto /kɒn'hʌntəʊ/ ▶ **noun** (pl. **conjuntos**) (in Latin America or Hispanic communities) a small musical group or band.
– ORIGIN Spanish, literally 'an ensemble, group'.

conjuration /ˌkʌndʒə'reɪʃ(ə)n, ˌkɒndʒʊ(ə)-/ ▶ **noun** a magic incantation or spell. ■ [mass noun] the performance of something supernatural by means of a magic incantation or spell.
– ORIGIN late Middle English (also in the sense 'conspiracy, the swearing of an oath together'): via Old French from Latin *conjuratio(n-)*, from *conjurare* (see CONJURE).

conjure /'kʌndʒə/ ▶ **verb 1** [with obj.] (often **conjure something up**) cause (a spirit or ghost) to appear by means of a magic ritual: *they hoped to conjure up the spirit of their dead friend.* ■ make (something) appear unexpectedly or seemingly from nowhere: *Anne conjured up a delicious home-made hotpot.* ■ call (an image) to the mind: *she had forgotten how to conjure up the image of her mother's face.* ■ (of a word, sound, smell, etc.) cause someone to think of (something): *a special tune that conjures up a particular time and place.*
2 /kən'dʒʊə, kən'dʒɔː/ [with obj. and infinitive] archaic implore (someone) to do something.
– PHRASES **a name to conjure with** used to indicate that a particular person is very important or well regarded: *on the merger scene his is a name to conjure with.*
– ORIGIN Middle English (also in the sense 'oblige by oath'): from Old French *conjurer* 'to plot or exorcise', from Latin *conjurare* 'band together by an oath, conspire' (in medieval Latin 'invoke'), from *con-* 'together' + *jurare* 'swear'.

conjuring ▶ **noun** [mass noun] the performance of tricks which are seemingly magical, typically involving sleight of hand: [as modifier] *a conjuring trick.*

conjuror (also **conjurer**) ▶ **noun** a performer of conjuring tricks.
– ORIGIN Middle English: partly from CONJURE, partly from Old French *conjureor, conjurere*, from medieval Latin *conjurator*, from Latin *conjurare* 'conspire' (see CONJURE).

conk[1] ▶ **verb** [no obj.] (**conk out**) informal (of a machine) break down: *my car conked out.* ■ (of a person) faint or go to sleep: *he conked out on the rear seat.* ■ die.
– ORIGIN First World War: of unknown origin.

conk[2] informal ▶ **noun 1** Brit. a person's nose.
2 dated a person's head. ■ a blow to the head.
▶ **verb** [with obj.] hit (someone) on the head: *the clown conked him.*
– ORIGIN early 19th cent.: perhaps an alteration of CONCH.

conker ▶ **noun** Brit. the hard, shiny dark brown nut of a horse chestnut tree. ■ (**conkers**) [treated as sing.] a children's game in which each has a conker on the end of a string and takes turns in trying to break another's with it.
– ORIGIN mid 19th cent. (a dialect word denoting a snail shell, with which the game, or a form of it, was originally played): perhaps from CONCH, but associated with (and frequently spelled) CONQUER in the 19th and early 20th cents: an alternative name was *conquerors*.

conman ▶ **noun** informal a man who cheats or tricks someone by means of a confidence trick.

con moto /kɒn 'məʊtəʊ/ ▶ **adverb** Music (especially as a direction) with movement: *andante con moto.*
– ORIGIN Italian.

conn ▶ **verb** US spelling of CON[4].

Conn. ▶ **abbreviation** Connecticut.

Connacht /'kɒnɔːt/ (also **Connaught**) a province in the west of the Republic of Ireland.

connate /'kɒneɪt/ ▶ **adjective 1** Philosophy (especially of ideas or principles) existing in a person or thing from birth; innate.
2 Biology (of parts) united so as to form a single part.
3 Geology (of water) trapped in sedimentary rock during its deposition.
– ORIGIN mid 17th cent.: from late Latin *connatus*, past participle of *connasci*, from *con-* 'together' + *nasci* 'be born'.

connatural ▶ **adjective** belonging naturally; innate.
– ORIGIN late 16th cent.: from late Latin *connaturalis*, from *con-* 'together' + Latin *naturalis* 'natural'.

Connaught variant spelling of CONNACHT.

connect ▶ **verb** [with obj.] **1** bring together or into contact so that a real or notional link is established: *the electrodes were* ***connected to*** *a recording device* | (as adj. **connected**) *a connected series of cargo holds.* ■ join together so as to provide access and communication: *all the buildings are connected by underground passages* | [no obj.] *the motorway* ***connects with*** *major routes from all parts of the country.* ■ link to a power or water supply: *by 1892 most of the village had been* ***connected to*** *the mains.* ■ put (someone) into contact by telephone: *I was quickly* ***connected to*** *the police.* ■ [no obj.] (of a train, bus, aircraft, etc.) be timed to arrive at its destination just before another train, bus, etc., departs so that passengers can transfer: *the bus* ***connects with*** *trains from Windermere station* | (as adj. **connecting**) *we missed the connecting flight to the USA.*
2 associate or relate (something) in some respect: *employees are rewarded with bonuses* ***connected to*** *their firm's performance | jobs* ***connected with*** *the environment.* ■ provide or have a link or relationship with: *there was no evidence to* ***connect*** *Jefferson with the theft* | [no obj.] *the desire for religious faith* ***connects up with*** *profound needs at the core of our existence.* ■ [no obj.] form a relationship or feel an affinity: *he can't* ***connect with*** *anyone any more.*
3 [no obj.] informal (of a blow) hit the intended target: *the blow connected and he felt a burst of pain.*
– DERIVATIVES **connectable** adjective, **connectedly** adverb, **connectedness** noun.
– ORIGIN late Middle English (in the sense 'be united physically'; rare before the 18th cent.): from Latin *connectere*, from *con-* 'together' + *nectere* 'bind'.

Connecticut /kə'nɛtɪkət/ **1** a state in the north-eastern US, on the Atlantic coast; capital, Hartford; pop. 3,501,252 (est. 2008). It was one of the original thirteen states of the Union and ratified the draft US Constitution in 1788.
2 the longest river in New England, rising in northern New Hampshire and flowing south for 655 km (407 miles) to enter Long Island Sound.

connecting rod ▶ **noun** a rod connecting two moving parts in a mechanism, especially that between the piston and the crankpin (or equivalent parts) in an engine or pump.

connection (Brit. also **connexion**) ▶ **noun 1** a relationship in which a person or thing is linked or associated with something else: *the* ***connections*** ***between*** *social attitudes and productivity | sufferers deny that their problems have any* ***connection with*** *drugs.* ■ [mass noun] the action of linking one thing with another: *connection to the Internet.* ■ [mass noun] the placing of parts of an electric circuit in contact so that a current may flow. ■ a link between electrical components or pipes: *ensure that all connections between the wires are properly made.* ■ a link between two telephones: *she replaced the receiver before the connection was made.* ■ an arrangement or opportunity for catching a connecting train, bus, aircraft, etc.: *ferry connections are sporadic in the low season.* ■ a connecting train, bus, etc.: *we had to wait for our connection to Frankfurt.* ■ (**connections**) people with whom one has social or professional contact or to whom one is related, especially those with influence and able to offer one help: *he had connections with the music industry.*
2 informal, chiefly N. Amer. a supplier of narcotics. ■ a narcotics sale or purchase.
3 chiefly historical an association of Methodist Churches.
– PHRASES **in connection with** with reference to; concerning: *detectives are questioning two men in connection with alleged criminal damage.* **in this** (or **that**) **connection** with reference to this (or that): *the local Marine Surveyor should be able to assist in this connection.*
– DERIVATIVES **connectional** adjective.
– ORIGIN late Middle English: from Latin *connexio(n-)*, from *connectere* (see CONNECT). The spelling *-ct* (18th cent.) is from *connect*, on the pattern of pairs such as *collect, collection*.

connectionism ▶ **noun** [mass noun] an artificial intelligence approach to cognition in which multiple connections between nodes (equivalent to brain cells) form a massive interactive network in which many processes take place simultaneously and certain processes, operating in parallel, are grouped together in hierarchies that bring about results such as thought or action. Also called PARALLEL DISTRIBUTED PROCESSING.

connective ▶ **adjective** connecting: *connective words and phrases.*
▶ **noun 1** Grammar a word or phrase whose function is to link other linguistic units.
2 Anatomy a bundle of nerve fibres connecting two nerve centres or ganglia, especially in invertebrate animals.

connective tissue ▶ **noun** [mass noun] Anatomy tissue that connects, supports, binds, or separates other tissues or organs, typically having relatively few cells embedded in an amorphous matrix, often with collagen or other fibres, and including cartilaginous, fatty, and elastic tissues.

connectivity ▶ **noun** [mass noun] the state of being connected or interconnected. ■ Computing capacity for the interconnection of platforms, systems, and applications.

connector ▸ noun a thing which links two or more things together: *a pipe connector.* ■ a device for keeping two parts of an electric circuit in contact.

Connemara /ˌkɒnɪˈmɑːrə/ a mountainous coastal region of Galway, in the west of the Republic of Ireland.

Connery /ˈkɒnəri/, Sir Sean (b.1930), Scottish film actor best known for his portrayal of James Bond; born *Thomas Connery*.

connexion ▸ noun variant spelling of CONNECTION.

conning tower /ˈkɒnɪŋ/ ▸ noun the superstructure of a submarine, from which it can be commanded when on the surface and which contains the periscope.

conniption /kəˈnɪpʃ(ə)n/ ▸ noun N. Amer. informal a fit of rage or hysterics: *his client was **having conniptions** on the phone.*
– ORIGIN mid 19th cent.: probably an invented word.

connivance ▸ noun [mass noun] willingness to allow or be secretly involved in an immoral or illegal act: *this infringement of the law had taken place with the **connivance of** officials.*
– ORIGIN late 16th cent. (also in the Latin sense 'winking'): from French *connivence* or Latin *conniventia*, from *connivere* 'shut the eyes (to)' (see CONNIVE).

connive /kəˈnʌɪv/ ▸ verb [no obj.] (**connive at/in**) secretly allow (something immoral, illegal, or harmful) to occur: *government officials were prepared to connive in impeding the course of justice.* ■ (usu. **connive to do something**) conspire to do something immoral, illegal, or harmful: *she **connived with** a senior official to rig the results of last year's election.*
– DERIVATIVES **conniver** noun.
– ORIGIN early 17th cent.: from French *conniver* or Latin *connivere* 'shut the eyes (to)', from *con-* 'together' + an unrecorded word related to *nictare* 'to wink'.

conniving /kəˈnʌɪvɪŋ/ ▸ adjective given to or involved in conspiring to do something immoral, illegal, or harmful: *a heartless and conniving woman.*

connoisseur /ˌkɒnəˈsəː/ ▸ noun an expert judge in matters of taste: *a **connoisseur of** music.*
– DERIVATIVES **connoisseurship** noun.
– ORIGIN early 18th cent.: from obsolete French, from *conoistre* 'know'.

Connolly[1] /ˈkɒnəli/, Cyril (Vernon) (1903–74), English writer and journalist. His works include one novel, *The Rock Pool* (1936), and collections of essays, aphorisms, and reflections, among which are *Enemies of Promise* (1938) and *The Unquiet Grave* (1944).

Connolly[2] /ˈkɒnəli/, Maureen Catherine (1934–69), American tennis player; known as **Little Mo**. She was 16 when she first won the US singles title and 17 when she took the Wimbledon title. In 1953 she became the first woman to win the grand slam before being forced to retire in 1954 after a riding accident.

connotation /kɒnəˈteɪʃ(ə)n/ ▸ noun an idea or feeling which a word invokes for a person in addition to its literal or primary meaning: *the word 'discipline' has unhappy connotations of punishment and repression.* ■ [mass noun] the implying of such ideas or feelings: *the work functions both by analogy and by connotation.* ■ Philosophy the abstract meaning or intension of a term, which forms a principle determining which objects or concepts it applies to. Often contrasted with DENOTATION.
– ORIGIN mid 16th cent.: from medieval Latin *connotatio(n-)*, from *connotare* 'mark in addition' (see CONNOTE).

connote /kəˈnəʊt/ ▸ verb [with obj.] (of a word) imply or suggest (an idea or feeling) in addition to the literal or primary meaning: *the term 'modern science' usually connotes a complete openness to empirical testing.* ■ (of a fact) imply as a consequence or condition: *spinsterhood connoted failure.*
– DERIVATIVES **connotative** /ˈkɒnəteɪtɪv, kəˈnəʊtətɪv/ adjective.
– ORIGIN mid 17th cent.: from medieval Latin *connotare* 'mark in addition', from *con-* 'together with' + *notare* 'to note' (from *nota* 'a mark').

USAGE **Connote** does not mean the same as **denote**. Whereas **denote** refers to the literal, primary meaning of something, **connote** refers to other characteristics suggested or implied by that thing. Thus, one might say that a word like **mother** *denotes* 'a woman who is a parent' but *connotes* qualities such as protection and affection.

connubial /kəˈnjuːbɪəl/ ▸ adjective literary relating to marriage or the relationship of husband and wife; conjugal: *their connubial bed.*
– DERIVATIVES **connubiality** noun,.
– ORIGIN mid 17th cent.: from Latin *connubialis*, from *connubium* 'marriage', from *con-* 'with' + *nubere* 'marry'.

conodont /ˈkəʊnədɒnt/ ▸ noun (also **conodont animal**) a fossil marine animal of the Cambrian to Triassic periods, having a long worm-like body, numerous small teeth, and a pair of eyes. It is now believed to be the earliest vertebrate. ● Class Conodonta, phylum Chordata: numerous families.
■ (also **conodont element**) a tooth of the conodont, often found as a fossil.
– ORIGIN mid 19th cent.: from modern Latin *Conodonta* (plural), from Greek *kōnos* 'cone' + *odous, odont-* 'tooth'.

conoid /ˈkəʊnɔɪd/ chiefly Zoology ▸ adjective (also **conoidal**) approximately conical in shape.
▸ noun a conoid object.

conquer ▸ verb [with obj.] overcome and take control of (a place or people) by military force: *he conquered Cyprus* | figurative *they've conquered new markets in Japan.* ■ successfully overcome (a problem or weakness): *a fear she never managed to conquer.* ■ climb (a mountain) successfully: *the second Briton to conquer Everest.* ■ gain the love, admiration, or respect of (a person or group of people): *the Beatles were to leave Liverpool and conquer the world.*
– DERIVATIVES **conquerable** adjective.
– ORIGIN Middle English (also in the general sense 'acquire, attain'): from Old French *conquerre*, based on Latin *conquirere* 'gain, win', from *con-* (expressing completion) + *quaerere* 'seek'.

conqueror ▸ noun a person who conquers a place or people; a vanquisher: *a people ruled over by a foreign conqueror* | figurative *a chance for revenge against his Olympic conqueror.*

conquest ▸ noun [mass noun] the subjugation and assumption of control of a place or people by military force: *the conquest of the Aztecs by the Spanish.* ■ [count noun] a territory which has been gained in such a way: *colonial conquests.* ■ (**the Conquest**) the invasion and assumption of control of England by William of Normandy in 1066. ■ the overcoming of a problem or weakness: *the conquest of inflation.* ■ the successful ascent of a mountain, especially one not previously climbed: *the conquest of Everest.* ■ [count noun] a person whose affection or favour has been won.
– ORIGIN Middle English: from Old French *conquest(e)*, based on Latin *conquirere* (see CONQUER).

conquistador /kɒnˈkwɪstədɔː, -ˈkɪst-/ ▸ noun (pl. **conquistadores** /-ˈdɔːreɪz/ or **conquistadors**) a conqueror, especially one of the Spanish conquerors of Mexico and Peru in the 16th century.
– ORIGIN mid 19th cent.: Spanish.

Conrad, Joseph (1857–1924), Polish-born British novelist; born *Józef Teodor Konrad Korzeniowski.* Much of his work, including his story *Heart of Darkness* (1902) and the novel *Nostromo* (1904), explores the darkness within human nature.

con rod ▸ noun Brit. informal term for CONNECTING ROD.

Cons. ▸ abbreviation Conservative.

consanguine /kɒnˈsaŋgwɪn/ ▸ adjective another term for CONSANGUINEOUS.

consanguineous /ˌkɒnsaŋˈgwɪnɪəs/ ▸ adjective relating to or denoting people descended from the same ancestor: *consanguineous marriages may give rise to recessive syndromes.*
– DERIVATIVES **consanguinity** noun.
– ORIGIN early 17th cent.: from Latin *consanguineus* 'of the same blood' (from *con-* 'together' + *sanguis* 'blood') + -OUS.

conscience ▸ noun a person's moral sense of right and wrong, viewed as acting as a guide to one's behaviour: *he had a **guilty conscience** about his desires* | [mass noun] *Ben was suffering a pang of conscience.*
– PHRASES **in (all) conscience** given the fact that this is probably wrong; in fairness: *how can we in all conscience justify the charging of fees for such a service?* **on one's conscience** weighing heavily and guiltily on one's mind: *an act of providence had prevented him from having a death on his conscience.*
– DERIVATIVES **conscienceless** adjective.
– ORIGIN Middle English (also in the sense 'inner thoughts or knowledge'): via Old French from Latin *conscientia*, from *conscient-* 'being privy to', from the verb *conscire*, from *con-* 'with' + *scire* 'know'.

conscience clause ▸ noun chiefly N. Amer. a clause in a law providing for exemption or other allowances on the grounds of moral or religious conscience.

conscience money ▸ noun [mass noun] money paid because of feelings of guilt, especially about a payment that one has evaded.

conscience-stricken ▸ adjective made uneasy by a guilty conscience: *she was still conscience-stricken over her outburst.*

conscientious /ˌkɒnʃɪˈɛnʃəs/ ▸ adjective **1** wishing to do one's work or duty well and thoroughly: *a conscientious man, he took his duties very seriously.* **2** relating to a person's conscience: *the individual is denied even the opportunity to break the law on conscientious grounds.*
– DERIVATIVES **conscientiously** adverb, **conscientiousness** noun.
– ORIGIN early 17th cent.: from French *consciencieux*, from medieval Latin *conscientiosus*, from Latin *conscientia* (see CONSCIENCE).

conscientious objector ▸ noun a person who for reasons of conscience objects to serving in the armed forces.
– DERIVATIVES **conscientious objection** noun.

conscious ▸ adjective **1** aware of and responding to one's surroundings: *although I was in pain, I was conscious.* **2** having knowledge of something: *we are **conscious of** the extent of the problem.* ■ [in combination] concerned with or worried about a particular matter: *they were growing increasingly security-conscious.* **3** (of an action or feeling) deliberate and intentional: *a conscious effort to walk properly.* ■ (of the mind or a thought) directly perceptible to and under the control of the person concerned.
– DERIVATIVES **consciously** adverb.
– ORIGIN late 16th cent. (in the sense 'being aware of wrongdoing'): from Latin *conscius* 'knowing with others or in oneself' (from *conscire* 'be privy to') + -OUS.

consciousness ▸ noun **1** [mass noun] the state of being aware of and responsive to one's surroundings: *she failed to regain consciousness and died two days later.* **2** a person's awareness or perception of something: *her acute consciousness of Luke's presence.* ■ the fact of awareness by the mind of itself and the world.

consciousness-raising ▸ noun [mass noun] the activity of seeking to make people more aware of personal, social, or political issues: [as modifier] *a consciousness-raising group.*

conscript ▸ verb /kənˈskrɪpt/ [with obj.] enlist (someone) compulsorily, typically into the armed services: *they were **conscripted into** the army.*
▸ noun /ˈkɒnskrɪpt/ a person enlisted compulsorily.
– ORIGIN late 18th cent. (as a noun): from French *conscrit*, from Latin *conscriptus*, past participle of *conscribere* 'enrol'. The verb is a back-formation from CONSCRIPTION.

conscription ▸ noun [mass noun] compulsory enlistment for state service, typically into the armed forces.
– ORIGIN early 19th cent.: via French (conscription was introduced in France in 1798), from late Latin *conscriptio(n-)* 'levying of troops', from Latin *conscribere* 'write down together, enrol', from *con-* 'together' + *scribere* 'write'.

consecrate /ˈkɒnsɪkreɪt/ ▸ verb [with obj.] make or declare (something, typically a church) sacred; dedicate formally to a religious purpose: *the present Holy Trinity church was consecrated in 1845* | (as adj. **consecrated**) *consecrated ground.* ■ (in Christian belief) declare (bread and wine) to be or represent the body and blood of Christ: (as adj. **consecrated**) *they received the host but not the consecrated wine.* ■ ordain (someone) to a sacred office, typically that of bishop: [with obj. and complement] *he was consecrated bishop of York.* ■ informal devote (something) exclusively to a particular purpose: *the gun room was a male preserve, **consecrated to** sport.*
– DERIVATIVES **consecration** noun, **consecrator** noun, **consecratory** adjective.
– ORIGIN late Middle English: from Latin *consecrat-* 'dedicated, devoted as sacred', from the verb *consecrare*, from *con-* (expressing intensive force) + *sacrare* 'dedicate', from *sacer* 'sacred'.

consecutive /kənˈsɛkjʊtɪv/ ▸ adjective **1** following each other continuously: *five consecutive months of serious decline.* ■ in unbroken or logical sequence. **2** Grammar expressing consequence or result: *a consecutive clause.*

3 Music denoting intervals of the same kind (especially fifths or octaves) occurring in succession between two parts or voices.
– DERIVATIVES **consecutively** adverb, **consecutiveness** noun.
– ORIGIN early 17th cent.: from French *consécutif, -ive*, from medieval Latin *consecutivus*, from Latin *consecut-* 'followed closely', from the verb *consequi*.

consensual /kən'sɛnsjʊəl, -ʃʊəl/ ▶ **adjective** relating to or involving consent or consensus: *consensual sexual activity*.
– DERIVATIVES **consensually** adverb.
– ORIGIN mid 18th cent.: from Latin *consensus* 'agreement' (from *consens-* 'felt together, agreed', from the verb *consentire*) + **-AL**.

consensus /kən'sɛnsəs/ ▶ **noun** [usu. in sing.] a general agreement: [with clause] *there is a growing consensus that the current regime has failed* | [as modifier] *a consensus view*.
– ORIGIN mid 17th cent.: from Latin, 'agreement', from *consens-* 'agreed', from the verb *consentire*.

consensus sequence ▶ **noun** Biochemistry a sequence of DNA having similar structure and function in different organisms.

consent ▶ **noun** [mass noun] permission for something to happen or agreement to do something: *no change may be made without the consent of all the partners*.
▶ **verb** [no obj.] give permission for something to happen: *he consented to a search by a detective*. ■ [with infinitive] agree to do something: *he had consented to serve as external assessor on the panel*.
– PHRASES **by common consent** with the agreement of all. **informed consent** permission granted in full knowledge of the possible consequences, typically that which is given by a patient to a doctor for treatment with knowledge of the possible risks and benefits.
– ORIGIN Middle English: from Old French *consente* (noun), *consentir* (verb), from Latin *consentire*, from *con-* 'together' + *sentire* 'feel'.

consentient /kən'sɛnʃ(ə)nt/ ▶ **adjective** archaic of the same opinion in a matter; in agreement.
– ORIGIN early 17th cent.: from Latin *consentient-* 'agreeing', from the verb *consentire* (see **CONSENT**).

consenting adult ▶ **noun** an adult who willingly agrees to engage in a sexual act.

consequence ▶ **noun 1** a result or effect, typically one that is unwelcome or unpleasant: *abrupt withdrawal of drug treatment can have serious consequences* | *many have been laid off from work* **as a consequence of** *government policies*.
2 [mass noun] [usu. with negative] importance or relevance: *the past is* **of no consequence**. ■ dated social distinction: *a woman* **of consequence**.
3 (**consequences**) [treated as sing.] a game in which a narrative is made up by the players in turn, each ignorant of what has already been contributed.
– PHRASES **in consequence** as a result. **take** (or **bear**) **the consequences** accept responsibility for the negative results or effects of one's choice or action.
– ORIGIN late Middle English: via Old French from Latin *consequentia*, from *consequent-* 'following closely', from the verb *consequi*.

consequent ▶ **adjective 1** following as a result or effect: *the social problems of pupils and their consequent educational difficulties* | *you've got a university place* **consequent on** *your exam results*. ■ archaic logically consistent.
2 Geology (of a stream or valley) having a direction or character determined by the original slope of the land before erosion.
▶ **noun 1** Logic the second part of a conditional proposition, whose truth is stated to be implied by that of the antecedent.
2 Music the second or imitating voice or part in a canon.
– ORIGIN late Middle English: via Old French from Latin *consequent-* 'overtaking, following closely', from the verb *consequi*.

consequential ▶ **adjective 1** following as a result or effect: *a loss of confidence and a consequential withdrawal of funds*. ■ Law resulting from an act, but not immediately and directly: *consequential damages*.
2 important; significant: *the new congress lacked consequential leaders*.
– DERIVATIVES **consequentiality** noun, **consequentially** adverb.
– ORIGIN early 17th cent.: from Latin *consequentia* (see **CONSEQUENCE**) + **-AL**.

consequentialism ▶ **noun** [mass noun] Philosophy the doctrine that the morality of an action is to be judged solely by its consequences.
– DERIVATIVES **consequentialist** adjective & noun.

consequently ▶ **adverb** as a result: *flexible workers find themselves in great demand, and consequently gain high salaries*.

conservancy /kən'səːv(ə)nsi/ ▶ **noun** (pl. **conservancies**) **1** [in names] a body concerned with the preservation of natural resources: *the Nature Conservancy*. ■ a commission controlling a port, river, or catchment area.
2 [mass noun] the conservation of wildlife and the environment.
– ORIGIN mid 18th cent.: alteration of obsolete *conservacy*, from Anglo-Norman French *conservacie*, via Anglo-Latin from Latin *conservatio* (see **CONSERVATION**).

conservation ▶ **noun** [mass noun] **1** the action of conserving something, in particular: ■ preservation, protection, or restoration of the natural environment and of wildlife. ■ preservation and repair of archaeological, historical, and cultural sites and artefacts. ■ prevention of wasteful use of a resource.
2 Physics the principle by which the total value of a physical quantity or parameter (such as energy, mass, linear or angular momentum) remains constant in a system which is not subject to external influence.
– DERIVATIVES **conservational** adjective.
– ORIGIN late Middle English: from Latin *conservatio(n-)*, from the verb *conservare* (see **CONSERVE**).

conservation area ▶ **noun** Brit. an area of notable environmental or historical interest or importance which is protected by law against undesirable changes.

conservationist ▶ **noun** a person who advocates or acts for the protection and preservation of the environment and wildlife: [as modifier] *conservationist groups*.

conservative ▶ **adjective 1** averse to change or innovation and holding traditional values: *they were very conservative in their outlook*. ■ (of dress or taste) sober and conventional: *a conservative suit*.
2 (in a political context) favouring free enterprise, private ownership, and socially conservative ideas. ■ (**Conservative**) relating to the Conservative Party of Great Britain or a similar party elsewhere.
3 (of an estimate) purposely low for the sake of caution: *police placed the value of the haul at a conservative £500,000*.
4 (of surgery or medical treatment) intended to control rather than eliminate a condition, with existing tissue preserved as far as possible.
▶ **noun 1** a person who is averse to change and holds traditional values.
2 (**Conservative**) a supporter or member of the Conservative Party of Great Britain or a similar party elsewhere.
– PHRASES **conservative with a small 'c'** said of someone who is conservative in outlook but does not necessarily vote for or support a Conservative party: *I think there are a good number of teachers who are instinctively conservative with a small c*.
– DERIVATIVES **conservatism** noun, **conservatively** adverb, **conservativeness** noun.
– ORIGIN late Middle English (in the sense 'aiming to preserve'): from late Latin *conservativus*, from *conservat-* 'conserved', from the verb *conservare* (see **CONSERVE**). Current senses date from the mid 19th cent.

Conservative Judaism ▶ **noun** [mass noun] a form of Judaism, particularly prevalent in North America, which seeks to preserve Jewish tradition and ritual but has a more flexible approach to the interpretation of the law than Orthodox Judaism.

Conservative Party ▶ **noun** a political party promoting free enterprise and private ownership, in particular a major British party that since the Second World War has been in power 1951–64, 1970–4, and 1979–97. It emerged from the old Tory Party under Sir Robert Peel in the 1830s and 1840s.

conservatoire /kən'səːvətwɑː/ ▶ **noun** Brit. a college for the study of classical music or other arts, typically in the continental European tradition.
– ORIGIN late 18th cent.: French, from Italian *conservatorio*, from late Latin *conservatorium*, from *conservare* 'to preserve' (see **CONSERVE**). Compare with **CONSERVATORY**.

conservator /'kɒnsə,veɪtə, kən'səːvətə/ ▶ **noun** a person responsible for the repair and preservation of things of cultural or environmental interest, such as buildings or works of art.

conservatorium /kən,səːvə'tɔːrɪəm/ ▶ **noun** (pl. **conservatoriums** or **conservatoria**) Australian term for **CONSERVATOIRE**.
– ORIGIN mid 19th cent.: from German *Konservatorium* and modern Latin.

conservatory ▶ **noun** (pl. **conservatories**) **1** Brit. a room with a glass roof and walls, attached to a house at one side and used as a sun lounge or for growing delicate plants.
2 N. Amer. another term for **CONSERVATOIRE**.
– ORIGIN mid 16th cent. (denoting something that preserves): from late Latin *conservatorium*, from *conservare* 'to preserve' (see **CONSERVE**).

conserve /kən'səːv/ ▶ **verb** [with obj.] protect (something, especially something of environmental or cultural importance) from harm or destruction: *the funds raised will help conserve endangered meadowlands*. ■ prevent the wasteful overuse of (a resource): *industry should conserve more water*. ■ Physics maintain (a quantity such as energy) at a constant overall total. ■ Biochemistry retain (a particular amino acid, nucleotide, or sequence of these) unchanged in different protein or DNA molecules.
▶ **noun** also /'kɒnsəːv/ [mass noun] a preparation made by preserving fruit with sugar; jam or marmalade.
– ORIGIN late Middle English: from Old French *conserver* (verb), *conserve* (noun), from Latin *conservare* 'to preserve', from *con-* 'together' + *servare* 'to keep'.

consider ▶ **verb** [with obj.] **1** think carefully about (something), typically before making a decision: *each application is considered on its merits* | (as adj. **considered**) *I may not have time to give a considered reply to suggestions*. ■ believe to be; think: [with obj. and infinitive] *at first women were considered to be at low risk from HIV* | [with clause] *I don't consider that I'm to blame*. ■ [with obj. and complement] regard (someone or something) as having a specified quality: *I consider him irresponsible*. ■ take (something) into account when making a judgement: *one service area is not enough when you consider the number of cars using this motorway*.
2 look attentively at: *the old man considered his granddaughter thoughtfully*.
– PHRASES **all things considered** taking everything into account.
– ORIGIN late Middle English: from Old French *considerer*, from Latin *considerare* 'examine', perhaps based on *sidus, sider-* 'star'.

considerable ▶ **adjective** notably large in size, amount, or extent: *a position of considerable influence*. ■ (of a person) having merit or distinction: *Snow was a limited, but still considerable, novelist*.
– ORIGIN late Middle English (in the sense 'capable of being considered'): from medieval Latin *considerabilis* 'worthy of consideration', from Latin *considerare* (see **CONSIDER**).

considerably ▶ **adverb** by a notably large amount or to a notably large extent; greatly: *things have improved considerably over the last few years* | [as submodifier] *a considerably higher density*.

considerate ▶ **adjective 1** careful not to inconvenience or harm others: *she was unfailingly kind and considerate*.
2 archaic showing careful thought: *be considerate over your handwriting*.
– DERIVATIVES **considerately** adverb, **considerateness** noun.
– ORIGIN late 16th cent. (in the sense 'showing careful thought'): from Latin *consideratus*, past participle of *considerare* 'examine' (see **CONSIDER**).

consideration ▶ **noun 1** [mass noun] careful thought, typically over a period of time. ■ [count noun] a fact or a motive taken into account in deciding something: *the idea was motivated by political considerations*. ■ thoughtfulness and sensitivity towards others: *companies should show more consideration for their employees*.
2 a payment or reward: *you can buy the books for a small consideration*. ■ Law (in a contractual agreement) anything given or promised or forborne by one party in exchange for the promise or undertaking of another.
3 archaic importance; esteem.
– PHRASES **in consideration of** in return for; on account of: *he paid them in consideration of their services*. **take into consideration** take into account. **under consideration** being thought about: *the abolition of the House of Lords was under consideration*.
– ORIGIN late Middle English: via Old French from Latin *consideratio(n-)*, from *considerare* 'examine'.

C

considering ▶ preposition & conjunction taking into consideration: [as prep.] *considering the circumstances, Simon was remarkably phlegmatic* | [as conjunction] ***considering that** he was the youngest on the field he played well.*
▶ **adverb** informal taking everything into account: *they weren't feeling too bad, considering.*

consigliere /ˌkɒnsɪˈljɛːreɪ/ ▶ noun (pl. **consiglieri** pronunc. **same**) a member of a Mafia family who serves as an adviser to the leader and resolves disputes within the family.
– ORIGIN Italian, literally 'a member of a council'.

consign /kənˈsʌɪn/ ▶ verb [with obj.] deliver (something) to a person's keeping: *he **consigned** three paintings **to** Sotheby's.* ■ send (goods) by a public carrier. ■ (**consign someone/thing to**) put someone or something in (a place) in order to be rid of it or them: *she consigned the letter to the waste-paper basket.*
– DERIVATIVES **consignee** noun, **consignor** noun.
– ORIGIN late Middle English (in the sense 'mark with the sign of the cross', especially at baptism or confirmation, as a sign of dedication to God): from French *consigner* or Latin *consignare* 'mark with a seal'.

consignment ▶ noun a batch of goods destined for or delivered to someone: *a consignment of drugs.* ■ [mass noun] the action of consigning or delivering something.

consignment store ▶ noun N. Amer. a shop that sells second-hand items on behalf of the original owner, who receives a percentage of the selling price.

consilience /kənˈsɪlɪəns/ ▶ noun [mass noun] agreement between the approaches to a topic of different academic subjects, especially science and the humanities.
– DERIVATIVES **consilient** adjective.
– ORIGIN mid 19th cent.: from **CON-** + Latin *-silient-, -siliens* 'jumping' (as in *resilient*- **RESILIENT**), after **CONCURRENT**.

consist ▶ verb /kənˈsɪst/ [no obj.] **1** (**consist of**) be composed or made up of: *the crew consists of five men.* ■ (**consist in**) have as an essential feature: *his poetry consisted in the use of emotive language.*
2 (**consist with**) archaic be consistent with: *the information perfectly consists with our friend's account.*
▶ **noun** /ˈkɒnsɪst/ Railways the set of vehicles forming a complete train.
– ORIGIN late Middle English (in the sense 'be located or inherent in'): from Latin *consistere* 'stand firm or still, exist', from *con-* 'together' + *sistere* 'stand (still)'.

consistency (also **consistence**) ▶ noun (pl. **consistencies**) [mass noun] **1** consistent behaviour or treatment: *the consistency of measurement techniques.* ■ the quality of achieving a level of performance which does not vary greatly in quality over time.
2 the way in which a substance holds together; thickness or viscosity: *the sauce has the consistency of creamed butter.*
– ORIGIN late 16th cent. (denoting permanence of form): from late Latin *consistentia*, from *consistent-* 'standing firm' (see **CONSISTENT**).

consistent ▶ adjective **1** acting or done in the same way over time, especially so as to be fair or accurate: *the parents are being consistent and firm in their reactions* | *a consistent worldwide application of its policies.* ■ unchanging in nature, standard, or effect over time: *he is Rangers' most consistent player this season* | *the mixtures are of consistent quality.*
2 (of an argument or set of ideas) not containing any logical contradictions: *a consistent explanation.*
3 [predic.] compatible or in agreement with something: *the injuries are **consistent with** falling from a great height.*
– DERIVATIVES **consistently** adverb.
– ORIGIN late 16th cent. (in the sense 'consisting or composed of'): from Latin *consistent-* 'standing firm or still, existing', from the verb *consistere* (see **CONSIST**).

consistory /kənˈsɪst(ə)ri/ ▶ noun (pl. **consistories**) a church council or court, in particular: ■ (in the Roman Catholic Church) the council of cardinals, with or without the Pope. ■ (also **consistory court**) (in the Church of England) a court presided over by a bishop, for the administration of ecclesiastical law in a diocese. ■ (in other Churches) a local administrative body.
– DERIVATIVES **consistorial** /ˌkɒnsɪˈstɔːrɪəl/ adjective.
– ORIGIN Middle English (originally denoting a non-ecclesiastical council): from Anglo-Norman French *consistorie*, from late Latin *consistorium*, from *consistere* 'stand firm' (see **CONSIST**).

consociation ▶ noun **1** a political system formed by the cooperation of different, especially antagonistic, social groups on the basis of shared power. ■ Ecology a small climax community of plants having a characteristic dominant species. ■ Zoology a group of animals of the same species which interact more or less equally with each other.
2 [mass noun] dated close association or fellowship.
– DERIVATIVES **consociational** adjective, **consociationalism** noun.
– ORIGIN late 16th cent. (in the sense 'associating, combination'): from Latin *consociatio(n-)*, from the verb *consociare*, from *con-* 'together' + *sociare* 'to associate' (from *socius* 'fellow').

consolation /ˌkɒnsəˈleɪʃ(ə)n/ ▶ noun [mass noun] the comfort received by a person after a loss or disappointment: *there was consolation in knowing that others were worse off.* ■ [count noun] a person or thing providing consolation: *the Church was the main consolation in a short and hard life.* ■ (also **consolation goal**) [count noun] Brit. (in sport) a goal scored at a point when it is no longer possible for the scoring team to win: *two minutes from time Moore grabbed a consolation goal for the losers.*
– DERIVATIVES **consolatory** /kənˈsɒlət(ə)ri, -ˈsəʊl-/ adjective.
– ORIGIN late Middle English: via Old French from Latin *consolatio(n-)*, from the verb *consolari* (see **CONSOLE¹**).

consolation prize ▶ noun a prize given to a competitor who just fails to win or who has come last.

console¹ /kənˈsəʊl/ ▶ verb [with obj.] comfort (someone) at a time of grief or disappointment: *she tried to console him but he pushed her gently away* | *you can **console yourself with** the thought that you did your best* | (as adj. **consoling**) *he put a consoling arm around her shoulder.*
– DERIVATIVES **consolable** adjective, **consoler** noun, **consolingly** adverb.
– ORIGIN mid 17th cent. (replacing earlier *consolate*): from French *consoler*, from Latin *consolari*, from *con-* 'with' + *solari* 'soothe'.

console² /ˈkɒnsəʊl/ ▶ noun **1** a panel or unit accommodating a set of controls for electronic or mechanical equipment. ■ (also **games console**) a small electronic device for playing computerized video games. ■ a cabinet for television or radio equipment. ■ the cabinet or enclosure containing the keyboards, stops, pedals, etc., of an organ.
2 an ornamented bracket or corbel supporting a shelf or table top.
– ORIGIN mid 17th cent. (in sense 2): from French, perhaps from *consolider*, from Latin *consolidare* (see **CONSOLIDATE**).

console table ▶ noun a table top supported by ornamented brackets against a wall.

consolidate /kənˈsɒlɪdeɪt/ ▶ verb [with obj.] **1** make (something) physically stronger or more solid: *the first phase of the project is to consolidate the outside walls.* ■ strengthen (one's position or power): *the company consolidated its position in the international market.*
2 combine (a number of things) into a single more effective or coherent whole: *all manufacturing activities have been consolidated in new premises.* ■ combine (a number of financial accounts or funds) into a single overall account or set of accounts. ■ chiefly Brit. combine (separate pieces of legislation) into a single legislative act.
– DERIVATIVES **consolidation** noun, **consolidator** noun.
– ORIGIN early 16th cent. (in the sense 'combine into a whole'): from Latin *consolidare*, from *con-* 'together' + *solidare* 'make firm' (from *solidus* 'solid').

Consolidated Fund the account held by the Exchequer of the British government at the Bank of England into which public monies (such as tax receipts) are paid and from which major payments are made, other than those dependent on periodic parliamentary approval.

Consols /ˈkɒns(ə)lz/ ▶ plural noun British government securities without redemption date and with fixed annual interest.
– ORIGIN late 18th cent.: contraction of *consolidated annuities*.

consommé /kənˈsɒmeɪ/ ▶ noun [mass noun] a clear soup made with concentrated stock.
– ORIGIN French, past participle of *consommer* 'consume or consummate', from Latin *consummare* 'make complete' (see **CONSUMMATE**).

consonance /ˈkɒns(ə)nəns/ ▶ noun [mass noun] agreement or compatibility between opinions or actions: *consonance between conservation measures and existing agricultural practice* | *a constitution **in consonance with** the people's customs.* ■ the recurrence of similar-sounding consonants in close proximity, especially in prosody. ■ Music a combination of notes which are in harmony with each other due to the relationship between their frequencies.
– ORIGIN late Middle English: from Old French, or from Latin *consonantia*, from *consonant-* 'sounding together', from the verb *consonare* (see **CONSONANT**).

consonant /ˈkɒns(ə)nənt/ ▶ noun a basic speech sound in which the breath is at least partly obstructed and which can be combined with a vowel to form a syllable. Contrasted with **VOWEL**. ■ a letter representing a consonant.
▶ **adjective 1** [attrib.] denoting or relating to a consonant: *a consonant phoneme.*
2 (**consonant with**) in agreement or harmony with: *the findings are consonant with other research.* ■ Music making a harmonious interval or chord: *the bass is consonant with all the upper notes.*
– DERIVATIVES **consonantal** adjective, **consonantly** adverb.
– ORIGIN Middle English (in the sense 'letter representing a consonant'): via Old French from Latin *consonare* 'sound together', from *con-* 'with' + *sonare* 'to sound' (from *sonus* 'sound').

con sordino /ˌkɒn sɔːˈdiːnəʊ/ ▶ adverb Music (especially as a direction) with the use of a mute.
– ORIGIN Italian.

consort¹ ▶ noun /ˈkɒnsɔːt/ **1** a wife, husband, or companion, in particular the spouse of a reigning monarch.
2 a ship sailing in company with another.
▶ **verb** /kənˈsɔːt/ [no obj.] (**consort with**) habitually associate with (someone), typically with the disapproval of others: *you chose to consort with the enemy.* ■ (**consort with/to**) archaic agree or be in harmony with.
– ORIGIN late Middle English (denoting a companion or colleague): via French from Latin *consors* 'sharing, partner', from *con-* 'together with' + *sors, sort-* 'lot, destiny'. The verb senses are probably influenced by similar senses (now obsolete) of the verb *sort*.

consort² /ˈkɒnsɔːt/ ▶ noun a small group of musicians performing together, typically playing instrumental music of the Renaissance period.
– ORIGIN late 16th cent.: earlier form of **CONCERT**.

consortium /kənˈsɔːtɪəm/ ▶ noun (pl. **consortia** /-tɪə, -ʃə/ or **consortiums**) **1** an association, typically of several companies.
2 [mass noun] Law the right of association and companionship with one's husband or wife.
– ORIGIN early 19th cent. (in the sense 'partnership'): from Latin, from *consors* 'sharing, partner' (see **CONSORT¹**).

conspecific /kɒnspəˈsɪfɪk/ Biology ▶ adjective (of animals or plants) belonging to the same species.
▶ **noun** (usu. **conspecifics**) a member of the same species: *the rabbit was isolated from male conspecifics.*
– DERIVATIVES **conspecificity** noun.

conspectus /kənˈspɛktəs/ ▶ noun a summary or overview of a subject.
– ORIGIN mid 19th cent.: from Latin, past participle (used as a noun) of *conspicere* 'look at attentively'.

conspicuous /kənˈspɪkjʊəs/ ▶ adjective clearly visible: *he was very thin, with a conspicuous Adam's apple.* ■ attracting notice or attention: *he showed conspicuous bravery.*
– PHRASES **conspicuous by one's absence** obviously not present where one or it should be. [from a speech made by Lord John Russell in an address to electors (1859): taken from Tacitus (*Annals* iii. 76).]
– DERIVATIVES **conspicuity** noun, **conspicuously** adverb, **conspicuousness** noun.
– ORIGIN mid 16th cent.: from Latin *conspicuus* (from *conspicere* 'look at attentively', from *con-* (expressing intensive force) + *spicere* 'look at') + **-OUS**.

conspiracist ▶ noun a person who supports a conspiracy theory.

conspiracy ▶ noun (pl. **conspiracies**) a secret plan by a group to do something unlawful or harmful: *a conspiracy to destroy the government.* ■ [mass noun] the action of plotting or conspiring: *they were cleared of conspiracy to pervert the course of justice.*
– PHRASES **a conspiracy of silence** an agreement to say nothing about an issue that should be generally known.

– ORIGIN late Middle English: from Anglo-Norman French *conspiracie*, alteration of Old French *conspiration*, based on Latin *conspirare* 'agree, plot' (see CONSPIRE).

conspiracy theory ▸ noun a belief that some covert but influential organization is responsible for an unexplained event.

conspirator ▸ noun a person who takes part in a conspiracy.
– DERIVATIVES **conspiratorial** adjective, **conspiratorially** adverb.
– ORIGIN late Middle English: from Old French *conspirateur*, from Latin *conspirator*, from *conspirat-* 'agreed, plotted', from the verb *conspirare* (see CONSPIRE).

conspire ▸ verb [no obj.] make secret plans jointly to commit an unlawful or harmful act: *they conspired against him* | [with infinitive] *they deny conspiring to defraud the Inland Revenue.* ■ [with infinitive] (of events or circumstances) seem to be working together to bring about a particular negative result: *everything conspires to exacerbate the situation.*
– ORIGIN late Middle English: from Old French *conspirer*, from Latin *conspirare* 'agree, plot', from *con-* 'together with' + *spirare* 'breathe'.

Const. ▸ abbreviation constable.

Constable /ˈkʌnstəb(ə)l, ˈkɒn-/, John (1776–1837), English painter. Among his best-known works are early paintings such as *Flatford Mill* (1817) and *The Hay Wain* (1821), inspired by the landscape of his native Suffolk.

constable /ˈkʌnstəb(ə)l, ˈkɒn-/ ▸ noun **1** Brit. a police officer. ■ (also **police constable**) a police officer of the lowest rank.
2 the governor of a royal castle. ■ historical the highest-ranking official in a royal household.
– ORIGIN Middle English (in sense 2): from Old French *conestable*, from late Latin *comes stabuli* 'count (head officer) of the stable'. Sense 1 dates from the mid 19th cent.

constabulary /kənˈstabjʊləri/ ▸ noun (pl. **constabularies**) Brit. a police force covering a particular area or city: *the Royal Irish Constabulary.*
– ORIGIN late 15th cent. (denoting the district under the charge of a constable): from medieval Latin *constabularia (dignitas)* '(rank) of constable', from *constabulus*, based on Latin *comes stabuli* (see CONSTABLE).

Constance, Lake a lake in SE Germany on the north side of the Swiss Alps, at the meeting point of Germany, Switzerland, and Austria, forming part of the course of the River Rhine. German name **BODENSEE**.

constancy ▸ noun [mass noun] the quality of being faithful and dependable. ■ the quality of being enduring and unchanging: *the constancy of the tradition.*
– ORIGIN late 15th cent.: from Latin *constantia*, from *constant-* 'standing firm' (see CONSTANT).

constant ▸ adjective occurring continuously over a period of time: *the constant background noise of the city.* ■ remaining the same over a period of time: *these discs rotate at a constant speed.* ■ (of a person) unchangingly faithful and dependable.
▸ noun a situation that does not change: *the condition of struggle remained a constant.* ■ Mathematics a quantity or parameter that does not change its value whatever the value of the variables, under a given set of conditions. ■ Physics a number expressing a relation or property which remains the same in all circumstances, or for the same substance under the same conditions.
– ORIGIN late Middle English (in the sense 'staying resolute or faithful'): from Old French, from Latin *constant-* 'standing firm', from the verb *constare*, from *con-* 'with' + *stare* 'stand'. The noun senses date from the mid 19th cent.

Constanţa /kɒnˈstantsə/ (also **Constanza**) the chief port of Romania, on the Black Sea; pop. 305,550 (2006). Founded in the 7th century BC by the Greeks, it was under Roman rule from 72 BC. Formerly called Tomis, it was renamed after Constantine the Great in the 4th century.

constantan /ˈkɒnst(ə)ntan/ ▸ noun [mass noun] a copper–nickel alloy used in electrical work for its high resistance.
– ORIGIN early 20th cent.: from CONSTANT + -AN.

Constantine[1] /ˈkɒnstəntʌɪn/ a city in NE Algeria; pop. 462,800 (est. 2009). The capital of the Roman province of Numidia, it was destroyed in 311 but rebuilt by Constantine the Great and given his name.

Constantine[2] /ˈkɒnstəntʌɪn/ (c.274–337), Roman emperor 306–37; known as **Constantine the Great**. He was the first Roman emperor to be converted to Christianity and in 324 made Christianity a state religion. In 330 he moved his capital from Rome to Byzantium, renaming it Constantinopolis (Constantinople). In the Orthodox Church he is venerated as a saint.

Constantinople /ˌkɒnstantɪˈnəʊp(ə)l/ the former name for Istanbul from AD 330 (when it was given its name by Constantine the Great) to the capture of the city by the Turks in 1453.

constantly ▸ adverb continuously over a period of time; always: *the world is constantly changing* | *he was constantly on her mind.*

Constanza variant spelling of CONSTANŢA.

constative /ˈkɒnstətɪv, kənˈsteɪtɪv/ Linguistics
▸ adjective denoting a speech act or sentence that is a statement declaring something to be the case. Often contrasted with PERFORMATIVE.
▸ noun a constative speech act or sentence.
– ORIGIN early 20th cent.: from Latin *constat-* 'established' (from the verb *constare*) + -IVE.

constellate /ˈkɒnstəleɪt/ ▸ verb literary form or cause to form into a cluster or group; gather together: [no obj.] *the towns and valleys where people constellate* | [with obj.] *their stories were never constellated.*
– ORIGIN mid 17th cent.: from late Latin *constellatus*, from *con-* 'together' + *stellatus* 'arranged like a star'.

constellation ▸ noun a group of stars forming a recognizable pattern that is traditionally named after its apparent form or identified with a mythological figure. ■ a group of associated or similar people or things: *no two patients ever show exactly the same **constellation of** symptoms.*
– ORIGIN Middle English (as an astrological term denoting the relative positions of the 'stars' (planets), supposed to influence events): via Old French from late Latin *constellatio(n-)*, based on Latin *stella* 'star'.

consternate /ˈkɒnstəneɪt/ ▸ verb [with obj.] fill (someone) with anxiety: (as adj. **consternated**) *'Oh dear,' said Georgiana, looking a little consternated.*
– ORIGIN mid 17th cent.: from Latin *consternat-* 'terrified, prostrated', from the verb *consternare*.

consternation ▸ noun [mass noun] a feeling of anxiety or dismay, typically at something unexpected: ***to her consternation** her car wouldn't start.*
– ORIGIN early 17th cent.: from Latin *consternatio(n-)*, from the verb *consternare* 'lay prostrate, terrify' (see CONSTERNATE).

constipated /ˈkɒnstɪpeɪtɪd/ ▸ adjective affected with constipation. ■ repressed or inhibited: *he's one of those emotionally constipated, stiff-upper-lip types.*
– DERIVATIVES **constipate** verb.
– ORIGIN mid 16th cent.: from Latin *constipat-* 'crowded or pressed together', from the verb *constipare*, from *con-* 'together' + *stipare* 'press, cram'.

constipation ▸ noun [mass noun] a condition in which there is difficulty in emptying the bowels, usually associated with hardened faeces. ■ a high level of constraint or restriction: *literary constipation.*
– ORIGIN late Middle English (in the sense 'contraction of body tissues'): from late Latin *constipatio(n-)*, from the verb *constipare* (see CONSTIPATED).

constituency /kənˈstɪtjʊənsi/ ▸ noun (pl. **constituencies**) a group of voters in a specified area who elect a representative to a legislative body: *most politicians are more interested in the voice of their constituency.* ■ chiefly Brit. the area represented in this way: *a parliamentary candidate in the Hampstead and Highgate constituency.* ■ a group of people with shared interests or political opinions: *the right needed to move beyond its blue-blood constituency.*

constituent ▸ adjective [attrib.] **1** being a part of a whole: *the constituent minerals of the rock.*
2 being a voting member of an organization and having the power to appoint or elect: *the constituent body has a right of veto.* ■ able to make or change a political constitution: *a constituent assembly.*
▸ noun **1** a member of an area which elects a representative to a legislative body.
2 a component part of something: *the essential constituents of the human diet.*
– ORIGIN late 15th cent. (as a noun denoting a person who appoints another as agent): from Latin *constituent-* (partly via French *constituant*) 'establishing, appointing', from the verb *constituere* (see CONSTITUTE).

constitute /ˈkɒnstɪtjuːt/ ▸ verb [with obj.] **1** be (a part) of a whole: *lone parents constitute a great proportion of the poor.* ■ combine to form (a whole): *there were enough members present to constitute a quorum.* ■ be or be equivalent to (something): *his failure to act constituted a breach of duty.*
2 give legal or constitutional form to (an institution); establish by law.
– ORIGIN late Middle English: from Latin *constitut-* 'established, appointed', from the verb *constituere*, from *con-* 'together' + *statuere* 'set up'.

constitution ▸ noun **1** a body of fundamental principles or established precedents according to which a state or other organization is acknowledged to be governed. ■ (**the Constitution**) the basic written set of principles and precedents of federal government in the US, which came into operation in 1789 and has since been modified by twenty-six amendments. ■ historical a decree, ordinance, or law.
2 [mass noun] the composition of something: *the genetic constitution of a species.* ■ the action of forming or establishing something: *the constitution of a police authority.*
3 a person's physical state as regards vitality, health, and strength: *pregnancy had weakened her constitution.* ■ a person's character.
– ORIGIN Middle English (denoting a law, or a body of laws or customs): from Latin *constitutio(n-)*, from *constituere* 'establish, appoint' (see CONSTITUTE).

constitutional ▸ adjective **1** relating to an established set of principles governing a state: *a constitutional amendment.* ■ in accordance with a constitution: *a constitutional monarchy.*
2 relating to someone's nature or physical condition: *a constitutional weakness.*
▸ noun dated a walk taken regularly to maintain or restore good health.
– DERIVATIVES **constitutionality** noun, **constitutionally** adverb.

constitutionalism ▸ noun [mass noun] constitutional government. ■ adherence to a constitutional system of government.
– DERIVATIVES **constitutionalist** noun.

constitutionalize (also **constitutionalise**) ▸ verb [with obj.] N. Amer. make subject to the provisions of a country's constitution: *divorce is not constitutionalized.*

Constitution State informal name for CONNECTICUT.

constitutive ▸ adjective **1** having the power to establish or give organized existence to something: *the state began to exercise a new and constitutive function.*
2 forming a part or constituent of something: *poverty is a constitutive element of a particular form of economic growth.* ■ forming an essential element of something: *language is **constitutive of** thought.*
3 Biochemistry relating to an enzyme or enzyme system that is continuously produced in an organism, regardless of the needs of cells.
– DERIVATIVES **constitutively** adverb.

constrain ▸ verb [with obj.] compel or force (someone) to follow a particular course of action: [with obj. and infinitive] *children are constrained to work in the way the book dictates.* ■ (as adj. **constrained**) appearing forced or overly controlled: *he was acting in a constrained manner.* ■ severely restrict the scope, extent, or activity of: *agricultural development is considerably constrained by climate.* ■ archaic bring about (something) by compulsion: *Calypso in her caves constrained his stay.* ■ literary confine forcibly; imprison.
– DERIVATIVES **constrainedly** adverb.
– ORIGIN Middle English: from Old French *constraindre*, from Latin *constringere* 'bind tightly together'.

constraint ▸ noun a limitation or restriction: *time constraints make it impossible to do everything* | *the availability of water is the main **constraint on** food production.* ■ [mass noun] stiffness of manner and inhibition in relations between people: *they would be able to talk without constraint.*
– ORIGIN late Middle English (in the sense 'coercion'): from Old French *constreinte*, feminine past participle of *constraindre* (see CONSTRAIN).

constrict ▸ verb [with obj.] make narrower, especially by encircling pressure: *chemicals that constrict the blood vessels* | (as adj. **constricted**) *constricted air passages.* ■ [no obj.] become narrower: *he felt his throat constrict.* ■ (of a snake) coil round (prey) in order to asphyxiate it. ■ inhibit or restrict: *the fear and the reality of crime constrict many people's lives.*
– DERIVATIVES **constrictive** adjective.

C

– ORIGIN mid 18th cent.: from Latin *constrict-* 'bound tightly together', from the verb *constringere* (see CONSTRAIN).

constriction ▶ noun [mass noun] the action of making something narrower by pressure or of becoming narrower; tightening: *asthma is a constriction of the airways.* ■ [count noun] a place where something has become tighter or narrower; an obstruction: *flow was impeded at bends and constrictions.*

constrictor ▶ noun 1 a snake that kills by coiling round its prey and asphyxiating it. ● Families Boidae and Pythonidae, and some members of other families (in particular Colubridae).
2 (also **constrictor muscle**) Anatomy a muscle whose contraction narrows a vessel or passage. ■ each of the muscles which constrict the pharynx.
– ORIGIN early 18th cent.: modern Latin, from *constrict-* 'bound tightly together', from the verb *constringere* (see CONSTRAIN).

construct ▶ verb /kən'strʌkt/ [with obj.] build or make (something, typically a building, road, or machine): *a company that constructs oil rigs.* ■ form (an idea or theory) by bringing together various conceptual elements: *poetics should construct a theory of literary discourse.* ■ Grammar form (a sentence) according to grammatical rules. ■ Geometry draw or delineate (a geometrical figure) accurately to given conditions.
▶ noun /'kɒnstrʌkt/ an idea or theory containing various conceptual elements, typically one considered to be subjective and not based on empirical evidence: *history is largely an ideological construct.* ■ Linguistics a group of words forming a phrase. ■ a physical thing which is deliberately built or formed.
– DERIVATIVES **constructor** noun.
– ORIGIN late Middle English: from Latin *construct-* 'heaped together, built', from the verb *construere*, from *con-* 'together' + *struere* 'pile, build'.

construction ▶ noun [mass noun] 1 the action of building something, typically a large structure: *there was a skyscraper **under construction**.* ■ the industry of constructing buildings, roads, etc. ■ the style or method used in the building of something: *the mill is of brick construction.* ■ [count noun] a building or other structure.
2 the creation of an abstract entity: *language plays a large part in our construction of reality.* ■ [count noun] an interpretation or explanation: *you could **put an honest construction upon** their conduct.* ■ Grammar the arrangement of words according to syntactical rules: *sentence construction.*
– DERIVATIVES **constructional** adjective, **constructionally** adverb.
– ORIGIN late Middle English: via Old French from Latin *constructio(n-)*, from *construere* 'heap together' (see CONSTRUCT).

constructionism ▶ noun another term for CONSTRUCTIVISM.

constructionist ▶ noun 1 another term for CONSTRUCTIVIST (see CONSTRUCTIVISM).
2 US a person who puts a particular interpretation upon a legal document, especially the US Constitution.

construction paper ▶ noun [mass noun] N. Amer. a type of thick coloured paper used for making models, designs, and other craftwork.

construction site ▶ noun a building site.

constructive ▶ adjective 1 having or intended to have a useful or beneficial purpose: *constructive advice.*
2 Law not obvious or stated explicitly; derived by inference: *constructive liability.*
3 Mathematics relating to, based on, or denoting mathematical proofs which show how an entity may in principle be constructed or arrived at in a finite number of steps.
– DERIVATIVES **constructively** adverb, **constructiveness** noun.
– ORIGIN mid 17th cent. (in sense 2): from late Latin *constructivus*, from Latin *construct-* 'heap together', from the verb *construere* (see CONSTRUCT).

constructive dismissal ▶ noun [mass noun] the changing of an employee's job or working conditions with the aim of forcing their resignation.

constructivism ▶ noun [mass noun] 1 Art a style or movement in which assorted mechanical objects are combined into abstract mobile structural forms. The movement originated in Russia in the 1920s and has influenced many aspects of modern architecture and design. [transliterating Russian *konstruktivizm*.]
2 Mathematics a view which admits as valid only constructive proofs and entities demonstrable by them, implying that the latter have no independent existence.
– DERIVATIVES **constructivist** noun & adjective.

construe ▶ verb (**construes, construing, construed**) [with obj.] 1 interpret (a word or action) in a particular way: *his words could hardly be **construed as** an apology.*
2 dated analyse the syntax of (a text, sentence, or word): *both verbs can be **construed with** either infinitive.* ■ translate (a passage or author) word for word, typically aloud.
– DERIVATIVES **construable** adjective, **construal** noun.
– ORIGIN late Middle English: from Latin *construere* (see CONSTRUCT), in late Latin 'analyse the construction of a sentence'.

consubstantial ▶ adjective of the same substance or essence (used especially of the three persons of the Trinity in Christian theology): *Christ is **consubstantial with** the Father.*
– DERIVATIVES **consubstantiality** noun.
– ORIGIN late Middle English: from ecclesiastical Latin *consubstantialis* (translating Greek *homoousios* 'of one substance'), from *con-* 'with' + *substantialis* (see SUBSTANTIAL).

consubstantiation /ˌkɒnsəbstanʃɪ'eɪʃ(ə)n, -sɪ-/ ▶ noun [mass noun] Christian Theology the doctrine, especially in Lutheran belief, that the substance of the bread and wine coexists with the body and blood of Christ in the Eucharist. Compare with TRANSUBSTANTIATION.
– ORIGIN late 16th cent.: from modern Latin *consubstantiatio(n-)*, from *con-* 'together', on the pattern of *transubstantiatio(n-)* 'transubstantiation'.

consuetude /'kɒnswɪtjuːd/ ▶ noun chiefly Scottish a custom, especially one having legal force.
– DERIVATIVES **consuetudinary** /-'tjuːdɪn(ə)ri/ adjective.
– ORIGIN late Middle English: from Old French, or from Latin *consuetudo* (see CUSTOM).

consul /'kɒns(ə)l/ ▶ noun 1 an official appointed by a state to live in a foreign city and protect the state's citizens and interests there.
2 (in ancient Rome) each of the two annually elected chief magistrates who jointly ruled the republic. ■ any of the three chief magistrates of the first French republic (1799–1804).
– DERIVATIVES **consular** /'kɒnsjʊlə/ adjective, **consulship** noun.
– ORIGIN late Middle English (denoting an ancient Roman magistrate): from Latin, related to *consulere* 'take counsel'.

consulate ▶ noun 1 the building in which a consul's duties are carried out. ■ the office or position of a consul.
2 historical the period of office of a Roman consul. ■ (**the consulate**) the system of government by consuls in ancient Rome.
3 (**the Consulate**) the government of the first French republic (1799–1804) by three consuls.
– ORIGIN late Middle English (denoting the government of Rome by consuls): from Latin *consulatus*, from *consul* (see CONSUL).

consul general ▶ noun (pl. **consuls general**) a consul of the highest status.

consult ▶ verb [with obj.] seek information or advice from (someone, especially an expert or professional): *if you consult a solicitor, making a will is a simple procedure.* ■ have discussions with (someone), typically before undertaking a course of action: *patients are entitled to be consulted about their treatment* | [no obj.] *the government must **consult with** interested bodies.* ■ refer for information to (a book, diary, or watch).
– DERIVATIVES **consultative** adjective.
– ORIGIN early 16th cent. (in the sense 'confer'): from French *consulter*, from Latin *consultare*, frequentative of *consulere* 'take counsel'.

consultancy ▶ noun (pl. **consultancies**) a professional practice that gives expert advice within a particular field: [as modifier] *a management consultancy firm.* ■ [mass noun] the work of giving such advice.

consultant ▶ noun 1 a person who provides expert advice professionally.
2 [often as modifier] Brit. a hospital doctor of senior rank within a specific field: *a consultant paediatrician.*
– ORIGIN late 17th cent. (in the sense 'a person who consults'): probably from French, from Latin *consultare* (see CONSULT).

consultation ▶ noun [mass noun] the action or process of formally consulting or discussing: *they improved standards **in consultation with** consumer representatives* | [count noun] *consultations between all sections of the party.* ■ [count noun] a meeting with an expert, such as a medical doctor, in order to seek advice.
– ORIGIN late Middle English: from Latin *consultatio(n-)*, from the verb *consultare* (see CONSULT).

consultee ▶ noun a person who is formally consulted or asked for advice on a matter.

consulting ▶ adjective engaged in the business of giving expert advice to people working in a professional or technical field: *a consulting engineer.*
▶ noun [mass noun] the business of giving expert advice to other professionals.

consulting room ▶ noun a room in which a doctor or other therapeutic practitioner examines patients.

consumable ▶ adjective (of an item for sale) intended to be used up and then replaced.
▶ noun (usu. **consumables**) a commodity that is intended to be used up relatively quickly: *drugs and other medical consumables.*

consume ▶ verb [with obj.] 1 eat, drink, or ingest (food or drink): *people consume a good deal of sugar in drinks.* ■ (of a fire) completely destroy: *the fire spread rapidly, consuming many homes.* ■ use up (a resource): *this process consumes enormous amounts of energy.*
2 buy (goods or services).
3 (of a feeling) completely fill the mind of (someone): *Carolyn was consumed with guilt.*
– ORIGIN late Middle English: from Latin *consumere*, from *con-* 'altogether' + *sumere* 'take up'; reinforced by French *consumer*.

consumer ▶ noun a person who purchases goods and services for personal use: [as modifier] *consumer demand.* ■ a person or thing that eats or uses something.

consumer durables ▶ plural noun Brit. manufactured items, typically cars or household appliances, that are expected to have a relatively long useful life after purchase.

consumer goods ▶ plural noun goods bought and used by consumers, rather than by manufacturers for producing other goods. Often contrasted with CAPITAL GOODS.

consumerism ▶ noun [mass noun] 1 the protection or promotion of the interests of consumers.
2 often derogatory the preoccupation of society with the acquisition of consumer goods.
– DERIVATIVES **consumerist** adjective & noun, **consumeristic** adjective.

consumer price index ▶ noun (in the US) an index of the variation in prices for retail goods and other items.

consumer society ▶ noun chiefly derogatory a society in which the buying and selling of goods and services is the most important social and economic activity.

consumer unit ▶ noun an apparatus in the electrical supply at the point it enters a domestic property, which contains devices such as a switch and circuit-breakers.

consuming ▶ adjective (of a feeling) completely filling one's mind and attention; absorbing: *a consuming passion.*
– DERIVATIVES **consumingly** adverb.

consummate ▶ verb /'kɒnsjʊmeɪt, -sə-/ [with obj.] make (a marriage or relationship) complete by having sexual intercourse: *his first wife refused to consummate their marriage.* ■ complete (a transaction): *the property sale is consummated.*
▶ adjective /kən'sʌmət, 'kɒnsʌmət/ showing great skill and flair: *she dressed with consummate elegance.*
– DERIVATIVES **consummately** adverb, **consummator** noun.
– ORIGIN late Middle English (as an adjective in the sense 'completed, accomplished'): from Latin *consummat-* 'brought to completion', from the verb *consummare*, from *con-* 'altogether' + *summa* 'sum total', feminine of *summus* 'highest, supreme'.

consummation ▶ noun the action of making a marriage or relationship complete by having sexual intercourse: *the eager consummation that follows a long and passionate seduction.* ■ [mass noun] the point at which something is complete or finalized: ***the consummation of** a sale.*
– ORIGIN late Middle English: from Latin *consummatio(n-)*, from the verb *consummare* (see CONSUMMATE).

consumption ▶ noun [mass noun] 1 the action of using up a resource: *industrialized countries should reduce their energy consumption.* ■ the action of eating or drinking something: *liquor is sold for consumption*

off the premises. ■ [in sing.] an amount of something which is used up or ingested: *a daily consumption of 15 cigarettes.* ■ the purchase of goods and services by the public. ■ the reception of information or entertainment by a mass audience: *his confidential speech was not meant for public consumption.*
2 dated a wasting disease, especially pulmonary tuberculosis.
– ORIGIN late Middle English: from Latin *consumptio(n-)*, from the verb *consumere* (see CONSUME).

consumptive ▶ **adjective 1** dated affected with a wasting disease, especially pulmonary tuberculosis.
2 chiefly derogatory relating to the using up of resources: *tourism represents an insidious form of consumptive activity.*
▶ **noun** dated a person with a wasting disease, especially pulmonary tuberculosis.
– DERIVATIVES **consumptively** adverb.
– ORIGIN mid 17th cent.: from medieval Latin *consumptivus*, from Latin *consumpt-* 'consumed', from the verb *consumere* (see CONSUME).

cont. ▶ **abbreviation** ■ contents. ■ continued.

contact ▶ **noun** /ˈkɒntakt/ **1** [mass noun] the state of physical touching: *equipment **in contact with** water can benefit from rubber lining.* ■ [as modifier] caused by or operating through physical touch: *contact dermatitis.* ■ (**contacts**) contact lenses.
2 [mass noun] the action of communicating or meeting: *she had little contact with family members.* ■ [count noun] a meeting, communication, or relationship with someone: *they have forged contacts with key people in business.* ■ [count noun] a person who may be approached for information or assistance, especially with regard to one's job: *Francesca had good contacts.* ■ [count noun] a person who has associated with a patient with a contagious disease (and so may carry the infection).
3 [count noun] a connection for the passage of an electric current from one thing to another, or a part or device by which such a connection is made: *the sliding contact of the potentiometer.*
▶ **verb** /ˈkɒntakt, kənˈtakt/ [with obj.] **1** communicate with (someone), typically in order to give or receive information.
2 touch: *I winced as my blister contacted the floor.*
– DERIVATIVES **contactable** adjective.
– ORIGIN early 17th cent.: from Latin *contactus*, from *contact-* 'touched, grasped, bordered on', from the verb *contingere*, from *con-* 'together with' + *tangere* 'to touch'.

contact-breaker ▶ **noun** another term for CIRCUIT BREAKER.

contact clause ▶ **noun** Grammar a relative clause appended without a relative pronoun to the noun phrase that governs it, as in *the man I saw yesterday.*

contactee ▶ **noun** a person who claims to have been contacted by alien beings, especially through an abduction.

contact flight (also **contact flying**) ▶ **noun** [mass noun] navigation of an aircraft by the observation of landmarks.

contact lens ▶ **noun** a thin plastic lens placed directly on the surface of the eye to correct visual defects.

contactless ▶ **adjective** denoting a smart card that uses radio signals to provide a wireless connection to a card reader, with no physical contact being necessary.

contact metamorphism ▶ **noun** [mass noun] Geology metamorphism due to contact with or proximity to an igneous intrusion.

contact print ▶ **noun** a photographic print made by placing a negative directly on to sensitized paper, glass, or film and illuminating it.
▶ **verb** (**contact-print**) [with obj.] make a photograph from (a negative) in this way.

contact process ▶ **noun** the major industrial process used to make sulphuric acid, by oxidizing sulphur dioxide in the presence of a solid catalyst and absorbing the resulting sulphur trioxide in water.

contact sheet ▶ **noun** a piece of photographic paper on to which several or all of the negatives on a film have been contact-printed.

contact sport ▶ **noun** a sport in which the participants necessarily come into bodily contact with one another.

contadina /ˌkɒntəˈdiːnə/ ▶ **noun** (pl. **contadine** /-neɪ/ or **contadinas**) an Italian peasant girl or peasant woman.
– ORIGIN Italian.

contadino /ˌkɒntəˈdiːnəʊ/ ▶ **noun** (pl. **contadini** /-ni/ or **contadinos**) an Italian peasant or countryman.
– ORIGIN Italian, from *contado*, denoting the peasant population around a city.

contagion /kənˈteɪdʒ(ə)n/ ▶ **noun** [mass noun] the communication of disease from one person or organism to another by close contact: *the rooms held no risk of contagion.* ■ [count noun] dated a disease spread in such a way: *through personal hygiene the spread of common contagions is discouraged.*
– ORIGIN late Middle English (denoting a contagious disease): from Latin *contagio(n-)*, from *con-* 'together with' + the base of *tangere* 'to touch'.

contagious ▶ **adjective 1** (of a disease) spread from one person or organism to another, typically by direct contact: *a contagious disease.* ■ (of a person) having a disease that can be transmitted by contact with other people: *precautions are taken with anyone who seems contagious.*
2 (of an emotion, feeling, or attitude) likely to spread to and affect others: *her enthusiasm is contagious.*
– DERIVATIVES **contagiously** adverb, **contagiousness** noun.
– ORIGIN late Middle English: from late Latin *contagiosus*, from *contagio* (see CONTAGION).

> **USAGE** Strictly, a **contagious** disease is one transmitted by physical contact, whereas an **infectious** one is transmitted via microorganisms in the air or water. In practice there is little or no difference in meaning between **contagious** and **infectious** when applied to disease or its spread. In figurative senses **contagious** may describe the spread of good things such as laughter and enthusiasm or bad ones such as violence or panic, whereas **infectious** usually refers to the spread of positive things, such as good humour or optimism.

contagious abortion ▶ **noun** [mass noun] a type of brucellosis which causes spontaneous abortion in cattle.

contain ▶ **verb** [with obj.] **1** have or hold (someone or something) within: *the cigarettes were thought to contain cannabis.* ■ be made up of (a number of things): *documents containing both text and simple graphics can be created.* ■ (of a number) be divisible by (a factor) without a remainder.
2 control or restrain (oneself or a feeling): *he must contain his hatred.* ■ prevent (a severe problem) from spreading or intensifying: *the government has already taken steps to contain the disease.*
– DERIVATIVES **containable** adjective.
– ORIGIN Middle English: from Old French *contenir*, from Latin *continere*, from *con-* 'altogether' + *tenere* 'to hold'.

container ▶ **noun** an object for holding or transporting something. ■ a large metal box of a standard design and size used for the transport of goods by road, rail, sea, or air: [as modifier] *a container lorry.*

containerize (also **containerise**) ▶ **verb** [with obj.] (usu. as adj. **containerized**) pack into or transport by container.
– DERIVATIVES **containerization** noun.

container ship ▶ **noun** a ship which is designed to carry goods stored in containers.

containment ▶ **noun** [mass noun] the action of keeping something harmful under control or within limits: *the containment of the AIDS epidemic.* ■ the action or policy of preventing the expansion of a hostile country or influence: *a policy of containment and negotiation was the appropriate course of action.*

contaminate ▶ **verb** [with obj.] make (something) impure by exposure to or addition of a poisonous or polluting substance: *the site was found to be contaminated by radioactivity* | figurative *celebrity has contaminated every aspect of public life* | (as adj. **contaminated**) *contaminated blood products.*
– DERIVATIVES **contaminant** noun, **contamination** noun, **contaminator** noun.
– ORIGIN late Middle English: from Latin *contaminat-* 'made impure', from the verb *contaminare*, from *contamen* 'contact, pollution', from *con-* 'together with' + the base of *tangere* 'to touch'.

contango /kənˈtaŋgəʊ/ ▶ **noun** [mass noun] Brit. Stock Exchange the normal situation in which the spot or cash price of a commodity is lower than the forward price. Often contrasted with BACKWARDATION. ■ historical a percentage paid by a buyer of stock to postpone transfer to a future settling day.
– ORIGIN mid 19th cent.: probably an arbitrary formation on the pattern of Latin verb forms ending in *-o*
in the first person singular, perhaps with the idea 'I make contingent' (see CONTINGENT).

conte /kɒnt/, French /kɔ̃t/ ▶ **noun** a short story as a form of literary composition. ■ a medieval narrative tale.
– ORIGIN French, based on Latin *computare* 'reckon, sum up'.

Conté /ˈkɒnteɪ/ ▶ **noun** [mass noun] a kind of hard, grease-free crayon used as a medium for artwork: [as modifier] *Conté pastels.*
– ORIGIN mid 19th cent.: named after Nicolas J. *Conté* (1755–1805), the French inventor who developed it.

contemn /kənˈtɛm/ ▶ **verb** [with obj.] archaic treat or regard with contempt.
– DERIVATIVES **contemner** /-ˈtɛmə, -ˈtɛmnə/ noun.
– ORIGIN late Middle English: from Latin *contemnere*, from *con-* (expressing intensive force) + *temnere* 'despise'.

contemplate /ˈkɒntɛmpleɪt, -təm-/ ▶ **verb** [with obj.] look thoughtfully for a long time at: *he contemplated his image in the mirrors.* ■ think about: *she couldn't even begin to contemplate the future.* ■ [no obj.] think deeply and at length. ■ have in view as a probable intention: *he was contemplating action for damages.*
– DERIVATIVES **contemplator** noun.
– ORIGIN late 16th cent.: from Latin *contemplat-* 'surveyed, observed, contemplated', from the verb *contemplari*, based on *templum* 'place for observation'.

contemplation ▶ **noun** [mass noun] the action of looking thoughtfully at something for a long time: *the road is too busy for leisurely contemplation of the scenery.* ■ deep reflective thought: *he would retire to his room for study or contemplation.* ■ the state of being considered or planned: *substantial fitting work is **in contemplation**.* ■ religious meditation. ■ a form of Christian prayer or meditation in which a person seeks to pass beyond mental images and concepts to a direct experience of the divine.
– ORIGIN Middle English: from Old French, from Latin *contemplatio(n-)*, from the verb *contemplari* (see CONTEMPLATE).

contemplative /kənˈtɛmplətɪv/ ▶ **adjective** expressing or involving prolonged thought: *she regarded me with a contemplative eye.* ■ involving or given to deep silent prayer or religious meditation: *contemplative knowledge of God.*
▶ **noun** a person whose life is devoted primarily to prayer, especially in a monastery or convent.
– DERIVATIVES **contemplatively** adverb.

contemporaneous /kənˌtɛmpəˈreɪnɪəs, kɒn-/ ▶ **adjective** existing at or occurring in the same period of time: *Pythagoras was **contemporaneous with** Buddha.*
– DERIVATIVES **contemporaneity** noun, **contemporaneously** adverb, **contemporaneousness** noun.
– ORIGIN mid 17th cent.: from Latin, from *con-* 'together with' + *temporaneus* (from **tempus, tempor-** 'time') + **-ous**.

contemporary /kənˈtɛmp(ə)r(ər)i/ ▶ **adjective**
1 living or occurring at the same time: *the event was recorded by a contemporary historian.* ■ dating from the same time: *this series of paintings is **contemporary with** other works in an early style.*
2 belonging to or occurring in the present: *the tension and complexities of our contemporary society.* ■ following modern ideas in style or design: *contemporary ceramics by leading potters.*
▶ **noun** (pl. **contemporaries**) a person or thing living or existing at the same time as another: *he was a contemporary of Darwin.* ■ a person of roughly the same age as another: *my contemporaries at school.*
– DERIVATIVES **contemporarily** adverb, **contemporariness** noun.
– ORIGIN mid 17th cent.: from medieval Latin *contemporarius*, from *con-* 'together with' + *tempus, tempor-* 'time' (on the pattern of Latin *contemporaneus* and late Latin *contemporalis*).

contempt ▶ **noun** [mass noun] the feeling that a person or a thing is worthless or deserving scorn: *Pam stared at the girl with total contempt* | *he wouldn't answer a woman he held in such contempt.* ■ disregard for something that should be considered: *this action displays an arrogant **contempt for** the wishes of the majority.* ■ (also **contempt of court**) the offence of being disobedient to or disrespectful of a court of law and its officers.
– PHRASES **beneath contempt** utterly worthless or despicable. **hold someone in contempt** judge someone to have committed the offence of contempt of court. **hold someone/thing in contempt** consider someone or something to be unworthy of respect or attention: *the speed limit is held in contempt by many drivers.*

– ORIGIN late Middle English: from Latin *contemptus*, from *contemnere* (see CONTEMN).

contemptible ▶ adjective deserving contempt; despicable: *a display of contemptible cowardice.*
– DERIVATIVES **contemptibly** adverb.
– ORIGIN late Middle English: from Old French, or from late Latin *contemptibilis*, from Latin *contemnere* (see CONTEMN).

C

contemptuous ▶ adjective showing contempt; scornful: *she was intolerant and* ***contemptuous of*** *the majority of the human race.*
– DERIVATIVES **contemptuously** adverb, **contemptuousness** noun.
– ORIGIN mid 16th cent. (in the sense 'despising law and order'): from medieval Latin *contemptuosus*, from Latin *contemptus* 'contempt', from *contemnere* (see CONTEMN).

contend ▶ verb **1** [no obj.] (**contend with/against**) struggle to surmount (a difficulty): *she had to contend with his uncertain temper.* ■ (**contend for**) compete with others in a struggle to achieve (something): *factions within the government were contending for the succession to the presidency.*
2 [with clause] assert something as a position in an argument: *he contends that the judge was wrong.*
– DERIVATIVES **contender** noun.
– ORIGIN late Middle English (in the sense 'compete for (something)'): from Old French *contendre* or Latin *contendere*, from *con-* 'with' + *tendere* 'stretch, strive'.

content[1] /kənˈtɛnt/ ▶ adjective in a state of peaceful happiness: *he seemed more content, less bitter.* ■ willing to accept something; satisfied: *he had to be* ***content with*** *third place* | [with infinitive] *the duke was content to act as Regent.*
▶ verb [with obj.] satisfy (someone): *nothing would content her apart from going off to Barcelona.* ■ (**content oneself with**) accept as adequate despite wanting more or better: *we contented ourselves with a few small purchases.*
▶ noun **1** [mass noun] a state of satisfaction: *the greater part of the century was a time of content.*
2 a member of the British House of Lords who votes for a particular motion.
– ORIGIN late Middle English: via Old French from Latin *contentus* 'satisfied', past participle of *continere* (see CONTAIN).

content[2] /ˈkɒntɛnt/ ▶ noun (also **contents**) the things that are held or included in something: *she unscrewed the top of the flask and drank the contents.* ■ [in sing.] [with modifier] the amount of a particular constituent occurring in a substance: *soya milk has a low fat content.* ■ (**contents**) a list of the chapters or sections given at the front of a book or periodical: [as modifier] *the contents page.* ■ [mass noun] the material dealt with in a speech, literary work, etc. as distinct from its form or style: *the tone, if not the content, of his book is familiar.* ■ information made available by a website or other electronic medium: [as modifier] *online content providers.*
– DERIVATIVES **contentless** adjective.
– ORIGIN late Middle English: from medieval Latin *contentum* (plural *contenta* 'things contained'), neuter past participle of *continere* (see CONTAIN).

contented ▶ adjective feeling or expressing happiness or satisfaction: *I felt warm and contented* | *she gave a contented little smile.* ■ willing to accept something; satisfied: *I was never* ***contented with*** *half measures.*
– DERIVATIVES **contentedly** adverb, **contentedness** noun.

contention ▶ noun **1** [mass noun] heated disagreement: *the captured territory was the main area of contention between the two countries.*
2 [count noun] an assertion, especially one maintained in argument: *Freud's contention that all dreams were wish fulfilment.*
– PHRASES **in** (or **out of**) **contention** having (or not having) a good chance of success in a contest.
– ORIGIN late Middle English: from Latin *contentio(n-)*, from *contendere* 'strive with' (see CONTEND).

contentious ▶ adjective causing or likely to cause an argument; controversial: *a contentious issue.* ■ involving heated argument: *the socio-economic plan had been the subject of contentious debate.* ■ (of a person) given to provoking argument. ■ Law relating to or involving differences between contending parties.
– DERIVATIVES **contentiously** adverb, **contentiousness** noun.
– ORIGIN late Middle English: from Old French *contentieux*, from Latin *contentiosus*, from *content-* 'striven', from the verb *contendere.*

contentment ▶ noun [mass noun] a state of happiness and satisfaction: *he found contentment in living a simple life in the country.*
– ORIGIN late Middle English (denoting the payment of a claim): from French *contentement*, from Latin *contentus* (see CONTENT[1]).

content provider ▶ noun an organization that supplies information for use on a website.

conterminous /kɒnˈtəːmɪnəs/ ▶ adjective sharing a common boundary: *the forty-eight conterminous United States.* ■ having the same area, context, or meaning: *a genealogy* ***conterminous with*** *the history of the USA.*
– DERIVATIVES **conterminously** adverb.
– ORIGIN mid 17th cent.: from Latin *conterminus* (from *con-* 'with' + *terminus* 'boundary') + **-ous**. Compare with COTERMINOUS.

contessa /kɒnˈtɛsə/ ▶ noun an Italian countess.
– ORIGIN Italian, from late Latin *comitissa* (see COUNTESS).

contest ▶ noun /ˈkɒntɛst/ an event in which people compete for supremacy in a sport or other activity, or in a quality: *a tennis contest.* ■ a competition for a political position: *a leadership contest.* ■ a dispute or conflict: *a contest between traditional and liberal views.*
▶ verb /kənˈtɛst/ [with obj.] **1** engage in competition to attain (a position of power): *she declared her intention to contest the presidency.* ■ take part in (a competition or election): *a coalition was formed to contest the presidential elections.*
2 oppose (an action or theory) as mistaken or wrong: *the former chairman contests his dismissal.* ■ engage in dispute about: *the issues have been hotly contested.*
– PHRASES **no contest 1** chiefly US another term for NOLO CONTENDERE. **2** a decision by the referee to declare a boxing match invalid on the grounds that one or both of the boxers are not making serious efforts. ■ a competition, comparison, or choice of which the outcome is a foregone conclusion: *when the two teams faced each other it was no contest.*
– DERIVATIVES **contestability** noun, **contestable** adjective, **contester** noun.
– ORIGIN late 16th cent. (as a verb in the sense 'swear to, attest'): from Latin *contestari* 'call upon to witness, initiate (by calling witnesses)', from *con-* 'together' + *testare* 'to witness'. The senses 'wrangle, struggle for' arose in the early 17th cent., whence the current noun and verb senses.

contestant ▶ noun a person who takes part in a contest or competition.
– ORIGIN mid 17th cent.: from French, present participle of *contester*, from Latin *contestari* 'call upon to witness' (see CONTEST).

contestation ▶ noun [mass noun] formal the action or process of disputing or arguing.
– ORIGIN mid 16th cent. (in the sense 'solemn appeal or protest'): from Latin *contestatio(n-)*, from *contestari* 'call upon to witness' (see CONTEST); reinforced by French *contestation.*

context /ˈkɒntɛkst/ ▶ noun the circumstances that form the setting for an event, statement, or idea, and in terms of which it can be fully understood: *the proposals need to be considered in the context of new European directives.* ■ the parts of something written or spoken that immediately precede and follow a word or passage and clarify its meaning.
– PHRASES **in context** considered together with the surrounding words or circumstances. **out of context** without the surrounding words or circumstances and so not fully understandable.
– DERIVATIVES **contextual** adjective, **contextually** adverb.
– ORIGIN late Middle English (denoting the construction of a text): from Latin *contextus*, from *con-* 'together' + *texere* 'to weave'.

contextualism ▶ noun [mass noun] Philosophy a doctrine which emphasizes the importance of the context of enquiry in a particular question.
– DERIVATIVES **contextualist** noun.

contextualize (also **contextualise**) ▶ verb [with obj.] place or study in context: *the excellent introduction summarizes and contextualizes Bowen's career.*
– DERIVATIVES **contextualization** noun.

contiguity /ˌkɒntɪˈgjuːɪti/ ▶ noun [mass noun] the state of bordering or being in contact with something: *nations bound together by geographical contiguity.* ■ Psychology the sequential occurrence or proximity of stimulus and response, causing their association in the mind.
– ORIGIN early 16th cent.: from late Latin *contiguitas*, from Latin *contiguus* 'touching' (see CONTIGUOUS).

contiguous /kənˈtɪgjʊəs/ ▶ adjective sharing a common border; touching: *the Southern Ocean is* ***contiguous with*** *the Atlantic.* ■ next or together in sequence.
– DERIVATIVES **contiguously** adverb.
– ORIGIN early 16th cent.: from Latin *contiguus* 'touching', from the verb *contingere* 'be in contact, befall' (see CONTINGENT), + **-ous**.

continent[1] ▶ noun any of the world's main continuous expanses of land (Europe, Asia, Africa, North and South America, Australia, Antarctica). ■ (also **the Continent**) the mainland of Europe as distinct from the British Isles.
– ORIGIN mid 16th cent. (denoting a continuous tract of land): from Latin *terra continens* 'continuous land'.

continent[2] ▶ adjective **1** able to control movements of the bowels and bladder.
2 exercising self-restraint, especially sexually.
– DERIVATIVES **continence** noun, **continently** adverb.
– ORIGIN late Middle English (in sense 2): from Latin *continent-* 'holding together, restraining oneself', from *continere* (see CONTAIN).

continental ▶ adjective **1** [attrib.] forming or belonging to a continent: *continental Antarctica.*
2 (also **Continental**) in, from, or characteristic of mainland Europe: *a continental holiday.*
▶ noun an inhabitant of mainland Europe.
– DERIVATIVES **continentally** adverb.

Continental Army (in the US) the army raised by the Continental Congress of 1775, with George Washington as commander.

continental breakfast ▶ noun a light breakfast, typically consisting of coffee and bread rolls with butter and jam.

continental climate ▶ noun a relatively dry climate with very hot summers and very cold winters, characteristic of the central parts of Asia and North America.

Continental Congress (in the US) each of the three congresses held by the American colonies in revolt against British rule in 1774, 1775, and 1776 respectively. The second Congress, convened in the wake of the battles at Lexington and Concord, created a Continental Army, which fought and eventually won the American War of Independence.

continental crust ▶ noun Geology the relatively thick part of the earth's crust which forms the large land masses. It is generally older and more complex than the oceanic crust.

continental day ▶ noun Brit. a school day lasting from early morning to early afternoon.

Continental Divide the main series of mountain ridges in North America, chiefly the crests of the Rocky Mountains, which form a watershed separating the rivers flowing eastwards into the Atlantic Ocean or the Gulf of Mexico from those flowing westwards into the Pacific. Also called GREAT DIVIDE.

continental drift ▶ noun [mass noun] the gradual movement of the continents across the earth's surface through geological time.

> The reality of continental drift was confirmed in the 1960s, leading to the theory of plate tectonics. It is believed that a single supercontinent called Pangaea broke up to form Gondwana and Laurasia, which further split to form the present-day continents. Such movement continues today: South America and Africa, for example, are moving apart at a rate of a few centimetres per year.

continental quilt ▶ noun British term for DUVET.

continental shelf ▶ noun the area of seabed around a large land mass where the sea is relatively shallow compared with the open ocean. The continental shelf is geologically part of the continental crust.

continental slope ▶ noun the slope between the outer edge of the continental shelf and the deep ocean floor.

Continental System Napoleon's strategy of blockading Britain (1806–13), by which British ships were prohibited from entering the ports of France and her allies.

contingency /kənˈtɪndʒ(ə)nsi/ ▶ noun (pl. **contingencies**) a future event or circumstance which is possible but cannot be predicted with certainty: *a detailed contract which attempts to provide for all possible contingencies.* ■ a provision for a possible

event or circumstance: *stores were kept as a contingency against a blockade.* ■ an incidental expense. ■ [mass noun] the absence of certainty in events: *the island's public affairs can occasionally be seen to be invaded by contingency.* ■ [mass noun] Philosophy the absence of necessity; the fact of being so without having to be so.
– ORIGIN mid 16th cent. (in the philosophical sense): from late Latin *contingentia* (in its medieval Latin sense 'circumstance'), from *contingere* 'befall' (see CONTINGENT).

contingency fee ▶ **noun** (in the US) a sum of money that a lawyer receives as a fee only if the case is won.

contingency fund ▶ **noun** a reserve of money set aside to cover possible unforeseen future expenses.

contingency plan ▶ **noun** a plan designed to take account of a possible future event or circumstance.

contingency table ▶ **noun** Statistics a table showing the distribution of one variable in rows and another in columns, used to study the correlation between the two variables.

contingent /kən'tɪndʒ(ə)nt/ ▶ **adjective 1** subject to chance: *the contingent nature of the job.* ■ (of losses, liabilities, etc.) that can be anticipated to arise if a particular event occurs.
2 (**contingent on/upon**) occurring or existing only if (certain circumstances) are the case; dependent on: *his fees were contingent on the success of his search.*
3 Philosophy true by virtue of the way things in fact are and not by logical necessity.
▶ **noun** a group of people sharing a common feature, forming part of a larger group. ■ a body of troops or police sent to join a larger force.
– DERIVATIVES **contingently adverb**.
– ORIGIN late Middle English (in the sense 'of uncertain occurrence'): from Latin *contingere* 'befall', from *con-* 'together with' + *tangere* 'to touch'. The noun sense was originally 'something happening by chance', then 'a person's share resulting from a division, a quota'; the current sense dates from the early 18th cent.

continual ▶ **adjective** forming a sequence in which the same action or event is repeated frequently: *his plane went down after continual attacks.* ■ having no interruptions: *some patients need continual safeguarding.*
– ORIGIN Middle English: from Old French *continuel*, from *continuer* 'continue', from Latin *continuare*, from *continuus* (see CONTINUOUS).

> **USAGE** For an explanation of the difference between **continual** and **continuous**, see **USAGE** at **CONTINUOUS**.

continually ▶ **adverb 1** repeated frequently in the same way; regularly: *this information is continually updated.*
2 without interruption; constantly: *I was continually moving around.*

continuance ▶ **noun 1** [mass noun] formal the state of remaining in existence or operation: *his interests encouraged him to favour the continuance of war.* ■ the time for which a situation or action lasts: *the trademarks shall be used only during the continuance of this agreement.* ■ the state of remaining in a particular position or condition: *the king's ministers depended on his favour for their continuance in office.*
2 US Law a postponement or an adjournment.
– ORIGIN late Middle English: from Old French, from *continuer* 'continue', from Latin *continuare*, from *continuus* (see CONTINUOUS).

continuant ▶ **noun 1** Phonetics a consonant which is sounded with the vocal tract only partly closed, allowing the breath to pass through and the sound to be prolonged (as with *f, l, m, n, r, s, v*).
2 Philosophy & Psychology a thing that retains its identity even though its states and relations may change.
▶ **adjective** relating to or denoting a continuant.
– ORIGIN early 17th cent. (as an adjective in the general sense 'continuing'): from French, from *continuer*, reinforced by Latin *continuant-* 'continuing', from the verb *continuare*, from *continuus* (see CONTINUOUS). Current senses date from the 19th cent.

continuation ▶ **noun** [mass noun] the action of carrying something on over time or the state of being carried on: *the continuation of discussions about a permanent peace.* ■ the state of remaining in a particular position or condition. ■ [count noun] [usu. in sing.] a part that is attached to and is an extension of something else: *once a separate village, it is now a continuation of the suburbs.*
– ORIGIN late Middle English: via Old French from Latin *continuatio(n-)*, from *continuare* 'continue', from *continuus* (see CONTINUOUS).

continuative /kən'tɪnjʊətɪv/ Linguistics ▶ **adjective** (of a word or phrase) having the function of moving a discourse or conversation forward.
▶ **noun** a word or phrase of this type (e.g. *yes, well, as I was saying*).
– ORIGIN mid 16th cent. (as a noun denoting something which brings about continuity): from late Latin *continuativus*, from *continuat-* 'continued', from the verb *continuare* (see CONTINUE).

continuator ▶ **noun** a person or thing that continues something or maintains continuity. ■ a person who writes a continuation of another's work.

continue ▶ **verb** (**continues, continuing, continued**)
1 [no obj.] persist in an activity or process: *he was unable to continue with his job* | [with infinitive] *prices continued to fall during April.* ■ remain in existence or operation: *discussions continued throughout the year.* ■ remain in a specified position or state: *they have indicated their willingness to continue in office* | [with complement] *the weather continued warm and pleasant* | (as adj. **continuing**) *a continuing controversy.* ■ [with obj.] carry on with (something that one has begun): *the Archive has continued its programme of research* | (as adj. **continued**) *he asked for their continued support.* ■ [with adverbial of direction] carry on travelling in the same direction: *they continued northwards to Glasgow.*
2 recommence or resume after interruption: [with obj.] *we continue the story from the point reached in Chapter 1* | [no obj.] *the trial continues tomorrow.* ■ [no obj.] carry on speaking after a pause or interruption: *I told him he was obstructing the enquiry and he let me continue* | [with direct speech] *'Pleased to make your acquaintance,' he continued.* ■ [with obj.] US Law postpone or adjourn (a legal proceeding): *the case was continued without a finding until August 2.*
– DERIVATIVES **continuer noun**.
– ORIGIN Middle English: from Old French *continuer*, from Latin *continuare*, from *continuus* (see CONTINUOUS).

continued fraction ▶ **noun** Mathematics a fraction of infinite length whose denominator is a quantity plus a fraction, which latter fraction has a similar denominator, and so on.

continuing education ▶ **noun** [mass noun] education provided for adults after they have left the formal education system, consisting typically of short or part-time courses.

continuity /ˌkɒntɪ'njuːɪti/ ▶ **noun** (pl. **continuities**) [mass noun] **1** the unbroken and consistent existence or operation of something over time: *a consensus favouring continuity of policy.* ■ a state of stability and the absence of disruption: *they have provided the country with a measure of continuity.* ■ a connection or line of development with no sharp breaks: *a firm line of continuity between pre-war and post-war Britain.*
2 the maintenance of continuous action and self-consistent detail in the various scenes of a film or broadcast: [as modifier] *a continuity error.* ■ the linking of broadcast items by a spoken commentary: [as modifier] *the BBC continuity announcer.*
– ORIGIN late Middle English: from Old French *continuite*, from Latin *continuitas*, from *continuare* 'continue', from *continuus* (see CONTINUOUS).

continuo /kən'tɪnjʊəʊ/ (also **basso continuo**) ▶ **noun** (pl. **continuos**) [mass noun] (in baroque music) an accompanying part which includes a bass line and harmonies, typically played on a keyboard instrument and with other instruments such as cello or lute.
– ORIGIN early 18th cent.: Italian *basso continuo* 'continuous bass'.

continuous ▶ **adjective 1** forming an unbroken whole; without interruption: *the whole performance is enacted in one continuous movement.* ■ forming a series with no exceptions or reversals: *there are continuous advances in design and production.*
2 Grammar another term for PROGRESSIVE (sense 3 of the adjective).
3 Mathematics (of a function) of which the graph is a smooth unbroken curve, i.e. one such that as the value of x approaches any given value a, the value of $f(x)$ approaches that of $f(a)$ as a limit.
– DERIVATIVES **continuously adverb**, **continuousness noun**.
– ORIGIN mid 17th cent.: from Latin *continuus* 'uninterrupted', from *continere* 'hang together' (from *con-* 'together with' + *tenere* 'hold') + **-ous**.

> **USAGE** There is some overlap in meaning between **continuous** and **continual**, but the two words are not wholly synonymous. Both can mean roughly 'without interruption' (*a long and **continual** war; five years of **continuous** warfare*), but **continuous** is much more prominent in this sense and, unlike **continual**, can be used to refer to space as well as time, as in *the development forms a **continuous** line along the coast.* **Continual**, on the other hand, typically means 'happening frequently, with intervals between', as in *the bus service has been disrupted by **continual** breakdowns.* Overall, **continuous** occurs much more frequently than **continual** (almost five times more often in the Oxford English Corpus).

C

continuous assessment ▶ **noun** [mass noun] Brit. the evaluation of a pupil's progress throughout a course of study, as distinct from by examination.

continuous creation ▶ **noun** [mass noun] the creation of matter as a continuing process throughout time, especially as postulated in steady state theories of the universe.

continuous spectrum ▶ **noun** Physics an emission spectrum that consists of a continuum of wavelengths.

continuous wave ▶ **noun** an electromagnetic wave, especially a radio wave, having a constant amplitude.

continuum ▶ **noun** (pl. **continua**) a continuous sequence in which adjacent elements are not perceptibly different from each other, but the extremes are quite distinct.
– ORIGIN mid 17th cent.: from Latin, neuter of *continuus* (see CONTINUOUS).

contort /kən'tɔːt/ ▶ **verb** twist or bend out of the normal shape: [with obj.] *a spasm of pain contorted his face* | [no obj.] *her face contorted with anger* | (as adj. **contorted**) *contorted limbs* | figurative *a contorted version of the truth.*
– DERIVATIVES **contortion noun**.
– ORIGIN late Middle English: from Latin *contort-* 'twisted round, brandished', from the verb *contorquere*, from *con-* 'together' + *torquere* 'twist'.

contortionist ▶ **noun** an entertainer who twists and bends their body into strange and unnatural positions.

contour ▶ **noun 1** (usu. **contours**) an outline representing or bounding the shape or form of something: *she traced the contours of his face with her finger* | figurative *challenges that have shaped the contours of European integration.* ■ short for CONTOUR LINE. ■ a line joining points on a diagram at which some property has the same value.
2 a way in which something varies, especially the pitch of music or the pattern of tones in an utterance.
▶ **verb** [with obj.] **1** mould into a specific shape, especially one designed to fit into something else: *the compartment has been contoured with smooth rounded corners* | (as adj. **contoured**) *the contoured leather seats.*
2 mark (a map or diagram) with contour lines: (as adj. **contoured**) *a huge contoured map.*
3 (of a road or railway) follow the outline of (a topographical feature), especially along a contour line: *the road contours the hillside.*
– ORIGIN mid 17th cent.: from French, from Italian *contorno*, from *contornare* 'draw in outline', from *con-* 'together' + *tornare* 'to turn'.

contour feather ▶ **noun** any of the mainly small feathers which form the outline of an adult bird's plumage.

contour line ▶ **noun** a line on a map joining points of equal height above or below sea level.

contour map ▶ **noun** a map marked with contour lines.

contour ploughing ▶ **noun** [mass noun] ploughing along the contours of the land in order to minimize soil erosion.

Contra /'kɒntrə/ ▶ **noun** a member of a guerrilla force in Nicaragua which opposed the left-wing Sandinista government 1979–90, and was supported by the US for much of that time.
– ORIGIN abbreviation of Spanish *contrarevolucionario* 'counter-revolutionary'.

contra- /'kɒntrə/ ▶ **prefix 1** against; opposite: *contraception* | *contraflow.*
2 Music (of an instrument or organ stop) pitched an octave below: *contrabass.*
– ORIGIN from Latin *contra* 'against'.

contraband /'kɒntrəband/ ▶ **noun** [mass noun] goods that have been imported or exported illegally: *customs men had searched the carriages for contraband.*

C

■ trade in smuggled goods: *the salt trade (and contraband in it) were very active in the town.* ■ (also **contraband of war**) goods forbidden to be supplied by neutrals to those engaged in war.
▶ **adjective** imported or exported illegally, either in defiance of a total ban or without payment of duty: *contraband brandy.* ■ relating to traffic in illegal goods: *the contraband market.*
– DERIVATIVES **contrabandist** noun.
– ORIGIN late 16th cent.: from Spanish *contrabanda*, from Italian *contrabando*, from *contra-* 'against' + *bando* 'proclamation, ban'.

contrabass ▶ **noun** another term for DOUBLE BASS.
▶ **adjective** denoting a musical instrument with a range an octave lower than the normal bass range: *a contrabass clarinet.*
– ORIGIN late 18th cent.: from Italian *contrabasso*, from *contra-* 'pitched an octave below' + *basso* (see BASS[1]).

contrabassoon ▶ **noun** another term for DOUBLE BASSOON.

contraception ▶ **noun** [mass noun] the deliberate use of artificial methods or other techniques to prevent pregnancy as a consequence of sexual intercourse. The major forms of artificial contraception are: barrier methods, of which the commonest is the condom or sheath; the contraceptive pill, which contains synthetic sex hormones which prevent ovulation in the female; intrauterine devices, such as the coil, which prevent the fertilized ovum from implanting in the uterus; and male or female sterilization.
– ORIGIN late 19th cent.: from CONTRA- 'against' + a shortened form of CONCEPTION.

contraceptive ▶ **adjective** (of a method or device) serving to prevent pregnancy: *the contraceptive pill.* ■ relating to contraception: *a book popularizing contraceptive knowledge.*
▶ **noun** a device or drug serving to prevent pregnancy.

contract ▶ **noun** /ˈkɒntrakt/ a written or spoken agreement, especially one concerning employment, sales, or tenancy, that is intended to be enforceable by law: *he has just signed a contract keeping him with the club* | [mass noun] *much of the produce is grown **under contract**.* ■ [mass noun] the branch of law concerned with the making and observation of contracts. ■ informal an arrangement for someone to be killed by a hired assassin: *smuggling bosses routinely put out contracts on witnesses.* ■ Bridge the declarer's undertaking to win the number of tricks bid with a stated suit as trumps: *South can **make the contract** with correct play.* ■ dated a formal agreement to marry.
▶ **verb** /kənˈtrakt/ **1** [no obj.] decrease in size, number, or range: *glass contracts as it cools.* ■ (of a muscle) become shorter and tighter in order to effect movement of part of the body: *the heart contracts about seventy times a minute* | [with obj.] *exhale and slowly contract your abdominal muscles.* ■ [with obj.] shorten (a word or phrase) by combination or elision.
2 [no obj.] enter into a formal and legally binding agreement: *the local authority **will contract with** a wide range of agencies to provide services.* ■ (**contract in/into**) Brit. choose to be involved in (a scheme): *politically committed members contract into paying the levy.* ■ (**contract out**) Brit. choose to withdraw from or not become involved in a scheme: *plans to encourage people to **contract out of** the pension scheme.* ■ secure specified rights or undertake specified obligations in a formal and legally binding agreement: *a buyer may **contract for the right** to withhold payment* | [with infinitive] *the paper had contracted to publish extracts from the diaries.* ■ [with obj. and infinitive] impose an obligation on (someone) to do something by means of a formal agreement: *health authorities contract a hospital to treat a specific number of patients.* ■ [with obj.] (**contract something out**) arrange for work to be done by another organization. ■ [with obj.] formally enter into (a marriage). ■ [with obj.] enter into (a friendship or other relationship): *the patterns of social relationships contracted by men and women differ.*
3 [with obj.] catch or develop (a disease or infectious agent): *three people contracted a killer virus.*
4 [with obj.] become liable to pay (a debt): *he contracted a debt of £3,300.*
– DERIVATIVES **contractee** noun, **contractive** adjective.
– ORIGIN Middle English: via Old French from Latin *contractus*, from *contract-* 'drawn together, tightened', from the verb *contrahere*, from *con-* 'together' + *trahere* 'draw'.

contractable ▶ **adjective** (of a disease) able to be caught.

contract bridge ▶ **noun** [mass noun] the standard form of the card game bridge, in which only tricks bid and won count towards the game, as opposed to auction bridge.

contractible ▶ **adjective** able to be shrunk or capable of contracting.

contractile /kənˈtraktʌɪl/ ▶ **adjective** Biology & Physiology capable of or producing contraction: *the contractile activity of the human colon.*
– DERIVATIVES **contractility** noun.

contractile vacuole ▶ **noun** Zoology a vacuole in some protozoans which expels excess liquid on contraction.

contraction ▶ **noun** [mass noun] the process of becoming smaller: *the general contraction of the industry did further damage to morale* | [count noun] *the manufacturing sector suffered a severe contraction.* ■ the process in which a muscle becomes or is made shorter and tighter: *neurons control the contraction of muscles.* ■ [count noun] (usu. **contractions**) a shortening of the uterine muscles occurring at intervals before and during childbirth. ■ the process of shortening a word by combination or elision. ■ [count noun] a word or group of words resulting from shortening an original form: *'goodbye' is a contraction of 'God be with you'.*
– ORIGIN late Middle English: via Old French from Latin *contractio(n-)*, from *contrahere* 'draw together' (see CONTRACT).

contract note ▶ **noun** a certificate confirming the terms of a sale of specified assets or securities between two parties.

contractor ▶ **noun** a person or firm that undertakes a contract to provide materials or labour to perform a service or do a job.

contractorization (also **contractorisation**) ▶ **noun** [mass noun] Brit. the provision of a service, especially a public one, by an external contractor rather than by the employees of the body responsible for the service.

contractual ▶ **adjective** agreed in a contract: *a contractual obligation.* ■ having similar characteristics to a contract: *the contractual nature of the shareholder's rights.*
– DERIVATIVES **contractually** adverb.

contractural ▶ **adjective 1** Medicine relating to or involving contracture.
2 another term for CONTRACTUAL.

contracture /kənˈtraktʃə/ ▶ **noun** [mass noun] Medicine a condition of shortening and hardening of muscles, tendons, or other tissue, often leading to deformity and rigidity of joints.
– ORIGIN mid 17th cent.: from French, or from Latin *contractura*, from Latin *contract-* 'drawn together', from the verb *contrahere*.

contradance ▶ **noun** a country dance in which the couples form lines facing each other.
– ORIGIN early 19th cent.: variant of CONTREDANSE.

contradict ▶ **verb** [with obj.] deny the truth of (a statement) by asserting the opposite: *the survey appears to contradict the industry's claims* | [with clause] *he did not contradict what he said last week.* ■ assert the opposite of a statement made by (someone): *he did not contradict her but just said nothing* | *within five minutes he had contradicted himself twice.* ■ be in conflict with: *the existing layout of the city contradicted the logic of the new centre.*
– DERIVATIVES **contradictor** noun.
– ORIGIN late 16th cent.: from Latin *contradict-* 'spoken against', from the verb *contradicere*, originally *contra dicere* 'speak against'.

contradiction ▶ **noun** a combination of statements, ideas, or features which are opposed to one another: *the proposed new system suffers from a set of internal contradictions.* ■ a situation in which inconsistent elements are present: *the paradox of using force to overcome force is a real contradiction.* ■ [mass noun] the statement of a position opposite to one already made: *the second sentence appears to be in flat contradiction of the first* | [count noun] *the experiment provides a contradiction of the hypothesis.*
– PHRASES **contradiction in terms** a statement or group of words associating incompatible objects or ideas.
– ORIGIN late Middle English: via Old French from Latin *contradictio(n-)*, from the verb *contradicere* (see CONTRADICT).

contradictory ▶ **adjective** mutually opposed or inconsistent: *the two studies came to contradictory conclusions.* ■ containing elements which are inconsistent: *politically he exhibited contradictory behaviour.* ■ Logic (of two propositions) so related that one and only one must be true. Compare with CONTRARY.
▶ **noun** (pl. **contradictories**) Logic a contradictory proposition.
– DERIVATIVES **contradictorily** adverb, **contradictoriness** noun.
– ORIGIN late Middle English (as a term in logic): from late Latin *contradictorius*, from Latin *contradict-* 'spoken against', from the verb *contradicere* (see CONTRADICT).

contradistinction ▶ **noun** [mass noun] distinction made by contrasting the different qualities of two things: *such a process is known as induction, **in contradistinction to** the deduction process.*

contradistinguish ▶ **verb** [with obj.] archaic distinguish between (two things) by contrasting them.

contrafactive ▶ **adjective** Linguistics denoting a verb that assigns to its object (normally a clausal object) the status of not being true, e.g. *pretend* and *wish*. Contrasted with FACTIVE, NON-FACTIVE.

contrafactual /kɒntrəˈfaktʃʊəl, -tjʊəl/ ▶ **adjective** another term for COUNTERFACTUAL.

contraflow ▶ **noun** Brit. a temporary arrangement where traffic on a road is transferred from its usual side to share the other half of the carriageway with traffic moving in the opposite direction.

contrail /ˈkɒntreɪl/ ▶ **noun** chiefly N. Amer. another term for VAPOUR TRAIL.
– ORIGIN 1940s: abbreviation of *condensation trail*.

contraindicate ▶ **verb** [with obj.] Medicine (of a condition or circumstance) suggest or indicate that (a particular technique or drug) should not be used in the case in question.
– DERIVATIVES **contraindication** noun.

contralateral /ˌkɒntrəˈlat(ə)r(ə)l/ ▶ **adjective** Medicine relating to or denoting the side of the body opposite to that on which a particular structure or condition occurs: *the symptom develops in the hand **contralateral to** the lesion.*

contralto /kənˈtraltəʊ/ ▶ **noun** (pl. **contraltos**) the lowest female singing voice: *she sang in a high contralto.* ■ a singer with such a voice. ■ a part written for such a voice.
– ORIGIN mid 18th cent.: Italian, from *contra-* (in the sense 'counter to') + ALTO. Compare with COUNTERTENOR.

contra mundum /ˌkɒntrə ˈmʌndəm/ ▶ **adverb** defying or opposing everyone else.
– ORIGIN Latin, 'against the world'.

contraposition ▶ **noun** [mass noun] Logic conversion of a proposition from *all A is B* to *all not-B is not-A*.
– DERIVATIVES **contrapositive** adjective & noun.
– ORIGIN mid 16th cent.: from late Latin *contrapositio(n-)*, from the verb *contraponere*, from *contra-* 'against' + *ponere* 'to place'.

contrapposto /ˌkɒntrəˈpɒstəʊ/ ▶ **noun** (pl. **contrapposti** /-ti/) Sculpture an asymmetrical arrangement of the human figure in which the line of the arms and shoulders contrasts with, while balancing, those of the hips and legs.
– ORIGIN Italian, past participle of *contrapporre*, from Latin *contraponere* 'place against'.

contra proferentem /ˌkɒntrə prɒfəˈrɛntɛm/ ▶ **adverb** Law (of the interpretation of an ambiguous contract) against the party which proposed or drafted the contract or clause.
– ORIGIN Latin, 'against (the person) mentioning'.

contraption ▶ **noun** a machine or device that appears strange or unnecessarily complicated, and often badly made or unsafe: *repairing stereos and making contraptions out of spare electronic bits.*
– ORIGIN early 19th cent.: perhaps from CONTRIVE (on the pattern of pairs such as *conceive, conception*), by association with TRAP[1].

contrapuntal /ˌkɒntrəˈpʌnt(ə)l/ ▶ **adjective** Music of or in counterpoint.
– DERIVATIVES **contrapuntally** adverb, **contrapuntist** noun.
– ORIGIN mid 19th cent.: from Italian *contrapunto* (see COUNTERPOINT) + -AL.

contrarian /kənˈtrɛːrɪən/ ▶ **noun** a person who opposes or rejects popular opinion, especially in stock exchange dealing.
▶ **adjective** opposing or rejecting popular opinion or current practice: *the comment came more from a contrarian disposition than moral conviction.*
– DERIVATIVES **contrarianism** noun.

contrariety /ˌkɒntrəˈrʌɪəti/ ▶ **noun** [mass noun] **1** Logic contrary opposition.
2 opposition or inconsistency between two things.
– ORIGIN late Middle English: from Old French *contrariete*, from late Latin *contrarietas*, from *contrarius* (see **CONTRARY**).

contrariwise /kənˈtrɛːrɪwʌɪz, ˈkɒntrərɪˌwʌɪz/ ▶ **adverb** in the opposite way or order: *it worked contrariwise—first you dialled the number then you put the money in.* ■ in contrast to something that has just been stated or mentioned: *contrariwise, a registered person may vote, even if not entitled to be registered.*

contra-rotating ▶ **adjective** rotating in the opposite direction or in opposite directions, especially about the same shaft.

contrary /ˈkɒntrəri/ ▶ **adjective 1** opposite in nature, direction, or meaning: *he ignored contrary advice and agreed on the deal.* ■ (of two or more statements, beliefs, etc.) opposed to one another: *his mother had given him contrary messages.* ■ (of a wind) blowing in the opposite direction to one's course; unfavourable. ■ Logic (of two propositions) so related that one or neither but not both must be true. Compare with **CONTRADICTORY**.
2 /kənˈtrɛːri/ perversely inclined to disagree or to do the opposite of what is expected or desired: *she is sulky and contrary where her work is concerned.*
▶ **noun** (pl. **contraries**) **1** (**the contrary**) the opposite: *an Act applies only to the United Kingdom unless the contrary is expressed.*
2 Logic a contrary proposition.
– PHRASES **contrary to** conflicting with or running counter to: *contrary to his expectations, he found the atmosphere exciting.* **on** (or **quite**) **the contrary** used to intensify a denial of what has just been implied or stated by suggesting that the opposite is the case: *there was no malice in her; on the contrary, she was very kind.* **to the contrary** with the opposite meaning or implication: *he continued to drink despite medical advice to the contrary.*
– DERIVATIVES **contrarily** /ˈkɒntrərɪli, kənˈtrɛːrɪli/ **adverb**, **contrariness** /ˈkɒntrərɪnɪs, kənˈtrɛːrɪnɪs/ **noun**.
– ORIGIN Middle English: from Anglo-Norman French *contrarie*, from Latin *contrarius*, from *contra* 'against'.

contrast ▶ **noun** /ˈkɒntrɑːst/ [mass noun] the state of being strikingly different from something else in juxtaposition or close association: *the day began cold and blustery,* ***in contrast to*** *almost two weeks of uninterrupted sunshine* | [count noun] ***a contrast between*** *rural and urban trends* | *Kos is an island of contrasts.* ■ differences in colour, tone, or shape that contribute to the visual effect of a design or image. ■ the difference between tones in a television picture, photograph, etc. ■ [in sing.] a thing or person having qualities noticeably different from another: *the castle is quite a* ***contrast to*** *other places where the singer has performed.*
▶ **verb** /kənˈtrɑːst/ [no obj.] differ strikingly: *his friend's success* ***contrasted with*** *his own failure* | (as adj. **contrasting**) *a contrasting view.* ■ [with obj.] compare in such a way as to emphasize differences: *people contrasted her* ***with*** *her sister.*
– DERIVATIVES **contrastingly** **adverb**, **contrastive** **adjective**.
– ORIGIN late 17th cent. (as a term in fine art, in the sense 'juxtapose so as to bring out differences in form and colour'): from French *contraste* (noun), *contraster* (verb), via Italian from medieval Latin *contrastare*, from Latin *contra-* 'against' + *stare* 'stand'.

contrast medium ▶ **noun** Medicine a substance introduced into a part of the body in order to improve the visibility of internal structures during radiography.

contrasty ▶ **adjective** informal (of a photograph, film, or television picture) showing a high degree of contrast.

contrate wheel /ˈkɒntreɪt/ ▶ **noun** another term for **CROWN WHEEL**.
– ORIGIN late 17th cent.: *contrate* (a rare adjective meaning 'opposed, contrary') from medieval Latin *contrata* 'lying opposite', from Latin *contra* 'against'.

contravene /ˌkɒntrəˈviːn/ ▶ **verb** [with obj.] offend against the prohibition or order of (a law, treaty, or code of conduct): *he contravened the Official Secrets Act.* ■ conflict with (a right, principle, etc.), especially to its detriment: *the Privy Council held that the prosecution contravened the rights of the individual.*
– DERIVATIVES **contravener** **noun**.
– ORIGIN mid 16th cent.: from late Latin *contravenire*, from Latin *contra-* 'against' + *venire* 'come'.

contravention ▶ **noun** an action which offends against a law, treaty, or other ruling: *the publishing of misleading advertisements was a contravention of the Act* | [mass noun] *contravention of parking restrictions* | *there were repeated raids by one side upon the other* ***in contravention of*** *treaty terms.*
– ORIGIN mid 16th cent.: via French from medieval Latin *contraventio(n-)*, from late Latin *contravenire* (see **CONTRAVENE**).

contredanse /ˈkɒntrədɑːns, -dɒ̃s/ ▶ **noun** (pl. pronunc. **same**) a French form of country dance, originating in the 18th century and related to the quadrille. ■ another term for **CONTRADANCE**.
– ORIGIN French, alteration of English **COUNTRY DANCE**, by association with *contre* 'against, opposite'.

contre-jour /ˈkɒ̃trəˌʒʊə/, French /kɔ̃tʀəʒuʀ/ ▶ **adjective & adverb** Photography having or involving the sun or other light source behind the subject: [as adj.] *a glorious contre-jour effect.*
– ORIGIN early 20th cent.: French, from *contre* 'against' + *jour* 'daylight'.

contretemps /ˈkɒntrətɒ̃/ ▶ **noun** (pl. **same** /-tɒ̃z/) a minor dispute or disagreement: *she had occasional contretemps with her staff.* ■ an unexpected and unfortunate occurrence.
– ORIGIN late 17th cent. (originally as a fencing term, denoting a thrust made at an inopportune moment): French, originally 'motion out of time', from *contre-* 'against' + *temps* 'time'.

contribute /kənˈtrɪbjuːt, ˈkɒntrɪbjuːt/ ▶ **verb** [with obj.] give (something, especially money) in order to help achieve or provide something: *taxpayers had* ***contributed*** *£141.8 million* ***towards*** *the cost of local services* | [no obj.] ***he contributed to*** *a private pension.* ■ [no obj.] (**contribute to**) help to cause or bring about: *the government imposed a tax on fuels which contributed to global warming.* ■ supply (an article) for publication in a newspaper, magazine, or journal: *he* ***contributed*** *articles* ***to*** *the magazine.* ■ [no obj.] give one's views in a discussion: *he did not* ***contribute to*** *the meetings.*
– DERIVATIVES **contributive** /kənˈtrɪb-/ **adjective**.
– ORIGIN mid 16th cent.: from Latin *contribut-* 'brought together, added', from the verb *contribuere*, from *con-* 'with' + *tribuere* 'bestow'.

> **USAGE** There are two possible pronunciations of the word **contribute**, one which puts the stress on the **-tri-** and one which puts it on the **con-**. The first is held to be the standard, correct pronunciation even though the pronunciation with stress on the **con-** is older.

contribution /kɒntrɪˈbjuːʃ(ə)n/ ▶ **noun** a gift or payment to a common fund or collection: *the agency is mainly financed from voluntary contributions.* ■ the part played by a person or thing in bringing about a result or helping something to advance: *the major contribution of social scientists to the understanding of political life.* ■ a piece of writing submitted for publication in a journal, book, etc.
– ORIGIN late Middle English (denoting a tax or levy): from late Latin *contributio(n-)*, from Latin *contribuere* 'bring together, add' (see **CONTRIBUTE**).

contributor /kənˈtrɪbjʊtə/ ▶ **noun** a person or thing that contributes something, in particular: ■ a person who writes articles for a magazine or newspaper. ■ a person who donates to a cause. ■ a causal factor in the existence or occurrence of something: *stress is a major* ***contributor to*** *most diseases.*

contributory /kənˈtrɪbjʊt(ə)ri/ ▶ **adjective 1** playing a part in bringing something about: *smoking may be a contributory cause of the disease.*
2 (of a pension or insurance scheme) operated by means of a fund into which people pay: *contributory benefits.*
▶ **noun** (pl. **contributories**) Law, Brit. a person liable to give money towards the payment of a wound-up company's debts.
– ORIGIN late Middle English (in the sense 'contributing to a fund'): from medieval Latin *contributorius*, from Latin *contribut-* 'added' (see **CONTRIBUTION**).

contributory negligence ▶ **noun** [mass noun] Law failure of an injured party to act prudently, considered to be a contributory factor in the injury which they have suffered.

con trick ▶ **noun** Brit. informal term for **CONFIDENCE TRICK**.

contrite /kənˈtrʌɪt, ˈkɒntrʌɪt/ ▶ **adjective** feeling or expressing remorse at the recognition that one has done wrong: *a contrite tone.*
– DERIVATIVES **contritely** **adverb**, **contriteness** **noun**.
– ORIGIN Middle English: from Old French *contrit*, from Latin *contritus*, past participle of *conterere* 'grind down, wear away', from *con-* 'together' + *terere* 'rub'.

contrition ▶ **noun** [mass noun] the state of feeling remorseful and penitent. ■ (in the Roman Catholic Church) the repentance of past sins during or after confession.
– ORIGIN Middle English: via Old French from late Latin *contritio(n-)*, from *contrit-* 'ground down', from the verb *conterere* (see **CONTRITE**).

C

contrivance ▶ **noun 1** [mass noun] the use of skill to create or bring about something, especially with a consequent effect of artificiality: *the requirements of the system, by happy chance and some contrivance, can be summed up in an acronym.*
2 [count noun] a device, especially in literary or artistic composition, which gives a sense of artificiality. ■ a thing which is created skilfully and inventively to serve a particular purpose: *an assortment of electronic equipment and mechanical contrivances.*

contrive /kənˈtrʌɪv/ ▶ **verb** [with obj.] create or bring about (an object or a situation) by deliberate use of skill and artifice: *his opponents contrived a cabinet crisis* | [with infinitive] *you contrived to be alone with me despite the supervision.* ■ [with infinitive] manage to do something foolish or create an undesirable situation: *he contrived to flood the flat three times.*
– DERIVATIVES **contriver** **noun**.
– ORIGIN Middle English: from Old French *controeve*, stressed stem of *controver* 'imagine, invent', from medieval Latin *contropare* 'compare'.

contrived ▶ **adjective** deliberately created rather than arising naturally or spontaneously. ■ created or arranged in a way that seems artificial and unrealistic: *the ending of the novel is too pat and contrived.*

control ▶ **noun 1** [mass noun] the power to influence or direct people's behaviour or the course of events: *the whole operation is* ***under the control of*** *a production manager* | *the situation was slipping* ***out of*** *her* ***control.*** ■ the ability to manage a machine, vehicle, or other moving object: *he* ***lost control of*** *his car* | *improve your ball control.* ■ the restriction of an activity, tendency, or phenomenon: *crime control.* ■ the ability to restrain one's own emotions or actions: *she was goaded beyond control.* ■ [count noun] (often **controls**) a means of limiting or regulating something: *growing* ***controls on*** *local spending.* ■ [count noun] a switch or other device by which a device or vehicle is regulated: *he had the chance to take the controls and fly the glider* | *the volume control.* ■ [with modifier] the place from which a system or activity is directed or where a particular item is verified: *passport control.* ■ Computing short for **CONTROL KEY**.
2 a person or thing used as a standard of comparison for checking the results of a survey or experiment: *platelet activity was higher in patients with the disease than in the controls.*
3 a member of an intelligence organization who personally directs the activities of a spy.
4 Bridge a high card that will prevent the opponents from establishing a particular suit.
▶ **verb** (**controls, controlling, controlled**) **1** [with obj.] determine the behaviour or supervise the running of: *he was appointed to control the company's marketing strategy.* ■ maintain influence or authority over: *there were never enough masters to control the unruly mobs of boys.* ■ limit the level, intensity, or numbers of: *he had to control his temper.* ■ (**control oneself**) remain calm and reasonable despite provocation. ■ regulate (a mechanical or scientific process): *the airflow is controlled by a fan.* ■ (as adj. **controlled**) (of a drug) restricted by law in respect of use and possession: *a sentence for possessing controlled substances.*
2 [no obj.] (**control for**) take into account (an extraneous factor that might affect the results of an experiment): *no attempt was made to control for variations* | (as adj. **controlled**) *a controlled trial.*
– PHRASES **in control** able to direct a situation, person, or activity. **out of control** no longer possible to manage. **under control** (of a danger or emergency) such that people are able to deal with it successfully: *it took two hours to bring the blaze under control.*
– DERIVATIVES **controllability** **noun**, **controllable** **adjective**, **controllably** **adverb**.
– ORIGIN late Middle English (as a verb in the sense 'check or verify accounts', especially by referring to a duplicate register): from Anglo-Norman French *contreroller* 'keep a copy of a roll of accounts', from medieval Latin *contrarotulare*, from *contrarotulus*

'copy of a roll', from *contra-* 'against' + *rotulus* 'a roll'. The noun is perhaps via French *contrôle*.

control account ▸ **noun** an account used to record the balances on a number of subsidiary accounts and to provide a cross-check on them.

control character ▸ **noun** Computing a character that does not represent a printable character but serves to initiate a particular action.

C

control freak ▸ **noun** informal a person who feels an obsessive need to exercise control over themselves and others and to take command of any situation.
– DERIVATIVES **control freakery** noun.

control key ▸ **noun** Computing a key which alters the function of another key if the two are pressed at the same time.

controller ▸ **noun** a person or thing that directs or regulates something: *the Controller of BBC Television Programmes | a temperature controller.* ■ a person in charge of an organization's finances.
– DERIVATIVES **controllership** noun.
– ORIGIN Middle English (denoting a person who kept a duplicate register of accounts): from Anglo-Norman *contrerollour*, from *contreroller* 'keep a copy of a roll of accounts' (see **CONTROL**). Compare with **COMPTROLLER**.

controlling interest ▸ **noun** the holding by one person or group of a majority of the stock of a business, giving the holder a means of exercising control: *the purchase of a* **controlling interest** *in a company in California.*

control rod ▸ **noun** a rod of a neutron-absorbing substance used to vary the output power of a nuclear reactor.

control tower ▸ **noun** a tall building at an airport from which the movements of air traffic are controlled.

controversial ▸ **adjective** giving rise or likely to give rise to controversy or public disagreement: *years of wrangling over a controversial bypass.*
– DERIVATIVES **controversialist** noun, **controversially** adverb.
– ORIGIN late 16th cent.: from late Latin *controversialis*, from *controversia* (see **CONTROVERSY**).

controversy /ˈkɒntrəvəːsi, kənˈtrɒvəsi/ ▸ **noun** (pl. **controversies**) [mass noun] prolonged public disagreement or heated discussion: *the design of the building has caused controversy* | [count noun] *the announcement ended a protracted controversy.*
– ORIGIN late Middle English: from Latin *controversia*, from *controversus* 'turned against, disputed', from *contro-* (variant of *contra-* 'against') + *versus*, past participle of *vertere* 'to turn'.

> **USAGE** There are two possible pronunciations of the word **controversy**: one puts the stress on the **con-** and the other puts it on the **-trov-**. The second pronunciation, though common, is still widely held to be incorrect in standard English.

controvert ▸ **verb** [with obj.] deny the truth of (something): *subsequent work from the same laboratory controverted these results.*
– DERIVATIVES **controvertible** adjective.
– ORIGIN mid 16th cent.: from Latin *controversus* (see **CONTROVERSY**), on the pattern of pairs such as *adversus* (see **ADVERSE**), *advertere* (see **ADVERT²**).

contumacious /ˌkɒntjʊˈmeɪʃəs/ ▸ **adjective** archaic or Law (especially of a defendant's behaviour) stubbornly or wilfully disobedient to authority.
– DERIVATIVES **contumaciously** adverb.
– ORIGIN late 16th cent.: from Latin *contumax*, *contumac-* (perhaps from *con-* 'with' + *tumere* 'to swell') + **-IOUS**.

contumacy /ˈkɒntjʊməsi/ ▸ **noun** [mass noun] archaic or Law stubborn refusal to obey or comply with authority, especially disobedience to a court order or summons.
– ORIGIN Middle English: from Latin *contumacia* 'inflexibility', from *contumax* (see **CONTUMACIOUS**).

contumelious /ˌkɒntjʊˈmiːlɪəs/ ▸ **adjective** archaic (of behaviour) scornful and insulting; insolent.
– DERIVATIVES **contumeliously** adverb.
– ORIGIN late Middle English: from Old French *contumelieus*, from Latin *contumeliosus*, from *contumelia* 'abuse, insult' (see **CONTUMELY**).

contumely /ˈkɒntjuːmɪli, -tjʊmli/ ▸ **noun** (pl. **contumelies**) [mass noun] archaic insolent or insulting language or treatment: *the Church should not be exposed to gossip and contumely.*
– ORIGIN late Middle English: from Old French *contumelie*, from Latin *contumelia*, perhaps from *con-* 'with' + *tumere* 'to swell'.

contuse /kənˈtjuːz/ ▸ **verb** [with obj.] Medicine injure (a part of the body) without breaking the skin, forming a bruise.
– ORIGIN late Middle English: from Latin *contus-* 'bruised, crushed', from the verb *contundere*, from *con-* 'together' + *tundere* 'beat, thump'.

contusion /kənˈtjuːʒ(ə)n/ ▸ **noun** Medicine a region of injured tissue or skin in which blood capillaries have been ruptured; a bruise.
– ORIGIN late Middle English: from French, from Latin *contusio(n-)*, from the verb *contundere* (see **CONTUSE**).

conundrum /kəˈnʌndrəm/ ▸ **noun** (pl. **conundrums**) a confusing and difficult problem or question: *one of the most difficult conundrums for the experts.* ■ a question asked for amusement, typically one with a pun in its answer; a riddle.
– ORIGIN late 16th cent.: of unknown origin, but first recorded in a work by Thomas Nashe, as a term of abuse for a crank or pedant, later coming to denote a whim or fancy, also a pun. Current senses date from the late 17th cent.

conurbation /ˌkɒnəˈbeɪʃ(ə)n/ ▸ **noun** an extended urban area, typically consisting of several towns merging with the suburbs of a central city.
– ORIGIN early 20th cent.: from **CON-** 'together' + Latin *urbs*, *urb-* 'city' + **-ATION**.

conure /ˈkɒnjʊə/ ▸ **noun** a Central and South American parakeet that typically has green plumage with patches of other colours. ● *Aratinga*, *Pyrrhura*, and other genera, family Psittacidae: numerous species.
– ORIGIN mid 19th cent.: from modern Latin *conurus* (former genus name), from Greek *kōnos* 'cone' + *oura* 'tail'.

conus /ˈkəʊnəs/ ▸ **noun** (pl. **coni** /-nʌɪ/) Anatomy **1** (in full **conus arteriosus** /ɑːˌtɪərɪˈəʊsəs/) the upper front part of the right ventricle of the heart.
2 (in full **conus medullaris** /ˌmɛdəˈlɑːrɪs/) the conical lower extremity of the spinal cord.
– ORIGIN late 19th cent.: from Latin, literally 'cone'.

convalesce /ˌkɒnvəˈlɛs/ ▸ **verb** [no obj.] recover one's health and strength over a period of time after an illness or medical treatment: *he spent eight months convalescing after the stroke.*
– ORIGIN late 15th cent.: from Latin *convalescere*, from *con-* 'altogether' + *valescere* 'grow strong' (from *valere* 'be well').

convalescence ▸ **noun** [mass noun] time spent recovering from an illness or medical treatment; recuperation: *a period of convalescence* | [count noun] *I had a long convalescence ahead.*

convalescent ▸ **adjective** (of a person) recovering from an illness or medical treatment. ■ [attrib.] relating to convalescence: *a convalescent home.*
▸ **noun** a person who is recovering after an illness or medical treatment.
– ORIGIN mid 17th cent.: from Latin *convalescent-* 'growing strong, recovering', from the verb *convalescere* (see **CONVALESCE**).

convect /kənˈvɛkt/ ▸ **verb** [with obj.] transport (heat or material) by convection: *this gas fire convects heat efficiently* | (as adj. **convected**) *convected warmth.* ■ [no obj.] (of a fluid or fluid body) undergo convection: *the fluid starts to convect* | (as adj. **convecting**) *the convecting layer.*
– ORIGIN late 19th cent.: back-formation from **CONVECTION**.

convection ▸ **noun** [mass noun] the movement caused within a fluid by the tendency of hotter and therefore less dense material to rise, and colder, denser material to sink under the influence of gravity, which consequently results in transfer of heat.
– DERIVATIVES **convectional** adjective, **convective** adjective.
– ORIGIN mid 19th cent.: from late Latin *convectio(n-)*, from Latin *convehere*, from *con-* 'together' + *vehere* 'carry'.

convection cell ▸ **noun** a self-contained area in a fluid in which upward motion of warmer fluid in the centre is balanced by downward motion of cooler fluid at the periphery.

convection current ▸ **noun** a current in a fluid that results from convection.

convector ▸ **noun** a heating appliance that circulates warm air by convection.

convenance /ˈkɒnvəˌnɑːns/ ▸ **noun** [mass noun] (also **convenances**) archaic conventional propriety.
– ORIGIN French, from *convenir* 'be fitting', from Latin *convenire* (see **CONVENE**).

convene /kənˈviːn/ ▸ **verb** come or bring together for a meeting or activity; assemble: [with obj.] *he had convened a secret meeting of military personnel* | [no obj.] *the committee had convened for its final plenary session.*
– ORIGIN late Middle English: from Latin *convenire* 'assemble, agree, fit', from *con-* 'together' + *venire* 'come'.

convener (also **convenor**) ▸ **noun** a person whose job it is to call people together for meetings of a committee. ■ Brit. a senior trade union official at a workplace. ■ the chairman and civic head of some regional Scottish councils.

convenience ▸ **noun 1** [mass noun] the state of being able to proceed with something without difficulty: *services should be run to suit the convenience of customers, not of staff.* ■ the quality of being useful, easy, or suitable for someone: *the success of the food halls in large stores is due to their convenience.* ■ [count noun] a thing that contributes to an easy and effortless way of life: *voicemail was seen as one of the desktop conveniences of the electronic office.*
2 [count noun] Brit. a public toilet.
– PHRASES **at one's convenience** at a time or place that suits one. **at one's earliest convenience** as soon as one can without difficulty.
– ORIGIN late Middle English: from Latin *convenientia*, from *convenient-* 'assembling, agreeing', from the verb *convenire* (see **CONVENE**).

convenience food ▸ **noun** a food, typically a complete meal, that has been pre-prepared commercially and so requires minimum further preparation by the consumer.

convenience store ▸ **noun** chiefly N. Amer. a shop with extended opening hours, stocking a limited range of household goods and groceries.

conveniency ▸ **noun** rare term for **CONVENIENCE** (sense 1).

convenient ▸ **adjective** fitting in well with a person's needs, activities, and plans: *I phoned your office to confirm that this date is convenient.* ■ involving little trouble or effort: *the new car park will make shopping much more convenient.* ■ (**convenient for**) situated so as to allow easy access to: *the site would have to be convenient for London.* ■ helpfully placed or occurring: *guests were relaxing beneath a convenient palm tree.*
– DERIVATIVES **conveniently** adverb [sentence adverb] *he lived, conveniently, in Paris.*
– ORIGIN late Middle English (in the sense 'befitting, becoming, suitable'): from Latin *convenient-* 'assembling, agreeing, fitting', from the verb *convenire* (see **CONVENE**).

convenor ▸ **noun** variant spelling of **CONVENER**.

convent ▸ **noun** a Christian community of nuns living together under monastic vows. ■ (also **convent school**) a school attached to and run by a convent.
– ORIGIN Middle English: from Old French, from Latin *conventus* 'assembly, company', from the verb *convenire* (see **CONVENE**). The original spelling was *covent* (surviving in the place name *Covent Garden*); the modern form dates from the 16th cent.

conventicle /kənˈvɛntɪk(ə)l/ ▸ **noun** historical a secret or unlawful religious meeting, typically of nonconformists.
– ORIGIN late Middle English (in the general sense 'assembly, meeting', particularly a clandestine or illegal one): from Latin *conventiculum* '(place of) assembly', diminutive of *conventus* 'assembly, company', from the verb *convenire* (see **CONVENE**).

convention ▸ **noun 1** a way in which something is usually done: *to attract the best patrons the movie houses had to ape the conventions and the standards of theatres.* ■ [mass noun] behaviour that is considered acceptable or polite to most members of a society: *he was an upholder of convention and correct form* | [count noun] *the law is felt to express social conventions.*
2 an agreement between states covering particular matters, especially one less formal than a treaty.
3 a large meeting or conference, especially of members of a political party or a particular profession or group: *the party held its biennial convention.* ■ N. Amer. an assembly of the delegates of a political party to select candidates for office. ■ a body set up by agreement to deal with a particular issue. ■ historical a meeting of Parliament without a summons from the sovereign.
4 Bridge a bid or system of bidding by which the bidder tries to convey specific information about the

hand to their partner, as opposed to seeking to win the auction.
– ORIGIN late Middle English (in sense 3): via Old French from Latin *conventio(n-)* 'meeting, covenant', from the verb *convenire* (see **CONVENE**). Sense 1 dates from the late 18th cent.

conventional ▸ adjective 1 based on or in accordance with what is generally done or believed: *a conventional morality had dictated behaviour.* ■ (of a person) greatly or overly concerned with what is generally held to be socially acceptable. ■ (of a work of art or literature) following traditional forms and genres. ■ (of weapons or power) non-nuclear.
2 Bridge (of a bid) intended to convey a particular meaning according to an agreed convention. Often contrasted with **NATURAL**.
– DERIVATIVES **conventionalism** noun, **conventionalist** noun, **conventionality** noun, **conventionalize** (also **conventionalise**) verb, **conventionally** adverb.
– ORIGIN late 15th cent. (in the sense 'relating to a formal agreement or convention'): from French *conventionnel* or late Latin *conventionalis*, from Latin *conventio(n-)* 'meeting, covenant', from the verb *convenire* (see **CONVENE**).

conventioneer ▸ noun N. Amer. a person attending a convention.

conventual /kən'vɛntʃʊəl/ ▸ adjective relating or belonging to a convent: *the conventual life.* ■ relating to the less strict order of the Franciscans, living in large convents.
▸ noun a person who lives in or is a member of a convent.
– ORIGIN late Middle English: from medieval Latin *conventualis*, from Latin *conventus* 'assembly, company' (see **CONVENT**).

converge /kən'vəːdʒ/ ▸ verb [no obj.] 1 (of lines) tend to meet at a point: *a pair of lines of longitude are parallel at the equator but converge toward the poles.* ■ come together from different directions so as eventually to meet: *convoys from America and the UK traversed thousands of miles to converge in the Atlantic.* ■ (**converge on/upon**) come from different directions and meet at (a place): *half a million sports fans will converge on the capital for the London Marathon.* ■ (of a number of things) gradually change so as to become similar or develop something in common: *the aims of the two developments can and should converge.*
2 Mathematics (of a series) approximate in the sum of its terms towards a definite limit.
– ORIGIN late 17th cent.: from late Latin *convergere*, from *con-* 'together' + Latin *vergere* 'incline'.

convergence (also **convergency**) ▸ noun [mass noun] the process or state of converging: *the convergence of lines in the distance.* ■ Biology the tendency of unrelated animals and plants to evolve superficially similar characteristics under similar environmental conditions. ■ (also **convergence zone**) a location where airflows or ocean currents meet, characteristically marked by upwelling (of air) or downwelling (of water).

convergent ▸ adjective 1 coming closer together; converging: *a convergent boundary | there are a number of convergent reasons for the growth of interest in pragmatics.* ■ Psychology (of thought) tending to follow only well-established patterns. ■ Biology relating to or denoting evolutionary convergence.
2 Mathematics (of a series) approaching a definite limit as more of its terms are added.
– ORIGIN early 18th cent.: from late Latin *convergent-* 'inclining together', from the verb *convergere* (see **CONVERGE**).

conversant ▸ adjective [predic.] familiar with or knowledgeable about something: *you need someone who is **conversant with** the new technology.*
– DERIVATIVES **conversance** noun, **conversancy** noun.
– ORIGIN Middle English: from Old French, present participle of *converser* (see **CONVERSE¹**). The original sense was 'habitually spending time in a particular place or with a particular person'.

conversation ▸ noun a talk, especially an informal one, between two or more people, in which news and ideas are exchanged: *she picked up the phone and **held a conversation** in French | [mass noun] the two men were **deep in conversation**.*
– PHRASES **make conversation** talk for the sake of politeness without having anything to say.
– ORIGIN Middle English (in the sense 'living among, familiarity, intimacy'): via Old French from Latin *conversatio(n-)*, from the verb *conversari* (see **CONVERSE¹**).

conversational ▸ adjective as used in conversation; not formal: *she spoke fluent, conversational English.* ■ consisting of or relating to conversation: *conversational skills.*
– DERIVATIVES **conversationally** adverb.

conversationalist ▸ noun a person who is good at or fond of engaging in conversation.

conversation piece ▸ noun 1 a painting of a genre in which groups of figures are posed in a landscape or domestic setting, popular especially in the 18th century.
2 an object whose unusual quality makes it a topic of conversation.

conversation-stopper ▸ noun informal a remark which is so surprising or embarrassing that it is difficult to find a polite reply.

conversazione /ˌkɒnvəsatsɪ'əʊneɪ/ ▸ noun (pl. **conversaziones** or **conversazioni** /-ni/) a scholarly social gathering held for discussion of literature and the arts.
– ORIGIN Italian, from Latin *conversatio* (see **CONVERSATION**).

converse¹ ▸ verb /kən'vəːs/ [no obj.] engage in conversation: *she was withdrawn and preoccupied, hardly able to **converse with** her mother.*
▸ noun /'kɒnvəːs/ [mass noun] archaic conversation.
– ORIGIN late Middle English (in the sense 'live among, be familiar with'): from Old French *converser*, from Latin *conversari* 'keep company (with)', from *con-* 'with' + *versare*, frequentative of *vertere* 'to turn'. The current sense of the verb dates from the early 17th cent.

converse² /'kɒnvəːs/ ▸ noun a situation, object, or statement that is the reverse of another or corresponds to it but with certain terms transposed: *if spirituality is properly political, the converse is also true: politics is properly spiritual.* ■ Mathematics a theorem whose hypothesis and conclusion are the conclusion and hypothesis of another.
▸ adjective having characteristics which are the reverse of something else already mentioned: *the only mode of change will be the slow process of growth and the converse process of decay.*
– ORIGIN late Middle English: from Latin *conversus* 'turned about', past participle of *convertere* (see **CONVERT**).

conversely ▸ adverb introducing a statement or idea which reverses one that has just been made or referred to: *he would have preferred his wife not to work, although conversely he was also proud of what she did.*

conversion ▸ noun [mass noun] 1 the process of changing or causing something to change from one form to another: *the conversion of food into body tissues.* ■ the adaptation of a building or part of a building for a new use: *the conversion of a house into flats | [count noun] they were carrying out a loft conversion.* ■ [count noun] Brit. a building that has been adapted for a new use: *high-quality cottages and barn conversions.* ■ Law the changing of real property into personalty, or of joint into separate property, or vice versa. ■ Logic the transposition of the subject and predicate of a proposition according to certain rules to form a new proposition by inference.
2 the fact of changing one's religion or beliefs or the action of persuading someone else to change theirs. ■ Christian Theology repentance and change to a godly life.
3 [count noun] Rugby a successful kick at goal after a try, scoring two points. ■ American Football an act of converting a touchdown or a down.
4 Law the action of wrongfully dealing with goods in a manner inconsistent with the owner's rights: *he was found guilty of the **fraudulent conversion** of clients' monies.*
5 Psychiatry the manifestation of a mental disturbance as a physical disorder or disease.
– ORIGIN Middle English (in the sense 'turning of sinners to God'): via Old French from Latin *conversio(n-)*, from *convers-* 'turned about', from the verb *convertere* (see **CONVERT**).

conversion factor ▸ noun 1 an arithmetical multiplier for converting a quantity expressed in one set of units into an equivalent expressed in another.
2 Economics the manufacturing cost of a product relative to the cost of raw materials.

conversion van ▸ noun N. Amer. a motor vehicle in which the area behind the driver has been converted into a living space.

convert ▸ verb /kən'vəːt/ 1 [with obj.] change the form, character, or function of something: *modernization has **converted** the country **from** a primitive society **to** a near-industrial one.* ■ [no obj.] be able to change from one form to another: *the seating **converts to** a double or two single beds.* ■ change (money, stocks, or units in which a quantity is expressed) into others of a different kind. ■ adapt (a building) to make it suitable for a new purpose: *the company converted a disused cinema to house twelve machinists | (as adj. **converted**) a converted Victorian property.* ■ Logic transpose the subject and predicate of (a proposition) according to certain rules to form a new proposition by inference.
2 [no obj.] change one's religious faith or other belief: *at sixteen he **converted to** Catholicism.* ■ [with obj.] persuade (someone) to change their religious faith or other belief: *he was **converted** in his later years **to** the socialist cause.*
3 [with obj.] score from (a penalty kick, pass, or other opportunity) in a sport or game. ■ Rugby score extra points after (a try) by a successful kick at goal. ■ American Football advance the ball far enough after (a down) to get another try for a first down. ■ American Football make an extra score after (a touchdown) by kicking a goal (one point) or running another play into the end zone (two points).
▸ noun /'kɒnvəːt/ a person who has been persuaded to change their religious faith or other belief: *he is a recent **convert to** the Church.*
– PHRASES **convert something to one's own use** Law wrongfully make use of another's property.
– ORIGIN Middle English (in the sense 'turn round, send in a different direction'): from Old French *convertir*, based on Latin *convertere* 'turn about', from *con-* 'altogether' + *vertere* 'turn'.

converted rice ▸ noun [mass noun] N. Amer. (trademark in the US) white rice prepared from brown rice that has been soaked, steamed under pressure, and then dried and milled.

converter (also **convertor**) ▸ noun a person or thing that converts something: *the would-be converter of a building to domestic use.* ■ a device for altering the nature of an electric current or signal, especially from AC to DC or vice versa, or from analogue to digital or vice versa. ■ a retort used in steel-making. ■ short for **CATALYTIC CONVERTER**. ■ Computing a program that converts data from one format to another. ■ a camera lens which changes the focal length of another lens by a set amount.

converter reactor ▸ noun a nuclear reactor that converts fertile material into fissile material.

convertible ▸ adjective able to be changed in form, function, or character: *a convertible sofa | nationalism is too easily **convertible into** bitterness and selfishness.* ■ (of currency) able to be converted into other forms, especially into gold or US dollars. ■ (of a bond or stock) able to be converted into ordinary or preference shares. ■ (of a car) having a folding or detachable roof. ■ Logic (of terms) synonymous.
▸ noun 1 a car with a folding or detachable roof.
2 (usu. **convertibles**) a convertible security.
– DERIVATIVES **convertibility** noun.
– ORIGIN late Middle English (in the sense 'interchangeable'): from Old French, from Latin *convertibilis*, from *convertere* 'turn about' (see **CONVERT**).

convex /'kɒnvɛks/ ▸ adjective 1 having an outline or surface curved like the exterior of a circle or sphere. Compare with **CONCAVE**.
2 (of a polygon) not having any interior angles greater than 180°.
– DERIVATIVES **convexity** noun, **convexly** adverb.
– ORIGIN late 16th cent.: from Latin *convexus* 'vaulted, arched'.

convexo-concave /kən'vɛksəʊ/ ▸ adjective (of a lens) convex on one side and concave on the other and thickest in the centre.

convey /kən'veɪ/ ▸ verb 1 [with obj.] transport or carry to a place: *pipes were laid to **convey** water **to** the house.* ■ make (an idea, impression, or feeling) known or understandable: *the real virtues and diversity of America had never been conveyed in the movies | [with clause] it's impossible to convey how lost I felt.* ■ communicate (a message or information): *Mr Harvey and his daughter have asked me to convey their very kind regards.*
2 Law transfer the title to (property).
– ORIGIN Middle English (in the sense 'escort'; compare with **CONVOY**): from Old French *conveier*, from medieval Latin *conviare*, from *con-* 'together' + Latin *via* 'way'.

conveyance ▸ noun [mass noun] 1 the action or process of transporting or carrying someone or something from one place to another: *a busy centre for the*

C

C

conveyance of agricultural produce from the Billingshurst area. ■ [count noun] formal or humorous a means of transport; a vehicle: *adventurers attempt the trail using all manner of conveyances, including mountain bikes and motorcycles.* ■ the action of making an idea, feeling, or impression known or understandable to someone: *a role that demands much more than the conveyance of simple emotions.*
2 Law the legal process of transferring property from one owner to another. ■ [count noun] a legal document effecting such a process in the case of an unregistered title.

conveyancing ▸ **noun** [mass noun] the branch of law concerned with the preparation of documents for the conveyance of property. ■ the action of preparing documents for the conveyance of property.
– DERIVATIVES **conveyancer noun.**

conveyor (also **conveyer**) ▸ **noun** a person or thing that transports or communicates something: *a conveyor of information.* ■ a conveyor belt.

conveyor belt ▸ **noun** a continuous moving band of fabric, rubber, or metal used for transporting objects from one place to another.

convict ▸ **verb** /kənˈvɪkt/ declare (someone) to be guilty of a criminal offence by the verdict of a jury or the decision of a judge in a court of law: *her former boyfriend was **convicted of** assaulting her* | (as adj. **convicted**) *a convicted murderer.*
▸ **noun** /ˈkɒnvɪkt/ a person found guilty of a criminal offence and serving a sentence of imprisonment.
– ORIGIN Middle English: from Latin *convict-* 'demonstrated, refuted, convicted', from the verb *convincere* (see **CONVINCE**). The noun is from obsolete *convict* 'convicted'.

conviction ▸ **noun 1** a formal declaration by the verdict of a jury or the decision of a judge in a court of law that someone is guilty of a criminal offence: *she had a previous conviction for a similar offence.*
2 a firmly held belief or opinion: *she takes pride in stating her political convictions* | [with clause] *his conviction that the death was no accident was stronger.* ■ [mass noun] the quality of showing that one is firmly convinced of what one believes or says: *she had been speaking for some five minutes with force and conviction.*
– ORIGIN late Middle English: from Latin *convictio(n-)*, from the verb *convincere* (see **CONVINCE**).

convince ▸ **verb** [with obj.] cause (someone) to believe firmly in the truth of something: *Robert's expression had obviously **convinced** her **of** his innocence* | [with obj. and clause] *we had to convince politicians that they needed to do something.* ■ [with obj. and infinitive] persuade (someone) to do something: *she convinced my father to branch out on his own.*
– DERIVATIVES **convincer noun.**
– ORIGIN mid 16th cent. (in the sense 'overcome, defeat in argument'): from Latin *convincere*, from *con-* 'with' + *vincere* 'conquer'. Compare with **CONVICT**.

> **USAGE** Convince used (with an infinitive) as a synonym for **persuade** first became common in the 1950s in the US, as in *she **convinced** my father **to** branch out on his own.* Some traditionalists deplore the blurring of distinction between **convince** and **persuade**, maintaining that **convince** should be reserved for situations in which someone's belief is changed but no action is taken as a result (*he **convinced** me that he was right*) while **persuade** should be used for situations in which action results (*he **persuaded** me* rather than *he **convinced** me to seek more advice*). In practice the newer use is well established.

convinced ▸ **adjective** completely certain about something: *she was not entirely **convinced of** the soundness of his motives* | [with clause] *I am convinced the war will be over in a matter of months.* ■ [attrib.] firm in one's belief with regard to a particular cause or issue: *a convinced pacifist.*

convincing ▸ **adjective** capable of causing someone to believe that something is true or real: *there is no convincing evidence that advertising influences total alcohol consumption.* ■ (of a victory or a winner) leaving no margin of doubt; clear: *Wales cruised to a convincing win over Ireland.*
– DERIVATIVES **convincingly adverb.**

convivial /kənˈvɪvɪəl/ ▸ **adjective** (of an atmosphere or event) friendly, lively, and enjoyable: *a convivial cocktail party.* ■ (of a person) cheerful and friendly; jovial: *she was relaxed and convivial.*
– DERIVATIVES **convivially adverb.**
– ORIGIN mid 17th cent. (in the sense 'fit for a feast, festive'): from Latin *convivialis*, from *convivium* 'a feast', from *con-* 'with' + *vivere* 'live'.

conviviality /kənˌvɪvɪˈalɪti/ ▸ **noun** [mass noun] the quality of being friendly and lively; friendliness: *the conviviality of the evening.*

convo ▸ **noun** (pl. **convos**) informal, chiefly Austral. a conversation: *I struck up a convo with the girl sitting next to me.*

convocation /ˌkɒnvəˈkeɪʃ(ə)n/ ▸ **noun 1** a large formal assembly of people, in particular: ■ (in the Church of England) a representative assembly of clergy of the province of Canterbury or York. ■ Brit. a legislative or deliberative assembly of a university. ■ N. Amer. a formal ceremony for the conferment of university awards.
2 [mass noun] the action of calling people together for a large formal assembly.
– DERIVATIVES **convocational adjective.**
– ORIGIN late Middle English: from Latin *convocatio(n-)*, from the verb *convocare* (see **CONVOKE**).

convoke /kənˈvəʊk/ ▸ **verb** [with obj.] formal call together or summon (an assembly or meeting): *she sent messages convoking a Council of Ministers.*
– ORIGIN late 16th cent.: from Latin *convocare*, from *con-* 'together' + *vocare* 'call'.

convoluted /ˌkɒnvəˈl(j)uːtɪd/ ▸ **adjective 1** (especially of an argument, story, or sentence) extremely complex and difficult to follow: *the film is let down by a convoluted plot in which nothing really happens.*
2 chiefly technical intricately folded, twisted, or coiled: *walnuts come in hard and convoluted shells.*
– DERIVATIVES **convolute verb.**
– ORIGIN late 18th cent.: past participle of *convolute*, from Latin *convolutus*, past participle of *convolvere* 'roll together, intertwine' (see **CONVOLVE**).

convolution ▸ **noun 1** a coil or twist: *crosses adorned with elaborate convolutions.* ■ [mass noun] the state of being or process of becoming coiled or twisted.
2 a thing that is complex and difficult to follow: *the convolutions of farm policy.*
3 a sinuous fold in the surface of the brain.
4 (also **convolution integral**) Mathematics a function derived from two given functions by integration which expresses how the shape of one is modified by the other. ■ a method of determination of the sum of two random variables by integration or summation.
– DERIVATIVES **convolutional adjective.**
– ORIGIN mid 16th cent.: from medieval Latin *convolutio(n-)*, from *convolvere* 'roll together' (see **CONVOLVE**).

convolve /kənˈvɒlv/ ▸ **verb** [with obj.] **1** rare roll or coil together; entwine.
2 Mathematics combine (one function or series) with another by forming their convolution.
– ORIGIN late 16th cent. (in the sense 'enclose in folds'): from Latin *convolvere* 'roll together', from *con-* 'together' + *volvere* 'roll'.

convolvulus /kənˈvɒlvjʊləs/ ▸ **noun** (pl. **convolvuluses**) a twining plant with trumpet-shaped flowers, of which some kinds are invasive weeds (see also **BINDWEED**), and others are cultivated for their bright flowers. ● Genus *Convolvulus*, family Convolvulaceae.
– ORIGIN Latin, 'bindweed', from *convolvere* 'roll together' (see **CONVOLVE**).

convoy /ˈkɒnvɔɪ/ ▸ **noun** a group of ships or vehicles travelling together, typically one accompanied by armed troops, warships, or other vehicles for protection: *a convoy of lorries.*
▸ **verb** [with obj.] (of a warship or armed troops) accompany (a group of ships or vehicles) for protection.
– PHRASES **in convoy** as a group; together: *the army trucks had passed through in convoy the previous evening.*
– ORIGIN late Middle English (originally Scots, as a verb in the senses 'convey', 'conduct', and 'act as escort'): from French *convoyer*, from medieval Latin *conviare* (see **CONVEY**).

convulsant ▸ **adjective** (chiefly of drugs) producing sudden and involuntary muscle contractions.
▸ **noun** a convulsant drug.
– ORIGIN late 19th cent.: from French, from *convulser*, from Latin *convuls-* 'pulled violently, wrenched', from the verb *convellere* (see **CONVULSE**).

convulse /kənˈvʌls/ ▸ **verb 1** [no obj.] suffer violent involuntary contraction of the muscles, producing contortion of the body or limbs: *she convulsed, collapsing to the floor with the pain.* ■ [with obj.] (of an emotion, laughter, or physical stimulus) cause (someone) to make sudden, violent, uncontrollable movements: *she rocked backwards and forwards, convulsed with helpless mirth.*
2 [with obj.] throw (a country) into violent social or political upheaval: *a wave of mass strikes convulsed the Ruhr, Berlin, and central Germany.*
– ORIGIN mid 17th cent.: from Latin *convuls-* 'pulled violently, wrenched', from the verb *convellere*, from *con-* 'together' + *vellere* 'to pull'.

convulsion ▸ **noun** (often **convulsions**) **1** a sudden, violent, irregular movement of the body, caused by involuntary contraction of muscles and associated especially with brain disorders such as epilepsy, the presence of certain toxins or other agents in the blood, or fever in children. ■ (**convulsions**) uncontrollable laughter: *the audience collapsed in convulsions.* ■ an earthquake or other violent or major movement of the earth's crust: *the violent convulsions of tectonic plates.*
2 a violent social or political upheaval: *the convulsions of 1939–45.*
– ORIGIN mid 16th cent. (originally in the sense 'cramp, spasm'): from Latin *convulsio(n-)*, from the verb *convellere* (see **CONVULSE**).

convulsive ▸ **adjective** producing or consisting of convulsions: *a convulsive disease* | *she gave a convulsive sob.*
– DERIVATIVES **convulsively adverb.**

Conwy /ˈkɒnwi/ (also **Conway**) a market town and county in North Wales, on the River Conwy; town pop. 3,900 (est. 2009). A railway bridge built by Stephenson in 1848 and a suspension bridge built by Telford in 1826 span the river here.

cony ▸ **noun** (pl. **conies**) variant spelling of **CONEY**.

coo[1] ▸ **verb** (**coos, cooing, cooed**) [no obj.] (of a pigeon or dove) make a soft murmuring sound: *ringdoves cooed among the branches.* ■ (of a person) speak in a soft gentle voice: *she cooed with delight as he unpacked the bags* | [with direct speech] *'I knew I could count on you,' she cooed.*
▸ **noun** a soft murmuring sound made by a dove or pigeon.
– ORIGIN mid 17th cent.: imitative.

coo[2] ▸ **exclamation** Brit. informal used to express surprise: *'Coo, ain't it high!' Mary squeaked.*
– ORIGIN early 20th cent.: imitative.

co-occur ▸ **verb** [no obj.] occur together or simultaneously.
– DERIVATIVES **co-occurrence noun.**

cooee informal ▸ **exclamation** used to attract attention, especially at a distance: *'Cooee!' The call brought all three heads round.*
▸ **verb** (**cooees, cooeeing, cooeed**) [no obj.] make a call to attract attention.
– PHRASES **within cooee** Austral./NZ within reach; near: *there's loads of cheap accommodation **within cooee of** the airport.*
– ORIGIN late 18th cent.: imitative of a signal used by Australian Aborigines and copied by settlers.

Cook[1], Captain James (1728–79), English explorer. On his first expedition to the Pacific (1768–71), he charted the coasts of New Zealand and New Guinea as well as exploring the east coast of Australia and claiming it for Britain. He made two more voyages to the Pacific before being killed in a skirmish with indigenous people in Hawaii.

Cook[2], Peter (Edward) (1937–95), English comedian and actor. A writer and performer of the revue *Beyond the Fringe* (1959–64), he is remembered also for his television partnership with Dudley Moore. He had a long association with the satirical magazine *Private Eye.*

Cook[3], Thomas (1808–92), English founder of the travel firm Thomas Cook. In 1841 he organized the first publicly advertised excursion train in England; the success of this venture led him to organize further excursions both in Britain and abroad, laying the foundations for the tourist and travel-agent industry.

cook ▸ **verb 1** [with obj.] prepare (food, a dish, or a meal) by mixing, combining, and heating the ingredients: *shall I cook dinner tonight?* | [with two objs] *she cooked me eggs and bacon* | (as adj. **cooked**) *a cooked breakfast.* ■ [no obj.] (of food) be heated so that the state required for eating is reached: *while the rice is cooking, add the saffron to the stock.*
2 [with obj.] informal alter dishonestly; falsify: *a narcotics team who cooked the evidence.*
3 [no obj.] (**be cooking**) informal be happening or planned: *what's cooking on the alternative fuels front?*
4 [no obj.] N. Amer. informal perform or proceed vigorously or very well: *the band used to get up on the bandstand and really cook.*

▶ noun a person who prepares and cooks food, especially as a job or in a specified way: *Susan was a school cook | I'm a good cook.*
– PHRASES **cook the books** informal alter facts or figures dishonestly or illegally. **cook someone's goose** informal spoil someone's plans; cause someone's downfall. **too many cooks spoil the broth** proverb if too many people are involved in a task or activity, it will not be done well.
– PHRASAL VERBS **cook something up** concoct a clever or devious story, excuse, or plan: *I've had plenty of time to cook up an outlandish conspiracy theory.*
– ORIGIN Old English *cōc* (noun), from popular Latin *cocus*, from Latin *coquus*.

Cook, Mount the highest peak in New Zealand, in the Southern Alps in the South Island, rising to a height of 3,764 m (12,349 ft). It is named after Captain James Cook. Official name AORAKI/MOUNT COOK.

cookbook ▶ noun a cookery book.

cook-chill ▶ adjective [attrib.] Brit. relating to or denoting a procedure whereby food is cooked and refrigerated by the manufacturer ready for reheating by the consumer: *cook-chill food | cook-chill processes.*

Cooke, Sir William Fothergill (1806–79), English inventor. With Sir Charles Wheatstone he invented the electric telegraph alarm.

cooker ▶ noun Brit. **1** an appliance used for cooking food, typically consisting of an oven, hob, and grill and powered by gas or electricity.
2 informal an apple or other fruit that is more suitable for cooking than for eating raw.

cookery ▶ noun (pl. **cookeries**) **1** [mass noun] the practice or skill of preparing and cooking food.
2 N. Amer. a place in which food is cooked; a kitchen.

cookery book ▶ noun chiefly Brit. a book containing recipes and other information about the preparation and cooking of food.

cookhouse ▶ noun **1** a kitchen or dining hall in a military camp.
2 an outdoor kitchen in a warm country.

cookie ▶ noun (pl. **cookies**) **1** N. Amer. a sweet biscuit.
2 [with adj.] informal a person of a specified kind: *she's a tough cookie.*
3 Scottish a plain bun.
4 Computing a packet of data sent by an Internet server to a browser, which is returned by the browser each time it subsequently accesses the same server, used to identify the user or track their access to the server.
– PHRASES **that's the way the cookie crumbles** informal, chiefly N. Amer. that's the way the situation is, and it must be accepted, however undesirable.
– ORIGIN early 18th cent.: from Dutch *koekje* 'little cake', diminutive of *koek*.

cookie cutter ▶ noun N. Amer. a device with sharp edges for cutting biscuit dough into a particular shape. ■ [as modifier] denoting something mass-produced or lacking any distinguishing characteristics: *a cookie-cutter apartment in a high-rise building.*

cookie jar ▶ noun N. Amer. a jar for biscuits or small cakes.
– PHRASES **with one's hand in the cookie jar** engaged in surreptitious theft from one's employer: *they got caught with their hands in the cookie jar.*

cookie sheet ▶ noun N. Amer. a flat metal tray on which biscuits or cakes may be cooked.

cooking ▶ noun [mass noun] the process of preparing food by heating it. ■ food that has been prepared in a particular way: *authentic Italian cooking.* ■ [as modifier] suitable for or used in cooking: *cooking chocolate.*

Cook Islands a group of fifteen islands in the SW Pacific Ocean between Tonga and French Polynesia, which have the status of a self-governing territory in free association with New Zealand; pop. 11,900 (est. 2009); languages, English (official), Rarotongan (a Polynesian language); capital, Avarua, on Rarotonga.
– ORIGIN named after Captain James Cook (see COOK[1]), who visited them in 1773.

cookout ▶ noun N. Amer. a party or gathering where a meal is cooked and eaten outdoors.

cookshop ▶ noun **1** archaic a shop selling cooked food.
2 Brit. a shop selling cooking equipment.

Cook's tour ▶ noun informal a rapid tour of many places: *let me give you the Cook's tour of the works here* | figurative *he then took me on a Cook's tour of his scientific theories.*
– ORIGIN early 20th cent.: from the name of the travel agent Thomas Cook (see COOK[3]).

Cook Strait the strait separating the South Island and the North Island of New Zealand. It was named after Captain James Cook, who visited it in 1770.

cooktop ▶ noun N. Amer. a cooking unit, usually with hot plates or burners, built into or fixed on the top of a cabinet or other surface.

cookware ▶ noun [mass noun] pots, pans, or dishes in which food can be cooked: *cast-iron cookware.*

cool ▶ adjective **1** of or at a fairly low temperature: *it'll be a cool afternoon | the wind kept them cool.* ■ soothing or refreshing because of its low temperature: *a long, cool glass of orange juice.* ■ (especially of clothing) keeping one from becoming too hot: *a cool cotton dress.* ■ (of a colour) containing pale blue, green, or grey tones: *the bathroom was all glass and cool, muted blues.*
2 showing no friendliness towards a person or enthusiasm for an idea or project: *he gave a cool reception to the suggestion for a research centre.* ■ free from excitement, anxiety, or excessive emotion: *he prided himself on **keeping a cool head** | she seems **cool, calm, and collected**.* ■ (of jazz) restrained and relaxed.
3 informal fashionably attractive or impressive: *youngsters are turning to smoking because they think it makes them appear cool.* ■ excellent: [as exclamation] *our office was a sunny room with a computer you didn't even have to plug in. Cool!* ■ used to express acceptance of or agreement with something: *if people want to freak out at our clubs, that's cool.*
4 (**a cool ——**) informal used to emphasize the size of an amount of money: *research for a new drug can cost a cool £50 million.*
▶ noun [mass noun] **1** (**the cool**) a fairly low temperature: *the cool of the night air.* ■ a time or place at which the temperature is pleasantly low: *the cool of the day.*
2 calmness; composure: *he recovered his cool and then started laughing at us.*
3 the quality of being fashionably attractive or impressive: *all the cool of high fashion.*
▶ verb become or make less hot: [no obj.] *we dived into the river to **cool off** |* [with obj.] *cool the pastry for five minutes.* ■ become or make calm or less excited: [no obj.] *after I'd **cooled off**, I realized I was being irrational |* [with obj.] *George was trying to **cool him down**.* ■ [no obj.] (**cool out**) chiefly W. Indian relax: *a dreamy spot full of sunshine and sea where you could cool out and detox.*
– PHRASES **cool it!** informal behave in a less excitable manner: *cool it and tell me why you're so ecstatic.* **cool one's heels** see HEEL[1]. **keep** (or **lose**) **one's cool** informal maintain (or fail to maintain) a calm and controlled attitude: *he finally lost his cool with a photographer and threatened to hit him.* **too cool for school** informal very cool or fashionable: *he has no brains, no looks, no personality, but he still thinks he's too cool for school.*
– DERIVATIVES **cooled** adjective [in combination] *a water-cooled engine*, **coolish** adjective, **coolly** adverb, **coolness** noun.
– ORIGIN Old English *cōl* (noun), *cōlian* (verb), of Germanic origin; related to Dutch *koel*, also to COLD.

WORD TRENDS Cool hasn't just meant 'chilly' since the 1920s, when it started being used by black Americans to describe someone or something fashionable, stylish, and impressive. This sense became more widely known in the 1940s, with the popularity of jazz and beatnik culture, and was then particularly 'cool' in the 1960s. As is often the fate of popular slang, the word itself became 'uncool' for a couple of decades, before reclaiming its place as a favourite way of expressing positive feelings (*there's a lot of cool stuff happening in Manchester | winning awards is such a cool thing*) or agreement (*if you want to use mine, that's cool*). The Oxford English Corpus shows that this use is now just as common as the word's original sense of 'at a fairly low temperature'. See also STUFF.

coolabah /ˈkuːləbɑː/ ▶ noun variant spelling of COOLIBAH.

coolant ▶ noun a liquid or gas that is used to remove heat from something.
– ORIGIN 1930s: from COOL, on the pattern of *lubricant*.

cool bag ▶ noun Brit. a soft insulated container for keeping food and drink cool.

cool box (also **cool bag**) ▶ noun Brit. a rigid insulated container for keeping food and drink cool.

cooldrink ▶ noun S. African a soft drink.

cooler ▶ noun **1** a container for keeping food or bottles cool.
2 N. Amer. a refrigerator.
3 chiefly N. Amer. a long drink, especially a mixture of wine, fruit juice, and soda water.
4 (**the cooler**) informal prison or a prison cell.

Cooley's anaemia /ˈkuːlɪz/ ▶ noun another term for THALASSAEMIA.
– ORIGIN 1930s: named after Thomas B. *Cooley* (1871–1945), American paediatrician.

cool-headed ▶ adjective not easily worried or excited.

cool hunter ▶ noun informal a person whose job is to make observations or predictions about new styles and trends.
– DERIVATIVES **cool hunting** noun.

coolibah /ˈkuːlɪbɑː/ (also **coolabah**) ▶ noun a North Australian gum tree which typically grows near watercourses and yields very strong, hard timber.
● *Eucalyptus microtheca*, family Myrtaceae.
– ORIGIN late 19th cent.: from Kamilaroi (and related languages) *gulubaa*.

Coolidge /ˈkuːlɪdʒ/, (John) Calvin (1872–1933), American Republican statesman, 30th President of the US 1923–9.

coolie /ˈkuːli/ ▶ noun (pl. **coolies**) dated an unskilled native labourer in India, China, and some other Asian countries. ■ offensive a person from South or East Asia.
– ORIGIN mid 17th cent.: from Hindi and Telugu *kūlī* 'day labourer', probably associated with Urdu *ḳulī* 'slave'.

coolie hat ▶ noun a broad conical hat as worn by labourers in some Asian countries.

cooling-off period ▶ noun an interval during which two sides in a disagreement can try to settle their differences before taking further action. ■ a period of time after a sale contract is agreed during which the buyer can cancel the contract without incurring a penalty.

cooling tower ▶ noun a tall, open-topped, cylindrical concrete tower, used for cooling water or condensing steam from an industrial process.

CoolMax ▶ noun [mass noun] trademark a polyester fabric which draws perspiration along its fibres away from the skin, used chiefly in sportswear.
– ORIGIN 1980s: an invented name, probably from COOL + MAX.

coolth /kuːlθ/ ▶ noun [mass noun] **1** pleasantly low temperature: *the coolth of the evening.*
2 informal the quality of being fashionable: *the pinnacle of 1960s coolth.*
– ORIGIN mid 16th cent. (but rare before the 20th cent.): from COOL + -TH[2].

coomb (also **coombe**) ▶ noun variant spelling of COMBE.

coon ▶ noun **1** N. Amer. short for RACCOON.
2 informal, offensive a black person. [slang use of sense 1, from an earlier sense '(sly) fellow'.]
– PHRASES **for** (or **in**) **a coon's age** N. Amer. informal, dated for a very long time.

cooncan /ˈkuːnkan/ ▶ noun [mass noun] a card game for two players, originally from Mexico, similar to rummy.
– ORIGIN late 19th cent.: probably from Spanish *con quién* 'with whom?'.

coonhound ▶ noun a dog of a black and tan American breed, used to hunt raccoons.

coonskin ▶ noun the pelt of a raccoon.

coop ▶ noun a cage or pen in which poultry are kept. ■ Brit. a basket used in catching fish.
▶ verb [with obj.] **1** (usu. **be cooped up**) confine in a small space: *being cooped up indoors all day makes him fidgety.*
2 put or keep (poultry) in a cage or pen.
– ORIGIN Middle English *cowpe*; related to Dutch *kuip* 'vat' and German *Kufe* 'cask', based on Latin *cupa*. Compare with COOPER.

co-op /ˈkəʊɒp/ ▶ noun informal a cooperative society, shop, business, or farm.
– ORIGIN mid 19th cent.: abbreviation.

Cooper[1], Gary (1901–61), American actor; born *Frank James Cooper*. He is noted for his performances in such westerns as *The Virginian* (1929) and *High Noon* (1952).

Cooper[2], Sir Henry (b.1934), English boxer, the only man to win a Lonsdale belt outright three times. He knocked down Muhammad Ali (then Cassius Clay) in 1963, but a bad cut inflicted by the same opponent in 1966 in his only world title fight hastened his retirement in 1971.

Cooper[3], James Fenimore (1789–1851), American novelist. He is renowned for his tales of American

Indians and frontier life, in particular *The Last of the Mohicans* (1826).

cooper ▶ **noun** a maker or repairer of casks and barrels.
▶ **verb** [with obj.] make or repair (a cask or barrel).
– ORIGIN Middle English *cowper*, from Middle Dutch, Middle Low German *kūper*, from *kūpe* 'tub, vat', based on Latin *cupa*. Compare with **COOP**.

C

cooperage ▶ **noun** a cooper's business or premises. ■ [mass noun] the making of barrels and casks.

cooperate /kəʊˈɒpəreɪt/ (also **co-operate**) ▶ **verb** [no obj.] work jointly towards the same end: *the leaders promised to* ***cooperate in*** *ending the civil war* | *staff need to* ***cooperate with each other***. ■ assist someone or comply with their requests: *his captor threatened to kill him if he didn't cooperate*.
– DERIVATIVES **cooperant** noun, **cooperator** noun.
– ORIGIN late 16th cent.: from ecclesiastical Latin *cooperat-* 'worked together', from the verb *cooperari*, from *co-* 'together' + *operari* 'to work'.

cooperation (also **co-operation**) ▶ **noun** [mass noun] the action or process of working together to the same end: *they worked* ***in close cooperation with*** *the British Tourist Authority*. ■ assistance, especially by complying readily with requests: *we should like to ask for your cooperation in the survey*. ■ Economics the formation and operation of cooperatives.
– ORIGIN late Middle English: from Latin *cooperatio(n-)*, from the verb *cooperari* (see **COOPERATE**); later reinforced by French *coopération*.

cooperative (also **co-operative**) ▶ **adjective** involving mutual assistance in working towards a common goal: *every member has clearly defined tasks in a cooperative enterprise*. ■ willing to be of assistance: *they have been extremely considerate, polite, and cooperative*. ■ (of a farm, business, etc.) owned and run jointly by its members, with profits or benefits shared among them.
▶ **noun** a farm, business, or other organization which is owned and run jointly by its members, who share the profits or benefits.
– DERIVATIVES **cooperatively** adverb, **cooperativeness** noun.
– ORIGIN early 17th cent.: from late Latin *cooperativus*, from Latin *cooperat-* 'worked together', from the verb *cooperari* (see **COOPERATE**).

cooperative movement ▶ **noun** a movement originating in the industrial areas of northern England and Scotland in the late 18th century, based on the belief that industries and commercial concerns should be owned and controlled by the people working in them, for joint economic benefit.

Cooperative Republic of Guyana official name for **GUYANA**.

Cooper pair ▶ **noun** Physics a loosely bound pair of electrons with opposite spins and moving with the same speed in opposite directions, held to be responsible for the phenomenon of superconductivity. ■ a similar bound pair of atoms in a superfluid.
– ORIGIN 1960s: named after Leon N. *Cooper* (born 1930), American physicist.

coopery ▶ **noun** (pl. **cooperies**) another term for **COOPERAGE**.

coopetition /ˌkəʊɒpəˈtɪʃ(ə)n/ ▶ **noun** [mass noun] collaboration between business competitors, in the hope of mutually beneficial results.
– ORIGIN 1980s: from **COOPERATIVE** + **COMPETITION**.

co-opt ▶ **verb** [with obj.] appoint to membership of a committee or other body by invitation of the existing members. ■ divert to or use in a role different from the usual or original one: [with obj. and infinitive] *social scientists were co-opted to work with the development agencies*. ■ adopt (an idea or policy) for one's own use: *the green parties have had most of their ideas co-opted by bigger parties*.
– DERIVATIVES **co-optation** noun, **co-option** noun, **co-optive** adjective.
– ORIGIN mid 17th cent.: from Latin *cooptare*, from *co-* 'together' + *optare* 'choose'.

coordinate (also **co-ordinate**) ▶ **verb** /kəʊˈɔːdɪneɪt/ [with obj.] **1** bring the different elements of (a complex activity or organization) into a harmonious or efficient relationship: *he had responsibility for coordinating London's transport services*. ■ [no obj.] negotiate with others in order to work together effectively: *you will* ***coordinate with*** *consultants and other departments on a variety of projects*. ■ [no obj.] match or harmonize attractively: *the stud fastenings are coloured to* ***coordinate with*** *the shirt* | (as adj. **coordinating**) *a variety of coordinating colours*.
2 Chemistry form a coordinate bond to (an atom or molecule).
▶ **adjective** /kəʊˈɔːdɪnət/ **1** equal in rank or importance: *cross references in the catalogue link subjects which may be coordinate*. ■ Grammar (of parts of a compound sentence) equal in rank and fulfilling identical functions.
2 Chemistry denoting a type of covalent bond in which one atom provides both the shared electrons.
▶ **noun** /kəʊˈɔːdɪnət/ **1** each of a group of numbers used to indicate the position of a point, line, or plane.
2 (**coordinates**) matching items of clothing.
– DERIVATIVES **coordinative** adjective, **coordinator** noun.
– ORIGIN mid 17th cent. (in the senses 'of the same rank' and 'place in the same rank'): from **co-** 'together' + Latin *ordinare* (from *ordo* 'order'), on the pattern of *subordinate*.

Coordinated Universal Time another term for **GREENWICH MEAN TIME**.

coordinating conjunction ▶ **noun** a conjunction placed between words, phrases, clauses, or sentences of equal rank, e.g. *and*, *but*, *or*. Contrasted with **SUBORDINATING CONJUNCTION**.

coordination /kəʊˌɔːdɪˈneɪʃ(ə)n/ ▶ **noun** [mass noun] **1** the organization of the different elements of a complex body or activity so as to enable them to work together effectively: *an important managerial task is the control and coordination of activities*. ■ cooperative effort resulting in an effective relationship: *action groups work* ***in coordination with*** *local groups to end rainforest destruction*.
2 the ability to use different parts of the body together smoothly and efficiently: *changing from one foot position to another requires coordination and balance*.
3 Chemistry the linking of atoms by coordinate bonds.
– ORIGIN mid 17th cent. (in the sense 'placing in the same rank'): from French or from late Latin *coordinatio(n-)*, based on Latin *ordo*, *ordin-* 'order'.

coordination compound ▶ **noun** Chemistry a compound containing coordinate bonds, typically between a central metal atom and a number of other atoms or groups.

coordination number ▶ **noun** Chemistry the number of atoms or ions immediately surrounding a central atom in a complex or crystal.

coot ▶ **noun 1** (pl. **same**) an aquatic bird of the rail family, with blackish plumage, lobed feet, and a bill that extends back on to the forehead as a horny shield. ● Genus *Fulica*, family Rallidae: several species, in particular the widespread *F. atra*, which has a white bill and frontal shield.
2 (usu. **old coot**) informal a stupid or eccentric person, typically an old man.
– ORIGIN Middle English: probably of Dutch or Low German origin and related to Dutch *koet*.

cooter ▶ **noun** a North American river turtle with a dull brown shell and typically having yellow stripes on the head. ● Genus *Pseudemys*, family Emydidae: several species, in particular *P. concinna*, some races of which are known as sliders.
– ORIGIN early 19th cent.: of unknown origin.

cootie /ˈkuːti/ ▶ **noun** N. Amer. informal a body louse.
– ORIGIN First World War: perhaps from Malay *kutu*, denoting a parasitic biting insect.

co-own ▶ **verb** [with obj.] own (something) jointly.
– DERIVATIVES **co-owner** noun, **co-ownership** noun.

cooze /kuːz/ ▶ **noun** N. Amer. vulgar slang a woman's genitals. ■ a woman, especially one regarded as sexually attractive or promiscuous.
– ORIGIN 1950s: origin uncertain.

cop[1] informal ▶ **noun 1** a police officer.
2 (also **cop-on**) [mass noun] Irish shrewdness; practical intelligence: *he had the cop-on to stay clear of Hugh Thornley*.
▶ **verb** (**cops**, **copping**, **copped**) [with obj.] **1** catch or arrest (an offender): *he was copped for speeding*. ■ incur (something unwelcome): *England's captain copped most of the blame*. ■ (**cop it**) Brit. get into trouble: *will you cop it from your dad if you get back late?* ■ (**cop it**) Brit. be killed: *he almost copped it in a horrific accident*.
2 receive or attain (something welcome): *she copped an award for her role in the film*. ■ US obtain (an illegal drug).
3 N. Amer. strike (an attitude or pose): *I copped an attitude—I acted real tough*.
– PHRASES **cop hold of** [usu. in imperative] Brit. take hold of: *cop hold of the suitcase, I'm off*. **cop a plea** N. Amer. engage in plea bargaining. **good cop, bad cop** used to refer to a police interrogation technique in which one officer feigns a sympathetic or protective attitude while another adopts an aggressive approach: *questioners often* ***play good cop, bad cop*** | figurative *the prime minister and chancellor were involved in a classic good cop, bad cop routine*. **it's a fair cop** see **FAIR**[1]. **not much cop** Brit. not very good: *they say he's not much cop as a coach*.
– PHRASAL VERBS **cop off** Brit. have a sexual encounter: *loads of girls think that guys just want to* ***cop off with any girl***. **cop on** Irish become aware of something: *she never copped on—you've no idea of the guilt I went through*. ■ [as imperative] used as a way of telling someone not to be so stupid: *ah, cop on, I was only messin'*. **cop out** avoid doing something that one ought to do: *he would not* ***cop out of*** *the difficult tax decisions*. **cop to** US accept or admit to: *there are a lot of people in the world who don't cop to their past*.
– ORIGIN early 18th cent. (as a verb): perhaps from obsolete *cap* 'arrest', from Old French *caper* 'seize', from Latin *capere*. The noun is from **COPPER**[2].

cop[2] ▶ **noun** a conical mass of thread wound on to a spindle.
– ORIGIN late 18th cent.: possibly from Old English *cop* 'summit, top'.

Copacabana Beach /ˌkɒpəkəˈbanə/ a resort on the Atlantic coast of Brazil near Rio de Janeiro.

copacetic /ˌkəʊpəˈsɛtɪk, -ˈsiːt-/ ▶ **adjective** N. Amer. informal in excellent order.
– ORIGIN early 20th cent.: of unknown origin.

copaiba /kəʊˈpʌɪbə/ ▶ **noun** [mass noun] an aromatic plant oil or resin used in medicines and perfumes. ● These resins are obtained from plants of the genus *Copaifera*.
– ORIGIN early 17th cent.: via Portuguese from Tupi *copaiba*, Guarani *cupaiba*.

copal /ˈkəʊp(ə)l/ ▶ **noun** [mass noun] resin from any of a number of tropical trees, used to make varnish. ● The resin is obtained from trees in the families Leguminosae (genera *Guibourtia*, *Copaifera*, and *Trachylobium*) and Araucariaceae (genus *Agathis*).
– ORIGIN late 16th cent.: via Spanish from Nahuatl *copalli* 'incense'.

Copán /kəʊˈpan/ an ancient Mayan city, in western Honduras near the Guatemalan frontier, the southernmost point of the Mayan empire.

coparcenary /kəʊˈpɑːs(ə)n(ə)ri/ ▶ **noun** (pl. **coparcenaries**) [mass noun] English Law joint heirship; the status of a coparcener.
– ORIGIN early 16th cent.: from **co-** 'together' + *parcenary*, legal term in the same sense, from Anglo-Norman French *parcenarie*, from *parcener* 'coparcener' (see **COPARCENER**).

coparcener /kəʊˈpɑːs(ə)nə/ ▶ **noun** English Law a person who shares equally with others in the inheritance of an undivided estate or in the rights to it (in the UK now as equitable interests).
– ORIGIN late Middle English: from **co-** 'together' + *parcener*, legal term in the same (see **PARTNER**).

co-parent ▶ **verb** [with obj.] (often as noun **co-parenting**) (especially of a separated or unmarried couple) share the duties of bringing up (a child).
▶ **noun** a person who co-parents a child.

co-partner ▶ **noun** a partner or associate, especially an equal partner in a business.
– DERIVATIVES **co-partnership** noun.

COPD ▶ **abbreviation** Medicine chronic obstructive pulmonary disease, involving constriction of the airways and difficulty or discomfort in breathing.

cope[1] ▶ **verb** [no obj.] (of a person) deal effectively with something difficult: *his ability to* ***cope with*** *stress* | *it all got too much for me and I couldn't cope*. ■ (of a machine or system) have the capacity to deal successfully with: *the roads are barely adequate to* ***cope with*** *the present traffic*.
– ORIGIN Middle English (in the sense 'meet in battle, come to blows'): from Old French *coper*, *colper*, from *cop*, *colp* 'a blow', via Latin from Greek *kolaphos* 'blow with the fist'.

cope[2] ▶ **noun** a long, loose cloak worn by a priest or bishop on ceremonial occasions. ■ technical or literary a thing resembling or likened to a cloak: *the outer shell of clay is called the cope*.
▶ **verb** [with obj.] (in building) cover (a joint or structure) with a coping: (as adj. **coped**) *a coped joint*.
– ORIGIN Middle English (denoting a long outdoor cloak): from medieval Latin *capa*, variant of late Latin *cappa* (see **CAP**[1] and **CAPE**[1]).

copeck ▶ **noun** variant spelling of **KOPEK**.

Copenhagen /ˌkəʊpənˈheɪg(ə)n, -ˈhɑːg(ə)n/ the capital and chief port of Denmark, a city occupying the eastern part of Zealand and northern part of the island of Amager; pop. 518,574 (2009). Danish name **KØBENHAVN**.

copepod /ˈkəʊpɪpɒd/ ▶ **noun** Zoology a small or microscopic aquatic crustacean of the large class Copepoda.

Copepoda /ˌkəʊpɪˈpəʊdə/ ▶ **plural noun** Zoology a large class of small aquatic crustaceans, many of which occur in plankton and some of which are parasitic on larger aquatic animals.
– ORIGIN modern Latin, from Greek *kōpē* 'handle, oar' + *pous, pod-* 'foot' (because of its paddle-like feet).

coper¹ (also **horse-coper**) ▶ **noun** archaic a horse-dealer.
– ORIGIN mid 16th cent.: from Middle English *cope* 'buy', from Dutch, Low German *kōpen*; related to German *kaufen*, also to **CHEAP**.

coper² ▶ **noun** a person who deals effectively with difficult situations: *Emma was always going to be fine. She was one of life's copers.*

Copernican system /kəˈpəːnɪk(ə)n/ (also **Copernican theory**) ▶ **noun** Astronomy the theory that the sun is the centre of the solar system, with the planets (including the earth) orbiting round it. Compare with **PTOLEMAIC SYSTEM**.
– ORIGIN mid 17th cent.: named after **COPERNICUS**.

Copernicus /kəˈpəːnɪkəs/, Nicolaus (1473–1543), Polish astronomer; Latinized name of *Mikołaj Kopernik*. He proposed a model of the solar system in which the planets orbited in perfect circles around the sun, and his work ultimately led to the overthrow of the established geocentric cosmology. He published his astronomical theories in *De Revolutionibus Orbium Coelestium* (1543).
– DERIVATIVES **Copernican** adjective.

copestone ▶ **noun** old-fashioned term for **COPING STONE**.
– ORIGIN mid 16th cent.: from **COPE²** + **STONE**.

copiable ▶ **adjective** able to be copied, especially legitimately.

copier ▶ **noun** a machine that makes exact copies of something, especially documents, video or audio recordings, or software.

co-pilot ▶ **noun** a second pilot in an aircraft.
▶ **verb** [with obj.] act as the co-pilot of (an aircraft).

coping ▶ **noun** the top, typically curved or sloping, course of a brick or stone wall.
– ORIGIN mid 16th cent.: from the verb **COPE²**, originally meaning 'dress in a cope', hence 'to cover'.

coping saw ▶ **noun** a saw with a very narrow blade stretched across a D-shaped frame, used for cutting curves in wood.
– ORIGIN 1920s: *coping* from **COPE²**, used to describe likeness to a vault, arch, canopy, etc.

coping stone ▶ **noun** chiefly Brit. a flat stone forming part of a coping. ■ the highest stone in a building, wall, or structure. ■ a finishing touch or crowning achievement.

copious ▶ **adjective** abundant in supply or quantity: *she took copious notes.* ■ archaic profuse in speech or ideas.
– DERIVATIVES **copiously** adverb, **copiousness** noun.
– ORIGIN late Middle English: from Old French *copieux* or Latin *copiosus*, from *copia* 'plenty'.

copita /kəˈpiːtə/ ▶ **noun** a slim stemmed glass that narrows slightly towards the top, used for sherry.
– ORIGIN mid 19th cent.: from Spanish, diminutive of *copa* 'cup', from popular Latin *cuppa* (see **CUP**).

coplanar /kəʊˈpleɪnə/ ▶ **adjective** Geometry in the same plane.
– DERIVATIVES **coplanarity** noun.

Copland /ˈkəʊplənd/, Aaron (1900–90), American composer, pianist, and conductor, of Lithuanian descent. He established a distinctive American style in his compositions, borrowing from jazz, folk, and other traditional music. Notable works: *Music for the Theater* (1925), *Appalachian Spring* (1944), *Fanfare for the Common Man* (1942).

Copley /ˈkɒpli/, John Singleton (1738–1815), American painter. He is noted for his portraits and for paintings such as *The Death of Chatham* (1779–80), one of the first large-scale paintings of contemporary events.

copolymer /kəʊˈpɒlɪmə/ ▶ **noun** Chemistry a polymer made by reaction of two different monomers, with units of more than one kind.

copolymerize (also **copolymerise**) ▶ **verb** [with obj.] Chemistry polymerize together to form a copolymer.
– DERIVATIVES **copolymerization** noun.

cop-out ▶ **noun** informal an instance of avoiding a commitment or responsibility.

copper¹ ▶ **noun 1** [mass noun] a red-brown metal, the chemical element of atomic number 29. (Symbol: **Cu**)

> Copper was the earliest metal to be used by humans, first by itself and then later alloyed with tin to form bronze. A ductile easily worked metal, it is a very good conductor of heat and electricity and is used especially for electrical wiring.

2 (**coppers**) Brit. brown coins of low value made of copper or bronze.
3 dated a large copper or iron container for boiling laundry.
4 [mass noun] a reddish-brown colour like that of copper.
5 [with modifier] a small butterfly with bright reddish-brown wings. ● Genus *Lycaena*, family Lycaenidae: many species.
▶ **verb** [with obj.] cover or coat (something) with copper.
– ORIGIN Old English *copor, coper* (related to Dutch *koper* and German *Kupfer*), based on late Latin *cuprum*, from Latin *cyprium aes* 'Cyprus metal' (so named because Cyprus was the chief source).

copper² ▶ **noun** Brit. informal a police officer.
– ORIGIN mid 19th cent.: from **COP¹** + **-ER¹**.

Copper Age Archaeology the Chalcolithic period, especially in SE Europe.

copperas /ˈkɒp(ə)rəs/ ▶ **noun** [mass noun] green crystals of hydrated ferrous sulphate, especially as an industrial product.
– ORIGIN late Middle English *coperose*, from Old French *couperose*, from medieval Latin *cuperosa*, literally 'flower of copper', from late Latin *cuprum* (see **COPPER¹**) + *rosa* 'rose', translating Greek *khalkanthon*.

copper beech ▶ **noun** a beech tree of a variety with purplish-brown leaves.

Copperbelt a mining region of central Zambia with rich deposits of copper, cobalt, and uranium; chief town, Ndola.

copper-bottomed ▶ **adjective** Brit. thoroughly reliable; certain not to fail: *a copper-bottomed guarantee*. [from earlier usage referring to the copper sheathing of the bottom of a ship.]

copper-fasten ▶ **verb** [with obj.] make (an undertaking or agreement) firm or binding.

copperhead ▶ **noun** any of a number of stout-bodied venomous snakes with coppery-pink or reddish-brown coloration, in particular: ● a North American pit viper (*Agkistrodon contortrix*, family Viperidae). Also called **HIGHLAND MOCCASIN** ● an Australian snake of the cobra family (genus *Austrelaps*, family Elapidae, in particular *A. superbus*).

coppering ▶ **noun** [mass noun] Brit. informal the work of a police officer: *he doesn't do his coppering by the book.*

coppernob ▶ **noun** informal a red-haired person.

copperplate ▶ **noun 1** a polished copper plate with a design engraved or etched into it. ■ a print made from such a plate.
2 [mass noun] a style of neat, round handwriting, usually slanted and looped, the thick and thin strokes being made by pressure with a flexible metal nib. [the copybooks for this writing were originally printed from copperplates.]
▶ **adjective** of or in copperplate writing.

copper pyrites ▶ **noun** another term for **CHALCOPYRITE**.

coppersmith ▶ **noun 1** a person who makes things out of copper.
2 (also **coppersmith barbet**) the crimson-breasted barbet of SE Asia, which has a red breast band, a streaked belly, and a repetitive metallic call. ● *Megalaima haemacephala*, family Capitonidae.

copper sulphate ▶ **noun** [mass noun] a blue crystalline solid used in electroplating and as a fungicide. ● Chem. formula: $CuSO_4.5H_2O$.

coppery ▶ **adjective** like copper, especially in colour: *his hair was fine and coppery.*

coppice ▶ **noun** an area of woodland in which the trees or shrubs are periodically cut back to ground level to stimulate growth and provide firewood or timber.
▶ **verb** [with obj.] cut back (a tree or shrub) to ground level periodically to stimulate growth: (as adj. **coppiced**) *coppiced timber.*
– ORIGIN late Middle English: from Old French *copeiz*, based on medieval Latin *colpus* 'a blow' (see **COPE¹**). Compare with **COPSE**.
– PHRASES **coppice with standards** chiefly historical managed woodland consisting of coppiced shrubs or trees, with scattered trees that are allowed to reach full height.

Coppola /ˈkɒpələ/, Francis Ford (b.1939), American film director, writer, and producer. Notable films: *The Godfather* (1972) and its two sequels; *Apocalypse Now* (1979).

copra /ˈkɒprə/ ▶ **noun** [mass noun] dried coconut kernels, from which oil is obtained.
– ORIGIN late 16th cent.: via Portuguese and Spanish from Malayalam *koppara* 'coconut'.

co-precipitation ▶ **noun** [mass noun] Chemistry the simultaneous precipitation of more than one compound from a solution.
– DERIVATIVES **co-precipitate** verb.

copro- ▶ **combining form** relating to dung or faeces: *coprophagous* | *coprophilia*.
– ORIGIN from Greek *kopros* 'dung'.

coprocessor ▶ **noun** Computing a microprocessor designed to supplement the capabilities of the primary processor.

co-produce ▶ **verb** [with obj.] produce (a theatrical work or a radio or television programme) jointly.
– DERIVATIVES **co-producer** noun, **co-production** noun.

coprolalia /ˌkɒprə(ʊ)ˈleɪlɪə/ ▶ **noun** [mass noun] Psychiatry the involuntary and repetitive use of obscene language, as a symptom of mental illness or organic brain disease.
– ORIGIN late 19th cent.: from Greek *kopros* 'dung' + *lalia* 'speech, chatter'.

coprolite /ˈkɒprə(ʊ)lʌɪt/ ▶ **noun** Palaeontology a piece of fossilized dung.

coprophagy /kɒˈprɒfədʒi/ (also **coprophagia** /ˌkɒprə(ʊ)ˈfeɪdʒɪə/) ▶ **noun** [mass noun] Zoology the eating of faeces or dung.
– DERIVATIVES **coprophagic** adjective, **coprophagous** adjective.

coprophilia /ˌkɒprə(ʊ)ˈfɪlɪə/ ▶ **noun** [mass noun] abnormal interest and pleasure in faeces and defecation.

copse ▶ **noun** a small group of trees.
– ORIGIN late 16th cent.: shortened from **COPPICE**.

cop shop ▶ **noun** Brit. informal a police station.

Copt /kɒpt/ ▶ **noun 1** a native Egyptian in the Hellenistic and Roman periods.
2 a member of the Coptic Church.
– ORIGIN from French *Copte* or modern Latin *Coptus*, from Arabic *al-qibṭ, al-qubṭ* 'Copts', from Coptic *Gyptios*, from Greek *Aiguptios* 'Egyptian'.

copter ▶ **noun** informal term for **HELICOPTER**.

Coptic ▶ **noun** [mass noun] the language of the Copts, which represents the final stage of ancient Egyptian. It now survives only as the liturgical language of the Coptic Church.
▶ **adjective** relating to the Copts or their language.

Coptic Church the native Christian Church in Egypt, traditionally founded by St Mark, and adhering to the Monophysite doctrine rejected by the Council of Chalcedon. Long persecuted after the Muslim Arab conquest of Egypt in the 7th century, the Coptic community now make up about 5 per cent of Egypt's population.

copula /ˈkɒpjʊlə/ ▶ **noun** Logic & Grammar a connecting word, in particular a form of the verb *be* connecting a subject and complement.
– DERIVATIVES **copular** adjective.
– ORIGIN early 17th cent.: from Latin, 'connection, linking of words', from *co-* 'together' + *apere* 'fasten'.

copulate /ˈkɒpjʊleɪt/ ▶ **verb** [no obj.] have sexual intercourse.
– DERIVATIVES **copulatory** adjective.
– ORIGIN late Middle English (in the sense 'join'): from Latin *copulat-* 'fastened together', from the verb *copulare*, from *copula* (see **COPULA**).

copulation /ˌkɒpjʊˈleɪʃ(ə)n/ ▶ **noun** [mass noun] sexual intercourse: *males may seek copulation with the breeding female.*

copulative ▶ **adjective 1** Grammar (of a word) connecting words or clauses linked in sense. Compare with **DISJUNCTIVE**. ■ connecting a subject and predicate.
2 relating to sexual intercourse.
– ORIGIN late Middle English: from Old French *copulatif, -ive* or late Latin *copulativus*, from *copulat-* 'coupled', from the verb *copulare* (see **COPULATE**).

copy ▶ **noun** (pl. **copies**) **1** a thing made to be similar or identical to another: *the problem is telling which is the original document and which the copy.*

C

2 a single specimen of a particular book, record, or other publication or issue: *the record has sold more than a million copies.*
3 [mass noun] matter to be printed: *copy for the next issue must be submitted by the beginning of the month.* ▪ material for a newspaper or magazine article: *it is an unfortunate truth of today's media that bad news makes good copy.* ▪ the text of an advertisement.
▸ **verb** (**copies, copying, copied**) [with obj.] **1** make a similar or identical version of; reproduce: *each form had to be copied and sent to a different department.* ▪ Computing reproduce (data stored in one location) in another location: *the command will copy a file from one disc to another.* ▪ write out information that one has read or heard: *he copied the details into his notebook* | *I began to* **copy out** *the addresses.* ▪ (**copy something to**) send a copy of a letter or an email to (a third party). ▪ (**copy someone in**) send someone a copy of an email that is addressed to a third party: *I attached the document and copied him in so he'd know it had been sent.*
2 imitate the style or behaviour of: *lifestyles that were* **copied from** *Miami and Fifth Avenue* | [no obj.] *art students* **copied from** *approved old masters.*
3 [no obj.] hear or understand someone speaking on a radio transmitter: *this is Edwards, do you copy, over.*
– ORIGIN Middle English (denoting a transcript or copy of a document): from Old French *copie* (noun), *copier* (verb), from Latin *copia* 'abundance' (in medieval Latin 'transcript', from such phrases as *copiam describendi facere* 'give permission to transcribe').

copybook ▸ **noun** a book containing models of handwriting for learners to imitate.
▸ **adjective** [attrib.] exactly in accordance with established criteria; perfect.

copycat ▸ **noun** informal, derogatory (especially in children's use) a person who copies another's behaviour, dress, or ideas. ▪ [as modifier] denoting an action, typically a crime, carried out in imitation of another: *copycat killings.*

copydesk ▸ **noun** N. Amer. a desk in a newspaper office at which copy is edited for printing.

copy-edit ▸ **verb** [with obj.] edit (text to be printed) by checking its consistency and accuracy.
– DERIVATIVES **copy editor** noun.

copyhold ▸ **noun** [mass noun] Brit. historical tenure of land based on manorial records.

copyholder ▸ **noun 1** Brit. historical a person who held land in copyhold.
2 a clasp or stand for holding sheets of text while it is keyed or typed.

copyist ▸ **noun** a person who makes copies, especially of handwritten documents or music. ▪ a person who imitates the styles of others, especially in art or music: *Beatles copyists.*
– ORIGIN mid 17th cent.: from **COPY** + **-IST**; replacing earlier *copist*, from French *copiste* or medieval Latin *copista*, from *copiare* 'to copy', from *copia* (see **COPY**).

copyleft ▸ **noun** [mass noun] an arrangement whereby software or artistic work may be used, modified, and distributed freely on condition that anything derived from it is bound by the same conditions.
– DERIVATIVES **copylefted** adjective.
– ORIGIN 1980s: after **COPYRIGHT**.

copyread ▸ **verb** [with obj.] read and edit (text) for a newspaper, magazine, or book.
– DERIVATIVES **copyreader** noun.

copyright ▸ **noun** [mass noun] the exclusive and assignable legal right, given to the originator for a fixed number of years, to print, publish, perform, film, or record literary, artistic, or musical material: *he issued a writ for breach of copyright* | [count noun] *works whose copyrights had lapsed.* ▪ [count noun] a particular literary, artistic, or musical work that is covered by copyright.
▸ **adjective** protected by copyright: *permission to reproduce photographs and other copyright material.*
▸ **verb** [with obj.] secure copyright for (material): (as adj. **copyrighted**) *copyrighted music downloaded illegally from the Internet.*

copyright library ▸ **noun** a library entitled to a free copy of each book published in the UK. The copyright libraries in the British Isles are the British Library, the Bodleian Library, Cambridge University Library, the National Library of Wales, the National Library of Scotland, and the library of Trinity College, Dublin.

copy typist ▸ **noun** a person whose job is to type transcripts of written drafts.

copywriter ▸ **noun** a person who writes the text of advertisements or publicity material.
– DERIVATIVES **copywriting** noun.

coq au vin /ˌkɒk əʊ ˈvã/ ▸ **noun** [mass noun] a casserole of chicken pieces cooked in red wine.
– ORIGIN French, literally 'cock in wine'.

coquetry /ˈkɒkɪtri, ˈkəʊ-/ ▸ **noun** [mass noun] flirtatious behaviour.
– ORIGIN mid 17th cent.: from French *coquetterie*, from *coqueter* 'to flirt', from *coquet* 'wanton' (see **COQUETTE**).

coquette /kɒˈkɛt/ ▸ **noun 1** a flirtatious woman.
2 a crested Central and South American hummingbird, typically with green plumage, a reddish crest, and elongated cheek feathers. ● *Lophornis* and two other genera, family Trochilidae: several species.
– ORIGIN mid 17th cent.: French, feminine of *coquet* 'wanton', diminutive of *coq* 'cock'.

coquettish /kəˈkɛtɪʃ/ ▸ **adjective** behaving in such a way as to suggest a playful sexual attraction; flirtatious: *a coquettish grin.*
– DERIVATIVES **coquettishly** adverb, **coquettishness** noun.

coquina /kɒˈkiːnə/ ▸ **noun 1** [mass noun] a soft limestone of broken shells, used in road-making in the Caribbean and Florida.
2 (also **coquina clam**) a small bivalve mollusc with a wedge-shaped shell which has a wide variety of colours and patterns. ● Genus *Donax*, family Donacidae: several species.
– ORIGIN mid 19th cent.: from Spanish, literally 'cockle', based on Latin *concha* (see **CONCH**).

coquito /kɒˈkiːtəʊ/ ▸ **noun** (pl. **coquitos**) a thick-trunked Chilean palm tree which yields large amounts of sweet sap (palm honey) and fibre. ● *Jubaea chilensis*, family Palmae.
– ORIGIN mid 19th cent.: from Spanish, diminutive of *coco* 'coconut'.

cor ▸ **exclamation** Brit. informal expressing surprise, excitement, admiration, or alarm: *Cor! That's a beautiful black eye you've got!*
– PHRASES **cor blimey** see **BLIMEY**.
– ORIGIN 1930s: alteration of **GOD**.

Cor. ▸ **abbreviation** ▪ US coroner. ▪ Epistle to the Corinthians (in biblical references).

cor- ▸ **prefix** variant spelling of **COM-** assimilated before *r* (as in *corrode, corrugate*).

Cora /ˈkɔːrə/ ▸ **noun 1** a member of an American Indian people of western Mexico.
2 [mass noun] the Uto-Aztecan language of the Coras, with about 15,000 speakers.
▸ **adjective** relating to the Coras or their language.

coracle /ˈkɒrək(ə)l/ ▸ **noun** (especially in Wales and Ireland) a small round boat made of wickerwork covered with a watertight material, propelled with a paddle.
– ORIGIN mid 16th cent.: from Welsh *corwgl, cwrwgl*, related to Scottish Gaelic and Irish *curach* 'small boat'; compare with **CURRACH**.

coracoid /ˈkɒrəkɔɪd/ (also **coracoid process**) ▸ **noun** Anatomy a short projection from the shoulder blade in mammals, to which part of the biceps is attached.
– ORIGIN mid 18th cent.: from modern Latin *coracoides*, from Greek *korakoeidēs* 'raven-like', from *korax* 'raven' (because of the resemblance to a raven's beak).

coral ▸ **noun 1** [mass noun] a hard stony substance secreted by certain marine coelenterates as an external skeleton, typically forming large reefs in warm seas. ▪ precious red coral, used in jewellery. ▪ the pinkish-red colour of red coral.
2 a sedentary coelenterate of warm and tropical seas, with a calcareous, horny, or soft skeleton. Most corals are colonial and many rely on the presence of green algae in their tissues to obtain energy from sunlight. ● Several orders in the class Anthozoa, including the 'true' or **stony corals** (order Scleractinia or Madreporaria), which form reefs, the **soft corals** (order Alcyonacea), which form leathery or fleshy colonies, and the **horny corals** (order Gorgonacea).
3 [mass noun] the unfertilized roe of a lobster or scallop, which is used as food and becomes reddish when cooked.
– DERIVATIVES **coralloid** adjective (chiefly Biology & Zoology).
– ORIGIN Middle English: via Old French from Latin *corallum*, from Greek *korallion, kouralion*.

coralberry ▸ **noun** (pl. **coralberries**) an evergreen North American shrub of the honeysuckle family, which has fragrant white flowers followed by deep red berries. ● *Symphoricarpos orbiculatus*, family Caprifoliaceae.

coral fungus ▸ **noun** a fungus which produces a fruiting body composed of upright branching finger-like projections which resemble coral, found in both Eurasia and North America. ● Genus *Clavulina*, family Clavariaceae, class Hymenomycetes.

Corallian /kɒˈralɪən/ ▸ **adjective & noun** another term for **OXFORDIAN** (sense 1 of the adjective, sense 1 of the noun).
– ORIGIN from Latin *corallium* 'coral' (with reference to the coral-derived limestone deposits) + **-AN**.

coralline /ˈkɒrəlʌɪn/ ▸ **noun** (also **coralline alga** or **coralline seaweed**) a branching reddish seaweed with a calcareous jointed stem. ● Family Corallinaceae, division Rhodophyta, in particular *Corallina officinalis*, which is common on the coasts of the North Atlantic.
▪ (in general use) a sedentary colonial marine animal, especially a bryozoan.
▸ **adjective** Geology derived or formed from coral: *the islands were volcanic rather than coralline in origin.* ▪ of the pinkish-red colour of precious red coral. ▪ resembling coral: *coralline sponges.*
– ORIGIN mid 16th cent.: the noun from Italian *corallina*, diminutive of *corallo* 'coral', the adjective (mid 17th cent.) from French *corallin* or late Latin *corallinus*, both based on Latin *corallum* 'coral'.

corallita /ˌkɒrəˈliːtə/ (also **coralita**) ▸ **noun** a pink-flowered climbing vine native to Mexico and the Caribbean, grown as an ornamental. ● *Antigonon leptopus*, family Polygonaceae.
– ORIGIN late 19th cent.: from American Spanish *coralito*, diminutive of Spanish *coral* 'coral'.

corallite /ˈkɒrəlʌɪt/ ▸ **noun** Palaeontology the cup-like calcareous skeleton of a single coral polyp. ▪ a fossil coral.
– ORIGIN early 19th cent.: from Latin *corallum* 'coral' + **-ITE**[1].

coral rag ▸ **noun** [mass noun] rubbly limestone composed chiefly of petrified coral.

coralroot ▸ **noun 1** (also **coralroot orchid**) a leafless orchid which has inconspicuous flowers and lacks chlorophyll. It has a pale knobbly rhizome which obtains nourishment from decaying organic matter. ● Genus *Corallorhiza*, family Orchidaceae: several species, including the widespread *C. trifida*.
▪ another term for **COCKSCOMB** (sense 3).
2 (also **coralroot bittercress**) a Eurasian woodland plant with purple flowers and bud-like swellings (bulbils) at the base of the stem. ● *Cardamine bulbifera*, family Cruciferae.

Coral Sea a part of the western Pacific lying between Australia, New Guinea, and Vanuatu, the scene of a naval battle between US and Japanese carriers in 1942.

coral snake ▸ **noun** a brightly coloured venomous snake of the cobra family, typically having conspicuous bands of red, yellow, white, and black. ● *Micrurus* and other genera in the family Elapidae: numerous species.

coral spot (also **coral spot disease**) ▸ **noun** [mass noun] a common fungal disease of trees and shrubs, appearing as numerous minute pink or dark red cushion-like bodies on the twigs and branches and causing dieback. ● *Nectria cinnabarina*, family Hypocreaceae, subdivision Ascomycotina.

coral tree ▸ **noun** a tropical or subtropical thorny shrub or tree with showy red or orange flowers. ● Genus *Erythrina*, family Leguminosae.

coram populo /ˌkɔːrəm ˈpɒpjʊləʊ/ ▸ **adverb** in public.
– ORIGIN Latin, literally 'in the presence of the people'.

cor anglais /kɔːr ˈɑːŋɡleɪ, ˈɒŋɡleɪ/ ▸ **noun** (pl. **cors anglais** pronunc. **same**) Music an alto woodwind instrument of the oboe family, having a bulbous bell and sounding a fifth lower than the oboe. Also called **ENGLISH HORN**. ▪ an organ stop with the quality of a cor anglais.
– ORIGIN late 19th cent.: French, literally 'English horn'.

corbeil /ˈkɔːbeɪl/ ▸ **noun** Architecture a representation in stone of a basket of flowers.
– ORIGIN early 18th cent.: from French *corbeille* 'basket', from late Latin *corbicula* 'small basket', diminutive of *corbis*.

corbeille /kɔːˈbeɪ/ ▸ **noun** an elegant basket of flowers or fruit.
– ORIGIN early 19th cent.: French, 'basket' (see also **CORBEIL**).

corbel /ˈkɔːb(ə)l/ ▸ **noun** a projection jutting out from a wall to support a structure above it.
▸ **verb** (**corbels, corbelling, corbelled**; US **corbels, corbeling, corbeled**) [with obj.] support (a structure) on corbels: (as adj. **corbelled**) *a very high corbelled vault.*

– ORIGIN late Middle English: from Old French, diminutive of *corp* 'crow', from Latin *corvus* 'raven' (perhaps because of the shape of a corbel, resembling a crow's beak).

corbel table ▶ **noun** a projecting course of bricks or stones resting on corbels.

corbicula /kɔːˈbɪkjʊlə/ ▶ **noun** (pl. **corbiculae** /-liː/) Entomology another term for **POLLEN BASKET**.
– ORIGIN early 19th cent.: from late Latin.

corbie /ˈkɔːbi/ ▶ **noun** (pl. **corbies**) Scottish a raven, crow, or rook.
– ORIGIN late Middle English: from Old French *corb*, variant of *corp* 'crow' (see **CORBEL**).

corbie steps ▶ **plural noun** Scottish term for **CROW STEPS**.

Corbusian /kɔːˈbjuːzɪən/ ▶ **adjective** relating to the architect Le Corbusier.

Corcovado /ˌkɔːkəˈvɑːdəʊ/ a peak rising to 711 m (2,310 ft) on the south side of Rio de Janeiro. A gigantic statue of Christ, 40 m (131 ft) high, named 'Christ the Redeemer', stands on its summit.

Corcyra /kɔːˈsʌɪərə/ ancient Greek name for **CORFU**.

cord ▶ **noun 1** [mass noun] thin, flexible string or rope made from several twisted strands: *her feet were tied with cord.* ■ [count noun] a length of cord: *a dressing-gown cord.* ■ [count noun] an anatomical structure resembling a length of cord (e.g. the spinal cord, the umbilical cord). ■ [count noun] an electric flex.
2 [mass noun] ribbed fabric, especially corduroy. ■ (**cords**) corduroy trousers: *he was dressed in faded black cords.* ■ a cord-like rib on fabric.
3 a measure of cut wood (usually 128 cu. ft, 3.62 cubic metres).
▶ **verb** [with obj.] attach a cord to.
– PHRASES **cut the (umbilical) cord** cease to rely on someone or something protective or supportive and begin to act independently.
– ORIGIN Middle English: from Old French *corde*, from Latin *chorda*, from Greek *khordē* 'gut, string of a musical instrument'.

> **USAGE** See **USAGE** at **CHORD**[2].

cordage ▶ **noun** [mass noun] cords or ropes, especially in a ship's rigging.
– ORIGIN late 15th cent.: from Old French, from *corde* 'rope' (see **CORD**).

cordate /ˈkɔːdeɪt/ ▶ **adjective** Botany & Zoology heart-shaped.
– ORIGIN mid 17th cent. (in the sense 'wise, prudent'): from Latin *cordatus* 'wise' (in modern Latin 'heart-shaped'), from *cor, cord-* 'heart'.

Corday /kɔːˈdeɪ/, Charlotte (1768–93), French political assassin; full name *Marie Anne Charlotte Corday d'Armont*. She became involved with the Girondists and in 1793 assassinated the revolutionary leader Jean Paul Marat in his bath; she was found guilty of treason and guillotined.

corded ▶ **adjective 1** (of cloth) ribbed. ■ (of a tensed muscle) standing out so as to resemble a piece of cord.
2 equipped with a cord or flex: *corded and cordless phones.*

Cordelier /ˌkɔːdəˈlɪə/ ▶ **noun** a Franciscan Observant.
– ORIGIN late Middle English: from Old French, from *cordelle* 'small rope', diminutive of *corde* (see **CORD**). The name derives from the knotted cord worn by the Cordeliers around the waist.

cordgrass ▶ **noun** [mass noun] a coarse wiry coastal grass which is sometimes used to stabilize mudflats. ● Genus *Spartina*, family Gramineae.

cordial ▶ **adjective 1** warm and friendly: *the atmosphere was cordial and relaxed.*
2 strongly felt: *I earned his cordial loathing.*
▶ **noun 1** Brit. a sweet fruit-flavoured drink. ■ N. Amer. another term for **LIQUEUR**.
2 a pleasant-tasting medicine.
– DERIVATIVES **cordiality** noun, **cordially** adverb.
– ORIGIN Middle English (also in the sense 'belonging to the heart'): from medieval Latin *cordialis*, from Latin *cor, cord-* 'heart'.

cordierite /ˈkɔːdɪərʌɪt/ ▶ **noun** [mass noun] a dark blue mineral occurring chiefly in metamorphic rocks. It consists of an aluminosilicate of magnesium and iron, and also occurs as a dichroic gem variety.
– ORIGIN early 19th cent.: named after Pierre L. A. *Cordier* (1777–1861), French geologist, + **-ITE**[1].

cordillera /ˌkɔːdɪˈljɛːrə/ ▶ **noun** a system or group of parallel mountain ranges together with the intervening plateaux and other features, especially in the Andes or the Rockies.
– ORIGIN early 18th cent.: from Spanish, from *cordilla*, diminutive of *cuerda* 'cord', from Latin *chorda* (see **CORD**).

cording ▶ **noun** [mass noun] cord or braid, especially that used as a decorative fabric trimming.

cordite ▶ **noun** [mass noun] a smokeless explosive made from nitrocellulose, nitroglycerine, and petroleum jelly, used in ammunition.
– ORIGIN late 19th cent.: from **CORD** (because of its string-like appearance) + **-ITE**[1].

cordless ▶ **adjective** (of an electrical appliance or telephone) working without connection to a mains supply or central unit.

Cordoba /ˈkɔːdəbə/ (also **Cordova**) **1** a city in Andalusia, southern Spain; pop. 325,453 (2008). Founded by the Carthaginians, it was under Moorish rule from 711 to 1236, and was renowned for its architecture, particularly the Great Mosque. Spanish name **Córdoba** /ˈkəɔrðəβa/.
2 a city in central Argentina; pop. 1,319,000 (est. 2005).

cordoba /ˈkɔːdəbə/ ▶ **noun** the basic monetary unit of Nicaragua, equal to 100 centavos.
– ORIGIN named after F. Fernández de *Córdoba*, a 16th-cent. Spanish governor of Nicaragua.

cordon /ˈkɔːd(ə)n/ ▶ **noun 1** a line or circle of police, soldiers, or guards preventing access to or from an area or building: *the crowd was halted in front of the police cordon.*
2 a fruit tree trained to grow as a single stem.
3 Architecture a projecting course of brick or stone on the face of a wall.
▶ **verb** [with obj.] (**cordon something off**) prevent access to or from an area or building by surrounding it with police or other guards: *the city centre was cordoned off after fires were discovered in two stores.*
– ORIGIN late Middle English (denoting an ornamental braid): from Italian *cordone*, augmentative of *corda*, and French *cordon*, diminutive of *corde*, both from Latin *chorda* 'string, rope' (see **CORD**). Sense 3 of the noun, the earliest of the current noun senses, dates from the early 18th cent.

cordon bleu /ˌkɔːdɒ̃ ˈbləː/ ▶ **adjective** Cookery of the highest class: *a cordon bleu chef.* ■ [postpositive] denoting a dish consisting of an escalope of veal or chicken rolled, filled with cheese and ham, and then fried in breadcrumbs.
▶ **noun 1** a cook of the highest class.
2 (**cordon-bleu** or **cordon-bleu finch**) an African waxbill that is popular as a cage bird. The male has a blue face, breast, and tail, a brown back, and a red bill. ● Genus *Uraeginthus*, family Estrildidae: three species.
– ORIGIN mid 18th cent. (as a noun, often specifically denoting a first-class cook): French, literally 'blue ribbon'. The blue ribbon once signified the highest order of chivalry in the reign of the Bourbon kings.

cordon sanitaire /kɔːˌdɒ̃ sanɪˈtɛː/ ▶ **noun** (pl. **cordons sanitaires** pronunc. **same**) a guarded line preventing anyone from leaving an area infected by a disease and thus spreading it. ■ a measure designed to prevent communication or the spread of undesirable influences: *these rules help to reinforce the cordon sanitaire around Whitehall.*
– ORIGIN mid 19th cent.: French, from *cordon* 'line, border' (see **CORDON**) + *sanitaire* 'sanitary'.

Cordova /ˈkɔːdəvə/ variant spelling of **CORDOBA**.

cordovan /ˈkɔːdəv(ə)n/ ▶ **noun** [mass noun] a kind of soft leather made originally from goatskin and now from horse hide.
– ORIGIN late 16th cent.: from Spanish *cordován*, former spelling of *cordobán* 'of Cordoba', where it was originally made.

Cordtex ▶ **noun** [mass noun] trademark fuse cable consisting of a core of explosive material in a plastic and textile sheath.
– ORIGIN 1930s: from the noun **CORD** + **TEXTILE**.

Cordura /kɔːˈdjʊərə/ ▶ **noun** [mass noun] trademark a durable synthetic fabric.

corduroy /ˈkɔːdərɔɪ, -djʊ-/ ▶ **noun** [mass noun] a thick cotton fabric with velvety ribs. ■ (**corduroys**) trousers made of corduroy.
▶ **verb** [with obj.] make (a road) out of tree trunks.
– ORIGIN late 18th cent.: probably from **CORD** 'ribbed fabric' + *duroy*, denoting a kind of lightweight worsted formerly made in the West of England, of unknown origin.

corduroy road ▶ **noun** a road made of tree trunks laid across a swamp.

cordwainer /ˈkɔːdweɪnə/ ▶ **noun** archaic a shoemaker (still used in the names of guilds): *the Cordwainers' Company.*
– ORIGIN Middle English: from Anglo-Norman French *cordewaner*, from Old French *cordewan*, 'of Cordoba' (see **CORDOVAN**).

cordwood ▶ **noun** [mass noun] wood that has been cut into uniform lengths, used especially as firewood or for building.

CORE ▶ **abbreviation** (in the US) Congress of Racial Equality.

core ▶ **noun 1** the tough central part of various fruits, containing the seeds: *an apple core.*
2 the part of something that is central to its existence or character: *the plan has the interests of children at its core* | [as modifier] *managers can concentrate on their core activities.* ■ an important or unchanging group of people forming the central part of a larger body.
3 the dense central region of a planet, especially the nickel–iron inner part of the earth. ■ the central part of a nuclear reactor, which contains the fissile material. ■ a tiny ring of magnetic material used in a computer memory to store one bit of data, now superseded by semiconductor memories. ■ the inner strand of an electric cable or rope. ■ a piece of soft iron forming the centre of an electromagnet or an induction coil. ■ an internal mould filling a space to be left hollow in a casting. ■ a cylindrical sample of rock, ice, or other material obtained by boring with a hollow drill. ■ Archaeology a piece of flint from which flakes or blades have been removed.
▶ **verb** [with obj.] remove the tough central part and seeds from (a fruit): *peel and core the pears.*
– PHRASES **to the core** to the depths of one's being: *she was shaken to the core by his words.* ■ used to indicate that someone possesses a characteristic to a very high degree: *he is a politician to the core.*
– DERIVATIVES **corer** noun.
– ORIGIN Middle English: of unknown origin.

-core ▶ **combining form** denoting types of rock or dance music that have an aggressive presentation: *emocore.*
– ORIGIN from **CORE**, on the pattern of *hardcore*.

core dump ▶ **noun** Computing a dump of the contents of main memory, carried out typically as an aid to debugging.

coreferential ▶ **adjective** Linguistics (of two elements or units) having the same reference.
– DERIVATIVES **coreference** noun.

co-religionist (also **coreligionist**) ▶ **noun** an adherent of the same religion as another person.

corella /kəˈrɛlə/ ▶ **noun** a white Australasian cockatoo with some pink feathers on the face, bare blue skin around the eye, and typically a long bill. ● Genus *Cacatua*, family Cacatuidae (or Psittacidae): three species, in particular the widespread **little corella** (*C. sanguinea*).
ORIGIN late 19th cent.: from Wiradhuri.

Corelli[1] /kəˈrɛli/, Arcangelo (1653–1713), Italian violinist and composer. His best-known works are his trio and solo sonatas for the violin and his concerti grossi (published posthumously in 1714), especially the 'Christmas' concerto.

Corelli[2] /kəˈrɛli/, Marie (1855–1924), English writer of romantic fiction; pseudonym of *Mary Mackay*. The sales of her novels *Thelma* (1887), *Barabbas* (1893), and *The Sorrows of Satan* (1895) broke all existing records for book sales, although popularity was not matched by critical acclaim.

coreopsis /ˌkɒrɪˈɒpsɪs/ ▶ **noun** (pl. **coreopses**) a plant of the daisy family, which is cultivated for its rayed, typically yellow, flowers. Also called **TICKSEED**. ● Genus *Coreopsis*, family Compositae.
– ORIGIN modern Latin, from Greek *koris* 'bug' + *opsis* 'appearance' (because of the shape of the seed).

co-respondent (also **corespondent**) ▶ **noun** a person cited in a divorce case as having committed adultery with the respondent.

co-respondent shoes ▶ **plural noun** dated, humorous men's two-toned shoes.

core time ▶ **noun** [mass noun] Brit. the central part of the working day in a flexitime system, when an employee must be present.

corf /kɔːf/ ▶ **noun** (pl. **corves**) Brit. a wagon or large basket formerly used for bringing coal out of a mine.
– ORIGIN late Middle English (in the general sense 'basket'): from Middle Low German and Middle Dutch *korf*, from Latin *corbis* 'basket'.

Corfu /kɔːˈf(j)uː/ a Greek island, one of the largest of the Ionian Islands, off the west coast of mainland

C

C

Greece. It was known in ancient times as Corcyra; pop. 127,900 (est. 2009). Greek name **Kérkira**.

corgi (also **Welsh corgi**) ▶ **noun** (pl. **corgis**) a dog of a short-legged breed with a foxlike head.
– ORIGIN 1920s: from Welsh, from *cor* 'dwarf' + *ci* 'dog'.

coriaceous /ˌkɒrɪˈeɪʃəs/ ▶ **adjective** technical resembling or having the texture of leather: *coriaceous leaves*.
– ORIGIN late 17th cent.: from late Latin *coriaceus* (from Latin *corium* 'leather') + **-ous**.

coriander /ˌkɒrɪˈandə/ ▶ **noun** [mass noun] an aromatic Mediterranean plant of the parsley family, the leaves and seeds of which are used as culinary herbs.
● *Coriandrum sativum*, family Umbelliferae.
– ORIGIN Middle English: from Old French *coriandre*, from Latin *coriandrum*, from Greek *koriannon*.

Corinth /ˈkɒrɪnθ/ a city on the north coast of the Peloponnese, Greece; pop. 27,600 (est. 2009). The modern city, built in 1858, is a little to the north-east of the site of an ancient city of the same name, which was a prominent city-state in ancient Greece. Greek name **Kórinthos**.

Corinth, Gulf of an inlet of the Ionian Sea extending between the Peloponnese and central Greece. Also called **Lepanto, Gulf of**.

Corinth, Isthmus of a narrow neck of land linking the Peloponnese with central Greece and separating the Gulf of Corinth from the Saronic Gulf.

Corinth Canal a man-made shipping channel across the narrowest part of the Isthmus of Corinth (a distance of 6.4 km, or 4 miles). Opened in 1893, it links the Gulf of Corinth and the Saronic Gulf.

Corinthian /kəˈrɪnθɪən/ ▶ **adjective** **1** belonging or relating to Corinth, especially the ancient city.
■ relating to or denoting the most ornate of the classical orders of architecture (used especially by the Romans), characterized by flared capitals with rows of acanthus leaves.
2 involving the highest standards of amateur sportsmanship.
▶ **noun** **1** a native of Corinth.
2 [mass noun] the Corinthian order of architecture.

Corinthians, Epistle to the either of two books of the New Testament, epistles of St Paul to the Church at Corinth.

Coriolanus /ˌkɒrɪəˈleɪnəs/, Gaius (or Gnaeus) Marcius (5th century BC), Roman general, who got his name from the capture of the Volscian town of Corioli. According to legend, after his banishment from Rome he led a Volscian army against the city and was only turned back by the pleas of his mother and wife.

Coriolis effect /ˌkɒrɪˈəʊlɪs/ ▶ **noun** Physics an effect whereby a mass moving in a rotating system experiences a force (the **Coriolis force**) acting perpendicular to the direction of motion and to the axis of rotation. On the earth, the effect tends to deflect moving objects to the right in the northern hemisphere and to the left in the southern and is important in the formation of cyclonic weather systems.
– ORIGIN early 20th cent.: named after Gaspard *Coriolis* (1792–1843), French engineer.

corium /ˈkɔːrɪəm/ ▶ **noun** chiefly Zoology another term for **dermis**.
– ORIGIN early 19th cent.: from Latin, 'skin'.

Cork a county of the Republic of Ireland, on the south coast in the province of Munster. ■ its county town, a port on the River Lee; pop. 190,384 (2006).

cork ▶ **noun** **1** [mass noun] a buoyant light brown substance obtained from the outer layer of the bark of the cork oak. ■ Botany a protective layer of dead cells immediately below the bark of woody plants.
2 a bottle stopper made of cork or a similar material. ■ a piece of cork used as a float for a fishing line or net.
▶ **verb** [with obj.] **1** close or seal (a bottle) with a cork: *the bottles were tightly corked and wired*. ■ (as adj. **corked**) (of wine) spoilt by tannin from the cork.
2 draw with burnt cork.
3 illicitly hollow out (a baseball bat) and fill it with cork to make it lighter.
– ORIGIN Middle English: from Dutch and Low German *kork*, from Spanish *alcorque* 'cork-soled sandal', from Arabic *al-* 'the' and (probably) Spanish Arabic *qurq*, *qorq*, based on Latin *quercus* 'oak, cork oak'.

corkage ▶ **noun** [mass noun] a charge made by a restaurant or hotel for serving wine that has been brought in by a customer.

cork cambium ▶ **noun** [mass noun] Botany tissue in the stem of a plant that gives rise to cork on its outer surface and a layer of cells containing chlorophyll on its inner.

corker informal ▶ **noun** an excellent or astonishing person or thing: *it was the season's first goal, and a corker*.
▶ **adjective** NZ very good; excellent.

corking ▶ **adjective** Brit. informal, dated very good; excellent: *cars in corking condition*.

cork oak ▶ **noun** an evergreen Mediterranean oak, the outer layer of the bark of which is the source of cork, which can be stripped without harming the tree. ● *Quercus suber*, family Fagaceae.

corkscrew ▶ **noun** a device for pulling corks from bottles, consisting of a spiral metal rod that is inserted into the cork, and a handle that extracts it. ■ [usu. as modifier] a thing with a spiral shape or movement: *a girl with corkscrew curls*.
▶ **verb** [no obj.] move or twist in a spiral motion: *the plane was corkscrewing towards the earth*.

corkwood ▶ **noun** a shrub or tree which yields light porous timber, in particular: ● a small American tree which produces timber used for fishing floats (*Leitneria floridana*, family Leitneriaceae). ● a similar tree native to New Zealand (*Entelea arborescens, family Tiliaceae*).

corky ▶ **adjective** (**corkier**, **corkiest**) **1** resembling cork: *corky lesions on apples*.
2 (of wine) corked.

corm ▶ **noun** a rounded underground storage organ present in plants such as crocuses, gladioli, and cyclamens, consisting of a swollen stem base covered with scale leaves. Compare with **bulb** (sense 1).
– ORIGIN mid 19th cent.: from modern Latin *cormus*, from Greek *kormos* 'trunk stripped of its boughs'.

cormel /ˈkɔːm(ə)l/ ▶ **noun** a small corm growing at the side of a mature corm.

cormorant /ˈkɔːm(ə)r(ə)nt/ ▶ **noun** a rather large diving bird with a long neck, long hooked bill, short legs, and mainly dark plumage. It typically breeds on coastal cliffs. ● Genus *Phalacrocorax* (and *Nannopterum*), family Phalacrocoracidae: numerous species, in particular the widespread (**great**) **cormorant** (*P. carbo*).
– ORIGIN Middle English: from Old French *cormaran*, from medieval Latin *corvus marinus* 'sea raven'. The final *-t* is on the pattern of words such as *peasant*.

corn[1] ▶ **noun** [mass noun] **1** Brit. the chief cereal crop of a district, especially (in England) wheat or (in Scotland) oats. ■ the grain of a cereal crop. ■ North American, Australian, and New Zealand term for **maize**.
2 informal something banal or sentimental: *the film is pure corn*.
– PHRASES **corn on the cob** maize when cooked and eaten straight from the cob.
– ORIGIN Old English, of Germanic origin; related to Dutch *koren* and German *Korn*.

corn[2] ▶ **noun** a small, painful area of thickened skin on the foot, especially on the toes, caused by pressure.
– ORIGIN late Middle English: via Anglo-Norman French from Latin *cornu* 'horn'.

cornball N. Amer. informal ▶ **adjective** trite and sentimental: *a cornball movie*.
▶ **noun** a person with trite or sentimental ideas.

corn beef ▶ **noun** [mass noun] corned beef.

corn borer ▶ **noun** a moth whose larvae feed upon and bore into maize. ● Several species in the family Pyralidae, in particular the **European corn borer** (*Ostrinia nubilalis*), which was accidentally introduced into North America, and *Diatraea* (or *Zeadiatraea*) *grandiosella* of the southern US.

cornbrash ▶ **noun** [mass noun] Geology an earthy fossiliferous limestone occurring widely in England in a thin formation of Jurassic age.
– ORIGIN early 19th cent.: from **corn**[1] + **brash**[2].

cornbread ▶ **noun** [mass noun] a type of bread made from maize meal.

corn bunting ▶ **noun** a large thickset Eurasian bunting with brown streaked plumage and a jangling song, inhabiting open grassland and arable land.
● *Emberiza* (or *Miliaria*) *calandra*, family Emberizidae (subfamily Emberizinae).

corn circle ▶ **noun** another term for **crop circle**.

corncob ▶ **noun** see **cob**[1] (sense 2).

corncob pipe ▶ **noun** US a tobacco pipe with a bowl made from a dried corncob.

corncockle ▶ **noun** a pink-flowered Mediterranean plant introduced into Britain, where it became a cornfield weed. It has since been almost eradicated because its poisonous seeds contaminate flour.
● *Agrostemma githago*, family Caryophyllaceae.
– ORIGIN early 18th cent.: from **corn**[1] + *cockle* (from Old English *coccul* 'corncockle', perhaps via Latin from Greek *kokkos* 'berry').

corncrake ▶ **noun** a secretive Eurasian crake inhabiting coarse grasslands, with mainly brown streaked plumage and a distinctive double rasping call. Due to changes in agricultural practices it is now much rarer in the British Isles than formerly. Also called **landrail**. ● *Crex crex*, family Rallidae.

corn dodger ▶ **noun** US a small fried or baked cornmeal cake.

corn dog ▶ **noun** N. Amer. a hot dog covered in maize-flour batter, fried, and served on a stick.

corn dolly ▶ **noun** Brit. a symbolic or decorative model of a human figure, made of plaited straw.

cornea /ˈkɔːnɪə/ ▶ **noun** the transparent layer forming the front of the eye.
– DERIVATIVES **corneal** **adjective**.
– ORIGIN late Middle English: from medieval Latin *cornea tela* 'horny tissue', from Latin *cornu* 'horn'.

corn earworm ▶ **noun** an American moth caterpillar which is a pest of both maize and cotton. Also called **bollworm**, **cotton bollworm**. ● *Heliothis zea*, family Noctuidae.

corned ▶ **adjective** (of food) preserved in brine: *corned ham*.

corned beef ▶ **noun** [mass noun] **1** Brit. beef preserved in brine, chopped and pressed and sold in tins.
2 N. Amer. beef brisket cured in brine and boiled, typically served cold.

Corneille /kɔːˈneɪ/, French /kɔʀnɛj/, Pierre (1606–84), French dramatist, generally regarded as the founder of classical French tragedy. Notable plays: *Le Cid* (1637), *Cinna* (1641), and *Polyeucte* (1643).

cornel /ˈkɔːn(ə)l/ ▶ **noun** a dogwood, especially of a dwarf variety. ● Genus *Cornus*, family Cornaceae: several species, including the dwarf *C. suecica*.
– ORIGIN late Middle English (denoting the wood of the cornelian cherry): from Old French *corneille*, from Latin *cornus*.

cornelian /kɔːˈniːlɪən/ ▶ **noun** variant spelling of **carnelian**.

cornelian cherry ▶ **noun** a Eurasian flowering shrub or small tree of the dogwood family, cultivated as an ornamental. ● *Cornus mas*, family Cornaceae.
■ the edible oval red berry of the cornelian cherry.
– ORIGIN early 17th cent.: *cornelian* from **cornel** + **-ian**.

corneous /ˈkɔːnɪəs/ ▶ **adjective** formal horn-like; horny: *the skeleton is formed of a corneous substance*.
– ORIGIN mid 17th cent.: from Latin *corneus* (from *cornu* 'horn') + **-ous**.

corner ▶ **noun** **1** a place or angle where two sides or edges meet: *Jan sat at one corner of the table*. ■ the area inside a room or other space near the place where two walls or other surfaces meet: *the colour TV in the corner of the room*. ■ a place where two or more streets meet: *the huge bookshop **on the corner***. ■ a sharp bend in a road: *they took the corner in a skidding turn*. ■ Climbing, Brit. a place where two planes of rock meet at an angle of between 60° and 120°.
2 a location or area, especially one regarded as secluded or remote: *fountains are discovered in quiet corners and sleepy squares* | *dance professionals from all corners of the globe attended the five-day festival* | figurative *she couldn't bear journalists prying into every corner of her life*.
3 a position in which one dominates the supply of a particular commodity: *London doesn't have a corner on film festivals*.
4 a difficult or awkward situation: *I didn't wait for the prosecutor to try to get me in a corner*.
5 (also **corner kick**) Soccer a place kick taken by the attacking side from a corner of the field after the ball has been sent over the byline by a defender. ■ a free hit in field hockey, taken from the corner of the field.
6 Boxing & Wrestling each of the diagonally opposite ends of the ring, where a contestant rests between rounds. ■ a contestant's supporters or seconds: *Hodkinson was encouraged by his corner*.
7 Brit. a triangular cut from the hind end of a side of bacon.
▶ **verb** [with obj.] **1** force (a person or animal) into a place or situation from which it is hard to escape: *the man was eventually cornered by police dogs*. ■ detain (someone) in conversation: *I managed to corner Gary for fifteen minutes*.

2 control (a market) by dominating the supply of a particular commodity: *whether they will corner the market in graphics software remains to be seen.* ▪ establish a corner in (a commodity): *you cornered vanadium and made a killing.*
3 [no obj.] (of a vehicle) go round a bend in a road: *no squeal is evident from the tyres when cornering fast.*
– PHRASES **(just) around** (or **round**) **the corner** very near: *there's a chemist round the corner.* **fight one's corner** defend one's position or interests: *we need someone in the cabinet to fight our corner.* **in someone's corner** on someone's side; giving someone support and encouragement. **on** (or **at** or **in**) **every corner** everywhere: *there are saloons on every corner.* **see someone/thing out of** (or **from**) **the corner of one's eye** see someone or something at the edge of one's field of vision.
– ORIGIN Middle English: from Anglo-Norman French, based on Latin *cornu* 'horn, tip, corner'.

cornerback ▸ noun American Football a defensive back positioned to the outside of the linebackers.

corner boy ▸ noun chiefly Irish a disreputable man or youth who spends his time loitering on the street.

corner dairy ▸ noun see **DAIRY** (sense 2 of the noun).

cornered ▸ adjective 1 [in combination] having a specified number of corners: *young boys in six-cornered hats.* ▪ having a specified number of parties involved: *a three-cornered meeting was being arranged in Hong Kong.*
2 (of a person or animal) forced into a place or situation from which it is hard to escape: *nothing is more dangerous than a cornered wild beast.*

corner forward ▸ noun (in hurling) a player in an attacking position on the wing.

corner kick ▸ noun another term for **CORNER** (sense 5 of the noun).

cornerman ▸ noun (pl. **cornermen**) a person whose job is to assist a boxer or wrestler at the corner between rounds.

corner shop ▸ noun Brit. a small shop selling groceries and general goods in a mainly residential area.

cornerstone ▸ noun 1 an important quality or feature on which a particular thing depends or is based: *a national minimum wage remained the cornerstone of policy.*
2 a stone that forms the base of a corner of a building, joining two walls.

cornerwise ▸ adverb at an angle of approximately 45°; diagonally: *he laid the cloth cornerwise on the polished table.*

cornet[1] /ˈkɔːnɪt/ ▸ noun 1 Music a brass instrument resembling a trumpet but shorter and wider. ▪ a compound organ stop with a powerful treble sound.
2 Brit. a cone-shaped wafer filled with ice cream.
– DERIVATIVES **cornetist** /kɔːˈnɛtɪst/ (also **cornettist**) noun.
– ORIGIN late Middle English (originally denoting a wind instrument made of a horn): from Old French, diminutive of a variant of Latin *cornu* 'horn'.

cornet[2] /ˈkɔːnɪt/ ▸ noun chiefly historical the fifth grade of commissioned officer in a cavalry troop, who carried the colours. It is still used in some British cavalry regiments for officers of the rank of second lieutenant.
– DERIVATIVES **cornetcy** noun (pl. **cornetcies**).
– ORIGIN mid 16th cent.: from French *cornette*, diminutive of *corne* (originally a collective term), based on Latin *cornua* 'horns'. The word originally denoted a kind of woman's headdress, or a strip of lace hanging down from a headdress against the cheeks; later it referred to the pennon of a cavalry troop, hence the officer who carried the colours.

cornetfish ▸ noun (pl. **same** or **cornetfishes**) a large marine fish with a long, narrow flute-like snout, an elongated body, and a whip-like extension to the tail. It is common in shallow tropical waters of the Atlantic and Indo-Pacific region. ● Family Fistulariidae and genus *Fistularia*: several species.

cornetto /kɔːˈnɛtəʊ/ (also **cornett** /ˈkɔːnɪt, kɔːˈnɛt/) ▸ noun (pl. **cornetti** or **cornetts**) a woodwind instrument of the 16th and 17th centuries, typically curved, with finger holes and a cup-shaped mouthpiece.
– ORIGIN late 19th cent.: from Italian, diminutive of *corno* 'horn', from Latin *cornu*. Compare with **CORNET**[1].

corn exchange ▸ noun (in the UK) a building where corn is or was traded, typically a hall now converted for other public use.

corn-fed ▸ adjective fed on grain, especially maize: *corn-fed chickens.* ▪ US informal plump; well fed. ▪ US informal provincial; unsophisticated: *a backward, corn-fed Heartland town.*

cornfield ▸ noun a field in which corn is being grown.

cornflakes ▸ plural noun a breakfast cereal consisting of toasted flakes made from maize flour.

cornflour ▸ noun [mass noun] Brit. finely ground maize flour, used for thickening sauces.

cornflower ▸ noun a slender Eurasian plant related to the knapweeds, with flowers that are typically a deep, vivid blue. ● Genus *Centaurea*, family Compositae: several species, including the annual *Centaurea cyaneus* (also called **BLUEBOTTLE**), formerly a common weed of cornfields, and the perennial *C. montana*, grown in gardens.
▪ (also **cornflower blue**) [mass noun] a deep, vivid blue colour.

Cornhusker State informal name for **NEBRASKA**.

cornice /ˈkɔːnɪs/ ▸ noun 1 an ornamental moulding round the wall of a room just below the ceiling. ▪ a horizontal moulded projection crowning a building or structure, especially the uppermost member of the entablature of an order, surmounting the frieze.
2 an overhanging mass of hardened snow at the edge of a mountain precipice.
– DERIVATIVES **corniced** adjective, **cornicing** noun.
– ORIGIN mid 16th cent.: from French *corniche*, from Italian *cornice*, perhaps from Latin *cornix* 'crow' (compare with **CORBEL**), but influenced by Greek *korōnis* 'coping stone'.

corniche /ˈkɔːnɪʃ, kɔːˈniːʃ/ ▸ noun a road cut into the edge of a cliff, especially one running along a coast.
– ORIGIN mid 19th cent.: from French (see **CORNICE**).

Cornish ▸ adjective relating to Cornwall or its people or language.
▸ noun 1 (as plural noun **the Cornish**) the people of Cornwall collectively.
2 [mass noun] the ancient Celtic language of Cornwall, belonging to the Brythonic branch of the Celtic language group. It gradually died out in the 17th and 18th centuries, although attempts have been made to revive it.
– DERIVATIVES **Cornishman** noun (pl. **Cornishmen**), **Cornishwoman** noun (pl. **Cornishwomen**).
– ORIGIN late Middle English: from the first element of **CORNWALL** + **-ISH**[1].

Cornish cream ▸ noun [mass noun] Brit. clotted cream.

Cornish hen (also **Cornish game hen**) ▸ noun another term for **ROCK CORNISH**.

Cornish pasty ▸ noun Brit. a pasty containing seasoned meat and vegetables, especially potato.

Corn Laws (in the UK) a series of 19th-century laws introduced to protect British farmers from foreign competition by allowing grain to be imported only after the price of home-grown wheat had risen above a certain level. They had the unintended effect of forcing up bread prices and were eventually repealed in 1846.

corn marigold ▸ noun a daisy-like yellow-flowered Eurasian plant which was formerly a common weed of cornfields. ● *Chrysanthemum segetum*, family Compositae.

cornmeal ▸ noun [mass noun] meal made from corn, especially (in the US) maize flour or (in Scotland) oatmeal.

corn oil ▸ noun [mass noun] an oil obtained from the germ of maize, used in cookery and salad dressings.

corn pone N. Amer. ▸ noun [mass noun] unleavened maize bread.
▸ adjective (**corn-pone**) informal rustic; unsophisticated: *country music and corn-pone humor.*

corn roast ▸ noun Canadian a party at which green maize is roasted and eaten.

cornrows ▸ plural noun (especially among black people) a style of braiding and plaiting the hair in narrow strips to form geometric patterns on the scalp.

corn salad ▸ noun another term for **LAMB'S LETTUCE**.

cornsilk N. Amer. ▸ noun [mass noun] the fine thread-like styles on an ear of maize.
▸ adjective (of hair) fine and blonde, like cornsilk.

corn snake ▸ noun a long North American rat snake with a spear-shaped mark between the eyes. ● *Elaphe guttata*, family Colubridae.
– ORIGIN late 17th cent.: so named because often found in cornfields.

corn snow ▸ noun [mass noun] chiefly N. Amer. snow with a rough granular surface resulting from alternate thawing and freezing.
– ORIGIN from *corn* in the dialect sense 'granule'.

cornstarch ▸ noun North American term for **CORNFLOUR**.

cornstone ▸ noun [mass noun] Geology a mottled red and green limestone characteristic of the Old and the New Red Sandstone in Britain.

corn syrup ▸ noun [mass noun] chiefly US glucose syrup, especially when made from cornflour.

cornu /ˈkɔːnjuː/ ▸ noun (pl. **cornua** /-njʊə/) Anatomy 1 a horn-shaped projection of the thyroid cartilage or of certain bones (such as the hyoid and the coccyx).
2 either of the two lateral cavities of the womb, into which the fallopian tubes pass.
3 each of three elongated parts of the lateral ventricles of the brain.
– DERIVATIVES **cornual** adjective.
– ORIGIN late 17th cent.: from Latin, 'horn'.

cornucopia /ˌkɔːnjʊˈkəʊpɪə/ ▸ noun a symbol of plenty consisting of a goat's horn overflowing with flowers, fruit, and corn. ▪ an ornamental container shaped like a goat's horn. ▪ an abundant supply of good things of a specified kind: ***the festival offers a cornucopia of pleasures.***
– DERIVATIVES **cornucopian** adjective.
– ORIGIN early 16th cent.: from late Latin, from Latin *cornu copiae* 'horn of plenty' (a mythical horn able to provide whatever is desired).

cornus /ˈkɔːnəs/ ▸ noun a plant of a genus that comprises the dogwoods. ● Genus *Cornus*, family Cornaceae.
– ORIGIN modern Latin, from Latin, 'dogwood'.

Cornwall a county occupying the extreme south-western peninsula of England; county town, Truro.

Cornwall, Duchy of an estate vested in the Prince of Wales, consisting of properties in Cornwall and elsewhere in SW England.

corny ▸ adjective (**cornier**, **corniest**) informal trite, banal, or mawkishly sentimental: *it sounds corny, but as soon as I saw her I knew she was the one.*
– DERIVATIVES **cornily** adverb, **corniness** noun.
– ORIGIN 1930s: from an earlier sense 'rustic, appealing to country folk'.

corolla /kəˈrɒlə/ ▸ noun Botany the petals of a flower, typically forming a whorl within the sepals and enclosing the reproductive organs. Compare with **CALYX**.
– ORIGIN late 17th cent. (in the sense 'little crown'): from Latin, diminutive of *corona* 'wreath, crown, chaplet'.

corollary /kəˈrɒləri/ ▸ noun (pl. **corollaries**) a proposition that follows from (and is often appended to) one already proved. ▪ a direct or natural consequence or result: ***the huge increases in unemployment were the corollary of expenditure cuts.***
▸ adjective forming a proposition that follows from one already proved. ▪ associated or supplementary: *the court did not answer a corollary question.*
– ORIGIN late Middle English: from Latin *corollarium* 'money paid for a garland or chaplet; gratuity' (in late Latin 'deduction'), from *corolla*, diminutive of *corona* 'wreath, crown, chaplet'.

coromandel /ˌkɒrəˈmand(ə)l/ ▸ noun 1 (also **coromandel wood** or **coromandel ebony**) [mass noun] a fine-grained, greyish brown ebony streaked with black, used in furniture. Also called **CALAMANDER**.
2 the Sri Lankan tree that yields coromandel ebony. ● *Diospyros quaesita*, family Ebenaceae.
▸ adjective denoting a form of oriental lacquerware with intaglio designs.
– ORIGIN from **COROMANDEL COAST**, from which oriental lacquerware was originally transported.

Coromandel Coast /ˌkɒrəˈmand(ə)l/ the southern part of the east coast of India, from Point Calimere to the mouth of the Krishna River.

corona[1] /kəˈrəʊnə/ ▸ noun (pl. **coronae** /-niː/)
1 Astronomy the rarefied gaseous envelope of the sun and other stars. The sun's corona is normally visible only during a total solar eclipse, when it is seen as an irregularly shaped pearly glow surrounding the darkened disc of the moon. ▪ (also **corona discharge**) Physics the glow around a conductor at high potential. ▪ a small circle of light seen round the sun or moon, due to diffraction by water droplets.
2 Anatomy a crown or crown-like structure.
3 Botany the cup-shaped or trumpet-shaped outgrowth at the centre of a daffodil or narcissus flower.
4 a circular chandelier in a church.

5 Architecture a part of a cornice having a broad vertical face.
– ORIGIN mid 16th cent. (in sense 5): from Latin, 'wreath, crown'.

corona[2] /kəˈrəʊnə/ ▶ **noun** a long, straight-sided cigar.
– ORIGIN late 19th cent.: from Spanish *La Corona*, literally 'the crown', originally a proprietary name.

Corona Australis /kəˌrəʊnə ɒˈstreɪlɪs/ Astronomy a small southern constellation (the Southern Crown), with no bright stars.
– ORIGIN Latin.

Corona Borealis /ˌbɔːrɪˈeɪlɪs/ Astronomy a northern constellation (the Northern Crown), in which the main stars form a small but prominent arc.
– ORIGIN Latin.

coronach /ˈkɒrənək, -x/ ▶ **noun** (in Scotland or Ireland) a funeral song.
– ORIGIN early 16th cent. (originally Scots, denoting the outcry of a crowd): from Scottish Gaelic *corranach* (Irish *coranach*), from *comh-* 'together' + *rànach* 'outcry'.

corona discharge ▶ **noun** see CORONA[1] (sense 1).

coronagraph ▶ **noun** an instrument that blocks out light emitted by the sun's actual surface so that the corona can be observed.

coronal[1] /kəˈrəʊn(ə)l, ˈkɒr(ə)n(ə)l/ ▶ **adjective 1** Astronomy relating to the corona of the sun or another star.
2 Anatomy relating to the crown of the head.
3 Anatomy of or in the coronal plane.
4 Phonetics (of a consonant) formed by raising the tip or blade of the tongue towards the hard palate.
▶ **noun** Phonetics a coronal consonant.
– ORIGIN late Middle English (in sense 2 of the adjective): from Latin *coronalis*, from *corona* 'crown'.

coronal[2] /ˈkɒr(ə)n(ə)l/ ▶ **noun** a garland or wreath for the head. ■ literary a small crown; a coronet.
– ORIGIN Middle English: apparently from Anglo-Norman French, from *corune* 'crown, wreath' (see CROWN).

coronal bone ▶ **noun** former term for FRONTAL BONE.

coronal plane ▶ **noun** Anatomy an imaginary plane dividing the body into dorsal and ventral parts.

coronal suture ▶ **noun** Anatomy the transverse suture in the skull separating the frontal bone from the parietal bones.

coronary ▶ **adjective** Anatomy relating to or denoting the arteries which surround and supply the heart. ■ relating to or denoting a structure which encircles a part of the body.
▶ **noun** (pl. **coronaries**) short for CORONARY THROMBOSIS.
– ORIGIN mid 17th cent. (in the sense 'resembling a crown'): from Latin *coronarius*, from *corona* 'wreath, crown'.

coronary thrombosis ▶ **noun** a blockage of the flow of blood to the heart, caused by a blood clot in a coronary artery.

coronation ▶ **noun** the ceremony of crowning a sovereign or a sovereign's consort.
– ORIGIN late Middle English: via Old French from medieval Latin *coronatio(n-)*, from *coronare* 'to crown, adorn with a garland', from *corona* (see CROWN).

coronation chicken ▶ **noun** [mass noun] a cold dish of cooked chicken served in a sauce flavoured with apricots and curry powder.
– ORIGIN so named because the dish was created for the coronation of Queen Elizabeth II in 1953.

Coronation stone another term for STONE OF SCONE.

coronavirus /kəˈrəʊnəˌvʌɪrəs/ ▶ **noun** Medicine any of a group of RNA viruses that cause a variety of diseases in humans and other animals.

coroner /ˈkɒr(ə)nə/ ▶ **noun** an official who holds inquests into violent, sudden, or suspicious deaths, and (in Britain) inquiries into cases of treasure trove. ■ historical an official responsible for safeguarding the private property of the Crown.
– ORIGIN Middle English: from Anglo-Norman French *coruner*, from *corune* 'a crown' (see CROWN); reflecting the Latin title *custos placitorum coronae* 'guardian of the pleas of the Crown'.

coronet /ˈkɒr(ə)nɪt/ ▶ **noun 1** a small or relatively simple crown, especially as worn by lesser royalty and peers or peeresses. ■ a circular decoration for the head, especially one made of flowers.
2 a ring of bone at the base of a deer's antler.
3 the band of tissue on the lowest part of a horse's pastern, containing the horn-producing cells from which the hoof grows.
– DERIVATIVES **coroneted** adjective.
– ORIGIN late Middle English: from Old French *coronete* 'small crown or garland', diminutive of *corone* (see CROWN).

coronial /kəˈrəʊnɪəl/ ▶ **adjective** relating to a coroner.

coronoid process ▶ **noun** Anatomy **1** a flattened triangular projection above the angle of the jaw where the temporalis muscle is attached.
2 a projection from the front of the ulna forming part of the articulation of the elbow.
– ORIGIN mid 18th cent.: *coronoid* from Greek *korōnē* (denoting something hooked) + -OID.

Corot /ˈkɒrəʊ/, French /kɔʀo/, (Jean-Baptiste) Camille (1796–1875), French landscape painter, who worked in an essentially classical style despite his contact with the Barbizon School. Corot had a significant influence on the Impressionists.

Corp. ▶ **abbreviation** ■ N. Amer. Corporation: *IBM Corp.* ■ (**Corp**) informal Corporal: *been abroad before, Corp?*

corpora plural form of CORPUS.

corporal[1] ▶ **noun 1** a rank of non-commissioned officer in the army, above lance corporal or private first class and below sergeant.
2 (also **ship's corporal**) Brit. historical a petty officer who attended solely to police matters, under the master-at-arms.
3 North American term for FALLFISH.
– ORIGIN mid 16th cent.: from French, obsolete variant of *caporal*, from Italian *caporale*, probably based on Latin *corpus*, *corpor-* 'body (of troops)', with a change of spelling in Italian due to association with *capo* 'head'.

corporal[2] ▶ **adjective** relating to the human body.
– DERIVATIVES **corporally** adverb.
– ORIGIN late Middle English: via Old French from Latin *corporalis*, from *corpus*, *corpor-* 'body'.

corporal[3] ▶ **noun** a cloth on which the chalice and paten are placed during the celebration of the Eucharist.
– ORIGIN Middle English: from medieval Latin *corporale (pallium)* 'body (cloth)', from Latin *corpus*, *corpor-* 'body'.

corporality ▶ **noun** [mass noun] rare material or corporeal existence.
– ORIGIN late Middle English: from late Latin *corporalitas*, from Latin *corporalis* 'relating to the body' (see CORPORAL[2]).

corporal punishment ▶ **noun** [mass noun] physical punishment, such as caning or flogging.

corporate ▶ **adjective** relating to a large company or group: *airlines are very keen on their corporate identity.* ■ Law (of a large company or group) authorized to act as a single entity and recognized as such in law. ■ of or shared by all the members of a group: *the service emphasizes the corporate responsibility of the congregation.*
▶ **noun** a corporate company or group.
– DERIVATIVES **corporately** adverb.
– ORIGIN late 15th cent.: from Latin *corporatus*, past participle of *corporare* 'form into a body', from *corpus*, *corpor-* 'body'.

corporate hospitality ▶ **noun** [mass noun] the entertaining of clients by companies in order to promote business, especially at sporting or other public events.

corporate raider ▶ **noun** a financier who makes a practice of making hostile takeover bids for companies, either to control their policies or to resell them for a profit.

corporate state ▶ **noun** a state governed by representatives not of geographical areas but of vocational corporations of the employers and employees in each trade, profession, or industry.

corporation ▶ **noun 1** a large company or group of companies authorized to act as a single entity and recognized as such in law.
2 Brit. a group of people elected to govern a city, town, or borough.
3 dated, humorous a paunch.
– ORIGIN late Middle English: from late Latin *corporatio(n-)*, from Latin *corporare* 'combine in one body' (see CORPORATE).

corporation tax ▶ **noun** [mass noun] Brit. tax levied on companies' profits.

corporatism ▶ **noun** [mass noun] the control of a state or organization by large interest groups.
– DERIVATIVES **corporatist** adjective & noun.

corporative ▶ **adjective** relating to or denoting a state, typically a fascist one, organized into corporations representing employers and employees in various trades or professions.
– DERIVATIVES **corporativism** noun, **corporativist** adjective & noun.

corporatize (also **corporatise**) ▶ **verb** [with obj.] convert (a state organization) into an independent commercial company.
– DERIVATIVES **corporatization** noun.

corporator ▶ **noun** Indian an elected member of a municipal corporation.

corporeal /kɔːˈpɔːrɪəl/ ▶ **adjective** relating to a person's body, especially as opposed to their spirit: *he was frank about his corporeal appetites.* ■ having a body: *a corporeal God.* ■ Law consisting of material objects.
– DERIVATIVES **corporeality** /-ˈalɪti/ noun, **corporeally** adverb.
– ORIGIN late Middle English (in the sense 'material'): from late Latin *corporealis*, from Latin *corporeus* 'bodily, physical', from *corpus*, *corpor-* 'body'.

corporeity /ˌkɔːpəˈriːɪti, -ˈreɪɪti/ ▶ **noun** [mass noun] rare the quality of having a physical body or existence.
– ORIGIN early 17th cent.: from French *corporéité* or medieval Latin *corporeitas*, from Latin *corporeus* 'composed of flesh', from *corpus*, *corpor-* 'body'.

corposant /ˈkɔːpəzant/ ▶ **noun** archaic an appearance of St Elmo's fire on a mast, rigging, or other structure.
– ORIGIN mid 16th cent.: from Old Spanish, Portuguese, and Italian *corpo santo* 'holy body'.

corps /kɔː/ ▶ **noun** (pl. **corps** /kɔːz/) [often in names] a main subdivision of an army in the field, consisting of two or more divisions: *the 5th Army Corps.* ■ a branch of an army assigned to a particular kind of work: *the Royal Army Medical Corps.* ■ [with adj. or noun modifier] a body of people engaged in a particular activity: *the press corps.* ■ short for CORPS DE BALLET.
– ORIGIN late 16th cent.: from French, from Latin *corpus* 'body'.

corps de ballet /ˌkɔː də ˈbaleɪ/ ▶ **noun** [treated as sing. or pl.] the members of a ballet company who dance together as a group. ■ the members of the lowest rank of dancers in a ballet company.
– ORIGIN early 19th cent.: French.

corps d'elite /ˌkɔː deɪˈliːt/ ▶ **noun** a select group of people.
– ORIGIN French.

corpse ▶ **noun** a dead body, especially of a human being rather than an animal.
▶ **verb** [no obj.] theatrical slang spoil a piece of acting by forgetting one's lines or laughing uncontrollably. ■ [with obj.] cause (an actor) to do this.
– ORIGIN Middle English (denoting the living body of a person or animal): alteration of CORSE by association with Latin *corpus*, a change which also took place in French (Old French *cors* becoming *corps*). The *p* was originally silent, as in French; the final *e* was rare before the 19th cent., but now distinguishes *corpse* from *corps*.

corpse candle ▶ **noun** a lambent flame seen just above the ground in a churchyard or over a grave, superstitiously regarded as an omen of death.

corpulence /ˈkɔːpjʊləns/ ▶ **noun** [mass noun] the state of being fat; obesity: *her corpulence is the butt of every joke.*
– DERIVATIVES **corpulency** noun.

corpulent /ˈkɔːpjʊl(ə)nt/ ▶ **adjective** (of a person) fat: *a short, somewhat corpulent man.*
– ORIGIN late Middle English: from Latin *corpulentus*, from *corpus* 'body'.

cor pulmonale /ˌkɔː pʌlməˈnɑːli, -ˈneɪli/ ▶ **noun** [mass noun] Medicine abnormal enlargement of the right side of the heart as a result of disease of the lungs or the pulmonary blood vessels.
– ORIGIN mid 19th cent.: from Latin *cor* 'heart' and modern Latin *pulmonalis* (from Latin *pulmo(n-)* 'lung').

corpus /ˈkɔːpəs/ ▶ **noun** (pl. **corpora** or **corpuses**) **1** a collection of written texts, especially the entire works of a particular author or a body of writing on a particular subject: *the Darwinian corpus.* ■ a collection of written or spoken material in machine-readable form, assembled for the purpose of linguistic research.
2 Anatomy the main body or mass of a structure. ■ the central part of the stomach, between the fundus and the antrum.
– ORIGIN late Middle English (denoting a human or animal body): from Latin, literally 'body'. Sense 1 dates from the early 18th cent.

corpus callosum /kəˈləʊsəm/ ▶ noun (pl. **corpora callosa** /-sə/) Anatomy a broad band of nerve fibres joining the two hemispheres of the brain.
– ORIGIN early 18th cent.: from **CORPUS** and Latin *callosum*, neuter of *callosus* 'tough'.

corpus cavernosum /ˌkavəˈnəʊsəm/ ▶ noun (pl. **corpora cavernosa** /-sə/) Anatomy either of two masses of erectile tissue forming the bulk of the penis and the clitoris.
– ORIGIN from **CORPUS** and Latin *cavernosum*, neuter of *cavernosus* 'containing hollows'.

Corpus Christi[1] /ˌkɔːpəs ˈkrɪsti/ ▶ noun a feast of the Western Christian Church commemorating the institution of the Eucharist, observed on the Thursday after Trinity Sunday.
– ORIGIN Latin, literally 'body of Christ'.

Corpus Christi[2] /ˌkɔːpəs ˈkrɪsti/ a city and port in southern Texas; pop. 286,462 (est. 2008). It is situated on Corpus Christi Bay, an inlet of the Gulf of Mexico.

corpuscle /ˈkɔːpʌs(ə)l/ ▶ noun Biology a minute body or cell in an organism, especially a red or white cell in the blood of vertebrates. ■ historical a minute particle regarded as the basic constituent of matter or light.
– DERIVATIVES **corpuscular** /kɔːˈpʌskjʊlə/ adjective.
– ORIGIN mid 17th cent.: from Latin *corpusculum* 'small body', diminutive of *corpus*.

corpus delicti /dɪˈlɪktʌɪ/ ▶ noun Law the facts and circumstances constituting a crime. ■ concrete evidence of a crime, such as a corpse.
– ORIGIN Latin, literally 'body of offence'.

corpus luteum /ˈluːtɪəm/ ▶ noun (pl. **corpora lutea** /ˈluːtɪə/) Anatomy a hormone-secreting structure that develops in an ovary after an ovum has been discharged but degenerates after a few days unless pregnancy has begun.
– ORIGIN late 18th cent.: from **CORPUS** and Latin *luteum*, neuter of *luteus* 'yellow'.

corpus spongiosum /ˌspʌndʒɪˈəʊsəm/ ▶ noun (pl. **corpora spongiosa** /-sə/) Anatomy a mass of erectile tissue alongside the corpora cavernosa of the penis and terminating in the glans.
– ORIGIN from **CORPUS** and Latin *spongiosum*, neuter of *spongiosus* 'porous'.

corpus striatum /strʌɪˈeɪtəm/ ▶ noun (pl. **corpora striata** /-tə/) Anatomy part of the basal ganglia of the brain, comprising the caudate and lentiform nuclei.
– ORIGIN from **CORPUS** and Latin *striatum*, neuter of *striatus* 'grooved'.

corral /kəˈrɑːl/ ▶ noun N. Amer. **1** a pen for livestock, especially cattle or horses, on a farm or ranch.
2 historical a defensive enclosure formed of wagons in an encampment.
▶ verb (**corrals, corralling, corralled**) [with obj.] **1** chiefly N. Amer. put or keep (livestock) in a corral. ■ gather (a group of people or things) together: *the organizers were corralling the crowd into marching formation.*
2 N. Amer. historical form (wagons) into a corral.
– ORIGIN late 16th cent.: from Spanish and Old Portuguese (now *curral*), perhaps based on Latin *currere* 'to run'. Compare with **KRAAL**.

correct ▶ adjective free from error; in accordance with fact or truth: *make sure you have been given the correct information.* ■ [predic.] not mistaken in one's opinion or judgement; right: [with infinitive] *the government was correct to follow a course of defeating inflation.* ■ meeting the requirements of or most appropriate for a particular situation or activity: *cut the top and bottom tracks to the correct length with a hacksaw.* ■ (of a person or their appearance or behaviour) conforming to accepted social standards; proper: *he was a polite man, invariably correct and pleasant with Mrs Collins.* ■ chiefly N. Amer. conforming to a particular political or ideological orthodoxy. See also **POLITICALLY CORRECT**.
▶ verb [with obj.] put right (an error or fault): *the Council issued a statement correcting some points in the press reports.* ■ mark the errors in (a written or printed text): *he corrected Dixon's writing for publication.* ■ tell (someone) that they are mistaken: *he had assumed she was married and she had not corrected him.* ■ counteract or rectify: *the steel industry's current overcapacity will be corrected this year.* ■ adjust (an instrument) to function accurately or accord with a standard: *motorists can have their headlights tested and corrected at a reduced price on Saturday.* ■ adjust (a numerical result or reading) to allow for departure from standard conditions: *data were corrected for radionuclide decay.*
– DERIVATIVES **correctable** adjective, **correctness** noun, **corrector** noun.
– ORIGIN Middle English (as a verb): from Latin *correct-* 'made straight, amended', from the verb *corrigere*, from *cor-* 'together' + *regere* 'guide'. The adjective is via French.

correction ▶ noun [mass noun] the action or process of correcting something: *I checked the typing for errors and sent it back for correction.* ■ [count noun] a change that rectifies an error or inaccuracy: *he made a few corrections to my homework.* ■ used to introduce an amended version of something one has just said: *I once dated a guy – correction – had one date with a guy.* ■ [count noun] a quantity adjusting a numerical result to allow for a departure from standard conditions. ■ N. Amer. or dated punishment, especially that of criminals in prison intended to rectify their behaviour.
– ORIGIN Middle English: via Old French from Latin *correctio(n-)*, from *corrigere* 'make straight, bring into order' (see **CORRECT**).

correctional ▶ adjective chiefly N. Amer. relating to the punishment of criminals in a way intended to rectify their behaviour: *a correctional institution.*

correction fluid ▶ noun [mass noun] an opaque liquid painted over a typed or written error so as to allow for the insertion of the correct character.

correctitude /kəˈrɛktɪtjuːd/ ▶ noun [mass noun] correctness, especially conscious correctness in one's behaviour.
– ORIGIN late 19th cent.: blend of **CORRECT** and **RECTITUDE**.

corrective ▶ adjective designed to correct or counteract something harmful or undesirable: *management were informed so that corrective action could be taken.*
▶ noun a thing intended to correct or counteract something else: *the move might be a **corrective to** some inefficient practices within hospitals.*
– DERIVATIVES **correctively** adverb.
– ORIGIN mid 16th cent.: from French *correctif, -ive* or late Latin *correctivus*, from Latin *correct-* 'brought into order' from the verb *corrigere* (see **CORRECT**).

correctly ▶ adverb in a way that is true, factual or appropriate; accurately: *she correctly answered eight questions.* ■ in a way that is socially acceptable; properly: *she had acted correctly.*

Correggio /kɒˈrɛdʒɪəʊ/, Antonio Allegri da (*c.*1494–1534), Italian painter; born *Antonio Allegri*. The soft, sensual style of his devotional and mythological paintings influenced the rococo of the 18th century. He is best known for his frescoes in Parma cathedral.

correlate /ˈkɒrəleɪt, -rɪ-/ ▶ verb [no obj.] have a mutual relationship or connection, in which one thing affects or depends on another: *the study found that success in the educational system **correlates** highly **with** class.* ■ [with obj.] establish such a relationship or connection between: *we should **correlate** general trends in public opinion **with** trends in the content of television news.*
▶ noun each of two or more related or complementary things: *strategies to promote health should pay greater attention to financial hardship and other correlates of poverty.*
– ORIGIN mid 17th cent. (as a noun): back-formation from **CORRELATION** and **CORRELATIVE**.

correlation ▶ noun a mutual relationship or connection between two or more things: *research showed a clear correlation between recession and levels of property crime* | [mass noun] *there was no correlation between the number of visits to the clinic and the treatment outcome.* ■ [mass noun] the process of establishing a relationship or connection between two or more things. ■ [mass noun] Statistics interdependence of variable quantities. ■ Statistics a quantity measuring the extent of such interdependence.
– DERIVATIVES **correlational** adjective.
– ORIGIN mid 16th cent.: from medieval Latin *correlatio(n-)*, from *cor-* 'together' + *relatio* (see **RELATION**).

correlation coefficient ▶ noun Statistics a number between +1 and −1 calculated so as to represent the linear interdependence of two variables or sets of data. (Symbol: **r**)

correlative /kəˈrɛlətɪv/ ▶ adjective having a mutual relationship; corresponding: *rights, whether moral or legal, can involve correlative duties.* ■ Grammar (of words such as *neither* and *nor*) corresponding to each other and regularly used together.
▶ noun a word or concept that has a mutual relationship with another word or concept: *the child's right to education is a correlative of the parent's duty to send the child to school.*
– DERIVATIVES **correlatively** adverb, **correlativity** noun.
– ORIGIN mid 16th cent.: from medieval Latin *correlativus*, from *cor-* 'together' + late Latin *relativus* (see **RELATIVE**).

correspond ▶ verb [no obj.] **1** have a close similarity; match or agree almost exactly: *the carved heads described in the poem **correspond to** a drawing of Edgcote House* | *communication is successful when the ideas in the minds of the speaker and hearer correspond.* ■ be analogous or equivalent in character, form, or function: *the rank of Feldwebel in the German forces nominally **corresponded to** the British rank of sergeant.*
2 communicate by exchanging letters: *Margaret **corresponded with** him until his death* | *the doctor and I corresponded for more than two decades.*
– ORIGIN late Middle English: from Old French *correspondre*, from medieval Latin *correspondere*, from *cor-* 'together' + Latin *respondere* (see **RESPOND**).

correspondence ▶ noun **1** a close similarity, connection, or equivalence: *there is a simple **correspondence between** the distance of a focused object from the eye and the size of its image on the retina.*
2 [mass noun] communication by exchanging letters: *the organization engaged in detailed **correspondence with** local MPs.* ■ letters sent or received: *his wife dealt with his private correspondence.*
– ORIGIN late Middle English: via Old French from medieval Latin *correspondentia*, from *correspondent-* 'corresponding' (see **CORRESPONDENT**).

correspondence college (also **correspondence school**) ▶ noun a college offering correspondence courses.

correspondence column ▶ noun Brit. the part of a newspaper, magazine, or journal that contains letters from readers.

correspondence course ▶ noun a course of study in which student and tutors communicate by post.

correspondence principle Physics ▶ noun the principle that states that for very large quantum numbers the laws of quantum theory merge with those of classical physics.

correspondence school ▶ noun another term for **CORRESPONDENCE COLLEGE**.

correspondence theory Philosophy ▶ noun the theory that states that the definition or criterion of truth is that true propositions correspond to the facts.

correspondent ▶ noun **1** a person who writes letters on a regular basis: *she wasn't much of a correspondent.*
2 [often with adj. or noun modifier] a person employed to report for a newspaper or broadcasting organization: *a cricket correspondent.*
▶ adjective corresponding.
– ORIGIN late Middle English (as an adjective): from Old French *correspondant* or medieval Latin *correspondent-* 'corresponding', from the verb *correspondere* (see **CORRESPOND**).

corresponding ▶ adjective analogous or equivalent in character, form, or function; comparable: *the corresponding Jamaican word is 'bada'.*
– DERIVATIVES **correspondingly** adverb.

corresponding angles ▶ plural noun Mathematics the angles which occupy the same relative position at each intersection where a straight line crosses two others. If the two lines are parallel, the corresponding angles are equal.

corresponding member ▶ noun an honorary member of a learned society who has no voice in the society's affairs, especially one living some distance from its headquarters.

corrida /kɒˈriːdə/ ▶ noun a bullfight.
– ORIGIN late 19th cent.: from Spanish *corrida de toros* 'running of bulls'.

corridor ▶ noun a long passage in a building from which doors lead into rooms. ■ Brit. a passage along the side of some railway carriages, from which doors lead into compartments. ■ a belt of land linking two other areas or following a road or river: *the security forces established corridors for humanitarian supplies.*
– PHRASES **the corridors of power** the senior levels of government or administration. [from the name of C. P. Snow's novel *The Corridors of Power* (1964).]
– ORIGIN late 16th cent. (as a military term denoting a strip of land along the outer edge of a ditch, protected by a parapet): from French, from Italian *corridore*, alteration (by association with *corridore* 'runner') of *corridoio* 'running place', from *correre*

'to run', from Latin *currere*. The current sense dates from the early 19th cent.

corrie /ˈkɒri/ ▶ **noun** (pl. **corries**) a cirque, especially one in the mountains of Scotland.
– ORIGIN mid 16th cent.: from Scottish Gaelic and Irish *coire* 'cauldron, hollow'.

Corriedale /ˈkɒrɪdeɪl/ ▶ **noun** a sheep of a New Zealand breed kept for both wool and meat.
– ORIGIN early 20th cent.: named after an estate in northern Otago, New Zealand.

corrigendum /ˌkɒrɪˈdʒɛndəm/ ▶ **noun** (pl. **corrigenda** /-də/) a thing to be corrected, typically an error in a printed book.
– ORIGIN early 19th cent.: Latin, neuter gerundive of *corrigere* 'bring into order' (see CORRECT).

corrigible /ˈkɒrɪdʒɪb(ə)l/ ▶ **adjective** capable of being corrected, rectified, or reformed.
– DERIVATIVES **corrigibility** noun.
– ORIGIN late Middle English (in the sense 'liable to or deserving punishment'): via French from medieval Latin *corrigibilis*, from Latin *corrigere* 'to correct'.

corroborate /kəˈrɒbəreɪt/ ▶ **verb** [with obj.] confirm or give support to (a statement, theory, or finding): *the witness had corroborated the boy's account of the attack*.
– DERIVATIVES **corroborative** adjective, **corroborator** noun, **corroboratory** adjective.
– ORIGIN mid 16th cent. (in the sense 'make physically stronger'): from Latin *corroborat-* 'strengthened', from the verb *corroborare*, from *cor-* 'together' + *roborare*, from *robur* 'strength'.

corroboration /kəˌrɒbəˈreɪʃ(ə)n/ ▶ **noun** [mass noun] evidence which confirms or supports a statement, theory, or finding; confirmation: *there is no independent corroboration for this*.

corroboree /kəˈrɒbəri/ ▶ **noun** an Australian Aboriginal dance ceremony which may take the form of a sacred ritual or an informal gathering. ■ chiefly Austral. a party or other lively social gathering.
– ORIGIN from Dharuk *garaabara*, denoting a style of dancing.

corrode /kəˈrəʊd/ ▶ **verb** [with obj.] **1** destroy or damage (metal, stone, or other materials) slowly by chemical action: *acid rain poisons fish and corrodes buildings*. ■ [no obj.] (of metal or other materials) be destroyed or damaged in this way: *over the years copper pipework corrodes*.
2 destroy or weaken (something) gradually: *the self-centred climate corrodes ideals and concerns about social justice*.
– DERIVATIVES **corrodible** adjective.
– ORIGIN late Middle English: from Latin *corrodere*, from *cor-* (expressing intensive force) + *rodere* 'gnaw'.

corrody /ˈkɒrədi/ ▶ **noun** (pl. **corrodies**) historical a pension or provision for maintenance, especially as given regularly by a religious house.
– ORIGIN late Middle English: from Anglo-Norman French *corodie*, from a Romance word meaning 'preparation'.

corrosion ▶ **noun** [mass noun] the process of corroding or being corroded: *each aircraft part is sprayed with oil to prevent corrosion*. ■ damage caused by such a process: *engineers found the corrosion when checking the bridge*.
– ORIGIN late Middle English: from Old French, or from late Latin *corrosio(n-)*, from Latin *corrodere* 'gnaw through' (see CORRODE).

corrosive ▶ **adjective** tending to cause corrosion: *the corrosive effects of salt water*.
▶ **noun** a corrosive substance.
– DERIVATIVES **corrosively** adverb, **corrosiveness** noun.
– ORIGIN late Middle English: from Old French *corosif, -ive*, from medieval Latin *corrosivus*, from Latin *corros-* 'gnawed through', from the verb *corrodere* (see CORRODE).

corrosive sublimate ▶ **noun** old-fashioned term for MERCURIC CHLORIDE.

corrugate /ˈkɒrʊgeɪt/ ▶ **verb** contract or cause to contract into wrinkles or folds: [no obj.] *Micky's brow corrugated in a simian frown*.
– ORIGIN late Middle English: from Latin *corrugat-* 'wrinkled', from the verb *corrugare*, from *cor-* (expressing intensive force) + *rugare* (from *ruga* 'a wrinkle').

corrugated ▶ **adjective** (of a material or surface) shaped into a series of parallel ridges and grooves so as to give added rigidity and strength: *corrugated cardboard*.
– DERIVATIVES **corrugation** noun.

corrugated iron ▶ **noun** [mass noun] a building material consisting of iron or steel sheeting bent into a corrugated form.

corrupt ▶ **adjective 1** having or showing a willingness to act dishonestly in return for money or personal gain: *unscrupulous logging companies assisted by corrupt officials*. ■ evil or morally depraved: *the old corrupt order*.
2 (of a text or a computer database or program) made unreliable by errors or alterations.
3 archaic (of organic or inorganic matter) in a state of decay; rotten or putrid.
▶ **verb** [with obj.] **1** cause to act dishonestly in return for money or personal gain: *there is a continuing fear of firms corrupting politicians in the search for contracts*. ■ cause to become morally depraved: *he has corrupted the boy*.
2 change or debase by making errors or unintentional alterations: *a backup copy will be needed if the original copy becomes corrupted | Epicurus's teachings have since been much corrupted*.
3 archaic infect; contaminate.
– DERIVATIVES **corrupter** noun, **corruptibility** noun, **corruptible** adjective, **corruptive** adjective, **corruptly** adverb, **corruptness** noun.
– ORIGIN Middle English: from Latin *corruptus*, past participle of *corrumpere* 'mar, bribe, destroy', from *cor-* 'altogether' + *rumpere* 'to break'.

corruption ▶ **noun** [mass noun] **1** dishonest or fraudulent conduct by those in power, typically involving bribery: *the journalist who wants to expose corruption in high places*. ■ the action or effect of making someone or something morally depraved.
2 the process by which a word or expression is changed from its original state to one regarded as erroneous or debased: *a record of a word's corruption* | [count noun] *the term 'hobgoblin' is thought to be a corruption of 'Robgoblin'*. ■ the process by which a computer database or program becomes debased by alteration or the introduction of errors.
3 archaic the process of decay; putrefaction.
– ORIGIN Middle English: via Old French from Latin *corruptio(n-)*, from *corrumpere* 'mar, bribe, destroy' (see CORRUPT).

corrupt practice ▶ **noun** a fraudulent activity, especially an attempt to rig an election.

corsac fox /ˈkɔːsak/ ▶ **noun** a russet-grey fox found on the steppes of central Asia. ● *Vulpes corsac*, family Canidae.
– ORIGIN mid 19th cent.: *corsac* from Russian *korsak*, from Turkic *karsak*.

corsage /kɔːˈsɑːʒ, ˈkɔːsɑːʒ/ ▶ **noun 1** a spray of flowers worn pinned to a woman's clothes.
2 the upper part of a woman's dress.
– ORIGIN early 19th cent. (in sense 2): French, from Old French *cors* 'body', from Latin *corpus*.

corsair /kɔːˈsɛː, ˈkɔːsɛː/ ▶ **noun** archaic a pirate. ■ a pirate ship. ■ a privateer, especially one operating along the southern shore of the Mediterranean in the 16th–18th centuries.
– ORIGIN mid 16th cent.: from French *corsaire*, from medieval Latin *cursarius*, from *cursus* 'a raid, plunder', special use of Latin *cursus* 'course', from *currere* 'to run'.

Corse /kɔʀs/ French name for CORSICA.

corse /kɔːs/ ▶ **noun** archaic a corpse.
– ORIGIN Middle English: from Old French *cors* 'body', from Latin *corpus*. Compare with CORPSE.

corselet ▶ **noun 1** /ˈkɔːs(ə)lɪt/ historical a piece of armour covering the trunk.
2 variant spelling of CORSELETTE.
– ORIGIN late 15th cent.: from Old French *corslet*, diminutive of *cors* 'body'.

corselette /kɔːs(ə)ˈlɛt, ˈkɔːs(ə)lɛt/ (also **corselet**) ▶ **noun** a woman's foundation garment combining corset and bra.
– ORIGIN 1920s: from *corselet* (see CORSELET).

corset ▶ **noun** a woman's tightly fitting undergarment extending from below the chest to the hips, worn to shape the figure. ■ a similar garment worn by men or women to support a weak or injured back. ■ historical a tightly fitting laced or stiffened outer bodice.
– DERIVATIVES **corseted** adjective, **corsetry** noun.
– ORIGIN Middle English: from Old French, diminutive of *cors* 'body', from Latin *corpus*. The sense 'close-fitting undergarment' dates from the late 18th cent., by which time the sense 'bodice' had mainly historical reference.

corsetière /ˈkɔːsɪtjɛː/ ▶ **noun** a woman who makes or fits corsets.
– ORIGIN mid 19th cent.: French, feminine of *corsetier*, from *corset* (see CORSET).

Corsica /ˈkɔːsɪkə/ a mountainous island off the west coast of Italy, forming an administrative region of France; pop. 273,000 (est. 2004); chief towns, Bastia (northern department) and Ajaccio (southern department). It was the birthplace of Napoleon I. French name CORSE.

Corsican ▶ **adjective** relating to Corsica, its people, or their language.
▶ **noun 1** a native or inhabitant of Corsica.
2 [mass noun] the language of Corsica, which originated as a dialect of Italian.

corso /ˈkɔːsəʊ/ ▶ **noun** (pl. **corsos**) (in Italy and some other Mediterranean countries) a social promenade. ■ a street used for social promenades, or where races and parades were formerly held.
– ORIGIN Italian, 'main street', from Latin *cursus* 'a course'.

Cort /kɔːt/, Henry (1740–1800), English ironmaster. He patented a process for producing iron bars by passing iron through grooved rollers, thus avoiding a hammering stage.

cortège /kɔːˈteɪʒ, -ˈtɛʒ/ ▶ **noun** a solemn procession, especially for a funeral. ■ a person's entourage or retinue.
– ORIGIN mid 17th cent.: from French, from Italian *corteggio*, from *corteggiare* 'attend court', from *corte* 'court', from Latin *cohors, cohort-* 'retinue'.

Cortes /ˈkɔːtɛs, -z/, Spanish /ˈkaoɾtes/ the legislative assembly of Spain and formerly of Portugal.
– ORIGIN Spanish and Portuguese, plural of *corte* 'court', from Latin *cohors, cohort-* 'yard, retinue'.

Cortés /ˈkɔːtɛz/, Spanish /kaoɾˈtes/ (also **Cortez**), Hernando (1485–1547), first of the Spanish conquistadores. Cortés overthrew the Aztec empire, conquering its capital, Tenochtitlán, in 1519 and deposing the emperor, Montezuma. In 1521 he destroyed Tenochtitlán completely and established Mexico City as the new capital of Mexico (then called New Spain).

cortex /ˈkɔːtɛks/ ▶ **noun** (pl. **cortices** /-tɪˌsiːz/) **1** Anatomy the outer layer of the cerebrum (the **cerebral cortex**), composed of folded grey matter and playing an important role in consciousness. ■ an outer layer of another organ or body part such as a kidney (the **renal cortex**), the cerebellum, or a hair.
2 Botany an outer layer of tissue immediately below the epidermis of a stem or root.
– DERIVATIVES **cortical** adjective.
– ORIGIN late Middle English: from Latin, literally 'bark'.

corticate /ˈkɔːtɪkeɪt/ ▶ **adjective** Botany having a cortex, bark, or rind.
– ORIGIN mid 19th cent.: from Latin *corticatus*, from *cortex, cortic-* 'bark'.

cortico- ▶ **combining form** representing CORTEX, used especially with reference to the adrenal and cerebral cortices.
– ORIGIN from Latin *cortex, cortic-* 'bark'.

corticofugal /ˌkɔːtɪkəʊˈfjuːg(ə)l/ (also **corticifugal** /ˌkɔːtɪˈsɪfjuːg(ə)l/) ▶ **adjective** Anatomy (of a nerve fibre) originating in and running from the cerebral cortex.
– ORIGIN late 19th cent.: from CORTICO- 'cortex' + Latin *fugere* 'run from'.

corticosteroid /ˌkɔːtɪkəʊˈstɪərɔɪd, -ˈstɛrɔɪd/ ▶ **noun** Biochemistry any of a group of steroid hormones produced in the adrenal cortex or made synthetically. There are two kinds: glucocorticoids and mineralocorticoids. They have various metabolic functions and some are used to treat inflammation.

corticosterone /ˌkɔːtɪkəʊˈstɛrəʊn/ ▶ **noun** [mass noun] Biochemistry a hormone secreted by the adrenal cortex, one of the glucocorticoids.

corticotrophin /ˌkɔːtɪkə(ʊ)ˈtrəʊfɪn/ (also **corticotropin** /-pɪn/) ▶ **noun** Biochemistry another term for ADRENOCORTICOTROPHIC HORMONE.

cortile /kɔːˈtiːleɪ/, Italian /korˈtile/ ▶ **noun** (pl. **cortili** /-li/ or **cortiles**) (in Italy) an enclosed area, typically roofless and arcaded, within or attached to a building.
– ORIGIN Italian, derivative of *corte* 'court'.

cortina /kɔːˈtʌɪnə, -ˈtiːnə/ ▶ **noun** Botany (in some toadstools) a thin web-like veil extending from the edge of the cap to the stalk.
– ORIGIN mid 19th cent.: from late Latin, literally 'curtain'.

cortisol /ˈkɔːtɪsɒl/ ▶ **noun** Biochemistry another term for HYDROCORTISONE.

cortisone /ˈkɔːtɪzəʊn/ ▸ **noun** [mass noun] Biochemistry a hormone produced by the adrenal cortex. One of the glucocorticoids, it is also made synthetically for use as an anti-inflammatory and anti-allergy agent.
– ORIGIN 1940s: from elements of its chemical name *17-hydroxy-11-dehydrocorticosterone*.

corundum /kəˈrʌndəm/ ▸ **noun** [mass noun] extremely hard crystallized alumina, used as an abrasive. Ruby and sapphire are varieties of corundum.
– ORIGIN early 18th cent.: from Tamil *kuruntam* and Telugu *kuruvindam*.

Corunna /kəˈrʌnə/ a port in NW Spain; pop. 245,164 (2008). It was the point of departure for the Armada in 1588 and the site of a battle in 1809 in the Peninsular War, at which British forces under Sir John Moore defeated the French. Spanish name **LA CORUÑA**.

coruscant /kɒˈrʌsk(ə)nt/ ▸ **adjective** literary glittering; sparkling.
– ORIGIN late 15th cent.: from Latin *coruscant-* 'vibrating, glittering', from the verb *coruscare*.

coruscate /ˈkɒrəskeɪt/ ▸ **verb** [no obj.] literary (of light) flash or sparkle: *the light was coruscating through the walls*.
– DERIVATIVES **coruscation** noun.
– ORIGIN early 18th cent.: from Latin *coruscat-* 'glittered', from the verb *coruscare*.

coruscating /ˈkɒrəskeɪtɪŋ/ ▸ **adjective** flashing; sparkling: *a coruscating kaleidoscope of colours*. ▪ brilliant or striking in content or style: *the play's coruscating wit*.

corvée /ˈkɔːveɪ/ ▸ **noun** historical a day's unpaid labour owed by a vassal to his feudal lord. ▪ [mass noun] forced labour exacted in lieu of taxes, in particular that on public roads in France before 1776.
– ORIGIN Middle English: from Old French, based on Latin *corrogare* 'ask for, collect'. Rare in English before the late 18th cent.

corves plural form of **CORF**.

corvette /kɔːˈvɛt/ ▸ **noun** a small warship designed for convoy escort duty. ▪ historical a type of sailing warship with one tier of guns.
– ORIGIN mid 17th cent.: from French, from Dutch *korf*, denoting a kind of ship, + the diminutive suffix *-ette*.

corvid /ˈkɔːvɪd/ ▸ **noun** Ornithology a bird of the crow family (Corvidae); a crow.
– ORIGIN mid 20th cent.: from modern Latin *Corvidae* (plural), from Latin *corvus* 'raven'.

corvina[1] /kɔːˈviːnə/ ▸ **noun** [mass noun] a variety of wine grape native to the Veneto region of NE Italy, used to make Valpolicella and Bardolino.
– ORIGIN Italian (feminine adjective), literally 'raven-black'.

corvina[2] /kɔːˈviːnə/ ▸ **noun** a marine food and game fish of the drum family, found on the Pacific coasts of California and Mexico and sometimes living in fresh water. ● Genus *Cynoscion*, family Sciaenidae: two species.
– ORIGIN late 18th cent.: from Spanish and Portuguese.

corvine /ˈkɔːvʌɪn/ ▸ **adjective** of or like a raven or crow, especially in colour.
– ORIGIN mid 17th cent.: from Latin *corvinus*, from *corvus* 'raven'.

Corvus /ˈkɔːvəs/ Astronomy a small southern constellation (the Crow or Raven), south of Virgo.
– ORIGIN Latin.

corybantic /ˌkɒrɪˈbantɪk/ ▸ **adjective** wild; frenzied.
– ORIGIN mid 17th cent.: from *Corybantes*, Latin name of the priests of Cybele, a Phrygian goddess of nature, who performed wild dances, from Greek *Korubantes* + **-IC**.

corydalis /kəˈrɪdəlɪs/ ▸ **noun** a herbaceous plant with spurred tubular flowers, found in north temperate regions. ● Genus *Corydalis*, family Fumariaceae: many species, including **yellow corydalis** (*C. lutea*), a garden escape which has become naturalized in Britain.
– ORIGIN modern Latin, from Greek *korudallis* 'crested lark', alluding to a similarity between the flower and the bird's spur.

corymb /ˈkɒrɪmb/ ▸ **noun** Botany a flower cluster whose lower stalks are proportionally longer so that the flowers form a flat or slightly convex head.
– DERIVATIVES **corymbose** adjective.
– ORIGIN early 18th cent.: from French *corymbe* or Latin *corymbus*, from Greek *korumbos* 'cluster'.

corynebacterium /ˌkɒrɪnɪbakˈtɪərɪəm, kəˌrɪn-/ ▸ **noun** (pl. **corynebacteria** /-rɪə/) a bacterium which sometimes causes disease in humans and other animals, including diphtheria. ● Genus *Corynebacterium*; Gram-positive non-motile club-shaped rods.
– ORIGIN modern Latin, from Greek *korunē* 'club' + **BACTERIUM**.

coryphée /ˈkɒrɪfeɪ/ ▸ **noun** a leading dancer in a corps de ballet.
– ORIGIN French, via Latin from Greek *koruphaios* 'leader of a chorus', from *koruphē* 'head'.

coryza /kəˈrʌɪzə/ ▸ **noun** [mass noun] Medicine catarrhal inflammation of the mucous membrane in the nose, caused especially by a cold or by hay fever.
– ORIGIN early 16th cent.: from Latin, from Greek *koruza* 'nasal mucus'.

Cos variant spelling of **Kos**.

cos[1] /kɒs/ (also **cos lettuce**) ▸ **noun** Brit. a lettuce of a variety with crisp narrow leaves that form a tall head.
– ORIGIN late 17th cent.: named after the Aegean island of **Cos**, where it originated.

cos[2] /kɒz, kɒs/ ▸ **abbreviation** cosine.

cos[3] /kɒz, kəz/ (also **'cos** or **coz**) ▸ **conjunction** Brit. informal short for **BECAUSE**.

Cosa Nostra /ˌkəʊzə ˈnɒstrə/ a US criminal organization resembling and related to the Mafia.
– ORIGIN Italian, literally 'our affair'.

coscoroba swan /ˌkɒskəˈrəʊbə/ ▸ **noun** a small South American swan with white plumage and bright pink legs and feet. ● *Coscoroba coscoroba*, family Anatidae.
– ORIGIN early 19th cent.: *coscoroba* from the modern Latin taxonomic name, of unknown origin.

cosec /ˈkəʊsɛk/ ▸ **abbreviation** cosecant.

cosecant /kəʊˈsiːk(ə)nt, -ˈsɛk-/ ▸ **noun** Mathematics the ratio of the hypotenuse (in a right-angled triangle) to the side opposite an acute angle; the reciprocal of sine.
– ORIGIN early 18th cent.: from modern Latin *cosecant-*, from **co-** 'mutually' + Latin *secant-* 'cutting' (from the verb *secare*). Compare with **SECANT**.

coset /ˈkəʊsɛt/ ▸ **noun** Mathematics a set composed of all the products obtained by multiplying each element of a subgroup in turn by one particular element of the group containing the subgroup.

cosh[1] Brit. informal ▸ **noun** a thick, heavy stick or bar used as a weapon.
▸ **verb** [with obj.] hit (someone) on the head with a cosh.
– PHRASES **under the cosh** under pressure; in a difficult situation: *car dealers are under the cosh right now*.
– ORIGIN mid 19th cent.: of unknown origin.

cosh[2] /kɒʃ, kɒˈseɪtʃ/ ▸ **abbreviation** Mathematics hyperbolic cosine.
– ORIGIN from **cos[2]** + *-h* for *hyperbolic*. Compare with **COTH**.

COSHH ▸ **abbreviation** Brit. control of substances hazardous for health, a body of regulations introduced in Britain to govern the storage and use of such substances.

co-signatory ▸ **noun** a person or state signing a treaty or other document jointly with others.

Cosimo de' Medici /ˈkɒzɪməʊ/ (1389–1464), Italian statesman and banker; known as **Cosimo the Elder**. He laid the foundations for the Medici family's power in Florence, becoming the city's ruler in 1434 and using his considerable wealth to promote the arts and learning.

cosine /ˈkəʊsʌɪn/ ▸ **noun** Mathematics the trigonometric function that is equal to the ratio of the side adjacent to an acute angle (in a right-angled triangle) to the hypotenuse.

co-sleeping ▸ **noun** [mass noun] the practice of parents and young children sleeping in the same bed.
– DERIVATIVES **co-sleep** verb.

cosmeceutical /ˌkɒzməˈsuːtɪk(ə)l, -ˈsjuː-/ ▸ **noun** a cosmetic that has or is claimed to have medicinal properties.
– ORIGIN 1980s: blend of **COSMETIC** and **PHARMACEUTICAL**.

cosmetic ▸ **adjective 1** relating to treatment intended to restore or improve a person's appearance: *cosmetic surgery*. ▪ serving to improve the appearance of the body, especially the face: *cosmetic creams*.
2 affecting only the appearance of something rather than its substance: *the reform package was merely a cosmetic exercise*.
▸ **noun** (usu. **cosmetics**) a preparation applied to the body, especially the face, to improve its appearance.
– DERIVATIVES **cosmetically** adverb.
– ORIGIN early 17th cent. (as a noun denoting the art of beautifying the body): from French *cosmétique*, from Greek *kosmētikos*, from *kosmein* 'arrange or adorn', from *kosmos* 'order or adornment'.

cosmetician /ˌkɒzməˈtɪʃ(ə)n/ ▸ **noun** N. Amer. a person who sells or applies cosmetics as an occupation.

cosmetology /ˌkɒzmɪˈtɒlədʒi/ ▸ **noun** [mass noun] the professional skill or practice of beautifying the face, hair, and skin.
– DERIVATIVES **cosmetological** adjective, **cosmetologist** noun.

cosmic ▸ **adjective** relating to the universe or cosmos, especially as distinct from the earth: *cosmic matter* | *the cosmic void*. ▪ inconceivably vast: *the song is a masterpiece of cosmic proportions*.
– DERIVATIVES **cosmical** adjective, **cosmically** adverb.

cosmic dust ▸ **noun** [mass noun] small particles of matter distributed throughout space.

cosmic radiation ▸ **noun** [mass noun] radiation consisting of cosmic rays.

cosmic ray ▸ **noun** a highly energetic atomic nucleus or other particle travelling through space at a speed approaching that of light.

cosmic string ▸ **noun** see **STRING** (sense 6 of the noun).

cosmo- /ˈkɒzməʊ/ ▸ **combining form** relating to the world or the universe: *cosmodrome* | *cosmography*.
– ORIGIN from Greek *kosmos* 'order, world'.

cosmodrome /ˈkɒzmədrəʊm/ ▸ **noun** (in the countries of the former Soviet Union) a launching site for spacecraft.
– ORIGIN 1950s: from **COSMO-** + **DROME**, on the pattern of *aerodrome*.

cosmogenesis /ˌkɒzmə(ʊ)ˈdʒɛnɪsɪs/ ▸ **noun** the origin or evolution of the universe.
– DERIVATIVES **cosmogenetic** adjective, **cosmogenic** adjective.

cosmogeny /kɒzˈmɒdʒəni/ ▸ **noun** (pl. **cosmogenies**) the origin or evolution of the universe.

cosmogony /kɒzˈmɒɡəni/ ▸ **noun** (pl. **cosmogonies**) [mass noun] the branch of science that deals with the origin of the universe, especially the solar system. ▪ [count noun] a theory regarding the origin of the universe: *in their cosmogony, the world was thought to be a square, flat surface*.
– DERIVATIVES **cosmogonic** /-məˈɡɒnɪk/ adjective, **cosmogonical** /-məˈɡɒnɪk(ə)l/ adjective, **cosmogonist** noun.
– ORIGIN late 17th cent.: from Greek *kosmogonia*, from *kosmos* 'order or world' + *-gonia* '-begetting'.

cosmography ▸ **noun** (pl. **cosmographies**) [mass noun] the branch of science which deals with the general features of the universe, including the earth. ▪ [count noun] a description or representation of the universe or the earth.
– DERIVATIVES **cosmographer** noun, **cosmographic** adjective, **cosmographical** adjective.
– ORIGIN late Middle English: from French *cosmographie*, or via late Latin from Greek *kosmographia*, from *kosmos* (see **COSMOS[1]**) + *-graphia* 'writing'.

cosmological argument ▸ **noun** Philosophy an argument for the existence of God which claims that all things in nature depend on something else for their existence (i.e. are contingent), and that the whole cosmos must therefore itself depend on a being which exists independently or necessarily. Compare with **ONTOLOGICAL ARGUMENT** and **TELEOLOGICAL ARGUMENT**.

cosmological constant ▸ **noun** Physics an arbitrary constant in the field equations of general relativity.

cosmology ▸ **noun** (pl. **cosmologies**) [mass noun] the science of the origin and development of the universe. Modern cosmology is dominated by the Big Bang theory, which brings together observational astronomy and particle physics. ▪ [count noun] an account or theory of the origin of the universe.
– DERIVATIVES **cosmological** adjective, **cosmologist** noun.
– ORIGIN mid 17th cent.: from French *cosmologie* or modern Latin *cosmologia*, from Greek *kosmos* 'order or world' + *-logia* 'discourse'.

cosmonaut ▸ **noun** a Russian astronaut.
– ORIGIN 1950s: from **COSMOS[1]**, on the pattern of *astronaut* and Russian *kosmonavt*.

cosmopolis /kɒzˈmɒp(ə)lɪs/ ▸ **noun** a city inhabited by people from many different countries.
– ORIGIN mid 19th cent.: from Greek *kosmos* 'world' + *polis* 'city'.

C

C

cosmopolitan /ˌkɒzməˈpɒlɪt(ə)n/ ▶ **adjective 1** familiar with and at ease in many different countries and cultures: *his knowledge of French, Italian, and Spanish made him genuinely cosmopolitan.* ■ including people from many different countries: *immigration transformed the city into a cosmopolitan metropolis.* ■ having an exciting and glamorous character associated with travel and a mixture of cultures: *their designs became a byword for cosmopolitan chic.*
2 (of a plant or animal) found all over the world.
▶ **noun 1** a cosmopolitan person.
2 a cosmopolitan plant or animal.
3 a cocktail made with Cointreau, lemon vodka, cranberry juice, and lime juice.
– DERIVATIVES **cosmopolitanism** noun, **cosmopolitanize** (also **cosmopolitanise**) verb.
– ORIGIN mid 17th cent. (as a noun): from COSMOPOLITE + -AN.

cosmopolite /kɒzˈmɒp(ə)lʌɪt/ ▶ **noun 1** a cosmopolitan person.
2 Ecology another term for COSMOPOLITAN (sense 2 of the noun).
– ORIGIN early 17th cent.: from French, from Greek *kosmopolitēs*, from *kosmos* 'world' + *politēs* 'citizen'.

cosmos[1] ▶ **noun** (**the cosmos**) the universe seen as a well-ordered whole: *he sat staring deep into the void, reminding himself of man's place in the cosmos.* ■ a system of thought: *the new gender-free intellectual cosmos.*
– ORIGIN Middle English: from Greek *kosmos* 'order or world'.

cosmos[2] ▶ **noun** an ornamental plant of the daisy family, which bears single dahlia-like flowers and is native to Mexico and warm regions of America.
● Genus *Cosmos*, family Compositae.
– ORIGIN from Greek *kosmos* in the sense 'ornament'.

COSPAR /ˈkəʊspɑː/ ▶ **abbreviation** Committee on Space Research.

cosplay /ˈkɒzpleɪ/ ▶ **noun** [mass noun] the practice of dressing up as a character from a film, book, or video game, especially one from the Japanese genres of manga or anime.
▶ **verb** [no obj.] engage in cosplay.
– DERIVATIVES **cosplayer** noun.
– ORIGIN 1990s: blend of COSTUME and PLAY.

Cossack /ˈkɒsak/ ▶ **noun** a member of a people of southern Russia, Ukraine, and Siberia, noted for their horsemanship and military skill. ■ a member of a Cossack military unit.

> The Cossacks had their origins in the 15th century when refugees from religious persecution, outlaws, adventurers, and escaped serfs banded together in settlements for protection. Under the tsars they were allowed considerable autonomy in return for protecting the frontiers; with the collapse of Soviet rule Cossack groups have reasserted their identity in both Russia and Ukraine.

▶ **adjective** relating to or characteristic of the Cossacks.
– ORIGIN from Russian *kazak* from Turkic, 'vagabond, nomad'; later influenced by French *Cosaque* (see also KAZAKH).

cosset ▶ **verb** (**cossets, cosseting, cosseted**) [with obj.] care for and protect in an overindulgent way: *all her life she'd been cosseted by her family.*
– ORIGIN mid 16th cent. (as a noun denoting a lamb brought up by hand, later a spoiled child): probably from Anglo-Norman French *coscet* 'cottager', from Old English *cotsǣta* 'cottar'.

cossie (also **cozzie**) ▶ **noun** (pl. **cossies**) informal a swimming costume or a pair of swimming trunks.
– ORIGIN early 20th cent.: alteration of the first element of COSTUME.

Cossyra /kəˈsʌɪərə/ Roman name for PANTELLERIA.

cost ▶ **verb** (past and past participle **cost**) [with obj.] **1** (of an object or action) require the payment of (a specified sum of money) before it can be acquired or done: *each issue of the magazine costs £1* | [with two objs] *the journey will cost her £25.* ■ cause the loss or unpleasant consequence of: [with two objs] *driving at more than double the speed limit cost the woman her driving licence.* ■ informal be expensive for (someone): *if you want to own an island, it'll cost you.*
2 (past and past participle **costed**) estimate the price of: *it is their job to plan and cost a media schedule for the campaign.*
▶ **noun** an amount that has to be paid or spent to buy or obtain something: *we are able to cover the cost of the event* | *health-care costs* | [mass noun] *the tunnel has been built at no cost to the state.* ■ the effort, loss, or sacrifice necessary to achieve or obtain something: *the government succeeded in diverting resources away from consumption at considerable cost to its political popularity.* ■ (**costs** (or N. Amer. also **court costs**)) legal expenses, especially those allowed in favour of the winning party or against the losing party in a suit.
– PHRASES **at all costs** (or **at any cost**) regardless of the price to be paid or the effort needed: *he was anxious to avoid war at all costs.* **at cost** at cost price; without profit to the seller. **cost an arm and a leg** see ARM[1]. **cost someone dear** (or **dearly**) involve someone in a serious loss or a heavy penalty: *they were really bad mistakes on my part and they cost us dear.* **to someone's cost** with loss or disadvantage to someone: *without programmes to play on it, the cleverest machine is useless—as some hardware manufacturers already know to their cost.*
– ORIGIN Middle English: from Old French *coust* (noun), *couster* (verb), based on Latin *constare* 'stand firm, stand at a price'.

costa ▶ **noun** (pl. **costae** /ˈkɒstiː/) Botany & Zoology a rib, midrib, or rib-like structure. ■ Entomology the main vein running along the leading edge of an insect's wing.
– ORIGIN mid 19th cent.: from Latin.

Costa Blanca /ˌkɒstə ˈblaŋkə/ a resort region on the Mediterranean coast of SE Spain.
– ORIGIN Spanish, literally 'white coast'.

Costa Brava /ˈbrɑːvə/, Spanish /ˈbraβa/ a resort region to the north of Barcelona, on the Mediterranean coast of NE Spain.
– ORIGIN Spanish, literally 'wild coast'.

cost accounting ▶ **noun** [mass noun] the recording of all the costs incurred in a business in a way that can be used to improve its management.
– DERIVATIVES **cost accountant** noun.

Costa del Sol /dɛl ˈsɒl/ a resort region on the Mediterranean coast of southern Spain.
– ORIGIN Spanish, literally 'coast of the sun'.

costal /ˈkɒst(ə)l/ ▶ **adjective** relating to the ribs.
■ Anatomy & Zoology relating to a costa.
– ORIGIN mid 17th cent.: from French, from modern Latin *costalis*, from Latin *costa* 'rib'.

co-star ▶ **noun** a cinema or stage star appearing with another or others of equal importance.
▶ **verb** [no obj.] appear in a production as a co-star: *Rickman co-starred with Bruce Willis in the movie.* ■ [with obj.] (of a production) include as a co-star: *his new TV show co-stars John Schneider.*

Costard /ˈkɒstəd, ˈkʌst-/ ▶ **noun 1** Brit. a cooking apple of a large ribbed variety.
2 archaic, humorous a person's head.
– ORIGIN Middle English: from Anglo-Norman French, from *coste* 'rib', from Latin *costa*.

Costa Rica /ˈriːkə/ a republic in Central America on the Isthmus of Panama; pop. 4,253,900 (est. 2009); official language, Spanish; capital, San José.

> Colonized by Spain in the early 16th century, Costa Rica achieved independence in 1823 and emerged as a separate country in 1838 after fourteen years within the United Provinces of Central America.

– DERIVATIVES **Costa Rican** adjective & noun.
– ORIGIN Spanish, literally 'rich coast'.

costate /ˈkɒsteɪt/ ▶ **adjective** Botany & Zoology ribbed; possessing a costa.
– ORIGIN early 19th cent.: from Latin *costatus*, from *costa* 'rib'.

cost–benefit ▶ **adjective** relating to or denoting a process that assesses the relation between the cost of an undertaking and the value of the resulting benefits: *a cost–benefit analysis.*

cost centre ▶ **noun** a part of an organization to which costs may be charged for accounting purposes.

cost-cutting ▶ **noun** [mass noun] the reduction of costs, especially in a business.
– DERIVATIVES **cost-cutter** noun.

cost-effective ▶ **adjective** effective or productive in relation to its cost: *the most cost-effective way to invest in the stock market.*
– DERIVATIVES **cost-effectively** adverb, **cost-effectiveness** noun.

cost-efficient ▶ **adjective** another term for COST-EFFECTIVE.
– DERIVATIVES **cost-efficiency** noun.

coster ▶ **noun** short for COSTERMONGER.

costermonger /ˈkɒstəmʌŋgə/ ▶ **noun** Brit. dated a person who sells goods, especially fruit and vegetables, from a handcart in the street.
– ORIGIN early 16th cent. (denoting an apple seller): from COSTARD + -MONGER.

costing ▶ **noun** (often **costings**) the proposed or estimated cost of producing or undertaking something: *he obtained costings for manual keyboarding of the records.* ■ [mass noun] the process of determining such a cost: *detailed costing can make the difference between an excellent idea and a ruinous one.*

costive /ˈkɒstɪv/ ▶ **adjective 1** constipated.
2 slow or reluctant in speech or action; unforthcoming: *if he did ask her she would become costive.*
– DERIVATIVES **costively** adverb, **costiveness** noun.
– ORIGIN late Middle English: via Old French from Latin *constipatus* 'pressed together' (see CONSTIPATED).

costly ▶ **adjective** (**costlier, costliest**) costing a lot; expensive: *major problems requiring costly repairs.* ■ causing suffering, loss, or disadvantage: *the government's biggest and most costly mistake.*
– DERIVATIVES **costliness** noun.

costmary /ˈkɒstmɛːri/ ▶ **noun** (pl. **costmaries**) an aromatic plant of the daisy family, formerly used in medicine and for flavouring ale prior to the use of hops. Also called ALECOST. ● *Balsamita major*, family Compositae.
– ORIGIN late Middle English: from obsolete *cost* (via Latin from Greek *kostos*, via Arabic from Sanskrit *kuṣṭha*, denoting an aromatic plant) + *Mary*, the mother of Christ (with whom it was associated in medieval times because of its medicinal qualities).

cost-of-carry ▶ **noun** Finance the difference between the cost and the financial benefit of holding a particular asset for a specified period.

cost of living ▶ **noun** the level of prices relating to a range of everyday items.

cost-of-living index ▶ **noun** another term for RETAIL PRICE INDEX.

cost-plus ▶ **adjective** relating to or denoting a method of pricing a service or product in which a fixed profit factor is added to the costs.

cost price ▶ **noun** the price at which goods are or have been bought by a merchant or retailer.

cost-push ▶ **adjective** relating to or denoting inflation caused by increased labour or raw material costs. Contrasted with DEMAND-PULL.

costume ▶ **noun** a set of clothes in a style typical of a particular country or historical period: *authentic Elizabethan costumes* | [mass noun] *dancers in national costume.* ■ a set of clothes worn by an actor or performer for a particular role. ■ Brit. a swimming costume. ■ Brit. dated a woman's matching jacket and skirt: *a chic black costume and white fur wrap.*
▶ **verb** [with obj.] dress (someone) in a particular set of clothes: *an all-woman troupe elaborately costumed in clinging silver lamé.*
– ORIGIN early 18th cent.: from French, from Italian *costume* 'custom, fashion, habit', from Latin *consuetudo* (see CUSTOM).

costume drama ▶ **noun** a television or cinema production set in a particular historical period, in which the actors wear costumes typical of that period.

costume jewellery ▶ **noun** [mass noun] jewellery made with inexpensive materials or imitation gems.

costumier /kɒˈstjuːmɪə/ (US also **costumer** /-mə/) ▶ **noun** Brit. a person or company that makes or supplies theatrical or fancy-dress costumes.
– ORIGIN mid 19th cent.: French, from *costumer* 'dress in a costume' (see COSTUME).

cosy (US **cozy**) ▶ **adjective** (**cosier, cosiest; cozier, coziest**) giving a feeling of comfort, warmth, and relaxation: *the flickering lamp gave the room a cosy lived-in air.* ■ (of a relationship or conversation) intimate and relaxed. ■ not seeking or offering challenge or difficulty; complacent: *a cosy assumption among audit firms that they would never go bust.* ■ informal, derogatory (of a transaction or arrangement) beneficial to all those involved and possibly somewhat corrupt: *a cosy deal.*
▶ **noun** (pl. **cosies**) **1** a cover to keep a teapot or a boiled egg hot.
2 Brit. a canopied corner seat for two.
▶ **verb** (**cosies, cosying, cosied**) [with obj.] informal make (someone) feel comfortable or complacent: *she cosied him and made out she found him irresistible.* ■ [no obj.] (**cosy up to**) snuggle up to. ■ [no obj.] (**cosy up to**) ingratiate oneself with: *he decided to resign rather than cosy up to hardliners in the party.*
– DERIVATIVES **cosily** adverb, **cosiness** noun.
– ORIGIN early 18th cent. (originally Scots): of unknown origin.

C

cot[1] ▸ noun Brit. a small bed with high barred sides for a baby or very young child. ■ a plain narrow bed. ■ N. Amer. a camp bed. ■ Nautical a bed resembling a hammock hung from deck beams, formerly used by officers.
– ORIGIN mid 17th cent. (originally Anglo-Indian, denoting a light bedstead): from Hindi *khāṭ* 'bedstead, hammock'.

cot[2] ▸ noun 1 a small shelter for livestock.
2 archaic a small, simple cottage.
– ORIGIN Old English, of Germanic origin; compare with Old Norse *kytja* 'hovel'; related to COTE.

cot[3] ▸ abbreviation Mathematics cotangent.

cotangent /kəʊˈtandʒ(ə)nt/ ▸ noun Mathematics (in a right-angled triangle) the ratio of the side (other than the hypotenuse) adjacent to a particular acute angle to the side opposite the angle.

cot-case ▸ noun Austral./NZ informal a person who is too ill to leave their bed. ■ a person who is incapacitated by alcohol. ■ an eccentric or mad person.

cot death ▸ noun Brit. the unexplained death of a baby in its sleep.

cote ▸ noun a shelter for mammals or birds, especially pigeons.
– ORIGIN Old English (in the sense 'cottage'), of Germanic origin; related to COT[2].

Côte d'Azur /ˌkəʊt dəˈzjʊə/ a coastal area of south-eastern France which includes Nice, Cannes, and Saint Tropez, and the principality of Monaco.

Côte d'Ivoire /ˌkəʊt diːˈvwɑː, kəʊt divwaʀ/ a country in West Africa, on the Gulf of Guinea; pop. 20,617,100 (est. 2009); languages, French (official), West African languages; capital, Yamoussoukro. Also called IVORY COAST.

> The area was explored by the Portuguese in the late 15th century. Subsequently it was disputed by traders from various European countries, who mainly sought ivory and slaves. It was made a French protectorate in 1842 and became a fully independent republic in 1960.

cote-hardie /ˈkəʊtˌhɑːdi/ ▸ noun (pl. **cote-hardies**) historical a medieval close-fitting tunic with sleeves, worn by both sexes.
– ORIGIN Middle English: from Old French, from *cote* 'coat' + *hardie* (feminine) 'bold'.

coterie /ˈkəʊt(ə)ri/ ▸ noun (pl. **coteries**) a small group of people with shared interests or tastes, especially one that is exclusive of other people: *a coterie of friends and advisers*.
– ORIGIN early 18th cent.: from French, earlier denoting an association of tenants, based on Middle Low German *kote* 'cote'.

coterminous /kəʊˈtəːmɪnəs/ ▸ adjective having the same boundaries or extent in space, time, or meaning: *the coterminous Borough and Parliamentary Constituency of Blyth Valley*.
– ORIGIN late 18th cent.: alteration of CONTERMINOUS.

coth /kɒθ, kɒtˈeɪtʃ/ ▸ abbreviation hyperbolic cotangent.
– ORIGIN from COT[3] + *-h* for *hyperbolic*.

co-tidal line ▸ noun a line on a map connecting points at which a tidal level, especially high tide, occurs simultaneously.

cotillion /kəˈtɪljən/ ▸ noun 1 an elaborate 18th-century French dance based on the contredanse. ■ US a quadrille.
2 US a formal ball, especially one at which debutantes are presented.
– ORIGIN early 18th cent.: from French *cotillon*, literally 'petticoat dance', diminutive of *cotte*, from Old French *cote*.

cotinga /kəˈtɪŋgə/ ▸ noun a perching bird found in the forests of Central and South America, the male of which is frequently brilliantly coloured. ● Family Cotingidae (the **cotinga family**): several genera, especially *Cotinga*, and numerous species. The cotinga family also includes the bellbirds, umbrellabirds, and cocks-of-the-rock, and is sometimes placed within the family Tyrannidae.
– ORIGIN via French from Tupi *cutinga*.

Cotman /ˈkɒtmən/, John Sell (1782–1842), English watercolourist and landscape painter, regarded as one of the leading figures of the Norwich School.

cotoneaster /kəˌtəʊnɪˈastə/ ▸ noun a small-leaved shrub of the rose family, cultivated as a hedging plant or for its bright red berries which often remain on the plant throughout the winter. ● Genus *Cotoneaster*, family Rosaceae.
– ORIGIN mid 18th cent.: modern Latin, from Latin *cotoneum* (see QUINCE) + -ASTER.

Cotonou /ˌkɒtəˈnuː/ the largest city, chief port, and chief commercial and political centre of Benin, on the coast of West Africa; pop. 719,912 (2006).

Cotopaxi /ˌkɒtəˈpaksi/ the highest active volcano in the world, rising to 5,896 m (19,142 ft) in the Andes of central Ecuador. Its name is Quechuan and means 'shining peak'.

co-trimoxazole /ˌkəʊtrʌɪˈmɒksəzəʊl/ ▸ noun [mass noun] Medicine a mixture of the drugs sulphamethoxazole and trimethoprim, used to treat bacterial infections synergistically.

Cotswold /ˈkɒtswəʊld/ ▸ noun 1 a sheep of a breed with fine wool, often used to produce cross-bred lambs.
2 [mass noun] Double Gloucester cheese containing chives and onions.
▸ adjective relating to the Cotswolds.

Cotswold Hills (also **the Cotswolds**) a range of limestone hills in SW England, largely in the county of Gloucestershire.

cotta /ˈkɒtə/ ▸ noun a short garment resembling a surplice, worn typically by Catholic priests and servers.
– ORIGIN mid 19th cent.: from Italian; ultimately related to COAT.

cottage ▸ noun 1 a small house, typically one in the country. ■ a simple house forming part of a farm, used by a worker.
2 Brit. informal (in the context of casual homosexual encounters) a public toilet.
▸ verb [no obj.] (usu. as noun **cottaging**) Brit. informal perform homosexual acts in a public toilet.
– DERIVATIVES **cottagey** adjective.
– ORIGIN late Middle English: from Anglo-Norman French *cotage* and Anglo-Latin *cotagium*, from COT[2] or COTE.

cottage cheese ▸ noun [mass noun] soft, lumpy white cheese made from the curds of skimmed milk.

cottage garden ▸ noun an informal garden stocked typically with colourful flowering plants.

cottage hospital ▸ noun Brit. a small hospital in a country area.

cottage industry ▸ noun a business or manufacturing activity carried on in people's homes.

cottage loaf ▸ noun Brit. a loaf consisting of two round sections of bread, the smaller of which is on top of the larger.

cottage pie ▸ noun Brit. a dish of minced meat topped with browned mashed potato.

cottager ▸ noun Brit. a person living in a cottage. ■ N. Amer. a person holidaying in a cottage.

cottar /ˈkɒtə/ (also **cotter**) ▸ noun historical (in Scotland and Ireland) a farm labourer or tenant occupying a cottage in return for labour.
– ORIGIN late Old English, from COT[2] + -AR[4].

Cottbus /ˈkɒtbʊs/ an industrial city in SE Germany, in Brandenburg, on the River Spree; pop. 103,800 (est. 2006).

cotter pin (also **cotter**) ▸ noun a metal pin used to fasten two parts of a mechanism together. ■ a split pin that is opened out after being passed through a hole.
– ORIGIN mid 17th cent.: of unknown origin.

cottier /ˈkɒtɪə/ ▸ noun 1 archaic a rural labourer living in a cottage.
2 historical an Irish peasant holding land by cottier tenure.
– ORIGIN Middle English: from Old French *cotier*, ultimately of Germanic origin and related to COT[2].

cottier tenure ▸ noun [mass noun] historical (in Ireland) the letting of land in small portions direct to the labourers, at a rent fixed by competition.

cottise /ˈkɒtɪs/ (also **cotise**) ▸ noun Heraldry a narrow band adjacent and parallel to an ordinary such as a bend or chevron.
– ORIGIN late 16th cent.: from French *cotice* 'leather thong'.

cotton ▸ noun [mass noun] 1 a soft white fibrous substance which surrounds the seeds of the cotton plant and is made into textile fibre and thread for sewing. ■ [often as modifier] textile fabric made from cotton fibre: *a white cotton blouse*. ■ thread made from cotton fibre. ■ N. Amer. cotton wool.
2 (also **cotton plant**) the tropical and subtropical plant which is commercially grown to make cotton fabric and thread. Oil and a protein-rich flour are also obtained from the seeds. ● Genus *Gossypium*, family Malvaceae: many species and forms.
▸ verb [no obj.] informal 1 (**cotton on**) begin to understand: *he cottoned on to what I was trying to say*.
2 (**cotton to**) N. Amer. have a liking for: *his rivals didn't cotton to all the attention he was getting*.
– DERIVATIVES **cottony** adjective.
– ORIGIN late Middle English: from Old French *coton*, from Arabic *quṭn*.

cotton batting ▸ noun North American term for COTTON WOOL (sense 1).

cotton belt ▸ noun the cotton-producing region of the southern US.

cotton bud ▸ noun Brit. a small wad of cotton wool on a short, thin stick, used for cosmetic purposes or cleaning the ears.

cotton cake ▸ noun [mass noun] compressed cotton seed, used as food for cattle.

cotton candy ▸ noun North American term for CANDYFLOSS.

cotton gin ▸ noun a machine for separating cotton from its seeds.

cotton grass ▸ noun [mass noun] a sedge which typically grows on wet moorlands in the northern hemisphere, producing tufts of long white silky hairs which aid in the dispersal of the seeds. Also called BOG COTTON. ● Genus *Eriophorum*, family Cyperaceae.

cotton lavender ▸ noun a small aromatic shrubby plant of the daisy family, with silvery or greenish lavender-like foliage and yellow button flowers. Native to the Mediterranean area, it has insecticidal properties. ● Genus *Santolina*, family Compositae; several species, in particular *S. chamaecyparissus*.

cotton-leaf worm ▸ noun the larva of a migratory tropical moth which feeds on the leaves of the cotton plant and was formerly a major pest in North America. ● *Alabama argillacea*, family Noctuidae.

cottonmouth (also **cottonmouth moccasin**) ▸ noun a large, dangerous semiaquatic pit viper which inhabits lowland swamps and waterways of the south-eastern US. When threatening it opens its mouth wide to display the white interior. Also called WATER MOCCASIN. ● *Agkistrodon piscivorus*, family Viperidae.

cotton-picking ▸ adjective [attrib.] N. Amer. informal used for emphasis: *just a cotton-picking minute!*

cotton rat ▸ noun a short-tailed rat found in grassland and scrub from North America to Guyana. ● Genus *Sigmodon*, family Muridae: several species.

cotton spinner ▸ noun a dark sea cucumber of shallow seas which ejects long sticky threads from the anus when disturbed. ● *Holothuria forskali*, class Holothuroidea.

cotton stainer ▸ noun a North American bug which feeds on cotton bolls, causing reddish staining of the fibres. ● Genus *Dysdercus*, family Pyrrhocoridae, suborder Heteroptera: several species, in particular *D. suturellus*.

cotton state ▸ noun any of the states of the southern US of which cotton is or was a major product. ■ (**Cotton State**) informal name for ALABAMA.

cotton swab ▸ noun North American term for COTTON BUD.

cottontail ▸ noun an American rabbit which has a speckled brownish coat and a white underside to the tail. ● Genus *Sylvilagus*, family Leporidae: several species.

cotton waste ▸ noun [mass noun] scraps of waste cotton yarn, used typically to clean machinery.

cottonweed ▸ noun [mass noun] a yellow-flowered aromatic plant of the daisy family, with silvery felted leaves and stems. It grows on sandy beaches, chiefly in southern and western Europe. ● *Otanthus maritimus*, family Compositae.

cottonwood ▸ noun 1 a North American poplar with seeds covered in white cottony hairs. ● Genus *Populus*, family Salicaceae: several species, including *P. deltoides*.
2 any of a number of downy-leaved Australasian shrubs: ● an evergreen shrub of the buckthorn family (*Pomaderris phylicifolia*, family Rhamnaceae). ● a shrub of the daisy family (*Bedfordia salicina*, family Compositae).

cotton wool ▸ noun [mass noun] 1 Brit. fluffy wadding of a kind originally made from raw cotton, used for cleaning the skin or bathing wounds.
2 US raw cotton.
– PHRASES **wrap someone in cotton wool** be overprotective towards someone.

cottony-cushion scale ▸ noun [mass noun] an Australian scale insect with a large fluted cottony egg sac, infesting citrus trees. It threatened to destroy the Californian citrus industry until it was controlled by the introduction of the Australian vedalia beetle. ● *Icerya purchasi*, family Margarodidae, suborder Homoptera.

C

cotyledon /ˌkɒtɪˈliːd(ə)n/ ▶ **noun 1** Botany an embryonic leaf in seed-bearing plants, one or more of which are the first leaves to appear from a germinating seed.
2 a succulent plant of the stonecrop family, some kinds of which are grown as ornamentals. ● Genus *Cotyledon* and related genera, family Crassulaceae: several species.
– DERIVATIVES **cotyledonary** adjective.
– ORIGIN mid 16th cent. (denoting a patch of villi on the placenta of mammals): from Latin, 'navelwort' (which has cup-shaped leaves), from Greek *kotulēdōn* 'cup-shaped cavity', from *kotulē* 'cup'.

coucal /ˈkuːk(ə)l, ˈkʊkɑːl/ ▶ **noun** an ungainly long-tailed Old World bird that is a large ground-dwelling member of the cuckoo family. ● Genus *Centropus* (and *Coua*), family Cuculidae: numerous species, including the Australasian **pheasant coucal** (*Centropus phasianinus*).
– ORIGIN early 19th cent.: from French, perhaps a blend of *coucou* 'cuckoo' and *alouette* 'lark'.

couch¹ /kaʊtʃ/ ▶ **noun** a long upholstered piece of furniture for several people to sit on. ■ a reclining seat with a headrest at one end on which a psychoanalyst's subject or doctor's patient lies while undergoing treatment.
▶ **verb** [with obj.] **1** express (something) in language of a specified style: *the assurances were couched in general terms.*
2 literary lay down: *two fair creatures, couched side by side in deepest grass.*
3 archaic lower (a spear) to the position for attack.
4 (usu. as noun **couching**) chiefly historical treat (a cataract) by pushing the lens of the eye downwards and backwards, out of line with the pupil.
5 (in embroidery) fix (a thread) to a fabric by stitching it down flat with another thread: *gold and silver threads couched by hand.*
– PHRASES **on the couch** undergoing psychoanalysis or psychiatric treatment.
– ORIGIN Middle English (as a noun denoting something to sleep on; as a verb in the sense 'lay something down'): from Old French *couche* (noun), *coucher* (verb), from Latin *collocare* 'place together' (see COLLOCATE).

couch² /kaʊtʃ, kuːtʃ/ (also **couch grass**) ▶ **noun** [mass noun] a coarse grass with long creeping roots, which can be a serious weed in gardens. ● Genera *Elymus* and *Agropyron*, family Gramineae: several species, in particular the Eurasian **common couch** (*E. repens*).
– ORIGIN late 16th cent.: variant of QUITCH.

couchant /ˈkaʊtʃ(ə)nt/ ▶ **adjective** [usu. postpositive] Heraldry (of an animal) lying with the body resting on the legs and the head raised: *two lions couchant.*
– ORIGIN late Middle English: French, 'lying', present participle of *coucher* (see COUCH¹).

couchette /kuːˈʃɛt/ ▶ **noun** a railway carriage with seats convertible into sleeping berths. ■ a berth in such a carriage.
– ORIGIN 1920s: French, literally 'little bed', diminutive of *couche* 'a couch'.

couch potato ▶ **noun** informal a person who takes little or no exercise and watches a lot of television.

coudé /kuːˈdeɪ/ ▶ **adjective** relating to or denoting a telescope in which the rays are bent to a focus at a fixed point off the axis.
– ORIGIN late 19th cent.: French, literally 'bent at right angles', past participle of *couder*, from *coude* 'elbow', from Latin *cubitum*.

cougar /ˈkuːɡə/ ▶ **noun 1** North American term for PUMA.
2 informal an older woman seeking a sexual relationship with a younger man.
– ORIGIN late 18th cent.: from French *couguar*, abbreviation of modern Latin *cuguarcarana*, from Guarani *guaçuarana*.

cough ▶ **verb** [no obj.] expel air from the lungs with a sudden sharp sound: *he tried to speak and started to cough.* ■ (of an engine) make a sudden harsh noise, especially as a sign of malfunction. ■ [with obj.] force (something, especially blood) out of the lungs or throat by coughing: *he coughed up bloodstained fluid.* ■ [with obj.] (**cough something out**) say something in an abrupt way: *he coughed out his orders.* ■ Brit. informal reveal information; confess: *once he realized we knew, he was ready to cough fast enough.*
▶ **noun** an act or sound of coughing: *she gave a discreet cough.* ■ a condition of the respiratory organs causing coughing: *he looked feverish and had a bad cough.*
– PHRASAL VERBS **cough something up** (or **cough up**) informal give something reluctantly, especially money or information that is due or required: *the company coughed up $40 m. in settlement of the legal claims.*
– DERIVATIVES **cougher** noun.
– ORIGIN Middle English: of imitative origin; related to Dutch *kuchen* 'to cough' and German *keuchen* 'to pant'.

cough drop (also **cough sweet**) ▶ **noun** a medicated lozenge sucked to relieve a cough.

cough mixture ▶ **noun** [mass noun] Brit. liquid medicine taken to relieve a cough.

could ▶ **modal verb** past of CAN¹. ■ used to indicate possibility: *they could be right | I would go if I could afford it.* ■ used in making suggestions or polite requests: *you could always ring him up | could I use the phone?* ■ used to indicate annoyance because of something that has not been done: *they could have told me!* ■ used to indicate a strong inclination to do something: *he irritates me so much that I could scream.*

> **USAGE** For a discussion on the use of **could of** instead of **could have**, see USAGE at HAVE.

couldn't ▶ **contraction** could not.

coulee /ˈkuːli/ ▶ **noun** N. Amer. a deep ravine.
– ORIGIN early 19th cent.: from French *coulée* '(lava) flow', from *couler* 'to flow', from Latin *colare* 'to strain or flow', from *colum* 'strainer'.

coulibiac /ˌkuːlɪˈbjak/ (also **koulibiac**) ▶ **noun** a Russian pie of fish or meat, cabbage or other vegetables, and herbs.
– ORIGIN from Russian *kulebyaka*.

coulis /ˈkuːli/ ▶ **noun** (pl. **same**) a thin fruit or vegetable purée, used as a sauce.
– ORIGIN French, from *couler* 'to flow'.

coulisse /kuːˈliːs/ ▶ **noun** a flat piece of scenery at the side of the stage in a theatre. ■ (**the coulisses**) the spaces between these pieces of scenery; the wings.
– ORIGIN early 19th cent.: French, feminine of *coulis* 'sliding', based on Latin *colare* 'to flow'.

couloir /ˈkuːlwɑː/ ▶ **noun** a steep, narrow gully on a mountainside.
– ORIGIN early 19th cent.: French, 'gully or corridor', from *couler* 'to flow'.

coulomb /ˈkuːlɒm/ (abbrev.: **C**) ▶ **noun** Physics the SI unit of electric charge, equal to the quantity of electricity conveyed in one second by a current of one ampere.
– ORIGIN late 19th cent.: named after Charles-Augustin de *Coulomb* (1736–1806), French military engineer.

Coulomb's law /ˈkuːlɒmz/ ▶ **noun** Physics a law stating that like charges repel and opposite charges attract, with a force proportional to the product of the charges and inversely proportional to the square of the distance between them.
– ORIGIN late 18th cent.: named after C.-A. de *Coulomb* (see COULOMB).

coulrophobia /ˌkɒlrəˈfəʊbɪə/ ▶ **noun** [mass noun] rare extreme or irrational fear of clowns.
– ORIGIN 1980s: from Greek *kolobatheron* 'stilt' + -PHOBIA.

coulter /ˈkəʊltə/ (US **colter**) ▶ **noun** a vertical cutting blade fixed in front of a ploughshare. ■ the part of a seed drill that makes the furrow for the seed.
– ORIGIN Old English, from Latin *culter* 'knife or ploughshare'.

coumarin /ˈkuːmərɪn/ ▶ **noun** [mass noun] Chemistry a vanilla-scented compound found in many plants, formerly used for flavouring food. ● A bicyclic lactone; chem. formula: $C_9H_6O_2$.
■ [count noun] any derivative of this.
– ORIGIN mid 19th cent.: from French *coumarine*, from *coumarou*, via Portuguese and Spanish from Tupi *cumarú* 'tonka bean'.

coumarone /ˈkuːmərəʊn/ ▶ **noun** [mass noun] Chemistry an organic compound present in coal tar, used to make thermoplastic resins for paints and varnishes.
● A bicyclic compound with fused benzene and furan rings; chem. formula: C_8H_6O.
– ORIGIN late 19th cent.: from COUMARIN + -ONE.

council ▶ **noun** an advisory, deliberative, or administrative body of people formally constituted and meeting regularly: *an official human rights council.* ■ a body of people elected to manage the affairs of a city, county, or other municipal district. ■ [as modifier] Brit. denoting housing provided by a local council at a subsidized rent: *a council flat.* ■ an ecclesiastical assembly. ■ a meeting for consultation or advice: *that evening, she held a family council.*
– ORIGIN Old English (in the sense 'ecclesiastical assembly'): from Anglo-Norman French *cuncile*, from Latin *concilium* 'convocation, assembly', from *con-* 'together' + *calare* 'summon'. Compare with COUNSEL.

council estate ▶ **noun** Brit. an area of houses built and rented out to tenants by a local council.

Council for Mutual Economic Assistance historical fuller form of COMECON.
– ORIGIN translating Russian *Sovet ékonomicheskoĭ vzaimopomoshchi*.

council house ▶ **noun** Brit. a house owned by a local council and rented out to tenants.

councillor (US also **councilor**) ▶ **noun** a member of a council.
– ORIGIN late Middle English: alteration of COUNSELLOR, by association with COUNCIL.

> **USAGE** On the difference between councillor and counsellor, see USAGE at COUNSELLOR.

councilman (or **councilwoman**) ▶ **noun** (pl. **councilmen** or **councilwomen**) US a member of a council, especially a municipal one.

Council of Chalcedon, Council of Europe, etc. see CHALCEDON, COUNCIL OF; EUROPE, COUNCIL OF, etc.

council of war ▶ **noun** a gathering of military officers in wartime. ■ a meeting held to plan a response to an emergency.

council tax ▶ **noun** [mass noun] a tax levied on households by local authorities in Britain, based on the estimated value of a property and the number of people living in it.

counsel ▶ **noun 1** [mass noun] advice, especially that given formally. ■ archaic consultation, especially to seek or give advice.
2 (pl. **same**) a barrister or other legal adviser conducting a case: *the counsel for the defence.*
▶ **verb** (**counsels, counselling, counselled**; US **counsels, counseling, counseled**) [with obj.] give advice to (someone): *careers officers should counsel young people in making their career decisions.* ■ give professional help and advice to (someone) to resolve personal or psychological problems: *he was being counselled for depression.* ■ recommend (a course of action): *the athlete's coach counselled caution.*
– PHRASES **a counsel of despair** an action to be taken when all else fails. **a counsel of perfection** advice that is ideal but not feasible. **keep one's own counsel** say nothing about what one thinks or plans: *she doubted what he said but kept her own counsel.* **take counsel** discuss a problem.
– ORIGIN Middle English: via Old French *counseil* (noun), *conseiller* (verb), from Latin *consilium* 'consultation, advice', related to *consulere* (see CONSULT). Compare with COUNCIL.

counselling (US **counseling**) ▶ **noun** [mass noun] the provision of professional assistance and guidance in resolving personal or psychological problems: *bereavement counselling.*

counsellor (US **counselor**) ▶ **noun 1** a person trained to give guidance on personal or psychological problems: *a marriage counsellor.* ■ [with modifier] a person who gives advice on a specified subject: *a debt counsellor.*
2 a senior officer in the diplomatic service.
3 (also **counselor-at-law**) US & Irish a barrister.
4 N. Amer. a supervisor at a children's summer camp.
– ORIGIN Middle English (in the general sense 'adviser'): from Old French *conseillier*, from Latin *consiliarius*, and Old French *conseillour*, from Latin *consiliator*, both from *consilium* 'consultation or advice'.

> **USAGE** The words **counsellor** and **councillor** are often confused. A **counsellor** is a person who gives advice or counsel, especially on personal problems (*a marriage counsellor*), whereas a **councillor** is a member of a city, county, or other council (*she stood as a Labour candidate for city councillor*).

Counsellor of State ▶ **noun** (in the UK) a temporary regent during a sovereign's absence.

count¹ ▶ **verb 1** [with obj.] determine the total number of (a collection of items): *I started to count the stars I could see | they counted up their change.* ■ [no obj.] recite numbers in ascending order: *hold the position as you count to five.* ■ [no obj.] (**count down**) recite or display numbers backwards to zero to indicate the time remaining before the launch of a rocket or the start of an operation. ■ [no obj.] (**count down**) prepare for a significant event in the short time

remaining before it: *with more orders expected, the company is* ***counting down to*** *a bumper Christmas.*
2 [with obj.] take into account; include: *the staff has shrunk to four, or five if you count the European director.* ■ regard or be regarded as possessing a specified quality or fulfilling a specified role: *she met some rebuffs from people she had* ***counted as*** *her friends* | [with obj. and complement] *I count myself fortunate to have known him* | [no obj.] *results which are consistent with all models cannot* ***count as*** *evidence for any of them.*
3 [no obj.] be significant: *it did not matter what the audience thought—it was the critics that counted.* ■ (of a factor) play a part in influencing opinion for or against someone or something: *he hopes his sporting attitude will* ***count in his favour.*** ■ (**count for**) be worth (a specified amount): *he has no power base and his views count for little.* ■ (**count towards**) be included in an assessment of (a final result or amount): *reduced rate contributions do not count towards your pension.*
4 [no obj.] (**count on/upon**) rely on: *whatever you're doing, you can count on me.*
▶ **noun 1** an act of determining the total number of something: ***at the last count,*** *fifteen applications were still outstanding* | *the party's only candidate was eliminated at the first count.* ■ the total determined by counting: *there was a moderate increase in the white cell count in both patients.*
2 an act of reciting numbers in ascending order, up to the specified number: *hold the position for a count of seven.* ■ an act of reciting numbers up to ten by the referee when a boxer is knocked down, the boxer being considered knocked out if still down when ten is reached.
3 a point for discussion or consideration: *the programme remained vulnerable on a number of counts.* ■ Law a separate charge in an indictment: *he pleaded guilty to five counts of murder.*
4 the measure of the fineness of a yarn expressed as the weight of a given length or the length of a given weight. ■ a measure of the fineness of a woven fabric expressed as the number of warp or weft threads in a given length.
– PHRASES **—— and counting** used to say that a figure is constantly increasing: *nearly seven years later (and counting), Hackett remains undefeated.* **count one's blessings** be grateful for what one has. **count the cost** experience the adverse consequences of something, typically a foolish action. **count the days** (or **hours**) be impatient for time to pass: *they counted the days until they came home on leave.* **count something on the fingers of one hand** used to emphasize the small number of a particular thing: *you can count the exceptions on the fingers of one hand.* **count the pennies** see PENNY. **count sheep** see SHEEP. **don't count your chickens before they're hatched** proverb don't be too confident in anticipating success or good fortune before it is certain. **keep count** (or **a count**) take note of the number or amount of something: *you can protect yourself by keeping a count of what you drink.* **lose count** forget how many of something there are, especially because the number is so high: *I've lost count of the hundreds of miles I've covered.* **out** (or N. Amer. also **down**) **for the count** Boxing defeated by being knocked to the ground and unable to rise within ten seconds. ■ unconscious or soundly asleep. **take the count** Boxing be knocked out.
– PHRASAL VERBS **count someone in** informal include someone in an activity or the plans for it: *if the project gets started, count me in.* **count someone out 1** complete a count of ten seconds over a fallen boxer to indicate defeat. **2** not include someone in an activity: *if this is a guessing game you can count me out.* **count something out 1** take items one by one from a stock of something, especially money, keeping a note of how many one takes: *opening the wallet I counted out 19 dollars.* **2** Brit. procure the adjournment of the House of Commons when fewer than 40 members are present.
– ORIGIN Middle English (as a noun): from Old French *counte* (noun), *counter* (verb), from the verb *computare* 'calculate' (see COMPUTE).

count² ▶ **noun** a foreign nobleman whose rank corresponds to that of an earl.
– DERIVATIVES **countship** noun.
– ORIGIN late Middle English: from Old French *conte*, from Latin *comes, comit-* 'companion, overseer, attendant' (in late Latin 'person holding a state office'), from *com-* 'together with' + *it-* 'gone' (from the verb *ire* 'go').

countable ▶ **adjective** able to be counted.
– DERIVATIVES **countably** adverb.

countable noun ▶ **noun** another term for COUNT NOUN.

countback ▶ **noun** a method of deciding the winner of a tied game or competition by awarding it to the contestant with the better score in the later part.

countdown ▶ **noun** an act of counting numerals in reverse order to zero, especially before the launching of a rocket or missile: *the missiles' launch crews would begin their final countdown.* ■ the period of time leading up to a significant event and the procedures carried out during this time: *the* ***countdown to*** *your holiday.* ■ a digital display that counts down.

countenance /ˈkaʊnt(ə)nəns, -tɪn-/ ▶ **noun 1** a person's face or facial expression: *his impenetrable eyes and inscrutable countenance give little away.*
2 [mass noun] support or approval: *she was giving her specific countenance to the occasion.*
▶ **verb** [with obj.] admit as acceptable or possible: *he was reluctant to countenance the use of force.*
– PHRASES **keep one's countenance** maintain one's composure, especially by refraining from laughter. **keep someone in countenance** help someone to remain calm and confident. **out of countenance** disconcerted or unpleasantly surprised.
– ORIGIN Middle English: from Old French *contenance* 'bearing, behaviour', from *contenir* (see CONTAIN). The early sense was 'bearing, demeanour', also 'facial expression', hence 'the face'.

counter¹ ▶ **noun 1** a long flat-topped fitment across which business is conducted in a shop or bank or refreshments are served in a cafeteria. ■ N. Amer. a worktop.
2 a small disc used in board games for keeping the score or as a place marker. ■ a token representing a coin. ■ a factor used to give one party an advantage in negotiations: *the proposal has become a crucial bargaining counter over prices.*
3 a device used for counting: *the counter tells you how many pictures you have taken.* ■ a person who counts something, for example votes in an election. ■ Physics an apparatus used for counting individual ionizing particles or events.
– PHRASES **behind the counter** serving in a shop or bank. **over the counter** by ordinary retail purchase, with no need for a prescription or licence: [as modifier] *over-the-counter medicines.* ■ (of share transactions) taking place outside the stock exchange system. **under the counter** (or **table**) (with reference to goods bought or sold) surreptitiously and typically illegally: *hard porn is legally banned, but still available under the counter* | [as modifier] *an under-the-counter deal.*
– ORIGIN Middle English (in sense 2): from Old French *conteor*, from medieval Latin *computatorium*, from Latin *computare* (see COMPUTE).

counter² ▶ **verb** [with obj.] speak or act in opposition to: *the second argument is more difficult to counter.* ■ [no obj.] respond to hostile speech or action: *the possibility of the enemy being able to* ***counter with*** *similar missiles was remote.* ■ [no obj.] Boxing give a return blow while parrying: *he countered with a left hook.*
▶ **adverb** (**counter to**) in the opposite direction or in opposition to: *his writing* ***ran counter to*** *the dominant trends of the decade.*
▶ **adjective** responding to something of the same kind, especially in opposition: *after years of argument and counter argument there is no conclusive answer.* See also COUNTER-.
▶ **noun 1** [usu. in sing.] a thing which opposes or prevents something else: *the stimulus to employers' organization was partly a* ***counter to*** *growing union power.* ■ an answer to an argument or criticism: *he anticipates an objection and plans his counter.* ■ Boxing a blow given while parrying, a counterpunch.
2 the curved part of the stern of a ship projecting aft above the waterline.
3 Printing the white space enclosed by a letter such as *O* or *c*.
– PHRASES **go** (or Brit. **hunt** or **run**) **counter** run or ride against the direction taken by a quarry.
– ORIGIN late Middle English: from Old French *contre*, from Latin *contra* 'against', or directly from COUNTER-.

counter³ ▶ **noun** the back part of a shoe or boot, enclosing the heel.
– ORIGIN mid 19th cent.: abbreviation of *counterfort* 'buttress', from French *contrefort*.

counter- ▶ **prefix** denoting opposition, retaliation, or rivalry: *counter-attack* | *counter-espionage.* ■ denoting movement or effect in the opposite direction: *counterpoise.* ■ denoting correspondence, duplication, or substitution: *counterpart.*
– ORIGIN from Anglo-Norman French *countre-*, Old French *contre*, from Latin *contra* 'against'.

counteract ▶ **verb** [with obj.] act against (something) in order to reduce its force or neutralize it: *should we deliberately intervene in the climate system to counteract global warming?*
– DERIVATIVES **counteraction** noun, **counteractive** adjective.

C

counterargument ▶ **noun** an argument or set of reasons put forward to oppose an idea or theory developed in another argument: *the obvious counterargument to that dire prediction is that the recession has depressed earnings.*

counter-attack ▶ **noun** an attack made in response to one by an opponent.
▶ **verb** [no obj.] attack in response: *as deputies tried to dislodge him, he counter-attacked by forcing through elections.*
– DERIVATIVES **counter-attacker** noun.

counter-attraction ▶ **noun** a rival attraction: *it is a pity that this book may not triumph over the counter-attractions on the booksellers' shelves.*

counterbalance ▶ **noun** /ˈkaʊntəˌbal(ə)ns/ a weight that balances another weight. ■ a factor having the opposite effect to that of another and so preventing it from exercising a disproportionate influence: *his restoration to power was intended as a* ***counterbalance to*** *his rival's influence.*
▶ **verb** /ˌkaʊntəˈbal(ə)ns/ [with obj.] (of a weight) balance (another weight). ■ neutralize or cancel by exerting an opposite influence: *the extra cost of mail order may be counterbalanced by its convenience.*

counterblast ▶ **noun** a strongly worded reply to someone else's views: *a* ***counterblast to*** *the growing propaganda of the Left.*

counterbore ▶ **noun** a drilled hole that has a wider section at the top. ■ a drill whose bit has a uniform smaller diameter near the tip, for drilling counterbores in one operation.
▶ **verb** [with obj.] drill a counterbore in (an object).

counterchange ▶ **verb** [with obj.] literary chequer with contrasting colours. ■ Heraldry interchange the tinctures of (a charge) with that of a divided field.
▶ **noun** [mass noun] **1** change that is equivalent in degree but opposite in effect to a previous change.
2 patterning in which a dark motif on a light ground alternates with the same motif light on a dark ground.
– ORIGIN late Middle English (as a heraldic term): from French *contrechanger*, from *contre* (expressing substitution) + *changer* 'to change'.

countercharge ▶ **noun 1** an accusation made in turn by someone against their accuser: *charges and countercharges concerning producers, quotas, and affidavits.*
2 a charge by police or an armed force in response to one made against them.

countercheck ▶ **noun 1** a second check for security or accuracy.
2 archaic a restraint.
3 archaic a sharp or incisive retort.
▶ **verb** [with obj.] archaic stop (something) by acting to cancel or counteract it.

counterclaim ▶ **noun** a claim made to rebut a previous claim. ■ Law a claim made by a defendant against a plaintiff.
▶ **verb** [no obj.] chiefly Law make a counterclaim for something.

counterclockwise ▶ **adverb & adjective** North American term for ANTICLOCKWISE.

counter-conditioning ▶ **noun** [mass noun] a technique employed in animal training and the treatment of phobias and similar conditions in humans, in which behaviour incompatible with a habitual undesirable pattern is induced. Compare with DECONDITIONING.

counterculture ▶ **noun** a way of life and set of attitudes opposed to or at variance with the prevailing social norm: *the idealists of the 60s counterculture.*
– DERIVATIVES **countercultural** adjective.

countercurrent ▶ **noun** a current flowing in an opposite direction to another.
▶ **adverb** in or with opposite directions of flow.

counterdemonstration ▶ **noun** a public demonstration organized in order to express opposition to the aims of another demonstration: *an effort by right-wing elements to organize a counterdemonstration failed.*

counter-espionage ▶ **noun** [mass noun] activities designed to prevent or thwart spying by an enemy.

counterfactual Philosophy ▶ **adjective** relating to or expressing what has not happened or is not the case.
▶ **noun** a counterfactual conditional statement (e.g. *If kangaroos had no tails, they would topple over*).

counterfeit ▶ **adjective** made in exact imitation of something valuable with the intention to deceive or defraud: *counterfeit £10 notes*. ■ pretended; sham: *a counterfeit image of reality*.
▶ **noun** a fraudulent imitation of something else: *he knew the tapes to be counterfeits*.
▶ **verb** [with obj.] imitate fraudulently: *my signature is extremely hard to counterfeit*. ■ pretend to feel or possess (an emotion or quality): *no pretence could have counterfeited such terror*. ■ literary resemble closely: *sleep counterfeited Death so well*.
– DERIVATIVES **counterfeiter** noun.
– ORIGIN Middle English (as a verb): from Anglo-Norman French *countrefeter*, from Old French *contrefait*, past participle of *contrefaire*, from Latin *contra-* 'in opposition' + *facere* 'make'.

counterfoil ▶ **noun** Brit. the part of a cheque, receipt, ticket, or other document that is torn off and kept as a record by the person issuing it.

counter-insurgency ▶ **noun** [mass noun] military or political action taken against the activities of guerrillas or revolutionaries: [as modifier] *a counter-insurgency force*.

counter-intelligence ▶ **noun** another term for COUNTER-ESPIONAGE.

counter-intuitive ▶ **adjective** contrary to intuition or to common-sense expectation.
– DERIVATIVES **counter-intuitively** adverb.

counterirritant ▶ **noun** something such as heat or an ointment that is used to produce surface irritation of the skin, thereby counteracting underlying pain or discomfort.
– DERIVATIVES **counterirritation** noun.

counter-jumper ▶ **noun** informal, derogatory a shop assistant.

countermand /ˌkaʊntəˈmɑːnd/ ▶ **verb** [with obj.] revoke or cancel (an order): *an order to arrest the strike leaders had been countermanded*. ■ revoke or cancel an order issued by (another person): *he was already countermanding her*. ■ declare (a vote or election) invalid.
▶ **noun** an order revoking a previous one.
– ORIGIN late Middle English: from Old French *contremander* (verb), *contremand* (noun), from medieval Latin *contramandare*, from *contra-* 'against' + *mandare* 'to order'.

countermarch ▶ **verb** [no obj.] march in the opposite direction or back along the same route.
▶ **noun** an act or instance of marching in the opposite direction.

countermark ▶ **noun** an additional mark placed on something already marked, especially for increased security.

countermeasure ▶ **noun** an action taken to counteract a danger or threat.

countermelody ▶ **noun** (pl. **countermelodies**) a subordinate melody accompanying a principal one.

countermine ▶ **noun** Military an excavation dug to intercept another dug by an enemy.

countermove ▶ **noun** a move or other action made in opposition to another.
– DERIVATIVES **countermovement** noun.

counternarcotics ▶ **plural noun** [treated as sing.] measures or activities designed to prevent the use or distribution of illegal narcotic drugs.

counteroffensive ▶ **noun** an attack made in response to one from an enemy, typically on a large scale or for a prolonged period.

counter-offer ▶ **noun** an offer made in response to another.

counterpane ▶ **noun** dated a bedspread.
– ORIGIN early 17th cent.: alteration of COUNTERPOINT, from Old French *contrepointe*, based on medieval Latin *culcitra puncta* 'quilted mattress' (*puncta*, literally meaning 'pricked', from the verb *pungere*). The change in the ending was due to association with PANE in an obsolete sense 'cloth'.

counterpart ▶ **noun 1** a person or thing that corresponds to or has the same function as another person or thing in a different place or situation: *the minister held talks with his French counterpart*.
2 Law one of two copies of a legal document.

counterpart fund ▶ **noun** a sum of money accrued in a local currency arising from goods or services received from abroad.

counterparty ▶ **noun** an opposite party in a contract or financial transaction.

counterplot ▶ **noun** a plot intended to thwart another plot.

counterpoint ▶ **noun 1** [mass noun] Music the technique of setting, writing, or playing a melody or melodies in conjunction with another, according to fixed rules. ■ [count noun] a melody played in conjunction with another.
2 a thing that forms a pleasing or notable contrast to something else: *the sauce made a piquant **counterpoint to** the ham*.
▶ **verb** [with obj.] **1** Music add counterpoint to (a melody): *the orchestra counterpoints the vocal part*.
2 emphasize by contrast: *the cream walls and maple floors are counterpointed by black accents*.
– ORIGIN late Middle English: from Old French *contrepoint*, from medieval Latin *contrapunctum* '(song) pricked or marked over against (the original melody')', from *contra-* 'against' + *punctum*, from *pungere* 'to prick'.

counterpoise ▶ **noun** a factor or force that balances or neutralizes another: *the organization sees the power of Brussels as a **counterpoise to** that of London*. ■ a counterbalancing weight. ■ a state of equilibrium.
▶ **verb** [with obj.] have an opposing and balancing effect on: *they make a delightful couple, his gentle intellectuality counterpoised by her firm practicality*. ■ bring into contrast: *the stories counterpoise a young recruit with an old-timer*.
– ORIGIN late Middle English: from Old French *contrepois* from *contre* 'against' + *pois* from Latin *pensum* 'weight'. Compare with POISE[1]. The verb, originally *counterpeise*, from Old French *contrepeser*, was altered under the influence of the noun in the 16th cent.

counterpose ▶ **verb** [with obj.] set against or in opposition to.
– DERIVATIVES **counterposition** noun.

counterproductive ▶ **adjective** having the opposite of the desired effect: *child experts fear the Executive's plans may prove counterproductive*.

counterproliferation ▶ **noun** [mass noun] action intended to prevent an increase or spread in the possession of nuclear weapons.

counterproposal ▶ **noun** an alternative proposal made in response to a previous proposal that is regarded as unacceptable or unsatisfactory: *the union rejected the airline's counterproposal*.

counterpunch Boxing ▶ **noun** a punch thrown in return for one received.
▶ **verb** [no obj.] throw a counterpunch.
– DERIVATIVES **counterpuncher** noun.

Counter-Reformation the reform of the Church of Rome in the 16th and 17th centuries which was stimulated by the Protestant Reformation.

> Measures to oppose the spread of the Reformation were resolved on at the Council of Trent (1545–63) and the Jesuit order became the spearhead of the Counter-Reformation, both within Europe and abroad. Although most of northern Europe remained Protestant, southern Germany and Poland were brought back to the Roman Catholic Church.

counter-revolution ▶ **noun** a revolution opposing a former one or reversing its results.
– DERIVATIVES **counter-revolutionary** adjective & noun.

counterrotate ▶ **verb** [no obj.] rotate in opposite directions, especially about the same axis.
– DERIVATIVES **counterrotation** noun.

counterscarp ▶ **noun** the outer wall of a ditch in a fortification.
– ORIGIN late 16th cent.: from French *contrescarpe*, from Italian *controscarpa*; compare with SCARP.

countershading ▶ **noun** [mass noun] Zoology protective coloration used by some animals in which parts normally in shadow are light and those exposed to the sky are dark.
– DERIVATIVES **countershaded** adjective.

countershaft ▶ **noun** a machine driveshaft that transmits motion from the main shaft to where it is required, such as the drive axle in a vehicle.

countersign ▶ **verb** [with obj.] add a signature to (a document already signed by another person): *each cheque had to be signed and countersigned*.
▶ **noun** archaic a signal or password given in reply to a soldier on guard.
– DERIVATIVES **countersignature** noun.
– ORIGIN late 16th cent. (as a noun): from French *contresigner* (verb), *contresigne* (noun), from Italian *contrassegno*, based on Latin *signum* 'sign'.

countersink ▶ **verb** (past and past participle **countersunk**) [with obj.] enlarge and bevel the rim of (a drilled hole) so that a screw, nail, or bolt can be inserted flush with the surface. ■ drive (a screw, nail, or bolt) into such a hole.

counterspy /ˈkaʊntəspʌɪ/ ▶ **noun** (pl. **counterspies**) a spy engaged in counter-espionage.

counterstain Biology ▶ **noun** an additional dye used in a microscopy specimen to produce a contrasting background or to make clearer the distinction between different kinds of tissue.
▶ **verb** [with obj.] treat (a specimen) with a counterstain.

counterstroke ▶ **noun** an attack carried out in retaliation.

countersubject ▶ **noun** Music a second or subsidiary subject, especially accompanying the subject or its answer in a fugue.

countertenor ▶ **noun** Music the highest male adult singing voice (sometimes distinguished from the male alto voice by its strong, pure tone). ■ a singer with such a voice.
– ORIGIN late Middle English: from French *contre-teneur*, from obsolete Italian *contratenore*, based on Latin *tenor* (see TENOR[1]).

counterterrorism ▶ **noun** [mass noun] political or military activities designed to prevent or thwart terrorism.
– DERIVATIVES **counterterrorist** noun.

countertop ▶ **noun** North American term for WORKTOP.

countertrade ▶ **noun** [mass noun] international trade by exchange of goods rather than by currency purchase.

counter-transference ▶ **noun** [mass noun] Psychoanalysis the emotional reaction of the analyst to the subject's contribution.

countervail /ˌkaʊntəˈveɪl/ ▶ **verb** [with obj.] (usu. as adj. **countervailing**) offset the effect of (something) by countering it with something of equal force: *the dominance of the party was mediated by a number of countervailing factors*.
– ORIGIN late Middle English (in the sense 'be equivalent to in value'): from Anglo-Norman French *contrevaloir*, from Latin *contra valere* 'be of worth against'.

countervailing duty ▶ **noun** an import tax imposed on certain goods in order to prevent dumping or to counter export subsidies.

countervalue ▶ **noun** Brit. an equivalent or equal, especially in military strategy: [as modifier] *countervalue weapons*.

counterweight ▶ **noun** another term for COUNTERBALANCE.

countess ▶ **noun** the wife or widow of a count or earl. ■ a woman holding the rank of count or earl in her own right.
– ORIGIN Middle English: from Old French *contesse*, from late Latin *comitissa*, feminine of *comes* (see COUNT[2]).

countian ▶ **noun** [with modifier] chiefly US an inhabitant of a particular county: *Sussex countians*.

counting ▶ **preposition** taking account of when reaching a total; including: *there were three of us in the family, or four counting my pet rabbit* | *the college had 139 employees, **not counting** those engaged in routine clerical work*.

counting house ▶ **noun** historical an office or building in which the accounts and money of a person or company were kept.

countless ▶ **adjective** too many to be counted; very many: *she'd apologized countless times before*.

count noun ▶ **noun** Grammar a noun that can form a plural and, in the singular, can be used with the indefinite article (e.g. *books, a book*). Contrasted with MASS NOUN.

count palatine ▶ **noun** (pl. **counts palatine**) historical a feudal lord having royal authority within a region of a kingdom. ■ a high official of the Holy Roman Empire with royal authority within his domain.
– ORIGIN see PALATINE[1].

countrified (also **countryfied**) ▶ **adjective** reminiscent or characteristic of the country, especially in being unsophisticated: *a countrified cottage garden* | *her tweeds were far too countrified*.

– ORIGIN mid 17th cent.: past participle of *countrify* 'make rural'.

country ▸ noun (pl. **countries**) **1** a nation with its own government, occupying a particular territory: *the country's increasingly precarious economic position* | *Spain, Italy, and other European countries.* ■ **(the country)** the people of a nation: *the whole country took to the streets.*
2 (often **the country**) districts and small settlements outside large urban areas or the capital: *the airfield is right out in the country* | [as modifier] *a country lane.*
3 [mass noun] an area or region with regard to its physical features: *a tract of wild country.* ■ a region associated with a particular person, work, or television programme: *an old mansion in Stevenson's 'Kidnapped' country.*
4 short for COUNTRY MUSIC.
– PHRASES **across country** not keeping to roads. **go** (or **appeal**) **to the country** Brit. test public opinion by dissolving Parliament and holding a general election. **one's line of country** Brit. a subject in which one is skilled or knowledgeable: *anagrams are not in my line of country.*
– ORIGIN Middle English: from Old French *cuntree*, from medieval Latin *contrata (terra)* '(land) lying opposite', from Latin *contra* 'against, opposite'.

country and western ▸ noun another term for COUNTRY MUSIC.

country blues ▸ noun [mass noun] a simple form of blues in which the singer is accompanied by an acoustic guitar.

country club ▸ noun a club with sporting and social facilities, set in a rural area.

country cousin ▸ noun a person with an unsophisticated and provincial appearance or manners.

country dance ▸ noun a traditional type of social English dance, in particular one performed by couples facing each other in long lines.

countryfied ▸ adjective variant of COUNTRIFIED.

country-fried ▸ adjective N. Amer. (of an item of food) covered in batter, flour, or breadcrumbs and fried: *country-fried steak.* ■ informal rural or unsophisticated: *country-fried tunes.*

country gentleman ▸ noun a rich man of good social standing who owns and lives on an estate in a rural area.

country house ▸ noun Brit. a large house in the country, typically the seat of a wealthy or aristocratic family.

countrymade ▸ adjective Indian (especially of a weapon) manufactured by an illegal cottage industry.

countryman (or **countrywoman**) ▸ noun (pl. **countrymen** or **countrywomen**) **1** a person living or born in a rural area.
2 a person from the same country as someone else: *they trust a fellow countryman.*

country mile ▸ noun informal a very long way: *he hit the ball a country mile.*

country music ▸ noun [mass noun] a form of popular music originating in the rural southern US. It is a mixture of ballads and dance tunes played characteristically on fiddle, banjo, guitar, and pedal steel guitar. Also called COUNTRY AND WESTERN.

country party ▸ noun historical a political party supporting agricultural rather than manufacturing interests.

country rock[1] ▸ noun [mass noun] Geology the rock which encloses a mineral deposit, igneous intrusion, or other feature.

country rock[2] ▸ noun [mass noun] a type of popular music that is a blend of rock and country music.

country seat ▸ noun Brit. a large country house and estate belonging to an aristocratic family.

countryside ▸ noun [mass noun] the land and scenery of a rural area: *they explored the surrounding countryside.*

countrywide ▸ adjective & adverb extending throughout a nation: [as adj.] *a countrywide tour* | [as adv.] *these units travel countrywide.*

countrywoman ▸ noun see COUNTRYMAN.

county ▸ noun (pl. **counties**) a territorial division of some countries, forming the chief unit of local administration. ■ Brit. a sporting team playing for a county. ■ US a political and administrative division of a state. ■ [as modifier] Brit. relating to or characteristic of aristocratic people with an ancestral home in a particular county: *a county grande dame.*
– ORIGIN Middle English: from Old French *conte*, from Latin *comitatus*, from *comes, comit-* (see COUNT[2]). The word seems first to have denoted a periodical meeting held to transact shire business.

county borough ▸ noun (in Wales and formerly in England and Northern Ireland) a town having the administrative status of a county.

county clerk ▸ noun (in the US) an elected county official who is responsible for local elections and maintaining public records.

county corporate ▸ noun Brit. historical a city or town ranking as an administrative county.

county council ▸ noun (in the UK) the elected governing body of an administrative county.
– DERIVATIVES **county councillor** noun.

county court ▸ noun (in England and Wales) a judicial court for civil cases. ■ US a court for civil and criminal cases.

county cricket ▸ noun [mass noun] first-class cricket played in the UK between the eighteen professional teams contesting the County Championship.

County Durham see DURHAM.

County Palatine historical ▸ noun (in England and Ireland) a county in which royal privileges and exclusive rights of jurisdiction were held by its earl or lord.
– ORIGIN see PALATINE[1].

county school ▸ noun (in the UK) a school that is established and funded by the local education authority.

county town (N. Amer. **county seat**) ▸ noun the town that is the administrative capital of a county.

coup /kuː/ ▸ noun (pl. **coups** /kuːz/) **1** (also **coup d'état**) a sudden, violent, and illegal seizure of power from a government: *he was overthrown in an army coup.*
2 an instance of successfully achieving something difficult: *it was a major coup to get such a prestigious contract.* ■ an unusual or unexpected but successful tactic in card play.
3 Billiards a direct pocketing of the cue ball, which is a foul stroke.
4 historical (among North American Indians) an act of touching an enemy, as a deed of bravery, or an act of first touching an item of the enemy's in order to claim it.
– ORIGIN late 18th cent.: from French, from medieval Latin *colpus* 'blow' (see COPE[1]).

coup de foudre /ˌkuː də ˈfuːdr(ə)/, French /ku də fudʀ/ ▸ noun (pl. **coups de foudre** pronunc. **same**) a sudden unforeseen event, in particular an instance of love at first sight.
– ORIGIN French, literally 'stroke of lightning'.

coup de grâce /ˌkuː də ˈɡrɑːs/, French /ku də ɡʀɑs/ ▸ noun (pl. **coups de grâce** pronunc. **same**) a final blow or shot given to kill a wounded person or animal: *he administered the coup de grâce with a knife.* ■ an action or event that serves as the culmination of a bad or deteriorating situation: *Howarth delivered the coup de grâce with a penalty two minutes from time.*
– ORIGIN French, literally 'stroke of grace'.

coup de main /ˌkuː də ˈmã/, French /ku də mɛ̃/ ▸ noun (pl. **coups de main** pronunc. **same**) a sudden surprise attack, especially one made by an army during war.
– ORIGIN French, literally 'stroke of hand'.

coup de maître /ˌkuː də ˈmɛːtr(ə)/, French /ku də mɛtʀ/ ▸ noun (pl. **coups de maître** pronunc. **same**) a master stroke.
– ORIGIN French.

coup d'état /ˌkuː deɪˈtɑː/, French /ku deta/ ▸ noun (pl. **coups d'état** pronunc. **same**) another term for COUP (sense 1).
– ORIGIN French, literally 'blow of state'.

coup de théâtre /ˌkuː də teɪˈɑːtr(ə)/, French /ku də teɑtʀ/ ▸ noun (pl. **coups de théâtre** pronunc. **same**)
1 a dramatically sudden action or turn of events, especially in a play.
2 a successful theatrical production.
– ORIGIN French, literally 'blow of theatre'.

coup d'œil /kuː ˈdəːɪ/, French /ku dœj/ ▸ noun (pl. **coups d'œil** pronunc. **same**) a glance that takes in a comprehensive view.
– ORIGIN French, literally 'stroke of eye'.

coupe /kuːp/ ▸ noun a shallow glass or glass dish, typically with a stem, in which desserts or champagne are served. ■ a dessert served in such a dish.
– ORIGIN French, 'goblet'.

coupé /ˈkuːpeɪ/ (also **coupe** /kuːp/) ▸ noun **1** a car with a fixed roof, two doors, and a sloping rear.
2 historical a four-wheeled enclosed carriage for two passengers and a driver.
3 (in South Africa) an end compartment in a railway carriage, with seats on only one side.
– ORIGIN mid 19th cent. (in sense 2): from French *carrosse coupé*, literally 'cut carriage'. Sense 1 dates from the early 20th cent.

couped /kuːpt/ ▸ adjective [usu. postpositive] Heraldry cut off or truncated in a straight line.
– ORIGIN early 16th cent.: from French *couper* 'to cut' + -ED[2].

C

Couperin /ˈkuːpərã/, French /kupʀɛ̃/, François (1668–1733), French composer, organist, and harpsichordist. A composer at the court of Louis XIV, he is principally known for his harpsichord works.

couple ▸ noun **1** two people or things of the same sort considered together: ***a couple of*** *girls were playing marbles.* ■ a pair of partners in a dance or game. ■ (pl. **couple**) a pair of hunting dogs. ■ (**couples**) two collars joined together and used for holding hounds together. ■ a pair of rafters. ■ Mechanics a pair of equal and parallel forces acting in opposite directions, and tending to cause rotation about an axis perpendicular to the plane containing them.
2 [treated as sing. or pl.] two people who are married or otherwise closely associated romantically or sexually.
3 informal an indefinite small number: [as pronoun] *he hoped she'd be better in* ***a couple of*** *days* | *we got some eggs—would you like a couple?* | [as determiner] *just a couple more questions* | N. Amer. *clean the stains with a couple squirts dishwashing liquid.*
▸ verb **1** [with obj.] link or combine (something) with something else: *a sense of hope* ***is coupled with*** *a palpable sense of loss.* ■ connect (a railway vehicle or a piece of equipment) to another: *a cable is* ***coupled up*** *to one of the wheels.* ■ connect (two electrical components) using electromagnetic induction, electrostatic charge, or an optical link: (as adj. **coupled**) *networks of coupled oscillators.* ■ [no obj.] (**couple up**) join to form a pair.
2 [no obj.] mate or have sexual intercourse.
– DERIVATIVES **coupledom** noun.
– ORIGIN Middle English: from Old French *cople* (noun), *copler* (verb), from Latin *copula* (noun), *copulare* (verb), from *co-* 'together' + *apere* 'fasten'. Compare with COPULA and COPULATE.

coupler ▸ noun a thing that connects two things, especially mechanical components or systems: *a hydraulic coupler.* ■ Music a device in an organ for connecting two manuals, or a manual with pedals, so that they both sound when only one is played. ■ (also **octave coupler**) Music a device in an organ for connecting notes with their octaves above or below. ■ Photography a compound in a developer or an emulsion which combines with the products of development to form an insoluble dye, part of the image. ■ (also **acoustic coupler**) a modem which converts digital signals from a computer into audible sound signals and vice versa, so that the former can be transmitted and received over telephone lines.

couplet ▸ noun a pair of successive lines of verse, typically rhyming and of the same length.
– ORIGIN late 16th cent.: from French, diminutive of *couple*, from Old French *cople* (see COUPLE).

coupling ▸ noun **1** a device for connecting parts of machinery. ■ a fitting on the end of a railway vehicle for connecting it to another.
2 [mass noun] the pairing of two items: *the coupling of tribunals with ministerial enquiries.* ■ an interaction between two electrical components by electromagnetic induction, electrostatic charge, or optical link.
3 [mass noun] the action of mating or having sexual intercourse.
4 two people in a romantic relationship; a couple.

coupling constant ▸ noun Physics a constant representing the strength of the interaction between a particle and a field.

coupling rod ▸ noun a rod which couples the driving wheels of a locomotive, enabling them to act as a unit.

couply (also **coupley**) ▸ adjective informal, often derogatory relating to or characteristic of a couple in a romantic or sexual relationship, especially when the relationship is regarded as particularly intimate or socially exclusive.

coupon ▸ noun **1** a voucher entitling the holder to a discount off a particular product. ■ a detachable ticket entitling the holder to a ration of food, clothes, or other goods, especially in wartime. ■ a detachable portion of a bond which is given up in

return for a payment of interest. ■ the nominal rate of interest on a fixed-interest security.
2 a form in a newspaper or magazine which may be sent as an application for a purchase or information. ■ Brit. an entry form for a football pool or other competition.
3 Scottish & Irish a person's face: *he had a big beaming smile on his coupon.*
– ORIGIN early 19th cent. (denoting a detachable portion of a stock certificate): from French, literally 'piece cut off', from *couper* 'cut', from Old French *colper* (see COPE[1]).

coupon-clipper ▶ noun N. Amer. informal a person with a large number of interest-bearing bonds.

courage ▶ noun [mass noun] the ability to do something that frightens one; bravery: *she called on all her courage to face the ordeal.* ■ strength in the face of pain or grief: *he fought his illness with great courage.*
– PHRASES **have the courage of one's convictions** act on one's beliefs despite danger or disapproval. **pluck up** (or **screw up** or **take**) **courage** make an effort to do something that frightens one. **take one's courage in both hands** nerve oneself to do something that frightens one.
– ORIGIN Middle English (denoting the heart, as the seat of feelings): from Old French *corage*, from Latin *cor* 'heart'.

courageous ▶ adjective not deterred by danger or pain; brave: *her courageous human rights work.*
– DERIVATIVES **courageously** adverb, **courageousness** noun.
– ORIGIN Middle English: from Old French *corageus*, from *corage* (see COURAGE).

courant /kʊˈrant/ ▶ adjective [usu. postpositive] Heraldry represented as running.
– ORIGIN early 17th cent.: French, 'running', present participle of *courir*.

courante /kʊˈrɒ̃t, -rɑːnt/ ▶ noun a 16th-century court dance consisting of short advances and retreats, later developed into a rapid gliding dance in quick triple time. ■ a piece of music written for or in the style of such a dance, typically one forming a movement of a suite.
– ORIGIN late 16th cent.: French, literally 'running', feminine present participle of *courir*.

Courbet /ˈkʊəbeɪ/, French /kuʀbɛ/, Gustave (1819–77), French painter. A leader of the 19th-century realist school of painting, he favoured an unidealized choice of subject matter that did not exclude the ugly or vulgar. Notable works: *Burial at Ornans* (1850) and *Painter in his Studio* (1855).

courbette /kʊəˈbɛt/ ▶ noun (in classical riding) a movement in which the horse performs a series of jumps on the hind legs without the forelegs touching the ground.
– ORIGIN mid 17th cent.: French, from Italian *corvetta* 'little curve', based on Latin *curvus* 'curved'.

coureur de bois /kuːˌrəː də ˈbwʌ/ ▶ noun (pl. **coureurs de bois** pronunc. **same**) historical (in Canada and the northern US) a woodsman or trader of French origin.
– ORIGIN French, literally 'wood-runner'.

courgette /kʊəˈʒɛt/ ▶ noun Brit. the immature fruit of a vegetable marrow, in particular one of a variety developed for harvesting and eating at an early stage of growth. Called ZUCCHINI in North America.
– ORIGIN 1930s: from French, diminutive of *courge* 'gourd', from Latin *cucurbita*.

courier /ˈkʊrɪə/ ▶ noun 1 a company or employee of a company that transports commercial packages and documents: *the cheque was dispatched by courier* | [as modifier] *a courier service.* ■ a messenger for an underground or espionage organization.
2 chiefly Brit. a person employed to guide and assist a group of tourists.
▶ verb [with obj.] send (goods or documents) by courier: *your order can be couriered to you in three days.*
– ORIGIN late Middle English (denoting a person sent to run with a message): originally from Old French *coreor*; later from French *courier* (now *courrier*), from Italian *corriere*; based on Latin *currere* 'to run'.

courol /ˈkuːrɒl/ ▶ noun another term for CUCKOO-ROLLER.
– ORIGIN contraction.

Courrèges /kʊəˈreɪʒ, -ˈrɛʒ/, French /kuʀɛʒ/, André (b.1923), French fashion designer. He is famous for his futuristic and youth-oriented styles, in particular the use of plastic and metal and unisex fashion such as trouser suits for women.

course ▶ noun 1 the route or direction followed by a ship, aircraft, road, or river: *the road adopts a tortuous course along the coast* | *the new fleet* **changed course** *to join the other ships.* ■ the way in which something progresses or develops: *the course of history.* ■ (also **course of action**) [count noun] a procedure adopted to deal with a situation: *my decision had seemed to be the wisest course open to me at the time.*
2 a dish, or a set of dishes served together, forming one of the successive parts of a meal: *guests are offered a choice of main course* | [in combination] *a four-course meal.*
3 an area of land set aside and prepared for racing, golf, or another sport.
4 a series of lectures or lessons in a particular subject, leading to an examination or qualification: *a business studies course.* ■ Medicine a series of repeated treatments or doses of medication: *the doctor prescribed a course of antibiotics.* ■ Bell-ringing a series of changes which brings the bells back to their original order, or the changes of a particular bell.
5 a continuous horizontal layer of brick, stone, or other material in a wall.
6 a pursuit of game (especially hares) with greyhounds by sight rather than scent.
7 a sail on the lowest yards of a square-rigged ship.
8 a set of adjacent strings on a guitar, lute, etc., tuned to the same note.
▶ verb 1 [no obj., with adverbial of direction] (of liquid) move without obstruction; flow: *tears were coursing down her cheeks* | figurative *exultation coursed through him.*
2 [with obj.] pursue (game, especially hares) with greyhounds using sight rather than scent: *many of the hares coursed escaped unharmed* | [no obj.] *she would course for hares with her greyhounds.*
– PHRASES **course of action** see COURSE (sense 1 of the noun). **the course of nature** events or processes which are normal and to be expected: *each man would, in the course of nature, have his private opinions.* **in (the) course of —— 1** undergoing the specified process: *a new text book was in course of preparation.* **2** during the specified period or activity: *he was a friend to many people in the course of his life.* **in** (or **over**) **the course of time** as time goes by: *the property will deteriorate in the course of time.* **of course** used to introduce an idea or action as being obvious or to be expected: *the point is of course that the puzzle itself is misleading.* ■ used to give or emphasize agreement or permission: *'Can I see you for a minute?' 'Of course.'* ■ introducing a qualification or admission: *of course we've been in touch by phone, but I wanted to see things for myself.* **off course** not following the intended route. **on course** following the intended route: *he battled to keep the ship on course* | figurative *we need to spend money to get the economy back on course.* ■ (**on course for/to do something**) likely to achieve something: *he was on course for victory.* **run** (or **take**) **its course** complete its natural development without interference: *his illness had to run its course to the crisis.*
– ORIGIN Middle English: from Old French *cours*, from Latin *cursus*, from *curs-* 'run', from the verb *currere*.

coursebook ▶ noun Brit. a textbook designed for use on a particular course of study.

courser[1] ▶ noun literary a swift horse.
– ORIGIN Middle English: from Old French *corsier*, based on Latin *cursus* (see COURSE).

courser[2] ▶ noun a fast-running plover-like bird related to the pratincoles, typically found in open country in Africa and Asia. ● Genera *Cursorius* and *Rhinoptilus*, family Glareolidae: several species, in particular the desert-dwelling **cream-coloured courser** (*C. cursor*).
– ORIGIN mid 18th cent.: from modern Latin *Cursorius* 'adapted for running', from *cursor* 'runner', from the verb *currere* (see COURSE).

courser[3] ▶ noun a person who hunts animals such as hares with greyhounds using sight rather than scent.
– ORIGIN early 17th cent.: from COURSER[1].

courseware ▶ noun [mass noun] computer programs or other material designed for use in an educational or training course.

coursework ▶ noun [mass noun] written or practical work done by a student during a course of study, usually assessed in order to count towards a final mark or grade.

coursing ▶ noun [mass noun] the sport of hunting game animals such as hares with greyhounds using sight rather than scent.

court ▶ noun 1 (also **court of law**) a body of people presided over by a judge, judges, or magistrate, and acting as a tribunal in civil and criminal cases: *she will take the matter to court* | [as modifier] *a court case.* ■ the place where a court meets.
2 a quadrangular area, either open or covered, marked out for ball games such as tennis or squash: *a squash court.* ■ a quadrangular area surrounded by a building or group of buildings. ■ (**Court**) used in the names of large houses or blocks of flats: *Hampton Court.*
3 the courtiers, retinue, and household of a sovereign: *the emperor is shown with his court.* ■ a sovereign and his or her councillors, constituting a ruling power: *relations between the king and the imperial court.* ■ a sovereign's residence.
4 the qualified members of a company or a corporation. ■ a meeting of the members of a company or a corporation.
▶ verb 1 [with obj.] dated be involved with (someone) romantically, with the intention of marrying: *he was courting a girl from the neighbouring farm* | [no obj.] *we went to the cinema when we were courting.* ■ (of a male bird or other animal) try to attract (a mate).
2 pay special attention to (someone) in an attempt to win their support or favour: *Western politicians courted the leaders of the newly independent states.* ■ try hard to win (favourable attention): *he never had to court the approval of the political elite.* ■ risk incurring (misfortune) because of one's behaviour: *he has often courted controversy.*
– PHRASES **go to court** take legal action. **have one's day in court** have a chance to make one's case in a court of law: *victims of violence should have their day in court.* **in court** appearing as a party or an advocate in a court of law. **out of court 1** before a legal hearing can take place: *they are trying to settle the squabble out of court* | [as modifier] *an out-of-court settlement.* **2** not worthy of consideration: *the price would put it out of court for most private buyers.* **pay court to** pay flattering attention to (someone) in order to win favour.
– ORIGIN Middle English: from Old French *cort*, from Latin *cohors*, *cohort-* 'yard or retinue'. The verb is influenced by Old Italian *corteare*, Old French *courtoyer*. Compare with COHORT.

Courtauld /ˈkɔːtəʊld/, Samuel (1876–1947), English industrialist. He was a director of his family's silk firm and a collector of French Impressionist and post-Impressionist paintings. He presented his collection to the University of London, endowed the Courtauld Institute of Art, and bequeathed to it his house in Portman Square, London.

court bouillon /kɔːt ˈbuːjɒn/ ▶ noun [mass noun] a stock made from wine and vegetables, typically used in fish dishes.
– ORIGIN French, from *court* 'short' and BOUILLON.

court card ▶ noun Brit. a playing card that is a king, queen, or jack of a suit.
– ORIGIN mid 17th cent.: alteration of 16th-cent. *coat card*, so named because of the decorative dress of the figures depicted.

court circular ▶ noun (usu. **the Court Circular**) Brit. a daily report of the activities and public engagements of royal family members, published in some newspapers.

court costs ▶ plural noun see COST (noun).

court cupboard ▶ noun a 16th- or 17th-century sideboard for displaying plate and other decorative objects, especially one consisting of three open shelves and sometimes a small cupboard in the upper half.

courteous /ˈkəːtjəs/ ▶ adjective polite, respectful, or considerate in manner.
– DERIVATIVES **courteously** adverb, **courteousness** noun.
– ORIGIN Middle English (meaning 'having manners fit for a royal court'): from Old French *corteis*, based on Latin *cohors* 'yard, retinue' (see COURT). The change in the ending in the 16th cent. was due to association with words ending in **-EOUS**.

courtesan /ˌkɔːtɪˈzan, ˈkɔːtɪ-/ ▶ noun chiefly literary a prostitute, especially one with wealthy or upper-class clients.
– ORIGIN mid 16th cent.: from French *courtisane*, from obsolete Italian *cortigiana*, feminine of *cortigiano* 'courtier', from *corte* (see COURT).

courtesy /ˈkəːtɪsi/ ▶ noun (pl. **courtesies**) 1 [mass noun] the showing of politeness in one's attitude and behaviour towards others: *he treated the players with courtesy and good humour.* ■ [as modifier] (especially of transport) supplied free of charge to people who are already paying for another service: *a courtesy car.*
2 archaic a curtsy.
– PHRASES **by courtesy** as a favour rather than by right. **(by) courtesy of** given or allowed by: *photograph courtesy of the Evening Star.* ■ informal as a

result of: *he booked his place in the final courtesy of a remarkable victory*.
– ORIGIN Middle English: from Old French *cortesie*, from *corteis* (see COURTEOUS).

courtesy light ▶ noun a small light in a car that is automatically switched on when one of the doors is opened.

courtesy title ▶ noun a title given to someone, especially the son or daughter of a peer, that has no legal validity.

courthouse ▶ noun **1** a building in which a judicial court is held.
2 US a building containing the administrative offices of a county.

courtier /'kɔːtɪə/ ▶ noun a person who attends a royal court as a companion or adviser to the king or queen.
– ORIGIN Middle English: via Anglo-Norman French from Old French *cortoyer* 'be present at court', from *cort* (see COURT).

court leet ▶ noun (pl. **courts leet**) see LEET[1].

courtly ▶ adjective (**courtlier**, **courtliest**) very polite or refined, as befitting a royal court: *he gave a courtly bow*.
– DERIVATIVES **courtliness** noun.

courtly love ▶ noun [mass noun] a highly conventionalized medieval tradition of love between a knight and a married noblewoman, first developed by the troubadours of southern France and extensively employed in European literature of the time. The love of the knight for his lady was regarded as an ennobling passion and the relationship was typically unconsummated.

court martial ▶ noun (pl. **courts martial** or **court martials**) a judicial court for trying members of the armed services accused of offences against military law.
▶ verb (**court-martial**) (**court-martials**, **court-martialling**, **court-martialled**; US **court-martials**, **court-martialing**, **court-martialed**) [with obj.] try (someone) by a court martial: *they were court-martialled and imprisoned*.

Court of Appeal ▶ noun (in England and Wales) a court of law that hears appeals against both civil and criminal judgements from the Crown Courts, High Court, and County Courts. ■ (**court of appeals**) US a court of law in a federal circuit or state to which appeals are taken.

Court of Claims ▶ noun US a federal court that tries claims against the government.

court of first instance ▶ noun a court in which legal proceedings are begun or first heard.

court of inquiry ▶ noun a tribunal appointed to investigate a matter and decide whether a court martial is warranted.

court of law ▶ noun see COURT (sense 1 of the noun).

Court of Protection an English court with jurisdiction over the affairs of people who are mentally ill or disabled, created in 2005.

court of record ▶ noun a court whose proceedings are recorded and available as evidence of fact.

court of review ▶ noun a court before which sentences previously imposed come for revision.

Court of St James's the British sovereign's court.

Court of Session the supreme civil court in Scotland.

court of summary jurisdiction ▶ noun Brit. a court, especially a magistrate's court, that tries summary offences without a jury.

court order ▶ noun a direction issued by a court or a judge requiring a person to do or not do something.

court plaster ▶ noun [mass noun] historical sticking plaster made of silk or other cloth with an adhesive such as isinglass.
– ORIGIN late 18th cent.: so named because it was formerly used by ladies at court for beauty spots.

Courtrai /kuʀtʀɛ/ French name for **KORTRIJK**.

court record ▶ noun see RECORD (sense 1 of the noun).

court roll ▶ noun Brit. historical the record kept by a manorial court of rent paid and property held by tenants.

courtroom ▶ noun the place or room in which a court of law meets.

courtship ▶ noun a period during which a couple develop a romantic relationship before getting married. ■ [mass noun] behaviour designed to persuade someone to marry or develop a romantic relationship with one. ■ [mass noun] the behaviour of male birds and other animals aimed at attracting a mate. ■ [mass noun] the action of attempting to win a person's favour or support: *the country's courtship of foreign investors*.

court shoe ▶ noun Brit. a woman's plain, lightweight shoe that has a low-cut upper, no fastening, and typically a medium heel.

court tennis ▶ noun North American term for REAL TENNIS.

courtyard ▶ noun an unroofed area that is completely or partially enclosed by walls or buildings, typically one forming part of a castle or large house.

couscous /'kʊskʊs, 'kuːskuːs/ ▶ noun [mass noun] a type of North African semolina in granules made from crushed durum wheat. ■ a spicy dish made by steaming or soaking couscous and adding meat, vegetables, or fruit.
– ORIGIN early 17th cent.: from French, from Arabic *kuskus*, from *kaskasa* 'to pound', probably of Berber origin.

cousin ▶ noun (also **first cousin**) a child of one's uncle or aunt. ■ a person belonging to the same extended family. ■ a thing related or analogous to another: *the new motorbikes are not proving as popular as their four-wheeled cousins*. ■ (usu. **cousins**) a person of a kindred race or nation: *our American cousins*. ■ historical a title formerly used by a sovereign in addressing another sovereign or a noble of their own country.
– PHRASES **first cousin once removed 1** a child of one's first cousin. **2** one's parent's first cousin. **first cousin twice removed 1** a grandchild of one's first cousin. **2** one's grandparent's first cousin. **second cousin** a child of one's parent's first cousin. **second cousin once removed 1** a child of one's second cousin. **2** one's parent's second cousin. **third cousin** a child of one's parent's second cousin.
– DERIVATIVES **cousinhood** noun, **cousinly** adjective, **cousinship** noun.
– ORIGIN Middle English: from Old French *cosin*, from Latin *consobrinus* 'mother's sister's child', from *con-* 'with' + *sobrinus* 'second cousin' (from *soror* 'sister').

cousin-german ▶ noun (pl. **cousins-german**) old-fashioned term for COUSIN.
– ORIGIN Middle English: from French *cousin germain* (see COUSIN, GERMAN).

Cousteau /'kuːstəʊ/, French /kusto/, Jacques-Yves (1910–97), French oceanographer and film director. He devised the scuba apparatus, but is known primarily for several feature films and popular television series on marine life.

couth /kuːθ/ humorous ▶ adjective cultured, refined, and well mannered: *it is more couth to hold your shrimp genteelly by the tail when eating*.
▶ noun [mass noun] good manners; refinement: *he has no couth, no brains and doesn't know the meaning of the word diplomacy*.
– ORIGIN late 19th cent.: back-formation from UNCOUTH.

couthy /'kuːθi/ (also **couthie**) ▶ adjective Scottish (of a person) warm and friendly. ■ (of a place) cosy and comfortable: *a couthy wee tavern*.
– ORIGIN early 18th cent.: apparently from Old English *cūth* 'known' + -Y[1] (also -IE).

couture /kuː'tjʊə/ ▶ noun [mass noun] the design and manufacture of fashionable clothes to a client's specific requirements and measurements. ■ fashionable made-to-measure clothes: *they were dressed in size eight printed-silk couture*.
– ORIGIN 1920s: French, 'sewing, dressmaking'.

couturier /kuː'tjʊərɪeɪ/ ▶ noun a fashion designer who manufactures and sells clothes that have been tailored to a client's specific requirements and measurements.
– ORIGIN late 19th cent.: French, from COUTURE.

couturière /kuː'tjʊərɪɛː/ ▶ noun a female couturier.

couvade /kuː'vɑːd/ ▶ noun [mass noun] the custom in some cultures in which a man takes to his bed and goes through certain rituals when his child is being born, as though he were physically affected by the birth.
– ORIGIN mid 19th cent.: French, from *couver* 'to hatch', from Latin *cubare* 'lie down'. The adoption of the term in French was due to a misunderstanding of the phrase *faire la couvade* 'sit doing nothing', used by earlier writers.

couvert /kuː'vɛː/ ▶ noun another term for COVER (sense 5 of the noun).
– ORIGIN mid 18th cent.: French, past participle (used as a noun) of *couvrir* 'to cover'.

couverture /'kuːvətjʊə/ ▶ noun [mass noun] chocolate made with extra cocoa butter to give a high gloss, used for covering sweets and cakes.
– ORIGIN 1930s: French, literally 'covering', from *couvrir* 'to cover'.

covalent /kəʊ'veɪl(ə)nt/ ▶ adjective Chemistry relating to or denoting chemical bonds formed by the sharing of electrons between atoms. Often contrasted with IONIC.
– DERIVATIVES **covalence** noun, **covalency** noun, **covalently** adverb.

covariance /kəʊ'vɛːrɪəns/ ▶ noun **1** [mass noun] Mathematics the property of a function of retaining its form when the variables are linearly transformed.
2 Statistics the mean value of the product of the deviations of two variates from their respective means.

covariant Mathematics ▶ noun a function of the coefficients and variables of a given function which is invariant under a linear transformation except for a factor equal to a power of the determinant of the transformation.
▶ adjective changing in such a way that mathematical interrelations with another simultaneously changing quantity or set of quantities remain unchanged.

covariation ▶ noun [mass noun] Mathematics correlated variation.

cove[1] ▶ noun **1** a small sheltered bay. ■ dialect a sheltered recess among hills or in the side of a mountain.
2 Architecture a concave arch or arched moulding, especially one formed at the junction of a wall with a ceiling.
▶ verb [with obj.] (usu. as adj. **coved**) Architecture provide (a room, ceiling, etc.) with a cove.
– ORIGIN Old English *cofa* 'chamber, cave', of Germanic origin; related to German *Koben* 'pigsty, pen'. Sense 1 of the noun dates from the late 16th cent.

cove[2] ▶ noun Brit. informal, dated a man: *he is a perfectly amiable cove*.
– ORIGIN mid 16th cent.: perhaps from Romany *kova* 'thing or person'.

covelline /kəʊ'vɛlʌɪn/ ▶ noun another term for COVELLITE.

covellite /kəʊ'vɛlʌɪt/ ▶ noun [mass noun] a blue mineral consisting of copper sulphide, typically occurring as a coating on other copper minerals.
– ORIGIN mid 19th cent.: named after Nicolò *Covelli* (1790–1829), Italian chemist, + -ITE[1].

coven /'kʌv(ə)n/ ▶ noun a group or meeting of witches. ■ often derogatory a secret or close-knit group of associates: *covens of militants within the party*.
– ORIGIN mid 17th cent.: variant of COVIN.

covenant /'kʌv(ə)nənt/ ▶ noun an agreement. ■ Law a formal agreement, contract, or promise in writing, especially one undertaking to make regular payments to a charity. ■ Law a clause in a contract drawn up by deed. ■ Theology an agreement which brings about a relationship of commitment between God and his people. The Jewish faith is based on the biblical covenants made with Abraham, Moses, and David.
▶ verb [no obj.] agree by lease, deed, or other legal contract: [with infinitive] *the landlord covenants to repair the property*. ■ [with obj.] Brit. undertake to give (a sum of money) regularly to charity by means of a covenant.
– PHRASES **Old Covenant** Christian Theology the covenant between God and Israel in the Old Testament. **New Covenant** Christian Theology the covenant between God and the followers of Christ.
– DERIVATIVES **covenantal** adjective, **covenantor** noun.
– ORIGIN Middle English: from Old French, present participle of *covenir* 'agree', from Latin *convenire* (see CONVENE).

Covenanter /'kʌv(ə)nəntə/ ▶ noun (in 17th-century Scotland) an adherent of the National Covenant (1638) or of the Solemn League and Covenant (1643), upholding the organization of the Scottish Presbyterian Church.

covenant of grace ▶ noun (in Reformation theology) the covenant between God and humanity which was established by Christ at the Atonement.

Covent Garden a district in central London, originally the convent garden of the Abbey of Westminster. It was the site for 300 years of London's chief fruit and vegetable market, which in 1974 was moved to Nine Elms, Battersea. The first Covent Garden Theatre was opened in 1732; since 1946 it has been the home of the national opera and ballet companies, based at the Royal Opera House (built 1888).

C

Coventry /ˈkɒv(ə)ntri, ˈkʌv-/ an industrial city in the west Midlands of England; pop. 271,100 (est. 2009).
– PHRASES **send someone to Coventry** chiefly Brit. refuse to associate with or speak to someone. [mid 18th cent.: sometimes said to stem from the extreme unpopularity of soldiers stationed in *Coventry*, who were cut off socially by the citizens, or because Royalist prisoners were sent there during the English Civil War, the city being staunchly Parliamentarian.]

cover ▶ **verb 1** put something on top of or in front of (something) in order to protect or conceal it: *the table had been **covered with** a checked tablecloth* | *her husband had **covered up** his bald patch.* ■ envelop in a layer of something, especially dirt: *he was covered in mud* | figurative *she was covered in confusion.* ■ scatter a layer of loose material over (a floor or other surface), leaving it obscured: *the barn floor was covered in straw.* ■ lie over or adhere to (a surface), as decoration or to conceal something: *masonry paint will cover hairline cracks.*
2 extend over (an area): *the grounds covered eight acres.* ■ travel (a specified distance): *it took them four days to cover 150 miles.*
3 deal with (a subject) by describing or analysing its most important aspects or events: *a sequence of novels that will cover the period from 1968 to the present.* ■ investigate, report on, or show pictures of (an event): *Channel 4 are covering the match.* ■ have responsibility for or provide services to (a particular area): *development officers whose work would cover a large area.* ■ (of a rule or law) apply to (a person or situation).
4 (of a sum of money) be enough to pay (a cost): *there are grants to cover the cost of materials for loft insulation.* ■ (of insurance) protect against a liability, loss, or accident involving financial consequences: *your contents are now **covered against** accidental loss or damage in transit.* ■ (**cover oneself**) take precautionary measures so as to protect oneself against future blame or liability: *one reason doctors take temperatures is to **cover** themselves **against** negligence claims.*
5 disguise the sound or fact of (something) with another sound or action: *Louise laughed to cover her embarrassment.* ■ [no obj.] (**cover for**) disguise the illicit absence or wrongdoing of (someone) in order to spare them punishment: *if the sergeant wants to know where you are, I'll cover for you.* ■ [no obj.] (**cover for**) temporarily take over the job of (a colleague) in their absence.
6 aim a gun at (someone) in order to prevent them from moving or escaping. ■ protect (an exposed person) by shooting at an enemy: (as adj. **covering**) *we retreated behind spurts of **covering** fire.* ■ (of a fortress, gun, or cannon) have (an area) within range. ■ chiefly Cricket stand behind (another player) to stop any missed balls. ■ (in team games) take up a position ready to defend against (an opposing player). ■ Baseball be in position at (a base) ready to catch the ball.
7 record or perform a new version of (a song) originally performed by someone else: *other artists who have covered the song include U2.*
8 (of a male animal, especially a stallion) copulate with (a female animal).
9 Bridge play a higher card on (a high card) in a trick.
▶ **noun 1** a thing which lies on, over, or around something, especially in order to protect or conceal it: *a seat cover* | *a duvet cover.* ■ a thin solid object that seals a container or hole; a lid: *a manhole cover.* ■ a thick protective outer part or page of a book or magazine: *the year that Crime and Punishment appeared in hard covers.* ■ (**the covers**) bedclothes: *she burrowed down beneath the covers.*
2 [mass noun] shelter or protection sought by people in danger: *the sirens wailed and we ran for cover.* ■ undergrowth or trees used as a shelter by animals: *the standing crops of game cover.* See also COVERT (sense 1 of the noun). ■ military support given when someone is being attacked: *they agreed to provide additional naval cover.* ■ an activity or organization used as a means of concealing an illegal or secret activity: *the restaurant was run as a **cover for** a money-laundering operation.* ■ [in sing.] an identity adopted by a spy to conceal their true activities: *he was worried that their cover was blown.*
3 [mass noun] Brit. protection by insurance against a liability, loss, or accident: *your policy provides **cover against** damage by subsidence.*
4 (also **cover version**) a recording or performance of a song previously recorded by a different artist.
5 a place setting at a table in a restaurant. [rendering French *couvert*.]
6 Cricket short for COVER POINT. ■ (**the covers**) an area of the field consisting of cover point and extra cover.
7 Ecology the amount of ground covered by a vertical projection of the vegetation, usually expressed as a percentage.
– PHRASES **break cover** suddenly leave a place of shelter, especially vegetation, when being hunted or pursued. **cover all the bases** informal deal with something thoroughly: *we thought our legal department had covered all the bases in our terms and conditions.* **cover one's back** (or N. Amer. **ass**) informal foresee and avoid the possibility of attack or criticism. **cover oneself in** (or **with**) **glory** [often negative] perform very well: *we didn't exactly cover ourselves in glory with our batting.* **cover one's position** purchase securities in order to be able to fulfil a commitment to sell. **cover one's tracks** conceal evidence of one's activities. **cover the waterfront** N. Amer. informal cover every aspect of something: *while half the dishes are Italian, the kitchen covers the waterfront from Greece to Morocco.* **from cover to cover** from beginning to end of a book or magazine. **take cover** protect oneself from attack by ducking down into or under a shelter: *if the bombing starts, take cover in the basement.* **under cover** under a roof or other shelter. **under cover of** concealed by: *the yacht made landfall under cover of darkness.* ■ while pretending to do: *Moran watched every move under cover of reading the newspaper.* **under plain cover** in an envelope or parcel without any marks to identify the sender. **under separate cover** in a separate envelope.
– PHRASAL VERBS **cover something up** try to hide the fact of illegal or illicit activity: *the prime minister was accused of trying to cover up the scandal.*
– DERIVATIVES **coverable** adjective.
– ORIGIN Middle English: from Old French *covrir*, from Latin *cooperire*, from *co-* (expressing intensive force) + *operire* 'to cover'. The noun is partly a variant of COVERT.

coverage ▶ **noun** [mass noun] **1** the extent to which something deals with something else: *the grammar did not offer total coverage of the language.* ■ the treatment of an issue by the media: *the programme won an award for its news coverage.* ■ the area reached by a broadcasting station or advertising medium: *a network of eighty transmitters would give nationwide coverage.*
2 the area that can be covered by a specified volume or weight of a substance: *coverage is 6.5 square metres per litre.*
3 US the amount of protection given by an insurance policy.
4 American Football the manner in which a defender or a defensive team cover a player, an area, or a play.

coverall ▶ **noun** (usu. **coveralls**) N. Amer. overalls.

cover charge ▶ **noun** a flat fee paid for admission to a restaurant, bar, club, etc.

cover crop ▶ **noun** a crop grown for the protection and enrichment of the soil.

Coverdale /ˈkʌvədeɪl/, Miles (1488–1568), English biblical scholar. He translated the first complete printed English Bible (1535), published in Zurich while he was in exile for preaching against confession and images. He also edited the Great Bible of 1539.

cover drive ▶ **noun** Cricket a drive past cover point.

cover girl ▶ **noun** a female model whose picture appears on magazine covers.

cover glass ▶ **noun** another term for COVERSLIP.

covering ▶ **noun** a thing used to protect, decorate, or conceal something else: *a vinyl floor covering.* ■ [usu. in sing.] a layer of something that covers something else: *the sky was obscured by a covering of cloud.*

covering letter (also **covering note**, N. Amer. **cover letter**) ▶ **noun** Brit. a letter sent with, and explaining the contents of, another document or a parcel of goods.

coverlet ▶ **noun** a bedspread.
– ORIGIN Middle English: from Anglo-Norman French *covrelet*, from Old French *covrir* 'to cover' + *lit* 'bed'.

cover note ▶ **noun** Brit. a temporary certificate showing that a person has a current insurance policy.

cover point ▶ **noun** Cricket a fielding position a little in front of the batsman on the off side and halfway to the boundary. ■ a fielder at this position.

coverslip ▶ **noun** a small, thin piece of glass used to cover and protect a specimen on a microscope slide.

cover story ▶ **noun 1** a magazine article that is illustrated or advertised on the front cover.
2 a fictitious account invented to conceal a person's identity or reasons for doing something.

covert ▶ **adjective** /ˈkʌvət, ˈkəʊvəːt/ not openly acknowledged or displayed: *covert operations against the dictatorship.*
▶ **noun** /ˈkʌvət, ˈkʌvə/ **1** a thicket in which game can hide.
2 Ornithology a feather covering the base of a main flight or tail feather of a bird.
– DERIVATIVES **covertly** adverb, **covertness** noun.
– ORIGIN Middle English (in the general senses 'covered' and 'a cover'): from Old French, 'covered', past participle of *covrir* (see COVER).

covert coat ▶ **noun** Brit. a short, light overcoat designed to be worn for outdoor sports such as shooting and riding.

coverture /ˈkʌvətjʊə/ ▶ **noun 1** [mass noun] literary protective or concealing covering.
2 Law, historical the legal status of a married woman, considered to be under her husband's protection and authority.
– ORIGIN Middle English (originally denoting a coverlet or garment): from Old French, from *covrir* 'to cover'.

cover-up ▶ **noun 1** an attempt to prevent people discovering the truth about a serious mistake or crime.
2 a loose outer garment, as worn over a swimsuit or exercise outfit.

cover version ▶ **noun** see COVER (sense 4 of the noun).

covet /ˈkʌvɪt/ ▶ **verb** (**covets, coveting, coveted**) [with obj.] yearn to possess (something, especially something belonging to another): *I covet one of their smart bags* | (as adj. **coveted**) *I gave up a coveted job, that of editor-in-chief.*
– DERIVATIVES **covetable** adjective.
– ORIGIN Middle English: from Old French *cuveitier*, based on Latin *cupiditas* (see CUPIDITY).

covetous ▶ **adjective** having or showing a great desire to possess something belonging to someone else: *she fingered the linen with covetous hands.*
– DERIVATIVES **covetously** adverb, **covetousness** noun.
– ORIGIN Middle English: from Old French *coveitous*, based on Latin *cupiditas* (see CUPIDITY).

covey /ˈkʌvi/ ▶ **noun** (pl. **coveys**) a small flock of birds, especially partridge. ■ a small group of people or things: *coveys of actors rushed through the rooms.*
– ORIGIN Middle English: from Old French *covee*, feminine past participle of *cover*, from Latin *cubare* 'lie down'.

covin /ˈkʌvɪn/ (also **covine**) ▶ **noun** [mass noun] archaic fraud; deception.
– ORIGIN Middle English (denoting a company or band): from Old French, from medieval Latin *convenium*, from Latin *convenire* (see CONVENE). Compare with COVEN.

coving ▶ **noun** another term for COVE[1] (sense 2 of the noun).

cow[1] ▶ **noun 1** a fully grown female animal of a domesticated breed of ox, kept to produce milk or beef: *a dairy cow.* ■ (loosely) a domestic bovine animal, regardless of sex or age. ■ (in farming) a female domestic bovine animal which has borne more than one calf. Compare with HEIFER. ■ the female of certain other large animals, for example elephant, rhinoceros, whale, or seal.
2 informal an unpleasant or disliked woman. ■ Austral./NZ an unpleasant person or thing.
– PHRASES **have a cow** N. Amer. informal become angry, excited, or agitated: *don't have a cow—it's no big deal.* **till the cows come home** informal for an indefinitely long time: *those two could talk till the cows came home.*
– ORIGIN Old English *cū*, of Germanic origin; related to Dutch *koe* and German *Kuh*, from an Indo-European root shared by Latin *bos* and Greek *bous*.

cow[2] ▶ **verb** [with obj.] cause (someone) to submit to one's wishes by intimidation: *the intellectuals had been **cowed into** silence.*
– ORIGIN late 16th cent.: probably from Old Norse *kúga* 'oppress'.

cowabunga /ˌkaʊəˈbʌŋgə, ˌkɑːwə-/ ▶ **exclamation** informal used to express delight or satisfaction: *Cowabunga! It's an actor's dream.*
– ORIGIN 1950s: first popularized by a character on the US television programme *Howdy Doody* (1947–60). It later became associated with surfing culture and was further popularized by use on the US television cartoon programme *Teenage Mutant Ninja Turtles* (1987–96).

Coward, Sir Noël (Pierce) (1899–1973), English dramatist, actor, and composer. He is remembered for witty, satirical plays, such as *Hay Fever* (1925) and *Private Lives* (1930), as well as revues and musicals featuring songs such as 'Mad Dogs and Englishmen' (1932).

coward ▶ noun a person who is contemptibly lacking in the courage to do or endure dangerous or unpleasant things.
▶ adjective **1** literary excessively afraid of danger or pain. **2** Heraldry (of an animal) depicted with the tail between the hind legs.
– ORIGIN Middle English: from Old French *couard*, based on Latin *cauda* 'tail', possibly with reference to a frightened animal with its tail between its legs, reflected in sense 2 of the adjective (early 16th cent.).

cowardice ▶ noun [mass noun] lack of bravery.
– ORIGIN Middle English: from Old French *couardise*, from *couard* (see COWARD).

cowardly ▶ adjective lacking courage: *he was a weak, cowardly man.* ■ (of an action) carried out against a person who is unable to retaliate: *a cowardly attack on a helpless victim.*
▶ adverb archaic in a way which shows a lack of courage.
– DERIVATIVES **cowardliness** noun.

cowardy ▶ adjective (in phrase **cowardy custard**) Brit. informal a cowardly person (often used as a taunt by children).

cowbane ▶ noun any of a number of tall poisonous plants of the parsley family, growing in swampy or wet habitats. ● another term for WATER HEMLOCK ● a North American plant (*Oxypolis rigidior, family Umbelliferae).*
– ORIGIN late 18th cent.: from COW¹ + BANE, because it is poisonous to grazing cattle.

cowbell ▶ noun a bell hung round a cow's neck to indicate its whereabouts. ■ a similar bell used as a percussion instrument, typically without a clapper and struck with a stick.

cowberry ▶ noun (pl. **cowberries**) a low-growing evergreen dwarf shrub of the heather family, which bears dark red berries and grows in northern upland habitats. See also LINGONBERRY. ● *Vaccinium vitis-idaea*, family Ericaceae.
■ the edible acid berry of the cowberry plant.

cowbird ▶ noun a New World songbird with dark plumage and a relatively short bill, typically laying its eggs in other birds' nests. ● Genus *Molothrus* (and *Scaphidura*), family Icteridae: several species, in particular the widespread **brown-headed** (or **common**) **cowbird** (*M. ater*).

cowboy ▶ noun **1** (especially in the western US) a man who herds and tends cattle, performing much of his work on horseback.
2 Brit. informal a dishonest or careless person in business, especially an unqualified one.
▶ verb [no obj.] N. Amer. informal work as a cowboy.

cowboy boot ▶ noun a high-heeled boot of a style originally worn by cowboys, typically with a pointed toe and decorative stitching.

cow camp ▶ noun N. Amer. a seasonal camp apart from the main buildings of a ranch, used during a cattle round-up.

cowcatcher ▶ noun N. Amer. a metal frame at the front of a locomotive for pushing aside cattle or other obstacles on the line.

cow chip ▶ noun N. Amer. a dried cowpat.

cow cocky ▶ noun (pl. **cow cockies**) Austral./NZ informal a small dairy farmer.
– ORIGIN from COW¹ + COCKY².

Cowen /ˈkaʊən/, Brian (b.1960), Irish Fianna Fáil statesman, Taoiseach (Prime Minister) since 2008.

cower ▶ verb [no obj.] crouch down in fear: *children cowered in terror as the shoot-out erupted.*
– ORIGIN Middle English: from Middle Low German *kūren* 'lie in wait', of unknown ultimate origin.

Cowes /kaʊz/ a town on the Isle of Wight, southern England; pop. 19,900 (est. 2009). It is internationally famous as a yachting centre.

cowfish ▶ noun (pl. **same** or **cowfishes**) **1** a boxfish with horn-like spines on the head. ● Several genera and species in the family Ostraciontidae, in particular *Lactoria diaphana*.
2 a marine mammal, especially a manatee.

cow flop (also **cow flap**) ▶ noun informal, chiefly N. Amer. a cowpat.

cowgirl ▶ noun a woman who herds and tends cattle; a female cowboy.

cowherd ▶ noun a person who tends grazing cattle.
– ORIGIN Old English, from COW¹ + obsolete *herd* 'herdsman'.

cowhide ▶ noun a cow's hide. ■ [mass noun] leather made from the hide of a cow. ■ a whip made from cowhide.

cow-house ▶ noun Brit. a shed or shelter for cows.

Cowichan sweater /ˈkaʊɪtʃən/ ▶ noun (in Canada) a thick sweater made with unbleached wool and decorated with symbols taken from the mythology of the Cowichan Indians of southern Vancouver Island.

cowl ▶ noun **1** a large loose hood, especially one forming part of a monk's habit. ■ a monk's hooded, sleeveless habit. ■ a cloak with wide sleeves worn by members of Benedictine orders.
2 the hood-shaped covering of a chimney or ventilation shaft.
3 another term for COWLING.
– DERIVATIVES **cowled** adjective.
– ORIGIN Old English *cugele, cūle*, from ecclesiastical Latin *cuculla*, from Latin *cucullus* 'hood of a cloak'.

cowlick ▶ noun a lock of hair hanging or projecting over a person's forehead.

cowling ▶ noun the removable cover of a vehicle or aircraft engine.

cowl neck ▶ noun a neckline on a woman's garment that hangs in draped folds.

cowman ▶ noun (pl. **cowmen**) a person who is employed to tend grazing cattle. ■ N. Amer. a cowboy.

co-worker ▶ noun a fellow worker.

cow parsley ▶ noun a European hedgerow plant of the parsley family, which has fern-like leaves and large heads of tiny white flowers, giving the appearance of lace. Also called QUEEN ANNE'S LACE. ● *Anthriscus sylvestris*, family Umbelliferae.

cow parsnip ▶ noun another term for HOGWEED.

cowpat ▶ noun Brit. a flat round deposit of cow dung.

cowpea ▶ noun a plant of the pea family native to the Old World tropics, cultivated for its edible pods and seeds. ● *Vigna unguiculata*, family Leguminosae.
■ the seed of the cowpea as food.

Cowper /ˈkuːpə/, William (1731–1800), English poet, best known for his long poem *The Task* (1785) and the comic ballad *John Gilpin* (1782). In 1779 he wrote *Olney Hymns* with the evangelical minister John Newton (1725–1807).

Cowper's gland ▶ noun Anatomy either of a pair of small glands which open into the urethra at the base of the penis and secrete a constituent of seminal fluid.
– ORIGIN mid 18th cent.: named after William *Cowper* (1666–1709), English anatomist.

cow pie ▶ noun N. Amer. a cowpat.

cowpoke ▶ noun N. Amer. informal a cowboy.

cowpox ▶ noun [mass noun] a viral disease of cows' udders which, when contracted by humans through contact, resembles mild smallpox, and was the basis of the first smallpox vaccines.

cowpuncher ▶ noun N. Amer. informal a cowboy.

cowrie /ˈkaʊ(ə)ri/ (also **cowry**) ▶ noun (pl. **cowries**) a marine mollusc which has a glossy, brightly patterned domed shell with a long, narrow opening. ● Genus *Cypraea*, family Cypraeidae, class Gastropoda: numerous species, including the small **money cowrie** (*C. moneta*).
■ the flattened yellowish shell of the money cowrie, formerly used as money in parts of Africa and the Indo-Pacific area.
– ORIGIN mid 17th cent.: from Hindi *kauṛī*.

co-write ▶ verb [with obj.] write (something) together with another person.
– DERIVATIVES **co-writer** noun.

cow shark ▶ noun a dull grey or brown shark that lives mainly in deep water, especially in the North Atlantic and Mediterranean. ● *Hexanchus griseus*, family Hexanchidae.

cowshed ▶ noun a farm building in which cattle are kept when not at pasture, or in which they are milked.

cowslip ▶ noun **1** a European primula with clusters of drooping fragrant yellow flowers in spring, growing on dry grassy banks and in pasture. ● *Primula veris*, family Primulaceae.
2 any of a number of herbaceous plants, in particular: ● North American term for MARSH MARIGOLD ● (also **Virginia cowslip**) a North American plant with blue flowers (*Mertensia virginica*, family Boraginaceae).
– ORIGIN Old English *cūslyppe*, from *cū* 'cow' + *slipa*, *slyppe* 'slime', i.e. cow slobber or dung.

cow town ▶ noun N. Amer. a town or city in a cattle-raising area of western North America. ■ a small, isolated, or unsophisticated town.

cow tree ▶ noun a tropical American tree yielding a juice which looks and tastes like cow's milk. ● Several species, in particular the Venezuelan *Brosimum utile* (family Moraceae).

cow wheat ▶ noun a yellowish-flowered plant of the figwort family, partly parasitic on the roots of other plants and found in both Eurasia and North America. ● Genus *Melampyrum*, family Scrophulariaceae: several species, including **common cow wheat** (*M. pratense*).

C

Cox (in full **Cox's orange pippin**) ▶ noun an English eating apple of a variety with a red-tinged green skin.
– ORIGIN mid 19th cent.: named after R. *Cox* (died 1845), the English amateur fruit grower who first grew it (1825).

cox ▶ noun a coxswain, especially of a racing boat.
▶ verb [with obj.] act as a coxswain for (a racing boat or crew): *the winning eight was coxed by a woman* | (as adj. **coxed**) *the coxed pairs.*
– DERIVATIVES **coxless** adjective.
– ORIGIN mid 19th cent.: abbreviation.

coxa /ˈkɒksə/ ▶ noun (pl. **coxae** /-siː/) **1** Anatomy the hip bone or hip joint.
2 Entomology the first or basal segment of the leg of an insect.
– DERIVATIVES **coxal** adjective.
– ORIGIN late 17th cent.: from Latin, 'hip'.

coxcomb /ˈkɒkskəʊm/ ▶ noun **1** archaic a vain and conceited man; a dandy.
2 variant spelling of COCKSCOMB (sense 2).
– DERIVATIVES **coxcombry** /-kəmri/ noun (pl. **coxcombries**) (sense 1).
– ORIGIN mid 16th cent. (denoting a simpleton): variant of COCKSCOMB, in the sense 'jester's cap' (resembling a cockscomb), hence 'a jester, a fool'.

coxopodite /kɒkˈsɒpədʌɪt/ ▶ noun Zoology the segment nearest the body in the leg of an arthropod, especially a crustacean.
– ORIGIN late 19th cent.: from Latin *coxa* 'hip' + Greek *pous, pod-* 'foot' + -ITE¹.

Coxsackie virus /kɒkˈsaki, kʊk-/ ▶ noun Medicine any of a group of enteroviruses which cause various respiratory, neurological, and muscular diseases in humans.
– ORIGIN 1940s: named after *Coxsackie*, New York State, where the first cases were diagnosed.

Cox's Bazar a port and resort town on the Bay of Bengal, near Chittagong, southern Bangladesh; pop. 114,700 (est. 2009).

Cox's orange pippin ▶ noun see Cox.

coxswain /ˈkɒks(ə)n/ ▶ noun the person who steers a ship's boat, racing boat, or other boat. ■ the helmsman and skipper of a lifeboat. ■ the senior petty officer in a small ship or submarine in the Royal Navy.
– ORIGIN Middle English: from obsolete *cock* (see COCKBOAT) + SWAIN. Compare with BOATSWAIN.

Coy ▶ abbreviation chiefly Military Company.

coy ▶ adjective (**coyer, coyest**) **1** (especially with reference to a woman) making a pretence of shyness or modesty which is intended to be alluring: *she treated him to a coy smile of invitation.*
2 reluctant to give details about something regarded as sensitive: *he is coy about his age.*
– DERIVATIVES **coyly** adverb.
– ORIGIN Middle English: from Old French *coi, quei*, from Latin *quietus* (see QUIET). The original sense was 'quiet, still' (especially in behaviour), later 'modestly retiring', and hence (of a woman) 'affecting to be unresponsive to advances'.

coydog ▶ noun N. Amer. a hybrid between a coyote and a dog.

coyness ▶ noun [mass noun] **1** (especially in a woman) the quality of feigning shyness or modesty in an attempt to seem alluring.
2 the quality of being reluctant to give details about something regarded as sensitive; reticence: *his coyness about his sexual orientation.*

coyote /ˈkɔɪəʊt, kɔɪˈəʊti/ ▶ noun (pl. **same** or **coyotes**) **1** a wolf-like wild dog native to North America. Also called BRUSH WOLF or PRAIRIE WOLF in North America. ● *Canis latrans*, family Canidae.
2 N. Amer. informal a person who smuggles people from Latin America across the US border, typically for a very high fee.
– ORIGIN mid 18th cent.: from Mexican Spanish, from Nahuatl *coyotl*.

Coyote State informal name for SOUTH DAKOTA.

coypu /ˈkɔɪpuː/ ▸ noun (pl. **coypus**) a large semi-aquatic beaver-like rodent, native to South America. It is kept in captivity for its fur and has become naturalized in many other areas. ● *Myocastor coypus*, the only member of the family Myocastoridae.
– ORIGIN late 18th cent.: from Araucanian.

coz[1] /kʌz/ ▸ noun archaic or N. Amer. an informal word for 'cousin', used especially as a term of address.
– ORIGIN mid 16th cent.: abbreviation.

coz[2] /kɒz, kəz/ ▸ conjunction variant spelling of COS[3].

cozen /ˈkʌz(ə)n/ ▸ verb [with obj.] literary trick or deceive: *do not think to cozen your contemporaries.* ■ obtain by deception: *he was able to cozen a profit.*
– DERIVATIVES **cozenage** noun, **cozener** noun.
– ORIGIN late 16th cent.: perhaps from obsolete Italian *cozzonare* 'to cheat', from *cozzone* 'middleman, broker', from Latin *cocio* 'dealer'.

Cozumel /ˌkəʊzəˈmɛl/ a resort island in the Caribbean, off the NE coast of the Yucatán Peninsula of Mexico.

cozy ▸ adjective US spelling of COSY.

cozzie ▸ noun (pl. **cozzies**) variant spelling of COSSIE.

CP ▸ abbreviation ■ cerebral palsy. ■ Finance commercial paper. ■ Law, historical (Rolls of the Court of) Common Pleas. ■ Communist Party. ■ (in South Africa) Conservative Party.

cp. ▸ abbreviation compare.

c.p. ▸ abbreviation candlepower.

CPA ▸ abbreviation US certified public accountant.

CPI ▸ abbreviation (in the US) consumer price index.

Cpl ▸ abbreviation Corporal.

CPO ▸ abbreviation Chief Petty Officer.

CPR ▸ abbreviation cardiopulmonary resuscitation.

CPS ▸ abbreviation (in the UK) Crown Prosecution Service.

cps (also **c.p.s.**) ▸ abbreviation ■ Computing characters per second. ■ cycles per second.

CPU ▸ abbreviation Computing central processing unit.

CPVC ▸ abbreviation chlorinated polyvinyl chloride, a plastic material used to make water pipes.

CPVE ▸ abbreviation (in the UK) Certificate of Pre-Vocational Education.

CR ▸ abbreviation ■ Community of the Resurrection. ■ Costa Rica (international vehicle registration).

Cr[1] ▸ symbol the chemical element chromium.

Cr[2] ▸ abbreviation ■ Councillor. ■ credit.

crab[1] ▸ noun **1** a crustacean, found chiefly on seashores, with a broad carapace, stalked eyes, and five pairs of legs, the first pair of which are modified as pincers. ● Many families in the order Decapoda, class Malacostraca.
■ [mass noun] the flesh of a crab as food. ■ (**the Crab**) the zodiacal sign or constellation Cancer.
2 (also **crab louse**) a louse that infests human body hair, especially in the genital region, causing extreme irritation. ● *Phthirus pubis*, family Pediculidae, order Anoplura.
■ (**crabs**) informal an infestation of crab lice.
3 a machine with pincer-like arms for lifting heavy weights.
▸ verb (**crabs, crabbing, crabbed**) **1** [no obj., with adverbial of direction] move sideways or obliquely: *he began crabbing sideways across the roof.* ■ [with obj.] steer (an aircraft or ship) slightly sideways to compensate for a crosswind or current.
2 [no obj.] fish for crabs.
– PHRASES **catch a crab** Rowing make a faulty stroke in which the oar is jammed under water or misses the water altogether.
– DERIVATIVES **crabber** noun, **crablike** adjective & adverb.
– ORIGIN Old English *crabba*, of Germanic origin; related to Dutch *krabbe*, and more distantly to Dutch *kreeft* and German *Krebs*; also to CRAB[3].

crab[2] ▸ noun short for CRAB APPLE.

crab[3] ▸ verb (**crabs, crabbing, crabbed**) informal **1** [no obj.] grumble about something petty: *on picnics, I would crab about sand in my food.*
2 [with obj.] dated act so as to spoil (something).
– ORIGIN late 16th cent. (referring to hawks, meaning 'claw or fight each other'): from Low German *krabben*; related to CRAB[1].

crab apple ▸ noun (also **crab**) **1** a small sour apple.
2 (also **crab tree** or **crab-apple tree**) the small tree that bears the crab apple. ● Genus *Malus*, family Rosaceae: several species and hybrids, in particular the wild **Eurasian crab apple** (*M. sylvestris*).
– ORIGIN late Middle English: *crab* perhaps an alteration (influenced by CRAB[1] or CRABBED) of Scots and northern English *scrab*, in the same sense, probably of Scandinavian origin.

Crabbe /krab/, George (1754–1832), English poet, best known for grimly realistic narrative poems, such as 'The Village' (1783) and 'The Borough' (1810); the latter included tales of Peter Grimes and Ellen Orford and later provided the subject matter for Benjamin Britten's opera *Peter Grimes* (1945).

crabbed ▸ adjective **1** (of handwriting) very small and difficult to decipher. ■ (of style) contorted and difficult to understand: *crabbed legal language.*
2 bad-tempered: *a crabbed, unhappy middle age.*
– DERIVATIVES **crabbedly** adverb, **crabbedness** noun.
– ORIGIN Middle English (in the sense 'perverse, wayward'): from CRAB[1], because of the crab's sideways gait and habit of snapping.

crabby ▸ adjective (**crabbier, crabbiest**) irritable.
– DERIVATIVES **crabbily** adverb, **crabbiness** noun.

crab canon ▸ noun another term for CANON CANCRIZANS.

crabeater seal ▸ noun a slender grey Antarctic seal which lives on the pack ice, feeding mainly on krill. ● *Lobodon carcinophagus*, family Phocidae.

crabgrass ▸ noun [mass noun] N. Amer. a creeping grass that can become a serious weed. ● *Digitaria* and other genera, family Gramineae: several species, in particular *D. sanguinalis* and *D. ciliaris*.

crab louse ▸ noun see CRAB[1] (sense 2 of the noun).

crabmeat ▸ noun [mass noun] the flesh of a crab as food.

Crab Nebula Astronomy an irregular patch of luminous gas in the constellation Taurus, believed to be the remnant of a supernova explosion seen by Chinese astronomers in 1054. At its centre is the first pulsar to be observed visually, and the nebula is a strong source of high-energy radiation.

crab pot ▸ noun a wicker trap for crabs.

crab spider ▸ noun a spider with long front legs, moving with a crablike sideways motion and typically lying in wait in vegetation and flowers for passing prey. ● Family Thomisidae: several genera.

crab stick ▸ noun a stick of mixed compressed fish pieces, rectangular in section, and including and flavoured with crab.

crab tree ▸ noun see CRAB APPLE (sense 2).

crabwise ▸ adverb & adjective (of movement) sideways, typically in an awkward way: [as adv.] *supermarket trolleys that only go crabwise* | [as adj.] *crabwise steps.*

crack ▸ noun **1** a line on the surface of something along which it has split without breaking apart: *a hairline crack down the middle of the glass.* ■ a narrow space between two surfaces which have broken or been moved apart: *he climbed into a crack between two rocks* | *the door opened a tiny crack.* ■ a vulnerable point; a flaw: *the company spotted a crack in their rival's defences.*
2 a sudden sharp or explosive noise: *a loud crack of thunder.* ■ a sharp audible blow: *she gave the thief a crack over the head with her rolling pin.*
3 informal a joke, typically a critical or unkind one.
4 (also **craic**) [mass noun] chiefly Irish enjoyable social activity; a good time: *he loved the crack, the laughing.* ■ [count noun] Scottish & N. English a conversation: *they are having a great crack about shooting.*
5 [in sing.] informal an attempt to achieve something: *I fancy* ***having a crack at*** *winning a fourth title.* ■ a chance to attack or compete with someone: *he wanted to* ***have a crack at*** *the enemy.*
6 (also **crack cocaine**) [mass noun] a potent hard crystalline form of cocaine broken into small pieces and inhaled or smoked.
▸ verb **1** break or cause to break without a complete separation of the parts: [no obj.] *the ice all over the bog had cracked* | [with obj.] *take care not to crack the glass.* ■ break or cause to break open or apart: [no obj., with adverbial] *a chunk of the cliff had* ***cracked off*** *in a storm* | figurative *his face cracked into a smile* | [with obj.] *she cracked an egg into the frying pan.* ■ give way or cause to give way under torture, pressure, or strain: [no obj.] *the witnesses cracked and the truth came out* | [with obj.] *no one can crack them—they believe their cover story.*
2 make or cause to make a sudden sharp or explosive sound: [no obj.] *a shot cracked across the ridge* | [with obj.] *he cracked his whip and galloped away.* ■ [no obj.] knock hard against something: *she winced as her knees cracked against metal.* ■ [with obj.] hit (someone or something) hard: *she cracked him across the forehead.* ■ [no obj.] (of a person's voice) suddenly change in pitch, especially through strain: *'I want to get away,' she said, her voice cracking.*
3 [with obj.] informal find a solution to; decipher or interpret: *the code will help you crack the messages.* ■ break into (a safe).
4 [with obj.] tell (a joke).
5 [with obj.] decompose (hydrocarbons) by heat and pressure with or without a catalyst to produce lighter hydrocarbons, especially in oil refining.
▸ adjective [attrib.] very good or skilful: *he is a crack shot* | *crack troops.*
– PHRASES **crack a book** N. Amer. informal open a book and read it; study. **crack (open) a bottle** open a bottle, especially of wine, and drink from it. **crack a crib** archaic, informal break into a house. **crack of dawn** a time very early in the morning; daybreak. **crack of doom** a peal of thunder announcing the Day of Judgement. **crack of the whip** Brit. informal a chance to try or participate in something: *individuals who feel that they have not had a fair crack of the whip.* **be cracked up to be** [with negative] informal be asserted to be (used to indicate that someone or something has been described too favourably): *life on tour is not as glamorous as it's cracked up to be.* **crack wise** N. Amer. informal make jokes. **get cracking** informal act quickly and decisively: *most tickets have been snapped up, so get cracking if you want one.* **slip** (or **fall**) **through the cracks** another way of saying SLIP THROUGH THE NET (see NET[1]).
– PHRASAL VERBS **crack down on** informal take severe measures against: *the police will crack down on criminals.* **crack on** Brit. informal proceed or progress quickly: *we'll* ***crack on with*** *the rest of the job this month.* **crack on to** Austral. informal seek to form a sexual relationship with (someone). **crack up 1** informal suffer an emotional breakdown under pressure: *I feel I'm cracking up, always on the verge of tears.* **2** informal burst into laughter: *she tries to keep a straight face, but she keeps cracking up.*
– DERIVATIVES **cracky** adjective.
– ORIGIN Old English *cracian* 'make an explosive noise'; of Germanic origin; related to Dutch *kraken* and German *krachen*. Sense 4 of the noun is from Irish *craic* 'entertaining conversation'.

crackbrained ▸ adjective informal extremely foolish; crazy: *a crackbrained idea.*

crackdown ▸ noun [usu. in sing.] a series of severe measures to restrict undesirable or illegal people or behaviour: *a crackdown on car crime.*

cracked ▸ adjective **1** damaged and showing lines on the surface from having split without coming apart: *the old pipes were cracked and leaking.* ■ (of a person's voice) having an unusual harshness or pitch, especially through strain.
2 [predic.] informal crazy; insane: *you must think my family are cracked.*

cracked wheat ▸ noun [mass noun] grains of wheat that have been crushed into small pieces.

cracker ▸ noun **1** a person or thing that cracks. ■ an installation for cracking hydrocarbons. ■ a person who breaks into a computer system, typically for an illegal purpose.
2 a decorated paper cylinder which, when pulled apart, makes a sharp noise and releases a small toy or other novelty: *a Christmas cracker.* ■ a firework that explodes with a sharp noise.
3 a thin dry biscuit, typically eaten with cheese. ■ a light crisp made of rice or tapioca flour: *prawn crackers.*
4 Brit. informal a fine example of something: *don't miss this cracker of a CD.* ■ an attractive person, especially a woman.
5 US offensive another term for POOR WHITE.

cracker-barrel ▸ adjective [attrib.] N. Amer. (of an outlook or point of view) plain, simple, and unsophisticated: *his cracker-barrel philosophy.*
– ORIGIN late 19th cent.: with reference to the barrels of soda crackers once found in country stores, around which informal discussions would take place between customers.

crackerjack N. Amer. informal ▸ adjective exceptionally good: *a crackerjack eye surgeon.*
▸ noun an exceptionally good person or thing.

crackers ▸ adjective [predic.] Brit. informal insane: *if Luke wasn't here I'd go crackers.* ■ extremely angry: *when he saw the mess he went crackers.*

crackhead ▸ noun informal a person who habitually takes or is addicted to crack cocaine.

crack house ▶ noun informal a place where crack cocaine is bought and sold.

cracking ▶ adjective [attrib.] Brit. informal excellent: *he is in cracking form to win this race* | [as submodifier] *a cracking good story*. ■ fast and exciting: *the story rips along at a cracking pace*.

crack-jaw ▶ adjective archaic, informal (of a word) difficult to pronounce.

crackle ▶ verb [no obj.] make a rapid succession of short sharp noises: *the fire suddenly crackled and spat sparks*. ■ give a sense of great tension or animation: *attraction and antagonism were crackling between them*.
▶ noun **1** a sound made up of a rapid succession of short sharp noises: *there was a crackle and a whine from the microphone*.
2 [mass noun] a pattern of minute surface cracks on paintwork, varnish, glazed ceramics, or glass.
– DERIVATIVES **crackly** adjective (**cracklier**, **crackliest**).
– ORIGIN late Middle English: from CRACK + -LE[4].

crackling ▶ noun [mass noun] **1** (US also **cracklings**) the crisp fatty skin of roast pork.
2 Brit. informal, offensive attractive women regarded collectively as objects of sexual desire.

cracknel /ˈkrakn(ə)l/ ▶ noun **1** a light, crisp, savoury biscuit.
2 a brittle sweet made from set melted sugar, typically containing nuts.
– ORIGIN late Middle English: alteration of Old French *craquelin*, from Middle Dutch *krākelinc*, from *krāken* 'to crack'.

crackpot informal ▶ noun an eccentric or foolish person.
▶ adjective [attrib.] eccentric; impractical: *his head's full of crackpot ideas*.

cracksman ▶ noun (pl. **cracksmen**) informal, dated a burglar, especially a safe-breaker.

crack-up ▶ noun [usu. in sing.] informal **1** an emotional breakdown.
2 an act of breaking up or splitting apart.

crack willow ▶ noun a large Eurasian willow with long glossy leaves, growing typically in damp or riverside habitats. The brittle branches break off easily, often taking root and producing new growth. ● *Salix fragilis*, family Salicaceae.

Cracow /ˈkrakaʊ/ an industrial and university city in southern Poland, on the River Vistula; pop. 754,624 (2008). It was the capital of Poland from 1320 until replaced by Warsaw in 1609. Polish name **KRAKÓW**.

-cracy ▶ combining form denoting a particular form of government, rule, or influence: *autocracy* | *democracy*.
– ORIGIN from French *-cratie*, via medieval Latin from Greek *-kratia* 'power, rule'.

cradle ▶ noun **1** a baby's bed or cot, typically one mounted on rockers. ■ (**the cradle**) infancy: *the welfare state was set up to provide care **from the cradle to the grave***. ■ (**the cradle of**) a place or process in which something originates or flourishes: *the Middle East is generally held to be the cradle of agriculture*.
2 a framework resembling a cradle, in particular: ■ a framework on which a boat rests during construction or repairs. ■ Brit. a framework on which a worker is suspended to work on a ceiling, ship, or the side of a high building. ■ the part of a telephone on which the receiver rests when not in use.
▶ verb [with obj.] **1** hold gently and protectively: *she cradled his head in her arms*.
2 place (a telephone receiver) in its cradle.
– ORIGIN Old English *cradol*, of uncertain origin; perhaps related to German *Kratte* 'basket'.

cradleboard ▶ noun (among North American Indians) a board to which an infant is strapped.

cradle cap ▶ noun [mass noun] a skin condition sometimes seen in babies caused by excessive production of sebum, characterized by areas of yellowish or brownish scales on the top of the head.

cradle-snatcher ▶ noun derogatory a person who marries or has a sexual relationship with a much younger person.

cradle song ▶ noun a lullaby.

cradling ▶ noun Architecture a wooden or iron framework, typically one used as a structural support in a ceiling.

craft ▶ noun **1** an activity involving skill in making things by hand: *the craft of cobbling* | [mass noun] *art and craft*. ■ (**crafts**) work or objects made by hand: *the shop sells local crafts* | (as modifier **craft**) *a craft fair*. ■ [in sing.] the skills in carrying out one's work: *the artist learned his craft in Holland*. ■ the members of a skilled profession. ■ (**the Craft**) the brotherhood of Freemasons.
2 [mass noun] skill used in deceiving others: *her cousin was not her equal in guile and evasive craft*.
3 (pl. **same**) a boat or ship: *sailing craft*. ■ an aircraft or spaceship.
▶ verb [with obj.] exercise skill in making (something): *he crafted the chair lovingly* | (as adj., with submodifier **crafted**) *a beautifully crafted object*.
– DERIVATIVES **crafter** noun.
– ORIGIN Old English *cræft* 'strength, skill', of Germanic origin; related to Dutch *kracht*, German *Kraft*, and Swedish *kraft* 'strength'. Sense 3 of the noun, originally in the expression *small craft* 'small trading vessels', may be elliptical, referring to vessels requiring a small amount of 'craft' or skill to handle, as opposed to large ocean-going ships.

craft beer (also **craft brew**) ▶ noun US a beer with a distinctive flavour, produced and distributed in a particular region.

craft guild ▶ noun historical an association of workers of the same trade for mutual benefit.

craft knife ▶ noun Brit. another term for **UTILITY KNIFE**.

craftsman (or **craftswoman**) ▶ noun (pl. **craftsmen** or **craftswomen**) a worker skilled in a particular craft. ■ [usu. as title] (in the UK) a qualified private soldier in the Royal Electrical and Mechanical Engineers. *Craftsman Browne*.

craftsmanship ▶ noun [mass noun] skill in a particular craft: *I admire his engineering skills and craftsmanship*. ■ the quality of design and work shown in something made by hand; artistry: *a piece of fine craftsmanship*.

craftsperson ▶ noun (pl. **craftspeople**) a person who is skilled at making things by hand (used as a neutral alternative).

craft union ▶ noun a trade union of people of the same skilled craft.

craftwork ▶ noun [mass noun] the making of things by hand as a profession or leisure activity. ■ work produced in such a way.
– DERIVATIVES **craftworker** noun.

crafty ▶ adjective (**craftier**, **craftiest**) **1** clever at achieving one's aims by indirect or deceitful methods: *a crafty crook faked an injury to escape from prison*. ■ involving or relating to indirect or deceitful methods: *he sneaked off to a toilet for a crafty smoke*.
2 informal involving or relating to the making of objects by hand: *a market full of crafty pots and interesting earrings*.
– DERIVATIVES **craftily** adverb, **craftiness** noun.
– ORIGIN Old English *cræftig* 'strong, powerful', later 'skilful' (see **CRAFT**, **-Y**[1]).

crag ▶ noun **1** a steep or rugged cliff or rock face.
2 [mass noun] Geology a shelly sandstone occurring in eastern England.
– ORIGIN Middle English: of Celtic origin. Sense 2, dating from the mid 18th cent., may have been a different word originally.

crag and tail ▶ noun Geology a rocky outcrop with a tapering ridge of glacial deposits extending to one side.

craggy ▶ adjective (**craggier**, **craggiest**) (of a landscape) having many crags: *a craggy coastline*. ■ (of a cliff or rock face) rough and uneven. ■ (of a man's face) rugged and rough-textured in an attractive way.
– DERIVATIVES **craggily** adverb, **cragginess** noun.

cragsman ▶ noun (pl. **cragsmen**) a skilled rock climber.

craic ▶ noun variant spelling of **CRACK** (sense 4 of the noun).

Craiova /krəˈjəʊvə/ a city in SW Romania; pop. 300,587 (2006).

crake ▶ noun a bird of the rail family with a short bill, such as the corncrake. ● Family Rallidae: several genera, in particular *Porzana*, and numerous species.
■ the rasping cry of the corncrake.
– ORIGIN Middle English (originally denoting a crow or raven): from Old Norse *kráka*, *krákr*, of imitative origin.

cram ▶ verb (**crams**, **cramming**, **crammed**) **1** [with obj.] completely fill (a place or container) to the point of overflowing: *the ashtray by the bed was **crammed with** cigarette butts*. ■ force (people or things) into a place or container that is or appears to be too small to contain them: *it's amazing how you've managed to **cram** everyone **in*** | figurative *he had **crammed** so much into his short life*. ■ [no obj.] (of a number of people) enter a place that is too small to accommodate all of them: *they all crammed into the car*.
2 [no obj.] study intensively over a short period of time just before an examination: *lectures were called off so students could cram for the semester finals*.
– ORIGIN Old English *crammian*, of Germanic origin; related to Dutch *krammen* 'to cramp or clamp'.

crambo ▶ noun [mass noun] a game in which a player gives a word or line of verse to which each of the other players must find a rhyme.
– ORIGIN early 17th cent. (denoting a particular fashion in drinking): from earlier *crambe* 'cabbage', used figuratively to denote something distasteful that is repeated, apparently from Latin *crambe repetita* 'cabbage served up again', applied by Juvenal to any distasteful repetition.

cram-full ▶ adjective [predic.] very full; packed: *all the roads were cram-full of cars*.

crammer ▶ noun Brit. a person or institution that prepares pupils for an examination intensively over a short period of time.

cramp ▶ noun **1** [mass noun] painful involuntary contraction of a muscle or muscles, typically caused by fatigue or strain: *an attack of cramp* | [count noun] *he suffered severe cramps in his foot*. ■ (**cramps**) N. Amer. abdominal pain caused by menstruation.
2 a tool, typically shaped like a capital G, for clamping two objects together for gluing or other work.
■ (also **cramp-iron**) a metal bar with bent ends for holding masonry together.
▶ verb **1** [with obj.] inhibit the development of: *tighter rules will cramp economic growth*.
2 [with obj.] fasten with a cramp or cramps: *cramp the gates to the posts*.
3 [no obj.] suffer from sudden and painful contractions of a muscle or muscles.
– PHRASES **cramp someone's style** informal prevent a person from acting freely or naturally.
– ORIGIN late Middle English: from Middle Low German and Middle Dutch *krampe*; sense 1 of the noun is via Old French *crampe*.

cramp balls ▶ plural noun a European fungus which produces a shiny spherical black fruiting body on dead or dying wood, especially ash. Also called **KING ALFRED'S CAKES**. ● *Daldinia concentrica*, family Xylariaceae, subdivision Ascomycotina.
– ORIGIN so named because it was once believed to be a charm against cramp and ague.

cramped ▶ adjective **1** suffering from cramp.
2 uncomfortably small or restricted: *staff had to work in cramped conditions*. ■ inhibiting the development of someone or something: *he felt cramped in a large organization*. ■ (of handwriting) small and difficult to read.

crampon /ˈkrampɒn, -pən/ ▶ noun (usu. **crampons**) **1** a metal plate with spikes fixed to a boot for walking on ice or rock climbing.
2 archaic term for **GRAPPLING HOOK**.
– ORIGIN Middle English (in sense 2): from Old French, of Germanic origin.

cran ▶ noun historical a measure of fresh herrings, equivalent to 37½ gallons.
– ORIGIN late 18th cent.: from Scottish Gaelic *crann*, perhaps the same word as *crann* 'lot', denoting the share of fish given to each member of the crew.

Cranach /ˈkranək/, German /ˈkraːnax/ two German painters. **Lucas** (1472–1553, known as **Cranach the Elder**) was a member of the Danube School who was noted for his early religious pictures, such as *The Rest on the Flight into Egypt* (1504). He also painted portraits, including several of Martin Luther. His son **Lucas** (1515–86, known as **Cranach the Younger**) continued working in the same tradition as his father.

cranage /ˈkreɪnɪdʒ/ ▶ noun [mass noun] the use of a crane or cranes. ■ fees paid for using a crane or cranes.

cranberry ▶ noun (pl. **cranberries**) **1** a small red acid berry used in cooking.
2 the evergreen dwarf shrub of the heather family which yields the cranberry. ● Genus *Vaccinium*, family Ericaceae: several species.
– ORIGIN mid 17th cent. (originally North American): from German *Kranbeere* or Low German *kranebeere* 'crane-berry'.

cranberry bush ▶ noun chiefly N. Amer. a shrub of the honeysuckle family, with round clusters of white flowers followed by red berries. ● Genus *Viburnum*, family Caprifoliaceae: the **American cranberry bush**

(*V. trilobum*), with edible berries, and the guelder rose or **European cranberry bush**.

Crane[1], (Harold) Hart (1899–1932), American poet. He published only two books before committing suicide: the collection *White Buildings* (1926) and *The Bridge* (1930), a mystical epic poem concerned with American life and consciousness.

Crane[2], Stephen (1871–1900), American writer. His reputation rests on his novel *The Red Badge of Courage* (1895), a study of an inexperienced soldier in the American Civil War. It was hailed as a masterpiece of psychological realism, even though Crane himself had no personal experience of war.

crane[1] ▶ **noun** a large, tall machine used for moving heavy objects by suspending them from a projecting arm or beam. ■ a moving platform supporting a television or film camera.
▶ **verb 1** [no obj., with adverbial of direction] stretch out one's body or neck in order to see something: *she craned forward to look more clearly.* ■ [with obj.] stretch out (one's neck) so as to see something.
2 [with obj. and adverbial] move (a heavy object) with a crane: *the wheelhouse module is craned into position on the hull.*
– ORIGIN Middle English: figuratively from CRANE[2] (the same sense development occurred in the related German *Kran* and Dutch *kraan* (see CRANE[2]), and in French *grue*). The verb dates from the late 16th cent.

crane[2] ▶ **noun** a tall, long-legged, long-necked bird, typically with white or grey plumage and often with tail plumes and patches of bare red skin on the head. Cranes are noted for their elaborate courtship dances. ● Family Gruidae: four genera, in particular *Grus*, and several species, including the Eurasian **common crane** (*G. grus*).
– ORIGIN Old English, of Germanic origin; related to Dutch *kraan* and German *Kran*, from an Indo-European root shared by Latin *grus* and Greek *geranos*.

crane fly ▶ **noun** a slender two-winged fly with very long legs. The larva of some kinds is the leatherjacket. Also called DADDY-LONG-LEGS in Britain. ● Family Tipulidae: many genera and species, in particular the large and common *Tipula maxima*.

cranesbill ▶ **noun** a herbaceous plant which typically has lobed leaves and purple, violet, or pink five-petalled flowers. ● Genus *Geranium*, family Geraniaceae: several species, including the common bluish-purple flowered **meadow cranesbill** (*G. pratense*).
– ORIGIN mid 16th cent.: so named because of the long spur on the fruit, thought to resemble a crane's beak.

cranial /ˈkreɪnɪəl/ ▶ **adjective** Anatomy relating to the skull or cranium.
– ORIGIN early 19th cent.: from CRANIUM + -AL.

cranial index ▶ **noun** another term for CEPHALIC INDEX.

cranial nerve ▶ **noun** Anatomy each of twelve pairs of nerves which arise directly from the brain, not from the spinal cord, and pass through separate apertures in the skull.

> They are (with conventional Roman numbering) the olfactory (I), optic (II), oculomotor (III), trochlear (IV), trigeminal (V), abducens (VI), facial (VII), vestibulocochlear (VIII), glossopharyngeal (IX), vagus (X), accessory (XI), and hypoglossal (XII) nerves.

craniate /ˈkreɪnɪət/ Zoology ▶ **noun** an animal that possesses a skull. Compare with VERTEBRATE. ● Subphylum Craniata, phylum Chordata; used instead of Vertebrata in some classification schemes.
▶ **adjective** relating to the craniates.
– ORIGIN late 19th cent.: from modern Latin *craniatus*, from medieval Latin *cranium* (see CRANIUM).

cranio- /ˈkreɪnɪəʊ/ ▶ **combining form** relating to the cranium: *craniotomy*.
– ORIGIN from Greek *kranion* 'skull'.

craniofacial /ˌkreɪnɪə(ʊ)ˈfeɪʃ(ə)l/ ▶ **adjective** Anatomy relating to the cranium and the face: *craniofacial surgery*.

craniology /ˌkreɪnɪˈɒlədʒi/ ▶ **noun** [mass noun] historical the scientific study of the shape and size of the skulls of different human races. ■ another term for PHRENOLOGY.
– DERIVATIVES **craniological** adjective, **craniologist** noun.

craniometry /ˌkreɪnɪˈɒmɪtri/ ▶ **noun** [mass noun] historical the scientific measurement of skulls, especially in relation to craniology.
– DERIVATIVES **craniometric** adjective.

craniopagus /kreɪnɪˈɒpəgəs/ ▶ **noun** (pl. **craniopagi** /-gʌɪ/) [usu. as modifier] a pair of conjoined twins attached at the head.
– ORIGIN late 19th cent.: from CRANIO- + Greek 'that which is fixed'.

craniosacral therapy /ˌkreɪnɪəʊˈseɪkr(ə)l, -ˈsak-/ ▶ **noun** [mass noun] a system of alternative medicine intended to relieve pain and tension by gentle manipulations of the skull regarded as harmonizing with a natural rhythm in the central nervous system.

craniotomy /ˌkreɪnɪˈɒtəmi/ ▶ **noun** [mass noun] surgical removal of a portion of the skull. ■ surgical perforation of the skull of a dead fetus to ease delivery.

cranium /ˈkreɪnɪəm/ ▶ **noun** (pl. **craniums** or **crania** /-nɪə/) Anatomy the skull, especially the part enclosing the brain.
– ORIGIN late Middle English: via medieval Latin from Greek *kranion* 'skull'.

crank[1] ▶ **verb** [with obj.] **1** turn the crankshaft of (an internal-combustion engine) in order to start the engine. ■ turn (a handle) in order to start an engine. ■ (**crank something up**) informal increase the intensity of something: *the volume is cranked up a notch.* ■ (**crank something out**) informal, derogatory produce something regularly and routinely: *an army of researchers cranked out worthy studies.*
2 (usu. as adj. **cranked**) give a bend to (a shaft, bar, etc.).
3 [no obj.] informal inject a narcotic drug: *he's been cranking up on smack.*
▶ **noun 1** a part of an axle or shaft bent out at right angles, for converting reciprocal to circular motion and vice versa.
2 [mass noun] informal the drug methamphetamine.
– ORIGIN Old English *cranc* (recorded in *crancstæf*, denoting a weaver's implement), related to *crincan* (see CRINGE).

crank[2] ▶ **noun 1** an eccentric person, especially one who is obsessed by a particular subject: *when he first started to air his views, they labelled him a crank* | [as modifier] *I am used to getting crank calls from conspiracy theorists.* ■ N. Amer. a bad-tempered person. [mid 19th cent.: back-formation from CRANKY.]
2 literary a fanciful turn of speech. [late 16th cent.: perhaps from a base meaning 'bent together, curled up', shared by Old English *cranc* (see CRANK[1]).]

crank[3] ▶ **adjective** Nautical, archaic (of a sailing ship) liable to heel over.
– ORIGIN early 17th cent.: perhaps from dialect *crank* 'weak, shaky' (compare with CRANKY or CRANK[1]).

crankcase ▶ **noun** a case or covering enclosing a crankshaft.

crankpin ▶ **noun** a pin by which a connecting rod is attached to a crank.

crankshaft ▶ **noun** a shaft driven by a crank.

cranky ▶ **adjective** (**crankier**, **crankiest**) **1** Brit. informal eccentric or strange: *a cranky scheme to pipe ground-level ozone into the stratosphere.*
2 chiefly N. Amer. bad-tempered; irritable: *he was cranky after eight hours of working.*
3 (of a machine) working erratically: *after a juddering landing the cranky plane eased up the runway.*
– DERIVATIVES **crankily** adverb, **crankiness** noun.
– ORIGIN late 18th cent. (in the sense 'sickly, in poor health'): perhaps from obsolete (*counterfeit*) *crank* 'a rogue feigning sickness', from Dutch or German *krank* 'sick'.

Cranmer /ˈkranmə/, Thomas (1489–1556), English Protestant cleric and martyr. After helping to negotiate Henry VIII's divorce from Catherine of Aragon, he was appointed the first Protestant Archbishop of Canterbury in 1532. He was responsible for liturgical reform and the compilation of the Book of Common Prayer (1549). In the reign of Mary Tudor Cranmer was tried for treason and heresy and burnt at the stake.

crannog /ˈkranəg/ ▶ **noun** an ancient fortified dwelling constructed in a lake or marsh in Scotland or Ireland.
– ORIGIN early 17th cent.: from Irish *crannóg*, Scottish Gaelic *crannag* 'timber structure', from *crann* 'tree, beam'.

cranny ▶ **noun** (pl. **crannies**) a small, narrow space or opening.
– PHRASES **every nook and cranny** see NOOK.
– DERIVATIVES **crannied** adjective.
– ORIGIN late Middle English: from Old French *crane* 'notched', from *cran*, from popular Latin *crena* 'notch'.

crap[1] vulgar slang ▶ **noun** [mass noun] **1** something of extremely poor quality. ■ nonsense. ■ unwanted articles; rubbish.
2 excrement. ■ [in sing.] an act of defecation.
▶ **verb** (**craps**, **crapping**, **crapped**) [no obj.] **1** defecate.
2 (**crap on**) talk at length in a foolish or boring way.
▶ **adjective** Brit. extremely poor in quality.
– ORIGIN Middle English: related to Dutch *krappe*, from *krappen* 'pluck or cut off', and perhaps also to Old French *crappe* 'siftings', Anglo-Latin *crappa* 'chaff'. The original sense was 'chaff', later 'residue from rendering fat', also 'dregs of beer'. Current senses date from the late 19th cent.

crap[2] N. Amer. ▶ **noun** a losing throw of 2, 3, or 12 in craps.
▶ **verb** [no obj.] (**crap out**) informal make a losing throw at craps. ■ give up an activity because of fear or fatigue: *when entrepreneurs get to $1 billion they crap out and turn their companies over to others.* ■ fail in an attempt: *the Rams almost crapped out late in the game.* ■ (of a machine) break down: *his teleprompter crapped out.*
– ORIGIN early 20th cent.: from CRAPS.

crape ▶ **noun** [mass noun] **1** variant spelling of CRÊPE.
2 black silk, formerly used for mourning clothes. ■ [count noun] a band of black silk formerly worn round a person's hat as a sign of mourning.
– DERIVATIVES **crapy** adjective.
– ORIGIN early 16th cent.: from French *crêpe* (see CRÊPE).

crape fern ▶ **noun** a tall New Zealand fern with dark green fronds. ● *Leptopteris superba*, family Osmundaceae.

crape hair ▶ **noun** [mass noun] Brit. artificial hair used by actors, chiefly for false beards and moustaches.

crape myrtle (also **crepe myrtle**) ▶ **noun** an ornamental Chinese shrub or small tree with pink, white, or purplish crinkled petals. ● *Lagerstroemia indica*, family Lythraceae.

crap game ▶ **noun** N. Amer. a game of craps.

crap hat ▶ **noun** vulgar slang (in the British army) a term used by paratroopers and commandos to refer to a soldier from a regiment in the rest of the army.
– ORIGIN probably with derogatory reference to the standard khaki-coloured (now dark blue) berets, in contrast to the prized red and green berets of the special regiments.

crapola /kraˈpəʊlə/ ▶ **noun** [mass noun] N. Amer. vulgar slang nonsense; rubbish.
– ORIGIN 1920s: from CRAP[1] and *-ola*, a suffix used humorously to extend standard words.

crapper ▶ **noun** vulgar slang a toilet.

crappie ▶ **noun** (pl. **crappies**) a North American freshwater fish of the sunfish family, the male of which builds a nest and guards the eggs and young. ● Genus *Pomoxis*, family Centrarchidae: several species, including the **white crappie** (*P. annularis*).
– ORIGIN mid 19th cent.: of unknown origin.

crappy ▶ **adjective** (**crappier**, **crappiest**) vulgar slang of extremely poor quality. ■ ill; unwell: *I feel really crappy today.*

craps ▶ **plural noun** [treated as sing.] a gambling game played with two dice, chiefly in North America. A throw of 7 or 11 is a winning throw, 2, 3, or 12 is a losing throw. See also CRAP[2].
– ORIGIN early 19th cent.: perhaps from CRAB[1] or *crab's eyes*, denoting the lowest throw (two ones) at dice.

crapshoot ▶ **noun** N. Amer. a game of craps. ■ informal a risky or uncertain matter: *skiing here can be a bit of a crapshoot at any time.*
– DERIVATIVES **crapshooter** noun.

crapulent /ˈkrapjʊl(ə)nt/ ▶ **adjective** literary relating to the drinking of alcohol or drunkenness.
– DERIVATIVES **crapulence** noun, **crapulous** adjective.
– ORIGIN mid 17th cent.: from late Latin *crapulentus* 'very drunk', from Latin *crapula* 'inebriation', from Greek *kraipalē* 'drunken headache'.

craquelure /ˈkrakljʊə, krakˈljʊə/ ▶ **noun** [mass noun] a network of fine cracks in the paint or varnish of a painting.
– ORIGIN early 20th cent.: French, from *craqueler* 'to crackle'.

crash[1] ▶ **verb 1** [no obj.] (of a vehicle) collide violently with an obstacle or another vehicle: *a racing car had crashed, wrecking a safety barrier* | *the stolen car she was riding in crashed into a tree.* ■ [with obj.] cause (a vehicle) to collide violently with something. ■ (of an aircraft) fall from the sky and hit the land or sea: *a jet crashed 200 yards from the school.* ■ [with obj.] cause (an aircraft) to fall from the sky.
2 move or cause to move with force, speed, and sudden loud noise: [no obj., with adverbial of direction] *huge waves crashed down on to us* | [with obj. and adverbial of direction] *she crashed down the telephone receiver.* ■ [no obj.] make a sudden loud noise: *the thunder crashed.*

3 [no obj.] informal (of shares, a business, etc.) suddenly drop in value or fail: *the shares crashed to 329p.* ■ be heavily defeated in a sporting competition: *Barcelona crashed out of the European Cup.*
4 [no obj.] (of a computer, computing system, or software) fail suddenly. ■ chiefly N. Amer. (of a patient) suffer a cardiac arrest.
5 [with obj.] informal enter (a party) without an invitation; gatecrash. ■ illegally pass (a red traffic light).
6 [no obj.] informal go to sleep, especially suddenly or in an improvised setting: *what was it you said just before I **crashed out**?*
▶ **noun 1** a violent collision, typically of one vehicle with another or with an object: *a car crash.* ■ an instance of an aircraft falling from the sky to hit the land or sea.
2 a sudden loud noise as of something breaking or hitting another object: *he slammed the phone down with a crash.*
3 a sudden disastrous drop in the value or price of something: *the 1987 stock-market crash.* ■ the sudden failure of a business.
4 a sudden failure which puts a computer system out of action.
▶ **adjective** [attrib.] done rapidly or urgently and involving a concentrated effort: *a crash course in Italian.*
▶ **adverb** with a sudden loud sound: *crash went the bolt.*
– PHRASES **crash and burn** informal come to grief or fail spectacularly.
– ORIGIN late Middle English: imitative, perhaps partly suggested by CRAZE and DASH.

crash^{2} ▶ **noun** [mass noun] dated a coarse plain linen, woollen, or cotton fabric.
– ORIGIN early 19th cent.: from Russian *krashenina* 'dyed coarse linen'.

crash barrier ▶ **noun** Brit. a strong fence at the side of a road or in the middle of a dual carriageway or motorway, intended to reduce the risk of serious accidents.

crash diet ▶ **noun** a weight-loss diet undertaken on an urgent, short-term basis with the aim of achieving very rapid results.
▶ **verb** (**crash-diet**) [no obj.] embark on a crash diet: *some climbers crash-diet for three days before major ascents.*

crash-dive ▶ **verb** [no obj.] (of a submarine) dive rapidly and steeply to a deeper level in an emergency. ■ (of an aircraft) plunge steeply downwards into a crash.
▶ **noun** (**crash dive**) a steep dive by a submarine or aircraft.

crash helmet ▶ **noun** a helmet worn by a motorcyclist to protect the head in case of a crash.

crashing ▶ **adjective** informal complete; total (used for emphasis): *a crashing bore.*
– DERIVATIVES **crashingly** adverb.

crash-land ▶ **verb** [no obj.] (of an aircraft) land roughly in an emergency, typically without lowering the undercarriage. (as noun **crash-landing**) *his plane made a crash-landing on a motorway.*

crash pad ▶ **noun 1** informal a place to sleep, especially for a single night or in an emergency.
2 a thick piece of shock-absorbing material for the protection of the occupants of an aircraft cockpit or motor vehicle.

crash team ▶ **noun** (in a hospital) a team of medical practitioners that stand by to resuscitate patients who have suffered cardiac or respiratory failure.

crash-test ▶ **verb** [with obj.] deliberately crash (a new vehicle) under controlled conditions in order to evaluate and improve its ability to withstand impact.
▶ **noun** (**crash test**) an instance of crash-testing a vehicle.

crash trolley (N. Amer. **crash cart**) ▶ **noun** (in a hospital) a trolley carrying medicine and equipment for use in emergency resuscitations.

crashworthiness ▶ **noun** [mass noun] the degree to which a vehicle will protect its occupants from the effects of an accident.
– DERIVATIVES **crashworthy** adjective.

crasis /'kreɪsɪs/ ▶ **noun** (pl. **crases** /-siːz/) Phonetics a contraction of two adjacent vowels into one long vowel or diphthong, for example the reduction of words in ancient Greek from three syllables to two.
– ORIGIN mid 16th cent. (as a medical term denoting the blending of physical qualities giving rise to a particular state of health): from Greek *krasis* 'mixture'.

crass ▶ **adjective** showing no intelligence or sensitivity: *the crass assumptions that men make about women* | *an act of crass stupidity.*
– DERIVATIVES **crassly** adverb, **crassness** noun.
– ORIGIN late 15th cent. (in the sense 'dense or coarse'): from Latin *crassus* 'solid, thick'.

Crassus /'krasəs/, Marcus Licinius (*c.*115–53 BC), Roman politician. After defeating Spartacus in 71 BC, Crassus joined Caesar and Pompey in the First Triumvirate in 60. In 55 he was made consul and given a special command in Syria, where, after some successes, he was defeated and killed.

-crat ▶ **combining form** denoting a member or supporter of a particular form of government or rule: *plutocrat* | *technocrat.*
– ORIGIN from French *-crate*, from adjectives ending in *-cratique* (see -CRATIC).

cratch ▶ **noun** dialect a long open trough or rack used for holding food for farm animals out of doors.
– ORIGIN Middle English: from Old French *creche*; ultimately of Germanic origin and related to CRIB.

crate ▶ **noun 1** a slatted wooden case used for transporting goods: *a crate of bananas.* ■ a square rigid container divided into small units, used for transporting or storing bottles: *a milk crate.*
2 informal an old and dilapidated vehicle.
▶ **verb** [with obj.] pack (something) in a crate for transportation.
– DERIVATIVES **crateful** noun (pl. **cratefuls**).
– ORIGIN late Middle English: perhaps related to Dutch *krat* 'tailboard of a wagon', earlier 'box of a coach', of unknown origin.

Crater /'kreɪtə/ Astronomy a small and faint southern constellation (the Cup), between Hydra and Leo, said to represent the goblet of Apollo.
– ORIGIN Latin, from Greek, 'mixing bowl'.

crater ▶ **noun 1** a large bowl-shaped cavity in the ground or on a celestial object, typically one caused by an explosion or the impact of a meteorite. ■ a large hollow forming the mouth of a volcano.
2 a large bowl used in ancient Greece for mixing wine.
▶ **verb** [with obj.] form a crater in (the ground or a planet): *pilots returned to the airfields to crater the runways* | (as adj. **cratered**) *the heavily cratered areas of the moon.*
– ORIGIN early 17th cent. (denoting the hollow forming the mouth of a volcano): via Latin from Greek *kratēr* 'mixing-bowl', from *krasis* 'mixture'.

Crater Lake a lake filling a volcanic crater in the Cascade mountains of SW Oregon. With a depth of more than 600 m (1,968 ft) it is the deepest lake in the US.

-cratic ▶ **combining form** relating to a particular kind of government or rule: *bureaucratic* | *democratic.*
– DERIVATIVES **-cratically** combining form in corresponding adverbs.
– ORIGIN from French *-cratique*, from *-cratie* (see -CRACY).

C rations ▶ **plural noun** N. Amer. a type of tinned food formerly used by American soldiers.
– ORIGIN C for *combat.*

craton /'kratɒn/ ▶ **noun** Geology a large stable block of the earth's crust forming the nucleus of a continent.
– DERIVATIVES **cratonic** adjective.
– ORIGIN 1930s: alteration of *kratogen* in the same sense, from Greek *kratos* 'strength'.

cratur /'kreɪtʃə/ ▶ **noun** non-standard spelling of CREATURE, used in representing Irish speech: *choked to death on her dentures, poor cratur.*

cravat ▶ **noun** a short, wide strip of fabric worn by men round the neck and tucked inside an open-necked shirt.
– DERIVATIVES **cravatted** adjective.
– ORIGIN mid 17th cent.: from French *cravate*, from *Cravate* 'Croat' (from German *Krabat*, from Serbian and Croatian *Hrvat*), because of the scarf worn by Croatian mercenaries in France.

crave ▶ **verb** [with obj.] feel a powerful desire for (something): *if only she had shown her daughter the love she craved* | [no obj.] ***Will craved for** family life.* ■ archaic ask for: *I must crave your indulgence.*
– DERIVATIVES **craver** noun.
– ORIGIN Old English *crafian* (in the sense 'demand, claim as a right'), of Germanic origin; related to Swedish *kräva*, Danish *kræve* 'demand'. The current sense dates from late Middle English.

craven ▶ **adjective** contemptibly lacking in courage; cowardly: *a craven abdication of his moral duty.*
▶ **noun** archaic a cowardly person.
– DERIVATIVES **cravenly** adverb, **cravenness** noun.
– ORIGIN Middle English *cravant* 'defeated', perhaps via Anglo-Norman French from Old French *cravante*, past participle of *cravanter* 'crush, overwhelm', based on Latin *crepare* 'burst'. The change in the ending in the 17th cent. was due to association with past participles ending in *-en* (see -EN^{3}).

craving ▶ **noun** a powerful desire for something: *a **craving for** chocolate.*

craw ▶ **noun** dated the crop of a bird or insect.
– PHRASES **stick in one's craw** see STICK^{2}.
– ORIGIN late Middle English: from or related to Middle Dutch *crāghe* or Middle Low German *krage* 'neck, throat'.

crawdad /'krɔːdad/ ▶ **noun** N. Amer. a freshwater crayfish.
– ORIGIN early 20th cent.: fanciful alteration of CRAWFISH.

crawfish ▶ **noun** (pl. **same** or **crawfishes**) another term for SPINY LOBSTER. ■ chiefly N. Amer. a freshwater crayfish.
▶ **verb** [no obj.] US informal retreat from a position.
– ORIGIN early 17th cent.: variant of CRAYFISH.

Crawford /'krɔːfəd/, Joan (1908–77), American actress; born *Lucille le Sueur*. Her film career lasted for over forty years, during which she played the female lead in films such as *Mildred Pierce* (1945) and in later years mature roles such as that in the horror film *Whatever Happened to Baby Jane?* (1962).

crawl ▶ **verb 1** [no obj., with adverbial of direction] move forward on the hands and knees or by dragging the body close to the ground: *they crawled from under the table.* ■ (of an insect or small animal) move slowly along a surface: *the tiny spider was crawling up Nicky's arm.* ■ (of a vehicle) move at an unusually slow pace: *the traffic was crawling along.* ■ technical (of paint or other liquid) move after application to form an uneven layer over the surface below.
2 [no obj.] informal behave obsequiously or ingratiatingly in the hope of gaining someone's favour: *a reporter's job can involve **crawling to** objectionable people.*
3 (**be crawling with**) be covered or crowded with (insects or people), to an extent that is objectionable: *the floor was dirty and crawling with bugs.*
▶ **noun** [in sing.] **1** an act of moving on one's hands and knees or dragging one's body along the ground: *they began the crawl back to their own lines.* ■ a slow rate of movement, typically that of a vehicle: *he reduced his speed to a crawl.*
2 a swimming stroke involving alternate overarm movements and rapid kicks of the legs.
– PHRASES **make someone's skin crawl** cause someone to feel an unpleasant sensation resembling something moving over the skin, as a symptom of fear or disgust.
– DERIVATIVES **crawlingly** adverb, **crawly** adjective.
– ORIGIN Middle English: of unknown origin; possibly related to Swedish *kravla* and Danish *kravle*.

crawler ▶ **noun 1** a thing that crawls or moves at a slow pace, especially an insect. ■ a tractor or other vehicle moving on an endless caterpillar track. ■ Computing a program that searches the Internet in order to create an index of data.
2 Brit. informal a person who behaves obsequiously in the hope of gaining favour.

crawling peg ▶ **noun** a point on a scale of exchange rates in which a currency's value is allowed to go up or down frequently by small amounts within overall limits.

crawl space ▶ **noun** an area of limited height under a floor or roof, giving access to wiring and plumbing.

cray ▶ **noun** Austral./NZ a crayfish.
– ORIGIN early 20th cent.: abbreviation.

crayfish ▶ **noun** (pl. **same** or **crayfishes**) (also **freshwater crayfish**) a nocturnal freshwater crustacean that resembles a small lobster and inhabits streams and rivers. ● Several genera in the infraorder Astacidea, class Malacostraca, including *Astacus* of Europe and *Cambarus* of North America.
■ (also **marine crayfish**) another term for SPINY LOBSTER.
– ORIGIN Middle English: from Old French *crevice*, of Germanic origin and related to German *Krebs* (see CRAB^{1}). In the 16th cent. or earlier the second syllable was altered by association with FISH^{1}.

crayon ▶ **noun** a pencil or stick of coloured chalk or wax, used for drawing.
▶ **verb** [with obj.] draw with a crayon or crayons: *Will crayoned a picture on a legal pad* | [no obj.] *a child crayoning in a colouring book.*
– ORIGIN mid 17th cent.: from French, from *craie* 'chalk', from Latin *creta*.

craze ▸ **noun** an enthusiasm for a particular activity or object which appears suddenly and achieves widespread but short-lived popularity: *the new craze for step aerobics.*
▸ **verb** [with obj.] **1** (usu. as adj. **crazed**) make (someone) wildly insane or out of control: *a crazed killer.*
2 produce a network of fine cracks on (a surface): *the loch was frozen over but crazed with cracks.* ■ [no obj.] develop fine cracks.
– ORIGIN late Middle English (in the sense 'break, produce cracks'): perhaps of Scandinavian origin and related to Swedish *krasa* 'crunch'.

crazy informal ▸ **adjective** (**crazier**, **craziest**) **1** mad, especially as manifested in wild or aggressive behaviour: *Stella **went crazy** and assaulted a visitor | a crazy look.* ■ extremely angry: *the noise was **driving me crazy**.* ■ foolish: *it was **crazy to** hope that good might come out of this mess.*
2 extremely enthusiastic: *I'm **crazy about** Cindy* | [in combination] *a football-crazy bunch of boys.*
3 (of an angle) appearing absurdly out of place or unlikely: *the monument leant at a crazy angle.* ■ archaic (of a ship or building) full of cracks or flaws; unsound.
▸ **noun** (pl. **crazies**) chiefly N. Amer. a mad person.
– PHRASES **like crazy** to a great degree; very intensely: *we are just working like crazy.* ■ in a very fast or unrestrained way: *another driver, who was driving like crazy, ran him off the road.*
– DERIVATIVES **crazily** adverb, **craziness** noun.

crazy bone ▸ **noun** US term for FUNNY BONE.

Crazy Horse (*c.*1849–77), Sioux chief; Sioux name *Ta-Sunko-Witko*. A leading figure in the resistance to white settlement on American Indian land, he was at the centre of the confederation that defeated General Custer at Little Bighorn (1876). He surrendered in 1877 and was killed in custody.

crazy paving ▸ **noun** [mass noun] Brit. paving made of irregular pieces of flat stone.

crazy quilt ▸ **noun** a patchwork quilt of a type traditionally made in North America, with patches of randomly varying sizes, shapes, colours, and fabrics. ■ a disorganized collection of things: *colonial America was a crazy quilt of laws.*

CRC ▸ **abbreviation** ■ (in printing) camera-ready copy. ■ (in computing) cyclic redundancy check or code.

creak ▸ **verb** [no obj.] **1** (of an object, typically a wooden one) make a scraping or squeaking sound when being moved or when pressure is applied: *the stairs creaked as she went up them* | [with complement] *the garden gate creaked open.*
2 show weakness or frailty under strain: *the system started to creak.*
▸ **noun** a scraping or squeaking sound.
– DERIVATIVES **creakingly** adverb.
– ORIGIN Middle English (as a verb in the sense 'croak'): imitative.

creaky ▸ **adjective** (**creakier**, **creakiest**) **1** making or liable to make a creaking sound when being moved or when pressure is applied: *I climbed the creaky stairs.* ■ (of a voice) producing a harsh, high-pitched sound.
2 old-fashioned or decrepit: *the country's creaky legal system.*
– DERIVATIVES **creakily** adverb, **creakiness** noun.

cream ▸ **noun** [mass noun] **1** the thick white or pale yellow fatty liquid which rises to the top when milk is left to stand and which can be eaten as an accompaniment to desserts or used as a cooking ingredient: *strawberries and cream* | [as modifier] *a cream cake.* ■ a sauce, soup, dessert, or other dish containing cream or having a creamy consistency: *a tin of **cream of** mushroom soup.* ■ [count noun] a sweet of a specified flavour which is creamy in texture: *a peppermint cream.* ■ [count noun] a biscuit with a creamy filling: *a custard cream.*
2 a thick liquid or semi-solid cosmetic or medical preparation applied to the skin: *shaving cream* | [count noun] *moisturizing creams.*
3 the very best of a group of people or things: *the paper's readership is **the cream of** American society.*
4 a very pale yellow or off-white colour: *the dress is available in white or cream* | [as modifier] *a cream linen jacket.*
▸ **verb** [with obj.] **1** work (butter, typically with sugar) to form a smooth paste. ■ (usu. as adj. **creamed**) mash (a cooked vegetable) with milk or cream: *creamed turnips.* ■ add cream to (coffee).
2 rub a cosmetic cream into (the skin): *Madge was creaming her face in front of the mirror.*
3 informal, chiefly N. Amer. defeat (someone) heavily in a sporting contest. ■ collide heavily with (someone), especially in a car: *she got creamed by a speeding car.*
4 [no obj.] vulgar slang (of a person) be sexually aroused to the point of producing sexual secretions.
– PHRASAL VERBS **cream something off** take the best of (a group of people or things), especially in a way that is considered unfair: *the schools cream off some of the more able pupils.* ■ make (an excessive profit) on a transaction.
– ORIGIN Middle English: from Old French *cresme*, from a blend of late Latin *cramum* (probably of Gaulish origin) and ecclesiastical Latin *chrisma* (see CHRISM).

cream bun ▸ **noun** Brit. a bun filled or topped with cream.

cream cheese ▸ **noun** [mass noun] soft, rich cheese made from unskimmed milk and cream.

cream cracker ▸ **noun** Brit. a dry unsweetened biscuit eaten chiefly with cheese.

cream-crackered ▸ **adjective** Brit. informal extremely tired.
– ORIGIN 1980s: rhyming slang for 'knackered'.

creamer ▸ **noun 1** [mass noun] a cream or milk substitute for adding to coffee or tea.
2 N. Amer. a jug for cream.
3 historical a flat dish used for skimming the cream off milk.
4 a machine used for separating cream from milk.

creamery ▸ **noun** (pl. **creameries**) a factory that produces butter and cheese. ■ dated a shop where dairy products are sold.
– ORIGIN mid 19th cent.: from CREAM, on the pattern of French *crémerie*.

cream horn ▸ **noun** a pastry shaped like a horn and filled with cream and jam.

cream of tartar ▸ **noun** [mass noun] a white crystalline acidic compound obtained as a by-product of wine fermentation and used chiefly in baking powder.
● Alternative name: **potassium hydrogen tartrate**; chem. formula: HOOC(CHOH)$_2$COOK.

cream puff ▸ **noun 1** a cake made of puff pastry filled with cream.
2 informal a weak or ineffectual person. ■ derogatory a male homosexual.
3 [as modifier] US denoting something of little consequence or difficulty: *a cream-puff assignment.*
4 N. Amer. informal a second-hand car or other item maintained in excellent condition.

cream sherry ▸ **noun** [mass noun] a full-bodied mellow sweet sherry.

cream soda ▸ **noun** [mass noun] chiefly N. Amer. a carbonated vanilla-flavoured soft drink.

cream tea ▸ **noun** Brit. a meal taken in the afternoon consisting of tea to drink with scones, jam, and cream.

creamware ▸ **noun** [mass noun] glazed earthenware pottery of a rich cream colour, developed by Josiah Wedgwood in about 1760.

creamy ▸ **adjective** (**creamier**, **creamiest**) resembling cream in consistency or colour: *beat the sugar and egg yolks together until thick and creamy | creamy white flowers.* ■ containing a lot of cream: *a thick, creamy dressing.*
– DERIVATIVES **creamily** adverb, **creaminess** noun.

creance /ˈkriːəns/ ▸ **noun** Falconry a long fine cord attached to a hawk's leash to prevent escape during training.
– ORIGIN late 15th cent.: from French *créance* 'faith', also denoting a cord to retain a bird of *peu de créance* ('of little faith' i.e. which cannot yet be relied upon).

crease ▸ **noun 1** a line or ridge produced on paper or cloth by folding, pressing, or crushing: *khaki trousers with knife-edge creases.* ■ a wrinkle or furrow in the skin, especially of the face, caused by age or a particular facial expression.
2 Cricket any of a number of lines marked on the pitch at specified places. See POPPING CREASE, BOWLING CREASE, RETURN CREASE. ■ (**the crease**) the position of a batsman during their innings: *England were 15 for 3 overnight, with Stewart and Russell at the crease.*
3 (**the crease**) an area around the goal in ice hockey or lacrosse which the players may not enter unless the puck or the ball has already done so.
▸ **verb** [with obj.] **1** make a crease in (cloth or paper): *he sank into the chair, careful not to crease his dinner jacket* | (as adj. **creased**) *a creased piece of paper.* ■ [no obj.] (of a facial feature) be marked by creases, typically as an expression of an emotion: *his eyes creased in amusement.*
2 (**crease up** or **crease someone up**) Brit. informal burst out or cause to burst out laughing: [no obj.] *Jo could imitate anybody and always made him crease up.*
3 Brit. informal hit or punch (someone) hard: *clap or I'll crease you.*
4 (of a bullet) graze (someone or something): *a bullet creased his thigh.*
– ORIGIN late 16th cent.: probably a variant of CREST.

create ▸ **verb 1** [with obj.] bring (something) into existence: *he created a thirty-acre lake | over 170 jobs were created.* ■ cause (something) to happen as a result of one's actions: *divorce created only problems for children.* ■ (of an actor) originate (a role) by playing a character for the first time. ■ [with obj. and complement] invest (someone) with a title of nobility: *he was created a baronet.*
2 [no obj.] Brit. informal make a fuss; complain: *little kids create because they hate being ignored.*
– DERIVATIVES **creatable** adjective.
– ORIGIN late Middle English (in the sense 'form out of nothing', used of a divine or supernatural being): from Latin *creat-* 'produced', from the verb *creare*.

creatine /ˈkriːətiːn/ ▸ **noun** [mass noun] Biochemistry a compound formed in protein metabolism and present in much living tissue. It is involved in the supply of energy for muscular contraction. ● A guanidine derivative, usually present as a phosphate; chem. formula: $C_4H_9N_3O_2$.
– ORIGIN mid 19th cent.: formed irregularly from Greek *kreas* 'meat' + -INE[4].

creatinine /kriˈatɪniːn/ ▸ **noun** [mass noun] Biochemistry a compound which is produced by metabolism of creatine and excreted in the urine. ● An anhydride of creatine; chem. formula: $C_4H_7N_3O$.

creation ▸ **noun** [mass noun] **1** the action or process of bringing something into existence: *creation of a coalition government | job creation.* ■ [count noun] a thing which has been made or invented, especially something showing artistic talent: *she treats fictional creations as if they were real people.*
2 (**the Creation**) the creating of the universe, especially when regarded as an act of God. ■ [mass noun] everything created; the universe: *our alienation from the rest of Creation.*
3 the action of investing someone with a title of nobility.
– ORIGIN late Middle English: via Old French from Latin *creatio(n-)*, from the verb *creare* (see CREATE).

creationism ▸ **noun** [mass noun] the belief that the universe and living organisms originate from specific acts of divine creation, as in the biblical account, rather than by natural processes such as evolution. ■ another term for CREATION SCIENCE.
– DERIVATIVES **creationist** noun & adjective.

creation science ▸ **noun** [mass noun] the reinterpretation of scientific knowledge in accord with belief in the literal truth of the Bible, especially regarding the origin of matter, life, and humankind.

creative ▸ **adjective** relating to or involving the use of the imagination or original ideas to create something: *change unleashes people's creative energy | creative writing.* ■ having good imagination or original ideas: *a creative team of designers.*
▸ **noun** informal a person whose job involves creative work.
– DERIVATIVES **creatively** adverb, **creativeness** noun.

creative accountancy (also **creative accounting**) ▸ **noun** [mass noun] informal the exploitation of loopholes in financial regulation in order to gain advantage or present figures in a misleadingly favourable light.

creativity ▸ **noun** [mass noun] the use of imagination or original ideas to create something; inventiveness: *firms are keen to encourage creativity.*

creator ▸ **noun** a person or thing that brings something into existence. ■ (**the Creator**) used as a name for God.

creature ▸ **noun 1** an animal, as distinct from a human being: *night sounds of birds and other creatures.* ■ an animal or person: *as fellow creatures on this planet, animals deserve respect.* ■ a fictional or imaginary being: *a creature from outer space.* ■ [with adj.] a person of a specified kind: *you heartless creature!*
2 a person or organization considered to be under the complete control of another: *the village teacher was expected to be the creature of his employer.*
3 archaic anything living or existing: *dress, jewels, and other transitory creatures.*
– PHRASES **creature of habit** a person who follows an unvarying routine: *he's a creature of habit—he keeps to the places he knows.*

– DERIVATIVES **creaturely** adjective.
– ORIGIN Middle English (in the sense 'something created'): via Old French from late Latin *creatura*, from the verb *creare* (see CREATE).

creature comforts ▶ plural noun material comforts that contribute to physical ease and well-being, such as good food and accommodation.

crèche /krɛʃ, kreɪʃ/ ▶ noun **1** Brit. a nursery where babies and young children are cared for during the working day.
2 N. Amer. a representation of the nativity scene.
– ORIGIN late 18th cent. (in sense 2): French (see also CRATCH).

Crécy, Battle of /ˈkrɛsi/ a battle between the English and the French in 1346 near the village of Crécy-en-Ponthieu in Picardy, at which the forces of Edward III defeated those of Philip VI. It was the first major English victory of the Hundred Years War.

cred ▶ noun informal term for STREET CREDIBILITY.

credal /ˈkriːd(ə)l/ (also **creedal**) ▶ adjective relating to a statement of Christian or other religious belief.

credence /ˈkriːd(ə)ns/ ▶ noun **1** [mass noun] belief in or acceptance of something as true: *psychoanalysis finds little credence among laymen.* ■ the likelihood of something being true; plausibility: *being called upon by the media as an expert **lends credence** to one's opinions.*
2 [usu. as modifier] a small side table, shelf, or niche in a church for holding the elements of the Eucharist before they are consecrated: *a credence table.*
– ORIGIN Middle English: via Old French from medieval Latin *credentia*, from Latin *credent-* 'believing', from the verb *credere*.

credential /krɪˈdɛnʃ(ə)l/ ▶ noun (usu. **credentials**) a qualification, achievement, quality, or aspect of a person's background, especially when used to indicate their suitability for something: *recruitment is based mainly on academic credentials.* ■ a document proving a person's identity or qualifications. ■ a letter of introduction given by a government to an ambassador before a new posting.
▶ verb [with obj.] (usu. as adj. **credentialed**) chiefly N. Amer. provide with credentials.
– ORIGIN late Middle English: from medieval Latin *credentialis*, from *credentia* (see CREDENCE). The original use was as an adjective in the sense 'giving credence to, recommending', frequently in *credential letters* or *papers*, hence *credentials* (mid 17th cent.).

credenza /krɪˈdɛnzə/ ▶ noun a sideboard or cupboard.
– ORIGIN late 19th cent.: Italian, from medieval Latin *credentia* (see CREDENCE).

credibility ▶ noun [mass noun] the quality of being trusted and believed in: *the government's loss of credibility.* ■ the quality of being convincing or believable: *the book's anecdotes have scant regard for credibility.*
– ORIGIN mid 16th cent.: from medieval Latin *credibilitas*, from Latin *credibilis* (see CREDIBLE).

credibility gap ▶ noun an apparent difference between what is said or promised and what happens or is true.

credible ▶ adjective able to be believed; convincing: *few people found his story credible | a credible witness.* ■ capable of persuading people that something will happen or be successful: *a credible threat.*
– DERIVATIVES **credibly** adverb.
– ORIGIN late Middle English: from Latin *credibilis*, from *credere* 'believe'.

> **USAGE** Confusion often arises between the words **credible** and **creditable**. **Credible** chiefly means 'able to be believed; convincing' (*few people found his story credible*), while **creditable** means 'deserving acknowledgement and praise but not necessarily outstanding' (*a very creditable 2–4 defeat*).

credit ▶ noun **1** [mass noun] the ability of a customer to obtain goods or services before payment, based on the trust that payment will be made in the future: *I've got unlimited credit.* ■ the money lent or borrowed under a credit arrangement: *the bank refused to extend their credit | [as modifier] he exceeded his credit limit.*
2 an entry recording a sum received, listed on the right-hand side or column of an account. The opposite of DEBIT. ■ a payment received: *you need to record debits or credits made to your account.*
3 [mass noun] public acknowledgement or praise, given or received when a person's responsibility for an action or idea becomes apparent: *the Prime Minister was quick to claim the credit for abolishing the tax.* ■ [in sing.] a source of pride: *the fans are a credit to the club.* ■ (also **credit title**) [count noun] (usu. **credits**) an item in a list displayed at the beginning or end of a film or television programme, acknowledging a contributor's role: *the closing credits finished rolling.*
4 [mass noun] chiefly N. Amer. the acknowledgement of a student's completion of a course or activity that counts towards a degree or diploma as maintained in a school's records: *a student can earn one unit of academic credit.* ■ [count noun] a unit of study counting towards a degree or diploma: *the National Certificate consists of twelve credits.* ■ [count noun] Brit. a grade above a pass in an examination. ■ acknowledgement of merit in an examination which is reflected in the marks awarded: *candidates will receive credit for accuracy and style.*
5 [mass noun] archaic the quality of being believed or credited: *the abstract philosophy of Cicero has lost its credit.* ■ good reputation.
▶ verb (**credits, crediting, credited**) [with obj.] **1** publicly acknowledge a contributor's role in the production of (something published or broadcast): *the screenplay is **credited to** one American and two Japanese writers.* ■ (**credit someone with**) ascribe (an achievement or good quality) to someone: *he is credited with painting one hundred and twenty-five canvases.*
2 add (an amount of money) to an account: *this deferred tax can be **credited to** the profit and loss account.*
3 [often with modal] Brit. believe (something surprising or unlikely): *you would hardly credit it—but it was true.*
– PHRASES **be in credit** (of an account) have money in it. **credit where credit is due** praise given when it is deserved, even if one is reluctant to give it. **do someone credit** (or **do credit to someone**) make someone worthy of praise or respect: *your concern does you credit.* **give someone credit for** commend someone for (a quality or achievement), especially with reluctance or surprise: *please give me credit for some sense.* **have something to one's credit** have achieved something notable: *he has 65 Tournament wins to his credit.* **on credit** with an arrangement to pay later. **on the credit side** as a good aspect of the situation: *on the credit side, the text is highly readable.* **to one's credit** used to indicate that something praiseworthy has been achieved, especially despite difficulties: *to his credit, he'd made a real effort with the carving.*
– ORIGIN mid 16th cent. (originally in the senses 'belief', 'credibility'): from French *crédit*, probably via Italian *credito* from Latin *creditum*, neuter past participle of *credere* 'believe, trust'.

creditable ▶ adjective (of a performance, effort, or action) deserving public acknowledgement and praise but not necessarily outstanding or successful: *a very creditable 2–4 defeat.*
– DERIVATIVES **creditability** noun, **creditably** adverb.

> **USAGE** On the difference between creditable and credible, see USAGE at CREDIBLE.

credit account ▶ noun Brit. another term for CHARGE ACCOUNT.

credit agency ▶ noun see CREDIT REFERENCE AGENCY.

credit card ▶ noun a small plastic card issued by a bank, building society, etc., allowing the holder to purchase goods or services on credit.

credit crunch ▶ noun a sudden sharp reduction in the availability of money or credit from banks and other lenders: *the beleaguered company has become the latest victim of the credit crunch.*

credit insurance ▶ noun [mass noun] insurance taken out to protect against bad debts.

credit line ▶ noun another term for LINE OF CREDIT (see LINE[1] (noun)).

credit note ▶ noun Brit. a receipt given by a shop to a customer who has returned goods, which can be offset against future purchases.

creditor ▶ noun a person or company to whom money is owing.

credit rating ▶ noun an estimate of the ability of a person or organization to fulfil their financial commitments, based on previous dealings. ■ [mass noun] the process of assessing this.

credit reference agency (also **credit agency**) ▶ noun a company which collects information relating to the credit ratings of individuals and makes it available to banks, finance companies, etc.

credit standing ▶ noun the reputation of a person or organization with regard to capability and promptness in meeting financial obligations.

credit title ▶ noun see CREDIT (sense 3 of the noun).

credit transfer ▶ noun [mass noun] **1** a system whereby successfully completed units of study contributing towards a degree or diploma can be transferred from one course to another.
2 Brit. a direct payment of money from one bank account to another.

credit union ▶ noun a non-profit-making money cooperative whose members can borrow from pooled deposits at low interest rates.

C

creditworthy ▶ adjective (of a person or company) considered suitable to receive credit, especially because of being reliable in paying money back in the past.
– DERIVATIVES **creditworthiness** noun.

credo /ˈkriːdəʊ, ˈkreɪ-/ ▶ noun (pl. **credos**) a statement of the beliefs or aims which guide someone's actions: *he announced his credo in his first editorial.* ■ (**Credo**) a creed of the Christian Church in Latin. ■ (**Credo**) a musical setting of the Nicene Creed, typically as part of a mass.
– ORIGIN Middle English: Latin, 'I believe'. Compare with CREED.

credulity /krɪˈdjuːlɪti/ ▶ noun [mass noun] a tendency to be too ready to believe that something is real or true.

credulous /ˈkrɛdjʊləs/ ▶ adjective having or showing too great a readiness to believe things.
– DERIVATIVES **credulously** adverb, **credulousness** noun.
– ORIGIN late 16th cent. (in the general sense 'inclined to believe'): from Latin *credulus* (from *credere* 'believe') + **-ous**.

Cree /kriː/ ▶ noun (pl. **same** or **Crees**) **1** a member of an American Indian people living in a vast area of central Canada.
2 [mass noun] the Algonquian language of the Cree, closely related to Montagnais. It has about 60,000 speakers.
▶ adjective relating to the Cree or their language.
– ORIGIN from Canadian French *Cris*, abbreviation of *Cristinaux*, from Algonquian.

creed ▶ noun a system of religious belief; a faith: *people of many creeds and cultures.* ■ (often **the Creed**) a formal statement of Christian beliefs, especially the Apostles' Creed or the Nicene Creed. ■ a set of beliefs or aims which guide someone's actions: *liberalism was more than a political creed.*
– ORIGIN Old English, from Latin CREDO.

creedal ▶ adjective variant spelling of CREDAL.

Creek /kriːk/ ▶ noun (pl. **same**) **1** a member of a confederacy of American Indian peoples of the south-eastern US in the 16th to 19th centuries; their descendants now live mainly in Oklahoma.
2 [mass noun] the Muskogean language that was spoken by members of the Creek confederacy.
▶ adjective relating to or denoting this confederacy.
– ORIGIN from CREEK, because they lived beside the waterways of the flatlands of Georgia and Alabama.

creek ▶ noun chiefly Brit. a narrow, sheltered waterway, especially an inlet in a shoreline or channel in a marsh. ■ N. Amer. & Austral./NZ a stream or minor tributary of a river.
– PHRASES **be up the creek** informal **1** (also **be up the creek without a paddle**) be in severe difficulty or trouble, especially with no means of extricating oneself from it. **2** Brit. be stupid or misguided. **be up shit creek** see SHIT.
– ORIGIN Middle English: from Old French *crique* or from Old Norse *kriki* 'nook'; perhaps reinforced by Middle Dutch *krēke*; of unknown ultimate origin.

creel ▶ noun **1** a large wicker basket for holding fish. ■ an angler's fishing basket.
2 a rack holding bobbins or spools when spinning.
– ORIGIN Middle English (in sense 1; originally Scots and northern English): of unknown origin. Sense 2 dates from the mid 19th cent.

creep ▶ verb (past and past participle **crept** /krɛpt/) [no obj.] **1** [usu. with adverbial of direction] move slowly and carefully in order to avoid being heard or noticed: *he crept downstairs, hardly making any noise | they were taught how to **creep up on** an enemy.* ■ (of a thing) move very slowly and inexorably: *the fog was creeping up from the marsh.* ■ (of a plant) grow along the ground or other surface by means of extending stems or branches. ■ (of a plastic solid) undergo gradual deformation under stress.
2 (**creep in/into**) (of a negative characteristic or fact) occur or develop gradually and almost imperceptibly: *errors crept into his game* | (as adj. **creeping**) *the creeping privatization of the health*

service. ■ **(creep up)** increase slowly but steadily in number or amount: *gas prices have been creeping up for a while.*
▶ **noun 1** informal a detestable person. ■ a person who behaves obsequiously in the hope of advancement.
2 [mass noun] slow steady movement, especially when imperceptible: *an attempt to prevent this slow creep of costs.* ■ the tendency of a car with automatic transmission to move when in gear without the accelerator being pressed. ■ the gradual downward movement of disintegrated rock or soil due to gravity. ■ the gradual deformation of a plastic solid under stress.
3 Brit. an opening in a hedge or wall for an animal to pass through. ■ a feeding enclosure for young animals, with a long, narrow entrance.
4 [mass noun] Brit. solid food given to young farm animals in order to wean them.
– PHRASES **give someone the creeps** informal induce a feeling of revulsion or fear in someone. **make one's flesh creep** cause one to feel disgust and have a sensation like that of something crawling over the skin.
– PHRASAL VERBS **creep someone out** (past and past participle **creeped**) informal give someone an unpleasant feeling of fear or unease: *an anonymous note like that would creep me out.* **creep to** Brit. informal behave obsequiously towards (someone) in the hope of advancement.
– ORIGIN Old English *crēopan* 'move with the body close to the ground', of Germanic origin; related to Dutch *kruipen*. Sense 1 of the verb dates from Middle English.

creeper ▶ **noun 1** Botany any plant that grows along the ground, around another plant, or up a wall by means of extending stems or branches.
2 [with modifier] any of a number of small birds that creep around in trees or vegetation: ● **(brown creeper)** N. Amer. the American treecreeper (*Certhia americana*, family Certhiidae). ● **(brown creeper)** NZ a New Zealand songbird (*Mohoua (or Finschia) novaeseelandiae, family Pachycephalidae or Acanthizidae).* ● a Philippine songbird (family Rhabdornithidae and genus *Rhabdornis*: two species). ● a Hawaiian honeycreeper (genus *Paroreomyza, family Drepanididae: three species).*
3 informal **(creepers)** short for BROTHEL CREEPERS.

creepie ▶ **noun** (pl. **creepies**) chiefly Scottish a low stool.
– ORIGIN mid 17th cent.: from the verb CREEP + -IE.

creeping Jenny ▶ **noun** a trailing evergreen European plant with round glossy leaves and yellow flowers, growing in damp places and by water. Also called MONEYWORT. ● *Lysimachia nummularia*, family Primulaceae.

creeping Jesus ▶ **noun** Brit. informal a person who is obsequious or hypocritically pious.

creeping paralysis ▶ **noun** less technical term for LOCOMOTOR ATAXIA.

creepy ▶ **adjective** (**creepier**, **creepiest**) informal causing an unpleasant feeling of fear or unease: *the creepy feelings one often gets in a strange house.*
– DERIVATIVES **creepily** adverb, **creepiness** noun.

creepy-crawly ▶ **noun** (pl. **creepy-crawlies**) informal a spider, worm, or other small flightless creature, especially when considered unpleasant or frightening.

creese ▶ **noun** archaic spelling of KRIS.

crema /ˈkrɛmə/ ▶ **noun** [mass noun] a brownish foam that forms on the top of freshly made espresso coffee.
– ORIGIN Italian, literally 'cream'.

cremaster /krɪˈmastə/ ▶ **noun 1** (also **cremaster muscle**) Anatomy the muscle of the spermatic cord, by which the testicle can be partially raised.
2 Entomology the hook-like tip of a butterfly pupa, serving as an anchorage point.
– ORIGIN late 17th cent.: from Greek *kremastēr*, from *krema-* 'hang'.

cremate ▶ **verb** dispose of (a dead person's body) by burning it to ashes, typically after a funeral ceremony: *she had refused to have her husband cremated.*
– DERIVATIVES **cremation** noun, **cremator** noun.
– ORIGIN late 19th cent. (as *cremation*): from Latin *cremare* 'burn'.

crematorium /ˌkrɛməˈtɔːrɪəm/ ▶ **noun** (pl. **crematoria** or **crematoriums**) a place where a dead person's body is cremated.
– ORIGIN late 19th cent.: modern Latin, from *cremare* 'burn'.

crematory /ˈkrɛmət(ə)ri/ ▶ **adjective** relating to cremation.
▶ **noun** (pl. **crematories**) North American term for CREMATORIUM.

creme /kriːm/ ▶ **noun** a substance or product with a thick, creamy consistency: *self-tanning creme.*
– ORIGIN from French *crème*, 'cream'.

crème anglaise /ˌkrɛm ɒ̃ˈɡleɪz/ ▶ **noun** [mass noun] a rich egg custard.
– ORIGIN French, literally 'English cream'.

crème brûlée /ˌkrɛm bruːˈleɪ/ ▶ **noun** (pl. **crèmes brûlées** pronunc. **same** or **crème brûlées** /-ˈleɪz/) [mass noun] a dessert of custard topped with caramelized sugar.
– ORIGIN French, literally 'burnt cream'.

crème caramel /krɛm ˌkarəˈmɛl, ˈkarəmɛl/ ▶ **noun** (pl. **crèmes caramel** pronunc. **same** or **crème caramels**) [mass noun] a custard dessert made with whipped cream and eggs and topped with caramel.
– ORIGIN French.

crème de cacao /ˌkrɛm də kəˈkeɪəʊ, -ˈkaʊ/ ▶ **noun** [mass noun] a chocolate-flavoured liqueur.
– ORIGIN French, literally 'cream of cacao'.

crème de cassis /ˌkrɛm də kaˈsiːs/ ▶ **noun** see CASSIS[1].
– ORIGIN French, literally 'cream of blackcurrant'.

crème de la crème /ˌkrɛm də la ˈkrɛm/, French /kʀɛm də la kʀɛm/ ▶ **noun** the best person or thing of a particular kind: *the crème de la crème of the dancers have left the country.*
– ORIGIN French, literally 'cream of the cream'.

crème de menthe /ˌkrɛm də ˈmɒnθ, ˈmɒ̃t/ ▶ **noun** [mass noun] a peppermint-flavoured liqueur.
– ORIGIN French, literally 'cream of mint'.

crème fraiche /krɛm ˈfrɛʃ/ ▶ **noun** [mass noun] a type of thick cream made from double cream with the addition of buttermilk, sour cream, or yogurt.
– ORIGIN from French *crème fraîche*, literally 'fresh cream'.

Cremona /krɪˈməʊnə, krɛ-/ a city in Lombardy, in northern Italy; pop. 72,267 (2008). Between the 16th and the 18th century the city was home to three renowned families of violin-makers: the Amati, the Guarneri, and the Stradivari.

crenate /ˈkriːneɪt/ ▶ **adjective** Botany & Zoology (especially of a leaf or shell) having a round-toothed or scalloped edge. Compare with CRENULATE.
– DERIVATIVES **crenated** adjective, **crenation** noun.
– ORIGIN late 18th cent. (earlier as *crenated*): from modern Latin *crenatus*, from popular Latin *crena* 'notch'.

crenel /ˈkrɛn(ə)l/ (also **crenelle** /krɪˈnɛl/) ▶ **noun** an indentation in the battlements of a fort or castle, used for shooting or firing missiles through.
– ORIGIN late 15th cent.: from Old French, based on popular Latin *crena* 'notch'.

crenellate /ˈkrɛn(ə)leɪt/ (also **crenelate**) ▶ **verb** [with obj.] (usu. as adj. **crenellated**) chiefly historical provide (a wall of a building) with battlements.
– ORIGIN early 19th cent.: from French *créneler*, from Old French *crenel* (see CRENEL).

crenellations ▶ **plural noun** the battlements of a castle or other building.

crenulate /ˈkrɛnjʊleɪt/ ▶ **adjective** technical (especially of a leaf, shell, or shoreline) having a finely scalloped or notched outline or edge. Compare with CRENATE.
– DERIVATIVES **crenulated** adjective, **crenulation** noun.
– ORIGIN late 18th cent.: from modern Latin *crenulatus*, from *crenula*, diminutive of *crena* 'notch'.

creodont /ˈkriːədɒnt/ ▶ **noun** a fossil carnivorous mammal of the early Tertiary period, ancestral to modern carnivores. ● Order Creodonta: several families.
– ORIGIN late 19th cent.: from modern Latin *Creodonta* (plural), from Greek *kreas* 'flesh' + *odous, odont-* 'tooth'.

Creole /ˈkriːəʊl/ (also **creole**) ▶ **noun 1** a person of mixed European and black descent, especially in the Caribbean.
2 a descendant of Spanish or other European settlers in the Caribbean or Central or South America. ■ a white descendant of French settlers in Louisiana and other parts of the southern US.
3 a mother tongue formed from the contact of a European language (especially English, French, Spanish, or Portuguese) with local languages (especially African languages spoken by slaves in the West Indies): *a Portuguese-based Creole.*
▶ **adjective** relating to a Creole or Creoles.
– ORIGIN from French *créole, criole*, from Spanish *criollo*, probably from Portuguese *crioulo* 'black person born in Brazil', from *criar* 'to breed', from Latin *creare* 'produce, create'.

creolize /ˈkriːə(ʊ)lʌɪz, ˈkriːɒl-/ (also **creolise**) ▶ **verb** [with obj.] form (a Creole language) from the contact of a European language with a local language: (as adj. **creolized**) *a creolized variety of French.*
– DERIVATIVES **creolization** /-ˈzeɪʃ(ə)n/ noun.

creosol /ˈkriːəsɒl/ ▶ **noun** [mass noun] Chemistry a colourless liquid which is the chief constituent of wood-tar creosote. ● Alternative name: **2-methoxy-4-methylphenol**; chem. formula: $C_8H_{10}O_2$.
– ORIGIN mid 19th cent.: from CREOSOTE + -OL.

creosote ▶ **noun** (also **creosote oil**) [mass noun] a dark brown oil containing various phenols and other organic compounds, distilled from coal tar and used as a wood preservative. ■ a colourless, pungent, oily liquid, containing creosol and other compounds, distilled from wood tar and used as an antiseptic.
▶ **verb** [with obj.] treat (wood) with creosote.
– ORIGIN mid 19th cent.: coined in German from Greek *kreas* 'flesh' + *sōtēr* 'preserver', with reference to its antiseptic properties.

creosote bush ▶ **noun** a shrub native to arid parts of Mexico and the western US. Its leaves smell of creosote and when steeped in boiling water they yield an antiseptic lotion. ● *Larrea tridentata*, family Zygophyllaceae.

crêpe /kreɪp/ ▶ **noun 1** [mass noun] (also **crape**) a light, thin fabric with a wrinkled surface: [as modifier] *a crêpe bandage.* ■ (also **crêpe rubber**) hard-wearing wrinkled rubber, used for the soles of shoes.
2 also /krɛp/ a thin pancake.
– DERIVATIVES **crêpey** (also **crêpy**) adjective.
– ORIGIN late 18th cent.: French, from Old French *crespe* 'curled, frizzed', from Latin *crispus*.

crêpe de Chine /də ˈʃiːn/ ▶ **noun** [mass noun] a fine crêpe of silk or similar fabric.
– ORIGIN late 19th cent.: French, literally 'crêpe of China'.

crepe myrtle ▶ **noun** variant spelling of CRAPE MYRTLE.

crêpe paper ▶ **noun** [mass noun] thin, crinkled paper resembling crêpe, used especially for making decorations.

crêperie /ˈkreɪpəri, ˈkrɛp-/, French /kʀɛpʀi/ ▶ **noun** (pl. **crêperies**) a small restaurant, typically one in France, in which a variety of crêpes are served.
– ORIGIN French.

crêpe Suzette ▶ **noun** (pl. **crêpes Suzette** pronunc. **same**) a thin dessert pancake flamed and served in alcohol.

crépinette /ˌkreɪpɪˈnɛt/, French /kʀepinɛt/ ▶ **noun** a flat sausage consisting of minced meat and savoury stuffing wrapped in pieces of pork caul.
– ORIGIN French, diminutive of *crépine* 'caul'.

crepitate /ˈkrɛpɪteɪt/ ▶ **verb** [no obj.] make a crackling sound: *the night crepitates with an airy whistling cacophony.*
– DERIVATIVES **crepitant** adjective.
– ORIGIN early 17th cent. (in the sense 'break wind'): from Latin *crepitat-* 'crackled, rustled', from the verb *crepitare*, from *crepare* 'to rattle'.

crepitation ▶ **noun 1** a crackling or rattling sound: *pistol-like crepitations.* ■ Medicine a crackling sound made when breathing with an inflamed lung, detected using a stethoscope.
2 [mass noun] Entomology the explosive ejection of irritant fluid from the abdomen of a bombardier beetle.
– ORIGIN mid 17th cent.: from French *crépitation* or Latin *crepitatio(n-)*, from the verb *crepitare* (see CREPITATE).

crepitus /ˈkrɛpɪtəs/ ▶ **noun** [mass noun] Medicine a grating sound or sensation produced by friction between bone and cartilage or the fractured parts of a bone. ■ the production of crepitations in the lungs; rale.
– ORIGIN early 19th cent.: from Latin, from *crepare* 'rattle'.

crépon /ˈkreɪpɒn/ ▶ **noun** [mass noun] a fabric resembling crêpe, but heavier and with a more pronounced crinkled effect.
– ORIGIN late 19th cent.: French.

crept past and past participle of CREEP.

crepuscular /krɪˈpʌskjʊlə, krɛ-/ ▶ **adjective** resembling or relating to twilight. ■ Zoology (of an animal) appearing or active in twilight.
– ORIGIN mid 17th cent.: from Latin *crepusculum* 'twilight' + -AR[1].

Cres. ▶ **abbreviation** crescent.

cresc. (also **cres.**) ▶ **abbreviation** Music crescendo.

crescendo /krɪˈʃɛndəʊ/ ▶ **noun 1** (pl. **crescendos** or **crescendi** /-di/) Music a gradual increase in loudness in a piece of music. ■ Music a passage of music marked or performed with a crescendo. ■ the loudest point

reached in a gradually increasing sound: *the port engine revs rose **to a crescendo**.*
2 a progressive increase in intensity: *a crescendo of misery.* ■ the most intense point reached: *the hysteria **reached a crescendo** around the spring festival.*
▶ **adverb & adjective** Music with a gradual increase in loudness.
▶ **verb** (**crescendoes**, **crescendoing**, **crescendoed**) [no obj.] increase in loudness or intensity: *the reluctant cheers began to crescendo.*
– ORIGIN late 18th cent.: Italian, present participle of *crescere* 'to increase', from Latin *crescere* 'grow'.

crescent /ˈkrɛz(ə)nt, -s-/ ▶ **noun** **1** the curved sickle shape of the waxing or waning moon. ■ a representation of a crescent used as an emblem of Islam or of Turkey. ■ (**the Crescent**) chiefly historical the political power of Islam or of the Ottoman Empire.
2 a thing which has the shape of a single curve that is broad in the centre and tapers to a point at each end: *a three-mile crescent of golden sand.* ■ [usu. in names] chiefly Brit. a street or terrace of houses forming an arc: *we lived at Westway Crescent.* ■ Heraldry a charge in the form of a crescent, typically with the points upward.
3 a moth or butterfly which bears crescent-shaped markings on the wings, in particular: ● an orange or brown American butterfly with a silvery mark on the underside of the hindwing (genus *Phyciodes*, subfamily Melitaeinae, family Nymphalidae). ● a brownish European moth with a pale mark on the forewing (several species in the family Noctuidae, in particular *Celaena leucostigma*).
▶ **adjective** **1** [attrib.] having the shape of a crescent: *a crescent moon.*
2 literary growing, increasing, or developing.
– DERIVATIVES **crescentic** /-ˈsɛntɪk/ **adjective**.
– ORIGIN late Middle English *cressant*, from Old French *creissant*, from Latin *crescere* 'grow'. The spelling change in the 17th century was due to the influence of the Latin.

crescent wrench ▶ **noun** N. Amer. an adjustable spanner designed to grip hexagonal nuts, with an adjusting screw fitted in the crescent-shaped head of the spanner.

cresol /ˈkriːsɒl/ ▶ **noun** Chemistry each of three isomeric crystalline compounds present in coal-tar creosote, used as disinfectants. ● the *ortho-*, *meta-*, and *para-*methyl derivatives of phenol; chem. formula: $CH_3C_6H_4OH$.
– ORIGIN mid 19th cent.: from CREOSOTE + -OL.

cress ▶ **noun** [mass noun] a plant of the cabbage family, typically having small white flowers and pungent leaves. Some kinds are edible and are eaten raw as salad. ● *Barbarea* and other genera, family Cruciferae: several species, including **garden cress** (used in mustard and cress) and **watercress**.
– ORIGIN Old English *cresse*, *cærse*, of West Germanic origin; related to Dutch *kers* and German *Kresse*.

cresset /ˈkrɛsɪt/ ▶ **noun** historical a metal container of oil, grease, wood, or coal set alight for illumination and typically mounted on a pole.
– ORIGIN late Middle English: from Old French, from *craisse*, variant of *graisse* 'oil, grease'.

Cressida /ˈkrɛsɪdə/ (in medieval legends of the Trojan War) the daughter of Calchas, a priest. She was faithless to her lover Troilus, a son of Priam.

Crest (in the UK) a computer system for buying and selling shares, introduced in 1996.
– ORIGIN an arbitrary formation.

crest ▶ **noun** **1** a comb or tuft of feathers, fur, or skin on the head of a bird or other animal. ■ a plume of feathers on a helmet.
2 the top of a mountain or hill: *she reached the crest of the hill.* ■ Anatomy a ridge along the surface of a bone. ■ the upper line of the neck of a horse or other mammal.
3 the curling foamy top of a wave.
4 Heraldry a distinctive device representing a family or corporate body, borne above the shield of a coat of arms (originally as worn on a helmet) or separately reproduced, for example on writing paper.
▶ **verb** **1** [with obj.] reach the top of (a hill or wave). ■ [no obj.] US (of a river, flood, etc.) rise to its highest level.
2 [no obj.] (of a wave) form a curling foamy top.
3 (**be crested with**) have attached at the top: *his helmet was crested with a fan of spikes.*
– PHRASES **on the crest of a wave** at a very successful point: *his career is on the crest of a wave at present.*
– DERIVATIVES **crestless** **adjective**.
– ORIGIN Middle English: from Old French *creste*, from Latin *crista* 'tuft, plume'.

Cresta Run a hazardously winding, steeply banked channel of ice built each year at the Cresta Valley, St Moritz, Switzerland, as a tobogganing course, on which competitors race on light toboggans in a characteristic head-first position. Such a run was first built in 1884.

crested ▶ **adjective** **1** (of a bird or other animal) having a comb or tuft of feathers, fur, or skin on the head: *the crested drake mandarin duck* | [in combination] *a plush-crested jay.*
2 emblazoned with a coat of arms or other emblem: *crested notepaper.*

crested newt (also **great crested newt**) ▶ **noun** a large Eurasian newt, the male of which has a tall crest along the back and tail during the breeding season. Also called WARTY NEWT. ● *Triturus cristatus*, family Salamandridae.

crested tit ▶ **noun** a small European tit (songbird) with a short crest, living chiefly in coniferous woodland. ● *Parus cristatus*, family Paridae.

crested wood ibis ▶ **noun** see WOOD IBIS (sense 2).

crestfallen ▶ **adjective** sad and disappointed: *he came back empty-handed and crestfallen.*
– ORIGIN late 16th cent.: originally with reference to a mammal or bird having a fallen or drooping crest.

crestfish ▶ **noun** (pl. **same** or **crestfishes**) a very elongated silvery marine fish with a crimson dorsal fin running the full length of its body and a forehead that projects forward into a long filament. ● *Lophotus lacepedei*, family Lophotidae.

cresting ▶ **noun** [mass noun] an ornamental decoration at the ridge of a roof or top of a wall.

cresyl /ˈkriːsʌɪl, -sɪl/ ▶ **noun** [as modifier] Chemistry of or denoting a radical $-OC_6H_4CH_3$, derived from a cresol.

Cretaceous /krɪˈteɪʃəs/ ▶ **adjective** Geology relating to or denoting the last period of the Mesozoic era, between the Jurassic and Tertiary periods. ■ (as noun **the Cretaceous**) the Cretaceous period or the system of rocks deposited during it.

> The Cretaceous lasted from about 146 to 65 million years ago. The climate was warm and the sea level rose; the period is characterized especially in NW Europe by the deposition of chalk. The first flowering plants emerged and the domination of the dinosaurs continued, although they died out quite abruptly towards the end of it.

– ORIGIN late 17th cent.: from Latin *cretaceus* (from *creta* 'chalk') + -OUS.

Cretaceous–Tertiary boundary (also **K/T boundary**) Geology the division between the Cretaceous and Tertiary periods, about 65 million years ago.

> A widespread layer of sediment dating from this time has been shown since 1980 to be enriched in iridium and other elements and to contain minerals showing evidence of thermal shock and carbon deposits indicative of extensive fires. This appears to indicate the catastrophic impact of one or more large meteorites, and geologists have identified a formation at Chicxulub in the Yucatán Peninsula, Mexico, as a probable impact site. A resulting drastic climate change has been suggested as the cause of the extinction of dinosaurs and many other organisms at this time, but this remains controversial.

Crete /kriːt/ a Greek island in the eastern Mediterranean; pop. 630,000 (est. 2009); capital, Heraklion. It is noted for the remains of the Minoan civilization which flourished there in the 2nd millennium BC. It fell to Rome in 67 BC and was subsequently ruled by Byzantines, Venetians, and Turks. Crete played an important role in the Greek struggle for independence from the Turks in the late 19th and early 20th centuries, becoming administratively part of an independent Greece in 1913. Greek name **Kríti**.
– DERIVATIVES **Cretan** **adjective & noun**.

cretic /ˈkriːtɪk/ ▶ **noun** Prosody a metrical foot containing one short or unstressed syllable between two long or stressed ones.
– ORIGIN late 16th cent.: from Latin *Creticus*, from Greek *Krētikos*, from *Krētē* 'Crete'.

cretin /ˈkrɛtɪn/ ▶ **noun** **1** a stupid person (used as a general term of abuse).
2 Medicine, dated a person who is physically deformed and has learning difficulties because of congenital thyroid deficiency.
– DERIVATIVES **cretinism** **noun**, **cretinous** **adjective**.
– ORIGIN late 18th cent.: from French *crétin*, from Swiss French *crestin* 'Christian' (from Latin *Christianus*), here used to mean 'human being', apparently as a reminder that, though deformed, cretins were human and not beasts.

cretonne /krɛˈtɒn, ˈkrɛtɒn/ ▶ **noun** [mass noun] a heavy cotton fabric, typically with a floral pattern printed on one or both sides, used for upholstery.
– ORIGIN late 19th cent.: from French, of unknown origin.

Creutzfeldt–Jakob disease /ˌkrɔɪtsfɛltˈjakɒb/ ▶ **noun** [mass noun] a fatal degenerative disease affecting nerve cells in the brain, causing mental, physical, and sensory disturbances such as dementia and seizures. It is believed to be caused by prions and hence to be related to BSE and other spongiform encephalopathies such as kuru and scrapie.
– PHRASES **new variant Creutzfeldt–Jakob disease** a form of the disease characterized by an early age of onset and possibly linked to BSE.
– ORIGIN 1930s: named after H. G. *Creutzfeldt* (1885–1964) and A. *Jakob* (1882–1927), the German neurologists who first described cases of the disease in 1920–1. Creutzfeldt is credited with the first description of the disease in 1920, although the case is atypical by current diagnostic criteria; a year later Jakob described four cases, at least two of whom had clinical features suggestive of CJD as it is currently described.

crevasse /krɪˈvas/ ▶ **noun** a deep open crack, especially one in a glacier. ■ N. Amer. a breach in the embankment of a river or canal.
– ORIGIN early 19th cent.: from French, from Old French *crevace* (see CREVICE).

crevette /krəˈvɛt/ ▶ **noun** a shrimp or prawn, especially as an item on a menu.
– ORIGIN French.

crevice /ˈkrɛvɪs/ ▶ **noun** a narrow opening or fissure, especially in a rock or wall.
– ORIGIN Middle English: from Old French *crevace*, from *crever* 'to burst', from Latin *crepare* 'to rattle, crack'.

crew[1] ▶ **noun** **1** [treated as sing. or pl.] a group of people who work on and operate a ship, aircraft, train, etc. ■ such a group other than the officers: *the ship's captain and crew may be brought to trial.* ■ [mass noun] US the sport of rowing.
2 a group of people who work closely together: *a film crew.* ■ informal, often derogatory a group of people associated in some way: *a crew of assorted computer geeks.* ■ informal, chiefly US a group of rappers, break dancers, or graffiti artists performing or operating together.
▶ **verb** [with obj.] provide (a craft or vehicle) with a group of people to operate it: *normally the boat is crewed by five people.* ■ [no obj.] act as a member of a crew, subordinate to a captain: *I've never crewed for a world-famous yachtsman before.*
– DERIVATIVES **crewman** **noun** (pl. **crewmen**).
– ORIGIN late Middle English: from Old French *creue* 'augmentation, increase', feminine past participle of *croistre* 'grow', from Latin *crescere*. The original sense was 'band of soldiers serving as reinforcements'; hence it came to denote any organized armed band or, generally, a company of people (late 16th cent.).

crew[2] past of CROW[2].

crew cut ▶ **noun** a very short haircut for men and boys.
– ORIGIN 1940s: apparently first adopted as a style by boat crews of Harvard and Yale universities.

Crewe /kruː/ a town and major railway junction in Cheshire, west central England; pop. 77,700 (est. 2009).

crewel /ˈkruːəl/ ▶ **noun** a thin, loosely twisted, worsted yarn used for tapestry and embroidery.
– ORIGIN late 15th cent.: of unknown origin.

crewel work ▶ **noun** [mass noun] embroidery or tapestry worked in crewels on linen or cloth.

crew neck ▶ **noun** a close-fitting round neckline on a sweater or T-shirt: [as modifier] *a crew-neck sweater.* ■ a sweater with a crew neck.
– DERIVATIVES **crew-necked** **adjective**.

crib ▶ **noun** **1** chiefly N. Amer. a child's bed with barred or latticed sides; a cot. ■ a barred container or rack for animal fodder; a manger. ■ Brit. a model of the Nativity of Christ, with a manger as a bed.
2 informal a translation of a text for use by students, especially in a surreptitious way: *an English crib of Caesar's Gallic Wars.* ■ a thing that has been plagiarized: *is the song a crib from Mozart's 'Don Giovanni'?*
3 informal, chiefly N. Amer. a person's apartment or house.
4 [mass noun] short for CRIBBAGE. ■ [count noun] the cards discarded by the players at cribbage, counting to the dealer.

C

C

5 (also **cribwork**) a heavy timber framework used in foundations for a building or to line a mineshaft.
6 Austral./NZ a light meal; a snack.
▸ **verb** (**cribs, cribbing, cribbed**) [with obj.] **1** Brit. informal copy (another person's work) illicitly or without acknowledgement: *he was doing an exam and didn't want anybody to crib the answers from him* | [no obj.] *he often **cribbed from** other researchers.* ■ archaic steal.
2 archaic restrain: *he had been so cabined, cribbed, and confined by office.*
3 [no obj.] Brit. dated or Indian grumble: *those guys have nothing to crib about.*
– DERIVATIVES **cribber** noun.
– ORIGIN Old English (in the sense 'manger'), of Germanic origin; related to Dutch *krib, kribbe* and German *Krippe*.

cribbage ▸ **noun** [mass noun] a card game, usually for two players, in which the objective is to play so that the pip value of one's cards played reaches exactly 15 or 31.
– ORIGIN mid 17th cent.: related to CRIB; the game is said to have been invented by the English poet Sir John Suckling; it seems to have been developed from an older game called Noddy.

cribbage board ▸ **noun** a board with pegs and holes, used for scoring at cribbage.

crib-biting ▸ **noun** [mass noun] a repetitive habit of some horses which involves the biting and chewing of wood in the stable, causing excessive wear to the front teeth.

crib death ▸ **noun** North American term for COT DEATH.

cribellum /krɪˈbɛləm/ ▸ **noun** (pl. **cribella** /-lə/) Zoology (in some spiders) an additional spinning organ with numerous fine pores, situated in front of the spinnerets.
– DERIVATIVES **cribellate** adjective.
– ORIGIN late 19th cent.: from late Latin, diminutive of *cribrum* 'sieve'.

cribo /ˈkriːbəʊ, ˈkrʌɪbəʊ/ ▸ **noun** (pl. **cribos**) another term for INDIGO SNAKE.
– ORIGIN late 19th cent.: of unknown origin.

cribriform /ˈkrɪbrɪfɔːm/ ▸ **adjective** Anatomy denoting an anatomical structure that is pierced by numerous small holes, in particular the plate of the ethmoid bone through which the olfactory nerves pass.
– ORIGIN mid 18th cent.: from Latin *cribrum* 'sieve' + -IFORM.

cribwork ▸ **noun** see CRIB (sense 5 of the noun).

Crichton /ˈkrʌɪt(ə)n/, James (1560–*c*.1585), Scottish adventurer; known as **the Admirable Crichton**. Crichton was an accomplished swordsman, poet, and scholar. He served in the French army and made a considerable impression on French and Italian universities with his skills as a polyglot orator.

Crick, Francis Harry Compton (1916–2004), English biophysicist. Together with J. D. Watson he proposed the double helix structure of the DNA molecule, thus broadly explaining how genetic information is carried in living organisms and how genes replicate. Nobel Prize for Physiology or Medicine (1962, shared with Watson and M. H. F. Wilkins).

crick ▸ **noun** a painful stiff feeling in the neck or back.
▸ **verb** [with obj.] twist or strain (one's neck or back), causing painful stiffness: (as adj. **cricked**) *he suffered a cricked neck during tackling practice.*
– ORIGIN late Middle English: of unknown origin.

cricket[1] ▸ **noun** [mass noun] an open-air game played on a large grass field with ball, bats, and two wickets, between teams of eleven players, the object of the game being to score more runs than the opposition.

> Cricket is played mainly in Britain and in territories formerly under British rule, such as Australia, South Africa, the West Indies, New Zealand, and the Indian subcontinent. The full game with two innings per side can last several days; shorter single-innings matches are usual at amateur level and have become popular at professional level since the 1960s.

– PHRASES **a cricket score** Brit. informal (in sports other than cricket) an unusually high score: *England looked set to run up a cricket score when they went four tries ahead.* **not cricket** Brit. informal something contrary to traditional standards of fairness or rectitude.
– DERIVATIVES **cricketer** noun, **cricketing** adjective.
– ORIGIN late 16th cent.: of unknown origin.

cricket[2] ▸ **noun** an insect related to the grasshoppers but with shorter legs. The male produces a characteristic musical chirping sound. ● Family Gryllidae: many genera and species, including the **field cricket** and the **house cricket**.
■ used in names of insects of related families, e.g. **bush cricket, mole cricket**.
– ORIGIN Middle English: from Old French *criquet*, from *criquer* 'to crackle', of imitative origin.

cricoid /ˈkrʌɪkɔɪd/ ▸ **noun** (also **cricoid cartilage**) Anatomy the ring-shaped cartilage of the larynx.
– ORIGIN mid 18th cent.: from modern Latin *cricoides* 'ring-shaped', from Greek *krikoeidēs*, from *krikos* 'ring'.

cricothyroid /ˌkrʌɪkə(ʊ)ˈθʌɪrɔɪd/ ▸ **adjective** Anatomy relating to the cricoid and thyroid cartilages.
– ORIGIN mid 19th cent.: from Greek *kriko-* (combining form of *krikos* 'ring') + THYROID.

cri de cœur /ˌkriː də ˈkəː/, French /kʀi də kœʀ/ ▸ **noun** (pl. **cris de cœur** pronunc. **same**) a passionate appeal, complaint, or protest.
– ORIGIN French, 'cry from the heart'.

cried past and past participle of CRY.

crier ▸ **noun** an officer who makes public announcements in a court of justice. ■ short for TOWN CRIER.
– ORIGIN late Middle English: from Old French *criere*, from *crier* 'to shout'.

crikey ▸ **exclamation** Brit. informal an expression of surprise: *Crikey! I never thought I'd see you again.*
– ORIGIN mid 19th cent.: euphemism for CHRIST.

crim ▸ **noun & adjective** informal, chiefly Austral./NZ short for CRIMINAL.

Crimbo ▸ **noun** variant spelling of CHRIMBO.

crime ▸ **noun** an action or omission which constitutes an offence and is punishable by law: *shoplifting was a serious crime.* ■ [mass noun] illegal activities: *the victims of crime.* ■ an action or activity considered to be evil, shameful, or wrong: *they condemned apartheid as a **crime against humanity** | it's a crime to keep a creature like Willy in a tank.*
▸ **verb** [with obj.] Brit. informal (especially in the army) charge with or find guilty of an offence: *they found the note and I got crimed for it.*
– ORIGIN Middle English (in the sense 'wickedness, sin'): via Old French from Latin *crimen* 'judgement, offence', based on *cernere* 'to judge'.

Crimea /krʌɪˈmiːə/ (usu. **the Crimea**) a peninsula of Ukraine lying between the Sea of Azov and the Black Sea. It was the scene of the Crimean War in the 1850s. The majority of the population is Russian.
– DERIVATIVES **Crimean** adjective.

Crimean War a war (1853–6) between Russia and an alliance of Great Britain, France, Sardinia, and Turkey. Russian aggression against Turkey led to war in 1853, with Turkey's European allies intervening to destroy Russian naval power in the Black Sea in 1854 and eventually capture the fortress city of Sebastopol in 1855 after a lengthy siege.

crime-fighting ▸ **noun** [mass noun] the action of working to reduce the incidence of crime.
– DERIVATIVES **crime-fighter** noun.

crimen injuria /ˌkrʌɪmən ɪnˈdʒuːrɪə/ ▸ **noun** S. African Law a wilful injury to someone's dignity, caused by the use of obscene or racially offensive language or gestures.
– ORIGIN Latin, from *crimen* 'accusation' + *injuria* 'indignity'.

crime passionnel /ˌkriːm pasjəˈnɛl/ ▸ **noun** (pl. **crimes passionnels** pronunc. **same**) a crime, typically a murder, committed in a fit of sexual jealousy.
– ORIGIN French, 'crime of passion'.

crime sheet ▸ **noun** Brit. a form on which police record details of a reported crime. ■ (in the armed forces) a record of someone's offences and punishments under military law.

crime wave ▸ **noun** a sudden increase in the number of crimes committed in a country or area.

crime writer ▸ **noun** a writer of detective stories or thrillers.

criminal ▸ **noun** a person who has committed a crime: *these men are dangerous criminals.*
▸ **adjective 1** relating to crime: *he is charged with conspiracy to commit criminal damage.* ■ Law relating to crime as opposed to civil matters: *a criminal court.*
2 informal (of an action or situation) deplorable and shocking: *he may never fulfil his potential, and that would be a criminal waste.*
– DERIVATIVES **criminality** /-ˈnalɪti/ noun, **criminally** adverb.
– ORIGIN late Middle English (as an adjective): from late Latin *criminalis*, from Latin *crimen, crimin-* (see CRIME).

criminal conversation ▸ **noun** [mass noun] historical adultery, especially as formerly constituting grounds for the recovery of legal damages by a husband from his wife's adulterous partner.

criminalistics ▸ **plural noun** [treated as sing.] another term for FORENSICS.

criminalize (also **criminalise**) ▸ **verb** [with obj.] turn (an activity) into a criminal offence by making it illegal: *his view is that the state should not criminalize drug use but discourage it.* ■ turn (someone) into a criminal by making their activities illegal: *these punitive measures would further criminalize travellers for their way of life.*
– DERIVATIVES **criminalization** /-ˈzeɪʃ(ə)n/ noun.

criminal law ▸ **noun** [mass noun] a system of law concerned with the punishment of offenders. Contrasted with CIVIL LAW.

criminal libel ▸ **noun** [mass noun] Law the offence of making a malicious defamatory statement in a permanent form.

criminal record ▸ **noun** a list of a person's previous criminal convictions: *the caution wouldn't go on his criminal record.* ■ a history of being convicted for crime: *he admits he has a criminal record.*

criminogenic /ˌkrɪmɪnəˈdʒɛnɪk/ ▸ **adjective** (of a system, situation, or place) causing or likely to cause criminal behaviour: *the criminogenic nature of homelessness.*

criminology /ˌkrɪmɪˈnɒlədʒi/ ▸ **noun** [mass noun] the scientific study of crime and criminals.
– DERIVATIVES **criminological** adjective, **criminologist** noun.
– ORIGIN late 19th cent.: from Latin *crimen, crimin-* 'crime' + -LOGY.

criminy /ˈkrɪmɪni/ ▸ **exclamation** US informal used to express surprise or disbelief: *criminy, what is this world coming to?*
– ORIGIN late 17th cent. (as *crimine*): origin uncertain; perhaps an alteration of CHRIST, perhaps from Italian *crimine* 'crime'.

crimp ▸ **verb** [with obj.] **1** compress (something) into small folds or ridges: *she crimped the edge of the pie.* ■ connect (a wire or cable) by squeezing the end or ends: *pliers will crimp wires together.* ■ (often as adj. **crimped**) make waves in (someone's hair) with a hot iron: *crimped blonde hair.*
2 N. Amer. informal have a limiting or adverse effect on (something): *his zeal about his career can crimp the rest of his life.*
▸ **noun 1** a folded or compressed edge. ■ a small connecting piece for crimping wires or lines together.
2 N. Amer. informal a restriction or limitation: *the crimp on take-home pay has been even tighter since taxes were raised.*
– PHRASES **put a crimp in** N. Amer. informal have an adverse effect on: *well, that puts a crimp in my theory.*
– DERIVATIVES **crimpy** adjective.
– ORIGIN Old English *gecrympan*, of Germanic origin; related to Dutch *krimpen* 'shrink, wrinkle'. Of rare occurrence before the 18th cent., the word was perhaps reintroduced from Low German or Dutch.

crimper ▸ **noun 1** a person or thing that crimps.
2 informal a hairdresser.

Crimplene /ˈkrɪmpliːn/ ▸ **noun** [mass noun] trademark a synthetic crease-resistant fibre and fabric.
– ORIGIN 1950s: perhaps from the name of the *Crimple* valley in Yorkshire, site of the ICI laboratory where the fabric was developed, + -ENE.

crimson /ˈkrɪmz(ə)n/ ▸ **adjective** of a rich deep red colour inclining to purple: *she blushed crimson with embarrassment.*
▸ **noun** [mass noun] a rich deep red colour inclining to purple.
▸ **verb** [no obj.] (of a person's face) become flushed, especially through embarrassment: *my face crimsoned and my hands began to shake.*
– ORIGIN late Middle English: from obsolete French *cramoisin* or Old Spanish *cremesin*, based on Arabic *qirmizī*, from *qirmiz* (see KERMES). Compare with CARMINE.

cringe /krɪn(d)ʒ/ ▸ **verb** (**cringes, cringing, cringed**) [no obj.] bend one's head and body in fear or apprehension or in a servile manner: *he **cringed away from** the blow* | (as adj. **cringing**) *we are surrounded by cringing yes-men and sycophants.* ■ experience an inward shiver of embarrassment or disgust: *I cringed at the fellow's stupidity.*
▸ **noun** an act of cringing.
– DERIVATIVES **cringer** noun.

– ORIGIN Middle English *crenge, crenche*, related to Old English *cringan, crincan* 'bend, yield, fall in battle', of Germanic origin and related to Dutch *krengen* 'heel over' and German *krank* 'sick', also to CRANK[1].

cringe-making ▶ adjective another term for CRINGEWORTHY.

cringeworthy ▶ adjective informal causing feelings of embarrassment or awkwardness: *the play's cast was excellent, but the dialogue was unforgivably cringeworthy.*

cringingly ▶ adverb in a servile or sycophantic way: *Carfax shrank cringingly to one side.* ■ [usu. as submodifier] informal so as to make one feel embarrassed or disgusted: *their early performances were cringingly awkward.*

cringle ▶ noun Sailing a ring of rope containing a thimble, for another rope to pass through.
– ORIGIN early 17th cent.: from Low German *kringel*, diminutive of *kring* 'ring'.

crinkle ▶ verb form into small surface creases or wrinkles: [no obj.] *Rose's face crinkled in bewilderment* | [with obj.] *he smiled boyishly, crinkling his eyes* | (as adj. **crinkled**) *a skirt in crinkled fabric.*
▶ noun a wrinkle or crease on the surface of something: *there was a crinkle of suspicion on her forehead.*
– ORIGIN late Middle English: related to Old English *crincan* (see CRINGE).

crinkle-cut ▶ adjective (especially of chips) cut with wavy edges.

crinkly ▶ adjective (**crinklier**, **crinkliest**) full of creases or wrinkles; wrinkled: *brown crinkly paper.*

crinkum-crankum /krɪŋkəmˈkraŋkəm/ ▶ noun [mass noun] archaic elaborate decoration or detail.
– ORIGIN mid 17th cent.: fanciful reduplication of the nouns CRANK[1] and CRANK[2].

crinoid /ˈkrʌmɔɪd, ˈkrɪnɔɪd/ Zoology ▶ noun an echinoderm of the class Crinoidea, which comprises the sea lilies and feather stars.
▶ adjective relating to or denoting crinoids.
– DERIVATIVES **crinoidal** /-ˈnɔɪd(ə)l/ adjective.

Crinoidea /krʌɪˈnɔɪdɪə/ ▶ plural noun Zoology a class of echinoderms that comprises the sea lilies and feather stars. They have slender feathery arms and (in some kinds) a stalk for attachment, and were abundant in the Palaeozoic era.
– ORIGIN modern Latin (plural), from Greek *krinoeidēs* 'lily-like', from *krinon* 'lily'.

crinoline /ˈkrɪn(ə)lɪn/ ▶ noun historical **1** a stiffened or hooped petticoat worn to make a long skirt stand out.
2 [mass noun] a stiff fabric made of horsehair and cotton or linen thread, used for stiffening petticoats or as a lining.
– ORIGIN mid 19th cent. (originally in sense 2, early crinolines being made of such material): from French, formed irregularly from Latin *crinis* 'hair' + *linum* 'thread'.

criollo /krɪˈɒləʊ, -ɒljəʊ/ ▶ noun (pl. **criollos**) **1** a person from Spanish South or Central America, especially one of pure Spanish descent. ■ a horse or other domestic animal of a South or Central American breed.
2 (also **criollo tree**) a cacao tree of a variety producing thin-shelled beans of high quality.
– ORIGIN late 19th cent.: Spanish, literally 'native to the locality' (see CREOLE).

crip ▶ noun **1** offensive, chiefly N. Amer. a disabled person.
2 (usu. **Crip**) a member of a Los Angeles street gang.
– ORIGIN early 20th cent.: abbreviation of CRIPPLE.

cripes /krʌɪps/ ▶ exclamation informal used as a euphemism for Christ.
– ORIGIN early 20th cent.: alteration of CHRIST.

Crippen /ˈkrɪpɪn/, Hawley Harvey (1862–1910), American-born British murderer; known as **Doctor Crippen**. Crippen poisoned his wife at their London home and sailed to Canada with his former secretary. His arrest in Canada was achieved through the intervention of radio-telegraphy, the first case of its use in apprehending a criminal; Crippen was later hanged.

cripple ▶ noun dated or offensive a person who is unable to walk or move properly through disability or because of injury to their back or legs. ■ a person with a severe limitation of a specified kind: *an emotional cripple.*
▶ verb [with obj.] **1** cause (someone) to become unable to walk or move properly: *a young student was crippled for life* | (as adj. **crippling**) *a crippling disease.* ■ cause severe and disabling damage to (a machine).
2 cause a severe and almost insuperable problem for: *developing countries are crippled by their debts.*
– DERIVATIVES **crippler** noun, **cripplingly** adverb.
– ORIGIN Old English: from two words, *crypel* and *crēopel*, both of Germanic origin and related to CREEP.

> **USAGE** The word **cripple** has long been in use to refer to 'a person unable to walk through illness or disability' and is recorded (in the *Lindisfarne Gospels*) as early as AD 950. In the 20th century the term acquired offensive connotations and has now been largely replaced by broader terms such as 'disabled person'.

crippled ▶ adjective (of a person) unable to walk or move properly; disabled: *a crippled old man.* ■ (of a machine) severely damaged: *the pilot displayed skill and nerve in landing the crippled plane.*

> **USAGE** See USAGE at CRIPPLE.

crise de nerfs /ˌkriːz də ˈnɛː(f)/, French /kriz də nɛrf/ ▶ noun (pl. **crises de nerfs** pronunc. **same**) dated an attack of anxiety: *I had a crise de nerfs before the first performance.*
– ORIGIN French, literally 'crisis of nerves'.

crisis ▶ noun (pl. **crises**) a time of intense difficulty or danger: *the current economic crisis* | [mass noun] *the monarchy was in crisis.* ■ a time when a difficult or important decision must be made: [as modifier] *the situation has reached crisis point.* ■ the turning point of a disease when an important change takes place, indicating either recovery or death.
– ORIGIN late Middle English (denoting the turning point of a disease): medical Latin, from Greek *krisis* 'decision', from *krinein* 'decide'. The general sense 'decisive point' dates from the early 17th cent.

crisis management ▶ noun [mass noun] the process by which a business or other organization deals with a sudden emergency situation.

crisp ▶ adjective **1** (of a substance) firm, dry, and brittle: *crisp bacon* | *the snow is lovely and crisp.* ■ (of a fruit or vegetable) firm and juicy: *a crisp lettuce.* ■ (of paper or cloth) stiff and uncreased: *£65 in crisp new notes.* ■ (of hair) having tight curls.
2 (of the weather) cool, fresh, and invigorating: *a crisp autumn day.*
3 (of a way of speaking) briskly decisive and matter-of-fact, without hesitation or unnecessary detail: *her answer was crisp.*
▶ noun **1** (also **potato crisp**) Brit. a wafer-thin slice of potato fried or baked until crisp and eaten as a snack.
2 a dessert of fruit baked with a crunchy topping of brown sugar, butter, and flour: *rhubarb crisp.*
▶ verb [with obj.] **1** give (something, especially food) a crisp surface by placing it in an oven or under a grill: *crisp the pitta in the oven.* ■ [no obj.] (of food) acquire a crisp surface in this way.
2 archaic curl (something) into short, stiff, wavy folds or crinkles.
– PHRASES **burn something to a crisp** burn something completely, leaving only a charred remnant.
– DERIVATIVES **crisply** adverb, **crispness** noun.
– ORIGIN Old English (referring to hair in the sense 'curly'): from Latin *crispus* 'curled'. Other senses may result from symbolic interpretation of the sound of the word.

crispate ▶ adjective Botany (especially of a leaf) having a wavy or curly edge.
– ORIGIN mid 19th cent.: from Latin *crispatus*, past participle of *crispare* 'to curl'.

crispbread ▶ noun a thin, crisp biscuit made from crushed rye or wheat.

crisper ▶ noun a compartment at the bottom of a refrigerator for storing fruit and vegetables.

crispy ▶ adjective (**crispier**, **crispiest**) (of food) having a firm, dry, and brittle surface or texture: *crispy fried bacon.*
– DERIVATIVES **crispiness** noun.

criss ▶ adjective W. Indian smart or fashionable.
– ORIGIN alteration of CRISP.

crissal thrasher /ˈkrɪs(ə)l/ ▶ noun a large grey thrasher (songbird) with a red patch under the tail, found in the south-western US and Mexico.
● *Toxostoma dorsale* (or *crissale*), family Mimidae.
– ORIGIN late 19th cent.: *crissal* from modern Latin *crissum* (denoting the vent region of a bird) + -AL.

criss-cross ▶ noun a pattern of intersecting straight lines or paths: *the blotting paper was marked with a criss-cross of different inks.*
▶ adjective containing a number of straight lines or paths which intersect each other: *the streets ran in a regular criss-cross pattern* | [as adv.] *the swords were strung criss-cross on his back.*
▶ verb [with obj.] form a pattern of intersecting lines or paths on (a place): *the green hill was criss-crossed with a network of sheep tracks* | [no obj.] *the smaller streets criss-crossed in a grid pattern.* ■ move or travel around (a place) by going back and forth repeatedly: *the President criss-crossed America.*
– ORIGIN early 17th cent. (denoting a figure of a cross preceding the alphabet in a hornbook): from *Christ-cross* (in the same sense in late Middle English), from *Christ's cross*. The form was later treated as a reduplication of CROSS.

crista /ˈkrɪstə/ ▶ noun (pl. **cristae** /-tiː/) **1** Anatomy & Zoology a ridge or crest.
2 Biology each of the partial partitions in a mitochondrion formed by infolding of the inner membrane.
– DERIVATIVES **cristate** adjective.
– ORIGIN mid 19th cent.: from Latin, 'tuft, plume, crest'.

cristobalite /krɪˈstəʊbəlʌɪt/ ▶ noun [mass noun] a form of silica which is the main component of opal and also occurs as small octahedral crystals.
– ORIGIN late 19th cent.: named after *Cerro San Cristóbal* in Mexico, where it was discovered, + -ITE[1].

crit ▶ noun informal short for CRITICISM or CRITIC. ■ Brit. a review of a literary or artistic work or production.

criterion /krʌɪˈtɪərɪən/ ▶ noun (pl. **criteria** /-rɪə/) a principle or standard by which something may be judged or decided: *they award a green label to products that meet certain environmental criteria.*
– DERIVATIVES **criterial** adjective.
– ORIGIN early 17th cent.: from Greek *kritērion* 'means of judging', from *kritēs* (see CRITIC).

> **USAGE** Strictly speaking, the singular form (following the original Greek) is **criterion** and the plural form is **criteria**. It is a common mistake to use **criteria** as if it were a singular, as in *a further **criteria** needs to be considered.*

critic ▶ noun **1** a person who expresses an unfavourable opinion of something: *critics of the new legislation say it is too broad.*
2 a person who judges the merits of literary or artistic works, especially one who does so professionally: *a film critic.*
– ORIGIN late 16th cent.: from Latin *criticus*, from Greek *kritikos*, from *kritēs* 'a judge', from *krinein* 'judge, decide'.

critical ▶ adjective **1** expressing adverse or disapproving comments or judgements: *I was very **critical** of the previous regime.*
2 expressing or involving an analysis of the merits and faults of a work of literature, music, or art: *she never won the critical acclaim she sought.* ■ (of a text) incorporating a detailed and scholarly analysis and commentary: *a critical edition of a Bach sonata.* ■ involving the objective analysis and evaluation of an issue in order to form a judgement: *professors often find it difficult to encourage critical thinking amongst their students.*
3 (of a situation or problem) having the potential to become disastrous; at a point of crisis: *the floodwaters had not receded and the situation was still critical.* ■ extremely ill and at risk of death: *she was critical but stable in Middlesbrough General Hospital.* ■ having a decisive or crucial importance in the success or failure of something: *temperature is a critical factor in successful fruit storage* | [in combination] *time-critical tasks.*
4 Mathematics & Physics relating to or denoting a point of transition from one state to another.
5 (of a nuclear reactor or fuel) maintaining a self-sustaining chain reaction: *the reactor is due to go critical in October.*
– DERIVATIVES **criticality** noun (sense 3, sense 4), **critically** adverb [as submodifier] *he's critically ill*, **criticalness** noun.
– ORIGIN mid 16th cent. (in the sense 'relating to the crisis of a disease'): from late Latin *criticus* (see CRITIC).

critical angle ▶ noun Optics the angle of incidence beyond which rays of light passing through a denser medium to the surface of a less dense medium are no longer refracted but totally reflected.

critical apparatus ▶ noun see APPARATUS (sense 3).

critical damping ▶ noun [mass noun] Physics damping just sufficient to prevent oscillations.

critical list ▶ noun [in sing.] a list of those who are critically ill in hospital.

critical mass ▶ noun [in sing.] **1** Physics the minimum amount of fissile material needed to maintain a nuclear chain reaction.

C

2 the minimum size or amount of resources required to start or maintain a venture: *some of our new industries are now reaching critical mass.*

critical path ▶ **noun** the sequence of stages determining the minimum time needed for an operation, especially when analysed on a computer for a large organization.

critical path analysis ▶ **noun** [mass noun] the mathematical network analysis technique of planning complex working procedures with reference to the critical path of each alternative system.

critical period ▶ **noun** Psychology a period during someone's development in which a particular skill or characteristic is believed to be most readily acquired.

critical point ▶ **noun 1** Chemistry a point on a phase diagram at which both the liquid and gas phases of a substance have the same density, and are therefore indistinguishable.
2 Mathematics US term for **STATIONARY POINT**.

critical pressure ▶ **noun** Chemistry the pressure of a gas or vapour in its critical state.

critical state ▶ **noun** [mass noun] Chemistry the state of a substance when it is at the critical point, i.e. at critical temperature and pressure.

critical temperature ▶ **noun** Chemistry the temperature of a gas in its critical state, above which it cannot be liquefied by pressure alone.

critical theory ▶ **noun** [mass noun] a philosophical approach to culture, and especially to literature, that considers the social, historical, and ideological forces and structures which produce and constrain it.

critical volume ▶ **noun** Chemistry the volume occupied by a unit mass of a gas or vapour in its critical state.

criticaster /ˌkrɪtɪˈkastə, ˈkrɪtɪˌkastə/ ▶ **noun** rare a minor or inferior critic.
– ORIGIN late 17th cent.: from **CRITIC** + **-ASTER**.

criticism ▶ **noun** [mass noun] **1** the expression of disapproval of someone or something on the basis of perceived faults or mistakes: *he received a lot of criticism* | [count noun] *he ignored the criticisms of his friends.*
2 the analysis and judgement of the merits and faults of a literary or artistic work: *alternative methods of criticism supported by well-developed literary theories.* ■ the scholarly investigation of literary or historical texts to determine their origin or intended form.
– ORIGIN early 17th cent.: from **CRITIC** or Latin *criticus* + **-ISM**.

criticize (also **criticise**) ▶ **verb** [with obj.] **1** indicate the faults of (someone or something) in a disapproving way: *the opposition criticized the government's failure to consult adequately* | *technicians were criticized for defective workmanship.*
2 form and express a judgement of (a literary or artistic work): *a literary text may be criticized on two grounds: the semantic and the expressive.*
– DERIVATIVES **criticizable** adjective, **criticizer** noun.

critique /krɪˈtiːk/ ▶ **noun** a detailed analysis and assessment of something, especially a literary, philosophical, or political theory.
▶ **verb** (**critiques**, **critiquing**, **critiqued**) [with obj.] evaluate (a theory or practice) in a detailed and analytical way: *the authors critique the methods and practices used in the research.*
– ORIGIN mid 17th cent. (as a noun): from French, based on Greek *kritikē tekhnē* 'critical art'.

critter ▶ **noun** informal or dialect, chiefly N. Amer. a living creature; an animal. ■ [usu. with adj.] a person of a particular kind: *the old critter used to live in a shack.*
– ORIGIN early 19th cent.: variant of **CREATURE**.

CRM ▶ **abbreviation** customer relationship management, denoting strategies and software that enable a company to optimize its customer relations.

croak ▶ **noun** a characteristic deep hoarse sound made by a frog or a crow. ■ a sound resembling a croak: *Lorton tried to laugh—it came out as a croak.*
▶ **verb** [no obj.] **1** (of a frog or crow) make a characteristic deep hoarse sound. ■ (of a person) make a sound similar to a croak when speaking or laughing: [with direct speech] *'Thank you,' I croaked.*
2 informal die: *the dog finally croaked in 1987.* ■ [with obj.] kill (someone): *there are a few people down there who'd like to croak him.*
– ORIGIN Middle English (as a verb): imitative.

croaker ▶ **noun** a person or animal that croaks. ■ another term for **DRUM**³.

croaky ▶ **adjective** (**croakier**, **croakiest**) (of a person's voice) deep and hoarse.
– DERIVATIVES **croakily** adverb.

Croat /ˈkrəʊat/ ▶ **noun 1** a native or inhabitant of Croatia, or a person of Croatian descent.
2 [mass noun] the Southern Slavic language of the Croats, almost identical to Serbian but written in the Roman alphabet. See **SERBO-CROAT**.
▶ **adjective** relating to the Croats or their language.
– ORIGIN from modern Latin *Croatae* (plural), from Serbian and Croatian *Hrvat*.

Croatia /krəʊˈeɪʃə/ a country in SE Europe, formerly a constituent republic of Yugoslavia; pop. 4,489,400 (est. 2009); language, Croatian; capital, Zagreb. Croatian name **HRVATSKA**.

> Apart from a period of Turkish rule in the 16th–17th centuries, Croatia largely remained linked with Hungary until 1918, when it joined the Kingdom of the Serbs, Croats, and Slovenes (later Yugoslavia). After a period in the Second World War as a Nazi puppet state (1941–5), Croatia became part of Yugoslavia once more and remained a constituent republic until it declared itself independent in 1991. The secession of Croatia led to war between Croats and the Serb minority, and with Serbia; a ceasefire was called in 1992.

Croatian ▶ **noun & adjective** another term for **CROAT**.

croc ▶ **noun** informal a crocodile.
– ORIGIN late 19th cent.: abbreviation.

Croce /ˈkrəʊtʃeɪ/, Italian /ˈkrɔtʃe/, Benedetto (1866–1952), Italian philosopher and politician. In his 'Philosophy of Spirit' he denied the physical reality of a work of art and identified philosophical endeavour with a methodological approach to history. A former Minister of Education, he helped to rebuild democracy in Italy after the fall of Mussolini.

crochet /ˈkrəʊʃeɪ, -ʃi/ ▶ **noun** [mass noun] a handicraft in which yarn is made up into a textured fabric by means of a hooked needle: [as modifier] *a crochet hook.* ■ crocheted fabric or items: *the bikini is tiny, three triangles of cotton crochet.*
▶ **verb** (**crochets** /ˈkrəʊʃeɪz/, **crocheting** /-ʃeɪɪŋ/, **crocheted** /-ʃeɪd/) [with obj.] make (a garment or piece of fabric) using crochet: *she had crocheted the shawl herself* | [no obj.] *her mother had stopped crocheting.*
– DERIVATIVES **crocheter** /ˈkrəʊʃeɪə/ noun.
– ORIGIN mid 19th cent.: from French, diminutive of *croc* 'hook', from Old Norse *krókr*.

croci plural form of **CROCUS**.

crocidolite /krə(ʊ)ˈsɪdəlʌɪt/ ▶ **noun** [mass noun] a fibrous blue or green mineral consisting of a silicate of iron and sodium. Also called **BLUE ASBESTOS**.
– ORIGIN mid 19th cent.: from Greek *krokis*, *krokid-* 'nap of cloth' + **-LITE**.

crock¹ informal ▶ **noun** Brit. an old person who is considered to be feeble and useless. ■ an old and worn-out vehicle.
▶ **verb** [with obj.] Brit. injure (part of the body): *he crocked a shoulder in the test against South Africa.* ■ (as adj. **crocked**) N. Amer. drunk: *his party guests were pretty crocked.*
– ORIGIN late Middle English: perhaps from Flemish, and probably related to **CRACK**. Originally a Scots term for an old ewe, it came in the late 19th cent. to denote an old or broken-down horse.

crock² ▶ **noun 1** an earthenware pot or jar. ■ a broken piece of earthenware. ■ a plate, cup, or other item of crockery.
2 (also vulgar slang **crock of shit**) chiefly N. Amer. something considered to be complete nonsense.
– ORIGIN Old English *croc*, *crocca*, of Germanic origin; related to Old Norse *krukka* and probably to Dutch *kruik* and German *Krug*.

crockery ▶ **noun** [mass noun] plates, dishes, cups, and other similar items, especially ones made of earthenware or china.
– ORIGIN early 18th cent.: from obsolete *crocker* 'potter', from **CROCK**².

crocket /ˈkrɒkɪt/ ▶ **noun** (in Gothic architecture) a small carved ornament, typically a bud or curled leaf, on the inclined side of a pinnacle, arch, etc.
– ORIGIN Middle English (denoting a curl or roll of hair): from Old Northern French, variant of Old French *crochet* (see **CROTCHET**). The current sense dates from the late 17th cent., but *crotchet* was used in the same sense from late Middle English until the 19th cent.

Crockett /ˈkrɒkɪt/, Davy (1786–1836), American frontiersman, soldier, and politician; full name *David Crockett*. He was a member of the House of Representatives 1827–35 and cultivated the image of a rough backwoods legislator. On leaving politics he returned to the frontier, where he took up the cause of Texan independence and was killed at the siege of the Alamo.

Crockford Crockford's Clerical Directory, a reference book of Anglican clergy in the British Isles first issued in 1860.
– ORIGIN named after John *Crockford* (1823–65), its first publisher.

Crockpot ▶ **noun** N. Amer. trademark a large electric cooking pot, used to cook stews and other dishes slowly.

crocodile ▶ **noun 1** a large predatory semiaquatic reptile with long jaws, long tail, short legs, and a horny textured skin. ● Family Crocodylidae: three genera, in particular *Crocodylus*, and several species. ■ [mass noun] leather made from crocodile skin, used especially to make bags and shoes.
2 Brit. informal a line of schoolchildren walking in pairs.
– ORIGIN Middle English *cocodrille*, *cokadrill*, from Old French *cocodrille*, via medieval Latin from Latin *crocodilus*, from Greek *krokodilos* 'worm of the stones', from *krokē* 'pebble' + *drilos* 'worm'. The spelling was changed in the 16th cent. to conform with the Latin and Greek forms.

crocodile bird ▶ **noun** the Egyptian plover, which is said to feed on insects parasitic on crocodiles.

crocodile clip ▶ **noun** chiefly Brit. a sprung metal clip with long, serrated jaws, used attached to an electric cable for making a temporary connection to a battery or other component.

crocodile tears ▶ **plural noun** tears or expressions of sorrow that are insincere.
– ORIGIN mid 16th cent.: said to be so named from a belief that crocodiles wept while devouring or luring their prey.

crocodilian /ˌkrɒkəˈdɪlɪən/ ▶ **noun** Zoology a large predatory semiaquatic reptile of an order that comprises the crocodiles, alligators, caimans, and gharial. Crocodilians are distinguished by long jaws, short legs, and a powerful tail. ● Order Crocodylia: three families.
▶ **adjective** relating to crocodilians.

crocoite /ˈkrəʊkəʊʌɪt/ ▶ **noun** [mass noun] a rare bright orange mineral consisting of lead chromate.
– ORIGIN mid 19th cent.: originally as French *crocoise*, from Greek *krokoeis* 'saffron-coloured', from *krokos* 'crocus'. The spelling was altered to *crocoisite*, then *crocoite*.

crocosmia /krə(ʊ)ˈkɒzmɪə/ ▶ **noun** a plant of a genus that includes montbretia. ● Genus *Crocosmia*, family Iridaceae.
– ORIGIN modern Latin, from Greek *krokos* 'saffron'.

crocus /ˈkrəʊkəs/ ▶ **noun** (pl. **crocuses** or **croci** /-kʌɪ, -kiː/) a small spring-flowering Eurasian plant of the iris family, which grows from a corm and bears bright yellow, purple, or white flowers. See also **AUTUMN CROCUS**. ● Genus *Crocus*, family Iridaceae.
– ORIGIN late Middle English (also denoting saffron, obtained from a species of crocus): via Latin from Greek *krokos*, of Semitic origin and related to Hebrew *karkōm* and Arabic *kurkum*.

croeso /ˈkrɔɪsɔː/ ▶ **exclamation** Welsh welcome!
– ORIGIN Welsh.

Croesus /ˈkriːsəs/ (6th century BC), last king of Lydia *c.*560–546 BC. Renowned for his great wealth, he subjugated the Greek cities on the coast of Asia Minor before being overthrown by Cyrus the Great. ■ (as noun **a Croesus**) a person of great wealth.

croft Brit. ▶ **noun** a small rented farm, especially one in Scotland, comprising a plot of arable land attached to a house and with a right of pasturage held in common with other such farms. ■ an enclosed field used for tillage or pasture, typically attached to a house and worked by the occupier.
▶ **verb** [with obj.] farm (land) as a croft or crofts.
– ORIGIN Old English: of unknown origin.

crofter ▶ **noun** Brit. a person who farms a croft.

crofting ▶ **noun** [mass noun] Brit. the practice or system of farming in crofts: [as modifier] *a crofting community.*

Crohn's disease /ˈkrəʊnz/ ▶ **noun** [mass noun] a chronic inflammatory disease of the intestines, especially the colon and ileum, associated with ulcers and fistulae.
– ORIGIN 1930s: named after Burrill B. *Crohn* (1884–1983), American pathologist, who was among the first to describe it.

croissant /ˈkrwasɒ̃/ ▶ **noun** a French crescent-shaped roll made of sweet flaky yeast dough, eaten for breakfast.

– ORIGIN late 19th cent.: French (see **CRESCENT**). The term had occasionally been recorded earlier as a variant of *crescent*.

Cro-Magnon man /krəʊˈmanjɔ̃ man, -ˈmagnən/ ▶ **noun** [mass noun] the earliest form of modern human in Europe, associated with the Aurignacian flint industry. The group's appearance *c.*35,000 years ago marked the beginning of the Upper Palaeolithic and the apparent decline and disappearance of Neanderthal man; the group persisted at least into the Neolithic period.
– ORIGIN *Cro-Magnon*, the name of a hill in the Dordogne, France, where remains were found in 1868.

Cromarty Firth /ˈkrɒməti/ an inlet of the Moray Firth on the coast of Highland region, northern Scotland. The shipping forecast area **Cromarty** extends far beyond this, covering Scottish coastal waters roughly from Aberdeen in the south to John o'Groats in the north.

crombec /ˈkrɒmbɛk/ ▶ **noun** a small African warbler with a very short tail, and grey or green upper parts with rufous or white underparts. ● Genus *Sylvietta*, family Sylviidae: several species, in particular the (**northern**) **crombec** (*S. brachyura*).
– ORIGIN early 20th cent.: from French, from Dutch *krom* 'crooked' + *bek* 'beak'.

Crome /krəʊm/, John (1768–1821), English painter. Founder and leading member of the Norwich School, he later developed a distinctive romantic style of his own, exemplified in such landscapes as *Slate Quarries* (undated).

Cromerian /krəʊˈmɪərɪən/ ▶ **adjective** Geology relating to or denoting an interglacial period in the Middle Pleistocene of Britain and northern Europe, preceding the Elster (Anglian) glaciation. ■ (as noun **the Cromerian**) the Cromerian interglacial period or the system of fossil-rich deposits laid down during it.
– ORIGIN early 20th cent.: from *Cromer*, in Norfolk, site of an outcrop of fossil-rich deposits from this period, + **-IAN**.

cromlech /ˈkrɒmlɛk/ ▶ **noun 1** (in Wales) a megalithic tomb consisting of a large flat stone laid on upright ones; a dolmen.
2 (in Brittany) a circle of standing stones.
– ORIGIN Welsh, from *crom*, feminine of *crwm* 'arched' + *llech* 'flat stone'; sense 2 is via French from Breton *krommlec'h*.

cromoglycate /ˌkrəʊmə(ʊ)ˈglʌɪseɪt/ (also **sodium cromoglycate**) ▶ **noun** [mass noun] Medicine a synthetic non-steroidal anti-inflammatory drug, inhaled to prevent asthmatic attacks and allergic reactions.
– ORIGIN mid 20th cent.: from an alteration of *chromone* (a bicyclic ketone) + *glyc(erol)* + **-ATE**[1].

Crompton[1] /ˈkrɒmpt(ə)n/, Richmal (1890–1969), English writer; pseudonym of *Richmal Crompton Lamburn*. She made her name with *Just William* (1922), a collection of stories for children about a mischievous schoolboy, William Brown. She published a further thirty-seven collections based on the same character, as well as some fifty books for adults.

Crompton[2] /ˈkrɒmpt(ə)n/, Samuel (1753–1827), English inventor. Famed for his invention of the spinning mule, he lacked the means to obtain a patent and sold his rights to a Bolton industrialist for £67. The House of Commons subsequently gave him £5,000 in compensation.

Cromwell[1] /ˈkrɒmwɛl/, Oliver (1599–1658), English general and statesman, Lord Protector of the Commonwealth 1653–8. Cromwell was the leader of the victorious Parliamentary forces (or Roundheads) in the English Civil War. As head of state he styled himself Lord Protector, and refused Parliament's offer of the Crown in 1657. His rule was notable for its puritan reforms in the Church of England. He was briefly succeeded by his son **Richard** (1626–1712), who was forced into exile in 1659.
– DERIVATIVES **Cromwellian** adjective.

Cromwell[2] /ˈkrɒmwɛl/, Thomas (*c.*1485–1540), English statesman, chief minister to Henry VIII 1531–40. He presided over the king's divorce from Catherine of Aragon (1533) and his break with the Roman Catholic Church as well as the dissolution of the monasteries and the 1534 Act of Supremacy. He fell from favour over Henry's marriage to Anne of Cleves and was executed on a charge of treason.

cron ▶ **noun** [usu. as modifier] Computing a command to an operating system or server for a job that is to be executed at a specified time: *a cron job*.
– ORIGIN 1990s: from **CHRONOLOGICAL**.

crone ▶ **noun** an ugly old woman.
– ORIGIN late Middle English: via Middle Dutch *croonje*, *caroonje* 'carcass, old ewe' from Old Northern French *caroigne* 'carrion, cantankerous woman' (see **CARRION**).

Cronin /ˈkrəʊnɪn/, A. J. (1896–1981), Scottish novelist; full name *Archibald Joseph Cronin*. His novels, including *The Citadel* (1937), often reflect his early experiences as a doctor and were successfully adapted for radio and television as *Dr Finlay's Casebook* in the 1960s and 1990s.

croning /ˈkrəʊnɪŋ/ ▶ **noun** (especially among feminists in the US and Australasia) a celebration or ceremony to honour older women.
– ORIGIN 1990s: blend of **CRONE** + *crowning* from **CROWN**.

cronk ▶ **adjective** Austral./NZ informal, dated unfit or unsound. ■ fraudulent.
– ORIGIN late 19th cent.: probably related to **CRANK**[3].

Cronus /ˈkrɒnəs, ˈkrəʊn-/ (also **Kronos**) Greek Mythology the supreme god until dethroned by Zeus. The youngest son of Uranus (Heaven) and Gaia (Earth), Cronus overthrew and castrated his father and then married his sister Rhea. Because he was fated to be overcome by one of his male children, Cronus swallowed all of them as soon as they were born, but when Zeus was born Rhea deceived him and hid the baby away. Roman equivalent **SATURN**.

crony /ˈkrəʊni/ ▶ **noun** (pl. **cronies**) informal, often derogatory a close friend or companion: *he went gambling with his cronies*.
– ORIGIN mid 17th cent. (originally Cambridge university slang): from Greek *khronios* 'long-lasting' (here used to mean 'contemporary'), from *khronos* 'time'. Compare with **CHUM**[1].

cronyism (also **croneyism**) ▶ **noun** [mass noun] derogatory the appointment of friends and associates to positions of authority, without proper regard to their qualifications.

crook ▶ **noun 1** the hooked staff of a shepherd. ■ a bishop's crozier. ■ a bend in something, especially at the elbow in a person's arm: *her head was cradled in **the crook of** Luke's left arm*. ■ a piece of extra tubing which can be fitted to a brass instrument to lower the pitch by a set interval.
2 informal a person who is dishonest or a criminal.
▶ **verb** [with obj.] bend (something, especially a finger as a signal): *he crooked a finger for the waitress*.
▶ **adjective** Austral./NZ informal bad, unpleasant, or unsatisfactory: *it was pretty crook on the land in the early 1970s*. ■ (of a person or a part of the body) unwell or injured: *a crook knee*. ■ dishonest; illegal: *some pretty crook things went on there*.
– PHRASES **be crook on** Austral./NZ informal be annoyed by: *you're crook on me because I didn't walk out with you*. **go crook** Austral./NZ informal lose one's temper.
– DERIVATIVES **crookery** noun.
– ORIGIN Middle English (in the sense 'hooked tool or weapon'): from Old Norse *krókr* 'hook'. A noun sense 'deceit, guile, trickery' (compare with **CROOKED**) was recorded in Middle English but was obsolete by the 17th cent. The Australian senses are abbreviations of **CROOKED**.

crookback ▶ **noun** archaic a person with a hunchback.
– DERIVATIVES **crookbacked** adjective.

crooked /ˈkrʊkɪd/ ▶ **adjective** (**crookeder**, **crookedest**) **1** bent or twisted out of shape or out of place: *his teeth were yellow and crooked*.
2 informal dishonest; illegal: *a crooked business deal*.
3 (usu. **crooked on**) Austral./NZ informal annoyed; exasperated: *'It's not you I'm **crooked on**,' he assured Vivien*. [1940s: from the phrase *go crook* 'become angry'.]
– DERIVATIVES **crookedly** adverb, **crookedness** noun.
– ORIGIN Middle English: from **CROOK**, probably modelled on Old Norse *krókóttr* 'crooked, cunning'.

crookneck (also **crookneck squash**) ▶ **noun** N. Amer. a squash of a club-shaped variety with a curved neck and warty skin.

croon ▶ **verb** [no obj.] hum or sing in a soft, low voice, especially in a sentimental manner: *she was crooning to the child* | [with obj.] *the female vocalist crooned smoky blues into the microphone*. ■ [with direct speech] say in a soft, low voice: *'Goodbye, you lovely darling,' she crooned*.
▶ **noun** [in sing.] a soft, low voice or tone: *he sang in a gentle, highly expressive croon*.
– ORIGIN late 15th cent. (originally Scots and northern English): from Middle Low German and Middle Dutch *krōnen* 'groan, lament'. The use of *croon* in standard English was probably popularized by Robert Burns.

crooner ▶ **noun** a singer, typically a male one, who sings sentimental songs in a soft, low voice.

crop ▶ **noun 1** a cultivated plant that is grown on a large scale commercially, especially a cereal, fruit, or vegetable: *the main crops were oats and barley*. ■ an amount of produce harvested at one time: *a heavy crop of fruit*. ■ an abundance of something, especially a person's hair: *he had a thick **crop of** wiry hair*. ■ the total number of young farm animals born in a particular year on one farm.
2 a group or amount of related people or things appearing or occurring at one time: *the current crop of politicians*.
3 a hairstyle in which the hair is cut very short.
4 short for **RIDING CROP** or **HUNTING CROP**.
5 a pouch in a bird's gullet where food is stored or prepared for digestion. ■ an organ resembling a pouch in an insect or earthworm.
6 the entire tanned hide of an animal.
▶ **verb** (**crops**, **cropping**, **cropped**) **1** [with obj.] cut (something, especially a person's hair) very short: (as adj. **cropped**) *cropped blonde hair*. ■ (of an animal) bite off and eat the tops of (plants): *the horse was gratefully cropping the grass*. ■ cut the edges of (a photograph) in order to produce a better picture or to fit a given space.
2 [with obj.] harvest (plants or their produce) from a particular area: *hay would have been cropped several times through the summer*. ■ sow or plant (land) with plants that will produce food or fodder, especially on a large commercial scale: *the southern areas are cropped in cotton* | (as adj., with submodifier **cropped**) *intensively cropped areas*. ■ [no obj.] (of land or a plant) yield a harvest of plants or produce: *the parsley will need protection to continue cropping through the winter*.
– PHRASAL VERBS **crop out** (of rock) appear or be exposed at the surface of the earth. **crop up** appear, occur, or come to one's notice unexpectedly: *some urgent business had cropped up*.
– ORIGIN Old English, of Germanic origin; related to German *Kropf*. From Old English to the late 18th cent. there existed a sense 'flower head, ear of corn', giving rise to sense 1 of the noun and senses referring to the top of something, whence sense 4 of the noun.

crop circle ▶ **noun** an area of standing crops which has been flattened in the form of a circle or more complex pattern. No general cause of crop circles has been identified although various natural and unorthodox explanations have been put forward; many are known to have been hoaxes.

crop dusting ▶ **noun** [mass noun] the spraying of powdered insecticide or fertilizer on crops, especially from the air.
– DERIVATIVES **crop duster** noun.

crop-eared ▶ **adjective** historical **1** having the tops of the ears cut off.
2 (especially of a Roundhead in the English Civil War) having the hair cut very short.

cropland ▶ **noun** [mass noun] (also **croplands**) land used for growing crops.

crop-over ▶ **noun** [mass noun] a West Indian celebration marking the end of the sugar-cane harvest.

cropper ▶ **noun 1** a plant which yields a specified crop: *the white-fleshed varieties are the heaviest croppers*.
2 a machine or person that cuts or trims something.
3 chiefly US a person who raises a crop, especially as a sharecropper.
– PHRASES **come a cropper** Brit. informal fall heavily. ■ suffer a defeat or disaster: *the club's challenge for the championship has come a cropper*.

crop rotation ▶ **noun** see **ROTATION**.

crop top (also **cropped top**) ▶ **noun** a woman's casual sleeveless or short-sleeved garment or undergarment for the upper body, cut short so that it reveals the stomach.

croquembouche /ˌkrɒkɒmˈbuːʃ/ ▶ **noun** a decorative dessert consisting of choux pastry and crystallized fruit or other confectionery items arranged in a cone and held together by a caramel sauce.
– ORIGIN French, literally 'crunch in the mouth'.

croque-monsieur /ˌkrɒk məˈsjəː/ ▶ **noun** a fried or grilled cheese and ham sandwich.
– ORIGIN French, literally 'bite (a) man'.

croquet /ˈkrəʊkeɪ, -ki/ ▶ **noun** [mass noun] a game played on a lawn, in which wooden balls are driven through a series of square-topped hoops by means of mallets: [as modifier] *a croquet lawn*. ■ [count noun] an act of croqueting a ball.

▶ **verb** (**croquets** /ˈkrəʊkeɪz/, **croqueting** /-keɪɪŋ/, **croqueted** /-keɪd/) [with obj.] drive away (an opponent's ball) by holding one's own ball against it and striking this with the mallet. A player is entitled to do this after their ball has struck an opponent's.
– ORIGIN mid 19th cent.: perhaps a dialect form of French *crochet* 'hook'.

C

croquette /krə(ʊ)ˈkɛt/ ▶ **noun** a small ball or roll of vegetables, minced meat, or fish, fried in breadcrumbs: *a potato croquette*.
– ORIGIN French, from *croquer* 'to crunch'.

crore /krɔː/ ▶ **noun** (pl. **same** or **crores**) Indian ten million; one hundred lakhs, especially of rupees, units of measurement, or people.
– ORIGIN from Hindi *karoṛ*, based on Sanskrit *koṭi* 'ten millions'.

Crosby, Bing (1904–77), American singer and actor; born *Harry Lillis Crosby*. His songs include 'White Christmas' (from the film *Holiday Inn*, 1942). He also starred in a series of films (1940–62) with Bob Hope and Dorothy Lamour (1914–96).

crosier /ˈkrəʊzɪə, -ʒə/ ▶ **noun** variant spelling of **CROZIER**.

cross ▶ **noun 1** a mark, object, or figure formed by two short intersecting lines or pieces (+ or ×): *place a cross against the preferred choice*. ■ a cross (×) used to show that something is incorrect or unsatisfactory.
2 an upright post with a transverse bar, as used in antiquity for crucifixion. ■ **(the Cross)** the cross on which Christ was crucified. ■ a cross as an emblem of Christianity: *she wore a cross around her neck*. ■ short for **SIGN OF THE CROSS** (see **SIGN**). ■ a staff surmounted by a cross carried in religious processions and on ceremonial occasions before an archbishop.
3 something unavoidable that has to be endured: *she's just a cross we have to bear*.
4 a cross-shaped decoration awarded for personal valour or indicating rank in some orders of knighthood: *the Military Cross*.
5 (**the Cross**) the constellation Crux. Also called **SOUTHERN CROSS**.
6 an animal or plant resulting from cross-breeding; a hybrid: *a Galloway and shorthorn cross*. ■ **(a cross between)** a mixture or compromise of two things: *the system is a cross between a monorail and a conventional railway*.
7 Soccer a pass of the ball across the field towards the centre close to one's opponents' goal.
8 Boxing a blow given with a crosswise movement of the fist: *a right cross*.
▶ **verb** [with obj.] **1** go or extend across or to the other side of (an area, stretch of water, etc.): *she has crossed the Atlantic twice* | *two paths crossed the field* | figurative *a shadow of apprehension crossed her face* | [no obj.] *we crossed over the bridge*. ■ go across or climb over (an obstacle or boundary): *he attempted to cross the border into Jordan* | [no obj.] *we crossed over a stile*. ■ [no obj.] **(cross over)** (especially of an artist or an artistic style or work) begin to appeal to a different audience, especially a wider one: *a talented animator who crossed over to live action*.
2 [no obj.] pass in an opposite or different direction; intersect: *the two lines cross at 90°*. ■ [with obj.] cause to intersect or lie crosswise: *cross the cables in opposing directions* | *Michele sat back and crossed her arms*. ■ (of a letter) be dispatched before receipt of another from the person being written to: *our letters crossed*.
3 draw a line or lines across; mark with a cross: *voters should ask one question before they cross today's ballot paper*. ■ Brit. mark or annotate (a cheque), typically by drawing a pair of parallel lines across it, to indicate that it must be paid into a named bank account. ■ **(cross someone/thing off)** delete a name or item on a list as being no longer required or involved: *Liz crossed off the days on the calendar*. ■ **(cross something out/through)** delete an incorrect or inapplicable word or phrase by drawing a line through it.
4 (**cross oneself**) (of a person) make the sign of the cross in front of one's chest as a sign of Christian reverence or to invoke divine protection.
5 Soccer pass (the ball) across the field towards the centre when attacking.
6 cause (an animal of one species, breed, or variety) to breed with one of another species, breed, or variety: *many animals of the breed were crossed with the closely related Guernsey*. ■ cross-fertilize (a plant): *a hybrid tea was crossed with a polyantha rose*.
7 oppose or stand in the way of (someone): *no one dared cross him*.
▶ **adjective** annoyed: *he seemed to be very cross about something*.
– PHRASES **as cross as two sticks** Brit. very annoyed or irritated. **at cross purposes** misunderstanding or having different aims from one another: *we had been talking at cross purposes*. **cross one's fingers** (or **keep one's fingers crossed**) put one finger across another as a sign of hoping for good luck. **cross the floor** Brit. join the opposing side in Parliament. **cross my heart** (**and hope to die**) used to emphasize the truthfulness and sincerity of what one is saying. **cross one's legs** place one leg over the other while seated: *I crossed my my legs and leaned back in my chair*. **cross one's mind** (of a thought) occur to one, especially transiently: *it had not crossed Flora's mind that they might need payment*. **cross someone's palm with silver** humorous pay someone for a favour or service, especially before having one's fortune told. **cross someone's path** be met or encountered. **cross swords** have an argument or dispute. **crossed line** a telephone connection that has been wrongly made with the result that another call or calls can be heard. **get one's wires** (or **lines**) **crossed** become wrongly connected by telephone. ■ have a misunderstanding. **have a/one's cross to bear** have a difficult problem or responsibility one has to deal with: *as a smoker, I can tell you it's a horrible habit, but that's my cross to bear*.
– DERIVATIVES **crosser** noun, **crossly** adverb, **crossness** noun.
– ORIGIN late Old English (in the sense 'monument in the form of a cross'): from Old Norse *kross*, from Old Irish *cros*, from Latin *crux*.

cross- ▶ **combining form 1** denoting movement or position across something: *cross-channel*. ■ denoting interaction: *cross-pollinate*. ■ passing from side to side; transverse: *crosspiece*.
2 describing the form or figure of a cross: *crossbones*.

cross-assembler ▶ **noun** Computing an assembler which can convert instructions into machine code for a computer other than that on which it is run.

crossbar ▶ **noun 1** the horizontal bar between the two upright posts of a goal in football, rugby, hockey, etc.
2 the horizontal metal bar between the handlebars and saddle on a man's or boy's bicycle.

cross-beam ▶ **noun** a transverse beam.

cross-bedding ▶ **noun** [mass noun] Geology layering within a stratum and at an angle to the main bedding plane.

cross bench ▶ **noun** (in the House of Lords and some other legislatures) a bench occupied by members who are independent of any political party.
– DERIVATIVES **cross-bencher** noun.

crossbill ▶ **noun** a thickset finch with a crossed bill adapted for extracting seeds from the cones of conifers. The plumage is typically red in the male and olive green in the female. ● Genus *Loxia*, family Fringillidae: four species, in particular the widespread **red** (or **common**) **crossbill** (*L. curvirostra*).

crossbones ▶ **noun** see **SKULL AND CROSSBONES** at **SKULL**.

cross-border ▶ **adjective** involving movement or activity across a border between two countries: *cross-border trade*.

crossbow ▶ **noun** a medieval bow of a kind that is fixed across a wooden support and has a groove for the bolt and a mechanism for drawing and releasing the string.
– DERIVATIVES **crossbowman** noun (pl. **crossbowmen**).

cross-breed ▶ **verb** [with obj.] produce (an animal or plant) by mating or hybridizing two different species, breeds, or varieties: (as adj. **cross-bred**) *a cross-bred puppy*. ■ hybridize (a breed, species, or variety) with another. ■ [no obj.] (of an animal or plant) breed with a different breed, species, or variety.
▶ **noun** an animal or plant produced by cross-breeding: [as modifier] *a cross-breed Labrador*.

cross-check ▶ **verb** [with obj.] **1** verify (figures or information) by using an alternative source or method: *always try to cross-check your bearings* | (as noun **cross-checking**) *no cross-checking has been done*.
2 Ice Hockey obstruct (an opponent) illegally with the stick held horizontally in both hands.
▶ **noun** an instance of cross-checking figures or information: *as a cross-check they were also asked to give their date of birth*.

cross-colour (US **cross-color**) ▶ **noun** [mass noun] coloured flashes of interference in a colour television receiver caused by the misinterpretation of high-frequency luminance detail as colour information.

cross-compiler ▶ **noun** Computing a compiler which can convert instructions into machine code or low-level code for a computer other than that on which it is run.

cross-connection ▶ **noun** a connection made between two or more distinct things, typically parts of different networks or circuits.

cross-contamination ▶ **noun** [mass noun] the process by which bacteria or other microorganisms are unintentionally transferred from one substance or object to another, with harmful effect.
– DERIVATIVES **cross-contaminate** verb.

cross-correlate ▶ **verb** [with obj.] compare (a sequence of data) against another.
– DERIVATIVES **cross-correlation** noun.

cross-country ▶ **adjective 1** across fields or countryside, as opposed to on roads or tracks: *cross-country walking*. ■ relating to or denoting skiing over relatively flat countryside, as opposed to down mountain slopes.
2 not keeping to main or direct roads, routes, or railway lines: *an awkward, cross-country journey by train* | [as adv.] *we drove cross-country to a family reunion*. ■ chiefly US travelling to many different parts of a country: *a whirlwind cross-country tour*.
▶ **noun** [mass noun] the sport of cross-country running, riding, skiing, or motoring: *skiing in the Rockies is a pleasant mix of downhill and cross-country*.

cross-court ▶ **adverb & adjective** (of a stroke in tennis and other racket sports) hit diagonally across the court: [as adj.] *a cross-court volley*.

cross cousin ▶ **noun** each of two cousins who are children of a brother and sister.

cross-cultural ▶ **adjective** relating to different cultures or comparison between them: *cross-cultural understanding*.

cross-current ▶ **noun 1** a current in a river or sea which flows across another.
2 a situation or tendency marked by conflict with another: *strong cross-currents of debate*.

cross-curricular ▶ **adjective** Brit. involving curricula in more than one educational subject.

cross-cut ▶ **verb** [with obj.] **1** cut (wood or stone) across its main grain or axis.
2 alternate (one sequence) with another when editing a film.
▶ **noun 1** a diagonal cut, especially one across the main grain or axis of wood or stone.
2 an instance of alternating between two or more sequences when editing a film.
▶ **adjective** (of a file) having two sets of grooves crossing each other diagonally.

cross-cut saw ▶ **noun** a saw with a handle at each end, used by two people for cutting across the grain of timber.

cross-dating ▶ **noun** [mass noun] Archaeology the dating of objects by correlation with the chronology of another culture or site.

cross-dress ▶ **verb** [no obj.] wear clothing typical of the opposite sex.
– DERIVATIVES **cross-dresser** noun.

crosse /krɒs/ ▶ **noun** the stick used in women's field lacrosse.
– ORIGIN mid 19th cent.: from French, from Old French *croce* 'bishop's crook', ultimately of Germanic origin and related to **CRUTCH**.

cross-examine ▶ **verb** [with obj.] question (a witness called by the other party) in a court of law to challenge or extend testimony already given. Compare with **EXAMINATION-IN-CHIEF**. ■ question (someone) aggressively or in great detail: *I was cross-examined over the breakfast table*.
– DERIVATIVES **cross-examination** noun, **cross-examiner** noun.

cross-eyed ▶ **adjective** having one or both eyes turned inwards towards the nose, either from focusing on something very close, through temporary loss of control of focus, or as a permanent condition (convergent strabismus).

cross-fade ▶ **verb** [no obj.] (in sound or film editing) make a picture or sound appear or be heard gradually as another disappears or becomes silent.
▶ **noun** an instance of cross-fading.

cross-fertilize (also **cross-fertilise**) ▶ **verb 1** [with obj.] fertilize (a plant) using pollen from another plant of the same species. ■ [no obj.] (of two plants) fertilize each other.
2 stimulate the development of (something) with an exchange of ideas or information: *sessions between*

the two groups cross-fertilize ideas and provide insights.
– DERIVATIVES **cross-fertilization** noun.

crossfire ▸ noun [mass noun] gunfire from two or more directions passing through the same area: *a photographer was killed in crossfire* | figurative *the sponsors are caught in the crossfire of the battle between the world champion and his team boss.*

crossflow ▸ noun a type of engine cylinder head where the intake ports are on the opposite side of the engine from the exhaust ports.

cross-grain ▸ adjective [attrib.] running across the regular grain in timber: *cross-grain swelling.*

cross-grained ▸ adjective **1** (of timber) having a grain that runs across the regular grain.
2 stubbornly contrary or bad-tempered: *Bruce was a cross-grained and boastful individual.*

cross guard ▸ noun a guard on a sword or dagger consisting of a short transverse bar.

cross hairs ▸ plural noun a pair of fine wires crossing at right angles at the focus of an optical instrument or gunsight, for use in positioning, aiming, or measuring.

cross-hatch ▸ verb [with obj.] (often as noun **cross-hatching**) (in drawing or graphics) shade (an area) with intersecting sets of parallel lines.

cross head ▸ noun **1** a bar or block between the piston rod and connecting rod in a steam engine.
2 a screw with an indented cross shape in its head.
3 (also **cross heading**) a heading to a paragraph printed across a column in the body of a newspaper article.

cross index ▸ noun a note or cross reference in a book or list which refers the reader to other material.
▸ verb (**cross-index**) [with obj.] index (something) under another heading as a cross reference: (as adj. **cross-indexed**) *a cross-indexed file.*

cross infection ▸ noun [mass noun] the transfer of infection, especially to a hospital patient with a different infection or between different species of animal or plant.

crossing ▸ noun **1** a place where roads or railway lines cross.
2 a place at which one may safely cross something, especially a street.
3 [mass noun] the action of crossing something: *the crossing of the Pennines.* ■ a journey across water in a ship: *a short ferry crossing.*
4 Architecture the intersection of a church nave and the transepts.

crossing over ▸ noun [mass noun] Genetics the exchange of genes between homologous chromosomes, resulting in a mixture of parental characteristics in offspring.

cross-legged ▸ adjective & adverb (of a seated person) with the legs crossed at the ankles and the knees bent outwards: [as adv.] *John sat cross-legged on the floor.*

cross-license ▸ verb [with obj.] give one party a licence to use (patented or copyright material) in return for a similar licence: *the two companies have agreed to cross-license their intellectual property.*

cross light ▸ noun a light positioned to illuminate the parts of a photographic subject which the main lighting leaves in shade.

cross link ▸ noun a chemical bond between different chains of atoms in a polymer or other complex molecule.
▸ verb (**cross-link**) make or become linked with a cross link. ■ [with obj.] connect (something) by a series of transverse links.
– DERIVATIVES **cross-linkage** noun.

crossmatch Medicine ▸ verb [with obj.] test the compatibility of (a donor's and a recipient's blood or tissue).
▸ noun an instance of crossmatching.

cross member ▸ noun a transverse piece which adds support to a structure.

cross of Lorraine ▸ noun another term for LORRAINE CROSS.

crossopterygian /ˌkrɒsɒptəˈrɪdʒɪən/ Zoology ▸ noun a lobe-finned fish, such as the coelacanth.
▸ adjective relating to such fishes.
– ORIGIN mid 19th cent.: from modern Latin *Crossopterygii*, from Greek *krossos* 'tassel' + *pterux, pterug-* 'fin'.

crossover ▸ noun **1** a point or place of crossing from one side to the other.
2 [mass noun] the process of achieving success in a different field or style, especially in popular music: [as modifier] *a jazz–classical crossover album.*
3 [as modifier] relating to or denoting trials of medical treatment in which experimental subjects and control groups are exchanged after a set period: *a crossover study.*

crossover distortion ▸ noun [mass noun] Electronics distortion occurring where a signal changes from positive to negative or vice versa.

crossover network ▸ noun a filter in a loudspeaker unit that divides the signal and delivers different parts to bass and treble speakers.

cross-ownership ▸ noun [mass noun] the ownership by one corporation of different companies with related interests or commercial aims.

cross-party ▸ adjective involving or relating to two or more political parties: *a cross-party committee of MPs.*

crosspatch ▸ noun informal a bad-tempered person.
– ORIGIN early 18th cent.: from the adjective CROSS + obsolete *patch* 'fool, clown', perhaps from Italian *pazzo* 'madman'.

cross peen (also **cross pein**) ▸ noun a hammer having a peen that lies crossways to the length of the shaft.

crosspiece ▸ noun a beam or bar fixed or placed across something else.

cross-platform ▸ adjective Computing able to be used on different types of computers or with different software packages: *a cross-platform game.*

cross-ply ▸ adjective Brit. (of a tyre) having fabric layers with their threads running diagonally, crosswise to each other.

cross-point ▸ adjective (of a screwdriver) having a cross-shaped point for turning cross-head screws.

cross-pollinate ▸ verb [with obj.] pollinate (a flower or plant) with pollen from another flower or plant.
– DERIVATIVES **cross-pollination** noun.

cross-posting ▸ noun [mass noun] **1** the transfer of an employee or officer to a different department, industry, or regiment.
2 the simultaneous sending of a message to more than one newsgroup on the Internet in such a way that the receiving software at individual sites can detect and ignore duplicates.
– DERIVATIVES **cross-post** verb & noun.

cross-pressure ▸ verb [with obj.] N. Amer. expose (someone) to different, incompatible opinions: *the executive has been cross-pressured by the interests of the states and the electorate.*

cross product ▸ noun another term for VECTOR PRODUCT.

cross-promotion ▸ noun [mass noun] the cooperative marketing by two or more companies of one another's products.
– DERIVATIVES **cross-promote** verb.

cross-question ▸ verb [with obj.] question (someone) in great detail: *the Chancellor was cross-questioned by the finance committee* | (as noun **cross-questioning**) *the cross-questioning of Lopez.*

cross-rate ▸ noun an exchange rate between two currencies computed by reference to a third currency, usually the US dollar.

cross-reaction ▸ noun Biochemistry the reaction of an antibody with an antigen other than the one which gave rise to it.

cross-refer ▸ verb refer to another text or part of a text, typically in order to elaborate on a point: [no obj.] *the database cross-refers to the printed book* | [with obj.] *the entry cross-refers readers to 'Style'.*

cross reference ▸ noun a reference to another text or part of a text, typically given in order to elaborate on a point.
▸ verb (**cross-reference**) [with obj.] provide with cross references: *entries are fully cross-referenced.*

cross-rhythm ▸ noun Music a rhythm used simultaneously with another rhythm or rhythms.

crossroads ▸ noun (pl. **same**) **1** an intersection of two or more roads. ■ (**crossroad**) N. Amer. a road that crosses a main road or joins two main roads.
2 a point at which a crucial decision must be made which will have far-reaching consequences: *by 1998 I was at the crossroads.*

cross-ruff ▸ noun a sequence of play in bridge or whist in which partners alternately trump each other's leads.
▸ verb [no obj.] alternately trump particular suits in such a way.

cross section ▸ noun **1** a surface or shape exposed by making a straight cut through something, especially at right angles to an axis: *the cross section of an octahedron is a square* | *in cross section the sailfish's body looks like a tapering spear.* ■ a thin strip of organic tissue or other material removed by making two such cuts.
2 a typical or representative sample of a larger group: *a cross section of our senior managers.*
3 Physics a quantity having the dimensions of an area which expresses the probability of a given interaction between particles.
▸ verb (**cross-section**) [with obj.] make a cross section of.
– DERIVATIVES **cross-sectional** adjective.

cross-sectoral ▸ adjective relating to or affecting more than one group, area, or section: *cross-sectoral collaboration.*

cross-sell ▸ verb [with obj.] sell (a different product or service) to an existing customer: *their database is used to cross-sell financial services.*

cross-slide ▸ noun a sliding part on a lathe or planing machine which is supported by the saddle and carries the tool in a direction at right angles to the bed of the machine.

cross-stitch Needlework ▸ noun a stitch formed of two stitches crossing each other. ■ [mass noun] needlework done using cross-stitches.
▸ verb [with obj.] sew or embroider using cross-stitch: (as adj. **cross-stitched**) *a cross-stitched pillow.*

cross street ▸ noun chiefly N. Amer. a street that crosses another street or connects two streets.

cross-subsidize (also **cross-subsidise**) ▸ verb [with obj.] subsidize (a business or activity) out of the profits of another business or activity.
– DERIVATIVES **cross-subsidization** noun, **cross-subsidy** noun.

crosstalk ▸ noun [mass noun] **1** unwanted transfer of signals between communication channels.
2 witty conversation; repartee.

cross tie ▸ noun US a railway sleeper.

cross-town ▸ adjective & adverb extending or travelling from one side of a town to the other: [as adj.] *the cross-town traffic.*

cross-train ▸ verb [no obj.] learn another skill, especially one related to one's current job.

cross-training ▸ noun [mass noun] training in two or more sports in order to improve fitness and performance, especially in a main sport.

crosstrees ▸ plural noun a pair of horizontal struts attached to a sailing ship's mast to spread the rigging, especially at the head of a topmast.

cross-voting ▸ noun [mass noun] (especially in a parliament) voting for a party one does not belong to, or for more than one party.

crosswalk ▸ noun North American and Australian term for PEDESTRIAN CROSSING.

crossways ▸ adverb another term for CROSSWISE.

crosswind ▸ noun a wind blowing across one's direction of travel.

crosswise ▸ adverb in the form of a cross: *their arms were held out crosswise.* ■ diagonally or transversely: *wash the potatoes and halve them crosswise.*

crossword (also **crossword puzzle**) ▸ noun a puzzle consisting of a grid of squares and blanks into which words crossing vertically and horizontally are written according to clues.
– ORIGIN said to have been invented by the journalist Arthur Wynne, whose puzzle (called a 'word-cross') appeared in a Sunday newspaper, the *New York World*, on 21 December 1913.

crosswort /ˈkrɒswəːt/ ▸ noun a yellow-flowered European plant related to the bedstraws, with leaves arranged in a cross or whorl of four. ● *Cruciata laevipes*, family Rubiaceae.

crostini /krɒˈstiːni/ ▸ plural noun small pieces of toasted or fried bread served with a topping as a starter or canapé.
– ORIGIN Italian, plural of *crostino* 'little crust'.

crotal ▸ noun variant spelling of CROTTLE.

crotale /ˈkrəʊt(ə)l/ ▸ noun (usu. **crotales**) a small tuned cymbal.
– ORIGIN 1930s: French, from Latin *crotalum*, denoting an ancient type of castanet, from Greek *krotalon*.

crotch ▸ noun **1** the part of the human body between the legs where they join the torso. ■ the part of a garment that passes between the legs.

C

2 a fork in a tree, road, or river.
– DERIVATIVES **crotched** adjective.
– ORIGIN mid 16th cent. (denoting an agricultural or garden fork, also a crutch): perhaps related to Old French *croche* 'crozier, shepherd's crook', based on Old Norse *krókr* 'hook'; partly also a variant of CRUTCH.

crotchet /ˈkrɒtʃɪt/ ▸ noun **1** Music, Brit. a note having the time value of a quarter of a semibreve or half a minim, represented by a large solid dot with a plain stem. Also called QUARTER NOTE.
2 a perverse or unfounded belief or notion: *the natural crotchets of inveterate bachelors*.
– ORIGIN Middle English (in the sense 'hook'): from Old French *crochet*, diminutive of *croc* 'hook', from Old Norse *krókr*.

crotchety ▸ adjective irritable: *he was tired and crotchety*.
– DERIVATIVES **crotchetiness** noun.
– ORIGIN early 19th cent.: from CROTCHET (sense 2) + -Y[1].

crotchless ▸ adjective (of a garment) leaving the genitals uncovered.

croton /ˈkrəʊt(ə)n/ ▸ noun **1** a strong-scented tree, shrub, or herbaceous plant of the spurge family, native to tropical and warm regions. Several kinds yield timber and other commercially important products. ● Genus *Croton*, family Euphorbiaceae: numerous species, including *C. laccifer*, the host plant for the lac insect.
2 a small evergreen tree or shrub of the Indo-Pacific region, which is grown for its colourful ornamental foliage. ● Genus *Codiaeum*, family Euphorbiaceae: several species.
– ORIGIN modern Latin, from Greek *krotōn* 'sheep tick' (from the shape of the seeds of the croton in sense 1).

croton oil ▸ noun [mass noun] a foul-smelling oil, formerly used as a purgative, obtained from the seeds of a tropical Asian croton tree. ● The tree is *Croton tiglium* (family Euphorbiaceae).

crottin /ˈkrɒtã/ ▸ noun (pl. pronunc. **same**) a small, round cheese made from goat's milk.
– ORIGIN French, literally 'piece of horse dung'.

crottle /ˈkrɒt(ə)l/ (also **crotal**) ▸ noun a common lichen found on rocks, used in Scotland to make a golden-brown or reddish-brown dye for staining wool for making tweed. ● *Parmelia saxatilis* (order Parmeliales) and other species.
– ORIGIN mid 18th cent.: from Scottish Gaelic and Irish *crotal*, *crotan*.

crouch ▸ verb [no obj.] adopt a position where the knees are bent and the upper body is brought forward and down, typically in order to avoid detection or to defend oneself: *we **crouched down** in the trench* | (**be crouched**) *Leo was crouched before the fire*.
▸ noun [in sing.] a crouching stance or posture.
– ORIGIN late Middle English: perhaps from Old French *crochir* 'be bent', from *croche* (see CROTCH).

croup[1] /kruːp/ ▸ noun [mass noun] inflammation of the larynx and trachea in children, associated with infection and causing breathing difficulties.
– DERIVATIVES **croupy** adjective.
– ORIGIN mid 18th cent.: from dialect *croup* 'to croak', of imitative origin.

croup[2] /kruːp/ ▸ noun the rump or hindquarters, especially of a horse.
– ORIGIN Middle English: from Old French *croupe*, ultimately of Germanic origin and related to CROP.

croupade /krʊˈpeɪd/ ▸ noun a movement performed in classical riding, in which the horse leaps from the ground with its legs tucked under its body.
– ORIGIN mid 17th cent.: French, from Italian *groppata*, from *groppa* 'croup'.

croupier /ˈkruːpɪə, -pɪeɪ/ ▸ noun **1** the person in charge of a gaming table, responsible for gathering in and paying out money or tokens.
2 historical the assistant chairman at a public dinner, seated at the lower end of the table.
– ORIGIN early 18th cent. (denoting a person standing behind a gambler to give advice): French, from Old French *cropier* 'pillion rider, rider on the croup', related to Old French *croupe* (see CROUP[2]). Compare with CRUPPER.

croustade /krʊˈstɑːd/ ▸ noun a crisp piece of bread or pastry hollowed to receive a savoury filling.
– ORIGIN French, from Old French *crouste* or Italian *crostata* 'tart' (from *crosta* 'crust').

croute /kruːt/ ▸ noun a piece of toasted bread on which savoury snacks can be served. See also EN CROUTE.
– ORIGIN French *croûte* (see CRUST).

crouton /ˈkruːtɒn/ ▸ noun a small piece of fried or toasted bread served with soup or used as a garnish.
– ORIGIN from French *croûton*, from *croûte* (see CRUST).

Crow ▸ noun (pl. **same** or **Crows**) **1** a member of an American Indian people inhabiting eastern Montana.
2 [mass noun] the Siouan language of the Crow, with about 5,000 speakers.
▸ adjective relating to the Crow or their language.
– ORIGIN suggested by French *gens de corbeaux*, translating Siouan *apsáaloke* 'crow people'.

crow[1] ▸ noun **1** a large perching bird with mostly glossy black plumage, a heavy bill, and a raucous voice. ● Genus *Corvus*, family Corvidae (the **crow family**): several species, including the **carrion crow** (*C. corone*) and the **American crow** (*C. brachyrhynchos*). The crow family also includes the ravens, jays, magpies, choughs, and nutcrackers.
2 informal, derogatory an old or ugly woman.
– PHRASES **as the crow flies** in a straight line: *Easingwold was 22 miles away as the crow flies*. **eat crow** N. Amer. informal be humiliated by having to admit one's defeats or mistakes.
– ORIGIN Old English *crāwe*, of West Germanic origin; related to Dutch *kraai* and German *Krähe*, also to CROW[2].

crow[2] ▸ verb (past **crowed** or **crew**) [no obj.] **1** (of a cock) utter its characteristic loud cry.
2 (of a person) express great pride or triumph, especially in a tone of gloating satisfaction: *Ruby crowed with delight* | *avoid crowing about your success* | [with direct speech] *'I knew you 'd be back,' she crowed*.
▸ noun **1** [usu. in sing.] the cry of a cock.
2 a sound made by a person expressing great pride or triumph: *she gave a little crow of triumph*.
– ORIGIN Old English *crāwan*, of West Germanic origin; related to German *krähen*, also to CROW[1]; ultimately imitative.

crowbait ▸ noun N. Amer. informal, derogatory an old horse.

crowbar ▸ noun an iron bar with a flattened end, used as a lever.
▸ verb (**crowbars**, **crowbarring**, **crowbarred**) [with obj. and complement] use a crowbar to open (something): *he crowbarred the box open*.

crowberry ▸ noun (pl. **crowberries**) a creeping heather-like dwarf shrub with small leaves and black berries, growing on moorland. ● *Empetrum nigrum*, family Empetraceae.
■ the edible but flavourless black berry of the crowberry.

crowd ▸ noun a large number of people gathered together in a disorganized or unruly way: *a huge crowd gathered in the street outside*. ■ an audience, especially one at a sporting event: *they played before a 25,000 crowd* | [as modifier] *a match marred by crowd trouble*. ■ informal, often derogatory a group of people who are linked by a common interest or activity: *I've broken away from that whole junkie crowd*.
■ (**the crowd**) the mass or multitude of ordinary people: *make yourself stand out from the crowd* | *free-thinkers who don't follow the crowd*. ■ a large number of things regarded collectively: *the crowd of tall buildings*.
▸ verb [with obj.] **1** (of a number of people) fill (a space) almost completely, leaving little or no room for movement: *the dance floor was crowded with revellers*. ■ [no obj.] (**crowd into**) (of a number of people) move into (a restricted space): *they crowded into the cockpit*. ■ [no obj.] (**crowd round**) (of a group of people) form a tightly packed mass around: *photographers crowded round him*.
2 move too close to (someone): *don't crowd her, she needs air*. ■ [no obj.] (**crowd in on**) overwhelm and preoccupy (someone): *as demands crowd in on you it becomes difficult to keep things in perspective*.
3 (**crowd someone/thing out**) exclude someone or something by taking their place: *rampant plants will crowd out the less vigorous*.
– ORIGIN Old English *crūdan* 'press, hasten', of Germanic origin; related to Dutch *kruien* 'push in a wheelbarrow'. In Middle English the senses 'move by pushing' and 'push one's way' arose, leading to the sense 'congregate', and hence (mid 16th cent.) to the noun.

crowded ▸ adjective (of a space) full of people, leaving little or no room for movement; packed: *a very crowded room* | *the crowded streets of Southwark*.
– DERIVATIVES **crowdedness** noun.

crowdie /ˈkraʊdi/ (also **crowdy**) ▸ noun [mass noun] a soft Scottish cheese made from buttermilk or sour milk.
– ORIGIN early 19th cent.: from CRUD + -IE.

crowd-pleaser ▸ noun a person or thing with great popular appeal: *once again, the group has produced an album which is bound to be a crowd-pleaser*.
– DERIVATIVES **crowd-pleasing** adjective.

crowd-puller ▸ noun informal an event, person, or display that attracts a large audience.
– DERIVATIVES **crowd-pulling** adjective.

crowdsourcing ▸ noun [mass noun] the practice whereby an organization enlists a variety of freelancers, paid or unpaid, to work on a specific task or problem.

crowd-surf ▸ verb [no obj.] be passed in a prone position over the heads of the audience at a rock concert, typically after having jumped from the stage.

croweater ▸ noun Austral. informal a South Australian.

crowfoot ▸ noun (pl. **crowfoots**) a herbaceous plant related to the buttercups, typically having lobed or divided leaves and white or yellow flowers. Many kinds are aquatic with flowers held above the water. ● Genus *Ranunculus*, family Ranunculaceae: many species, in particular the European **water crowfoot** (*R. aquatilis*).

crow hop ▸ noun a short jump with both feet together.

crown ▸ noun **1** a circular ornamental headdress worn by a monarch as a symbol of authority, usually made of or decorated with precious metals and jewels.
■ (**the Crown**) the monarchy or reigning monarch: *their loyalty to the Church came before their loyalty to the Crown*. ■ an ornament, emblem, or badge shaped like a crown. ■ a wreath of leaves or flowers, especially that worn as an emblem of victory in ancient Greece or Rome.
2 an award or distinction gained by a victory or achievement, especially in sport: *the world heavyweight crown*.
3 the top or highest part of something: *the crown of the hill*. ■ the top part of a person's head or a hat. ■ the part of a plant just above and below the ground from which the roots and shoots branch out. ■ the upper branching or spreading part of a tree or other plant. ■ the upper part of a cut gem, above the girdle.
4 the part of a tooth projecting from the gum. ■ an artificial replacement or covering for the upper part of a tooth.
5 (also **crown piece**) a British coin with a face value of five shillings or 25 pence, now minted only for commemorative purposes. ■ a foreign coin with a name meaning 'crown', especially the krona or krone.
6 (in full **metric crown**) [mass noun] a paper size, 384 × 504 mm. ■ (in full **crown octavo**) a book size, 186 × 123 mm. ■ (in full **crown quarto**) a book size, 246 × 189 mm.
▸ verb [with obj.] **1** ceremonially place a crown on the head of (someone) in order to invest them as a monarch: *he went to Rome to be crowned* | [with complement] *she was crowned queen in 1953*. ■ [with obj. and complement] declare or acknowledge (someone) as the best, especially at a sport: *he was crowned world champion last September*. ■ (in draughts) promote (a piece) to king by placing another on top of it.
2 rest on or form the top of: *the distant knoll was crowned with trees*.
3 be the triumphant culmination of (an effort or endeavour, especially a prolonged one): *years of struggle were crowned by a state visit to Paris* | (as adj. **crowning**) *the crowning moment of a worthy career*.
4 fit a crown to (a tooth).
5 informal hit on the head: *she contained the urge to crown him*.
6 [no obj.] (of a baby's head during labour) fully appear in the vaginal opening prior to emerging.
– PHRASES **crowning glory** the best and most notable aspect of something: *the scene is the crowning glory of this marvellously entertaining show*. ■ chiefly humorous a person's hair. **to crown it all** Brit. as the final event in a series of particularly fortunate or unfortunate events: *it was cold and raining, and, to crown it all, we had to walk home*.
– ORIGIN Middle English: from Anglo-Norman French *corune* (noun), *coruner* (verb), Old French *corone* (noun), *coroner* (verb), from Latin *corona* 'wreath, chaplet'.

Crown Agents ▸ plural noun a body appointed by the British government to provide commercial and financial services, originally to British colonies, now to foreign governments and international bodies. It is responsible to the Minister for Overseas Development and its full title (as re-established in 1979) is the Crown Agents for Overseas Governments and Administrations.

crown and anchor ▶ **noun** [mass noun] a gambling game played with three dice each bearing a crown, an anchor, and the four card suits, and played on a board similarly marked.

Crown attorney ▶ **noun** Canadian term for **CROWN PROSECUTOR**.

crown cap ▶ **noun** another term for **CROWN CORK**.

Crown Colony ▶ **noun** a British colony whose legislature and administration is controlled by the Crown, represented by a governor.

crown cork ▶ **noun** a metal bottle cap with a crimped edge.

Crown Court ▶ **noun** (in England and Wales) a court of criminal jurisdiction, which deals with serious offences and appeals referred from the magistrates' courts.

Crown Derby ▶ **noun** [mass noun] a kind of soft-paste porcelain made at Derby and often marked with a crown above the letter 'D'.

crowned crane ▶ **noun** an African crane with a yellowish bristly crest, a mainly black or dark grey body, much white on the wings, and pink and white cheeks. ● Genus *Balearica*, family Gruidae: two species, in particular the **(black) crowned crane** (*B. pavonina*).

crowned head ▶ **noun** a king or queen.

crowned pigeon ▶ **noun** the largest known pigeon, which has mainly bluish plumage and a tall erect crest, found in New Guinea. Also called **GOURA**. ● Genus *Goura*, family Columbidae: three species.

crown ether ▶ **noun** Chemistry any of a class of organic compounds whose molecules are large rings containing a number of ether linkages.

crown fire ▶ **noun** a forest fire that spreads from treetop to treetop.

crown gall ▶ **noun** [mass noun] a bacterial disease of plants, especially fruit bushes and trees, which is characterized by large tumour-like galls on the roots and lower trunk. ● This disease is caused by the soil bacterium *Agrobacterium tumefaciens*.
■ [count noun] a gall of this type.

crown glass ▶ **noun** [mass noun] glass made without lead or iron, originally in a circular sheet. Formerly used in windows, it is now used as optical glass of low refractive index.

crown green ▶ **noun** Brit. a kind of bowling green which rises slightly towards the middle: [as modifier] *crown green bowls*.

crown imperial ▶ **noun** an Asian fritillary (plant) with a cluster of bell-like flowers at the top of a tall, largely bare stem. ● *Fritillaria imperialis*, family Liliaceae.

Crown Jewels ▶ **plural noun** the crown and other ornaments and jewellery worn or carried by the sovereign on certain state occasions.

Crown land ▶ **noun** [mass noun] (also **Crown lands**) land belonging to the British Crown. ■ land belonging to the state in some parts of the Commonwealth.

crown moulding ▶ **noun** US term for **CORNICE** (sense 1).

Crown Office (in full **Crown Office and Procurator Fiscal Service**) ▶ **noun** a Scottish law court responsible for listing cases to be tried in Scotland.

crown of thorns ▶ **noun 1** a large spiky starfish of the tropical Indo-Pacific, feeding on coral and sometimes causing great damage to reefs. ● *Acanthaster planci*, class Asteroidea.
2 a Madagascan shrub of the spurge family, with bright red flowers and many slender thorns. It is a popular houseplant and is sometimes used for hedging in the tropics. Also called **CHRIST'S THORN**. ● *Euphorbia milii*, family Euphorbiaceae.
■ any of a number of thorny plants, especially Christ's thorn (*Ziziphus spina-christi*).
– ORIGIN by association with Christ's crown of thorns.

crown piece ▶ **noun** see **CROWN** (sense 5 of the noun).

crown prince ▶ **noun** (in some countries) a male heir to a throne.

crown princess ▶ **noun** the wife of a crown prince. ■ (in some countries) a female heir to a throne.

Crown Prosecution Service (abbrev.: **CPS**) (in England and Wales) an independent organization which decides whether cases brought by the police proceed to the criminal court. Its head is the Director of Public Prosecutions, with each region having its own Chief Crown Prosecutor.

Crown prosecutor ▶ **noun** (in England, Wales, and Canada) a lawyer who acts for the Crown, especially a prosecutor in a criminal court. In Canada also called **CROWN ATTORNEY**.

crown roast ▶ **noun** a roast of rib pieces of pork or lamb arranged like a crown in a circle with the bones pointing upwards.

crown saw ▶ **noun** another term for **HOLE SAW**.

crown wheel ▶ **noun** a gearwheel or cogwheel with teeth that project from the face of the wheel at right angles, used especially in the gears of motor vehicles.

crow-pheasant ▶ **noun** a coucal (bird), especially the greater coucal, which has black plumage with chestnut wings and back and is found in southern Asia. ● Genus *Centropus*, family Cuculidae, especially *C. sinensis*.

crow quill ▶ **noun** a quill pen made from a large feather of a crow's wing, formerly used for fine writing. ■ (also **crow-quill pen**) a small, fine pen for map drawing.

crow's foot ▶ **noun** (pl. **crow's feet**) **1** a branching wrinkle at the outer corner of a person's eye.
2 a mark, symbol, or design formed of lines diverging from a point, resembling a bird's footprint.
3 historical a military caltrop.

crowsfoot spanner ▶ **noun** an adjustable spanner.

crow's-nest ▶ **noun** a shelter or platform fixed at the masthead of a vessel as a place for a lookout to stand.

crow steps ▶ **plural noun** step-like projections on the sloping part of a gable, common in Flemish architecture and 16th- and 17th-century Scottish buildings.
– DERIVATIVES **crow-stepped** adjective.

croze /krəʊz/ ▶ **noun** a groove at the end of a cask or barrel to receive the edge of the head. ■ a cooper's tool for making croze grooves.
– ORIGIN early 17th cent.: perhaps from French *creux, creuse* 'hollow'.

Crozet Islands /krəʊˈzeɪ/ a group of five small islands in the southern Indian Ocean, under French administration.

crozier /ˈkrəʊzɪə/ (also **crosier**) ▶ **noun 1** a hooked staff carried by a bishop as a symbol of pastoral office.
2 the curled top of a young fern.
– ORIGIN Middle English (originally denoting the person who carried a processional cross in front of an archbishop): partly from Old French *croisier* 'cross-bearer', from *crois* 'cross', based on Latin *crux*; reinforced by Old French *crocier* 'bearer of a bishop's crook', from *croce* (see **CROSSE**).

CRT ▶ **abbreviation** cathode ray tube.

cru /kruː/, French /kʀy/ ▶ **noun** (pl. **crus** pronunc. **same**) (in France) a vineyard or group of vineyards, especially one of recognized superior quality. See also **GRAND CRU, PREMIER CRU**.
– ORIGIN French, from *crû*, literally 'growth', past participle of *croître*.

crubeen /ˈkruːbiːn/ ▶ **noun** Irish a boiled pig's trotter as food.
– ORIGIN mid 19th cent.: from Irish *crúibín*, diminutive of *crúb* 'claw, hoof'.

cruces plural form of **CRUX**.

crucial /ˈkruːʃ(ə)l/ ▶ **adjective** decisive or critical, especially in the success or failure of something: *negotiations were at a crucial stage*. ■ of great importance: *this game is **crucial** to our survival*. ■ informal excellent.
– DERIVATIVES **cruciality** /-ʃɪˈalɪti/ noun, **crucially** adverb.
– ORIGIN early 18th cent. (in the sense 'cross-shaped'): from French, from Latin *crux, cruc-* 'cross'. The sense 'decisive' is from Francis Bacon's Latin phrase *instantia crucis* 'crucial instance', which he explained as a metaphor from a *crux* or fingerpost marking a fork at a crossroad; Newton and Boyle took up the metaphor in *experimentum crucis* 'crucial experiment'.

crucian /ˈkruːʃ(ə)n/ (also **crucian carp**) ▶ **noun** a small olive-green to reddish-brown European carp of still or slow-moving waters, important as a farmed fish in eastern Europe. ● *Carassius carassius*, family Cyprinidae.
– ORIGIN mid 18th cent.: from Low German *karusse, karutze*, perhaps based on Latin *coracinus*, from Greek *korax* 'raven', also denoting a black fish found in the Nile.

cruciate /ˈkruːʃɪət, -eɪt/ ▶ **adjective** Anatomy & Botany cross-shaped.
– ORIGIN early 19th cent.: from Latin *cruciatus*, from *crux, cruc-* 'cross'.

cruciate ligament ▶ **noun** Anatomy either of a pair of ligaments in the knee which cross each other and connect the femur to the tibia.

crucible /ˈkruːsɪb(ə)l/ ▶ **noun** a ceramic or metal container in which metals or other substances may be melted or subjected to very high temperatures.
■ a situation of severe trial, or in which different elements interact, leading to the creation of something new: *their relationship was forged in the crucible of war*.
– ORIGIN late Middle English: from medieval Latin *crucibulum* 'night lamp, crucible' (perhaps originally a lamp hanging in front of a crucifix), from Latin *crux, cruc-* 'cross'.

crucifer /ˈkruːsɪfə/ ▶ **noun 1** Botany a cruciferous plant, with four petals arranged in a cross.
2 a person carrying a cross or crucifix in a procession.
– ORIGIN mid 16th cent.: from Christian Latin, from Latin *crux, cruc-* 'cross'.

cruciferous /kruːˈsɪf(ə)rəs/ ▶ **adjective** Botany relating to or denoting plants of the cabbage family (Cruciferae).
– ORIGIN mid 19th cent.: from modern Latin *Cruciferae* (plural), from Latin *crux, cruc-* 'cross' + *-fer* 'bearing' (because the flowers have four equal petals arranged crosswise), + **-OUS**.

crucifix /ˈkruːsɪfɪks/ ▶ **noun** a representation of a cross with a figure of Christ on it.
– ORIGIN Middle English: via Old French from ecclesiastical Latin *crucifixus*, from Latin *cruci fixus* 'fixed to a cross'. Compare with **CRUCIFY**.

crucifixion /kruːsɪˈfɪkʃ(ə)n/ ▶ **noun** [mass noun] an ancient form of execution in which a person was nailed or bound to a cross. ■ (**the Crucifixion**) the killing of Jesus Christ by crucifixion. ■ (**Crucifixion**) an artistic representation or musical composition based on the Crucifixion.
– ORIGIN late Middle English: from ecclesiastical Latin *crucifixio(n-)*, from the verb *crucifigere* (see **CRUCIFY**).

cruciform /ˈkruːsɪfɔːm/ ▶ **adjective** having the shape of a cross: *a cruciform sword*. ■ (of a church) having a cross-shaped plan with a nave and transepts.
▶ **noun** a thing shaped like a cross.
– ORIGIN mid 17th cent.: from Latin *crux, cruc-* 'cross' + **-IFORM**.

crucify /ˈkruːsɪfʌɪ/ ▶ **verb** (**crucifies, crucifying, crucified**) [with obj.] **1** historical put (someone) to death by nailing or binding them to a cross: *two thieves were crucified with Jesus*. ■ cause anguish to (someone): *she'd been crucified by his departure*.
2 informal criticize (someone) severely and unrelentingly: *our fans would crucify us if we lost*.
– DERIVATIVES **crucifier** noun.
– ORIGIN Middle English: from Old French *crucifier*, from late Latin *crucifigere*, from Latin *crux, cruc-* 'cross' + *figere* 'fix'. Compare with **CRUCIFIX**.

cruciverbalist /kruːsɪˈvəːb(ə)lɪst/ ▶ **noun** a person who enjoys or is skilled at solving crosswords.
– ORIGIN 1970s: from Latin *crux, cruci-* 'cross' and **VERBALIST**.

cruck /krʌk/ ▶ **noun** Brit. either of a pair of curved timbers extending from ground level to the transverse beam or ridge of a roof and forming a structure frame in a medieval timber-framed house: [as modifier] *a cruck barn*.
– ORIGIN late 16th cent.: variant of **CROOK**.

crud ▶ **noun** [mass noun] informal **1** a substance which is considered unpleasant or disgusting, typically because of its dirtiness. ■ heavy snow on which it is difficult to ski.
2 nonsense: *the usual crud which passes itself off as a smart twenty-something comedy*.
3 [count noun] a contemptible person.
– DERIVATIVES **cruddy** adjective (**cruddier, cruddiest**).
– ORIGIN late Middle English: variant of **CURD** (the original sense). The earliest modern senses, 'filth' and 'nonsense' (originally US), date from the 1940s.

crude ▶ **adjective 1** in a natural or raw state; not yet processed or refined: *crude oil*. ■ Statistics (of figures) not adjusted or corrected: *the crude mortality rate*. ■ (of an estimate or guess) likely to be only approximately accurate.
2 constructed in a rudimentary or makeshift way: *a relatively crude nuclear weapon*. ■ (of an action) showing little finesse or subtlety and as a result unlikely to succeed: *the measure was condemned by economists as crude and ill-conceived*.
3 offensively coarse or rude, especially in relation to sexual matters: *a crude joke*.
▶ **noun** [mass noun] natural mineral oil: *the ship was carrying 80,000 tonnes of crude*.
– DERIVATIVES **crudely** adverb, **crudeness** noun.
– ORIGIN late Middle English: from Latin *crudus* 'raw, rough'.

C

crude turpentine ▸ noun see TURPENTINE (sense 1 of the noun).

crudités /ˈkruːdɪteɪ/ ▸ plural noun mixed raw vegetables served as an hors d'oeuvre, typically with a sauce into which they may be dipped.
– ORIGIN plural of French *crudité* 'rawness, crudity', from Latin *crudus* 'raw, rough'.

crudity ▸ noun [mass noun] **1** the quality of being rudimentary or makeshift; primitiveness: *he criticises the crudity of design.*
2 the quality of being offensively coarse or rude; vulgarity: *the crudity of the language.*

cruel ▸ adjective (**crueller**, **cruellest**; US **crueler**, **cruelest**) wilfully causing pain or suffering to others, or feeling no concern about it: *people who are **cruel to animals** | a cruel remark.* ■ causing pain or suffering: *the winters are long, hard, and cruel.*
▸ verb (**cruels**, **cruelling**, **cruelled**) [with obj.] Austral. informal spoil or ruin (an opportunity or a chance of success): *Ernie nearly cruelled the whole thing by laughing.* [late 19th cent.: perhaps influenced by the idiom *queer someone's pitch* (see QUEER).]
– PHRASES **be cruel to be kind** act towards someone in a way which seems harsh but will ultimately be of benefit to them. **cruel and unusual punishment** a category of excessively severe punishment banned under the Eighth Amendment of the US Constitution (and originally under the English Bill of Rights).
– DERIVATIVES **cruelly** adverb.
– ORIGIN Middle English: via Old French from Latin *crudelis*, related to *crudus* (see CRUDE).

cruelty ▸ noun (pl. **cruelties**) [mass noun] cruel behaviour or attitudes: *he has treated her with extreme cruelty | we can't stand **cruelty to animals** |* [count noun] *the cruelties of forced assimilation and genocide.* ■ Law behaviour which causes physical or mental harm to another, especially a spouse, whether intentionally or not.
– ORIGIN Middle English: from Old French *crualte*, based on Latin *crudelitas*, from *crudelis* (see CRUEL).

cruelty-free ▸ adjective (of cosmetics or other commercial products) manufactured or developed by methods which do not involve cruelty to animals.

cruet /ˈkruːɪt/ ▸ noun **1** a small container or set of containers for salt, pepper, oil, or vinegar for use at a dining table.
2 (in church use) a small container for the wine or water to be used in the celebration of the Eucharist.
– ORIGIN Middle English (in sense 2): from Anglo-Norman French, diminutive of Old French *crue* 'pot', from Old Saxon *krūka*; related to CROCK².

Cruft /krʌft/, Charles (1852–1939), English showman. In 1886 he initiated the first dog show in London. The Crufts dog shows are now held annually.

Cruikshank /ˈkrʊkʃaŋk/, George (1792–1878), English painter, illustrator, and caricaturist. The most eminent political cartoonist of his day, he was known for exposing the private life of the Prince Regent. His later work includes illustrations for Charles Dickens's *Sketches by Boz* (1836), and a series of etchings supporting the temperance movement.

cruise ▸ verb **1** [no obj., with adverbial] sail about in an area without a precise destination, especially for pleasure: *they were cruising off the California coast |* [with obj.] *she cruised the canals of France in a barge.* ■ take a holiday on a ship or boat following a predetermined course, usually calling in at several places. ■ travel or move slowly around without a specific destination in mind: *a police van cruised past us |* [with obj.] *teenagers were aimlessly cruising the mall.*
2 [no obj.] (of a motor vehicle or aircraft) travel smoothly at a moderate or economical speed.
3 [no obj., with adverbial] achieve an objective with ease, especially in sport: *Millwall **cruised to** a 2–0 win over Leicester.*
4 [no obj.] informal wander about in search of a sexual partner: *he spends his time cruising and just hanging out in New Orleans |* [with obj.] *he cruised the gay bars of Los Angeles.*
▸ noun a voyage on a ship or boat taken for pleasure or as a holiday and usually calling in at several places: *a cruise down the Nile |* [as modifier] *a cruise liner.*
– PHRASES **cruising for a bruising** informal heading or looking for trouble.
– ORIGIN mid 17th cent. (as a verb): probably from Dutch *kruisen* 'to cross', from *kruis* 'cross', from Latin *crux*.

cruise control ▸ noun a device in a motor vehicle which can be switched on to maintain a selected constant speed without the use of the accelerator pedal. ■ used in reference to actions performed with little effort: *the team went **on cruise control** during the second half.*

cruise missile ▸ noun a low-flying missile which is guided to its target by an on-board computer.

cruiser ▸ noun **1** a relatively fast warship larger than a destroyer and less heavily armed than a battleship.
2 a yacht or motor boat with passenger accommodation, designed for leisure use. ■ a person who goes on a pleasure cruise.
3 N. Amer. a police patrol car.
– ORIGIN late 17th cent.: from Dutch *kruiser*, from *kruisen* (see CRUISE).

cruiserweight ▸ noun chiefly Brit. another term for LIGHT HEAVYWEIGHT.

cruisie ▸ noun variant spelling of CRUSIE.

cruising chute ▸ noun Sailing a type of spinnaker that is designed to be more stable but less efficient than a normal spinnaker.

cruising speed ▸ noun a speed for a particular vehicle, ship, or aircraft, usually somewhat below maximum, that is comfortable and economical.

cruiskeen /kruːʃkiːn/ ▸ noun Irish a small jug.
– ORIGIN Irish *crúiscín*.

cruisy ▸ adjective (**cruisier**, **cruisiest**) informal **1** Austral./NZ relaxed or easy-going: *I spent three cruisy days with my folks.*
2 (of a place) used by people searching for gay sexual partners: *he was assaulted near a cruisy park.*

cruller /ˈkrʌlə/ ▸ noun N. Amer. a small cake made of rich dough twisted or curled and fried in deep fat.
– ORIGIN early 19th cent.: from Dutch *kruller*, from *krullen* 'to curl'.

crumb ▸ noun **1** a small fragment of bread, cake, or biscuit. ■ [mass noun] the soft inner part of a loaf of bread.
2 a very small amount of something: *the Budget provided few crumbs of comfort.*
3 informal, chiefly N. Amer. an objectionable or contemptible person: *he's an absolute crumb.*
4 (also **crumb rubber**) [mass noun] granulated rubber, usually made from recycled car tyres.
▸ verb [with obj.] cover (food) with breadcrumbs: (as adj. **crumbed**) *crispy crumbed mushrooms with garlic dip.*
– PHRASES **crumbs from ——'s table** an unfair and inadequate share of something large.
– ORIGIN Old English *cruma*, of Germanic origin; related to Dutch *kruim* and German *Krume*. The final *-b* was added in the 16th cent., perhaps from CRUMBLE but also influenced by words such as *dumb*, where the original final *-b* is retained although no longer pronounced.

crumble ▸ verb [no obj.] break or fall apart into small fragments, especially as part of a process of deterioration: *the plaster started to crumble |* (as adj. **crumbling**) *their crumbling ancestral home.* ■ [with obj.] cause (something) to break apart into small fragments: *the easiest way to crumble blue cheese.* ■ (of something abstract) disintegrate gradually over a period of time: *the party's fragile unity began to crumble.*
▸ noun [mass noun] Brit. a mixture of flour and fat that is rubbed to the texture of breadcrumbs and cooked as a topping for fruit. ■ a pudding made with crumble and fruit: *apple crumble.*
– ORIGIN late Middle English: probably from an Old English word related to CRUMB.

crumbly ▸ adjective (**crumblier**, **crumbliest**) consisting of or easily breaking into small fragments: *the cheese has a sharp flavour and is crumbly and moist.*
▸ noun (pl. **crumblies**) informal, humorous or derogatory an old person: *the high proportion of crumblies in the population.*
– DERIVATIVES **crumbliness** noun.

crumbs ▸ exclamation Brit. informal used to express dismay or surprise: *'Crumbs,' said Emily, 'how embarrassing.'.*
– ORIGIN late 19th cent.: euphemism for *Christ*.

crumb structure ▸ noun [mass noun] the porous structure or condition of soil when its particles are moderately aggregated.

crumby ▸ adjective (**crumbier**, **crumbiest**) **1** resembling or covered in crumbs.
2 variant spelling of CRUMMY.

crumhorn ▸ noun variant spelling of KRUMMHORN.

crummy (also **crumby**) informal ▸ adjective (**crummier**, **crummiest**; **crumbier**, **crumbiest**) dirty, unpleasant, or of poor quality: *a crummy little room.* ■ unwell: *I've been feeling pretty crummy the last few days.*
▸ noun N. Amer. a truck used to transport loggers to and from work.
– DERIVATIVES **crumminess** noun.
– ORIGIN mid 19th cent. (earlier in the literal senses 'crumbly' and 'like or covered with crumbs'): variant of CRUMBY.

crump ▸ noun a loud thudding sound, especially one made by an exploding bomb or shell.
▸ verb [no obj.] make such a sound.
– ORIGIN mid 17th cent.: imitative. The original sense (as a verb) was 'munch, crunch', later 'hit hard' (used initially as a term in the game of cricket), and then the military sense 'bombard' (First World War).

crumpet ▸ noun **1** a thick, flat, savoury cake with a soft, porous texture, made from a yeast mixture cooked on a griddle and eaten toasted and buttered.
2 [mass noun] Brit. informal people, especially women, regarded as objects of sexual desire: *fat chance of our running into any crumpet |* [in sing.] *he's the thinking woman's crumpet.*
3 archaic, informal a person's head.
– ORIGIN late 17th cent.: of unknown origin. Sense 2 dates from the 1930s.

crumple ▸ verb [with obj.] crush (something, typically paper or cloth) so that it becomes creased and wrinkled: *he **crumpled up** the paper bag |* (as adj. **crumpled**) *a crumpled sheet.* ■ [no obj.] become creased, bent, or crooked: *the bumper crumpled as it glanced off the wall.* ■ [no obj.] (of a person) suddenly flop down to the ground: *she crumpled to the floor in a dead faint |* figurative *her composure crumpled.* ■ [no obj.] (of a person's face) suddenly sag and show an expression of desolation: *the child's face crumpled and he began to howl.*
▸ noun a crushed fold, crease, or wrinkle.
– DERIVATIVES **crumply** adjective.
– ORIGIN Middle English: from obsolete *crump* 'make or become curved', from Old English *crump* 'bent, crooked', of West Germanic origin; related to German *krumm*.

crumple zone ▸ noun a part of a motor vehicle, especially the extreme front and rear, designed to crumple easily in a crash and absorb the main force of an impact.

crunch ▸ verb [with obj.] **1** crush (a hard or brittle foodstuff) with the teeth, making a loud but muffled grinding sound: *she paused to crunch a ginger biscuit.* ■ [no obj.] make a crunching sound, especially when walking or driving over gravel or an icy surface.
2 (especially of a computer) process (large quantities of information): *the program crunches data from 14,000 sensors to decipher evolving patterns.*
▸ noun **1** [usu. in sing.] a loud muffled grinding sound like that of something hard or brittle being crushed: *Marco's fist struck Brian's nose with a crunch.*
2 (**the crunch**) informal a crucial point or situation, typically one at which a decision with important consequences must be made: *when it comes to the crunch you chicken out.* ■ a severe shortage of money or credit: *the agencies are facing a financial crunch.*
3 a physical exercise designed to strengthen the abdominal muscles; a sit-up.
– ORIGIN early 19th cent. (as a verb): variant of 17th-cent. *cranch* (probably imitative), by association with CRUSH and MUNCH.

cruncher ▸ noun informal **1** a critical or vital point; a crucial or difficult question.
2 a computer, system, or person able to perform very large or complex operations: *a global information cruncher.* See also NUMBER CRUNCHER.

crunchy ▸ adjective (**crunchier**, **crunchiest**) **1** making a sharp noise when bitten or crushed: *bake until the topping is crunchy.*
2 N. Amer. informal politically liberal and environmentally aware: *a song that incorporates whale-singing seems pretty crunchy.*
– DERIVATIVES **crunchily** adverb, **crunchiness** noun.

crupper /ˈkrʌpə/ ▸ noun a strap buckled to the back of a saddle and looped under the horse's tail to prevent the saddle or harness from slipping forward.
– ORIGIN Middle English: from Old French *cropiere*, related to *croupe* (see CROUP²). Compare with CROUPIER.

crura plural form of CRUS.

crura cerebri plural form of CRUS CEREBRI.

crural /ˈkrʊər(ə)l/ ▸ adjective Anatomy & Zoology relating to the leg or the thigh. ■ relating to any part called 'crus', for example, the crura cerebri.
– ORIGIN late 16th cent.: from Latin *cruralis*, from *crus*, *crur-* 'leg'.

crus /krʌs/ ▶ **noun** (pl. **crura** /ˈkrʊərə/) Anatomy an elongated part of an anatomical structure, especially one which occurs in the body as a pair. See **CRUS CEREBRI**.
– ORIGIN early 18th cent.: from Latin, 'leg'.

crusade /kruːˈseɪd/ ▶ **noun 1** (**Crusade**) each of a series of medieval military expeditions made by Europeans to recover the Holy Land from the Muslims in the 11th, 12th, and 13th centuries. ■ a war instigated for alleged religious ends.
2 a vigorous campaign for political, social, or religious change: *a **crusade against** crime.*
▶ **verb** [no obj.] (often as adj. **crusading**) lead or take part in a vigorous campaign for social, political, or religious change: *a crusading stance on poverty.*
– ORIGIN late 16th cent. (originally as *croisade*): from French *croisade*, an alteration (influenced by Spanish *cruzado*) of earlier *croisée*, literally 'the state of being marked with the cross', based on Latin *crux*, *cruc-* 'cross'; in the 17th cent. the form *crusado*, from Spanish *cruzado*, was introduced. The blending of these two forms led to the current spelling, first recorded in the early 18th cent.

crusader /kruːˈseɪdə/ ▶ **noun 1** (**Crusader**) a fighter in the medieval Crusades.
2 a person who campaigns vigorously for political, social, or religious change; a campaigner: ***crusaders for** early detection and treatment of mental illnesses.*

crus cerebri /ˈsɛrɪbrʌɪ/ ▶ **noun** (pl. **crura cerebri**) Anatomy either of two symmetrical tracts of nerve fibres at the base of the midbrain, linking the pons and the cerebral hemispheres.
– ORIGIN early 18th cent.: from Latin, literally 'leg of the brain'.

cruse /kruːz/ ▶ **noun** archaic an earthenware pot or jar.
– ORIGIN Old English *crūse*, of Germanic origin; related to Dutch *kroes* and German *Krause*; reinforced in Middle English by Low German *krūs*.

crush ▶ **verb** [with obj.] **1** deform, pulverize, or force inwards by compressing forcefully: *you can crush a pill between two spoons | a labourer was crushed to death by a lorry |* (as adj. **crushed**) *the crushed remains of a Ford Cortina.* ■ crease or crumple (cloth or paper).
2 violently subdue (opposition or a rebellion): *the government had taken elaborate precautions to crush any resistance.*
3 make (someone) feel overwhelmingly disappointed or embarrassed: *I was crushed—was I not good enough? |* (as adj. **crushing**) *the news came as a crushing blow.*
▶ **noun 1** [usu. in sing.] a crowd of people pressed closely together: *a number of youngsters fainted in the crush.*
2 informal a brief but intense infatuation for someone: *she did **have a crush on** Dr Russell.*
3 [mass noun] a drink made from the juice of pressed fruit: *lemon crush.*
4 (also **crush pen**) a fenced passage with one narrow end, used for handling cattle or sheep.
– PHRASAL VERBS **crush on** US informal be infatuated with: *he's awesome, so it wasn't too surprising that other girls were crushing on him.*
– DERIVATIVES **crushable** adjective, **crusher** noun, **crushingly** adverb.
– ORIGIN Middle English: from Old French *cruissir*, 'gnash (teeth) or crack', of unknown origin.

crush bar ▶ **noun** Brit. a bar in a theatre or opera house selling drinks to the audience in the interval.

crush barrier ▶ **noun** Brit. a barrier, especially a temporary one, for restraining a crowd.

crushed velvet ▶ **noun** [mass noun] velvet which has its nap pointing in different directions in irregular patches.

crush zone ▶ **noun** another term for **CRUMPLE ZONE**.

crusie /ˈkruːzi/ (also **cruisie**) ▶ **noun** (pl. **crusies**) Scottish historical a small oil lamp with a handle. ■ a triangular candlestick.
– ORIGIN early 16th cent.: perhaps representing French *creuset* 'crucible'.

crust ▶ **noun 1** the tough outer part of a loaf of bread: *a sandwich with the crusts cut off |* [mass noun] *I tore off several pieces of crust from the loaf.* ■ a hard, dry scrap of bread: *a kindly old woman might give her a crust.*
2 a hardened layer, coating, or deposit on the surface of something soft: *a crust of snow.* ■ a layer of pastry covering a pie. ■ the outermost layer of rock of which a planet consists, especially the part of the earth above the mantle: *the earth's crust.* ■ a deposit of tartrates and other substances formed in wine aged in the bottle, especially port.
3 Brit. informal a living or livelihood: *I've been **earning a crust** wherever I can.*
▶ **verb** [no obj.] form into a hard outer layer: *the blisters eventually crust over.* ■ [with obj.] cover with a hard outer layer: *the burns crusted his cheek.*
– DERIVATIVES **crustal** adjective (Geology).
– ORIGIN Middle English: from Old French *crouste*, from Latin *crusta* 'rind, shell, crust'.

Crustacea /krʌˈsteɪʃ(ə)/ ▶ **plural noun** Zoology a large group of mainly aquatic arthropods which include crabs, lobsters, shrimps, woodlice, barnacles, and many minute forms. They are very diverse, but most have four or more pairs of limbs and several other appendages. ● Subphylum (or phylum) Crustacea.
■ (**crustacea**) arthropods of this group.
– ORIGIN modern Latin (plural), from *crusta* (see **CRUST**).

crustacean Zoology ▶ **noun** an arthropod of the large, mainly aquatic group Crustacea, such as a crab, lobster, shrimp, or barnacle.
▶ **adjective** relating to or denoting crustaceans.
– DERIVATIVES **crustaceous** adjective.

crusted ▶ **adjective 1** having or forming a hard outer layer: *she washed away the crusted blood.* ■ denoting a style of unfiltered, blended port which deposits a sediment in the bottle.
2 old-fashioned or venerable: *a crusted establishment figure.*

crustose /ˈkrʌstəʊs/ ▶ **adjective** Botany (of a lichen or alga) forming or resembling a crust.
– ORIGIN late 19th cent.: from Latin *crustosus*, from *crusta* (see **CRUST**).

crusty ▶ **adjective** (**crustier**, **crustiest**) **1** having or acting as a hard outer layer or covering: *crusty bread | Lake Manyara was ringed by crusty salt deposits.*
2 (especially of an old person) easily irritated: *a crusty old Scots judge.*
▶ **noun** (also **crustie**) (pl. **crusties**) informal a young person who is homeless or travels constantly, has a shabby appearance, and rejects conventional values.
– DERIVATIVES **crustily** adverb, **crustiness** noun.

crutch ▶ **noun 1** a long stick with a crosspiece at the top, used as a support under the armpit by a lame person. ■ [in sing.] a thing used for support or reassurance: *they use the Internet as a crutch for their loneliness.*
2 the crotch of the body or a garment.
– ORIGIN Old English *crycc*, *cryc*, of Germanic origin; related to Dutch *kruk* and German *Krücke*.

Crutched Friars an order of mendicant friars established in Italy by 1169, which spread to England, France, and the Low Countries in the 13th century and was suppressed in 1656.
– ORIGIN *crutched* (earlier *crouched*), from Latin *crux*, *cruc-* 'cross', referring to the cross worn on the top of their staves, and later on the front of their habits.

Crux /krʌks/ Astronomy the smallest constellation (the Cross or Southern Cross), but the most familiar one to observers in the southern hemisphere. It contains the bright star Acrux, the 'Jewel Box' star cluster, and most of the Coalsack nebula. Formerly called **Crux Australis**.
– ORIGIN Latin.

crux /krʌks/ ▶ **noun** (pl. **cruxes** or **cruces** /ˈkruːsiːz/) (**the crux**) the decisive or most important point at issue: *the crux of the matter is that attitudes have changed.* ■ a particular point of difficulty: *both cruces can be resolved by a consideration of the manuscripts.*
– ORIGIN mid 17th cent. (denoting a representation of a cross, chiefly in *crux ansata* 'ankh', literally 'cross with a handle'): from Latin, literally 'cross'.

Cruyff /krɔɪf/, Johan (b.1947), Dutch footballer and football manager. An attacking midfielder, he was a member of the Ajax team that won three consecutive European Cup Finals (1971–3) and captained the Netherlands in their World Cup Final defeat by West Germany (1974).

cry ▶ **verb** (**cries**, **crying**, **cried**) [no obj.] **1** shed tears in distress, pain, or sorrow: *don't cry—it'll be all right |* [with obj.] *you'll cry tears of joy.*
2 shout or scream in fear, pain, or grief: *the little girl fell down and cried for mummy.* ■ [with direct speech] say something loudly in an excited or anguished tone of voice: *'Where will it end?' he **cried out**.* ■ [with obj.] (of a hawker) proclaim (wares) for sale in the street.
3 (of a bird or other animal) make a loud characteristic call: *the wild birds **cried out** over the water.*
▶ **noun** (pl. **cries**) **1** a loud inarticulate shout or scream expressing a powerful feeling or emotion: *a cry of despair.* ■ a loud excited utterance of a word or words: *there was a cry of 'Silence!'.* ■ the call of a hawker selling wares on the street. ■ an urgent appeal or entreaty: *fund-raisers have issued a cry for help.* ■ a demand or opinion expressed by many people: *peace became the popular cry.*
2 the loud characteristic call of a bird or other animal.
3 a spell of shedding tears: *I still have a cry, sometimes, when I realize that my mother is dead.*
– PHRASES **cry one's eyes** (or **heart**) **out** weep bitterly and at length. **cry for the moon** ask for what is unattainable or impossible. **cry foul** protest strongly about a real or imagined wrong or injustice. **cry from the heart** a passionate and honest appeal or protest. **cry stinking fish** Brit. disparage one's own efforts or products. **cry wolf** see **WOLF**. **for crying out loud** informal used to express one's irritation or impatience: *why do you have to take everything so personally, for crying out loud?* **in full cry** (of hounds) baying in keen pursuit. ■ expressing an opinion loudly and forcefully: *the prime minister was in full cry with warnings against the plots of the Americans.* **it's no use crying over spilt milk** see **MILK**.
– PHRASAL VERBS **cry someone/thing up** (or **down**) dated praise (or disparage) someone or something: *when one of them does something wrong, they cry down the lot.* **cry off** Brit. informal go back on a promise or fail to keep to an arrangement: *we were going to Spain together and he cried off at the last moment.* **cry out for** demand as a self-evident requirement or solution: *the scheme cries out for reform.*
– ORIGIN Middle English (in the sense 'ask for earnestly or loudly'): from Old French *crier* (verb), *cri* (noun), from Latin *quiritare* 'raise a public outcry', literally 'call on the *Quirites* (Roman citizens) for help'.

crybaby ▶ **noun** (pl. **crybabies**) a person, especially a child, who sheds tears frequently or readily.

cryer ▶ **noun** archaic spelling of **CRIER**.

crying ▶ **adjective** [attrib.] very great: *it would be **a crying shame** to let some other woman have it.*

cryo- /ˈkrʌɪəʊ/ ▶ **combining form** involving or producing cold, especially extreme cold: *cryostat | cryosurgery.*
– ORIGIN from Greek *kruos* 'frost'.

cryobiology ▶ **noun** [mass noun] the branch of biology which deals with the properties of organisms and tissues at low temperatures.
– DERIVATIVES **cryobiologist** noun.

cryogen /ˈkrʌɪə(ʊ)dʒ(ə)n/ ▶ **noun** a substance used to produce very low temperatures.

cryogenics /ˌkrʌɪə(ʊ)ˈdʒɛnɪks/ ▶ **plural noun** [treated as sing.] **1** the branch of physics dealing with the production and effects of very low temperatures.
2 another term for **CRYONICS**.
– DERIVATIVES **cryogenic** adjective.

cryoglobulin /ˌkrʌɪə(ʊ)ˈglɒbjʊlɪn/ ▶ **noun** Biochemistry a protein which occurs in the blood in certain disorders. It can be precipitated out of solution below 10°C, causing obstruction in the fingers and toes.

cryolite /ˈkrʌɪəlʌɪt/ ▶ **noun** [mass noun] a white or colourless mineral consisting of a fluoride of sodium and aluminium. It is added to bauxite as a flux in aluminium smelting.
– ORIGIN early 19th cent.: from **CRYO-** 'cold, frost' (because the main deposits are found in Greenland) + **-LITE**.

cryonics /krʌɪˈɒnɪks/ ▶ **plural noun** [treated as sing.] the practice or technique of deep-freezing the bodies of those who have died of an incurable disease, in the hope of a future cure.
– DERIVATIVES **cryonic** adjective.
– ORIGIN 1960s: contraction of **CRYOGENICS**.

cryoprecipitate /ˌkrʌɪəʊprɪˈsɪpɪtət/ ▶ **noun** chiefly Biochemistry a substance precipitated from a solution, especially from the blood, at low temperatures.
■ [mass noun] Medicine an extract rich in a blood-clotting factor obtained as a residue when frozen blood plasma is thawed.

cryopreserve ▶ **verb** [with obj.] Biology & Medicine preserve (cells or tissues) by cooling them below the freezing point of water.
– DERIVATIVES **cryopreservation** noun.

cryoprotectant ▶ **noun** Physiology a substance that prevents the freezing of tissues, or prevents damage to cells during freezing.

cryostat /ˈkrʌɪə(ʊ)stat/ ▶ **noun 1** an apparatus for maintaining a very low temperature.
2 a cold chamber in which frozen tissue is divided with a microtome.

C

cryosurgery ▶ noun [mass noun] surgery using the local application of intense cold to destroy unwanted tissue.

cryotherapy ▶ noun [mass noun] the use of extreme cold in surgery or other medical treatment.

crypt ▶ noun **1** an underground room or vault beneath a church, used as a chapel or burial place.
2 Anatomy a small tubular gland, pit, or recess.
– ORIGIN late Middle English (in the sense 'cavern'): from Latin *crypta*, from Greek *kruptē* 'a vault', from *kruptos* 'hidden'.

cryptanalysis ▶ noun [mass noun] the art or process of deciphering coded messages without being told the key.
– DERIVATIVES **cryptanalyst** noun, **cryptanalytic** adjective, **cryptanalytical** adjective.
– ORIGIN 1920s: from CRYPTO- + ANALYSIS.

cryptic ▶ adjective **1** having a meaning that is mysterious or obscure: *he found his boss's utterances too cryptic.* ■ (of a crossword) having difficult clues which indicate the solutions indirectly.
2 Zoology (of coloration or markings) serving to camouflage an animal in its natural environment.
– DERIVATIVES **cryptically** adverb.
– ORIGIN early 17th cent.: from late Latin *crypticus*, from Greek *kruptikos*, from *kruptos* 'hidden'. Sense 2 dates from the late 19th cent.

cryptid /ˈkrɪptɪd/ ▶ noun an animal whose existence or survival is disputed or unsubstantiated, such as the yeti.
– ORIGIN 1990s: from CRYPTO- + -ID³.

crypto- /ˈkrɪptəʊ/ ▶ combining form concealed; secret: *cryptogram*.
– ORIGIN from Greek *kruptos* 'hidden'.

cryptobiosis /ˌkrɪptə(ʊ)bʌɪˈəʊsɪs/ ▶ noun [mass noun] Biology a physiological state in which metabolic activity is reduced to an undetectable level without disappearing altogether. It is known in certain plant and animal groups adapted to survive periods of extremely dry conditions.

cryptobiotic ▶ adjective Biology **1** relating to or capable of cryptobiosis.
2 denoting primitive organisms of the kind presumed to have existed in earlier geological periods but to have left no trace of their existence.

cryptococcosis /ˌkrɪptə(ʊ)kəˈkəʊsɪs/ ▶ noun [mass noun] Medicine infestation with a yeast-like fungus, resulting in tumours in the lungs and sometimes spreading to the brain. It occurs chiefly in the United States. Also called TORULOSIS. ● The fungus is *Cryptococcus neoformans*, subdivision Deuteromycotina (or class Teliomycetes).
– DERIVATIVES **cryptococcal** adjective.
– ORIGIN 1930s: from modern Latin *Cryptococcus* (part of the binomial of the fungus) + -OSIS.

cryptocrystalline ▶ adjective having a crystalline structure visible only when magnified.

cryptogam /ˈkrɪptə(ʊ)gam/ ▶ noun Botany, dated a plant that has no true flowers or seeds, including ferns, mosses, liverworts, lichens, algae, and fungi.
– DERIVATIVES **cryptogamous** adjective.
– ORIGIN mid 19th cent.: from French *cryptogame*, from modern Latin *cryptogamae (plantae)*, denoting non-flowering plants, from Greek *kruptos* 'hidden' + *gamos* 'marriage' (because the means of reproduction was not apparent).

cryptogamic ▶ adjective **1** Botany relating to or denoting cryptogams.
2 Ecology (of a desert soil or surface crust) covered with or consisting of a fragile black layer of cyanobacteria, mosses, and lichens, which is often important in preventing erosion.

cryptogenic /ˌkrɪptəʊˈdʒɛnɪk/ ▶ adjective (of a disease) of obscure or uncertain origin.

cryptogram /ˈkrɪptə(ʊ)gram/ ▶ noun a text written in code.

cryptography ▶ noun [mass noun] the art of writing or solving codes.
– DERIVATIVES **cryptographer** noun, **cryptographic** adjective, **cryptographically** adverb.

cryptology ▶ noun [mass noun] the study of codes, or the art of writing and solving them.
– DERIVATIVES **cryptological** adjective, **cryptologist** noun.

cryptomeria /ˌkrɪptə(ʊ)ˈmɪərɪə/ ▶ noun a tall conical coniferous tree with long, curved, spirally arranged leaves and short cones. Native to China and Japan, it is grown for timber in Japan. Also called JAPANESE CEDAR. ● *Cryptomeria japonica*, family Taxodiaceae.
– ORIGIN modern Latin, from CRYPTO- 'hidden' + Greek *meros* 'part' (because the seeds are concealed by scales).

cryptonym /ˈkrɪptənɪm/ ▶ noun a code name.
– ORIGIN late 19th cent.: from CRYPTO- 'hidden' + -ONYM.

cryptorchid /ˌkrɪpˈtɔːkɪd/ ▶ noun Medicine a person suffering from cryptorchidism.

cryptorchidism ▶ noun [mass noun] Medicine a condition in which one or both of the testes fail to descend from the abdomen into the scrotum.
– ORIGIN late 19th cent.: from CRYPTO- 'hidden' + Greek *orkhis, orkhid-* 'testicle' + -ISM.

cryptosporidiosis /ˌkrɪptə(ʊ)spərɪdɪˈəʊsɪs/ ▶ noun [mass noun] Medicine an intestinal condition caused by infection with cryptosporidium, causing diarrhoea and vomiting.

cryptosporidium /ˌkrɪptə(ʊ)spɒˈrɪdɪəm/ ▶ noun (pl. **cryptosporidia**) a parasitic coccidian protozoan found in the intestinal tract of many vertebrates, where it sometimes causes disease. ● Genus *Cryptosporidium*, phylum Sporozoa.
– ORIGIN early 20th cent.: from CRYPTO- 'concealed' + modern Latin *sporidium* 'small spore'.

Cryptozoic /ˌkrɪptəˈzəʊɪk/ ▶ adjective Geology relating to or denoting the period (the Precambrian) in which rocks contain no, or only slight, traces of living organisms. Compare with PHANEROZOIC.
– ORIGIN early 20th cent.: from Greek *kruptos* 'hidden' + *zōē* 'life' + -IC.

cryptozoic /ˌkrɪptəˈzəʊɪk/ ▶ adjective Ecology (of small invertebrates) living on the ground but hidden in the leaf litter under stones or pieces of wood.
– DERIVATIVES **cryptozoa** plural noun.
– ORIGIN late 19th cent.: from Greek *kruptos* 'hidden' + *zōē* 'life' + -IC.

cryptozoology ▶ noun [mass noun] the search for and study of animals whose existence or survival is disputed or unsubstantiated, such as the Loch Ness monster and the yeti.
– DERIVATIVES **cryptozoological** adjective, **cryptozoologist** noun.

crystal ▶ noun **1** a piece of a homogeneous solid substance having a natural geometrically regular form with symmetrically arranged plane faces. ■ Chemistry any solid consisting of a symmetrical, ordered, three-dimensional aggregation of atoms or molecules. ■ Electronics a crystalline piece of semiconductor used as an oscillator or transducer. ■ [mass noun] a clear transparent mineral, especially quartz. ■ a piece of crystalline substance believed to have healing powers.
2 (also **crystal glass**) [mass noun] highly transparent glass with a high refractive index: [as modifier] *a crystal chandelier.* ■ articles made of crystal glass: *a collection of crystal.* ■ [count noun] the glass over a watch face.
3 [as modifier] clear and transparent like crystal: *the clean crystal waters of the lake.*
– PHRASES **crystal clear** completely transparent and unclouded. ■ unambiguous; easily understood.
– ORIGIN late Old English (denoting ice or a mineral resembling it), from Old French *cristal*, from Latin *crystallum*, from Greek *krustallos* 'ice, crystal'. The chemistry sense dates from the early 17th cent.

crystal axis ▶ noun each of three axes used to define the edges of the unit cell of a crystal.

crystal ball ▶ noun a solid globe of glass or rock crystal, used by fortune-tellers and clairvoyants for crystal-gazing.

crystal class ▶ noun each of thirty-two categories of crystals classified according to the possible combinations of symmetry elements possessed by the crystal lattice.

crystal form ▶ noun a set of crystal faces defined according to their relationship to the crystal axes.

crystal-gazing ▶ noun [mass noun] looking intently into a crystal ball with the aim of seeing images relating to future or distant events. ■ attempting to forecast the future.

crystal healing (also **crystal therapy**) ▶ noun [mass noun] the use of the supposed healing powers of crystals in alternative medicine.

crystal lattice ▶ noun the symmetrical three-dimensional arrangement of atoms inside a crystal.

crystallin /ˈkrɪst(ə)lɪn/ ▶ noun [mass noun] Biochemistry a protein of the globulin class present in the lens of the eye.
– ORIGIN mid 19th cent.: from Latin *crystallum* 'crystal' + -IN¹.

crystalline /ˈkrɪst(ə)lʌɪn/ ▶ adjective having the structure and form of a crystal; composed of crystals: *a crystalline rock.* ■ literary very clear: *he writes a crystalline prose.*
– DERIVATIVES **crystallinity** noun.
– ORIGIN Middle English: from Old French *cristallin*, via Latin from Greek *krustallinos*, from *krustallos* (see CRYSTAL).

crystalline lens ▶ noun the transparent elastic structure behind the iris by which light is focused on to the retina of the eye.

crystalline sphere ▶ noun historical (in ancient and medieval astronomy) a transparent sphere of the heavens postulated to lie between the fixed stars and the *primum mobile* and to account for the precession of the equinox and other motions.

crystallite /ˈkrɪst(ə)lʌɪt/ ▶ noun an individual perfect crystal or region of regular crystalline structure in the substance of a material, typically of a metal or a partly crystalline polymer. ■ a very small crystal.

crystallize (also **crystallise**) ▶ verb **1** form or cause to form crystals: [no obj.] *when most liquids freeze they crystallize.*
2 (usu. as adj. **crystallized**) coat and impregnate (fruit or petals) with sugar as a means of preserving them: *a box of crystallized fruits.*
3 make or become definite and clear: *vague feelings of unrest **crystallized into** something more concrete* | [with obj.] *writing can help to crystallize your thoughts.*
4 Finance convert or be converted from a floating charge into a fixed charge.
– DERIVATIVES **crystallizable** adjective, **crystallization** noun.

crystallography /ˌkrɪstəˈlɒgrəfi/ ▶ noun [mass noun] the branch of science concerned with the structure and properties of crystals.
– DERIVATIVES **crystallographer** noun, **crystallographic** adjective, **crystallographically** adverb.

crystalloid ▶ adjective resembling a crystal in shape or structure.
▶ noun **1** Botany a small crystal-like mass of protein in a plant cell.
2 Chemistry a substance that, when dissolved, forms a true solution rather than a colloid and is able to pass through a semipermeable membrane.

crystal meth ▶ noun see METH (sense 1).

Crystal Palace a large building of prefabricated iron and glass resembling a giant greenhouse, designed by Joseph Paxton for the Great Exhibition of 1851 in Hyde Park, London, and re-erected at Sydenham near Croydon; it was accidentally burnt down in 1936.

crystal set (also **crystal radio**) ▶ noun a simple early form of radio receiver with a crystal touching a metal wire as the rectifier (instead of a valve or transistor), and no amplifier or loudspeaker, necessitating headphones or an earphone.

crystal system ▶ noun each of seven categories of crystals (cubic, tetragonal, orthorhombic, trigonal, hexagonal, monoclinic, and triclinic) classified according to the possible relations of the crystal axes.

crystal therapy ▶ noun another term for CRYSTAL HEALING.

crystal violet ▶ noun [mass noun] a synthetic violet dye, related to rosaniline, used as a stain in microscopy and as an antiseptic in the treatment of skin infections.

CS ▶ abbreviation Brit. ■ chartered surveyor. ■ Civil Service. ■ Court of Session.

Cs ▶ symbol the chemical element caesium.

c/s ▶ abbreviation cycles per second.

CSA ▶ abbreviation Child Support Agency.

csardas /ˈtʃɑːdaʃ, ˈzɑːdəs/ (also **czardas**) ▶ noun (pl. **same**) a Hungarian dance with a slow introduction and a fast, wild finish.
– ORIGIN mid 19th cent.: from Hungarian *csárdás*, from *csárda* 'inn'.

CSC ▶ abbreviation Brit. Civil Service Commission.

CSE ▶ abbreviation historical Certificate of Secondary Education.

C-section ▶ noun N. Amer. a caesarean section.

CS gas ▶ noun [mass noun] a powerful form of tear gas used particularly in the control of riots.
– ORIGIN 1960s: from the initials of Ben B. *Corson* (1896–1987) and Roger W. *Stoughton* (1906–57), the

American chemists who discovered the properties of the chemical in 1928.

CSIRO ▸ abbreviation (in Australia) Commonwealth Scientific and Industrial Research Organization.

CSM ▸ abbreviation ■ command and service modules (see COMMAND MODULE). ■ (in the UK) Committee on Safety of Medicines. ■ Company Sergeant Major.

CST ▸ abbreviation Central Standard Time (see CENTRAL TIME).

CT ▸ abbreviation ■ computerized (or computed) tomography. ■ Connecticut (in official postal use).

ct ▸ abbreviation ■ carat: *18 ct gold.* ■ cent.

CTC ▸ abbreviation ■ City Technology College. ■ (in the UK) Cyclists' Touring Club.

ctenidium /tɪˈnɪdɪəm/ ▸ noun (pl. **ctenidia** /-dɪə/) Zoology a comb-like structure, especially a respiratory organ or gill in a mollusc, consisting of an axis with a row of projecting filaments.
– ORIGIN late 19th cent.; modern Latin, from Greek *ktenidion*, diminutive of *kteis, kten-* 'comb'.

ctenoid /ˈtiːnɔɪd/ ▸ adjective Zoology (of fish scales) having many tiny projections on the edge like the teeth of a comb, as in many bony fishes. Compare with GANOID and PLACOID.
– ORIGIN mid 19th cent.: from Greek *kteis, kten-* 'comb' + -OID.

Ctenophora /tiːˈnɒfərə, tɛ-/ ▸ plural noun Zoology a small phylum of aquatic invertebrates that comprises the comb jellies.
– ORIGIN modern Latin (plural), from Greek *kteis, kten-* 'comb' + *pherein* 'to bear'.

ctenophore /ˈtiːnəfɔː, ˈtɛ-/ ▸ noun Zoology an aquatic invertebrate of the phylum Ctenophora, which comprises the comb jellies.

Ctesiphon /ˈtɛsɪf(ə)n/ an ancient city on the Tigris near Baghdad, capital of the Parthian kingdom from *c.*224 and then of Persia under the Sassanian dynasty. It was taken by the Arabs in 636 and destroyed in the 8th century.

C2C ▸ abbreviation consumer-to-consumer, denoting transactions conducted via the Internet between consumers.

CTS ▸ abbreviation carpal tunnel syndrome.

CTT ▸ abbreviation capital transfer tax.

CU ▸ abbreviation ■ Christian Union. ■ informal see you.

Cu ▸ symbol the chemical element copper.
– ORIGIN from late Latin *cuprum*.

cu. ▸ abbreviation cubic (in units of measurement: for example, cu. ft. = cubic feet).

cuadrilla /kwɒˈdriːljə, -ˈdriːjə/ ▸ noun a matador's team.
– ORIGIN mid 19th cent.: Spanish.

cuatro /ˈkwatrəʊ/ ▸ noun (pl. **cuatros**) a small guitar, typically with four (or five) single or paired strings, used in Latin American and Caribbean folk music, especially in Puerto Rico.
– ORIGIN Latin American Spanish, literally 'four'.

cub ▸ noun **1** the young of a fox, bear, lion, or other carnivorous mammal. ■ archaic a young man, especially one who is awkward or bad-mannered.
2 (**Cubs**) a junior branch of the Scout Association, for boys aged about 8 to 11. ■ (also **Cub Scout**) a member of this organization.
▸ verb (**cubs, cubbing, cubbed**) [no obj.] **1** give birth to cubs: *both share the same earth during the first ten days after cubbing.*
2 hunt fox cubs: *members of the Grafton Hunt were out cubbing.*
– DERIVATIVES **cubhood** noun.
– ORIGIN mid 16th cent.: of unknown origin.

Cuba /ˈkjuːbə/ a Caribbean country, the largest and furthest west of the islands of the West Indies, situated at the mouth of the Gulf of Mexico; pop. 11,451,700 (est. 2009); official language, Spanish; capital, Havana.

> A Spanish colony, Cuba became nominally independent after the Spanish–American War of 1898 and achieved full autonomy in 1934. Fidel Castro led a communist revolution in 1959, and held the presidency until replaced by his brother Raúl Castro in 2008. The country suffered under a U.S. trade embargo and, after the collapse of the Soviet Union and the Eastern bloc, lost much of its trade.

– DERIVATIVES **Cuban** adjective & noun.

cubage ▸ noun cubic content or capacity.

Cuba libre /ˌk(j)uːbə ˈliːbreɪ/ ▸ noun (pl. **Cuba libres**) a long drink typically containing lime juice and rum.
– ORIGIN American Spanish, 'free Cuba'.

Cubango /kjuːˈbaŋgəʊ/ another name for OKAVANGO.

Cuban heel ▸ noun a moderately high straight-sided heel on a shoe or boot.

Cuban Missile Crisis an international crisis in October 1962, the closest approach to nuclear war at any time between the US and the USSR. When the US discovered Soviet nuclear missiles on Cuba, President John F. Kennedy demanded their removal and announced a naval blockade of the island; the Soviet leader Khrushchev acceded to the US demands a week later.

cubature /ˈkjuːbətʃə/ ▸ noun [mass noun] the determination of the volume of a solid.
– ORIGIN late 17th cent.: from the verb CUBE, on the pattern of *quadrature*.

cubby ▸ noun (pl. **cubbies**) chiefly N. Amer. a cubbyhole.
– ORIGIN mid 17th cent. (originally Scots, denoting a straw basket): related to dialect *cub* 'stall, pen, hutch', of Low German origin.

cubbyhole ▸ noun a small enclosed space or room. ■ S. African a glove compartment in a car.

cube ▸ noun **1** a symmetrical three-dimensional shape, either solid or hollow, contained by six equal squares. ■ a block of something with six sides: *a sugar cube.* ■ a partitioned-off area in an office containing a desk; a cubicle.
2 Mathematics the product of a number multiplied by its square, represented by a superscript figure 3: *a body increasing in weight by the cube of its length*
▸ verb [with obj.] **1** Mathematics raise (a number or value) to its cube.
2 cut (food) into small cubes: *I bought sirloin from the butcher and cubed it myself.*
– ORIGIN mid 16th cent.: from Old French, or via Latin from Greek *kubos*.

cubeb /ˈkjuːbɛb/ ▸ noun a tropical shrub of the pepper family, which bears pungent berries. ● Genus *Piper*, family Piperaceae: several species.
■ [mass noun] the dried unripe berries of the cubeb, used medicinally and to flavour cigarettes.
– ORIGIN Middle English: from Old French *cubebe*, from Spanish Arabic *kubēba*, from Arabic *kubāba*.

cube farm ▸ noun chiefly US a large office divided into cubicles for individual workers.

cube root ▸ noun the number which produces a given number when cubed.

cubic /ˈkjuːbɪk/ ▸ adjective **1** having the shape of a cube: *a cubic room.* ■ denoting a crystal system or three-dimensional geometrical arrangement having three equal axes at right angles.
2 denoting a unit of measurement equal to the volume of a cube whose side is one of the linear units specified: *15 billion cubic metres of water.*
3 involving the cube (and no higher power) of a quantity or variable: *a cubic equation.*
▸ noun Mathematics a cubic equation, or a curve described by one.
– DERIVATIVES **cubical** adjective, **cubically** adverb.
– ORIGIN late 15th cent. (in the sense 'involving the cube (and no higher power)'): from Old French *cubique*, or via Latin from Greek *kubikos*, from *kobos* 'cube'.

cubic capacity ▸ noun the volume contained by a hollow structure, expressed in litres, cubic centimetres, or other cubic units.

cubic content ▸ noun the volume of a solid, often expressed in cubic metres.

cubicle ▸ noun a small partitioned-off area of a room, for example one containing a shower or toilet, or a desk in an office.
– ORIGIN late Middle English (in the sense 'bedroom'): from Latin *cubiculum*, from *cubare* 'lie down'.

cubiform ▸ adjective technical cube-shaped: *the columns are thick and have cubiform capitals.*

cubism ▸ noun [mass noun] an early 20th-century style and movement in art, especially painting, in which perspective with a single viewpoint was abandoned and use was made of simple geometric shapes, interlocking planes, and, later, collage.

> Cubism was a reaction against traditional modes of representation and Impressionist concerns with light and colour. The style, created by Picasso and Braque and first named by the French critic Louis Vauxcelles in 1908, was inspired by the later work of Cézanne and by African sculpture.

– DERIVATIVES **cubist** noun & adjective.
– ORIGIN early 20th cent.: from French *cubisme*, from *cube* (see CUBE).

cubit /ˈkjuːbɪt/ ▸ noun an ancient measure of length, approximately equal to the length of a forearm. It was typically about 18 inches or 44 cm, though there was a **long cubit** of about 21 inches or 52 cm.
– ORIGIN Middle English: from Latin *cubitum* 'elbow, forearm, cubit'.

cubital /ˈkjuːbɪt(ə)l/ ▸ adjective **1** Anatomy of the forearm or the elbow: *the cubital vein.*
2 Entomology of the cubitus.
– ORIGIN late Middle English: from Latin *cubitalis*, from *cubitus* 'cubit'.

cubitus /ˈkjuːbɪtəs/ ▸ noun Entomology the fifth longitudinal vein from the anterior edge of an insect's wing.
– ORIGIN early 19th cent.: from Latin.

cuboid /ˈkjuːbɔɪd/ ▸ adjective more or less cubic in shape: *the school was a hideous cuboid erection of brick and glass.*
▸ noun **1** Geometry a solid which has six rectangular faces at right angles to each other.
2 (also **cuboid bone**) Anatomy a squat tarsal bone on the outer side of the foot, articulating with the heel bone and the fourth and fifth metatarsals.
– DERIVATIVES **cuboidal** adjective.
– ORIGIN early 19th cent.: from modern Latin *cuboides*, from Greek *kuboeidēs*, from *kubos* (see CUBE).

cub reporter ▸ noun informal a young or inexperienced newspaper reporter.

Cub Scout ▸ noun see CUB (sense 2 of the noun).

cucking-stool /ˈkʌkɪŋstuːl/ ▸ noun historical a chair to which disorderly women were tied and then ducked into water or subjected to public ridicule as a punishment.
– ORIGIN Middle English: from obsolete *cuck* 'defecate', of Scandinavian origin; so named because a stool containing a chamber pot was often used for the purpose.

cuckold /ˈkʌk(ə)ld/ ▸ noun dated the husband of an adulteress, often regarded as an object of derision.
▸ verb [with obj.] (of a man) make (another man) a cuckold by having a sexual relationship with his wife. ■ (of a man's wife) make (her husband) a cuckold.
– DERIVATIVES **cuckoldry** noun.
– ORIGIN late Old English, from Old French *cucuault*, from *cucu* 'cuckoo' (from the cuckoo's habit of laying its egg in another bird's nest). The equivalent words in French and other languages applied to both the bird and the adulterer; *cuckold* has never been applied to the bird in English.

cuckoo ▸ noun **1** a long-tailed, medium-sized bird, typically with a grey or brown back and barred or pale underparts. Many cuckoos lay their eggs in the nests of small songbirds. ● Family Cuculidae (the **cuckoo family**): numerous genera and species, especially the (**Eurasian**) **cuckoo** (*Cuculus canorus*), the male of which has a well-known two-note call. The cuckoo family also includes the coucals, roadrunners, malkohas, and anis.
2 informal a mad person.
▸ adjective informal mad; crazy: *people think you're cuckoo.*
– PHRASES **cuckoo in the nest** an unwelcome intruder in a place or situation.
– ORIGIN Middle English: from Old French *cucu*, imitative of its call.

cuckoo bee ▸ noun a bee which lays its eggs in the nest of another kind of bee, the young being raised and fed by the host. ● *Nomada* and related genera (which parasitize solitary bees), and *Psithyrus* (which parasitize bumblebees), family Apidae.

cuckoo clock ▸ noun a clock that strikes the hour with a sound like a cuckoo's call and typically has a mechanical cuckoo that emerges with each note.

cuckooflower ▸ noun a spring-flowering herbaceous European plant with pale lilac flowers, growing in damp meadows and by streams. Also called LADY'S SMOCK. ● *Cardamine pratensis*, family Cruciferae.
– ORIGIN late 16th cent.: so named because it flowers at the time of year when the cuckoo is first heard calling.

cuckoo pint ▸ noun the common European wild arum of woodland and hedgerows, with a pale spathe and a purple or green spadix followed by bright red berries. Also called LORDS AND LADIES or JACK-IN-THE-PULPIT. ● *Arum maculatum*, family Araceae.
– ORIGIN late Middle English: from earlier *cuckoo-pintle*, from PINTLE in the obsolete sense 'penis' (because of the shape of the spadix).

cuckoo-roller ▸ noun a bird resembling a roller, with an iridescent green cap, back, wings, and tail, found only in Madagascar. Also called COUROL. ● *Leptosomus discolor*, the only member of the family Leptosomatidae.

C

cuckoo-shrike ▸ **noun** a shrike-like Old World songbird, somewhat resembling a cuckoo when in flight, and typically with grey, black, or white plumage. ● Family Campephagidae (the **cuckoo-shrike family**): several genera, especially *Coracina* and *Campephaga*, and numerous species. The cuckoo-shrike family also includes the cicadabirds, greybirds, minivets, and trillers.

cuckoo spit ▸ **noun** [mass noun] whitish froth found in compact masses on leaves and plant stems, exuded by the larvae of froghoppers.

cuckoo wasp ▸ **noun** a wasp which lays its eggs in the nest of a bee or another kind of wasp, in particular: ● a ruby-tailed wasp. ● a true wasp lacking a worker caste, whose larvae are fed by the social wasp host (several species in the family Vespidae, including *Vespula austriaca*).

cucumber ▸ **noun 1** a long, green-skinned fruit with watery flesh, usually eaten raw in salads or pickled. **2** the climbing plant of the gourd family which yields cucumbers, native to the Chinese Himalayan region. It is widely cultivated but very rare in the wild. ● *Cucumis sativus*, family Cucurbitaceae.
– PHRASES **(as) cool as a cucumber** untroubled by heat or exertion. ■ calm and relaxed.
– ORIGIN late Middle English: from Old French *cocombre, coucombre*, from Latin *cucumis, cucumer-*.

cucumber mosaic ▸ **noun** [mass noun] a virus disease affecting plants of the gourd family, spread by beetles and aphids and causing mottling and stunting.

cucurbit /kjʊˈkəːbɪt/ ▸ **noun** chiefly US a plant of the gourd family (Cucurbitaceae), which includes melon, pumpkin, squash, and cucumber.
– DERIVATIVES **cucurbitaceous adjective**.
– ORIGIN late Middle English: from Old French *cucurbite*, from Latin *cucurbita*.

cud ▸ **noun** [mass noun] partly digested food returned from the first stomach of ruminants to the mouth for further chewing.
– PHRASES **chew the cud 1** (of a ruminant animal) further chew partly digested food. **2** think or talk reflectively.
– ORIGIN Old English *cwidu, cudu*, of Germanic origin; related to German *Kitt* 'cement, putty' and Swedish *kåda* 'resin'.

cuddle ▸ **verb** [with obj.] hold close in one's arms as a way of showing love or affection: *he cuddles the baby close* | *they were cuddling each other in the back seat* | [no obj.] *the pair have been spotted kissing and cuddling*. ■ [no obj., with adverbial] lie or sit close: *Rebecca cuddled up to Mum* | *they cuddled together to keep out the cold*. ■ [no obj.] (**cuddle up to**) informal ingratiate oneself with: *they start cuddling up to the Liberals for support*.
▸ **noun** a prolonged and affectionate hug.
– ORIGIN early 16th cent. (rare before the 18th cent.): of unknown origin.

cuddlesome ▸ **adjective** endearing and pleasant to cuddle: *cuddlesome lion cubs and strokeable deer*.

cuddly ▸ **adjective** (**cuddlier, cuddliest**) endearing and pleasant to cuddle, especially as a result of being soft or plump: *she was short and cuddly*. ■ Brit. denoting a toy, especially a model of an animal, that is padded or spongy and covered in soft fabric.

cuddy ▸ **noun** (pl. **cuddies**) dialect, chiefly Scottish **1** a donkey.
2 a stupid person: *you great soft cuddy!*
– ORIGIN early 18th cent.: perhaps a pet form of the given name *Cuthbert*, once popular in Scotland and northern England.

cudgel /ˈkʌdʒ(ə)l/ ▸ **noun** a short, thick stick used as a weapon.
▸ **verb** (**cudgels, cudgelling, cudgelled**; US **cudgels, cudgeling, cudgeled**) [with obj.] beat with a cudgel.
– PHRASES **cudgel one's brain** (or **brains**) Brit. think hard about a problem. **take up the cudgels** start to defend or support someone or something strongly: *there was no one else to take up the cudgels on their behalf*.
– ORIGIN Old English *cycgel*, of unknown origin.

Cudlipp /ˈkʌdlɪp/, Hugh, Baron Cudlipp of Aldingbourne (1913–98), British newspaper editor. Editorial director of the *Daily Mirror*, he introduced the formula that combined sensationalized reporting of sex and crime with populist politics, dramatically increasing the paper's circulation.

cudweed ▸ **noun** [mass noun] a plant of the daisy family, with hairy or downy leaves and inconspicuous flowers. ● Genera *Gnaphalium* and *Filago*, family Compositae.
– ORIGIN mid 16th cent.: from CUD + WEED, said to be given to cattle who had lost their cud.

cue[1] ▸ **noun 1** a thing said or done that serves as a signal to an actor or other performer to enter or to begin their speech or performance. ■ a signal for action: *his success was the cue for the rest of Fleet Street to forge ahead*. ■ a circumstance or piece of information which aids the memory in retrieving details not recalled spontaneously. ■ Psychology a feature of something perceived that is used in the brain's interpretation of the perception: *expectancy is communicated both by auditory and visual cues*. ■ a hint or indication about how to behave in particular circumstances: *my teacher joked about such attitudes and I followed her cue*.
2 [mass noun] a facility for playing through an audio or video recording very rapidly until a desired starting point is reached.
▸ **verb** (**cues, cueing** or **cuing, cued**) [with obj.] **1** give a cue to or for: *Ros and Guil, cued by Hamlet, also bow deeply*. ■ act as a prompt or reminder: *have a list of needs and questions on paper to cue you*.
2 set a piece of audio or video equipment in readiness to play (a particular part of the recorded material): *there was a pause while she cued up the next tape*.
– PHRASES **on cue** at the correct moment: *right on cue the door opened*. **take one's cue from** follow the example or advice of: *McGee did not move and Julia took her cue from him*.
– ORIGIN mid 16th cent.: of unknown origin.

cue[2] ▸ **noun** a long straight tapering wooden rod for striking the ball in snooker, billiards, etc.
▸ **verb** (**cues, cueing** or **cuing, cued**) [no obj.] use a cue to strike the ball.
– ORIGIN mid 18th cent. (denoting a long plait or pigtail): variant of QUEUE.

cue ball ▸ **noun** the ball, usually a white one, that is to be struck with the cue in snooker, billiards, etc.

cue bid ▸ **noun** Bridge a bid intended to give specific information about the content of the hand to the bidder's partner rather than to advance the auction.

cueca /ˈkwɛkə/ ▸ **noun** a lively South American dance.
– ORIGIN early 20th cent.: American Spanish, from *zamacueca*, also denoting a dance performed especially in Chile.

cue card ▸ **noun** a card held beside a camera for a television broadcaster to read from while appearing as if looking into the camera.

Cuenca /ˈkwɛŋkə/ a city in the Andes in southern Ecuador; pop. 374,200 (est. 2008). Founded in 1557, it is known as the 'marble city' because of its many fine buildings.

Cuernavaca /ˌkwɛːnəˈvakə/, Spanish /kwernaˈβaka/ a resort town in central Mexico, at an altitude of 1,542 m (5,060 ft), capital of the state of Morelos; pop. 332,197 (2005).

cuesta /ˈkwɛstə/ ▸ **noun** Geology a ridge with a gentle slope (dip) on one side and a steep slope (scarp) on the other.
– ORIGIN early 19th cent. (originally a US term for a steep slope at the edge of a plain): from Spanish, 'slope', from Latin *costa* 'rib, flank'.

cuff[1] ▸ **noun 1** the end part of a sleeve, where the material of the sleeve is turned back or a separate band is sewn on. ■ the part of a glove covering the wrist. ■ N. Amer. a trouser turn-up. ■ the top part of a boot, typically padded or turned down.
2 (**cuffs**) informal handcuffs.
3 an inflatable bag wrapped round the arm when blood pressure is measured.
▸ **verb** [with obj.] informal secure with handcuffs: *the man's hands were cuffed behind his back*.
– PHRASES **off the cuff** informal without preparation: *they posed some difficult questions to answer off the cuff* | [as modifier] *an off-the-cuff remark*. [as if from impromptu notes made on one's shirt cuffs.]
– DERIVATIVES **cuffed adjective**.
– ORIGIN late Middle English (denoting a glove or mitten): of unknown origin.

cuff[2] ▸ **verb** [with obj.] strike (someone) with an open hand, especially on the head: *he cuffed him playfully on the ear*.
▸ **noun** [usu. in sing.] a blow given with an open hand.
– ORIGIN mid 16th cent.: of unknown origin.

cufflink ▸ **noun** (usu. **cufflinks**) a device for fastening together the sides of a shirt cuff, typically a pair of linked studs or a single plate connected to a short swivelling rod, passed through a hole in each side of the cuff.

Cufic ▸ **noun & adjective** variant spelling of KUFIC.

Cuiabá /ˌkuːjəˈbɑː/ **1** a river port in west central Brazil, on the Cuiabá River, capital of the state of Mato Grosso; pop. 526,831 (2007).
2 a river of western Brazil, which rises in the Mato Grosso plateau and flows for 483 km (300 miles) to join the São Lourenço River near the border with Bolivia.

cui bono? /kwiː ˈbɒnəʊ, ˈbəʊ-/ ▸ **exclamation** who stands, or stood, to gain (from a crime, and so might have been responsible for it)?
– ORIGIN Latin, 'to whom (is it) a benefit?'

cuirass /kwɪˈras/ ▸ **noun 1** historical a piece of armour consisting of breastplate and backplate fastened together.
2 Medicine an artificial ventilator which encloses the body, leaving the limbs free, and forces air in and out of the lungs by changes in pressure.
– ORIGIN late Middle English: from Old French *cuirace*, based on late Latin *coriaceus* (adjective), from *corium* 'leather' (of which a cuirass was originally made).

cuirassier /ˌkwɪrəˈsɪə/, French /kɥiʀasje/ ▸ **noun** historical a cavalry soldier wearing a cuirass.
– ORIGIN mid 16th cent.: French, from *cuirasse*, from Old French *cuirace* (see CUIRASS).

cuisine /kwɪˈziːn/ ▸ **noun** [mass noun] a style or method of cooking, especially as characteristic of a particular country, region, or establishment: *much Venetian cuisine is based on seafood*. ■ food cooked in a certain way: *we spent the evening sampling the local cuisine*.
– ORIGIN late 18th cent.: French, literally 'kitchen', from Latin *coquina*, from *coquere* 'to cook'.

cuisse /kwɪs/ (also **cuish** /kwɪʃ/) ▸ **noun** (usu. **cuisses** or **cuishes**) historical a piece of armour for the thigh.
– ORIGIN Middle English (originally in the plural): from Old French *cuisseaux*, plural of *cuissel*, from late Latin *coxale*, from *coxa* 'hip'.

cuke /kjuːk/ ▸ **noun** informal a cucumber.

culch ▸ **noun** variant spelling of CULTCH.

culchie /ˈkʌl(t)ʃi/ ▸ **noun** (pl. **culchies**) Irish informal an unsophisticated country person.
– ORIGIN apparently an alteration of *Kiltimagh* (Irish *Coillte Mach*), the name of a country town in County Mayo, Ireland.

Culdee /kʌlˈdiː/ ▸ **noun** an Irish or Scottish monk of the 8th to 12th centuries, living as a recluse usually in a group of thirteen (on the analogy of Christ and his Apostles). The tradition ceased as the Celtic Church was brought under Roman Catholic rule.
– ORIGIN late Middle English: from medieval Latin *culdeus*, alteration, influenced by Latin *cultores Dei* 'worshippers of God', of *kelledei* (plural, found in early Scottish records), from Old Irish *céle dé*, literally 'companion of God'.

cul-de-sac /ˈkʌldəˌsak, ˈkʊl-/ ▸ **noun** (pl. **culs-de-sac** or **cul-de-sacs** pronunc. **same** or /-ˌsaks/) a street or passage closed at one end. ■ a route or course leading nowhere: *was the new post a career cul-de-sac?* ■ Anatomy a vessel, tube, or sac open at only one end.
– ORIGIN mid 18th cent. (originally in anatomy): French, literally 'bottom of a sack'.

-cule ▸ **suffix** forming nouns such as *molecule, reticule*, which were originally diminutives.
– ORIGIN from French *-cule* or Latin *-culus, -cula, -culum*.

culex /ˈkjuːlɛks/ (also **culex mosquito**) ▸ **noun** (pl. **culices** /-lɪsiːz/) a mosquito of a genus which includes a number of kinds commonly found in cooler regions. They do not transmit malaria, but can pass on a variety of other parasites including those causing filariasis. Compare with ANOPHELES. ● Genus *Culex*, subfamily Culicinae, family Culicidae.
– DERIVATIVES **culicine** /ˈkjuːlɪsʌɪn, -siːn/ **adjective & noun**.
– ORIGIN Latin, 'gnat'.

Culiacán Rosales /ˌkʊljəˌkɑːn rəʊˈzɑːlɛz/ a city in NW Mexico, capital of the state of Sinaloa; pop. 540,800 (2005).

culinary ▸ **adjective** of or for cooking: *culinary skills* | *savour the culinary delights of the region*.
– DERIVATIVES **culinarily adverb**.
– ORIGIN mid 17th cent.: from Latin *culinarius*, from *culina* 'kitchen'.

cull ▸ **verb** [with obj.] **1** reduce the population of (a wild animal) by selective slaughter: *some of the culled deer will be used for scientific research* | (as noun **culling**) *kangaroo culling*. ■ send (an inferior or surplus farm animal) to be slaughtered.

2 select from a large quantity; obtain from a variety of sources: *anecdotes culled from Greek and Roman history*.
▶ **noun** a selective slaughter of animals. ■ an inferior or surplus livestock animal selected for culling.
– DERIVATIVES **culler** noun.
– ORIGIN Middle English: from Old French *coillier*, based on Latin *colligere* (see COLLECT[1]).

Cullen skink ▶ **noun** [mass noun] a Scottish soup made from smoked haddock, potatoes, onions, and milk.
– ORIGIN from the name of *Cullen*, a village on the Moray Firth in NE Scotland, + Scots *skink* 'soup made from shin of beef', probably from Middle Low German *Schinke* 'ham'.

cullet /ˈkʌlɪt/ ▶ **noun** [mass noun] recycled broken or waste glass used in glass-making.
– ORIGIN early 19th cent.: variant of COLLET, in the obsolete sense 'glass left on the blowing-iron when the finished article is removed'.

Culloden, Battle of /kəˈlɒd(ə)n/ the final engagement of the Jacobite uprising of 1745–6, fought on a moor near Inverness, the last pitched battle on British soil. The Hanoverian army under the Duke of Cumberland crushed the small and poorly supplied Jacobite army of Charles Edward Stuart, and a ruthless pursuit after the battle effectively prevented any chance of saving the Jacobite cause.

cully /ˈkʌli/ ▶ **noun** (pl. **cullies**) archaic, informal (often as a form of address) a man; a friend.
– ORIGIN mid 17th cent. (denoting a person who is imposed upon): of unknown origin.

Culm /kʌlm/ ▶ **noun** [mass noun] **1** Geology a series of Carboniferous strata in SW England, mainly shale and limestone with some thin coal seams.
2 (**culm**) archaic coal dust or slack.
– ORIGIN Middle English (in the sense 'soot, smut', now only Scots): probably related to COAL.

culm /kʌlm/ ▶ **noun** the hollow stem of a grass or cereal plant, especially that bearing the flower.
– ORIGIN mid 17th cent.: from Latin *culmus* 'stalk'.

culmen /ˈkʌlmɛn/ ▶ **noun** (pl. **culmina** /-mɪnə/)
1 Ornithology the upper ridge of a bird's bill.
2 Anatomy a small region in the brain on the anterior surface of the cerebellum.
– ORIGIN mid 17th cent. (in the sense 'top, summit'): from Latin, contraction of *columen* 'top, summit'.

culminant ▶ **adjective** at or forming the top or highest point.

culminate /ˈkʌlmɪneɪt/ ▶ **verb** [no obj.] **1** reach a climax or point of highest development: *weeks of violence culminated in the brutal murder of a magistrate*.
■ [with obj.] be the climax or point of highest development of: *her book culminated a research project on the symmetry studies of Escher*.
2 archaic or Astrology (of a celestial body) reach or be at the meridian.
– ORIGIN mid 17th cent. (in astronomy and astrology): from late Latin *culminat-* 'exalted', from the verb *culminare*, from *culmen* 'summit'.

culmination ▶ **noun** [usu. in sing.] **1** the highest or climactic point of something, especially as attained after a long time: *the deal marked the culmination of years of negotiation*.
2 archaic or Astrology the reaching of the meridian by a celestial body.

culottes /kjuːˈlɒt(s)/ ▶ **plural noun** women's knee-length trousers, cut with full legs to resemble a skirt.
– ORIGIN mid 19th cent.: French, 'knee breeches', diminutive of *cul* 'rump', from Latin *culus*.

culpability ▶ **noun** [mass noun] responsibility for a fault or wrong; blame: *a level of moral culpability*.

culpable ▶ **adjective** deserving blame: *mercy killings are less culpable than 'ordinary' murders*.
– DERIVATIVES **culpably** adverb.
– ORIGIN Middle English (in the sense 'deserving punishment'): from Old French *coupable, culpable*, from Latin *culpabilis*, from *culpare* 'to blame', from *culpa* 'fault, blame'.

culpable homicide ▶ **noun** [mass noun] Law (in some jurisdictions, including Scotland, South Africa, and India) an act which has resulted in a person's death but is held not to amount to murder.

Culpeper /ˈkʌlpɛpə/, Nicholas (1616–54), English herbalist. His *Complete Herbal* (1653) popularized herbalism and, despite embracing ideas of astrology and the doctrine of signatures, was important in the development of botany and pharmacology.

culprit ▶ **noun** a person who is responsible for a crime or other misdeed. ■ the cause of a problem or defect: *low-level ozone pollution is the real culprit*.
– ORIGIN late 17th cent. (originally in the formula *Culprit, how will you be tried?*, said by the Clerk of the Crown to a prisoner pleading not guilty): perhaps from a misinterpretation of the written abbreviation *cul. prist* for Anglo-Norman French *Culpable: prest d'averrer notre bille* '(You are) guilty: (We are) ready to prove our indictment'; in later use influenced by Latin *culpa* 'fault, blame'.

cult ▶ **noun 1** a system of religious veneration and devotion directed towards a particular figure or object: *the cult of St Olaf*. ■ a relatively small group of people having religious beliefs or practices regarded by others as strange or as imposing excessive control over members: *a network of Satan-worshipping cults*. ■ a misplaced or excessive admiration for a particular thing: *the cult of the pursuit of money as an end in itself*.
2 a person or thing that is popular or fashionable among a particular group or section of society: *the series has become a bit of a cult in the UK* | [as modifier] *a cult film*.
– DERIVATIVES **cultic** adjective, **cultish** adjective, **cultishness** noun, **cultism** noun, **cultist** noun.
– ORIGIN early 17th cent. (originally denoting homage paid to a divinity): from French *culte* or Latin *cultus* 'worship', from *cult-* 'inhabited, cultivated, worshipped', from the verb *colere*.

cultch /kʌltʃ/ (also **culch**) ▶ **noun** [mass noun] the mass of stones, broken shells, and grit of which an oyster bed is formed.
– ORIGIN mid 17th cent.: of unknown origin.

cultigen /ˈkʌltɪdʒ(ə)n/ ▶ **noun** Botany a plant species or variety known only in cultivation, especially one with no known wild ancestor.
– ORIGIN early 20th cent.: from *cultivated* (past participle of CULTIVATE) + -GEN.

cultivar /ˈkʌltɪvɑː/ ▶ **noun** Botany a plant variety that has been produced in cultivation by selective breeding. Cultivars are usually designated in the style *Taxus baccata* 'Variegata'. See also VARIETY (sense 2).
– ORIGIN 1920s: blend of CULTIVATE and VARIETY.

cultivate ▶ **verb** [with obj.] **1** prepare and use (land) for crops or gardening. ■ break up (soil) in preparation for sowing or planting. ■ raise or grow (plants), especially on a large scale for commercial purposes.
2 Biology grow or maintain (living cells or tissue) in culture.
3 try to acquire or develop (a quality or skill): *he cultivated an air of indifference*. ■ try to win the friendship or favour of (someone): *it helps if you go out of your way to cultivate the local people*. ■ try to improve or develop (one's mind).
– DERIVATIVES **cultivable** adjective, **cultivatable** adjective.
– ORIGIN mid 17th cent.: from medieval Latin *cultivat-* 'prepared for crops', from the verb *cultivare*, from *cultiva (terra)* 'arable (land)', from *colere* 'cultivate, inhabit'.

cultivated ▶ **adjective** refined and well educated: *he was a remarkably cultivated and educated man*.

cultivation ▶ **noun** [mass noun] **1** the action of cultivating land, or the state of being cultivated: *the cultivation of arable crops* | *the economy was based largely on rice cultivation*.
2 the process of trying to acquire or develop a quality or skill: *the cultivation of good staff–management relations*.
3 refinement and good education: *a man of cultivation and taste*.

cultivator ▶ **noun** a person or thing that cultivates something: *they were herders of cattle and cultivators of corn*. ■ a mechanical implement for breaking up the ground and uprooting weeds.

cultural ▶ **adjective 1** relating to the ideas, customs, and social behaviour of a society: *the cultural diversity of British society*.
2 relating to the arts and to intellectual achievements: *a cultural festival*.
– DERIVATIVES **culturally** adverb.
– ORIGIN mid 19th cent.: from Latin *cultura* 'tillage' + -AL.

cultural anthropology ▶ **noun** see ANTHROPOLOGY.

cultural attaché ▶ **noun** an embassy official whose function is to promote cultural relations between their own country and the one to which they are accredited.

Cultural Revolution a political upheaval in China between 1966 and 1976 intended to bring about a return to revolutionary Maoist beliefs. Largely carried forward by the Red Guard, it resulted in attacks on intellectuals, a large-scale purge in party posts, and the appearance of a personality cult around Mao Zedong. It led to considerable economic dislocation and was gradually brought to a halt by premier Zhou Enlai.

culturati /ˌkʌltʃəˈrɑːti/ ▶ **plural noun** well-educated people who appreciate the arts.
– ORIGIN 1980s: blend of CULTURE and LITERATI.

culture ▶ **noun** [mass noun] **1** the arts and other manifestations of human intellectual achievement regarded collectively: *20th century popular culture*. ■ a refined understanding or appreciation of culture: *men of culture*.
2 the ideas, customs, and social behaviour of a particular people or society: *Afro-Caribbean culture* | [count noun] *people from many different cultures*. ■ [with modifier] the attitudes and behaviour characteristic of a particular social group: *the emerging drug culture*.
3 Biology the cultivation of bacteria, tissue cells, etc. in an artificial medium containing nutrients: *the cells proliferate readily in culture*. ■ [count noun] a preparation of cells obtained by culture: *the bacterium was isolated in two blood cultures*.
4 the cultivation of plants: *this variety of lettuce is popular for its ease of culture*.
▶ **verb** [with obj.] Biology maintain (tissue cells, bacteria, etc.) in conditions suitable for growth.
– ORIGIN Middle English (denoting a cultivated piece of land): the noun from French *culture* or directly from Latin *cultura* 'growing, cultivation'; the verb from obsolete French *culturer* or medieval Latin *culturare*, both based on Latin *colere* 'tend, cultivate' (see CULTIVATE). In late Middle English the sense was 'cultivation of the soil' and from this (early 16th cent.), arose 'cultivation (of the mind, faculties, or manners)'; sense 1 of the noun dates from the early 19th cent.

cultured ▶ **adjective 1** characterized by refined taste and manners and good education: *a cultured and intelligent man*.
2 Biology (of tissue cells, bacteria, etc.) grown or propagated in an artificial medium.
3 (of a pearl) formed round a foreign body inserted into an oyster.

culture jamming ▶ **noun** [mass noun] the practice of criticizing and subverting advertising and consumerism in the mass media, by methods such as producing advertisements parodying those of global brands.

culture shock ▶ **noun** [mass noun] the feeling of disorientation experienced by someone when they are suddenly subjected to an unfamiliar culture, way of life, or set of attitudes.

culture vulture ▶ **noun** informal a person who is very interested in the arts.

culture war ▶ **noun** a conflict between groups with different ideals, beliefs, philosophies, etc.

cultus /ˈkʌltəs/ ▶ **noun** technical a system or variety of religious worship.
– ORIGIN mid 19th cent.: Latin (see CULT).

culverin /ˈkʌlv(ə)rɪn/ ▶ **noun 1** a 16th- or 17th-century cannon with a relatively long barrel for its bore.
2 a kind of handgun of the 15th and 16th centuries.
– ORIGIN late 15th cent. (in sense 2): from Old French *coulevrine*, from *couleuvre* 'snake', based on Latin *colubra*.

culvert /ˈkʌlvət/ ▶ **noun** a tunnel carrying a stream or open drain under a road or railway.
▶ **verb** [with obj.] channel (a stream or drain) through a culvert.
– ORIGIN late 18th cent.: of unknown origin.

cum[1] /kʌm/ ▶ **preposition** [usu. in combination] combined with; also used as (used to describe things with a dual nature or function): *a study-cum-bedroom*.
– ORIGIN late 19th cent.: Latin.

cum[2] /kʌm/ ▶ **noun** informal variant spelling of COME.

cumber /ˈkʌmbə/ ▶ **verb** [with obj.] dated hamper or hinder: *they were cumbered with greatcoats and swords*. ■ obstruct (a path or space): *the road was clean and dry and not still cumbered by slush*.
▶ **noun** archaic a hindrance, obstruction, or burden: *a cumber of limestone rocks*.
– ORIGIN Middle English (in the sense 'overthrow, destroy'): probably from ENCUMBER.

Cumberland[1] /ˈkʌmbələnd/ a former county of NW England. In 1974 it was united with Westmorland and part of Lancashire to form Cumbria.

Cumberland[2] /ˈkʌmbələnd/, William Augustus, Duke of (1721–65), English military commander, third son of George II. He gained great notoriety (and his nickname 'the Butcher') for the severity of

C

his suppression of the Jacobite clans in the aftermath of his victory at the Battle of Culloden (1746).

Cumberland sauce ▶ noun [mass noun] a piquant sauce served as a relish with game and cold meats. It is typically made from redcurrant jelly flavoured with orange, mustard, and port.

Cumberland sausage ▶ noun [mass noun] Brit. a type of coarse sausage traditionally made in a continuous strip and cooked and served as a spiral.

Cumbernauld /ˌkʌmbəˈnɔːld/ a town in central Scotland, in North Lanarkshire; pop. 54,000 (est. 2009). It was built as a new town in 1955.

cumbersome ▶ adjective large or heavy and therefore difficult to carry or use; unwieldy: *cumbersome diving suits.* ■ slow or complicated and therefore inefficient: *organizations with cumbersome hierarchical structures.*
– DERIVATIVES **cumbersomely** adverb, **cumbersomeness** noun.
– ORIGIN late Middle English (in the sense 'difficult to get through'): from CUMBER + -SOME[1].

cumbia /ˈkʊmbɪə/ ▶ noun [mass noun] a kind of dance music of Colombian origin, similar to salsa. ■ [count noun] a dance performed to cumbia.
– ORIGIN 1940s: from Colombian Spanish, perhaps from Spanish *cumbé.*

Cumbria /ˈkʌmbrɪə/ a county of NW England; county town, Carlisle. Cumbria was an ancient British kingdom, and the name continued to be used for the hilly north-western region of England containing the Lake District. The county of Cumbria was formed in 1974, largely from the former counties of Westmorland and Cumberland.
– DERIVATIVES **Cumbrian** adjective & noun.
– ORIGIN from medieval Latin, from Welsh *Cymry* 'Welshman'.

cumbrous /ˈkʌmbrəs/ ▶ adjective literary term for CUMBERSOME.
– DERIVATIVES **cumbrously** adverb, **cumbrousness** noun.
– ORIGIN late Middle English (in the sense 'difficult to get through'): from CUMBER + -OUS.

cum dividend ▶ adverb (of share purchases) with a dividend about to be paid.

cumec ▶ noun a cubic metre per second, as a unit of rate of flow of water.
– ORIGIN 1950s: from *cu*bic *me*tres per se*c*ond.

cumene /ˈkjuːmiːn/ ▶ noun [mass noun] Chemistry a liquid hydrocarbon made catalytically from benzene, chiefly as an intermediate in phenol synthesis. ● Alternative name: **isopropyl benzene**; chem. formula: $C_6H_5CH(CH_3)_2$.
– ORIGIN mid 19th cent.: from Latin *cuminum* 'cumin' + -ENE.

cum grano salis /kʌm ˌɡraːnəʊ ˈsɑːlɪs/ ▶ adverb (in phrase **take something cum grano salis**) another way of saying TAKE SOMETHING WITH A PINCH OF SALT (see SALT).
– ORIGIN Latin, 'with a grain of salt'.

cumin /ˈkjuːmɪn/ (also **cummin**) ▶ noun [mass noun]
1 the aromatic seeds of a plant of the parsley family, used as a spice, especially ground and used in curry powder.
2 the small, slender plant which bears cumin seeds, occurring from the Mediterranean to central Asia. ● *Cuminum cyminum*, family Umbelliferae.
– ORIGIN Old English *cymen*, from Latin *cuminum*, from Greek *kuminon*, probably of Semitic origin and related to Hebrew *kammōn* and Arabic *kammūn*; superseded in Middle English by forms from Old French *cumon, comin*, also from Latin.

cum laude /kʌm ˈlɔːdi, kʊm ˈlaʊdeɪ/ ▶ adverb & adjective chiefly N. Amer. with distinction (with reference to university degrees and diplomas).
– ORIGIN Latin, literally 'with praise'.

cummerbund /ˈkʌməbʌnd/ ▶ noun a sash worn around the waist, especially as part of a man's formal evening suit.
– ORIGIN early 17th cent.: from Urdu and Persian *kamar-band*, from *kamar* 'waist, loins' and *-bandi* 'band'. The sash was formerly worn in the Indian subcontinent by domestic workers and low-status office workers.

cummings, e. e. (1894–1962), American poet and novelist; full name *Edward Estlin Cummings*. His poems are characterized by their experimental typography (most notably in the avoidance of capital letters), technical skill, frank vocabulary, and the sharpness of his satire.

cummingtonite /ˈkʌmɪŋtənʌɪt/ ▶ noun [mass noun] a mineral occurring typically as brownish fibrous crystals in some metamorphic rocks. It is a magnesium-rich iron silicate of the amphibole group.
– ORIGIN early 19th cent.: named after *Cummington*, a town in Massachusetts, US, + -ITE[1].

cumquat ▶ noun variant spelling of KUMQUAT.

cumulate ▶ verb /ˈkjuːmjʊleɪt/ 1 [with obj.] gather together and combine: *the systems cumulate data over a period of years.* ■ [no obj.] be gathered together and combined: *all unpaid dividend payments cumulate and are paid when earnings are sufficient.*
2 (as adj. **cumulated**) Chemistry denoting two double bonds attached to the same carbon atom.
▶ noun /ˈkjuːmjʊlət/ Geology an igneous rock formed by gravitational settling of particles in a magma.
– DERIVATIVES **cumulation** noun.
– ORIGIN mid 16th cent. (as a verb in the sense 'gather in a heap'): from Latin *cumulat-* 'heaped', from the verb *cumulare*, from *cumulus* 'a heap'. Current senses date from the early 20th cent.

cumulative ▶ adjective increasing or increased in quantity, degree, or force by successive additions: *the cumulative effect of two years of drought.*
– DERIVATIVES **cumulatively** adverb, **cumulativeness** noun.

cumulative distribution function ▶ noun Statistics a function whose value is the probability that a corresponding continuous random variable has a value less than or equal to the argument of the function.

cumulative error ▶ noun Statistics an error that increases with the size of the sample revealing it.

cumulative preference share ▶ noun a preference share whose annual fixed-rate dividend, if it cannot be paid in any year, accrues until it can.

cumulative voting ▶ noun [mass noun] a system of voting in an election in which each voter is allowed a number of votes, and may give them all to one candidate or divide them among several.

cumulonimbus /ˌkjuːmjʊləʊˈnɪmbəs/ ▶ noun (pl. **cumulonimbi** /-bʌɪ/) [mass noun] Meteorology cloud forming a towering mass with a flat base at fairly low altitude and often a flat top, as in thunderstorms.

cumulus /ˈkjuːmjʊləs/ ▶ noun (pl. **cumuli** /-lʌɪ, -liː/) [mass noun] Meteorology cloud forming rounded masses heaped on each other above a flat base at fairly low altitude.
– ORIGIN mid 17th cent. (denoting a heap or an accumulation): from Latin, 'heap'.

Cuna ▶ noun & adjective variant spelling of KUNA.

Cunard /kjuːˈnɑːd/, Sir Samuel (1787–1865), Canadian-born British shipowner. One of the pioneers of the regular transatlantic passenger service, he founded the steamship company which still bears his name with the aid of a contract to carry the mail between Britain and Canada. The first such voyage for the company was made in 1840.

cuneate /ˈkjuːnɪət/ ▶ adjective chiefly Anatomy & Botany wedge-shaped.
– ORIGIN early 19th cent.: from Latin *cuneus* 'wedge' + -ATE[2].

cuneiform /ˈkjuːnɪfɔːm, kjuːˈneɪɪfɔːm/ ▶ adjective 1 denoting or relating to the wedge-shaped characters used in the ancient writing systems of Mesopotamia, Persia, and Ugarit, surviving mainly on clay tablets: *a cuneiform inscription.*
2 Anatomy denoting three bones of the tarsus (ankle) between the navicular bone and the metatarsals.
3 chiefly Biology wedge-shaped: *the eggs are cuneiform.*
▶ noun [mass noun] cuneiform writing.
– ORIGIN late 17th cent.: from French *cunéiforme* or modern Latin *cuneiformis*, from Latin *cuneus* 'wedge'.

Cunene /kjuːˈneɪnə/ a river of Angola, which rises near the city of Huambo and flows 250 km (156 miles) southwards as far as the frontier with Namibia, which then follows it westwards to the Atlantic.

cu-nim ▶ noun short for CUMULONIMBUS.

cunjevoi /ˈkʌndʒɪvɔɪ/ ▶ noun 1 a tall Australian plant of the arum family, with edible corms. ● *Alocasia macrorrhiza*, family Araceae.
2 an Australian sea squirt used as fishing bait. ● *Pyura praeputialis*, class Ascidiacea.
– ORIGIN late 19th cent. (in sense 1): of Aboriginal (probably Queensland) origin. Sense 2 dates from the early 20th cent.

cunner /ˈkʌnə/ ▶ noun an edible greenish-grey wrasse (fish) which lives along the Atlantic coast of North America. ● *Tautogolabrus adspersus*, family Labridae.
– ORIGIN early 17th cent.: perhaps associated with archaic *conder*, denoting a lookout who alerts the crew of fishing boats to the direction taken by shoals of herring.

cunnilingus /ˌkʌnɪˈlɪŋɡəs/ ▶ noun [mass noun] stimulation of the female genitals using the tongue or lips.
– ORIGIN late 19th cent.: from Latin, from *cunnus* 'vulva' + *lingere* 'lick'.

cunning ▶ adjective 1 having or showing skill in achieving one's ends by deceit or evasion: *a cunning look came into his eyes.* ■ ingenious: *plants have evolved cunning defences.*
2 N. Amer. attractive or quaint: *Baby will look too cunning for anything in that pink print.*
▶ noun [mass noun] skill in achieving one's ends by deceit: *a statesman to whom cunning had come as second nature.* ■ ingenuity: *what resources of energy and cunning it took just to survive.*
– DERIVATIVES **cunningly** adverb, **cunningness** noun.
– ORIGIN Middle English: perhaps from Old Norse *kunnandi* 'knowledge', from *kunna* 'know' (related to CAN[1]), or perhaps from Middle English *cunne*, an obsolete variant of CAN[1]. The original sense was '(possessing) erudition or skill' and had no implication of deceit; the sense 'deceitfulness' dates from late Middle English.

Cunningham /ˈkʌnɪŋəm/, Merce (1919–2009), American dancer and choreographer. A dancer with the Martha Graham Dance Company (1939–45), he formed his own company in 1953 and explored new abstract directions for modern dance.

Cunobelinus /ˌkjuːnə(ʊ)bəˈlʌɪnəs/ variant of CYMBELINE.

cunt ▶ noun vulgar slang a woman's genitals. ■ an unpleasant or stupid person.
– ORIGIN Middle English: of Germanic origin; related to Norwegian and Swedish dialect *kunta*, and Middle Low German, Middle Dutch, and Danish dialect *kunte.*

CUP ▶ abbreviation Cambridge University Press.

cup ▶ noun 1 a small bowl-shaped container for drinking from, typically having a handle. ■ the contents of a cup: ***a cup of tea.*** ■ chiefly N. Amer. a measure of capacity used in cookery, equal to half a US pint (0.237 litre): ***a cup of butter.*** ■ (in church use) a chalice used at the Eucharist.
2 an ornamental trophy in the form of a cup, usually made of gold or silver and having a stem and two handles, awarded as a prize in a sports contest. ■ (**Cup**) a contest in which the winners are awarded a cup: *playing in the Cup is the best thing ever.*
3 a cup-shaped thing. ■ either of the two parts of a bra shaped to contain or support one breast: *she had grown from an A to a C cup in just six months.* ■ Golf the hole on a putting green, or the metal container in it.
4 [mass noun] a mixed drink made from fruit juices and typically containing wine or cider.
5 (**cups**) one of the suits in a tarot pack.
▶ verb (**cups, cupping, cupped**) [with obj.] 1 form (one's hand or hands) into the curved shape of a cup: *'Hey!' Dad shouted, with his hands cupped around his mouth.* ■ place the curved hand or hands around: *he cupped her face in his hands.*
2 Medicine, historical bleed (someone) by using a glass in which a partial vacuum is formed by heating: *Dr Ross ordered me to be cupped.*
– PHRASES **in one's cups** informal drunk. **not one's cup of tea** informal not what one likes or is interested in: *cats were not her cup of tea.*
– DERIVATIVES **cupful** noun (pl. **cupfuls**).
– ORIGIN Old English: from popular Latin *cuppa*, probably from Latin *cupa* 'tub'.

cup-and-ring ▶ adjective denoting marks cut in megalithic monuments consisting of a circular depression surrounded by concentric rings.

cup-bearer ▶ noun chiefly historical a person who serves wine, especially in a royal or noble household.

cupboard ▶ noun a recess or piece of furniture with a door and usually shelves, used for storage: *a broom cupboard.*
– ORIGIN late Middle English (denoting a table or sideboard on which cups, plates, etc. were displayed): from CUP + BOARD.

cupboard love ▶ noun [mass noun] Brit. affection that is feigned in order to obtain something.

cupcake ▶ noun 1 a small cake baked in a cup-shaped foil or paper container and typically iced.
2 US informal an attractive woman (often as a term of address). ■ a weak or effeminate man.

cup coral ▶ **noun** a small brightly coloured solitary coral with tentacles that end in small knobs, sometimes found in colder seas. ● Genus *Caryophyllia*, order Scleractinia (or Madreporaria): several species.

cupel /ˈkjuːp(ə)l/ ▶ **noun** a shallow, porous container in which gold or silver can be refined or assayed by melting with a blast of hot air which oxidizes lead or other base metals.
▶ **verb** (**cupels**, **cupelling**, **cupelled**; US **cupels**, **cupeling**, **cupeled**) [with obj.] assay or refine (a metal) in a cupel.
– DERIVATIVES **cupellation** noun.
– ORIGIN early 17th cent. (as a noun): from French *coupelle*, diminutive of *coupe* 'goblet'.

Cup Final ▶ **noun** Brit. the final match in a sports competition in which the winners are awarded a cup.

cup fungus ▶ **noun** a fungus in which the spore-producing layer forms the lining of a shallow cup. ● Several families in the orders Helotiales and Pezizales, subdivision Ascomycotina.

cupholder ▶ **noun** a device for holding a plastic cup or other drinking container.

Cupid Roman Mythology the god of love. He is represented as a naked winged boy with a bow and arrows, with which he wounds his victims. Greek equivalent **Eros**. ■ (as noun also **cupid**) a representation of a naked winged child, typically carrying a bow.
– ORIGIN from Latin *Cupido*, personification of *cupido* 'love, desire', from *cupere* 'to desire'.

cupidity /kjuːˈpɪdɪti/ ▶ **noun** [mass noun] greed for money or possessions.
– ORIGIN late Middle English: from Old French *cupidite* or Latin *cupiditas*, from *cupidus* 'desirous', from *cupere* 'to desire'. Compare with **covet**.

Cupid's bow ▶ **noun** a shape like that of the double-curved bow often shown carried by Cupid, especially at the top edge of a person's upper lip.

cupid's dart ▶ **noun** a herbaceous plant of the daisy family, with white, blue, or lilac flowers. ● *Catananche caerulea*, family Compositae.

cup lichen ▶ **noun** a greenish-grey lichen with small cup-like structures arising from its spreading lobes, found typically on heathland and moorland. ● Genus *Cladonia*, order Cladoniales: many species.

cupola /ˈkjuːpələ/ ▶ **noun 1** a rounded dome forming or adorning a roof or ceiling.
2 a gun turret.
3 (also **cupola furnace**) a cylindrical furnace for refining metals, with openings at the bottom for blowing in air and originally with a dome leading to a chimney above.
– DERIVATIVES **cupolaed** /-ləd/ adjective.
– ORIGIN mid 16th cent.: Italian, from late Latin *cupula* 'small cask or burying vault', diminutive of *cupa* 'cask'.

cuppa Brit. informal ▶ **noun** a cup of tea: *a good strong cuppa*.
▶ **contraction** cup of. *let's have another cuppa tea*.
– ORIGIN 1920s: alteration.

cupping ▶ **noun** [mass noun] (in Chinese medicine) a therapy in which heated glass cups are applied to the skin along the meridians of the body, creating suction and believed to stimulate the flow of energy.

cuppy ▶ **adjective** (of ground) full of shallow depressions.

cupr- ▶ **combining form** variant spelling of **cupro-**. shortened before a vowel (as in *cuprammonium*).

cuprammonium /ˌkjuːprəˈməʊnɪəm/ ▶ **noun** [as modifier] Chemistry a complex ion, $Cu(NH_3)_4^{2+}$, formed in solution when ammonia is added to copper salts. The solution is deep blue and is used to dissolve cellulose.

cupreous /ˈkjuːprɪəs/ ▶ **adjective** of or like copper.
– ORIGIN mid 17th cent.: from late Latin *cupreus* (from *cuprum* 'copper') + **-ous**.

cupric /ˈkjuːprɪk/ ▶ **adjective** Chemistry of copper with a valency of two; of copper(II). Compare with **cuprous**.
– ORIGIN late 18th cent.: from late Latin *cuprum* 'copper' + **-ic**.

cuprite /ˈkjuːprʌɪt/ ▶ **noun** [mass noun] a dark red or brownish black mineral consisting of cuprous oxide.

cupro /ˈk(j)uːprəʊ/ ▶ **noun** [mass noun] a type of rayon made by dissolving cotton cellulose with cuprammonium salts and spinning the resulting solution into filaments.
– ORIGIN 1980s: an invented word, probably from **cuprammonium**.

cupro- /ˈkjuːprəʊ/ (also **cupr-**) ▶ **combining form** relating to copper: *cupro-nickel*.
– ORIGIN from late Latin *cuprum*.

cupro-nickel ▶ **noun** [mass noun] an alloy of copper and nickel, especially in the proportions 3:1 as used in 'silver' coins.

cuprous /ˈkjuːprəs/ ▶ **adjective** Chemistry of copper with a valency of one; of copper(I).
– ORIGIN mid 17th cent.: partly directly from late Latin *cuprum* 'copper' (reinforced by **cupric**) + **-ous**.

cup tie ▶ **noun** Brit. a match in a competition for which the prize is a cup.

cup-tied ▶ **adjective** Brit. (of a soccer player) ineligible to play for one's club in a cup competition as a result of having played for another club in an earlier round.

cupule /ˈkjuːpjuːl/ ▶ **noun** Botany & Zoology a cup-shaped organ, structure, or receptacle in a plant or animal.
– ORIGIN late Middle English: from late Latin *cupula* (see **cupola**).

cur /kəː/ ▶ **noun** an aggressive or unkempt dog, especially a mongrel. ■ informal a contemptible man.
– ORIGIN Middle English (in the general sense 'dog'): probably originally in *cur-dog*, perhaps from Old Norse *kurr* 'grumbling'.

curable ▶ **adjective 1** (of a disease or condition) able to be cured: *most skin cancers are completely curable*.
2 (of plastic, varnish, etc.) able to be hardened by some additive or other agent.
– DERIVATIVES **curability** noun.
– ORIGIN late Middle English: from Old French, or from late Latin *curabilis*, from Latin *curare* (see **cure**).

Curaçao /ˌkjʊərəˈsəʊ, -ˈseɪəʊ/ the largest island of the Netherlands Antilles, situated in the Caribbean Sea 60 km (37 miles) north of the Venezuelan coast; pop. 141,766 (2009); chief town, Willemstad.

curaçao /ˌkjʊərəˈsəʊ/ ▶ **noun** (pl. **curaçaos**) [mass noun] a liqueur flavoured with the peel of bitter oranges.
– ORIGIN early 19th cent.: named after **Curaçao**, where the oranges are grown.

curacy ▶ **noun** (pl. **curacies**) the office of a curate, or the tenure of this: *he served his curacy in Northampton*.

curandero /ˌkjʊərənˈdɛːrəʊ/, Spanish /kuranˈðerao/ ▶ **noun** (pl. **curanderos** fem. **curandera** /-ˈdɛːrə/, Spanish /-ˈðera/) (in Spain and Latin America) a healer who uses folk remedies.
– ORIGIN Spanish, from *curar* 'to cure', from Latin *curare*.

curare /kjʊˈrɑːri/ ▶ **noun** [mass noun] a bitter resinous substance obtained from the bark and stems of some South American plants. It paralyses the motor nerves and is traditionally used by some Indian peoples to poison their arrows and blowpipe darts. ● Curare is obtained from *Curarea* species and *Chondodendron tomentosum* (family Menispermaceae), and *Strychnos toxifera* (family Loganiaceae).
– ORIGIN late 18th cent.: from a Carib word, partly via Spanish and Portuguese.

curassow /ˈkjʊərəsəʊ/ ▶ **noun** a large crested pheasant-like bird of the guan family, found in tropical American forests. The male is typically black in colour. ● Genus *Crax* (and *Nothocrax*), family Cracidae: several species.
– ORIGIN late 17th cent.: anglicized form of **Curaçao**.

curate[1] /ˈkjʊərət/ ▶ **noun** (also **assistant curate**) a member of the clergy engaged as assistant to a vicar, rector, or parish priest. ■ archaic a minister with pastoral responsibility.
– ORIGIN Middle English: from medieval Latin *curatus*, from Latin *cura* 'care'.

curate[2] /kjʊ(ə)ˈreɪt/ ▶ **verb** [with obj.] select, organize, and look after the items in (a collection or exhibition): *both exhibitions are curated by the Centre's director*. ■ select acts to perform at (a music festival): *in past years the festival has been curated by the likes of David Bowie*.
– DERIVATIVES **curation** noun.
– ORIGIN late 19th cent.: back-formation from **curator**.

curate-in-charge ▶ **noun** another term for **priest-in-charge**.

curate's egg ▶ **noun** Brit. a thing that is partly good and partly bad: *this book is a bit of a curate's egg*.
– ORIGIN early 20th cent.: from a cartoon in *Punch* (1895) depicting a meek curate who, given a stale egg at the bishop's table, assures his host that 'parts of it are excellent'.

curative ▶ **adjective** able to cure disease: *the curative properties of herbs*.
▶ **noun** a curative medicine or agent.
– DERIVATIVES **curatively** adverb.
– ORIGIN late Middle English (in the sense 'relating to cures'): from French *curatif*, *-ive*, from medieval Latin *curativus*, from Latin *curare* (see **cure**).

curator ▶ **noun** a keeper or custodian of a museum or other collection. ■ a person who selects acts to perform at a music festival.
– DERIVATIVES **curatorial** adjective, **curatorship** noun.
– ORIGIN late Middle English (denoting an ecclesiastical pastor, also (still a Scots legal term) the guardian of a minor): from Old French *curateur* or, in later use, directly from Latin *curator*, from *curare* (see **cure**). The current sense dates from the mid 17th cent.

C

curb ▶ **noun 1** a check or restraint on something: *plans to introduce tougher curbs on insider dealing*.
2 (also **curb bit**) a type of bit with a strap or chain attached which passes under a horse's lower jaw, used as a check.
3 N. Amer. variant spelling of **kerb**.
4 a swelling on the back of a horse's hock, caused by spraining a ligament.
▶ **verb** [with obj.] restrain or keep in check: *she promised she would curb her temper*. ■ restrain (a horse) by means of a curb.
– ORIGIN late 15th cent. (denoting a strap fastened to the bit): from Old French *courber* 'bend, bow', from Latin *curvare* (see **curve**).

curb chain ▶ **noun** a small chain which is attached to a curb bit and lies in the groove on a horse's chin.

curb cut ▶ **noun** North American term for **dropped kerb**.

curb roof ▶ **noun** a roof of which each face has two slopes, the lower one steeper than the upper. ■ Brit. a mansard roof.

curbside ▶ **adjective** US spelling of **kerbside**.

curbstone ▶ **noun** US spelling of **kerbstone**. ■ [as modifier] informal unqualified; amateur: *curbstone commentators*.

curculio /kəːˈkjuːlɪəʊ/ ▶ **noun** (pl. **curculios**) chiefly N. Amer. a beetle of the weevil family, especially one which is a pest of fruit trees. ● Several genera and species in the family Curculionidae, including the **plum curculio** (*Conotrachelus nenuphar*).
– ORIGIN modern Latin, used as the genus name for weevils in the 18th cent., now restricted to the nut weevils.

curcuma /ˈkəːkjʊmə/ ▶ **noun** a tropical Asian plant of a genus that includes turmeric, zedoary, and other species that yield spices, dyes, and medicinal products. ● Genus *Curcuma*, family Zingiberaceae.
– ORIGIN modern Latin, from Arabic *kurkum* 'saffron', from Sanskrit *kuṅkuma* (so named because the colour of the spices resembles that of saffron).

curd ▶ **noun 1** [mass noun] (also **curds**) a soft, white substance formed when milk coagulates, used as the basis for cheese. ■ a fatty substance found between the flakes of poached salmon.
2 the edible head of a cauliflower.
– DERIVATIVES **curdy** adjective.
– ORIGIN late Middle English: of unknown origin.

curd cheese ▶ **noun** [mass noun] chiefly Brit. a mild, soft, smooth cheese made from skimmed milk curd.

curdle ▶ **verb** separate or cause to separate into curds or lumps: [no obj.] *take care not to let the soup boil or it will curdle* | [with obj.] *rennet is used for making cheese by curdling milk*.
– PHRASES **make one's blood curdle** fill one with horror.
– DERIVATIVES **curdler** noun.
– ORIGIN late 16th cent.: frequentative of obsolete *curd* 'congeal'.

cure ▶ **verb** [with obj.] **1** relieve (a person or animal) of the symptoms of a disease or condition: *he was cured of the disease*. ■ eliminate (a disease or condition) with medical treatment: *this technology could be used to cure diabetes*. ■ solve (a problem): *a bid to trace and cure the gearbox problems*.
2 preserve (meat, fish, tobacco, or an animal skin) by salting, drying, or smoking: (as adj., in combination **-cured**) *home-cured ham*. ■ harden (rubber, plastic, concrete, etc.) after manufacture by a chemical process such as vulcanization. ■ [no obj.] undergo hardening by a chemical process.
▶ **noun 1** a substance or treatment that cures a disease or condition: *the search for a cure for the common cold*. ■ [mass noun] restoration to health: *he was beyond cure*. ■ a solution to a problem: *the cure is to improve the clutch operation*.
2 [mass noun] the process of curing rubber, plastic, or other material.

C

3 [mass noun] a Christian minister's pastoral charge or area of responsibility for spiritual ministry: *a benefice involving the cure of souls.* ▪ [count noun] a parish.
– DERIVATIVES **curer** noun.
– ORIGIN Middle English (as a noun): from Old French *curer* (verb), *cure* (noun), both from Latin *curare* 'take care of', from *cura* 'care'. The original noun senses were 'care, concern, responsibility', in particular spiritual care (hence sense 3 of the noun). In late Middle English the senses 'medical care' and 'successful medical treatment' arose, and hence 'remedy'.

curé /ˈkjʊəreɪ/, French /kyʀe/ ▶ **noun** a parish priest in a French-speaking country.
– ORIGIN French, from medieval Latin *curatus* (see CURATE[1]).

cure-all ▶ **noun** a medicine or other remedy that will supposedly cure any ailment. ▪ a solution to any problem.

curettage /kjʊəˈrɛtɪdʒ, ˌkjʊərɪˈtɑːʒ/ ▶ **noun** [mass noun] Surgery the use of a curette, especially on the lining of the uterus. See DILATATION AND CURETTAGE.
– ORIGIN late 19th cent.: from French, from CURETTE.

curette /kjʊəˈrɛt/ ▶ **noun** a small surgical instrument used to remove material by a scraping action, especially from the uterus.
▶ **verb** [with obj.] clean or scrape with a curette.
– ORIGIN mid 18th cent. (as a noun): from French, from *curer* 'cleanse', from Latin *curare* (see CURE).

curfew /ˈkəːfjuː/ ▶ **noun** a regulation requiring people to remain indoors between specified hours, typically at night: *a dusk-to-dawn curfew* | [mass noun] *the whole area was immediately placed* ***under curfew***. ▪ the hour designated as the beginning of a curfew.
– ORIGIN Middle English (denoting a regulation requiring people to extinguish fires at a fixed hour in the evening, or a bell rung at that hour): from Old French *cuevrefeu*, from *cuvrir* 'to cover' + *feu* 'fire'. The current sense dates from the late 19th cent.

Curia /ˈkjʊərɪə/ the papal court at the Vatican, by which the Roman Catholic Church is governed. It comprises various Congregations, Tribunals, and other commissions and departments.
– DERIVATIVES **Curial** adjective.
– ORIGIN mid 19th cent.: from Latin *curia*, denoting a division of an ancient Roman tribe, also (by extension) the senate of cities other than Rome; later the term came to denote a feudal or Roman Catholic court of justice, whence the current sense.

Curie /ˈkjʊəri/, Marie (1867–1934), Polish-born French physicist, and Pierre (1859–1906), French physicist, pioneers of radioactivity. Working together on the mineral pitchblende, they discovered the elements polonium and radium, for which they shared the 1903 Nobel Prize for Physics with A.-H. Becquerel. After her husband's accidental death Marie received another Nobel Prize (for chemistry) in 1911 for her isolation of radium. She died of leukaemia, caused by prolonged exposure to radioactive materials.

curie /ˈkjʊəri/ (abbrev.: **Ci**) ▶ **noun** (pl. **curies**) a unit of radioactivity, corresponding to 3.7×10^{10} disintegrations per second. ▪ the quantity of radioactive substance that emits one curie of activity.
– ORIGIN early 20th cent.: named after Pierre and Marie CURIE.

curio /ˈkjʊərɪəʊ/ ▶ **noun** (pl. **curios**) a rare, unusual, or intriguing object.
– ORIGIN mid 19th cent.: abbreviation of CURIOSITY.

curiosa /ˌkjʊərɪˈəʊsə/ ▶ **plural noun** curiosities, especially erotic or pornographic books or articles.
– ORIGIN late 19th cent.: from Latin, neuter plural of *curiosus* (see CURIOUS).

curiosity ▶ **noun** (pl. **curiosities**) **1** [mass noun] a strong desire to know or learn something: *filled with curiosity, she peered through the window* | ***curiosity got the better of me****, so I called him.*
2 an unusual or interesting object or fact: *he showed them some of the curiosities of the house.*
– PHRASES **curiosity killed the cat** proverb being inquisitive about other people's affairs may get you into trouble.
– ORIGIN late Middle English: from Old French *curiousete*, from Latin *curiositas*, from *curiosus* (see CURIOUS).

curious ▶ **adjective 1** eager to know or learn something: *I began to be curious about the whereabouts of the bride and groom* | *she was* ***curious to know*** *what had happened.* ▪ expressing curiosity: *a curious stare.*
2 strange; unusual: *a curious sensation overwhelmed her.* ▪ euphemistic (of books) erotic or pornographic.
– DERIVATIVES **curiously** adverb [sentence adverb] *curiously, I find snooker riveting*, **curiousness** noun.
– ORIGIN Middle English: from Old French *curios*, from Latin *curiosus* 'careful', from *cura* 'care'. Sense 2 dates from the early 18th cent.

Curitiba /ˌkʊərɪˈtiːbə/ a city in southern Brazil, capital of the state of Paraná; pop. 1,797,408 (2007).

curium /ˈkjʊərɪəm/ ▶ **noun** [mass noun] the chemical element of atomic number 96, a radioactive metal of the actinide series. Curium does not occur naturally and was first made by bombarding plutonium with helium ions. (Symbol: **Cm**)
– ORIGIN 1940s: modern Latin, from the name of Marie and Pierre CURIE.

curl ▶ **verb 1** form or cause to form into a curved or spiral shape: [no obj.] *her fingers curled round the microphone* | *a slice of ham had begun to* ***curl up*** *at the edges* | [with obj.] *she used to curl her hair with rags.* ▪ [no obj.] (**curl up**) sit or lie with the knees drawn up: *she curled up and went to sleep.* ▪ move or cause to move in a spiral or curved course: [no obj., with adverbial of direction] *a wisp of smoke curling across the sky.* ▪ (with reference to one's mouth or upper lip) raise or cause to raise slightly on one side as an expression of contempt or disapproval: [no obj.] *Maria saw his lip curl sardonically.*
2 (in weight training) lift (a weight) using only the hands, wrists, and forearms.
3 [no obj.] play at the game of curling.
▶ **noun 1** something in the shape of a spiral or coil, especially a lock of hair: *her blonde hair was a mass of tangled curls* | *a curl of blue smoke.* ▪ a curling movement: *the sneering curl of his lip.* ▪ (with reference to a person's hair) a state or condition of being curled: *your hair has a natural curl* | [mass noun] *large perm rods give volume and control rather than lots of curl.* ▪ see LEAF CURL.
2 a weightlifting exercise involving movement of only the hands, wrists, and forearms: *a dumb-bell curl.*
3 Mathematics a function giving a measure of the rotation of a vector field.
– PHRASES **make someone's hair curl** informal shock or horrify someone.
– ORIGIN late Middle English: from obsolete *crulle* 'curly', from Middle Dutch *krul.*

curler ▶ **noun 1** (usu. **curlers**) a roller or clasp around which a lock of hair is wrapped to curl it.
2 a player in the game of curling.

curlew /ˈkəːl(j)uː/ ▶ **noun** (pl. **same** or **curlews**) a large wading bird of the sandpiper family, with a long downcurved bill, brown streaked plumage, and frequently a distinctive ascending two-note call. See also STONE CURLEW. ● Genus *Numenius*, family Scolopacidae: several species, in particular *N. arquata* of Eurasia.
– ORIGIN Middle English: from Old French *courlieu*, alteration (by association with *courliu* 'courier', from *courre* 'run' + *lieu* 'place') of imitative *courlis.*

curlicue /ˈkəːlɪkjuː/ ▶ **noun** a decorative curl or twist in calligraphy or in the design of an object.
– ORIGIN mid 19th cent.: from CURLY + CUE[2] (in the sense 'pigtail'), or *-cue* representing the letter *q.*

curling ▶ **noun** [mass noun] a game played on ice, especially in Scotland and Canada, in which large round flat stones are slid across the surface towards a mark. Members of a team use brooms to sweep the surface of the ice in the path of the stone to control its speed and direction.

curling stone ▶ **noun** a large polished circular stone, with a handle on top, used in the game of curling.

curling tongs (also **curling iron** or **curling pins**) ▶ **plural noun** a device incorporating a heated rod used for rolling a person's hair into curls.

curly ▶ **adjective** (**curlier**, **curliest**) made, growing, or arranged in curls or curves: *my hair is just naturally thick and curly.*
– DERIVATIVES **curliness** noun.

curly bracket ▶ **noun** another term for BRACE (sense 4 of the noun).

curly endive ▶ **noun** see ENDIVE.

curly kale ▶ **noun** [mass noun] kale of a variety with dark green tightly curled leaves.

curly-wurly ▶ **adjective** informal twisting and curling.
– ORIGIN late 18th cent.: reduplication of CURLY.

curmudgeon /kəːˈmʌdʒ(ə)n/ ▶ **noun** a bad-tempered or surly person.
– DERIVATIVES **curmudgeonliness** noun, **curmudgeonly** adjective.
– ORIGIN late 16th cent.: of unknown origin.

currach /ˈkʌrə(x)/ (also **curragh**) ▶ **noun** Irish and Scottish term for CORACLE.
– ORIGIN late Middle English: from Irish and Scottish Gaelic *curach* 'small boat'. Compare with CORACLE.

curragh[1] ▶ **noun** variant spelling of CURRACH.

curragh[2] /ˈkʌrə(x)/ ▶ **noun** (in Ireland and the Isle of Man) a stretch of marshy waste ground. ▪ (**the Curragh**) a level stretch of open ground in County Kildare, Ireland, famous for its racecourse and military camp.
– ORIGIN mid 17th cent.: from Irish *currach* 'marsh', Manx *curragh* 'bog, fen'.

currajong ▶ **noun** variant spelling of KURRAJONG.

currant ▶ **noun 1** a small dried fruit made from a small seedless variety of grape originally grown in the eastern Mediterranean region and much used in cookery.
2 a Eurasian shrub which produces small edible black, red, or white berries. ● Genus *Ribes*, family Grossulariaceae: several species, including **blackcurrant** and **redcurrant**.
▪ a berry from a currant shrub.
– ORIGIN Middle English *raisons of Corauntz*, translating Anglo-Norman French *raisins de Corauntz* 'grapes of Corinth' (the original source).

currant gall ▶ **noun** a spherical red or purple gall which forms on the leaves or male catkins of oak trees in response to the developing larva of a gall wasp. It results from eggs laid in the spring and alternates within the annual cycle with the spangle gall.
● The wasp is *Neuroterus quercusbaccarum*, family Cynipidae.

currawong /ˈkʌrəwɒŋ/ ▶ **noun** a crow-like songbird of the Australian butcher-bird family, with mainly black or grey plumage, a robust straight bill, and a resonant call. Also called BELL MAGPIE. ● Genus *Strepera*, family Cracticidae: three species.
– ORIGIN 1920s: from an Aboriginal word.

currency ▶ **noun** (pl. **currencies**) **1** a system of money in general use in a particular country: *the dollar was a strong currency* | [mass noun] *travellers cheques in foreign currency.*
2 [mass noun] the fact or quality of being generally accepted or in use: *the term gained wider currency after the turn of the century.* ▪ the time during which something is in use or operation: *no claim had been made during the currency of the policy.*

current ▶ **adjective** belonging to the present time; happening or being used or done now: *keep abreast of current events* | *I started my current job in 2001.* ▪ in common or general use: *the other meaning of the word is still current.*
▶ **noun 1** a body of water or air moving in a definite direction, especially through a surrounding body of water or air in which there is less movement: *ocean currents.*
2 a flow of electricity which results from the ordered directional movement of electrically charged particles. ▪ a quantity representing the rate of flow of electric charge, usually measured in amperes.
3 the general tendency or course of events or opinion: *the student movement formed a distinct current of protest.*
– ORIGIN Middle English (in the adjective sense 'running, flowing'): from Old French *corant* 'running', from *courre* 'run', from Latin *currere* 'run'.

current account ▶ **noun** Brit. an account with a bank or building society from which money may be withdrawn without notice, typically an active account catering for frequent deposits and withdrawals by cheque.

current affairs ▶ **plural noun** events of political or social interest and importance happening in the world at the present time.

current assets ▶ **plural noun** cash and other assets that are expected to be converted to cash within a year. Compare with FIXED ASSETS.

current cost accounting ▶ **noun** [mass noun] a method of accounting in which assets are valued on the basis of their current replacement cost, and increases in their value as a result of inflation are excluded from calculations of profit.

current density ▶ **noun** Physics the amount of electric current flowing per unit cross-sectional area of a material.

current liabilities ▶ **plural noun** amounts due to be paid to creditors within twelve months.

currently ▶ **adverb** at the present time: *the EC is currently attempting greater economic integration.*

curricle /ˈkʌrɪk(ə)l/ ▶ **noun** historical a light, open, two-wheeled carriage pulled by two horses side by side.

– ORIGIN mid 18th cent.: from Latin *curriculum* 'course, racing chariot', from *currere* 'to run'.

curriculum /kəˈrɪkjʊləm/ ▶ **noun** (pl. **curricula** or **curriculums**) the subjects comprising a course of study in a school or college.
– DERIVATIVES **curricular** adjective.
– ORIGIN early 19th cent.: from Latin (see CURRICLE).

curriculum vitae /ˈviːtʌɪ, ˈvʌɪtiː/ (abbrev.: **CV**) ▶ **noun** (pl. **curricula vitae**) a brief account of a person's education, qualifications, and previous occupations, typically sent with a job application.
– ORIGIN early 20th cent.: Latin, 'course of life'.

currier /ˈkʌrɪə/ ▶ **noun** a person who curries leather.
– ORIGIN late Middle English: from Old French *corier*, from Latin *coriarius*, from *corium* 'leather'.

currish /ˈkəːrɪʃ/ ▶ **adjective** archaic like a cur; bad-tempered.
– DERIVATIVES **currishly** adverb,.

curry[1] ▶ **noun** (pl. **curries**) a dish of meat, vegetables, etc., cooked in an Indian-style sauce of strong spices.
▶ **verb** (**curries, currying, curried**) [with obj.] (usu. as adj. **curried**) prepare or flavour with a sauce of hot-tasting spices: *curried chicken*.
– ORIGIN late 16th cent.: from Tamil *kaṟi*.

curry[2] ▶ **verb** (**curries, currying, curried**) [with obj.]
1 chiefly N. Amer. groom (a horse) with a curry comb.
2 historical treat (tanned leather) to improve its properties.
3 archaic thrash; beat.
– PHRASES **curry favour** ingratiate oneself with someone through obsequious behaviour: *a wimpish attempt to* ***curry favour with*** *the new bosses*. [alteration of Middle English *curry favel*, from the name (*Favel* or *Fauvel*) of a chestnut horse in a 14th-cent. French romance who became a symbol of cunning and duplicity; hence 'to curry (or groom) Favel' meant to use the cunning which he personified.]
– ORIGIN Middle English: from Old French *correier*, ultimately of Germanic origin.

curry comb ▶ **noun** a metal device with serrated ridges, used for removing dirt from a body brush with which a horse is being groomed. ■ a similar device of flexible rubber, used for grooming horses.

curry leaf ▶ **noun** a shrub or small tree native to India and Sri Lanka, the leaves of which are widely used in Indian cooking. ● *Murraya koenigii*, family Rutaceae.

curry plant ▶ **noun** a small shrubby plant of the daisy family, which has narrow silver-grey leaves and small yellow flowers and emits a strong smell of curry.
● *Helichrysum angustifolium*, family Compositae.

curry powder ▶ **noun** [mass noun] a mixture of finely ground spices, such as turmeric, ginger, and coriander, used for making curry.

curse ▶ **noun 1** a solemn utterance intended to invoke a supernatural power to inflict harm or punishment on someone or something: *she'd* ***put a curse on*** *him*. ■ [usu. in sing.] a cause of harm or misery: *impatience is the curse of our day and age*.
2 an offensive word or phrase used to express anger or annoyance: *at every blow there was a curse*.
3 (**the curse**) informal menstruation.
▶ **verb 1** [with obj.] invoke or use a curse against: *it often seemed as if the family had been cursed*. ■ (**be cursed with**) be afflicted with: *many owners have been cursed with a series of bankruptcies*.
2 [no obj.] utter offensive words in anger or annoyance: *he cursed loudly as he burned his hand*. ■ [with obj.] address with offensive words: *I cursed myself for my carelessness*.
– DERIVATIVES **curser** noun.
– ORIGIN Old English, of unknown origin.

cursed /ˈkəːsɪd, kəːst/ ▶ **adjective** [attrib.] informal, dated used to express annoyance or irritation: *his cursed tidy-mindedness*.
– DERIVATIVES **cursedly** adverb, **cursedness** noun.

cursillo /kəːˈsiːjəʊ, -ˈsiːljəʊ/ ▶ **noun** (pl. **cursillos**) a short informal spiritual retreat by a group of Roman Catholics, especially in Spain or Latin America.
– ORIGIN 1950s: Spanish, 'little course'.

cursive /ˈkəːsɪv/ ▶ **adjective** written with the characters joined: *cursive script*.
▶ **noun** [mass noun] cursive writing.
– DERIVATIVES **cursively** adverb.
– ORIGIN late 18th cent.: from medieval Latin *cursivus*, from Latin *curs-* 'run', from the verb *currere*.

cursor ▶ **noun 1** a movable indicator on a computer screen identifying the point that will be affected by input from the user.
2 chiefly historical the transparent slide engraved with a hairline that is part of a slide rule and is used for marking a point on the rule while bringing a point on the central sliding portion up to it.
– ORIGIN Middle English (denoting a runner or running messenger): from Latin, 'runner', from *curs-* (see CURSIVE). Sense 2 dates from the late 16th cent.

cursorial /kəːˈsɔːrɪəl/ ▶ **adjective** Zoology having limbs adapted for running.
– ORIGIN mid 19th cent.: from Latin *cursor* (see CURSOR) + -IAL.

cursory /ˈkəːs(ə)ri/ ▶ **adjective** hasty and therefore not thorough or detailed: *a cursory glance at the figures*.
– DERIVATIVES **cursorily** adverb, **cursoriness** noun.
– ORIGIN early 17th cent.: from Latin *cursorius* 'of a runner', from *cursor* (see CURSOR).

curst ▶ **adjective** archaic spelling of CURSED.

curt ▶ **adjective** rudely brief: *his reply was curt*.
– DERIVATIVES **curtly** adverb, **curtness** noun.
– ORIGIN late Middle English (in the sense 'short, shortened'): from Latin *curtus* 'cut short, abridged'.

curtail /kəːˈteɪl/ ▶ **verb** [with obj.] reduce in extent or quantity; impose a restriction on: *civil liberties were further curtailed*. ■ (**curtail someone of**) archaic deprive someone of (something): *I that am curtailed of this fair proportion*.
– ORIGIN late 15th cent.: from obsolete *curtal* 'horse with a docked tail', from French *courtault*, from *court* 'short', from Latin *curtus*. The change in the ending was due to association with TAIL[1] and perhaps also with French *tailler* 'to cut'.

curtailment /kəˈteɪlm(ə)nt/ ▶ **noun** [mass noun] the action or fact of reducing or restricting something: *the curtailment of human rights*.

curtain ▶ **noun 1** a piece of material suspended at the top to form a screen, typically movable sideways along a rail and found as one of a pair at a window: *she drew the curtains and lit the fire* | figurative *through the curtain of falling snow, she could just make out gravestones*.
2 (**the curtain**) a screen of heavy cloth or other material that can be raised or lowered at the front of a stage. ■ a raising or lowering of the curtain at the beginning or end of an act or scene: *the art is to hold your audience right from the opening curtain*.
3 (**curtains**) informal a disastrous outcome: *it looked like* ***curtains for*** *me*.
▶ **verb** [with obj.] (often as adj. **curtained**) provide with a curtain or curtains: *a curtained window*. ■ conceal or screen with a curtain: *a curtained-off side room*.
– PHRASES **bring down the curtain on** bring to an end: *her decision brought down the curtain on a glittering 30-year career*.
– ORIGIN Middle English: from Old French *cortine*, from late Latin *cortina*, translation of Greek *aulaia*, from *aulē* 'court'.

curtain call ▶ **noun** the appearance of one or more performers on stage after a performance to acknowledge the audience's applause.

curtain fire (also chiefly US **curtain of fire**) ▶ **noun** [mass noun] Brit. rapid, continuous artillery or machine-gun fire on a designated line or area.

curtain lecture ▶ **noun** dated an instance of a wife reprimanding her husband in private.
– ORIGIN mid 17th cent.: originally a reprimand given behind bed curtains.

curtain-raiser ▶ **noun** an entertainment or other event happening just before a longer or more important one: *Bach's Sinfonia in B flat was an ideal* ***curtain-raiser to*** *Mozart's last piano concerto*.
– ORIGIN late 19th cent.: originally used in the theatre to denote a short opening piece performed before a play.

curtain ring ▶ **noun** a ring, typically one of brass or wood, used to fasten a curtain to a rail or rod.

curtain-sider ▶ **noun** a lorry or trailer having fabric sides.

curtain speech ▶ **noun** a speech of thanks or appreciation to an audience, made after a performance by an actor playing a leading role, typically from the front of the stage with the curtains closed.

curtain-up ▶ **noun** [in sing.] the beginning of a stage performance: *curtain-up is at 8 p.m.*

curtain wall ▶ **noun** a fortified wall around a medieval castle, typically one linking towers together. ■ a wall which encloses the space within a building but does not support the roof.

curtal /ˈkəːt(ə)l/ ▶ **adjective** archaic shortened, abridged, or curtailed.
▶ **noun** historical a dulcian or bassoon of the late 16th to early 18th century.
– ORIGIN late 15th cent. (denoting a short-barrelled cannon): from French *courtault*, from *court* 'short' + the pejorative suffix *-ault*. In both English and French the noun denoted various items characterized by something short, especially an animal with a docked tail, which probably gave rise to the adjective sense.

curtana /kəːˈtɑːnə, -ˈteɪnə/ ▶ **noun** Brit. the unpointed sword carried in front of English sovereigns at their coronation to represent mercy.
– ORIGIN Middle English: from Anglo-Latin *curtana* (*spatha*) 'shortened (sword)', from Old French *cortain*, the name of the sword belonging to ROLAND (the point of which was damaged when it was thrust into a block of steel), from *cort* 'short', from Latin *curtus* 'cut short'.

curtilage /ˈkəːt(ɪ)lɪdʒ/ ▶ **noun** an area of land attached to a house and forming one enclosure with it: *the roads* ***within the curtilage of*** *the development site*.
– ORIGIN Middle English: from Anglo-Norman French, variant of Old French *courtillage*, from *courtil* 'small court', from *cort* 'court'.

Curtin /ˈkəːtɪn/, John (Joseph Ambrose) (1885–1945), Australian Labor statesman, Prime Minister 1941–5.

Curtiss /ˈkəːtɪs/, Glenn (Hammond) (1878–1930), American air pioneer and aircraft designer. In 1908 Curtiss made the first public American flight of 1.0 km (0.6 miles). He built his first aeroplane in 1909, and invented the aileron and demonstrated the first practical seaplane two years later.

curtsy (also **curtsey**) ▶ **noun** (pl. **curtsies** or **curtseys**) a woman's or girl's formal greeting made by bending the knees with one foot in front of the other: *she* ***bobbed a curtsy*** *to him*.
▶ **verb** (**curtsies, curtsying, curtsied** or **curtseys, curtseying, curtseyed**) [no obj.] perform a curtsy: *his sisters had* ***curtsied to*** *the vicar*.
– ORIGIN early 16th cent.: variant of COURTESY. Both forms were used to denote the expression of respect or courtesy by a gesture, especially in phrases such as *do courtesy, make courtesy*, and from this arose the current use (late 16th cent.).

curule /ˈkjʊəruːl/ ▶ **adjective** historical denoting or relating to the authority exercised by the senior magistrates in ancient Rome, chiefly the consul and praetor, who were entitled to use the *sella curulis* ('curule seat', a kind of folding chair).
– ORIGIN early 17th cent.: from Latin *curulis*, from *currus* 'chariot' (in which the chief magistrate was conveyed to the seat of office), from *currere* 'to run'.

curvaceous /kəːˈveɪʃəs/ ▶ **adjective** (especially of a woman or a woman's figure) having an attractively curved shape.
– DERIVATIVES **curvaceously** adverb, **curvaceousness** noun.

curvature /ˈkəːvətʃə/ ▶ **noun** [mass noun] the fact of being curved or the degree to which something is curved: *spinal curvature* | *the curvature of the earth*. ■ Geometry the degree to which a curve deviates from a straight line, or a curved surface deviates from a plane. ■ a numerical quantity expressing curvature.
– ORIGIN late Middle English: via Old French from Latin *curvatura*, from *curvare* (see CURVE).

curve ▶ **noun** a line or outline which gradually deviates from being straight for some or all of its length: *the parapet wall sweeps down in a bold curve*. ■ N. Amer. a place where a road deviates from a straight path: *the vehicle rounded a curve*. ■ (**curves**) a curving contour of a woman's figure. ■ a line on a graph (whether straight or curved) showing how one quantity varies with respect to another: *the population curve*. ■ (also **curve ball**) Baseball a delivery in which the pitcher causes the ball to deviate from a straight path by imparting spin.
▶ **verb** form or cause to form a curve: [no obj.] *her mouth curved in a smile* | [with obj.] *starting with arms outstretched, curve the body sideways*.
– PHRASES **ahead of** (or **behind**) **the curve** (especially of a business or politician) ahead of (or lagging behind) current thinking or trends: *we are continually looking for ways to stay ahead of the curve and provide added value to our consumers*.
– ORIGIN late Middle English: from Latin *curvare* 'to bend', from *curvus* 'bent'. The noun dates from the late 17th cent.

curved ▶ **adjective** having the form of a curve; bent: *birds with long curved bills*.

curvet /kəːˈvɛt/ ▶ **verb** (**curvets, curvetting, curvetted** or **curvets, curveting, curveted**) [no obj.] (of a horse) perform a courbette. ■ leap gracefully or energetically.

C

C

▸ noun a graceful or energetic leap.
– ORIGIN late 16th cent.: from Italian *corvetta*, diminutive of *corva*, earlier form of *curva* 'a curve', from Latin *curvus* 'bent'.

curvilinear /ˌkəːvɪˈlɪnɪə/ ▸ adjective contained by or consisting of a curved line or lines: *these designs employ flowing, curvilinear forms.*
– DERIVATIVES **curvilinearly** adverb.
– ORIGIN early 18th cent.: from Latin *curvus* 'bent, curved', on the pattern of *rectilinear*.

curvy ▸ adjective (**curvier**, **curviest**) having curves: *curvy lines.* ■ informal (of a woman's figure) shapely and voluptuous.
– DERIVATIVES **curviness** noun.

cuscus /ˈkʌskʌs/ ▸ noun a tree-dwelling marsupial with a rounded head and prehensile tail, native to New Guinea and northern Australia. ● Four genera in the family Phalangeridae: several species, including the **spotted cuscus** (*Spilocuscus maculatus*) and the **grey cuscus** (*Phalanger orientalis*). See also PHALANGER.
– ORIGIN mid 17th cent.: via French and Dutch from a local name in the Molucca Islands.

cusec /ˈkjuːsɛk/ ▸ noun a unit of flow (especially of water) equal to one cubic foot per second.
– ORIGIN early 20th cent.: abbreviation of *cubic foot per second*.

Cush /kʊʃ/ **1** (in the Bible) the eldest son of Ham and grandson of Noah (Gen. 10:6).
2 the southern part of ancient Nubia, first mentioned in Egyptian records of the Middle Kingdom. In the Bible it is the country of the descendants of Cush.

cush /kʊʃ/ ▸ noun informal a cushion on a billiard table.
– ORIGIN late 19th cent.: abbreviation.

cushat /ˈkʌʃət/ ▸ noun dialect, chiefly Scottish a wood pigeon.
– ORIGIN Old English, of unknown origin.

cushaw /kʊˈʃɔː, ˈkuːʃɔː/ (also **cushaw squash**) ▸ noun US a large winter squash of a variety with a curved neck.
– ORIGIN late 16th cent.: of unknown origin.

Cushing's disease ▸ noun [mass noun] Cushing's syndrome as caused by a tumour of the pituitary gland.

Cushing's syndrome ▸ noun [mass noun] Medicine a metabolic disorder caused by overproduction of corticosteroid hormones by the adrenal cortex and often involving obesity and high blood pressure.
– ORIGIN 1930s: named after Harvey W. *Cushing* (1869–1939), American surgeon.

cushion ▸ noun **1** a bag of cloth stuffed with a mass of soft material, used as a comfortable support for sitting or leaning on.
2 something providing support or protection against impact: *underlay forms a cushion between carpet and floor.* ■ the elastic lining of the sides of a billiard table, from which the ball rebounds. ■ the layer of air supporting a hovercraft or similar vehicle.
▸ verb [with obj.] **1** soften the effect of an impact on: *the bag cushions equipment from inevitable knocks.*
2 mitigate the adverse effects of: *to **cushion the blow**, wages and pensions were increased.*
– DERIVATIVES **cushioned** adjective, **cushiony** adjective.
– ORIGIN Middle English: from Old French *cuissin*, based on a Latin word meaning 'cushion for the hip', from *coxa* 'hip, thigh'. The Romans also had a word *cubital* 'elbow cushion', from *cubitus* 'elbow'.

cushion capital ▸ noun Architecture a capital resembling a cushion pressed down by a weight, seen particularly in Romanesque churches.

cushion star ▸ noun a small shallow-water starfish with a broad body and very short blunt arms. Also called STARLET. ● *Asterina* and related genera, class Asteroidea, in particular *A. gibbosa* of the NE Atlantic.

Cushitic /kʊˈʃɪtɪk/ ▸ noun [mass noun] a group of East African languages of the Afro-Asiatic family spoken mainly in Ethiopia and Somalia, including Somali and Oromo.
▸ adjective relating to this group of languages.
– ORIGIN early 20th cent.: from CUSH + -ITIC.

cushty /ˈkʊʃti/ ▸ adjective Brit. informal very good or pleasing: *he's got a cushty set-up.*
– ORIGIN 1920s: from Romany *kushto*, *kushti* 'good', perhaps influenced by CUSHY.

cushy ▸ adjective (**cushier**, **cushiest**) informal **1** (of a job or situation) undemanding, easy, or secure: *he doesn't have anything like the cushy life you professors have | the Caribbean posting is not a cushy number.*
2 N. Amer. (of furniture) comfortable.
– DERIVATIVES **cushiness** noun.
– ORIGIN First World War (originally Anglo-Indian): from Urdu *ḵushī* 'pleasure', from Persian *ḵuš*.

cusk /kʌsk/ ▸ noun another term for TORSK.
– ORIGIN early 17th cent.: of unknown origin.

cusk-eel ▸ noun a small eel-like fish with a tapering body and fins that form a pointed tail, typically found in deep water. ● Family Ophidiidae: numerous genera.

cusp /kʌsp/ ▸ noun **1** a pointed end where two curves meet, in particular: ■ Architecture a moulded projection at the point of a small arch in Gothic tracery. ■ a cone-shaped prominence on the surface of a tooth. ■ Anatomy a pocket or fold in the wall of the heart or a major blood vessel that fills and distends if the blood flows backwards, so forming part of a valve. ■ Mathematics a point at which the direction of a curve is abruptly reversed. ■ each of the pointed ends of the crescent moon. ■ Botany a sharp rigid point of a leaf.
2 Astrology the initial point of an astrological sign or house: *he was Aries **on the cusp** with Taurus.*
3 a point of transition between two different states: *those **on the cusp of** adulthood.*
– DERIVATIVES **cuspate** adjective, **cusped** adjective, **cuspidate** adjective, **cuspidal** adjective.
– ORIGIN late 16th cent. (in sense 2): from Latin *cuspis* 'point or apex'.

cuspid ▸ noun a tooth with a single cusp or point; a canine tooth.
– ORIGIN mid 18th cent.: from Latin *cuspis*, *cuspid-* 'point or apex'.

cuspidor /ˈkʌspɪdɔː/ ▸ noun US a spittoon.
– ORIGIN mid 18th cent.: from Portuguese, 'spitter', from *cuspir* 'to spit', from Latin *conspuere*.

cusping ▸ noun [mass noun] Architecture a formation consisting of cusps.

cuss informal ▸ noun **1** an annoying or stubborn person or animal: *he was certainly an unsociable cuss.*
2 another term for CURSE (sense 2 of the noun).
▸ verb another term for CURSE (sense 2 of the verb).

cussed /ˈkʌsɪd/ ▸ adjective informal awkward; annoying: *why do you have to be so cussed?*
– DERIVATIVES **cussedly** adverb, **cussedness** noun.
– ORIGIN mid 19th cent. (originally US): variant of CURSED.

cuss word ▸ noun informal a swear word.

custard ▸ noun [mass noun] a dessert or sweet sauce made with milk and eggs, or milk and a proprietary powder.
– ORIGIN late Middle English *crustarde*, *custarde* (denoting an open pie containing meat or fruit in a spiced or sweetened sauce thickened with eggs), from Old French *crouste* (see CRUST).

custard apple ▸ noun **1** a large fleshy tropical fruit with a sweet yellow pulp. See also CHERIMOYA, BULLOCK'S HEART, SWEETSOP.
2 the tree which bears the custard apple, native to Central and South America. ● Genus *Annona*, family Annonaceae: several species.

custard cream ▸ noun Brit. a biscuit with a vanilla-flavoured cream filling.

custard marrow ▸ noun Brit. a summer squash of a variety which has flattened round fruits with scalloped edges.

custard pie ▸ noun an open pie containing cold set custard. ■ a custard pie, or a flat container of foam, used for throwing in someone's face in slapstick comedy.

custard powder ▸ noun [mass noun] a preparation of flavoured cornflour for making custard.

Custer /ˈkʌstə/, George (Armstrong) (1839–76), American cavalry general. He served with distinction in the American Civil War but led his men to their deaths in a clash (popularly known as Custer's Last Stand) with the Sioux at Little Bighorn in Montana.

custodian /kʌˈstəʊdɪən/ ▸ noun a person who has responsibility for taking care of or protecting something: *the custodians of pension and insurance funds.* ■ US a person employed to clean and maintain a building. ■ Brit. humorous a goalkeeper or wicketkeeper.
– DERIVATIVES **custodianship** noun.
– ORIGIN late 18th cent.: from CUSTODY, on the pattern of *guardian*.

custody /ˈkʌstədi/ ▸ noun [mass noun] **1** the protective care or guardianship of someone or something: *the property was placed in the custody of a trustee.* ■ Law parental responsibility, especially as allocated to one of two divorcing parents: *he was trying to get custody of their child.*
2 imprisonment: *my father was being **taken into custody**.*
– DERIVATIVES **custodial** /kʌˈstəʊdɪəl/ adjective.
– ORIGIN late Middle English: from Latin *custodia*, from *custos* 'guardian'.

custom ▸ noun **1** a traditional and widely accepted way of behaving or doing something that is specific to a particular society, place, or time: *the old English custom of dancing round the maypole* | [mass noun] *custom demanded that a person should have gifts for the child.* ■ [in sing.] a thing that one does habitually: *it is our custom to visit the Lake District in October.* ■ Law established usage having the force of law or right.
2 [mass noun] Brit. regular dealings with a shop or business by customers: *if you keep me waiting, I will take my custom elsewhere.*
▸ adjective [attrib.] N. Amer. made or done to order; custom-made: *a custom guitar.*
– ORIGIN Middle English: from Old French *coustume*, based on Latin *consuetudo*, from *consuetus*, past participle of *consuescere* 'accustom', from *con-* (expressing intensive force) + *suescere* 'become accustomed'.

customal /ˈkʌstəm(ə)l/ ▸ noun variant spelling of CUSTUMAL.

customarily ▸ adverb in a way which follows customs or usual practices; usually: *the leaves are customarily used for animal fodder.*

customary ▸ adjective according to the customs or usual practices associated with a particular society, place, or set of circumstances: *it is customary to mark an occasion like this with a toast.* ■ [attrib.] according to a person's habitual practice: *I put the kettle on for our customary cup of coffee.* ■ Law established by or based on custom rather than common law or statute. ■ (in South Africa) relating to black African traditional custom or law.
▸ noun (pl. **customaries**) historical another term for CUSTUMAL.
– ORIGIN late Middle English (as a noun): from medieval Latin *custumarius*, from *custuma*, from Anglo-Norman French *custume* (see CUSTOM).

custom-built ▸ adjective built or made to a particular customer's order.

customer ▸ noun **1** a person who buys goods or services from a shop or business: *Mr Harrison was a regular customer at the Golden Lion.*
2 [with adj.] a person of a specified kind with whom one has to deal: *he's a tough customer.*

customer-facing ▸ adjective dealing directly with customers: *a customer-facing role.*

custom house (also **customs house**) ▸ noun chiefly historical the office at a port or frontier where customs duty is collected.

customize (also **customise**) ▸ verb [with obj.] modify (something) to suit a particular individual or task: *the software can be customized to the developing needs of your students* | (as adj. **customized**) *many caterers offer private tastings and customized menus.*
– DERIVATIVES **customizable** adjective, **customization** noun.

custom-made ▸ adjective made or done to order for a particular customer.

customs ▸ plural noun the official department that administers and collects the duties levied by a government on imported goods: *cocaine seizures by customs have risen this year* | [as modifier] *a customs officer.* ■ the place at a port, airport, or frontier where officials check incoming goods, travellers, or luggage: *we were through customs with a minimum of formalities.* ■ (usu. **customs duties**) the duties levied by a government on imported goods.
– ORIGIN late Middle English: originally in the singular, denoting a customary due paid to a ruler, later duty levied on goods on their way to market.

customs union ▸ noun a group of states that have agreed to charge the same import duties as each other and usually to allow free trade between themselves.

custos rotulorum /ˌkʌstɒs ˌrəʊtjʊˈlɔːrəm/ ▸ noun (pl. **custodes rotulorum** /kʌˈstəʊdiːz/) (in England and Wales) the principal Justice of the Peace of a county, who has nominal custody of the records of the commission of the peace. The function is usually fulfilled by the Lord Lieutenant.
– ORIGIN Latin.

custumal /ˈkʌstjʊm(ə)l/ (also **customal**) ▸ noun historical a written account of the customs of a manor or other local community or large establishment.

– ORIGIN late 16th cent.: from medieval Latin *custumale* 'customs book', neuter of *custumalis*, from *custuma* 'custom'.

cut ▶ verb (**cutting**; past and past participle **cut**) [with obj.] **1** make an opening, incision, or wound in (something) with a sharp-edged tool or object: *he cut his big toe on a sharp stone* | *when fruit is* ***cut open****, it goes brown.*
2 remove (something) from something larger by using a sharp implement: *I cut his photograph* ***out of*** *the paper* | *some prisoners had their right hands* ***cut off****.* ■ castrate (an animal, especially a horse). ■ (**cut something out**) make something by cutting: *I cut out some squares of paper.* ■ (**cut something out**) remove, exclude, or stop eating or doing something undesirable: *start today by cutting out fatty foods.* ■ (**cut something out**) N. Amer. separate an animal from the main herd.
3 divide into pieces with a knife or other sharp implement: ***cut*** *the beef* ***into*** *thin slices* | *he* ***cut*** *his food* ***up*** *into teeny pieces.* ■ make divisions in (something): *land that has been* ***cut up*** *by streams into forested areas.* ■ separate (something) into two; sever: *they cut the rope before he choked.* ■ (**cut something down**) cause something to fall by cutting it through at the base. ■ (**cut someone down**) (of a weapon, bullet, or disease) kill or injure someone: *Barker had been cut down by a sniper's bullet.*
4 make or form (something) by using a sharp tool to remove material: *workmen* ***cut a hole in*** *the pipe.* ■ make or design (a garment) in a particular way: (as adj., with submodifier **cut**) *an impeccably cut suit.* ■ make (a path, tunnel, or other route) by excavation, digging, or chopping: *plans to cut a road through a rainforest* | [no obj.] *investigators called for a machete to* ***cut through*** *the bush.* ■ make (a sound recording).
5 trim or reduce the length of (grass, hair, etc.) by using a sharp implement: *Ted was cutting the lawn* | ***cut back*** *all the year's growth to about four leaves.*
6 reduce the amount or quantity of: *buyers will bargain hard to* ***cut the cost of*** *the house they want* | *I should* ***cut down*** *my sugar intake* | [no obj.] *they've* ***cut back on*** *costs.* ■ abridge (a text, film, or performance) by removing material: *he had to cut unnecessary additions made to the opening scene.* ■ Computing delete (part of a text or other display) so as to insert a copy of it elsewhere. See also **CUT AND PASTE** below. ■ end or interrupt the provision of (a supply): *we resolved to cut oil supplies to territories controlled by the rebels* | *if the pump develops a fault, the electrical supply is immediately* ***cut off****.* ■ switch off (an engine or a light). ■ N. Amer. absent oneself from (something one should normally attend, especially school): *Rodney was cutting class.*
7 (**cut something off**) block the usual means of access to a place: *the caves were* ***cut off from*** *the outside world by a landslide.*
8 informal ignore or refuse to recognize (someone): *they cut her in public.*
9 (of a line) cross or intersect (another line). ■ [no obj.] (**cut across**) pass or traverse, especially so as to shorten one's route: *the following aircraft cut across to join him.* ■ [no obj.] (**cut across**) have an effect regardless of (divisions or boundaries between groups): *subcultures which cut across national and political boundaries.* ■ [no obj.] (**cut along**) informal, dated leave or move hurriedly.
10 [no obj., often in imperative] stop filming or recording. ■ [with adverbial] move to another shot in a film: *cut to a dentist's surgery.* ■ [with obj.] make (a film) into a coherent whole by removing parts or placing them in a different order.
11 [no obj.] divide a pack of playing cards by lifting a portion from the top, either to reveal a card at random or to place the top portion under the bottom portion.
12 strike or kick (a ball) with an abrupt, typically downward motion: *Cook cut the ball back to him.* ■ Golf slice (the ball). ■ Cricket hit (the ball) to the off side with the bat held almost horizontally; play such a stroke against (the bowler). ■ [no obj.] Cricket (of the ball) turn sharply on pitching.
13 mix (an illegal drug) with another substance: *speed* ***cut with*** *rat poison.*
14 (**cut it**) N. Amer. informal come up to expectations; meet requirements: *this CD player doesn't quite cut it.* [shortened form of the idiom *cut the mustard*.]
▶ noun **1** an act of cutting, in particular: ■ [in sing.] a haircut: *his hair was in need of a cut.* ■ a stroke or blow given by a sharp-edged implement or by a whip or cane: *he could skin an animal with a single cut of the knife.* ■ a wounding remark or act. ■ [often with modifier] a reduction in amount or size: *she took a 20% pay cut* | *a* ***cut in*** *interest rates.* ■ Brit. a power cut. ■ an act of cutting part of a book, play, etc.: *they would not publish the book unless the author was willing to* ***make cuts****.* ■ an immediate transition from one scene to another in a film. ■ Golf the halfway point of a golf tournament, where half of the players are eliminated. ■ Tennis & Cricket a stroke made with an abrupt, typically horizontal or downward action.
2 a result of cutting something, in particular: ■ a long, narrow incision in the skin made by something sharp: *blood ran from a cut on his jaw.* ■ a long, narrow opening or incision made in a surface or piece of material: *make a single cut along the top of each potato.* ■ a piece of meat cut from a carcass: *a good lean cut of beef.* ■ [in sing.] informal a share of the profits from something: *the directors are demanding their cut.* ■ a recording of a piece of music: *a cut from his forthcoming album.* ■ a version of a film after editing. ■ a passage cut or dug out, as a railway cutting or a new channel made for a river or other waterway.
3 [in sing.] the way or style in which something, especially a garment or someone's hair, is cut: *the elegant cut of his dinner jacket.*

– PHRASES **be cut out for** (or **to be**) [usu. with negative] informal have exactly the right qualities for a particular role or job: *I'm just not cut out to be a policeman.* **a cut above** informal noticeably superior to: *she's a cut above the rest.* **cut and dried** [often with negative] (of a situation) completely settled: *the championship is not as cut and dried as everyone thinks.* [early 18th cent.: originally used to distinguish the herbs of herbalists' shops from growing herbs.] **cut and paste** Computing move (text) by cutting it from one part of the text and inserting it in another. **cut and run** informal make a speedy departure from a difficult situation rather than deal with it. [originally a nautical phrase, meaning 'cut the anchor cable because of some emergency and make sail immediately'.] **cut and thrust** a lively and competitive atmosphere or environment: *the cut and thrust of political debate.* ■ a situation or sphere of activity regarded as carried out under adversarial conditions: *the ruthless cut and thrust of the business world.* [originally a phrase in fencing.] **cut both ways** (of a point or statement) serve both sides of an argument. ■ (of an action or process) have both good and bad effects: *the triumphs of civilization cut both ways.* **cut the corner** take the shortest course by going across and not around a corner. **cut corners** do something perfunctorily so as to save time or money. **cut a dash** Brit. be stylish or impressive in one's dress or behaviour. **cut someone dead** completely ignore someone. **cut a deal** N. Amer. informal come to an arrangement, especially in business; make a deal. **cut someone down to size** informal deflate someone's exaggerated sense of self-worth. **cut something down to size** reduce the size or power of something, for example an organization, which is regarded as having become too large or powerful. **cut a —— figure** present oneself or appear in a particular way: *David has cut a dashing figure on the international social scene.* **cut from the same cloth** of the same nature; similar. **cut in line** N. Amer. jump the queue. **cut it fine** see **FINE**[1]. **cut it out** [usu. in imperative] informal used to ask someone to stop doing or saying something that is annoying or offensive. **cut loose** distance or free oneself from a person, group, or system: *he was a young teenager, already* ***cutting loose from*** *his family.* ■ begin to act without restraint: *when Mannion cut loose the home side collapsed to 127 all out.* **cut someone/thing loose** (or **free**) free someone or something from something which holds or restricts them: *he'd cut loose the horses.* **cut one's losses** abandon an enterprise or course of action that is clearly going to be unprofitable or unsuccessful before one suffers more loss or harm. **cut the mustard** informal come up to expectations; reach the required standard: *I didn't cut the mustard as a hockey player.* **cut no ice** informal have no influence or effect: *your holier-than-thou attitude* ***cuts no ice with*** *me.* **cut someone off** (or **down**) **in their prime** bring someone's life or career to an abrupt end while they are at the peak of their abilities. **cut someone/thing short** interrupt someone or something; bring an abrupt or premature end to something said or done: *Peter cut him short rudely.* **cut someone to pieces** kill or severely injure someone. ■ totally defeat someone. **cut a** (or **the**) **rug** N. Amer. informal dance, especially in an energetic or accomplished way. **cut one's teeth** acquire initial practice or experience of a particular sphere of activity: *the brothers cut their professional teeth at Lusardi's before starting their own restaurant.* **cut a tooth** (of a baby) have a tooth appear through the gum. **cut to the chase** N. Amer. informal come to the point: *cut to the chase—what is it you want us to do?* [*cut* in the sense 'move to another part of the film', expressing the notion of ignoring any preliminaries.] **cut up rough** Brit. informal behave in an aggressive, quarrelsome, or awkward way. **cut up well** archaic bequeath a large fortune. **cut your coat according to your cloth** proverb undertake only what you have the money or ability to do and no more. **have one's work cut out** see **WORK**. **make the cut** [usu. with negative] Golf equal or better a required score, thus avoiding elimination from the last two rounds of a four-round tournament. **miss the cut** Golf fail to equal or better a required score, thus being eliminated from the last two rounds of a four-round tournament.

– PHRASAL VERBS **cut in 1** interrupt someone while they are speaking: *'It's urgent,' Raoul cut in.* **2** pull in too closely in front of another vehicle after having overtaken it: *she* ***cut in on*** *a station wagon, forcing the driver to brake.* **3** (of a motor or other mechanical device) begin operating, especially when triggered automatically by an electrical signal. **4** dated interrupt a dancing couple to take over from one partner. **cut someone in** informal include someone in a deal and give them a share of the profits. **cut into** interrupt the course of: *Victoria's words cut into her thoughts.* **cut someone off 1** interrupt someone while they are speaking. ■ interrupt someone during a telephone call by breaking the connection. **2** prevent someone from receiving or being provided with something, especially power or water. **3** reject someone as one's heir; disinherit someone: *Gabrielle's family* ***cut her off without a penny****.* **4** prevent someone from having access to somewhere or someone; isolate someone from something they previously had connections with: *the couple were cut off by a fast-moving tide.* **cut out 1** (of a motor or engine) suddenly stop operating. **2** N. Amer. informal (of a person) leave quickly, especially so as to avoid a boring or awkward situation. **cut someone out** exclude someone: *his mother cut him out of her will.* **cut up 1** N. Amer. informal behave in a mischievous or unruly manner: *kids cutting up in a classroom.* **2** informal (of a horse race) have a particular selection of runners: *the race has* ***cut up badly*** *with no other opposition from England.* **cut someone up 1** informal (of a driver) overtake someone and pull in too closely in front of them. **2** N. Amer. informal criticize someone severely: *my kids cut him up about his appetite all the time.*

– ORIGIN Middle English (probably existing, although not recorded, in Old English); probably of Germanic origin and related to Norwegian *kutte* and Icelandic *kuta* 'cut with a small knife', *kuti* 'small blunt knife'.

cut-and-come-again ▶ noun [usu. as modifier] a garden plant, especially a green vegetable or a flower, that can be repeatedly cut or harvested: *cut-and-come-again spinach.*

cut-and-cover ▶ noun [mass noun] a method of building a tunnel by making a cutting which is then lined and covered over.

cutaneous /kjuːˈteɪnɪəs/ ▶ adjective relating to or affecting the skin: *cutaneous pigmentation.*
– ORIGIN late 16th cent.: from modern Latin *cutaneus* (from Latin *cutis* 'skin') + **-OUS**.

cutaway ▶ noun [often as modifier] **1** a coat or jacket with the front cut away below the waist.
2 a diagram or drawing with some external parts left out to reveal the interior.
3 a shot or scene in a film which is of a different subject from those to which it is joined in editing.

cutback ▶ noun an act or instance of reducing something, especially expenditure: ***cutbacks in*** *defence spending.*

cutch /kʌtʃ/ ▶ noun see **CATECHU**.

cut-down ▶ adjective reduced in scope or length: *it's a cut-down version of a DTP program.*

cute ▶ adjective **1** attractive in a pretty or endearing way: *she had a cute little nose.* ■ N. Amer. informal sexually attractive.
2 N. Amer. informal clever or cunning, especially in a self-seeking or superficial way: *she had a real cute idea* | *the two brothers were cute enough to find a couple of rich women and marry them.*
– DERIVATIVES **cutely** adverb, **cuteness** noun.
– ORIGIN early 18th cent. (in the sense 'clever, shrewd'): shortening of **ACUTE**.

cutesy ▶ adjective (**cutesier**, **cutesiest**) informal cute to a sentimental or mawkish extent: *the film's cutesy shots of children playing in the streets.*

cut glass ▶ noun [mass noun] **1** glass ornamented with patterns cut into it by grinding and polishing.
2 [as modifier] characterized by precise and careful enunciation: *a cut-glass accent.*

C

C

Cuthbert, St (d.687), English monk. He lived as a hermit on Farne Island before becoming bishop of Lindisfarne. Feast day, 20 March.

cuticle /ˈkjuːtɪk(ə)l/ ▶ **noun 1** the dead skin at the base of a fingernail or toenail.
2 the outer cellular layer of a hair.
3 Botany & Zoology a protective and waxy or hard layer covering the epidermis of a plant, invertebrate, or shell. ■ Zoology another term for **EPIDERMIS**.
– DERIVATIVES **cuticular** /-ˈtɪkjʊlə/ **adjective**.
– ORIGIN late 15th cent. (denoting a membrane of the body): from Latin *cuticula*, diminutive of *cutis* 'skin'.

cutie ▶ **noun** (pl. **cuties**) informal an attractive or endearing person, especially a young woman.

cutin /ˈkjuːtɪn/ ▶ **noun** [mass noun] Biochemistry a waxy water-repellent substance in the cuticle of plants, consisting of highly polymerized esters of fatty acids.
– ORIGIN mid 19th cent.: from **CUTIS** + **-IN**[1].

cut-in ▶ **noun** a shot in a film that is edited into another shot or scene.

cutis /ˈkjuːtɪs/ ▶ **noun** [mass noun] Anatomy the true skin or dermis.
– ORIGIN early 17th cent.: from Latin, 'skin'.

cutlass /ˈkʌtləs/ ▶ **noun** a short sword with a slightly curved blade, formerly used by sailors.
– ORIGIN late 16th cent.: from French *coutelas*, based on Latin *cultellus* 'small knife' (see **CUTLER**).

cutlassfish ▶ **noun** (pl. **same** or **cutlassfishes**) a long, slender marine fish with sharp teeth and a dorsal fin running the length of the back. ● Family Trichiuridae: several species, including the Atlantic *Trichiurus lepturus* (also called **SNAKEFISH**), an important food fish in the tropics.

cutler ▶ **noun** a person who makes or sells cutlery.
– ORIGIN Middle English: from Old French *coutelier*, from *coutel* 'knife', from Latin *cultellus*, diminutive of *culter* 'knife, ploughshare'. Compare with **COULTER**.

cutlery ▶ **noun** [mass noun] knives, forks, and spoons used for eating or serving food. ■ N. Amer. cutting utensils, especially knives.
– ORIGIN Middle English: from Old French *coutellerie*, from *coutelier* (see **CUTLER**).

cutlet ▶ **noun** a portion of meat, usually served grilled or fried and often covered in breadcrumbs. ■ Brit. a lamb or veal chop from just behind the neck. ■ a flat croquette of minced meat, nuts, or pulses, typically covered in breadcrumbs and shaped like a veal chop.
– ORIGIN early 18th cent.: from French *côtelette*, earlier *costelette*, diminutive of *coste* 'rib', from Latin *costa*.

cutline ▶ **noun 1** N. Amer. the caption to a photograph or other illustration.
2 (in squash) the line above which a served ball must strike the front wall.

cut lunch ▶ **noun** Austral./NZ a packed lunch.

cut-off ▶ **noun 1** a point or level which is a designated limit of something: *2,500 g is the standard cut-off below which infants are categorized as 'low birth-weight'* | [as modifier] *the cut-off date to register is July 2.*
2 an act of stopping or interrupting the supply of something: *a cut-off of aid would be a disaster.* ■ a device for producing an interruption in flow of a power or fuel supply. ■ a sudden drop in amplification or responsiveness of an electric device at a certain frequency. ■ [mass noun] the stopping of the supply of steam to the cylinders of a steam engine when the piston has travelled a set percentage of its stroke.
3 (**cut-offs**) shorts made by cutting off the legs of a pair of jeans or other trousers and leaving the edges unhemmed.
4 N. Amer. a short cut.

cut-out ▶ **noun 1** a shape cut out of board or another material. ■ a person perceived as characterless or lacking in individuality: *this film's protagonists are cardboard cut-outs.*
2 a hole cut in something for decoration or to allow the insertion of something else.
3 a device that automatically breaks an electric circuit for safety and either resets itself or can be reset.

cutover ▶ **noun** a rapid transition from one phase of a business enterprise or project to another.
▶ **adjective** (of land) having had its saleable timber felled and removed.

cut-price (N. Amer. also **cut-rate**) ▶ **adjective** for sale at a reduced or unusually low price: *cut-price footwear.* ■ offering goods at reduced prices: *cut-price supermarkets.*

cutpurse ▶ **noun** archaic term for **PICKPOCKET**.
– ORIGIN late Middle English: with reference to stealing by cutting purses suspended from a waistband.

cutscene ▶ **noun** (in computer games) a scene that develops the storyline and is often shown on completion of a certain level, or when the player's character dies.

cutter ▶ **noun 1** a person or thing that cuts something, in particular: ■ [often with adj. or noun modifier] a tool for cutting something, especially one intended for cutting a particular thing or for producing a particular shape: *a biscuit cutter* | (**cutters**) *a pair of bolt cutters.* ■ a person who cuts or edits film. ■ a person in a tailoring establishment who takes measurements and cuts the cloth.
2 a light, fast coastal patrol boat. ■ a ship's boat used for carrying light stores or passengers. ■ historical a small fore-and-aft rigged sailing boat with one mast, more than one headsail, and a running bowsprit, used as a fast auxiliary. ■ a yacht with one mainsail and two foresails.
3 Cricket & Baseball a ball that deviates sharply on pitching.
4 N. Amer. a light horse-drawn sleigh.
5 a pig heavier than a porker but lighter than a baconer.

cut-throat ▶ **noun 1** dated a murderer or other violent criminal.
2 short for **CUT-THROAT RAZOR**.
3 (also **cut-throat trout**) a trout of western North America, with red or orange markings under the jaw. ● *Salmo clarki*, family Salmonidae.
▶ **adjective 1** (of a competitive situation or activity) fierce and intense; involving the use of ruthless measures: *the cut-throat world of fashion.* ■ (of a person) using ruthless methods in a competitive situation: *the greedy cut-throat manufacturers he worked for.*
2 denoting a form of whist (or other card game normally for four) played by three players.

cut-throat razor ▶ **noun** Brit. a razor having a long blade set in a handle, usually folding like a penknife.

cutting ▶ **noun 1** [mass noun] the action of cutting something: *the cutting of the cake* | *tax-cutting.*
2 (often **cuttings**) a piece cut off from something, especially what remains when something is being trimmed or prepared: *grass cuttings.* ■ Brit. an article or other piece cut from a newspaper or periodical. ■ a piece cut from a plant for propagation.
3 Brit. an open passage excavated through higher ground for a railway, road, or canal.
▶ **adjective** capable of cutting something: *the cutting blades of the hedge trimmer.* ■ (of a comment) causing emotional pain; hurtful: *a cutting remark.* ■ (of the wind) bitterly cold.
– DERIVATIVES **cuttingly adverb**.

cutting edge ▶ **noun 1** the edge of a tool's blade.
2 [in sing.] the latest or most advanced stage in the development of something: *researchers **at the cutting edge of** molecular biology.*
3 [in sing.] a dynamic or invigorating quality: *the party's campaign began to lose its cutting edge.*
▶ **adjective** (**cutting-edge**) highly advanced; innovative or pioneering: *cutting-edge technology.*

cutting grass ▶ **noun 1** [mass noun] an Australian and New Zealand sedge with sharp-edged leaves or stems. ● Genus *Gahnia*, family Cyperaceae.
2 another term for **CANE RAT**.

cutting horse ▶ **noun** N. Amer. a horse trained in separating cattle from a herd.

cutting room ▶ **noun** a room in a film studio where film is cut and edited: [as modifier] *such a scene would **end up on the cutting-room floor**.*

cuttle ▶ **noun** a cuttlefish.
– ORIGIN Old English *cudele* 'cuttlefish', of Germanic origin; related to *codd* 'bag', with reference to its ink bag.

cuttlebone ▶ **noun** the flattened oval internal skeleton of the cuttlefish, which is made of white lightweight chalky material. It is used as a dietary supplement for cage birds and for making casts for precious metal items.

cuttlefish ▶ **noun** (pl. **same** or **cuttlefishes**) a swimming marine mollusc that resembles a broad-bodied squid, having eight arms and two long tentacles that are used for grabbing prey. Its internal skeleton is the familiar cuttlebone, which it uses for adjusting buoyancy. ● Order Sepioidea, class Cephalopoda: *Sepia* and other genera.
– ORIGIN late 16th cent.: from **CUTTLE** + **FISH**[1].

cutty Scottish & N. English ▶ **adjective** short, either naturally so or through being cut down: *they carried wee cutty ladders.*
▶ **noun** (pl. **cutties**) a short tobacco pipe.

Cutty Sark /ˌkʌtɪ ˈsɑːk/ the only survivor of the British tea clippers, launched in 1869 and now preserved as a museum ship at Greenwich, London.
– ORIGIN from Robert Burns's *Tam o' Shanter*, a poem about a Scottish farmer chased by a young witch who wore only her 'cutty sark' (= short shift).

cutty-stool ▶ **noun** Scottish historical a stool on which an offender was publicly rebuked during a church service.

cut up ▶ **adjective** [predic.] **1** (of soft ground) rutted and uneven after the passage of heavy vehicles or animals.
2 informal (of a person) very distressed: *she was pretty cut up about them leaving.*
▶ **noun** (**cut-up**) **1** a film or sound recording made by cutting and editing material from pre-existing recordings.
2 N. Amer. informal a person who is fond of making jokes or playing the fool.

cutwater ▶ **noun 1** the forward edge of a ship's prow.
2 a wedge-shaped projection on the pier of a bridge, which divides the flow of water and prevents debris from becoming trapped against the pier.

cutwork ▶ **noun** [mass noun] embroidery in which parts of the fabric ground are cut out and the edges oversewn or elaborately stitched.

cutworm ▶ **noun** a moth caterpillar that lives in the upper layers of the soil and eats through the stems of young plants at ground level. ● Several species in the family Noctuidae, in particular the large yellow underwing (see **YELLOW UNDERWING**).

cuvée /ˈkjuːveɪ/, French /kyve/ ▶ **noun** a type, blend, or batch of wine, especially champagne.
– ORIGIN mid 19th cent.: French, 'vatful', from *cuve* 'cask', from Latin *cupa*.

cuvette /kjuːˈvɛt/ ▶ **noun** Biochemistry a straight-sided clear container for holding liquid samples in a spectrophotometer or other instrument.
– ORIGIN early 18th cent.: from French, diminutive of *cuve* 'cask', from Latin *cupa*.

Cuvier /ˈkuːvɪeɪ/, French /kyvje/, Georges Léopold Chrétien Frédéric Dagobert, Baron (1769–1832), French naturalist. Cuvier founded the science of palaeontology and made pioneering studies in comparative anatomy and classification.

Cuzco /ˈkʊskəʊ/, Spanish /ˈkusko, ˈkuθko/ a city in the Andes in southern Peru; pop. 348,900 (est. 2007). It was the capital of the Inca empire until the Spanish conquest in 1533.

CV ▶ **abbreviation** curriculum vitae.

cv. ▶ **abbreviation** cultivated variety.

CVO ▶ **abbreviation** (in the UK) Commander of the Royal Victorian Order.

CVS ▶ **abbreviation** chorionic villus sampling.

CVT ▶ **abbreviation** continuously variable transmission.

Cwlth ▶ **abbreviation** Commonwealth.

cwm /kʊm/ ▶ **noun** a cirque, especially one in the mountains of Wales.
– ORIGIN mid 19th cent.: Welsh; related to **COMBE**.

Cwmbran /kʊmˈbrɑːn/ a town in SE Wales, administrative centre of Monmouthshire; pop. 49,400 (est. 2009).

CWO ▶ **abbreviation** Chief Warrant Officer.

c.w.o. ▶ **abbreviation** cash with order.

cwr ▶ **abbreviation** continuous welded rail.

CWS ▶ **abbreviation** Cooperative Wholesale Society.

cwt ▶ **abbreviation** hundredweight.
– ORIGIN from Latin *centum* 'a hundred'.

cwtch /kʊtʃ/ ▶ **noun** Welsh **1** a cupboard or cubbyhole.
2 a cuddle or hug.
– ORIGIN Welsh, from *cwts*, related to **COUCH**[1].

CY ▶ **abbreviation** Cyprus (international vehicle registration).

-cy ▶ **suffix 1** denoting state or condition: *bankruptcy.*
2 denoting rank or status: *baronetcy.*
– ORIGIN from Latin *-cia*, *-tia* and Greek *-k(e)ia*, *-t(e)ia*.

cyan /ˈsʌɪən/ ▶ **noun** [mass noun] a greenish-blue colour which is one of the primary subtractive colours, complementary to red.
– ORIGIN late 19th cent.: from Greek *kuaneos* 'dark blue'.

cyanamide /sʌɪˈanəmʌɪd/ ▶ **noun** [mass noun] Chemistry a weakly acidic crystalline compound made as an inter-

mediate in the production of ammonia. ● Alternative name: **cyanogen amide**; chem. formula: CH_2N_2.
■ a salt of this containing the anion CN_2^{2-}, especially the calcium salt used as a fertilizer.
– ORIGIN mid 19th cent.: blend of CYANOGEN and AMIDE.

cyanate /ˈsʌɪəneɪt/ ▶ **noun** Chemistry a salt or ester of cyanic acid.

cyanic /sʌɪˈanɪk/ ▶ **adjective 1** Chemistry of cyanogen.
2 rare blue; azure.
– ORIGIN early 19th cent.: from CYAN + -IC.

cyanic acid ▶ **noun** [mass noun] Chemistry a colourless, poisonous, volatile, strongly acidic liquid. ● Chem. formula: HOCN. See also FULMINIC ACID, ISOCYANIC ACID.
– ORIGIN early 19th cent.: from CYANOGEN.

cyanide /ˈsʌɪənʌɪd/ ▶ **noun** Chemistry a salt or ester of hydrocyanic acid, containing the anion CN^- or the group –CN. The salts are generally extremely toxic. Compare with NITRILE. ■ [mass noun] sodium or potassium cyanide used as a poison or in the extraction of gold and silver.
– ORIGIN early 19th cent.: from CYANOGEN + -IDE.

cyano- ▶ **combining form 1** relating to the colour blue, especially dark blue: *cyanosis*.
2 representing CYANIDE.
– ORIGIN from Greek *kuan(e)os* 'dark blue'.

cyanoacrylate /ˌsʌɪənəʊˈakrɪleɪt/ ▶ **noun** Chemistry any of a class of compounds which are cyanide derivatives of acrylates. They are easily polymerized and are used to make quick-setting adhesives.

Cyanobacteria /ˌsʌɪənəʊbakˈtɪərɪə/ ▶ **plural noun** Biology a division of microorganisms that are related to the bacteria but are capable of photosynthesis. They are prokaryotic and represent the earliest known form of life on the earth. ● Division Cyanobacteria, kingdom Monera.
■ (**cyanobacteria**) microorganisms of the Cyanobacteria division; blue-green algae.
– DERIVATIVES **cyanobacterial** adjective.
– ORIGIN modern Latin (plural), from Greek *kuaneos* 'dark blue' + plural of BACTERIUM.

cyanocobalamin /ˌsʌɪənə(ʊ)kəˈbaləmɪn/ ▶ **noun** [mass noun] a vitamin derived from foods of animal origin such as liver, fish, and eggs, a deficiency of which can cause pernicious anaemia. It contains a cyanide group bonded to the central cobalt atom of a cobalamin molecule. Also called VITAMIN B_{12}.
– ORIGIN 1950s: from CYANOGEN and *cobalamin* (blend of COBALT and VITAMIN).

cyanogen /sʌɪˈanədʒ(ə)n/ ▶ **noun** [mass noun] Chemistry a colourless flammable highly poisonous gas made by oxidizing hydrogen cyanide. ● Chem. formula: C_2N_2.
– ORIGIN early 19th cent.: from French *cyanogène*, from Greek *kuanos* 'dark blue mineral' + *-gène* (see -GEN), so named because it is a constituent of Prussian blue.

cyanogenesis /ˌsʌɪənə(ʊ)ˈdʒɛnɪsɪs/ ▶ **noun** [mass noun] Botany the production of hydrogen cyanide by certain plants, such as cherry laurel and bracken, as a response to wounding or a deterrent to herbivores.

cyanogenic /ˌsʌɪənəˈdʒɛnɪk/ ▶ **adjective** Botany (of a plant) capable of cyanogenesis. ■ Biochemistry containing a cyanide group in the molecule.

cyanohydrin /ˌsʌɪənə(ʊ)ˈhʌɪdrɪn/ ▶ **noun** Chemistry an organic compound containing a carbon atom linked to both a cyanide group and a hydroxyl group.

cyanophyte /ˈsʌɪənə(ʊ)fʌɪt/ ▶ **noun** Biology a microorganism of the division Cyanobacteria.

cyanosis /ˌsʌɪəˈnəʊsɪs/ ▶ **noun** [mass noun] Medicine a bluish discoloration of the skin due to poor circulation or inadequate oxygenation of the blood.
– DERIVATIVES **cyanotic** adjective.
– ORIGIN mid 19th cent.: modern Latin, from Greek *kuanōsis* 'blueness', from *kuaneos* 'dark blue'.

cyanotype /ˈsʌɪənə(ʊ)tʌɪp/ ▶ **noun** a photographic blueprint.

cyathium /sʌɪˈaθɪəm/ ▶ **noun** (pl. **cyathia** /-ɪə/) Botany the characteristic inflorescence of the spurges, resembling a single flower. It consists of a cup-shaped involucre of fused bracts enclosing several greatly reduced male flowers and a single female flower.
– ORIGIN late 19th cent.: modern Latin, from Greek *kuathion*, diminutive of *kuathos* 'cup'.

Cybele /ˈsɪbɪli/ Mythology a mother goddess worshipped especially in Phrygia and later in Greece (where she was associated with Demeter), Rome, and the Roman provinces, with her consort Attis.

cyber /ˈsʌɪbə/ ▶ **adjective** relating to or characteristic of the culture of computers, information technology, and virtual reality: *the cyber age*.
– ORIGIN 1980s: abbreviation of CYBERNETICS.

cyber- /ˈsʌɪbə/ ▶ **combining form** relating to electronic communication networks and virtual reality: *cyberpunk | cyberspace*.
– ORIGIN back-formation from CYBERNETICS.

WORD TRENDS Cyber- seems to be a thoroughly modern prefix, summoning up images of advanced technology, supercomputers, and virtual reality. However, in striving to be so very up to date it has developed a whiff of the old-fashioned. The word's rise in popularity is part of the problem—it seems to be added to almost anything to give a high-tech twist. The Oxford English Corpus contains examples of *cyberartist, cybertalk, cyberfiction, cyberculture, cyber-economy, cyber-activist, cyberpiracy, cybercriminal, cyber-cinema*, and so on. Using **cyber-** like this draws attention to the use of technology and the Internet, implying that such a notion is unusual or remarkable. As these resources become an ever more integral part of our lives, the use of computers in almost every aspect of life will be assumed, eventually making the addition of **cyber-** redundant.

cyberattack ▶ **noun** an attempt by hackers to damage or destroy a computer network or system.

cybercafe ▶ **noun** another term for INTERNET CAFE.

cybercrime ▶ **noun** [mass noun] criminal activities carried out by means of computers or the Internet.
– DERIVATIVES **cybercriminal** noun.

cybernaut ▶ **noun 1** an expert or habitual user of the Internet.
2 a person who uses computer technology and sensory devices to experience virtual reality.
– ORIGIN 1960s (in the senses 'robot' and 'cyborg'): from CYBER-, on the pattern of *astronaut*.

cybernetics ▶ **plural noun** [treated as sing.] the science of communications and automatic control systems in both machines and living things.
– DERIVATIVES **cybernetic** adjective, **cybernetician** noun, **cyberneticist** noun.
– ORIGIN 1940s: from Greek *kubernētēs* 'steersman', from *kubernan* 'to steer'.

cyberphobia ▶ **noun** [mass noun] extreme or irrational fear of computers or technology.

cyberpunk ▶ **noun** [mass noun] a genre of science fiction set in a lawless subculture of an oppressive society dominated by computer technology.

cybersex ▶ **noun** [mass noun] sexual arousal using computer technology, especially by wearing virtual reality equipment or by exchanging messages with another person via the Internet.

cyberspace ▶ **noun** [mass noun] the notional environment in which communication over computer networks occurs.

cybersquatting ▶ **noun** [mass noun] the practice of registering names, especially well-known company or brand names, as Internet domains, in the hope of reselling them at a profit.
– DERIVATIVES **cybersquatter** noun.

cyberstalking ▶ **noun** [mass noun] the repeated use of electronic communications to harass or frighten someone, for example by sending threatening emails.
– DERIVATIVES **cyberstalker** noun.

cyberterrorism ▶ **noun** [mass noun] the politically motivated use of computers and information technology to cause severe disruption or widespread fear.
– DERIVATIVES **cyberterrorist** noun.

cyberwar ▶ **noun** [mass noun] the use of computers to disrupt the activities of an enemy country, especially the deliberate attacking of communication systems.

cyborg /ˈsʌɪbɔːg/ ▶ **noun** a fictional or hypothetical person whose physical abilities are extended beyond normal human limitations by mechanical elements built into the body.
– ORIGIN 1960s: blend of CYBER- and ORGANISM.

cycad /ˈsʌɪkad/ ▶ **noun** a palm-like plant of tropical and subtropical regions, bearing large male or female cones. Cycads were abundant during the Triassic and Jurassic eras, but have since been in decline. ● Class Cycadopsida, subdivision Gymnospermae: twenty species in the genus *Cycas* and family Cycadaceae.
– ORIGIN mid 19th cent.: from modern Latin *Cycas*, *Cycad-* (order name), from supposed Greek *kukas*, scribal error for *koikas*, plural of *koix* 'Egyptian palm'.

Cyclades /ˈsɪklədiːz/ a large group of islands in the southern Aegean Sea, regarded in antiquity as circling around the sacred island of Delos. The Cyclades form a department of modern Greece. Greek name KIKLÁDHES.
– ORIGIN Latin, based on Greek *kuklos* 'circle'.

Cycladic /sɪˈkladɪk, sʌɪ-/ ▶ **adjective** relating to the Cyclades. ■ Archaeology relating to or denoting a Bronze Age civilization that flourished in the Cyclades, dated to c.3000 to c.1050 BC. ■ (as noun **the Cycladic**) the Cycladic culture or period.

cyclamate /ˈsɪkləmeɪt, ˈsʌɪk-/ ▶ **noun** Chemistry a salt of a synthetic acid which is a cyclohexyl derivative of sulphamic acid. Sodium and calcium cyclamates were formerly used as artificial sweeteners.
– ORIGIN 1950s: contraction of *cyclohexylsulphamate*.

cyclamen /ˈsɪkləmən/ ▶ **noun** (pl. **same** or **cyclamens**) a European plant of the primrose family, having pink, red, or white flowers with backward-curving petals and grown as a winter-flowering pot plant. ● Genus *Cyclamen*, family Primulaceae: several species.
■ [mass noun] a pinkish-purple colour.
– ORIGIN modern Latin, from Latin *cyclaminos*, from Greek *kuklaminos*, perhaps from *kuklos* 'circle', with reference to its bulbous roots.

cycle ▶ **noun 1** [often with adj. or noun modifier] a series of events that are regularly repeated in the same order: *the recurrent cycle of harvest failure, food shortages, and price increases*. ■ the period of time taken to complete a cycle of events: *the cells are shed over a cycle of twenty-eight days*. ■ technical a recurring series of successive operations or states, such as in the working of an internal-combustion engine, or in the alternation of an electric current or a wave. ■ Biology a recurring series of events or metabolic processes in the lifetime of a plant or animal: *the storks' breeding cycle*. ■ Biochemistry a series of successive metabolic reactions in which one of the products is regenerated and reused. ■ Ecology the movement of a simple substance through the soil, rocks, water, atmosphere, and living organisms of the earth. See CARBON CYCLE, NITROGEN CYCLE. ■ Computing a single set of hardware operations, especially that by which memory is accessed and an item is transferred to or from it, to the point at which the memory may be accessed again. ■ Physics a cycle per second; one hertz.
2 a complete set or series: *the painting is one of a cycle of seven*. ■ a series of songs, stories, plays, or poems composed around a particular theme, and usually intended to be performed or read in sequence: *Wagner's Ring Cycle*.
3 a bicycle or tricycle. ■ [in sing.] a ride on a bicycle: *a 112-mile cycle*.
▶ **verb 1** [no obj., with adverbial of direction] ride a bicycle: *she cycled to work every day*.
2 [no obj.] move in or follow a regularly repeated sequence of events: *economies cycle regularly between boom and slump*.
– ORIGIN late Middle English: from Old French, from late Latin *cyclus*, from Greek *kuklos* 'circle'.

cycle lane ▶ **noun** Brit. a division of a road marked off with painted lines, for use by cyclists.

cycle of erosion ▶ **noun** Geology, dated an idealized course of landscape evolution, passing from youthful stages, marked by steep gradients, to old age, when the landscape is reduced to a peneplain.

cycle rickshaw (also **bicycle rickshaw**) ▶ **noun** (in South Asia) a three-wheeled bicycle for public hire, with a covered seat for passengers behind the driver.

cycle track (also **cycleway**, **cycle path**) ▶ **noun** Brit. a path or road for bicycles and not motor vehicles.

cyclic /ˈsʌɪklɪk, ˈsɪk-/ ▶ **adjective 1** occurring in cycles; regularly repeated: *the cyclic pattern of the last two decades*. ■ Mathematics (of a group) having the property that each element of the group can be expressed as a power of one particular element. ■ denoting a musical or literary composition with a recurrent theme or structural device.
2 Mathematics relating to a circle or other closed curve. ■ Geometry (of a polygon) having all its vertices lying on a circle.
3 Chemistry (of a compound) having a molecular structure containing one or more closed rings of atoms.
4 Botany (of a flower) having its parts arranged in whorls.
– ORIGIN late 18th cent.: from French *cyclique* or Latin *cyclicus*, from Greek *kuklikos*, from *kuklos* 'circle'.

cyclical /ˈsɪklɪk(ə)l/ ▶ **adjective** occurring in cycles; recurrent: *the cyclical nature of the cement industry*.
– DERIVATIVES **cyclically** adverb.

cyclic AMP ▶ **noun** [mass noun] Biochemistry a cyclic form of adenosine monophosphate (adenylic acid) which

C

C

plays a major role in controlling many enzyme-catalysed processes in living cells.

cyclic redundancy check (also **cyclic redundancy code**) (abbrev.: **CRC**) ▶ **noun** Computing a code added to data which is used to detect errors occurring during transmission, storage, or retrieval.

cyclin /ˈsʌɪklɪn/ ▶ **noun** Biochemistry any of a number of proteins associated with the cycle of cell division which are thought to initiate certain processes of mitosis.
– ORIGIN 1980s: from CYCLE + -IN[1].

cycling ▶ **noun** [mass noun] the sport or activity of riding a bicycle. Cycle racing has three main forms: road racing (typically over long distances), pursuit (on an oval track), and cyclo-cross (over rough, open country).

Cycliophora /sɪklɪˈɒphərə/ ▶ **plural noun** Zoology a new phylum that has been proposed for a minute marine invertebrate (*Symbion pandora*) that was discovered in 1995 attached to the mouthparts of lobsters. It is related to the phyla Bryozoa and Entoprocta.
– ORIGIN modern Latin (plural), from Greek *kuklios* 'circular' + *pherein* 'to bear'.

cyclist ▶ **noun** a person who rides a bicycle.

cyclize /ˈsʌɪklʌɪz/ (also **cyclise**) ▶ **verb** Chemistry undergo or cause to undergo a reaction in which one part of a molecule becomes linked to another to form a closed ring.
– DERIVATIVES **cyclization** noun.

cyclo- /ˈsʌɪkləʊ/ ▶ **combining form 1** circular: *cyclorama*.
2 relating to a cycle or cycling: *cyclo-cross*.
3 cyclic: *cycloalkane*.
– ORIGIN from Greek *kuklos* 'circle', or directly from CYCLE or CYCLIC.

cycloaddition ▶ **noun** Chemistry an addition reaction in which a cyclic molecule is formed.

cycloalkane ▶ **noun** Chemistry a hydrocarbon with a molecule containing a ring of carbon atoms joined by single bonds.

cyclo-cross ▶ **noun** [mass noun] cross-country racing on bicycles.

cyclohexane ▶ **noun** [mass noun] Chemistry a colourless flammable liquid cycloalkane obtained from petroleum or by hydrogenating benzene, and used as a solvent and paint remover. ● Chem. formula: C_6H_{12}.

cyclohexyl /ˌsʌɪklə(ʊ)ˈhɛksʌɪl, -sɪl/ ▶ **noun** [as modifier] Chemistry of or denoting the cyclic hydrocarbon radical $-C_6H_{11}$, derived from cyclohexane.

cycloid /ˈsʌɪklɔɪd/ ▶ **noun** Mathematics a curve (resembling a series of arches) traced by a point on a circle being rolled along a straight line.
– DERIVATIVES **cycloidal** adjective.
– ORIGIN mid 17th cent.: from Greek *kukloeidēs* 'circular', from *kuklos* 'circle'.

cyclometer /sʌɪˈklɒmɪtə/ ▶ **noun 1** an instrument for measuring circular arcs.
2 an instrument attached to a bicycle for measuring the distance it travels.

cyclone /ˈsʌɪkləʊn/ ▶ **noun** Meteorology a system of winds rotating inwards to an area of low barometric pressure, with an anticlockwise (northern hemisphere) or clockwise (southern hemisphere) circulation; a depression. ■ another term for TROPICAL STORM.
– DERIVATIVES **cyclonic** adjective, **cyclonically** adverb.
– ORIGIN mid 19th cent.: probably from Greek *kuklōma* 'wheel, coil of a snake', from *kuklos* 'circle'. The change of spelling from *-m* to *-n* is unexplained.

cycloparaffin ▶ **noun** Chemistry another term for CYCLOALKANE.

cyclopean /ˌsʌɪkləˈpiːən, sʌɪˈkləʊpɪən/ (also **cyclopian**) ▶ **adjective 1** denoting a type of ancient masonry made with massive irregular blocks: *cyclopean stone walls*. [by association with the great size of the Cyclops.]
2 of or resembling a Cyclops: *a cyclopean eye*.

cyclopedia /sʌɪklə(ʊ)ˈpiːdɪə/ (also **cyclopaedia**) ▶ **noun** archaic (except in book titles) an encyclopedia: *Bailey's Cyclopedia of Horticulture*.
– ORIGIN late 17th cent.: shortening of ENCYCLOPEDIA.

cyclophosphamide /ˌsʌɪklə(ʊ)ˈfɒsfəmʌɪd/ ▶ **noun** [mass noun] Medicine a synthetic cytotoxic drug used in treating leukaemia and lymphoma and as an immunosuppressive agent.

cyclopropane ▶ **noun** [mass noun] Chemistry a flammable gaseous synthetic compound whose molecule contains a ring of three carbon atoms. It has some use as a general anaesthetic. ● Chem. formula: C_3H_6.

Cyclops /ˈsʌɪklɒps/ ▶ **noun 1** (pl. **Cyclops** or **Cyclopes** /sʌɪˈkləpiːz/) Greek Mythology a member of a race of savage one-eyed giants. In the Odyssey, Odysseus escaped death by blinding the Cyclops Polyphemus.
2 (**cyclops**) a minute predatory freshwater crustacean which has a cylindrical body with a single central eye. ● Genus *Cyclops* and other genera, order Cyclopoida.
– ORIGIN via Latin from Greek *Kuklōps*, literally 'round-eyed', from *kuklos* 'circle' + *ōps* 'eye'.

cyclorama /ˌsʌɪkləˈrɑːmə/ ▶ **noun** a circular picture of a 360° scene, viewed from inside. ■ a cloth stretched tight in an arc around the back of a stage set, often used to depict the sky.
– ORIGIN mid 19th cent.: from CYCLO-, on the pattern of words such as *panorama*.

cyclosporin /ˌsʌɪklə(ʊ)ˈspɔːrɪn/ (also **cyclosporin A**, **cyclosporine**) ▶ **noun** [mass noun] Medicine a drug with immunosuppressive properties used to prevent the rejection of grafts and transplants. A cyclic peptide, it is obtained from a fungus. ● This drug is obtained from the fungus *Trichoderma polysporum*.
– ORIGIN 1970s: from CYCLO- + *-sporin* (from Latin *spora* 'spore') + -IN[1].

cyclostome /ˈsʌɪklə(ʊ)stəʊm/ ▶ **noun** Zoology an eel-like jawless vertebrate with a round sucking mouth, of a former group that included the lampreys and hagfishes. ● Subclass Cyclostomata, now incorporated in the superclass Agnatha.
– ORIGIN mid 19th cent.: from CYCLO- + Greek *stoma* 'mouth'.

cyclostyle /ˈsʌɪklə(ʊ)stʌɪl/ ▶ **noun** an early device for duplicating handwriting, in which a pen with a small toothed wheel pricks holes in a sheet of waxed paper, which is then used as a stencil.
▶ **verb** [with obj.] (usu. as adj. **cyclostyled**) duplicate with a cyclostyle: *a cyclostyled leaflet*.
– ORIGIN late 19th cent.: from CYCLO- 'circular' + the noun STYLE.

cyclothymia /ˌsʌɪklə(ʊ)ˈθʌɪmɪə/ ▶ **noun** [mass noun] Psychiatry, dated a mental state characterized by marked swings of mood between depression and elation; manic-depressive tendency.
– DERIVATIVES **cyclothymic** adjective.
– ORIGIN 1920s: from CYCLO- + Greek *thumos* 'temper'.

cyclotron /ˈsʌɪklətrɒn/ ▶ **noun** Physics an apparatus in which charged atomic and subatomic particles are accelerated by an alternating electric field while following an outward spiral or circular path in a magnetic field.

cyder ▶ **noun** archaic spelling of CIDER.

cygnet /ˈsɪɡnɪt/ ▶ **noun** a young swan.
– ORIGIN late Middle English: from Anglo-Norman French *cignet*, diminutive of Old French *cigne* 'swan', based on Latin *cycnus*, from Greek *kuknos*.

Cygnus /ˈsɪɡnəs/ Astronomy a prominent northern constellation (the Swan), said to represent a flying swan that was the form adopted by Zeus on one occasion. It contains the bright star Deneb.
– ORIGIN Latin.

cylinder /ˈsɪlɪndə/ ▶ **noun 1** a solid geometrical figure with straight parallel sides and a circular or oval section.
2 a solid or hollow body, object, or part having the shape of a cylinder.
3 a piston chamber in a steam or internal-combustion engine.
4 a cylindrical container for liquefied gas under pressure.
5 a rotating metal roller in a printing press.
6 Archaeology a cylinder seal.
– DERIVATIVES **cylindric** adjective, **cylindrical** adjective, **cylindrically** /-ˈlɪndrɪk(ə)li/ adverb.
– ORIGIN late 16th cent.: from Latin *cylindrus*, from Greek *kulindros* 'roller', from *kulindein* 'to roll'.

cylinder block ▶ **noun** see BLOCK (sense 1 of the noun).

cylinder head ▶ **noun** the end cover of a cylinder in an internal-combustion engine, against which the piston compresses the cylinder's contents.

cylinder liner ▶ **noun** see LINER[2].

cylinder lock ▶ **noun** a lock with the keyhole and tumbler mechanism contained in a cylinder.

cylinder seal ▶ **noun** Archaeology a small barrel-shaped stone object with a hole down the centre and bearing an incised design or cuneiform inscription, originally for rolling on clay when soft to indicate ownership or authenticate a document, used chiefly in Mesopotamia from the late 4th to the 1st millennium BC.

cymbal /ˈsɪmb(ə)l/ ▶ **noun** a musical instrument consisting of a slightly concave round brass plate which is either struck against another one or struck with a stick to make a ringing or clashing sound.
– DERIVATIVES **cymbalist** noun.
– ORIGIN Old English, from Latin *cymbalum*, from Greek *kumbalon*, from *kumbē* 'cup'; readopted in Middle English from Old French *cymbale*.

Cymbeline /ˈsɪmbəliːn/ (also **Cunobelinus**) (died *c.*42 AD), British chieftain. A powerful ruler, he made Camulodunum (Colchester) his capital, and established a mint there. He was the subject of a medieval fable used by Shakespeare for his play *Cymbeline*.

cymbidium /sɪmˈbɪdɪəm/ ▶ **noun** (pl. **cymbidiums**) a tropical orchid with long, narrow leaves and arching stems bearing several flowers, growing chiefly as an epiphyte from Asia to Australasia and widely grown for buttonholes. ● Genus *Cymbidium*, family Orchidaceae.
– ORIGIN modern Latin, from Greek *kumbē* 'cup'.

cyme /sʌɪm/ ▶ **noun** Botany a flower cluster with a central stem bearing a single terminal flower that develops first, the other flowers in the cluster developing as terminal buds of lateral stems. Compare with RACEME.
– DERIVATIVES **cymose** adjective.
– ORIGIN early 18th cent. (denoting the unopened head of a plant): from French, literally 'summit', from a popular variant of Latin *cyma*.

Cymraeg /ˈkʌmrʌɪɡ/ ▶ **noun** [mass noun] the Welsh language.
– ORIGIN Welsh.

Cymric /ˈkɪmrɪk/ ▶ **adjective** Welsh in language or culture.
▶ **noun** [mass noun] the Welsh language.
– ORIGIN mid 19th cent.: from Welsh *Cymru* 'Wales', *Cymry* 'the Welsh', + -IC.

Cymru /ˈkʌmri/ Welsh name for WALES.

Cynewulf /ˈkɪnɪwʊlf/ (late 8th–9th centuries), Anglo-Saxon poet. Modern scholarship attributes four poems to him: *Juliana, Elene, The Fates of the Apostles*, and *Christ II*.

cynic /ˈsɪnɪk/ ▶ **noun 1** a person who believes that people are motivated purely by self-interest rather than acting for honourable or unselfish reasons: *some cynics thought that the controversy was all a publicity stunt*. ■ a person who questions whether something will happen or whether it is worthwhile: *the cynics were silenced when the factory opened*.
2 (**Cynic**) a member of a school of ancient Greek philosophers founded by Antisthenes, marked by an ostentatious contempt for ease and pleasure. The movement flourished in the 3rd century BC and revived in the 1st century AD.
– ORIGIN mid 16th cent. (in sense 2): from Latin *cynicus*, from Greek *kunikos*; probably originally from *Kunosarges*, the name of a gymnasium where Antisthenes taught, but popularly taken to mean 'doglike, churlish', *kuōn, kun-*, 'dog' becoming a nickname for a Cynic.

cynical ▶ **adjective 1** believing that people are motivated purely by self-interest; distrustful of human sincerity or integrity: *he was brutally cynical and hardened to every sob story under the sun*. ■ doubtful as to whether something will happen or whether it is worthwhile: *most residents are cynical about efforts to clean mobsters out of their city*. ■ contemptuous; mocking: *he gave a cynical laugh*.
2 concerned only with one's own interests and typically disregarding accepted standards in order to achieve them: *a cynical manipulation of public opinion*.
– DERIVATIVES **cynically** adverb.

cynicism /ˈsɪnɪsɪz(ə)m/ ▶ **noun** [mass noun] **1** an inclination to believe that people are motivated purely by self-interest; scepticism: *public cynicism about politics*. ■ an inclination to question whether something will happen or whether it is worthwhile; pessimism: *cynicism about the future*.
2 (**Cynicism**) a school of ancient Greek philosophers, the Cynics.

cyno- /sʌɪnəʊ/ ▶ **combining form** relating to dogs: *cynodont*.
– ORIGIN from Greek *kuōn, kun-* 'dog'.

cynodont /ˈsʌɪnə(ʊ)dɒnt/ ▶ **noun** a fossil carnivorous mammal-like reptile of the late Permian and Triassic periods, with well-developed specialized teeth. ● Suborder Cynodontia, order Therapsida: several families.
– ORIGIN late 19th cent.: from Greek *kuōn, kun-* 'dog' + *odous, odont-* 'tooth'.

cynosure /ˈsɪnəzjʊə, ˈsʌɪn-, -sjʊə/ ▶ **noun** [in sing.] a person or thing that is the centre of attention or admiration: *Kirk was the cynosure of all eyes*.

– ORIGIN late 16th cent.: from French, or from Latin *cynosura*, from Greek *kunosoura* 'dog's tail' (also 'Ursa Minor'), from *kuōn, kun-* 'dog' + *oura* 'tail'. The term originally denoted the constellation Ursa Minor, or the pole star which it contains, long used as a guide by navigators.

cyphel /ˈsʌɪf(ə)l/ (also **mossy cyphel**) ▸ noun a European mountain plant of the pink family, which forms cushion-like mounds and bears small greenish flowers. ● *Minuartia sedoides*, family Caryophyllaceae.
– ORIGIN late Middle English (denoting the houseleek): apparently from Greek *kuphella* 'hollows of the ears'.

cypher ▸ noun variant spelling of CIPHER[1].

cypherpunk ▸ noun a person who uses encryption when accessing a computer network in order to ensure privacy, especially from government authorities.
– ORIGIN 1990s: on the pattern of *cyberpunk*.

cy-pres /siː ˈpreɪ/ ▸ adverb & adjective Law as near as possible to the testator's or donor's intentions when these cannot be precisely followed.
– ORIGIN early 19th cent.: from a late Anglo-Norman French variant of French *si près* 'so near'.

cypress ▸ noun (also **cypress tree**) an evergreen coniferous tree with small rounded woody cones and flattened shoots bearing small scale-like leaves. ● *Cupressus, Chamaecyparis*, and other genera, family Cupressaceae: many species, including the columnar **Italian cypress** (*Cupressus sempervirens*), common throughout southern Europe.
■ a cypress tree, or branches from it, as a symbol of mourning. ■ used in names of coniferous trees of other families that resemble the cypress, e.g. **swamp cypress**.
– ORIGIN Middle English: from Old French *cipres*, from late Latin *cypressus*, from Greek *kuparissos*.

Cyprian, St /ˈsɪprɪən/ (d.258), Carthaginian bishop and martyr. The author of a work on the nature of true unity in the Church in its relation to the episcopate, he was martyred in the reign of the Roman emperor Valerian. Feast day, 16 or 26 September.

cyprinid /ˈsɪprɪnɪd/ ▸ noun Zoology a fish of the carp family (Cyprinidae).
– ORIGIN late 19th cent.: from modern Latin *Cyprinidae* (plural), based on Greek *kuprinos* 'carp'.

cyprinoid /ˈsɪprɪnɔɪd/ Zoology ▸ noun a fish of a large group which includes the carps, suckers, and loaches, and (in some classification schemes) the characins. ● Order Cypriniformes or superfamily Cyprinoidea.
▸ adjective relating to fish of the cyprinoid group.
– ORIGIN mid 19th cent.: from modern Latin *Cyprinoidea*, based on Latin *cyprinus* 'carp' (from Greek *kuprinos*).

Cypriot ▸ noun 1 a native or inhabitant of Cyprus. 2 [mass noun] the dialect of Greek used in Cyprus.
▸ adjective relating to Cyprus or its people or the Greek dialect used there. ■ denoting an ancient syllabic script related to the Minoan and Mycenaean scripts, which was used to write the Cypriot dialect of Greek from the 6th to the 3rd centuries BC.
– ORIGIN from Greek *Kupriōtes*, from *Kupros* 'Cyprus'.

cypripedium /ˌsɪprɪˈpiːdɪəm/ ▸ noun (pl. **cypripediums**) an orchid of a genus which comprises the lady's slippers. ● Genus *Cypripedium*, family Orchidaceae.
– ORIGIN modern Latin, from Greek *Kupris* 'Aphrodite' + *pedilon* 'slipper'.

Cyprus /ˈsʌɪprəs/ an island lying in the eastern Mediterranean about 80 km (50 miles) south of the Turkish coast; pop. 1,084,700 (est. 2009); official languages, Greek and Turkish; capital, Nicosia.

> A Greek colony in ancient times, Cyprus was held by the Turks from 1571 until 1878, when it was placed under British administration. After virtual civil war between the Greek Cypriots (some of whom favour enosis or union with Greece) and the Turkish Cypriots, Cyprus became an independent Commonwealth republic in 1960. In 1974 Turkish forces took over the northern part of the island, which proclaimed itself the independent Turkish Republic of Northern Cyprus in 1983 but has not received international recognition. The Greek Cypriot–controlled Republic of Cyprus joined the EU in May 2004.

cypsela /ˈsɪpsɪlə/ ▸ noun (pl. **cypselae** /-liː/) Botany a dry single-seeded fruit formed from a double ovary of which only one develops into a seed, as in the daisy family.
– ORIGIN late 19th cent.: modern Latin, from Greek *kupselē* 'hollow vessel'.

Cyrano de Bergerac /ˌsɪrənəʊ də ˈbɛːʒərak/, French /siʀanɔ də bɛʀʒəʀak/, Savinien (1619–55), French soldier, duellist, and writer. He is chiefly remembered for the large number of duels that he fought (many on account of his proverbially large nose), as immortalized in a play by Edmond Rostand (*Cyrano de Bergerac*, 1897).

Cyrenaic /ˌsʌɪrɪˈneɪɪk/ ▸ adjective denoting the hedonistic school of philosophy founded c.400 BC by Aristippus the Elder of Cyrene, which holds that pleasure is the highest good and that virtue is to be equated with the ability to enjoy.
▸ noun a follower of the Cyrenaic school of philosophy.
– DERIVATIVES **Cyrenaicism** noun.

Cyrenaica /ˌsʌɪərɪˈneɪɪkə/ a region of NE Libya, bordering on the Mediterranean Sea, settled by the Greeks c.640 BC.

Cyrene /sʌɪˈriːni/ an ancient Greek city in North Africa, near the coast in Cyrenaica. From the 4th century BC it was a great intellectual centre with a noted medical school.

Cyril, St (826–69), Greek missionary. The invention of the Cyrillic alphabet is ascribed to him. Feast day (in the Eastern Church) 11 May; (in the Western Church) 14 February.

Cyrillic /sɪˈrɪlɪk/ ▸ adjective denoting the alphabet used by many Slavic peoples, chiefly those with a historical allegiance to the Orthodox Church. Ultimately derived from Greek uncials, it is now used for Russian, Bulgarian, Serbian, Ukrainian, and some other Slavic languages.
▸ noun [mass noun] the Cyrillic alphabet.
– ORIGIN early 19th cent.: named after St *Cyril* (see CYRIL, ST).

Cyril of Alexandria, St (d.444), Doctor of the Church and patriarch of Alexandria. A champion of orthodoxy, he is best known for his vehement opposition to the views of the patriarch of Constantinople, Nestorius, whose condemnation he secured at the Council of Ephesus in 431. Feast day, 9 February.

Cyrus[1] /ˈsʌɪrəs/ (died c.530 BC), king of Persia 559–530 BC and founder of the Achaemenid dynasty, father of Cambyses; known as **Cyrus the Great**. He defeated the Median empire in 550 BC and went on to conquer Asia Minor, Babylonia, Syria, Palestine, and most of the Iranian plateau.

Cyrus[2] /ˈsʌɪrəs/ (d.401 BC), Persian prince; known as **Cyrus the Younger**. On the death of his father, Darius II, in 405 BC, Cyrus led an army of mercenaries against his elder brother, who had succeeded to the throne as Artaxerxes II. His campaign is recounted by the historian Xenophon.

cyst /sɪst/ ▸ noun 1 Biology a thin-walled hollow organ or cavity in an animal or plant, containing a liquid secretion; a sac, vesicle, or bladder.
2 Medicine a membranous sac or cavity of abnormal character in the body, containing fluid.
3 a tough protective capsule enclosing the larva of a parasitic worm or the resting stage of an organism. Zoology
– ORIGIN early 18th cent.: from late Latin *cystis*, from Greek *kustis* 'bladder'.

cystectomy /sɪsˈtɛktəmi/ ▸ noun (pl. **cystectomies**)
1 a surgical operation to remove the urinary bladder.
2 a surgical operation to remove an abnormal cyst: *an ovarian cystectomy*.

cysteine /ˈsɪstɪiːn, -tɪn, -teɪn, -tiːn/ ▸ noun [mass noun] Biochemistry a sulphur-containing amino acid which occurs in keratins and other proteins, often in the form of cystine, and is a constituent of many enzymes. ● Chem. formula: $HSCH_2CH(NH_2)COOH$.
– ORIGIN late 19th cent.: from CYSTINE + *-eine* (variant of -INE[4]).

cystic ▸ adjective 1 Medicine relating to or characterized by cysts. ■ Zoology (of a parasite or other organism) enclosed in a cyst.
2 relating to the urinary bladder or the gall bladder: *the cystic artery*.
– ORIGIN mid 17th cent. (originally referring to the gall bladder): from French *cystique* or modern Latin *cysticus*, from late Latin *cystis* (see CYST).

cysticercus /ˌsɪstɪˈsəːkəs/ ▸ noun (pl. **cysticerci** /-sʌɪ/) Zoology a larval tapeworm at a stage in which the scolex is inverted in a sac, typically found encysted in the muscle tissue of the host.
– ORIGIN mid 19th cent.: modern Latin (originally the name of a supposed genus), from Greek *kustis* 'bladder' + *kerkos* 'tail'.

cystic fibrosis ▸ noun [mass noun] a hereditary disorder affecting the exocrine glands. It causes the production of abnormally thick mucus, leading to the blockage of the pancreatic ducts, intestines, and bronchi and often resulting in respiratory infection.

cystine /ˈsɪstiːn, -tɪn/ ▸ noun [mass noun] Biochemistry a compound which is an oxidized dimer of cysteine and is the form in which cysteine often occurs in organic tissue. ● Chem. formula: $C_6H_{12}N_2O_4S_2$.
– ORIGIN mid 19th cent.: from Greek *kustis* 'bladder' (because it was first isolated from urinary calculi) + -INE[4].

C

cystitis /sɪˈstʌɪtɪs/ ▸ noun [mass noun] Medicine inflammation of the urinary bladder. It is often caused by infection and is usually accompanied by frequent painful urination.

cysto- /ˈsɪstəʊ/ ▸ combining form relating to the urinary bladder: *cystotomy*.
– ORIGIN from Greek *kustis* 'bladder'.

cystoscope /ˈsɪstəskəʊp/ ▸ noun Medicine an instrument inserted into the urethra for examining the urinary bladder.
– DERIVATIVES **cystoscopic** adjective, **cystoscopy** noun.

cystotomy /sɪˈstɒtəmi/ ▸ noun (pl. **cystotomies**) a surgical incision into the urinary bladder.

-cyte ▸ combining form Biology denoting a mature cell: *lymphocyte*. Compare with -BLAST.
– ORIGIN from Greek *kutos* 'vessel'.

Cytherea /ˌsɪθəˈriːə/ ▸ noun another name for APHRODITE.
– ORIGIN from Latin *Cythera* 'Kithira', the name of an Ionian island.

Cytherean /ˌsɪθəˈriːən/ ▸ adjective Astronomy relating to the planet Venus: *the Cytherean atmosphere*.
■ Mythology relating to the goddess Cytherea.

cytidine /ˈsʌɪtɪdiːn/ ▸ noun [mass noun] Biochemistry a nucleoside composed of cytosine linked to ribose, obtained from RNA by hydrolysis.
– ORIGIN early 20th cent.: from CYTO- + -IDE + -INE[4].

cytisus /sʌɪˈtɪsəs, ˈsɪtɪsəs/ ▸ noun a plant of a large genus of shrubs, mostly native to southern Europe, which includes some brooms. ● Genus *Cytisus*, family Leguminosae.
– ORIGIN modern Latin, from Greek *kutisos*.

cyto- /ˈsʌɪtəʊ/ ▸ combining form Biology of a cell or cells: *cytology* | *cytoplasm*.
– ORIGIN from Greek *kutos* 'vessel'.

cytoarchitectonics /ˌsʌɪtəʊˌɑːkɪtɛkˈtɒnɪks/ ▸ plural noun [treated as sing. or pl.] another term for CYTOARCHITECTURE.

cytoarchitecture /ˌsʌɪtəʊˈɑːkɪtɛktʃə/ ▸ noun [mass noun] Anatomy the arrangement of cells in a tissue, especially in specific areas of the cerebral cortex characterized by the arrangement of their cells and each associated with particular functions. Also called CYTOARCHITECTONICS. ■ the study of cytoarchitecture.
– DERIVATIVES **cytoarchitectural** adjective.

cytocentrifuge /ˌsʌɪtəʊˈsɛntrɪfjuːdʒ/ Biology ▸ noun a centrifuge used for depositing cells suspended in a liquid on a slide for microscopic examination.
▸ verb [with obj.] deposit (cells) on a slide using a cytocentrifuge.

cytochrome ▸ noun [mass noun] Biochemistry any of a number of compounds consisting of haem bonded to a protein. Cytochromes function as electron transfer agents in many metabolic pathways, especially cellular respiration.

cytogenetics /ˌsʌɪtəʊdʒəˈnɛtɪks/ ▸ plural noun [treated as sing.] Biology the study of inheritance in relation to the structure and function of chromosomes.
– DERIVATIVES **cytogenetic** adjective, **cytogenetical** adjective, **cytogenetically** adverb, **cytogeneticist** noun.

cytokine /ˈsʌɪtə(ʊ)kʌɪn/ ▸ noun Physiology any of a number of substances, such as interferon, interleukin, and growth factors, which are secreted by certain cells of the immune system and have an effect on other cells.

cytokinesis /ˌsʌɪtə(ʊ)kʌɪˈniːsɪs/ ▸ noun [mass noun] Biology the cytoplasmic division of a cell at the end of mitosis or meiosis, bringing about the separation into two daughter cells.

cytokinin /ˌsʌɪtəʊˈkʌɪnɪn/ ▸ noun another term for KININ (sense 2).

cytology /sʌɪˈtɒlədʒi/ ▸ noun [mass noun] the branches of biology and medicine concerned with the structure and function of plant and animal cells.
– DERIVATIVES **cytological** adjective, **cytologically** adverb, **cytologist** noun.

C

cytolysis /sʌɪˈtɒlɪsɪs/ ▶ **noun** [mass noun] Biology the dissolution or disruption of cells, especially by an external agent.
– DERIVATIVES **cytolytic** adjective.

cytomegalic /ˌsʌɪtə(ʊ)mɪˈɡalɪk/ ▶ **adjective** Medicine characterized by enlarged cells, especially with reference to a disease caused by a cytomegalovirus.

cytomegalovirus /ˌsʌɪtə(ʊ)ˈmɛɡ(ə)lə(ʊ)ˌvʌɪrəs/ (abbrev.: **CMV**) ▶ **noun** Medicine a kind of herpesvirus which usually produces very mild symptoms in an infected person but may cause severe neurological damage in people with weakened immune systems and in the newborn.

cytophotometry /ˌsʌɪtə(ʊ)fə(ʊ)ˈtɒmɪtri/ ▶ **noun** [mass noun] Biology the investigation of the contents of cells by measuring the light they allow through after staining.
– DERIVATIVES **cytophotometric** adjective.

cytoplasm /ˈsʌɪtə(ʊ)plaz(ə)m/ ▶ **noun** [mass noun] Biology the material or protoplasm within a living cell, excluding the nucleus.
– DERIVATIVES **cytoplasmic** adjective.

cytoplasmic inheritance ▶ **noun** [mass noun] inheritance of traits, usually via the maternal line, controlled by an extrachromosomal element.

cytosine /ˈsʌɪtəsiːn/ ▶ **noun** [mass noun] Biochemistry a compound found in living tissue as a constituent base of DNA. It is paired with guanine in double-stranded DNA. ● A pyrimidine derivative; chem. formula: $C_4H_5N_3O$.

cytoskeleton ▶ **noun** Biology a microscopic network of protein filaments and tubules in the cytoplasm of many living cells, giving them shape and coherence.
– DERIVATIVES **cytoskeletal** adjective.

cytosol /ˈsʌɪtə(ʊ)sɒl/ ▶ **noun** [mass noun] Biology the aqueous component of the cytoplasm of a cell, within which various organelles and particles are suspended.
– DERIVATIVES **cytosolic** adjective.

cytotoxic ▶ **adjective** toxic to living cells.
– DERIVATIVES **cytotoxicity** noun.

czar etc. ▶ **noun** variant spelling of TSAR etc.

czardas ▶ **noun** variant spelling of CSARDAS.

Czech /tʃɛk/ ▶ **noun 1** a native or inhabitant of the Czech Republic or (formerly) Czechoslovakia, or a person of Czech descent.
2 [mass noun] the Western Slavic language spoken in the Czech Republic, closely related to Slovak. It has over 10 million speakers.
▶ **adjective** relating to the Czechs or their language.
– ORIGIN Polish spelling of Czech *Čech*.

Czechoslovakia /ˌtʃɛkə(ʊ)sləˈvakɪə/ a former country in central Europe, now divided between the Czech Republic and Slovakia; capital, Prague.

Czechoslovakia was created out of the northern part of the Austro-Hungarian Empire at the end of the First World War. It was crushed by the Nazi takeover of the Sudetenland in 1938 and the rest of the country in 1939. After the Second World War Czechoslovakia fell under Soviet domination, an attempt at liberalization being crushed by military intervention in 1968, until the 'velvet revolution' of 1989. The two parts separated on 1 January 1993.

– DERIVATIVES **Czechoslovak** /-ˈsləʊvak/ noun & adjective, **Czechoslovakian** adjective & noun.

Czech Republic a country in central Europe; pop. 10,211,900 (est. 2009); official language, Czech; capital, Prague.

Formerly one of the two constituent republics of Czechoslovakia, the Czech Republic became independent on the partition of that country on 1 January 1993. It comprises the former provinces of Bohemia, Silesia, and Moravia.

Czerny /ˈtʃɛːni/, Karl (1791–1857), Austrian pianist, teacher, and composer. The bulk of his output is made up of more than 1,000 exercises and studies for the piano.

Częstochowa /ˌtʃɛnstəˈkəʊvə/ an industrial city in south central Poland; pop. 244,137 (2007). It is famous for its shrine housing a painting of the black Madonna.

D[1] (also **d**) ▶ **noun** (pl. **Ds** or **D's**) **1** the fourth letter of the alphabet. ■ denoting the fourth in a set of items, categories, sizes, etc. ■ the fourth-highest category of academic mark. ■ **(d)** Chess denoting the fourth file from the left, as viewed from White's side of the board. ■ denoting the second lowest earning socio-economic category for marketing purposes, including semi-skilled and unskilled personnel.
2 **(D)** (also **dee**) a shape like that of a capital D: [in combination] *the D-shaped handle*. ■ **(D)** a semicircle marked on a billiard table in the baulk area, with its diameter part of the baulk line, within which a player must place the cue ball when breaking off or restarting from hand.
3 (usu. **D**) Music the second note of the diatonic scale of C major. ■ a key based on a scale with D as its keynote.
4 the Roman numeral for 500. [understood as half of CIↃ, an earlier form of M (= 1,000).]

D[2] ▶ **abbreviation** ■ (in the US) Democrat or Democratic. ■ depth (in the sense of the dimension of an object from front to back). ■ Chemistry dextrorotatory: *D-glucose*. ■ (with a numeral) dimension(s) or dimensional: *a 3-D model*. ■ (in tables of sports results) drawn. ■ (on an automatic gear shift) drive. ■ Germany (international vehicle registration). [from German *Deutschland*.]
▶ **symbol** ■ Physics electric flux density. ■ Chemistry the hydrogen isotope deuterium.

d ▶ **abbreviation** ■ (in genealogies) daughter. ■ day(s). ■ [in combination] (in units of measurement) deci-. ■ (in travel timetables) departs. ■ **(d.)** died (used to indicate a date of death): *Barents, Willem (d.1597)*. ■ Brit. penny or pence (of pre-decimal currency): *£20 10s 6d*. [from Latin *denarius* 'penny'.] ■ Chemistry denoting electrons and orbitals possessing two units of angular momentum: *d-electrons*. [*d* from *diffuse*, originally applied to lines in atomic spectra.]
▶ **symbol** ■ Mathematics diameter. ■ Mathematics denoting a small increment in a given variable: *dy/dx*.

'd ▶ **contraction** had: *they'd already gone*. ■ would: *I'd expect that*.

DA ▶ **abbreviation** ■ US district attorney. ■ informal duck's arse (a man's hairstyle of the 1950s).

da[1] ▶ **determiner** non-standard spelling of **THE**, used in representing informal American speech.

da[2] ▶ **abbreviation** [in combination] (in units of measurement) deca-.

D/A ▶ **abbreviation** Electronics digital to analogue.

DAB ▶ **abbreviation** digital audio broadcasting.

dab[1] ▶ **verb** (**dabs, dabbing, dabbed**) [with obj.] **1** press against (something) lightly several times with a piece of absorbent material in order to clean or dry it or to apply a substance: *he dabbed his mouth with his napkin* | [no obj.] *she* ***dabbed at*** *her eyes with a handkerchief*. ■ apply (a substance) with light quick strokes: *she* ***dabbed*** *disinfectant* ***on*** *the cut*.
2 dialect strike with a light blow.
▶ **noun 1** a small amount of something: *she licked* ***a dab of*** *chocolate from her finger*. ■ a brief application of a piece of absorbent material to a surface: *apply concealer with light dabs*.
2 (**dabs**) Brit. informal fingerprints.
– ORIGIN Middle English: symbolic of a light striking movement; compare with **DABBLE** and **DIB**.

dab[2] ▶ **noun** a small, commercially important flatfish found chiefly in the North Atlantic. ● *Limanda* and other genera, family Pleuronectidae (several species, in particular the European *L. limanda*).
– ORIGIN late Middle English: of unknown origin.

dabber ▶ **noun** a rounded pad used in printing to apply ink to a surface.

dabberlocks /ˈdabəlɒks/ ▶ **noun** variant spelling of **BADDERLOCKS**.

dabble ▶ **verb 1** [with obj.] immerse (one's hands or feet) partially in water and move them around gently: *they dabbled their feet in the rock pools*. ■ [no obj.] (of a duck or other waterbird) move the bill around in shallow water while feeding: *teal dabble in the shallows*.
2 [no obj.] take part in an activity in a casual or superficial way: *he* ***dabbled in*** *left-wing politics*.
– DERIVATIVES **dabbler** noun.
– ORIGIN mid 16th cent.: from obsolete Dutch *dabbelen*, or a frequentative of the verb **DAB**[1].

dabbling duck ▶ **noun** a freshwater duck which typically feeds in shallow water by dabbling and upending, such as the mallard, teal, and pintail. Compare with **DIVING DUCK**. ● Tribe Anatini, family Anatidae: genus *Anas* (numerous species).

dabchick ▶ **noun** a small grebe, especially the little grebe. ● Genera *Tachybaptus* and *Podilymbus*, family Podicipedidae: several species.
– ORIGIN mid 16th cent. (as *dapchick* or *dopchick*): the first element is perhaps related to **DIP** and **DEEP**.

dab hand ▶ **noun** Brit. informal a person who is an expert at a particular activity: *Liam is a dab hand at golf*.
– ORIGIN early 19th cent.: of unknown origin.

DAC ▶ **abbreviation** Electronics digital to analogue converter.

da capo /dɑː ˈkɑːpəʊ/ Music ▶ **adverb** (especially as a direction) repeat from the beginning. Compare with **DAL SEGNO**.
▶ **adjective** [attrib.] including the repetition of a passage at the beginning: *da capo arias*.
– ORIGIN Italian, literally 'from the head'.

Dacca variant spelling of **DHAKA**.

dace /deɪs/ ▶ **noun** (pl. **same**) a small freshwater fish related to the carp, typically living in running water. ● *Leuciscus* and other genera, family Cyprinidae: several species, in particular *L. leuciscus* of northern Eurasia.
– ORIGIN late Middle English: from Old French *dars* (see **DART**).

dacha /ˈdatʃə/ (also **datcha**) ▶ **noun** a country house or cottage in Russia, typically used as a second or holiday home.
– ORIGIN Russian, originally 'grant (of land)'.

Dachau /ˈdakaʊ/, German /ˈdaxaʊ/ a Nazi concentration camp in southern Bavaria, from 1933 to 1945.

dachshund /ˈdakshʊnd, -s(ə)nd/ ▶ **noun** a dog of a very short-legged, long-bodied breed.
– ORIGIN late 19th cent.: from German, literally 'badger dog' (the breed being originally used to dig badgers out of their setts).

Dacia /ˈdeɪʃə, ˈdeɪsɪə/ an ancient country of SE Europe in what is now NW Romania. It was annexed by Trajan in AD 106 as a province of the Roman Empire.
– DERIVATIVES **Dacian** adjective & noun.

dacite /ˈdeɪsʌɪt/ ▶ **noun** [mass noun] Geology a volcanic rock resembling andesite but containing free quartz.
– DERIVATIVES **dacitic** adjective.
– ORIGIN late 18th cent.: from the name of the Roman province of **DACIA** (as it was first found in the Carpathian Mountains) + **-ITE**[1].

dacoit /dəˈkɔɪt/ ▶ **noun** (in India or Burma (Myanmar)) a member of a band of armed robbers.
– ORIGIN from Hindi *ḍakait*, from *ḍakaitī* 'robbery by a gang'.

dacoity /dəˈkɔɪti/ ▶ **noun** (pl. **dacoities**) (in India or Burma (Myanmar)) an act of violent robbery committed by an armed gang.
– ORIGIN from Hindi *ḍakaitī*.

Dacron /ˈdakrɒn/ ▶ **noun** [mass noun] trademark a synthetic polyester (polyethylene terephthalate) with tough, elastic properties, used as a textile fabric.
– ORIGIN 1950s: an invented name.

dactyl /ˈdaktɪl/ ▶ **noun** Prosody a metrical foot consisting of one stressed syllable followed by two unstressed syllables or (in Greek and Latin) one long syllable followed by two short syllables.
– ORIGIN late Middle English: via Latin from Greek *daktulos*, literally 'finger' (the three bones of the finger corresponding to the three syllables).

dactylic Prosody ▶ **adjective** of or using dactyls: *dactylic rhythm*.
▶ **noun** (usu. **dactylics**) dactylic verse.

dactylic hexameter ▶ **noun** Prosody a hexameter consisting of five dactyls and either a spondee or trochee, in which any of the first four dactyls, and sometimes the fifth, may be replaced by a spondee.

dad ▶ **noun** informal one's father.
– ORIGIN mid 16th cent.: perhaps imitative of a young child's first syllables *da, da*.

Dada /ˈdɑːdɑː/ ▶ **noun** an early 20th-century movement in art, literature, music, and film, repudiating and mocking artistic and social conventions and emphasizing the illogical and absurd.

> Dada was launched in Zurich in 1916 by Tristan Tzara and others, soon merging with a similar group in New York. It favoured montage, collage, and the ready-made. Leading figures: Jean Arp, André Breton, Max Ernst, Man Ray, and Marcel Duchamp.

– DERIVATIVES **Dadaism** noun, **Dadaist** noun & adjective, **Dadaistic** adjective.
– ORIGIN French, literally 'hobby horse', the title of a review published in Zurich in 1916.

dada[1] /ˈdadə/ ▶ **noun** informal one's father.
– ORIGIN late 17th cent.: perhaps imitative of a young child's first syllables (see **DAD**).

dada[2] /ˈdɑːdɑː/ ▶ **noun** Indian an older brother or male cousin. ■ a respectful form of address for an older male.
– ORIGIN from Hindi *dādā*.

dadah /ˈdɑːdɑː/ ▶ **noun** [mass noun] (in Malaysia) illegal drugs.
– ORIGIN Malay, 'medicine, drugs'.

Dadd, Richard (1817–86), English painter. After killing his father while suffering a mental breakdown, he was confined in asylums, where he produced a series of visionary paintings.

daddy ▶ **noun** (pl. **daddies**) informal one's father. ■ the oldest, best, or biggest example of something: *the daddy of all potholes*. ■ **(the daddy)** the best or most

D

successful person: *it's you who's calling the shots now—you're the daddy.*
– ORIGIN early 16th cent.: from **DAD** + **-Y²**.

daddy-long-legs ▸ noun (pl. **same**) informal **1** Brit. a crane fly.
2 N. Amer. a harvestman.

daddy's girl ▸ noun informal a girl or woman who is particularly attached to, and indulged by, her father.

dado /ˈdeɪdəʊ/ ▸ noun (pl. **dados**) **1** the lower part of the wall of a room, below about waist height, when decorated differently from the upper part. ■ short for **DADO RAIL**.
2 N. Amer. a groove cut in the face of a board, into which the edge of another board is fixed.
3 Architecture the part of a pedestal between the base and the cornice.
– ORIGIN mid 17th cent. (denoting the main part of a pedestal, above the base): from Italian, literally 'dice or cube', from Latin *datum* 'something given, starting point' (see **DATUM**).

dado rail ▸ noun a decorative waist-high moulding round the wall of a room, which also protects the wall from damage.

Dadra and Nagar Haveli /ˈdɑːdrə, ˌnɑːgə həˈveɪli/ a Union Territory in western India, on the Arabian Sea; pop. 303,200 (est. 2009); capital, Silvassa.

Daedalic /ˈdiːdəlɪk/ ▸ adjective relating to or denoting an ancient Greek (chiefly Dorian) sculptural style of the 7th century BC.
– ORIGIN from the name **DAEDALUS** + **-IC**.

Daedalus /ˈdiːdələs/ Greek Mythology a craftsman, considered the inventor of carpentry, who is said to have built the labyrinth for Minos, king of Crete. Minos imprisoned him and his son Icarus, but they escaped using wings which Daedalus made and fastened with wax. Icarus, however, flew too near the sun and was killed.

daemon¹ /ˈdiːmən/ (also **daimon**) ▸ noun **1** (in ancient Greek belief) a divinity or supernatural being of a nature between gods and humans. ■ an inner or attendant spirit or inspiring force.
2 archaic spelling of **DEMON¹**.
– DERIVATIVES **daemonic** adjective.
– ORIGIN mid 16th cent.: common spelling of **DEMON¹** until the 19th cent.

daemon² /ˈdiːmən/ (also **demon**) ▸ noun Computing a background process that handles requests for services such as print spooling and file transfers, and is dormant when not required.
– ORIGIN 1980s: perhaps from *d(isk) a(nd) e(xecution) mon(itor)* or from *de(vice) mon(itor)*, or a transferred use of **DEMON¹**.

daffodil ▸ noun a bulbous European plant which typically bears bright yellow flowers with a long trumpet-shaped centre (corona). ● Genus *Narcissus*, family Liliaceae (or Amaryllidaceae): several species, in particular the common *Narcissus pseudonarcissus* and its varieties.
– ORIGIN mid 16th cent.: from late Middle English *affodill*, from medieval Latin *affodilus*, variant of Latin *asphodilus* (see **ASPHODEL**). The initial *d-* is unexplained.

daffy ▸ adjective (**daffier**, **daffiest**) informal silly; mildly eccentric: *another one of his daffy dad's catchphrases.*
– DERIVATIVES **daffiness** noun.
– ORIGIN late 19th cent.: from northern English dialect *daff* 'simpleton' + **-Y¹**; perhaps related to **DAFT**.

daft ▸ adjective Brit. informal silly; foolish: *don't ask such daft questions.* ■ (**daft about**) infatuated with: *I was daft about him.*
– DERIVATIVES **daftness** noun.
– ORIGIN Old English *gedæfte* 'mild, meek', of Germanic origin; related to Gothic *gabadan* 'become or be fitting'.

dag ▸ noun **1** (usu. **dags**) Austral./NZ a lock of wool matted with dung hanging from the hindquarters of a sheep.
2 Austral./NZ informal an entertainingly eccentric person; a character.
3 Austral. informal a conservative or unfashionable person. ■ an untidy or dirty-looking person. ■ an awkward adolescent.
▸ verb (**dags**, **dagging**, **dagged**) [with obj.] Austral./NZ cut dags from (a sheep).
– PHRASES **rattle one's dags** Austral./NZ informal hurry up.
– ORIGIN late Middle English (denoting a hanging pointed part of something): possibly related to **TAG¹**. Sense 1 of the noun dates from the early 17th cent.; sense 2 of the noun is a transferred use of English dialect meaning 'a challenge'.

da Gama /də ˈgɑːmə/, Vasco (*c.*1469–1524), Portuguese explorer. He led the first European expedition round the Cape of Good Hope in 1497, sighting and naming Natal on Christmas Day before crossing the Indian Ocean and arriving in Calicut (now Kozhikode) in 1498. He also established colonies in Mozambique.

Dagestan /ˌdagɪˈstɑːn, -ˈstan/ an autonomous republic in SW Russia, on the western shore of the Caspian Sea; pop. 2,707,900 (est. 2009); capital, Makhachkala.
– DERIVATIVES **Dagestani** noun & adjective, **Dagestanian** noun & adjective.

dagga /ˈdaxə/ ▸ noun [mass noun] S. African cannabis.
– ORIGIN late 17th cent.: from Afrikaans, from Khoikhoi *dachab*.

dagger ▸ noun **1** a short knife with a pointed and edged blade, used as a weapon. ■ Printing another term for **OBELUS**.
2 a moth with a dark dagger-shaped marking on the forewing. ● Genus *Acronicta*, family Noctuidae: several species.
– PHRASES **be at daggers drawn** Brit. (of two people) be bitterly hostile towards each other. **look** (or **glare**) **daggers at** glare very angrily at.
– ORIGIN late Middle English: perhaps from obsolete *dag* 'pierce, stab', influenced by Old French *dague* 'long dagger'.

daggerboard ▸ noun a kind of centreboard which slides vertically through the keel of a sailing boat.

daggy ▸ adjective (**daggier**, **daggiest**) informal, chiefly Austral./NZ (especially of clothes) scruffy. ■ not stylish; unfashionable: *a daggy disco track.*

dago /ˈdeɪgəʊ/ ▸ noun (pl. **dagos** or **dagoes**) informal, offensive a Spanish, Portuguese, or Italian-speaking person.
– ORIGIN mid 19th cent.: from the Spanish given name *Diego* (equivalent to *James*).

Dagon /ˈdeɪgɒn/ (in the Bible) a national deity of the ancient Philistines, represented as a fish-tailed man.
– ORIGIN via Latin and Greek from Hebrew *dāgōn*, perhaps from *dāgān* 'corn', but said (according to folk etymology) to be from *dāg* 'fish'.

Daguerre /dəˈgɛː/, French /dagɛʀ/, Louis-Jacques-Mandé (1789–1851), French physicist, painter, and inventor of the first practical photographic process. He went into partnership with **Joseph-Nicéphore Niépce** (1765–1833) to improve the latter's heliography process, and in 1839 he presented his daguerreotype process to the French Academy of Sciences.

daguerreotype /dəˈgɛrətʌɪp/ (also **daguerrotype**) ▸ noun a photograph taken by an early photographic process employing an iodine-sensitized silvered plate and mercury vapour.
– ORIGIN mid 19th cent.: from French *daguerréotype*, named after L.-J.-M. **DAGUERRE**.

Dagwood sandwich (also **Dagwood**) ▸ noun US a thick sandwich with a variety of different fillings.
– ORIGIN 1970s: named after *Dagwood* Bumstead, a comic-strip character who makes and eats this type of sandwich.

dah /dɑː/ ▸ noun (in the Morse system) another term for **DASH**.
– ORIGIN Second World War: imitative.

dahabeeyah /ˌdɑːhəˈbiːjə/ ▸ noun a large passenger boat used on the Nile, typically with lateen sails.
– ORIGIN mid 19th cent.: from Arabic, literally 'golden', denoting the gilded state barge formerly used by the Muslim rulers of Egypt.

dahi /ˈdəhiː/ ▸ noun Indian term for **YOGURT**.
– ORIGIN from Hindi *dahī* 'curds'.

Dahl /dɑːl/, Roald (1916–90), British writer, of Norwegian descent. His fiction and drama, such as the short-story collection *Tales of the Unexpected* (1979), typically include macabre plots and unexpected outcomes. Notable works for children: *Charlie and the Chocolate Factory* (1964), *The BFG* (1982).

dahlia /ˈdeɪlɪə/ ▸ noun a tuberous-rooted Mexican plant of the daisy family, which is cultivated for its brightly coloured single or double flowers. ● Genus *Dahlia*, family Compositae.
– ORIGIN modern Latin, named in honour of Andreas *Dahl* (1751–89), Swedish botanist.

Dahomey /dəˈhəʊmi/ former name (until 1975) for **BENIN**.

dai /dʌɪ/ ▸ noun (pl. **dais**) Indian a midwife or wet nurse.
– ORIGIN from Urdu, from Persian *dāyah*.

daikon /ˈdʌɪk(ə)n, -kɒn/ ▸ noun another term for **MOOLI**.
– ORIGIN Japanese, from *dai* 'large' + *kon* 'root'.

Dáil /dɔɪl/, Irish /daːlʲ/ (in full **Dáil Éireann** /ˈɛːr(ə)n/, Irish /ˈeːrʲən/) the lower house of Parliament in the Republic of Ireland, composed of 166 members (called **Teachtai Dála**). It was first established in 1919, when Irish republicans proclaimed an Irish state.
– ORIGIN Irish, 'assembly (of Ireland)'.

daily ▸ adjective done, produced, or occurring every day or every weekday: *a daily newspaper.* ■ relating to the period of a single day: *boats can be hired for a daily rate.*
▸ adverb every day: *the museum is open daily.*
▸ noun (pl. **dailies**) informal **1** a newspaper published every day except Sunday.
2 (also **daily help**) Brit. dated a woman who is employed to clean someone else's house each day.
3 (**dailies**) the first prints from cinematographic takes; the rushes.
– PHRASES **daily life** the activities and experiences that constitute a person's normal existence: *the routines of my daily life.*
– ORIGIN late Middle English: from **DAY** + **-LY¹**, **-LY²**.

daily double ▸ noun Horse Racing a single bet on the winners of two named races in a day.

daily dozen ▸ noun informal, dated regular exercises, especially those done first thing in the morning.

Daimler /ˈdeɪmlə/, German /ˈdaɪmlɐ/, Gottlieb (1834–1900), German engineer and motor manufacturer. An employee of Nikolaus Otto, he produced a small engine using the Otto cycle in 1884 and made it propel a bicycle using petrol vapour. He founded the Daimler motor company in 1890.

daimon /ˈdʌɪməʊn/ ▸ noun variant spelling of **DAEMON¹**.
– DERIVATIVES **daimonic** /-ˈməʊnɪk, -ˈmɒnɪk/ adjective.

daimyo /ˈdʌɪmɪəʊ, ˈdʌɪmjəʊ/ (also **daimio**) ▸ noun (pl. **same** or **daimyos**) (in feudal Japan) one of the great lords who were vassals of the shogun.
– ORIGIN Japanese, from *dai* 'great' + *myō* 'name'.

dainty ▸ adjective (**daintier**, **daintiest**) **1** delicately small and pretty: *a dainty lace handkerchief | the china cup seemed too dainty in his large hands.* ■ (of a person) delicate and graceful in build or movement. ■ (of food) particularly good to eat and served in a small portion: *a dainty morsel.*
2 fastidious, especially concerning food: *a dainty appetite.*
▸ noun (pl. **dainties**) something good to eat; a delicacy.
– DERIVATIVES **daintily** adverb, **daintiness** noun.
– ORIGIN Middle English (as noun): from Old French *daintie*, *deintie* 'choice morsel, pleasure', from Latin *dignitas* 'worthiness or beauty', from *dignus* 'worthy'.

daiquiri /ˈdʌɪkɪri, ˈdak-/ ▸ noun (pl. **daiquiris**) a cocktail containing rum and lime juice.
– ORIGIN named after *Daiquiri*, a rum-producing district in Cuba.

Dairen /dʌɪˈrɛn/ former name for **DALIAN**.

dairy ▸ noun (pl. **dairies**) **1** a building or room for the processing, storage, and distribution of milk and milk products. ■ a shop where milk and milk products are sold. ■ [mass noun] milk and milk products collectively: *I rely on soya as a substitute for dairy.*
2 (also **corner dairy**) NZ a small grocery shop.
▸ adjective [attrib.] containing or made from milk: *dairy products.* ■ concerned with the production of milk: *a dairy farmer.*
– ORIGIN Middle English *deierie*, from *deie* 'dairymaid' (in Old English *dǣge* 'female servant'), of Germanic origin; related to Old Norse *deigja*, also to **DOUGH** and to the second element of Old English *hlǣfdige* (see **LADY**).

dairying ▸ noun [mass noun] the business of producing, storing, and distributing milk and its products.

dairymaid ▸ noun archaic a woman employed in a dairy.

dairyman ▸ noun (pl. **dairymen**) a man who is employed in a dairy or sells dairy products.

dais /ˈdeɪɪs, deɪs/ ▸ noun a low platform for a lectern or throne.
– ORIGIN Middle English (originally denoting a raised table for distinguished guests): from Old French *deis*, from Latin *discus* 'disc or dish' (later 'table'). Little used after the Middle English period, the word was revived by antiquarians in the early 19th cent. with the disyllabic pronunciation.

daisy ▸ noun (pl. **daisies**) a small European grassland plant which has flowers with a yellow disc and white

rays. ● *Bellis perennis*, family Compositae (or Asteraceae; the **daisy family**). The plants of this large family (known as composites) are distinguished by having composite flower heads consisting of numerous disc florets, ray florets, or both; they include many weeds (dandelions, thistles) and garden flowers (asters, chrysanthemums, dahlias).
■ used in names of other plants of the same family, e.g. **Michaelmas daisy, Shasta daisy**.
– PHRASES **be (as) fresh as a daisy** be healthy and full of energy. **be pushing up (the) daisies** informal be dead and buried.
– ORIGIN Old English *dæges ēage* 'day's eye' (because the flower opens in the morning and closes at night).

daisy bush ▸ noun a shrubby evergreen Australasian plant of the daisy family, which typically has grey-green leaves and bears fragrant flower heads. ● Genus *Olearia*, family Compositae.

daisy chain ▸ noun a string of daisies threaded together by their stems. ■ a series of associated or connected people or things: *a daisy chain of coloured lights*.
▸ verb (**daisy-chain**) [with obj.] Computing connect (several devices) together in a linear series.
– DERIVATIVES **daisy-chainable** adjective.

daisy-cutter ▸ noun informal **1** (in sport) a ball hit or bowled so as to roll along the ground.
2 an immensely powerful aerial thermobaric bomb.

daisy wheel ▸ noun a device used as a printer in some word processors, consisting of a disc of spokes each terminating in a printing character.

dak /dɑːk, dɔːk/ ▸ noun [mass noun] the postal service in the Indian subcontinent, originally delivered by a system of relay runners.
– ORIGIN Hindi *ḍāk*.

Dak. ▸ abbreviation Dakota.

Dakar /ˈdakɑː/ the capital of Senegal, a port on the Atlantic coast of West Africa; pop. 2,604,000 (est. 2007).

dak bungalow ▸ noun a travellers' rest house in the Indian subcontinent, originally on a dak route.

Dakota[1] /dəˈkəʊtə/ a former territory of the US, organized in 1889 into the states of North Dakota and South Dakota.
– DERIVATIVES **Dakotan** noun & adjective.

Dakota[2] /dəˈkəʊtə/ ▸ noun (pl. **same** or **Dakotas**) **1** a member of a North American Indian people of the northern Mississippi valley and the surrounding plains.
2 [mass noun] the Siouan language of the Dakota, spoken by about 15,000 people. Also called **SIOUX**.
▸ adjective relating to the Dakota or their language.
– ORIGIN the name in Dakota, literally 'allies'.

daks ▸ plural noun Austral./NZ informal trousers.
– ORIGIN a proprietary name.

dal[1] /dɑːl/ (also **dhal**) ▸ noun [mass noun] (in Indian cookery) split pulses, in particular lentils. ■ a dish made with these.
– ORIGIN Hindi *dāl*.

dal[2] ▸ abbreviation decalitre(s).

Dalai Lama /ˌdalʌɪ ˈlɑːmə/ ▸ noun the spiritual head of Tibetan Buddhism and, until the establishment of Chinese communist rule, the spiritual and temporal ruler of Tibet.

> Each Dalai Lama is believed to be the reincarnation of the bodhisattva Avalokitesvara, reappearing in a child when the incumbent Dalai Lama dies. The present Dalai Lama, the fourteenth incarnation, escaped to India in 1959 following the Chinese invasion of Tibet and was awarded the Nobel Peace Prize in 1989.

– ORIGIN from Tibetan, literally 'ocean monk', so named because he is regarded as 'the ocean of compassion'.

dalasi /dɑːˈlɑːsiː/ ▸ noun (pl. **same** or **dalasis**) the basic monetary unit of Gambia, equal to 100 butut.
– ORIGIN a local word.

Dalcroze see **JAQUES-DALCROZE**.

dale ▸ noun a valley, especially in northern England.
– ORIGIN Old English *dæl*, of Germanic origin; related to Old Norse *dalr*, Dutch *dal*, and German *Tal*, also to **DELL**.

dalek /ˈdɑːlɛk/ ▸ noun a member of a race of hostile alien machine-organisms which appeared in the BBC television science-fiction series *Doctor Who* from 1963.
– ORIGIN a word invented by the author Terry Nation after a volume of an encyclopedia covering the alphabetical sequence *dal–lek*.

d'Alembert /ˈdaləmbɛː/, French /dalɑ̃bɛʀ/, Jean le Rond (1717–83), French mathematician, physicist, and philosopher. His most famous work was the *Traité de dynamique* (1743), in which he developed his own laws of motion. From 1746 to 1758 he was Diderot's chief collaborator on the *Encyclopédie*.

Dalesman ▸ noun (pl. **Dalesmen**) an inhabitant of the Yorkshire Dales in northern England.

Dales pony ▸ noun Brit. a large stocky pony of a breed which is typically black.

Dalhousie /dalˈhaʊzi/, James Andrew Broun Ramsay, 1st Marquess of (1812–60), British colonial administrator, a progressive Governor General of India 1847–56.

Dalí /ˈdɑːli/, Salvador (1904–89), Spanish painter. A surrealist, he portrayed dream images with almost photographic realism against backgrounds of arid Catalan landscapes. Dalí also collaborated with Buñuel in the production of the film *Un Chien andalou* (1928). Notable works: *The Persistence of Memory* (1931).
– DERIVATIVES **Daliesque** adjective.

Dalian /ˌdɑːlɪˈan/ a port and shipbuilding centre on the Liaodong Peninsula in NE China, now part of the urban complex of Luda. Former name **DAIREN**.

Dalit /ˈdʌlɪt/ ▸ noun (in the traditional Indian caste system) a member of the lowest caste. See also **UNTOUCHABLE, SCHEDULED CASTE**.
– ORIGIN via Hindi from Sanskrit *dalita* 'oppressed'.

Dallas /ˈdaləs/ a city in NE Texas, noted as a centre of the oil industry; pop. 1,279,910 (est. 2008).

dalliance /ˈdalɪəns/ ▸ noun a casual romantic or sexual relationship. ■ a period of brief or casual involvement with something: *Berkeley was my last **dalliance with** the education system*.
– ORIGIN Middle English (in the sense 'conversation'): from **DALLY** + **-ANCE**.

Dall sheep /dɑːl/ (also **Dall's sheep**) ▸ noun a wild North American sheep found in mountainous country from Alaska to British Columbia. Also called **WHITE SHEEP**. ● *Ovis dalli*, family Bovidae.
– ORIGIN early 20th cent.: named after William H. Dall (1845–1927), American naturalist.

dally ▸ verb (**dallies, dallying, dallied**) [no obj.] **1** act or move slowly: *she'd dallied upstairs long enough to put on a little make-up*.
2 (**dally with**) have a casual romantic or sexual liaison with: *he should stop dallying with film stars*. ■ show a casual interest in: *the company was dallying with the idea of opening a new office*.
– ORIGIN Middle English: from Old French *dalier* 'to chat', of unknown origin.

Dalmatia /dalˈmeɪʃə/ an ancient region in what is now SW Croatia, comprising mountains and a narrow coastal plain along the Adriatic, together with offshore islands. It once formed part of the Roman province of Illyricum.

Dalmatian ▸ noun **1** a dog of a large, white short-haired breed with dark spots.
2 a native or inhabitant of Dalmatia.
▸ adjective relating to Dalmatia.
– ORIGIN late 16th cent. (in sense 2 of the noun): the dog is believed to have originated in Dalmatia in the 18th cent.

dalmatic /dalˈmatɪk/ ▸ noun a wide-sleeved long, loose vestment open at the sides, worn by deacons and bishops, and by monarchs at their coronation.
– ORIGIN late Middle English: from Old French *dalmatique* or late Latin *dalmatica*, from *dalmatica* (*vestis*) '(robe) of (white) Dalmatian wool', from *Dalmaticus* 'of Dalmatia'.

Dalradian /dalˈreɪdɪən/ ▸ adjective Geology relating to or denoting a series of late Precambrian metamorphic rocks, occurring in Scotland and Ireland. ■ (as noun **the Dalradian**) the Dalradian series of rocks.
– ORIGIN late 19th cent.: from *Dalrad-*, from **DALRIADA** (by alteration), + **-IAN**.

Dalriada /dalˈrɪədə/ an ancient Gaelic kingdom in northern Ireland whose people (the Scots) established a colony in SW Scotland from about the late 5th century. By the 9th century Irish Dalriada had declined but the people of Scottish Dalriada gradually acquired dominion over the whole of Scotland.

dal segno /dal ˈsɛnjəʊ/ ▸ adverb & adjective Music (especially as a direction) repeat from the point marked by a sign. Compare with **DA CAPO**.
– ORIGIN Italian, 'from the sign'.

Dalton /ˈdɔːlt(ə)n/, John (1766–1844), English chemist, father of modern atomic theory. He defined an atom as the smallest part of a substance that could participate in a chemical reaction and argued that elements are composed of atoms. He stated that elements combine in definite proportion and produced the first table of comparative atomic weights.

dalton /ˈdɔːlt(ə)n/ ▸ noun Chemistry a unit used in expressing the molecular weight of proteins, equivalent to atomic mass unit.
– ORIGIN 1930s: named after John **DALTON**.

daltonism ▸ noun another term for **PROTANOPIA**, a form of colour blindness.
– ORIGIN mid 19th cent.: from the name of John **DALTON** + **-ISM**.

D

Dalton's law ▸ noun Chemistry a law stating that the pressure exerted by a mixture of gases in a fixed volume is equal to the sum of the pressures that would be exerted by each gas alone in the same volume.

dam[1] ▸ abbreviation decametre(s).

dam[2] ▸ noun **1** a barrier constructed to hold back water and raise its level, forming a reservoir used to generate electricity or as a water supply. ■ a barrier of branches in a stream, constructed by a beaver to provide a deep pool and a lodge. ■ chiefly S. African an artificial pond or reservoir where rain or spring water is collected for storage.
2 (also **dental dam**) a rubber sheet used to keep saliva from the teeth during dental operations, or as a prophylactic device during cunnilingus and anilingus.
▸ verb (**dams, damming, dammed**) [with obj.] build a dam across (a river or lake). ■ hold back or obstruct (something): *the closed lock gates **dammed up** the canal*.
– ORIGIN Middle English: from Middle Low German or Middle Dutch; related to Dutch *dam* and German *Damm*, also to Old English *fordemman* 'close up'.

dam[3] ▸ noun the female parent of an animal, especially a domestic mammal.
– ORIGIN late Middle English (denoting a human mother): alteration of **DAME**.

dama gazelle /ˈdɑːmə/ ▸ noun a large long-legged gazelle with a mainly whitish coat, native to the southern and western Sahara (where it is now very rare). Also called **ADDRA GAZELLE**. ● *Gazella dama*, family Bovidae.
– ORIGIN modern Latin *dama* 'fallow deer' (the specific epithet of its Latin name).

damage ▸ noun **1** [mass noun] physical harm that impairs the value, usefulness, or normal function of something. ■ detrimental effects: *the **damage to** his reputation was considerable*.
2 (**damages**) a sum of money claimed or awarded in compensation for a loss or an injury: *she was awarded $284,000 in damages*.
▸ verb [with obj.] inflict physical harm on (something) so as to impair its value, usefulness, or normal function: *the car was badly damaged in the accident*. ■ have a detrimental effect on: *the scandal could seriously damage his career*.
– PHRASES **the damage is done** used to indicate that it is too late to prevent the occurrence of something unfortunate or undesirable. **what's the damage?** informal, humorous used to ask the cost of something.
– ORIGIN Middle English: from Old French, from *dam*, *damne* 'loss or damage', from Latin *damnum* 'loss or hurt'; compare with **DAMN**.

damage control ▸ noun chiefly N. Amer. another term for **DAMAGE LIMITATION**.

damaged goods ▸ plural noun informal a person who is regarded as inadequate or impaired in some way.

damage feasant /ˈfiːz(ə)nt/ English Law ▸ noun [mass noun] damage done on one person's land by another person's trespassing animal, which justifies the landowner in retaining the animal until compensated.
▸ adverb on grounds of damage caused to land or property.
– ORIGIN late 16th cent.: from Old French *damage fesant* 'doing damage'.

damage limitation ▸ noun [mass noun] action taken to limit the damaging effects of an accident or error.

damaging ▸ adjective causing physical damage: *new cars are less **damaging to** the environment*. ■ having a detrimental effect on someone or something: *damaging allegations of corruption*.
– DERIVATIVES **damagingly** adverb.

Daman and Diu /dəˈmɑːn, ˈdiːuː/ a Union Territory in India, on the west coast north of Mumbai (Bombay); pop. 217,500 (est. 2009); capital, Daman. It consists of the district of Daman and the island of Diu, and until 1987 was administered with Goa.

damar /ˈdamə/ ▸ **noun & adjective** variant spelling of **DAMMAR**.

Damara /dəˈmɑːrə/ ▸ **noun** (pl. **same** or **Damaras**) a member of a people inhabiting mountainous parts of Namibia and speaking the Nama language.
▸ **adjective** relating to the Damara.
– ORIGIN the name in Nama.

Damaraland /dəˈmɑːrəland/ a plateau region of central Namibia inhabited chiefly by the Damara and Herero peoples.

D

Damascene /ˈdaməsiːn, ˌdaməˈsiːn/ ▸ **adjective** **1** relating to the city of Damascus. ■ relating to or resembling the conversion of St Paul on the road to Damascus: *a transformation of Damascene proportions*.
2 historical relating to Damascus steel or its manufacture.
3 (often **damascene**) relating to or denoting a process of inlaying a metal object with gold or silver decoration.
▸ **noun** a native or inhabitant of Damascus.
– ORIGIN late Middle English (as a noun): via Latin from Greek *Damaskēnos* 'of Damascus'.

damascened /ˈdaməsiːnd, ˌdaməˈsiːnd/ ▸ **adjective** **1** (of iron or steel) given a wavy pattern by hammer-welding and repeated heating and forging.
2 (of a metal object) inlaid with gold or silver decoration.

Damascus /dəˈmɑːskəs, -ˈmaskəs/ the capital of Syria since the country's independence in 1946; pop. 1,614,300 (est. 2009). It has existed as a city for over 4,000 years.

Damascus steel ▸ **noun** [mass noun] historical steel given a wavy pattern by hammer-welding strips of steel and iron followed by repeated heating and forging, used chiefly for knife and sword blades. Such items were often marketed in Damascus during the medieval period.

damask /ˈdaməsk/ ▸ **noun** **1** [mass noun] a rich, heavy silk or linen fabric with a pattern woven into it, used for table linen and upholstery.
2 short for **DAMASK ROSE**.
3 (also **damask steel**) [mass noun] historical another term for **DAMASCUS STEEL**.
▸ **adjective** literary having the velvety pink or light red colour of a damask rose.
▸ **verb** [with obj.] literary decorate with or as if with a variegated pattern: *flowers damask the fragrant seat*.
– ORIGIN late Middle English: from *Damaske*, early form of the name of *Damascus*, where the fabric was first produced.

damask rose ▸ **noun** a sweet-scented rose of an old variety, having pink or light red velvety petals which are used to make attar. ● *Rosa damascena*, family Rosaceae.

dame ▸ **noun** **1** (**Dame**) (in the UK) the title given to a woman with the rank of Knight Commander or holder of the Grand Cross in the Orders of Chivalry.
2 archaic or humorous an elderly or mature woman. ■ N. Amer. informal a woman. ■ (also **pantomime dame**) Brit. a comic middle-aged female character in modern pantomime, usually played by a man.
– ORIGIN Middle English (denoting a female ruler): via Old French from Latin *domina* 'mistress'.

dame school ▸ **noun** historical a small primary school run by elderly women, especially in their own homes.

damfool informal, dated ▸ **adjective** [attrib.] thoroughly foolish.
▸ **noun** a foolish person.

damiana /ˌdeɪmɪˈɑːnə/ ▸ **noun** a small shrub native to tropical America, whose leaves are used in herbal medicine and in the production of a liqueur, and also reputedly possess aphrodisiac qualities. ● *Turnera diffusa*, family Turneraceae.
– ORIGIN American Spanish.

Damietta /ˌdamɪˈɛtə/ the eastern branch of the Nile delta. Arabic name **DUMYAT**. ■ a port at the mouth of the Damietta; pop. 206,700 (est. 2006).

dammar /ˈdamə/ (also **damar**) ▸ **noun** [mass noun] resin obtained from any of a number of tropical, chiefly Indo-Malaysian trees, used to make varnish. ● The resin is obtained from trees in the families Araucariaceae (genus *Agathis*), Dipterocarpaceae (genera *Hopea*, *Shorea*, and *Vatica*), and Burseraceae (genus *Canarium*).
– ORIGIN late 17th cent.: from Malay *damar* 'resin'.

dammit ▸ **exclamation** informal used to express anger or frustration.
– PHRASES **as near as dammit** as close to being accurate as makes no difference.
– ORIGIN mid 19th cent.: alteration of *damn it*.

damn /dam/ ▸ **verb** [with obj.] **1** (**be damned**) (in Christian belief) be condemned by God to suffer eternal punishment in hell. ■ be doomed to misfortune or failure: *the enterprise was damned*.
2 criticize strongly: *the book damns her husband*. ■ curse (someone or something): *she cleared her throat, damning it for its huskiness | damn him for making this sound trivial*.
▸ **exclamation** informal expressing anger or frustration: *Damn! I completely forgot!*
▸ **adjective** [attrib.] informal used for emphasis, especially to express anger or frustration: *turn that damn thing off! |* [as submodifier] *don't be so damn silly!*
– PHRASES **as near as damn it** as close to being accurate as makes no difference. —— **be damned** used to express defiance or rejection of someone or something previously mentioned: *glory be damned!* **damn all** Brit. informal nothing at all. **damn someone/thing with faint praise** praise someone or something so unenthusiastically as to imply condemnation. **I'm** (or **I'll be**) **damned if** informal used to express a strong negative: *I'm damned if I know*. **not be worth a damn** informal have no value at all. **not give a damn** see **GIVE**. **well I'll be** (or **I'm**) **damned** informal used to express surprise.
– ORIGIN Middle English: from Old French *dam(p)ner*, from Latin *dam(p)nare* 'inflict loss on', from *damnum* 'loss, damage'.

damna /ˈdamnə/ plural form of **DAMNUM**.

damnable /ˈdamnəb(ə)l/ ▸ **adjective** **1** very bad or unpleasant: *leave this damnable place behind*.
2 subject to or worthy of divine condemnation: *suicide was thought damnable in the Middle Ages*.
– DERIVATIVES **damnably** adverb.
– ORIGIN Middle English (in sense 2): from Old French *dam(p)nable*, from Latin *dam(p)nabilis*, from *dam(p)nare* 'inflict loss on' (see **DAMN**).

damnation /damˈneɪʃ(ə)n/ ▸ **noun** [mass noun] condemnation to eternal punishment in hell.
▸ **exclamation** expressing anger or frustration.
– ORIGIN Middle English: via Old French from Latin *dam(p)natio(n-)*, from the verb *dam(p)nare* 'inflict loss on' (see **DAMN**).

damnatory /ˈdamnəˌt(ə)ri/ ▸ **adjective** conveying or causing censure or damnation.
– ORIGIN late 17th cent.: from Latin *damnatorius*, from *dam(p)nat-* 'caused to suffer loss', from the verb *dam(p)nare* (see **DAMN**).

damned /damd/ ▸ **adjective** **1** (in Christian belief) condemned by God to suffer eternal punishment in hell: *damned sinners |* (as plural noun **the damned**) *the spirits of the damned*.
2 [attrib.] informal used for emphasis, especially to express anger or frustration: *it's none of your damned business |* [as submodifier] *she's too damned arrogant*. ■ (**damnedest**) N. Amer. used to emphasize the surprising nature of something: *the damnedest thing I ever saw*.
– PHRASES **do** (or **try**) **one's damnedest** informal do or try one's utmost.

damnify /ˈdamnɪfʌɪ/ ▸ **verb** (**damnifies, damnifying, damnified**) [with obj.] English Law, rare cause injury to.
– DERIVATIVES **damnification** noun.
– ORIGIN early 16th cent.: from Old French *damnefier*, *dam(p)nifier*, from late Latin *damnificare* 'injure, condemn', from Latin *damnificus* 'hurtful', from *damnus* 'loss, damage'.

damning ▸ **adjective** (of a circumstance or piece of evidence) strongly suggesting guilt or error. ■ extremely critical: *a damning indictment of the government's record*.
– DERIVATIVES **damningly** adverb.

damnum /ˈdamnəm/ ▸ **noun** (pl. **damna** /-nə/) Law a loss.
– ORIGIN Latin, 'hurt, harm, or damage'.

Damocles /ˈdaməkliːz/ a legendary courtier who extravagantly praised the happiness of Dionysius I, ruler of Syracuse. To show him how precarious this happiness was, Dionysius seated him at a banquet with a sword hung by a single hair over his head.
– PHRASES **sword of Damocles** used to refer to an extremely precarious situation.
– DERIVATIVES **Damoclean** adjective.

Damon /ˈdeɪmən/ a legendary Syracusan of the 4th century BC whose friend Pythias (also called Phintias) was sentenced to death by Dionysius I. Damon stood bail for Pythias, who returned just in time to save him, and was himself reprieved.

damp ▸ **adjective** slightly wet: *her hair was still damp from the shower*.
▸ **noun** **1** [mass noun] moisture diffused through the air or a solid substance or condensed on a surface, typically with detrimental or unpleasant effects. ■ short for **FIREDAMP**. ■ (**damps**) archaic damp air or atmosphere.
2 archaic a discouragement or check: *shame gave a damp to her triumph*.
▸ **verb** [with obj.] **1** make (something) slightly wet: *damp a small area with water*.
2 (**damp something down**) make a fire burn less strongly by reducing the flow of air to it. ■ control or restrain a feeling or a situation: *she tried to damp down her feelings of despair*.
3 reduce or stop the vibration of (the strings of a piano or other musical instrument) so as to reduce the volume of sound. ■ Physics progressively reduce the amplitude of (an oscillation or vibration).
– DERIVATIVES **dampish** adjective, **damply** adverb.
– ORIGIN Middle English (in the noun sense 'noxious inhalation'): of West Germanic origin; related to a Middle Low German word meaning 'vapour, steam, smoke'.

damp course (also **damp-proof course**) ▸ **noun** Brit. a layer of waterproof material in the wall of a building near the ground, to prevent rising damp.

damp-dry ▸ **verb** [with obj.] dry (something wet) until it is only damp.

dampen ▸ **verb** [with obj.] **1** make slightly wet: *the fine rain dampened her face*.
2 make less strong or intense: *nothing could dampen her enthusiasm*. ■ reduce the amplitude of (a sound source): *slider switches on the mixers can dampen the drums*.

dampener ▸ **noun** a thing that has a restraining or subduing effect: *television and booze, those twin dampeners of the revolutionary spirit*.
– PHRASES **put a dampener on** another way of saying **PUT A DAMPER ON** (see **DAMPER**).

damper ▸ **noun** **1** a person or thing that has a subduing or inhibiting effect. ■ Music a pad silencing a piano string except when removed by means of a pedal or by the note being struck. ■ a device for reducing mechanical vibration, in particular a shock absorber on a motor vehicle. ■ a conductor used to reduce oscillation in an electric motor or generator. ■ a movable metal plate in a flue or chimney, used to regulate the draught and so control the rate of combustion.
2 chiefly Austral./NZ an unleavened loaf or cake of flour and water baked in wood ashes. [in the sense 'something that takes the edge off the appetite'.]
– PHRASES **put a damper on** have a subduing or inhibiting effect on: *he put a damper on her youthful excitement*.

Dampier /ˈdampɪə/, William (1652–1715), English explorer and adventurer. He is notable for having sailed round the world twice. In 1683 he set out from Panama, crossing the Pacific and reaching England again in 1691; in 1699 the government commissioned him to explore the NW coast of Australia.

damping ▸ **noun** [mass noun] **1** technical a reduction in the amplitude of an oscillation as a result of energy being drained from the system to overcome frictional or other resistive forces. ■ a method of bringing about a reduction in oscillatory peaks in an electric current or voltage using an energy-absorbing or resistance circuit.
2 (**damping off**) the death of young seedlings as a result of a fungal infection encouraged by damp conditions. ● The disease is caused by fungi of the genera *Pythium* (subdivision Mastigomycotina) or *Fusarium* (subdivision Deuteromycotina).

dampness ▸ **noun** [mass noun] the state or condition of being slightly wet: *the dampness in the air*.

damp-proof ▸ **adjective** impervious to damp.
▸ **verb** [with obj.] make impervious to damp by using a damp course.

damp squib ▸ **noun** Brit. a situation or event which is much less impressive than expected.

damsel /ˈdamz(ə)l/ ▸ **noun** archaic or literary a young unmarried woman.
– PHRASES **damsel in distress** humorous a young woman in trouble.
– ORIGIN Middle English: from Old French *dameisele*, *damisele*, based on Latin *domina* 'mistress'.

damsel bug ▸ **noun** a slender long-legged bug that is a predator of other insects. ● Family Nabidae, suborder Heteroptera: several genera.

damselfish ▸ **noun** (pl. **same** or **damselfishes**) a small brightly coloured tropical marine fish that lives in or near coral reefs. ● *Chromis* and other genera, family Pomacentridae: numerous species.

damselfly ▸ noun (pl. **damselflies**) a slender insect related to the dragonflies, typically resting with the wings folded back along the body. ● Suborder Zygoptera, order Odonata: several families.

damson /ˈdamz(ə)n/ ▸ noun **1** a small purple-black plum-like fruit. ■ [mass noun] a dark purple colour.
2 (also **damson tree**) the small deciduous tree which bears damsons, probably derived from the bullace. ● *Prunus domestica* subsp. *insititia* (or *P. damascena*), family Rosaceae.
– ORIGIN late Middle English *damascene*, from Latin *damascenum (prunum)* '(plum) of Damascus'. Compare with DAMASCENE and DAMASK.

damson cheese ▸ noun [mass noun] a solid preserve made from damsons and sugar.

Dan (in the Bible) a Hebrew patriarch, son of Jacob and Bilhah (Gen. 30:6). ■ the tribe of Israel traditionally descended from Dan. ■ an ancient town in the north of Canaan, where the tribe of Dan settled. It marked the northern limit of the ancient Hebrew kingdom of Israel (Judges 20).

dan[1] ▸ noun any of ten degrees of advanced proficiency in judo or karate. ■ a person who has achieved a dan.
– ORIGIN 1940s: from Japanese.

dan[2] (also **dan buoy**) ▸ noun a small temporary marker buoy with a lightweight flagpole.
– ORIGIN late 17th cent.: of unknown origin.

Dan. ▸ abbreviation Daniel (in biblical references).

Dana[1] /ˈdeɪnə/, James Dwight (1813–95), American naturalist, geologist, and mineralogist. He founded an important classification of minerals based on chemistry and physics. His view of the earth as a unit was an evolutionary one, but he was slow to accept Darwin's theory of evolution.

Dana[2] /ˈdeɪnə/, Richard Henry (1815–82), American adventurer, lawyer, and writer, known for his account of his voyage from Boston round Cape Horn to California, *Two Years before the Mast* (1840).

Danae /ˈdaneɪiː/ Greek Mythology the daughter of Acrisius, king of Argos. An oracle foretold that she would bear a son who would kill her father. Attempting to evade this Acrisius imprisoned her, but Zeus visited her in the form of a shower of gold and she conceived Perseus, who killed Acrisius by accident.

danaid /ˈdaneɪɪd/ ▸ noun Entomology a large strikingly marked butterfly of a group that includes the monarch (milkweed) and plain tiger, found chiefly in the tropics of Africa and East Asia. ● Subfamily Danainae, family Nymphalidae (formerly family Danaidae).
– ORIGIN late 19th cent.: from modern Latin *Danaidae*, arbitrary use of the Latin name of the daughters of Danaus.

Danaids /ˈdaneɪɪdz/ Greek Mythology the daughters of Danaus, king of Argos, who were compelled to marry the sons of his brother Aegyptus but murdered their husbands on the wedding night, except for one, Hypermnestra, who helped her husband to escape. The remaining Danaids were punished in Hades by being set to fill a leaky jar with water.

Danakil /ˈdanəkɪl, dəˈnɑːk(ə)l/ ▸ noun & adjective another term for AFAR.
– ORIGIN from Arabic *danāqil*, plural of *danqalī*.

Danakil Depression a long low-lying desert region of NE Ethiopia and northern Djibouti, between the Red Sea and the Great Rift Valley.

Da Nang /dɑː ˈnaŋ/ a port and city in central Vietnam, on the South China Sea; pop. 770,500 (est. 2009). During the Vietnam War it was used as a US military base. Former name TOURANE.

dance ▸ verb [no obj.] **1** move rhythmically to music, typically following a set sequence of steps: *all the men wanted her to dance with them*. ■ [with obj.] perform (a particular dance or a role in a ballet): *they danced a tango*. ■ [with obj. and adverbial of direction] lead (a dancing partner) in a particular direction: *I danced her out of the room*.
2 [with adverbial of direction] (of a person) move in a quick and lively way: *Sheila danced in gaily*. ■ move up and down lightly and quickly in the air: *midges danced over the stream*. ■ (of someone's eyes) sparkle with pleasure or excitement.
▸ noun a series of steps and movements that match the speed and rhythm of a piece of music. ■ an act of dancing: *they rolled back the carpet and had a dance*. ■ a particular sequence of steps and movements constituting a particular form of dancing. ■ [mass noun] steps and movements of this type considered as an activity or art form: *the rules of classical dance*. ■ a social gathering at which people dance. ■ a piece of music for dancing to: *the last dance had been played*. ■ (also **dance music**) [mass noun] a type of popular music intended for dancing to in clubs, typically having a repetitive beat and a synthesized backing track that features sound samples.
– PHRASES **dance attendance on** chiefly Brit. do one's utmost to please someone by attending to all their requests. **dance to someone's tune** comply completely with someone's demands. **lead someone a dance** (or **a merry dance**) Brit. cause someone a great deal of trouble or worry.
– DERIVATIVES **danceable** adjective, **dancey** adjective.
– ORIGIN Middle English: from Old French *dancer* (verb), *dance* (noun), of unknown origin.

dance band ▸ noun a band that plays music suitable for dancing to, especially swing.

dance card ▸ noun dated a card bearing the names of a woman's prospective partners at a formal dance.

dance floor ▸ noun an area of uncarpeted floor in a nightclub, disco, or restaurant reserved for dancing. ■ [as modifier] denoting a type of music particularly popular as an accompaniment to dancing.

dance hall ▸ noun **1** a large public hall or building where people pay to enter and dance.
2 (**dancehall**) [mass noun] an uptempo style of dance music derived from reggae, in which a DJ improvises lyrics over a recorded backing track or to the accompaniment of live musicians.

dance of death ▸ noun a medieval allegorical representation in which a personified Death leads all types of people to the grave, intended to emphasize the equality of all before death.

dancer ▸ noun a person who dances or whose profession is dancing.

dancercise (also **dancercize**) ▸ noun [mass noun] a system of aerobic exercise using dance movements.
– ORIGIN 1960s: blend of DANCE and EXERCISE.

dancetté /ˈdɑːnsəteɪ/ (also **dancetty**) ▸ adjective [usu. postpositive] Heraldry having deep zigzag indentations.
– ORIGIN early 17th cent.: alteration of French *denché*, based on Latin *dens*, *dent-* 'tooth'.

dancing ▸ noun [mass noun] the activity of dancing for pleasure or in order to entertain others.

dancing dervish ▸ noun see DERVISH.

dancing girl ▸ noun a female professional dancer, especially a member of the chorus in a musical.

danda /ˈdʌndə/ ▸ noun (in South Asia) a large stick used as a weapon by a policeman or guard.
– ORIGIN from Hindi *ḍaṇḍā*, from Sanskrit *daṇḍa*.

D and C ▸ abbreviation dilatation and curettage.

dandelion ▸ noun a widely distributed weed of the daisy family, with a rosette of leaves and large bright yellow flowers followed by globular heads of seeds with downy tufts. ● Genus *Taraxacum*, family Compositae: several species, in particular *T. officinale*, which has edible leaves.
– ORIGIN late Middle English: from French *dent-de-lion*, translation of medieval Latin *dens leonis* 'lion's tooth' (because of the jagged shape of the leaves).

dandelion clock ▸ noun Brit. the downy spherical seed head of a dandelion.
– ORIGIN from the child's game of blowing away the seeds to find out what time it is.

dandelion coffee ▸ noun [mass noun] a hot drink made from dried and powdered dandelion roots.

dandelion greens ▸ plural noun N. Amer. fresh dandelion leaves used as a salad vegetable or herb.

dander[1] ▸ noun (in phrase **get/have one's dander up**) informal lose one's temper.
– ORIGIN mid 19th cent. (originally US): of unknown origin.

dander[2] ▸ noun [mass noun] flakes of skin in an animal's fur or hair.
– ORIGIN late 18th cent.: related to DANDRUFF.

dander[3] chiefly Scottish ▸ noun a stroll.
▸ verb [no obj., with adverbial of direction] stroll: *he dandered in to change his coat*.
– ORIGIN late 16th cent.: frequentative form; perhaps related to dialect *dadder* 'quake' and *daddle* 'dawdle'.

dandiacal /danˈdʌɪək(ə)l/ ▸ adjective relating to or characteristic of a dandy.

Dandie Dinmont /ˌdandɪ ˈdɪnmɒnt/ ▸ noun a terrier of a breed from the Scottish Borders, with short legs, a long body, and a rough coat.
– ORIGIN early 19th cent.: named after a character in Sir Walter Scott's *Guy Mannering* who owned a special breed of terriers.

dandified ▸ adjective (of a man) showing excessive concern about his clothes or appearance. ■ self-consciously sophisticated or elaborate: *he writes a dandified prose*.

dandiprat ▸ noun archaic, informal a young or insignificant person.
– ORIGIN early 16th cent. (denoting a coin worth three halfpence): of unknown origin.

dandiya raas /ˈdandɪə rɑːs/ ▸ noun [mass noun] a type of traditional Gujarati dance in which pairs of dancers hold a short stick in each hand and strike one another's sticks in time to the music.
– ORIGIN Gujarati, from *dandiya* 'sticks' (from *daṇḍi* 'stick') and *raas* 'dance'.

dandle ▸ verb [with obj.] move (a baby or young child) up and down in a playful or affectionate way. ■ move (something) lightly up and down: *dandling the halter rope, he gently urged the pony's head up*.
– ORIGIN mid 16th cent.: of unknown origin.

Dandong /danˈdʊŋ/ a port in Liaoning province, NE China, near the mouth of the Yalu River, on the border with North Korea; pop. 597,900 (est. 2006). Former name ANTUNG.

dandruff ▸ noun [mass noun] small pieces of dead skin in a person's hair.
– DERIVATIVES **dandruffy** adjective.
– ORIGIN mid 16th cent.: the first element is unknown; the second (*-ruff*) is perhaps related to Middle English *rove* 'quality of being scurfy'.

dandy ▸ noun (pl. **dandies**) **1** a man unduly concerned with looking stylish and fashionable.
2 informal, dated an excellent thing of its kind.
▸ adjective (**dandier**, **dandiest**) **1** N. Amer. informal excellent: *things are all fine and dandy*.
2 relating to or characteristic of a dandy.
– DERIVATIVES **dandyish** adjective, **dandyism** noun.
– ORIGIN late 18th cent.: perhaps a shortened form of 17th-cent. *Jack-a-dandy* 'conceited fellow' (the last element representing *Dandy*, a pet form of the given name *Andrew*).

dandy brush ▸ noun a coarse brush used for grooming a horse.

Dane ▸ noun a native or inhabitant of Denmark, or a person of Danish descent. ■ historical one of the Viking invaders of the British Isles in the 9th–11th centuries.
– ORIGIN Old English *Dene*; superseded in Middle English by forms influenced by Old Norse *Danir* and late Latin *Dani* (both plural).

Danegeld /ˈdeɪngɛld/ ▸ noun [mass noun] historical a land tax levied in Anglo-Saxon England during the reign of King Ethelred to raise funds for protection against Danish invaders. ■ taxes collected for national defence by the Norman kings until 1162.
– ORIGIN late Old English, from Old Norse *Danir* 'Danes' + *gjald* 'payment'.

Danelaw /ˈdeɪnlɔː/ the part of northern and eastern England occupied or administered by Danes from the late 9th century until after the Norman Conquest.
– ORIGIN late Old English *Dena lagu* 'Danes' law'.

danewort /ˈdeɪnwəːt/ ▸ noun a dwarf Eurasian elder with a strong, unpleasant smell and berries yielding a blue dye. ● *Sambucus ebulus*, family Caprifoliaceae.
– ORIGIN early 16th cent.: so named from the folklore that the plant sprang up where Danish blood was spilt in battle.

Danforth anchor /ˈdanfəθ/ ▸ noun a type of lightweight anchor with flat flukes.

dang ▸ adjective, exclamation, & verb N. Amer. informal euphemism for DAMN: [as adj.] *just get the dang car started!*

danger ▸ noun [mass noun] the possibility of suffering harm or injury: *his life was **in danger***. ■ [count noun] a cause or likely cause of harm or injury: *the dangers of smoking*. ■ the possibility of something unwelcome or unpleasant happening: *she was **in danger of** being exploited | there was no danger of the champagne running out*. ■ Brit. the status of a railway signal indicating that the line is not clear and that a train should not proceed.
– PHRASES **out of danger** (of a person who has suffered a serious injury or illness) not expected to die.
– ORIGIN Middle English (in the sense 'jurisdiction or power', specifically 'power to harm'): from Old French *dangier*, based on Latin *dominus* 'lord'.

D

danger list ▶ noun Brit. a list of those who are dangerously ill in hospital: *he is now **off the danger list** | the 28-year-old is still **on the danger list**.*

danger money (N. Amer. **danger pay**) ▶ noun [mass noun] extra payment for working under dangerous conditions.

dangerous ▶ adjective able or likely to cause harm or injury: *a dangerous animal | insecticides which are dangerous to the environment.* ■ likely to cause problems or to have adverse consequences: *it is dangerous to convict on his evidence.*
– DERIVATIVES **dangerously** adverb, **dangerousness** noun.
– ORIGIN Middle English (in the senses 'arrogant', 'fastidious', and 'difficult to please'): from Old French *dangereus*, from *dangier* (see DANGER).

dangle ▶ verb [no obj., with adverbial of place] hang or swing loosely: *saucepans dangled from a rail* | [with obj.] *they were dangling their legs over the water.* ■ [with obj.] offer (an enticing incentive) to someone: *the defence portfolio could be the carrot to **dangle before** him.*
– PHRASES **keep someone dangling** keep someone in an uncertain position.
– DERIVATIVES **dangler** noun, **dangly** adjective.
– ORIGIN late 16th cent.: symbolic of something loose and pendulous, corresponding to Danish *dangle*, Swedish *dangla*, but the origin is unclear.

dangling ▶ adjective hanging or swinging loosely: *a pair of dangling earrings.*

dangling participle ▶ noun Grammar a participle intended to modify a noun which is not actually present in the text.

> **USAGE** A **participle** is a word formed as an inflection of the verb, such as *arriving* or *arrived*. A **dangling participle** is one which is left 'hanging' because, in the grammar of the clause, it does not relate to the noun it should. In the sentence ***arriving** at the station, **she** picked up her case* the construction is correct because the participle **arriving** and the subject **she** relate to each other (**she** is the one doing the **arriving**). But in the following sentence, a **dangling participle** has been created: ***arriving** at the station, **the sun** came out*. We know, logically, that it is not **the sun** which is **arriving** but grammatically that is exactly the link which has been created. Such errors are frequent, even in written English, and can give rise to genuine confusion.

Daniel a Hebrew prophet (6th century BC), who spent his life as a captive at the court of Babylon. In the Bible he interpreted the dreams of Nebuchadnezzar and was delivered by God from the lions' den into which he had been thrown as the result of a trick; in the apocryphal Book of Susanna he is portrayed as a wise judge (Sus. 45–64). ■ a book of the Bible containing Daniel's prophecies. It was probably written at the outbreak of persecution of the Jews under Seleucid rule *c.*167 BC.

Daniell cell /ˈdanj(ə)l/ ▶ noun a primary voltaic cell with a copper anode and a zinc-amalgam cathode, giving a standard electromotive force when either copper sulphate or sulphuric acid is used as the electrolyte.
– ORIGIN mid 19th cent.: named after John *Daniell* (1790–1845), the British physicist who invented it.

danio /ˈdanɪəʊ/ ▶ noun (pl. **danios**) a small, brightly coloured freshwater fish of South and SE Asia.
● Genera *Danio* and *Brachydanio*, family Cyprinidae: several species.
– ORIGIN modern Latin (genus name).

Danish /ˈdeɪnɪʃ/ ▶ adjective relating to Denmark or its people or language.
▶ noun **1** [mass noun] the Scandinavian language spoken in Denmark, which is also the official language of Greenland and the Faroes. It is spoken by over 5 million people.
2 (as plural noun **the Danish**) the people of Denmark.
3 informal a Danish pastry.
– ORIGIN Old English *Denisc*, of Germanic origin; superseded in Middle English by forms influenced by Old French *daneis* and medieval Latin *Danensis* (from late Latin *Dani* 'Danes').

Danish blue ▶ noun [mass noun] a soft, salty, strongly flavoured white cheese with blue veins.

Danish oil ▶ noun [mass noun] a mixture of tung oil, other vegetable oils, and chemicals to quicken drying, used to treat wood.

Danish pastry ▶ noun a cake of sweetened yeast pastry with toppings or fillings such as icing, fruit, or nuts.

dank ▶ adjective unpleasantly damp and cold: *huge dank caverns.*
– DERIVATIVES **dankly** adverb, **dankness** noun.
– ORIGIN Middle English: probably of Scandinavian origin and related to Swedish *dank* 'marshy spot'.

Danmark /ˈdanmarg/ Danish name for DENMARK.

d'Annunzio /daˈnʊntsɪəʊ/, Gabriele (1863–1938), Italian novelist, dramatist, and poet. He is best known for his 'Romances of the Rose' trilogy, including *The Triumph of Death* (1894), which shows the influence of Nietzsche.

Dano-Norwegian /ˌdeɪnəʊnɔːˈwiːdʒ(ə)n/ ▶ noun another term for BOKMÅL.

danse macabre /ˌdɑːns məˈkɑːbr(ə)/ ▶ noun another term for DANCE OF DEATH.
– ORIGIN French, recorded from late Middle English in anglicized forms such as *dance of Machabray, dance of Macaber* (see also MACABRE).

danseur /dɒ̃ˈsəː/ ▶ noun a male ballet dancer.
– ORIGIN French, from *danser* 'to dance'.

danseur noble /dɒ̃ˌsəː ˈnɒbl(ə)/ ▶ noun a principal male ballet dancer, especially one who is particularly suited by bearing or physique to princely roles.
– ORIGIN French, literally 'noble dancer'.

danseuse /dɒ̃ˈsəːz/ ▶ noun a female ballet dancer.
– ORIGIN French, 'female dancer'.

Dante /ˈdanteɪ/ (1265–1321), Italian poet; full name *Dante Alighieri*. His reputation rests chiefly on *The Divine Comedy* (*c.*1309–20), an epic poem describing his spiritual journey through Hell and Purgatory and finally to Paradise. His love for Beatrice Portinari is described in *Vita nuova* (*c.*1290–4).

Dantean /ˈdantɪən, danˈtiːən/ ▶ adjective of or reminiscent of the poetry of Dante, especially in invoking his vision of hell in *The Divine Comedy*.
▶ noun an admirer or student of Dante or his writing.

Dantesque /ˌdantɪˈɛsk/ (also **Dante-esque**) ▶ adjective another term for DANTEAN.

danthonia /danˈθəʊnɪə/ ▶ noun [mass noun] a widely distributed tufted grass that grows on poor soils and is of low palatability to grazing animals. ● Genus *Danthonia*, family Gramineae.
– ORIGIN modern Latin, named after Étienne *Danthoine*, 19th-cent. French botanist.

Danton /ˈdantən/, French /dɑ̃tɔ̃/, Georges (Jacques) (1759–94), French revolutionary. A noted orator, he won great popularity in the early days of the French Revolution. He was initially an ally of Robespierre but later revolted against the severity of the Revolutionary Tribunal and was executed on Robespierre's orders.

Danube /ˈdanjuːb/ a river which rises in the Black Forest in SW Germany and flows about 2,850 km (1,770 miles) into the Black Sea. It is the second-longest river in Europe after the Volga; the cities of Vienna, Budapest, and Belgrade are situated on it. German name DONAU[1].
– DERIVATIVES **Danubian** /daˈnjuːbɪən/ adjective.

Danube School a group of landscape painters working in the Danube region in the early 16th century. Its members included Altdorfer and Cranach the Elder.

Danubian principalities the former European principalities of Moldavia and Wallachia. In 1861 they united to form the state of Romania.

Danzig /ˈdantsɪç/ German name for GDAŃSK.

dap ▶ verb (**daps, dapping, dapped**) [no obj.] fish by letting the fly (but not the line) bob lightly on the water.
▶ noun **1** (usu. **the dap**) a fishing fly used in this way.
2 (**daps**) dialect rubber-soled shoes.
– ORIGIN mid 17th cent. (as a verb): symbolic of a flicking movement, similar to DAB[1].

Daphne /ˈdafni/ Greek Mythology a nymph who was turned into a laurel bush to save her from the amorous pursuit of Apollo.

daphne /ˈdafni/ ▶ noun a small, typically evergreen Eurasian shrub with sweet-scented flowers. ● Genus *Daphne*, family Thymelaeaceae: several species.
– ORIGIN late Middle English (denoting the laurel or bay tree): from Greek *daphnē*, from the name of the nymph DAPHNE.

daphnia /ˈdafnɪə/ ▶ noun (pl. **same**) a minute semi-transparent freshwater crustacean with long antennae and a prominent single eye. Also called WATER FLEA. ● Genus *Daphnia*, order Cladocera.
– ORIGIN modern Latin, from Greek *Daphnē*, from the name of the nymph DAPHNE.

Daphnis /ˈdafnɪs/ Greek Mythology a Sicilian shepherd who, according to one version of the legend, was struck with blindness for his infidelity to the nymph Echenaïs. He consoled himself with pastoral poetry, of which he was the originator.

Da Ponte /dɑː ˈpɒnteɪ/, Lorenzo (1749–1838), Italian poet and librettist; born *Emmanuele Conegliano*. He became poet to the Court Opera in Vienna in 1784 and wrote the libretti for Mozart's *Marriage of Figaro* (1786), *Don Giovanni* (1787), and *Così fan tutte* (1790).

dapper ▶ adjective (of a man) neat and trim in dress and appearance: *he looked very dapper in a dark silk suit.*
– DERIVATIVES **dapperly** adverb, **dapperness** noun.
– ORIGIN late Middle English: probably from a Middle Low German or Middle Dutch word meaning 'strong, stout'.

dapple ▶ verb [with obj.] mark with spots or rounded patches: *the floor was dappled with pale moonlight.*
▶ noun **1** a patch or spot of colour or light.
2 an animal with a dappled coat.
– ORIGIN late 16th cent. (earlier as an adjective): perhaps related to Old Norse *depill* 'spot'.

dappled ▶ adjective marked with spots or rounded patches: *the horse's dappled flank.*

dapple grey ▶ adjective (of a horse) grey or white with darker ring-like markings.
▶ noun a dapple-grey horse.

Dapsang /dʌpˈsʌŋ/ another name for **K2**.

dapsone /ˈdapsəʊn/ ▶ noun [mass noun] Medicine a sulphur compound with bacteriostatic action, used in the treatment of leprosy. ● Chem. formula: $(H_2NC_6H_4)_2SO_2$.
– ORIGIN 1950s: from elements of its alternative systematic name *dipara-aminophenyl sulphone*.

Daqing /dɑːˈtʃɪŋ/ (also **Taching**) a major industrial city in NE China, in Heilongjiang province; pop. 976,200 (est. 2006).

DAR ▶ abbreviation Daughters of the American Revolution.

darbies /ˈdɑːbɪz/ ▶ plural noun archaic, informal handcuffs.
– ORIGIN late 17th cent.: allusive use of *Father Darby's bands*, a rigid form of agreement which put debtors in the power of moneylenders, possibly from the name of a 16th-cent. usurer.

Darby and Joan ▶ noun Brit. a devoted old married couple.
– ORIGIN late 18th cent.: from a poem (1735) in the *Gentleman's Magazine*, which contained the lines 'Old Darby, with Joan by his side ... They're never happy asunder.'

Darby and Joan club ▶ noun Brit. a club for senior citizens.

Dard /dɑːd/ ▶ noun **1** a member of a group of peoples inhabiting eastern Afghanistan, northern Pakistan, and Kashmir.
2 [mass noun] the group of Indic languages spoken by the Dards, including Kashmiri.
▶ adjective relating to the Dards or their languages.
– DERIVATIVES **Dardic** noun & adjective.
– ORIGIN the name in Dard.

Dardanelles /ˌdɑːdəˈnɛlz/ a narrow strait between Europe and Asiatic Turkey (called the Hellespont in classical times), linking the Sea of Marmara with the Aegean Sea. It is 60 km (38 miles) long. In 1915 it was the scene of an unsuccessful attack on Turkey by Allied troops (see GALLIPOLI).

dare ▶ verb (3rd sing. present usu. **dare** before an expressed or implied infinitive) **1** (as modal usu. with infinitive with or without **to** often with negative) have the courage to do something: *a story he dare not write down | she leaned forward as far as she dared.* ■ (**how dare you**) used to express indignation at something: *how dare you talk to me like that!* ■ (**don't you dare**) used to order someone threateningly not to do something: *don't you dare touch me.*
2 [with obj. and infinitive] defy or challenge (someone) to do something: *she was daring him to disagree* | [with obj.] *swap with me, I dare you.*
3 [with obj.] literary take the risk of; brave: *few dared his wrath.*
▶ noun a challenge, especially to prove courage: *she ran across a main road **for a dare**.*
– PHRASES **I dare say** (or **daresay**) used to indicate that one believes something is probable: *I dare say you've heard about her.*
– DERIVATIVES **darer** noun.
– ORIGIN Old English *durran*, of Germanic origin; related to Gothic *gadaursan*, from an Indo-European root shared by Greek *tharsein* and Sanskrit *dhṛṣ-* 'be bold'.

daredevil ▸ noun a reckless person who enjoys doing dangerous things.
▸ adjective reckless and daring.
– DERIVATIVES **daredevilry** noun.

Dar es Salaam /ˌdɑːr ɛs səˈlɑːm/ the chief port and former capital of Tanzania; pop. 2,930,000 (est. 2007). It was founded in 1866 by the sultan of Zanzibar. Its Arabic name means 'haven of peace'.

Darfur /dɑːˈfʊə/ a region in the west of Sudan, an independent kingdom until 1874. In 2003 a rebellion against the Sudanese government began, and many thousands have died or been displaced in the subsequent conflict.

dargah /ˈdʊəgɑː/ ▸ noun the tomb or shrine of a Muslim saint.
– ORIGIN from Urdu, from Persian.

Dari /ˈdɑːriː/ ▸ noun [mass noun] the form of Persian spoken in Afghanistan.
– ORIGIN from Persian.

Darien /ˈdɛːrɪən, ˈdar-/ a sparsely populated province of eastern Panama. The name was formerly applied to the whole of the Isthmus of Panama.

Darien, Gulf of part of the Caribbean Sea between Panama and Colombia.

daring ▸ adjective (of a person or action) adventurous or audaciously bold: *a daring crime*. ▪ causing outrage or surprise by being boldly unconventional: *a pretty girl in daring clothes*.
▸ noun [mass noun] adventurous courage.
– DERIVATIVES **daringly** adverb.

dariole /ˈdarɪəʊl/ ▸ noun (also **dariole mould**) (in French cooking) a small, flowerpot-shaped mould in which an individual sweet or savoury dish is cooked and served. ▪ an individual savoury or sweet dish cooked and served in a dariole mould.
– ORIGIN late Middle English: from Old French.

Darius I /dəˈrʌɪəs/ (*c*.550–486 BC), king of Persia 521–486 BC; known as **Darius the Great**. After a revolt by the Greek cities in Ionia (499–494 BC) he invaded Greece but was defeated at Marathon (490 BC).

Darjeeling[1] /dɑːˈdʒiːlɪŋ/ (also **Darjiling**) a hill station at an altitude of 2,150 m (7,054 ft) in West Bengal, NE India, near the Sikkim border; pop. 141,200 (est. 2009).

Darjeeling[2] /dɑːˈdʒiːlɪŋ/ ▸ noun [mass noun] a high-quality tea grown in the mountainous regions of northern India.

dark ▸ adjective **1** with little or no light: *it's too dark to see much*. ▪ (of a theatre) closed; not in use.
2 (of a colour or object) not reflecting much light; approaching black in shade: *dark green*. ▪ (of someone's skin, hair, or eyes) brown or black in colour. ▪ (of a person) having such skin, hair, or eyes.
3 (of a period or situation) characterized by great unhappiness or unpleasantness: *the dark days of the war*. ▪ deeply pessimistic: *a dark vision of the future*. ▪ (of an expression) angry. ▪ suggestive of or arising from evil; sinister: *so many dark deeds had been committed*.
4 hidden from knowledge; mysterious: *a dark secret*. ▪ (**darkest**) humorous (of a region) most remote, inaccessible, or uncivilized: *he lives somewhere in darkest Essex*. ▪ archaic ignorant; unenlightened: *he is dark on certain points of scripture*.
5 Phonetics denoting a velarized form of the sound of the letter *l* (as in *pull* in south-eastern English speech). Often contrasted with CLEAR.
▸ noun **1** (**the dark**) the absence of light in a place: *Carolyn was sitting in the dark*. ▪ [mass noun] nightfall: *I'll be home before dark*.
2 a dark colour or shade, especially in a painting.
– PHRASES **the darkest hour is just before the dawn** proverb when things seem to be at their worst they are about to start improving. **in the dark** in a state of ignorance. **keep something dark** Brit. keep something secret. **a shot** (or **stab**) **in the dark** an act whose outcome cannot be foreseen; a guess.
– DERIVATIVES **darkish** adjective, **darksome** adjective (literary).
– ORIGIN Old English *deorc*, of Germanic origin, probably distantly related to German *tarnen* 'conceal'.

dark adaptation ▸ noun [mass noun] the adjustment of the eye to low light intensities, involving reflex dilation of the pupil and activation of the rod cells in preference to the cone cells.
– DERIVATIVES **dark-adapted** adjective.

Dark Ages 1 the period in western Europe between the fall of the Roman Empire and the high Middle Ages, *c*.500–1100 AD, during which Germanic tribes swept through Europe and North Africa, often attacking and destroying towns and settlements. It was judged to have been a time of relative unenlightenment, though scholarship was kept alive in the monasteries and learning was encouraged at the courts of Charlemagne and Alfred the Great. ▪ a period of supposed unenlightenment: *a throwback to the dark ages of computing*. ▪ (**the dark ages**) humorous or derogatory an obscure or little-regarded period in the past, especially as characterizing an outdated attitude or practice: *the judge is living in the dark ages*.
2 Archaeology a period in Greece and the Aegean from the end of the Bronze Age until the beginning of the historical period. There was no building of palaces and fortresses, and the art of writing was apparently lost.

dark chocolate ▸ noun another term for PLAIN CHOCOLATE.

Dark Continent historical a name given to Africa at a time when it was little known to Europeans.

dark current ▸ noun the residual electric current flowing in a photoelectric device when there is no incident illumination.

darken ▸ verb **1** make or become dark or darker: [no obj.] *the sky was darkening rapidly* | [with obj.] *darken the eyebrows with black powder* | (as adj. **darkened**) *a darkened room*.
2 make or become angry, unhappy, or gloomy: [no obj.] *his mood darkened* | [with obj.] *the abuse darkened the rest of their lives*. ▪ [no obj.] (of someone's eyes or expression) show anger or another strong negative emotion. ▪ [with obj.] (of such an emotion) show in (someone's eyes or expression): *misery darkened her gaze*.
– PHRASES **never darken someone's door** keep away from someone's home permanently.
– DERIVATIVES **darkener** noun.

dark energy ▸ noun [mass noun] Physics a theoretical form of energy postulated to act in opposition to gravity and to occupy the entire universe, accounting for most of the energy in it and causing its expansion to accelerate.

dark-field microscopy ▸ noun [mass noun] a type of light microscopy which produces brightly illuminated objects on a dark background.

dark glasses ▸ plural noun glasses with tinted lenses, worn to protect or conceal a person's eyes.

Darkhan /dɑːˈkɑːn/ an industrial and mining city in northern Mongolia, established in 1961; pop. 78,300 (est. 2009).

dark horse ▸ noun a candidate or competitor about whom little is known but who unexpectedly wins or succeeds.
– ORIGIN early 19th cent.: originally racing slang.

darkie (also **darky**) ▸ noun (pl. **darkies**) offensive, informal a black person.

dark line ▸ noun Physics an absorption line in an electromagnetic spectrum, appearing as a black line at visible wavelengths.

darkling ▸ adjective literary growing dark or characterized by darkness: *the darkling sky*.

darkling beetle ▸ noun a dark-coloured nocturnal beetle, typically with reduced or absent wings.
● Family Tenebrionidae: numerous genera and species.

darkly ▸ adverb **1** in a threatening, mysterious, or ominous way: *'You can't trust him,' said Jacob darkly*. ▪ in a pessimistic way: *I wondered darkly if I was wasting my time*.
2 with a dark colour: *a figure silhouetted darkly against the trees*.

dark matter ▸ noun [mass noun] Astronomy (in some cosmological theories) non-luminous material which is postulated to exist in space and which could take either of two forms: weakly interacting particles (**cold dark matter**) or high-energy randomly moving particles created soon after the Big Bang (**hot dark matter**).

dark nebula ▸ noun Astronomy a non-luminous nebula of dust and gas which is observable because it obscures light from other sources.

darkness ▸ noun [mass noun] **1** the partial or total absence of light: *the office was in darkness*. ▪ night: *they began to make camp before darkness fell*. ▪ the quality of being dark in colour: *the darkness of his jacket*.
2 wickedness or evil: *the forces of darkness*. ▪ unhappiness or gloom: *moments of darkness were rare*. ▪ secrecy or mystery: *they drew a veil of darkness across the proceedings*.

darknet ▸ noun Computing a computer network with restricted access that is used chiefly for illegal peer-to-peer file sharing.

dark night of the soul ▸ noun a period of spiritual desolation suffered by a mystic in which all sense of consolation is removed.
– ORIGIN mid 19th cent.: used to translate Spanish *Noche oscura*, the title of a poem by the mystic St John of the Cross.

dark reaction ▸ noun Biochemistry the cycle of reactions (the Calvin cycle) which occurs in the second phase of photosynthesis and does not require the presence of light. It involves the fixation of carbon dioxide and its reduction to carbohydrate and the dissociation of water, using chemical energy stored in ATP.

darkroom ▸ noun a room for developing photographs, in which normal light is excluded.

dark star ▸ noun Astronomy a starlike object which emits little or no visible light. Its existence is inferred from other evidence, such as the eclipsing of other stars.

darky ▸ noun variant spelling of DARKIE.

Darling, Grace (1815–42), English heroine. The daughter of a lighthouse keeper on the Farne Islands off the coast of Northumberland, she achieved fame in September 1838 when she and her father rowed through a storm to rescue the survivors of the wrecked ship *Forfarshire*.

darling ▸ noun used as an affectionate form of address to a beloved person: *good night, darling*. ▪ a lovable or endearing person: *he's such a darling*. ▪ a person who is particularly popular with a certain group: *he is* ***the darling of*** *Labour's left wing*.
▸ adjective beloved: *his darling wife*. ▪ (in affected use) pretty; charming: *a darling little pillbox hat*.
– ORIGIN Old English *dēorling* (see DEAR, -LING).

Darling River a river of SE Australia, flowing 2,757 km (1,712 miles) in a generally south-westward course to join the Murray River.

Darlington an industrial town in County Durham, NE England; pop. 87,000 (est. 2009).

Darmstadt /ˈdɑːmʃtat/, German /ˈdarmʃtat/ an industrial town in Hesse, western Germany; pop. 141,300 (est. 2006).

darmstadtium /dɑːmˈstatɪəm/ ▸ noun [mass noun] the chemical element of atomic number 110, a radioactive element produced artificially. (Symbol: **Ds**)
– ORIGIN early 21st cent.: named after the German city of *Darmstadt* (where it was discovered) + -IUM.

darn[1] ▸ verb [with obj.] mend (a hole in knitted material) by interweaving yarn with a needle: *I don't expect you to darn my socks*. ▪ embroider (material) with a large running stitch.
▸ noun a place in a garment that has been darned.
– ORIGIN early 17th cent.: perhaps from dialect *dern* 'to hide', which is from Old English *diernan*, of West Germanic origin; compare with Middle Dutch *dernen* 'stop holes in (a dyke)'.

darn[2] (US also **durn**) ▸ verb, adjective, & exclamation informal, chiefly N. Amer. euphemism for DAMN: [as verb] *darn it all, Poppa* | [as adj.] *he was a darn sight younger than Jill*.

darned (US also **durned**) ▸ adjective informal, chiefly N. Amer. euphemism for DAMNED: *you have to work a darned sight harder*.
– DERIVATIVES **darnedest** adjective.

darnel /ˈdɑːn(ə)l/ ▸ noun a Eurasian ryegrass. ● Genus *Lolium*, family Gramineae: several species.
– ORIGIN Middle English: of unknown origin; apparently related to French (Walloon dialect) *darnelle*.

darner ▸ noun N. Amer. a large slender-bodied dragonfly. Also called DARNING NEEDLE, DEVIL'S DARNING NEEDLE.
● Family Aeshnidae: several genera.

darning ▸ noun [mass noun] the skill or activity of darning. ▪ articles being darned or needing to be darned.

darning mushroom (also **darning egg**) ▸ noun a mushroom-shaped (or egg-shaped) piece of wood or other smooth hard material used to stretch and support material being darned.

darning needle ▸ noun **1** a long sewing needle with a large eye, used in darning.
2 N. Amer. another term for DARNER.

Darnley /ˈdɑːnli/, Henry Stewart (or Stuart), Lord (1545–67), Scottish nobleman, second husband of Mary, Queen of Scots and father of James I of England. He was implicated in the murder of his wife's

D

secretary Rizzio in 1566, and was later killed in a mysterious gunpowder explosion in Edinburgh.

DARPA /ˈdɑːpə/ ▶ **abbreviation** US Defense Advanced Research Projects Agency.

darshan /ˈdɑːʃ(ə)n/ ▶ **noun** Hinduism an opportunity to see or an occasion of seeing a holy person or the image of a deity.
– ORIGIN via Hindi from Sanskrit *darśana* 'sight or seeing'.

Dart, Raymond Arthur (1893–1988), Australian-born South African anthropologist and anatomist. In 1925 he found the first specimen of a hominid for which he coined the genus name *Australopithecus*.

D

dart ▶ **noun 1** a small pointed missile that can be thrown or fired. ■ a small pointed missile with a feather or plastic flight, used in the game of darts. ■ Zoology a dart-like calcareous organ of a snail forming part of the reproductive system, exchanged during copulation.
2 an act of running somewhere suddenly and rapidly: *the cat* ***made a dart for*** *the door*. ■ a sudden, intense pang of a particular emotion: *a dart of panic*.
3 a tapered tuck stitched in a garment in order to shape it.
▶ **verb 1** [no obj., with adverbial of direction] move or run somewhere suddenly or rapidly: *she darted across the street*. ■ [with obj. and adverbial of direction] cast (a look or one's eyes) suddenly and rapidly in a particular direction: *she darted a glance across the table*.
2 [with obj.] shoot (an animal) with a dart, typically in order to administer a drug. ■ archaic throw (a missile).
– ORIGIN Middle English: from Old French, accusative of *darz, dars*, from a West Germanic word meaning 'spear, lance'.

dartboard ▶ **noun** a circular board marked with numbered segments, used as a target in the game of darts.

darter ▶ **noun 1** a long-necked fish-eating bird related to the cormorants, typically found in fresh water, where they frequently swim submerged to the neck. Also called ANHINGA, SNAKEBIRD. ● Family Anhingidae and genus *Anhinga*: four species.
2 a small fast-moving North American freshwater fish. ● Genera *Etheostoma* and *Percina*, family Percidae: numerous species.
3 (also **darter dragonfly**) a broad-bodied dragonfly that typically darts out from a perch to grab prey. ● Libellulidae and related families: several genera.

Dartford warbler /ˈdɑːtfəd/ ▶ **noun** a long-tailed non-migratory warbler with grey upper parts and purplish-brown underparts, found in western Europe and North Africa. ● *Sylvia undata*, family Sylviidae.
– ORIGIN late 18th cent.: from *Dartford* in Kent, England, where the bird was first seen.

Dartmoor /ˈdɑːtmɔː, -mʊə/ a moorland district in Devon that was a royal forest in Saxon times, now a national park.

Dartmoor pony ▶ **noun** a pony of a small hardy breed with a long shaggy coat in winter.

Dartmouth /ˈdɑːtməθ/ a port in Devon, SW England; pop. 6,000 (est. 2009). It is the site of the Royal Naval College.

darts ▶ **plural noun** [usu. treated as sing.] an indoor game in which small pointed missiles with feather or plastic flights are thrown at a circular target marked with numbers in order to score points.

Darwin[1] /ˈdɑːwɪn/ the capital of Northern Territory, Australia; pop. 120,652 (2008).

Darwin[2] /ˈdɑːwɪn/, Charles (Robert) (1809–82), English natural historian and geologist, proponent of the theory of evolution by natural selection. Darwin was the naturalist on HMS *Beagle* for her voyage around the southern hemisphere (1831–6), during which he collected the material which became the basis for his ideas on natural selection. His works *On the Origin of Species* (1859) and *The Descent of Man* (1871) had a fundamental effect on our concepts of nature and humanity's place within it.

Darwin[3] /ˈdɑːwɪn/, Erasmus (1731–1802), English physician, scientist, inventor, and poet. Darwin is chiefly remembered for his scientific and technical writing, much of which appeared in the form of long poems. These include *Zoonomia* (1794–96), which proposed a Lamarckian view of evolution. He was the grandfather of Charles Darwin and Francis Galton.

Darwinian ▶ **adjective** relating to Darwinism.
▶ **noun** an adherent of Darwinism.

Darwinism ▶ **noun** [mass noun] the theory of the evolution of species by natural selection advanced by Charles Darwin.

> Darwin argued that since offspring tend to vary slightly from their parents, mutations which make an organism better adapted to its environment will be encouraged and developed by the pressures of natural selection, leading to the evolution of new species differing widely from one another and from their common ancestors. Darwinism was later developed by the findings of Mendelian genetics (see NEO-DARWINIAN).

– DERIVATIVES **Darwinist** noun & adjective.

Darwin's finches ▶ **plural noun** a group of songbirds related to the buntings and found on the Galapagos Islands, discovered by Charles Darwin and used by him to illustrate his theory of natural selection. They are believed to have evolved from a common ancestor and have developed a variety of bills to suit various modes of life. Also called GALAPAGOS FINCHES. ● Family Emberizidae (subfamily Emberizinae): four to six genera, especially *Geospiza* (the **ground finches**) and *Camarhynchus* (the **tree finches**).

Dasehra /ˈdaʃərə/ ▶ **noun** variant spelling of DUSSEHRA.

Dasein /ˈdɑːzʌɪn/ ▶ **noun** [mass noun] Philosophy (in Hegelianism) existence or determinate being; (in existentialism) human existence.
– ORIGIN mid 19th cent.: German, from *dasein* 'exist', from *da* 'there' + *sein* 'be'.

dash ▶ **verb 1** [no obj., usu. with adverbial of direction] run or travel somewhere in a great hurry: *I dashed into the garden | I must dash, I'm late*.
2 [with obj. and adverbial of direction] strike or fling (something) somewhere with great force, especially so as to have a destructive effect; hurl: *the ship was dashed upon the rocks*. ■ [no obj., with adverbial of direction] strike forcefully against something: *a gust of rain dashed against the bricks*. ■ [with obj.] destroy or frustrate (hopes or expectations): *the budget dashed hopes of an increase in funding*. ■ [with obj.] cause (someone) to lose confidence; dispirit: *I won't tell Stuart—I think he'd be dashed*.
▶ **exclamation** Brit. informal used to express mild annoyance: *dash it all, I am in charge*.
▶ **noun 1** an act of running somewhere suddenly and hastily: *she* ***made a dash for*** *the door*. ■ a journey or period of time characterized by urgency or eager haste: *a 20-mile dash to the airport*. ■ N. Amer. a short, fast race run in one heat; a sprint.
2 a small quantity of a liquid added to something else: *whisky with* ***a dash of*** *soda*. ■ a small amount of a quality that adds piquancy or distinctiveness to something else: *a casual atmosphere with* ***a dash of*** *sophistication*.
3 a horizontal stroke in writing or printing to mark a pause or break in sense or to represent omitted letters or words. ■ the longer signal of the two used in Morse code. Compare with DOT[1]. ■ Music a short vertical mark placed above or beneath a note to indicate that it is to be performed in a very staccato manner.
4 [mass noun] impetuous or flamboyant vigour and confidence; panache.
5 informal short for DASHBOARD.
– PHRASAL VERBS **dash something off** write something hurriedly and without much premeditation: *I dashed off a quick letter*.
– DERIVATIVES **dasher** noun.
– ORIGIN Middle English (in the sense 'strike forcibly against'): probably symbolic of forceful movement and related to Swedish and Danish *daska*.

dashboard ▶ **noun 1** the panel facing the driver of a vehicle or the pilot of an aircraft, containing instruments and controls.
2 historical a board of wood or leather in front of a carriage, to keep out mud.

dashed ▶ **adjective** [attrib.] Brit. informal, dated used for emphasis: *it's a dashed shame* | [as submodifier] *she was dashed rude*.

dasheen /daˈʃiːn/ ▶ **noun** another term for TARO.
– ORIGIN late 19th cent. (originally West Indian): of unknown origin.

dashiki /ˈdɑːʃɪki/ ▶ **noun** (pl. **dashikis**) a loose brightly coloured shirt or tunic, originally from West Africa.
– ORIGIN from Yoruba or Hausa.

dashing ▶ **adjective** (of a man) attractive, adventurous, and full of confidence: *a dashing young pilot*. ■ stylish and fashionable: *a dashing black fedora*.
– DERIVATIVES **dashingly** adverb.

dashpot ▶ **noun** a device for damping shock or vibration.

dassie /ˈdasi/ ▶ **noun** (pl. **dassies**) **1** a hyrax (mammal), especially the rock hyrax of southern Africa. ● Family Procaviidae, in particular *Procavia capensis*.
2 S. African a silvery marine fish with dark fins and a black spot on the tail, found around African and Mediterranean coasts. ● *Diplodus sargus*, family Sparidae.
– ORIGIN late 18th cent.: from Afrikaans, from South African Dutch *dasje*, diminutive of Dutch *das* 'badger'; the fish is said to have been named because of a perceived resemblance (in its habit of frequenting rocks, or from its shy nature) to the rock hyrax.

dastard /ˈdastəd, ˈdɑː-/ ▶ **noun** dated or humorous a dishonourable or despicable man.
– ORIGIN late Middle English (in the sense 'stupid person'): probably from *dazed*, influenced by *dotard* and *bastard*.

dastardly ▶ **adjective** dated or humorous wicked and cruel: *pirates and their dastardly deeds*.
– DERIVATIVES **dastardliness** noun.
– ORIGIN mid 16th cent. (in the sense 'dull or stupid'): from DASTARD in the obsolete sense 'base coward'.

dastur /dəˈstʊə/ (also **dastoor**) ▶ **noun** Indian a chief priest of the Parsees.
– ORIGIN Persian, from Old Persian *dastōbār*.

dasyure /ˈdasɪjʊə/ ▶ **noun** another term for QUOLL.
– ORIGIN mid 19th cent.: from French, from modern Latin *dasyurus*, from Greek *dasus* 'rough, hairy' + *oura* 'tail'.

DAT ▶ **abbreviation** digital audiotape.

data /ˈdeɪtə/ ▶ **noun** [mass noun] facts and statistics collected together for reference or analysis: *there is very little data available*. ■ the quantities, characters, or symbols on which operations are performed by a computer, which may be stored and transmitted in the form of electrical signals and recorded on magnetic, optical, or mechanical recording media. ■ Philosophy things known or assumed as facts, making the basis of reasoning or calculation.
– ORIGIN mid 17th cent. (as a term in philosophy): from Latin, plural of DATUM.

> **USAGE** In Latin, **data** is the plural of **datum** and, historically and in specialized scientific fields, it is also treated as a plural in English, taking a plural verb, as in *the data were collected and classified*. In modern non-scientific use, however, it is generally not treated as a plural. Instead, it is treated as a mass noun, similar to a word like **information**, which takes a singular verb. Sentences such as ***data was*** *collected over a number of years* are now widely accepted in standard English.

databank ▶ **noun** a large repository of computer data on a particular topic, sometimes formed from more than one database, and accessible by many users.

database ▶ **noun** a structured set of data held in a computer, especially one that is accessible in various ways.

database management system ▶ **noun** Computing software that handles the storage, retrieval, and updating of data in a computer system.

datable (also **dateable**) ▶ **adjective** able to be dated to a particular time: *the mosaic is* ***datable to*** *the second century*.

data capture ▶ **noun** [mass noun] Computing the action or process of gathering data, especially from an automatic device, control system, or sensor.

data centre ▶ **noun** a large group of networked computer servers typically used by organizations for the remote storage, processing, or distribution of large amounts of data.

datacomms (also **datacoms**) ▶ **plural noun** data communications.

data dictionary ▶ **noun** Computing a set of information describing the contents, format, and structure of a database and the relationship between its elements, used to control access to and manipulation of the database.

dataglove ▶ **noun** Computing a device worn like a glove, which allows the manual manipulation of images in virtual reality.

data link ▶ **noun** a telecommunications link over which data is transmitted.

data mining ▶ **noun** [mass noun] Computing the practice of examining large pre-existing databases in order to generate new information.

data processing ▶ **noun** [mass noun] the carrying out of operations on data, especially by a computer, to retrieve, transform, or classify information.
– DERIVATIVES **data processor** noun.

data protection ▸ noun [mass noun] legal control over access to and use of data stored in computers.

data set ▸ noun Computing a collection of related sets of information that is composed of separate elements but can be manipulated as a unit by a computer.

data smog ▸ noun [mass noun] informal an overwhelming excess of information, especially that obtained as the result of an Internet search.

data terminal ▸ noun a terminal at which a person can enter data into a computer-based system or receive data from one.

dataveillance ▸ noun [mass noun] the practice of monitoring the online activity of a person or group.
– ORIGIN late 20th cent.: blend of DATA and SURVEILLANCE.

data warehouse ▸ noun a large store of data accumulated from a wide range of sources within a company and used to guide management decisions.
– DERIVATIVES **data warehousing** noun.

datcha /ˈdatʃə/ ▸ noun variant spelling of DACHA.

date[1] ▸ noun **1** the day of the month or year as specified by a number: *what's the date today?* | *please give your name, address, and date of birth.* ■ a particular day or year when a given event occurred or will occur: *1066 is the most famous date in English history.* ■ (**dates**) the years of a particular person's birth and death or of the beginning and end of a particular period or event. ■ the period of time to which an artefact or structure belongs: *the church is the largest of its date.*
2 a social or romantic appointment or engagement. ■ a person with whom one has a date: *my date isn't going to show, it seems.* ■ a musical or theatrical engagement or performance, especially as part of a tour.
▸ verb [with obj.] **1** establish or ascertain the date of (an object or event): *they **date** the paintings **to** 1460–70.* ■ mark with a date: *sign and date the document.* ■ [no obj.] (**date from** or **back to**) originate at a particular time; have existed since: *the controversy dates back to 1986.*
2 reveal (someone) as being old-fashioned: *jazzy—does that word date me?* ■ [no obj.] seem old-fashioned: *the coat may be pricey but it will never date.*
3 go out with (someone in whom one is romantically or sexually interested): *my sister's pretty judgemental about the girls I date* | [no obj.] *they have been dating for more than a year.*
– PHRASES **to date** (Indian also **till date**) until now: *their finest work to date.*
– ORIGIN Middle English: via Old French from medieval Latin *data*, feminine past participle of *dare* 'give'; from the Latin formula used in dating letters, *data (epistola)* '(letter) given or delivered', to record a particular time or place.

date[2] ▸ noun **1** a sweet, dark brown oval fruit containing a hard stone, usually eaten dried.
2 (also **date palm**) a tall palm tree which bears clusters of dates, native to western Asia and North Africa. ● *Phoenix dactylifera*, family Palmae.
– ORIGIN Middle English: from Old French, via Latin from Greek *daktulos* 'finger' (because of the finger-like shape of its leaves).

dateable ▸ adjective variant spelling of DATABLE.

datebook ▸ noun N. Amer. an engagement diary.

dated ▸ adjective **1** marked with a date: *a signed and dated painting.*
2 old-fashioned: *a dated expression.*

dateless ▸ adjective **1** not clearly belonging to any particular period, therefore not likely to go out of date.
2 having no marked date.

dateline ▸ noun a line at the head of a dispatch or newspaper article showing the date and place of writing.
▸ verb [with obj.] mark (a dispatch or article) with a dateline.

Date Line (also **International Date Line**) an imaginary North–South line through the Pacific Ocean, adopted in 1884, to the east of which the date is a day earlier than it is to the west. It lies chiefly along the meridian furthest from Greenwich (i.e. longitude 180°), with diversions to pass around some island groups.

date mussel ▸ noun a brown, cigar-shaped bivalve mollusc which bores into limestone and coral. ● Genus *Lithophaga*, family Mytilidae.

date plum ▸ noun another term for PERSIMMON.

date rape ▸ noun [mass noun] rape of a woman by the man she is dating, or with whom she has gone on a date.
▸ verb [with obj.] rape (a woman) in this way.

date stamp ▸ noun a stamped mark indicating a date, used on food packaging, posted envelopes, etc. ■ an adjustable stamp used to make a date stamp.
▸ verb (**date-stamp**) [with obj.] mark with a date stamp.

dating agency ▸ noun a service which arranges introductions for people seeking romantic partners.

dative /ˈdeɪtɪv/ Grammar ▸ adjective (in Latin, Greek, German, and some other languages) denoting a case of nouns and pronouns, and words in grammatical agreement with them, indicating an indirect object or recipient.
▸ noun a noun or other word in the dative case. ■ (**the dative**) the dative case.
– ORIGIN late Middle English: from Latin *(casus) dativus* '(case) of giving', from *dat-* 'given', from the verb *dare.*

Datong /dɑːˈtʊŋ/ a city in northern China in Shanxi province; pop. 1,105,100 (est. 2006).

Datuk /ˈdɑːtək/ ▸ noun (in Malaysia) a title of respect.
– ORIGIN Malay.

datum /ˈdeɪtəm/ ▸ noun (pl. **data**) See also DATA. **1** a piece of information. ■ an assumption or premise from which inferences may be drawn. See also SENSE DATUM.
2 a fixed starting point of a scale or operation. See also ORDNANCE DATUM.
– ORIGIN mid 18th cent.: from Latin, literally 'something given', neuter past participle of *dare* 'give'.

datum line (also **datum level**) ▸ noun a standard of comparison or point of reference. ■ Surveying an assumed surface used as a reference for the measurement of heights and depths. ■ a line to which dimensions are referred on engineering drawings, and from which measurements are calculated.

datura /dəˈtjʊərə/ ▸ noun a shrubby annual plant with large, erect, trumpet-shaped flowers, native to southern North America. They contain toxic or narcotic alkaloids and are used as hallucinogens by some American Indian peoples. ● Genus *Datura*, family Solanaceae: several species, including the thorn apple or jimson weed.
– ORIGIN modern Latin, from Hindi *dhatūrā*, from Sanskrit *dhustur.*

daub /dɔːb/ ▸ verb [with obj.] carelessly coat or smear (a surface) with a thick or sticky substance: *the walls **were daubed with** splashes of paint.* ■ spread (a thick or sticky substance) on a surface in such a way: *a canvas with paint **daubed on** it.* ■ paint (words or drawings) on a surface in such a way: *they **daubed** graffiti **on** the walls.*
▸ noun **1** a patch or smear of a thick or sticky substance: *a daub of paint.* ■ a painting executed without much skill.
2 [mass noun] plaster, clay, or another substance used for coating a surface, especially when mixed with straw and applied to laths or wattles to form a wall.
– DERIVATIVES **dauber** noun.
– ORIGIN late Middle English: from Old French *dauber*, from Latin *dealbare* 'whiten, whitewash', based on *albus* 'white'.

daube /dəʊb/ ▸ noun a stew of meat, typically beef, braised slowly in wine.
– PHRASES **en daube** (of meat) braised slowly in wine.
– ORIGIN French; compare with Italian *addobbo* 'seasoning'.

Daubenton's bat /ˈdɔːbəntənz, dɔːˈbɛntənz/ ▸ noun a small brown myotis bat that typically flies low over water, found throughout Eurasia. ● *Myotis daubentonii*, family Vespertilionidae.
– ORIGIN late 19th cent.: named after Louis-Jean-Marie *Daubenton* (1716–1800), French naturalist and physician.

Daubigny /ˈdəʊbɪnji/, French /dobiɲi/, Charles François (1817–78), French landscape painter. He was a member of the Barbizon School and is often regarded as a linking figure between this group and the Impressionists.

Daudet /ˈdəʊdeɪ/, French /dodɛ/, Alphonse (1840–97), French novelist and dramatist. He is best known for his sketches of life in his native Provence, particularly the *Lettres de mon moulin* (1869).

daughter ▸ noun **1** a girl or woman in relation to either or both of her parents. ■ a female offspring of an animal. ■ a female descendant: *we are the sons and daughters of Adam.* ■ a woman considered as the product of a particular person, influence, or environment: *she was a daughter of the vicarage in manner and appearance.* ■ archaic used as a term of affectionate address to a woman or girl, typically by an older person.
2 Physics a nuclide formed by the radioactive decay of another.
– DERIVATIVES **daughterhood** noun, **daughterly** adjective.
– ORIGIN Old English *dohtor*, of Germanic origin; related to Dutch *dochter* and German *Tochter*, from an Indo-European root shared by Greek *thugatēr.*

D

daughterboard (also **daughtercard**) ▸ noun Electronics a small printed circuit board that attaches to a larger one.

daughter cell ▸ noun Biology a cell formed by the division or budding of another.

daughter-in-law ▸ noun (pl. **daughters-in-law**) the wife of one's son.

Daughters of the American Revolution (abbrev.: **DAR**) (in the US) a patriotic society whose aims include encouraging education and the study of US history and which tends to be politically conservative. Membership is limited to female descendants of those who aided the cause of independence.

Daumier /ˈdəʊmɪeɪ/, French /domje/, Honoré (1808–78), French painter and lithographer. From the 1830s he worked as a cartoonist for periodicals such as *Charivari*, where he produced lithographs satirizing French society and politics.

daunorubicin /ˌdɔːnə(ʊ)ˈruːbɪsɪn/ ▸ noun [mass noun] Medicine a synthetic antibiotic that interferes with DNA synthesis and is used in the treatment of acute leukaemia and other cancers.
– ORIGIN 1960s: from *Daunia*, in southern Italy where it was developed, + *-rubi-* 'red' + -MYCIN.

daunt /dɔːnt/ ▸ verb [with obj.] make (someone) feel intimidated or apprehensive: *some people are daunted by technology.*
– PHRASES **nothing daunted** without having been made fearful or apprehensive: *nothing daunted, the committee set to work.*
– ORIGIN Middle English: from Old French *danter*, from Latin *domitare*, frequentative of *domare* 'to tame'.

daunting ▸ adjective seeming difficult to deal with in prospect; intimidating: *a daunting task.*
– DERIVATIVES **dauntingly** adverb.

dauntless ▸ adjective showing fearlessness and determination: *dauntless bravery.*
– DERIVATIVES **dauntlessly** adverb, **dauntlessness** noun.

dauphin /ˈdɔːfɪn, ˈdəʊfã/, French /dofɛ̃/ ▸ noun historical the eldest son of the King of France.
– ORIGIN French, from the family name of the lords of the Dauphiné, an area of SE France: ultimately a nickname meaning 'dolphin'. In 1349 the future Charles V acquired the lands and the title; when king he ceded them to his eldest son, establishing the practice of passing both title and lands to the Crown Prince.

Dauphiné /ˈdəʊfɪneɪ/, French /dofine/ a region and former province of SE France. Its capital was Grenoble.

dauphinois /ˌdəʊfɪˈnwʌ/ (also **dauphinoise** /-ˈnwʌz/) ▸ adjective (of potatoes or other vegetables) sliced and cooked in milk, typically with a topping of cheese.
– ORIGIN French, 'from the province of Dauphiné'.

Davao /dɑːˈvɑːəʊ/ a seaport in the southern Philippines, on the island of Mindanao; pop. 785,700 (est. 2007). Founded in 1849, it is the largest city on the island and the third-largest city in the Philippines.

daven /ˈdɑːv(ə)n/ ▸ verb (**davens**, **davening**, **davened**) [no obj.] (in Judaism) recite the prescribed liturgical prayers.
– ORIGIN Yiddish.

davenport /ˈdav(ə)npɔːt/ ▸ noun **1** Brit. an ornamental writing desk with drawers and a sloping surface for writing. [probably named after Captain *Davenport*, for whom early examples of this type of desk were made in the late 18th cent.]
2 N. Amer. a large heavily upholstered sofa. [perhaps from a manufacturer's name.]

David[1] /ˈdeɪvɪd/ (died c.962 BC), king of Judah and Israel c.1000–c.962 BC. In the biblical account he was the youngest son of Jesse and killed the Philistine Goliath; on Saul's death, he became king, making Jerusalem his capital. He is traditionally regarded as the author of the Psalms, though this has been disputed.

David² /ˈdeɪvɪd/ the name of two kings of Scotland: ■ **David I** (*c.*1084–1153), sixth son of Malcolm III, reigned 1124–53. In 1136 he invaded England in support of his niece Matilda's claim to the throne, but was defeated at the Battle of the Standard in 1138. ■ **David II** (1324–71), son of Robert the Bruce, reigned 1329–71. His reign witnessed a renewal of fighting with England, with Edward III supporting the pretender Edward de Baliol. His death without issue left the throne to the Stuarts.

D

David³ /ˈdeɪvɪd/, Elizabeth (1913–92), British cookery writer. She played a leading role in introducing Mediterranean cuisine to Britain in the 1950s and 1960s.

David⁴ /daˈviːd/, French /david/, Jacques-Louis (1748–1825), French painter, famous for neoclassical paintings such as *The Oath of the Horatii* (1784). He became actively involved in the French Revolution, voting for the death of Louis XVI and supporting Robespierre.

David, St (6th century), Welsh monk; Welsh name **Dewi**. Since the 12th century he has been regarded as the patron saint of Wales. Little is known of his life, but it is generally accepted that he transferred the centre of Welsh ecclesiastical administration from Caerleon to Mynyw (now St David's). Feast day, 1 March.

Davies¹, Sir Peter Maxwell (b.1934), English composer and conductor, influenced particularly by serialism and early English music. Notable works: *Eight Songs for a Mad King* (1969) and *Taverner* (1970).

Davies², W. H. (1871–1940), Welsh poet; full name *William Henry Davies*. He emigrated to the US and lived as a vagrant and labourer, writing *The Autobiography of a Super-Tramp* (1908) about his experiences.

Davies³, (William) Robertson (1913–95), Canadian novelist, dramatist, and journalist. He won international recognition with his Deptford trilogy of novels, comprising *Fifth Business* (1970), *The Manticore* (1972), and *World of Wonders* (1975).

da Vinci, Leonardo, see **LEONARDO DA VINCI**.

Davis¹, Bette (1908–89), American actress; born *Ruth Elizabeth Davis*. She established her Hollywood career playing a number of strong, independent female characters in such films as *Dangerous* (1935). Her flair for suggesting the macabre and menacing emerged in later films, such as *Whatever Happened to Baby Jane?* (1962).

Davis² the name of two English billiards and snooker players. **Joe** (1901–78) held the world championship from 1927 until his retirement in 1946. He was also world billiards champion 1928–32. His brother **Fred** (1913–98) was world snooker champion (1948–9; 1951–6) and world billiards champion (1980).

Davis³, Miles (Dewey) (1926–91), American jazz trumpeter, composer, and bandleader. In the 1950s he played and recorded arrangements in a new style which became known as 'cool' jazz, heard on albums such as *Kind of Blue* (1959). In the 1960s he pioneered the fusion of jazz and rock.

Davis⁴, Steve (b.1957), English snooker player. He was UK Professional Champion (1980–1; 1984–7) and World Professional Champion (1981; 1983–4; 1987–9).

Davis Cup an annual tennis championship for men, first held in 1900, between teams from different countries.
– ORIGIN named after Dwight F. *Davis* (1879–1945), the American doubles champion who donated the trophy.

Davis Strait a sea passage 645 km (400 miles) long separating Greenland from Baffin Island and connecting Baffin Bay with the Atlantic Ocean.
– ORIGIN named after John *Davis* (1550–1605), the English explorer who sailed through it in 1587.

davit /ˈdavɪt, ˈdeɪv-/ ▶ **noun** a small crane on board a ship, especially one of a pair for suspending or lowering a lifeboat.
– ORIGIN late 15th cent.: from Old French *daviot*, diminutive of *david*, denoting a kind of carpenter's tool.

Davos /dɑːˈvɒs/ a resort and winter-sports centre in eastern Switzerland; pop. 10,686 (2007).

Davy, Sir Humphry (1778–1829), English chemist, a pioneer of electrochemistry. He discovered nitrous oxide (laughing gas) and the elements sodium, potassium, magnesium, calcium, strontium, and barium. He also identified and named the element chlorine, determined the properties of iodine, and demonstrated that diamond was a form of carbon. In 1815 he invented the miner's safety lamp.

Davy Jones's locker ▶ **noun** informal the bottom of the sea, especially regarded as the grave of those drowned at sea.
– ORIGIN extension of early 18th-cent. nautical slang *Davy Jones*, denoting the evil spirit of the sea.

Davy lamp ▶ **noun** a miner's portable safety lamp with the flame enclosed by wire gauze to reduce the risk of an explosion of gas.

daw ▶ **noun** another term for **JACKDAW**.
– ORIGIN late Middle English: of Germanic origin; related to German *Dohle*.

dawdle ▶ **verb** [no obj.] waste time; be slow: *she mustn't dawdle—she had to make the call now*. ■ [with adverbial of direction] move slowly and idly in a particular direction: *Ruth dawdled back through the wood*.
– DERIVATIVES **dawdler** noun.
– ORIGIN mid 17th cent.: related to dialect *daddle*, *doddle* 'dally'.

dawg /dɔːg/ ▶ **noun** non-standard spelling of **DOG**, used especially to represent American speech.

Dawkins, Richard (b.1941), English biologist. Dawkins's book *The Selfish Gene* (1976) did much to popularize the theory of sociobiology. In *The Blind Watchmaker* (1986) Dawkins discussed evolution by natural selection and suggested that the theory could answer the fundamental question of why life exists.

dawn ▶ **noun** the first appearance of light in the sky before sunrise: *he set off at dawn*. ■ the beginning of a phenomenon or period of time, especially one perceived as auspicious: *the dawn of civilization*.
▶ **verb** [no obj.] **1** (of a day) begin: [with complement] *Thursday dawned bright and sunny*. ■ come into existence: *a new age was dawning in the Tory party*.
2 become evident to the mind; be perceived or understood: *the awful truth was beginning to* **dawn on** *him* | (as adj. **dawning**) *he smiled with dawning recognition*.
– ORIGIN late 15th cent. (as a verb): back-formation from Middle English **DAWNING**.

dawn chorus ▶ **noun** Brit. the singing of a large number of birds before dawn each day, particularly during the breeding season.

dawning ▶ **noun** literary dawn. ■ the beginning or first appearance of something: *the dawnings of civilization*.
– ORIGIN Middle English: alteration of earlier *dawing*, from Old English *dagian* 'to dawn', of Germanic origin; related to Dutch *dagen* and German *tagen*, also to **DAY**.

dawn raid ▶ **noun** a surprise visit at dawn, especially by police searching for criminals or illicit goods. ■ Stock Exchange, Brit. an attempt to acquire a substantial portion of a company's shares at the start of a day's trading, typically as a preliminary to a takeover bid.

dawn redwood ▶ **noun** a coniferous tree with deciduous needles, known only as a fossil until it was found growing in SW China in 1941. ● *Metasequoia glyptostroboides*, family Taxodiaceae.

DAX /daks/ ▶ **abbreviation** Deutsche Aktienindex, the German stock exchange.

Day, Doris (b.1924), American actress and singer; born *Doris Kappelhoff*. She became a film star in the 1950s with roles in light-hearted musicals, comedies, and romances such as *Calamity Jane* (1953) and *Pillow Talk* (1959).

day ▶ **noun 1** each of the twenty-four-hour periods, reckoned from one midnight to the next, into which a week, month, or year is divided, and corresponding to a rotation of the earth on its axis. ■ the part of a day when it is light; the time between sunrise and sunset: *the animals hunt* **by day**. ■ the part of a day spent working: *he works an eight-hour day*. ■ Astronomy a single rotation of a planet in relation to its primary. ■ Astronomy the period on a planet when its primary star is above the horizon. ■ [mass noun] archaic or literary daylight: *by the time they had all gone it was broad day*.
2 (also **days**) a particular period of the past; an era: *in Shakespeare's day* | *the laws were very strict in those days*. ■ (**the day**) the present time: *the political issues of the day*. ■ (usu. with modifier **days**) a particular period in a person's life or career: *my student days*. ■ (**one's day**) the most active or successful period of a person's life or career: *he had been a star in his day*. ■ (**one's days**) the remaining period of someone's life: *she cared for him* **for the rest of his days**.
– PHRASES **all in a day's work** (of something unusual or difficult) accepted as part of someone's normal routine or as a matter of course: *dodging sharks is all in a day's work for some scientists*. **any day** informal **1** at any time or under any circumstances (used to express a strong opinion or preference): *they could outfight the police any day*. **2** very soon: *she's expected to give birth any day now*. **at the end of the day** see **END**. **by the day** gradually and steadily: *the campaign is growing by the day*. **call it a day** decide or agree to stop doing something. **day after day** on each successive day over a long period: *the rain poured down day after day*. **day and night** all the time: *the district is patrolled day and night*. **day by day** on each successive day; gradually and steadily. **day in, day out** continuously or repeatedly over a long period of time. **day of reckoning** the time when past mistakes or misdeeds must be punished or paid for. [with allusion to Judgement Day, on which (in some beliefs) the judgement of mankind is expected to take place.] **don't give up the day job** informal used as a humorous way of recommending someone not to pursue something at which they are unlikely to be successful. **from day one** from the very beginning: *children need a firm hand from day one*. **have had one's** (or **its**) **day** be no longer popular, successful, or influential: *power dressing has had its day*. **if he** (or **she** etc.) **is a day** at least (appended to a statement about a person's age): *he must be seventy if he's a day*. **in this day and age** at the present time. **not someone's day** used to convey that someone has experienced a day of successive misfortunes. **one day** (or **some day** or **one of these days**) at some time in the future: *our wishes will come true one of these days*. **one of those days** a day when several things go wrong. **that will be the day** informal that is very unlikely. **these days** at present: *he's drinking far too much these days*. **those were the days** used to assert that a particular past time was better than the present. **to the day** exactly: *it's four years to the day since he was killed*. **to this day** at the present time as in the past; still: *the tradition continues to this day*.
– ORIGIN Old English *dæg*, of Germanic origin; related to Dutch *dag* and German *Tag*.

Dayak /ˈdʌɪak/ (also **Dyak**) ▶ **noun** (pl. **same** or **Dayaks**) **1** a member of a group of indigenous peoples inhabiting parts of Borneo, including the Iban (or **Sea Dayak**) of the north, the **Land Dayak** of the south-west, and the Punan.
2 [mass noun] the group of Austronesian languages spoken by the Dayak.
▶ **adjective** relating to the Dayak or their languages.
– ORIGIN Malay, literally 'up-country'.

Dayan /daˈjɑːn/, Moshe (1915–81), Israeli statesman and general. As Minister of Defence he oversaw Israel's victory in the Six Day War and as Foreign Minister he played a prominent role in negotiations towards the Camp David agreements of 1979.

dayan /daˈjɑːn/ (also **Dayan**) ▶ **noun** (pl. **dayanim** /daˈjɑːnɪm/) Judaism a senior rabbi, especially one who acts as a religious judge in a Jewish community.
– ORIGIN from Hebrew *dayyān*, from *dān* 'to judge'.

daybed ▶ **noun** N. Amer. a couch that can be made up into a bed.

dayboat ▶ **noun** another term for **DAYSAILOR**.

daybook ▶ **noun 1** an account book in which a day's transactions are entered for later transfer to a ledger. **2** N. Amer. a diary.

day boy ▶ **noun** Brit. a boy who lives at home but attends a school where other pupils board.

daybreak ▶ **noun** the time in the morning when daylight first appears; dawn: *she set off* **at daybreak**.

day care ▶ **noun** [mass noun] daytime care for people who cannot be fully independent, such as children or elderly people. ■ [count noun] (**daycare**) N. Amer. a day centre.

day centre (also **day-care centre**) ▶ **noun** Brit. a place providing care and recreation facilities for those who cannot be fully independent.

daydream ▶ **noun** a series of pleasant thoughts that distract one's attention from the present.
▶ **verb** [no obj.] indulge in a daydream: *stop daydreaming and pay attention*.
– DERIVATIVES **daydreamer** noun.

day flower ▶ **noun** a plant of warm climates with short-lived flowers that are typically blue. ● Genus *Commelina*, family Commelinaceae.

day girl ▸ noun Brit. a girl who lives at home but attends a school where other pupils board.

Day-Glo (also **dayglo**) ▸ noun [mass noun] trademark a fluorescent paint or other colouring.
▸ adjective very bright or fluorescent in colour.
– ORIGIN 1950s: blend of DAY and GLOW.

day labourer ▸ noun an unskilled labourer paid by the day.

Day Lewis, C. (1904–72), English poet and critic; full name *Cecil Day Lewis*. His early verse, such as *Transitional Poems* (1929), reflects the influence of revolutionary thinking. After 1940, however, he increasingly became a figure of the Establishment and was Poet Laureate 1968–72.

daylight ▸ noun [mass noun] the natural light of the day: [as modifier] *the daylight hours.* ■ the first appearance of light in the morning; dawn: *I returned at daylight.* ■ an appreciable distance or difference between one person or thing and another: *their views on education are so close that it's difficult to see daylight between them.*
– PHRASES **—— the living daylights out of** do the specified thing to (someone) with great severity: *he beat the living daylights out of them.* [from *daylights* meaning 'eyes', hence 'any vital organ'.] **see daylight** **1** gain public exposure or attention: *old photographs that rarely see daylight.* **2** begin to understand what was previously puzzling or unclear.

daylighting ▸ noun [mass noun] the illumination of buildings by natural light.

daylight robbery ▸ noun [mass noun] Brit. informal blatant and unfair overcharging.

daylight saving time (also **daylight time**) ▸ noun [mass noun] N. Amer. time as adjusted to achieve longer evening daylight in summer by setting the clocks an hour ahead of the standard time. Compare with SUMMER TIME.

day lily ▸ noun a Eurasian lily which bears large yellow, red, or orange flowers, each flower lasting only one day. ● Genus *Hemerocallis*, family Liliaceae.

day-long ▸ adjective lasting a whole day: *a day-long seminar.*

daymare ▸ noun a frightening hallucinatory condition experienced while awake.

day nursery ▸ noun see NURSERY.

Day of Atonement another term for YOM KIPPUR.

day off ▸ noun (pl. **days off**) a day's holiday from work or school, on what would normally be a working day.

Day of Judgement another term for JUDGEMENT DAY.

day of rest ▸ noun a day in the week set aside from normal work or activity, typically Sunday on religious grounds.

day out ▸ noun (pl. **days out**) Brit. a trip or excursion for a day.

daypack ▸ noun a small rucksack.

day release ▸ noun [mass noun] Brit. a system of allowing employees days off work to go on educational courses: *she goes to college on day release.*

day return ▸ noun Brit. a reduced-price fare for a journey on public transport out and back in one day.

day room ▸ noun a room, especially a communal room in an institution, used during the day.

daysack ▸ noun Brit. another term for DAYPACK.

daysail ▸ verb [no obj.] sail a yacht for a single day.

daysailor (US also **daysailer**) ▸ noun a sailing boat without a cabin, designed for use during the day only.

day school ▸ noun **1** a non-residential school, typically a fee-paying one.
2 Brit. a short educational course on a particular subject.

day shift ▸ noun a period of time worked during the daylight hours in a hospital, factory, etc. ■ [treated as sing. or pl.] the employees who work during the day shift.

dayside ▸ noun Astronomy the side of a planet that is facing its primary star.

Days of Awe ▸ plural noun another term for HIGH HOLIDAYS.

dayspring ▸ noun archaic dawn.

day surgery ▸ noun [mass noun] minor surgery that does not require the patient to stay in hospital overnight.

daytime ▸ noun the time of the day between sunrise and sunset: *she was alone in the daytime* | [as modifier] *a daytime telephone number.*

daytimer ▸ noun trademark, chiefly N. Amer. an appointment diary or an electronic organizer.

day-to-day ▸ adjective [attrib.] happening regularly every day: *the day-to-day management of the classroom* | *he is battling the disease on a day-to-day basis.* ■ ordinary; everyday: *our day-to-day domestic life.* ■ short-term; without consideration for the future: *the struggle for day-to-day survival.*
▸ adverb on a daily basis: *the information to be traded is determined day-to-day.*

Dayton /ˈdeɪt(ə)n/ a city in western Ohio; pop. 154,200 (est. 2008). It was the home of the aviation pioneers the Wright brothers and is still a centre of aerospace research.

day trading ▸ noun [mass noun] Stock Exchange a form of share dealing in which individuals buy and sell shares over the Internet over a period of a single day's trading, with the intention of profiting from small price fluctuations.
– DERIVATIVES **day trader** noun.

day trip ▸ noun a journey or excursion completed in one day.
– DERIVATIVES **day tripper** noun (Brit.).

daywear ▸ noun [mass noun] articles of casual clothing suitable for informal or everyday occasions.

daywork ▸ noun [mass noun] casual work paid for on a daily basis.
– DERIVATIVES **dayworker** noun.

daze ▸ verb [with obj.] (especially of an emotional or physical shock) make (someone) unable to think or react properly: *she was dazed by his revelations* | (as adj. **dazed**) *a dazed expression.*
▸ noun [in sing.] a state of stunned confusion or bewilderment: *he was walking around in a daze.*
– DERIVATIVES **dazedly** /-zɪdli/ adverb.
– ORIGIN Middle English: back-formation from *dazed* (adjective), from Old Norse *dasathr* 'weary'; compare with Swedish *dasa* 'lie idle'.

dazibao /ˈdɑːdzəbaʊ/ ▸ noun (pl. **same**) (in the People's Republic of China) a wall poster written in large characters, expressing a political opinion.
– ORIGIN Chinese, from *dà* 'big' + *zì* 'character' + *bào* 'newspaper or poster'.

dazzle ▸ verb [with obj.] (of a bright light) blind (a person or their eyes) temporarily: *she was dazzled by the headlights.* ■ amaze or overwhelm (someone) with a particular impressive quality: *I was dazzled by the beauty and breadth of the exhibition.*
▸ noun [mass noun] brightness that blinds someone temporarily: *I screwed my eyes up against the dazzle.*
– DERIVATIVES **dazzlement** noun.
– ORIGIN late 15th cent. (in the sense 'be dazzled'): frequentative of the verb DAZE.

dazzler ▸ noun a person or thing that dazzles, in particular a person who is highly impressive or skilful.

dazzling ▸ adjective extremely bright, especially so as to blind the eyes temporarily: *the sunlight was dazzling* | figurative *a dazzling smile.* ■ extremely impressive, beautiful, or skilful: *a dazzling display of football.*
– DERIVATIVES **dazzlingly** adverb.

Db ▸ symbol the chemical element dubnium.

dB ▸ abbreviation decibel(s).

dba ▸ abbreviation doing business as: *Bruce Newman, dba Newman Graphics.*

DBE ▸ abbreviation (in the UK) Dame Commander of the Order of the British Empire.

DBMS ▸ abbreviation database management system.

DBS ▸ abbreviation ■ direct broadcasting by satellite. ■ direct-broadcast satellite.

dbx ▸ noun [mass noun] trademark electronic circuitry designed to increase the dynamic range of reproduced sound and reduce noise in the system.
– ORIGIN 1970s: from DB 'decibel' + *x* (representing *expander*).

DC ▸ abbreviation ■ Music da capo. ■ (also **d.c.**) direct current. ■ District of Columbia: *Washington DC.* ■ District Commissioner.

DCB ▸ abbreviation (in the UK) Dame Commander of the Order of the Bath.

DCL ▸ abbreviation (in the UK) Doctor of Civil Law.

DCM ▸ abbreviation (in the UK) Distinguished Conduct Medal, awarded for bravery.

DCMG ▸ abbreviation (in the UK) Dame Commander of the Order of St Michael and St George.

DCMS ▸ abbreviation (in the UK) Department for Culture, Media, and Sport.

DCVO ▸ abbreviation (in the UK) Dame Commander of the Royal Victorian Order.

DD ▸ abbreviation Doctor of Divinity.

D-Day ▸ noun the day (6 June 1944) in the Second World War on which Allied forces invaded northern France by means of beach landings in Normandy. ■ the day on which an important operation is to begin or a change to take effect.
– ORIGIN from *D* for *day* + DAY. Compare with H-HOUR.

DDC ▸ abbreviation dideoxycytidine.

DDE ▸ noun Computing a standard allowing data to be shared between different programs.
– ORIGIN 1980s: abbreviation of *Dynamic Data Exchange.*

DDI ▸ abbreviation ■ dideoxyinosine. ■ divisional detective inspector.

DDoS ▸ abbreviation Computing distributed denial of service, denoting the intentional paralysing of a computer network by flooding it with data sent simultaneously from many individual computers.

DDR ▸ abbreviation German Democratic Republic.
– ORIGIN abbreviation of German *Deutsche Demokratische Republik.*

DDT ▸ abbreviation dichlorodiphenyltrichloroethane, a synthetic organic compound used as an insecticide. Like other chlorinated aromatic hydrocarbons, DDT tends to persist in the environment and become concentrated in animals at the head of the food chain. Its use is now banned in many countries. ● Chem. formula: $CCl_3CH(C_6H_4Cl)_2$.

DE ▸ abbreviation ■ Delaware (in official postal use). ■ (formerly in the UK) Department of Employment.

de- ▸ prefix **1** (forming verbs and their derivatives) down; away: *descend* | *deduct.* ■ completely: *denude* | *derelict.*
2 (added to verbs and their derivatives) denoting removal or reversal: *deaerate* | *de-ice.*
3 denoting formation from: *deverbal.*
– ORIGIN from Latin *de* 'off, from'; sense 2 via Old French *des-* from Latin *dis-*.

DEA ▸ abbreviation US Drug Enforcement Administration.

deaccession /ˌdiːəkˈsɛʃ(ə)n/ ▸ verb [with obj.] officially remove (an item) from a library, museum, or art gallery in order to sell it.
▸ noun [mass noun] the official removal of an item from a library, museum, or art gallery in order to sell it.

deacon /ˈdiːk(ə)n/ ▸ noun (in Catholic, Anglican, and Orthodox Churches) an ordained minister of an order ranking below that of priest. ■ (in some Nonconformist Churches) a lay officer appointed to assist a minister, especially in secular affairs. ■ historical (in the early church) a minister appointed to administer charity.
▸ verb [with obj.] appoint or ordain as a deacon.
– DERIVATIVES **deaconship** noun.
– ORIGIN Old English *diacon*, via ecclesiastical Latin from Greek *diakonos* 'servant' (in ecclesiastical Greek 'Christian minister').

deaconess /ˌdiːkəˈnɛs/ ▸ noun (in the early Church and some modern Churches) a woman with duties similar to those of a deacon.

deactivate ▸ verb [with obj.] make (something) inactive by disconnecting or destroying it: *the switch deactivates the alarm.* ■ Military remove from active duty.
– DERIVATIVES **deactivation** noun, **deactivator** noun.

dead ▸ adjective **1** no longer alive: *a dead body* | [as complement] *he was shot dead by terrorists* | (as plural noun **the dead**) *there was no time to bury the dead with decency.* ■ (of a part of the body) having lost sensation; numb. ■ lacking emotion, sympathy, or sensitivity: *a cold, dead voice.* ■ no longer current, relevant, or important: *pollution had become a dead issue.* ■ devoid of living things: *a dead planet.* ■ (of a place or time) characterized by a lack of activity or excitement: *Brussels isn't dead after dark, if you know where to look.* ■ (of money) not financially productive. ■ (of sound) without resonance; dull. ■ (of a colour) not glossy or bright. ■ (of a piece of equipment) no longer functioning: *the phone had gone dead.* ■ (of an electric circuit or conductor) carrying or transmitting no current: *the batteries are dead.* ■ no longer alight: *the fire had been dead for some days.* ■ (of a glass or bottle) empty or no longer

D

being used. ■ (of the ball in a game) out of play. See also **DEAD BALL**. ■ (of a cricket pitch or other surface) lacking springiness or bounce.
2 [attrib.] complete; absolute: *we sat in dead silence.*
▶ **adverb** [often as submodifier] absolutely; completely: *you're dead right* | *he was dead against the idea.* ■ exactly: *they arrived dead on time.* ■ straight; directly: *red flares were seen dead ahead.* ■ Brit. informal very: *omelettes are dead easy to prepare.*
– PHRASES **dead and buried** over; finished: *the incident is dead and buried.* **(as) dead as a** (or **the**) **dodo** see **DODO**. **(as) dead as a doornail** see **DOORNAIL**. **(as) dead as mutton** see **MUTTON**. **dead from the neck up** informal stupid. **dead in the water** (of a ship) unable to move. ■ unable to function effectively: *the economy is dead in the water.* **dead meat** informal used to suggest someone is in serious trouble: *if anyone finds out, you're dead meat.* **the dead of night** the quietest, darkest part of the night. **the dead of winter** the coldest part of winter. **dead on** exactly right: *her judgement was dead on.* **dead on one's feet** informal extremely tired. **dead to the world** informal fast asleep. **from the dead** from a state of death: *according to Christian belief, Jesus rose from the dead three days later.* ■ from a period of obscurity or inactivity: *the cartoon brought animation back from the dead.* **make a dead set at** see **SET**[2]. **more dead than alive** (of a person) hurt and in a very poor state: *he was breathing, but more dead than alive.* **over my dead body** see **BODY**. **wouldn't be seen** (or **caught**) **dead** informal used to express strong dislike for a particular thing: *I wouldn't be seen dead in a navy suit* | *she wouldn't be seen dead shopping with her mother.*
– DERIVATIVES **deadness** noun.
– ORIGIN Old English *dēad*, of Germanic origin: related to Dutch *dood* and German *tot*, also to **DIE**[1].

dead air ▶ **noun** [mass noun] a period during which the signal of a television or radio broadcast is unintentionally interrupted, so that no material is transmitted.

dead ball ▶ **noun** (in ball games) a ball that has gone out of play or is declared to be out of play. ■ [as modifier] Soccer involving a restart of the game by kicking a stationary ball, e.g. by a free kick: *dead-ball situations.*

dead-ball line ▶ **noun 1** Rugby a line behind the goal line, beyond which the ball is out of play.
2 Soccer the byline.

dead bat ▶ **noun** Cricket a bat held loosely so that the ball falls to the ground immediately when struck.

deadbeat ▶ **adjective 1** (**dead beat**) informal completely exhausted: *I must go to bed—I'm dead beat.*
2 (of a clock escapement or other mechanism) without recoil.
▶ **noun** informal an idle, feckless, or disreputable person. ■ N. Amer. a person who tries to evade paying their debts.

deadbolt ▶ **noun** a bolt engaged by turning a knob or key, rather than by spring action.

dead cat bounce ▶ **noun** Stock Exchange a temporary recovery in share prices after a substantial fall, caused by speculators buying in order to cover their positions.

dead centre ▶ **noun** the exact centre of something: *Kansas, the dead centre of the USA.* ■ the position of a crank when it is in line with the connecting rod and not exerting torque.

dead duck ▶ **noun** informal a person or thing that is defunct or has no chance of success: *travel promotions are a dead duck as far as marketing directors are concerned.*
– ORIGIN from the old saying 'never waste powder on a dead duck'.

deaden ▶ **verb** [with obj.] make (a noise or sensation) less strong or intense: *ether was used to deaden the pain.* ■ deprive of the power of sensation: *diabetes can deaden the nerve endings.* ■ deprive of force or vitality; stultify: *the syllabus has deadened the teaching process* | (as adj. **deadening**) *a deadening routine.* ■ make (someone) insensitive to something: *laughter might **deaden** us **to** the moral issue.*
– DERIVATIVES **deadener** noun.

dead end ▶ **noun** an end of a road or passage from which no exit is possible: *the path came to a dead end.* ■ a road or passage having such an end. ■ a situation offering no prospects of progress or development: *their relationship had reached a dead end* | [as modifier] *a dead-end street.*
▶ **verb** [no obj.] (**dead-end**) N. Amer. (of a road or passage) come to a dead end: *he kept walking, until the corridor dead-ended.*

deadeye ▶ **noun 1** Sailing a circular wooden block with a groove round the circumference to take a lanyard, used singly or in pairs to tighten a shroud.
2 informal, chiefly N. Amer. an expert marksman.

deadfall ▶ **noun** N. Amer. **1** a trap consisting of a heavy weight positioned to fall on an animal.
2 [mass noun] a tangled mass of fallen trees and brush. ■ [count noun] a fallen tree.
3 informal a disreputable drinking place.

dead hand ▶ **noun** an undesirable persisting influence: *the dead hand of state control.*

deadhead ▶ **noun 1** Brit. a faded flower head.
2 informal a boring or unenterprising person. ■ chiefly N. Amer. a passenger or member of an audience with a free ticket.
3 a sunken or partially submerged log.
4 (**Deadhead**) informal a fan of the rock group the Grateful Dead.
▶ **verb 1** [with obj.] remove dead flower heads from (a plant): *deadhead and spray rose bushes.*
2 [no obj.] N. Amer. informal (of a commercial driver) complete a trip in a train or other vehicle with no passengers or cargo: *they deadhead back to Denver on eastbound trains.*

dead heat ▶ **noun** a situation in which two or more competitors in a race are exactly level.
▶ **verb** (**dead-heat**) [no obj.] run or finish a race exactly level.

dead leg ▶ **noun 1** an injury caused by a numbing blow with the knee to a person's upper leg.
2 a length of pipe running from a hot water cylinder to the hot taps.
▶ **verb** (**dead-leg**) [with obj.] informal give (someone) a numbing blow to the upper leg with one's knee.

dead letter ▶ **noun 1** a law or treaty which has not been repealed but is ineffectual or defunct in practice. ■ a thing which is unimportant or obsolete: *theoretical reasoning is a dead letter to a child.*
2 chiefly N. Amer. an unclaimed or undelivered piece of mail.

dead letter box ▶ **noun** a place where messages can be left and collected without the sender and recipient meeting.

dead lift ▶ **noun** Weightlifting a lift made from a standing position, without the use of a bench or other equipment.

deadlight ▶ **noun 1** a protective cover or shutter fitted over a porthole or window on a ship.
2 US a skylight designed not to be opened.

deadline ▶ **noun 1** the latest time or date by which something should be completed.
2 historical a line drawn around a prison beyond which prisoners were liable to be shot.

dead load ▶ **noun** the intrinsic weight of a structure or vehicle, excluding the weight of passengers or goods. Often contrasted with **LIVE LOAD**.

deadlock ▶ **noun 1** [in sing.] a situation, typically one involving opposing parties, in which no progress can be made. ■ a situation in a game or match where the scores are level: *Ashton **broke the deadlock** with a penalty after 15 minutes.*
2 Brit. a type of lock requiring a key to open and close it, as distinct from a spring lock.
▶ **verb** [with obj.] **1** [no obj.] cause (a situation or opposing parties) to come to a point where no progress can be made because of fundamental disagreement: *the meeting is deadlocked.* ■ (**be deadlocked**) (of a game or match) be tied, with the score level.
2 Brit. secure (a door) with a deadlock.

dead loss ▶ **noun** a venture or situation which produces no profit. ■ informal, chiefly Brit. a person or thing that is completely useless.

deadly ▶ **adjective** (**deadlier**, **deadliest**) **1** causing or able to cause death: *a deadly weapon.* ■ filled with hate: *his voice was cold and deadly.* ■ extremely accurate, effective, or skilful: *his aim is deadly.* ■ Brit. informal extremely boring: *my end of the theatre is deadly at the moment.* ■ [attrib.] complete; total: *she was in deadly earnest.*
2 Irish & Austral. informal very good; excellent: *it's a great town and the pubs are deadly.*
▶ **adverb** [as submodifier] in a way resembling or suggesting death; as if dead: *her skin was deadly pale.* ■ extremely: *a deadly serious remark.*
– DERIVATIVES **deadliness** noun.
– ORIGIN Old English *dēadlic* 'mortal, in danger of death' (see **DEAD**, **-LY**[1]).

deadly nightshade ▶ **noun** a poisonous bushy Eurasian plant with drooping purple flowers and black cherry-like fruit. Also called **BELLADONNA**. ● *Atropa belladonna*, family Solanaceae.

deadly sin ▶ **noun** (in Christian tradition) a sin regarded as leading to damnation, especially one of a traditional list of seven. See **THE SEVEN DEADLY SINS** at **SEVEN**.

dead man ▶ **noun 1** informal a bottle after the contents have been drunk.
2 (also **deadman**) an object buried in or secured to the ground for the purpose of providing anchorage or leverage.

dead man's fingers ▶ **plural noun 1** a European colonial soft coral which has spongy lobes stiffened by calcareous spines, said to resemble the fingers of a corpse. ● *Alcyonium digitatum*, order Alcyonacea.
2 a fungus that produces clumps of dull black, irregular, finger-like fruiting bodies at the bases of dead tree stumps in Eurasia and North America. ● *Xylaria polymorpha*, family Xylariaceae, subdivision Ascomycotina.
3 informal the finger-like divisions of a lobster's or crab's gills.

dead man's handle (also **dead man's pedal**) ▶ **noun** (in a train) a lever which acts as a safety device by shutting off power when not held in place by the driver.

dead march ▶ **noun** a slow, solemn piece of music suitable for a funeral procession.

dead-nettle ▶ **noun** a Eurasian and North African plant of the mint family, with leaves that resemble those of a nettle but lack stinging hairs. ● *Lamium* and related genera, family Labiatae: several species, including the common **white dead-nettle** (*L. album*).

deadpan ▶ **adjective** impassive or expressionless: *she delivered her monologue in a deadpan voice.*
▶ **adverb** in a deadpan manner.
▶ **verb** (**dead-pan**) (**dead-pans**, **dead-panning**, **dead-panned**) [with direct speech] say something amusing while affecting a serious manner: *'I'm an undercover dentist,' he dead-panned.*

dead reckoning ▶ **noun** [mass noun] the process of calculating one's position, especially at sea, by estimating the direction and distance travelled rather than by using landmarks or astronomical observations.

dead ringer ▶ **noun** see **RINGER**.

deadrise ▶ **noun** the vertical distance between a line horizontal to the keel of a boat and its chine.

Dead Sea a salt lake or inland sea in the Jordan valley, on the Israel–Jordan border. Its surface is 400 m (1,300 ft) below sea level.

Dead Sea scrolls a collection of Hebrew and Aramaic manuscripts discovered in pottery storage jars in caves near Qumran between 1947 and 1956. Thought to have been hidden by the Essenes or a similar Jewish sect shortly before the revolt against Roman rule AD 66–70, the scrolls include texts of many books of the Old Testament; they are some 1,000 years older than previously known versions.

dead set ▶ **noun** see **SET**[2] (sense 2 of the noun).

dead shot ▶ **noun** an extremely accurate marksman or markswoman.

deadstick landing ▶ **noun** an unpowered landing of an aircraft.

deadstock ▶ **noun** [mass noun] the machinery used on a farm, as opposed to the livestock.
– ORIGIN mid 19th cent.: on the pattern of *livestock*.

dead time ▶ **noun** [mass noun] time in which someone or something is inactive or unable to act productively. ■ Physics the period after the recording of a particle or pulse when a detector is unable to record another.

dead water ▶ **noun** [mass noun] chiefly N. Amer. still water without any current.

dead weight ▶ **noun** the weight of an inert person or thing. ■ a heavy or oppressive burden. ■ the total weight of cargo, stores, etc. which a ship carries or can carry. ■ another term for **DEAD LOAD**. ■ [mass noun] Farming animals sold by the estimated weight of saleable meat that they will yield. ■ [usu. as modifier] Economics losses incurred because of the inefficient allocation of resources, especially through taxation or restriction: *a dead-weight burden.* ■ [usu. as modifier] a debt not covered by assets.

dead white ▶ **noun** [mass noun] a flat, lustreless white.

dead white European male (also **dead white male**) ▶ **noun** informal a writer, philosopher, or other significant figure whose importance and talents may have been exaggerated by virtue of his belonging to a historically dominant gender and ethnic group.

dead wood ▸ **noun** [mass noun] parts of a tree or branch which are dead. ■ people or things that are no longer useful or productive: *a lot of the company's dead wood was removed by voluntary redundancy.*

dead zone ▸ **noun 1** a place or period in which nothing happens or in which no life exists: *the week before Christmas is always a dead zone at work.* ■ an area of the ocean that is depleted of oxygen, frequently due to pollution.
2 a place where it is not possible to receive a mobile phone or radio signal.

deaerate /diːˈɛːreɪt/ ▸ **verb** [with obj.] remove dissolved air from (a substance).
– DERIVATIVES **deaeration** noun.

deaf ▸ **adjective** lacking the power of hearing or having impaired hearing: *I'm a bit deaf so you'll have to speak up | deaf children.* ■ unwilling or unable to hear or pay attention to something: *she is* ***deaf to*** *all advice.*
– PHRASES **(as) deaf as a post** having very bad hearing. **fall on deaf ears** (of a statement or request) be ignored. **turn a deaf ear** refuse to listen or respond to a statement or request.
– DERIVATIVES **deafness** noun.
– ORIGIN Old English *dēaf*, of Germanic origin; related to Dutch *doof* and German *taub*, from an Indo-European root shared by Greek *tuphlos* 'blind'.

deaf aid ▸ **noun** Brit. a hearing aid.

deaf-blind ▸ **adjective** having a severe impairment of both hearing and vision.

deafen ▸ **verb** [with obj.] cause (someone) to lose the power of hearing permanently or temporarily: *we were deafened by the explosion.* ■ **(deafen someone to)** cause someone to be unaware of (other sounds): *the noise deafened him to Ron's approach.*

deafening ▸ **adjective** (of a noise) so loud as to make it impossible to hear anything else: *the music reached a deafening crescendo.*
– DERIVATIVES **deafeningly** adverb.

deafferentation /diːˌaf(ə)r(ə)nˈteɪʃ(ə)n/ ▸ **noun** [mass noun] Biology the interruption or destruction of the afferent connections of nerve cells, performed especially in animal experiments to demonstrate the spontaneity of locomotor movement.
– DERIVATIVES **deafferented** adjective.

deaf mute ▸ **noun** a person who is both deaf and unable to speak.
▸ **adjective** (of a person) both deaf and unable to speak.

> **USAGE** In modern use **deaf mute** has acquired offensive connotations (implying, wrongly, that such people are without the capacity for communication). It should be avoided in favour of other terms such as **profoundly deaf**.

Deakin /ˈdiːkɪn/, Alfred (1856–1919), Australian Liberal statesman, Prime Minister 1903–4, 1905–8, and 1909–10.

deal[1] ▸ **verb** (past and past participle **dealt**) **1** [with obj.] distribute (cards) in an orderly rotation to players for a game or round: *the cards were dealt for the last hand* | [with two objs] figurative *fate dealt her a different hand* | [no obj.] *he shuffled and dealt.* ■ **(deal someone in)** include a new player in a card game by giving them cards. ■ distribute or mete out (something) to a person or group: *the punishments* ***dealt out*** *to the rioters were hideous.*
2 [no obj.] take part in commercial trading of a particular commodity: *directors were prohibited from* ***dealing in*** *the company's shares.* ■ be concerned with: *journalism that* ***deals in*** *small-town chit-chat.* ■ informal buy and sell illegal drugs.
3 [no obj.] **(deal with)** take measures concerning (someone or something), especially with the intention of putting something right: *the government had been unable to deal with the economic crisis.* ■ cope with or control (a difficult person or situation): *you'll have to find a way of dealing with those feelings.* ■ [with adverbial] treat (someone) in a particular way: *life had dealt very harshly with her.* ■ have commercial relations with: *the bank deals directly with the private sector.* ■ have as a subject; discuss: *the novel deals with several different topics.*
4 [with two objs] inflict (a blow) on (someone or something): *hopes of an economic recovery were dealt another blow.*
▸ **noun 1** an agreement entered into by two or more parties for their mutual benefit, especially in a business or political context: *the government was ready to do a deal with the opposition.* ■ [with adj.] a particular form of treatment given or received: *working mothers get a bad deal.*
2 [in sing.] the process of distributing the cards to players in a card game. ■ a player's turn to distribute cards. ■ the round of play following this. ■ the set of hands dealt to the players.
– PHRASES **a big deal** informal [usu. with negative] a thing considered important: *they don't make a big deal out of minor irritations.* ■ **(big deal)** used to express one's contempt for something regarded as impressive or important by another person. **a deal of** dated a large amount of: *he lost a deal of blood.* **a good** (or **great**) **deal** a large amount: *I don't know a great deal about politics.* ■ to a considerable extent: *she had got to know him a good deal better.* **a square deal** a fair arrangement. **it's a deal** informal used to express one's assent to an agreement.
– ORIGIN Old English *dǣlan* 'divide', 'participate', of Germanic origin; related to Dutch *deel* and German *Teil* 'part' (noun), also to **DOLE[1]**. The sense 'divide' gave rise to 'distribute', hence sense 1 of the verb, sense 4 of the verb; the sense 'participate' gave rise to 'have dealings with', hence sense 2 of the verb, sense 3 of the verb.

deal[2] ▸ **noun** [mass noun] fir or pine wood as a building material. ■ [count noun] a plank of such wood.
– ORIGIN Middle English: from Middle Low German and Middle Dutch *dele* 'plank'.

deal-breaker ▸ **noun** (in business and politics) a factor or issue which, if unresolved during negotiations, would cause one party to withdraw from a deal.

de-alcoholize (also **de-alcoholise**) ▸ **verb** [with obj.] remove the alcohol from (a normally alcoholic drink).
– DERIVATIVES **de-alcoholization** noun.

dealer ▸ **noun 1** a person who buys and sells goods: *a dealer in foreign stamps.* ■ a person who buys and sells shares, securities, or other financial assets as a principal (rather than as a broker or agent). See also **BROKER-DEALER**. ■ informal a person who buys and sells drugs: *he posed as a dealer willing to buy heroin.*
2 the player who distributes the cards at the start of a game.
– DERIVATIVES **dealership** noun (sense 1).

dealfish ▸ **noun** (pl. **same** or **dealfishes**) a long, slender silvery fish with a dorsal fin running the length of the body, living in the NE Atlantic. ● *Trachipterus arcticus*, family Trachipteridae.
– ORIGIN mid 19th cent.: from **DEAL[2]** in the sense 'board' (with reference to its shape) + **FISH[1]**.

dealign ▸ **verb** [no obj.] (of a voter) withdraw allegiance to a political party.
– DERIVATIVES **dealignment** noun.

dealing ▸ **noun 1 (dealings)** business relations or transactions: *they had dealings with an insurance company.* ■ a personal connection or association with someone: *my dealings with the gentler sex.*
2 the activity of buying and selling a particular commodity: *share dealings | drug dealing.*

dealmaker ▸ **noun** a person who is skilled at bringing commercial or political deals to a satisfactory conclusion.
– DERIVATIVES **dealmaking** noun.

dealt past participle of **DEAL[1]**.

deamination /dɪˈamɪneɪʃ(ə)n/ ▸ **noun** [mass noun] Biochemistry the removal of an amino group from an amino acid or other compound.
– DERIVATIVES **deaminated** adjective.

Dean, James (1931–55), American actor; born *James Byron*. Although he starred in only three films before dying in a car accident, he became a cult figure closely identified with the title role of *Rebel Without a Cause* (1955), symbolizing for many the disaffected youth of the post-war era.

dean[1] ▸ **noun 1** the head of the chapter of a cathedral or collegiate church. ■ (also **rural dean, area dean**) Brit. a member of the clergy exercising supervision over a group of parochial clergy within a division of an archdeaconry.
2 the head of a university faculty or department or of a medical school. ■ (in a college or university, especially Oxford or Cambridge) a senior member of a college, with disciplinary and advisory functions.
– ORIGIN Middle English: from Old French *deien*, from late Latin *decanus* 'chief of a group of ten', from *decem* 'ten'. Compare with **DOYEN**.

dean[2] ▸ **noun** variant spelling of **DENE[1]**.

deanery ▸ **noun** (pl. **deaneries**) **1** Brit. the group of parishes presided over by a rural dean.
2 the official residence of a dean. ■ the position or office of a dean.

de-anglicize (also **de-anglicise**) ▸ **verb** [with obj.] remove English characteristics or influence from.
– DERIVATIVES **de-anglicization** noun.

Dean of Faculty ▸ **noun** the president of the Faculty of Advocates in Scotland.

dean's list ▸ **noun** N. Amer. a list of students recognized for academic achievement during a term by the dean of the college they attend.

dear ▸ **adjective 1** regarded with deep affection: *a dear friend | he is very* ***dear to*** *me.* ■ used in speech as a polite or affectionate form of address: *Martin, my dear fellow.* ■ used in the polite form of address at the start of a letter. ■ endearing; sweet: *a dear little puppy.*
2 chiefly Brit. expensive: *five pounds—that's a bit dear!*
▸ **noun** used as an affectionate or friendly form of address: *don't you worry, dear.* ■ a sweet or endearing person: *Harry's a dear.*
▸ **adverb** chiefly Brit. at a high cost: *they buy property cheaply and sell dear.*
▸ **exclamation** used in expressions of surprise, dismay, or sympathy: *oh dear, I've upset you.*
– PHRASES **for dear life** see **LIFE**.
– DERIVATIVES **dearness** noun.
– ORIGIN Old English *dēore*, of Germanic origin; related to Dutch *dier* 'beloved', also to Dutch *duur* and German *teuer* 'expensive'.

dearest ▸ **adjective 1** most loved or cherished: *one of my dearest friends.*
2 Brit. most expensive: *beer is dearest in Germany.*
▸ **noun** used as an affectionate form of address.

dearie ▸ **noun** (pl. **dearies**) informal, chiefly Brit. used as a friendly or condescending form of address.
– PHRASES **dearie me!** used to express surprise or dismay.

Dear John letter (also **Dear John**) ▸ **noun** informal a letter from a woman to a man, ending a romantic or sexual relationship.

dearly ▸ **adverb 1** very much: *he loved his parents dearly.*
2 with much loss or suffering; at great cost: *freedom to worship our religion has been bought dearly.*

dearth /dəːθ/ ▸ **noun** a scarcity or lack of something: *there is* ***a dearth of*** *evidence.* ■ archaic a situation where food is in short supply.
– ORIGIN Middle English *derthe* (see **DEAR, -TH[2]**).

deasil /ˈdɛs(ə)l, ˈdjɛʃ(ə)l/ (also **deisal**) ▸ **adverb** dated, chiefly Scottish in the direction of the sun's apparent course, considered as lucky; clockwise.
– ORIGIN late 18th cent.: from Scottish Gaelic *deiseil*.

death ▸ **noun** [mass noun] the action or fact of dying or being killed; the end of the life of a person or organism: *he had been depressed since the death of his father* | [count noun] *an increase in deaths from skin cancer | I don't believe in life after death.* ■ the state of being dead: *even in death, she was beautiful.* ■ the permanent ending of vital processes in a cell or tissue. ■ **(Death)** the personification of the power that destroys life, often represented in art and literature as a skeleton or an old man holding a scythe. Also called **THE GRIM REAPER**. ■ the destruction or permanent end of something: *the death of her hopes.* ■ a damaging or destructive state of affairs: *to be driven to a dance by one's father would be social death.*
– PHRASES **as sure as death** quite certain. **at death's door** (especially in hyperbolic use) so ill that one may die. **be the death of** (often used hyperbolically or humorously) cause someone's death: *you'll be the death of me with all your questions.* **be in at the death** be present when a hunted animal is caught and killed. ■ be present when something fails or comes to an end. **catch one's death (of cold)** informal catch a severe cold or chill. **do someone to death** kill someone. **do something to death** perform or repeat something so frequently that it becomes tediously familiar: *a subject that has been done to death by generations of painters.* **a fate worse than death** a terrible experience. **like death warmed up** (or N. Amer. **over**) informal extremely tired or ill. **a matter of life and death** see **LIFE**. **put someone to death** kill someone, especially with official sanction. **to death** used of a particular action or process that results in someone's death: *he was stabbed to death.* ■ used to emphasize the extreme nature of a specific action, feeling, or state of mind: *I'm sick to death of you | I've got used to speaking in public but it used to scare me to death.* **to the death** until dead: *a fight to the death.*
– DERIVATIVES **deathlike** adjective.

D

– ORIGIN Old English *dēath*, of Germanic origin; related to Dutch *dood* and German *Tod*, also to DIE[1].

death adder ▶ noun a venomous Australian snake which has a thin worm-like tail that it uses to lure birds and other prey. ● Genus *Acanthophis*, family Elapidae: three species.

deathbed ▶ noun the bed where someone is dying or has died. ■ used in reference to the time when someone is dying or died: [as modifier] *a deathbed confession*.

death blow ▶ noun a stroke with a hand or weapon that causes death. ■ an event or circumstance which abruptly ends something: *this feature of quantum mechanics* ***dealt a death blow to*** *the theory*.

death camp ▶ noun a prison camp for political prisoners or prisoners of war in which many die from poor conditions and treatment.

death cap ▶ noun a deadly poisonous toadstool with a pale olive-green cap and white gills, growing in broadleaved woodland in both Eurasia and North America. ● *Amanita phalloides*, family Amanitaceae, class Hymenomycetes.

death cell ▶ noun a cell occupied by a prisoner who has been condemned to death or who awaits execution.

death certificate ▶ noun an official statement, signed by a doctor, of the cause, date, and place of a person's death.

death-dealing ▶ adjective capable of causing death: *death-dealing drugs*.

death duty ▶ noun [mass noun] (in the UK) a tax levied on property after the owner's death (replaced officially in 1975 by capital transfer tax and in 1986 by inheritance tax).

death futures ▶ plural noun US informal life insurance policies of terminally ill people, purchased by a third party at less than their mature value as a form of short-term investment. See also VIATICAL SETTLEMENT.

death grant ▶ noun (in the UK) a state grant towards funeral expenses (abolished under the Social Security Act 1986).

death house ▶ noun a house in which someone has died. ■ a place for storing bodies prior to burial or cremation. ■ US informal the building in which prisoners are kept in preparation for execution.

death instinct ▶ noun Psychoanalysis an innate desire for self-annihilation, proposed by certain psychologists. Compare with LIFE INSTINCT.

death knell ▶ noun the tolling of a bell to mark someone's death. ■ used to refer to the imminent destruction or failure of something: *the chaos may* ***sound the death knell for*** *the UN peace plan*.

deathless ▶ adjective chiefly literary or humorous immortal: *pages of deathless prose*.

– DERIVATIVES **deathlessness** noun.

deathly ▶ adjective (**deathlier**, **deathliest**) resembling or suggestive of death: *a deathly hush fell over the breakfast table* | [as submodifier] *his face was deathly pale*. ■ archaic or literary relating to or causing death: *an eagle carrying a snake in its deathly grasp*.

death mask ▶ noun a plaster cast taken of a dead person's face, used to make a mask or model.

death match ▶ noun **1** (in wrestling) a match in which many of the normal rules do not apply, typically leading to a more violent contest.
2 (in computer gaming) a mode of play in which the aim is to kill the characters controlled by other players.

death metal ▶ noun [mass noun] a form of heavy metal music using lyrics preoccupied with death, suffering, and destruction.

death-or-glory ▶ adjective brave to the point of foolhardiness; reckless: *a death-or-glory approach to political problems*.

death penalty ▶ noun (**the death penalty**) punishment by execution.

death rate ▶ noun the ratio of deaths to the population of a particular area or during a particular period of time, usually calculated as the number of deaths per one thousand people per year.

death rattle ▶ noun a gurgling sound sometimes heard in a dying person's throat.

death ray ▶ noun (in science fiction) a beam or ray capable of killing.

death roll ▶ noun Brit. old-fashioned term for DEATH TOLL.

death row ▶ noun a prison block or section for those sentenced to death: *a convicted killer* ***on death row***.

death's head ▶ noun a human skull as a symbol of mortality.

death's head hawkmoth ▶ noun a large dark European hawkmoth which has a skull-like marking on the thorax. ● *Acherontia atropos*, family Sphingidae.

death song ▶ noun a song sung before or after someone's death or to commemorate the dead.

death squad ▶ noun an armed paramilitary group formed to kill political opponents.

death tax ▶ noun US term for INHERITANCE TAX.

death toll ▶ noun the number of deaths resulting from a particular cause.

deathtrap ▶ noun a place, structure, or vehicle that is potentially very dangerous.

Death Valley a deep arid desert basin below sea level in SE California and SW Nevada, the hottest and driest part of North America.

death warrant ▶ noun an official order for the execution of a condemned person: *he signed the king's death warrant in 1649* | figurative *he signed his own death warrant by being seen as a peacemaker*.

death-watch beetle ▶ noun a small beetle whose larvae bore into dead wood and structural timbers, causing considerable damage. The adult makes a tapping sound like a watch ticking, formerly believed to portend death. ● *Xestobium rufovillosum*, family Anobiidae.

death wish ▶ noun an unconscious desire for one's own death.

deb ▶ noun informal short for DEBUTANTE.

debacle /deɪˈbɑːk(ə)l/ ▶ noun a sudden and ignominious failure; a fiasco.

– ORIGIN early 19th cent.: from French *débâcle*, from *débâcler* 'unleash', from *dé-* 'un-' + *bâcler* 'to bar' (from Latin *baculum* 'staff').

debag /diːˈbag/ ▶ verb (**debags**, **debagging**, **debagged**) [with obj.] Brit. informal take the trousers off (someone) as a joke or punishment.

debar ▶ verb (**debars**, **debarring**, **debarred**) [with obj.] exclude or prohibit (someone) officially from doing something: *first-round candidates were* ***debarred from*** *standing*.

– DERIVATIVES **debarment** noun.

– ORIGIN late Middle English: from French *débarrer*, from Old French *desbarrer* 'unbar', from *des-* (expressing reversal) + *barrer* 'to bar'.

debark[1] ▶ verb [no obj.] leave a ship or aircraft. ■ [with obj.] unload (cargo or troops) from a ship or aircraft.

– DERIVATIVES **debarkation** noun.

– ORIGIN mid 17th cent.: from French *débarquer*.

debark[2] ▶ verb [with obj.] remove (the bark) from a tree.

debase /dɪˈbeɪs/ ▶ verb **1** [with obj.] reduce (something) in quality or value; degrade: *the love episodes debase the dignity of the drama*. ■ lower the moral character of (someone): *war debases people*.
2 historical lower the value of (coinage) by reducing the content of precious metal.

– DERIVATIVES **debasement** noun, **debaser** noun.

– ORIGIN mid 16th cent. (in the sense 'humiliate, belittle'): from DE- 'down' + the obsolete verb *base* (compare with ABASE), expressing the notion 'bring down completely'.

debased ▶ adjective reduced in quality or value: *the debased traditions of sportsmanship*.

debatable ▶ adjective open to discussion or argument: *it is debatable whether the country is coming out of recession*. ■ historical (of land) on the border between two countries and claimed by each.

– DERIVATIVES **debatably** adverb.

debate ▶ noun a formal discussion on a particular matter in a public meeting or legislative assembly, in which opposing arguments are put forward and which usually ends with a vote. ■ an argument about a particular subject, especially one in which many people are involved: *the national* ***debate on*** *abortion* | [mass noun] *there has been much debate about prices*.
▶ verb [with obj.] argue about (a subject), especially in a formal manner: *MPs debated the issue in the Commons* | [no obj.] *members of the society debated for five nights*. ■ [with clause] consider a possible course of action in one's mind before reaching a decision: *he debated whether he should leave the matter alone or speak to her*.

– PHRASES **be open to debate** be unproven and requiring further discussion. **under debate** being discussed or disputed.

– DERIVATIVES **debater** noun.

– ORIGIN Middle English: via Old French from Latin *dis-* (expressing reversal) + *battere* 'to fight'.

debauch /dɪˈbɔːtʃ/ ▶ verb [with obj.] destroy or debase the moral purity of; corrupt. ■ dated seduce (a woman).
▶ noun a bout of excessive indulgence in sex, alcohol, or drugs.

– DERIVATIVES **debaucher** noun.

– ORIGIN late 16th cent.: from French *débaucher* (verb) 'turn away from one's duty', from Old French *desbaucher*, of uncertain ultimate origin.

debauched ▶ adjective indulging in or characterized by excessive indulgence in sex, alcohol, or drugs: *a debauched lifestyle*.

debauchee /ˌdɪbɔːˈtʃiː, -ˈʃiː/ ▶ noun a person given to excessive indulgence in sex, alcohol, or drugs.

– ORIGIN mid 17th cent.: from French *débauché* 'turned away from duty', past participle of *débaucher* (see DEBAUCH).

debauchery ▶ noun [mass noun] excessive indulgence in sex, alcohol, or drugs.

debby ▶ adjective informal characteristic of a debutante: *a debby girlfriend*.

debeak ▶ verb [with obj.] remove the upper part of the beak of (a bird) to prevent it injuring other birds.

de Beauvoir /də ˈbəʊvwɑː/, French /də boʊvwaʀ/, Simone (1908–86), French existentialist philosopher, novelist, and feminist. Her best-known work is *The Second Sex* (1949), a central book of the 'second wave' of feminism. She had a lifelong association with Jean-Paul Sartre.

debenture /dɪˈbɛntʃə/ ▶ noun Brit. a long-term security yielding a fixed rate of interest, issued by a company and secured against assets. ■ (also **debenture bond**) N. Amer. an unsecured loan certificate issued by a company.

– ORIGIN late Middle English (denoting a voucher issued by a royal household, giving the right to claim payment for goods or services): from Latin *debentur* 'are owing' (from *debere* 'owe'), used as the first word of a certificate recording a debt. The current sense dates from the mid 19th cent.

debilitate /dɪˈbɪlɪteɪt/ ▶ verb [with obj.] make (someone) very weak and infirm: *he was severely debilitated by a stomach upset* | (as adj. **debilitated**) *a debilitated patient*. ■ hinder, delay, or weaken: *hard drugs destroy families and debilitate communities*.

– DERIVATIVES **debilitation** noun, **debilitative** adjective.

– ORIGIN mid 16th cent.: from Latin *debilitat-* 'weakened', from the verb *debilitare*, from *debilitas* (see DEBILITY).

debilitating ▶ adjective (of a disease or condition) making someone very weak and infirm: *debilitating back pain*. ■ tending to weaken something: *the debilitating effects of underinvestment*.

– DERIVATIVES **debilitatingly** adverb.

debility ▶ noun (pl. **debilities**) [mass noun] physical weakness, especially as a result of illness.

– ORIGIN late Middle English: from Old French *debilite*, from Latin *debilitas*, from *debilis* 'weak'.

debit ▶ noun an entry recording a sum owed, listed on the left-hand side or column of an account. The opposite of CREDIT. ■ a payment made or owed.
▶ verb (**debits**, **debiting**, **debited**) [with obj.] (of a bank or other financial organization) remove (an amount of money) from a customer's account: *$10,000 was debited from their account*. ■ remove an amount of money from (a bank account): *cash terminals automatically debit a customer's bank account*.

– PHRASES **be in debit** (of an account) show a net balance of money owed to others. **the debit side** the unsatisfactory aspect of a situation: *on the debit side, they predict a rise in book prices*.

– ORIGIN late Middle English (in the sense 'debt'): from French *débit*, from Latin *debitum* 'something owed' (see DEBT). The verb sense dates from the 17th cent.; the current noun sense from the late 18th cent.

debitage /ˌdɛbɪˈtɑːʒ/ ▶ noun [mass noun] Archaeology waste material produced in the making of prehistoric stone implements.

– ORIGIN mid 20th cent.: from French *débitage* 'cutting of stone', from *débiter* 'discharge, dispense'.

debit card ▶ noun a card allowing the holder to transfer money electronically from their bank account when making a purchase.

deblur ▶ verb (**deblurs**, **deblurring**, **deblurred**) [with obj.] technical make (a blurred image) sharper.

debonair ▸ adjective (of a man) confident, stylish, and charming.
– DERIVATIVES **debonairly** adverb.
– ORIGIN Middle English (in the sense 'meek or courteous'): from Old French *debonaire*, from *de bon aire* 'of good disposition'.

debone ▸ verb [with obj.] (often as adj. **deboned**) remove the bones from (meat or fish) before cooking.

Deborah /ˈdɛbərə, ˈdɛbrə/ a biblical prophet and leader who inspired the Israelite army to defeat the Canaanites (Judges 4–5). The 'Song of Deborah', a song of victory attributed to her, is thought to be one of the oldest sections of the Bible.

debouch /dɪˈbaʊtʃ, -ˈbuːʃ/ ▸ verb [no obj., with adverbial of direction] emerge from a confined space into a wide, open area: *the stream finally debouches into a silent pool.*
– DERIVATIVES **debouchment** noun.
– ORIGIN mid 18th cent.: from French *déboucher*, from *dé-* (expressing removal) + *bouche* 'mouth' (from Latin *bucca* 'cheek').

Debrecen /ˈdɛbrətsɛn/ an industrial and commercial city in eastern Hungary; pop. 206,225 (2009).

Debrett /dəˈbrɛt/, John (*c.*1750–1822), English publisher. He compiled *The Peerage of England, Scotland, and Ireland* (first issued in 1803), which is regarded as the authority on the British nobility; it is published today as *Debrett's Peerage and Baronetage*, but is often known just as **Debrett's**.

debridement /deɪˈbriːdmɒ̃, dɪˈbriːdm(ə)nt/ ▸ noun [mass noun] Medicine the removal of damaged tissue or foreign objects from a wound.
– DERIVATIVES **debride** verb.
– ORIGIN mid 19th cent.: from French, from *débrider*, literally 'remove the bridle from', based on *bride* 'bridle' (of Germanic origin).

debrief ▸ verb [with obj.] question (someone, typically a soldier or spy) about a completed mission or undertaking: *the government debriefed him over a span of four years* | (as noun **debriefing**) *during his debriefing he exposed two Russian spies.*
▸ noun a series of questions about a completed mission or undertaking.
– DERIVATIVES **debriefer** noun.

debris /ˈdɛbriː, ˈdeɪbriː/ ▸ noun [mass noun] scattered pieces of rubbish or remains. ■ loose natural material consisting especially of broken pieces of rock.
– ORIGIN early 18th cent.: from French *débris*, from obsolete *débriser* 'break down'.

de Broglie /də ˈbrəʊgli/, French /də bʀɔj/, Louis-Victor, Prince (1892–1987), French physicist. He was the first to suggest that subatomic particles can also have the properties of waves, and his name is now applied to such a wave. He further developed the study of wave mechanics, which was fundamental to the subsequent development of quantum mechanics. Nobel Prize for Physics (1929).

debruise /dɪˈbruːz/ ▸ verb [with obj.] Heraldry partly obscure (another charge).
– ORIGIN Middle English: from Old French *debruisier*, *debrisier*, from **DE-** + *bruiser*, *brisier* (modern *briser*), 'break'.

debt ▸ noun a sum of money that is owed or due: *I paid off my debts* | [mass noun] *a way to reduce Third World debt.* ■ [mass noun] the state of owing money: *the firm is heavily in debt.* ■ a feeling of gratitude for a service or favour: *I would like to acknowledge my debt to my teachers.*
– PHRASES **be in someone's debt** owe gratitude to someone for a service or favour.
– ORIGIN Middle English *dette*: from Old French, based on Latin *debitum* 'something owed', past participle of *debere* 'owe'. The spelling change in French and English was by association with the Latin word.

debt collector ▸ noun a person who is employed to collect debts for creditors.

debt counsellor ▸ noun a person who offers professional advice on methods of debt repayment.

debt of honour ▸ noun a debt that is not legally recoverable, especially a sum lost in gambling. ■ a feeling of great gratitude: *we owe a debt of honour to miners who have died from these terrible diseases.*

debtor ▸ noun a person, country, or organization that owes money.

debt relief ▸ noun [mass noun] the partial or total remission of debts, especially those owed by developing countries to external creditors.

debt security ▸ noun a negotiable or tradable liability or loan.

debt swap (also **debt-for-nature swap**) ▸ noun an arrangement whereby a foreign debt owed by a developing country is transferred to a particular organization, typically in return for the country's committing itself to specified conservation measures.

debug ▸ verb (**debugs**, **debugging**, **debugged**) [with obj.] **1** identify and remove errors from (computer hardware or software): *games are the worst to debug* | (as noun **debugging**) *software debugging.*
2 detect and remove concealed microphones from (an area).
3 N. Amer. remove insects from (something), especially with a pesticide.
▸ noun [mass noun] the process of identifying and removing errors from computer hardware or software.

debugger ▸ noun a computer program that assists in the detection and correction of errors in other computer programs.

debunk ▸ verb [with obj.] expose the falseness or hollowness of (an idea or belief): *she debunks all the usual rubbish about acting.* ■ reduce the inflated reputation of (someone): *comedy takes delight in debunking heroes.*
– DERIVATIVES **debunker** noun, **debunkery** noun.

deburr /diːˈbəː/ (also **debur**) ▸ verb (**deburrs**, **deburring**, **deburred**) [with obj.] neaten and smooth the rough edges or ridges of (an object, typically one made of metal).

debus /diːˈbʌs/ ▸ verb (**debuses**, **debussing**, **debussed**) [no obj.] Brit., chiefly military slang alight from a motor vehicle. ■ [with obj.] unload (personnel or stores) from a vehicle.

Debussy /dəˈb(j)uːsi/, French /dəbysi/, (Achille) Claude (1862–1918), French composer and critic. Debussy carried the ideas of Impressionist art and symbolist poetry into music, using melodies based on the whole-tone scale and delicate harmonies exploiting overtones. Notable works: *Prélude à l'après-midi d'un faune* (1894).

debut /ˈdeɪbjuː, -buː/ ▸ noun a person's first appearance or performance in a particular capacity or role: *the film marked his debut as a director.* ■ [as modifier] denoting the first recording or publication of a group, singer, or writer: *a debut album.* ■ dated the first appearance of a debutante in society.
▸ verb [no obj., with adverbial] perform in public for the first time: *the Rolling Stones debuted at the Marquee.* ■ (of a new product) be launched: *the model is expected to debut at $19,000.* ■ [with obj.] (of a company) launch (a new product): *the company is to debut new software.*
– ORIGIN mid 18th cent.: from French *début*, from *débuter* 'lead off'.

debutant /ˈdɛbjuːtɒ̃, ˈdeɪ-/ ▸ noun a man making his first public appearance, especially in sport.
– ORIGIN early 19th cent.: from French *débutant* 'leading off', from the verb *débuter*.

debutante /ˈdɛbjʊtɑːnt, ˈdeɪ-/ ▸ noun an upper-class young woman making her first appearance in fashionable society. ■ a woman making her first public appearance, especially in sport.
– ORIGIN early 19th cent.: from French *débutante* (feminine) 'leading off', from the verb *débuter*.

Debye /dəˈbʌɪ/, Peter Joseph William (1884–1966), Dutch-born American chemical physicist. Debye is best known for establishing the existence of permanent electric dipole moments in many molecules, demonstrating the use of these to determine molecular size and shape, and modifying Einstein's theory of specific heats as applied to solids. Nobel Prize for Chemistry (1936).

debye /dəˈbʌɪ/ (also **debye unit**) ▸ noun Chemistry a unit used to express electric dipole moments of molecules. One debye is equal to 3.336×10^{-30} coulomb metre.
– ORIGIN early 20th cent.: named after P. J. **DEBYE**.

Dec. ▸ abbreviation December.

dec. ▸ abbreviation ■ deceased. ■ Cricket declared.

deca- /ˈdɛkə/ (also **dec-** before a vowel) ▸ combining form (used commonly in units of measurement) ten; having ten: *decahedron* | *decane.*
– ORIGIN from Greek *deka* 'ten'.

decade /ˈdɛkeɪd, dɪˈkeɪd/ ▸ noun **1** a period of ten years. ■ a period of ten years beginning with a year ending in 0.
2 each of the five divisions of each chapter of the rosary.
3 a range of electrical resistances, frequencies, or other quantities spanning from one to ten times a base value.
– DERIVATIVES **decadal** adjective.
– ORIGIN late Middle English (denoting each of ten parts of a literary work): via Old French and late Latin from Greek *deka* 'ten'. Sense 1 dates from the early 17th cent.

> **USAGE** There are two possible pronunciations for **decade**: one puts the stress on the **dec-** while the other puts the stress on the **-cade** (sounds like **decayed**). The second pronunciation is disapproved of by some traditionalists but is now regarded as a standard, acceptable alternative.

D

decadence /ˈdɛkəd(ə)ns/ ▸ noun [mass noun] moral or cultural decline as characterized by excessive indulgence in pleasure or luxury: *he denounced Western decadence.* ■ luxurious self-indulgence: *cream cakes on a Wednesday—pure decadence.*
– ORIGIN mid 16th cent.: from French *décadence*, from medieval Latin *decadentia*; related to **DECAY**.

decadent ▸ adjective characterized by or reflecting a state of moral or cultural decline. ■ luxuriously self-indulgent: *a decadent soak in a scented bath.*
▸ noun a person who is luxuriously self-indulgent. ■ (often **Decadent**) a member of a group of late 19th-century French and English poets associated with the Aesthetic Movement.
– DERIVATIVES **decadently** adverb.
– ORIGIN mid 19th cent.: from French *décadent*, from medieval Latin *decadentia* (see **DECADENCE**).

decaf /ˈdiːkaf/ (also **decaff**) ▸ noun [mass noun] informal (trademark in the UK) decaffeinated coffee.
– ORIGIN 1960s: abbreviation.

decaffeinated /diːˈkafɪneɪtɪd/ ▸ adjective (of coffee or tea) having had most or all of the caffeine removed.
– DERIVATIVES **decaffeinate** verb, **decaffeination** noun.

decagon /ˈdɛkəg(ə)n/ ▸ noun a plane figure with ten straight sides and angles.
– DERIVATIVES **decagonal** adjective.
– ORIGIN mid 17th cent.: via medieval Latin from Greek *dekagōnon*, neuter (used as a noun) of *dekagōnos* 'ten-angled'.

decahedron /ˌdɛkəˈhiːdr(ə)n, -ˈhɛd-/ ▸ noun (pl. **decahedra** or **decahedrons**) a solid figure with ten plane faces.
– DERIVATIVES **decahedral** adjective.
– ORIGIN early 19th cent.: from **DECA-** 'ten' + **-HEDRON**, on the pattern of words such as *polyhedron*.

decal /ˈdiːkal/ ▸ noun a design prepared on special paper for durable transfer on to another surface such as glass or porcelain.
– ORIGIN 1950s: abbreviation of **DECALCOMANIA**.

decalcified ▸ adjective (of rock or bone) containing a reduced quantity of calcium salts.
– DERIVATIVES **decalcification** noun, **decalcifier** noun, **decalcify** verb (**decalcifies**, **decalcifying**, **decalcified**).

decalcomania /dɪˌkalkə(ʊ)ˈmeɪnɪə/ ▸ noun [mass noun] the process of transferring designs from prepared paper on to glass or porcelain. ■ a technique used by some surrealist artists which involves pressing paint between sheets of paper.
– ORIGIN mid 19th cent.: from French *décalcomanie*, from *décalquer* 'transfer a tracing' + *-manie* '-mania' (with reference to the enthusiasm for the process in the 1860s).

decalitre (US **decaliter**, **dekaliter**) (abbrev.: **dal**; US also **dkl**) ▸ noun a metric unit of capacity, equal to 10 litres.

Decalogue /ˈdɛkəlɒg/ ▸ noun (**the Decalogue**) the Ten Commandments.
– ORIGIN late Middle English: via French and ecclesiastical Latin from Greek *dekalogos* (*biblos*) '(book of) the Ten Commandments', from *hoi deka logoi* 'the Ten Commandments' (literally 'the ten sayings').

Decameron /dɪˈkamərən/ a work by Boccaccio, written between 1348 and 1358, containing a hundred tales supposedly told in ten days by a party of ten young people who had fled from the Black Death in Florence. The work was influential on later writers such as Chaucer and Shakespeare.

decametre (US **decameter**, **dekameter**) (abbrev.: **dam**; US also **dkm**) ▸ noun a metric unit of length, equal to 10 metres.
– DERIVATIVES **decametric** adjective.

decamp ▸ verb [no obj.] **1** leave a place suddenly or secretly: *now he has decamped to Hollywood.*

D

2 break up or leave a military camp.
– DERIVATIVES **decampment** noun.
– ORIGIN late 17th cent.: from French *décamper*, from *dé-* (expressing removal) + *camp* 'camp'.

decan /ˈdɛk(ə)n/ ▶ **noun** Astrology each of three equal ten-degree divisions of a sign of the zodiac.
– ORIGIN late 16th cent.: from late Latin *decanus* 'chief of a group of ten' (see DEAN[1]).

decanal /dɪˈkeɪn(ə)l, ˈdɛk(ə)n(ə)l/ ▶ **adjective** relating to a dean or deanery. ■ relating to or denoting the south side of the choir of a church, the side on which the dean sits. The opposite of CANTORIAL.
– ORIGIN early 18th cent.: from medieval Latin *decanalis*, from late Latin *decanus* (see DEAN[1]).

decane /ˈdɛkeɪn/ ▶ **noun** [mass noun] Chemistry a colourless liquid hydrocarbon of the alkane series, present in petroleum spirit. ● Chem. formula: $C_{10}H_{22}$.

decani /dɪˈkeɪnʌɪ/ ▶ **noun** the section of a church or cathedral choir conventionally placed on the south side and taking the first or higher part in antiphonal singing. The opposite of CANTORIS.
– ORIGIN mid 18th cent.: from Latin, literally 'of the dean' (see DEAN[1]).

decant /dɪˈkant/ ▶ **verb** [with obj.] gradually pour (wine, port, or another liquid) from one container into another, typically in order to separate out sediment: *he decanted the rich red liquid into some glasses.* ■ Brit. temporarily transfer (people) to another place: *tour coaches decant eager customers directly into the store.*
– ORIGIN mid 17th cent.: from medieval Latin *decanthare*, from Latin *de-* 'away from' + *canthus* 'edge, rim' (used to denote the angular lip of a beaker), from Greek *kanthos* 'corner of the eye'.

decanter ▶ **noun** a stoppered glass container into which wine or spirit is decanted.

decapitate /dɪˈkapɪteɪt/ ▶ **verb** [with obj.] cut off the head of (someone): (as adj. **decapitated**) *a decapitated body.* ■ attempt to undermine (a group or organization) by removing its leaders: *the Church had been decapitated by the arrest and deportation of all its bishops.*
– DERIVATIVES **decapitation** noun, **decapitator** noun.
– ORIGIN early 17th cent.: from late Latin *decapitat-* 'decapitated', from the verb *decapitare*, from *de-* (expressing removal) + *caput*, *capit-* 'head'.

decapod /ˈdɛkəpɒd/ Zoology ▶ **noun** a crustacean of the order Decapoda, such as a shrimp, crab, or lobster.
▶ **adjective** relating to or denoting decapods.

Decapoda /ˌdɛkəˈpəʊdə/ ▶ **plural noun** Zoology **1** an order of crustaceans which includes shrimps, crabs, and lobsters. They have five pairs of walking legs and are typically marine.
2 a former order of cephalopod molluscs which includes squids and cuttlefishes, which have eight arms and two long tentacles. Compare with OCTOPODA.
– ORIGIN modern Latin (plural), from DECA- 'ten' + Greek *pous*, *pod-* 'foot'.

decapsulate ▶ **verb** [with obj.] Surgery remove the capsule or covering from (a kidney or other organ).

decarbonize (also **decarbonise**) ▶ **verb** [with obj.] reduce the amount of gaseous carbon compounds released in or as a result of (an environment or process): *policies to decarbonize the UK economy.* ■ remove carbon or carbonaceous deposits from (an engine or other metal object).
– DERIVATIVES **decarbonization** noun.

decarboxylase /ˌdiːkɑːˈbɒksɪleɪz/ ▶ **noun** Biochemistry an enzyme that catalyses the decarboxylation of a particular organic molecule.

decarboxylate /ˌdiːkɑːˈbɒksɪleɪt/ ▶ **verb** [with obj.] Chemistry eliminate a carboxylic acid group from (an organic compound).
– DERIVATIVES **decarboxylation** noun.

decarburize /diːˈkɑːbjʊrʌɪz/ (also **decarburise**) ▶ **verb** [with obj.] Metallurgy remove carbon from (iron or steel).
– DERIVATIVES **decarburization** noun.
– ORIGIN mid 19th cent.: from DE- (expressing removal) + CARBURIZE, on the pattern of French *décarburer*.

decastyle /ˈdɛkəstʌɪl/ Architecture ▶ **adjective** (of a temple or portico) having ten columns.
▶ **noun** a ten-columned portico.
– ORIGIN early 18th cent.: from Greek *dekastulos* 'having ten columns', from *deka* 'ten' + *stulos* 'column'.

decasyllabic /ˌdɛkəsɪˈlabɪk/ ▶ **adjective** Prosody (of a metrical line) consisting of ten syllables.

decasyllable ▶ **noun** a metrical line of ten syllables.

decathlon /dɪˈkaθlɒn, -lən/ ▶ **noun** an athletic event taking place over two days, in which each competitor takes part in the same prescribed ten events (100 metres sprint, long jump, shot-put, high jump, 400 metres, 110 metres hurdles, discus, pole vault, javelin, and 1,500 metres).
– DERIVATIVES **decathlete** noun.
– ORIGIN early 20th cent.: from DECA- 'ten' + Greek *athlon* 'contest'.

decay ▶ **verb** [no obj.] (of organic matter) rot or decompose through the action of bacteria and fungi: *the body had begun to decay* | (as adj. **decayed**) *decayed animal and plant matter* | (as adj. **decaying**) *the odour of decaying fish.* ■ [with obj.] cause to rot or decompose: *the fungus will decay soft timber.* ■ fall into disrepair; deteriorate: *facilities decay when money is not spent on refurbishment.* ■ decline in quality, power, or vigour: *the moral authority of the party was decaying.* ■ Physics (of a radioactive substance, particle, etc.) undergo change to a different form by emitting radiation. ■ technical (of a physical quantity) undergo a gradual decrease.
▶ **noun** [mass noun] the state or process of rotting or decomposition: *hardwood is more resistant to decay than softwood* | *tooth decay.* ■ rotten matter or tissue: *fluoride heals small spots of decay.* ■ structural or physical deterioration: *the old barn rapidly **fell into decay**.* ■ the process of declining in quality, power, or vigour: *the problems of urban decay.* ■ Physics the change of a radioactive substance, particle, etc. into another by the emission of radiation. ■ technical gradual decrease in the magnitude of a physical quantity.
– ORIGIN late Middle English: from Old French *decair*, based on Latin *decidere* 'fall down or off', from *de-* 'from' + *cadere* 'fall'.

Deccan /ˈdɛkən/ a triangular plateau in southern India, bounded by the Malabar Coast in the west, the Coromandel Coast in the east, and by the Vindhaya mountains in the north.

decease ▶ **noun** [in sing.] formal or Law a person's death: *he held the post until his untimely decease in 1991.*
▶ **verb** [no obj.] archaic die.
– ORIGIN Middle English: from Old French *deces*, from Latin *decessus* 'death', past participle (used as a noun) of *decedere* 'to die'.

deceased formal or Law ▶ **noun** (**the deceased**) the recently dead person in question.
▶ **adjective** recently dead: *the deceased man's family* | [postpositive] *the will of Christopher Smith deceased.*

decedent /dɪˈsiːd(ə)nt/ ▶ **noun** US Law a deceased person.
– ORIGIN late 16th cent.: from Latin *decedent-* 'dying', from the verb *decedere* (see DECEASE).

deceit ▶ **noun** [mass noun] the action or practice of deceiving someone by concealing or misrepresenting the truth: *a web of deceit* | [count noun] *a series of lies and deceits.*
– ORIGIN Middle English: from Old French, past participle (used as a noun) of *deceveir* 'deceive'.

deceitful ▶ **adjective** guilty of or involving deceit; deceiving or misleading others: *a deceitful politician* | *such an act would have been deceitful and irresponsible.*
– DERIVATIVES **deceitfully** adverb, **deceitfulness** noun.

deceive ▶ **verb** [with obj.] deliberately cause (someone) to believe something that is not true, especially for personal gain: *I didn't intend to **deceive** people **into** thinking it was French champagne.* ■ (of a thing) give (someone) a mistaken impression: *the area may seem to offer nothing of interest, but don't be deceived.* ■ (**deceive oneself**) fail to admit to oneself that something is true. ■ be sexually unfaithful to (one's regular partner): *he had deceived her with another woman.*
– DERIVATIVES **deceivable** adjective, **deceiver** noun.
– ORIGIN Middle English: from Old French *deceivre*, from Latin *decipere* 'catch, ensnare, cheat'.

decelerate /diːˈsɛləreɪt/ ▶ **verb** reduce or cause to reduce in speed: [no obj.] *the train began to decelerate.*
– DERIVATIVES **deceleration** noun, **decelerator** noun.
– ORIGIN late 19th cent.: from DE- (expressing removal) + a shortened form of ACCELERATE.

December ▶ **noun** the twelfth month of the year, in the northern hemisphere usually considered the first month of winter: *the fuel shortage worsened during December.*
– ORIGIN Middle English: from Latin, from *decem* 'ten' (being originally the tenth month of the Roman year).

Decembrist /dɪˈsɛmbrɪst/ ▶ **noun** a member of a group of Russian revolutionaries who in December 1825 led an unsuccessful revolt against Tsar Nicholas I.

decency ▶ **noun** (pl. **decencies**) **1** [mass noun] behaviour that conforms to accepted standards of morality or respectability: *she **had the decency to** come and confess.* ■ behaviour or appearance that avoids impropriety or immodesty: *a loose dress, rather too low-cut for decency.* ■ (**decencies**) the requirements of accepted or respectable behaviour: *an appeal to common decencies.*
2 (**decencies**) things required for a reasonable standard of life: *I can't afford any of the decencies of life.*
– ORIGIN mid 16th cent. (in the sense 'appropriateness, fitness'): from Latin *decentia*, from *decent-* 'being fitting' (see DECENT).

decennial /dɪˈsɛnɪəl/ ▶ **adjective** recurring every ten years: *the decennial census.* ■ lasting for or relating to a period of ten years: *decennial insurance.*
– DERIVATIVES **decennially** adverb.
– ORIGIN mid 17th cent.: from Latin *decennium* 'a decade', from *decennis* 'of ten years' (from *decem* 'ten' + *annus* 'year'), + -AL.

decennium ▶ **noun** (pl. **decennia** or **decenniums**) rare a decade.
– ORIGIN late 17th cent.: from Latin, from *decem* 'ten' + *annus* 'year'.

decent ▶ **adjective 1** conforming with generally accepted standards of respectable or moral behaviour: *a decent clean-living individual.* ■ appropriate; fitting: *they would meet again after a decent interval.* ■ not likely to shock or embarrass others: *a decent high-necked dress.* ■ informal sufficiently clothed to see visitors: *'Hello, miss? Are you decent?'.*
2 [attrib.] of an acceptable standard; satisfactory: *people need decent homes.* ■ good: *there's a few decent players in the team.* ■ Brit. informal kind, obliging, or generous: *that's awfully decent of you.*
– PHRASES **do the decent thing** take the most honourable or appropriate course of action, even if is not necessarily in one's own interests: *after his defeat he should do the decent thing and step down.*
– DERIVATIVES **decently** adverb.
– ORIGIN mid 16th cent. (in the sense 'suitable, appropriate'): from Latin *decent-* 'being fitting', from the verb *decere.*

decentralize (also **decentralise**) ▶ **verb** [with obj.] (often as adj. **decentralized**) transfer (authority) from central to local government: *Canada has one of the most decentralized governments in the world.* ■ move departments of (a large organization) away from a single administrative centre to other locations.
– DERIVATIVES **decentralist** noun & adjective, **decentralization** noun.

decentre (US **decenter**) ▶ **verb** [with obj.] displace from the centre or from a central position.

deception ▶ **noun** [mass noun] the action of deceiving someone: *obtaining property by deception.* ■ [count noun] a thing that deceives: *a range of elaborate deceptions.*
– ORIGIN late Middle English: from late Latin *deceptio(n-)*, from *decipere* 'deceive'.

deceptive ▶ **adjective** giving an appearance or impression different from the true one; misleading: *he put the question with deceptive casualness.*
– DERIVATIVES **deceptiveness** noun.

deceptively ▶ **adverb** [usu. as submodifier] in a way or to an extent that gives a misleading impression: ■ to a lesser extent than appears the case: *the idea was deceptively simple.* ■ to a greater extent than appears the case: *the airy and deceptively spacious lounge.*

> **USAGE** **Deceptively** belongs to a very small set of words whose meaning is genuinely ambiguous. It can be used in similar contexts to mean both one thing and also its complete opposite. A ***deceptively smooth** surface* is one which appears smooth but in fact is not smooth at all, while a ***deceptively spacious** room* is one that does not look spacious but is in fact **more** spacious than it appears. But what is a ***deceptively steep** gradient*? Or a person who is described as ***deceptively strong***? To avoid confusion, it is probably best to reword and not to use **deceptively** in such contexts at all.

decerebrate /diːˈsɛrɪbreɪt/ ▶ **verb** [with obj.] (usu. as adj. **decerebrated**) Biology remove the cerebrum from (a laboratory animal).
– DERIVATIVES **decerebration** noun.

decertify ▶ **verb** (**decertifies, decertifying, decertified**) [with obj.] remove a certificate or certification from.
– DERIVATIVES **decertification** noun.

de-Christianize (also **de-Christianise**) ▶ **verb** [with obj.] remove Christian influences or characteristics from.
– DERIVATIVES **de-Christianization** noun.

deci- ▶ **combining form** (used commonly in units of measurement) one tenth: *decilitre*.
– ORIGIN from Latin *decimus* 'tenth'.

decibel /ˈdɛsɪbɛl/ (abbrev.: **dB**) ▶ **noun** a unit used to measure the intensity of a sound or the power level of an electrical signal by comparing it with a given level on a logarithmic scale. ■ (in general use) a degree of loudness: *his voice went up several decibels*.
– ORIGIN early 20th cent.: from DECI- 'ten' + BEL (the unit being one tenth of a bel).

decide ▶ **verb** [with obj.] come or bring to a resolution in the mind as a result of consideration: [with clause] *she decided that she liked him* | [with infinitive] *I've decided to stay on a bit* | *this business about the letter decided me*. ■ [no obj.] make a choice from a number of alternatives: *she had **decided on** her plan of action* | *I've **decided against** having children*. ■ [no obj.] give a judgement concerning a matter or legal case: *the courts decided in favour of the New York claimants* | [with obj.] *the judge will decide the case*. ■ come to a decision about (something): *the council will decide the fate of the homes*. ■ resolve or settle (a question or contest): *an exciting game was decided by a 65th-minute goal*.
– DERIVATIVES **decidable** adjective.
– ORIGIN late Middle English (in the sense 'bring to a settlement'): from French *décider*, from Latin *decidere* 'determine', from *de-* 'off' + *caedere* 'cut'.

decided ▶ **adjective** [attrib.] (of a quality) definite; unquestionable: *the sunshine is a decided improvement*. ■ (of a person) having clear opinions; resolute. ■ (of a legal case) having been resolved.
– DERIVATIVES **decidedness** noun.

decidedly ▶ **adverb 1** [usu. as submodifier] undoubtedly; undeniably: *he looked decidedly uncomfortable*.
2 Brit. in a decisive and confident way: *'No,' Donna said decidedly*.

decider ▶ **noun** a game, goal, point, etc. that settles a contest or series of contests: *a tense promotion decider*.

deciding ▶ **adjective** serving to resolve or settle something: *taxes could be the **deciding factor** for millions of floating voters*.

decidua /dɪˈsɪdjʊə/ ▶ **noun** [mass noun] Physiology the thick layer of modified mucous membrane which lines the uterus during pregnancy and is shed with the afterbirth.
– DERIVATIVES **decidual** adjective.
– ORIGIN late 18th cent.: from modern Latin *decidua* (*membrana*), literally 'falling off (membrane)'.

deciduous /dɪˈsɪdjʊəs/ ▶ **adjective** (of a tree or shrub) shedding its leaves annually. Often contrasted with EVERGREEN. ■ informal (of a tree or shrub) broadleaved. ■ denoting the milk teeth of a mammal, which are shed after a time.
– DERIVATIVES **deciduously** adverb, **deciduousness** noun.
– ORIGIN late 17th cent.: from Latin *deciduus* (from *decidere* 'fall down or off') + -OUS.

decigram /ˈdɛsɪgram/ (also **decigramme**) (abbrev.: **dg**) ▶ **noun** a metric unit of mass, equal to one tenth of a gram.

decile /ˈdɛsʌɪl/ ▶ **noun** Statistics each of ten equal groups into which a population can be divided according to the distribution of values of a particular variable: *the lowest income decile of the population*. ■ each of the nine values of the random variable which divide a population into ten such groups.
– ORIGIN late 17th cent.: from French *décile*, from a medieval Latin derivative of Latin *decem* 'ten'.

decilitre (US **deciliter**) (abbrev.: **dl**) ▶ **noun** a metric unit of capacity, equal to one tenth of a litre.

decimal ▶ **adjective** relating to or denoting a system of numbers and arithmetic based on the number ten, tenth parts, and powers of ten: *decimal arithmetic*. ■ relating to or denoting a system of currency, weights and measures, or other units in which the smaller units are related to the principal units as powers of ten: *decimal coinage*.
▶ **noun** (also **decimal fraction**) a fraction whose denominator is a power of ten and whose numerator is expressed by figures placed to the right of a decimal point. ■ [mass noun] the system of decimal numerical notation.
– DERIVATIVES **decimally** adverb.
– ORIGIN early 17th cent.: from modern Latin *decimalis* (adjective), from Latin *decimus* 'tenth'.

decimalize (also **decimalise**) ▶ **verb** [with obj.] convert (a system of coinage or weights and measures) to a decimal system.
– DERIVATIVES **decimalization** noun.

decimal place ▶ **noun** the position of a digit to the right of a decimal point.

decimal point ▶ **noun** a full point or dot placed after the figure representing units in a decimal fraction.

decimate /ˈdɛsɪmeɪt/ ▶ **verb** [with obj.] **1** kill, destroy, or remove a large proportion of: *the inhabitants of the country had been decimated*. ■ drastically reduce the strength or effectiveness of (something): *public transport has been decimated*.
2 historical kill one in every ten of (a group of people, originally a mutinous Roman legion) as a punishment for the whole group.
– DERIVATIVES **decimation** noun, **decimator** noun.
– ORIGIN late Middle English: from Latin *decimat-* 'taken as a tenth', from the verb *decimare*, from *decimus* 'tenth'. In Middle English the term *decimation* denoted the levying of a tithe, and later the tax imposed by Cromwell on the Royalists (1655).

> **USAGE** Historically, the meaning of the word **decimate** is 'kill one in every ten of (a group of people)'. This sense has been more or less totally superseded by the later, more general sense 'kill, destroy, or remove a large proportion of', as in *the virus has **decimated** the population*. Some traditionalists argue that this is incorrect, but it is clear that it is now part of standard English.

decimetre (US **decimeter**) (abbrev.: **dm**) ▶ **noun** a metric unit of length, equal to one tenth of a metre.
– DERIVATIVES **decimetric** adjective.

decipher /dɪˈsʌɪfə/ ▶ **verb** [with obj.] convert (a text written in code, or a coded signal) into normal language. ■ succeed in understanding, interpreting, or identifying (something): [with clause] *visual signals help us **decipher** what is being communicated*.
– DERIVATIVES **decipherable** adjective, **decipherment** noun.
– ORIGIN early 16th cent.: from DE- (expressing reversal) + CIPHER[1], on the pattern of French *déchiffrer*.

decision ▶ **noun** a conclusion or resolution reached after consideration: *I'll make the decision on my own* | *the editor's decision is final*. ■ [mass noun] the action or process of deciding something or of resolving a question: *the information was used as the basis for decision*. ■ [mass noun] the ability or tendency to make decisions quickly; decisiveness: *she was a woman of decision*.
– ORIGIN late Middle English: from Latin *decisio(n-)*, from *decidere* 'determine' (see DECIDE).

decision-making ▶ **noun** [mass noun] the action or process of making important decisions: [as modifier] *the decision-making process*.
– DERIVATIVES **decision-maker** noun.

decision problem ▶ **noun** Logic the problem of finding a way to decide whether a formula or class of formulas is true or provable within a given system of axioms.
– ORIGIN 1930s: translation of German *Entscheidungsproblem*.

decision support system ▶ **noun** Computing a set of related computer programs and the data required to assist with analysis and decision-making within an organization.

decision theory ▶ **noun** [mass noun] the mathematical study of strategies for optimal decision-making between options involving different risks or expectations of gain or loss depending on the outcome. Compare with GAME THEORY.

decisive ▶ **adjective 1** settling an issue; producing a definite result: *the archers played a decisive part in the victory* | *a decisive battle*.
2 having or showing the ability to make decisions quickly and effectively.
– DERIVATIVES **decisively** adverb, **decisiveness** noun.
– ORIGIN early 17th cent.: from French *décisif, -ive*, from medieval Latin *decisivus*, from *decis-* 'determined', from the verb *decidere* (see DECIDE).

Decius /ˈdiːsɪəs/, Gaius Messius Quintus Trajanus (*c.*201–51), Roman emperor 249–51. He was the first Roman emperor to promote systematic persecution of the Christians in the empire.
– DERIVATIVES **Decian** adjective.

deck ▶ **noun 1** a floor of a ship, especially the upper, open level extending for the full length of the vessel: *he stood on the deck of his flagship* | *the lower decks*. ■ a floor or platform resembling or compared to a ship's deck: *the upper deck of the car park*. ■ a floor of a double-decker bus. ■ N. Amer. short for SUN DECK (sense 2). ■ (**the deck**) informal the ground or floor: *there was a big thud when I **hit the deck***. ■ the flat part of a skateboard or snowboard.
2 a component or unit for playing or recording records, tapes, or compact discs: *a cassette deck* | *every serious DJ needs a set of decks*.
3 chiefly N. Amer. a pack of cards. ■ N. Amer. informal a packet of narcotics.
▶ **verb** [with obj.] **1** decorate or adorn brightly or festively: *Ingrid was **decked out** in her Sunday best*.
2 informal knock (someone) to the ground with a punch.
– PHRASES **not playing with a full deck** N. Amer. informal mentally deficient. **on deck** on or on to a ship's main deck: *she stood on deck for hours*. ■ N. Amer. informal ready for action or work.
– DERIVATIVES **decked** adjective [in combination] *a three-decked vessel*.
– ORIGIN late Middle English: from Middle Dutch *dec* 'covering, roof, cloak', *dekken* 'to cover'. Originally denoting canvas used to make a covering (especially on a ship), the term came to mean the covering itself, later denoting a solid surface serving as roof and floor.

deckchair ▶ **noun** a folding chair of wood and canvas, typically used by the sea or on the deck of passenger ships.

-decker ▶ **combining form** having a specified number of decks or layers: *double-decker*.

deckhand ▶ **noun** a member of a ship's crew whose duties include cleaning, mooring, and cargo handling.

deckhead ▶ **noun** the underside of the deck of a ship.

deckhouse ▶ **noun** a cabin on the deck of a ship or boat, used for navigation or accommodation.

decking ▶ **noun** [mass noun] the material of the deck of a ship, floor, or platform.

deckle /ˈdɛk(ə)l/ ▶ **noun** (also **deckle strap**) a device in a papermaking machine for limiting the size of the sheet, consisting of a continuous belt on either side of the wire. ■ a frame on the mould used to shape the pulp when making paper by hand.
– ORIGIN mid 18th cent.: from German *Deckel*, diminutive of *Decke* 'covering'.

deckle edge ▶ **noun** the rough uncut edge of a sheet of paper, formed by a deckle.
– DERIVATIVES **deckle-edged** adjective.

deck quoits ▶ **plural noun** [treated as sing.] Brit. a game in which rope quoits are aimed at a peg, played especially on cruise ships.

deck shoe ▶ **noun** a flat canvas or leather shoe with rubber soles.

deck tennis ▶ **noun** a game in which a quoit of rope or rubber is tossed to and fro over a net, played especially on cruise ships.

declaim ▶ **verb** [reporting verb] utter or deliver words in a rhetorical or impassioned way, as if to an audience: [with obj.] *she declaimed her views* | [no obj.] *a preacher declaiming from the pulpit* | *an opportunity to **declaim against** the evils of society*.
– DERIVATIVES **declaimer** noun.
– ORIGIN late Middle English: from French *déclamer* or Latin *declamare*, from *de-* (expressing thoroughness) + *clamare* 'to shout'.

declamation ▶ **noun** [mass noun] the action or art of declaiming: *Shakespearean declamation* | [count noun] *declamations of patriotism*. ■ [count noun] a rhetorical exercise or set speech.
– ORIGIN late Middle English (in the sense 'a set speech'): from Latin *declamatio(n-)*, from the verb *declamare* (see DECLAIM).

declamatory /dɪˈklamət(ə)ri/ ▶ **adjective** vehement or impassioned in expression: *a long declamatory speech*.

declarant /dɪˈklɛːr(ə)nt/ chiefly Law ▶ **noun** a person or party who makes a formal declaration.
▶ **adjective** making or having made a formal declaration.
– ORIGIN late 17th cent.: from French *déclarant*, present participle of *déclarer*, from Latin *declarare* 'make quite clear' (see DECLARE).

declaration ▶ **noun 1** a formal or explicit statement or announcement: *a declaration of love*. ■ the formal announcement of the beginning of a state or

D

condition: *the declaration of war.* ■ a written public announcement of intentions or of the terms of an agreement. ■ (also **declaration of the poll**) Brit. a public official announcement of the votes cast for candidates in an election. ■ Law a plaintiff's statement of claims in proceedings. ■ Law an affirmation made in place of an oath. ■ the naming of trumps in bridge, whist, or a similar card game. ■ an announcement of a combination held in certain card games.
2 Cricket an act of declaring an innings closed.
– ORIGIN late Middle English: from Latin *declaratio(n-)*, from *declarare* 'make quite clear' (see DECLARE).

Declaration of Independence a document declaring the US to be independent of the British Crown, signed on 4 July 1776 by the Congressional representatives of thirteen states, including Thomas Jefferson, Benjamin Franklin, and John Adams.

Declaration of Rights a statute passed by the English Parliament in 1689, which established the joint monarchy of William and Mary and which was designed to ensure that the Crown would not act without Parliament's consent. It was later incorporated in the Bill of Rights.

declarative /dɪˈklarətɪv/ ▶ **adjective 1** of the nature of or making a declaration: *declarative statements.* ■ Grammar (of a sentence or phrase) taking the form of a simple statement.
2 Computing denoting high-level programming languages which can be used to solve problems without requiring the programmer to specify an exact procedure to be followed.
▶ **noun** a statement in the form of a declaration. ■ Grammar a declarative sentence or phrase.
– DERIVATIVES **declaratively** adverb.

declarator /dɪˈklarətə/ (also **action for declarator**) ▶ **noun** Scots Law an action whereby a legal right or status is declared but nothing further is done.

declare ▶ **verb 1** [reporting verb] say something in a solemn and emphatic manner: [with clause] *the prime minister declared that the programme of austerity had paid off* | [with direct speech] *'I was under too much pressure,' he declared.* ■ [with obj.] formally announce the beginning of (a state or condition): *Spain **declared war on** Britain in 1796.* ■ [with obj. and complement] pronounce or assert (a person or thing) to be something specified: *the mansion was declared a fire hazard.* ■ [no obj.] (**declare for/against**) Brit. openly align oneself for or against (a party or position) in a dispute: *the president had declared for denuclearization of Europe.* ■ (**declare oneself**) reveal one's intentions or identity. ■ [no obj.] announce oneself as a candidate for an election: *he declared last April.* ■ (**declare oneself**) archaic express feelings of love to someone: *she waited in vain for him to declare himself.*
2 [with obj.] acknowledge possession of (taxable income or dutiable goods).
3 [no obj.] Cricket close an innings voluntarily before all the wickets have fallen: *Pakistan declared at 446 for four.*
4 [with obj.] announce that one holds (certain combinations of cards) in a card game. ■ name (the trump suit) in a card game.
– PHRASES **well, I declare** (or **I do declare**) an exclamation of incredulity, surprise, or vexation.
– DERIVATIVES **declarable** adjective, **declaratory** adjective, **declared** adjective, **declaredly** adverb.
– ORIGIN Middle English: from Latin *declarare*, from *de-* 'thoroughly' + *clarare* 'make clear' (from *clarus* 'clear').

declarer ▶ **noun** Bridge the player whose bid establishes the suit of the contract and who must therefore play both their own hand and the exposed hand of the dummy.

declass ▶ **verb** [with obj.] remove (someone) from their original social class.

déclassé /deɪˈklaseɪ/ (also **déclassée**) ▶ **adjective** having fallen in social status: *his parents were poor and déclassé.*
– ORIGIN late 19th cent.: French, 'removed from one's class, degraded', past participle of *déclasser*.

declassify ▶ **verb** (**declassifies, declassifying, declassified**) [with obj.] **1** officially declare (information or documents) to be no longer secret: *government documents were declassified.*
2 reassign to a lower classification: *she called for vigorous research before any moves are made to declassify the drug in Ireland.*
– DERIVATIVES **declassification** noun.

declaw /diːˈklɔː/ ▶ **verb** [with obj.] remove the claws from (an animal, typically a cat).

declension /dɪˈklɛnʃ(ə)n/ ▶ **noun** [mass noun] **1** (in the grammar of Latin, Greek, and certain other languages) the variation of the form of a noun, pronoun, or adjective, by which its grammatical case, number, and gender are identified. ■ [count noun] the class to which a noun or adjective is assigned according to the manner of this variation.
2 archaic a condition of decline or moral deterioration: *the declension of the new generation.*
– DERIVATIVES **declensional** adjective.
– ORIGIN late Middle English *declinson*, from Old French *declinaison*, from *decliner* 'to decline'. The change in the ending was probably due to association with words such as *ascension*.

de Clerambault's syndrome /də ˈklɛrəmbəʊz/ ▶ **noun** Psychiatry another term for EROTOMANIA.
– ORIGIN from the name of Gatin *de Clérambault* (1872–1934), French psychiatrist, who first described it.

declination /ˌdɛklɪˈneɪʃ(ə)n/ ▶ **noun 1** Astronomy the angular distance of a point north or south of the celestial equator. Compare with RIGHT ASCENSION and CELESTIAL LATITUDE. ■ the angular deviation of a compass needle from true north (because the magnetic north pole and the geographic north pole do not coincide).
2 Linguistics another term for DOWNDRIFT.
3 US formal refusal: [as modifier] *the mandatory vaccine declination form.*
– ORIGIN late Middle English: from Latin *declinatio(n-)*, from the verb *declinare* (see DECLINE).

declination axis ▶ **noun** Astronomy the axis of an equatorially mounted telescope which is at right angles to the polar axis, about which the telescope is turned in order to view points at different declinations but at a constant right ascension.

decline ▶ **verb 1** [no obj.] (typically of something regarded as good) become smaller, fewer, or less; decrease: *the birth rate continued to decline.* ■ diminish in strength or quality; deteriorate: *her health began to decline* | (as adj. **declining**) *declining industries.*
2 [with obj.] politely refuse (an invitation or offer): *Caroline declined the coffee* | [with infinitive] *the company declined to comment.*
3 [no obj.] (especially of the sun) move downwards. ■ archaic bend down; droop.
4 [with obj.] (in the grammar of Latin, Greek, and certain other languages) state the forms of (a noun, pronoun, or adjective) corresponding to case, number, and gender.
▶ **noun** a gradual and continuous loss of strength, numbers, or value: *a serious **decline** in bird numbers* | [mass noun] *a civilization **in decline**.* ■ archaic the sun's gradual setting. ■ archaic a disease in which the bodily strength gradually fails, especially tuberculosis.
– PHRASES **declining years** the period of one's old age. ■ the period leading up to the end of an enterprise or institution: *the declining years of the Austro-Hungarian empire.*
– DERIVATIVES **declinable** adjective, **decliner** noun.
– ORIGIN late Middle English: from Old French *decliner*, from Latin *declinare* 'bend down, turn aside', from *de-* 'down' + *clinare* 'to bend'.

declivity /dɪˈklɪvɪti/ ▶ **noun** (pl. **declivities**) formal a downward slope: *a thickly wooded declivity.*
– DERIVATIVES **declivitous** adjective.
– ORIGIN early 17th cent.: from Latin *declivitas*, from *declivis* 'sloping down', from *de-* 'down' + *clivus* 'a slope'.

declutch ▶ **verb** [no obj.] disengage the clutch of a motor. See also DOUBLE-DECLUTCH.

declutter ▶ **verb** [with obj.] remove unnecessary items from (an untidy or overcrowded place): *there's no better time to declutter your home.*

deco ▶ **noun 1** /ˈdɛkəʊ/ short for ART DECO.
2 /ˈdiːkəʊ/ (in scuba diving) short for DECOMPRESSION.

decoct /dɪˈkɒkt/ ▶ **verb** [with obj.] extract the essence from (something) by heating or boiling it.
– ORIGIN late Middle English (in the sense 'cook, heat up'): from Latin *decoct-* 'boiled down', from the verb *decoquere*, from *de-* 'down' + *coquere* 'cook'.

decoction ▶ **noun** a concentrated liquor resulting from heating or boiling a substance, especially a medicinal preparation made from a plant: *a decoction of a root.* ■ [mass noun] the action or process of extracting the essence of something.
– ORIGIN late Middle English: from late Latin *decoctio(n-)*, from *decoquere* 'boil down' (see DECOCT).

decode ▶ **verb** [with obj.] convert (a coded message) into intelligible language. ■ analyse and interpret (a communication or image): *a handbook to help parents decode street language.* ■ convert (audio or video signals) into a different or usable form, for example to analogue from digital in sound reproduction.
– DERIVATIVES **decodable** adjective, **decoder** noun.

decoke ▶ **verb** /diːˈkəʊk/ [with obj.] Brit. remove carbon or carbonaceous material from (an internal-combustion engine).

decollate[1] /dɪˈkɒleɪt, ˈdɛkəleɪt/ ▶ **verb** [with obj.] archaic behead (someone).
– ORIGIN late Middle English: from Latin *decollat-* 'beheaded', from the verb *decollare*, from *de-* (expressing removal) + *collum* 'neck'.

decollate[2] /ˌdiːkəˈleɪt/ ▶ **verb** [no obj.] mechanically separate sheets of paper into different piles.
– DERIVATIVES **decollation** noun.
– ORIGIN 1960s: from DE- 'away from' + COLLATE.

decollement /deɪˈkɒlmɔ̃/ ▶ **noun** [mass noun] Geology a process in which some strata become partly detached from those underneath and slide over them, causing folding and deformation. ■ (also **decollement zone**) [count noun] a boundary separating deformed strata from underlying strata which are not similarly deformed.
– ORIGIN mid 19th cent.: from French, from *décoller* 'unstick'.

décolletage /ˌdeɪkɒlɪˈtɑːʒ, deɪˈkɒltɑːʒ/ ▶ **noun** a low neckline on a woman's dress or top. ■ a woman's cleavage as revealed by such a neckline.
– ORIGIN late 19th cent.: French, from *décolleter* 'expose the neck', from *dé-* (expressing removal) + *collet* 'collar of a dress'.

décolleté /deɪˈkɒlteɪ/ (also **décolletée**) ▶ **adjective** (of a woman's dress or top) having a low neckline.
▶ **noun** a low neckline on a woman's dress or top.
– ORIGIN mid 19th cent.: French, past participle of *décolleter* 'expose the neck'.

decolonize (also **decolonise**) ▶ **verb** [with obj.] (of a state) withdraw from (a colony), leaving it independent: *Spain seemed in no hurry to decolonize those lands.*
– DERIVATIVES **decolonization** noun.

decolorize (also **decolorise**) ▶ **verb** [with obj.] remove the colour from.
– DERIVATIVES **decolorization** noun.

decommission ▶ **verb** [with obj.] withdraw (something, especially weapons or military equipment) from service. ■ make (a nuclear reactor) inoperative and dismantle it safely.

decompensation ▶ **noun 1** [mass noun] Medicine the failure of an organ (especially the liver or heart) to compensate for the functional overload resulting from disease.
2 Psychiatry the failure to generate effective psychological coping mechanisms in response to stress, resulting in personality disturbance.
– DERIVATIVES **decompensated** adjective.

decompile ▶ **verb** [with obj.] produce source code from (compiled code).
– DERIVATIVES **decompilation** noun, **decompiler** noun.

decompose ▶ **verb** (with reference to a dead body or other organic matter) make or become rotten; decay or cause to decay: [no obj.] *the body had begun to decompose* | (as adj. **decomposing**) *decomposing fungi* | [with obj.] *dead plant matter can be completely decomposed by micro-organisms.* ■ (with reference to a chemical compound) break down or cause to break down into component elements or simpler constituents. ■ [with obj.] Mathematics express (a number or function) as a combination of simpler components.
– DERIVATIVES **decomposable** adjective, **decomposer** noun.
– ORIGIN mid 18th cent. (in the sense 'separate into simpler constituents'): from French *décomposer*, from *de-* (expressing reversal) + *composer*.

decomposition ▶ **noun** [mass noun] the state or process of rotting; decay: *the decomposition of organic waste.*

decompress /ˌdiːkəmˈprɛs/ ▶ **verb** [with obj.] **1** [with obj.] relieve of compressing forces, in particular: ■ subject (a diver) to decompression. ■ expand (compressed data) to its normal size so that it can be read and processed by a computer.
2 [no obj.] N. Amer. informal calm down and relax: *Michael sits for a minute to decompress before walking home.*

decompression ▶ **noun** [mass noun] **1** reduction in air pressure: *decompression of the aircraft cabin.* ■ a gradual reduction of air pressure on a person who has been experiencing high pressure while diving.

2 the process of expanding computer data to its normal size so that it can be read by a computer.

decompression chamber ▶ **noun** a small room in which the air pressure can be varied, used chiefly to allow deep-sea divers to adjust gradually to normal air pressure.

decompression sickness ▶ **noun** [mass noun] a condition that results when too rapid decompression causes nitrogen bubbles to form in the tissues of the body. It is suffered particularly by divers (who often call it **the bends**), and can cause pain in the muscles and joints, cramp, numbness, nausea, and paralysis. Also called CAISSON DISEASE.

decompressor ▶ **noun** Brit. a device for reducing pressure in the engine of a motor vehicle.

deconditioned ▶ **adjective** having lost fitness or muscle tone, especially through lack of exercise.
– DERIVATIVES **decondition** verb.

deconditioning ▶ **noun** Psychiatry the reform or reversal of previously conditioned behaviour, especially in the treatment of phobia and other anxiety disorders in which the fear response to certain stimuli is brought under control. Compare with COUNTER-CONDITIONING.

deconflict /ˌdiːkənˈflɪkt/ ▶ **verb** [with obj.] Military reduce the risk of collision between (aircraft, airborne weaponry, etc.) in an area by coordinating their movements.
– DERIVATIVES **deconfliction** noun.

decongest ▶ **verb** [with obj.] relieve the congestion of (something).
– DERIVATIVES **decongestion** noun.

decongestant ▶ **adjective** (chiefly of a medicine) used to relieve nasal congestion.
▶ **noun** a decongestant medicine.

deconsecrate ▶ **verb** [with obj.] transfer (a building) from sacred to secular use: *the church was deconsecrated in the early nineteenth century.*
– DERIVATIVES **deconsecration** noun.

deconstruct /ˌdiːk(ə)nˈstrʌkt/ ▶ **verb** [with obj.] analyse (a text or linguistic or conceptual system) by deconstruction. ■ reduce (something) to its constituent parts in order to reinterpret it: *I want to deconstruct this myth that poverty breeds crime.*
– DERIVATIVES **deconstructive** adjective.
– ORIGIN late 19th cent.: back-formation from DECONSTRUCTION.

deconstruction ▶ **noun** [mass noun] a method of critical analysis of philosophical and literary language which emphasizes the internal workings of language and conceptual systems, the relational quality of meaning, and the assumptions implicit in forms of expression.

> Deconstruction focuses on a text as such rather than as an expression of the author's intention, stressing the limitlessness (or impossibility) of interpretation and rejecting the Western philosophical tradition of seeking certainty through reasoning by privileging certain types of interpretation and repressing others. It was effectively named and popularized by the French philosopher Jacques Derrida from the late 1960s and taken up particularly by US literary critics.

– DERIVATIVES **deconstructionism** noun, **deconstructionist** adjective & noun.
– ORIGIN late 19th cent. (originally in the general sense 'taking to pieces'): from DE- (expressing reversal) + CONSTRUCTION.

decontaminate ▶ **verb** [with obj.] neutralize or remove dangerous substances, radioactivity, or germs from (an area, object, or person): *they tried to decontaminate nearby villages.*
– DERIVATIVES **decontamination** noun.

decontextualize (also **decontextualise**) ▶ **verb** [with obj.] (usu. as adj. **decontextualized**) consider (something) in isolation from its context.
– DERIVATIVES **decontextualization** noun.

decontrol ▶ **verb** (**decontrols, decontrolling, decontrolled**) [with obj.] release (a commodity, market, etc.) from controls or restrictions.
▶ **noun** [mass noun] the action of decontrolling something.

deconvolution ▶ **noun** [mass noun] a process of resolving something into its constituent elements or removing complication. ■ Mathematics the resolution of a convolution function into the functions from which it was formed in order to separate their effects. ■ (also **deconvolution analysis**) the improvement of resolution of images or other data by a mathematical algorithm designed to separate the information from artefacts which result from the method of collecting it.

decor /ˈdeɪkɔː, ˈdɛ-/ ▶ **noun** the furnishing and decoration of a room. ■ the decoration and scenery of a stage.
– ORIGIN late 19th cent.: from French *décor*, from the verb *décorer*, from Latin *decorare* 'embellish' (see DECORATE).

decorate ▶ **verb** [with obj.] **1** make (something) look more attractive by adding extra items or images to it: *the town was decorated with Christmas lights.* ■ chiefly Brit. apply paint or wallpaper in (a room or building): *the five bedrooms are individually decorated.*
2 confer an award or medal on (a member of the armed forces): *he was decorated for outstanding bravery.*
– ORIGIN mid 16th cent. (in the sense 'to grace or honour'): from Latin *decoratus* 'embellished' (past participle of *decorare*), from *decus*, *decor-* 'beauty, honour, or embellishment'.

Decorated ▶ **adjective** denoting a stage of English Gothic church architecture typical of the 14th century (between Early English and Perpendicular), with increasing use of decoration and geometrical, curvilinear, and reticulated tracery.

decoration ▶ **noun 1** [mass noun] the process or art of decorating something: *the lavish decoration of cloth with gilt* | *interior decoration.* ■ ornamentation: *inside there was little decoration.* ■ chiefly Brit. paint or wallpaper applied when decorating a room: *an authority on English furniture and decoration.* ■ [count noun] a thing that serves as an ornament: *Christmas tree decorations.*
2 a medal or award conferred as an honour.
– ORIGIN late Middle English: from late Latin *decoratio(n-)*, from the verb *decorare* (see DECORATE).

Decoration Day ▶ **noun** US another term for MEMORIAL DAY.

decorative /ˈdɛk(ə)rətɪv/ ▶ **adjective** serving to make something look more attractive; ornamental: *a well-appointed house with original decorative features.* ■ relating to decoration: *a decorative artist.* ■ informal (of a woman) attractive.
– DERIVATIVES **decoratively** adverb, **decorativeness** noun.

decorative arts ▶ **plural noun** the arts concerned with the production of objects which are both useful and beautiful.

decorator ▶ **noun** a person who decorates, in particular: ■ chiefly Brit. a person whose job is to decorate the interior of buildings by painting the walls and hanging wallpaper. ■ chiefly N. Amer. a person whose job is to design the interior of houses by choosing colours, carpets, and furnishings.

decorous /ˈdɛk(ə)rəs/ ▶ **adjective** in keeping with good taste and propriety; polite and restrained: *Charlotte gave David a decorous kiss.*
– DERIVATIVES **decorously** adverb, **decorousness** noun.
– ORIGIN mid 17th cent. (in the sense 'appropriate, seemly'): from Latin *decorus* 'seemly' + -OUS.

decorticate /diːˈkɔːtɪkeɪt/ ▶ **verb** [with obj.] **1** technical remove the bark, rind, or husk from.
2 subject to surgical decortication.
▶ **adjective** Biology & Psychology (of an animal) having had the cortex of the brain removed or separated.
– ORIGIN early 17th cent.: from Latin *decorticat-* 'stripped of its bark', from the verb *decorticare*, from *de-* (expressing removal) + *cortex*, *cortic-* 'bark'.

decortication ▶ **noun** [mass noun] the removal of the outer layer or cortex from a structure, especially the kidney, brain, or other organ. ■ Medicine the operation of removing fibrous scar tissue that prevents expansion of the lung.

decorum /dɪˈkɔːrəm/ ▶ **noun** [mass noun] behaviour in keeping with good taste and propriety. ■ etiquette: *he had no idea of funeral decorum.* ■ (**decorums**) archaic particular requirements of good taste and propriety.
– ORIGIN mid 16th cent. (as a literary term, denoting suitability of style): from Latin, neuter of the adjective *decorus* 'seemly'.

découpage /ˌdeɪkuːˈpɑːʒ, dɪˈkuːpɑːʒ/ ▶ **noun** [mass noun] the decoration of the surface of an object with paper cut-outs.
– ORIGIN 1960s: French, from *découper* 'cut out'.

decouple ▶ **verb** [with obj.] **1** separate, disengage, or dissociate (something) from something else. ■ make the interaction between (electrical components) so weak that there is little transfer of energy between them, especially to remove unwanted AC distortion or oscillations in circuits with a common power supply.
2 muffle the sound or shock of (a nuclear explosion) by causing it to take place in an underground cavity.

decoy ▶ **noun** /ˈdiːkɔɪ, dɪˈkɔɪ/ **1** a bird or mammal, or an imitation of one, used by hunters to attract other birds or mammals: [as modifier] *a decoy duck.* ■ a person or thing used to mislead or lure someone into a trap.
2 a pond from which narrow netted channels lead, into which wild duck may be enticed for capture.
▶ **verb** /dɪˈkɔɪ, ˈdiːkɔɪ/ [with obj. and adverbial of direction] lure or entice (a person or animal) away from their intended course, typically into a trap: *they would try to decoy the enemy towards the hidden group.*
– ORIGIN mid 16th cent. (earlier as *coy*): from Dutch *de kooi* 'the decoy', from Middle Dutch *de kouw* 'the cage', from Latin *cavea* 'cage'. Sense 2 of the noun is from the practice of using tamed ducks to lead wild ones along channels into captivity.

D

decrease ▶ **verb** /dɪˈkriːs/ make or become smaller or fewer in size, amount, intensity, or degree: [no obj.] *the population of the area has decreased radically* | [with obj.] *the aisles were decreased in height.*
▶ **noun** /ˈdiːkriːs/ an instance of becoming smaller or fewer: ***a decrease in births*** | [mass noun] *the rate of decrease became greater.*
– PHRASES **on the decrease** becoming less common or widespread; decreasing.
– DERIVATIVES **decreasingly** adverb [as submodifier] *voters have proved decreasingly willing to support the party*
– ORIGIN late Middle English: from Old French *decreis* (noun), *decreistre* (verb), based on Latin *decrescere*, from *de-* 'down' + *crescere* 'grow'.

decree ▶ **noun** an official order that has the force of law. ■ [mass noun] the issuing of a decree: *the king **ruled by decree**.* ■ a judgement or decision of certain law courts, especially in matrimonial cases.
▶ **verb** (**decrees, decreeing, decreed**) [with obj.] order (something) by decree: [with clause] *the president decreed that the military was to be streamlined.*
– ORIGIN Middle English (denoting an edict issued by an ecclesiastical council to settle a point of doctrine or discipline): from Old French *decre*, *decret*, from Latin *decretum* 'something decided', from *decernere* 'decide'.

decree absolute ▶ **noun** (pl. **decrees absolute**) English Law a court of law's final order officially ending a marriage, enabling either party to remarry.

decree nisi ▶ **noun** (pl. **decrees nisi**) English Law an order by a court of law stating the date on which a marriage will end unless a good reason not to grant a divorce is produced.
– ORIGIN late 19th cent.: Latin *nisi* 'unless'.

decrement /ˈdɛkrɪm(ə)nt/ ▶ **noun** technical a reduction or diminution. ■ an amount by which something is reduced or diminished: *the dose was reduced by 10 mg weekly decrements.* ■ Physics the ratio of the amplitudes in successive cycles of a damped oscillation.
▶ **verb** [with obj.] chiefly Computing cause a discrete reduction in (a numerical quantity).
– ORIGIN early 17th cent. (as a noun): from Latin *decrementum* 'diminution', from the stem of *decrescere* 'to decrease'.

decrepit /dɪˈkrɛpɪt/ ▶ **adjective** worn out or ruined because of age or neglect: *a row of decrepit houses.* ■ (of a person) elderly and infirm: *a rather decrepit old man.*
– ORIGIN late Middle English: from Latin *decrepitus*, from *de-* 'down' + *crepitus*, past participle of *crepare* 'rattle, creak'.

decrepitate /dɪˈkrɛpɪteɪt/ ▶ **verb** [no obj.] technical (of a solid, especially a crystal) disintegrate audibly when heated.
– DERIVATIVES **decrepitation** noun.
– ORIGIN mid 17th cent.: from DE- 'away' + Latin *crepitat-* 'crackled', from the verb *crepitare*, frequentative of *crepare* 'rattle' (see DECREPIT).

decrepitude ▶ **noun** [mass noun] the state of being decrepit: *he had passed directly from middle age into decrepitude.*

decrescendo /ˌdiːkrɪˈʃɛndəʊ/ ▶ **noun** (pl. **decrescendos**), **adverb & adjective** another term for DIMINUENDO.
– ORIGIN early 19th cent.: Italian, literally 'decreasing'.

decrescent /dɪˈkrɛs(ə)nt/ ▶ **adjective** (of the moon) waning.
– ORIGIN early 17th cent.: from Latin *decrescent-* 'growing less', from the verb *decrescere* (see DECREASE).

D

decretal /dɪˈkriːt(ə)l/ ▶ **noun** a papal decree concerning a point of canon law.
▶ **adjective** of the nature of a decree.
– ORIGIN Middle English: from late Latin *decretale*, neuter of *decretalis* (adjective), from Latin *decret-* 'decided', from the verb *decernere*.

Decretum /dɪˈkriːtəm/ ▶ **noun** a collection of decisions and judgements in canon law.
– ORIGIN Latin, literally 'something decreed'.

decriminalize (also **decriminalise**) ▶ **verb** [with obj.] cease to treat (something) as illegal: *a battle to decriminalize cannabis*.
– DERIVATIVES **decriminalization** noun.

decry /dɪˈkrʌɪ/ ▶ **verb** (**decries, decrying, decried**) [with obj.] publicly denounce: *they decried human rights abuses*.
– ORIGIN early 17th cent. (in the sense 'decrease the value of coins by royal proclamation'): from DE- 'down' + CRY, on the pattern of French *décrier* 'cry down'.

decrypt /diːˈkrɪpt/ ▶ **verb** [with obj.] make (a coded or unclear message) intelligible: *the computer can be used to encrypt and decrypt sensitive transmissions*.
▶ **noun** a text that has been decoded.
– DERIVATIVES **decryption** noun.
– ORIGIN 1930s: from DE- (expressing reversal) + *crypt* as in *encrypt*.

decubitus /dɪˈkjuːbɪtəs/ ▶ **noun** [mass noun] chiefly Medicine the posture adopted by a person who is lying down: [as modifier] *lumbar puncture with the patient in the lateral decubitus position*.
– ORIGIN late 19th cent.: modern Latin, from Latin *decumbere* 'lie down', on the pattern of words such as *accubitus* 'reclining at table'.

decubitus ulcer ▶ **noun** technical term for BEDSORE.

decumbent /dɪˈkʌmb(ə)nt/ ▶ **adjective** Botany (of a plant) lying along the ground or along a surface, with the extremity curving upwards.
– ORIGIN late 18th cent.: from Latin *decumbent-* 'lying down', from the verb *decumbere*, based on *de-* 'down' + a verb related to *cubare* 'to lie'.

decurrent /dɪˈkʌr(ə)nt/ ▶ **adjective** Botany (of a fungus gill, leaf, etc.) extending down the stem below the point of attachment. ■ (of a shrub or the crown of a tree) having several roughly equal branches.
– ORIGIN mid 18th cent.: from Latin *decurrent-* 'running down', from the verb *decurrere*.

decurved ▶ **adjective** Biology (especially of a bird's bill) curved downwards.

decussate technical ▶ **verb** /dɪˈkʌseɪt, ˈdɛkəseɪt/ [no obj.] (of two or more things) cross or intersect each other to form an X.
▶ **adjective** /dɪˈkʌsət/ shaped like an X. ■ Botany (of leaves) arranged in opposite pairs, each pair being at right angles to the pair below.
– DERIVATIVES **decussation** noun.
– ORIGIN mid 17th cent. (as a verb): from Latin *decussatus*, past participle of *decussare* 'divide crosswise', from *decussis* (describing the figure X, i.e. the Roman numeral for the number 10), from *decem* 'ten'.

decyl /ˈdɛsʌɪl, -sɪl/ ▶ **noun** [as modifier] Chemistry of or denoting an alkyl radical $-C_{10}H_{21}$, derived from decane.
– ORIGIN mid 19th cent.: from Greek *deka-* 'ten' + -YL.

dedans /dəˈdɒ̃/ ▶ **noun** (in real tennis) an open gallery for spectators at the service side of a court.
– ORIGIN early 18th cent.: French, literally 'inside'.

Dedekind /ˈdeɪdəkɪnd/, German /ˈdeːdəkɪnt/, Richard (1831–1916), German mathematician, one of the founders of abstract algebra and modern mathematics.

dedendum /dɪˈdɛndəm/ ▶ **noun** Engineering the radial distance from the pitch circle of a cogwheel or wormwheel to the bottom of the tooth space or groove. Compare with ADDENDUM.
– ORIGIN early 20th cent.: from Latin, 'thing that can be surrendered', neuter gerundive of *dedere*.

dedicate ▶ **verb** [with obj.] (often **dedicate something to**) devote (time or effort) to a particular task or purpose: *Joan has dedicated her life to animals*.
■ devote (something) to a particular subject: *volume four is dedicated to wasps*. ■ cite or nominate (a book or other artistic work) as being issued or performed in someone's honour: *the novel is dedicated to the memory of my mother*. ■ formally open or unveil (a building or monument): *today the President dedicates the new Second World War memorial in Washington*.
■ ceremonially assign (a church or other building) to a deity or saint: *the parish church is dedicated to St Paul*.
– DERIVATIVES **dedicatee** noun, **dedicator** noun, **dedicatory** adjective.
– ORIGIN late Middle English (in the sense 'devote to sacred use by solemn rites'): from Latin *dedicat-* 'devoted, consecrated', from the verb *dedicare*.

dedicated ▶ **adjective 1** devoted to a task or purpose: *a team of dedicated doctors*.
2 exclusively allocated to or intended for a particular purpose: *a dedicated high-speed rail link from the Channel Tunnel*.
– DERIVATIVES **dedicatedly** adverb.

dedication ▶ **noun** [mass noun] **1** the quality of being dedicated or committed to a task or purpose: *his dedication to his duties*.
2 the action of dedicating a church or other building: *the dedication of a new city church*. ■ [count noun] an inscription or form of words dedicating a building, book, etc. to a person or deity.
– ORIGIN late Middle English: from Latin *dedicatio(n-)*, from *dedicare* 'devote, consecrate' (see DEDICATE).

de dicto /deɪ ˈdɪktəʊ, diː/ ▶ **adjective** Philosophy relating to the form of an assertion or expression itself, rather than any property of a thing it refers to. Compare with DE RE.
– ORIGIN Latin, 'from what is said'.

dedifferentiate /ˌdiːdɪfəˈrɛnʃɪeɪt/ ▶ **verb** [no obj.] Biology (of a cell or tissue) undergo a reversal of differentiation and lose specialized characteristics.
– DERIVATIVES **dedifferentiation** noun.

deduce ▶ **verb** [with obj.] **1** arrive at (a fact or a conclusion) by reasoning; draw as a logical conclusion: *little can be safely **deduced from** these figures* | [with clause] *they **deduced that** the fish died because of water pollution*.
2 archaic trace the course or derivation of: *he cannot deduce his descent wholly by heirs male*.
– DERIVATIVES **deducible** adjective.
– ORIGIN late Middle English (in the sense 'lead or convey'): from Latin *deducere*, from *de-* 'down' + *ducere* 'lead'.

deduct ▶ **verb** [with obj.] subtract or take away (an amount or part) from a total: *tax has been **deducted from** the payments*.
– ORIGIN late Middle English: from Latin *deduct-* 'taken or led away', from the verb *deducere*. *Deduct* and *deduce* were not distinguished in sense until the mid 17th cent.

deductible ▶ **adjective** able to be deducted, especially from taxable income or tax to be paid. See also TAX-DEDUCTIBLE.
▶ **noun** N. Amer. the part of an insurance claim to be paid by the insured; an excess.
– DERIVATIVES **deductibility** noun.

deduction ▶ **noun** [mass noun] **1** the action of deducting or subtracting something: *the dividend will be paid without deduction of tax*. ■ [count noun] an amount that is or may be deducted from something, especially from taxable income or tax to be paid: *tax deductions*.
2 the inference of particular instances by reference to a general law or principle: *the detective must uncover the murderer by deduction from facts* | [count noun] *we do not yet know if these deductions are correct*. Often contrasted with INDUCTION.
– ORIGIN late Middle English: from Latin *deductio(n-)*, from the verb *deducere* (see DEDUCE).

deductive ▶ **adjective** characterized by or based on the inference of particular instances from a general law: *deductive reasoning* | *I used my deductive powers*.
– DERIVATIVES **deductively** adverb.
– ORIGIN mid 17th cent.: from medieval Latin *deductivus*, from *deduct-* 'deduced', from the verb *deducere* (see DEDUCE).

de Duve /də ˈduːv/, French /də dyv/, Christian René (b.1917), British-born Belgian biochemist. A pioneer in the study of cell biology, he won the Nobel Prize for Physiology or Medicine in 1974.

Dee[1] **1** a river in NE Scotland, which rises in the Grampian Mountains and flows eastwards past Balmoral Castle to the North Sea at Aberdeen.
2 a river which rises in North Wales and flows past Chester and on into the Irish Sea.

Dee[2], John (1527–1608), English alchemist, mathematician, and geographer. He was Elizabeth I's astrologer and in later life he absorbed himself in alchemy and acquired notoriety as a sorcerer.

dee ▶ **noun** the letter D.

deed ▶ **noun 1** chiefly literary an action that is performed intentionally or consciously: *doing good deeds*. ■ a brave or noble act: *their deeds will live on in song*.
■ [mass noun] action or performance: *she had erred in both deed and manner*.
2 (often **deeds**) a legal document that is signed and delivered, especially one regarding the ownership of property or legal rights. See also TITLE DEED.
▶ **verb** [with obj.] N. Amer. convey or transfer (property or rights) by legal deed.
– ORIGIN Old English *dēd*, *dǣd*, of Germanic origin; related to Dutch *daad* and German *Tat*, from an Indo-European root shared by DO[1].

deed of covenant ▶ **noun** Brit. an agreement to pay a regular amount of money, particularly when this enables the recipient (typically a charity) to reclaim any tax paid by the donor on the amount.

deed poll ▶ **noun** English Law a legal deed made and executed by one party only, especially to formalize a change of a person's name: *he changed his name by deed poll*.
– ORIGIN late 16th cent.: so named because the parchment was 'polled' or cut cleanly, not indented at the edges as in the case of a deed made by two parties.

deedy ▶ **adjective** dialect or archaic industrious, effective, or earnest.

deejay informal ▶ **noun** a disc jockey.
▶ **verb** [no obj.] perform as a disc jockey, typically in a club.
– ORIGIN 1950s (originally US): representing the pronunciation of *DJ*.

deem ▶ **verb** [with obj. and complement] formal regard or consider in a specified way: *the event was deemed a great success* | [with obj. and infinitive] *the strike was deemed to be illegal*.
– ORIGIN Old English *dēman* (also in the sense 'act as judge'), of Germanic origin; related to Dutch *doemen*, also to DOOM.

de-emphasize (also **de-emphasise**) ▶ **verb** [with obj.] reduce the importance or prominence given to (something).
– DERIVATIVES **de-emphasis** noun.

deemster /ˈdiːmstə/ ▶ **noun** a judge (of whom there are two) in the Isle of Man judiciary.
– ORIGIN Middle English (originally a general word for a judge): from DEEM + -STER. The current sense dates from the early 17th cent.

de-energize (also **de-energise**) ▶ **verb** [with obj.] disconnect (an electric circuit) from a power supply.

deep ▶ **adjective 1** extending far down from the top or surface: *a deep gorge* | *the lake was deep and cold*.
■ extending or situated far in from the outer edge or surface: *a deep alcove* | ***deep in** the woods*. ■ [predic.] (after a measurement and in questions) extending a specified distance from the top, surface, or outer edge: *the well was 200 feet deep*. ■ [in combination] as far up or down as a specified point: *they stood waist-deep in the water*. ■ [predic.] in a specified number of ranks one behind another: [in combination] *they were standing three-deep at the bar*. ■ taking in or giving out a lot of air: *she took a deep breath*. ■ Cricket (of a fielding position) relatively distant from the batsman; near the boundary: *deep midwicket*. ■ (in ball games) to or from a position far down or across the field: *a deep cross from Neill*.
2 very intense or extreme: *she was in deep trouble* | *a deep sleep*. ■ (of an emotion or feeling) intensely felt: *deep disappointment*. ■ profound or penetrating in awareness or understanding: *a deep analysis*. ■ difficult to understand: *this is all getting too deep for me*.
■ (**deep in**) fully absorbed or involved in (a state or activity): *they were deep in their own thoughts*. ■ (of a person) unpredictable and secretive: *that Thomas is a deep one*.
3 (of sound) low in pitch and full in tone; not shrill: *a deep, resonant voice*.
4 (of colour) dark and intense: *a deep pink*.
▶ **noun 1** (**the deep**) literary the sea: *denizens of the deep*.
■ (usu. **deeps**) a deep part of the sea: *the dark and menacing deeps* | figurative *the deeps of her imagination*.
2 (**the deep**) Cricket the part of the field distant from the batsman.
▶ **adverb** far down or in; deeply: *he travelled deep into the forest*. ■ (in sport) distant from the batsman or forward line of one's team: *he swung the ball in deep*.
– PHRASES **the deep end** the end of a swimming pool where the water is deepest. **dig deep** informal use one's physical, mental, or financial resources. **go off the deep end** informal give way immediately to an emotional outburst, especially of anger. ■ chiefly US go mad; behave extremely strangely: *they looked*

at me as if I had gone off the deep end. **go** (or **run**) **deep** (of emotions, beliefs, etc.) be strongly and wholeheartedly felt or held: *his passion runs deep.* **in deep** inextricably involved in or committed to a situation. **in deep water** (or **waters**) informal in trouble or difficulty: *he landed in deep water when he began the affair.* **jump** (or **be thrown**) **in at the deep end** informal face a difficult problem or undertaking with little or no preparation or prior experience.
– DERIVATIVES **deepness** noun.
– ORIGIN Old English *dēop* (adjective), *dīope, dēope* (adverb), of Germanic origin; related to Dutch *diep* and German *tief*, also to DIP.

Deepavali /diːpəˈvɑːli/ ▸ noun another term for DIWALI.
– ORIGIN respelling of Sanskrit *dīpāvali* (see DIWALI).

deep-bodied ▸ adjective (of an animal, especially a fish) having a body which is deeper (from back to belly) than it is wide.

deep-cycle ▸ adjective N. Amer. denoting a type of electric battery that can be totally discharged and recharged several times.

deep-discount ▸ adjective denoting financial securities carrying a low rate of interest relative to prevailing market rates and issued at a discount to their redemption value, so mainly providing capital gain rather than income. ■ N. Amer. heavily discounted; greatly reduced in price: *deep-discount pricing has kept air fares affordable.*

deep-dish ▸ adjective chiefly N. Amer. **1** (of a pie) baked in a deep dish to allow for a large filling: *deep-dish apple pie.* ■ (also **deep-pan**) (of a pizza) cooked in a deep dish and having a thick dough base.
2 informal extreme or thoroughgoing: *deep-dish conservatism.*

deep-drawn ▸ adjective (of metal) shaped by being forced through a die when cold.

deep-dyed ▸ adjective informal thoroughgoing; complete: *a deep-dyed Beatles fan.*

deep ecology ▸ noun [mass noun] an environmental movement and philosophy which regards human life as just one of many equal components of a global ecosystem.

deepen ▸ verb make or become deep or deeper: [no obj.] *the crisis deepened* | (as adj. **deepening**) *a deepening depression.*

deep freeze ▸ noun (also **deep freezer**) a refrigerator in which food can be quickly frozen and kept for long periods at a very low temperature.
▸ verb (**deep-freeze**) [with obj.] (often as adj. **deep-frozen**) store (something) in a deep freeze.

deep-fry ▸ verb [with obj.] (often as adj. **deep-fried**) fry (food) in an amount of fat or oil sufficient to cover it completely: *deep-fried scampi.*

deep kiss ▸ noun dated a kiss involving insertion of the tongue into the partner's mouth.

deep-laid ▸ adjective (of a scheme) elaborate and secret: *a deep-laid plot.*

deeply ▸ adverb **1** far down or in: *he breathed deeply.*
2 intensely: *Richard felt her loss very deeply* | [as submodifier] *she was deeply hurt.*

deep-mined ▸ adjective (of coal) obtained from far below the surface of the ground, not from opencast mines.
– DERIVATIVES **deep mining** noun.

deep mourning ▸ noun [mass noun] a state of mourning, conventionally expressed by wearing only black clothing. ■ the black clothing worn by someone in deep mourning.

deep-mouthed ▸ adjective archaic (of a dog) having a deep-sounding bark.

deep-pan ▸ adjective see DEEP-DISH.

deep-rooted ▸ adjective firmly embedded in thought, behaviour, or culture, and so having a persistent influence: *her deep-rooted fears and anxieties.*
– DERIVATIVES **deep-rootedness** noun.

deep sea ▸ noun [usu. as modifier] the deeper parts of the ocean, especially those beyond the edge of the continental shelf: *deep-sea diving.*

deep-seated ▸ adjective firmly established at a deep or profound level: *an opportunity for tackling the deep-seated causes of crime.*

deep-set ▸ adjective **1** embedded or positioned firmly or deeply: *the young man had deep-set eyes.*
2 long-established and profound: *the deep-set interrelations between religion and politics.*

deep-six ▸ verb [with obj.] N. Amer. informal destroy or dispose of (something) irretrievably: *someone had deliberately deep-sixed evidence.*
– ORIGIN 1920s (as *the deep six* 'the grave'): perhaps from the custom of burial at sea at a depth of six fathoms.

Deep South the south-eastern region of the US regarded as embodying traditional Southern culture and traditions.

deep space ▸ noun another term for OUTER SPACE.

deep structure ▸ noun [mass noun] (in transformational grammar) the underlying logical relationships of the elements of a phrase or sentence. Contrasted with SURFACE STRUCTURE.

deep throat ▸ noun a person who anonymously supplies information about covert or illegal action in the organization where they work.
– ORIGIN 1970s: the title of a pornographic film of 1972, first applied in this sense as the name ('Deep Throat') of an informant in the Watergate scandal.

deep-vein thrombosis ▸ noun [mass noun] thrombosis in a vein lying deep below the skin, especially in the legs, often precipitated by immobility during illness or long-distance travel.

deer ▸ noun (pl. **same**) a hoofed grazing or browsing animal, with branched bony antlers that are shed annually and typically borne only by the male.
● Family Cervidae: several genera and many species.
– ORIGIN Old English *dēor*, also originally denoting any quadruped, used in the (now archaic) phrase *small deer* meaning 'small creatures collectively'; of Germanic origin; related to Dutch *dier*, German *Tier*.

deer fly ▸ noun **1** a bloodsucking louse fly which is a parasite of deer. It loses its wings on finding a host, and the female gives birth to fully grown larvae.
● *Lipoptena cervi*, family Hippoboscidae.
2 a bloodsucking horsefly which attacks humans and other large mammals. It can transmit various diseases, including tularaemia. ● Genus *Chrysops*, family Tabanidae: several species, including *C. callidus*, widespread throughout North America.

deergrass ▸ noun a small sedge related to cotton grass, growing in tufts on wet moors and bogs.
● *Trichophorum cespitosum* (or *Scirpus cespitosus*), family Cyperaceae.

deerhound ▸ noun a large dog of a rough-haired breed, resembling the greyhound.

deer lick ▸ noun N. Amer. a place where deer come to lick salt.

deer mouse ▸ noun a mainly nocturnal mouse found in a wide range of habitats in North and Central America. ● Genus *Peromyscus*, family Muridae: numerous species.

deer park ▸ noun a large enclosed area of ground attached to a country house, in which deer are kept.

deerskin ▸ noun [mass noun] leather made from deer's skin.

deerstalker ▸ noun **1** a soft cloth cap, originally worn for hunting, with peaks in front and behind and ear flaps which can be tied together over the top.
2 a person who stalks deer.

de-escalate ▸ verb [with obj.] reduce the intensity of (a conflict or potentially violent situation).
– DERIVATIVES **de-escalation** noun.

def ▸ adjective chiefly black slang excellent: *a truly def tattoo.*
– ORIGIN 1980s: probably an alteration of DEATH (used in Jamaican English as an intensifier), or shortened from DEFINITIVE or DEFINITE.

deface ▸ verb [with obj.] spoil the surface or appearance of (something), for example by drawing or writing on it: *he defaced library books.*
– DERIVATIVES **defacement** noun, **defacer** noun.
– ORIGIN Middle English: from Old French *desfacier*, from *des-* (expressing removal) + *face* 'face'.

de facto /deɪ ˈfaktəʊ, diː/ ▸ adverb in fact, whether by right or not: *the country was de facto divided between two states.* Often contrasted with DE JURE.
▸ adjective existing or holding a specified position in fact but not necessarily by legal right: *a de facto one-party system.*
– ORIGIN Latin, literally 'of fact'.

defaecate ▸ verb Brit. variant spelling of DEFECATE.

defalcate /ˈdiːfalkeɪt/ ▸ verb [with obj.] formal embezzle (funds with which one has been entrusted).
– DERIVATIVES **defalcation** noun.
– ORIGIN mid 16th cent. (in the sense 'deduct, subtract'): from medieval Latin *defalcat-* 'lopped', from the verb *defalcare*, from *de-* 'away from, off' + Latin *falx, falc-* 'sickle'.

de Falla, Manuel, see FALLA.

defamation /ˌdɛfəˈmeɪʃ(ə)n/ ▸ noun [mass noun] the action of damaging the good reputation of someone; slander or libel: *she sued him for defamation.*

defamatory /dɪˈfamət(ə)ri/ ▸ adjective (of remarks, writing, etc.) damaging the good reputation of someone; slanderous or libellous: *a defamatory allegation.*

defame ▸ verb [with obj.] damage the good reputation of (someone); slander or libel: *he claimed that the article defamed his family.*
– DERIVATIVES **defamer** noun.
– ORIGIN Middle English: from Old French *diffamer*, from Latin *diffamare* 'spread evil report', from *dis-* (expressing removal) + *fama* 'report'.

defamiliarize (also **defamiliarise**) ▸ verb [with obj.] make (something) unfamiliar or strange: *art serves to defamiliarize our experience of our own present.*

defang ▸ verb [with obj.] make (something) harmless or ineffectual: *the president had largely defanged the opposition.*

defat ▸ verb (**defats, defatting, defatted**) [with obj.] (usu. as adj. **defatted**) remove fat from (food).

default ▸ noun **1** [mass noun] failure to fulfil an obligation, especially to repay a loan or appear in a law court: *the company will have to restructure its debts to avoid default.*
2 [in sing.] a preselected option adopted by a computer program or other mechanism when no alternative is specified by the user or programmer.
▸ verb [no obj.] **1** fail to fulfil an obligation, especially to repay a loan or to appear in a law court: *some had defaulted on student loans.* ■ [with obj.] declare (a party) to have defaulted and give judgement against that party: *two semi-finalists were defaulted.*
2 (**default to**) (of a computer program or other mechanism) revert automatically to (a preselected option): *when you start a fresh letter the system will default to its own style.*
– PHRASES **by default** because of a lack of opposition. ■ through lack of positive action rather than conscious choice: *he became an actor by default.* **in default** guilty of failing to repay a loan or appear in a law court. **in default of** in the absence of: *in default of agreement the rent was to be determined by a surveyor.*
– ORIGIN Middle English: from Old French *defaut*, from *defaillir* 'to fail', based on Latin *fallere* 'disappoint, deceive'.

defaulter ▸ noun a person who fails to fulfil a duty, obligation, or undertaking. ■ chiefly Brit. a member of the armed forces guilty of a military offence.

defeasance /dɪˈfiːz(ə)ns/ ▸ noun [mass noun] Law the action or process of rendering something null and void. ■ [count noun] a clause or condition which, if fulfilled, renders a deed or contract null and void.
– ORIGIN late Middle English (as a legal term): from Old French *defesance*, from *defaire, desfaire* 'undo' (see DEFEAT).

defeasible /dɪˈfiːzɪb(ə)l/ ▸ adjective chiefly Law & Philosophy open in principle to revision, valid objection, forfeiture, or annulment.
– DERIVATIVES **defeasibility** noun, **defeasibly** adverb.
– ORIGIN Middle English: via Anglo-Norman French from the stem of Old French *desfesant* 'undoing' (see also DEFEASANCE).

defeat ▸ verb [with obj.] win a victory over (someone) in a battle or other contest; overcome or beat: *Garibaldi defeated the Neapolitan army.* ■ prevent (someone) from achieving an aim: *she was defeated by the last steep hill.* ■ prevent (an aim) from being achieved: *don't cheat by allowing your body to droop—this defeats the object of the exercise.* ■ reject or block (a motion or proposal): *the amendment was defeated.* ■ be impossible for (someone) to understand: *this line of reasoning defeats me, I must confess.* ■ Law render null and void; annul.
▸ noun an instance of defeating or being defeated: *a 1–0 defeat by Grimsby* | [mass noun] *she had still not quite admitted defeat.*
– ORIGIN late Middle English (in the sense 'undo, destroy, annul'): from Old French *desfait* 'undone', past participle of *desfaire*, from medieval Latin *disfacere* 'undo'.

defeated ▸ adjective having been beaten in a battle or other contest: *the defeated army.* ■ demoralized and overcome by adversity.
– DERIVATIVES **defeatedly** adverb.

D

defeatist ▸ noun a person who expects or is excessively ready to accept failure.
▸ adjective demonstrating expectation or acceptance of failure: *we have a duty not to be so defeatist*.
– DERIVATIVES **defeatism** noun.
– ORIGIN early 20th cent.: from French *défaitiste*, from *défaite* 'defeat'.

defecate /ˈdɛfɪkeɪt, ˈdiːf-/ (Brit. also **defaecate**) ▸ verb [no obj.] discharge faeces from the body.
– DERIVATIVES **defecator** noun, **defecatory** adjective.
– ORIGIN late Middle English (in the sense 'clear of dregs, purify'): from Latin *defaecat-* 'cleared of dregs', from the verb *defaecare*, from *de-* (expressing removal) + *faex, faec-* 'dregs'. The current sense dates from the mid 19th cent.

defecation /ˌdɛfɪˈkeɪʃ(ə)n/ (Brit. also **defaecation**) ▸ noun [mass noun] the discharge of faeces from the body.

defect[1] ▸ noun /ˈdiːfɛkt, dɪˈfɛkt/ a shortcoming, imperfection, or lack: *genetic defects* | [mass noun] *the property is free from defect*.
– ORIGIN late Middle English (as a noun, influenced by Old French *defect* 'deficiency'): from Latin *defectus*, past participle of *deficere* 'desert or fail', from *de-* (expressing reversal) + *facere* 'do'.

defect[2] /dɪˈfɛkt/ ▸ verb [no obj.] abandon one's country or cause in favour of an opposing one: *he defected to the Soviet Union after the war*.
– DERIVATIVES **defector** noun.
– ORIGIN late 16th cent.: from Latin *defect-* 'failed', from the verb *deficere* (see DEFECT[1]).

defection ▸ noun [mass noun] the desertion of one's country or cause in favour of an opposing one: *his defection from the Labour Party* | [count noun] *a number of defections by leading ballet dancers*.

defective ▸ adjective **1** imperfect or faulty: *complaints over defective goods*. ■ lacking or deficient: *dystrophin is commonly **defective** in muscle tissue*. ■ Grammar (of a word) not having all the inflections normal for the part of speech.
2 dated or offensive having mental disabilities.
▸ noun dated or offensive a person with mental disabilities.
– DERIVATIVES **defectively** adverb, **defectiveness** noun.

defeminize (also **defeminise**) ▸ verb [with obj.] deprive of feminine characteristics.

defence (US **defense**) ▸ noun **1** [mass noun] the action of defending from or resisting attack: *methods of defence against this kind of attack* | *she **came to the defence of** the eccentric professor* | *he spoke **in defence of** a disciplined approach*. ■ [count noun] an instance of defending a title or seat in a contest or election: *his first title defence against Jones*. ■ military measures or resources for protecting a country: *the minister of defence* | [as modifier] *defence policy*. ■ a means of protecting something from attack: *wire netting is the best defence against rabbits*. ■ (**defences**) fortifications or barriers against attack: *coastal defences*.
2 the case presented by or on behalf of the party accused of a crime or being sued in a civil lawsuit. ■ (**the defence**) [treated as sing. or pl.] the counsel for the defendant in a lawsuit: *the defence requested more time to prepare their case*.
3 (in sport) the action or role of defending one's goal or wicket against the opposition: *Wolves were pressed back into defence*. ■ (**the defence**) the players in a team who defend the goal.
– PHRASES **defence in depth** the arrangement of defensive lines or fortifications so that they can defend each other.
– ORIGIN Middle English: from Old French *defens*, from late Latin *defensum* (neuter), *defensa* (feminine), past participles of *defendere* 'defend'.

Defence Force the South African armed services, consisting of the army, navy, air force, and medical service.

defenceless (US **defenseless**) ▸ adjective without defence or protection; totally vulnerable: *attacks on defenceless civilians*.
– DERIVATIVES **defencelessness** noun.

defenceman (US **defenseman**) ▸ noun (pl. **defencemen**) (in ice hockey and lacrosse) a player in a defensive position.

defence mechanism ▸ noun an automatic reaction of the body against disease-causing organisms. ■ a mental process initiated unconsciously to avoid experiencing conflict or anxiety.

defend ▸ verb [with obj.] **1** resist an attack made on (someone or something); protect from harm or danger: *we shall defend our island, whatever the cost*. ■ speak or write in favour of (an action or person); attempt to justify: *he defended his policy of imposing high rates*. ■ compete to retain (a title or seat) in a contest or election: *he won the party's nomination to defend the Welsh seat* | (as adj. **defending**) *the defending champion*.
2 conduct the case for (the party being accused or sued) in a lawsuit: *he is a lawyer who specializes in defending political prisoners*.
3 [no obj.] (in sport) protect one's goal or wicket rather than attempt to score against one's opponents.
– DERIVATIVES **defendable** adjective.
– ORIGIN Middle English: from Old French *defendre*, from Latin *defendere*, from *de-* 'off' + *-fendere* 'to strike'. Compare with OFFEND.

defendant ▸ noun an individual, company, or institution sued or accused in a court of law. Compare with PLAINTIFF.

defender ▸ noun **1** a person who defends someone or something: *a determined defender of British interests*. ■ Bridge either member of the partnership that did not win the auction. Compare with DECLARER.
2 (in sport) a player whose task it is to protect their own side's goal.
3 Scots Law another term for DEFENDANT.

Defender of the Faith ▸ noun a title conferred on Henry VIII by Pope Leo X in 1521. It was recognized by Parliament as an official title of the English monarch in 1544, and has been borne by all subsequent sovereigns.
– ORIGIN translation of Latin *Fidei Defensor*.

defenestration ▸ noun [mass noun] formal or humorous the action of throwing someone out of a window. ■ (**the Defenestration of Prague**) see PRAGUE.
– DERIVATIVES **defenestrate** verb.
– ORIGIN early 17th cent.: from modern Latin *defenestratio(n-)*, from *de-* 'down from' + Latin *fenestra* 'window'.

defense etc. ▸ noun US spelling of DEFENCE etc.

defensible ▸ adjective **1** justifiable by argument: *a morally defensible penal system*.
2 able to be protected: *a fort with a defensible yard at its feet*.
– DERIVATIVES **defensibility** noun, **defensibly** adverb.
– ORIGIN Middle English (in the sense 'capable of giving protective defence'): from late Latin *defensibilis*, from Latin *defendere* (see DEFEND).

defensive ▸ adjective **1** used or intended to defend or protect: *defensive barriers*. ■ (in sport) relating to or intended as defence.
2 very anxious to challenge or avoid criticism: *he was very defensive about that side of his life*.
– PHRASES **on the defensive** expecting or resisting criticism or attack: *British forces were on the defensive*.
– DERIVATIVES **defensively** adverb, **defensiveness** noun.
– ORIGIN late Middle English: from Old French *défensif, -ive*, from medieval Latin *defensivus*, from Latin *defens-* 'warded off', from the verb *defendere* (see DEFEND).

defensive end ▸ noun American Football either of the two defensive players positioned at the end of the line of the scrimmage.

defer[1] /dɪˈfəː/ ▸ verb (**defers, deferring, deferred**) [with obj.] put off (an action or event) to a later time; postpone: *they deferred the decision until February*. ■ Law (of a judge) postpone (a sentence) so that the circumstances or conduct of the defendant can be further assessed: *the judge deferred sentence until 5 April for background reports*. ■ US historical postpone the conscription of (someone).
– DERIVATIVES **deferrable** adjective, **deferral** noun.
– ORIGIN late Middle English (also in the sense 'put on one side'): from Old French *differer* 'defer or differ', from Latin *differre*, from *dis-* 'apart' + *ferre* 'bring, carry'. Compare with DEFER[2] and DIFFER.

defer[2] /dɪˈfəː/ ▸ verb (**defers, deferring, deferred**) [no obj.] (**defer to**) submit to or acknowledge the merit of: *he deferred to Tim's superior knowledge*.
– DERIVATIVES **deferrer** noun.
– ORIGIN late Middle English: from Old French *deferer*, from Latin *deferre* 'carry away, refer (a matter)', from *de-* 'away from' + *ferre* 'bring, carry'. Compare with DEFER[1].

deference ▸ noun [mass noun] polite submission and respect: *he addressed her with the deference due to age*.
– PHRASES **in deference to** out of respect for; in consideration of.
– ORIGIN mid 17th cent.: from French *déférence*, from *déférer* 'refer' (see DEFER[2]).

deferent[1] /ˈdɛf(ə)r(ə)nt/ ▸ adjective another term for DEFERENTIAL.
– ORIGIN early 19th cent.: from DEFER[2] and DEFERENCE.

deferent[2] /ˈdɛf(ə)r(ə)nt/ ▸ noun (in the Ptolemaic system of astronomy) the large circular orbit followed by the centre of the small epicycle in which a planet was thought to move.
– ORIGIN late Middle English: from medieval Latin *deferent-* 'carrying away', from the verb *deferre*.

deferential ▸ adjective showing deference; respectful: *people were always **deferential to** him*.
– DERIVATIVES **deferentially** adverb.
– ORIGIN early 19th cent.: from DEFERENCE, on the pattern of pairs such as *prudence, prudential*.

deferment ▸ noun [mass noun] the action or fact of putting something off to a later time; postponement: *deferment of the decision*. ■ US historical the postponement of a person's conscription: [count noun] *he was granted five deferments from the draft*.

deferred annuity ▸ noun an annuity which commences only after a lapse of some specified time after the final purchase premium has been paid.

defervescence /ˌdɪfəˈvɛs(ə)ns/ ▸ noun [mass noun] Medicine the abatement of a fever as indicated by a decrease in bodily temperature.
– ORIGIN early 18th cent.: from Latin *defervescent-* 'ceasing to boil', from the verb *defervescere*.

deffo ▸ adverb Brit. informal definitely; certainly: *Tyler is by far the best—he should deffo win*.
– ORIGIN 1990s: abbreviation.

defiance ▸ noun [mass noun] open resistance; bold disobedience: *an act of defiance* | *the demonstration was held **in defiance of** official warnings*.
– ORIGIN Middle English (denoting the renunciation of an allegiance or friendship): from Old French, from *defier* 'defy'.

defiant ▸ adjective showing defiance: *a defiant gesture*.
– DERIVATIVES **defiantly** adverb.

defibrillation /ˌdiːfɪbrɪˈleɪʃ(ə)n/ ▸ noun [mass noun] Medicine the stopping of fibrillation of the heart by administering a controlled electric shock, to allow restoration of the normal rhythm.
– DERIVATIVES **defibrillate** verb.

defibrillator ▸ noun Medicine an apparatus used to control heart fibrillation by application of an electric current to the chest wall or heart.

deficiency ▸ noun (pl. **deficiencies**) a lack or shortage: ***deficiencies in** material resources*. ■ a failing or shortcoming: *for all its deficiencies it remains his most powerful play*. ■ the amount by which something, especially revenue, falls short; a deficit: *a budget deficiency of $96 billion*.

deficiency disease ▸ noun a disease caused by the lack of an element in the diet, usually a particular vitamin or mineral.

deficiency payment ▸ noun a payment made, typically by a government body, to cover a financial deficit incurred in the course of an activity such as farming.

deficient /dɪˈfɪʃ(ə)nt/ ▸ adjective **1** not having enough of a specified quality or ingredient: *this diet is **deficient in** vitamin B*. ■ insufficient or inadequate: *the documentary evidence is deficient*.
2 (also **mentally deficient**) offensive having mental disabilities.
– DERIVATIVES **deficiently** adverb.
– ORIGIN late 16th cent. (originally in the theological phrase *deficient cause*, denoting a failure or deficiency that has a particular consequence): from Latin *deficient-* 'failing', from the verb *deficere* (see DEFECT[1]).

deficit /ˈdɛfɪsɪt, ˈdiː-/ ▸ noun the amount by which something, especially a sum of money, is too small. ■ an excess of expenditure or liabilities over income or assets in a given period: *an annual operating deficit* | [mass noun] *the balance of payments is again **in deficit***. ■ (in sport) the amount or score by which a team or individual is losing: *a 3–0 deficit*. ■ technical a deficiency or failing, especially in a neurological or psychological function: *deficits in speech comprehension*.
– ORIGIN late 18th cent.: via French from Latin *deficit* 'it is lacking', from the verb *deficere* (see DEFECT[1]).

deficit financing ▸ noun [mass noun] government funding of spending by borrowing.

deficit spending ▸ noun [mass noun] government spending, in excess of revenue, of funds raised by borrowing rather than from taxation.

defilade /ˌdɛfɪˈleɪd/ Military ▸ noun [mass noun] the protection of forces against enemy observation or gunfire.
▸ verb [with obj.] protect (forces) against enemy observation or gunfire.
– ORIGIN early 19th cent.: from French *défiler* 'protect from the enemy' + **-ADE**[1].

defile[1] /dɪˈfʌɪl/ ▸ verb [with obj.] damage the purity or appearance of; mar or spoil: *the land was defiled by a previous owner.* ■ desecrate or profane (something sacred): *the tomb had been defiled and looted.* ■ archaic rape or sexually assault (a woman).
– DERIVATIVES **defiler** noun.
– ORIGIN late Middle English: alteration of obsolete *defoul*, from Old French *defouler* 'trample down', influenced by obsolete *befile* 'befoul, defile'.

defile[2] /dɪˈfʌɪl/ ▸ noun also /ˈdiːfʌɪl/ a steep-sided narrow gorge or passage (originally one requiring troops to march in single file).
▸ verb [no obj., with adverbial of direction] archaic (of troops) march in single file.
– ORIGIN late 17th cent.: from French *défilé* (noun), *défiler* (verb), from *dé* 'away from' + *file* 'column, file'.

defilement ▸ noun [mass noun] the action of defiling or the state of being defiled.

definable ▸ adjective able to be defined: *it may not serve a definable purpose.*

define ▸ verb [with obj.] **1** state or describe exactly the nature, scope, or meaning of: *the contract will seek to define the client's obligations.* ■ give the meaning of (a word or phrase), especially in a dictionary. ■ make up or establish the character or essence of: *for some, the football club defines their identity.*
2 mark out the boundary or limits of: (as adj. **defined**) *clearly defined boundaries.* ■ make clear the outline of; delineate: *she defined her eyes by applying eyeshadow to her eyelids.*
– DERIVATIVES **definer** noun.
– ORIGIN late Middle English (also in the sense 'bring to an end'): from Old French *definer*, from a variant of Latin *definire*, from *de-* (expressing completion) + *finire* 'finish' (from *finis* 'end').

definiendum /dɪˌfɪnɪˈɛndəm/ ▸ noun (pl. **definienda**) a word, phrase, or symbol which is the subject of a definition, especially in a dictionary entry, or which is introduced into a logical system by being defined. Contrasted with **DEFINIENS**.
– ORIGIN late 19th cent.: from Latin, 'that which is to be defined', from the verb *definire* (see **DEFINE**).

definiens /dɪˈfɪnɪɛnz/ ▸ noun (pl. **definientia**) a word, phrase, or symbolic expression used to define something, especially in a dictionary entry, or introducing a word or symbol into a logical system by providing a statement of its meaning. Contrasted with **DEFINIENDUM**.
– ORIGIN late 19th cent.: from medieval Latin, 'defining', present participle of *definire* (see **DEFINE**).

defining moment ▸ noun an event which typifies or determines all subsequent related occurrences.

definite ▸ adjective clearly stated or decided; not vague or doubtful: *we had no definite plans.* ■ clearly true or real; unambiguous: *no definite proof has emerged.* ■ [predic.] (of a person) certain or sure about something: *you're very definite about that!* ■ clear or undeniable (used for emphasis): *under the circumstances, air conditioning is a definite asset.* ■ having exact and discernible physical limits or form.
– DERIVATIVES **definiteness** noun.
– ORIGIN mid 16th cent.: from Latin *definitus* 'defined, set within limits', past participle of *definire* (see **DEFINE**).

> **USAGE** For an explanation of the difference between **definite** and **definitive**, see **USAGE** at **DEFINITIVE**.

definite article ▸ noun Grammar a determiner (*the* in English) that introduces a noun phrase and implies that the thing mentioned has already been mentioned, or is common knowledge, or is about to be defined (as in *the book on the table*; *the art of government*; *the famous public school in Berkshire*). Compare with **INDEFINITE ARTICLE**.

definite description ▸ noun chiefly Philosophy a noun phrase introduced by the definite article or its equivalent, and denoting a particular entity or phenomenon.

definite integral ▸ noun Mathematics an integral expressed as the difference between the values of the integral at specified upper and lower limits of the independent variable.

definitely ▸ adverb without doubt (used for emphasis): *I shall definitely be at the airport to meet you.*

definition ▸ noun **1** a statement of the exact meaning of a word, especially in a dictionary. ■ an exact statement or description of the nature, scope, or meaning of something: *our definition of what constitutes poetry.* ■ [mass noun] the action or process of defining something.
2 [mass noun] the degree of distinctness in outline of an object, image, or sound. ■ the capacity of a device to make images distinct in outline: [in combination] *high-definition television.*
– PHRASES **by definition** by its very nature; intrinsically: *the assumption is that travel will, by definition, lead to creative insight.*
– DERIVATIVES **definitional** adjective, **definitionally** adverb.
– ORIGIN late Middle English: from Latin *definitio(n-)*, from the verb *definire* 'set bounds to' (see **DEFINE**).

definitive ▸ adjective **1** (of a conclusion or agreement) done or reached decisively and with authority: *a definitive decision.* ■ (of a book or other text) the most authoritative of its kind: *the definitive biography of Prince Charles.*
2 (of a postage stamp) for general use and typically of standard design, not special or commemorative.
▸ noun a definitive postage stamp.
– DERIVATIVES **definitively** adverb.
– ORIGIN late Middle English: from Old French *definitif, -ive*, from Latin *definitivus*, from *definit-* 'set within limits', from the verb *definire* (see **DEFINE**).

> **USAGE** **Definitive** is often used, rather imprecisely, when **definite** is actually intended, to mean simply 'clearly decided'. Although **definitive** and **definite** have a clear overlap in meaning, **definitive** has the additional sense of 'having an authoritative basis'. Thus, *a* ***definitive*** *decision* is one which is not only conclusive but also carries the stamp of authority or is a benchmark for the future, while *a* ***definite*** *decision* is simply one which has been made clearly and is without doubt.

definitive host ▸ noun Biology an organism which supports the adult or sexually reproductive form of a parasite. Compare with **INTERMEDIATE HOST**.

deflagrate /ˈdɛfləgreɪt/ ▸ verb Chemistry, dated burn or cause to burn away with a sudden flame and rapid, sharp combustion: [with obj.] *the current will deflagrate some of the particles.*
– ORIGIN early 18th cent.: from Latin *deflagrat-* 'burnt up', from the verb *deflagrare*, from *de-* 'away, thoroughly' + *flagrare* 'to burn'.

deflagration ▸ noun [mass noun] the action of heating a substance until it burns away rapidly. ■ technical combustion which propagates through a gas or across the surface of an explosive at subsonic speeds, driven by the transfer of heat. Compare with **DETONATION**.
– ORIGIN early 17th cent.: from Latin *deflagratio(n-)*, from the verb *deflagrare* (see **DEFLAGRATE**).

deflate ▸ verb [with obj.] **1** let air or gas out of (a tyre, balloon, or similar object): *he deflated one of the tyres.* ■ [no obj.] be emptied of air or gas: *the balloon deflated.*
2 make (someone) suddenly lose confidence or feel dispirited: (as adj. **deflated**) *the news left him feeling utterly deflated.*
3 Economics bring about a general reduction of price levels in (an economy).
– DERIVATIVES **deflator** noun.
– ORIGIN late 19th cent.: from **DE-** (expressing reversal) + *flate* (as in *inflate*).

deflation ▸ noun [mass noun] **1** the action or process of deflating or being deflated: *the deflation of the illusion that the 1960s were a perpetual party.*
2 Economics reduction of the general level of prices in an economy.
3 Geology the removal of particles of rock, sand, etc. by the wind.
– DERIVATIVES **deflationist** noun & adjective.
– ORIGIN late 19th cent. (in the sense 'release of air from something inflated'): from **DEFLATE**; sense 3 via German from Latin *deflat-* 'blown away', from the verb *deflare*.

deflationary ▸ adjective characterized by or tending to cause economic deflation.

deflect ▸ verb [with obj., and usu. with adverbial of direction] cause (something) to change direction; turn aside from a straight course: *the bullet was deflected harmlessly into the ceiling* | figurative *he attempted to deflect attention away from his private life.* ■ [no obj., with adverbial of direction] (of an object) change direction after hitting something: *the ball deflected off Knight's body.* ■ cause (someone) to deviate from an intended purpose: *she refused to be **deflected from** anything she had set her mind on.*
– ORIGIN mid 16th cent.: from Latin *deflectere*, from *de-* 'away from' + *flectere* 'to bend'.

deflection (also **deflexion**) ▸ noun [mass noun] the action or process of deflecting or being deflected: *the deflection of the light beam* | [count noun] ***his volley took a deflection off a United defender.***
– ORIGIN early 17th cent.: from late Latin *deflexio(n-)*, from *deflectere* 'bend away' (see **DEFLECT**).

D

deflector ▸ noun a device that deflects something, in particular: ■ a plate or other attachment for deflecting a flow of air, water, heat, etc. ■ an electrode in a cathode ray tube whose magnetic field is used to deflect a beam of electrons on to a phosphor screen to form an image.

deflesh ▸ verb [with obj.] remove the flesh from.

deflexed ▸ adjective technical bent or curving downwards or backwards: *a deflexed beak.*
– ORIGIN early 19th cent. (earlier as *deflex*): from Latin *deflexus* 'bent away' (past participle of *deflectere*) + **-ED**[1].

deflocculate /diːˈflɒkjʊleɪt/ ▸ verb [with obj.] Chemistry break up the floccules of (a substance suspended in a liquid) into fine particles, producing a dispersion.

defloration /ˌdiːflɔːˈreɪʃ(ə)n/ ▸ noun [mass noun] dated or literary the taking of a woman's virginity.
– ORIGIN late Middle English: from late Latin *defloratio(n-)*, from the verb *deflorare* (see **DEFLOWER**).

deflower ▸ verb [with obj.] dated or literary deprive (a woman) of her virginity.
– ORIGIN late Middle English: from Old French *desflourer*, from a variant of late Latin *deflorare*, from *de-* (expressing removal) + Latin *flos, flor-* 'a flower'.

defocus ▸ verb (**defocuses, defocusing, defocused** or **defocusses, defocussing, defocussed**) [with obj.] cause (an image, lens, or beam) to go out of focus.

Defoe /dɪˈfəʊ/, Daniel (1660–1731), English novelist and journalist. His best-known novel, *Robinson Crusoe* (1719), is loosely based on the true story of the shipwrecked sailor Alexander Selkirk; it has a claim to being the first English novel. Other notable works: *Moll Flanders* (novel, 1722) and *A Journal of the Plague Year* (historical fiction, 1722).

defogger ▸ noun N. Amer. a device for demisting a vehicle windscreen.

defoliant ▸ noun a chemical that removes the leaves from trees and plants, used in warfare.

defoliate /diːˈfəʊlɪeɪt/ ▸ verb [with obj.] remove leaves from (a tree, plant, or area of land), for agricultural purposes or as a military tactic.
– DERIVATIVES **defoliation** noun.
– ORIGIN late 18th cent.: from late Latin *defoliat-* 'stripped of leaves', from the verb *defoliare*, from *de-* (expressing removal) + *folium* 'leaf'.

defoliator ▸ noun **1** an adult or larval insect which strips all the leaves from a tree or shrub.
2 a machine that removes the leaves from a root crop.

deforce /dɪˈfɔːs/ ▸ verb [with obj.] Law deprive (someone) wrongfully or forcibly of their rightful property.
– ORIGIN late Middle English: from Anglo-Norman French *deforcer*, from *de-* (expressing removal) + *forcer* 'to force'.

deforest ▸ verb [with obj.] clear (an area) of forests or trees.

deform ▸ verb [with obj.] distort the shape or form of; make misshapen: *he was physically deformed by a rare bone disease.* ■ [no obj.] become distorted or misshapen; undergo deformation.
– DERIVATIVES **deformable** adjective.
– ORIGIN late Middle English: from Old French *desformer*, via medieval Latin from Latin *deformare*, from *de-* (expressing reversal) + *forma* 'a shape'.

deformation /ˌdiːfɔːˈmeɪʃ(ə)n/ ▸ noun [mass noun] the action or process of deforming or distorting. ■ the result of a distorting process: *the deformation will be temporary.* ■ [count noun] an altered form of a word, especially one used to avoid overt profanity (e.g. *dang* for *damn*).
– DERIVATIVES **deformational** adjective.

deformed ▸ adjective (of a person or part of the body) not having the normal or natural shape or form; misshapen: *his deformed hands.*

deformity ▶ **noun** (pl. **deformities**) a deformed part, especially of the body; a malformation: *deformities of the hands or feet.* ▪ [mass noun] the state of being deformed or misshapen: *respiratory problems caused by spinal deformity.*
– ORIGIN late Middle English: from Old French *desformite*, from Latin *deformitas*, from *deformis* 'misshapen'.

DEFRA ▶ **abbreviation** (in the UK) Department for Environment, Food, and Rural Affairs.

defrag ▶ **verb** (**defrags, defragging, defragged**) Computing short for **DEFRAGMENT**.

defragment /ˌdiːfragˈmɛnt/ ▶ **verb** [with obj.] Computing reduce the fragmentation of (a file) by concatenating parts stored in separate locations on a disk.
– DERIVATIVES **defragmentation** noun, **defragmenter** noun.

defraud ▶ **verb** [with obj.] illegally obtain money from (someone) by deception: *he used a second identity to* **defraud** *the bank* **of** *thousands of pounds.*
– DERIVATIVES **defrauder** noun.
– ORIGIN late Middle English: from Old French *defrauder* or Latin *defraudare*, from *de-* 'from' + *fraudare* 'to cheat' (from *fraus, fraud-* 'fraud').

defray /dɪˈfreɪ/ ▶ **verb** [with obj.] provide money to pay (a cost or expense): *the proceeds from the raffle help to defray the expenses of the evening.*
– DERIVATIVES **defrayable** adjective, **defrayal** noun, **defrayment** noun.
– ORIGIN late Middle English (in the general sense 'spend money'): from French *défrayer*, from *dé-* (expressing removal) + obsolete *frai* 'cost, expenses' (from medieval Latin *fredum* 'a fine for breach of the peace').

defriend ▶ **verb** another term for **UNFRIEND**.

defrock ▶ **verb** [with obj.] deprive (a person in holy orders) of ecclesiastical status. ▪ deprive (someone) of professional status or membership of a prestigious group.
– ORIGIN early 17th cent.: from French *défroquer*, from *dé-* (expressing removal) + *froc* 'frock'.

defrost ▶ **verb** [with obj.] free (the interior of a refrigerator or freezer) of accumulated ice, usually by turning it off for a period. ▪ [no obj.] (of a refrigerator or freezer) become free of accumulated ice in this way: *she opened the door to let the fridge defrost.* ▪ thaw (frozen food) before cooking it: *defrost the turkey slowly.* ▪ N. Amer. remove frost or ice from (the windscreen of a motor vehicle).
– DERIVATIVES **defroster** noun.

deft ▶ **adjective** neatly skilful and quick in one's movements: *a deft piece of footwork.* ▪ demonstrating skill and cleverness: *the script was both deft and literate.*
– DERIVATIVES **deftly** adverb, **deftness** noun.
– ORIGIN Middle English: variant of **DAFT**, in the obsolete sense 'meek'.

defterdar /ˌdɛftəˈdɑː/ ▶ **noun** (in the Ottoman Empire and modern Turkey) a finance officer or treasurer, especially a provincial accountant general.
– ORIGIN Turkish, from Persian *daftardār*, from *daftar* 'register' + *-dār* 'holder'.

defunct /dɪˈfʌŋ(k)t/ ▶ **adjective** no longer existing or functioning: *the now defunct Somerset & Dorset railway line.*
– ORIGIN mid 16th cent. (in the sense 'deceased'): from Latin *defunctus* 'dead', past participle of *defungi* 'carry out, finish', from *de-* (expressing reversal) + *fungi* 'perform'.

defund ▶ **verb** [with obj.] US prevent from continuing to receive funds: *the California Legislature has defunded the Industrial Welfare Commission.*

defuse ▶ **verb** [with obj.] remove the fuse from (an explosive device) in order to prevent it from exploding. ▪ make (a situation) less tense or dangerous: *a scheme that teaches officers how to defuse potentially explosive situations.*

> **USAGE** On the potential confusion between **defuse** and **diffuse**, see **USAGE** at **DIFFUSE**.

defy ▶ **verb** (**defies, defying, defied**) **1** [with obj.] openly resist or refuse to obey: *a woman who defies convention.* ▪ be of such a kind or nature that (a specified attitude or action) is almost impossible: *his actions defy belief | the outfit defied adequate description.*
2 [with obj. and infinitive] appear to be challenging (someone) to do or prove something: *he glowered at her, defying her to mock him.* ▪ archaic challenge (someone) to fight.
– DERIVATIVES **defier** noun.
– ORIGIN Middle English (in the senses 'renounce an allegiance' and 'challenge to combat'): from Old French *desfier*, based on Latin *dis-* (expressing reversal) + *fidus* 'faithful'.

deg. ▶ **abbreviation** degree(s).

dégagé /deɪˈgɑːʒeɪ, -ˈgaʒeɪ/ ▶ **adjective** unconcerned or unconstrained; relaxed.
▶ **noun** (pl. pronunc. **same**) Ballet a movement in which weight is shifted from one foot to the other in preparation for the execution of a step.
– ORIGIN late 17th cent.: French, past participle of *dégager* 'set free'.

Degas /ˈdeɪgɑː/, French /dəga/, (Hilaire Germain) Edgar (1834–1917), French painter and sculptor. An Impressionist painter, Degas is best known for his paintings of ballet dancers.

degas /diːˈgas/ ▶ **verb** (**degases, degassing, degassed**) make or become free of unwanted or excess gas.

de Gaulle /də ˈgəʊl/, French /də gol/, Charles (André Joseph Marie) (1890–1970), French general and statesman, head of government 1944–6, President 1959–69. A wartime organizer of the Free French movement, he is remembered particularly for his assertive foreign policy and for quelling the student uprisings and strikes of May 1968.

degauss /diːˈgaʊs/ ▶ **verb** [with obj.] **1** Electronics remove unwanted magnetism from (a television or monitor) in order to correct colour disturbance.
2 historical neutralize the magnetic field of (a ship) by encircling it with a conductor carrying electric currents.
– DERIVATIVES **degausser** noun.
– ORIGIN mid 20th cent.: from **DE-** + **GAUSS**.

degeneracy ▶ **noun** [mass noun] the state or quality of being degenerate: *the degeneracy of later Roman work.*

degenerate ▶ **adjective** /dɪˈdʒɛn(ə)rət/ **1** having lost the physical, mental, or moral qualities considered normal and desirable; showing evidence of decline: *a degenerate form of a higher civilization.*
2 technical lacking some usual or expected property or quality, in particular: ▪ Mathematics (of a type of equation, curve, etc.) equivalent to a simpler type, especially when a variable or parameter is set to zero. ▪ Physics (of an energy level) corresponding to more than one quantum state. ▪ Physics (of matter) at densities so high that gravitational contraction is counteracted, either by the Pauli exclusion principle or by an analogous quantum effect between closely packed neutrons. ▪ Biology having reverted to a simpler form as a result of losing a complex or adaptive structure present in the ancestral form.
▶ **noun** /dɪˈdʒɛn(ə)rət/ an immoral or corrupt person.
▶ **verb** /dɪˈdʒɛnəreɪt/ [no obj.] decline or deteriorate physically, mentally, or morally: *the quality of life had degenerated | the debate* **degenerated into** *a brawl.*
– DERIVATIVES **degenerately** adverb.
– ORIGIN late 15th cent.: from Latin *degeneratus* 'no longer of its kind', from the verb *degenerare*, from *degener* 'debased', from *de-* 'away from' + *genus, gener-* 'race, kind'.

degeneration ▶ **noun** [mass noun] the state or process of being or becoming degenerate; decline or deterioration: *overgrazing has caused serious degeneration of grassland.* ▪ Medicine deterioration and loss of function in the cells of a tissue or organ: *degeneration of the muscle fibres.*

degenerative /dɪˈdʒɛn(ə)rətɪv/ ▶ **adjective** (of a disease) characterized by progressive deterioration and loss of function in the organs or tissues.

degenerescence /dɪˌdʒɛnəˈrɛs(ə)ns/ ▶ **noun** another term for **DEGENERATION**.
– ORIGIN mid 19th cent.: from French *dégénérescence*, from *dégénérer* 'to degenerate'.

deglaciation /ˌdiːgleɪsɪˈeɪʃ(ə)n/ ▶ **noun** [mass noun] Geology the disappearance of ice from a previously glaciated region.

deglamorize (also **deglamorise**) ▶ **verb** [with obj.] make less glamorous or attractive.

deglaze ▶ **verb** [with obj.] make a gravy or sauce by adding liquid to the cooking juices and food particles in (a pan in which meat has been cooked).
– ORIGIN late 19th cent.: from French *déglacer*.

deglutition /ˌdiːgluːˈtɪʃ(ə)n/ ▶ **noun** [mass noun] technical the action or process of swallowing.
– ORIGIN mid 17th cent.: from French *déglutition* or modern Latin *deglutitio(n-)*, from *deglutire* 'swallow down'.

degradation /ˌdɛgrəˈdeɪʃ(ə)n/ ▶ **noun** [mass noun] **1** the condition or process of degrading or being degraded: *a trail of human misery and degradation.*
2 Geology the wearing down of rock by disintegration.
– ORIGIN mid 16th cent.: from Old French, or from ecclesiastical Latin *degradatio(n-)*, from the verb *degradare* (see **DEGRADE**).

degrade ▶ **verb** [with obj.] **1** treat or regard (someone) with contempt or disrespect: *she thought that many supposedly erotic pictures degraded women.* ▪ lower the character or quality of: *vast areas of natural habitats have been degraded.*
2 break down or deteriorate chemically: *the bacteria will degrade hydrocarbons.* ▪ Physics reduce (energy) to a less readily convertible form. ▪ Geology wear down (rock) and cause it to disintegrate.
3 archaic reduce (someone) to a lower rank, especially as a punishment.
– DERIVATIVES **degradability** noun, **degradable** adjective, **degradative** adjective, **degrader** noun.
– ORIGIN late Middle English: from Old French *degrader*, from ecclesiastical Latin *degradare*, from *de-* 'down, away from' + Latin *gradus* 'step or grade'.

degraded ▶ **adjective** treated or regarded with contempt or disrespect: *she had felt cheap and degraded.* ▪ reduced in quality; inferior: *it will grow successfully even on degraded land.*

degrading ▶ **adjective** causing a loss of self-respect; humiliating: *the prisoners were subjected to cruel and degrading treatment.*
– DERIVATIVES **degradingly** adverb.

degranulate ▶ **verb** [no obj.] Physiology (of a cell) lose or release granules of a substance, typically as part of an immune reaction.
– DERIVATIVES **degranulation** noun.

degrease ▶ **verb** [with obj.] remove excess grease or fat from.
– DERIVATIVES **degreasant** noun, **degreaser** noun.

degree ▶ **noun 1** the amount, level, or extent to which something happens or is present: *a degree of caution is probably wise | [mass noun] a question of degree.*
2 a unit of measurement of angles, one ninetieth of a right angle or the angle subtended by one three-hundred-and-sixtieth of the circumference of a circle: *set at an angle of 45 degrees.* (Symbol: °)
3 a unit in any of various scales of temperature, intensity, or hardness: *water boils at 100 degrees Celsius.* (Symbol: °)
4 a stage in a scale or series, in particular: ▪ [in combination] each of a set of grades (usually three) used to classify burns according to their severity. See **FIRST-DEGREE, SECOND-DEGREE, THIRD-DEGREE.** ▪ [in combination] a legal grade of crime or offence, especially murder: *second-degree murder.* ▪ [often in combination] a step in direct genealogical descent: *second-degree relatives.* ▪ Music a position in a musical scale, counting upwards from the tonic or fundamental note: *the lowered third degree of the scale.* ▪ Mathematics the class into which an equation falls according to the highest power of unknowns or variables present: *an equation of the second degree.* ▪ Grammar any of the three steps on the scale of comparison of gradable adjectives and adverbs, namely positive, comparative, and superlative. ▪ a rank in an order of freemasonry.
5 an academic rank conferred by a college or university after examination or after completion of a course, or conferred as an honour on a distinguished person: *a degree in zoology.*
6 [mass noun] archaic social or official rank: *persons of unequal degree.*
– PHRASES **by degrees** a little at a time; gradually. **to a degree** to some extent: *to a degree, it is possible to educate oneself.* ▪ dated to a considerable extent: *the pressure you were put under must have been frustrating to a degree.*
– ORIGIN Middle English (in the senses 'step', 'tier', 'rank', or 'relative state'): from Old French, based on Latin *de-* 'down' + *gradus* 'step or grade'.

degree day ▶ **noun 1** a day on which academic degrees are formally awarded.
2 a unit used to determine the heating requirements of buildings, representing a fall of one degree below a specified average outdoor temperature (usually 18°C or 65°F) for one day.

degree of freedom ▶ **noun** each of a number of independently variable factors affecting the range of states in which a system may exist, in particular any of the directions in which independent motion can occur.

degressive /dɪˈɡrɛsɪv/ ▸ **adjective** reducing by gradual amounts. ■ (of taxation) at successively lower rates on lower amounts.
– ORIGIN late 19th cent.: from Latin *degress-* 'descended' (from the verb *degredi*, from *de-* 'down' + *gradi* 'walk') + **-IVE**.

degu /ˈdeɪɡuː/ ▸ **noun** a rat-like rodent with a long silky coat, found in southern South America. ● Genus *Octodon*, family Octodontidae: three species.
– ORIGIN mid 19th cent.: from American Spanish, from South American Indian *deuñ*.

degust /dɪˈɡʌst/ ▸ **verb** [with obj.] rare taste (something) carefully to appreciate it fully.
– DERIVATIVES **degustation** noun.
– ORIGIN early 17th cent.: from Latin *degustare*, from *de-* 'completely' + *gustare* 'to taste'.

de haut en bas /də ˌəʊt ɒ̃ ˈbɑː/, French /də ot ɑ̃ ba/ ▸ **adverb & adjective** in a condescending or superior manner: [as adv.] *he never addressed his students de haut en bas*.
– ORIGIN French, 'from above to below'.

de Havilland /də ˈhavɪlənd/, Sir Geoffrey (1882–1965), English aircraft designer and manufacturer. He designed and built many aircraft, including the Mosquito of the Second World War.

dehisce /dɪˈhɪs/ ▸ **verb** [no obj.] technical (of a pod or seed vessel, or a cut or wound) gape or burst open.
– DERIVATIVES **dehiscence** noun, **dehiscent** adjective.
– ORIGIN mid 17th cent.: from Latin *dehiscere*, from *de-* 'away' + *hiscere* 'begin to gape' (from *hiare* 'gape').

de Hooch /də ˈhuːtʃ/ (also **de Hoogh**), Pieter (*c.*1629–*c.*1684), Dutch genre painter. He is noted for his depictions of domestic interior and courtyard scenes.

dehorn ▸ **verb** [with obj.] remove the horns from (an animal).

dehors /dəˈɔː, dəˈhɔː/ ▸ **preposition** Law other than, not including, or outside the scope of.
– ORIGIN early 18th cent.: from an Old French usage as a preposition (in modern French functioning as an adverb and noun).

Dehra Dun /ˌdɛːrə ˈduːn/ (also **Dehradun**) a city in northern India, capital of the state of Uttarakhand; pop. 551,300 (est. 2009).

dehull ▸ **verb** another term for **HULL²**.

dehumanize (also **dehumanise**) ▸ **verb** [with obj.] deprive of positive human qualities: (as adj. **dehumanizing**) *the dehumanizing effects of war*.
– DERIVATIVES **dehumanization** noun.

dehumidify ▸ **verb** (**dehumidifies**, **dehumidifying**, **dehumidified**) [with obj.] remove moisture from (the air or a gas).
– DERIVATIVES **dehumidification** noun, **dehumidifier** noun.

dehusk ▸ **verb** [with obj.] remove the husk or husks from (grain).

dehydrate /diːhʌɪˈdreɪt, diːˈhʌɪdreɪt/ ▸ **verb** [with obj.] (often as adj. **dehydrated**) cause (a person or their body) to lose a large amount of water: *his body temperature was high and he had become dehydrated*. ■ [no obj.] lose a large amount of water from the body. ■ remove water from (food) in order to preserve and store it: *dehydrated mashed potatoes*.
– DERIVATIVES **dehydration** noun, **dehydrator** noun.
– ORIGIN late 19th cent.: from **DE-** (expressing removal) + Greek *hudros*, *hudr-* 'water'.

dehydrocholesterol /diːˌhʌɪdrə(ʊ)kəˈlɛstərɒl/ ▸ **noun** [mass noun] Biochemistry a derivative of cholesterol present in the skin. It can be converted to cholecalciferol (vitamin D_3) by the action of ultraviolet radiation. ● Chem. formula: $C_{27}H_{44}O$.
– ORIGIN 1930s: from *dehydro-* 'that has lost hydrogen' + **CHOLESTEROL**.

dehydrogenase /ˌdiːhʌɪˈdrɒdʒəneɪz/ ▸ **noun** Biochemistry an enzyme that catalyses the removal of hydrogen atoms from a particular molecule, particularly in the electron transport chain reactions of cell respiration in conjunction with the coenzymes NAD and FAD.
– ORIGIN early 20th cent.: from **DE-** (expressing removal) + **HYDROGEN** + **-ASE**.

dehydrogenate ▸ **verb** [with obj.] Chemistry remove a hydrogen atom or atoms from (a compound).
– DERIVATIVES **dehydrogenation** noun.
– ORIGIN mid 19th cent.: from **DE-** (expressing removal) + **HYDROGEN** + **-ATE³**.

Deianira /ˌdiːəˈnʌɪrə/ Greek Mythology the wife of Hercules, who was tricked into smearing poison on a garment thereby causing his death.

de-ice ▸ **verb** [with obj.] remove ice from.
– DERIVATIVES **de-icer** noun.

deicide /ˈdeɪɪsʌɪd, ˈdiːɪ-/ ▸ **noun** the killer of a god. ■ [mass noun] the killing of a god.
– DERIVATIVES **deicidal** adjective.
– ORIGIN early 17th cent.: from ecclesiastical Latin *deicida* 'killer of a god', or directly from Latin *deus* 'god' + **-CIDE**.

deictic /ˈdeɪktɪk, ˈdʌɪktɪk/ Linguistics ▸ **adjective** relating to or denoting a word or expression whose meaning is dependent on the context in which it is used (such as *here*, *you*, *me*, *that one there*, or *next Tuesday*). Also called **INDEXICAL**.
▸ **noun** a deictic word or expression.
– DERIVATIVES **deictically** adverb.
– ORIGIN early 19th cent.: from Greek *deiktikos*, *deiktos* 'capable of proof', from *deiknunai* 'to show'.

deid /diːd/ ▸ **adjective** Scottish form of **DEAD**.

deify /ˈdeɪɪfʌɪ, ˈdiːɪ-/ ▸ **verb** (**deifies**, **deifying**, **deified**) [with obj.] worship or regard as a god: *she was deified by the early Romans as a fertility goddess*.
– DERIVATIVES **deification** noun.
– ORIGIN Middle English (in the sense 'make godlike in character'): from Old French *deifier*, from ecclesiastical Latin *deificare*, from *deus* 'god'.

deign /deɪn/ ▸ **verb** [no obj., with infinitive] do something that one considers to be beneath one's dignity: *she did not deign to answer the maid's question*. ■ [with obj.] archaic condescend to give (something): *he had deigned an apology*.
– ORIGIN Middle English: from Old French *degnier*, from Latin *dignare*, *dignari* 'deem worthy', from *dignus* 'worthy'.

Dei gratia /ˌdeɪiː ˈɡrɑːtɪə, -ʃɪə/ ▸ **adverb** by the grace of God.
– ORIGIN Latin.

deil /diːl/ ▸ **noun** Scottish form of **DEVIL**.

Deimos /ˈdeɪmɒs/ Astronomy the outer of the two small satellites of Mars, discovered in 1877 (15 km long and 12 km across).
– ORIGIN named after one of the sons of Ares in Greek mythology.

de-index ▸ **verb** [with obj.] end the indexation to inflation of (pensions or other benefits).

deindustrialization (also **deindustrialisation**) ▸ **noun** [mass noun] the reduction of industrial activity or capacity in a region or economy.
– DERIVATIVES **deindustrialize** verb.

deink ▸ **verb** [with obj.] remove ink from (paper being recycled).

deinonychus /dʌɪˈnɒnɪkəs/ ▸ **noun** a dromaeosaurid dinosaur of the mid Cretaceous period, growing up to 3.3 m (11 ft) in length. ● Genus *Deinonychus*, family Dromaeosauridae, suborder Theropoda.
– ORIGIN modern Latin, from Greek *deinos* 'terrible' + *onux*, *onukh-* 'claw'.

deinotherium /ˌdʌɪnə(ʊ)ˈθɪərɪəm/ (also **deinothere** /ˈdʌɪnə(ʊ)θɪə/) ▸ **noun** (pl. **deinotheria** or **deinotheriums**) a fossil elephant-like mammal found mainly in the Pliocene epoch, that had tusks in the lower jaw that curved downwards and backwards. ● Genus *Deinotherium*, suborder Deinotherioidea, order Proboscidea.
– ORIGIN modern Latin, from Greek *deinos* 'terrible' + *thērion* 'wild beast'.

deinstall (also **deinstal**) ▸ **verb** (**deinstalls** or **deinstals**, **deinstalling**, **deinstalled**) [with obj.] remove (an application or file) from a computer.
– DERIVATIVES **deinstallation** noun.

deinstitutionalize (also **deinstitutionalise**) ▸ **verb** [with obj.] discharge (a long-term inmate) from an institution such as a psychiatric hospital or prison.
– DERIVATIVES **deinstitutionalization** noun.

deionize /diːˈʌɪənʌɪz/ (also **deionise**) ▸ **verb** [with obj.] remove the ions or ionic constituents from (a substance, especially water).
– DERIVATIVES **deionization** noun, **deionizer** noun.

Deirdre /ˈdɪədri/ Irish Mythology a tragic heroine of whom it was prophesied that her beauty would bring banishment and death to heroes. King Conchobar of Ulster wanted to marry her, but she fell in love with Naoise, son of Usnach, who with his brothers carried her off to Scotland. They were lured back by Conchobar and treacherously slain, and Deirdre took her own life.

deisal ▸ **adverb** variant spelling of **DEASIL**.

deism /ˈdeɪɪz(ə)m, ˈdiːɪ-/ ▸ **noun** [mass noun] belief in the existence of a supreme being, specifically of a creator who does not intervene in the universe. Compare with **THEISM**.
– DERIVATIVES **deist** noun, **deistic** adjective, **deistical** adjective.
– ORIGIN late 17th cent.: from Latin *deus* 'god' + **-ISM**.

deity /ˈdeɪɪti, ˈdiːɪ-/ ▸ **noun** (pl. **deities**) a god or goddess (in a polytheistic religion): *a deity of ancient Greece*. ■ [mass noun] divine status, quality, or nature: *a ruler driven by delusions of deity*. ■ (usu. **the Deity**) the creator and supreme being (in a monotheistic religion such as Christianity).
– ORIGIN Middle English (denoting the divine nature of God): from Old French *deite*, from ecclesiastical Latin *deitas* (translating Greek *theotēs*), from *deus* 'god'.

D

deixis /ˈdeɪksɪs, ˈdʌɪksɪs/ ▸ **noun** [mass noun] Linguistics the function or use of deictic words, forms, or expressions.
– ORIGIN 1940s: from Greek, literally 'reference', from *deiknunai* 'to show'.

déjà vu /deɪʒɑː ˈvuː/, French /deʒa vy/ ▸ **noun** [mass noun] a feeling of having already experienced the present situation.
– ORIGIN early 20th cent.: French, literally 'already seen'.

deject ▸ **verb** [with obj.] archaic make sad or dispirited; depress: *nothing dejects a trader like the interruption of his profits*.
– ORIGIN late Middle English (also in the sense 'overthrow, abase, degrade'): from Latin *deject-* 'thrown down', from the verb *deicere*, from *de-* 'down' + *jacere* 'to throw'.

dejected ▸ **adjective** sad and depressed; dispirited: *he stood in the street looking dejected*.
– DERIVATIVES **dejectedly** adverb.

dejection ▸ **noun** [mass noun] a sad and depressed state; low spirits: *he was slumped in deep dejection*.
– ORIGIN late Middle English: from Latin *dejectio(n-)*, from *deicere* 'throw down' (see **DEJECT**).

dejunk ▸ **verb** [with obj.] informal clear (a room or other space) by disposing of clutter and unwanted possessions: *dejunk the house before you move*.

de jure /deɪ ˈjʊəreɪ, diː ˈdʒʊəri/ ▸ **adverb** according to rightful entitlement or claim; by right. Often contrasted with **DE FACTO**.
▸ **adjective** existing or holding a specified position by legal right: *he had been de jure king since his father's death*.
– ORIGIN Latin, literally 'of law'.

dekaliter ▸ **noun** US variant spelling of **DECALITRE**.

dekameter ▸ **noun** US variant spelling of **DECAMETRE**.

deke /diːk/ Ice Hockey ▸ **noun** a deceptive movement or feint that induces an opponent to move out of position.
▸ **verb** [with obj. and adverbial] draw (a player) out of position by such a movement.
– ORIGIN 1960s: shortened form of **DECOY**.

Dekker /ˈdɛkə/, Thomas (*c.*1570–1632), English dramatist, author of the revenge tragedy *The Witch of Edmonton* (1623), in which he collaborated with John Ford and William Rowley, and *The Honest Whore* (1604; 1630) with Thomas Middleton.

dekko /ˈdɛkəʊ/ ▸ **noun** [in sing.] Brit. informal a quick look or glance: *come and have a dekko at this*.
– ORIGIN late 19th cent. (originally used by the British army in India): from Hindi *dekho* 'look!', imperative of *dekhnā*.

de Klerk /də ˈklɛːk/, F. W. (b.1936), South African statesman, State President 1989–94; full name *Frederik Willem de Klerk*. As State President he freed Nelson Mandela in 1990, lifted the ban on membership of the ANC, and opened the negotiations that led to the first democratic elections in 1994. Nobel Peace Prize with Nelson Mandela (1993).

de Kooning /də ˈkuːnɪŋ/, Willem (1904–97), Dutch-born American painter, a leading exponent of abstract expressionism. The female form became a central theme in his later work, notably in the *Women* series (1950–3).

del ▸ **noun** Mathematics an operator used in vector analysis. (Symbol: ∇) ● del is defined as $\mathbf{i}^{\partial}/_{\partial x} + \mathbf{j}^{\partial}/_{\partial y} + \mathbf{k}^{\partial}/_{\partial z}$, where **i**, **j**, and **k** are vectors directed respectively along the Cartesian axes *x*, *y*, and *z*.
– ORIGIN early 20th cent.: abbreviation of **DELTA¹**, from the representation of the operator as an inverted capital delta.

Del. ▸ **abbreviation** Delaware.

Delacroix /ˌdɛləˈkrwɑː/, French /dəlakʀwa/, (Ferdinand Victor) Eugène (1798–1863), French painter, the chief painter of the French romantic school. He is known for his use of vivid colour, free drawing, and exotic, violent, or macabre subject matter. Notable works: *The Massacre at Chios* (1824).

de la Mare /ˌdə la ˈmɛː/, Walter (John) (1873–1956), English poet, known particularly for his verse for children. Notable works: *The Listeners* (1912).

delaminate /diːˈlamɪneɪt/ ▶ **verb** [with obj.] technical divide into layers.
– DERIVATIVES **delamination** noun.
– ORIGIN late 19th cent.: from **DE-** 'away' + Latin *lamina* 'thin plate' + **-ATE**³.

D

delate /dɪˈleɪt/ ▶ **verb** [with obj.] archaic report (an offence or crime). ■ inform against or denounce (someone): *they deliberated together on delating her as a witch*.
– DERIVATIVES **delation** noun, **delator** noun.
– ORIGIN late 15th cent.: from Latin *delat-* 'referred, carried away', from the verb *deferre* (see **DEFER**²).

Delaunay /dəˈlɔːneɪ/, French /dəlonε/, Robert (1885–1941), French painter. For most of his career he experimented with the abstract qualities of colour, and he painted some of the first purely abstract pictures. He was one of the founder members of Orphism together with Sonia Delaunay-Terk.

Delaunay-Terk /dəˌlɔːneɪˈtɛːk/, French /dəlonetεrk/, Sonia (1885–1979), Russian-born French painter and textile designer, wife of Robert Delaunay. She created abstract paintings based on harmonies of form and colour.

Delaware¹ /ˈdɛləwɛː/ **1** a river of the north-eastern US. Rising in the Catskill Mountains in New York State, it flows some 450 km (280 miles) southwards to northern Delaware, where it meets the Atlantic at Delaware Bay. For much of its length it forms the eastern border of Pennsylvania.
2 a state of the US on the Atlantic coast, one of the original thirteen states of the Union (1787); pop. 873,092 (est. 2008); capital, Dover.
– DERIVATIVES **Delawarean** noun & adjective.

Delaware² /ˈdɛləwɛː/ ▶ **noun** (pl. **same** or **Delawares**) **1** a member of an American Indian people formerly inhabiting the Delaware River valley of New Jersey and eastern Pennsylvania.
2 [mass noun] either of two Algonquian languages (Munsi and Unami), both now extinct, spoken by the Delaware.
▶ **adjective** relating to the Delaware or their languages.
– ORIGIN named after the River *Delaware* (see **DELAWARE**¹).

delay ▶ **verb** [with obj.] make (someone or something) late or slow: *the train was delayed*. ■ [no obj.] be late or slow; loiter: *time being of the essence, they delayed no longer*. ■ postpone or defer (an action): *he may decide to delay the next cut in interest rates*.
▶ **noun** a period of time by which something is late or postponed: *a two-hour delay* | *long delays in obtaining passports*. ■ [mass noun] the action of delaying or being delayed: *I set off without delay*. ■ Electronics the time interval between the propagation of an electrical signal and its reception. ■ an electronic device which introduces a delay, especially in an audio signal.
– DERIVATIVES **delayer** noun.
– ORIGIN Middle English: from Old French *delayer* (verb).

delayed-action ▶ **adjective** [attrib.] operating or effective after a predetermined length of time: *delayed-action bombs*.

delayering ▶ **noun** [mass noun] the action or process of reducing the number of levels in the hierarchy of employees in an organization.
– DERIVATIVES **delayer** verb.

delaying tactics ▶ **plural noun** tactics designed to defer or postpone something in order to gain an advantage for oneself.

delay line ▶ **noun** a device producing a specific desired delay in the transmission of a signal.

dele /ˈdiːli/ ▶ **verb** (**deles, deleing, deled**) [with obj.] delete or mark (a part of a text) for deletion.
▶ **noun** a proofreader's sign indicating matter to be deleted.
– ORIGIN Latin, 'blot out! efface!', imperative of *delere*.

delectable ▶ **adjective** (of food or drink) delicious: *delectable handmade chocolates*. ■ humorous extremely attractive: *the delectable Ms Davis*.
– DERIVATIVES **delectability** noun, **delectably** adverb.
– ORIGIN late Middle English: via Old French from Latin *delectabilis*, from *delectare* 'to charm' (see **DELIGHT**).

delectation /ˌdiːlɛkˈteɪʃ(ə)n/ ▶ **noun** [mass noun] formal, chiefly humorous pleasure and delight: *they had all manner of rock 'n' roll goodies for our delectation*.
– ORIGIN late Middle English: via Old French from Latin *delectatio(n-)*, from *delectare* 'to charm' (see **DELIGHT**).

delegacy /ˈdɛlɪɡəsi/ ▶ **noun** (pl. **delegacies**) [treated as sing. or pl.] a body of delegates; a committee or delegation.
– ORIGIN late Middle English: from **DELEGATE**, on the pattern of the pair *prelate, prelacy*.

delegate ▶ **noun** /ˈdɛlɪɡət/ a person sent or authorized to represent others, in particular an elected representative sent to a conference. ■ a member of a committee.
▶ **verb** /ˈdɛlɪɡeɪt/ [with obj.] entrust (a task or responsibility) to another person, typically one who is less senior than oneself: *she must delegate duties so as to free herself for more important tasks* | *the power delegated to him must never be misused*. ■ [with obj. and infinitive] send or authorize (someone) to do something as a representative: *Edward was delegated to meet new arrivals*.
– DERIVATIVES **delegable** /ˈdɛlɪɡəb(ə)l/ adjective, **delegator** noun.
– ORIGIN late Middle English: from Latin *delegatus* 'sent on a commission', from the verb *delegare*, from *de-* 'down' + *legare* 'depute'.

delegation ▶ **noun 1** [treated as sing. or pl.] a body of delegates or representatives; a deputation: *a delegation of teachers*.
2 [mass noun] the action or process of delegating or being delegated: *the delegation of power to the district councils*.
– ORIGIN early 17th cent. (denoting the action or process of delegating; also in the sense 'delegated power'): from Latin *delegatio(n-)*, from *delegare* 'send on a commission' (see **DELEGATE**).

delegitimate ▶ **verb** another term for **DELEGITIMIZE**.

delegitimatize (also **delegitimatise**) ▶ **verb** another term for **DELEGITIMIZE**.

delegitimize (also **delegitimise**) ▶ **verb** [with obj.] withdraw legitimate status or authority from: *the country has been delegitimized by the world community*.
– DERIVATIVES **delegitimization** noun.

de Lenclos, Ninon, see **LENCLOS**.

delete ▶ **verb** [with obj.] remove or obliterate (written or printed matter), especially by drawing a line through it: *the passage was deleted*. ■ remove (data) from a computer's memory. ■ remove (a product, especially a recording) from the catalogue of those available for purchase: *their EMI release has already been deleted*. ■ (**be deleted**) Genetics (of a section of genetic code, or its product) be lost or excised from a nucleic acid or protein sequence.
▶ **noun** a command or key on a computer which erases text.
– DERIVATIVES **deletion** noun.
– ORIGIN late Middle English (in the sense 'destroy'): from Latin *delet-* 'blotted out, effaced', from the verb *delere*.

deleterious /ˌdɛlɪˈtɪərɪəs/ ▶ **adjective** formal causing harm or damage: *divorce is assumed to have deleterious effects on children*.
– DERIVATIVES **deleteriously** adverb.
– ORIGIN mid 17th cent.: via medieval Latin from Greek *dēlētērios* 'noxious' + **-OUS**.

deleveraging /diːˈliːv(ə)rɪdʒɪŋ/ ▶ **noun** [mass noun] Finance the process or practice of reducing the level of one's debt by rapidly selling one's assets.
– DERIVATIVES **deleverage** noun & verb.

delexical /diːˈlɛksɪk(ə)l/ ▶ **adjective** Linguistics (of a verb) having little or no meaning in its own right, for example *take* in *take a photograph*.

Delft /dɛlft/ a town in the Netherlands, in the province of South Holland; pop. 96,168 (2008). The home of the painters Pieter de Hooch and Jan Vermeer, it is noted for its pottery.
– ORIGIN originally *Delf*, from Dutch *delf* 'ditch', still the name of the town's main canal.

delft /dɛlft/ ▶ **noun** [mass noun] English or Dutch tin-glazed earthenware, typically decorated by hand in blue on a white background.
– DERIVATIVES **delftware** noun.
– ORIGIN late 17th cent. (originally *Delf ware*): see **DELFT**, where the pottery originated.

Delhi /ˈdɛli/ (also **Old Delhi**) a walled city on the River Jumna in north central India, which was made the capital of the Mogul empire in 1638 by Shah Jahan (1592–1666). See also **NEW DELHI**.

Delhi belly ▶ **noun** [mass noun] informal an upset stomach accompanied by diarrhoea, especially as suffered by visitors to India.

deli ▶ **noun** (pl. **delis**) informal short for **DELICATESSEN**.

Delian /ˈdiːlɪən/ ▶ **adjective** relating to Delos.
▶ **noun** a native or inhabitant of Delos.

Delian League an alliance of ancient Greek city-states, dominated by Athens, that joined in 478–447 BC against the Persians. The league was disbanded on the defeat of Athens in the Peloponnesian War (404 BC), but again united under Athens' leadership against Spartan aggression in 377–338 BC. Also called the **ATHENIAN EMPIRE**.

deliberate ▶ **adjective** /dɪˈlɪb(ə)rət/ **1** done consciously and intentionally: *a deliberate attempt to provoke conflict*.
2 careful and unhurried: *a conscientious and deliberate worker*. ■ fully considered; not impulsive: *a deliberate decision*.
▶ **verb** /dɪˈlɪbəreɪt/ [no obj.] engage in long and careful consideration: *she deliberated over the menu*. ■ [with obj.] consider (a question) carefully: *jurors deliberated the fate of those charged* | [with clause] *they deliberated what they should do with him*.
– DERIVATIVES **deliberateness** noun, **deliberator** noun.
– ORIGIN late Middle English (as an adjective): from Latin *deliberatus*, 'considered carefully', past participle of *deliberare*, from *de-* 'down' + *librare* 'weigh' (from *libra* 'scales').

deliberately ▶ **adverb 1** consciously and intentionally; on purpose: *the fire was started deliberately*.
2 in a careful and unhurried way: *slowly and deliberately he rose from the armchair*.

deliberation ▶ **noun** [mass noun] **1** long and careful consideration or discussion: *after much deliberation we arrived at a compromise* | [count noun] *the commission's deliberations*.
2 slow and careful movement or thought: *he replaced the glass on the table with deliberation*.
– ORIGIN late Middle English: via Old French from Latin *deliberatio(n-)*, from *deliberare* 'consider carefully' (see **DELIBERATE**).

deliberative ▶ **adjective** relating to or intended for consideration or discussion: *a deliberative assembly*.
– DERIVATIVES **deliberatively** adverb.

Delibes /dəˈliːb/, French /dəlib/, (Clément Philibert) Léo (1836–91), French composer and organist. His best-known works are the ballets *Coppélia* (1870) and *Sylvia* (1876).

delicacy ▶ **noun** (pl. **delicacies**) [mass noun] **1** fineness or intricacy of texture or structure: *miniature pearls of exquisite delicacy*.
2 susceptibility to illness or adverse conditions; fragility.
3 tact and consideration: *I have to treat this matter with the utmost delicacy*. ■ the quality of requiring discretion or sensitivity: *the delicacy of the situation*.
4 [count noun] a choice or expensive food: *traditional Japanese delicacies*.
– ORIGIN late Middle English (in the senses 'voluptuousness' and 'luxuriousness'): from **DELICATE** + **-ACY**.

delicate ▶ **adjective 1** very fine in texture or structure; of intricate workmanship or quality: *a delicate lace shawl*. ■ (of colour) subtle and subdued: *delicate pastel shades*. ■ (of food or drink) subtly and pleasantly flavoured: *a delicate, sweet flavour*.
2 easily broken or damaged; fragile: *delicate china*. ■ susceptible to illness or adverse conditions: *his delicate health*. ■ (of a state or condition) easily upset or affected: *owls have a delicate balance with their habitat*.
3 requiring sensitive or careful handling: *delicate negotiations*. ■ tactful and considerate: *a delicate approach is needed*. ■ skilful and finely judged; deft: *his delicate ball-playing skills*. ■ (of an instrument) highly sensitive.
▶ **noun** informal a delicate fabric or garment.
– PHRASES **in a delicate condition** archaic pregnant.
– DERIVATIVES **delicately** adverb, **delicateness** noun.
– ORIGIN late Middle English (in the sense 'delightful, charming'): from French *délicat* or Latin *delicatus*, of unknown origin. Senses also expressed in Middle English (now obsolete) include 'voluptuous', 'self-indulgent', 'fastidious', and 'effeminate'.

delicatessen /ˌdɛlɪkəˈtɛs(ə)n/ ▶ **noun** a shop selling cooked meats, cheeses, and unusual or foreign prepared foods.

– ORIGIN late 19th cent. (originally US, denoting prepared foods for sale): from German *Delikatessen* or Dutch *delicatessen*, from French *délicatesse* 'delicateness', from *délicat* (see DELICATE).

delicense (also **delicence**) ▶ **verb** [with obj.] deprive of a licence.

delicious ▶ **adjective** highly pleasant to the taste: *delicious home-baked brown bread.* ■ delightful: *a delicious irony.*
– DERIVATIVES **deliciously** adverb, **deliciousness** noun.
– ORIGIN Middle English (also in the sense 'characterized by sensuous indulgence'): via Old French from late Latin *deliciosus*, from Latin *deliciae* (plural) 'delight, pleasure'.

delict /dɪˈlɪkt, ˈdiːlɪkt/ ▶ **noun** Law a violation of the law; a tort.
– ORIGIN late Middle English: from Latin *delictum* 'something showing fault', neuter past participle of *delinquere* (see DELINQUENT).

delight ▶ **verb** [with obj.] please (someone) greatly: *an experience guaranteed to delight both young and old.* ■ [no obj.] (**delight in**) take great pleasure in: *they delight in playing tricks.*
▶ **noun** [mass noun] great pleasure: *she took great delight in telling your story.* ■ [count noun] a cause or source of great pleasure: *the trees here are a delight.*
– ORIGIN Middle English: from Old French *delitier* (verb), *delit* (noun), from Latin *delectare* 'to charm', frequentative of *delicere*. The *-gh-* was added in the 16th cent. by association with LIGHT[1].

delighted ▶ **adjective** feeling or showing great pleasure: *a delighted smile* | [with infinitive] *we were delighted to see her.*
– DERIVATIVES **delightedly** adverb.

delightful ▶ **adjective** causing delight; charming: *a delightful secluded garden.*
– DERIVATIVES **delightfully** adverb, **delightfulness** noun.

Delilah /dɪˈlʌɪlə/ (in the Bible) a woman who betrayed Samson to the Philistines (Judges 16) by revealing to them that the secret of his strength lay in his long hair.

delimit /dɪˈlɪmɪt/ ▶ **verb** (**delimits, delimiting, delimited**) [with obj.] determine the limits or boundaries of: *agreements delimiting fishing zones.*
– DERIVATIVES **delimitation** noun, **delimiter** noun.
– ORIGIN mid 19th cent.: from French *délimiter*, from Latin *delimitare*, from *de-* 'down, completely' + *limitare* (from *limes, limit-* 'boundary, limit').

delineate /dɪˈlɪnɪeɪt/ ▶ **verb** [with obj.] **1** describe or portray (something) precisely: *the law should delineate and prohibit behaviour which is socially abhorrent.*
2 indicate the exact position of (a border or boundary).
– DERIVATIVES **delineator** noun.
– ORIGIN mid 16th cent. (in the sense 'trace the outline of something'): from Latin *delineat-* 'outlined', from the verb *delineare*, from *de-* 'out, completely' + *lineare* (from *linea* 'line').

delineation /dɪˌlɪnɪˈeɪʃ(ə)n/ ▶ **noun** [mass noun] **1** the action of describing or portraying something precisely: *the artist's exquisite delineation of costume and jewellery.*
2 the action of indicating the exact position of a border or boundary.

delink ▶ **verb** [with obj.] (often as noun **delinking**) break the connection between (something) and something else: *the possibility of delinking from the international economic system.*

delinquency ▶ **noun** (pl. **delinquencies**) [mass noun] **1** minor crime, especially that committed by young people: *social causes of crime and delinquency.*
2 formal neglect of one's duty. ■ [count noun] chiefly US a failure to pay an outstanding debt by the due date.
– ORIGIN mid 17th cent.: from ecclesiastical Latin *delinquentia*, from Latin *delinquent-* 'offending' (see DELINQUENT).

delinquent /dɪˈlɪŋkw(ə)nt/ ▶ **adjective 1** (typically of a young person) tending to commit crime, particularly minor crime: *delinquent teenagers.*
2 formal failing in one's duty. ■ N. Amer. in arrears: *delinquent accounts.*
▶ **noun** a delinquent person: *juvenile delinquents.*
– DERIVATIVES **delinquently** adverb.
– ORIGIN late 15th cent.: from Latin *delinquent-* 'offending', from the verb *delinquere*, from *de-* 'away' + *linquere* 'to leave'.

deliquesce /ˌdɛlɪˈkwɛs/ ▶ **verb** [no obj.] (of organic matter) become liquid, typically during decomposition. ■ Chemistry (of a solid) become liquid by absorbing moisture from the air.
– ORIGIN mid 18th cent.: from Latin *deliquescere* 'dissolve', from *de-* 'down' + *liquescere* 'become liquid' (from *liquere* 'be liquid').

deliquescent ▶ **adjective** becoming liquid, or having a tendency to become liquid. ■ Chemistry (of a solid) tending to absorb moisture from the air and dissolve in it.
– DERIVATIVES **deliquescence** noun.
– ORIGIN late 18th cent.: from Latin *deliquescent-* 'dissolving', from the verb *deliquescere* (see DELIQUESCE).

delirious ▶ **adjective** in an acutely disturbed state of mind characterized by restlessness, illusions, and incoherence; affected by delirium. ■ in a state of wild excitement or ecstasy: *there was a great roar from the delirious crowd.*
– DERIVATIVES **deliriously** adverb [as submodifier] *Rose was deliriously happy.*

delirium /dɪˈlɪrɪəm/ ▶ **noun** [mass noun] an acutely disturbed state of mind characterized by restlessness, illusions, and incoherence, occurring in intoxication, fever, and other disorders. ■ wild excitement or ecstasy.
– ORIGIN mid 16th cent.: from Latin, from *delirare* 'deviate, be deranged' (literally 'deviate from the furrow'), from *de-* 'away' + *lira* 'ridge between furrows'.

delirium tremens /ˈtriːmɛnz, ˈtrɛ-/ ▶ **noun** [mass noun] a psychotic condition typical of withdrawal in chronic alcoholics, involving tremors, hallucinations, anxiety, and disorientation.
– ORIGIN early 19th cent.: from Latin, 'trembling delirium'.

delish ▶ **adjective** informal delicious.

delist ▶ **verb** [with obj.] remove from a list, in particular: ■ remove (a security) from the official register of a stock exchange. ■ remove (a product) from the list of those sold by a particular retailer.

Delius /ˈdiːlɪəs/, Frederick (1862–1934), English composer, of German and Scandinavian descent. He is best known for pastoral works such as *Brigg Fair* (1907), but he also wrote songs, concertos, and choral and theatre music.

deliver ▶ **verb** [with obj.] **1** bring and hand over (a letter, parcel, or goods) to the proper recipient or address: *the products should be delivered on time* | [no obj.] *we'll deliver direct to your door.*
2 provide (something promised or expected): *he had been able to deliver votes in huge numbers* | [no obj.] *she's waiting for him to* **deliver on** *his promise.* ■ formally hand over (someone): *there was a reward if you were delivered unharmed to the nearest British post.* ■ (**deliver someone/thing up**) surrender someone or something: *had he feared she would deliver him up to the police?* ■ Law acknowledge that one intends to be bound by (a deed), either explicitly by declaration or implicitly by formal handover.
3 launch or aim (a blow, ball, or attack): *he delivered a punch to the man's belly* | figurative *the company has delivered a body blow to this city.*
4 state in a formal manner: *he will deliver a lecture on endangered species* | *he* **delivered himself of** *a sermon.* ■ (of a judge or court) give (a judgement or verdict): *the court was due to deliver its verdict.*
5 assist in the birth of: *the village midwife delivered the baby.* ■ (also archaic **be delivered of**) give birth to: *she was delivered of her second child.* ■ assist (a woman) in giving birth.
6 (**deliver someone/thing from**) save, rescue, or set someone or something free from: *deliver us from the nightmare of junk mail.*
– PHRASES **deliver the goods** informal provide that which is promised or expected.
– DERIVATIVES **deliverer** noun.
– ORIGIN Middle English: from Old French *delivrer*, based on Latin *de-* 'away' + *liberare* 'set free'.

deliverable ▶ **adjective** able to be delivered: *goods in a deliverable state.*
▶ **noun** (usu. **deliverables**) a thing able to be provided, especially as a product of a development process.

deliverance ▶ **noun 1** [mass noun] the action of being rescued or set free: *prayers for deliverance.*
2 a formal or authoritative utterance.
– ORIGIN Middle English: from Old French *delivrance*, from the verb *delivrer* (see DELIVER).

delivery ▶ **noun** (pl. **deliveries**) [mass noun] **1** the action of delivering letters, parcels, or goods: *allow up to 28 days for delivery* | [count noun] *there will be around 15 deliveries a week.* ■ [count noun] an item or items delivered on a particular occasion: *new deliveries are stacked behind older stock.*
2 the process of giving birth: *injuries sustained during delivery* | [count noun] *practically all deliveries take place in hospital.*
3 [count noun] an act of throwing, bowling, or kicking a ball, especially a cricket ball: *he reached 59 runs off only 42 deliveries.*
4 the manner or style of giving a speech: *her delivery was stilted.*
5 the supply or provision of something: *a mechanism for rapid delivery of bile into the duodenum.*
6 Law the acknowledgement by the maker of a deed that they intend to be bound by it.
– PHRASES **take delivery of** receive (something purchased): *we took delivery of the software in February.*
– ORIGIN late Middle English: from Anglo-Norman French *delivree*, feminine past participle of *delivrer* (see DELIVER).

D

dell ▶ **noun** literary a small valley, usually among trees: *lush green valleys and wooded dells.*
– ORIGIN Old English, of Germanic origin; related to Dutch *del* and German dialect *Telle*, also to DALE.

della Francesca see PIERO DELLA FRANCESCA.

della Quercia /ˌdɛlə ˈkwɛːtʃə/, Italian /ˌdella ˈkwertʃa/, Jacopo (*c.*1374–1438), Italian sculptor. He is noted for his tomb of Ilaria del Carretto in Lucca cathedral (*c.*1406) and for the biblical reliefs on the portal of San Petronio in Bologna (1425–35).

della Robbia /ˈrɒbɪə/, Luca (1400–82), Italian sculptor and ceramicist. He is best known for his relief panels in Florence cathedral and his colour-glazed terracotta figures.

delocalize (also **delocalise**) ▶ **verb** [with obj.] detach or remove from a particular place or location: (as adj. **delocalized**) *delocalized cortical activity.* ■ (**be delocalized**) Chemistry (of electrons) be shared among more than two atoms in a molecule.
– DERIVATIVES **delocalization** noun.

Delors /dəˈlɔː/, French /dəlɔr/, Jacques (Lucien Jean) (b.1925), French socialist politician, president of the European Commission 1985–94. During his presidency he pressed for closer European union and oversaw the introduction of a single market within the European Community, which came into effect on 1 January 1993.

Delos /ˈdiːlɒs/ a small Greek island in the Aegean Sea, regarded as the centre of the Cyclades. Now virtually uninhabited, in classical times it was considered to be sacred to Apollo, and according to legend was the birthplace of Apollo and Artemis. Greek name **Dhílos**.

delouse /diːˈlaʊs/ ▶ **verb** [with obj.] treat (a person or animal) to rid them of lice and other parasitic insects.

delph ▶ **noun** [mass noun] Irish plates, dishes, and other similar items; crockery.
– ORIGIN variant of DELFT.

Delphi /ˈdɛlfi, -fʌɪ/ one of the most important religious sanctuaries of the ancient Greek world, dedicated to Apollo and situated on the lower southern slopes of Mount Parnassus above the Gulf of Corinth. It was the seat of the Delphic Oracle, whose riddling responses to a wide range of questions were delivered by the Pythia. Greek name **Dhelfoí**.

Delphic /ˈdɛlfɪk/ (also **Delphian** /-fɪən/)
▶ **adjective** relating to the ancient Greek oracle at Delphi. ■ deliberately obscure or ambiguous.

delphinium /dɛlˈfɪnɪəm/ ▶ **noun** (pl. **delphiniums**) a popular garden plant of the buttercup family, which bears tall spikes of blue flowers. ● Genus *Delphinium*, family Ranunculaceae.
– ORIGIN modern Latin, from Greek *delphinion* 'larkspur', from *delphin* 'dolphin' (because of the shape of the spur, thought to resemble a dolphin's back).

Delphinus /dɛlˈfʌɪnəs/ Astronomy a small constellation (the Dolphin), just north of the celestial equator near Cygnus.
– ORIGIN Latin.

del Sarto, Andrea, see SARTO.

delta[1] ▶ **noun 1** the fourth letter of the Greek alphabet (Δ, δ), transliterated as 'd'. ■ Brit. a fourth-class mark given for an essay, examination paper, or other piece of work. ■ [as modifier] the fourth in a series of items, categories, etc.: *delta hepatitis.* ■ (**Delta**) [followed by Latin genitive] Astronomy the fourth (usually fourth-brightest) star in a constellation: *Delta Cephei.*
2 a code word representing the letter D, used in radio communication.

D

3 (also **delta connection**) a triangular arrangement of electrical three-phase windings.
▶ **symbol** ■ (δ) Mathematics variation of a variable or function. ■ (Δ) Mathematics a finite increment. ■ (δ) Astronomy declination.
– ORIGIN Greek, from Phoenician *daleth*.

delta² ▶ **noun** a triangular tract of sediment deposited at the mouth of a river, typically where it diverges into several outlets.
– DERIVATIVES **deltaic** adjective.
– ORIGIN mid 16th cent.: originally specifically as *the Delta* (of the River Nile), from the shape of the Greek letter (see DELTA¹).

Delta Force an elite American military force whose main responsibilities are rescue operations and special forces work.

delta rays ▶ **plural noun** Physics rays of low penetrative power consisting of slow electrons or other particles ejected from atoms by the impact of ionizing radiation.

delta rhythm ▶ **noun** [mass noun] electrical activity of the brain at a frequency of around 1–8 Hz, typical of sleep. The resulting oscillations, detected using an electroencephalograph, are called **delta waves**.

delta-v (also **delta-vee**) ▶ **noun** [mass noun] informal acceleration: *four hundred knots of delta-v*.
– ORIGIN late 20th cent.: from DELTA¹ (as a mathematical symbol denoting variation) + *v* for *velocity*.

delta wing ▶ **noun** a single triangular swept-back wing fitted on some jet aircraft.
– DERIVATIVES **delta-winged** adjective.

deltiologist /ˌdɛltɪˈɒlədʒɪst/ ▶ **noun** a person who collects postcards as a hobby.
– ORIGIN 1940s: from Greek *deltion* (diminutive of *deltos* 'writing tablet') + -LOGIST.

deltoid /ˈdɛltɔɪd/ ▶ **adjective** technical triangular: *a tree with large deltoid leaves*.
▶ **noun** (also **deltoid muscle**) a thick triangular muscle covering the shoulder joint and used for raising the arm away from the body. ■ each of the three parts of a deltoid muscle, attached at the front, side, and rear of the shoulder: *the anterior deltoid*.
– ORIGIN mid 18th cent.: from French *deltoïde*, or via modern Latin from Greek *deltoeidēs*.

delude /dɪˈl(j)uːd/ ▶ **verb** [with obj.] make (someone) believe something that is not true: *too many theorists have deluded the public* | (as adj. **deluded**) *the poor deluded creature*.
– DERIVATIVES **deludedly** adverb, **deluder** noun.
– ORIGIN late Middle English: from Latin *deludere* 'to mock', from *de-* (with pejorative force) + *ludere* 'to play'.

deluge /ˈdɛljuːdʒ/ ▶ **noun** a severe flood. ■ (**the Deluge**) the biblical Flood (recorded in Genesis 6–8). ■ a heavy fall of rain: ***a deluge of** rain hit the plains*. ■ a great quantity of something arriving at the same time: ***a deluge of** complaints*.
▶ **verb** [with obj.] overwhelm with a flood. ■ inundate with a great quantity of something: *he has been **deluged with** offers of work*.
– ORIGIN late Middle English: from Old French, variant of *diluve*, from Latin *diluvium*, from *diluere* 'wash away'.

delusion ▶ **noun** an idiosyncratic belief or impression maintained despite being contradicted by reality or rational argument, typically as a symptom of mental disorder: *the delusion of being watched*. ■ [mass noun] the action of deluding or the state of being deluded: *what a capacity television has for delusion*.
– PHRASES **delusions of grandeur** a false impression of one's own importance.
– DERIVATIVES **delusional** adjective.
– ORIGIN late Middle English (in the sense 'act of deluding or of being deluded'): from late Latin *delusio(n-)*, from the verb *deludere* (see DELUDE).

delusive ▶ **adjective** giving a false or misleading impression: *a delusive perception of opportunity for all*.
– DERIVATIVES **delusively** adverb.

delusory /dɪˈl(j)uːs(ə)ri, -z-/ ▶ **adjective** another term for DELUSIVE.

delustre (US **deluster**) ▶ **verb** [with obj.] remove the lustre from (a textile), typically by chemical treatment.

deluxe /dɪˈlʌks, ˈlʊks/ ▶ **adjective** luxurious or sumptuous; of a superior kind: *a deluxe hotel*.
– ORIGIN early 19th cent.: French *de luxe*, literally 'of luxury'.

delve ▶ **verb** [no obj.] **1** reach inside a receptacle and search for something: *she delved in her pocket*. ■ research or make painstaking enquiries into something: *the society is determined to delve deeper into the matter*.
2 archaic dig; excavate.
– DERIVATIVES **delver** noun.
– ORIGIN Old English *delfan* 'dig', of West Germanic origin; related to Dutch *delven*.

Dem. ▶ **abbreviation** US Democrat.

demagnetize (also **demagnetise**) ▶ **verb** [with obj.] remove magnetic properties from.
– DERIVATIVES **demagnetization** noun, **demagnetizer** noun.

demagogue /ˈdɛməgɒg/ ▶ **noun** a political leader who seeks support by appealing to popular desires and prejudices rather than by using rational argument. ■ (in ancient Greece and Rome) a leader or orator who espoused the cause of the common people.
– DERIVATIVES **demagogic** /-ˈgɒgɪk/ adjective, **demagoguery** /-ˈgɒg(ə)ri/ noun, **demagogy** noun.
– ORIGIN mid 17th cent.: from Greek *dēmagōgos*, from *dēmos* 'the people' + *agōgos* 'leading' (from *agein* 'to lead').

de Maintenon see MAINTENON.

demand ▶ **noun** an insistent and peremptory request, made as of right: *a series of **demands for** far-reaching reforms*. ■ (usu. **demands**) pressing requirements: *he's got enough **demands on** his time already*. ■ [mass noun] the desire of consumers, clients, employers, etc. for a particular commodity, service, or other item: *a recent slump in demand* | [count noun] *a demand for specialists*.
▶ **verb** [reporting verb] ask authoritatively or brusquely: [with direct speech] *'Where is she?' he demanded* | [with clause] *the police demanded that he give them the names*. ■ [with obj.] insist on having: *an outraged public demanded retribution* | *too much was being **demanded of** the top players*. ■ require; need: *a complex activity demanding detailed knowledge*.
– PHRASES **in demand** sought after: *all these skills are much in demand*. **on demand** as soon as or whenever required: *a combination boiler provides hot water on demand* | [as modifier] *an on-demand movie service on broadband*.
– DERIVATIVES **demander** noun.
– ORIGIN Middle English (as a noun): from Old French *demande* (noun), *demander* (verb), from Latin *demandare* 'hand over, entrust' (in medieval Latin 'demand'), from *de-* 'formally' + *mandare* 'to order'.

demand curve ▶ **noun** a graph showing how the demand for a commodity or service varies with changes in its price.

demand draft (also **demand note**) ▶ **noun** chiefly Indian a financial draft payable on demand.

demanding ▶ **adjective** (of a task) requiring much skill or effort: *she has a busy and demanding job*. ■ (of a person) making others work hard or meet high standards; not easily satisfied.
– DERIVATIVES **demandingly** adverb.

demand-led (also **demand-driven**) ▶ **adjective** Economics caused or determined by demand from consumers or clients.

demand-pull ▶ **adjective** relating to or denoting inflation caused by an excess of demand over supply. Contrasted with COST-PUSH.

demantoid /dɪˈmantɔɪd/ ▶ **noun** [mass noun] a lustrous green variety of andradite (garnet).
– ORIGIN late 19th cent.: from German, from *Demant* 'diamond'.

demarcate /ˈdiːmɑːkeɪt/ ▶ **verb** [with obj.] set the boundaries or limits of: *plots of land demarcated by barbed wire*. ■ separate or distinguish from: *art was being demarcated from the more objective science*.
– ORIGIN early 19th cent.: back-formation from DEMARCATION.

demarcation ▶ **noun** [mass noun] the action of fixing the boundary or limits of something: *the demarcation of the maritime border*. ■ [count noun] a dividing line. ■ Brit. the practice of requiring that specific jobs be assigned to members of particular trade unions: *strikes over job demarcation*.
– DERIVATIVES **demarcator** noun.
– ORIGIN early 18th cent.: from Spanish *demarcación*, from *demarcar* 'mark the bounds of', ultimately of Germanic origin and related to MARK¹. Originally used in the phrase *line of demarcation* (Spanish *línea de demarcación*, Portuguese *linha de demarcação*), the word denoted a line dividing the New World between the Spanish and Portuguese, laid down by the Pope in 1493.

demarcation dispute ▶ **noun** Brit. a dispute between trade unions about who should do a particular job.

démarche /deɪˈmɑːʃ/ ▶ **noun** a political step or initiative: *foreign policy démarches*.
– ORIGIN mid 17th cent.: French, from *démarcher* 'take steps'.

demark /diːˈmɑːk/ ▶ **verb** another term for DEMARCATE.
– ORIGIN mid 19th cent.: from DEMARCATION, on the pattern of the verb *mark*.

dematerialize (also **dematerialise**) ▶ **verb** [no obj.] become free of physical substance. ■ (in science fiction) disappear by means of some imagined technological process: *he watched the time machine dematerialize*. ■ [with obj.] replace (physical records or certificates) with a paperless computerized system.
– DERIVATIVES **dematerialization** noun.

de Maupassant, Guy, see MAUPASSANT.

deme /diːm/ ▶ **noun** **1** a political division of Attica in ancient Greece. ■ an administrative division in modern Greece.
2 Biology a subdivision of a population consisting of closely related plants, animals, or people, typically breeding mainly within the group.
– ORIGIN from Greek *dēmos* 'people'; sense 2 is an extended use dating from the 1930s.

demean¹ /dɪˈmiːn/ ▶ **verb** [with obj.] cause a severe loss in the dignity of and respect for (someone or something): *I had demeaned the profession*. ■ (**demean oneself**) do something that is beneath one's dignity.
– ORIGIN early 17th cent.: from DE- 'away, down' + the adjective MEAN², on the pattern of *debase*.

demean² /dɪˈmiːn/ ▶ **verb** (**demean oneself**) archaic conduct oneself in a particular way: *no man demeaned himself so honourably*.
– ORIGIN Middle English (also in the sense 'manage, control'): from Old French *demener* 'to lead', based on Latin *de-* 'away' + *minare* 'drive (animals), drive on with threats' (from *minari* 'threaten').

demeaning ▶ **adjective** causing someone to lose their dignity and the respect of others: *the poster was not **demeaning to** women*.
– DERIVATIVES **demeaningly** adverb.

demeanour (US **demeanor**) ▶ **noun** [mass noun] outward behaviour or bearing: *his happy demeanour*.
– ORIGIN late 15th cent.: from DEMEAN², probably influenced by obsolete *havour* 'behaviour'.

de' Medici¹ see MEDICI.

de' Medici², Catherine, see CATHERINE DE' MEDICI.

de' Medici³, Cosimo, see COSIMO DE' MEDICI.

de' Medici⁴, Giovanni, the name of Pope Leo X (see LEO¹).

de' Medici⁵, Lorenzo, see LORENZO DE' MEDICI.

de Médicis, Marie, see MARIE DE MÉDICIS.

dement /dɪˈmɛnt/ ▶ **noun** archaic a person suffering from dementia.
– ORIGIN late 15th cent. (as an adjective in the sense 'demented'): from French *dément* or Latin *demens*, *dement-* 'insane'. The noun use dates from the late 19th cent.

demented ▶ **adjective** suffering from dementia. ■ informal, chiefly Brit. behaving irrationally due to anger, distress, or excitement: *she was demented with worry*.
– DERIVATIVES **dementedly** adverb, **dementedness** noun.
– ORIGIN mid 17th cent.: past participle of earlier *dement* 'drive mad', from Old French *dementer* or late Latin *dementare*, from *demens* 'out of one's mind'.

démenti /deɪˈmɒ̃ti/ ▶ **noun** an official denial of a published statement.
– ORIGIN French, from *démentir* 'contradict or accuse of lying'.

dementia /dɪˈmɛnʃə/ ▶ **noun** [mass noun] Medicine a chronic or persistent disorder of the mental processes caused by brain disease or injury and marked by memory disorders, personality changes, and impaired reasoning.
– ORIGIN late 18th cent.: from Latin, from *demens*, *dement-* 'out of one's mind'.

dementia praecox /ˈpriːkɒks/ ▶ **noun** archaic term for SCHIZOPHRENIA.
– ORIGIN Latin, literally 'early insanity'.

Demerara /ˌdɛməˈrɛːrə, -ˈrɑːrə/ **1** a river of northern Guyana. Rising in the Guiana Highlands, it flows about 320 km (200 miles) northwards to the Atlantic. **2** a former Dutch colony in South America, now part of Guyana.

demerara /ˌdɛməˈrɛːrə, -ˈrɑːrə/ ▶ **noun** [mass noun]
1 (also **demerara sugar**) Brit. light brown cane sugar coming originally and chiefly from Guyana.
2 (also **demerara rum**) a dark rum fermented from molasses, made in Guyana.
– ORIGIN mid 19th cent.: named after the region of DEMERARA.

demerge ▶ **verb** [with obj.] Brit. separate (a business) from another, particularly to dissolve an earlier merger.

demerger ▶ **noun** Brit. the separation of a large company into two or more smaller organizations, particularly as the dissolution of an earlier merger.

demerit ▶ **noun 1** a fault or disadvantage: *the merits and demerits of these proposals.*
2 N. Amer. a mark awarded against someone for a fault or offence.
– DERIVATIVES **demeritorious** /-ˈtɔːrɪəs/ **adjective.**
– ORIGIN late Middle English (also in the sense 'merit'): from Old French *desmerite* or Latin *demeritum* 'something deserved', neuter past participle of *demereri*, from *de-* 'thoroughly' (also understood in medieval Latin as denoting reversal) + *mereri* 'to merit'.

Demerol /ˈdɛmərɒl/ ▶ **noun** trademark for PETHIDINE.
– ORIGIN 1940s: of unknown origin.

demersal /dɪˈməːs(ə)l/ ▶ **adjective** (chiefly of fish) living close to the floor of the sea or a lake. Often contrasted with PELAGIC.
– ORIGIN late 19th cent.: from Latin *demersus* (past participle of *demergere* 'submerge, sink', from *de-* 'down' + *mergere* 'plunge') + -AL.

demesne /dɪˈmeɪn, dɪˈmiːn/ ▶ **noun** historical **1** a piece of land attached to a manor and retained by the owner for their own use. ▪ the lands of an estate. ▪ archaic a region or domain: *she may one day queen it over that fair demesne.*
2 [mass noun] Law possession of real property in one's own right.
– PHRASES **held in demesne** (of an estate) occupied by the owner, not by tenants.
– ORIGIN Middle English: from Old French *demeine* (later Anglo-Norman French *demesne*) 'belonging to a lord', from Latin *dominicus*, from *dominus* 'lord, master'. Compare with DOMAIN.

Demeter /dɪˈmiːtə/ Greek Mythology the corn goddess, daughter of Cronus and Rhea and mother of Persephone. She is associated with Cybele and her symbol is typically an ear of corn. The Eleusinian mysteries were held in honour of her. Roman equivalent CERES. See also PERSEPHONE.

demi- ▶ **prefix 1** half; half-size: *demisemiquaver.*
2 partially; in an inferior degree: *demigod.*
– ORIGIN via French from medieval Latin *dimedius* 'half', from earlier *dimidius*.

demi-caractère /ˌdɛmɪkarakˈtɛː/ ▶ **noun** (pl. **same**) [mass noun] a style of ballet having elements of character dance, but executed with steps based on the classical technique.
– ORIGIN French, literally 'half character'.

demi-glace /ˈdɛmɪglas/ (also **demi-glaze**) ▶ **noun** a rich, glossy brown sauce from which the liquid has been partly evaporated, typically flavoured with wine and served with meat.
– ORIGIN French, literally 'half glaze'.

demigod (or **demigoddess**) ▶ **noun** a being with partial or lesser divine status, such as a minor deity, the offspring of a god and a mortal, or a mortal raised to divine rank.
– ORIGIN mid 16th cent.: translating Latin *semideus*.

demijohn ▶ **noun** a bulbous narrow-necked bottle holding from 3 to 10 gallons of liquid, typically enclosed in a wicker cover.
– ORIGIN mid 18th cent.: probably an alteration of French *dame-jeanne* 'Lady Jane', by association with DEMI- 'half-sized' and the given name *John*.

demilitarize (also **demilitarise**) ▶ **verb** [with obj.] (usu. as adj. **demilitarized**) remove all military forces from (an area): *a demilitarized zone.*
– DERIVATIVES **demilitarization** **noun.**

de Mille /də ˈmɪl/, Cecil B. (1881–1959), American film producer and director, famous for his spectacular epics; full name *Cecil Blount de Mille*. Notable films: *The Ten Commandments* (1923; remade 1956) and *Samson and Delilah* (1949).

demilune /ˈdɛmɪluːn/ ▶ **noun** a crescent or half-circle, or a thing of this shape.
– ORIGIN early 18th cent.: from French *demi-lune*, literally 'half-moon'.

demi-mondaine /ˈdɛmɪmɒnˌdeɪn/, French /dəmimɔ̃dɛn/ ▶ **noun** a woman considered to belong to the demi-monde.
– ORIGIN French.

demi-monde /ˌdɛmɪˈmɒnd/, French /dəmimɔ̃d/ ▶ **noun** (in 19th-century France) a class of women considered to be of doubtful social standing and morality. ▪ a group of people on the fringes of respectable society: *the demi-monde of arms deals.*
– ORIGIN French, literally 'half-world'.

demine ▶ **verb** [with obj.] remove explosive mines from: *the army is working to demine the border.*
– DERIVATIVES **deminer** **noun.**

demineralize (also **demineralise**) ▶ **verb** [with obj.] (often as adj. **demineralized**) remove salts from (water). ▪ deprive (teeth or bones) of essential minerals.
– DERIVATIVES **demineralization** **noun.**

demi-pension /ˌdɛmɪˈpɒ̃sjɒ̃/ ▶ **noun** [mass noun] hotel accommodation with bed, breakfast, and one main meal per day.
– ORIGIN French, literally 'half board'.

demirep /ˈdɛmɪrɛp/ ▶ **noun** archaic a woman whose chastity is considered doubtful.
– ORIGIN mid 18th cent.: abbreviation of *demi-reputable*.

demise /dɪˈmʌɪz/ ▶ **noun** [in sing.] **1** a person's death: *Mr Grisenthwaite's tragic demise.* ▪ the end or failure of an enterprise or institution: *the demise of industry.*
2 [mass noun] Law conveyance or transfer of property or a title by will or lease.
▶ **verb** [with obj.] Law convey or grant (an estate) by will or lease. ▪ transmit (a sovereign's title) by death or abdication.
– ORIGIN late Middle English (as a legal term): from Anglo-Norman French, past participle (used as a noun) of Old French *desmettre* 'dismiss', (in reflexive) 'abdicate', based on Latin *dimittere* (see DISMISS).

demi-sec /dɛmɪˈsɛk/, French /dəmisɛk/ ▶ **adjective** (of wine) medium dry.
– ORIGIN French, literally 'half-dry'.

demisemiquaver /ˌdɛmɪˈsɛmɪˌkweɪvə/ ▶ **noun** Music, chiefly Brit. a note having the time value of half a semiquaver, represented by a large dot with a three-hooked stem. Also called THIRTY-SECOND NOTE.

demist /diːˈmɪst/ ▶ **verb** [with obj.] Brit. clear condensation from (a vehicle's windscreen).
– DERIVATIVES **demister** **noun.**

demit /dɪˈmɪt/ ▶ **verb** (**demits, demitting, demitted**) [with obj.] formal resign from (an office or position).
– DERIVATIVES **demission** **noun.**
– ORIGIN early 16th cent. (in the sense 'dismiss'): from French *démettre*, from *dé-* 'away from' + *mettre* 'put'.

demitasse /ˈdɛmɪtas/ ▶ **noun** a small coffee cup.
– ORIGIN mid 19th cent.: from French, literally 'half-cup'.

demiurge /ˈdiːmɪəːdʒ, ˈdɛm-/ ▶ **noun** a being responsible for the creation of the universe, in particular: ▪ (in Platonic philosophy) the Maker or Creator of the world. ▪ (in Gnosticism and other theological systems) a heavenly being, subordinate to the Supreme Being, that is considered to be the controller of the material world and antagonistic to all that is purely spiritual.
– DERIVATIVES **demiurgic** /-ˈəːdʒɪk/ **adjective,** **demiurgical** **adjective.**
– ORIGIN early 17th cent. (denoting a magistrate in certain ancient Greek states): via ecclesiastical Latin from Greek *dēmiourgos* 'craftsman', from *dēmios* 'public' (from *dēmos* 'people') + *-ergos* 'working'.

demo informal ▶ **noun** (pl. **demos**) **1** chiefly Brit. a public demonstration: *a peace demo.*
2 a demonstration of the capabilities of something, typically computer software or a musical group: [as modifier] *a demo tape.*
▶ **verb** (**demos, demoing, demoed**) [with obj.] demonstrate the capabilities of (software or equipment). ▪ record (a song) for demonstration purposes: *they've already demoed twelve new songs.*

demob /diːˈmɒb/ Brit. informal ▶ **verb** (**demobs, demobbing, demobbed**) [with obj.] demobilize (troops).
▶ **noun** [mass noun] demobilization: *we were waiting for our demob.*
– ORIGIN 1920s (following the First World War): abbreviation.

demob-happy ▶ **adjective** Brit. informal feeling elated because one is about to leave a stressful or responsible job or situation: *he's looking a little more relaxed these days, though he's not demob-happy quite yet.*

demobilize /diːˈməʊbɪlʌɪz/ (also **demobilise**) ▶ **verb** [with obj.] take (troops) out of active service, typically at the end of a war: *he was demobilized in February 1946.* ▪ [no obj.] cease military operations: *Germany demanded that they demobilize within twelve hours.*
– DERIVATIVES **demobilization** **noun.**
– ORIGIN late 19th cent.: from French *démobiliser*, from *dé-* (expressing reversal) + *mobiliser* 'mobilize'.

democracy /dɪˈmɒkrəsi/ ▶ **noun** (pl. **democracies**) [mass noun] a system of government by the whole population or all the eligible members of a state, typically through elected representatives: *a system of parliamentary democracy.* ▪ [count noun] a state governed in such a way: *a multiparty democracy.* ▪ control of an organization or group by the majority of its members: *the intended extension of industrial democracy.* ▪ the practice or principles of social equality: *demands for greater democracy.*
– ORIGIN late 16th cent.: from French *démocratie*, via late Latin from Greek *dēmokratia*, from *dēmos* 'the people' + *-kratia* 'power, rule'.

D

democrat ▶ **noun 1** an advocate or supporter of democracy.
2 (**Democrat**) (in the US) a member of the Democratic Party.
– ORIGIN late 18th cent. (originally denoting an opponent of the aristocrats in the French Revolution of 1790): from French *démocrate*, on the pattern of *aristocrate* 'aristocrat'.

democratic ▶ **adjective 1** relating to or supporting democracy or its principles: *democratic countries | democratic government.* ▪ favouring or characterized by social equality; egalitarian: *cycling is a very democratic activity which can be enjoyed by anyone.*
2 (**Democratic**) (in the US) relating to the Democratic Party.
– DERIVATIVES **democratically** **adverb.**
– ORIGIN early 17th cent.: from French *démocratique*, via medieval Latin from Greek *dēmokratikos*, from *dēmokratia* (see DEMOCRACY).

democratic centralism ▶ **noun** [mass noun] the Leninist organizational system in which policy is decided centrally and is binding on all members.

Democratic Party one of the two main US political parties (the other being the Republican Party), which follows a broadly liberal programme, tending to support social reform and minority rights.

Democratic Republican Party a US political party founded in 1792 by Thomas Jefferson, a forerunner of the modern Democratic Party.

democratize /dɪˈmɒkrətʌɪz/ (also **democratise**) ▶ **verb** [with obj.] introduce a democratic system or democratic principles to: *public institutions need to be democratized.* ▪ make (something) accessible to everyone: *mass production has not democratized fashion.*
– DERIVATIVES **democratization** **noun.**
– ORIGIN late 18th cent.: from French *démocratiser*.

Democritus /dɪˈmɒkrɪtəs/ (c.460–c.370 BC), Greek philosopher. He developed the atomic theory originated by his teacher, Leucippus, which explained natural phenomena in terms of the arrangement and rearrangement of atoms moving in a void.

démodé /deɪˈməʊdeɪ/ ▶ **adjective** out of fashion.
– ORIGIN French, past participle of *démoder* 'go out of fashion'.

demodectic mange /ˌdiːmə(ʊ)ˈdɛktɪk/ ▶ **noun** [mass noun] a form of mange caused by follicle mites and tending to affect chiefly the head and foreparts. Compare with SARCOPTIC MANGE.
– ORIGIN late 19th cent.: *demodectic* from modern Latin *Demodex* (from Greek *dēmos* 'fat' + *dēx* 'woodworm') + -IC.

demodulate ▶ **verb** [with obj.] Electronics extract or separate (a modulating signal) from its carrier.
– DERIVATIVES **demodulation** **noun,** **demodulator** **noun.**

demographic /ˌdɛməˈgrafɪk/ ▶ **adjective** relating to the structure of populations: *the demographic trend is towards an older population.*
▶ **noun** a particular sector of a population: *the drink is popular with a young demographic.*
– DERIVATIVES **demographical** **adjective,** **demographically** **adverb.**

demographics ▶ **plural noun** statistical data relating to the population and particular groups within it: *the demographics of book buyers.*

demography /dɪˈmɒgrəfi/ ▶ **noun** [mass noun] the study of statistics such as births, deaths, income, or the incidence of disease, which illustrate the changing

structure of human populations. ■ the composition of a particular human population: *Europe's demography is changing.*
– DERIVATIVES **demographer** noun.
– ORIGIN late 19th cent.: from Greek *dēmos* 'the people' + -GRAPHY.

demoi plural form of DEMOS.

demoiselle /ˌdɛmwɑːˈzɛl/ ▶ noun **1** (also **demoiselle crane**) a small Old World crane with a black head and breast and white ear tufts, breeding in SE Europe and central Asia. ● *Anthropoides virgo*, family Gruidae.

2 a damselfly, especially an agrion.
3 a damselfish.
4 archaic or literary a young woman.
– ORIGIN early 16th cent. (in sense 4): from French, from Old French *dameisele* 'damsel'.

de Moivre's theorem /də ˈmwɑːvr(ə)/ ▶ noun Mathematics a theorem which states that $(\cos \theta + i \sin \theta)^n = \cos n\theta + i \sin n\theta$, where i is the square root of -1.
– ORIGIN early 18th cent.: named after Abraham *de Moivre* (1667–1754), French-born mathematician, fellow of the Royal Society.

demolish /dɪˈmɒlɪʃ/ ▶ verb [with obj.] pull or knock down (a building). ■ comprehensively refute (an argument or its proponent): *I looked forward keenly to demolishing my opponent.* ■ informal overwhelmingly defeat (a player or team): *Arsenal demolished City 3–0.* ■ Brit. humorous eat up (food) quickly: *Brown was busy demolishing a sausage roll.*
– DERIVATIVES **demolisher** noun.
– ORIGIN mid 16th cent.: from French *démoliss-*, lengthened stem of *démolir*, from Latin *demoliri*, from *de-* (expressing reversal) + *moliri* 'construct' (from *moles* 'mass').

demolition ▶ noun [mass noun] the action or process of demolishing or being demolished: *the monument was saved from demolition.* ■ informal an overwhelming defeat.
– DERIVATIVES **demolitionist** noun.
– ORIGIN mid 16th cent.: via French from Latin *demolitio(n-)*, from the verb *demoliri* (see DEMOLISH).

demolition derby ▶ noun N. Amer. a competition in which cars are driven into each other until only one car is left running.

demon[1] ▶ noun **1** an evil spirit or devil, especially one thought to possess a person or act as a tormentor in hell. ■ a cruel, evil, or unmanageable person: *I was a little demon, I can tell you.* ■ a powerful, often destructive compulsion or obsession: *he is plagued by demons which go back to his childhood.* ■ something very insidious and harmful: *the demon of sexism* | [as modifier] *the demon drink.*
2 [often as modifier] a forceful or skilful performer of a specified activity: *a friend of mine is a demon cook.*
3 another term for DAEMON[1] (sense 1).
– PHRASES **like a demon** in a very forceful, fierce, or skilful way: *he worked like a demon.*
– ORIGIN Middle English: from medieval Latin, from Latin *daemon*, from Greek *daimōn* 'deity, genius'; in sense 1 also from Latin *daemonium* 'lesser or evil spirit', from Greek *daemonion*, diminutive of *daimōn*.

demon[2] ▶ noun Austral./NZ informal a police officer.
– ORIGIN late 19th cent.: perhaps from Van *Diemen*'s Land, an early name for Tasmania, or based on *dee* (slang term for *detective*) + MAN.

demon[3] ▶ noun variant spelling of DAEMON[2].

demonetize /diːˈmʌnɪtʌɪz, -mɒn-/ (also **demonetise**) ▶ verb [with obj.] deprive (a coin or precious metal) of its status as money.
– DERIVATIVES **demonetization** noun.
– ORIGIN mid 19th cent.: from French *démonétiser*, from *dé-* (expressing reversal) + Latin *moneta* 'money'.

demoniac /dɪˈməʊnɪak/ ▶ adjective relating to or characteristic of a demon or demons: *a goddess with both divine and demoniac qualities* | *demoniac rage.*
▶ noun a person supposedly possessed by an evil spirit.
– DERIVATIVES **demoniacal** /ˌdiːməˈnʌɪək(ə)l/ adjective, **demoniacally** adverb.
– ORIGIN late Middle English: from Old French *demoniaque*, from ecclesiastical Latin *daemoniacus*, from *daemonium* 'lesser or evil spirit' (see DEMON[1]).

demonic /dɪˈmɒnɪk/ ▶ adjective relating to or characteristic of demons or evil spirits: *demonic possession* | *her laughter was demonic.*
– DERIVATIVES **demonically** adverb.
– ORIGIN mid 17th cent.: via late Latin from Greek *daimonikos*, from *daimōn* (see DEMON[1]).

demonism /ˈdiːmənɪz(ə)m/ ▶ noun [mass noun] **1** belief in the power of demons.
2 action or behaviour that seems too cruel or wicked to be human: *the demonism of warfare.*

demonize (also **demonise**) ▶ verb [with obj.] portray as wicked and threatening: *he was demonized by the right-wing press.*
– DERIVATIVES **demonization** noun.

demono- /ˈdiːmənəʊ/ ▶ combining form relating to demons: *demonolatry.*
– ORIGIN from Greek *daimōn* 'demon'.

demonolatry /ˌdiːməˈnɒlətri/ ▶ noun [mass noun] the worship of demons.

demonology ▶ noun (pl. **demonologies**) [mass noun] the study of demons or demonic belief. ■ a set of beliefs about people or things regarded as harmful or unwelcome.
– DERIVATIVES **demonological** adjective, **demonologist** noun.

demonstrable /dɪˈmɒnstrəb(ə)l, ˈdɛmən-/ ▶ adjective clearly apparent or capable of being logically proved: *the demonstrable injustices of racism.*
– DERIVATIVES **demonstrability** noun, **demonstrably** /ˈdɛmənstrəbli/ adverb.
– ORIGIN late Middle English: from Latin *demonstrabilis*, from *demonstrare* 'point out'.

demonstrate ▶ verb **1** [with obj.] clearly show the existence or truth of (something) by giving proof or evidence: *their shameful silence demonstrates their ineptitude.* ■ show (a feeling or quality) by one's actions: *she began to demonstrate a new-found confidence.*
2 [with obj.] give a practical exhibition and explanation of (how a machine, skill, or craft works or is performed): *computerized design methods will be demonstrated* | [with clause] *she demonstrated how to cook chops.*
3 [no obj.] take part in a public demonstration: *thousands demonstrated in favour of the government.*
– ORIGIN mid 16th cent. (in the sense 'point out'): from Latin *demonstrat-* 'pointed out', from the verb *demonstrare.*

demonstration ▶ noun **1** an act of showing that something exists or is true by giving proof or evidence: *his demonstration of the need for computer corpora in language study is convincing* | [mass noun] *acts of faith are not capable of mathematical demonstration.* ■ an outward show of a feeling or quality: *physical demonstrations of affection.*
2 a practical exhibition and explanation of how something works or is performed: *a microwave cookery demonstration.*
3 a public meeting or march protesting against something or expressing views on a political issue.
– DERIVATIVES **demonstrational** adjective.
– ORIGIN late Middle English (also in the senses 'proof provided by logic' and 'sign, indication'): from Latin *demonstratio(n-)*, from *demonstrare* 'point out' (see DEMONSTRATE). Sense 3 dates from the mid 19th cent.

demonstrative /dɪˈmɒnstrətɪv/ ▶ adjective **1** (of a person) unrestrained in showing feelings, especially those of affection.
2 serving as conclusive evidence of something. ■ involving demonstration, especially by scientific means: *the possibility of a demonstrative science of ethics.*
3 Grammar (of a determiner or pronoun) indicating the person or thing referred to (e.g. *this, that, those*).
▶ noun Grammar a demonstrative determiner or pronoun.
– DERIVATIVES **demonstratively** adverb, **demonstrativeness** noun.
– ORIGIN late Middle English (in the senses 'serving as conclusive evidence of' and 'making manifest'): from Old French *demonstratif, -ive*, from Latin *demonstrativus*, from *demonstrare* 'point out' (see DEMONSTRATE).

demonstrator ▶ noun **1** a participant in a public protest meeting or march.
2 a person who shows how a piece of equipment works or how a skill or craft is performed. ■ a piece of merchandise which can be tested by potential buyers.

de Montespan, Marquise de, see MONTESPAN.

de Montfort, Simon, see MONTFORT[1].

demoralize (also **demoralise**) ▶ verb [with obj.]
1 cause (someone) to lose confidence or hope: *the General Strike had demoralized the trade unions.*
2 archaic corrupt the morals of (someone).
– DERIVATIVES **demoralization** noun, **demoralizing** adjective, **demoralizingly** adverb.
– ORIGIN late 18th cent.: from French *démoraliser* (a word of the French Revolution), from *dé-* (expressing reversal) + *moral* 'moral', from Latin *moralis.*

demoralized (also **demoralised**) ▶ adjective having lost confidence or hope; disheartened: *a weak and demoralized president.*

De Morgan's laws ▶ plural noun Mathematics two laws in Boolean algebra and set theory which state that AND and OR, or union and intersection, are dual. They are used to simplify the design of electronic circuits. ● The laws can be expressed in Boolean logic as: NOT (*a* AND *b*) = NOT *a* OR NOT *b*; NOT (*a* OR *b*) = NOT *a* AND NOT *b*.
– ORIGIN early 20th cent.: named after Augustus De *Morgan* (1806–71), English mathematician, but already known (by logicians) as principles in the Middle Ages.

demos /ˈdiːmɒs/ ▶ noun (pl. **demoi** /ˈdiːmɔɪ/) the common people of an ancient Greek state. ■ the populace of a democracy as a political unit.
– ORIGIN from Greek *dēmos.*

Demosthenes /dɪˈmɒsθəniːz/ (384–322 BC), Athenian orator and statesman. He is best known for his political speeches on the need to resist the aggressive tendencies of Philip II of Macedon (the *Philippics*).

demote ▶ verb [with obj.] move (someone) to a lower position or rank, usually as a punishment: *the head of the army was demoted to deputy defence secretary.*
– ORIGIN late 19th cent.: from DE- 'down' + a shortened form of PROMOTE.

demotic /dɪˈmɒtɪk/ ▶ adjective denoting or relating to the kind of language used by ordinary people; colloquial: *a demotic idiom.* ■ relating to or denoting the form of modern Greek used in everyday speech and writing. Compare with KATHAREVOUSA. ■ relating to or denoting a simplified, cursive form of ancient Egyptian script, dating from *c.*650 BC and replaced by Greek in the Ptolemaic period. Compare with HIERATIC.
▶ noun [mass noun] ordinary colloquial speech. ■ demotic Greek. ■ demotic Egyptian script.
– ORIGIN early 19th cent. (in the sense 'relating to the Egyptian demotic'): from Greek *dēmotikos* 'popular', from *dēmotēs* 'one of the people', from *dēmos* 'the people'.

demotion ▶ noun [mass noun] reduction in rank or status: *she could remain on the staff if she accepted demotion to ordinary lecturer* | [count noun] *too many demotions would weaken morale.*
– ORIGIN early 20th cent.: from DEMOTE, on the pattern of *promotion.*

demotivate ▶ verb [with obj.] make (someone) less eager to work or study: *some children disrupt classes and demotivate other pupils.*
– DERIVATIVES **demotivation** noun.

demountable ▶ adjective able to be dismantled or removed from its setting and readily reassembled or repositioned.
– DERIVATIVES **demount** verb.

Dempsey /ˈdɛmpsi/, Jack (1895–1983), American boxer; full name *William Harrison Dempsey.* He was world heavyweight champion 1919–26.

demulcent /dɪˈmʌls(ə)nt/ Medicine ▶ adjective (of a substance) relieving inflammation or irritation.
▶ noun a substance that relieves irritation of the mucous membranes in the mouth by forming a protective film.
– ORIGIN mid 18th cent.: from Latin *demulcent-* 'stroking caressingly', from the verb *demulcere*, from *de-* 'away' + *mulcere* 'soothe'.

demur /dɪˈməː/ ▶ verb (**demurs, demurring, demurred**) [no obj.] raise objections or show reluctance: *normally she would have accepted the challenge, but she demurred.* ■ Law, dated put forward a demurrer.
▶ noun [mass noun] [usu. with negative] the action of objecting to or hesitating over something: *they accepted this ruling without demur.*
– ORIGIN Middle English (in the sense 'linger, delay'): from Old French *demourer* (verb), *demeure* (noun), based on Latin *de-* 'away, completely' + *morari* 'delay'.

demure /dɪˈmjʊə, dɪˈmjɔː/ ▶ adjective (**demurer, demurest**) (of a woman or her behaviour) reserved, modest, and shy. ■ (of clothing) suggesting that a woman is demure.
– DERIVATIVES **demurely** adverb, **demureness** noun.
– ORIGIN late Middle English (in the sense 'sober, serious, reserved'): perhaps from Old French *demoure*,

past participle of *demourer* 'remain' (see **DEMUR**); influenced by Old French *mur* 'grave', from Latin *maturus* 'ripe or mature'. The sense 'reserved, shy' dates from the late 17th cent.

demurrable /dɪˈməːrəb(ə)l/ ▶ **adjective** dated, chiefly Law open to demurrer.

demurrage /dɪˈmʌrɪdʒ/ ▶ **noun** [mass noun] Law a charge payable to the owner of a chartered ship on failure to load or discharge the ship within the time agreed.
– ORIGIN mid 17th cent. (also in the general sense 'delay'): from Old French *demourage*, from the verb *demourer* (see **DEMUR**).

demurral /dɪˈməːr(ə)l/ ▶ **noun** [mass noun] the action of demurring: *words of demurral.*

demurrer /dɪˈməːrə/ ▶ **noun** Law, dated an objection granting the factual basis of an opponent's point but dismissing it as irrelevant or invalid. ■ formal an objection.
– ORIGIN early 16th cent.: from Anglo-Norman French (infinitive used as a noun), from Old French *demourer* 'remain, stay' (see **DEMUR**).

demutualize /diːˈmjuːtʃʊəlʌɪz, -tjʊə-/ (also **demutualise**) ▶ **verb** [no obj.] (of a mutual organization such as a building society) change from being owned by its members to a different kind of ownership.
– DERIVATIVES **demutualization** noun.

demy /dɪˈmʌɪ/ (also **metric demy**) ▶ **noun** [mass noun] a paper size, 564 × 444 mm. ■ (also **demy octavo**) a book size, 216 × 138 mm. ■ (also **demy quarto**) a book size, 276 × 219 mm.
– ORIGIN late Middle English (as an adjective in the sense 'half-sized'): from **DEMI-**, or from its source, French *demi* 'half'.

demyelinate /diːˈmʌɪəlɪneɪt/ ▶ **verb** [with obj.] (usu. as adj. **demyelinating**) Medicine cause the loss or destruction of myelin in (nerve tissue): *a chronic demyelinating disease.*
– DERIVATIVES **demyelination** noun.

demystify ▶ **verb** (**demystifies, demystifying, demystified**) [with obj.] make (a difficult subject) clearer and easier to understand: *this book attempts to demystify technology.*
– DERIVATIVES **demystification** noun.

demythologize (also **demythologise**) ▶ **verb** [with obj.] reinterpret (a subject) so that it is free of mythical elements: *the biographer undertakes to demythologize a man who is for many a modern saint.* ■ reinterpret what are considered to be mythological elements of (the Bible).

den ▶ **noun 1** a wild mammal's hidden home; a lair. ■ informal a room or hideout where a person can go to relax or be private. ■ a place where people meet in secret, typically to engage in an illicit activity: *an opium den | a den of iniquity.*
2 chiefly US a small subdivision of a Cub Scout pack.
▶ **verb** (**dens, denning, denned**) [no obj.] (of a wild animal) live in a den: *the cubs denned in the late autumn.*
– ORIGIN Old English *denn*, of Germanic origin; related to German *Tenne* 'threshing floor', also to **DENE[1]**.

Denali /dɪˈnɑːli/ another name for Mount McKinley (see **MCKINLEY, MOUNT**).

denar /ˈdiːnə/ ▶ **noun** the basic monetary unit of the republic of Macedonia.
– ORIGIN based on Latin *denarius*; compare with **DINAR**.

denarius /dɪˈnɛːrɪəs, dɪˈnɑːrɪəs/ ▶ **noun** (pl. **denarii** /-rɪʌɪ, -rɪiː/) an ancient Roman silver coin, originally worth ten asses. ■ a unit of weight equal to that of a silver denarius. ■ an ancient Roman gold coin worth 25 silver denarii.
– ORIGIN Latin, literally 'containing ten', from the phrase *denarius nummus* 'coin worth ten asses' (see **AS[2]**), from *deni* 'in tens', from *decem* 'ten'.

denary /ˈdiːn(ə)ri/ ▶ **adjective** less common term for **DECIMAL**: *denary numbers.*
– ORIGIN mid 19th cent.: from Latin *denarius* 'containing ten' (see **DENARIUS**).

denationalize (also **denationalise**) ▶ **verb** [with obj.] **1** transfer (a nationalized industry or institution) from public to private ownership.
2 deprive (a country or person) of nationality or national characteristics.
– DERIVATIVES **denationalization** noun.
– ORIGIN early 19th cent. (in sense 2): from French *dénationaliser* (a word of the French Revolution), from *dé-* (expressing reversal) + *nationaliser* 'nationalize'.

denaturalize (also **denaturalise**) ▶ **verb** [with obj.] **1** make (something) unnatural.
2 deprive (someone) of citizenship of a country.
– DERIVATIVES **denaturalization** noun.

denaturant /diːˈneɪtʃər(ə)nt/ ▶ **noun 1** a substance which causes denaturation of proteins or other biological compounds.
2 a toxic or foul-smelling substance added to alcohol to make it unfit for drinking.

denature /diːˈneɪtʃə/ ▶ **verb** [with obj.] **1** (often as adj. **denatured**) take away or alter the natural qualities of: *many forms of packaged and denatured culture.*
2 make (alcohol) unfit for drinking by the addition of toxic or foul-tasting substances.
3 Biochemistry destroy the characteristic properties of (a protein or other biological macromolecule) by heat, acidity, or other effect which disrupts its molecular conformation.
– DERIVATIVES **denaturation** noun.
– ORIGIN late 17th cent.: from French *dénaturer*, from *dé-* (expressing reversal) + *nature* 'nature'.

denazify ▶ **verb** (**denazifies, denazifying, denazified**) [with obj.] remove Nazi influence from.
– DERIVATIVES **denazification** noun.

Denbighshire /ˈdɛnbɪʃɪə, -ʃə/ a county of North Wales; administrative centre, Ruthin. It was divided between Clwyd and Gwynedd between 1974 and 1996.

Dench /dɛntʃ/, Dame Judi (b.1934), English actress; full name *Judith Olivia Dench*. She has performed with the Old Vic Company (1957–61) and the Royal Shakespeare Company, and appeared in numerous West End, film, and television productions; she won an Oscar for her role in *Shakespeare in Love* (1999).

dendrimer /ˈdɛndrɪmə/ ▶ **noun** a synthetic polymer with a branching, tree-like structure.
– ORIGIN 1990s: from Greek *dendron* 'tree' + **-I-** + **-MER**.

dendrite /ˈdɛndrʌɪt/ ▶ **noun 1** Physiology a short branched extension of a nerve cell, along which impulses received from other cells at synapses are transmitted to the cell body. Compare with **AXON**.
2 a crystal or crystalline mass with a branching, tree-like structure. ■ a natural tree-like or moss-like marking on a rock or mineral.
– ORIGIN early 18th cent.: from French, from Greek *dendritēs* 'tree-like', from *dendron* 'tree'.

dendritic /dɛnˈdrɪtɪk/ ▶ **adjective** technical having a branched form resembling a tree. ■ Physiology relating to a dendrite or dendrites. ■ (of a solid) consisting of crystalline dendrites: *dendritic salt.*

dendro- /ˈdɛndrəʊ/ ▶ **combining form** relating to a tree or trees: *dendrology.*
– ORIGIN from Greek *dendron* 'tree'.

dendrochronology ▶ **noun** [mass noun] the science or technique of dating events, environmental change, and archaeological artefacts by using the characteristic patterns of annual growth rings in timber and tree trunks.
– DERIVATIVES **dendrochronological** adjective, **dendrochronologist** noun.

dendrogram /ˈdɛndrə(ʊ)gram/ ▶ **noun** a tree diagram, especially one showing taxonomic relationships.

dendroid /ˈdɛndrɔɪd/ ▶ **adjective** Biology (of a plant, marine invertebrate, or structure) tree-shaped; branching.
▶ **noun** Palaeontology a graptolite of a type that formed much-branched colonies, found chiefly in the Ordovician and Silurian periods. ● Order Dendroidea, class Graptolithina.
– ORIGIN mid 19th cent.: from **DENDRO-** 'tree' + **-OID**.

dendrology /dɛnˈdrɒlədʒi/ ▶ **noun** [mass noun] the scientific study of trees.
– DERIVATIVES **dendrological** adjective, **dendrologist** noun.

dendron /ˈdɛndrɒn/ ▶ **noun** another term for **DENDRITE** (sense 1).
– ORIGIN late 19th cent.: from **DENDRITE**, on the pattern of words such as *axon.*

Dene /ˈdɛneɪ, ˈdɛni/ ▶ **noun** (pl. **same**) **1** a member of a group of American Indian peoples of the Canadian North-West and Alaska.
2 [mass noun] any of the Athabaskan languages of the Dene.
▶ **adjective** relating to the Dene or their languages.
– ORIGIN from French *Déné*, from an Athabaskan word meaning 'people'.

dene[1] /diːn/ (also **dean**) ▶ **noun** [usu. in place names] Brit. a vale, especially the deep, narrow, wooded valley of a small river: *Rottingdean | Deepdene.*
– ORIGIN Old English *denu*, of Germanic origin; related to **DEN**.

dene[2] /diːn/ ▶ **noun** dialect a bare sandy tract or low sandhill by the sea.
– ORIGIN Middle English: perhaps of Germanic origin and related to **DUNE**.

Deneb /ˈdɛnɛb/ Astronomy the brightest star in the constellation Cygnus, a yellow supergiant.
– ORIGIN from Arabic, literally 'tail' (i.e. of the 'swan').

Denebola /dɪˈnɛbələ/ Astronomy the second-brightest star in the constellation Leo.
– ORIGIN from Arabic *dhanab al(-asad)* '(lion's) tail'.

denervate /diːˈnəːveɪt/ ▶ **verb** [with obj.] Medicine remove or cut off the nerve supply from (a body part or organ): (as adj. **denervated**) *the denervated muscle fibres.*
– DERIVATIVES **denervation** noun.

Deneuve /dəˈnəːv/, French /dənœv/, Catherine (b.1943), French actress; born *Catherine Dorléac*. Notable films: *Repulsion* (1965) and *Belle de jour* (1967).

dengue /ˈdɛŋgi/ (also **dengue fever**) ▶ **noun** [mass noun] a debilitating viral disease of the tropics, transmitted by mosquitoes, and causing sudden fever and acute pains in the joints.
– ORIGIN early 19th cent.: from West Indian Spanish, from Kiswahili *dinga* (in full *kidingapopo*), influenced by Spanish *dengue* 'fastidiousness' (with reference to the dislike of movement by affected patients).

Deng Xiaoping /ˌdɛŋ ʃaʊˈpɪŋ, ˌdʌŋ/ (also **Teng Hsiao-p'ing**) (1904–97), Chinese communist statesman, Vice-Premier 1973–6 and 1977–80; Vice Chairman of the Central Committee of the Chinese Communist Party 1977–80. Discredited during the Cultural Revolution, he was reinstated in 1977, becoming the effective leader of China. He worked to modernize the economy and improve relations with the West, although in 1989 his orders led to the killing of pro-democracy demonstrators in Beijing's Tiananmen Square.

Den Haag /dɛn ˈhɑːg/, Dutch /dɛn ˈhaːx/ Dutch name for The Hague (see **HAGUE**).

deni /ˈdɛniː/ ▶ **noun** a monetary unit of the republic of Macedonia, equal to one hundredth of a denar.
– ORIGIN Macedonian, from **DENAR**.

deniable ▶ **adjective** able to be denied.
– DERIVATIVES **deniability** noun, **deniably** adverb.

denial ▶ **noun** [mass noun] the action of denying something: *she shook her head **in denial**.* ■ [count noun] a statement that something is not true: *his pious denials of responsibility.* ■ the refusal of something requested or desired: *the denial of insurance to people with certain medical conditions.* ■ refusal to acknowledge an unacceptable truth or emotion or to admit it into consciousness, used as a defence mechanism: *I was an addict **in denial**.*

> **WORD TRENDS** In 1991 the British historian David Irving was convicted in Germany of Holocaust **denial**—claiming that the mass murder of the Jews and other groups by the Nazis in the Second World War never happened. In 2006 he was imprisoned on a similar charge in Austria. *Holocaust denial* is not a crime under UK law, but in the 21st century it is often considered taboo to deny the truth of certain concepts. After *Holocaust*, the commonest modifiers of **denier** in the Oxford English Corpus reflect some highly contentious modern issues: *climate change, evolution,* and *global warming*. Refusal to acknowledge the existence of these things is now seen as so dangerous that some green activists have called for *climate change denial* to be made illegal.

denial of service (abbr.: **DoS**) ▶ **noun** Computing an interruption in an authorized user's access to a computer network, typically one caused with malicious intent.

denier[1] /ˈdɛnɪə/ ▶ **noun 1** a unit of weight by which the fineness of silk, rayon, or nylon yarn is measured, equal to the weight in grams of 9,000 metres of the yarn and often used to describe the thickness of hosiery: *15-denier stockings.*
2 a former French coin, equal to one twelfth of a sou, which was withdrawn in the 19th century.
– ORIGIN late Middle English: via Old French from Latin *denarius* (see **DENARIUS**). Sense 1 dates from the mid 19th cent.

denier² /dɪˈnʌɪə/ ▶ **noun** a person who denies something: *a prominent denier of global warming.*

denigrate /ˈdɛnɪɡreɪt/ ▶ **verb** [with obj.] criticize unfairly; disparage: *doom and gloom merchants who denigrate their own country.*
– DERIVATIVES **denigration** noun, **denigrator** noun, **denigratory** /-ˈɡreɪt(ə)ri/ adjective.
– ORIGIN late Middle English (in the sense 'blacken, make dark'): from Latin *denigrat-* 'blackened', from the verb *denigrare*, from *de-* 'away, completely' + *nigrare* (from *niger* 'black').

D

denim ▶ **noun** [mass noun] a hard-wearing cotton twill fabric, typically blue and used for jeans and other clothing. ■ (**denims**) jeans or other garments made of denim: *a pair of denims.*
– ORIGIN late 17th cent. (as *serge denim*): from French *serge de Nîmes*, denoting a kind of serge from the town of **NÎMES**.

De Niro /də ˈnɪərəʊ/, Robert (b.1943), American actor. He has starred in many films, often playing tough characters and frequently working with director Martin Scorsese. He has won Oscars for *The Godfather Part II* (1974) and *Raging Bull* (1980).

Denis /dəˈniː/, French /dəni/, Maurice (1870–1943), French painter, designer, and art theorist. A member of the Nabi Group, he wrote many works on art, including *Théories* (1913) and *Nouvelles Théories* (1921).

Denis, St /ˈdɛnɪs/, French /dəni/ (also **Denys**) (died *c.*250), Italian-born French bishop, patron saint of France; Roman name *Dionysius*. According to tradition he was one of a group of seven missionaries sent from Rome to convert Gaul; he became bishop of Paris and was martyred in the reign of the emperor Valerian. Feast day, 9 October.

denitrify /diːˈnʌɪtrɪfʌɪ/ ▶ **verb** (**denitrifies, denitrifying, denitrified**) [with obj.] (chiefly of bacteria) remove the nitrates or nitrites from (soil, air, or water) by chemical reduction.
– DERIVATIVES **denitrification** noun.

denizen /ˈdɛnɪz(ə)n/ ▶ **noun** formal or humorous a person, animal, or plant that lives or is found in a particular place: *denizens of field and forest.* ■ Brit. historical a foreigner allowed certain rights in their adopted country.
– DERIVATIVES **denizenship** noun.
– ORIGIN late Middle English *deynseyn*, via Anglo-Norman French from Old French *deinz* 'within' (from Latin *de* 'from' + *intus* 'within') + *-ein* (from Latin *-aneus* '-aneous'). The change in the form of the word was due to association with **CITIZEN**.

Denmark a Scandinavian country consisting of the greater part of the Jutland peninsula and several neighbouring islands, between the North Sea and the Baltic; pop. 5,500,500 (est. 2009); official language, Danish; capital, Copenhagen. Danish name **DANMARK**.

> Denmark emerged as a separate country during the Viking period of the 10th and 11th centuries. In the 14th century Denmark and Norway were united under a Danish king, the union being joined between 1389–97 and 1523 by Sweden; Norway was ceded to Sweden in 1814. Although neutral, Denmark was occupied by Germany for much of the Second World War. Denmark joined the EC in 1973.

den mother ▶ **noun** US the female leader of a den of Cub Scouts.

denominal /dɪˈnɒmɪnəl/ ▶ **adjective** (of a word) derived from a noun.
▶ **noun** a word that is derived from a noun.
– ORIGIN 1930s: from **DE-** (sense 3) + **NOMINAL**.

denominate /dɪˈnɒmɪneɪt/ ▶ **verb 1** (**be denominated**) (of sums of money) be expressed in a specified monetary unit: *the borrowings were **denominated in** US dollars.*
2 [with obj. and complement] formal call; name.
– ORIGIN late Middle English (in sense 2): from Latin *denominat-* 'named', from the verb *denominare*, from *de-* 'away, formally' + *nominare* 'to name' (from *nomen, nomin-* 'name'). Sense 1 dates from the mid 20th cent.

denomination ▶ **noun 1** a recognized autonomous branch of the Christian Church. ■ a branch of any religion: *Orthodox Jewish denominations.*
2 the face value of a banknote, coin, or postage stamp: [as modifier] *high-denomination banknotes.* ■ the rank of a playing card within a suit, or of a suit relative to others: *two cards of the same denomination.*
3 formal a name or designation. ■ [mass noun] the action of naming or classifying something.
– ORIGIN late Middle English (in sense 3): from Latin *denominatio(n-)*, from the verb *denominare* (see **DENOMINATE**). Sense 1 dates from the mid 17th cent.

denominational ▶ **adjective** relating to or according to the principles of a particular religious denomination: *denominational schools.*
– DERIVATIVES **denominationalism** noun.

denominative /dɪˈnɒmɪnətɪv/ ▶ **adjective** old-fashioned term for **DENOMINAL**.
– ORIGIN late 16th cent. (as a noun in the grammatical sense): from late Latin *denominativus*, from *denominat-* 'named', from the verb *denominare* (see **DENOMINATE**).

denominator ▶ **noun** Mathematics the number below the line in a vulgar fraction; a divisor. ■ a figure representing the total population in terms of which statistical values are expressed.

de nos jours /ˌdə nəʊ ˈʒʊə/, French /də no ʒuʀ/ ▶ **adjective** [postpositive] contemporary: *he is a kind of Oscar Wilde de nos jours.*
– ORIGIN French, 'of our days'.

denotation ▶ **noun** the literal or primary meaning of a word, in contrast to the feelings or ideas that the word suggests. ■ [mass noun] the action of indicating or referring to something by means of a word, symbol, etc. ■ Philosophy the object or concept to which a term refers, or the set of objects of which a predicate is true. Often contrasted with **CONNOTATION**.
– DERIVATIVES **denotational** adjective.

denote /dɪˈnəʊt/ ▶ **verb** [with obj.] be a sign of; indicate: *this mark denotes purity and quality.* ■ stand as a name or symbol for: *the level of output per firm is denoted by X.*
– DERIVATIVES **denotative** /-tətɪv/ adjective.
– ORIGIN late 16th cent. (in the sense 'be a sign of, mark out'): from French *dénoter* or Latin *denotare*, from *de-* 'away, thoroughly' + *notare* 'observe, note' (from *nota* 'a mark').

> **USAGE** For an explanation of the difference between denote and connote, see **USAGE** at **CONNOTE**.

denouement /deɪˈnuːmɒ̃/ (also **dénouement**) ▶ **noun** the final part of a play, film, or narrative in which the strands of the plot are drawn together and matters are explained or resolved. ■ the outcome of a situation, when something is decided or made clear: *I waited by the eighteenth green to see the denouement.*
– ORIGIN mid 18th cent.: French *dénouement*, from *dénouer* 'unknot'.

denounce ▶ **verb** [with obj.] publicly declare to be wrong or evil: *the Assembly denounced the use of violence | he was widely **denounced as** a traitor.* ■ inform against: *priests **denounced** him **to** the King **for** heresy.*
– DERIVATIVES **denouncement** noun, **denouncer** noun.
– ORIGIN Middle English (originally in the sense 'proclaim', also 'proclaim someone to be wicked, a rebel, etc.'): from Old French *denoncier*, from Latin *denuntiare* 'give official information', based on *nuntius* 'messenger'.

de novo /deɪ ˈnəʊvəʊ, diː/ ▶ **adverb & adjective** starting from the beginning; anew: [as adv.] *in a pure meritocracy, everyone must begin de novo* | [as adj.] *a general strategy for de novo protein design.*
– ORIGIN Latin, literally 'from new'.

Denpasar /dɛnˈpɑːsɑː/ the chief city of the island of Bali, a seaport on the south coast; pop. 424,300 (est. 2009).

dense ▶ **adjective 1** closely compacted in substance: *as the storm cleared, a dense fog came down.* ■ having the constituent parts crowded closely together: *she made her way through the dense undergrowth.*
2 informal (of a person) stupid.
3 (of a text) hard to understand because of its complexity of ideas.
– DERIVATIVES **densely** adverb, **denseness** noun.
– ORIGIN late Middle English: from Latin *densus*.

densify ▶ **verb** (**densifies, densifying, densified**) [with obj.] (often as adj. **densified**) make (something) more dense: *densified hardboard.*
– DERIVATIVES **densification** noun.

densimeter /dɛnˈsɪmɪtə/ ▶ **noun** an instrument for measuring density, especially of liquids.
– ORIGIN mid 19th cent.: from Latin *densus* 'dense' + **-METER**.

densitometer /ˌdɛnsɪˈtɒmɪtə/ ▶ **noun 1** a device for measuring the density of a material.
2 an instrument for measuring the photographic density of an image on a film or photographic print.
– DERIVATIVES **densitometric** adjective, **densitometrically** adverb, **densitometry** noun.

density ▶ **noun** (pl. **densities**) [mass noun] **1** the degree of compactness of a substance: *a reduction in bone density.* ■ (also **packing density**) Computing a measure of the amount of information on a storage medium: [as modifier, in combination] *a low-density floppy disk.* ■ Physics the quantity of mass per unit volume of a substance. ■ the opacity of a photographic image.
2 the quantity of people or things in a given area or space: *areas of low population density* | [count noun] *a density of 10,000 per square mile.*
– ORIGIN early 17th cent.: from French *densité* or Latin *densitas*, from *densus* 'dense'.

density function ▶ **noun** short for **PROBABILITY DENSITY FUNCTION**.

dent ▶ **noun 1** a slight hollow in a hard even surface made by a blow or pressure.
2 a reduction in amount or size: *he has barely **made a dent in** the poverty rate.*
▶ **verb** [with obj.] **1** mark with a dent: *he hit a concrete bollard, denting the wing.*
2 have an adverse effect on; diminish: *this neither deterred him nor dented his enthusiasm.*
– ORIGIN Middle English (designating a blow with a weapon): variant of **DINT**.

dental ▶ **adjective 1** [attrib.] relating to the teeth: *dental health.* ■ relating to dentistry.
2 Phonetics (of a consonant) pronounced with the tip of the tongue against the upper front teeth (as *th*) or the alveolar ridge (as *n, d, t*).
▶ **noun** Phonetics a dental consonant.
– DERIVATIVES **dentalize** (also **dentalise**) verb (Phonetics), **dentally** adverb.
– ORIGIN late 16th cent.: from late Latin *dentalis*, from Latin *dens, dent-* 'tooth'.

dental dam ▶ **noun** see **DAM²**.

dental floss ▶ **noun** [mass noun] a soft thread of floss silk or similar material used to clean between the teeth.

dental formula ▶ **noun** Zoology a formula expressing the number and kinds of teeth possessed by a mammal. A dental formula is usually written in the form of four 'fractions', one for each type of tooth, with the upper and lower lines describing the upper and lower jaws respectively.

dental hygienist ▶ **noun** an ancillary dental worker specializing in scaling and polishing teeth, and giving advice on oral hygiene.
– DERIVATIVES **dental hygiene** noun.

dentalium /dɛnˈteɪlɪəm/ ▶ **noun** ■ [mass noun] tusk shells used as ornaments or (formerly) as currency, especially by some American Indian peoples.
– ORIGIN modern Latin, from late Latin *dentalis* (see **DENTAL**).

dental nurse ▶ **noun** a person whose job is to assist a dentist in the treatment of patients.

dental surgeon ▶ **noun** a dentist.

dental technician (also **dental mechanic**) ▶ **noun** a person who makes and repairs artificial teeth.

dentary /ˈdɛnt(ə)ri/ ▶ **noun** (pl. **dentaries**) Zoology the anterior bone of the lower jaw which bears the teeth. In mammals it forms the whole of the lower jaw (or mandible).
– ORIGIN mid 19th cent.: from late Latin *dentarius*, from Latin *dens, dent-* 'tooth'.

dentate /ˈdɛnteɪt/ ▶ **adjective** Botany & Zoology having a tooth-like or serrated edge.
– ORIGIN late Middle English: from Latin *dentatus*, from *dens, dent-* 'tooth'.

dentelle /dɛnˈtɛl/ ▶ **noun** (pl. pronunc. **same**) [mass noun] ornamental tooling used in bookbinding, resembling lace edging.
– ORIGIN mid 19th cent.: from French, 'lace', from *dent* 'tooth' + the diminutive suffix *-elle*.

dentex ▶ **noun** (pl. **same** or **dentexes**) a sea bream of the genus *Dentex*, especially *D. dentex* of the Mediterranean and the North African Atlantic coast.
– ORIGIN modern Latin (genus name), from Latin.

denticle /ˈdɛntɪk(ə)l/ ▶ **noun** Zoology a small tooth or tooth-like projection.
– ORIGIN late Middle English (denoting a pointer on an astrolabe): from Latin *denticulus*, diminutive of *dens, dent-* 'tooth'.

denticulate /dɛnˈtɪkjʊlət/ ▶ **adjective** having small teeth or tooth-like projections; finely toothed.
– DERIVATIVES **denticulated** adjective.
– ORIGIN mid 17th cent.: from Latin *denticulatus*, from *denticulus* 'small tooth' (see **DENTICLE**).

dentifrice /ˈdɛntɪfrɪs/ ▸ **noun** a paste or powder for cleaning the teeth.
– ORIGIN late Middle English: from French, from Latin *dentifricium*, from *dens, dent-* 'tooth' + *fricare* 'to rub'.

dentil /ˈdɛntɪl/ ▸ **noun** [often as modifier] (in classical architecture) one of a number of small rectangular blocks resembling teeth, used as a decoration under the moulding of a cornice: *a dentil frieze*.
– ORIGIN late 16th cent.: from Italian *dentello* or obsolete French *dentille*, diminutive of *dent* 'tooth', from Latin *dens, dent-*.

dentilingual /ˌdɛntɪˈlɪŋgw(ə)l/ ▸ **adjective** Phonetics (of a consonant) pronounced with the teeth and the tongue; dental.
– ORIGIN late 19th cent.: from Latin *dens, dent-* 'tooth' + **LINGUAL**.

dentine /ˈdɛntiːn/ (US **dentin** /-tɪn/) ▸ **noun** [mass noun] hard dense bony tissue forming the bulk of a tooth, beneath the enamel.
– DERIVATIVES **dentinal** /ˈdɛntɪn(ə)l/ **adjective**.
– ORIGIN mid 19th cent.: from Latin *dens, dent-* 'tooth' + **-INE**[4].

dentist ▸ **noun** a person who is qualified to treat diseases and other conditions that affect the teeth and gums, especially the repair and extraction of teeth and the insertion of artificial ones.
– DERIVATIVES **dentistry** noun.
– ORIGIN mid 18th cent.: from French *dentiste*, from *dent* 'tooth', from Latin *dens, dent-*.

dentition /dɛnˈtɪʃ(ə)n/ ▸ **noun** [mass noun] the arrangement or condition of the teeth in a particular species or individual.
– ORIGIN late 16th cent. (denoting the development of teeth): from Latin *dentitio(n-)*, from *dentire* 'teethe', from *dens, dent-* 'tooth'.

denture /ˈdɛntʃə/ ▸ **noun** (usu. **dentures**) a removable plate or frame holding one or more artificial teeth.
– ORIGIN late 19th cent.: from French, from *dent* 'tooth', from Latin *dens, dent-*.

denturist ▸ **noun** a person who makes dentures.

denuclearize (also **denuclearise**) ▸ **verb** [with obj.] remove nuclear weapons from.
– DERIVATIVES **denuclearization** noun.

denude ▸ **verb** [with obj.] strip (something) of its covering, possessions, or assets: *almost overnight the Arctic was* ***denuded of*** *animals*.
– DERIVATIVES **denudation** noun.
– ORIGIN late Middle English: from Latin *denudare*, from *de-* 'completely' + *nudare* 'to bare' (from *nudus* 'naked').

denumerable /dɪˈnjuːm(ə)rəb(ə)l/ ▸ **adjective** Mathematics able to be counted by a one-to-one correspondence with the infinite set of integers.
– DERIVATIVES **denumerably** adverb.
– ORIGIN early 20th cent.: from late Latin *denumerare* 'count out' + **-ABLE**.

denunciation /dɪˌnʌnsɪˈeɪʃ(ə)n/ ▸ **noun** [mass noun] public condemnation of someone or something. ■ the action of informing against someone.
– DERIVATIVES **denunciator** noun, **denunciatory** adjective.
– ORIGIN late Middle English: from Latin *denuntiatio(n-)*, from the verb *denuntiare* (see **DENOUNCE**). The original sense was 'public announcement', also 'formal accusation'; the main sense dates from the mid 19th cent.

Denver /ˈdɛnvə/ a city in Colorado, the state capital; pop. 598,707 (est. 2008). Situated at an altitude of 1,608 m (5,280 ft) on the eastern side of the Rocky Mountains, Denver was developed in the 1870s as a silver-mining town.

Denver boot ▸ **noun** N. Amer. a wheel clamp.

deny /dɪˈnʌɪ/ ▸ **verb** (**denies, denying, denied**) [with obj.] state that one refuses to admit the truth or existence of: *both firms deny any responsibility for the tragedy*. ■ [with two objs] refuse to give (something requested or desired) to (someone): *the inquiry was denied access to intelligence sources*. ■ (**deny oneself**) refuse to let oneself have something that one desires: *he had denied himself sexually for years*. ■ archaic refuse access to (someone).
– ORIGIN Middle English: from Old French *deni-*, stressed stem of *deneier*, from Latin *denegare*, from *de-* 'formally' + *negare* 'say no'.

Denys, St see **DENIS, ST**.

deoch an doris /ˌdɒx (ə)n ˈdɒrɪs, dɒk/ (also **doch an dorris**) ▸ **noun** Scottish & Irish a final drink taken before parting.
– ORIGIN late 17th cent.: from Scottish Gaelic *deoch an doruis* 'drink at the door'.

deodar /ˈdiːə(ʊ)dɑː/ ▸ **noun** a tall, broadly conical cedar which has drooping branches and bears large barrel-shaped cones, native to the Himalayas. ● *Cedrus deodara*, family Pinaceae.
– ORIGIN early 19th cent.: from Hindi *deodār*, from Sanskrit *devadāru* 'divine tree'.

deodorant /dɪˈəʊd(ə)r(ə)nt/ ▸ **noun** a substance which removes or conceals unpleasant smells, especially bodily odours.
– ORIGIN mid 19th cent.: from **DE-** (expressing removal) + Latin *odor* 'smell' + **-ANT**.

deodorize (also **deodorise**) ▸ **verb** [with obj.] remove or conceal an unpleasant smell in: *people used dried flowers to deodorize their homes*.
– DERIVATIVES **deodorization** noun, **deodorizer** noun.
– ORIGIN mid 19th cent.: from **DE-** (expressing removal) + Latin *odor* 'smell' + **-IZE**.

Deo gratias /ˌdeɪəʊ ˈgrɑːtɪəs, -ʃɪəs/ ▸ **exclamation** thanks be to God.
– ORIGIN Latin.

deontic /dɪˈɒntɪk/ ▸ **adjective** Philosophy relating to duty and obligation as ethical concepts. ■ Linguistics expressing duty or obligation.
– ORIGIN mid 19th cent. (as noun *deontics*): from Greek *deont-* 'being right' (from *dei* 'it is right') + **-IC**.

deontology /ˌdiːɒnˈtɒlədʒi/ ▸ **noun** [mass noun] Philosophy the study of the nature of duty and obligation.
– DERIVATIVES **deontological** adjective, **deontologist** noun.
– ORIGIN early 19th cent.: from Greek *deont-* 'being right' (from *dei* 'it is right') + **-LOGY**.

Deo volente /ˌdeɪəʊ vɒˈlɛnteɪ/ ▸ **adverb** God willing; if nothing prevents it.
– ORIGIN Latin.

deoxidize /diːˈɒksɪdʌɪz/ (also **deoxidise**) ▸ **verb** [with obj.] remove combined oxygen from (a substance, usually a metal).
– DERIVATIVES **deoxidation** noun, **deoxidizer** noun.

deoxycorticosterone /diːˌɒksɪˌkɔːtɪkəʊˈstɛrəʊn/ ▸ **noun** [mass noun] Biochemistry a corticosteroid hormone involved in regulating the salt and water balance of the body.

deoxygenate /diːˈɒksɪdʒəneɪt/ ▸ **verb** [with obj.] (usu. as adj. **deoxygenated**) remove oxygen from: *deoxygenated air*.
– DERIVATIVES **deoxygenation** noun.

deoxyribonuclease /diːˌɒksɪrʌɪbəʊˈnjuːklɪeɪz/ ▸ **noun** Biochemistry another term for **DNASE**.

deoxyribonucleic acid /dɪˌɒksɪrʌɪbəʊnjuːˈkleɪɪk/ ▸ **noun** see **DNA**.
– ORIGIN 1930s: *deoxyribonucleic* from a blend of **DEOXYRIBOSE** and **NUCLEIC ACID**.

deoxyribose /dɪˌɒksɪˈrʌɪbəʊz, -s/ ▸ **noun** [mass noun] Biochemistry a sugar derived from ribose by replacement of a hydroxyl group by hydrogen. ● Chem. formula; $C_5H_{10}O_4$. There are several isomers; the isomer **2-deoxyribose** is a constituent of DNA.
– ORIGIN 1930s: from **DE-** (expressing reduction) + **OXY-**[2] + **RIBOSE**.

dep. ▸ **abbreviation** ■ departs. ■ deputy.

Depardieu /ˈdɛpɑːdjəː/, French /dəpaʀdjø/, Gérard (b.1948), French actor. Notable films: *Danton* (1982), *Jean de Florette* (1986), and *Cyrano de Bergerac* (1990).

depart ▸ **verb** [no obj.] leave, especially in order to start a journey: *they* ***departed for*** *Germany* | *a contingent* ***was departing from*** *Cairo*. ■ (**depart from**) deviate from (an accepted, prescribed, or usual course of action): *he departed from the precedent set by many*. ■ [with obj.] N. Amer. leave (one's job).
– PHRASES **depart this life** archaic die.
– ORIGIN Middle English: from Old French *departir*, based on Latin *dispertire* 'to divide'. The original sense was 'separate', also 'take leave of each other', hence 'go away'.

departed ▸ **adjective** dead: *a dear departed relative* | (as noun **the departed**) *prayers for the departed*.

department ▸ **noun** a division of a large organization such as a government, university, or business, dealing with a specific area of activity: *the council's finance department*. ■ an administrative district in France and other countries. ■ (**one's department**) informal an area of special expertise or responsibility: *that's not my department*. ■ [with modifier] informal a specified aspect or quality: *he was a bit lacking in the height department*.
– ORIGIN late Middle English: from Old French *departement*, from *departir* (see **DEPART**). The original sense was 'division or distribution', later 'separation', hence 'a separate part' (core sense, mid 18th cent.).

departmental ▸ **adjective** concerned with or belonging to a department of an organization: *a departmental meeting*.
– DERIVATIVES **departmentally** adverb.

departmentalism ▸ **noun** [mass noun] adherence to departmental methods or structure.

departmentalize (also **departmentalise**) ▸ **verb** [with obj.] divide (an organization or its work) into departments.
– DERIVATIVES **departmentalization** noun.

department store ▸ **noun** a large shop stocking many varieties of goods in different departments.

departure ▸ **noun** [mass noun] the action of leaving, especially to start a journey: *the day of departure* | [count noun] *she made a hasty departure*. ■ [count noun] a deviation from an accepted, prescribed, or usual course of action: *the album is not a radical* ***departure from*** *the band's previous work*. ■ Nautical the amount of a ship's change of longitude.
– ORIGIN late Middle English: from Old French *departeure*, from the verb *departir* (see **DEPART**).

depasture ▸ **verb** [with obj.] Brit. put (an animal) to graze on pasture.
– DERIVATIVES **depasturage** noun.

depauperate /dɪˈpɔːp(ə)rət/ ▸ **adjective** Biology (of a flora, fauna, or ecosystem) lacking in numbers or variety of species: *oceanic islands are generally depauperate in mayflies*. ■ (of a plant or animal) imperfectly developed.
– ORIGIN late Middle English (in the sense 'impoverished'): from medieval Latin *depauperatus*, past participle of *depauperare*, from *de-* 'completely' + *pauperare* 'make poor' (from *pauper* 'poor').

dépaysé /deɪˈpeɪzeɪ/, French /depeize/ (also **dépaysée**) ▸ **adjective** removed from one's habitual surroundings.
– ORIGIN French, '(removed) from one's own country'.

depend ▸ **verb** [no obj.] **1** (**depend on/upon**) be controlled or determined by: *differences in earnings depended on a wide variety of factors*.
2 (**depend on/upon**) be able to trust; rely on: *we can depend on her to deliver a quality product*. ■ need for financial or other support: *a town which had depended heavily upon the wool industry*. ■ be grammatically dependent on.
3 archaic or literary hang down: *his tongue* ***depended from*** *open jaws*.
– PHRASES **depending on** according to: *makes 8–10 burgers (depending on size)*. **it** (or **that**) (**all**) **depends** used to express uncertainty in answering a question: *How many people use each screen? It all depends*.
– ORIGIN late Middle English (in sense 3; also in the sense 'wait or be in suspense'): from Old French *dependre*, from Latin *dependere*, from *de-* 'down' + *pendere* 'hang'.

> **USAGE** In informal use, it is quite common for the **on** to be dropped in sentences such as *it all* ***depends how*** *you look at it* (rather than *it all* ***depends on how*** *you look at it*), but in well-formed written English the **on** should be retained.

dependable ▸ **adjective** trustworthy and reliable.
– DERIVATIVES **dependability** noun, **dependably** adverb.

dependant (also **dependent**) ▸ **noun** a person who relies on another, especially a family member, for financial support.
– ORIGIN late Middle English (denoting a dependency): from Old French, literally 'hanging down from', present participle of *dependre* (see **DEPEND**).

> **USAGE** Until recently the only correct spelling of the noun in British English was **dependant**, as in *a single man with no* ***dependants***. However, the variant **dependent** is now standard, and indeed it is now as common as **dependant** in the Oxford English Corpus. In US English **dependent** is the standard form for the noun. The adjective is spelled **-ent**, not **-ant**, as in *we are* ***dependent*** *on his goodwill*.

dependence ▸ **noun** [mass noun] the state of relying on or being controlled by someone or something else: *Japan's dependence on imported oil*. ■ reliance on someone or something for financial support: *the*

dependence of our medical schools on grant funds. ■ addiction to drink or drugs: *alcohol dependence.*
– ORIGIN late Middle English (in the sense 'hanging down or something that hangs down'): from Old French *dependance*, from the verb *dependre* (see DEPEND).

dependency ▶ noun (pl. **dependencies**) **1** a country or province controlled by another.
2 [mass noun] dependence: *the country's **dependency on** the oil industry.*

dependency culture ▶ noun a way of life characterized by dependency on state benefits.

dependent ▶ adjective **1** (**dependent on/upon**) contingent on or determined by: *the various benefits will be dependent on length of service.*
2 requiring someone or something for financial or other support: *an economy heavily **dependent on** oil exports | households with dependent children.* ■ unable to do without: *people **dependent on** drugs.*
3 Grammar (of a clause, phrase, or word) subordinate to another clause, phrase, or word.
▶ noun variant spelling of DEPENDANT.
– DERIVATIVES **dependently** adverb.
– ORIGIN late Middle English *dependant* 'hanging down', from Old French, present participle of *dependre* (see DEPEND). The spelling change in the 16th cent. was due to association with the Latin participial stem *dependent-*.

> **USAGE** On the distinction between **dependent** and **dependant**, see **USAGE** at **DEPENDANT**.

dependent variable ▶ noun Mathematics a variable (often denoted by *y*) whose value depends on that of another. Also called RESPONSE VARIABLE.

depersonalization /diːˌpəːs(ə)n(ə)lʌɪˈzeɪʃ(ə)n/ (also **depersonalisation**) ▶ noun [mass noun] the action of divesting someone or something of human characteristics or individuality. ■ Psychiatry a state in which one's thoughts and feelings seem unreal or not to belong to oneself.

depersonalize (also **depersonalise**) ▶ verb [with obj.] divest of human characteristics or individuality.

dephlogisticated /ˌdiːfləˈdʒɪstɪkeɪtɪd/ ▶ adjective Chemistry, historical deprived of 'phlogiston'. Oxygen was originally called **dephlogisticated air** by Joseph Priestley.

depict /dɪˈpɪkt/ ▶ verb [with obj.] represent by a drawing, painting, or other art form. ■ portray in words; describe: *youth is **depicted as** a time of vitality and good health.*
– DERIVATIVES **depicter** noun, **depictive** adjective.
– ORIGIN late Middle English: from Latin *depict-* 'portrayed', from the verb *depingere*, from *de-* 'completely' + *pingere* 'to paint'.

depiction ▶ noun [mass noun] the action of depicting something, especially in a work of art: *the painting's horrific depiction of war* | [count noun] *Michelangelo's depictions of the male nude.*

depigment /diːˈpɪgm(ə)nt/ ▶ verb [with obj.] (usu. as adj. **depigmented**) reduce or remove the pigmentation of (the skin).
– DERIVATIVES **depigmentation** noun.

depilate /ˈdɛpɪleɪt/ ▶ verb [with obj.] remove the hair from: *they scrubbed and depilated her* | (as adj. **depilated**) *his permanently depilated and tattooed skull.*
– DERIVATIVES **depilation** noun, **depilator** noun.
– ORIGIN mid 16th cent. (earlier (late Middle English) as *depilation*): from Latin *depilat-* 'stripped of hair', from the verb *depilare*, from *de-* (expressing removal) + *pilare* (from *pilus* 'hair').

depilatory /dɪˈpɪlət(ə)ri/ ▶ adjective used to remove unwanted hair.
▶ noun (pl. **depilatories**) a cream or lotion for removing unwanted hair.
– ORIGIN early 17th cent.: from Latin *depilatorius*, from *depilat-* 'stripped of hair', from the verb *depilare* (see DEPILATE).

de Pisan /də ˈpiːzan/ (also **de Pizan**), Christine (*c.*1364–*c.*1430), Italian writer, resident in France from 1369. The first professional woman writer in France, she is best known for her works in defence of women's virtues and achievements, such as *Le Livre des trois vertus* (1406).

deplane ▶ verb [no obj.] N. Amer. disembark from an aircraft: *we landed and deplaned.*

deplete /dɪˈpliːt/ ▶ verb [with obj.] (often as adj. **depleted**) use up the supply or resources of: *fish stocks are severely depleted | Mansfield started the game with a heavily depleted side.* ■ [no obj.] diminish in number or quantity: *supplies are depleting fast.*
– DERIVATIVES **depleter** noun.
– ORIGIN early 19th cent. (earlier (mid. 17th cent.) as *depletion*): from Latin *deplet-* 'emptied out', from the verb *deplere*, from *de-* (expressing reversal) + *plere* 'fill' (from *plenus* 'full').

depleted uranium ▶ noun [mass noun] uranium from which most of the fissile isotope uranium-235 has been removed.

depletion ▶ noun [mass noun] reduction in the number or quantity of something: *the depletion of the ozone layer.*

depletion allowance ▶ noun N. Amer. a tax concession allowable to a company whose normal business activities (in particular oil extraction) reduce the value of its own assets.

deplorable /dɪˈplɔːrəb(ə)l/ ▶ adjective deserving strong condemnation; completely unacceptable: *children living in deplorable conditions.* ■ shockingly bad in quality: *her spelling was deplorable.*
– DERIVATIVES **deplorably** adverb.
– ORIGIN early 17th cent.: from French *déplorable* or late Latin *deplorabilis*, from the verb *deplorare* (see DEPLORE).

deplore /dɪˈplɔː/ ▶ verb [with obj.] feel or express strong condemnation of (something): *we deplore all violence.*
– DERIVATIVES **deploringly** adverb.
– ORIGIN mid 16th cent. (in the sense 'weep for, regret deeply'): from French *déplorer* or Italian *deplorare*, from Latin *deplorare*, from *de-* 'away, thoroughly' + *plorare* 'bewail'.

deploy /dɪˈplɔɪ/ ▶ verb [with obj.] **1** move (troops) into position for military action: *forces were deployed at strategic locations.* ■ [no obj.] (of troops) move into position for military action: *the air force began to deploy forward.*
2 bring into effective action: *small states can often deploy resources more freely.*
– DERIVATIVES **deployable** adjective, **deployment** noun.
– ORIGIN late 18th cent.: from French *déployer*, from Latin *displicare* and late Latin *deplicare* 'unfold or explain', from *dis-*, *de-* 'un-' + *plicare* 'to fold'. Compare with DISPLAY.

deplume ▶ verb [with obj.] remove feathers from (a bird).
– ORIGIN late Middle English: from Old French *desplumer* or medieval Latin *deplumare*, from *des-*, *de-* (expressing reversal) + Latin *pluma* 'feather'.

depolarize /diːˈpəʊlərʌɪz/ (also **depolarise**) ▶ verb [with obj.] Physics reduce or remove the polarization of: *the threshold necessary to depolarize the membrane.*
– DERIVATIVES **depolarization** noun.

depoliticize (also **depoliticise**) ▶ verb [with obj.] remove from political activity or influence: *we have to depoliticize sex education.*
– DERIVATIVES **depoliticization** noun.

depolymerize /diːˈpɒlɪmərʌɪz/ (also **depolymerise**) ▶ verb [with obj.] Chemistry break (a polymer) down into monomers or other smaller units. ■ [no obj.] undergo this process.
– DERIVATIVES **depolymerization** noun.

deponent /dɪˈpəʊnənt/ ▶ adjective Grammar (of a verb, especially in Latin or Greek) passive or middle in form but active in meaning.
▶ noun **1** Grammar a deponent verb.
2 Law a person who makes a deposition or affidavit under oath.
– ORIGIN late Middle English: from Latin *deponent-* 'laying aside, putting down' (in medieval Latin 'testifying'), from the verb *deponere*, from *de-* 'down' + *ponere* 'place'. The use in grammar arose from the notion that the verb had 'laid aside' the passive sense (although in fact these verbs were originally reflexive).

depopulate ▶ verb [with obj.] substantially reduce the population of (an area): *the disease could depopulate a town the size of Bournemouth.*
– DERIVATIVES **depopulation** noun.
– ORIGIN mid 16th cent. (in the sense 'ravage, lay waste'): from Latin *depopulat-* 'ravaged', from the verb *depopulari*, from *de-* 'completely' + *populari* 'lay waste' (from *populus* 'people').

deport ▶ verb **1** [with obj.] expel (a foreigner) from a country, typically on the grounds of illegal status or for having committed a crime: *he was deported for violation of immigration laws.* ■ exile (a native) to another country.
2 (**deport oneself**) archaic conduct oneself in a specified manner: *he has deported himself with great dignity.*
– DERIVATIVES **deportable** adjective.
– ORIGIN late 16th cent. (in sense 2): from French *déporter*, from Latin *deportare*, from *de-* 'away' + *portare* 'carry'.

deportation ▶ noun [mass noun] the action of deporting a foreigner from a country: *asylum seekers facing deportation* | [as modifier] *a deportation order.*

deportee /ˌdiːpɔːˈtiː/ ▶ noun a person who has been or is being expelled from a country.

deportment ▶ noun [mass noun] **1** Brit. the way a person stands and walks, particularly as an element of etiquette: *poise is directly concerned with good deportment.*
2 chiefly N. Amer. a person's behaviour or manners: *there are team rules governing deportment on and off the field.*
– ORIGIN early 17th cent. (denoting behaviour in general): from French *déportement*, from the verb *déporter* (see DEPORT).

depose ▶ verb [with obj.] **1** remove from office suddenly and forcefully: *he had been deposed by a military coup.*
2 Law testify to or give (evidence) under oath, typically in a written statement: *every affidavit shall state which of the facts **deposed to** are within the deponent's knowledge.*
– ORIGIN Middle English: from Old French *deposer*, from Latin *deponere* (see DEPONENT), but influenced by Latin *depositus* and Old French *poser* 'to place'.

deposit ▶ noun **1** a sum of money paid into a bank or building society account.
2 a sum payable as a first instalment on the purchase of something or as a pledge for a contract, the balance being payable later: *we've saved enough for a **deposit on** a house.* ■ a returnable sum payable on the hire or rental of something, to cover possible loss or damage. ■ (in the UK) a sum of money lodged by an election candidate and forfeited if they fail to receive a certain proportion of the votes.
3 a layer or mass of accumulated matter: *the deposits of salt on the paintwork.* ■ a natural underground layer of rock, coal, or other material.
4 [mass noun] the action of placing something in a specified place.
▶ verb (**deposits**, **depositing**, **deposited**) **1** [with obj. and usu. with adverbial of place] put or set down (something or someone) in a specific place: *he deposited a pile of school books on the kitchen table.* ■ (of water, the wind, or other natural agency) lay down (matter) gradually as a layer or covering: *beds where salt is deposited by the tide.* ■ lay (an egg).
2 [with obj.] place (something) somewhere for safekeeping: *a vault in which guests may deposit valuable property.* ■ pay (a sum of money) into a bank or building society account: *the money had been deposited in a Swiss bank account.* ■ pay (a sum) as a first instalment or as a pledge for a contract: *I had to deposit 10% of the price of the house.*
– PHRASES **on deposit** (of money) placed in a deposit account.
– ORIGIN late 16th cent. (especially in the phrases *in deposit* or *on deposit*): from Latin *depositum* (noun), medieval Latin *depositare* (verb), both from Latin *deposit-* 'laid aside', from the verb *deponere*.

deposit account ▶ noun Brit. a bank account that pays interest and is usually not able to be drawn on without notice or loss of interest.

depositary (also **depository**) ▶ noun (pl. **depositaries**) a person to whom something is lodged in trust.
– ORIGIN early 17th cent.: from late Latin *depositarius*, from the verb *deponere* (see DEPOSIT).

deposition /ˌdɛpəˈzɪʃ(ə)n, diː-/ ▶ noun [mass noun] **1** the action of deposing someone, especially a monarch: *Edward V's deposition.*
2 Law the giving of sworn evidence: *the deposition of four expert witnesses.* ■ [count noun] a formal, usually written, statement to be used as evidence.
3 the action of depositing something: *pebbles formed by the deposition of calcium in solution.*
4 (**the Deposition**) the removal of the body of Christ from the Cross.
– ORIGIN late Middle English: from Latin *depositio(n-)*, from the verb *deponere* (see DEPOSIT).

depositor ▶ noun a person who keeps money in a bank or building society account.

depository ▶ noun (pl. **depositories**) **1** a place where things are stored.
2 variant spelling of DEPOSITARY.

– ORIGIN mid 17th cent. (denoting a depositary): from late Latin *depositorium*, from *deposit-* 'laid aside', from the verb *deponere* (see DEPOSIT).

depot /ˈdɛpəʊ/ ▶ **noun 1** a place for the storage of large quantities of equipment, food, or goods: *an arms depot.*
2 a place where buses, trains, or other vehicles are housed and maintained and from which they are dispatched for service. ■ N. Amer. a railway or bus station.
3 Military a place where recruits are trained or other troops are assembled.
– ORIGIN late 18th cent. (in the sense 'act of depositing'): from French *dépôt*, from Latin *depositum* 'something deposited' (see DEPOSIT).

depower ▶ **verb** [with obj.] Sailing adjust or alter (a sail) so that the wind no longer fills it.

deprave /dɪˈpreɪv/ ▶ **verb** [with obj.] make (someone) immoral or wicked: *this book would deprave and corrupt young children.*
– DERIVATIVES **depravation** noun.
– ORIGIN late Middle English (in the sense 'pervert the meaning or intention of something'): from Old French *depraver* or Latin *depravare*, from *de-* 'down, thoroughly' + *pravus* 'crooked, perverse'.

depraved ▶ **adjective** morally corrupt; wicked: *he was a depraved lecher | this city is depraved.*

depravity /dɪˈpravɪti/ ▶ **noun** (pl. **depravities**) [mass noun] moral corruption; wickedness: *a tale of depravity hard to credit* | [count noun] *I wondered what depravities had occurred in that place.* ■ Christian Theology the innate corruption of human nature, due to original sin.
– ORIGIN mid 17th cent.: alteration (influenced by DEPRAVE) of obsolete *pravity*, from Latin *pravitas*, from *pravus* 'crooked, perverse'.

deprecate /ˈdɛprɪkeɪt/ ▶ **verb** [with obj.] **1** express disapproval of: *what I deprecate is persistent indulgence* | (as adj. **deprecating**) *he sniffed in a deprecating way.*
2 another term for DEPRECIATE (sense 2): *he deprecates the value of children's television.*
– DERIVATIVES **deprecatingly** adverb, **deprecation** noun, **deprecative** /ˈdɛprɪkətɪv/ adjective, **deprecator** noun.
– ORIGIN early 17th cent. (in the sense 'pray against'): from Latin *deprecat-* 'prayed against (as being evil)', from the verb *deprecari*, from *de-* (expressing reversal) + *precari* 'pray'.

deprecatory ▶ **adjective** expressing disapproval; disapproving. ■ apologetic or appeasing: *a deprecatory smile.*

depreciate /dɪˈpriːʃɪeɪt, -sɪ-/ ▶ **verb 1** [no obj.] diminish in value over a period of time: *the latest cars will depreciate heavily in the first year.* ■ [with obj.] reduce the recorded value in a company's books of (an asset) each year over a predetermined period.
2 [with obj.] disparage or belittle (something): *she was already depreciating her own aesthetic taste.*
– DERIVATIVES **depreciable** adjective, **depreciative** adjective, **depreciatory** adjective.
– ORIGIN late Middle English (in sense 2): from late Latin *depreciat-* 'lowered in price, undervalued', from the verb *depreciare*, from Latin *de-* 'down' + *pretium* 'price'.

depreciation ▶ **noun** [mass noun] a reduction in the value of an asset over time, due in particular to wear and tear. ■ a decrease in the value of a currency relative to other currencies.

depredation /ˌdɛprɪˈdeɪʃ(ə)n/ ▶ **noun** (usu. **depredations**) an act of attacking or plundering: *protecting grain from the depredations of rats and mice.*
– ORIGIN late 15th cent. (in the sense 'plundering, robbery', (plural) 'ravages'): from French *déprédation*, from late Latin *depraedatio(n-)*, from *depraedari* 'plunder'.

depredator /ˈdɛprɪdeɪtə/ ▶ **noun** archaic a person or thing that makes depredations, especially a predatory animal.
– DERIVATIVES **depredatory** /ˈdɛprɪdeɪt(ə)ri, dɪˈprɛdət(ə)ri/ adjective.

depress ▶ **verb** [with obj.] **1** make (someone) feel utterly dispirited or dejected: *that first day at school depressed me.*
2 reduce the level or strength of activity in (something, especially an economic or biological system): *fear of inflation in America depressed bond markets | alcohol depresses the nervous system.*
3 push or pull (something) down into a lower position: *depress the lever.*
– DERIVATIVES **depressible** adjective.
– ORIGIN late Middle English: from Old French *depresser*, from late Latin *depressare*, frequentative of *deprimere* 'press down'.

depressant ▶ **adjective** (chiefly of a drug) reducing functional or nervous activity.
▶ **noun** a depressant drug. ■ an influence that depresses economic activity: *higher taxation is a depressant.*

depressed ▶ **adjective 1** (of a person) in a state of unhappiness or despondency. ■ (of a person) suffering from clinical depression.
2 (of a place or economic activity) suffering the damaging effects of a lack of demand or employment: *depressed inner-city areas.*
3 (of an object or part of an object) in a lower position, having been pushed down: *a depressed fracture of the skull.*

depressing ▶ **adjective 1** causing or resulting in a feeling of miserable dejection: *that thought is too depressing for words.*
2 causing a damaging reduction in economic activity: *the mortgage rate increase will have a depressing effect on the housing market.*
– DERIVATIVES **depressingly** adverb.

depression ▶ **noun 1** [mass noun] severe, typically prolonged, feelings of despondency and dejection. ■ Medicine a mental condition characterized by severe feelings of hopelessness and inadequacy, typically accompanied by a lack of energy and interest in life: *she suffered from clinical depression.*
2 a long and severe recession in an economy or market: *the depression in the housing market.* ■ (**the Depression** or **the Great Depression**) the financial and industrial slump of 1929 and subsequent years.
3 [mass noun] the action of lowering something or pressing something down: *depression of the plunger delivers two units of insulin.* ■ [count noun] a sunken place or hollow on a surface: *the original shallow depressions were slowly converted to creeks.*
4 Meteorology a region of lower atmospheric pressure, especially a cyclonic weather system.
5 Astronomy & Geography the angular distance of an object below the horizon or a horizontal plane.
– ORIGIN late Middle English: from Latin *depressio(n-)*, from *deprimere* 'press down' (see DEPRESS).

depressive ▶ **adjective** causing feelings of severe despondency and dejection. ■ Medicine relating to or tending to suffer from clinical depression: *a depressive illness.* ■ causing a reduction in strength, effectiveness, or value: *steroids have a depressive effect on the immune system.*
▶ **noun** Medicine a person suffering from or with a tendency to suffer from depression.

depressor ▶ **noun 1** Anatomy (also **depressor muscle**) a muscle whose contraction pulls down a part of the body. ■ any of several specific muscles in the face: [followed by Latin genitive] *depressor anguli oris.*
2 Physiology a nerve whose stimulation results in a lowering of blood pressure.
3 an instrument for pressing something down.

depressurize (also **depressurise**) ▶ **verb** [with obj.] release the pressure of the gas inside (a pressurized vehicle or container). ■ [no obj.] (of a pressurized vehicle or container) lose pressure.
– DERIVATIVES **depressurization** noun.

Deprez variant spelling of DES PREZ.

deprivation /dɛprɪˈveɪʃ(ə)n/ ▶ **noun** [mass noun] the damaging lack of material benefits considered to be basic necessities in a society: *low wages mean that 3.75 million people suffer serious deprivation.* ■ the lack or denial of something considered to be a necessity: *sleep deprivation.* ■ archaic the action of depriving someone of office, especially an ecclesiastical office.
– ORIGIN late Middle English (in the sense 'removal from office'): from medieval Latin *deprivatio(n-)*, from the verb *deprivare* (see DEPRIVE).

deprive /dɪˈprʌɪv/ ▶ **verb** [with obj.] prevent (a person or place) from having or using something: *the city was deprived of its water supplies.* ■ archaic depose (someone, especially a clergyman) from office.
– DERIVATIVES **deprival** noun.
– ORIGIN Middle English (in the sense 'depose from office'): from Old French *depriver*, from medieval Latin *deprivare*, from *de-* 'away, completely' + *privare* (see PRIVATE).

deprived ▶ **adjective** suffering a severe and damaging lack of basic material and cultural benefits: *the charity cares for destitute and deprived children.* ■ (of a person) lacking a specified benefit that is considered important: *the men felt sexually deprived.*

de profundis /ˌdeɪ prəˈfʊndɪs/ ▶ **adverb** used to convey that one's most heartfelt feelings of sorrow or anguish are being expressed.
▶ **noun** a heartfelt cry of appeal.
– ORIGIN Latin, 'from the depths', the opening words of Psalm 130.

deprogramme (US **deprogram**) ▶ **verb** (**deprogrammes, deprogramming, deprogrammed**; US **deprograms, deprograming, deprogramed**) [with obj.] release (someone) from apparent brainwashing, typically that of a religious cult, by the systematic reindoctrination of conventional values.

deproteinize /diːˈprəʊtiːnʌɪz/ (also **deproteinise**) ▶ **verb** [with obj.] remove the protein from (a substance), usually as a stage in chemical purification.
– DERIVATIVES **deproteinization** noun.

Dept ▶ **abbreviation** Department.

depth ▶ **noun** [mass noun] **1** the distance from the top or surface to the bottom of something: *water of no more than 12 feet* ***in depth.*** ■ the distance from the front to the back of something: *the depth of the wardrobe.* ■ the distance from the top or surface of something to a specified lower point within it: [in sing.] *loosen the soil to* ***a depth of*** *8 inches.* ■ the apparent existence of three dimensions in a picture or other two-dimensional representation: *texture in a picture gives it depth.*
2 the quality of being intense or extreme: *he was surprised by the depth of Eloise's vindictiveness | the government failed to understand the depth of the problems.* ■ complexity and profundity of thought: *the book has unexpected depth.* ■ extensive and detailed study or knowledge: *third-year courses typically go into more depth.*
3 intensity of colour: *strong lighting will accentuate the depth of colour.*
4 (**the depths**) a point far below the surface: *he lifted the manhole cover and peered into the depths beneath.* ■ a time considered to be the worst point within a bad period: *4 a.m.* ***in the depths of winter.*** ■ a time when one's negative feelings are at their most intense: *she was* ***in the depths of despair.*** ■ a remote and inaccessible place: *I wish I didn't live in the depths of Devon.*
– PHRASES **hidden depths** admirable but previously unnoticed qualities: *his solo spots reveal hidden depths.* **in depth** comprehensively and thoroughly: *research students pursue a specific aspect of a subject in depth.* See also IN-DEPTH. **out of one's depth** in water too deep to stand in. ■ in a situation that is beyond one's capabilities: *they soon realized they were out of their depth in Division One.*
– ORIGIN late Middle English: from DEEP + -TH², on the pattern of pairs such as *long, length.*

depth charge ▶ **noun** an explosive charge designed to be dropped from a ship or aircraft and to explode under water at a preset depth, used for attacking submarines.

depth finder ▶ **noun** an echo sounder or other device for measuring water depth.

depth gauge ▶ **noun** a device fitted to a drill bit to ensure that the hole drilled does not exceed the required depth.

depthless ▶ **adjective 1** too deep to be measured: *a depthless gorge.*
2 shallow and superficial.
– DERIVATIVES **depthlessly** adverb.

depth of field ▶ **noun** (in photography) the distance between the nearest and the furthest objects giving a focused image.

depth of focus ▶ **noun 1** another term for DEPTH OF FIELD.
2 the distance between the two extreme axial points behind a lens at which an image is judged to be in focus.

depth psychology ▶ **noun** [mass noun] the study of unconscious mental processes and motives, especially in psychoanalytic theory and practice.

depth sounder ▶ **noun** another term for ECHO SOUNDER.

depuration /dɪpjʊəˈreɪʃ(ə)n, dɛpjʊˈreɪʃ(ə)n/ ▶ **noun** [mass noun] technical the action or process of freeing something of impurities.
– DERIVATIVES **depurate** verb, **depurative** adjective & noun.
– ORIGIN early 17th cent.: from Latin *depuratio(n-)*, from the verb *depurare*, from *de-* 'completely' + *purare* 'purify' (from *purus* 'pure').

deputation ▶ **noun** a group of people appointed to undertake a mission or take part in a formal process

D

on behalf of a larger group: *he had been a member of a deputation to Napoleon III.*
– ORIGIN late Middle English (in the sense 'appointment to an office or function'): from late Latin *deputatio(n-)*, from the verb *deputare* (see DEPUTE).

depute ▶ verb /dɪˈpjuːt/ [with obj. and infinitive] appoint or instruct (someone) to perform a task for which one is responsible: *she was deputed to look after him while Clare was away.* ■ [with obj.] delegate (authority or a task).
▶ noun /ˈdɛpjuːt/ Scottish a person appointed to act in an official capacity or as a representative of another official: [as modifier] *a depute chairman.*
– ORIGIN late Middle English: via Old French from Latin *deputare* 'consider to be, assign', from *de-* 'away' + *putare* 'consider'.

D

deputize /ˈdɛpjʊtʌɪz/ (also **deputise**) ▶ verb [no obj.] temporarily act or speak on behalf of someone else: *the post-holder is required to **deputize for** the manager in their absence.* ■ [with obj.] N. Amer. make (someone) a deputy.

deputy ▶ noun (pl. **deputies**) a person who is appointed to undertake the duties of a superior in the superior's absence. ■ a parliamentary representative in certain countries. ■ Brit. a coal mine official responsible for safety.
– PHRASES **by deputy** historical instructing another person to act in one's stead; by proxy.
– DERIVATIVES **deputyship** noun.
– ORIGIN late Middle English: from Old French *depute*, from late Latin *deputatus*, past participle of *deputare* (see DEPUTE).

deputy lieutenant ▶ noun (in the UK) the deputy of the Lord Lieutenant of a county.

dequeue ▶ verb (**dequeues**, **dequeuing** or **dequeueing**, **dequeued**) [with obj.] Computing remove (an item of data awaiting processing) from a queue of such items.

De Quincey /də ˈkwɪnsi/, Thomas (1785–1859), English essayist and critic. He achieved fame with his *Confessions of an English Opium Eater* (1822), a study of his addiction to opium and its psychological effects.

deracinate /dɪˈrasɪneɪt/ ▶ verb [with obj.] (usu. as adj. **deracinated**) uproot (someone) from their natural geographical, social, or cultural environment: *a deracinated writer who has complicated relations with his working-class background.*
– DERIVATIVES **deracination** noun.
– ORIGIN late 16th cent.: from French *déraciner*, from *dé-* (expressing removal) + *racine* 'root' (based on Latin *radix*).

déraciné /deɪˈrasɪneɪ/, French /deʀasine/ ▶ adjective (of a person) deracinated: *the self-consciousness of déraciné Americans.*
▶ noun a person who has been or feels deracinated.
– ORIGIN French, 'uprooted'.

derail ▶ verb [with obj.] cause (a train or tram) to leave its tracks accidentally: *a train was derailed after it collided with a herd of cattle.* ■ [no obj.] (of a train or tram) accidentally leave the tracks. ■ [with obj.] obstruct (a process) by diverting it from its intended course: *the plot is seen by some as an attempt to derail the negotiations.*
– DERIVATIVES **derailment** noun.
– ORIGIN mid 19th cent.: from French *dérailler*, from *dé-* (expressing removal) + *rail* 'rail'.

derailleur /dɪˈreɪl(j)ə/ ▶ noun a bicycle gear which works by lifting the chain from one sprocket wheel to another of a different size.
– ORIGIN 1930s: from French, from *dérailler* 'derail'.

Derain /ˈdərã/, French /dəʀɛ̃/, André (1880–1954), French painter, one of the exponents of Fauvism. He also designed theatre sets and costumes, notably for the Ballets Russes.

derange ▶ verb [with obj.] **1** make (someone) insane: *that business last month must have deranged him a bit.* ■ cause (something) to act irregularly: *stress deranges the immune system.*
2 archaic intrude on; disturb: *I am sorry to have deranged you for so small a matter.*
– DERIVATIVES **derangement** noun.
– ORIGIN late 18th cent.: from French *déranger*, from Old French *desrengier*, literally 'move from orderly rows'.

deranged ▶ adjective mad; insane: *a deranged gunman.*

derate ▶ verb [with obj.] **1** Brit. (under the former rates system) remove part or all of the burden of rates from (a property or business).
2 reduce the power rating of (a component or device): *the engines were derated to 90 horse power.*

deration ▶ verb [with obj.] free (a commodity) of rationing restrictions.

Derbent /dəˈbɛnt/ a city in southern Russia, in Dagestan on the western shore of the Caspian Sea; pop. 109,000 (est. 2008).

Derby[1] /ˈdɑːbi/ a city in the Midlands of England, on the River Derwent; pop. 244,700 (est. 2009).

Derby[2] /ˈdɑːbi/, Edward George Geoffrey Smith Stanley, 14th Earl of (1799–1869), British Conservative statesman, Prime Minister 1852, 1858–9, and 1866–8. In his last term as Prime Minister he carried the second Reform Act (1867) through Parliament.

Derby[3] /ˈdɑːbi/ ▶ noun (pl. **Derbies**) **1** an annual flat race for three-year-old horses, founded in 1780 by the 12th Earl of Derby and run on Epsom Downs in England in late May or early June. ■ a similar race elsewhere: *the Irish Derby.* ■ [often in names] (also **derby**) an important sporting contest: *the showjumping Derby at Hickstead.* ■ (**derby**; also **local derby**) Brit. a sports match between two rival teams from the same area.
2 (**derby**) N. Amer. a bowler hat. [said to be from American demand for a hat of the type worn at the Epsom Derby.]
3 a boot or shoe having the eyelet tabs stitched on top of the vamp.

Derby[4] /ˈdɑːbi/ ▶ noun [mass noun] a hard cheese made from skimmed milk, chiefly in Derbyshire.

Derby Day ▶ noun the day on which the Derby is run.

Derbyshire /ˈdɑːbɪʃɪə, -ʃə/ a county of north central England; county town, Matlock.

de re /deɪ ˈreɪ, diː/ ▶ adjective Philosophy relating to the properties of things mentioned in an assertion or expression, rather than to the assertion or expression itself. Compare with DE DICTO.
– ORIGIN Latin, literally 'about the thing'.

derealization (also **derealisation**) ▶ noun [mass noun] a feeling that one's surroundings are not real, especially as a symptom of mental disturbance.

derecho /dɪˈreɪtʃəʊ/ ▶ noun (pl. **derechos**) US a storm system that moves a long distance rapidly and brings winds which can devastate an area several miles wide.
– ORIGIN late 19th cent.: Spanish, literally 'direct, straight'.

derecognize (also **derecognise**) ▶ verb [with obj.] withdraw recognition of (an organization or country).
– DERIVATIVES **derecognition** noun.

dereference /diːˈrɛfərəns/ ▶ verb [with obj.] Computing obtain the address of a data item held in another location from (a pointer).

deregister ▶ verb [with obj.] remove from a register: *scores of patients have been deregistered by the practices.* ■ [no obj.] remove one's name from a register.
– DERIVATIVES **deregistration** noun.

de règle /də ˈrɛgl(ə)/, French /də ʀɛgl/ ▶ adjective required by custom; proper: *it shall be de règle for guests to come in afternoon dresses.*
– ORIGIN French, literally 'of rule'.

deregulate ▶ verb [with obj.] remove regulations or restrictions from: *the trucking industry was deregulated in the early 1980s.*
– DERIVATIVES **deregulation** noun, **deregulatory** adjective.

derelict ▶ adjective **1** in a very poor condition as a result of disuse and neglect: *a derelict Georgian mansion | the barge **lay derelict** for years.*
2 chiefly N. Amer. shamefully negligent of one's duties or obligations: *he was **derelict in** his duty to his country.*
▶ noun **1** a person without a home, job, or property.
2 a ship or other piece of property abandoned by the owner and in poor condition.
– ORIGIN mid 17th cent.: from Latin *derelictus* 'abandoned', past participle of *derelinquere*, from *de-* 'completely' + *relinquere* 'forsake'.

dereliction ▶ noun [mass noun] **1** the state of having been abandoned and become dilapidated: *a 15th-century farmhouse has been saved from dereliction.*
2 (**dereliction of duty**) the shameful failure to fulfil one's obligations.
– ORIGIN late 16th cent.: from Latin *derelictio(n-)*, from the verb *derelinquere* (see DERELICT).

derepress /ˌdiːrɪˈprɛs/ ▶ verb [with obj.] Biochemistry & Genetics activate (enzymes, genes, etc.) from an inoperative or latent state.
– DERIVATIVES **derepression** noun.

derequisition ▶ verb [with obj.] dated return (requisitioned property) to its former owner.

derestrict ▶ verb [with obj.] remove restrictions from.
– DERIVATIVES **derestriction** noun.

deride /dɪˈrʌɪd/ ▶ verb [with obj.] express contempt for; ridicule: *the decision was derided by environmentalists.*
– DERIVATIVES **derider** noun.
– ORIGIN mid 16th cent.: from Latin *deridere* 'scoff at'.

de rigueur /ˌdə rɪˈgəː/ ▶ adjective required by etiquette or current fashion: *it was de rigueur for bands to grow their hair long.*
– ORIGIN mid 19th cent.: French, literally 'in strictness'.

derision /dɪˈrɪʒ(ə)n/ ▶ noun [mass noun] contemptuous ridicule or mockery: *my stories were greeted with derision and disbelief.*
– PHRASES **hold** (or **have**) **in derision** archaic regard with mockery.
– DERIVATIVES **derisible** /dɪˈrɪzɪb(ə)l/ adjective.
– ORIGIN late Middle English: via Old French from late Latin *derisio(n-)*, from *deridere* 'scoff at'.

derisive /dɪˈrʌɪsɪv, -z-/ ▶ adjective expressing contempt or ridicule: *he gave a harsh, derisive laugh.*
– DERIVATIVES **derisively** adverb, **derisiveness** noun.
– ORIGIN mid 17th cent.: from DERISION, on the pattern of the pair *decision, decisive.*

derisory /dɪˈrʌɪs(ə)ri, -z-/ ▶ adjective **1** ridiculously small or inadequate: *they were given a derisory pay rise.*
2 another term for DERISIVE: *his derisory gaze swept over her.*
– ORIGIN early 17th cent. (in the sense 'derisive'): from late Latin *derisorius*, from *deris-* 'scoffed at', from the verb *deridere* (see DERISION).

> **USAGE** Although the words **derisory** and **derisive** share similar roots they have different core meanings. **Derisory** usually means 'ridiculously small or inadequate', as in *a **derisory** pay offer* or *the security arrangements were **derisory***. **Derisive**, on the other hand, is used to mean 'showing contempt', as in *he gave a **derisive** laugh.*

derivate /ˈdɛrɪvət, -eɪt/ ▶ noun something derived, especially a product obtained chemically from a raw material.
– ORIGIN late Middle English: from Latin *derivat-* 'derived', from the verb *derivare* (see DERIVE).

derivation ▶ noun [mass noun] **1** the action of obtaining something from a source or origin: *the **derivation of** scientific laws **from** observation.* ■ the formation of a word from another word or from a root in the same or another language. ■ origin; extraction: *music of primarily Turkish derivation.* ■ [count noun] something derived; a derivative.
2 Linguistics the set of stages that link a sentence in a natural language to its underlying logical form.
3 Mathematics the process of deducing a new formula, theorem, etc., from previously accepted statements. ■ [count noun] a sequence of statements showing that a formula, theorem, etc., is a consequence of previously accepted statements.
– DERIVATIVES **derivational** adjective.
– ORIGIN late Middle English (denoting the drawing of a fluid, especially pus or blood; also in the sense 'formation of a word from another word'): from Latin *derivatio(n-)*, from the verb *derivare* (see DERIVE).

derivative /dɪˈrɪvətɪv/ ▶ adjective **1** imitative of the work of another artist, writer, etc., and usually disapproved of for that reason: *an artist who is not in the slightest bit derivative.* ■ originating from, based on, or influenced by: *Darwin's work is **derivative of** the moral philosophers.*
2 [attrib.] (of a financial product) having a value deriving from an underlying variable asset: *equity-based derivative products.*
▶ noun **1** something which is based on another source: *the aircraft is a derivative of the Falcon 20G.* ■ a word derived from another or from a root in the same or another language. ■ a substance that is derived chemically from a specified compound: *crack is a highly addictive cocaine derivative.*
2 (often **derivatives**) a financial product (such as a future, option, or warrant) whose value derives from and is dependent on the value of an underlying asset.
3 Mathematics an expression representing the rate of change of a function with respect to an independent variable.
– DERIVATIVES **derivatively** adverb.
– ORIGIN late Middle English (in the adjective sense 'having the power to draw off', and in the noun

sense 'a word derived from another'): from French *dérivatif, -ive*, from Latin *derivativus*, from *derivare* (see DERIVE).

derive /dɪˈrʌɪv/ ▶ **verb** [with obj.] (**derive something from**) obtain something from (a specified source): *they derived great comfort from this assurance.* ■ (**derive something from**) base a concept on an extension or modification of (another concept): *some maintain that he derived the idea of civil disobedience from Thoreau.* ■ [no obj.] (**derive from**) (of a word) have (a specified word, usually of another language) as a root or origin: *the word 'punch' derives from the Hindustani 'pancha'* | [with obj.] *the word 'man' is derived from the Sanskrit 'manas'.* ■ [no obj.] (**derive from**) arise from or originate in (a specified source): *words whose spelling derives from Dr Johnson's incorrect etymology.* ■ (**be derived from**) Linguistics (of a sentence in a natural language) be linked by a set of stages to (its underlying logical form). ■ (**be derived from**) (of a substance) be formed or prepared by (a chemical or physical process affecting another substance): *strong acids are derived from the combustion of fossil fuels.* ■ Mathematics obtain (a function or equation) from another by a sequence of logical steps, for example by differentiation.
– DERIVATIVES **derivable** adjective.
– ORIGIN late Middle English (in the sense 'draw a fluid through or into a channel'): from Old French *deriver* or Latin *derivare*, from *de-* 'down, away' + *rivus* 'brook, stream'.

derived demand ▶ **noun** Economics a demand for a commodity, service, etc. which is a consequence of the demand for something else.

derived fossil ▶ **noun** a fossil redeposited in a sediment which is younger than the one in which it first occurred.

derm /dəːm/ ▶ **noun** another term for DERMIS.

derma /ˈdəːmə/ ▶ **noun** another term for DERMIS.
– ORIGIN early 18th cent.: modern Latin, from Greek 'skin'.

dermabrasion /ˌdəːməˈbreɪʒ(ə)n/ ▶ **noun** [mass noun] (in cosmetic surgery) the removal of superficial layers of skin with a rapidly revolving abrasive tool.
– ORIGIN 1950s: from Greek *derma* 'skin' + ABRASION.

Dermaptera /dəːˈmaptərə/ ▶ **plural noun** Entomology an order of insects that comprises the earwigs.
– DERIVATIVES **dermapteran** noun & adjective.
– ORIGIN modern Latin (plural), from Greek *derma* 'skin' + *pteron* 'wing'.

dermatitis /ˌdəːməˈtʌɪtɪs/ ▶ **noun** [mass noun] a condition of the skin in which it becomes red, swollen, and sore, sometimes with small blisters, resulting from direct irritation of the skin by an external agent or an allergic reaction to it. Compare with ECZEMA.
– ORIGIN late 19th cent.: from Greek *derma, dermat-* 'skin' + -ITIS.

dermato- /ˈdəːmətəʊ/ ▶ **combining form** relating to the skin: *dermatomycosis*.
– ORIGIN from Greek *derma, dermat-* 'skin, hide'.

dermatoglyphics /ˌdəːmətə(ʊ)ˈglɪfɪks/ ▶ **plural noun** [treated as sing.] the study of skin markings or patterns on fingers, hands, and feet, and its application, especially in criminology.
– DERIVATIVES **dermatoglyphic** adjective.
– ORIGIN 1920s: from DERMATO- 'skin' + Greek *gluphikos* 'carved' (from *gluphē* 'carving').

dermatology /ˌdəːməˈtɒlədʒi/ ▶ **noun** [mass noun] the branch of medicine concerned with the diagnosis and treatment of skin disorders.
– DERIVATIVES **dermatologic** adjective, **dermatological** adjective, **dermatologically** adverb, **dermatologist** noun.

dermatome /ˈdəːmətəʊm/ ▶ **noun** Embryology the lateral wall of each somite in a vertebrate embryo, giving rise to the connective tissue of the skin. Compare with MYOTOME, SCLEROTOME. ■ Physiology an area of the skin supplied by nerves from a single spinal root.

dermatomycosis /ˌdəːmətə(ʊ)mʌɪˈkəʊsɪs/ ▶ **noun** (pl. **dermatomycoses** /-siːz/) [mass noun] a fungal infection of the skin, especially by a dermatophyte.

dermatomyositis /ˌdəːmətə(ʊ)mʌɪə(ʊ)ˈsʌɪtɪs/ ▶ **noun** [mass noun] Medicine inflammation of the skin and underlying muscle tissue, involving degeneration of collagen, discoloration, and swelling, typically occurring as an autoimmune condition or associated with internal cancer.

dermatophyte /ˈdəːmətə(ʊ)fʌɪt/ ▶ **noun** a pathogenic fungus that grows on skin, mucous membranes, hair, nails, feathers, and other body surfaces, causing ringworm and related diseases. ● *Trichophyton* and other genera, subdivision Deuteromycotina.
– DERIVATIVES **dermatophytic** adjective.

dermatophytosis /ˌdəːmətə(ʊ)fʌɪˈtəʊsɪs/ ▶ **noun** (pl. **dermatophytoses** /-siːz/) another term for DERMATOMYCOSIS.

dermatosis /ˌdəːməˈtəʊsɪs/ ▶ **noun** (pl. **dermatoses** /-siːz/) [mass noun] a disease of the skin, especially one that does not cause inflammation.

dermestid /dəːˈmɛstɪd/ ▶ **noun** Entomology a small beetle of a family (Dermestidae) that includes many kinds which are destructive (especially as larvae) to hides, skin, fur, wool, and other animal substances.
– ORIGIN late 19th cent.: from modern Latin *Dermestidae* (plural), from the genus name *Dermestes*, formed irregularly from Greek *derma* 'skin' + *esthiein* 'eat'.

dermis /ˈdəːmɪs/ ▶ **noun** [mass noun] technical the skin. ■ Anatomy the thick layer of living tissue below the epidermis which forms the true skin, containing blood capillaries, nerve endings, sweat glands, hair follicles, and other structures.
– DERIVATIVES **dermal** adjective.
– ORIGIN mid 19th cent.: modern Latin, suggested by *epidermis*.

dermoid cyst ▶ **noun** Medicine an abnormal growth (teratoma) containing epidermis, hair follicles, and sebaceous glands, derived from residual embryonic cells.

Dermoptera /dəːˈmɒptərə/ ▶ **plural noun** Zoology a small order of mammals which comprises the flying lemurs or colugos.
– DERIVATIVES **dermopteran** noun & adjective.
– ORIGIN modern Latin (plural), from Greek *derma* 'skin' + *pteron* 'wing'.

dernier cri /dɛːnjeɪ ˈkriː/ ▶ **noun** (**the/le dernier cri**) the very latest fashion.
– ORIGIN late 19th cent.: French, literally 'last cry'.

derogate /ˈdɛrəgeɪt/ ▶ **verb** formal **1** [no obj.] (**derogate from**) detract from: *this does not derogate from his duty to act honestly and faithfully.*
2 [no obj.] (**derogate from**) deviate from (a set of rules or agreed form of behaviour): *one country has derogated from the Rome Convention.*
3 [with obj.] disparage (someone or something): *it is typical of him to derogate the powers of reason.*
– DERIVATIVES **derogative** adjective.
– ORIGIN late Middle English: from Latin *derogat-* 'abrogated', from the verb *derogare*, from *de-* 'aside, away' + *rogare* 'ask'.

derogation ▶ **noun 1** an exemption from or relaxation of a rule or law: *countries assuming a derogation from EC law.*
2 [mass noun] the perception or treatment of someone or something as being of little worth: *the derogation of women.*
– ORIGIN late Middle English (in the sense 'impairment of the force of'): from Latin *derogatio(n-)*, from the verb *derogare* (see DEROGATE).

derogatory /dɪˈrɒgət(ə)ri/ ▶ **adjective** showing a critical or disrespectful attitude: *she tells me I'm fat and is always making derogatory remarks.*
– DERIVATIVES **derogatorily** adverb.
– ORIGIN early 16th cent. (in the sense 'impairing in force or effect'): from late Latin *derogatorius*, from *derogat-* 'abrogated', from the verb *derogare* (see DEROGATE).

derrick /ˈdɛrɪk/ ▶ **noun 1** a kind of crane with a movable pivoted arm for moving heavy weights, especially on a ship.
2 the framework over an oil well or similar boring, holding the drilling machinery.
– ORIGIN early 17th cent. (denoting a hangman, also the gallows): from *Derrick*, the surname of a London hangman.

Derrida /ˈdɛrɪdə/, French /dɛrida/, Jacques (1930–2004), French philosopher and critic, the most important figure in deconstructionism. Notable works: *Of Grammatology* (1967) and *Writing and Difference* (1967).
– DERIVATIVES **Derridean** /ˌdɛrɪˈdɪən/ adjective & noun.

derrière /ˌdɛrɪˈɛː/ ▶ **noun** euphemistic a person's buttocks.
– ORIGIN late 18th cent.: French, literally 'behind'.

derring-do /ˌdɛrɪŋˈduː/ ▶ **noun** [mass noun] dated or humorous action displaying heroic courage: *tales of derring-do.*
– ORIGIN late 16th cent.: from late Middle English *dorryng do* 'daring to do', used by Chaucer, and, in a passage by Lydgate based on Chaucer's work, misprinted in 16th-cent. editions as *derrynge do*; this was misinterpreted by Spenser to mean 'manhood, chivalry', and subsequently taken up and popularized by Sir Walter Scott.

derringer /ˈdɛrɪn(d)ʒə/ ▶ **noun** a small pistol with a large bore, which is very effective at close range.
– ORIGIN mid 19th cent.: named after Henry *Deringer* (1786–1868), the American gunsmith who invented it.

derris /ˈdɛrɪs/ ▶ **noun 1** [mass noun] an insecticide containing rotenone, made from the powdered roots of certain tropical plants.
2 a woody climbing plant of the pea family, which has tuberous roots from which the insecticide derris is obtained. ● Genus *Derris*, family Leguminosae.
– ORIGIN mid 19th cent. (in sense 2): modern Latin (genus name), from Greek, 'leather covering' (referring to the plant's leathery pods).

D

derro /ˈdɛrəʊ/ ▶ **noun** (pl. **derros**) Austral./NZ informal a vagrant, especially one who is dependent on alcohol.
– ORIGIN 1970s: abbreviation of DERELICT + -O.

Derry see LONDONDERRY.

derry ▶ **noun** (in phrase **have a derry on**) Austral./NZ informal have a strong dislike for.
– ORIGIN late 19th cent.: apparently from the song refrain *derry down*, used humorously for *down* in the sense 'dislike'.

derv (also **DERV**) ▶ **noun** [mass noun] Brit. diesel oil for road vehicles.
– ORIGIN 1940s (apparently Second World War forces' slang): acronym from *diesel-engined road vehicle*.

dervish /ˈdəːvɪʃ/ ▶ **noun** a member of a Muslim (specifically Sufi) religious order who has taken vows of poverty and austerity. Dervishes first appeared in the 12th century; they were noted for their wild or ecstatic rituals and were known as **dancing**, **whirling**, or **howling dervishes** according to the practice of their order.
– ORIGIN from Turkish *derviş*, from Persian *darvīš* 'poor', (as a noun) 'religious mendicant'.

DES ▶ **abbreviation** ■ Computing data encryption standard. ■ (formerly in the UK) Department of Education and Science.

desacralize /diːˈsakrəlʌɪz/ (also **desacralise**) ▶ **verb** [with obj.] remove the religious or sacred status or significance from.
– DERIVATIVES **desacralization** noun.

de Sade, Marquis, see SADE.

desalinate /diːˈsalɪneɪt/ ▶ **verb** [with obj.] (usu. as adj. **desalinated**) remove salt from (seawater).
– DERIVATIVES **desalination** noun, **desalinator** noun.

desalinize ▶ **verb** US term for DESALINATE.
– DERIVATIVES **desalinization** noun.

desalt ▶ **verb** another term for DESALINATE.

desaparecido /ˌdɛzəpærəˈsiːdəʊ/, Spanish /desapareˈsiðo, -ˈθiðo/ ▶ **noun** (pl. **desaparecidos**) (especially in South America) a person who has disappeared, presumed killed by members of the armed services or the police.
– ORIGIN Spanish, literally 'disappeared'.

desaturate ▶ **verb** [with obj.] make unsaturated or less saturated.
– DERIVATIVES **desaturation** noun.

descale ▶ **verb** [with obj.] Brit. remove deposits of scale from.
– DERIVATIVES **descaler** noun.

descamisado /dɛsˌkamɪˈsɑːdəʊ/ ▶ **noun** (pl. **descamisados**) (in Latin America) a very poor person.
– ORIGIN Spanish, literally 'shirtless'.

descant ▶ **noun** /ˈdɛskant/ **1** Music an independent treble melody sung or played above a basic melody. ■ archaic or literary a melodious song.
2 literary a discourse on a theme: *his descant of deprivation.*
▶ **verb** /dɪˈskant, dɛ-/ [no obj.] literary talk tediously or at length: *I have descanted on this subject before.*
– ORIGIN late Middle English: from Old French *deschant*, from medieval Latin *discantus* 'part-song, refrain'.

descant recorder ▶ **noun** the most common size of recorder (musical instrument), with a range of two octaves from the C above middle C upwards.

Descartes /ˈdeɪkɑːt/, French /dekaʀt/, René (1596–1650), French philosopher, mathematician, and man of science.

Aiming to reach totally secure foundations for knowledge, Descartes concluded that everything was open to doubt except his own conscious experience, and his existence as a necessary condition of this: '*Cogito, ergo sum*' (I think, therefore I am). From this certainty he developed a dualistic theory regarding mind and matter as separate though interacting. In mathematics Descartes developed the use of coordinates to locate a point in two or three dimensions.

D

descend ▸ verb [no obj.] **1** move or fall downwards: *the aircraft began to descend.* ■ [with obj.] move down (a slope or stairs): *the vehicle descended a ramp.* ■ (of a road, path, or flight of steps) slope or lead downwards: *a side road descended into the forest* | [with obj.] *a flight of stairs descended a steep slope.* ■ move down a scale of quality: (as adj. **descending**) *the categories are listed in descending order of usefulness.* ■ Music (of sound) become lower in pitch: (as adj. **descending**) *a passage of descending chords.* ■ (**descend to**) act in a shameful way that is far below one's usual standards: *he was scrupulous in refusing to descend to misrepresentation.* ■ (**descend into**) (of a situation or group of people) reach (an undesirable state): *the army had descended into chaos.*
2 (**descend on/upon**) make a sudden attack on: *the militia descended on Rye.* ■ (**descend on/upon**) make an unexpected visit to: *groups of visiting supporters descended on a local pub.* ■ (of a feeling) develop suddenly and affect a place or person: *an air of gloom descended on Labour Party headquarters.* ■ (of night or darkness) begin to occur: *as the winter darkness descended, the fighting ceased.*
3 (**be descended from**) be a blood relative of (a specified ancestor): *John Dalrymple* ***was descended from*** *an ancient Ayrshire family.* ■ (of an asset) pass by inheritance, typically from parent to child: *his lands* ***descended to*** *his eldest son.*
– DERIVATIVES **descendent** adjective.
– ORIGIN Middle English: from Old French *descendre*, from Latin *descendere*, from *de-* 'down' + *scandere* 'to climb'.

descendant ▸ noun a person, plant, or animal that is descended from a particular ancestor: *she's a descendant of Charles Darwin.* ■ a machine, artefact, system, etc., that has developed from an earlier, more rudimentary version: *house music is a descendant of disco.*
– ORIGIN late Middle English (as an adjective in the sense 'descending'): from French, present participle of *descendre* 'to descend' (see DESCEND). The noun dates from the early 17th cent.

USAGE The correct spelling for the noun meaning 'person descended from a particular ancestor' is **descendant**, not **-ent**. **Descendent** is a less common adjective meaning 'descending from an ancestor'. Almost 15 per cent of the citations for the term in the Oxford English Corpus use the wrong spelling.

descender ▸ noun a part of a letter that extends below the level of the base of a letter such as *x* (as in *g* and *p*). ■ a letter having a descender.

descendeur /dɪˈsɛndə/ ▸ noun Climbing a piece of metal around which a rope is passed, which makes use of friction to slow descent during abseiling.
– ORIGIN late 20th cent.: from French, literally 'descender'.

descendible ▸ adjective Law (of property) eligible to be inherited by a descendant.

descending colon ▸ noun Anatomy the part of the large intestine which passes downwards on the left side of the abdomen towards the rectum.

descent ▸ noun **1** [usu. in sing.] an act of moving downwards, dropping, or falling: *the plane had gone into a steep descent.* ■ a downward slope: *a steep, badly eroded descent.* ■ a moral, social, or psychological decline: *the ancient empire's slow* ***descent into*** *barbarism.*
2 [mass noun] the origin or background of a person in terms of family or nationality: *the settlers were* ***of*** *Cornish* ***descent.*** ■ the transmission of qualities, property, or privileges by inheritance.
3 (**descent on**) a sudden violent attack: *a descent on the Channel ports.* ■ an unexpected visit.
– ORIGIN Middle English: from Old French *descente*, from *descendre* 'to descend' (see DESCEND).

descramble ▸ verb [with obj.] convert or restore (a signal) to intelligible form.
– DERIVATIVES **descrambler** noun.

describe ▸ verb [with obj.] **1** give a detailed account in words of: *he described his experiences in a letter to his parents.*
2 mark out or draw (a geometrical figure): *on the diameter of a circle an equilateral triangle is described.* ■ move in a way which follows the outline of (an imaginary geometrical figure): *a single light is seen to describe a circle.*
– DERIVATIVES **describable** adjective, **describer** noun.
– ORIGIN late Middle English: from Latin *describere*, from *de-* 'down' + *scribere* 'write'.

description ▸ noun **1** a spoken or written account of a person, object, or event: *people who had seen him were able to give a description.* ■ [mass noun] the action of giving a spoken or written account: *the emphasis was placed on explanation rather than description.*
2 a type or class of people or things: *it is laughably easy to buy drugs* ***of all descriptions.***
– PHRASES **beyond description** to a great and astonishing extent: *his face was swollen beyond description.* **defy description** be so unusual or remarkable as to be impossible to describe.
– ORIGIN late Middle English: via Old French from Latin *descriptio(n-)*, from *describere* 'write down'.

descriptive ▸ adjective **1** serving or seeking to describe: *the text contains some good descriptive passages.* ■ Grammar (of an adjective) assigning a quality rather than restricting the application of the expression modified, e.g. *blue* as distinct from *few*.
2 describing or classifying in an objective and non-judgemental way. ■ Linguistics denoting or relating to an approach to language analysis that describes accents, forms, structures, and usage without making value judgements. Often contrasted with PRESCRIPTIVE.
– DERIVATIVES **descriptively** adverb, **descriptiveness** noun.
– ORIGIN mid 18th cent.: from late Latin *descriptivus*, from *descript-* 'written down', from the verb *describere* (see DESCRIBE).

descriptivism ▸ noun [mass noun] Philosophy the doctrine that the meanings of ethical or aesthetic terms and statements are purely descriptive rather than prescriptive, evaluative, or emotive.
– DERIVATIVES **descriptivist** noun & adjective.

descriptor ▸ noun **1** Linguistics a word or expression used to describe or identify something.
2 Computing a piece of stored data that indicates how other data is stored.

descry /dɪˈskrʌɪ/ ▸ verb (**descries, descrying, descried**) [with obj.] literary catch sight of: *she descried two figures.*
– ORIGIN Middle English: Old French *descrier* 'publish, proclaim', perhaps confused with obsolete *descry* 'describe'.

desecrate /ˈdɛsɪkreɪt/ ▸ verb [with obj.] treat (a sacred place or thing) with violent disrespect: *more than 300 graves were desecrated.* ■ spoil (something which is valued or respected): *many lanes are desecrated with yellow lines.*
– DERIVATIVES **desecrator** noun.
– ORIGIN late 17th cent.: from DE- (expressing reversal) + a shortened form of CONSECRATE.

desecration ▸ noun [mass noun] the action of desecrating something: *the desecration of a grave.*

deseed ▸ verb [with obj.] (usu. as adj. **deseeded**) remove the seeds from (a plant, vegetable, or fruit).

desegregate ▸ verb [with obj.] end a policy of racial segregation in: *actions to desegregate schools.*
– DERIVATIVES **desegregation** noun.

deselect ▸ verb [with obj.] **1** Brit. (of a local branch of a political party) reject (an existing MP) as a candidate in a forthcoming election.
2 turn off (a selected feature) on a list of options on a computer menu.
– DERIVATIVES **deselection** noun.

desensitize (also **desensitise**) ▸ verb [with obj.] make less sensitive: *creams to desensitize the skin at the site of the injection.* ■ make (someone) less likely to feel shock or distress at scenes of cruelty or suffering by overexposure to such images: (as adj. **desensitized**) *people who view such movies become* ***desensitized to*** *violence.* ■ free (someone) from a phobia or neurosis by gradually exposing them to the thing that is feared. See SYSTEMATIC DESENSITIZATION.
– DERIVATIVES **desensitization** noun, **desensitizer** noun.

desert[1] /dɪˈzəːt/ ▸ verb [with obj.] abandon (a person, cause, or organization) in a way considered disloyal or treacherous: *he deserted his wife and daughter and went back to England.* ■ (of people) leave (a place), causing it to appear empty: *the tourists have deserted the beaches.* ■ (of a quality or ability) fail (someone) when most needed: *her luck deserted her.* ■ [no obj.] Military illegally leave the armed forces.
– ORIGIN late Middle English: from Old French *deserter*, from late Latin *desertare*, from Latin *desertus* 'left waste' (see DESERT[2]).

desert[2] /ˈdɛzət/ ▸ noun a waterless, desolate area of land with little or no vegetation, typically one covered with sand. ■ a situation or place considered dull and uninteresting: *a cultural desert.*
▸ adjective [attrib.] like a desert: *overgrazing has created desert conditions.* ■ uninhabited and desolate: *desert wastes.*
– ORIGIN Middle English: via Old French from late Latin *desertum* 'something left waste', neuter past participle of *deserere* 'leave, forsake'.

desert boot ▸ noun a lightweight boot with the upper made from suede.

deserted ▸ adjective (of a place) empty of people: *deserted beaches of soft sand.*

deserter ▸ noun a member of the armed forces who deserts: *deserters from the army.*

desertification /dɛˌzəːtɪfɪˈkeɪʃ(ə)n/ ▸ noun [mass noun] the process by which fertile land becomes desert, typically as a result of drought, deforestation, or inappropriate agriculture.

desertion ▸ noun [mass noun] the action of deserting a person, cause, or organization: *her guilt over her desertion of her husband.* ■ Military the action of illegally leaving the armed forces: *three officers were shot for desertion* | [count noun] *the number of desertions was rising.*

desert island ▸ noun a remote tropical island, typically an uninhabited one.

desert oak ▸ noun an Australian casuarina tree, which typically grows in arid regions. ● *Casuarina decaisneana*, family Casuarinaceae.

desert pavement ▸ noun Geology a surface layer of closely packed or cemented pebbles, rock fragments, etc., from which fine material has been removed by the wind in arid regions.

desert rat ▸ noun informal a soldier of the 7th British armoured division (with the jerboa as a badge) in the North African desert campaign of 1941–2.

desert rose ▸ noun **1** a flower-like aggregate of crystals of a mineral, occurring in arid areas.
2 a succulent plant with pink tubular flowers and a woody stem containing toxic milky sap, native to East Africa and Arabia. ● *Adenium obesum*, family Apocynaceae.
3 (also **Sturt's desert rose**) a dense shrub with pinkish-lilac flowers and black spotted leaves and fruit, native to arid regions of Australia. ● *Gossypium sturtianum*, family Malvaceae.

deserts /dɪˈzəːts/ ▸ plural noun what a person deserves with regard to reward or (more usually) punishment: *the penal system fails to punish offenders in accordance with their deserts.*
– PHRASES **get** (or **receive**) **one's just deserts** receive what one deserves, especially appropriate punishment: *those who caused great torment to others rarely got their just deserts.*
– ORIGIN Middle English: via Old French *desert*, from *deservir* 'serve well' (see DESERVE).

USAGE If a person gets their **just deserts** they get what they deserve. **Deserts** here is related to **deserve**, and is spelled with one *-s-* in the middle; a **dessert** is a sweet course eaten at the end of a meal. The *-ss-* spelling in the sense 'what a person deserves' is regarded as an error, although in the Oxford English Corpus it is almost as common as the correct spelling.

desert varnish ▸ noun [mass noun] Geology a dark hard film of oxides formed on exposed rock surfaces in arid regions.

deserve ▸ verb [with obj.] do something or have or show qualities worthy of (a reaction which rewards or punishes as appropriate): *the referee deserves a pat on the back* | [with infinitive] *we didn't deserve to win.*
– PHRASES **deserve a medal** have done something considered especially praiseworthy or heroic.
– ORIGIN Middle English: from Old French *deservir*, from Latin *deservire* 'serve well or zealously'.

deserved ▸ adjective rightfully earned because of something done or qualities shown; merited: *a deserved standing ovation.*

deservedly /dɪˈzəːvɪdli/ ▸ adverb in the way that is deserved; rightfully: *a deservedly popular sitcom* | *they are top of the league, and* ***deservedly so.***

deserving ▸ adjective worthy of being treated in a particular way, typically of being given assistance: *the deserving poor.*
– DERIVATIVES **deservingly** adverb, **deservingness** noun.

desex ▶ **verb** [with obj.] (usu. as adj. **desexed**) **1** deprive (someone) of sexual qualities or attraction: *Lawrence portrays feminists as shrill, humourless, and desexed.*
2 castrate or spay (an animal).

desexualize (also **desexualise**) ▶ **verb** [with obj.] deprive of sexual character or the distinctive qualities of a sex.
– DERIVATIVES **desexualization** noun.

desh /dɛʃ/ ▶ **noun** [mass noun] Indian a person's or a people's native land: *contrary to my visit in December, I have a very positive view about desh now.*
– ORIGIN from Hindi *deś*.

déshabillé /ˌdɛzaˈbiːjeɪ/ (also **dishabille**) ▶ **noun** [mass noun] the state of being only partly or scantily clothed: *the paintings of Venus all shared the same state of déshabillé.*
– ORIGIN French, 'undressed'.

desi /ˈdeɪsi/ (also **deshi** /ˈdeɪʃ(i)/) Indian ▶ **adjective**
1 local; indigenous: *desi liquor.* ■ derogatory rustic; unsophisticated.
2 unadulterated or pure: *desi ghee.*
▶ **noun** a person of Indian, Pakistani, or Bangladeshi birth or descent who lives abroad.
– ORIGIN via Hindi from Sanskrit *deśa* 'country, land'.

De Sica /də ˈsiːkə/, Vittorio (1901–74), Italian film director and actor, a key figure in Italian neo-realist cinema. Notable films: *Bicycle Thieves* (1948) and *Two Women* (1960), both of which won Oscars.

desiccant ▶ **noun** a hygroscopic substance used as a drying agent.
– ORIGIN late 17th cent.: from Latin *desiccant-* 'making thoroughly dry', from the verb *desiccare*.

desiccate /ˈdɛsɪkeɪt/ ▶ **verb** [with obj.] **1** (usu. as adj. **desiccated**) remove the moisture from (something), typically in order to preserve it: *desiccated coconut.*
2 (as adj. **desiccated**) lacking interest, passion, or energy: *a desiccated history of ideas.*
– DERIVATIVES **desiccation** noun.
– ORIGIN late 16th cent.: from Latin *desiccat-* 'made thoroughly dry', from the verb *desiccare*.

desiccator ▶ **noun** a glass container or other apparatus holding a drying agent for removing moisture from specimens and protecting them from water vapour in the air.

desiderate /dɪˈzɪdəreɪt, -ˈsɪd-/ ▶ **verb** [with obj.] archaic feel a keen desire for (something lacking or absent): *I desiderate the resources of a family.*
– ORIGIN mid 17th cent.: from Latin *desiderat-* 'desired', from the verb *desiderare*, perhaps from *de-* 'down' + *sidus, sider-* 'star'. Compare with **CONSIDER**.

desiderative /dɪˈzɪd(ə)rətɪv, -ˈsɪd-/ ▶ **adjective** Grammar (in Latin and other inflected languages) denoting a verb formed from another and expressing a desire to do the act denoted by the root verb (such as Latin *esurire* 'want to eat', from *edere* 'eat'). ■ having, expressing, or relating to desire.
– ORIGIN mid 16th cent.: from late Latin *desiderativus*, from Latin *desiderat-* 'desired', from the verb *desiderare* (see **DESIDERATE**).

desideratum /dɪˌzɪdəˈrɑːtəm, -ˈreɪtəm, -ˌsɪd-/ ▶ **noun** (pl. **desiderata** /-tə/) something that is needed or wanted: *integrity was a desideratum.*
– ORIGIN mid 17th cent.: from Latin, 'something desired', neuter past participle of *desiderare* (see **DESIDERATE**).

design ▶ **noun 1** a plan or drawing produced to show the look and function or workings of a building, garment, or other object before it is made: *he has just unveiled his design for the new museum.* ■ [mass noun] the art or action of conceiving of and producing a plan or drawing of something before it is made: *good design can help the reader understand complicated information.* ■ [mass noun] the arrangement of the features of an artefact, as produced from following a plan or drawing: *inside, the design reverts to turn-of-the-century luxe.*
2 a decorative pattern: *pottery with a lovely blue and white design.*
3 [mass noun] purpose or planning that exists behind an action, fact, or object: *the appearance of design in the universe.*
▶ **verb** [with obj.] decide upon the look and functioning of (a building, garment, or other object), by making a detailed drawing of it: *a number of architectural students were designing a factory* | (as adj., with submodifier **designed**) *specially designed buildings.* ■ do or plan (something) with a specific purpose in mind: [with obj. and infinitive] *the tax changes were designed to stimulate economic growth.*
– PHRASES **by design** as a result of a plan; intentionally: *I became a presenter by default rather than by design.* **have designs on** aim to obtain (something), typically in an underhand way: *he suspected her of having designs on the family fortune.* ■ informal have an undisclosed sexual interest in.
– ORIGIN late Middle English (as a verb in the sense 'to designate'): from Latin *designare* 'to designate', reinforced by French *désigner*. The noun is via French from Italian.

designate ▶ **verb** /ˈdɛzɪɡneɪt/ [with obj.] appoint (someone) to a specified office or post: *he was designated as prime minister.* ■ officially give a specified status or name to: [with obj. and complement] *the Wye Valley is designated an area of outstanding natural beauty* | *certain schools are designated 'science schools'.*
▶ **adjective** /ˈdɛzɪɡnət/ [postpositive] appointed to an office or post but not yet installed: *the Director designate.*
– DERIVATIVES **designator** noun.
– ORIGIN mid 17th cent. (as an adjective): from Latin *designatus* 'designated', past participle of *designare*, based on *signum* 'a mark'.

designated driver ▶ **noun** a person who abstains from alcohol at a social gathering so as to be fit to drive others home.

designated hitter ▶ **noun** Baseball a non-fielding player named before the start of a game to bat instead of the pitcher anywhere in the batting order.

designation ▶ **noun** [mass noun] the action of choosing someone to hold an office or post: *a leader's designation of his own successor.* ■ the action of choosing a place for a special purpose or giving it a special status: *Dibden Bay's designation as a Site of Special Scientific Interest.* ■ [count noun] an official name, description, or title: *quality designations such as 'Premier Cru'.*
– ORIGIN late Middle English (in the sense 'the action of marking'): from Latin *designatio(n-)*, from the verb *designare* (see **DESIGNATE**).

designedly ▶ **adverb** deliberately in order to produce a specific effect: *the goblet designedly left for him.*

designer ▶ **noun** a person who plans the look or workings of something prior to it being made, by preparing drawings or plans: *a leading car designer.* ■ [as modifier] made by a famous and prestigious fashion designer: *designer clothes.* ■ [as modifier] fashionable: *designer food.*

designer baby ▶ **noun** a baby whose genetic make-up has been selected in order to eradicate a particular defect, or to ensure that a particular gene is present.

designer drug ▶ **noun** a synthetic analogue of a legally restricted or prohibited drug, devised to circumvent drug laws.

designing ▶ **adjective** [attrib.] acting in a calculating, deceitful way: *a designing little minx.*

desirability ▶ **noun** [mass noun] the quality of being desirable: *we agree on the desirability of a negotiated settlement.*

desirable ▶ **adjective** wished for as being an attractive, useful, or necessary course of action: [with infinitive] *it is desirable to check that nothing has been forgotten.* ■ (of a person) arousing sexual desire: *you're a very desirable woman.*
▶ **noun** a desirable person or thing: *the store sells various desirables.*
– DERIVATIVES **desirableness** noun, **desirably** adverb.
– ORIGIN late Middle English: from Old French, suggested by Latin *desiderabilis*, from *desiderare* 'to desire' (see **DESIDERATE**).

desire ▶ **noun** a strong feeling of wanting to have something or wishing for something to happen: *he resisted public desires for choice in education.* ■ [mass noun] strong sexual feeling or appetite: *they were clinging together in fierce desire.* ■ something desired.
▶ **verb** [with obj.] strongly wish for or want (something): *he never achieved the status he so desired* | (as adj. **desired**) *the bribe had its desired effect.* ■ want (someone) sexually. ■ archaic express a wish to.
– ORIGIN Middle English: from Old French *desir* (noun), *desirer* (verb), from Latin *desiderare* (see **DESIDERATE**).

Desiree /dɪˈzɪəreɪ/ ▶ **noun** a potato of a pink-skinned variety with yellow waxy flesh.

desirous /dɪˈzʌɪərəs/ ▶ **adjective** [predic.] having or characterized by desire: *the pope was desirous of peace in Europe.*
– ORIGIN Middle English: from Old French *desireus*, based on Latin *desiderare* 'to desire' (see **DESIDERATE**).

desist /dɪˈzɪst, dɪˈsɪst/ ▶ **verb** [no obj.] stop doing something; cease or abstain: *each pledged to desist from acts of sabotage.*
– ORIGIN late Middle English: from Old French *desister*, from Latin *desistere*, from *de-* 'down from' + *sistere* 'to stop' (reduplication of *stare* 'to stand').

desk ▶ **noun 1** a piece of furniture with a flat or sloping surface and typically with drawers, at which one can read, write, or do other work.
2 a counter in a hotel, bank, or airport at which a customer may check in or obtain information: *the reception desk.*
3 [with modifier] a specified section of a newspaper or broadcasting organization: *he landed a job on the sports desk.*
4 Music a position in an orchestra at which two players share a music stand: *an extra desk of first and second violins.*
– ORIGIN late Middle English: from medieval Latin *desca*, probably based on Provençal *desca* 'basket' or Italian *desco* 'table, butcher's block', both based on Latin *discus* (see **DISCUS**).

desk-bound ▶ **adjective** restricted to working in an office, rather than in an active, physical capacity: *his contempt for the desk-bound staff behind the lines.*

desk diary ▶ **noun** a large diary designed for use in an office.

desk dictionary ▶ **noun** N. Amer. a one-volume dictionary of medium size.

deskill ▶ **verb** [with obj.] reduce the level of skill required to carry out (a job): *advances in technology had deskilled numerous working-class jobs.* ■ make the skills of (a worker) obsolete.

desk job ▶ **noun** a job based at a desk, especially as opposed to one in active military service.

desk jockey ▶ **noun** N. Amer. informal, chiefly derogatory a person who works at a desk; an office worker.

desk sergeant ▶ **noun** a sergeant in administrative charge of a police station.

desktop ▶ **noun** the working surface of a desk. ■ (also **desktop computer**) a computer suitable for use at an ordinary desk. ■ the working area of a computer screen regarded as a representation of a notional desktop and containing icons representing items such as files.

desktop publishing (abbreviation: **DTP**) ▶ **noun** [mass noun] the production of printed matter by means of a printer linked to a desktop computer, with special software. The system enables reports, advertising matter, etc., to be produced cheaply with a layout and print quality similar to that of typeset books.

desman /ˈdɛzmən/ ▶ **noun** a small semiaquatic European mammal related to the mole, with a long tubular muzzle and webbed toes. ● Family Talpidae: the **Russian desman** (*Desmana moschata*) and the **Pyrenean desman** (*Galemys pyrenaicus*).
– ORIGIN late 18th cent.: via French and German from Swedish *desman-råtta* 'muskrat', from *desman* 'musk'.

desmid /ˈdɛzmɪd/ ▶ **noun** Biology a single-celled freshwater alga which appears to be composed of two rigid cells with a shared nucleus. The presence of desmids is usually an indicator of unpolluted water. ● Family Desmidiaceae, division Chlorophyta (or phylum Gamophyta, kingdom Protista).
– ORIGIN mid 19th cent.: from modern Latin *Desmidium* (genus name), from Greek *desmos* 'band, chain' (because the algae are often found united in chains or masses).

desmoid /ˈdɛzmɔɪd/ ▶ **adjective** Medicine denoting a type of fibrous tumour of muscle and connective tissue, typically in the abdomen.
– ORIGIN mid 19th cent.: from Greek *desmos* 'bond' or *desmē* 'bundle' + **-OID**.

Des Moines /deɪ ˈmɔɪn/ the state capital and largest city of Iowa; pop. 197,052 (est. 2008).

desmosome /ˈdɛzməsəʊm/ ▶ **noun** Biology a structure by which two adjacent cells are attached, formed from protein plaques in the cell membranes linked by filaments.
– DERIVATIVES **desmosomal** adjective.
– ORIGIN 1930s: from Greek *desmos* 'bond, chain' + **-SOME**[3].

desolate ▶ **adjective** /ˈdɛs(ə)lət/ **1** (of a place) uninhabited and giving an impression of bleak emptiness: *a desolate Pennine moor.*
2 feeling or showing great unhappiness or loneliness: *I suddenly felt desolate and bereft.*

D

▸ **verb** /ˈdɛsəleɪt/ [with obj.] **1** make (a place) appear bleakly empty: *the droughts that desolated the dry plains.*
2 make (someone) feel utterly wretched and unhappy: *he was desolated by the deaths of his treasured friends.*
– DERIVATIVES **desolately** adverb, **desolateness** noun, **desolator** noun.
– ORIGIN late Middle English: from Latin *desolatus* 'abandoned', past participle of *desolare*, from *de-* 'thoroughly' + *solus* 'alone'.

desolation ▸ **noun** [mass noun] **1** a state of complete emptiness or destruction: *the stony desolation of the desert.*
2 great unhappiness or loneliness: *in choked desolation, she watched him leave.*
– ORIGIN late Middle English: from late Latin *desolatio(n-)*, from Latin *desolare* 'to abandon' (see DESOLATE).

desolder ▸ **verb** [with obj.] remove solder from.

desorb /diːˈsɔːb/ ▸ **verb** [with obj.] Chemistry cause the release of (an adsorbed substance) from a surface. ■ [no obj.] (of an adsorbed substance) become released.
– DERIVATIVES **desorbent** adjective & noun, **desorber** noun, **desorption** noun.
– ORIGIN 1920s: back-formation from *desorption* (from *de-* 'away' + *adsorption*).

despair ▸ **noun** [mass noun] the complete loss or absence of hope: *a voice full of self-hatred and despair* | *in despair, I hit the bottle.*
▸ **verb** [no obj.] lose or be without hope: *we should not despair* | *she **despaired of** finding a good restaurant nearby.*
– PHRASES **be the despair of** cause to lose hope: *such students can be the despair of conscientious teachers.*
– ORIGIN Middle English: the noun via Anglo-Norman French from Old French *desespeir*; the verb from Old French *desperer*, from Latin *desperare*, from *de-* 'down from' + *sperare* 'to hope'.

despairing ▸ **adjective** showing the loss of all hope: *he gave a despairing little shrug.*
– DERIVATIVES **despairingly** adverb.

despatch ▸ **verb & noun** Brit. variant spelling of DISPATCH.

desperado /ˌdɛspəˈrɑːdəʊ/ ▸ **noun** (pl. **desperadoes** or **desperados**) dated a desperate or reckless person, especially a criminal.
– ORIGIN early 17th cent.: pseudo-Spanish alteration of the obsolete noun *desperate*. Both *desperate* and *desperado* originally denoted a person in despair or in a desperate situation, hence someone made reckless by despair.

desperate ▸ **adjective 1** feeling or showing a hopeless sense that a situation is so bad as to be impossible to deal with: *a desperate sadness enveloped Ruth.* ■ (of an act) tried in despair or when everything else has failed: *drugs used in a desperate attempt to save his life.* ■ (of a situation) extremely serious or dangerous: *there is a desperate shortage of teachers.* ■ (of a person) violent or dangerous: *a desperate criminal.* ■ Irish informal very bad: *that beer's desperate—it's a wonder you've the nerve to offer it for sale.*
2 [predic.] (of a person) having a great need or desire for something: *I am **desperate for** a cigarette* | [with infinitive] *other women are desperate to get back to work.*
– PHRASES **desperate diseases must have desperate remedies** proverb extreme measures are justified as a response to a difficult or dangerous situation.
– DERIVATIVES **desperateness** noun.
– ORIGIN late Middle English (in the sense 'in despair'): from Latin *desperatus* 'deprived of hope', past participle of *desperare* (see DESPAIR).

desperately ▸ **adverb** in a way that shows despair: *he looked around desperately.* ■ used to emphasize the extreme degree of something: *he desperately needed a drink* | [as submodifier] *I am desperately disappointed.*

desperation ▸ **noun** [mass noun] a state of despair, typically one which results in rash or extreme behaviour: *she wrote to him **in desperation**.*
– ORIGIN late Middle English: from Old French, from Latin *desperatio(n-)*, from the verb *desperare* (see DESPAIR).

despicable /dɪˈspɪkəb(ə)l, ˈdɛspɪk-/ ▸ **adjective** deserving hatred and contempt: *a despicable crime.*
– DERIVATIVES **despicably** adverb.
– ORIGIN mid 16th cent.: from late Latin *despicabilis*, from *despicari* 'look down on'.

de Spinoza, Baruch, see SPINOZA.

despise /dɪˈspʌɪz/ ▸ **verb** [with obj.] feel contempt or a deep repugnance for: *he **despised** himself **for** being selfish.*
– DERIVATIVES **despiser** noun.
– ORIGIN Middle English: from Old French *despire*, from Latin *despicere*, from *de-* 'down' + *specere* 'look at'.

despite /dɪˈspʌɪt/ ▸ **preposition** without being affected by; in spite of: *he remains a great leader despite age and infirmity.*
▸ **noun** [mass noun] archaic **1** contemptuous treatment or behaviour; outrage: *the despite done by him to the holy relics.*
2 contempt; disdain: *the theatre only earns my despite.*
– PHRASES **despite oneself** used to indicate that one did not intend to do the thing mentioned: *despite herself Frau Nordern laughed.*
– DERIVATIVES **despiteful** adjective (archaic).
– ORIGIN Middle English (originally used as a noun meaning 'contempt, scorn' in the phrase *in despite of*): from Old French *despit*, from Latin *despectus* 'looking down on', past participle (used as a noun) of *despicere* (see DESPISE).

despoil /dɪˈspɔɪl/ ▸ **verb** [with obj.] steal or violently remove valuable possessions from; plunder: *the church was **despoiled of** its marble wall covering.*
– DERIVATIVES **despoiler** noun, **despoilment** noun.
– ORIGIN Middle English: from Old French *despoillier*, from Latin *despoliare* 'rob, plunder' (from *spolia* 'spoil').

despoliation /dɪˌspəʊlɪˈeɪʃ(ə)n/ ▸ **noun** [mass noun] the action of despoiling or the condition of being despoiled; plunder: *the despoliation of the resources of the natural world.*

despond /dɪˈspɒnd/ ▸ **verb** [no obj.] archaic become dejected and lose confidence.
– ORIGIN mid 17th cent.: from Latin *despondere* 'give up, abandon', from *de-* 'away' + *spondere* 'to promise'. The word was originally used as a noun in SLOUGH OF DESPOND.

despondency ▸ **noun** [mass noun] low spirits from loss of hope or courage; dejection: *an air of despondency.*

despondent ▸ **adjective** in low spirits from loss of hope or courage: *she grew more and more despondent.*
– DERIVATIVES **despondence** noun, **despondently** adverb.

despot /ˈdɛspɒt/ ▸ **noun** a ruler or other person who holds absolute power, typically one who exercises it in a cruel or oppressive way.
– ORIGIN mid 16th cent.: from French *despote*, via medieval Latin from Greek *despotēs* 'master, absolute ruler'. Originally (after the Turkish conquest of Constantinople) the term denoted a minor Christian ruler under the Turkish empire. The current sense dates from the late 18th cent.

despotic ▸ **adjective** of or typical of a despot; tyrannical: *a despotic regime.*
– DERIVATIVES **despotically** adverb.

despotism /ˈdɛspətɪz(ə)m/ ▸ **noun** [mass noun] the exercise of absolute power, especially in a cruel and oppressive way: *the ideology of enlightened despotism.* ■ [count noun] a country or political system where the ruler holds absolute power.
– ORIGIN early 18th cent.: from French *despotisme*, from *despote* (see DESPOT).

des Prez /deɪ ˈpreɪ/ (also **des Prés** or **Deprez**), Josquin (*c.*1440–1521), Flemish musician. A leading Renaissance composer, he wrote eighteen complete masses, 112 motets, and some seventy songs.

desquamate /ˈdɛskwəmeɪt/ ▸ **verb** [no obj.] (usu. as adj. **desquamated**) (of a layer of cells, e.g. of the skin) come off in scales or flakes: *desquamated cells.*
– DERIVATIVES **desquamation** noun, **desquamative** /-ˈskwamətɪv/ adjective.
– ORIGIN early 18th cent. (in the sense 'remove the scales from'): from Latin *desquamat-* 'scaled', from the verb *desquamare*, from *de-* 'away from' + *squama* 'a scale'.

des res /dɛz ˈrɛz/ ▸ **noun** Brit. informal a desirable residence (used as a humorous allusion to the language used in housing advertisements).
– ORIGIN 1980s: abbreviation.

Dessau /ˈdɛsaʊ/ an industrial city in Germany, on the River Mulde, in Anhalt about 112 km (70 miles) south-west of Berlin; pop. 77,400 (est. 2006).

dessert /dɪˈzəːt/ ▸ **noun** the sweet course eaten at the end of a meal: *a dessert of chocolate mousse.*
– ORIGIN mid 16th cent.: from French, past participle of *desservir* 'clear the table', from *des-* (expressing removal) + *servir* 'to serve'.

USAGE See USAGE at DESERTS.

dessertspoon ▸ **noun** a spoon used for dessert, smaller than a tablespoon and larger than a teaspoon. ■ the amount held by a dessertspoon, in the UK considered to be 11.8 millilitres when used as a measurement in cookery.
– DERIVATIVES **dessertspoonful** noun (pl. **dessertspoonfuls**).

dessert wine ▸ **noun** a sweet wine drunk with or following dessert.

destabilize (also **destabilise**) ▸ **verb** [with obj.] upset the stability of; cause unrest in: *the discovery of an affair can destabilize a relationship.*
– DERIVATIVES **destabilization** noun.

de Staël /də ˈstɑːl/, French /də stal/, Madame (1766–1817), French novelist and critic, a precursor of the French romantics, born *Anne Louise Germaine Necker*. Her best-known critical work, *De l'Allemagne* (1810), introduced late 18th-century German writers and thinkers to France.

destain ▸ **verb** [with obj.] Biology selectively remove stain from (a specimen for microscopy, a chromatography gel, etc.) after it has previously been stained.

De Stijl /də ˈstʌɪl/ a 20th-century Dutch art movement founded in 1917 by Theo van Doesburg (1883–1931) and Piet Mondrian. The movement favoured an abstract, economical style and was influential on the Bauhaus and constructivist movements.
– ORIGIN Dutch, literally 'the style', originally the name of the movement's periodical.

destination ▸ **noun** the place to which someone or something is going or being sent: *Delft is an ideal destination for a relaxing weekend.* ■ [as modifier] denoting a place that people will make a special trip to visit: *a destination restaurant.*
– ORIGIN late Middle English: from Latin *destinatio(n-)*, from *destinare* 'make firm, establish'. The original sense was 'the action of intending someone or something for a purpose', later 'being destined for a place', hence (from the early 19th cent.) the place itself.

destine /ˈdɛstɪn/ ▸ **verb** [with obj.] intend or choose for a particular purpose or end.
– ORIGIN Middle English (in the sense 'predetermine, decree'): from Old French *destiner*, from Latin *destinare* 'make firm, establish'.

destined ▸ **adjective** [predic.] (of a person's future) regarded as developing as though according to a pre-existing plan: *he was **destined for** great things* | [with infinitive] *they were destined to become diplomats.* ■ (**destined to**) certain to meet (a particular fate): *the Act seems destined to failure.* ■ (**destined for**) intended for or travelling towards (a particular place): *the shipment of illegal drugs destined for American and European markets.* ■ [attrib.] preordained: *your heroine will be united with her destined mate.*

destiny ▸ **noun** (pl. **destinies**) the events that will necessarily happen to a particular person or thing in the future: *she was unable to control her own destiny.* ■ [mass noun] the hidden power believed to control future events; fate: *he believed in destiny.*
– ORIGIN Middle English: from Old French *destinee*, from Latin *destinata*, feminine past participle of *destinare* 'make firm, establish'.

destitute /ˈdɛstɪtjuːt/ ▸ **adjective** extremely poor and lacking the means to provide for oneself: *the charity cares for destitute children.* ■ (**destitute of**) not having: *towns destitute of commerce.*
– ORIGIN late Middle English (in the sense 'deserted, abandoned, empty'): from Latin *destitutus*, past participle of *destituere* 'forsake', from *de-* 'away from' + *statuere* 'to place'.

destitution ▸ **noun** [mass noun] poverty so extreme that one lacks the means to provide for oneself: *the family faced eviction and destitution.*

destock ▸ **verb** [no obj.] Brit. (of a retailer) reduce the quantity of stock held.

de-stress ▸ **verb** [no obj.] relax after a period of work or tension.

destrier /ˈdɛstrɪə, dɛˈstriːə/ ▸ **noun** a medieval knight's warhorse.
– ORIGIN Middle English: from Old French, based on Latin *dextera* 'the right hand', from *dexter* 'on the right' (because the squire led the knight's horse with his right hand).

destroy ▶ **verb** [with obj.] end the existence of (something) by damaging or attacking it: *the room had been destroyed by fire.* ■ ruin (someone) emotionally or spiritually: *he has been determined to destroy her.* ■ defeat (someone) utterly: *Northants have the batting to destroy anyone.* ■ kill (a sick, savage, or unwanted animal) by humane means: *their terrier was destroyed after the attack.*
– ORIGIN Middle English: from Old French *destruire*, based on Latin *destruere*, from *de-* (expressing reversal) + *struere* 'build'.

destroyer ▶ **noun 1** a small, fast warship, especially one equipped for a defensive role against submarines and aircraft.
2 a person or thing that destroys something: *CFCs are the chief destroyers of the ozone layer.*

destroying angel ▶ **noun** a deadly poisonous white toadstool which grows in woodland, native to Eurasia and North America. ● *Amanita virosa*, family Amanitaceae, class Hymenomycetes.

destruct ▶ **verb** [with obj.] cause deliberate, terminal damage to.
▶ **noun** [in sing.] [usu. as modifier] the deliberate causing of terminal damage: *press the destruct button.*
– DERIVATIVES **destructor** noun.
– ORIGIN 1950s (originally US): back-formation from DESTRUCTION.

destructible ▶ **adjective** able to be destroyed: *destructible plastic labels.*
– DERIVATIVES **destructibility** noun.
– ORIGIN mid 18th cent. (earlier in *indestructible*): from French, from late Latin *destructibilis*, from Latin *destruct-* 'destroyed', from the verb *destruere* (see DESTROY).

destruction ▶ **noun** [mass noun] the action or process of causing so much damage to something that it no longer exists or cannot be repaired: *the destruction of the rainforest* | *the avalanche left a trail of destruction.* ■ the action or process of killing or being killed: *the wanton destruction of human life.* ■ [in sing.] a cause of someone's ruin: *gambling was his destruction.*
– ORIGIN Middle English: from Latin *destructio(n-)*, from the verb *destruere* (see DESTROY).

destructive ▶ **adjective** causing great and irreparable damage: *the destructive power of weapons.* ■ negative and unhelpful: *destructive criticism.*
– DERIVATIVES **destructively** adverb, **destructiveness** noun.

destructive distillation ▶ **noun** [mass noun] Chemistry decomposition of a solid by heating it in a closed container and collecting the volatile constituents given off.

desuetude /ˈdɛswɪtjuːd, dəˈsjuːətjuːd/ ▶ **noun** [mass noun] formal a state of disuse: *the docks* ***fell into desuetude.***
– ORIGIN early 17th cent. (in the sense 'cessation'): from French, from Latin *desuetudo*, from *desuet-* 'made unaccustomed', from the verb *desuescere*, from *de-* (expressing reversal) + *suescere* 'be accustomed'.

desulphurize (also **desulphurise**, US **desulfurize**) ▶ **verb** [with obj.] remove sulphur or sulphur compounds from (a substance).
– DERIVATIVES **desulphurization** noun.

desultory /ˈdɛs(ə)lt(ə)ri, -z-/ ▶ **adjective** lacking a plan, purpose, or enthusiasm: *a few people were left, dancing in a desultory fashion.* ■ (of conversation or speech) going from one subject to another in a half-hearted way: *the desultory conversation faded.* ■ occurring randomly or occasionally: *desultory passengers were appearing.*
– DERIVATIVES **desultorily** adverb, **desultoriness** noun.
– ORIGIN late 16th cent. (also in the literal sense 'skipping about'): from Latin *desultorius* 'superficial' (literally 'relating to a vaulter'), from *desultor* 'vaulter', from the verb *desilire*.

desuperheater ▶ **noun** a container for reducing the temperature of steam to make it less superheated.

desynchronize (also **desynchronise**) ▶ **verb** [with obj.] disturb the synchronization of; put out of step or phase.
– DERIVATIVES **desynchronization** noun.

detach ▶ **verb** [with obj.] **1** disengage (something or part of something) and remove it: *he detached the front lamp* ***from*** *its bracket* | figurative *a willingness to detach comment from political allegiance.* ■ [no obj.] be easily removable: *the screen detaches from the keyboard.*
2 (**detach oneself from**) leave or separate oneself from (a group or place): *a figure in brown detached itself from the shadows* | figurative *the newspaper detached itself from the political parties.* ■ (**be detached**) Military (of a group of soldiers or ships) be sent on a separate mission.
– DERIVATIVES **detachability** noun, **detachable** adjective.
– ORIGIN late 16th cent. (in the sense 'discharge a gun'): from French *détacher*, earlier *destacher*, from *des-* (expressing reversal) + *attacher* 'attach'.

detached ▶ **adjective 1** separate or disconnected, in particular: ■ (of a house or other building) not joined to another on either side: *a four-bedroomed detached house.* ■ (of a social worker or social work) operating or based in the community rather than in an office: *detached youth workers.*
2 aloof and objective: *he is a detached observer of his own actions.*
– DERIVATIVES **detachedly** adverb.

detached retina ▶ **noun** a retina that has become separated from the underlying choroid tissue at the back of the eye, causing loss of vision in the affected area.

detachment ▶ **noun 1** [mass noun] the state of being objective or aloof: *he felt a sense of detachment from what was going on.*
2 Military a group of troops, aircraft, or ships sent away on a separate mission: *a detachment of Marines* | [mass noun] *the Squadron went* ***on detachment*** *to Malta.* ■ a party of people separated from a larger group: *a truck containing a detachment of villagers.*
3 [mass noun] the action or process of detaching; separation: *structural problems resulted in cracking and detachment of the wall.*
– ORIGIN mid 17th cent.: from French *détachement*, from *détacher* 'to detach' (see DETACH).

detail ▶ **noun 1** an individual fact or item: *we shall consider every detail of the Bill* | [mass noun] *her meticulous* ***attention to detail.*** ■ a less significant item or fact: *he didn't want them to get sidetracked on a detail of policy.* ■ a minor decorative feature of a building or work of art: *a detail on Charlemagne's tomb.* ■ [mass noun] the style or treatment of minor decorative features: *the classical French detail of the building's facade.* ■ a small part of a picture that is reproduced separately for close study. ■ (**details**) itemized information about someone: *the official asked for my father's details.*
2 a small detachment of troops or police officers given a special duty: *the governor's security detail.* ■ [often with modifier] a special duty assigned to a detachment of troops or police officers.
▶ **verb** [with obj.] **1** give full information about: *the report details proposals to improve public transport.*
2 [with obj. and infinitive] assign (someone) to undertake a particular task: *the ships were detailed to keep watch.*
3 US clean (a motor vehicle) thoroughly.
– PHRASES **go into detail** give a full account of something. **in detail** as regards every feature or aspect; fully: *we will have to examine the proposals in detail.*
– ORIGIN early 17th cent. (in the sense 'minor items or events regarded collectively'): from French *détail* (noun), *détailler* (verb), from *dé-* (expressing separation) + *tailler* 'to cut' (based on Latin *talea* 'twig, cutting').

detailed ▶ **adjective** having many details or facts; showing attention to detail: *more detailed information was needed.* ■ (of a work of art) executed with many minor decorative features: *an exquisitely detailed carving.*

detailing ▶ **noun** [mass noun] small decorative features on a building, garment, or work of art.

detain ▶ **verb** [with obj.] keep (someone) from proceeding by holding them back or making claims on their attention: *she made to open the door, but he detained her.* ■ keep (someone) in official custody, typically for questioning about a crime or in a politically sensitive situation: *she was detained without trial for two years.* ■ officially seize and hold (goods).
– DERIVATIVES **detainment** noun.
– ORIGIN late Middle English (in the sense 'be afflicted with sickness or infirmity'): from Old French *detenir*, from a variant of Latin *detinere*, from *de-* 'away, aside' + *tenere* 'to hold'.

detainee /ˌdiːteɪˈniː, ˌdiː-/ ▶ **noun** a person held in custody, especially for political reasons.

detainer ▶ **noun** Law **1** [mass noun] the action of detaining or withholding property. ■ the detention of a person in custody. ■ [count noun] an order authorizing the continued detention of a person in custody.
2 a person who detains someone or something.
– ORIGIN early 17th cent.: from Anglo-Norman French *detener* 'detain' (used as a noun), variant of Old French *detenir* (see DETAIN).

detangle ▶ **verb** [with obj.] remove tangles from (hair).

detect ▶ **verb** [with obj.] discover or identify the presence or existence of: *cancer may soon be detected in its earliest stages.* ■ discern (something intangible or barely perceptible): *Paul detected a faint note of weariness in his father's voice.* ■ discover or investigate (a crime or its perpetrators): *the public can help the police to detect crime.*
– DERIVATIVES **detectable** adjective, **detectably** adverb.
– ORIGIN late Middle English: from Latin *detect-* 'uncovered', from the verb *detegere*, from *de-* (expressing reversal) + *tegere* 'to cover'. The original senses were 'uncover, expose' and 'give someone away', later 'expose the real or hidden nature of'; hence the current (partly influenced by DETECTIVE).

D

detection ▶ **noun** [mass noun] the action or process of identifying the presence of something concealed: *the early detection of fetal abnormalities.* ■ the work of a detective in investigating a crime: *modern technology is essential to crime detection.*
– ORIGIN late 15th cent. (in the sense 'revelation of what is concealed'): from late Latin *detectio(n-)*, from Latin *detegere* 'uncover' (see DETECT).

detective ▶ **noun** a person, especially a police officer, whose occupation is to investigate and solve crimes. ■ [as modifier] denoting a rank of police officer with investigative duties: *a detective inspector.* ■ [as modifier] concerning crime and its investigation: *detective work.*
– ORIGIN mid 19th cent.: from DETECT. The noun was originally short for *detective policeman*, from an adjectival use of the word in the sense 'serving to detect'.

detective story (also **detective novel**) ▶ **noun** a story whose plot revolves around the investigation and solving of a crime.

detector ▶ **noun** [often with modifier] a device or instrument designed to detect the presence of a particular object or substance: *methane detectors.*

detectorist ▶ **noun** a person who uses a metal detector for a hobby.

detent /dɪˈtɛnt/ ▶ **noun** a catch in a machine which prevents motion until released. ■ a catch that regulates striking in a clock.
– ORIGIN late 17th cent. (denoting a catch in a clock): from French *détente*, from Old French *destente*, from *destendre* 'slacken', from *des-* (expressing reversal) + Latin *tendere* 'to stretch'.

détente /deɪˈtɑːnt/ ▶ **noun** [mass noun] the easing of hostility or strained relations, especially between countries: *his policy of arms control and detente with the Soviet Union.*
– ORIGIN early 20th cent.: French, 'loosening, relaxation'.

detention ▶ **noun** [mass noun] the action of detaining someone or the state of being detained in official custody: *the fifteen people arrested were still in police detention.* ■ the punishment of being kept in school after hours: *teachers were divided as to the effectiveness of detention* | [count noun] *masters gave lines or detentions.*
– ORIGIN late Middle English (in the sense 'withholding of what is claimed or due'): from late Latin *detentio(n-)*, from Latin *detinere* 'hold back' (see DETAIN).

detention centre ▶ **noun** an institution for the short-term detention of illegal immigrants, refugees, people awaiting trial or sentence, or (formerly in the UK) young offenders.

detenu /dɪˈtenjuː/ (also **detenue**) ▶ **noun** Indian a person held in custody; a detainee.
– ORIGIN early 19th cent. (in British use): from French *détenu*.

deter /dɪˈtəː/ ▶ **verb** (**deters**, **deterring**, **deterred**) [with obj.] discourage (someone) from doing something by instilling doubt or fear of the consequences: *only a health problem would* ***deter*** *him* ***from*** *seeking re-election.* ■ prevent the occurrence of: *strategists think not only about how to deter war, but about how war might occur.*
– ORIGIN mid 16th cent.: from Latin *deterrere*, from *de-* 'away from' + *terrere* 'frighten'.

deterge /dɪˈtəːdʒ/ ▶ **verb** [with obj.] rare cleanse thoroughly.
– ORIGIN early 17th cent.: from French *déterger* or Latin *detergere* 'wipe away'.

D

detergent ▸ noun a water-soluble cleansing agent which combines with impurities and dirt to make them more soluble, and differs from soap in not forming a scum with the salts in hard water. ■ any additive with a similar action to a detergent, e.g. an oil-soluble substance which holds dirt in suspension in lubricating oil.
▸ adjective relating to detergents or their action.
– DERIVATIVES **detergence** noun, **detergency** noun.
– ORIGIN early 17th cent. (as an adjective): from Latin *detergent-* 'wiping away', from the verb *detergere*, from *de-* 'away from' + *tergere* 'to wipe'.

deteriorate /dɪˈtɪərɪəreɪt/ ▸ verb [no obj.] become progressively worse: *relations between the countries had deteriorated sharply* | (as adj. **deteriorating**) *deteriorating economic conditions.*
– DERIVATIVES **deteriorative** adjective.
– ORIGIN late 16th cent. (in the sense 'make worse'): from late Latin *deteriorat-* 'worsened', from the verb *deteriorare*, from Latin *deterior* 'worse'.

deterioration ▸ noun [mass noun] the process of becoming progressively worse: *a deterioration in the condition of the patient.*

determinable ▸ adjective **1** able to be definitely decided or ascertained: *a readily determinable market value.*
2 Law capable of being brought to an end under given conditions.
– ORIGIN late Middle English: via Old French from late Latin *determinabilis* 'finite', from the verb *determinare* (see DETERMINE).

determinant /dɪˈtəːmɪnənt/ ▸ noun **1** a factor which decisively affects the nature or outcome of something: *pure force of will was the main determinant of his success.* ■ Biology a gene or other factor which determines the character and development of a cell or cells in an organism, a set of which forms an individual's idiotype.
2 Mathematics a quantity obtained by the addition of products of the elements of a square matrix according to a given rule.
▸ adjective serving to determine or decide something.
– ORIGIN early 17th cent.: from Latin *determinant-* 'determining', from the verb *determinare* (see DETERMINE).

determinate /dɪˈtəːmɪnət/ ▸ adjective having exact and discernible limits or form: *the longest determinate prison sentence ever upheld by English courts.* ■ Botany (of a flowering shoot) having the main axis ending in a flower bud and therefore no longer extending in length, as in a cyme.
– DERIVATIVES **determinacy** noun, **determinately** adverb, **determinateness** noun.
– ORIGIN late Middle English: from Latin *determinatus* 'limited, determined', past participle of *determinare* (see DETERMINE).

determination ▸ noun [mass noun] **1** the quality of being determined; firmness of purpose: *those who succeed because of sheer grit and determination.*
2 the process of establishing something exactly by calculation or research: *determination of molecular structures.* ■ Law the settlement of a dispute by the authoritative decision of a judge or arbitrator. ■ [count noun] Law a judicial decision or sentence.
3 the controlling or deciding of the nature or outcome of something: *genetic sex determination.*
4 Law the cessation of an estate or interest.
5 archaic a tendency to move in a fixed direction.
– ORIGIN late Middle English (in the senses 'settlement of a controversy by a judge or by reasoning' and 'authoritative opinion'): via Old French from Latin *determinatio(n-)*, from the verb *determinare* (see DETERMINE).

determinative /dɪˈtəːmɪnətɪv/ ▸ adjective [predic.] chiefly Law serving to define, qualify, or direct: *the employer's view is not determinative of the issue.*
▸ noun Grammar another term for DETERMINER.

determine /dɪˈtəːmɪn/ ▸ verb [with obj.] **1** cause (something) to occur in a particular way or to have a particular nature: *it will be her mental attitude that determines her future.*
2 ascertain or establish exactly by research or calculation: *the inquest is entrusted with the task of determining the cause of death* | [with clause] *the point of our study was to **determine what** is true, not what is practicable.* ■ Mathematics specify the value, position, or form of (a mathematical or geometrical object) uniquely.
3 [no obj.] firmly decide: *he **determined on** a withdrawal of his forces* | [with infinitive] *she determined to tackle Stephen the next day.*
4 Law, archaic bring or come to an end.
– ORIGIN late Middle English: from Old French *determiner*, from Latin *determinare* 'limit, fix', from *de-* 'completely' + *terminare* 'terminate'.

determined ▸ adjective having made a firm decision and being resolved not to change it: [with infinitive] *Alina was determined to be heard.* ■ possessing or displaying resolve: *Helen was a determined little girl* | *a determined effort to reduce inflation.*
– DERIVATIVES **determinedly** adverb, **determinedness** noun.

determiner ▸ noun **1** a person or thing that determines or decides something.
2 Grammar a modifying word that determines the kind of reference a noun or noun group has, for example *a, the, every.* See also ARTICLE.

determining ▸ adjective causing something to occur or be done in a particular way; serving to decide something: *money may have been the determining factor in his decision.*

determinism ▸ noun [mass noun] Philosophy the doctrine that all events, including human action, are ultimately determined by causes regarded as external to the will. Some philosophers have taken determinism to imply that individual human beings have no free will and cannot be held morally responsible for their actions.
– DERIVATIVES **determinist** noun & adjective, **deterministic** adjective, **deterministically** adverb.

deterrent /dɪˈtɛr(ə)nt/ ▸ noun a thing that discourages or is intended to discourage someone from doing something: *cameras are a major **deterrent to** crime.* ■ a nuclear weapon or weapons system regarded as deterring an enemy from attack.
▸ adjective able or intended to deter: *the deterrent effect of heavy prison sentences.*
– DERIVATIVES **deterrence** noun.
– ORIGIN early 19th cent.: from Latin *deterrent-* 'deterring', from the verb *deterrere* (see DETER).

detest ▸ verb [with obj.] dislike intensely: *she really did detest his mockery.*
– DERIVATIVES **detester** noun.
– ORIGIN late 15th cent.: from Latin *detestari*, from *de-* 'down' + *testari* 'witness, call upon to witness' (from *testis* 'a witness').

detestable ▸ adjective deserving intense dislike: *I found the film's violence detestable.*
– DERIVATIVES **detestably** adverb.
– ORIGIN late Middle English: from Old French, or from Latin *detestabilis*, from the verb *detestari* (see DETEST).

detestation /ˌdiːtɛˈsteɪʃ(ə)n/ ▸ noun [mass noun] intense dislike: *Wordsworth's detestation of aristocracy.* ■ [count noun] archaic a detested person or thing: *he is the detestation of the neighbourhood.*
– ORIGIN late Middle English: via Old French from Latin *detestatio(n-)*, from the verb *detestari* (see DETEST).

dethrone ▸ verb [with obj.] remove (a monarch) from power. ■ remove from a position of authority or dominance: *he dethroned the defending title-holder.*
– DERIVATIVES **dethronement** noun.

detinue /ˈdɛtɪnjuː/ ▸ noun [mass noun] Law the crime of wrongful detention of goods or personal possessions (replaced in the UK by the tort of wrongful interference of goods).
– ORIGIN late Middle English: from Old French *detenue*, past participle (used as a noun) of *detenir* 'detain'.

detonate /ˈdɛtəneɪt/ ▸ verb explode or cause to explode: [no obj.] *two other bombs failed to detonate* | [with obj.] *a trigger that can detonate nuclear weapons.*
– DERIVATIVES **detonative** adjective.
– ORIGIN early 18th cent.: from Latin *detonat-* 'thundered down or forth', from the verb *detonare*, from *de-* 'down' + *tonare* 'to thunder'.

detonation ▸ noun [mass noun] the action of causing a bomb or explosive device to explode. ■ [count noun] a loud explosion: *a series of deafening detonations was heard.* ■ technical combustion of a substance which is initiated suddenly and propagates extremely rapidly, giving rise to a shock wave. Compare with DEFLAGRATION. ■ the premature combustion of fuel in an internal-combustion engine, causing pinking.
– ORIGIN late 17th cent.: from French *détonation*, from the verb *détoner*, from Latin *detonare* 'thunder down' (see DETONATE).

detonator ▸ noun a device or small sensitive charge used to detonate an explosive. ■ Brit. another term for FOG SIGNAL.

detorsion /dɪˈtɔːʃ(ə)n/ ▸ noun [mass noun] Zoology (in gastropod molluscs) the evolutionary reversion of a group to a primitive linear body plan. Compare with TORSION.

detour ▸ noun a long or roundabout route that is taken to avoid something or to visit somewhere along the way: *he had **made a detour to** a cafe.* ■ an alternative route for use by traffic when the usual road is temporarily closed.
▸ verb [no obj., with adverbial of direction] chiefly N. Amer. take a long or roundabout route: *he detoured around the walls.* ■ [with obj.] avoid by taking a detour: *I would detour the endless stream of motor homes.*
– ORIGIN mid 18th cent. (as a noun): from French *détour* 'change of direction', from *détourner* 'turn away'.

detox informal ▸ noun /ˈdiːtɒks/ [mass noun] detoxification: *he ended up **in detox** for three months.*
▸ verb /diːˈtɒks/ detoxify.

detoxicate /diːˈtɒksɪkeɪt/ ▸ verb another term for DETOXIFY.
– DERIVATIVES **detoxication** noun.
– ORIGIN mid 19th cent.: from DE- (expressing removal) + Latin *toxicum* 'poison', on the pattern of *intoxicate*.

detoxification ▸ noun [mass noun] the process of removing toxic substances. ■ medical treatment of an alcoholic or drug addict involving abstention from drink or drugs until the bloodstream is free of toxins.

detoxify /diːˈtɒksɪfʌɪ/ ▸ verb (**detoxifies, detoxifying, detoxified**) [with obj.] remove toxic substances from: *the process uses chemical reagents to detoxify the oil.* ■ abstain or help to abstain from drink and drugs until the bloodstream is free of toxins, in order to overcome alcoholism or drug addiction. ■ [no obj.] become free of harmful substances: *you can help your body detoxify by cutting down on coffee.*
– DERIVATIVES **detoxifier** noun.
– ORIGIN early 20th cent.: from DE- (expressing removal) + Latin *toxicum* 'poison' + -FY.

detract ▸ verb [no obj.] (**detract from**) diminish the worth or value of (a quality or achievement): *these quibbles in no way detract from her achievement.* ■ [with obj.] take away (a specified amount) from the worth or value of a quality or achievement.
– DERIVATIVES **detraction** noun, **detractive** adjective.
– ORIGIN late Middle English: from Latin *detract-* 'drawn away', from the verb *detrahere*, from *de-* 'away from' + *trahere* 'draw'.

detractor ▸ noun a person who disparages someone or something.

detrain ▸ verb leave or cause to leave a train.
– DERIVATIVES **detrainment** noun.

detribalize (also **detribalise**) ▸ verb [with obj.] (usu. as adj. **detribalized**) remove (someone) from a traditional tribal social structure.
– DERIVATIVES **detribalization** noun.

detriment /ˈdɛtrɪm(ə)nt/ ▸ noun [mass noun] the state of being harmed or damaged: *he is engrossed in his work **to the detriment of** his married life* | *light industry can be carried out in a residential area **without detriment to** its amenities.* ■ [count noun] a cause of harm or damage: *such tests are **a detriment to** good education.*
– ORIGIN late Middle English in the sense 'loss sustained by damage': from Old French, from Latin *detrimentum*, from *detri-*, stem of *deterere* 'wear away'.

detrimental ▸ adjective tending to cause harm: *recent policies have been **detrimental to** the interests of many old people* | *moving her could have a **detrimental effect on** her health.*
– DERIVATIVES **detrimentally** adverb.

detrition /dɪˈtrɪʃ(ə)n/ ▸ noun [mass noun] rare the action of wearing something away by friction.
– ORIGIN late 17th cent.: from medieval Latin *detritio(n-)*, from *detri-*, stem of *deterere* 'wear away'.

detritivore /dɪˈtrɪtɪvɔː/ ▸ noun Zoology an animal which feeds on dead organic material, especially plant detritus.
– DERIVATIVES **detritivorous** /ˌdɛtrɪˈtɪv(ə)rəs/ adjective.
– ORIGIN 1960s: from DETRITUS + *-vore* 'eating' (see -VOROUS).

detritus /dɪˈtrʌɪtəs/ ▸ noun [mass noun] waste or debris of any kind: *the streets were foul with detritus.* ■ gravel, sand, silt, or other material produced by erosion. ■ organic matter produced by the decomposition of organisms.
– DERIVATIVES **detrital** adjective.

– ORIGIN late 18th cent. (in the sense 'detrition'): from French *détritus*, from Latin *detritus*, from *deterere* 'wear away'.

Detroit /dɪˈtrɔɪt/ a major industrial city and Great Lakes shipping centre in SE Michigan; pop. 912,062 (est. 2008). It is the centre of the US automobile industry, containing the headquarters of Ford, Chrysler, and General Motors.

de trop /də ˈtrəʊ/, French /də tʀo/ ▶ **adjective** not wanted; unwelcome: *she had no grasp of the conversation and felt herself de trop.*
– ORIGIN mid 18th cent.: French, literally 'excessive'.

de Troyes, Chrétien, see **Chrétien de Troyes**.

detrusor /dɪˈtruːsə/ (also **detrusor muscle**) ▶ **noun** Anatomy a muscle which forms a layer of the wall of the bladder.
– ORIGIN mid 18th cent.: modern Latin, from Latin *detrus-* 'thrust down', from the verb *detrudere*.

Dettol /ˈdɛtɒl, -t(ə)l/ ▶ **noun** [mass noun] trademark a type of surgical or household disinfectant.
– ORIGIN 1930s: an invented name.

detumescence /ˌdiːtjʊˈmɛs(ə)ns/ ▶ **noun** [mass noun] the process of subsiding from a state of tension, swelling, or (especially) sexual arousal.
– DERIVATIVES **detumesce** verb, **detumescent** adjective.
– ORIGIN late 17th cent.: from Latin *detumescere*, from *de-* 'down, away' + *tumescere* 'to swell'.

detune ▶ **verb** [with obj.] **1** cause (a musical instrument) to become out of tune.
2 (usu. as adj. **detuned**) reduce the performance or efficiency of (a motor vehicle or engine) by adjustment.
3 change the frequency of (an oscillatory system such as a laser) away from a state of resonance.

Deucalion /djuːˈkeɪlɪən/ Greek Mythology the son of Prometheus. With his wife Pyrrha he survived a flood sent by Zeus to punish human wickedness; they were then instructed to throw stones over their shoulders, and these turned into humans to repopulate the world.

deuce[1] /djuːs/ ▶ **noun 1** N. Amer. a thing representing, or represented by, the number two, in particular: ■ the two on dice or playing cards. ■ a throw of two at dice. ■ informal, dated a two-dollar bill.
2 Tennis the score of 40 all in a game, at which each player needs two consecutive points to win the game.
– ORIGIN late 15th cent.: from Old French *deus* 'two', from Latin *duos*.

deuce[2] /djuːs/ ▶ **noun** (**the deuce**) informal used as a euphemism for 'devil' in expressions of annoyance, impatience, surprise, etc.: ***how the deuce** are we to make a profit?* | ***what the deuce** are you trying to do?*
– PHRASES **a** (or **the**) **deuce of a ——** used to emphasize how bad, difficult, or serious something is.
– ORIGIN mid 17th cent.: from Low German *duus*, probably of the same origin as **deuce**[1] (two aces at dice being the worst throw).

deuced /ˈdjuːsɪd, djuːst/ informal, dated ▶ **adjective** [attrib.] used for emphasis, especially to express disapproval or frustration: *I sound like a deuced newspaper reporter* | [as submodifier] *I'm so deuced fond of you.*
– DERIVATIVES **deucedly** adverb [as submodifier] *they're deucedly hard to find.*

deurmekaar /ˌdjəːməˈkɑː/ ▶ **adjective** [predic.] S. African informal in a state of muddle or confusion.
– ORIGIN Afrikaans, from Dutch dialect variants of *door elkaar*, literally 'through one another, interchangeable'.

deus ex machina /ˌdeɪʊs ɛks ˈmakɪnə, ˌdiːəs ɛks məˈʃiːnə/ ▶ **noun** an unexpected power or event saving a seemingly hopeless situation, especially as a contrived plot device in a play or novel.
– ORIGIN late 17th cent.: modern Latin, translation of Greek *theos ek mēkhanēs*, 'god from the machinery'. In Greek theatre, actors representing gods were suspended above the stage, the denouement of the play being brought about by their intervention.

Deut. ▶ **abbreviation** Deuteronomy (in biblical references).

deuteragonist /ˌdjuːtəˈragənɪst/ ▶ **noun** the person second in importance to the protagonist in a drama.
– ORIGIN mid 19th cent.: from Greek *deuteragōnistēs*, from *deuteros* 'second' + *agōnistēs* 'actor'.

deuteranope /ˈdjuːt(ə)rənəʊp/ ▶ **noun** a person suffering from deuteranopia.

deuteranopia /ˌdjuːt(ə)rəˈnəʊpɪə/ ▶ **noun** [mass noun] colour blindness resulting from insensitivity to green light, causing confusion of greens, reds, and yellows. Compare with **protanopia**.
– ORIGIN early 20th cent.: from **deutero-** 'second' (the colour green being regarded as the second component of colour vision) + **an-**[1] + **-opia**.

deuterated /ˈdjuːtəreɪtɪd/ (also **deuteriated** /djuːˈtɪərɪeɪtɪd/) ▶ **adjective** Chemistry (of a compound) in which the ordinary isotope of hydrogen has been replaced with deuterium.
– DERIVATIVES **deuteration** noun.

deuteric /ˈdjuːtərɪk/ ▶ **adjective** Geology relating to or denoting alteration of the minerals of an igneous rock during the later stages of consolidation.
– ORIGIN early 20th cent.: from **deutero-** 'secondary' + **-ic**.

deuterium /djuːˈtɪərɪəm/ ▶ **noun** [mass noun] Chemistry a stable isotope of hydrogen with a mass approximately twice that of the usual isotope. (Symbol: **D**)

> Deuterium atoms have a neutron as well as a proton in the nucleus, and the isotope is present to about 1 part in 6,000 in naturally occurring hydrogen. It is used as a fuel in thermonuclear bombs, and heavy water (D_2O) is used as a moderator in nuclear reactors.

– ORIGIN 1930s: modern Latin, from Greek *deuteros* 'second'.

deutero- /ˈdjuːtərəʊ/ ▶ **combining form** second: *Deutero-Isaiah.* ■ secondary: *deuterocanonical.*
– ORIGIN from Greek *deuteros* 'second'.

deuterocanonical /ˌdjuːtərəʊkəˈnɒnɪk(ə)l/ ▶ **adjective** (of sacred books or literary works) forming a secondary canon.

Deutero-Isaiah /ˌdjuːtərəʊʌɪˈzʌɪə/ the supposed later author of Isaiah 40–55.

deuteron /ˈdjuːtərɒn/ ▶ **noun** the nucleus of a deuterium atom, consisting of a proton and a neutron.
– ORIGIN 1930s: from Greek *deuteros* 'second', on the pattern of *proton*.

Deuteronomy /ˌdjuːtəˈrɒnəmi/ the fifth book of the Bible, containing a recapitulation of the Ten Commandments and much of the Mosaic law.

Deutschland /ˈdɔʏtʃlant/ German name for **Germany**.

Deutschmark /ˈdɔɪtʃmɑːk/ (also **Deutsche Mark** /ˈdɔɪtʃə mɑːk/, German /ˌdɔʏtʃə ˈmark/) ▶ **noun** (until the introduction of the euro in 2002) the basic monetary unit of Germany, equal to 100 pfennig.
– ORIGIN from German *deutsche Mark* 'German mark'.

deutzia /ˈdjuːtsɪə, ˈdɔɪt-/ ▶ **noun** an ornamental shrub with white or pinkish flowers, native to Asia and Central America. ● Genus *Deutzia*, family Hydrangeaceae.
– ORIGIN modern Latin, named after Johann van der *Deutz*, 18th-cent. Dutch patron of botany.

deva /ˈdeɪvə/ ▶ **noun** a member of a class of divine beings in the Vedic period, which in Indian religion are benevolent and in Zoroastrianism are evil. Compare with **asura**. ■ Indian (in general use) a god.
– ORIGIN from Sanskrit, literally 'shining one', later 'god'.

devadasi /ˌdeɪvəˈdɑːsi/ ▶ **noun** (pl. **devadasis**) a hereditary female dancer in a Hindu temple.
– ORIGIN from Sanskrit *devadāsī*, literally 'female servant of a god'.

de Valera /ˌdə vəˈlɛːrə/, Eamon (1882–1975), American-born Irish statesman, Taoiseach (Prime Minister) 1937–48, 1951–4, and 1957–9 and President of the Republic of Ireland 1959–73. He was the leader of Sinn Fein 1917–26 and the founder of the Fianna Fáil Party in 1926. As President of the Irish Free State from 1932, de Valera was largely responsible for the new constitution of 1937 which created the state of Eire.

de Valois /də ˈvalwɑː/, Dame Ninette (1898–2001), Irish choreographer, ballet dancer, and teacher; born *Edris Stannus*. A former soloist with Diaghilev's Ballets Russes, she formed the Vic-Wells Ballet (which eventually became the Royal Ballet) and the Sadler's Wells ballet school.

devalorize /diːˈvalərʌɪz/ (also **devalorise**) ▶ **verb** [with obj.] rare devalue.
– DERIVATIVES **devalorization** noun.
– ORIGIN early 20th cent.: from French *dévaloriser*.

devalue ▶ **verb** (**devalues, devaluing, devalued**) [with obj.] reduce or underestimate the worth or importance of: *I resent the way people seem to devalue my achievement.* ■ Economics reduce the official value of (a currency) in relation to other currencies: *the dinar was devalued by 20 per cent.*
– DERIVATIVES **devaluation** noun.

Devanagari /ˌdeɪvəˈnɑːg(ə)ri, dɛv-/ ▶ **noun** [mass noun] the alphabet used for Sanskrit, Hindi, and other Indian languages.
– ORIGIN from Sanskrit, literally 'divine town script', from *deva* 'god' + *nāgarī* (from *nagara* 'town'), an earlier name of the script.

devastate /ˈdɛvəsteɪt/ ▶ **verb** [with obj.] **1** destroy or ruin: *the city was devastated by a huge earthquake.*
2 cause (someone) severe and overwhelming shock or grief: *she was devastated by the loss of Damian.*
– DERIVATIVES **devastator** noun.
– ORIGIN mid 17th cent.: from Latin *devastat-* 'laid waste', from the verb *devastare*, from *de-* 'thoroughly' + *vastare* 'lay waste'.

D

devastating ▶ **adjective 1** highly destructive or damaging: *a devastating cyclone.*
2 causing severe shock, distress, or grief: *the news came as a devastating blow.*
3 informal extremely impressive or effective: *she had a devastating wit.*
– DERIVATIVES **devastatingly** adverb [as submodifier] *a devastatingly attractive man.*

devastation ▶ **noun** [mass noun] **1** great destruction or damage: *the floods caused widespread devastation.*
2 severe and overwhelming shock or grief: *she spoke of her devastation at his death.*

devein ▶ **verb** [with obj.] remove the main central vein from (a shrimp or prawn).

develop ▶ **verb** (**develops, developing, developed**)
1 grow or cause to grow and become more mature, advanced, or elaborate: [no obj.] *motion pictures were to **develop into** mass entertainment* | (as adj. **developing**) *this is a rapidly developing field* | [with obj.] *enabling individuals to develop their personal skills.* ■ [with obj.] convert (land) to a new purpose by constructing buildings or making other use of its resources. ■ [with obj.] elaborate (a musical theme) by modification of the melody, harmony, or rhythm.
2 start to exist, experience, or possess: [no obj.] *a strange closeness developed* | [with obj.] *I developed an interest in law* | *call the doctor if your child develops a rash.*
3 [with obj.] treat (a photographic film) with chemicals to make a visible image.
4 [with obj.] Chess bring (a piece) into play from its initial position on a player's back rank.
– ORIGIN mid 17th cent. (in the sense 'unfold, unfurl'): from French *développer*, based on Latin *dis-* 'un-' + a second element of unknown origin found also in **envelop**.

developable ▶ **adjective 1** (of land or property) able to be adapted or improved so as to become profitable.
2 Geometry (of a curved surface) capable of being flattened into a plane without overlap or separation, as with a cylinder.
3 Mathematics (of a function or expression) capable of being expanded as a series.

developed ▶ **adjective** advanced or elaborated to a specified degree: *a fully developed system of public law.* ■ (of a person or part of the body) having specified physical proportions: *a strongman with well-developed muscles.* ■ (of a country or region) advanced economically and socially: *the developed world.*

developer ▶ **noun** a person or thing that develops something: *a property developer* | *software developers.* ■ [with adj.] a person who grows or matures at a specified time or rate: *I was a slow developer.* ■ [mass noun] a chemical agent used for treating photographic film to make a visible image.

developing country ▶ **noun** a poor agricultural country that is seeking to become more advanced economically and socially.

development ▶ **noun** [mass noun] **1** the process of developing or being developed: *she traces the development of the novel* | *the paintings provide evidence of his artistic development.* ■ a specified state of growth or advancement: *the wings attain their full development several hours after birth.* ■ [count noun] a new and advanced product or idea: *the latest developments in information technology.*
2 [count noun] an event constituting a new stage in a changing situation: *I don't think there have been any new developments since yesterday.*
3 the process of converting land to a new purpose by constructing buildings or making use of its resources: *land suitable for development.* ■ [count noun] an area of land with new buildings on it: *a major housing development in Essex.*
4 the process of starting to be affected by an ailment or feeling: *the development of brittle bones.*

D

5 the process of treating photographic film with chemicals to make a visible image.
6 Chess the process of bringing one's pieces into play in the opening phase of a game.

developmental ▶ **adjective** concerned with the development of someone or something: *developmental problems | developmental psychology.* ■ concerned with ontogenetic development, especially embryonic development in animals: *developmental biology.*
– DERIVATIVES **developmentally** adverb.

developmental delay ▶ **noun** [mass noun] the condition of a child being less developed mentally or physically than is normal for its age.

development area ▶ **noun** (in the UK) an area in which government assistance is available to encourage business investment, in order to counteract unemployment.

development education ▶ **noun** [mass noun] education aimed at giving an understanding of developing countries and their place in the global socio-economic situation.

development system ▶ **noun** Computing a system of software and hardware designed to assist in the development of new software or products.

développé /ˌdeɪv(ə)lɒˈpeɪ/ ▶ **noun** (pl. **développés** pronunc. **same**) Ballet a movement in which one leg is raised and then kept in a fully extended position.
– ORIGIN French, past participle of *développer* 'stretch out, develop'.

Devensian /dɪˈvɛnzɪən/ ▶ **adjective** Geology relating to or denoting the most recent Pleistocene glaciation in Britain, identified with the Weichselian of northern Europe. ■ (as noun **the Devensian**) the Devensian glaciation or the system of deposits laid down during it.
– ORIGIN 1960s: from Latin *Devenses* 'people dwelling near the River Dee' (see **DEE**[1] (sense 2)) + **-IAN**.

deverbal /diːˈvəːb(ə)l/ ▶ **adjective** (of a noun or adjective) derived from a verb.
▶ **noun** a deverbal noun or adjective.

Devi /ˈdeɪvi/ Hinduism the supreme goddess, often identified with Parvati and Sakti. ■ (**devi**) Indian (in general use) a goddess. ■ Indian used after the first name of a Hindu woman as a form of respect: *Deval Devi.*
– ORIGIN from Sanskrit.

deviance ▶ **noun** [mass noun] the fact or state of diverging from usual or accepted standards, especially in social or sexual behaviour.
– DERIVATIVES **deviancy** noun.

deviant ▶ **adjective** departing from usual or accepted standards, especially in social or sexual behaviour: *deviant behaviour | a deviant ideology.* ■ derogatory homosexual.
▶ **noun** a deviant person or thing.
– ORIGIN late Middle English: from late Latin *deviant-* 'turning out of the way', from the verb *deviare* (see **DEVIATE**).

deviate ▶ **verb** /ˈdiːvɪeɪt/ [no obj.] (usu. **deviate from**) depart from an established course: *you must not deviate from the agreed route.* ■ depart from usual or accepted standards: *those who deviate from society's values.*
▶ **noun & adjective** /ˈdiːvɪət/ old-fashioned term for **DEVIANT**.
– DERIVATIVES **deviator** noun.
– ORIGIN mid 16th cent. (as an adjective in the sense 'remote'): from late Latin *deviat-* 'turned out of the way', from the verb *deviare*, from *de-* 'away from' + *via* 'way'. The verb dates from the mid 17th cent.

deviation ▶ **noun** [mass noun] **1** the action of departing from an established course or accepted standard: ***deviation from a norm** | sexual deviation* | [count noun] ***deviations from** Standard English.*
2 Statistics the amount by which a single measurement differs from a fixed value such as the mean.
3 the deflection of a ship's compass needle caused by iron in the ship.
– DERIVATIVES **deviationism** noun, **deviationist** noun.
– ORIGIN late Middle English: via French from medieval Latin *deviatio(n-)*, from Latin *deviare* (see **DEVIATE**).

device ▶ **noun 1** a thing made or adapted for a particular purpose, especially a piece of mechanical or electronic equipment: *a measuring device.* ■ a bomb or other explosive weapon: *an incendiary device.*
2 a plan, method, or trick with a particular aim: *writing a letter to a newspaper is a traditional device for signalling dissent.* ■ a form of words intended to produce a particular effect in speech or a literary work: *a rhetorical device.*
3 a drawing or design: *the decorative device on the invitations.* ■ an emblematic or heraldic design: *their shields bear the device of the Blazing Sun.* ■ [mass noun] archaic the design or look of something: *works of strange device.*
– PHRASES **leave someone to their own devices** leave someone to do as they wish without supervision.
– ORIGIN Middle English: from Old French *devis*, based on Latin *divis-* 'divided', from the verb *dividere*. The original sense was 'desire or intention', found now only in *leave someone to their own devices* (which has become associated with sense 2).

devil ▶ **noun 1** (usu. **the Devil**) (in Christian and Jewish belief) the supreme spirit of evil; Satan. ■ an evil spirit; a demon. ■ a very wicked or cruel person: *they prefer voting for devils than for decent men.* ■ (**the devil**) fighting spirit; wildness: *he was dangerous when the devil was in him.* ■ (**the devil**) a thing that is very difficult or awkward to do or deal with: *it's going to be **the very devil** to disentangle.*
2 [with adj.] informal a person with specified characteristics: *the cunning old devil | you lucky devil.*
3 (**the devil**) expressing surprise or annoyance in various questions or exclamations: *'Where the devil is he?'.*
4 an instrument or machine fitted with sharp teeth or spikes, used for tearing or other destructive work.
5 informal, dated a junior assistant of a barrister or other professional. See also **PRINTER'S DEVIL**.
▶ **verb** (**devils, devilling, devilled**; US **devils, deviling, deviled**) **1** [no obj.] informal, dated act as a junior assistant for a barrister or other professional.
2 [with obj.] N. Amer. harass or worry (someone): *he was deviled by a new-found fear.*
– PHRASES **be a devil!** Brit. informal said when encouraging someone to do something that they are hesitating to do: *'Go on, be a devil and stop being so staid!'.* **between the devil and the deep blue sea** in a difficult situation where there are two equally unpleasant choices. **devil a ——** archaic not even one or any: *the devil a man of you stirred himself over it.* **the devil can quote scripture for his purpose** proverb people may conceal unworthy motives by reciting words that sound morally authoritative. [with allusion to the Temptation.] **the devil finds work for idle hands to do** proverb if someone doesn't have enough work to occupy them, they are liable to cause or get into trouble. **the devil looks after his own** proverb success or good fortune often seem to come to those who least deserve it. **a devil of a ——** informal used to emphasize great size or degree: *photographic equipment costs a devil of a lot.* **the devil's dozen** thirteen. **the devil's in the detail** the details of a matter are its most problematic aspect. **the devil's own ——** informal used to emphasize the difficulty or seriousness of something: *it was the devil's own job to get her to give me money.* **the devil to pay** serious trouble to be dealt with. **every man for himself and the devil take the hindmost** see **MAN**. **give the devil his due** proverb if someone or something generally considered bad or undeserving has any redeeming features these should be acknowledged. **like the devil** with great speed or energy: *he drove like the devil.* **play the devil with** have a damaging or disruptive effect on: *this brandy plays the devil with one's emotions!* **speak** (or **talk**) **of the devil** said when a person appears just after being mentioned. [from the superstition that the devil will appear if his name is spoken.]
– ORIGIN Old English *dēofol* (related to Dutch *duivel* and German *Teufel*), via late Latin from Greek *diabolos* 'accuser, slanderer' (used in the Septuagint to translate Hebrew *śāṭān* 'Satan'), from *diaballein* 'to slander', from *dia* 'across' + *ballein* 'to throw'.

devil dance ▶ **noun** a dance performed as part of Buddhist ritual in Sri Lanka and Tibet, for the invocation, propitiation, or exorcism of spirits.
– DERIVATIVES **devil dancer** noun.

devilfish ▶ **noun** (pl. **same** or **devilfishes**) any of a number of marine creatures that are perceived as having a sinister appearance, in particular a devil ray, a stonefish, or an octopus or squid.

devilish ▶ **adjective** like or appropriate to a devil in evil and cruelty: *devilish tortures.* ■ mischievous and rakish: *a wide, devilish grin.* ■ very difficult to deal with or use: *it turned out to be a devilish job.*
▶ **adverb** [as submodifier] informal, dated very; extremely: *a devilish clever chap.*
– DERIVATIVES **devilishly** adverb, **devilishness** noun.

devilled ▶ **adjective** (of food) cooked with hot seasoning: *devilled kidneys.*

devilling float ▶ **noun** a wooden or plastic block with tips of nails just protruding through its base, used to scratch the surface of plaster lightly to enable more plaster to adhere to it.

devil-may-care ▶ **adjective** cheerful and reckless: *light-hearted, devil-may-care young pilots.*

devilment ▶ **noun** [mass noun] reckless mischief; wild spirits: *his eyes were blazing with devilment.*

devil ray ▶ **noun** a large long-tailed ray which has a fleshy horn-like projection on each side of the mouth. It occurs on or near the surface of warm seas and feeds on plankton. ● Family Mobulidae: two genera and several species, including the manta.

devilry ▶ **noun** [mass noun] wicked activity: *some devilry was afoot.* ■ reckless mischief: *a perverse sense of devilry urged her to lead him on.* ■ black magic; dealings with the devil.

devil's advocate ▶ **noun** a person who expresses a contentious opinion in order to provoke debate or test the strength of the opposing arguments. ■ historical a person appointed by the Roman Catholic Church to challenge a proposed beatification or canonization, or the verification of a miracle.

devil's bit ▶ **noun** any of a number of wild plants with a very short rootstock, said in folklore to have been bitten off by the devil, in particular: ● (also **devil's bit scabious**) a blue-flowered plant native to Eurasia and North Africa (*Succisa pratensis*, family Dipsacaceae). ● N. Amer. the blazing star (*Chamaelirium luteum*, family Liliaceae).

devil's claw ▶ **noun** a plant whose seed pods bear claw-like hooks which can harm livestock. ● Two genera in the family Pedaliaceae: genus *Proboscidea* of warm regions of America, used in basketry or grown for their fruit, and *Harpagophytum procumbens* of southern Africa and Madagascar, used in herbal medicine.

devil's club ▶ **noun** a very spiny straggling shrub of western North America. ● *Oplopanax horridus*, family Araliaceae.

devil's coach-horse ▶ **noun** Brit. a large black predatory rove beetle which raises its hind end and opens its jaws in a threatening manner when disturbed. ● *Staphylinus olens*, family Staphylinidae.

devil's darning needle ▶ **noun** N. Amer. another term for **DARNER**.

devil's food cake ▶ **noun** chiefly N. Amer. a rich chocolate cake.

devil's grip ▶ **noun** informal term for **BORNHOLM DISEASE**.

Devil's Island a rocky island off the coast of French Guiana, used from 1852 as a penal settlement, especially for political prisoners. The last prisoner was released in 1953.

devils on horseback ▶ **plural noun** chiefly Brit. a savoury snack of prunes individually wrapped in slices of bacon, served on toast or croutons.

devil's paintbrush ▶ **noun** N. Amer. the European orange hawkweed, which has become naturalized in North America. ● *Hieracium aurantiacum*, family Compositae.

devil's walking stick ▶ **noun** a prickly angelica tree native to the eastern US. Also called **HERCULES' CLUB**. ● *Aralia spinosa*, family Araliaceae.

deviltry ▶ **noun** archaic variant of **DEVILRY**.

devious /ˈdiːvɪəs/ ▶ **adjective 1** showing a skilful use of underhand tactics to achieve goals: *he's as devious as a politician needs to be | they have devious ways of making money.*
2 (of a route or journey) longer and less direct than the most straightforward way.
– DERIVATIVES **deviously** adverb, **deviousness** noun.
– ORIGIN late 16th cent.: from Latin *devius* (from *de-* 'away from' + *via* 'way') + **-OUS**. The original sense was 'remote'; the later sense 'departing from the direct route' gave rise to the figurative sense 'deviating from the straight way' and hence 'skilled in underhand tactics'.

devise /dɪˈvʌɪz/ ▶ **verb** [with obj.] **1** plan or invent (a complex procedure, system, or mechanism) by careful thought: *a training programme should be devised | a complicated game **of his own devising**.*
2 Law leave (something, especially real estate) to someone by the terms of a will.
▶ **noun** Law a clause in a will leaving something, especially real estate, to someone.
– DERIVATIVES **devisable** adjective, **devisee** noun (sense 2 of the verb), **deviser** noun, **devisor** noun (sense 2 of the verb).

– ORIGIN Middle English: the verb from Old French *deviser*, from Latin *divis-* 'divided', from the verb *dividere* (this sense being reflected in the original English sense of the verb); the noun is a variant of DEVICE (in the early sense 'will, desire').

devitalize (also **devitalise**) ▸ verb [with obj.] (usu. as adj. **devitalized**) deprive of strength and vigour: *an effective product to treat devitalized skin.*
– DERIVATIVES **devitalization** noun.

devitrify ▸ verb (**devitrifies, devitrifying, devitrified**) (with reference to glass or vitreous rock) become or make hard, opaque, and crystalline.
– DERIVATIVES **devitrification** noun.

devoice ▸ verb [with obj.] Phonetics make (a vowel or voiced consonant) voiceless.

devoid /dɪˈvɔɪd/ ▸ adjective (**devoid of**) entirely lacking or free from: *Lisa kept her voice devoid of emotion.*
– ORIGIN late Middle English: past participle of obsolete *devoid* 'cast out', from Old French *devoidier*.

devoir /dəˈvwɑː/ ▸ noun archaic a person's duty: *you have **done your devoir** right well.*
– PHRASES **pay one's devoirs** pay one's respects formally.
– ORIGIN Middle English: from Old French *deveir*, from Latin *debere* 'owe'. The spelling, and subsequently the pronunciation, was changed under the influence of modern French *devoir*.

devolution /ˌdiːvəˈluːʃ(ə)n, ˌdɛv-/ ▸ noun [mass noun] **1** the transfer or delegation of power to a lower level, especially by central government to local or regional administration. ■ Law the legal transfer of property from one owner to another.
2 formal descent to a lower or worse state: *the **devolution** of the gentlemanly ideal **into** a glorification of drunkenness.* ■ Biology evolutionary degeneration.
– DERIVATIVES **devolutionary** adjective, **devolutionist** noun.
– ORIGIN late 15th cent. (in the sense 'transference by default'): from late Latin *devolutio(n-)*, from Latin *devolvere* 'roll down' (see DEVOLVE).

devolve /dɪˈvɒlv/ ▸ verb **1** [with obj.] transfer or delegate (power) to a lower level, especially from central government to local or regional administration: *measures to **devolve** power **to** a Scottish assembly* | (as adj. **devolved**) *devolved and decentralized government.* ■ [no obj.] (**devolve on/upon/to**) (of duties or responsibility) pass to (a body or person at a lower level): *his duties devolved on a comrade.* ■ [no obj.] (**devolve on/upon/to**) Law (of property) be transferred from one owner to (another), especially by inheritance.
2 [no obj.] (**devolve into**) formal pass into (a different state, especially a worse one); degenerate: *the Empire devolved into separate warring states.*
– DERIVATIVES **devolvement** noun.
– ORIGIN late Middle English (in the sense 'roll down'): from Latin *devolvere*, from *de-* 'down' + *volvere* 'to roll'.

Devon[1] (also **Devonshire**) a county of SW England; county town, Exeter.
– ORIGIN from medieval Latin *Devonia* 'Devonshire'.

Devon[2] ▸ noun an animal of a breed of red beef cattle.
– ORIGIN mid 19th cent.: named after the county of Devon (see DEVON[1]).

Devonian /dɛˈvəʊnɪən, dɪ-/ ▸ adjective **1** relating to Devon.
2 Geology relating to or denoting the fourth period of the Palaeozoic era, between the Silurian and Carboniferous periods.

> The Devonian period lasted from about 409 to 363 million years ago. During this period fish became abundant, the first amphibians evolved, and the first forests appeared.

▸ noun **1** a native or inhabitant of Devon.
2 (**the Devonian**) Geology the Devonian period or the system of rocks deposited during it.

devoré /dəˈvɔːreɪ/ (also **devore**) ▸ noun [usu. as modifier] a velvet fabric with a pattern formed by burning the pile away with acid: *a devoré top.*
– ORIGIN 1990s: from French *dévoré*, literally 'devoured', past participle of *dévorer*.

devote ▸ verb [with obj.] **1** (**devote something to**) give all or most of one's time or resources to (a person or activity): *I wanted to devote more time to my family* | *she devoted herself to fundraising.* ■ use a certain amount of space or time to cover (a topic).
2 archaic invoke or pronounce a curse upon.
– ORIGIN late 16th cent. (in the sense 'dedicate formally, consecrate'): from Latin *devot-* 'consecrated', from the verb *devovere*, from *de-* 'formally' + *vovere* 'to vow'.

devoted ▸ adjective **1** very loving or loyal: *he was a devoted husband* | *Leo was **devoted to** his job.*
2 (**devoted to**) given over to the display, study, or discussion of: *there is a museum devoted to her work.*
– DERIVATIVES **devotedly** adverb (sense 1), **devotedness** noun (sense 1).

devotee /ˌdɛvə(ʊ)ˈtiː/ ▸ noun a person who is very interested in and enthusiastic about someone or something: *a devotee of Lewis Carroll.* ■ a strong believer in a particular religion or god: *devotees of Krishna.*

devotion ▸ noun [mass noun] love, loyalty, or enthusiasm for a person or activity: *his **devotion to** duty never wavered* | *she was the epitome of wifely devotion.* ■ religious worship or observance: *the order's aim was to live a life of devotion.* ■ (**devotions**) prayers or religious observances.
– ORIGIN Middle English: from Latin *devotio(n-)*, from *devovere* 'consecrate' (see DEVOTE).

devotional ▸ adjective of or used in religious worship: *devotional books.*
– DERIVATIVES **devotionally** adverb.

devour /dɪˈvaʊə/ ▸ verb [with obj.] **1** eat (food or prey) hungrily or quickly: *he devoured half of his burger in one bite.* ■ (of fire or a similar force) destroy completely: *the hungry flames devoured the old house.*
2 read quickly and eagerly: *she spent her evenings devouring the classics.*
3 (**be devoured**) be totally absorbed by a powerful feeling: *she was devoured by need.*
– DERIVATIVES **devourer** noun.
– ORIGIN Middle English: from Old French *devorer*, from Latin *devorare*, from *de-* 'down' + *vorare* 'to swallow'.

devout /dɪˈvaʊt/ ▸ adjective having or showing deep religious feeling or commitment: *she was a devout Catholic* | *a rabbi's devout prayers.* ■ totally committed to a cause or belief: *the most devout environmentalist.*
– DERIVATIVES **devoutly** adverb, **devoutness** noun.
– ORIGIN Middle English: from Old French *devot*, from Latin *devotus* 'devoted', past participle of *devovere* (see DEVOTE).

DEW ▸ abbreviation distant early warning, a radar system in North America for the early detection of a missile attack.

dew ▸ noun [mass noun] tiny drops of water that form on cool surfaces at night, when atmospheric vapour condenses: *the grass was wet with dew* | [in sing.] *a cold, heavy dew dripped from the leaves.* ■ [in sing.] a beaded or glistening liquid resembling dew: *her body had broken out in a fine dew of perspiration.*
▸ verb [with obj.] literary moisten with drops of liquid: *sweat dewed her lashes.*
ORIGIN Old English *dēaw*, of Germanic origin; related to Dutch *dauw* and German *Tau* (noun), *tauen* (verb).

dewan /dɪˈwɑːn/ ▸ noun variant spelling of DIWAN.

Dewar /ˈdjuːə/, Sir James (1842–1923), Scottish chemist and physicist. He is chiefly remembered for his work in cryogenics, in which he devised the vacuum flask, achieved temperatures close to absolute zero, and was the first to produce liquid oxygen and hydrogen in quantity.

dewar /ˈdjuːə/ ▸ noun a double-walled flask of metal or silvered glass with a vacuum between the walls, used to hold liquids at well below ambient temperature.
ORIGIN late 19th cent.: named after Sir James DEWAR.

dewater ▸ verb [with obj.] drain (a waterlogged or flooded area). ■ remove water from (sediment or waste materials).

dewax ▸ verb [with obj.] remove wax from: *linoleum needs to be dewaxed using a strong solvent.*

dewberry ▸ noun (pl. **dewberries**) a trailing European bramble with soft prickles and edible fruit resembling the blackberry, which have a dewy white bloom on the skin. ● *Rubus caesius*, family Rosaceae. ■ N. Amer. any of a number of trailing brambles. ■ the blue-black fruit of the dewberry.

dewclaw ▸ noun a rudimentary inner toe present in some dogs. ■ a false hoof on an animal such as a deer, which is formed by its rudimentary side toes.
– ORIGIN late 16th cent.: apparently from DEW and CLAW.

dewdrop ▸ noun a drop of dew.

Dewey decimal classification (also **Dewey system**) ▸ noun an internationally applied decimal system of library classification which uses a three-figure code from 000 to 999 to represent the major branches of knowledge, and allows finer classification to be made by the addition of further figures after a decimal point.
– ORIGIN late 19th cent.: named after Melvil *Dewey* (1851–1931), American librarian.

dewfall ▸ noun [mass noun] literary the formation of dew, or the time of the evening when dew begins to form. ■ the film of dew covering an area.

Dewi /ˈdewi/ Welsh name for St David (see DAVID, ST).

D

dewlap ▸ noun a fold of loose skin hanging from the neck or throat of an animal or bird, especially that present in many cattle.
– ORIGIN Middle English: from DEW and LAP[1], perhaps influenced by a Scandinavian word (compare with Danish *doglæp*).

deworm ▸ verb [with obj.] treat (an animal) to free it of worms.
– DERIVATIVES **dewormer** noun.

dew point ▸ noun the atmospheric temperature (varying according to pressure and humidity) below which water droplets begin to condense and dew can form.

dew pond ▸ noun Brit. a shallow pond, especially an artificial one made on downs where the water supply from springs or surface drainage is inadequate.

Dewsbury /ˈdjuːzb(ə)ri/ a textile manufacturing town in West Yorkshire, northern England; pop. 53,300 (est. 2009).

dew worm ▸ noun N. Amer. an earthworm, in particular one that is used as fishing bait.
– ORIGIN Old English *deaw-wyrm* 'ringworm'; compare with East Frisian *dauworm*, denoting both ringworm and the earthworm.

dewy ▸ adjective (**dewier, dewiest**) **1** wet with dew.
2 (of a person's skin) appearing soft and lustrous. ■ youthful and fresh: *the girls have yet to lose their dewy charm.*
– DERIVATIVES **dewily** adverb, **dewiness** noun.
– ORIGIN Old English *dēawig* (see DEW, -Y[1]).

dewy-eyed ▸ adjective having eyes that are moist with tears (used typically to indicate that a person is nostalgic, naive, or sentimental): *she gets slightly dewy-eyed as she talks about her family.*

dex ▸ noun informal short for DEXEDRINE.

dexamethasone /ˌdɛksəˈmɛθəsəʊn, -zəʊn/ ▸ noun [mass noun] Medicine a synthetic drug of the corticosteroid type, used especially as an anti-inflammatory agent.
– ORIGIN 1950s: from *dexa-* (blend of DECA- and HEXA-) + *meth(yl)* + *-a-* + *(cortis)one*.

Dexedrine /ˈdɛksədriːn, -drɪn/ ▸ noun trademark a form of amphetamine (see AMPHETAMINE).
– ORIGIN 1940s: probably from DEXTRO-, on the pattern of *Benzedrine*.

dexter[1] /ˈdɛkstə/ ▸ adjective [attrib.] archaic & Heraldry on or towards the right-hand side (in a coat of arms, from the bearer's point of view, i.e. the left as it is depicted). The opposite of SINISTER.
– ORIGIN mid 16th cent.: from Latin, 'on the right'.

dexter[2] /ˈdɛkstə/ ▸ noun an animal of a small, hardy breed of Irish cattle.
– ORIGIN late 19th cent.: said to have been named after the breeder.

dexterity /dɛkˈstɛrɪti/ ▸ noun [mass noun] skill in performing tasks, especially with the hands: *her dexterity with chopsticks* | *his record testifies to a certain dexterity in politics.*
– ORIGIN early 16th cent. (in the sense 'mental adroitness'): from French *dextérité*, from Latin *dexteritas*, from *dexter* 'on the right'.

dexterous /ˈdɛkst(ə)rəs/ (also **dextrous**) ▸ adjective showing or having skill, especially with the hands: *a dexterous keyboard player.*
– DERIVATIVES **dexterously** adverb, **dexterousness** noun.
– ORIGIN early 17th cent. (in the sense 'mentally adroit'): from Latin *dexter* 'on the right' + -OUS.

dextral /ˈdɛkstr(ə)l/ ▸ adjective of or on the right side or the right hand (the opposite of SINISTRAL). ■ right-handed. ■ Geology relating to or denoting a strike-slip fault in which the motion of the block on the further side of the fault from an observer is towards the right. ■ Zoology (of a spiral mollusc shell) with whorls rising to the right and coiling in an anticlockwise direction.

▶ noun a right-handed person.
– DERIVATIVES **dextrality** /-ˈstralɪti/ noun, **dextrally** adverb.
– ORIGIN mid 17th cent.: from medieval Latin *dextralis*, from Latin *dextra* 'the right hand', from *dexter* 'on the right'.

dextran /ˈdɛkstran/ ▶ noun [mass noun] Chemistry a carbohydrate gum formed by the fermentation of sugars and consisting of polymers of glucose. ■ Medicine a solution containing a hydrolysed form of dextran, used as a substitute for blood plasma.
– ORIGIN late 19th cent.: from DEXTRO- + -AN.

D

dextrin /ˈdɛkstrɪn/ ▶ noun [mass noun] a soluble gummy substance obtained by hydrolysis of starch, used as a thickening agent and in adhesives and dietary supplements.
– ORIGIN mid 19th cent.: from DEXTRO- + -IN[1].

dextro- ▶ combining form on or to the right: *dextrorotatory*.
– ORIGIN from Latin *dexter, dextr-* 'right'.

dextrorotatory /ˌdɛkstrəʊˈrəʊtət(ə)ri/ ▶ adjective Chemistry (of a compound) having the property of rotating the plane of a polarized light ray to the right, i.e. clockwise facing the oncoming radiation. The opposite of LAEVOROTATORY.

dextrose /ˈdɛkstrəʊz, -s/ ▶ noun [mass noun] Chemistry the dextrorotatory form of glucose (and the predominant naturally occurring form).
– ORIGIN mid 19th cent.: from Latin *dexter, dextr-* 'on the right' + -OSE[2].

dextrous ▶ adjective variant spelling of DEXTEROUS.

dexy /ˈdɛksi/ ▶ noun (pl. **dexies**) [mass noun] informal Dexedrine. ■ [count noun] a tablet of Dexedrine.
– ORIGIN 1950s: abbreviation.

dezincification /diːˌzɪŋkɪfɪˈkeɪʃ(ə)n/ ▶ noun [mass noun] a form of corrosion and weakening of brass objects in which zinc is dissolved out of the brass alloy.

DF ▶ abbreviation ■ Defender of the Faith. [from Latin *Defensor Fidei*.] ■ direction finder.

DFC ▶ abbreviation (in the UK) Distinguished Flying Cross, a decoration for distinguished active service awarded to members of the RAF, instituted in 1918.

DFID ▶ abbreviation (in the UK) Department for International Development.

Dfl ▶ abbreviation Dutch florins.

DFM ▶ abbreviation (in the UK) Distinguished Flying Medal, a decoration awarded to RAF personnel for acts of courage or devotion to duty when not in action against an enemy, instituted in 1918.

DfT ▶ abbreviation (in the UK) Department for Transport.

DG ▶ abbreviation ■ Dei gratia, by the grace of God. ■ Deo gratias, thanks be to God. ■ (in the UK) director general.

dg ▶ abbreviation decigram(s).

DH Baseball ▶ abbreviation designated hitter.
▶ verb (**DH's**, **DHing**, **DH'd**) [no obj.] act as a designated hitter.

dhaba /ˈdɑːbə/ ▶ noun Indian a roadside food stall.
– ORIGIN from Hindi *ḍhābā*.

Dhaka /ˈdakə/ (also **Dacca**) the capital of Bangladesh, on the Ganges delta; pop. 7,000,940 (2008).
– DERIVATIVES **Dhakai** adjective.

dhal ▶ noun variant spelling of DAL[1].

dhamma /ˈdɑːmə, ˈdʌmə/ ▶ noun another term for DHARMA, especially among Theravada Buddhists.
– ORIGIN Pali, from Sanskrit *dharma* 'decree or custom'.

Dhanbad /ˈdɑːnbad/ a city in Jharkhand, NE India; pop. 241,800 (est. 2009).

dhansak /ˈdʌnsɑːk/ ▶ noun [mass noun] an Indian dish of meat or vegetables cooked with lentils and occasionally spinach: *chicken dhansak*.
– ORIGIN Gujarati.

dharma /ˈdɑːmə, ˈdəːmə/ ▶ noun [mass noun] (in Indian religion) the eternal law of the cosmos, inherent in the very nature of things.

> In Hinduism, dharma is seen as the cosmic law both upheld by the gods and expressed in right behaviour by humans, including adherence to the social order. In Buddhism (termed *dhamma*), it is interpreted as universal truth or law, especially as proclaimed by the Buddha. In Jainism, it is conceived both as virtue and as a kind of fundamental substance, the medium of motion.

– ORIGIN Sanskrit, literally 'decree or custom'.

dharmashala /ˈdɑːməˌʃɑːlə/ (also **dharmsala** /ˈdɑːmˌsɑːlə/, **dharamshala** /ˈdɑːrəmˌʃɑːlə/) ▶ noun (in South Asia) a building devoted to religious or charitable purposes, especially a rest house for travellers.
– ORIGIN from Sanskrit *dharmaśālā*, from *dharma* 'virtue' + *śālā* 'house'.

dharna /ˈdəːnə, -ɑː/ ▶ noun [mass noun] Indian a mode of compelling payment or compliance, by sitting at the debtor's or offender's door until the demand is complied with. ■ [count noun] a peaceful demonstration.
– ORIGIN from Hindi *dharnā* 'sitting in restraint, placing'.

Dharuk /ˈdʌrʊk/ ▶ noun [mass noun] an Aboriginal language of the area around Sydney, Australia, now extinct.

Dhaulagiri /ˌdaʊləˈɡɪəri/ a mountain massif in the Himalayas, in Nepal, with six peaks, rising to 8,172 m (26,810 ft) at its highest point.

Dhelfoí /ðɛlˈfi/ Greek name for DELPHI.

dhikr /ˈðɪk(ə)r/ (also **zikr** /ˈzɪk(ə)r/) ▶ noun [mass noun] Islam a form of devotion, associated chiefly with Sufism, in which the worshipper is absorbed in the rhythmic repetition of the name of God or his attributes. ■ [count noun] a Sufi ceremony in which dhikr is practised.
– ORIGIN from Arabic *ḏikr* 'remembrance'.

Dhílos /ˈðilɔs/ Greek name for DELOS.

dhobi /ˈdəʊbi/ ▶ noun (pl. **dhobis**) (in South Asia) a washerman or washerwoman.
– ORIGIN from Hindi *dhobī*, from *dhob* 'washing'.

dhobi itch ▶ noun [mass noun] informal itching inflammation of the skin, especially in the groin region, suffered particularly in the tropics and typically caused by certain types of ringworm infection or by allergic dermatitis.

Dhofar /dəʊˈfɑː/ the fertile southern province of Oman.

dhol /dəʊl/ ▶ noun a large, barrel-shaped or cylindrical wooden drum, typically two-headed, used in South Asia.
– ORIGIN from Hindi *ḍhol*.

dholak /ˈdəʊlək/ ▶ noun a medium-sized dhol.
– ORIGIN Hindi, from *ḍhol* (see DHOL) + the diminutive suffix *-ak*.

dhole /dəʊl/ ▶ noun an Asian wild dog with a sandy coat and a black bushy tail, living in packs. Also called RED DOG. ● *Cuon alpinus*, family Canidae.
– ORIGIN early 19th cent.: of unknown origin.

dhoni /ˈdəʊni/ ▶ noun (pl. **dhonis**) a small wooden sailing vessel used in India and SE Asia.
– ORIGIN from Telugu *doni*; compare with Persian *dōnī* 'yacht'.

dhoti /ˈdəʊti/ ▶ noun (pl. **dhotis**) a garment worn by male Hindus, consisting of a piece of material tied around the waist and extending to cover most of the legs.
– ORIGIN Hindi *dhotī*.

dhow /daʊ/ ▶ noun a lateen-rigged ship with one or two masts, used chiefly in the Arabian region.
– ORIGIN late 18th cent.: from Arabic *dāwa*, probably related to Marathi *dāw*.

DHSS ▶ abbreviation (formerly in the UK) Department of Health and Social Security.

DHT ▶ abbreviation dihydrotestosterone.

DHTML ▶ abbreviation Computing dynamic HTML.

dhurrie /ˈdʌri/ (also **durrie**) ▶ noun (pl. **dhurries**) a heavy cotton rug of Indian origin.
– ORIGIN from Hindi *darī*.

dhyana /dɪˈɑːnə/ ▶ noun [mass noun] (in Hindu and Buddhist practice) profound meditation which is the penultimate stage of yoga.
– ORIGIN from Sanskrit *dhyāna*.

DI ▶ abbreviation ■ (in the UK) Defence Intelligence. ■ (in the UK) Detective Inspector. ■ direct injection.

di-[1] /dʌɪ, di/ ▶ combining form twice; two-; double: *dichromatic*. ■ Chemistry containing two atoms, molecules, or groups of a specified kind: *dioxide*.
– ORIGIN from Greek *dis* 'twice'.

di-[2] /di, dʌɪ/ ▶ prefix variant spelling of DIS- shortened before *l, m, n, r, s* (followed by a consonant), and *v*; also often shortened before *g*, and sometimes before *j*.
– ORIGIN from Latin.

di-[3] /dʌɪ/ ▶ prefix variant spelling of DIA- shortened before a vowel (as in *dielectric*).

dia. ▶ abbreviation diameter.

dia- (also **di-** before a vowel) ▶ prefix **1** through; across: *diameter* | *diaphanous* | *diuretic*. **2** apart: *diakinesis*.
– ORIGIN from Greek *dia* 'through'.

diabase /ˈdʌɪəbeɪs/ ▶ noun Geology another term for DOLERITE.
– ORIGIN mid 19th cent. (originally denoting diorite): from French, formed irregularly as if from *di-* 'two' + *base* 'base' (thus 'rock with two bases', referring to the base minerals of diorite), but associated later perhaps with Greek *diabasis* 'transition'.

diabetes /ˌdʌɪəˈbiːtiːz/ ▶ noun [mass noun] a disorder of the metabolism causing excessive thirst and the production of large amounts of urine.
– ORIGIN mid 16th cent.: via Latin from Greek, literally 'siphon', from *diabainein* 'go through'.

diabetes insipidus /ɪnˈsɪpɪdəs/ ▶ noun [mass noun] a rare form of diabetes caused by a deficiency of the pituitary hormone vasopressin, which regulates kidney function.
– ORIGIN late 19th cent.: from DIABETES + Latin *insipidus* 'insipid'.

diabetes mellitus /mɪˈlʌɪtəs/ ▶ noun [mass noun] the commonest form of diabetes, caused by a deficiency of the pancreatic hormone insulin, which results in a failure to metabolize sugars and starch. Sugars accumulate in the blood and urine, and the by-products of alternative fat metabolism disturb the acid–base balance of the blood, causing a risk of convulsions and coma.
– ORIGIN late 19th cent.: from DIABETES + Latin *mellitus* 'sweet'.

diabetic ▶ adjective having diabetes. ■ relating to or designed to relieve diabetes: *a diabetic clinic* | *a diabetic diet*.
▶ noun a person suffering from diabetes.

diablerie /dɪˈɑːbləri/ ▶ noun [mass noun] the quality of being reckless or wild in a charismatic way. ■ archaic sorcery supposedly assisted by the devil.
– ORIGIN mid 18th cent.: from French, from *diable*, from ecclesiastical Latin *diabolus* 'devil'.

diabolic /ˌdʌɪəˈbɒlɪk/ ▶ adjective relating to or characteristic of the Devil: *the darkness of a diabolic world*.
– ORIGIN late Middle English: from Old French *diabolique* or ecclesiastical Latin *diabolicus*, from *diabolus* 'devil'.

diabolical ▶ adjective **1** characteristic of the Devil, or so evil as to recall the Devil: *his diabolical cunning*. **2** Brit. informal disgracefully bad or unpleasant: *a singer with an absolutely diabolical voice*.
– DERIVATIVES **diabolically** adverb [as submodifier] *a diabolically clever scheme*.

diabolism /dʌɪˈabəlɪz(ə)m/ ▶ noun [mass noun] worship of the Devil.
– DERIVATIVES **diabolist** noun.
– ORIGIN early 17th cent.: from ecclesiastical Latin *diabolus* or Greek *diabolos* 'devil' + -ISM.

diabolize /dʌɪˈabəlʌɪz/ (also **diabolise**) ▶ verb [with obj.] archaic represent as diabolical.

diabolo /dɪˈabələʊ, dʌɪ-/ ▶ noun (pl. **diabolos**) [mass noun] a game in which a two-headed top is thrown up and caught with a string stretched between two sticks. ■ [count noun] the wooden top used in the game of diabolo.
– ORIGIN early 20th cent.: from Italian, from ecclesiastical Latin *diabolus* 'devil'; the game was formerly called *devil on two sticks*.

diacetylmorphine /dʌɪˌasɪtʌɪlˈmɔːfiːn/ ▶ noun technical term for HEROIN.

diachronic /ˌdʌɪəˈkrɒnɪk/ ▶ adjective concerned with the way in which something, especially language, has developed and evolved through time. Often contrasted with SYNCHRONIC.
– DERIVATIVES **diachroneity** /ˌdʌɪəkrəˈniːɪti, -ˈneɪɪti/ noun, **diachronically** adverb, **diachronistic** /dʌɪˌakrəˈnɪstɪk/ adjective, **diachrony** /dʌɪˈakrəni/ noun.
– ORIGIN mid 19th cent.: from DIA- 'through' + Greek *khronos* 'time' + -IC.

diachronism /dʌɪˈakrənɪz(ə)m/ ▶ noun [mass noun] Geology the occurrence of a feature or phenomenon in different geological periods.
– DERIVATIVES **diachronous** adjective, **diachronously** adverb.

diaconal /dʌɪˈak(ə)n(ə)l/ ▶ adjective relating to a deacon, or to the role of a deacon.
– ORIGIN early 17th cent.: from ecclesiastical Latin *diaconalis*, from *diaconus* (see DEACON).

diaconate /dʌɪˈakənеɪt, -ət/ ▶ noun the office of deacon, or a person's tenure of it. ■ a body of deacons collectively.
– ORIGIN early 18th cent.: from ecclesiastical Latin *diaconatus*, from *diaconus* (see DEACON).

diacritic /ˌdʌɪəˈkrɪtɪk/ ▶ noun a sign, such as an accent or cedilla, which when written above or below a letter indicates a difference in pronunciation from the same letter when unmarked or differently marked.
▶ adjective (of a mark or sign) indicating a difference in pronunciation.
– DERIVATIVES **diacritical** adjective, **diacritically** adverb.
– ORIGIN late 17th cent.: from Greek *diakritikos*, from *diakrinein* 'distinguish', from *dia-* 'through' + *krinein* 'to separate'.

diadelphous /ˌdʌɪəˈdɛlfəs/ ▶ adjective Botany (of stamens) united by their filaments so as to form two groups.
– ORIGIN early 19th cent.: from DI-[1] 'two' + Greek *adelphos* 'brother' + -OUS.

diadem /ˈdʌɪədɛm/ ▶ noun a jewelled crown or headband worn as a symbol of sovereignty. ■ (**the diadem**) archaic the authority or dignity symbolized by a crown.
– DERIVATIVES **diademed** adjective.
– ORIGIN Middle English: from Old French *diademe*, via Latin from Greek *diadēma* 'the regal headband of the Persian kings', from *diadein* 'bind round'.

Diadochi /dʌɪˈadəki/ the six Macedonian generals of Alexander the Great (Antigonus, Antipater, Cassander, Lysimachus, Ptolemy, and Seleucus), among whom his empire was eventually divided after his death in 323 BC.
– ORIGIN from Greek *diadokhoi* 'successors'.

diaeresis /dʌɪˈɪərɪsɪs, -ˈɛr-/ (US **dieresis**) ▶ noun (pl. **diaereses** /-siːz/) **1** a mark (¨) placed over a vowel to indicate that it is sounded separately, as in *naïve*, *Brontë*. ■ [mass noun] the division of a sound into two syllables, especially by sounding a diphthong as two vowels.
2 Prosody a natural rhythmic break in a line of verse where the end of a metrical foot coincides with the end of a phrase.
– ORIGIN late 16th cent. (denoting the division of one syllable into two): via Latin from Greek *diairesis* 'separation', from *diairein* 'take apart', from *dia* 'apart' + *hairein* 'take'.

diagenesis /ˌdʌɪəˈdʒɛnɪsɪs/ ▶ noun [mass noun] Geology the physical and chemical changes occurring during the conversion of sediment to sedimentary rock.
– DERIVATIVES **diagenetic** adjective, **diagenetically** adverb.

Diaghilev /dɪˈagɪlɛf/, Sergei (Pavlovich) (1872–1929), Russian ballet impresario. In 1909 he formed the Ballets Russes, which he directed until his death.

diagnose /ˈdʌɪəgnəʊz, -ˈnəʊz/ ▶ verb [with obj.] identify the nature of (an illness or other problem) by examination of the symptoms: *two doctors failed to diagnose a punctured lung*. ■ identify the nature of the medical condition of: *she was finally* ***diagnosed as*** *having epilepsy* | *20,000 men are* ***diagnosed with*** *skin cancer every year*.
– DERIVATIVES **diagnosable** adjective.
– ORIGIN mid 19th cent.: back-formation from DIAGNOSIS.

diagnosis /ˌdʌɪəgˈnəʊsɪs/ ▶ noun (pl. **diagnoses** /-siːz/) [mass noun] **1** the identification of the nature of an illness or other problem by examination of the symptoms: *early diagnosis and treatment are essential* | [count noun] *a diagnosis of Crohn's disease was made*.
2 the distinctive characterization in precise terms of a genus, species, or phenomenon.
– ORIGIN late 17th cent.: modern Latin, from Greek, from *diagignōskein* 'distinguish, discern', from *dia* 'apart' + *gignōskein* 'recognize, know'.

diagnostic /dʌɪəgˈnɒstɪk/ ▶ adjective **1** concerned with the diagnosis of illness or other problems: *a diagnostic tool*. ■ (of a symptom) distinctive, and so indicating the nature of an illness: *there are fifteen infections which are* ***diagnostic of*** *AIDS*.
2 characteristic of a particular species, genus, or phenomenon: *the diagnostic character of having not one but two pairs of antennae*.
▶ noun **1** a distinctive symptom or characteristic. ■ Computing a program or routine that helps a user to identify errors.
2 (**diagnostics**) the practice or techniques of diagnosis: *advanced medical diagnostics*.
– DERIVATIVES **diagnostically** adverb, **diagnostician** /-nɒˈstɪʃ(ə)n/ noun.
– ORIGIN early 17th cent.: from Greek *diagnōstikos* 'able to distinguish', from *diagignōskein* 'distinguish'; the noun from *hē diagnōstikē tekhnē* 'the art of distinguishing (disease)'.

diagonal /dʌɪˈag(ə)n(ə)l/ ▶ adjective (of a straight line) joining two opposite corners of a square, rectangle, or other straight-sided shape. ■ (of a line) straight and at an angle; slanting: *a tie with diagonal stripes*.
▶ noun a straight line joining two opposite corners of a square, rectangle, or other straight-sided shape. ■ Mathematics the set of elements of a matrix that lie on a line joining two opposite corners. ■ a slanting straight line: *the bars of light made diagonals across the entrance* | *tiles can be laid* ***on the diagonal***. ■ Chess a slanting row of squares whose colour is the same.
– ORIGIN mid 16th cent.: from Latin *diagonalis*, from Greek *diagōnios* 'from angle to angle', from *dia* 'through' + *gōnia* 'angle'.

diagonally ▶ adverb in a diagonal direction: *now walk diagonally across the field towards a farmhouse*.

diagonal matrix ▶ noun Mathematics a matrix having non-zero elements only in the diagonal running from the upper left to the lower right.

diagram /ˈdʌɪəgram/ ▶ noun a simplified drawing showing the appearance, structure, or workings of something; a schematic representation: *a diagram of the living room*. ■ Geometry a figure composed of lines that is used to illustrate a definition or statement or to aid in the proof of a proposition. ■ Brit. a graphical schedule for operating railway locomotives and rolling stock in order to provide a desired service.
▶ verb (**diagrams**, **diagramming**, **diagrammed**; US **diagrams**, **diagraming**, **diagramed**) [with obj.] represent (something) in graphic form: *the experiment is diagrammed on page fourteen*. ■ Brit. schedule the operations of (a locomotive or train) according to a diagram.
– ORIGIN early 17th cent.: from Latin *diagramma*, from Greek, from *diagraphein* 'mark out by lines', from *dia* 'through' + *graphein* 'write'.

diagrammatic /ˌdʌɪəgrəˈmatɪk/ ▶ adjective of or in the form of a diagram: *a diagrammatic representation of the system*.
– DERIVATIVES **diagrammatically** adverb.

diagrid /ˈdʌɪəgrɪd/ ▶ noun Brit. a supporting framework in a building formed with diagonally intersecting ribs of metal or concrete.
– ORIGIN 1940s: from DIAGONAL + GRID.

diakinesis /ˌdʌɪəkʌɪˈniːsɪs/ ▶ noun (pl. **diakineses** /-siːz/) [mass noun] Biology the fifth and last stage of the prophase of meiosis, following diplotene, when the separation of homologous chromosomes is complete and crossing over has occurred.
– ORIGIN early 20th cent.: from DIA- 'through, across' + Greek *kinēsis* 'motion'.

dial ▶ noun a face of a clock or watch that is marked to show units of time. ■ a similar face or flat plate with a scale and pointer for showing measurements of weight, volume, or pressure. ■ a disc with numbered finger holes on a telephone, rotated a particular distance for each digit of the number being called. ■ a plate or disc turned to select a setting on a radio, cooker, or other piece of equipment. ■ Brit. informal a person's face.
▶ verb (**dials**, **dialling**, **dialled**; US **dials**, **dialing**, **dialed**) [with obj.] **1** call (a telephone number) by turning a dial or using a keypad: *she dialled 999* | [no obj.] *company employees* ***dial out from*** *their office*. ■ (**dial something up**) gain access to a service using a telephone line: *plans to enable customers to dial up videos from their living room*.
2 indicate or regulate by means of a dial: *you're expected to* ***dial in*** *volume and tone settings*. ■ include or add: *the car has a lot of understeer* ***dialled into*** *the suspension*.
– PHRASES **be** (or **get**) **dialled in** informal be or become so focused that one is able to perform to the best of one's abilities: *I didn't really get dialled in until the final qualifying session*.
– ORIGIN Middle English (denoting a mariner's compass): from medieval Latin *diale* 'clock dial', based on Latin *dies* 'day'.

dial-a- ▶ combining form denoting a service available for booking by telephone: *dial-a-ride*.

dialect /ˈdʌɪəlɛkt/ ▶ noun a particular form of a language which is peculiar to a specific region or social group: *the Lancashire dialect seemed like a foreign language*. ■ Computing a particular version of a programming language.
– DERIVATIVES **dialectal** /-ˈlɛkt(ə)l/ adjective, **dialectally** adverb.
– ORIGIN mid 16th cent. (denoting the art of investigating the truth of opinions): from French *dialecte*, or via Latin from Greek *dialektos* 'discourse, way of speaking', from *dialegesthai* 'converse with' (see DIALOGUE).

dialectic /ˌdʌɪəˈlɛktɪk/ Philosophy ▶ noun [mass noun] (also **dialectics**) [usu. treated as sing.] **1** the art of investigating or discussing the truth of opinions.
2 enquiry into metaphysical contradictions and their solutions. ■ the existence or action of opposing social forces, concepts, etc.

> The ancient Greeks used the term dialectic to refer to various methods of reasoning and discussion in order to discover the truth. More recently, Kant applied the term to the criticism of the contradictions which arise from supposing knowledge of objects beyond the limits of experience, e.g. the soul. Hegel applied the term to the process of thought by which apparent contradictions (which he termed thesis and antithesis) are seen to be part of a higher truth (synthesis).

▶ adjective relating to dialectic or dialectics; dialectical.
– ORIGIN late Middle English: from Old French *dialectique* or Latin *dialectica*, from Greek *dialektikē* (*tekhnē*) '(art) of debate', from *dialegesthai* 'converse with' (see DIALOGUE).

dialectical ▶ adjective **1** relating to the logical discussion of ideas and opinions: *dialectical ingenuity*.
2 concerned with or acting through opposing forces: *a dialectical opposition between social convention and individual libertarianism*.
– DERIVATIVES **dialectically** adverb.

dialectical materialism ▶ noun [mass noun] the Marxist theory (adopted as the official philosophy of the Soviet communists) that political and historical events result from the conflict of social forces and are interpretable as a series of contradictions and their solutions. The conflict is seen as caused by material needs.
– DERIVATIVES **dialectical materialist** noun & adjective.

dialectician /ˌdʌɪəlɛkˈtɪʃ(ə)n/ ▶ noun a person skilled in philosophical debate.
– ORIGIN mid 16th cent.: from French *dialecticien*, from Latin *dialecticus*, based on Greek *dialegesthai* 'converse with'.

dialectology /ˌdʌɪəlɛkˈtɒlədʒi/ ▶ noun [mass noun] the branch of linguistics concerned with the study of dialects.
– DERIVATIVES **dialectological** /-təˈlɒdʒɪk(ə)l/ adjective, **dialectologist** noun.

dial-in ▶ adjective another term for DIAL-UP.

dialler (US **dialer**) ▶ noun a device or piece of software for calling telephone numbers automatically: *a handheld computer phone dialler*.

dialling code ▶ noun Brit. a sequence of numbers dialled to connect a telephone to an exchange in another area or country.

dialling tone (N. Amer. **dial tone**) ▶ noun a sound produced by a telephone that indicates that a caller may start to dial.

dialog box (Brit. also **dialogue box**) ▶ noun Computing a small area on screen in which the user is prompted to provide information or select commands.

dialogic /ˌdʌɪəˈlɒdʒɪk/ ▶ adjective relating to or in the form of dialogue.
– DERIVATIVES **dialogical** adjective.
– ORIGIN mid 19th cent.: via late Latin from Greek *dialogikos*, from *dialogos* (see DIALOGUE).

dialogism /dʌɪˈalədʒɪz(ə)m/ ▶ noun [mass noun] the use in a text of different tones or viewpoints, whose interaction or contradiction are important to the text's interpretation.
– ORIGIN mid 16th cent.: from late Latin *dialogismos*, from Greek *dialogizesthai* 'to converse', from *dialogos* 'discourse' (see DIALOGUE).

dialogue (US also **dialog**) ▶ noun a conversation between two or more people as a feature of a book, play, or film: *the book consisted of a series of dialogues* | [mass noun] *passages of dialogue*. ■ a discussion between two or more people or groups, especially one directed towards exploration of a particular subject or resolution of a problem: *the USA would enter into a direct dialogue with Vietnam* | [mass noun] *interfaith dialogue*.

▶ **verb** [no obj.] chiefly N. Amer. take part in a conversation or discussion to resolve a problem: *he stated that he wasn't going to **dialogue with** the guerrillas.* ■ [with obj.] provide (a film or play) with a dialogue.
– PHRASES **dialogue of the deaf** a discussion in which each party is unresponsive to what the others say.
– ORIGIN Middle English: from Old French *dialoge*, via Latin from Greek *dialogos*, from *dialegesthai* 'converse with', from *dia* 'through' + *legein* 'speak'.

dial tone ▶ **noun** North American term for DIALLING TONE.

D

dial-up ▶ **adjective** (of a computer system or service) used remotely via a telephone line.

dialysate /dʌɪˈalɪzeɪt/ (US also **dialyzate**) ▶ **noun** [mass noun] the part of a mixture which passes through the membrane in dialysis. ■ the solution the dialysate forms with the fluid on the other side of the membrane. ■ the fluid used on the other side of the membrane during dialysis to remove impurities.
– ORIGIN late 19th cent.: from DIALYSIS + -ATE[1]; the term originally denoted the part of the mixture which does *not* pass through the membrane.

dialyse /ˈdʌɪəlʌɪz/ (US **dialyze**) ▶ **verb** [with obj.] purify (a mixture) by means of dialysis. ■ treat (a patient) by means of dialysis.
– ORIGIN mid 19th cent.: from DIALYSIS, on the pattern of *analyse*.

dialysis /dʌɪˈalɪsɪs/ ▶ **noun** (pl. **dialyses** /-siːz/) [mass noun] Chemistry the separation of particles in a liquid on the basis of differences in their ability to pass through a membrane. ■ Medicine the clinical purification of blood by dialysis, as a substitute for the normal function of the kidney.
– DERIVATIVES **dialytic** adjective.
– ORIGIN mid 19th cent.: via Latin from Greek *dialusis*, from *dialuein* 'split, separate', from *dia* 'apart' + *luein* 'set free'.

diamagnetic ▶ **adjective** Physics (of a substance or body) tending to become magnetized in a direction at 180° to the applied magnetic field.
– DERIVATIVES **diamagnetically** adverb, **diamagnetism** noun.
– ORIGIN 1846: coined by Faraday, from Greek *dia* 'through, across' + MAGNETIC.

diamanté /dɪəˈmɒnteɪ/ ▶ **adjective** decorated with glass cut to resemble diamonds: *a diamanté brooch.*
▶ **noun** [mass noun] costume jewellery or fabric made or decorated with glass that is cut to resemble diamonds.
– ORIGIN early 20th cent.: French, literally 'set with diamonds', past participle of *diamanter*, from *diamant* 'diamond'.

diamantine /ˌdʌɪəˈmantɪn, -iːn/ ▶ **adjective** made from or reminiscent of diamonds.
– ORIGIN mid 16th cent. (in the sense 'hard as diamond'): from French *diamantin*, from *diamant* 'diamond'.

diameter /dʌɪˈamɪtə/ ▶ **noun 1** a straight line passing from side to side through the centre of a body or figure, especially a circle or sphere. ■ a transverse measurement of something; width or thickness.
2 a unit of linear measurement of magnifying power.
– DERIVATIVES **diametral** adjective.
– ORIGIN late Middle English: from Old French *diametre*, via Latin from Greek *diametros (grammē)* '(line) measuring across', from *dia* 'across' + *metron* 'measure'.

diametrical /ˌdʌɪəˈmɛtrɪk(ə)l/ ▶ **adjective 1** (of opposites) complete; absolute: *he's the diametrical opposite of Gabriel.*
2 of or along a diameter.
– DERIVATIVES **diametric** adjective.
– ORIGIN mid 16th cent. (in sense 2): from Greek *diametrikos* (from *diametros* 'measuring across': see DIAMETER) + -AL.

diametrically ▶ **adverb** (with reference to opposition) completely; directly: [as submodifier] *two **diametrically opposed** viewpoints.*

diamine /dʌɪˈeɪmiːn, dʌɪˈam-, ˈdʌɪəmiːn/ ▶ **noun** Chemistry a compound whose molecule contains two amino groups, especially when not part of amide groups.

diamond ▶ **noun 1** a precious stone consisting of a clear and colourless crystalline form of pure carbon, the hardest naturally occurring substance: [as modifier] *a diamond ring.* ■ a tool with a small diamond for cutting glass. ■ **(a diamond)** Brit. informal an excellent or very special person or thing: *Fred's a diamond.*

Diamonds occur in some igneous rock formations (kimberlite) and alluvial deposits. They are typically octahedral in shape but can be cut in many ways to enhance the internal reflection and refraction of light, producing jewels of sparkling brilliance. Diamonds are also used in cutting tools and abrasives.

2 [often as modifier] a figure with four straight sides of equal length forming two opposite acute angles and two opposite obtuse angles; a rhombus: *a sweater with a pale-blue diamond pattern.* ■ **(diamonds)** one of the four suits in a conventional pack of playing cards, denoted by a red diamond. ■ a card of the suit of diamonds.
3 the area delimited by the four bases of a baseball field, forming a square shape. ■ a baseball field.
4 [usu. as modifier] a railway crossing in which two tracks cross over each other at an acute angle.
– PHRASES **diamond cut diamond** used to describe a situation in which a sharp-witted person meets their match. **diamond in the rough** North American term for ROUGH DIAMOND.
– DERIVATIVES **diamondiferous** /-ˈdɪf(ə)rəs/ adjective.
– ORIGIN Middle English: from Old French *diamant*, from medieval Latin *diamas, diamant-*, variant of Latin *adamans* (see ADAMANT).

diamondback ▶ **noun** N. Amer. **1** (also **diamondback rattlesnake**) a common large North American rattlesnake with diamond-shaped markings. Also called DIAMOND RATTLESNAKE. ● Genus *Crotalus*, family Viperidae: two species.
2 another term for TERRAPIN (sense 2).

diamondback moth ▶ **noun** a small greyish moth which displays a pattern of diamonds along its back when the wings are folded. The caterpillar can be a pest of brassicas and other cultivated vegetables. ● *Plutella xylostella*, family Yponomeutidae.

diamond-bird ▶ **noun** Austral. a pardalote, which typically has rows of small white spots on the dark parts of its plumage.

diamond-cut ▶ **adjective 1** cut with facets like a diamond.
2 cut into the shape of a diamond.

Diamond Head an extinct volcano overlooking the port of Honolulu on the Hawaiian island of Oahu.

diamond jubilee ▶ **noun** the sixtieth anniversary of a notable event, especially a sovereign's accession or the foundation of an organization.

diamond python ▶ **noun** a carpet python of a race occurring in the coastal areas of New South Wales. ● *Morelia spilota spilota*, family Pythonidae.

diamond rattlesnake ▶ **noun** another term for DIAMONDBACK (sense 1).

Diamond State informal name for the state of DELAWARE[1].

diamond wedding ▶ **noun** Brit. the sixtieth anniversary of a wedding.

diamond willow ▶ **noun** N. Amer. a willow tree with diamond-shaped depressions on the trunk as a result of fungal attack, resulting in timber with a diamond-shaped pattern of pale sapwood and darker heartwood. ● Several species in the genus *Salix* are affected, in particular *S. bebbiana*.

diamorphine /dʌɪˈmɔːfiːn/ ▶ **noun** short for DIACETYLMORPHINE (heroin).

Diana /dʌɪˈanə/ Roman Mythology an early Italian goddess associated with hunting, virginity, and, in later literature, with the moon. Greek equivalent ARTEMIS.

diana /dʌɪˈanə/ ▶ **noun** a North American fritillary (butterfly), the male of which is orange and black and the female blue and black. ● *Speyeria diana*, subfamily Argynninae, family Nymphalidae.
– ORIGIN modern Latin; associated with the goddess of the moon, because of the silvery crescents on the wings.

Diana, Princess of Wales (1961–97), former wife of Prince Charles; title before marriage *Lady Diana Frances Spencer*. The daughter of the 8th Earl Spencer, she married Prince Charles in 1981; the couple were divorced in 1996. She became a popular figure through her charity work and glamorous media appearances, and her death in a car crash in Paris gave rise to intense national mourning.

Diana monkey ▶ **noun** a West African monkey that has a black face with a white crescent on the forehead. ● *Cercopithecus diana*, family Cercopithecidae.
– ORIGIN early 19th cent.: named after the Roman moon goddess DIANA.

Dianetics /ˌdʌɪəˈnɛtɪks/ ▶ **plural noun** [treated as sing.] a system developed by the founder of the Church of Scientology, L. Ron Hubbard, which aims to relieve psychosomatic disorder by cleansing the mind of harmful mental images.
– ORIGIN 1950s: from Greek *dianoētikos* 'relating to thought' + -ICS.

dianthus /dʌɪˈanθəs/ ▶ **noun** (pl. **dianthuses**) a flowering plant of a genus that includes the pinks and carnations. ● Genus *Dianthus*, family Caryophyllaceae.
– ORIGIN from Greek *Dios* 'of Zeus' + *anthos* 'a flower'.

diapason /ˌdʌɪəˈpeɪs(ə)n, -z-/ ▶ **noun 1** (also **open diapason** or **stopped diapason**) an organ stop sounding a main register of flue pipes, typically of eight-foot pitch.
2 a grand swelling burst of harmony.
– ORIGIN late Middle English (denoting the interval of an octave): via Latin from Greek *dia pasōn (khordōn)* 'through all (notes)'.

diapause /ˈdʌɪəpɔːz/ Zoology ▶ **noun** [mass noun] a period of suspended development in an insect, other invertebrate, or mammal embryo, especially during unfavourable environmental conditions.
▶ **verb** [no obj.] (usu. as adj. **diapausing**) (of an insect or other animal) undergo a period of suspended development.
– ORIGIN late 19th cent.: from DIA- 'through' + the noun PAUSE.

diapedesis /ˌdʌɪəpəˈdiːsɪs/ ▶ **noun** [mass noun] Medicine the passage of blood cells through the intact walls of the capillaries, typically accompanying inflammation.
– ORIGIN early 17th cent.: modern Latin, based on Greek *dia* 'through' + *pēdan* 'throb or leap'.

diaper /ˈdʌɪəpə/ ▶ **noun 1** N. Amer. a baby's nappy.
2 [mass noun] a linen or cotton fabric woven in a repeating pattern of small diamonds. ■ a repeating geometrical or floral pattern used to decorate a surface.
▶ **verb** [with obj.] **1** N. Amer. put a nappy on (a baby).
2 decorate (a surface) with a repeating geometrical or floral pattern.
– ORIGIN Middle English: from Old French *diapre*, from medieval Latin *diasprum*, from medieval Greek *diaspros* (adjective), from *dia* 'across' + *aspros* 'white'. The term seems originally to have denoted a costly fabric, but after the 15th cent. it was used as in sense 2 of the noun; babies' nappies were originally made from pieces of this fabric, hence sense 1 of the noun (late 16th cent.).

diaphanous /dʌɪˈaf(ə)nəs/ ▶ **adjective** (especially of fabric) light, delicate, and translucent: *a diaphanous dress of pale gold.*
– ORIGIN early 17th cent.: from medieval Latin *diaphanus*, from Greek *diaphanēs*, from *dia* 'through' + *phainein* 'to show'.

diaphone /ˈdʌɪəfəʊn/ ▶ **noun** a low-pitched fog signal operated by compressed air, characterized by the 'grunt' which ends each note.
– ORIGIN early 20th cent.: from Greek *dia* 'through' + *phōnē* 'sound'.

diaphorase /dʌɪˈafəreɪz/ ▶ **noun** [mass noun] Biochemistry an enzyme of the flavoprotein type, able to oxidize a reduced form of the coenzyme NAD.
– ORIGIN 1930s: from Greek *diaphoros* 'different' + -ASE.

diaphoresis /ˌdʌɪəfəˈriːsɪs/ ▶ **noun** [mass noun] technical sweating, especially to an unusual degree as a symptom of disease or a side effect of a drug.
– ORIGIN late 17th cent.: via late Latin from Greek, from *diaphorein* 'carry off, sweat out', from *dia* 'through' + *phorein* 'carry'.

diaphoretic /ˌdʌɪəfəˈrɛtɪk/ ▶ **adjective** Medicine (chiefly of a drug) inducing perspiration. ■ (of a person) sweating heavily.
– ORIGIN late Middle English: via late Latin from Greek *diaphorētikos*, from *diaphorein* 'sweat out'.

diaphragm /ˈdʌɪəfram/ ▶ **noun 1** a dome-shaped muscular partition separating the thorax from the abdomen in mammals. It plays a major role in breathing, as its contraction increases the volume of the thorax and so inflates the lungs.
2 a thin sheet of material forming a partition. ■ a taut flexible membrane in mechanical or acoustic systems.
3 a thin contraceptive cap fitting over the cervix.
4 a device for varying the effective aperture of the lens in a camera or other optical system.
– DERIVATIVES **diaphragmatic** adjective.
– ORIGIN late Middle English: from late Latin *diaphragma*, from Greek, from *dia* 'through, apart' + *phragma* 'a fence'.

diddle ▶ **verb** informal **1** [with obj.] cheat or swindle (someone) so as to deprive them of something: *he thought he'd been* ***diddled out of*** *his change.* ■ deliberately falsify: *he diddled his income tax returns.*
2 [no obj.] chiefly N. Amer. pass time aimlessly or unproductively: *I felt sorry for her,* ***diddling around*** *in her room while her friends were having a good time.*
3 [with obj.] vulgar slang, chiefly N. Amer. (of a man) have sexual intercourse with. [originally in Scots dialect use in the sense 'jerk from side to side', apparently corresponding to dialect *didder* 'tremble'.]
– DERIVATIVES **diddler** **noun**.
– ORIGIN early 19th cent.: probably from the name of Jeremy *Diddler*, a character in the farce *Raising the Wind* (1803) by the Irish dramatist James Kenney (1780–1849). Diddler constantly borrowed and failed to repay small sums of money: the name may be based on an earlier verb *diddle* 'walk unsteadily'.

diddly-squat /ˈdɪdlɪˌskwɒt/ (also **doodly-squat**) ▶ **pronoun** [usu. with negative] informal anything: *Hiram didn't care diddly-squat about what Darrel thought.*
– ORIGIN 1960s: probably from US slang *doodle* 'excrement' + SQUAT in the sense 'defecate'.

diddums /ˈdɪdəmz/ ▶ **exclamation** Brit. informal used to express commiseration to a child or, ironically, to an adult.
– ORIGIN late 19th cent.: from *did 'em*, i.e. 'did they?' (tease you, do that to you, etc.).

diddy[1] ▶ **noun** (pl. **diddies**) Brit. informal a fool.
– ORIGIN late 18th cent.: alteration of TITTY.

diddy[2] ▶ **adjective** Brit. informal little: *a little diddy baby hedgehog.*
– ORIGIN probably a child's corruption of LITTLE.

dideoxycytidine /ˌdʌɪdɪɒksɪˈsʌɪtɪdiːn/ (abbrev.: **DDC** or **ddC**) ▶ **noun** [mass noun] Medicine a drug which inhibits the replication of HIV and is used in the treatment of AIDS, especially in combination with zidovudine. It is a synthetic analogue of a pyrimidine nucleoside.

dideoxyinosine /ˌdʌɪdɪɒksɪˈɪnəʊsiːn/ (abbrev.: **DDI** or **ddI**) ▶ **noun** [mass noun] Medicine a drug which inhibits the replication of HIV and is used in the treatment of AIDS, especially in combination with zidovudine. It is a synthetic analogue of a purine nucleoside.
– ORIGIN 1970s: from DI-[1] 'two' + *deoxy-* (in the sense 'that has lost oxygen') + INOSINE.

Diderot /ˈdiːdərəʊ/, French /didəʀo/, Denis (1713–84), French philosopher, writer, and critic. A leading figure of the Enlightenment in France, he was principal editor of the *Encyclopédie* (1751–76), through which he disseminated and popularized philosophy and scientific knowledge. Other notable works: *Le Rêve de D'Alembert* (1782) and *Le Neveu de Rameau* (1805).

didgeridoo /ˌdɪdʒ(ə)rɪˈduː/ (also **didjeridu**) ▶ **noun** an Australian Aboriginal wind instrument in the form of a long wooden tube, traditionally made from a hollow branch, which is blown to produce a deep, resonant sound, varied by rhythmic accents of timbre and volume.
– ORIGIN 1920s: imitative; from an Aboriginal language of Arnhem Land.

didi /ˈdiːdiː/ ▶ **noun** Indian an older sister or older female cousin (often as a proper name or form of address): *'Just have a look at this luggage, didi.'* ■ a respectful form of address to any older woman familiar to the speaker.
– ORIGIN from Hindi *dīdī*.

didicoi /ˈdɪdɪkɔɪ/ ▶ **noun** (pl. **didicois**) dialect a Gypsy or other nomadic person.
– ORIGIN mid 19th cent.: perhaps an alteration of Romany *dik akei* 'look here'.

didn't ▶ **contraction** did not.

Dido /ˈdʌɪdəʊ/ (in the *Aeneid*) the queen and founder of Carthage, who fell in love with the shipwrecked Aeneas and killed herself when he deserted her.

dido /ˈdʌɪdəʊ/ ▶ **noun** (pl. **didoes** or **didos**) N. Amer. informal (in phrase **cut/cut up didoes**) perform mischievous tricks or deeds.
– ORIGIN early 19th cent.: of unknown origin.

didst archaic second person singular past of DO[1].

Didyma /ˈdɪdɪmə/ an ancient sanctuary of Apollo, site of one of the most famous oracles of the Aegean region, close to the west coast of Asia Minor.

didymium /dɪˈdɪmɪəm/ ▶ **noun** [mass noun] Chemistry a mixture containing the rare earth elements praseodymium and neodymium, used to colour glass for optical filters. It was originally regarded as a single element.
– ORIGIN mid 19th cent.: from Greek *didumos* 'twin' (because it was closely associated with lanthanum) + *-ium* (used as a suffix for new metals).

die[1] ▶ **verb** (**dies, dying, died**) [no obj.] **1** (of a person, animal, or plant) stop living: *he* ***died of*** *AIDS | trees are* ***dying from*** *acid rain* | [with obj.] *the king died a violent death.* ■ (**die out**) become extinct: *many species died out.* ■ be forgotten: *her genius has assured her name will never die.* ■ [with adverbial] become less loud or strong: *after a while, the noise* ***died down*** *| at last the storm* ***died away.*** ■ (**die back**) (of a plant) decay from the tip toward the root: *rhubarb dies back to a crown of buds each winter.* ■ (**die off**) die one after another until few or none are left: *the original founders died off or retired.* ■ (of a fire or light) stop burning or gleaming. ■ informal (of a machine) stop functioning: *three toasters have died on me.*
2 informal be very eager for something: *they must be* ***dying for*** *a drink* | [with infinitive] *he's dying to meet you.* ■ used to emphasize how strongly one is affected by a particular feeling or emotion: *only the thought of Matilda prevented him from* ***dying of*** *boredom | we nearly died laughing when he told us.*
3 archaic have an orgasm.
– PHRASES **die a** (or **the**) **death** Brit. informal come to an end; cease or fail to be popular or successful: *the craze for cycling shorts is dying a death.* **die hard** disappear or change very slowly: *old habits die hard.* **die in harness** die before retirement. **die like flies** see FLY[2]. **die on one's feet** informal come to a sudden or premature end: *critics said the show would die on its feet.* **die on the vine** be unsuccessful at an early stage. **die with one's boots on** see BOOT[1]. **never say die** used to encourage someone not to give up hope in a difficult situation. **to die for** informal extremely good or desirable: *the ice creams are to die for.*
– ORIGIN Middle English: from Old Norse *deyja*, of Germanic origin; related to DEAD.

die[2] ▶ **noun 1** singular form of DICE.
2 (pl. **dies**) a device for cutting or moulding metal into a particular shape. ■ an engraved device for stamping a design on coins or medals.
3 Architecture the cubical part of a pedestal between the base and the cornice; a dado or plinth.
– PHRASES **the die is cast** an event has happened or a decision has been taken that cannot be changed. (**as**) **straight as a die** absolutely straight. ■ entirely open and honest.
– ORIGIN Middle English: from Old French *de*, from Latin *datum* 'something given or played', neuter past participle of *dare*.

USAGE In modern standard English, the singular **die** (rather than **dice**) is uncommon. **Dice** is used for both the singular and the plural.

dieback ▶ **noun** [mass noun] a condition in which a tree or shrub begins to die from the tip of its leaves or roots backwards, owing to disease or an unfavourable environment.

die-cast ▶ **adjective** (of a metal object) formed by pouring molten metal into a reusable mould: *a die-cast aluminium loudspeaker chassis.*
▶ **verb** [with obj.] (usu. as noun **die-casting**) make (a metal object) by pouring molten metal into a mould.

dieffenbachia /ˌdiːf(ə)nˈbakɪə/ ▶ **noun** a plant of a genus that includes dumb cane and its relatives.
● Genus *Dieffenbachia*, family Araceae.
– ORIGIN modern Latin, named after Ernst *Dieffenbach* (1811–55), German horticulturalist.

diegesis /ˌdʌɪəˈdʒiːsɪs/ ▶ **noun** (pl. **diegeses** /-siːz/) a narrative or plot, typically in a film.
– DERIVATIVES **diegetic** /-ˈdʒɛtɪk/ **adjective**.
– ORIGIN early 19th cent.: from Greek *diēgēsis* 'narrative'.

Diego Garcia /dɪˌeɪɡəʊ ɡɑːˈsiːə/ the largest island of the Chagos Archipelago in the middle of the Indian Ocean, site of a strategic Anglo-American naval base established in 1973.

diehard ▶ **noun** [often as modifier] a person who strongly opposes change or who continues to support something in spite of opposition: *my stepfather was a diehard Republican | a diehard Yankees fan.*
– ORIGIN mid 19th cent.: from *die hard* (see DIE[1]).

diel /ˈdiːl/ ▶ **adjective** Biology denoting or involving a period of twenty-four hours: *tidal and diel cycles.*
– ORIGIN 1930s: from Latin *dies* 'day' + *-(a)l* (see -AL).

dieldrin /ˈdiːldrɪn/ ▶ **noun** [mass noun] a toxic insecticide produced by the oxidation of aldrin, now largely banned because of its persistence in the environment. ● A chlorinated epoxide; chem. formula: $C_{12}H_8Cl_6O$.
– ORIGIN 1940s: blend of the name *Diels* (see DIELS–ALDER REACTION) + ALDRIN.

dielectric /ˌdʌɪɪˈlɛktrɪk/ Physics ▶ **adjective** having the property of transmitting electric force without conduction; insulating.
▶ **noun** a medium or substance with a dielectric property; an insulator.
– DERIVATIVES **dielectrically** **adverb**.
– ORIGIN mid 19th cent.: from DI-[3] + ELECTRIC, literally 'across which electricity is transmitted (without conduction)'.

dielectric constant ▶ **noun** Physics a quantity measuring the ability of a substance to store electrical energy in an electric field.

dielectrophoresis /dʌɪˌlɛktrəfəˈriːsɪs/ ▶ **noun** [mass noun] Physics the migration of uncharged particles towards the position of maximum field strength in a non-uniform electric field.
– ORIGIN mid 20th cent.: blend of DIELECTRIC and ELECTROPHORESIS.

die link ▶ **noun** an established connection between coins struck from the same die.
▶ **verb** [with obj.] (**die-link**) establish a connection between (coins).

Diels–Alder reaction /diːlzˈɔːldə/ ▶ **noun** Chemistry an addition reaction in which a conjugated diene reacts with a compound with a double or triple bond so as to form a six-membered ring.
– ORIGIN 1940s: named after Otto *Diels* (1876–1954), and Kurt *Alder* (1902–58), German chemists.

Dien Bien Phu /ˌdjɛn bjɛn ˈfuː/ a village in NW Vietnam, in 1954 the site of a French military post which was captured by the Vietminh after a 55-day siege.

diencephalon /ˌdʌɪɛnˈsɛf(ə)lɒn, -ˈkɛf-/ ▶ **noun** Anatomy the caudal (posterior) part of the forebrain, containing the epithalamus, thalamus, hypothalamus, and ventral thalamus and the third ventricle. Compare with TELENCEPHALON.
– DERIVATIVES **diencephalic** **adjective**.
– ORIGIN late 19th cent.: from DI-[3] 'across' + Greek *enkephalos* 'brain'.

diene /ˈdʌɪiːn/ ▶ **noun** Chemistry an unsaturated hydrocarbon containing two double bonds between carbon atoms.
– ORIGIN early 20th cent.: from DI-[1] 'two' + -ENE.

Dieppe /dɪˈɛp/, French /djɛp/ a channel port in northern France, from which ferries run to Newhaven and elsewhere; pop. 34,670 (2006). In August 1942 it was the scene of an unsuccessful amphibious raid by a joint force of British and Canadian troops to destroy the German-held port and airfield.

dieresis ▶ **noun** US spelling of DIAERESIS.

Diesel /ˈdiːz(ə)l/, Rudolf (Christian Karl) (1858–1913), French-born German engineer, inventor of the diesel engine. In 1892 he patented a design for a new, more efficient internal-combustion engine and developed it, exhibiting the prototype in 1897.

diesel /ˈdiːz(ə)l/ ▶ **noun** (also **diesel engine**) an internal-combustion engine in which heat produced by the compression of air in the cylinder is used to ignite the fuel: [as modifier] *a diesel locomotive.* ■ [mass noun] (also **diesel oil**) a heavy petroleum fraction used as fuel in diesel engines: *eleven litres of diesel.*
– DERIVATIVES **dieselize** (also **dieselise**) **verb**.
– ORIGIN late 19th cent.: named after R. DIESEL.

diesel-electric ▶ **adjective** denoting or relating to a locomotive driven by the electric current produced by a diesel-engined generator.
▶ **noun** a diesel-electric locomotive.

diesel-hydraulic ▶ **adjective** denoting or relating to a locomotive driven by a hydraulic transmission system powered by a diesel engine.
▶ **noun** a diesel-hydraulic locomotive.

die-sinker ▶ **noun** a person who engraves dies used to stamp designs on coins or medals.
– DERIVATIVES **die-sinking** **noun**.

Dies Irae /ˌdiːeɪz ˈɪərʌɪ, ˈɪəreɪ/ ▶ **noun** a Latin hymn sung in a Mass for the dead.
– ORIGIN Latin, 'day of wrath' (the opening words of the hymn).

diesis /ˈdʌɪɪsɪs/ ▶ **noun** (pl. **dieses** /-ɪsiːz/) Printing the double dagger symbol ‡.
– ORIGIN late Middle English: Latin, from Greek *diesis*, from *diienai* 'send through', from *dia* 'through' + *ienai* 'send'.

dies non /ˌdiːeɪz ˈnɒn/ ▶ **noun** (pl. **same**) a day on which no legal business can be done, or which does not count for legal purposes.

– ORIGIN Latin, short for *dies non juridicus* 'non-judicial day'.

die-stamping ▶ **noun** [mass noun] a method of embossing paper or another surface using a die. ■ a method of printing using an inked die to produce raised print.

diestock ▶ **noun** a hand tool used in the cutting of external screw threads, consisting of a holder for the die which is turned using long handles.

diestrus ▶ **noun** US spelling of **DIOESTRUS**.

diet[1] ▶ **noun 1** the kinds of food that a person, animal, or community habitually eats: *a vegetarian diet.* ■ the activities, pastimes, etc. in which a person or group habitually engages: *screen violence is becoming the staple diet of the video generation.*
2 a special course of food to which a person restricts themselves, either to lose weight or for medical reasons: *I'm **going on a diet**.* ■ [as modifier] (of food or drink) with reduced fat or sugar content: *diet soft drinks.*
▶ **verb** (**diets, dieting, dieted**) [no obj.] restrict oneself to small amounts or special kinds of food in order to lose weight: *I began dieting again.* ■ [with obj.] put (a person or animal) on a special diet.
– DERIVATIVES **dieter** noun.
– ORIGIN Middle English: from Old French *diete* (noun), *dieter* (verb), via Latin from Greek *diaita* 'a way of life'.

diet[2] ▶ **noun** a legislative assembly in certain countries. ■ historical a regular meeting of the states of a confederation. ■ Scots Law a meeting or session of a court.
– ORIGIN late Middle English: from medieval Latin *dieta* 'day's work, wages, etc.', also 'meeting of councillors'.

dietary ▶ **adjective** relating to or provided by diet: *dietary advice for healthy skin and hair.*
▶ **noun** (pl. **dietaries**) dated a regulated or restricted diet.
– ORIGIN late Middle English (as a noun): from medieval Latin *dietarium*, from Latin *diaeta* (see **DIET**[1]).

dietetic /ˌdʌɪəˈtɛtɪk/ ▶ **adjective** concerned with diet and nutrition: *experienced dietetic advice.*
– DERIVATIVES **dietetically** adverb.
– ORIGIN mid 16th cent. (as a noun in the sense 'dietetics'): via Latin from Greek *diaitētikos*, from *diaita* 'a way of life'.

dietetics ▶ **plural noun** [treated as sing.] the branch of knowledge concerned with the diet and its effects on health, especially with the practical application of a scientific understanding of nutrition.

diethylene glycol /dʌɪˈɛθɪliːn, -θ(ə)l-/ ▶ **noun** [mass noun] Chemistry a colourless soluble liquid used as a solvent and antifreeze. ● Chem. formula: $(C_2H_4OH)_2O$.

diethyl ether /dʌɪˈiːθʌɪl/ ▶ **noun** see **ETHER** (sense 1).

diethylstilboestrol /dʌɪˌiːθʌɪlstɪlˈbiːstrɒl, -ˈɛθɪl/ (US **diethylstilbestrol**) ▶ **noun** another term for **STILBOESTROL**.

dietitian /dʌɪəˈtɪʃ(ə)n/ (also **dietician**) ▶ **noun** an expert on diet and nutrition.

Diet of Worms a meeting of the Holy Roman emperor Charles V's imperial diet at Worms in 1521, at which Martin Luther was summoned to appear. Luther committed himself there to the cause of Protestant reform, and his teaching was formally condemned in the Edict of Worms.

Dietrich /ˈdiːtrɪx/, Marlene (1901–92), German-born American actress and singer; born *Maria Magdelene Dietrich*. She became famous for her part as Lola in *The Blue Angel* (1930), one of many films she made with Josef von Sternberg. From the 1950s she was also successful as an international cabaret star.

Dieu et mon droit /ˌdjəː eɪ mɔ̃ ˈdrwɑː/ ▶ **noun** God and my right (the motto of the British monarch).
– ORIGIN French.

dif- ▶ **prefix** variant spelling of **DIS-** assimilated before *f* (as in *diffraction, diffuse.*).
– ORIGIN from Latin, variant of **DIS-**.

differ ▶ **verb** [no obj.] be unlike or dissimilar: *the second set of data **differed from** the first* | *tastes differ, especially in cars* | (as adj. **differing**) *widely differing circumstances.* ■ disagree: *he **differed from** his contemporaries in ethical matters.*
– PHRASES **agree to differ** cease to argue about something because neither party will compromise or be persuaded. **beg to differ** politely disagree.
– ORIGIN late Middle English (also in the sense 'put off, defer'): from Old French *differer* 'differ, defer', from Latin *differre*, from *dis-* 'from, away' + *ferre* 'bring, carry'. Compare with **DEFER**[1].

difference ▶ **noun 1** a point or way in which people or things are dissimilar: *the **differences between** men and women.* ■ [mass noun] the state or condition of being dissimilar: *their **difference from** one another.* ■ a quantity by which amounts differ; the remainder left after subtraction of one value from another: *the insurance company will pay the difference.* ■ Heraldry an alteration in a coat of arms to distinguish members or branches of a family.
2 a disagreement, quarrel, or dispute: *the couple are patching up their differences.*
▶ **verb** [with obj.] Heraldry alter (a coat of arms) to distinguish members or branches of a family.
– PHRASES **make a** (or **no**) **difference** have a significant effect (or no effect) on a person or situation: *the Act will **make no difference to** my business.* **with a difference** having a new or unusual feature or treatment: *a fashion show with a difference.*
– ORIGIN Middle English: via Old French from Latin *differentia* (see **DIFFERENTIA**).

difference threshold ▶ **noun** the least amount by which two sensory stimuli can differ for an individual to perceive them as different.

different ▶ **adjective 1** not the same as another or each other; unlike in nature, form, or quality: *you can play this game in different ways* | *the car's **different from** anything else on the market.* ■ informal novel and unusual: *try something deliciously different.*
2 distinct; separate: *on two different occasions.*
– PHRASES **different strokes for different folks** proverb different things appeal to different people.
– DERIVATIVES **differently** adverb, **differentness** noun.
– ORIGIN late Middle English: via Old French from Latin *different-* 'carrying away, differing', from the verb *differre* (see **DIFFER**).

> **USAGE** **Different from, different than,** and **different to:** are there any distinctions between these three constructions, and is one more correct than the others? In practice, **different from** is both the most common structure, both in British and US English, and the most accepted. **Different than** is used chiefly in North America, although its use is increasing in British English. It has the advantage that it can be followed by a clause, and so is sometimes more concise than **different from:** compare *things are definitely different than they were one year ago* with *things are definitely different from the way they were one year ago.* **Different to** is common in Britain, but is disliked by traditionalists. The argument against it is based on the relation of **different** to **differ,** which is used with **from;** but this is a flawed argument which is contradicted by other pairs of words such as **accord (with)** and **according (to).**

differentia /ˌdɪfəˈrɛnʃɪə/ ▶ **noun** (pl. **differentiae** /-ʃiː/) a distinguishing mark or characteristic. ■ chiefly Philosophy an attribute that distinguishes a species of thing from other species of the same genus.
– ORIGIN late 17th cent.: from Latin, literally 'difference', from *different-* 'carrying away' (see **DIFFERENT**).

differentiable /ˌdɪfəˈrɛnʃɪəb(ə)l/ ▶ **adjective** able to be differentiated.
– DERIVATIVES **differentiability** noun.
– ORIGIN mid 19th cent.: from **DIFFERENTIATE**, on the pattern of pairs such as *depreciate, depreciable.*

differential /ˌdɪfəˈrɛnʃ(ə)l/ chiefly technical ▶ **adjective** [attrib.] of, showing, or depending on a difference; varying according to circumstances or relevant factors: *the differential achievements of boys and girls.* ■ constituting a specific difference; distinctive: *the differential features between benign and malignant tumours.* ■ Mathematics relating to infinitesimal differences or to the derivatives of functions. ■ relating to a difference in a physical quantity: *a differential amplifier.*
▶ **noun** a difference between amounts of things: *the **differential between** petrol and diesel prices.* ■ Brit. a difference in wages between industries or between categories of employees in the same industry: *regional differentials in pay.* ■ Mathematics an infinitesimal difference between successive values of a variable. ■ (also **differential gear**) a gear allowing a vehicle's driven wheels to revolve at different speeds in cornering.
– DERIVATIVES **differentially** adverb.
– ORIGIN mid 17th cent.: from medieval Latin *differentialis*, from Latin *differentia* 'difference' (see **DIFFERENTIA**).

differential calculus ▶ **noun** [mass noun] a branch of mathematics concerned with the determination, properties, and application of derivatives and differentials. Compare with **INTEGRAL CALCULUS**.

differential coefficient ▶ **noun** Mathematics another term for **DERIVATIVE**.

differential diagnosis ▶ **noun** Medicine the process of differentiating between two or more conditions which share similar signs or symptoms.

differential equation ▶ **noun** an equation involving derivatives of a function or functions.

differential lock ▶ **noun** a device which disables the differential of a motor vehicle in slippery conditions to improve grip.

differential operator ▶ **noun** Mathematics another term for **DEL**.

differentiate /ˌdɪfəˈrɛnʃɪeɪt/ ▶ **verb** [with obj.] **1** recognize or ascertain what makes (someone or something) different: *children can **differentiate** the past **from** the present.* ■ [no obj.] (**differentiate between**) identify differences between (two or more things or people): *he is unable to differentiate between fantasy and reality.* ■ make (someone or something) appear different or distinct: *little now **differentiates** the firm's products **from** its rivals.*
2 technical make or become different in the process of growth or development: [with obj.] *the receptors are developed and differentiated into sense organs* | [no obj.] *the cells differentiate into a wide variety of cell types.*
3 Mathematics transform (a function) into its derivative.
– DERIVATIVES **differentiator** noun.
– ORIGIN early 19th cent.: from medieval Latin *differentiat-* 'carried away from', from the verb *differentiare*, from *differentia* (see **DIFFERENTIA**).

differentiation ▶ **noun** [mass noun] the action or process of differentiating: *packaging can be a source of product differentiation.*

differently abled ▶ **adjective** chiefly N. Amer. disabled.

> **USAGE** **Differently abled** was first proposed (in the 1980s) as an alternative to **disabled, handicapped,** etc. on the grounds that it gave a more positive message and so avoided discrimination towards people with disabilities. The term has gained little currency, however, and has been criticized as both over-euphemistic and condescending. The accepted term in general use is still **disabled.**

difficult ▶ **adjective** needing much effort or skill to accomplish, deal with, or understand: *she had a difficult decision to make* | *the questions are too **difficult for** the children.* ■ characterized by or causing hardships or problems: *a difficult economic climate.* ■ (of a person) not easy to please or satisfy; awkward: *Lily could be difficult.*
– DERIVATIVES **difficultly** adverb (rare), **difficultness** noun.
– ORIGIN late Middle English: back-formation from **DIFFICULTY**.

difficulty ▶ **noun** (pl. **difficulties**) [mass noun] the state or condition of being difficult: *Guy **had no difficulty in** making friends* | *I managed **with difficulty** to struggle upright.* ■ [count noun] a thing that is hard to accomplish, deal with, or understand: *there is a practical difficulty* | *a club with financial difficulties.* ■ (**difficulties**) a situation that is difficult or dangerous: *they went for a swim but **got into difficulties**.*
– ORIGIN late Middle English (in the senses 'requiring effort or skill' and 'something difficult'): from Latin *difficultas*, from *dis-* (expressing reversal) + *facultas* 'ability, opportunity'.

diffidence ▶ **noun** [mass noun] modesty or shyness resulting from a lack of self-confidence: *I say this with some diffidence.*

diffident ▶ **adjective** modest or shy because of a lack of self-confidence: *a diffident youth.*
– DERIVATIVES **diffidently** adverb.
– ORIGIN late Middle English (in the sense 'lacking confidence or trust in someone or something'): from Latin *diffident-* 'failing in trust', from the verb *diffidere*, from *dis-* (expressing reversal) + *fidere* 'to trust'.

diffract /dɪˈfrakt/ ▶ **verb** [with obj.] Physics cause to undergo diffraction.
– DERIVATIVES **diffractive** adjective.
– ORIGIN early 19th cent.: from Latin *diffract-* 'broken in pieces', from the verb *diffringere*, from *dis-* 'away, from' + *frangere* 'to break'.

diffraction ▶ **noun** [mass noun] the process by which a beam of light or other system of waves is spread out as a result of passing through a narrow aperture or across an edge, typically accompanied by interference between the wave forms produced.

diffraction grating ▸ **noun** a plate of glass or metal ruled with very close parallel lines, producing a spectrum by diffraction and interference of light.

diffractometer /ˌdɪfrakˈtɒmɪtə/ ▸ **noun** an instrument for measuring diffraction, chiefly used to determine the structure of a crystal by analysis of the diffraction of X-rays.

diffuse ▸ **verb** /dɪˈfjuːz/ spread over a wide area or between a large number of people: [no obj.] *technologies diffuse rapidly* | [with obj.] *the problem is how to diffuse power without creating anarchy* ■ Physics intermingle with another substance by movement, typically in a specified direction or at specified speed: [no obj.] *oxygen molecules **diffuse across** the membrane* | [with obj.] *gas is **diffused into** the bladder.* ■ [with obj.] cause (light) to spread evenly to reduce glare and harsh shadows.
▸ **adjective** /dɪˈfjuːs/ **1** spread out over a large area; not concentrated: *the diffuse community which centred on the church* | *the light is more diffuse.* ■ (of disease) not localized in the body: *diffuse hyperplasia.*
2 lacking clarity or conciseness: *the second argument is more diffuse.*
– DERIVATIVES **diffusely** /dɪˈfjuːsli/ **adverb**, **diffuseness** /dɪˈfjuːsnɪs/ **noun**.
– ORIGIN late Middle English: from Latin *diffus-* 'poured out', from the verb *diffundere*, from *dis-* 'away' + *fundere* 'pour'; the adjective via French *diffus* or Latin *diffusus* 'extensive', from *diffundere*.

> **USAGE** The verbs **diffuse** and **defuse** sound similar but have different meanings. **Diffuse** means, broadly, 'disperse', while the non-literal meaning of **defuse** is 'reduce the danger or tension in'. Thus sentences such as *Cooper successfully **diffused** the situation* are regarded as incorrect, while *Cooper successfully **defused** the situation* would be correct. However, such uses of **diffuse** are widespread, and can make sense: the image in, for example, *only peaceful dialogue between the two countries could diffuse tension* is not of making a bomb safe but of reducing something dangerous to particles and dispersing them harmlessly.

diffuser (also **diffusor**) ▸ **noun** a thing that diffuses something, in particular: ■ an attachment or duct for broadening an airflow and reducing its speed.
■ Photography a device which spreads the light from a light source evenly and reduces harsh shadows.

diffusible /dɪˈfjuːzɪb(ə)l/ ▸ **adjective** able to intermingle by diffusion: *diffusible factors in the cytoplasm.*

diffusion ▸ **noun** [mass noun] the spreading of something more widely: *the rapid diffusion of ideas and technology.* ■ the action of spreading the light from a light source evenly to reduce glare and harsh shadows. ■ Physics the intermingling of substances by the natural movement of their particles: *the rate of diffusion of a gas.* ■ Anthropology the dissemination of elements of culture to another region or people.
– DERIVATIVES **diffusionism** **noun** (Anthropology), **diffusionist** **adjective & noun** (Anthropology), **diffusive** **adjective** (Physics).
– ORIGIN late Middle English (in the sense 'pouring out, effusion'): from Latin *diffusio(n-)*, from *diffundere* 'pour out'.

diffusion line (also **diffusion range**) ▸ **noun** a range of relatively inexpensive ready-to-wear garments produced for the mass market by a fashion designer.

diffusivity /ˌdɪfjuːˈsɪvɪti/ ▸ **noun** (pl. **diffusivities**) Physics a measure of the capability of a substance or energy to be diffused or to allow something to pass by diffusion.

dig ▸ **verb** (**digging**; past and past participle **dug**) **1** [no obj.] break up and move earth with a tool or machine, or with hands, paws, snout, etc.: *the boar had been **digging for** roots* | [with obj.] *she had to dig the garden* | *authorities cause chaos by **digging up** roads.* ■ [with obj.] make (a hole, grave, etc.) by digging: *he took a spade and dug a hole* | (as adj. **dug**) *the newly dug grave.* ■ [with obj. and adverbial] extract from the ground by breaking up and moving earth: *the water board came and dug the cable up.* ■ (**dig in**) (of a soldier) protect oneself by digging a trench or similar ground defence. ■ (**dig in**) informal begin eating heartily.
■ [with obj.] excavate (an archaeological site).
2 [with obj.] push or poke sharply: *he dug his hands into his pockets.* ■ [no obj., with adverbial] search or rummage in a specified place: *Catherine dug into her handbag and produced her card.* ■ [no obj.] engage in research; conduct an investigation: *he had no compunction about digging into her private affairs.* ■ (**dig something up/out**) bring out or discover something after a search or investigation: *they dug out last year's notes* | *have you **dug up** any information on the captain?*
3 [with obj.] informal like, appreciate, or understand: *I really dig heavy rock.*
▸ **noun 1** [in sing.] an act or spell of digging: *a thorough dig of the whole plot.* ■ [count noun] an archaeological excavation.
2 a push or poke with one's elbow, finger, etc.: *Ginnie gave her sister **a dig in the ribs**.* ■ informal a remark intended to mock or criticize: *she never missed an opportunity to have a dig at him.*
– PHRASES **dig the dirt** (or **dig up dirt**) informal discover and reveal damaging information about someone. **dig a hole for oneself** (or **dig oneself into a hole**) get oneself into an awkward or restrictive situation. **dig in one's heels** (or **toes** or **feet**) resist stubbornly; refuse to give in: *officials dug their heels in on particular points.* **dig a pit for** see PIT[1]. **dig's one's own grave** see GRAVE[1].
– ORIGIN Middle English: perhaps from Old English *dīc* 'ditch'.

Digambara /dɪˈɡʌmbərə/ ▸ **noun** a member of one of two principal sects of Jainism, which was formed as a result of doctrinal schism in about AD 80 and continues today in parts of southern India. Male ascetic members of the sect traditionally reject property ownership and do not wear clothes. See also SVETAMBARA.
– ORIGIN from Sanskrit *Digāmbara*, literally 'sky-clad'.

digamma /dʌɪˈɡamə/ ▸ **noun** the sixth letter of the early Greek alphabet (Ϝ, ϝ), probably pronounced as 'w'. It became obsolete before the Classical period.
– ORIGIN late 17th cent.: via Latin from Greek, from *di-* 'twice' + GAMMA (because of the shape of the letter, resembling gamma (Γ) with an extra stroke).

digastric /dʌɪˈɡastrɪk/ (also **digastric muscle**) ▸ **noun** Anatomy each of a pair of muscles which run under the jaw and act to open it.
– ORIGIN late 17th cent.: from modern Latin *digastricus*, from *di-* 'twice' + Greek *gastēr* 'belly' (because the muscle has two fleshy parts or 'bellies' at an angle, connected by a tendon).

digenean /ˌdʌɪdʒɪˈniːən, dʌɪˈdʒɛnɪən/ Zoology
▸ **adjective** relating to a group of flukes which are internal parasites needing two to four hosts to complete their life cycle. Compare with MONOGENEAN.
▸ **noun** a digenean fluke; a trematode. ● Subclass Digenea, class Trematoda.
– ORIGIN 1960s: from modern Latin *Digenea* (from Greek *di-* 'twice' + *genea* 'generation, race') + -AN.

digerati /ˌdɪdʒəˈrɑːti/ ▸ **plural noun** people with expertise or professional involvement in information technology.
– ORIGIN 1990s: blend of DIGITAL and LITERATI.

digest ▸ **verb** /dʌɪˈdʒɛst, dɪ-/ [with obj.] **1** break down (food) in the stomach and intestines into substances that can be used by the body. ■ Chemistry treat (a substance) with heat, enzymes, or a solvent in order to decompose it or extract essential components.
2 understand or assimilate (information) by a period of reflection: *Leonora digested this piece of news with mixed feelings.* ■ arrange in a systematic or convenient order, especially by reduction: *the computer **digested** your labours **into** a form understandable by a program.*
▸ **noun** /ˈdʌɪdʒɛst/ **1** a compilation or summary of material or information: *a digest of their findings.*
■ a periodical consisting of condensed versions of pieces of writing or news published elsewhere.
■ a methodical summary of a body of laws. ■ (**the Digest**) the compendium of Roman law compiled in the reign of Justinian.
2 Chemistry a substance or mixture obtained by digestion: *a digest of cloned DNA.*
– ORIGIN late Middle English: from Latin *digest-* 'distributed, dissolved, digested', from the verb *digerere*, from *di-* 'apart' + *gerere* 'carry'; the noun from Latin *digesta* 'matters methodically arranged', from *digestus* 'divided', from *digerere*.

digester ▸ **noun** Chemistry a container in which substances are treated with heat, enzymes, or a solvent in order to promote decomposition or extract essential components.

digestible ▸ **adjective 1** (of food) able to be digested.
2 (of information) easy to understand or follow: *her books convey philosophical issues in a lucid and digestible form.*
– DERIVATIVES **digestibility** **noun**.
– ORIGIN late Middle English: via Old French from Latin *digestibilis*, from *digest-* 'digested', from the verb *digerere* (see DIGEST).

digestif /dʌɪˈdʒɛstɪf, ˌdiːʒɛˈstiːf/ ▸ **noun** a drink, especially an alcoholic one, drunk before or after a meal in order to aid the digestion.
– ORIGIN French, literally 'digestive'.

digestion ▸ **noun** [mass noun] the process of digesting food. ■ [count noun] a person's capacity to digest food: *he suffered with his digestion.* ■ Chemistry the process of treating a substance with heat, enzymes, or a solvent to promote decomposition or extract essential components.
– ORIGIN late Middle English: via Old French from Latin *digestio(n-)*, from the verb *digerere* (see DIGEST).

digestive ▸ **adjective** relating to the process of digesting food: *digestive disorders.* ■ (of food or medicine) aiding or promoting the process of digestion: *tubes of digestive mints.*
▸ **noun 1** a food, drink, or medicine that aids or promotes the digestion of food.
2 (also **digestive biscuit**) Brit. a round semi-sweet biscuit made of wholemeal flour.
– DERIVATIVES **digestively** **adverb**.
– ORIGIN late Middle English: from Old French *digestif, -ive* or Latin *digestivus*, from *digest-* 'digested', from the verb *digerere* (see DIGEST).

digestive gland ▸ **noun** Zoology a glandular organ of digestion present in crustaceans, molluscs, and certain other invertebrates.

digestivo /dɪdʒesˈtiːvəʊ/ ▸ **noun** (pl. **digestivi** /-vi/) another term for DIGESTIF.
– ORIGIN Italian, from *digerire* 'to digest'.

digger ▸ **noun 1** a person, animal, or large machine that digs earth. ■ a miner. ■ a person who excavates archaeological sites.
2 (**Digger**) a member of a group of radical dissenters formed in England in 1649 as an offshoot of the Levellers, believing in a form of agrarian communism in which common land would be made available to the poor.
3 Austral./NZ informal a man, especially a private soldier (often used as a friendly form of address): *how are you, Digger?* [early 20th cent.: from *digger* 'miner', reinforced by association with the digging of trenches on the battlefields.]

digger wasp ▸ **noun** a solitary wasp which typically excavates a burrow in sandy soil, filling it with one or more paralysed insects or spiders for its larvae to feed on. ● Families Sphecidae (which includes sand wasps) and Pompilidae (which includes spider-hunting wasps).

diggings ▸ **plural noun 1** a site such as a mine or goldfield that has been excavated: *hills scarred with peat diggings.* ■ material that has been dug from the ground.
2 Brit. informal, dated lodgings.

digging stick ▸ **noun** a primitive digging implement consisting of a pointed stick, sometimes weighted by a stone.

dight /dʌɪt/ ▸ **adjective** archaic clothed or equipped.
▸ **verb** [with obj.] literary make ready for a use or purpose; prepare. ■ Scottish & N. English wipe clean or dry. ■ Scottish & N. English winnow (corn).
– ORIGIN Middle English: past participle of archaic *dight* 'order, deal with', based on Latin *dictare* 'compose (in language), order'. The wide and varied use of the word in Middle English is reflected dialectally.

digicam ▸ **noun** trademark a digital camera.

digipak /ˈdɪdʒɪpak/ ▸ **noun** trademark a type of packaging for CDs or DVDs, typically made from cardboard with an internal plastic holder for one or more discs.
– ORIGIN 1980s: from DIGITAL and PACK[1], probably on the pattern of TETRA PAK.

digit /ˈdɪdʒɪt/ ▸ **noun 1** any of the numerals from 0 to 9, especially when forming part of a number.
2 a finger or thumb. ■ Zoology a structure equivalent to a finger or thumb at the end of the limbs of many higher vertebrates.
– ORIGIN late Middle English: from Latin *digitus* 'finger, toe'; sense 1 arose from the practice of counting on the fingers.

digital ▸ **adjective 1** relating to or using signals or information represented by discrete values of a physical quantity such as voltage or magnetic polarization: *digital TV.* Often contrasted with ANALOGUE.
■ involving or relating to the use of computer technology: *the digital revolution.*
2 (of a clock or watch) showing the time by means of displayed digits rather than hands or a pointer.
3 relating to a finger or fingers.
– DERIVATIVES **digitally** **adverb**.
– ORIGIN late 15th cent.: from Latin *digitalis*, from *digitus* 'finger, toe'.

digital audiotape (abbrev.: **DAT**) ▶ **noun** [mass noun] magnetic tape which is used to make digital sound recordings of very high quality.

digital camera ▶ **noun** a camera which produces digital images that can be stored in a computer and displayed on screen.

digital divide ▶ **noun** the gulf between those who have ready access to computers and the Internet, and those who do not.

digitalin /ˌdɪdʒɪˈteɪlɪn/ ▶ **noun** [mass noun] a drug containing the active constituents of digitalis.
– ORIGIN mid 19th cent.: from DIGITALIS + -IN[1].

D

digitalis /ˌdɪdʒɪˈteɪlɪs/ ▶ **noun** [mass noun] a drug prepared from the dried leaves of foxgloves and containing substances (notably digoxin and digitoxin) that stimulate the heart muscle.
– ORIGIN late 18th cent.: from the modern Latin genus name of the foxglove, from *digitalis (herba)* '(plant) relating to the finger', from *digitus* 'finger, toe'; suggested by German *Fingerhut* 'thimble or foxglove'.

digitalize[1] (also **digitalise**) ▶ **verb** another term for DIGITIZE.
– DERIVATIVES **digitalization** noun.

digitalize[2] (also **digitalise**) ▶ **verb** [with obj.] Medicine administer digitalis or digoxin to (a patient with a heart complaint).
– DERIVATIVES **digitalization** noun.

digital signature ▶ **noun** Computing a digital code (generated and authenticated by public key encryption) which is attached to an electronically transmitted document to verify its contents and the sender's identity.

digital-to-analogue converter ▶ **noun** an electronic device for converting digital signals to analogue form.

digitate /ˈdɪdʒɪteɪt, -eɪt/ ▶ **adjective** technical shaped like a spread hand: *digitate leaves | a digitate delta*.
– ORIGIN mid 17th cent.: from Latin *digitatus*, from *digitus* 'finger, toe'.

digitation ▶ **noun** Zoology & Botany a finger-like protuberance or division.

digitigrade /ˈdɪdʒɪtɪˌɡreɪd/ ▶ **adjective** Zoology (of a mammal) walking on its toes and not touching the ground with its heels, as a dog, cat, or rodent. Compare with PLANTIGRADE.
– ORIGIN mid 19th cent.: from Latin *digitus* 'finger, toe' + *-gradus* '-walking'.

digitize (also **digitise**) ▶ **verb** [with obj.] (usu. as adj. **digitized**) convert (pictures or sound) into a digital form that can be processed by a computer.
– DERIVATIVES **digitization** noun, **digitizer** noun.

digitoxin /ˌdɪdʒɪˈtɒksɪn/ ▶ **noun** [mass noun] Chemistry a compound with similar properties to digoxin and found with it in the foxglove and similar plants.

diglossia /dʌɪˈɡlɒsɪə/ ▶ **noun** [mass noun] Linguistics a situation in which two languages (or two varieties of the same language) are used under different conditions within a community, often by the same speakers. The term is usually applied to languages with distinct 'high' and 'low' (colloquial) varieties, such as Arabic.
– DERIVATIVES **diglossic** adjective.
– ORIGIN 1950s: from Greek *diglōssos* 'bilingual', on the pattern of French *diglossie*.

dignified ▶ **adjective** having or showing a composed or serious manner that is worthy of respect: *she maintained a dignified silence | a dignified old lady*.
– DERIVATIVES **dignifiedly** adverb.

dignify ▶ **verb** (**dignifies, dignifying, dignified**) [with obj.] make (something) seem worthy and impressive: *the Americans had dignified their departure with a ceremony*. ■ give an impressive name to (someone or something unworthy of it): *dumps are increasingly dignified as landfills*.
– ORIGIN late Middle English: from Old French *dignefier*, from late Latin *dignificare*, from Latin *dignus* 'worthy'.

dignitary /ˈdɪɡnɪt(ə)ri/ ▶ **noun** (pl. **dignitaries**) a person considered to be important because of high rank or office.
– ORIGIN late 17th cent.: from DIGNITY, on the pattern of the pairs *propriety, proprietary*.

dignity ▶ **noun** (pl. **dignities**) [mass noun] **1** the state or quality of being worthy of honour or respect: *the dignity of labour*. ■ [count noun] a high rank or position: *he promised dignities to the nobles in return for his rival's murder*.
2 a composed or serious manner or style: *he bowed with great dignity*. ■ a sense of pride in oneself; self-respect: *it was beneath his dignity to shout*.
– PHRASES **stand on one's dignity** insist on being treated with due respect.
– ORIGIN Middle English: from Old French *dignete*, from Latin *dignitas*, from *dignus* 'worthy'.

digoxin /dɪˈdʒɒksɪn/ ▶ **noun** [mass noun] Chemistry a poisonous compound present in the foxglove and other plants. It is a steroid glycoside and is used in small doses as a cardiac stimulant.
– ORIGIN 1930s: contraction of DIGITOXIN.

digraph /ˈdʌɪɡrɑːf/ ▶ **noun** a combination of two letters representing one sound, as in *ph* and *ey*. ■ Printing a character consisting of two joined letters; a ligature.
– DERIVATIVES **digraphic** adjective.

digress /dʌɪˈɡrɛs/ ▶ **verb** [no obj.] leave the main subject temporarily in speech or writing: *I have digressed a little from my original plan*.
– DERIVATIVES **digresser** noun.
– ORIGIN early 16th cent.: from Latin *digress-* 'stepped away', from the verb *digredi*, from *di-* 'aside' + *gradi* 'to walk'.

digression ▶ **noun** a temporary departure from the main subject in speech or writing: *let's return to the main topic after that brief digression*.

digressive ▶ **adjective** characterized by digression; tending to depart from the subject.
– DERIVATIVES **digressively** adverb, **digressiveness** noun.

digs ▶ **plural noun** informal lodgings.
– ORIGIN late 19th cent.: short for DIGGINGS, used in the same sense, probably referring to the land where a farmer digs, i.e. works and, by extension, lives.

dihedral /dʌɪˈhiːdr(ə)l/ ▶ **adjective** having or contained by two plane faces: *a dihedral angle*.
▶ **noun 1** an angle formed by two plane faces.
2 [mass noun] Aeronautics inclination of an aircraft's wing from the horizontal, especially upwards away from the fuselage. Compare with ANHEDRAL.
3 N. Amer. Climbing a place where two planes of rock meet at an angle of between 60° and 120°.
– ORIGIN late 18th cent.: from DI-[1] 'two' + *-hedral* (see -HEDRON).

dihybrid /dʌɪˈhʌɪbrɪd/ ▶ **noun** Genetics a hybrid that is heterozygous for alleles of two different genes: [as modifier] *a dihybrid cross*.

dihydric /dʌɪˈhʌɪdrɪk/ ▶ **adjective** Chemistry (of an alcohol) containing two hydroxyl groups.
– ORIGIN late 19th cent.: from DI-[1] 'two' + HYDROGEN + -IC.

dihydrotestosterone /dʌɪˌhʌɪdrəʊtɛsˈtɒstərəʊn/ ▶ **noun** [mass noun] Biochemistry a male sex hormone which is the active form of testosterone, formed from testosterone in bodily tissue.
– ORIGIN 1950s: from *dihydro-* (in the sense 'containing two hydrogen atoms in the molecule') + TESTOSTERONE.

dihydroxyacetone /ˌdʌɪhʌɪdrɒksɪˈasɪtəʊn/ ▶ **noun** [mass noun] Chemistry a synthetic compound with strong reducing properties, used in lotions for colouring the skin in sunlight. ● Chem. formula: $(CH_2OH)CO$.
– ORIGIN late 19th cent.: from *dihydroxy-* (in the sense 'containing two hydroxyl groups in the molecule') + ACETONE.

Dijon /ˈdiːʒɒ̃/, French /diʒɔ̃/ an industrial city in east central France, the former capital of Burgundy; pop. 155,340 (2006).

dik-dik /ˈdɪkdɪk/ ▶ **noun** (pl. **same** or **dik-diks**) a dwarf antelope found on the dry savannah of Africa, the female of which is larger than the male. ● Genus *Madoqua*, family Bovidae: several species.
– ORIGIN late 19th cent.: a local word in East Africa, imitative of its call.

dike[1] ▶ **noun** variant spelling of DYKE[1].

dike[2] ▶ **noun** variant spelling of DYKE[2].

dikkop /ˈdɪkəp/ ▶ **noun** S. African a stone curlew. ● The **Cape dikkop** is the spotted stone curlew (*Burhinus capensis*).
– ORIGIN mid 19th cent.: from Afrikaans, from *dik* 'thick' + *kop* 'head'.

diktat /ˈdɪktat/ ▶ **noun** an order or decree imposed by someone in power without popular consent: *a diktat from the Bundestag* | [mass noun] *he can disband the legislature and rule by diktat*.
– ORIGIN 1930s: from German, from Latin *dictatum* 'something dictated', neuter past participle of *dictare*.

DIL ▶ **abbreviation** Electronics dual in-line (package). See **DIP**.

Dilantin /dʌɪˈlantɪn/ ▶ **noun** US trademark for PHENYTOIN.
– ORIGIN 1930s: from DI-[1] 'two' + *-l-* + *(hyd)ant(o)in*.

dilapidate /dɪˈlapɪdeɪt/ ▶ **verb** [with obj.] archaic cause (something) to fall into disrepair or ruin.
– ORIGIN early 16th cent. (in the sense 'waste, squander'): from Latin *dilapidat-* 'demolished, squandered', from the verb *dilapidare*, literally 'scatter as if throwing stones', from *di-* 'apart, abroad' + *lapis, lapid-* 'stone'.

dilapidated ▶ **adjective** (of a building or object) in a state of disrepair or ruin as a result of age or neglect.

dilapidation ▶ **noun** [mass noun] the state or process of falling into decay or being in disrepair: *the mill was in a state of dilapidation*. ■ (**dilapidations**) repairs required during or at the end of a tenancy or lease. ■ [count noun] Law a cause of action to force a tenant to pay for such repairs. ■ (in church use) a sum charged against an incumbent for wear and tear during a tenancy.
– ORIGIN late Middle English (also in the sense 'squandering, waste'): from late Latin *dilapidatio(n-)*, from Latin *dilapidare* 'demolish, squander' (see DILAPIDATE).

dilatancy /dʌɪˈleɪt(ə)nsi, dɪ-/ ▶ **noun** [mass noun] Chemistry the phenomenon exhibited by some fluids, sols, and gels in which they become more viscous or solid under pressure.

dilatation /ˌdʌɪleɪˈteɪʃ(ə)n, dɪ-, -lə-/ ▶ **noun** [mass noun] chiefly Medicine & Physiology the action of dilating a vessel or opening or the process of becoming dilated. ■ [count noun] a dilated part of a hollow organ or vessel.
– ORIGIN late Middle English: via Old French from late Latin *dilatatio(n-)*, from the verb *dilatare* (see DILATE).

dilatation and curettage (abbrev.: **D and C**) ▶ **noun** a surgical procedure involving dilatation of the cervix and curettage of the uterus, performed after a miscarriage or for the removal of cysts or tumours.

dilate /dʌɪˈleɪt, dɪ-/ ▶ **verb 1** make or become wider, larger, or more open: [no obj.] *her eyes dilated with horror* | [with obj.] *the woman dilated her nostrils*.
2 [no obj.] (**dilate on**) speak or write at length on (a subject).
– DERIVATIVES **dilatable** adjective, **dilation** noun.
– ORIGIN late Middle English: from Old French *dilater*, from Latin *dilatare* 'spread out', from *di-* 'apart' + *latus* 'wide'.

dilator ▶ **noun** a thing that dilates something, in particular: ■ (also **dilator muscle**) Anatomy a muscle whose contraction dilates an organ or aperture, such as the pupil of the eye. ■ a surgical instrument for dilating a tube or cavity in the body. ■ a vasodilatory drug.

dilatory /ˈdɪlət(ə)ri/ ▶ **adjective** slow to act: *he had been dilatory in appointing a solicitor*. ■ intended to cause delay: *they resorted to dilatory tactics, forcing a postponement of peace talks*.
– DERIVATIVES **dilatorily** adverb, **dilatoriness** noun.
– ORIGIN late Middle English: from late Latin *dilatorius* 'delaying', from Latin *dilator* 'delayer', from *dilat-* 'deferred', from the verb *differre*.

dildo ▶ **noun** (pl. **dildos** or **dildoes**) **1** an object shaped like an erect penis used for sexual stimulation.
2 vulgar slang a stupid or ridiculous person.
– ORIGIN late 16th cent.: of unknown origin.

dilemma /dɪˈlɛmə, dʌɪ-/ ▶ **noun** a situation in which a difficult choice has to be made between two or more alternatives, especially ones that are equally undesirable: *he wants to make money, but he also disapproves of it: Den's dilemma in a nutshell*. ■ a difficult situation or problem: *the insoluble dilemma of adolescence*. ■ Logic an argument forcing an opponent to choose either of two unfavourable alternatives.
– ORIGIN early 16th cent. (denoting a form of argument involving a choice between equally unfavourable alternatives): via Latin from Greek *dilēmma*, from *di-* 'twice' + *lēmma* 'premise'.

> **USAGE** At its core, a **dilemma** is a situation in which a difficult choice has to be made between two or more alternatives. More informally, it can mean 'a difficult situation or problem' (as in *the insoluble* ***dilemma*** *of adolescence*). Some traditionalists object to this weakened use, but it is recorded as early as the first part of the 17th century, and is now widespread and generally acceptable.

dilettante /ˌdɪlɪˈtanteɪ, -ti/ ▶ **noun** (pl. **dilettanti** /-ti/ or **dilettantes**) a person who cultivates an area of interest, such as the arts, without real commitment

or knowledge. ■ archaic a person with an amateur interest in the arts.
– DERIVATIVES **dilettantish** adjective, **dilettantism** noun.
– ORIGIN mid 18th cent.: from Italian, 'person loving the arts', from *dilettare* 'to delight', from Latin *delectare*.

Dili /ˈdiːliː/ the capital and chief port of East Timor, on the northern coast of the island; pop. 171,400 (est. 2009).

diligence[1] /ˈdɪlɪdʒ(ə)ns/ ▶ noun [mass noun] careful and persistent work or effort.
– ORIGIN Middle English (in the sense 'close attention, caution'): via Old French from Latin *diligentia*, from *diligent-* 'assiduous' (see DILIGENT).

diligence[2] /ˈdɪlɪdʒ(ə)ns/ ▶ noun historical a public stagecoach.
– ORIGIN late 17th cent.: from French, shortened from *carrosse de diligence* 'coach of speed'.

diligent ▶ adjective having or showing care and conscientiousness in one's work or duties: *after diligent searching, he found a parcel.*
– DERIVATIVES **diligently** adverb.
– ORIGIN Middle English: via Old French from Latin *diligens, diligent-* 'assiduous', from *diligere* 'love, take delight in'.

dill[1] (also **dill weed**) ▶ noun [mass noun] an aromatic annual herb of the parsley family, with fine blue-green leaves and yellow flowers. The leaves or seeds are used for flavouring and for medicinal purposes. ● *Anethum graveolens*, family Umbelliferae.
– ORIGIN Old English *dile, dyle*; related to Dutch *dille* and German *Dill*; of unknown ultimate origin.

dill[2] ▶ noun Austral./NZ informal a naive or foolish person.
– ORIGIN 1940s: apparently a back-formation from DILLY[2].

dill pickle ▶ noun [mass noun] pickled cucumber flavoured with dill.

dill water ▶ noun [mass noun] an extract distilled from dill, used to relieve flatulence.

dilly[1] ▶ noun (pl. **dillies**) [usu. in sing.] N. Amer. informal an excellent example of a particular type of person or thing: *that's a dilly of a breakfast recipe.*
– ORIGIN late 19th cent. (as an adjective in the sense 'delightful'): alteration of the first syllable of DELIGHTFUL or DELICIOUS.

dilly[2] ▶ adjective (**dillier, dilliest**) Austral./NZ informal, dated odd; foolish.
– ORIGIN late 19th cent.: perhaps a blend of DAFT and SILLY.

dillybag (also **dilly**) ▶ noun Austral. a bag or basket of traditional Aboriginal design, made from woven grass or fibre.
– ORIGIN from Yagara (an extinct Aboriginal language of Queensland) *dili* 'coarse grass or reeds; a bag woven of this' + BAG.

dilly-dally ▶ verb (**dilly-dallies, dilly-dallying, dilly-dallied**) [no obj.] informal waste time through aimless wandering or indecision: *don't dilly-dally for too long.*
– ORIGIN early 17th cent.: reduplication of DALLY.

dilophosaurus /dʌɪˌləʊfə(ʊ)ˈsɔːrəs/ ▶ noun the earliest of the large bipedal dinosaurs, which had two long crests on the head and occurred in the early Jurassic period. ● Genus *Dilophosaurus*, infraorder Carnosauria, suborder Theropoda.
– ORIGIN modern Latin, from Greek *dilophos* 'two-crested' + *sauros* 'lizard'.

diluent /ˈdɪljʊənt/ technical ▶ noun a substance used to dilute something.
▶ adjective acting to cause dilution.
– ORIGIN early 18th cent. (denoting a medicine used to increase the proportion of water in the blood): from Latin *diluent-* 'dissolving', from the verb *diluere*.

dilute /dʌɪˈl(j)uːt, dɪ-/ ▶ verb [with obj.] make (a liquid) thinner or weaker by adding water or another solvent to it: *bleach can be diluted with cold water* | (as adj. **diluted**) *diluted fruit juice.* ■ make (something) weaker in force, content, or value by modification or the addition of other elements: *the reforms have been diluted* | (as adj. **diluted**) *the report was published in a diluted form.*
▶ adjective also /dʌɪˈluːt/ (of a liquid) made thinner or weaker by having had water or another solvent added to it. ■ Chemistry (of a solution) having a relatively low concentration of solute: *a dilute solution of potassium permanganate.*
– DERIVATIVES **diluter** noun.
– ORIGIN mid 16th cent.: from Latin *dilut-* 'washed away, dissolved', from the verb *diluere*.

dilution ▶ noun [mass noun] the action of making a liquid more dilute. ■ the action of making something weaker in force, content, or value: *he is resisting any dilution of dogma.* ■ [count noun] a liquid that has been diluted. ■ [count noun] the degree to which a solution has been diluted: *the antibody was applied at a dilution of 1:50.*
– DERIVATIVES **dilutive** adjective (chiefly Finance).

diluvial /dʌɪˈl(j)uːvɪəl, dɪ-/ ▶ adjective relating to a flood or floods, especially the biblical Flood.
– ORIGIN mid 17th cent.: from late Latin *diluvialis*, from *diluvium* 'deluge', from *diluere* 'wash away'.

diluvian /dʌɪˈl(j)uːvɪən, dɪ-/ ▶ adjective another term for DILUVIAL.

dim ▶ adjective (**dimmer, dimmest**) **1** (of a light, colour, or illuminated object) not shining brightly or clearly: *the dim glow of the fire.* ■ (of an object or shape) made difficult to see by darkness, shade, or distance: *a dim figure in the dark kitchen.* ■ (of a room or other space) made difficult to see in by darkness: *long dim corridors.* ■ (of the eyes) unable to see clearly. ■ (of a sound) indistinct or muffled: *the dim drone of their voices.* ■ not clearly recalled or formulated in the mind: *dim memories* | *the matter was in the dim and distant past.*
2 (of a situation) not giving cause for hope or optimism: *their prospects for the future looked fairly dim.*
3 informal stupid or slow to understand.
▶ verb (**dims, dimming, dimmed**) make or become less bright or distinct: [with obj.] *a smoky inferno that dimmed the sun* | [no obj.] *the lights dimmed and the curtains parted.* ■ [with obj.] lower the beam of (a vehicle's headlights) to avoid dazzling oncoming drivers. ■ make or become less intense: [with obj.] *the difficulty in sleeping couldn't dim her happiness.* ■ make or become less able to see clearly: [no obj.] *his eyes dimmed.*
– PHRASES **take a dim view of** regard with disapproval.
– DERIVATIVES **dimly** adverb, **dimmable** adjective, **dimmish** adjective, **dimness** noun.
– ORIGIN Old English *dim, dimm*, of Germanic origin; related to German dialect *timmer*.

dim. ▶ abbreviation diminuendo.

DiMaggio /dɪˈmadʒɪəʊ/, Joe (1914–99), American baseball player; full name *Joseph Paul DiMaggio*. Star of the New York Yankees team 1936–51, he was renowned for his outstanding batting ability and for his outfield play. He was briefly married to Marilyn Monroe in 1954.

Dimbleby /ˈdɪmb(ə)lbi/, (Frederick) Richard (1913–65), English broadcaster. He was the BBC's first news correspondent (1936) and was particularly noted for his radio and television commentaries on royal, national, and international events. His sons **David** (b.1938) and **Jonathan** (b.1944) have both followed their father into careers in news broadcasting.

dime /dʌɪm/ ▶ noun N. Amer. a ten-cent coin. ■ informal a small amount of money: *he didn't have a dime.*
– PHRASES **a dime a dozen** informal very common and of no particular value: *experts in this field are a dime a dozen.* **drop a** (or **the**) **dime on someone** informal inform on someone. **get off the dime** informal be decisive and show initiative. **on a dime** informal used to refer to a manoeuvre that can be performed within a small area or short distance: *boats that can turn on a dime.*
– ORIGIN late Middle English: from Old French *disme*, from Latin *decima pars* 'tenth part'. The word originally denoted a tithe or tenth part; the modern sense 'ten cent coin' dates from the late 18th cent.

dime bag ▶ noun N. Amer. informal a specified amount of an illegal drug, packaged and sold for a fixed price.

dime novel ▶ noun N. Amer. dated a cheap, popular novel, typically a melodramatic romance or adventure story.

dimension /dɪˈmɛnʃ(ə)n, dʌɪ-/ ▶ noun **1** (usu. **dimensions**) a measurable extent of a particular kind, such as length, breadth, depth, or height: *the final dimensions of the pond were 14 ft x 8 ft* | [mass noun] *the drawing must be precise in dimension.* ■ a mode of linear extension of which there are three in space and two on a flat surface, which corresponds to one of a set of coordinates specifying the position of a point. ■ Physics an expression for a derived physical quantity in terms of fundamental quantities such as mass, length, or time, raised to the appropriate power (acceleration, for example, having the dimension of $length \times time^{-2}$).
2 an aspect or feature of a situation: *we must focus on the cultural dimensions of the problem.*
▶ verb [with obj.] cut or shape (something) to particular measurements. ■ (usu. as adj. **dimensioned**) mark (a diagram) with measurements.
– DERIVATIVES **dimensional** adjective [in combination] *multi-dimensional scaling*, **dimensionless** adjective.
– ORIGIN late Middle English (in sense 1 of the noun): via Old French from Latin *dimensio(n-)*, from *dimetiri* 'measure out'. Sense 2 of the noun dates from the 1920s.

dimensional analysis ▶ noun [mass noun] Mathematics analysis using the fact that physical quantities added to or equated with each other must be expressed in terms of the same fundamental quantities (such as mass, length, or time) for inferences to be made about the relations between them.

D

dimer /ˈdʌɪmə/ ▶ noun Chemistry a molecule or molecular complex consisting of two identical molecules linked together.
– DERIVATIVES **dimeric** adjective.
– ORIGIN 1930s: from DI-[1] 'two', on the pattern of *polymer*.

dimercaprol /ˌdʌɪməˈkaprɒl/ ▶ noun [mass noun] Chemistry a colourless, oily liquid with an unpleasant smell, used as an antidote for poisoning by mercury, arsenic, lead, and other heavy metals. ● Alternative name: **2,3,-dimercapto-1-propanol**; chem. formula: $CH_2(SH)CH(SH)CH_2OH$.
– ORIGIN 1940s: from elements of the systematic name (see above).

dimerize /ˈdʌɪmərʌɪz/ (also **dimerise**) ▶ verb [no obj.] Chemistry combine with a similar molecule to form a dimer.
– DERIVATIVES **dimerization** noun.

dimerous /ˈdɪm(ə)rəs/ ▶ adjective Botany & Zoology having parts arranged in groups of two. ■ consisting of two joints or parts.
– ORIGIN early 19th cent.: from modern Latin *dimerus* (from Greek *dimerēs* 'bipartite') + -OUS.

dime store ▶ noun N. Amer. a shop selling cheap merchandise (originally one where the maximum price was a dime). ■ [as modifier] cheap and inferior: *plastic dime-store toys.* ■ [as modifier] trite; simplistic: *the dime-store moralism of yesteryear.*

dimeter /ˈdɪmɪtə/ ▶ noun Prosody a line of verse consisting of two metrical feet.
– ORIGIN late 16th cent.: via late Latin from Greek *dimetros* 'of two measures', from *di-* 'twice' + *metron* 'a measure'.

dimethoate /dʌɪˈmiːθəʊeɪt/ ▶ noun [mass noun] a crystalline synthetic organophosphorus compound used in solution as an insecticide.
– ORIGIN 1960s: from DI-[1] 'two' + METHYL + THIO- + -ATE[1].

dimethyl sulphoxide /dʌɪˌmiːθʌɪl sʌlˈfɒksʌɪd, -ˌmɛθ-, -θɪl/ (US **dimethyl sulfoxide**) (abbrev.: **DMSO**) ▶ noun [mass noun] Chemistry a colourless liquid used as a solvent and synthetic reagent. It is readily able to penetrate the skin and is used in medicinal preparations for skin application. ● Chem. formula: $(CH_3)_2SO$.

dimetric /dʌɪˈmɛtrɪk/ ▶ adjective (in technical drawing) denoting or incorporating a method of showing projection or perspective using a set of three geometrical axes of which two are of the same scale or dimension but the third is of another.
– ORIGIN mid 19th cent.: from DI-[1] 'two' + Greek *metron* 'measure' + -IC.

dimetrodon /dʌɪˈmiːtrədɒn/ ▶ noun a large fossil carnivorous mammal-like reptile of the Permian period, with long spines on its back supporting a sail-like crest. ● Genus *Dimetrodon*, order Pelycosauria, subclass Synapsida.
– ORIGIN modern Latin, from *di-* 'twice' + Greek *metron* 'measure' + *odous, odont-* 'tooth' (taken in the sense 'two long teeth').

dimidiate /dɪˈmɪdɪeɪt/ ▶ verb [with obj.] Heraldry (of a coat of arms or charge) adjoin (another) so that only half of each is visible. ■ (as adj. **dimidiated**) (of a charge) having only one half depicted.
– ORIGIN late 16th cent.: from Latin *dimidiat-* 'halved', from the verb *dimidiare*, from *dimidium* 'half'.

dimidiation ▶ noun [mass noun] Heraldry the combination of two coats of arms by juxtaposing the dexter half of one and the sinister half of the other on a single shield (a practice largely superseded by impalement).

diminish ▶ verb make or become less: [with obj.] *the new law is expected to diminish the government's chances* | [no obj.] *the pain will gradually diminish.* ■ [with obj.] cause to seem less impressive or valuable: *the trial has aged and diminished him.*

– PHRASES **(the law of) diminishing returns** used to refer to a point at which the level of profits or benefits gained is less than the amount of money or energy invested.
– ORIGIN late Middle English: blend of archaic *minish* 'diminish' (based on Latin *minutia* 'smallness') and obsolete *diminue* 'speak disparagingly' (based on Latin *deminuere* 'lessen' (in late Latin *diminuere*), from *minuere* 'make small').

diminished ▸ **adjective 1** made smaller or less: *a diminished role for local government.* ■ [predic.] made to seem less impressive or valuable: *she felt diminished by the report.*
2 [attrib.] Music denoting or containing an interval which is one semitone less than the corresponding minor or perfect interval: *a diminished fifth.*

D

diminished responsibility ▸ **noun** [mass noun] English Law an unbalanced mental state which is considered to make a person less answerable for murder, being recognized as grounds to reduce the charge to that of manslaughter.

diminished seventh ▸ **noun** Music **1** the interval which is a semitone less than a minor seventh, e.g. from A to G flat (which in equal tuning sounds the same as a major sixth).
2 (also **diminished seventh chord**) a chord formed by a note together with those above it at intervals of a minor third, a diminished fifth, and a diminished seventh. The resulting chord consists entirely of superimposed minor thirds, and is much used in modern music in modulating between keys.

diminuendo /dɪˌmɪnjʊˈɛndəʊ/ Music ▸ **noun** (pl. **diminuendos** or **diminuendi** /-di/) a decrease in loudness in a piece of music. ■ a passage to be performed with a decrease in loudness.
▸ **adverb & adjective** (especially as a direction) with a decrease in loudness: [as adj.] *the diminuendo chorus before the final tumult.*
▸ **verb** (**diminuendos, diminuendoing, diminuendoed**) [no obj.] decrease in loudness or intensity.
– ORIGIN Italian, literally 'diminishing', from *diminuire*, from Latin *deminuere* 'lessen' (see DIMINISH).

diminution /ˌdɪmɪˈnjuːʃ(ə)n/ ▸ **noun** a reduction in the size, extent, or importance of something: *a permanent diminution in value* | [mass noun] *the disease shows no signs of diminution.* ■ Music the shortening of the time values of notes in a melodic part.
– ORIGIN Middle English: via Old French from Latin *deminutio(n-)*, from the verb *deminuere* (see DIMINISH).

diminutive /dɪˈmɪnjʊtɪv/ ▸ **adjective** extremely or unusually small: *a diminutive figure dressed in black.* ■ (of a word, name, or suffix) implying smallness, either actual or imputed to convey affection, scorn, etc. (e.g. *teeny, -let, -kins*).
▸ **noun** a smaller or shorter thing, in particular: ■ a diminutive word or suffix. ■ a shortened form of a name, typically used informally: *'Nick' is a diminutive of 'Nicholas'.* ■ Heraldry a charge of the same form as an ordinary but of lesser size or width.
– DERIVATIVES **diminutively** adverb, **diminutiveness** noun.
– ORIGIN late Middle English (as a grammatical term): from Old French *diminutif, -ive*, from late Latin *diminutivus*, from Latin *deminut-* 'diminished', from the verb *deminuere* (see DIMINISH).

dimissory /ˈdɪmɪs(ə)ri/ ▸ **adjective** (in the Christian Church) denoting formal permission from a bishop (**letters dimissory**) for a person from one diocese to be ordained in another, or (formerly) for an ordained person to leave one diocese for another.
– ORIGIN late Middle English (as a plural noun): from late Latin *dimissorius*, from *dimiss-* 'sent away', from the verb *dimittere*. The adjective dates from the late 16th cent., the original sense being 'valedictory'.

dimity /ˈdɪmɪti/ ▸ **noun** [mass noun] a hard-wearing cotton fabric woven with stripes or checks.
– ORIGIN late Middle English: from Italian *dimito* or medieval Latin *dimitum*, from Greek *dimitos*, from *di-* 'twice' + *mitos* 'warp thread'; the origin of the final *-y* is unknown.

DIMM ▸ **abbreviation** Computing dual in-line memory module.

dimmer ▸ **noun 1** (also **dimmer switch**) a device for varying the brightness of an electric light.
2 US a headlight with a low beam. ■ (**dimmers**) small parking lights on a motor vehicle.

dimorphic /dʌɪˈmɔːfɪk/ ▸ **adjective** chiefly Biology occurring in or representing two distinct forms: *in this sexually dimorphic species only the males have wings.*
– DERIVATIVES **dimorphism** noun.
– ORIGIN mid 19th cent.: from Greek *dimorphos* (from *di-* 'twice' + *morphē* 'form') + -IC.

dimple ▸ **noun** a small depression in the flesh, either one that exists permanently or one that forms in the cheeks when one smiles. ■ a slight depression in the surface of an object: [as modifier] *a new golf ball, with a different dimple pattern.*
▸ **verb** [with obj.] produce a dimple or dimples in the surface of: *rain began to fall, dimpling the water.* ■ [no obj.] form or show a dimple or dimples: *she dimpled at Auguste* | (as adj. **dimpled**) *her dimpled thighs.*
– DERIVATIVES **dimply** adjective (**dimplier, dimpliest**).
– ORIGIN Middle English: of Germanic origin; related to German *Tümpel* 'pond'.

dim sum /dɪm ˈsʌm/ (also **dim sim** /ˈsɪm/) ▸ **noun** [mass noun] a Chinese dish of small steamed or fried savoury dumplings containing various fillings.
– ORIGIN from Chinese (Cantonese dialect) *tim sam*, from *tim* 'dot' and *sam* 'heart'.

dimwit ▸ **noun** informal a stupid or silly person.

dim-witted ▸ **adjective** informal stupid or silly: *a dim-witted waiter.*
– DERIVATIVES **dim-wittedly** adverb, **dim-wittedness** noun.

DIN ▸ **noun** any of a series of technical standards originating in Germany and used internationally, especially to designate electrical connections, film speeds, and paper sizes: [as modifier] *a DIN socket.*
– ORIGIN early 20th cent.: acronym from *Deutsche Industrie-Norm* 'German Industrial Standard' (as laid down by the *Deutsches Institut für Normung* 'German Institute for Standards').

din ▸ **noun** [in sing.] a loud, unpleasant, and prolonged noise: *the fans made an awful din.*
▸ **verb** (**dins, dinning, dinned**) **1** [with obj.] (**din something into**) make (someone) learn or remember an idea by constant repetition: *a runner-up, he dinned into them, was a loser.*
2 [no obj.] make a loud, unpleasant, and prolonged noise: *the sound dinned irritatingly into Marian's head.*
– ORIGIN Old English *dyne, dynn* (noun), *dynian* (verb), of Germanic origin; related to Old High German *tuni* (noun) and Old Norse *dynr* (noun), *dynja* 'come rumbling down'.

dinar /ˈdiːnɑː/ ▸ **noun 1** the basic monetary unit of Serbia, equal to 100 paras.
2 the basic monetary unit of certain countries of the Middle East and North Africa, equal to 1000 fils in Jordan, Bahrain, and Iraq, 1000 dirhams in Libya, and 100 centimes in Algeria.
3 a monetary unit of Iran, equal to one hundredth of a rial.
– ORIGIN from Arabic and Persian *dīnār*, Turkish and Serbian *dinar*, via late Greek from Latin *denarius* (see DENARIUS).

Dinaric Alps /dɪˈnarɪk/ a mountain range in the Balkans, running parallel to the Adriatic coast from Slovenia in the north-west, through Croatia, Bosnia, and Montenegro, to Albania in the south-east.

din-dins (also **din-din**) ▸ **noun** [mass noun] a child's word for dinner.

dine ▸ **verb** [no obj.] eat dinner: *we dined at a restaurant* | (as noun **dining**) *a dining area.* ■ (**dine out**) eat dinner in a restaurant. ■ (**dine out on**) regularly entertain friends with (a humorous story or interesting fact). ■ [with obj.] take (someone) to dinner.
– ORIGIN Middle English: from Old French *disner*, probably from *desjëuner* 'to break fast', from *des-* (expressing reversal) + *jëun* 'fasting' (from Latin *jejunus*).

diner ▸ **noun 1** a person who is eating, typically a customer in a restaurant.
2 a dining car on a train. ■ N. Amer. a small roadside restaurant with a long counter and booths.

dinero /dɪˈnɛːrəʊ/ ▸ **noun** [mass noun] N. Amer. informal money: *their pockets full of dinero.*
– ORIGIN Spanish, 'coin, money'.

Dinesen /ˈdɪnɪs(ə)n/, Isak, see BLIXEN.

dinette /dʌɪˈnɛt/ ▸ **noun** a small room or part of a room used for eating meals. ■ N. Amer. a set of table and chairs for a dining area.
– ORIGIN 1930s: formed irregularly from DINE + -ETTE.

ding[1] ▸ **verb** [no obj.] make a ringing sound: *cash registers were dinging softly.*
▸ **exclamation** used to imitate a metallic ringing sound resembling a bell.
– ORIGIN early 17th cent.: imitative.

ding[2] ▸ **noun** Austral. informal a lively party or celebration.
– ORIGIN 1950s: perhaps from DING-DONG or WINGDING.

ding[3] ▸ **noun** informal, chiefly N. Amer. a mark or dent on the bodywork of a car, boat, or other vehicle. ■ Scottish or dialect a blow on the head.
▸ **verb** [with obj.] dent (something). ■ hit (someone), especially on the head: *I dinged him one.* ■ [no obj.] (**ding into**) Scottish bump into.
– ORIGIN Middle English: probably of Scandinavian origin; compare with Danish *dænge* 'beat, bang'.

ding-a-ling ▸ **noun 1** [in sing.] the ringing sound of a bell.
2 N. Amer. informal an eccentric or stupid person.
– ORIGIN late 19th cent.: imitative.

Ding an sich /ˌdɪŋ an ˈzɪx/, German /ˌdɪŋ an ˈzɪç/ ▸ **noun** (in Kant's philosophy) a thing as it is in itself, not mediated through perception by the senses or conceptualization, and therefore unknowable.
– ORIGIN German.

dingbat /ˈdɪŋbat/ ▸ **noun** informal **1** N. Amer. & Austral./NZ a stupid or eccentric person.
2 (**dingbats**) Austral./NZ delusions or feelings of unease, particularly those induced by delirium tremens.
3 a typographical device other than a letter or numeral (such as an asterisk), used to signal divisions in text or to replace letters in a euphemistically presented vulgar word.
– ORIGIN mid 19th cent. (in early use applied to various vaguely specified objects): origin uncertain; perhaps based on DING[3]. Sense 2 is probably by association with *have bats in the belfry.*

ding-dong ▸ **noun** informal **1** [in sing.] Brit. a fierce argument or fight: *they had a bit of a ding-dong.*
2 dated a riotous party.
3 N. Amer. a silly or foolish person.
▸ **adverb & adjective 1** with the simple alternate chimes of or as of a bell: [as adv.] *the church bells go ding-dong* | [as adj.] *he heard the ding-dong tones on the aircraft.* ■ [as adv.] Brit. energetically or wildly: *her biological clock is going ding-dong.*
2 [as adj.] Brit. informal (of a contest) evenly matched and hard fought: *the game was an exciting ding-dong battle.*
– ORIGIN mid 16th cent.: imitative.

dinger /ˈdɪŋə/ ▸ **noun** Baseball, informal a home run. ■ US informal, dated a thing outstanding of its kind: *it was going to be a dinger of a night.*
– ORIGIN late 19th cent.: shortening of HUMDINGER.

dinges ▸ **noun** South African spelling of DINGUS.

dinghy /ˈdɪŋgi, ˈdɪŋi/ ▸ **noun** (pl. **dinghies**) a small boat for recreation or racing, especially an open boat with a mast and sails. ■ a small inflatable rubber boat.
– ORIGIN early 19th cent. (denoting a rowing boat used on rivers in India): from Hindi *ḍiṅgī*. The *-gh* in English serves to indicate the hard *g*.

dingle ▸ **noun** literary or dialect a deep wooded valley or dell.
– ORIGIN Middle English (denoting a deep abyss): of unknown origin. The current sense dates from the mid 17th cent.

dingleberry ▸ **noun** (pl. **dingleberries**) **1** US informal a foolish or inept person.
2 vulgar slang a particle of faecal matter attached to anal hair.
– ORIGIN mid 20th cent.: from *dingle* of unknown origin + BERRY.

dingo /ˈdɪŋgəʊ/ ▸ **noun** (pl. **dingoes** or **dingos**) **1** a wild or half-domesticated dog with a sandy-coloured coat, found in Australia. ● *Canis dingo*, family Canidae.
2 Austral. informal a cowardly or treacherous person.
– ORIGIN late 18th cent.: from Dharuk *din-gu* 'domesticated dingo'; sense 2 dates from the mid 19th cent. and alludes to the treachery popularly associated with the dingo.

dingus /ˈdɪŋəs/ (S. African also **dinges** pronounced same) ▸ **noun** (pl. **dinguses**) N. Amer. & S. African informal used to refer to something one cannot or does not wish to name specifically.
– ORIGIN late 19th cent.: via Afrikaans from Dutch *ding* 'thing'.

dingy /ˈdɪn(d)ʒi/ ▸ **adjective** (**dingier, dingiest**) gloomy and drab: *a dingy room.*
– DERIVATIVES **dingily** adverb, **dinginess** noun.
– ORIGIN mid 18th cent.: perhaps based on Old English *dynge* 'dung'.

dining car ▸ **noun** a railway carriage equipped as a restaurant.

dining hall ▶ noun a large room, typically in a school or other institution, in which people eat meals together.

dining room ▶ noun a room in a house or hotel in which meals are eaten.

dining table ▶ noun a table on which meals are served in a dining room.

dinitrogen tetroxide /dʌɪˈnʌɪtrə(ʊ)dʒ(ə)n/ ▶ noun see NITROGEN DIOXIDE.

dink[1] ▶ noun another term for DINKY[2].

dink[2] ▶ noun (in sport) a softly hit pass which drops abruptly to the ground. ■ Tennis a drop shot.
▶ verb [with obj.] hit (the ball) with a dink.
– ORIGIN 1930s (originally a North American usage): symbolic of the light action.

Dinka /ˈdɪŋkə/ ▶ noun (pl. **same** or **Dinkas**) **1** a member of a Sudanese people of the Nile basin.
2 [mass noun] the Nilotic language of the Dinka, with about 1.4 million speakers.
▶ adjective relating to the Dinka or their language.
– ORIGIN from the local word *Jieng* 'people'.

dinkum /ˈdɪŋkəm/ Austral./NZ informal ▶ adjective (of an article or person) genuine, honest, true: *a real dinkum bloke.*
▶ adverb really, truly, honestly.
– PHRASES **fair dinkum** used to emphasize or seek confirmation of the genuineness or truth of something: *Eric and his assistant are fair dinkum magicians | 'Burt's just told me he's packing up in a month.' 'Fair dinkum?'.*
– ORIGIN late 19th cent.: of unknown origin.

Dinky ▶ noun [as modifier] trademark denoting a miniature motor vehicle of die-cast metal.

dinky[1] ▶ adjective (**dinkier**, **dinkiest**) informal **1** Brit. (of an object or place) attractively small and neat: *a dinky little restaurant.*
2 N. Amer. disappointingly small; insignificant: *I can't believe the dinky salaries they pay here.*
– ORIGIN late 18th cent.: from Scots and northern English dialect *dink* 'neat, trim', of unknown origin.

dinky[2] ▶ noun (pl. **dinkies**) informal a partner in a well-off working couple with no children.
– ORIGIN 1980s: acronym from *double income, no kids*, on the pattern of *yuppy*.

dinky-di /ˌdɪŋkɪˈdʌɪ/ (also **dinki-di**) ▶ adjective Austral./NZ informal another term for DINKUM.
– ORIGIN early 20th cent.: from DINKUM, with a nonsensical final element.

dinna (also **dinnae**) ▶ verb non-standard spelling of DON'T, used in representing Scottish speech.
– PHRASES **dinna fash** see FASH.

dinner ▶ noun the main meal of the day, taken either around midday or in the evening. ■ a formal evening meal, typically one in honour of a person or event.
– PHRASES **done like (a) dinner** Austral./NZ & Canadian informal utterly defeated or outwitted. **more —— than someone has had hot dinners** Brit. informal used to emphasize someone's wide experience of a specified activity or phenomenon: *he's seen more battles than you've had hot dinners.*
– ORIGIN Middle English: from Old French *disner* (infinitive used as a noun: see DINE).

dinner dance ▶ noun a formal social event in which guests have dinner, followed by dancing.

dinner jacket ▶ noun a man's jacket without tails, typically black, worn with a bow tie for formal occasions in the evening.

dinner lady ▶ noun Brit. a woman who serves meals to children in a school.

dinner pail ▶ noun dated, chiefly US a pail in which a labourer's or schoolchild's dinner is carried and kept warm.
– PHRASES **hand in one's dinner pail** informal die.

dinner party ▶ noun a social occasion at which guests eat dinner together.

dinner service (also **dinner set**) ▶ noun a set of matching crockery for serving a meal.

dinner suit ▶ noun a dinner jacket and trousers, worn with a bow tie on formal occasions.

dinner theatre ▶ noun N. Amer. a theatre in which a meal is included in the price of a ticket.

dinner time ▶ noun the time at which dinner is customarily eaten, either around midday or in the evening: *I'll be back at dinner time.*

dinnerware ▶ noun [mass noun] N. Amer. dishes, utensils, and glassware used at table; tableware.

dinoflagellate /ˌdʌɪnə(ʊ)ˈfladʒəleɪt/ ▶ noun Biology a single-celled organism with two flagella, occurring in large numbers in marine plankton and also found in fresh water. Some produce toxins that can accumulate in shellfish, resulting in poisoning when eaten. ● Division Dinophyta or class Dinophyceae, division Chromophycota (or phylum Dinophyta, kingdom Protista).
– ORIGIN late 19th cent. (as an adjective): from modern Latin *Dinoflagellata* (plural), from Greek *dinos* 'whirling' + Latin *flagellum* 'small whip' (see FLAGELLUM).

dinosaur /ˈdʌɪnəsɔː/ ▶ noun **1** a fossil reptile of the Mesozoic era, often reaching an enormous size.

> The dinosaurs are placed, according to their hip structure, in two distantly related orders (see ORNITHISCHIAN and SAURISCHIAN). Some of them may have been warm-blooded, and their closest living relatives are the birds. Dinosaurs were all extinct by the end of the Cretaceous period (65 million years ago), possibly as a result of a catastrophic asteroid impact in the Gulf of Mexico.

2 a person or thing that is outdated or has become obsolete because of failure to adapt to changing circumstances.
– DERIVATIVES **dinosaurian** adjective & noun.
– ORIGIN mid 19th cent.: from modern Latin *dinosaurus*, from Greek *deinos* 'terrible' + *sauros* 'lizard'.

dint ▶ noun **1** a dent or hollow in a surface: *the soft dints at the top of a coconut.*
2 archaic a blow or stroke, typically one made with a weapon in fighting. ■ [mass noun] force of attack; impact: *I perceive you feel the dint of pity.*
▶ verb [with obj.] mark (a surface) with dents or hollows.
– PHRASES **by dint of** by means of: *he had got to where he was today by dint of sheer hard work.*
– ORIGIN Old English *dynt* 'stroke with a weapon', reinforced in Middle English by the related Old Norse word *dyntr*; of unknown ultimate origin. Compare with DENT.

diocesan /dʌɪˈɒsɪs(ə)n/ ▶ adjective of or concerning a diocese.
▶ noun the bishop of a diocese.
– ORIGIN late Middle English: from French *diocésain*, from medieval Latin *diocesanus*, from Latin *dioecesis* (see DIOCESE).

diocesan quota ▶ noun see QUOTA.

diocese /ˈdʌɪəsɪs/ ▶ noun (pl. **dioceses** /ˈdʌɪəsiːz, -siːzɪz/) a district under the pastoral care of a bishop in the Christian Church.
– ORIGIN Middle English: from Old French *diocise*, from late Latin *diocesis*, from Latin *dioecesis* 'governor's jurisdiction, diocese', from Greek *dioikēsis* 'administration, diocese', from *dioikein* 'keep house, administer'.

dioch /ˈdʌɪək/ ▶ noun a quelea (weaver bird). ● The **black-faced** (or **Sudan**) **dioch** is the red-billed quelea (*Quelea quelea*).
– ORIGIN late 19th cent.: probably a local African name.

Diocletian /ˌdʌɪəˈkliːʃ(ə)n/ (245–313), Roman emperor 284–305; full name *Gaius Aurelius Valerius Diocletianus*. Faced with mounting military problems, in 286 he divided the empire between himself in the east and Maximian in the west. Diocletian launched the final persecution of the Christians (303).

diode /ˈdʌɪəʊd/ ▶ noun Electronics a semiconductor device with two terminals, typically allowing the flow of current in one direction only. ■ a thermionic valve having two electrodes (an anode and a cathode).
– ORIGIN early 20th cent.: from DI-[1] 'two' + a shortened form of ELECTRODE.

dioecious /dʌɪˈiːʃəs/ ▶ adjective Biology (of a plant or invertebrate animal) having the male and female reproductive organs in separate individuals. Compare with MONOECIOUS.
– DERIVATIVES **dioecy** noun.
– ORIGIN mid 18th cent.: from modern Latin *Dioecia* (a class in Linnaeus's sexual system), from DI-[1] 'two' + Greek *-oikos* 'house'.

dioestrus /dʌɪˈiːstrəs/ (US **diestrus**) ▶ noun [mass noun] Zoology (in most female mammals) a period of sexual inactivity between recurrent periods of oestrus.

Diogenes /dʌɪˈɒdʒɪniːz/ (*c.*400–*c.*325 BC), Greek philosopher. The most famous of the Cynics, he lived ascetically in Athens (according to legend, he lived in a tub) and was accordingly nicknamed *Kuōn* ('the dog'), from which the Cynics derived their name. He emphasized self-sufficiency and the need for natural, uninhibited behaviour, regardless of social conventions.

diogenite /dʌɪˈɒdʒənʌɪt/ ▶ noun a stony meteorite of a kind consisting largely of pyroxenes and plagioclase.
– ORIGIN late 19th cent.: from Greek *Diogenēs* 'descended from Zeus' + -ITE[1].

diol /ˈdʌɪɒl/ ▶ noun Chemistry an alcohol containing two hydroxyl groups in its molecule.
– ORIGIN 1920s: from DI-[1] 'two' + -OL.

Dione /dʌɪˈəʊni/ Astronomy a satellite of Saturn, the twelfth closest to the planet, discovered by Cassini in 1684, being icy with a partly cratered and partly smooth surface (diameter 1,120 km).
– ORIGIN named after a Titan, the mother of Aphrodite, in Greek mythology.

Dionysiac /ˌdʌɪəˈnɪzɪak/ (also **Dionysian** /-zɪən/) ▶ adjective **1** Greek Mythology relating to the god Dionysus.
2 relating to the sensual, spontaneous, and emotional aspects of human nature. Compare with APOLLONIAN.

Dionysius /ˌdʌɪəˈnɪsɪəs/ the name of two rulers of Syracuse: ■ **Dionysius I** (*c.*430–367 BC), ruled 405–367; known as **Dionysius the Elder**. A tyrannical ruler, he waged three wars against the Carthaginians for control of Sicily, later becoming the principal power in Greek Italy after the capture of Rhegium (386) and other Greek cities in southern Italy. ■ **Dionysius II** (*c.*397–*c.*344 BC), son of Dionysius I, ruled 367–357 and 346–344; known as **Dionysius the Younger**. He lacked his father's military ambitions and signed a peace treaty with Carthage in 367. Despite his patronage of philosophers, he resisted the attempt by Plato to turn him into a philosopher king.

Dionysius Exiguus /ɪɡˈzɪɡjʊəs/ (died *c.*556), Scythian monk and scholar. He is famous for introducing the system of dates BC and AD that is still in use today, accepting 753 AUC as the year of the Incarnation; this has since been shown to be mistaken. He is said to have taken the nickname *Exiguus* ('little') as a sign of humility.

Dionysius of Halicarnassus (1st century BC), Greek historian, literary critic, and rhetorician. He lived in Rome from 30 BC and is best known for his detailed history of the city, written in Greek; this covers the period from the earliest times until the outbreak of the first Punic War (264 BC).

Dionysius the Areopagite /ˌarɪˈɒpəɡʌɪt/ (1st century AD), Greek churchman. His conversion by St Paul is recorded in Acts 17:34 and according to tradition he went on to become the first bishop of Athens. He was later confused with St Denis and with a mystical theologian, Pseudo-Dionysius the Areopagite, who exercised a profound influence on medieval theology.

Dionysus /ˌdʌɪəˈnʌɪsəs/ Greek Mythology a Greek god, son of Zeus and Semele; his worship entered Greece from Thrace *c.*1000 BC. Originally a god of the fertility of nature, associated with wild and ecstatic religious rites, in later traditions he is a god of wine who loosens inhibitions and inspires creativity in music and poetry. Also called BACCHUS.

Diophantine equation /ˌdʌɪəˈfantɪn, -tʌɪn/ ▶ noun Mathematics a polynomial equation with integral coefficients for which integral solutions are required.
– ORIGIN early 18th cent.: named after DIOPHANTUS.

Diophantus /ˌdʌɪəˈfantəs/ (*fl. c.*250 AD), Greek mathematician. Diophantus was the first to attempt an algebraical notation, showing in *Arithmetica* how to solve simple and quadratic equations. His work led to Pierre de Fermat's discoveries in the theory of numbers.

diopside /dʌɪˈɒpsʌɪd/ ▶ noun [mass noun] a mineral occurring as white to pale green crystals in metamorphic and basic igneous rocks. It consists of a calcium and magnesium silicate of the pyroxene group, often also containing iron and chromium.
– ORIGIN early 19th cent.: from French, formed irregularly from DI-[3] 'through' + Greek *opsis* 'aspect', later interpreted as derived from Greek *diopsis* 'a view through'.

dioptase /dʌɪˈɒpteɪz/ ▶ noun [mass noun] a rare mineral occurring as emerald green or blue-green crystals. It consists of a hydrated silicate of copper.
– ORIGIN early 19th cent.: from French, formed irregularly from Greek *dioptos* 'transparent'.

dioptre /dʌɪˈɒptə/ (US **diopter**) ▶ noun a unit of refractive power, which is equal to the reciprocal of the focal length (in metres) of a given lens.

– ORIGIN late 16th cent. (originally as *diopter*, denoting an alidade): from French, from Latin *dioptra*, from Greek, from *di-* 'through' + *optos* 'visible'. The term was used in the early 17th cent. to denote an ancient form of theodolite; the current sense dates from the late 19th cent.

dioptric /dʌɪˈɒptrɪk/ ▸ **adjective** relating to the refraction of light, especially in the organs of sight or in devices which aid or improve the vision.
– ORIGIN mid 17th cent.: from Greek *dioptrikos*, from *dioptra*, a kind of theodolite (see **DIOPTRE**).

D

dioptrics ▸ **plural noun** [treated as sing.] the branch of optics that deals with refraction.

Dior /ˈdiːɔː/, French /djɔʀ/, Christian (1905–57), French couturier. His first collection (1947), featured narrow-waisted tightly fitted bodices and full pleated skirts; this became known as the New Look. He later created the first A-line garments.

diorama /ˌdʌɪəˈrɑːmə/ ▸ **noun** a model representing a scene with three-dimensional figures, either in miniature or as a large-scale museum exhibit. ■ chiefly historical a scenic painting, viewed through a peephole, in which changes in colour and direction of illumination simulate changes in the weather, time of day, etc. ■ a miniature film set used for special effects or animation.
– ORIGIN early 19th cent.: coined in French from **DIA-** 'through', on the pattern of *panorama*.

diorite /ˈdʌɪərʌɪt/ ▸ **noun** [mass noun] Geology a speckled, coarse-grained igneous rock consisting essentially of plagioclase, feldspar, and hornblende or other mafic minerals.
– DERIVATIVES **dioritic** adjective.
– ORIGIN early 19th cent.: coined in French, formed irregularly from Greek *diorizein* 'distinguish' + **-ITE**[1].

Dioscuri /ˌdʌɪɒˈskjʊəri, dʌɪˈɒskjʊri/ Greek & Roman Mythology the twins Castor and Pollux, born to Leda after her seduction by Zeus. Castor was mortal, but Pollux was immortal; at Pollux's request they shared his immortality between them, spending half their time below the earth in Hades and the other half on Olympus. They are often identified with the constellation Gemini.
– ORIGIN from Greek *Dioskouroi* 'sons of Zeus'.

diosgenin /dʌɪˈɒsdʒənɪn/ ▸ **noun** [mass noun] Chemistry a steroid compound obtained from Mexican yams and used in the synthesis of steroid hormones.
– ORIGIN 1930s: from *dios-* (from the modern Latin genus name *Dioscorea*) + *genin*, denoting steroids that occur as the non-sugar part of certain glycosides.

dioxane /dʌɪˈɒkseɪn/ (also **dioxan** /-an/) ▸ **noun** [mass noun] Chemistry a colourless toxic liquid used as an organic solvent. ● A heterocyclic compound with a ring of four carbon and two oxygen atoms; chem. formula: $C_4H_8O_2$.
– ORIGIN early 20th cent.: from **DI-**[1] 'two' + **OX-** 'oxygen' + **-AN** (or **-ANE**[2]).

dioxide /dʌɪˈɒksʌɪd/ ▸ **noun** Chemistry an oxide containing two atoms of oxygen in its molecule or empirical formula.

dioxin /dʌɪˈɒksɪn/ ▸ **noun** [mass noun] a highly toxic compound produced as a by-product in some manufacturing processes, notably herbicide production and paper bleaching. It is a serious and persistent environmental pollutant. ● A heterocyclic organochlorine compound; alternative name: **2,3,7,8-tetrachlorodibenzo-paradioxin** (abbrev.: **TCDD**); chem. formula: $C_{12}H_4O_2Cl_4$. ■ [count noun] any of the class of compounds to which dioxin belongs.
– ORIGIN early 20th cent.: from **DI-**[1] 'two' + **OX-** 'oxygen' + **-IN**[1].

DIP ▸ **abbreviation** ■ Computing document image processing, a system for the digital storage and retrieval of documents as scanned images. ■ Electronics dual in-line package, a package for an integrated circuit consisting of a rectangular sealed unit with two parallel rows of downward-pointing pins.

dip ▸ **verb** (**dips, dipping, dipped**) **1** [with obj.] (**dip something in/into**) put or let something down quickly or briefly in or into (liquid): *he dipped a brush in the paint.* ■ immerse (sheep) in a chemical solution that kills parasites. ■ make (a candle) by immersing a wick repeatedly in hot wax. ■ informal, dated baptize (someone) by immersion in water.
2 [no obj.] (**dip into**) put a hand or implement into (a bag or container) in order to take something out: *Ian dipped into his briefcase and pulled out a photograph.* ■ spend from or make use of (one's financial resources): *you won't have to dip into your savings.* ■ read only parts of (a publication or document): *a reference work to dip into time and time again.*
3 [no obj.] sink, drop, or slope downwards: *the sun had dipped below the horizon | the road dipped down to the bridge.* ■ (of a level or amount) become lower or smaller, typically temporarily: *the president's popularity has dipped | audiences dipped below 600,000 for the match.* ■ [with obj.] lower or move (something) downwards: *the plane dipped its wings.* ■ [with obj.] Brit. lower the beam of (a vehicle's headlights).
4 [no obj.] (**dip out**) Austral./NZ informal miss an opportunity; fail.
5 [with obj.] informal, dated pick (someone's pocket).
▸ **noun 1** a brief swim: *they cooled off by taking a dip in the pool.* ■ a brief immersion in liquid. ■ short for **SHEEP DIP**.
2 [mass noun] a thick sauce in which pieces of food are dipped before eating: *tasty garlic dip.*
3 a brief downward slope followed by an upward one: *the big hedge at the bottom of the dip.* ■ an act of sinking or dropping briefly before rising again: *a dip in the share price.*
4 [mass noun] technical the extent to which something is angled downward from the horizontal, in particular: ■ (also **magnetic dip**) the angle made with the horizontal at any point by the earth's magnetic field, or by a magnetic needle in response to this. ■ Geology the angle a stratum makes with the horizontal. ■ Astronomy & Surveying the apparent depression of the horizon from the line of observation, due to the curvature of the earth.
5 informal, dated a pickpocket.
6 N. Amer. informal a stupid or foolish person.
7 archaic a candle made by immersing a wick repeatedly in hot wax.
– PHRASES **dip one's toe into** (or **in**) put one's toe briefly in (water), typically to check the temperature. ■ begin to do or test (something) cautiously: *the company has already dipped its toe into the market.*
– ORIGIN Old English *dyppan*, of Germanic origin; related to **DEEP**.

Dip. ▸ **abbreviation** diploma.

DipAD ▸ **abbreviation** (in the UK) Diploma in Art and Design.

dip-dye ▸ **verb** [with obj.] immerse (a yarn or fabric) in a special solution in order to colour it.

DipEd ▸ **abbreviation** (in the UK) Diploma in Education.

dipeptide /dʌɪˈpɛptʌɪd/ ▸ **noun** Biochemistry a peptide composed of two amino-acid residues.

DipHE ▸ **abbreviation** (in the UK) Diploma of Higher Education.

diphenhydramine /ˌdʌɪfɛnˈhʌɪdrəmiːn/ ▸ **noun** [mass noun] Medicine an antihistamine compound used for the symptomatic relief of allergies. ● A synthetic amine, usually used as a hydrochloride salt; chem. formula: $C_{17}H_{21}NO$.
– ORIGIN 1940s: from *diphen-* (denoting the presence of two phenyl groups) + **HYDR-** + **AMINE**.

diphenylamine /dʌɪˈfiːnʌɪləˌmiːn, -ˈfɛnɪl-/ ▸ **noun** [mass noun] Chemistry a synthetic crystalline compound with basic properties, used in making azo dyes and as an insecticide and larvicide. ● Chem. formula: $(C_6H_5)_2NH$.

diphtheria /dɪfˈθɪərɪə, dɪp-/ ▸ **noun** [mass noun] an acute and highly contagious bacterial disease causing inflammation of the mucous membranes, formation of a false membrane in the throat which hinders breathing and swallowing, and potentially fatal heart and nerve damage by a bacterial toxin in the blood. It is now rare in developed countries owing to immunization. ● The disease is caused by *Corynebacterium diphtheriae*: see **KLEBS–LÖFFLER BACILLUS**.
– DERIVATIVES **diphtheritic** /-θəˈrɪtɪk/ adjective.
– ORIGIN mid 19th cent.: modern Latin, from French *diphthérie* (earlier *diphthérite*), from Greek *diphthera* 'skin, hide'.

> **USAGE** In the past **diphtheria** was pronounced with an **f** sound representing the two letters **ph** (as in **telephone**, **sulphur**, and other **ph** words derived from Greek). In recent years the pronunciation has shifted and today the most common pronunciation, no longer incorrect in standard English, is with a **p** sound. A very similar shift has taken place with the word **diphthong**, which is now also widely pronounced with a **p** rather than an **f** sound.

diphtheroid /ˈdɪfθərɔɪd, ˈdɪp-/ ▸ **noun** Microbiology any bacterium of a genus that includes the diphtheria bacillus, especially one that does not cause disease. See **CORYNEBACTERIUM**.
▸ **adjective** [attrib.] Medicine similar to diphtheria.

diphthong /ˈdɪfθɒŋ, ˈdɪp-/ ▸ **noun** a sound formed by the combination of two vowels in a single syllable, in which the sound begins as one vowel and moves towards another (as in *coin*, *loud*, and *side*). Often contrasted with **MONOPHTHONG, TRIPHTHONG**. ■ a digraph representing the sound of a diphthong or single vowel (as in *feat*). ■ a compound vowel character; a ligature (such as *æ*).
– DERIVATIVES **diphthongal** /-ˈθɒŋg(ə)l/ adjective.
– ORIGIN late Middle English: from French *diphtongue*, via late Latin from Greek *diphthongos*, from *di-* 'twice' + *phthongos* 'voice, sound'.

> **USAGE** For a discussion of the pronunciation of **diphthong**, see **USAGE** at **DIPHTHERIA**.

diphthongize /ˈdɪfθɒŋʌɪz, ˈdɪp-/ (also **diphthongise**) ▸ **verb** [with obj.] change (a vowel) into a diphthong.
– DERIVATIVES **diphthongization** noun.

diphycercal /ˌdɪfɪˈsəːk(ə)l/ ▸ **adjective** Zoology (of a fish's tail) approximately symmetrical and with the vertebral column continuing to the tip, as in lampreys. Contrasted with **HETEROCERCAL, HOMOCERCAL**.
– ORIGIN mid 19th cent.: from Greek *diphu-* 'of double form' + *kerkos* 'tail' + **-AL**.

diplegia /dʌɪˈpliːdʒə/ ▸ **noun** [mass noun] Medicine paralysis of corresponding parts on both sides of the body, typically affecting the legs more severely than the arms.
– ORIGIN late 19th cent.: from **DI-**[1] 'two', on the pattern of *hemiplegia* and *paraplegia*.

diplo- ▸ **combining form 1** double: *diplococcus*.
2 Genetics diploid.
– ORIGIN from Greek *diplous* 'double'.

diploblastic /ˌdɪplə(ʊ)ˈblastɪk/ ▸ **adjective** Zoology having a body derived from only two embryonic cell layers (ectoderm and endoderm, but no mesoderm), as in sponges and coelenterates.

diplococcus /ˌdɪplə(ʊ)ˈkɒkəs/ ▸ **noun** (pl. **diplococci** /-k(s)ʌɪ, -k(s)iː/) a bacterium that occurs as pairs of cocci, e.g. pneumococcus.

diplodocus /dɪˈplɒdəkəs, ˌdɪplə(ʊ)ˈdəʊkəs/ ▸ **noun** a huge herbivorous dinosaur of the late Jurassic period, with a long slender neck and tail. ● Genus *Diplodocus*, infraorder Sauropoda, order Saurischia.
– ORIGIN modern Latin, from **DIPLO-** 'double' + Greek *dokos* 'wooden beam'.

diploid /ˈdɪplɔɪd/ Genetics ▸ **adjective** (of a cell or nucleus) containing two complete sets of chromosomes, one from each parent. Compare with **HAPLOID**. ■ (of an organism or part) composed of diploid cells.
▸ **noun** a diploid cell, organism, or species.
– DERIVATIVES **diploidy** noun.
– ORIGIN late 19th cent.: from Greek *diplous* 'double' + **-OID**.

diploid number ▸ **noun** Genetics the number of chromosomes present in the body cells of a diploid organism.

diploma ▸ **noun 1** a certificate awarded by an educational establishment to show that someone has successfully completed a course of study.
2 historical an official document or charter.
– ORIGIN mid 17th cent. (in the sense 'state paper'): via Latin from Greek *diplōma* 'folded paper', from *diploun* 'to fold', from *diplous* 'double'.

diplomacy ▸ **noun** [mass noun] the profession, activity, or skill of managing international relations, typically by a country's representatives abroad: *an extensive round of diplomacy in the Middle East.* ■ the art of dealing with people in a sensitive and tactful way: *with perfect diplomacy, he divided his attention between Meryl and Anthea.*
– ORIGIN late 18th cent.: from French *diplomatie*, from *diplomatique* 'diplomatic', on the pattern of *aristocratie* 'aristocracy'.

diplomat ▸ **noun** an official representing a country abroad. ■ a person who can deal with others in a sensitive and tactful way.
– ORIGIN early 19th cent.: from French *diplomate*, back-formation from *diplomatique* 'diplomatic', from Latin *diploma* (see **DIPLOMA**).

diplomate /ˈdɪpləmeɪt/ ▸ **noun** chiefly US a person who holds a diploma, especially a doctor certified as a specialist by a board of examiners.

diplomatic ▸ **adjective 1** of or concerning diplomacy: *diplomatic relations with Britain were broken.* ■ having or showing an ability to deal with people in a sensitive and tactful way: *he tried his best to be diplomatic.*
2 (of an edition or copy) exactly reproducing an original version: *a diplomatic transcription.*
– DERIVATIVES **diplomatically** adverb.
– ORIGIN early 18th cent. (in the sense 'relating to official documents'): from modern Latin *diplomati-*

cus and French *diplomatique*, from Latin *diploma* (see DIPLOMA). Sense 1 (late 18th cent.) is probably due to the publication of the *Codex Juris Gentium Diplomaticus* (1695), a collection of originals of important public documents, many of which dealt with international affairs.

diplomatic bag ▶ noun Brit. a container in which official mail is sent to or from an embassy, which is not subject to customs inspection.

diplomatic corps ▶ noun the body of diplomats representing other countries in a particular state.

diplomatic immunity ▶ noun [mass noun] the privilege of exemption from certain laws and taxes granted to diplomats by the state in which they are working.

diplomatic pouch ▶ noun US term for DIPLOMATIC BAG.

diplomatic recognition ▶ noun see RECOGNITION.

diplomatic service ▶ noun the government department concerned with the representation of a country abroad.

diplomatist ▶ noun old-fashioned term for DIPLOMAT.

diplopia /dɪˈpləʊpɪə/ ▶ noun technical term for DOUBLE VISION.

Diplopoda /ˌdɪpləˈpəʊdə/ ▶ plural noun Zoology a class of myriapod arthropods that comprises the millipedes.
– DERIVATIVES **diplopod** /ˈdɪpləpɒd/ noun.
– ORIGIN modern Latin (plural), from Greek *diploos* 'double' + *pous, pod-* 'foot'.

diplotene /ˈdɪplətiːn/ ▶ noun [mass noun] Biology the fourth stage of the prophase of meiosis, following pachytene, during which the paired chromosomes begin to separate into two pairs of chromatids.
– ORIGIN 1920s: from DIPLO- 'double' + Greek *tainia* 'band'.

Diplura /dɪˈplʊərə/ ▶ plural noun Entomology an order of small primitive wingless insects which resemble the true bristletails but have two bristles at the end of the abdomen. ● Order Diplura, subclass Apterygota, class Insecta (or Hexapoda).
– DERIVATIVES **dipluran** noun & adjective.
– ORIGIN modern Latin (plural), from DI-[1] 'two' + Greek *pleura* 'side of the body'.

dip net chiefly N. Amer. ▶ noun a small fishing net with a long handle.
▶ verb (**dip-net**) [with obj.] catch (fish) using a dip net.

dipole /ˈdʌɪpəʊl/ ▶ noun **1** Physics a pair of equal and oppositely charged or magnetized poles separated by a distance. ■ Chemistry a molecule in which a concentration of positive electric charge is separated from a concentration of negative charge.
2 an aerial consisting of a horizontal metal rod with a connecting wire at its centre.
– DERIVATIVES **dipolar** adjective.

dipole moment ▶ noun Physics & Chemistry the mathematical product of the separation of the ends of a dipole and the magnitude of the charges.

dip pen ▶ noun a pen that has to be dipped in ink.

dipper ▶ noun **1** a short-tailed songbird related to the wrens, frequenting fast-flowing streams and able to swim, dive, and walk under water to feed. ● Family Cinclidae and genus *Cinclus*: five species, in particular the white-throated Eurasian *C. cinclus*.
2 a ladle or scoop.
3 a person who dips something in liquid.
4 informal a pickpocket.
5 archaic, informal a Baptist or Anabaptist.

dippy ▶ adjective (**dippier**, **dippiest**) informal silly and eccentric or scatterbrained: *dippy ideas.*
– ORIGIN early 20th cent.: of unknown origin.

dipshit ▶ noun vulgar slang, chiefly N. Amer. a contemptible or inept person.
– ORIGIN 1970s: perhaps a blend of DIPPY and SHIT.

dip slope ▶ noun a gentle slope in the land that follows that of the underlying strata, especially the gentler slope of a cuesta. Often contrasted with SCARP SLOPE.

dipso ▶ noun (pl. **dipsos**) informal a person suffering from dipsomania; an alcoholic.

dipsomania /ˌdɪpsə(ʊ)ˈmeɪnɪə/ ▶ noun [mass noun] alcoholism, specifically in a form characterized by intermittent bouts of craving for alcohol.
– DERIVATIVES **dipsomaniac** noun.
– ORIGIN mid 19th cent.: from Greek *dipso-* (from *dipsa* 'thirst') + -MANIA.

dipstick ▶ noun **1** a graduated rod for measuring the depth of a liquid, especially oil in a vehicle's engine.
2 informal a stupid or inept person.

DIP switch ▶ noun Computing an arrangement of switches in a dual in-line package used to select the operating mode of a device such as a printer.

dip switch ▶ noun Brit. a switch for lowering a vehicle's headlight beams.

Diptera /ˈdɪpt(ə)rə/ ▶ plural noun Entomology a large order of insects that comprises the two-winged or true flies, which have the hindwings reduced to form balancing organs (halteres). It includes many biting forms such as mosquitoes and tsetse flies that are vectors of disease. ■ (**diptera**) insects of the order Diptera; flies.
– ORIGIN modern Latin (plural), from Greek *diptera*, neuter plural of *dipteros* 'two-winged', from *di-* 'two' + *pteron* 'wing'.

dipteral /ˈdɪpt(ə)r(ə)l/ ▶ adjective Architecture having a double peristyle.
– ORIGIN early 19th cent.: from Latin *dipteros* (from Greek, from *di-* 'twice' + *pteron* 'wing') + -AL.

dipteran /ˈdɪpt(ə)r(ə)n/ Entomology ▶ noun an insect of the large order Diptera; a fly.
▶ adjective relating to or denoting dipterans.

dipterist /ˈdɪpt(ə)rɪst/ ▶ noun a person who studies or collects flies.
– ORIGIN late 19th cent.: from DIPTERA + -IST.

dipterocarp /ˈdɪpt(ə)rə(ʊ)ˌkɑːp/ ▶ noun a tall forest tree from which are obtained resins and timber for the export trade, occurring mainly in SE Asia. ● Family Dipterocarpaceae: numerous species.
– ORIGIN late 19th cent.: from modern Latin *Dipterocarpus*, from Greek *dipteros* 'two-winged' + *karpos* 'fruit'.

dipterous /ˈdɪpt(ə)rəs/ ▶ adjective **1** Entomology relating to flies of the order Diptera.
2 Botany having two wing-like appendages.
– ORIGIN late 18th cent.: from modern Latin *dipterus* (from Greek *dipteros* 'two-winged') + -OUS.

diptych /ˈdɪptɪk/ ▶ noun **1** a painting, especially an altarpiece, on two hinged wooden panels which may be closed like a book.
2 an ancient writing tablet consisting of two hinged leaves with waxed inner sides.
– ORIGIN early 17th cent.: via late Latin from late Greek *diptukha* 'pair of writing tablets', neuter plural of Greek *diptukhos* 'folded in two', from *di-* 'twice' + *ptukhē* 'a fold'.

dipyridamole /ˌdʌɪpɪˈrɪdəməʊl/ ▶ noun [mass noun] Medicine a synthetic drug used as a coronary vasodilator to treat angina, and to reduce platelet aggregation and hence the chance of thrombosis.
– ORIGIN mid 20th cent.: from DI-[1] 'two' + *pyr(imidine)* + *(piper)id(ine)* + *am(ino-)* + -OL.

diquat /ˈdʌɪkwɒt/ ▶ noun [mass noun] a synthetic compound used in controlling plant growth, often as a non-persistent contact herbicide. ● A bromide of a quaternary amine; chem. formula: $(C_5H_4NCH_2)_2Br_2$.
– ORIGIN 1960s: from DI-[1] 'two' + QUATERNARY.

Dirac /dɪˈrak/, Paul Adrian Maurice (1902–84), English theoretical physicist. He described the properties of the electron, including its spin, and postulated the existence of the positron by applying Einstein's theory of relativity to quantum mechanics. Nobel Prize for Physics (1933).

diram /ˈdɪərəm/ ▶ noun a monetary unit of Tajikistan, equal to one hundredth of a somoni.
– ORIGIN Tajik.

dire ▶ adjective **1** extremely serious or urgent: *misuse of drugs can have dire consequences | he was in dire need of help.* ■ (of a warning or threat) presaging disaster: *there were dire warnings from the traffic organizations.*
2 Brit. informal of a very poor quality: *the concert was dire.*
– DERIVATIVES **direly** adverb, **direness** noun.
– ORIGIN mid 16th cent.: from Latin *dirus* 'fearful, threatening'.

direct /dɪˈrɛkt, dʌɪ-/ ▶ adjective **1** extending or moving from one place to another without changing direction or stopping: *there was no direct flight that day.* ■ Astronomy & Astrology (of apparent planetary motion) proceeding from west to east in accord with actual motion.
2 without intervening factors or intermediaries: *the complications are a direct result of bacteria spreading | I had no direct contact with Mr Clark.* ■ (of light or heat) proceeding from a source without being reflected or blocked: *ferns like a bright position out of direct sunlight.* ■ (of genealogy) proceeding in continuous succession from parent to child: *a direct descendant of Edward III.* ■ (of a quotation) taken from someone's words without being changed. ■ (of taxation) levied on income or profits rather than on goods or services. ■ complete (used for emphasis): *attitudes which were in direct contrast to the confrontational perspectives of the past.*
3 (of a person or their behaviour) going straight to the point; frank: *he is very direct and honest.* ■ (of evidence or proof) bearing immediately and unambiguously upon the facts at issue: *there is no direct evidence that officials accepted bribes.*
4 perpendicular to a surface; not oblique: *a direct butt joint between surfaces of steel.*
▶ adverb with no one or nothing in between: *they seem reluctant to deal with me direct.* ■ by a straight route or without breaking a journey: *Austrian Airlines are flying direct to Innsbruck again.*
▶ verb [with obj.] **1** control the operations of; manage or govern: *an economic elite directed the nation's affairs.* ■ supervise and control (a film, play, or other production, or the actors in it). ■ train and conduct (a group of musicians).
2 [with obj. and adverbial of direction] aim (something) in a particular direction or at a particular person: *heating ducts to direct warm air to rear-seat passengers | his smile was directed at Lois.* ■ tell or show (someone) how to get somewhere: *can you direct me to the railway station, please?* ■ address or give instructions for the delivery of (a letter or parcel). ■ focus (one's thoughts) on or address (one's efforts) towards something. ■ (**direct something at/to**) address a comment to or aim a criticism at: *his criticism was directed at the wastage of ammunition | I suggest that he direct his remarks to the council.* ■ (**direct something at**) target a product or advertisement specifically at (someone): *the book is directed at the younger reader.* ■ archaic guide or advise in a course or decision: *the conscience of the credulous prince was directed by saints and bishops.*
3 [with obj. and infinitive] give (someone) an official order or authoritative instruction: *the judge directed him to perform community service* | [with clause] *he* ***directed*** ***that*** *no picture from his collection could be sold.*
– DERIVATIVES **directness** noun.
– ORIGIN late Middle English: from Latin *directus*, past participle of *dirigere*, from *di-* 'distinctly' or *de-* 'down' + *regere* 'put straight'.

direct access ▶ noun [mass noun] the facility of retrieving data immediately from any part of a computer file, without having to read the file from the beginning. Compare with RANDOM ACCESS and SEQUENTIAL ACCESS.

direct action ▶ noun [mass noun] the use of strikes, demonstrations, or other public forms of protest rather than negotiation to achieve one's demands.

direct banking ▶ noun another term for TELEBANKING.

direct current (abbrev.: **DC** or **dc**) ▶ noun an electric current flowing in one direction only. Compare with ALTERNATING CURRENT.

direct debit ▶ noun an arrangement made with a bank that allows a third party to transfer money from a person's account on agreed dates, typically in order to pay bills.

direct deposit ▶ noun [mass noun] N. Amer. the electronic transfer of money from one bank account to another.

direct dialling ▶ noun [mass noun] the facility of making a telephone call without connection by the operator.
– DERIVATIVES **direct-dial** adjective.

direct discourse ▶ noun chiefly N. Amer. another term for DIRECT SPEECH.

direct-drive ▶ adjective denoting or relating to mechanical parts driven directly by a motor, without a belt or other device to transmit power.

direct examination ▶ noun another term for EXAMINATION-IN-CHIEF.

direct-grant school ▶ noun historical (in the UK) a fee-paying school that received funds from the government in return for the admission of non-paying pupils nominated by the local authority.

direct injection ▶ noun [mass noun] (in diesel engines) the use of a pump to spray fuel into the cylinder at high pressure, without the use of compressed air.

direction /dɪˈrɛkʃ(ə)n, dʌɪ-/ ▶ noun **1** a course along which someone or something moves: *she set off in the opposite direction* | [mass noun] *he had a terrible sense of direction.* ■ the course which must be taken in order to reach a destination: *the village is over the moors*

D

in a northerly direction. ■ a point to or from which a person or thing moves or faces: *a house with views in all directions.* ■ a general way in which someone or something is developing; a trend or tendency: *new directions in painting and architecture | any dialogue between them is **a step in the right direction**.* ■ [mass noun] general aim or purpose: *the campaign's lack of direction.*
2 [mass noun] the management or guidance of someone or something: *under his direction, the college has developed an international reputation.* ■ the work of directing the actors and other staff in a film, play, or other production. ■ (**directions**) instructions on how to reach a destination or about how to do something: *Preston gave him directions to a restaurant not far from the studio.*

D

– PHRASES **sense of direction** a person's ability to know without explicit guidance the direction in which they are or should be moving.
– ORIGIN late Middle English (in sense 2): from Latin *directio(n-)*, from the verb *dirigere* (see DIRECT).

directional ▶ adjective **1** relating to or indicating the direction in which someone or something is situated or moving: *directional signs wherever two paths joined.* ■ relating to, influencing, or exemplifying the latest trends in fashion: *a directional womenswear designer.*
2 having a particular direction of motion, progression, or orientation: *coiling the wire permits directional flow of the magnetic flux.* ■ relating to, denoting, or designed for the projection, transmission, or reception of light, radio, or sound waves in or from a particular direction or directions: *a directional microphone.*
– DERIVATIVES **directionality** /-ˈnalɪti/ noun, **directionally** adverb.

direction finder ▶ noun a system of aerials for locating the source of radio signals, used as an aid to navigation.

directionless ▶ adjective lacking in general aim or purpose: *music which bordered on directionless experimentalism.*

directive ▶ noun an official or authoritative instruction: *a new EC directive.*
▶ adjective involving the management or guidance of operations: *the authority is seeking a directive role in energy policy.*
– ORIGIN late Middle English (as an adjective): from medieval Latin *directivus*, from *direct-* 'guided, put straight', from the verb *dirigere* (see DIRECT).

direct labour ▶ noun [mass noun] **1** labour involved in production rather than administration, maintenance, and other support services.
2 labour employed by the authority commissioning the work, not by a contractor.

directly ▶ adverb **1** without changing direction or stopping: *they went directly to the restaurant.* ■ at once; immediately: *I went directly after breakfast.* ■ dated in a little while; soon: *I'll be back directly.*
2 with nothing or no one in between: *the decisions directly affect people's health | the security forces were directly responsible for the massacre.* ■ exactly in a specified position: *the ceiling directly above the door | the houses directly opposite.*
3 in a frank way: *she spoke simply and directly.*
▶ conjunction Brit. as soon as: *she fell asleep directly she got into bed.*

direct mail ▶ noun [mass noun] unsolicited commercial literature sent to prospective customers through the post.
– DERIVATIVES **direct mailing** noun.

direct marketing ▶ noun [mass noun] the business of selling products or services directly to the public, e.g. by mail order or telephone selling, rather than through retailers.

direct method ▶ noun [in sing.] a system of teaching a foreign language using only that language and without emphasis on the study of grammar.

direct object ▶ noun a noun phrase denoting a person or thing that is the recipient of the action of a transitive verb, for example *the dog* in *Jeremy fed the dog*. Compare with INDIRECT OBJECT.

Directoire /dɪˈrɛktwɑː/, French /diʀɛktwaʀ/ ▶ adjective relating to a neoclassical decorative style intermediate between the more ornate Louis XVI style and the Empire style, prevalent during the French Directory (1795–9).
– ORIGIN French.

Directoire drawers (also **Directoire knickers**) ▶ plural noun Brit. historical knickers which are straight, full, and knee-length.

director ▶ noun a person who is in charge of an activity, department, or organization: *the sales director.* ■ a member of the board of people that manages or oversees the affairs of a business. ■ a person who supervises the actors and other staff in a film, play, or similar production. ■ short for MUSICAL DIRECTOR.
– DERIVATIVES **directorial** adjective, **directorship** noun.
– ORIGIN late Middle English: from Anglo-Norman French *directour*, from late Latin *director* 'governor', from *dirigere* 'to guide'.

directorate ▶ noun [treated as sing. or pl.] **1** the board of directors of a company.
2 a section of a government department in charge of a particular activity: *the Food Safety Directorate.*

director general ▶ noun chiefly Brit. the chief executive of a large organization.

Director of Public Prosecutions (abbrev.: **DPP**) ▶ noun (in the UK) a senior law officer who is head of the Crown Prosecution Service.

director's cut ▶ noun a version of a film that reflects the director's original intentions, released after the first studio version.

directory ▶ noun (pl. **directories**) **1** a book or website listing individuals or organizations alphabetically or thematically with details such as names, addresses, and telephone numbers. ■ a board in an organization or large store listing names and locations of departments, individuals, etc. ■ Computing a file which consists solely of a set of other files (which may themselves be directories).
2 chiefly historical a book of directions for the conduct of Christian worship, especially in Presbyterian and Roman Catholic Churches.
3 (**the Directory**) the revolutionary government in France 1795–9, comprising two councils and a five-member executive. It maintained an aggressive foreign policy, but could not control events at home and was overthrown by Napoleon Bonaparte.
– ORIGIN late Middle English (in the general sense 'something that directs'): from late Latin *directorium*, from *director* 'governor', from *dirigere* 'to guide'.

directory enquiries (N. Amer. **directory assistance**) ▶ plural noun a telephone service used to find out someone's telephone number.

direct proportion (also **direct ratio**) ▶ noun [mass noun] the relation between quantities whose ratio is constant: *sensors emit an electronic signal **in direct proportion to** the amount of light detected.*

directress (also **directrice**) ▶ noun a female director.
– ORIGIN early 17th cent.: from DIRECTOR + -ESS[1]; the variant *directrice* is an adopted French form.

directrix /dɪˈrɛktrɪks, dʌɪ-/ ▶ noun (pl. **directrices** /-trɪsiːz/) Geometry a fixed line used in describing a curve or surface.
– ORIGIN early 18th cent.: from medieval Latin, literally 'directress', based on Latin *dirigere* 'to guide'.

direct rule ▶ noun [mass noun] a system of government in which a province is controlled by a central government.

direct speech ▶ noun [mass noun] the reporting of speech by repeating the actual words of a speaker, for example *'I'm going', she said.* Contrasted with REPORTED SPEECH.

direct tax ▶ noun a tax, such as income tax, which is levied on the income or profits of the person who pays it, rather than on goods or services.

direful ▶ adjective archaic or literary extremely bad; dreadful.
– DERIVATIVES **direfully** adverb.
– ORIGIN late 16th cent.: from DIRE + -FUL.

dire wolf ▶ noun a large extinct wolf of the Pleistocene epoch, which preyed on large mammals. ● *Canis dirus*, family Canidae.
– ORIGIN *dire* in the sense 'threatening', translating the modern Latin taxonomic name.

dirge /dəːdʒ/ ▶ noun a lament for the dead, especially one forming part of a funeral rite. ■ a mournful song, piece of music, or sound. ■ informal a song or piece of music that is considered too slow, miserable, or boring.
– DERIVATIVES **dirgeful** adjective.
– ORIGIN Middle English (denoting the Office for the Dead): from Latin *dirige!* (imperative) 'direct!', the first word of an antiphon (Ps. 5:8) formerly used in the Latin Office for the Dead.

dirham /ˈdɪər(h)əm/ ▶ noun **1** the basic monetary unit of Morocco and the United Arab Emirates, equal to 100 centimes in Morocco and 100 fils in the United Arab Emirates.
2 a monetary unit of Libya and Qatar, equal to one thousandth of a dinar in Libya and one hundredth of a riyal in Qatar.
– ORIGIN from Arabic, from Greek *drakhmē*, denoting an Attic weight or coin. Compare with DRACHMA.

dirigible /ˈdɪrɪdʒɪb(ə)l/ ▶ noun an airship.
▶ adjective capable of being steered, guided, or directed: *a dirigible spotlight.*
– ORIGIN late 16th cent.: from Latin *dirigere* 'to direct' + -IBLE.

dirigisme /ˈdɪrɪʒɪz(ə)m/ ▶ noun [mass noun] state control of economic and social matters.
– DERIVATIVES **dirigiste** adjective.
– ORIGIN 1950s: from French, from the verb *diriger*, from Latin *dirigere* 'to direct'.

diriment impediment /ˈdɪrɪm(ə)nt/ ▶ noun (in ecclesiastical law) a factor which invalidates a marriage, such as the existence of a prior marriage.
– ORIGIN mid 19th cent.: *diriment* from Latin *diriment-* 'interrupting', from the verb *dirimere*.

dirk /dəːk/ ▶ noun a short dagger of a kind formerly carried by Scottish Highlanders.
– ORIGIN mid 16th cent.: of unknown origin.

dirndl /ˈdəːnd(ə)l/ ▶ noun **1** (also **dirndl skirt**) a full, wide skirt with a tight waistband.
2 a woman's dress in the style of Alpine peasant costume, with a dirndl skirt and a close-fitting bodice.
– ORIGIN 1930s: from south German dialect, diminutive of *Dirne* 'girl'.

dirt ▶ noun [mass noun] **1** a substance, such as mud or dust, that soils someone or something: *Jo wiped the dirt off her face.* ■ soil or earth: *Michael threw a handful of dirt on to the coffin | [as modifier] a dirt road.* ■ informal excrement: *a lawn covered in dog dirt.* ■ a state or quality of uncleanliness: *the sweat and dirt of industry.*
2 informal information about someone's activities or private life that could prove damaging if revealed: *is there any **dirt on** Desmond?*
– PHRASES **do someone dirt** (also **do dirt to**) informal harm someone's reputation maliciously. **drag the name of someone/thing through the dirt** informal give someone or something a bad reputation through bad behaviour or damaging revelations. **eat dirt** informal suffer insults or humiliation. **treat someone like dirt** treat someone with a complete lack of respect.
– ORIGIN Middle English: from Old Norse *drit* 'excrement', an early sense in English.

dirtbag ▶ noun US informal a very unkempt or unpleasant person.

dirt bike ▶ noun a motorcycle designed for use on rough terrain, such as unsurfaced roads or tracks, and used especially in scrambling.

dirt cheap ▶ adverb & adjective informal extremely cheap: [as adv.] *the auctioneers let us have the stuff dirt cheap* | [as adj.] *a dirt-cheap price.*

dirt farmer ▶ noun N. Amer. a farmer who ekes out a living from a farm on poor land, typically without the help of hired labour.
– DERIVATIVES **dirt farm** noun.

dirt poor ▶ adjective extremely poor: *dirt-poor villages.*

dirt track ▶ noun a course made of rolled cinders for motorcycle racing or of earth for flat racing.
– DERIVATIVES **dirt tracker** noun.

dirty ▶ adjective (**dirtier**, **dirtiest**) **1** covered or marked with an unclean substance: *a tray of dirty cups and saucers | her boots were dirty.* ■ causing a person or place to become unclean: *farming is a hard, dirty job.* ■ (of a nuclear weapon) producing considerable radioactive fallout.
2 (of an activity) dishonest; dishonourable: *he had a reputation for dirty dealing.* ■ US informal using illegal drugs. ■ [attrib.] informal used to emphasize one's disgust for someone or something: *you dirty rat!*
3 concerned with sex in a lewd or obscene way: *he told a stream of dirty jokes.*
4 (of weather) rough, stormy, and unpleasant.
5 (of a colour) not bright or pure; dull: *the sea was a waste of dirty grey.* ■ (of popular music) having a distorted or rasping tone: *Nirvana's dirty guitar sound.*
▶ adverb [as submodifier] Brit. informal used for emphasis: *a dirty great slab of stone.*
▶ verb (**dirties**, **dirtying**, **dirtied**) [with obj.] make dirty: *she didn't like him dirtying her nice clean towels.*
– PHRASES **the dirty end of the stick** informal the difficult or unpleasant part of a task or situation. **do the dirty on someone** Brit. informal cheat or betray

someone. **get one's hands dirty** (or **dirty one's hands**) do manual, menial, or other hard work. ■ informal become involved in dishonest or dishonourable activity. **play dirty** informal act in a dishonest or unfair way. **talk dirty** informal talk about sex in a coarse or salacious way.
– DERIVATIVES **dirtily** adverb, **dirtiness** noun.

dirty bomb ▶ noun a conventional bomb that contains radioactive material.

dirty look ▶ noun informal a facial expression of disapproval, disgust, or anger: *they were giving me dirty looks for taking up so much room at the bar.*

dirty money ▶ noun [mass noun] money obtained unlawfully or immorally.

dirty old man ▶ noun informal an older man who is sexually interested in younger women or girls.

dirty rice ▶ noun [mass noun] a Cajun dish consisting of white rice cooked with onions, peppers, chicken livers, and herbs.

dirty trick ▶ noun a dishonest or unkind act. ■ (**dirty tricks**) underhand political or commercial activity designed to discredit an opponent.

dirty weekend ▶ noun Brit. informal a weekend spent away, especially in secret, with a lover.

dirty word ▶ noun an offensive or indecent word. ■ a thing regarded with dislike or disapproval: *VAT is a dirty word among small businesses.*

dirty work ▶ noun [mass noun] activities or tasks that are unpleasant or dishonest and given to someone else to undertake.

dis /dɪs/ (also **diss**) informal ▶ verb (**disses, dissing, dissed**) [with obj.] speak disrespectfully to or criticize: *I don't like her dissing my friends | a campaign of forum postings and emails dissing the company.*
▶ noun [mass noun] disrespectful talk.
– ORIGIN 1980s: abbreviation of DISRESPECT.

dis- /dɪs/ ▶ prefix **1** expressing negation: *disadvantage | disbelieve.*
2 denoting reversal or absence of an action or state: *diseconomy | disaffirm.*
3 denoting removal of something: *disbud.* ■ denoting separation: *discarnate.* ■ denoting expulsion: *disbar.*
4 expressing completeness or intensification of an unpleasant or unattractive action: *disgruntled.*
– ORIGIN from Latin, sometimes via Old French *des-*.

disability ▶ noun (pl. **disabilities**) **1** a physical or mental condition that limits a person's movements, senses, or activities: *children with severe physical disabilities* | [mass noun] *differing types of disability.*
2 a disadvantage or handicap, especially one imposed or recognized by the law: *the plaintiff was **under a disability**.*

disable ▶ verb [with obj.] (of a disease, injury, or accident) limit (someone) in their movements, senses, or activities: *it's an injury that could disable somebody for life* | (as adj. **disabling**) *a progressively disabling disease.* ■ put out of action: *the raiders tried to disable the alarm system.* ■ (of an action or circumstance) prevent or discourage (someone) from doing something: *their choice **disables** them **from** pursuing certain avenues.*
– DERIVATIVES **disablement** noun.

disabled ▶ adjective (of a person) having a physical or mental condition that limits their movements, senses, or activities: *facilities for disabled people.* ■ relating to or specifically designed for people with a physical or mental disability: *disabled access is available at all venues.*

> **USAGE** The word **disabled** came to be used as the standard term in referring to people with physical or mental disabilities in the second half of the 20th century, and it remains the most generally accepted term in both British and US English today. It superseded outmoded, now often offensive, terms such as **crippled**, **defective**, and **handicapped** and has not been overtaken itself by newer coinages such as **differently abled** or **physically challenged**.
> Although the usage is very widespread, some people regard the use of the adjective as a plural noun (as in *the needs of the disabled*) as dehumanizing because it tends to treat people with disabilities as an undifferentiated group, defined merely by their capabilities. To avoid offence, a more acceptable term would be **people with disabilities**.

disablist ▶ adjective discriminating or prejudiced against people who are disabled.

disabuse /ˌdɪsəˈbjuːz/ ▶ verb [with obj.] persuade (someone) that an idea or belief is mistaken: *he quickly **disabused** me **of** my fanciful notions.*

disaccharide /dʌɪˈsakərʌɪd/ ▶ noun Chemistry any of a class of sugars whose molecules contain two monosaccharide residues.

disaccord rare ▶ noun [mass noun] lack of agreement or harmony.
▶ verb [no obj.] disagree; be at variance.

disadvantage ▶ noun an unfavourable circumstance or condition that reduces the chances of success or effectiveness: *a major disadvantage is the limited nature of the data* | [mass noun] *situations of serious social and economic disadvantage.*
▶ verb [with obj.] put in an unfavourable position in relation to someone or something else: *the pension scheme tends to disadvantage women.*
– PHRASES **at a disadvantage** in an unfavourable position relative to someone or something else: *stringent regulations have **put** British farmers **at a disadvantage**.* **to one's disadvantage** so as to cause harm to one's interests or standing: *his poor educational track record inevitably worked to his disadvantage.*
– ORIGIN late Middle English: from Old French *desavantage*, from *des-* (expressing reversal) + *avantage* 'advantage'.

disadvantaged ▶ adjective (of a person or area) in unfavourable circumstances, especially with regard to financial or social opportunities: *disadvantaged groups such as the unemployed* | (as plural noun **the disadvantaged**) *we began to help the disadvantaged.*

disadvantageous ▶ adjective involving or creating unfavourable circumstances that reduce the chances of success or effectiveness: *the new employment scheme is disadvantageous to women.*
– DERIVATIVES **disadvantageously** adverb.

disaffected ▶ adjective dissatisfied, especially with people in authority or a system of control: *a military plot by disaffected elements in the army.*
– DERIVATIVES **disaffectedly** adverb.
– ORIGIN mid 17th cent.: past participle of *disaffect*, originally in the sense 'dislike or disorder' from DIS- (expressing reversal) + AFFECT².

disaffection ▶ noun [mass noun] a state or feeling of being dissatisfied, especially with people in authority or a system of control: *there is growing **disaffection with** large corporations.*

disaffiliate /ˌdɪsəˈfɪlɪeɪt/ ▶ verb [with obj.] (of a group or organization) end its official connection with (a subsidiary group): *the party disaffiliated the Socialist League.* ■ [no obj.] (of a subsidiary group) end an official connection with an organization: *students' unions who wish to **disaffiliate from** the NUS.*
– DERIVATIVES **disaffiliation** noun.

disaffirm ▶ verb [with obj.] Law reverse (a previous decision). ■ repudiate (a settlement).

disafforest /ˌdɪsəˈfɒrɪst/ ▶ verb [with obj.] **1** another term for DEFOREST.
2 English Law, historical reduce (a district) from the legal status of forest to that of ordinary land.
– DERIVATIVES **disafforestation** noun.
– ORIGIN late Middle English (in sense 2): from Anglo-Latin *disafforestare*.

disaggregate /dɪsˈagrɪgeɪt/ ▶ verb [with obj.] separate (something) into its component parts: *a method for disaggregating cells.*
– DERIVATIVES **disaggregation** noun.

disagree ▶ verb (**disagrees, disagreeing, disagreed**) [no obj.] **1** have or express a different opinion: *no one was willing to **disagree with** him | historians often disagree.* ■ (**disagree with**) disapprove of: *she disagreed with the system of apartheid.*
2 (of statements or accounts) be inconsistent or fail to correspond: *results which disagree with the findings reported so far.* ■ (**disagree with**) (of food, climate, or an experience) have an adverse effect on: *the sea crossing disagreed with her.*
– ORIGIN late 15th cent. (in sense 2, also in the sense 'refuse to agree to'): from Old French *desagreer*.

disagreeable ▶ adjective unpleasant or unenjoyable: *a disagreeable thought | aspects of his work are **disagreeable to** him.* ■ unfriendly and bad-tempered: *Henry was always a very disagreeable boy.*
– DERIVATIVES **disagreeableness** noun, **disagreeably** adverb.
– ORIGIN late Middle English (in the sense 'discordant, incongruous'): from Old French *desagreable*, based on *agreer* 'agree'.

disagreement ▶ noun [mass noun] lack of consensus or approval: *there was some disagreement about the details* | [count noun] *disagreements between parents and adolescents.* ■ lack of consistency or correspondence: *disagreement between the results of the two assessments.*

disallow ▶ verb [with obj.] refuse to declare valid: *he was offside and the goal was disallowed.*
– DERIVATIVES **disallowance** noun.
– ORIGIN late Middle English (in the sense 'disown, refuse to accept'): from Old French *desalouer*.

disambiguate ▶ verb [with obj.] remove uncertainty of meaning from (an ambiguous sentence, phrase, or other linguistic unit).
– DERIVATIVES **disambiguation** noun.

disamenity /ˌdɪsəˈmiːnɪti, -ˈmɛnɪti/ ▶ noun (pl. **disamenities**) [mass noun] the unpleasant quality or character of something: *two rapidly growing sources of disamenity are air travel and tourism.*

disappear ▶ verb [no obj.] cease to be visible: *he **disappeared into** the trees | the sun had disappeared.* ■ cease to exist or be in use: *the tension had completely disappeared.* ■ (of a thing) be mislaid: *my wallet seems to have disappeared.* ■ (of a person) go missing or (in coded political language) be killed: *the family disappeared after being taken into custody.*
– ORIGIN late Middle English: from DIS- (expressing reversal) + APPEAR, on the pattern of French *disparaître*.

disappearance ▶ noun [usu. in sing.] an act of someone or something ceasing to be visible. ■ an act or the fact of someone or something going missing: *the police were investigating her disappearance.* ■ [mass noun] the process of something ceasing to exist or be in use: *the disappearance of grammar schools.*

disappearing act ▶ noun informal an instance of someone being impossible to find, especially when they are required to face something unpleasant.

disapply ▶ verb (**disapplies, disapplying, disapplied**) [with obj.] treat (something) as inapplicable: *British courts are under obligation to disapply Acts where they conflict with European law.*
– DERIVATIVES **disapplication** noun.

disappoint ▶ verb [with obj.] fail to fulfil the hopes or expectations of: *I have no wish to disappoint everyone by postponing the visit.* ■ prevent (hopes or expectations) from being realized: *the governing coalition had bitterly disappointed the hopes of its voters.*
– ORIGIN late Middle English (in the sense 'deprive of a position'): from Old French *desappointer*.

disappointed ▶ adjective sad or displeased because someone or something has failed to fulfil one's hopes or expectations: *I'm **disappointed in** you, Mary | thousands of disappointed customers were kept waiting.* ■ (of hopes or expectations) prevented from being realized.
– DERIVATIVES **disappointedly** adverb.

disappointing ▶ adjective failing to fulfil someone's hopes or expectations: *the team made a disappointing start* | [with clause] *it was **disappointing that** there were relatively few possibilities.*
– DERIVATIVES **disappointingly** adverb [as submodifier] *there was disappointingly little change* | [sentence adverb] *disappointingly, my German failed to improve.*

disappointment ▶ noun [mass noun] sadness or displeasure caused by the non-fulfilment of one's hopes or expectations: ***to her disappointment**, there was no chance to talk privately with Luke.* ■ [count noun] a person or thing that causes disappointment: *the job proved a disappointment | I was a big **disappointment to** her.*

disapprobation /dɪsˌaprəˈbeɪʃ(ə)n/ ▶ noun [mass noun] strong disapproval, typically on moral grounds: *she braved her mother's disapprobation and slipped out to enjoy herself.*

disapproval ▶ noun [mass noun] possession or expression of an unfavourable opinion: *Jill replied with a hint of disapproval in her voice.*

disapprove ▶ verb [no obj.] have or express an unfavourable opinion: *Bob strongly **disapproved of** drinking and driving.* ■ [with obj.] officially refuse to agree to: *a company may take power to disapprove the transfer of shares.*
– DERIVATIVES **disapprover** noun.

disapproving ▶ adjective expressing an unfavourable opinion: *he shot a disapproving glance at her.*
– DERIVATIVES **disapprovingly** adverb.

disarm ▶ verb [with obj.] **1** take a weapon or weapons away from (a person, force, or country): *guerrillas had completely disarmed their forces.* ■ [no obj.] (of a country or force) give up or reduce its armed forces or weapons: *the other militias had disarmed by the*

agreed deadline. ■ remove the fuse from (a bomb), making it safe.
2 allay the hostility or suspicions of: *his tact and political skills will disarm critics.* ■ deprive of the power to hurt: *camp humour acts to provoke rather than disarm moral indignation.*
▶ **noun** [in sing.] Fencing an act of taking a weapon away from someone: *a well-executed disarm.*
– ORIGIN late Middle English: from Old French *desarmer.*

disarmament /dɪsˈɑːməm(ə)nt/ ▶ **noun** [mass noun] the reduction or withdrawal of military forces and weapons.

disarmer ▶ **noun** a person who advocates or campaigns for the withdrawal of nuclear weapons.

disarming ▶ **adjective** (of manner or behaviour) having the effect of allaying suspicion or hostility, especially through charm: *he gave her a disarming smile.*
– DERIVATIVES **disarmingly** adverb.

disarrange ▶ **verb** [with obj.] make untidy or disordered: *had any of the statues been removed or disarranged?*
– DERIVATIVES **disarrangement** noun.

disarray ▶ **noun** [mass noun] a state of disorganization or untidiness: *her grey hair was* ***in disarray*** | *his plans have been* ***thrown into disarray.***
▶ **verb** [with obj.] **1** throw into a state of disorganization or untidiness: *the inspection disarrayed the usual schedule.*
2 literary undress (someone): *attendant damsels to help to disarray her.*
– ORIGIN late Middle English: from Anglo-Norman French *dissairay.*

disarticulate ▶ **verb** [with obj.] **1** separate (bones) at the joints: *the African egg-eating snake can disarticulate its lower jaw from its upper.*
2 disrupt the logic of (an argument or opinion): *novels disarticulate theories.*
– DERIVATIVES **disarticulation** noun.

disassemble ▶ **verb** [with obj.] take (something) to pieces: *the piston can be disassembled for transport.* ■ Computing translate (a program) from machine code into a symbolic language.
– DERIVATIVES **disassembly** noun.

disassembler ▶ **noun** Computing a program for converting machine code into a low-level symbolic language.

disassociate ▶ **verb** another term for **DISSOCIATE.**
– DERIVATIVES **disassociation** noun.

disaster ▶ **noun** a sudden accident or a natural catastrophe that causes great damage or loss of life: *159 people died in the disaster* | [mass noun] *disaster struck within minutes of take-off.* ■ [as modifier] denoting a genre of films that use natural or accidental catastrophe as the mainspring of plot and setting: *a disaster movie.* ■ an event or fact that has unfortunate consequences: *a string of personal disasters* | [mass noun] *reduced legal aid could spell financial disaster.* ■ informal a person or thing that is a complete failure: *lunch had turned out to be a total disaster.*
– ORIGIN late 16th cent.: from Italian *disastro* 'ill-starred event', from *dis-* (expressing negation) + *astro* 'star' (from Latin *astrum*).

disaster area ▶ **noun** an area in which a major disaster has recently occurred: *the vicinity of the explosion was declared a disaster area.* ■ informal a thing that is regarded as chaotic or highly unsuccessful: *football has long been a disaster area for investors.*

disastrous ▶ **adjective** causing great damage: *a disastrous fire swept through the museum.* ■ informal highly unsuccessful: *United made a disastrous start to the season.*
– DERIVATIVES **disastrously** adverb.
– ORIGIN late 16th cent. (in the sense 'ill-fated'): from French *désastreux,* from Italian *disastroso,* from *disastro* 'disaster'.

disavow ▶ **verb** [with obj.] deny any responsibility or support for: *the union leaders resisted pressure to disavow picket-line violence.*
– ORIGIN late Middle English: from Old French *desavouer.*

disavowal ▶ **noun** [mass noun] the denial of any responsibility or support for something; repudiation: *his disavowal of his previous writings* | [count noun] *they know this, despite their disavowals.*

disband ▶ **verb** (with reference to an organized group) break up or cause to break up.
– DERIVATIVES **disbandment** noun.
– ORIGIN late 16th cent.: from obsolete French *desbander.*

disbar ▶ **verb** (**disbars, disbarring, disbarred**) [with obj.] **1** expel (a barrister) from the Bar, so that they no longer have the right to practise law.
2 exclude (someone) from something: *competitors wearing rings will be* ***disbarred from*** *competition.*
– DERIVATIVES **disbarment** noun.
– ORIGIN mid 16th cent. (in sense 2): from **DIS-** 'away' + **BAR**[1].

disbelief ▶ **noun** [mass noun] inability or refusal to accept that something is true or real: *Laura shook her head in disbelief.* ■ lack of faith: *I'll burn in hell for disbelief.*

disbelieve ▶ **verb** [with obj.] be unable to believe: *he seemed to disbelieve her.* ■ [no obj.] have no religious faith: *to disbelieve is as much an act of faith as belief.*

disbeliever ▶ **noun** a person who refuses to believe something or who lacks religious faith: *she intends to prove the disbelievers wrong.*

disbelieving ▶ **adjective** feeling or expressing disbelief: *the disbelieving look in her eyes.*
– DERIVATIVES **disbelievingly** adverb.

disbenefit ▶ **noun** Brit. a disadvantage or loss resulting from something.

disbound ▶ **adjective** (of a portion of a book) removed from a bound volume.

disbud ▶ **verb** (**disbuds, disbudding, disbudded**) [with obj.] remove superfluous or unwanted buds from (a plant). ■ Farming remove the horn buds from (a young animal).

disburden ▶ **verb** [with obj.] relieve (someone or something) of a burden or responsibility: *I decided to disburden myself of the task.* ■ archaic relieve (someone's mind) of worries.

disburse /dɪsˈbəːs/ ▶ **verb** [with obj.] pay out (money from a fund): *$67 million of the pledged aid had already been disbursed.*
– DERIVATIVES **disbursal** noun, **disburser** noun.
– ORIGIN mid 16th cent.: from Old French *desbourser,* from *des-* (expressing removal) + *bourse* 'purse'.

disbursement ▶ **noun** [mass noun] the payment of money from a fund. ■ [count noun] a payment, especially one made by a solicitor to a third party and then claimed back from the client.

disc (US also **disk**) ▶ **noun 1** a flat, thin circular object: *coins were made by striking a blank disc of metal* | *a man's body with an identity disc around the neck.* ■ (**disk**) an information storage device for a computer in the shape of a round flat plate which can be rotated to give access to all parts of the surface. The data may be stored either magnetically (in a **magnetic disk**) or optically (in an **optical disk** such as a CD-ROM). ■ a CD or record. ■ (**discs**) one of the suits in some tarot packs, corresponding to coins in others.
2 an object or part resembling a disc in shape or appearance: *the smudged yellow disc of the moon.* ■ (also **intervertebral disc**) a layer of cartilage separating adjacent vertebrae in the spine: *he suffered a prolapsed disc.* ■ Botany the central part of the flower of a daisy or other composite plant, consisting of a close-packed cluster of tubular florets.
– ORIGIN mid 17th cent. (originally referring to the seemingly flat circular form of the sun or moon): from French *disque* or Latin *discus* (see **DISCUS**).

> **USAGE** Generally speaking, the British spelling is **disc** and the US spelling is **disk**, although there is much overlap and variation between the two. In particular, the spelling for senses relating to computers is nearly always **disk**, as in **floppy disk, disk drive,** and so on.

discalced /dɪsˈkalst/ ▶ **adjective** denoting or belonging to one of several strict orders of Catholic friars or nuns who go barefoot or are shod only in sandals.
– ORIGIN mid 17th cent.: variant, influenced by French *déchaux,* of earlier *discalceated,* from Latin *discalceatus,* from *dis-* (expressing removal) + *calceus* (from *calceus* 'shoe').

discard ▶ **verb** /dɪˈskɑːd/ [with obj.] get rid of (someone or something) as no longer useful or desirable: *Hilary bundled up the clothes she had discarded.* ■ (in bridge, whist, and similar card games) play (a card that is neither of the suit led nor a trump), when one is unable to follow suit.
▶ **noun** /ˈdɪskɑːd/ a thing rejected as no longer useful or desirable. ■ (in bridge, whist, and similar card games) a card played which is neither of the suit led nor a trump, when one is unable to follow suit.
– DERIVATIVES **discardable** /dɪsˈkɑːdəb(ə)l/ adjective.
– ORIGIN late 16th cent. (originally in the sense 'reject (a playing card)'): from **DIS-** (expressing removal) + the noun **CARD**[1].

discarnate /dɪsˈkɑːnət/ ▶ **adjective** (of a person or being) not having a physical body.
– ORIGIN late 19th cent.: from **DIS-** 'without' + Latin *caro, carn-* 'flesh' or late Latin *carnatus* 'fleshy'.

disc brake ▶ **noun** a type of vehicle brake employing the friction of pads against a disc which is attached to the wheel.

disc drive ▶ **noun** variant spelling of **DISK DRIVE.**

discectomy /dɪsˈkɛktəmi/ ▶ **noun** [mass noun] surgical removal of the whole or a part of an intervertebral disc.

discern /dɪˈsəːn/ ▶ **verb** [with obj.] recognize or find out: *I can discern no difference between the two policies* | [with clause] ***pupils quickly discern what is acceptable to the teacher.*** ■ distinguish (someone or something) with difficulty by sight or with the other senses: *she could faintly discern the shape of a skull.*
– DERIVATIVES **discerner** noun.
– ORIGIN late Middle English: via Old French from Latin *discernere,* from *dis-* 'apart' + *cernere* 'to separate'.

discernible ▶ **adjective** able to be discerned; perceptible: *the scandal had no discernible effect on his career.*
– DERIVATIVES **discernibly** adverb.

discerning ▶ **adjective** having or showing good judgement: *the brasserie attracts discerning customers.*
– DERIVATIVES **discerningly** adverb.

discernment ▶ **noun** [mass noun] the ability to judge well: *an astonishing lack of discernment.*

discerption /dɪˈsəːpʃ(ə)n/ ▶ **noun** [mass noun] archaic the action of pulling something apart.
– DERIVATIVES **discerptible** adjective.
– ORIGIN mid 17th cent.: from late Latin *discerptio(n-),* from Latin *discerpere* 'pluck to pieces'.

disc floret ▶ **noun** Botany (in a composite flower head of the daisy family) any of a number of small tubular and usually fertile florets that form the disc. In rayless plants such as the tansy the flower head is composed entirely of disc florets. Compare with **RAY FLORET.**

discharge ▶ **verb** /dɪsˈtʃɑːdʒ/ [with obj.] **1** tell (someone) officially that they can or must leave, in particular: ■ allow (a patient) to leave hospital because they are judged fit. ■ dismiss from the armed forces or police. ■ release from the custody or restraint of the law: *she was conditionally discharged for two years at Oxford Crown Court.* ■ relieve (a juror or jury) from serving in a case.
2 allow (a liquid, gas, or other substance) to flow out from where it has been confined: *industrial plants* ***discharge*** *highly toxic materials* ***into*** *rivers* | [no obj.] *the overflow should discharge in an obvious place.* ■ (of an orifice or diseased tissue) emit (pus or other liquid). ■ Physics release or neutralize the electric charge of (an electric field, battery, or other object). ■ (of a person) fire (a gun or missile). ■ [no obj.] (of a firearm) be fired: *there was a dull thud as the gun discharged.* ■ unload (goods or passengers) from a ship: *the ferry was discharging passengers* | [no obj.] *ninety ships were queuing to discharge.* ■ allow (an emotion) to be expressed: *he discharged his resentment in the harmless form of memoirs.*
3 do all that is required to perform (a duty) or fulfil (a responsibility). ■ pay off (a debt). ■ release (a party) from a contract or obligation: *the insurer is discharged from liability from the day of breach.* ■ Law relieve (a bankrupt) of residual liability.
4 Law (of a judge or court) cancel (an order of a court). ■ cancel (a contract) because of completion or breach: *an existing mortgage to be discharged on completion.*
▶ **noun** /ˈdɪstʃɑːdʒ, dɪsˈtʃɑːdʒ/ [mass noun] **1** the action of discharging someone from a hospital or from the armed forces or police: *referrals can be discussed before discharge from hospital* | [count noun] *offending policemen receive a dishonourable discharge.* ■ [count noun] an act of releasing someone from the custody or restraint of the law: *she was given an absolute discharge after admitting breaking a smoking ban.*
2 the action of discharging a liquid, gas, or other substance: *those germs might lead to vaginal discharge.* ■ a substance that has been discharged: *industrial discharge has turned the river into an open sewer* | [count noun] *a greeny-yellow nasal discharge.* ■ Physics the release of electricity from a charged object: *slow discharge of a condenser is fundamental to oscillatory circuits.* ■ [count noun] a flow of electricity through air or other gas, especially when accompanied by emission of light: *a sizzling discharge between sky and turret.* ■ the action of firing a gun or missile: *a police*

permit for discharge of an air gun | [count noun] *sounds like discharges of artillery.* ■ the action of unloading a ship.
3 the action of doing all that is required to fulfil a responsibility or perform a duty: *directors must use skill in the discharge of their duties.* ■ the payment of a debt: *money paid **in discharge of** a claim.* ■ Law the relief of a bankrupt from residual liability.
4 Law the cancellation of an order of a court.
– DERIVATIVES **dischargeable** adjective.
– ORIGIN Middle English (in the sense 'relieve of an obligation'): from Old French *descharger*, from late Latin *discarricare* 'unload', from *dis-* (expressing reversal) + *carricare* 'to load' (see CHARGE).

discharge lamp ▶ noun a lamp in which the light is produced by a discharge tube.

discharger ▶ noun a person or thing that discharges something, in particular: ■ a person or organization that allows industrial waste or other harmful substances to be released into the environment. ■ a device that releases nerve gas or other substances for military purposes. ■ an apparatus for releasing or neutralizing an electric charge.

discharge tube ▶ noun a tube containing charged electrodes and filled with a gas in which ionization is induced by an electric field. The gas molecules emit light as they return to the ground state.

disc harrow ▶ noun a harrow with cutting edges consisting of a row of concave discs set at an oblique angle.

disciple /dɪˈsʌɪp(ə)l/ ▶ noun a personal follower of Christ during his life, especially one of the twelve Apostles. ■ a follower or pupil of a teacher, leader, or philosopher: *a disciple of Rousseau.*
– DERIVATIVES **discipleship** noun, **disciplic** adjective, **discipular** /dɪˈsɪpjʊlə/ adjective.
– ORIGIN Old English, from Latin *discipulus* 'learner', from *discere* 'learn'; reinforced by Old French *deciple*.

Disciples of Christ a Protestant denomination, originating among American Presbyterians in the early 19th century and found chiefly in the US, which rejects creeds and regards the Bible as the only basis of faith.

disciplinarian ▶ noun a person who believes in or practises firm discipline.

disciplinary ▶ adjective concerning or enforcing discipline: *a soldier will face disciplinary action after going absent without leave.*
– ORIGIN late 15th cent. (originally with reference to ecclesiastical order): from medieval Latin *disciplinarius*, from Latin *disciplina*, from *discipulus* 'learner' (see DISCIPLE).

discipline /ˈdɪsɪplɪn/ ▶ noun **1** [mass noun] the practice of training people to obey rules or a code of behaviour, using punishment to correct disobedience: *a lack of proper parental and school discipline.* ■ the controlled behaviour resulting from such training: *he was able to maintain discipline among his men.* ■ activity that provides mental or physical training: *the tariqa offered spiritual discipline* | [count noun] *Kung fu is a discipline open to old and young.* ■ [count noun] a system of rules of conduct: *he doesn't have to submit to normal disciplines.*
2 a branch of knowledge, typically one studied in higher education: *sociology is a fairly new discipline.*
▶ verb [with obj.] train (someone) to obey rules or a code of behaviour, using punishment to correct disobedience: *many parents have been afraid to discipline their children.* ■ punish or rebuke formally for an offence: *a member of staff was to be disciplined by management.* ■ **(discipline oneself to do something)** train oneself to do something in a controlled and habitual way: *every month discipline yourself to go through the file.*
– DERIVATIVES **disciplinable** adjective, **disciplinal** /ˌdɪsɪˈplʌɪn(ə)l, ˈdɪsɪˌplɪn(ə)l/ adjective.
– ORIGIN Middle English (in the sense 'mortification by scourging oneself'): via Old French from Latin *disciplina* 'instruction, knowledge', from *discipulus* (see DISCIPLE).

disciplined ▶ adjective showing a controlled form of behaviour or way of working: *a disciplined approach to management.*

disc jockey ▶ noun a person who introduces and plays recorded popular music, especially on radio or at a club.

disclaim ▶ verb [with obj.] refuse to acknowledge; deny: *the school disclaimed any responsibility for his death.* ■ Law renounce a legal claim to (a property or title).
– ORIGIN late Middle English (in legal contexts): from Anglo-Norman French *desclamer*, from *des-* (expressing reversal) + *clamer* 'to claim' (see CLAIM).

disclaimer ▶ noun a statement that denies something, especially responsibility: *the novel carries a disclaimer about the characters bearing no relation to living persons.* ■ Law an act of repudiating a claim, warranty, or bequest.

disclose ▶ verb [with obj.] make (secret or new information) known: *they **disclosed** her name **to** the press.* ■ allow (something hidden) to be seen: *he cleared away the grass and disclosed a narrow opening descending into the darkness.*
– DERIVATIVES **discloser** noun.
– ORIGIN late Middle English: from Old French *desclos-*, stem of *desclore*, based on Latin *claudere* 'to close'.

disclosure ▶ noun [mass noun] the action of making new or secret information known: *a judge ordered the disclosure of the government documents.* ■ [count noun] a fact, especially a secret, that is made known: *the government's disclosures about missile programmes.*
– ORIGIN late 16th cent.: from DISCLOSE, on the pattern of *closure*.

disco ▶ noun (pl. **discos**) **1** a club or party at which people dance to pop music. ■ the lighting and sound equipment used at a disco: *no one knows how to waltz so I've ordered a disco.*
2 short for DISCO MUSIC.
▶ verb (**discoes, discoing, discoed**) [no obj.] attend or dance at a disco: *she filled every hour of the day playing tennis, or discoing with friends.*
– ORIGIN 1960s (originally US): abbreviation of DISCOTHEQUE.

discobolus /dɪˈskɒbələs/ ▶ noun (pl. **discoboli** /-lʌɪ/) a discus-thrower in ancient Greece.
– ORIGIN early 18th cent.: via Latin from Greek *diskobolos*, from *diskos* 'discus' + *-bolos* '-throwing' (from *ballein* 'to throw').

discography /dɪˈskɒgrəfi/ ▶ noun (pl. **discographies**) a descriptive catalogue of musical recordings, particularly those of a particular performer or composer. ■ all of a performer's or composer's recordings considered as a body of work: *his discography is overwhelmingly classical.* ■ [mass noun] the study of musical recordings and compilation of descriptive catalogues.
– DERIVATIVES **discographer** noun.
– ORIGIN 1930s: from DISC + -GRAPHY, on the pattern of *biography*.

discoid /ˈdɪskɔɪd/ ▶ adjective technical shaped like a disc.
▶ noun a thing that is shaped like a disc, particularly a type of ancient stone tool.
– DERIVATIVES **discoidal** adjective.
– ORIGIN late 18th cent.: from Greek *diskoeidēs*, from *diskos* (see DISCUS).

discoloration (also **discolouration**) ▶ noun the process of changing to a different, less attractive colour: *a bluish **discoloration of** the skin.*

discolour (US **discolor**) ▶ verb change or cause to change to a different, less attractive colour: [no obj.] *do not over-knead the dough or it will discolour* | [with obj.] *too much aluminium can discolour water.*
– ORIGIN late Middle English: from Old French *descolorer* or medieval Latin *discolorare*, from *des-*, *dis-* (expressing reversal) + Latin *colorare* 'to colour'.

discoloured (US **discolored**) ▶ adjective changed in colour in a way that is less attractive: *her beauty was marred by discoloured teeth.*

discombobulate /ˌdɪskəmˈbɒbjʊleɪt/ ▶ verb [with obj.] humorous, chiefly N. Amer. disconcert or confuse (someone): (as adj. **discombobulated**) *he is looking a little pained and discombobulated.*
– DERIVATIVES **discombobulation** noun.
– ORIGIN mid 19th cent.: probably based on DISCOMPOSE or DISCOMFIT.

discomfit /dɪsˈkʌmfɪt/ ▶ verb (**discomfits, discomfiting, discomfited**) [with obj.] make (someone) feel uneasy or embarrassed: *he was not noticeably discomfited by her tone.*
– ORIGIN Middle English (in the sense 'defeat in battle'): from Old French *desconfit*, past participle of *desconfire*, based on Latin *dis-* (expressing reversal) + *conficere* 'put together' (see CONFECTION).

> **USAGE** The words **discomfit** and **discomfort** are etymologically unrelated but in modern use their principal meanings as a verb have collapsed into one: 'make someone feel uneasy'.

discomfiture /dɪsˈkʌmfɪtʃə(r)/ ▶ noun [mass noun] a feeling of unease or embarrassment; awkwardness: *much to the discomfiture of the organisers.*

discomfort ▶ noun [mass noun] slight pain: *the patient complained of discomfort in the left calf.* ■ worry or embarrassment: *his remarks caused her discomfort.* ■ [count noun] something that causes one to feel uncomfortable: *the discomforts of too much sun in summer.*
▶ verb [with obj.] make (someone) feel anxious or embarrassed: *the unknown leaker's purpose was to discomfort the Prime Minister.* ■ (often as adj. **discomforting**) cause (someone) slight pain: *if the patient's condition has discomforting symptoms, these should be controlled.*
– ORIGIN Middle English (as a verb in the sense 'dishearten'): from Old French *desconforter* (verb), *desconfort* (noun), from *des-* (expressing reversal) + *conforter* 'to comfort' (see COMFORT).

D

discommode /ˌdɪskəˈməʊd/ ▶ verb [with obj.] formal cause (someone) trouble or inconvenience: *I am sorry to have discommoded you.*
– DERIVATIVES **discommodious** adjective, **discommodity** noun.
– ORIGIN early 18th cent.: from obsolete French *discommoder*, variant of *incommoder* (see INCOMMODE).

discompose ▶ verb [with obj.] (often as adj. **discomposed**) disturb or agitate (someone): *she looked a little discomposed as she spoke.*

discomposure ▶ noun [mass noun] the state or feeling of being disturbed or agitated; agitation: *she laughed to mask her discomposure.*

disco music ▶ noun [mass noun] pop music intended mainly for dancing to at discos, typically soul-influenced and melodic with a regular bass beat and popular particularly in the late 1970s.

disconcert /ˌdɪskənˈsəːt/ ▶ verb [with obj.] disturb the composure of; unsettle: *the abrupt change of subject disconcerted her* | (as adj. **disconcerted**) *Keith looked momentarily disconcerted.*
– DERIVATIVES **disconcertedly** adverb, **disconcertion** noun.
– ORIGIN late 17th cent. (in the sense 'upset the progress of'): from obsolete French *desconcerter*, from *des-* (expressing reversal) + *concerter* 'bring together'.

disconcerting ▶ adjective causing one to feel unsettled: *he had a disconcerting habit of offering jobs to people he met at dinner parties.*
– DERIVATIVES **disconcertingly** adverb.

disconfirm ▶ verb [with obj.] show that (a belief or hypothesis) is not or may not be true.
– DERIVATIVES **disconfirmation** /ˌdɪskɒnfəˈmeɪʃ(ə)n/ noun, **disconfirmatory** adjective.

disconformity ▶ noun (pl. **disconformities**) **1** [mass noun] lack of conformity.
2 Geology a break in a sedimentary sequence which does not involve a difference of inclination between the strata on each side of the break. Compare with UNCONFORMITY.

disconnect ▶ verb [with obj.] break the connection of or between: *if the axle unit is partially disconnected from the body, the car should not be driven.* ■ put (an electrical device) out of action by detaching it from a power supply. ■ interrupt or terminate (a telephone conversation) by breaking the connection: *I phoned them in Edinburgh but we got disconnected.* ■ terminate the connection of (a household) to water, electricity, gas, or telephone, typically because of non-payment of bills.
▶ noun an instance of disconnecting or being disconnected: [as modifier] *a disconnect message.* ■ a discrepancy or lack of connection: *there can be a disconnect between boardrooms and IT departments when it comes to technology.*
– DERIVATIVES **disconnection** (also **disconnexion**) noun.

disconnected ▶ adjective having had a connection broken: *he expected the disconnected phone to start ringing.* ■ [predic.] (of a person) lacking contact with reality: *I drove away, feeling **disconnected from** the real world.* ■ (of speech, writing, or thought) lacking a logical sequence: *a disconnected narrative.*
– DERIVATIVES **disconnectedly** adverb, **disconnectedness** noun.

disconsolate /dɪsˈkɒns(ə)lət/ ▶ adjective very unhappy and unable to be comforted: *she left Fritz looking disconsolate.*
– DERIVATIVES **disconsolately** adverb, **disconsolation** noun.

– ORIGIN late Middle English: from medieval Latin *disconsolatus*, from *dis-* (expressing reversal) + Latin *consolatus* (past participle of *consolari* 'to console').

discontent ▶ **noun** [mass noun] dissatisfaction with one's circumstances; lack of contentment: *voters voiced **discontent with** both parties* | [count noun] *the discontents of the working class.* ■ [count noun] a person who is dissatisfied, typically with the prevailing social or political situation: *the cause attracted a motley crew of discontents and zealots.*
▶ **adjective** dissatisfied.
– DERIVATIVES **discontentment** noun.

discontented ▶ **adjective** dissatisfied, especially with one's circumstances: *I am so **discontented with** my work* | *a discontented housewife* | (as plural noun **the discontented**) *the ranks of the discontented were swelled by returning soldiers.*
– DERIVATIVES **discontentedly** adverb, **discontentedness** noun.

discontinue ▶ **verb** (**discontinues, discontinuing, discontinued**) [with obj.] cease from doing or providing (something), especially something that has been provided on a regular basis: *the ferry service was discontinued by the proprietors* | *he discontinued his visits.* ■ stop making (a particular product). ■ cease taking (a newspaper or periodical) or paying (a subscription).
– DERIVATIVES **discontinuance** noun, **discontinuation** noun.
– ORIGIN late Middle English (in the sense 'interrupt, disrupt'): via Old French from medieval Latin *discontinuare*, from Latin *dis-* 'not' + *continuare* (see CONTINUE).

discontinued ▶ **adjective** (of a product) no longer available or produced: *discontinued fabrics.*

discontinuity ▶ **noun** (pl. **discontinuities**) [mass noun] the state of having intervals or gaps; lack of continuity: *there is no significant discontinuity between modern and primitive societies.* ■ [count noun] a break in or lack of continuity: *changes in government have resulted in discontinuities in policy.*
– ORIGIN late 16th cent.: from medieval Latin *discontinuitas*, from *discontinuus* (see DISCONTINUOUS).

discontinuous ▶ **adjective** having intervals or gaps: *a person with a discontinuous employment record.*
– DERIVATIVES **discontinuously** adverb.
– ORIGIN mid 17th cent. (in the sense 'producing discontinuity'): from medieval Latin *discontinuus*, from *dis-* 'not' + *continuus* (see CONTINUOUS).

discord ▶ **noun** /ˈdɪskɔːd/ [mass noun] **1** disagreement between people: *a prosperous family who showed no signs of discord.* ■ lack of agreement or harmony between things: *the discord between indigenous and Western cultures.*
2 Music lack of harmony between notes sounding together: *the music faded in discord.* ■ [count noun] a chord which (in conventional harmonic terms) is regarded as unpleasing or requiring resolution by another. ■ [count noun] any interval except unison, an octave, a perfect fifth or fourth, a major or minor third and sixth, or their octaves. ■ [count noun] a single note dissonant with another.
▶ **verb** /dɪsˈkɔːd/ [no obj.] archaic (of people) disagree: *we discorded commonly on two points.* ■ (of things) be different: *the party's views were apt to **discord with** those of the leading members of the government.*
– ORIGIN Middle English: from Old French *descord* (noun), *descorder* (verb), from Latin *discordare*, from *discors* 'discordant', from *dis-* (expressing negation, reversal) + *cor, cord-* 'heart'.

discordant ▶ **adjective 1** disagreeing or incongruous: *the operative principle of democracy is a balance of discordant qualities.* ■ characterized by conflict: *a study of children in discordant homes.*
2 (of sounds) harsh and jarring because of a lack of harmony: *the singers continued their discordant chanting.*
– PHRASES **strike a discordant note** appear strange and out of place.
– DERIVATIVES **discordance** noun, **discordancy** noun, **discordantly** adverb.
– ORIGIN late Middle English: from Old French *descordant*, present participle of *descorder* (see DISCORD).

discotheque /ˈdɪskətɛk/ ▶ **noun** another term for DISCO (sense 1 of the noun).
– ORIGIN 1950s: from French *discothèque*, originally 'record library', on the pattern of *bibliothèque* 'library'.

discount ▶ **noun** /ˈdɪskaʊnt/ a deduction from the usual cost of something: *rail commuters get a discount on season tickets* | [mass noun] *we introduced a standard level of discount for everyone.* ■ Finance a percentage deducted from the face value of a bill of exchange or promissory note when it changes hands before the due date.
▶ **verb** /dɪsˈkaʊnt/ [with obj.] **1** deduct an amount from (the usual price of something): *a product may carry a price which cannot easily be discounted.* ■ reduce (a product or service) in price: *one shop has discounted children's trainers.* ■ buy or sell (a bill of exchange) before its due date at less than its maturity value.
2 regard (a possibility or fact) as being unworthy of consideration because it lacks credibility: *I'd heard rumours, but discounted them.*
– PHRASES **at a discount** below the nominal or usual price. Compare with AT A PREMIUM (see PREMIUM).
– DERIVATIVES **discountable** /dɪsˈkaʊntəb(ə)l/ adjective, **discounter** /dɪsˈkaʊntə/ noun.
– ORIGIN early 17th cent.: from obsolete French *descompte* (noun), *descompter* (verb), or (in commercial contexts) from Italian *(di)scontare*, both from medieval Latin *discomputare*, from Latin *dis-* (expressing reversal) + *computare* (see COMPUTE).

discounted cash flow ▶ **noun** [mass noun] Finance a method of assessing investments taking into account the expected accumulation of interest.

discountenance ▶ **verb** [with obj.] **1** refuse to approve of: *the best solution to alcohol abuse is a healthy family life where alcohol consumption is discountenanced.*
2 disturb the composure of: *Amanda was not discountenanced by the accusation.*

discount house ▶ **noun 1** Brit. a company that buys and sells bills of exchange.
2 N. Amer. another term for DISCOUNT STORE.

discount market ▶ **noun** the section of the financial market which deals in discounted bills of exchange.

discount rate ▶ **noun** Finance **1** the minimum interest rate set by the US Federal Reserve (and some other national banks) for lending to other banks.
2 a rate used for discounting bills of exchange.

discount store ▶ **noun** a shop that sells goods at less than the normal retail price.

discourage ▶ **verb** [with obj.] cause (someone) to lose confidence or enthusiasm: *tedious regulations could discourage investors.* ■ prevent or try to prevent (something) by showing disapproval or creating difficulties: *the plan is designed to discourage the use of private cars.* ■ persuade (someone) against an action: *we want to **discourage** children **from** smoking.*
– ORIGIN late Middle English: from Old French *descouragier*, from *des-* (expressing reversal) + *corage* 'courage'.

discouraged ▶ **adjective** having lost confidence or enthusiasm; disheartened: *he must be feeling pretty discouraged.*

discouragement ▶ **noun 1** [mass noun] a loss of confidence or enthusiasm; dispiritedness: *do not give in to discouragement.*
2 an attempt to prevent something by showing disapproval or creating difficulties; deterrent: *the discouragement of crime.*

discouraging ▶ **adjective** causing someone to lose confidence or enthusiasm; depressing: *a discouraging experience.*
– DERIVATIVES **discouragingly** adverb.

discourse ▶ **noun** /ˈdɪskɔːs, -ˈkɔːs/ written or spoken communication or debate: [mass noun] *the language of political discourse* | [count noun] *an imagined discourse between two people.* ■ [count noun] a formal discussion of a topic in speech or writing: *a discourse on critical theory.* ■ Linguistics a connected series of utterances; a text or conversation.
▶ **verb** /dɪsˈkɔːs/ [no obj.] speak or write authoritatively about a topic: *she could **discourse** at great length **on** the history of Europe.* ■ engage in conversation: *he spent an hour **discoursing with** his supporters.*
– ORIGIN late Middle English (denoting the process of reasoning): from Old French *discours*, from Latin *discursus* 'running to and fro' (in medieval Latin 'argument'), from the verb *discurrere*, from *dis-* 'away' + *currere* 'to run'; the verb influenced by French *discourir*.

discourse marker ▶ **noun** Grammar a word or phrase whose function is to organize discourse into segments, for example *well* or *I mean*.

discourteous ▶ **adjective** showing rudeness and a lack of consideration for other people: *it would be unkind and discourteous to decline a visit.*
– DERIVATIVES **discourteously** adverb, **discourteousness** noun.

discourtesy ▶ **noun** (pl. **discourtesies**) [mass noun] rude and inconsiderate behaviour: *he was able to discourage visitors without obvious discourtesy.* ■ [count noun] an impolite act or remark: *the fact that MPs were not kept informed was an extraordinary discourtesy.*

discover ▶ **verb** [with obj.] **1** find unexpectedly or during a search: *firemen discovered a body in the debris* | *she discovered her lover in the arms of another woman.* ■ become aware of (a fact or situation): *the courage to discover the truth and possibly be disappointed* | [with clause] *it was a relief to discover that he wasn't in.* ■ be the first to find or observe (a place, substance, or scientific phenomenon): *Fleming discovered penicillin early in the twentieth century.* ■ show interest in (an activity or subject) for the first time: *a teenager who has recently discovered fashion.* ■ be the first to recognize the potential of (an actor or performer): *I discovered the band back in the mid 70s.*
2 archaic divulge (a secret). ■ disclose the identity of (someone): *she at last discovered herself to me.* ■ display (a quality or feeling): *with what agility did these military men discover their skill in feats of war.*
– DERIVATIVES **discoverability** noun, **discoverable** adjective.
– ORIGIN Middle English (in the sense 'make known'): from Old French *descovrir*, from late Latin *discooperire*, from Latin *dis-* (expressing reversal) + *cooperire* 'cover completely' (see COVER).

discovered check ▶ **noun** Chess a check which results when a player moves a piece or pawn so as to put the opponent's king in check from another piece.

discoverer ▶ **noun** the first person to find or explore a place. ■ the first person to find or observe a substance or scientific phenomenon: *many chemical processes are named after their original discoverers.*

Discovery ▶ **noun** a dessert apple of a variety with crisp flesh and bright red skin.

discovery ▶ **noun** (pl. **discoveries**) [mass noun] **1** the action or process of discovering or being discovered: *the discovery of the body* | [count noun] *he made some startling discoveries.* ■ [count noun] a person or thing discovered: *the drug is not a new discovery.*
2 Law the compulsory disclosure, by one party to an action to another, of relevant testimony or documents.
– ORIGIN mid 16th cent.: from DISCOVER, on the pattern of the pair *recover, recovery*.

discovery well ▶ **noun** the first successful oil well in a new field.

discredit ▶ **verb** (**discredits, discrediting, discredited**) [with obj.] harm the good reputation of: *his remarks were taken out of context in an effort to discredit him* | (as adj. **discredited**) *a discredited government.* ■ cause (an idea or account) to seem false or unreliable: *his explanation for the phenomenon was soon discredited.*
▶ **noun** [mass noun] loss or lack of reputation or respect: *they committed crimes which brought discredit upon the administration.* ■ [count noun] a person or thing that is a source of disgrace: *the ships were a **discredit** to the country.*
– ORIGIN mid 16th cent.: from DIS- (expressing reversal) + CREDIT, on the pattern of Italian *(di)scredito* (noun), *(di)screditare* (verb), and French *discrédit* (noun), *discréditer* (verb).

discreditable ▶ **adjective** tending to bring harm to a reputation: *allegations of discreditable conduct.*
– DERIVATIVES **discreditably** adverb.

discreet /dɪˈskriːt/ ▶ **adjective** (**discreeter, discreetest**) careful and prudent in one's speech or actions, especially in order to keep something confidential or to avoid embarrassment: *we made some discreet inquiries.* ■ intentionally unobtrusive: *a discreet cough.*
– DERIVATIVES **discreetly** adverb, **discreetness** noun.
– ORIGIN Middle English: from Old French *discret*, from Latin *discretus* 'separate', past participle of *discernere* 'discern', the sense arising from late Latin *discretio* (see DISCRETION). Compare with DISCRETE.

> **USAGE** The words **discrete** and **discreet** are pronounced in the same way and share the same origin but they do not mean the same thing. **Discrete** means 'separate', as in *a finite number of **discrete** categories*, while **discreet** means 'careful and circumspect', as in *you can rely on him to be **discreet**.*

discrepancy /dɪsˈkrɛp(ə)nsi/ ▶ **noun** (pl. **discrepancies**) an illogical or surprising lack of compatibility or similarity between two or more facts: *there's a **discrepancy between** your account and his.*

– DERIVATIVES **discrepant** adjective.
– ORIGIN early 17th cent.: from Latin *discrepantia*, from *discrepare* 'be discordant', from *dis-* 'apart, away' + *crepare* 'to creak'.

discrete /dɪˈskriːt/ ▶ adjective individually separate and distinct: *speech sounds are produced as a continuous sound signal rather than discrete units.*
– DERIVATIVES **discretely** adverb, **discreteness** noun.
– ORIGIN late Middle English: from Latin *discretus* 'separate'; compare with DISCREET.

discretion ▶ noun [mass noun] **1** the quality of behaving or speaking in such a way as to avoid causing offence or revealing confidential information: *she knew she could rely on his discretion | I'll be **the soul of discretion**.*
2 the freedom to decide what should be done in a particular situation: *local authorities should **use their discretion** in setting the charges | honorary fellowships may be awarded **at the discretion of** the council.*
– PHRASES **discretion is the better part of valour** proverb it's better to avoid a dangerous situation than to confront it.
– ORIGIN Middle English (in the sense 'discernment'): via Old French from Latin *discretio(n-)* 'separation' (in late Latin 'discernment'), from *discernere* (see DISCERN).

discretionary ▶ adjective available for use at the discretion of the user: *there has been an increase in year-end discretionary bonuses.* ■ denoting or relating to investment funds placed with a broker or manager who has discretion to invest them on the client's behalf: *discretionary portfolios.*

discretionary income ▶ noun [mass noun] income remaining after deduction of taxes, social security charges, and basic living costs. Compare with DISPOSABLE INCOME.

discretionary trust ▶ noun a trust in which the number of shares of each beneficiary are not fixed by the settlor in the trust deed, but at the discretion of the trustees.

discretize /dɪˈskriːtʌɪz/ (also **discretise**) ▶ verb [with obj.] Mathematics represent or approximate (a quantity or series) using a discrete quantity or quantities.
– DERIVATIVES **discretization** noun.

discriminable /dɪˈskrɪmɪnəb(ə)l/ ▶ adjective able to be discriminated; distinguishable: *the target contours will not be discriminable from their background.*
– DERIVATIVES **discriminability** noun.
– ORIGIN mid 18th cent.: from DISCRIMINATE, on the pattern of the pair *separate, separable.*

discriminant /dɪˈskrɪmɪnənt/ ▶ noun a distinguishing feature or characteristic: *anaemia is commonly present in patients with both conditions, and is therefore not a helpful discriminant.* ■ Mathematics a function of the coefficients of a polynomial equation whose value gives information about the roots of the polynomial. See also DISCRIMINANT FUNCTION.
– ORIGIN mid 19th cent. (in the sense 'showing discernment'): from Latin *discriminant-* 'distinguishing between', from the verb *discriminare* (see DISCRIMINATE).

discriminant analysis ▶ noun [mass noun] statistical analysis using a discriminant function to assign data to one of two or more groups.

discriminant function ▶ noun Statistics a function of several variates used to assign items into one of two or more groups. The function for a particular set of items is obtained from measurements of the variates of items which belong to a known group.

discriminate /dɪˈskrɪmɪneɪt/ ▶ verb [no obj.] **1** recognize a distinction; differentiate: *babies can **discriminate between** different facial expressions.* ■ [with obj.] perceive or constitute the difference in or between: *features that **discriminate** this species **from** other gastropods.*
2 make an unjust or prejudicial distinction in the treatment of different categories of people, especially on the grounds of race, sex, or age: *existing employment policies **discriminate against** women.*
– DERIVATIVES **discriminately** adverb, **discriminative** adjective.
– ORIGIN early 17th cent.: from Latin *discriminat-* 'distinguished between', from the verb *discriminare*, from *discrimen* 'distinction', from the verb *discernere* (see DISCERN).

discriminating ▶ adjective having or showing refined taste or good judgement: *he became a discriminating collector and patron of the arts.*
– DERIVATIVES **discriminatingly** adverb.

discrimination ▶ noun [mass noun] **1** the unjust or prejudicial treatment of different categories of people, especially on the grounds of race, age, or sex: *victims of racial discrimination | **discrimination against** homosexuals.*
2 recognition and understanding of the difference between one thing and another: *discrimination between right and wrong* | [count noun] *young children have difficulties in making fine discriminations.* ■ the ability to judge what is of high quality; good judgement or taste: *those who could afford to buy showed little taste or discrimination.*
3 Electronics the selection of a signal having a required characteristic, such as frequency or amplitude, by means of a discriminator.

discriminator ▶ noun **1** a characteristic which enables people or things to be distinguished from one another: *age should not be used as a primary discriminator in recruitment.*
2 Electronics a circuit or device which only produces an output when the input exceeds a fixed value. ■ a circuit which converts a frequency-modulated signal into an amplitude-modulated one.

discriminatory /dɪˈskrɪmɪnˌt(ə)ri, dɪˌskrɪmɪˈneɪt(ə)ri/ ▶ adjective making or showing an unfair or prejudicial distinction between different categories of people or things, especially on the grounds of race, age, or sex: *discriminatory employment practices.*

discursive /dɪsˈkəːsɪv/ ▶ adjective **1** digressing from subject to subject: *students often write dull, second-hand, discursive prose.* ■ (of a style of speech or writing) fluent and expansive: *the short story is concentrated, whereas the novel is discursive.*
2 relating to discourse or modes of discourse: *the attempt to transform utterances from one discursive context to another.*
3 Philosophy, archaic proceeding by argument or reasoning rather than by intuition.
– DERIVATIVES **discursively** adverb, **discursiveness** noun.
– ORIGIN late 16th cent.: from medieval Latin *discursivus*, from Latin *discurs-*, literally 'gone hastily to and fro', from the verb *discurrere* (see DISCOURSE).

discus /ˈdɪskəs/ ▶ noun (pl. **discuses**) **1** a heavy thick-centred disc thrown by an athlete, in ancient Greek games or in modern field events.
2 a small colourful South American freshwater fish with a rounded laterally compressed body, native to South America and popular in aquariums. ● Genus *Symphysodon*, family Cichlidae: several species.
– ORIGIN via Latin from Greek *diskos*.

discuss ▶ verb [with obj.] talk about (something) with a person or people: *I discussed the matter with my wife* | [with clause] *they were discussing where to go for a drink.* ■ talk or write about (a topic) in detail, taking into account different issues or ideas: *in Chapter Six I discuss problems that arise in applying Darwin's ideas.*
– DERIVATIVES **discussable** adjective, **discusser** noun.
– ORIGIN late Middle English (in the sense 'dispel, disperse', also 'examine by argument'): from Latin *discuss-* 'dashed to pieces', later 'investigated', from the verb *discutere*, from *dis-* 'apart' + *quatere* 'shake'.

discussant ▶ noun a person who takes part in a discussion, especially a prearranged one.

discussion ▶ noun [mass noun] the action or process of talking about something in order to reach a decision or to exchange ideas: *the committee acts as a forum for discussion | the EC directive is currently **under discussion**.* ■ [count noun] a conversation or debate about a specific topic: *discussions about environmental improvement.* ■ [count noun] a detailed treatment of a topic in speech or writing.
– ORIGIN Middle English (denoting judicial examination): via Old French from late Latin *discussio(n-)*, from *discutere* 'investigate' (see DISCUSS).

discussion board ▶ noun another term for MESSAGE BOARD.

disc wheel ▶ noun a bicycle wheel with a central disc in place of spokes.

disdain ▶ noun [mass noun] the feeling that someone or something is unworthy of one's consideration or respect: *her upper lip curled in disdain | an aristocratic **disdain for** manual labour.*
▶ verb [with obj.] consider to be unworthy of one's consideration: *he disdained his patients as an inferior rabble.* ■ refuse to do (something) from feelings of pride or superiority: *she remained standing, pointedly disdaining his invitation to sit down* | [with infinitive] *he disdained to discuss the matter further.*
– ORIGIN Middle English: from Old French *desdeign* (noun), *desdeignier* (verb), based on Latin *dedignari*, from *de-* (expressing reversal) + *dignari* 'consider worthy' (from *dignus* 'worthy').

disdainful ▶ adjective showing contempt or lack of respect: *with a last disdainful look, she turned towards the door.*
– DERIVATIVES **disdainfully** adverb, **disdainfulness** noun.

disease ▶ noun a disorder of structure or function in a human, animal, or plant, especially one that produces specific symptoms or that affects a specific location and is not simply a direct result of physical injury: *bacterial meningitis is quite a rare disease* | [mass noun] *heart disease.* ■ a particular quality or disposition regarded as adversely affecting a person or group of people: *we are suffering from the British disease of self-deprecation.*
– ORIGIN Middle English (in the sense 'lack of ease; inconvenience'): from Old French *desaise* 'lack of ease', from *des-* (expressing reversal) + *aise* 'ease'.

diseased ▶ adjective suffering from disease: *diseased trees.* ■ abnormal and corrupt: *I cannot bear your diseased view of mankind.*

diseconomy ▶ noun (pl. **diseconomies**) Economics an economic disadvantage such as an increase in cost arising from an increase in the size of an organization: *in an ideal world, these **diseconomies of scale** would be minimized.*

disembark ▶ verb [no obj.] leave a ship, aircraft, or train: *the passengers began to disembark.*
– DERIVATIVES **disembarkation** noun.
– ORIGIN late 16th cent.: from French *désembarquer*, Spanish *desembarcar*, or Italian *disimbarcare*, based on Latin *barca* 'ship's boat'.

disembarrass ▶ verb (**disembarrass oneself of/from**) free oneself of (a burden or nuisance): *shouldn't empires disembarrass themselves of elements which no longer serve a purpose?* ■ [with obj.] rare free from embarrassment.

disembodied ▶ adjective separated from or existing without the body: *a disembodied ghost.* ■ (of a sound) lacking any obvious physical source: *a disembodied voice at the end of the phone.*

disembody ▶ verb (**disembodies, disembodying, disembodied**) [with obj.] separate (something) from its material form: *the play of light off the dome's glass further served to disembody it.*
– DERIVATIVES **disembodiment** noun.

disembogue /ˌdɪsɪmˈbəʊg, ˌdɪsɛm-/ ▶ verb (**disembogues, disemboguing, disembogued**) [no obj.] literary (of a river or stream) emerge or be discharged in quantity; pour out.
– ORIGIN late 16th cent.: from Spanish *desembocar*, from *des-* (expressing reversal) + *embocar* 'run into a creek or strait' (based on *boca* 'mouth').

disembowel /ˌdɪsɪmˈbaʊəl, ˌdɪsɛm-/ ▶ verb (**disembowels, disembowelling, disembowelled**; US **disembowels, disemboweling, disemboweled**) [with obj.] cut open and remove the internal organs of.
– DERIVATIVES **disembowelment** noun.

disembroil /ˌdɪsɪmˈbrɔɪl, ˌdɪsɛm-/ ▶ verb [with obj.] archaic free from confusion: *to disembroil a subject that seems to have perplexed even Antiquity.*

disempower ▶ verb [with obj.] make (a person or group) less powerful or confident: *the experience of hospital invariably disempowers women.*
DERIVATIVES **disempowerment** noun.

disenchant ▶ verb [with obj.] cause (someone) to be disappointed: *he may have been disenchanted by the loss of his huge following.*
– DERIVATIVES **disenchanting** adjective.
– ORIGIN late 16th cent.: from French *désenchanter*, from *dés-* (expressing reversal) + *enchanter* (see ENCHANT).

disenchanted ▶ adjective disappointed by someone or something previously respected or admired; disillusioned: *he became **disenchanted with** his erstwhile ally | there are a lot of disenchanted music fans out there.*

disenchantment ▶ noun [mass noun] a feeling of disappointment about someone or something you previously respected or admired; disillusionment: *their growing **disenchantment with** the leadership.*

disencumber ▶ verb [with obj.] free from or relieve of an encumbrance: *the sect claims to disencumber adherents of the untoward effects of past traumas.*

disendow ▶ verb [with obj.] deprive (someone or something) of an endowment, in particular deprive (a Church) of the property and funds that it receives from the state.
– DERIVATIVES **disendowment** noun.

D

D

disenfranchise /ˌdɪsɪnˈfran(t)ʃʌɪz, ˌdɪsɛn-/ (also **disfranchise**) ▶ **verb** [with obj.] deprive (someone) of the right to vote: *the law disenfranchised some 3,000 voters on the basis of a residence qualification.* ■ deprive (someone) of a right or privilege: *we strongly oppose any measure which would disenfranchise people from access to legal advice.* ■ archaic deprive (a place) of the right to send a representative to Parliament.
– DERIVATIVES **disenfranchisement** noun.

disengage /ˌdɪsɪnˈɡeɪdʒ, ˌdɪsɛn-/ ▶ **verb 1** [with obj.] separate or release (someone or something) from something to which they are attached or connected: *I **disengaged** his hand **from** mine | they clung together for a moment, then she **disengaged herself**.* ■ [no obj.] become released: *the clutch will not disengage.*
2 remove (troops) from an area of conflict: *the ceasefire gave the commanders a chance to disengage their forces* | [no obj.] *plans were already afoot for the Americans to **disengage from** the city.*
3 [no obj.] Fencing pass the point of one's sword over or under the opponent's sword to change the line of attack.
▶ **noun** Fencing a disengaging movement.

disengaged ▶ **adjective** emotionally detached: *the students were oddly disengaged, as if they didn't believe they could control their lives.*

disengagement ▶ **noun** [mass noun] **1** the action or process of withdrawing from involvement in an activity, situation, or group: *his **disengagement from** the provisional government.* ■ the withdrawal of military forces or the renunciation of military or political influence in an area. ■ the process of separating or releasing something or of becoming separated or released: *the mechanism prevents accidental disengagement.* ■ archaic the breaking off of an engagement to be married.
2 emotional detachment; objectivity: *contemporary criticism can afford neutral disengagement.*
3 Fencing another term for DISENGAGE.

disentailment ▶ **noun** [mass noun] Law the action of freeing property from entail: *the disentailment of the Church's landed property.*

disentangle ▶ **verb** [with obj.] free (something or someone) from something that they are entangled with: *'I must go,' she said, **disentangling** her fingers **from** Gabriel's* | figurative *it was difficult to **disentangle** fact **from** fiction.* ■ remove knots or tangles from (wool, rope, or hair).
– DERIVATIVES **disentanglement** noun.

disenthral /ˌdɪsɪnˈθrɔːl, ˌdɪsɛn-/ (US **disenthrall**) ▶ **verb** (**disenthrals**, **disenthralling**, **disenthralled**) [with obj.] literary set free: *I disenthral my mind from theories.*
– DERIVATIVES **disenthralment** noun.

disentitle ▶ **verb** [with obj.] deprive (someone) of a right: *she was **disentitled to** a redundancy payment.*
– DERIVATIVES **disentitlement** noun.

disentomb ▶ **verb** [with obj.] remove (something) from a tomb: *a mummy which we saw disentombed* | figurative *he disentombed a great part of the early history of England.*
– DERIVATIVES **disentombment** noun.

disequilibrium /dɪsiːkwɪˈlɪbrɪəm, ˌdɪsɛk-/ ▶ **noun** [mass noun] a loss or lack of equilibrium or stability, especially in relation to supply, demand, and prices.

disestablish ▶ **verb** [with obj.] deprive (an organization, especially a national Church) of its official status.
– DERIVATIVES **disestablishment** noun.

disesteem ▶ **noun** [mass noun] low esteem or regard: *her disesteem for institutionalized medicine now heightened to aversion.*
▶ **verb** [with obj.] formal have a low opinion of: *novels and short stories have been disesteemed.*

diseuse /diːˈzəːz/ ▶ **noun** a female artiste who entertains with spoken monologues.
– ORIGIN French, literally 'talker', feminine of *diseur*, from *dire* 'to say'.

disfavour (US **disfavor**) ▶ **noun** [mass noun] disapproval or dislike: *the headmaster regarded her with disfavour.* ■ the state of being disliked: *coal fell into disfavour because steam engines are noisy and polluting.*
▶ **verb** [with obj.] put at a disadvantage or treat as undesirable: *the system favours those who employ less labour and disfavours those who employ more.*

disfellowship ▶ **noun** [mass noun] exclusion from fellowship, especially as a form of discipline in some Protestant and Mormon Churches.
▶ **verb** (**disfellowships**, **disfellowshipping**, **disfellowshipped**) [with obj.] exclude (someone) from fellowship.

disfigure ▶ **verb** [with obj.] spoil the appearance of: *litter disfigures the countryside* | (as adj. **disfiguring**) *a disfiguring birthmark.*
– DERIVATIVES **disfiguration** noun.
– ORIGIN late Middle English: from Old French *desfigurer*, based on Latin *figura* 'figure'.

disfigurement ▶ **noun** [mass noun] the action of spoiling the appearance of something or someone; defacement: *the **disfigurement of** this very pleasant area.* ■ something which spoils the appearance of someone or something; a blemish: *a severe facial disfigurement.*

disforest ▶ **verb** another term for DISAFFOREST.
– DERIVATIVES **disforestation** noun.

disfranchise ▶ **verb** another term for DISENFRANCHISE.

disgorge ▶ **verb** [with obj.] **1** pour (something) out: *the combine disgorged a steady stream of grain.* ■ (of a building or vehicle) discharge (the occupants): *an aircraft disgorging paratroopers.* ■ bring up or vomit (food). ■ yield or give up (funds, especially when dishonestly acquired): *they were made to disgorge all the profits made from the record.* ■ [no obj.] (of a river) empty into a sea: *the Nile disgorges into the sea at Rashid.*
2 remove the sediment from (a sparkling wine) after fermentation.
– DERIVATIVES **disgorgement** noun.
– ORIGIN late 15th cent.: from Old French *desgorger*, from *des-* (expressing removal) + *gorge* 'throat'.

disgorger ▶ **noun** Fishing a device for extracting a hook from a fish's throat.

disgrace ▶ **noun** [mass noun] loss of reputation or respect as the result of a dishonourable action: *he left the army **in disgrace** | if he'd gone back it would have brought disgrace on the family.* ■ [in sing.] a person or thing regarded as shameful and unacceptable: *he's **a disgrace to** the legal profession.*
▶ **verb** [with obj.] bring shame or discredit on: *you have disgraced the family name | John stiffened his jaw so he wouldn't **disgrace himself** by crying.* ■ cause (someone) to fall from favour or a position of power or honour: *he has been publicly disgraced for offences for which he was not guilty.*
– ORIGIN mid 16th cent. (as a verb): via French from Italian *disgrazia* (noun), *disgraziare* (verb), from *dis-* (expressing reversal) + Latin *gratia* 'grace'.

disgraced ▶ **adjective** having fallen from favour or a position of power or honour; discredited: *the disgraced city financier.*

disgraceful ▶ **adjective** shockingly unacceptable: *a disgraceful waste of money* | [with clause] *it is disgraceful that they should be denied unemployment benefits.*
– DERIVATIVES **disgracefully** adverb.

disgruntled ▶ **adjective** angry or dissatisfied: *judges receive letters from disgruntled members of the public.*
– DERIVATIVES **disgruntlement** noun.
– ORIGIN mid 17th cent.: from DIS- (as an intensifier) + dialect *gruntle* 'utter little grunts', from GRUNT.

disguise ▶ **verb** [with obj.] give (someone or oneself) a different appearance in order to conceal one's identity: *he **disguised himself as** a girl | Bryn was disguised as a priest* | (as adj. **disguised**) *a disguised reporter.* ■ make (something) unrecognizable by altering its appearance, sound, taste, or smell: *does holding a handkerchief over the mouthpiece really disguise your voice?* ■ conceal the nature or existence of (a feeling or situation): *he made no effort to disguise his contempt* | (as adj. **disguised**) *his voice was heavy with barely disguised emotion.*
▶ **noun** a means of altering one's appearance to conceal one's identity: *I put on dark glasses as a disguise.* ■ [mass noun] the state of having altered one's appearance in order to conceal one's identity: *I told them you were a policewoman **in disguise**.* ■ [mass noun] the concealing of one's true intentions or feelings: *the children looked at her without disguise.*
– ORIGIN Middle English (meaning 'change one's usual style of dress', with no implication of concealing one's identity): from Old French *desguisier*.

disgust ▶ **noun** [mass noun] a feeling of revulsion or strong disapproval aroused by something unpleasant or offensive: *the sight filled her with disgust | some of the audience walked out **in disgust**.*
▶ **verb** [with obj.] cause (someone) to feel revulsion or strong disapproval: *they were disgusted by the violence* | (as adj. **disgusted**) *a disgusted look.*
– DERIVATIVES **disgustedly** adverb.
– ORIGIN late 16th cent.: from early modern French *desgoust* or Italian *disgusto*, from Latin *dis-* (expressing reversal) + *gustus* 'taste'.

disgustful ▶ **adjective** old-fashioned term for DISGUSTING.

disgusting ▶ **adjective** arousing revulsion or strong indignation: *he had the most disgusting rotten teeth | I think the decision is disgusting.*
– DERIVATIVES **disgustingly** adverb, **disgustingness** noun.

dish ▶ **noun 1** a shallow, flat-bottomed container for cooking or serving food: *an ovenproof dish.* ■ the food contained or served in a dish: *a **dish of** sauté potatoes.* ■ a particular variety or preparation of food served as part of a meal: *fresh fish dishes.* ■ (**the dishes**) all the items that have been used in the preparation, serving, and eating of a meal: *I left the children to do the dishes.*
2 [usu. with modifier] a shallow, concave receptacle, especially one intended to hold a particular substance: *a soap dish.* ■ (also **dish aerial**) a bowl-shaped radio aerial. See also SATELLITE DISH.
3 informal a sexually attractive person: *I gather he's quite a dish.* ■ (**one's dish**) dated a thing that one enjoys or does well: *as a public relations man this was my dish and the campaign was right up my street.*
4 (**the dish**) informal information which is not generally known or available: *if he has the real dish I wish he'd tell us.*
5 [mass noun] concavity of a spoked wheel resulting from a difference in spoke tension on each side and consequent sideways displacement of the rim in relation to the hub.
▶ **verb** [with obj.] **1** (**dish something out/up**) put food on to a plate or plates before a meal: *Steve was dishing up vegetables.* ■ (**dish something out**) dispense something in a casual or indiscriminate way: *the banks dished out loans to all and sundry.* ■ (**dish something up**) offer or present something, especially something regarded as substandard: *is your ISP short-changing you by dishing up outdated and perhaps incorrect information?* ■ (**dish it out**) informal subject others to criticism or punishment: *you can dish it out but you can't take it.* ■ [no obj.] N. Amer. informal gossip or share intimate information: *groups gather to dish about romances.*
2 informal, chiefly Brit. utterly destroy or defeat: *the election interview dished Labour's chances.*
3 give concavity to (a wheel) by tensioning the spokes.
– PHRASES **dish the dirt** informal reveal or spread scandal or gossip.
– DERIVATIVES **dishful** noun (pl. **dishfuls**).
– ORIGIN Old English *disc* 'plate, bowl' (related to Dutch *dis*, German *Tisch* 'table'), based on Latin *discus* (see DISCUS).

dishabille /ˌdɪsaˈbiːl, -ˈbiː/ ▶ **noun** variant spelling of DÉSHABILLÉ.

disharmony ▶ **noun** [mass noun] lack of harmony or agreement.
– DERIVATIVES **disharmonious** adjective, **disharmoniously** adverb.

dishcloth ▶ **noun** a cloth for washing or drying dishes.

dishcloth gourd ▶ **noun** North American term for LOOFAH.

dishdasha /ˈdɪʃˌdaʃə/ (also **dishdash**) ▶ **noun** a long robe with long sleeves, worn by men from the Arabian peninsula.
– ORIGIN late 19th cent.: from Arabic *dišdāša*.

dishearten ▶ **verb** [with obj.] cause (someone) to lose determination or confidence: *the farmer was disheartened by the damage to his crops* | (as adj. **disheartened**) *a disheartened tone of voice.*
– DERIVATIVES **dishearteningly** adverb, **disheartenment** noun.

dished ▶ **adjective** having the shape of a dish; concave: *overloaded timber floors are likely to sag, producing a dished or sloping floor surface.*

dishevel ▶ **verb** (**dishevels**, **dishevelling**, **dishevelled**; US **dishevels**, **disheveling**, **disheveled**) [with obj.] make (a person's hair or clothes) untidy.
– ORIGIN probably a back-formation from DISHEVELLED.

dishevelled /dɪˈʃɛv(ə)ld/ (US **disheveled**) ▶ **adjective** (of a person's hair, clothes, or appearance) untidy; disordered: *a man with long dishevelled hair.*
– DERIVATIVES **dishevelment** noun.
– ORIGIN late Middle English: from obsolete *dishevely*, from Old French *deschevele*, past participle of *descheveler* (based on *chevel* 'hair', from Latin *capillus*). The original sense was 'having the hair uncovered';

later, referring to the hair itself, 'hanging loose', hence 'disordered, untidy'. Compare with UNKEMPT.

dishonest ▶ adjective behaving or prone to behave in an untrustworthy, deceitful, or insincere way: *he was a dishonest hypocrite prepared to exploit his family.* ■ intended to mislead or cheat: *he gave the editor a dishonest account of events.*
– DERIVATIVES **dishonestly** adverb.
– ORIGIN late Middle English (in the sense 'dishonourable, unchaste'): from Old French *deshoneste*, Latin *dehonestus*.

dishonesty ▶ noun (pl. **dishonesties**) [mass noun] deceitfulness shown in someone's character or behaviour: *the dismissal of thirty civil servants for dishonesty and misconduct.* ■ [count noun] a fraudulent or deceitful act: *they are tackling the divisions and dishonesties on the campus.*
– ORIGIN late Middle English (in the sense 'dishonour, sexual misconduct'): from Old French *deshoneste* 'indecency' (see DISHONEST).

dishonour (US **dishonor**) ▶ noun [mass noun] a state of shame or disgrace: *the incident brought dishonour upon the police.*
▶ verb [with obj.] **1** bring shame or disgrace on: *the ceremony was undertaken if a pupil had done something to dishonour the school.* ■ archaic violate the chastity of (a woman); rape.
2 fail to observe or respect (an agreement or principle): *the community has its own principles it can itself honour or dishonour.* ■ refuse to accept or pay (a cheque or a bill of exchange).
– ORIGIN Middle English: from Old French *deshonor* (noun), *deshonorer* (verb), based on Latin *honor* 'honour'.

dishonourable (US **dishonorable**) ▶ adjective bringing shame or disgrace on someone or something: *his crimes are petty and dishonourable.*
– DERIVATIVES **dishonourableness** noun, **dishonourably** adverb.

dishonourable discharge ▶ noun the dismissal of someone from the armed forces as a result of criminal or morally unacceptable actions.

dishpan ▶ noun N. Amer. a bowl in which dishes are washed.

dishrag ▶ noun N. Amer. a dishcloth.

dishwasher ▶ noun **1** a machine for washing dishes automatically.
2 a person employed to wash dishes.
– DERIVATIVES **dishwashing** noun & adjective.

dishwater ▶ noun [mass noun] dirty water in which dishes have been washed: *as for the coffee, dishwater would probably have tasted better.*
– PHRASES **dull as dishwater** see DULL.

dishy ▶ adjective (**dishier**, **dishiest**) informal **1** chiefly Brit. (of a man) sexually attractive.
2 N. Amer. scandalous or gossipy: *she's the perfect candidate for a dishy biography.*

disillusion /ˌdɪsɪˈl(j)uːʒ(ə)n/ ▶ noun [mass noun] disappointment resulting from the discovery that something is not as good as one believed it to be.
▶ verb [with obj.] cause (someone) to realize that a belief they hold is false: *if they think we have a magic formula to solve the problem, don't disillusion them.*

disillusioned ▶ adjective disappointed in someone or something that one discovers to be less good than one had believed: *the minority groups were completely **disillusioned with** the party.*

disillusionment ▶ noun [mass noun] a feeling of disappointment resulting from the discovery that something is not as good as one believed it to be: *the high abstention rate at the election reflected the voters' growing **disillusionment with** politics.*

disincarnate /ˌdɪsɪŋˈkɑːnət/ ▶ adjective another term for DISCARNATE.

disincentive ▶ noun a factor, especially a financial disadvantage, that discourages a particular action: *spiralling house prices are beginning to act as a disincentive to development.*
▶ adjective tending to discourage.

disincentivize (also **disincentivise**) ▶ verb [with obj.] discourage (a person or course of action) by removing an incentive: *such policies disincentivize those on average incomes.*

disinclination ▶ noun [in sing.] a reluctance or lack of enthusiasm: *Lucy felt a strong **disinclination to** talk about her engagement.*

disinclined ▶ adjective [predic., with infinitive] unwilling; reluctant: *the rural community was disinclined to abandon the old ways.*

disincorporate ▶ verb [with obj.] dissolve (a corporate body).

disinfect ▶ verb [with obj.] clean (something) with a disinfectant in order to destroy bacteria: *he disinfected and dressed the cut on his forehead.*
– DERIVATIVES **disinfection** noun.
– ORIGIN late 16th cent. (in the sense 'rid of infection'): from French *désinfecter*, from *dés-* (expressing reversal) + *infecter* 'to infect'.

disinfectant ▶ noun [mass noun] a chemical liquid that destroys bacteria.
▶ adjective causing disinfection: *cleansing and disinfectant products.*

disinfest ▶ verb [with obj.] rid (someone or something) of infesting vermin.
– DERIVATIVES **disinfestation** noun.

disinflation ▶ noun [mass noun] Economics reduction in the rate of inflation.
– DERIVATIVES **disinflationary** adjective.

disinformation ▶ noun [mass noun] false information which is intended to mislead, especially propaganda issued by a government organization to a rival power or the media.
– ORIGIN 1950s: formed on the pattern of Russian *dezinformatsiya*.

disingenuous /ˌdɪsɪnˈdʒɛnjʊəs/ ▶ adjective not candid or sincere, typically by pretending that one knows less about something than one really does: *this journalist was being somewhat disingenuous as well as cynical.*
– DERIVATIVES **disingenuity** noun, **disingenuously** adverb, **disingenuousness** noun.

disinherit ▶ verb (**disinherits**, **disinheriting**, **disinherited**) [with obj.] change one's will or take other steps to prevent (someone) from inheriting one's property.
– DERIVATIVES **disinheritance** noun.
– ORIGIN late Middle English (superseding earlier *disherit*): from DIS- (expressing removal) + *inherit* in the obsolete sense 'make someone an heir'.

disinhibit ▶ verb (**disinhibits**, **disinhibiting**, **disinhibited**) [with obj.] make less inhibited: *as well as disinhibiting me, he educated me.*
– DERIVATIVES **disinhibition** noun.

disintegrate /dɪsˈɪntɪɡreɪt/ ▶ verb [no obj.] **1** break up into small parts as the result of impact or decay: *our shoes had to last until they disintegrated on our feet.* ■ Physics undergo or cause to undergo disintegration at a subatomic level.
2 lose strength or cohesion and gradually fail: *their marriage disintegrated.*
– DERIVATIVES **disintegrative** adjective, **disintegrator** noun.

disintegration ▶ noun [mass noun] **1** the process of losing cohesion or strength: *the twin problems of economic failure and social disintegration.*
2 the process of coming to pieces: *the disintegration of infected cells.* ■ Physics a process in which a nucleus or other subatomic particle emits a smaller particle or divides into smaller particles.

disinter /ˌdɪsɪnˈtəː/ ▶ verb (**disinters**, **disinterring**, **disinterred**) [with obj.] dig up (something that has been buried, especially a corpse). ■ discover (something that is well hidden): *he has disinterred an important collection of writings.*
– DERIVATIVES **disinterment** noun.
– ORIGIN early 17th cent.: from French *désenterrer*, from *dis-* (expressing reversal) + *enterrer* 'to inter'.

disinterest ▶ noun [mass noun] **1** the state of not being influenced by personal involvement in something; impartiality: *I do not claim any scholarly disinterest with this book.*
2 lack of interest in something: *he chided Dennis for his **disinterest in** anything that is not his own idea.*

disinterested ▶ adjective **1** not influenced by considerations of personal advantage: *a banker is under an obligation to give disinterested advice.*
2 having or feeling no interest in something: *her father was so disinterested in her progress that he only visited the school once.*
– DERIVATIVES **disinterestedly** adverb, **disinterestedness** noun.
– ORIGIN early 17th cent.: past participle of the rare verb *disinterest* 'rid of interest or concern', from DIS- (expressing removal) + INTEREST.

> **USAGE** Nowhere are the battle lines more deeply drawn in usage questions than over the difference between **disinterested** and **uninterested**. According to traditional guidelines, **disinterested** should never be used to mean 'not interested' (i.e. it is not a synonym for **uninterested**) but only to mean 'impartial', as in *the judgements of **disinterested** outsiders are likely to be more useful*. Ironically, the earliest recorded sense of **disinterested** is for the disputed sense. Today, the 'incorrect' use of **disinterested** is widespread: around a quarter of citations in the Oxford English Corpus for **disinterested** are for this sense.

disintermediation /ˌdɪsɪntəmiːdɪˈeɪʃ(ə)n/ ▶ noun [mass noun] Economics reduction in the use of intermediaries between producers and consumers, for example by investing directly in the securities market rather than through a bank.
– DERIVATIVES **disintermediate** verb.

disinvent ▶ verb [with obj.] undo the invention of: *you can't disinvent nuclear power.*

disinvest ▶ verb [no obj.] withdraw or reduce an investment: *the oil industry began to disinvest, and oil share prices have fallen* | [with obj.] *they opposed the move to disinvest shares.*
– DERIVATIVES **disinvestment** noun.

disinvite ▶ verb [with obj.] withdraw or cancel an invitation to: *the White House called to disinvite him from the President's party.*

disinvoltura /ˌdɪsɪnvɒlˈtjʊərə/ ▶ noun [mass noun] literary self-assurance; lack of constraint.
– ORIGIN mid 19th cent.: from Italian, from *disinvolto* 'unembarrassed', from *disinvolgere* 'unwind'.

disjecta membra /dɪsˌdʒɛktə ˈmɛmbrə/ ▶ plural noun scattered fragments, especially of written work.
– ORIGIN Latin, alteration of *disjecti membra poetae* (used by Horace) 'limbs of a dismembered poet'.

disjoin ▶ verb [with obj.] separate or disunite: *they asked that their parish be disjoined from Lewis and added to Harris.*
– ORIGIN late Middle English: from Old French *desjoindre*, from Latin *disjungere*, from *dis-* (expressing reversal) + *jungere* 'to join'.

disjoint ▶ verb [with obj.] **1** disturb the cohesion or organization of: *the loss of the area disjointed military plans.*
2 dated take apart at the joints.
▶ adjective Mathematics (of two or more sets) having no elements in common.
– ORIGIN late Middle English (as an adjective in the sense 'disjointed'): from Old French *desjoint* 'separated', from the verb *desjoindre* (see DISJOIN).

disjointed ▶ adjective lacking a coherent sequence or connection: *piecing together disjointed fragments of information.*
– DERIVATIVES **disjointedly** adverb, **disjointedness** noun.

disjunct /ˈdɪsdʒʌŋ(k)t/ ▶ noun **1** Logic each of the terms of a disjunctive proposition.
2 Grammar another term for SENTENCE ADVERB.
▶ adjective disjoined and distinct from one another: *a series of disjunct chords.*
– ORIGIN late Middle English: from Latin *disjunctus* 'disjoined, separated', from the verb *disjungere*.

disjunction ▶ noun **1** a lack of correspondence or consistency: *there is a **disjunction between** the skills taught in education and those demanded in the labour market.*
2 [mass noun] Logic the relation of two distinct alternatives. ■ [count noun] a statement expressing the relation of two distinct alternatives (especially one using the word 'or').
– ORIGIN late Middle English: from Latin *disjunctio(n-)*, from *disjungere* 'disjoin' (see DISJUNCT).

disjunctive ▶ adjective **1** lacking connection or consistency: *the novel's disjunctive detail.*
2 Grammar (of a conjunction) expressing a choice between two mutually exclusive possibilities, for example *or* in *she asked if he was going or staying*. Compare with COPULATIVE. ■ Logic (of a proposition) expressing alternatives.
▶ noun Grammar a disjunctive conjunction or other word. ■ Logic a disjunctive proposition.
– DERIVATIVES **disjunctively** adverb.
– ORIGIN late Middle English (in sense 2 of the adjective): from Latin *disjunctivus*, from *disjunct-* 'disjoined' (see DISJUNCT).

disjuncture ▶ noun a separation or disconnection: *the monstrous disjuncture between his private and his public life.*
– ORIGIN late Middle English: from medieval Latin *disjunctura*, from Latin *disjunct-* 'disjoined' (see DISJUNCT).

disk ▶ noun US spelling of DISC, also widely used in computing contexts.

disk drive ▶ noun a device which allows a computer to read from and write on to computer disks.

diskette ▶ noun another term for FLOPPY.

Disko /ˈdɪskəʊ/ an island with extensive coal deposits on the west coast of Greenland. Its chief settlement is Godhavn.

disk operating system ▶ noun see **DOS**.

dislike ▶ verb [with obj.] feel distaste for or hostility towards: *she disliked any kind of unnecessary rudeness.*
▶ noun [mass noun] a feeling of distaste or hostility: *he made no secret of his dislike of the police | they had **taken a dislike to** each other.* ■ [count noun] a thing to which one feels aversion: *I know all his likes and dislikes.*
– DERIVATIVES **dislikeable** (also **dislikable**) adjective, **disliker** noun.

dislocate /ˈdɪsləkeɪt/ ▶ verb [with obj.] disturb the normal position of (a bone in a joint): *he dislocated his shoulder in training.* ■ disturb the organization of; disrupt: *trade was dislocated by a famine.* ■ move from its proper place or position: *the symbol is dislocated from its political context.*
– ORIGIN late 16th cent.: probably a back-formation from DISLOCATION, but perhaps from medieval Latin *dislocatus* 'moved from a former position', from the verb *dislocare*.

dislocation /ˌdɪslə(ʊ)ˈkeɪʃ(ə)n/ ▶ noun [mass noun] disturbance from a proper, original, or usual place or state: *rapid urban and industrial development brought immense social dislocation in its wake.* ■ injury or disability caused when the normal position of a joint or other part of the body is disturbed: *congenital dislocation of the hip | [count noun] dealing with fractures and dislocations.* ■ [count noun] Crystallography a displacement of part of a crystal lattice structure.
– ORIGIN late Middle English: from Old French, or from medieval Latin *dislocatio(n-)*, from the verb *dislocare* (see DISLOCATE), based on Latin *locare* 'to place'.

dislodge ▶ verb [with obj.] knock or force out of position: *the hoofs of their horses dislodged loose stones.* ■ remove from a position of power or authority: *government opponents failed to dislodge the Prime Minister.*
– DERIVATIVES **dislodgeable** adjective, **dislodgement** noun.
– ORIGIN late Middle English: from Old French *desloger*, from *des-* (expressing reversal) + *logier* 'encamp', from *loge* (see LODGE).

disloyal ▶ adjective failing to be loyal to a person, country, or organization to which one has obligations: *she was accused of being **disloyal to** the government.* ■ (of a remark or thought) demonstrating a lack of loyalty: *disloyal mutterings about his leadership.*
– DERIVATIVES **disloyally** adverb.
– ORIGIN late 15th cent.: from Old French *desloial*, from *des-* (expressing negation) + *loial* 'loyal'.

disloyalty ▶ noun [mass noun] the quality of not being loyal to a person, country, or organization; unfaithfulness: *an accusation of disloyalty and betrayal.*

dismal /ˈdɪzm(ə)l/ ▶ adjective causing a mood of gloom or depression: *the dismal weather made the late afternoon seem like evening.* ■ (of a person or their mood) gloomy. ■ informal pitifully or disgracefully bad: *he shuddered as he watched his team's dismal performance.*
– PHRASES **the dismals** archaic, informal low spirits: *a fit of the dismals.* **the dismal science** humorous economics.
– DERIVATIVES **dismally** adverb, **dismalness** noun.
– ORIGIN late Middle English: from earlier *dismal* (noun), denoting the two days in each month which in medieval times were believed to be unlucky, from Anglo-Norman French *dis mal*, from medieval Latin *dies mali* 'evil days'.

Dismal Swamp another name for GREAT DISMAL SWAMP.

dismantle ▶ verb [with obj.] take (a machine or structure) to pieces: *the engines were dismantled and the bits piled into a heap | figurative the old regime was dismantled.*
– DERIVATIVES **dismantlement** noun, **dismantler** noun.
– ORIGIN late 16th cent. (in the sense 'destroy the defensive capability of a fortification'): from Old French *desmanteler*, from *des-* (expressing reversal) + *manteler* 'fortify' (from Latin *mantellum* 'cloak').

dismast ▶ verb [with obj.] break or force down the mast or masts of (a ship): (as adj. **dismasted**) *a dismasted ship wallowing in stormy seas.*

dismay ▶ noun [mass noun] concern and distress caused by something unexpected: ***to his dismay**, she left him.*
▶ verb [with obj.] cause (someone) to feel concern and distress: *they were dismayed by the U-turn in policy | (as adj. **dismaying**) to most experts, such findings have been somewhat dismaying.*
– DERIVATIVES **dismayingly** adverb.
– ORIGIN Middle English: from Old French, based on Latin *dis-* (expressing negation) + the Germanic base of MAY[1].

dismember /dɪsˈmɛmbə/ ▶ verb [with obj.] **1** cut off the limbs of (a person or animal): *he watched a doctor dismember the body | (as adj. **dismembered**) a dismembered corpse.*
2 partition or divide up (a territory or organization): *the winning powers of World War I set out to dismember the Ottoman Empire.*
– DERIVATIVES **dismemberment** noun.
– ORIGIN Middle English: from Old French *desmembrer*, based on Latin *dis-* 'apart' + *membrum* 'limb'.

dismiss ▶ verb [with obj.] **1** order or allow to leave; send away: *she dismissed the taxi at the corner of the road.* ■ remove from employment or office, typically on the grounds of unsatisfactory performance: *the prime minister dismissed five members of his cabinet.* ■ [no obj.] (of a group assembled under someone's authority) disperse: *he told his company to dismiss.* ■ Cricket end the innings of (a batsman or a side): *Australia were dismissed for 118.*
2 treat as unworthy of serious consideration: *it would be easy to **dismiss** him as all brawn and no brain.* ■ deliberately cease to think about: *he suspected a double meaning in her words, but dismissed the thought.* ■ Law refuse further hearing to (a case): *the judge dismissed the case for lack of evidence.*
– DERIVATIVES **dismissible** adjective.
– ORIGIN late Middle English: from medieval Latin *dismiss-*, variant of Latin *dimiss-* 'sent away', from the verb *dimittere*.

dismissal ▶ noun **1** the act of ordering or allowing someone to leave: *their controversial **dismissal from** the competition.* ■ the act of removing someone from employment or office; discharge: *the dismissal of an employee | a claim for unfair dismissal.* ■ Cricket an instance of ending a batsman's innings or of having one's innings ended: *the dismissal of a batsman.*
2 the act of treating something as unworthy of serious consideration; rejection: *the government's dismissal of the report.* ■ Law a decision not to continue hearing a case: *the dismissal of the appeal.*

dismissive ▶ adjective feeling or showing that something is unworthy of consideration: *monetarist theory is dismissive of the need to control local spending | his dismissive attitude towards women left him isolated.*
– DERIVATIVES **dismissively** adverb, **dismissiveness** noun.

dismount ▶ verb **1** [no obj.] get off a horse, bicycle, or anything that one is riding. ■ [with obj.] cause to fall off a horse, bicycle, etc.: *his escort had dismounted a trooper.*
2 [with obj.] remove (something) from its support: *we have to dismount the pump.* ■ Computing make (a disk or disk drive) unavailable for use.
▶ noun Gymnastics a move in which a gymnast jumps off an apparatus or completes a floor exercise.
– ORIGIN mid 16th cent.: from DIS- + MOUNT[1], probably on the pattern of Old French *desmonter*, medieval Latin *dismontare*.

Disney, Walt (1901–66), American animator and film producer; full name *Walter Elias Disney*. He made his name with the creation of cartoon characters such as Mickey Mouse, Donald Duck, Goofy, and Pluto. *Snow White and the Seven Dwarfs* (1937) was the first full-length cartoon feature film with sound and colour. Other notable films: *Pinocchio* (1940), *Dumbo* (1941), and *Bambi* (1942).

disobedience ▶ noun [mass noun] failure or refusal to obey rules or someone in authority: *disobedience to law is sometimes justified.*

disobedient ▶ adjective refusing to obey rules or someone in authority: *Larry was stern with disobedient employees.*
– DERIVATIVES **disobediently** adverb.
– ORIGIN late Middle English: from Old French *desobedient*, based on Latin *oboedient-* 'obeying' (see OBEDIENT).

disobey ▶ verb [with obj.] fail to obey (rules, a command, or someone in authority): *around 1,000 soldiers had disobeyed orders and surrendered.*
– DERIVATIVES **disobeyer** noun.
– ORIGIN late Middle English: from Old French *desobeir*, based on Latin *oboedire* 'obey' (see OBEY).

disoblige ▶ verb [with obj.] offend (someone) by not acting in accordance with their wishes: *one didn't disoblige them if one could help it.*
– ORIGIN late 16th cent. (in the sense 'release from an obligation'): from French *désobliger*, based on Latin *obligare* 'oblige'.

disobliging ▶ adjective deliberately unhelpful; uncooperative. ■ unkind: *disobliging remarks about colleagues.*

disomy /dʌɪˈsəʊmi/ ▶ noun [mass noun] Genetics the condition of having a chromosome represented twice in a chromosomal complement.
– DERIVATIVES **disomic** adjective.
– ORIGIN late 20th cent.: from DI-[1] 'two' + -SOME[3] + -Y[3].

disorder ▶ noun [mass noun] a state of confusion: *the world's currency markets were in disorder.* ■ the breakdown of peaceful and law-abiding public behaviour: *recurrent food crises led to outbreaks of disorder.* ■ [count noun] Medicine an illness that disrupts normal physical or mental functions: *skin disorders | [mass noun] an improved understanding of mental disorder.*
▶ verb [with obj.] (usu. as adj. **disordered**) disrupt the systematic functioning or neat arrangement of: *she went to comb her disordered hair | his sleep is disordered.* ■ Medicine disrupt the normal functioning of: *a patient who is mentally disordered.*
– ORIGIN late 15th cent. (as a verb): alteration, influenced by ORDER, of earlier *disordain*, from Old French *desordener*, ultimately based on Latin *ordinare* 'ordain'.

disorderly ▶ adjective lacking organization; untidy: *his life was as disorderly as ever | a disorderly pile of books.* ■ involving or contributing to a breakdown of peaceful and law-abiding behaviour: *they had no intention of staging a disorderly protest.*
– DERIVATIVES **disorderliness** noun.

disorderly conduct ▶ noun [mass noun] Law unruly behaviour constituting a minor offence.

disorderly house ▶ noun Law or archaic a brothel.

disorganized (also **disorganised**) ▶ adjective not properly planned and controlled: *the campaign was hopelessly disorganized.* ■ unable to plan one's activities efficiently: *she's very muddled and disorganized.*
– DERIVATIVES **disorganization** noun, **disorganize** verb.

disorient /dɪsˈɔːrɪɛnt/ ▶ verb another term for DISORIENTATE.
– ORIGIN mid 17th cent.: from French *désorienter* 'turn from the east'.

disorientate ▶ verb [with obj.] (often as adj. **disorientated**) Brit. cause (someone) to lose their sense of direction: *when he emerged into the street he was totally disorientated.* ■ make (someone) feel confused: *being near him made her feel weak and disorientated.*
– DERIVATIVES **disorientation** noun.

disown ▶ verb [with obj.] refuse to acknowledge or maintain any connection with: *Lovell's rich family had disowned him because of his marriage.*
– DERIVATIVES **disownment** noun.

disparage /dɪˈsparɪdʒ/ ▶ verb [with obj.] regard or represent as being of little worth: *he never missed an opportunity to disparage his competitors.*
– DERIVATIVES **disparagement** noun.
– ORIGIN late Middle English (in the sense 'marry someone of unequal rank', also 'bring discredit on'): from Old French *desparagier* 'marry someone of unequal rank', based on Latin *par* 'equal'.

disparaging /dɪˈsparɪdʒɪŋ/ ▶ adjective expressing the opinion that something is of little worth; derogatory: *disparaging remarks about council houses.*
– DERIVATIVES **disparagingly** adverb.

disparate /ˈdɪsp(ə)rət/ ▶ adjective essentially different in kind; not able to be compared: *they inhabit disparate worlds of thought.* ■ containing elements very different from one another: *a culturally disparate country.*
▶ noun (**disparates**) archaic things so unlike that there is no basis for comparison.
– DERIVATIVES **disparately** adverb, **disparateness** noun.
– ORIGIN late Middle English: from Latin *disparatus* 'separated', from the verb *disparare*, from *dis-*

'apart' + *parare* 'to prepare'; influenced in sense by Latin *dispar* 'unequal'.

disparity ▶ noun (pl. **disparities**) a great difference: *economic* ***disparities between*** *different regions of the country* | [mass noun] *the arrangements could lead to disparity of treatment between companies.*
– ORIGIN mid 16th cent.: from French *disparité*, from late Latin *disparitas*, based on Latin *paritas* 'parity'.

dispassionate ▶ adjective not influenced by strong emotion, and so able to be rational and impartial: *she dealt with life's disasters in a calm, dispassionate way.*
– DERIVATIVES **dispassion** noun, **dispassionately** adverb, **dispassionateness** noun.

dispatch (also **despatch**) ▶ verb [with obj.] **1** send off to a destination or for a purpose: *he dispatched messages back to base* | [with obj. and infinitive] *the government dispatched 150 police to restore order.*
2 deal with (a task or opponent) quickly and efficiently: *the Welsh team were dispatched comfortably by the opposition.* ■ kill: *he dispatched the animal with one blow.*
▶ noun **1** [mass noun] the sending of someone or something to a destination or for a purpose: *a resolution authorizing the dispatch of a peacekeeping force.* ■ promptness and efficiency: *the situation might change, so he should proceed* ***with dispatch.***
2 an official report on state or military affairs: *in his battle dispatch he described the gunner's bravery.* ■ a report sent in from abroad by a journalist.
3 [mass noun] the killing of someone or something: *the executioner's merciful dispatch of his victims.*
– DERIVATIVES **dispatcher** noun.
– ORIGIN early 16th cent.: from Italian *dispacciare* or Spanish *despachar* 'expedite', from *dis-*, *des-* (expressing reversal) + the base of Italian *impacciare*, Spanish *empachar* 'hinder'.

dispatch box ▶ noun **1** (also **dispatch case**) chiefly Brit. a container for official state or military dispatches.
2 (**the Dispatch Box**) a box in the House of Commons next to which ministers stand when speaking.

dispatch rider ▶ noun Brit. a messenger who delivers urgent business documents or military dispatches by motorcycle or (formerly) on horseback.

dispel /dɪˈspɛl/ ▶ verb (**dispels**, **dispelling**, **dispelled**) [with obj.] make (a doubt, feeling, or belief) disappear: *the brightness of the day did nothing to dispel Elaine's dejection.*
– DERIVATIVES **dispeller** noun.
– ORIGIN late Middle English: from Latin *dispellere*, from *dis-* 'apart' + *pellere* 'to drive'.

dispensable ▶ adjective able to be replaced or done without; superfluous: *the captain's loss of form made him dispensable.* ■ (of a law or other rule) not mandatory but susceptible of being waived in special cases.
– DERIVATIVES **dispensability** noun.
– ORIGIN early 16th cent. (in the sense 'permissible in special circumstances'): from medieval Latin *dispensabilis*, from Latin *dispensare* (see DISPENSE).

dispensary /dɪˈspɛns(ə)ri/ ▶ noun (pl. **dispensaries**) **1** a room where medicines are prepared and provided.
2 a clinic provided by public or charitable funds.
– ORIGIN late 17th cent.: from medieval Latin *dispensarium*, neuter (used as a noun) of *dispensarius*, from Latin *dispensare* (see DISPENSE).

dispensation ▶ noun **1** [mass noun] exemption from a rule or usual requirement: *although she was too young, she was given special dispensation to play before her birthday.* ■ permission to be exempted from the laws or observances of the Church: *he received papal dispensation to hold a number of benefices* | [count noun] *the pope granted Henry a dispensation to marry Elizabeth of York.*
2 a political, religious, or social system prevailing at a particular time: *scholarship is conveyed to a wider audience than under the old dispensation.* ■ (in Christian theology) a divinely ordained system prevailing at a particular period of history: *the Mosaic dispensation.* ■ archaic an act of divine providence: *the laws to which the creator in all his dispensations conforms.*
3 [mass noun] the action of distributing or supplying something: *regulations controlling dispensation of medications.*
– DERIVATIVES **dispensational** adjective.
– ORIGIN late Middle English: from Latin *dispensatio(n-)*, from the verb *dispensare* (see DISPENSE).

dispensationalism ▶ noun [mass noun] Christian Theology belief in a system of historical progression, as revealed in the Bible, consisting of a series of stages in God's self-revelation and plan of salvation.
– DERIVATIVES **dispensationalist** noun.

dispense /dɪˈspɛns/ ▶ verb **1** [with obj.] distribute or provide (a service or information) to a number of people: *orderlies went round dispensing drinks.* ■ (of a machine or container) supply or release (a product or cash): *the machines dispense a range of drinks* | (as adj. **dispensing**) *a dispensing machine.* ■ (of a chemist) make up and give out (medicine) according to a doctor's prescription.
2 [no obj.] (**dispense with**) manage without or get rid of: *let's dispense with the formalities, shall we?* ■ give special exemption from (a law or rule): *the Secretary of State was empowered to dispense with the nationality requirement in individual cases.* ■ [with obj.] grant (someone) an exemption from a religious obligation: *the Pope personally nominated him as bishop,* ***dispensing him from*** *his impediment.*
– PHRASES **dispense with someone's services** dismiss someone from a job.
– ORIGIN late Middle English: via Old French from Latin *dispensare* 'continue to weigh out or disburse', from the verb *dispendere*, based on *pendere* 'weigh'.

dispenser ▶ noun a person or thing that dispenses something: *his role as protector of the weak and dispenser of justice.* ■ a person who prepares medicines in a dispensary. ■ [usu. with modifier] an automatic machine or container which is designed to release a specific amount of something: *a paper towel dispenser.*

dispensing chemist ▶ noun Brit. a person qualified to make up, advise on, and dispense medicine.

dispensing optician ▶ noun Brit. a person qualified to prescribe and dispense as well as to make glasses and contact lenses.

dispersal ▶ noun [mass noun] the action or process of distributing or spreading things or people over a wide area: *dispersal of pollen by the wind* | [count noun] *dispersals of archaic populations.* ■ the splitting up of a group of people, causing them to leave in different directions: *the dispersal of the crowd by mounted police.* ■ the splitting up and selling off of a collection of artefacts or books.

dispersant ▶ noun a liquid or gas used to disperse small particles in a medium.

disperse /dɪˈspəːs/ ▶ verb [with obj.] distribute or spread over a wide area: *storms can disperse seeds via high altitudes* | *caravan sites could be* ***dispersed among*** *trees so as to be out of sight.* ■ go or cause to go in different directions: [no obj.] *the crowd dispersed* | [with obj.] *the police used tear gas to disperse the protesters.* ■ (with reference to gas, smoke, mist, or cloud) thin out or cause to thin out and disappear: [no obj.] *the earlier mist had dispersed* | [with obj.] *winds dispersed the radioactive cloud high in the atmosphere.* ■ Physics divide (light) into constituents of different wavelengths.
▶ adjective [attrib.] Chemistry denoting a phase dispersed in another phase, as in a colloid.
– DERIVATIVES **disperser** noun, **dispersible** adjective, **dispersive** adjective.
– ORIGIN late Middle English: from Latin *dispers-* 'scattered', from the verb *dispergere*, from *dis-* 'widely' + *spargere* 'scatter, strew'.

dispersion ▶ noun [mass noun] **1** the action or process of distributing things or people over a wide area: *some seeds rely on birds for dispersion.* ■ the state of being dispersed: *the study looks at the dispersion of earnings with OECD member countries.* ■ Ecology the pattern of distribution of individuals within a habitat. ■ (also **the Dispersion**) another term for DIASPORA. ■ [count noun] a mixture of one substance dispersed in another medium: *the virus is transmitted in the dispersion of droplets which results from sneezing or coughing.*
2 Physics the separation of white light into colours or of any radiation according to wavelength.
3 Statistics the extent to which values of a variable differ from a fixed value such as the mean.
– ORIGIN late Middle English: from late Latin *dispersio(n-)*, from Latin *dispergere* (see DISPERSE).

dispirit /dɪˈspɪrɪt/ ▶ verb [with obj.] cause (someone) to lose enthusiasm or hope: *the army was dispirited by the uncomfortable winter conditions.*

dispirited /dɪˈspɪrɪtɪd/ ▶ adjective having lost enthusiasm and hope; disheartened: *she was determined to appear unworried in front of her dispirited family.*
– DERIVATIVES **dispiritedly** adverb, **dispiritedness** noun.

dispiriting /dɪˈspɪrɪtɪŋ/ ▶ adjective causing someone to lose enthusiasm and hope; disheartening: *it was a dispiriting occasion.*
– DERIVATIVES **dispiritingly** adverb.

displace ▶ verb [with obj.] take over the place, position, or role of: *he believes that books may be displaced by the electronic word.* ■ move (something) from its proper or usual position: *he seems to have displaced some vertebrae.* ■ force (someone) to leave their home, typically because of war, persecution, or natural disaster: *thousands of people have been displaced by the civil war.* ■ remove (someone) from a job or position of authority: *his aides were discredited and displaced.*
– DERIVATIVES **displacer** noun.
– ORIGIN mid 16th cent.: from Old French *desplacer*.

D

displaced person ▶ noun a person who is forced to leave their home country because of war or persecution; a refugee.

displacement ▶ noun [mass noun] **1** the action of moving something from its place or position: *vertical displacement of the shoreline* | [count noun] *a displacement of the vertebra at the bottom of the spine.* ■ the removal of someone or something by someone or something else which takes their place: *males may be able to resist displacement by other males.* ■ the enforced departure of people from their homes, typically because of war, persecution, or natural disaster: *the displacement of farmers by guerrilla activity.* ■ [count noun] the amount by which a thing is moved from a position: *a displacement of 6.8 metres along the San Andreas fault.*
2 the occupation by a submerged body or part of a body of a volume which would otherwise be occupied by a fluid. ■ the volume or weight of fluid that would fill the volume displaced by a floating ship, used as a measure of the ship's size: *the submarine has a surface displacement of 2,185 tons.* ■ technical the volume swept by a reciprocating system, as in a pump or engine.
3 Psychoanalysis the unconscious transfer of an intense emotion from one object to another: *this phobia was linked with the displacement of fear of his father.*
4 Physics the component of an electric field due to free separated charges, regardless of any polarizing effects. ■ the vector representing such a component. ■ the flux density of such an electric field.

displacement activity ▶ noun Psychology an animal or human activity that seems inappropriate, such as head-scratching when confused, considered to arise unconsciously when a conflict between antagonistic urges cannot be resolved.

displacement pump ▶ noun a pump in which liquid is moved out of the pump chamber by a moving surface or by the introduction of compressed air or gas.

displacement ton ▶ noun see TON[1] (sense 1 of the noun).

display ▶ verb [with obj.] put (something) in a prominent place in order that it may readily be seen: *the palace used to display a series of tapestries* | *a notice was displayed in the booking office.* ■ show (data or an image) on a computer, television, or other screen. ■ give a clear demonstration of (a quality, emotion, or skill): *both players displayed a great deal of spirit.* ■ [no obj.] (of a male bird, reptile, or fish) engage in a specialized pattern of behaviour that is intended to attract a mate.
▶ noun **1** a performance, show, or event staged for public entertainment: *a display of fireworks* | [as modifier] *an aerobatic display team.* ■ a collection of objects arranged for public viewing: *the museum houses an informative display of rocks* | [mass noun] *the latest in computer gadgetry was* ***on display.*** ■ a clear demonstration of an emotion, skill, or quality: *a hint of malice underlay his display of concern.* ■ [mass noun] the conspicuous exhibition of one's wealth; ostentation: *every clansman was determined to outdo the Campbells in display.* ■ a specialized pattern of behaviour by the males of certain species of birds, reptiles, and fish that is intended to attract a mate: *the teal were indulging in delightful courtship displays.* ■ [mass noun] Printing the arrangement and choice of type in a style intended to attract attention.
2 an electronic device for the visual presentation of data or images: *the colour display now costs £400.* ■ [mass noun] the process or facility of presenting data on a computer screen or other device. ■ the data or images shown on a computer screen or other device.
– DERIVATIVES **displayer** noun.
– ORIGIN Middle English (in the sense 'unfurl, unfold'): from Old French *despleier*, from Latin

displicare 'scatter, disperse' (in medieval Latin 'unfold'). Compare with DEPLOY.

display case (also **display cabinet**) ▸ noun a case, made all or partly of glass, for displaying items in a shop or museum for observation or inspection.

displayed ▸ adjective **1** (of information) shown on a computer screen or other device.
2 Heraldry (of a bird of prey) depicted with the wings extended. ▪ (of the wings of a bird of prey) extended.

display type ▸ noun [mass noun] large, bold, or eye-catching type used for headings or advertisements.

displease ▸ verb [with obj.] make (someone) feel annoyed or upset: *the tone of the letter displeased him* | (as adj. **displeasing**) *it was not entirely displeasing to be the centre of such a drama.*
– DERIVATIVES **displeasingly** adverb.
– ORIGIN late Middle English: from Old French *desplaisir*, from *des-* (expressing reversal) + *plaisir* 'to please', from Latin *placere*.

displeased ▸ adjective feeling or showing annoyance and displeasure: *he was **displeased with** your work.*

displeasure ▸ noun [mass noun] a feeling of annoyance or disapproval: *he started hanging around the local pubs, much to the displeasure of his mother.*
▸ verb [with obj.] archaic annoy; displease: *not for worlds would I do aught that might displeasure thee.*
– ORIGIN late Middle English: from Old French *desplaisir* (see DISPLEASE), influenced by PLEASURE.

disport ▸ verb [no obj.] archaic or humorous enjoy oneself unrestrainedly; frolic: *a painting of ladies **disporting themselves** by a lake.*
▸ noun [mass noun] archaic diversion from work or serious matters; recreation or amusement: *the King and all his Court were met for solace and disport.* ▪ [count noun] archaic a pastime, game, or sport.
– ORIGIN late Middle English: from Old French *desporter*, from *des-* 'away' + *porter* 'carry' (from Latin *portare*).

disposable ▸ adjective **1** (of an article) intended to be thrown away after use: *disposable nappies* | *a disposable razor.* ▪ (of a person or idea) able to be dispensed with; easily dismissed: *the poor performer is motivated by the fear that he or she is highly disposable.*
2 (chiefly of financial assets) readily available for the owner's use as required: *he made a mental inventory of his disposable assets.*
▸ noun an article designed to be thrown away after use: *don't buy disposables, such as cups and plates.*
– DERIVATIVES **disposability** noun.

disposable income ▸ noun [mass noun] income remaining after deduction of taxes and social security charges, available to be spent or saved as one wishes. Compare with DISCRETIONARY INCOME.

disposal ▸ noun [mass noun] **1** the action or process of getting rid of something: *the disposal of radioactive waste* | [count noun] *consents for disposals at sea.* ▪ [count noun] N. Amer. informal a waste-disposal unit: *garbage disposals that never worked.* ▪ the action of overcoming a rival or threat: *England's 4-0 disposal of Turkey.*
2 the sale of shares, property, or other assets.
3 literary the arrangement of something: *she brushed her hair carefully, as if her success lay in the sleek disposal of each gleaming black thread.*
– PHRASES **at one's disposal** available for one to use whenever or however one wishes: *a helicopter was put at their disposal.* **at someone's disposal** ready to assist the person concerned in any way they wish: *I am at your disposal until Sunday.*

dispose ▸ verb **1** [no obj.] (**dispose of**) get rid of by throwing away or giving or selling to someone else: *the waste is disposed of in the North Sea* | *people now have substantial assets to dispose of after their death.* ▪ informal kill: *she came up with schemes for disposing of her husband.* ▪ overcome (a rival or threat): *the Scottish champions were buoyant after they disposed of English champions Leeds.* ▪ informal consume (food or drink) quickly or enthusiastically: *she watched him dispose of a large slice of cheese.*
2 incline (someone) towards a particular activity or mood: *prolactin, a calming hormone, is released, **disposing** you **towards** sleep* | [with obj. and infinitive] *if you touch the female readers' hearts, it might dispose their husbands to be charitable.*
3 [with obj. and adverbial] arrange in a particular position: *the chief disposed his attendants in a circle.* ▪ [no obj.] literary determine the course of events: *the government proposed, but the trade union movement disposed.* [from the proverb 'Man proposes, (but) God disposes', translating Latin *Homo proponit, sed Deus disponit* (Thomas à Kempis's *De Imitatione Christi* I. xix).]
– DERIVATIVES **disposer** noun.
– ORIGIN late Middle English: from Old French *disposer*, from Latin *disponere* 'arrange', influenced by *dispositus* 'arranged' and Old French *poser* 'to place'.

disposed ▸ adjective [predic., usu. with infinitive] inclined or willing: *James didn't seem disposed to take the hint.* ▪ [with submodifier] having a specified attitude to or towards: *he is favourably **disposed towards** the proposals.*

disposition ▸ noun **1** a person's inherent qualities of mind and character: *a sweet-natured girl of a placid disposition* | *he has the disposition of a saint.* ▪ [often with infinitive] an inclination or tendency: *the Prime Minister has shown a disposition to alter policies* | *the judge's **disposition to** clemency.*
2 [mass noun] the way in which something is placed or arranged, especially in relation to other things: *the plan shows the disposition of the rooms.* ▪ the action of arranging people or things in a particular way: *the prerogative gives the state widespread powers regarding the disposition and control of the armed forces.* ▪ (**dispositions**) the stationing of troops ready for military action: *the new strategic dispositions of our forces.*
3 [mass noun] Law the distribution or transfer of property or money to someone, especially by bequest: *this is a tax which affects the disposition of assets on death.*
4 the power to deal with something as one pleases: *if Napoleon had had railways **at his disposition**, he would have been invincible.* ▪ archaic the determination of events by divine power.
– ORIGIN late Middle English: via Old French from Latin *dispositio(n-)*, from *disponere* 'arrange' (see DISPOSE).

dispositive /dɪsˈpɒzətɪv/ ▸ adjective relating to or bringing about the settlement of an issue or the disposition of property: *such litigation will rarely be dispositive of any question.* ▪ (in Scots and US law) dealing with the disposition of property by deed or will: *the testator had to make his signature after making the dispositive provisions.* ▪ (in US law) producing a final settlement or determination. ▪ dealing with the settling of international conflicts by an agreed disposition of disputed territories.
– ORIGIN late Middle English (in the sense 'contributory, conducive'): from Old French, or from medieval Latin *dispositivus*, from Latin *disposit-* 'arranged, disposed', from the verb *disponere* (see DISPOSE).

dispositor /dɪˈspɒzɪtə/ ▸ noun Astrology the planet which rules the sign in which another planet is located in a particular chart.

dispossess ▸ verb [with obj.] deprive (someone) of land, property, or other possessions: *they were **dispossessed of** lands and properties during the Reformation* | (as plural noun **the dispossessed**) *a champion of the poor and the dispossessed.* ▪ (in sport) deprive (a player) of the ball: *he dispossessed Hendrie and set off on a solo run.*
– DERIVATIVES **dispossession** noun.
– ORIGIN late 15th cent.: from Old French *despossesser*, from *des-* (expressing reversal) + *possesser* 'possess'.

dispraise ▸ noun [mass noun] censure; criticism: *this engraving has on occasion elicited dispraise for Raphael.*
▸ verb [with obj.] archaic express censure or criticism of: *men cannot praise Dryden without dispraising Coleridge.*
– ORIGIN Middle English: from Old French *despreisier*, based on late Latin *depreciare* (see DEPRECIATE).

disproof ▸ noun [mass noun] a set of facts that prove that something is untrue: *Rex was living disproof of the youth-preserving powers imputed to life in the college.* ▪ the action of proving that something is untrue: *the answer ought to turn on considerations that are susceptible to verification or disproof.*

disproportion ▸ noun an instance of being out of proportion with something else: *there is a disproportion between the scale of expenditure and any benefit that could possibly result.*
– DERIVATIVES **disproportional** adjective, **disproportionality** noun, **disproportionally** adverb.
– ORIGIN mid 16th cent.: from DIS- (expressing absence) + PROPORTION, on the pattern of French *disproportion*.

disproportionate¹ /ˌdɪsprəˈpɔːʃ(ə)nət/ ▸ adjective too large or too small in comparison with something else: *people on lower incomes spend a disproportionate amount of their income on fuel* | *persistent offenders were given sentences that were disproportionate to the offences they had committed.*
– DERIVATIVES **disproportionately** adverb, **disproportionateness** noun.
– ORIGIN mid 16th cent.: from DIS- (expressing absence) + PROPORTIONATE, on the pattern of French *disproportionné*.

disproportionate² /ˌdɪsprəˈpɔːʃ(ə)neɪt/ ▸ verb [no obj.] Chemistry undergo disproportionation: *water disproportionates to oxygen and hydrogen.*

disproportionation ▸ noun [mass noun] Chemistry a reaction in which a substance is simultaneously oxidized and reduced, giving two different products.

disprove ▸ verb [with obj.] prove that (something) is false: *he has given the Department of Transport two months to disprove the allegation.*
– DERIVATIVES **disprovable** adjective.
– ORIGIN late Middle English: from Old French *desprover*.

Dispur /dɪsˈpʊə/ a city in NE India, capital of the state of Assam; pop. 9,800 (est. 2009).

disputable ▸ adjective not established as a fact, and so open to question or debate: *whether it can be described as art criticism may be disputable.*
– DERIVATIVES **disputably** adverb.
– ORIGIN late 15th cent.: from Latin *disputabilis*, from the verb *disputare* 'to estimate', later 'to dispute' (see DISPUTE).

disputation ▸ noun [mass noun] debate or argument: *promoting consensus rather than disputation* | [count noun] *a lengthy disputation about the rights and wrongs of a particular request.* ▪ formal academic debate: *the founding father of logical disputation* | [count noun] *scholastic disputations.*
– DERIVATIVES **disputative** adjective.
– ORIGIN late Middle English: from Latin *disputatio(n-)*, from the verb *disputare* (see DISPUTE).

disputatious ▸ adjective fond of having heated arguments: *it's a congenial hang-out for disputatious academics.*
– DERIVATIVES **disputatiously** adverb, **disputatiousness** noun.

dispute ▸ noun /dɪˈspjuːt, ˈdɪspjuːt/ a disagreement or argument: *a territorial dispute between the two countries* | [mass noun] *the Commission is **in dispute with** the government.* ▪ a disagreement between management and employees that leads to industrial action: *an industrial dispute.*
▸ verb /dɪˈspjuːt/ [with obj.] **1** argue about (something): *the point has been much disputed* | [no obj.] *he taught and **disputed with** local poets.* ▪ question whether (a statement or alleged fact) is true or valid: *the accusations are not disputed* | [with clause] *the estate disputes that it is responsible for the embankment.*
2 compete for; strive to win: *the two drivers crashed while disputing the lead.* ▪ archaic resist (a landing or advance): *I formed my line and prepared to dispute the advance of the foe.*
– PHRASES **beyond** (or **without**) **dispute** certain or certainly: *the main part of his argument was beyond dispute.* **open to dispute** not definitely decided.
– DERIVATIVES **disputant** noun, **disputer** noun.
– ORIGIN Middle English: via Old French from Latin *disputare* 'to estimate' (in late Latin 'to dispute'), from *dis-* 'apart' + *putare* 'reckon'.

disqualification ▸ noun [mass noun] the action of disqualifying or the state of being disqualified. ▪ [count noun] a fact that disqualifies someone from a position or activity: *such an offence is no longer a disqualification for office.*

disqualify ▸ verb (**disqualifies**, **disqualifying**, **disqualified**) [with obj.] declare (someone) ineligible for an office, activity, or competition because of an offence or infringement: *he was **disqualified from** driving for six months* | *she was disqualified after failing a drugs test* | (as adj. **disqualified**) *he was hit by a disqualified driver.* ▪ (of a feature or characteristic) make (someone) unsuitable for an office or activity: *a heart murmur disqualified him for military service.*

disquiet ▸ noun [mass noun] a feeling of worry or unease: *public disquiet about animal testing.*
▸ verb [with obj.] (usu. as adj. **disquieted**) make (someone) worried or uneasy: *she felt disquieted at the lack of interest the girl had shown.*

disquieting ▸ adjective inducing feelings of anxiety or worry: *he found Jean's gaze disquieting.*
– DERIVATIVES **disquietingly** adverb.

disquietude ▸ noun [mass noun] a state of uneasiness or anxiety.

disquisition /ˌdɪskwɪˈzɪʃ(ə)n/ ▸ **noun** a long or elaborate essay or discussion on a particular subject: *nothing can kill a radio show quicker than a disquisition on intertextual analysis.*
– DERIVATIVES **disquisitional adjective** (archaic).
– ORIGIN late 15th cent.: via French from Latin *disquisitio(n-)* 'investigation', based on *quaerere* 'seek'. The original sense was 'topic for investigation', whence 'discourse in which a subject is investigated' (mid 17th cent.).

Disraeli /dɪzˈreɪli/, Benjamin, 1st Earl of Beaconsfield (1804–81), British Conservative statesman; Prime Minister 1868 and 1874–80. He was largely responsible for the introduction of the second Reform Act (1867). He also ensured that Britain bought a controlling interest in the Suez Canal (1875) and made Queen Victoria Empress of India.

disrate /dɪsˈreɪt/ ▸ **verb** [with obj.] reduce (a sailor) to a lower rank.

disregard ▸ **verb** [with obj.] pay no attention to; ignore: *the body of evidence is too substantial to disregard.*
▸ **noun** [mass noun] the action or state of paying no attention to something: *blatant* ***disregard for*** *the law.*
– DERIVATIVES **disregardful adjective.**

disrelish archaic ▸ **noun** [mass noun] a feeling of dislike or distaste: *disrelish for any pursuit is ample reason for abandoning it.*
▸ **verb** [with obj.] regard with dislike or distaste: *I am not surprised that some members of the House should disrelish your report.*

disremember ▸ **verb** [with obj.] US dialect fail to remember: *mostly what you disremember ain't worth the trouble to call to mind.*

disrepair ▸ **noun** [mass noun] poor condition of a building or structure due to neglect: *the station gradually* ***fell into disrepair.***

disreputable ▸ **adjective** not considered to be respectable in character or appearance: *he was heavy, grubby, and vaguely disreputable.*
– DERIVATIVES **disreputableness noun, disreputably adverb.**

disrepute /ˌdɪsrɪˈpjuːt/ ▸ **noun** [mass noun] the state of being held in low esteem by the public: *one of the top clubs in the country is bringing the game* ***into disrepute.***

disrespect ▸ **noun** [mass noun] lack of respect or courtesy: *growing disrespect for the rule of law.*
▸ **verb** [with obj.] informal, chiefly N. Amer. show a lack of respect for; insult: *a young brave who disrespects his elders.*

disrespectful ▸ **adjective** showing a lack of respect or courtesy; impolite: *a deeply disrespectful attitude towards women.*
– DERIVATIVES **disrespectfully adverb.**

disrobe ▸ **verb** [no obj.] take off one's clothes: *she began to disrobe.* ■ take off official vestments or regalia: *they walked to the vestry to disrobe.* ■ [with obj.] undress (someone).
– ORIGIN late Middle English: from **DIS-** (expressing reversal) + **ROBE**, perhaps on the pattern of French *desrober.*

disrupt ▸ **verb** [with obj.] interrupt (an event, activity, or process) by causing a disturbance or problem: *flooding disrupted rail services.* ■ drastically alter or destroy the structure of: *alcohol can disrupt the chromosomes of an unfertilized egg.*
– DERIVATIVES **disrupter** (also **disruptor**) **noun.**
– ORIGIN late Middle English: from Latin *disrupt-* 'broken apart', from the verb *disrumpere.*

disruption ▸ **noun** [mass noun] disturbance or problems which interrupt an event, activity, or process: *the scheme was planned to minimize disruption* | [count noun] *there had been no delays or* ***disruptions to*** *flights.*

disruptive ▸ **adjective** causing or tending to cause disruption: *disruptive pupils* | *the hours of work are* ***disruptive to*** *home life.* ■ innovative or groundbreaking: *breaking a disruptive technology into the market is never easy.*
– DERIVATIVES **disruptively adverb, disruptiveness noun.**

> **WORD TRENDS** Is it bad to be *disruptive*? The Oxford English Corpus would suggest it is, with *violent, destructive, dangerous,* and *antisocial* all commonly paired with the word. However, a new form of **disruption** is emerging—one that many people are welcoming and even encouraging. *Disruptive behaviour* may be the most common combination in the Corpus, but it is closely followed by *disruptive technology*, a concept first described in 1995. The new sense refers to innovations that improve products or services in an unexpected way, and thus disrupt the established market: *a market ripe for breakout disruptive technologies* | *disruptive innovations often see failure before success.*

diss ▸ **verb & noun** variant spelling of **DIS.**

dissatisfaction ▸ **noun** [mass noun] lack of satisfaction: *widespread public* ***dissatisfaction with*** *incumbent politicians.*

dissatisfied ▸ **adjective** not content or happy with something: *his parents are* ***dissatisfied with*** *the quality of tuition on offer* | *dissatisfied customers.*
– DERIVATIVES **dissatisfiedly adverb.**

dissatisfy ▸ **verb** (**dissatisfies, dissatisfying, dissatisfied**) [with obj.] fail to satisfy (someone): *what is it about these words that dissatisfies you?*

dissaving ▸ **noun** [mass noun] chiefly N. Amer. the action of spending more than one has earned in a given period. ■ (**dissavings**) the excess amount spent.

dissect /dʌɪˈsɛkt, dɪ-/ ▸ **verb** [with obj.] methodically cut up (a body or plant) in order to study its internal parts. ■ analyse (a text or idea) in minute detail: *he dissected the Prime Minister's statement and revealed the truth behind it.*
– DERIVATIVES **dissector noun.**
– ORIGIN late 16th cent.: from Latin *dissect-* 'cut up', from the verb *dissecare*, from *dis-* 'apart' + *secare* 'to cut'.

dissected ▸ **adjective 1** having been cut up for anatomical study.
2 having a divided form or structure, in particular: ■ Botany (of a leaf) divided into many deep lobes. ■ Geology (of a plateau or upland) divided by a number of deep valleys.

dissection ▸ **noun** [mass noun] the action of dissecting a body or plant to study its internal parts: *the dissection of animals for scientific research.* ■ very detailed analysis of a text or idea: *this dissection of modern relationships.*

dissemble /dɪˈsɛmb(ə)l/ ▸ **verb** [no obj.] conceal or disguise one's true feelings or beliefs: *an honest, sincere person with no need to dissemble.* ■ [with obj.] disguise or conceal (a feeling or intention): *she smiled, dissembling her true emotion.*
– DERIVATIVES **dissemblance noun, dissembler noun.**
– ORIGIN late Middle English: alteration (suggested by **SEMBLANCE**) of obsolete *dissimule*, via Old French from Latin *dissimulare* 'disguise, conceal'.

disseminate /dɪˈsɛmɪneɪt/ ▸ **verb** [with obj.] spread (something, especially information) widely: *health authorities should foster good practice by disseminating information.* ■ (usu. as adj. **disseminated**) spread throughout an organ or the body: *disseminated colonic cancer.*
– DERIVATIVES **disseminator noun.**
– ORIGIN late Middle English: from Latin *disseminat-* 'scattered', from the verb *disseminare*, from *dis-* 'abroad' + *semen, semin-* 'seed'.

disseminated sclerosis ▸ **noun** see **SCLEROSIS.**

dissemination /dɪˌsɛmɪˈneɪʃn/ ▸ **noun** [mass noun] the act of spreading something, especially information, widely; circulation: *dissemination of public information.*

disseminule /dɪˈsɛmɪnjuːl/ ▸ **noun** Botany a part of a plant that serves to propagate it, such as a seed or a fruit.
– ORIGIN early 20th cent.: formed irregularly from *dissemination* (see **DISSEMINATE**) + **-ULE.**

dissension /dɪˈsɛnʃ(ə)n/ ▸ **noun** [mass noun] disagreement that leads to discord: *this manoeuvre caused dissension within feminist ranks* | [count noun] *the mill was the cause of a dissension in 1620.*
– ORIGIN Middle English: via Old French from Latin *dissensio(n-)*, from the verb *dissentire* (see **DISSENT**).

dissensus /dɪˈsɛnsəs/ ▸ **noun** [mass noun] widespread dissent: *the 'shame' attached to being held responsible for social dissensus.*
– ORIGIN 1960s: from **DIS-** (expressing reversal) + a shortened form of **CONSENSUS**, or from Latin *dissensus* 'disagreement'.

dissent /dɪˈsɛnt/ ▸ **noun** [mass noun] the holding or expression of opinions at variance with those commonly or officially held: *there was no* ***dissent from*** *this view.* ■ (also **Dissent**) refusal to accept the doctrines of an established or orthodox Church; nonconformity. ■ (in sport) the offence of expressing disagreement with the referee's decision: *he was sent off for dissent.* ■ [count noun] US a statement by a judge giving reasons as to why he or she disagrees with a decision made by the other judges in a court case.
▸ **verb** [no obj.] hold or express opinions that are at variance with those commonly or officially held: *two members* ***dissented from*** *the majority* | (as adj. **dissenting**) *there were a couple of dissenting voices.* ■ disagree with the doctrine of an established or orthodox Church.
– ORIGIN late Middle English: from Latin *dissentire* 'differ in sentiment'.

dissenter ▸ **noun** a person who dissents. ■ (**Dissenter**) Brit. historical a member of a non-established Church; a Nonconformist.

dissentient /dɪˈsɛnʃɪənt, -ʃ(ə)nt/ ▸ **adjective** in opposition to a majority or official opinion: *dissentient voices were castigated as 'hopeless bureaucrats'.*
▸ **noun** a person who opposes a majority or official opinion.
– ORIGIN early 17th cent.: from Latin *dissentient-* 'differing in opinion', from the verb *dissentire.*

dissepiment /dɪˈsɛpɪm(ə)nt/ ▸ **noun** Botany & Zoology a partition in a part or organ; a septum.
– ORIGIN early 18th cent.: from Latin *dissaepimentum*, from *dissaepire* 'make separate', from *dis-* (expressing separation) + *saepire* 'divide by a hedge'.

dissertation /ˌdɪsəˈteɪʃ(ə)n/ ▸ **noun** a long essay on a particular subject, especially one written for a university degree or diploma.
– ORIGIN early 17th cent. (in the sense 'discussion, debate'): from Latin *dissertatio(n-)*, from *dissertare* 'continue to discuss', from *disserere* 'examine, discuss'.

disservice ▸ **noun** [usu. in sing.] a harmful action: *you have* ***done a disservice to*** *the African people by ignoring this fact.*

dissever /dɪ(s)ˈsɛvə/ ▸ **verb** [with obj.] rare divide or sever (something): *a European tradition which had not been willing to dissever reason from the law of nature.*
– DERIVATIVES **disseverance noun, disseverment noun.**
– ORIGIN Middle English (in the sense 'separate'): from Old French *dessevrer*, from late Latin *disseparare*, from *dis-* (expressing intensive force) + Latin *separare* 'to separate'.

dissidence /ˈdɪsɪd(ə)ns/ ▸ **noun** [mass noun] protest against official policy.
– ORIGIN mid 17th cent.: from Latin *dissidentia*, from *dissident-* 'sitting apart' (see **DISSIDENT**).

dissident /ˈdɪsɪd(ə)nt/ ▸ **noun** a person who opposes official policy, especially that of an authoritarian state.
▸ **adjective** in opposition to official policy: *the measure was supported by dissident Tories.*
– ORIGIN mid 16th cent. (in the sense 'differing in opinion or character'): from Latin *dissident-* 'sitting apart, disagreeing', from *dis-* 'apart' + *sedere* 'sit'.

dissimilar ▸ **adjective** not the same; different: *a collection of dissimilar nations lacking overall homogeneity* | *the pleasures of the romance novel are* ***not dissimilar from*** *those of the chocolate bar.*
– DERIVATIVES **dissimilarly adverb.**
– ORIGIN late 16th cent.: from **DIS-** (expressing reversal) + **SIMILAR**, on the pattern of Latin *dissimilis*, French *dissimilaire.*

dissimilarity ▸ **noun** difference; variance: *the similarity or* ***dissimilarity between*** *humans and other animals.*

dissimilate /dɪˈsɪmɪleɪt/ ▸ **verb** [with obj.] Linguistics change (a sound or sounds in a word) to another when the word originally had identical sounds near each other (e.g. in *taper*, which derives from *papyrus*, the *p* is dissimilated to *t*). ■ [no obj.] (of a sound) undergo such a change: *the first 'r' dissimilates to 'l'.*
– DERIVATIVES **dissimilation noun, dissimilatory** /dɪˈsɪmɪlət(ə)ri/ **adjective.**
– ORIGIN mid 19th cent.: from **DIS-** (expressing reversal) + Latin *similis* 'like, similar', on the pattern of *assimilate.*

dissimilitude /ˌdɪsɪˈmɪlɪtjuːd/ ▸ **noun** [mass noun] formal dissimilarity or diversity.
– ORIGIN late Middle English: from Latin *dissimilitudo*, from *dissimilis* 'unlike', from *dis-* (expressing reversal) + *similis* 'like, similar'.

dissimulate /dɪˈsɪmjʊleɪt/ ▸ **verb** [with obj.] conceal or disguise (one's thoughts, feelings, or character): *a country gentleman who dissimulates his wealth beneath ragged pullovers* | [no obj.] *now that they have power, they no longer need to dissimulate.*
– DERIVATIVES **dissimulator noun.**

D

D

– ORIGIN late Middle English: from Latin *dissimulat-* 'hidden, concealed', from the verb *dissimulare*.

dissimulation /dɪˌsɪmjʊˈleɪʃ(ə)n/ ▶ noun [mass noun] concealment of one's thoughts, feelings, or character; pretence: *an attempt at dissimulation*.

dissipate /ˈdɪsɪpeɪt/ ▶ verb **1** (with reference to a feeling or emotion) disappear or cause to disappear: [no obj.] *the concern she'd felt for him had wholly dissipated* | [with obj.] *he wanted to dissipate his anger*. ■ disperse or scatter: *the cloud of smoke dissipated*.
2 [with obj.] waste or fritter away (money, energy, or resources). ■ Physics cause (energy) to be lost through its conversion to heat.
– DERIVATIVES **dissipative** adjective, **dissipator** (also **dissipater**) noun.
– ORIGIN late Middle English: from Latin *dissipat-* 'scattered', from the verb *dissipare*, from *dis-* 'apart, widely' + *supare* 'to throw'.

dissipated ▶ adjective (of a person or way of life) overindulging in sensual pleasures: *dissipated behaviour*.

dissipation ▶ noun [mass noun] **1** dissipated living: *a descent into drunkenness and sexual dissipation*.
2 the squandering of money, energy, or resources: *the dissipation of the country's mineral wealth*. ■ Physics loss of energy through its conversion into heat.
– ORIGIN late Middle English (in the sense 'complete disintegration'): from Latin *dissipatio(n-)*, from the verb *dissipare* (see DISSIPATE).

dissociable ▶ adjective able to be dissociated; separable: *language and cognition are not dissociable*.
– ORIGIN mid 19th cent.: from French, from Latin *dissociabilis*, from *dissociare* 'to separate'.

dissociate /dɪˈsəʊʃɪeɪt, -sɪ-/ ▶ verb [with obj.] **1** (especially in abstract contexts) disconnect or separate: *the word 'spiritual' has become for many dissociated from religion*. ■ (**dissociate oneself from**) declare that one is not connected with or a supporter of (someone or something): *he took pains to dissociate himself from the religious radicals*. ■ Psychiatry split off (a component of mental activity) to act as an independent part of mental life.
2 Chemistry (with reference to a molecule) split into separate smaller atoms, ions, or molecules, especially reversibly: [with obj.] *these compounds are dissociated by solar radiation to yield atoms of chlorine*.
– DERIVATIVES **dissociative** adjective.
– ORIGIN mid 16th cent.: from Latin *dissociat-* 'separated', from the verb *dissociare*, from *dis-* (expressing reversal) + *sociare* 'join together' (from *socius* 'companion').

dissociated personality ▶ noun another term for MULTIPLE-PERSONALITY DISORDER.

dissociation /dɪˌsəʊʃɪˈeɪʃ(ə)n, -sɪ-/ ▶ noun [mass noun] the action of disconnecting or separating or the state of being disconnected: *we in the West honour a long-standing dissociation between church and state*. ■ Chemistry the splitting of a molecule into smaller molecules, atoms, or ions, especially by a reversible process. ■ Psychiatry separation of normally related mental processes, resulting in one group functioning independently from the rest, leading in extreme cases to disorders such as multiple personality: [count noun] *the dissociations that one can observe in neuropsychological patients*.

dissociation constant ▶ noun Chemistry a quantity expressing the extent to which a particular substance in solution is dissociated into ions, equal to the product of the concentrations of the respective ions divided by the concentration of the undissociated molecule.

dissoluble ▶ adjective able to be dissolved, loosened, or disconnected: *permitting divorce would render every marriage dissoluble*.
– DERIVATIVES **dissolubility** noun.
– ORIGIN mid 16th cent.: from Latin *dissolubilis*, from the verb *dissolvere* (see DISSOLVE).

dissolute /ˈdɪsəluːt/ ▶ adjective (of a person or a way of life) overindulging in sensual pleasures: *unfortunately, his heir was feckless and dissolute*.
– DERIVATIVES **dissolutely** adverb, **dissoluteness** noun.
– ORIGIN late Middle English: from Latin *dissolutus* 'disconnected, loose', from the verb *dissolvere* (see DISSOLVE).

dissolution ▶ noun [mass noun] **1** the action of formally ending or dismissing an assembly, partnership, or official body: *the dissolution of their marriage* | [count noun] *the Prime Minister asked the queen for a dissolution of Parliament*. ■ technical the action or process of dissolving or being dissolved: *minerals susceptible to dissolution*. ■ disintegration; decomposition: *the dissolution of the flesh*. ■ archaic death.
2 debauched living; dissipation: *an advanced state of dissolution*.
– ORIGIN late Middle English: from Latin *dissolutio(n-)*, from the verb *dissolvere* (see DISSOLVE).

dissolution of the monasteries the abolition of monasteries in England and Wales by Henry VIII under two Acts (1536, 1539), in order to replenish his treasury by vesting monastic assets in the Crown and to establish royal supremacy in ecclesiastical affairs.

dissolve ▶ verb **1** (with reference to a solid) become or cause to become incorporated into a liquid so as to form a solution: [no obj.] *glucose dissolves easily in water* | [with obj.] *dissolve a stock cube in a pint of hot water*. ■ [no obj.] disappear: *my courage dissolved*. ■ [no obj.] (**dissolve into/in**) subside uncontrollably into (an expression of strong feelings): *she suddenly dissolved into floods of tears*. ■ [no obj.] (**dissolve into/to**) (of an image or scene in a film) change gradually to (another): *the scene dissolves into a series of shots of the Morgan family*.
2 [with obj.] close down or dismiss (an assembly or official body). ■ annul or end (a partnership or marriage).
▶ noun an act or instance of moving gradually from one image or scene in a film to another.
– DERIVATIVES **dissolvable** adjective.
– ORIGIN late Middle English (also in the sense 'break down into component parts'): from Latin *dissolvere*, from *dis-* 'apart' + *solvere* 'loosen or solve'.

dissolvent ▶ noun a substance that dissolves something else: *the experience of death could strengthen family ties, rather than act as a dissolvent*.
– ORIGIN mid 17th cent.: from Latin *dissolvent-* 'dissolving', from the verb *dissolvere* (see DISSOLVE).

dissonance /ˈdɪs(ə)nəns/ ▶ noun [mass noun] Music lack of harmony among musical notes: *an unusual degree of dissonance for such choral styles* | [count noun] *a session full of jangling dissonances*. ■ lack of agreement or harmony between people or things: *the party faithful might be willing to put up with such dissonance among their candidates*.
– ORIGIN late Middle English: from Old French, from late Latin *dissonantia*, from Latin *dissonant-* 'disagreeing in sound', from the verb *dissonare*.

dissonant ▶ adjective Music lacking harmony: *irregular, dissonant chords*. ■ unsuitable or unusual in combination; clashing: *Jackson employs both harmonious and dissonant colour choices*.
– DERIVATIVES **dissonantly** adverb.
– ORIGIN late Middle English (in the sense 'clashing'): from Old French, or from Latin *dissonant-* 'being discordant', from the verb *dissonare*, from *dis-* 'apart' + *sonare* 'to sound'.

dissuade /dɪˈsweɪd/ ▶ verb [with obj.] persuade (someone) not to take a particular course of action: *his friends tried to* ***dissuade*** *him* ***from*** *flying*.
– DERIVATIVES **dissuader** noun, **dissuasion** noun, **dissuasive** adjective.
– ORIGIN late 15th cent. (in the sense 'advise against'): from Latin *dissuadere*, from *dis-* (expressing reversal) + *suadere* 'advise, persuade'.

dissyllable /dɪˈsɪləb(ə)l/ ▶ noun variant spelling of DISYLLABLE.
– DERIVATIVES **dissyllabic** adjective.

dissymmetry ▶ noun (pl. **dissymmetries**) [mass noun] lack of symmetry. ■ technical the symmetrical relation of mirror images, the left and right hands, or crystals with two corresponding forms.
– DERIVATIVES **dissymmetric** adjective, **dissymmetrical** adjective.

distaff /ˈdɪstɑːf/ ▶ noun **1** a stick or spindle on to which wool or flax is wound for spinning.
2 [as modifier] of or concerning women: *marriage is still the passport to distaff power*.
– PHRASES **the distaff side** the female side of a family: *the family title could be passed down through the distaff side*. The opposite of THE SPEAR SIDE.
– ORIGIN Old English *distæf*: the first element is apparently related to Middle Low German *dise*, *disene* 'distaff, bunch of flax'; the second is STAFF[1]. Sense 2 arose because spinning was traditionally done by women.

distal /ˈdɪst(ə)l/ ▶ adjective Anatomy situated away from the centre of the body or from the point of attachment: *the distal end of the tibia*. The opposite of PROXIMAL. ■ Geology relating to or denoting the outer part of an area affected by geological activity.
– DERIVATIVES **distally** adverb.
– ORIGIN early 19th cent.: from DISTANT, on the pattern of words such as *dorsal*.

distance ▶ noun **1** the length of the space between two points: *I cycled the short distance home* | *you may have to walk long distances*. ■ [mass noun] the condition of being far off; remoteness: *distance makes things look small*. ■ a far-off point: *watching them* ***from a distance***. ■ (**the distance**) the more remote part of what is visible or discernible: *I heard police sirens* ***in the distance*** | *they sped off* ***into the distance***. ■ an interval of time: *the sort of goal which remains in the memory even at a distance of six years*.
2 the full length of a race: *he claimed the 100 m title in only his second race over the distance*. ■ Brit. Horse Racing a space of more than twenty lengths between two finishers in a race: *he stormed home by a distance in the Handicap Chase*. ■ (**the distance**) Brit. a length of 240 yards from the winning post on a racecourse. ■ N. Amer. Horse Racing the distance from the winning post which a horse must have reached when the winner finishes in order to qualify for a subsequent heat. ■ (**the distance**) Boxing the scheduled length of a fight: *he has won his first five fights* ***inside the distance***.
3 [mass noun] the avoidance of familiarity; reserve: *a mix of warmth and distance makes a good neighbour*.
▶ verb [with obj.] **1** make (someone or something) far off or remote in position or nature: *her mother wished to* ***distance*** *her* ***from*** *the rough village children*. ■ (**distance oneself from**) declare that one is not connected with or a supporter of (someone or something): *he sought to distance himself from the proposals*.
2 N. Amer. Horse Racing beat (a horse) by a distance.
– PHRASES **distance lends enchantment to the view** proverb things look better from further away. **go the distance** Boxing complete a fight without being knocked out. ■ (of a boxing match) last the scheduled length. ■ Baseball pitch for the entire length of a game. ■ last for a long time: *this amplifier system should go the distance*. **keep one's distance** stay far away. ■ maintain one's reserve: *you had to say nothing and keep your distance*. **within —— distance** near enough to reach by the means specified: *her flat is within walking distance*. **within spitting** (or US **shouting**) **distance** within a very short distance. **within striking distance** near enough to hit or achieve something: *we are within striking distance of our goal*.
– ORIGIN Middle English (in the sense 'discord, debate'): from Old French or from Latin *distantia*, from *distant-* 'standing apart', from the verb *distare* (see DISTANT).

distance learning ▶ noun [mass noun] a method of studying in which lectures are broadcast or lessons are conducted by correspondence, without the student needing to attend a school or college.

distance post ▶ noun N. Amer. a post placed at a specified distance before the finishing post on a racecourse, which a horse must have passed when the winner finishes in order to qualify for a subsequent heat.

distance runner ▶ noun an athlete who competes in long- or middle-distance races.

distant ▶ adjective **1** far away in space or time: *distant parts of the world* | *I remember that distant afternoon*. ■ [predic.] (after a measurement) at a specified distance: *the star is 30,000 light years* ***distant from*** *Earth* | *the town lay half a mile distant*. ■ (of a sound) faint because far away: *the distant bark of some farm dog*. ■ remote or far apart in resemblance or relationship: *a distant acquaintance*. ■ [attrib.] (of a person) not closely related: *a distant cousin of the King*.
2 (of a person) not intimate; cool or reserved: *his children found him strangely distant* | *she and my father were* ***distant with*** *each other*. ■ not paying attention; remote: *a distant look in his eyes*.
– ORIGIN late Middle English: from Latin *distant-* 'standing apart', from the verb *distare*, from *dis-* 'apart' + *stare* 'stand'.

distantiate /dɪˈstanʃɪeɪt/ ▶ verb [with obj.] set or keep (something) at a distance, especially mentally: *Austen's aesthetic forms distantiate ideology*.
– DERIVATIVES **distantiation** noun.
– ORIGIN 1940s: based on Latin *distantia* 'distance'.

distantly ▶ adverb far away: *distantly he heard shouts*. ■ not closely: *they are distantly related to the elephants*. ■ coolly or remotely: *she smiled distantly*.

distant signal ▶ noun a railway signal giving a warning of the condition of the next home signal.

distaste ▶ **noun** [in sing.] mild dislike or aversion: *Harry nurtured a **distaste for** all things athletic* | [mass noun] *his mouth twisted with distaste.*
– ORIGIN late 16th cent.: from **DIS-** (expressing reversal) + **TASTE**, on the pattern of early modern French *desgout*, Italian *disgusto*. Compare with **DISGUST**.

distasteful ▶ **adjective** causing dislike or aversion; disagreeable or unpleasant: *he found such cynicism distasteful.*
– DERIVATIVES **distastefully** adverb, **distastefulness** noun.

Di Stefano /dɪ ˈstɛfənəʊ/, Alfredo (b.1926), Argentinian-born Spanish footballer. He played as a forward in Argentina and Colombia, then for Spain and Real Madrid, with whom he won the European Cup in each of its first five seasons (1956–60).

distemper[1] /dɪˈstɛmpə/ ▶ **noun** [mass noun] a kind of paint using glue or size instead of an oil base, for use on walls or for scene-painting. ■ a method of mural and poster painting using distemper.
▶ **verb** [with obj.] (often as adj. **distempered**) paint with distemper: *the distempered roof timbers.*
– ORIGIN late Middle English (originally as a verb in the senses 'dilute' and 'steep'): from Old French *destremper* or late Latin *distemperare* 'soak'.

distemper[2] /dɪˈstɛmpə/ ▶ **noun** [mass noun] **1** a viral disease of some animals, especially dogs, causing fever, coughing, and catarrh.
2 archaic political disorder: *an attempt to illuminate the moral roots of the modern world's distemper.*
– ORIGIN mid 16th cent. (originally in the sense 'bad temper', later 'illness'): from Middle English *distemper* 'upset, derange', from late Latin *distemperare* 'soak, mix in the wrong proportions', from *dis-* 'thoroughly' + *temperare* 'mingle'. Compare with **TEMPER**. Sense 1 dates from the mid 18th cent.

distempered ▶ **adjective** literary emotionally or psychologically disturbed. ■ symptomatic of a general moral and psychological debility: *this distempered fog, this old corruption of the nation.*

distend /dɪˈstɛnd/ ▶ **verb** swell or cause to swell by pressure from inside: [no obj.] *the abdomen distended rapidly* | [with obj.] *air is introduced into the stomach to distend it.*
– DERIVATIVES **distensibility** noun, **distensible** adjective, **distension** noun.
– ORIGIN late Middle English: from Latin *distendere*, from *dis-* 'apart' + *tendere* 'to stretch'.

distended /dɪˈstɛndɪd/ ▶ **adjective** swollen due to pressure from inside; bloated: *a distended belly.*

distich /ˈdɪstɪk/ ▶ **noun** Prosody a pair of verse lines; a couplet.
– ORIGIN early 16th cent.: via Latin from Greek *distikhon (metron)* '(measure) of two lines', neuter of *distikhos*, from *di-* 'twice' + *stikhos* 'line'.

distichous /ˈdɪstɪkəs/ ▶ **adjective** Botany (of parts) arranged alternately in two opposite vertical rows.
– DERIVATIVES **distichously** adverb.
– ORIGIN mid 18th cent.: via Latin from Greek *distikhos* (see **DISTICH**) + **-OUS**.

distil /dɪˈstɪl/ (US **distill**) ▶ **verb** (**distils**, **distilling**, **distilled**) [with obj.] **1** purify (a liquid) by heating it so that it vaporizes, then cooling and condensing the vapour and collecting the resulting liquid: *they managed to distil a small quantity of water* | (as adj. **distilled**) *distilled water.* ■ make (spirits or an essence) by distilling: *whisky is **distilled from** a mash of grains* | (as noun **distilling**) *the distilling industry.* ■ extract the essence of (something) by heating it with a solvent: *distil the leaves of some agrimony.* ■ remove (a volatile constituent) of a mixture by heating: *coal tar is made by **distilling out** the volatile products in coal.* ■ [no obj.] literary emanate as a vapour or in minute drops: *she drew back from the dank breath that distilled out of the earth.*
2 extract the essential meaning or most important aspects of: *my travel notes were **distilled into** a book* | (as adj. **distilled**) *the report is a distilled version of the main accounts.*
– DERIVATIVES **distillatory** adjective.
– ORIGIN late Middle English: from Latin *distillare*, variant of *destillare*, from *de-* 'down, away' + *stillare* (from *stilla* 'a drop').

distillate /ˈdɪstɪleɪt/ ▶ **noun** something formed by distillation: *petroleum distillates* | [mass noun] *natural gas mixed with distillate.*
– ORIGIN mid 19th cent.: from Latin *distillatus* 'fallen in drops', from the verb *distillare* (see **DISTIL**).

distillation ▶ **noun** [mass noun] **1** the action of purifying a liquid by a process of heating and cooling: *the petroleum distillation process.*
2 the extraction of the essential meaning or most important aspects of something: *this book represents the distillation of years of experience in the private sector* | [count noun] *the film is a distillation of personal experiences.*

distiller ▶ **noun** a person or company that manufactures spirits: *a family-owned whisky distiller.*

distillery ▶ **noun** (pl. **distilleries**) a place where spirits are manufactured.

distinct ▶ **adjective 1** recognizably different in nature from something else of a similar type: *the patterns of spoken language are **distinct from** those of writing* | *there are two distinct types of sickle cell disease.* ■ physically separate: *the gallery is divided into five distinct spaces.*
2 readily distinguishable by the senses: *a distinct smell of nicotine.* ■ [attrib.] (used for emphasis) so clearly apparent to the mind as to be unmistakable; definite: *he got the distinct impression that Melissa wasn't best pleased.*
– DERIVATIVES **distinctness** noun.
– ORIGIN late Middle English (in the sense 'differentiated'): from Latin *distinctus* 'separated, distinguished', from the verb *distinguere* (see **DISTINGUISH**).

distinction ▶ **noun 1** a difference or contrast between similar things or people: *there is a sharp distinction between domestic politics and international politics* | *I was completely unaware of class distinctions.* ■ [mass noun] the separation of people or things into different groups according to their characteristics: *high interest rates strike down, without distinction, small businesses and the unemployed.*
2 [mass noun] excellence that sets someone or something apart from others: *a novelist of distinction.* ■ [count noun] a decoration or honour awarded to someone: *he gained the highest distinction awarded for excellence in photography.* ■ [count noun] a grade in an examination denoting excellence: *she gained a distinction in her diploma.* Compare with **MERIT**.
– ORIGIN Middle English (in the sense 'subdivision, category'): via Old French from Latin *distinctio(n-)*, from the verb *distinguere* (see **DISTINGUISH**).

distinctive ▶ **adjective** characteristic of one person or thing, and so serving to distinguish it from others: *juniper berries give gin its distinctive flavour.*
– DERIVATIVES **distinctively** adverb, **distinctiveness** noun.
– ORIGIN late Middle English (in the sense 'serving to differentiate'): from late Latin *distinctivus*, from Latin *distinct-* 'distinguished' (see **DISTINCT**).

distinctly ▶ **adverb** in a way that is readily distinguishable by the senses; clearly: *reading each word slowly and distinctly.* ■ [as submodifier] (used for emphasis) in a way that is very noticeable or apparent; decidedly: *two distinctly different cultures* | *he looked distinctly uncomfortable.*

distingué /dɪˈstaŋgeɪ/ ▶ **adjective** (fem. **distinguée** pronunc. **same**) having a distinguished manner or appearance: *he was lean and distingué, with a small goatee.*
– ORIGIN French, 'distinguished', from the verb *distinguer*.

distinguish /dɪˈstɪŋgwɪʃ/ ▶ **verb** [with obj.] **1** recognize or treat (someone or something) as different: *the child is perfectly capable of **distinguishing** reality **from** fantasy.* ■ [no obj.] recognize or point out a difference: *we must **distinguish between** two kinds of holiday.* ■ be an identifying characteristic or mark of: *what **distinguishes** sport **from** games?*
2 manage to discern (something barely perceptible): *it was too dark to distinguish anything more than their vague shapes.*
3 (**distinguish oneself**) make oneself worthy of respect by one's behaviour or achievements: *many distinguished themselves in the fight against Hitler.*
– ORIGIN late 16th cent.: formed irregularly from French *distinguer* or Latin *distinguere*, from *dis-* 'apart' + *stinguere* 'put out' (from a base meaning 'prick').

distinguishable /dɪˈstɪŋgwɪʃəb(ə)l/ ▶ **adjective** clear enough to be recognized or identified as different; discernible: *distinguishable features* | *this particular case is **distinguishable from** others.* ■ clear enough to be discerned or perceived: *his words were barely distinguishable.*

distinguished ▶ **adjective** very successful, authoritative, and commanding great respect: *a distinguished American educationist.* ■ dignified and noble in appearance or manner: *that hairstyle makes you look quite distinguished.*

Distinguished Flying Cross ▶ **noun** see **DFC**.

Distinguished Service Order ▶ **noun** see **DSO**.

distinguishing /dɪˈstɪŋgwɪʃɪŋ/ ▶ **adjective** characteristic of one thing or person, so serving to identify it; distinctive: *a house with no distinguishing features.*

distort /dɪˈstɔːt/ ▶ **verb** [with obj.] **1** pull or twist out of shape: *a grimace distorted her fine mouth.* ■ [no obj.] become twisted out of shape: *the pipe will distort as you bend it.*
2 give a misleading or false account or impression of: *many factors can distort the results.*
3 change the form of (an electrical signal or sound wave) during transmission, amplification, or other processing: *you're distorting the sound by overdriving the amp.*
– ORIGIN late 15th cent. (in the sense 'twist to one side'): from Latin *distort-* 'twisted apart', from the verb *distorquere*, from *dis-* 'apart' + *torquere* 'to twist'.

distorted /dɪˈstɔːtɪd/ ▶ **adjective 1** pulled or twisted out of shape; contorted.
2 giving a misleading or false account or impression; misrepresented: *his report gives a distorted view of the meeting.*
3 affected by electrical distortion: *distorted guitars.*
– DERIVATIVES **distortedly** adverb, **distortedness** noun.

distortion ▶ **noun** [mass noun] **1** the action of distorting or the state of being distorted: *the virus causes distortion of the leaves* | [count noun] *deliberate distortions of pitch and timbre.* ■ [count noun] a distorted form or part: *a distortion in the eye's shape or structure.*
2 the action of giving a misleading account or impression: *we're fed up with the media's continuing distortion of our issues.*
3 change in the form of an electrical signal or sound wave during processing.
– DERIVATIVES **distortional** adjective, **distortionless** adjective.

distract /dɪˈstrakt/ ▶ **verb** [with obj.] prevent (someone) from concentrating on something: *don't allow noise to **distract** you **from** your work.* ■ divert (attention) from something: *it was another attempt to **distract** attention **from** the truth.* ■ (**distract oneself**) divert one's attention from something unpleasant by doing something different or more pleasurable: *I tried to distract myself by concentrating on Jane.* ■ archaic perplex and bewilder: *horror and doubt distract His troubl'd thoughts.*
– ORIGIN late Middle English (also in the sense 'pull in different directions'): from Latin *distract-* 'drawn apart', from the verb *distrahere*, from *dis-* 'apart' + *trahere* 'to draw, drag'.

distracted ▶ **adjective** unable to concentrate because one is preoccupied by something worrying or unpleasant: *Charlotte seemed too distracted to give him much attention.*
– DERIVATIVES **distractedly** adverb.

distracting ▶ **adjective** preventing concentration or diverting attention; disturbing: *she found his nearness distracting.*
– DERIVATIVES **distractingly** adverb [as submodifier] *some of my classmates are distractingly pretty.*

distraction ▶ **noun 1** a thing that prevents someone from concentrating on something else: *the firm found passenger travel **a distraction from** the main business of moving freight.* ■ a diversion or recreation: *there are plenty of distractions such as sailing* | [mass noun] *he roved the district in search of distraction.*
2 [mass noun] extreme agitation of the mind: *her uncharacteristic air of distraction.*
– PHRASES **to distraction** almost to a state of madness: *she loved him to distraction.*
– ORIGIN late Middle English: from Latin *distractio(n-)*, from the verb *distrahere* (see **DISTRACT**).

distractor ▶ **noun** a person or thing that distracts: *the visual channel is capable of being a powerful distractor.* ■ an incorrect option in a multiple choice question.

distrain /dɪˈstreɪn/ ▶ **verb** [with obj.] Law seize (someone's property) in order to obtain payment of rent or other money owed: *legislation has restricted the right to distrain goods found upon the premises.* ■ seize the property of (someone) in order to obtain payment of money owed: *the Crown applied political pressure by distraining debtors.*
– DERIVATIVES **distrainer** noun, **distrainment** noun.

D

– ORIGIN Middle English: from Old French *destreindre*, from Latin *distringere* 'stretch apart', from *dis-* 'apart' + *stringere* 'tighten'.

distraint /dɪˈstreɪnt/ ▶ **noun** [mass noun] Law the seizure of someone's property in order to obtain payment of money owed, especially rent: *many faced heavy fines and the distraint of goods.*

– ORIGIN mid 18th cent.: from DISTRAIN, on the pattern of *constraint*.

distrait /dɪˈstreɪ, ˈdɪstreɪ/ ▶ **adjective** (fem. **distraite** /-ˈstreɪt/) [predic.] distracted or absent-minded: *he seemed oddly distrait.*

– ORIGIN mid 18th cent.: French, from Old French *destrait*, past participle of *destraire* 'distract', from Latin *distrahere* 'pull apart' (see DISTRACT).

distraught /dɪˈstrɔːt/ ▶ **adjective** very worried and upset: *a distraught woman sobbed and screamed for help | he is terribly distraught.*

– ORIGIN late Middle English: alteration of the obsolete adjective *distract* (from Latin *distractus* 'pulled apart'), influenced by *straught*, archaic past participle of STRETCH.

distress ▶ **noun** [mass noun] **1** extreme anxiety, sorrow, or pain: *to his distress he saw that she was trembling | her fingers flew to her throat in* **distress**. ■ the state of a ship or aircraft when in danger or difficulty and needing help: *vessels* **in distress** *on or near the coast |* [as modifier] *a distress call.* ■ difficulty caused by lack of money: *a company* **in financial distress**. ■ Medicine a state of physical strain, especially difficulty in breathing: *they said the baby was in distress.*
2 Law another term for DISTRAINT.
▶ **verb** [with obj.] **1** cause (someone) anxiety, sorrow, or pain: *I didn't mean to distress you | please don't* **distress yourself**.
2 give (furniture or clothing) simulated marks of age and wear: *the manner in which leather jackets are industrially distressed.*

– DERIVATIVES **distressful** adjective.

– ORIGIN Middle English: from Old French *destresce* (noun), *destrecier* (verb), based on Latin *distringere* 'stretch apart'.

distressed ▶ **adjective 1** suffering from extreme anxiety, sorrow, or pain: *I was distressed at the news of his death | the distressed relatives of his victims.* ■ dated impoverished: *women in distressed circumstances.* ■ informal, chiefly US (of property) offered for sale cheaply due to mortgage foreclosure or because it is part of an insolvent estate.
2 (of furniture or clothing) having simulated marks of age and wear: *a distressed leather jacket.*

distressed area ▶ **noun** a region of high unemployment and poverty.

distressing ▶ **adjective** causing anxiety, sorrow or pain; upsetting: *some very distressing news.*

– DERIVATIVES **distressingly** adverb [as submodifier] *the pattern was distressingly familiar.*

distress rocket ▶ **noun** a rocket fired as a distress signal.

distress signal ▶ **noun** a signal from a ship or aircraft that is in danger.

distress warrant ▶ **noun** Law a warrant authorizing distraint.

distributary /dɪˈstrɪbjʊt(ə)ri/ ▶ **noun** (pl. **distributaries**) a branch of a river that does not return to the main stream after leaving it (as in a delta).

distribute /dɪˈstrɪbjuːt, ˈdɪstrɪbjuːt/ ▶ **verb** [with obj.] **1** give a share or a unit of (something) to each of a number of recipients: *information leaflets are being distributed to hotels.* ■ supply (goods) to retailers: *the journal is distributed worldwide.* ■ Printing separate (metal type that has been set up) and return the characters to their separate compartments in a type case.
2 (**be distributed**) occur throughout an area: *the birds are mainly distributed in marshes and river valleys.* ■ spread (a load) over an area: *the seat is designed to ensure the weight of the passenger is evenly distributed.* ■ (as adj. **distributed**) Computing (of a computer system) spread over several machines, especially over a network.
3 Logic use (a term) to include every individual of the class to which it refers.

– DERIVATIVES **distributable** adjective.

– ORIGIN late Middle English: from Latin *distribut-* 'divided up', from the verb *distribuere*, from *dis-* 'apart' + *tribuere* 'assign'.

> **USAGE** The word **distribute** is pronounced either with the stress on the **-stri-** or with the stress on the **dis-**. Until recently the latter, with the stress on the first syllable, was considered incorrect in standard British English, but now both pronunciations are standard.

distribution ▶ **noun** [mass noun] **1** the action of sharing something out among a number of recipients: *the government released about 74,000 tonnes of rice for distribution among people affected by the cyclone |* [count noun] *unequal distributions of income and wealth.* ■ the action or process of supplying goods to retailers. ■ Bridge the different number of cards of each suit in a player's hand.
2 the way in which something is shared out among a group or spread over an area: *changes undergone by the area have affected the distribution of its wildlife.*

– DERIVATIVES **distributional** adjective.

– ORIGIN late Middle English: from Latin *distributio(n-)*, from the verb *distribuere* (see DISTRIBUTE).

distribution board ▶ **noun** a panel carrying the fuses, terminals, and other components of a number of subsidiary electric circuits.

distributive /dɪˈstrɪbjʊtɪv/ ▶ **adjective 1** concerned with the supply of goods to retailers: *transport and distributive industries.* ■ concerned with the way in which things are shared between people: *the distributive effects of public expenditure.*
2 Grammar (of a determiner or pronoun) referring to each individual of a class, not to the class collectively, e.g. *each*, *either*.
3 Mathematics (of an operation) fulfilling the condition that, when it is performed on two or more quantities already combined by another operation, the result is the same as when it is performed on each quantity individually and the products then combined.
▶ **noun** Grammar a distributive word.

– DERIVATIVES **distributively** adverb.

– ORIGIN late Middle English: from Old French *distributif, -ive* or late Latin *distributivus*, from Latin *distribut-* 'divided up', from the verb *distribuere* (see DISTRIBUTE).

distributor /dɪˈstrɪbjʊtə/ ▶ **noun 1** an agent who supplies goods to retailers: *a sports goods distributor.*
2 a device in a petrol engine for passing electric current to each spark plug in turn.

district ▶ **noun** an area of a country or city, especially one characterized by a particular feature or activity: *a coal-mining district.* ■ [often as modifier] a region defined for an administrative purpose: *a district health authority.* ■ Brit. a division of a county or region that elects its own councillors.
▶ **verb** [with obj.] N. Amer. divide into areas: (as noun **districting**) *the province's system of electoral districting.*

– ORIGIN early 17th cent. (denoting the territory under the jurisdiction of a feudal lord): from French, from medieval Latin *districtus* '(territory of) jurisdiction', from Latin *distringere* 'draw apart'.

district attorney (abbrev.: **DA**) ▶ **noun** (in the US) a public official who acts as prosecutor for the state in a particular district.

district auditor ▶ **noun** (in the UK) a civil servant responsible for auditing the accounts of local authorities.

district court ▶ **noun** (in most US jurisdictions) the federal or state trial court.

district heating ▶ **noun** [mass noun] the supply of heat or hot water from one source to a district or a group of buildings.

district nurse ▶ **noun** (in the UK) a nurse who visits and treats patients in their homes, operating in a specific area or in association with a particular general practice surgery or health centre.

District of Columbia (abbrev.: **DC**) a federal district of the US, coextensive with the city of Washington, situated on the Potomac River with boundaries on the states of Virginia and Maryland.

district surgeon ▶ **noun** (in South Africa) a doctor appointed to serve a particular district.

distro ▶ **noun** (pl. **distros**) informal a computer software distribution package.

distrust ▶ **noun** [mass noun] the feeling that someone or something cannot be relied upon: *the public's distrust of politicians.*
▶ **verb** [with obj.] doubt the honesty or reliability of; regard with suspicion: *speculation remained that the Army distrusted the peace process.*

– DERIVATIVES **distruster** noun.

distrustful ▶ **adjective** feeling or showing distrust of someone or something: *I have grown up to be distrustful of men.*

– DERIVATIVES **distrustfully** adverb.

disturb ▶ **verb** [with obj.] **1** interfere with the normal arrangement or functioning of: *take the rollers out carefully so as not to disturb the curls too much.*
2 interrupt the sleep, relaxation, or privacy of: *I'll see my patient now and we are not to be disturbed.*
3 make (someone) anxious: *I am disturbed by the document I have just read.*

– DERIVATIVES **disturber** noun.

– ORIGIN Middle English: from Old French *destourber*, from Latin *disturbare*, from *dis-* 'utterly' + *turbare* 'disturb' (from *turba* 'tumult').

disturbance ▶ **noun 1** [mass noun] the interruption of a settled and peaceful condition: *a helicopter landing can cause disturbance to residents.* ■ [count noun] a breakdown of peaceful and law-abiding behaviour: *the disturbances were precipitated when four men were refused bail.* ■ Law interference with rights or property.
2 a state in which normal mental or physical functioning is disrupted: *children with learning difficulty and personality disturbance.*

– ORIGIN Middle English: from Old French *destourbance*, from *destourber* (see DISTURB).

disturbed ▶ **adjective 1** having had the normal pattern or functioning disrupted: *disturbed sleep.*
2 having or resulting from emotional and mental problems: *the treatment of disturbed children | disturbed behaviour.*

disturbing ▶ **adjective** causing anxiety; worrying: *disturbing unemployment figures.*

– DERIVATIVES **disturbingly** adverb [as submodifier] *a woman who looked disturbingly familiar.*

disubstituted /dʌɪˈsʌbstɪtjuːtɪd/ ▶ **adjective** Chemistry (of a molecule) having two substituent groups.

disulfiram /dʌɪˈsʌlfɪram/ ▶ **noun** [mass noun] Medicine a synthetic compound used in the treatment of alcoholics to make drinking alcohol produce unpleasant after-effects. Also called ANTABUSE (trademark). ● Alternative name: **tetraethylthiuram disulphide**; chem. formula: $(C_2H_5)_2NCSSCN(C_2H_5)_2$.

– ORIGIN 1940s: blend of *disulfide* (see DISULPHIDE) and *thiuram* (from THIO- + UREA + AMIDE).

disulphide /dʌɪˈsʌlfʌɪd/ (US **disulfide**) ▶ **noun** Chemistry a sulphide containing two atoms of sulphur in its molecule or empirical formula. ■ an organic compound containing the group –S–S– bonded to other groups.

disunion ▶ **noun** [mass noun] the breaking up of something such as a federation: *his rejection of disunion was consistent with his nationalism.*

disunited ▶ **adjective** lacking unity: *a disunited nation.*

disunity /dɪsˈjuːnɪti/ ▶ **noun** [mass noun] disagreement and conflict within a group: *the disunity among opposition parties.*

disuse /dɪsˈjuːs/ ▶ **noun** [mass noun] the state of not being used: *his voice was croaky with disuse.*

disused ▶ **adjective** no longer being used: *they held an exhibition in a disused warehouse.*

disutility /ˌdɪsjuːˈtɪlɪti/ ▶ **noun** [mass noun] Economics the adverse or harmful effects associated with a particular activity or process, especially when carried out over a long period.

disvalue ▶ **verb** [with obj.] undervalue (something or someone): *I'm not going to disvalue the way they feel.*
▶ **noun** a negative value or worth: *a story in which exhibitionism is a disvalue.*

– DERIVATIVES **disvaluation** noun.

disyllabic /ˌdʌɪsɪˈlabɪk/ (also **dissyllabic**) ▶ **adjective** (of a word or metrical foot) consisting of two syllables. ■ (of a bird's characteristic call) consisting of two distinct sounds, such as the call of the cuckoo.

– ORIGIN mid 17th cent.: from French *dissyllabique*, via Latin from Greek *disullabos* 'of two syllables'.

disyllable /dʌɪˈsɪləb(ə)l, ˈdʌɪsɪl-/ (also **dissyllable** /dɪˈsɪləb(ə)l/) ▶ **noun** Prosody a word or metrical foot consisting of two syllables.

– ORIGIN late 16th cent.: alteration (influenced by SYLLABLE) of French *disyllabe*, via Latin from Greek *disullabos* 'of two syllables', from *di-* 'two' + *sullabē* 'syllable'.

dit ▶ **noun** (in the Morse system) another term for DOT[1].

– ORIGIN Second World War: imitative.

ditch ▶ **noun** a narrow channel dug at the side of a road or field, to hold or carry away water.

▶ **verb** [with obj.] **1** provide with a ditch or ditches. ■ [no obj.] make or repair ditches: (as noun **ditching**) *they would have to pay for hedging and ditching.*
2 informal get rid of or give up: *plans for the road were ditched following a public inquiry.* ■ end a relationship with (someone) peremptorily: *she ditched her husband to marry the window cleaner.* ■ N. Amer. play truant from (school): *maybe she could ditch school and run away.*
3 bring (an aircraft) down on water in an emergency: *he was picked up by a gunboat after ditching his plane in the Mediterranean.* ■ [no obj.] (of an aircraft) make a forced landing on water: *the aircraft was obliged to ditch in the sea off the North African coast.* ■ US derail (a train).
– DERIVATIVES **ditcher** noun.
– ORIGIN Old English *dīc*, of Germanic origin; related to Dutch *dijk* 'ditch, dyke' and German *Teich* 'pond, pool', also to **DYKE**[1].

ditchwater ▶ **noun** [mass noun] stagnant water in a ditch.

diterpene /dʌɪˈtəːpiːn/ ▶ **noun** Chemistry any of a group of terpenes found in plant gums and resins, having unsaturated molecules based on a unit with the formula $C_{20}H_{32}$.
– DERIVATIVES **diterpenoid** adjective & noun.

ditheism /ˈdʌɪθɪɪz(ə)m/ ▶ **noun** [mass noun] a belief in two gods, especially as independent and opposed principles of good and evil.

dither ▶ **verb** [no obj.] **1** be indecisive: *I can't bear people who dither* | *he was dithering about the election date.*
2 [with obj.] add white noise to (a digital recording) to reduce distortion of low-amplitude signals. ■ display or print (a colour image) in such a way that it appears to contain more colours than are really available: (as adj. **dithered**) *dithered bitmaps.*
▶ **noun 1** [mass noun] informal indecisive behaviour: *after months of dither ministers had still not agreed.*
2 [in sing.] a state of agitation: ***all of a dither**, he prophesied instant chaos.*
– DERIVATIVES **ditherer** noun, **dithery** adjective.
– ORIGIN mid 17th cent. (in the dialect sense 'tremble, quiver'): variant of dialect *didder*; related to **DODDER**[1].

dithionite /dʌɪˈθʌɪənʌɪt/ ▶ **noun** Chemistry a salt containing the anion $S_2O_4^{2-}$.
– ORIGIN mid 20th cent.: from **DI-**[1] 'two' + Greek *theion* 'sulphur' + **-ITE**[1].

dithizone /dʌɪˈθʌɪzəʊn/ ▶ **noun** [mass noun] Chemistry a synthetic compound used as a reagent for the analysis and separation of lead and other metals.
● Alternative name: **diphenylthiocarbazone**; chem. formula: $C_{13}H_{12}N_4S$.
– ORIGIN 1920s: from elements of the systematic name (see above).

dithyramb /ˈdɪθɪram(b)/ ▶ **noun** a wild choral hymn of ancient Greece, especially one dedicated to Dionysus. ■ a passionate or inflated speech, poem, or other writing.
– DERIVATIVES **dithyrambic** adjective.
– ORIGIN early 17th cent.: via Latin from Greek *dithurambos*, of unknown ultimate origin.

ditransitive /dʌɪˈtransɪtɪv, -ˈtrɑː-, -nz-/ ▶ **adjective** Grammar denoting a verb that takes two objects, for example *give* as in *I gave her the book.*

ditsy ▶ **adjective** variant spelling of **DITZY**.

dittany /ˈdɪtəni/ ▶ **noun** [mass noun] (pl. **dittanies**) any of a number of aromatic herbaceous or shrubby plants: ● (also **dittany of Crete**) a dwarf shrub with white woolly leaves and pink flowers, native to Crete and Greece (*Origanum dictamnus*, family Labiatae). ● (also **American dittany**) an American herb used in cookery and herbal medicine (genus *Cunila*, family Labiatae). ● another term for **GAS PLANT**.
– ORIGIN late Middle English: from Old French *ditain* or medieval Latin *ditaneum*, from Latin *dictamnus*, *dictamnum*, from Greek *diktamnon*, perhaps from *Diktē*, the name of a mountain in Crete.

ditto ▶ **noun** (pl. **dittos**) the same thing again (used in lists and accounts and often indicated by a ditto mark under the word or figure to be repeated).
■ informal used to indicate that something already said is applicable a second time: *if one folds his arms, so does the other; if one crosses his legs, ditto.*
– ORIGIN early 17th cent. (in the sense 'in the aforesaid month'): from Tuscan dialect, variant of Italian *detto* 'said', from Latin *dictus* 'said'.

dittography /dɪˈtɒgrəfi/ ▶ **noun** (pl. **dittographies**) a mistaken repetition of a letter, word, or phrase by a copyist.
– ORIGIN late 19th cent.: from Greek *dittos* 'double' + **-GRAPHY**.

ditto marks ▶ **plural noun** two apostrophes (") representing 'ditto'.

ditty ▶ **noun** (pl. **ditties**) a short, simple song: *a lovely little music-hall ditty.*
– ORIGIN Middle English: from Old French *dite* 'composition', from Latin *dictatum* (neuter) 'something dictated', from *dictare* 'to dictate'.

ditty bag (also **ditty box**) ▶ **noun** a receptacle for odds and ends, especially one used by sailors or fishermen.
– ORIGIN mid 19th cent.: of unknown origin.

ditz ▶ **noun** N. Amer. informal a scatterbrained person.
– ORIGIN 1970s: back-formation from **DITZY**.

ditzy (also **ditsy**) ▶ **adjective** (**ditzier**, **ditziest**; **ditsier**, **ditsiest**) N. Amer. informal silly or scatterbrained: *don't tell me my ditzy secretary didn't send you an invitation!*
– DERIVATIVES **ditziness** noun.
– ORIGIN 1970s: of unknown origin.

diuresis /ˌdʌɪjʊ(ə)ˈriːsɪs/ ▶ **noun** [mass noun] Medicine increased or excessive production of urine. Compare with **POLYURIA**.
– ORIGIN late 17th cent.: modern Latin, from **DI-**[3] 'through' + Greek *ourēsis* 'urination'.

diuretic /ˌdʌɪjʊ(ə)ˈrɛtɪk/ Medicine ▶ **adjective** (chiefly of drugs) causing increased passing of urine.
▶ **noun** a diuretic drug.
– ORIGIN late Middle English: from Old French *diuretique*, or via late Latin from Greek *diourētikos*, from *diourein* 'urinate', from *dia* 'through' + *ouron* 'urine'.

diurnal /dʌɪˈəːn(ə)l/ ▶ **adjective 1** of or during the day. ■ Zoology (of animals) active in the daytime. ■ Botany (of flowers) open only during the day.
2 daily; of each day: *diurnal rhythms.* ■ Astronomy of or resulting from the daily rotation of the earth: *diurnal aberration.*
– DERIVATIVES **diurnally** adverb.
– ORIGIN late Middle English (as a term in astronomy): from late Latin *diurnalis*, from Latin *diurnus* 'daily', from *dies* 'day'.

div[1] ▶ **abbreviation** divergence (in mathematical equations).

div[2] ▶ **noun** another term for **DIVVY**[2].

Div. ▶ **abbreviation** Division.

diva /ˈdiːvə/ ▶ **noun** a celebrated female opera singer. ■ a famous female singer of popular music: *a pop diva.* ■ a woman regarded as temperamental or haughty.
– ORIGIN late 19th cent.: via Italian from Latin, literally 'goddess'.

divagate /ˈdʌɪvəgeɪt/ ▶ **verb** [no obj.] literary stray or digress: *Yeats divagated into Virgil's territory only once.*
– DERIVATIVES **divagation** noun.
– ORIGIN late 16th cent.: from Latin *divagat-* 'wandered about', from the verb *divagari*, from *di-* 'widely' + *vagari* 'wander'.

divalent /dʌɪˈveɪl(ə)nt/ ▶ **adjective** Chemistry having a valency of two.

Divali ▶ **noun** variant spelling of **DIWALI**.

divan /dɪˈvan, dʌɪˈvan, ˈdʌɪvan/ ▶ **noun 1** (also **divan bed**) Brit. a bed consisting of a base and mattress but no footboard or headboard.
2 a long, low sofa without a back or arms.
3 historical a legislative body, council chamber, or court of justice in the Ottoman Empire or elsewhere in the Middle East.
– ORIGIN late 16th cent. (in sense 3): via French or Italian from Turkish *dīvān*, from Persian *dīwān* 'anthology, register, court, or bench'; compare with **DIWAN**. As a piece of furniture, a *divan* was originally (early 18th cent.) a low bench or raised section of floor against an interior wall, used as a long seat and common in Middle Eastern countries; European imitation of this led to the sense 'low flat sofa or bed' (late 19th cent.).

divaricate /dʌɪˈvarɪkeɪt, dɪ-/ ▶ **verb** [no obj.] technical or literary stretch or spread apart; diverge widely: *her crow's feet are divaricating like deltas.*
▶ **adjective** Botany (of a branch) coming off the stem almost at a right angle.
– DERIVATIVES **divarication** noun.
– ORIGIN early 17th cent.: from Latin *divaricat-* 'stretched apart', from the verb *divaricare*, from *di-* (expressing intensive force) + *varicare* 'stretch the legs apart' (from *varicus* 'straddling').

dive ▶ **verb** (past and past participle **dived**; US also **dove** /dəʊv/) [no obj.] **1** [with adverbial of direction] plunge head first into water with one's arms raised over one's head: *she walked to the deep end, then she dived in* | *he dived off the bridge for a bet.* ■ (of a fish or submarine) go to a deeper level in water: *the fish dive down to about 1,400 feet.* ■ swim under water using breathing equipment: *he had been diving in the area to test equipment.*
2 (of an aircraft or bird) plunge steeply downwards through the air: *arctic skuas which dive at your head as you walk near their territories.* ■ move quickly or suddenly in a specified direction: *a bullet passed close to his head and he dived for cover* | (as adj. **diving**) *he scored with a diving header.* ■ (of prices or profits) drop suddenly: *profits before tax dived by 61 per cent.* ■ informal put one's hand quickly into a pocket or bag in order to find something: *she **dived into** her bag and extracted a card.* ■ Soccer (of a player) deliberately fall when challenged in order to deceive the referee into awarding a foul.
▶ **noun 1** a plunge head first into water: *he hit the sea in a shallow dive.* ■ an instance of swimming or going deeper under water: *divers should have a good intake of fluid before each dive.*
2 a steep descent by an aircraft or bird: *the jumbo jet went into a dive.* ■ a sudden movement in a specified direction: *she **made a dive for** the fridge to quench her thirst.* ■ a sudden marked fall in prices or profits: *an 11 per cent dive in profits.* ■ Soccer a deliberate fall by a player, intended to deceive the referee into awarding a foul.
3 informal a disreputable nightclub or bar: *he got into a fight in some dive.*
– PHRASES **take a dive** Boxing pretend to be knocked down or out. ■ (of prices, hopes, fortunes, etc.) fall suddenly: *profits could take a dive as easily as they could soar.*
– PHRASAL VERBS **dive in** help oneself to food. **dive into** occupy oneself suddenly and enthusiastically with (a meal, or an engrossing subject or activity): *I'm not quite ready to dive into that discussion.*
– ORIGIN Old English *dūfan* 'dive, sink' and *dȳfan* 'immerse', of Germanic origin; related to **DEEP** and **DIP**.

dive-bomb ▶ **verb** [with obj.] bomb (a target) while diving steeply downwards in an aircraft: *planes were dive-bombing the aerodrome.* ■ (of a bird or flying insect) attack (something) by swooping down on it: *the crow folded its wings and dive-bombed the vulture.*
– DERIVATIVES **dive-bomber** noun.

divemaster ▶ **noun** a person who is in charge of an underwater diving expedition.

diver ▶ **noun 1** a person who dives as a sport: *an Olympic diver.* ■ a person who wears a diving suit to work under water: *a police diver.*
2 a large diving waterbird of northern latitudes, with a sleek black or grey head, a straight pointed bill, and short legs set far back under the body. Called **LOON**[2] in North America. ● Family Gaviidae and genus *Gavia*: five species, including the **great northern diver** or common loon (*G. immer*) of both Canada and Eurasia.

diverge /dʌɪˈvəːdʒ, dɪ-/ ▶ **verb** [no obj.] **1** (of a road, route, or line) separate from another route and go in a different direction: *the flight path **diverged from** the original flight plan* | figurative *their ways had diverged at university.* ■ (of an opinion, theory, or approach) differ: *the coverage by the columnists **diverged from** that in the main news stories* | (as adj. **diverging**) *diverging concepts of nation-building.* ■ (**diverge from**) depart from (a set course or standard): *suddenly he diverged from his text.* ■ develop in a different direction: *English Gothic architecture began to **diverge from** that on the Continent.*
2 Mathematics (of a series) increase indefinitely as more of its terms are added.
– ORIGIN mid 17th cent.: from medieval Latin *divergere*, from Latin *dis-* 'in two ways' + *vergere* 'to turn or incline'.

divergence ▶ **noun** [mass noun] **1** the process or state of diverging: *the divergence between primates and other groups.* ■ [count noun] a difference in opinions, interests, etc.: *a fundamental divergence of attitude.* ■ [count noun] a place where airflows or ocean currents diverge, typically marked by downwelling (of air) or upwelling (of water).
2 Mathematics the scalar product of the operator del and a given vector, which gives a measure of the quantity of flux emanating from any point of the vector field or the rate of loss of mass, heat, etc., from it.

divergent ▶ **adjective 1** tending to be different or develop in different directions: *divergent interpretations* | *varieties of English can remain astonishingly **divergent from** one another.* ■ Psychology (of thought) using a variety of premises, especially unfamiliar

D

premises, as bases for inference, and avoiding common limiting assumptions in making deductions.
2 Mathematics (of a series) increasing indefinitely as more of its terms are added.
– DERIVATIVES **divergency** noun, **divergently** adverb.

divers /ˈdʌɪvəz/ ▸ **adjective** archaic or literary of varying types; several: *in divers places*.
– ORIGIN Middle English: via Old French from Latin *diversus* 'diverse', from *divertere* 'turn in separate ways' (see **DIVERT**).

D

diverse /dʌɪˈvəːs, ˈdʌɪvəːs/ ▸ **adjective** showing a great deal of variety; very different: *a culturally diverse population | subjects as diverse as architecture, language teaching, and the physical sciences*.
– DERIVATIVES **diversely** adverb.
– ORIGIN Middle English: variant of **DIVERS**.

diversify /dʌɪˈvəːsɪfʌɪ, dɪ-/ ▸ **verb** (**diversifies**, **diversifying**, **diversified**) make or become more diverse or varied: [no obj.] *the trilobites* ***diversified into*** *a great number of species* | [with obj.] *new plants will diversify the habitat*. ■ [no obj.] (of a company) enlarge or vary its range of products or field of operation: *the company expanded rapidly and* ***diversified into*** *computers*. ■ [with obj.] (often as adj. **diversified**) enlarge or vary the range of products or the field of operation of (a company): *the rise of the diversified corporation*.
– DERIVATIVES **diversification** noun.
– ORIGIN late Middle English (in the sense 'show diversity'): via Old French from medieval Latin *diversificare* 'make dissimilar', from Latin *diversus*, past participle of *divertere* (see **DIVERT**).

diversion /dʌɪˈvəːʃ(ə)n, dɪ-/ ▸ **noun 1** [mass noun] the action of turning something aside from its course: *the diversion of resources from defence to civil research*. ■ the action of reallocating something: *the diversion of funds to the Contras*. ■ [count noun] Brit. an alternative route for use by traffic when the usual road is temporarily closed: *the road was closed and diversions put into operation*.
2 an activity that diverts the mind from tedious or serious concerns; a recreation or pastime: *our chief diversion was reading* | [mass noun] *people in search of diversion*. ■ something intended to distract attention from something more important: *a subsidiary raid was carried out on the airfield to create a diversion*.
– DERIVATIVES **diversionary** adjective.
– ORIGIN late Middle English: from late Latin *diversio(n-)*, from Latin *divertere* 'turn aside' (see **DIVERT**).

diversity /dʌɪˈvəːsɪti, dɪ-/ ▸ **noun** (pl. **diversities**) [mass noun] the state of being diverse: *there was considerable diversity in the style of the reports*. ■ [in sing.] a range of different things: *newspapers were obliged to allow a diversity of views to be printed*.
– ORIGIN Middle English: from Old French *diversite*, from Latin *diversitas*, from *diversus* 'diverse', past participle of *divertere* 'turn aside' (see **DIVERT**).

divert /dʌɪˈvəːt, dɪ-/ ▸ **verb** [with obj.] **1** cause (someone or something) to change course or turn from one direction to another: *a scheme to* ***divert*** *water* ***from*** *the river to irrigate agricultural land*. ■ [no obj.] (of a vehicle or person) change course: *an aircraft has diverted and will be with you shortly*. ■ reallocate (money or resources) to a different purpose: *more of their advertising budget was* ***diverted into*** *promotions*.
2 distract (someone) from something: *she managed to* ***divert*** *Rose* ***from*** *the dangerous topic of Lady Usk*. ■ (usu. as adj. **diverting**) draw the attention of (someone) away from tedious or serious concerns; entertain or amuse: *a diverting book*.
– DERIVATIVES **divertingly** adverb.
– ORIGIN late Middle English: via French from Latin *divertere*, from *di-* 'aside' + *vertere* 'to turn'.

diverticula plural form of **DIVERTICULUM**.

diverticular /ˌdʌɪvəˈtɪkjʊlə/ ▸ **adjective** Medicine relating to diverticula.

diverticular disease ▸ **noun** [mass noun] a condition in which muscle spasm in the colon (lower intestine) in the presence of diverticula causes abdominal pain and disturbance of bowel function without inflammation.

diverticulitis /ˌdʌɪvətɪkjʊˈlʌɪtɪs/ ▸ **noun** [mass noun] Medicine inflammation of a diverticulum, especially in the colon, causing pain and disturbance of bowel function. Compare with **DIVERTICULOSIS**.

diverticulosis /ˌdʌɪvətɪkjʊˈləʊsɪs/ ▸ **noun** [mass noun] Medicine a condition in which diverticula are present in the intestine without signs of inflammation. Compare with **DIVERTICULITIS**.

diverticulum /ˌdʌɪvəˈtɪkjʊləm/ ▸ **noun** (pl. **diverticula** /-lə/) Anatomy & Zoology a blind tube leading from a cavity or passage. ■ Medicine an abnormal sac or pouch formed at a weak point in the wall of the alimentary tract.
– ORIGIN early 19th cent.: from medieval Latin, variant of Latin *deverticulum* 'byway', from *devertere* 'turn down or aside'.

divertimento /dɪˌvəːtɪˈmɛntəʊ, -ˌvɛːt-/ ▸ **noun** (pl. **divertimenti** /-ti/ or **divertimentos**) Music a light and entertaining composition, typically one in the form of a suite for chamber orchestra.
– ORIGIN mid 18th cent. (denoting a diversion or amusement): Italian, literally 'diversion'.

divertissement /dɪˈvəːtɪsmənt, ˌdiːvɛːˈtiːsmɒ̃/ ▸ **noun** a minor entertainment or diversion: *the intellectual divertissements of working men*. ■ Ballet a short dance within a ballet that displays a dancer's technical skill without advancing the plot or character development.
– ORIGIN early 18th cent. (specifically denoting a short ballet): French, from *divertiss-*, stem of *divertir*, from Latin *divertere* 'turn in separate ways'.

Dives /ˈdʌɪviːz/ ▸ **noun** literary used to refer to a typical or hypothetical rich man: *there must be rich and poor, Dives says, smacking his claret*.
– ORIGIN late Middle English: from late Latin, used in the Vulgate translation of the Bible (Luke 16).

divest /dʌɪˈvɛst, dɪ-/ ▸ **verb** [with obj.] (**divest someone/thing of**) deprive someone of (power, rights, or possessions): *men are unlikely to be divested of power without a struggle*. ■ deprive something of (a particular quality): *he has divested the original play of its charm*. ■ rid oneself of (a business interest or investment): *the government's policy of divesting itself of state holdings*. ■ dated or humorous relieve someone of (a garment): *she divested him of his coat*.
– ORIGIN early 17th cent.: alteration of *devest*, from Old French *desvestir*, from *des-* (expressing removal) + Latin *vestire* (from *vestis* 'garment').

divestiture (also **divesture**) ▸ **noun** another term for **DIVESTMENT**.
– ORIGIN early 17th cent.: from medieval Latin *divestit-* 'divested' (from the verb *divestire*) + **-URE**.

divestment ▸ **noun** [mass noun] the action or process of selling off subsidiary business interests or investments: *the importance of divestment* | [count noun] *proceeds from divestments*.

divi ▸ **noun** (pl. **divis**) variant spelling of **DIVVY**[1].

divide ▸ **verb 1** separate or be separated into parts: [with obj.] *consumer magazines can be* ***divided into*** *a number of categories* | [no obj.] *the cell clusters began to divide rapidly*. ■ [with obj.] separate (something) into portions and share out among a number of people: *Jack* ***divided up*** *the rest of the cash | profits from his single were* ***divided between*** *a number of charities*. ■ [with obj.] allocate (different parts of one's time or efforts) to different activities or places: *the last years of her life were* ***divided between*** *Bermuda and Paris*. ■ [with obj.] form a boundary between (two people or things): *glass panels* ***divide*** *the bar* ***from*** *the TV room*. ■ (of a legislative assembly) separate or be separated into two groups for voting: [no obj.] *the House divided: Ayes 287, Noes 196* | [with obj.] *the Party decided to put down an amendment and thus divide the House*.
2 disagree or cause to disagree: [with obj.] *the question had divided Frenchmen since the Revolution* | (as adj. **divided**) *a divided party leadership* | [no obj.] *cities where politicians frequently divide along racial lines*.
3 [with obj.] Mathematics find how many times (a number) contains another: *36* ***divided by*** *2 equals 18*. ■ [no obj.] (of a number) be susceptible of division without a remainder: *30 does not divide by 8*. ■ find how many times (a number) is contained in another: *divide 4 into 20*.
▸ **noun** a difference or disagreement between two groups, typically producing tension: *there was still a profound cultural* ***divide between*** *the parties*. ■ a boundary between two things: *symbolically, the difference of sex is a divide*. ■ chiefly US a ridge or line of high ground forming the division between two valleys or river systems.
– PHRASES **divide and rule** (or **conquer**) the policy of maintaining control over one's subordinates or opponents by encouraging dissent between them, thereby preventing them from uniting in opposition. **divided against itself** (of a group which should be coherent) split by factional interests: *the regime is profoundly divided against itself*.
– ORIGIN Middle English (as a verb): from Latin *dividere* 'force apart, remove'. The noun dates from the mid 17th cent.

divided highway ▸ **noun** N. Amer. a dual carriageway.

divided skirt ▸ **noun** dated culottes.

dividend /ˈdɪvɪdɛnd/ ▸ **noun 1** a sum of money paid regularly (typically annually) by a company to its shareholders out of its profits (or reserves). ■ a payment divided among a number of people, e.g. winners in a football pool or members of a cooperative. ■ an individual's share of a dividend. ■ (**dividends**) a benefit from an action or policy: *buying a rail pass may still* ***pay dividends***.
2 Mathematics a number to be divided by another number.
– ORIGIN late 15th cent. (in the general sense 'portion, share'): from Anglo-Norman French *dividende*, from Latin *dividendum* 'something to be divided', from the verb *dividere* (see **DIVIDE**).

dividend cover ▸ **noun** the ratio of a company's net profits to the total sum allotted in dividends to ordinary shareholders.

dividend warrant (US **dividend check**) ▸ **noun** a document that shows that a shareholder is entitled to a dividend.

dividend yield ▸ **noun** a dividend expressed as a percentage of a current share price.

divider ▸ **noun 1** a person or thing that divides a whole into parts. ■ (also **room divider**) a screen or piece of furniture that divides a room into two parts. ■ an issue on which opinions are divided: *on the Labour side, the big divider was still nuclear weapons*.
2 (**dividers**) a measuring compass, especially one with a screw for making fine adjustments.

dividing line ▸ **noun** the boundary between two areas. ■ a distinction or set of distinctions marking the difference between two things that are closely related: *the smudged dividing line between drama and reality*.

divi-divi /ˈdɪvɪˌdɪvi/ ▸ **noun** (pl. **divi-divis**) a small tropical American tree of the pea family. ● *Caesalpinia coriaria*, family Leguminosae.
■ [mass noun] the curled pods of the divi-divi tree, used as a source of tannin.
– ORIGIN mid 19th cent.: via American Spanish from Carib.

divination /ˌdɪvɪˈneɪʃ(ə)n/ ▸ **noun** [mass noun] the practice of seeking knowledge of the future or the unknown by supernatural means.
– DERIVATIVES **divinatory** adjective.
– ORIGIN late Middle English: from Latin *divinatio(n-)*, from *divinare* 'predict' (see **DIVINE**[2]).

divine[1] ▸ **adjective** (**diviner**, **divinest**) **1** of or like God or a god: *heroes with divine powers | paintings of shipwrecks being prevented by divine intervention*. ■ devoted to God; sacred: *divine liturgy*.
2 informal very pleasing; delightful: *he had the most divine smile*.
▸ **noun 1** dated a cleric or theologian.
2 (**the Divine**) providence or God.
– DERIVATIVES **divinely** adverb, **divineness** noun.
– ORIGIN late Middle English: via Old French from Latin *divinus*, from *divus* 'godlike' (related to *deus* 'god').

divine[2] ▸ **verb** [with obj.] **1** discover (something) by guesswork or intuition: *mum had divined my state of mind* | [with clause] *they had divined that he was a fake*.
2 have supernatural or magical insight into (future events): *frauds who claimed to divine the future in chickens' entrails*. ■ discover (water) by dowsing.
– DERIVATIVES **diviner** noun.
– ORIGIN late Middle English: from Old French *deviner* 'predict', from Latin *divinare*, from *divinus* (see **DIVINE**[1]).

Divine Office ▸ **noun** see **OFFICE** (sense 4).

divine right of kings ▸ **noun** the doctrine that kings derive their authority from God not their subjects, from which it follows that rebellion is the worst of political crimes. It was enunciated in Britain in the 16th and 17th centuries under the Stuarts and is also associated with the absolutism of Louis XIV of France.

divine service ▸ **noun** [mass noun] public Christian worship.

diving ▸ **noun** [mass noun] **1** the sport or activity of swimming or exploring under water.
2 the sport or activity of diving into water from a diving board.

diving beetle ▸ **noun** a predatory water beetle which has fringed back legs for swimming and which stores air under its wing cases while diving. ● Family Dytiscidae: numerous genera and species, including the **great diving beetle** (*Dytiscus marginalis*).

diving bell ▶ noun an open-bottomed chamber supplied with air, in which a person can be let down under water.

diving board ▶ noun an elevated board projecting over a swimming pool or other body of water, from which people dive or jump in.

diving duck ▶ noun a duck of a type which dives under water for food, such as the pochard, scaup, tufted duck, and goldeneye. Compare with DABBLING DUCK. ● Tribes Aythyini and Mergini, family Anatidae: several genera, in particular *Aythya* and *Bucephala*.

diving suit ▶ noun a watertight suit, typically with a helmet and an air supply, worn for working or exploring deep under water.

divining rod ▶ noun a stick or rod used for dowsing.

divinity /dɪˈvɪnɪti/ ▶ noun (pl. **divinities**) [mass noun] **1** the state or quality of being divine: *Christ's divinity.* ■ [count noun] a divine being; a god or goddess: *busts of Roman divinities.* ■ (**the Divinity**) God. **2** the study of religion; theology: *a doctor of divinity.*
– ORIGIN Middle English: from Old French *divinite*, from Latin *divinitas*, from *divinus* 'belonging to a deity' (see DIVINE[1]).

divinize /ˈdɪvɪnʌɪz/ (also **divinise**) ▶ verb [with obj.] make (someone) divine; deify.
– ORIGIN mid 17th cent.: from French *diviniser*, from *divin* 'divine'.

divisi /dɪˈviːsi/ ▶ adjective a musical direction indicating that a section of players should be divided into two or more groups each playing a different part: [postpositive] *violas divisi.*
▶ noun (pl. **same**) a passage written or played in this manner.
– ORIGIN Italian, literally 'divided' (plural), from *dividere* 'to divide'.

divisible /dɪˈvɪzɪb(ə)l/ ▶ adjective **1** capable of being divided: *the marine environment is **divisible into** a number of areas.* **2** Mathematics (of a number) containing another number a number of times without a remainder: *24 is **divisible by** 4.*
– DERIVATIVES **divisibility** noun.
– ORIGIN late Middle English: from late Latin *divisibilis*, from *divis-* 'divided', from the verb *dividere* (see DIVIDE).

division ▶ noun [mass noun] **1** the action of separating something into parts or the process of being separated: *the **division** of the land **into** small fields | a gene that helps regulate cell division.* ■ the distribution of something separated into parts: *the **division** of his estates **between** the two branches of his family.* ■ [count noun] an instance of members of a legislative body separating into two groups to vote: *the new clause was agreed without a division.* ■ Logic the action of dividing a wider class into two or more subclasses. **2** difference or disagreement between two or more groups, typically producing tension: *a growing sense of **division between** north and south* | [count noun] *a country with ethnic and cultural divisions.* **3** the process of dividing one number by another. ■ Mathematics the process of dividing a matrix, vector, or other quantity by another under specific rules to obtain a quotient. **4** [count noun] each of the parts into which something is divided: *the main divisions of the book.* ■ a major section of an organization, with responsibility for a particular area of activity: *a retail division.* ■ a group of army brigades or regiments: *an infantry division.* ■ a number of teams or competitors grouped together in a sport for competitive purposes according to such characteristics as ability or weight: *the club will finish second in Division One.* ■ a part of a county, country, or city defined for administrative or political purposes: *a licensing division of a district.* ■ Brit. a part of a county or borough forming a parliamentary constituency. ■ Botany a principal taxonomic category that ranks above class and below kingdom, equivalent to the phylum in zoology. ■ Zoology any subsidiary category between major levels of classification. **5** [count noun] a partition: *the villagers lived in a communal building and there were no solid divisions between neighbours.*
– PHRASES **division of labour** the assignment of different parts of a manufacturing process or task to different people in order to improve efficiency.
– ORIGIN late Middle English: from Old French *devision*, from Latin *divisio(n-)*, from the verb *dividere* (see DIVIDE).

divisional ▶ adjective **1** relating to an organizational or administrative division: *a divisional manager.* **2** forming a partition: *divisional walls.*
– DERIVATIVES **divisionally** adverb.

divisionalize /dɪˈvɪʒ(ə)n(ə)lʌɪz/ (also **divisionalise**) ▶ verb [with obj.] (usu. as adj. **divisionalized**) subdivide (an organization) into a number of divisions: *a large divisionalized Western corporation.*
– DERIVATIVES **divisionalization** noun.

division bell ▶ noun (in Britain) a bell rung in Parliament to announce an imminent division.

divisionism ▶ noun another term for POINTILLISM.

division lobby ▶ noun see LOBBY (sense 2 of the noun).

division sign ▶ noun the sign ÷, placed between two numbers showing that the first is to be divided by the second, as in *6 ÷ 3 = 2*.

divisive /dɪˈvʌɪsɪv/ ▶ adjective tending to cause disagreement or hostility between people: *the highly divisive issue of abortion.*
– DERIVATIVES **divisively** adverb, **divisiveness** noun.
– ORIGIN mid 16th cent. (as a noun denoting something that divides or separates): from late Latin *divisivus*, from Latin *dividere* (see DIVIDE).

divisor /dɪˈvʌɪzə/ ▶ noun Mathematics a number by which another number is to be divided. ■ a number that divides into another without a remainder.
– ORIGIN late Middle English: from French *diviseur* or Latin *divisor*, from *dividere* (see DIVIDE).

divorce ▶ noun the legal dissolution of a marriage by a court or other competent body: *her **divorce from** her first husband* | [mass noun] *one in three marriages ends in divorce.* ■ a legal decree dissolving a marriage. ■ [in sing.] a separation between things which were or ought to be connected: ***a divorce between** ownership and control in the typical large company.*
▶ verb [with obj.] legally dissolve one's marriage with (someone): *she divorced him in 1965* | [no obj.] *they divorced eight years later.* ■ separate or dissociate (something) from something else, typically with an undesirable effect: *religion cannot be **divorced from** morality.* ■ (**divorce oneself from**) dissociate oneself from (something): *a desire to divorce myself from history.*
– DERIVATIVES **divorcement** noun.
– ORIGIN late Middle English: the noun from Old French *divorce*, from Latin *divortium*, based on *divertere* (see DIVERT); the verb from Old French *divorcer*, from late Latin *divortiare*, from *divortium*.

divorcee /ˌdɪvɔːˈsiː/ ▶ noun (US masc. **divorcé**, fem. **divorcée** /-ˈseɪ/) a divorced person.
– ORIGIN early 19th cent.: from French *divorcé(e)* 'divorced man (or woman)'.

divot /ˈdɪvət/ ▶ noun **1** a piece of turf cut out of the ground by a golf club in making a stroke or by a sports player's boot. ■ a small hole made in such a way. **2** chiefly Scottish a piece of turf, as formerly used for roofing cottages.
– ORIGIN early 16th cent.: of unknown origin.

divulge /dʌɪˈvʌldʒ, dɪ-/ ▶ verb [with obj.] make known (private or sensitive information): *I am too much of a gentleman to divulge her age.*
– DERIVATIVES **divulgation** noun, **divulgence** noun.
– ORIGIN late Middle English (in the sense 'announce publicly'): from Latin *divulgare*, from *di-* 'widely' + *vulgare* 'publish' (from *vulgus* 'common people').

divvy[1] informal ▶ noun (also **divi**) (pl. **divvies**) Brit. a dividend or share, especially of profits earned by a cooperative: *the divvy is being held at 8.8p.*
▶ verb (**divvies**, **divvying**, **divvied**) [with obj.] share out: *they **divvied up** the proceeds.*
– ORIGIN late 19th cent.: abbreviation of DIVIDEND.

divvy[2] Brit. informal ▶ noun (pl. **divvies**) a foolish or stupid person.
▶ adjective foolish; stupid.
– ORIGIN 1970s: of unknown origin.

Diwali /dɪˈwɑːli/ (also **Divali**) ▶ noun a Hindu festival with lights, held in the period October to November. It is particularly associated with Lakshmi, the goddess of prosperity, and marks the beginning of the financial year in India.
– ORIGIN from Hindi *dīvālī*, from Sanskrit *dīpāvali* 'row of lights', from *dīpa* 'lamp' + *vali* 'row'.

diwan /dɪˈwɑːn/ (also **dewan**) ▶ noun **1** (in Islamic societies) a central finance department, chief administrative office, or regional governing body. **2** historical a chief treasury official, finance minister, or Prime Minister in some Indian states.
– ORIGIN Urdu, from Persian *dīwān* 'fiscal register'; compare with DIVAN.

Dixie an informal name for the Southern states of the US. It was used in the song 'Dixie' (1859), a marching song popular with Confederate soldiers in the American Civil War.
– PHRASES **whistle Dixie** US engage in unrealistic fantasies; waste one's time.

dixie ▶ noun (pl. **dixies**) a large iron cooking pot used by campers or soldiers.
– ORIGIN early 20th cent.: from Hindi *degcī* 'cooking pot', from Persian *degča*, diminutive of *deg* 'pot'.

D

Dixiecrat /ˈdɪksɪkrat/ ▶ noun US informal any of the Southern Democrats who seceded from the party in 1948 in opposition to its policy of extending civil rights.

Dixieland ▶ noun [mass noun] a kind of jazz with a strong two-beat rhythm and collective improvisation, which originated in New Orleans in the early 20th century.

DIY chiefly Brit. ▶ noun [mass noun] the activity of decorating, building, and making fixtures and repairs at home by oneself rather than employing a professional.
▶ adjective [attrib.] relating to DIY: *a DIY store.* ■ done in person by someone without the relevant qualifications: *we intend to have DIY funerals.*
– DERIVATIVES **DIY'er** noun.
– ORIGIN 1950s: abbreviation of DO-IT-YOURSELF.

diya /ˈdiːjə/ ▶ noun Indian a small cup-shaped oil lamp made of baked clay.
– ORIGIN from Hindi *diyā*.

Diyarbakir /dɪˈjɑːbəˌkɪə/ a city in SE Turkey, capital of a province of the same name; pop. 592,600 (est. 2007).

dizygotic /ˌdʌɪzʌɪˈgɒtɪk/ ▶ adjective (of twins) derived from two separate ova, and so not identical.

dizygous /dʌɪˈzʌɪgəs/ ▶ adjective another term for DIZYGOTIC.

dizzy ▶ adjective (**dizzier**, **dizziest**) having or involving a sensation of spinning around and losing one's balance: *Jonathan had begun to suffer dizzy spells* | figurative *he looked around, dizzy with happiness.* ■ causing a spinning sensation: *a sheer, dizzy drop* | figurative *a dizzy range of hues.* ■ informal (of a woman) silly: *a dizzy blonde.*
▶ verb (**dizzies**, **dizzying**, **dizzied**) [with obj.] (usu. as adj. **dizzying**) make (someone) feel unsteady, confused, or amazed: *the dizzying rate of change | her nearness dizzied him.*
– PHRASES **the dizzy heights** informal a position of great importance: *the dizzy heights of TV stardom.*
– DERIVATIVES **dizzily** adverb, **dizziness** noun.
– ORIGIN Old English *dysig* 'foolish', of West Germanic origin; related to Low German *dusig*, *dösig* 'giddy' and Old High German *tusic* 'foolish, weak'.

DJ[1] ▶ noun (pl. **DJs**) a disc jockey. ■ a person who uses samples of recorded music to make dance music.
▶ verb (**DJ's**, **DJ'ing**, **DJ'd**) [no obj.] perform as a disc jockey, typically in a club.

DJ[2] ▶ noun (pl. **DJs**) Brit. a dinner jacket.

Djakarta variant spelling of JAKARTA.

djebel ▶ noun variant spelling of JEBEL.

djellaba /ˈdʒɛləbə/ (also **djellabah** or **jellaba**) ▶ noun a loose hooded woollen cloak of a kind traditionally worn by Arabs.
– ORIGIN early 19th cent.: from Moroccan Arabic *jellāba*, *jellābiyya*.

djembe /ˈʒɛmbə, ˈʒɛmbeɪ/ ▶ noun a kind of goblet shaped hand drum originating in West Africa.
– ORIGIN French *djembé*, from Mande *jembe*.

Djerba /ˈdʒəːbə/ (also **Jerba**) a resort island in the Gulf of Gabès off the coast of Tunisia.

djibba (also **djibbah**) ▶ noun variant spelling of JIBBA.

Djibouti /dʒɪˈbuːti/ (also **Jibuti**) a country on the NE coast of Africa; pop. 724,600 (est. 2009); languages, Arabic (official), French (official), Somali and other Cushitic languages. ■ the capital of Djibouti, a port at the western end of the Gulf of Aden; pop. 583,000 (est. 2007).

> The territory became a French protectorate under the name of French Somaliland in 1897. It was renamed the French Territory of the Afars and Issas in 1946, the Afars and the Issas forming the two main ethnic groups. In 1977 the country achieved independence as the Republic of Djibouti.

– DERIVATIVES **Djiboutian** adjective & noun.

djinn ▸ noun variant spelling of JINN.

DK ▸ abbreviation Denmark (international vehicle registration).

dkl ▸ abbreviation US dekaliter(s).

dkm ▸ abbreviation US dekameter(s).

DL ▸ abbreviation ■ Deputy Lieutenant. ■ N. Amer. disabled list, a list of injured sports players who are temporarily unable to play.

dl ▸ abbreviation decilitre(s).

D-layer ▸ noun the lowest layer of the ionosphere, able to reflect low-frequency radio waves.
– ORIGIN 1930s: from an arbitrary use of the letter *D*.

DLitt ▸ abbreviation Doctor of Letters.
– ORIGIN from Latin *Doctor Litterarum*.

DLL ▸ abbreviation Computing dynamic linked library, a collection of subroutines stored on disk, which can be loaded into memory and executed when accessed by a running program.

D-lock ▸ noun a mechanism used to secure a bicycle or motorbike when parked, consisting of a U-shaped bar which is locked to a crosspiece of solid metal.

dlr ▸ abbreviation dollar.

DM ▸ abbreviation Deutschmark.

dm ▸ abbreviation decimetre(s).

DMA ▸ abbreviation direct memory access, a method allowing a peripheral device to transfer data to or from the memory of a computer system using operations not under the control of the central processor.

D-mark ▸ noun short for DEUTSCHMARK.

DMD ▸ abbreviation Duchenne muscular dystrophy.

DMs ▸ abbreviation Dr Martens.

DMSO ▸ abbreviation Chemistry dimethyl sulphoxide.

dmu ▸ abbreviation Brit. diesel multiple unit.

DMus ▸ abbreviation Doctor of Music.

DMV ▸ abbreviation (in the US) Department of Motor Vehicles.

DMZ ▸ abbreviation N. Amer. demilitarized zone, an area from which warring parties agree to remove their military forces.

DNA ▸ noun [mass noun] Biochemistry deoxyribonucleic acid, a self-replicating material which is present in nearly all living organisms as the main constituent of chromosomes. It is the carrier of genetic information.

> Each molecule of DNA consists of two strands coiled round each other to form a double helix, a structure like a spiral ladder. Each rung of the ladder consists of a pair of chemical groups called bases (of which there are four types), which combine in specific pairs so that the sequence on one strand of the double helix is complementary to that on the other: it is the specific sequence of bases which constitutes the genetic information. ■ the fundamental and distinctive characteristics or qualities of someone or something, especially when regarded as unchangeable: *diversity is part of the company's DNA | men just don't get shopping—it's not in our DNA.*

DNA fingerprinting (also **DNA profiling**) ▸ noun another term for GENETIC FINGERPRINTING.

DNase /ˌdiːɛnˈeɪz/ ▸ noun [mass noun] Biochemistry an enzyme which catalyses the hydrolysis of DNA into oligonucleotides and smaller molecules. Also called DEOXYRIBONUCLEASE.
– ORIGIN 1940s: from **DNA** + **-ASE**.

DNA virus ▸ noun a virus in which the genetic information is stored in the form of DNA (as opposed to RNA).

DNB ▸ abbreviation Dictionary of National Biography.

Dnieper /ˈdniːpə/ a river of eastern Europe, rising in Russia west of Moscow and flowing southwards some 2,200 km (1,370 miles) through Ukraine to the Black Sea. Ukrainian name **Dnipro** /dniːˈprəʊ/.

Dniester /ˈdniːstə/ a river of eastern Europe, rising in the Carpathian Mountains in western Ukraine and flowing 1,410 km (876 miles) to the Black Sea near Odessa. Russian name **Dnestr** /dnʲiˈstʲer/.

Dniprodzerzhinsk /ˌdniːprədzəˈʒɪnsk/ an industrial city and river port in Ukraine, on the River Dnieper; pop. 245,100 (est. 2009). Former name (until 1936) KAMENSKOYE.

Dnipropetrovsk /ˌdniːprəpɛˈtrɒfsk/ an industrial city and river port in Ukraine, on the River Dnieper; pop. 1,017,500 (est. 2009). It was known as Yekaterinoslav (Ekaterinoslav) until 1926. Russian name **Dnepropetrovsk** /ˌdnʲɪprəpʲɪˈtrofsk/.

D-notice ▸ noun Brit. a government notice issued to news editors requiring them not to publicize certain information for reasons of national security.
– ORIGIN Second World War: *D* for *defence*.

DNR ▸ abbreviation ■ (in the US) Department of Natural Resources. ■ do not resuscitate, denoting an instruction not to attempt the resuscitation of a terminally ill patient after cardiac arrest in hospital.

DNS ▸ abbreviation Computing ■ domain name server, the system that automatically translates Internet addresses to the numeric machine addresses that computers use. ■ domain name system, the hierarchical method by which Internet addresses are constructed.

do[1] ▸ verb (**does**; **doing**; past **did**; past participle **done**)
1 [with obj.] perform (an action, the precise nature of which is often unspecified): *something must be done about the city's traffic | she knew what she was doing | what can I do for you? | Brian was looking at the girl, and had been doing so for most of the hearing.* ■ perform (a particular task): *Dad always did the washing up on Sundays.* ■ work on (something) to bring it to completion or to a required state: *it takes them longer to do their hair than me | she's the secretary and does the publicity.* ■ [no obj.] Brit. informal do the cleaning for a person or household: *Florrie usually did for the Shermans in the mornings.* ■ make or have available and provide: *many hotels don't do single rooms at all | [with two objs] he decided to do her a pastel sketch of himself.* ■ solve; work out: *Joe was doing sums aloud.* ■ cook (food) to completion or to a specified degree: *if a knife inserted into the centre comes out clean, then your pie is done.* ■ (often in questions) work at for a living: *what does she do?* ■ learn or study; take as one's subject: *I'm doing English, German, and History.* ■ produce or give a performance of (a particular play, opera, etc.): *the Royal Shakespeare Company are doing Macbeth next month.* ■ informal imitate (a particular person) in order to entertain people: *he not only does Schwarzenegger and Groucho, he becomes them.* ■ informal take (a narcotic drug): *he doesn't smoke, drink, or do drugs.* ■ attend to (someone): *the barber said he'd do me next.* ■ vulgar slang have sexual intercourse with. ■ (**do it**) informal have sexual intercourse. ■ (**do it**) informal urinate or defecate.
2 [with obj.] achieve or complete, in particular: ■ travel (a specified distance): *one car I looked at had done 112,000 miles.* ■ travel at (a specified speed): *I was speeding, doing seventy-five.* ■ make (a particular journey): *last time I did Oxford–York return by train it was £50.* ■ informal visit as a tourist, especially in a superficial or hurried way: *the Americans are allotted only a day to do the Yorkshire Moors.* ■ spend (a specified period of time) in prison or in a particular occupation: *he did five years for manslaughter | Peter has done thirteen years in the RAF.* ■ [no obj.] informal finish: *you must sit there and wait till I've done | [with present participle] we've done arguing.* ■ (**be done**) be over: *the special formula continues to beautify your tan when the day is done.* ■ (**be/have done with**) Brit. give up concern for; have finished with: *I should sell the place and* ***be done with it*** *| Steve was not done with her.*
3 [no obj., with adverbial] act or behave in a specified way: *they are free to do as they please | you did well to bring her back.* ■ make progress or perform in a specified way; get on or fare: *when a team is doing badly, it's not easy for a new player to settle in | Mrs Walters, how're you doing?* ■ [with obj. and complement] have a specified effect on: *the walk will do me good.* ■ [with obj.] result in: *the years of stagnation did a lot of harm to the younger generation.*
4 [no obj.] be suitable or acceptable: *if he's anything like you, he'll do | [with obj.] a couple of quid'll do me.* ■ suffice or be usable: *a strip of white cotton about 20 yards long did for a fence.*
5 [with obj.] informal beat up or kill: *one day I'll do him.* ■ (**be done**) be ruined: *once you falter, you're done.* ■ rob (a place): *this would be an easy place to do and there was plenty of money lying around.* ■ Brit. informal swindle: *a thousand pounds for one set of photos—Jacqui had been done.*
6 [with obj.] (usu. **be/get done for**) Brit. informal prosecute or convict: *we got done for conspiracy to cause GBH.*
▸ **auxiliary verb 1** used before a verb (except *be, can, may, ought, shall, will*) in questions and negative statements: *do you have any pets? | did he see me? | I don't smoke | it does not matter.* ■ used to make tag questions: *you write poetry, don't you? | I never seem to say the right thing, do I?* ■ used in negative commands: *don't be silly | do not forget.*
2 used to refer back to a verb already mentioned: *he looks better than he did before | you wanted to enjoy yourself, and you did | as they get smarter, so do the crooks.*
3 used to give emphasis to a positive verb: *I do want to act on this | he did look tired.* ■ used in positive commands to give polite encouragement: *do tell me! | do sit down.*
4 used with inversion of a subject and verb when an adverbial phrase begins a clause for emphasis: *only rarely did they succumb | not only did the play close, the theatre closed.*
▸ **noun** (pl. **dos** or **do's**) **1** Brit. informal a party or other social event: *the soccer club Christmas do.*
2 (also **'do**) informal, chiefly N. Amer. short for HAIRDO.
3 archaic, informal a swindle or hoax.
– PHRASES **be nothing to do with** be no business or concern of: *it's my decision—it's nothing to do with you.* ■ be unconnected with: *he says his departure is nothing to do with the resignation calls.* **be to do with** be concerned or connected with: *the problems are usually to do with family tension.* **do a —** informal behave in a manner characteristic of (a specified person): *he did a Garbo after his flop in the play.* **do battle** enter into a conflict. **don't — me** informal do not use the word — to me: *'Don't morning me. Where the hell've you been all night?'* **do one** [in imperative] N. English informal go away: *look, just do one, will you!* **do or die** persist, even if death is the result. ■ used to describe a critical situation where one's actions may result in victory or defeat: *the 72nd hole was do or die.* **dos and don'ts** rules of behaviour: *I have no knowledge of the political dos and don'ts.* **do well for oneself** become successful or wealthy. **do well out of** make a profit out of; benefit from: *they're doing well out of scrap metal.* **have (got) — to do with** be connected with (someone or something) to the extent specified: *John's got nothing to do with that terrible murder.* ■ (**have nothing to do with**) have no contact or dealings with: *Billy and his father have had nothing to do with each other for nearly twenty years.* **it isn't done** Brit. used to express the opinion that a particular thing contravenes custom or propriety: *in such a society it is not done to admit to taking religion seriously.* **it won't do** Brit. used to express the opinion that a particular person's behaviour is unsatisfactory and cannot be allowed to continue: *Can't have that kind of talk—I've told you before, it won't do.* **no you don't!** informal used to indicate that one intends to prevent someone from doing what they were about to do: *Sharon went to get in the taxi. 'Oh no you don't', said Steve.* **that does it!** informal used to indicate that one will not tolerate a particular thing any longer: *That does it! Let's go!* **that's done it!** informal used to express dismay or anger when something has gone wrong.
– PHRASAL VERBS **do away with** informal put an end to; remove: *the desire to do away with racism.* ■ kill: *he didn't have the courage to do away with her.* **do by** dated treat or deal with in a specified way: *do as you would be done by | she did well by them.* **do someone/thing down** Brit. informal get the better of someone, typically in an underhand way. ■ criticize someone or something: *they're always moaning and doing British industry down.* **do for** informal defeat, ruin, or kill: *without that contract we're done for | it was the cold that did for him in the end.* **do something (or nothing) for** informal enhance (or detract from) the appearance or quality of: *whatever the new forum does for industry, it certainly does something for the Minister | that scarf does nothing for you.* **do someone in** informal kill someone. ■ (**be done in**) informal be tired out: *there was 1 minute 4 seconds to play and the Lions were done in.* **do something in** informal injure something: *I did my back in a few years ago.* **do someone out of** informal deprive someone of (something) in an underhand or unfair way. **do something out** Brit. informal decorate or furnish a room or building in a particular style, colour, or material: *the basement is* ***done out in*** *limed oak.* **do someone over** Brit. informal beat someone up. **do something over 1** Brit. informal ransack a place, especially while searching for something worth stealing. **2** informal decorate or furnish a room or building. **3** N. Amer. informal repeat something: *to absorb the lesson, I had to do it over and over.* **do up** be able to be fastened: *a shirt so tight that not all of the buttons did up.* **do someone up** dress someone up, especially in an elaborate or impressive way: *Agnes was all done up in a slinky black number.* **do something up 1** fasten something: *she drew on her coat and did up the buttons.* ■ arrange one's hair in a particular way, especially so as to be pulled back from one's face or shoulders: *her dark hair was done up in a pony tail.* ■ wrap something up: *unwieldy packs all done up with string.* **2** Brit. informal renovate or redecorate a room or building: *Mrs Hamilton did*

the place up for letting. **do with** [with modal] would find useful or would like to have or do: *I could do with a cup of coffee.* ■ **(can't/won't be doing with)** Brit. be unwilling to tolerate or be bothered with: *she couldn't be doing with meals for one.* **do without** [with modal] manage without: *she could do without food for a day.* ■ informal would prefer not to have: *I can do without your carping first thing in the morning.*
– ORIGIN Old English *dōn*, of Germanic origin; related to Dutch *doen* and German *tun*, from an Indo-European root shared by Greek *tithēmi* 'I place' and Latin *facere* 'make, do'.

do[2] ▸ **noun** variant spelling of **DOH**[1].

do. ▸ **abbreviation** dated ditto.

DOA ▸ **abbreviation** dead on arrival, used to describe a person who is declared dead immediately upon their arrival at a hospital.

doable /ˈduːəb(ə)l/ ▸ **adjective** informal within one's powers; feasible: *none of the jobs were fun, but they were doable.*

dob ▸ **verb (dobs, dobbing, dobbed)** [with obj.] Austral./NZ informal **1 (dob someone in)** inform against someone: *Helen dobbed me in to Mum.* ■ [no obj.] **(dob on)** inform on; betray.
2 (dob something in) contribute money to a common cause: *everyone dobbed in a few dollars.*
3 (dob someone in) impose on someone to do something: *I dobbed him in to do the cleaning.*
– DERIVATIVES **dobber** noun.
– ORIGIN 1950s: figurative use of dialect *dob* 'put down abruptly', later 'throw something at a target'.

d.o.b. ▸ **abbreviation** date of birth.

dobbin ▸ **noun** a pet name for a draught horse or a farm horse.
– ORIGIN late 16th cent.: pet form of the given name *Robert*.

dobby ▸ **noun** (pl. **dobbies**) a mechanism attached to a loom for weaving small patterns similar to but simpler than those produced by a Jacquard loom.
– ORIGIN late 19th cent.: perhaps an application of the given name *Dobbie*, from *Dob* (alteration of the given name *Rob*). The usage is probably an extension of the earlier sense 'benevolent elf' (who performed household tasks secretly).

dobe /ˈdəʊbi/ ▸ **noun** [mass noun] US informal adobe.
– ORIGIN mid 19th cent.: abbreviation.

Dobermann /ˈdəʊbəmən/ (also **Dobermann pinscher** /ˈpɪnʃə/) (chiefly N. Amer. also **Doberman**) ▸ **noun** a large dog of a German breed with powerful jaws and a smooth coat, typically black with tan markings.
– ORIGIN early 20th cent.: from the name of Ludwig *Dobermann*, 19th-cent. German dog breeder + German *Pinscher* 'terrier'.

dobra /ˈdɒbrə/ ▸ **noun** the basic monetary unit of São Tomé and Principe, equal to 100 centavos.
– ORIGIN from Portuguese *dóbra* 'doubloon'.

Dobrich /ˈdɒbrɪtʃ/ a city in NE Bulgaria, the centre for an agricultural region; pop. 93,163 (2008). It was named Tolbukhin 1949–91 after the Soviet marshal Fyodor Ivanovich Tolbukhin.

dobro /ˈdɒbrəʊ/ ▸ **noun** (pl. **dobros**) trademark a type of acoustic guitar with steel resonating discs inside the body under the bridge.
– ORIGIN 1950s: from *Do(pěra) Bro(thers)*, the Czech-American inventors of the instrument.

Dobruja /ˈdɒbrʊdʒə/ a district of eastern Romania and NE Bulgaria on the Black Sea coast, bounded on the north and west by the River Danube.

dobsonfly /ˈdɒbs(ə)nflʌɪ/ ▸ **noun** (pl. **dobsonflies**) a large grey North American winged insect related to the alderflies. Its predatory aquatic larva (the hellgrammite) is often used as fishing bait. ● Family Corydalidae, order Neuroptera: several genera and species, in particular *Corydalis cornutus*.
– ORIGIN early 20th cent.: of unknown origin.

Dobsonian /dɒbˈsəʊnɪən/ ▸ **adjective** relating to or denoting a low-cost Newtonian reflecting telescope with large aperture and short focal length, or the simple altazimuth mount used for it.
– ORIGIN 1980s: from the name of John *Dobson*, American amateur astronomer, + **-IAN**.

Dobson unit (abbrev.: **DU**) ▸ **noun** a unit of measurement for the total amount of ozone in the atmosphere above a point on the earth's surface, one Dobson unit being equivalent to a layer of pure ozone 0.01 mm thick at standard temperature and pressure.
– ORIGIN 1980s: from the name of G. M. B. *Dobson* (1889–1976), British meteorologist.

doc ▸ **abbreviation** informal ■ doctor. ■ Computing document.

docent /ˈdəʊs(ə)nt/ ▸ **noun 1** (in certain US and European universities and colleges) a member of the teaching staff immediately below professorial rank.
2 a person who acts as a guide, typically on a voluntary basis, in a museum, art gallery, or zoo.
– ORIGIN late 19th cent.: via German from Latin *docent-* 'teaching', from *docere* 'teach'.

Docetism /dəˈsiːtɪz(ə)m, ˈdəʊsɪˌtɪz(ə)m/ ▸ **noun** [mass noun] the doctrine, important in Gnosticism, that Christ's body was not human but either a phantasm or of real but celestial substance, and that therefore his sufferings were only apparent.
– DERIVATIVES **Docetist** noun.
– ORIGIN mid 19th cent.: from medieval Latin *Docetae* (the name, based on Greek *dokein* 'seem', given to a group of 2nd-cent. Christian heretics) + **-ISM**.

doch an dorris ▸ **noun** variant spelling of **DEOCH AN DORIS**.

docile /ˈdəʊsʌɪl/ ▸ **adjective** ready to accept control or instruction; submissive: *a cheap and docile workforce* | *she's a black Labrador, gentle and docile.*
– DERIVATIVES **docilely** adverb, **docility** noun.
– ORIGIN late 15th cent. (in the sense 'apt or willing to learn'): from Latin *docilis*, from *docere* 'teach'.

dock[1] ▸ **noun** an enclosed area of water in a port for the loading, unloading, and repair of ships.
■ **(docks)** a group of docks along with wharves and associated buildings. ■ short for **DRY DOCK**. ■ N. Amer. a jetty or pier where a ship may moor. ■ (also **loading dock**) a platform for loading lorries or goods trains.
▸ **verb** [no obj.] (of a ship) come into a dock and tie up at a wharf: *the ship docked at Southampton.* ■ [with obj.] bring (a ship or boat) into a dock: *the yard where the boats were docked and maintained.* ■ (of a spacecraft) join with a space station or another spacecraft in space. ■ attach (a piece of equipment) to another: *the user wants to dock a portable into a desktop computer.*
– PHRASES **in dock** (of a ship) moored in a dock. ■ Brit. informal (of a person) not fully fit and out of action: *he grazed my arm and put me in dock for a couple of days.*
– ORIGIN late Middle English: from Middle Dutch, Middle Low German *docke*, of unknown origin.

dock[2] ▸ **noun** the enclosure in a criminal court where a defendant stands or sits: *the nine others **in the dock** face a combination of charges.*
– ORIGIN late 16th cent.: probably originally slang and related to Flemish *dok* 'chicken coop, rabbit hutch', of unknown origin.

dock[3] ▸ **noun** a coarse weed of temperate regions, with inconspicuous greenish or reddish flowers. The leaves are used to relieve nettle stings. ● Genus *Rumex*, family Polygonaceae.
– ORIGIN Old English *docce*, of Germanic origin; related to Dutch dialect *dokke*.

dock[4] ▸ **verb** [with obj.] **1** deduct (something, especially an amount of money or a point in a game): *the agency enforce payments by docking money from the father's salary* | [with two objs] *he was docked a penalty point.*
2 cut short (an animal's tail): *their tails were docked.*
▸ **noun** the solid bony or fleshy part of an animal's tail, excluding the hair. ■ the stump left after a tail has been docked.
– ORIGIN late Middle English: perhaps related to Frisian *dok* 'bunch, ball (of string etc.)' and German *Docke* 'doll'. The original noun sense was 'the solid part of an animal's tail', whence the verb sense 'cut short an animal's tail', later generalized to 'reduce, deduct'.

dockage ▸ **noun** [mass noun] accommodation or berthing of ships in docks.

dock brief ▸ **noun** chiefly historical a brief given directly to a barrister selected from a panel of those present by a prisoner in the dock, without the agency of a solicitor.

docken /ˈdɒk(ə)n/ ▸ **noun** chiefly Scottish another term for **DOCK**[3] (the plant).
– ORIGIN late Middle English: apparently from Old English *doccan*, plural of *docce* (see **DOCK**[3]).

docker ▸ **noun** a person employed in a port to load and unload ships.

docket ▸ **noun 1** Brit. a document or label listing the contents of a consignment or package. ■ a customs warrant certifying that duty has been paid on goods entering a country. ■ a voucher entitling the holder to receive or obtain delivery of goods ordered.
2 N. Amer. a list of cases for trial or people having cases pending. ■ an agenda or list of things to be done.
▸ **verb (dockets, docketing, docketed)** [with obj.] **1** mark (a consignment or package) with a document or label listing the contents.
2 N. Amer. enter (a case) on a list of those due to be heard.
– ORIGIN late 15th cent.: perhaps from **DOCK**[4]. The word originally denoted a short summary or abstract; hence, in the early 18th cent., 'a document giving particulars of a consignment'.

docking station ▸ **noun** a device to which a portable computer is connected so that it can be used like a desktop computer, with an external power supply, monitor, data transfer capability, etc.

dockland ▸ **noun** [mass noun] (also **docklands**) Brit. the area containing a city's docks: *an old fishing village just west of dockland* | *plans to redevelop London's docklands.*

dockominium /ˌdɒkəˈmɪnɪəm/ ▸ **noun** (pl. **dockominiums**) US a waterfront condominium with a private mooring. ■ a privately owned landing stage at a marina.
– ORIGIN 1980s: from **DOCK**[1], on the pattern of *condominium.*

dockside ▸ **noun** the area immediately adjacent to a dock.

dockyard ▸ **noun** an area with docks and equipment for repairing and maintaining ships.

Doc Martens ▸ **plural noun** see **DR MARTENS**.

doco ▸ **noun** (pl. **docos**) Austral./NZ informal a documentary: *a doco on the D-Day landings.*

doctor ▸ **noun 1** a person who is qualified to treat people who are ill: [as title] *Doctor Thornhill.* ■ N. Amer. a qualified dentist or veterinary surgeon. ■ [with modifier] informal a person employed to make improvements or give advice: *the script doctor rewrote the original.*
2 (Doctor) a person who holds the highest university degree: *he was made a Doctor of Divinity.*
■ short for **DOCTOR OF THE CHURCH**. ■ archaic a teacher or learned person: *the wisest doctor is gravelled by the inquisitiveness of a child.*
3 Angling an artificial fishing fly.
▸ **verb** [with obj.] **1** change the content or appearance of (a document or picture) in order to deceive; falsify: *the reports could have been doctored.* ■ alter the content of (food or drink) by adding strong or harmful ingredients: *he denied doctoring Stephen's drinks.*
■ Cricket & Baseball tamper with (a ball) so as to affect its flight when bowled or pitched.
2 (usu. as noun **doctoring**) informal treat (someone) medically: *he contemplated giving up doctoring.*
■ remove the sexual organs of (an animal) so that it cannot reproduce. ■ repair (a machine).
– PHRASES **be (just) what the doctor ordered** informal be very beneficial or desirable under the circumstances: *a 2-0 victory is just what the doctor ordered.* **go for the doctor** Austral./NZ informal make an all-out effort: *he will go for the doctor in Parliament next week.*
– DERIVATIVES **doctorly** adjective.
– ORIGIN Middle English (in the senses 'learned person' and 'Doctor of the Church'): via Old French from Latin *doctor* 'teacher' (from *docere* 'teach').

doctoral /ˈdɒkt(ə)r(ə)l/ ▸ **adjective** [attrib.] relating to or designed to achieve a doctorate: *a doctoral thesis.*

doctorate /ˈdɒkt(ə)rət/ ▸ **noun** the highest degree awarded by a university faculty or other approved educational organization: *a doctorate in art history.*
– ORIGIN mid 17th cent.: from medieval Latin *doctoratus* 'made a doctor'.

Doctor Martens ▸ **plural noun** see **DR MARTENS**.

Doctor of Philosophy (abbrev.: **PhD** or **DPhil**) ▸ **noun** a doctorate in any faculty except medicine or sometimes theology. ■ a person holding such a degree.

Doctor of the Church ▸ **noun** one of the early Christian theologians regarded as especially authoritative in the Western Church (particularly St Augustine of Hippo, St Jerome, St Ambrose, and St Gregory the Great) or later so designated by the Pope (e.g. St Thomas Aquinas, St Teresa of Ávila). Compare with **FATHERS OF THE CHURCH** (see **FATHER** (sense 3 of the noun)).

doctrinaire /ˌdɒktrɪˈnɛː/ ▸ **adjective** seeking to impose a doctrine in all circumstances without regard to practical considerations: *the administration's doctrinaire economic policy.*
▸ **noun** a doctrinaire person.
– ORIGIN early 19th cent.: from French, from *doctrine* (see **DOCTRINE**).

D

doctrinal /dɒkˈtrʌɪn(ə)l/ ▶ adjective concerned with a doctrine or doctrines: *doctrinal disputes.*
– DERIVATIVES **doctrinally** adverb.
– ORIGIN late Middle English: from late Latin *doctrinalis*, from *doctrina* 'teaching, learning' (see DOCTRINE).

doctrine /ˈdɒktrɪn/ ▶ noun a belief or set of beliefs held and taught by a Church, political party, or other group: *the doctrine of predestination.* ■ US a stated principle of government policy, mainly in foreign or military affairs: *the Truman Doctrine.*
– ORIGIN late Middle English: from Old French, from Latin *doctrina* 'teaching, learning', from *doctor* 'teacher', from *docere* 'teach'.

docudrama /ˈdɒkjʊˌdrɑːmə/ ▶ noun a dramatized television film based on real events.
– ORIGIN 1960s: blend of DOCUMENTARY and DRAMA.

document ▶ noun /ˈdɒkjʊm(ə)nt/ a piece of written, printed, or electronic matter that provides information or evidence or that serves as an official record.
▶ verb /ˈdɒkjʊmɛnt/ [with obj.] record (something) in written, photographic, or other form: *the photographer spent years documenting the lives of miners.* ■ support or accompany with documentation.
– DERIVATIVES **documentable** adjective, **documental** /-ˈmɛnt(ə)l/ adjective, **documentative** adjective.
– ORIGIN late Middle English: from Old French, from Latin *documentum* 'lesson, proof' (in medieval Latin 'written instruction, official paper'), from *docere* 'teach'.

documentalist ▶ noun a person engaged in keeping records and providing information.

documentarian /ˌdɒkjʊmɛnˈtɛːrɪən/ ▶ noun **1** (also **documentarist**) a photographer specializing in producing a factual record. ■ a director or producer of documentaries.
2 an expert analyst of historical documents.

documentary ▶ adjective **1** consisting of or based on official documents: *documentary evidence of regular payments from the company.*
2 using pictures or interviews with people involved in real events to provide a factual report on a particular subject: *a documentary programme about Manchester United.*
▶ noun (pl. **documentaries**) a film or television or radio programme that provides a factual report on a particular subject.

documentation ▶ noun [mass noun] **1** material that provides official information or evidence or that serves as a record: *you will have to complete the relevant documentation.* ■ the written specification and instructions accompanying a product, especially a computer program or hardware.
2 the process of classifying and annotating texts, photographs, etc.: *she arranged the collection and documentation of photographs.*

document case ▶ noun a lightweight, typically flexible case for carrying papers.

docusoap ▶ noun a documentary following people in a particular occupation or location over a period of time.
– ORIGIN 1990s: blend of DOCUMENTARY and SOAP.

docutainment /ˌdɒkjʊˈteɪnmənt/ ▶ noun [mass noun] N. Amer. entertainment provided by films or other presentations that is intended both to inform and entertain.
– ORIGIN 1970s: blend of DOCUMENTARY and ENTERTAINMENT.

DOD ▶ abbreviation (in the US) Department of Defense.

dodder¹ ▶ verb [no obj.] (often as adj. **doddering**) tremble or totter, typically because of old age: *that doddering old fool.*
– DERIVATIVES **dodderer** noun.
– ORIGIN early 17th cent.: variant of obsolete dialect *dadder*; related to DITHER.

dodder² ▶ noun a widely distributed parasitic climbing plant of the convolvulus family, with leafless thread-like stems that are attached to the host plant by means of suckers. ● Genus *Cuscuta*, family Convolvulaceae.
– ORIGIN Middle English: related to Middle Low German *doder*, *dodder*, Middle High German *toter*.

doddery ▶ adjective slow and unsteady in movement because of weakness in old age.

doddle ▶ noun [in sing.] Brit. informal a very easy task: *this printer's a doddle to set up and use.*
– ORIGIN 1930s: perhaps from dialect *doddle* 'toddle', of unknown origin.

dodeca- /ˈdəʊdɛkə/ ▶ combining form (used chiefly in scientific and musical terms) twelve; having twelve: *dodecahedron* | *dodecaphonic.*
– ORIGIN from Greek.

dodecagon /dəʊˈdɛkəg(ə)n/ ▶ noun a plane figure with twelve straight sides and angles.
– DERIVATIVES **dodecagonal** /dəʊdɪˈkag(ə)n(ə)l/ adjective.
– ORIGIN late 17th cent.: from Greek *dōdekagōnon*, neuter (used as a noun) of *dōdekagōnos* 'twelve-angled'.

dodecahedron /ˌdəʊdɛkəˈhiːdr(ə)n, -ˈhɛd-/ ▶ noun (pl. **dodecahedra** /-drə/ or **dodecahedrons**) a three-dimensional shape having twelve plane faces, in particular a regular solid figure with twelve equal pentagonal faces.
– DERIVATIVES **dodecahedral** adjective.
– ORIGIN late 16th cent.: from Greek *dōdekaedron*, neuter (used as a noun) of *dōdekaedros* 'twelve-faced'.

Dodecanese /ˌdəʊdɪkəˈniːz/ a group of twelve islands in the SE Aegean, of which the largest is Rhodes.

dodecaphonic /ˌdəʊdɛkəˈfɒnɪk/ ▶ adjective Music another term for TWELVE-NOTE.

dodge ▶ verb [with obj.] **1** avoid (someone or something) by a sudden quick movement: *marchers had to dodge missiles thrown by loyalists.* ■ [no obj., with adverbial of direction] move quickly to one side or out of the way: *Adam dodged between the cars.* ■ avoid (something) in a cunning or dishonest way: *he'd caught her dodging fares on the underground.*
2 (often as noun **dodging**) Photography expose (one area of a print) less than the rest during processing or enlarging.
3 [no obj.] Bell-ringing (of a bell in change-ringing) move one place contrary to the normal sequence, and then back again in the following round.
▶ noun **1** a sudden quick movement to avoid someone or something. ■ informal a cunning trick or dishonest act, in particular one intended to avoid something unpleasant: *the grant system's widespread use as a tax dodge.*
2 Bell-ringing the dodging of a bell in change-ringing.
– ORIGIN mid 16th cent. (in the senses 'dither' and 'haggle'): of unknown origin.

dodgeball ▶ noun [mass noun] N. Amer. a game in which players, in teams, form a circle and try to hit opponents with a large ball.

Dodge City a city in SW Kansas; pop. 25,689 (est. 2008). Established in 1872 as a railhead on the Santa Fe Trail, it rapidly gained a reputation as a rowdy frontier town.

dodgem (also **dodgem car**) ▶ noun Brit. a small electrically powered car with rubber bumpers all round, driven in an enclosure at a funfair with the aim of bumping into other such cars.
– ORIGIN 1920s: US proprietary name (as *Dodg'em*), from the phrase *dodge them.*

dodger ▶ noun **1** [often with modifier] informal a person who engages in cunning tricks or dishonest practices to avoid something unpleasant: *tax dodgers.* ■ [in combination] Brit. humorous a person who dislikes or avoids a specified thing: *a greasy-haired soap-dodger.*
2 Nautical a canvas screen on a ship giving protection from spray.

Dodgson, Charles Lutwidge, see CARROLL.

dodgy ▶ adjective (**dodgier**, **dodgiest**) Brit. informal dishonest or unreliable: *a dodgy second-hand car salesman.* ■ potentially dangerous: *activities like these could be dodgy for your heart.* ■ of low quality: *Spurs' dodgy defence had thrown away a 2-0 lead.*
– DERIVATIVES **dodgily** adverb, **dodginess** noun.

dodo /ˈdəʊdəʊ/ ▶ noun (pl. **dodos** or **dodoes**) a large extinct flightless bird with a stout body, stumpy wings, a large head, and a heavy hooked bill. It was found on Mauritius until the end of the 17th century. ● *Raphus cucullatus*, family Raphidae.
■ informal an old-fashioned and ineffective person.
– PHRASES **(as) dead as a** (or **the**) **dodo** informal completely dead or extinct. ■ no longer effective, valid, or interesting: *the campaign was as dead as a dodo.*
– ORIGIN early 17th cent.: from Portuguese *doudo* 'simpleton' (because the bird had no fear of man and was easily killed). Compare with DOTTEREL.

Dodoma /dəʊˈdəʊmə/ the capital of Tanzania, in the centre of the country; pop. 183,000 (est. 2007).

DoE ▶ abbreviation (formerly in the UK) Department of the Environment.

doe ▶ noun a female deer, especially a female roe, fallow deer, or reindeer. ■ a female hare, rabbit, rat, ferret, or kangaroo.
– ORIGIN Old English *dā*, of unknown origin.

doe-eyed ▶ adjective (especially of a woman) having large, gentle dark eyes: *doe-eyed waifs.*

doek /dʊk/ ▶ noun S. African a headscarf.
– ORIGIN South African Dutch, from Dutch, 'cloth'.

doer ▶ noun the person who does something: *the doer of the action.* ■ a person who acts rather than merely talking or thinking: *I'm a doer, not a moaner.* ■ (also **hard doer**) Austral./NZ a person who is admired because of their courage and toughness.

does third person singular present of DO¹.

doeskin /ˈdəʊskɪn/ ▶ noun [mass noun] leather made from the skin of a doe fallow deer. ■ a fine satin-weave woollen cloth resembling doeskin.

doesn't ▶ contraction does not.

doest archaic second person singular present of DO¹.

doeth archaic third person singular present of DO¹.

dof /dɒf/ ▶ adjective S. African informal stupid; uninformed.
– ORIGIN Afrikaans.

doff ▶ verb [with obj.] remove (an item of clothing). ■ take off or raise (one's hat) as a greeting or token of respect: *the manager doffed his hat to her.*
– ORIGIN late Middle English: contraction of *do off*. Compare with DON².

dog ▶ noun **1** a domesticated carnivorous mammal that typically has a long snout, an acute sense of smell, non-retractile claws, and a barking, howling, or whining voice. ● *Canis familiaris*, family Canidae (the **dog family**); probably domesticated from the wolf in the Mesolithic period. The dog family also includes the wolves, coyotes, jackals, and foxes.
■ a wild animal of the dog family. ■ the male of an animal of the dog family, or of some other mammals such as the otter: [as modifier] *a dog fox.* ■ **(the dogs)** Brit. informal greyhound racing: *a night at the dogs.*
2 informal an unpleasant, contemptible, or wicked man. ■ [with adj.] dated used to refer to a person of a specified kind in a tone of playful reproof, commiseration, or congratulation: *your historian is a dull dog* | *you lucky dog!* ■ used to refer to someone who is abject or miserable, especially because they have been treated harshly: *I make him work like a dog* | *Rab was treated like a dog.* ■ informal, offensive an unattractive woman. ■ Austral./NZ informal an informer or traitor: *one day she's going to turn dog on you.* ■ informal, chiefly N. Amer. a thing of poor quality: *a dog of a film.* ■ informal a horse that is slow or difficult to handle.
3 used in names of dogfishes, e.g. **sandy dog**, **spur-dog**.
4 a mechanical device for gripping.
5 (**dogs**) N. Amer. informal feet.
6 (**dogs**) Horse Racing, US barriers used to keep horses off a particular part of the track.
▶ verb (**dogs**, **dogging**, **dogged**) [with obj.] **1** follow (someone) closely and persistently: *photographers seemed to dog her every step.* ■ (of a problem) cause continual trouble for: *the twenty-nine-year-old has constantly been dogged by controversy.*
2 (**dog it**) informal, chiefly N. Amer. act lazily; fail to try one's hardest.
3 grip (something) with a mechanical device: [with obj. and complement] *she has dogged the door shut.*
– PHRASES **dog and bone** Brit. rhyming slang a telephone. **dog-and-pony show** N. Amer. informal an elaborate display or presentation. **dog eat dog** used to refer to a situation of fierce competition in which people are willing to harm each other in order to succeed: *New York is a dog-eat-dog society.* **dog in the manger** a person who prevents others from having or using things that they do not need themselves. [alluding to the fable of the dog that lay in a manger to prevent the ox and horse from eating the hay.] **a dog's age** N. Amer. informal a very long time: *the best I've seen in a dog's age.* **dogs bark, but the caravans move on** proverb people may make a fuss, but it won't change the situation. **the dog's bollocks** Brit. vulgar slang a person or thing that is the best of its kind. **a dog's dinner** (or **breakfast**) Brit. informal a poor piece of work; a mess: *we made a real dog's breakfast of it.* **a dog's life** an unhappy existence, full of problems or unfair treatment: *he led poor Amy a dog's life.* **the dogs of war** literary the havoc accompanying military conflict. [from Shakespeare's *Julius Caesar* (III. 1. 274).] **dressed (up) like a dog's dinner** Brit. informal wearing ridiculously smart or ostentatious clothes. **every dog has his** (or **its**) **day** proverb everyone will have good luck or success at some point in their lives. **give a dog a bad name and hang him** proverb

it's very difficult to lose a bad reputation, even if it's unjustified. **go to the dogs** informal deteriorate shockingly: *the country is going to the dogs*. **like a dog with two tails** used to emphasize how delighted someone is: *'Is he pleased?' 'Like a dog with two tails.'* **not a dog's chance** no chance at all. **put on the dog** N. Amer. informal behave in a pretentious or ostentatious way: *we have to put on the dog for Anne Marie*. **throw someone to the dogs** discard someone as worthless: *young people look upon the older person as someone to be thrown to the dogs*. **you can't teach an old dog new tricks** proverb you cannot make people change their ways. **why keep a dog and bark yourself?** proverb why pay someone to work for you and then do the work yourself?
– DERIVATIVES **dogdom** noun, **doggish** adjective, **doglike** adjective.
– ORIGIN Old English *docga*, of unknown origin.

dogbane /'dɒgbeɪn/ ▸ noun a shrubby North American plant, typically having bell-shaped flowers and reputed to be poisonous to dogs. ● Genus *Apocynum*, family Apocynaceae.

dogberry ▸ noun (pl. **dogberries**) informal the fruit of the dogwood. ■ (also **dogberry tree**) the dogwood. ■ a fruit of poor eating quality from any of a number of other shrubs or small trees, e.g. the American rowan.

dog biscuit ▸ noun a hard, thick biscuit for feeding to dogs.

dogbox ▸ noun Austral. informal a compartment in a railway carriage without a corridor.
– PHRASES **in the dogbox** NZ & S. African informal in disfavour.
– ORIGIN early 19th cent.: originally denoting a box for a dog to lie in, later denoting a railway compartment for transporting dogs.

dog cart ▸ noun a two-wheeled cart for driving in, with cross seats back to back, originally incorporating a box under the seat for sportsmen's dogs.

dog clutch ▸ noun a device for coupling two shafts in order to transmit motion, one part having teeth which engage with slots in another.

dog cockle ▸ noun a burrowing bivalve mollusc which has a highly convex, almost spherical, shell. ● Family Glycimeridae: many species.

dog collar ▸ noun informal a clerical collar.

dog days ▸ plural noun chiefly literary the hottest period of the year (reckoned in antiquity from the heliacal rising of Sirius, the Dog Star). ■ a period of inactivity or decline: *these are indeed dog days for British film production*.

doge /dəʊdʒ/ ▸ noun historical the chief magistrate of Venice or Genoa.
– ORIGIN mid 16th cent.: from French, from Venetian Italian *doze*, based on Latin *dux*, *duc-* 'leader'.

dog-eared ▸ adjective (of an object made from paper) having the corners worn or battered with use.

dog-end ▸ noun Brit. informal a cigarette end. ■ the last and least pleasing part of something: *the dog-end of a hard day*.

dogface ▸ noun US informal, dated a US soldier, especially an infantryman.

dogfight ▸ noun a close combat between military aircraft. ■ a ferocious struggle for supremacy between interested parties: *the meeting deteriorated into a dogfight*.
– DERIVATIVES **dogfighter** noun, **dogfighting** noun.

dogfish ▸ noun (pl. **same** or **dogfishes**) **1** a small sand-coloured bottom-dwelling shark with a long tail, common on European coasts. Also called **ROUGH HOUND, SANDY DOG**. ● *Scyliorhinus canicula*, family Scyliorhinidae.
2 [with modifier] a small shark that resembles or is related to the dogfish, sometimes caught for food. ● Several genera in the families Scyliorhinidae, Squalidae, and Triakidae.

dogged /'dɒgɪd/ ▸ adjective having or showing tenacity and grim persistence: *success required dogged determination*.
– DERIVATIVES **doggedly** adverb, **doggedness** noun.

dogger[1] ▸ noun historical a two-masted bluff-bowed Dutch sailing boat, used for fishing.
– ORIGIN Middle English: from Middle Dutch.

dogger[2] ▸ noun Geology a large spherical concretion occurring in sedimentary rock.
– ORIGIN late 17th cent. (originally a dialect word denoting a kind of ironstone): perhaps from **DOG**.

Dogger Bank a submerged sandbank in the North Sea, about 115 km (70 miles) off the NE coast of England. This part of the central North Sea is covered by the shipping forecast area **Dogger**.

doggerel /'dɒg(ə)r(ə)l/ ▸ noun [mass noun] comic verse composed in irregular rhythm. ■ verse or words that are badly written or expressed: *the last stanza deteriorates into doggerel*.
– ORIGIN late Middle English (as an adjective describing such verse): apparently from **DOG** (used contemptuously, as in **DOG LATIN**) + **-REL**.

Doggett's Coat and Badge /'dɒgɪts/ an orange livery with a silver badge offered as a trophy in an annual rowing contest among Thames watermen in London. It was instituted in 1715 by an Irish comic actor, Thomas Doggett (1620–1721).

dogging ▸ noun [mass noun] Brit. informal the practice of watching or engaging in exhibitionist sexual activity in a public place.
– ORIGIN 1980s: probably from **DOG** (verb) + **-ING**[1].

doggo ▸ adverb (in phrase **lie doggo**) informal remain motionless and quiet to escape detection: *a dozen officers had been lying doggo for hours*.
– ORIGIN late 19th cent.: of obscure origin; apparently from **DOG** + **-O**.

doggone /'dɒgɒn/ N. Amer. informal ▸ adjective [attrib.] used to express feelings of annoyance, surprise, or pleasure: *now just a doggone minute* | [as submodifier] *it's doggone good to be home*.
▸ verb [with obj.] damn; darn (used to express surprise, irritation, or anger): *from that moment, doggone it if I didn't see a motivation in Joey!* | ***I'll be doggoned if** every fourth kid is affected*.
– ORIGIN early 19th cent.: probably from *dog on it*, euphemism for *God damn it*.

doggy ▸ adjective (**doggier**, **doggiest**) of or like a dog: *his doggy brown eyes*. ■ informal fond of dogs: *it was a doggy household*.
▸ noun (also **doggie**) (pl. **doggies**) a child's word for a dog.
– DERIVATIVES **dogginess** noun.

doggy bag ▸ noun a bag used by a restaurant customer or party guest to take home leftover food, supposedly for their dog.

doggy-paddle ▸ noun an elementary swimming stroke in which the swimmer beats at the water with the hands in a manner resembling a swimming dog.
▸ verb [no obj.] swim using doggy-paddle.

doggy style (also **doggy fashion**) ▸ noun a sexual position in which the woman, usually supporting herself on her hands and knees, is penetrated from behind by the man.

dog handler ▸ noun a person who works with trained dogs: *a police dog handler*.
– DERIVATIVES **dog-handling** noun.

doghouse ▸ noun N. Amer. a dog's kennel. ■ Sailing a raised area at the after end of a yacht's coachroof, providing standing room.
– PHRASES **be in the doghouse** informal be in disgrace or disfavour.

dogie /'dəʊgi/ ▸ noun (pl. **dogies**) N. Amer. a motherless or neglected calf.
– ORIGIN late 19th cent.: of unknown origin.

dog Latin ▸ noun [mass noun] a debased form of Latin.

dog-leg ▸ noun a thing that bends sharply, in particular a sharp bend in a road or route. ■ Golf a hole where the fairway has a bend.

dog-leg stair (also **dog-leg staircase**) ▸ noun a staircase which has no well and a bend of 180° in it, usually at a landing halfway between floors.

dogma /'dɒgmə/ ▸ noun a principle or set of principles laid down by an authority as incontrovertibly true: *the dogmas of faith* | [mass noun] *the rejection of political dogma*.
– ORIGIN mid 16th cent.: via late Latin from Greek *dogma* 'opinion', from *dokein* 'seem good, think'.

dogman ▸ noun (pl. **dogmen**) Austral./NZ a person giving directional signals to the operator of a crane, typically while sitting on the crane's load.
– ORIGIN 1940s: from **DOG** (sense 4 of the noun) + **MAN**.

dogmatic /dɒg'matɪk/ ▸ adjective inclined to lay down principles as undeniably true: *she was not tempted to be dogmatic about what she believed*.
– DERIVATIVES **dogmatically** adverb.
– ORIGIN early 17th cent. (as a noun denoting a philosopher or physician of a school based on a priori assumptions): via late Latin from Greek *dogmatikos*, from *dogma*, *dogmat-* (see **DOGMA**).

dogmatics ▸ plural noun [treated as sing.] a system of principles laid down by an authority, especially the Roman Catholic Church, as undeniably true: *it is a work of analysis, not of dogmatics*.

dogmatism ▸ noun [mass noun] the tendency to lay down principles as undeniably true, without consideration of evidence or the opinions of others: *a culture of dogmatism and fanaticism*.
– DERIVATIVES **dogmatist** noun.
– ORIGIN early 17th cent.: via French from medieval Latin *dogmatismus*, from Latin *dogma* (see **DOGMA**).

dogmatize /'dɒgmətʌɪz/ (also **dogmatise**) ▸ verb [with obj.] represent as an undeniable truth: *I find views dogmatized to the point of absurdity*.
– ORIGIN early 17th cent.: via French and late Latin from Greek *dogmatizein* 'lay down one's opinion', from *dogma* (see **DOGMA**).

dognap ▸ verb (**dognaps**, **dognapping**, **dognapped**) [with obj.] informal steal (a dog), especially in order to sell it.
– DERIVATIVES **dognapper** noun.

do-gooder ▸ noun a well-meaning but unrealistic or interfering philanthropist or reformer.
– DERIVATIVES **do-good** adjective & noun, **do-goodery** noun, **do-gooding** noun, **do-goodism** noun.

dog-paddle ▸ noun & verb chiefly N. Amer. another term for **DOGGY-PADDLE**.

dog racing ▸ noun another term for **GREYHOUND RACING**.

Dogrib /'dɒgrɪb/ ▸ noun **1** a member of a Dene people of NW Canada.
2 [mass noun] the Athabaskan language of the Dogrib, with about 2,000 speakers.
▸ adjective relating to the Dogrib or their language.
– ORIGIN translation of Dogrib *Thlingchadinne* 'dog's flank', from the legend that the people's common ancestor was a dog.

dog-robber ▸ noun informal, chiefly US an army or navy officer's orderly.

dog rose ▸ noun a delicately scented Eurasian wild rose with pink or white flowers, which commonly grows in hedgerows. ● Genus *Rosa*, family Rosaceae: several closely related species, in particular *R. canina*.

dogsbody ▸ noun (pl. **dogsbodies**) Brit. informal a person who is given menial tasks to do, especially a junior in an office: *I got myself a job as typist and general dogsbody on a small magazine*.
– DERIVATIVES **dogsbodying** noun.

dogshore ▸ noun each of a pair of blocks of timber positioned on each side of a ship on a slipway to prevent it sliding down before launching.

dogskin ▸ noun [mass noun] leather made of or imitating dog's skin, especially as used for gloves.

dog sled ▸ noun N. Amer. a sled designed to be pulled by dogs.

dog's mercury ▸ noun a Eurasian plant of the spurge family, with hairy stems and small green flowers, found as a dominant plant of old woodland. ● *Mercurialis perennis*, family Euphorbiaceae.
– ORIGIN late 16th cent.: translating modern Latin *Mercurialis canina* (former taxonomic name); the plant is poisonous and is contrasted with *Mercurialis annua* 'annual mercury', useful in medicine.

dogstail (also **dog's-tail**) ▸ noun an Old World fodder grass with spiky flower heads. ● Genus *Cynosurus*, family Gramineae: several species, in particular **crested dogstail** (*C. cristatus*), a common pasture grass.

Dog Star the star Sirius.
– ORIGIN translating Greek *kuon* or Latin *canicula* 'small dog', both names of the star; so named as it appears to follow at the heels of Orion (the hunter).

dog's-tooth violet ▸ noun a plant of the lily family which has backward-curving pointed petals. ● Genus *Erythronium*, family Liliaceae: several species, in particular the Eurasian *E. dens-canis*, with speckled leaves and pinkish-purple flowers.

dog tag ▸ noun a metal tag attached to a dog's collar, typically giving its name and owner's address. ■ N. Amer. informal a soldier's metal identity tag.

dog-tired ▸ adjective extremely tired; worn out: *he'd gone to bed dog-tired*.

dog-tooth ▸ noun **1** Architecture a small pointed ornament or moulding forming one of a series radiating like petals from a raised centre, typical of Norman and Early English styles.
2 (also **dogstooth**) [mass noun] a small check pattern with notched corners suggestive of a canine tooth, used in cloth for jackets and suits.

dogtrot ▶ **noun** [in sing.] a gentle easy trot.
▶ **verb** [no obj.] move at a dogtrot.

dog violet ▶ **noun** a scentless wild violet, typically having purple or lilac flowers. ● Genus *Viola*, family Violaceae: several species.

dogwatch ▶ **noun** either of two short watches on a ship (4–6 or 6–8 p.m.).

dog-weary ▶ **adjective** another term for **DOG-TIRED**.

dog whelk ▶ **noun** a predatory marine mollusc that typically occurs on the shore or in shallow waters. ● Family Nassariidae, class Gastropoda: *Nucella* and other genera.

D

dogwood ▶ **noun** a shrub or small tree of north temperate regions, which yields hard timber and is grown for its decorative foliage, red stems, or colourful berries. ● Genus *Cornus*, family Cornaceae: many species. ■ used in names of trees which resemble the dogwood or yield similar hard timber.
– ORIGIN so named because the wood was formerly used to make 'dogs' (i.e. skewers).

DoH ▶ **abbreviation** (in the UK) Department of Health.

doh¹ /dəʊ/ (also **do**) ▶ **noun** Music (in tonic sol-fa) the first and eighth note of a major scale. ■ the note C in the fixed-doh system.
– ORIGIN mid 18th cent.: from Italian *do*, an arbitrarily chosen syllable replacing *ut*, taken from a Latin hymn (see **SOLMIZATION**).

doh² /dəʊ/ ▶ **exclamation** informal used to comment on a foolish or stupid action, especially one's own: *I keep crashing cars. Doh! What a dummy!*

Doha /ˈdəʊhɑː/ the capital of Qatar; pop 385,000 (est. 2007).

DOHC ▶ **abbreviation** double overhead camshaft.

dohyo /ˈdəʊjəʊ/ ▶ **noun** (pl. **dohyos**) the ring within which sumo wrestling takes place.
– ORIGIN Japanese, abbreviation of *dohyōba* 'wrestling arena'.

DOI ▶ **abbreviation** Computing digital object identifier, a unique string of characters allocated to a website, file, or other piece of digital information.

doily /ˈdɔɪli/ ▶ **noun** (pl. **doilies**) a small ornamental mat made of lace or paper with a lace pattern, put on a plate under cakes or other sweet food.
– ORIGIN late 17th cent.: from *Doiley* or *Doyley*, the name of a 17th-cent. London draper. The word originally denoted a woollen material used for summer wear, said to have been introduced by this draper. The current sense (originally *doily napkin*) dates from the early 18th cent.

doing ▶ **noun 1** (usu. **doings**) the activities in which a particular person engages: *the latest doings of television stars*. ■ informal excrement, especially that of a domestic animal. ■ [in sing.] informal a beating or scolding: *someone had given her a doing*.
2 (**doings**) [treated as sing. or pl.] informal used to refer to things when one has forgotten their name or when no one word easily covers them: *the drawer where he kept the doings*.
– PHRASES **be someone's doing** be the creation or fault of the person named: *he looked at Lisa as though it was all her doing*. **take some doing** be difficult to achieve: *it would take some doing to calm him down*.

Doisneau /ˈdwʌnəʊ/, French /dwanəo/, Robert (1912–94), French photographer, best known for his photos of the city and inhabitants of Paris, such as 'The Kiss at the Hôtel de Ville' (1950).

doit /dɔɪt/ ▶ **noun** [in sing.] archaic a very small amount of money.
– ORIGIN late 16th cent.: from Middle Low German *doyt*, Middle Dutch *duit*, of unknown origin.

doited /ˈdɔɪtɪd/ ▶ **adjective** Scottish archaic having the faculties impaired, especially by age.
– ORIGIN late Middle English: perhaps an alteration of *doted*, past participle of **DOTE**.

do-it-yourself ▶ **noun & adjective** full form of **DIY**.
– DERIVATIVES **do-it-yourselfer** noun.

dojo /ˈdəʊdʒəʊ/ ▶ **noun** (pl. **dojos**) a room or hall in which judo and other martial arts are practised.
– ORIGIN Japanese, from *dō* 'way, pursuit' + *jō* 'a place'.

dol. ▶ **abbreviation** dollar or dollars.

Dolby /ˈdɒlbi, ˈdəʊl-/ ▶ **noun** [mass noun] trademark an electronic noise-reduction system used in tape recording to reduce hiss. ■ an electronic system used to provide stereophonic sound for cinemas and television sets.
– ORIGIN 1960s: named after Ray M. *Dolby* (born 1933), the American engineer who devised it.

dolce /ˈdɒltʃeɪ/ ▶ **adverb & adjective** Music (especially as a direction) sweetly and softly.
– ORIGIN Italian, literally 'sweet'.

dolce far niente /ˌdɒltʃeɪ fɑː nɪˈɛnteɪ/ ▶ **noun** [mass noun] pleasant idleness.
– ORIGIN Italian, 'sweet doing nothing'.

Dolcelatte /ˌdɒltʃəˈlɑːteɪ, -ˈlati/ ▶ **noun** [mass noun] trademark a kind of soft creamy blue-veined cheese from Italy.
– ORIGIN Italian, literally 'sweet milk'.

dolce vita /ˌdɒltʃeɪ ˈviːtə/ ▶ **noun** (usu. **la dolce vita**) a life of heedless pleasure and luxury.
– ORIGIN Italian, literally 'sweet life'.

doldrums /ˈdɒldrəmz/ ▶ **plural noun** (**the doldrums**)
1 a state or period of stagnation or depression: *the mortgage market has been in the doldrums for three years*.
2 an equatorial region of the Atlantic Ocean with calms, sudden storms, and light unpredictable winds.
– ORIGIN late 18th cent. (as *doldrum* 'dull, sluggish person'): perhaps from **DULL**, on the pattern of *tantrums*.

dole¹ ▶ **noun 1** [mass noun] (usu. **the dole**) Brit. informal benefit paid by the state to the unemployed: ***I was on the dole for three years*** | [as modifier] ***my next dole cheque***. ■ [count noun] dated a charitable gift of food, clothes, or money.
2 literary a person's lot or destiny.
▶ **verb** [with obj.] (**dole something out**) distribute shares of something: *the scanty portions of food **doled out** to them*.
– ORIGIN Old English *dāl* 'division, portion, or share', of Germanic origin; related to **DEAL¹**. The sense 'distribution of charitable gifts' dates from Middle English; the sense 'unemployment benefit' dates from the early 20th cent.

dole² ▶ **noun** [mass noun] archaic or literary sorrow; mourning.
– ORIGIN Middle English: from Old French *doel* 'mourning', from popular Latin *dolus*, from Latin *dolere* 'grieve'.

dole-bludger ▶ **noun** Austral./NZ informal a person who chooses to receive unemployment benefit rather than work.

doleful ▶ **adjective** expressing sorrow; mournful: *a doleful look*. ■ causing grief or misfortune: *he could be struck off, with doleful consequences*.
– DERIVATIVES **dolefully** adverb, **dolefulness** noun.

dolerite /ˈdɒlərʌɪt/ ▶ **noun** [mass noun] Geology a dark, medium-grained igneous rock, typically with ophitic texture, containing plagioclase, pyroxene, and olivine. It typically occurs in dykes and sills. Also called **DIABASE**.
– ORIGIN mid 19th cent.: from French *dolérite*, from Greek *doleros* 'deceptive' (because it is difficult to distinguish from diorite).

doli capax /ˌdɒlɪ ˈkapaks/ ▶ **adjective** Law deemed capable of forming the intent to commit a crime or tort, especially by reason of age (ten years old or older).
– ORIGIN Latin, 'capable of evil'.

dolichocephalic /ˌdɒlɪkə(ʊ)sɪˈfalɪk, -keˈfalɪk-/ ▶ **adjective** Anatomy having a relatively long skull (typically with the breadth less than 80 (or 75) per cent of the length). Often contrasted with **BRACHYCEPHALIC**.
– DERIVATIVES **dolichocephaly** noun.
– ORIGIN mid 19th cent.: from Greek *dolikhos* 'long' + **-CEPHALIC**.

doli incapax /ˈdɒlɪ ɪnˈkapaks/ ▶ **adjective** Law deemed incapable of forming the intent to commit a crime or tort, especially by reason of age (under ten years old).
– ORIGIN Latin, literally 'incapable of evil'.

Dolin /ˈdəʊlɪn, ˈdɒl-/, Sir Anton (1904–83), English ballet dancer and choreographer; born *Sydney Francis Patrick Chippendall Healey-Kay*. He was the first artistic director of the London Festival Ballet (1950–61), as well as first soloist.

doline /dɒˈliːn/ (also **dolina** /dɒˈliːnə/) ▶ **noun** Geology a hollow or basin in a karstic region, typically funnel-shaped.
– ORIGIN late 19th cent.: via German from Slovene *dolina* 'valley'.

D'Oliveira /ˌdɒlɪˈvɪərə/, Basil (Lewis) (b.1931), British cricketer and coach, born in South Africa and of Cape coloured origin. South Africa's refusal to allow him into the country led to the cancellation of England's 1968–9 tour and to South Africa's subsequent banishment from Test cricket until the end of apartheid.

Doll, Sir (William) Richard (Shaboe) (1912–2005), English physician. With **Sir A. Bradford Hill** (1897–1991) he was the first to show a statistical link between smoking and lung cancer.

doll¹ ▶ **noun** a small model of a human figure, typically one of a baby or girl, used as a child's toy. ■ informal, chiefly N. Amer. an attractive young woman. ■ N. Amer. informal a generous or considerate person: *would you be a doll and set the table?*
▶ **verb** [with obj.] (**doll someone up**) informal dress someone smartly and attractively: *I got all **dolled up** for a party*.
– ORIGIN mid 16th cent. (denoting a mistress): pet form of the given name *Dorothy*. The sense 'small model of a human figure' dates from the late 17th cent.

doll² Horse Racing, Brit. ▶ **noun** a temporary barrier on a racecourse or gallop.
▶ **verb** [with obj.] place a barrier in front of (a jump or other part of the course that is to be omitted from a race).
– ORIGIN 1940s: perhaps a variant of archaic *dool* 'boundary marker'.

dollar ▶ **noun** the basic monetary unit of the US, Canada, Australia, and certain countries in the Pacific, Caribbean, SE Asia, Africa, and South America.
– PHRASES **dollars to doughnuts** N. Amer. informal used to emphasize one's certainty: *I'd **bet dollars to doughnuts** he's a medical student*.
– ORIGIN from early Flemish or Low German *daler*, from German *T(h)aler*, short for *Joachimsthaler*, a coin from the silver mine of *Joachimsthal* ('Joachim's valley'), now *Jáchymov* in the Czech Republic. The term was later applied to a coin used in the Spanish-American colonies, which was also widely used in the British North American colonies at the time of the American War of Independence, hence adopted as the name of the US monetary unit in the late 18th cent.

dollar area ▶ **noun** the area of the world in which currency is linked to the US dollar.

dollarbird ▶ **noun** the eastern broad-billed roller of Asia and Australasia, which has a conspicuous white coin-like mark on the wing that is visible in flight. ● *Eyrystomus orientalis*, family Coraciidae.

dollar diplomacy ▶ **noun** [mass noun] the use of a country's financial power to extend its international influence.

dollar gap ▶ **noun** the amount by which a country's import trade with the dollar area exceeds the corresponding export trade.

dollarization (also **dollarisation**) ▶ **noun** [mass noun] the process of aligning a country's currency with the US dollar. ■ the dominating effect of the US on the economy of a country.

dollar sign (also **dollar mark**) ▶ **noun** the sign $, representing a dollar.

Dollfuss /ˈdɒlfʊs/, Engelbert (1892–1934), Austrian statesman, Chancellor of Austria 1932–4. From 1933 Dollfuss attempted to block Austrian Nazi plans to force the *Anschluss* by governing without Parliament. He was assassinated by Austrian Nazis.

dollop ▶ **noun** informal a large, shapeless mass of something, especially soft food: *great **dollops** of cream* | figurative *a **dollop** of romance here and there*.
▶ **verb** (**dollops, dolloping, dolloped**) [with obj. and adverbial of direction] add (a large mass of something) casually and without measuring: *she stopped him from dolloping cream into his coffee*.
– ORIGIN late 16th cent. (denoting a clump of grass or weeds in a field): perhaps of Scandinavian origin and related to Norwegian dialect *dolp* 'lump'.

doll's house (N. Amer. **dollhouse**) ▶ **noun** a miniature toy house used for playing with dolls.

dolly ▶ **noun** (pl. **dollies**) **1** a child's word for a doll. ■ informal, dated an attractive but unintelligent young woman.
2 a small platform on wheels used for holding heavy objects, typically film or television cameras.
3 Cricket, informal an easy catch.
4 historical a short wooden pole for stirring clothes in a washtub.
▶ **verb** (**dollies, dollying, dollied**) [no obj., with adverbial of direction] (of a film or television camera) be moved on a mobile platform in a specified direction: *the camera dollies back to reveal hundreds of people*.

dolly bird ▶ **noun** Brit. informal an attractive but unintelligent young woman.

dolly mixtures ▶ **plural noun** Brit. a mixture of small variously shaped and coloured sweets.

dolly switch ▸ noun an electrical on-off switch whose external operating mechanism is a short pivoted lever terminating in a rounded knob, rather than a spring-loaded rocker.

dolly tub ▸ noun historical a washtub.
– ORIGIN late 19th cent.: from dialect *dolly* (used as a term for various contrivances thought to resemble a doll in some way) and TUB.

Dolly Varden /ˈvɑːd(ə)n/ ▸ noun 1 (also **Dolly Varden hat**) a large hat with one side drooping and with a floral trimming, formerly worn by women.
2 a brightly spotted edible charr (fish) occurring in fresh water on both sides of the North Pacific.
• *Salvelinus malma*, family Salmonidae.
– ORIGIN late 19th cent.: from the name of a character in Dickens's *Barnaby Rudge*, who wore a similar hat.

dolma /ˈdɒlmə/ ▸ noun (pl. **dolmas** or **dolmades** /-ˈmɑːdɛz, -ˈmɑːðɛz/) a Greek and Turkish delicacy in which ingredients such as spiced rice, meat, and bread are wrapped in vine or cabbage leaves.
– ORIGIN from modern Greek *ntolmas* or its source, Turkish *dolma*, from *dolmak* 'fill, be filled'.

dolman /ˈdɒlmən/ ▸ noun a long Turkish robe open in front. ■ a woman's loose cloak with cape-like sleeves.
– ORIGIN late 16th cent.: based on Turkish *dolama*, *dolaman*.

dolman sleeve ▸ noun a loose sleeve cut in one piece with the body of a garment.

dolmen /ˈdɒlmɛn/ ▸ noun a megalithic tomb with a large flat stone laid on upright ones, found chiefly in Britain and France.
– ORIGIN mid 19th cent.: from French, perhaps via Breton from Cornish *tolmen* 'hole of a stone'.

dolmus /ˈdɒlmʊʃ/ ▸ noun (in Turkey) a shared taxi.
– ORIGIN from Turkish *dolmuş*, literally 'filled'.

dolomite /ˈdɒləmʌɪt/ ▸ noun [mass noun] a translucent mineral consisting of a carbonate of calcium and magnesium, usually also containing iron. ■ a sedimentary rock formed chiefly of dolomite.
– DERIVATIVES **dolomitic** adjective.
– ORIGIN late 18th cent.: from French, from the name of *Dolomieu* (1750–1801), the French geologist who discovered it, + -ITE[1].

Dolomite Mountains (also **the Dolomites**) a range of the Alps in northern Italy, so named because the characteristic rock of the region is dolomitic limestone.

dolorimeter /ˌdɒləˈrɪmɪtə/ ▸ noun an instrument for measuring sensitivity to, or levels of, pain.
– DERIVATIVES **dolorimetry** noun.

dolorous /ˈdɒl(ə)rəs/ ▸ adjective literary feeling or expressing great sorrow or distress.
– DERIVATIVES **dolorously** adverb.
– ORIGIN late Middle English: from Old French *doleros*, from late Latin *dolorosus*, from Latin *dolor* 'pain, grief'.

dolostone /ˈdɒləstəʊn/ ▸ noun [mass noun] Geology rock consisting of dolomite.
– ORIGIN mid 20th cent.: from DOLOMITE + STONE.

dolour /ˈdɒlə/ (US **dolor**) ▸ noun [mass noun] literary a state of great sorrow or distress: *they squatted, hunched in their habitual dolour*.
– ORIGIN Middle English (denoting both physical and mental pain or distress): via Old French from Latin *dolor* 'pain, grief'.

dolphin ▸ noun 1 a small gregarious toothed whale which typically has a beak-like snout and a curved fin on the back. Dolphins have become well known for their sociable nature and high intelligence. • Families Delphinidae (marine) and Platanistidae (the **river dolphins**): several genera and many species.
2 (also **dolphinfish**) another term for DORADO (sense 1).
3 a bollard, pile, or buoy for mooring boats.
4 a structure for protecting the pier of a bridge.
– ORIGIN late Middle English: from Old French *dauphin*, from Provençal *dalfin*, from Latin *delphinus*, from Greek *delphin*.

dolphinarium /ˌdɒlfɪˈnɛːrɪəm/ ▸ noun (pl. **dolphinariums** or **dolphinaria**) an aquarium in which dolphins are kept and trained for public entertainment.

dolt /dəʊlt/ ▸ noun a stupid person.
– ORIGIN mid 16th cent.: perhaps a variant of *dulled*, past participle of DULL.

doltish /ˈdəʊltɪʃ/ ▸ adjective (of a person) stupid; idiotic: *a doltish character*.
– DERIVATIVES **doltishly** adverb, **doltishness** noun.

Dom /dɒm/ ▸ noun 1 a title prefixed to the names of some Roman Catholic dignitaries and Benedictine and Carthusian monks: *Dom Bede Griffiths*.
2 Portuguese form of DON[1] (sense 2).
– ORIGIN from Latin *dominus* 'master'.

-dom ▸ suffix forming nouns: 1 denoting a state or condition: *freedom*.
2 denoting rank or status: *earldom*.
3 denoting a domain: *fiefdom*.
4 denoting a class of people or the attitudes associated with them, regarded collectively: *officialdom*.
– ORIGIN Old English *-dōm*, originally meaning 'decree, judgement'.

domain /də(ʊ)ˈmeɪn/ ▸ noun 1 an area of territory owned or controlled by a particular ruler or government: *the French domains of the Plantagenets*. ■ a specified sphere of activity or knowledge: *the country's isolation in the domain of sport*.
2 Computing a distinct subset of the Internet with addresses sharing a common suffix or under the control of a particular organization or individual.
3 Physics a discrete region of magnetism in ferromagnetic material.
4 Mathematics the set of possible values of the independent variable or variables of a function.
5 Biochemistry a distinct region of a complex molecule or structure.
– ORIGIN late Middle English (denoting heritable or landed property): from French *domaine*, alteration (by association with Latin *dominus* 'lord') of Old French *demeine* 'belonging to a lord' (see DEMESNE).

domaine /dəˈmeɪn/ ▸ noun a vineyard.
– ORIGIN French, literally 'estate' (see DOMAIN).

domain name ▸ noun Computing the part of a network address which identifies it as belonging to a particular domain.

domal /ˈdəʊm(ə)l/ ▸ adjective (chiefly of geological features) having the form of a dome.

domanial /dəˈmeɪnɪəl/ ▸ adjective relating to the control or ownership of an area of territory by a ruler or government.
– ORIGIN early 19th cent.: from French, from medieval Latin *domanialis*, from *domanium* 'lordship'.

dome ▸ noun 1 a rounded vault forming the roof of a building or structure, typically with a circular base: *the dome of St Paul's Cathedral*. ■ the revolving openable hemispherical roof of an observatory. ■ [in names] N. Amer. a sports stadium with a domed roof.
2 a thing shaped like a dome, in particular: ■ a natural vault or canopy, such as that of the sky or trees: *the dome of the sky*. ■ Geology a rounded uplifted landform or underground structure. ■ informal the top of the head: *her Mohican projected from her shaved dome*.
3 literary a stately building.
▸ verb [no obj.] (often as noun **doming**) (of stratified rock or a surface) become rounded in formation; swell.
– DERIVATIVES **dome-like** adjective.
– ORIGIN early 16th cent. (in sense 3 of the noun): from Latin *domus*; other senses are via French *dôme*, from Italian *duomo* 'cathedral, dome'.

domed ▸ adjective covered with or shaped like a rounded vault: *his domed forehead* | [in combination] *a glass-domed roof*.

dome fastener ▸ noun a press stud consisting of a rounded portion which clips into a socket, used especially as a fastener for gloves.

Dome of the Rock an Islamic shrine in Jerusalem, for Muslims the third most holy place after Mecca and Medina. It surrounds the sacred rock on which, according to tradition, Abraham prepared to sacrifice his son Isaac and from which the prophet Muhammad made his miraculous midnight ascent into heaven (the Night Journey).

Domesday /ˈduːmzdeɪ/ (also **Domesday Book**) ▸ noun a comprehensive record of the extent, value, ownership, and liabilities of land in England, made in 1086 by order of William I.
– ORIGIN Middle English: an old spelling of DOOMSDAY, which was apparently applied because the book was regarded as a final authority.

domestic ▸ adjective 1 relating to the running of a home or to family relations: *domestic chores* | *domestic violence*. ■ of or for use in the home rather than in an industrial or office environment: *domestic water supplies*. ■ (of an animal) tame and kept by humans: *domestic dogs*. ■ (of a person) fond of family life and running a home: *she was not at all domestic*.
2 existing or occurring inside a particular country; not foreign or international: *Egypt's domestic affairs*.
▸ noun 1 (also **domestic worker** or **domestic help**) a person who is paid to help with cleaning and other menial tasks in a person's home.
2 Brit. informal a violent quarrel between family members, especially husband and wife: *they are often called to sort out a domestic*.
3 N. Amer. a product not made abroad.
– DERIVATIVES **domestically** adverb.
– ORIGIN late Middle English: from French *domestique*, from Latin *domesticus*, from *domus* 'house'.

domesticate ▸ verb [with obj.] tame (an animal) and keep it as a pet or on a farm: *mammals were first domesticated for their milk*. ■ cultivate (a plant) for food. ■ humorous make (someone) fond of and good at home life and the tasks that it involves: *you've quite domesticated him*.
– DERIVATIVES **domesticable** adjective, **domestication** noun.
– ORIGIN mid 17th cent.: from medieval Latin *domesticat-* 'domesticated', from the verb *domesticare*, from Latin *domesticus* 'belonging to the house' (see DOMESTIC).

D

domesticated ▸ adjective (of an animal) tame and kept as a pet or on a farm: *domesticated dogs*. ■ (of a plant) cultivated for food; naturalized: *domesticated crops*. ■ humorous (of a man) fond of home life and housework: *he is thoroughly domesticated*.

domestic bursar ▸ noun the person responsible for the administration of the domestic establishment of a college or university.

domesticity ▸ noun [mass noun] home or family life: *the atmosphere is one of happy domesticity*.

domestic partner ▸ noun N. Amer. a person who is living with another in a close personal and sexual relationship.
– DERIVATIVES **domestic partnership** noun.

domestic pigeon ▸ noun see PIGEON[1] (sense 1).

domestic science ▸ noun Brit. dated the study of household skills such as cooking or sewing, especially as taught at school; home economics.

domical /ˈdəʊmɪk(ə)l/ ▸ adjective another term for DOMED: *an octagonal, domical vault*.

domicile /ˈdɒmɪsʌɪl, -sɪl/ ▸ noun formal or Law the country that a person treats as their permanent home, or lives in and has a substantial connection with: *his wife has a **domicile of origin** in Germany*. Compare with RESIDENCE. ■ chiefly US a person's residence or home: *the builder I've hired to renovate my new domicile*. ■ the place at which a company or other body is registered, especially for tax purposes.
▸ verb [with adverbial of place] (**be domiciled**) formal or Law treat a specified country as a permanent home: *the tenant is domiciled in the United Kingdom*. Compare with RESIDE. ■ chiefly US reside or be based: *he was domiciled in a frame house in the outskirts of Bogotá*.
– ORIGIN late Middle English: via Old French from Latin *domicilium* 'dwelling', from *domus* 'home'.

domiciliary /ˌdɒmɪˈsɪlɪəri/ ▸ adjective concerned with or occurring in someone's home: *a study compared domiciliary care with hospital care*.
– ORIGIN late 19th cent.: from French *domiciliaire*, from medieval Latin *domiciliarius*, from Latin *domicilium* 'dwelling' (see DOMICILE).

dominance ▸ noun [mass noun] power and influence over others: *the worldwide dominance of Hollywood*. ■ Genetics the phenomenon whereby, in an individual containing two allelic forms of a gene, one is expressed to the exclusion of the other. ■ Ecology the predominance of one or more species in a plant (or animal) community.
– DERIVATIVES **dominancy** noun.

dominant ▸ adjective having power and influence over others: *they are now in an even more dominant position in the market*. ■ (of a high place) overlooking others. ■ Genetics relating to or denoting heritable characteristics which are controlled by genes that are expressed in offspring even when inherited from only one parent. Often contrasted with RECESSIVE. ■ Ecology denoting the predominant species in a plant (or animal) community. ■ (in decision theory) denoting a choice that is at least as good as the alternatives in all circumstances, and better in some: *holding back is here a dominant strategy*.
▸ noun 1 Genetics a dominant trait or gene. ■ Ecology a dominant species in a plant (or animal) community.
2 Music the fifth note of the diatonic scale of any key, or the key based on this, considered in relation to the key of the tonic.
– DERIVATIVES **dominantly** adverb.

D

– ORIGIN late Middle English: via Old French from Latin *dominant-* 'ruling, governing', from the verb *dominari* (see DOMINATE).

dominant seventh ▸ noun Music the common chord of the dominant note in a key, plus the diminished seventh from that note (e.g. in the key of C, a chord of G-B-D-F). It is important in conventional harmony, as it naturally resolves to the tonic or subdominant.

dominate /ˈdɒmɪneɪt/ ▸ verb [with obj.] have power and influence over: *the company dominates the market for operating system software*. ■ be the most important or conspicuous person or thing in: *the race was dominated by the 1998 champion*. ■ have a commanding position over; overlook: *a picturesque city dominated by the cathedral tower*.
– DERIVATIVES **dominator** noun.
– ORIGIN early 17th cent.: from Latin *dominat-* 'ruled, governed', from the verb *dominari*, from *dominus* 'lord, master'.

domination ▸ noun [mass noun] **1** the exercise of power or influence over someone or something, or the state of being so controlled: *the imperial domination of India*.
2 (**dominations**) (in traditional Christian angelology) the fourth-highest order of the ninefold celestial hierarchy.
– ORIGIN late Middle English: via Old French from Latin *dominatio(n-)*, from the verb *dominari* (see DOMINATE).

dominatrix /ˌdɒmɪˈneɪtrɪks/ ▸ noun (pl. **dominatrices** /-trɪsiːz/ or **dominatrixes**) a dominating woman, especially one who takes the sadistic role in sadomasochistic sexual activities.
– ORIGIN mid 16th cent. (rare before the late 20th cent.): from Latin, feminine of *dominator*, from *dominat-* 'ruled', from the verb *dominari* (see DOMINATE).

dominee /ˈdɒmɪni/ ▸ noun S. African a minister of the Dutch Reformed Church.
– ORIGIN Afrikaans and Dutch, from the Latin vocative *domine!* 'master!'.

domineer /ˌdɒmɪˈnɪə/ ▸ verb [no obj.] (usu. as adj. **domineering**) assert one's will over another in an arrogant way: *Cathy had been a martyr to her gruff, domineering husband*.
– DERIVATIVES **domineeringly** adverb.
– ORIGIN late 16th cent.: from Dutch *dominieren*, from French *dominer*, from Latin *dominari* (see DOMINATE).

Domingo /dəˈmɪŋɡəʊ/, Placido (b.1941), Spanish-born tenor. His performances in operas by Verdi and Puccini have met with particular acclaim.

Dominic, St /ˈdɒmɪnɪk/ (*c*.1170–1221), Spanish priest and friar; Spanish name *Domingo de Guzmán*. In 1216 he founded the Order of Friars Preachers at Toulouse in France; its members became known as Dominicans or Black Friars. Feast day, 8 August.

Dominica /ˌdɒmɪˈniːkə, dəˈmɪnɪkə/ a mountainous island in the Caribbean, the loftiest of the Lesser Antilles and the northernmost and largest of the Windward Islands; pop. 72,700 (est. 2009); languages, English (official), Creole; capital, Roseau. The island came into British possession at the end of the 18th century, becoming an independent republic within the Commonwealth in 1978.
– ORIGIN named by Columbus, who discovered it on a Sunday (Latin *dies dominica* 'the Lord's day') in 1493.

dominical /dəˈmɪnɪk(ə)l/ ▸ adjective **1** of Sunday as the Lord's day.
2 of Jesus Christ as the lord.
– ORIGIN Middle English: from late Latin *dominicalis*, from Latin *dominicus*, from *dominus* 'lord, master'.

dominical letter ▸ noun any of the seven letters A–G used in Church calendars to indicate the date (1–7 January) on which the first Sunday in the year falls, and hence in dating movable feasts.

Dominican[1] /dəˈmɪnɪk(ə)n/ ▸ noun a member of the Roman Catholic order of preaching friars founded by St Dominic, or of a religious order for women founded on similar principles.
▸ adjective relating to St Dominic or the Dominicans.
– ORIGIN late 16th cent.: from medieval Latin *Dominicanus*, from *Dominicus*, the Latin name of *Domingo de Guzmán* (see DOMINIC, ST).

Dominican[2] /dəˈmɪnɪk(ə)n/ ▸ adjective relating to the Dominican Republic or its people.
▸ noun a native or inhabitant of the Dominican Republic.
– ORIGIN from Spanish *Dominicana*, influenced by SANTO DOMINGO.

Dominican[3] /ˌdɒmɪˈniːk(ə)n, dəˈmɪnɪk(ə)n/ ▸ adjective relating to the island of Dominica or its people.
▸ noun a native or inhabitant of the island of Dominica.

Dominican Republic /dəˈmɪnɪkən/ a country in the Caribbean occupying the eastern part of the island of Hispaniola; pop. 9,650,100 (est. 2009); official language, Spanish; capital, Santo Domingo. The Dominican Republic is the former Spanish colony of Santo Domingo, the part of Hispaniola which Spain retained when it ceded the western portion (now Haiti) to France in 1697. It was proclaimed a republic in 1844.

dominie /ˈdɒmɪni/ ▸ noun (pl. **dominies**) **1** Scottish a schoolmaster.
2 chiefly US a pastor or clergyman.
– ORIGIN late 17th cent.: alteration of Latin *domine!* (vocative) 'master!, sir!', from *dominus* 'lord' (formerly used as a polite form of address to a clergyman or member of one of the professions).

dominion ▸ noun **1** [mass noun] sovereignty or control: *man's attempt to establish **dominion over** nature*. ■ another term for DOMINIUM.
2 (usu. **dominions**) the territory of a sovereign or government: *the Angevin dominions*. ■ (**Dominion**) historical each of the self-governing territories of the British Commonwealth.
3 (**dominions**) another term for DOMINATION (sense 2).
– ORIGIN Middle English: via Old French from medieval Latin *dominio(n-)*, from Latin *dominium*, from *dominus* 'lord, master'.

dominium /dəˈmɪnɪəm/ ▸ noun [mass noun] Law, chiefly US ownership and control of property.
– ORIGIN mid 18th cent.: from Latin.

Domino /ˈdɒmɪnəʊ/, Fats (b.1928), American pianist, singer, and songwriter; born *Antoine Domino*. His music represents part of the transition from rhythm and blues to rock and roll. Notable songs: 'Ain't That a Shame' (1955) and 'Blueberry Hill' (1956).

domino /ˈdɒmɪnəʊ/ ▸ noun (pl. **dominoes**) **1** any of 28 small oblong pieces marked with 0–6 pips in each half. ■ (**dominoes**) [treated as sing.] the game played with dominoes, in which they are laid down to form a line, each player in turn trying to find and lay down a domino with a value matched by that of a piece at either end of the line already formed.
2 historical a loose cloak, worn with a mask for the upper part of the face at masquerades.
– ORIGIN late 17th cent.: from French, denoting a hood worn by priests in winter, probably based on Latin *dominus* 'lord, master'.

domino effect ▸ noun the effect of the domino theory.

domino theory ▸ noun the theory that a political event in one country will cause similar events in neighbouring countries, like a falling domino causing an entire row of upended dominoes to fall.

Domitian /dəˈmɪʃ(ə)n/ (AD 51–96), son of Vespasian, Roman emperor 81–96; full name *Titus Flavius Domitianus*. An energetic but autocratic ruler, he embarked on a major building programme, but was assassinated following a lengthy period of terror.

dom palm ▸ noun variant spelling of DOUM PALM.

Don /dɒn/ **1** a river in Russia which rises near Tula, south-east of Moscow, and flows for a distance of 1,958 km (1,224 miles) to the Sea of Azov.
2 a river in Scotland which rises in the Grampians and flows 131 km (82 miles) eastwards to the North Sea at Aberdeen.
3 a river in northern England which rises in the Pennines and flows 112 km (70 miles) eastwards to join the Ouse shortly before it, in turn, joins the Humber.

don[1] ▸ noun **1** Brit. a university teacher, especially a senior member of a college at Oxford or Cambridge.
2 (**Don**) a Spanish title prefixed to a male forename. ■ a Spanish gentleman. ■ N. Amer. informal a high-ranking member of the Mafia.
– DERIVATIVES **donship** noun.
– ORIGIN early 16th cent. (in sense 2): from Spanish, from Latin *dominus* 'lord, master'.

don[2] ▸ verb (**dons, donning, donned**) [with obj.] put on (an item of clothing): *in the dressing room the players donned their football shirts*.
– ORIGIN late Middle English: contraction of *do on*. Compare with DOFF.

donate ▸ verb [with obj.] give (money or goods) for a good cause, for example to a charity: *the proceeds will be donated to an AIDS awareness charity*. ■ allow the removal of (blood or an organ) from one's body for transplantation, transfusion, or research. ■ Chemistry & Physics provide or contribute (electrons or protons).
– DERIVATIVES **donator** noun.
– ORIGIN late 18th cent.: back-formation from DONATION.

Donatello /ˌdɒnəˈtɛləʊ/ (1386–1466), Italian sculptor; born *Donato di Betto Bardi*. He was one of the pioneers of scientific perspective, and is especially famous for his lifelike sculptures, including the bronze *David* (*c*.1430–60).

donatio mortis causa /dəˌneɪʃɪəʊ ˌmɔːtɪs ˈkɔːzə/ ▸ noun (pl. **donationes mortis causa** /dəˌneɪʃɪˈəʊniːz/) Law a gift of personal property made by someone who expects to die in the immediate future, taking full effect only after the donor dies.
– ORIGIN Latin, literally 'gift by reason of death'.

donation ▸ noun something that is given to a charity, especially a sum of money: *please send your donation of £20 to the Disaster Appeal*. ■ [mass noun] the action of donating something.
– ORIGIN late Middle English: via Old French from Latin *donatio(n-)*, from the verb *donare*, based on *donum* 'gift'.

Donatist /ˈdəʊnətɪst/ ▸ noun a member of a schismatic Christian group in North Africa, formed in 311, who held that only those living a blameless life belonged in the Church. They survived until the 7th century.
– DERIVATIVES **Donatism** noun.
– ORIGIN from *Donatus* (died *c*.355), a Christian prelate in Carthage and the group's leader, + -IST.

donative /ˈdəʊnətɪv/ rare ▸ noun a donation, especially one given formally or officially as a largesse.
▸ adjective given as a donation. ■ historical (of a benefice) given directly, not presentative.
– ORIGIN late Middle English: from Latin *donativum* 'gift, largesse', from *donat-* 'given', from the verb *donare* (see DONATION).

Donatus /dəˈneɪtəs/, Aelius (4th century), Roman grammarian. The *Ars Grammatica*, containing his treatises on Latin grammar, was used in schools in the Middle Ages.

Donau[1] /ˈdəʊnaʊ/ German name for DANUBE.

Donau[2] /ˈdɒnəʊ/ ▸ noun [usu. as modifier] Geology a series of Lower Pleistocene glaciations in the Alps, preceding the Günz. ■ the system of deposits laid down during this period.
– ORIGIN German, 'Danube'.

Donbas /dɒnˈbɑːs/ Ukrainian name for DONETS BASIN.

Doncaster /ˈdɒŋkəstə/ an industrial town in South Yorkshire, northern England; pop. 63,800 (est. 2009).

done past participle of DO[1]. ▸ adjective **1** (of food) cooked thoroughly: *the turkey will be **done to a turn***.
2 no longer happening or existing: *her hunting days were done*.
3 Brit. informal socially acceptable: *therapy was **not the done thing** then*.
▸ exclamation used to indicate that the speaker accepts the terms of an offer: *'I'll give ten to one he misses by a mile!' called Reilly. 'Done!', said the conductor*.
– PHRASES **a done deal** an agreement that has been finalized. **done for** informal in a situation so bad that it is impossible to get out: *if the guard sees us, we're done for*. **done in** (or **up**) informal extremely tired: *you look done in*.
– DERIVATIVES **doneness** noun informal (sense 1 of the adjective).

donee /dəʊˈniː/ ▸ noun a person who receives a gift. ■ Law a person who is given a power of appointment.
– ORIGIN early 16th cent.: from DONOR + -EE.

Donegal[1] /ˌdɒnɪˈɡɔːl/ a county in the extreme north-west of the Republic of Ireland, part of the old province of Ulster; capital, Lifford.

Donegal[2] (also **Donegal tweed**) ▸ noun [mass noun] a tweed characterized by bright flecks randomly distributed on a background that is typically light grey, as originally woven in County Donegal.

doner kebab /ˈdɒnə, ˈdəʊnə/ ▸ noun a Turkish dish consisting of spiced lamb cooked on a spit and served in slices, typically with pitta bread.
– ORIGIN from Turkish *döner kebap*, from *döner* 'rotating' and *kebap* 'roast meat'.

Donets /dɒˈnjɛts/ a river in eastern Europe, rising near Belgorod in southern Russia and flowing south-eastwards for some 1,000 km (630 miles) through Ukraine before re-entering Russia and joining the Don near Rostov.

Donets Basin a coal-mining and industrial region of SE Ukraine, stretching between the valleys of the

Donets and lower Dnieper Rivers. Ukrainian name **Donbas**.

Donetsk /dɒˈnjɛtsk/ the leading city of the Donets Basin in Ukraine; pop. 974,600 (est. 2009). The city was called Yuzovka from 1872 until 1924, and Stalin or Stalino from 1924 until 1961.

dong[1] ▶ **verb 1** [no obj.] (of a bell) make a deep, resonant sound.
2 [with obj.] Austral./NZ informal hit or punch (someone).
▶ **noun 1** the deep, resonant sound of a large bell.
2 Austral./NZ a blow; a punch.
3 vulgar slang a man's penis.
– ORIGIN late 16th cent.: imitative.

dong[2] ▶ **noun** the basic monetary unit of Vietnam, equal to 100 xu.
– ORIGIN from Vietnamese *đông* 'coin'.

donga /ˈdɒŋgə/ ▶ **noun 1** S. African & Austral./NZ a dry gully, formed by the eroding action of running water.
2 Austral. a temporary, usually transportable, dwelling.
3 Austral. the bush; the remote countryside.
– ORIGIN Sense 1 from Xhosa and Zulu *udonga*; sense 2 is said to stem from an extended usage of the term in the Boer War.

dongle /ˈdɒŋg(ə)l/ ▶ **noun** a device that is connected to a computer to allow access to wireless broadband or use of protected software.
– ORIGIN 1980s: an arbitrary formation.

dong quai /dɒŋ ˈkwɛɪ, ˈkwʌɪ/ ▶ **noun** [mass noun] an aromatic herb native to China and Japan, the root of which is used by herbalists to treat premenstrual syndrome and menopausal symptoms. ● *Angelica sinensis*, family Umbelliferae.
– ORIGIN from Chinese *dāngguī*.

Donizetti /ˌdɒnɪˈtsɛti/, Gaetano (1797–1848), Italian composer. His operas include tragedies such as *Lucia di Lammermoor* (1835) and comedies such as *Don Pasquale* (1843).

donjon /ˈdɒndʒ(ə)n, ˈdʌn-/ ▶ **noun** the great tower or innermost keep of a castle.
– ORIGIN Middle English: variant of **dungeon**.

Don Juan /dɒn ˈhwɑːn, dɒn ˈdʒuːən/ a legendary Spanish nobleman of dissolute life, famous for seducing women. ■ (as noun **a Don Juan**) a seducer of women; a libertine.

donkey ▶ **noun** (pl. **donkeys**) **1** a domesticated hoofed mammal of the horse family with long ears and a braying call, used as a beast of burden; an ass. ● *Equus asinus*, family Equidae, descended from the wild ass of Africa.
2 informal a stupid or inept person.
3 informal an engine.
4 (also **donkey stool**) a low stool on which an artist sits astride, especially in an art school.
5 [mass noun] a children's card game involving exchanging cards.
– PHRASES **donkey's years** Brit. informal a very long time: *we've been close friends for donkey's years.*
– ORIGIN late 18th cent. (originally pronounced to rhyme with *monkey*): perhaps from **dun**[1], or from the given name *Duncan*.

donkey derby ▶ **noun** a race between competitors riding donkeys.

donkey engine ▶ **noun** a small auxiliary engine.

donkey jacket ▶ **noun** Brit. a heavy jacket which has a patch of waterproof leather or plastic across the shoulders, worn typically by building workers.

donkeyman ▶ **noun** (pl. **donkeymen**) a man with responsibilities in a ship's engine room: [as modifier] *a donkeyman greaser.*

donkey work ▶ **noun** [mass noun] Brit. informal the boring or laborious part of a job; drudgery: *supervisors who get a research student to do the donkey work.*

Donkin /ˈdɒŋkɪn/, Bryan (1768–1855), English engineer. He developed a method of food preservation by heat sterilization, sealing the food inside a container made of sheet steel and so producing the first tin can.

Donna /ˈdɒnə/ ▶ **noun** a title or form of address for an Italian woman.
– ORIGIN early 17th cent.: from Italian, from Latin *domina* 'mistress', feminine of *dominus* 'lord, master'.

Donnan equilibrium /ˈdɒn(ə)n/ ▶ **noun** [mass noun] Chemistry the equilibrium reached between two ionic solutions separated by a semipermeable membrane when one or more of the kinds of ion present cannot pass through the membrane. The result is a difference in osmotic pressure and electrical potential between the solutions.
– ORIGIN early 20th cent.: named after Frederick G. Donnan (1870–1956), British physical chemist.

Donne /dʌn/, John (1572–1631), English poet and preacher. A metaphysical poet, he is most famous for his *Satires* and *Elegies* (*c.*1590–9) and his love poems. He also wrote religious poems and, as dean of St Paul's from 1621, was one of the most celebrated preachers of his age.

donnée /ˈdɒneɪ/ (also **donné**) ▶ **noun 1** a subject or theme of a narrative.
2 a basic fact or assumption.
– ORIGIN French, 'given'.

donnish ▶ **adjective** Brit. resembling a college don, particularly because of having a pedantic, scholarly manner.
– DERIVATIVES **donnishly** adverb, **donnishness** noun.

donnybrook /ˈdɒnɪbrʊk/ ▶ **noun** N. Amer. & Austral./NZ a scene of uproar and disorder; a heated argument: *raucous ideological donnybrooks.*
– ORIGIN mid 19th cent.: from the name of a suburb of Dublin, Ireland, formerly famous for its annual fair.

donor /ˈdəʊnə, -nɔː/ ▶ **noun** a person who donates something, especially money to charity: *an anonymous donor has given £25* | [as modifier] *loans from rich donor countries.* ■ a person who provides blood, an organ, or semen for transplantation, transfusion, etc. ■ Chemistry an atom or molecule that provides a pair of electrons in forming a coordinate bond. ■ Physics an impurity atom in a semiconductor which contributes a conducting electron to the material.
– ORIGIN Middle English: from Old French *doneur*, from Latin *donator*, from *donare* 'give'.

donor card ▶ **noun** a card which a person carries to indicate consent to the use of their organs for transplant surgery in the event of their death.

donor fatigue ▶ **noun** [mass noun] another term for **compassion fatigue**.

do-nothing informal ▶ **adjective** taking no action; doing nothing: *a weak, divided, do-nothing government.*
▶ **noun** an idle or feckless person: *a shiftless lot of do-nothings.*

Don Quixote /dɒn kiːˈhəʊti, dɒn ˈkwɪksəʊt/ the hero of a romance (1605–15) by Cervantes, a satirical account of chivalric beliefs and conduct. The character of Don Quixote is typified by a romantic vision and naive, unworldly idealism.

don't ▶ **contraction** do not.
– PHRASES **dos and don'ts** see **do**[1].

don't-know ▶ **noun** a person who disclaims knowledge, especially one who is undecided when replying to an opinion poll or questionnaire.

donut ▶ **noun** US spelling of **doughnut**.

doobie ▶ **noun** informal a cannabis cigarette.
– ORIGIN 1960s (originally US): of unknown origin.

doobry (also **doobrey** or **doobrie** /ˈduːbri/) ▶ **noun** (pl. **doobries** or **doobreys** /ˈduːbrɪz/) Brit. informal another term for **doodah**: *you know, the little plastic doobry that covers the connector.*
– ORIGIN 1950s: of unknown origin.

doodad /ˈduːdad/ ▶ **noun** North American term for **doodah**.
– ORIGIN early 20th cent.: of unknown origin.

doodah /ˈduːdɑː/ ▶ **noun** Brit. informal used to refer to something that the speaker cannot name precisely: *from the poshest pot pourri to the humblest dangly doodah.*
– PHRASES **all of a doodah** very agitated: *they'll be all of a doodah because of the bombs.*
– ORIGIN early 20th cent. (in the phrase *all of a doodah*): perhaps from the refrain of the song *Camptown Races*.

doodle ▶ **verb** [no obj.] scribble absent-mindedly: *he was only doodling in the margin.*
▶ **noun** a rough drawing made absent-mindedly.
– DERIVATIVES **doodler** noun.
– ORIGIN early 17th cent. (originally as a noun denoting a fool, later as a verb in the sense 'make a fool of, cheat'): from Low German *dudeltopf*, *dudeldopp* 'simpleton'. Current senses date from the 1930s.

doodlebug ▶ **noun** informal **1** Brit. informal term for **V-1**.
2 N. Amer. the larva of an ant lion.
3 US an unscientific device for locating oil or minerals; a divining rod. ■ a prospector for oil or minerals.
4 a small car or other vehicle.
– ORIGIN mid 19th cent. (in sense 2): from 17th-cent. *doodle* 'ninny' + **bug**.

doodly-squat ▶ **noun** another term for **diddly-squat**.

doo-doo ▶ **noun** a child's word for excrement, used euphemistically in other contexts: *when our fax machine isn't working, we're* ***in deep doo-doo.***

doofus /ˈduːfʌs/ (also **dufus**) ▶ **noun** (pl. **doofuses**) N. Amer. informal a stupid person.
– ORIGIN 1960s: perhaps an alteration of **goofus**, or from Scots *doof* 'dolt'.

doohickey /ˈduːhɪki/ ▶ **noun** (pl. **doohickeys**) N. Amer. informal a small object or gadget, especially one whose precise name the speaker cannot recall: *a garage filled with electronic parts and other valuable doohickeys.*
– ORIGIN early 20th cent. (originally servicemen's slang): blend of **doodad** and **hickey**.

doojigger /ˈduːdʒɪgə/ ▶ **noun** US another term for **doohickey**.
– ORIGIN 1920s: blend of **doodad** and **jigger**[1].

doolally /duːˈlali/ ▶ **adjective** Brit. informal temporarily deranged or feeble-minded: *Uncle's gone doolally again.* ■ transported with excitement or pleasure: *a return on capital that the City would go doolally over.*
– ORIGIN early 20th cent.: originally *doolally tap*, Indian army slang, from *Deolali* (the name of a town with a military sanatorium and a transit camp) + Urdu *tap* 'fever'.

Doolittle /ˈduːlɪt(ə)l/, Hilda (1886–1961), American poet; pseudonym **H.D.** Her work shows the influence of Ezra Pound and other imagist poets. Notable works: *Sea Garden* (1916).

doom ▶ **noun** [mass noun] death, destruction, or some other terrible fate: *the aircraft was sent crashing to its doom in the water.* ■ [in sing.] archaic (in Christian belief) the Last Judgement. See also **crack of doom** at **crack**.
▶ **verb** [with obj.] condemn to certain death or destruction: *fuel was spilling out of the damaged wing and the aircraft was doomed.* ■ cause to have an unfortunate and inescapable outcome: *her plan was* ***doomed to*** *failure.*
– PHRASES **doom and gloom** (also **gloom and doom**) a general feeling of pessimism or despondency: *the national feeling of doom and gloom.*
– ORIGIN Old English *dōm* 'statute, judgement', of Germanic origin, from a base meaning 'to put in place'; related to **do**[1].

doomed ▶ **adjective** likely to have an unfortunate and inescapable outcome; ill-fated: *the moving story of their doomed love affair.*

doom-laden ▶ **adjective** conveying a sense of tragedy: *a doom-laden speech.*

doomsayer ▶ **noun** chiefly N. Amer. a person who predicts disaster.
– DERIVATIVES **doomsaying** noun.

doomsday ▶ **noun** the last day of the world's existence. ■ (in religious belief) the day of the Last Judgement. ■ a time or event of crisis or great danger: [as modifier] *in all the concern over greenhouse warming, one doomsday scenario stands out.*
– PHRASES **till doomsday** informal forever: *we'll be here till doomsday if you go blethering on.*
– ORIGIN Old English *dōmes dæg* (see **doom**, **day**).

Doomsday Book ▶ **noun** see **Domesday**.

doomster ▶ **noun** Brit. another term for **doomsayer**.

doomwatch ▶ **noun** an organized campaign of vigilance to alert people to the dangers of environmental pollution.

doomy ▶ **adjective** (**doomier**, **doomiest**) suggesting or predicting disaster; ominous: *doomy forecasts.*
– DERIVATIVES **doomily** adverb, **doominess** noun.

doona /ˈduːnə/ ▶ **noun** Austral. trademark a quilted eiderdown or duvet.
– ORIGIN 1970s: perhaps from Swedish *dun* (see **down**[2]).

door ▶ **noun** a hinged, sliding, or revolving barrier at the entrance to a building, room, or vehicle, or in the framework of a cupboard. ■ a doorway: *she walked through the door.* ■ used to refer to the distance from one building in a row to another: *he lives just a few doors away from the Strongs.*
– PHRASES **as one door closes, another opens** proverb you shouldn't be discouraged by failure, as other opportunities will soon present themselves. **at the door** on admission to an event rather than in advance: *tickets will be available at the door.* **close** (or **shut**) **the door on** (or **to**) exclude the opportunity for: *she had closed the door on ever finding out what he was feeling.* **(from) door to door 1** from start to finish of a journey: *the trip from door to door could take more than four hours.* **2** visiting all the houses in an

D

area to sell or publicize something: *he went from door to door selling insurance policies* | [as modifier] *a door-to-door salesman.* **lay something at someone's door** regard someone as responsible for something: *the failure is laid at the door of the government.* **leave the door open** ensure that there is still an opportunity for something: *he is leaving the door open for future change.* **on the door 1** monitoring admission to a building or event: *the uniformed commissionaires on the door.* **2** another way of saying **AT THE DOOR. open the door to** create an opportunity for: *her research has opened the door to a deeper understanding of the subject.* **out of doors** in or into the open air: *food tastes even better out of doors.*
– DERIVATIVES **doored** adjective [in combination] *a glass-doored desk.*
– ORIGIN Old English *duru, dor*, of Germanic origin; related to Dutch *deur* 'door' and German *Tür* 'door', *Tor* 'gate'; from an Indo-European root shared by Latin *foris* 'gate' and Greek *thura* 'door'.

doorbell ▶ noun a bell in a building which can be rung by visitors outside to signal their arrival.

do-or-die ▶ adjective showing or requiring a determination not to compromise or be deterred: *the mercenaries fought with a do-or-die fanaticism.*

door frame (also **doorcase**) ▶ noun the frame in a doorway into which a door is fitted.

door furniture ▶ noun [mass noun] the handles, lock, and other fixtures on a door.

door head ▶ noun the upper part of a door frame.

doorkeeper ▶ noun a person on duty at the entrance to a building.

doorknob ▶ noun a handle on a door that is turned to release the latch.

doorknock Austral./NZ ▶ noun a campaign of door-to-door house visits to collect for a charity or to appeal for support for a political candidate: [as modifier] *a doorknock appeal.*
▶ verb [no obj.] campaign by making door-to-door house visits.

doorman ▶ noun (pl. **doormen**) a man such as a porter, bouncer, or janitor who is on duty at the entrance to a large building.

doormat ▶ noun a mat placed in a doorway, on which people can wipe their shoes on entering a building. ■ a submissive person who allows others to dominate them: *to put up with such treatment you must be either a saint or a doormat.*

doornail ▶ noun a stud set in a door for strength or as an ornament.
– PHRASES **(as) dead as a doornail** quite dead.

Doornik /'dəʊːrnɪk/ Flemish name for **TOURNAI**.

door plate ▶ noun a plate on the door of a house or room which gives information about the occupant.

doorpost ▶ noun each of the two upright parts of a door frame.

door prize ▶ noun a prize which each person present at an event has a chance to win, usually by means of a draw or raffle.

doorstep ▶ noun a step leading up to the outer door of a house. ■ Brit. informal a thick slice of bread: [as modifier] *doorstep sandwiches.*
▶ verb (**doorsteps, doorstepping, doorstepped**) [with obj.] Brit. informal (of a journalist) wait uninvited outside the home of (someone) in order to obtain an interview or photograph: *he was being doorstepped by the tabloids.*
– PHRASES **on one's** (or **the**) **doorstep** situated very close by: *the airport is on my doorstep so flying is easy.*

doorstop (also **doorstopper**) ▶ noun a fixed or heavy object that keeps a door open or stops it from banging against a wall. ■ a heavy or bulky object, especially a thick book: *his sixth novel is a thumping 400-page doorstop.*

doorway ▶ noun an entrance to a room or building through a door: *Beth stood there in the doorway* | figurative *the doorway to success.*

dooryard ▶ noun N. Amer. a yard or garden by the door of a house.

doo-wop /'duːwɒp/ ▶ noun [mass noun] a style of pop music marked by the use of close harmony vocals using nonsense phrases, originating in the US in the 1950s.
– ORIGIN imitative.

doozy /'duːzi/ (also **doozie**) ▶ noun (pl. **doozies**) informal, chiefly N. Amer. something outstanding or unique of its kind: *it's gonna be a doozy of a black eye.*
– ORIGIN early 20th cent.: of unknown origin.

dop /dɒp/ ▶ noun S. African informal a drink, especially of brandy or other spirits.
– ORIGIN South African Dutch, 'shell, husk'.

dopa /'dəʊpə/ ▶ noun [mass noun] Biochemistry a compound which is present in nervous tissue as a precursor of dopamine, used in the treatment of Parkinson's disease. See also **L-DOPA**. ● An amino acid; alternative name: dihydroxyphenylalanine; chem. formula: $C_9H_{11}NO_4$.
– ORIGIN early 20th cent.: from German, acronym from the systematic name.

dopamine /'dəʊpəmiːn/ ▶ noun [mass noun] Biochemistry a compound present in the body as a neurotransmitter and a precursor of other substances including adrenalin. ● Alternative name: **3,4-dihydroxyphenylethylamine**; chem. formula: $C_8H_{11}NO_2$.
– ORIGIN 1950s: blend of **DOPA** and **AMINE**.

dopaminergic /ˌdəʊpəmiː'nəːdʒɪk/ ▶ adjective Biochemistry releasing or involving dopamine as a neurotransmitter.
– ORIGIN 1960s: from **DOPAMINE** + Greek *ergon* 'work' + **-IC**.

dopant /'dəʊp(ə)nt/ ▶ noun Electronics a substance used to produce a desired electrical characteristic in a semiconductor.
– ORIGIN 1960s: from the verb **DOPE** + **-ANT**.

dope ▶ noun [mass noun] **1** informal a drug taken illegally for recreational purposes, especially cannabis or (US) heroin. ■ a drug given to a racehorse or greyhound to inhibit or enhance its performance. ■ a drug taken by an athlete to improve performance: [as modifier] *he failed a dope test.*
2 [count noun] informal a stupid person: *though he wasn't an intellectual giant, he was no dope either.*
3 informal information about a subject, especially if not generally known: *our reviewer will give you the dope on hot spots around the town.*
4 a varnish formerly applied to fabric surfaces of aircraft to strengthen them and keep them airtight. ■ a thick liquid used as a lubricant. ■ a substance added to petrol to increase its effectiveness.
▶ verb [with obj.] **1** administer drugs to (a racehorse, greyhound, or athlete) in order to inhibit or enhance sporting performance: *the horse was doped before the race.* ■ **(be doped up)** informal be heavily under the influence of drugs, typically illegal ones: *he was so doped up that he can't remember a thing.* ■ treat (food or drink) with drugs: *maybe they had doped her Perrier.* ■ [no obj.] informal, dated regularly take illegal drugs.
2 smear or cover with varnish or other thick liquid: *she doped the surface with photographic emulsion.*
3 Electronics add an impurity to (a semiconductor) to produce a desired electrical characteristic.
▶ adjective black slang very good: *that suit is dope!*
– PHRASAL VERBS **dope something out** informal, dated work out something: *they met to dope out plans for covering the event.*
– DERIVATIVES **doper** noun.
– ORIGIN early 19th cent. (in the sense 'thick liquid'): from Dutch *doop* 'sauce', from *doopen* 'to dip, mix'.

dopester /'dəʊpstə/ ▶ noun N. Amer. informal a person who collects and supplies information, typically on sporting events or elections: *they are inside dopesters with special access to the racing world.*

dopey (also **dopy**) ▶ adjective (**dopier, dopiest**) informal stupefied by sleep or a drug: *she was under sedation and a bit dopey.* ■ idiotic: *did you ever hear such dopey names?*
– DERIVATIVES **dopily** adverb, **dopiness** noun.

dopiaza /'dəʊpɪɑːʒə/ ▶ noun [mass noun] an Indian dish consisting of meat cooked with onions and garnished with raw or fried onions: *chicken dopiaza.*
– ORIGIN from Hindi *do* 'two' + *pyāz* 'onion'.

doppelgänger /'dɒp(ə)lˌɡaŋə, -ˌɡɛŋə/ ▶ noun an apparition or double of a living person.
– ORIGIN mid 19th cent.: from German, literally 'double-goer'.

Dopper /'dɒpə/ ▶ noun (in South Africa) a member of the Gereformeerde Kerk, a strictly orthodox Calvinistic denomination.
– ORIGIN Afrikaans, of unknown origin.

doppie /'dɒpi/ ▶ noun S. African informal a tot of spirits.
– ORIGIN Afrikaans, diminutive of *dop* (see **DOP**).

Doppler /'dɒplə/, Johann Christian (1803–53), Austrian physicist, famous for his discovery, in 1842, of what is now known as the Doppler effect.

Doppler broadening ▶ noun [mass noun] Physics the broadening of spectral lines as a result of the different velocities of the emitting atoms giving rise to different Doppler shifts.

Doppler effect ▶ noun Physics an increase (or decrease) in the frequency of sound, light, or other waves as the source and observer move towards (or away from) each other. The effect causes the sudden change in pitch noticeable in a passing siren, as well as the red shift seen by astronomers.

Doppler shift ▶ noun Physics a change in frequency due to the Doppler effect.

dopy ▶ adjective variant spelling of **DOPEY**.

dor /dɔː/ (also **dor beetle**) ▶ noun a large black dung beetle that makes a droning sound in flight and excavates burrows in which its young develop.
● Family Geotrupidae: several genera and species, including the common *Geotrupes stercorarius.*
– ORIGIN Old English (denoting a bee or buzzing fly), probably imitative.

Dorado /də'rɑːdəʊ/ Astronomy a southern constellation (the Goldfish), containing most of the Large Magellanic Cloud.
– ORIGIN Spanish (see **DORADO**).

dorado /də'rɑːdəʊ/ ▶ noun (pl. **dorados**) **1** an edible marine fish of warm seas, with silver and bright blue or green coloration when alive. Also called **DOLPHIN**.
● Family Coryphaenidae and genus *Coryphaena*: two species, in particular the large *C. hippurus.*
2 a South American freshwater fish with a golden body and red fins, popular as a game fish. ● *Salminus maxillosus*, family Characidae.
– ORIGIN early 17th cent.: from Spanish, literally 'gilded', from late Latin *deauratus*, from *deaurare* 'to gild over' (see also **DORY**[1]).

do-rag /'duːraɡ/ ▶ noun US black slang a scarf or cloth worn to protect one's hairstyle.
– ORIGIN 1990s: from **HAIRDO**.

dorcas gazelle /'dɔːkəs/ ▶ noun a small gazelle found on semi-desert plains in North Africa and western Asia. ● *Gazella dorcas*, family Bovidae.
– ORIGIN early 19th cent.: from modern Latin *Gazella dorcas* (from Greek *dorkas* 'gazelle').

Dorchester /'dɔːtʃɪstə/ a town in southern England, the county town of Dorset; pop. 17,700 (est. 2009).

Dordogne /dɔː'dɔɪn/, French /dɔRdɔɲ/ a river of western France which rises in the Auvergne and flows 472 km (297 miles) westwards to meet the Garonne and form the Gironde estuary. ■ a department of SW France. It contains caves that have yielded abundant remains of early humans and their artefacts and art, such as that at Lascaux.

Dordrecht /dɔː'drɛxt/ an industrial city and river port in the Netherlands, near the mouth of the Rhine (there called the Waal), 20 km (12 miles) south-east of Rotterdam; pop. 118,182 (2008). Also called **DORT**.

Doré /'dɔːreɪ/, French /dɔRe/, Gustave (1832–83), French book illustrator, known for his woodcut illustrations of books such as Dante's *Inferno* (1861), Cervantes' *Don Quixote* (1863), and the Bible (1865–6).

doré /'dɔːreɪ, -riː/ ▶ noun Canadian term for **WALL EYE** (sense 2).
– ORIGIN late 18th cent.: French, literally 'gilded'.

Dorian /'dɔːrɪən/ ▶ noun a member of a Hellenic people speaking the Doric dialect of Greek, thought to have entered Greece from the north *c.*1100 BC. They settled in the Peloponnese and later colonized Sicily and southern Italy.
▶ adjective relating to the Dorians or to Doris in central Greece.
– ORIGIN via Latin from Greek *Dōrios* 'of Doris' + **-IAN**.

Dorian mode ▶ noun Music the mode represented by the natural diatonic scale D–D (containing a minor 3rd and minor 7th).

Doric /'dɒrɪk/ ▶ adjective **1** relating to or denoting a classical order of architecture characterized by a sturdy fluted column and a thick square abacus resting on a rounded moulding.
2 relating to the ancient Greek dialect of the Dorians. ■ archaic (of a dialect) broad; rustic.
▶ noun [mass noun] **1** the Doric order of architecture.
2 the ancient Greek dialect of the Dorians. ■ a broad or rustic dialect, especially the dialect spoken in the north-east of Scotland.
– ORIGIN via Latin from Greek *Dōrikos*, from *Dōrios* (see **DORIAN**).

dorje /'dɔːdʒeɪ/ ▶ noun (in Tibetan Buddhism) a representation of a thunderbolt in the form of a short double trident or sceptre, symbolizing the male aspect of the spirit and held during invocations and prayers. Compare with **VAJRA**.
– ORIGIN Tibetan.

dork ▸ noun **1** informal a contemptible, socially inept person.
2 N. Amer. vulgar slang a man's penis.
– DERIVATIVES **dorkiness** noun, **dorky** adjective (**dorkier**, **dorkiest**).
– ORIGIN 1960s (originally US): perhaps a variant of DIRK, influenced by DICK[1].

dorm ▸ noun informal a dormitory.
– ORIGIN early 20th cent.: abbreviation.

dormant ▸ adjective (of an animal) having normal physical functions suspended or slowed down for a period of time; in or as if in a deep sleep: *dormant butterflies* | figurative *the event evoked memories that she would rather had **lain dormant**.* ■ (of a plant or bud) alive but not actively growing. ■ (of a volcano) temporarily inactive. ■ (of a disease) causing no symptoms but not cured and liable to recur. ■ [usu. postpositive] Heraldry (of an animal) depicted lying with its head on its paws.
– DERIVATIVES **dormancy** noun.
– ORIGIN late Middle English (in the senses 'fixed in position' and 'latent'): from Old French, 'sleeping', present participle of *dormir*, from Latin *dormire* 'to sleep'.

dormer (also **dormer window**) ▸ noun a window that projects vertically from a sloping roof.
– ORIGIN late 16th cent. (denoting the window of a dormitory or bedroom): from Old French *dormeor* 'dormitory', from *dormir* 'to sleep'.

Dormition /dɔːˈmɪʃ(ə)n/ ▸ noun (in the Orthodox Church) the passing of the Virgin Mary from earthly life. ■ the feast held in honour of this on 15 August, corresponding to the Assumption in the Western Church.
– ORIGIN late 15th cent.: from French, from Latin *dormitio(n-)* 'falling asleep', from *dormire* 'to sleep'.

dormitory /ˈdɔːmɪt(ə)ri/ ▸ noun (pl. **dormitories**) a large bedroom for a number of people in a school or institution. ■ N. Amer. a university or college hall of residence or hostel. ■ [usu. as modifier] chiefly Brit. a small town or suburb providing a residential area for those who work in a nearby city: *a dormitory town*.
– ORIGIN late Middle English: from Latin *dormitorium*, neuter (used as a noun) of *dormitorius*, from *dormire* 'to sleep'.

Dormobile /ˈdɔːməbiːl/ ▸ noun Brit. trademark a motor caravan that can be used for sleeping in.
– ORIGIN 1950s: blend of DORMITORY and AUTOMOBILE.

dormouse ▸ noun (pl. **dormice**) an agile mouse-like rodent with a hairy or bushy tail, found in Africa and Eurasia. Some kinds are noted for spending long periods in hibernation. ● Family Myoxidae: several genera and species, including the **common** (or **hazel**) **dormouse** (*Muscardinus avellanarius*) and the **fat dormouse**.
– ORIGIN late Middle English: of unknown origin, but associated with French *dormir* or Latin *dormire* 'to sleep' and MOUSE.

dormy /ˈdɔːmi/ ▸ adjective Golf (of a player in match play) ahead by a specified number of holes when the same number of holes remain to be played, and thus in a position at least to draw the match (used preceding a numeral): *he reached the 17th hole dormy two*.
– ORIGIN mid 19th cent.: of unknown origin.

doronicum /dəˈrɒnɪkəm/ ▸ noun (pl. **doronicums**) a plant of the genus *Doronicum* in the daisy family, especially (in gardening) leopard's bane.
– ORIGIN modern Latin (Linnaeus), from modern Greek *dōronikon*, from Persian *darūnak*.

dorp /dɔːp/ ▸ noun S. African a small rural town or village (often used to suggest that a place is backward or unimpressive): *dreary little dorps*.
– ORIGIN Dutch, 'village' (see THORP).

dorsal /ˈdɔːs(ə)l/ ▸ adjective Anatomy, Zoology, & Botany on or relating to the upper side or back of an animal, plant, or organ: *a dorsal view of the body* | *the dorsal aorta*. Compare with VENTRAL.
– DERIVATIVES **dorsally** adverb.
– ORIGIN late Middle English: from late Latin *dorsalis*, from Latin *dorsum* 'back'.

dorsal fin ▸ noun Zoology an unpaired fin on the back of a fish or whale, e.g. the tall triangular fin of a shark or killer whale.

Dorset[1] /ˈdɔːsɪt/ a county of SW England; county town, Dorchester.

Dorset[2] /ˈdɔːsɪt/ ▸ noun [usu. as modifier] Archaeology a prehistoric culture which flourished in the American Arctic during the 1st millennium AD and was displaced by the Thule culture.
– ORIGIN 1930s: from the name of Cape *Dorset*, Baffin Island.

Dorset Down ▸ noun a sheep of a breed with a brown face and legs.

Dorset Horn ▸ noun a sheep of a breed with a white face and horns on both the ewe and the ram.

dorsi- ▸ combining form towards or on the back: *dorsiventral*.
– ORIGIN from Latin *dorsum* 'back'.

dorsiflex /ˈdɔːsɪflɛks/ ▸ verb [with obj.] Physiology bend (something, typically the hand or foot) dorsally or towards its upper surface.
– DERIVATIVES **dorsiflexion** noun.

dorsiflexor /ˈdɔːsɪˌflɛksə/ ▸ noun Anatomy a muscle whose contraction dorsiflexes the hand or foot.

dorsiventral /ˌdɔːsɪˈvɛntr(ə)l/ ▸ adjective chiefly Botany (of a leaf or other part of a plant) having dissimilar dorsal and ventral surfaces. ■ another term for DORSOVENTRAL.
– DERIVATIVES **dorsiventrality** noun, **dorsiventrally** adverb.

dorso- ▸ combining form relating to the back: *dorsoventral*.
– ORIGIN from Latin *dorsum* 'back'.

dorsolateral /ˌdɔːsə(ʊ)ˈlat(ə)r(ə)l/ ▸ adjective Anatomy & Biology relating to or involving the dorsal and lateral surfaces.
– DERIVATIVES **dorsolaterally** adverb.

dorsoventral /ˌdɔːsə(ʊ)ˈvɛntr(ə)l/ ▸ adjective Anatomy & Biology of, denoting, or extending along an axis joining the dorsal and ventral surfaces.
– DERIVATIVES **dorsoventrally** adverb.

dorsum /ˈdɔːsəm/ ▸ noun (pl. **dorsa**) Anatomy & Zoology the dorsal part of an organism or structure.
– ORIGIN late 18th cent. (denoting a long hill or ridge): from Latin, 'back'.

Dort /dɔːt/ another name for DORDRECHT.

Dortmund /ˈdɔːtmʊnd/, German /ˈdɔrtmʊnt/ an industrial city in NW Germany, in North Rhine-Westphalia; pop. 587,600 (est. 2006).

dory[1] /ˈdɔːri/ ▸ noun (pl. **dories**) a narrow deep-bodied fish with a mouth that can be opened very wide. ● Several genera and species in the families Zeidae and Oreosomatidae. See also JOHN DORY.
– ORIGIN late Middle English: from French *dorée*, feminine past participle of *dorer* 'gild', from late Latin *deaurare* 'gild over', based on Latin *aurum* 'gold'. Compare with DORADO.

dory[2] /ˈdɔːri/ ▸ noun (pl. **dories**) a small flat-bottomed rowing boat with a high bow and stern, originally of a kind used for fishing in New England.
– ORIGIN early 18th cent.: perhaps from Miskito *dóri* 'dugout'.

doryphore /ˈdɒrɪfɔː/ ▸ noun rare a pedantic and annoyingly persistent critic.
– ORIGIN 1950s (introduced by Sir Harold Nicolson): from French, literally 'Colorado beetle', from Greek *doruphoros* 'spear carrier'.

DOS ▸ abbreviation Computing disk operating system, an operating system originally developed for IBM personal computers.

DoS ▸ abbreviation Computing denial of service.

dosa /ˈdəʊsə/ ▸ noun (pl. **dosas** or **dosai** /ˈdəʊsʌɪ/) (in southern Indian cooking) a pancake made from rice flour and ground pulses, typically served with a spiced vegetable filling.
– ORIGIN from Tamil *tōcai*.

dos-à-dos /ˌdəʊzəˈdəʊ/ ▸ adjective (of two books) bound together with a shared central board and facing in opposite directions.
▸ noun (pl. **same**) a seat or carriage in which the occupants sit back to back.
– ORIGIN French, 'back to back'.

dosage ▸ noun the size or frequency of a dose of a medicine or drug: *a dosage of 450 milligrams a day* | [mass noun] *there are recommendations about dosage in elderly patients*. ■ a level of exposure to or absorption of ionizing radiation.

dose ▸ noun a quantity of a medicine or drug taken or recommended to be taken at a particular time: *he took **a dose of** cough mixture*. ■ an amount of ionizing radiation received or absorbed at one time or over a specified period: ***a dose of** radiation exceeding safety limits*. ■ informal a venereal infection. ■ informal a quantity of something unpleasant but necessary: *I wanted to give you **a dose of** the hell you put me through*.
▸ verb [with obj.] administer a dose to (a person or animal): *he **dosed** himself **with** vitamins*. ■ adulterate or blend (a substance) with another substance: *the petrol is **dosed with** lead*.
– PHRASES **in small doses** informal when experienced or engaged in a little at a time: *computer games are great in small doses*. **like a dose of salts** Brit. informal very fast and efficiently: *we'll go through this place like a dose of salts and scrub it from top to bottom*. [from the use of Epsom salts as a laxative.]
– ORIGIN late Middle English: from French, via late Latin from Greek *dosis* 'gift', from *didonai* 'give'.

dose equivalent ▸ noun an estimate of the biological effect of a dose of ionizing radiation, calculated by multiplying the dose received by a factor depending on the type of radiation. It is measured in sieverts.

dose-response curve ▸ noun Medicine the relationship between the size of a dose and the extent of the response to it.

dosh ▸ noun [mass noun] Brit. informal money: *cycling saves you a heap of dosh*.
– ORIGIN 1950s: of unknown origin.

dosha /ˈdɒʃə, ˈdəʊʃə/ ▸ noun (in Ayurvedic medicine) each of three energies believed to circulate in the body and govern physiological activity, their differing proportions determining individual temperament and physical constitution and (when unbalanced) causing a disposition to particular physical and mental disorders.
– ORIGIN Sanskrit *dosa*, literally 'fault, disease'.

do-si-do /ˌdəʊzɪˈdəʊ, -sɪ-/ (also **do-se-do**) ▸ noun (pl. **do-si-dos**) (in country dancing) a figure in which two dancers pass round each other back to back and return to their original positions.
▸ verb [no obj.] dance a do-si-do.
– ORIGIN 1920s (originally US): alteration of DOS-À-DOS.

dosimeter /dəʊˈsɪmɪtə/ ▸ noun a device used to measure an absorbed dose of ionizing radiation.
– DERIVATIVES **dosimetric** adjective, **dosimetry** noun.

Dos Passos /dɒs ˈpasɒs/, John (Roderigo) (1896–1970), American novelist, chiefly known for his portrayal of American life in such novels as *Manhattan Transfer* (1925) and *USA* (1938).

doss Brit. informal ▸ verb [no obj.] **1** sleep in rough accommodation or on an improvised bed: *he **dossed down** on a friend's floor*.
2 spend time idly: *all I've seen her do so far is **doss around***.
▸ noun **1** an instance of sleeping in rough accommodation or on an improvised bed. ■ archaic a bed in a cheap lodging house.
2 a situation giving the opportunity for being extremely idle: *they thought being a student was a great doss*.
– ORIGIN late 18th cent.: perhaps based on Latin *dorsum* 'back'.

dossal /ˈdɒs(ə)l/ ▸ noun an ornamental cloth hung behind an altar in a church or at the sides of a chancel.
– ORIGIN mid 17th cent. (denoting an ornamental cloth for covering the back of a seat): from medieval Latin *dossale*, from late Latin *dorsalis* 'on the back' (see DORSAL).

dosser ▸ noun Brit. informal, derogatory **1** a person who sleeps rough; a tramp.
2 an idle person.

dosseret /ˈdɒsərɛt/ ▸ noun Architecture an additional block of stone placed above an abacus in the columns of a Byzantine or Romanesque arcade.
– ORIGIN mid 19th cent.: from French, diminutive of *dossier* 'back' (denoting a supporting structure).

dosshouse ▸ noun Brit. informal a cheap lodging house for homeless people and tramps.

dossier /ˈdɒsɪə, -ɪeɪ, -jeɪ/ ▸ noun a collection of documents about a particular person, event, or subject: *we have **a dossier on** him* | ***a dossier of** complaints*.
– ORIGIN late 19th cent.: from French, denoting a bundle of papers with a label on the back, from *dos* 'back', based on Latin *dorsum*.

dost /dʌst/ archaic second person singular present of DO[1].

Dostoevsky /ˌdɒstɔɪˈɛfski/ (also **Dostoyevsky**), Fyodor (Mikhailovich) (1821–81), Russian novelist. Dostoevsky's novels reveal his psychological insight, savage humour, and concern with the religious, political, and moral problems posed by human suffering. Notable novels: *Crime and Punishment* (1866), *The Idiot* (1868), and *The Brothers Karamazov* (1880).

DOT ▸ abbreviation directly observed therapy, a method of supervising patients to ensure that they take medication as directed.

D

D

DoT ▸ abbreviation ■ (in Canada and formerly in the UK) Department of Transport. ■ (in the US) Department of Transportation.

dot¹ ▸ noun a small round mark or spot: *a symbol depicted in coloured dots.* ■ such a mark written or printed as part of an *i* or *j*, as one of a series of marks to signify omission, or as a full stop. ■ Music such a mark used to denote the lengthening of a note or rest by half, or to indicate staccato. ■ the shorter signal of the two used in Morse code. Compare with DASH (sense 3 of the noun). ■ used to refer to an object that appears tiny because it is far away: *they were mere dots on the horizon now.* ■ used to indicate the punctuation separating parts of an email or website address: *OUP dot com.*
▸ verb (**dots, dotting, dotted**) [with obj.] **1** mark with a small spot or spots: *wet spots of rain began to dot his shirt.* ■ (of a number of items) be scattered over (an area): *churches dot the countryside* | (**be dotted**) *there appear to be a number of airfields **dotted about**.* ■ place a dot over (a letter): *you need to dot the i.* ■ Music mark (a note or rest) to show that the time value is increased by half: (as adj. **dotted**) *a dotted minim.*
2 Brit. informal hit (someone): *'You want to **dot him one**,' he said.*
– PHRASES **dot the i's and cross the t's** informal ensure that all details are correct. **on the dot** informal exactly on time: *he arrived on the dot at nine o'clock.* **the year dot** Brit. informal a very long time ago: *that wallpaper has been there since the year dot.*
– DERIVATIVES **dotter** noun.
– ORIGIN Old English *dott* 'head of a boil'. The word is recorded only once in Old English, then not until the late 16th cent., when it is found in the sense 'a small lump or clot', perhaps influenced by Dutch *dot* 'a knot'. The sense 'small mark or spot' dates from the mid 17th cent.

dot² ▸ noun archaic a dowry from which only the interest or annual income was available to the husband.
– ORIGIN from French, from Latin *dos, dot-* 'dowry' (see DOWER).

dotage /ˈdəʊtɪdʒ/ ▸ noun the period of life in which a person is old and weak: *you could live here and look after me **in my dotage**.*
– ORIGIN late Middle English: from DOTE + -AGE.

dotard /ˈdəʊtəd/ ▸ noun an old person, especially one who has become weak or senile.
– ORIGIN late Middle English: from DOTE + -ARD.

dot-com (also **dot.com**) ▸ noun a company that conducts its business on the Internet.
– ORIGIN 1990s: from '.com' in an Internet address, indicating a commercial site.

dote ▸ verb [no obj.] **1** (**dote on/upon**) be extremely and uncritically fond of: *she doted on her two young children.*
2 archaic be silly or feeble-minded, especially as a result of old age: *the parson is now old and dotes.*
▸ noun Irish informal a sweet or adorable person: *he's gorgeous and the twins are dotes.*
– DERIVATIVES **doter** noun.
– ORIGIN Middle English (in the sense 'act or talk foolishly'): of uncertain origin; related to Middle Dutch *doten* 'be silly'.

doth /dʌθ/ archaic third person singular present of DO¹.

doting ▸ adjective extremely and uncritically fond of someone; adoring: *she was spoiled outrageously by her doting father.*
– DERIVATIVES **dotingly** adverb.

dotish ▸ adjective archaic or W. Indian stupid or silly: *dotish foreign TV programmes.*
– ORIGIN early 16th cent.: from obsolete *dote* 'folly' + -ISH¹.

dot matrix ▸ noun [usu. as modifier] a grid of dots which are filled selectively to produce an image on a screen or paper: *a dot matrix printer.*

dot-org (also **dot.org**) ▸ noun a non-profit-making organization that conducts its business on the Internet.
– ORIGIN 1990s: from '.org' in an Internet address, indicating a non-commercial site.

dot plant ▸ noun a garden plant that is planted singly to stand out against the surrounding plants.

dot product ▸ noun another term for SCALAR PRODUCT.

dotted line ▸ noun a line made up of dots or dashes (often used in reference to the space left for a signature on a contract): *Adam **signed on the dotted line** with a flourish.*

dotted note ▸ noun Music a note written with a dot after it, which has one and a half times the length of the same note without a dot.

dotted rhythm ▸ noun Music rhythm in which the beat is unequally subdivided into a long dotted note and a short note.

dotterel /ˈdɒt(ə)r(ə)l/ ▸ noun (pl. **same** or **dotterels**) a small plover with a brown streaked back and a chestnut or buff belly with black below, breeding in mountainous areas and in the tundra. ● Genus *Eudromias*, family Charadriidae: two species.
■ [with modifier] Austral./NZ any small plover, especially one of the genus *Charadrius.*
– ORIGIN Middle English: from DOTE (so named because it is easily caught) + -REL. Compare with DODO.

dottle /ˈdɒt(ə)l/ ▸ noun a remnant of tobacco left in a pipe after smoking.
– ORIGIN late Middle English (denoting a plug for a barrel or other container): from DOT¹ + -LE¹.

dotty ▸ adjective (**dottier, dottiest**) Brit. informal eccentric or slightly mad: *a dotty old lady.* ■ (**dotty about**) infatuated with: *she's dotty about her husband.*
– DERIVATIVES **dottily** adverb, **dottiness** noun.
– ORIGIN late 19th cent.: perhaps from obsolete *dote* 'simpleton, fool', apparently from Dutch *dote* 'folly'.

Douala /duːˈɑːlə/ the chief port and largest city of Cameroon; pop. 1,776,000 (est. 2007).

Douay Bible /ˈduːeɪ, ˈdaʊeɪ/ (also **Douay version**) ▸ noun an English translation of the Bible formerly used in the Roman Catholic Church, completed at Douai in France early in the 17th century.

double ▸ adjective **1** consisting of two equal, identical, or similar parts or things: *double doors.* ■ having twice the usual size, quantity, or strength: *she sipped a double brandy.* ■ designed to be used by two people: *a double bed.* ■ having two different roles or interpretations, especially in order to deceive or confuse: *the furtive double life of a terrorist.* ■ (of a letter or number) occurring twice in succession: *'otter' is spelled with a double t.* ■ (of a flower) having more than one circle of petals: *large double blooms.* ■ (of a domino) having the same number of pips on each half.
2 Music lower in pitch by an octave.
▸ predeterminer twice as much or as many: *the jail now houses almost double the number of prisoners it was designed for* | *I'll pay double what I paid last time.*
▸ adverb at or to twice the amount or extent: *you have to be careful, and this counts double for older people.*
▸ noun **1** a thing which is twice as large as usual or is made up of two standard units or things: *join the two sleeping bags together to make a double.* ■ a double measure of spirits. ■ a system of betting in which the winnings and stake from the first bet are transferred to a second. ■ Bridge a call that will increase the penalty points won by the defenders if the declarer fails to make the contract. ■ Darts a hit on the narrow ring enclosed by the two outer circles of a dartboard, scoring double.
2 a person who looks exactly like another: *you could pass yourself off as his double.* ■ a person who stands in for an actor in a film. ■ an apparition of a living person: *she had seen her husband's double.*
3 (**doubles**) (especially in tennis and badminton) a game or competition involving sides made up of two players: *the semi-finals of the doubles.*
4 Bell-ringing a system of change-ringing using five bells, with two pairs changing places each time.
5 a pair of victories in the same sport in two different competitions: *Manchester United won the double twice.* ■ Brit. a home and away victory over the same team in one season or competition: *Oldham **did the double over** Forest last season.*
▸ pronoun a number or amount which is twice as large as a contrasting or usual number or amount: *he paid double and had a room all to himself.*
▸ verb **1** [no obj.] become twice as much or as many: *profits doubled in one year.* ■ [with obj.] make twice as much or as many of (something): *Clare doubled her income overnight.* ■ [with obj.] archaic amount to twice as much as: *thy fifty yet doth double five and twenty.* ■ (**double up**) use the winnings from a bet as stake for another bet. ■ Military move at twice the usual speed; run: *I doubled across the deck to join the others.* ■ (**double up**) share a room: *'Where's Jimmy going to sleep?' 'He can **double up with** Bertie.'* ■ Bridge make a call increasing the value of the penalty points to be scored on an opponent's bid if it wins the auction and is not fulfilled.
2 [with obj.] fold or bend (paper, cloth, or other material) over on itself: *the muslin is doubled and then laid in a sieve over the bowl.* ■ [no obj.] (**double up**) bend over or curl up, typically because one is overcome with pain or mirth: *Billy started to double up with laughter.* ■ clench (a fist). ■ [no obj.] (usu. **double back**) go back in the direction one has come: *he had to double back to collect them.* ■ Snooker pot (a ball) by making it rebound off a cushion. ■ Nautical sail round (a headland): *we struck out seaward to double the headland of the cape.*
3 [no obj.] be used in or play another, different role: *a laser printer **doubles as** a photocopier.* ■ [with obj.] (of an actor) play (two parts) in the same piece. ■ Music play two or more musical instruments. ■ [with obj.] Music add the same note in a higher or lower octave to (a note).
– PHRASES **at the double** (US **on the double**) at running speed; very fast: *he disappeared at the double.* **bend double** bend over into a stooping position. **be seeing double** seem to see two images of one object. **double or quits** (US **double or nothing**) a gamble to decide whether a loss or debt should be doubled or cancelled.
– DERIVATIVES **doubleness** noun, **doubler** noun.
– ORIGIN Middle English: via Old French from Latin *duplus* (see DUPLE). The verb is from Old French *dobler*, from late Latin *duplare*, from *duplus.*

double acrostic ▸ noun an acrostic in which the first and last letters of each line form a hidden word or words.

double act ▸ noun a performance involving two people. ■ a pair of entertainers who perform a double act: *my father was part of a double act with his brother.*

double-acting ▸ adjective **1** (of a device or product) combining two different functions.
2 (of an engine) having pistons pushed from both sides alternately.

double-action ▸ adjective **1** combining two different functions; double-acting.
2 (of a gun) needing to be cocked and fired as two separate actions.

double agent ▸ noun an agent who pretends to act as a spy for one country or organization while in fact acting on behalf of an enemy.

double axe ▸ noun an axe with two blades.

double-bank ▸ verb [with obj.] chiefly Brit. arrange in two similar or parallel lines; double.

double bar ▸ noun a pair of closely spaced bar lines marking the end of a piece or section of music.

double-barrelled ▸ adjective **1** (of a gun) having two barrels. ■ having two parts or aspects.
2 Brit. (of a surname) having two parts joined by a hyphen.

double bass ▸ noun the largest and lowest-pitched instrument of the violin family, providing the bass line of the orchestral string section and also used in jazz and some country music.

double bassoon ▸ noun a bassoon that is larger and longer than the normal type and sounds an octave lower in pitch.

double bill ▸ noun a programme of entertainment with two main items: *a double bill of horror movies.*

double bind ▸ noun a situation in which a person is confronted with two irreconcilable demands or a choice between two undesirable courses of action.

double-bitted axe ▸ noun chiefly N. Amer. another term for DOUBLE AXE.

double-blind ▸ adjective denoting a test or trial, especially of a drug, in which any information which may influence the behaviour of the tester or the subject is withheld until after the test.

double bluff ▸ noun an action or statement that is intended to appear as a bluff but is in fact genuine.

double bogey Golf ▸ noun a score of two strokes over par for a hole.
▸ verb (**double-bogey**) [with obj.] complete (a hole) in two strokes over par.

double boiler ▸ noun a saucepan with a detachable upper compartment heated by boiling water in the lower one.

double bond ▸ noun a chemical bond in which two pairs of electrons are shared between two atoms.

double-book ▸ verb [with obj.] inadvertently reserve (something, especially a seat or a hotel room) for two different customers or parties at the same time: *the hotel was double-booked.*

double-breasted ▶ adjective (of a jacket or coat) having a substantial overlap of material at the front and showing two rows of buttons when fastened.

double bridle ▶ noun a bridle which has both a curb and a snaffle bit, each with its own set of reins.

double-check ▶ verb [with obj.] check (something) for a second time to ensure that it is accurate or safe: *he double-checked our credentials* | [with clause] *double-check that all windows are firmly locked.*

double chin ▶ noun a roll of fatty flesh below a person's chin.
– DERIVATIVES **double-chinned** adjective.

double-click ▶ verb [no obj.] press a computer mouse button twice in quick succession to select a file, program, or function: *to run a window just* ***double-click on the icon*** | [with obj.] *when you double-click this file it should open.*

double-clutch ▶ verb North American term for DOUBLE-DECLUTCH.

double coconut ▶ noun another term for COCO DE MER.

double concerto ▶ noun a concerto for two solo instruments.

double cream ▶ noun [mass noun] Brit. thick cream that contains a lot of milk fat.

double-cross ▶ verb [with obj.] deceive or betray (a person with whom one is supposedly cooperating): *he was blackmailed into double-crossing his own government.*
▶ noun a betrayal of someone with whom one is supposedly cooperating.
– DERIVATIVES **double-crosser** noun.

double-cut ▶ adjective another term for CROSS-CUT.

double dagger (also **double obelus**, **double obelisk**) ▶ noun a symbol (‡) used in printed text to introduce an annotation.

double-dealing ▶ noun [mass noun] the practice of working to people's disadvantage behind their backs.
▶ adjective working deceitfully to injure others: *she is a back-stabbing, double-dealing twister.*
– DERIVATIVES **double-dealer** noun.

double-decker ▶ noun something, especially a bus, that has two floors or levels: [as modifier] *a double-decker bus* | *double-decker sandwiches.*

double-declutch ▶ verb [no obj.] Brit. release and re-engage the clutch of a vehicle twice when changing gear.

double decomposition ▶ noun Chemistry a reaction in which two compounds exchange ions, typically with precipitation of an insoluble product.

double digging ▶ noun [mass noun] (in gardening) digging of an area in parallel trenches two spits deep, burying the soil of each upper spit in the bottom of the next trench.

double-digit ▶ adjective (of a number or variable) between 10 and 99.
▶ noun (**double digits**) N. Amer. another term for DOUBLE FIGURES.

double-dip ▶ verb [no obj.] N. Amer. informal obtain an income from two different sources, typically in an illicit way.
– DERIVATIVES **double-dipper** noun.

double dot Music ▶ noun two dots placed side by side after a note to indicate that it is to be lengthened by three quarters of its value.
▶ verb (**double-dot**) [with obj.] write or perform (music) with a rhythm of alternating long and short notes in a ratio of seven to one, producing a more marked effect than ordinary dotted rhythm.

double Dutch ▶ noun [mass noun] **1** Brit. informal language that is impossible to understand; gibberish: *instructions written in double Dutch.*
2 N. Amer. a jumping game played with two skipping ropes swung in opposite directions so that they cross rhythmically.

double-dyed ▶ adjective (of clothing) dyed twice in order to give a very deep colour. ■ (of a person) thoroughly imbued with a particular quality: *a double-dyed liberal.*

double eagle ▶ noun **1** a representation of a two-headed eagle. ■ US a gold coin worth twenty dollars.
2 Golf a score of three strokes under par at a hole. Also called ALBATROSS.

double-edged ▶ adjective (of a knife or sword) having two cutting edges. ■ having two contradictory aspects or possible outcomes: *the consequences can be double-edged.*
– PHRASES **a double-edged sword** a situation or course of action having both positive and negative effects.

double effect ▶ noun [mass noun] the good and bad effect of an action, compared according to a principle which seeks to justify the action if the bad effect, though foreseen, is outweighed by the good effect.

double-ender ▶ noun a boat in which stern and bow are similarly tapered.

double entendre /ˌduːb(ə)l ɒ̃ˈtɒ̃dr(ə)/ ▶ noun (pl. **double entendres** pronunc. **same**) a word or phrase open to two interpretations, one of which is usually risqué or indecent. ■ [mass noun] humour using such words or phrases.
– ORIGIN late 17th cent.: from obsolete French (now *double entente*), 'double understanding'.

double-entry ▶ adjective denoting a system of bookkeeping in which each transaction is entered as a debit in one account and a credit in another.

double exposure ▶ noun [mass noun] the repeated exposure of a photographic plate or film to light, often producing ghost images.

double-faced ▶ adjective **1** having two faces: *a double-faced clock.* ■ (of a fabric or material) finished on both sides so that either may be used as the right side.
2 tending to say one thing and do another; deceitful.

double fault ▶ noun Tennis an instance of two consecutive faults in serving, counting as a point against the server.
▶ verb (**double-fault**) [no obj.] serve a double fault.

double feature ▶ noun chiefly N. Amer. a cinema programme with two full-length films.

double figures ▶ plural noun chiefly Brit. a number or amount between 10 and 99: *inflation was* ***in double figures.***

double first ▶ noun Brit. a university degree with first-class honours in two subjects or two major examinations.

double flat ▶ noun a sign (𝄫) placed before a musical note to indicate that it is to be lowered two semitones. ■ a note so marked or lowered.

double-fronted ▶ adjective (of a house) with principal windows on either side of the front door.

double fugue ▶ noun Music a fugue with two subjects, each similarly treated.

double glazing ▶ noun [mass noun] chiefly Brit. windows which have two layers of glass with a space between them, designed to reduce loss of heat and exclude noise.
– DERIVATIVES **double-glaze** verb.

Double Gloucester ▶ noun [mass noun] a kind of hard cheese originally made in Gloucestershire.
– ORIGIN so named because the curd is processed twice.

double-handed ▶ adjective made to be lifted or held with two hands: *double-handed war axes.* ■ using both hands: *a double-handed backhand.*

double harness ▶ noun a harness worn by two horses working together.

double-headed ▶ adjective **1** (of a train) pulled by two locomotives.
2 (of a weapon) having two cutting implements, typically one at each end of the shaft: *a double-headed axe.*

double-header ▶ noun **1** a train pulled by two locomotives coupled together.
2 chiefly N. Amer. a sporting event in which two games or contests are played in succession at the same venue, typically between the same teams or players.

double helix ▶ noun a pair of parallel helices intertwined about a common axis, especially that in the structure of the DNA molecule.

double-hung ▶ adjective (of a window) consisting of two sliding vertical sashes.

double indemnity ▶ noun [mass noun] chiefly N. Amer. provision for payment of double the face amount of an insurance policy under certain conditions, e.g. when death occurs as a result of an accident.

double jeopardy ▶ noun [mass noun] Law, chiefly N. Amer. the prosecution or punishment of a person twice for the same offence. ■ risk or disadvantage incurred from two sources simultaneously: *he is* ***in double jeopardy****, unable to speak either language adequately.*

double-jointed ▶ adjective (of a person) having unusually flexible joints, typically those of the fingers, arms, or legs.
– DERIVATIVES **double-jointedness** noun.

double knitting ▶ noun [mass noun] a grade of yarn of medium thickness, typically used in hand knitting.
– ORIGIN mid 19th cent.: *double* with reference to the 'doubling' of the yarn to four-ply.

double lock ▶ noun a type of spring lock which may be used as a deadlock by an extra turn of the key.
▶ verb (**double-lock**) [with obj.] fasten (a door) with two locks, or with a double lock.

double napoleon ▶ noun historical a gold forty-franc French coin.

D

double negation ▶ noun Philosophy the result of negating the negation of a proposition, and the principle (not admitted in intuitionist logic) that this is equivalent to the proposition itself.

double negative ▶ noun Grammar a negative statement containing two negative elements (for example *he didn't say nothing*). ■ a positive statement in which two negative elements are used to produce the positive force, usually for some particular rhetorical effect, for example *there is not nothing to worry about!*

> **USAGE** According to standard English grammar, a **double negative** used to express a single negative, such as *I don't know nothing* (rather than *I don't know anything*), is incorrect. The rules dictate that the two negative elements cancel each other out to give an affirmative statement, so that *I don't know nothing* would be interpreted as *I know something*.
> In practice this sort of double negative is widespread in dialect and other non-standard usage and rarely gives rise to confusion as to the intended meaning. Double negatives are standard in certain other languages such as Spanish and they have not always been unacceptable in English, either. The double negative was normal in Old English and Middle English and did not come to be frowned upon until some time after the 16th century, when attempts were made to relate the rules of language to the rules of formal logic.
> Modern (correct) uses of the double negative give an added subtlety to statements: saying *I am* ***not unconvinced*** *by his argument* suggests reservations in the speaker's mind that are not present in its 'logical' equivalent: *I am* ***convinced*** *by his argument.*

double obelus (also **double obelisk**) ▶ noun another term for DOUBLE DAGGER.

double-park ▶ verb [with obj.] park (a vehicle) alongside one that is already parked at the side of the road.

double play ▶ noun Baseball a defensive play in which two runners are put out.

double pneumonia ▶ noun [mass noun] pneumonia affecting both lungs.

double precision ▶ noun [mass noun] Computing the use of twice the usual number of bits to represent a number, giving greater arithmetic accuracy.

double quick ▶ adjective & adverb Brit. informal very quick or quickly: [as adj.] *I got changed* ***in double quick time*** | [as adv.] *you get upstairs double quick!*

double reed ▶ noun Music a reed with two slightly separated blades, used for playing a wind instrument such as an oboe or bassoon.

double refraction ▶ noun [mass noun] Physics division of a single incident light ray or other electromagnetic wave into two separate rays in an anisotropic medium.

double rhyme ▶ noun a rhyme involving two syllables in each rhyming line.

double salt ▶ noun Chemistry a crystalline salt having the composition of a mixture of two simple salts but with a different crystal structure from either.

double saucepan ▶ noun British term for DOUBLE BOILER.

double sharp ▶ noun a sign (𝄪) placed before a musical note to indicate that it is to be raised two semitones. ■ a note so marked or raised.

double shuffle ▶ noun a dance in which a person makes shuffling movements twice with each foot alternately.

double-sided ▶ adjective using or able to be used on both sides: *double-sided tape.*

doublespeak ▶ noun [mass noun] deliberately euphemistic, ambiguous, or obscure language: *the art of political doublespeak.*
– ORIGIN 1950s: often attributed incorrectly to George Orwell's novel *Nineteen Eighty-Four.*

double standard ▸ noun a rule or principle which is unfairly applied in different ways to different people or groups: *the double standards employed to deal with ordinary people and those in the City.*

double star ▸ noun two stars actually or apparently very close together.

double steal ▸ noun Baseball a play in which two base runners each steal or attempt to steal a base.

double-stopping ▸ noun [mass noun] the sounding of two strings at once on a violin or similar bowed instrument.
– DERIVATIVES **double stop** noun.

D

Double Summer Time daylight saving time in which clocks are set two hours ahead of standard time, used in Britain during the Second World War.

doublet ▸ noun **1** a pair of similar things, in particular two words of the same derivation but having different meanings, for example *fashion* and *faction*, *cloak* and *clock*. ■ (**doublets**) the same number on two dice thrown at once. ■ Physics & Chemistry a pair of associated lines close together in a spectrum or electrophoretic gel. ■ a combination of two simple lenses.
2 a man's short close-fitting padded jacket, commonly worn from the 14th to the 17th century.
– ORIGIN Middle English: from Old French, 'something folded', also denoting a fur-lined coat, from *double* 'double'.

double take ▸ noun a delayed reaction to something unexpected, immediately after one's first reaction: *Tony glanced at her, then* ***did a double take.***

double-talk ▸ noun chiefly N. Amer. another term for **DOUBLESPEAK**.

double-team N. Amer. ▸ verb [with obj.] (in ball games) block (an opponent) with two players.
▸ noun an act of double-teaming.

doublethink ▸ noun [mass noun] the acceptance of contrary opinions or beliefs at the same time, especially as a result of political indoctrination.
– ORIGIN 1949: coined by George Orwell in his novel *Nineteen Eighty-Four*.

double time ▸ noun [mass noun] **1** a rate of pay equal to double the standard rate, sometimes paid for working on holidays or outside normal working hours.
2 Military a regulation running pace.
3 Music a rhythm that is twice as fast as an earlier one.

doubleton /ˈdʌb(ə)lt(ə)n/ ▸ noun (in card games, especially bridge) a pair of cards which are the only cards of their suit in a hand. ■ a pair of people or things.
– ORIGIN early 20th cent.: from **DOUBLE**, on the pattern of *singleton*.

double tonguing ▸ noun [mass noun] Music the use of two alternating movements of the tongue (usually as in sounding *t* and *k*) in playing rapid passages on a wind instrument.

double top ▸ noun Darts a score of double twenty.

doubletree ▸ noun N. Amer. a crossbar in front of a wagon with a swingletree at each end, enabling two horses to be harnessed.
– ORIGIN mid 19th cent.: from **DOUBLE**, on the pattern of *singletree*.

double vision ▸ noun [mass noun] the simultaneous perception of two images, usually overlapping, of a single scene or object.

double whammy ▸ noun informal a twofold blow or setback: *a double whammy of taxation and price increases.*
ORIGIN 1950s: originally with reference to the comic strip *Li'l Abner* (see **WHAMMY**).

double-wide ▸ noun N. Amer. a semi-permanent mobile home consisting of two separate units connected on site.

double yellow line ▸ noun (in the UK) a pair of yellow lines painted at the side of a road to indicate that parking is not permitted at most times of day.

doubloon /dʌˈbluːn/ ▸ noun historical a Spanish gold coin.
– ORIGIN early 17th cent.: from French *doublon* or its source, Spanish *doblón*, from *doble* 'double' (so named because the coin was worth double the value of a pistole).

doublure /duːˈbljʊə/ ▸ noun an ornamental lining, especially one made of leather, on the inside of a book cover.
– ORIGIN French, 'lining', from *doubler* 'to line'.

doubly ▸ adverb [often as submodifier] to twice the normal extent or degree; especially: *we're going to have to work doubly hard.* ■ two times or in two ways: *doubly mutant cells.*

doubt ▸ noun [mass noun] a feeling of uncertainty or lack of conviction: *some* ***doubt*** *has been* ***cast upon*** *the authenticity of this account* | [count noun] *they had doubts that they would ever win.*
▸ verb **1** [with obj.] feel uncertain about: *I doubt my ability to do the job* | [with clause] *I doubt if anyone slept that night.* ■ question the truth or fact of (something): *who can doubt the value and necessity of these services?* ■ disbelieve or lack faith in (someone): *I have no reason to doubt him.* ■ [no obj.] feel uncertain, especially about one's religious beliefs.
2 [with clause] archaic fear; be afraid: *I doubt not any ones contradicting this Journal.*
– PHRASES **beyond doubt** allowing no uncertainty: *you've proved it beyond doubt.* **in doubt** open to question: *the outcome is no longer in doubt.* ■ feeling uncertain about something: *by the age of 14 he was in no doubt about his career aims.* **no doubt** used to indicate the speaker's firm belief that something is true: *those who left were attracted, no doubt, by higher pay.* ■ used to introduce a concession which is subsequently dismissed as unimportant or irrelevant: *they no doubt did what they could to help her, but their best proved insufficient.* **without (a) doubt** indisputably: *he was without doubt the very worst kind of reporter.*
– DERIVATIVES **doubtable** adjective, **doubting** adjective, **doubtingly** adverb.
– ORIGIN Middle English: from Old French *doute* (noun), *douter* (verb), from Latin *dubitare* 'hesitate', from *dubius* 'doubtful' (see **DUBIOUS**).

doubter ▸ noun a person who questions or lacks faith in something; a sceptic: *he had proved all his doubters wrong.*

doubtful ▸ adjective **1** feeling uncertain about something: *he looked doubtful, but gave a nod* | *I was* ***doubtful of*** *my judgement.*
2 not known with certainty: *the fire was of doubtful origin.* ■ improbable: [with clause] *it is doubtful whether these schemes have any lasting effect.* ■ not established as genuine or acceptable: *of doubtful legality.*
– DERIVATIVES **doubtfully** adverb, **doubtfulness** noun.

doubting Thomas ▸ noun a person who is sceptical and refuses to believe something without proof.
– ORIGIN early 17th cent.: with biblical allusion to the apostle Thomas (John 20:24–29).

doubtless ▸ adverb [sentence adverb] certainly; without doubt: *the company would doubtless find the reduced competition to their liking.* ■ presumably or very probably: *doubtless you'll solve the problem.*
– DERIVATIVES **doubtlessly** adverb.

douce /duːs/ ▸ adjective chiefly Scottish sober and sedate: *stories which would have outraged their douce minds.*
– ORIGIN Middle English (in the sense 'pleasant, sweet'): from Old French *dous, douce*, from Latin *dulcis* 'sweet'.

douceur /duːˈsəː/, French /dusœʀ/ ▸ noun a financial inducement; a bribe: *Pericles gave a handsome douceur to the Spartan commanders to withdraw without fighting.*
– ORIGIN French, literally 'sweetness'.

douceur de vivre /duːˌsəː də ˈviːvr(ə)/, French /dusœʀ də vivʀ/ (also **douceur de vie** /viː/, French /vi/) ▸ noun [mass noun] a way of living that is pleasant and free from worries.
– ORIGIN French, literally 'sweetness of living (or life)'.

douche /duːʃ/ ▸ noun a shower of water: *I felt better for taking a daily douche.* ■ a jet of liquid applied to part of the body for cleansing or medicinal purposes. ■ a device for washing out the vagina as a contraceptive measure.
▸ verb [with obj.] spray or shower with water. ■ [no obj.] use a douche as a method of contraception.
– ORIGIN mid 18th cent. (as a noun): via French from Italian *doccia* 'conduit pipe', from *docciare* 'pour by drops', based on Latin *ductus* 'leading' (see **DUCT**).

douche bag ▸ noun a small syringe for douching the vagina, especially as a contraceptive measure. ■ N. Amer. informal a loathsome or contemptible person.

douc langur /duːk/ (also **douc monkey**) ▸ noun a langur with black, white, and orange fur, native to the tropical rainforests of SE Asia. ● *Pygathrix nemaeus*, family Cercopithecidae.
– ORIGIN late 18th cent.: *douc* via French from Vietnamese.

doudou /ˈduːduː/ ▸ noun W. Indian a term of endearment.
– ORIGIN French Creole, from French *doux* 'sweet'.

dough ▸ noun [mass noun] **1** a thick, malleable mixture of flour and liquid, used for baking into bread or pastry.
2 informal money: *lots of dough.*
– DERIVATIVES **doughiness** noun, **doughy** adjective (**doughier, doughiest**).
– ORIGIN Old English *dāg*, of Germanic origin; related to Dutch *deeg* and German *Teig*, from an Indo-European root meaning 'smear, knead'.

doughboy ▸ noun **1** a boiled or deep-fried dumpling.
2 US informal a United States infantryman, especially one in the First World War. [said to have been a term applied in the Civil War to the large globular brass buttons on the infantry uniform; also said to derive from the use of pipe clay 'dough' to clean the white belts worn by infantrymen.]

doughnut (US also **donut**) ▸ noun a small fried cake of sweetened dough, typically in the shape of a ball or ring. ■ a ring-shaped object, in particular a vacuum chamber in some types of particle accelerator.

doughty /ˈdaʊti/ ▸ adjective (**doughtier, doughtiest**) archaic or humorous brave and persistent: *his doughty spirit kept him going.*
– DERIVATIVES **doughtily** adverb, **doughtiness** noun.
– ORIGIN late Old English *dohtig*, variant of *dyhtig*, of Germanic origin; related to Dutch *duchtig* and German *tüchtig*.

Douglas /ˈdʌgləs/ the capital of the Isle of Man; pop. 27,200 (est. 2009).

Douglas fir ▸ noun a tall, slender conifer with soft foliage and, in mature trees, deeply fissured bark. It is widely planted as a timber tree. ● Genus *Pseudotsuga*, family Pinaceae: several species.
– ORIGIN mid 19th cent.: named after David *Douglas* (1798–1834), the Scottish botanist and explorer who introduced it to Europe from North America.

Douglas-Home /ˌdʌgləsˈhjuːm/, Sir Alec, Baron Home of the Hirsel of Coldstream (1903–95), British Conservative statesman, Prime Minister 1963–4; born *Alexander Frederick Douglas-Home*. When Douglas-Home became Prime Minister he relinquished his hereditary peerage.

doula /ˈduːlə/ ▸ noun a woman who gives support, help, and advice to another woman during pregnancy and during and after the birth.
– ORIGIN 1960s: modern Greek, from Greek *doulē* 'female slave'.

Doulton /ˈdəʊlt(ə)n/ (also **Royal Doulton**) ▸ noun [mass noun] trademark fine decorative pottery or porcelain made at the factories of John Doulton (1793–1873) or his successors.

doum palm /duːm/ (also **dom palm**) ▸ noun a palm tree with a forked trunk, producing edible fruit and a vegetable ivory substitute. It is native to the Nile region of Upper Egypt. ● *Hyphaene thebaica*, family Palmae.
– ORIGIN early 18th cent.: *doum* from Arabic *dawm, dūm*.

dour /ˈdʊə, ˈdaʊə/ ▸ adjective relentlessly severe, stern, or gloomy in manner or appearance: *a hard, dour, humourless fanatic.*
– DERIVATIVES **dourly** adverb, **dourness** noun.
– ORIGIN late Middle English (originally Scots): probably from Scottish Gaelic *dúr* 'dull, obstinate, stupid', perhaps from Latin *durus* 'hard'.

Douro /ˈdʊəruː/ a river of the Iberian peninsula, rising in central Spain and flowing west for 900 km (556 miles) through Portugal to the Atlantic Ocean near Oporto. Spanish name **DUERO**.

douroucouli /ˌdʊərʊˈkuːli/ ▸ noun (pl. **douroucoulis**) a large-eyed chiefly nocturnal monkey found in South America. Also called **NIGHT MONKEY, OWL MONKEY**. ● Genus *Aotus*, family Cebidae: two or more species.
– ORIGIN mid 19th cent.: probably a South American Indian name.

douse /daʊs/ ▸ verb [with obj.] **1** pour a liquid over; drench: *he doused the car with petrol and set it on fire.*
2 extinguish (a fire or light): *stewards appeared and the fire was doused* | figurative *nothing could douse her sudden euphoria.*
3 Sailing lower (a sail) quickly.
– ORIGIN early 17th cent.: perhaps imitative, influenced by **SOUSE**, or perhaps from dialect *douse* 'strike, beat', from Middle Dutch and Low German *dossen*.

dout /daʊt/ (also **dowt**) chiefly Scottish ▸ verb [with obj.] extinguish (a fire or light).
▸ noun a cigarette end.
– ORIGIN early 16th cent. (as a verb): contraction of *do out*. The noun dates from the 1940s.

dove¹ /dʌv/ ▶ **noun 1** a stocky bird with a small head, short legs, and a cooing voice, feeding on seeds or fruit. Doves are generally smaller and more delicate than pigeons, but many kinds have been given both names. ● Family Columbidae: numerous genera and species; white doves are a variety of the domestic pigeon.
2 a person who advocates peaceful or conciliatory policies, especially in foreign affairs. Compare with HAWK¹ (sense 2 of the noun).
3 (**Dove**) (in Christian art and poetry) the Holy Spirit (as represented in John 1:32).
– DERIVATIVES **dovelike** adjective, **dovish** adjective (sense 2).
– ORIGIN Middle English: from Old Norse *dúfa*.

dove² /dəʊv/ N. Amer. past of DIVE.

dovecote /ˈdʌvkɒt/ (also **dovecot**) ▶ **noun** a shelter with nest holes for domesticated pigeons.
– PHRASES **flutter the dovecotes** (also **cause a flutter among the dovecotes**) startle or upset a sedate or conventionally minded community.

dove grey ▶ **noun** [mass noun] a light grey.

dovekie /ˈdʌvki/ ▶ **noun** chiefly N. Amer. another term for LITTLE AUK.
– ORIGIN early 19th cent. (originally denoting the black guillemot, *Cepphus grylle*, also formerly called the *Greenland dove*): from a Scots diminutive of DOVE¹.

Dover 1 a ferry port in Kent, in England, on the coast of the English Channel; pop. 35,200 (est. 2009). It is mainland Britain's nearest point to the Continent, being only 35 km (22 miles) from Calais. ■ a shipping forecast area covering the Strait of Dover.
2 the state capital of Delaware; pop. 36,107 (est. 2008).

Dover, Strait of a sea passage between England and France, connecting the English Channel with the North Sea.

Dover sole ▶ **noun** either of two flatfishes which are highly valued as food: ● a true sole that is common in European waters (*Solea solea*, family Soleidae). ● N. Amer. a relative of the lemon sole found in the East Pacific (*Microstomus pacificus*, family Pleuronectidae).

dove's-foot cranesbill ▶ **noun** a European cranesbill which has white downy hairs on the leaves and spreading stems. The leaves supposedly resemble the foot of a bird. ● *Geranium molle*, family Geraniaceae.

dove shell ▶ **noun** a small mollusc with a robust shell, occurring in tropical and subtropical seas. ● Family Pyrenidae (or Columbellidae), class Gastropoda: *Pyrene* and other genera.

dovetail ▶ **noun** a joint formed by one or more tapered projections (tenons) on one piece which interlock with corresponding notches or recesses (mortises) in another. ■ a tenon used in a dovetail joint, typically wider at its extremity.
▶ **verb 1** [with obj.] join together by means of a dovetail.
2 fit or cause to fit together easily and conveniently: [with obj.] *plan to enable parents to dovetail their career and family commitments* | [no obj.] *flights that* ***dovetail with*** *the working day.*

dovetail saw ▶ **noun** a tenon saw with a small blade and fine teeth, used mainly for making joints.

dove tree ▶ **noun** a slender deciduous Chinese tree with flowers that bear large white bracts said to resemble doves' wings, grown as an ornamental. ● *Davidia involucrata*, family Nyssaceae.

Dow /daʊ/ short for **DOW JONES INDEX**: *the Dow fell sharply that summer.*

dowager /ˈdaʊədʒə/ ▶ **noun** a widow with a title or property derived from her late husband: [as modifier] *the dowager duchess* | [postpositive] *the queen dowager.* ■ informal a dignified elderly woman.
– ORIGIN mid 16th cent.: from Old French *douagiere*, from *douage* 'dower', from *douer* 'endow', from Latin *dotare* 'endow' (see DOWER).

dowager's hump ▶ **noun** [mass noun] forward curvature of the spine resulting in a stoop, typically in women with osteoporosis, caused by collapse of the front edges of the thoracic vertebrae.

dowd /daʊd/ ▶ **noun** a person, typically a woman, of dull, unfashionable appearance.
– ORIGIN Middle English: of unknown origin. Perhaps reintroduced in the early 19th cent. as a back-formation from DOWDY.

Dowding /ˈdaʊdɪŋ/, Hugh (Caswall Tremenheere), Baron (1882–1970), British Marshal of the RAF. He was Commander-in-Chief of the British air defence forces that defeated the Luftwaffe during the Battle of Britain in 1940.

dowdy ▶ **adjective** (**dowdier**, **dowdiest**) (of a person, typically a woman, or their clothes) unfashionable and unstylish in appearance: *she could achieve the kind of casual chic which made every other woman around her look dowdy.*
– DERIVATIVES **dowdily** adverb, **dowdiness** noun.
– ORIGIN late 16th cent. (as a noun): from DOWD.

dowel /ˈdaʊəl/ ▶ **noun** a projecting peg used for holding together components of a structure.
▶ **verb** (**dowels**, **dowelling**, **dowelled**; US **dowels**, **doweling**, **doweled**) [with obj.] fasten with a dowel or dowels.
– ORIGIN Middle English: perhaps from Middle Low German *dovel*.

dowelling (US **doweling**) ▶ **noun** [mass noun] cylindrical rods for cutting into dowels.

dower /ˈdaʊə/ ▶ **noun** a widow's share for life of her husband's estate. ■ archaic a dowry.
▶ **verb** [with obj.] archaic give a dowry to.
– ORIGIN late Middle English: from Old French *douaire*, from medieval Latin *dotarium*, from Latin *dotare* 'endow', from *dos*, *dot-* 'dowry'; related to *dare* 'give'.

dower house ▶ **noun** Brit. a house intended as the residence of a widow, typically one near the main house on her late husband's estate.

dowitcher /ˈdaʊɪtʃə/ ▶ **noun** a wading bird of the sandpiper family, with a long straight bill, breeding in arctic and subarctic North America and eastern Asia. ● Genus *Limnodromus*, family Scolopacidae: three species.
– ORIGIN mid 19th cent.: from Iroquoian.

Dow Jones index /daʊˈdʒəʊnz/ (also **Dow Jones average**) an index of figures indicating the relative price of shares on the New York Stock Exchange, based on the average price of selected stocks.
– ORIGIN from the name of *Dow Jones & Co, Inc.*, a financial news agency founded by Charles H. *Dow* (1851–1902) and Edward D. *Jones* (*c.*1855–1920), American economists whose company compiled the first average of US stock prices in 1884.

Down one of the Six Counties of Northern Ireland, since 1973 an administrative district; chief town, Downpatrick.

down¹ ▶ **adverb 1** towards or in a lower place or position, especially to or on the ground or another surface: *she looked down* | *the sun started to go down* | *he put his glass down* | *he swung the axe to chop down the tree.* ■ at or to a specified distance below: *you can plainly see the bottom 35 feet down.* ■ downstairs: *I went down to put the kettle on.* ■ expressing movement or position away from the north: *they're living down south.* ■ to or at a place perceived as lower (often expressing casualness or lack of hurry): *I'd rather be down at the villa* | *I'm going down to the pub.* ■ Brit. away from the capital or major city: *there are eight trains a day, four up and four down.* ■ Brit. away from a university, especially Oxford or Cambridge. ■ (with reference to food or drink swallowed) in or into the stomach: *she couldn't keep anything down.* ■ so as to lie or be fixed flush or flat: *she stuck down a Christmas label.* ■ [as exclamation] used as a command to a person or animal to sit or lie down: *down, boy!* ■ referring to a crossword answer which reads vertically: *how many letters in fifteen down?*
2 to or at a lower level of intensity, volume, or activity: *keep the noise down* | *the panic was dying down* | *at night it would cool down.* ■ to or at a lower price, value, or rank: *output was down by 20 per cent* | *soup is down from 59p to 49p.* ■ to a finer consistency, a smaller amount or size, or a simpler or more basic state: *I must slim down a bit* | *a formal statement that can't be edited down* | *thin down an oil-based paint with spirits.* ■ from an earlier to a later point in time or order: *buildings in England* ***down to*** *1540* | *everyone, from the President* ***down to*** *the bloke selling hot dogs, wants her dead.*
3 in or into a weaker or worse position, mood, or condition: *the scandal brought down the government* | *he was* ***down with*** *the flu.* ■ losing or at a disadvantage by a specified amount: *United were 3–0 down.* ■ used to express progress through a series of tasks or items: *one down and only six more to go.* ■ (of a computer system) out of action or unavailable for use: *the system went down yesterday.* ■ (**down with ——**) shouted to express strong dislike of a specified person or thing: *crowds chanted 'Down with America!'.*
4 in or into writing: *Graham noted the numbers down carefully* | *taking down notes.* ■ on or on to a list, schedule, or record: *I'll put you* ***down for*** *the evening shift.*
5 (with reference to partial payment of a sum of money) made initially or on the spot: *pay £5 down and the rest at the end of the month.*
6 (of sailing) with the current or the wind. ■ (of a ship's helm) moved round to leeward so that the rudder is to windward.
7 American Football (of the ball or a player in possession) not in play, typically through progress being stopped.
▶ **preposition 1** from a higher to a lower point of (something): *up and down the stairs* | *tears streaming down her face.* ■ at or to the part of (a river or stream) that is nearer the sea: *a dozen miles or so down the Thames.* ■ moving or at a point further along the course of (something): *he lived down the street* | *I wandered down the road.* ■ informal at or to (a place): *she was tired of going down the pub every night.*
2 throughout (a period of time): *astrologers down the ages.*
▶ **adjective 1** [attrib.] directed or moving towards a lower place or position: *the down escalator* | *click on the down arrow.* ■ relating to or denoting trains travelling away from the main terminus: *we travelled on the first down train.* ■ Physics denoting a flavour of quark having a charge of $-{}^1/_3$. Protons and neutrons are thought to be composed of combinations of up and down quarks.
2 [predic.] unhappy; depressed: *he's been so down lately.*
3 [predic.] (of a computer system) temporarily out of action or unavailable: *sorry, but the computer's down.*
4 [predic.] US black slang supporting or going along with someone or something: *you got to be* ***down with*** *me.* ■ aware of and following the latest fashion: *a seriously down, hip-hop homie.*
▶ **verb** [with obj.] informal **1** knock or bring to the ground: *175 enemy aircraft had been downed* | *he struck Slater on the face, downing him.*
2 consume (something, typically a drink): *he downed five pints of cider.* ■ Golf sink (a putt).
▶ **noun 1** American Football a chance for a team to advance the ball, ending when the ball carrier is tackled or the ball becomes out of play. A team must advance at least ten yards in a series of four downs in order to keep possession.
2 (**downs**) informal unwelcome experiences or events: *there had been more downs than ups during his years at Ferrari.*
3 informal a feeling or period of unhappiness or depression: *everyone gets their downs, their depressive periods.*
– PHRASES **be** (or **have a**) **down on** Brit. informal feel hostile or antagonistic towards. **be down to 1** be attributable to (a particular factor or circumstance): *he claimed his problems were down to the media.* ■ be the responsibility of (a particular person): *it's down to you to make sure the boiler receives regular servicing.* **2** be left with only (the specified amount): *I'm down to my last few pounds.* **down in the mouth** informal unhappy; dejected. **down on one's luck** informal experiencing a period of bad luck. **down tools** Brit. informal stop work, especially as a form of industrial action: *the union instructed its members to down tools.* **down to the ground** informal completely; totally. **down town** into or in the centre of a town: *I went down town to do a few errands.* **have** (or **put**) **someone/thing down as** judge someone or something to be (a particular type): *I never had Jake down as a ladies' man.*
– ORIGIN Old English *dūn*, *dūne*, shortened from *adūne* 'downward', from the phrase *of dūne* 'off the hill' (see DOWN³).

down² ▶ **noun** [mass noun] soft, fine, fluffy feathers which form the first covering of a young bird or an insulating layer below the contour feathers of an adult bird. ■ such feathers taken from ducks or their nests and used for stuffing cushions, quilts, etc. ■ fine, soft hair on the face or body of a person: *the little girl had a covering of golden down on her head.* ■ short, soft hairs on some leaves, fruit, or seeds.
– ORIGIN Middle English: from Old Norse *dúnn*.

down³ ▶ **noun 1** (usu. **downs**) a gently rolling hill: *the gentle green contours of the downs.* ■ (**the Downs**) ridges of undulating chalk and limestone hills in southern England, used mainly for pasture.
2 (**the Downs**) a stretch of sea off the east coast of Kent, sheltered by the Goodwin Sands.
– ORIGIN Old English *dūn* 'hill' (related to Dutch *duin* 'dune'), perhaps ultimately of Celtic origin and related to Old Irish *dún* and obsolete Welsh *din* 'fort', which are from an Indo-European root shared by TOWN.

D

down and dirty N. Amer. informal ▶ adjective **1** highly competitive or unprincipled: *he's willing to get down and dirty, slinging mud at will and knowing that some of it will stick.*
2 explicit; direct: *I won't bore you with the down-and-dirty details.*

down and out ▶ adjective **1** (of a person) without money, a job, or a place to live; destitute: *a novel about being down and out in London.*
2 (of a boxer) knocked down and unable to continue fighting. ■ (of a competitor) facing certain defeat.
▶ noun (**down-and-out**) a person without money, a job, or a place to live: *a hostel for down-and-outs.*

down at heel ▶ adjective **1** (of a shoe) with the heel worn down.
2 having a poor, shabby appearance: *down-at-heel areas.*

downbeat ▶ adjective **1** pessimistic or gloomy: *the assessment of the UK's economic prospects is downbeat.*
2 relaxed and understated: *he responds to her enthusiasm with downbeat bemusement.*
▶ noun Music an accented beat, usually the first of the bar.

downburst /ˈdaʊnbəːst/ ▶ noun a strong downward current of air from a cumulonimbus cloud, which is usually accompanied by intense rain or a thunderstorm.

downcase ▶ verb [with obj.] change (an upper-case letter) to a lower-case one.

downcast ▶ adjective **1** (of a person's eyes) looking downwards: *her modestly downcast eyes.*
2 (of a person) feeling despondent.
▶ noun a shaft dug in a mine for extra ventilation.

downchange ▶ noun a change to a lower gear in a motor vehicle.
▶ verb [with obj.] put (a vehicle) into a lower gear. ■ [no obj.] change to a lower gear.

downcomer ▶ noun a pipe for the downward transport of water or gas from the top of a furnace or boiler.

downconverter ▶ noun Electronics a device that converts a signal to a lower frequency, especially in television reception.
– DERIVATIVES **downconversion** noun.

downcountry ▶ adjective & adverb chiefly N. Amer. in, into, or relating to the low-lying and generally more densely settled part of a country as opposed to hilly regions: [as adj.] *a downcountry upstart* | [as adv.] *the land rolled away a hundred miles downcountry.*

downcurved ▶ adjective curved downwards.

downcut ▶ verb (**downcuts**, **downcutting**, past and past participle **downcut**) [no obj.] Geology (of a river) erode downwards through its bed.

downdraught (US **downdraft**) ▶ noun a downward current or draught of air.

downdrift ▶ noun [mass noun] a tendency in certain languages or kinds of utterance for pitch to fall near the end of a phrase, clause, or sentence.

downer ▶ noun informal **1** (usu. **downers**) a depressant or tranquillizing drug, especially a barbiturate.
2 a dispiriting or depressing experience or factor: *the thought of the danger his son was in put something of a downer on the situation.*
3 a cow or other animal that has fallen down and cannot get to its feet unaided.

downfall ▶ noun **1** a loss of power, prosperity, or status: *the crisis led to the downfall of the government.* ■ the cause of a loss of power, prosperity, or status: *his intractability will prove to be his downfall.*
2 a heavy fall of rain or snow.

downfield ▶ adverb **1** N. Amer. another term for UPFIELD (sense 1).
2 Physics in a direction corresponding to decreasing field strength.

downfold ▶ noun Geology a syncline.

downforce ▶ noun a force, produced by a combination of air resistance and gravity, that acts on a moving vehicle, having the effect of pressing it down towards the ground and giving it increased stability.

downgrade ▶ verb [with obj.] reduce to a lower grade, rank, or level of importance: *some jobs had gradually been downgraded from skilled to semi-skilled.*
▶ noun **1** an instance of reducing someone or something's rank, status, or level of importance.
2 N. Amer. a downward gradient on a railway or road.
– PHRASES **on the downgrade** N. Amer. in decline: *profits are on the downgrade.*

downhaul ▶ noun Nautical a rope used for hauling down a sail, spar, etc.

downhearted ▶ adjective discouraged; in low spirits: *fans must not be downhearted even though we lost.*
– DERIVATIVES **downheartedly** adverb, **downheartedness** noun.

downhill ▶ adverb /daʊnˈhɪl/ towards the bottom of a slope: *he ran downhill* | *follow the road downhill.* ■ into a steadily worsening situation: *her marriage continued to slide downhill* | *the business is going downhill fast.*
▶ adjective leading down towards the bottom of a slope: *the route is downhill for part of the way.* ■ relating to the sport of skiing downhill: *the world downhill champion.* ■ leading to a steadily worsening situation: *the downhill road to delinquency.* ■ without difficulty or challenge: *we can take the easy road, the downhill road, or we can put America on the path to greatness again.*
▶ noun /ˈdaʊnhɪl/ **1** a downward slope.
2 Skiing a downhill race. ■ [mass noun] the activity of downhill skiing.
– PHRASES **be downhill all the way 1** be easy in comparison with what came before: *two-nil up—it should have been downhill all the way.* **2** become worse or less successful: *that had been the start of the present trouble—downhill all the way since then.*

downhiller ▶ noun a skier or cyclist who takes part in downhill races.

downhole ▶ adjective & adverb (in the oil industry) used, occurring, or performed in a well or borehole.

down-home ▶ adjective N. Amer. connected with an unpretentious way of life, especially that of rural peoples or areas: *some good down-home cooking.*

Downing Street a street in Westminster, London, between Whitehall and St James's Park. No. 10 is the official residence of the Prime Minister; No. 11 is the home of the Chancellor of the Exchequer. ■ used allusively for the British government or the Prime Minister: *Downing Street flatly refused to confirm that the summit was off.*

downland ▶ noun [mass noun] (also **downlands**) gently rolling hill country, especially in southern England.

downlighter (also **downlight**) ▶ noun a light placed or designed so as to throw illumination downwards.
– DERIVATIVES **downlighting** noun.

downlink ▶ noun a telecommunications link for signals coming to the earth from a satellite, spacecraft, or aircraft.
▶ verb [with obj.] relay to the earth (a telecommunications signal or the information it conveys): *any TV station can downlink just about any game.*

download Computing ▶ verb [with obj.] copy (data) from one computer system to another or to a disk.
▶ noun [mass noun] the act or process of copying data in such a way: [as modifier] *a download and upload routine.* ■ [count noun] a computer file transferred in such a way: *a popular download from bulletin boards.*
– DERIVATIVES **downloadable** adjective, **downloader** noun.

down-low ▶ noun (in phrase **on the down-low**) chiefly black slang on the quiet; in secret: *he kept his status as a Hell's Angel on the down-low.* ■ (of a man) concealing his homosexual tendencies.

downmarket ▶ adjective & adverb chiefly Brit. towards or relating to the cheaper or less prestigious sector of the market: [as adj.] *an interview for the downmarket tabloids* | [as adv.] *competition threatens to drive broadcasters further downmarket.*

downmost ▶ adjective & adverb chiefly Brit. the furthest down; at or towards the bottom.

down payment ▶ noun an initial payment made when something is bought on credit.

downpipe ▶ noun Brit. a pipe to carry rainwater from a roof to a drain or to ground level.

downplay ▶ verb [with obj.] make (something) appear less important than it really is: *this report downplays the seriousness of global warming.*

downpour ▶ noun a heavy fall of rain: *a sudden downpour had filled the gutters and drains.*

downrate ▶ verb [with obj.] make lower in value, standard, or importance: *he notched up five kills although Fighter Command downrated them to four probables.*

downright ▶ adjective **1** [attrib.] (of something bad or unpleasant) utter; complete (used for emphasis): *it's a downright disgrace.*
2 so direct in manner as to be blunt: *her common sense and downright attitude to life surprised him.*
▶ adverb [as submodifier] to an extreme degree; thoroughly: *he was downright rude.*

downriver ▶ adverb & adjective towards or situated at a point nearer the mouth of a river: [as adv.] *the cabin cruiser started to drift downriver* | [as adj.] *the downriver side of the bridge.*

downscale N. Amer. ▶ verb [with obj.] reduce in size, scale, or extent: *he was unable to downscale his strongly unionized workforce.*
▶ adjective at the lower end of a scale, especially a social scale; downmarket: *these brands appeal to downscale shoppers who are looking for a low price.*

downshift ▶ verb [no obj.] **1** N. Amer. change to a lower gear in a motor vehicle or bicycle. ■ slow down; slacken off: *well before the country slipped into recession, business was downshifting.*
2 change a financially rewarding but stressful career or lifestyle for a less pressured and less highly paid but more fulfilling one: *increasing numbers of men want to downshift from full-time work.*
▶ noun **1** N. Amer. a change to a lower gear in a motor vehicle or bicycle.
2 an instance of changing to a less pressured and less highly paid but more fulfilling career or lifestyle.

downside ▶ noun the negative aspect of something otherwise regarded as good or desirable: *a magazine feature on the downside of fashion modelling.*

downsize ▶ verb [with obj.] **1** N. Amer. make (something) smaller: *I downsized the rear wheel to 26 inches.*
2 make (a company or organization) smaller by shedding staff. ■ [no obj.] (of a company) shed staff: *recession forced many companies to downsize.*

downslope ▶ adverb at or towards a lower point on a slope.
▶ adjective caused by, occurring, or acting on a downward slope: *they can produce strong downslope winds.*
▶ noun a downward slope.

downspout ▶ noun N. Amer. a downpipe.

Down's syndrome ▶ noun [mass noun] Medicine a congenital disorder arising from a chromosome defect, causing intellectual impairment and physical abnormalities including short stature and a broad facial profile. It arises from a defect involving chromosome 21, usually an extra copy (trisomy-21).
– ORIGIN 1960s: named after John L. H. *Down* (1828–96), the English physician who first described it.

> **USAGE** Of relatively recent coinage, **Down's syndrome** is the accepted term in modern use, and former terms such as **mongol** and **mongolism**, which are likely to cause offence, should be avoided.

downstage ▶ adjective & adverb at or towards the front of a stage: [as adv.] *all four run for their lives downstage* | [as adj.] *the downstage area.*

downstairs ▶ adverb down a flight of stairs: *I tripped over the cat and fell downstairs.* ■ on or to a lower floor: *we were waiting for you downstairs* | *she called him downstairs.*
▶ adjective [attrib.] situated downstairs: *the downstairs loo.*
▶ noun the ground floor or lower floors of a building: *the downstairs was hardly damaged at all.*

downstate US ▶ adjective & adverb of, in, or to a part of a state that is remote from its large cities, especially the southern part.
▶ noun [mass noun] a remote part of a state.
– DERIVATIVES **downstater** noun.

downstream ▶ adverb & adjective situated or moving in the direction in which a stream or river flows: [as adv.] *the bridge spanned the river just **downstream of the rail line*** | [as adj.] *deforestation could have disastrous consequences for downstream regions.* ■ Biology situated in or towards the part of a sequence of genetic material where transcription takes place later than at a given point. ■ at a stage in the process of gas or oil extraction and production after the raw material is ready for refining.

downstroke ▶ noun a stroke made downwards: *he writes the figure seven with a line through the downstroke.*

downswing ▶ noun **1** another term for DOWNTURN.
2 Golf the downward movement of a club when the player is about to hit the ball.

downtempo ▶ adjective & adverb Music played at a slow tempo.

down-the-line ▶ adjective informal thorough and uncompromising: *the party avoids down-the-line support of unions.*

downthrow Geology ▶ verb (past **downthrew**; past participle **downthrown**) [with obj.] displace (a rock formation) downwards.
▶ noun a downward displacement of rock strata.

downtime ▶ noun [mass noun] time during which a machine, especially a computer, is out of action or unavailable for use. ■ N. Amer. time when one is not working or active: *everyone needs downtime to unwind.*

down to earth ▶ adjective with no illusions or pretensions; practical and realistic: *a down-to-earth view of marriage.*
– DERIVATIVES **down-to-earthness** noun.

downtown chiefly N. Amer. ▶ adjective in or relating to the central part or main business and commercial area of a town or city: *downtown Chicago | a downtown bar.*
▶ adverb in or into a such an area: *I drove downtown.*
▶ noun the downtown area of a town or city: *the heart of Pittsburgh's downtown.*
– DERIVATIVES **downtowner** noun.

downtrend ▶ noun a downward tendency, especially in economic matters.

downtrodden ▶ adjective oppressed or treated badly by people in power: *a downtrodden proletarian struggling for social justice.*

downturn ▶ noun a decline in economic, business, or other activity: *a downturn in the housing market.*
▶ verb [with obj.] (usu. as adj. **downturned**) turn (something) downwards: *his downturned mouth.*

down under informal ▶ adverb in or to Australia or New Zealand: *take a flight down under in September.*
▶ noun (also **Down Under**) Australia and New Zealand: *a girl from down under.*
– ORIGIN late 19th cent.: with reference to the position of these countries on a globe.

downward ▶ adverb (also **downwards**) towards a lower place or level: *he was lying face downward | the floor sloped downwards.*
▶ adjective moving or leading towards a lower place or level: *a downward trend in inflation.*
– ORIGIN Middle English: shortening of Old English *adūnweard.*

downwardly ▶ adverb towards a lower level; in a downward direction.
– PHRASES **downwardly mobile** see MOBILE.

downwarp /ˈdaʊnwɔːp/ Geology ▶ noun a broad depression of the earth's surface.
▶ verb [with obj.] displace (a rock formation) downwards so as to form a downwarp.

downwash ▶ noun [mass noun] the downward deflection of an airstream by an aircraft wing or helicopter rotor blade.

downwelling ▶ noun [mass noun] the downward movement of fluid, especially in the sea, the atmosphere, or deep in the earth.
▶ adjective characterized by or undergoing downwelling.

downwind ▶ adverb & adjective in the direction in which the wind is blowing: [as adv.] *warnings were issued to people living downwind of the fire* | [as adj.] *downwind landings.*

downwinder /daʊnˈwɪndə/ ▶ noun chiefly US a person living downwind of a nuclear test site or reactor, where the risk from fallout or radiation leaks is greatest.

downy ▶ adjective (**downier**, **downiest**) **1** covered with fine, soft hair or feathers: *the baby's downy cheek.* ■ soft and fluffy: *pale downy hair.* ■ filled with soft feathers: *a downy pillow.*
2 dated (of a person) shrewd; sharp: *I told you she was a downy one.*

downy mildew ▶ noun [mass noun] mildew on a plant which is marked by a whitish down composed of spore-forming hyphae, penetrating more deeply into the plant than powdery mildew. ● Family Peronosporaceae, subdivision Mastigomycotina.

downzone ▶ verb [with obj.] N. Amer. assign (land or property) to a zoning grade under which the permitted density of housing and development is reduced.

dowry /ˈdaʊ(ə)ri/ ▶ noun (pl. **dowries**) an amount of property or money brought by a bride to her husband on their marriage.
– ORIGIN Middle English (denoting a widow's life interest in her husband's estate): from Anglo-Norman French *dowarie*, from medieval Latin *dotarium* (see DOWER).

dowse /daʊz/ ▶ verb [no obj.] practise dowsing: *water is easy to dowse for.* ■ [with obj.] search for or discover by dowsing: *he dowsed a spiral of energy on the stone.*
– DERIVATIVES **dowser** noun.
– ORIGIN late 17th cent.: of unknown origin.

dowsing ▶ noun [mass noun] a technique for searching for underground water, minerals, ley lines, or anything invisible, by observing the motion of a pointer (traditionally a forked stick, now often paired bent wires) or the changes in direction of a pendulum, supposedly in response to unseen influences: [as modifier] *a dowsing rod.*

Dowson /ˈdaʊs(ə)n/, Ernest (Christopher) (1867–1900), English poet, associated with the 'decadent' school of Oscar Wilde and Aubrey Beardsley. His two books of poems, *Verses* (1896) and *Decorations* (1899), deal with themes of ennui and world-weariness.

doxastic /dɒkˈsastɪk/ ▶ adjective Philosophy relating to an individual's beliefs: *doxastic worlds.*
– ORIGIN late 18th cent.: from Greek *doxastikos* 'conjectural', from *doxazein* 'to conjecture'.

doxology /dɒkˈsɒlədʒi/ ▶ noun (pl. **doxologies**) a liturgical formula of praise to God.
– DERIVATIVES **doxological** adjective.
– ORIGIN mid 17th cent.: via medieval Latin from Greek *doxologia*, from *doxa* 'appearance, glory' (from *dokein* 'seem') + *-logia* (see -LOGY).

doxorubicin /ˌdɒksəʊˈruːbɪsɪn/ ▶ noun [mass noun] Medicine a bacterial antibiotic that is widely used to treat leukaemia and various other forms of cancer. ● This is produced by the streptomycete bacterium *Streptomyces peucetius caesius.*
– ORIGIN 1970s: from *deoxy-* (in the sense 'that has lost oxygen') + Latin *rubus* 'red' + -MYCIN.

doxy /ˈdɒksi/ ▶ noun (pl. **doxies**) archaic a lover or mistress. ■ a prostitute.
– ORIGIN mid 16th cent. (originally slang): of unknown origin.

doxycycline /ˌdɒksɪˈsʌɪkliːn/ ▶ noun [mass noun] Medicine a broad-spectrum antibiotic of the tetracycline group, which has a long half-life in the body.
– ORIGIN 1960s: from *d(e)oxy-* + TETRACYCLINE.

doyen /ˈdɔɪən, ˈdwɑːjã/ ▶ noun the most respected or prominent person in a particular field: *he became the doyen of British physicists.*
– ORIGIN late 17th cent.: via French from Old French *deien* (see DEAN[1]).

doyenne /ˈdɔɪɛn, dɔɪˈɛn, dwʌˈjɛn/ ▶ noun the most respected or prominent woman in a particular field: *she became a doyenne of the London Irish music scene.*
– ORIGIN mid 19th cent.: from French, feminine of *doyen* (see DOYEN).

Doyenne du Comice /ˈdɔɪɛn d(j)uː kɒˈmɪs, dɔɪˈɛn, dwʌˈjɛn/ ▶ noun fuller term for COMICE.

Doyle /dɔɪl/, Sir Arthur Conan (1859–1930), Scottish novelist and short-story writer, chiefly remembered for his creation of the private detective Sherlock Holmes. Holmes first appeared (with his friend Dr Watson, the narrator of the stories) in *A Study in Scarlet* (1887), and featured in more than fifty stories and in novels such as *The Hound of the Baskervilles* (1902).

D'Oyly Carte /ˌdɔɪli ˈkɑːt/, Richard (1844–1901), English impresario and producer. He brought together the librettist Sir W. S. Gilbert and the composer Sir Arthur Sullivan, producing many of their operettas in London's Savoy Theatre, which he had established in 1881.

doz. ▶ abbreviation dozen.

doze ▶ verb [no obj.] sleep lightly: *he found his mother dozing by the fire.* ■ (**doze off**) fall lightly asleep: *I dozed off for a few seconds.*
▶ noun a short, light sleep.
– ORIGIN mid 17th cent. (in the sense 'stupefy, bewilder, or make drowsy'): perhaps related to Danish *døse* 'make drowsy'.

dozen ▶ noun **1** (pl. **same**) a group or set of twelve: *a dozen bottles of sherry.* ■ (**dozens**) informal a lot: *she has dozens of admirers.*
2 (**the dozens**) an exchange of insults engaged in as a game or ritual among black Americans.
– PHRASES **by the dozen** in large quantities. **talk nineteen to the dozen** Brit. talk incessantly.
– DERIVATIVES **dozenth** adjective.
– ORIGIN Middle English: from Old French *dozeine*, based on Latin *duodecim* 'twelve'.

dozer ▶ noun informal short for BULLDOZER.

dozy ▶ adjective (**dozier**, **doziest**) feeling drowsy and lazy: *he grew dozy at the end of a long day.* ■ Brit. informal sluggish and not alert; stupid: *at breakfast, a dozy waitress brings the wrong things.*
– DERIVATIVES **dozily** adverb, **doziness** noun.

DP ▶ abbreviation ■ data processing. ■ displaced person.

dpc ▶ abbreviation damp-proof course.

DPhil ▶ abbreviation (in the UK) Doctor of Philosophy.

dpi ▶ abbreviation Computing dots per inch, a measure of the resolution of printers, scanners, etc.

D

dpm ▶ abbreviation damp-proof membrane, a sheet of material used to make a structure such as a solid concrete floor damp-proof.

DPP ▶ abbreviation (in the UK) Director of Public Prosecutions.

DPT ▶ abbreviation diphtheria, pertussis (whooping cough), and tetanus, a combined vaccine given to small children.

Dr ▶ abbreviation ■ debit. [formerly representing *debtor.*] ■ (as a title) Doctor: *Dr Michael Russell.* ■ (in street names) Drive.

dr. ▶ abbreviation ■ drachm or drachms. ■ drachma or drachmas. ■ dram or drams.

drab[1] ▶ adjective (**drabber**, **drabbest**) **1** lacking brightness or interest; drearily dull: *the landscape was drab and grey | her drab suburban existence.*
2 of a dull light brown colour: *drab camouflage uniforms.*
▶ noun [mass noun] fabric of a dull light brown colour. ■ (**drabs**) clothes, especially trousers, made of drab: *a young man dressed in drabs.*
– DERIVATIVES **drably** adverb, **drabness** noun.
– ORIGIN mid 16th cent. (as a noun denoting undyed cloth): probably from Old French *drap* 'cloth' (see DRAPE).

drab[2] ▶ noun archaic **1** a slovenly woman.
2 a prostitute.
– ORIGIN early 16th cent.: perhaps related to Low German *drabbe* 'mire' and Dutch *drab* 'dregs'.

drabble ▶ verb archaic make or become wet and dirty by movement into or through muddy water.
– ORIGIN Middle English: from Low German *drabbelen* 'paddle in water or mire', from *drabbe* 'mire'.

dracaena /drəˈsiːnə/ ▶ noun a tropical palm-like shrub or tree with ornamental foliage, popular as a greenhouse or indoor plant. ● Genera *Dracaena* and *Cordyline*, family Agavaceae.
– ORIGIN modern Latin, from Greek *drakaina*, feminine of *drakōn* 'serpent, dragon' (the genus *Dracaena* includes *Dracaena draco*, the dragon tree).

drachm /dram/ (abbrev.: **dr.**) ▶ noun a unit of weight formerly used by apothecaries, equivalent to 60 grains or one eighth of an ounce. ■ (also **fluid drachm**) a liquid measure formerly used by apothecaries, equivalent to 60 minims or one eighth of a fluid ounce.
– ORIGIN late Middle English (denoting the ancient Greek drachma): from Old French *dragme* or late Latin *dragma*, via Latin from Greek *drakhmē* (see DRACHMA).

drachma /ˈdrakmə/ ▶ noun (pl. **drachmas** or **drachmae** /-miː/) a former monetary unit of Greece, notionally equal to 100 lepta, replaced in 2002 by the euro. ■ a silver coin of ancient Greece.
– ORIGIN via Latin from Greek *drakhmē*, an Attic weight and coin. Compare with DIRHAM and DRACHM.

drack /drak/ ▶ adjective Austral. informal (especially of a woman) unattractive or slovenly. ■ dreary and dull.
– ORIGIN 1940s: said to be from the name of the 1930s film *Dracula's Daughter*, but possibly related to DRECK.

Draco[1] /ˈdreɪkəʊ/ Astronomy a large northern constellation (the Dragon), stretching around the north celestial pole and said to represent the dragon killed by Hercules. It has no bright stars.
– ORIGIN Latin.

Draco[2] /ˈdreɪkəʊ/ (7th century BC), Athenian legislator. His codification of Athenian law was notorious for its severity in that the death penalty was imposed even for trivial crimes.

dracone /ˈdrakəʊn/ ▶ noun a large flexible sausage-shaped container used for transporting oil and other liquids on water.
– ORIGIN 1950s: from Latin *draco*, *dracon-*, from Greek *drakōn* 'serpent' (because of its shape).

draconian /drəˈkəʊnɪən, dreɪ-/ ▶ adjective (of laws or their application) excessively harsh and severe.

– DERIVATIVES **draconic** /-ˈkɒnɪk/ adjective.
– ORIGIN late 19th cent.: from the name of *Draco* (see **DRACO**[2]) + **-IAN**.

Dracula /ˈdrakjʊlə/ the Transylvanian vampire in Bram Stoker's novel *Dracula* (1897).
– ORIGIN variant of *Drakula, Dragwlya*, names given to Vlad Țepeș (Vlad the Impaler), a 15th-cent. prince of Wallachia renowned for his cruelty.

draegerman /ˈdreɪgəmən/ ▶ **noun** (pl. **draegermen**) Canadian a member of a crew trained for underground rescue work.
– ORIGIN early 20th cent.: the first element from the name of A. B. *Dräger* (1870–1928), German inventor of a type of breathing apparatus.

D

draff /draf/ ▶ **noun** [mass noun] literary dregs or refuse.
– ORIGIN Middle English: perhaps from an unrecorded Old English word related to German *Treber, Träber* 'husks, grains', and perhaps also to **DRIVEL**.

draft ▶ **noun 1** a preliminary version of a piece of writing: *the first draft of the party's manifesto* | [as modifier] *a draft document*. ■ a plan, sketch, or rough drawing. ■ [mass noun] Computing a mode of operation of a printer in which text is produced rapidly but with relatively low definition.
2 a written order to pay a specified sum.
3 (**the draft**) US compulsory recruitment for military service: *25 million men were subject to the draft*. ■ N. Amer. a procedure whereby sports players are made available for selection or reselection by the teams in a league, usually with the earlier choices being given to the weaker teams. ■ rare a group or individual selected from a larger group for a special duty, e.g. for military service.
4 US spelling of **DRAUGHT**.
▶ **verb** [with obj.] **1** prepare a preliminary version of (a document): *I drafted a letter of resignation*.
2 select (a person or group of people) and bring them somewhere for a certain purpose: *riot police were* **drafted in** *to break up the blockade*. ■ US conscript (someone) for military service. ■ N. Amer. select (a player) for a sports team through the draft.
– DERIVATIVES **drafter** noun.
– ORIGIN mid 16th cent.: phonetic spelling of **DRAUGHT**.

draft dodger ▶ **noun** N. Amer. derogatory a person who has avoided compulsory military service.
– DERIVATIVES **draft dodging** noun.

draftee ▶ **noun** US a person conscripted for military service.

draft pick ▶ **noun** N. Amer. the right of a sports team to select a player during the annual selection process. ■ a player selected during the draft.

draftsman ▶ **noun** (pl. **draftsmen**) **1** a person who drafts legal documents.
2 chiefly N. Amer. variant spelling of **DRAUGHTSMAN**.

drafty ▶ **adjective** US spelling of **DRAUGHTY**.

drag ▶ **verb** (**drags, dragging, dragged**) **1** [with obj. and adverbial of direction] pull (someone or something) along forcefully, roughly, or with difficulty: *we dragged the boat up the beach*. ■ take (someone) to or from a place or event, despite their reluctance: *my girlfriend is dragging me off to Rhodes for a week*. ■ (**drag oneself**) go somewhere wearily, reluctantly, or with difficulty: *I have to drag myself out of bed each day*. ■ move (an image or highlighted text) across a computer screen using a tool such as a mouse. ■ [no obj.] (of a person's clothes or an animal's tail) trail along the ground: *the nuns walked in meditation, their habits dragging on the grassy verge*. ■ [no obj.] (**drag at**) catch hold of and pull (something): *desperately, Jinny dragged at his arm*. ■ [with obj.] (of a ship) trail (an anchor) along the seabed, drifting in the process. ■ [no obj.] (of an anchor) fail to hold, causing a ship or boat to drift. ■ [with obj.] search the bottom of (a river, lake, or the sea) with grapnels or nets: *frogmen had dragged the local river*.
2 [no obj.] (of time) pass slowly and tediously: *the day dragged—eventually it was time for bed*. ■ (**drag on**) (of a process or situation) continue at tedious and unnecessary length: *the dispute between the two families dragged on for some years*. ■ [with obj.] (**drag something out**) protract something unnecessarily: *he dragged out the process of serving them*.
▶ **noun 1** [mass noun] the action of pulling something forcefully or with difficulty: *the drag of the current*. ■ the longitudinal retarding force exerted by air or other fluid surrounding a moving object. ■ [in sing.] a person or thing that impedes progress or development: *Larry was turning out to be* **a drag on** *her career*. ■ Angling unnatural motion of a fishing fly caused by the pull of the line. ■ [count noun] archaic an iron shoe that can be applied as a brake to the wheel of a cart or wagon.
2 [in sing.] informal a boring or tiresome person or thing: *working nine to five can be a drag*.
3 informal an act of inhaling smoke from a cigarette: *he took a long drag on his cigarette*.
4 [mass noun] clothing more conventionally worn by the opposite sex, especially women's clothes worn by a man: *a fashion show, complete with men* **in drag**.
5 informal a street or road: *the main drag is wide but there are few vehicles*.
6 historical a private vehicle like a stagecoach, drawn by four horses. ■ Brit. informal, dated a car: *a stately great drag with a smart chauffeur*.
7 short for **DRAG RACE**.
8 a thing that is pulled along the ground or through water, in particular: ■ historical a harrow used for breaking up the surface of land. ■ an apparatus for dredging or for recovering objects from the bottom of a river or lake. ■ another term for **DRAGNET**.
9 a strong-smelling lure drawn before hounds as a substitute for a fox. ■ a hunt using such a lure.
10 [mass noun] N. Amer. informal influence over other people: *they had the education but they didn't have the drag*.
11 Music one of the basic patterns (rudiments) of drumming, consisting of a stroke preceded by two grace notes usually played with the other stick. See also **RUFF**[4].
– PHRASES **drag and drop** Computing move (an image or highlighted text) to another part of the screen using a mouse or similar device. **drag one's feet** walk slowly and wearily or with difficulty. ■ (also **drag one's heels**) be deliberately slow or reluctant to act: *the government has dragged its heels over permanent legislation*. **drag someone/thing through the mud** see **MUD**.
– PHRASAL VERBS **drag someone/thing down** bring someone or something to a lower level or standard: *the economy will be dragged down by inefficient firms*. **drag something in/into** introduce an irrelevant or inappropriate subject: *politics were never dragged into the conversation*. **drag someone/thing into** involve someone or something in (a situation or matter), typically when such involvement is inappropriate or unnecessary: *he had no right to drag you into this sort of thing*. **drag on** informal inhale the smoke from (a cigarette). **drag something out** extract information from someone against their will: *the truth was being* **dragged out of** *us*. **drag up** informal dress up in clothes more conventionally worn by the opposite sex. **drag something up** informal deliberately mention an unwelcome or unpleasant fact: *pieces of evidence about his early life were dragged up*. **drag someone up** Brit. informal bring up a child badly: *would you have her dragged up by a succession of au pairs?*
– ORIGIN Middle English: from Old English *dragan* or Old Norse *draga* 'to draw'; the noun partly from Middle Low German *dragge* 'grapnel'.

drag anchor ▶ **noun** another term for **SEA ANCHOR**.

drag chain ▶ **noun** a chain used to slow down or steady the motion of a vehicle.

dragée /ˈdrɑːʒeɪ/ ▶ **noun** a sweet consisting of a centre covered with a coating, such as a sugared almond. ■ a small silver ball for decorating a cake.
– ORIGIN late 17th cent. (also denoting a mixture of spices): French, from Old French *dragie* (see **DREDGE**[2]).

dragger ▶ **noun** N. Amer. a fishing boat that uses a dragnet.

dragging brush ▶ **noun** another term for **FLOGGER**.

draggle ▶ **verb** [with obj.] make (something) dirty or wet, typically by trailing it through mud or water: (as adj. **draggled**) *she wore a draggled skirt*. ■ [no obj.] hang untidily: *red hairs draggled dispiritedly from her chignon*. ■ [no obj.] archaic trail behind others; lag behind.
– ORIGIN early 16th cent.: diminutive and frequentative of **DRAG**.

draggle-tailed ▶ **adjective** archaic having untidily trailing skirts: *a draggle-tailed wench*.

draggy ▶ **adjective** (**draggier, draggiest**) informal dreary and lacking liveliness: *a long, draggy, boring Friday afternoon*.

drag hound ▶ **noun** a hound used to hunt with a drag.

drag lift ▶ **noun** a type of ski lift which pulls skiers up a slope on their skis.

dragline ▶ **noun 1** a large excavator with a bucket pulled in by a wire cable.
2 a line of silk produced by a spider and acting as a safety line or (in newly hatched spiders) a parachute.

dragnet ▶ **noun** a net drawn through a river or across ground to trap fish or game.

dragoman /ˈdragə(ʊ)mən/ ▶ **noun** (pl. **dragomans** or **dragomen**) an interpreter or guide, especially in countries speaking Arabic, Turkish, or Persian.
– ORIGIN late Middle English: from obsolete French, from Italian *dragomanno*, from medieval Greek *dragoumanos*, from Arabic *tarjumān* 'interpreter'.

dragon ▶ **noun 1** a mythical monster like a giant reptile. In European tradition the dragon is typically fire-breathing and tends to symbolize chaos or evil, whereas in East Asia it is usually a beneficent symbol of fertility, associated with water and the heavens. ■ derogatory a fierce and intimidating woman: *his wife is a real dragon*.
2 (also **flying dragon**) another term for **FLYING LIZARD**. ■ Austral. any lizard of the agama family.
– PHRASES **chase the dragon** informal smoke heroin.
– ORIGIN Middle English (also denoting a large serpent): from Old French, via Latin from Greek *drakōn* 'serpent'.

dragon arum ▶ **noun** an arum of the eastern Mediterranean, with a deep purple spathe and spadix and an unpleasant smell. ● *Dracunculus vulgaris*, family Araceae.

dragon boat ▶ **noun 1** a boat of a traditional Chinese design, typically decorated to resemble a dragon, propelled with paddles by a large crew and used for racing.
2 another term for **DRAGON SHIP**.

dragonet /ˈdrag(ə)nɪt/ ▶ **noun** a marine fish which often lies partly buried in the seabed. The male is brightly coloured. ● Two genera in the family Callionymidae: several species, in particular the European *Callionymus lyra*.
– ORIGIN Middle English (denoting a small dragon): from Old French, diminutive of *dragon* 'dragon'.

dragonfish ▶ **noun** (pl. **same** or **dragonfishes**) a deep-sea fish with a long slender body: ● a fish with fang-like teeth, a barbel on the chin, and luminous organs on the body (families Stomiatidae and Idiacanthidae). ● (**Antarctic dragonfish**) a fish of southern polar seas with a flattened head (family Bathydraconidae).

dragonfly ▶ **noun** (pl. **dragonflies**) a fast-flying long-bodied predatory insect with two pairs of large transparent wings which are spread out sideways at rest. The voracious aquatic larvae take up to five years to reach adulthood. Compare with **DAMSELFLY**. ● Suborder Anisoptera, order Odonata: several families.

dragonnade /ˌdragəˈneɪd/ ▶ **noun** a form of persecution directed by Louis XIV against French Protestants, in which troops were quartered on them.
– ORIGIN early 18th cent.: from French, from *dragon* 'dragon' (see **DRAGOON**).

dragon's blood ▶ **noun** [mass noun] a red gum or powder that is derived from the fruit of certain palm trees and from the stem of the dragon tree and related plants.

dragon's head ▶ **noun** Astrology the ascending or north node of the moon's orbit, used in drawing up an astrological chart.

dragon ship ▶ **noun** a Viking longship ornamented with a beaked prow.

dragon's tail ▶ **noun** Astrology the descending or south node of the moon's orbit, used in drawing up an astrological chart.

dragon's teeth ▶ **plural noun** Brit. informal concrete obstacles pointing upwards from the ground in rows, used against tanks in the Second World War.
– PHRASES **sow** (or **plant**) **dragon's teeth** take action that is intended to prevent trouble, but which actually brings it about.
– ORIGIN with allusion to the teeth of the dragon killed by Cadmus.

dragon tree ▶ **noun** a slow-growing palm-like tree of the agave family, which is native to the Canary Islands and yields dragon's blood. ● *Dracaena draco*, family Agavaceae.

dragoon /drəˈguːn/ ▶ **noun** a member of any of several cavalry regiments in the British army. ■ historical a mounted infantryman armed with a carbine.
▶ **verb** [with obj.] coerce (someone) into doing something: *she had been* **dragooned into** *helping with the housework*.
– ORIGIN early 17th cent. (denoting a kind of carbine or musket, thought of as breathing fire): from French *dragon* 'dragon'.

drag queen ▸ noun informal a man who ostentatiously dresses up in women's clothes.

drag race ▸ noun a race between two cars over a short distance, usually a quarter of a mile, as a test of acceleration.
– DERIVATIVES **drag racer** noun, **drag racing** noun.

dragster ▸ noun a car built or modified to take part in drag races.

drail /dreɪl/ ▸ noun Angling a fish hook and line weighted with lead for dragging below the surface of the water.
– ORIGIN late 16th cent. (denoting part of a plough): from the obsolete verb *drail*, an alteration of TRAIL.

drain ▸ verb [with obj.] **1** cause the water or other liquid in (something) to run out, leaving it empty or dry: *we drained the swimming pool.* ■ cause or allow (liquid) to run off or out of something: *fry the pork and **drain off** any excess fat.* ■ make (land) drier by providing channels for water to flow away in: *the land was drained and the boggy ground reclaimed.* ■ (of a river) carry off the superfluous water from (an area): *the stream drains a wide moorland above the waterfall.* ■ [no obj., with adverbial of direction] (of water or another liquid) flow away from, out of, or into something: *the river drains into the Pacific* | figurative *Polly felt the blood drain from her face.* ■ [no obj.] become dry or drier as liquid runs off or away: *dishes left to drain.* ■ drink the entire contents of (a glass or other container): *the stranger drained his glass of beer.*
2 deprive of strength or vitality: *his limbs were **drained of** all energy* | *Ruth slumped down in her seat, drained by all that had happened.* ■ cause (a valuable resource) to be lost or used up: *my mother's hospital bills are draining my income.* ■ [no obj., with adverbial] (of a valuable resource) be lost or used up: *votes and campaign funds drained away from the Republican candidate.*
3 Golf, informal (of a player) hole (a putt).
▸ noun **1** a channel or pipe carrying off surplus liquid, especially rainwater or liquid waste. ■ Brit. a frame of metal bars set in a road over the opening to a rainwater channel. ■ a tube for drawing off accumulating fluid from a body cavity or an abscess. ■ Electronics the part of a field-effect transistor to which the charge carriers flow after passing the gate.
2 [in sing.] a thing that uses up a particular resource: *nuclear power is **a serious drain on** the public purse.* ■ the continuous loss or expenditure of a particular resource: *the drain of talented staff to the United States.*
– PHRASES **go down the drain** informal be totally wasted: *the government must stop public money going down the drain.*
– ORIGIN Old English *drēahnian*, *drēhnian* 'strain (liquid)', of Germanic origin; related to DRY.

drainage ▸ noun [mass noun] the action or process of draining something: *the pot must have holes in the base for good drainage* | *the drainage of wetlands.* ■ a system of drains.

drainboard ▸ noun North American term for DRAINING BOARD.

draincock ▸ noun a valve for draining the water from a boiler.

drainer ▸ noun **1** a device used for draining things, in particular: ■ a rack placed on a draining board to hold crockery and cutlery while it drains. ■ a draining board.
2 a person who drains a flooded area.

draining board ▸ noun Brit. a sloping grooved board or surface on which washed dishes are left to drain into an adjacent sink.

drainpipe ▸ noun a pipe for carrying off rainwater or liquid refuse from a building. ■ (**drainpipes** or **drainpipe trousers**) trousers with very narrow legs.

Draize test ▸ noun a pharmacological test in which a substance is introduced into the eye or applied to the skin of a laboratory animal in order to ascertain the likely effect of that substance on the corresponding human tissue.
– ORIGIN 1970s: named after John H. Draize (1900–92), the American pharmacologist who helped to develop this type of test.

Drake, Sir Francis (*c.*1540–96), English sailor and explorer. He was the first Englishman to circumnavigate the globe (1577–80), in his ship the *Golden Hind*. He played an important part in the defeat of the Spanish Armada.

drake[1] ▸ noun a male duck: [as modifier] *a drake mallard.*
– ORIGIN Middle English: of West Germanic origin; related to Low German *drake* and German *Enterich*.

drake[2] ▸ noun (in fishing) a natural or artificial mayfly, especially a subadult or a gravid female.
– ORIGIN Old English *draca*, from Latin *draco* 'dragon'.

Drake equation ▸ noun Astronomy a speculative equation which gives an estimate of the likelihood of discovering intelligent extraterrestrial life in the galaxy, formulated by the US astronomer Frank Drake in 1961.

Drakensberg Mountains /ˈdrɑːkənzˌbəːg/ a range of mountains in southern Africa, stretching in a NE–SW direction for a distance of 1,126 km (700 miles) through Lesotho and parts of South Africa. The highest peak is Thabana Ntlenyana (3,482 m, 11,425 ft).

Drake Passage an area of ocean, noted for its violent storms, connecting the South Atlantic with the South Pacific and separating the southern tip of South America (Cape Horn) from the Antarctic Peninsula.
– ORIGIN named after Sir Francis DRAKE.

Dralon /ˈdreɪlɒn/ ▸ noun [mass noun] trademark, chiefly Brit. a synthetic textile made from acrylic fibre and used for curtains and upholstery.
– ORIGIN 1950s: on the pattern of *nylon*.

DRAM ▸ noun Electronics a memory chip that depends upon an applied voltage to keep the stored data.
– ORIGIN acronym from *dynamic random-access memory*.

dram[1] /dram/ ▸ noun **1** chiefly Scottish a small drink of whisky or other spirits: *a wee dram to ward off the winter chill.*
2 another term for DRACHM.
– ORIGIN late Middle English (in sense 2): from Old French *drame* or medieval Latin *drama*, variants of *dragme* and *dragma* (see DRACHM).

dram[2] /drɑːm/ ▸ noun the basic monetary unit of Armenia, equal to 100 luma.
– ORIGIN Armenian, literally 'coin, money', from Greek *drakhmē* DRACHMA.

drama ▸ noun **1** a play for theatre, radio, or television: *a gritty urban drama about growing up in Harlem.* ■ [mass noun] such works as a genre or style of literature: *Renaissance drama.* ■ [mass noun] the activity of acting: *teachers who use drama are working in partnership with pupils* | [as modifier] *drama school.*
2 an exciting, emotional, or unexpected event or circumstance: *a hostage drama* | [mass noun] *an afternoon of high drama at Wembley.*
– PHRASES **make a drama out of** informal exaggerate the importance of (a minor problem or incident).
– ORIGIN early 16th cent.: via late Latin from Greek *drama*, from *dran* 'do, act'.

drama-documentary ▸ noun a television film based on real events.

Dramamine /ˈdraməmiːn/ ▸ noun [mass noun] trademark an antihistamine compound used to counter nausea (especially travel sickness), also used as a recreational drug.
– ORIGIN 1940s: from *dram-* (of unknown origin) + AMINE.

drama queen ▸ noun informal a person who habitually responds to situations in a melodramatic way.

dramatic ▸ adjective **1** [attrib.] relating to drama or the performance or study of drama: *the dramatic arts* | *a dramatic society.*
2 (of an event or circumstance) sudden and striking: *a dramatic increase in recorded crime.* ■ exciting or impressive: *he recalled his dramatic escape from the building* | *dramatic mountain peaks.* ■ (of a person or their behaviour) intending or intended to create an effect; theatrical: *with a dramatic gesture, she put a hand to her brow.*
– DERIVATIVES **dramatically** adverb.
– ORIGIN late 16th cent.: via late Latin from Greek *dramatikos*, from *drama*, *dramat-* (see DRAMA).

dramatic irony ▸ noun see IRONY[1].

dramatic monologue ▸ noun a poem in the form of a speech or narrative by an imagined person, in which the speaker inadvertently reveals aspects of their character while describing a particular situation or series of events.

dramatics ▸ plural noun **1** [treated as sing. or pl.] the study or practice of acting in and producing plays: *amateur dramatics.*
2 theatrically exaggerated or overemotional behaviour: *cut out the dramatics.*

dramatis personae /ˌdramətɪs pəːˈsəʊnʌɪ, -niː/ ▸ plural noun [treated as sing. or pl.] the characters of a play, novel, or narrative.
– ORIGIN mid 18th cent.: from Latin, literally 'persons of the drama'.

dramatist ▸ noun a person who writes plays.

dramatize (also **dramatise**) ▸ verb [with obj.] adapt (a novel) or present (a particular incident) as a play or film: *his play dramatized the plight of Maureen, a pregnant young woman.* ■ exaggerate the seriousness or importance of (an incident or situation): *she had a tendency to dramatize things.*
– DERIVATIVES **dramatization** /-ˈzeɪʃ(ə)n/ noun.

dramaturge /ˈdramətəːdʒ/ (also **dramaturg**) ▸ noun **1** a dramatist.
2 a literary editor on the staff of a theatre who liaises with authors and edits texts.
– ORIGIN mid 19th cent.: via French and German from Greek *dramatourgos*, from *drama*, *dramat-* 'drama' + *-ergos* 'worker'.

dramaturgy /ˈdraməˌtəːdʒi/ ▸ noun [mass noun] the theory and practice of dramatic composition: *studies of Shakespeare's dramaturgy.*
– DERIVATIVES **dramaturgic** adjective, **dramaturgical** adjective, **dramaturgically** adverb.

Drambuie /dramˈbuːi, -ˈbjʊi/ ▸ noun [mass noun] trademark a sweet Scotch whisky liqueur.
– ORIGIN from Scottish Gaelic *dram buidheach* 'satisfying drink'.

dramedy /ˈdrɑːmɪdi/ ▸ noun (pl. **dramedies**) a television programme or film in which the comic elements derive mainly from character and plot development.
– ORIGIN early 20th cent.: blend of DRAMA and COMEDY.

Drammen /ˈdrɑːmən/ a seaport in SE Norway, on an inlet of Oslofjord; pop. 93,006 (2007).

Drang nach Osten /ˌdraŋ nax ˈɒst(ə)n/, German /ˌdraŋ naːx ˈɔstn/ ▸ noun the former German policy of eastward expansion, especially that espoused under Nazi rule.
– ORIGIN German, literally 'pressure towards the east'.

drank past of DRINK.

drape ▸ verb [with obj. and adverbial] arrange (cloth or clothing) loosely or casually on or round something: *she draped a shawl around her shoulders.* ■ cover or wrap loosely with folds of cloth: *the body was draped in a blanket.* ■ let (oneself or a part of one's body) rest somewhere in a casual or relaxed way: *he draped an arm around her shoulders.* ■ [no obj.] (of fabric) hang in loose, graceful folds: *velvet drapes beautifully.*
▸ noun **1** (**drapes**) N. Amer. long curtains: *Katherine pulled back the heavy velvet drapes.* ■ [usu. as modifier] a man's suit consisting of a long jacket and narrow trousers, as worn by a Teddy boy: *a drape jacket.* ■ a cloth for covering parts of a patient's body other than that part on which a surgical operation is being performed.
2 [in sing.] the way in which a garment or fabric hangs: *by fixing the band lower down you obtain a fuller drape in the fabric.*
– DERIVATIVES **drapey** adjective.
– ORIGIN mid 19th cent.: back-formation from DRAPERY, influenced by French *draper* 'to drape'. The noun senses date from the early 20th cent.

draper ▸ noun Brit. dated a person who sells textile fabrics.
– ORIGIN late Middle English (denoting a maker of woollen cloth): from Old French *drapier*, from *drap* 'cloth', from late Latin *drappus*.

drapery ▸ noun (pl. **draperies**) [mass noun] cloth, curtains, or clothing hanging in loose folds: *the hall of the school was hung with green drapery.* ■ the depiction of folds of cloth in sculpture or painting: *the effigy is notable for its flowing drapery.*
– ORIGIN Middle English (in the sense 'cloth, fabrics'): from Old French *draperie*, from *drap* 'cloth' (see DRAPER).

drastic /ˈdrastɪk, ˈdrɑː-/ ▸ adjective likely to have a strong or far-reaching effect; radical and extreme: *a drastic reduction of staffing levels.*
– DERIVATIVES **drastically** adverb.
– ORIGIN late 17th cent. (originally applied to the effect of medicine): from Greek *drastikos*, from *dran* 'do'.

drat ▸ exclamation (often **drat someone/something**) a fairly mild expression of anger or annoyance: *'Oh, drat Feargal and his suspicions!'*
– DERIVATIVES **dratted** adjective.
– ORIGIN early 19th cent.: shortening of *od rat*, euphemism for *God rot*.

draught /drɑːft/ (US **draft**) ▸ noun **1** a current of cool air in a room or other confined space: *heavy curtains at the windows cut out draughts.*

2 a single act of drinking or inhaling: *she downed the remaining beer in one draught.* ■ the amount swallowed or inhaled in a draught: *he took deep draughts of oxygen into his lungs.* ■ literary or archaic a quantity of a liquid with medicinal properties: *a sleeping draught.*
3 the depth of water needed to float a ship: *the shallow draught enabled her to get close inshore.*
4 the drawing in of a fishing net. ■ the fish taken at one drawing; a catch.
▸ **verb** variant spelling of DRAFT.
▸ **adjective** [attrib.] **1** denoting beer or cider served from a barrel or tank rather than from a bottle or can: *draught ale.*
2 denoting an animal used for pulling heavy loads: *a draught horse.*
– PHRASES **feel the draught** informal experience an adverse change in one's financial circumstances. **on draught** (of beer or cider) ready to be drawn from a barrel or tank; not bottled or canned.
– ORIGIN Middle English (in the sense 'drawing, pulling'; also 'something drawn, a load'): from Old Norse *dráttr*, of Germanic origin; related to German *Tracht*, also to DRAW. Compare with DRAFT.

draughtboard ▸ **noun** Brit. a square chequered board of 64 small squares identical to a chessboard and used for playing draughts.

draught excluder ▸ **noun** a strip of foam rubber, metal, or other material inserted in a door or window frame to keep out draughts.

draughtproof ▸ **adjective** sealed so as to keep out draughts.
▸ **verb** [with obj.] make (a building, door, or window) draughtproof: (as noun **draughtproofing**) *simple draughtproofing is relatively inexpensive.*

draughts ▸ **noun** Brit. a board game for two players, played on a draughtboard. Each player starts with twelve disc-shaped pieces in three rows along one side of the board, and moves them diagonally with the aim of capturing all the opponent's pieces.
– ORIGIN late Middle English: from DRAUGHT; related to obsolete *draught* in the sense 'move' (in chess or any similar game); compare with French *trait*, from Latin *tractus* 'a dragging'.

draughtsman (or **draughtswoman**) ▸ **noun** (pl. **draughtsmen** or **draughtswomen**) **1** a person who makes detailed technical plans or drawings.
2 an artist skilled in drawing.
3 variant spelling of DRAFTSMAN.
– DERIVATIVES **draughtsmanship** noun.

draughtsperson (US **draftsperson**) ▸ **noun** (pl. **draughtspeople**) a draughtsman or draughtswoman (used as a neutral alternative).

draughty (US **drafty**) ▸ **adjective** (**draughtier**, **draughtiest**; **draftier**, **draftiest**) (of an enclosed space) cold and uncomfortable because of currents of cool air: *anyone would get pneumonia living in that draughty old house.* ■ (of a door or window) ill-fitting and allowing in currents of cool air.
– DERIVATIVES **draughtiness** noun.

Dravidian /drəˈvɪdɪən/ ▸ **adjective** relating to or denoting a family of languages spoken in southern India and Sri Lanka, or the peoples who speak them.
▸ **noun 1** [mass noun] the Dravidian family of languages.
2 a member of any of the peoples speaking a Dravidian language.

> Dravidian languages were once spoken throughout the Indian subcontinent, but were restricted to the south following the arrival of speakers of Indic languages c.1000 BC. Those still used, by over 160 million people, include Tamil, Kannada, Malayalam, and Telugu.

– ORIGIN from Sanskrit *drāviḍa* 'relating to the Tamils' (from *Draviḍa* 'Tamil') + -IAN.

draw ▸ **verb** (past **drew**; past participle **drawn**) [with obj.] **1** produce (a picture or diagram) by making lines and marks on paper with a pencil, pen, etc.: *he drew a map.* ■ produce an image of (someone or something) by making lines and marks on paper: *I asked her to draw me* | [no obj.] *you're at art college, you must be able to draw.* ■ trace or produce (a line or mark) on a surface: *she drew a wavering line down the board.*
2 pull or drag (something such as a vehicle) so as to make it follow behind: *a cart drawn by two horses.* ■ [with obj. and adverbial of direction] pull or move (something) in a specified direction: *I drew back the blanket and uncovered the body.* ■ [with obj. and adverbial of direction] gently pull or guide (someone) in a specified direction: *'David,' she whispered, drawing him aside.* ■ [no obj., with adverbial of direction] move somewhere in a slow steady way: *the train drew in to the station.* ■ [no obj., with adverbial] come to or arrive at a point in time or in a process: *the campaign* ***drew to a close.*** ■ pull (curtains) shut or open: *do you want me to draw the curtains?* ■ make (wire) by pulling a piece of metal through successively smaller holes.
3 extract (an object) from a container or receptacle: *he drew his gun and peered into the gloomy apartment.*
4 take or obtain (liquid) from a container or receptacle: *a wheel was built to draw water from the well* | *he drew off a pint of bitter.* ■ run (a bath): *I would have been drawing his bath.* ■ (**draw something from**) obtain something from (a particular source): *an independent panel of judges drawn from members of the public.* ■ (**draw on**) use (one's experience, talents, or skills) as a resource: *Sue has a lot of past experience to draw on.* ■ obtain or withdraw (money) from a bank or other source. ■ Hunting search (cover) for game. ■ Bridge (of the declarer) force the defenders to play (cards in a particular suit) by leading cards in that suit. ■ (**draw on**) suck smoke from (a cigarette or pipe). ■ [no obj.] (of a chimney, flue, or fire) allow air to flow in and upwards freely, so that a fire can burn: *failure of a fire to draw properly can have a number of causes.* ■ take in (a breath): *Mrs Feather drew a long breath.* ■ [no obj.] (of tea) be left standing so that the flavour is extracted from the leaves: *a pot of tea is allowed to draw.* ■ disembowel: *after a mockery of a trial he was* ***hanged, drawn, and quartered.***
5 be the cause of (a specified response): *he drew criticism for his lavish spending.* ■ attract (someone) to come to a place or an event: *you really drew the crowds with your playing.* ■ induce (someone) to reveal or do something: *he refused to be* ***drawn on*** *what would happen.* ■ direct or attract (someone's attention) to something: *it was an outrage and we had to draw people's attention to it* | *a bright red instantly draws the eye.* ■ reach (a conclusion) by deduction or inference from a set of circumstances: *the moral to be drawn is that spending wins votes.* ■ formulate or perceive (a comparison or distinction): *the law drew a clear distinction between innocent and fraudulent misrepresentation.*
6 finish (a contest or game) with an even score: [with obj. and complement] *Brazil had drawn a stormy match 1–1* | [no obj., with complement] *they drew 0–0 in 1974.*
7 Bowls cause (a bowl) to travel in a curve determined by its bias to the desired point. ■ Golf hit (the ball) so that it deviates slightly, usually as a result of spin. Compare with FADE.
8 (of a ship) require (a specified depth of water) to float in: *boats that draw only a few inches of water.*
9 [no obj.] (of a sail) be filled with wind.
▸ **noun 1** an act of selecting names randomly to decide winners in a lottery, opponents in a sporting contest, etc.: *the draw has been made for this year's tournament.*
2 an even score at the conclusion of a game or match: *he scored twice to force a 4–4 draw.* ■ Cricket a game which is left incomplete for lack of time, regardless of the scores. Compare with TIE.
3 a person or thing that is very attractive or interesting: *the museum has turned out to be a big draw for school children in the city.*
4 an act of drawing on a cigarette. ■ [mass noun] Brit. informal cannabis: *they're dropping Es and smoking draw.*
5 an act of pulling a gun from its holster in order to shoot.
6 Golf a shot causing the ball to deviate slightly.
– PHRASES **draw a bead on** see BEAD. **draw a blank** see BLANK. **draw blood** cause someone to bleed, especially in the course of a fight: *the blow drew blood from the corner of his mouth.* **draw someone's fire** attract hostile criticism away from a more important target: *the concession will go some way to draw the fire of the government's critics.* **draw the line at** set a limit of what one is willing to do or accept: *she drew the line at prostitution.* **draw lots** see LOT. **draw the short straw** see STRAW. **draw stumps** Cricket take the stumps out of the ground at close of play. **quick on the draw** very fast in taking one's gun from its holster. ■ very fast in acting or reacting.
– PHRASAL VERBS **draw back** choose not to do something that one was expected to do: *the government has* ***drawn back from*** *attempting reform.* **draw in** (of successive days) become shorter because of the changing seasons. ■ (of a day) approach its end. ■ (of successive evenings or nights) start earlier because of the changing seasons: *the nights were drawing in fast.* **draw on** (of a period of time) pass by and approach its end: *he remembered sitting in silence with his grandmother as evening drew on.* **draw something on** put an item of clothing on: *he drew on his dressing gown.* **draw out** (of successive days) become longer because of the changing seasons. **draw someone out** gently or subtly persuade someone to talk or become more expansive: *she drew me out and flattered me.* **draw something out** make something last longer: *the transition was long and drawn out.* **draw up** come to a halt: *drivers drew up at the lights.* **draw something up** prepare a plan, agreement, or other document in detail: *they instructed an attorney to draw up a sales agreement.* **draw oneself up** make oneself stand in a stiffly upright manner.
– ORIGIN Old English *dragan*, of Germanic origin; related to Dutch *dragen* and German *tragen*, also to DRAUGHT.

> **USAGE** On the confusion of **draw** and **drawer**, see **USAGE** at **DRAWER**.

drawback ▸ **noun 1** a feature that renders something less acceptable; a disadvantage or problem: *the main drawback of fitting catalytic converters is the cost.*
2 (also **duty drawback**) an amount of excise or import duty remitted on goods exported.

drawbar ▸ **noun 1** a bar on a vehicle to which something can be attached to pull it or be pulled.
2 a bar in a structure that can be removed to allow someone through or to let other parts move.
3 one of a number of bars that may be pulled out to control harmonics on an electric organ.

drawbridge ▸ **noun** historical a bridge, especially one over a castle's moat, which is hinged at one end so that it may be raised to prevent people crossing or to allow vessels to pass under it.

drawcard ▸ **noun** informal a quality or feature that evokes interest or liking; an attraction: *most described natural beauty as the country's main drawcard.*

drawcord ▸ **noun** another term for DRAWSTRING.

drawdown ▸ **noun 1** a reduction in the volume of water in a lake or reservoir. ■ a reduction in the size or presence of a military force: *the unit is the first to leave Germany as part of the drawdown.*
2 an act of drawing on available loan facilities.

drawee /drɔː(r)ˈiː/ ▸ **noun** the person or organization, typically a bank, who must pay a draft or bill.

drawer ▸ **noun 1** /drɔː/ a box-like storage compartment without a lid, made to slide horizontally in and out of a desk, chest, or other piece of furniture.
2 (**drawers** /drɔːz/) dated or humorous knickers or underpants.
3 /ˈdrɔː(r)ə/ a person who writes a cheque.
4 /ˈdrɔː(r)ə/ a person who produces a drawing or design.
– DERIVATIVES **drawerful** noun (pl. **drawerfuls**).

> **USAGE** The word **drawer** is often spelled incorrectly as **draw**. As a noun, **draw** chiefly means 'an act of selecting names randomly to decide winners' or 'an even score at the conclusion of a game', whereas **drawer** mainly means 'a sliding storage compartment'.

draw hoe ▸ **noun** a hoe designed to be used with a pulling action.

drawing ▸ **noun** a picture or diagram made with a pencil, pen, or crayon rather than paint: *a series of charcoal drawings on white paper.* ■ [mass noun] the art or activity of making drawings: *she took lessons in drawing.*

drawing board ▸ **noun** a large flat board on which paper may be spread for artists or designers to work on.
– PHRASES **back to the drawing board** used to indicate that an idea, scheme, or proposal has been unsuccessful and that a new one must be devised: *the government must go back to the drawing board and review the whole issue of youth training.* **on the drawing board** (of an idea, scheme, or proposal) under consideration and not yet ready to put into practice: *there are plans to enlarge the runway, but at present all this remains on the drawing board.*

drawing pin ▸ **noun** Brit. a short flat-headed pin, used for fastening paper to a wall or other surface.

drawing room ▸ **noun** a room in a large private house in which guests can be received and entertained. ■ [as modifier] (of a song or play) characterized by a polite observance of social proprieties: *a stock figure of Thirties drawing-room comedy.*
– ORIGIN mid 17th cent. (denoting a private room attached to a more public one): abbreviation of 16th-cent. *withdrawing-room* 'a room to withdraw to'.

drawknife ▶ noun (pl. **drawknives**) a knife consisting of a blade with a handle at each end at right angles to it, which is drawn towards the user to remove wood from a surface.

drawl ▶ verb [no obj.] speak in a slow, lazy way with prolonged vowel sounds: [with direct speech] *'Suits me fine,' he drawled.*
▶ noun [in sing.] a slow, lazy way of speaking or an accent with prolonged vowel sounds: *a strong Texan drawl.*
– DERIVATIVES **drawly** adjective.
– ORIGIN late 16th cent.: probably originally slang, from Low German or Dutch *dralen* 'delay, linger'.

drawn past participle of DRAW. ▶ adjective (of a person) looking strained from illness, exhaustion, anxiety, or pain: *Cathy was pale and drawn and she looked tired out.*

drawn butter ▶ noun [mass noun] N. Amer. melted butter.

drawn-out ▶ adjective lasting or seeming to last longer than is necessary: *after the long drawn-out years of waiting the end of the war was in sight.*

drawn work (also **drawn-thread-work**) ▶ noun [mass noun] ornamental work on linen or other fabric, in which threads are drawn out of the fabric to create a pattern of openings and holes.

draw-off (also **draw-off pipe**) ▶ noun a pipe which takes water from the plumbing system to a tap or other points of use.

draw reins ▶ plural noun a pair of reins that are attached to a horse's saddle or girth and pass through the bit rings to the rider's hands.

draw sheet ▶ noun **1** a sheet that is placed in such a way that it can be taken from under a patient or invalid without disturbing the bedclothes.
2 a list of matches to be played in a tournament.

drawstring ▶ noun a string in the seam of the material of a garment or a bag, which can be pulled to tighten or close it.

dray ▶ noun a truck or cart without sides, for delivering beer barrels or other heavy loads. ■ Austral./NZ a two-wheeled cart.
– ORIGIN late Middle English (denoting a sledge): perhaps from Old English *dræge* 'dragnet', related to *dragan* 'to pull' (see DRAW).

dray horse ▶ noun a large, powerful horse used to pull heavy loads.

drayman ▶ noun (pl. **draymen**) a person who delivers beer for a brewery.

DRC ▶ abbreviation Democratic Republic of the Congo.

dread ▶ verb [with obj.] **1** anticipate with great apprehension or fear: *Jane was dreading the party* | [with infinitive] *I **dread to think** what Russell will say.*
2 archaic regard with great awe or reverence.
▶ noun **1** [mass noun] great fear or apprehension: *the thought of returning to London filled her with dread* | [in sing.] *I used to have a dread of Friday afternoons.*
2 a sudden take-off and flight of a flock of gulls or other birds.
3 informal a person with dreadlocks: *the band appeals to dreads and baldheads alike.* ■ (**dreads**) dreadlocks.
▶ adjective [attrib.] **1** greatly feared; dreadful: *he was stricken with the dread disease and died.*
2 archaic regarded with awe; greatly revered: *that dread being we dare oppose.*
– ORIGIN Old English *ādrǣdan*, *ondrǣdan*, of West Germanic origin; related to Old High German *intrātan*.

dreaded ▶ adjective [attrib.] regarded with great fear or apprehension: *the dreaded news came that Joe had been wounded* | humorous *the dreaded fax machine.*

dreadful ▶ adjective **1** causing or involving great suffering, fear, or unhappiness, extremely bad or serious: *there's been a dreadful accident.* ■ extremely disagreeable: *the weather was dreadful.* ■ (of a person) unwell or troubled: *I feel dreadful—I hate myself* | *she looked quite dreadful and she was struggling for breath.*
2 [attrib.] used to emphasize the degree to which something is the case, especially something regarded with sadness or disapproval: *this was all a dreadful mistake* | *you're a dreadful flirt.*
– DERIVATIVES **dreadfulness** noun.

dreadfully chiefly Brit. ▶ adverb **1** [often as submodifier] extremely: *you're dreadfully thin* | *I'm dreadfully sorry!* ■ very much: *I'll miss you dreadfully.*
2 very badly: *the company has performed dreadfully.*

dreadlocks ▶ plural noun a Rastafarian hairstyle in which the hair is washed but not combed and twisted while wet into tight braids or ringlets hanging down on all sides.
– DERIVATIVES **dreadlocked** adjective.

dreadnought /ˈdrɛdnɔːt/ ▶ noun **1** historical a type of battleship introduced in the early 20th century, larger and faster than its predecessors and equipped entirely with large-calibre guns. [named after Britain's HMS *Dreadnought*, which was the first to be completed (1906).]
2 archaic a fearless person.
3 archaic a heavy overcoat for stormy weather.

dream ▶ noun **1** a series of thoughts, images, and sensations occurring in a person's mind during sleep: *I had a recurrent dream about falling from great heights.* ■ [in sing.] a state of mind in which someone is or seems to be unaware of their immediate surroundings: *he had been walking around **in a dream** all day.*
2 a cherished aspiration, ambition, or ideal: *I fulfilled a childhood dream when I became champion.* ■ an unrealistic or self-deluding fantasy: *maybe he could get a job and earn some money—but he knew this was just a dream.* ■ a person or thing perceived as wonderful or perfect: *her new man's an absolute dream* | *it was **a dream of a** backhand.*
▶ verb (past and past participle **dreamed** /drɛmt, driːmd/ or **dreamt** /drɛmt/) [no obj.] **1** experience dreams during sleep: *I **dreamed about** her last night.* ■ [with obj.] see, hear, or feel (something) in a dream: *maybe you dreamed it* | [with clause] *I dreamed that I was going to be executed.*
2 indulge in daydreams or fantasies about something greatly desired: *she had **dreamed of** a trip to America.*
3 [with negative] contemplate the possibility of doing something or that something might be the case: *I wouldn't **dream of** foisting myself on you* | [with clause] *I never dreamed anyone would take offence.*
– PHRASES **beyond one's wildest dreams** bigger or better than could be reasonably expected: *stockbrokers command salaries beyond the wildest dreams of most workers.* **in your dreams** used ironically to assert that something desired is never likely to happen. **in one's wildest dreams** [with negative] used to emphasize that a situation is beyond the scope of one's imagination: *she could never in her wildest dreams have imagined the summer weather in New York.* **like a dream** informal very well or successfully: *the car is still running like a dream.*
– PHRASAL VERBS **dream on** [in imperative] informal used as an ironic comment on the unlikely nature of a plan or aspiration: *Dean thinks he's going to get the job. Dream on, Babe.* **dream something up** imagine or invent something: *he's been dreaming up new ways of attracting customers.*
– DERIVATIVES **dreamful** adjective (literary), **dreamless** adjective.
– ORIGIN Middle English: of Germanic origin, related to Dutch *droom* and German *Traum*, and probably also to Old English *drēam* 'joy, music'.

dreamboat ▶ noun informal a very attractive person, especially a man.

dreamcatcher ▶ noun a small hoop containing a horsehair mesh decorated with feathers and beads, believed by American Indians to give its owner good dreams.

dreamer ▶ noun **1** a person who dreams or is dreaming.
2 a person who is unpractical or idealistic: *a rebellious young dreamer.*

Dreaming ▶ noun (in the mythology of some Australian Aboriginal peoples) Dreamtime or Alcheringa, especially as manifested in the natural world and celebrated in ritual.

dreamland ▶ noun **1** [mass noun] sleep regarded as a world of dreams: *she tries to lull herself into dreamland.*
2 an imagined and unrealistically ideal world: *a digital dreamland where you'll pay bills with a click of the mouse.*

dreamlike ▶ adjective having the qualities of a dream; unreal: *she snapped out of her dreamlike state.*

dreamscape ▶ noun a landscape or scene with the strangeness or mystery characteristic of dreams.

dream team ▶ noun a team of people perceived as the perfect combination for a particular purpose: *the two have been linked as the dream team that will revitalize New York Democrats.*

dream ticket ▶ noun Brit. a pair of candidates standing together for political office who are ideally matched to attract widespread support.

Dreamtime ▶ noun another term for ALCHERINGA.

dreamwork ▶ noun [mass noun] Psychoanalysis the processes by which the unconscious mind alters the manifest content of dreams in order to conceal their real meaning from the dreamer.

dreamworld ▶ noun a fantastic or idealized view of life: *somebody who can live in a romantic dreamworld.*

dreamy ▶ adjective (**dreamier**, **dreamiest**) **1** having a magical or pleasantly unreal quality; dreamlike: *the atmosphere is tranquil and dreamy* | *a slow dreamy melody.* ■ informal delightful; gorgeous: *I bet he was really dreamy.*
2 given to or indulging in daydreaming: *a dreamy boy who grew up absorbed in poetry.*
– DERIVATIVES **dreamily** adverb, **dreaminess** noun.

D

drear /drɪə/ ▶ adjective literary term for DREARY.
– ORIGIN early 17th cent.: abbreviation.

dreary ▶ adjective (**drearier**, **dreariest**) depressingly dull and bleak or repetitive: *the dreary round of working, eating, and trying to sleep.*
– DERIVATIVES **drearily** adverb, **dreariness** noun.
– ORIGIN Old English *drēorig* 'gory, cruel', also 'melancholy', from *drēor* 'gore', of Germanic origin; related to German *traurig* 'sorrowful', also to DROWSY, and probably to DRIZZLE.

dreck /drɛk/ (also **drek**) ▶ noun [mass noun] informal rubbish; trash: *this so-called art is pure dreck.*
– DERIVATIVES **dreckish** adjective, **drecky** adjective.
– ORIGIN early 20th cent.: from Yiddish *drek* 'filth, dregs', from a Germanic base shared by Old English *threax*; probably related to Greek *skatos* 'dung'.

dredge[1] ▶ verb [with obj.] clear the bed of (a harbour, river, or other area of water) by scooping out mud, weeds, and rubbish with a dredge. ■ bring up or clear (something) from a river, harbour, or other area of water with a dredge: *mud was dredged out of the harbour* | [no obj.] *they start to **dredge for** oysters in November.* ■ (**dredge something up**) bring something unwelcome and forgotten or obscure to people's attention: *I don't understand why you had to dredge up this story.*
▶ noun an apparatus for bringing up objects or mud from a river or seabed by scooping or dragging.
– ORIGIN late 15th cent. (as a noun; originally in *dredge-boat*): perhaps related to Middle Dutch *dreghe* 'grappling hook'.

dredge[2] ▶ verb [with obj.] sprinkle (food) with a powdered substance such as flour or sugar: *dredge the bananas with sugar and cinnamon.*
– ORIGIN late 16th cent.: from obsolete *dredge* 'sweetmeat, mixture of spices', from Old French *dragie*, perhaps via Latin from Greek *tragēmata* 'spices'. Compare with DRAGÉE.

dredger ▶ noun a boat designed for dredging harbours or other bodies of water.

dree /driː/ ▶ verb (**drees**, **dreeing**, **dreed**) [with obj.] Scottish or archaic endure (something burdensome or painful).
– PHRASES **dree one's weird** submit to one's destiny.
– ORIGIN Old English *drēogan*, of Germanic origin; related to Old Norse *drýgja* 'practise, perpetrate'.

D-region ▶ noun another term for D-LAYER.

dregs ▶ plural noun the remnants of a liquid left in a container, together with any sediment: *coffee dregs* ■ the most worthless part or parts of something: *the dregs of society.*
– DERIVATIVES **dreggy** adjective.
– ORIGIN Middle English: probably of Scandinavian origin and related to Swedish *drägg* (plural).

dreich /driːx/ ▶ adjective Scottish (especially of weather) dreary; bleak: *a cold, dreich early April day.*
– ORIGIN Middle English (in the sense 'patient, long-suffering'): of Germanic origin, corresponding to Old Norse *drjúgr* 'enduring, lasting'.

dreidel /ˈdreɪd(ə)l/ (also **dreidl**) ▶ noun N. Amer. a small four-sided spinning top with a Hebrew letter on each side, used in Jewish gambling games, especially at Hanukkah.
– ORIGIN 1930s: from Yiddish *dreydl*; compare with German *drehen* 'to turn'.

drek ▶ noun variant spelling of DRECK.

drench ▶ verb [with obj.] **1** wet thoroughly; soak: *I fell in the stream and was drenched.* ■ cover (something) liberally or thoroughly: *cool patios drenched in flowers.*
2 forcibly administer a drug in liquid form orally to (an animal).
▶ noun a dose of medicine administered to an animal. ■ archaic a draught of a medicinal or poisonous liquid.

– ORIGIN Old English *drencan* 'force to drink', *drenc* 'a drink or draught', of Germanic origin; related to German *tränken* (verb), *Trank* (noun), also to DRINK.

Drenthe /'drɛntə/ a sparsely populated agricultural province in the NE Netherlands; capital, Assen.

Dresden[1] /'drɛzdən/, German /'dreːsdn/ a city in eastern Germany, the capital of Saxony, on the River Elbe; pop. 504,800 (est. 2006). Famous for its baroque architecture, it was almost totally destroyed by Allied bombing in 1945.

Dresden[2] /'drɛzd(ə)n/ (also **Dresden china**) ▶ **noun** [mass noun] porcelain ware with elaborate decoration and delicate colourings, made originally at Dresden and (since 1710) at nearby Meissen.

dress ▶ **verb 1** [no obj.] put on one's clothes: *Graham showered and dressed quickly* | *I'll go and* ***get dressed***. ■ [with adverbial] wear clothes in a particular way or of a particular type: *she's nice-looking and dresses well* | (**be dressed**) *he was dressed in jeans and a thick sweater*. ■ [with obj.] put clothes on (someone): *they dressed her in a white hospital gown*. ■ put on clothes appropriate for a formal occasion: *we* ***dressed for dinner*** *every night*.
2 [with obj.] decorate (something) in an artistic or attractive way: *she'd enjoyed dressing the tree when the children were little*. ■ decorate (a ship) with flags for a special occasion.
3 [with obj.] treat or prepare (something) in a certain way, in particular: ■ clean, treat, or apply a dressing to (a wound). ■ clean and prepare (food, especially poultry or shellfish) for cooking or eating: (as adj. **dressed**) *dressed crab*. ■ add a dressing to (a salad). ■ apply a fertilizer to (an area of ground or a plant). ■ complete the preparation or manufacture of (leather or fabric) by treating its surface in some way. ■ smooth the surface of (stone): (as adj. **dressed**) *dressed Cotswold stone*. ■ arrange or style (hair).
4 [with obj.] Military draw up (troops) in the proper alignment. ■ [no obj.] (of troops) come into proper alignment.
5 (of a man) have the genitals habitually on one or the other side of the fork of the trousers: *do you dress to the left?*
6 [with obj.] make (an artificial fly) for use in fishing.
▶ **noun 1** a one-piece garment for a woman or girl that covers the body and extends down over the legs.
2 [mass noun] clothing of a specified kind for men or women: *traditional African dress*. ■ [as modifier] denoting military uniform or other clothing used on formal or ceremonial occasions: *a dress suit*.
– PHRASES **dressed overall** (of a ship) decorated with a continuous line of flags from bow to stern. **dressed to kill** wearing glamorous clothes intended to create a striking impression.
– PHRASAL VERBS **dress down** dress informally: *Sue dressed down in old jeans and a white blouse*. **dress someone down** informal reprimand someone. **dress up** dress in smart or formal clothes. ■ dress in a special costume for fun or as part of an entertainment: *he dressed up as a gorilla*. **dress something up** present something in such a way that it appears better than it really is: *the company dressed up the figures a little*.
– ORIGIN Middle English (in the sense 'put straight'): from Old French *dresser* 'arrange, prepare', based on Latin *directus* 'direct, straight'.

dressage /'drɛsɑː(d)ʒ/ ▶ **noun** [mass noun] the art of riding and training a horse in a manner that develops obedience, flexibility, and balance.
– ORIGIN 1930s: from French, literally 'training', from *dresser* 'to train'.

dress circle ▶ **noun** Brit. the first level of seats above the ground floor in a theatre.

dress coat ▶ **noun** a coat with long tails at the back, worn by men on very formal occasions.

dresser[1] ▶ **noun** a sideboard with shelves above for storing and displaying plates and kitchen utensils. ■ N. Amer. a chest of drawers.
– ORIGIN late Middle English (denoting a kitchen sideboard or table on which food was prepared): from Old French *dresseur*, from *dresser* 'prepare' (see DRESS).

dresser[2] ▶ **noun 1** [with adj.] a person who dresses in a specified way: *a snappy dresser*.
2 a person whose job is to look after theatrical costumes and help actors to dress.
3 Brit. a person who assists a surgeon during operations.
4 a person who prepares, treats, or finishes a material or piece of equipment.

dressing ▶ **noun 1** (also **salad dressing**) [mass noun] a sauce for salads, typically one consisting of oil and vinegar with herbs or other flavourings. ■ N. Amer. stuffing: *turkey with apple dressing*.
2 a piece of material used to cover and protect a wound.
3 [mass noun] size or stiffening used in the finishing of fabrics.
4 a fertilizing substance such as compost or manure spread over or ploughed into land.

dressing case ▶ **noun** historical a case used for toiletries.

dressing-down ▶ **noun** [in sing.] informal a severe reprimand: *the secretary received a public dressing-down*.

dressing gown ▶ **noun** a long, loose robe, typically worn after getting out of bed or bathing.

dressing room ▶ **noun** a room in which actors or sports players change clothes before and after their performance or game. ■ a small room attached to a bedroom, used for dressing in and to store clothes.

dressing station ▶ **noun** a place for giving emergency treatment to troops injured in battle.

dressing table ▶ **noun** a table with a mirror and drawers, used while dressing or applying make-up.

dress length ▶ **noun** a piece of material long enough to make a dress.

dressmaker ▶ **noun** a person whose job is making women's clothes.
– DERIVATIVES **dressmaking** noun.

dress parade ▶ **noun** a military parade in full dress uniform.

dress rehearsal ▶ **noun** the final rehearsal of a live show, in which everything is done as it would be in a real performance.

dress sense ▶ **noun** [mass noun] a good instinct for selecting garments which suit the wearer.

dress shield (also **dress preserver**) ▶ **noun** a piece of waterproof material fastened in the armpit of a dress to protect it from perspiration.

dress shirt ▶ **noun** a man's white shirt worn with a bow tie and a dinner jacket on formal occasions. ■ N. Amer. a man's long-sleeved shirt, suitable for wearing with a tie.

dressy ▶ **adjective** (**dressier**, **dressiest**) (of clothes) suitable for a smart or formal occasion. ■ requiring or given to wearing such clothes: *the sweater can be worn under a blazer for more dressy events*.

drew past of DRAW.

drey /dreɪ/ ▶ **noun** (pl. **dreys**) the nest of a squirrel, typically in the form of a mass of twigs in a tree.
– ORIGIN early 17th cent.: of unknown origin.

Dreyfus /'dreɪfəs/, Alfred (1859–1935), French army officer, of Jewish descent. In 1894 he was falsely accused of providing military secrets to the Germans; his trial and imprisonment caused a major political crisis in France. He was eventually rehabilitated in 1906.

dribble ▶ **verb 1** [no obj. and usu. with adverbial of direction] (of a liquid) fall slowly in drops or a thin stream: *rain dribbled down the window*. ■ [with obj. and adverbial of direction] pour (a liquid) slowly in a thin stream: *he dribbled cream into his coffee*. ■ [no obj.] allow saliva to run from the mouth: *his mouth was open and he was dribbling*.
2 [with obj. and adverbial of direction] (in soccer, hockey, and basketball) take (the ball) forwards past opponents with slight touches of the feet or the stick, or (in basketball) by continuous bouncing: *he attempted to dribble the ball from the goal area*.
▶ **noun 1** a thin stream of liquid; a trickle: *a dribble of blood*. ■ [mass noun] saliva running from the mouth.
2 (in soccer, hockey, and basketball) an act of taking the ball forward with repeated slight touches or bounces.
– DERIVATIVES **dribbler** noun, **dribbly** adjective.
– ORIGIN mid 16th cent.: frequentative of obsolete *drib*, variant of DRIP. The original sense was 'shoot an arrow short or wide of its target', which was also a sense of *drib*.

driblet ▶ **noun** a thin stream or small drop of liquid: *driblets of spittle run from her mouth*. ■ a small or insignificant amount: *the prisoners were let out in driblets*.
– ORIGIN late 16th cent. (in the sense 'small sum of money'): from obsolete *drib* (see DRIBBLE) + -LET.

dribs and drabs ▶ **plural noun** (**in dribs and drabs**) informal in small scattered or sporadic amounts: *more folk followed in dribs and drabs*.
– ORIGIN mid 19th cent.: from obsolete *drib* (see DRIBBLE) and *drab* (by reduplication).

dried past and past participle of DRY.

drier[1] ▶ **adjective** comparative of DRY.

drier[2] ▶ **noun** variant spelling of DRYER.

driest ▶ **adjective** superlative of DRY.

drift ▶ **verb** [no obj.] **1** be carried slowly by a current of air or water: *the cabin cruiser started to drift downstream* | figurative *excited voices drifted down the hall*. ■ [with adverbial of direction] walk slowly, aimlessly, or casually: *people began to drift away*. ■ [with adverbial] move passively, aimlessly, or involuntarily into a certain situation or condition: *I was* ***drifting off to sleep***. ■ (of a person or their attention) digress or stray to another subject: *I noticed my audience's attention drifting*.
2 (especially of snow or leaves) be blown into heaps by the wind: *fallen leaves start to drift in the gutters* | (as adj. **drifting**) *long stretches of drifting snow*.
▶ **noun 1** [in sing.] a continuous slow movement from one place to another: *there was a drift to the towns*. ■ [mass noun] the deviation of a vessel, aircraft, or projectile from its intended or expected course as the result of currents or winds: *the pilot had not noticed any appreciable drift*. ■ a steady movement or development from one thing towards another that is perceived as unwelcome: *the drift towards a more repressive style of policing*. ■ [mass noun] a state of inaction or indecision. ■ Motor Racing a controlled skid, used in taking bends at high speeds.
2 [in sing.] the general intention or meaning of an argument or someone's remarks: *maybe I'm too close to the forest to see the trees,* ***if you catch my drift***.
3 a large mass of snow, leaves, or other material piled up or carried along by the wind. ■ [mass noun] Geology glacial and fluvioglacial deposits left by retreating ice sheets. ■ a large spread of flowering plants growing together: *a drift of daffodils*.
4 Mining a horizontal or inclined passage following a mineral vein or coal seam.
5 Brit. historical an act of driving cattle or sheep. ■ an act of herding cattle within a forest to a particular place on an appointed day in order to determine ownership or to levy fines.
6 S. African a ford.
– PHRASAL VERBS **drift apart** (of two or more people) gradually become less intimate or friendly: *Lewis and his father drifted apart*.
– DERIVATIVES **drifty** adjective (**driftier**, **driftiest**).
– ORIGIN Middle English (in the sense 'mass of snow, leaves, etc.'): originally from Old Norse *drift* 'snowdrift, something driven'; in later use from Middle Dutch *drift* 'course, current', and (in sense 6 of the noun) South African Dutch *drift* 'ford'; related to DRIVE.

drifter ▶ **noun 1** a person who is continually moving from place to place, without any fixed home or job.
2 a fishing boat equipped with a drift net.

driftfish ▶ **noun** (pl. **same** or **driftfishes**) a slender-bodied bottom-dwelling fish found in the deeper waters of warm seas. ● Family Nomeidae (or Stromateidae): several genera, in particular *Ariomma*.

drift ice ▶ **noun** [mass noun] detached pieces of ice drifting with the wind or ocean currents.

drift net ▶ **noun** a large net for herring and similar fish, kept upright by weights at the bottom and floats at the top and allowed to drift with the tide.
– DERIVATIVES **drift netter** noun, **drift netting** noun.

drift pin ▶ **noun** a steel pin driven into a hole in a piece of metal to enlarge, shape, or align the hole.

driftway ▶ **noun** Brit. historical a broad route along which cattle or sheep used to be driven to market.

driftwood ▶ **noun** [mass noun] pieces of wood which are floating on the sea or have been washed ashore.

drill[1] ▶ **noun 1** a tool or machine with a rotating cutting tip or reciprocating hammer or chisel, used for making holes. ■ a tool with a rotating tip used by a dentist for cutting away part of a tooth before filling it.
2 [mass noun] instruction or training in military exercises: *parade-ground drill*. ■ intensive instruction or training in something, typically by means of repeated exercises: *tables can be mastered by drill and practice* | [count noun] *language-learning drills*. ■ [count noun] a rehearsal of the procedure to be followed in an emergency: *air-raid drills*. ■ (**the drill**) informal the correct or recognized procedure or way of doing something: *he didn't know the drill*.
3 a predatory mollusc that bores into the shells of other molluscs in order to feed on the soft tissue.

● Family Muricidae, class Gastropoda: several genera and species, in particular the American **oyster drill** (*Urosalpinx cinerea*), which is a serious pest of oyster beds.
▸ verb [with obj.] **1** produce (a hole) in something by or as if by boring with a drill: *drill holes through the tiles for the masonry pins.* ■ make a hole in (something) by boring with a drill: *a power tool for drilling wood.* ■ [no obj., with adverbial of direction] make a hole in or through something by using a drill: *do not attempt to drill through a joist* | figurative *his eyes drilled into her.* ■ [no obj.] sink a borehole in order to obtain oil or water: *BP has been licensed to **drill for** oil in the area* | (as noun **drilling**) *drilling should begin next year.* ■ (of a dentist) cut away part of (a tooth) before filling it. ■ [with obj. and adverbial of direction] informal (of a sports player) hit (a shot) hard and in a straight line: *he drilled a right-foot volley into the back of the net.*
2 subject (someone) to military training exercises: *a sergeant was drilling new recruits.* ■ [no obj.] (of a person) take part in military training exercises: *the troops were drilling.* ■ instruct (someone) in something by the means of repeated exercises or practice: *I reacted instinctively because I had been drilled to do just that.* ■ (**drill something into**) cause (someone) to learn something by repeating it regularly: *his mother had drilled into him the need to pay for one's sins.*
– PHRASAL VERBS **drill down** Computing access data which is in a lower level of a hierarchically structured database: *just click on a button and drill down until you find the level of detail you require* | [as modifier] *a drill-down menu of topics.*
– DERIVATIVES **driller** noun.
– ORIGIN early 17th cent.: from Middle Dutch *drillen* 'bore, turn in a circle'.

drill[2] ▸ noun a machine which makes small furrows, sows seed in them, and then covers the seed with earth. ■ a small furrow made by a drill. ■ a row of plants sown in a drill: *drills of lettuces.*
▸ verb [with obj.] sow (seed) with a drill: *crops drilled in autumn.* ■ plant (the ground) in furrows: (as noun **drilling**) *accurate ridging and drilling make hoeing much easier.*
– ORIGIN early 18th cent. (as a noun in the sense 'small furrow'): perhaps from DRILL[1].

drill[3] ▸ noun a dark brown baboon with a short tail and a naked blue or purple rump, found in the rainforests of West Africa. ● *Mandrillus leucophaeus*, family Cercopithecidae.
– ORIGIN mid 17th cent.: probably a local word. Compare with MANDRILL.

drill[4] ▸ noun [mass noun] a coarse twilled cotton or linen fabric.
– ORIGIN early 18th cent.: abbreviation of earlier *drilling*, from German *Drillich*, from Latin *trilix* 'triple-twilled', from *tri-* 'three' + *licium* 'thread'.

drilling rig ▸ noun a large structure with equipment for drilling an oil well.

drill press ▸ noun a machine tool for drilling holes, set on a fixed stand.

drill sergeant ▸ noun a non-commissioned officer who trains soldiers in military parade exercises.

drill stem ▸ noun a rotating rod or cylinder used in drilling.

drill string ▸ noun a structure consisting of coupled lengths of pipe or casing, which occupies the hole made in drilling for oil or gas.

drily /ˈdrʌɪli/ (also **dryly**) ▸ adverb **1** in a matter-of-fact or ironically humorous way: *'How very observant', he said drily.*
2 in a dry way or condition: *Evans swallowed drily.*

drink ▸ verb (past **drank**; past participle **drunk**) [with obj.] **1** take (a liquid) into the mouth and swallow: *we sat by the fire, drinking our tea* | [no obj.] *he drank thirstily.* ■ [no obj.] consume or be in the habit of consuming alcohol: *she doesn't drink or smoke* | (as noun **drinking**) *Les was ordered to cut down his drinking.* ■ [no obj.] (**drink up**) quickly consume the rest of a drink. ■ informal (of a plant or a porous substance) absorb (moisture). ■ [no obj.] (of wine) have a specified flavour or character when drunk: *this wine is really drinking beautifully.*
2 (**drink something in**) watch or listen to something with eager pleasure or interest: *she strolled to the window to drink in the view.*
▸ noun a liquid that can be swallowed as refreshment or nourishment: *fizzy drinks* | [mass noun] *a table covered with food and drink.* ■ a quantity of liquid swallowed at one go: *he had a drink of water.* ■ [mass noun] alcohol, or the habitual or excessive consumption of alcohol: *the effects of too much drink* | *they both **took to drink**.* ■ a glass of liquid, especially when alcoholic: *we went for a drink.* ■ (**drinks**) a social gathering at which alcoholic drinks are served: *would you like to come for drinks on Sunday?* ■ (**the drink**) informal the sea or another large area of water.
– PHRASES **be drinking in the last chance saloon** Brit. informal be in a difficult situation in which there is one final chance to put it right. **drink and drive** drive a vehicle while under the influence of alcohol. **drink deep** take a large draught or draughts of something: figurative *he learnt to **drink deep of** the Catholic tradition.* **drink someone's health** express one's good wishes for someone by raising one's glass and drinking a small amount. **drink (a toast) to** celebrate or wish for the good fortune of someone or something by raising one's glass and drinking a small amount. **drink someone under the table** informal consume as much alcohol as one's drinking companion without becoming as drunk. **drive someone to drink** often humorous trouble or disturb someone so much that they start to drink alcohol heavily: *a job with enough management crises and near-disasters to drive any sane person to drink.* **I'll drink to that** uttered to express one's agreement with or approval of a statement. **in drink** when intoxicated: *we've hit each other before, in drink.*
– ORIGIN Old English *drincan* (verb), *drinc* (noun), of Germanic origin; related to Dutch *drinken* and German *trinken*.

drinkable ▸ adjective (of a liquid) fit to drink; potable: *a supply of drinkable water.* ■ informal (of a drink) pleasant to taste; palatable: *a very drinkable red wine.*

drink-driving ▸ noun [mass noun] Brit. the crime of driving a vehicle with an excess of alcohol in the blood.
– DERIVATIVES **drink-driver** noun.

drinker ▸ noun **1** a person who drinks a particular drink: *coffee drinkers.* ■ a person who drinks alcohol, especially to excess: *a heavy drinker.*
2 (also **drinker moth**) a large brownish European moth, the caterpillar of which bears irritant hairs and is noted for drinking dew. ● *Euthrix potatoria*, family Lasiocampidae.
3 a container from which an animal can drink.

drinking chocolate ▸ noun [mass noun] Brit. a mixture of cocoa powder, milk solids, and sugar, added to hot milk to make a chocolate drink.

drinking fountain ▸ noun a device producing a small jet of water for drinking.

drinking horn ▸ noun chiefly historical a drinking container carved from an animal's horn.

drinking song ▸ noun a hearty song, typically concerning drink and having bawdy lyrics, which is sung while drinking alcohol.

drinking-up time ▸ noun [mass noun] (in the UK) a short period (now twenty minutes) legally allowed for finishing drinks bought before closing time in a pub or bar.

drinking water ▸ noun [mass noun] water pure enough for drinking.

drip ▸ verb (**drips, dripping, dripped**) [no obj.] let fall or be so wet as to shed small drops of liquid: *the tap won't stop dripping* | *his hands were **dripping with** blood.* ■ [with adverbial] (of liquid) fall in small drops: *water dripped from her clothing.* ■ [with obj.] cause or allow (a liquid) to fall in small drops: *the candle was dripping wax down one side.* ■ display a copious amount or degree of a particular quality or thing: *the women were **dripping with** gold and diamonds* | [with obj.] *his voice dripped sarcasm.*
▸ noun **1** a small drop of a liquid: *she put the bucket on top of the dresser to catch the drips.* ■ the action or sound of liquid falling steadily in small drops: *the drip, drip, drip of the leak in the roof.* ■ (also **drip feed**) Medicine an apparatus which passes fluid, nutrients, or drugs drop by drop into a patient's body on a continuous basis, usually intravenously: *he had been **on a drip** for several days.*
2 informal a weak and ineffectual person.
3 Architecture a projection on a moulding, channelled to prevent rain from running down the wall below. Compare with DRIPSTONE.
– ORIGIN Old English *dryppan*, *drȳpen*, of Germanic origin; related to Danish *dryppe*, also to DROP.

drip-dry ▸ adjective (of a fabric or garment) capable of drying without creasing when hung up after washing: *drip-dry shirts.*
▸ verb [no obj.] (of fabric or a garment) become dry without forming creases when hung up after washing. ■ [with obj.] dry (fabric or a garment) without creases by hanging it up: *it's easy to wash and simple to drip-dry.*

drip feed ▸ noun a device for introducing fluid drop by drop into a system, for example lubricating oil into an engine. ■ a medicinal drip.
▸ verb (**drip-feed**) [with obj.] introduce (fluid) drop by drop: *the oiler drip-feeds oil on to all drive chains.* ■ supply (a patient) with fluid, nutrients, or drugs through a drip. ■ provide gradually and in small amounts: *their correspondence is being drip-fed to newspapers.*

drip mat ▸ noun Brit. a small mat placed under a glass to protect the surface on which the glass is resting.

D

drip moulding ▸ noun another term for DRIPSTONE (sense 1).

dripping ▸ noun [mass noun] (US **drippings**) fat that has melted and dripped from roasting meat, used in cooking or eaten cold as a spread. ■ (**drippings**) US wax, fat, or other liquid produced from something by the effect of heat.
▸ adjective very wet: [as submodifier] ***dripping wet** hair.*

drippy ▸ adjective (**drippier, drippiest**) **1** informal weak, ineffectual, or sloppily sentimental: *a drippy love song.*
2 tending to drip: *drippy food.*
– DERIVATIVES **drippily** adverb, **drippiness** noun.

dripstone ▸ noun **1** Architecture a moulding over a door or window which deflects rain.
2 [mass noun] Geology rock deposited by precipitation from dripping water, such as that which forms stalactites and stalagmites.

drive ▸ verb (past **drove**; past participle **driven**) **1** [no obj., usu. with adverbial of direction] operate and control the direction and speed of a motor vehicle: *he got into his car and drove off* | *they drove back into town.* ■ (of a motor vehicle) travel under the control of a driver: *a car drives up, and a man gets out* | *a stream of black cars drove by.* ■ [with obj.] own or use (a specified type of car): *Sue drives an estate car.* ■ [no obj.] be licensed or competent to drive a motor vehicle: *I take it you can drive?* ■ [with obj.] convey (someone) in a vehicle, especially a private car: *his wife drove him to Regent's Park.*
2 [with obj. and adverbial of direction] propel or carry along by force in a specified direction: *the wind will drive you onshore.* ■ [no obj.] (of wind, rain, or snow) move or fall with great force: *the snow drove against him.* ■ [with obj.] (of a source of power) provide the energy to set and keep (an engine or piece of machinery) in motion: *turbines driven by steam.* ■ [with obj.] Electronics (of a device) power or operate (another device): *the interface can be used to drive a printer.* ■ [with obj.] force (a stake or nail) into place by hitting or pushing it: *nails are driven through the boards.* ■ [with obj. and adverbial] bore (a tunnel). ■ [with obj.] (in ball games) hit or kick (the ball) hard with a free swing of the bat, racket, or foot. ■ [with obj.] Golf strike (a ball) from the tee, typically with a driver.
3 [with obj. and adverbial of direction] urge or force (animals or people) to move in a specified direction: *they drove a flock of sheep through the centre of the city* | *the French infantry were driven back.* ■ compel to leave: *troops drove out the demonstrators* | *he wanted to drive me away.*
4 [with obj.] (of a fact or feeling) compel (someone) to act in a particular way, especially one that is considered undesirable or inappropriate: *he was driven by ambition* | [with obj. and infinitive] *some people are driven to murder their tormentors.* ■ [with obj.] bring (someone) forcibly into a specified negative state: *the thought **drove** him **to despair*** | [with obj. and complement] *my laziness drives my wife crazy.* ■ [with obj.] force (someone) to work to an excessive extent: *you're **driving yourself** too hard.* ■ cause (something abstract) to happen or develop: *the consumer has been driving the economy for a number of years* | *we need to allow market forces to drive growth in the telecommunications sector.*
▸ noun **1** a trip or journey in a car: *they **went for a drive** in the country.* ■ [in names] a street or road: *Hammond Drive.* ■ (also **driveway**) a short road leading from a public road to a house or other building.
2 Psychology an innate, biologically determined urge to attain a goal or satisfy a need: *her emotional and sexual drives.* ■ [mass noun] determination and ambition to achieve something: *his drive helped Leeds to four Cup finals.*
3 an organized effort by a number of people to achieve a purpose: *a recruitment drive by the police.* ■ Brit. an organized gathering to play whist or another game, involving many players: *a whist drive.*

4 [mass noun] the transmission of power to machinery or to the wheels of a motor vehicle. ■ (in a car with automatic transmission) the position of the gear selector in which the car will move forward, changing gears automatically as required: *he threw the car into drive*. ■ [count noun] Computing short for **DISK DRIVE**.
5 (in ball games) a forceful stroke made with a free swing of the bat, racket, or foot against the ball. ■ Golf a shot from the tee.
6 an act of driving a group of animals to a particular destination.
– PHRASES **drive something home** see **HOME**. **drive a nail into the coffin of** severely harm (something that is already in a poor state): *companies will be pushed to the brink, driving another nail in the coffin of British manufacturing*. **what someone is driving at** the point that someone is attempting to make: *I don't understand what you're driving at*.
– DERIVATIVES **drivability** (also **driveability**) noun, **drivable** (also **driveable**) adjective.
– ORIGIN Old English *drīfan* 'urge (a person or animal) to go forward', of Germanic origin; related to Dutch *drijven* and German *treiben*.

drive bay ▶ noun Computing a space inside a computer in which a floppy disk, hard disk, or disk drive can be accommodated.

drive belt ▶ noun a belt that transmits drive from a motor, engine, or line shaft to a moving part or machine tool.

drive-by chiefly N. Amer. ▶ adjective (of a shooting or other act) carried out from a passing vehicle: *a drive-by shooting*.
▶ noun a shooting carried out from a passing vehicle.

drive-by-wire (also **steer-by-wire**) ▶ noun [mass noun] [usu. as modifier] a semi-automatic and typically computer-regulated system for controlling the engine, handling, suspension, and other functions of a motor vehicle.

drive chain ▶ noun an endless chain with links that engage with toothed wheels in order to transmit power from one shaft to another in an engine or machine tool.

drive-in ▶ adjective denoting a facility such as a cinema or restaurant that one can visit without leaving one's car: *a drive-in cinema*.
▶ noun a drive-in facility.

drivel /ˈdrɪv(ə)l/ ▶ noun [mass noun] nonsense: *don't talk such drivel!*
▶ verb (**drivels**, **drivelling**, **drivelled**; US **drivels**, **driveling**, **driveled**) [no obj.] 1 talk nonsense: *he was drivelling on about the glory days*.
2 archaic let saliva or mucus flow from the mouth or nose.
– DERIVATIVES **driveller** (US **driveler**) noun.
– ORIGIN Old English *dreflian* (in sense 2 of the verb), of uncertain origin; perhaps related to **DRAFF**.

driveline /ˈdrʌɪvlʌɪn/ ▶ noun another term for **DRIVETRAIN**.

driven past participle of **DRIVE**. ▶ adjective 1 [in combination] operated, moved, or controlled by a specified person or source of power: *a chauffeur-driven limousine | wind-driven sand*. ■ motivated or determined by a specified factor or feeling: *a market-driven response to customer needs*. ■ (of a person) relentlessly compelled by the need to accomplish a goal; very hard-working and ambitious: *my husband is a driven man*.
2 (of snow) piled into drifts or made smooth by the wind.

drive-on (also **drive-on/drive-off**) ▶ adjective denoting a ferry or train on to and from which motor vehicles may be driven.

driver ▶ noun 1 a person who drives a vehicle: *a taxi driver | learner drivers*. ■ a person who drives a specified kind of animal: *mule drivers*.
2 a wheel or other part in a mechanism that receives power directly and transmits motion to other parts. ■ Electronics a device or part of a circuit that provides power for output. ■ Computing a program that controls the operation of a device such as a printer or scanner.
3 a factor which causes a particular phenomenon to happen or develop: *the hope of achieving such monopolies becomes the main driver of investment*.
4 a golf club with a flat face and wooden head, used for driving from the tee.
– PHRASES **in the driver's seat** see **IN THE DRIVING SEAT** at **DRIVING**.
– DERIVATIVES **driverless** adjective.

driver ant ▶ noun another term for **ARMY ANT**.

driver's license ▶ noun North American term for **DRIVING LICENCE**.

driver's test ▶ noun North American term for **DRIVING TEST**.

driveshaft ▶ noun a rotating shaft which transmits torque in an engine.

drive-through N. Amer. ▶ adjective denoting a restaurant or other facility in which one can be served without leaving one's car.
▶ noun a drive-through facility.

drive time ▶ noun (especially in broadcasting) the parts of the day when many people commute by car: [as modifier] *drive-time radio*.

drivetrain ▶ noun the system in a motor vehicle which connects the transmission to the drive axles.

driveway ▶ noun see **DRIVE** (sense 1 of the noun).

driving ▶ adjective (of rain or snow) blown by the wind with great force: *driving rain*. ■ having a strong and controlling influence: *he was the* **driving force** *behind the plan | a driving ambition*.
▶ noun [mass noun] the control and operation of a motor vehicle: *he was convicted of reckless driving*.
– PHRASES **in the driving** (or **driver's**) **seat** in control of a situation.

driving licence (N. Amer. **driver's license**) ▶ noun a document permitting a person to drive a motor vehicle: *I've got a full, clean driving licence*.

driving range ▶ noun an area where golfers can practise drives.

driving test (N. Amer. **driver's test**) ▶ noun an official test of a motorist's competence which must be passed in order to get a driving licence.

driving wheel ▶ noun 1 any of the large wheels of a locomotive, to which power is applied either directly or via coupling rods.
2 a wheel transmitting motive power in machinery.

drizzle ▶ noun 1 [mass noun] light rain falling in very fine drops: *Scotland will be cloudy with patchy drizzle* | [in sing.] *a steady drizzle has been falling since 3 a.m.*
2 [in sing.] Cookery a thin stream of a liquid ingredient trickled over something.
▶ verb 1 [no obj.] (**it drizzles**, **it is drizzling**, etc.) rain lightly: *it's started to drizzle*.
2 [with obj.] Cookery cause a thin stream of (a liquid ingredient) to trickle over food: *drizzle the clarified butter over the top*.
– DERIVATIVES **drizzly** adjective (**drizzlier**, **drizzliest**).
– ORIGIN mid 16th cent.: probably based on Old English *drēosan* 'to fall', of Germanic origin; probably related to **DREARY**.

DRM ▶ abbreviation digital rights management.

Dr Martens /ˈmɑːtɪnz/ (also **Doc Martens** or **DMs**) ▶ plural noun trademark a type of heavy lace-up boot or shoe with an air-cushioned sole.
– ORIGIN 1970s: named after Klaus *Maertens*, German inventor of the sole.

Drogheda /ˈdrɔɪɪdə/ a port in the NE Republic of Ireland; pop. 35,090 (2006). In 1649 the inhabitants were massacred after refusing to surrender to Oliver Cromwell's forces.

drogue /drəʊɡ/ ▶ noun a conical or funnel-shaped device with open ends, towed behind a boat, aircraft, or other moving object to reduce speed or improve stability. ■ an object resembling a drogue, used as an aerial target for gunnery practice or as a windsock. ■ (in tanker aircraft) a funnel-shaped part on the end of the hose into which a probe is inserted by an aircraft being refuelled in flight. ■ (also **drogue parachute**) a small parachute used as a brake or to pull out a larger parachute or other object from an aircraft in flight or a fast-moving vehicle.
– ORIGIN early 18th cent. (originally a whaling term denoting a piece of stout board attached to a harpoon line, used to slow down or mark the position of a harpooned whale): perhaps related to **DRAG**.

droid /drɔɪd/ ▶ noun (in science fiction) a robot. ■ a person regarded as lifeless or mechanical: *a marketing droid*.
– ORIGIN 1970s: shortening of **ANDROID**.

droit /drɔɪt/ ▶ noun Law, historical a right or due.
– ORIGIN late Middle English: from Old French, based on Latin *directus* 'straight, right, direct'.

droit de seigneur /ˌdrwʌ də sɛnˈjəː/ ▶ noun [mass noun] the alleged right of a medieval feudal lord to have sexual intercourse with a vassal's bride on her wedding night.
– ORIGIN French, literally 'lord's right'.

droll /drəʊl/ ▶ adjective curious or unusual in a way that provokes dry amusement: *his unique brand of droll self-mockery*.
▶ noun archaic a jester or entertainer; a buffoon.
– DERIVATIVES **drollery** noun, **drollness** noun, **drolly** /ˈdrəʊlli/ adverb.
– ORIGIN early 17th cent. (as an adjective): from French *drôle*, perhaps from Middle Dutch *drolle* 'imp, goblin'.

dromaeosaurid /ˌdrəʊmɪə(ʊ)ˈsɔːrɪd/ (also **dromaeosaur** /ˈdrəʊmɪə(ʊ)sɔː/) ▶ noun a carnivorous bipedal dinosaur of a late Cretaceous family which included deinonychus and the velociraptors. They had a large slashing claw on each hind foot. ● Family Dromaeosauridae, suborder Theropoda, order Saurischia.
– ORIGIN 1970s: from modern Latin *Dromaeosauridae*, based on Greek *dromaios* 'swift-running' + *sauros* 'lizard'.

drome ▶ noun informal, dated an aerodrome.
– ORIGIN early 20th cent.: shortened form.

-drome ▶ combining form 1 denoting a place for running or racing: *aerodrome*.
2 denoting something that runs or proceeds in a certain way: *palindrome*.
– ORIGIN from Greek *dromos* 'course, running' (see **DROMOS**).

dromedary /ˈdrɒmɪd(ə)ri, ˈdrʌm-/ ▶ noun (pl. **dromedaries**) an Arabian camel, especially one of a light and swift breed trained for riding or racing.
– ORIGIN Middle English: from Old French *dromedaire* or late Latin *dromedarius* (*camelus*) 'swift camel', based on Greek *dromas*, *dromad-* 'runner'.

dromond /ˈdrɒmənd, ˈdrʌm-/ ▶ noun historical a large medieval ship of a kind used for war or commerce, chiefly in the Mediterranean.
– ORIGIN Middle English: via Old French and late Latin from late Greek *dromōn* 'light vessel', from Greek *dromos* 'running'.

dromos /ˈdrɒmɒs/ ▶ noun (pl. **dromoi** /-mɔɪ/) an avenue or passage leading into an ancient Greek temple or tomb, especially one between rows of columns or statues.
– ORIGIN Greek, 'course, running, avenue'; related to *dramein* 'to run'.

drone ▶ verb [no obj.] make a continuous low humming sound: *in the far distance a machine droned*. ■ speak tediously in a dull monotonous tone: *he reached for another beer while Jim* **droned on**. ■ [with adverbial of direction] move with a continuous humming sound: *traffic droned up and down the street*.
▶ noun 1 a continuous low humming sound: *he nodded off to the drone of the car engine*. ■ informal a monotonous speech: *only twenty minutes of the hour-long drone had passed*.
2 a continuous musical note of low pitch. ■ a musical instrument, or part of one, sounding a continuous note of low pitch, in particular (also **drone pipe**) a pipe in a bagpipe or (also **drone string**) a string in an instrument such as a hurdy-gurdy or a sitar.
3 a male bee in a colony of social bees, which does no work but can fertilize a queen. ■ a person who does no useful work and lives off others.
4 a remote-controlled pilotless aircraft or missile.
– ORIGIN Old English *drān*, *drǣn* 'male bee', from a West Germanic verb meaning 'resound, boom'; related to Dutch *dreunen* 'to drone', German *dröhnen* 'to roar', and Swedish *dröna* 'to drowse'.

drone fly ▶ noun a hoverfly that resembles a honeybee. Its larva is the rat-tailed maggot. ● *Eristalis tenax*, family Syrphidae.

drongo /ˈdrɒŋɡəʊ/ ▶ noun (pl. **drongos** or **drongoes**) 1 a songbird with glossy black plumage and typically a long forked tail and a crest, found in Africa, southern Asia, and Australia. ● Family Dicruridae and genus *Dicrurus*: several species.
2 informal, chiefly Austral./NZ a stupid or incompetent person.
– ORIGIN mid 19th cent.: from Malagasy. Sense 2 is said to be from the name of an Australian racehorse of the 1920s which consistently finished last or near last.

droob /druːb/ ▶ noun Austral. informal an unprepossessing or contemptible person.
– ORIGIN 1930s: perhaps related to **DROOP**.

droog /druːɡ/ ▶ noun informal a young man belonging to a street gang.
– ORIGIN 1962: coined by Anthony Burgess in *A Clockwork Orange*; alteration of Russian *drug* 'friend'.

drookit /ˈdrʊkɪt/ (also **droukit**) ▶ adjective Scottish extremely wet; drenched.

– ORIGIN early 16th cent.: origin uncertain; cf. Old Norse *drukna* 'to be drowned'.

drool ▶ verb [no obj.] drop saliva uncontrollably from the mouth: *the baby begins to drool, then to cough.* ■ informal make an excessive and obvious show of pleasure or desire: *I could imagine him as a schoolmaster being **drooled over** by the girls.*
▶ noun [mass noun] saliva falling from the mouth.
– ORIGIN early 19th cent.: contraction of DRIVEL.

droop ▶ verb [no obj.] bend or hang downwards limply: *a long black cloak drooped from his shoulders.* ■ sag down from or as if from weariness or dejection: *his eyelids drooped and he became drowsy.* ■ [with obj.] cause to bend or hang downwards: *James hid his face in his hands and drooped his head.*
▶ noun [in sing.] an act or instance of drooping; a limp or weary attitude: *the exhausted droop of her shoulders.*
– ORIGIN Middle English: from Old Norse *drúpa* 'hang the head'; related to DRIP and DROP.

droop-snoot ▶ noun informal a downward-sloping nose of an aircraft or motor vehicle, especially one that is of variable pitch, giving an efficient aerodynamic profile.

droopy ▶ adjective (**droopier**, **droopiest**) hanging down limply; drooping: *a droopy moustache.* ■ lacking strength or spirit: *she was a lovely girl in a rather droopy, Pre-Raphaelite way.*
– DERIVATIVES **droopily** adverb, **droopiness** noun.

drop ▶ verb (**drops**, **dropping**, **dropped**) [with obj.]
1 let or make (something) fall vertically: *the fire was caused by someone dropping a lighted cigarette | they dropped bombs on Caen during the raid.* ■ deliver (supplies or troops) by parachute: *the airlift dropped food into the camp.* ■ Rugby score (a goal) by a drop kick: (as adj. **dropped**) *Botha responded with a superb dropped goal.* ■ (of an animal) give birth to (young). ■ informal take (a drug, especially LSD) orally: *he dropped a lot of acid in the Sixties.*
2 [no obj. and usu. with adverbial] fall vertically: *the spoon dropped with a clatter from her hand.* ■ (of a person) allow oneself to fall; let oneself down without jumping: *they escaped by climbing out of the window and dropping to the ground.* ■ (of a person or animal) sink to or towards the ground: *he dropped to his knees in the mud.* ■ informal collapse or die from exhaustion: *he looked **ready to drop**.* ■ (of ground) slope steeply down: *the land drops away to the river.*
3 make or become lower, weaker, or less: [with obj.] *he dropped his voice as she came into the room* | [no obj.] *pre-tax profits dropped by 37 per cent | tourism has **dropped off** in the last few years.*
4 abandon or discontinue (a course of action or study): *the charges against him were dropped last year.* ■ discard or exclude (someone or something): *they were dropped from the team in the reshuffle.* ■ informal stop associating with: *I was under pressure from family and friends to drop Barbara.*
5 set down or unload (a passenger or goods), especially on the way to somewhere else: *he **dropped** the load **off** at a dealer's | his mum dropped him outside and drove off to work.* ■ [with obj. and adverbial] put or leave in a particular place without ceremony or formality: *just drop it in the post when you've got time.* ■ mention in passing, typically in order to impress: *she dropped a remark about having been included in the selection.* ■ Brit. informal (of a DJ) select and play (a record): *various guest DJs drop quality tunes both old and new.* ■ informal release (a musical recording).
6 (in sport) fail to win (a point or a match): *the club have yet to drop a point in the Second Division.* ■ informal lose (money) through gambling: *he reckoned I'd dropped forty thousand pounds.*
7 Bridge force or be forced to play (a relatively high card) as a loser under an opponent's higher card, because it is the only card in its suit held in the hand.
▶ noun **1** a small round or pear-shaped portion of liquid that hangs or falls or adheres to a surface: *the first **drops of rain** splashed on the ground.* ■ [often with negative] a very small amount of liquid: *there was not a drop of water in sight.* ■ [usu. with negative] a small drink of spirits: *he doesn't touch a drop during the week.* ■ (**drops**) liquid medication to be measured or applied in very small amounts: *eye drops.*
2 [usu. in sing.] an instance of falling or dropping: *they left within five minutes of the drop of the curtain.* ■ an act of dropping supplies or troops by parachute: *the planes finally managed to make the drop.* ■ a fall in amount, quality, or rate: *a significant **drop in** consumer spending.* ■ an abrupt or steep fall or slope: *standing on the lip of a sixty-foot drop.* ■ (**the drop**) informal the relegation of a sports team to a lower league or division. ■ (**the drop**) Bridge the playing of a high card underneath an opponent's higher card, because it is the only card in its suit held in the hand.
3 something that drops or is dropped, in particular: ■ a section of theatrical scenery lowered from the flies; a drop cloth or drop curtain. ■ a trapdoor on a gallows, the opening of which causes the prisoner to fall and thus be hanged. ■ (**the drop**) execution by hanging.
4 ■ [usu. with modifier] a sweet or lozenge: *a chocolate drop.*
5 informal a delivery: *I got to the depot and made the drop.* ■ US a letter box. ■ a hiding place for stolen, illicit, or secret things: *the lavatory's water cistern could be used as a letter drop.*
– PHRASES **at the drop of a hat** informal without hesitation or good reason: *he used to be very bashful, blushing at the drop of a hat.* **drop one's aitches** omit the 'h' sound from the beginning of words. **drop asleep** fall gently asleep, especially without intending to. **drop the ball** N. Amer. informal make a mistake; mishandle things: *I really dropped the ball on this one.* **drop a brick** Brit. informal make an indiscreet or embarrassing remark: *he dropped a brick when he admitted that he knew where we were going.* **drop a curtsy** Brit. make a curtsy. **drop dead** die suddenly and unexpectedly: *she had seen her father drop dead of a heart attack.* ■ [in imperative] informal used as an expression of intense scorn or dislike. **drop a** (or **the**) **dime on** see DIME. **drop one's guard** abandon one's habitual defensive or protective stance. **drop a hint** (or **drop hints**) give a hint or hints as if casually or unconsciously: *he was dropping hints that in future he would be taking a back seat in politics.* **a drop in the ocean** (or N. Amer. **bucket**) a very small amount compared with what is needed or expected: *the £550 million saving is likely to be a drop in the ocean.* **drop someone a line** send someone a note or letter in a casual manner: *drop me a line at the usual address.* **drop names** another term for NAME-DROP (see NAME-DROPPING). **drop one's serve** (in tennis) lose a game in which one is serving. **drop a stitch** let a stitch fall off the end of a knitting needle. **drop one's trousers** deliberately let one's trousers fall down, especially in a public place. **have the drop on** informal have the advantage over: *if your enemy gets the drop on you he can kill you.* **have had a drop too much** informal be drunk: *obstreperous squaddies who have had a drop too much.*
– PHRASAL VERBS **drop back/behind** fall back or get left behind: *the colt was struggling to stay with the pace and started to drop back.* **drop by/in** call informally and briefly as a visitor: *they would unexpectedly drop in on us.* **drop into 1** call casually and informally at (a place): *he'd actually considered dropping into one of the pickup bars.* **2** pass quickly and easily into (a habitual state or manner): *she couldn't help dropping into a Geordie accent.* **drop off** fall asleep easily, especially without intending to: *struggle as she might, she kept dropping off.* **drop out 1** cease to participate in a race or competition. **2** abandon a course of study: *she had **dropped out of** college.* **3** reject conventional society to pursue an alternative lifestyle. **4** Rugby restart play with a drop kick. ■ score a drop goal.
– DERIVATIVES **droppable** adjective.
– ORIGIN Old English *dropa* (noun), *droppian* (verb), of Germanic origin; related to German *Tropfen* 'a drop', *tropfen* 'to drip', also to DRIP and DROOP.

drop capital (also **drop initial**) ▶ noun a large capital letter at the beginning of a section of text, occupying more than the depth of one line.

drop cloth ▶ noun **1** another term for DROP CURTAIN. **2** North American term for DUST SHEET.

drop curtain ▶ noun a curtain or painted cloth lowered vertically on to a theatre stage.

drop-dead ▶ adjective informal used to emphasize how attractive someone or something is: *her drop-dead good looks* | [as submodifier] ***a drop-dead gorgeous** Hollywood icon.*

drop-down ▶ adjective dropping down or unfolding when required: *a drop-down bed.* ■ Computing (of a menu) appearing below a menu title when it is selected, and remaining until used or dismissed. Compare with PULL-DOWN.

drop-forged ▶ adjective (of a metal object) made by forcing hot metal into or through a die with a drop hammer.
– DERIVATIVES **drop-forging** noun.

drop goal ▶ noun Rugby a goal scored in open play by drop-kicking the ball over the crossbar, scoring three points (rugby union) or one point (rugby league).

drop hammer ▶ noun a large, heavy weight raised mechanically and allowed to drop, as used in drop-forging and piledriving.

drop handlebars (also **dropped handlebars**) ▶ plural noun bicycle handlebars of which the handles are bent below the rest of the bar, used especially on racing cycles.

drophead ▶ noun Brit. a car having a fabric roof that can be folded down; a convertible.

drop-in ▶ adjective **1** visited on an informal basis without booking or appointments: *a drop-in disco.* **2** (of an object such as a chair seat) designed to drop into position.

D

drop-in centre ▶ noun a place run by a welfare agency or charity where people may call casually for advice or assistance.

drop initial ▶ noun another term for DROP CAPITAL.

drop kick ▶ noun (chiefly in rugby) a kick made by dropping the ball and kicking it as it bounces up from the ground. ■ (chiefly in martial arts) a flying kick made against an opponent while dropping to the ground.
▶ verb (**drop-kick**) [with obj.] kick using a drop kick.

drop-leaf ▶ adjective (of a table) having a hinged flap.

droplet ▶ noun a very small drop of a liquid: *droplets of water.*

drop-off ▶ noun **1** a decline or decrease: *a sudden **drop-off in** tourism.* **2** N. Amer. a sheer downward slope; a cliff: *dizzy drop-offs on either side.*

dropout ▶ noun **1** a person who has abandoned a course of study or who has rejected conventional society to pursue an alternative lifestyle: *a college dropout.* **2** Rugby the restarting of play with a drop kick. **3** a momentary loss of recorded audio signal or an error in reading data on a magnetic tape or disk, usually due to a flaw in the coating. **4** (usu. **dropouts**) a U-shaped slot at the end of a fork or stay on a bicycle, made to receive the axle and enabling the wheel to be changed rapidly.

dropped kerb ▶ noun Brit. a small ramp built into the kerb of a pavement to make it easier for people using pushchairs or wheelchairs to pass from the pavement to the road.

dropper ▶ noun **1** a short glass tube with a rubber bulb at one end and a tiny hole at the other, for measuring out drops of medicine or other liquids. **2** Austral./NZ & S. African a light vertical stave in a fence, especially a lath used to separate the wires of a wire fence. **3** Fishing a subsidiary line or loop of filament attached to a main line or leader.
– ORIGIN mid 17th cent. (in the sense 'a person who lets something drop'); sense 1 is first recorded in the late 19th cent.

droppings ▶ plural noun the excrement of certain animals, such as rodents, sheep, birds, and insects.

drop scene ▶ noun a drop curtain used as part of stage scenery, especially one in front of which a scene is played while the setting is changed behind. ■ the last scene of a play.

drop scone ▶ noun a small, thick pancake made by dropping spoonfuls of batter on to a griddle or other heated surface.

dropseed ▶ noun [mass noun] a grass that readily drops its seeds. ● Genus *Sporobolus*, family Gramineae: several species, including the widespread North American **sand dropseed** (*S. cryptandrus*), which has a high yield of edible grain.

drop-ship ▶ verb (**drop-ships**, **drop-shipping**, **drop-shipped**) [with obj.] provide (goods) by direct delivery from the manufacturer to the retailer or customer.
– DERIVATIVES **drop shipment** noun.

drop shot ▶ noun (chiefly in tennis or squash) a softly hit shot, usually with backspin, which drops abruptly to the ground.

drop shoulder (also **dropped shoulder**) ▶ noun a style of shoulder on a garment cut so that the seam is positioned on the upper arm rather than the shoulder.

dropsical /ˈdrɒpsɪk(ə)l/ ▶ adjective affected with or characteristic of dropsy; oedematous.
– ORIGIN late 17th cent.: from DROPSY[1], replacing earlier *hydropic(al)*, via Latin from Greek *hudrōps* 'dropsy'.

dropside ▶ adjective (of a cot or a truck) having a side that drops down to open.
▶ noun a side that drops down in this way.

D

drop-stitch ▸ adjective denoting an openwork pattern in knitted garments made by dropping a made stitch at intervals.

dropsy[1] /ˈdrɒpsi/ ▸ noun (pl. **dropsies**) old-fashioned or less technical term for **OEDEMA**.
– ORIGIN Middle English: shortening of *idropesie*, earlier form of obsolete *hydropsy*, via Old French and Latin from Greek *hudrōps* 'dropsy', from *hudōr* 'water'.

dropsy[2] /ˈdrɒpsi/ ▸ noun (pl. **dropsies**) Brit. informal a tip or bribe: *McCloy's little dropsy for services rendered.*
– ORIGIN 1930s: slang, elaborated form of slang *drop* 'a bribe'.

drop tank ▸ noun an external fuel tank on an aircraft which can be jettisoned when empty.

drop test ▸ noun a test of the strength of an object, in which it is dropped under standard conditions or a set weight is dropped on it from a given height.
– DERIVATIVES **drop-testing** noun.

drop-top ▸ noun another term for **DROPHEAD**.

drop waist (also **dropped waist**) ▸ noun a style of waistline on a dress cut so that the seam is positioned at the hips rather than the waist.

dropwort ▸ noun a Eurasian grassland plant with small white flowers and divided leaves, related to meadowsweet. ● *Filipendula vulgaris*, family Rosaceae.
– ORIGIN Middle English: so named because it has small drop-like fibrous tubers on its roots.

drop zone (also **dropping zone**) ▸ noun a designated area into which troops or supplies are dropped by parachute or in which skydivers land.

drosera /ˈdrɒs(ə)rə/ ▸ noun a sundew (insectivorous plant). ● Genus *Drosera*, family Droseraceae.
– ORIGIN modern Latin, from Greek *droseros* 'dewy' (from the appearance of the glistening hairs on the leaves).

droshky /ˈdrɒʃki/ ▸ noun (pl. **droshkies**) historical a low four-wheeled open carriage of a kind formerly used in Russia.
– ORIGIN early 19th cent.: from Russian *drozhki*, diminutive of *drogi* 'wagon', from *droga* 'shaft, carriage pole'.

drosophila /drɒˈsɒfɪlə/ ▸ noun a small fruit fly, used extensively in genetic research because of its large chromosomes, numerous varieties, and rapid rate of reproduction. ● Genus *Drosophila*, family Drosophilidae: several species, in particular *D. melanogaster*.
– ORIGIN modern Latin, from Greek *drosos* 'dew, moisture' + *philos* 'loving'.

dross ▸ noun [mass noun] **1** something regarded as worthless; rubbish: *there are bargains if you have the patience to sift through the dross.*
2 foreign matter, dregs, or mineral waste, in particular scum formed on the surface of molten metal.
– DERIVATIVES **drossy** adjective (**drossier**, **drossiest**).
– ORIGIN Old English *drōs* (in the sense 'scum on molten metal'); related to Dutch *droesem* and German *Drusen* 'dregs, lees'.

Drottningholm /ˈdrɒtnɪŋˌhɒlm/ the winter palace of the Swedish royal family, on an island to the west of Stockholm.

drought /draʊt/ ▸ noun a prolonged period of abnormally low rainfall, leading to a shortage of water. ■ [usu. with modifier] a prolonged absence of something specified: *he ended a five-game goal drought.* ■ [mass noun] archaic thirst.
– ORIGIN late Old English *drūgath* 'dryness', of Germanic origin; compare with Dutch *droogte*; related to **DRY**.

drouth /draʊθ/ ▸ noun dialect or literary form of **DROUGHT**.
– DERIVATIVES **drouthy** adjective.

Drouzhba /ˈdruːʒbə/ a resort town on the Black Sea coast of Bulgaria. Also called **SVETI KONSTANTIN**.

drove[1] past of **DRIVE**.

drove[2] ▸ noun a herd or flock of animals being driven in a body: *a drove of cattle.* ■ a large number of people or things doing or undergoing the same thing: *tourists have stayed away in droves this summer.*
▸ verb [with obj.] historical drive (livestock, especially cattle) to market.
– DERIVATIVES **drover** noun.
– ORIGIN Old English *drāf*, related to *drifan* 'to drive'.

drove road ▸ noun an ancient roadway along which cattle were driven to market.

drown ▸ verb [no obj.] die through submersion in and inhalation of water: *a motorist drowned when her car plunged off the edge of a quay* | (**be drowned**) *two fishermen were drowned when their motor boat capsized.* ■ [with obj.] deliberately kill (a person or animal) by drowning: *he immediately drowned four of the dogs.* ■ [with obj.] submerge or flood (an area): *when the ice melted the valleys were drowned.* ■ [with obj.] (of a sound) make (another sound) inaudible by being much louder: *his voice was **drowned out** by the approaching engine noise.* ■ [no obj.] (**be drowning in**) be overwhelmed by a large amount of something: *both business and household sectors are drowning in debt* | *art dealers are still **drowning in a sea of** paperwork.* ■ [with obj.] (**drown something in**) cover or immerse food in: *good pizza is not eight inches thick and drowned in tomato sauce.*
– PHRASES **drown one's sorrows** forget one's problems by getting drunk. **like a drowned rat** extremely wet and bedraggled.
– ORIGIN Middle English (originally northern): related to Old Norse *drukkna* 'to be drowned', also to **DRINK**.

drowned valley ▸ noun a valley partly or wholly submerged by a rise in sea level.

drowse /draʊz/ ▸ verb [no obj.] be half asleep; doze intermittently: *he was beginning to drowse in his chair.* ■ [with obj.] archaic make sleepy. ■ archaic be sluggish or inactive.
▸ noun [in sing.] a light sleep; a condition of being half asleep.
– ORIGIN late 16th cent.: back-formation from **DROWSY**.

drowsiness ▸ noun [mass noun] a feeling of being sleepy and lethargic; sleepiness: *this drug can cause drowsiness.*

drowsy ▸ adjective (**drowsier**, **drowsiest**) sleepy and lethargic; half asleep: *the wine had made her drowsy.* ■ causing sleepiness: *the drowsy heat of the meadows.* ■ (of a place) peaceful and quiet: *a drowsy suburb called Surrey Hills.*
– DERIVATIVES **drowsily** adverb.
– ORIGIN late 15th cent.: probably from the stem of Old English *drūsian* 'be languid or slow', of Germanic origin; related to **DREARY**.

drub ▸ verb (**drubs**, **drubbing**, **drubbed**) [with obj.] hit or beat (someone) repeatedly. ■ informal defeat thoroughly in a match or contest: *the Cleveland Indians drubbed Baltimore 9–0.*
– ORIGIN early 17th cent.: probably from Arabic *ḍaraba* 'to beat, bastinado'. The first recorded uses in English are by travellers in the Near East referring specifically to the punishment of bastinado.

drubbing ▸ noun a beating; a thrashing: *I'll give the scoundrels a drubbing if I can!* ■ informal a resounding defeat in a match or contest.

drudge ▸ noun a person made to do hard menial or dull work: *she was little more than a drudge round the house.*
▸ verb [no obj.] archaic do hard menial work.
– ORIGIN Middle English (as a noun): of unknown origin; perhaps related to **DRAG**.

drudgery ▸ noun [mass noun] hard menial or dull work: *domestic drudgery.*

drug ▸ noun a medicine or other substance which has a physiological effect when ingested or otherwise introduced into the body: *a new drug aimed at sufferers from Parkinson's disease.* ■ a substance taken for its narcotic or stimulant effects, often illegally.
▸ verb (**drugs**, **drugging**, **drugged**) [with obj.] administer a drug to (someone) in order to induce stupor or insensibility: *they were drugged to keep them quiet.* ■ add a drug to (food or drink). ■ [no obj.] informal take illegally obtained drugs: *she was convinced he was out drinking and drugging.*
– PHRASES **do drugs** informal take illegal drugs. **on drugs** taking medically prescribed drugs: *on drugs for high blood pressure.* ■ under the influence of or habitually taking illegal drugs.
– ORIGIN Middle English: from Old French *drogue*, possibly from Middle Dutch *droge vate*, literally 'dry vats', referring to the contents (i.e. dry goods).

drug abuse ▸ noun [mass noun] the habitual taking of illegal drugs.

drug addict ▸ noun a person who is addicted to an illegal drug.

drug baron (also **drugs baron**) ▸ noun a person who controls an organization dealing in illegal drugs.

drugged ▸ adjective (of a person) unconscious or in a stupor as a result of taking or being given a drug: *in his drugged state.* ■ (of food or drink) adulterated with a drug: *he offered them drugged wine.*

drugget /ˈdrʌɡɪt/ ▸ noun a floor covering made of a coarse woven fabric. ■ [mass noun] the fabric used for such coverings.
– ORIGIN mid 16th cent.: from French *droguet*, from *drogue* in the sense 'poor-quality article'.

druggist ▸ noun N. Amer. a pharmacist or retailer of medicinal drugs.
– ORIGIN early 17th cent.: from French *droguiste*, from *drogue* 'drug'.

druggy informal ▸ adjective (**druggier**, **druggiest**) caused by, involving, or given to taking illegal drugs: *a druggy haze* | *the druggy world of rock and roll.*
▸ noun (also **druggie**) (pl. **druggies**) a drug addict or habitual user of drugs.
– ORIGIN late 16th cent. (as an adjective): from **DRUG** + **-Y**[1]. The noun dates from the 1960s.

drug squad (also **drugs squad**) ▸ noun chiefly Brit. a division of a police force investigating crimes involving illegal drugs.

drugstore ▸ noun N. Amer. a pharmacy which also sells toiletries and other articles.

drugstore beetle ▸ noun another term for **BISCUIT BEETLE**.

drug test ▸ noun a test performed on blood or urine to determine the presence or absence of proscribed drugs and used especially to detect athletes using performance-enhancing drugs such as steroids.

Druid /ˈdruːɪd/ ▸ noun a priest, magician, or soothsayer in the ancient Celtic religion. ■ a member of a present-day group claiming to represent or be derived from this religion.
– DERIVATIVES **Druidic** adjective, **Druidical** adjective, **Druidism** noun.
– ORIGIN from Latin *druidae*, *druides* (plural), from Gaulish; related to Irish *draoidh* 'magician, sorcerer'.

drum[1] ▸ noun **1** a percussion instrument sounded by being struck with sticks or the hands, typically cylindrical, barrel-shaped, or bowl-shaped, with a taut membrane over one or both ends. ■ (**drums**) a drum kit. ■ (**drums**) the percussion section of a band or orchestra. ■ [in sing.] a sound made by or resembling that of a drum: *the drum of their feet.* ■ historical a military drummer.
2 a cylindrical container or receptacle: *a drum of powdered bleach.* ■ a rotating cylindrical part in a washing machine, in which the washing is placed. ■ Architecture the circular vertical wall supporting a dome. ■ Architecture a stone block forming part of a column. ■ Austral./NZ a tramp's bundle of belongings.
3 Brit. informal a house or flat.
4 an evening or afternoon tea party of a kind that was popular in the late 18th and early 19th century.
5 Austral./NZ informal a piece of reliable inside information: *he had got the drum that the police wouldn't lock us up.* [early 20th cent.: perhaps by association with the musical instrument used to give a signal.]
▸ verb (**drums**, **drumming**, **drummed**) **1** [no obj.] play on a drum. ■ make a continuous rhythmic noise: *she felt the blood drumming in her ears* | (as noun **drumming**) *the drumming of hooves.* ■ [with obj.] beat (the fingers, feet, etc.) repeatedly on a surface, especially as a sign of impatience or annoyance: *waiting around an empty table, drumming their fingers.* ■ (of a woodpecker) strike the bill rapidly on a dead trunk or branch, especially as a sound indicating a territorial claim. ■ (of a snipe) vibrate the outer tail feathers in a diving display flight, making a throbbing sound.
2 [with obj.] Austral./NZ informal, dated give (someone) reliable information or a warning: *I'm drumming you, if they come I'm going.* [see sense 5 of the noun.]
– PHRASES **beat** (or **bang**) **the drum of** (or **for**) be ostentatiously in support of: *he bangs the drum of the free market.* **drum something home** another way of saying **DRUM SOMETHING INTO**: *they keep drumming this point home.*
– PHRASAL VERBS **drum something into** make (someone) learn something by constant repetition: *it had been drummed into them to dress correctly.* **drum someone out** expel or dismiss someone with ignominy from a place or institution: *he was **drummed out** of the air force.* [with allusion to the formal military drum beat accompanying dismissal from a regiment.] **drum something up** attempt to obtain something by canvassing or soliciting: *the organizers are hoping to drum up support from local businesses.*
– ORIGIN Middle English: from Middle Dutch or Low German *tromme*, of imitative origin.

drum[2] ▸ noun Scottish & Irish a long, narrow hill, especially one separating two parallel valleys.
– ORIGIN early 18th cent.: from Scottish Gaelic and Irish *druim* 'ridge'.

drum³ (also **drumfish**) ▶ noun (pl. **same** or **drums**) a fish that makes a drumming sound by vibrating its swim bladder, found mainly in estuarine and shallow coastal waters. Also called CROAKER. ● Family Sciaenidae (the **drum family**): many species, including the **black drum** (*Pogonias cromis*) of the western Atlantic. The drum family also includes the mulloway and a number of marine fishes that resemble salmon (e.g. the weakfish).

drum and bass ▶ noun [mass noun] a type of dance music characterized by bare instrumentation consisting largely of electronic drums and bass, originating in Britain during the early 1990s.

drumbeat ▶ noun a stroke or pattern of strokes on a drum: *she was aware of a constant, faint drumbeat.*

drum brake ▶ noun a type of vehicle brake in which brake shoes press against the inside of a drum on the wheel.

drumfire ▶ noun [mass noun] heavy continuous rapid artillery fire.

drumfish ▶ noun (pl. **same** or **drumfishes**) see DRUM³.

drumhead ▶ noun **1** the membrane or skin of a drum.
2 a winter cabbage of a flat-topped variety.
3 chiefly historical the circular top of a ship's capstan, with holes into which bars are placed to turn it.
▶ adjective [attrib.] carried out by or as if by an army in the field; improvised or summary: *a drumhead court martial.*

drum kit ▶ noun a set of drums, cymbals, and other percussion instruments, used with drumsticks in jazz and popular music. The most basic components are a foot-operated bass drum, a snare drum, a suspended cymbal, and one or more tom-toms.

drumlin /ˈdrʌmlɪn/ ▶ noun Geology a low oval mound or small hill, typically one of a group, consisting of compacted boulder clay moulded by past glacial action.
– ORIGIN mid 19th cent.: probably from DRUM² + *-lin* from -LING.

drum machine ▶ noun a programmable electronic device able to imitate the sounds of a drum kit.

drum major ▶ noun **1** a non-commissioned officer commanding the drummers of a regimental band.
2 the male leader of a marching band, who often twirls a baton. ■ a male member of a baton-twirling parading group.

drum majorette ▶ noun the female leader of a marching band, who often twirls a baton. ■ a female member of a marching band or other parading group.

drummer ▶ noun **1** a person who plays a drum or drums.
2 informal, chiefly US a travelling sales representative: *a drummer in electronic software.* [from DRUM SOMETHING UP (see DRUM¹).]
3 (also **silver drummer**) a deep-bodied marine fish with dark longitudinal stripes, found in shallow coastal waters of Australia. ● *Kyphosus sydneyanus*, family Kyphosidae.
4 Brit. informal, dated a thief or burglar.

drum pad ▶ noun an electronic device with one or more flat pads which imitate the sounds of a drum kit when struck.

drum roll ▶ noun a rapid succession of beats sounded on a drum, often used to introduce an announcement or event.

drumstick ▶ noun **1** a stick, typically with a shaped or padded head, used for beating a drum.
2 the lower joint of the leg of a cooked chicken, turkey, or other fowl.

drumstick primrose (also **drumstick primula**) ▶ noun a Himalayan primula with a globular head of flowers on an erect stem. ● *Primula denticulata*, family Primulaceae.

drunk past participle of DRINK. ▶ adjective [predic.] affected by alcohol to the extent of losing control of one's faculties or behaviour: *he was so drunk he lurched from wall to wall | she was* ***drunk on*** *vodka.* ■ (**drunk with**) overcome with (a strong emotion): *the crowd was high on euphoria and drunk with patriotism.*
▶ noun a person who is drunk or who habitually drinks to excess. ■ informal a drinking bout; a period of drunkenness: *he used to go on these blind drunks.*
– PHRASES **drunk and disorderly** creating a public disturbance under the influence of alcohol. (**as**) **drunk as a lord** (or **skunk**) extremely drunk.

drunkard ▶ noun a person who is habitually drunk.
– ORIGIN Middle English: from Middle Low German *drunkert*.

drunk driving (also **drunken driving**) ▶ noun North American term for DRINK-DRIVING.
– DERIVATIVES **drunk driver** noun.

drunken ▶ adjective [attrib.] drunk or intoxicated: *gangs of drunken youths roamed the streets.* ■ habitually or frequently drunk: *his violent, drunken father.* ■ caused by or showing the effects of drink: *the man's drunken, slurred speech.*
– DERIVATIVES **drunkenly** adverb.
– ORIGIN Old English, archaic past participle of DRINK.

drunkenness ▶ noun [mass noun] the state of being drunk; intoxication: *a growing problem of drunkenness.*

drunk tank ▶ noun N. Amer. informal a large prison cell for the detention of drunks.

drupe /druːp/ ▶ noun **1** Botany a fleshy fruit with thin skin and a central stone containing the seed, e.g. a plum, cherry, almond, or olive.
2 a small marine mollusc with a thick knobbly shell, found mainly in the Indo-Pacific. ● Genus *Drupa*, family Muricidae, class Gastropoda.
– DERIVATIVES **drupaceous** adjective (sense 1).
– ORIGIN mid 18th cent.: from Latin *drupa* 'overripe olive', from Greek *druppa* 'olive'.

drupel /ˈdruːp(ə)l/ ▶ noun Botany any of the small individual drupes forming a fleshy aggregate fruit such as a blackberry or raspberry.
– ORIGIN mid 19th cent.: from modern Latin *drupella*, diminutive of *drupa* 'overripe olive' (see DRUPE).

drupelet /ˈdruːplɪt/ ▶ noun another term for DRUPEL.

Drury Lane /ˈdrʊəri/ the site in London of the Theatre Royal, one of London's most famous theatres.

druse /druːz/ ▶ noun **1** Geology a rock cavity lined with a crust of projecting crystals. ■ the crust of crystals lining such a cavity.
2 Botany a rounded cluster of calcium oxalate crystals found in some plant cells.
– DERIVATIVES **drusy** adjective (Geology).
– ORIGIN early 19th cent.: via French from German *Druse* 'weathered ore'.

druther /ˈdrʌðə/ N. Amer. informal ▶ noun (usu. **one's druthers**) one's preference in a matter: *if I had my druthers, I would prefer to be a writer.*
▶ adverb rather; by preference.
– ORIGIN late 19th cent.: from a US regional pronunciation of *I'd rather*, contraction of *would rather*.

Druze /druːz/ (also **Druse**) ▶ noun (pl. **same**, **Druzes**, or **Druses**) a member of a political and religious sect of Islamic origin, living chiefly in Lebanon and Syria. The Druze broke away from the Ismaili Muslims in the 11th century; they are regarded as heretical by the Muslim community at large.
– ORIGIN from French, from Arabic *durūz* (plural), from the name of one of their founders, Muhammad ibn Ismail *al-Darazī* (died 1019).

dry ▶ adjective (**drier**, **driest**) **1** free from moisture or liquid; not wet or moist: *the jacket kept me warm and dry | he wiped the table dry with his shirt.* ■ (of paint, ink, etc.) having lost all wetness or moisture over a period of time: *wait until the paint is dry.* ■ for use without liquid: *the conversion of dry latrines into the flushing type.* ■ with little or no rainfall or humidity: *the West Coast has had two dry winters in a row.* ■ (of a river, lake, or stream) empty of water as a result of lack of rainfall: *the river is always dry at this time of year.* ■ (of a source) not yielding a supply of water or oil: *a dry well.* ■ thirsty or thirst-making: *working in the hot sun is making me dry.* ■ (of a cow or other domestic animal) no longer producing milk. ■ without grease or other moisturizer or lubricator: *cream conditioners for dry hair.* ■ (of bread or toast) without butter or other spreads: *only dry bread and water.*
2 (of information, writing, etc.) dully factual: *the dry facts of the matter.* ■ unemotional, undemonstrative, or impassive: *it transformed him from a dry administrator into the people's hero.*
3 (of a joke or sense of humour) subtle and expressed in a matter-of-fact way: *he delighted his friends with a dry, covert sense of humour.*
4 prohibiting the sale or consumption of alcoholic drink: *the country is strictly dry, in accordance with Islamic law.* ■ (of a person) no longer addicted to or drinking alcohol: *I heard much talk about how sobriety was more than staying straight or dry.*
5 (of an alcoholic drink) not sweet: *a dry, medium-bodied red wine.*
6 Brit. relating to political 'dries' sense 3 of the noun; rigidly monetarist.
▶ verb (**dries**, **drying**, **dried**) [no obj.] **1** become dry: *waiting for the paint to dry | do not let the soil dry out | pools are left as the rivers* ***dry up.*** ■ [with obj.] cause to become dry: *they had washed and dried their hair.* ■ [with obj.] wipe tears from (the eyes): *she dried her eyes and blew her nose.* ■ (also Brit. **dry up**) wipe dishes dry with a cloth after they have been washed. ■ [with obj.] (usu. as adj. **dried**) preserve by allowing or encouraging evaporation of moisture from: *dried flowers.*
2 theatrical slang forget one's lines: *a colleague of mine once dried in the middle of a scene.*
▶ noun (pl. **dries** or **drys**) **1** the process or an instance of drying.
2 (**the dry**) a dry or covered place. ■ chiefly Austral. the dry season: *the grass was yellowing and the dry had started.* ■ Austral. a tract of waterless country: *the forty-mile dry.*
3 (usu. **dries**) Brit. a Conservative politician (especially in the 1980s) in favour of strict monetarist policies.
4 US a person in favour of the prohibition of alcohol.
– PHRASES **come up dry** N. Amer. be unsuccessful: *experiments have so far come up dry.* (**as**) **dry as a bone** extremely dry. (**as**) **dry as dust** extremely dry. ■ extremely dull; lacking emotion, expression, or interest: *what the students learned was as dry as dust.* **there wasn't a dry eye** (**in the house**) (with reference to a play, film, or similar event) everyone in the audience was moved to tears.
– PHRASAL VERBS **dry an animal off** cease milking and reduce the rations of a cow or other animal so that it stops producing milk. **dry out** informal overcome alcoholism: *he intends to dry out and get his life back together again.* **dry up 1** informal cease talking: *then he dried up, and Phil couldn't get another word out of him.* **2** (of something perceived as a continuous flow or source) decrease and stop: *his commissions began to dry up.*
– DERIVATIVES **dryish** adjective, **dryness** noun.
– ORIGIN Old English *drȳge* (adjective), *drȳgan* (verb), of Germanic origin; related to Middle Low German *dröge*, Dutch *droog*, and German *trocken*.

dryad /ˈdrʌɪəd, -ad/ ▶ noun **1** (in folklore and Greek mythology) a nymph inhabiting a tree or wood.
2 a dark brown Eurasian butterfly with two prominent bluish eyespots on each forewing. ● *Minois dryas*, subfamily Satyrinae, family Nymphalidae.
– ORIGIN via Old French and Latin from Greek *druas*, *druad-* 'tree nymph', from *drus* 'tree'.

dryad's saddle ▶ noun a common bracket fungus having a scaly yellowish-brown upper surface, found in both Eurasia and North America and edible when young. ● *Polyporus squamosus*, family Polyporaceae, class Hymenomycetes.

dryas /ˈdrʌɪəs/ ▶ noun **1** a plant of a genus that comprises the mountain avens. ● Genus *Dryas*, family Rosaceae.
2 (**Dryas**) Geology the first and third climatic stages of the late-glacial period in northern Europe, in which cold conditions prevailed and plants of the genus *Dryas* were abundant. The **Older Dryas** (about 15,000 to 12,000 years ago) followed the last ice retreat, and the **Younger Dryas** (about 10,800 to 10,000 years ago) followed the Allerød stage.
– ORIGIN modern Latin, from Greek *druas* (see DRYAD). The plant (sense 1) has leaves that resemble those of the oak (hence the association with dryads, being originally nymphs of the oak).

dry battery ▶ noun an electric battery consisting of one or more dry cells.

dry bulb ▶ noun an ordinary exposed thermometer bulb, especially as used in conjunction with a wet bulb.

dry cell ▶ noun an electric cell in which the electrolyte is absorbed in a solid to form a paste, preventing spillage.

dry-clean ▶ verb [with obj.] clean (a garment) with an organic solvent, without using water: *I had my winter coat dry-cleaned recently* | (as noun **dry-cleaning**) *premises which offered dry-cleaning.*
– DERIVATIVES **dry-cleaner** noun.

dry cough ▶ noun a cough not accompanied by phlegm production.

dry-cure ▶ verb [with obj.] cure (meat or fish) with salt rather than in liquid.

Dryden /ˈdrʌɪd(ə)n/, John (1631–1700), English poet, critic, and dramatist of the Augustan Age. He is best known for *Marriage à la mode* (comedy, 1673), *All for Love* (a tragedy based on Shakespeare's *Antony and Cleopatra*, 1678), and *Absalom and Achitophel* (verse satire in heroic couplets, 1681).

dry distillation ▶ noun another term for DESTRUCTIVE DISTILLATION.

dry dock ▸ noun a dock which can be drained of water to allow the inspection and repair of a ship's hull.
▸ verb (**dry-dock**) [with obj.] place (a ship) in a dry dock.

dryer (also **drier**) ▸ noun **1** a machine or device for drying something, especially the hair or laundry.
2 a substance mixed with oil paint or ink to promote drying.

dry eye ▸ noun [mass noun] Medicine inflammation of the conjunctiva and cornea of the eye, due to inadequate tear secretion.

D

dry-eyed ▸ adjective (of a person) not crying: *Jill was dry-eyed and stoical under assault.*

dry farming ▸ noun another term for DRYLAND FARMING.

dry fly ▸ noun an artificial fishing fly which is made to float lightly on the water.

dry-fry ▸ verb [with obj.] fry (food) in a pan without fat or oil.

dry goods ▸ plural noun **1** solid commodities traded in bulk, such as tea, sugar, and grain.
2 N. Amer. drapery and haberdashery.

dry hole ▸ noun a well drilled for oil or gas but yielding none.

dry ice ▸ noun [mass noun] solid carbon dioxide. ■ the cold dense white mist produced by this in air, used for theatrical effects.

drying oil ▸ noun an oil that thickens or hardens on exposure to air, especially one used by artists in mixing paint.

dry land ▸ noun [mass noun] land as opposed to the sea or another body of water.

dryland farming (also **dry farming**) ▸ noun [mass noun] chiefly N. Amer. a method of farming in semi-arid areas using drought-resistant crops and conserving moisture.

drylands ▸ plural noun chiefly N. Amer. an arid area; a region with low rainfall.

dry lease ▸ noun an arrangement covering the hire of an aircraft which does not include provision of a flight crew.
▸ verb (**dry-lease**) [with obj.] hire (an aircraft) on the basis of a dry lease.

dry lining ▸ noun a lining to an interior wall that does not need to be plastered.

dryly ▸ adverb variant spelling of DRILY.

dry measure ▸ noun a measure of volume for loose dry goods such as grain, tea, and sugar.

dry milk ▸ noun [mass noun] US milk that has been preserved by evaporation and reduction to powder.

dry mounting ▸ noun [mass noun] Photography a process in which a print is bonded to a mount using a layer of shellac in a hot press.

dry-nurse ▸ noun archaic a woman who looks after a baby but does not breastfeed it.

Dryopithecus /ˌdrʌɪəˈpɪθɪkəs/ ▸ noun a fossil anthropoid ape of the middle Miocene to early Pliocene periods, of a genus including the supposed common ancestor of gorillas, chimpanzees, and humans.
● Genus *Dryopithecus*, family Pongidae.
– DERIVATIVES **dryopithecine** /-ɪsiːn/ noun & adjective.
– ORIGIN modern Latin, from Greek *drus* 'tree' + *pithēkos* 'ape'.

dry painting ▸ noun another term for SAND PAINTING.

dry plate ▸ noun Photography a glass plate coated with a light-sensitive gelatin-based emulsion, used formerly as an improvement on the earlier wet plate.

dry point ▸ noun a steel needle for engraving on a bare copper plate without acid. ■ an engraving or print produced with a dry point needle. ■ [mass noun] engraving by means of a dry point needle.

dry-roasted (also **dry-roast**) ▸ adjective roasted without fat or oil: *dry-roasted peanuts.*

dry rot ▸ noun **1** [mass noun] fungal timber decay occurring in poorly ventilated conditions in buildings, resulting in cracking and powdering of the wood.
2 (also **dry rot fungus**) the fungus that causes dry rot decay. ● *Serpula lacrymans*, family Corticiaceae, class Hymenomycetes.

dry run ▸ noun informal a rehearsal of a performance or procedure before the real one: *the president went through a dry run of his speech.*

dry-salt ▸ verb another term for DRY-CURE.

dry-salter ▸ noun Brit. historical a dealer in dyes, gums, and drugs, and sometimes also in pickles and other preserved foodstuffs.

dry shampoo ▸ noun [mass noun] a shampoo in powder form, used without the addition of water.

dry shave ▸ noun a shave without using shaving foam, typically one using an electric razor.
▸ verb (**dry-shave**) [no obj.] shave without using shaving foam.
– DERIVATIVES **dry-shaver** noun.

dry-shod ▸ adjective & adverb without wetting one's shoes.

dry sink ▸ noun N. Amer. an antique kitchen cabinet with an inset basin.

dry slope (also **dry-ski slope**) ▸ noun an artificial ski slope used for practice and training.

drystone ▸ adjective [attrib.] Brit. (of a stone wall) built without using mortar.

drysuit ▸ noun a waterproof rubber suit worn for water sports and diving, under which warm clothes can be worn.

dry valley ▸ noun a valley cut by water erosion but containing no permanent surface stream, typically one occurring in an area of porous rock such as limestone.

drywall ▸ noun [mass noun] N. Amer. plasterboard.

dry wash ▸ noun US the dry bed of an intermittent stream.

dry well ▸ noun **1** a shaft or chamber constructed in the ground in order to aid drainage, sometimes containing pumping equipment.
2 another term for DRY HOLE.

DS ▸ abbreviation ■ Music dal segno. ■ Military directing staff. ■ document signed.

Ds ▸ symbol the chemical element darmstadtium.

DSC ▸ abbreviation (in the UK) Distinguished Service Cross, a decoration for distinguished active service at sea, instituted in 1914.

DSc ▸ abbreviation Doctor of Science.

DSL ▸ abbreviation digital subscriber line, a technology for the high-speed transmission of digital information over standard telephone lines.

DSM ▸ abbreviation (in the UK) Distinguished Service Medal, a medal for distinguished service at sea, instituted in 1914.

DSO ▸ abbreviation (in the UK) Distinguished Service Order, a decoration for distinguished service awarded to officers of the army and navy, instituted in 1886.

DSP ▸ abbreviation ■ (in genealogy) died without issue. [from Latin *decessit sine prole.*] ■ (in computing and sound reproduction) digital signal processor or processing.

DSS ▸ abbreviation ■ decision support system. ■ (formerly in the UK) Department of Social Security.

DST ▸ abbreviation daylight saving time.

DTD ▸ abbreviation Computing document type definition, a document that defines the tagging structure of an SGML or XML document.

DTI ▸ abbreviation (in the UK) Department of Trade and Industry.

DTP ▸ abbreviation desktop publishing.

DTs ▸ plural noun (usu. **the DTs**) informal delirium tremens.
– ORIGIN mid 19th cent.: abbreviation, originally in the singular form *DT* (now rare).

DTT ▸ abbreviation digital terrestrial television.

DTV ▸ abbreviation digital television.

DU ▸ abbreviation ■ depleted uranium. ■ Dobson unit(s).

dual ▸ adjective **1** [attrib.] consisting of two parts, elements, or aspects: *their dual role at work and home | dual-language texts in English and Italian.* ■ Grammar (in some languages) denoting an inflection that refers to exactly two people or things (as distinct from singular and plural). ■ (in an aircraft) using dual controls.
2 (often **dual to**) Mathematics (of a theorem, expression, etc.) related to another by the interchange of particular pairs of terms, such as 'point' and 'line'.
▸ noun **1** Grammar a dual form of a word. ■ [mass noun] the dual number.
2 Mathematics a theorem, expression, etc., that is dual to another.
▸ verb (**duals, dualling, dualled**) [with obj.] Brit. convert (a road) into a dual carriageway.
– DERIVATIVES **dualize** (also **dualise**) verb, **dually** adverb.
– ORIGIN late Middle English (as a noun denoting either of the two middle incisor teeth in each jaw): from Latin *dualis*, from *duo* 'two'.

dual aspect ▸ noun a layout in a room or building in which windows on adjacent walls allow for views in more than one direction: [as modifier] *a dual-aspect master bedroom.*

dual carriageway ▸ noun Brit. a road with a dividing strip between the traffic in opposite directions and usually two or more lanes in each direction.

dual control ▸ adjective (of an aircraft or vehicle) having two sets of controls, one of which is used by the instructor: *a dual-control pilot trainer.*
▸ noun (usu. **dual controls**) two such sets of controls in an aircraft or vehicle.

dual heritage ▸ noun [mass noun] the fact of having parents from different ethnic or cultural backgrounds.

dual in-line package ▸ noun see DIP.

dualism ▸ noun [mass noun] **1** the division of something conceptually into two opposed or contrasted aspects, or the state of being so divided: *a dualism between man and nature.* ■ Philosophy a theory or system of thought that regards a domain of reality in terms of two independent principles, especially mind and matter (**Cartesian dualism**). Compare with IDEALISM, MATERIALISM, MONISM. ■ the religious doctrine that the universe contains opposed powers of good and evil, especially seen as balanced equals. ■ (in Christian theology) the doctrine that Christ had two coexisting natures, human and divine.
2 the quality or condition of being dual; duality.
– DERIVATIVES **dualist** noun & adjective, **dualistic** adjective, **dualistically** adverb.
– ORIGIN late 18th cent.: from DUAL, on the pattern of French *dualisme*.

duality ▸ noun (pl. **dualities**) **1** [mass noun] the quality or condition of being dual: *this duality of purpose was discernible in the appointments.* ■ Mathematics the property of two theorems, expressions, etc., of being dual to each other. ■ Physics the quantum-mechanical property of being regardable as both a wave and a particle.
2 an instance of opposition or contrast between two concepts or two aspects of something; a dualism: *his photographs capitalize on the dualities of light and dark, stillness and movement.*
– ORIGIN late Middle English: from late Latin *dualitas*, from *dualis* (see DUAL).

dual nationality ▸ noun [mass noun] citizenship of two countries concurrently.

dual-purpose ▸ adjective serving two purposes or functions: *a dual-purpose hand and nail cream.*

dual-use ▸ adjective chiefly US (of technology or equipment) designed or suitable for both civilian and military purposes.

dub[1] ▸ verb (**dubs, dubbing, dubbed**) **1** [with obj. and complement] give an unofficial name or nickname to: *the media dubbed anorexia 'the slimming disease'.* ■ make (someone) a knight by the ritual touching of the shoulder with a sword: *he should be dubbed Sir Hubert.*
2 [with obj.] dress (an artificial fishing fly) with strands of fur or wool or with other material. ■ incorporate (fur, wool, or other materials) into a fishing fly.
3 [with obj.] smear (leather) with grease. Compare with DUBBIN.
– ORIGIN late Old English (in the sense 'make a knight'): from Old French *adober* 'equip with armour', of unknown origin. Sense 2 is from the obsolete meaning 'dress or adorn'.

dub[2] ▸ verb (**dubs, dubbing, dubbed**) [with obj.]
1 provide (a film) with a soundtrack in a different language from the original: *the film will be **dubbed into** French and Flemish.* ■ add (sound effects or music) to a film or recording: *background sound can **be dubbed in** at the editing stage.*
2 make a copy of (a sound or video recording). ■ transfer (a recording) from one medium to another. ■ combine (two or more sound recordings) into one composite soundtrack.
▸ noun **1** an instance of dubbing sound effects or music: *the level of the dub can be controlled manually.*
2 [mass noun] a style of popular music originating from the remixing of recorded music (especially reggae), typically with the removal of some vocals and instruments and the accentuation of bass guitar.
– DERIVATIVES **dubby** adjective.
– ORIGIN 1920s: abbreviation of DOUBLE.

dub[3] informal ▶ **noun** US an inexperienced or unskilful person.
▶ **verb** (**dubs, dubbing, dubbed**) [with obj.] Golf misplay (a shot).
– ORIGIN late 19th cent.: perhaps from DUB[1] in the obsolete technical sense 'make blunt'.

dub[4] ▶ **verb** (**dubs, dubbing, dubbed**) [no obj.] (**dub in/up**) N. English informal pay up; make a contribution.
– ORIGIN early 19th cent.: of unknown origin.

Dubai /d(j)uː'bʌɪ/ a member state of the United Arab Emirates; pop. 1,775,000 (est. 2009). ■ its capital city, a port on the Persian Gulf; pop. 1,770,500 (est. 2009).

Du Barry /d(j)uː 'bari/, French /dy baʀi/, Marie Jeanne Bécu, Comtesse (1743–93), French courtier and mistress of Louis XV. During the French Revolution she was arrested by the Revolutionary Tribunal and guillotined.

dubbin /'dʌbɪn/ Brit. ▶ **noun** [mass noun] prepared grease used for softening and waterproofing leather.
▶ **verb** (**dubbins, dubbining, dubbined**) [with obj.] apply dubbin to (leather).
– ORIGIN early 19th cent.: alteration of *dubbing*, present participle of DUB[1] (sense 3).

dubbing ▶ **noun** [mass noun] material used for the bodies of artificial fishing flies, especially fur or wool on waxed silk.
– ORIGIN late 17th cent.: from DUB[1] + -ING[1].

Dubček /'dʊbtʃɛk/, Alexander (1921–92), Czechoslovak statesman, First Secretary of the Czechoslovak Communist Party 1968–9. Dubček was the driving force behind the political reforms of 1968, which prompted the Soviet invasion of Czechoslovakia in 1968 and his removal from office. After the collapse of communism in 1989 he was elected speaker of the Federal Assembly in the new Czechoslovak parliament.

dubiety /djuː'bʌɪɪti/ ▶ **noun** [mass noun] formal the state or quality of being doubtful; uncertainty: *his enemies made much of the dubiety of his paternity.*
– ORIGIN mid 18th cent.: from late Latin *dubietas*, from Latin *dubium* 'a doubt'.

dubious /'djuːbɪəs/ ▶ **adjective 1** hesitating or doubting: *I was rather* ***dubious about*** *the whole idea.*
2 not to be relied upon; suspect: *extremely dubious assumptions.* ■ morally suspect: *timeshare has been brought into disrepute by dubious sales methods.* ■ of questionable value: *he holds the dubious distinction of being relegated with every club he has played for.*
– DERIVATIVES **dubiously** adverb, **dubiousness** noun.
– ORIGIN mid 16th cent. (in sense 2): from Latin *dubiosus*, from *dubium* 'a doubt', neuter of *dubius* 'doubtful'.

dubitable /'djuːbɪtəb(ə)l/ ▶ **adjective** rare (of a belief, conclusion, etc.) open to doubt.
– ORIGIN early 17th cent.: from Latin *dubitabilis*, from *dubitare* 'to doubt'.

dubitation /ˌdjuːbɪ'teɪʃ(ə)n/ ▶ **noun** [mass noun] formal doubt or hesitation: *a judgement fenced around with proper scholarly dubitation.*
– DERIVATIVES **dubitative** adjective.
– ORIGIN late Middle English: from Latin *dubitatio(n-)*, from *dubitare* 'to doubt'.

Dublin /'dʌblɪn/ the capital city of the Republic of Ireland, situated on the Irish Sea at the mouth of the River Liffey; pop. 506,211 (2006). It was the birthplace of many writers, including Jonathan Swift, Oscar Wilde, and James Joyce. Irish name BAILE ÁTHA CLIATH. ■ a county of the Republic of Ireland, in the province of Leinster; county town, Dublin.
– DERIVATIVES **Dubliner** noun.

Dublin Bay prawn ▶ **noun** another term for NORWAY LOBSTER. ■ (**Dublin Bay prawns**) scampi.

dubnium /'dʌbnɪəm/ ▶ **noun** [mass noun] the chemical element of atomic number 105, a very unstable element made by high-energy atomic collisions. (Symbol: **Db**) See also HAHNIUM, JOLIOTIUM.
– ORIGIN 1990s: modern Latin, from *Dubna* in Russia, site of the Joint Nuclear Institute.

Du Bois /duː 'bɔɪz/, W. E. B. (1868–1963), American writer, sociologist, and political activist; full name *William Edward Burghardt Du Bois*. He was an important figure in campaigning for equality for black Americans and co-founded the National Association for the Advancement of Colored People in 1909.

Dubonnet /d(j)uː'bɒneɪ/ ▶ **noun** [mass noun] trademark a type of sweet red vermouth made in France.
– ORIGIN from the name of a family of French wine merchants.

Dubrovnik /dʊ'brɒvnɪk/ a port and resort on the Adriatic coast of Croatia; pop. 26,500 (est. 2009). Its historic centre was damaged by Serb bombardment in the war of 1991–2, but has been restored. Italian name (until 1918) RAGUSA.

dubstep ▶ **noun** [mass noun] a form of dance music, typically instrumental, characterized by a sparse, syncopated rhythm and a strong bassline.

Dubuffet /duː'buːfeɪ/, French /dybyfɛ/, Jean (1901–85), French painter. He rejected traditional techniques, incorporating materials such as sand and plaster in his paintings and producing sculptures made from rubbish.

ducal /'djuːk(ə)l/ ▶ **adjective** like or relating to a duke or dukedom: *the ducal palace in Rouen.*
– ORIGIN late 15th cent.: from Old French, from *duc* 'duke'.

ducat /'dʌkət/ ▶ **noun 1** a gold coin formerly current in most European countries. ■ (**ducats**) informal money.
2 N. Amer. informal an admission ticket.
– ORIGIN from Italian *ducato*, originally referring to a silver coin minted by the Duke of Apulia in 1190: from medieval Latin *ducatus* (see DUCHY). Sense 2 dates from the late 19th cent.

Duccio /'duːtʃɪəʊ/, Italian /'duttʃjo/ (*c.*1255–*c.*1320), Italian painter, founder of the Sienese school of painting; full name *Duccio di Buoninsegna*. The only fully documented surviving work by him is the *Maestà* for the high altar of Siena cathedral (completed 1311).

Duce /'duːtʃeɪ/ (**Il Duce**) the title assumed by Benito Mussolini in 1922.
– ORIGIN Italian, literally 'leader'.

duces plural form of DUX.

Duchamp /djuː'ʃɒ̃/, French /dyʃɑ̃/, Marcel (1887–1968), French-born artist, a US citizen from 1955. A leading figure of the Dada movement and originator of conceptual art, he invented 'ready-mades', mass-produced articles selected at random and displayed as works of art—most famously a bicycle wheel and a urinal.

Duchenne muscular dystrophy /duː'ʃɛn/ (abbrev.: **DMD**) ▶ **noun** [mass noun] a severe form of muscular dystrophy caused by a genetic defect and usually affecting boys.
– ORIGIN late 19th cent.: named after G. B. A. *Duchenne* (1806–75), the French neurologist who first described it.

duchess ▶ **noun** the wife or widow of a duke. ■ a woman holding a rank equivalent to duke in her own right. ■ Brit. informal (especially among cockneys) an affectionate form of address used by a man to a girl or woman.
– ORIGIN late Middle English: via Old French from medieval Latin *ducissa*, from Latin *dux, duc-* (see DUKE).

duchesse /duː'ʃɛs, 'dʌtʃɪs, -ɛs/ ▶ **noun 1** (also **duchesse satin**) [mass noun] a soft, heavy, glossy kind of satin, usually of silk.
2 a chaise longue resembling two armchairs linked by a stool.
3 (also **duchesse dressing table**) a dressing table with a pivoting mirror.
– ORIGIN late 18th cent. (in sense 2): from French, literally 'duchess'.

duchesse lace ▶ **noun** [mass noun] a kind of Brussels pillow lace characterized by bold floral patterns worked with a fine thread.

duchesse potatoes ▶ **plural noun** mashed potatoes mixed with egg yolk, formed into small shapes and baked.

duchy /'dʌtʃi/ ▶ **noun** (pl. **duchies**) the territory of a duke or duchess; a dukedom. ■ (**the Duchy**) the royal dukedom of Cornwall or Lancaster.
– ORIGIN Middle English: from Old French *duche*, from medieval Latin *ducatus*, from Latin *dux, duc-* (see DUKE).

duck[1] ▶ **noun** (pl. **same** or **ducks**) **1** a waterbird with a broad blunt bill, short legs, webbed feet, and a waddling gait. ● Family Anatidae (the **duck family**); domesticated ducks are mainly descended from the mallard or **wild duck**. The duck family also includes geese and swans, from which ducks are distinguished by their generally smaller size and shorter necks.
■ a female duck. Contrasted with DRAKE[1]. ■ a duck as food: [mass noun] *a tangy stew of duck, lamb, and sausage.*
2 a pure white thin-shelled bivalve mollusc found off the Atlantic coasts of America. ● Genus *Anatina*, family Mactridae.
3 another term for **DUKW**.
– PHRASES **get** (or **have**) **one's ducks in a row** N. Amer. informal get (or have) one's facts straight; get (or have) everything organized. **like water off a duck's back** referring to a potentially hurtful remark which has no apparent effect on the person involved: *it was like water off a duck's back to Nick, but I'm sure it upset Paul.* **take to something like a duck to water** take to something very readily: *he shows every sign of taking to University politics like a duck to water.*
– ORIGIN Old English *duce*, from the Germanic base of DUCK[2] (expressing the notion of 'diving bird').

duck[2] ▶ **verb 1** [no obj.] lower the head or the body quickly to avoid a blow or missile or so as not to be seen: *spectators ducked for cover* | [with obj.] *he ducked his head and entered.* ■ [with obj.] avoid (a blow or missile) by moving quickly: *he ducked a punch from an angry first baseman.* ■ [with obj.] informal evade or avoid (an unwelcome duty or undertaking): *a responsibility which a less courageous man might well have ducked* | [no obj.] *I was engaged twice and* ***ducked out*** *both times.*
2 [with obj.] push or plunge (someone) under water, either playfully or as a punishment: *Rufus grabbed him from behind to duck him under the surface.*
3 [no obj.] Bridge refrain from playing a winning card on a particular trick for tactical reasons.
▶ **noun** [in sing.] a quick lowering of the head.
– PHRASES **duck and dive** Brit. use one's ingenuity to deal with or evade a situation.
– DERIVATIVES **ducker** noun.
– ORIGIN Middle English: of Germanic origin; related to Dutch *duiken* and German *tauchen* 'dive, dip, plunge', also to DUCK[1].

duck[3] ▶ **noun** Cricket a batsman's score of nought: *he was out for a duck.*
– PHRASES **break one's duck** Cricket score the first run of one's innings. ■ Brit. make one's first score or achieve a particular feat for the first time.
– ORIGIN mid 19th cent.: short for *duck's egg*, used for the figure 0 because of its similar outline.

duck[4] (also **ducks**) ▶ **noun** Brit. informal dear; darling (used as an informal or affectionate form of address, especially among cockneys).
– ORIGIN late 16th cent.: from DUCK[1].

duck[5] ▶ **noun** [mass noun] a strong linen or cotton fabric, used chiefly for work clothes and sails. ■ (**ducks**) trousers made of such a fabric.
– ORIGIN mid 17th cent.: from Middle Dutch *doek* 'linen, linen cloth'; related to German *Tuch* 'cloth'.

duckbill ▶ **noun** an animal with jaws resembling a duck's bill, e.g. a platypus or a duck-billed dinosaur.
▶ **adjective** [attrib.] shaped like a duck's bill: *duckbill pliers.*

duck-billed dinosaur ▶ **noun** another term for HADROSAUR.

duck-billed platypus ▶ **noun** see PLATYPUS.

duckboard ▶ **noun** (usu. **duckboards**) a board consisting of a number of wooden slats joined together, placed so as to form a path over muddy ground or in a trench.

duck-dive ▶ **verb** [no obj.] dive head first under the water while swimming.
▶ **noun** a dive made head first while swimming.

duck-egg blue ▶ **noun** [mass noun] a soft, turquoise-blue shade.

duck hawk ▶ **noun** N. Amer. dated the peregrine falcon.

ducking stool ▶ **noun** historical a chair fastened to the end of a pole, used formerly to plunge offenders into a pond or river as a punishment.

duckling ▶ **noun** a young duck. ■ [mass noun] the flesh of a young duck as food.

duck mussel ▶ **noun** a freshwater bivalve mollusc that is smaller and darker than the related swan mussel, found in rivers with sandy or gravelly beds. ● *Anodonta anatina*, family Unionidae.

duckpin ▶ **noun** US a short, squat bowling pin. ■ (**duckpins**) [treated as sing.] a game played with duckpins.

ducks and drakes ▶ **noun** [mass noun] a game of throwing flat stones so that they skim along the surface of water.
– PHRASES **play ducks and drakes with** trifle with; treat frivolously.

D

– ORIGIN late 16th cent.: from the movement of the stone over the water.

duck's arse (N. Amer. **duck's ass**) (abbrev.: **DA**) ▶ **noun** informal a man's hairstyle, associated especially with the 1950s, in which the hair is slicked back on both sides and tapered at the nape.

duck-shove ▶ **verb** [with obj.] Austral./NZ informal avoid or evade (a responsibility or issue).

duck soup ▶ **noun** [mass noun] N. Amer. informal an easy task, or someone easy to overcome: *we had some great battles, but against me he was duck soup.*

ducktail ▶ **noun** North American term for **DUCK'S ARSE**.

duckwalk ▶ **verb** [no obj.] walk with the body in a squatting posture.
▶ **noun** a walk with the body in a squatting posture.

duckweed ▶ **noun** [mass noun] a tiny aquatic flowering plant that floats in large quantities on still water, often forming an apparently continuous green layer on the surface. ● Family Lemnaceae, in particular the genus *Lemna*.

Duckworth–Lewis ▶ **adjective** denoting a method of determining the runs total needed to win a one-day cricket match that is affected by rain or other interruptions.
– ORIGIN named after the English statisticians Frank *Duckworth* (born 1939) and Tony *Lewis* (born 1942), who invented the method.

ducky informal ▶ **noun** (pl. **duckies**) Brit. dear (used as a form of address): *come and sit down, ducky.*
▶ **adjective** chiefly N. Amer. charming; delightful: *everything here is just ducky.*
– ORIGIN early 19th cent.: from **DUCK**[4].

duct ▶ **noun** a tube or passageway in a building or machine for air, liquid, cables, etc. ■ (in the body) a vessel for conveying lymph or glandular secretions such as tears or bile. ■ (in a plant) a vessel for conveying water, sap, or air.
▶ **verb** [with obj.] convey through a duct: *a ventilation system that must be ducted through the wall.*
– DERIVATIVES **ductal** adjective.
– ORIGIN mid 17th cent. (in the sense 'course' or 'direction'): from Latin *ductus* 'leading, aqueduct' from *duct-* 'led', from the verb *ducere*.

ductile /ˈdʌktʌɪl/ ▶ **adjective** (of a metal) able to be drawn out into a thin wire. ■ able to be deformed without losing toughness; pliable, not brittle.
– DERIVATIVES **ductility** noun.
– ORIGIN Middle English (in the sense 'malleable'): from Latin *ductilis*, from *duct-* 'led', from the verb *ducere*.

ducting ▶ **noun** [mass noun] a system of ducts. ■ tubing or piping forming such a system.

ductless ▶ **adjective** Anatomy denoting a gland that secretes directly into the bloodstream, such as an endocrine gland or a lymph gland.

duct tape ▶ **noun** [mass noun] N. Amer. strong cloth-backed waterproof adhesive tape.
– ORIGIN 1970s: originally used for repairing leaks in ducted ventilation and heating systems.

ductule /ˈdʌktjuːl/ ▶ **noun** Anatomy a minute duct.
– DERIVATIVES **ductular** adjective.
– ORIGIN late 19th cent.: Latin, diminutive of *ductus* 'leading'.

ductus /ˈdʌktəs/ ▶ **noun** (pl. **ducti**) Anatomy a duct.
– ORIGIN mid 17th cent.: from Latin, literally 'leading'.

ductwork ▶ **noun** [mass noun] a system or network of ducts.

dud informal ▶ **noun 1** a thing that fails to work properly or is otherwise unsatisfactory or worthless: *all three bombs were duds.* ■ an ineffectual person.
2 (**duds**) clothes: *buy yourself some new duds.*
▶ **adjective** not working or meeting standards; faulty: *a dud ignition switch.* ■ counterfeit: *she was charged with issuing dud cheques.*
– ORIGIN Middle English (in the sense 'item of clothing'): of unknown origin.

dude /d(j)uːd/ informal, chiefly N. Amer. ▶ **noun** a man; a guy (often as a form of address): *hey dude, what's up?* | *if some dude smacked me, I'd smack him back.* ■ a stylish and confident person: *cool dudes.* ■ dated a dandy.
▶ **verb** [no obj.] (**dude up**) dress up elaborately: *my brother was all duded up in silver and burgundy.*
– DERIVATIVES **dudish** adjective.
– ORIGIN late 19th cent. (denoting a dandy): probably from German dialect *Dude* 'fool'.

dude ranch ▶ **noun** (in the western US) a cattle ranch converted to a holiday centre for tourists.

dudgeon /ˈdʌdʒ(ə)n/ ▶ **noun** [mass noun] a feeling of offence or deep resentment: *the manager walked out in high dudgeon.*
– ORIGIN late 16th cent.: of unknown origin.

Dudley[1] /ˈdʌdli/ an industrial town in the west Midlands of England, near Birmingham; pop. 193,200 (est. 2009).

Dudley[2] /ˈdʌdli/, Robert, Earl of Leicester (*c.*1532–88), English nobleman, military commander, and favourite of Elizabeth I.

due ▶ **adjective 1** [predic.] expected at or planned for at a certain time: *the baby's due in August* | *he is due back soon* | [with infinitive] *talks are due to adjourn tomorrow.* ■ (of a payment) required at a certain time: *the May instalment was due.* ■ (of a person) having reached a point where the thing mentioned is required or owed: *she was* ***due for*** *a rise.* ■ (of a thing) required or owed as a legal or moral obligation: *he was only taking back what was* ***due to*** *him* | *you must pay any income tax due.*
2 [attrib.] of the proper quality or extent: *driving without due care and attention.*
▶ **noun 1** (**one's due/dues**) one's right; what is owed to one: *he thought it was his due.*
2 (**dues**) an obligatory payment; a fee: *he had paid trade union dues for years.*
▶ **adverb** (with reference to a point of the compass) exactly; directly: *we'll head due south again on the same road.*
– PHRASES **due to 1** caused by or ascribable to: *his death was not due to any lack of care.* **2** because of; owing to: *he had to withdraw due to a knee injury.* **give someone their due** be fair to someone. **in due course** at the appropriate time: *the range will be extended in due course.* **pay one's dues** fulfil one's obligations. ■ experience difficulties before achieving success: *this drummer has paid his dues with the best.*
– ORIGIN Middle English (in the sense 'payable'): from Old French *deu* 'owed', based on Latin *debitus* 'owed', from *debere* 'owe'.

> **USAGE** Due to in the sense 'because of', as in *he had to retire* ***due to*** *an injury*, has been condemned as incorrect on the grounds that **due** is an adjective and should not be used as a preposition; **owing to** is often recommended as a better alternative. However, the prepositional use, first recorded at the end of the 19th century, is now common in all types of literature and is regarded as part of standard English.

due date ▶ **noun** the date on which something falls due, especially the payment of a bill or the expected birth of a baby.

due diligence ▶ **noun** [mass noun] Law reasonable steps taken by a person to avoid committing a tort or offence. ■ a comprehensive appraisal of a business undertaken by a prospective buyer, especially to establish its assets and liabilities and evaluate its commercial potential.

duel ▶ **noun** chiefly historical a prearranged contest with deadly weapons between two people in order to settle a point of honour. ■ (in modern use) a contest between two parties: *he won by a short head after a great final-furlong duel.*
▶ **verb** (**duels, duelling, duelled**; US **duels, dueling, dueled**) [no obj.] fight a duel or duels.
– DERIVATIVES **dueller** (US **dueler**) noun, **duellist** (US **duelist**) noun.
– ORIGIN late 15th cent.: from Latin *duellum*, archaic and literary form of *bellum* 'war', used in medieval Latin with the meaning 'combat between two persons', partly influenced by *dualis* 'of two'. The original sense was 'single combat used to decide a judicial dispute'; the sense 'contest to decide a point of honour' dates from the early 17th cent.

duende /duːˈɛndeɪ/ ▶ **noun** [mass noun] a quality of passion and inspiration. ■ [count noun] a spirit.
– ORIGIN 1920s: from Spanish, contraction of *duen de casa*, from *dueño de casa* 'owner of the house'.

duenna /duːˈɛnə/ ▶ **noun** an older woman acting as a governess and companion in charge of girls, especially in a Spanish family; a chaperone.
– ORIGIN mid 17th cent.: earlier form of Spanish *dueña*, from Latin *domina* 'lady, mistress'.

due process (also **due process of law**) ▶ **noun** [mass noun] fair treatment through the normal judicial system, especially a citizen's entitlement to notice of a charge and a hearing before an impartial judge.

Duero /ˈdwerəʊ/ Spanish name for **DOURO**.

duet ▶ **noun** a performance by two singers, instrumentalists, or dancers. ■ a musical composition for two performers.
▶ **verb** (**duets, duetting, duetted**) [no obj.] perform a duet.
– DERIVATIVES **duettist** noun.
– ORIGIN mid 18th cent.: from Italian *duetto*, diminutive of *duo* 'duet', from Latin *duo* 'two'.

Dufay /djuːˈfʌɪ/, French /dyfaj/, Guillaume (*c.*1400–74), French composer. He made a significant contribution to the development of Renaissance polyphony.

duff[1] ▶ **noun** [usu. with modifier] a flour pudding boiled or steamed in a cloth bag: *a currant duff.*
– ORIGIN mid 19th cent.: northern English form of **DOUGH**.

duff[2] ▶ **adjective** Brit. informal of very poor quality: *duff lyrics.* ■ incorrect or false: *she played a couple of duff notes.*
▶ **noun** [mass noun] N. Amer. & Scottish decaying vegetable matter covering the ground under trees.
– ORIGIN late 18th cent. (denoting something worthless): of unknown origin.

duff[3] ▶ **verb** [with obj.] informal **1** (**duff someone up**) Brit. beat someone up.
2 Austral. steal and alter brands on (cattle).
3 Golf, Brit. mishit (a shot).
– ORIGIN early 19th cent.: of uncertain origin; sense 2 and sense 3 are probably back-formations from **DUFFER**[2] and **DUFFER**[1].

duff[4] ▶ **noun** N. Amer. informal a person's buttocks: *I did not get where I am today by sitting on my duff.*
– ORIGIN mid 19th cent.: of unknown origin.

duff[5] ▶ **noun** (in phrase **up the duff**) Brit. informal pregnant: *it looks like he's got her up the duff.*
– ORIGIN 1940s (originally Australian): perhaps related to **DUFF**[1].

duffel (also **duffle**) ▶ **noun** [mass noun] **1** a coarse woollen cloth with a thick nap.
2 N. Amer. sporting or camping equipment.
– ORIGIN mid 17th cent.: from *Duffel*, the name of a town in Belgium where the cloth was originally made.

duffel bag ▶ **noun** a cylindrical canvas bag closed by a drawstring and carried over the shoulder.
– ORIGIN early 20th cent. (originally US): from **DUFFEL** (sense 2), originally denoting a bag for equipment.

duffel coat ▶ **noun** a coat made of duffel, typically hooded and fastened with toggles.

duffer[1] ▶ **noun** informal **1** an incompetent or stupid person: *a complete duffer at languages.*
2 Austral./NZ an unproductive mine.
– ORIGIN mid 19th cent.: from Scots *dowfart* 'stupid person', from *douf* 'spiritless'.

duffer[2] ▶ **noun** Austral. informal a person who steals and alters the brands on cattle.
– ORIGIN mid 19th cent.: of unknown origin; in use earlier as thieves' slang for 'someone who sells trashy articles as if they were valuable'.

Duffy, Carol Ann (b.1955), Scottish poet, Poet Laureate since 2009. She is the first woman to hold the post.

Du Fu /duː/ variant of **TU FU**.

dufus ▶ **noun** variant spelling of **DOOFUS**.

Dufy /ˈdjuːfi/, French /dyfi/, Raoul (1877–1953), French painter and textile designer. His characteristic style involved calligraphic outlines sketched on brilliant background washes.

dug[1] past and past participle of **DIG**.

dug[2] ▶ **noun** (usu. **dugs**) the udder, teat, or nipple of a female animal. ■ archaic a woman's breast.
– ORIGIN mid 16th cent.: possibly of Old Norse origin and related to Swedish *dägga*, Danish *dægge* 'suckle'.

dugite /ˈdjuːgʌɪt/ ▶ **noun** a highly venomous snake found in SW Australia, similar to the related brown snakes. ● *Pseudonaja affinis*, family Elapidae.
– ORIGIN late 19th cent.: from Nyungar *dukayj*.

dugong /ˈduːgɒŋ, ˈdjuː-/ ▶ **noun** (pl. **same** or **dugongs**) a sea cow found on the coasts of the Indian Ocean from eastern Africa to northern Australia. It is distinguished from the manatees by its forked tail. ● *Dugong dugon*, family Dugongidae.
– ORIGIN early 19th cent.: based on Malay *duyong*.

dugout ▶ **noun 1** a trench that is dug and roofed over as a shelter for troops. ■ an underground air-raid or nuclear shelter. ■ a low shelter at the side of a sports field for a team's coaches and substitutes.
2 (also **dugout canoe**) a canoe made from a hollowed tree trunk.

duh /də:/ ▶ **exclamation** another way of saying **DOH²**.

DUI ▶ **abbreviation** US driving under the influence (of drugs or alcohol).

duiker /ˈdʌɪkə/ ▶ **noun** (pl. **same** or **duikers**) **1** a small African antelope that typically has a tuft of hair between the horns, found mainly in forests. ● *Cephalophus* and other genera, family Bovidae: several species, including the **common duiker** (*Sylvicapra grimmia*), which is unusual in occurring in open savannah, and the very small **blue duiker** (*Philantomba monticola*), prized for its skin.
2 S. African a cormorant. ● Genus *Phalacrocorax*, family Phalacrocoracidae; several species, in particular the long-tailed cormorant, *P. africanus*.
– ORIGIN late 18th cent.: from South African Dutch, from Dutch, literally 'diver', from the antelope's habit of plunging through bushes when pursued; related to **DUCK²**.

Duisburg /ˈdjuːsbəːɡ/, German /ˈdysbʊrk/ an industrial city in NW Germany, in North Rhine-Westphalia; pop. 499,100 (est. 2006).

du jour /d(j)uː ˈʒʊə/, French /dy ʒuʀ/ ▶ **adjective** [postpositive] informal used to describe something that is enjoying great but probably short-lived popularity or publicity: *black comedy is the genre du jour*.
– ORIGIN French, literally 'of the day'.

duke ▶ **noun 1** a male holding the highest hereditary title in the British and certain other peerages. ■ chiefly historical (in some parts of Europe) a male ruler of a small independent state.
2 (**dukes**) informal the fists, especially when raised in a fighting attitude. [from rhyming slang *Duke of Yorks* 'forks' (= fingers).]
▶ **verb** [no obj.] (**duke it out**) N. Amer. informal fight it out.
– ORIGIN Old English (denoting the ruler of a duchy), from Old French *duc*, from Latin *dux, duc-* 'leader'; related to *ducere* 'to lead'.

duke cherry ▶ **noun** a cultivated cherry which is a hybrid between the sweet cherry and the sour cherry. ● *Prunus × gondouinii*, family Rosaceae.

dukedom ▶ **noun** a territory ruled by a duke. ■ the rank of duke.

Duke of Argyll's tea tree ▶ **noun** see **TEA TREE** (sense 2).

dukun /ˈduːkʌn/ ▶ **noun** SE Asian a traditional healer believed to have spiritual and occult powers; a shaman.
– ORIGIN Indonesian.

DUKW ▶ **noun** an amphibious transport vehicle, especially as used by the Allies during the Second World War. Also called **DUCK¹**.
– ORIGIN an official designation, being a combination of factory-applied letters referring to features of the vehicle.

dulcamara /ˌdʌlkəˈmɛːrə/ ▶ **noun** [mass noun] an extract of woody nightshade, used in homeopathy especially for treating skin diseases and chest complaints.
– ORIGIN late 16th cent.: from medieval Latin (used as a specific epithet in *Solanum dulcamara*), from Latin *dulcis* 'sweet' + *amara* 'bitter'.

dulcet /ˈdʌlsɪt/ ▶ **adjective** (especially of sound) sweet and soothing (often used ironically): *record the dulcet tones of your family and friends*.
– ORIGIN late Middle English *doucet*, from Old French *doucet*, diminutive of *doux*, from Latin *dulcis* 'sweet'. The Latin form influenced the modern spelling.

dulcian /ˈdʌlsɪən/ ▶ **noun 1** an early type of bassoon made in one piece.
2 any of various organ stops, typically with 8-foot funnel-shaped flue pipes or 8- or 16-foot reed pipes.
– ORIGIN mid 19th cent.: from German *Dulzian*, or a variant of **DULCIANA**.

dulciana /ˌdʌlsɪˈɑːnə/ ▶ **noun** an organ stop, typically with small conical open metal pipes.
– ORIGIN late 18th cent.: via medieval Latin from Latin *dulcis* 'sweet'.

dulcify /ˈdʌlsɪfʌɪ/ ▶ **verb** (**dulcifies, dulcifying, dulcified**) [with obj.] rare sweeten: *cider pap dulcified with molasses*. ■ calm or soothe: *the exquisite melody dulcifies whatever pain the singer's words express*.
– ORIGIN late 16th cent. (in the sense 'sweeten'): from Latin *dulcificare* 'sweeten', from *dulcis* 'sweet'.

dulcimer /ˈdʌlsɪmə/ ▶ **noun** a musical instrument with a sounding board or box, typically trapezoid in shape, over which strings of graduated length are stretched, played by plucking or especially by being struck with handheld hammers. The term **hammered dulcimer** is sometimes used, especially in the US, to distinguish these from plucked instruments such as the **Appalachian dulcimer**.
– ORIGIN late 15th cent.: from Old French *doulcemer*, probably from Latin *dulce melos* 'sweet melody'.

dulcitone /ˈdʌlsɪtəʊn/ ▶ **noun** a musical keyboard instrument in which a series of steel tuning forks are struck by hammers. It was invented in the late 19th century and was superseded by the celesta.
– ORIGIN late 19th cent.: coined by T. Machell, the instrument's inventor, from Latin *dulcis* 'sweet' + *tonus* 'tone'.

dulia /djʊˈlʌɪə/ ▶ **noun** [mass noun] (in Roman Catholic theology) the reverence accorded to saints and angels. Compare with **LATRIA**.
– ORIGIN late Middle English: via medieval Latin from Greek *douleia* 'servitude', from *doulos* 'slave'.

dull ▶ **adjective 1** lacking interest or excitement: *your diet doesn't have to be dull and boring*. ■ archaic (of a person) feeling bored and dispirited.
2 lacking brightness, vividness, or sheen: *his face glowed in the dull lamplight* | *his black hair looked dull*. ■ (of the weather) overcast; gloomy: *next morning dawned dull*. ■ (of sound) not clear; muffled: *a dull thud of hooves*. ■ (of pain) indistinctly felt; not acute: *there was a dull pain in his lower jaw*. ■ (of an edge or blade) blunt. ■ (of activity) sluggish or slow-moving: *shares closed weaker after a day of dull trading*.
3 (of a person) slow to understand; stupid: *the voice of a teacher talking to a rather dull child*. ■ archaic (of a person's senses) not perceiving things distinctly.
▶ **verb** make or become dull or less intense: [with obj.] *time dulls the memory* | [no obj.] *Albert's eyes dulled a little*.
– PHRASES (**as**) **dull as dishwater** (or **ditchwater**) Brit. extremely dull. **dull the edge of** cause to be less keenly felt; reduce the intensity of: *she'd have to find something to dull the edges of the pain*.
– DERIVATIVES **dullish** adjective, **dullness** (also **dulness**) noun, **dully** /ˈdʌl,li/ adverb.
– ORIGIN Old English *dol* 'stupid', of Germanic origin; related to Dutch *dol* 'crazy' and German *toll* 'mad, fantastic, wonderful'.

dullard /ˈdʌləd/ ▶ **noun** a slow or stupid person.
– ORIGIN Middle English: from Middle Dutch *dullaert*, from *dul* 'dull'.

Dulles /ˈdʌlɪs/, John Foster (1888–1959), American Republican statesman and international lawyer. He was the US adviser at the founding of the United Nations in 1945 and negotiated the peace treaty with Japan in 1951.

dullsville informal, chiefly N. Amer. ▶ **noun** [mass noun] a dull or monotonous place or condition.
▶ **adjective** dull or monotonous: *she has transformed their dullsville life*.

dull-witted ▶ **adjective** slow to understand; stupid.

dulosis /djʊːˈləʊsɪs/ ▶ **noun** [mass noun] Entomology the practice by slave-making ants of capturing the pupae of other ant species and rearing them as workers of their own colony.
– ORIGIN early 20th cent.: from Greek *doulōsis* 'slavery', from *doulos* 'slave'.

dulse /dʌls/ ▶ **noun** [mass noun] a dark red edible seaweed with flattened branching fronds. ● *Rhodymenia palmata*, division Rhodophyta.
– ORIGIN early 17th cent.: from Irish and Scottish Gaelic *duileasg*.

Duluth /dəˈluːθ/ a port in NE Minnesota, at the western end of Lake Superior; pop. 84,284 (est. 2008).

duly ▶ **adverb** in accordance with what is required or appropriate; following proper procedure or arrangement: *a document duly signed and authorized by the inspector* | *the ceremony duly began at midnight*. ■ as might be expected or predicted: *I used the tent and was duly impressed*.

dum /dʌm/ ▶ **adjective** Indian cooked with steam: *dum aloo*.
– ORIGIN from Hindi *dam*.

Duma /ˈduːmə/ ▶ **noun** a legislative body in the ruling assembly of Russia and of some other republics of the former Soviet Union.

> 'Duma' originally denoted pre-19th century advisory municipal councils in Russia. It later referred to any of four elected legislative bodies established due to popular demand in Russia between 1906 and 1917. After the collapse of communism in 1991 a new Duma was set up as the lower chamber of the Russian parliament.

Dumas /ˈdjuːmɑː/, French /dymɑ/ the name of two French novelists and dramatists: ■ **Alexandre** (1802–70); known as **Dumas** *père*. Although he was a pioneer of the romantic theatre in France, his reputation now rests on his historical adventure novels *The Three Musketeers* (1844–5) and *The Count of Monte Cristo* (1844–5). ■ **Alexandre** (1824–95), son of Dumas *père*; known as **Dumas** *fils*. He wrote the novel (and play) *La Dame aux camélias* (1848), which formed the basis of Verdi's opera *La Traviata* (1853).

Du Maurier¹ /djuː ˈmɒrɪeɪ/, Dame Daphne (1907–89), English novelist, granddaughter of George du Maurier. Many of her popular novels and period romances are set in the West Country of England, where she spent most of her life. Notable works: *Jamaica Inn* (1936) and *Rebecca* (1938).

Du Maurier² /djuː ˈmɒrɪeɪ/, George (Louis Palmella Busson) (1834–96), French-born novelist, cartoonist, and illustrator. He is chiefly remembered for his novel *Trilby* (1894), which included the character Svengali and gave rise to the word *Svengali* for a person with a hypnotic influence on another.

dumb ▶ **adjective 1** (of a person) unable to speak, most typically because of congenital deafness: *he was born deaf, dumb, and blind*. ■ (of animals) unable to speak as a natural state and thus regarded as helpless or deserving pity. ■ [predic.] temporarily unable or unwilling to speak: *she stood dumb while he poured out a stream of abuse*. ■ [attrib.] resulting in or expressed by speechlessness: *they stared in dumb amazement*.
2 informal, chiefly N. Amer. stupid: *a dumb question*.
3 (of a computer terminal) able only to transmit data to or receive data from a computer; having no independent processing capability. Often contrasted with **INTELLIGENT**.
▶ **verb** [with obj.] **1** (**dumb something down**) informal simplify or reduce the intellectual content of something so as to make it accessible to a larger number of people: *the producers categorically deny that they're dumbing down the show*. ■ [no obj.] (**dumb down**) become less intellectually challenging: *the need to dumb down for mass audiences*.
2 literary make dumb or unheard; silence: *a splendour that dazed the mind and dumbed the tongue*.
– PHRASES **dumb luck** pure chance: *finally, through dumb luck, it worked and I got a network connection*. **play dumb** pretend to be unintelligent or unaware in order to deceive someone or gain an advantage: *'Hide what?' Aubrey said, still playing dumb*.
– DERIVATIVES **dumbly** adverb, **dumbness** noun.
– ORIGIN Old English, of Germanic origin; related to Old Norse *dumbr* and Gothic *dumbs* 'mute', also to Dutch *dom* 'stupid' and German *dumm* 'stupid'.

> **USAGE** Although **dumb** meaning 'not able to speak' is the older sense, it has been overwhelmed by the newer sense (meaning 'stupid') to such an extent that the use of the first sense is now almost certain to cause offence. Alternatives such as **speech-impaired** should be used instead.

Dumbarton /dʌmˈbɑːt(ə)n/ a town in Scotland on the Clyde west of Glasgow, in West Dunbartonshire; pop. 19,500 (est. 2009).

Dumbartonshire variant spelling of **DUNBARTONSHIRE**.

dumb-ass ▶ **adjective** [attrib.] N. Amer. informal stupid; brainless: *dumb-ass politicians*.

dumb-bell ▶ **noun 1** a short bar with a weight at each end, used typically in pairs for exercise or muscle-building. ■ [as modifier] shaped like a dumb-bell: *a dumb-bell molecule*.
2 N. Amer. informal a stupid person.
– ORIGIN early 18th cent.: originally denoting an apparatus similar to that used to ring a church bell (but without the bell, so noiseless or 'dumb'); sense 2 (dating from the 1920s) is an extended use by association with **DUMB** 'stupid'.

dumb blonde ▶ **noun** informal a blonde-haired woman perceived in a stereotypical way as being attractive but unintelligent.

dumb cane ▶ **noun** a thick-stemmed plant with large variegated leaves, native to tropical America and widely grown as a houseplant. ● Genus *Dieffenbachia*, family Araceae: several species, in particular the Caribbean *D. seguine*, which has a poisonous sap that swells the tongue and destroys the power of speech.

dumbfound ▶ **verb** [with obj.] greatly astonish or amaze: *she was dumbfounded at the sight that met her eyes* | [as adj] *a dumbfounded look on her face*.
– ORIGIN mid 17th cent.: blend of **DUMB** and **CONFOUND**.

dumbhead ▶ **noun** N. Amer. informal a stupid person.

D

dumb iron ▸ noun historical a curved side piece of a vehicle chassis, to which the front springs are attached.

dumbo ▸ noun (pl. **dumbos**) informal a stupid person.
– ORIGIN 1950s (originally US): from DUMB + -O, popularized by the 1941 cartoon film *Dumbo*.

dumb piano ▸ noun a dummy piano keyboard for exercising the fingers.

dumbshow ▸ noun [mass noun] gestures used to convey a meaning or message without speech; mime: *they demonstrated **in dumbshow** how the tea should be made.* ▪ [count noun] a piece of dramatic mime: *there were gags, spoofs, and dumbshows.* ▪ [count noun] (especially in English drama of the 16th and 17th centuries) a part of a play acted in mime to summarize, supplement, or comment on the main action.

D

dumbsize ▸ verb [no obj.] chiefly US (of a company) reduce staff numbers to levels so low that work can no longer be carried out effectively.
– ORIGIN 1990s: humorously, on the pattern of *downsize*.

dumbstruck ▸ adjective so shocked or surprised as to be unable to speak: *he was dumbstruck with terror.*

dumb waiter ▸ noun **1** a small lift for carrying things, especially food and crockery, between the floors of a building.
2 Brit. a movable table, typically with revolving shelves, used in a dining room.

dumdum (also **dumdum bullet**) ▸ noun a kind of soft-nosed bullet that expands on impact and inflicts laceration.
– ORIGIN late 19th cent.: from *Dum Dum*, name of a town and arsenal in eastern India where such bullets were first produced.

dum-dum ▸ noun informal a stupid person.
– ORIGIN 1970s (originally US): reduplication of DUMB.

Dumfries /dʌmˈfriːs/ a market town in SW Scotland, administrative centre of Dumfries and Galloway; pop. 30,900 (est. 2009).

Dumfries and Galloway a council area in SW Scotland, formed in 1975; administrative centre, Dumfries.

Dumfriesshire /dʌmˈfriːsʃɪə, -ʃə/ a former county of SW Scotland, which became part of Dumfries and Galloway region in 1975.

dumka /ˈdʊmkə/ ▸ noun (pl. **dumkas** or **dumky** /ˈdʊmki/) a piece of Slavic music, originating as a folk ballad or lament, typically melancholy with contrasting lively sections.
– ORIGIN late 19th cent.: via Czech and Polish from Ukrainian.

dummy ▸ noun (pl. **dummies**) **1** a model or replica of a human being: *a waxwork dummy.* ▪ a figure used for displaying or fitting clothes: *a tailor's dummy.* ▪ a ventriloquist's doll.
2 an object designed to resemble and serve as a substitute for the real or usual one: *tests using stuffed owls and wooden dummies* | [as modifier] *a dummy torpedo.* ▪ Brit. a rubber or plastic teat for a baby to suck on. ▪ a prototype or mock-up, especially of a book or the layout of a page. ▪ a blank round of ammunition. ▪ [as modifier] Grammar denoting a word that has no semantic content but is used to maintain grammatical structure: *a dummy subject as in 'it is' or 'there are'.*
3 (chiefly in rugby and soccer) a feigned pass or kick intended to deceive an opponent.
4 informal, chiefly N. Amer. a stupid person.
5 Bridge the declarer's partner, whose cards are exposed on the table after the opening lead and played by the declarer. ▪ Bridge the exposed hand of the declarer's partner. ▪ an imaginary fourth player in whist: [as modifier] *dummy whist.*
▸ verb (**dummies, dummying, dummied**) [no obj.] (chiefly in rugby and soccer) feign a pass or kick in order to deceive an opponent: *Blanco dummied past a static defence.*
– PHRASES **sell someone a dummy** (chiefly in rugby and soccer) deceive an opponent by feigning a pass or kick.
– PHRASAL VERBS **dummy up** N. Amer. informal keep quiet; give no information.
– ORIGIN late 16th cent.: from DUMB + -Y[1]. The original sense was 'a person who cannot speak', then 'an imaginary fourth player in whist' (mid 18th cent.), whence 'a substitute for the real thing' and 'a model of a human being' (mid 19th cent.).

dummy run ▸ noun Brit. a practice or trial.

dumortierite /djuːˈmɔːtɪərʌɪt/ ▸ noun [mass noun] a rare blue or violet mineral occurring typically as needles and fibrous masses in gneiss and schist. It consists of an aluminium and iron borosilicate.
– ORIGIN late 19th cent.: from the name of V.-E. *Dumortier* (1802–76), French geologist, + -ITE[1].

dump ▸ noun **1** a site for depositing rubbish. ▪ [usu. with modifier] a place where a particular kind of waste, especially dangerous waste, is left: *a nuclear waste dump.* ▪ a heap of rubbish left at a dump.
2 informal an unpleasant or dreary place: *why are you living in a dump like this?*
3 Computing a copying of stored data to a different location, performed typically as a protection against loss. ▪ a printout or list of the contents of a computer's memory, occurring typically after a system failure.
4 informal an act of defecation.
▸ verb [with obj.] **1** deposit or dispose of (rubbish, waste, or unwanted material), typically in a careless or hurried way: *trucks dumped 1,900 tons of refuse here.* ▪ abandon (something) hurriedly in order to make an escape: *the couple dumped the car and fled.* ▪ put (something) down heavily or carelessly: *she dumped her knapsack on the floor.* ▪ informal abandon or desert (someone): *Zoë was heartbroken when her boyfriend dumped her.* ▪ send (goods unsaleable in the home market) to a foreign market for sale at a low price: *these countries have been **dumping** cheap fertilizers **on the UK market**.* ▪ informal sell off (assets) rapidly: *investors dumped shares in scores of other consumer-goods firms.*
2 Computing copy (stored data) to a different location, especially so as to protect against loss. ▪ print out or list the contents of (a store), especially after a system failure.
– PHRASAL VERBS **dump on** N. Amer. informal criticize or abuse (someone); treat badly: *you get dumped on just because of your name.*
– ORIGIN Middle English: perhaps from Old Norse; related to Danish *dumpe* and Norwegian *dumpa* 'fall suddenly' (the original sense in English); in later use partly imitative; compare with THUMP.

dump bin ▸ noun a promotional box in a shop for displaying books or other items.

dumper ▸ noun **1** a person or thing that dumps something. ▪ (also **dumper truck**) Brit. a truck with a body that tilts or opens at the back for unloading. ▪ Austral./NZ a large wave that breaks and hurls the swimmer or surfer on to the beach.
2 N. Amer. a large metal container for rubbish. ▪ (**the dumper**) informal used in reference to a bad or unwanted state: *his career's **in the dumper**.*

dumping ground ▸ noun a place where rubbish or unwanted material is left.

dumping syndrome ▸ noun [mass noun] Medicine a group of symptoms, including weakness, abdominal discomfort, and sometimes abnormally rapid bowel evacuation, occurring after meals in some patients who have undergone gastric surgery.

dumpling ▸ noun a small savoury ball of dough (usually made with suet) which may be boiled, fried, or baked in a casserole. ▪ a pudding consisting of apple or other fruit enclosed in a sweet dough and baked. ▪ a small, fat person: *he was a 250-pound dumpling.*
– ORIGIN early 17th cent.: apparently from the rare adjective *dump* 'of the consistency of dough', although *dumpling* is recorded much earlier.

dumps ▸ plural noun (in phrase (**down**) **in the dumps**) informal (of a person) depressed or unhappy.
– ORIGIN early 16th cent. (originally singular in the sense 'a dazed or puzzled state'): probably a figurative use of Middle Dutch *domp* 'haze, mist'.

dumpster ▸ noun N. Amer. a very large container for rubbish; a skip.
– ORIGIN 1930s: originally *Dempster Dumpster*, proprietary name (based on DUMP) given by the American manufacturers, Dempster Brothers of Knoxville, Tennessee.

dump truck ▸ noun N. Amer. a dumper truck.

dumpy ▸ adjective (**dumpier, dumpiest**) (of a person) short and stout: *her plain, dumpy sister.*
– DERIVATIVES **dumpiness** noun.
– ORIGIN mid 18th cent.: from DUMPLING + -Y[1].

Dumyat /dʊmˈjɑːt/ Arabic name for DAMIETTA.

dun[1] ▸ adjective of a dull greyish-brown colour: *a dun cow.* ▪ literary dark or dusky: *when the dun evening comes.*
▸ noun **1** [mass noun] a dull greyish-brown colour.
2 a horse with a sandy or sandy-grey coat, black mane, tail, and lower legs, and a dark dorsal stripe.
3 a subadult mayfly, which has drab coloration and opaque wings. ▪ an artificial fishing fly imitating this.
– ORIGIN Old English *dun, dunn*, of Germanic origin; probably related to DUSK.

dun[2] ▸ verb (**duns, dunning, dunned**) [with obj.] make persistent demands on (someone), especially for payment of a debt.
▸ noun archaic a debt collector or an insistent creditor. ▪ a demand for payment.
– ORIGIN early 17th cent. (as a noun): from obsolete *Dunkirk privateer*, from the French port of DUNKIRK.

dun[3] ▸ noun Archaeology a stone-built fortified settlement in Scotland or Ireland, of a kind built from the late Iron Age to the early Middle Ages. The word is a frequent place-name element in Scotland and Ireland.
– ORIGIN late 18th cent.: from Irish *dún*, Scottish Gaelic *dùn* 'hill or hill fort'.

dunam /ˈdʊnəm/ ▸ noun a measure of land area used in parts of the former Turkish empire, including Israel (where it is equal to about 900 square metres).
– ORIGIN from modern Hebrew *dûnām* or Arabic *dūnum*, from Turkish *dönüm*, from *dönmek* 'go round'.

Dunbar /dʌnˈbɑː/, William (*c.*1456–*c.*1513), Scottish poet. He was the author of satires such as the political allegory 'The Thrissill and the Rois' ('The Thistle and the Rose', 1503) and of elegies such as 'Lament for the Makaris'.

dun-bar /dʌnˈbɑː/ ▸ noun a variable European moth with darker lines and bands on the wings, found in wooded districts. ● *Cosmia trapezina*, family Noctuidae.

Dunbartonshire /dʌnˈbɑːt(ə)nʃɪə, -ʃə/ (also **Dumbartonshire**) a former county of west central Scotland, on the Clyde, divided into **East Dunbartonshire** and **West Dunbartonshire** council areas.

Duncan, Isadora (1878–1927), American dancer and teacher. She was a pioneer of modern dance, famous for her 'free' barefoot dancing. She died through being accidentally strangled when her scarf became entangled in the wheels of a car.

Duncan I (*c.*1010–40), king of Scotland 1034–40. He was killed in battle by Macbeth.

dunce ▸ noun a person who is slow at learning; a stupid person.
– ORIGIN early 16th cent.: originally an epithet for a follower of John DUNS SCOTUS, whose followers were ridiculed by 16th-cent. humanists and reformers as enemies of learning.

dunce's cap (N. Amer. also **dunce cap**) ▸ noun a paper cone formerly put on the head of a dunce at school as a mark of disgrace.

Dundalk /dʌnˈdɔːk/ the county town of Louth, in the Republic of Ireland, a port on the east coast; pop. 29,037 (2006).

Dundee a city in eastern Scotland, on the north side of the Firth of Tay; pop. 141,600 (est. 2009).

Dundee cake ▸ noun chiefly Brit. a rich fruit cake, typically decorated on top with almonds.

dunderhead ▸ noun informal a stupid person.
– DERIVATIVES **dunderheaded** adjective.
– ORIGIN early 17th cent.: compare with obsolete Scots *dunder, dunner* 'resounding noise'; related to DIN.

dune ▸ noun a mound or ridge of sand or other loose sediment formed by the wind, especially on the sea coast or in a desert: *a sand dune.*
– ORIGIN late 18th cent.: from French, from Middle Dutch *dūne*; related to Old English *dūn* 'hill' (see DOWN[3]).

dune buggy ▸ noun another term for BEACH BUGGY.

Dunedin /dʌˈniːdɪn/ a city and port in the South Island, New Zealand, founded in 1848 by Scottish settlers; pop. 118,683 (2006).

Dunfermline /dʌnˈfəːmlɪn/ a town in Fife, Scotland, near the Firth of Forth; pop. 51,500 (est. 2009).

dung ▸ noun [mass noun] the excrement of animals; manure.
▸ verb [no obj.] (of an animal) defecate. ▪ [with obj.] drop or spread dung on (a piece of ground).
– ORIGIN Old English, of Germanic origin; related to German *Dung*, Swedish *dynga*, Icelandic *dyngja* 'dung, dunghill, heap', and Danish *dynge* 'heap'.

dungaree /ˌdʌŋgəˈriː/ ▸ noun **1** (**dungarees**) chiefly Brit. a garment consisting of trousers with a bib held up by straps over the shoulders, made of calico, denim,

or a similar material and worn as casual or working clothes. ■ N. Amer. hard-wearing denim trousers.
2 [mass noun] a kind of coarse Indian calico.
– ORIGIN late 17th cent. (in sense 2): from Hindi *duṅgrī*.

Dungarvan /dʌnˈgɑːv(ə)n/ a town on the south coast of the Republic of Ireland, the administrative centre of Waterford; pop. 7,813 (2006).

dung beetle ▸ **noun** a beetle whose larvae feed on dung, especially a scarab. The larger kinds place the dung in a hole before the eggs are laid, and some of them roll it along in a ball. ● Superfamily Scarabaeoidea, in particular families Scarabaeidae and Geotrupidae.

Dungeness crab /ˌdʌndʒəˈnɛs/ ▸ **noun** a large crab found off the west coast of North America, where it is popular as food. ● *Cancer magister*, family Cancridae.
– ORIGIN mid 20th cent.: from *Dungeness*, the name of a fishing village on the coast of Washington State.

dungeon ▸ **noun 1** a strong underground prison cell, especially in a castle.
2 archaic term for **DONJON**.
▸ **verb** [with obj.] literary imprison (someone) in a dungeon.
– ORIGIN Middle English (also with the sense 'castle keep'): from Old French (perhaps originally with the sense 'lord's tower' or 'mistress tower'), based on Latin *dominus* 'lord, master'. Compare with **DONJON**.

Dungeons and Dragons ▸ **noun** [mass noun] trademark a fantasy role-playing game set in an imaginary world based loosely on medieval myth.

dung fly ▸ **noun** a hairy fly that lays its eggs in fresh dung. ● Families Scathophagidae and Sphaeroceridae: several species.

dunghill (also **dungheap**) ▸ **noun** a heap of dung or refuse, especially in a farmyard.

dungworm ▸ **noun** an earthworm found in dung or compost, used by anglers as bait.

Dunhuang /dʊnˈhwaŋ/ a town in NW China, in Gansu province, located on the old Silk Road near the site of the earliest known Buddhist cave shrines (4th century AD).

dunite /ˈdʌnʌɪt/ ▸ **noun** [mass noun] Geology a green to brownish coarse-grained igneous rock consisting largely of olivine.
– ORIGIN mid 19th cent.: from the name of *Dun* Mountain, New Zealand, + **-ITE**[1].

dunk ▸ **verb 1** [with obj.] dip (bread or other food) into a drink or soup before eating it: *I dunked a biscuit into the cup of scalding tea.* ■ immerse or dip in water: *he was dunked head first in the cold swimming pool.*
2 [no obj.] Basketball score by shooting the ball down through the basket with the hands above the rim.
▸ **noun** Basketball a shot downwards into the basket with the hands above the rim.
– DERIVATIVES **dunker** noun.
– ORIGIN early 20th cent.: from Pennsylvanian German *dunke* 'dip', from German *tunken* 'dip or plunge'.

Dunkard /ˈdʌŋkəd/ ▸ **noun** another term for **DUNKER**.

Dunker /ˈdʌŋkə/ ▸ **noun** a member of the German Baptist Brethren, a sect of Baptist Christians founded in 1708 but living in the US since the 1720s.
– ORIGIN early 18th cent.: from Pennsylvanian German, from *dunke* (see **DUNK**).

Dunkirk /dʌnˈkəːk/ a port in northern France; pop. 70,654 (2006). French name **Dunkerque** /dœ̃kɛrk/.

> Dunkirk was the scene of the evacuation of the British Expeditionary Force in 1940. Forced to retreat to the Channel by the German breakthrough at Sedan, 335,000 Allied troops were evacuated by warships, requisitioned civilian ships, and a host of small boats, under constant attack from the air.

Dunkirk spirit ▸ **noun** Brit. stoicism and determination in a difficult or dangerous situation, especially as displayed by a group of people: *Yorkshire flood victims showed the Dunkirk spirit as they battled the rising water.*

Dun Laoghaire /dʌn ˈlɪəri, ˈlɛːrə/, Irish /duːn ˈliːrʲə/ a ferry port and resort town in the Republic of Ireland, near Dublin; pop. 114,166 (2006).

dunlin /ˈdʌnlɪn/ ▸ **noun** (pl. **same** or **dunlins**) a migratory sandpiper with a downcurved bill and (in the breeding season) a reddish-brown back and black belly. It is the commonest small wader of the northern hemisphere. ● *Calidris alpina*, family Scolopacidae.
– ORIGIN mid 16th cent.: probably from **DUN**[1] + **-LING**, from the greyish-brown winter colouring of its upper parts.

Dunlop[1] /ˈdʌnlɒp/, John Boyd (1840–1921), Scottish inventor. He developed the first successful pneumatic bicycle tyre (1888), manufactured by the company named after him.

Dunlop[2] /ˈdʌnlɒp, dʌnˈlɒp/ (also **Dunlop cheese**) ▸ **noun** [mass noun] a full-cream hard cheese originally made in Dunlop, near Ayr in Scotland.

Dunmow flitch /ˈdʌnməʊ/ a side of bacon awarded at Great Dunmow in Essex on Whit Monday to any married couple who will swear that they have not quarrelled or repented of their marriage vows for at least a year and a day.

dunnage /ˈdʌnɪdʒ/ ▸ **noun** [mass noun] **1** loose wood, matting, or similar material used to keep a cargo in position in a ship's hold.
2 informal a person's belongings, especially those brought on board ship.
– ORIGIN Middle English: of unknown origin.

dunnage bag ▸ **noun** a kitbag.

dunnart /ˈdʌnɑːt/ ▸ **noun** a mouse-like insectivorous marsupial with a pointed snout and prominent eyes, found in Australia and New Guinea. Also called **MARSUPIAL MOUSE**. ● Genus *Sminthopsis*, family Dasyuridae: many species, including the **common dunnart** (*S. murina*).
– ORIGIN 1920s: from Nyungar *danart*.

Dunnet Head /ˈdʌnɪt/ a headland on the north coast of Scotland, between Thurso and John o'Groats. It is the most northerly point on the British mainland.

dunno /ˈdʌnəʊ, dəˈnəʊ/ ▸ **contraction** (I) do not know.
– ORIGIN mid 19th cent.: representing an informal pronunciation.

dunnock /ˈdʌnək/ ▸ **noun** a small European songbird of the accentor family, with a dark grey head and a reddish-brown back. Also called **HEDGE SPARROW**. ● *Prunella modularis*, family Prunellidae.
– ORIGIN Middle English: apparently from **DUN**[1] (from its brown and grey plumage) + **-OCK**.

dunny /ˈdʌni/ ▸ **noun** (pl. **dunnies**) **1** Scottish an underground passage or cellar, especially in a tenement.
2 Austral./NZ informal a toilet.
– ORIGIN early 19th cent. (in the sense 'dung'): from dialect *dunnekin* 'privy', probably from **DUNG** + archaic slang *ken* 'house'. Sense 1 is perhaps a different word.

Duns Scotus /dʌnz ˈskəʊtəs/, John (*c.*1265–1308), Scottish theologian and scholar. A profoundly influential figure in the Middle Ages, he was the first major theologian to defend the theory of the Immaculate Conception, and opposed St Thomas Aquinas in arguing that faith was a matter of will rather than something dependent on logical proofs.

Dunstable /ˈdʌnstəb(ə)l/, John (*c.*1390–1453), English composer. He was a significant early exponent of counterpoint.

Dunstan, St /ˈdʌnstən/ (*c.*909–88), Anglo-Saxon prelate. As Archbishop of Canterbury he introduced the strict Benedictine rule into England and succeeded in restoring monastic life. Feast day, 19 May.

dunt /dʌnt/ chiefly N. Amer. & Scottish ▸ **verb** [with obj.] bump into or hit heavily.
▸ **noun** a heavy dull-sounding blow.
– ORIGIN late Middle English: perhaps a variant of **DINT**.

duo ▸ **noun** (pl. **duos**) **1** a pair of people or things, especially in music or entertainment: *the comedy duo Laurel and Hardy.*
2 Music a duet: *two duos for violin and viola.*
– ORIGIN late 16th cent. (in sense 2): via Italian from Latin *duo* 'two'.

duo- ▸ **combining form** two; having two: *duopoly* | *duotone*.
– ORIGIN from Latin.

duodecimal /ˌdjuːə(ʊ)ˈdɛsɪm(ə)l/ ▸ **adjective** relating to or denoting a system of counting or numerical notation that has twelve as a base.
▸ **noun** [mass noun] the system of duodecimal notation.
– DERIVATIVES **duodecimally** adverb.
– ORIGIN late 17th cent.: from Latin *duodecimus* 'twelfth' (from *duodecim* 'twelve') + **-AL**.

duodecimo /ˌdjuːə(ʊ)ˈdɛsɪməʊ/ ▸ **noun** (pl. **duodecimos**) a size of book in which each leaf is one twelfth of the size of the printing sheet. ■ a book of this size.
– ORIGIN mid 17th cent.: from Latin (*in*) *duodecimo* 'in a twelfth', from *duodecimus* 'twelfth'.

duodenary /ˌdjuːəˈdiːnəri/ ▸ **adjective** rare relating to or based on the number twelve.
– ORIGIN mid 19th cent.: from Latin *duodenarius* 'containing twelve', based on *duodecim* 'twelve'.

duodenitis /ˌdjuːədiːˈnʌɪtɪs/ ▸ **noun** [mass noun] Medicine inflammation of the duodenum.

duodeno- /ˌdjuːəˈdiːnəʊ/ (also **duoden-** before a vowel) ▸ **combining form** Anatomy & Medicine relating to the duodenum: *duodenitis*.

duodenum /ˌdjuːəˈdiːnəm/ ▸ **noun** (pl. **duodenums** or **duodena** /-ˈdiːnə/) Anatomy the first part of the small intestine immediately beyond the stomach, leading to the jejunum.
– DERIVATIVES **duodenal** adjective.
– ORIGIN late Middle English: from medieval Latin, from *duodeni* 'in twelves', its length being equivalent to the breadth of approximately twelve fingers.

duologue /ˈdjuːəlɒg/ ▸ **noun** a play or part of a play with speaking roles for only two actors.
– ORIGIN mid 18th cent.: from **DUO-**, on the pattern of *monologue*.

duomo /ˈdwəʊməʊ/ ▸ **noun** (pl. **duomos**) an Italian cathedral.
– ORIGIN Italian, literally 'dome'.

duopoly /djuˈɒpəli/ ▸ **noun** (pl. **duopolies**) a situation in which two suppliers dominate the market for a commodity or service.
– DERIVATIVES **duopolistic** adjective.
– ORIGIN 1920s: from **DUO-**, on the pattern of *monopoly*.

duotone /ˈdjuːətəʊn/ ▸ **noun** a half-tone illustration made from a single original with two different colours at different screen angles. ■ [mass noun] the technique or process of making such illustrations: *the best images that duotone can produce.*

dupatta /dʊˈpʌtə/ ▸ **noun** a length of material worn arranged in two folds over the chest and thrown back around the shoulders, typically with a salwar kameez, by women from South Asia.
– ORIGIN from Hindi *dupaṭṭā*.

dupe[1] ▸ **verb** [with obj.] deceive; trick: *the newspaper was duped into publishing an untrue story.*
▸ **noun** a victim of deception: *men who were simply the dupes of their unscrupulous leaders.*
– DERIVATIVES **dupable** adjective, **duper** noun, **dupery** noun.
ORIGIN late 17th cent.: from dialect French *dupe* 'hoopoe', from the bird's supposedly stupid appearance.

dupe[2] ▸ **verb & noun** short for **DUPLICATE**, especially in photography.

dupion /ˈdjuːpɪən/ (also **silk dupion**) ▸ **noun** [mass noun] a rough slubbed silk fabric woven from the threads of double cocoons. ■ an imitation of this with other fibres.
– ORIGIN early 19th cent. (in the sense 'double cocoon'): from French *doupion*, from Italian *doppione*, from *doppio* 'double'.

duple /ˈdjuːp(ə)l/ ▸ **adjective** Music (of rhythm) based on two main beats to the bar: *duple time.*
– ORIGIN mid 16th cent.: from Latin *duplus*, from *duo* 'two'.

duplet /ˈdjuːplɪt/ ▸ **noun** a set of two things. ■ Music a pair of equal notes to be performed in the time of three.
– ORIGIN mid 17th cent. (as a dicing term in the sense of *doublets* (see **DOUBLET**): from Latin *duplus* 'duple', on the pattern of *doublet*. Current senses date from the 1920s.

duplex /ˈdjuːplɛks/ ▸ **noun 1** N. Amer. a residential building divided into two apartments. ■ a flat on two floors. ■ chiefly N. Amer. & Austral. a semi-detached house.
2 Biochemistry a double-stranded polynucleotide molecule.
▸ **adjective 1** having two parts, in particular: ■ N. Amer. (of a house) consisting of two flats. ■ N. Amer. (of a flat) on two floors. ■ (of paper or board) having two differently coloured layers or sides. ■ (of a printer or its software) capable of printing on both sides of the paper.
2 (of a communications system, computer circuit, etc.) allowing the transmission of two signals simultaneously in opposite directions.
– ORIGIN mid 16th cent. (as an adjective): from Latin *duplex, duplic-*, from *duo* 'two' + *plicare* 'to fold'. The noun dates from the 1920s.

duplicate ▸ **adjective** /ˈdjuːplɪkət/ [attrib.] **1** exactly like something else, especially through having been copied: *a duplicate set of keys.*
2 technical having two corresponding or identical parts.
▸ **noun** /ˈdjuːplɪkət/ **1** one of two or more identical things: *books may be disposed of if they are duplicates.* ■ a copy of an original: *locksmiths can make duplicates of most keys.*
2 short for **DUPLICATE BRIDGE**.
3 archaic a pawnbroker's ticket.
▸ **verb** /ˈdjuːplɪkeɪt/ [with obj.] make or be an exact copy of: *information sheets had to be typed and duplicated* |

they have not been able to duplicate his successes. ■ multiply by two; double: *the normal amount of DNA has been duplicated thousands of times.* ■ do (something) again unnecessarily: *most of these proposals duplicated work already done.*
– PHRASES **in duplicate** twice in exactly the same way. ■ consisting of two exact copies: *forms to complete in duplicate.*
– DERIVATIVES **duplicable** adjective.
– ORIGIN late Middle English (in the sense 'having two corresponding parts'): from Latin *duplicat-* 'doubled', from the verb *duplicare*, from *duplic-* 'twofold' (see DUPLEX).

D

duplicate bridge ▶ noun [mass noun] a competitive form of bridge in which the same hands are played successively by different partnerships.

duplication ▶ noun [mass noun] the action or process of duplicating something: *an attempt to avoid unnecessary duplication of effort.* ■ [count noun] Genetics a DNA segment in a chromosome which is a copy of another segment.
– ORIGIN late Middle English (used in the mathematical sense 'multiplication by two'): from Old French, or from Latin *duplicatio(n-)*, from *duplicare* 'to double' (see DUPLICATE).

duplicator ▶ noun a machine or device for making copies of something, in particular a machine that makes copies of documents by means of fluid ink and a stencil.

duplicitous ▶ adjective **1** deceitful: *a duplicitous philanderer.*
2 Law (of a charge or plea) containing more than one allegation.
– DERIVATIVES **duplicitously** adverb.

duplicity /djuːˈplɪsɪti, djʊ-/ ▶ noun [mass noun] **1** deceitfulness: *the president was accused of duplicity in his dealings with Congress.*
2 archaic the state of being double.
– ORIGIN late Middle English: from Old French *duplicite* or late Latin *duplicitas*, from Latin *duplic-* 'twofold' (see DUPLEX).

dupondius /djuːˈpɒndɪəs/ ▶ noun (pl. **dupondii** /-dɪʌɪ/) a bronze or brass coin of the Roman Empire, equal to two asses or half a sesterce.
– ORIGIN Latin, from *duo* 'two' + *pondo* 'by weight'.

duppy /ˈdʌpi/ ▶ noun (pl. **duppies**) W. Indian a malevolent spirit or ghost.
– ORIGIN late 18th cent.: probably of West African origin.

du Pré /d(j)uː ˈpreɪ/, Jacqueline (1945–87), English cellist. She made her solo debut at the age of 16 and became famous for her interpretations of cello concertos. Her performing career was halted in 1972 by multiple sclerosis.

Dupuytren's contracture /dʊːˈpwiːtrəns/ (also **Dupuytren's disease**) ▶ noun [mass noun] Medicine a condition in which there is fixed forward curvature of one or more fingers, caused by the development of a fibrous connection between the finger tendons and the skin of the palm.
– ORIGIN late 19th cent.: named after Baron Guillaume *Dupuytren* (1777–1835), the French surgeon who first described the condition.

Duque de Caxias /ˌduːkeɪ də kəˈʃiːəʃ/ a city in SE Brazil, a suburb of Rio de Janeiro; pop. 842,686 (2007).

dur /dəː/ ▶ exclamation informal another way of saying DOH[2].

dura[1] /ˈdjʊərə/ (in full **dura mater**) ▶ noun Anatomy the tough outermost membrane enveloping the brain and spinal cord.
– DERIVATIVES **dural** adjective.
– ORIGIN late 19th cent.: from medieval Latin, literally 'hard mother', translation of Arabic *al-'umm al-jāfiya* 'coarse mother'.

dura[2] ▶ noun variant spelling of DURRA.

durability ▶ noun [mass noun] the ability to withstand wear, pressure, or damage: *the reliability and durability of plastics.*

durable ▶ adjective able to withstand wear, pressure, or damage; hard-wearing: *porcelain enamel is strong and durable* | figurative *a durable peace can be achieved.* ■ informal (of a person) having endurance: *the durable Smith lasted the full eight rounds.*
▶ noun (**durables**) short for CONSUMER DURABLES.
– DERIVATIVES **durably** adverb.
– ORIGIN Middle English (in the sense 'steadfast'): via Old French from Latin *durabilis*, from *durare* 'to last' (see DURATION).

durable goods ▶ plural noun North American term for CONSUMER DURABLES.

Duralumin /djʊˈraljʊmɪn/ ▶ noun [mass noun] trademark a hard, light alloy of aluminium with copper and other elements.
– ORIGIN early 20th cent.: perhaps from Latin *durus* 'hard' + ALUMINIUM, but probably influenced by *Düren*, the name of the Rhineland town where such alloys were first produced.

dura mater /ˌdjʊərə ˈmeɪtə/ ▶ noun see DURA[1].

duramen /djʊˈreɪmɛn/ ▶ noun [mass noun] Botany the heartwood of a tree.
– ORIGIN mid 19th cent.: from Latin, literally 'hardness', from *durare* 'harden'.

durance ▶ noun [mass noun] archaic imprisonment or confinement.
– ORIGIN late Middle English (in the sense 'continuance'): from Old French, from *durer* 'to last', from Latin *durare*. The sense 'imprisonment' is first recorded in the early 16th cent.

Durango /djʊˈraŋgəʊ/ a state of north central Mexico. ■ its capital city; pop. 463,830 (2005). Full name VICTORIA DE DURANGO.

Duras /ˈdjʊərɑː/, French /dyʀa/, Marguerite (1914–96), French novelist, film director, and dramatist; pseudonym of *Marguerite Donnadieu*. She is best known for the screenplay to Alain Resnais' film *Hiroshima mon amour* (1959) and for her semi-autobiographical novel *L'Amant* (1984).

duration ▶ noun the time during which something continues: *bicycle hire for the duration of your holiday* | *a flight of over eight hours' duration.*
– PHRASES **for the duration** until the end of something, especially a war. ■ informal for a very long time: *once she sits down on that settee, she'll be there for the duration.*
– DERIVATIVES **durational** adjective.
– ORIGIN late Middle English: via Old French from medieval Latin *duratio(n-)*, from *durare* 'to last', from *durus* 'hard'.

durative /ˈdjʊərətɪv/ ▶ adjective Grammar denoting or relating to continuing action. Contrasted with PUNCTUAL.

Durazzo /duˈrattsəo/ Italian name for DURRËS.

Durban a seaport and resort in South Africa, on the coast of KwaZulu-Natal; pop. 3,409,100 (est. 2009). Former name (until 1835) PORT NATAL.

durbar /ˈdəːbɑː/ ▶ noun historical the court of an Indian ruler. ■ a public reception held by an Indian prince or a British governor or viceroy in India.
– ORIGIN Urdu, from Persian *darbār* 'court'.

durchkomponiert /ˌdʊəxˈkɒmpɒnɪət/, German /ˌdʊrçkɔmpəʊˈniːrt/ ▶ adjective Music (of a composition, especially a song) not based on repeated sections or verses, especially having different music for each verse. Also called THROUGH-COMPOSED.
– ORIGIN from German, from *durch* 'through' + *komponiert* 'composed' (because the music is different throughout).

Dürer /ˈdjʊərə/, German /ˈdyːrɐ/, Albrecht (1471–1528), German engraver and painter. He was the leading German artist of the Renaissance, important for his technically advanced woodcuts and copper engravings and also noted for his watercolours and drawings.

duress /djʊ(ə)ˈrɛs, ˈdjʊərɛs/ ▶ noun [mass noun] threats, violence, constraints, or other action used to coerce someone into doing something against their will or better judgement: *confessions extracted **under duress**.* ■ Law constraint illegally exercised to force someone to perform an act. ■ archaic forcible restraint or imprisonment.
– ORIGIN Middle English (in the sense 'harshness, severity, cruel treatment'): via Old French from Latin *duritia*, from *durus* 'hard'.

Durex ▶ noun (pl. **same**) Brit. trademark a contraceptive sheath; a condom.
– ORIGIN 1930s: name invented by the manufacturers, probably based on Latin *durare* 'to last'.

Durey /djʊəˈreɪ/, French /dyʀɛ/, Louis (1888–1979), French composer. A member until 1921 of the group Les Six, he later wrote music of a deliberate mass appeal, in accordance with communist doctrines on art. Notable works: *La Longue marche* (cantata, 1949).

Durga /ˈdʊəgɑ/ Hinduism a fierce goddess, wife of Shiva, often identified with Kali. She is usually depicted riding a tiger or lion and slaying the buffalo demon, and with eight or ten arms.

Durgapur /ˌdʊəgəˈpʊə/ a city in NE India, in the state of West Bengal; pop. 543,900 (est. 2009).

durgon /ˈdəːgɒn/ ▶ noun see BLACK DURGON.

Durham /ˈdʌrəm/ a city on the River Wear; pop. 42,100 (est. 2009). It is famous for its 11th-century cathedral, which contains the tomb of the Venerable Bede, and its university. ■ (also **County Durham**) a county of NE England; county town, Durham.

Durham quilt ▶ noun a quilt made by sewing together a piece of fabric, an inner wad, and a lining, the stitches making decorative patterns.

durian /ˈdʊərɪən/ ▶ noun **1** a spiny oval tropical fruit containing a creamy pulp. Despite its fetid smell it is highly valued for its flavour.
2 (also **durian tree**) the large tree that bears the durian, native to Malaysia. ● *Durio zibethinus*, family Bombaceae.
– ORIGIN late 16th cent.: from Malay *durian*, from *duri* 'thorn'.

duricrust /ˈdjʊərɪkrʌst/ ▶ noun Geology a hard mineral crust formed at or near the surface of soil in semi-arid regions by the evaporation of groundwater.
– ORIGIN 1920s: from Latin *durus* 'hard' + CRUST.

during ▶ preposition throughout the course or duration of (a period of time): *the restaurant is open during the day* | *the period during which he grew to adulthood.* ■ at a particular point in the course of: *the stabbing took place during a row at a party.*
– ORIGIN late Middle English: present participle of the obsolete verb *dure* 'last, endure, extend', via Old French from Latin *durare* 'to last' (see DURATION).

Durkheim /ˈdəːkhʌɪm/, French /dyʀkɛm/, Émile (1858–1917), French sociologist, one of the founders of modern sociology. He became the first professor of sociology at the Sorbonne (1913). Notable works: *The Division of Labour in Society* (1893) and *Suicide* (1897).

durmast oak /ˈdəːmɑːst/ ▶ noun another term for SESSILE OAK.
– ORIGIN late 18th cent.: *durmast* perhaps originally an error for *dunmast*, from DUN[1] + MAST[2].

durn ▶ verb, exclamation, adjective & adverb US dialect form of DARN[2].

durned ▶ adjective & adverb US dialect form of DARNED.

Duroc /ˈdjʊərɒk/ ▶ noun a pig of a reddish breed developed in North America.
– ORIGIN early 19th cent.: from the name of a stallion that is said to have been bought by the breeder Isaac Frink on the same day as the pigs from which he developed the breed.

durra /ˈdʊrə, ˈdʊərə/ ▶ noun [mass noun] grain sorghum of the principal variety grown from NE Africa to India. ● *Sorghum bicolor* var. *durra*, family Gramineae; **white durra** is var. *cernuum*.
– ORIGIN late 18th cent.: from Arabic *ḏura*, *ḏurra*.

Durrell[1] /ˈdʌrəl/, Gerald (Malcolm) (1925–95), English zoologist and writer, younger brother of Lawrence Durrell. In 1958 he founded a zoo (later the Jersey Wildlife Preservation Trust) devoted to the conservation and captive breeding of endangered species. Notable works: *My Family and Other Animals* (1956).

Durrell[2] /ˈdʌrəl/, Lawrence (George) (1912–90), English novelist, poet, and travel writer, brother of Gerald Durrell. He spent much of his life abroad, particularly in the Mediterranean. Notable works: *Alexandria Quartet* (four novels, 1957–60) and *Prospero's Cell* (travel, 1945).

Durrës /ˈdʊrəs/ a port and resort in Albania, on the Adriatic coast; pop. 132,700 (est. 2009). Italian name DURAZZO.

durrie ▶ noun (pl. **durries**) variant spelling of DHURRIE.

durry ▶ noun Austral./NZ informal a cigarette.
– ORIGIN 1940s: of unknown origin.

durst archaic or regional past of DARE.

durum /ˈdjʊərəm/ (also **durum wheat**) ▶ noun [mass noun] a kind of hard wheat grown in arid regions, having bearded ears and yielding flour that is used to make pasta. ● *Triticum durum*, family Gramineae.
– ORIGIN early 20th cent.: from Latin, neuter of *durus* 'hard', used in the species name since 1798.

durwan /dəːˈwɑːn/ ▶ noun Indian a porter or doorkeeper.
– ORIGIN late 18th cent.: Urdu *darwān*, from Persian.

durzi /ˈdəːzi/ ▶ noun (pl. **durzis**) Indian a tailor.
– ORIGIN Urdu, from Persian *darzī*, from *darz* 'sewing'.

Dushanbe /duːˈʃanbeɪ/ the capital of Tajikistan; pop. 553,000 (est. 2007). Former name (1929–61) STALINABAD.

dusk ▶ noun the darker stage of twilight: *dusk was falling rapidly* | *working the land* ***from dawn to dusk.*** ■ [mass noun] literary semi-darkness: *the dusk of the vestry.*
▶ verb [no obj.] literary grow dark: (as adj. **dusking**) *he saw the lights blaze in the dusking sky.*
▶ adjective literary shadowy, dim, or dark.
– ORIGIN Old English *dox* 'dark, swarthy' and *doxian* 'darken in colour', of Germanic origin; related to Old High German *tusin* 'darkish'; compare with DUN[1] The noun dates from the early 17th cent. The change in form from *-x* to *-sk* occurred in Middle English.

dusky ▶ adjective (**duskier**, **duskiest**) darkish in colour: *dusky red* | *a dusky complexion.* ■ dated used in euphemistic or poetic reference to black or other dark-skinned people: *a dusky Moorish maiden.* ■ literary dim: *dusky light came from a small window.* ■ [attrib.] used in names of animals with dark coloration, e.g. **dusky dolphin**, **dusky warbler**.
– DERIVATIVES **duskily** adverb, **duskiness** noun.

Dussehra /ˈdʌʃərə/ (also **Dasehra**, **Dusserah**) ▶ noun the tenth and final day of the Hindu festival of Navaratri, usually in October. In southern India it especially commemorates the victory of the god Rama over the demon king Ravana.
– ORIGIN from Hindi *daśahrā*, from Sanskrit *daśaharā*.

Düsseldorf /ˈdʊs(ə)ldɔːf/, German /ˈdʏsldɔrf/ an industrial city of NW Germany, on the Rhine, capital of North Rhine-Westphalia; pop. 577,500 (est. 2006).

dust ▶ noun **1** [mass noun] fine, dry powder consisting of tiny particles of earth or waste matter lying on the ground or on surfaces or carried in the air: *the car sent up clouds of dust.* ■ [with modifier] any material in the form of tiny particles: *coal dust.* ■ [in sing.] a fine powder: *he ground it into a fine dust.* ■ [in sing.] a cloud of dust. ■ literary a dead person's remains: *scatter my dust and ashes.* ■ literary the mortal human body: *the soul, that dwells within your dust.*
2 [in sing.] an act of dusting: *a quick dust, to get rid of the cobwebs.*
▶ verb [with obj.] **1** remove the dust or dirt from the surface of (something) by wiping or brushing it: *I broke the vase I had been dusting* | *pick yourself up and* ***dust yourself down*** | [no obj.] *she washed and dusted and tidied.* ■ (**dust something down/off**) bring something out for use again after a long period of neglect: *a number of aircraft will be dusted off and returned to flight.*
2 cover lightly with a powdered substance: *roll out on a surface dusted with icing sugar.* ■ sprinkle (a powdered substance) on to something: *orange powder was dusted over the upper body.*
3 US informal beat up or kill someone: *the officers dusted him up a little bit.*
– PHRASES **be done and dusted** informal (of a project) be completely finished or ready. **dust and ashes** used to convey a feeling of great disappointment or disillusion about something: *the party would be dust and ashes if he couldn't come.* **the dust settles** things quieten down: *she hoped that the dust would settle quickly and the episode be forgotten.* **eat someone's dust** N. Amer. informal fall far behind someone in a competitive situation. **gather** (or **collect**) **dust** remain unused: *some professors let their computers gather dust.* **leave someone/thing in the dust** surpass someone or something easily: *today's modems leave their predecessors in the dust.* **not see someone for dust** find that a person has made a hasty departure. **kick up (a) dust** informal create a disturbance.
– DERIVATIVES **dustless** adjective.
– ORIGIN Old English *dūst*, of Germanic origin; related to Dutch *duist* 'chaff'.

dustball ▶ noun N. Amer. a ball of dust and fluff.

dust bath ▶ noun a bird's act of rolling in dust to clean its feathers.

dustbin ▶ noun Brit. a container for household refuse, especially one kept outside.

dustbin man ▶ noun (pl. **dustbin men**) Brit. a dustman.

dust bowl ▶ noun an area of land where vegetation has been lost and soil reduced to dust and eroded, especially as a consequence of drought or unsuitable farming practice. ■ (**the Dust Bowl**) an area of Oklahoma and other prairie states of the US affected by severe soil erosion in the early 1930s.

dust bunny ▶ noun N. Amer. informal a ball of dust and fluff.

Dustbuster ▶ noun trademark, chiefly N. Amer. a handheld vacuum cleaner.

dustcart ▶ noun Brit. a vehicle used for collecting household refuse.

dustcoat ▶ noun a coat worn for protection against dust. ■ another term for DUSTER (sense 2).

dust cover ▶ noun a dust jacket or dust sheet.

dust devil ▶ noun a small whirlwind or air vortex over land, visible as a column of dust and debris.

duster ▶ noun **1** a cloth or pad for dusting furniture.
2 (also **duster coat**) a woman's loose, lightweight full-length coat without buttons, of a style originally worn in the 1920s when travelling in an open car. ■ N. Amer. a short, light housecoat.
3 US informal a dust storm.

dustheap ▶ noun a heap of household refuse.

dusting powder ▶ noun [mass noun] powder for dusting over something, in particular talcum powder.

dust jacket ▶ noun a removable paper cover, generally with a decorative design, used to protect a book from dirt or damage.

dustman ▶ noun (pl. **dustmen**) Brit. a man employed to remove household refuse from dustbins.

dustpan ▶ noun a flat handheld receptacle into which dust and waste can be swept from the floor.

dust sheet ▶ noun Brit. a large sheet for covering furniture or flooring to protect it from dust or while decorating.

dust shot ▶ noun [mass noun] the smallest size of gunshot.

dust storm ▶ noun a strong, turbulent wind which carries clouds of fine dust, soil, and sand over a large area.

dust trap ▶ noun something on, in, or under which dust readily gathers.

dust-up ▶ noun informal a fight or quarrel: *he'd had a dust-up with Vera.*

dust wrapper ▶ noun another term for DUST JACKET.

dusty ▶ adjective (**dustier**, **dustiest**) covered with, full of, or resembling dust: *dusty old records* | *a hot, dusty road.* ■ (of a colour) dull or muted: *patches of pale gold and dusty pink.* ■ staid and uninteresting: *a dusty old bore.*
– PHRASES **a dusty answer** Brit. a curt and unhelpful reply. **not so dusty** Brit. informal, dated (of a person's health or situation) fairly good.
– DERIVATIVES **dustily** adverb, **dustiness** noun.

dusty miller ▶ noun a plant of the daisy family with whitish or greyish foliage. ● Several species in the family Compositae, in particular the cultivated *Artemisia stellerana* of North America and *Senecio cineraria* of the Mediterranean.
– ORIGIN early 19th cent.: named from the fine powder on the flowers and leaves.

Dutch ▶ adjective relating to the Netherlands or its people or their language.
▶ noun **1** [mass noun] the language of the Netherlands, spoken by some 20 million people.
2 (as plural noun **the Dutch**) the people of the Netherlands collectively.

> Dutch belongs to the West Germanic branch of Indo-European languages and is most closely related to German and English. It is also the official language of Suriname and the Netherlands Antilles, and is spoken in northern Belgium, where it is called Flemish.

– PHRASES **go Dutch** share the cost of something, especially a meal, equally. **in Dutch** US informal, dated in trouble: *he's been getting in Dutch at school.*
– ORIGIN from Middle Dutch *dutsch* 'Dutch, Netherlandish, German': the English word originally denoted speakers of both High and Low German, but became more specific after the United Provinces adopted the Low German of Holland as the national language on independence in 1579.

dutch ▶ noun (usu. **one's old dutch**) Brit. informal (especially among cockneys) one's wife.
– ORIGIN late 19th cent.: abbreviation of DUCHESS.

Dutch auction ▶ noun a method of selling in which the price is reduced until a buyer is found.

Dutch barn ▶ noun Brit. a farm building with a curved roof set over a steel, timber, or concrete frame without walls, used for storing hay.

Dutch cap ▶ noun **1** a woman's lace cap with triangular flaps on each side, worn as part of Dutch traditional dress.
2 see CAP[1] (sense 4 of the noun).

Dutch clover ▶ noun another term for WHITE CLOVER.

Dutch courage ▶ noun [mass noun] strength or confidence gained from drinking alcohol: *I'll have a couple of drinks to give me Dutch courage.*

Dutch doll ▶ noun Brit. a jointed wooden doll.

Dutch door ▶ noun N. Amer. a stable door.

Dutch East India Company a Dutch trading company founded in 1602 to protect Dutch trading interests in the Indian Ocean.

Dutch East Indies former name (until 1949) for INDONESIA.

Dutch elm disease ▶ noun [mass noun] a fungal disease of elm trees that is spread by elm bark beetles. A virulent strain of the fungus which arose in North America has destroyed the majority of elms in southern Britain. ● The fungus is *Ceratocystis ulmi*, subdivision Ascomycotina.

Dutch Guiana former name (until 1948) for SURINAME.

Dutch hoe ▶ noun a hoe used with a pushing action just under the surface of the soil.

dutchie ▶ noun W. Indian a large, heavy cooking pot.
– ORIGIN from DUTCH OVEN.

Dutch interior ▶ noun a painting of the interior of a Dutch house in a style characteristic of the work of 17th-century genre painters.

Dutch light ▶ noun a cold frame in which the glass is a single large pane.

Dutchman (or **Dutchwoman**) ▶ noun (pl. **Dutchmen** or **Dutchwomen**) a native or inhabitant of the Netherlands, or a person of Dutch descent. ■ S. African derogatory an Afrikaner.
– PHRASES **I'm a Dutchman** Brit. used to express one's disbelief or as a way of underlining an emphatic assertion: *if she's seventeen, I'm a Dutchman.*

Dutchman's breeches ▶ noun chiefly N. Amer. a plant related to bleeding heart, but typically having pale yellow flowers. ● Genus *Dicentra*, family Fumariaceae: several species, in particular *D. spectabilis*.
– ORIGIN mid 19th cent.: so named because of the shape of the spurred flower.

Dutchman's pipe ▶ noun a vigorous climbing vine with hooked tubular flowers, native to eastern North America. ● *Aristolochia durior*, family Aristolochiaceae.

Dutch metal ▶ noun [mass noun] an alloy of copper and zinc used in imitation of gold leaf.

Dutch New Guinea former name (until 1963) for PAPUA (sense 1).

Dutch oven ▶ noun a covered earthenware or cast-iron container for cooking casseroles. ■ chiefly historical a large cooking pot or metal box serving as a simple oven, heated by being placed under or next to hot coals. ■ S. African a brick or clay oven traditionally built into the side of a kitchen hearth or as a free-standing structure outside a house.

Dutch Reformed Church a branch of the Protestant Church in the Netherlands, formed during the Reformation. It was replaced in 1816 by the Netherlands Reformed Church. ■ the dominant branch of the Protestant Church among Afrikaners in South Africa.

Dutch tile ▶ noun a kind of glazed white tile painted with traditional Dutch motifs in blue or brown.
▶ verb [with obj.] (usu. as adj. **Dutch-tiled**) decorate with such tiles: *Dutch-tiled fireplaces.*

Dutch treat ▶ noun an outing, meal, or other special occasion at which each participant pays for their share of the expenses.

Dutch uncle ▶ noun informal, chiefly N. Amer. a person giving firm but benevolent advice.

Dutch West India Company a Dutch trading company founded in 1621 to develop Dutch trading interests in western India, South America, and West Africa.

Dutch wife ▶ noun a bolster used for resting the legs in bed.
– ORIGIN late 19th cent.: extended use of the term, earlier describing a rattan open frame used in the Dutch Indies to support the limbs in bed.

Dutchwoman ▶ noun see DUTCHMAN.

duteous /ˈdjuːtɪəs/ ▶ adjective archaic dutiful: *a duteous vassal.*
– DERIVATIVES **duteously** adverb.
– ORIGIN late 16th cent.: from DUTY, on the pattern of words such as *bounteous.*

dutiable /ˈdjuːtɪəb(ə)l/ ▶ adjective liable to customs or other duties: *dutiable goods.*

dutiful ▸ adjective conscientiously or obediently fulfilling one's duty: *a dutiful daughter.* ▪ motivated by duty rather than desire or enthusiasm: *dutiful applause* | *a dutiful visit.*
– DERIVATIVES **dutifully** adverb, **dutifulness** noun.

duty ▸ noun (pl. **duties**) **1** a moral or legal obligation; a responsibility: *it's my duty to uphold the law* | *she was determined to* ***do her duty*** *as a citizen* | [mass noun] *a strong sense of duty.* ▪ [as modifier] (of a visit or other undertaking) done from a sense of moral obligation rather than for pleasure: *a fifteen-minute duty visit.* **2** (often **duties**) a task or action that one is required to perform as part of one's job: *the queen's official duties* | *your duties will include operating the switchboard* | [mass noun] *Juliet reported for duty.* ▪ [mass noun] military service: *combat duty in the army.* ▪ [as modifier] (of a person) engaged in their regular work: *a duty nurse.* ▪ [mass noun] (also **duties**) performance of prescribed church services by a priest or minister: *he was willing to take Sunday duties.* **3** a payment levied on the import, export, manufacture, or sale of goods: *a 6 per cent* ***duty on imports*** | [mass noun] *goods subject to excise duty.* ▪ Brit. a payment levied on the transfer of property, for licences, and for the legal recognition of documents. **4** technical the measure of an engine's effectiveness in units of work done per unit of fuel.
– PHRASES **do duty as** (or **for**) serve or act as a substitute for something else: *the rusting shack which did duty as the bridge.* **on** (or **off**) **duty** engaged (or not engaged) in one's regular work: *the doorman had gone off duty and the lobby was unattended.*
– ORIGIN late Middle English: from Anglo-Norman French *duete*, from Old French *deu* (see DUE).

duty-bound ▸ adjective [with infinitive] morally or legally obliged to do something: *legitimate news stories which the press is duty-bound to report.*

duty cycle ▸ noun the cycle of operation of a machine or other device which operates intermittently rather than continuously.

duty drawback ▸ noun see DRAWBACK (sense 2).

duty-free ▸ adjective & adverb exempt from payment of duty: [as adj.] *the permitted number of duty-free goods* | [as adv.] *most EC goods enter almost duty-free.* ▪ [as adj.] (of a shop or area) selling or trading in goods that are exempt from payment of duty.
▸ noun [mass noun] (also **duty-frees**) goods that are exempt from payment of duty: *a bag of duty-free.*

duty officer ▸ noun an officer, especially in the police or armed forces, who is on duty at a particular time.

duty-paid ▸ adjective on which the cost of duty has been met: *limits on duty-paid goods.*

duumvir /djuːˈʌmvə/ ▸ noun (in ancient Rome) each of two magistrates or officials holding a joint office.
– ORIGIN Latin, from *duum virum* 'of the two men'.

duumvirate /djuːˈʌmvɪrət/ ▸ noun a coalition of two people having joint authority or influence.
– ORIGIN mid 17th cent.: from Latin *duumviratus.*

Duvalier /djuːˈvalɪeɪ/, François (1907–71), Haitian statesman, President 1957–71; known as **Papa Doc**. His regime was noted for its oppressive nature, opponents being assassinated or forced into exile by his security force, the Tontons Macoutes. He was succeeded by his son Jean-Claude (b.1951), known as **Baby Doc**, who was overthrown in 1986.

duvet /ˈd(j)uːveɪ/ ▸ noun chiefly Brit. a soft quilt filled with down, feathers, or a synthetic fibre, used instead of an upper sheet and blankets. ▪ (also **duvet jacket**) a thick down-filled jacket worn by mountaineers.
– ORIGIN mid 18th cent.: from French, literally 'down' (see DOWN²).

duvet day ▸ noun informal an unscheduled extra day's leave from work, taken to alleviate stress or pressure and sanctioned by one's employer.

dux /dʌks/ ▸ noun (pl. **duces** /ˈdjuːsiːz/) chiefly Scottish the top pupil in a school or class.
– ORIGIN mid 18th cent. (denoting the leading voice or instrument in a fugue or canon): from Latin, 'leader'.

duxelles /ˈdʌks(ə)lz, dʊkˈsɛl/ ▸ noun [mass noun] a preparation of mushrooms sautéed with onions, shallots, garlic, and parsley and used to make stuffing or sauce.
– ORIGIN named after the Marquis *d'Uxelles*, a 17th-cent. French nobleman.

DV ▸ abbreviation formal Deo volente: *this time next week (DV) I shall be among the mountains.*

DVD ▸ noun (pl. **DVDs**) a type of compact disc able to store large amounts of data, especially high-resolution audiovisual material.
– ORIGIN 1990s: abbreviation of *digital versatile disc* (originally of *digital video disc*).

DVD-R ▸ noun a DVD which can be recorded on once only.
– ORIGIN abbreviation of *DVD recordable.*

DVD-ROM ▸ noun a DVD used in a computer for displaying data.
– ORIGIN abbreviation from *DVD read-only memory.*

DVD-RW (also **DVD-RAM**) ▸ noun a DVD on which recordings can be made and erased a number of times.
– ORIGIN abbreviation of *DVD rewritable (or random-access memory).*

DVLA ▸ abbreviation Driver and Vehicle Licensing Agency.

DVM ▸ abbreviation Doctor of Veterinary Medicine.

Dvořák /ˈdvɔːʒak, -ʒɑːk/, Antonín (1841–1904), Czech composer. Combining folk elements with the Viennese musical tradition, he wrote chamber music, operas, and songs, but is best known for his ninth symphony ('From the New World', 1892–5).

DVR ▸ abbreviation digital video recorder.

DVT ▸ abbreviation deep-vein thrombosis.

dwaal /dwɑːl/ ▸ noun S. African informal a dreamy, dazed, or absent-minded state: *you're* ***in a real dwaal!***
– ORIGIN Afrikaans.

dwale /dweɪl/ ▸ noun [mass noun] archaic deadly nightshade or belladonna. ▪ a soporific drink formerly made from this.
– ORIGIN Middle English: probably of Scandinavian origin and related to Danish *dvale* 'deep sleep, stupor', *dvaledrik* 'sleeping draught'.

dwam /dwɑːm/ ▸ noun chiefly Scottish a state of semi-consciousness or reverie.
– ORIGIN early 16th cent.: from the Germanic base of DWELL; compare with Middle Dutch *dwelm* 'stupefaction', also with Old English *dwolma* 'confusion'.

dwarf ▸ noun (pl. **dwarfs** or **dwarves**) **1** (in folklore or fantasy literature) a member of a mythical race of short, stocky human-like creatures who are generally skilled in mining and metalworking. ▪ an abnormally small person. ▪ [as modifier] denoting something, especially an animal or plant, which is much smaller than the usual size for its type or species: *a dwarf conifer.* **2** (also **dwarf star**) Astronomy a star of relatively small size and low luminosity, including the majority of main sequence stars.
▸ verb [with obj.] cause to seem small or insignificant in comparison: *the buildings surround and dwarf All Saints church.* ▪ stunt the growth or development of: (as adj. **dwarfed**) *the dwarfed but solid branch of a tree.*
– DERIVATIVES **dwarfish** adjective.
– ORIGIN Old English *dweorg, dweorh*, of Germanic origin; related to Dutch *dwerg* and German *Zwerg.*

> **USAGE** In the sense 'an abnormally small person', **dwarf** is normally considered offensive. However, there are no accepted alternatives in the general language, since terms such as **person of restricted growth** have gained little currency.

dwarfism ▸ noun [mass noun] (in medical or technical contexts) unusually or abnormally low stature or small size.

dwarf planet ▸ noun Astronomy a celestial body resembling a small planet but lacking certain technical criteria that are required for it to be classed as such.

dweeb ▸ noun N. Amer. informal a boring, studious, or socially inept person.
– DERIVATIVES **dweebish** adjective, **dweeby** adjective (**dweebier, dweebiest**).
– ORIGIN 1980s: perhaps a blend of DWARF and early 20th-cent. *feeb* 'a feeble-minded person' (from FEEBLE).

dwell ▸ verb (past and past participle **dwelt** or **dwelled**) [no obj.] **1** [with adverbial of place] formal live in or at a specified place: *groups of gypsies still dwell in these caves* | (as adj., in combination **-dwelling**) *bottom-dwelling fish.* **2** (**dwell on/upon**) think, speak, or write at length about (a particular subject, especially one that is a source of unhappiness, anxiety, or dissatisfaction): *I've got better things to do than dwell on the past.* ▪ (**dwell on/upon**) (of one's eyes or attention) linger on (a particular object or place): *she let her eyes dwell on them for a moment.*
▸ noun technical a slight regular pause in the motion of a machine.
– DERIVATIVES **dweller** noun [in combination] *city-dwellers.*
– ORIGIN Old English *dwellan* 'lead astray, hinder, delay' (in Middle English 'tarry, remain in a place'), of Germanic origin; related to Middle Dutch *dwellen* 'stun, perplex' and Old Norse *dvelja* 'delay, tarry, stay'.

dwelling (also **dwelling place**) ▸ noun formal a house, flat, or other place of residence.

dwelling house ▸ noun Law a house used as a residence rather than for business.

dwell time ▸ noun [mass noun] technical time spent in the same position, area, stage of a process, etc.

DWEM ▸ abbreviation dead white European male.

DWI ▸ abbreviation US driving while intoxicated.

dwindle ▸ verb [no obj.] diminish gradually in size, amount, or strength: *traffic has dwindled to a trickle* | (as adj. **dwindling**) *dwindling resources.*
– ORIGIN late 16th cent.: frequentative of Scots and dialect *dwine* 'fade away', from Old English *dwīnan*, of Germanic origin; related to Middle Dutch *dwīnen* and Old Norse *dvína.*

DWM ▸ abbreviation dead white male.

DWP ▸ abbreviation (in the UK) Department for Work and Pensions.

dwt ▸ abbreviation ▪ deadweight tonnage: *a 40,000 dwt slipway.* ▪ pennyweight.

DY ▸ abbreviation Benin (international vehicle registration).
– ORIGIN from DAHOMEY.

Dy ▸ symbol the chemical element dysprosium.

dyad /ˈdʌɪad/ ▸ noun technical something that consists of two elements or parts. ▪ Mathematics an operator which is a combination of two vectors.
– DERIVATIVES **dyadic** adjective.
– ORIGIN late 17th cent. (originally denoting the number two or a pair): from late Latin *dyas, dyad-*, from Greek *duas*, from *duo* 'two'. Current senses date from the late 19th cent.

Dyak /ˈdʌɪak/ ▸ noun & adjective variant spelling of DAYAK.

dyarchy ▸ noun (pl. **dyarchies**) variant spelling of DIARCHY.

dybbuk /ˈdɪbʊk/ ▸ noun (pl. **dybbuks** or **dybbukim** /-kɪm/) (in Jewish folklore) a malevolent wandering spirit that enters and possesses the body of a living person until exorcised.
– ORIGIN from Yiddish *dibek*, from Hebrew *dibbūq*, from *dāḇaq* 'cling'.

dye ▸ noun [mass noun] a natural or synthetic substance used to add a colour to or change the colour of something: *blonde hair dye* | [count noun] *a black dye.*
▸ verb (**dyes, dyeing, dyed**) [with obj.] add a colour to or change the colour of (something) by soaking it in a solution impregnated with a dye: [with complement] *I dyed my hair blonde* | (as adj. **dyed**) *dyed black hair.* ▪ [no obj.] take colour well or badly during such a process: *it's good material—it should dye well.*
– PHRASES **dyed in the wool** unchanging in a particular belief or opinion; inveterate: *she's a true blue dyed-in-the-wool Conservative.* [with allusion to the fact that yarn was dyed in the raw state, producing a more even and permanent colour.]
– DERIVATIVES **dyeable** adjective.
– ORIGIN Old English *dēag* (noun), *dēagian* (verb). The noun is not recorded from Old English to the late 16th cent., when it was re-formed from the verb.

dye laser ▸ noun a tunable laser using the fluorescence of an organic dye.

dyeline ▸ noun [usu. as modifier] a diazo copying or colouring process.

dyer ▸ noun a person whose trade is the dyeing of cloth or other material.

dyer's greenweed ▸ noun [mass noun] a bushy yellow-flowered Eurasian plant of the pea family, which has become naturalized in North America. The flowers were formerly used to make a yellow or green dye.
● *Genista tinctoria*, family Leguminosae.

dyer's oak ▸ noun another term for VALONIA.

dyer's rocket ▸ noun another term for WELD².

dyestuff ▸ noun a substance yielding a dye or that can be used as a dye, especially when in solution.

Dyfed /ˈdʌvɛd/ a former county of SW Wales 1974–96, which included the present counties of Ceredigion, Carmarthenshire, and Pembrokeshire.

dying ▶ **adjective** on the point of death: *he visited his dying mother.* ■ occurring at or connected with the time that someone dies: *he strained to catch her dying words.* ■ gradually ceasing to exist or function; in decline and about to disappear: *the making of valves is a dying art | the dying embers of the fire.* ■ (of a period of time) final; closing: *the dying moments of the match.*
– PHRASES **to** (or **until**) **one's dying day** for the rest of one's life: *he will regret that decision to his dying day.*
– ORIGIN late 16th cent.: present participle of **DIE**[1].

dyke[1] (also **dike**) ▶ **noun 1** a long wall or embankment built to prevent flooding from the sea. ■ [often in place names] a low wall or earthwork serving as a boundary or defence: *Offa's Dyke.* ■ a causeway.
2 a ditch or watercourse.
3 Geology an intrusion of igneous rock cutting across existing strata. Compare with **SILL**.
4 Austral./NZ informal, dated a toilet.
▶ **verb** [with obj.] (often as adj. **dyked**) provide (land) with a wall or embankment to prevent flooding.
– PHRASES **put one's finger in the dyke** attempt to stem the advance of something undesirable. [from a story of a small Dutch boy who saved his community from flooding, by placing his finger in a hole in a dyke.]
– ORIGIN Middle English (denoting a trench or ditch): from Old Norse *dík*, related to **DITCH**. Sense 1 of the noun has been influenced by Middle Low German *dīk* 'dam' and Middle Dutch *dijc* 'ditch, dam'.

dyke[2] (also **dike**) ▶ **noun** informal a lesbian.
– DERIVATIVES **dykey** adjective (**dykier, dykiest**).
– ORIGIN 1940s (earlier as **BULLDYKE**): of unknown origin.

Dylan /ˈdɪlən/, Bob (b.1941), American singer and songwriter; born *Robert Allen Zimmerman.* The leader of an urban folk-music revival in the 1960s, he became known for political and protest songs such as 'The Times They Are A-Changin' (1964). Notable albums: *Highway 61 Revisited* (1965) and *Blood on the Tracks* (1975).

dyn ▶ **abbreviation** dyne.

dynamic /dʌɪˈnamɪk/ ▶ **adjective 1** (of a process or system) characterized by constant change, activity, or progress: *a dynamic economy.* ■ Physics relating to forces producing motion. Often contrasted with **STATIC**. ■ Linguistics (of a verb) expressing an action, activity, event, or process. Contrasted with **STATIVE**. ■ denoting or relating to web pages that update frequently or are generated according to an individual's search terms: *the dynamic content of these sites keeps their audience informed and up to date.*
2 ■ (of a person) positive in attitude and full of energy and new ideas: *a dynamic young advertising executive.*
3 Electronics (of a memory device) needing to be refreshed by the periodic application of a voltage.
4 Music relating to the volume of sound produced by an instrument, voice, or recording.
▶ **noun 1** a force that stimulates change or progress within a system or process: *evaluation is part of the basic dynamic of the project.*
2 Music another term for **DYNAMICS** (sense 3).
– DERIVATIVES **dynamical** adjective, **dynamically** adverb.
– ORIGIN early 19th cent. (as a term in physics): from French *dynamique*, from Greek *dunamikos*, from *dunamis* 'power'.

dynamic equilibrium ▶ **noun** a state of balance between continuing processes.

dynamic metamorphism ▶ **noun** [mass noun] Geology metamorphism produced by mechanical forces.

dynamic pricing ▶ **noun** [mass noun] the practice of pricing items at a level determined by a particular customer's perceived ability to pay.

dynamic range ▶ **noun** the range of acceptable or possible volumes of sound occurring in the course of a piece of music or a performance. ■ the ratio of the largest to the smallest intensity of sound that can be reliably transmitted or reproduced by a particular sound system, measured in decibels.

dynamics ▶ **plural noun 1** [treated as sing.] the branch of mechanics concerned with the motion of bodies under the action of forces. Compare with **STATICS**. ■ [usu. with modifier] the branch of any science in which forces or changes are considered: *chemical dynamics.*
2 the forces or properties which stimulate growth, development, or change within a system or process: *the dynamics of changing social relations.*
3 Music the varying levels of volume of sound in different parts of a musical performance.
– DERIVATIVES **dynamicist** noun (sense 1).

dynamic viscosity ▶ **noun** a quantity measuring the force needed to overcome internal friction in a fluid.

dynamism ▶ **noun** [mass noun] **1** the quality of being characterized by vigorous activity and progress: *the dynamism and strength of the economy.* ■ the quality of being dynamic and positive in attitude: *he was known for his dynamism and strong views.*
2 Philosophy, chiefly historical the theory that phenomena of matter or mind are due to the action of forces rather than to motion or matter.
– DERIVATIVES **dynamist** noun.
– ORIGIN mid 19th cent.: from Greek *dunamis* 'power' + **-ISM**.

dynamite ▶ **noun** [mass noun] a high explosive consisting of nitroglycerine mixed with an absorbent material and typically moulded into sticks. ■ something that could generate extreme reactions or have devastating repercussions: *that roads policy is political dynamite.* ■ informal an extremely impressive or exciting person or thing: *both her albums are dynamite* | [as modifier] *a chick with a dynamite figure.* ■ informal, dated a narcotic, especially heroin.
▶ **verb** [with obj.] blow up (something) with dynamite.
– DERIVATIVES **dynamiter** noun.
– ORIGIN mid 19th cent.: from Greek *dunamis* 'power' + **-ITE**[1].

dynamize (also **dynamise**) ▶ **verb** [with obj.] give power or energy to; make dynamic.
– DERIVATIVES **dynamization** noun.

dynamo ▶ **noun** (pl. **dynamos**) chiefly Brit. a machine for converting mechanical energy into electrical energy, typically by means of rotating coils of copper wire in a magnetic field. ■ informal an extremely energetic person: *she was a dynamo in London politics.*
– ORIGIN late 19th cent.: abbreviation of *dynamo-electric machine*, from Greek *dunamis* 'power'.

dynamometer /ˌdʌɪnəˈmɒmɪtə/ ▶ **noun** an instrument which measures the power output of an engine.
– ORIGIN early 19th cent.: from French *dynamomètre*, from Greek *dunamis* 'power' + French *-mètre* '(instrument) measuring'.

dynast /ˈdɪnəst, ˈdʌɪnəst, -nast/ ▶ **noun** a member of a powerful family, especially a hereditary ruler.
– ORIGIN mid 17th cent.: via Latin from Greek *dunastēs*, from *dunasthai* 'be able'.

dynasty /ˈdɪnəsti/ ▶ **noun** (pl. **dynasties**) a line of hereditary rulers of a country: *the Tang dynasty.* ■ a succession of people from the same family who play a prominent role in business, politics, or another field: *the Guinness dynasty.*
– DERIVATIVES **dynastic** /dɪˈnastɪk, dʌɪˈnastɪk/ adjective, **dynastically** adverb.
– ORIGIN late Middle English: from French *dynastie*, or via late Latin from Greek *dunasteia* 'lordship, power', from *dunastēs* (see **DYNAST**).

dyne /dʌɪn/ ▶ **noun** Physics a unit of force that, acting on a mass of one gram, increases its velocity by one centimetre per second every second along the direction that it acts.
– ORIGIN late 19th cent.: from French, from Greek *dunamis* 'force, power'.

dyno ▶ **noun** (pl. **dynos**) **1** short for **DYNAMOMETER**.
2 Climbing a rapid move across a rock face in order to reach a hold.
▶ **verb** (**dynos, dynoing, dyno'd** or **dynoed**) **1** [with obj.] measure (the output of an engine) with a dynamometer.
2 [no obj.] (in mountaineering) climb using dynos.

dynode /ˈdʌɪnəʊd/ ▶ **noun** Electronics an intermediate electrode which emits additional electrons in a photomultiplier or similar amplifying device.
– ORIGIN 1930s: from Greek *dunamis* 'power' + **-ODE**[2].

dys- /dɪs/ ▶ **combining form** bad; difficult (used especially in medical terms): *dyspepsia | dysphasia.*
– ORIGIN from Greek *dus-*; related to German *zer-*, also to Old English *to-*.

dysaesthesia /dɪsɪsˈθiːzɪə/ (US **dysesthesia**) ▶ **noun** (pl. **dysaesthesiae** /-ziːi:/ or **dysaesthesias**) Medicine an abnormal unpleasant sensation felt when touched, caused by damage to peripheral nerves.
– ORIGIN early 18th cent.: modern Latin, from Greek *dusaisthēsia*, from **DYS-** 'bad' + *aisthēsis* 'sensation' + **-IA**[1].

dysarthria /dɪsˈɑːθrɪə/ ▶ **noun** [mass noun] Medicine difficult or unclear articulation of speech that is otherwise linguistically normal.
– ORIGIN late 19th cent.: from **DYS-** 'difficult' + Greek *arthron* 'joint or articulation'.

dyscalculia /ˌdɪskalˈkjuːlɪə/ ▶ **noun** [mass noun] Psychiatry severe difficulty in making arithmetical calculations, as a result of brain disorder.

dyscrasia /dɪsˈkreɪzɪə/ ▶ **noun** [mass noun] Medicine an abnormal or disordered state of the body or of a bodily part.
– ORIGIN late Middle English (denoting an imbalance of physical qualities): via late Latin from Greek *duskrasia* 'bad combination', from *dus-* 'bad' + *krasis* 'mixture'.

dysentery /ˈdɪs(ə)nt(ə)ri/ ▶ **noun** [mass noun] infection of the intestines resulting in severe diarrhoea with the presence of blood and mucus in the faeces.
● **Amoebic dysentery** is caused by the protozoan *Entamoeba histolytica*, mainly in warm climates, and spread by contaminated water and food; **bacterial dysentery** is caused by bacteria of the genus *Shigella* and can also spread by contact (see **SHIGELLA**).
– DERIVATIVES **dysenteric** /-ˈtɛrɪk/ adjective.
– ORIGIN late Middle English: from Old French *dissenterie*, or via Latin from Greek *dusenteria*, from *dusenteros* 'afflicted in the bowels', from *dus-* 'bad' + *entera* 'bowels'.

dysesthesia ▶ **noun** US spelling of **DYSAESTHESIA**.

dysfunction ▶ **noun** [mass noun] abnormality or impairment in the operation of a specified bodily organ or system: *bowel dysfunction.* ■ disruption of normal social relations: *inner-city dysfunction.*

dysfunctional ▶ **adjective** not operating normally or properly: *the telephones are dysfunctional.* ■ unable to deal adequately with normal social relations: *an emotionally dysfunctional businessman | dysfunctional families.*
– DERIVATIVES **dysfunctionality** noun, **dysfunctionally** adverb.

dysgenic /dɪsˈdʒɛnɪk/ ▶ **adjective** exerting a detrimental effect on later generations through the inheritance of undesirable characteristics: *dysgenic breeding.*

dysgraphia /dɪsˈgrafɪə/ ▶ **noun** [mass noun] Psychiatry inability to write coherently, as a symptom of brain disease or damage.
– DERIVATIVES **dysgraphic** adjective.
– ORIGIN 1930s: from **DYS-** 'difficult' + Greek *-graphia* 'writing'.

dyskinesia /ˌdɪskɪˈniːzɪə, -kʌɪ-/ ▶ **noun** [mass noun] Medicine abnormality or impairment of voluntary movement.

dyslalia /dɪsˈleɪlɪə/ ▶ **noun** [mass noun] Medicine inability to articulate comprehensible speech, especially when associated with the use of private words or sounds.
– ORIGIN mid 19th cent.: from **DYS-** 'difficult' + Greek *lalia* 'speech'.

dyslexia /dɪsˈlɛksɪə/ ▶ **noun** [mass noun] a general term for disorders that involve difficulty in learning to read or interpret words, letters, and other symbols, but that do not affect general intelligence.
– DERIVATIVES **dyslectic** adjective & noun, **dyslexic** adjective & noun.
– ORIGIN late 19th cent.: coined in German from **DYS-** 'difficult' + Greek *lexis* 'speech' (apparently by confusion of Greek *legein* 'to speak' and Latin *legere* 'to read').

dysmenorrhoea /ˌdɪsmɛnəˈriːə/ (US **dysmenorrhea**) ▶ **noun** [mass noun] Medicine painful menstruation, typically involving abdominal cramps.

dysmorphia /dɪsˈmɔːfɪə/ ▶ **noun** [mass noun] Medicine deformity or abnormality in the shape or size of a specified part of the body: *muscle dysmorphia.*
– DERIVATIVES **dysmorphic** adjective.
– ORIGIN late 19th cent.: from Greek *dusmorphia* 'misshapenness, ugliness', from *dus-* **DYS-** + *morphē* 'form'.

dyspareunia /ˌdɪspəˈruːnɪə/ ▶ **noun** [mass noun] Medicine difficult or painful sexual intercourse.
– ORIGIN late 19th cent.: from **DYS-** 'difficult' + Greek *pareunos* 'lying with'.

dyspepsia /dɪsˈpɛpsɪə/ ▶ **noun** [mass noun] indigestion.
– ORIGIN early 18th cent.: via Latin from Greek *duspepsia*, from *duspeptos* 'difficult to digest'.

dyspeptic ▶ **adjective** having indigestion or a consequent air of irritable bad temper.
▶ **noun** a person who suffers from indigestion or bad temper.

dysphagia /dɪsˈfeɪdʒɪə/ ▶ **noun** [mass noun] Medicine difficulty or discomfort in swallowing, as a symptom of disease: *progressive dysphagia.*

D

D

dysphasia /dɪsˈfeɪzɪə/ ▶ **noun** [mass noun] Psychiatry language disorder marked by deficiency in the generation of speech, and sometimes also in its comprehension, due to brain disease or damage.
– DERIVATIVES **dysphasic** adjective.
– ORIGIN late 19th cent.: from Greek *dusphatos* 'hard to utter', from *dus-* 'difficult' + *phatos* 'spoken'.

dysphemism /ˈdɪsfɪmɪz(ə)m/ ▶ **noun** a derogatory or unpleasant term used instead of a pleasant or neutral one. The opposite of **EUPHEMISM**.

dysphonia /dɪsˈfəʊnɪə/ ▶ **noun** [mass noun] Medicine difficulty in speaking due to a physical disorder of the mouth, tongue, throat, or vocal cords.

dysphoria /dɪsˈfɔːrɪə/ ▶ **noun** [mass noun] Psychiatry a state of unease or generalized dissatisfaction with life. The opposite of **EUPHORIA**.
– DERIVATIVES **dysphoric** adjective & noun.
– ORIGIN mid 19th cent.: from Greek *dusphoria*, from *dusphoros* 'hard to bear'.

dysplasia /dɪsˈpleɪzɪə/ ▶ **noun** [mass noun] Medicine the enlargement of an organ or tissue by the proliferation of cells of an abnormal type, as a developmental disorder or an early stage in the development of cancer.
– DERIVATIVES **dysplastic** adjective.
– ORIGIN 1930s: from **DYS-** 'bad' + Greek *plasis* 'formation'.

dyspnoea /dɪspˈniːə/ (US **dyspnea**) ▶ **noun** [mass noun] Medicine difficult or laboured breathing.
– DERIVATIVES **dyspnoeic** adjective.
– ORIGIN mid 17th cent.: via Latin from Greek *duspnoia*, from *dus-* 'difficult' + *pnoē* 'breathing'.

dyspraxia /dɪsˈpraksɪə/ ▶ **noun** [mass noun] Medicine a developmental disorder of the brain in childhood causing difficulty in activities requiring coordination and movement.
– ORIGIN early 20th cent.: from Greek *dus-* 'bad or difficult' + *praxis* 'action'.

dysprosium /dɪsˈprəʊzɪəm/ ▶ **noun** [mass noun] the chemical element of atomic number 66, a soft silvery-white metal of the lanthanide series. (Symbol: **Dy**)
– ORIGIN late 19th cent.: from Greek *dusprositos* 'hard to get at' + **-IUM**.

dysrhythmia /dɪsˈrɪðmɪə/ ▶ **noun** [mass noun] Medicine abnormality in a physiological rhythm, especially in the activity of the brain or heart.
– DERIVATIVES **dysrhythmic** adjective.

dysthymia /dɪsˈθʌɪmɪə/ ▶ **noun** [mass noun] Psychiatry persistent mild depression.
– DERIVATIVES **dysthymic** adjective & noun.
– ORIGIN mid 19th cent.: from Greek *dusthumia*.

dystocia /dɪsˈtəʊʃə/ ▶ **noun** [mass noun] Medicine & Veterinary Medicine difficult birth, typically caused by a large or awkwardly positioned fetus, by smallness of the maternal pelvis, or by failure of the uterus and cervix to contract and expand normally.
– ORIGIN early 18th cent.: from Greek *dustokia*, from *dus-* 'difficult' + *tokos* 'childbirth'.

dystonia /dɪsˈtəʊnɪə/ ▶ **noun** [mass noun] Medicine a state of abnormal muscle tone resulting in muscular spasm and abnormal posture, typically due to neurological disease or a side effect of drug therapy.
– DERIVATIVES **dystonic** adjective.

dystopia /dɪsˈtəʊpɪə/ ▶ **noun** an imagined place or state in which everything is unpleasant or bad, typically a totalitarian or environmentally degraded one. The opposite of **UTOPIA**.
– DERIVATIVES **dystopian** (also **dystopic**) adjective & noun.
– ORIGIN late 18th cent.: from **DYS-** 'bad' + **UTOPIA**.

dystrophia myotonica /dɪsˌtrəʊfɪə mʌɪəˈtɒnɪkə/ ▶ **noun** [mass noun] Medicine a form of muscular dystrophy in which myotonia also occurs.

dystrophic /dɪsˈtrəʊfɪk, -ˈtrɒfɪk/ ▶ **adjective 1** Medicine affected by or relating to dystrophy, especially muscular dystrophy.
2 Ecology (of a lake) having brown acidic water that is low in oxygen and supports little life, owing to high levels of dissolved humus. Compare with **EUTROPHIC** and **OLIGOTROPHIC**.
– ORIGIN late 19th cent.: from Greek *dus-* 'bad' + *-trophia* 'nourishment' + **-IC**.

dystrophin /dɪsˈtrəʊfɪn/ ▶ **noun** [mass noun] Biochemistry a protein found in skeletal muscle, which is absent in sufferers from muscular dystrophy.

dystrophy /ˈdɪstrəfi/ ▶ **noun** [mass noun] Medicine & Veterinary Medicine a disorder in which an organ or tissue of the body wastes away. See also **MUSCULAR DYSTROPHY**.
– ORIGIN late 19th cent.: from modern Latin *dystrophia*, from Greek *dus-* 'bad' + *-trophia* 'nourishment'.

dysuria /dɪsˈjʊərɪə/ ▶ **noun** [mass noun] Medicine painful or difficult urination.
– ORIGIN late Middle English: via late Latin from Greek *dusouria*, from *dus-* 'difficult' + *ouron* 'urine'.

DZ ▶ **abbreviation** ■ Algeria (international vehicle registration). [from Arabic *Djazïr*.] ■ drop zone.

Dzaoudzi /ˈdzaʊdzi/ the former capital of the French island of Mayotte and of the Comoros; pop. 15,300 (est. 2007).

Dzaudzhikau /ˌdzaʊdʒɪˈkaʊ/ former name (1944–54) for **VLADIKAVKAZ**.

Dzerzhinsk /dzəːˈʒɪnsk/ a city in west central Russia, west of Nizhni Novgorod; pop. 247,500 (est. 2008). Former names **CHERNORECHYE** and **RASTYAPINO**.

Dzerzhinsky /dzəːˈʒɪnski/, Feliks (Edmundovich) (1877–1926), Russian Bolshevik leader, of Polish descent. He was the organizer and first head of the post-revolutionary Soviet security police (the Cheka, later the OGPU).

dzo /ʒəʊ, zəʊ/ (also **dzho** or **zho**) ▶ **noun** (pl. **same** or **dzos**) a hybrid of a cow and a yak.
– ORIGIN mid 19th cent.: from Tibetan *m̥dso*.

Dzongkha /ˈzɒŋkə/ ▶ **noun** [mass noun] the official language of Bhutan, closely related to Tibetan.
– ORIGIN Tibetan.

Ee

E^{1} (also **e**) ▶ **noun** (pl. **Es** or **E's**) **1** the fifth letter of the alphabet. ■ denoting the fifth in a set of items, categories, sizes, etc. ■ the fifth-highest class of academic mark. ■ (**e**) Chess denoting the fifth file from the left, as viewed from White's side of the board. ■ denoting the lowest-earning socio-economic category for marketing purposes.
2 (**E**) a shape like that of a capital E: [in combination] *an E-shaped stately home.*
3 (**E**) Music the third note of the diatonic scale of C major. ■ a key based on a scale with E as its keynote.

E^{2} ▶ **abbreviation** ■ East or Eastern: *139° E.* ■ informal the drug Ecstasy or a tablet of Ecstasy. ■ [in combination] denoting products, in particular food additives, which comply with EU regulations. See also **E-NUMBER.** ■ [in combination] (in units of measurement) exa- (10^{18}). ■ Spain (international vehicle registration). [from Spanish *España*.]
▶ **symbol** Physics ■ electric field strength. ■ electromotive force. ■ energy: $E = mc^2$.
– PHRASES **the three Es** economy, efficiency, and effectiveness.

e ▶ **symbol** ■ (€) euro or euros. ■ (also **e$^-$**) Chemistry an electron. ■ (*e*) Mathematics the transcendental number that is the base of Napierian or natural logarithms, approximately equal to 2.71828.

e-^{1} ▶ **prefix** variant spelling of **EX-^{1}** (as in *elect, emit*).

e-^{2} ▶ **prefix** denoting the use of electronic data transfer in cyberspace, especially through the Internet: *e-cash* | *e-zine.*
– ORIGIN from **ELECTRONIC**, on the pattern of *email.*

ea. ▶ **abbreviation** each: *T-shirts for £9.95 ea.*

each ▶ **determiner & pronoun** used to refer to every one of two or more people or things, regarded and identified separately: [as determiner] *each battery is in a separate compartment* | ***each one** of us was asked what went on* | [as pronoun] *Derek had money from **each of** his five uncles* | *they each have their own personality.*
▶ **adverb** to, for, or by every one of a group (used after a noun or an amount): *the cameras cost £35 each* | *Paul and Bill have a glass each.*
– PHRASES **each and every** every single (used for emphasis): *taking each and every opportunity* | *I look forward to seeing **each and every one of** you.*
– ORIGIN Old English *ǣlc*; related to Dutch *elk* and German *jeglich*, based on a West Germanic phrase meaning 'ever alike' (see **AYE^{2}**, **ALIKE**).

each other ▶ **pronoun** used to refer to each member of a group when each does something to or for other members: *they communicate with each other in French.*

each-way ▶ **adjective & adverb** Brit. (of a bet) divided into two equal wagers, one backing a horse or other competitor to win and the other backing it to finish in the first three. ■ [as adj.] to come first, second, or third in a race, considered from a betting point of view: *Travado has an each-way chance.*

Eadwig /ˈɛdwɪɡ/ variant spelling of **EDWY.**

eager ▶ **adjective** strongly wanting to do or have something: *the man was eager to please* | *young intellectuals **eager for** knowledge.* ■ (of a person's expression or tone of voice) keenly expectant or interested: *small eager faces looked up and listened.*
– PHRASES **eager beaver** informal a keen and enthusiastic person who works very hard.
– DERIVATIVES **eagerly** adverb.
– ORIGIN Middle English (also in the sense 'pungent, sour'): from Old French *aigre* 'keen', from Latin *acer, acr-* 'sharp, pungent'.

eagerness ▶ **noun** [mass noun] enthusiasm to do or to have something; keenness: *the player showed eagerness to play.*

eagle ▶ **noun 1** a large bird of prey with a massive hooked bill and long broad wings, known for its keen sight and powerful soaring flight. ● Family Accipitridae: several genera, in particular *Aquila.*
■ a figure of an eagle, especially as a symbol of the US.
2 Golf a score of two strokes under par at a hole. [suggested by **BIRDIE.**]
3 US a former gold coin worth ten dollars.
▶ **verb** [with obj.] Golf play (a hole) in two strokes under par: *he eagled the last to share fourth place.*
– ORIGIN Middle English: from Old French *aigle*, from Latin *aquila.*

eagle eye ▶ **noun** a keen or close watch: *she was **keeping an eagle eye on** Leni.*
– DERIVATIVES **eagle-eyed** adjective.

eagle owl ▶ **noun** a very large Old World owl with ear tufts and a deep hoot. ● Genus *Bubo*, family Strigidae: several species.

eagle ray ▶ **noun** a large marine ray with long pointed pectoral fins, a long tail, and a distinct head. ● Family Myliobatidae: genera *Myliobatis* and *Aetobatus*, and several species.

eaglet ▶ **noun** a young eagle.

eagre /ˈeɪɡə, ˈiː-/ ▶ **noun** dialect term for **BORE^{3}.**
– ORIGIN early 17th cent.: of unknown origin.

EAK ▶ **abbreviation** Kenya (international vehicle registration).
– ORIGIN from *East Africa Kenya.*

Eakins /ˈiːkɪnz/, Thomas (1844–1916), American painter and photographer noted for his portraits and genre pictures of life in Philadelphia. His picture *The Gross Clinic* (1875) aroused controversy because of its explicit depiction of surgery.

Ealing Studios a film studio in Ealing, West London, active 1929–55, but remembered chiefly for the comedies it made in the post-war decade.

-ean ▶ **suffix** forming adjectives and nouns such as *Antipodean* and *Pythagorean.*
– ORIGIN from Latin *-aeus, -eus* or Greek *aios, -eios*, + **-AN.**

ear^{1} ▶ **noun** the organ of hearing and balance in humans and other vertebrates, especially the external part of this. ■ an organ sensitive to sound in other animals. ■ [in sing.] an ability to recognize, appreciate, and reproduce sounds, especially music or language: ***an ear for** rhythm and melody.* ■ used to refer to a person's willingness to listen to others: *she offers a sympathetic ear to worried pet owners.*

> The ear of a mammal is composed of three parts. The outer or external ear consists of a fleshy external flap and a tube leading to the eardrum or tympanum. The middle ear is an air-filled cavity connected to the throat, containing three small linked bones that transmit vibrations from the eardrum to the inner ear. The inner ear is a complex fluid-filled labyrinth including the spiral cochlea (where vibrations are converted to nerve impulses) and the three semicircular canals (forming the organ of balance).

– PHRASES **be all ears** informal be listening eagerly. **bring something (down) about one's ears** bring misfortune on oneself: *she brought her world crashing about her ears.* **one's ears are burning** one is subconsciously aware of being talked about or criticized. **grin** (or **smile**) **from ear to ear** smile broadly. **have something coming out of one's ears** informal have a substantial amount of something: *that man's got money coming out of his ears.* **have someone's ear** have access to and influence with someone: *he claimed to have the prime minister's ear.* **have** (or **keep**) **an ear to the ground** be well informed about events and trends. **in one ear and out the other** heard but quickly forgotten: *whatever he tells me seems to go in one ear and out the other.* **listen with half an ear** not give one's full attention. **be out on one's ear** informal be dismissed ignominiously. **reach someone's ears** be heard or heard about by someone: *the sound of running feet reached my ears* | *one of those stories reached our ears.* **up to one's ears in** informal very busy with: *I'm up to my ears in work here.*
– DERIVATIVES **eared** adjective [in combination] *long-eared*, **earless** adjective.
– ORIGIN Old English *ēare*, of Germanic origin; related to Dutch *oor* and German *Ohr*, from an Indo-European root shared by Latin *auris* and Greek *ous.*

ear^{2} ▶ **noun** the seed-bearing head or spike of a cereal plant. ■ N. Amer. a head of maize.
– ORIGIN Old English *ēar*, of Germanic origin; related to Dutch *aar* and German *Ähre.*

earache ▶ **noun** [mass noun] pain inside the ear. Also called **OTALGIA.**

earbashing ▶ **noun** informal a lengthy and reproachful speech: *I picked up the phone and gave him an earbashing.*

earbud ▶ **noun** (usu. **earbuds**) a very small headphone, worn inside the ear.

ear candy ▶ **noun** [mass noun] informal light popular music that is pleasant and entertaining but intellectually undemanding.

ear defenders ▶ **plural noun** plugs or earmuffs which protect the eardrums from loud or persistent noise.

eardrum ▶ **noun** the membrane of the middle ear, which vibrates in response to sound waves; the tympanic membrane.

eared seal ▶ **noun** see **SEAL^{2}.**

ear flap ▶ **noun 1** a flap of material on a hat or cap, covering the ear.
2 a part of an animal's outer ear which extends out from the head as a fleshy flap or lobe.

earful ▶ **noun** [in sing.] informal **1** a prolonged and angry reprimand: *executives **got an earful** about poor rail connections.*
2 a loud blast of sound: *an earful of white noise.*

Earhart /ˈɛːhɑːt/, Amelia (1898–1937), American aviator. In 1932 she became the first woman to fly across the Atlantic solo. Her aircraft disappeared over the Pacific Ocean during a subsequent round-the-world flight with the loss of Earhart and her navigator.

earhole ▶ **noun** the external opening of the ear. ■ informal a person's ear: *a clip round the earhole.*

earl ▶ **noun** a British nobleman ranking above a viscount and below a marquess.
– ORIGIN Old English *eorl*, of Germanic origin. The word *earl* originally denoted a man of noble rank, as opposed to a churl, also specifically a hereditary

nobleman next above the rank of thane. It was later an equivalent of **JARL** and, under Canute and his successors, applied to the governor of divisions of England such as Wessex. In the late Old English period, as the Saxon court came under Norman influence, the word was applied to any nobleman bearing the continental title of count.

earldom ▸ noun the rank or title of an earl. ■ historical the territory governed by an earl.

earless lizard ▸ noun a small, long-legged burrowing lizard without visible external ear openings, native to North America. ● *Holbrookia texana*, family Iguanidae.

Earl Grey ▸ noun [mass noun] a kind of China tea flavoured with bergamot.
– ORIGIN probably named after the 2nd *Earl Grey* (1764–1845), said to have been given the recipe by a Chinese mandarin.

E

Earl Marshal ▸ noun (in the UK) the officer presiding over the College of Arms, with ceremonial duties on various royal occasions.

earlobe ▸ noun a soft, rounded fleshy part hanging from the lower margin of the ear.

earlock ▸ noun a lock of hair over or above the ear.

earl palatine ▸ noun (pl. **earls palatine**) historical an earl having royal authority within his country or domain.

early ▸ adjective (**earlier**, **earliest**) **1** happening or done before the usual or expected time: *we ate an early lunch.*
2 belonging or happening near the beginning of a particular period: *an early goal secured victory* | *she's in her early fifties.* ■ done or occurring near the beginning of the day: *we agreed to meet at 6 am to get an early start.* ■ denoting or belonging to the beginning of a historical period or cultural movement: *early Impressionism.* ■ occurring at the beginning of a sequence: *the earlier chapters of the book.* ■ (of a plant or crop) flowering or ripening before other varieties: *early potatoes.*
▸ adverb before the usual or expected time: *I want to finish work early today.* ■ near the beginning of a period: *we lost a couple of games early in the season.* ■ near the beginning of the day: *I wrote this piece early one morning.* ■ (**earlier**) before the present time or before the time one is referring to: *you met my husband earlier.*
▸ noun (**earlies**) **1** potatoes which are ready to be harvested before the main crop.
2 informal early shifts: *she is **on earlies**.*
– PHRASES **at the earliest** not before the time or date specified. **early bird** humorous a person who rises, arrives, or acts before the usual or expected time. **the early bird catches the worm** proverb the person who takes the earliest opportunity to do something will gain the advantage over others. **early doors** Brit. informal early on, especially in a game or contest: *you should try to wind up their star player early doors.* [apparently originally with reference to admission to a music hall some time before the start of the performance.] **an early grave** a premature or untimely death: *he worked himself into an early grave.* **the early hours** the time after midnight and before dawn. **an early night** an occasion when someone goes to bed before the usual time. **early** (or **earlier**) **on** at an early (or earlier) stage in a period: *they discovered early on that the published data were wrong.* **it's** (or **these are**) **early days** Brit. informal it is too soon to be sure how a situation will develop.
– DERIVATIVES **earliness** noun.
– ORIGIN Old English (as an adverb) *ǣrlīce* (see **ERE**, **-LY²**), influenced by Old Norse *árliga*. The adjective use dates from Middle English.

early adopter ▸ noun a person who starts using a product or technology as soon as it becomes available.

early closing ▸ noun [mass noun] Brit. the practice of shutting business premises on a particular afternoon every week.

Early English ▸ adjective denoting the earliest stage of English Gothic church architecture, typical of the late 12th and 13th centuries and marked by the use of pointed arches and simple lancet windows without tracery.

early leaver ▸ noun a person who leaves early, especially a person who abandons a pension plan before the expected date.

early music ▸ noun [mass noun] medieval, Renaissance, and early baroque music, especially as revived and played on period instruments.

early retirement ▸ noun [mass noun] the practice of leaving employment before the statutory age, especially on favourable financial terms.

earmark ▸ verb [with obj.] **1** designate (funds or resources) for a particular purpose: *the cash had been **earmarked for** a big expansion of the programme.* ■ designate a particular outcome for (someone or something): *the yard has been **earmarked for** a complete overhaul.*
2 mark the ear of (a domesticated animal) as a sign of ownership or identity.
▸ noun **1** a characteristic or identifying feature: *this car has all the earmarks of a classic.*
2 US a congressional directive that funds should be spent on a specific project.
3 a mark on the ear of a domesticated animal indicating ownership or identity.

earmuffs ▸ plural noun a pair of soft fabric coverings, connected by a band across the top of the head, that are worn over the ears to protect them from cold or noise.

earn ▸ verb [with obj.] **1** obtain (money) in return for labour or services: *he **earns his living** as a lorry driver* | [with two objs] *earn yourself a few pounds.* ■ [with two objs] (of an activity) cause (someone) to obtain (money): *this latest win earned them $50,000 in prize money.* ■ (of capital invested) gain (money) as interest or profit.
2 gain deservedly in return for one's behaviour or achievements: *through the years she has earned affection and esteem.*
– PHRASES **earn one's corn** Brit. informal put in a lot of effort to show that one deserves one's wages. **earn one's keep** work in return for food and accommodation. ■ be worth the time or money spent on one.
– PHRASAL VERBS **earn something out** (of an author, book, recording artist, etc.) generate sufficient income through sales to equal the amount paid in an advance or royalty.
– ORIGIN Old English *earnian*, of West Germanic origin, from a base shared by Old English *esne* 'labourer'.

earned income ▸ noun [mass noun] money derived from paid work.

earned run ▸ noun Baseball a run scored without the aid of errors by the team in the field (i.e. by hits, walks, and outs that advance base runners).

earner ▸ noun [with adj. or noun modifier] a person who obtains money of a specified kind or level in return for labour or services: *higher rates of income tax for high earners.* ■ an activity or product that brings in income of a specified kind or level: *tobacco is a major foreign currency earner.*
– PHRASES **a nice little earner** Brit. informal a profitable activity.

earnest¹ /ˈəːnɪst/ ▸ adjective resulting from or showing sincere and intense conviction: *an earnest student* | *two girls were in earnest conversation.*
– PHRASES **in earnest** to a greater extent or more intensely than before: *work began again in earnest.* ■ (of a person) sincere and serious in intention.
– DERIVATIVES **earnestness** noun.
– ORIGIN Old English *eornoste* (adjective), *eornost* (noun), of Germanic origin; related to German *Ernst* (noun).

earnest² /ˈəːnɪst/ ▸ noun [in sing.] a thing intended or regarded as a sign or promise of what is to come: *the very deliberateness of their disguise is an earnest of their real aloofness.*
– ORIGIN Middle English *ernes*, literally 'instalment paid to confirm a contract', based on Old French *erres*, from Latin *arra*, shortened form of *arrabo* 'a pledge'. The spelling was influenced by words ending in **-NESS**; the final *-t* is probably by association with **EARNEST¹**.

earnestly /ˈəːnɪstli/ ▸ adverb with sincere and intense conviction; seriously: *they earnestly hope to come back in the summer.*

earnest money ▸ noun [mass noun] chiefly US money paid to confirm a contract.

earnings ▸ plural noun money obtained in return for labour or services. ■ income derived from an investment or product: *export earnings.*

earn-out ▸ noun a provision written into some financial transactions whereby the seller of a business will receive additional payments based on the future performance of the business sold.

Earp /əːp/, Wyatt (Berry Stapp) (1848–1929), American gambler and marshal. He is famous for the gunfight at the OK Corral (1881), in which Wyatt with his brothers and his friend Doc Holliday fought the Clanton brothers at Tombstone, Arizona.

earphone ▸ noun (usu. **earphones**) an electrical device worn on the ear to receive radio or telephone communications or to listen to a radio, MP3 player, etc.

earpiece ▸ noun **1** the part of a telephone, radio receiver, or other aural device that is applied to the ear during use.
2 the part of a pair of glasses that fits around the ear.

ear-piercing ▸ adjective loud and shrill: *the alarm emits an ear-piercing screech.*
▸ noun [mass noun] the practice of making holes in the lobes or edges of the ears to allow the wearing of earrings.

earplug ▸ noun (usu. **earplugs**) a piece of wax, rubber, or cotton wool placed in the ear as protection against noise, water, or cold air.

earring ▸ noun a piece of jewellery worn on the lobe or edge of the ear.

ear shell ▸ noun another term for **ABALONE**.

earshot ▸ noun [mass noun] the range or distance over which one can hear or be heard: *she waited until he was **out of earshot** before continuing.*

ear-splitting ▸ adjective extremely loud: *an ear-splitting crack of thunder.*

earth ▸ noun **1** (also **Earth**) the planet on which we live; the world: *the diversity of life **on earth**.* ■ the surface of the world as distinct from the sky or the sea: *the pilot brought the plane gently back to earth.* ■ the present abode of humankind, as distinct from heaven or hell.

> The earth is the third planet from the sun in the solar system, orbiting between Venus and Mars at an average distance of 149.6 million km from the sun, and has one natural satellite, the moon. It has an equatorial diameter of 12,756 km, an average density 5.5 times that of water, and is believed to have formed about 4,600 million years ago. The earth, which is three-quarters covered by oceans and has a dense atmosphere of nitrogen and oxygen, is the only planet known to support life.

2 [mass noun] the substance of the land surface; soil: *a layer of earth.* ■ [count noun] used in names of stable, dense, non-volatile inorganic substances, e.g. **fuller's earth**. ■ literary the substance of the human body.
3 [mass noun] Brit. electrical connection to the ground, regarded as having zero electrical potential: *ensure metal fittings are electrically bonded to earth.*
4 the underground lair of a badger or fox.
5 one of the four elements in ancient and medieval philosophy and in astrology (considered essential to the nature of the signs Taurus, Virgo, and Capricorn).
▸ verb [with obj.] **1** Brit. connect (an electrical device) with the ground: *the front metal panels must be soundly earthed.*
2 Hunting drive (a fox) to its underground lair. ■ [no obj.] (of a fox) run to its underground lair.
3 (**earth something up**) cover the root and lower stem of a plant with heaped-up earth.
– PHRASES **bring** (or **come**) **back** (**down**) **to earth** cause to return (or return) to reality after a period of daydreaming or excitement. **the earth** Brit. a very large amount: *her hat cost the earth.* **the earth moved** (or **did the earth move for you?**) humorous one had (or did you have?) an orgasm. **go to earth** (of a hunted animal) hide in an underground burrow. ■ go into hiding: *he'd gone to earth after that meeting.* **like nothing on earth** informal very strange: *they looked like nothing on earth.* **on earth** used for emphasis, especially in questions and negative statements: *who on earth would venture out in weather like this?*
– ORIGIN Old English *eorthe*, of Germanic origin; related to Dutch *aarde* and German *Erde*.

earth ball ▸ noun a fungus that forms a leathery yellowish-brown warty sphere which ruptures when mature to release the spores, growing typically on acid sandy soil in both Eurasia and North America. ● Genus *Scleroderma*, family Sclerodermataceae, class Gasteromycetes: several species.

earthbound ▸ adjective **1** restricted to the earth: *a flightless earthbound bird.* ■ limited to material existence as distinct from a spiritual or heavenly one: *her earthbound view of the sacrament.*
2 moving towards the earth: *an earthbound spaceship.*

earth closet ▸ noun Brit. a basic type of toilet with dry earth used to cover excrement.

earthen ▶ adjective [attrib.] (of a floor or structure) made of compressed earth: *earthen mounds.* ■ (of a pot) made of baked or fired clay.

earthenware ▶ noun [mass noun] [often as modifier] pottery made of clay fired to a porous state which can be made impervious to liquids by the use of a glaze: *an earthenware jug.*

earthlight ▶ noun another term for **EARTHSHINE**.

earthling ▶ noun (in science fiction) a word used by aliens to refer to an inhabitant of the earth.

earth loop ▶ noun an unwanted electric current path in a circuit resulting in stray signals or interference, occurring for example when two earthed points in the same circuit have different potentials.

earthly ▶ adjective (**earthlier**, **earthliest**) **1** relating to the earth or human life: *water is liquid at normal earthly temperatures.* ■ relating to humankind's material existence as distinct from a spiritual or heavenly one: *all earthly happiness is but vanity.*
2 [with negative] informal used for emphasis: *there was no earthly reason why she should not come too.*
– PHRASES **not stand** (or **have**) **an earthly** Brit. informal have no chance at all: *she wouldn't stand an earthly if she tried to outrun him.*
– DERIVATIVES **earthliness** noun.

earth mother ▶ noun (in mythology and primitive religion) a goddess symbolizing fertility and the source of life. ■ an archetypally nurturing and maternal woman.

earth mover ▶ noun a vehicle or machine designed to excavate large quantities of soil.
– DERIVATIVES **earth moving** noun.

earthnut ▶ noun **1** a Eurasian plant of the parsley family, which has an edible roundish tuber and is found in woodland and acid pasture. Also called **PIGNUT**, **HOGNUT**. ● *Conopodium majus*, family Umbelliferae. ■ the almond-flavoured tuber of the earthnut.
2 Brit. another term for **PEANUT**.

earthquake ▶ noun a sudden violent shaking of the ground, typically causing great destruction, as a result of movements within the earth's crust or volcanic action. ■ a great upheaval: *a political earthquake.*

earth science ▶ noun [mass noun] the branch of science dealing with the physical constitution of the earth and its atmosphere. ■ (**earth sciences**) the various branches of earth science, e.g. geology or meteorology.

earth-shattering (also **earth-shaking**) ▶ adjective (in hyperbolic use) very important, shocking, or traumatic: *tell me this earth-shattering news of yours.*
– DERIVATIVES **earth-shatteringly** adverb.

earthshine (also **earthlight**) ▶ noun [mass noun] Astronomy the glow caused by sunlight reflected by the earth on the darker portion of a crescent moon.

earthstar ▶ noun a brownish woodland fungus with a spherical spore-containing fruiting body surrounded by a fleshy star-shaped structure, found in both Eurasia and North America. ● Family Geastraceae, class Gasteromycetes: *Geastrum* and other genera.

earth station ▶ noun a radio station located on the earth and used for relaying signals from satellites.

earth tremor ▶ noun see **TREMOR**.

earthward (also **earthwards**) ▶ adverb & adjective towards the earth. [as adv.] *when his parachute failed to open he fell earthward at 120 mph* | [as adj.] *the bird's earthward plummet.*

earthwork ▶ noun a large artificial bank of soil, especially one made as a defence in ancient times.

earthworm ▶ noun a burrowing annelid worm that lives in the soil, important in aerating and draining the soil and in burying organic matter. ● Family Lumbricidae, class Oligochaeta: *Lumbricus*, *Allolobophora*, and other genera.

earthy ▶ adjective (**earthier**, **earthiest**) **1** resembling or suggestive of earth or soil: *an earthy smell.*
2 (of a person or their language) direct and uninhibited, especially about sexual subjects or bodily functions.
– DERIVATIVES **earthily** adverb, **earthiness** noun.

ear trumpet ▶ noun a trumpet-shaped device formerly used as a hearing aid.

ear tuft ▶ noun each of a pair of tufts of longer feathers on the top of the head of some owls.

earwax ▶ noun [mass noun] the protective yellow waxy substance secreted in the passage of the outer ear. Also called **CERUMEN**.

earwig ▶ noun a small elongated insect with a pair of terminal appendages that resemble pincers. ● Order Dermaptera: several families.
▶ verb (**earwigs**, **earwigging**, **earwigged**) [no obj.] Brit. informal eavesdrop on a conversation: *he looked behind him to see if anyone was earwigging.* ■ [with obj.] archaic influence (someone) by secret means.
– ORIGIN Old English *ēarwicga*, from *ēare* 'ear' + *wicga* 'earwig' (probably related to *wiggle*); the insect was once thought to crawl into the human ear.

earwitness ▶ noun chiefly N. Amer. a witness whose testimony is based on what they personally heard.

earworm ▶ noun a catchy song or tune that runs continually through someone's mind.

ease ▶ noun [mass noun] absence of difficulty or effort: *she gave up smoking with ease* | *ease of use.* ■ absence of rigidity or discomfort; poise: *I was always vexed by her self-contained ease.* ■ freedom from worries or problems: *a life of wealth and ease.*
▶ verb **1** [with obj.] make (something unpleasant or intense) less serious or severe: *a huge road-building programme to ease congestion.* ■ [no obj.] become less serious or severe: *the pain doesn't usually **ease off** for several hours.* ■ [no obj.] (**ease off/up**) do something with more moderation: *I'd **ease up on** the hard stuff if I were you.* ■ make (something) happen more easily; facilitate: *Tokyo's dominance of government was deemed to ease efficient contact-making.*
2 [no obj., with adverbial of direction] move carefully or gradually: *I eased down the slope with care* | [with obj. and adverbial of direction] *she eased off her shoes.* ■ [with obj.] (**ease someone into**) introduce someone gradually to (an activity): *he brought in someone new and eased them into the job.* ■ [with obj.] (**ease someone out**) gradually exclude someone from a post, especially by devious or subtle manoeuvres: *after the scandal he was eased out of his job.* ■ (**ease something away/down/off**) Nautical slacken a rope or sail slowly or gently.
3 [no obj.] (of share prices, interest rates, etc.) decrease in value or amount: *shares eased 6p to 224p.*
– PHRASES **at (one's) ease** free from worry or awkwardness; relaxed: *she was never quite **at ease with** Phil.* ■ (**at ease**) Military in a relaxed attitude with the feet apart and the hands behind the back (often as a command). **ease someone's mind** alleviate someone's anxiety.
– DERIVATIVES **easer** noun.
– ORIGIN Middle English: from Old French *aise*, based on Latin *adjacens* 'lying close by', present participle of *adjacere*. The verb is originally from Old French *aisier*, from the phrase *a aise* 'at ease'; in later use from the noun.

easeful ▶ adjective literary providing comfort or peace: *life was easeful at that time.*

easel /ˈiːz(ə)l/ ▶ noun a wooden frame for holding an artist's work while it is being painted or drawn.
– ORIGIN late 16th cent.: from Dutch *ezel* 'ass'. The word 'horse' is used in English in a similar way to denote a supporting frame.

easement /ˈiːzm(ə)nt/ ▶ noun **1** Law a right to cross or otherwise use someone else's land for a specified purpose.
2 [mass noun] literary the state or feeling of comfort or peace: *time brings easement.*
– ORIGIN late Middle English: from Old French *aisement*, from *aisier* (see **EASE**).

easily ▶ adverb **1** without difficulty or effort: *he climbed the mountain easily* | *Bradford is easily accessible by road.* ■ more quickly or frequently than is usual: *they get bored easily.*
2 without doubt; by far: *he was easily the bravest man I've ever met.* ■ very probably: *the body could easily be that of an actress.*

east ▶ noun (usu. **the east**) **1** the direction towards the point of the horizon where the sun rises at the equinoxes, on the right-hand side of a person facing north: *a gale was blowing from the east* | *the Atlantic Ocean **to the east of** Florida.* ■ the compass point corresponding to this.
2 the eastern part of the world or of a specified country, region, or town: *a factory in the east of the city.* ■ (**the East**) the regions or countries lying to the east of Europe, especially China, Japan, and India: *the protection of trade routes to the East.* ■ (**the East**) historical the former communist states of eastern Europe.
3 (**East**) [as name] Bridge the player sitting to the left of North and partnering West.
▶ adjective [attrib.] **1** lying towards, near, or facing the east: *the hospital's east wing.* ■ (of a wind) blowing from the east.
2 of or denoting the eastern part of a specified region, town, or country: *East Fife* | *East African.*
3 situated in the part of a church containing the altar or high altar, usually the actual east.
▶ adverb to or towards the east: *travelling east, he met two men* | *the river rises **east of** Brentford.*
– ORIGIN Old English *ēast-*, of Germanic origin; related to Dutch *oost* and German *ost*, from an Indo-European root shared by Latin *aurora*, Greek *auōs* 'dawn'.

East Africa the eastern part of the African continent, especially the countries of Kenya, Uganda, and Tanzania.

East Anglia /ˈaŋglɪə/ a region of eastern England consisting of the counties of Norfolk, Suffolk, and parts of Essex and Cambridgeshire.

East Asia the eastern part of the Asian continent, including China and Japan.
– DERIVATIVES **East Asian** adjective.

East Bengal the part of the former Indian province of Bengal that was ceded to Pakistan in 1947, forming the greater part of the province of East Pakistan. It gained independence as Bangladesh in 1971.

eastbound ▶ adjective leading or travelling towards the east: *eastbound trains.*

Eastbourne a town on the south coast of England, in East Sussex; pop. 108,200 (est. 2009).

East Cape a peninsular region of the North Island, New Zealand. Its tip forms the most easterly point of the island.

East China Sea see **CHINA SEA**.

East Coast Fever ▶ noun [mass noun] a feverish disease of cattle, prevalent in Africa and usually fatal. ● This disease is caused by a parasitic protozoan of the genus *Theileria* (phylum Sporozoa, kingdom Protista), which lives in the host's blood cells and is transmitted by the bite of the tick *Rhipicephalus appendiculatus* (family Ixodidae).

East End the part of London east of the City as far as the River Lea, including the Docklands.
– DERIVATIVES **East Ender** noun.

Easter ▶ noun the most important and oldest festival of the Christian Church, celebrating the resurrection of Christ and held (in the Western Church) between 21 March and 25 April, on the first Sunday after the first full moon following the northern spring equinox. ■ the weekend from Good Friday to Easter Monday.
– ORIGIN Old English *ēastre*; of Germanic origin and related to German *Ostern* and **EAST**; perhaps from *Ēastre*, the name of a goddess associated with spring.

Easter bunny ▶ noun an imaginary rabbit said to bring gifts to children at Easter.

Easter Day (also **Easter Sunday**) ▶ noun the day on which the festival of Easter is celebrated.

Easter egg ▶ noun **1** an artificial chocolate egg or decorated hard-boiled egg given at Easter.
2 an unexpected or undocumented feature in a piece of computer software or on a DVD, included as a joke or a bonus.

Easter Eve ▶ noun the day immediately preceding Easter Day. Also called **HOLY SATURDAY**.

Easter Island an island in the SE Pacific west of Chile; pop. 3,300 (est. 2009). It has been administered by Chile since 1888. The island, first settled by Polynesians in about AD 400, is famous for its large monolithic statues of human heads, believed to date from the period 1000 to 1600.

Easter lily ▶ noun N. Amer. a spring-flowering lily. ● Genus *Lilium*, family Liliaceae: several species, in particular the tall, white-flowered Japanese lily *L. longiflorum*.

easterly ▶ adjective & adverb in an eastward position or direction: [as adj.] *he ordered an easterly course.* ■ (of a wind) blowing from the east: [as adj.] *the light easterly breeze.*
▶ noun (pl. **easterlies**) a wind blowing from the east.

Easter Monday ▶ noun the day after Easter Sunday, a public holiday in several countries.

eastern ▶ adjective **1** [attrib.] situated in, directed towards, or facing the east: *the eastern slopes of the mountain* | *eastern Spain.* ■ (of a wind) blowing from the east.
2 (**Eastern**) living in or originating from the regions or countries to the east of Europe: *an Eastern mystic.* ■ relating to or characteristic of the East or its inhabitants: *Eastern philosophy and culture.*
– DERIVATIVES **easternmost** adjective.
– ORIGIN Old English *ēasterne* (as **EAST**, **-ERN**).

E

E

Eastern bloc the countries of eastern and central Europe which were under Soviet domination from the end of the Second World War until the collapse of the Soviet communist system in 1989–91.

Eastern Cape a province of south-eastern South Africa, formerly part of Cape Province; capital, Bhisho.

Eastern Church (also **Eastern Orthodox Church**) another name for ORTHODOX CHURCH. ■ any of the Christian Churches originating in eastern Europe and the Middle East.

Eastern Desert another name for ARABIAN DESERT.

Eastern Empire the eastern part of the Roman Empire, after its division in AD 395. See also BYZANTINE EMPIRE.

easterner ▶ noun a native or inhabitant of the east of a region or country, especially of Europe or the US.

Eastern Ghats see GHATS.

eastern hemisphere the half of the earth containing Europe, Asia, and Africa.

Eastern time 1 the standard time in a zone including the eastern states of the US and parts of Canada, specifically: ● (**Eastern Standard Time**, abbrev.: **EST**) standard time based on the mean solar time at the meridian 75° W, five hours behind GMT. ● (**Eastern Daylight Time**, abbrev.: **EDT**) Eastern time during daylight saving time, four hours behind GMT.
2 the standard time in a zone including eastern Australia, based on the mean solar time at the meridian 150° E. It is ten hours ahead of GMT, or nine hours ahead when summer time is observed.

Eastern Zhou see ZHOU.

Easter Rising the uprising in Dublin and other cities in Ireland against British rule, Easter 1916. It ended with the surrender of the protesters, most of whose leaders were subsequently executed, but was a contributory factor in the establishment of the Irish Free State (1922).

Easter Saturday ▶ noun (in general use) the Saturday preceding Easter Day. In formal church use called HOLY SATURDAY or EASTER EVE.

Easter Sunday ▶ noun another term for EASTER DAY.

Eastertide ▶ noun the Easter period.

East Flanders a province of northern Belgium; capital, Ghent. See also FLANDERS.

East Frisian Islands see FRISIAN ISLANDS.

East Germanic ▶ noun the extinct eastern group of Germanic languages, including Gothic.
▶ adjective relating to this group of languages.

East Germany see GERMANY.

East India another name for EAST INDIES (sense 2).

East India Company a trading company formed in 1600 to develop commerce in the newly colonized areas of SE Asia and India. In the 18th century it took administrative control of Bengal and other areas of India, and held it until the British Crown took over in 1858 in the wake of the Indian Mutiny.

East Indiaman ▶ noun historical a trading ship belonging to the East India Company.

East Indies 1 the islands of SE Asia, especially the Malay Archipelago.
2 archaic the whole of SE Asia to the east of and including India.
– DERIVATIVES **East Indian** adjective.

easting ▶ noun [mass noun] distance travelled or measured eastward, especially at sea. ■ [count noun] a figure or line representing eastward distance on a map (expressed by convention as the first part of a grid reference, before northing).

East Kilbride /kɪlˈbrʌɪd/ a town in west central Scotland, in South Lanarkshire; pop. 74,600 (est. 2009).

East London a port and resort in South Africa, on the coast of Eastern Cape; pop. 452,200 (est. 2009).

East Lothian a council area and former county of east central Scotland.

Eastman, George (1854–1932), American inventor and manufacturer of photographic equipment. He invented flexible roll film coated with light-sensitive emulsion, and, in 1888, the Kodak camera for use with it.

east-north-east ▶ noun the direction or compass point midway between east and north-east.

East Prussia the north-eastern part of the former kingdom of Prussia, on the Baltic coast, later part of Germany and divided after the Second World War between the Soviet Union and Poland.

East Riding of Yorkshire a unitary authority in NE England, formerly one of the traditional ridings or divisions of the county of Yorkshire.

East River an arm of the Hudson River in New York City, separating Manhattan and the Bronx from Brooklyn and Queens.

East Sea the name in Korea for the JAPAN, SEA OF.

East Siberian Sea a part of the Arctic Ocean lying between the New Siberian Islands and Wrangel Island, to the north of eastern Siberia.

East Side a part of Manhattan in New York City, lying between the East River and Fifth Avenue.

east-south-east ▶ noun the direction or compass point midway between east and south-east.

East Sussex a county of SE England; county town, Lewes.

East Timor a country occupying the eastern part of the island of Timor in the southern Malay Archipelago; pop. 1,131,600 (est. 2009); capital, Dili; languages, Portuguese, Indonesian, English, and indigenous languages. Official name TIMOR LESTE.

> Formerly a Portuguese colony, the region declared itself independent in 1975. In 1976 it was invaded by Indonesia, which annexed and claimed it as the 27th state of Indonesia, a claim which was never recognized by the United Nations. The region became the scene of bitter fighting and of alleged mass killings by the Indonesian government and military forces. East Timor gained full independence following a referendum in 1999 and a formal declaration by the United Nations in 2002.

– DERIVATIVES **East Timorese** noun & adjective.

eastward ▶ adjective lying towards, near, or facing the east.
▶ adverb (also **eastwards**) towards the east: *limestone plateaux extend eastward towards the river.*
▶ noun (**the eastward**) the direction or region towards the east: *the wind has come round to the eastward.*
– DERIVATIVES **eastwardly** adverb.

Eastwood, Clint (b.1930), American film actor and director. He became famous with his role in *A Fistful of Dollars* (1964), the first cult spaghetti western; other successful films include *Dirty Harry* (1971). Films directed include *Bird* (1988) and the western *Unforgiven* (1992).

easy ▶ adjective (**easier**, **easiest**) 1 achieved without great effort; presenting few difficulties: *an easy way of retrieving information.*
2 (of a period of time or way of life) free from worries or problems: *promises of an easy life in the New World.* ■ (of a person) lacking anxiety or awkwardness; relaxed: *her easy and agreeable manner* | *he never felt easy with her.*
3 [attrib.] (of an object of attack or criticism) having no defence; vulnerable: *as a taxi driver he was an easy target.* ■ informal, derogatory (of a woman) very receptive to sexual advances: *her reputation at school for being easy.*
▶ adverb archaic or US without difficulty or effort: *we all scared real easy in those days.*
▶ exclamation be careful: *easy, girl—you'll knock me over!*
– PHRASES **be easier said than done** be more easily talked about than put into practice: *going on an economy drive is easier said than done.* **(as) easy as pie** see PIE[1]. **easy come, easy go** used especially in spoken English to indicate that a relationship or possession acquired without effort may be abandoned or lost without regret. **easy does it** used especially in spoken English to advise someone to approach a task carefully and slowly. **easy on the eye** (or **ear**) informal pleasant to look at (or listen to). **go** (or **be**) **easy on** informal **1** refrain from being harsh with or critical of (someone). **2** be sparing in one's use or consumption of: *go easy on fatty foods.* **have it easy** informal have no difficulties; be fortunate. **I'm easy** informal said by someone when offered a choice to indicate that they have no particular preference. **of easy virtue** dated or humorous (of a woman) sexually promiscuous. **sleep** (or **rest**) **easy** go to sleep without (or be untroubled by) worries: *this insurance policy will let you rest easy.* **stand easy!** Military used to instruct soldiers standing at ease that they may relax their attitude further. **take the easy way out** extricate oneself from a difficult situation by choosing the simplest rather than the most honourable course of action. **take it easy 1** proceed in a calm and relaxed manner. **2** make little effort; rest.
– DERIVATIVES **easiness** noun.
– ORIGIN Middle English (also in the sense 'comfortable, tranquil'): from Old French *aisie*, past participle of *aisier* 'put at ease, facilitate' (see EASE).

easy-care ▶ adjective [attrib.] (chiefly of man-made fabrics) requiring little effort to launder, and typically no ironing.

easy chair ▶ noun a large, comfortable chair, typically an armchair.

easy game ▶ noun another term for EASY MEAT (see MEAT).

easy-going ▶ adjective relaxed and tolerant in attitude or manner: *a relaxed, easy-going atmosphere.*

easy listening ▶ noun [mass noun] popular music that is tuneful and undemanding.

easy money ▶ noun [mass noun] money obtained by dubious means or for little work.

easy-peasy ▶ adjective Brit. informal very straightforward and easy (used by or as if by children): *easy-peasy questions.*
– ORIGIN 1970s: reduplication of EASY.

easy street ▶ noun [mass noun] informal a state of financial comfort or security: *£50,000 a year will put one on easy street.*

easy touch ▶ noun another term for SOFT TOUCH (see SOFT).

EAT ▶ abbreviation Tanzania (international vehicle registration).
– ORIGIN from *East Africa Tanzania* (formerly *Tanganyika*).

eat ▶ verb (past **ate** /ɛt, eɪt/; past participle **eaten**) [with obj.] put (food) into the mouth and chew and swallow it: *he was eating a hot dog* | *eat up all your peas* | [no obj.] *she watched her son as he ate.* ■ have (a meal): *we ate dinner in a noisy cafe.* ■ [no obj.] (**eat out**) have a meal in a restaurant. ■ [no obj.] (**eat in**) have a meal at home. ■ vulgar slang, chiefly US perform fellatio or cunnilingus on (someone).
▶ noun (**eats**) informal light food or snacks.
– PHRASES **eat someone alive** informal (of insects) bite someone many times: *we were eaten alive by mosquitoes.* ■ exploit someone's weakness and completely dominate them. **eat crow** see CROW[1]. **eat dirt** see DIRT. **eat someone's dust** see DUST. **eat one's heart out** suffer from excessive longing for someone or something unattainable. ■ [in imperative] informal used to indicate that one thinks someone will feel great jealousy or regret: *eat your heart out, those who missed the trip.* **eat humble pie** see HUMBLE. **eat like a bird** (or **a horse**) informal eat very little (or a lot). **eat someone out of house and home** informal eat a lot of someone else's food. **eat one's words** retract what one has said, especially in a humiliated way: *they will eat their words when I win.* **have someone eating out of one's hand** have someone completely under one's control. **I'll eat my hat** informal used to indicate that one thinks that something is extremely unlikely to happen: *if he comes back, I'll eat my hat.* **what's eating you** (or **him** or **her**)? informal what is worrying or annoying you (or him or her)?
– PHRASAL VERBS **eat something away** (or **eat away at**) erode or destroy something gradually: *the acid began to eat away at the edge of her tunic* | figurative *the knowledge of his affair still ate away at her.* **eat into** another way of saying EAT AWAY AT. ■ use up (profits, resources, or time): *sales were hard hit by high interest rates eating into disposable income.* **eat someone up** (usu. as adj. **eaten up**) dominate the thoughts of someone completely: *I'm eaten up with guilt.* **eat something up** use resources or time in very large quantities: *an operating system that eats up 200Mb of disk space.*
– ORIGIN Old English *etan*, of Germanic origin; related to Dutch *eten* and German *essen*, from an Indo-European root shared by Latin *edere* and Greek *edein*.

eatable ▶ adjective fit to be consumed as food: *eatable fruits.*
▶ noun (**eatables**) items of food: *parcels of eatables and gifts.*

eater ▶ noun 1 [with adj. or noun modifier] a person or animal who consumes food in a specified way or of a specified kind: *I'm still a big eater.*
2 Brit. informal an eating apple.

eatery ▶ noun (pl. **eateries**) informal a restaurant or cafe.

eat-in ▶ adjective N. Amer. (of a kitchen) designed for eating in as well as cooking.

eating apple ▶ noun an apple that is suitable for eating raw.

eating disorder ▶ noun any of a range of psychological disorders characterized by abnormal or disturbed eating habits (such as anorexia nervosa).

eating house ▶ noun a restaurant.

EAU ▶ abbreviation Uganda (international vehicle registration).
– ORIGIN from *East Africa Uganda*.

eau de cologne /ˌəʊ də kəˈləʊn/ ▶ noun (pl. **eaux de cologne** pronunc. **same**) [mass noun] a toilet water with a strong scent, originally made in Cologne.
– ORIGIN early 19th cent.: French, literally 'water of Cologne'.

eau de Nil /əʊ də ˈniːl/ ▶ noun [mass noun] a pale greenish colour.
– ORIGIN late 19th cent.: from French *eau-de-Nil*, literally 'water of the Nile' (from the supposed resemblance in colour).

eau de toilette /əʊ də twɑːˈlet/ ▶ noun (pl. **eaux de toilette** pronunc. **same**) [mass noun] a dilute form of perfume; toilet water.
– ORIGIN early 20th cent.: French, 'toilet water'.

eau de vie /əʊ də ˈviː/ ▶ noun (pl. **eaux de vie** pronunc. **same**) [mass noun] brandy.
– ORIGIN from French *eau-de-vie*, literally 'water of life'.

eaves ▶ plural noun the part of a roof that meets or overhangs the walls of a building.
– ORIGIN Old English *efes* (singular); of Germanic origin; related to German dialect *Obsen*, also probably to **OVER**.

eavesdrop ▶ verb (**eavesdrops**, **eavesdropping**, **eavesdropped**) [no obj.] secretly listen to a conversation: *my father **eavesdropped on** my phone calls.*
– DERIVATIVES **eavesdropper** noun.
– ORIGIN early 17th cent.: back-formation from *eavesdropper* (late Middle English) 'a person who listens from under the eaves', from the obsolete noun *eavesdrop* 'the ground on to which water drips from the eaves', probably from Old Norse *upsardropi*, from *ups* 'eaves' + *dropi* 'a drop'.

eavestrough ▶ noun Canadian a gutter fixed beneath the edge of a roof.

Eb (also **EB**) ▶ abbreviation exabyte(s).

eBay ▶ verb [with obj.] buy or sell (goods) through the eBay website.
– DERIVATIVES **eBayer** noun.
– ORIGIN 1997: from the proprietary name of the website *eBay* (from Echo *Bay* Technology Group, the name of a company run by eBay's founder, Pierre Omidyar).

ebb ▶ noun (usu. **the ebb**) the movement of the tide out to sea: *the tide was **on the ebb*** | [as modifier] *the ebb tide.*
▶ verb [no obj.] **1** (of tidewater) move away from the land; recede: *the tide began to ebb.* Compare with **FLOW**.
2 (of an emotion or quality) gradually decrease: *my enthusiasm was ebbing away.*
– PHRASES **at a low ebb** in a weakened or depressed state: *the country was at a low ebb due to the recent war.* **ebb and flow** a recurrent pattern of coming and going or decline and regrowth.
– ORIGIN Old English *ebba* (noun), *ebbian* (verb), of West Germanic origin; related to Dutch *ebbe* (noun), *ebben* (verb), and ultimately to **OF** which had the primary sense 'away from'.

EBD ▶ abbreviation emotional and behavioural difficulties (or disorder).

e-billing ▶ noun [mass noun] the practice by which invoices or bills are electronically delivered or presented to customers, rather than being sent by post.

EBIT ▶ abbreviation earnings before interest and tax.

EBITDA ▶ abbreviation earnings before interest, taxes, depreciation, and amortization.

Ebla /ˈɛblə/ a city in ancient Syria, situated to the south-west of Aleppo. It became very powerful in the mid 3rd millennium BC, when it dominated a region corresponding to modern Lebanon, northern Syria, and SE Turkey.

E-boat ▶ noun a German torpedo boat used in the Second World War.
– ORIGIN from *E-* for *enemy* + **BOAT**.

Ebola fever /iːˈbəʊlə, əˈbəʊlə/ ▶ noun [mass noun] an infectious and generally fatal disease marked by fever and severe internal bleeding, spread through contact with infected body fluids by a filovirus (**Ebola virus**), whose normal host species is unknown.
– ORIGIN 1976: named after a river in the Democratic Republic of the Congo (Zaire), near which the disease was first observed.

ebon /ˈɛb(ə)n/ ▶ noun [mass noun] literary dark brown or black; ebony: [as modifier] *the ebon acid of the Styx.*

Ebonics /ɛˈbɒnɪks/ ▶ plural noun [treated as sing.] American black English regarded as a language in its own right rather than as a dialect of standard English.
– ORIGIN 1970s: blend of **EBONY** and **PHONICS**.

ebonite ▶ noun another term for **VULCANITE**.
– ORIGIN mid 19th cent.: from **EBONY** + **-ITE**[1].

ebonized (also **ebonised**) ▶ adjective (of furniture) given the appearance of ebony: *an ebonized casket.*
– DERIVATIVES **ebonize** verb.

ebony /ˈɛb(ə)ni/ ▶ noun **1** [mass noun] heavy blackish or very dark brown timber from a mainly tropical tree. ■ [mass noun] a very dark brown or black colour: [as modifier] *his ebony hair.*
2 a tree of tropical and warm-temperate regions which produces such timber. ● Genera *Diospyros* and *Euclea*, family Ebenaceae: numerous species, in particular *D. ebenum*.
■ used in names of trees of other families which produce timber similar to ebony, e.g. **Jamaican** (or **American**) **ebony**.
– ORIGIN late Middle English: from earlier *ebon* (via Old French and Latin from Greek *ebenos* 'ebony tree'), perhaps on the pattern of *ivory*.

e-book ▶ noun an electronic version of a printed book which can be read on a computer or a specifically designed handheld device.

Eboracum /ɪˈbɔːrəkəm, ˌiːbəˈrɑːkəm/ Roman name for **YORK**.

EBRD ▶ abbreviation European Bank for Reconstruction and Development (founded in 1991 to provide financial assistance to the former communist countries of eastern Europe).

Ebro /ˈiːbrəʊ, ˈɛb-/ the principal river of NE Spain, rising in the mountains of Cantabria and flowing 910 km (570 miles) south-eastwards into the Mediterranean Sea.

ebullience /ɪˈbʊlɪəns/ ▶ noun [mass noun] the quality of being cheerful and full of energy; exuberance: *the ebullience of happy children.*

ebullient /ɪˈbʌljənt, -ˈbʊl-/ ▶ adjective **1** cheerful and full of energy: *she sounded ebullient and happy.*
2 archaic (of liquid or matter) boiling or agitated as if boiling: *misted and ebullient seas.*
– DERIVATIVES **ebulliently** adverb.
– ORIGIN late 16th cent. (in the sense 'boiling'): from Latin *ebullient-* 'boiling up', from the verb *ebullire*, from *e-* (variant of *ex-*) 'out' + *bullire* 'to boil'.

ebullition /ˌɛbəˈlɪʃ(ə)n, -bʊ-/ ▶ noun [mass noun] technical or archaic the action of bubbling or boiling. ■ [count noun] a sudden outburst of emotion or violence: *an ebullition of pure hatred.*
– ORIGIN late Middle English (denoting a state of agitation of the bodily humours): from late Latin *ebullitio(n-)*, from *ebullire* 'boil up' (see **EBULLIENT**).

e-business ▶ noun [mass noun] another term for **E-COMMERCE**. ■ [count noun] a company that does all or most of its transactions through the Internet.

EBV ▶ abbreviation Epstein–Barr virus.

EC ▶ abbreviation ■ East Central (London postal district). ■ Ecuador (international vehicle registration). ■ European Commission. ■ European Community. ■ executive committee.

ecad /ˈiːkad/ ▶ noun Ecology an organism that is modified by its environment.
– ORIGIN early 20th cent.: from Greek *oikos* 'house' + **-AD**[1].

écarté ▶ noun [mass noun] **1** /eɪˈkɑːteɪ/ a card game for two players, originating in 19th-century France, in which thirty two cards are used and certain cards may be discarded in exchange for others.
2 /ˌeɪkɑːˈteɪ/ Ballet a position in which the dancer, facing diagonally towards the audience, extends one leg in the air to the side with the arm of the same side raised above the head and the other arm extended to the side.
– ORIGIN early 19th cent.: French, past participle of *écarter* 'discard, throw out', from *é* 'out' + *carte* 'card'.

e-cash ▶ noun [mass noun] electronic financial transactions conducted in cyberspace via computer networks.

ECB ▶ abbreviation England and Wales Cricket Board.

Ecce Homo /ˌɛkeɪ ˈhɒməʊ, ˈhəʊməʊ/ ▶ noun Art a painting of Christ wearing the crown of thorns.
– ORIGIN Latin, 'behold the man', the words of Pontius Pilate to the Jews after Jesus was crowned with thorns (John 19:5).

eccentric /ɪkˈsɛntrɪk, ɛk-/ ▶ adjective **1** (of a person or their behaviour) unconventional and slightly strange: *he noted her eccentric appearance.*
2 technical not placed centrally or not having its axis or other part placed centrally: *a servo driving an eccentric cam.* ■ (of a circle) not centred on the same point as another. ■ (of an orbit) not circular.
▶ noun **1** a person of unconventional and slightly strange views or behaviour: *he's seen as a local eccentric.*
2 a disc or wheel mounted eccentrically on a revolving shaft in order to transform rotation into backward-and-forward motion, e.g. a cam in an internal-combustion engine.
– DERIVATIVES **eccentrically** adverb.
– ORIGIN late Middle English (as a noun denoting a circle or orbit not having the earth precisely at its centre): via late Latin from Greek *ekkentros*, from *ek* 'out of' + *kentron* 'centre'.

E

eccentric anomaly ▶ noun Astronomy the actual anomaly of a planet in an elliptical orbit. Compare with **MEAN ANOMALY**.

eccentricity /ˌɛksɛnˈtrɪsɪti/ ▶ noun (pl. **eccentricities**) [mass noun] **1** the quality of being eccentric. ■ [count noun] (usu. **eccentricities**) an eccentric act or habit: *her eccentricities were amusing rather than irritating.*
2 technical deviation of a curve or orbit from circularity. ■ [count noun] a measure of the extent of deviation from circularity: *Halley's Comet has an eccentricity of about 0.9675.*

ecchymosis /ˌɛkɪˈməʊsɪs/ ▶ noun (pl. **ecchymoses** /-siːz/) Medicine a discoloration of the skin resulting from bleeding underneath, typically caused by bruising.
– ORIGIN mid 16th cent.: modern Latin, from Greek *ekkhumōsis* 'escape of blood', from *ekkhumonathai* 'force out blood'.

Eccles /ˈɛk(ə)lz/, Sir John Carew (1903–97), Australian physiologist, who demonstrated the way in which nerve impulses are conducted by means of chemical neurotransmitters. Nobel Prize for Physiology or Medicine (1963).

Eccles. ▶ abbreviation Ecclesiastes (in biblical references).

Eccles cake ▶ noun Brit. a round flat cake of sweetened pastry filled with currants.
– ORIGIN named after the town of *Eccles* near Manchester, England.

ecclesial /ɪˈkliːzɪ(ə)l/ ▶ adjective formal relating to or constituting a Church or denomination: *the modernization of ecclesial buildings.*
– ORIGIN mid 17th cent. (rare before the 1960s): via Old French from Greek *ekklēsia* 'assembly, church' (see **ECCLESIASTIC**).

ecclesiarch /ɪkˈliːzɪɑːk/ ▶ noun archaic a ruler of a Church.
– ORIGIN late 18th cent.: from Greek *ekklēsia* 'church' + *arkhos* 'leader'.

Ecclesiastes /ɪˌkliːzɪˈastiːz/ a book of the Bible traditionally attributed to Solomon, consisting largely of reflections on the vanity of human life.

ecclesiastic formal ▶ noun a priest or clergyman.
▶ adjective another term for **ECCLESIASTICAL**.
– ORIGIN late Middle English: from French *ecclésiastique*, or via late Latin from Greek *ekklēsiastikos*, from *ekklēsiastēs* 'member of an assembly', from *ekklēsia* 'assembly, church', based on *ekkalein* 'summon out'.

ecclesiastical ▶ adjective relating to the Christian Church or its clergy: *the ecclesiastical hierarchy.*
– DERIVATIVES **ecclesiastically** adverb.

ecclesiasticism ▶ noun [mass noun] adherence or over-attention to details of Church practice: *the ecclesiasticism that so often gets in the way of the gospel.*

Ecclesiasticus /ɪˌkliːzɪˈastɪkəs/ a book of the Apocrypha containing moral and practical maxims, probably composed or compiled in the early 2nd century BC.

ecclesiology /ɪˌkliːzɪˈɒlədʒi/ ▶ noun [mass noun] **1** the study of churches, especially church building and decoration.
2 theology as applied to the nature and structure of the Christian Church.
– DERIVATIVES **ecclesiological** adjective, **ecclesiologist** noun.
– ORIGIN mid 19th cent.: from Greek *ekklēsia* 'assembly, church' + **-LOGY**.

Ecclus ▶ abbreviation Ecclesiasticus (in biblical references).

eccrine /ˈɛkrʌɪn, -krɪn/ ▶ adjective Medicine relating to or denoting multicellular glands which do not lose cytoplasm in their secretions, especially the sweat glands. Compare with **APOCRINE**.

– ORIGIN 1930s: from Greek *ekkrinein* 'secrete', from *ek-* 'out' + *krinein* 'sift, separate'.

ecdysiast /ɛk'dɪzɪast/ ▶ **noun** humorous a striptease performer.
– ORIGIN 1940s: from Greek *ekdusis* 'shedding', on the pattern of *enthusiast*.

ecdysis /'ɛkdɪsɪs, ɛk'dʌɪsɪs/ ▶ **noun** [mass noun] Zoology the process of shedding the old skin (in reptiles) or casting off the outer cuticle (in insects and other arthropods).
– DERIVATIVES **ecdysial** /ɛk'dɪzɪəl/ **adjective**.
– ORIGIN mid 19th cent.: from Greek *ekdusis*, from *ekduein* 'put off', from *ek-* 'out, off' + *duein* 'put'.

ecdysone /'ɛkdɪsəʊn, ɛk'dʌɪsəʊn/ ▶ **noun** [mass noun] Biochemistry a steroid hormone that controls moulting in insects and other arthropods.
– ORIGIN 1950s: from Greek *ekdusis* 'shedding' + **-ONE**.

E

ECG ▶ **abbreviation** electrocardiogram or electrocardiograph.

échappé /eɪ'ʃapeɪ/ ▶ **adjective** [postpositive] Ballet (of a movement) progressing from a closed position (first, third, or fifth) to an open position (second or fourth) of the feet.
– ORIGIN French, literally 'escaped'.

echelon /'ɛʃəlɒn, 'eɪʃ-/ ▶ **noun** 1 a level or rank in an organization, a profession, or society: *the upper echelons of the business world*.
2 Military a formation of troops, ships, aircraft, or vehicles in parallel rows with the end of each row projecting further than the one in front. ■ [often with modifier] a part of a military force differentiated by position in battle or by function: *the rear echelon*.
▶ **verb** [with obj.] Military arrange in an echelon formation.
– ORIGIN late 18th cent. (in sense 2 of the noun): from French *échelon*, from *échelle* 'ladder', from Latin *scala*.

echeveria /ˌɛtʃɪ'vɪərɪə/ ▶ **noun** a succulent plant with rosettes of fleshy colourful leaves, native to warm regions of America and popular as pot plants. ● Genus *Echeveria*, family Crassulaceae: numerous species and cultivars.
– ORIGIN modern Latin, named after Anastasio *Echeveri* or *Echeverría*, 19th-cent. Mexican botanical illustrator.

echidna /ɪ'kɪdnə/ ▶ **noun** a spiny insectivorous egg-laying mammal with a long snout and claws, native to Australia and New Guinea. Also called **SPINY ANTEATER**. ● Family Tachyglossidae, order Monotremata: two genera and species.
– ORIGIN mid 19th cent.: modern Latin, from Greek *ekhidna* 'viper', also the name of a mythical creature which gave birth to the Hydra; compare with *ekhinos* 'sea urchin, hedgehog'.

echinacea /ˌɛkɪ'neɪsɪə/ ▶ **noun** a North American plant of the daisy family, whose flowers have a raised cone-like centre which appears to consist of soft spines. It is used in herbal medicine, largely for its antibiotic and wound-healing properties. ● Genus *Echinacea*, family Compositae: several species.
– ORIGIN modern Latin, from Greek *ekhinos* 'hedgehog'.

echinoderm /ɪ'kʌɪnə(ʊ)dəːm, 'ɛkɪn-/ ▶ **noun** Zoology a marine invertebrate of the phylum Echinodermata, such as a starfish, sea urchin, or sea cucumber.

Echinodermata /ɪˌkʌɪnə(ʊ)də'mɑːtə, ˌɛkɪn-, -'dəːmətə/ ▶ **plural noun** Zoology a phylum of marine invertebrates which includes starfishes, sea urchins, brittlestars, crinoids, and sea cucumbers. They have fivefold radial symmetry, a calcareous skeleton, and tube feet operated by fluid pressure.
– ORIGIN modern Latin (plural), from Greek *ekhinos* 'hedgehog, sea urchin' + *derma* 'skin'.

echinoid /'ɛkɪnɔɪd/ Zoology ▶ **noun** an echinoderm of the class Echinoidea; a sea urchin.
▶ **adjective** relating to or denoting echinoids.

Echinoidea /ˌɛkɪ'nɔɪdɪə/ ▶ **plural noun** Zoology a class of echinoderms that comprises the sea urchins.
– ORIGIN modern Latin (plural), from **ECHINUS**.

echinus /ɪ'kʌɪnəs/ ▶ **noun** 1 Zoology a sea urchin. ● Genus *Echinus*, class Echinoidea: several species.
2 Architecture a rounded moulding below an abacus on a Doric or Ionic capital.
– ORIGIN late Middle English: via Latin from Greek *ekhinos* 'hedgehog, sea urchin'.

Echiura /ˌɛkɪ'jʊ(ə)rə/ ▶ **plural noun** Zoology a small phylum of worm-like marine invertebrates that comprises the spoonworms.
– DERIVATIVES **echiuran** noun & adjective.
– ORIGIN modern Latin (earlier *Echiuroidea*), from Greek *ekhis* 'viper' + *oura* 'tail'.

Echo /'ɛkəʊ/ Greek Mythology a nymph deprived of speech by Hera in order to stop her chatter, and left able only to repeat what others had said.

echo ▶ **noun** 1 (pl. **echoes**) a sound or sounds caused by the reflection of sound waves from a surface back to the listener: *the walls threw back the echoes of his footsteps*. ■ a reflected radio or radar beam. ■ [mass noun] the deliberate introduction of reverberation into a sound recording. ■ Linguistics the repetition in structure and content of one speaker's utterance by another.
2 a close parallel to an idea, feeling, or event: *his love for her* ***found an echo in*** *her own feelings*. ■ a characteristic that is suggestive of something else: *the cheese has a sharp rich aftertaste with echoes of salty, earthy pastures*.
3 archaic a person who slavishly repeats the words or opinions of another.
4 Bridge a play by a defender of a higher card in a suit followed by a lower one in a subsequent trick, used as a signal to request a further lead of that suit by their partner.
5 a code word representing the letter E, used in radio communication.
6 used in names of newspapers: *the South Wales Echo*.
▶ **verb** (**echoes, echoing, echoed**) 1 [no obj., with adverbial] (of a sound) be repeated or reverberate after the original sound has stopped: *their footsteps echoed on the metal catwalks*. ■ (of a place) resound with or reflect back a sound: *the house* ***echoed with*** *shouts*. ■ [with obj.] repeat (someone's words or opinions), typically to express agreement: *these criticisms are echoed in a number of other studies* | [with direct speech] *'A trip?' she echoed*.
2 [with obj.] (of an object or event) be reminiscent of or have shared characteristics with: *a blue suit that echoed the colour of her eyes*.
3 [with obj.] Computing send a copy of (an input signal or character) back to its source or to a screen for display.
4 [no obj.] Bridge (of a defender) play a higher card followed by a lower one in the same suit, as a signal to request one's partner to lead that suit.
– PHRASES **applaud** (or **cheer**) **someone to the echo** applaud (or cheer) someone enthusiastically.
– DERIVATIVES **echoer** noun, **echoey** adjective, **echoless** adjective.
– ORIGIN Middle English: from Old French or Latin, from Greek *ēkhō*, related to *ēkhē* 'a sound'.

echocardiogram /ˌɛkəʊ'kɑːdɪə(ʊ)gram/ ▶ **noun** a test of the action of the heart using ultrasound waves to produce a visual display, for the diagnosis or monitoring of heart disease.

echocardiography /ˌɛkəʊkɑːdɪ'ɒgrəfi/ ▶ **noun** [mass noun] the use of ultrasound waves to investigate the action of the heart.
– DERIVATIVES **echocardiograph** noun, **echocardiographic** adjective.

echo chamber ▶ **noun** an enclosed space for producing reverberation of sound.

echogram ▶ **noun** a recording of depth or distance under water made by an echo sounder.

echograph ▶ **noun** an instrument for recording echograms; an automated echo sounder.

echoic /ɛ'kəʊɪk/ ▶ **adjective** of or like an echo. ■ Linguistics representing a sound by imitation.
– DERIVATIVES **echoically** adverb.

echolalia /ˌɛkəʊ'leɪlɪə/ ▶ **noun** [mass noun] 1 Psychiatry meaningless repetition of another person's spoken words as a symptom of psychiatric disorder.
2 repetition of speech by a child learning to talk.
– ORIGIN late 19th cent.: modern Latin, from Greek *ēkhō* 'echo' + *lalia* 'speech'.

echolocation /'ɛkə(ʊ)lə(ʊ)ˌkeɪʃ(ə)n/ ▶ **noun** [mass noun] the location of objects by reflected sound, in particular that used by animals such as dolphins and bats.

echopraxia /ˌɛkəʊ'praksɪə/ ▶ **noun** [mass noun] Psychiatry meaningless repetition or imitation of the movements of others as a symptom of psychiatric disorder.
– ORIGIN early 20th cent.: modern Latin, from Greek *ēkhō* 'echo' + *praxis* 'action'.

echo sounder ▶ **noun** a device for determining the depth of the seabed or detecting objects in water by measuring the time taken for sound echoes to return to the listener.
– DERIVATIVES **echo-sounding** noun.

echovirus (also **ECHO virus**) ▶ **noun** Medicine any of a group of enteroviruses which can cause respiratory infections and a mild form of meningitis.
– ORIGIN 1950s: from *echo* (acronym from *enteric cytopathogenic human orphan*, because the virus was not originally assignable to any known disease) + **VIRUS**.

echt /ɛxt/ ▶ **adjective** authentic and typical: *Bart was an echt baseball fan*.
▶ **adverb** [as submodifier] authentically and typically: *echt-Viennese artists*.
– ORIGIN German.

eclair /eɪ'klɛː, ɪ-/ ▶ **noun** a long, thin individual cake of choux pastry filled with cream and topped with chocolate icing.
– ORIGIN mid 19th cent.: from French *éclair*, literally 'lightning'.

éclaircissement /ˌeɪklɛː'siːsmɒ̃/ ▶ **noun** literary an enlightening explanation of something that has hitherto been obscure or inexplicable.
– ORIGIN French, from *éclaircir* 'clear up', from *é* (expressing a change of state) + *clair* (see **CLEAR**).

eclampsia /ɪ'klam(p)sɪə/ ▶ **noun** [mass noun] Medicine a condition in which one or more convulsions occur in a pregnant woman suffering from high blood pressure, often followed by coma and posing a threat to the health of mother and baby. See also **PRE-ECLAMPSIA**.
– DERIVATIVES **eclamptic** adjective.
– ORIGIN mid 19th cent.: modern Latin, from French *éclampsie*, from Greek *eklampsis* 'sudden development', from *eklampein* 'shine out'.

éclat /eɪ'klɑː/ ▶ **noun** [mass noun] brilliant display or effect: *he finished his recital with great éclat*. ■ social distinction or conspicuous success: *she was quite unaware of the éclat of being ambassadress there*.
– ORIGIN late 17th cent.: from French, from *éclater* 'burst out'.

eclectic /ɪ'klɛktɪk/ ▶ **adjective** 1 deriving ideas, style, or taste from a broad and diverse range of sources: *universities offering an eclectic mix of courses*.
2 (**Eclectic**) Philosophy denoting or belonging to a class of ancient philosophers who did not belong to or found any recognized school of thought but selected doctrines from various schools of thought.
▶ **noun** a person who derives ideas, style, or taste from a broad and diverse range of sources.
– DERIVATIVES **eclectically** adverb, **eclecticism** noun.
– ORIGIN late 17th cent. (as a term in philosophy): from Greek *eklektikos*, from *eklegein* 'pick out', from *ek* 'out' + *legein* 'choose'.

eclipse /ɪ'klɪps/ ▶ **noun** 1 an obscuring of the light from one celestial body by the passage of another between it and the observer or between it and its source of illumination: *an eclipse of the sun*. ■ a loss of significance or power in relation to another person or thing: *the election result marked the eclipse of the traditional right*.
2 Ornithology a phase during which the distinctive markings of a bird (especially a male duck) are obscured by moulting of the breeding plumage.
▶ **verb** [with obj.] (of a celestial body) obscure the light from or to (another celestial body): *Jupiter was eclipsed by the Moon*. ■ deprive (someone or something) of significance or power: *the economy has eclipsed the environment as the main issue*. ■ literary obscure or block out (light): *a sea of blue sky violently eclipsed by showers*.
– PHRASES **in eclipse** 1 losing or having lost significance or power: *his political power was in eclipse*. 2 Ornithology (especially of a male duck) in its eclipse plumage.
– ORIGIN Middle English: from Old French *e(s)clipse* (noun), *eclipser* (verb), via Latin from Greek *ekleipsis*, from *ekleipein* 'fail to appear, be eclipsed', from *ek* 'out' + *leipein* 'to leave'.

eclipsing binary ▶ **noun** Astronomy a binary star whose brightness varies periodically as the two components pass one in front of the other.

ecliptic /ɪ'klɪptɪk/ ▶ **noun** Astronomy a great circle on the celestial sphere representing the sun's apparent path during the year, so called because lunar and solar eclipses can only occur when the moon crosses it.
▶ **adjective** of an eclipse or the ecliptic.
– ORIGIN late Middle English: via Latin from Greek *ekleiptikos*, from *ekleipein* 'fail to appear' (see **ECLIPSE**).

eclogite /'ɛklɒdʒʌɪt/ ▶ **noun** [mass noun] Geology a metamorphic rock containing granular minerals, typically garnet and pyroxene.
– ORIGIN mid 19th cent.: from French, from Greek *eklogē* 'selection' (with reference to the selective content of the rock) + **-ITE**[1].

eclogue /ˈɛklɒɡ/ ▸ **noun** a short poem, especially a pastoral dialogue.
– ORIGIN late Middle English: via Latin from Greek *eklogē* 'selection', from *eklegein* 'pick out'.

eclose /ɪˈkləʊz/ ▸ **verb** [no obj.] Entomology (of an insect) emerge as an adult from the pupa or as a larva from the egg.
– DERIVATIVES **eclosion** noun.
– ORIGIN late 19th cent. (as *eclosion*): from French *éclore* 'to hatch', based on Latin *ex-* 'out' + *claudere* 'to close'.

ECM ▸ **abbreviation** electronic countermeasures.

ECN ▸ **abbreviation** electronic communications network.

Eco /ˈɛkəʊ/, Umberto (b.1932), Italian novelist and semiotician. Notable works: *The Name of the Rose* (novel, 1981), *Travels in Hyperreality* (writings on semiotics, 1986), and *Foucault's Pendulum* (novel, 1989).

eco ▸ **adjective** informal not harming the environment; eco-friendly: *with its rustic bamboo construction and solar-heated shower, the accommodation looked eco enough.*

eco- /ˈiːkəʊ, ˈɛkəʊ/ ▸ **combining form** representing ECOLOGY, ECOLOGICAL, etc.

ecocentrism ▸ **noun** another term for BIOCENTRISM.
– DERIVATIVES **ecocentric** adjective.

ecocide ▸ **noun** [mass noun] destruction of the natural environment, especially when deliberate.

ecofeminism ▸ **noun** [mass noun] a philosophical and political theory and movement which combines ecological concerns with feminist ones, regarding both as resulting from male domination of society.
– DERIVATIVES **ecofeminist** noun.

ecofreak ▸ **noun** informal a person who is very concerned about preserving the environment.

eco-friendly ▸ **adjective** not harmful to the environment: *I use only eco-friendly products.*

eco-labelling ▸ **noun** [mass noun] the practice of marking products with a distinctive label so that consumers know that their manufacture conforms to recognized environmental standards.
– DERIVATIVES **eco-label** noun.

E. coli /ˈkəʊlʌɪ/ ▸ **noun** [mass noun] a bacterium commonly found in the intestines of humans and other animals, some strains of which can cause severe food poisoning. ● *Escherichia coli*; a motile Gram-negative bacillus.

ecolodge /ˈiːkəʊlɒdʒ/ ▸ **noun** a type of tourist accommodation designed to have the minimum possible impact on the natural environment in which it is situated.

ecological ▸ **adjective** relating to or concerned with the relation of living organisms to one another and to their physical surroundings: *pollution is posing a serious threat to the ecological balance of the oceans* | *one of the world's worst ecological disasters.*
– DERIVATIVES **ecologically** adverb.

ecological footprint ▸ **noun** the impact of a person or community on the environment, expressed as the amount of land required to sustain their use of natural resources.

ecology /ɪˈkɒlədʒi, ɛ-/ ▸ **noun** [mass noun] the branch of biology that deals with the relations of organisms to one another and to their physical surroundings. ■ (**Ecology**) the political movement concerned with protection of the environment.
– DERIVATIVES **ecologist** noun.
– ORIGIN late 19th cent. (originally as *oecology*): from Greek *oikos* 'house' + -LOGY.

e-commerce ▸ **noun** [mass noun] commercial transactions conducted electronically on the Internet.

econobox /ɪˈkɒnəbɒks/ ▸ **noun** N. Amer. informal a car that is small and economical rather than luxurious or stylish.

econometrics /ɪˌkɒnəˈmɛtrɪks/ ▸ **plural noun** [treated as sing.] the branch of economics concerned with the use of mathematical methods (especially statistics) in describing economic systems.
– DERIVATIVES **econometric** adjective, **econometrician** /-məˈtrɪʃ(ə)n/ noun, **econometrist** noun.
– ORIGIN 1930s: from ECONOMY, on the pattern of words such as *biometrics*.

economic /ˌiːkəˈnɒmɪk, ɛk-/ ▸ **adjective 1** relating to economics or the economy: *the government's economic policy.* ■ (of a subject) considered in relation to trade, industry, and the creation of wealth: *economic history.*
2 justified in terms of profitability: *many organizations must become larger if they are to remain economic.* ■ requiring fewer resources or costing less money: *solar power may provide a more economic solution.*
– ORIGIN late Middle English: via Old French and Latin from Greek *oikonomikos*, from *oikonomia* (see ECONOMY). Originally a noun, the word denoted household management or a person skilled in this, hence the early sense of the adjective (late 16th cent.) 'relating to household management'. Modern senses date from the mid 19th cent.

economical ▸ **adjective** giving good value or return in relation to the money, time, or effort expended: *a small, economical car.* ■ (of a person or lifestyle) careful not to waste money or resources. ■ using no more of something than is necessary: *the cast are economical with their actions.*
– PHRASES **be economical with the truth** euphemistic lie or deliberately withhold information. [from a statement given in evidence by Sir Robert Armstrong, British cabinet secretary, in the 'Spycatcher' trial (1986), conducted to prevent publication of a book by a former MI5 employee.]

economically ▸ **adverb 1** in a way that relates to economics or finance: [sentence adverb] *the region is important economically.*
2 in a way that involves careful use of money or resources: *the new building was erected as economically as possible.*
3 in a way that uses no more of something than is necessary.

Economic and Social Committee (abbrev.: **ESC**) a consultative body of the European Union, set up in 1957 and composed of representatives of the member states. It meets in Brussels.

economic good ▸ **noun** Economics a product or service which can command a price when sold.

economic indicator ▸ **noun** a statistic used to predict future trends in a nation's economy.

economic migrant ▸ **noun** a person who travels from one country or area to another in order to improve their standard of living.

economic rent ▸ **noun** Economics the extra amount earned by a resource (e.g. land, capital, or labour) by virtue of its present use.

economics ▸ **plural noun** [often treated as sing.] **1** the branch of knowledge concerned with the production, consumption, and transfer of wealth.
2 the condition of a region or group as regards material prosperity: *he is responsible for the island's modest economics.*

economism /ɪˈkɒnəmɪz(ə)m/ ▸ **noun** [mass noun] belief in the primacy of economic causes or factors.
– ORIGIN early 20th cent.: from French *économisme*, based on Greek *oikonomia* 'household management' (see ECONOMY).

economist ▸ **noun** an expert in economics.

economize (also **economise**) ▸ **verb** [no obj.] spend less; reduce one's expenses: *I have to economize where I can* | *people on low incomes may try to economize on fuel.*
– DERIVATIVES **economization** noun, **economizer** noun.

economy ▸ **noun** (pl. **economies**) **1** the state of a country or region in terms of the production and consumption of goods and services and the supply of money: *he favours tax cuts to stimulate the economy.* ■ a particular system or stage of an economy: *a free-market economy.*
2 [mass noun] careful management of available resources: *fuel economy.* ■ [as modifier] offering good value for money: *an economy pack of soap flakes.* ■ sparing or careful use of something: *a technique based on economy of effort.* ■ [count noun] (usu. **economies**) a financial saving: *there were many economies to be made by giving up our London offices.*
3 (also **economy class**) the cheapest class of air or rail travel.
– PHRASES **economy of scale** a proportionate saving in costs gained by an increased level of production. **economy of scope** a proportionate saving gained by producing two or more distinct goods, when the cost of doing so is less than that of producing each separately.
– ORIGIN late 15th cent. (in the sense 'management of material resources'): from French *économie*, or via Latin from Greek *oikonomia* 'household management', based on *oikos* 'house' + *nemein* 'manage'. Current senses date from the 17th cent.

economy-class syndrome ▸ **noun** [mass noun] deep-vein thrombosis said to be caused by periods of prolonged immobility on long-haul flights.

economy-size (also **economy-sized**) ▸ **adjective** of a size which offers a large quantity for a proportionally lower cost: *an economy-size container.*

e-content ▸ **noun** [mass noun] digital text and images designed for display on web pages.

écorché /ˌɛkɔːˈʃeɪ/ ▸ **noun** (pl. pronunc. **same**) a painting or sculpture of a human figure with the skin removed to display the musculature.
– ORIGIN French, literally 'flayed'.

ecoregion ▸ **noun** an area defined in terms of its natural features and environment.

ecosphere ▸ **noun** the biosphere of the earth or other planet, especially when the interaction between the living and non-living components is emphasized. ■ Astronomy the region of space around a star where conditions are such that planets are theoretically capable of sustaining life.

ecossaise /ˌɛkɒˈseɪz/ ▸ **noun** (pl. pronunc. **same**) an energetic country dance in duple time in which couples form lines facing each other.
– ORIGIN mid 19th cent.: from French, feminine of *écossais* 'Scottish'; the connection with Scotland is unclear.

ecosystem ▸ **noun** Ecology a biological community of interacting organisms and their physical environment.

ecotage /ˈiːkətɑːʒ, ˈɛ-/ ▸ **noun** [mass noun] sabotage carried out for ecological reasons.
– ORIGIN 1970s: blend of *ecological* (see ECOLOGY) and SABOTAGE.

ecoterrorism ▸ **noun** [mass noun] violence carried out to further environmentalist ends. ■ the action of causing deliberate environmental damage in order to further political ends.
– DERIVATIVES **ecoterrorist** noun.

ecotone /ˈiːkə(ʊ)təʊn, ˈɛk-/ ▸ **noun** Ecology a region of transition between two biological communities.
– DERIVATIVES **ecotonal** adjective.
– ORIGIN early 20th cent.: from ECO- + Greek *tonos* 'tension'.

ecotourism ▸ **noun** [mass noun] tourism directed towards exotic natural environments, intended to support conservation efforts and observe wildlife.
– DERIVATIVES **ecotour** noun & verb, **ecotourist** noun.

ecotown ▸ **noun** a new town designed to facilitate a lifestyle that has as little impact on the environment as possible.

ecotoxicology ▸ **noun** [mass noun] the branch of science that deals with the nature, effects, and interactions of substances that are harmful to the environment.
– DERIVATIVES **ecotoxicological** adjective, **ecotoxicologist** noun.

ecotype ▸ **noun** Botany & Zoology a distinct form or race of a plant or animal species occupying a particular habitat.

eco-warrior ▸ **noun** a person actively involved in preventing damage to the environment.

ecru /ˈeɪkruː, ɛˈkruː/ ▸ **noun** [mass noun] the light fawn colour of unbleached linen.
– ORIGIN mid 19th cent.: from French *écru* 'unbleached'.

ECSC ▸ **abbreviation** European Coal and Steel Community.

ecstasy /ˈɛkstəsi/ ▸ **noun** (pl. **ecstasies**) [mass noun] **1** an overwhelming feeling of great happiness or joyful excitement: *there was a look of ecstasy on his face* | [count noun] *they went into ecstasies over the view.*
2 an emotional or religious frenzy or trance-like state, originally one involving an experience of mystic self-transcendence.
3 (**Ecstasy**) an illegal amphetamine-based synthetic drug with euphoric effects, originally produced as an appetite suppressant. Also called **MDMA**.
– ORIGIN late Middle English (in sense 2): from Old French *extasie*, via late Latin from Greek *ekstasis* 'standing outside oneself', based on *ek-* 'out' + *histanai* 'to place'.

ecstatic /ɪkˈstatɪk, ɛk-/ ▸ **adjective 1** feeling or expressing overwhelming happiness or joyful excitement: *ecstatic fans filled the stadium.*
2 involving an experience of mystic self-transcendence: *an ecstatic vision of God.*
▸ **noun** a person subject to mystical experiences.
– DERIVATIVES **ecstatically** adverb.

E

ECT ▸ **abbreviation** electroconvulsive therapy.

ecto- ▸ **combining form** outer; external: *ectoderm*.
– ORIGIN from Greek *ektos* 'outside'.

ectoderm /ˈɛktə(ʊ)dəːm/ ▸ **noun** [mass noun] Zoology & Embryology the outermost layer of cells or tissue of an embryo in early development, or the parts derived from this, which include the epidermis, nerve tissue, and nephridia. Compare with **ENDODERM** and **MESODERM**.
– DERIVATIVES **ectodermal** adjective.
– ORIGIN mid 19th cent.: from **ECTO-** 'outside' + Greek *derma* 'skin'.

ectogenesis /ˌɛktə(ʊ)ˈdʒɛnɪsɪs/ ▸ **noun** [mass noun] (chiefly in science fiction) the development of embryos in artificial conditions outside the womb.

ectomorph /ˈɛktə(ʊ)mɔːf/ ▸ **noun** Physiology a person with a lean and delicate build of body. Compare with **ENDOMORPH** and **MESOMORPH**.
– DERIVATIVES **ectomorphic** adjective, **ectomorphy** noun.
– ORIGIN 1940s: *ecto-* from *ectodermal* (being the layer of the embryo giving rise to physical characteristics which predominate) + **-MORPH**.

-ectomy ▸ **combining form** denoting surgical removal of a specified part of the body: *appendectomy*.
– ORIGIN from Greek *ektomē* 'excision', from *ek* 'out' + *temnein* 'to cut'.

ectoparasite /ˌɛktəʊˈparəsʌɪt/ ▸ **noun** Biology a parasite, such as a flea, that lives on the outside of its host. Compare with **ENDOPARASITE**.
– DERIVATIVES **ectoparasitic** adjective.

ectopic /ɛkˈtɒpɪk/ ▸ **adjective** Medicine in an abnormal place or position.
▸ **noun** an ectopic pregnancy.
– ORIGIN late 19th cent.: from modern Latin *ectopia* 'presence of tissue, cells, etc. in an abnormal place' (from Greek *ektopos* 'out of place') + **-IC**.

ectopic beat ▸ **noun** another term for **EXTRASYSTOLE**.

ectopic pregnancy ▸ **noun** a pregnancy in which the fetus develops outside the womb, typically in a fallopian tube.

ectoplasm /ˈɛktə(ʊ)plaz(ə)m/ ▸ **noun** [mass noun]
1 Biology, dated the more viscous, clear outer layer of the cytoplasm in amoeboid cells. Compare with **ENDOPLASM**.
2 a supernatural viscous substance that supposedly exudes from the body of a medium during a spiritualistic trance and forms the material for the manifestation of spirits.
– DERIVATIVES **ectoplasmic** adjective.

Ectoprocta /ˌɛktə(ʊ)ˈprɒktə/ ▸ **plural noun** Zoology another term for **BRYOZOA**.
– DERIVATIVES **ectoproct** noun.
– ORIGIN modern Latin (plural), from *ektos* 'outside or external' + *prōktos* 'anus'.

ectotherm /ˈɛktəʊθəːm/ ▸ **noun** Zoology an animal that is dependent on external sources of body heat. Often contrasted with **ENDOTHERM**. Compare with **POIKILOTHERM**.
– DERIVATIVES **ectothermic** adjective, **ectothermy** noun.

ectropion /ɛkˈtrəʊpɪən/ ▸ **noun** [mass noun] Medicine a condition, typically a consequence of advanced age, in which the eyelid is turned outwards away from the eyeball.
– ORIGIN late 17th cent.: from Greek, from *ek-* 'out' + *trepein* 'to turn'.

ecu /ˈɛkjuː, ˈiː-, ˈeɪ-, -kuː/ (also **ECU**) ▸ **noun** (pl. **same** or **ecus**) former term for **EURO**[1].
– ORIGIN acronym from *European currency unit*.

Ecuador /ˈɛkwədɔː/, Spanish /ekwaˈðoɾ/ an equatorial republic in South America, on the Pacific coast; pop. 14,573,100 (est. 2009); languages, Spanish (official), Quechua; capital, Quito.

> Ranges and plateaux of the Andes separate the coastal plain from the tropical forests of the Amazon basin. Formerly part of the Inca empire, Ecuador was conquered by the Spanish in 1534 and remained part of Spain's American empire until, after the first uprising against Spanish rule in 1809, independence was gained in 1822.

– DERIVATIVES **Ecuadorian** (also **Ecuadorean**) adjective & noun.

ecumenical /ˌiːkjʊˈmɛnɪk(ə)l, ɛk-/ ▸ **adjective** representing a number of different Christian Churches. ■ promoting or relating to unity among the world's Christian Churches: *the ecumenical movement*.
– DERIVATIVES **ecumenically** adverb.
– ORIGIN late 16th cent. (in the sense 'belonging to the universal Church'): via late Latin from Greek *oikoumenikos* from *oikoumenē* 'the (inhabited) earth'.

Ecumenical Patriarch ▸ **noun** a title of the Orthodox Patriarch of Constantinople.

ecumenism /ɪˈkjuːmənɪz(ə)m/ ▸ **noun** [mass noun] the principle or aim of promoting unity among the world's Christian Churches.

eczema /ˈɛksɪmə, ˈɛkzɪmə/ ▸ **noun** [mass noun] a medical condition in which patches of skin become rough and inflamed with blisters which cause itching and bleeding.
– DERIVATIVES **eczematous** /ɛkˈziːmətəs, ɛkˈzɛm-/ adjective.
– ORIGIN mid 18th cent.: modern Latin, from Greek *ekzema*, from *ekzein* 'boil over, break out', from *ek-* 'out' + *zein* 'boil'.

ED ▸ **abbreviation** ■ chiefly US emergency department. ■ erectile dysfunction.

ed. ▸ **abbreviation** ■ edited by. ■ edition. ■ editor.

-ed[1] ▸ **suffix** forming adjectives: **1** (added to nouns) having; possessing; affected by: *talented* | *diseased*. ■ (added to nouns) characteristic of: *ragged*.
2 from phrases consisting of adjective and noun: *bad-tempered* | *three-sided*.
– ORIGIN Old English *-ede*.

-ed[2] ▸ **suffix** forming: **1** the past tense and past participle of weak verbs: *landed* | *walked*.
2 participial adjectives: *wounded*.
– ORIGIN Old English *-ed*, *-ad*, *-od*.

edacious /ɪˈdeɪʃəs/ ▸ **adjective** rare relating to or given to eating.
– DERIVATIVES **edacity** noun.
– ORIGIN early 19th cent.: from Latin *edax*, *edac-* (from *edere* 'eat') + **-IOUS**.

Edam[1] /ˈiːdam/ a town in the Netherlands, to the north-east of Amsterdam; pop. 28,448 (2008) (with Volendam).

Edam[2] /ˈiːdam/ ▸ **noun** [mass noun] a round Dutch cheese, typically pale yellow with a red wax coating.

edamame /ˌɛdəˈmɑːmeɪ/ ▸ **noun** [mass noun] a Japanese dish of salted green soybeans boiled in their pods, typically served as a snack or appetizer.
– ORIGIN Japanese, literally 'beans on a branch'.

edaphic /ɪˈdafɪk/ ▸ **adjective** Ecology of, produced by, or influenced by the soil.
– ORIGIN late 19th cent.: coined in German from Greek *edaphos* 'floor' + **-IC**.

edaphosaurus /ɪˈdafəsɔːrəs/ ▸ **noun** a large herbivorous synapsid reptile of the late Carboniferous and early Permian periods, with long knobbly spines on its back supporting a sail-like crest. ● Genus *Edaphosaurus*, order Pelycosauria, subclass Synapsida.
– ORIGIN modern Latin, from Greek *edaphos* 'floor' + *sauros* 'lizard'.

Edda /ˈɛdə/ either of two 13th-century Icelandic books, the **Elder** or **Poetic Edda** (a collection of Old Norse poems on Norse legends) and the **Younger** or **Prose Edda** (a handbook to Icelandic poetry by Snorri Sturluson). The Eddas are the chief source of knowledge of Scandinavian mythology.
– ORIGIN either from the name of a character in the Old Norse poem *Rigsthul*, or from Old Norse *óthr* 'poetry'.

Eddington, Sir Arthur Stanley (1882–1944), English astronomer, considered the founder of astrophysics. He used Einstein's theory of relativity to explain the bending of light by gravity that he observed in the 1919 solar eclipse.

eddo /ˈɛdəʊ/ ▸ **noun** (pl. **eddoes**) a taro corm or plant of a West Indian variety with many edible cormlets.
– ORIGIN late 17th cent.: of West African origin.

Eddy, Mary Baker (1821–1910), American religious leader and founder of the Christian Science movement. Long a victim to various ailments, she believed herself cured by a faith healer, Phineas Quimby, and later evolved her own system of spiritual healing.

eddy ▸ **noun** (pl. **eddies**) a circular movement of water causing a small whirlpool. ■ a circular movement of wind, fog, or smoke.
▸ **verb** (**eddies**, **eddying**, **eddied**) [no obj., with adverbial of direction] (of water, air, or smoke) move in a circular way: *the mists from the river eddied round the banks*.
– ORIGIN late Middle English: probably from the Germanic base of the Old English prefix *ed-* 'again, back'.

eddy current ▸ **noun** a localized electric current induced in a conductor by a varying magnetic field.

Eddystone Rocks /ˈɛdɪstən/ a rocky reef off the coast of Cornwall, 22 km (14 miles) SW of Plymouth. The reef was the site of the earliest lighthouse (1699) built on rocks fully exposed to the sea.

edelweiss /ˈeɪd(ə)lvʌɪs/ ▸ **noun** a European mountain plant which has woolly white bracts around its small flowers and downy grey-green leaves. ● *Leontopodium alpinum*, family Compositae.
– ORIGIN mid 19th cent.: from German, from *edel* 'noble' + *weiss* 'white'.

edema ▸ **noun** US spelling of **OEDEMA**.

Eden[1] /ˈiːd(ə)n/, (Robert) Anthony, 1st Earl of Avon (1897–1977), British Conservative statesman, Prime Minister 1955–7. His premiership was dominated by the Suez crisis of 1956; widespread opposition to Britain's role in this led to his resignation.

Eden[2] /ˈiːd(ə)n/ (also **Garden of Eden**) the place where Adam and Eve lived in the biblical account of the Creation, from which they were expelled for disobediently eating the fruit of the tree of knowledge. ■ (as noun **an Eden**) a place or state of great happiness; an unspoilt paradise: *the lost Eden of his childhood*.
– DERIVATIVES **Edenic** /ɪˈdɛnɪk/ adjective.
– ORIGIN from late Latin (Vulgate), Greek *Ēdēn* (Septuagint), and Hebrew *ʿĒḏen*; perhaps related to Akkadian *edinu*, from Sumerian *eden* 'plain, desert' (but believed to be related to Hebrew *ʿēḏen* 'delight').

Edentata /ˌiːdənˈtɑːtə, -ˈteɪtə/ ▸ **plural noun** Zoology another term for **XENARTHRA**.

edentate /ˈiːdənteɪt/ ▸ **noun** Zoology a mammal of an order distinguished by the lack of incisor and canine teeth, including the anteaters, sloths, and armadillos, all of which are native to Central and South America. ● Order Xenarthra (or Edentata).
– ORIGIN early 19th cent.: from Latin *edentatus*, past participle of *edentare* 'make toothless', from *e-* (variant of *ex-*) 'out' + *dens*, *dent-* 'tooth'.

edentulous /ɪˈdɛntjʊləs/ ▸ **adjective** Medicine & Zoology lacking teeth.
– ORIGIN early 18th cent.: from Latin *edentulus*, from *e-* (variant of *ex-*) 'out' + *dens*, *dent-* 'tooth' + **-ULOUS**.

Edgar /ˈɛdɡə/ (944–75), king of England 959–75, younger brother of Edwy. He became king of Northumbria and Mercia in 957 when these regions renounced their allegiance to Edwy, succeeding to the throne of England on Edwy's death.

edge ▸ **noun** **1** the outside limit of an object, area, or surface: *a willow tree at the water's edge* | *she perched on the edge of a desk*. ■ an area next to a steep drop: *the cliff edge*. ■ [in sing.] the point immediately before something unpleasant or momentous occurs: *the economy was teetering on **the edge of** recession*.
2 the sharpened side of the blade of a cutting implement or weapon. ■ [in sing.] an intense, sharp, or striking quality: *a flamenco singer brings a primitive edge to the music* | *there was an edge of menace in his voice*.
3 [in sing.] a quality or factor which gives superiority over close rivals: *his cars have **the edge over** his rivals'*.
4 the line along which two surfaces of a solid meet.
▸ **verb** [with obj.] **1** provide with a border or edge: *the pool is edged with paving*.
2 [with adverbial of direction] move or cause to move gradually or furtively in a particular direction: [no obj.] *she tried to edge away from him* | [with obj.] *Hazel quietly edged him away from the others*.
3 give an intense or sharp quality to: *the bitterness that edged her voice*.
4 Cricket strike (the ball) with the edge of the bat; strike a ball delivered by (the bowler) with the edge of the bat.
5 [no obj.] ski with one's weight on the edges of one's skis.
– PHRASES **on edge** tense, nervous, or irritable. **on the edge of one's seat** informal very excited and giving one's full attention to something. **set someone's teeth on edge** (especially of a harsh sound) cause someone to feel intense discomfort or irritation. **take the edge off** reduce the intensity or effect of (something unpleasant or severe): *the tablets will take the edge off the pain*.
– PHRASAL VERBS **edge someone out 1** narrowly defeat a rival or opponent: *Portugal edged out Holland in the semi-final*. **2** remove a person from an organization or role by indirect means: *she was edged out of the organization by the director*.
– DERIVATIVES **edged** adjective [in combination] *a black-edged handkerchief*, **edgeless** adjective, **edger** noun.
– ORIGIN Old English *ecg* 'sharpened side of a blade', of Germanic origin; related to Dutch *egge* and

German *Ecke*, also to Old Norse *eggja* (see EGG²), from an Indo-European root shared by Latin *acies* 'edge' and Greek *akis* 'point'.

edge city ▶ noun N. Amer. a relatively large urban area situated on the outskirts of a city, typically beside a major road.
– ORIGIN 1991: coined by J. Garreau in a book of the same name.

edge connector ▶ noun an electrical connector with a row of contacts, fitted to the edge of a printed circuit board to facilitate connection to external circuits.

Edgehill, Battle of /ɛdʒˈhɪl/ the first pitched battle of the English Civil War (1642), fought at the village of Edgehill in the west Midlands. The Parliamentary army attempted to halt the Royalist army's march on London; the battle ended with no clear winner and with heavy losses on both sides.

edge tool ▶ noun a handworked or machine-operated cutting tool.

edgeways (US **edgewise**) ▶ adverb with the edge uppermost or towards the viewer.
– PHRASES **get a word in edgeways** [usu. with negative] contribute to a conversation with difficulty because the other speaker talks incessantly.

Edgeworth /ˈɛdʒwəθ/, Maria (1767–1849), English-born Irish novelist. Notable works: *Castle Rackrent* (1800) and *Belinda* (1801).

edging ▶ noun [mass noun] something forming an edge or border: *a chemise with lace edging.* ■ the process of providing something with an edge or border.

edgy ▶ adjective (**edgier, edgiest**) **1** tense, nervous, or irritable: *he became edgy and defensive.* ■ (of a musical performance or piece of writing) having an intense or sharp quality.
2 informal at the forefront of a trend; experimental or avant-garde: *their songs combine good music and smart, edgy ideas.*
– DERIVATIVES **edgily** adverb, **edginess** noun.

edh /ɛð/ ▶ noun variant spelling of ETH.

EDI ▶ abbreviation electronic data interchange (a standard for exchanging information between computer systems).

edible /ˈɛdɪb(ə)l/ ▶ adjective fit to be eaten (often used to contrast with unpalatable or poisonous varieties): *the shrub has small edible berries.*
▶ noun (**edibles**) items of food.
– DERIVATIVES **edibility** noun.
ORIGIN late 16th cent.: from late Latin *edibilis*, from Latin *edere* 'eat'.

edible crab ▶ noun a large pinkish-brown European crab with black-tipped pincers, typically found in inshore waters and caught for food. ● *Cancer pagurus*, family Cancridae.

edible dormouse ▶ noun another term for FAT DORMOUSE.

edible frog ▶ noun a large green aquatic frog of mainland Europe, popular as food in some regions. ● *Rana esculenta*, family Ranidae.

edible-nest swiftlet ▶ noun a small Asian swift whose nest, constructed from solidified saliva, is used to make Chinese bird's-nest soup. ● Genus *Aerodramus* (or *Collocalia*), family Apodidae: two species.

edible snail ▶ noun a large snail which is widely collected or cultured for food, occurring chiefly in southern Europe. ● *Helix pomatia*, family Helicidae.

edict /ˈiːdɪkt/ ▶ noun an official order or proclamation issued by a person in authority.
– ORIGIN Middle English: from Latin *edictum* 'something proclaimed', neuter past participle of *edicere*, from *e-* (variant of *ex-*) 'out' + *dicere* 'say, tell'.

Edict of Nantes see NANTES, EDICT OF.

edification /ˌɛdɪfɪˈkeɪʃ(ə)n/ ▶ noun [mass noun] formal the moral or intellectual instruction or improvement of someone: *a video was filmed for the edification of clients.*
– ORIGIN late Middle English: from Latin *aedificatio(n-)*, from *aedificare* 'build' (see EDIFY).

edifice /ˈɛdɪfɪs/ ▶ noun formal **1** a large, imposing building.
2 a complex system of beliefs: *the concepts on which the edifice of capitalism was built.*
– ORIGIN late Middle English: via Old French from Latin *aedificium*, from *aedis* 'dwelling' + *facere* 'make'.

edify /ˈɛdɪfʌɪ/ ▶ verb (**edifies, edifying, edified**) [with obj.] formal instruct or improve (someone) morally or intellectually.
– ORIGIN Middle English: from Old French *edifier*, from Latin *aedificare* 'build', from *aedis* 'dwelling' + *facere* 'make' (compare with EDIFICE). The word originally meant 'construct a building', also 'strengthen', hence to 'build up' morally.

edifying ▶ adjective providing moral or intellectual instruction: *edifying literature.* ■ [with negative] used to express one's disapproval of something: *seeing a person blind drunk is not an edifying sight.*
– DERIVATIVES **edifyingly** adverb.

Edinburgh /ˈɛdɪnb(ə)rə/ the capital of Scotland, lying on the southern shore of the Firth of Forth; pop. 449,100 (est. 2009). The city grew up round the 11th-century castle built by Malcolm III on a rocky ridge which dominates the landscape.

Edinburgh, Duke of see PHILIP, PRINCE.

Edinburgh Festival (also **Edinburgh International Festival**) an international festival of the arts held annually in Edinburgh since 1947. In addition to the main programme a flourishing fringe festival has developed.

Edison /ˈɛdɪs(ə)n/, Thomas (Alva) (1847–1931), American inventor. He took out the first of more than a thousand patents at the age of 21. His inventions include automatic telegraph systems, the carbon microphone for telephones, the phonograph, and the carbon filament lamp.

edit ▶ verb (**edits, editing, edited**) [with obj.] **1** prepare (written material) for publication by correcting, condensing, or otherwise modifying it: *Volume I was edited by J. Johnson.* ■ choose material for (a film or radio or television programme) and arrange it to form a coherent whole: (as adj. **edited**) *edited highlights of the match.* ■ change (text) on a computer. ■ (**edit something out**) remove unnecessary or inappropriate material from a text, film, or radio or television programme.
2 be editor of (a newspaper or magazine).
▶ noun a change or correction made as a result of editing.
– ORIGIN late 18th cent. (as a verb): partly a back-formation from EDITOR, reinforced by French *éditer* 'to edit' (from *édition* 'edition').

editable ▶ adjective (of text or software) in a format that can be edited by the user.

edition ▶ noun **1** a particular form or version of a published text: *a paperback edition.* ■ a particular version of a text maintained by regular revision: *a first edition.*
2 the total number of copies of a book, newspaper, or other published material issued at one time.
3 a particular instance of a regular radio or television programme: *the Monday edition will be repeated on Wednesdays.*
– ORIGIN late Middle English: from French *édition*, from Latin *editio(n-)*, from *edere* 'put out', from *e-* (variant of *ex-*) 'out' + *dare* 'give'.

editio princeps /ɪˌdɪʃɪəʊ ˈprɪnsɛps/ ▶ noun (pl. **editiones principes** /ɪˌdɪʃɪˌəʊniːz ˈprɪnsɪpiːz/) the first printed edition of a book.
– ORIGIN Latin, from *editio(n-)* 'edition' and *princeps* 'chief, leader' (from *primus* 'first').

editor ▶ noun **1** a person who is in charge of and determines the final content of a newspaper, magazine, or multi-author book. ■ a person who commissions or prepares written or recorded material for publication or broadcast.
2 a computer program enabling the user to enter or alter text.
– DERIVATIVES **editorship** noun.
– ORIGIN mid 17th cent.: from Latin, 'producer (of games), publisher', from *edit-* 'produced, put out', from the verb *edere*.

editorial ▶ adjective relating to the commissioning or preparing of material for publication: *the editorial team.* ■ relating to the part of a newspaper or magazine which contains news, information, or comment as opposed to advertising.
▶ noun a newspaper article expressing the editor's opinion on a topical issue. ■ [mass noun] the parts of a newspaper or magazine which are not advertising.
– DERIVATIVES **editorialist** noun, **editorially** adverb.

editorialize (also **editorialise**) ▶ verb [no obj.] (of a newspaper, editor, or broadcasting organization) express opinions rather than just report the news.

editress ▶ noun dated or humorous a female editor.

editrix ▶ noun another term for EDITRESS.
– ORIGIN early 20th cent.: from EDITOR + -TRIX.

edit suite ▶ noun a room containing equipment, or a set of equipment, for electronically editing video-recorded material.

-edly ▶ suffix (forming adverbs) in a manner characterized by the action expressed by the formative verb: *agitatedly.*

Edmonton /ˈɛdmənt(ə)n/ the capital of Alberta, Canada; pop. 730,372 (2006).

Edmund /ˈɛdmənd/ the name of two kings of England: ■ **Edmund I** (921–46), reigned 939–46. After succeeding Athelstan Edmund spent much of his reign trying to win his northern lands back from Norse control. ■ **Edmund II** (*c.*980–1016), son of Ethelred the Unready, reigned 1016; known as **Edmund Ironside**. Edmund led the resistance to Canute's forces in 1015, but was eventually defeated and forced to divide the kingdom with Canute. On Edmund's death Canute became king of all England.

E

Edmund, St (*c.*1175–1240), English churchman and teacher, Archbishop of Canterbury 1234–40; born *Edmund Rich*. Feast day, 16 November.

Edmund Campion, St see CAMPION.

Edmund the Martyr, St (*c.*841–70), king of East Anglia 855–70. After the defeat of his army by the invading Danes in 870, tradition holds that he was captured and shot with arrows for refusing to reject the Christian faith or to share power with his pagan conqueror. Feast day, 20 November.

edn ▶ abbreviation edition.

Edo¹ former name for TOKYO.

Edo² /ˈɛdəʊ/ ▶ noun (pl. **same** or **Edos**) **1** a member of a people inhabiting the district of Benin in Nigeria.
2 [mass noun] the Benue-Congo language of the Edo, with about 1 million speakers.
▶ adjective relating to the Edo or their language.
– ORIGIN the name of Benin City in Edo.

Edomite /ˈiːdəmʌɪt/ ▶ noun a member of an ancient people living in Edom, a region south of the Dead Sea, in biblical times, traditionally believed to be descended from Esau.

EDP ▶ abbreviation electronic data processing.

EDT ▶ abbreviation Eastern Daylight Time (see EASTERN TIME).

EDTA ▶ abbreviation Chemistry ethylenediamine tetra-acetic acid, a crystalline acid with a strong tendency to form chelates with metal ions. ● Chem. formula: $(CH_2COOH)_2NCH_2CH_2N(CH_2COOH)_2$.

educable /ˈɛdʒʊkəb(ə)l/ ▶ adjective able to be educated: *we must have teachers who believe that every child is educable.*
– DERIVATIVES **educability** noun.

educate /ˈɛdjʊkeɪt/ ▶ verb [with obj.] give intellectual, moral, and social instruction to (someone), typically at a school or university: *she was educated at a boarding school.* ■ provide or pay for instruction for (one's child), especially at a school. ■ give (someone) training in or information on a particular subject: *a plan to **educate** the young **on** the dangers of drugs* | [with obj. and infinitive] *the need to educate people to conserve water.*
– ORIGIN late Middle English: from Latin *educat-* 'led out', from the verb *educare*, related to *educere* 'lead out' (see EDUCE).

educated ▶ adjective having been educated: [in combination] *a Harvard-educated lawyer.* ■ resulting from or having had a good education: *educated tastes.*

educated guess ▶ noun a guess based on knowledge and experience and therefore likely to be correct.

education ▶ noun [mass noun] **1** the process of receiving or giving systematic instruction, especially at a school or university: *a course of education.* ■ the theory and practice of teaching: *colleges of education.* ■ [count noun] a body of knowledge acquired while being educated: *his education is encyclopedic and eclectic.* ■ information about or training in a particular subject: *health education.*
2 (**an education**) an enlightening experience: *Petrus is a good workman—it is an education to watch him.*
– DERIVATIVES **educationist** noun.
– ORIGIN mid 16th cent.: from Latin *educatio(n-)*, from the verb *educare* (see EDUCATE).

educational ▶ adjective relating to the provision of education. ■ intended or serving to educate or enlighten: *seeing an analyst was a very educational experience.*
– DERIVATIVES **educationalist** noun, **educationally** adverb.

educative /ˈɛdʒʊkətɪv/ ▸ **adjective** intended or serving to educate or enlighten; educational: *a useful educative tool.*

educator /ˈɛdʒʊkeɪtə/ ▸ **noun** a person who provides instruction or education; a teacher: *the perspective of a professional educator.*

educe /ɪˈdjuːs/ ▸ **verb** [with obj.] formal bring out or develop (something latent or potential): *out of love obedience is to be educed.* ▪ infer (something) from data: *more information can be educed from these statistics.*
– DERIVATIVES **eduction noun.**
– ORIGIN late Middle English: from Latin *educere* 'lead out', from *e-* (variant of *ex-*) 'out' + *ducere* 'to lead'.

E

edulcorate /ɪˈdʌlkəreɪt/ ▸ **verb** [with obj.] rare make (something) more acceptable or palatable.
– ORIGIN mid 17th cent.: from medieval Latin *edulcorat-* 'sweetened', from the verb *edulcorare*, from Latin *e* (variant of *ex-*) 'out' + *dulcor* 'sweetness'.

edutainment /ˌɛdjʊˈteɪnm(ə)nt/ ▸ **noun** [mass noun] computer games, television programmes, or other material, intended to be both educational and enjoyable.
– ORIGIN 1980s: blend of EDUCATION and ENTERTAINMENT.

Edw. ▸ **abbreviation** Edward.

Edward the name of six kings of England and also one of Great Britain and Ireland and one of the United Kingdom: ▪ **Edward I** (1239–1307), son of Henry III, reigned 1272–1307; known as **the Hammer of the Scots.** His campaign against Prince Llewelyn ended with the annexation of Wales in 1284, but he failed to conquer Scotland, where resistance was led by Sir William Wallace and later Robert the Bruce. ▪ **Edward II** (1284–1327), son of Edward I, reigned 1307–27. In 1314 he was defeated by Robert the Bruce at Bannockburn. In 1326 Edward's wife, Isabella of France, and her lover, Roger de Mortimer, invaded England; Edward was deposed in favour of his son and murdered. ▪ **Edward III** (1312–77), son of Edward II, reigned 1327–77. In 1330 he took control of his kingdom, banishing Isabella and executing Mortimer. He supported Edward de Baliol, the pretender to the Scottish throne, and started the Hundred Years War. ▪ **Edward IV** (1442–83), son of Richard, Duke of York, reigned 1461–83. He became king after defeating the Lancastrian Henry VI. Edward was briefly forced into exile in 1470–1 by the Earl of Warwick but regained his position with victory at Tewkesbury in 1471. ▪ **Edward V** (1470–*c.*1483), son of Edward IV, reigned 1483 but not crowned. Edward and his brother Richard (known as the Princes in the Tower) were probably murdered and the throne was taken by their uncle, Richard III. ▪ **Edward VI** (1537–53), son of Henry VIII, reigned 1547–53. His reign saw the establishment of Protestantism as the state religion. ▪ **Edward VII** (1841–1910), son of Queen Victoria, reigned 1901–10. Although he played little part in government on coming to the throne, his popularity helped revitalize the monarchy. ▪ **Edward VIII** (1894–1972), son of George V, reigned 1936 but not crowned. Edward abdicated eleven months after coming to the throne in order to marry the American divorcee Mrs Wallis Simpson.

Edward, Lake a lake on the border between Uganda and the Democratic Republic of the Congo (Zaire), linked to Lake Albert by the Semliki River.

Edward, Prince, Edward Antony Richard Louis, Earl of Wessex (b.1964), third son of Elizabeth II. He married Sophie Rhys-Jones (b.1965) in 1999.

Edward, Prince of Wales see BLACK PRINCE.

Edwardian /ɛdˈwɔːdɪən/ ▸ **adjective** relating to or characteristic of the reign of King Edward VII: *the Edwardian era | a fine Edwardian house.*
▸ **noun** a person who lived during this period.

Edwardiana /ɛdˌwɔːdɪˈɑːnə/ ▸ **plural noun** articles, especially collectors' items, from the reign of Edward VII.

Edwards, Gareth (Owen) (b.1947), Welsh rugby union player. An international player from 1967 to 1978, he was the youngest-ever Welsh captain when appointed in 1968.

Edward the Confessor, St (*c.*1003–66), son of Ethelred the Unready, king of England 1042–66. Famed for his piety, Edward founded Westminster Abbey, where he was eventually buried. Feast day, 13 October.

Edward the Elder (*c.*870–924), son of Alfred the Great, king of Wessex 899–924. His military successes against the Danes made it possible for his son Athelstan to become the first king of all England in 925.

Edward the Martyr, St (*c.*963–78), son of Edgar, king of England 975–8. Edward was faced by a challenge for the throne from supporters of his half-brother, Ethelred, who eventually had him murdered at Corfe Castle in Dorset. Feast day, 18 March.

Edwy /ˈɛdwi/ (also **Eadwig**) , king of England 955–7. He was probably only 15 years old when he became king; after Mercia and Northumbria renounced him in favour of his brother Edgar, he ruled over only the lands south of the Thames.

ee ▸ **exclamation** northern English form of OH[1].

-ee ▸ **suffix** forming nouns: **1** denoting the person affected directly or indirectly by the action of the formative verb: *employee.*
2 denoting a person described as or concerned with: *absentee.*
3 denoting an object of relatively smaller size: *bootee.*
– ORIGIN from Anglo-Norman French *-é*, from Latin *-atus* (past participial ending). Some forms are anglicized modern French nouns (e.g. *refugee* from *réfugié*).

EEA ▸ **abbreviation** European Economic Area, a free-trade zone created in 1994, composed of the states of the European Union together with Iceland, Norway, and Liechtenstein.

EEC ▸ **abbreviation** European Economic Community.

EEG ▸ **abbreviation** electroencephalogram, electroencephalograph, or electroencephalography.

eejit /ˈiːdʒɪt/ ▸ **noun** informal Irish and Scottish form of IDIOT.

eek ▸ **exclamation** informal used to express alarm, horror, or surprise.

eel ▸ **noun** a snake-like fish with a slender elongated body and poorly developed fins, proverbial for its slipperiness. ● Order Anguilliformes: many families, in particular Anguillidae, which comprises mainly freshwater eels that breed in the sea, including the common *Anguilla anguilla* of Europe and *A. rostrata* of America.
▪ used in names of unrelated fishes that resemble the true eels, e.g. **electric eel, moray eel.**
– DERIVATIVES **eel-like adjective, eely adjective.**
– ORIGIN Old English *ǣl*, of Germanic origin; related to Dutch *aal* and German *Aal*.

Eelam /ˈiːləm/ the proposed homeland of the Tamil people of Sri Lanka, for which the Tamil Tigers separatist group have been fighting since the early 1980s.

eelgrass ▸ **noun** [mass noun] **1** a marine plant with long ribbon-like leaves which grows in European coastal waters. ● *Zostera marina*, family Zosteraceae.
2 North American term for TAPE-GRASS.

eelpout /ˈiːlpaʊt/ ▸ **noun** a small broad-headed fish of cool or cold seas, having an elongated body and the dorsal and anal fins continuous with the tail. ● Family Zoarcidae: numerous genera and species, including the northern European viviparous blenny (*Zoarces viviparus*).
– ORIGIN Old English *ǣlepūte* (see EEL, POUT[2]).

eelworm ▸ **noun** a nematode, especially a small soil nematode that can become a serious pest of crops and ornamental plants.

Eem /iːm/ ▸ **noun** [usu. as modifier] Geology the most recent interglacial period of the Pleistocene in northern Europe, preceding the Weichsel glaciation and corresponding to the Ipswichian in Britain. ▪ the system of deposits laid down at this time.
– DERIVATIVES **Eemian adjective & noun.**
– ORIGIN early 20th cent.: from the name of a river in the Netherlands.

e'en[1] /iːn/ ▸ **adverb** literary form of EVEN[1].

e'en[2] /iːn/ ▸ **noun** Scottish form of EVEN[2].

-een ▸ **suffix** Irish forming diminutive nouns such as *colleen.*
– ORIGIN from the Irish diminutive suffix *-ín*.

eensy /ˈiːnsi/ (also **eensy-weensy**) ▸ **adjective** informal extremely small; tiny.

EEPROM ▸ **noun** Computing a read-only memory whose contents can be erased and reprogrammed using a pulsed voltage.
– ORIGIN acronym from *electrically erasable programmable ROM.*

e'er /ɛː/ ▸ **adverb** literary form of EVER.

-eer ▸ **suffix 1** (forming nouns) denoting a person concerned with or engaged in an activity: *auctioneer.*
2 (forming verbs) denoting concern or involvement with an activity: *electioneer.*
– ORIGIN from French *-ier*, from Latin *-arius*; verbs are often back-formations (e.g. *electioneer* from *electioneering*).

eerie /ˈɪəri/ ▸ **adjective** (**eerier, eeriest**) strange and frightening: *an eerie green glow in the sky.*
– DERIVATIVES **eerily adverb** [as submodifier] *it was eerily quiet*, **eeriness noun.**
– ORIGIN Middle English (originally northern English and Scots in the sense 'fearful'): probably from Old English *earg* 'cowardly', of Germanic origin; related to German *arg*.

Eeyorish /ˈiːɔːrɪʃ/ (also **Eeyoreish**) ▸ **adjective** Brit. pessimistic or gloomy: *they were an Eeyorish bunch, always looking on the dark side of life.*
– ORIGIN 1990s: from *Eeyore*, the name of a donkey in A. A. Milne's *Winnie-the-Pooh* (1926), characterized by his gloomy outlook on life.

ef- ▸ **prefix** variant spelling of EX-[1] assimilated before *f* (as in *efface, effloresce*).

EFA ▸ **abbreviation** essential fatty acid.

eff ▸ **noun & verb** Brit. used as a euphemism for 'fuck'.
– PHRASES **eff and blind** informal use expletives; swear. [*blind* from its use in expletives such as *blind me* (see BLIMEY).]
– DERIVATIVES **effing adjective & adverb.**
– ORIGIN 1950s: the letter *F* represented as a word.

effable /ˈɛfəb(ə)l/ ▸ **adjective** rare able to be described in words.
– ORIGIN early 17th cent.: from Latin *effabilis*, from *effari* 'utter'.

efface /ɪˈfeɪs/ ▸ **verb** [with obj.] **1** erase (a mark) from a surface: *with time, the words are effaced by the rain.* ▪ cause (a memory or emotion) to disappear completely.
2 (**efface oneself**) make oneself appear insignificant or inconspicuous.
– DERIVATIVES **effacement noun.**
– ORIGIN late 15th cent. (in the sense 'pardon or be absolved from (an offence)'): from French *effacer*, from *e-* (from Latin *ex-* 'away from') + *face* 'face'.

effect ▸ **noun 1** a change which is a result or consequence of an action or other cause: *the lethal effects of hard drugs* | [mass noun] *politicians have some effect on the lives of ordinary people.* ▪ [mass noun] the state of being or becoming operative. ▪ [mass noun] the extent to which something succeeds or is operative: *wind power can be used to great effect.* ▪ [with modifier] Physics a physical phenomenon, typically named after its discoverer: *the Renner effect.* ▪ an impression produced in the mind of a person: *gentle music can have a soothing effect.*
2 (**effects**) the lighting, sound, or scenery used in a play, film, or broadcast: *the production relied too much on spectacular effects.*
3 (**effects**) personal belongings: *the insurance covers personal effects.*
▸ **verb** [with obj.] cause (something) to happen; bring about: *the prime minister effected many policy changes.*
– PHRASES **come into effect** come into force; start to apply: *similar legislation came into effect in Wales on the same date.* **for effect** in order to impress people: *I suspect he's controversial for effect.* **in effect** in force: *a moratorium in effect since 1985 has been lifted.* ▪ in practice, even if not formally acknowledged: *the minister's powers allow him, in effect, to ban programmes.* **put** (or **bring** or **carry**) **something into effect** cause something to apply or become operative: *they succeeded in putting their strategies into effect.* **take effect** come into force; start to apply: *the ban is to take effect in six months.* **to the effect that** used to refer to the general meaning of something written or spoken: *some comments to the effect that my essay was a little light on analysis.* **to that effect** having that result, purpose, or meaning: *she thought it a foolish rule and put a notice to that effect in a newspaper.* **with effect from** Brit. starting from (a specified date): *he resigned with effect from 1 June | the company said yesterday it would lay off all staff with immediate effect.*
– ORIGIN late Middle English: from Old French, or from Latin *effectus*, from *efficere* 'accomplish', from *ex-* 'out, thoroughly' + *facere* 'do, make'. Sense 3 of the noun, 'personal belongings', arose from the obsolete sense 'something acquired on completion of an action'.

USAGE For an explanation of the difference between **effect** and **affect**, see **USAGE** at **AFFECT[1]**.

effective ▸ **adjective 1** successful in producing a desired or intended result: *effective solutions to*

environmental problems. ■ (of a law, rule, or policy) operative: *the regulation will be effective from January.*
2 [attrib.] existing in fact, though not formally acknowledged as such: *she has been under effective house arrest since September.* ■ assessed according to actual rather than face value: *an effective price of £176 million.*
▸ **noun** a soldier fit and available for service.
– DERIVATIVES **effectivity** noun.
– ORIGIN late Middle English: from Latin *effectivus*, from *efficere* 'accomplish' (see EFFECT).

effective demand ▸ **noun** Economics the level of demand that represents a real intention to purchase by people with the means to pay.

effectively ▸ **adverb** in such a manner as to achieve a desired result: *make sure that resources are used effectively.* ■ actually but not officially or explicitly: *they were effectively controlled by the people they were supposed to be investigating* | [sentence adverb] *effectively, this means that companies will be able to avoid regulations.*

effectiveness ▸ **noun** [mass noun] the degree to which something is successful in producing a desired result; success: *the effectiveness of the treatment.*

effective temperature ▸ **noun** Physics the temperature of an object calculated from the radiation it emits, assuming black-body behaviour.

effector ▸ **noun** Biology an organ or cell that acts in response to a stimulus: [as modifier] *effector cells.*

effectual /ɪˈfɛktʃʊəl, -tjʊəl/ ▸ **adjective** (of something inanimate or abstract) successful in producing a desired or intended result; effective: *tobacco smoke is the most effectual protection against the midge.* ■ Law (of a legal document) valid or binding.
– DERIVATIVES **effectuality** noun, **effectually** adverb, **effectualness** noun.
– ORIGIN late Middle English: from medieval Latin *effectualis*, from Latin *effectus* (see EFFECT).

effectuate /ɪˈfɛktʃʊeɪt, -tjʊ-/ ▸ **verb** [with obj.] formal put into force or operation: *school choice would effectuate a transfer of power from government to individuals.*
– DERIVATIVES **effectuation** noun.
– ORIGIN late 16th cent.: from medieval Latin *effectuat-* 'caused to happen', from the verb *effectuare*, from Latin *effectus* (see EFFECT).

effeminate /ɪˈfɛmɪnət/ ▸ **adjective** derogatory (of a man) having characteristics regarded as typical of a woman; unmanly.
– DERIVATIVES **effeminacy** noun, **effeminately** adverb.
– ORIGIN late Middle English: from Latin *effeminatus*, past participle of *effeminare* 'make feminine', from *ex-* (expressing a change of state) + *femina* 'woman'.

effendi /ɛˈfɛndi/ ▸ **noun** (pl. **effendis**) a man of high education or social standing in an eastern Mediterranean or Arab country. ■ historical a title of respect or courtesy in Turkey.
– ORIGIN early 17th cent.: from Turkish *efendi*, from modern Greek *aphentēs*, from Greek *authentēs* 'lord, master'.

efferent /ˈɛf(ə)r(ə)nt/ ▸ **adjective** Physiology conducted or conducting outwards or away from something (for nerves, the central nervous system; for blood vessels, the organ supplied). The opposite of AFFERENT.
▸ **noun** an efferent nerve fibre or vessel.
– ORIGIN mid 19th cent.: from Latin *efferent-* 'carrying out', from the verb *efferre*, from *ex-* 'out' + *ferre* 'carry'.

effervesce /ˌɛfəˈvɛs/ ▸ **verb** [no obj.] **1** (of a liquid) give off bubbles.
2 be vivacious and enthusiastic.
– ORIGIN early 18th cent.: from Latin *effervescere*, from *ex-* 'out, up' + *fervescere* 'begin to boil' (from *fervere* 'be hot, boil').

effervescence ▸ **noun** [mass noun] **1** bubbles in a liquid; fizz: *the effervescence of sparkling wine.*
2 vivacity and enthusiasm: *he was filled with such effervescence.*

effervescent ▸ **adjective** **1** (of a liquid) giving off bubbles; fizzy.
2 vivacious and enthusiastic: *effervescent young people.*
– ORIGIN late 17th cent.: from Latin *effervescent-* 'boiling up', from the verb *effervescere* (see EFFERVESCE).

effete /ɪˈfiːt/ ▸ **adjective** affected, over-refined, and ineffectual: *effete trendies from art college.* ■ no longer capable of effective action: *the authority of an effete aristocracy began to dwindle.* ■ (of a man) weak or effeminate.
– DERIVATIVES **effetely** adverb, **effeteness** noun.
– ORIGIN early 17th cent. (in the sense 'no longer fertile'): from Latin *effetus* 'worn out by bearing young', from *ex-* 'out' + *fetus* 'breeding'; related to FETUS.

efficacious /ˌɛfɪˈkeɪʃəs/ ▸ **adjective** formal (of something inanimate or abstract) successful in producing a desired or intended result; effective: *this treatment was efficacious in some cases.*
– DERIVATIVES **efficaciously** adverb, **efficaciousness** noun.
– ORIGIN early 16th cent.: from Latin *efficax, efficac-* (from *efficere* 'accomplish': see EFFECT) + -IOUS.

efficacy /ˈɛfɪkəsi/ ▸ **noun** [mass noun] formal the ability to produce a desired or intended result: *there is little information on the efficacy of this treatment.*
– ORIGIN early 16th cent.: from Latin *efficacia*, from *efficax, efficac-* (see EFFICACIOUS).

efficiency ▸ **noun** (pl. **efficiencies**) [mass noun] the state or quality of being efficient: *greater energy efficiency.* ■ [count noun] an action designed to achieve efficiency: *the reforms will lead to efficiencies and savings.* ■ [count noun] technical the ratio of the useful work performed by a machine or in a process to the total energy expended or heat taken in.
– ORIGIN late 16th cent. (in the sense 'the fact of being an efficient cause'): from Latin *efficientia*, from *efficere* 'accomplish' (see EFFECT).

efficient ▸ **adjective** **1** (of a system or machine) achieving maximum productivity with minimum wasted effort or expense: *more efficient processing of information.* ■ [in combination] preventing the wasteful use of a particular resource: *an energy-efficient heating system.*
2 (of a person) working in a well-organized and competent way.
– DERIVATIVES **efficiently** adverb.
– ORIGIN late Middle English (in the sense 'making, causing', usually in EFFICIENT CAUSE): from Latin *efficient-* 'accomplishing', from the verb *efficere* (see EFFECT). The current sense dates from the late 18th cent.

efficient cause ▸ **noun** Philosophy an agent that brings a thing into being or initiates a change.

effigy /ˈɛfɪdʒi/ ▸ **noun** (pl. **effigies**) a sculpture or model of a person: *a tomb effigy of Eleanor of Aquitaine.* ■ a roughly made model of a person that is made in order to be damaged or destroyed as a protest.
– PHRASES **burn someone in effigy** burn a model of a person as a protest.
– ORIGIN mid 16th cent.: from Latin *effigies*, from *effingere* 'to fashion (artistically)', from *ex-* 'out' + *fingere* 'to shape'.

effleurage /ˌɛfləːˈrɑːʒ/ ▸ **noun** [mass noun] a form of massage involving a repeated circular stroking movement made with the palm of the hand.
▸ **verb** [with obj.] massage with a circular stroking movement: *effleurage the shoulders and press gently.*
– ORIGIN late 19th cent.: from French, from *effleurer* 'skim the surface, stroke lightly', literally 'remove the flower or 'outer beauty' of something'.

effloresce /ˌɛfləˈrɛs/ ▸ **verb** [no obj.] **1** (of a substance) lose moisture and turn to a fine powder on exposure to air. ■ (of salts) come to the surface of brickwork, rock, or other material and crystallize there. ■ (of a surface) become covered with salt particles.
2 reach an optimum stage of development: *simple concepts that effloresce into testable conclusions.*
– DERIVATIVES **efflorescence** noun, **efflorescent** adjective.
– ORIGIN late 18th cent.: from Latin *efflorescere*, from *e-* (variant of *ex-*) 'out' + *florescere* 'begin to bloom' (from *florere* 'to bloom', from *flos, flor-* 'flower').

effluence /ˈɛflʊəns/ ▸ **noun** a substance that flows out from something. ■ [mass noun] the action of flowing out.
– ORIGIN late Middle English: from medieval Latin *effluentia*, from Latin *effluere* 'flow out', from *ex-* 'out' + *fluere* 'to flow'.

effluent ▸ **noun** [mass noun] liquid waste or sewage discharged into a river or the sea: *industrial effluent* | [count noun] *contamination with trade effluents.*
– ORIGIN late Middle English (in the adjective sense 'flowing out'): from Latin *effluent-* 'flowing out', from the verb *effluere* (see EFFLUENCE). The noun dates from the mid 19th cent.

effluvium /ɪˈfluːvɪəm/ ▸ **noun** (pl. **effluvia** /-vɪə/) an unpleasant or harmful odour or discharge: *smoke and effluvia from factory chimneys.*
– ORIGIN mid 17th cent.: from Latin, from *effluere*: 'flow out'.

efflux /ˈɛflʌks/ ▸ **noun** [mass noun] technical the flowing out of a substance or particle. ■ material that is flowing out.
– ORIGIN mid 16th cent.: from medieval Latin *effluxus*, from *effluere* 'flow out'.

effluxion /ɪˈflʌkʃ(ə)n/ ▸ **noun** [mass noun] **1** Law the expiration of a limited-time agreement or contract.
2 archaic the action of flowing out.
– ORIGIN early 17th cent.: from French, or from late Latin *effluxio(n-)*, from *effluere* 'flow out'.

effort ▸ **noun** **1** a vigorous or determined attempt: *in an effort to reduce inflation, the government increased interest rates.* ■ the result of an attempt: *he was a keen gardener, winning many prizes for his efforts.* ■ [mass noun] strenuous physical or mental exertion: *achieving independence requires some effort and self-discipline.* ■ [with modifier] the activities of a group of people with a common purpose: *the war effort.*
2 technical a force exerted by a machine or in a process.
– PHRASES **make an effort** attempt to do something: *make an effort to do some kind of abdominal exercise.* **make every** (or **spare no**) **effort** try everything possible to achieve something: *the doctor spared no effort in helping my father.* **with effort** with physical difficulty: *'It's bad, sir', he said, controlling his voice with effort.*
– DERIVATIVES **effortful** adjective, **effortfully** adverb.
– ORIGIN late 15th cent.: from French, from Old French *esforcier*, based on Latin *ex-* 'out' + *fortis* 'strong'.

effortless ▸ **adjective** requiring no physical or mental exertion. ■ achieved with admirable ease: *her effortless sense of style.*
– DERIVATIVES **effortlessly** adverb, **effortlessness** noun.

effrontery /ɪˈfrʌnt(ə)ri/ ▸ **noun** [mass noun] insolent or impertinent behaviour: *one juror had the effrontery to challenge the coroner's decision.*
– ORIGIN late 17th cent.: from French *effronterie*, based on late Latin *effrons, effront-* 'shameless, barefaced', from *ex-* 'out' + *frons* 'forehead'.

effulgent /ɪˈfʌldʒ(ə)nt/ ▸ **adjective** literary shining brightly; radiant. ■ (of a person or their expression) emanating joy or goodness.
– DERIVATIVES **effulgence** noun, **effulgently** adverb.
– ORIGIN mid 18th cent. (earlier (mid 17th cent.) as *effulgence*): from Latin *effulgent-* 'shining brightly', from the verb *effulgere*, from *ex-* 'out' + *fulgere* 'to shine'.

effuse /ɪˈfjuːz/ ▸ **verb** **1** [with obj.] give off (a liquid, light, smell, or quality).
2 [no obj.] talk in an unrestrained, excited manner: *this was the type of material that they effused about.*
ORIGIN late Middle English: from Latin *effusus*, past participle of *effundere* 'pour out', from *ex-* 'out' + *fundere* 'pour'.

effusion ▸ **noun** **1** an instance of giving off something such as a liquid or gas: *a massive effusion of poisonous gas* | [mass noun] *he studied the rates of effusion of gases.* ■ Medicine an escape of fluid into a body cavity.
2 an act of talking or writing in an unrestrained or heartfelt way: *literary effusions.*
– ORIGIN late Middle English: from Latin *effusio(n-)*, from *effundere* 'pour out' (see EFFUSE).

effusive ▸ **adjective** **1** showing or expressing gratitude, pleasure, or approval in an unrestrained or heartfelt manner: *an effusive welcome.*
2 Geology (of igneous rock) poured out when molten and later solidified. ■ relating to the eruption of large volumes of molten rock: *effusive volcanism.*
– DERIVATIVES **effusively** adverb, **effusiveness** noun.

Efik /ˈɛfɪk/ ▸ **noun** (pl. **same**) **1** a member of a people of southern Nigeria.
2 [mass noun] the Benue-Congo language of the Efik, closely related to Ibibio. It is used as a lingua franca and has about 3.5 million speakers.
▸ **adjective** relating to the Efik or their language.
– ORIGIN the name in Efik.

e-fit ▸ **noun** Brit. an electronic picture of the face of a person being sought by the police, created by a computer program from composite photographs of facial features.
– ORIGIN 1980s: from E-[2] and FIT[1] (noun), on the pattern of PHOTOFIT.

EFL ▸ **abbreviation** English as a foreign language.

eft /ɛft/ ▸ **noun** dialect a newt. ■ Zoology the juvenile stage of a newt.

E

– ORIGIN Old English *efeta*, of unknown origin. Compare with NEWT.

EFTA ▸ abbreviation for European Free Trade Association.

EFTPOS /ˈɛftpɒz/ ▸ abbreviation electronic funds transfer at point of sale.

e.g. ▸ abbreviation for example.
– ORIGIN from Latin *exempli gratia* 'for the sake of example'.

egad /ɪˈgad/ ▸ exclamation archaic expressing surprise, anger, or affirmation.
– ORIGIN late 17th cent.: representing earlier *A God*.

E

egalitarian /ɪˌgalɪˈtɛːrɪən/ ▸ adjective believing in or based on the principle that all people are equal and deserve equal rights and opportunities: *a fairer, more egalitarian society*.
▸ noun a person who advocates or supports the principle of equality for all people.
– DERIVATIVES **egalitarianism** noun.
– ORIGIN late 19th cent.: from French *égalitaire*, from *égal* 'equal', from Latin *aequalis* (see EQUAL).

Egbert /ˈɛgbət/ (d.839), king of Wessex 802–39. In 825 he won a decisive victory that temporarily brought Mercian supremacy to an end and foreshadowed the supremacy that Wessex later secured over all England.

Eger /ˈɛgə/ a spa town in the north of Hungary, noted for the 'Bull's Blood' red wine produced in the surrounding region; pop. 56,429 (2009).

egest ▸ verb [with obj.] formal (of a cell or organism) excrete (waste matter).
– DERIVATIVES **egestion** noun.
– ORIGIN late Middle English (as *egestion*): from Latin *egest-*, from the verb *egerere* 'expel', from *e-* (variant of *ex-*) 'out' + *gerere* 'bear, carry'.

egg¹ ▸ noun **1** an oval or round object laid by a female bird, reptile, fish, or invertebrate, usually containing a developing embryo. The eggs of birds are enclosed in a chalky shell, while those of reptiles are in a leathery membrane. ■ an infertile bird's egg, especially one from a chicken, used for food. ■ a thing resembling a bird's egg in shape: *chocolate eggs*.
2 Biology the female reproductive cell in animals and plants; an ovum.
3 Architecture a decorative oval moulding, used alternately with triangular shapes: [as modifier] *egg and dart moulding*.
4 [with adj.] informal, dated a person of a specified kind: *the biography portrays him as a thoroughly bad egg*.
– PHRASES **don't put all your eggs in one basket** proverb don't risk everything on the success of one venture. **go suck an egg** [as imperative] N. Amer. informal used as an expression of anger or scorn. **kill the goose that lays the golden eggs** destroy a reliable and valuable source of income. [with allusion to one of Aesop's fables.] **lay an egg** N. Amer. informal be completely unsuccessful. **with egg on one's face** informal appearing foolish or ridiculous: *don't underestimate this team, or you'll be left with egg on your face*.
– DERIVATIVES **eggless** adjective.
– ORIGIN Middle English (superseding earlier *ey*, from Old English *ǣg*): from Old Norse.

egg² ▸ verb [with obj.] (**egg someone on**) encourage someone to do something foolish or risky.
– ORIGIN Middle English: from Old Norse *eggja* 'incite'.

egg-and-spoon race ▸ noun a race, typically run by children, in which each runner has to hold an egg balanced in a spoon.

eggar /ˈɛgə/ ▸ noun a large brownish moth which is often active during the day. ● Many species in the family Lasiocampidae, including the **oak eggar** (*L. quercus*).
– ORIGIN early 18th cent.: probably from EGG¹ (from the shape of the caterpillar's cocoon) + -ER¹.

egg beater ▸ noun **1** a kitchen utensil used for beating ingredients such as eggs or cream.
2 N. Amer. informal a helicopter.

egg-bound ▸ adjective (of a hen) unable through weakness or disease to expel its eggs.

eggcorn ▸ noun a word or phrase that results from a mishearing or misinterpretation of another, an element of the original being substituted for one which sounds very similar (e.g. *tow the line* instead of *toe the line*).
– ORIGIN early 21st cent.: with reference to a misinterpretation of ACORN.

egg cream ▸ noun US a drink consisting of milk and soda water, flavoured with syrup.

egg cup ▸ noun a small cup for holding a boiled egg upright while it is being eaten.

egg custard ▸ noun [mass noun] a custard made with milk and eggs, typically sweetened and baked.

egg-eating snake ▸ noun an Old World snake which swallows birds' eggs. ● Subfamily Dasypeltinae, family Colubridae: genus *Dasypeltis* (of Africa), and *Elachistodon westermanni* (of India).

egger ▸ noun a collector of birds' eggs.

egghead ▸ noun informal a highly academic or studious person; an intellectual.
– ORIGIN by analogy with a bald head.

eggnog (Brit. also **egg flip**) ▸ noun [mass noun] a drink consisting of rum, brandy, or other alcohol mixed with beaten egg, milk, and sugar.

eggplant ▸ noun N. Amer. another term for AUBERGINE.

egg roll ▸ noun N. Amer. a Chinese-style snack similar to a spring roll, consisting of diced meat or prawns and shredded vegetables wrapped in a dough made with egg and deep-fried.

eggs and bacon ▸ noun [mass noun] any of a number of plants with yellow flowers marked with orange, red, or brown, supposedly suggestive of eggs and bacon, in particular: ● bird's-foot trefoil. ● a shrubby Australian bush plant (*Bossiaea* and other genera, family Leguminosae).

eggs Benedict ▸ plural noun a dish consisting of poached eggs and sliced ham on toasted muffins, covered with hollandaise sauce.
– ORIGIN late 19th cent.: of uncertain origin.

eggshell ▸ noun **1** the thin, hard outer layer of an egg, especially a hen's egg.
2 [as modifier] (of china) of extreme thinness and delicacy: *eggshell porcelains*.
3 [mass noun] (also **eggshell paint**) a paint that dries with a slight sheen.

egg tempera ▸ noun [mass noun] an emulsion of pigment and egg yolk, used in tempera painting.

egg timer ▸ noun a device for timing the cooking of a boiled egg, traditionally a sealed glass container with a narrow neck in the middle through which, when the flask is inverted, sand flows for a fixed amount of time.

egg tooth ▸ noun a hard white protuberance on the beak or jaw of an embryo bird or reptile that is used for breaking out of the shell and is later lost.

egg white ▸ noun the clear, viscous substance round the yolk of an egg that turns white when cooked or beaten. Also called ALBUMEN.

eggy¹ ▸ adjective (**eggier**, **eggiest**) rich in or covered with egg: *cod fried in an eggy batter*.

eggy² ▸ adjective (**eggier**, **eggiest**) Brit. informal annoyed; irritated.
– ORIGIN 1930s: from EGG² + -Y¹.

eglantine /ˈɛgləntʌɪn/ ▸ noun another term for SWEET BRIAR.
– ORIGIN Middle English: from Old French, from Provençal *aiglentina*, based on Latin *acus* 'needle' or *aculeus* 'prickle'.

EGM ▸ abbreviation extraordinary general meeting.

Egmont, Mount /ˈɛgmənt/ a volcanic peak in the North Island, New Zealand, rising to a height of 2,518 m (8,260 ft). Official name TARANAKI.

ego /ˈiːgəʊ, ˈɛ-/ ▸ noun (pl. **egos**) a person's sense of self-esteem or self-importance: *he needed a boost to his ego*. ■ Psychoanalysis the part of the mind that mediates between the conscious and the unconscious and is responsible for reality testing and a sense of personal identity. Compare with ID and SUPEREGO. ■ Philosophy (in metaphysics) a conscious thinking subject.
– DERIVATIVES **egoless** adjective.
– ORIGIN early 19th cent.: from Latin, literally 'I'.

egocentric /ˌɛgə(ʊ)ˈsɛntrɪk, iː-/ ▸ adjective thinking only of oneself, without regard for the feelings or desires of others; self-centred: *egocentric loners with an overinflated sense of self-worth*. ■ centred in or arising from a person's own individual existence or perspective: *egocentric spatial perception*.
▸ noun an egocentric person.
– DERIVATIVES **egocentrically** adverb, **egocentricity** /-sɛnˈtrɪsɪti/ noun, **egocentrism** noun.
– ORIGIN early 20th cent.: from EGO, on the pattern of words such as *geocentric*.

ego-ideal ▸ noun Psychoanalysis (in Freudian theory) the part of the mind which imposes on itself concepts of ideal behaviour developed from parental and social standards.

egoism /ˈɛgəʊɪz(ə)m, ˈiː-/ ▸ noun [mass noun] **1** another term for EGOTISM.
2 Philosophy an ethical theory that treats self-interest as the foundation of morality.
– DERIVATIVES **egoist** noun, **egoistic** adjective, **egoistical** adjective, **egoistically** adverb.
– ORIGIN late 18th cent.: from French *égoïsme* and modern Latin *egoismus*, from Latin *ego* 'I'.

> **USAGE** The words **egoism** and **egotism** are frequently treated as interchangeable, but there are distinctions which are worth noting. **Egotism**, the more commonly used term, means 'the fact of being excessively conceited or absorbed in oneself'. Strictly speaking, **egoism** is a term used in Ethics to mean 'a theory that treats self-interest as the foundation of moral behaviour', although this sense is not dominant today; around 90 per cent of the citations for **egoism** in the Oxford English Corpus are for the meaning 'excessive conceit'.

egomania /ɛgə(ʊ)ˈmeɪnɪə, iː-/ ▸ noun [mass noun] obsessive egotism or self-centredness.
– DERIVATIVES **egomaniac** noun, **egomaniacal** adjective.

ego-psychology ▸ noun [mass noun] Psychology a system of psychoanalytic developmental psychology concerned especially with personality.
– DERIVATIVES **ego-psychologist** noun.

egosurf ▸ verb [no obj.] informal search the Internet for instances of one's own name or links to one's own website.

egotism /ˈɛgətɪz(ə)m, ˈiː-/ ▸ noun [mass noun] the fact of being excessively conceited or absorbed in oneself: *in his arrogance and egotism, he underestimated Gill*.
– ORIGIN early 18th cent.: from French *égoïste*, from Latin *ego* 'I'.

> **USAGE** On the difference between egotism and egoism, see USAGE at EGOISM.

egotist /ˈɛgətɪst/ ▸ noun a person who is excessively conceited or absorbed in themselves; self-seeker: *he is a self-absorbed egotist*.

egotistical /ˌɛgəˈtɪstɪk(ə)l/ ▸ adjective excessively conceited or absorbed in oneself; self-centred: *he's selfish, egotistical, and arrogant*.
– DERIVATIVES **egotistic** adjective, **egotistically** adverb.

ego trip ▸ noun informal an activity done in order to increase one's sense of self-importance: *driving that car was the biggest ego trip I'd ever had*.

egregious /ɪˈgriːdʒəs/ ▸ adjective **1** outstandingly bad; shocking: *egregious abuses of copyright*.
2 archaic remarkably good.
– DERIVATIVES **egregiously** adverb, **egregiousness** noun.
– ORIGIN mid 16th cent. (in sense 2): from Latin *egregius* 'illustrious', literally 'standing out from the flock', from *ex-* 'out' + *grex*, *greg-* 'flock'. Sense 1 (late 16th cent.) probably arose as an ironical use.

egress /ˈiːgrɛs/ ▸ noun [mass noun] **1** formal the action of going out of or leaving a place: *direct means of access and egress for passengers*. ■ [count noun] a way out: *a narrow egress*.
2 Astronomy another term for EMERSION.
▸ verb [with obj.] chiefly US go out of or leave (a place).
– DERIVATIVES **egression** noun.
– ORIGIN mid 16th cent.: from Latin *egressus* 'gone out', from the verb *egredi*, from *ex-* 'out' + *gradi* 'to step'.

egressive /ɪˈgrɛsɪv/ ▸ adjective Phonetics (of a speech sound) produced using the normal outward-flowing airstream.

egret /ˈiːgrɪt, ˈɛ-/ ▸ noun a heron with mainly white plumage, having long plumes in the breeding season. ● Genus *Egretta* (and *Bubulcus*), family Ardeidae: several species.
– ORIGIN Middle English: from Old French *aigrette*, from Provençal *aigreta*, from the Germanic base of HERON.

Egypt /ˈiːdʒɪpt/ a country in NE Africa bordering on the Mediterranean Sea; pop. 78,866,600 (est. 2009); official language, Arabic; capital, Cairo.

> The population of Egypt is concentrated chiefly along the fertile valley of the River Nile, the rest of the country being largely desert. Egypt's history spans 5,000 years: the ancient kingdoms of Upper and Lower Egypt were ruled successively by thirty-one dynasties, which may be divided into the Old Kingdom, the Middle Kingdom, and the New Kingdom. Egypt was a centre of Hellenistic culture and then a Roman province before coming under Islamic rule and then becoming part of the Ottoman

Empire. Modern Egypt became independent in 1922. From 1958 to 1961 Egypt was united with Syria as the United Arab Republic, a title it retained until 1971. Wars with Israel were fought in 1967 (the Six Day War) and 1973 (the Yom Kippur or October War); the countries signed a peace treaty in 1979.

Egyptian ▸ **adjective** relating to Egypt or its people. ▪ relating to the culture or language of ancient Egypt: *an Egyptian obelisk*.
▸ **noun 1** a native of ancient or modern Egypt, or a person of Egyptian descent.
2 [mass noun] the Afro-Asiatic language used in ancient Egypt, attested from *c.*3000 BC. It is represented in its oldest stages by hieroglyphic inscriptions and in its latest form by Coptic; it has been replaced in modern use by Arabic.

Egyptian cobra ▸ **noun** a large nocturnal African cobra with a thick body and large head. Also called ASP. ● *Naja haje*, family Elapidae.

Egyptian goose ▸ **noun** a large African goose with a dark patch around the eye and either reddish-brown or greyish-brown upper parts. ● *Alopochen aegyptiacus*, family Anatidae.

Egyptian mongoose ▸ **noun** a mongoose occurring over much of Africa and parts of SW Asia and Iberia, noted for its destruction of crocodile eggs. Also called ICHNEUMON. ● *Herpestes ichneumon*, family Herpestidae.

Egyptian plover ▸ **noun** an African bird of the courser family, with a striking pattern of black and white over a mainly bluish back and buff-coloured underparts. Also called CROCODILE BIRD. ● *Pluvianus aegyptius*, family Glareolidae.

Egyptian vulture ▸ **noun** a small white vulture with black wing tips, common in much of southern Eurasia and Africa. ● *Neophron percnopterus*, family Accipitridae.

Egyptology /ˌiːdʒɪpˈtɒlədʒi/ ▸ **noun** [mass noun] the study of the language, history, and culture of ancient Egypt.
– DERIVATIVES **Egyptological** adjective, **Egyptologist** noun.

eh ▸ **exclamation** used to represent a sound made in speech, especially one used to express enquiry, surprise, or to elicit agreement: *'Eh? What's this?'*
– PHRASES **eh up** N. English used as a greeting, to express surprise, or to attract someone's attention: *eh up, I'm talking to you!*
– ORIGIN natural utterance: first recorded in English in the mid 16th cent.

Ehrlich /ˈɛːlɪx/, German /ˈeːʁlɪç/, Paul (1854–1915), German medical scientist. One of the founders of modern immunology and chemotherapy, he developed techniques for staining specific tissues, believing that a disease organism could be destroyed by an appropriate magic bullet. The effective treatment of syphilis in 1911 proved his theories.

-eian /ɪən/ ▸ **suffix** forming adjectives and nouns corresponding to nouns ending in *-ey* or *-y* (such as *Bodleian* corresponding to *Bodley*).

Eichmann /ˈʌɪxmən/, German /ˈaɪçman/, (Karl) Adolf (1906–62), German Nazi administrator who was responsible for administering the concentration camps. In 1960 he was traced by Israeli agents and executed after trial in Israel.

eicosapentaenoic acid /ˌʌɪkɒsəˌpentiːˈnəʊɪk/ ▸ **noun** [mass noun] Chemistry a polyunsaturated fatty acid found especially in fish oils. ● Chem. formula: $C_{19}H_{29}COOH$.
– ORIGIN 1960s: from Greek *eicosa-* 'twenty' (the number of carbon atoms in the molecule) + PENTA- 'five' (the number of unsaturated bonds) + -ENE + *-oic* on the pattern of *methanoic*.

Eid /iːd/ (also **Id**) ▸ **noun** a Muslim festival, in particular: ▪ (in full **Eid ul-Fitr** /ˌiːdʊlˈfɪtrə/) the feast marking the end of the fast of Ramadan. Also called LESSER BAIRAM. ▪ (in full **Eid ul-Adha** /ˌiːdʊlˈɑːdə/) the festival marking the culmination of the annual pilgrimage to Mecca and commemorating the sacrifice of Abraham. Also called GREATER BAIRAM.
– ORIGIN from Arabic *ʿīd* 'feast', from Aramaic.

eider /ˈʌɪdə/ (also **eider duck**) ▸ **noun** (pl. **same** or **eiders**) a northern sea duck, of which the male is mainly black-and-white with a coloured head, and the female brown. ● Genus *Somateria* (and *Polysticta*), family Anatidae: four species.
– ORIGIN late 17th cent.: from Icelandic *æthur*, from Old Norse *æthr*.

eiderdown ▸ **noun 1** Brit. a quilt filled with down (originally from the eider) or some other soft material.
2 (**eider down**) [mass noun] small, soft feathers from the breast of the female eider.

eidetic /ʌɪˈdɛtɪk/ ▸ **adjective** Psychology relating to or denoting mental images having unusual vividness and detail, as if actually visible.
– DERIVATIVES **eidetically** adverb.
– ORIGIN 1920s: coined in German from Greek *eidētikos*, from *eidos* 'form'.

eidolon /ʌɪˈdəʊlɒn/ ▸ **noun** (pl. **eidolons** or **eidola** /-lə/) literary **1** an idealized person or thing.
2 a spectre or phantom.
– ORIGIN early 19th cent.: from Greek *eidōlon*, from *eidos* 'form'.

eidos /ˈʌɪdɒs/ ▸ **noun** [mass noun] Anthropology the distinctive expression of the cognitive or intellectual character of a culture or social group.
– ORIGIN 1930s: from Greek, literally 'form, type, idea', partly in contrast to ETHOS.

Eiffel /ˈʌɪf(ə)l/, French /ɛfɛl/, Alexandre Gustave (1832–1923), French engineer, best known as the designer and builder of the Eiffel Tower and architect of the inner structure of the Statue of Liberty.

Eiffel Tower a wrought-iron structure erected in Paris for the World Exhibition of 1889. With a height of 300 metres (984 ft), it was the tallest man made structure for many years.

eigen- /ˈʌɪɡ(ə)n/ ▸ **combining form** Mathematics & Physics proper; characteristic: *eigenfunction*.
– ORIGIN from German *eigen* 'own'.

eigenfrequency ▸ **noun** (pl. **eigenfrequencies**) Mathematics & Physics one of the natural resonant frequencies of a system.

eigenfunction ▸ **noun** Mathematics & Physics each of a set of independent functions which are the solutions to a given differential equation.

eigenstate ▸ **noun** Physics a quantum-mechanical state corresponding to an eigenvalue of a wave equation.

eigenvalue ▸ **noun** Mathematics & Physics **1** each of a set of values of a parameter for which a differential equation has a non-zero solution (an eigenfunction) under given conditions.
2 any number such that a given matrix minus that number times the identity matrix has zero determinant.

eigenvector ▸ **noun** Mathematics & Physics a vector which when operated on by a given operator gives a scalar multiple of itself.

Eiger /ˈʌɪɡə/ a mountain peak in the Bernese Alps of Switzerland, which rises to 3,970 m (13,101 ft).

Eigg /ɛɡ/ an island of the Inner Hebrides, off the west coast of Scotland to the south of Skye.

eight ▸ **cardinal number** equivalent to the product of two and four; one more than seven, or two less than ten; 8: *a committee of eight members | eight of them were unemployed | eight were acquitted*. (Roman numeral: **viii** or **VIII**) ▪ a group of eight people or things: *the win placed Canada closer to the final eight*. ▪ eight years old: *children as young as eight*. ▪ eight o'clock: *the play is to begin at eight*. ▪ a size of garment or other merchandise denoted by eight. ▪ an eight-oared rowing boat or its crew. ▪ a playing card with eight pips.
– PHRASES **have one over the eight** Brit. informal have one drink too many. [probably from the assumption that the average person can drink eight pints of beer without getting drunk.]
– ORIGIN Old English *ehta, eahta*, of Germanic origin; related to Dutch and German *acht*, from an Indo-European root shared by Latin *octo* and Greek *oktō*.

eight ball ▸ **noun** N. Amer. **1** (also **eight-ball pool**) [mass noun] a variety of the game of pool. ▪ [count noun] the black ball, numbered eight, in eight ball.
2 informal a portion of an illegal drug weighing an eighth of an ounce (3.54 g).
– PHRASES **behind the eight ball** informal at a disadvantage.

eighteen ▸ **cardinal number** equivalent to the product of two and nine; one more than seventeen, or eight more than ten; 18: *she wrote eighteen novels | out of sixty batches checked, eighteen were incorrect | eighteen of the guests were gathered*. (Roman numeral: **xviii** or **XVIII**) ▪ a set or team of eighteen individuals. ▪ eighteen years old: *he was barely eighteen*. ▪ a size of garment or other merchandise denoted by eighteen. ▪ (**18**) Brit. (of a film) classified as suitable for people of 18 years and over.
– DERIVATIVES **eighteenth** ordinal number.
– ORIGIN Old English *e(a)htatēne* (see EIGHT, -TEEN).

eighteenmo ▸ **noun** (pl. **eighteenmos**) another term for OCTODECIMO.

eightfold ▸ **adjective** eight times as great or as numerous: *an eightfold increase in expenditure*. ▪ having eight parts or elements: *an eightfold shape*.
▸ **adverb** by eight times; to eight times the number or amount: *claims have grown eightfold in ten years*.

eightfold path ▸ **noun** Buddhism the path to nirvana, comprising eight aspects in which an aspirant must become practised: right views, intention, speech, action, livelihood, effort, mindfulness, and concentration.

eighth ▸ **ordinal number 1** constituting number eight in a sequence; 8th: *in the eighth century | the eighth of September | seven men admitted conspiracy, an eighth admitted assisting an offender*. ▪ the eighth finisher or position in a race or competition: *she finished eighth of the eleven runners*.
2 each of eight equal parts into which something is or may be divided: *an eighth of an inch*.
– DERIVATIVES **eighthly** adverb.

E

eighth note ▸ **noun** Music, N. Amer. a quaver.

eights ▸ **plural noun** a race for eight-oared rowing boats.

eightsome (also **eightsome reel**) ▸ **noun** a lively Scottish dance for eight people.

eighty ▸ **cardinal number** (pl. **eighties**) equivalent to the product of eight and ten; ten less than ninety; 80: *eighty miles north | a buffet for eighty | eighty of the nurses fled*. (Roman numeral: **lxxx** or **LXXX**) ▪ (**eighties**) the numbers from 80 to 89, especially the years of a century or of a person's life: *his grandmother was in her eighties*. ▪ eighty years old: *he was over eighty at the time*. ▪ eighty miles an hour: *roaring down the highway doing eighty*.
– DERIVATIVES **eightieth** ordinal number, **eightyfold** adjective & adverb.
– ORIGIN Old English *hunde(a)htatig*, from *hund* (of uncertain origin) + *e(a)hta* 'eight' + *-tig* (see -TY[2]); the first element was lost early in the Middle English period.

eighty-six ▸ **verb** [with obj.] N. Amer. informal reject, discard, or destroy: *the only reason she hadn't eighty-sixed him before now was out of affection for his son*.
– ORIGIN 1930s (as a noun, used in restaurants and bars to indicate that a menu item is unavailable or that a customer is not to be served): perhaps rhyming slang for NIX[1].

Eilat /eɪˈlat/ (also **Elat**) a port and resort in Israel, at the head of the Gulf of Aqaba; pop. 46,600 (est. 2008). Founded in 1949 near the ruins of biblical Elath, it is Israel's only outlet to the Red Sea.

eina /ˈeɪnɑː/ S. African ▸ **exclamation** used as an expression of pain or distress.
▸ **noun** [mass noun] pain or trouble: *first aid without the eina*.
– ORIGIN Afrikaans, perhaps from Khoikhoi *llé*, interjection expressing pain, + *llná*, interjection expressing surprise, or perhaps from a nasalized pronunciation of Nama interjection *llei*.

Eindhoven /ˈʌɪndˌhəʊv(ə)n/ a city in the south of the Netherlands; pop. 210,333 (2008). The city is a major producer of electrical and electronic goods.

Einfühlung /ˈʌɪnˌfuːlʊŋ/, German /ˈaɪnˌfyːlʊŋ/ ▸ **noun** [mass noun] empathy.
– ORIGIN German, from *ein-* 'into' + *Fühlung* 'feeling'.

einkorn /ˈʌɪnkɔːn/ ▸ **noun** [mass noun] an old kind of wheat with small bearded ears and spikelets that each contain one slender grain, used as fodder in prehistoric times but now rarely grown. ● *Triticum monococcum*, family Gramineae.
– ORIGIN early 20th cent.: from German, from *ein* 'one' + *Korn* 'seed'.

Einstein /ˈʌɪnstʌɪn/, Albert (1879–1955), German-born American theoretical physicist, founder of the special and general theories of relativity. ▪ (as noun **an Einstein**) a genius.

Einstein is often regarded as the greatest scientist of the 20th century. In 1905 he published his special theory of relativity and in 1915 he succeeded in incorporating gravitation in his general theory of relativity, which was vindicated when one of its predictions was observed during the solar eclipse of 1919. However, Einstein searched without success for a unified field theory embracing electromagnetism, gravitation, relativity, and quantum mechanics. He influenced the decision to build an atom bomb but after the war he spoke out passionately against nuclear weapons.

– DERIVATIVES **Einsteinian** adjective.

einsteinium /ʌɪnˈstʌɪnɪəm/ ▶ noun [mass noun] the chemical element of atomic number 99, a radioactive metal of the actinide series. Einsteinium does not occur naturally and was discovered in 1953 in debris from the first hydrogen bomb explosion. (Symbol: **Es**)
– ORIGIN 1950s: from the name of Albert EINSTEIN + -IUM.

Eire /ˈɛːrə/ the Gaelic name for Ireland, the official name of the Republic of Ireland from 1937 to 1949.

Eirene /ʌɪˈriːni/ Greek Mythology the goddess of peace. Roman equivalent **PAX**.

E

eirenic ▶ adjective variant spelling of IRENIC.

eirenicon ▶ noun variant spelling of IRENICON.

Eisenhower /ˈʌɪz(ə)nˌhaʊə/, Dwight David (1890–1969), American general and Republican statesman, 34th President of the US 1953–61; known as **Ike**. In the Second World War he was Supreme Commander of Allied Expeditionary Forces in western Europe 1943–5. As President, he adopted a hard line towards communism.

Eisenstadt /ˈʌɪz(ə)nˌʃtat/ a city in eastern Austria, capital of the state of Burgenland; pop. 12,366 (2006).

Eisenstein /ˈʌɪz(ə)nˌstʌɪn/, Sergei (Mikhailovich) (1898–1948), Soviet film director, born in Latvia. He is chiefly known for *The Battleship Potemkin* (1925), a commemoration of the Russian Revolution of 1905 celebrated for its pioneering use of montage.

eisteddfod /ʌɪˈstɛdvəd/, Welsh /ʌɪˈstɛðvɒd/ ▶ noun (pl. **eisteddfods** or **eisteddfodau** /-ˈvɒdʌɪ/) a competitive festival of music and poetry in Wales.
– ORIGIN Welsh, literally 'session', from *eistedd* 'sit'.

Eiswein /ˈʌɪsvʌɪn/ ▶ noun (pl. **Eisweine** /-nə/ or **Eisweins**) [mass noun] wine made from ripe grapes picked while covered with frost.
– ORIGIN from German, from *Eis* 'ice' + *Wein* 'wine'.

either /ˈʌɪðə, ˈiː-/ ▶ conjunction & adverb **1** used before the first of two (or occasionally more) given alternatives (the other being introduced by 'or'): *either I accompany you to your room or I wait here | available in either black or white.*
2 [adverb, with negative] used to indicate a similarity or link with a statement just made: *You don't like him, do you? I don't either | it won't do any harm, but won't really help either.* ■ for that matter; moreover: *I was too tired to go. And I couldn't have paid, either.*
▶ determiner & pronoun one or the other of two people or things: [as determiner] *there were no children of either marriage* | [as pronoun] *their mortgage will be repaid if either of them dies.* ■ [determiner] each of two: *the road was straight, with fields on either side.*
– PHRASES **either way** whichever of two given alternatives is the case.
– ORIGIN Old English *ǣgther*, contracted form of *ǣg(e)hwæther*, of Germanic origin; ultimately related to AYE[1] and WHETHER.

USAGE In good English writing style, it is important that **either** and **or** are correctly placed so that the structures following each word balance and mirror each other. Thus, sentences such as ***either*** *I accompany you* ***or*** *I wait here* and *I'm going to buy* ***either*** *a new camera* ***or*** *a new video* are correct, whereas sentences such as ***either*** *I accompany you* ***or*** *John* and *I'm* ***either*** *going to buy a new camera* ***or*** *a video* are not well-balanced sentences and should not be used in written English.

either/or ▶ noun [usu. as modifier] an unavoidable choice between alternatives: *an either/or situation.*

eiusdem generis ▶ adjective variant spelling of EJUSDEM GENERIS.

ejaculate ▶ verb /ɪˈdʒakjʊleɪt/ **1** [no obj.] (of a man or male animal) eject semen from the body at the moment of sexual climax.
2 [with direct speech] dated say something quickly and suddenly: *'That will do!' he ejaculated.*
▶ noun /ɪˈdʒakjʊlət/ [mass noun] semen that has been ejected from the body.
– DERIVATIVES **ejaculator** noun, **ejaculatory** /ɪˈdʒakjʊlət(ə)ri/ adjective.
– ORIGIN late 16th cent.: from Latin *ejaculat-* 'darted out', from the verb *ejaculari*, from *e-* (variant of *ex-*) 'out' + *jaculari* 'to dart' (from *jaculum* 'dart, javelin', from *jacere* 'to throw').

ejaculation /ɪˌdʒakjʊˈleɪʃ(ə)n/ ▶ noun [mass noun] **1** the action of ejecting semen from the body.
2 dated something said quickly and suddenly.

eject ▶ verb [with obj.] **1** force or throw (something) out in a violent or sudden way: *lumps of viscous lava were* ***ejected from*** *the volcano.* ■ cause (something) to be expelled from a machine. ■ [no obj.] (of a pilot) escape from an aircraft by being explosively propelled out of it: *he put the plane in a nosedive and ejected.*
2 compel (someone) to leave a place: *angry supporters were forcibly* ***ejected from*** *the court.* ■ dismiss (someone) from office: *he was* ***ejected from*** *office in July.*
3 emit; give off: *plants utilize carbon dioxide in the atmosphere that animals eject.*
– ORIGIN late Middle English: from Latin *eject-* 'thrown out', from the verb *eicere*, from *e-* (variant of *ex-*) 'out' + *jacere* 'to throw'.

ejecta /ɪˈdʒɛktə/ ▶ plural noun [often treated as sing.] Geology & Astronomy material that is forced or thrown out, especially as a result of volcanic eruption, meteoritic impact, or stellar explosion.
– ORIGIN late 19th cent.: from Latin, 'things thrown out', neuter plural of *ejectus* 'thrown out', from *eicere* (see EJECT).

ejection ▶ noun [mass noun] **1** the action of forcing or throwing something out; emission: *an explosive ejection of ash.*
2 the action of forcing someone to leave a place or position; expulsion: *the forcible ejection of a table of rowdy drunks.*

ejection seat ▶ noun a device that causes the ejection of a pilot from an aircraft in an emergency.

ejective /ɪˈdʒɛktɪv/ Phonetics ▶ adjective denoting a type of consonant in some languages (e.g. Hausa) produced by sudden release of pressure from the glottis.
▶ noun an ejective consonant.

ejectment ▶ noun [mass noun] Law, chiefly historical the eviction of a tenant from property. ■ the process by which an evicted tenant seeks to recover possession and damages: *he brought* ***an action in ejectment*** *against the rector.*

ejector ▶ noun a device that causes something to be removed or to drop out.

ejector seat ▶ noun another term for EJECTION SEAT.

ejido /ɛˈhiːdəʊ/ ▶ noun (pl. **ejidos**) (in Mexico) a piece of land farmed communally under a system supported by the state.
– ORIGIN Mexican Spanish, from Spanish, denoting common land on the road leading out of the village.

ejusdem generis /eɪˌ(j)ʊsdɛm ˈdʒɛnɛrɪs/ (also **eiusdem generis**) ▶ adjective & adverb Law of or as the same kind. ■ [as adj.] denoting a rule for interpreting statutes and other writings by assuming that a general term describing a list of specific terms denotes other things that are like the specific elements.
– ORIGIN Latin.

Ekaterinburg /jɛˌkatəˈriːnbəːg/ variant spelling of YEKATERINBURG.

Ekaterinodar /jəˌkatəˈriːnədɑː/ variant spelling of YEKATERINODAR.

Ekaterinoslav /jəˌkatəˈriːnəslɑːf/ variant spelling of YEKATERINOSLAV.

ekdam /ɛkˈðʌm/ ▶ adverb Indian informal completely; totally: *his bravado was ekdam finished.*
– ORIGIN from Hindi *ek* 'one' + Urdu *dam* 'breath'.

eke[1] /iːk/ ▶ verb [with obj.] (**eke something out**) make an amount or supply of something last longer by using or consuming it frugally: *the remains of yesterday's stew could be eked out to make another meal.* ■ manage to make a living with difficulty: *many traders barely eked out a living.*
– ORIGIN Old English *ēacian, ēcan* (in the sense 'increase'), of Germanic origin; related to Old Norse *auka*.

eke[2] /iːk/ ▶ adverb archaic term for ALSO.
– ORIGIN Old English, of Germanic origin.

EKG ▶ abbreviation US electrocardiogram or electrocardiograph.
– ORIGIN early 20th cent.: from German *Elektrokardiogramm*.

ekka /ˈɛkə/ ▶ noun Indian a small one-horse vehicle.
– ORIGIN from Hindi *ikkā*, from Sanskrit *eka* 'one'.

El ▶ noun (**the El**) (in the US) an elevated railway, especially that in Chicago. ■ a train running on an elevated railway.

-el ▶ suffix variant spelling of -LE[2].

el-Aaiún /ˌɛlʌɪˈuːn/ Arabic name for LAAYOUNE.

elaborate ▶ adjective /ɪˈlab(ə)rət/ involving many carefully arranged parts or details; detailed and complicated in design and planning: *elaborate security precautions | elaborate wrought-iron gates.* ■ (of an action) lengthy and exaggerated: *he made an elaborate pretence of yawning.*
▶ verb /ɪˈlabəreɪt/ **1** [with obj.] develop or present (a theory, policy, or system) in further detail: *the theory was proposed by Cope and elaborated by Osborn.* ■ [no obj.] add more detail concerning what has already been said: *he would not* ***elaborate on*** *his news.*
2 [with obj.] Biology (of a natural agency) produce (a substance) from its elements or simpler constituents.
– DERIVATIVES **elaborately** adverb, **elaborateness** noun, **elaboration** noun, **elaborative** adjective, **elaborator** noun.
– ORIGIN late 16th cent. (in the sense 'produced by effort of labour', also in sense 2 of the verb): from Latin *elaborat-* 'worked out', from the verb *elaborare*, from *e-* (variant of *ex-*) 'out' + *labor* 'work'.

Elagabalus /ˌɛləˈgabələs/ variant spelling of HELIOGABALUS.

El Alamein, Battle of /ɛl ˈaləmeɪn/ a battle of the Second World War fought in 1942 at El Alamein in Egypt, 90 km (60 miles) west of Alexandria. The German Afrika Korps under Rommel was halted in its advance towards the Nile by the British 8th Army under Montgomery, giving a decisive British victory.

Elam /ˈiːlam/ an ancient state in SW Iran, established in the 4th millennium BC. Susa was one of its chief cities.

Elamite ▶ noun **1** a native or inhabitant of ancient Elam.
2 [mass noun] the agglutinative language spoken in ancient Elam from the 3rd millennium to the 4th century BC, of which a few records in pictographic and cuneiform script survive.
▶ adjective relating to the ancient Elamites or their language.

elan /eɪˈlɒ̃, eɪˈlan/ ▶ noun [mass noun] energy, style, and enthusiasm: *they performed with uncommon elan onstage.*
– ORIGIN mid 19th cent.: from French *élan*, from *élancer* 'to dart', from *é-* 'out' + *lancer* 'to throw'.

eland /ˈiːlənd/ ▶ noun a large spiral-horned African antelope which lives in open woodland and grassland. ● Genus *Tragelaphus*, family Bovidae: the **giant eland** (*T. derbianus*) and the **common eland** (*T. oryx*).
– ORIGIN late 18th cent.: via Afrikaans from Dutch, 'elk', from obsolete German *Elend*, from Lithuanian *élnis*.

elapse ▶ verb [no obj.] (of time) pass or go by: *weeks elapsed before anyone was charged with the attack.*
– ORIGIN late 16th cent. (in the sense 'slip away'): from Latin *elaps-* 'slipped away', from the verb *elabi*, from *e-* (variant of *ex-*) 'out, away' + *labi* 'to glide, slip'.

elasipod /ɪˈlasɪpɒd/ ▶ noun Zoology an aberrant deep-water sea cucumber that lacks a respiratory tree. Most live on the seabed and have leg-like appendages, while some swim by means of webbed papillae. ● Order Elasipodida, class Holothuroidea.
– ORIGIN late 19th cent.: from modern Latin *Elasipoda*, from Greek *elasmos* 'beaten metal' + *pous, pod-* 'foot'.

elasmobranch /ɪˈlazmə(ʊ)braŋk/ ▶ noun Zoology a cartilaginous fish of a group that comprises the sharks, rays, and skates. Compare with SELACHIAN. ● Subclass Elasmobranchii, class Chondrichthyes.
– ORIGIN late 19th cent.: from modern Latin *Elasmobranchii* (plural), from Greek *elasmos* 'beaten metal' + *brankhia* 'gills'.

elasmosaur /ɪˈlazmə(ʊ)sɔː/ ▶ noun a Cretaceous plesiosaur with a long neck shaped like that of a swan. ● Family Elasmosauridae, infraorder Plesiosauria: several genera, including *Elasmosaurus*.
– ORIGIN late 19th cent.: from modern Latin *Elasmosaurus*, from Greek *elasmos* 'beaten metal' + *sauros* 'lizard'.

elastane /ɪˈlasteɪn/ ▶ noun [mass noun] an elastic polyurethane material, used for hosiery, underwear, and other close-fitting clothing.
– ORIGIN 1970s: from ELASTIC + -ANE[2].

elastase /ɪˈlasteɪz/ ▶ noun [mass noun] Biochemistry a pancreatic enzyme which digests elastin.
– ORIGIN 1940s: from ELASTIC + -ASE.

elastic /ɪˈlastɪk/ ▶ adjective **1** (of an object or material) able to resume its normal shape spontaneously after being stretched or compressed.
2 able to encompass much variety and change; flexible and adaptable: *the definition of nationality is elastic in this cosmopolitan country.*

3 Economics (of demand or supply) sensitive to changes in price or income.
4 Physics (of a collision) involving no decrease of kinetic energy.
▸ noun [mass noun] cord, tape, or fabric, woven with strips of rubber, which returns to its original length or shape after being stretched.
– DERIVATIVES **elastically** adverb, **elasticize** (also **elasticise**) verb.
– ORIGIN mid 17th cent. (originally describing a gas in the sense 'expanding spontaneously to fill the available space'): from modern Latin *elasticus*, from Greek *elastikos* 'propulsive', from *elaunein* 'to drive'.

elasticated ▸ adjective Brit. (of a garment or material) made elastic by the insertion of rubber thread or tape: *trousers with elasticated waists.*

elastic band ▸ noun Brit. a rubber band.

elastic fibre ▸ noun Anatomy a yellowish fibre composed chiefly of elastin and occurring in networks or sheets which give elasticity to tissues in the body.

elasticity /ɛlaˈstɪsɪti, iː-, ɪ-/ ▸ noun [mass noun] 1 the ability of an object or material to resume its normal shape after being stretched or compressed; stretchiness: *aging can decrease the elasticity of your skin.*
2 ability to change and adapt; adaptability.
3 Economics the degree to which a demand or supply is sensitive to changes in price or income.

elastic limit ▸ noun Physics the maximum extent to which a solid may be stretched without permanent alteration of size or shape.

elastic modulus ▸ noun Physics the ratio of the force exerted upon a substance or body to the resultant deformation.

elastin /ɪˈlastɪn/ ▸ noun [mass noun] Biochemistry an elastic, fibrous glycoprotein found in connective tissue.
– ORIGIN late 19th cent.: from **ELASTIC** + **-IN**[1].

elastomer /ɪˈlastəmə/ ▸ noun a natural or synthetic polymer having elastic properties, e.g. rubber.
– DERIVATIVES **elastomeric** adjective.
– ORIGIN 1930s: from **ELASTIC** + **-MER**.

Elastoplast /ɪˈlastəplast, -plɑːst/ ▸ noun [mass noun] trademark adhesive sticking plaster for covering cuts and wounds.
– ORIGIN 1920s: from a blend of **ELASTIC** and **PLASTER**.

Elat variant spelling of **EILAT**.

elate /ɪˈleɪt/ ▸ verb [with obj.] (usu. as adj. **elated**) make (someone) ecstatically happy: *I felt elated at beating Dennis.*
▸ adjective archaic in high spirits; exultant or proud: *their elate and animated faces.*
– DERIVATIVES **elatedly** adverb, **elatedness** noun.
– ORIGIN late Middle English (as an adjective): from Latin *elat-* 'raised', from the verb *efferre*, from *ex-* 'out, from' + *ferre* 'to bear'. The verb dates from the late 16th cent.

elation ▸ noun [mass noun] great happiness and exhilaration: *Richard's **elation at** regaining his health was short-lived.*
– ORIGIN late Middle English: from Old French *elacion*, from Latin *elat-* 'raised', from the verb *efferre* (see **ELATE**).

E-layer ▸ noun a layer of the ionosphere able to reflect medium-frequency radio waves.
– ORIGIN 1930s: arbitrary use of the letter *E*, + **LAYER**.

Elba /ˈɛlbə/ a small island off the west coast of Italy, famous as the place of Napoleon's first exile (1814–15).

Elbasan /ˌɛlbəˈsɑːn/ an industrial town in central Albania; pop. 107,200 (est. 2009).

Elbe /ɛlb, ˈɛlbə/ a river of central Europe, flowing 1,159 km (720 miles) from the Czech Republic through Dresden, Magdeburg, and Hamburg to the North Sea.

el-Beqa'a another name for **BEKAA**.

Elbert, Mount /ˈɛlbət/ a mountain in Colorado, to the east of the resort town of Aspen. Rising to 4,399 m (14,431 ft), it is the highest peak in the Rocky Mountains.

elbow ▸ noun the joint between the forearm and the upper arm. ■ the part of the sleeve of a garment covering the elbow. ■ a thing resembling an elbow, in particular a piece of piping bent through an angle.
▸ verb [with obj. and adverbial] 1 push or strike (someone) with one's elbow: *one player had elbowed another in the face.* ■ [no obj., with adverbial of direction] move by pushing past people with one's elbows: *he **elbowed his way** through the crush.*
2 treat (a person or idea) dismissively: *the issues which concerned them tended to be elbowed aside by men.*
– PHRASES **at one's elbow** close at hand; nearby. **elbow-to-elbow** very close together. **give someone the elbow** Brit. informal reject or dismiss someone. **up to one's elbows in** informal with one's hands plunged in (something). ■ deeply involved in (a task or activity).
– ORIGIN Old English *elboga*, *elnboga*, of Germanic origin; related to Dutch *elleboog* and German *Ellenbogen* (see also **ELL**[1], **BOW**[1]).

elbow grease ▸ noun [mass noun] informal hard physical work, especially vigorous polishing or cleaning: *nothing would shift it however much elbow grease we used.*

elbow room ▸ noun [mass noun] informal adequate space to move or work in.

Elbrus /ɛlˈbruːs/ a peak in the Caucasus mountains, on the border between Russia and Georgia. Rising to 5,642 m (18,481 ft), it is the highest mountain in Europe.

Elburz Mountains /ɛlˈbʊəz/ a mountain range in NW Iran, close to the southern shore of the Caspian Sea. Damavand is the highest peak, rising to 5,604 m (18,386 ft).

Elche /ˈɛltʃeɪ/ a town in the province of Alicante in SE Spain; pop. 228,348 (2008).

El Cid, see **CID, EL**.

eld /ɛld/ ▸ noun [mass noun] literary old age. ■ former times; the past.
– ORIGIN Old English *ieldu*, *eldu*, of Germanic origin; related to **ELDER**[1] and **OLD**.

elder[1] ▸ adjective (of one or more out of a group of associated people) of a greater age: *my elder daughter* | *the elder of the two sons.* ■ (**the Elder**) used to distinguish between related famous people with the same name: *Pitt the Elder.*
▸ noun 1 (**one's elders**) people who are older than one: *schoolchildren were no less fascinated than their elders.* ■ (**one's elder**) a person who is older than one by a specified length of time: *she was two years his elder.*
2 (often **elders**) a leader or senior figure in a tribe or other group: *a council of village elders.* ■ an official in the early Christian Church, or of various Protestant Churches and sects. ■ historical a member of a senate or governing body.
– DERIVATIVES **eldership** noun.
– ORIGIN Old English *ieldra*, *eldra*, of Germanic origin; related to German *älter*, also to **ELD** and **OLD**.

elder[2] ▸ noun a small tree or shrub with pithy stems, white flowers, and bluish-black or red berries.
● Genus *Sambucus*, family Caprifoliaceae: numerous species, in particular the common Eurasian *S. nigra*.
■ used in names of plants that resemble the elder in leaf or flower, e.g. **ground elder**.
– ORIGIN Old English *ellærn*; related to Middle Low German *ellern*, *elderne*.

elderberry ▸ noun (pl. **elderberries**) 1 the bluish-black or red berry of the elder, used for making jelly or wine.
2 an elder tree or shrub.

Elder Brother ▸ noun (pl. **Elder Brethren**) (in the UK) each of the thirteen senior members of Trinity House.

eldercare ▸ noun [mass noun] N. Amer. the care of elderly people who are unable to look after themselves.

elderflower ▸ noun the flower of the elder, used to make wines, cordials, and other drinks.

elder hand ▸ noun (in card games for two players, e.g. piquet) the player dealt to.

elderly ▸ adjective (of a person) old or ageing: *an elderly relative* | (as plural noun **the elderly**) *specialist services for the elderly.*
– DERIVATIVES **elderliness** noun.

elder statesman ▸ noun an experienced and well-respected politician or other public figure.

eldest ▸ adjective (of one out of a group of related or otherwise associated people) of the greatest age; oldest: *Swift left the company to his eldest son, Charles.*
– ORIGIN Old English *ieldest*, *eldest*, of Germanic origin; related to German *ältest*, also to **ELD** and **OLD**.

eldest hand ▸ noun (in card games for three or more players) the first player dealt to, usually the player immediately to the left of the dealer.

el-Djem /ɛlˈdʒɛm/ a town in eastern Tunisia, noted for its well-preserved Roman amphitheatre.

El Dorado /ˌɛl dəˈrɑːdəʊ/ the name of a fictitious country or city abounding in gold, formerly believed to exist somewhere in the region of the Orinoco and Amazon Rivers. ■ [as noun] (also **eldorado**) (pl. **El Dorados** or **eldorados**) a place of great abundance.
– ORIGIN Spanish, literally 'the gilded one'.

eldritch /ˈɛl(d)rɪtʃ/ ▸ adjective weird and sinister or ghostly: *an eldritch screech.*
– ORIGIN early 16th cent. (originally Scots): perhaps related to **ELF**.

Eleanor of Aquitaine (*c.*1122–1204), daughter of the Duke of Aquitaine, queen of France 1137–52 and of England 1154–89. She was married to Louis VII of France from 1137; in 1152, with the annulment of their marriage, she married the future Henry II of England.

Eleatic /ˌɛlɪˈatɪk/ ▸ adjective relating to Elea, an ancient Greek city in SW Italy, or the school of philosophers which flourished there in about the 5th century BC, including Xenophanes, Parmenides, and Zeno.
▸ noun an Eleatic philosopher.
– ORIGIN late 17th cent.: from Latin *Eleaticus*, from *Elea*.

elecampane /ˌɛlɪkamˈpeɪn/ ▸ noun a plant which has yellow daisy-like flowers with long slender petals and bitter aromatic roots that are used in herbal medicine, native to central Asia. ● *Inula helenium*, family Compositae.
– ORIGIN late Middle English: from medieval Latin *enula* (from Greek *helenion* 'elecampane') + *campana* probably meaning 'of the fields' (from *campus* 'field').

elect /ɪˈlɛkt/ ▸ verb 1 [with obj.] choose (someone) to hold public office or some other position by voting: *he was **elected as** councillor* | *the members who were **elected to** the committee* | [with obj. and complement] *they elected him leader.* ■ Christian Theology (of God) choose (someone) in preference to others for salvation.
2 [with infinitive] opt for or choose to do something: *more people elected to work at home.*
▸ adjective (usu. as plural noun **the elect**) (of a person) chosen or singled out: *one of the century's elect.* ■ Christian Theology chosen by God for salvation. ■ [postpositive] chosen for a position but not yet in office: *the President-Elect.*
– DERIVATIVES **electability** noun, **electable** adjective.
– ORIGIN late Middle English: from Latin *elect-* 'picked out', from the verb *eligere*, from *e-* (variant of *ex-*) 'out' + *legere* 'to pick'.

election ▸ noun a formal and organized choice by vote of a person for a political office or other position: *the 2008 local elections* | [mass noun] *he agreed to **stand for election**.* ■ [mass noun] the action of electing or the fact of being elected: *his **election to** the House of Representatives.*
– ORIGIN Middle English: via Old French from Latin *electio(n-)*, from *eligere* 'pick out' (see **ELECT**).

electioneer ▸ verb [no obj.] (usu. as noun **electioneering**) (of a politician or political campaigner) take part actively and energetically in a campaign to be elected to public office: *the election will not be lost or won as the result of a few weeks of electioneering.*
▸ noun a campaigning politician during an election.

elective ▸ adjective 1 related to or working by means of election: *an elective democracy.* ■ (of a person or office) appointed or filled by election: *he had never held elective office* | *the National Assembly, with 125 elective members.* ■ (of a body or position) possessing or giving the power to elect: *powerful Emperors manipulated the elective body.*
2 (of surgical or medical treatment) chosen by the patient rather than urgently necessary. ■ (of a course of study) chosen by the student rather than compulsory.
▸ noun chiefly N. Amer. an optional course of study.
– DERIVATIVES **electively** adverb.
– ORIGIN late Middle English: from Old French *electif*, *-ive*, from late Latin *electivus*, from *elect-* 'picked out', from the verb *eligere* (see **ELECT**).

elective affinity ▸ noun a correspondence with, or feeling of sympathy or attraction towards, a particular idea, attitude, or person.
– ORIGIN mid 18th cent. (as *elective attraction*): originally a technical term for the preferential combination of chemical substances, it was widely used figuratively in the 19th cent., notably by Goethe (in his novel *Die Wahlverwandschaften* 'Elective Affinities') and by Weber (in describing the correspondence between aspects of Protestantism and capitalism).

elective mutism ▸ noun see **MUTISM**.

elector ▸ noun 1 a person who has the right to vote in an election, especially one for members of a national parliament. ■ (in the US) a member of the electoral college.

E

2 [usu. as title] historical a German prince entitled to take part in the election of the Holy Roman Emperor.
– DERIVATIVES **electorship** noun.

electoral ▶ adjective relating to elections or electors: *electoral reform.*
– DERIVATIVES **electorally** adverb.

electoral college ▶ noun a body of electors chosen by a larger group. ■ (in the US) a body of people representing the states of the US, who formally cast votes for the election of the President and Vice-President.

electoral roll (also **electoral register**) ▶ noun in the UK, an official list of the people in a district who are entitled to vote in an election.

electorate /ɪ'lɛkt(ə)rət/ ▶ noun **1** [treated as sing. or pl.] all the people in a country or area who are entitled to vote in an election.
2 Austral./NZ the area represented by one Member of Parliament.
3 historical the office or territories of a German elector.

Electra /ɪ'lɛktrə/ Greek Mythology the daughter of Agamemnon and Clytemnestra. She persuaded her brother Orestes to kill Clytemnestra and Aegisthus (their mother's lover) in revenge for the murder of Agamemnon.

Electra complex ▶ noun Psychoanalysis old-fashioned term for the Oedipus complex as manifested in young girls.

electress /ɪ'lɛktrɪs/ ▶ noun [usu. as title] historical the wife of a German elector.

electret /ɪ'lɛktrɪt/ ▶ noun Physics a permanently polarized piece of dielectric material, analogous to a permanent magnet.
– ORIGIN late 19th cent.: blend of **ELECTRICITY** and **MAGNET**.

electric /ɪ'lɛktrɪk/ ▶ adjective **1** of, worked by, charged with, or producing electricity: *an electric cooker.* ■ (of a musical instrument) amplified through a loudspeaker: *electric bass guitar.*
2 having or producing a sudden sense of thrilling excitement: *the atmosphere was electric.*
▶ noun **1** (**electrics**) Brit. the system of electric wiring and parts in a house or vehicle: *there's something wrong with the electrics.*
2 an electric train or other vehicle.
– ORIGIN mid 17th cent.: from modern Latin *electricus*, from Latin *electrum* 'amber', from Greek *ēlektron* (because rubbing amber causes electrostatic phenomena).

electrical ▶ adjective concerned with, operating by, or producing electricity: *electrical appliances.* ■ (of a company or shop) manufacturing or selling electrical appliances.
▶ noun (**electricals**) electrical equipment or circuitry. ■ shares in companies manufacturing electrical goods.
– DERIVATIVES **electrically** adverb.

electrical storm ▶ noun (also **electric storm**) a thunderstorm or other violent disturbance of the electrical condition of the atmosphere.

electric-arc furnace ▶ noun a furnace which uses an electric arc as a heat source, especially for steel-making.

electric blanket ▶ noun an electrically wired blanket used for heating a bed.

electric blue ▶ noun [mass noun] a steely or brilliant light blue.

electric chair ▶ noun a chair in which convicted criminals are executed by electrocution, especially in parts of the US.

electric eel ▶ noun a large eel-like freshwater fish of South America, using pulses of electricity to kill prey, assist in navigation, and for defence.
● *Electrophorus electricus*, the only member of the family Electrophoridae.

electric eye ▶ noun informal a photoelectric cell operating a relay when the beam of light illuminating it is obscured.

electric fence ▶ noun a fence through which an electric current can be passed, giving an electric shock to any person or animal touching it.

electric field ▶ noun Physics a region around a charged particle or object within which a force would be exerted on other charged particles or objects.

electric fire ▶ noun Brit. an electrically operated incandescent or convector heater, typically a portable one for domestic use.

electric guitar ▶ noun a guitar with a built-in pickup or pickups which convert sound vibrations into electrical signals for amplification.

electric hare ▶ noun see **HARE**.

electrician ▶ noun a person who installs and maintains electrical equipment.

electricity /ˌɪlɛk'trɪsɪti, ˌɛl-, ˌiːl-/ ▶ noun [mass noun] **1** a form of energy resulting from the existence of charged particles (such as electrons or protons), either statically as an accumulation of charge or dynamically as a current. ■ the supply of electric current to a building for heating, lighting, or powering appliances: *the electricity was back on* | [as modifier] *the regional electricity companies.*
2 a state or feeling of thrilling excitement: *the atmosphere was charged with a dangerous sexual electricity.*

electric organ ▶ noun **1** an organ (keyboard) in which the sound is produced electrically rather than by pipes.
2 Zoology an organ in certain fishes which is used to produce an electrical discharge for stunning prey, sense the surroundings, or as a defence.

electric ray ▶ noun a sluggish bottom-dwelling marine ray that typically lives in shallow water and can produce an electric shock for the capture of prey and for defence. Also called **TORPEDO RAY**.
● Family Torpedinidae: several genera, in particular *Torpedo*, and many species.

electric shaver (also **electric razor**) ▶ noun an electrical device for shaving, with oscillating or rotating blades behind a metal guard.

electric shock ▶ noun a sudden discharge of electricity through a part of the body.

electrify ▶ verb (**electrifies, electrifying, electrified**) [with obj.] **1** charge (a medium) with electricity; pass an electric current through: (as adj. **electrified**) *an electrified fence.* ■ convert (a machine or system, especially a railway line) to the use of electrical power.
2 (often as adj. **electrifying**) cause a sudden sense of thrilling excitement in (someone): *an electrifying performance.*
– DERIVATIVES **electrification** noun, **electrifier** noun.
– ORIGIN mid 18th cent.: from **ELECTRIC** + **-FY**.

electro /ɪ'lɛktrəʊ/ ▶ noun (pl. **electros**) **1** short for **ELECTROTYPE** or **ELECTROPLATE**.
2 [mass noun] a style of dance music with a fast beat and synthesized backing track.

electro- ▶ combining form **1** relating to or caused by electricity; involving electricity and ...: *electroconvulsive* | *electromagnetism.*
2 relating to music characterized by the use of synthesizers or electronically created sounds: *electro-pop.*

electro-acoustic ▶ adjective involving the direct conversion of electrical into acoustic energy or vice versa. ■ (of a guitar) having both a pickup and a reverberating hollow body.
▶ noun an electro-acoustic guitar.

electrocardiogram /ɪˌlɛktrəʊ'kɑːdɪəgram/ (abbrev.: **ECG**) ▶ noun Medicine a record or display of a person's heartbeat produced by electrocardiography.

electrocardiograph /ɪˌlɛktrəʊ'kɑːdɪəgrɑːf/ (abbrev.: **ECG**) ▶ noun a machine used for electrocardiography.

electrocardiography /ɪˌlɛktrəʊˌkɑːdɪ'ɒgrəfi/ ▶ noun [mass noun] the measurement of electrical activity in the heart and its recording as a visual trace (on paper or on an oscilloscope screen), using electrodes placed on the skin of the limbs and chest.
– DERIVATIVES **electrocardiographic** adjective.

electrocautery /ɪˌlɛktrəʊ'kɔːtəri/ ▶ noun [mass noun] cautery using a needle or other instrument that is electrically heated.

electrochemistry ▶ noun [mass noun] the branch of chemistry that deals with the relations between electrical and chemical phenomena.
– DERIVATIVES **electrochemical** adjective, **electrochemically** adverb, **electrochemist** noun.

electrochromism /ɪˌlɛktrə(ʊ)'krəʊmɪz(ə)m/ ▶ noun [mass noun] Chemistry the property of certain dyes of changing colour when placed in an electric field.
– DERIVATIVES **electrochromic** adjective.

electrocoagulation /ɪˌlɛktrəʊkəʊˌagjʊ'leɪʃ(ə)n/ ▶ noun [mass noun] the coagulation of blood or other tissues by the local application of an electric current to produce concentrated heat.

electroconvulsive ▶ adjective relating to the treatment of mental illness by the application of electric shocks to the brain.

electrocorticogram /ɪˌlɛktrə(ʊ)'kɔːtɪkə(ʊ)gram/ ▶ noun Physiology a chart or record of the electrical activity of the brain made using electrodes in direct contact with it.

electrocute ▶ verb [with obj.] injure or kill (someone) by electric shock: *a man was electrocuted on the rail track.*
– DERIVATIVES **electrocution** noun.
– ORIGIN late 19th cent.: from **ELECTRO-**, on the pattern of *execute.*

electrocyte /ɪ'lɛktrə(ʊ)sʌɪt/ ▶ noun Zoology a modified muscle or nerve cell that generates electricity in the electric organ of certain fishes.

electrode /ɪ'lɛktrəʊd/ ▶ noun a conductor through which electricity enters or leaves an object, substance, or region.
– ORIGIN mid 19th cent.: from **ELECTRIC** + Greek *hodos* 'way', on the pattern of *anode* and *cathode.*

electrodermal /ɪˌlɛktrə(ʊ)'dəːməl/ ▶ adjective relating to measurement of the electrical conductivity of the skin, especially as an indicator of someone's emotional responses.

electrodialysis /ɪˌlɛktrəʊdʌɪ'alɪsɪs/ ▶ noun [mass noun] Chemistry dialysis in which the movement of ions is aided by an electric field applied across the semipermeable membrane.

electrodynamics ▶ plural noun [usu. treated as sing.] the branch of mechanics concerned with the interaction of electric currents with magnetic fields or with other electric currents.
– DERIVATIVES **electrodynamic** adjective.

electroencephalogram /ɪˌlɛktrəʊɪn'sɛf(ə)ləgram, -'kɛf-/ ▶ noun a test or record of brain activity produced by electroencephalography.

electroencephalograph /ɪˌlɛktrəʊɪn'sɛf(ə)ləgrɑːf, -'kɛf-/ ▶ noun a machine used for electroencephalography.

electroencephalography /ɪˌlɛktrəʊɪnˌsɛfə'lɒgrəfi, -ˌkɛf-/ ▶ noun [mass noun] the measurement of electrical activity in different parts of the brain and its recording as a visual trace (on paper or on an oscilloscope screen).

electrofish ▶ verb [with obj.] fish (a stretch of water) using electrocution or a weak electric field.

electrogenic /ɪˌlɛktrə(ʊ)'dʒɛnɪk/ ▶ adjective Physiology producing a change in the electrical potential of a cell.

electrojet ▶ noun an intense electric current which occurs in a narrow belt in the lower ionosphere, especially in the region of strong auroral displays.

electrokinetic ▶ adjective relating to the flow of electricity.

electroless /ɪ'lɛktrəʊlɪs/ ▶ adjective relating to or denoting nickel plating using chemical means, as opposed to electroplating.

electrolier /ɪˌlɛktrə'lɪə/ ▶ noun a chandelier in which the lights are electrical.
– ORIGIN late 19th cent.: from **ELECTRO-**, on the pattern of *chandelier.*

electroluminescence /ɪˌlɛktrəʊluːmɪ'nɛs(ə)ns/ ▶ noun [mass noun] Chemistry luminescence produced electrically, especially by the application of a voltage.
– DERIVATIVES **electroluminescent** adjective.

electrolyse /ɪ'lɛktrəlʌɪz/ (US **electrolyze**) ▶ verb [with obj.] subject to or treat by electrolysis.
– DERIVATIVES **electrolyser** noun.
– ORIGIN mid 19th cent.: from **ELECTROLYSIS**, on the pattern of *analyse.*

electrolysis /ˌɪlɛk'trɒlɪsɪs, ˌɛl-/ ▶ noun [mass noun] **1** Chemistry chemical decomposition produced by passing an electric current through a liquid or solution containing ions.
2 the removal of hair roots or small blemishes on the skin by the application of heat using an electric current.
– DERIVATIVES **electrolytic** /ɪˌlɛktrə(ʊ)'lɪtɪk/ adjective, **electrolytical** adjective, **electrolytically** adverb.

electrolyte /ɪ'lɛktrəlʌɪt/ ▶ noun **1** a liquid or gel which contains ions and can be decomposed by electrolysis, e.g. that present in a battery.
2 (**electrolytes**) Physiology the ionized or ionizable constituents of a living cell, blood, or other organic matter.
– ORIGIN mid 19th cent.: from **ELECTRO-** + Greek *lutos* 'released' (from *luein* 'loosen').

electromagnet ▶ noun Physics a soft metal core made into a magnet by the passage of electric current through a coil surrounding it.

electromagnetic ▶ adjective relating to the interrelation of electric currents or fields and magnetic fields.
– DERIVATIVES **electromagnetically** adverb.

electromagnetic radiation ▶ noun [mass noun] Physics a kind of radiation including visible light, radio waves, gamma rays, and X-rays, in which electric and magnetic fields vary simultaneously.

electromagnetic spectrum ▶ noun [mass noun] Physics the range of wavelengths or frequencies over which electromagnetic radiation extends.

electromagnetic units ▶ plural noun Physics a largely disused system of electrical units derived primarily from the magnetic properties of electric currents.

electromagnetism ▶ noun [mass noun] the phenomenon of the interaction of electric currents or fields and magnetic fields. ■ the branch of physics concerned with electromagnetism.

electromechanical ▶ adjective relating to or denoting a mechanical device which is electrically operated.

electrometer /ˌɪlɛkˈtrɒmɪtə/ ▶ noun Physics an instrument for measuring electrical potential without drawing any current from the circuit.
– DERIVATIVES **electrometric** adjective, **electrometry** noun.

electromotive /ɪˌlɛktrəˈməʊtɪv/ ▶ adjective Physics producing or tending to produce an electric current.

electromotive force (abbrev.: **emf**) ▶ noun Physics a difference in potential that tends to give rise to an electric current.

electromyogram /ɪˌlɛktrə(ʊ)ˈmʌɪə(ʊ)gram/ ▶ noun Medicine a record or display produced by electromyography.

electromyography /ɪˌlɛktrə(ʊ)mʌɪˈɒgrəfi/ ▶ noun [mass noun] the recording of the electrical activity of muscle tissue, or its representation as a visual display or audible signal, using electrodes attached to the skin or inserted into the muscle.
– DERIVATIVES **electromyograph** noun, **electromyographic** adjective, **electromyographically** adverb.

electron /ɪˈlɛktrɒn/ ▶ noun Physics a stable subatomic particle with a charge of negative electricity, found in all atoms and acting as the primary carrier of electricity in solids.

> The electron's mass is about 9×10^{-28}g, 1,836 times less than that of the proton. Electrons orbit the positively charged nuclei of atoms and are responsible for binding atoms together in molecules, as well as for the electrical, thermal, optical, and magnetic properties of solids. Electric currents in metals and in semiconductors consist of a flow of electrons, and light, radio waves, X-rays, and much heat radiation are all produced by accelerating and decelerating electrons.

– ORIGIN late 19th cent.: from ELECTRIC + -ON.

electron beam ▶ noun Physics a stream of electrons in a gas or vacuum.

electron diffraction ▶ noun [mass noun] Physics the diffraction of a beam of electrons by atoms or molecules, used especially for determining crystal structures.

electronegative ▶ adjective 1 Physics electrically negative.
2 Chemistry (of an element) tending to acquire electrons and form negative ions in chemical reactions.
– DERIVATIVES **electronegativity** noun.

electron gun ▶ noun Physics a device for producing a narrow stream of electrons from a heated cathode.

electronic ▶ adjective 1 (of a device) having or operating with components such as microchips and transistors that control and direct electric currents: *an electronic calculator | an electronic organ.* ■ (of music) produced by electronic instruments. ■ relating to electronics: *a degree in electronic engineering.*
2 relating to electrons.
3 carried out or accessed by means of a computer or other electronic device, especially over a network: *the electronic edition of the newspaper | electronic banking.*
– DERIVATIVES **electronically** adverb.
– ORIGIN early 20th cent.: from ELECTRON + -IC.

electronica /ɪlɛkˈtrɒnɪkə/ ▶ noun [mass noun] 1 a popular style of music deriving from techno and rave and having a more ambient, esoteric, or cerebral quality.
2 electronic devices or technology considered collectively.
– ORIGIN 1990s: from ELECTRONIC + -A².

electronic flash ▶ noun Photography a flash from a gas-discharge tube, used in high-speed photography.

electronic mail ▶ noun another term for EMAIL.

electronic organizer ▶ noun a pocket-sized computer used for storing and retrieving information such as addresses and appointments.

electronic publishing ▶ noun [mass noun] the issuing of books and other material in machine-readable form rather than on paper.

electronics ▶ plural noun [usu. treated as sing.] the branch of physics and technology concerned with the design of circuits using transistors and microchips, and with the behaviour and movement of electrons in a semiconductor, conductor, vacuum, or gas. ■ [treated as pl.] circuits or devices using transistors, microchips, and other components.

electronic tagging ▶ noun [mass noun] the attaching of electronic markers to people or goods for monitoring purposes, e.g. to track offenders under house arrest or to deter shoplifters.

electron lens ▶ noun Physics a device for focusing a stream of electrons by means of electric or magnetic fields.

electron microscope ▶ noun Physics a microscope with high magnification and resolution, employing electron beams in place of light and using electron lenses.

electron optics ▶ plural noun [treated as sing.] the branch of physics that deals with the behaviour of electrons and electron beams in magnetic and electric fields.

electron pair ▶ noun 1 Chemistry two electrons occupying the same orbital in an atom or molecule.
2 Physics an electron and a positron produced in a high-energy reaction.

electron spin resonance (abbrev.: **ESR**) ▶ noun [mass noun] Physics a spectroscopic method of locating electrons within the molecules of a paramagnetic substance.

electron tube ▶ noun Physics an evacuated or gas-filled tube in which a current of electrons flows between electrodes.

electronvolt (abbrev.: **eV**) ▶ noun Physics a unit of energy equal to the work done on an electron in accelerating it through a potential difference of one volt.

electro-oculogram /ɪˌlɛktrəʊˈɒkjələ(ʊ)gram/ ▶ noun a record produced by electro-oculography.

electro-oculography /ɪˌlɛktrəʊɒkjəˈlɒgrəfi/ ▶ noun [mass noun] the measurement of the electrical potential between electrodes placed at points close to the eye, used to investigate eye movements especially in physiological research.
– DERIVATIVES **electro-oculographic** adjective.

electro-optics ▶ plural noun [treated as sing.] the branch of science that deals with the effect of electric fields on light and on the optical properties of substances.
– DERIVATIVES **electro-optic** adjective, **electro-optical** adjective.

electro-osmosis ▶ noun [mass noun] osmosis under the influence of an electric field.
– DERIVATIVES **electro-osmotic** adjective.

electrophilic /ɪˌlɛktrə(ʊ)ˈfɪlɪk/ ▶ adjective Chemistry (of a molecule or group) having a tendency to attract or acquire electrons. Often contrasted with NUCLEOPHILIC.
– DERIVATIVES **electrophile** noun.

electrophoresis /ɪˌlɛktrə(ʊ)fəˈriːsɪs/ ▶ noun [mass noun] Physics & Chemistry the movement of charged particles in a fluid or gel under the influence of an electric field.
– DERIVATIVES **electrophorese** verb, **electrophoretic** adjective, **electrophoretically** adverb.
– ORIGIN early 20th cent.: from ELECTRO- + Greek *phorēsis* 'being carried'.

electrophorus /ˌɪlɛkˈtrɒf(ə)rəs, ɛl-/ ▶ noun Physics a device for repeatedly generating static electricity by induction.
– ORIGIN late 18th cent.: from ELECTRO- + Greek *-phoros* 'bearing'.

electrophysiology /ɪˌlɛktrəʊfɪzɪˈɒlədʒi/ ▶ noun [mass noun] the branch of physiology that deals with the electrical phenomena associated with nervous and other bodily activity.
– DERIVATIVES **electrophysiological** adjective, **electrophysiologically** adverb, **electrophysiologist** noun.

electroplate /ɪˈlɛktrə(ʊ)pleɪt, ɪˌlɛktrə(ʊ)ˈpleɪt/ ▶ verb [with obj.] (usu. as noun **electroplating**) coat (a metal object) by electrolytic deposition with chromium, silver, or another metal.
▶ noun [mass noun] electroplated articles.
– DERIVATIVES **electroplater** noun.

electroplax /ɪˈlɛktrəʊplaks/ (also **electroplaque** /-plak/) ▶ noun Zoology each of a number of flattened plates of protoplasm that make up the electric organ of certain fishes, e.g. the electric eel.

electropolish /ɪˈlɛktrəʊˌpɒlɪʃ/ ▶ verb [with obj.] (often as noun **electropolishing**) give a shiny surface to (metal) using electrolysis.

electropop ▶ noun [mass noun] a style of popular music characterized by the use of electronically created sounds, with a synthesizer as the primary instrument.

electroporation /ɪˌlɛktrə(ʊ)pəˈreɪʃ(ə)n/ ▶ noun [mass noun] Biology the action or process of introducing DNA or chromosomes into bacteria or other cells using a pulse of electricity to open the pores in the cell membranes briefly.
– DERIVATIVES **electroporate** verb.

electropositive ▶ adjective 1 Physics electrically positive.
2 Chemistry (of an element) tending to lose electrons and form positive ions in chemical reactions.

electroreception ▶ noun [mass noun] the detection by an aquatic animal of electric fields or currents.
– DERIVATIVES **electroreceptor** noun.

electroretinogram /ɪˌlɛktrəʊˈrɛtɪnə(ʊ)gram/ ▶ noun a record of the electrical activity of the retina, used in medical diagnosis and research.

electroscope ▶ noun Physics an instrument for detecting and measuring electricity, especially as an indication of the ionization of air by radioactivity.

electro-selective pattern (abbrev.: **ESP**) ▶ noun Photography a mode of automatic light-metering in a camera which compensates for differences in the brightness of the central and peripheral portions of the image.

electroshock ▶ adjective denoting or relating to medical treatment by means of electric shocks: *electroshock therapy.*

electrostatic ▶ adjective Physics relating to stationary electric charges or fields as opposed to electric currents.
– DERIVATIVES **electrostatically** adverb.
– ORIGIN mid 19th cent.: from ELECTRO- + STATIC, on the pattern of *hydrostatic.*

electrostatic precipitator ▶ noun a device that removes suspended dust particles from a gas or exhaust by applying a high-voltage electrostatic charge and collecting the particles on charged plates.

electrostatics ▶ plural noun [treated as sing.] Physics the study of stationary electric charges or fields as opposed to electric currents.

electrostatic units ▶ plural noun a system of units based primarily on the forces between electric charges.

electrosurgery ▶ noun [mass noun] surgery using a high-frequency electric current to heat and so cut tissue with great precision.
– DERIVATIVES **electrosurgical** adjective.

electrotechnology ▶ noun [mass noun] the science of the application of electricity in technology.
– DERIVATIVES **electrotechnical** adjective, **electrotechnics** noun.

electrotherapy ▶ noun [mass noun] the use of electric currents passed through the body to stimulate nerves and muscles, chiefly in the treatment of various forms of paralysis.
– DERIVATIVES **electrotherapeutic** adjective, **electrotherapist** noun.

electrothermal ▶ adjective Physics relating to heat derived from electricity.

electrotype ▶ verb [with obj.] (often as noun **electrotyping**) make a copy of (something) by the electrolytic deposition of copper on a mould.
▶ noun an electrotyped copy.

electrovalent /ɪˌlɛktrə(ʊ)ˈveɪl(ə)nt/ ▶ adjective Chemistry (of bonding) resulting from electrostatic attraction between positive and negative ions; ionic.
– DERIVATIVES **electrovalence** noun.
– ORIGIN 1920s: from ELECTRO- + *-valent*, on the pattern of *trivalent.*

electroweak ▶ adjective Physics relating to or denoting electromagnetic and weak interactions regarded as manifestations of the same interaction.

E

electrum /ɪˈlɛktrəm/ ▸ **noun** [mass noun] a natural or artificial alloy of gold with at least 20 per cent of silver, used for jewellery, especially in ancient times.
– ORIGIN late Middle English: via Latin from Greek *ēlektron* 'amber, electrum'.

electuary /ɪˈlɛktjʊ(ə)ri/ ▸ **noun** (pl. **electuaries**) archaic a medicinal substance mixed with honey or another sweet substance.
– ORIGIN late Middle English: from late Latin *electuarium*, probably from Greek *ekleikton*, from *ekleikhein* 'lick up'.

eleemosynary /ˌɛliːˈmɒsɪnəri, -ˈmɒz-/ ▸ **adjective** formal relating to or dependent on charity; charitable.
– ORIGIN late 16th cent. (as a noun denoting a place where alms were distributed): from medieval Latin *eleemosynarius*, from late Latin *eleemosyna* 'alms', from Greek *eleēmosunē* 'compassion' (see **ALMS**).

E

elegance ▸ **noun** [mass noun] **1** the quality of being graceful and stylish in appearance or manner: *a slender woman with grace and elegance.*
2 the quality of being pleasingly ingenious and simple; neatness: *the simplicity and elegance of the solution.*

elegant ▸ **adjective 1** graceful and stylish in appearance or manner: *she will look elegant in black | an elegant, comfortable house.*
2 (of a scientific theory or solution to a problem) pleasingly ingenious and simple: *the grand unified theory is compact and elegant in mathematical terms.*
– DERIVATIVES **elegantly** adverb.
– ORIGIN late 15th cent.: from French, or from Latin *elegans*, *elegant-*, related to *eligere* 'choose, select' (see **ELECT**).

elegant variation ▸ **noun** [mass noun] the stylistic fault of studiedly finding different ways to denote the same thing in a piece of writing, merely to avoid repetition.

elegiac /ˌɛlɪˈdʒʌɪək/ ▸ **adjective** relating to or characteristic of an elegy: *haunting and elegiac poems.* ■ wistfully mournful.
▸ **plural noun** (**elegiacs**) verses in an elegiac metre.
– DERIVATIVES **elegiacally** adverb.
– ORIGIN late 16th cent.: from French *élégiaque*, or via late Latin, from Greek *elegeiakos*, from *elegeia* (see **ELEGY**).

elegiac couplet ▸ **noun** a pair of lines consisting of a dactylic hexameter and a pentameter, especially in Greek and Latin verse.

elegize /ˈɛlɪdʒʌɪz/ (also **elegise**) ▸ **verb** [no obj.] write in a wistfully mournful way.
– DERIVATIVES **elegist** noun.

elegy /ˈɛlɪdʒi/ ▸ **noun** (pl. **elegies**) **1** (in modern literature) a poem of serious reflection, typically a lament for the dead.
2 (in Greek and Latin verse) a poem written in elegiac couplets, as notably by Catullus and Propertius.
– ORIGIN early 16th cent.: from French *élégie*, or via Latin, from Greek *elegeia*, from *elegos* 'mournful poem'.

element ▸ **noun 1** an essential or characteristic part of something abstract: *the death had* **all the elements of** *a great tabloid story | there are four elements to the proposal.* ■ a small but significant amount of a feeling or quality: *it was the element of danger he loved in flying.* ■ (**elements**) the rudiments of a subject: *legal training may include the elements of economics and political science.* ■ (usu. with modifier often **elements**) a group of people of a particular kind within a larger group: *extreme right-wing elements in the army.* ■ Mathematics & Logic an entity that is a single member of a set.
2 (also **chemical element**) each of more than one hundred substances that cannot be chemically interconverted or broken down into simpler substances and are primary constituents of matter. Each element is distinguished by its atomic number, i.e. the number of protons in the nuclei of its atoms.
3 any of the four substances (earth, water, air, and fire) regarded as the fundamental constituents of the world in ancient and medieval philosophy.
4 (**the elements**) strong winds, heavy rain, or other kinds of bad weather: *there was no barrier against the elements.*
5 a person's or animal's natural or preferred environment: *raised in Hawaii, the sea is his natural element.*
6 a part in an electric kettle, heater, or cooker which contains a wire through which an electric current is passed to provide heat.
7 (**elements**) (in church use) the bread and wine of the Eucharist.
– PHRASES **be in** (or **out of**) **one's element** be in (or not in) a situation or environment that one particularly likes and in which one can perform well: *he was always in his element when working around the house.*
– ORIGIN Middle English (denoting fundamental constituents of the world or celestial objects): via Old French from Latin *elementum* 'principle, rudiment', translating Greek *stoikheion* 'step, component part'.

elemental /ˌɛlɪˈmɛnt(ə)l/ ▸ **adjective 1** forming an essential or typical feature; fundamental: *failure is always apparent at this elemental level.* ■ concerned with chemical elements or other basic components: *elemental analysis.* ■ denoting uncombined chemical elements: *elemental sulphur.*
2 related to or embodying the powers of nature: *a thunderstorm is the inevitable outcome of battling elemental forces.* ■ (of an emotion) powerful and primitive: *a magical, elemental desire.*
▸ **noun** a supernatural entity or force thought to be physically manifested by occult means.
– DERIVATIVES **elementalism** noun, **elementally** adverb.
– ORIGIN late 15th cent.: from medieval Latin *elementalis*, from *elementum* 'principle, rudiment' (see **ELEMENT**).

elementary ▸ **adjective 1** relating to the rudiments of a subject: *an elementary astronomy course.* ■ of the most basic kind: *the elementary rights of citizenship.* ■ straightforward and uncomplicated: *a series of elementary exercises.*
2 not decomposable into elements or other primary constituents.
– DERIVATIVES **elementarily** adverb, **elementariness** noun.
– ORIGIN late Middle English (in the sense 'composed of the four elements, earth, air, fire, and water'): from Latin *elementarius*, from *elementum* 'principle, rudiment' (see **ELEMENT**). Current senses date from the mid 16th cent.

elementary particle ▸ **noun** see **PARTICLE** (sense 1).

elementary school ▸ **noun** N. Amer. a primary school for the first six or eight grades. ■ Brit. historical a school where children were taught between the ages of five and thirteen.

elemi /ˈɛləmi/ ▸ **noun** [mass noun] an oleoresin obtained from a tropical tree and used in varnishes, ointments, and aromatherapy. ● This resin is obtained from several trees in the family Burseraceae, in particular *Bursera simaruba* (producing **American elemi**) and *Canarium luzanicum* (producing **Manila elemi**).
– ORIGIN mid 16th cent.: perhaps from Arabic *al-lāmī*.

elenchus /ɪˈlɛŋkəs/ ▸ **noun** (pl. **elenchi** /-kʌɪ/) Logic a logical refutation. ■ (also **Socratic elenchus**) [mass noun] the Socratic method of eliciting truth by question and answer, especially as used to refute an argument.
– ORIGIN mid 17th cent. (superseding late Middle English *elench*): via Latin from Greek *elenkhos*.

Eleonora's falcon /ˌɛlɪəˈnɔːrəz/ ▸ **noun** a long-winged falcon that breeds on rocky islands and cliffs in the Mediterranean area, either resembling a dark hobby or with all-black plumage. ● *Falco eleonorae*, family Falconidae.
– ORIGIN mid 19th cent.: named after *Eleonora* of Arborea (*c.*1350–1404), a princess of Sardinia.

elephant ▸ **noun** (pl. **same** or **elephants**) **1** a very large plant-eating mammal with a prehensile trunk, long curved ivory tusks, and large ears, native to Africa and southern Asia. It is the largest living land animal. ● Family Elephantidae, order Proboscidea: two species. See **AFRICAN ELEPHANT, INDIAN ELEPHANT.**
2 a size of paper, typically 28 × 23 inches (approximately 711 × 584 mm).
– PHRASES **the elephant in the room** a major problem or controversial issue which is obviously present but is avoided as a subject for discussion: *they've steadfastly ignored the elephant in the room: the ever-growing debt burden on graduates.*
– DERIVATIVES **elephantoid** /ˌɛlɪˈfantɔɪd/ adjective.
– ORIGIN Middle English: from Old French *elefant*, via Latin from Greek *elephas*, *elephant-* 'ivory, elephant'.

elephant bird ▸ **noun** a heavily built giant flightless bird, found in Madagascar until it was exterminated in about AD 1000. The eggs, which are still found occasionally, are the largest known. Also called **AEPYORNIS.** ● Family Aepyornithidae, genera *Aepyornis* and *Mullerornis*: several species, including *A. maximus*, which is the heaviest known bird.

elephant fish ▸ **noun** a fish with a trunk-like snout or proboscis. ● a chimaera with a hook-like process on the snout (family Callorhinchidae and genus *Callorhinchus*). ● another term for **ELEPHANT-SNOUT FISH.**

elephant grass ▸ **noun** [mass noun] a tall robust tropical African grass which is used for fodder and paper. ● *Pennisetum purpureum*, family Gramineae.

elephant hawkmoth ▸ **noun** a large pinkish hawkmoth with greenish-bronze markings. The foreparts of the caterpillar have eyespots and sometimes resemble an elephant's trunk. ● Genus *Deilephila*, family Sphingidae: several species, in particular the common *D. elpenor*.

elephantiasis /ˌɛlɪf(ə)nˈtʌɪəsɪs/ ▸ **noun** [mass noun] Medicine a condition in which a limb or other part of the body becomes grossly enlarged due to obstruction of the lymphatic vessels, typically by the nematode parasites which cause filariasis.
– ORIGIN mid 16th cent.: via Latin from Greek, from *elephas*, *elephant-* 'elephant' + **-IASIS**.

elephantine /ˌɛlɪˈfantʌɪn/ ▸ **adjective** of, resembling, or characteristic of an elephant or elephants, especially in being large, clumsy, or awkward: *there was an elephantine thud from the bathroom.*
– ORIGIN early 17th cent.: via Latin from Greek *elephantinos*, from *elephas*, *elephant-* 'elephant'.

Elephant Pass a narrow strip of land at the north end of Sri Lanka, linking the Jaffna peninsula with the rest of the island.

elephant seal ▸ **noun** a large seal that breeds on the west coast of North America and the islands around Antarctica. The male is much larger than the female and has a very thick neck and an inflatable snout. ● Genus *Mirounga*, family Phocidae: two species.

elephant shrew ▸ **noun** a small insectivorous African mammal with a long mobile snout, long hindlimbs, and a rat-like tail. ● Family Macroscelididae and order Macroscelidea: four genera and many species; sometimes placed in the order Insectivora.

elephant-snout fish ▸ **noun** an edible African freshwater fish with a downcurved snout that is typically elongated and trunk-like. Also called **ELEPHANT FISH.** ● Family Mormyridae: several genera, in particular *Mormyrus*.

Eleusinian mysteries /ˌɛljuːˈsɪnɪən/ ▸ **plural noun** the annual rites performed by the ancient Greeks at the village of Eleusis near Athens in honour of Demeter and Persephone.

elevate /ˈɛlɪveɪt/ ▸ **verb** [with obj.] **1** raise or lift (something) to a higher position: *the exercise will naturally elevate your chest and head.* ■ (of a priest) hold up (a consecrated host or chalice) for adoration. ■ raise the axis of (a piece of artillery) to increase its range.
2 raise to a more important or impressive level: *he was* **elevated to** *Secretary of State | he has* **elevated** *bad taste* **into** *an art form.* ■ increase the level of (something).
– DERIVATIVES **elevatory** adjective.
– ORIGIN late Middle English: from Latin *elevat-* 'raised', from the verb *elevare*, from *e-* (variant of *ex-*) 'out, away' + *levare* 'lighten' (from *levis* 'light').

elevated ▸ **adjective** situated or placed higher than the surrounding area: *this hotel has an elevated position above the village | the elevated section of the M4.* ■ (of a level or amount) higher or greater than normal: *an elevated temperature.* ■ of a high intellectual or moral level: *the elevated canon of great literary texts.* ■ having a high rank or social standing: *these parish gentry were conscious of their elevated status.*

elevation ▸ **noun 1** [mass noun] the action or fact of raising or being raised to a higher or more important level, state, or position: *her sudden elevation to the cabinet.* ■ increase in the level of something. ■ the raising of the consecrated elements for adoration at Mass. ■ Ballet the ability of a dancer to attain height in jumps.
2 [mass noun] height above a given level, especially sea level: *the area has a topography that ranges from 1,500 to 3,000 metres* **in elevation.** ■ [count noun] a high place or position: *an elevation of 300 metres.* ■ the angle of something with the horizontal, especially of a gun or of the direction of a celestial object.
3 a particular side of a building: *a burglar alarm was displayed on the front elevation.* ■ a scale drawing showing the vertical projection of one side of a building. Compare with **PLAN** (sense 3 of the noun).
– DERIVATIVES **elevational** adjective.
– ORIGIN late Middle English: from Latin *elevatio(n-)*, from *elevare* 'raise' (see **ELEVATE**).

elevator ▸ **noun 1** North American term for **LIFT** (sense 1 of the noun).
2 a machine consisting of an endless belt with scoops attached, used for raising grain to an upper storey for storage: *a grain elevator.* ■ N. Amer. a tall building used for storing grain.

3 a hinged flap on the tailplane of an aircraft, typically one of a pair, used to control the motion of the aircraft about its lateral axis.
4 a muscle whose contraction raises a part of the body: *elevators of the upper lip*.
5 (also **elevator shoe**) a shoe with a raised insole designed to make the wearer appear taller.
– ORIGIN mid 17th cent. (denoting a muscle): modern Latin, from Latin *elevare* 'raise'; in later use directly from ELEVATE.

elevator music ▶ **noun** [mass noun] chiefly N. Amer. bland recorded background music played in public places.

elevator pitch ▶ **noun** informal, chiefly US a succinct and persuasive sales pitch.
– ORIGIN from the idea of having to impress a senior executive during a brief ride in a lift (elevator).

eleven ▶ **cardinal number** equivalent to the sum of six and five; one more than ten; 11: *the room was about eleven feet wide | eighteen schools were founded, eleven of them in London*. (Roman numeral: **xi** or **XI**)
■ eleven years old: *the eldest is only eleven*. ■ eleven o'clock: *she often worked until eleven at night*. ■ a size of garment or other merchandise denoted by eleven. ■ a group or unit of eleven people or things. ■ a sports team of eleven players: *at cricket I played in the first eleven*.
– DERIVATIVES **elevenfold** adjective & adverb
– ORIGIN Old English *endleofon*, from the base of ONE + a second element (probably expressing the sense 'left over') occurring also in TWELVE; of Germanic origin and related to Dutch and German *elf*.

eleven-plus ▶ **noun** chiefly historical (in the UK) an examination taken at the age of 11–12 to determine the type of secondary school a child should enter.

elevenses ▶ **plural noun** Brit. informal a short break for light refreshments, usually with tea or coffee, taken at about eleven o'clock in the morning.

eleventh ▶ **ordinal number 1** constituting number eleven in a sequence; 11th: *the eleventh century | February the eleventh*. ■ Music an interval or chord spanning an octave and a fourth in the diatonic scale, or a note separated from another by this interval.
2 each of eleven equal parts into which something is or may be divided.
– PHRASES **the eleventh hour** the latest possible moment: *the decision to send Eddie with the team was made at the eleventh hour*.

elevon /ˈɛlɪvɒn/ ▶ **noun** Aeronautics the movable part of the trailing edge of a delta wing.
– ORIGIN 1940s: blend of ELEVATOR and AILERON (because the elevon combines the functions of both).

ELF ▶ **abbreviation** extremely low frequency.

elf ▶ **noun** (pl. **elves**) a supernatural creature of folk tales, typically represented as a small, delicate, elusive figure in human form with pointed ears, magical powers, and a capricious nature.
– DERIVATIVES **elfish** adjective, **elven** adjective (literary), **elvish** adjective.
– ORIGIN Old English, of Germanic origin; related to German *Alp* 'nightmare'.

elf cup (also **scarlet elf cup**) ▶ **noun** a fungus of decaying wood, producing small groups of shallow short-stemmed cups with a scarlet interior, found in both Eurasia and North America. ● *Sarcoscypha coccinea*, family Sarcosomataceae, subdivision Ascomycotina.

elfin ▶ **adjective 1** (of a person or their face) small and delicate, typically with a mischievous charm: *her black hair suited her elfin face*.
2 relating to elves: *an enchanted world of fairies in elfin glades*.
▶ **noun 1** archaic an elf.
2 a small North American butterfly that is typically brownish with markings on the wing margins that give the impression of scalloped edges. ● Genus *Incisalia*, family Lycaenidae.
– ORIGIN late 16th cent.: from ELF, probably suggested by Middle English *elvene* 'of elves', and by *Elphin*, the name of a character in Arthurian romance.

elf owl ▶ **noun** a tiny owl that nests in cacti and trees in the arid country of the southern US and Mexico. ● *Micrathene whitneyi*, family Strigidae.

Elgar /ˈɛlgɑː/, Sir Edward (William) (1857–1934), English composer. He is known particularly for the *Enigma Variations* (1899), the oratorio *The Dream of Gerontius* (1900), and for patriotic pieces such as the five *Pomp and Circumstance* marches (1901–30).

Elgin Marbles a collection of classical Greek marble sculptures and architectural fragments, chiefly from the Parthenon in Athens, brought to England by the diplomat and art connoisseur Thomas Bruce (1766–1841), the 7th Earl of Elgin.

> Carved under the direction of Phidias in the 5th century BC, the sculptures were brought from Greece between 1803 and 1812, when the country was under Turkish control. They are currently housed in the British Museum, but are the subject of a repatriation request from the Greek government, who do not accept the legality of the Turkish sale.

el-Giza /ɛlˈdʒiːzə/ another name for GIZA.

Elgon, Mount /ˈɛlgɒn/ an extinct volcano on the border between Kenya and Uganda, rising to 4,321 m (14,178 ft).

El Greco /ɛl ˈgrɛkəʊ/ (1541–1614), Cretan-born Spanish painter; born *Domenikos Theotokopoulos*. El Greco's portraits and religious works are characterized by distorted perspective, elongated figures, and strident use of colour.
– ORIGIN Spanish, literally 'the Greek'.

Eli /ˈiːlʌɪ/ (in the Bible) a priest who acted as a teacher to the prophet Samuel (1 Sam. 1–3).

Elia /ˈiːlɪə/ the pseudonym adopted by Charles Lamb in his *Essays of Elia* (1823) and *Last Essays of Elia* (1833).

elicit /ɪˈlɪsɪt/ ▶ **verb** (**elicits, eliciting, elicited**) [with obj.] evoke or draw out (a reaction, answer, or fact) from someone. *I tried to **elicit** a smile **from** Joanna | the work elicited enormous public interest*. ■ archaic draw forth (something that is latent or potential) into existence: *a corrupt heart elicits in an hour all that is bad in us*.
– DERIVATIVES **elicitation** noun, **elicitor** noun.
– ORIGIN mid 17th cent.: from Latin *elicit-* 'drawn out by trickery or magic', from the verb *elicere*, from *e-* (variant of *ex-*) 'out' + *lacere* 'entice, deceive'.

elide /ɪˈlʌɪd/ ▶ **verb** [with obj.] **1** omit (a sound or syllable) when speaking: (as adj. **elided**) *elided consonants*.
2 join together; merge: *whole periods of time are **elided into** a few seconds of screen time*.
– ORIGIN mid 16th cent. (in the sense 'annul', chiefly as a Scots legal term): from Latin *elidere* 'crush out', from *e-* (variant of *ex-*) 'out' + *laedere* 'to dash'.

eligible /ˈɛlɪdʒɪb(ə)l/ ▶ **adjective** (often **eligible for/to do something**) having the right to do or obtain something; satisfying the appropriate conditions: *customers who are eligible for discounts | eligible candidates*. ■ (of a person) desirable or suitable as a partner in marriage: *the world's most eligible bachelor*.
– DERIVATIVES **eligibility** noun, **eligibly** adverb.
– ORIGIN late Middle English: via French from late Latin *eligibilis*, from Latin *eligere* 'choose' (see ELECT).

Elijah /ɪˈlʌɪdʒə/ (9th century BC), a Hebrew prophet in the time of Jezebel who maintained the worship of Jehovah against that of Baal and other pagan gods.

eliminate /ɪˈlɪmɪneɪt/ ▶ **verb** [with obj.] **1** completely remove or get rid of (something): *a policy that would eliminate inflation*. ■ exclude (someone or something) from consideration or further participation: *the police have **eliminated** Lawrence **from** their inquiries* | (as adj. **eliminating**) *teams who had fought their way through the eliminating rounds*.
2 expel (waste matter) from the body: *this diet claims to eliminate toxins from the body*.
3 Mathematics remove (a variable) from an equation, typically by substituting another which is shown by another equation to be equivalent.
4 Chemistry generate (a simple substance) as a product in the course of a reaction involving larger molecules.
– DERIVATIVES **eliminable** adjective, **elimination** noun, **eliminator** noun, **eliminatory** adjective.
– ORIGIN mid 16th cent. (in the sense 'drive out'): from Latin *eliminat-* 'turned out of doors', from the verb *eliminare*, from *e-* (variant of *ex-*) 'out' + *limen, limin-* 'threshold'.

elimination diet ▶ **noun** a procedure used to identify foods which a person is intolerant of, in which all suspected foods are excluded from the diet and then reintroduced one at a time.

ELINT /ɪˈlɪnt/ ▶ **noun** [mass noun] covert intelligence-gathering by electronic means.
– ORIGIN 1960s (originally US): blend of ELECTRONIC and INTELLIGENCE.

Eliot[1] /ˈɛlɪət/, George (1819–80), English novelist; pseudonym of *Mary Ann Evans*. Her novels of provincial life are characterized by their exploration of moral problems and their development of the psychological analysis that marks the modern novel. Notable works: *Adam Bede* (1859), *The Mill on the Floss* (1860), and *Middlemarch* (1871–2).

Eliot[2] /ˈɛlɪət/, T. S. (1888–1965), American-born British poet, critic, and dramatist; full name *Thomas Stearns Eliot*. Associated with the rise of literary modernism, he was established as the voice of a disillusioned generation by *The Waste Land* (1922). *Four Quartets* (1943) revealed his increasing involvement with Christianity. Nobel Prize for Literature (1948).

ELISA /ɪˈlʌɪzə/ ▶ **noun** [mass noun] Biochemistry enzyme-linked immunosorbent assay.

Elisabethville /ɪˈlɪzəbəθ,vɪl/ former name (until 1966) for LUBUMBASHI.

Elisha /ɪˈlʌɪʃə/ (9th century BC), a Hebrew prophet, disciple and successor of Elijah.

elision /ɪˈlɪʒ(ə)n/ ▶ **noun** [mass noun] **1** the omission of a sound or syllable when speaking (as in *I'm, let's*). ■ [count noun] an omission of a passage in a book, speech, or film: *the movie's elisions and distortions have been carefully thought out*.
2 the process of joining together or merging things, especially abstract ideas: *unease at the elision of so many vital questions*.
– ORIGIN late 16th cent.: from late Latin *elisio(n-)*, from Latin *elidere* 'crush out' (see ELIDE).

Elista /ɛˈlɪstə/ a city in SW Russia, capital of the autonomous republic of Kalmykia; pop. 102,700 (est. 2008).

elite /eɪˈliːt, ɪ-/ ▶ **noun 1** a group of people considered to be superior in a particular society or organization: *the country's educated elite* | [as modifier] *an elite combat force*.
2 [mass noun] a size of letter in typewriting, with 12 characters to the inch (about 4.7 to the centimetre).
– ORIGIN late 18th cent.: from French *élite* 'selection, choice', from *élire* 'to elect', from a variant of Latin *eligere* (see ELECT). Sense 2 dates from the early 20th cent.

elitism ▶ **noun** [mass noun] the belief that a society or system should be led by an elite. ■ the dominance of a society or system by an elite. ■ the superior attitude or behaviour associated with an elite: *he accused her of racism and white elitism*.
– DERIVATIVES **elitist** adjective & noun.

elixir /ɪˈlɪksə, -sɪə/ ▶ **noun 1** a magical or medicinal potion: *an elixir guaranteed to induce love*. ■ a preparation supposedly able to change metals into gold, sought by alchemists. ■ (also **elixir of life**) a preparation supposedly able to prolong life indefinitely.
2 a particular type of medicinal solution: *a cough elixir*.
– ORIGIN late Middle English: via medieval Latin from Arabic *al-'iksīr*, from *al* 'the' + *'iksīr* from Greek *xērion* 'powder for drying wounds' (from *xēros* 'dry').

Elizabeth I (1533–1603), daughter of Henry VIII, queen of England and Ireland 1558–1603. Succeeding her Catholic sister Mary I, Elizabeth re-established a moderate form of Protestantism as the state religion. Her reign was dominated by the threat of a Catholic restoration and by war with Spain, culminating in the Armada of 1588. Although frequently courted, she never married.

Elizabeth II (b.1926), daughter of George VI, queen of the United Kingdom since 1952; born *Princess Elizabeth Alexandra Mary*. She married Prince Philip in 1947; they have four children, Prince Charles, Princess Anne, Prince Andrew, and Prince Edward.

Elizabeth, the Queen Mother (1900–2002), wife of George VI; born *Lady Elizabeth Angela Marguerite Bowes-Lyon*. She married George VI in 1923, when he was Duke of York; they had two daughters, Elizabeth II and Princess Margaret.

Elizabethan /ɪ,lɪzəˈbiːθ(ə)n/ ▶ **adjective** relating to or characteristic of the reign of Queen Elizabeth I: *an Elizabethan manor house*.
▶ **noun** a person alive during the reign of Queen Elizabeth I.

Elizavetpol /jə,liːzəˈvjɛtpɒl/ variant spelling of YELIZAVETPOL.

elk /ɛlk/ ▶ **noun** (pl. **same** or **elks**) **1** British term for MOOSE.
2 North American term for WAPITI.
– ORIGIN late 15th cent.: probably from Old English *elh, eolh*, with substitution of *k* for *h*.

elkhorn coral ▶ **noun** a coral with sturdy antler-like branches, found in shallow waters throughout the Caribbean. ● *Acropora palmata*, order Scleractinia.

elkhound ▶ **noun** a large hunting dog of a Scandinavian breed with a shaggy grey coat.

E

ell[1] ▸ **noun** a former measure of length (equivalent to six hand breadths) used mainly for textiles, locally variable but typically about 45 inches in England and 37 inches in Scotland.
– ORIGIN Old English *eln*, of Germanic origin; from an Indo-European root shared by Latin *ulna* (see **ULNA**). Compare with **ELBOW** and also with **CUBIT** (the measure was originally linked to the length of the human arm or forearm).

ell[2] ▸ **noun** see **L**[1].

ellagic acid /ɛˈladʒɪk/ ▸ **noun** [mass noun] Chemistry a compound extracted from oak galls and various fruits and nuts. It has some ability to inhibit blood flow and retard the growth of cancer cells. ● A tetracyclic phenol; chem. formula: $C_{14}H_6O_8$.
– ORIGIN early 19th cent.: *ellagic* from French *ellagique* (an anagram of *galle* 'gall nut' + *-ique*), thus avoiding the form *gallique*, already in use.

Ellesmere Island /ˈɛlzmɪə/ the northernmost island of the Canadian Arctic.
– ORIGIN named after the British statesman Francis Egerton, Earl of Ellesmere (1800–57).

Ellesmere Port a port in NW England on the estuary of the River Mersey; pop. 66,400 (est. 2009).

Ellice Islands /ˈɛlɪs/ former name for **TUVALU**.

Ellington /ˈɛlɪŋtən/, Duke (1899–1974), American jazz pianist, composer, and bandleader; born *Edward Kennedy Ellington*. Coming to fame in the early 1930s, Ellington wrote over 900 compositions and was one of the first popular musicians to write extended pieces. Notable works: *Mood Indigo* (1930).

ellipse /ɪˈlɪps/ ▸ **noun** a regular oval shape, traced by a point moving in a plane so that the sum of its distances from two other points (the foci) is constant, or resulting when a cone is cut by an oblique plane which does not intersect the base.
– ORIGIN late 17th cent.: via French from Latin *ellipsis* (see **ELLIPSIS**).

ellipsis /ɪˈlɪpsɪs/ ▸ **noun** (pl. **ellipses** /-siːz/) the omission from speech or writing of a word or words that are superfluous or able to be understood from contextual clues. ■ a set of dots (...) indicating such an omission.
– ORIGIN mid 16th cent.: via Latin from Greek *elleipsis*, from *elleipein* 'leave out'.

ellipsoid /ɪˈlɪpsɔɪd/ ▸ **noun** a three-dimensional figure symmetrical about each of three perpendicular axes, whose plane sections normal to one axis are circles and all the other plane sections are ellipses.
– DERIVATIVES **ellipsoidal** adjective.

elliptic ▸ **adjective** relating to or having the form of an ellipse.
– DERIVATIVES **ellipticity** noun.
– ORIGIN early 18th cent.: from Greek *elleiptikos* 'defective', from *elleipein* 'leave out, fall short'.

elliptical ▸ **adjective 1** (of speech or writing) using or involving ellipsis, especially so as to be difficult to understand.
2 another term for **ELLIPTIC**.
– DERIVATIVES **elliptically** adverb.

Ellis, (Henry) Havelock (1859–1939), English psychologist and writer, remembered as the pioneer of the scientific study of sex. His major work was the six-volume *Studies in the Psychology of Sex* (1897–1910, with a seventh volume added in 1928).

Ellis Island an island in the bay of New York that from 1892 until 1943 served as an entry point for immigrants to the US, and later (until 1954) as a detention centre for people awaiting deportation.

Ellsworth Land a plateau region of Antarctica between the Walgreen Coast and Palmer Land. It rises at the Vinson Massif, the highest point in Antarctica, to 5,140 m (16,863 ft).

elm (also **elm tree**) ▸ **noun** a tall deciduous tree which typically has rough serrated leaves and propagates from root suckers. ● Genus *Ulmus*, family Ulmaceae: several species, including the **English elm** (*U. procera*).
– ORIGIN Old English, of Germanic origin; related to German dialect *Ilm*, and Swedish and Norwegian *alm*.

El Niño /ɛl ˈniːnjəʊ/ ▸ **noun** (pl. **El Niños**) an irregularly occurring and complex series of climatic changes affecting the equatorial Pacific region and beyond every few years, characterized by the appearance of unusually warm, nutrient-poor water off northern Peru and Ecuador, typically in late December. The effects of El Niño include reversal of wind patterns across the Pacific, drought in Australasia, and unseasonal heavy rain in South America.
– ORIGIN Spanish, literally 'the (Christ) child', because of the occurrence near Christmas.

elocution /ˌɛləˈkjuːʃ(ə)n/ ▸ **noun** [mass noun] the skill of clear and expressive speech, especially of distinct pronunciation and articulation.
– DERIVATIVES **elocutionary** adjective, **elocutionist** noun.
– ORIGIN late Middle English (denoting oratorical or literary style): from Latin *elocutio(n-)*, from *eloqui* 'speak out' (see **ELOQUENCE**).

elodea /ˌɛlə(ʊ)ˈdiːə, ɪˈləʊdɪə/ ▸ **noun** [mass noun] an aquatic plant of a genus that includes Canadian pondweed. ● Genus *Elodea*, family Hydrocharitaceae.
– ORIGIN modern Latin, from Greek *helōdēs* 'marshy'.

Elohim /ɛˈləʊhɪm, ˈɛləʊhiːm/ ▸ **noun** a name for God used frequently in the Hebrew Bible.
– ORIGIN from Hebrew *'ĕlōhīm* (plural).

Elohist /ɛˈləʊhɪst/ the postulated author or authors of parts of the Hexateuch in which God is regularly named Elohim. Compare with **YAHWIST**.
– ORIGIN from Hebrew *'ĕlōhīm* (see **ELOHIM**) + **-IST**.

elongate /ˈiːlɒŋgeɪt/ ▸ **verb** [with obj.] (usu. as adj. **elongated**) make (something) longer, especially unusually so in relation to its width: *a slender, elongated neck*. ■ [no obj.] chiefly Biology become longer.
▸ **adjective** Biology long in relation to width; elongated: *elongate fishes*.
– ORIGIN late Middle English (in the sense 'move away'): from late Latin *elongat-* 'placed at a distance', from the verb *elongare*, from Latin *e-* (variant of *ex-*) 'away' + *longe* 'far off', *longus* 'long'.

elongation ▸ **noun** [mass noun] **1** the action or process of lengthening something. ■ an elongated part. ■ the amount of extension of an object under stress, usually expressed as a percentage of the original length.
2 Astronomy the angular separation of a planet from the sun or of a satellite from a planet, as seen by an observer.
– ORIGIN late Middle English: from late Latin *elongatio(n-)*, from *elongare* 'place at a distance' (see **ELONGATE**).

elope ▸ **verb** [no obj.] run away secretly in order to get married: *later he* **eloped with** *one of the housemaids*.
– DERIVATIVES **elopement** noun, **eloper** noun.
– ORIGIN late 16th cent. (in the general sense 'abscond, run away'): from Anglo-Norman French *aloper*, perhaps related to **LEAP**.

eloquence /ˈɛləkwəns/ ▸ **noun** [mass noun] fluent or persuasive speaking or writing: *a preacher of great power and eloquence*.
– ORIGIN late Middle English: via Old French from Latin *eloquentia*, from *eloqui* 'speak out', from *e-* (variant of *ex-*) 'out' + *loqui* 'speak'.

eloquent ▸ **adjective** fluent or persuasive in speaking or writing: *an eloquent speech*. ■ clearly expressing or indicating something: *the bus journey alone is* **eloquent of** *class inequality*.
– DERIVATIVES **eloquently** adverb.
– ORIGIN late Middle English: via Old French from Latin *eloquent-* 'speaking out', from the verb *eloqui* (see **ELOQUENCE**).

El Paso /ɛl ˈpasəʊ/ a city in western Texas on the Rio Grande, on the border with Mexico; pop. 613,190 (est. 2008).

el-Qahira /ɛlˈkɑːhiːrɑː/ variant spelling of **AL-QAHIRA**.

El Salvador /ɛl ˈsalvədɔː/, Spanish /el salβaˈðoɾ/ a country in Central America, on the Pacific coast; pop. 7,185,200 (est. 2009); official language, Spanish; capital, San Salvador.

> The territory was conquered by the Spanish in 1524 and gained its independence in 1821. Between 1979 and 1992 the country was devastated by a civil war marked by the activities of right-wing death squads and resistance by left-wing guerrillas; a UN-brokered peace accord was agreed in 1992.

Elsan /ˈɛlsan/ ▸ **noun** Brit. trademark a type of transportable chemical toilet.
– ORIGIN 1930s: apparently from the initials of *Ephraim Louis* Jackson (its manufacturer) and **SANITATION**.

else ▸ **adverb 1** [with indefinite pronoun or adverb] in addition; besides: ***anything else*** *you need to know?* | ***what else*** *is there to do?* | *they will offer low prices* ***but little else***.
2 [with indefinite pronoun or adverb] different; instead: *isn't there* ***anyone else*** *you could ask?* | *it's fate, destiny, or* ***whatever else*** *you like to call it*.
– PHRASES **or else** used to introduce the second of two alternatives: *he always had a cold or else was getting over an earache*. ■ in circumstances different from those mentioned: *they can't want it, or else they'd request it*. ■ used as a warning or threat: *you go along with this or else you're going to jail* | *she'd better shape up, or else*.
– ORIGIN Old English *elles*, of Germanic origin; related to Middle Dutch *els* and Swedish *eljest*.

elsewhere ▸ **adverb** in, at, or to some other place or other places: *he is seeking employment elsewhere*.
▸ **pronoun** some other place: *all Hawaiian plants originally came from elsewhere*.
– ORIGIN Old English *elles hwǣr* (see **ELSE**, **WHERE**).

Elsinore /ˈɛlsɪnɔː/ a port on the NE coast of the island of Zealand, Denmark; pop. 61,053 (2009). It is the site of the 16th-century Kronborg Castle, which is the setting for Shakespeare's *Hamlet*. Danish name **HELSINGØR**.

Elster /ˈɛlstə/ ▸ **noun** [usu. as modifier] Geology a Pleistocene glaciation in northern Europe, corresponding to the Anglian of Britain (and possibly the Mindel of the Alps). ■ the system of deposits laid down at the time of the Elster glaciation.
– DERIVATIVES **Elsterian** /ɛlˈstɪərɪən/ adjective & noun.
– ORIGIN 1930s: the name of a tributary of the River Elbe in Germany.

ELT ▸ **abbreviation** English language teaching.

eluant ▸ **noun** variant spelling of **ELUENT**.

eluate /ˈɛljuːət, -eɪt/ ▸ **noun** Chemistry a solution obtained by elution.
– ORIGIN 1930s: from Latin *eluere* 'wash out' + **-ATE**[1].

elucidate /ɪˈl(j)uːsɪdeɪt/ ▸ **verb** [with obj.] make (something) clear; explain: *work such as theirs will help to elucidate this matter* | [with clause] *in what follows I shall try to elucidate what I believe the problems to be*.
– DERIVATIVES **elucidative** adjective, **elucidator** noun, **elucidatory** adjective.
– ORIGIN mid 16th cent.: from late Latin *elucidat-* 'made clear', from the verb *elucidare*, from *e-* (variant of *ex-*) 'out' + *lucidus* 'lucid'.

elucidation /ɪˌl(j)uːsɪˈdeɪʃ(ə)n/ ▸ **noun** [mass noun] explanation that makes something clear; clarification: *work that led to the elucidation of the structure of proteins*.

elude /ɪˈl(j)uːd/ ▸ **verb** [with obj.] **1** escape from or avoid (a danger, enemy, or pursuer), typically in a skilful or cunning way: *he tried to elude the security men by sneaking through a back door*. ■ avoid compliance with (a law or penalty).
2 (of an achievement or something desired) fail to be attained by (someone): *sleep still eluded her*. ■ (of an idea or fact) fail to be understood or remembered by (someone): *the logic of this eluded most people*.
– DERIVATIVES **elusion** noun.
– ORIGIN mid 16th cent. (in the sense 'delude, baffle'): from Latin *eludere*, from *e-* (variant of *ex-*) 'out, away from' + *ludere* 'to play'.

eluent /ˈɛljʊənt/ (also **eluant**) ▸ **noun** Chemistry a fluid used to elute a substance.
– ORIGIN 1940s: from Latin *eluent-* 'washing out', from the verb *eluere* (see **ELUTE**).

Elul /ˈiːlʌl, ˈɛlʌl/ ▸ **noun** (in the Jewish calendar) the twelfth month of the civil and sixth of the religious year, usually coinciding with parts of August and September.
– ORIGIN from Hebrew *'ĕlūl*.

el-Uqsur /ɛlˈʊksʊə/ (also **al-Uqsur**) Arabic name for **LUXOR**.

elusive ▸ **adjective** difficult to find, catch, or achieve: *success will become ever more elusive*. ■ difficult to remember: *the elusive thought he had had moments before*.
– DERIVATIVES **elusively** adverb, **elusiveness** noun.
– ORIGIN early 18th cent.: from Latin *elus-* 'eluded' (from the verb *eludere*) + **-IVE**.

elute /ɪˈl(j)uːt/ ▸ **verb** [with obj.] Chemistry remove (an adsorbed substance) by washing with a solvent, especially in chromatography.
– DERIVATIVES **elution** noun.
– ORIGIN 1920s: from Latin *elut-* 'washed out', from the verb *eluere*, suggested by German *eluieren*.

elutriate /ɪˈl(j)uːtrɪeɪt/ ▸ **verb** [with obj.] Chemistry separate (lighter and heavier particles in a mixture) by suspension in an upward flow of liquid or gas.
– DERIVATIVES **elutriation** noun.
– ORIGIN mid 18th cent.: from Latin *elutriat-* 'washed out', from the verb *elutriare*, from *e-* (variant of *ex-*) 'out' + *lutriare* 'to wash'.

elvan /ˈɛlv(ə)n/ ▸ **noun** [mass noun] Geology hard intrusive igneous rock found in Cornwall, typically quartz porphyry.

– ORIGIN early 18th cent.: perhaps via Cornish from Welsh *elfen* 'element'.

elver /ˈɛlvə/ ▶ **noun** a young eel, especially when undergoing mass migration upriver from the sea.
– ORIGIN mid 17th cent.: variant of dialect *eel-fare* 'the passage of young eels up a river', also 'a brood of young eels', from **EEL** + **FARE** in its original sense 'a journey'.

elves plural form of **ELF**.

Ely /ˈiːli/ a cathedral city in the fenland of Cambridgeshire, on the River Ouse; pop. 15,600 (est. 2009).

Ely, Isle of a former county of England extending over the northern part of present-day Cambridgeshire. Before widespread drainage it formed a fertile 'island' in the surrounding fenland.

Elysée Palace /eɪˈliːzeɪ/ a building in Paris which has been the official residence of the French President since 1870. It was built in 1718 and was occupied by Madame de Pompadour, Napoleon I, and Napoleon III. French name **PALAIS DE L'ÉLYSÉE**.

Elysian /ɪˈlɪzɪən/ ▶ **adjective** relating to or characteristic of heaven or paradise: *Elysian visions.*
– PHRASES **the Elysian Fields** another name for **ELYSIUM**.

Elysium /ɪˈlɪzɪəm/ Greek Mythology the place at the ends of the earth to which certain favoured heroes were conveyed by the gods after death. ■ (as noun **an Elysium**) a place or state of perfect happiness.
– ORIGIN via Latin from Greek *Elusion* (*pedion*) '(plain) of the blessed'.

elytron /ˈɛlɪtrɒn/ ▶ **noun** (pl. **elytra** /-trə/) Entomology each of the two wing cases of a beetle.
– ORIGIN mid 18th cent. (denoting a sheath or covering, specifically that of the spinal cord): from Greek *elutron* 'sheath'.

Elzevir /ˈɛlzəvɪə/ a family of Dutch printers. Fifteen members were active 1581–1712; **Bonaventure** (1583–1652) and **Abraham** (1592–1652) managed the firm in its prime.

em ▶ **noun** Printing a unit for measuring the width of printed matter, equal to the height of the type size being used. ■ a unit of measurement equal to twelve points.
– ORIGIN late 18th cent.: the letter *M* represented as a word, since it is approximately this width.

'em ▶ **pronoun** short for **THEM**, especially in informal use: *let 'em know who's boss.*
– ORIGIN Middle English: originally a form of *hem*, dative and accusative third person plural pronoun in Middle English; now regarded as an abbreviation of **THEM**.

em- /ɪm, ɛm/ ▶ **prefix** variant spelling of **EN-**[1], **EN-**[2] assimilated before *b*, *p* (as in *emblazon*, *emplacement*)

emaciated /ɪˈmeɪsɪeɪtɪd, ɪˈmeɪʃ-/ ▶ **adjective** abnormally thin or weak, especially because of illness or a lack of food: *she was so emaciated she could hardly stand.*
– ORIGIN early 17th cent.: from Latin *emaciat-* 'made thin', from the verb *emaciare*, from *e-* (variant of *ex-*, expressing a change of state) + *macies* 'leanness'.

emaciation /ɪˌmeɪsɪˈeɪʃ(ə)n/ ▶ **noun** [mass noun] the state of being abnormally thin or weak: *thin to the point of emaciation.*

email (also **e-mail**) ▶ **noun** [mass noun] messages distributed by electronic means from one computer user to one or more recipients via a network: *reading email has become the first task of the morning* | [count noun] *we received thousands of emails.* ■ the system of sending messages by electronic means: *a contract communicated by email.*
▶ **verb** [with obj.] send an email to (someone). ■ send (a message) by email.
– DERIVATIVES **emailer** noun.
– ORIGIN 1980s: abbreviation of **ELECTRONIC MAIL**.

emalangeni plural form of **LILANGENI**.

emanate /ˈɛməneɪt/ ▶ **verb** [no obj.] (**emanate from**) (of a feeling, quality, or sensation) issue or spread out from (a source): *warmth emanated from the fireplace* | *she felt an undeniable charm emanating from him.* ■ originate from; be produced by: *the proposals emanated from a committee.* ■ [with obj.] give out or emit (a feeling, quality, or sensation): *he emanated a powerful brooding air.*
– ORIGIN mid 18th cent.: from Latin *emanat-* 'flowed out', from the verb *emanare*, from *e-* (variant of *ex-*) 'out' + *manare* 'to flow'.

emanation ▶ **noun 1** something which originates or issues from a source: *she saw the insults as emanations of his own tortured personality* | *the commission is an emanation of the state.* ■ [mass noun] the action or process of issuing from a source: *the risk of radon gas emanation.* ■ a substance or form of radiation given off by something: *vaporous emanations wreathe the mill's foundations.* ■ Chemistry, archaic a radioactive gas formed by radioactive decay of a solid.
2 (in various mystical traditions) a being or force which is a manifestation of God.

emancipate /ɪˈmansɪpeɪt/ ▶ **verb** [with obj.] set free, especially from legal, social, or political restrictions: *the citizen must be* ***emancipated from*** *the obsessive secrecy of government.* ■ Law set (a child) free from the authority of its parents. ■ free (someone) from slavery.
– DERIVATIVES **emancipator** noun, **emancipatory** adjective.
– ORIGIN early 17th cent.: from Latin *emancipat-* 'transferred as property', from the verb *emancipare*, from *e-* (variant of *ex-*) 'out' + *mancipium* 'slave'.

emancipated /ɪˈmansɪpeɪtɪd/ ▶ **adjective** free from legal, social, or political restrictions; liberated: *emancipated young women.*

emancipation /ɪˌmansɪˈpeɪʃ(ə)n/ ▶ **noun** [mass noun] the fact or process of being set free from legal, social, or political restrictions; liberation: *the social and political emancipation of women.* ■ the freeing of someone from slavery.

Emancipation Proclamation (in the American Civil War) the announcement made by President Lincoln on 22 September 1862 emancipating all black slaves in states still engaged in rebellion against the Federal Union. Although implementation was strictly beyond Lincoln's powers, the declaration turned the war into a crusade against slavery.

emasculate /ɪˈmaskjʊleɪt/ ▶ **verb** [with obj.] **1** (usu. as adj. **emasculated**) deprive (a man) of his male role or identity: *he feels emasculated, because he cannot control his sons' behaviour.* ■ archaic castrate (a man or male animal). ■ Botany remove the anthers from (a flower).
2 make (someone or something) weaker or less effective: *the refusal to allow them to testify effectively emasculated the committee.*
– DERIVATIVES **emasculation** noun, **emasculator** noun, **emasculatory** /-lət(ə)ri/ adjective.
– ORIGIN early 17th cent.: from Latin *emasculat-* 'castrated', from the verb *emasculare*, from *e-* (variant of *ex-*, expressing a change of state) + *masculus* 'male'.

embalm /ɪmˈbɑːm, ɛm-/ ▶ **verb** [with obj.] **1** (often as noun **embalming**) preserve (a corpse) from decay, originally with spices and now usually by arterial injection of a preservative: *the Egyptian method of embalming.* ■ preserve (someone or something) in an unaltered state: *the band was all about revitalizing pop greats and embalming their legacy.*
2 archaic give a pleasant fragrance to: *the buxom air, embalm'd with odours.*
– DERIVATIVES **embalmer** noun, **embalmment** noun.
– ORIGIN Middle English: from Old French *embaumer*, from *em-* 'in' + *baume* 'balm', variant of *basme* (see **BALM**).

embank ▶ **verb** [with obj.] construct a wall or bank of earth or stone in order to contain the course or flow of (a river). ■ construct a bank of earth or stone to carry (a road or railway) over low ground.

embankment ▶ **noun** a wall or bank of earth or stone built to prevent a river flooding an area. ■ a bank of earth or stone built to carry a road or railway over an area of low ground.

embargo /ɛmˈbɑːɡəʊ, ɪm-/ ▶ **noun** (pl. **embargoes**)
1 an official ban on trade or other commercial activity with a particular country: *an embargo on grain sales* | *an arms embargo.* ■ an official ban on any activity.
2 historical an order of a state forbidding foreign ships to enter, or any ships to leave, its ports: *an embargo laid by our Emperor upon all vessels whatsoever.*
▶ **verb** (**embargoes**, **embargoing**, **embargoed**) [with obj.] **1** impose an official ban on (trade or a country or commodity): *all of these countries have been embargoed by the US.* ■ officially ban the publication of: *documents of national security importance are routinely embargoed.*
2 archaic seize (a ship or goods) for state service.
– ORIGIN early 17th cent.: from Spanish, from *embargar* 'arrest', based on Latin *in-* 'in, within' + *barra* 'a bar'.

embark ▶ **verb** [no obj.] **1** go on board a ship or aircraft: *he embarked for India in 1817.* ■ [with obj.] put or take on board a ship or aircraft: *the passengers were ready to be embarked.*
2 (**embark on**/**upon**) begin (a course of action): *she embarked on a new career.*
– DERIVATIVES **embarkation** noun.
– ORIGIN mid 16th cent.: from French *embarquer*, from *em-* 'in' + *barque* 'bark, ship'.

embarras de richesses /ɒmbaˌrɑː də riːˈʃɛs/ (also **embarras de choix** /ˈʃwɑː/) ▶ **noun** more options or resources than one knows what to do with: *he had presented us with an embarras de richesses of history and culture.*
– ORIGIN French, 'embarrassment of riches (or choice)'.

embarrass /ɪmˈbarəs, ɛm-/ ▶ **verb** [with obj.] **1** cause (someone) to feel awkward, self-conscious, or ashamed: *she wouldn't embarrass either of them by making a scene.* ■ (**be embarrassed**) be caused financial difficulties: *he would be embarrassed by estate duty.*
2 archaic hamper or impede (a person or action): *the state of the rivers will embarrass the enemy.* ■ archaic make difficult or intricate; complicate.
– ORIGIN early 17th cent. (in sense 2): from French *embarrasser*, from Spanish *embarazar*, probably from Portuguese *embaraçar* (from *baraço* 'halter').

embarrassed ▶ **adjective** feeling or showing embarrassment: *I felt quite embarrassed whenever I talked to her* | *an embarrassed silence.* ■ having or showing financial difficulties.
– DERIVATIVES **embarrassedly** adverb.

embarrassing ▶ **adjective** causing embarrassment: *an embarrassing muddle.*
– DERIVATIVES **embarrassingly** adverb.

embarrassment ▶ **noun** [mass noun] a feeling of self-consciousness, shame, or awkwardness: *I turned red with embarrassment.* ■ [count noun] a person or thing causing feelings of embarrassment: *he was an embarrassment who was safely left ignored* | *her extreme views might be an* ***embarrassment to*** *the movement.* ■ financial difficulty: *his temporary financial embarrassment.*
– PHRASES **an embarrassment of riches** (or **choice**) more options or resources than one knows what to do with: *picking a highlight from such an embarrassment of riches is hard.*

embassage /ˈɛmbəsɪdʒ/ ▶ **noun** archaic the business or message of an envoy. ■ a deputation sent to or on behalf of a head of state.
– ORIGIN late 15th cent. (denoting the action of sending an envoy): from Old French *ambasse* 'message or embassy' + **-AGE**.

embassy ▶ **noun** (pl. **embassies**) **1** the official residence or offices of an ambassador: *the Chilean embassy in Moscow.* ■ the staff working in such a building.
2 chiefly historical a deputation or mission sent by one ruler or state to another.
– ORIGIN late 16th cent. (originally also as *ambassy* denoting the position of ambassador): from Old French *ambasse*, based on Latin *ambactus* 'servant'. Compare with **AMBASSADOR**.

embattle ▶ **verb** [with obj.] archaic **1** make (an army) ready for battle: *it was three o'clock before the king's army was embattled.*
2 fortify (a building or place) against attack.
– ORIGIN Middle English: from Old French *embataillier*.

embattled ▶ **adjective 1** (of a place or people) involved in or prepared for war, especially because surrounded by enemy forces: *the embattled northern province.* ■ (of a person) beset by problems or difficulties: *the worst may not be over for the embattled Chancellor.*
2 (of a building or part of a building) having battlements: *the church has a low embattled tower.* ■ [postpositive] Heraldry divided or edged by a line of square notches like battlements in outline.

embay ▶ **verb** [with obj.] **1** (of the wind) force (a boat) into a bay: *ships were embayed between two headlands.*
2 chiefly Geology enclose (something) in a recess or hollow.
3 (as adj. **embayed**) formed into bays: *the embayed island.*

embayment ▶ **noun** a recess in a coastline forming a bay.

embed (also **imbed**) ▶ **verb** (**embeds**, **embedding**, **embedded**) [with obj.] **1** fix (an object) firmly and

E

deeply in a surrounding mass: *he had an operation to remove a nail* ***embedded in*** *his chest.* ■ implant (an idea or feeling) so that it becomes ingrained within a particular context: *the Victorian values* ***embedded in*** *Tennyson's poetry.* ■ Linguistics place (a phrase or clause) within another clause or sentence. ■ Computing incorporate (a text or code) within the body of a file or document. ■ (often as adj. **embedded**) design and build (a microprocessor) as an integral part of a system or device.
2 attach (a journalist) to a military unit during a conflict.
▶ **noun** a journalist who is attached to a military unit during a conflict.
– DERIVATIVES **embedment** noun.

E

embellish ▶ **verb** [with obj.] make (something) more attractive by the addition of decorative details or features: *blue silk embellished with golden embroidery.* ■ make (a statement or story) more interesting by adding extra details that are often untrue: *followers often embellish stories about their heroes.*
– DERIVATIVES **embellisher** noun.
– ORIGIN late Middle English: from Old French *embelliss-*, lengthened stem of *embellir*, based on *bel* 'handsome', from Latin *bellus*.

embellishment ▶ **noun** a decorative detail or feature added to something to make it more attractive: *architectural embellishments.* ■ a detail, especially one that is untrue, added to a statement or story to make it more interesting. ■ [mass noun] the action of adding decorative details.

ember /ˈɛmbə/ ▶ **noun** (usu. **embers**) a small piece of burning or glowing coal or wood in a dying fire: *the dying embers in the grate* | figurative *the flickering embers of nationalism.*
– ORIGIN Old English *ǣmyrge*, of Germanic origin; related to Old High German *eimuria* 'pyre', Danish *emmer*, Swedish *mörja* 'embers'. The *b* was added in English for ease of pronunciation.

Ember day ▶ **noun** any of a number of days reserved for fasting and prayer in the Western Christian Church. Ember days traditionally comprise the Wednesday, Friday, and Saturday following St Lucy's Day (13 December), the first Sunday in Lent, Pentecost (Whitsun), and Holy Cross Day (14 September), though other days are observed locally.
– ORIGIN Old English *ymbren*, perhaps an alteration of *ymbryne* 'period', from *ymb* 'about' + *ryne* 'course', perhaps influenced in part by ecclesiastical Latin *quatuor tempora* 'four periods' (on which the equivalent German *Quatember* is based).

embezzle ▶ **verb** [with obj.] steal or misappropriate (money placed in one's trust or belonging to the organization for which one works): *she had embezzled £5,600,000 in company funds.*
– DERIVATIVES **embezzler** noun.
– ORIGIN late Middle English (in the sense 'steal'): from Anglo-Norman French *embesiler*, from *besiler* in the same sense (compare with Old French *besillier* 'maltreat, ravage'), of unknown ultimate origin. The current sense dates from the late 16th cent.

embezzlement ▶ **noun** [mass noun] theft or misappropriation of funds placed in one's trust or belonging to one's employer: *charges of fraud and embezzlement.*

Embioptera /ˌɛmbʌɪˈɒptərə/ ▶ **plural noun** Entomology a small order of insects that comprises the webspinners.
– DERIVATIVES **embiopteran** noun & adjective.
– ORIGIN modern Latin (plural), from *Embia* (genus name) + Greek *pteron* 'wing'.

embitter ▶ **verb** [with obj.] (usu. as adj. **embittered**) make (someone) feel bitter or resentful: *he died an embittered man.*
– DERIVATIVES **embitterment** noun.

emblazon /ɪmˈbleɪz(ə)n, ɛm-/ ▶ **verb** [with obj. and adverbial of place] conspicuously inscribe or display a design on: *T-shirts* ***emblazoned with*** *the names of baseball teams.* ■ depict (a heraldic device) on something: *the Queen's coat of arms is emblazoned on the door panel.* ■ archaic celebrate or extol publicly: *their success was emblazoned.*
– DERIVATIVES **emblazonment** noun.

emblem /ˈɛmbləm/ ▶ **noun** a heraldic device or symbolic object as a distinctive badge of a nation, organization, or family: *America's national emblem, the bald eagle.* ■ (**emblem of**) a thing serving as a symbol of a particular quality or concept: *our child would be a dazzling emblem of our love.*
– ORIGIN late 16th cent. (as a verb): from Latin *emblema* 'inlaid work, raised ornament', from Greek *emblēma* 'insertion', from *emballein* 'throw in, insert', from *em-* 'in' + *ballein* 'to throw'.

emblematic /ˌɛmbləˈmatɪk/ ▶ **adjective** serving as a symbol of a particular quality or concept; symbolic: *this case is emblematic of a larger problem.*
– DERIVATIVES **emblematical** adjective, **emblematically** adverb.

emblematist /ɛmˈblɛmətɪst/ ▶ **noun** a creator or user of emblems, especially in allegorical pictures.

emblematize /ɛmˈblɛmətʌɪz/ (also **emblematise**) ▶ **verb** [with obj.] formal serve as a symbol of (a quality or concept).

emblem book ▶ **noun** a book of a kind popular in medieval and Renaissance Europe, containing drawings accompanied by allegorical interpretations.

emblements /ˈɛmblɪm(ə)nts/ ▶ **plural noun** Law, rare the profit from crops that one has sown, regarded as personal property.
– ORIGIN late 15th cent.: from Old French *emblaement*, from *emblaier* 'sow with corn' (based on *blé* 'corn').

embodiment ▶ **noun** a tangible or visible form of an idea, quality, or feeling: *she seemed to be a living embodiment of vitality.* ■ [mass noun] the representation or expression of something in a tangible or visible form: *it was in Germany alone that his hope seemed capable of embodiment.*

embody /ɪmˈbɒdi, ɛm-/ ▶ **verb** (**embodies, embodying, embodied**) [with obj.] **1** be an expression of or give a tangible or visible form to (an idea, quality, or feeling): *a national team that embodies competitive spirit and skill.* ■ provide (a spirit) with a physical form.
2 include or contain (something) as a constituent part: *the changes in law* ***embodied in*** *the Children Act.*
3 archaic form (people) into a body, especially for military purposes.
– ORIGIN mid 16th cent.: from **EM-** + **BODY**, on the pattern of Latin *incorporare*.

embolden ▶ **verb** [with obj.] **1** give (someone) the courage or confidence to do something: *emboldened by the claret, he pressed his knee against hers.*
2 cause (a piece of text) to appear in a bold typeface: *centre, embolden, and underline the heading.*

embolectomy /ˌɛmbəˈlɛktəmi/ ▶ **noun** (pl. **embolectomies**) [mass noun] surgical removal of an embolus.

embolism /ˈɛmbəlɪz(ə)m/ ▶ **noun** Medicine obstruction of an artery, typically by a clot of blood or an air bubble.
– ORIGIN mid 19th cent.: via late Latin from Greek *embolismos*, from *emballein* 'insert'.

embolization /ˌɛmbəlʌɪˈzeɪʃ(ə)n/ (also **embolisation**) ▶ **noun** [mass noun] Medicine the artificial or natural formation or development of an embolus.

embolus /ˈɛmbələs/ ▶ **noun** (pl. **emboli** /-lʌɪ, iː/) a blood clot, air bubble, piece of fatty deposit, or other object which has been carried in the bloodstream to lodge in a vessel and cause an embolism.
– DERIVATIVES **embolic** adjective.
– ORIGIN mid 17th cent. (denoting something inserted or moving within another, specifically the plunger of a syringe): from Latin, literally 'piston', from Greek *embolos* 'peg, stopper'. The current sense dates from the mid 19th cent.

embonpoint /ˌɒmbɒ̃ˈpwã/ ▶ **noun** the plump or fleshy part of a person's body, in particular a woman's bosom.
– ORIGIN late 17th cent.: from French *en bon point* 'in good condition'.

embosom ▶ **verb** [with obj.] literary take or press (someone or something) to one's bosom; embrace. ■ surround (something) protectively.

emboss ▶ **verb** [with obj.] (usu. as adj. **embossed**) carve or mould a design on (a surface) so that it stands out in relief: *an embossed brass dish.*
– DERIVATIVES **embosser** noun.
– ORIGIN late Middle English: from the Old French base of obsolete French *embosser*, from *em-* 'into' + *boce* 'protuberance'.

embouchure /ˌɒmbʊˈʃʊə/ ▶ **noun 1** [mass noun] Music the way in which a player applies their mouth to the mouthpiece of a brass or wind instrument, especially as it affects the production of the sound. ■ [count noun] the mouthpiece of a flute or a similar instrument.
2 archaic the mouth of a river or valley.
– ORIGIN mid 18th cent.: French, from *s'emboucher* 'discharge itself by the mouth', from *emboucher* 'put in or to the mouth', from *em-* 'into' + *bouche* 'mouth'.

embourgeoisement /ɒ̃ˈbʊəʒwɑːzmɒ̃/, French /ɑ̃buʀʒwazmɑ̃/ ▶ **noun** the proliferation in a society of values perceived as characteristic of the middle class, especially of materialism.
– ORIGIN 1930s: French, from *embourgeoiser* 'become or make bourgeois'.

embowel /ɪmˈbaʊ(ə)l, ɛm-/ ▶ **verb** archaic term for **DISEMBOWEL**.
– ORIGIN early 16th cent.: from Old French *emboweler*, alteration of *esboueler*, from *es-* 'out' + *bouel* 'bowel'.

embower /ɪmˈbaʊə, ɛm-/ ▶ **verb** [with obj.] literary surround or shelter (a place or a person), especially with trees or climbing plants: *the house stood remote, embowered in trees.*

embrace ▶ **verb 1** [with obj.] hold (someone) closely in one's arms, especially as a sign of affection: *Aunt Sophie embraced her warmly* | [no obj.] *the two embraced, holding each other tightly.*
2 accept (a belief, theory, or change) willingly and enthusiastically: *besides traditional methods, artists are embracing new technology.*
3 include or contain (something) as a constituent part: *his career embraces a number of activities—composing, playing, and acting.*
▶ **noun 1** an act of holding someone closely in one's arms: *they were locked in an embrace.* ■ used to refer to something which is regarded as surrounding, holding, or restricting someone: *totalitarianism has meant that no interest falls outside the embrace of the state.*
2 [in sing.] an act of accepting something willingly or enthusiastically: *their eager embrace of foreign influences.*
– DERIVATIVES **embraceable** adjective, **embracement** noun, **embracer** noun.
– ORIGIN Middle English (in the sense 'encircle, surround, enclose'; formerly also as *imbrace*): from Old French *embracer*, based on Latin *in-* 'in' + *bracchium* 'arm'.

embrasure /ɪmˈbreɪʒə, ɛm-/ ▶ **noun** an opening in a wall or parapet which is bevelled or splayed out on the inside, typically one around a window or door.
– DERIVATIVES **embrasured** adjective.
– ORIGIN early 18th cent.: from French, from obsolete *embraser* (earlier form of *ébraser*) 'widen a door or window opening', of unknown ultimate origin.

embrittle ▶ **verb** make or become brittle.
– DERIVATIVES **embrittlement** noun.

embrocation /ˌɛmbrəˈkeɪʃ(ə)n/ ▶ **noun** [mass noun] a liquid used for rubbing on the body to relieve pain from sprains and strains.
– ORIGIN late Middle English: from medieval Latin *embrocatio(n-)*, from the verb *embrocare*, based on Greek *embrokhē* 'lotion'.

embroider ▶ **verb 1** [with obj.] decorate (cloth) by sewing patterns on it with thread: *she embroidered a tablecloth* | (as adj. **embroidered**) *an embroidered handkerchief* | [no obj.] *she was teaching the girls how to embroider.* ■ sew (a design) on cloth with thread: (as adj. **embroidered**) *a chunky sweater with embroidered flowers.*
2 add fictitious or exaggerated details to (an account) to make it more interesting: *she embroidered her stories with colourful detail.*
– DERIVATIVES **embroiderer** noun.
– ORIGIN late Middle English: from Anglo-Norman French *enbrouder*, from *en-* 'in, on' + Old French *brouder, broisder* 'decorate with embroidery', of Germanic origin.

embroidery ▶ **noun** (pl. **embroideries**) [mass noun] **1** the art or pastime of embroidering cloth. ■ cloth decorated with embroidered designs.
2 embellishment or exaggeration in the description of an event: *fanciful embroidery of the facts.*
– ORIGIN late Middle English: from Anglo-Norman French *enbrouderie*, from *enbrouder* 'embroider'.

embroil ▶ **verb** [with obj.] involve (someone) deeply in an argument, conflict, or difficult situation: *the organization is currently embroiled in running battles with pressure groups* | *the film's about a journalist who becomes* ***embroiled with*** *a nightclub owner.* ■ archaic bring into a state of confusion or disorder.
– DERIVATIVES **embroilment** noun.
– ORIGIN early 17th cent.: from French *embrouiller* 'to muddle'.

embryo /ˈɛmbrɪəʊ/ ▶ **noun** (pl. **embryos**) **1** an unborn or unhatched offspring in the process of development. ■ an unborn human, especially in the first eight weeks from conception, after implantation but before all the organs are developed. Compare with **FETUS**.

2 Botany the part of a seed which develops into a plant, consisting (in the mature embryo of a higher plant) of a plumule, a radicle, and one or two cotyledons.
3 a thing at a rudimentary stage that shows potential for development: *a simple commodity economy is merely the embryo of a capitalist economy* | [as modifier] *an embryo central bank.*
– PHRASES **in embryo** at a rudimentary stage with the potential for development.
– DERIVATIVES **embryonal** /'ɛmbrɪən(ə)l/ **adjective**, **embryoid adjective**.
– ORIGIN late Middle English: via late Latin from Greek *embruon* 'fetus', from *em-* 'into' + *bruein* 'swell, grow'.

embryo- ▸ **combining form** representing **EMBRYO**.

embryogenesis /,ɛmbrɪə(ʊ)'dʒɛnɪsɪs/ ▸ **noun** [mass noun] Biology the formation and development of an embryo.
– DERIVATIVES **embryogenic adjective**, **embryogeny** /,ɛmbrɪ'ɒdʒəni/ **noun**.

embryology /,ɛmbrɪ'ɒlədʒi/ ▸ **noun** [mass noun] the branch of biology and medicine concerned with the study of embryos and their development.
– DERIVATIVES **embryologic adjective**, **embryological adjective**, **embryologically adverb**, **embryologist noun**.

embryonic /,ɛmbrɪ'ɒnɪk/ ▸ **adjective 1** relating to an embryo.
2 (of a system, idea, or organization) in a rudimentary stage with potential for development: *the plan is still in its embryonic stages.*
– DERIVATIVES **embryonically adverb**.
– ORIGIN mid 19th cent.: from late Latin *embryo*, *embryon-* 'embryo' + **-IC**.

embus /ɪm'bʌs, ɛm-/ ▸ **verb** (**embuses, embusing, embused** or **embusses, embussing, embussed**) Military board or put onto a bus.

emcee /ɛm'siː/ informal ▸ **noun 1** a master of ceremonies.
2 an MC at a club or party.
▸ **verb** (**emcees, emceeing, emceed**) **1** [with obj.] act as a master of ceremonies at (an entertainment or large social occasion).
2 [no obj.] perform as an MC: (as noun **emceeing**) *a three-hour-long mix of DJ'ing and emceeing.*
– ORIGIN 1930s (originally US): representing a pronunciation of **MC**.

em dash ▸ **noun** another term for **EM RULE**.

-eme ▸ **suffix** Linguistics forming nouns denoting linguistic units that are in systemic contrast with one other: *grapheme* | *phoneme.*
– ORIGIN abstracted from **PHONEME**.

emend /ɪ'mɛnd/ ▸ **verb** [with obj.] make corrections and revisions to (a text). ■ alter (something that is incorrect): *the year of his death might need to be emended to 652.*
– ORIGIN late Middle English: from Latin *emendare*, from *e-* (variant of *ex-*) 'out of' + *menda* 'a fault'. Compare with **AMEND**.

emendation /,iːmɛn'deɪʃ(ə)n/ ▸ **noun** [mass noun] the process of making a revision or correction to a text. ■ [count noun] a correction or revision to a text: *here are some suggested emendations.*

emerald ▸ **noun 1** a bright green precious stone consisting of a chromium-rich variety of beryl: [as modifier] *an emerald necklace.*
2 [mass noun] (also **emerald green**) a bright green colour: *the sea glistened in shades of emerald and jade.*
3 (also **emerald moth**) a slender-bodied green moth, the colour of which tends to fade as the moth ages. ● Several genera in the family Geometridae.
4 a hawker dragonfly with a metallic green body. ● *Cordulia* and other genera, family Corduliidae.
5 a small hummingbird with bright metallic green plumage and darker wings and tail, found mainly in the area of the Caribbean and Central America. ● Three genera, in particular *Chlorostilbon* and *Amazilia*, family Trochilidae: numerous species.
▸ **adjective** bright green in colour: *beyond the airport lay emerald hills.*
– ORIGIN Middle English: from Old French *e(s)meraud*, ultimately via Latin from Greek *(s)maragdos*, via Prakrit from Semitic (compare with Hebrew *bāreqet*, from *bāraq* 'flash, sparkle').

emerald-cut ▸ **adjective** (of a gem) cut in a square shape with stepped facets.

Emerald Isle a name for Ireland.

emerge /ɪ'məːdʒ/ ▸ **verb** [no obj.] **1** move out of or away from something and become visible: *black ravens emerged from the fog.* ■ (of an insect or other invertebrate) break out from an egg, cocoon, or pupal case.
2 become apparent or prominent: *United have emerged as the bookies' clear favourite* | (as adj. **emerging**) *established and emerging artists.* ■ (of facts) become known: *reports of a deadlock emerged during preliminary discussions* | [with clause] *it **emerged that** the PM and the Chancellor are still at loggerheads.*
3 recover from or survive a difficult situation: *the economy has started to **emerge from** recession.*
– ORIGIN late 16th cent. (in the sense 'become known, come to light'): from Latin *emergere*, from *e-* (variant of *ex-*) 'out, forth' + *mergere* 'to dip'.

emergence ▸ **noun** [mass noun] **1** the process of becoming visible after being concealed: *I misjudged the timing of my emergence.* ■ the escape of an insect or other invertebrate from an egg, cocoon, or pupal case.
2 the process of coming into existence or prominence: *the emergence of the environmental movement.*
– ORIGIN mid 17th cent. (in the sense 'unforeseen occurrence'): from medieval Latin *emergentia*, from Latin *emergere* 'bring to light' (see **EMERGE**).

emergency ▸ **noun** (pl. **emergencies**) **1** a serious, unexpected, and often dangerous situation requiring immediate action: *personal alarms for use in an emergency* | [mass noun] *survival packs were carried in case of emergency.* ■ [as modifier] arising from or used in an emergency: *an emergency exit.* ■ a person with a medical condition requiring immediate treatment. ■ N. Amer. the department in a hospital which provides immediate treatment: *a doctor in emergency cleaned the wound.*
2 (**the Emergency**) Irish historical the Second World War.
3 Austral./NZ a reserve runner in horse racing.
– ORIGIN mid 17th cent.: from medieval Latin *emergentia*, from Latin *emergere* 'arise, bring to light' (see **EMERGE**).

emergency cord ▸ **noun** a cord or chain on a train which a passenger may pull in an emergency, causing the train to brake.

emergency room ▸ **noun** N. Amer. the casualty department of a hospital.

emergency services ▸ **plural noun** Brit. the public organizations that respond to and deal with emergencies when they occur, especially the ambulance service, the police, and the fire brigade.

emergent ▸ **adjective 1** in the process of coming into being or becoming prominent: *the emergent democracies of eastern Europe.* ■ Philosophy (of a property) arising as an effect of complex causes and not analysable simply as the sum of their effects.
2 Ecology of or denoting a plant which is taller than the surrounding vegetation, especially a tall tree in a forest. ■ of or denoting a water plant with leaves and flowers that appear above the water surface.
▸ **noun 1** Philosophy an emergent property.
2 Ecology an emergent tree or other plant.
– ORIGIN late Middle English (in the sense 'occurring unexpectedly'): from Latin *emergent-* 'arising from', from the verb *emergere* (see **EMERGE**).

emeritus /ɪ'mɛrɪtəs, iː-/ ▸ **adjective** (of the former holder of an office, especially a university professor) having retired but allowed to retain their title as an honour: *emeritus professor of microbiology* | [postpositive] *the National Gallery's director emeritus.*
– ORIGIN mid 18th cent.: from Latin, past participle of *emereri* 'earn one's discharge by service', from *e-* (variant of *ex-*) 'out of, from' + *mereri* 'earn'.

emerse /ɪ'məːs/ ▸ **adjective** Botany denoting or characteristic of an aquatic plant reaching above the surface of the water. Contrasted with **SUBMERSE**.
– DERIVATIVES **emersed adjective**.
– ORIGIN late 17th cent. (as *emersed*): from Latin *emersus* 'arisen', past participle of *emergere* (see **EMERGE**).

emersion ▸ **noun** [mass noun] **1** the process of emerging from water after being submerged.
2 Astronomy the reappearance of a celestial body after its eclipse or occultation.
– ORIGIN mid 17th cent.: from late Latin *emersio(n-)*, from Latin *emergere* (see **EMERGE**).

Emerson /'ɛməs(ə)n/, Ralph Waldo (1803–82), American philosopher and poet. He evolved the concept of Transcendentalism, which found expression in his essay *Nature* (1836).

emery /'ɛm(ə)ri/ ▸ **noun** [mass noun] a greyish-black form of corundum containing iron oxide or other impurities, used in powdered form as an abrasive. ■ [as modifier] denoting materials coated with emery for polishing, smoothing, or grinding: *emery paper.*
– ORIGIN late 15th cent.: from French *émeri*, from Old French *esmeri*, from Italian *smeriglio*, based on Greek *smuris*, *smiris* 'polishing powder'.

emery board ▸ **noun** a strip of thin wood or card coated with emery or another abrasive and used as a nail file.

Emesa /'ɛməsə/ a city in ancient Syria, on the River Orontes on the site of present-day Homs. It was famous for its temple to the sun god Elah-Gabal.

emesis /'ɛmɪsɪs/ ▸ **noun** [mass noun] technical the action or process of vomiting.
– ORIGIN late 19th cent.: from Greek, from *emein* 'to vomit'.

emetic /ɪ'mɛtɪk/ ▸ **adjective** (of a substance) causing vomiting.
▸ **noun** a medicine or other substance which causes vomiting.
– ORIGIN mid 17th cent.: from Greek *emetikos*, from *emein* 'to vomit'.

emetine /'ɛmɪtiːn/ ▸ **noun** [mass noun] an alkaloid present in ipecacuanha and formerly used in the treatment of amoebic infections and as an emetic in aversion therapy.
– ORIGIN early 19th cent.: from Greek *emetos* 'vomiting' + **-INE**[4].

EMF ▸ **abbreviation** ■ electromagnetic field(s). ■ (**emf**) electromotive force. ■ European Monetary Fund.

EMG ▸ **abbreviation** electromyogram or electromyography.

-emia ▸ **combining form** US spelling of **-AEMIA**.

emic /'iːmɪk/ ▸ **adjective** Anthropology studying or describing a particular language or culture in terms of its internal elements and their functioning rather than in terms of any existing external scheme. Often contrasted with **ETIC**.
– ORIGIN 1950s: abstracted from such words as *phonemic* (see **PHONEME**) and **SYSTEMIC**.

emigrant ▸ **noun** a person who leaves their own country in order to settle permanently in another.
– ORIGIN mid 18th cent.: from Latin *emigrant-* 'migrating from', from the verb *emigrare* (see **EMIGRATE**).

emigrate /'ɛmɪgreɪt/ ▸ **verb** [no obj.] leave one's own country in order to settle permanently in another: *Rose's parents **emigrated to** Australia.*
– ORIGIN late 18th cent.: from Latin *emigrat-* 'emigrated', from the verb *emigrare*, from *e-* (variant of *ex-*) 'out of' + *migrare* 'migrate'.

emigration /,ɛmɪ'greɪʃn/ ▸ **noun** [mass noun] the act of leaving one's own country to settle permanently in another; moving abroad: *mass emigration from Ireland to the United States.*

émigré /'ɛmɪgreɪ/ ▸ **noun** a person who has left their own country in order to settle in another, typically for political reasons.
– ORIGIN late 18th cent. (originally denoting a person escaping the French Revolution): French, past participle of *émigrer* 'emigrate'.

Emi Koussi /,eɪmi 'kuːsi/ a volcanic mountain in the Sahara, in northern Chad, the highest peak in the Tibesti Mountains.

Emilia-Romagna /ɛ,miːljərəʊ'mɑːnjə/, Italian /e'milia rɔ'maɲɲa/ a region of northern Italy; capital, Bologna.

eminence /'ɛmɪnəns/ ▸ **noun 1** [mass noun] fame or acknowledged superiority within a particular sphere: *her eminence in cinematography.*
2 [count noun] an important or distinguished person: *the Lord Chancellor canvassed the views of various legal eminences.* ■ (**His/Your Eminence**) a title or form of address given to a Roman Catholic cardinal: *His Eminence, Cardinal Thomas Wolsey.*
3 formal or literary a piece of rising ground: *an eminence commanding the River Emme.* ■ Anatomy a slight projection from the surface of the body.
– ORIGIN Middle English: from Latin *eminentia*, from *eminere* 'jut, project'.

éminence grise /,ɛmɪnɒs 'griːz/ ▸ **noun** (pl. **éminences grises** pronunc. **same**) a person who exercises power or influence in a certain sphere without holding an official position.
– ORIGIN 1930s: French, literally 'grey eminence'. The term was originally applied to Cardinal Richelieu's grey-cloaked private secretary, Père Joseph (1577–1638).

eminent ▸ **adjective 1** (of a person) famous and respected within a particular sphere: *one of the world's most eminent statisticians.*

2 [attrib.] (of a positive quality) present to a notable degree: *the book's scholarship and eminent readability.*
– ORIGIN late Middle English: from Latin *eminent-* 'jutting, projecting', from the verb *eminere.*

eminent domain ▶ **noun** [mass noun] Law the right of a government or its agent to expropriate private property for public use, with payment of compensation. In the UK it is used chiefly of international law, whereas in the US it is used of federal and state governments.

eminently ▶ **adverb** [often as submodifier] to a notable degree; very: *an eminently readable textbook.*

emir /ɛˈmɪːə/ (also **amir**) ▶ **noun** a title of various Muslim (mainly Arab) rulers: *HRH the Emir of Kuwait.* ■ historical a Muslim (usually Arab) military commander or local chief.
– ORIGIN late 16th cent. (denoting a male descendant of Muhammad): from French *émir*, from Arabic *'amīr* (see **AMIR**).

emirate /ˈɛmɪrət/ ▶ **noun** the rank, lands, or reign of an emir.

emissary /ˈɛmɪs(ə)ri/ ▶ **noun** (pl. **emissaries**) a person sent as a diplomatic representative on a special mission.
– ORIGIN early 17th cent.: from Latin *emissarius* 'scout, spy', from *emittere* 'send out' (see **EMIT**).

emission /ɪˈmɪʃ(ə)n/ ▶ **noun** [mass noun] the production and discharge of something, especially gas or radiation: *the effects of lead emission on health* | [count noun] *cuts in carbon dioxide emissions.* ■ [count noun] an ejaculation of semen.
– ORIGIN late Middle English (in the sense 'emanation'): from Latin *emissio(n-)*, from *emiss-* 'sent out', from the verb *emittere* (see **EMIT**).

emission nebula ▶ **noun** Astronomy a nebula that shines with its own light.

emission spectrum ▶ **noun** a spectrum of the electromagnetic radiation emitted by a source. Compare with **ABSORPTION SPECTRUM**.

emissions trading ▶ **noun** [mass noun] a system by which countries and organizations receive permits to produce a specified amount of carbon dioxide and other greenhouse gases, which they may trade with others.

emissive ▶ **adjective** technical having the power to radiate something, especially light, heat, or radiation.
– DERIVATIVES **emissivity** noun.
– ORIGIN mid 17th cent. (in the sense 'that is emitted'): from Latin *emiss-* 'emitted, sent out' (from the verb *emittere*) + **-IVE**.

emit ▶ **verb** (**emits, emitting, emitted**) [with obj.] produce and discharge (something, especially gas or radiation): *even the best cars emit carbon dioxide.* ■ make (a sound): *she emitted a sound like laughter.*
– ORIGIN early 17th cent.: from Latin *emittere*, from *e-* (variant of *ex-*) 'out of' + *mittere* 'send'.

emitter ▶ **noun** a thing which emits something. ■ Electronics the region in a bipolar transistor that produces carriers of current.

Emmanuel /ɪˈmanjʊəl/ (also **Immanuel**) the name given to Christ as the deliverer of Judah prophesied by Isaiah (Isa. 7:14, 8:8; Matt. 1:23).

emmenagogue /ɪˈmiːnəgɒg, ɛ-/ ▶ **noun** Medicine a substance that stimulates or increases menstrual flow.
– ORIGIN early 18th cent.: from Greek *emmēna* 'menses' + *agōgos* 'eliciting'.

Emmental /ˈɛməntaːl/ (also **Emmenthal**) ▶ **noun** [mass noun] a kind of hard Swiss cheese with many holes in it, similar to Gruyère.
– ORIGIN from German *Emmentaler*, from *Emmental*, the name of a valley in Switzerland where the cheese was originally made.

emmer /ˈɛmə/ ▶ **noun** [mass noun] a long-established species of wheat with bearded ears and spikelets that each contain two grains, now grown mainly for fodder and breakfast cereals. Compare with **EINKORN**, **SPELT²**. ● *Triticum dicoccum*, family Gramineae.
– ORIGIN early 20th cent.: from German, from Old High German *amer* 'spelt'.

emmet /ˈɛmɪt/ ▶ **noun** dialect an ant.
– ORIGIN Old English *ǣmete* (see **ANT**).

Emmy ▶ **noun** (pl. **Emmys**) (in the US) a statuette awarded annually to an outstanding television programme or performer.
– ORIGIN 1940s: said to be from *Immy*, short for *image orthicon tube* (a kind of television camera tube).

emo /ˈiːməʊ/ (also **emocore** /ˈiːməʊkɔː/) ▶ **noun** [mass noun] a style of rock music resembling punk but having more complex arrangements and lyrics that deal with more emotional subjects.
– ORIGIN 1990s: short for *emotional hardcore.*

emollient /ɪˈmɒlɪənt/ ▶ **adjective** **1** having the quality of softening or soothing the skin.
2 attempting to avoid confrontation or anger; calming or conciliatory: *the president's emollient approach to differences.*
▶ **noun** a preparation that softens the skin.
– DERIVATIVES **emollience** noun.
– ORIGIN mid 17th cent.: from Latin *emollient-* 'making soft', from the verb *emollire*, from *e-* (variant of *ex-* 'out') + *mollis* 'soft'.

emolument /ɪˈmɒljʊm(ə)nt, ɛ-/ ▶ **noun** (usu. **emoluments**) formal a salary, fee, or profit from employment or office: *the directors' emoluments.*
– ORIGIN late Middle English: from Latin *emolumentum*, originally probably 'payment to a miller for grinding corn', from *emolere* 'grind up', from *e-* (variant of *ex-*) 'out, thoroughly' + *molere* 'grind'.

Emona /ɪˈməʊnə/ Roman name for **LJUBLJANA**.

emote /ɪˈməʊt/ ▶ **verb** [no obj.] (especially of an actor) portray emotion in a theatrical manner.
– DERIVATIVES **emoter** noun.
– ORIGIN early 20th cent. (originally US): back-formation from **EMOTION**.

emoticon /ɪˈməʊtɪkɒn, -ˈmɒtɪ-/ ▶ **noun** a representation of a facial expression such as a smile or frown, formed by various combinations of keyboard characters and used in electronic communications to convey the writer's feelings or intended tone.
– ORIGIN 1990s: blend of **EMOTION** and **ICON**.

emotion ▶ **noun** a strong feeling deriving from one's circumstances, mood, or relationships with others: *she was attempting to control her emotions* | [mass noun] *his voice was shaky with emotion.* ■ [mass noun] instinctive or intuitive feeling as distinguished from reasoning or knowledge: *responses have to be based on historical insight, not simply on emotion.*
– ORIGIN mid 16th cent. (denoting a public disturbance): from French *émotion*, from *émouvoir* 'excite', based on Latin *emovere*, from *e-* (variant of *ex-*) 'out' + *movere* 'move'. The current sense dates from the early 19th cent.

emotional ▶ **adjective** relating to a person's emotions: *gaining emotional support from relatives.* ■ arousing or characterized by intense feeling: *an emotional speech.* ■ (of a person) having feelings that are easily excited and openly displayed: *he was a strongly emotional young man.*
– DERIVATIVES **emotionalism** noun, **emotionalist** noun & adjective, **emotionality** noun, **emotionalize** (also **emotionalise**) verb, **emotionally** adverb.

emotionless ▶ **adjective** not showing any emotion; unemotional: *her voice was flat and emotionless.*

emotive ▶ **adjective** arousing or able to arouse intense feeling: *animal experimentation is an emotive subject* | *the issue has proved highly emotive.* ■ expressing a person's feelings rather than being neutrally descriptive: *the comparisons are emotive rather than analytic.*
– DERIVATIVES **emotively** adverb, **emotiveness** noun, **emotivity** /ˌiːməʊˈtɪvɪti/ noun.
– ORIGIN mid 18th cent.: from Latin *emot-* 'moved', from the verb *emovere* (see **EMOTION**).

> **USAGE** The words **emotive** and **emotional** share similarities but are not simply interchangeable. **Emotive** is used to mean 'arousing intense feeling', while **emotional** tends to mean 'characterized by intense feeling'. Thus an ***emotive issue*** is one which is likely to arouse people's passions, while an ***emotional response*** is one which is itself full of passion. In sentences such as *we took our* ***emotive*** *farewells* the word **emotive** has been used in a context where **emotional** would be more appropriate.

emotivism ▶ **noun** [mass noun] Philosophy an ethical theory which regards ethical and value judgements as expressions of feeling or attitude and prescriptions of action, rather than assertions or reports of anything.
– DERIVATIVES **emotivist** noun.

empanada /ˌɛmpəˈnɑːdə/ ▶ **noun** a Spanish or Latin American pastry turnover filled with a variety of savoury ingredients and baked or fried.
– ORIGIN Spanish, feminine past participle (used as a noun) of *empanar* 'roll in pastry', based on Latin *panis* 'bread'.

empanel ▶ **verb** variant spelling of **IMPANEL**.
– DERIVATIVES **empanelment** noun.

empath /ˈɛmpaθ/ ▶ **noun** (chiefly in science fiction) a person with the paranormal ability to perceive the mental or emotional state of another individual.

empathize (also **empathise**) ▶ **verb** [no obj.] understand and share the feelings of another: *counsellors need to be able to* ***empathize with*** *people.*

empathy /ˈɛmpəθi/ ▶ **noun** [mass noun] the ability to understand and share the feelings of another.
– DERIVATIVES **empathetic** adjective, **empathetically** adverb, **empathic** /ɛmˈpaθɪk/ adjective, **empathically** adverb.
– ORIGIN early 20th cent.: from Greek *empatheia* (from *em-* 'in' + *pathos* 'feeling') translating German *Einfühlung.*

> **USAGE** People often confuse the words **empathy** and **sympathy**. **Empathy** means 'the ability to understand and share the feelings of another' (as in *both authors have the skill to make you feel empathy with their heroines*), whereas **sympathy** means 'feelings of pity and sorrow for someone else's misfortune' (as in *they had great sympathy for the flood victims*).

Empedocles /ɛmˈpɛdəkliːz/ (*c.*493–*c.*433 BC), Greek philosopher, born in Sicily. He taught that the universe is composed of fire, air, water, and earth, which mingle and separate under the influence of the opposing principles of Love and Strife. According to legend he leapt into the crater of Mount Etna in order that he might be thought a god.

empennage /ɛmˈpɛnɪdʒ/ ▶ **noun** Aeronautics an arrangement of stabilizing surfaces at the tail of an aircraft.
– ORIGIN early 20th cent.: from French, from *empenner* 'to feather an arrow', from *em-* 'in' + *penne* 'a feather' (from Latin *penna*).

emperor ▶ **noun** **1** a sovereign ruler of an empire.
2 an orange and brown North American butterfly with a swift dodging flight, breeding chiefly on hackberries. ● Genus *Asterocampa*, subfamily Apaturinae, family Nymphalidae: several species, in particular the **tawny emperor** (*A. clyton*). See also **PURPLE EMPEROR**.
– DERIVATIVES **emperorship** noun.
– ORIGIN Middle English (especially representing the title given to the head of the Roman Empire): from Old French *emperere*, from Latin *imperator* 'military commander', from *imperare* 'to command', from *in-* 'towards' + *parare* 'prepare, contrive'.

emperor moth ▶ **noun** a large moth of the silk moth family with eyespots on all four wings. ● *Saturnia* and other genera, family Saturniidae: several species, in particular the common European *S. pavonia*.

emperor penguin ▶ **noun** the largest penguin, which has a yellow patch on each side of the head and rears its young during the Antarctic winter. ● *Aptenodytes forsteri*, family Spheniscidae.

emphasis /ˈɛmfəsɪs/ ▶ **noun** (pl. **emphases** /-siːz/) [mass noun] **1** special importance, value, or prominence given to something: *they placed great emphasis on the individual's freedom* | [count noun] *different emphases and viewpoints.*
2 stress given to a word or words when speaking to indicate particular importance. ■ vigour or intensity of expression: *he spoke with emphasis and with complete conviction.*
– ORIGIN late 16th cent.: via Latin from Greek, originally 'appearance, show', later denoting a figure of speech in which more is implied than is said (the original sense in English), from *emphainein* 'exhibit', from *em-* 'in, within' + *phainein* 'to show'.

emphasize (also **emphasise**) ▶ **verb** [with obj.] **1** give special importance or value to (something) in speaking or writing: *they emphasize the need for daily, one-to-one contact between parent and child* | [with clause] *I would* ***emphasize that*** *I am not an economist.*
2 lay stress on (a word or phrase) when speaking.
3 make (something) more clearly defined: *a hip-length jacket which emphasized her shape.*

emphatic ▶ **adjective** **1** expressing something forcibly and clearly: *the children were* ***emphatic that*** *they would like to repeat the experience* | *an emphatic movement of his hand.* ■ (of an action or its result) definite and clear: *an emphatic World Cup win.*
2 (of a word or syllable) bearing the stress. ■ Linguistics (of certain Arabic consonants) pronounced with both dental articulation and constriction of the pharynx.
▶ **noun** Linguistics an emphatic consonant.
– ORIGIN early 18th cent.: via late Latin from Greek *emphatikos*, from *emphasis* (see **EMPHASIS**).

emphatically ▶ **adverb** in a forceful way. ■ [as submodifier] without doubt; clearly: *Jane, though born in California, feels emphatically English* | [sentence adverb] *Greg is emphatically not a slacker.*

emphysema /ˌɛmfɪˈsiːmə/ ▸ **noun** [mass noun] Medicine **1** (also **pulmonary emphysema**) a condition in which the air sacs of the lungs are damaged and enlarged, causing breathlessness.
2 a condition in which air is abnormally present within the body tissues.
– ORIGIN mid 17th cent. (in sense 2): via late Latin from Greek *emphusēma*, from *emphusan* 'puff up'.

empire ▸ **noun 1** an extensive group of states or countries ruled over by a single monarch, an oligarchy, or a sovereign state: [in names] *the Roman Empire.* ■ [mass noun] supreme political power over several countries when exercised by a single authority: *he encouraged the Greeks in their dream of empire in Asia Minor.*
2 an extensive sphere of activity controlled by one person or group: *the kitchen had once been the school dinner ladies' empire.* ■ a large commercial organization owned or controlled by one person or group: *her business empire grew.*
▸ **adjective** (**Empire**) [attrib.] **1** denoting a style of furniture, decoration, or dress fashionable chiefly during the First Empire in France. The decorative style was neoclassical but marked by an interest in Egyptian and other ancient motifs.
2 Brit. dated denoting produce from the Commonwealth.
– ORIGIN Middle English: via Old French from Latin *imperium*, related to *imperare* 'to command' (see **EMPEROR**).

empire-building ▸ **noun** [mass noun] the practice of obtaining more power, responsibility, or staff within an organization for the purposes of self-aggrandizement.
– DERIVATIVES **empire builder** noun.

Empire Day ▸ **noun** former name of **COMMONWEALTH DAY**.

empire line ▸ **noun** [usu. as modifier] a style of women's clothing characterized by a waistline cut just under the bust and typically a low neckline, first popular during the First Empire: *empire-line dresses.*

Empire State informal name for the state of **NEW YORK**.

Empire State Building a skyscraper on Fifth Avenue, New York City, which was for several years the tallest building in the world. When first erected in 1931 it measured 381 m (1,250 ft); the addition of a television mast in 1951 brought its height to 449 m (1,472 ft).

Empire State of the South informal name for the US state of **GEORGIA**.

empiric /ɛmˈpɪrɪk, ɪm-/ ▸ **adjective** another term for **EMPIRICAL**.
▸ **noun** archaic a person who, in medicine or other sciences, relies solely on observation and experiment. ■ a quack doctor.
– ORIGIN late Middle English: via Latin from Greek *empeirikos*, from *empeiria* 'experience', from *empeiros* 'skilled' (based on *peira* 'trial, experiment').

empirical ▸ **adjective** based on, concerned with, or verifiable by observation or experience rather than theory or pure logic: *they provided considerable empirical evidence to support their argument.*
– DERIVATIVES **empirically** adverb.

empirical formula ▸ **noun** Chemistry a formula giving the proportions of the elements present in a compound but not the actual numbers or arrangement of atoms.

empiricism /ɛmˈpɪrɪsɪz(ə)m/ ▸ **noun** [mass noun] Philosophy the theory that all knowledge is based on experience derived from the senses. Stimulated by the rise of experimental science, it developed in the 17th and 18th centuries, expounded in particular by John Locke, George Berkeley, and David Hume. Compare with **PHENOMENALISM**.
– DERIVATIVES **empiricist** noun & adjective.

emplacement ▸ **noun 1** a structure on or in which something is firmly placed. ■ a platform or defended position where a gun is placed for firing.
2 [mass noun] chiefly Geology the process or state of setting something in place or being set in place.
– DERIVATIVES **emplace** verb.
– ORIGIN early 19th cent.: from French, from *em-* 'in' + *place* 'a place'.

emplane (also **enplane**) ▸ **verb** go or put on board an aircraft.

employ ▸ **verb** [with obj.] **1** give work to (someone) and pay them for it: *the firm employs 150 people* | [with obj. and infinitive] *temporary staff can be employed to undertake the work* | (as adj. **employed**) *83 percent of employed people were working in full-time jobs.* ■ keep occupied: *the newcomers are employed in developing the technology into a product.*
2 make use of: *the methods they have employed to collect the data.*
▸ **noun** [in sing.] the state of being employed for wages or a salary. *I started work* ***in the employ of*** *a grocer.* ■ archaic employment: *her place of employ.*
– DERIVATIVES **employability** noun, **employable** adjective.
– ORIGIN late Middle English (formerly also as *imploy*): from Old French *employer*, based on Latin *implicari* 'be involved in or attached to', passive form of *implicare* (see **IMPLY**). In the 16th and 17th cent. the word also had the senses 'enfold, entangle' and 'imply', derived directly from Latin; compare with **IMPLICATE**.

employee ▸ **noun** a person employed for wages or salary, especially at non-executive level.

employer ▸ **noun** a person or organization that employs people.

employment ▸ **noun** [mass noun] **1** the state of having paid work: *a fall in the numbers* ***in full-time employment.*** ■ the action of giving work to someone. ■ [count noun] a person's trade or profession.
2 the utilization of something: *economies can be made by the full employment of existing facilities.*

employment agency ▸ **noun** a business that finds employers or employees for those seeking them.

employment office ▸ **noun** (in the UK) a government employment agency.

emporium /ɛmˈpɔːrɪəm, ɪm-/ ▸ **noun** (pl. **emporia** /-rɪə/ or **emporiums**) a large retail store selling a wide variety of goods. ■ archaic a centre of commerce; a market.
– ORIGIN late 16th cent.: from Latin, from Greek *emporion*, from *emporos* 'merchant', based on a stem meaning 'to journey'.

empower ▸ **verb** [with obj. and infinitive] give (someone) the authority or power to do something: *members are empowered to audit the accounts of limited companies.* ■ [with obj.] make (someone) stronger and more confident, especially in controlling their life and claiming their rights: *movements to empower the poor.*
– DERIVATIVES **empowerment** noun.

empress /ˈɛmprɪs/ ▸ **noun** a female emperor. ■ the wife or widow of an emperor.
– ORIGIN Middle English: from Old French *emperesse*, feminine of *emperere* (see **EMPEROR**).

empressement /ɒˈprɛsmɒ̃/ ▸ **noun** [mass noun] archaic animated eagerness or friendliness; effusion.
– ORIGIN from French, from *empresser* 'rush eagerly'.

Empson /ˈɛmps(ə)n/, Sir William (1906–84), English poet and literary critic. His influential literary criticism includes *Seven Types of Ambiguity* (1930).

emptiness ▸ **noun** [mass noun] **1** the state of containing nothing: *the vast emptiness of space.*
2 the quality of lacking meaning or sincerity; meaninglessness: *he realizes the emptiness of his statement.*
3 the quality of having no value or purpose; futility: *feelings of emptiness and loneliness.*

empty ▸ **adjective** (**emptier**, **emptiest**) **1** containing nothing; not filled or occupied: *she put down her empty cup* | *the room was* ***empty of*** *furniture.* ■ Mathematics (of a set) containing no members or elements.
2 (of words or a gesture) lacking meaning or sincerity.
3 having no value or purpose: *her life felt empty and meaningless.*
▸ **verb** (**empties**, **emptying**, **emptied**) [with obj.] remove all the contents of (a container): *we empty the till at closing time* | *pockets were* ***emptied of*** *loose change.* ■ remove (the contents) from a container: *he* ***emptied out*** *the contents of his briefcase.* ■ [no obj.] (of a place) be vacated by people in it: *the pub suddenly seemed to empty.* ■ [no obj.] (**empty into**) (of a river) flow into (the sea or a lake).
▸ **noun** (pl. **empties**) informal a bottle or glass left empty of its contents.
– PHRASES **be running on empty** have exhausted all of one's resources. **empty vessels make most noise** (or **sound**) proverb those with least wisdom or knowledge are always the most talkative. **on an empty stomach** see **STOMACH**.
– DERIVATIVES **emptily** adverb.
– ORIGIN Old English *ǣmtig*, *ǣmetig* 'at leisure, empty', from *ǣmetta* 'leisure', perhaps from *ā* 'no, not' + *mōt* 'meeting' (see **MOOT**).

empty calories ▸ **plural noun** calories derived from food containing no nutrients.

empty-handed ▸ **adjective** [predic.] having failed to obtain or achieve what one wanted: *the burglars fled empty-handed.*

empty-headed ▸ **adjective** unintelligent and foolish: *an empty-headed bimbo.*

empty nester ▸ **noun** informal, chiefly N. Amer. a parent whose children have grown up and left home.

Empty Quarter another name for **RUB' AL-KHALI**.

empty suit ▸ **noun** chiefly US an important or wealthy man regarded as lacking substance, personality, or ability: *they're a bunch of Ivy League empty suits.*

empurple ▸ **verb** make or become purple: [no obj.] *his face empurpled with fury.*

empyema /ˌɛmpʌɪˈiːmə/ ▸ **noun** Medicine the collection of pus in a cavity in the body, especially in the pleural cavity.
– ORIGIN late Middle English: via late Latin from Greek *empuēma*, from *empuein* 'suppurate', from *em-* 'in' + *puon* 'pus'.

empyrean /ˌɛmpʌɪˈriːən, -pɪ-, ɛmˈpɪrɪən/ ▸ **adjective** of or relating to heaven.
▸ **noun** (**the empyrean**) the highest part of heaven, thought by the ancients to be the realm of pure fire. ■ literary the visible heavens; the sky.
– DERIVATIVES **empyreal** /ˌɛmpʌɪˈriːəl, -pɪ-, ɛmˈpɪrɪəl/ adjective.
– ORIGIN late Middle English (as an adjective): via medieval Latin from Greek *empurios*, from *en-* 'in' + *pur* 'fire'. The noun dates from the mid 17th cent.

em rule /ˈɛm ruːl/ ▸ **noun** Brit. a long dash used in punctuation.

EMS ▸ **abbreviation** European Monetary System.

EMU ▸ **abbreviation** Economic and Monetary Union (or European Monetary Union).

emu[1] ▸ **noun** a large flightless fast-running Australian bird resembling the ostrich, with shaggy grey or brown plumage, bare blue skin on the head and neck, and three-toed feet. ● *Dromaius novaehollandiae*, the only member of the family Dromaiidae.
– ORIGIN early 17th cent.: from Portuguese *ema*. The word originally denoted the cassowary, later the greater rhea; current usage dates from the early 19th cent.

emu[2] ▸ **abbreviation** Brit. ■ electric multiple unit. ■ electromagnetic unit(s).

emu bush ▸ **noun** an Australian shrub that typically has reddish flowers and small oval fruits which are sometimes eaten by emus. ● Genus *Eremophila*, family Myoporaceae: several species.

emulate /ˈɛmjʊleɪt/ ▸ **verb** [with obj.] match or surpass (a person or achievement), typically by imitation: *most rulers wished to emulate Alexander the Great.* ■ imitate: *hers is not a hairstyle I wish to emulate.* ■ Computing reproduce the function or action of (a different computer, software system, etc.).
– DERIVATIVES **emulation** noun, **emulative** adjective, **emulator** noun.
– ORIGIN late 16th cent.: from Latin *aemulat-* 'rivalled, equalled', from the verb *aemulari*, from *aemulus* 'rival'.

emulous /ˈɛmjʊləs/ ▸ **adjective** formal seeking to emulate someone or something. ■ motivated by a spirit of rivalry: *emulous young writers.*
ORIGIN late Middle English (in the sense 'imitating'): from Latin *aemulus* 'rival'. Current senses date from the mid 16th cent.

emulsifier ▸ **noun 1** a substance that stabilizes an emulsion, in particular an additive used to stabilize processed foods.
2 an apparatus used for making an emulsion by stirring or shaking a substance.

emulsify /ɪˈmʌlsɪfʌɪ/ ▸ **verb** (**emulsifies**, **emulsifying**, **emulsified**) make into or become an emulsion: [with obj.] *mustard helps to emulsify a vinaigrette.*
– DERIVATIVES **emulsifiable** adjective, **emulsification** noun.

emulsion /ɪˈmʌlʃ(ə)n/ ▸ **noun 1** a fine dispersion of minute droplets of one liquid in another in which it is not soluble or miscible. ■ a fine dispersion of one liquid or puréed food substance in another: *ravioli with pea and ginger emulsion.*
2 (also **emulsion paint**) [mass noun] Brit. a type of paint used for walls, consisting of pigment bound in a synthetic resin which forms an emulsion with water. ■ a light-sensitive coating for photographic films and plates, containing crystals of a silver compound dispersed in a medium such as gelatin.
▸ **verb** [with obj.] Brit. informal paint with emulsion.
– DERIVATIVES **emulsive** adjective.

E

– ORIGIN early 17th cent. (denoting a milky liquid made by crushing almonds in water): from modern Latin *emulsio(n-)*, from the verb *emulgere* 'milk out', from *e-* (variant of *ex-*) 'out' + *mulgere* 'to milk'.

emu-wren ▶ **noun** a small Australian songbird of the fairy wren family, with a very long thin cocked tail consisting of only six feathers that have a coarse open structure resembling that of emu feathers.
● Genus *Stipiturus*, family Maluridae: three species.

en ▶ **noun** Printing a unit of measurement equal to half an em and approximately the average width of typeset characters, used especially for estimating the total amount of space a text will require.
– ORIGIN late 18th cent.: the letter *N* represented as a word, since it is approximately this width.

E

en-¹ (also **em-**) ▶ **prefix 1** (added to nouns) forming verbs meaning 'put into or on': *engulf* | *embed*.
2 (added to nouns and adjectives) forming verbs (often with the suffix *-en*) meaning 'bring into the condition of': *embolden* | *encrust*.
3 (added to verbs) in; into; on: *ensnare*. ■ as an intensifier: *entangle*.
– ORIGIN from French, from Latin *in-*. See also **IN-²**, a commonly found by-form.

en-² (also **em-**) ▶ **prefix** within; inside: *empathy* | *energy* | *enthusiasm*.
– ORIGIN from Greek.

-en¹ ▶ **suffix** forming verbs: **1** (from adjectives) denoting the development, creation, or intensification of a state: *widen* | *deepen*.
2 from nouns (such as *strengthen* from *strength*).
– ORIGIN Old English *-nian*, of Germanic origin.

-en² ▶ **suffix** (also **-n**) forming adjectives from nouns: **1** made or consisting of: *earthen* | *woollen*.
2 resembling: *golden*.
– ORIGIN Old English, of Germanic origin.

-en³ (also **-n**) ▶ **suffix** forming past participles of strong verbs: **1** as a regular inflection: *spoken*.
2 as an adjective: *mistaken* | *torn*.
– ORIGIN Old English, of Germanic origin.

-en⁴ ▶ **suffix** forming the plural of a few nouns such as *children*, *oxen*.
– ORIGIN Middle English reduction of the earlier suffix *-an*.

-en⁵ ▶ **suffix** forming diminutives of nouns (such as *chicken*, *maiden*).
– ORIGIN Old English, of Germanic origin.

-en⁶ ▶ **suffix 1** forming feminine nouns: *vixen*.
2 forming abstract nouns: *burden*.
– ORIGIN Old English, of Germanic origin.

enable ▶ **verb** [with obj.] **1** [with infinitive] give (someone) the authority or means to do something; make it possible for: *the evidence would enable us to arrive at firm conclusions*. ■ make (something) possible: *each of them has wheels to enable easy transportation*.
2 chiefly Computing make (a device or system) operational; activate. ■ (as adj., in combination **-enabled**) adapted for use with the specified application or system: *WAP-enabled mobile phones*.
– DERIVATIVES **enablement** noun, **enabler** noun.
– ORIGIN late Middle English (formerly also as *inable*): from **EN-¹**, **IN-²**, + **ABLE**.

enabling act ▶ **noun** a statute empowering a person or body to take certain action, especially to make regulations, rules, or orders.

enact ▶ **verb** [with obj.] **1** make (a bill or other proposal) law: *legislation was enacted to attract international companies*.
2 put into practice (an idea or suggestion).
3 act out (a role or play) on stage. ■ (**be enacted**) take place: *walkers stopped to watch, aware that some tragedy was being enacted*.
– DERIVATIVES **enactable** adjective, **enaction** noun, **enactive** adjective, **enactor** noun.
– ORIGIN late Middle English (formerly also as *inact*): from **EN-¹**, **IN-²**, + **ACT**, suggested by medieval Latin *inactare*, *inactitare*.

enactment ▶ **noun 1** [mass noun] the process of passing legislation. ■ [count noun] a law that is passed.
2 an instance of acting something out: *the story becomes an enactment of his fantasies*. ■ [mass noun] Psychoanalysis the controlled expression and acceptance of repressed emotions or impulses in behaviour during therapy.

enamel ▶ **noun** [mass noun] **1** an opaque or semi-transparent glossy substance that is a type of glass, applied by vitrification to metallic or other hard surfaces for ornament or as a protective coating. ■ [count noun] a work of art executed in enamel.
2 the hard glossy substance that covers the crown of a tooth.
3 (also **enamel paint**) a paint that dries to give a smooth, hard coat.
4 dated nail varnish.
▶ **verb** (**enamels**, **enamelling**, **enamelled**; US **enamels**, **enameling**, **enameled**) [with obj.] (often as adj. **enamelled**) coat or decorate (a metallic or hard object) with enamel: *an enamelled roasting tin*.
– DERIVATIVES **enameller** noun.
– ORIGIN late Middle English (originally as a verb; formerly also as *inamel*): from Anglo-Norman French *enamailler*, from *en-* 'in, on' + *amail* 'enamel', ultimately of Germanic origin.

enamelware ▶ **noun** [mass noun] enamelled kitchenware.

enamelwork ▶ **noun** [mass noun] the craft of inlaying or decorating metal objects with enamel.

enamour /ɪˈnamə, ɛ-/ (US **enamor**) ▶ **verb** (**be enamoured of/with/by**) be filled with love for: *it is not difficult to see why Edward is enamoured of her*. ■ have a liking or admiration for: *she was truly enamoured of New York*.
– ORIGIN Middle English (formerly also as *inamour*): from Old French *enamourer*, from *en-* 'in' + *amour* 'love'.

enanthema /ˌɛnanˈθiːmə/ ▶ **noun** Medicine an ulcer or eruption occurring on a mucus-secreting surface such as the inside of the mouth.
– ORIGIN mid 19th cent.: from **EN-²** 'within' + a shortened form of **EXANTHEMA**.

enantiodromia /ɪˌnantɪə(ʊ)ˈdrəʊmɪə, ɛ-/ ▶ **noun** [mass noun] rare the tendency of things to change into their opposites, especially as a supposed governing principle of natural cycles and of psychological development.
– ORIGIN early 20th cent.: from Greek, literally 'running in opposite ways'.

enantiomer /ɪˈnantɪə(ʊ)mə, ɛ-/ ▶ **noun** Chemistry each of a pair of molecules that are mirror images of each other.
– DERIVATIVES **enantiomeric** adjective, **enantiomerically** adverb.
– ORIGIN 1930s: from Greek *enantios* 'opposite' + **-MER**.

enantiomorph /ɪˈnantɪə(ʊ)mɔːf, ɛ-/ ▶ **noun** each of two crystalline or other geometrical forms which are mirror images of each other.
– DERIVATIVES **enantiomorphic** adjective, **enantiomorphism** noun, **enantiomorphous** adjective.
– ORIGIN late 19th cent.: from Greek *enantios* 'opposite' + **-MORPH**.

enargite /ˈɛnɑːɡʌɪt/ ▶ **noun** [mass noun] a dark grey mineral consisting of a sulphide of copper and arsenic.
– ORIGIN mid 19th cent.: from Greek *enargēs* 'clear' (referring to evident cleavage) + **-ITE¹**.

enarthrosis /ˌɛnɑːˈθrəʊsɪs/ ▶ **noun** (pl. **enarthroses** /-siːz/) Anatomy a ball-and-socket joint.
– ORIGIN late 16th cent.: from Greek *enarthrōsis*, from *enarthros* 'jointed', from *en-* 'inside' + *arthron* 'joint'.

enation /ɪˈneɪʃ(ə)n/ ▶ **noun** Botany an outgrowth from the surface of a leaf or other part of a plant.
– ORIGIN mid 19th cent.: from Latin *enatio(n-)*, from *enasci* 'issue forth'.

en bloc /ɒ̃ ˈblɒk/ ▶ **adverb** all together or all at the same time: *various private museums offered to purchase the trove en bloc*.
– ORIGIN mid 19th cent.: French.

en brosse /ɒ̃ ˈbrɒs/ ▶ **adjective** [postpositive] (of a person's hair) cut in a short and bristly style.
– ORIGIN French, 'in the form of a brush'.

enc. ▶ **abbreviation** ■ enclosed. ■ enclosure.

Encaenia /ɛnˈsiːnɪə/ ▶ **noun** an annual celebration at Oxford University in memory of founders and benefactors.
– ORIGIN late 17th cent.: via Latin from Greek *enkainia* 'dedication festival' (based on *kainos* 'new').

encage ▶ **verb** [with obj.] literary confine in or as in a cage.

encamp ▶ **verb** [no obj.] settle in or establish a camp: *we encamped for the night by a river*.

encampment ▶ **noun** a place with temporary accommodation consisting of huts or tents, typically for troops or nomads. ■ a prehistoric enclosed or fortified site, especially an Iron Age hill fort. ■ [mass noun] the action of setting up a camp.

encapsidate /ɪnˈkapsɪdeɪt, ɛn-/ ▶ **verb** [with obj.] Biochemistry enclose (a gene or virus particle) in a protein shell.
– DERIVATIVES **encapsidation** noun.
– ORIGIN late 20th cent.: from **EN-¹** + **CAPSID²** + **-ATE³**.

encapsulate /ɪnˈkapsjʊleɪt, ɛn-/ ▶ **verb** [with obj.] **1** enclose (something) in or as if in a capsule: *the company would encapsulate the asbestos waste in concrete pellets*. ■ Computing enclose (a message or signal) in a set of codes which allow transfer across networks. ■ Computing provide an interface for (a piece of software or hardware) to allow or simplify access for the user.
2 express the essential features of (something) succinctly: *the conclusion **is encapsulated in** one sentence*.
– DERIVATIVES **encapsulation** noun.
– ORIGIN late 19th cent. (also as *incapsulate*): from **EN-¹**, **IN-²** 'into' + Latin *capsula* (see **CAPSULE**).

encase (also **incase**) ▶ **verb** [with obj.] enclose or cover in a case or close-fitting surround: *each was encased in a plastic shrink-wrap*.
– DERIVATIVES **encasement** noun.

encash ▶ **verb** [with obj.] Brit. convert (a cheque, money order, bond, etc.) into money.
– DERIVATIVES **encashable** adjective, **encashment** noun.

encaustic /ɛnˈkɔːstɪk/ ▶ **adjective** (in painting and ceramics) decorated by burning in colours as an inlay, especially using coloured clays or pigments mixed with hot wax.
▶ **noun** [mass noun] the art or process of encaustic painting.
– ORIGIN late 16th cent.: via Latin from Greek *enkaustikos*, from *enkaiein* 'burn in', from *en-* 'in' + *kaiein* 'to burn'.

-ence ▶ **suffix** forming nouns: **1** denoting a quality or an instance of it: *impertinence*.
2 denoting an action or its result: *reference* | *reminiscence*.
– ORIGIN from French *-ence*, from Latin *-entia*, *-antia* (from present participial stems *-ent-*, *-ant-*). Since the 16th cent. many inconsistencies have occurred in the use of *-ence* and *-ance*.

enceinte¹ /ɒ̃ˈsãt/ ▶ **noun** archaic an enclosure or the enclosing wall of a fortified place.
– ORIGIN early 18th cent.: from French, from Latin *incincta*, feminine past participle of *incingere* 'gird in', from *in-* 'in' + *cingere* 'to gird'.

enceinte² /ɒ̃ˈsãt/ ▶ **adjective** archaic pregnant.
– ORIGIN early 17th cent.: from French.

Enceladus /ɛnˈsɛlədəs/ Astronomy a satellite of Saturn, the eighth closest to the planet and probably composed mainly of ice, discovered by W. Herschel in 1789 (diameter 500 km).
– ORIGIN named after a Greek mythological giant killed by Athene.

encephalic /ˌɛnsɪˈfalɪk, ɛnˈkɛf(ə)lɪk/ ▶ **adjective** Anatomy relating to, affecting, or situated in the brain.
– ORIGIN mid 19th cent.: from Greek *enkephalos* 'brain' (from *en-* 'in' + *kephalē* 'head') + **-IC**.

encephalin /ɛnˈsɛfəlɪn, -ˈkɛf-/ ▶ **noun** variant spelling of **ENKEPHALIN**.

encephalitis /ɛnˌsɛfəˈlʌɪtɪs, -ˌkɛfə-/ ▶ **noun** [mass noun] inflammation of the brain, caused by infection or an allergic reaction.
– DERIVATIVES **encephalitic** adjective.

encephalitis lethargica /lɪˈθɑːdʒɪkə/ ▶ **noun** [mass noun] a form of encephalitis caused by a virus and characterized by headache and drowsiness leading to coma. Also called **SLEEPY SICKNESS**.

encephalization (also **encephalisation**) ▶ **noun** [mass noun] Zoology an evolutionary increase in the complexity or relative size of the brain, involving a shift of function from non-cortical parts of the brain to the cortex.

encephalo- /ɛnˈsɛf(ə)ləʊ, -ˈkɛf-/ ▶ **combining form** relating to the brain: *encephalopathy*.
– ORIGIN from Greek *enkephalos*.

encephalogram /ɛnˈsɛf(ə)lə(ʊ)ɡram, -ˈkɛf-/ ▶ **noun** Medicine an image, trace, or other record of the structure or electrical activity of the brain.

encephalography /ɛnˌsɛfəˈlɒɡrəfi, -ˌkɛfə-/ ▶ **noun** [mass noun] Medicine any of various techniques for recording the structure or electrical activity of the brain.
– DERIVATIVES **encephalograph** noun, **encephalographic** adjective.

encephalomyelitis /ɛnˌsɛf(ə)ləʊmʌɪəˈlʌɪtɪs, -ˌkɛf-/ ▶ **noun** [mass noun] Medicine inflammation of the brain and spinal cord, typically due to acute viral infection.

encephalon /ɛnˈsɛfəlɒn, -ˈkɛf-/ ▶ **noun** Anatomy the brain.

– ORIGIN mid 18th cent.: from Greek *enkephalon* 'what is inside the head', from *en-* 'inside' + *kephalē* 'head'.

encephalopathy /ɛn,sɛfəˈlɒpəθi, -,kɛf-/ ▶ **noun** (pl. **encephalopathies**) Medicine a disease in which the functioning of the brain is affected by some agent or condition (such as viral infection or toxins in the blood).

enchain ▶ **verb** [with obj.] literary bind with or as with chains.
– DERIVATIVES **enchainment** noun.
– ORIGIN late Middle English: from Old French *enchainer*, based on Latin *catena* 'chain'.

enchaînement /õˈʃɛnmõ/ ▶ **noun** (pl. pronunc. **same**) Ballet a linked sequence of steps or movements constituting a phrase.
– ORIGIN mid 19th cent.: French, 'chaining together'.

enchant ▶ **verb** [with obj.] fill (someone) with great delight; charm: *Isabel was* ***enchanted with*** *the idea.* ■ (often as adj. **enchanted**) put (someone or something) under a spell: *an enchanted garden.*
– ORIGIN late Middle English (in the senses 'put under a spell' and 'delude'; formerly also as *inchant*): from French *enchanter*, from Latin *incantare*, from *in-* 'in' + *cantare* 'sing'.

enchanter ▶ **noun** a person who uses magic or sorcery, especially to put someone or something under a spell.

enchanter's nightshade ▶ **noun** a woodland plant with small white flowers and fruit with hooked bristles, native to Eurasia and the eastern US.
● *Circaea lutetiana*, family Onagraceae.
– ORIGIN late 16th cent.: believed by early botanists to be the herb used by Circe to charm Odysseus' companions.

enchanting ▶ **adjective** delightfully charming or attractive: *enchanting views | Dinah looked enchanting.*
– DERIVATIVES **enchantingly** adverb.

enchantment ▶ **noun** [mass noun] **1** a feeling of great pleasure; delight: *the enchantment of the mountains.*
2 the state of being under a spell; magic: *a world of mystery and enchantment.*

enchantress ▶ **noun** a woman who uses magic to put someone or something under a spell. ■ a woman who is captivatingly attractive.
– ORIGIN late Middle English: from Old French *enchanteresse*, from *enchanter* (see ENCHANT).

enchase /ɪnˈtʃeɪs, ɛn-/ ▶ **verb** [with obj.] decorate (a piece of jewellery or work of art) by inlaying, engraving, or carving.
– ORIGIN late Middle English: from Old French *enchasser* 'set gems, encase', from *en-* 'in' + *chasse* 'a case'.

enchilada /,ɛntʃɪˈlɑːdə/ ▶ **noun** a tortilla served with chilli sauce and a filling of meat or cheese.
– PHRASES **the big enchilada** N. Amer. informal a person or thing of great importance. **the whole enchilada** N. Amer. informal the whole situation; everything.
– ORIGIN Latin American Spanish, feminine past participle of *enchilar* 'season with chilli'.

enchiridion /,ɛnkʌɪˈrɪdɪən/ ▶ **noun** (pl. **enchiridions** or **enchiridia** /-dɪə/) formal a book containing essential information on a subject.
– ORIGIN late Middle English: via late Latin from Greek *enkheiridion*, from *en-* 'within' + *kheir* 'hand' + the diminutive suffix *-idion*.

encipher ▶ **verb** [with obj.] convert (a message or piece of text) into a coded form.
– DERIVATIVES **encipherment** noun.

encircle ▶ **verb** [with obj.] form a circle around; surround: *the town is encircled by fortified walls.*
– DERIVATIVES **encirclement** noun.

encl. (also **enc.**) ▶ **abbreviation** ■ enclosed. ■ enclosure.

en clair /õ ˈklɛː/ ▶ **adjective & adverb** (especially of a telegram or official message) in ordinary language, rather than in code or cipher.
– ORIGIN French, literally 'in clear'.

enclasp ▶ **verb** [with obj.] formal hold tightly in one's arms.

enclave /ˈɛnkleɪv/ ▶ **noun** a portion of territory surrounded by a larger territory whose inhabitants are culturally or ethnically distinct. ■ a place or group that is different in character from those surrounding it: *the engineering department is traditionally a male enclave.*
– ORIGIN mid 19th cent.: from French, from Old French *enclaver* 'enclose, dovetail', based on Latin *clavis* 'key'.

enclitic /ɪnˈklɪtɪk, ɛn-/ ▶ **noun** Linguistics a word pronounced with so little emphasis that it is shortened and forms part of the preceding word, for example *n't* in *can't*. Compare with PROCLITIC.
– ORIGIN mid 17th cent.: via late Latin from Greek *enklitikos*, from *enklinein* 'lean on', from *en-* 'in, on' + *klinein* 'to lean'.

enclose (also **inclose**) ▶ **verb** [with obj.] **1** surround or close off on all sides: *the entire estate was enclosed with walls* | (as adj. **enclosed**) *a dark enclosed space.* ■ historical fence in (common land) so as to make it private property. ■ (usu. as adj. **enclosed**) seclude (a religious order or other community) from the outside world.
2 place (something) in an envelope together with a letter.
3 (**enclose something in/within**) place an object inside (a container).
– ORIGIN Middle English (in the sense 'shut in, imprison'): from Old French *enclos*, past participle of *enclore*, based on Latin *includere* 'shut in'.

enclosure /ɪnˈkləʊʒə, ɛn-/ (also **inclosure**) ▶ **noun** **1** an area that is surrounded by a barrier: *a deer enclosure.* ■ Brit. a section of a racecourse for a specified activity or group of people: *the members' enclosure.* ■ a barrier that surrounds an area.
2 a document or object placed in an envelope together with a letter.
3 [mass noun] historical the process or policy of fencing in wasteland or common land so as to make it private property, as pursued in much of Britain in the 18th and early 19th centuries.
4 the state of being enclosed, especially in a religious community.
– ORIGIN late Middle English: from legal Anglo-Norman French and Old French, from *enclos* 'closed in' (see ENCLOSE).

encode ▶ **verb** [with obj.] convert into a coded form. ■ Computing convert (information or an instruction) into a particular form: *the amount of time required to encode a wav file to mp3 format.* ■ Biochemistry (of a gene) be responsible for producing (a substance or behaviour).
– DERIVATIVES **encoder** noun.

encomiast /ɛnˈkəʊmɪast/ ▶ **noun** formal a person who publicly praises or flatters someone else.
– DERIVATIVES **encomiastic** adjective.
– ORIGIN early 17th cent.: from Greek *enkōmiastēs*, from *enkōmiazein* 'to praise', from *enkōmion* (see ENCOMIUM).

encomienda /ɛn,kɒmɪˈɛndə/ ▶ **noun** historical a grant by the Spanish Crown to a colonist in America conferring the right to demand tribute and forced labour from the Indian inhabitants of an area.
– ORIGIN Spanish, 'commission, charge'.

encomium /ɛnˈkəʊmɪəm/ ▶ **noun** (pl. **encomiums** or **encomia**) formal a speech or piece of writing that praises someone or something highly.
– ORIGIN mid 16th cent.: Latin, from Greek *enkōmion* 'eulogy', from *en-* 'within' + *komos* 'revel'.

encompass /ɪnˈkʌmpəs, ɛn-/ ▶ **verb** **1** [with obj.] surround and have or hold within: *this area of London encompasses Piccadilly to the north and St James's Park to the south.* ■ include comprehensively: *no studies encompass all sectors of medical care.*
2 archaic cause to take place: *an act designed to encompass the death of the king.*
– DERIVATIVES **encompassment** noun.

encopresis /,ɛnkəʊˈpriːsɪs/ ▶ **noun** [mass noun] Medicine involuntary defecation, especially associated with emotional disturbance or psychiatric disorder.
– ORIGIN modern Latin, from Greek *en-* 'in' + *kopros* 'dung'.

encore /ˈɒŋkɔː/ ▶ **noun** a repeated or additional performance of an item at the end of a concert, as called for by an audience.
▶ **exclamation** again! (as called by an audience at the end of a concert).
▶ **verb** [with obj.] call for a repeated or additional performance of (an item) at the end of a concert. ■ [no obj.] (of a performer) give an encore.
– ORIGIN early 18th cent.: French, literally 'still, again'.

encounter ▶ **verb** [with obj.] **1** unexpectedly be faced with or experience (something hostile or difficult): *we have encountered one small problem.*
2 meet (someone) unexpectedly.
▶ **noun** an unexpected or casual meeting with someone or something: *she felt totally unnerved by the encounter.* ■ a confrontation or unpleasant struggle: *his close encounter with death.*
– ORIGIN Middle English (in the senses 'meet as an adversary' and 'a meeting of adversaries'; formerly also as *incounter*): from Old French *encontrer* (verb), *encontre* (noun), based on Latin *in-* 'in' + *contra* 'against'.

encounter group ▶ **noun** chiefly US a group of people who meet to gain psychological benefit through close contact with one another.

encourage ▶ **verb** [with obj.] give support, confidence, or hope to (someone): *we were encouraged by the success of this venture.* ■ [with obj. and infinitive] persuade (someone) to do or continue to do something by giving support and advice: *pupils are encouraged to be creative.* ■ stimulate the development of (an activity, state, or belief): *the intention is to encourage new writing talent.*
– DERIVATIVES **encourager** noun.
– ORIGIN Middle English (formerly also as *incourage*): from French *encourager*, from *en-* 'in' + *corage* 'courage'.

encouragement ▶ **noun** [mass noun] the action of giving someone support, confidence, or hope: *thank you for all your support and encouragement.* ■ persuasion to do or to continue something: *incentives and encouragement to play sports.* ■ the act of trying to stimulate the development of an activity, state, or belief: *the encouragement of foreign investment.*

encouraging ▶ **adjective** giving someone support or confidence; supportive: *she gave me an encouraging smile.* ■ positive and giving hope for future success; promising: *the results are very encouraging.*
– DERIVATIVES **encouragingly** adverb [as sentence adverb] *encouragingly, there is more research being done today* | [as submodifier] *the level of activity continues to be encouragingly high.*

encroach ▶ **verb** [no obj.] (usu. **encroach on/upon**) intrude on (a person's territory, rights, personal life, etc.): *rather than encroach on his privacy she might have kept to her room.* ■ advance gradually beyond usual or acceptable limits: *the sea has encroached all round the coast.*
– DERIVATIVES **encroacher** noun.
– ORIGIN late Middle English (in the sense 'obtain unlawfully, seize'; formerly also as *incroach*): from Old French *encrochier* 'seize, fasten upon', from *en-* 'in, on' + *crochier* (from *croc* 'hook', from Old Norse *krókr*).

encroachment ▶ **noun** [mass noun] intrusion on a person's territory, rights, etc.: *minor encroachments on our individual liberties.* ■ a gradual advance beyond usual or acceptable limits: *urban encroachment of habitat.*

en croute /õ ˈkruːt/ ▶ **adjective & adverb** in a pastry crust: [as postpositive adj.] *salmon en croute.*
– ORIGIN French *en croûte*.

encrust /ɪnˈkrʌst, ɛn-/ (also **incrust**) ▶ **verb** [with obj.] cover or decorate (something) with a hard surface layer: *the mussels encrust navigation buoys* | (as adj. **encrusted**) *the dried and encrusted blood.*
– ORIGIN early 17th cent. (in the sense 'cause to form a crust'): from French *incruster* or *encroûter*, both from Latin *incrustare*, from *in-* 'into' + *crusta* 'a crust'.

encrustation (also **incrustation**) ▶ **noun** [mass noun] the action of encrusting or state of being encrusted. ■ [count noun] a crust or hard coating on the surface of something. ■ [count noun] Architecture a facing of marble on a building.
– ORIGIN early 17th cent. (originally as *incrustation*): from late Latin *incrustatio(n-)*, from the verb *incrustare* (see ENCRUST).

encrypt /ɛnˈkrɪpt/ ▶ **verb** [with obj.] convert (information or data) into a code, especially to prevent unauthorized access. ■ (**encrypt something in**) conceal data in (something) by converting it into a code.
– DERIVATIVES **encryption** noun.
– ORIGIN 1950s (originally US): from EN-[1] 'in' + Greek *kruptos* 'hidden'.

enculturation ▶ **noun** variant spelling of INCULTURATION.

encumber /ɪnˈkʌmbə, ɛn-/ ▶ **verb** [with obj.] restrict or impede (someone or something) in such a way that free action or movement is difficult: *she was encumbered by her heavy skirts | they had arrived encumbered with families.*
– ORIGIN Middle English (in the sense 'cause trouble to, entangle'; formerly also as *incumber*): from Old French *encombrer* 'block up', from *en-* 'in' + *combre* 'river barrage'.

E

encumbrance ▶ **noun** an impediment or burden. ■ Law a mortgage or other claim on property or assets. ■ archaic a person, especially a child, who is dependent on someone else for support.
– ORIGIN Middle English (denoting an encumbered state; formerly also as *incumbrance*): from Old French *encombrance*, from *encombrer* 'block up' (see **ENCUMBER**).

-ency ▶ **suffix** forming nouns: **1** denoting a quality: *efficiency*.
2 denoting a state: *presidency*.
– ORIGIN from Latin *-entia* (compare with **-ENCE**).

encyclical /ɛnˈsɪklɪk(ə)l, ɪn-, -ˈsʌɪk-/ ▶ **noun** a papal letter sent to all bishops of the Roman Catholic Church.
– ORIGIN mid 17th cent. (as an adjective): via late Latin from Greek *enkuklios* 'circular, general', from *en-* 'in' + *kuklos* 'a circle'.

E

encyclopedia /ɛnˌsʌɪkləˈpiːdɪə, ɪn-/ (also **encyclopaedia**) ▶ **noun** a book or set of books giving information on many subjects or on many aspects of one subject and typically arranged alphabetically.
– ORIGIN mid 16th cent.: modern Latin, from pseudo-Greek *enkuklopaideia* for *enkuklios paideia* 'all-round education'.

encyclopedic /ɛnˌsʌɪkləˈpiːdɪk, ɪn-/ (also **encyclopaedic**) ▶ **adjective 1** comprehensive in terms of information: *he has an almost encyclopedic knowledge of food*.
2 relating to encyclopedias or information suitable for an encyclopedia: *a dictionary with encyclopedic material*.

encyclopedism (also **encyclopaedism**) ▶ **noun** [mass noun] comprehensive learning or knowledge.

encyclopedist (also **encyclopaedist**) ▶ **noun** a person who writes, edits, or contributes to an encyclopedia.

encyst /ɪnˈsɪst, ɛn-/ ▶ **verb** Zoology enclose or become enclosed in a cyst.
– DERIVATIVES **encystation** noun, **encystment** noun.

end ▶ **noun 1** a final part of something, especially a period of time, an activity, or a story: *the end of the year* | *Mario led the race* ***from beginning to end***. ■ a termination of a state or situation: *the party called for* ***an end to*** *violence* | *one notice will be effective to* ***bring*** *the tenancy* ***to an end***. ■ a person's death: *I saw him in hospital a few days before the end*. ■ archaic (in biblical use) an ultimate state or condition: *the end of that man is peace*.
2 the furthest or most extreme part of something: *the church at the end of the road* | [as modifier] *the end house*. ■ Brit. a small piece that is left after use: *an ashtray full of cigarette ends*. ■ a specified extreme of a scale: *homebuyers at the lower end of the market*. ■ either of two places linked by a telephone call, letter, or journey: *'Hello,' said a voice at the other end*. ■ either of the halves of a sports field or court defended by one team or player.
3 a part or person's share of an activity: *you're going to honour your end of the deal*.
4 a goal or desired result: *each would use the other to* ***further his own ends*** | ***to this end***, *schools were set up for peasant women*.
5 (in bowls and curling) a session of play in one particular direction across the playing area.
6 American Football a lineman positioned nearest the sideline.
▶ **verb** come or bring to a final point; finish: [no obj.] *when the war ended, policy changed* | *the chapter* ***ends with*** *a case study* | [with obj.] *she wanted to end the relationship*. ■ [no obj.] reach a point and go no further: *the surfaced road ends at the farm*. ■ [no obj.] perform a final act: *the man* ***ended by*** *attacking a police officer*. ■ [no obj.] (**end in**) have as its final part or result: *the match ended in a draw*. ■ [no obj.] (**end up**) eventually come to a specified place or situation: *I ended up in Eritrea* | *you could* ***end up with*** *a higher income*.
– PHRASES **all ends up** informal completely. **at the end of the day** Brit. informal when everything is taken into consideration: *at the end of the day I'm responsible for what happens in the school*. **be at** (or **have come to**) **an end** be finished or completed: *negotiations were virtually at an end*. ■ (of a supply of something) become exhausted: *our patience has come to an end*. **be at the end of** be close to having no more of (something): *she was at the end of her patience*. **be the end** Brit. informal be the limit of what one can tolerate: *you really are the end!* **come to** (or **meet**) **a sticky end** Brit. be led by one's own actions to ruin or an unpleasant death. **end one's days** (or **life**) spend the final part of one's life in a specified place or state: *she ended her days in London*. **an end in itself** a goal that is pursued in its own right to the exclusion of others. **end in tears** Brit. have an unhappy or unpleasant outcome: *this treaty will end in tears*. **end it all** commit suicide. **the end justifies the means** wrong or unfair methods may be used if the overall goal is good. **the end of the road** (or **line**) the point beyond which progress or survival cannot continue: *if the damages award is not lowered it could* ***be the end of the road for*** *the publisher*. **the end of one's tether** (or N. Amer. **rope**) Brit. having no patience or energy left to cope with something: *these individuals have* ***reached the end of their tether***. **the end of the world** the termination of life on the earth. ■ informal a complete disaster: ***it's not the end of the world*** *if we draw*. **end on** with the end of an object facing towards one: *seen end on, their sharp summits point like arrows*. ■ with the end of an object touching that of another: *stone tiles had been layered end on with incredible skill*. **end to end** in a row with the end of one object touching that of another. **get** (or **have**) **one's end away** Brit. vulgar slang have sexual intercourse. **in the end** eventually or on reflection: *in the end, I saw that she was right*. **keep** (or **hold**) **one's end up** Brit. informal perform well in a difficult or competitive situation. **make an end of** cause (someone or something) to stop existing or die. **make** (**both**) **ends meet** earn just enough money to live on. **never** (or **not**) **hear the end of** be continually reminded of (an unpleasant topic or cause of annoyance): *a criminal court which admitted such a defence would* ***never hear the end of it***. **no end** informal to a great extent; very much: *this cheered me up no end*. **no end of** informal a great deal of: *emotions can cause no end of problems*. **on end 1** continuing without stopping for a specified period of time: *sometimes they'll be gone for days on end*. **2** in an upright position: *he brushed his hair, leaving a tuft standing on end*. **put an end to** cause (someone or something) to stop existing or die: *injury put an end to his career* | *he decided to* ***put an end to himself***. **the sharp end** informal **1** the most important or influential part of an activity or process: *he was born at the sharp end of history*. ■ the most risky or unpleasant part of a system or activity: *businessmen* ***are at the sharp end of the recession***. **2** Brit. humorous the bow of a ship. **a —— to end all ——s** informal used to emphasize how impressive or successful something is of its kind: *she is going to throw a party to end all parties*. **without end** without a limit or boundary: *a war without end*.
– ORIGIN Old English *ende* (noun), *endian* (verb), of Germanic origin; related to Dutch *einde* (noun), *einden* (verb) and German *Ende* (noun), *enden* (verb).

-end ▶ **suffix** denoting a person or thing to be treated in a specified way: *dividend* | *reverend*.
– ORIGIN from Latin *-endus*, gerundive ending.

endanger ▶ **verb** [with obj.] put (someone or something) at risk or in danger: *he was driving in a manner likely to endanger life*.
– DERIVATIVES **endangerment** noun.

endangered ▶ **adjective** (of a species) seriously at risk of extinction.

end-around ▶ **noun** American Football an offensive play in which an end carries the ball round the opposing flank.

endarterectomy /ˌɛndɑːtəˈrɛktəmi/ ▶ **noun** (pl. **endarterectomies**) [mass noun] surgical removal of part of the inner lining of an artery, together with any obstructive deposits, most often carried out on the carotid artery or on vessels supplying the legs.

endarteritis /ˌɛndɑːtəˈrʌɪtɪs/ ▶ **noun** [mass noun] Medicine inflammation of the inner lining of an artery.

en dash ▶ **noun** another term for **EN RULE**.

endear /ɪnˈdɪə, ɛn-/ ▶ **verb** [with obj.] cause to be loved or liked: *Flora's spirit and character* ***endeared*** *her* ***to*** *everyone who met her*.

endearing ▶ **adjective** inspiring affection: *an endearing little grin*.
– DERIVATIVES **endearingly** adverb.

endearment ▶ **noun** a word or phrase expressing love or affection. ■ [mass noun] love or affection: *a term of endearment*.

endeavour /ɪnˈdɛvə, ɛn-/ (US **endeavor**) ▶ **verb** [no obj., with infinitive] try hard to do or achieve something: *he is endeavouring to help the Third World*.
▶ **noun** an attempt to achieve a goal: [with infinitive] *an endeavour to reduce serious injury*. ■ [mass noun] earnest, prolonged, and industrious effort: *enthusiasm is a vital ingredient in all human endeavour*. ■ an enterprise or undertaking: *a portfolio of business endeavours*.
– ORIGIN late Middle English (in the sense 'exert oneself'): from the phrase *put oneself in devoir* 'do one's utmost' (see **DEVOIR**).

endemic /ɛnˈdɛmɪk/ ▶ **adjective 1** (of a disease or condition) regularly found among particular people or in a certain area: *complacency is* ***endemic in*** *industry today*. ■ [attrib.] (of an area) in which a particular disease is regularly found: *the persistence of infection on pastures in endemic areas*.
2 (of a plant or animal) native or restricted to a certain place: *a marsupial* ***endemic to*** *north-eastern Australia*.
▶ **noun** an endemic plant or animal.
– DERIVATIVES **endemically** adverb, **endemicity** /ˌɛndɪˈmɪsɪti/ noun, **endemism** /ˈɛndɪmɪz(ə)m/ noun (sense 2 of the adjective).
– ORIGIN mid 17th cent. (as a noun): from French *endémique* or modern Latin *endemicus*, from Greek *endēmios* 'native' (based on *dēmos* 'people').

Enderby Land /ˈɛndəbi/ a part of Antarctica claimed by Australia.
– ORIGIN named by its discoverer, the English navigator John Biscoe (1794–1843), after the London whaling firm *Enderby* Brothers, where he was employed.

endergonic /ˌɛndəːˈɡɒnɪk/ ▶ **adjective** Biochemistry (of a metabolic or chemical process) accompanied by or requiring the absorption of energy, the products being of greater free energy than the reactants. The opposite of **EXERGONIC**.
– ORIGIN mid 20th cent.: from **ENDO-** 'within' + Greek *ergon* 'work' + **-IC**.

endgame ▶ **noun** the final stage of a game such as chess or bridge, when few pieces or cards remain.

endgate ▶ **noun** N. Amer. a tailboard.

end grain ▶ **noun** the grain of wood seen when it is cut across the growth rings.

endian ▶ **adjective** (usu. in phrase **big-endian** or **little-endian**) Computing denoting or relating to a system of ordering bytes in a word, or bits in a byte, in which the most significant (or least significant) item is put first.
– ORIGIN 1980s: from Swift's *Gulliver's Travels*, in which *big-endians* and *little-endians* ate boiled eggs by breaking the 'big' end or 'little' end respectively.

ending ▶ **noun** an end or final part of something: *the ending of the Cold War*. ■ the furthest part of something: *a nerve ending*. ■ the final part of a word, constituting a grammatical inflection or formative element.
– ORIGIN Old English *endung* 'termination, completion' (see **END**, **-ING**[1]).

endite /ˈɛndʌɪt/ ▶ **noun** Zoology an inwardly directed lobe on a limb segment of an arthropod, especially on the protopodite of a crustacean limb.
– ORIGIN late 19th cent.: from **ENDO-** 'within' + **-ITE**[1].

endive /ˈɛndʌɪv, -dɪv/ ▶ **noun 1** Brit. an edible Mediterranean plant, the bitter leaves of which may be used in salads. ● *Cichorium endivia*, family Compositae. The varieties of endive are placed in two groups: **curly endive**, with curled leaves, and **Batavian endive**, with smooth leaves.
2 (also **Belgian endive**) N. Amer. a chicory crown.
– ORIGIN late Middle English (also denoting the sowthistle): via Old French from medieval Latin *endivia*, based on Greek *entubon*.

endless ▶ **adjective** having or seeming to have no end or limit: *endless ocean wastes* | *the list is endless*. ■ countless; innumerable: *we smoked endless cigarettes*. ■ (of a belt, chain, or tape) having the ends joined to form a loop allowing continuous action.
– DERIVATIVES **endlessly** adverb, **endlessness** noun.
– ORIGIN Old English *endelēas* (see **END**, **-LESS**).

endless screw ▶ **noun** the threaded cylinder in a worm gear.

endmember ▶ **noun** Geology a mineral or rock representing one end of a series having a range of composition.

endmost ▶ **adjective** nearest to the end.

endnote ▶ **noun** a note printed at the end of a book or section of a book.

endo- ▶ **combining form** internal; within: *endoderm* | *endogenous*.
– ORIGIN from Greek *endon* 'within'.

endocardial /ˌɛndə(ʊ)ˈkɑːdɪəl/ ▶ **adjective** Anatomy & Medicine **1** relating to the endocardium.
2 inside the heart.

endocarditis /ˌɛndəʊkɑːˈdʌɪtɪs/ ▶ **noun** [mass noun] Medicine inflammation of the endocardium.
– DERIVATIVES **endocarditic** adjective.

endocardium /ˌɛndəʊˈkɑːdɪəm/ ▶ **noun** the thin, smooth membrane which lines the inside of the chambers of the heart and forms the surface of the valves.
– ORIGIN late 19th cent.: modern Latin, from **ENDO-** 'within' + Greek *kardia* 'heart'.

endocarp /ˈɛndə(ʊ)kɑːp/ ▶ **noun** Botany the innermost layer of the pericarp which surrounds a seed in a fruit. It may be membranous (as in apples) or woody (as in the stone of a peach or cherry).
– ORIGIN early 19th cent.: from **ENDO-** 'within' + a shortened form of **PERICARP**.

endocentric /ˌɛndəʊˈsɛntrɪk/ ▶ **adjective** Linguistics denoting or being a construction in which the whole has the same syntactic function as the head, for example *big black dogs*. Contrasted with **EXOCENTRIC**.

endocrine /ˈɛndə(ʊ)krʌɪn, -krɪn/ ▶ **adjective** Physiology relating to or denoting glands which secrete hormones or other products directly into the blood: *the endocrine system*.
– ORIGIN early 20th cent.: from **ENDO-** 'within' + Greek *krinein* 'sift'.

endocrinology /ˌɛndəʊkrɪˈnɒlədʒi/ ▶ **noun** [mass noun] the branch of physiology and medicine concerned with endocrine glands and hormones.
– DERIVATIVES **endocrinological** adjective, **endocrinologist** noun.

endocytosis /ˌɛndəʊsʌɪˈtəʊsɪs/ ▶ **noun** [mass noun] Biology the taking in of matter by a living cell by invagination of its membrane to form a vacuole.
– DERIVATIVES **endocytotic** adjective.

endoderm /ˈɛndə(ʊ)dəːm/ ▶ **noun** [mass noun] Zoology & Embryology the innermost layer of cells or tissue of an embryo in early development, or the parts derived from this, which include the lining of the gut and associated structures. Compare with **ECTODERM** and **MESODERM**.
– DERIVATIVES **endodermal** adjective.
– ORIGIN mid 19th cent.: from **ENDO-** 'within' + Greek *derma* 'skin'.

endodermis ▶ **noun** [mass noun] Botany an inner layer of cells in the cortex of a root and of some stems, surrounding a vascular bundle.
– ORIGIN early 20th cent.: from **ENDO-** 'within' + modern Latin *dermis* 'skin'.

endogamy /ɛnˈdɒgəmi/ ▶ **noun** [mass noun] **1** Anthropology the custom of marrying only within the limits of a local community, clan, or tribe. Compare with **EXOGAMY**.
2 Biology the fusion of reproductive cells from related individuals; inbreeding; self-pollination.
– DERIVATIVES **endogamous** adjective.
– ORIGIN mid 19th cent.: from **ENDO-** 'within' + Greek *gamos* 'marriage', on the pattern of *polygamy*.

endogenic /ˌɛndəʊˈdʒɛnɪk/ ▶ **adjective** Geology formed or occurring beneath the surface of the earth. Often contrasted with **EXOGENIC**.

endogenous /ɛnˈdɒdʒɪnəs, ɪn-/ ▶ **adjective** having an internal cause or origin. Often contrasted with **EXOGENOUS**. ■ Biology growing or originating from within an organism: *endogenous gene sequences*. ■ chiefly Psychiatry (of a disease or symptom) not attributable to any external or environmental factor: *endogenous depression*. ■ confined within a group or society.
– DERIVATIVES **endogenously** adverb.

endoglossic /ˌɛndə(ʊ)ˈglɒsɪk/ ▶ **adjective** Linguistics denoting or relating to an indigenous language that is used as the first or official language in a country or community. Compare with **EXOGLOSSIC**.
– ORIGIN 1980s: from **ENDO-**, Greek *glōssa* 'language, tongue', and **-IC**.

endolithic /ˌɛndə(ʊ)ˈlɪθɪk/ ▶ **adjective** Biology living in or penetrating into stone: *endolithic algae*.

endolymph /ˈɛndə(ʊ)lɪmf/ ▶ **noun** [mass noun] Anatomy the fluid in the membranous labyrinth of the ear.

endometriosis /ˌɛndə(ʊ)miːtrɪˈəʊsɪs/ ▶ **noun** [mass noun] Medicine a condition resulting from the appearance of endometrial tissue outside the womb and causing pelvic pain, especially associated with menstruation.

endometritis /ˌɛndə(ʊ)mɪˈtrʌɪtɪs/ ▶ **noun** [mass noun] Medicine inflammation of the endometrium.

endometrium /ˌɛndə(ʊ)ˈmiːtrɪəm/ ▶ **noun** Anatomy the mucous membrane lining the womb, which thickens during the menstrual cycle in preparation for possible implantation of an embryo.
– DERIVATIVES **endometrial** adjective.
– ORIGIN late 19th cent.: modern Latin, from **ENDO-** 'within' + Greek *mētra* 'womb'.

endomorph /ˈɛndə(ʊ)mɔːf/ ▶ **noun** Physiology a person with a soft round build of body and a high proportion of fat tissue. Compare with **ECTOMORPH** and **MESOMORPH**.
– DERIVATIVES **endomorphic** adjective, **endomorphy** noun.
– ORIGIN 1940s: *endo-* from *endodermal* (being the layer of the embryo giving rise to the physical characteristics which predominate) + **-MORPH**.

endonuclease /ˌɛndəʊˈnjuːklɪeɪz/ ▶ **noun** Biochemistry an enzyme which cleaves a polynucleotide chain by separating nucleotides other than the two end ones.

endoparasite ▶ **noun** Biology a parasite, such as a tapeworm, that lives inside its host. Compare with **ECTOPARASITE**.
– DERIVATIVES **endoparasitic** adjective.

endopeptidase /ˌɛndəʊˈpɛptɪdeɪz/ ▶ **noun** Biochemistry an enzyme which breaks peptide bonds other than terminal ones in a peptide chain.

endophora /ɛnˈdɒfərə/ ▶ **noun** [mass noun] Linguistics the set of relationships among words having the same reference within a text, contributing to textual cohesion; anaphora and cataphora. Compare with **EXOPHORA**.
– ORIGIN late 20th cent.: from **ENDO-** 'within', on the pattern of *anaphora*.

endophyte /ˈɛndəʊfʌɪt/ ▶ **noun** Botany a plant, especially a fungus, which lives inside another plant.
– DERIVATIVES **endophytic** adjective.

endoplasm /ˈɛndə(ʊ)plaz(ə)m/ ▶ **noun** [mass noun] Biology, dated the more fluid, granular inner layer of the cytoplasm in amoeboid cells. Compare with **ECTOPLASM** (sense 1).

endoplasmic reticulum /ˌɛndəʊˈplazmɪk/ ▶ **noun** [mass noun] Biology a network of membranous tubules within the cytoplasm of a eukaryotic cell, continuous with the nuclear membrane. It usually has ribosomes attached and is involved in protein and lipid synthesis.

endopodite /ɛnˈdɒpədʌɪt/ (also **endopod** /ˈɛndə(ʊ)pɒd/) ▶ **noun** Zoology the inner branch of the biramous limb or appendage of a crustacean. Compare with **EXOPODITE, PROTOPODITE**.
– ORIGIN late 19th cent.: from **ENDO-** 'within' + Greek *pous, pod-* 'foot' + **-ITE**[1].

end organ ▶ **noun 1** Anatomy a specialized, encapsulated ending of a peripheral sensory nerve, which acts as a receptor for a stimulus.
2 another term for **TARGET ORGAN**.

endorphin /ɛnˈdɔːfɪn/ ▶ **noun** Biochemistry any of a group of hormones secreted within the brain and nervous system and having a number of physiological functions. They are peptides which activate the body's opiate receptors, causing an analgesic effect.
– ORIGIN 1970s: blend of **ENDOGENOUS** and **MORPHINE**.

endorse /ɪnˈdɔːs, ɛn-/ (US & Law also **indorse**) ▶ **verb** [with obj.] **1** declare one's public approval or support of: *the report was endorsed by the college*. ■ recommend (a product) in an advertisement.
2 sign (a cheque or bill of exchange) on the back to make it payable to someone other than the stated payee or to accept responsibility for paying it. ■ write (a comment) on a document: *the speed and accuracy achieved will be endorsed on the certificate*.
3 (in the UK) mark (a driving licence) with the penalty points given as a punishment for a driving offence.
4 (**endorse someone out**) (in South Africa under apartheid) order a black person to leave an urban area for failing to meet certain requirements of the Native Laws Amendment Act.
– DERIVATIVES **endorsable** adjective, **endorser** noun.
– ORIGIN late 15th cent. (in the sense 'write on the back of'; formerly also as *indorse*): from medieval Latin *indorsare*, from Latin *in-* 'in, on' + *dorsum* 'back'.

endorsee /ˌɛndɔːˈsiː/ ▶ **noun** a person to whom a cheque or bill of exchange is made payable instead of the stated payee.

endorsement (US & Law also **indorsement**) ▶ **noun**
1 [mass noun] the action of endorsing someone or something.
2 (in the UK) a note on a driving licence recording the penalty points incurred for a driving offence.
3 a clause in an insurance policy detailing an exemption from or change in cover.

endoscope /ˈɛndəskəʊp/ ▶ **noun** Medicine an instrument which can be introduced into the body to give a view of its internal parts.
– DERIVATIVES **endoscopic** adjective, **endoscopically** adverb, **endoscopist** /ɛnˈdɒskəpɪst/ noun, **endoscopy** noun.

endoskeleton ▶ **noun** Zoology an internal skeleton, such as the bony or cartilaginous skeleton of vertebrates. Compare with **EXOSKELETON**.
– DERIVATIVES **endoskeletal** adjective.

endosperm ▶ **noun** [mass noun] Botany the part of a seed which acts as a food store for the developing plant embryo, usually containing starch with protein and other nutrients.

endospore ▶ **noun** Biology a resistant asexual spore that develops inside some bacteria cells. ■ the inner layer of the membrane or wall of some spores and pollen grains.

E

endosymbiosis /ˌɛndəʊˌsɪmbɪˈəʊsɪs, -bʌɪ-/ ▶ **noun** [mass noun] Biology symbiosis in which one of the symbiotic organisms lives inside the other.
– DERIVATIVES **endosymbiont** noun, **endosymbiotic** adjective.

endothelium /ˌɛndə(ʊ)ˈθiːlɪəm/ ▶ **noun** [mass noun] Anatomy the tissue which forms a single layer of cells lining various organs and cavities of the body, especially the blood vessels, heart, and lymphatic vessels. It is formed from the embryonic mesoderm. Compare with **EPITHELIUM**.
– DERIVATIVES **endothelial** adjective.
– ORIGIN late 19th cent.: modern Latin, from **ENDO-** 'within' + Greek *thēlē* 'nipple'.

endotherm /ˈɛndə(ʊ)θəːm/ ▶ **noun** Zoology an animal that is dependent on or capable of the internal generation of heat. Often contrasted with **ECTOTHERM**. Compare with **HOMEOTHERM**.
– DERIVATIVES **endothermy** noun.
– ORIGIN 1940s: from **ENDO-** 'within', on the pattern of *homeotherm*.

endothermic ▶ **adjective 1** Chemistry (of a reaction or process) accompanied by or requiring the absorption of heat. The opposite of **EXOTHERMIC**. ■ (of a compound) requiring a net input of heat for its formation from its constituent elements.
2 Zoology (of an animal) dependent on or capable of the internal generation of heat.
– DERIVATIVES **endothermal** adjective.

endotoxin /ˈɛndəʊˌtɒksɪn/ ▶ **noun** Microbiology a toxin present inside a bacterial cell that is released when it disintegrates. Compare with **EXOTOXIN**.

endotracheal /ˌɛndə(ʊ)ˈtreɪkɪəl, -trəˈkiːəl/ ▶ **adjective** Anatomy situated or occurring within or performed by way of the trachea.
– DERIVATIVES **endotracheally** adverb.

endow /ɪnˈdaʊ, ɛn-/ ▶ **verb** [with obj.] **1** give or bequeath an income or property to (a person or institution): *he endowed the Church with lands*. ■ establish (a university post, annual prize, etc.) by donating the funds needed to maintain it.
2 provide with a quality, ability, or asset: *he was endowed with tremendous physical strength*. ■ (**be endowed**) informal have breasts or a penis of specified size: *the girl on page three is well endowed*.
– DERIVATIVES **endower** noun.
– ORIGIN late Middle English (also in the sense 'provide a dower or dowry'; formerly also as *indow*): from legal Anglo-Norman French *endouer*, from *en-* 'in, towards' + Old French *douer* 'give as a gift' (from Latin *dotare*: see **DOWER**).

endowment ▶ **noun 1** [mass noun] the action of endowing something or someone: *he tried to promote the endowment of a Chair of Psychiatry*. ■ [count noun] an income or form of property given or bequeathed to someone.
2 (usu. **endowments**) a quality or ability possessed or inherited by someone.
3 [usu. as modifier] a form of life insurance involving payment of a fixed sum to the insured person on a specified date, or to their estate should they die before this date: *an endowment policy*.

endowment mortgage ▶ **noun** Brit. a mortgage linked to an endowment insurance policy which is intended to repay the capital sum on maturity.

endpaper ▶ **noun** a leaf of paper at the beginning or end of a book, especially one fixed to the inside of the cover.

end plate ▶ **noun 1** a flattened piece at or forming the end of something such as a motor or dynamo.
2 Anatomy each of the discoid expansions of a motor nerve where its branches terminate on a muscle fibre.

endplay Bridge ▸ **noun** a way of playing in the last few tricks which forces an opponent to make a disadvantageous lead.
▸ **verb** [with obj.] force (an opponent) to make an endplay.

end point ▸ **noun** the final stage of a period or process.

end product ▸ **noun** the final result of an activity or process, especially the finished article in a manufacturing process.

end result ▸ **noun** the final result or outcome of an activity or process.

endrin /ˈɛndrɪn/ ▸ **noun** [mass noun] a toxic insecticide which is a stereoisomer of dieldrin.
– ORIGIN mid 20th cent.: from **ENDO-** 'within' + a shortened form of **DIELDRIN**.

E

end run ▸ **noun** American Football an attempt by the ball carrier to run around the end of the defensive line.
■ N. Amer. an evasive tactic or manoeuvre.
▸ **verb** (**end-run**) [with obj.] N. Amer. evade; circumvent: *an attempt to end-run regulations for fire protection.*

end-scraper ▸ **noun** Archaeology a prehistoric flint tool with a single working edge at one end of a blade or flake, at right angles to the long axis.

end standard ▸ **noun** a standard of length in the form of a metal bar or block whose end faces are the standard distance apart.

end-stopped ▸ **adjective** (of verse) having a pause at the end of each line.

end times ▸ **plural noun** chiefly US (in some religious beliefs) the period leading up to Judgement Day.

endue /ɪnˈdjuː, ɛn-/ (also **indue**) ▸ **verb** (**endues**, **enduing**, **endued**) [with obj.] literary endow or provide with a quality or ability: *our sight would be endued with a far greater sharpness.*
– ORIGIN late Middle English (also in the sense 'induct into an ecclesiastical living'): from Old French *enduire*, partly from Latin *inducere* 'lead in' (see **INDUCE**), reinforced by the sense of Latin *induere* 'put on clothes'.

endurable ▸ **adjective** able to be endured; bearable: *my journey was long but endurable.*

endurance ▸ **noun** [mass noun] **1** the ability to endure an unpleasant or difficult process or situation without giving way: *she was close to the limit of her endurance.*
2 the capacity of something to last or to withstand wear and tear.
– ORIGIN late 15th cent. (in the sense 'continued existence, ability to last'; formerly also as *indurance*): from Old French, from *endurer* 'make hard' (see **ENDURE**).

endure /ɪnˈdjʊə, ɛn-, -ˈdjɔː/ ▸ **verb 1** [with obj.] suffer (something painful or difficult) patiently: *it seemed impossible that anyone could endure such pain.*
2 [no obj.] remain in existence; last: *these cities have endured through time.*
– ORIGIN Middle English: from Old French *endurer*, from Latin *indurare* 'harden', from *in-* 'in' + *durus* 'hard'.

enduring /ɪnˈdʒɔːrɪŋ, ɛn-/ ▸ **adjective** lasting over a period of time; durable: *he formed a number of enduring relationships with women.*
– DERIVATIVES **enduringly** adverb.

enduro /ɪnˈdjʊərəʊ, ɛn-/ ▸ **noun** (pl. **enduros**) a long-distance race for motor vehicles or bicycles, typically over rough terrain, designed to test endurance.
– ORIGIN 1950s: from **ENDURANCE** + the informal suffix **-O**.

end user ▸ **noun** the person who actually uses a particular product.

endways (also **endwise**) ▸ **adverb** with the end facing upwards, forwards, or towards the viewer: *a little town looking endways on to the river.* ■ in a row with the end of one object touching that of another: *strips of rubber cemented endways.*

Endymion /ɛnˈdɪmɪən/ Greek Mythology a remarkably beautiful young man, loved by the Moon (Selene). According to one story, he was put in an eternal sleep by Zeus for having fallen in love with Hera, and was then visited every night by Selene.

end zone ▸ **noun** American Football the rectangular area at the end of the field into which the ball must be carried or passed to score a touchdown.

ENE ▸ **abbreviation** east-north-east.

-ene ▸ **suffix 1** denoting an inhabitant: *Nazarene.*
2 Chemistry forming names of unsaturated hydrocarbons containing a double bond: *benzene.*
– ORIGIN from Greek *-ēnos*.

en échelon /ɒn ˈeɪʃ(ə)lɒ̃/ ▸ **adjective & adverb** chiefly Geology in approximately parallel formation at an oblique angle to a particular direction.
– ORIGIN French, literally 'in rung formation'.

enema /ˈɛnɪmə/ ▸ **noun** (pl. **enemas** or **enemata** /ɪˈnɛmətə/) a procedure in which liquid or gas is injected into the rectum, to expel its contents or to introduce drugs or permit X-ray imaging.
– ORIGIN late Middle English: via late Latin from Greek, from *enienai* 'send or put in', from *en-* 'in' + *hienai* 'send'.

enemy ▸ **noun** (pl. **enemies**) a person who is actively opposed or hostile to someone or something. ■ (**the enemy**) [treated as sing. or pl.] a hostile nation or its armed forces, especially in time of war: *the enemy shot down four helicopters* | [as modifier] *enemy aircraft.* ■ a thing that harms or weakens something else: *routine is the enemy of art.*
– PHRASES **be one's own worst enemy** act in a way contrary to one's own interests. **make an enemy of** cause (someone) to start feeling hostile to one: *you really don't want to make an enemy of your girlfriend's best mate.*
– ORIGIN Middle English: from Old French *enemi*, from Latin *inimicus*, from *in-* 'not' + *amicus* 'friend'.

Eneolithic /ˌiːnɪə(ʊ)ˈlɪθɪk/ ▸ **adjective & noun** another term for **CHALCOLITHIC**.
– ORIGIN early 20th cent.: from Latin *aeneus* 'of bronze or copper' + Greek *lithos* 'stone' + **-IC**.

energetic /ˌɛnəˈdʒɛtɪk/ ▸ **adjective 1** showing or involving great activity or vitality: *moderately energetic exercise.*
2 Physics relating to or characterized by energy (in the technical sense): *energetic X-rays.*
– DERIVATIVES **energetically** adverb.
– ORIGIN mid 17th cent. (in the sense 'powerfully effective'): from Greek *energētikos*, from *energein* 'operate, work in or upon' (based on *ergon* 'work').

energetics ▸ **plural noun 1** the properties of something in terms of energy.
2 [treated as sing.] the branch of science which deals with the properties of energy and the way in which it is redistributed in physical, chemical, or biological processes.

energize (also **energise**) ▸ **verb** [with obj.] give vitality and enthusiasm to: *people were energized by his ideas.* ■ supply energy, typically kinetic or electrical energy, to (something).
– DERIVATIVES **energizer** noun.

energumen /ˌɛnəˈgjuːmən/ ▸ **noun** archaic a person believed to be possessed by the devil or a spirit.
– ORIGIN early 18th cent. (also denoting an enthusiast or fanatic): via late Latin from Greek *energoumenos*, passive participle of *energein* 'work in or upon'.

energy ▸ **noun** (pl. **energies**) [mass noun] **1** the strength and vitality required for sustained physical or mental activity: *changes in the levels of vitamins can affect energy and well-being.* ■ (**energies**) a person's physical and mental powers.
2 power derived from the utilization of physical or chemical resources, especially to provide light and heat or to work machines: *nuclear energy.*
3 Physics the property of matter and radiation which is manifest as a capacity to perform work (such as causing motion or the interaction of molecules).
– ORIGIN mid 16th cent. (denoting force or vigour of expression): from French *énergie*, or via late Latin from Greek *energeia*, from *en-* 'in, within' + *ergon* 'work'.

energy audit ▸ **noun** an assessment of the energy needs and efficiency of a building or buildings.

enervate ▸ **verb** /ˈɛnəveɪt/ [with obj.] (often as adj. **enervated** or **enervating**) make (someone) feel drained of energy or vitality: *enervating heat.*
▸ **adjective** /ɪˈnəːvət/ literary lacking in energy or vitality: *the enervate slightness of his frail form.*
– ORIGIN early 17th cent.: from Latin *enervat-* 'weakened (by extraction of the sinews)', from the verb *enervare*, from *e-* (variant of *ex-*) 'out of' + *nervus* 'sinew'.

enervation /ɛnəˈveɪʃ(ə)n/ ▸ **noun** [mass noun] a feeling of being drained of energy or vitality; fatigue: *a sense of enervation.*

Enewetak variant spelling of **ENIWETOK**.

en face /ɒ̃ ˈfas/ ▸ **adverb & adjective** facing forwards.
– ORIGIN French.

en famille /ɒ̃ faˈmiː/ ▸ **adverb** with one's family, or as a family: *when they went out en famille, Steven always drove.*
– ORIGIN French, literally 'in family'.

enfant gâté /ˌɒ̃fɒ̃ ˈgateɪ/ ▸ **noun** dated a person who is excessively flattered or indulged.
– ORIGIN French, literally 'spoilt child'.

enfant terrible /ˌɒ̃fɒ̃ tɛˈriːbl(ə)/ ▸ **noun** (pl. **enfants terribles** pronunc. **same**) a person who behaves in an unconventional or controversial way.
– ORIGIN French, literally 'terrible child'.

enfeeble ▸ **verb** [with obj.] (often as adj. **enfeebled**) make weak or feeble: *trade unions are in an enfeebled state.*
– DERIVATIVES **enfeeblement** noun.
– ORIGIN Middle English: from Old French *enfeblir*, from *en-* (expressing a change of state) + *feble* 'feeble'.

enfeoff /ɪnˈfiːf, -ˈfɛf, ɛn-/ ▸ **verb** [with obj.] (under the feudal system) give (someone) freehold property or land in exchange for their pledged service.
– DERIVATIVES **enfeoffment** noun.
– ORIGIN late Middle English: from Anglo-Norman French *enfeoffer*, from Old French *en-* 'in' + *fief* 'fief'. Compare with **FEOFFMENT**.

en fête /ɒ̃ ˈfɛt/ ▸ **adverb & adjective** holding or prepared for a party or celebration.
– ORIGIN French, 'in festival'.

enfetter ▸ **verb** [with obj.] literary restrain (someone) with shackles.

enfilade /ˌɛnfɪˈleɪd/ ▸ **noun 1** a volley of gunfire directed along a line from end to end.
2 a suite of rooms with doorways in line with each other.
▸ **verb** [with obj.] direct a volley of gunfire along the length of (a target).
– ORIGIN early 18th cent. (denoting the position of a military post commanding the length of a line): from French, from *enfiler* 'thread on a string, pierce from end to end', from *en-* 'in, on' + *fil* 'thread'.

enflesh ▸ **verb** [with obj.] literary give bodily form to; make real or concrete.
– DERIVATIVES **enfleshment** noun.

enfleurage /ˌɒ̃fləˈrɑːʒ/ ▸ **noun** [mass noun] the extraction of essential oils and perfumes from flowers using odourless animal or vegetable fats.
– ORIGIN mid 19th cent.: French, from *enfleurer* 'saturate with the perfume from flowers'.

enflurane /ɛnˈflʊəreɪn/ ▸ **noun** [mass noun] Medicine a volatile organic liquid used as a general anaesthetic.
● A halogenated ether; chem. formula: CHF_2OCF_2CHFCl.
– ORIGIN 1970s: from *en-* (of unknown origin) + **FLUORO-** + **-ANE²**.

enfold /ɪnˈfəʊld, ɛn-/ ▸ **verb** [with obj.] surround; envelop: *he shut off the engine and silence enfolded them.* ■ hold or clasp (someone) lovingly in one's arms.
– ORIGIN late Middle English (in the sense 'involve, entail, imply'; formerly also as *infold*): from **EN-¹**, **IN-²** 'within' + **FOLD¹**.

enforce ▸ **verb** [with obj.] compel observance of or compliance with (a law, rule, or obligation): *the role of the police is to enforce the law.* ■ cause (something) to happen by necessity or force: *there is no outside agency to enforce cooperation between the players.* ■ archaic press home (a demand or argument).
– DERIVATIVES **enforceability** noun, **enforceable** adjective, **enforcer** noun.
– ORIGIN Middle English (in the senses 'strive' and 'impel by force'; formerly also as *inforce*): from Old French *enforcir*, *enforcier*, based on Latin *in-* 'in' + *fortis* 'strong'.

enforced ▸ **adjective** caused by necessity or force; compulsory: *a period of enforced idleness.*
– DERIVATIVES **enforcedly** adverb.

enforcement ▸ **noun** [mass noun] the act of compelling observance of or compliance with a law, rule, or obligation: *the strict enforcement of environmental regulations.*

enforcement notice ▸ **noun** English Law a notification to remedy a breach of planning legislation.

enfranchise /ɪnˈfran(t)ʃʌɪz, ɛn-/ ▸ **verb** [with obj.] **1** give the right to vote to: *a proposal that foreigners should be enfranchised for local elections.* ■ historical give (a town) the right to be represented in Parliament.
2 historical free (a slave).
– DERIVATIVES **enfranchisement** noun.
– ORIGIN late Middle English (formerly also as *infranchise*): from Old French *enfranchiss-*, lengthened stem of *enfranchir*, from *en-* (expressing a change of state) + *franc*, *franche* 'free'.

ENG ▸ **abbreviation** electronic news-gathering.

engage ▸ **verb 1** [with obj.] occupy or attract (someone's interest or attention): *he ploughed on, trying to*

outline his plans and engage Sutton's attention | I told him I was ***otherwise engaged****.* ■ (**engage someone in**) involve someone in (a conversation or discussion).
2 [no obj.] (**engage in** or **be engaged in**) participate or become involved in: *organizations engage in a variety of activities | some are actively engaged in crime.* ■ (**engage with**) establish a meaningful contact or connection with: *the teams needed to engage with local communities.*
3 [with obj.] arrange to employ or hire (someone): *he was engaged as a trainee copywriter.* ■ [with infinitive] pledge or enter into a contract to do something: *he engaged to pay them £10,000 against a bond.* ■ dated reserve (accommodation, a place, etc.) in advance.
4 (with reference to a part of a machine or engine) move into position so as to come into operation: [with obj.] *the clutch will not engage* | [with obj.] *the driver engaged the gears and pulled out into the road.*
5 [with obj.] (of fencers or swordsmen) bring (weapons) together preparatory to fighting. ■ [with obj.] enter into combat with (an enemy).
– ORIGIN late Middle English (formerly also as *ingage*): from French *engager*, ultimately from the base of **GAGE**[1]. The word originally meant 'to pawn or pledge something', later 'pledge oneself (to do something)', hence 'enter into a contract' (mid 16th cent.), 'involve oneself in an activity', 'enter into combat' (mid 17th cent.), giving rise to the notion 'involve someone or something else'.

engagé /ˌɒ̃ɡaˈʒeɪ/ ▶ **adjective** (of a writer or artist) committed to a particular aim or cause.
– ORIGIN French, past participle of *engager* (see **ENGAGE**).

engaged ▶ **adjective 1** [predic.] busy; occupied. ■ Brit. (of a telephone line) unavailable because already in use. ■ (of a toilet) already in use.
2 having formally agreed to marry.
3 Architecture (of a column) attached to or partly let into a wall.

engaged tone (also **engaged signal**) ▶ **noun** Brit. a sound indicating that a telephone line is engaged.

engagement ▶ **noun 1** a formal agreement to get married. ■ the duration of an agreement to get married: *a good long engagement to give you time to be sure.*
2 an arrangement to do something or go somewhere at a fixed time: *a dinner engagement.*
3 [mass noun] the action of engaging or being engaged: *Britain's continued* ***engagement in*** *open trading.*
4 a fight or battle between armed forces.
– ORIGIN early 17th cent. (in the general sense 'a legal or moral obligation'): French, from *engager* 'to pledge' (see **ENGAGE**).

engagement ring ▶ **noun** a ring given by a man to a woman when they agree to marry.

engaging ▶ **adjective** charming and attractive: *an engaging smile.*
– DERIVATIVES **engagingly** adverb.

Engelmann spruce /ˈɛŋɡ(ə)lmən/ (also **Engelmann's spruce**) ▶ **noun** a tall spruce found in the mountains of western North America and Mexico. ● *Picea engelmannii*, family Pinaceae.
– ORIGIN mid 19th cent.: named after George *Engelmann* (1809–84), American botanist.

Engels /ˈɛŋɡ(ə)lz/, Friedrich (1820–95), German socialist and political philosopher. He collaborated with Marx in the writing of the *Communist Manifesto* (1848) and translated and edited Marx's later work. Engels's own writings include *The Condition of the Working Classes in England in 1844* (1845).

engender /ɪnˈdʒɛndə, ɛn-/ ▶ **verb** [with obj.] cause or give rise to (a feeling, situation, or condition): *the issue engendered continuing controversy.* ■ archaic (of a father) beget (offspring).
– ORIGIN Middle English (formerly also as *ingender*): from Old French *engendrer*, from Latin *ingenerare*, from *in-* 'in' + *generare* 'beget' (see **GENERATE**).

engine ▶ **noun 1** a machine with moving parts that converts power into motion. ■ a thing that is the agent or instrument of a particular process: *exports used to be the engine of growth.*
2 (also **railway engine**) a locomotive. ■ a fire engine. ■ historical a mechanical device or instrument, especially one used in warfare: *a siege engine.*
– DERIVATIVES **engined** adjective [in combination] *a twin-engined helicopter*, **engineless** adjective.
– ORIGIN Middle English (formerly also as *ingine*): from Old French *engin*, from Latin *ingenium* 'talent, device', from *in-* 'in' + *gignere* 'beget'; compare with **INGENIOUS**. The original sense was 'ingenuity, cunning' (surviving in Scots as *ingine*), hence 'the product of ingenuity, a plot or snare', also 'tool, weapon', later specifically denoting a large mechanical weapon; whence a machine (mid 17th cent.), used commonly later in combinations such as *steam engine, internal-combustion engine.*

engine block ▶ **noun** see **BLOCK** (sense 1 of the noun).

engine driver ▶ **noun** Brit. dated a person who drives a railway locomotive.

engineer ▶ **noun 1** a person who designs, builds, or maintains engines, machines, or structures. ■ a person qualified in a branch of engineering, especially as a professional: *an aeronautical engineer.*
2 a person who controls an engine, especially on an aircraft or ship. ■ N. Amer. a train driver.
3 a skilful contriver or originator of something: *the prime engineer of the approach.*
▶ **verb** [with obj.] **1** design and build (a machine or structure): *the men who engineered the tunnel.* ■ modify (an organism) by manipulating its genetic material: (as adj., with submodifier **engineered**) *genetically engineered plants.*
2 skilfully arrange for (something) to occur: *she engineered another meeting with him.*
– ORIGIN Middle English (denoting a designer and constructor of fortifications and weapons; formerly also as *ingineer*): in early use from Old French *engigneor*, from medieval Latin *ingeniator*, from *ingeniare* 'contrive, devise', from Latin *ingenium* (see **ENGINE**); in later use from French *ingénieur* or Italian *ingegnere*, also based on Latin *ingenium*, with the ending influenced by **-EER**.

engineering ▶ **noun** [mass noun] **1** the branch of science and technology concerned with the design, building, and use of engines, machines, and structures. ■ a field of study or activity concerned with modification or development in a particular area: *software engineering.*
2 the action of working artfully to bring something about: *if not for his shrewd engineering, the election would have been lost.*

engineering brick ▶ **noun** a brick made of semi-vitreous material, which is strong and impervious to water or frost.

engineering science (also **engineering sciences**) ▶ **noun** [mass noun] the parts of science concerned with the physical and mathematical basis of engineering and machine technology.

engine room ▶ **noun** the part of a ship or building in which the engines are housed.

enginery /ˈɛndʒɪn(ə)ri/ ▶ **noun** [mass noun] archaic engines collectively; machinery.

engine turning ▶ **noun** [mass noun] the decoration of metal or ceramic objects with regular engraved patterns using a lathe.
– DERIVATIVES **engine-turned** adjective.

engirdle (also **engird**) ▶ **verb** [with obj.] literary surround; encircle: *railways engirdled this tract of country.*

englacial /ɪnˈɡleɪʃ(ə)l, -sɪəl, ɛn-/ ▶ **adjective** situated, occurring, or formed inside a glacier.

England a country forming the largest and southernmost part of Great Britain and of the United Kingdom, and containing the capital, London; pop. 51,446,000 (est. 2008).

> England was conquered by the Romans in the first century AD, when it was inhabited by Celtic peoples, and was a Roman province until the early 5th century. During the 3rd–7th centuries Germanic-speaking tribes, traditionally known as Angles, Saxons, and Jutes, established a number of independent kingdoms. England emerged as a distinct political entity in the 9th century before being conquered by William, Duke of Normandy, in 1066.

English ▶ **adjective** relating to England or its people or language.
▶ **noun 1** [mass noun] the language of England, now widely used in many varieties throughout the world.
2 (as plural noun **the English**) the people of England.
3 [mass noun] N. Amer. spin or side given to a ball, especially in pool or billiards.

> English is the principal language of Great Britain, the US, Ireland, Canada, Australia, New Zealand, and many other countries. There are some 400 million native speakers, and it is the medium of communication for many millions more: it is the most widely used second language in the world. It belongs to the West Germanic group of Indo-European languages, though its vocabulary has been much influenced by Norman French and Latin.

– DERIVATIVES **Englishness** noun.
– ORIGIN Old English *Englisc* (see **ANGLE**, **-ISH**[1]). The word originally denoted the early Germanic settlers of Britain (Angles, Saxons, and Jutes), or their language (now called **OLD ENGLISH**).

English bond ▶ **noun** [mass noun] Building a bond used in brickwork consisting of alternate courses of stretchers and headers.

English breakfast (also **full English breakfast**) ▶ **noun** a substantial breakfast including hot cooked food such as bacon and eggs.

English Canadian ▶ **noun** a Canadian whose principal language is English.
▶ **adjective** relating to English-speaking Canadians.

English Channel the sea channel separating southern England from northern France. It is 35 km (22 miles) wide at its narrowest point. A railway tunnel beneath it linking England and France was opened in 1994 (the Channel Tunnel).

English Civil War the war between Charles I and his Parliamentary opponents, 1642–9.

> Civil war broke out after Charles refused to accede to a series of demands made by Parliament. The king's forces (the Royalists or Cavaliers) were decisively defeated by the Parliamentary forces (or Roundheads) at the Battle of Naseby (1645), and an attempt by Charles to regain power in alliance with the Scots was defeated in 1648. Charles himself was tried and executed by Parliament in 1649.

English Heritage (in the UK) a body responsible since 1983 for England's ancient monuments, listed buildings, and conservation areas.

English horn ▶ **noun** chiefly N. Amer. another term for **COR ANGLAIS**.

Englishman ▶ **noun** (pl. **Englishmen**) a male native or inhabitant of England, or a man of English descent.
– PHRASES **an Englishman's home is his castle** Brit. proverb an English person's home is a place where they may do as they please and from which they may exclude anyone they choose.

English muffin ▶ **noun** North American term for **MUFFIN** (sense 2).

English mustard ▶ **noun** [mass noun] a kind of mustard made from mustard seeds milled to a powder, having a very hot taste and typically bright yellow in colour.

English Pale (also **the Pale**) **1** a small area round Calais, the only part of France remaining in English hands after the Hundred Years War. It was recaptured by France in 1558.
2 that part of Ireland over which England exercised jurisdiction before the whole country was conquered. Centred on Dublin, it varied in extent at different times from the reign of Henry II until the full conquest under Elizabeth I.
– ORIGIN *Pale* from **PALE**[2].

English rose ▶ **noun** an attractive English girl with a delicate, fair-skinned complexion regarded as typically English.

English setter ▶ **noun** a setter of a breed with a long white or partly white coat.

English springer ▶ **noun** see **SPRINGER** (sense 1).

Englishwoman ▶ **noun** (pl. **Englishwomen**) a female native or inhabitant of England, or a woman of English descent.

englobe ▶ **verb** [with obj.] literary enclose in or shape into a globe.

engorge /ɪnˈɡɔːdʒ, ɛn-/ ▶ **verb 1** [with obj.] cause to swell with blood, water, or another fluid: *the river was engorged by a day-long deluge.*
2 (**engorge oneself**) archaic eat to excess.
– DERIVATIVES **engorgement** noun.
– ORIGIN late 15th cent. (in the sense 'gorge; eat or fill to excess'): from Old French *engorgier* 'feed to excess', from *en-* 'into' + *gorge* 'throat'.

engraft (also **ingraft**) ▶ **verb** another term for **GRAFT**[1].
– DERIVATIVES **engraftment** noun.
– ORIGIN late 16th cent. (formerly also as *engraff, ingraft*): from **EN-**[1], **IN-**[2] 'into' + **GRAFT**[1].

engrailed ▶ **adjective** chiefly Heraldry having semicircular indentations along the edge. Compare with **INVECTED**.
– ORIGIN late Middle English (as verb *engrail*): from Old French *engresler* 'make thin', from *en-* (expressing a change of state) + *gresle* 'thin', from Latin *gracilis*.

engrain ▶ **verb** variant spelling of **INGRAIN**.

engrained ▶ **adjective** variant spelling of **INGRAINED**.

E

engram /ˈɛngram/ ▸ **noun** a hypothetical permanent change in the brain accounting for the existence of memory; a memory trace.
– DERIVATIVES **engrammatic adjective.**
– ORIGIN early 20th cent.: coined in German from Greek *en-* 'within' + *gramma* 'letter of the alphabet'.

engrave ▸ **verb** [with obj.] cut or carve (a text or design) on the surface of a hard object: *my name was engraved on the ring.* ■ cut or carve a text or design on (a hard object). ■ cut (a design) as lines on a metal plate for printing. ■ (**be engraved on** or **in**) be permanently fixed in (one's memory or mind): *the image would be forever engraved in his memory.*
– PHRASES **be engraved in stone** see **STONE.**
– DERIVATIVES **engraver noun.**
– ORIGIN late 15th cent. (formerly also as *ingrave*): from **EN-**[1], **IN-**[2] 'in, on' + **GRAVE**[3], influenced by obsolete French *engraver*.

engraving ▸ **noun** a print made from an engraved plate, block, or other surface. ■ [mass noun] the process or art of engraving a design on a hard surface, especially to make a print.

engross /ɪnˈɡrəʊs, ɛn-/ ▸ **verb** [with obj.] **1** (often **be engrossed in**) absorb all the attention or interest of: *they seemed to be engrossed in conversation* | *the notes totally engrossed him* | (as adj. **engrossing**) *the most engrossing parts of the book.* ■ archaic gain or keep exclusive possession of.
2 Law produce (a legal document, especially a deed or statute) in its final form.
– DERIVATIVES **engrossingly adverb.**
– ORIGIN late Middle English (formerly also as *ingross*): based on **EN-**[1], **IN-**[2] 'in' + late Latin *grossus* 'large'. Sense 1 is from Old French *en gros*, from medieval Latin *in grosso* 'wholesale'; sense 2 comes from Anglo-Norman French *engrosser*, medieval Latin *ingrossare*, from Old French *grosse*, medieval Latin *grossa* 'large writing', with reference to clerks writing out documents in large, clear writing.

engrossment ▸ **noun** Law the final version of a legal document, especially a deed or statute.

engulf ▸ **verb** [with obj.] **1** (of a natural force) sweep over (something) so as to surround or cover it completely: *the cafe was* **engulfed in** *flames* | figurative *Europe might be engulfed by war.*
2 powerfully affect (someone); overwhelm: *a feeling of anguish so great that it threatened to engulf him.*
– DERIVATIVES **engulfment noun.**
– ORIGIN mid 16th cent. (formerly also as *ingulf*): from **EN-**[1], **IN-**[2] 'in, on' + **GULF.**

enhance /ɪnˈhɑːns, -hans, ɛn-/ ▸ **verb** [with obj.] intensify, increase, or further improve the quality, value, or extent of: *his refusal does nothing to enhance his reputation.*
– ORIGIN Middle English (formerly also as *inhance*): from Anglo-Norman French *enhauncer*, based on Latin *in-* (expressing intensive force) + *altus* 'high'. The word originally meant 'elevate' (literally and figuratively), later 'exaggerate, make appear greater', also 'raise the value or price of something'. Current senses date from the early 16th cent.

enhancement /ɪnˈhɑːnsm(ə)nt, ɛn-/ ▸ **noun** an increase or improvement in quality, value, or extent: *this programme of enhancements will improve the daily experience of passengers* | [mass noun] *the enhancement of civic amenities.*

enhancer ▸ **noun** a person or thing that enhances something: *a sweetener and flavour enhancer.*
■ Genetics a DNA sequence that increases the level of transcription of a gene that is located nearby on the same chromosome.

enharmonic /ˌɛnhɑːˈmɒnɪk/ ▸ **adjective** Music relating to or denoting notes which are the same in pitch (in modern tuning) though bearing different names (e.g. F sharp and G flat or B and C flat). ■ of or having intervals smaller than a semitone (e.g. between notes such as F sharp and G flat, in systems of tuning which distinguish them).
– DERIVATIVES **enharmonically adverb.**
– ORIGIN early 17th cent. (designating ancient Greek music based on a tetrachord divided into two quarter-tones and a major third): via late Latin from Greek *enarmonikos*, from *en-* 'in' + *harmonia* 'harmony'.

enigma /ɪˈnɪɡmə/ ▸ **noun** a person or thing that is mysterious or difficult to understand: *Madeleine was still an enigma to him.*
– ORIGIN mid 16th cent.: via Latin from Greek *ainigma*, from *ainissesthai* 'speak allusively', from *ainos* 'fable'.

enigmatic /ˌɛnɪɡˈmatɪk/ ▸ **adjective** difficult to interpret or understand; mysterious: *he took the money with an enigmatic smile.*
– DERIVATIVES **enigmatical adjective, enigmatically adverb.**
– ORIGIN early 17th cent.: from French *énigmatique* or late Latin *aenigmaticus*, based on Greek *ainigma* 'riddle' (see **ENIGMA**).

enisle /ɛnˈʌɪl, ɪn-/ ▸ **verb** [with obj.] literary isolate on or as if on an island.

Eniwetok /ɛˈniːwəˌtɔːk, ˌɛnɪˈwiːtɔːk/ (also **Enewetak**) an uninhabited island in the North Pacific, one of the Marshall Islands. Cleared of its native population, it was used by the US as a testing ground for atom bombs from 1948 to 1954.

enjambed /ɪnˈdʒam, ɛn-/ ▸ **adjective** (of a line, couplet, or stanza of verse) ending part-way through a sentence or clause which continues in the next.
– ORIGIN late 19th cent.: from French *enjamber* 'stride over' + **-ED**[2].

enjambement /ɪnˈdʒam(b)m(ə)nt, ɛn-, ɒ̃ˈʒɒ̃bmɒ̃/ (also **enjambment**) ▸ **noun** [mass noun] (in verse) the continuation of a sentence without a pause beyond the end of a line, couplet, or stanza.
– ORIGIN mid 19th cent.: French, from *enjamber* 'stride over, go beyond', from *en-* 'in' + *jambe* 'leg'.

enjoin ▸ **verb** [with obj. and infinitive] instruct or urge (someone) to do something: *the code enjoined members to trade fairly.* ■ [with obj.] prescribe (an action or attitude) to be performed or adopted: *the charitable deeds* **enjoined on** *him by religion.* ■ [with obj.] (**enjoin someone from**) Law prohibit someone from performing (a particular action) by issuing an injunction.
– DERIVATIVES **enjoinment noun.**
– ORIGIN Middle English (formerly also as *injoin*): from Old French *enjoindre*, from Latin *injungere* 'join, attach, impose', from *in-* 'in, towards' + *jungere* 'to join'.

enjoinder ▸ **noun** Law a prohibition ordered by an injunction.

enjoy ▸ **verb** [with obj.] **1** take delight or pleasure in (an activity or occasion): *I enjoy watching good films.* ■ (**enjoy oneself**) have a pleasant time: *I could never enjoy myself, knowing you were in your room alone.* ■ [no obj., in imperative] informal, chiefly N. Amer. used to urge someone to take pleasure in what is being offered or is about to happen: *Bake until the filling starts to bubble and the crust turns golden brown. Enjoy!*
2 possess and benefit from: *the security forces enjoy legal immunity from prosecution.*
– DERIVATIVES **enjoyer noun.**
– ORIGIN late Middle English: from Old French *enjoier* 'give joy to' or *enjoïr* 'enjoy', both based on Latin *gaudere* 'rejoice'.

enjoyable ▸ **adjective** (of an activity or occasion) giving delight or pleasure: *they had an enjoyable afternoon.*
– DERIVATIVES **enjoyability noun, enjoyableness noun, enjoyably adverb.**

enjoyment ▸ **noun** [mass noun] **1** the state or process of taking pleasure in something: *the enjoyment of a good wine.* ■ [count noun] a thing that gives pleasure: *one of his particular enjoyments was campfire singing.*
2 the action of possessing and benefiting from something.

enkephalin /ɛnˈkɛf(ə)lɪn/ (also **encephalin**) ▸ **noun** Biochemistry either of two peptide compounds occurring naturally in the brain, related to the endorphins and having similar physiological effects.
– ORIGIN 1970s: from Greek *enkephalos* 'brain' (from *en-* 'in' + *kephalē* 'head') + **-IN**[1].

enkindle ▸ **verb** [with obj.] literary **1** set on fire.
2 arouse or inspire (an emotion): *fresh remembrance of vexation must still enkindle rage.*

enlace ▸ **verb** [with obj.] literary entwine or entangle.
– ORIGIN Middle English: from Old French *enlacier*, based on Latin *laqueus* 'noose'.

enlarge ▸ **verb** make or become larger or more extensive: [with obj.] *recently my son enlarged our garden pond* | (as adj. **enlarged**) *an enlarged spleen.* ■ [with obj.] develop a larger print of (a photograph).
– PHRASAL VERBS **enlarge on/upon** speak or write about (something) in greater detail: *I would like to enlarge on this theme.*
– ORIGIN Middle English (formerly also as *inlarge*): from Old French *enlarger*, from *en-* (expressing a change of state) + *large* 'large'.

enlargement ▸ **noun 1** [mass noun] the action or state of enlarging or being enlarged.
2 a photograph that is larger than the original negative or an earlier print.

enlarger ▸ **noun** Photography an apparatus for enlarging or reducing negatives or positives.

enlighten ▸ **verb** [with obj.] **1** give (someone) greater knowledge and understanding about a subject or situation: *Christopher had not enlightened Francis as to their relationship.* ■ give (someone) spiritual knowledge or insight.
2 archaic shed light on (an object).
– DERIVATIVES **enlightener noun.**
– ORIGIN Middle English (in the sense 'make luminous'; formerly also as *inlighten*): in early use from Old English *inlīhtan* 'to shine'; later from **EN-**[1], **IN-**[2] (as an intensifier) + **LIGHTEN**[2] or the noun **LIGHT**[1].

enlightened ▸ **adjective** having or showing a rational, modern, and well-informed outlook: *the more enlightened employers offer better terms.* ■ spiritually aware.

enlightenment ▸ **noun 1** [mass noun] the action of enlightening or the state of being enlightened: *Robbie looked to me for enlightenment.* ■ the action or state of attaining or having attained spiritual knowledge or insight, in particular (in Buddhism) that awareness which frees a person from the cycle of rebirth.
2 (**the Enlightenment**) a European intellectual movement of the late 17th and 18th centuries emphasizing reason and individualism rather than tradition. It was heavily influenced by 17th-century philosophers such as Descartes, Locke, and Newton, and its prominent figures included Kant, Goethe, Voltaire, Rousseau, and Adam Smith.

enlist ▸ **verb** enrol or be enrolled in the armed services: [no obj.] *he* **enlisted in** *the Royal Naval Air Service* | [with obj.] *hundreds of thousands of recruits had been enlisted.* ■ [with obj.] engage (a person or their help or support): *the company enlisted the help of independent consultants.*
– DERIVATIVES **enlistee noun, enlistment noun.**
– ORIGIN mid 16th cent. (formerly also as *inlist*): from **EN-**[1], **IN-**[2] 'in, on' + **LIST**[1], perhaps suggested by Dutch *inlijsten* 'put on a list'.

enlisted man ▸ **noun** US a member of the armed forces below the rank of officer.

enliven ▸ **verb** [with obj.] make (something) more entertaining, interesting, or appealing: *the wartime routine was enlivened by a series of concerts.* ■ make (someone) more cheerful or animated: *the visit had clearly enlivened my mother.*
– DERIVATIVES **enlivener noun, enlivenment noun.**
– ORIGIN mid 17th cent. (in the sense 'restore to life, give life to'; formerly also as *inliven*): from 16th-cent. *enlive, inlive* (in the same sense), from **EN-**[1], **IN-**[2] (as an intensifier) + **LIFE.**

en masse /ɒ̃ ˈmas/ ▸ **adverb** in a group; all together: *the cabinet immediately resigned en masse.*
– ORIGIN late 18th cent.: French, 'in a mass'.

enmesh ▸ **verb** [with obj.] (usu. **be enmeshed in**) cause to become entangled in something: *whales enmeshed in drift nets.* ■ involve (someone) in a difficult situation from which it is hard to escape: *he is enmeshed in an adulterous affair.*
– DERIVATIVES **enmeshment noun.**

enmity ▸ **noun** (pl. **enmities**) [mass noun] a state or feeling of active opposition or hostility: *decades of enmity between the two countries* | [count noun] *family feuds and enmities.*
– ORIGIN Middle English: from Old French *enemi(s)tie*, based on Latin *inimicus* (see **ENEMY**).

ennead /ˈɛnɪad/ ▸ **noun** rare a group or set of nine.
– ORIGIN mid 16th cent.: from Greek *enneas, ennead-*, from *ennea* 'nine'.

enneagram /ˈɛnɪəɡram/ ▸ **noun** a nine-sided figure used in a particular system of analysis to represent the spectrum of possible personality types.
– ORIGIN from Greek *ennea* 'nine' + **-GRAM**[1].

Ennis /ˈɛnɪs/ the county town of Clare, in the Republic of Ireland; pop. 20,142 (2006).

Enniskillen /ˌɛnɪsˈkɪlɪn/ a town in Northern Ireland; pop. 15,600 (est. 2009). The old spelling *Inniskilling* is preserved as a regimental name in the British army, commemorating the defence of Enniskillen by its townsmen against the supporters of the deposed King James II in 1689.

Ennius /ˈɛnɪəs/, Quintus (239–169 BC), Roman epic poet and dramatist. He was largely responsible for the creation of a native Roman literature based on Greek models, but only fragments of his many works survive.

ennoble ▸ **verb** [with obj.] **1** give (someone) a noble rank or title.
2 lend greater dignity or nobility of character to: *the theatre is a moral instrument to ennoble the mind.*
– DERIVATIVES **ennoblement** noun.
– ORIGIN late 15th cent. (formerly also as *innoble*): from French *ennoblir*, from *en-* (expressing a change of state) + *noble* 'noble'.

ennui /ɒn'wiː/ ▸ **noun** [mass noun] a feeling of listlessness and dissatisfaction arising from a lack of occupation or excitement.
– ORIGIN mid 18th cent.: French, from Latin *in odio(n-)*, from *mihi in odio est* 'it is hateful to me'. Compare with **ANNOY**.

Enoch /'iːnɒk/ **1** (in the Bible) the eldest son of Cain. ■ the first city, built by Cain (Gen. 4:17).
2 a Hebrew patriarch, father of Methuselah.

enoki /ɪ'nəʊki/ (also **enoki mushroom**) ▸ **noun** an edible Japanese mushroom, growing in clusters, with slender stems and small caps. ● *Flammulina velutipes*, family Agaricaceae, class Hymenomycetes.
– ORIGIN 1980s: from Japanese *enoki-take*, from *enoki* 'nettle tree' + *take* 'mushroom'.

enology ▸ **noun** US spelling of **OENOLOGY**.

enophile ▸ **noun** US spelling of **OENOPHILE**.

enormity ▸ **noun** (pl. **enormities**) **1** [mass noun] (**the enormity of**) the great or extreme scale, seriousness, or extent of something perceived as bad or morally wrong: *a thorough search disclosed the full enormity of the crime.* ■ (in neutral use) large size or scale: *I began to get a sense of the enormity of the task.*
2 a grave crime or sin: *the enormities of war.*
– ORIGIN late Middle English: via Old French from Latin *enormitas*, from *enormis*, from *e-* (variant of *ex-*) 'out of' + *norma* 'pattern, standard'. The word originally meant 'deviation from legal or moral rectitude' and 'transgression'. Current senses have been influenced by **ENORMOUS**.

> **USAGE** **Enormity** traditionally means 'the extreme scale or seriousness of something bad or morally wrong', as in *residents of the town were struggling to deal with the enormity of the crime.* Today, however, a more neutral sense as a synonym for **hugeness** or **immensity**, as in *he soon discovered the enormity of the task*, is common. Some people regard this use as wrong, arguing that **enormity** in its original sense meant 'a crime' and should therefore continue to be used only of contexts in which a negative moral judgement is implied. Nevertheless, the sense is now broadly accepted in standard English, although it generally relates to something difficult, such as a task, challenge, or achievement.

enormous ▸ **adjective** very large in size, quantity, or extent: *enormous sums of money* | *the possibilities are enormous.*
– DERIVATIVES **enormousness** noun.
– ORIGIN mid 16th cent.: from Latin *enormis* 'unusual, huge' (see **ENORMITY**) + **-OUS**.

enormously ▸ **adverb** to a very great degree or extent; considerably: *quality of life varies enormously from one place to another* | [as submodifier] *she has been enormously successful.*

enosis /ɪ'nəʊsɪs, 'ɛnəsɪs/ ▸ **noun** [mass noun] the political union of Cyprus and Greece, as an aim or ideal of certain Greeks and Cypriots.
– ORIGIN 1920s: from modern Greek *henōsis*, from *hena* 'one'.

enough ▸ **determiner & pronoun** as much or as many as required: [as determiner] *too much work and not* **enough** *people to do it* | *there was just* **enough** *room* **for** *two cars* | [as pronoun] *getting* **enough** *of the right things to eat* | [as postpositive adj.] *there will be time enough to tell you when we meet.* ■ used to indicate that one is unwilling to tolerate any more of something undesirable: [as determiner] *we've got enough problems without that* | [as pronoun] *I've* **had enough of** *this arguing* | **that's enough**, *pack it in.*
▸ **adverb** to the required degree or extent (used after an adjective, adverb, or verb): *before he was old* **enough** *to shave* | *you're not big* **enough for** *basketball.* ■ to a moderate degree; fairly: *he can get there easily enough* | *he seems nice enough.* ■ [with sentence adverb] used for emphasis: *curiously enough, there is no mention of him.*
– PHRASES **enough is as good as a feast** proverb moderation is more satisfying than excess. **enough is enough** no more will be tolerated. **enough said** there is no need to say more; all is understood.
– ORIGIN Old English *genōg*, of Germanic origin; related to Dutch *genoeg* and German *genug*.

en papillote /ɒ̃ 'papɪjɒt/ ▸ **adjective & adverb** (of food) cooked and served in a paper wrapper: [as postpositive adj.] *fish en papillote.*
– ORIGIN French.

en passant /ɒ̃ pa'sɑːnt, 'pasɒ̃/ ▸ **adverb** **1** by the way; incidentally: *the singular distinction of being mentioned, en passant, in an Act of Parliament.*
2 Chess by the en passant rule.
– PHRASES **en passant rule** (or **law**) Chess the rule that a pawn making a first move of two squares instead of one may nevertheless be immediately captured by an opposing pawn on the fifth rank.
– ORIGIN early 17th cent.: French, literally 'in passing'.

en pension /ɒ̃ 'pɒ̃sjɒ̃/ ▸ **adverb & adjective** as a boarder or lodger in a small hotel or private house.
– ORIGIN French (see **PENSION²**).

enplane ▸ **verb** variant spelling of **EMPLANE**.

en plein air /,ɒ̃ plɛn 'ɛː/ ▸ **adverb** (chiefly with reference to painting) in the open air. See also **PLEIN-AIR**.

en pointe ▸ **adjective & adverb** see **ON POINTE** at **POINTE**.

en poste /ɒ̃ pɒst/ ▸ **adverb** in an official diplomatic position at a particular place.
– ORIGIN French.

en primeur /,ɒ̃ prɪ'məː/, French /ɑ̃ pʀimœʀ/ ▸ **adjective & adverb** (of wine) newly produced and made available.
– ORIGIN French, literally 'as being new'.

enprint /'ɛnprɪnt/ ▸ **noun** Brit. a standard-sized photographic print produced by printing the whole of a negative to a moderate enlargement.
– ORIGIN mid 20th cent.: from *enlarged print.*

en prise /ɒ̃ 'priːz/ ▸ **adjective** [predic.] Chess (of a piece or pawn) in a position to be taken.
– ORIGIN early 19th cent.: French.

enqueue ▸ **verb** (**enqueues, enqueuing** or **enqueueing, enqueued**) [with obj.] Computing add (an item of data awaiting processing) to a queue of such items.

enquire ▸ **verb** chiefly Brit. **1** [reporting verb] ask for information from someone: [no obj.] ***he enquired about*** *cottages for sale* | [with clause] *I enquired where he lived* | [with direct speech] *'How well do you know Berlin?' he* **enquired of** *Hencke.* ■ [no obj.] (**enquire after**) ask about the health and well-being of (someone): *Angus enquired after her parents.* ■ [no obj.] (**enquire for**) ask to see or speak to (someone).
2 [no obj.] (**enquire into**) investigate; look into: *the task of political sociology is to enquire into the causes of political events.*
– DERIVATIVES **enquirer** noun.
– ORIGIN Middle English *enquere*, from Old French *enquerre*, based on Latin *inquirere* (based on *quaerere* 'seek').

> **USAGE** The traditional distinction between **enquire** and **inquire** is that **enquire** is used for general senses of 'ask' while **inquire** is reserved for uses meaning 'make a formal investigation'. In practice, however, there little discernible distinction in the way the two words are used today in British English, although **inquiry** is commoner than **enquiry** in the sense 'a formal investigation'. In all senses **inquire** and **inquiry** are the more usual forms in US English, whereas **enquire** and **enquiry** are chiefly restricted to British English.

enquiring ▸ **adjective** showing an interest in learning new things: *an open, enquiring mind.* ■ (of a look) suggesting that information is sought: *he sent her an enquiring glance.*
– DERIVATIVES **enquiringly** adverb.

enquiry ▸ **noun** (pl. **enquiries**) an act of asking for information: *the police were* **making enquiries** *in all the neighbouring pubs* | [mass noun] *her mind was buzzing with possible lines of enquiry.* ■ an official investigation.

enquiry agent ▸ **noun** Brit. dated a private detective.

enrage ▸ **verb** [with obj.] make (someone) very angry: *the students were enraged at these new rules.*
– ORIGIN late 15th cent. (formerly also as *inrage*): from French *enrager*, from *en-* 'into' + *rage* 'rage, anger'.

enraged ▸ **adjective** very angry; furious: *an enraged mob screamed abuse.*

en rapport /,ɒ̃ ra'pɔː/ ▸ **adverb** having a close and harmonious relationship.
– ORIGIN French (see **RAPPORT**).

enrapt ▸ **adjective** fascinated; enthralled: *the enrapt audience.*

enrapture ▸ **verb** [with obj.] give intense pleasure or joy to: *Ruth was enraptured by the sleeping child.*

enrich ▸ **verb** [with obj.] **1** improve or enhance the quality or value of: *her exposure to museums enriched her life in France.* ■ (usu. as adj. **enriched**) increase the proportion of a particular isotope in (an element), especially that of the fissile isotope U-235 in uranium, so as to make it more powerful or explosive. *enriched uranium.*
2 make (someone) wealthy or wealthier: *top party members had* **enriched themselves**.
– DERIVATIVES **enrichment** noun.
– ORIGIN late Middle English (in the sense 'make wealthy'): from Old French *enrichir*, from *en-* 'in' + *riche* 'rich'.

enrobe ▸ **verb** [with obj.] **1** formal dress in a robe or vestment.
2 coat (an item of food) in chocolate, a sauce, etc.

E

enrol /ɪn'rəʊl, ɛn-/ (US **enroll**) ▸ **verb** (**enrols, enrolling, enrolled**) **1** [no obj.] officially register as a member of an institution or a student on a course: *he* **enrolled in** *drama school* | [with obj.] *all entrants will be* **enrolled on** *new-style courses.* ■ [with obj.] recruit (someone) to perform a service: *a campaign to enrol more foster carers.* ■ archaic write the name of (someone) on a list or register.
2 [with obj.] Law, historical enter (a deed or other document) among the rolls of a court of justice.
– DERIVATIVES **enrollee** noun, **enroller** noun.
– ORIGIN late Middle English (formerly also as *inroll*): from Old French *enroller*, from *en-* 'in' + *rolle* 'a roll' (names being originally written on a roll of parchment).

enrolment (US **enrollment**) ▸ **noun** [mass noun] the action of enrolling or being enrolled: *the amount due must be paid on enrolment in October* | [count noun] *enrolments for teacher training have dropped off sharply.* ■ [count noun] N. Amer. the number of people enrolled at a school or college.

en route /ɒn 'ruːt/ ▸ **adverb** during the course of a journey; on the way: *he stopped in Turkey en route to Geneva.*
– ORIGIN late 18th cent.: French (see **ROUTE**).

en rule /'ɛn ruːl/ ▸ **noun** Brit. a short dash, the width of an en, used in punctuation.

ENSA /'ɛnsə/ an organization which arranged variety entertainment for the British armed services during the Second World War.
– ORIGIN acronym from *Entertainments National Service Association.*

Enschede /'ɛnskə,deɪ/ a city in the Netherlands; pop. 154,753 (2008).

ensconce /ɪn'skɒns, ɛn-/ ▸ **verb** [with obj. and adverbial of place] establish or settle (someone) in a comfortable, safe place: *Agnes* **ensconced herself** *in their bedroom.*
– ORIGIN late 16th cent. (in the senses 'fortify' and 'shelter within or behind a fortification'; formerly also as *insconce*): from **EN-¹**, **IN-²** 'in' + **SCONCE²**.

ensemble /ɒn'sɒmb(ə)l/ ▸ **noun** **1** a group of musicians, actors, or dancers who perform together: *a Bulgarian folk ensemble.* ■ a piece of music or passage written for performance by a whole cast, choir, or group of instruments. ■ [mass noun] the coordination between performers executing an ensemble passage: *a high level of tuning and ensemble is guaranteed.*
2 a group of items viewed as a whole rather than individually: *the buildings in the square present a charming provincial ensemble.* ■ [usu. in sing.] a set of clothes chosen to harmonize when worn together. ■ chiefly Physics a group of similar systems, or different states of the same system, often considered statistically.
– ORIGIN late Middle English (as an adverb (long rare) meaning 'at the same time'): from French, based on Latin *insimul*, from *in-* 'in' + *simul* 'at the same time'. The noun dates from the mid 18th cent.

ensheath ▸ **verb** [with obj.] chiefly Biology enclose (an organism, tissue, structure, etc.) in a sheath.

enshrine ▸ **verb** [with obj. and adverbial of place] place (a revered or precious object) in an appropriate receptacle: *relics are enshrined under altars.* ■ preserve (a right, tradition, or idea) in a form that ensures it will be protected and respected: *the right of all workers to strike was* **enshrined in** *the new constitution.*
– DERIVATIVES **enshrinement** noun.

enshroud /ɪn'ʃraʊd, ɛn-/ ▸ **verb** [with obj.] literary envelop completely and hide from view: *heavy grey clouds enshrouded the city.*

ensiform /'ɛnsɪfɔːm/ ▸ **adjective** chiefly Botany shaped like a sword blade; long and narrow with sharp edges and a pointed tip.

– ORIGIN mid 16th cent.: from Latin *ensis* 'sword' + -FORM.

ensiform cartilage ▶ noun another term for XIPHOID PROCESS.

ensign /ˈɛnsʌɪn/ ▶ noun **1** a flag or standard, especially a military or naval one indicating nationality. ■ archaic a sign or emblem of a particular thing: *all the ensigns of our greatness.*
2 historical a standard-bearer.
3 the lowest rank of commissioned officer in the US and some other navies, above chief warrant officer and below lieutenant. ■ historical the lowest rank of commissioned infantry officer in the British army.
– ORIGIN late Middle English: from Old French *enseigne*, from Latin *insignia* 'signs of office' (see INSIGNIA). Compare with ANCIENT².

E

ensilage /ˈɛnsɪlɪdʒ, ɛnˈsʌɪlɪdʒ/ ▶ noun another term for SILAGE.
▶ verb another term for ENSILE.
– ORIGIN late 19th cent.: from French, from *ensiler* (see ENSILE).

ensile /ɛnˈsʌɪl/ ▶ verb [with obj.] put (grass or another crop) into a silo or silage clamp in order to preserve it as silage.
– ORIGIN late 19th cent.: from French *ensiler*, from Spanish *ensilar*, from *en-* 'in' + *silo* 'silo'.

enslave ▶ verb [with obj.] make (someone) a slave. ■ cause (someone) to lose their freedom of choice or action: *they were enslaved by their need to take drugs.*
– DERIVATIVES **enslaver** noun.
– ORIGIN early 17th cent. (in the sense 'make (a person) subject to a superstition, passion, etc.'; formerly also as *inslave*): from EN-¹, IN-² (as an intensifier) + SLAVE.

enslavement ▶ noun [mass noun] the action of making someone a slave; subjugation: *the enslavement of millions of Africans.*

ensnare ▶ verb [with obj.] catch in or as in a trap: *they were ensnared in city centre traffic.*
– DERIVATIVES **ensnarement** noun.

ensnarl ▶ verb [with obj.] cause to become caught up in complex difficulties or problems.

Ensor /ˈɛnsɔː/, James (Sydney), Baron (1860–1949), Belgian painter and engraver, noted for his macabre subjects. His work is significant both for symbolism and for the development of 20th-century expressionism.

ensorcell /ɪnˈsɔːs(ə)l, ɛn-/ (US also **ensorcel**) ▶ verb (**ensorcells**, **ensorcelling**, **ensorcelled**; US **ensorcels**, **ensorceling**, **ensorceled**) [with obj.] literary enchant; fascinate.
– ORIGIN mid 16th cent.: from Old French *ensorceler*, alteration of *ensorcerer*, from *sorcier* 'sorcerer'.

ensoul ▶ verb [with obj.] endow with a soul.
– DERIVATIVES **ensoulment** noun.

enstatite /ˈɛnstətʌɪt/ ▶ noun [mass noun] a translucent crystalline mineral that occurs in some igneous rocks and stony meteorites. It consists of magnesium silicate and is a member of the pyroxene group.
– ORIGIN mid 19th cent.: from Greek *enstatēs* 'adversary' (because of its refractory nature) + -ITE¹.

ensue ▶ verb (**ensues**, **ensuing**, **ensued**) [no obj.] happen or occur afterwards or as a result: *the difficulties which **ensued from** their commitment to Cuba* | (as adj. **ensuing**) *there were repeated clashes in the ensuing days.*
– ORIGIN late Middle English (formerly also as *insue*): from Old French *ensivre*, from Latin *insequi*, based on *sequi* 'follow'.

en suite /ɒn ˈswiːt/ ▶ adjective & adverb Brit. (of a bathroom) immediately adjoining a bedroom and forming part of the same set of rooms.
– ORIGIN late 18th cent. (in the sense 'in agreement or harmony'): from French, literally 'in sequence'.

ensure /ɪnˈʃɔː, -ˈʃʊə, ɛn-/ ▶ verb [with obj.] make certain that (something) will occur or be the case: [with clause] *the client must ensure that accurate records are kept.* ■ make certain of obtaining or providing (something): *legislation to ensure equal opportunities for all.* ■ [no obj.] (**ensure against**) make sure that (a problem) does not occur.
– ORIGIN late Middle English (in the senses 'convince' and 'make safe'): from Anglo-Norman French *enseurer*, alteration of Old French *aseurer*, earlier form of *assurer* (see ASSURE). Compare with INSURE.

USAGE On the difference between **ensure** and **insure**, see **USAGE** at **INSURE**.

enswathe ▶ verb [with obj.] literary envelop or wrap in a garment or piece of fabric.

ENT ▶ abbreviation ear, nose, and throat (as a department in a hospital).

-ent ▶ suffix **1** (forming adjectives) denoting an occurrence of action: *refluent.* ■ denoting a state: *convenient.*
2 (forming nouns) denoting an agent: *coefficient.*
– ORIGIN from French, or from the Latin present participial verb stem *-ent-* (see also -ANT).

entablature /ɛnˈtablətʃə, ɪn-/ ▶ noun Architecture the upper part of a classical building supported by columns or a colonnade, comprising the architrave, frieze, and cornice.
– ORIGIN early 17th cent. (formerly also as *intablature*): from Italian *intavolatura* 'boarding' (partly via French *entablement* 'entablement'), from *intavolare* 'board up' (based on *tavola* 'table').

entablement /ɛnˈteɪb(ə)lm(ə)nt, ɪn-/ ▶ noun Architecture a platform supporting a statue, above the dado and base.
– ORIGIN mid 17th cent. (in the sense 'entablature'): from French, based on *table* 'table'.

entail ▶ verb [with obj.] **1** involve (something) as a necessary or inevitable part or consequence: *a situation which entails considerable risks.* ■ Logic have as a logically necessary consequence.
2 Law limit the inheritance of (property) over a number of generations so that ownership remains within a particular family or group: *her father's estate was **entailed on** a cousin.* ■ archaic cause to experience or possess (something) permanently or inescapably: *I cannot get rid of the disgrace which you have **entailed upon** us.*
▶ noun Law a limitation of the inheritance of property to certain heirs over a number of generations. ■ a property bequeathed under such conditions.
– DERIVATIVES **entailment** noun.
– ORIGIN late Middle English (referring to settlement of property; formerly also as *intail*): from EN-¹, IN-² 'into' + Old French *taille* 'notch, tax' (see TAIL²).

entamoeba /ˌɛntəˈmiːbə/ (US also **entameba**) ▶ noun (pl. **entamoebae** /-biː/ or **entamoebas**) an amoeba that typically lives harmlessly in the gut, though one kind can cause amoebic dysentery. ● Genus *Entamoeba*, phylum Rhizopoda, kingdom Protista.
– ORIGIN modern Latin, from Greek *entos* 'within' + AMOEBA.

entangle ▶ verb [with obj.] cause to become twisted together with or caught in: *fish attempt to swim through the mesh and become entangled.* ■ involve (someone) in difficulties or complicated circumstances from which it is difficult to escape: *they were suspicious of becoming entangled in a civil war.*

entanglement ▶ noun [mass noun] the action or fact of entangling or being entangled: *many dolphins die from entanglement in fishing nets.* ■ [count noun] a complicated or compromising relationship or situation: *romantic entanglements.* ■ [count noun] an extensive barrier, typically made of barbed wire and stakes, erected to impede enemy soldiers or vehicles.

entasis /ˈɛntəsɪs/ ▶ noun (pl. **entases**) Architecture a slight convex curve in the shaft of a column, introduced to correct the visual illusion of concavity produced by a straight shaft.
– ORIGIN mid 17th cent.: modern Latin, from Greek, from *enteinein* 'to stretch or strain'.

Entebbe /ɛnˈtɛbi/ a town in southern Uganda, on the north shore of Lake Victoria; pop. 73,100 (est. 2009). It was the capital of Uganda during the period of British rule, from 1894 to 1962.

entelechy /ɛnˈtɛləki, ɪn-/ ▶ noun (pl. **entelechies**) [mass noun] Philosophy the realization of potential. ■ the supposed vital principle that guides the development and functioning of an organism or other system or organization.
– ORIGIN late Middle English: via late Latin from Greek *entelekheia* (used by Aristotle), from *en-* 'within' + *telos* 'end, perfection' + *ekhein* 'be in a certain state'.

entellus /ɪnˈtɛləs, ɛn-/ (also **entellus monkey**) ▶ noun another term for HANUMAN.
– ORIGIN mid 19th cent.: from the name of an aged Trojan in Virgil's *Aeneid*.

entelodont /ɛnˈtɛlədɒnt/ ▶ noun a large pig-like mammal of the Oligocene epoch with two bony knobs on its lower jaw. ● Suborder Suina, order Artiodactyla.
– ORIGIN modern Latin, from Greek *entelēs* 'perfect' + *odous, odont-* 'tooth'.

entente /ɒnˈtɒnt, ɒ̃ˈtɒ̃t/ (also **entente cordiale** /ˌkɔːdɪˈɑːl/) ▶ noun a friendly understanding or informal alliance between states or factions: *the emperor hoped to bring about an entente with Russia.* ■ a group of states in an informal alliance. ■ (**the Entente Cordiale**) the understanding between Britain and France reached in 1904, forming the basis of Anglo-French cooperation in the First World War.
– ORIGIN mid 19th cent.: French *entente (cordiale)* '(friendly) understanding'.

enter ▶ verb [with obj.] **1** come or go into (a place): *she entered the kitchen* | [no obj.] *the door opened and Karl entered.* ■ [no obj.] used as a stage direction to indicate when a character comes on stage: *enter Hamlet.* ■ come or be introduced into: *the thought never entered my head.* ■ penetrate (something): *the bullet entered his stomach.* ■ (of a man) insert the penis into the vagina of (a woman).
2 begin to be involved in: *in 1941 America entered the war.* ■ become a member of or start working in (an institution or profession): *he entered the army as a cadet.* ■ register as a competitor or participant in a tournament, race, or examination: *they won every race they entered* | *the horse was entered in the Martell Cup at Aintree.* ■ start or reach (a stage or period of time) in an activity or situation: *the election campaign entered its final phase.* ■ [no obj.] (of a particular performer in an ensemble) start or resume playing or singing.
3 write or key (information) in a book, computer, etc.: *children can **enter** the data **into** the computer.*
4 Law submit (a statement) in an official capacity: *a solicitor entered a plea of guilty on her behalf.*
▶ noun (also **enter key**) a key on a computer keyboard which is used to perform various functions, such as executing a command or selecting options on a menu.
– PHRASES **enter one's head** (or **mind**) (of a thought or idea) occur to one: *the thought never entered my head!* **enter into force** come into effect: *the treaty entered into force in 1975.* **enter into the spirit of something** begin to enjoy and feel part of a lively event or atmosphere: *people **entered into the spirit of the occasion.*** **enter someone's life** (of a person or thing) start to play a significant part in someone's existence: *Shiona had been sixteen when Jake entered her life.*
– PHRASAL VERBS **enter into** become involved in (an activity or situation): *they have entered into a relationship.* ■ undertake to bind oneself by (an agreement or other commitment): *the council entered into an agreement with a private firm.* ■ form part of or be a factor in: *medical ethics also enter into the question.* **enter on/upon 1** formal begin (an activity or job); start to pursue (a particular course in life): *he entered upon a turbulent political career.* **2** Law (as a legal entitlement) go freely into (property) as or as if the owner.
– ORIGIN Middle English: from Old French *entrer*, from Latin *intrare*, from *intra* 'within'.

enteral /ˈɛntər(ə)l/ ▶ adjective Medicine involving or passing through the intestine, either naturally via the mouth and oesophagus, or through an artificial opening. Often contrasted with PARENTERAL.
– DERIVATIVES **enterally** adverb.
– ORIGIN early 20th cent.: from Greek *enteron* 'intestine' + -AL, partly as a back-formation from PARENTERAL.

enteric /ɛnˈtɛrɪk/ ▶ adjective relating to or occurring in the intestines.
– ORIGIN early 19th cent.: from Greek *enterikos*, from *enteron* 'intestine'.

enteric fever ▶ noun another term for TYPHOID or PARATYPHOID.

enteritis /ˌɛntəˈrʌɪtɪs/ ▶ noun [mass noun] Medicine inflammation of the intestine, especially the small intestine, usually accompanied by diarrhoea.

entero- ▶ combining form relating to the intestine: *enterovirus.*
– ORIGIN from Greek *enteron*.

enterococcus /ˌɛntərəʊˈkɒk(ə)s/ ▶ noun (pl. **enterococci** /-ˈkɒk(s)ʌɪ, -k(s)iː/) a streptococcus of a group that occurs naturally in the intestine but causes inflammation and blood infection if introduced elsewhere in the body (e.g. by injury or surgery). ● Genus *Streptococcus* (or *Enterococcus*); Gram-positive cocci.

enterocoel /ˈɛntərəʊˌsiːl/ ▶ noun Zoology a coelom or coelomic cavity, present in some invertebrates, which has developed from the wall of the archenteron.
– DERIVATIVES **enterocoely** noun.

enterocolitis /ˌɛntərəʊkəˈlʌɪtɪs/ ▶ **noun** [mass noun] Medicine inflammation of both the small intestine and the colon.

enterocyte /ˈɛntərə(ʊ)sʌɪt/ ▶ **noun** Physiology a cell of the intestinal lining.

enterohepatic /ˌɛntərəʊhɪˈpatɪk/ ▶ **adjective** Physiology relating to or denoting the circulation of bile salts and other secretions from the liver to the intestine, where they are reabsorbed into the blood and returned to the liver.

enteropathy /ˌɛntəˈrɒpəθi/ ▶ **noun** [mass noun] (pl. **enteropathies**) Medicine a disease of the intestine, especially the small intestine.

enterostomy /ˌɛntəˈrɒstəmi/ ▶ **noun** (pl. **enterostomies**) an ileostomy or similar surgical operation in which the small intestine is diverted to an artificial opening in the abdominal wall or in another part of the intestine. ■ an opening in the abdominal wall formed in this way.

enterotomy /ˌɛntəˈrɒtəmi/ ▶ **noun** [mass noun] rare the surgical cutting open of the intestine.

enterotoxaemia /ˌɛntərəʊtɒkˈsiːmiə/ (US **enterotoxemia**) ▶ **noun** [mass noun] chiefly Veterinary Medicine blood poisoning caused by an enterotoxin.

enterotoxigenic /ˌɛntərəʊˌtɒksɪˈdʒɛnɪk/ ▶ **adjective** Medicine (of bacteria) producing an enterotoxin.

enterotoxin /ˌɛntərəʊˈtɒksɪn/ ▶ **noun** Medicine a toxin produced in or affecting the intestines, such as those causing food poisoning or cholera.

enterovirus /ˈɛntərəʊˌvʌɪrəs/ ▶ **noun** Medicine any of a group of RNA viruses (including those causing polio and hepatitis A) which typically occur in the gastro-intestinal tract, sometimes spreading to the central nervous system or other parts of the body.

enterprise ▶ **noun 1** a project or undertaking, especially a bold or complex one: *a joint enterprise between French and Japanese companies.* ■ [mass noun] initiative and resourcefulness: *success came quickly, thanks to a mixture of talent, enterprise, and luck.*
2 a business or company: *a state-owned enterprise.* ■ [mass noun] entrepreneurial economic activity.
– DERIVATIVES **enterpriser** noun.
– ORIGIN late Middle English: from Old French, 'something undertaken', feminine past participle (used as a noun) of *entreprendre*, based on Latin *prendere, prehendere* 'to take'.

enterprise culture ▶ **noun** a capitalist society in which taking on financial risks in the hope of profit is encouraged.

enterprise zone ▶ **noun** an area in which state incentives such as tax concessions are offered to encourage business investment.

enterprising ▶ **adjective** having or showing initiative and resourcefulness: *some enterprising teachers have started their own recycling programmes.*
– DERIVATIVES **enterprisingly** adverb.

entertain ▶ **verb** [with obj.] **1** provide (someone) with amusement or enjoyment: *a tremendous game that thoroughly entertained the crowd.* ■ receive (someone) as a guest and provide them with food and drink: *a private dining room where members could entertain groups of friends.*
2 give attention or consideration to (an idea or feeling): *Washington entertained little hope of an early improvement in relations.*
– ORIGIN late Middle English: from French *entretenir*, based on Latin *inter* 'among' + *tenere* 'to hold'. The word originally meant 'maintain, continue', later 'maintain in a certain condition, treat in a certain way', also 'show hospitality' (late 15th cent.).

entertainer ▶ **noun** a person, such as a singer, dancer, or comedian, whose job is to entertain others.

entertaining ▶ **adjective** providing amusement or enjoyment: *a charming and entertaining companion.*
– DERIVATIVES **entertainingly** adverb.

entertainment ▶ **noun** [mass noun] the action of providing or being provided with amusement or enjoyment: *everyone just sits in front of the television for entertainment.* ■ [count noun] an event, performance, or activity designed to entertain others: *a theatrical entertainment.* ■ the action of receiving a guest or guests and providing them with food and drink.

enthalpy /ˈɛnθ(ə)lpi, ɛnˈθalpi/ ▶ **noun** Physics a thermodynamic quantity equivalent to the total heat content of a system. It is equal to the internal energy of the system plus the product of pressure and volume. (Symbol: **H**) ■ the change in enthalpy associated with a particular chemical process.
– ORIGIN 1920s: from Greek *enthalpein* 'warm in', from *en-* 'within' + *thalpein* 'to heat'.

enthral /ɪnˈθrɔːl, ɛn-/ (US **enthrall**) ▶ **verb** (**enthrals, enthralling, enthralled**) [with obj.] **1** capture the fascinated attention of: *she had been so enthralled by the adventure that she had hardly noticed the cold.*
2 (also **inthrall**) archaic enslave.
– DERIVATIVES **enthralment** (US **enthrallment**) noun.
– ORIGIN late Middle English (in the sense 'enslave'; formerly also as *inthrall*): from EN-[1], IN-[2] (as an intensifier) + THRALL.

enthralling /ɪnˈθrɔːlɪŋ, ɛn-/ ▶ **adjective** capturing and holding one's attention; fascinating: *an enthralling best-seller.*

enthrone ▶ **verb** [with obj.] install (a monarch or bishop) on a throne, especially during a ceremony to mark the beginning of their rule.
– DERIVATIVES **enthronement** noun.

enthuse /ɪnˈθjuːz, ɛn-/ ▶ **verb** [no obj.] express eager enjoyment, interest, or approval regarding something: *they both enthused over my new look.* ■ [with obj.] make (someone) interested and eagerly appreciative: *public art is a tonic that can enthuse alienated youth.*

enthusiasm ▶ **noun** [mass noun] **1** intense and eager enjoyment, interest, or approval: *her energy and enthusiasm for life | few expressed enthusiasm about the current leaders.* ■ [count noun] something that arouses enthusiasm: *the three enthusiasms of his life were politics, religion, and books.*
2 archaic, derogatory religious fervour supposedly resulting directly from divine inspiration, typically involving speaking in tongues and wild, uncoordinated movements of the body.
– ORIGIN early 17th cent. (in sense 2): from French *enthousiasme*, or via late Latin from Greek *enthousiasmos*, from *enthous* 'possessed by a god, inspired' (based on *theos* 'god').

enthusiast ▶ **noun 1** a person who is very interested in a particular activity or subject: *a sports car enthusiast.*
2 archaic, derogatory a person of intense and visionary Christian views.
– ORIGIN early 17th cent. (denoting a person believing that he or she is divinely inspired): from French *enthousiaste* or ecclesiastical Latin *enthusiastes* 'member of a heretical sect', from Greek *enthousiastēs* 'person inspired by a god', from the adjective *enthous* (see ENTHUSIASM).

enthusiastic ▶ **adjective** having or showing intense and eager enjoyment, interest, or approval: *he could be wildly enthusiastic about a project.*
– DERIVATIVES **enthusiastically** adverb.
– ORIGIN early 17th cent.: from Greek *enthousiastikos*, from *enthous* 'possessed by a god' (see ENTHUSIASM).

enthymeme /ˈɛnθɪmiːm/ ▶ **noun** Logic an argument in which one premise is not explicitly stated.
– ORIGIN mid 16th cent.: via Latin from Greek *enthumēma*, from *enthumeisthai* 'consider', from *en-* 'within' + *thumos* 'mind'.

entice /ɪnˈtʌɪs, ɛn-/ ▶ **verb** [with obj.] attract or tempt by offering pleasure or advantage: *a show which should entice a new audience into the theatre* | [with obj. and infinitive] *the treat is offered to entice the dog to eat.*
– DERIVATIVES **enticer** noun.
– ORIGIN Middle English (also in the sense 'incite, provoke'; formerly also as *intice*): from Old French *enticier*, probably from a base meaning 'set on fire', based on an alteration of Latin *titio* 'firebrand'.

enticement /ɪnˈtʌɪsm(ə)nt, ɛn-/ ▶ **noun** something used to attract or to tempt someone; a lure: *financial enticements.* ■ [mass noun] the quality of being attractive or tempting: *despite the enticement of low prices, sales fell sharply from 2000's record level.*

enticing /ɪnˈtʌɪsɪŋ, ɛn-/ ▶ **adjective** attractive or tempting; alluring: *an enticing prospect.*
– DERIVATIVES **enticingly** adverb.

entire /ɪnˈtʌɪə, ɛn-/ ▶ **adjective 1** [attrib.] with no part left out; whole: *my plans are to travel the entire world.* ■ without qualification or reservations; absolute: *an ideological system with which he is in entire agreement.*
2 not broken, damaged, or decayed.
3 (of a male horse) not castrated.
4 Botany (of a leaf) without indentations or division into leaflets.
▶ **noun** an uncastrated male horse.
– ORIGIN late Middle English (formerly also as *intire*): from Old French *entier*, based on Latin *integer* 'untouched, whole', from *in-* 'not' + *tangere* 'to touch'.

entirely ▶ **adverb** completely (often used for emphasis): *the traffic seemed to consist entirely of black cabs* | [as submodifier] *we have an entirely different outlook.* ■ solely: *eight coaches entirely for passenger transport.*

entirety ▶ **noun** [mass noun] the whole of something: *she would have to stay in her room for the entirety of the weekend.*
– PHRASES **in its entirety** as a whole; completely: *the poem is too long to quote in its entirety here.*
– ORIGIN Middle English: from Old French *entierete*, from Latin *integritas*, from *integer* 'untouched, whole' (see ENTIRE). Compare with INTEGRITY.

entisol /ˈɛntɪsɒl/ ▶ **noun** Soil Science a soil of an order comprising mineral soils that have not yet differentiated into distinct horizons.
– ORIGIN mid 20th cent.: from ENTIRE + -SOL.

E

entitle ▶ **verb** [with obj.] **1** (often **be entitled to**) give (someone) a legal right or a just claim to receive or do something: *employees are normally entitled to redundancy pay* | [with obj. and infinitive] *the landlord is entitled to require references.*
2 give (something) a particular title: *a satire entitled 'The Rise of the Meritocracy'.* ■ [with obj. and complement] archaic give (someone) a specified title expressing their rank, office, or character: *they entitled him Sultan.*
– ORIGIN late Middle English (formerly also as *intitle*): via Old French from late Latin *intitulare*, from *in-* 'in' + Latin *titulus* 'title'.

entitlement ▶ **noun** [mass noun] the fact of having a right to something: ***full entitlement** to fees and maintenance should be offered.* ■ the amount to which a person has a right: *annual leave entitlement.*

entity /ˈɛntɪti/ ▶ **noun** (pl. **entities**) a thing with distinct and independent existence: *Church and empire were fused in a single entity.* ■ [mass noun] existence; being: *entity and nonentity.*
– DERIVATIVES **entitative** adjective (chiefly Philosophy).
– ORIGIN late 15th cent. (denoting a thing's existence): from French *entité* or medieval Latin *entitas*, from late Latin *ens, ent-* 'being' (from *esse* 'be').

entomb /ɪnˈtuːm, ɛn-/ ▶ **verb** [with obj.] place (a dead body) in a tomb. ■ bury or trap within something: *many people died, most entombed in collapsed buildings.*
– ORIGIN late Middle English (formerly also as *intomb*): from Old French *entomber*, from *en-* 'in' + *tombe* 'tomb'.

entombment ▶ **noun** [mass noun] the placing of a dead body in a tomb; interment: *the entombment of Christ.*

entomo- /ˈɛntəməʊ/ ▶ **combining form** of an insect; relating to insects: *entomophagous.*
– ORIGIN from Greek *entomon*, neuter (denoting an insect) of *entomos* 'cut up, segmented'.

entomology /ˌɛntəˈmɒlədʒi/ ▶ **noun** [mass noun] the branch of zoology concerned with the study of insects.
– DERIVATIVES **entomological** /ˌɛntəməˈlɒdʒɪk(ə)l/ adjective, **entomologist** noun.
– ORIGIN mid 18th cent.: from French *entomologie* or modern Latin *entomologia*, from Greek *entomon* (denoting an insect) + *-logia* (see -LOGY).

entomophagy /ˌɛntəˈmɒfədʒi/ ▶ **noun** [mass noun] the practice of eating insects, especially by people.
– DERIVATIVES **entomophagous** adjective.

entomophilous /ˌɛntəˈmɒfɪləs/ ▶ **adjective** Botany (of a plant or flower) pollinated by insects.
– DERIVATIVES **entomophily** noun.

Entoprocta /ˌɛntə(ʊ)ˈprɒktə/ ▶ **plural noun** Zoology a small phylum of sedentary aquatic invertebrates that resemble moss animals. They have a rounded body on a long stalk, bearing a ring of tentacles for filtering food from the water.
– DERIVATIVES **entoproct** noun.
– ORIGIN modern Latin (plural), from Greek *entos* 'within' + *prōktos* 'anus', the anus being within the ring of tentacles.

entoptic /ɪnˈtɒptɪk, ɛn-/ ▶ **adjective** (of visual images) occurring or originating inside the eye.
– ORIGIN late 19th cent.: from Greek *entos* 'within' + OPTIC.

entourage /ˈɒntʊrɑːʒ, ˌɒntʊ(ə)ˈrɑːʒ/ ▶ **noun** a group of people attending or surrounding an important person: *an entourage of loyal courtiers.*
– ORIGIN mid 19th cent.: French, from *entourer* 'to surround'.

E

entr'acte /ˈɒntrakt, ˈɒ̃-/ ▶ **noun** an interval between two acts of a play or opera. ■ a piece of music or a dance performed during an interval.
– ORIGIN mid 19th cent.: French, from (earlier form of *entracte*), from *entre* 'between' + *acte* 'act'.

entrails ▶ **plural noun** a person's or animal's intestines or internal organs, especially when removed or exposed. ■ the innermost parts of something: *digging copper out of the entrails of the earth.*
– ORIGIN Middle English: from Old French *entrailles*, from medieval Latin *intralia*, alteration of Latin *interanea* 'internal things', based on *inter* 'among'.

entrain[1] /ɪnˈtreɪn, ɛn-/ ▶ **verb** [no obj.] formal board a train.

entrain[2] /ɪnˈtreɪn, ɛn-/ ▶ **verb** [with obj.] **1** (of a current or fluid) incorporate and sweep along in its flow. ■ formal cause or bring about as a consequence.
2 Biology (of a rhythm or something which varies rhythmically) cause (another) gradually to fall into synchronism with it.
– DERIVATIVES **entrainment** noun.
– ORIGIN mid 16th cent. (in the sense 'bring on as a consequence'): from French *entraîner*, from *en-* 'in' + *traîner* 'to drag'.

entrain[3] /ɒ̃ˈtrɑ̃/ ▶ **noun** [mass noun] rare enthusiasm or animation.
– ORIGIN French, from the phrase *être en train (de)* 'be in the process (of), be in action'.

entrammel /ɪnˈtram(ə)l, ɛn-/ ▶ **verb** (**entrammels, entrammelling, entrammelled**; US **entrammels, entrammeling, entrammeled**) [with obj.] literary entangle; trap.

entrance[1] /ˈɛntr(ə)ns/ ▶ **noun 1** an opening, such as a door, passage, or gate, that allows access to a place.
2 [usu. in sing.] an act or instance of entering somewhere: *at their abrupt entrance he rose to his feet* | *their entrance into the political arena.* ■ [usu. in sing.] the coming of an actor or performer on to a stage: *her final entrance is as a triumphant princess.* ■ [mass noun] the right, means, or opportunity to enter somewhere or be a member of an institution, society, or other body: *about fifty people attempted to gain entrance* | [as modifier] *an entrance examination.*
– PHRASES **make an** (or **one's**) **entrance** (of an actor or performer) come on stage. ■ enter somewhere in a conspicuous or impressive way: *she slowly counted to ten before making her entrance.*
– ORIGIN late 15th cent. (in the sense 'right or opportunity of admission'): from Old French, from *entrer* 'enter'.

entrance[2] /ɪnˈtrɑːns, ɛn-/ ▶ **verb** [with obj.] fill (someone) with wonder and delight, holding their entire attention: *I was entranced by the city's beauty* | (as adj. **entrancing**) *an entrancing girl.* ■ cast a spell on: *Orpheus entranced the wild beasts.*
– DERIVATIVES **entrancement** noun, **entrancingly** adverb.
– ORIGIN late 16th cent. (formerly also as *intrance*): from EN-[1], IN-[2] 'into' + TRANCE.

entranceway ▶ **noun** a door or corridor at the entrance to a building.

entrant ▶ **noun** a person or group that enters or takes part in something.
– ORIGIN early 17th cent. (denoting a person taking legal possession of land or property): from French, literally 'entering', present participle of *entrer* (see ENTER).

entrap ▶ **verb** (**entraps, entrapping, entrapped**) [with obj.] catch in or as in a trap: *discarded fishing lines can entrap wildlife.* ■ trick (someone) into committing a crime in order to secure their prosecution.
– DERIVATIVES **entrapment** noun.
– ORIGIN mid 16th cent.: from Old French *entraper*, from *en-* 'in' + *trappe* 'a trap'.

en travesti /ɒ̃ ˌtravɛˈstiː/ ▶ **adverb & adjective** dressed as a member of the opposite sex for a theatrical role.
– ORIGIN French, literally '(dressed) in disguise'.

entreat ▶ **verb 1** [reporting verb] ask someone earnestly or anxiously to do something: [with obj. and infinitive] *his friends entreated him not to go* | (as adj. **entreating**) *his entreating eyes.* ■ [with obj.] ask earnestly or anxiously for (something): *a message had been sent, entreating aid for the Navahos.*
2 [with obj. and adverbial] archaic treat (someone) in a specified manner: *the King, I fear, hath ill entreated her.*
– DERIVATIVES **entreatingly** adverb.
– ORIGIN late Middle English (in the sense 'treat, act towards (someone)'; formerly also as *intreat*): from Old French *entraitier*, based on *traitier* 'to treat', from Latin *tractare* 'to handle'.

entreaty ▶ **noun** (pl. **entreaties**) an earnest or humble request: *the king turned a deaf ear to his entreaties.*
– ORIGIN late Middle English (in the sense 'treatment, management'; formerly also as *intreaty*): from ENTREAT, on the pattern of *treaty*.

entrechat /ˈɒ̃trəʃɑː/ ▶ **noun** Ballet a vertical jump during which the dancer repeatedly crosses the feet and beats them together.
– ORIGIN French, from Italian *(capriola) intrecciata* 'complicated (caper)'.

entrecôte /ˈɒntrəkəʊt/ ▶ **noun** a boned steak cut off the sirloin.
– ORIGIN French, from *entre* 'between' + *côte* 'rib'.

entrée /ˈɒntreɪ/ ▶ **noun 1** the main course of a meal. ■ Brit. a dish served between the first and main courses at a formal dinner.
2 the right to enter or join a particular sphere or group: *an actress with an entrée into the intellectual society of Berlin.*
– ORIGIN early 18th cent. (denoting a piece of instrumental music forming the first part of a suite): French, feminine past participle of *entrer* 'enter' (see ENTRY).

entremets /ˌɒntrəˈmeɪ/ ▶ **noun** a light dish served between two courses of a formal meal.
– ORIGIN French, from *entre* 'between' + *mets* 'dish'.

entrench ▶ **verb 1** [with obj.] establish (an attitude, habit, or belief) so firmly that change is very difficult or unlikely: *ageism is **entrenched in** our society.* ■ establish (someone) in a position of great strength or security. ■ apply extra legal safeguards to (a right guaranteed by legislation).
2 [with obj.] establish (a military force) in trenches or other fortified positions.
3 [no obj.] (**entrench on/upon**) archaic encroach or trespass on.
– DERIVATIVES **entrenchment** noun.
– ORIGIN mid 16th cent. (in the sense 'place within a trench'): from EN-[1], IN-[2] 'into' + TRENCH.

entrenched ▶ **adjective** (of an attitude, habit, or belief) firmly established and difficult or unlikely to change; ingrained: *an entrenched resistance to change.*

entre nous /ˌɒ̃trə ˈnuː/ ▶ **adverb** between ourselves; privately: *entre nous, the old man's a bit of a case.*
– ORIGIN French.

entrepôt /ˈɒntrəpəʊ/ ▶ **noun** a port, city, or other centre to which goods are brought for import and export, and for collection and distribution.
– ORIGIN early 18th cent.: French, from *entreposer* 'to store', from *entre* 'among' + *poser* 'to place'.

entrepreneur /ˌɒntrəprəˈnəː/ ▶ **noun** a person who sets up a business or businesses, taking on financial risks in the hope of profit. ■ a promoter in the entertainment industry.
– DERIVATIVES **entrepreneurism** noun, **entrepreneurship** noun.
– ORIGIN early 19th cent. (denoting the director of a musical institution): from French, from *entreprendre* 'undertake' (see ENTERPRISE).

entrepreneurial /ˌɒntrəprəˈnəːrɪəl, -ˈnjʊərɪəl/ ▶ **adjective** characterized by the taking of financial risks in the hope of profit; enterprising: *an entrepreneurial culture* | *our entrepreneurial spirit thrives on meeting the next challenge.*
– DERIVATIVES **entrepreneurialism** noun, **entrepreneurially** adverb.

entresol /ˈɒntrəsɒl/ ▶ **noun** a low storey between the ground floor and the first floor of a building; a mezzanine floor.
– ORIGIN early 18th cent.: French, from Spanish *entresuelo*, from *entre* 'between' + *suelo* 'storey'.

entrism ▶ **noun** variant form of ENTRYISM.

entropion /ɪnˈtrəʊpɪən, ɛn-/ ▶ **noun** [mass noun] Medicine a condition in which the eyelid is rolled inward against the eyeball, typically caused by muscle spasm or by inflammation or scarring of the conjunctiva (as in diseases such as trachoma), and resulting in irritation of the eye by the lashes (trichiasis).
– ORIGIN late 19th cent.: from EN-[2] 'inside', on the pattern of *ectropion*.

entropy /ˈɛntrəpi/ ▶ **noun** [mass noun] **1** Physics a thermodynamic quantity representing the unavailability of a system's thermal energy for conversion into mechanical work, often interpreted as the degree of disorder or randomness in the system. (Symbol: **S**)
2 lack of order or predictability; gradual decline into disorder: *a marketplace where entropy reigns supreme.*
3 (in information theory) a logarithmic measure of the rate of transfer of information in a particular message or language.
– DERIVATIVES **entropic** /-ˈtrɒpɪk/ adjective, **entropically** adverb.
– ORIGIN mid 19th cent.: from EN-[2] 'inside' + Greek *tropē* 'transformation'.

entrust ▶ **verb** [with obj.] assign the responsibility for doing something to (someone): *I've been **entrusted with** the task of getting him safely back.* ■ put (something) into someone's care or protection: *you persuade people to **entrust** their savings **to** you.*
– DERIVATIVES **entrustment** noun.

entry ▶ **noun** (pl. **entries**) **1** an act of going or coming in: *the door was locked, but he forced an entry.* ■ a place of entrance, such as a door or lobby. ■ dialect a passage between buildings. ■ [mass noun] the right, means, or opportunity to enter a place or be a member of something: *people seeking entry to Australia.* ■ [mass noun] the action of entering something: *more young people are postponing their entry into full-time work.* ■ Music the point at which a particular performer in an ensemble starts or resumes playing or singing. ■ Bridge a card providing an opportunity to transfer the lead to a particular hand. ■ (also **entry into possession**) [mass noun] Law the action of taking up the legal right to property.
2 an item written or printed in a diary, list, account book, or reference book. ■ [mass noun] the action of recording an item in a diary, list, etc.: *sophisticated features to help ensure accurate data entry.*
3 a person or thing competing in a race or competition: *from the hundreds of entries we received, twelve winners were finally chosen.* ■ [in sing.] the number of competitors in a particular race or competition. ■ [mass noun] the action of participating in a race or competition.
4 the forward part of a ship's hull below the waterline, considered in terms of breadth or narrowness.
– ORIGIN Middle English: from Old French *entree*, based on Latin *intrata*, feminine past participle of *intrare* (see ENTER).

entry form ▶ **noun** an application form for a competition.

entryism (also **entrism**) ▶ **noun** [mass noun] the infiltration of a political party by members of another group, with the intention of subverting its policies or objectives.
– DERIVATIVES **entryist** noun.

entry-level ▶ **adjective** (of a product) suitable for a beginner or first-time user; basic: *entry-level computers.* ■ at the lowest level in an employment hierarchy.

entryphone ▶ **noun** Brit. trademark a type of intercom at the entrance to a building by which visitors are required to identify themselves before the door is unlocked by an internal device.

entryway ▶ **noun** N. Amer. a way in to somewhere or something; an entrance.

entry wound ▶ **noun** a wound made by a bullet or other missile at the point where it entered the body.

ents ▶ **plural noun** Brit. informal social and leisure activities organized for the benefit of students, holidaymakers, etc.: *getting involved in running ents can be fun.*
– ORIGIN 1970s: abbreviation of *entertainments*.

entwine ▶ **verb** [with obj.] wind or twist together; interweave: *they lay entwined in each other's arms* | figurative *the nations' histories were closely entwined.*
– DERIVATIVES **entwinement** noun.

enucleate /ɪˈnjuːklɪeɪt/ ▶ **verb** [with obj.] **1** Biology remove the nucleus from (a cell).
2 surgically remove (a tumour or gland, or the eyeball) intact from its surrounding capsule.
▶ **adjective** Biology (of a cell) lacking a nucleus.
– DERIVATIVES **enucleation** noun.
– ORIGIN mid 16th cent. (in the sense 'clarify, explain'): from Latin *enucleat-* 'extracted, made clear', from the verb *enucleare*, from *e-* (variant of *ex-*) 'out of' + *nucleus* 'kernel' (see NUCLEUS).

E-number ▶ **noun** Brit. a code number preceded by the letter E, denoting food additives numbered in accordance with EU directives. ■ informal a food additive.

enumerable /ɪˈnjuːm(ə)rəb(ə)l/ ▶ **adjective** Mathematics able to be counted by one-to-one correspondence with the set of all positive integers.

enumerate /ɪˈnjuːməreɪt/ ▶ **verb** [with obj.] mention (a number of things) one by one: *there is not space to enumerate all his works.* ■ formal establish the

number of: *6,079 residents were enumerated in 241 establishments.*
– DERIVATIVES **enumeration** noun, **enumerative** adjective.
– ORIGIN early 17th cent.: from Latin *enumerat-* 'counted out', from the verb *enumerare*, from *e-* (variant of *ex-*) 'out' + *numerus* 'number'.

enumerator ▸ noun a person employed in taking a census of the population.

enunciate /ɪˈnʌnsɪeɪt/ ▸ verb [with obj.] say or pronounce clearly: *she enunciated each word slowly.* ■ express (a proposition, theory, etc.) in clear or definite terms: *a written document enunciating this policy.*
– DERIVATIVES **enunciation** noun, **enunciative** adjective, **enunciator** noun.
– ORIGIN mid 16th cent. (as *enunciation*): from Latin *enuntiat-* 'announced clearly', from the verb *enuntiare*, from *e-* (variant of *ex-*) 'out' + *nuntiare* 'announce' (from *nuntius* 'messenger').

enure /ɪˈnjʊə, ɪˈnjɔː/ ▸ verb **1** [no obj.] (**enure for/to**) Law (of a right or other advantage) belong or be available to.
2 variant spelling of INURE.

enuresis /ˌɛnjʊəˈriːsɪs/ ▸ noun [mass noun] Medicine involuntary urination, especially by children at night.
– DERIVATIVES **enuretic** adjective & noun.
– ORIGIN early 19th cent.: modern Latin, from Greek *enourein* 'urinate in', from *en-* 'in' + *ouron* 'urine'.

envelop /ɪnˈvɛləp, ɛn-/ ▸ verb (**envelops**, **enveloping**, **enveloped**) [with obj.] wrap up, cover, or surround completely: *a figure enveloped in a black cloak* | figurative *a feeling of despair enveloped him.*
– DERIVATIVES **envelopment** noun.
– ORIGIN late Middle English (formerly also as *envelop(e)*): from Old French *envoluper*, from *en-* 'in' + a second element (also found in DEVELOP) of unknown origin.

> **USAGE** Envelop is a verb, stressed on the second syllable and meaning 'wrap completely'. The noun meaning 'paper container for a letter' is **envelope**, stressed on the first syllable.

envelope /ˈɛnvələʊp, ˈɒn-/ ▸ noun **1** a flat paper container with a sealable flap, used to enclose a letter or document.
2 a covering or containing structure or layer: *the external envelope of the swimming pool.* ■ the outer metal or glass housing of a vacuum tube, electric light, etc. ■ the structure within a balloon or nonrigid airship containing the gas. ■ Microbiology a membrane which forms the outer layer of certain viruses. ■ Electronics a curve joining the successive peaks of a modulated wave. ■ Mathematics a curve or surface tangent to each of a family of curves or surfaces.
– PHRASES **the back of an envelope** used in reference to calculations or plans of the most sketchy kind: *a proposal drawn up on the back of an envelope.* **push the envelope** (or **the edge of the envelope**) approach or extend the limits of what is possible: *these are extremely witty and clever stories that consistently push the envelope of TV comedy.* [originally aviation slang, relating to graphs of aerodynamic performance.]
– ORIGIN mid 16th cent. (in the sense 'wrapper, enveloping layer'; originally as *envelope*): from French *enveloppe*, from *envelopper* 'envelop'. The sense 'covering of a letter' dates from the early 18th cent.

envenom /ɪnˈvɛnəm, ɛn-/ ▸ verb [with obj.] archaic put poison on or into; make poisonous.
– ORIGIN Middle English (formerly also as *invenom*): from Old French *envenimer*, from *en-* 'in' + *venim* 'venom'.

envenomate ▸ verb [with obj.] Zoology & Medicine (of a snake, spider, insect, etc.) poison by biting or stinging.
– DERIVATIVES **envenomation** noun.

en ventre sa mère /ɒ̃ ˌvɒ̃trə sa ˈmɛː/ ▸ adverb & adjective Law in the mother's womb.
– ORIGIN French.

Enver Pasha /ˌɛnvə ˈpɑːʃə/ (1881–1922), Turkish political and military leader. A leader of the Young Turks in 1908, he came to power as part of a ruling triumvirate following a coup d'état in 1913.

enviable /ˈɛnvɪəb(ə)l/ ▸ adjective arousing or likely to arouse envy: *the firm is in the enviable position of having a full order book.*
– DERIVATIVES **enviably** adverb.

envious ▸ adjective feeling or showing envy: *I'm envious of their happiness* | *an envious glance.*
– DERIVATIVES **enviously** adverb.
– ORIGIN Middle English: from Old French *envieus*, from *envie* 'envy', on the pattern of Latin *invidiosus* 'invidious'.

enviro /ɪnˈvʌɪrəʊ/ ▸ noun (pl. **enviros**) short for ENVIRONMENTALIST.
▸ adjective short for ENVIRONMENTAL.

environ /ɪnˈvʌɪrən, ɛn-/ ▸ verb [with obj.] formal surround; enclose.
– ORIGIN Middle English (formerly also as *inviron*): from Old French *environer*, from *environ* 'surroundings', from *en* 'in' + *viron* 'circuit' (from *virer* 'to turn, veer').

environment ▸ noun **1** the surroundings or conditions in which a person, animal, or plant lives or operates: *survival in an often hostile environment.* ■ [usu. with modifier] the setting or conditions in which a particular activity is carried on: *a good learning environment.* ■ [with modifier] Computing the overall structure within which a user, computer, or program operates: *a desktop development environment.*
2 (**the environment**) the natural world, as a whole or in a particular geographical area, especially as affected by human activity.

environmental ▸ adjective **1** relating to the natural world and the impact of human activity on its condition: *acid rain may have caused major environmental damage.* ■ aiming or designed to promote the protection of the natural world: *environmental tourism.*
2 relating to or arising from a person's surroundings: *environmental noise.*
– DERIVATIVES **environmentally** adverb.

environmental audit ▸ noun an assessment of the extent to which an organization is observing practices which minimize harm to the environment.

environmentalist ▸ noun **1** a person who is concerned about protecting the environment.
2 a person who considers that environment, as opposed to heredity, has the primary influence on the development of a person or group.
– DERIVATIVES **environmentalism** noun.

environmentally friendly ▸ adverb not harmful to the environment: *cycling is an environmentally friendly form of transport.*

Environmentally Sensitive Area (abbrev.: **ESA**) ▸ noun (in the UK) an area officially designated as containing landscapes or wildlife that would be threatened by unrestricted development.

environs ▸ plural noun the surrounding area or district: *the picturesque environs of the loch.*
– ORIGIN mid 17th cent.: from French, plural of *environ* (see ENVIRON).

envisage /ɪnˈvɪzɪdʒ, ɛn-/ ▸ verb [with obj.] contemplate or conceive of as a possibility or a desirable future event: *the Rome Treaty envisaged free movement across frontiers.* ■ form a mental picture of (something not yet existing or known): *he knew what he liked but had difficulty envisaging it.*
– ORIGIN early 19th cent.: from French *envisager*, from *en-* 'in' + *visage* 'face'.

envision ▸ verb [with obj.] imagine as a future possibility; visualize: *she envisioned the admiring glances of guests seeing her home.*

envoi /ˈɛnvɔɪ/ (also **envoy**) ▸ noun **1** a short stanza concluding a ballade.
2 literary an author's concluding words.
– ORIGIN late Middle English: from Old French *envoi*, from *envoyer* 'send' (see ENVOY).

envoy /ˈɛnvɔɪ/ ▸ noun **1** a messenger or representative, especially one on a diplomatic mission.
2 (also **envoy extraordinary**) a minister plenipotentiary, ranking below ambassador and above chargé d'affaires.
– ORIGIN mid 17th cent.: from French *envoyé*, past participle of *envoyer* 'send', from *en voie* 'on the way', based on Latin *via* 'way'.

envy ▸ noun (pl. **envies**) [mass noun] a feeling of discontented or resentful longing aroused by someone else's possessions, qualities, or luck: *she felt a twinge of envy for the people on board.* ■ (**the envy of**) a person or thing that inspires envy: *France has a film industry that is the envy of Europe.*
▸ verb (**envies**, **envying**, **envied**) [with obj.] desire to have a quality, possession, or other desirable thing belonging to (someone else): *he envied people who did not have to work at the weekends* | [with two objs] *I envy Jane her happiness.* ■ desire for oneself (something belonging to another): *a lifestyle which most of us would envy.*
– DERIVATIVES **envier** noun.
– ORIGIN Middle English (also in the sense 'hostility, enmity'): from Old French *envie* (noun), *envier* (verb), from Latin *invidia*, from *invidere* 'regard maliciously, grudge', from *in-* 'into' + *videre* 'to see'.

enwrap ▸ verb (**enwraps**, **enwrapping**, **enwrapped**) [with obj.] wrap; envelop. ■ engross or absorb (someone): *they were enwrapped in conversation.*

enwreathe ▸ verb [with obj.] literary surround or envelop (something).

Enzed /ɛnˈzɛd/ ▸ noun Austral./NZ informal New Zealand or a New Zealander.
– DERIVATIVES **Enzedder** noun.
– ORIGIN representing a pronunciation of the initials *NZ*.

enzootic /ˌɛnzəʊˈɒtɪk/ ▸ adjective (of a disease) regularly affecting animals in a particular district or at a particular season. Compare with EPIZOOTIC, ENDEMIC (sense 1 of the adjective).
– ORIGIN late 19th cent.: from EN-[2] 'within' + Greek *zōion* 'animal' + -IC.

enzyme /ˈɛnzʌɪm/ ▸ noun Biochemistry a substance produced by a living organism which acts as a catalyst to bring about a specific biochemical reaction.

> Most enzymes are proteins with large complex molecules whose action depends on their particular molecular shape. Some enzymes control reactions within cells and some, such as the enzymes involved in digestion, outside them.

– DERIVATIVES **enzymatic** adjective, **enzymic** adjective.
– ORIGIN late 19th cent.: coined in German from modern Greek *enzumos* 'leavened', from *en-* 'within' + Greek *zumē* 'leaven'.

enzymology ▸ noun [mass noun] the branch of biochemistry concerned with enzymes.
– DERIVATIVES **enzymological** adjective, **enzymologist** noun.

EOC ▸ abbreviation (in the UK) Equal Opportunities Commission.

Eocene /ˈiːə(ʊ)siːn/ ▸ adjective Geology relating to or denoting the second epoch of the Tertiary period, between the Palaeocene and Oligocene epochs. ■ (as noun **the Eocene**) the Eocene epoch or the system of rocks deposited during it.

> The Eocene epoch lasted from 56.5 to 35.4 million years ago. It was a time of rising temperatures, and there was an abundance of mammals, including the first horses, bats, and whales.

– ORIGIN mid 19th cent.: from Greek *ēōs* 'dawn' + *kainos* 'new'.

EOF ▸ abbreviation Computing end of file.

eohippus /ˌiːəʊˈhɪpəs/ ▸ noun (pl. **eohippuses**) former term for HYRACOTHERIUM.
– ORIGIN late 19th cent.: from Greek *ēōs* 'dawn' + *hippos* 'horse'.

eo ipso /ˌeɪəʊ ˈɪpsəʊ/ ▸ adverb formal by that very act or quality; thereby: *such a grand theory would eo ipso give an account of how we communicate using language.*
– ORIGIN Latin, ablative of *id ipsum* 'the thing itself'.

EOKA /eɪˈəʊkə/ a Greek-Cypriot liberation movement active in Cyprus in the 1950s and in the early 1970s, which fought for the independence of Cyprus from Britain and for its eventual union with Greece.
– ORIGIN acronym from Greek *Ethnikē Organōsis Kupriakou Agōnos* 'National Organization of Cypriot Struggle'.

eolian ▸ adjective US spelling of AEOLIAN.

eolith /ˈiːə(ʊ)lɪθ/ ▸ noun Archaeology a roughly chipped flint found in Tertiary strata, originally thought to be an early artefact but probably of natural origin.
– ORIGIN late 19th cent.: from Greek *ēōs* 'dawn' + *lithos* 'stone'.

Eolithic /ˌiːə(ʊ)ˈlɪθɪk/ ▸ adjective Archaeology, dated relating to or denoting a period at the beginning of the Stone Age, preceding the Palaeolithic and characterized by the earliest crude stone tools. ■ (as noun **the Eolithic**) the Eolithic period.
– ORIGIN late 19th cent.: from French *éolithique*, from Greek *ēōs* 'dawn' + *lithikos* (from *lithos* 'stone').

eon ▸ noun US spelling of AEON.

Eos /ˈiːɒs/ Greek Mythology the Greek goddess of the dawn. Roman equivalent AURORA.

eosin /ˈiːə(ʊ)sɪn/ ▸ noun [mass noun] a red fluorescent dye that is a bromine derivative of fluorescein, or one of its salts or other derivatives.
– ORIGIN late 19th cent.: from Greek *ēōs* 'dawn' + -IN[1].

eosinophil /ˌiːə(ʊ)ˈsɪnəfɪl/ ▸ **noun** Physiology a white blood cell containing granules that are readily stained by eosin.

eosinophilia /ˌiːə(ʊ)ˌsɪnəˈfɪlɪə/ ▸ **noun** [mass noun] Medicine an increase in the number of eosinophils in the blood, occurring in response to some allergens, drugs, and parasites, and in some types of leukaemia.

eosinophilic ▸ **adjective 1** Physiology (of a cell or its contents) readily stained by eosin.
2 Medicine relating to or marked by eosinophilia.

EOT ▸ **abbreviation** ■ Computing end of tape. ■ Telecommunications end of transmission.

-eous ▸ **suffix** (forming adjectives) resembling; displaying the nature of: *aqueous* | *erroneous*.
– ORIGIN from the Latin suffix *-eus* + **-OUS**.

E

EP ▸ **abbreviation** ■ electroplate. ■ European Parliament. ■ extended-play (of a record or CD): *an EP of remixes*. ■ extreme pressure (used in grading lubricants).

Ep. ▸ **abbreviation** Epistle.

ep- /ɛp, ɪp, iːp/ ▸ **prefix** variant spelling of **EPI-** shortened before a vowel or *h* (as in *eparch*, *ephod*).

e.p. ▸ **abbreviation** Chess en passant.

EPA ▸ **abbreviation** (in the US) Environmental Protection Agency.

epact /ˈiːpakt/ ▸ **noun** the number of days by which the solar year exceeds the lunar year.
– ORIGIN mid 16th cent. (denoting the age of the moon in days at the beginning of the calendar year): from French *épacte*, via late Latin from Greek *epaktai (hēmerai)* 'intercalated (days)', from *epagein* 'bring in', from *epi* 'in addition' + *agein* 'bring'.

eparch /ˈɛpɑːk/ ▸ **noun** the chief bishop of an eparchy.
– ORIGIN mid 17th cent. (denoting the governor of an administrative division of Greece): from Greek *eparkhos*, from *epi* 'above' + *arkhos* 'ruler'.

eparchy /ˈɛpɑːki/ ▸ **noun** (pl. **eparchies**) a province of the Orthodox Church.
– ORIGIN late 18th cent.: from Greek *eparkhia*, from *eparkhos* (see **EPARCH**).

épater /eɪˈpateɪ/, French /epate/ ▸ **verb** (in phrase **épater les bourgeois**) shock people who have attitudes or views perceived as conventional or complacent.
– ORIGIN French.

epaulette /ˈɛpəlɛt, -pɔːl-, ˌɛpəˈlɛt/ (US also **epaulet**) ▸ **noun** an ornamental shoulder piece on an item of clothing, especially on the coat or jacket of a military uniform.
– ORIGIN late 18th cent.: from French *épaulette*, diminutive of *épaule* 'shoulder', from Latin *spatula* in the late Latin sense 'shoulder blade'.

epaxial /ɛˈpaksɪəl/ ▸ **adjective** Anatomy & Zoology situated on the dorsal side of an axis: *epaxial muscles*.

épée /ˈeɪpeɪ, ˈɛp-/ ▸ **noun** a sharp-pointed duelling sword, used, with the end blunted, in fencing.
– DERIVATIVES **épéeist** noun.
– ORIGIN late 19th cent.: French, 'sword', from Old French *espee* (see **SPAY**).

epeirogeny /ˌɪpʌɪˈrɒdʒəni/ ▸ **noun** [mass noun] Geology the regional uplift of an extensive area of the earth's crust.
– DERIVATIVES **epeirogenesis** noun, **epeirogenic** adjective.
– ORIGIN late 19th cent.: from Greek *ēpeiros* 'mainland' + **-GENY**.

ependyma /ɛˈpɛndɪmə/ ▸ **noun** [mass noun] Anatomy the thin membrane of glial cells lining the ventricles of the brain and the central canal of the spinal cord.
– DERIVATIVES **ependymal** adjective.
– ORIGIN late 19th cent.: from Greek *ependuma*, from *ependuein* 'put on over'.

epenthesis /ɛˈpɛnθɪsɪs/ ▸ **noun** (pl. **epentheses** /-siːz/) [mass noun] the insertion of a sound or letter within a word, e.g. the *b* in *thimble*.
– DERIVATIVES **epenthetic** adjective.
– ORIGIN mid 16th cent.: via late Latin from Greek, from *epentithenai* 'insert', from *epi* 'in addition' + *en-* 'within' + *tithenai* 'to place'.

epergne /ɪˈpəːn/ ▸ **noun** an ornamental centrepiece for a dining table, typically used for holding fruit or flowers.
– ORIGIN early 18th cent.: perhaps an altered form of French *épargne* 'saving, economy'.

epexegesis /ɛˌpɛksɪˈdʒiːsɪs/ ▸ **noun** (pl. **epexegeses** /-siːz/) [mass noun] the addition of words to clarify meaning.
– DERIVATIVES **epexegetical** adjective.
– ORIGIN late 16th cent.: from Greek *epexēgēsis*, from *epi* 'in addition' + *exēgēsis* 'explanation' (see **EXEGESIS**).

Eph. ▸ **abbreviation** Epistle to the Ephesians (in biblical references).

ephah /ˈiːfə/ ▸ **noun** an ancient Hebrew dry measure equivalent to the bath (of about 40 litres or 9 gallons).
– ORIGIN from Hebrew *'êpāh*, probably from Egyptian.

ephebe /ɛˈfiːb, ɪ-, ˈɛfiːb/ ▸ **noun** (in ancient Greece) a young man of 18–20 years undergoing military training.
– DERIVATIVES **ephebic** adjective.
– ORIGIN via Latin from Greek *ephēbos*, from *epi* 'near to' + *hēbē* 'early manhood'.

ephedra /ɛˈfɛdrə/ ▸ **noun** an evergreen shrub of warm arid regions which has trailing or climbing stems and tiny scale-like leaves. ● Family Ephedraceae and genus *Ephedra*.
– ORIGIN modern Latin, from Latin, 'equisetum' (which it resembles), from Greek.

ephedrine /ˈɛfədriːn/ ▸ **noun** [mass noun] Medicine a crystalline alkaloid drug obtained from some ephedras. It causes constriction of the blood vessels and widening of the bronchial passages, and is used to relieve asthma and hay fever. ● Chem. formula: $C_{10}H_{15}NO$.
– ORIGIN late 19th cent.: from **EPHEDRA** + **-INE**[4].

ephemera /ɪˈfɛm(ə)rə, -ˈfiːm-/ ▸ **plural noun** things that exist or are used or enjoyed for only a short time. ■ collectable items that were originally expected to have only short-term usefulness or popularity: *Mickey Mouse ephemera*.
– ORIGIN late 16th cent.: plural of *ephemeron*, from Greek, neuter of *ephēmeros* 'lasting only a day'. As a singular noun the word originally denoted a plant said by ancient writers to last only one day, or an insect with a short lifespan, and hence was applied (late 18th cent.) to a person or thing of short-lived interest. Current use has been influenced by plurals such as *trivia* and *memorabilia*.

ephemeral ▸ **adjective** lasting for a very short time. ■ (chiefly of plants) having a very short life cycle.
▸ **noun** an ephemeral plant.
– DERIVATIVES **ephemerality** noun, **ephemerally** adverb.
– ORIGIN late 16th cent.: from Greek *ephēmeros* (see **EPHEMERA**) + **-AL**.

ephemeris /ɪˈfɛm(ə)rɪs, -ˈfiːm-/ ▸ **noun** (pl. **ephemerides** /ˌɛfɪˈmɛrɪdiːz/) Astronomy & Astrology a table or data file giving the calculated positions of a celestial object at regular intervals throughout a period.
– ORIGIN early 16th cent.: from Latin, from Greek *ephēmeros* 'lasting only a day'.

ephemerist ▸ **noun** a person who collects ephemera.

ephemeris time ▸ **noun** time on a scale defined by the orbital period rather than the axial rotation of the earth.

Ephemeroptera /ɪˌfɛməˈrɒptərə, -ˌfiːm-/ ▸ **plural noun** Entomology an order of insects that comprises the mayflies. ■ (**ephemeroptera**) insects of the Ephemeroptera order; mayflies.
– DERIVATIVES **ephemeropteran** noun & adjective.
– ORIGIN modern Latin (plural), from *Ephemera* (genus name) + *pteron* 'wing'.

Ephesians, Epistle to the /ɪˈfiːʒ(ə)nz/ a book of the New Testament ascribed to St Paul consisting of an epistle to the Church at Ephesus.

Ephesus /ˈɛfɪsəs/ an ancient Greek city on the west coast of Asia Minor, in present-day Turkey, site of the temple of Diana, one of the Seven Wonders of the World. It was an important centre of early Christianity; St Paul preached there and St John is traditionally said to have lived there.

ephod /ˈiːfɒd, ˈɛfɒd/ ▸ **noun** (in ancient Israel) a sleeveless garment worn by Jewish priests.
– ORIGIN late Middle English: from Hebrew *'ēpōḏ*.

ephor /ˈɛfɔː/ ▸ **noun** (in ancient Greece) each of five senior Spartan magistrates.
– DERIVATIVES **ephorate** noun.
– ORIGIN from Greek *ephoros* 'overseer', from *epi* 'above' + the base of *horan* 'see'.

ephyra /ˈɛfɪrə/ ▸ **noun** (pl. **ephyrae** /-riː/) Zoology a larval jellyfish, after separation from the scyphistoma.
– ORIGIN mid 19th cent.: modern Latin, from Greek *Ephura*, denoting a Nereid and an Oceanid.

epi- (also **ep-**) ▸ **prefix 1** upon: *epigraph*.
2 above: *epicontinental*.
3 in addition: *epiphenomenon*.
– ORIGIN from Greek *epi* 'upon, near to, in addition'.

epibenthos /ˌɛpɪˈbɛnθɒs/ ▸ **noun** [mass noun] Ecology the flora and fauna living on the surface of the bottom of a sea or lake.
– DERIVATIVES **epibenthic** adjective.
– ORIGIN early 20th cent.: from Greek *epi* 'upon' + *benthos* 'depth of the sea'.

epiblast /ˈɛpɪblast/ ▸ **noun** Embryology the outermost layer of an embryo before it differentiates into ectoderm and mesoderm.

epic ▸ **noun 1** a long poem, typically one derived from ancient oral tradition, narrating the deeds and adventures of heroic or legendary figures or the past history of a nation. ■ [mass noun] the genre of epics: *the romances display gentler emotions not found in Greek epic*. ■ a long film, book, or other work portraying heroic deeds and adventures or covering an extended period of time: *a Hollywood biblical epic*.
2 informal an exceptionally long and arduous task or activity: *the business of getting hospital treatment soon became an epic*.
▸ **adjective 1** relating to or characteristic of an epic or epics: *our national epic poem Beowulf*.
2 heroic or grand in scale or character: *his epic journey around the world* | *a tragedy of epic proportions*.
– DERIVATIVES **epical** adjective, **epically** adverb.
– ORIGIN late 16th cent. (as an adjective): via Latin from Greek *epikos*, from *epos* 'word, song', related to *eipein* 'say'.

epicanthic ▸ **adjective** denoting a fold of skin from the upper eyelid covering the inner angle of the eye, typical in many peoples of eastern Asia and found as a congenital abnormality elsewhere.

epicardium /ˌɛpɪˈkɑːdɪəm/ ▸ **noun** [mass noun] Anatomy a serous membrane that forms the innermost layer of the pericardium, attached to the muscles of the wall of the heart.
– DERIVATIVES **epicardial** adjective.
– ORIGIN mid 19th cent.: from **EPI-** 'above' + Greek *kardia* 'heart', on the pattern of *pericardium*.

epicarp /ˈɛpɪkɑːp/ ▸ **noun** Botany the outermost layer of the pericarp.
– ORIGIN early 19th cent.: from **EPI-** + a shortened form of **PERICARP**.

epicedium /ˌɛpɪˈsiːdɪəm/ ▸ **noun** (pl. **epicedia** /-dɪə/) formal a funeral ode.
– DERIVATIVES **epicedian** adjective.
– ORIGIN mid 16th cent. (originally in the anglicized form *epicede* and the Greek form *epicedeon*): from Latin, from Greek *epikēdeion*, neuter of *epokēdeios* 'of a funeral' (based on *kēdos* 'care, grief').

epicene /ˈɛpɪsiːn/ ▸ **adjective** having characteristics of both sexes or no characteristics of either sex; of indeterminate sex: *the sort of epicene beauty peculiar to boys of a certain age*. ■ effeminate; effete: *the actor infused the role with an epicene languor*.
– ORIGIN late Middle English (as a grammatical term): via late Latin from Greek *epikoinos* (based on *koinos* 'common').

epicentre (US **epicenter**) ▸ **noun** the point on the earth's surface vertically above the focus of an earthquake. ■ the central point of something, typically a difficult or unpleasant situation: *the epicentre of labour militancy was the capital itself*.
– DERIVATIVES **epicentral** adjective.
– ORIGIN late 19th cent.: from Greek *epikentros* 'situated on a centre', from *epi* 'upon' + *kentron* 'centre'.

epicondyle /ˌɛpɪˈkɒndɪl/ ▸ **noun** Anatomy a protuberance above or on the condyle of a long bone, especially either of the two at the elbow end of the humerus.
– DERIVATIVES **epicondylar** adjective.
– ORIGIN mid 19th cent.: from French *épicondyle*, modern Latin *epicondylus* (see **EPI-**, **CONDYLE**).

epicondylitis /ˌɛpɪkɒndɪˈlʌɪtɪs/ ▸ **noun** [mass noun] Medicine a painful inflammation of tendons surrounding an epicondyle; tennis elbow.

epicontinental ▸ **adjective** denoting those areas of sea or ocean overlying the continental shelf.

epicormic /ˌɛpɪˈkɔːmɪk/ ▸ **adjective** Botany (of a shoot or branch) growing from a previously dormant bud on the trunk or a limb of a tree.
– ORIGIN early 20th cent.: from **EPI-** 'upon' + Greek *kormos* 'tree trunk'.

epicotyl /ˌɛpɪˈkɒtɪl/ ▸ **noun** Botany the region of an embryo or seedling stem above the cotyledon.

epicritic /ˌɛpɪˈkrɪtɪk/ ▸ **adjective** Physiology relating to or denoting those sensory nerve fibres of the skin which are capable of fine discrimination of touch or temperature stimuli. Often contrasted with **PROTOPATHIC**.

– ORIGIN early 20th cent.: from Greek *epikritikos* 'giving judgement over', from *epi* 'upon or over' + *krinein* 'to judge'.

Epictetus /ˌɛpɪkˈtiːtəs/ (*c*.55–*c*.135 AD), Greek philosopher. Originally a slave, he preached the common brotherhood of man and advocated a Stoic philosophy.

epicure /ˈɛpɪkjʊə, ˈɛpɪkjɔː/ ▶ **noun** a person who takes particular pleasure in fine food and drink.
– DERIVATIVES **epicurism** noun.
– ORIGIN late Middle English (denoting a disciple of EPICURUS): via medieval Latin from Greek *Epikouros* 'Epicurus'.

Epicurean /ˌɛpɪkjʊ(ə)ˈriːən/ ▶ **noun 1** a disciple or student of the Greek philosopher Epicurus.
2 (**epicurean**) a person devoted to sensual enjoyment, especially that derived from fine food and drink.
▶ **adjective 1** relating to Epicurus or his ideas: *Epicurean philosophers*.
2 (**epicurean**) relating to or suitable for an epicure: *epicurean feasts*.

Epicureanism /ˌɛpɪkjʊəˈriːəˌnɪz(ə)m/ ▶ **noun** [mass noun] an ancient school of philosophy founded in Athens by Epicurus. The school rejected determinism and advocated hedonism (pleasure as the highest good), but of a restrained kind: mental pleasure was regarded more highly than physical, and the ultimate pleasure was held to be freedom from anxiety and mental pain, especially that arising from needless fear of death and of the gods.

Epicurus /ˌɛpɪˈkjʊərəs/ (341–270 BC), Greek philosopher, founder of Epicureanism. His physics is based on Democritus' theory of a materialist universe composed of indestructible atoms moving in a void, unregulated by divine providence.

epicuticle /ˈɛpɪˌkjuːtɪk(ə)l/ ▶ **noun** [mass noun] Botany & Zoology the thin, waxy protective outer layer covering the surfaces of some plants, fungi, and insects and other arthropods.
– DERIVATIVES **epicuticular** adjective.

epicycle /ˈɛpɪˌsʌɪk(ə)l/ ▶ **noun** Geometry a small circle whose centre moves round the circumference of a larger one. ■ historical an epicycle used to describe planetary orbits in the Ptolemaic system.
– DERIVATIVES **epicyclic** adjective.
– ORIGIN late Middle English: from Old French, or via late Latin from Greek *epikuklos*, from *epi* 'upon' + *kuklos* 'circle'.

epicycloid /ˌɛpɪˈsʌɪklɔɪd/ ▶ **noun** Mathematics a curve traced by a point on the circumference of a circle rolling on the exterior of another circle.
– DERIVATIVES **epicycloidal** adjective.

Epidaurus /ˌɛpɪˈdɔːrəs/ an ancient Greek city and port on the NE coast of the Peloponnese. Greek name **Epídhavros** /ɛˈpiðavrɔs/.

epideictic /ˌɛpɪˈdeɪktɪk, -ˈdʌɪktɪk/ ▶ **adjective** formal characterized by or designed to display rhetorical or oratorical skill.
– ORIGIN late 18th cent.: from Greek *epideiktikos* (based on *deiknunai* 'to show').

epidemic ▶ **noun** a widespread occurrence of an infectious disease in a community at a particular time: *a flu epidemic*. ■ a sudden, widespread occurrence of an undesirable phenomenon: *an epidemic of violent crime*.
▶ **adjective** of the nature of an epidemic: *shoplifting has reached epidemic proportions*. Compare with ENDEMIC, PANDEMIC, EPIZOOTIC.
– ORIGIN early 17th cent. (as an adjective): from French *épidémique*, from *épidémie*, via late Latin from Greek *epidēmia* 'prevalence of disease', from *epidēmios* 'prevalent', from *epi* 'upon' + *dēmos* 'the people'.

epidemiology /ˌɛpɪdiːmɪˈɒlədʒi/ ▶ **noun** [mass noun] the branch of medicine which deals with the incidence, distribution, and possible control of diseases and other factors relating to health.
– DERIVATIVES **epidemiologic** adjective, **epidemiological** adjective, **epidemiologist** noun.
– ORIGIN late 19th cent.: from Greek *epidēmia* 'prevalence of disease' + -LOGY.

epidermis /ˌɛpɪˈdəːmɪs/ ▶ **noun** the outer layer of cells covering an organism, in particular: ■ Zoology & Anatomy the surface epithelium of the skin of an animal, overlying the dermis. ■ Botany the outer layer of tissue in a plant, except where it is replaced by periderm.
– DERIVATIVES **epidermal** adjective, **epidermic** adjective, **epidermoid** adjective.
– ORIGIN early 17th cent.: via late Latin from Greek, from *epi* 'upon' + *derma* 'skin'.

epidermolysis /ˌɛpɪdəːˈmɒlɪsɪs/ (also **epidermolysis bullosa** /bʊˈləʊsə/) ▶ **noun** [mass noun] Medicine loosening of the epidermis, with extensive blistering of the skin and mucous membranes, occurring either after injury or as a spontaneous and potentially dangerous condition, particularly in children.
– ORIGIN late 19th cent.: from Greek *epidermis* EPIDERMIS + -O- + *lusis* 'loosening'.

epidiascope /ˌɛpɪˈdʌɪəskəʊp/ ▶ **noun** an optical projector capable of giving images of both opaque and transparent objects.
– ORIGIN early 20th cent.: from EPI- + DIA- + -SCOPE.

epididymis /ˌɛpɪˈdɪdɪmɪs/ ▶ **noun** (pl. **epididymides** /ˌɛpɪdɪˈdɪmɪdiːz/) Anatomy a highly convoluted duct behind the testis, along which sperm passes to the vas deferens.
– DERIVATIVES **epididymal** adjective.
– ORIGIN early 17th cent.: from Greek *epididumis*, from *epi* 'upon' + *didumos* 'testicle' (from *duo* 'two').

epidote /ˈɛpɪdəʊt/ ▶ **noun** [mass noun] a lustrous yellow-green crystalline mineral, common in metamorphic rocks. It consists of a basic, hydrated silicate of calcium, aluminium, and iron.
– ORIGIN early 19th cent.: from French *épidote*, from Greek *epididonai* 'give additionally' (because of the length of the crystals).

epidural /ˌɛpɪˈdjʊər(ə)l/ ▶ **adjective** Anatomy & Medicine on or around the dura mater, in particular (of an anaesthetic) introduced into the space around the dura mater of the spinal cord.
▶ **noun** an epidural anaesthetic, used especially in childbirth to produce loss of sensation below the waist.
– ORIGIN late 19th cent.: from EPI- 'upon' + DURA[1] + -AL.

epifauna ▶ **noun** [mass noun] Ecology animals living on the surface of the seabed or a riverbed, or attached to submerged objects or aquatic animals or plants. Compare with INFAUNA.
– DERIVATIVES **epifaunal** adjective.

epifluorescence /ˌɛpɪflʊəˈrɛs(ə)ns, -flɔː-/ ▶ **noun** [mass noun] Optics the fluorescence of an object in an optical microscope when irradiated from the viewing side.

epigastrium /ˌɛpɪˈgastrɪəm/ ▶ **noun** (pl. **epigastria** /-rɪə/) Anatomy the part of the upper abdomen immediately over the stomach.
– DERIVATIVES **epigastric** adjective.
– ORIGIN late 17th cent.: via late Latin from Greek *epigastrion*, neuter of *epigastrios* 'over the belly', from *epi* 'upon' + *gastēr* 'belly'.

epigeal /ˌɛpɪˈdʒiːəl/ ▶ **adjective** Botany growing on or close to the ground. Compare with HYPOGEAL. ■ (of seed germination) with one or more seed leaves appearing above the ground.
– ORIGIN mid 19th cent.: from Greek *epigeios* (from *epi* 'upon' + *gē* 'earth') + -AL.

epigene /ˈɛpɪdʒiːn/ ▶ **adjective** Geology taking place or produced on the surface of the earth.
– ORIGIN early 19th cent.: from French *épigène*, from Greek *epigenēs*, from *epi* 'upon' + *genēs* (see -GEN).

epigenesis /ˌɛpɪˈdʒɛnɪsɪs/ ▶ **noun** [mass noun] Biology the theory, now generally held, that an embryo develops progressively from an undifferentiated egg cell. Often contrasted with PREFORMATION.
– DERIVATIVES **epigenesist** noun & adjective.
– ORIGIN mid 17th cent.: from EPI- 'in addition' + GENESIS.

epigenetic /ˌɛpɪdʒɪˈnɛtɪk/ ▶ **adjective 1** Biology resulting from external rather than genetic influences: *epigenetic carcinogens*. ■ relating to or of the nature of epigenesis.
2 Geology formed later than the surrounding or underlying rock formation.
– DERIVATIVES **epigenetically** adverb, **epigenetics** plural noun.

epiglottis /ˌɛpɪˈglɒtɪs/ ▶ **noun** a flap of cartilage behind the root of the tongue, which is depressed during swallowing to cover the opening of the windpipe.
– DERIVATIVES **epiglottal** adjective, **epiglottic** adjective.
– ORIGIN late Middle English: from Greek *epiglōttis*, from *epi* 'upon, near to' + *glōtta* 'tongue'.

epigone /ˈɛpɪgəʊn/ ▶ **noun** (pl. **epigones** or **epigoni** /ɪˈpɪgənʌɪ, ɛ-/) a less distinguished follower or imitator of someone, especially an artist or philosopher.
– ORIGIN mid 18th cent.: plurals from French *épigones* and Latin *epigoni*, from Greek *epigonoi* 'those born afterwards' (based on *gignesthai* 'be born').

epigram /ˈɛpɪgram/ ▶ **noun** a pithy saying or remark expressing an idea in a clever and amusing way. ■ a short poem, especially a satirical one, with a witty or ingenious ending.
– DERIVATIVES **epigrammatist** noun.
– ORIGIN late Middle English: from French *épigramme*, or Latin *epigramma*, from Greek, from *epi* 'upon, in addition' + *gramma* (see -GRAM[1]).

epigrammatic /ˌɛpɪgrəˈmatɪk/ ▶ **adjective** in the style of an epigram; concise, clever, and amusing: *an epigrammatic style*.
– DERIVATIVES **epigrammatically** adverb.

epigraph /ˈɛpɪgrɑːf/ ▶ **noun 1** an inscription on a building, statue, or coin.
2 a short quotation or saying at the beginning of a book or chapter, intended to suggest its theme.
– ORIGIN late 16th cent. (denoting the heading of a document or letter): from Greek *epigraphē*, from *epigraphein* 'write on'.

E

epigraphy /ɪˈpɪgrəfi, ɛ-/ ▶ **noun** [mass noun] the study and interpretation of ancient inscriptions. ■ epigraphs collectively.
– DERIVATIVES **epigrapher** noun, **epigraphic** adjective, **epigraphical** adjective, **epigraphically** adverb, **epigraphist** noun.

epigynous /ɪˈpɪdʒɪnəs, ɛ-/ ▶ **adjective** Botany (of a plant or flower) having the ovary enclosed in the receptacle, with the stamens and other floral parts situated above. Compare with HYPOGYNOUS, PERIGYNOUS.
– DERIVATIVES **epigyny** noun.
– ORIGIN mid 19th cent.: from modern Latin *epigynus*, from EPI- 'upon, above' + Greek *gunē* 'woman' + -OUS.

epilation /ˌɛpɪˈleɪʃ(ə)n/ ▶ **noun** [mass noun] the removal of hair by the roots.
– DERIVATIVES **epilate** verb, **epilator** noun.
– ORIGIN late 19th cent.: from French *épiler*, from *é-* (expressing removal) + Latin *pilus* 'strand of hair', on the pattern of *depilation*.

epilepsy /ˈɛpɪlɛpsi/ ▶ **noun** [mass noun] a neurological disorder marked by sudden recurrent episodes of sensory disturbance, loss of consciousness, or convulsions, associated with abnormal electrical activity in the brain.
– ORIGIN mid 16th cent.: from French *épilepsie*, or via late Latin from Greek *epilēpsia*, from *epilambanein* 'seize, attack', from *epi* 'upon' + *lambanein* 'take hold of'.

epileptic /ˌɛpɪˈlɛptɪk/ ▶ **adjective** relating to or suffering from epilepsy: *he had an epileptic fit*.
▶ **noun** a person who has epilepsy.
– ORIGIN early 17th cent.: from French *épileptique*, via late Latin from Greek *epilēptikos*, from *epilēpsia* (see EPILEPSY).

epileptogenic /ˌɛpɪlɛptə(ʊ)ˈdʒɛnɪk/ ▶ **adjective** Medicine capable of causing an epileptic attack.

epilimnion /ˌɛpɪˈlɪmnɪən/ ▶ **noun** (pl. **epilimnia** /-nɪə/) the upper layer of water in a stratified lake.
– ORIGIN early 20th cent.: from EPI- 'above' + Greek *limnion* (diminutive of *limnē* 'lake').

epilithic /ˌɛpɪˈlɪθɪk/ ▶ **adjective** Botany (of a plant) growing on the surface of rock.
– ORIGIN early 20th cent.: from EPI- 'upon' + Greek *lithos* 'stone' + -IC.

epilogue /ˈɛpɪlɒg/ (US also **epilog**) ▶ **noun** a section or speech at the end of a book or play that serves as a comment on or a conclusion to what has happened.
– ORIGIN late Middle English: from French *épilogue*, via Latin from Greek *epilogos*, from *epi* 'in addition' + *logos* 'speech'.

epimedium /ˌɛpɪˈmiːdɪəm/ ▶ **noun** (pl. **epimediums**) a creeping plant of a genus which includes barrenwort. ● Genus *Epimedium*, family Berberidaceae.
– ORIGIN modern Latin, from Greek *epimēdion*.

epimer /ˈɛpɪmə/ ▶ **noun** Chemistry each of two isomers with different configurations of atoms about one of several asymmetric carbon atoms present.
– DERIVATIVES **epimeric** /-ˈmɛrɪk/ adjective.

epimerize /ɪˈpɪmərʌɪz, ɛ-/ (also **epimerise**) ▶ **verb** [with obj.] Chemistry convert from one epimeric form into the other.

epimeron /ˌɛpɪˈmɪːrən/ ▶ **noun** (pl. **epimerons** or **epimera**) (in insects) the posterior part of the side wall of a thoracic segment.
– ORIGIN mid 19th cent.: from EPI- 'near' + Greek *mēros* 'thigh'.

epimysium /ˌɛpɪˈmɪsɪəm/ ▶ **noun** [mass noun] Anatomy a sheath of fibrous elastic tissue surrounding a muscle.
– ORIGIN modern Latin, from EPI- 'upon' + Greek *mus* 'muscle'.

epinephrine /ˌɛpɪˈnɛfrɪn, -riːn/ ▶ **noun** Biochemistry another term for ADRENALIN.

– ORIGIN late 19th cent.: from **EPI-** 'above' + Greek *nephros* 'kidney' + **-INE**[4].

epinician /ˌɛpɪˈnɪsɪən/ ▶ adjective denoting an ancient Greek lyric poem celebrating a victory.
– ORIGIN early 17th cent.: from Greek *epinikion*, neuter (used as a noun) of *epinikios* 'relating to victory', + **-AN**.

Epipalaeolithic /ˌɛpɪpalɪə(ʊ)ˈlɪθɪk/ (US **Epipaleolithic**) ▶ adjective Archaeology relating to or denoting a Stone Age period that shows features of both the Palaeolithic and the Mesolithic and may be transitional between them. ■ (as noun **the Epipalaeolithic**) the Epipalaeolithic period.
– ORIGIN early 20th cent.: from **EPI-** 'upon, in addition' + **PALAEOLITHIC**.

E

epiphany /ɪˈpɪf(ə)ni, ɛ-/ ▶ noun (pl. **epiphanies**) **1** (**Epiphany**) the manifestation of Christ to the Gentiles as represented by the Magi (Matthew 2:1–12). ■ the festival commemorating the Epiphany on 6 January.
2 a moment of sudden and great revelation or realization.
– DERIVATIVES **epiphanic** /ɛpɪˈfanɪk/ adjective.
– ORIGIN Middle English: from Greek *epiphainein* 'reveal'. The sense relating to the Christian festival is via Old French *epiphanie* and ecclesiastical Latin *epiphania*.

epiphenomenon /ˌɛpɪfəˈnɒmɪnən/ ▶ noun (pl. **epiphenomena** /-nə/) a secondary effect or by-product, in particular: ■ Medicine a secondary symptom, occurring simultaneously with a disease or condition but not directly related to it. ■ a mental state regarded as a by-product of brain activity.
– DERIVATIVES **epiphenomenal** adjective.

epiphora /ɪˈpɪf(ə)rə/ ▶ noun [mass noun] **1** Medicine excessive watering of the eye.
2 Rhetoric another term for **EPISTROPHE**.
– ORIGIN late 16th cent. (in sense 2): via Latin from Greek *epi* 'upon' + *pherein* 'to bear or carry'.

epiphyllum /ˌɛpɪˈfɪləm/ ▶ noun (pl. **epiphyllums**) a cactus with flattened stems and large, fragrant red or yellow flowers. ● Genus *Epiphyllum*, family Cactaceae: several species.
– ORIGIN modern Latin, from **EPI-** 'upon' + Greek *phullon* 'leaf'.

epiphysis /ɪˈpɪfɪsɪs, ɛ-/ ▶ noun (pl. **epiphyses**) **1** the end part of a long bone, initially growing separately from the shaft. Compare with **DIAPHYSIS**.
2 another term for **PINEAL**.
– DERIVATIVES **epiphyseal** adjective /ˌɛpɪˈfɪzɪəl/.
– ORIGIN mid 17th cent.: modern Latin, from Greek *epiphusis*, from *epi* 'upon, in addition' + *phusis* 'growth'.

epiphyte /ˈɛpɪfʌɪt/ ▶ noun Botany a plant that grows on another plant, especially one that is not parasitic, such as the numerous ferns, bromeliads, air plants, and orchids growing on tree trunks in tropical rainforests.
– DERIVATIVES **epiphytic** /-ˈfɪtɪk/ adjective.
– ORIGIN mid 19th cent.: from **EPI-** 'in addition' + Greek *phuton* 'plant'.

EPIRB ▶ abbreviation emergency position-indicating radio beacon.

Epirus /ɪˈpʌɪərəs/ a coastal region of NW Greece; capital, Ioánnina. Greek name **IPIROS**. ■ an ancient country of which the modern region of Epirus corresponds to the south-western part, extending northwards to Illyria and eastwards to Macedonia and Thessaly.

episcopacy /ɪˈpɪskəpəsi, ɛ-/ ▶ noun (pl. **episcopacies**) [mass noun] government of a Church by bishops. ■ (**the episcopacy**) the bishops of a region or church collectively. ■ the office of a bishop.
– ORIGIN mid 17th cent.: from ecclesiastical Latin *episcopatus* 'episcopate', on the pattern of *prelacy*.

episcopal /ɪˈpɪskəp(ə)l, ɛ-/ ▶ adjective of a bishop or bishops: *episcopal power*. ■ (of a Church) governed by or having bishops.
– DERIVATIVES **episcopalism** noun, **episcopally** adverb.
– ORIGIN late Middle English: from French *épiscopal* or ecclesiastical Latin *episcopalis*, from *episcopus* 'bishop', from Greek *episkopos* 'overseer' (see **BISHOP**).

Episcopal Church the Anglican Church in Scotland and the US.

episcopalian /ɪˌpɪskəˈpeɪlɪən, ɛ-/ ▶ adjective of or advocating government of a Church by bishops. ■ of or belonging to an episcopal Church.
▶ noun a person who advocates government of a Church by bishops. ■ (**Episcopalian**) a member of the Episcopal Church.
– DERIVATIVES **episcopalianism** noun.

episcopate /ɪˈpɪskəpət, ɛ-/ ▶ noun the office of a bishop. ■ (**the episcopate**) the bishops of a church or region collectively.
– ORIGIN mid 17th cent.: from ecclesiastical Latin *episcopatus* 'made a bishop', from *episcopus* 'bishop', from Greek *episkopos* 'overseer' (see **BISHOP**).

episcope /ˈɛpɪskəʊp/ ▶ noun an optical projector which gives images of opaque objects.

episematic /ˌɛpɪsɪˈmatɪk/ ▶ adjective Zoology (of coloration or markings) serving to help recognition by animals of other individuals of the same species.
– ORIGIN late 19th cent.: from **EPI-** 'upon' + Greek *sēma* 'sign' + **-ATIC**.

episiotomy /ɪˌpiːsɪˈɒtəmi, ɛ-/ ▶ noun (pl. **episiotomies**) a surgical cut made at the opening of the vagina during childbirth, to aid a difficult delivery and prevent rupture of tissues.
– ORIGIN late 19th cent.: from Greek *epision* 'pubic region' + **-TOMY**.

episode ▶ noun **1** an event or a group of events occurring as part of a sequence; an incident or period considered in isolation: *the whole episode has been a major embarrassment*. ■ a finite period in which someone is affected by a specified illness: *acute psychotic episodes*.
2 each of the separate instalments into which a serialized story or radio or television programme is divided. ■ Music a passage containing distinct material or introducing a new subject. ■ a section between two choric songs in Greek tragedy.
– ORIGIN late 17th cent. (denoting a section between songs in Greek tragedy): from Greek *epeisodion*, neuter of *epeisodios* 'coming in besides', from *epi* 'in addition' + *eisodos* 'entry' (from *eis* 'into' + *hodos* 'way').

episodic /ˌɛpɪˈsɒdɪk/ ▶ adjective **1** containing or consisting of a series of separate parts or events: *an episodic narrative*. ■ occurring occasionally and at irregular intervals: *volcanic activity is highly episodic in nature*.
2 (of a programme or story) broadcast or published as a series of instalments.
– DERIVATIVES **episodically** adverb.

episome /ˈɛpɪsəʊm/ ▶ noun Microbiology a genetic element inside some bacterial cells, especially the DNA of some bacteriophages, that can replicate independently of the host and also in association with a chromosome with which it becomes integrated. Compare with **PLASMID**.

epistasis /ɪˈpɪstəsɪs/ ▶ noun [mass noun] Genetics the interaction of genes that are not alleles, in particular the suppression of the effect of one such gene by another.
– DERIVATIVES **epistatic** /ˌɛpɪˈstatɪk/ adjective.
– ORIGIN early 19th cent.: from Greek, literally 'stoppage', from *ephistanai* 'to stop'.

epistaxis /ˌɛpɪˈstaksɪs/ ▶ noun [mass noun] Medicine bleeding from the nose.
– ORIGIN late 18th cent.: modern Latin, from Greek, from *epistazein* 'bleed from the nose', from *epi* 'upon, in addition' + *stazein* 'to drip'.

epistemic /ˌɛpɪˈstiːmɪk, -ˈstɛm-/ ▶ adjective relating to knowledge or to the degree of its validation.
– DERIVATIVES **epistemically** adverb.
– ORIGIN 1920s: from Greek *epistēmē* 'knowledge' (see **EPISTEMOLOGY**) + **-IC**.

epistemology /ɪˌpɪstɪˈmɒlədʒi, ɛ-/ ▶ noun [mass noun] Philosophy the theory of knowledge, especially with regard to its methods, validity, and scope, and the distinction between justified belief and opinion.
– DERIVATIVES **epistemological** adjective, **epistemologically** adverb, **epistemologist** noun.
– ORIGIN mid 19th cent.: from Greek *epistēmē* 'knowledge', from *epistasthai* 'know, know how to do'.

episternum /ˌɛpɪˈstəːnəm/ ▶ noun (pl. **episternums** or **episterna** /-nə/) Zoology a bone between the clavicles, especially (in mammals) the upper part of the sternum. ■ (in insects) the anterior part of the side wall of a thoracic segment.

epistle /ɪˈpɪs(ə)l/ ▶ noun formal or humorous a letter. ■ a poem or other literary work in the form of a letter or series of letters. ■ (**Epistle**) a book of the New Testament in the form of a letter from an Apostle: *St Paul's Epistle to the Romans*. ■ an extract from an Epistle (or another New Testament book not a Gospel) that is read in a church service.
– ORIGIN Old English, via Latin from Greek *epistolē*, from *epistellein* 'send news', from *epi* 'upon, in addition' + *stellein* 'send'. The word was reintroduced in Middle English from Old French.

Epistle to the Colossians, Epistle to the Ephesians, etc. see **COLOSSIANS, EPISTLE TO THE; EPHESIANS, EPISTLE TO THE**, etc.

epistolary /ɪˈpɪst(ə)ləri/ ▶ adjective relating to the writing of letters. ■ (of a literary work) in the form of letters: *an epistolary novel*.
– ORIGIN mid 17th cent.: from French *épistolaire* or Latin *epistolaris*, from *epistola* (see **EPISTLE**).

epistrophe /ɪˈpɪstrəfi, ɛ-/ ▶ noun [mass noun] the repetition of a word at the end of successive clauses or sentences.
– ORIGIN late 16th cent.: from Greek *epistrophē*, from *epistrephein* 'to turn around', from *epi* 'in addition' + *strephein* 'to turn'.

epistyle /ˈɛpɪstʌɪl/ ▶ noun Architecture an architrave.
– ORIGIN mid 16th cent. (in the Latin form *epistylium*): from French *épistyle* or via Latin, from Greek *epistulion*, from *epi* 'upon' + *stulos* 'pillar'.

epitaph /ˈɛpɪtɑːf, -taf/ ▶ noun a phrase or form of words written in memory of a person who has died, especially as an inscription on a tombstone. ■ something by which a person, time, or event will be remembered: *the story makes a sorry epitaph to a great career*.
– ORIGIN late Middle English: from Old French *epitaphe*, via Latin from Greek *epitaphion* 'funeral oration', neuter of *ephitaphios* 'over or at a tomb', from *epi* 'upon' + *taphos* 'tomb'.

epitaxy /ˈɛpɪtaksi/ ▶ noun [mass noun] Crystallography the natural or artificial growth of crystals on a crystalline substrate that determines their orientation.
– DERIVATIVES **epitaxial** adjective.
– ORIGIN 1930s: from French *épitaxie*, from Greek *epi* 'upon' + *taxis* 'arrangement'.

epithalamium /ˌɛpɪθəˈleɪmɪəm/ ▶ noun (pl. **epithalamiums** or **epithalamia**) a song or poem celebrating a marriage.
– DERIVATIVES **epithalamic** /-ˈlamɪk/ adjective.
– ORIGIN late 16th cent.: via Latin from Greek *epithalamion*, from *epi* 'upon' + *thalamos* 'bridal chamber'.

epithalamus /ˌɛpɪˈθaləməs/ ▶ noun (pl. **epithalami** /-mʌɪ, -miː/) Anatomy a part of the dorsal forebrain including the pineal gland and a region in the roof of the third ventricle.

epithelium /ˌɛpɪˈθiːlɪəm/ ▶ noun (pl. **epithelia** /-lɪə/) [mass noun] Anatomy the thin tissue forming the outer layer of a body's surface and lining the alimentary canal and other hollow structures. ■ the part of the epithelium derived from embryonic ectoderm and endoderm, as distinct from endothelium and mesothelium.
– DERIVATIVES **epithelial** adjective.
– ORIGIN mid 18th cent.: modern Latin, from **EPI-** 'above' + Greek *thēlē* 'teat'.

epithet /ˈɛpɪθɛt/ ▶ noun an adjective or phrase expressing a quality or attribute regarded as characteristic of the person or thing mentioned: *old men are often unfairly awarded the epithet 'dirty'*. ■ such a word or phrase as a term of abuse: *the woman begins to hurl racial epithets at them*.
– DERIVATIVES **epithetic** adjective, **epithetical** adjective.
– ORIGIN late 16th cent.: from French *épithète*, or via Latin from Greek *epitheton*, neuter of *epithetos* 'attributed', from *epitithenai* 'add', from *epi* 'upon' + *tithenai* 'to place'.

epitome /ɪˈpɪtəmi, ɛ-/ ▶ noun **1** (**the epitome of**) a person or thing that is a perfect example of a particular quality or type: *she looked the epitome of elegance and good taste*.
2 a summary of a written work; an abstract. ■ archaic a thing representing something else in miniature.
– ORIGIN early 16th cent.: via Latin from Greek *epitomē*, from *epitemnein* 'abridge', from *epi* 'in addition' + *temnein* 'to cut'.

epitomize (also **epitomise**) ▶ verb [with obj.] **1** be a perfect example of: *the company epitomized the problems faced by British industry*.
2 archaic give a summary of (a written work).
– DERIVATIVES **epitomization** noun.

epitope /ˈɛpɪtəʊp/ ▶ noun Biochemistry the part of an antigen molecule to which an antibody attaches itself. Also called **ANTIGENIC DETERMINANT**.
– ORIGIN 1960s: from **EPI-** 'upon' + Greek *topos* 'place'.

epizoic /ˌɛpɪˈzəʊɪk/ ▸ **adjective** Biology (of a plant or animal) growing or living non-parasitically on the exterior of a living animal.
– ORIGIN mid 19th cent.: from **EPI-** 'upon' + Greek *zōion* 'animal' + **-IC**.

epizoon /ˌɛpɪˈzəʊɒn/ ▸ **noun** (pl. **epizoa** /-ˈzəʊə/) Zoology an animal that lives on the body of another animal, especially as a parasite.
– ORIGIN mid 19th cent.: from **EPI-** 'upon' + Greek *zōion* 'animal'.

epizootic /ˌɛpɪzəʊˈɒtɪk/ ▸ **adjective** (of a disease) temporarily prevalent and widespread in an animal population. Compare with **ENZOOTIC**, **EPIDEMIC**.
– ORIGIN late 18th cent. (as an adjective): from French *épizootique*, from *épizootie*, from Greek *epi* 'upon' + *zōion* 'animal'.

EPLF ▸ **abbreviation** Eritrean People's Liberation Front.

e pluribus unum /eɪ ˌplʊərɪbʊs ˈjuːnʊm/ ▸ **noun** out of many, one (the motto of the US).
– ORIGIN Latin.

EPNS ▸ **abbreviation** electroplated nickel silver.

EPO ▸ **abbreviation** ▪ erythropoietin, especially when isolated as a drug for medical use or for illegal use by athletes. ▪ European Patent Office.

epoch /ˈiːpɒk, ˈɛpɒk/ ▸ **noun** a particular period of time in history or a person's life: *the Victorian epoch*. ▪ the beginning of a period in the history of someone or something. ▪ Geology a division of time that is a subdivision of a period and is itself subdivided into ages, corresponding to a series in chronostratigraphy: *the Pliocene epoch*. ▪ Astronomy an arbitrarily fixed date relative to which planetary or stellar measurements are expressed.
– ORIGIN early 17th cent. (in the Latin form *epocha*; originally in the general sense of a date from which succeeding years are numbered): from modern Latin *epocha*, from Greek *epokhē* 'stoppage, fixed point of time', from *epekhein* 'stop, take up a position', from *epi* 'upon, near to' + *ekhein* 'stay, be in a certain state'.

epochal /ˈɛpɒk(ə)l/ ▸ **adjective** forming or characterizing an epoch; epoch-making.

epoch-making ▸ **adjective** of major importance; likely to have a significant effect on a particular period of time.

epode /ˈɛpəʊd/ ▸ **noun 1** a form of lyric poem written in couplets, in which a long line is followed by a shorter one.
2 the third section of an ancient Greek choral ode, or of one division of such an ode.
– ORIGIN early 17th cent.: from French *épode*, or via Latin *epodos*, from Greek *epōidos*, from *epi* 'upon' + *ōidē* (see **ODE**).

eponym /ˈɛpənɪm/ ▸ **noun** a person after whom a discovery, invention, place, etc., is named or thought to be named. ▪ a name or noun formed after a person.
– ORIGIN mid 19th cent.: from Greek *epōnumos* 'given as a name, giving one's name to someone or something', from *epi* 'upon' + *onoma* 'name'.

eponymous /ɪˈpɒnɪməs/ ▸ **adjective** (of a person) giving their name to something: *the eponymous hero of the novel*. ▪ (of a thing) named after a particular person or group: *their eponymous debut LP*.
– DERIVATIVES **eponymously** adverb.

EPOS /ˈiːpɒz, ˈiːpɒs/ ▸ **abbreviation** electronic point of sale (used in reference to the electronic recording of information on goods sold by a retailer).

epoxide /ɪˈpɒksʌɪd/ ▸ **noun** Chemistry an organic compound whose molecule contains a three-membered ring involving an oxygen atom and two carbon atoms.
– ORIGIN 1930s: from **EPI-** 'in addition' + **OXIDE**.

epoxy /ɪˈpɒksi, ɛ-/ ▸ **noun** (pl. **epoxies**) (also **epoxy resin**) [mass noun] an adhesive, plastic, or other material made from a class of synthetic thermosetting polymers containing epoxide groups.
▸ **adjective** consisting of epoxy: *epoxy cement*.
▸ **verb** (**epoxies**, **epoxying**, **epoxied**) [with obj.] glue (something) using epoxy resin.
– ORIGIN early 20th cent.: from **EPI-** 'in addition' + **OXY-**[2].

EPROM /ˈiːprɒm/ ▸ **noun** Computing a read-only memory whose contents can be erased by ultraviolet light or other means and reprogrammed using a pulsed voltage.
– ORIGIN 1970s: acronym from *erasable programmable ROM*.

EPS ▸ **abbreviation** earnings per share.

epsilon /ˈɛpsɪlɒn, ɛpˈsʌɪlɒn/ ▸ **noun** the fifth letter of the Greek alphabet (Ε, ε), transliterated as 'e'. ▪ [as modifier] denoting the fifth in a series of items, categories, etc. ▪ (**Epsilon**) [followed by Latin genitive] Astronomy the fifth star in a constellation: *Epsilon Carinae*.
▸ **symbol** (ε) permittivity.
– ORIGIN Greek, 'bare or simple E', from *psilos* 'bare'.

Epsom /ˈɛpsəm/ a town in Surrey, SE England; pop. 35,000 (est. 2009). The annual Derby and Oaks horse races are held at its racecourse on Epsom Downs.

Epsom salts ▸ **plural noun** crystals of hydrated magnesium sulphate used as a purgative or for other medicinal use. ● Chem. formula: $MgSO_4.7H_2O$.
– ORIGIN mid 18th cent.: named after the town of **EPSOM**, where it was first found occurring naturally.

EPSRC ▸ **abbreviation** (in the UK) Engineering and Physical Sciences Research Council.

Epstein[1] /ˈɛpstʌɪn/, Brian (1934–67), English businessman and music journalist, manager of the Beatles.

Epstein[2] /ˈɛpstʌɪn/, Sir Jacob (1880–1959), American-born British sculptor. A founder member of the Vorticist group, he later had great success in his modelled portraits of the famous, in particular his *Einstein* (1933).

Epstein–Barr virus (abbrev.: **EBV**) ▸ **noun** Medicine a herpesvirus causing glandular fever and associated with certain cancers, for example Burkitt's lymphoma.
– ORIGIN 1960s: named after Michael A. *Epstein* (born 1921), British virologist, and Y. M. *Barr* (born 1932), Irish-born virologist.

epyllion /ɪˈpɪlɪən, ɛ-/ ▸ **noun** (pl. **epyllia**) a narrative poem that resembles an epic poem in style, but which is notably shorter.
– ORIGIN late 19th cent.: from Greek *epullion*, diminutive of *epos* 'word, song', from *eipein* 'say'.

EQ ▸ **abbreviation** (with reference to sound reproduction) equalizer or equalization.

equable /ˈɛkwəb(ə)l/ ▸ **adjective 1** not easily disturbed or angered; calm and even-tempered.
2 not varying or fluctuating greatly: *an equable climate*.
– DERIVATIVES **equability** noun, **equably** adverb.
– ORIGIN mid 17th cent. (in the sense 'fair, equitable'): from Latin *aequabilis*, from *aequare* 'make equal' (see **EQUATE**).

equal ▸ **adjective 1** being the same in quantity, size, degree, or value: *add equal amounts of water and flour* | *1 litre is roughly* ***equal to*** *1 quart*. ▪ (of people) having the same status, rights, or opportunities. ▪ uniform in application or effect; without discrimination on any grounds: *a dedicated campaigner for equal rights*. ▪ evenly or fairly balanced: *it was hardly an equal contest*.
2 (**equal to**) having the ability or resources to meet (a challenge): *the players proved equal to the task*.
▸ **noun** a person or thing that is the same as another in status or quality: *we all treat each other as equals* | *entertainment facilities* ***without equal*** *in the British Isles*.
▸ **verb** (**equals**, **equalling**, **equalled**; US **equals**, **equaling**, **equaled**) [with obj.] be the same as in number or amount: *four plus six divided by two equals five* | *the total debits should equal the total credits*. ▪ match or rival in performance or extent: *he equalled the world record of 9.93 seconds*. ▪ be equivalent to: *his work is concerned with why private property equals exploitation*.
– PHRASES (**the**) **first among equals** the person or thing having the highest status in a group. **on equal terms** with the same advantages and disadvantages: *all companies should be able to compete on equal terms*. **other** (or **all**) **things being equal** provided that other factors or circumstances remain the same: *it follows that, other things being equal, the price level will rise*. **some —— are more equal than others** although members of a society or group appear to be equal, in reality some receive better treatment than others: *evidently, some communities are more equal than others*.
– ORIGIN late Middle English: from Latin *aequalis*, from *aequus* 'even, level, equal'.

> **USAGE** It is widely held that adjectives such as **equal** and **unique** should not be modified and that it is incorrect to say **more equal** or **very unique**, on the grounds that these are adjectives which refer to a logical or mathematical absolute. For more discussion of this question, see **USAGE** at **UNIQUE**.

equalitarian /ɪˌkwɒlɪˈtɛːrɪən, iː-/ ▸ **noun** another term for **EGALITARIAN**.
– DERIVATIVES **equalitarianism** noun.

equality ▸ **noun 1** [mass noun] the state of being equal, especially in status, rights, or opportunities: *an organization aiming to promote racial equality*.
2 Mathematics a symbolic expression of the fact that two quantities are equal; an equation.
– ORIGIN late Middle English: via Old French from Latin *aequalitas*, from *aequalis* (see **EQUAL**).

Equality State informal name for **WYOMING**.

equalize (also **equalise**) ▸ **verb 1** [with obj.] make the same in quantity, size, or degree throughout a place or group: *the purpose is to equalize the workload among tutors*. ▪ make uniform in application or effect: *Britain is required to equalize pension rights between men and women*.
2 [no obj.] Brit. level the score in a match by scoring a goal: *Morgan equalized ten minutes into the second half*.
– DERIVATIVES **equalization** noun.
– ORIGIN late 16th cent. (in the sense 'be equal to'): from **EQUAL** + **-IZE**, partly suggested by French *égaliser*.

equalizer (also **equaliser**) ▸ **noun 1** a thing which has an equalizing effect: *education is the great equalizer*. ▪ Brit. a goal that levels the score in the game.
2 N. Amer. informal a weapon, especially a gun.
3 Electronics a passive network designed to modify a frequency response, especially to compensate for distortion.

equally ▸ **adverb** in the same manner or to the same extent: *all children should be treated equally* | [as submodifier] *follow-up discussion is equally important*. ▪ in amounts or parts that are the same in size: *the money can be divided equally between you*. ▪ [sentence adverb] in addition and having the same importance (used to introduce a further comment): *not all who live in inner cities are poor; equally, many poor people live outside inner cities*.

> **USAGE** The construction **equally as**, as in *follow-up discussion is* ***equally as*** *important*, is relatively common but is condemned on the grounds of redundancy. Either word can be used alone and be perfectly correct, e.g. *follow-up discussion is* **equally** *important* or *follow-up discussion is* **as** *important*.

equal opportunities (also **equal opportunity**) ▸ **plural noun** the right to be treated without discrimination, especially on the grounds of one's sex, race, or age.

equals sign (also **equal sign**) ▸ **noun** the symbol =.

equanimity /ˌɛkwəˈnɪmɪti, iː-/ ▸ **noun** [mass noun] calmness and composure, especially in a difficult situation: *she accepted both the good and the bad* ***with equanimity***.
– ORIGIN early 17th cent. (also in the sense 'fairness, impartiality'): from Latin *aequanimitas*, from *aequus* 'equal' + *animus* 'mind'.

equanimous /ɪˈkwanɪməs, iː-/ ▸ **adjective** calm and composed.
– ORIGIN mid 17th cent.: from Latin *aequanimus*, from *aequus* 'equal' + *animus* mind.

equant /ˈiːkwənt/ ▸ **noun** Astronomy, historical (in the Ptolemaic system) an imaginary circle introduced with the purpose of reconciling the planetary movements with the hypothesis of uniform circular motion.
▸ **adjective** Geology (of a crystal or particle) having its different diameters approximately equal, so as to be roughly cubic or spherical in shape.
– ORIGIN mid 16th cent.: from Latin *aequant-* 'making equal', from the verb *aequare*.

equate /ɪˈkweɪt/ ▸ **verb** [with obj.] (often **equate something to/with**) consider (one thing) to be the same as or equivalent to another: *customers equate their name with quality*. ▪ [no obj.] (**equate to/with**) (of one thing) be the same as or equivalent to (another): *that sum equates to half a million pounds today*. ▪ cause (two or more things) to be the same in quantity or value: *the level of prices will move to equate supply and demand*.
– DERIVATIVES **equatable** adjective.
– ORIGIN Middle English (in the sense 'make equal, balance'): from Latin *aequat-* 'made level or equal', from the verb *aequare*, from *aequus* (see **EQUAL**). Current senses date from the mid 19th cent.

equation /ɪˈkweɪʒ(ə)n/ ▸ **noun 1** Mathematics a statement that the values of two mathematical expressions are equal (indicated by the sign =).
2 [mass noun] the process of equating one thing with another: *the* ***equation of*** *science* ***with*** *objectivity*. ▪ (**the equation**) a situation in which several factors must be taken into account: *money also came into the equation*.

E

3 Chemistry a symbolic representation of the changes which occur in a chemical reaction, expressed in terms of the formulae of the molecules or other species involved.
– PHRASES **equation of the first** (or **second** etc.) **order** Mathematics an equation involving only the first derivative, second derivative, etc.
– ORIGIN late Middle English: from Latin *aequatio(n-)*, from *aequare* 'make equal' (see EQUATE).

equational ▸ adjective another term for EQUATIVE.

equation of state ▸ noun Chemistry an equation showing the relationship between the values of the pressure, volume, and temperature of a quantity of a particular substance.

E

equation of time ▸ noun the difference between mean solar time (as shown by clocks) and apparent solar time (indicated by sundials), which varies with the time of year.

equative /ɪˈkweɪtɪv/ ▸ adjective Grammar denoting or relating to a sentence or other structure in which one term is identified with another, as in *the winner is Jill*.

equator /ɪˈkweɪtə/ ▸ noun a line notionally drawn on the earth equidistant from the poles, dividing the earth into northern and southern hemispheres and constituting the parallel of latitude 0°. ■ Astronomy short for CELESTIAL EQUATOR.
– ORIGIN late Middle English: from medieval Latin *aequator*, in the phrase *circulus aequator diei et noctis* 'circle equalizing day and night', from Latin *aequare* 'make equal' (see EQUATE).

equatorial /ˌɛkwəˈtɔːrɪəl/ ▸ adjective of, at, or near the equator: *equatorial regions*.
– DERIVATIVES **equatorially** adverb.

Equatorial Guinea a small country of West Africa on the Gulf of Guinea, comprising several offshore islands and a coastal settlement between Cameroon and Gabon; pop. 633,400 (est. 2009); languages, Spanish (official), local Niger–Congo languages, pidgin; capital, Malabo (on the island of Bioko). Formerly a Spanish colony, the country became fully independent in 1968. It is the only independent Spanish-speaking state in the continent of Africa.
– DERIVATIVES **Equatorial Guinean** adjective & noun.

equatorial mount (also **equatorial mounting**) ▸ noun Astronomy a telescope mounting with one axis aligned to the celestial pole, which allows the movement of celestial objects to be followed by motion about this axis alone. Compare with ALTAZIMUTH (sense 1).

equatorial telescope ▸ noun an astronomical telescope on an equatorial mount.

equerry /ɪˈkwɛri, ˈɛkwəri/ ▸ noun (pl. **equerries**) an officer of the British royal household who attends or assists members of the royal family. ■ historical an officer of the household of a prince or noble who had charge over the stables.
– ORIGIN early 16th cent. (formerly also as *esquiry*): from Old French *esquierie* 'company of squires, prince's stables', from Old French *esquier* 'esquire', perhaps associated with Latin *equus* 'horse'. The historical sense is apparently based on Old French *esquier d'esquierie* 'squire of stables'.

eques /ˈɛkweɪz/ singular form of EQUITES.

equestrian /ɪˈkwɛstrɪən, ɛ-/ ▸ adjective relating to horse riding: *his amazing equestrian skills*. ■ depicting or representing a person on horseback: *an equestrian statue*.
▸ noun a rider or performer on horseback.
– ORIGIN mid 17th cent. (as an adjective): from Latin *equester* 'belonging to a horseman' (from *eques* 'horseman, knight', from *equus* 'horse') + -IAN.

equestrianism ▸ noun [mass noun] the skill or sport of horse riding. As an Olympic sport it is divided into three categories: showjumping, dressage, and three-day eventing (combining showjumping, dressage, and cross-country riding).

equestrienne /ɪˌkwɛstrɪˈɛn/ ▸ noun a female rider or performer on horseback.
– ORIGIN mid 19th cent.: alteration of EQUESTRIAN, on the pattern of feminine nouns such as *Parisienne*.

equi- /ˈiːkwi, ˈɛkwi/ ▸ combining form equal; equally: *equiangular | equidistant*.
– ORIGIN from Latin *aequi-*, from *aequus* 'equal'.

equiangular ▸ adjective having equal angles.

equiangular spiral ▸ noun Geometry a spiral such that the angle between the tangent and the radius vector is the same for all points of the spiral. Also called LOGARITHMIC SPIRAL.

equid /ˈɛkwɪd/ ▸ noun Zoology a mammal of the horse family (Equidae).
– ORIGIN late 19th cent.: from modern Latin *Equidae* (plural), from Latin *equus* 'horse'.

equidistant ▸ adjective at equal distances: *the line joins together all points which are equidistant from the two axes*.
– DERIVATIVES **equidistance** noun, **equidistantly** adverb.

equifinal /ˌɛkwɪˈfʌɪn(ə)l/ ▸ adjective technical having the same end or result.
– DERIVATIVES **equifinality** noun.

equilateral /ˌiːkwɪˈlat(ə)r(ə)l, ˌɛkwɪ-/ ▸ adjective having all its sides of the same length: *an equilateral triangle*.
– ORIGIN late 16th cent.: from French *équilatéral* or late Latin *aequilateralis*, from *aequilaterus* 'equal-sided' (based on Latin *latus, later-* 'side').

equilibrate /ˌiːkwɪˈlʌɪbreɪt, ɪˈkwɪlɪ-, iːˈkwɪlɪ-/ ▸ verb [with obj.] technical bring into or keep in equilibrium. ■ [no obj.] approach or attain a state of equilibrium.
– DERIVATIVES **equilibration** noun.
– ORIGIN mid 17th cent.: from late Latin *aequilibrat-* 'made to balance', from the verb *aequilibrare*, from *aequi-* 'equally' + *libra* 'balance'.

equilibrist /ɪˈkwɪlɪˌbrɪst, iːˈkwɪlɪ-, ˌiːkwɪˈlɪb-, ˌɛkwɪ-/ ▸ noun dated an acrobat who performs balancing feats, especially a tightrope walker.
– ORIGIN mid 18th cent.: from EQUILIBRIUM + -IST.

equilibrium /ˌiːkwɪˈlɪbrɪəm, ˌɛkwɪ-/ ▸ noun (pl. **equilibria** /-rɪə/) [mass noun] a state in which opposing forces or influences are balanced: *the task is the maintenance of social equilibrium*. ■ a state of physical balance: *I stumbled over a rock and recovered my equilibrium*. ■ a calm state of mind: *his intensity could unsettle his equilibrium*. ■ Chemistry a state in which a process and its reverse are occurring at equal rates so that no overall change is taking place: *ice is in* ***equilibrium with*** *water*. ■ Economics a situation in which supply and demand are matched and prices stable.
– DERIVATIVES **equilibrial** adjective.
– ORIGIN early 17th cent. (in the sense 'well-balanced state of mind'): from Latin *aequilibrium*, from *aequi-* 'equal' + *libra* 'balance'.

equine /ˈiːkwʌɪn, ˈɛ-/ ▸ adjective relating to or affecting horses or other members of the horse family: *equine infectious anaemia*. ■ resembling a horse: *her somewhat equine features*.
▸ noun a horse or other member of the horse family.
– ORIGIN late 18th cent.: from Latin *equinus*, from *equus* 'horse'.

equinoctial /ˌiːkwɪˈnɒkʃ(ə)l, ˌɛkwɪ-/ ▸ adjective happening at or near the time of an equinox. ■ having a day and night of equal length. ■ at or near the equator.
▸ noun (also **equinoctial line**) another term for CELESTIAL EQUATOR.
– ORIGIN late Middle English (in the sense 'relating to equal periods of day and night'): via Old French from Latin *aequinoctialis*, from *aequinoctium* (see EQUINOX).

equinoctial point ▸ noun either of two points at which the ecliptic cuts the celestial equator.

equinoctial year ▸ noun see YEAR (sense 1).

equinox /ˈiːkwɪnɒks, ˈɛkwɪ-/ ▸ noun the time or date (twice each year) at which the sun crosses the celestial equator, when day and night are of equal length (about 22 September and 20 March). ■ another term for EQUINOCTIAL POINT.
– ORIGIN late Middle English: from Old French *equinoxe* or Latin *aequinoctium*, from *aequi-* 'equal' + *nox, noct-* 'night'.

equip ▸ verb (**equips, equipping, equipped**) [with obj.] supply with the necessary items for a particular purpose: *all bedrooms are* ***equipped with*** *a colour TV | they* ***equipped*** *themselves* ***for*** *the campaign*. ■ prepare (someone) mentally for a particular situation or task: *I don't think he's equipped for the modern age*.
– ORIGIN early 16th cent.: from French *équiper*, probably from Old Norse *skipa* 'to man (a ship)', from *skip* 'ship'.

equipage /ˈɛkwɪpɪdʒ/ ▸ noun 1 [mass noun] archaic the equipment for a particular purpose.
2 historical a carriage and horses with attendants.
– ORIGIN mid 16th cent. (denoting the crew of a ship): from French *équipage*, from *équiper* 'equip'.

equipartition /ˌiːkwɪpɑːˈtɪʃ(ə)n/ (also **equipartition of energy**) ▸ noun [mass noun] Physics the equal distribution of the kinetic energy of a system among its various degrees of freedom. ■ the principle that equipartition exists for a system in thermal equilibrium.
– DERIVATIVES **equipartitioned** adjective.

equipment ▸ noun [mass noun] the necessary items for a particular purpose: *suppliers of office equipment*. ■ the process of supplying someone or something with necessary equipment: *the construction and equipment of new harbour facilities*. ■ mental resources: *they lacked the intellectual equipment to recognize the jokes*.
– ORIGIN early 18th cent.: from French *équipement*, from *équiper* 'equip'.

equipoise /ˈɛkwɪpɔɪz, ˈiːkwɪ-/ ▸ noun [mass noun] balance of forces or interests: *this temporary equipoise of power*. ■ [count noun] a counterbalance or balancing force: *capital flows act as an* ***equipoise to*** *international imbalances in savings*.
▸ verb [with obj.] balance or counterbalance (something).
– ORIGIN mid 17th cent.: from EQUI- 'equal' + the noun POISE[1], replacing the phrase *equal poise*.

equipollent /ˌiːkwɪˈpɒl(ə)nt, ˌɛkwɪ-/ ▸ adjective archaic equal or equivalent in power, effect, or significance.
– ORIGIN late Middle English: from Old French *equipolent*, from Latin *aequipollent-* 'of equal value', from *aequi-* 'equally' + *pollere* 'be strong'.

equipotent /ˌiːkwɪˈpəʊt(ə)nt, ˌɛkwɪ-/ ▸ adjective technical (chiefly of chemicals and medicines) equally powerful; having equal potencies.

equipotential ▸ adjective Physics (of a surface or line) composed of points all at the same potential.
▸ noun an equipotential line or surface.

equiprobable ▸ adjective Mathematics & Logic (of two or more things) equally likely to occur; having equal probability.
– DERIVATIVES **equiprobability** noun.

equisetum /ˌɛkwɪˈsiːtəm/ ▸ noun (pl. **equiseta** /-tə/ or **equisetums**) Botany a plant of a genus that comprises the horsetails. ● Genus *Equisetum*, family Equisetaceae.
– ORIGIN modern Latin, from Latin *equus* 'horse' + *saeta* 'bristle'.

equitable /ˈɛkwɪtəb(ə)l/ ▸ adjective 1 fair and impartial: *the equitable distribution of resources*.
2 Law valid in equity as distinct from law.
– DERIVATIVES **equitability** noun, **equitableness** noun, **equitably** adverb.
– ORIGIN mid 16th cent.: from French *équitable*, from *équité* (see EQUITY).

equitant /ˈɛkwɪt(ə)nt/ ▸ adjective Botany (of a leaf) having its base folded and partly enclosing the leaf next above it, as in an iris.
– ORIGIN late 18th cent.: from Latin *equitant-* 'riding on horseback', from the verb *equitare*.

equitation /ˌɛkwɪˈteɪʃ(ə)n/ ▸ noun [mass noun] formal the art and practice of horsemanship and horse riding.
– ORIGIN mid 16th cent.: from French *équitation* or Latin *equitatio(n-)*, from *equitare* 'ride a horse', from *eques, equit-* 'horseman' (from *equus* 'horse').

equites /ˈɛkwɪteɪz/ ▸ plural noun (sing. **eques**) (in ancient Rome) a class of citizens who originally formed the cavalry of the Roman army and at a later period were a wealthy class of great political importance.
– ORIGIN Latin, plural of *eques* 'horseman'.

equity /ˈɛkwɪti/ ▸ noun (pl. **equities**) [mass noun] 1 the quality of being fair and impartial: *equity of treatment*. ■ Law a branch of law that developed alongside common law and is concerned with fairness and justice, formerly administered in special courts.
2 the value of the shares issued by a company: *he owns 62% of the group's equity*. ■ (**equities**) stocks and shares that carry no fixed interest.
3 the value of a mortgaged property after deduction of charges against it.
4 (**Equity**) (in the UK, US, and several other countries) a trade union to which all professional actors must belong: [as modifier] *an Equity card*.
– ORIGIN Middle English: from Old French *equité*, from Latin *aequitas*, from *aequus* 'equal'.

equity of redemption ▸ noun [mass noun] Law the right of a mortgagor over the mortgaged property, especially the right to redeem the property on payment of the principal, interest, and costs.

equivalence /ɪˈkwɪv(ə)l(ə)ns/ ▸ noun [mass noun] the condition of being equal or equivalent in value, worth, function, etc.
– DERIVATIVES **equivalency** noun.

equivalence class ▸ noun Mathematics & Logic the class of all members of a set that are in a given equivalence relation.

equivalence principle ▶ **noun** Physics a basic postulate of general relativity, stating that at any point of space–time the effects of a gravitational field cannot be experimentally distinguished from those due to an accelerated frame of reference.

equivalence relation ▶ **noun** Mathematics & Logic a relation between elements of a set which is reflexive, symmetric, and transitive and which defines exclusive classes whose members bear the relation to each other and not to those in other classes.

equivalent /ɪˈkwɪv(ə)l(ə)nt/ ▶ **adjective** equal in value, amount, function, meaning, etc.: *one unit is equivalent to one glass of wine.* ■ (**equivalent to**) having the same or a similar effect as: *some regulations are equivalent to censorship.* ■ Mathematics belonging to the same equivalence class.
▶ **noun 1** a person or thing that is equal to or corresponds with another in value, amount, function, meaning, etc.: *the French equivalent of the Bank of England.*
2 (also **equivalent weight**) Chemistry the mass of a particular substance that can combine with or displace one gram of hydrogen or eight grams of oxygen, used in expressing combining powers, especially of elements.
– DERIVATIVES **equivalently** adverb.
– ORIGIN late Middle English (describing persons who were equal in power or rank): via Old French from late Latin *aequivalent*- 'being of equal worth', from the verb *aequivalere*, from *aequi*- 'equally' + *valere* 'be worth'.

equivocal /ɪˈkwɪvək(ə)l/ ▶ **adjective** open to more than one interpretation; ambiguous: *the equivocal nature of her remarks.* ■ (of a person) using ambiguous or evasive language: *he has always been equivocal about the meaning of his lyrics.* ■ uncertain or questionable in nature: *the results of the investigation were equivocal.*
– DERIVATIVES **equivocality** noun, **equivocally** adverb, **equivocalness** noun.
– ORIGIN mid 16th cent.: from late Latin *aequivocus*, from Latin *aequus* 'equally' + *vocare* 'to call'.

equivocate /ɪˈkwɪvəkeɪt/ ▶ **verb** [no obj.] use ambiguous language so as to conceal the truth or avoid committing oneself: *the government have equivocated too often in the past.*
– DERIVATIVES **equivocator** noun.
– ORIGIN late Middle English (in the sense 'use a word in more than one sense'): from late Latin *aequivocat*- 'called by the same name', from the verb *aequivocare*, from *aequivocus* (see EQUIVOCAL).

equivocation /ɪˌkwɪvəˈkeɪʃ(ə)n/ ▶ **noun** [mass noun] the use of ambiguous language to conceal the truth or to avoid committing oneself; prevarication: *I say this without equivocation.*

equivoque /ˈiːkwɪvəʊk, ˈɛkwɪ-/ (also **equivoke**) ▶ **noun** rare an expression capable of having more than one meaning; a pun. ■ [mass noun] the fact of having more than one meaning; ambiguity.
– ORIGIN late Middle English (as an adjective in the sense 'equivocal'): from Old French *equivoque* or late Latin *aequivocus* (see EQUIVOCAL).

Equuleus /ɛˈkwʊlɪəs/ Astronomy a small northern constellation (the Foal or Little Horse), perhaps representing the brother of Pegasus. It has no bright stars.
– ORIGIN Latin.

ER ▶ **abbreviation** ■ N. Amer. emergency room. ■ King Edward. [from Latin *Edwardus Rex.*] ■ Queen Elizabeth. [from Latin *Elizabetha Regina.*]

Er ▶ **symbol** the chemical element erbium.

er ▶ **exclamation** expressing hesitation: *'Would you like some tea?' 'Er … yes … thank you.'*
– ORIGIN natural utterance: first recorded in English in the mid 19th cent.

-er[1] ▶ **suffix 1** denoting a person or thing that performs a specified action or activity: *farmer | sprinkler.*
2 denoting a person or thing that has a specified attribute or form: *foreigner | two-wheeler.*
3 denoting a person concerned with a specified thing or subject: *milliner | philosopher.*
4 denoting a person belonging to a specified place or group: *city-dweller | New Yorker.*
– ORIGIN Old English *-ere*, of Germanic origin.

-er[2] ▶ **suffix** forming the comparative of adjectives (as in *bigger*) and adverbs (as in *faster*).
– ORIGIN Old English suffix *-ra* (adjectival), *-or* (adverbial), of Germanic origin.

-er[3] ▶ **suffix** forming nouns used informally, usually by distortion of the root word: *footer | rugger.*
– ORIGIN probably an extended use of -ER[1]; originally Rugby School slang, later adopted at Oxford University, then extended into general use.

-er[4] ▶ **suffix** forming frequentative verbs such as *glimmer, patter.*
– ORIGIN Old English *-erian, -rian*, of Germanic origin.

-er[5] ▶ **suffix** forming nouns: **1** such as *sampler*. Compare with -AR[1]. [ending corresponding to Latin *-aris.*] ■ such as *butler, danger*. [ending corresponding to Latin *-arius, -arium.*] ■ such as *border*. [ending corresponding (via Old French *-eure*) to Latin *-atura.*] ■ such as *laver*. See LAVER[2]. [ending corresponding (via Old French *-eor*) to Latin *-atorium.*]
2 equivalent to -OR[1].
– ORIGIN via Old French or Anglo-Norman French (see above).

-er[6] ▶ **suffix** chiefly Law (forming nouns) denoting verbal action or a document effecting such action: *disclaimer | misnomer.*
– ORIGIN from Anglo-Norman French (infinitive ending).

era /ˈɪərə/ ▶ **noun** a long and distinct period of history: *his death marked the end of an era | leading photographers of the Victorian era.* ■ a system of chronology dating from a particular event: *the dawn of the Christian era.* ■ Geology a major division of time that is a subdivision of an aeon and is itself subdivided into periods: *the Mesozoic era.* ■ archaic a date or event marking the beginning of a new and distinct period of time.
– ORIGIN mid 17th cent.: from late Latin *aera*, denoting a number used as a basis of reckoning, an epoch from which time is reckoned, plural of *aes, aer*- 'money, counter'.

eradicate /ɪˈradɪkeɪt/ ▶ **verb** [with obj.] destroy completely; put an end to: *this disease has been eradicated from the world.*
– DERIVATIVES **eradicable** adjective, **eradicant** noun, **eradicator** noun.
– ORIGIN late Middle English (in the sense 'pull up by the roots'): from Latin *eradicat*- 'torn up by the roots', from the verb *eradicare*, from *e*- (variant of *ex*-) 'out' + *radix, radic*- 'root'.

eradicated ▶ **adjective** [postpositive] Heraldry (of a tree or plant) depicted with the roots exposed.

eradication /ɪˌradɪˈkeɪʃ(ə)n/ ▶ **noun** [mass noun] the complete destruction of something: *the eradication of poverty.*

erase /ɪˈreɪz/ ▶ **verb** [with obj.] rub out or remove (writing or marks): *graffiti had been erased from the wall.* ■ remove all traces of; destroy or obliterate: *over twenty years the last vestiges of a rural economy were erased | the magic of the landscape erased all else from her mind.* ■ remove recorded material from (a magnetic tape or medium); delete (data) from a computer's memory.
– DERIVATIVES **erasable** adjective.
– ORIGIN late 16th cent. (originally as a heraldic term meaning 'represent the head or limb of an animal with a jagged edge'): from Latin *eras*- 'scraped away', from the verb *eradere*, from *e*- (variant of *ex*-) 'out' + *radere* 'scrape'.

erased ▶ **adjective** [postpositive] Heraldry (of a head or limb) depicted as cut off in a jagged line.

eraser ▶ **noun** a piece of soft rubber or plastic used to rub out something written.

Erasmus /ɪˈrazməs/, Desiderius (*c.*1469–1536), Dutch humanist and scholar; Dutch name *Gerhard Gerhards*. He was the foremost Renaissance scholar of northern Europe, paving the way for the Reformation with his satires on the Church, including the *Colloquia Familiaria* (1518). However, he opposed the violence of the Reformation and condemned Luther in *De Libero Arbitrio* (1523).

Erastianism /ɪˈrastɪəˌnɪz(ə)m/ ▶ **noun** [mass noun] the doctrine that the state should have supremacy over the Church in ecclesiastical matters (wrongly attributed to Erastus).
– DERIVATIVES **Erastian** noun & adjective.

Erastus /ɪˈrastəs/ (1524–83), Swiss theologian and physician; Swiss name *Thomas Lieber*; also *Liebler* or *Lüber*. Professor of medicine at Heidelberg from 1558, he opposed the imposition of a Calvinistic system of Church government in the city. The doctrine of Erastianism was later wrongly attributed to him.

erasure /ɪˈreɪʒə(r)/ ▶ **noun** [mass noun] the removal of writing, recorded material, or data. ■ the removal of all traces of something; obliteration: *the erasure of prior history.*

Erato /ˈɛrətəʊ/ Greek & Roman Mythology the Muse of lyric poetry and hymns.
– ORIGIN Greek, literally 'lovely'.

Eratosthenes /ˌɛrəˈtɒsθəniːz/ (*c.*275–194 BC), Greek scholar, geographer, and astronomer. The first systematic geographer of antiquity, he accurately calculated the circumference of the earth and attempted (less successfully) to determine the size and distance of the sun and of the moon.

erbium /ˈəːbɪəm/ ▶ **noun** [mass noun] the chemical element of atomic number 68, a soft silvery-white metal of the lanthanide series. (Symbol: **Er**)
– ORIGIN mid 19th cent.: modern Latin, from Ytt*erb*y, in Sweden, where it was first found. Compare with YTTERBIUM.

ere /ɛː/ ▶ **preposition & conjunction** literary or archaic before (in time): [as prep.] *we hope you will return ere long.*
– ORIGIN Old English *ǣr*, of Germanic origin; related to Dutch *eer* and German *eher*.

e-reader ▶ **noun** a device or application to facilitate or enhance the reading of electronic material.

Erebus /ˈɛrəbəs/ Greek Mythology the primeval god of darkness, son of Chaos.

Erebus, Mount a volcanic peak on Ross Island, Antarctica. Rising to 3,794 m (12,452 ft), it is the world's most southerly active volcano.
– ORIGIN named after the *Erebus*, the ship of Sir James Ross's expedition to the Antarctic.

Erech /ˈɛrɛk/ biblical name for URUK.

Erechtheum /ɪˈrɛkθɪəm/ a marble temple of the Ionic order built on the Acropolis in Athens *c.*421–406 BC, with shrines to Athene, Poseidon, and Erechtheus, a legendary king of Athens.

erect ▶ **adjective** rigidly upright or straight: *she stood erect with her arms by her sides.* ■ (of the penis, clitoris, or nipples) enlarged and rigid, especially in sexual excitement.
▶ **verb** [with obj.] put together and set upright (a building, wall, or other structure): *the guest house was erected in the eighteenth century | the police had erected roadblocks.* ■ create or establish (a theory or system): *the party that erected the welfare state.*
– DERIVATIVES **erectable** adjective, **erectly** adverb, **erectness** noun.
– ORIGIN late Middle English: from Latin *erect*- 'set up', from the verb *erigere*, from *e*- (variant of *ex*-) 'out' + *regere* 'to direct'.

erectile /ɪˈrɛktʌɪl/ ▶ **adjective** able to become erect: *erectile spines.* ■ denoting tissues which are capable of becoming temporarily engorged with blood, particularly those of the penis or other sexual organs. ■ relating to the capability of the penis or other sexual organs to become erect: *men with erectile dysfunction.*

erection ▶ **noun 1** [mass noun] the action of erecting a structure or object: *fees will be levied for the erection of monuments.* ■ [count noun] a building or other upright structure.
2 an enlarged and rigid state of the penis, typically in sexual excitement.
– ORIGIN late Middle English: from Latin *erectio(n-)*, from *erigere* 'set up' (see ERECT).

erector ▶ **noun** a person or thing that erects something. ■ a muscle which maintains an erect state of a part of the body or an erect posture of the body. ■ (**Erector**) N. Amer. trademark a construction toy consisting of components for making model buildings and vehicles.

E-region ▶ **noun** another term for E-LAYER.

eremite /ˈɛrɪmʌɪt/ ▶ **noun** a Christian hermit or recluse.
– DERIVATIVES **eremitic** adjective, **eremitical** adjective.
– ORIGIN Middle English: from Old French *eremite* from late Latin *eremita* (see HERMIT).

erethism /ˈɛrɪθɪz(ə)m/ ▶ **noun** [mass noun] **1** excessive sensitivity or rapid reaction to stimulation of a part of the body, especially the sexual organs.
2 a state of abnormal mental excitement or irritation.
– ORIGIN early 19th cent.: from French *éréthisme*, from Greek *erethismos*, from *erethizein* 'irritate'.

Erevan another name for YEREVAN.

erewhile /ɛːˈwʌɪl/ ▶ **adverb** archaic a while before; some time ago.
– ORIGIN Middle English: from ERE + WHILE.

erf /əːf/ ▶ **noun** (pl. **erfs** or **erven** /ˈəːv(ə)n/) S. African a plot of land.
– ORIGIN Dutch, originally in the sense 'inheritance'.

Erfurt /ˈɛːfʊət/, German /ˈɛrfʊrt/ an industrial city in central Germany, capital of Thuringia; pop. 202,700 (est. 2006).

erg[1] /əːɡ/ ▶ **noun** Physics a unit of work or energy, equal to the work done by a force of one dyne when its point of application moves one centimetre in the direction of action of the force.
– ORIGIN late 19th cent.: from Greek *ergon* 'work'.

erg[2] /əːɡ/ ▶ **noun** (pl. **ergs** or **areg** /ˈɑːrɛɡ/) an area of shifting sand dunes in the Sahara.
– ORIGIN late 19th cent.: from French, from Arabic *ʿirk, ʿerg*.

ergative /ˈəːɡətɪv/ Grammar ▶ **adjective** relating to or denoting a case of nouns (in some languages, e.g. Basque and Eskimo) that identifies the doer of an action as the object rather than the subject of a verb. ■ (in English) denoting verbs which can be used both transitively and intransitively to describe the same action, with the object in the former case being the subject in the latter, as in *I boiled the kettle* and *the kettle boiled*. Compare with **INCHOATIVE**.
▶ **noun** an ergative word. ■ (**the ergative**) the ergative case.
– DERIVATIVES **ergativity** noun.
– ORIGIN 1950s: from Greek *ergatēs* 'worker' (from *ergon* 'work') + **-IVE**.

ergo /ˈəːɡəʊ/ ▶ **adverb** therefore: *she was the sole beneficiary of the will, ergo the prime suspect.*
– ORIGIN Latin.

ergocalciferol /ˌəːɡə(ʊ)kalˈsɪfərɒl/ ▶ **noun** Biochemistry another term for **CALCIFEROL**, **VITAMIN** D_2.
– ORIGIN 1950s: blend of **ERGOT** and **CALCIFEROL**.

ergodic /əːˈɡɒdɪk/ ▶ **adjective** Mathematics relating to or denoting systems or processes with the property that, given sufficient time, they include or impinge on all points in a given space and can be represented statistically by a reasonably large selection of points.
– DERIVATIVES **ergodicity** noun.
– ORIGIN early 20th cent.: from German *ergoden*, from Greek *ergon* 'work' + *hodos* 'way' + **-IC**.

ergometer /əːˈɡɒmɪtə/ ▶ **noun** an apparatus which measures work or energy expended during a period of physical exercise.

ergometrine /ˌəːɡə(ʊ)ˈmɛtriːn/ ▶ **noun** [mass noun] Chemistry an alkaloid present in ergot. An amide of lysergic acid, it has oxytocic activity and is given to control bleeding after childbirth.
– ORIGIN 1930s: from **ERGOT** + Greek *mētra* 'womb' + **-INE**[4].

ergonomics /ˌəːɡəˈnɒmɪks/ ▶ **plural noun** [treated as sing.] the study of people's efficiency in their working environment.
– DERIVATIVES **ergonomic** adjective, **ergonomically** adverb, **ergonomist** noun.
– ORIGIN 1950s: from Greek *ergon* 'work', on the pattern of *economics*.

ergosphere /ˈəːɡəʊsfɪə/ ▶ **noun** Astronomy a postulated region round a black hole, from which energy could escape.

ergosterol /əːˈɡɒstərɒl/ ▶ **noun** [mass noun] Biochemistry a compound present in ergot and many other fungi. A steroid alcohol, it is converted to vitamin D_2 when irradiated with ultraviolet light.
– ORIGIN early 20th cent.: from **ERGOT**, on the pattern of *cholesterol*.

ergot /ˈəːɡɒt/ ▶ **noun 1** [mass noun] a fungal disease of rye and other cereals in which black elongated fruiting bodies grow in the ears of the cereal. Eating contaminated food can result in ergotism. ● The fungus is *Claviceps purpurea*, subdivision Ascomycotina. ■ the fruiting bodies of the ergot fungus, used as a source of certain medicinal alkaloids, especially for inducing uterine contractions or controlling postpartum bleeding.
2 a small horny protuberance on the back of each of a horse's fetlocks.
– ORIGIN late 17th cent.: from French, from Old French *argot* 'cock's spur' (because of the appearance produced by the disease).

ergotamine /əːˈɡɒtəmiːn/ ▶ **noun** [mass noun] Medicine a compound present in some kinds of ergot. An alkaloid, it causes constriction of blood vessels and is used in the treatment of migraine.

ergotism /ˈəːɡətɪz(ə)m/ ▶ **noun** [mass noun] poisoning produced by eating food affected by ergot, typically resulting in headache, vomiting, diarrhoea, and gangrene of the fingers and toes.

erhu /əːˈhuː/ (also **erh hu**) ▶ **noun** a Chinese two-stringed musical instrument held in the lap and played with a bow.
– ORIGIN early 20th cent.: Chinese, from *èr* 'two' + *hú* 'bowed instrument'.

erica /ˈɛrɪkə/ ▶ **noun** a plant of the genus *Erica* (family Ericaceae), especially (in gardening) heather.
– ORIGIN modern Latin, from Greek *ereikē*.

ericaceous /ˌɛrɪˈkeɪʃəs/ ▶ **adjective** Botany relating to or denoting plants of the heather family (Ericaceae). ■ (of compost) suitable for heathers and other lime-hating plants.
– ORIGIN mid 19th cent.: from modern Latin *Ericaceae* (plural), from the genus name *Erica* (see **ERICA**).

Ericsson[1] /ˈɛrɪks(ə)n/, John (1803–89), Swedish engineer whose inventions included a steam railway locomotive to rival Stephenson's *Rocket*, and the marine screw propeller (1836).

Ericsson[2] /ˈɛrɪks(ə)n/ (also **Ericson** or **Eriksson**), Leif (970–1020), Norse explorer, son of Eric the Red. He sailed westward from Greenland (*c.*1000) and visited land variously identified as Labrador, Newfoundland, or New England, which he named Vinland because of the vines he claimed to have found growing there.

Eric the Red (*c.*940–*c.*1010), Norse explorer. He left Iceland in 982 in search of land to the west, exploring Greenland and establishing a Norse settlement there in 986.

Eridanus /ɛˈrɪdənəs/ Astronomy a long straggling southern constellation (the River), said to represent the river into which Phaethon fell when struck by Zeus' thunderbolt.
– ORIGIN Latin.

Erie, Lake /ˈɪəri/ one of the five Great Lakes of North America, situated on the border between Canada and the US. It is linked to Lake Huron by the Detroit River and to Lake Ontario by the Welland Ship Canal and the Niagara River, which is its only natural outlet.

erigeron /ɪˈrɪdʒərɒn, ɛ-/ ▶ **noun** a widely distributed herbaceous plant of the daisy family, which is sometimes cultivated as an ornamental. ● Genus *Erigeron*, family Compositae.
– ORIGIN modern Latin, from Latin, 'groundsel' (the original sense in English), from Greek *ērigerōn*, from *ēri* 'early' + *gerōn* 'old man' (because the plant flowers early in the year, and some species bear grey down).

Eriksson variant spelling of **ERICSSON**[2].

Erin /ˈɛrɪn, ˈɪərɪn/ archaic or literary name for Ireland.

Erinys /ɛˈrɪnɪs/ ▶ **noun** (pl. **Erinyes** /ɛˈrɪniːz/) (in Greek mythology) a Fury.
– ORIGIN from Greek *Erinus*.

eristic /ɛˈrɪstɪk/ formal ▶ **adjective** of or characterized by debate or argument. ■ (of an argument or arguer) aiming at winning rather than at reaching the truth.
▶ **noun** a person given to debate or argument. ■ [mass noun] the art or practice of debate or argument.
– ORIGIN mid 17th cent.: from Greek *eristikos*, from *erizein* 'to wrangle', from *eris* 'strife'.

Eritrea /ˌɛrɪˈtreɪə/ an independent state in NE Africa, on the Red Sea; pop. 5,647,200 (est. 2009); language, Tigre and Cushitic languages; capital, Asmara.

> Eritrea was an Italian colony from 1890 to 1952, when it became part of Ethiopia. After a long guerrilla war it became internally self-governing in 1991 and fully independent in 1993.

– DERIVATIVES **Eritrean** adjective & noun.
– ORIGIN from Italian, from Latin *Mare Erythraeum* 'the Red Sea'.

erk /əːk/ ▶ **noun** Brit. informal, dated a male member of the RAF of the lowest rank.
▶ **exclamation** expressing panic or dismay: *Erk! What's that?*
– ORIGIN 1920s: of unknown origin.

Erlenmeyer flask /ˈəːlən,mʌɪə/ ▶ **noun** a conical flat-bottomed laboratory flask with a narrow neck.
– ORIGIN late 19th cent.: named after Emil *Erlenmeyer* (1825–1909), German chemist.

Erl King /ˈəːl kɪŋ/ ▶ **noun** (in Germanic mythology) a bearded giant or goblin believed to lure little children to the land of death.
– ORIGIN late 18th cent.: from German *Erlkönig* 'alder-king', a mistranslation of Danish *ellerkonge* 'king of the elves'.

ERM ▶ **abbreviation** Exchange Rate Mechanism.

ermine /ˈəːmɪn/ ▶ **noun** (pl. **same** or **ermines**) **1** a stoat, especially when in its white winter coat. ■ [mass noun] the white fur of the stoat, used for trimming garments, especially the ceremonial robes of judges or peers. ■ [mass noun] Heraldry fur represented as black spots on a white ground, as a heraldic tincture.
2 (also **ermine moth**) a stout-bodied moth that has cream or white wings with black spots. ● Genus *Spilosoma*, family Arctiidae: several species.
– DERIVATIVES **ermined** adjective.
– ORIGIN Middle English: from Old French *hermine*, probably from medieval Latin *(mus) Armenius* 'Armenian (mouse)'.

ermines /ˈəːmɪnz/ ▶ **noun** [mass noun] Heraldry fur resembling ermine but with white spots on a black ground.
– ORIGIN mid 16th cent.: perhaps from Old French *hermines*, plural of *herminet*, diminutive of *hermine* 'ermine'.

erminois /ˌəːmɪˈnɔɪz/ ▶ **noun** [mass noun] Heraldry fur resembling ermine but with black spots on a gold ground.
– ORIGIN mid 16th cent.: from Old French, from *hermine* 'ermine'.

-ern ▶ **suffix** forming adjectives such as *northern*.
– ORIGIN Old English *-erne*, of Germanic origin.

erne /əːn/ ▶ **noun** literary the sea eagle.
– ORIGIN Old English *earn* 'eagle', of Germanic origin; related to Dutch *arend*.

Ernie /ˈəːni/ ▶ **noun** (in the UK) the computer that randomly selects the prizewinning numbers of Premium Bonds.
– ORIGIN 1950s: acronym from *electronic random number indicator equipment*.

Ernst /əːnst, ɛːnst/, Max (1891–1976), German artist. He was a leader of the Dada movement and developed the techniques of collage, photomontage, and frottage. He is probably best known for surrealist paintings such as *L'Eléphant de Célèbes* (1921).

erode /ɪˈrəʊd/ ▶ **verb** [with obj.] (of wind, water, or other natural agents) gradually wear away (soil, rock, or land): *the cliffs on this coast have been eroded by the sea.* ■ [no obj.] (of soil, rock, or land) be gradually worn away by such natural agents. ■ gradually destroy or be gradually destroyed: [with obj.] *this humiliation has eroded what confidence Jean has.* ■ Medicine (of a disease) gradually destroy (bodily tissue).
– DERIVATIVES **erodible** adjective.
– ORIGIN early 17th cent.: from French *éroder* or Latin *erodere*, from *e-* (variant of *ex-*) 'out, away' + *rodere* 'gnaw'.

erogenous /ɪˈrɒdʒɪnəs, ɛ-/ ▶ **adjective** (of a part of the body) sensitive to sexual stimulation: *erogenous zones.*
– ORIGIN late 19th cent.: from **EROS** + **-GENOUS**.

Eros /ˈɪərɒs/ **1** Greek Mythology the god of love, son of Aphrodite. Roman equivalent **CUPID**. ■ [mass noun] sexual love or desire. ■ [mass noun] (in Freudian theory) the life instinct. Often contrasted with **THANATOS**. ■ [mass noun] (in Jungian psychology) the principle of personal relatedness in human activities, associated with the anima. Often contrasted with **LOGOS**.
2 Astronomy asteroid 433, discovered in 1898, which comes at times nearer to the earth than any celestial body except the moon.
– ORIGIN Latin, from Greek, literally 'sexual love'.

erosion /ɪˈrəʊʒ(ə)n/ ▶ **noun** [mass noun] the process of eroding or being eroded by wind, water, or other natural agents: *the problem of soil erosion.* ■ the gradual destruction or diminution of something: *the erosion of support for the party.* ■ Medicine the gradual destruction of tissue or tooth enamel by physical or chemical action. ■ [count noun] Medicine a place where surface tissue has been gradually destroyed: *patients with gastric erosions.*
– DERIVATIVES **erosional** adjective, **erosive** adjective.
– ORIGIN mid 16th cent.: via French from Latin *erosio(n-)*, from *erodere* 'wear or gnaw away' (see **ERODE**).

erotic /ɪˈrɒtɪk/ ▶ **adjective** relating to or tending to arouse sexual desire or excitement: *her book of erotic fantasies.*
– DERIVATIVES **erotically** adverb.
– ORIGIN mid 17th cent.: from French *érotique*, from Greek *erōtikos*, from *erōs*, *erōt-* 'sexual love'.

erotica ▶ **noun** [mass noun] erotic literature or art.
– ORIGIN mid 19th cent.: from Greek *erōtika*, neuter plural of *erōtikos* (see **EROTIC**).

eroticism ▶ **noun** [mass noun] the quality or character of being erotic: *a disturbing blend of violence and eroticism.* ■ sexual desire or excitement.

eroticize (also **eroticise**) ▶ **verb** [with obj.] give (something or someone) erotic qualities.
– DERIVATIVES **eroticization** noun.

erotism /ˈɛrətɪz(ə)m/ ▸ **noun** [mass noun] sexual desire or excitement; eroticism.
– ORIGIN mid 19th cent.: from Greek *erōs*, *erōt-* 'sexual love' + **-ISM**.

eroto- /ɪˈrɒtəʊ/ ▸ **combining form** relating to eroticism: *erotomania*.
– ORIGIN from Greek *erōs*, *erōt-* 'sexual love'.

erotogenic /ɪˌrɒtəˈdʒɛnɪk/ (also **erotogenous** /ˌɛrəˈtɒdʒɪnəs/) ▸ **adjective** another term for **EROGENOUS**.

erotology /ˌɛrəˈtɒlədʒi/ ▸ **noun** [mass noun] the study of sexual love and behaviour.

erotomania /ɪˌrɒtə(ʊ)ˈmeɪnɪə/ ▸ **noun** [mass noun] excessive sexual desire. ■ Psychiatry a delusion in which a person (typically a woman) believes that another person (typically of higher social status) is in love with them.
– DERIVATIVES **erotomaniac** noun.

ERP ▸ **abbreviation** enterprise resource planning, the management of all the information and resources involved in a company's operations by means of an integrated computer system.

err /əː/ ▸ **verb** [no obj.] formal be mistaken or incorrect; make a mistake: *the judge had* ***erred in*** *ruling that the evidence was inadmissible.* ■ (often as adj. **erring**) sin; do wrong: *he had been as solicitous as an erring husband.*
– PHRASES **err on the right side** act so that the least harmful of possible mistakes or errors is the most likely to occur. **err on the side of** display more rather than less of (a specified quality) in one's actions: *it is better to err on the side of caution.* **to err is human, to forgive divine** proverb it is human nature to make mistakes oneself while finding it hard to forgive others.
– ORIGIN Middle English (in the sense 'wander, go astray'): from Old French *errer*, from Latin *errare* 'to stray'.

errand ▸ **noun** a short journey undertaken in order to deliver or collect something, especially on someone else's behalf: *she asked Tim to* ***run an errand*** *for her.* ■ the purpose or object of an errand: *she knew that if she stated her errand she would not be able to see him.*
– PHRASES **errand of mercy** a journey or mission carried out to help someone in difficulty or danger.
– ORIGIN Old English *ǣrende* 'message, mission', of Germanic origin; related to Old High German *ārunti*, and obscurely to Swedish *ärende* and Danish *ærinde*.

errand boy ▸ **noun** dated a boy employed in a shop or office to make deliveries and run other errands.

errant /ˈɛr(ə)nt/ ▸ **adjective 1** formal or humorous erring or straying from the accepted course or standards: *an errant husband coming back from a night on the tiles.* ■ not in the right place; having moved from the correct position or course: *an errant strand of hair | fear of being hit by an errant bullet.*
2 [often postpositive] archaic or literary travelling in search of adventure: *that same lady errant.* See also **KNIGHT ERRANT**.
3 Zoology (of a polychaete worm) of a predatory kind that moves about actively and is not confined to a tube or burrow.
– DERIVATIVES **errancy** noun (sense 1), **errantry** noun (sense 2).
– ORIGIN Middle English (in sense 2): sense 1 from Latin *errant-* 'erring', from the verb *errare*; sense 2 from Old French *errant* 'travelling', present participle of *errer*, from late Latin *iterare* 'go on a journey', from *iter* 'journey'. Compare with **ARRANT**.

erratic /ɪˈratɪk/ ▸ **adjective** not even or regular in pattern or movement; unpredictable: *her breathing was erratic.*
▸ **noun** (also **erratic block** or **boulder**) Geology a rock or boulder that differs from the surrounding rock and is believed to have been brought from a distance by glacial action.
– DERIVATIVES **erratically** adverb, **erraticism** noun.
– ORIGIN late Middle English: from Old French *erratique*, from Latin *erraticus*, from *errare* 'to stray, err'.

erratum /ɛˈrɑːtəm/ ▸ **noun** (pl. **errata**) an error in printing or writing. ■ (**errata**) a list of corrected errors appended to a book or published in a subsequent issue of a journal.
– ORIGIN mid 16th cent.: from Latin, 'error', neuter past participle of *errare* 'err'.

Er Rif /ɛː ˈrɪf/ another name for **RIF MOUNTAINS**.

erroneous /ɪˈrəʊnɪəs, ɛ-/ ▸ **adjective** wrong; incorrect: *employers sometimes make erroneous assumptions.*
– DERIVATIVES **erroneously** adverb, **erroneousness** noun.
– ORIGIN late Middle English: from Latin *erroneus* (from *erro(n-)* 'vagabond', from *errare* 'to stray, err') + **-OUS**.

error ▸ **noun** a mistake: *spelling errors | an error of judgement.* ■ [mass noun] the state or condition of being wrong in conduct or judgement: *goods dispatched to your branch* ***in error*** *| the crash was caused by human error.* ■ [mass noun] technical a measure of the estimated difference between the observed or calculated value of a quantity and its true value.
– PHRASES **see the error of one's ways** realize or acknowledge one's wrongdoing.
– DERIVATIVES **errorless** adjective.
– ORIGIN Middle English: via Old French from Latin *error*, from *errare* 'to stray, err'.

error bar ▸ **noun** Mathematics a line through a point on a graph, parallel to one of the axes, which represents the uncertainty or error of the corresponding coordinate of the point.

error correction ▸ **noun** [mass noun] Computing the automatic correction of errors that arise from the incorrect transmission of digital data.

error message ▸ **noun** Computing a message displayed on a monitor screen or printout indicating that an incorrect instruction has been given or that there is an error resulting from faulty software or hardware.

-ers ▸ **suffix** forming colloquial nouns and adjectives such as *Twickers* (for *Twickenham*), *brekkers* (for *breakfast*), *preggers* (for *pregnant*), etc.
– ORIGIN extension of **-ER**[3].

ersatz /ˈəːsats, ˈɛː-/ ▸ **adjective** (of a product) made or used as a substitute, typically an inferior one, for something else: *ersatz coffee.* ■ not real or genuine: *ersatz emotion.*
– ORIGIN late 19th cent.: from German, literally 'replacement'.

Erse /əːs/ ▸ **noun** [mass noun] dated the Scottish or Irish Gaelic language.
– ORIGIN early Scots form of **IRISH**.

erst /əːst/ ▸ **adverb** archaic long ago; formerly: *the friends whom erst you knew.*
– ORIGIN Old English *ǣrest*, superlative of *ǣr* (see **ERE**).

erstwhile ▸ **adjective** [attrib.] former: *the erstwhile president of the company.*
▸ **adverb** archaic formerly: *Mary Anderson, erstwhile the queen of America's stage.*

Erté /ˈɛːteɪ/ (1892–1990), Russian-born French fashion designer and illustrator; born *Romain de Tirtoff*. During the First World War his garments became internationally famous through his decorative magazine illustrations, and in the 1920s he became a noted art deco designer.

Ertebølle /ˈɛːtəˌbəːlə/ ▸ **noun** [usu. as modifier] Archaeology a late Mesolithic culture in the western Baltic (4th millennium BC), the final phases of which show Neolithic influence in the form of permanent coastal fishing and collecting sites and the use of skin boats.
– ORIGIN named after *Ertebølle* in Jutland, Denmark.

erubescent /ˌɛrʊˈbɛs(ə)nt/ ▸ **adjective** rare reddening; blushing.
– ORIGIN mid 18th cent.: from Latin *erubescent-* 'blushing', from the verb *erubescere*, from *e-* (variant of *ex-*) 'out' + *rubescere* 'redden' (from *rubere* 'be red').

erucic acid /ɪˈruːsɪk/ ▸ **noun** [mass noun] Chemistry a solid compound present in mustard and rape seeds. ● An unsaturated fatty acid: chem. formula: $C_{21}H_{41}COOH$.
– ORIGIN mid 19th cent.: *erucic* from Latin *eruca* 'rocket' (denoting the plant) + **-IC**.

eructation /ˌiːrʌkˈteɪʃ(ə)n, ɪ-, ɛ-/ ▸ **noun** formal a belch.
– ORIGIN late Middle English: from Latin *eructatio(n-)*, from the verb *eructare*, from *e-* (variant of *ex-*) 'out' + *ructare* 'belch'.

erudite /ˈɛrʊdʌɪt/ ▸ **adjective** having or showing great knowledge or learning.
– DERIVATIVES **eruditely** adverb.
– ORIGIN late Middle English: from Latin *eruditus*, past participle of *erudire* 'instruct, train' (based on *rudis* 'rude, untrained').

erudition /ˌɛrʊˈdɪʃ(ə)n/ ▸ **noun** [mass noun] the quality of having or showing great knowledge or learning; scholarship: *he writes with great erudition.*

erupt ▸ **verb 1** [no obj.] (of a volcano) become active and eject lava, ash, and gases: *Mount Pinatubo began erupting in June.* ■ be ejected from an active volcano: *hot lava erupted from the crust.* ■ (of an object) explode with fire and noise: *smoke bombs erupted everywhere.*
2 break out suddenly and dramatically: *fierce fighting erupted between the army and guerrillas | noise erupted from the drawing room.*
3 give vent to anger, amusement, etc. in a sudden and noisy way: *the soldiers erupted in fits of laughter.*
4 (of a spot, rash, or other mark) suddenly appear on the skin. ■ (of the skin) suddenly develop a spot, rash, or mark.
5 (of a tooth) break through the gums during normal development.
– ORIGIN mid 17th cent.: from Latin *erupt-* 'broken out', from the verb *erumpere*, from *e-* (variant of *ex-*) 'out' + *rumpere* 'burst out, break'.

eruption ▸ **noun 1** an act or instance of erupting: *the eruption of Vesuvius.* ■ a sudden outbreak of something, typically something unwelcome or noisy: *a sudden eruption of street violence.*
2 a spot, rash, or other mark appearing suddenly on the skin.
– ORIGIN late Middle English: from Old French, or from Latin *eruptio(n-)*, from the verb *erumpere* (see **ERUPT**).

eruptive ▸ **adjective 1** relating to or formed by volcanic activity: *a history of the eruptive activity in an area.*
2 producing or characterized by eruptions: *an acute eruptive disease.*

eruv /ˈɛrʊv/ ▸ **noun** (pl. **eruvim**, **eruvs** /ˈɛrʊvɪm/) Judaism an urban area enclosed by a wire boundary which symbolically extends the private domain of Jewish households into public areas, permitting activities within it that are normally forbidden in public on the Sabbath.
– ORIGIN from Hebrew *'ērūḇ*, from a base meaning 'mixture'.

erven plural form of **ERF**.

-ery (also **-ry**) ▸ **suffix** forming nouns: **1** denoting a class or kind: *confectionery | greenery.*
2 denoting an occupation, a state, a condition, or behaviour: *archery | bravery | slavery.* ■ with depreciatory reference: *knavery | tomfoolery.*
3 denoting a place set aside for an activity or a grouping of things, animals, etc.: *orangery | rookery.*
– ORIGIN from French *-erie*, based on Latin *-arius* and *-ator*.

eryngium /ɪˈrɪndʒɪəm/ ▸ **noun** (pl. **eryngiums**) a plant of the genus *Eryngium* in the parsley family, especially (in gardening) sea holly.
– ORIGIN late 16th cent.: modern Latin, from Latin *eryngion*, from a diminutive of Greek *ērungos* 'sea holly'.

eryngo /ɪˈrɪŋgəʊ/ ▸ **noun** (pl. **eryngos** or **eryngoes**) another term for **SEA HOLLY** or **ERYNGIUM**.
– ORIGIN late 16th cent.: from Italian and Spanish *eringio*, from Latin *eryngion* (see **ERYNGIUM**).

erysipelas /ˌɛrɪˈsɪpɪləs/ ▸ **noun** [mass noun] Medicine an acute, sometimes recurrent disease caused by a bacterial infection, characterized by large raised red patches on the skin. ● This is caused by *Streptococcus pyogenes*, a Gram-positive coccus.
– ORIGIN late Middle English: via Latin from Greek *erusipelas*; perhaps related to *eruthros* 'red' and *pella* 'skin'.

erysipeloid /ˌɛrɪˈsɪpəlɔɪd/ ▸ **noun** [mass noun] Medicine dermatitis of the hands due to bacterial infection, occurring mainly among handlers of meat and fish products. ● This is caused by *Erysipelothrix rhusiopathiae*, a Gram-positive bacterium occurring either as slightly curved rods or as filaments.

erythema /ˌɛrɪˈθiːmə/ ▸ **noun** [mass noun] Medicine superficial reddening of the skin, usually in patches, as a result of injury or irritation causing dilatation of the blood capillaries.
– DERIVATIVES **erythemal** adjective, **erythematous** adjective.
– ORIGIN late 18th cent.: from Greek *eruthēma*, from *eruthainein* 'be red', from *eruthros* 'red'.

erythrism /ˈɛrɪθrɪz(ə)m/ ▸ **noun** [mass noun] Zoology a congenital condition of abnormal redness in an animal's fur, plumage, or skin.
– ORIGIN late 19th cent.: from Greek *eruthros* 'red' + **-ISM**.

erythritol /ɪˈrɪθrɪtɒl/ ▸ **noun** [mass noun] Chemistry a sweet substance extracted from certain lichens and algae. It is used medicinally as a vasodilator. ● A tetrahydric alcohol; chem. formula: $C_4H_{10}O_4$.
– ORIGIN late 19th cent.: from *erythrite* (earlier name for *erythritol*) + **-OL**.

erythro- ▸ **combining form** (used commonly in zoological and medical terms) red: *erythrocyte*.

– ORIGIN from Greek *eruthros* 'red'.

erythroblast /ɪˈrɪθrə(ʊ)blast/ ▶ **noun** Physiology an immature erythrocyte, containing a nucleus.
– DERIVATIVES **erythroblastic** adjective.

erythroblastosis /ɪˌrɪθrə(ʊ)blasˈtəʊsɪs/ ▶ **noun** [mass noun] Medicine the abnormal presence of erythroblasts in the blood. ■ (also **erythroblastosis fetalis**) another term for HAEMOLYTIC DISEASE OF THE NEWBORN.

erythrocyte /ɪˈrɪθrə(ʊ)sʌɪt/ ▶ **noun** a red blood cell, which (in humans) is typically a biconcave disc without a nucleus. Erythrocytes contain the pigment haemoglobin, which imparts the red colour to blood, and transport oxygen and carbon dioxide to and from the tissues.
– DERIVATIVES **erythrocytic** adjective.

E

erythrogenic /ɪˌrɪθrə(ʊ)ˈdʒɛnɪk/ ▶ **adjective** Medicine (of a bacterial toxin) causing inflammation and reddening of the skin.

erythroid /ˈɛrɪθrɔɪd/ ▶ **adjective** Physiology relating to erythrocytes.

erythroleukaemia /ɪˌrɪθrə(ʊ)luːˈkiːmɪə/ (US **erythroleukemia**) ▶ **noun** [mass noun] Medicine a rare acute form of leukaemia in which there is proliferation of immature red and white blood cells.

erythromycin /ɪˌrɪθrə(ʊ)ˈmʌɪsɪn/ ▶ **noun** [mass noun] Medicine an antibiotic used in the treatment of infections caused by Gram-positive bacteria. It is similar in its effects to penicillin. ● This is obtained from the streptomycete bacterium *Streptomyces erythreus*.
– ORIGIN 1950s: from elements of the modern Latin taxonomic name (see above) + -IN[1].

erythronium /ˌɛrɪˈθrəʊnɪəm/ ▶ **noun** (pl. **erythroniums** or **erythronia** /-ɪə/) a plant of a genus which includes dog's-tooth violet. ● Genus *Erythronium*, family Liliaceae.
– ORIGIN modern Latin, from Greek (*saturion*) *eruthronion* 'red-flowered (orchid)'.

erythropoiesis /ɪˌrɪθrə(ʊ)pɔɪˈiːsɪs/ ▶ **noun** [mass noun] Physiology the production of red blood cells.
– DERIVATIVES **erythropoietic** adjective.

erythropoietin /ɪˌrɪθrə(ʊ)pɔɪˈɛtɪn/ ▶ **noun** [mass noun] Biochemistry a hormone secreted by the kidneys that increases the rate of production of red blood cells in response to falling levels of oxygen in the tissues.

Erzgebirge /ˈɛːtsgəˌbɪəgə/, German /ˈeːɐtsgəˌbɪrgə, ˈɛrts-/ a range of mountains on the border between Germany and the Czech Republic. Also called the ORE MOUNTAINS.

Erzurum /ˈɛːzʊrʊm/ a city in NE Turkey, capital of a mountainous province of the same name; pop. 338,100 (est. 2007).

ES ▶ **abbreviation** El Salvador (international vehicle registration).

Es ▶ **symbol** the chemical element einsteinium.

-es[1] ▶ **suffix 1** forming plurals of nouns ending in sibilant sounds: *boxes* | *kisses*.
2 forming plurals of certain nouns ending in *-o*: *potatoes* | *heroes*.
– ORIGIN variant of -S[1].

-es[2] ▶ **suffix** forming the third person singular of the present tense: **1** in verbs ending in sibilant sounds: *pushes*.
2 in verbs ending in *-o* (but not *-oo*): *goes*.
– ORIGIN variant of -S[2].

ESA ▶ **abbreviation** ■ (in the UK) Environmentally Sensitive Area. ■ European Space Agency.

Esaki /ɛˈzɑːki/, Leo (b.1925), Japanese physicist. He investigated and pioneered the development of quantum-mechanical tunnelling of electrons in semiconductor devices, and designed the tunnel diode (also called the Esaki diode). Nobel Prize for Physics (1973).

Esau /ˈiːsɔː/ (in the Bible) the elder of the twin sons of Isaac and Rebecca, who sold his birthright to his brother Jacob and was tricked out of his father's blessing by his brother (Gen. 25, 27).

Esbjerg /ˈɛsbjəːg/ a port in Denmark, on the west coast of Jutland; pop. 71,025 (2009). It has ferry links with Britain and the Faroe Islands.

ESC ▶ **abbreviation** Economic and Social Committee.

escabeche /ˌɛskəˈbɛʃ, ˈɛskəbɛʃ/ ▶ **noun** [mass noun] a dish of fish that is fried then marinated in vinegar and spices.
– ORIGIN Spanish.

escadrille /ˌɛskəˈdrɪl/ ▶ **noun** a French squadron of aircraft.
– ORIGIN French, literally 'flotilla, flight'.

escalade /ˌɛskəˈleɪd/ ▶ **noun** [mass noun] historical the scaling of fortified walls using ladders, as a form of military attack.
– ORIGIN late 16th cent.: from French, or from Spanish *escalada*, *escalado*, from medieval Latin *scalare* 'to scale, climb', from Latin *scala* 'ladder'.

escalate /ˈɛskəleɪt/ ▶ **verb** [no obj.] increase rapidly: *the price of tickets escalated* | (as adj. **escalating**) *the escalating cost of health care*. ■ make or become more intense or serious: [no obj.] *the disturbance escalated into a full-scale riot* | [with obj.] *we do not want to escalate the war*.
– ORIGIN 1920s (in the sense 'travel on an escalator'): back-formation from ESCALATOR.

escalation /ɛskəˈleɪʃ(ə)n/ ▶ **noun** a rapid increase; a rise: *cost escalations*. ■ an increase in the intensity or seriousness of something; an intensification: *an escalation of violence* | [mass noun] *the present escalation of global warming*.

escalator ▶ **noun** a moving staircase consisting of an endlessly circulating belt of steps driven by a motor, which conveys people between the floors of a public building.
– ORIGIN early 20th cent. (originally US, as a trade name): from *escalade* 'climb a wall by ladder' (from ESCALADE), on the pattern of *elevator*.

escalator clause (also **escalation clause**) ▶ **noun** a clause in a contract that allows for a rise in wages or prices under certain conditions.

escallonia /ˌɛskəˈləʊnɪə/ ▶ **noun** an evergreen South American shrub with pink or white flowers. ● Genus *Escallonia*, family Grossulariaceae.
– ORIGIN modern Latin, named after *Escallon*, an 18th-cent. Spanish traveller who discovered the plants.

escallop /ɪˈskaləp, ɛ-, -ˈskɒl-/ ▶ **noun 1** variant spelling of ESCALOPE.
2 another term for SCALLOP (sense 2 of the noun).
3 Heraldry a scallop shell as a charge.
▶ **verb** (**escallops**, **escalloping**, **escalloped**) another term for SCALLOP (sense 3 of the verb).
– ORIGIN late 15th cent. (in sense 2 of the noun): from Old French *escalope* 'shell'. Compare with ESCALOPE and SCALLOP.

escalope /ɪˈskaləp, ɛ-, -ˈskɒl-, ˈɛskələʊp/ (also **escallop**) ▶ **noun** a thin slice of meat without any bone, typically a special cut of veal from the leg that is coated, fried, and served in a sauce.
– ORIGIN French; compare with ESCALLOP and SCALLOP.

escapade /ˈɛskəpeɪd, ˌɛskəˈpeɪd/ ▶ **noun** an act or incident involving excitement, daring, or adventure.
– ORIGIN mid 17th cent. (in the sense 'an escape'): from French, from Provençal or Spanish, from *escapar* 'to escape', based on medieval Latin *ex-* 'out of' + *cappa* 'cloak'. Compare with ESCAPE.

escape ▶ **verb 1** [no obj.] break free from confinement or control: *two burglars have just escaped from prison* | (as adj. **escaped**) *escaped convicts*. ■ [with obj.] elude or get free from (someone): *he drove along the dual carriageway to escape police*. ■ succeed in avoiding or eluding something dangerous or unpleasant: *the driver escaped with a broken knee* | [with obj.] *a baby boy narrowly escaped death*. ■ (of a gas, liquid, or heat) leak from a container: *the CFCs have escaped into the atmosphere*. ■ [with obj.] (of words or sounds) issue involuntarily or inadvertently from (someone): *a sob escaped her lips*.
2 [with obj.] fail to be noticed or remembered by (someone): *the name escaped him* | *it may have escaped your notice, but this is not a hotel*.
3 [with obj.] Computing interrupt (an operation) by means of the escape key. ■ cause (a subsequent character or characters) to be interpreted differently.
▶ **noun 1** an act of breaking free from confinement or control: *the gang had made their escape* | [mass noun] *he could think of no way of escape, short of rudeness*. ■ an act of avoiding something dangerous or unpleasant: *the baby was fine, but it was a lucky escape*. ■ a means of escaping from somewhere: [as modifier] *he had planned his escape route*. ■ a garden plant or pet animal that has gone wild and (especially in plants) become naturalized.
2 a form of temporary distraction from reality or routine: *romantic novels should present an escape from the dreary realities of life*.
3 a leakage of gas, liquid, or heat from a container.
4 (also **escape key**) Computing a key on a computer keyboard which either interrupts the current operation or causes subsequent characters to be interpreted differently.
– PHRASES **escape the clutches** (or **grip**) **of** break free from the control or grasp of. **make good one's escape** succeed in breaking free from confinement: *by the time they had given chase, she had made good her escape*.
– DERIVATIVES **escapable** adjective, **escaper** noun.
– ORIGIN Middle English: from Old French *eschaper*, based on medieval Latin *ex-* 'out' + *cappa* 'cloak'. Compare with ESCAPADE.

escape clause ▶ **noun** a contract provision which specifies the conditions under which a party can be freed from an obligation.

escapee /ˌɛskeɪˈpiː, ɪˈskeɪpiː/ ▶ **noun** a person who has escaped from somewhere, especially prison.

escape hatch ▶ **noun** a hatch for use as an emergency exit, especially from a submarine, ship, or aircraft. ■ a means of retreat from or avoidance of a difficulty or problem: *you shouldn't rush into marriage, looking at divorce as an escape hatch if things don't work out*.

escape mechanism ▶ **noun** Psychology a mental process which enables a person to avoid acknowledging unpleasant or threatening aspects of reality.

escapement /ɪˈskeɪpm(ə)nt, ɛ-/ ▶ **noun 1** a mechanism in a clock or watch that alternately checks and releases the train by a fixed amount and transmits a periodic impulse from the spring or weight to the balance wheel or pendulum.
2 a mechanism in a typewriter that shifts the carriage a small fixed amount to the left after a key is pressed and released.
3 the part of the mechanism in a piano that enables the hammer to fall back as soon as it has struck the string.
– ORIGIN late 18th cent.: from French *échappement*, from *échapper* 'to escape'.

escape road ▶ **noun** chiefly Brit. a slip road, especially on a racing circuit, for a vehicle to turn into if the driver is unable to negotiate a bend or slope safely.

escape velocity ▶ **noun** the lowest velocity which a body must have in order to escape the gravitational attraction of a particular planet or other object.

escape wheel ▶ **noun** a toothed wheel in the escapement of a watch or clock.

escapism ▶ **noun** [mass noun] the tendency to seek distraction and relief from unpleasant realities, especially by seeking entertainment or engaging in fantasy.
– DERIVATIVES **escapist** noun & adjective.

escapologist /ˌɛskəˈpɒlədʒɪst/ ▶ **noun** an entertainer specializing in freeing themselves from the confinement of such things as ropes, handcuffs, and chains.
– DERIVATIVES **escapology** noun.

escargot /ɛˈskɑːgəʊ, ɪ-/ ▶ **noun** the edible snail, especially as an item on a menu.
– ORIGIN French, from Old French *escargol*, from Provençal *escaragol*.

escarole /ˈɛskərəʊl/ ▶ **noun** [mass noun] N. Amer. an endive of a variety with broad undivided leaves and a slightly bitter flavour, used in salads.
– ORIGIN early 20th cent.: from French, from Italian *scar(i)ola*, based on Latin *esca* 'food'.

escarpment /ɪˈskɑːpm(ə)nt, ɛ-/ ▶ **noun** a long, steep slope, especially one at the edge of a plateau or separating areas of land at different heights.
– ORIGIN early 19th cent.: from French *escarpement*, *escarpe* 'scarp', from Italian *scarpa* 'slope'. Compare with SCARP.

Escaut /ɛsˈkəʊ/ French name for SCHELDT.

-esce ▶ **suffix** forming verbs, often denoting the initiation of action: *coalesce* | *effervesce*.
– ORIGIN from or suggested by Latin verbs ending in *-escere*.

-escent ▶ **suffix** forming adjectives denoting a developing state or action: *coalescent* | *fluorescent*.
– DERIVATIVES **-escence** suffix forming corresponding nouns.
– ORIGIN from French, or from Latin *-escent-* (present participial stem of verbs ending in *-escere*).

eschar /ˈɛskɑː/ ▶ **noun** Medicine a dry, dark scab or falling away of dead skin, typically caused by a burn, an insect bite, or infection with anthrax.
– ORIGIN late Middle English: from French *eschare* or late Latin *eschara* 'scar or scab', from Greek (see also SCAR).

eschatology /ˌɛskəˈtɒlədʒi/ ▶ **noun** [mass noun] the part of theology concerned with death, judgement, and the final destiny of the soul and of humankind.
– DERIVATIVES **eschatological** adjective, **eschatologist** noun.

– ORIGIN mid 19th cent.: from Greek *eskhatos* 'last' + **-LOGY**.

eschaton /ˈɛskətɒn/ ▶ **noun** (**the eschaton**) Theology the final event in the divine plan; the end of the world.
– ORIGIN 1930s: from Greek *eskhaton*, neuter of *eskhatos* 'last'.

escheat /ɪsˈtʃiːt, ɛs-/ chiefly historical ▶ **noun** [mass noun] the reversion of property to the state, or (in feudal law) to a lord, on the owner's dying without legal heirs. ■ [count noun] an item of property affected by escheat.
▶ **verb** [no obj.] (of land) revert to a lord or the state by escheat. ■ [with obj.] (usu. as adj. **escheated**) hand over (land) as an escheat.
– ORIGIN Middle English: from Old French *eschete*, based on Latin *excidere* 'fall away', from *ex-* 'out of, from' + *cadere* 'to fall'.

Escher /ˈɛʃə/, M. C. (1898–1972), Dutch graphic artist; full name *Maurits Corneille Escher*. His prints are characterized by their sophisticated use of visual illusion and paradoxical perspective.

eschew /ɪsˈtʃuː, ɛs-/ ▶ **verb** [with obj.] deliberately avoid using; abstain from: *he appealed to the crowd to eschew violence*.
– DERIVATIVES **eschewal** noun.
– ORIGIN late Middle English: from Old French *eschiver*, ultimately of Germanic origin and related to German *scheuen* 'shun', also to **SHY**[1].

eschscholzia /ɪsˈʃɒlzɪə, ɛʃˈʃɒlzɪə/ (also **eschscholtzia** /-tsɪə/) ▶ **noun** a North American poppy which is cultivated for its bright yellow, orange, or red flowers. ● Genus *Eschscholzia*, family Papaveraceae: several species, in particular the California poppy.
– ORIGIN modern Latin, named in honour of Johann Friedrich von *Eschscholtz* (1793–1831), Russian-born botanist and traveller.

Escoffier /ɛˈskɒfɪeɪ/, Georges-Auguste (1846–1935), French chef. He gained an international reputation while working in London at the Savoy Hotel (1890–9) and later at the Carlton (1899–1919).

escolar /ˌɛskəˈlɑː/ ▶ **noun** a large, elongated predatory fish occurring in tropical and temperate oceans throughout the world. Also called **SNAKE MACKEREL**. ● Family Gempylidae: several genera and species.
– ORIGIN mid 19th cent.: from Spanish, literally 'scholar', so named because the ringed markings around the eyes resemble spectacles.

Escorial /ˌɛskɒrɪˈɑːl/ a monastery and palace in central Spain, near Madrid, built in the late 16th century by Philip II.

escort ▶ **noun** /ˈɛskɔːt/ a person, vehicle, or group accompanying another for protection or as a mark of rank: *a police escort* | [mass noun] *he was driven away under armed escort*. ■ a man who accompanies a woman to a particular social event. ■ a person, typically a woman, who may be hired to accompany someone socially: [as modifier] *an escort agency*. ■ euphemistic a prostitute.
▶ **verb** /ɪˈskɔːt, ɛ-/ [with obj.] accompany (someone or something) somewhere as an escort: *he escorted her back to her hotel*.
– ORIGIN late 16th cent. (originally denoting a body of armed men escorting travellers): from French *escorte* (noun), *escorter* (verb), from Italian *scorta*, feminine past participle of *scorgere* 'to conduct, guide', based on Latin *ex-* 'out of' + *corrigere* 'set right' (see **CORRECT**).

escoveitch /ˈɛskəvɪtʃ/ (also **escovitch**) ▶ **noun** West Indian term for **ESCABECHE**.

escritoire /ˌɛskriːˈtwɑː/ ▶ **noun** a small writing desk with drawers and compartments.
– ORIGIN late 16th cent.: from French, from medieval Latin *scriptorium* 'writing room' (see **SCRIPTORIUM**).

escrow /ˈɛskrəʊ/ Law ▶ **noun** a bond, deed, or other document kept in the custody of a third party and taking effect only when a specified condition has been fulfilled. ■ [usu. as modifier] a deposit or fund held in trust or as a security: *an escrow account*. ■ [mass noun] the state of being kept in custody or trust until a specified condition has been fulfilled: *the board holds funds in escrow*.
▶ **verb** [with obj.] chiefly N. Amer. place in custody or trust until a specified condition has been fulfilled.
– ORIGIN late 16th cent.: from Old French *escroe* 'scrap, scroll', from medieval Latin *scroda*, of Germanic origin; related to **SHRED**.

escudo /ɛˈsk(j)uːdəʊ, ɛˈʃk-/ ▶ **noun** (pl. **escudos**) the basic monetary unit of Portugal and the Cape Verde Islands, equal to 100 centavos (replaced in Portugal by the euro in 2002).
– ORIGIN Spanish and Portuguese, from Latin *scutum* 'shield'.

esculent /ˈɛskjʊlənt/ formal ▶ **adjective** fit to be eaten; edible.
▶ **noun** a thing, especially a vegetable, which is fit to be eaten.
– ORIGIN early 17th cent.: from Latin *esculentus*, from *esca* 'food', from *esse* 'eat'.

escutcheon /ɪˈskʌtʃ(ə)n, ɛ-/ ▶ **noun 1** a shield or emblem bearing a coat of arms.
2 (also **escutcheon plate**) a flat piece of metal for protection and often ornamentation, around a keyhole, door handle, or light switch.
– PHRASES **a blot on one's escutcheon** a stain on one's reputation or character. **escutcheon of pretence** a small shield within a coat of arms, bearing another coat or device to which the bearer has a claim, especially one to which a man's wife is heiress.
– ORIGIN late 15th cent.: from Anglo-Norman French *escuchon*, based on Latin *scutum* 'shield'.

Esd. ▶ **abbreviation** Esdras, either in the Apocrypha or the Vulgate (in biblical references).

Esdras /ˈɛzdrəs/ **1** either of two books of the Apocrypha. The first is mainly a compilation from Chronicles, Nehemiah, and Ezra; the second is a record of angelic revelation.
2 (in the Vulgate) the books of Ezra and Nehemiah.

ESE ▶ **abbreviation** east-south-east.

-ese ▶ **suffix** forming adjectives and nouns: **1** denoting an inhabitant or language of a country or city: *Maltese* | *Viennese*.
2 often derogatory (especially with reference to language) denoting character or style: *journalese* | *officialese*.
– ORIGIN from Old French *-eis*, based on Latin *-ensis*.

esemplastic /ˌɛsɛmˈplastɪk/ ▶ **adjective** rare moulding into one; unifying.
– ORIGIN early 19th cent.: from Greek *es* 'into' + *hen* (neuter of *heis* 'one') + **-IC**; formed irregularly by Coleridge, probably suggested by German *Ineinsbildung*, in the same sense.

eserine /ˈɛsəriːn/ ▶ **noun** Chemistry another term for **PHYSOSTIGMINE**.
– ORIGIN mid 19th cent.: from French *ésérine*, from Efik *esere*.

Esfahan /ˌɛsfəˈhɑːn/ variant spelling of **ISFAHAN**.

esker /ˈɛskə/ ▶ **noun** Geology a long ridge of gravel and other sediment, typically having a winding course, deposited by meltwater from a retreating glacier or ice sheet.
– ORIGIN mid 19th cent.: from Irish *eiscir*.

Eskimo ▶ **noun** (pl. **same** or **Eskimos**) **1** a member of an indigenous people inhabiting northern Canada, Alaska, Greenland, and eastern Siberia, and traditionally living by hunting seals and other Arctic animals and birds and by fishing.
2 [mass noun] either of the two main languages of the Eskimo people (Inuit and Yupik), comprising a major division of the Eskimo-Aleut family.
▶ **adjective** relating to the Eskimos or their languages.
– ORIGIN via French *Esquimaux*, possibly from Spanish *esquimao*, *esquimal*, from Montagnais *ayaškimew* 'person who laces a snowshoe', probably applied first to the Micmac and later to the Eskimo (see **HUSKY**[2]).

> **USAGE** In recent years the word **Eskimo** has come to be regarded as offensive (partly through the associations of the now discredited etymology 'one who eats raw flesh'). The peoples inhabiting the regions from the central Canadian Arctic to western Greenland prefer to call themselves **Inuit**: see **USAGE** at **INUIT**. The term **Eskimo**, however, continues to be the only term which can be properly understood as applying to the people as a whole and is still widely used in anthropological and archaeological contexts.

Eskimo-Aleut ▶ **noun** [mass noun] the family of languages comprising Inuit, Yupik, and Aleut.
▶ **adjective** relating to this family of languages.

Eskimo curlew ▶ **noun** a small New World curlew with a striped head, formerly common in the arctic tundra but now close to extinction. ● *Numenius borealis*, family Scolopacidae.

Eskimo pie ▶ **noun** US trademark a bar of chocolate-coated ice cream.

Eskimo roll ▶ **noun** a complete rollover in canoeing, from upright to capsized to upright.

esky /ˈɛski/ ▶ **noun** (pl. **eskies**) Austral. trademark a portable insulated container for keeping food or drink cool.
– ORIGIN 1960s: probably from **ESKIMO**, by association with a cold climate.

ESL ▶ **abbreviation** English as a second language.

ESN ▶ **abbreviation** ■ dated educationally subnormal. ■ electronic serial number, a unique number programmed into a mobile phone which identifies it.

ESOL ▶ **abbreviation** English for speakers of other languages.

esophagus etc. ▶ **noun** US spelling of **OESOPHAGUS** etc.

esoteric /ˌɛsəˈtɛrɪk, ˌiːsə-/ ▶ **adjective** intended for or likely to be understood by only a small number of people with a specialized knowledge or interest: *esoteric philosophical debates*.
– DERIVATIVES **esoterically** adverb, **esotericism** noun, **esotericist** noun.
– ORIGIN mid 17th cent.: from Greek *esōterikos*, from *esōterō*, comparative of *esō* 'within', from *es*, *eis* 'into'. Compare with **EXOTERIC**.

esoterica /ˌɛsəˈtɛrɪkə, ˌiːsə-/ ▶ **noun** [mass noun] esoteric or highly specialized subjects or publications.
– ORIGIN early 20th cent.: from Greek *esōterika*, neuter plural of *esōterikos* 'esoteric'.

ESP ▶ **abbreviation** ■ Photography electro-selective pattern. ■ electrostatic precipitator. ■ extrasensory perception.

esp. ▶ **abbreviation** especially.

espada /ɛˈspɑːdə/ ▶ **noun** (pl. **same**) a scabbardfish, especially as caught for food in Madeira and elsewhere.
– ORIGIN via Portuguese from Spanish, from Latin *spatha* 'sword'.

espadrille /ˈɛspədrɪl, ˌɛspəˈdrɪl/ ▶ **noun** a light canvas shoe with a plaited fibre sole.
– ORIGIN late 19th cent.: from French, from Provençal *espardi(l)hos*, from *espart* 'esparto', from Latin *spartum* (see **ESPARTO**).

espalier /ɪˈspaljə, ɛ-/ ▶ **noun** a fruit tree or ornamental shrub whose branches are trained to grow flat against a wall, supported on a lattice. ■ a lattice for an espaliered tree or shrub.
▶ **verb** [with obj.] train (a tree or shrub) to grow flat against a wall.
– ORIGIN mid 17th cent.: from French, from Italian *spalliera*, from *spalla* 'shoulder', from Latin *spatula* (see **SPATULA**), in late Latin 'shoulder blade'.

España /esˈpaɲa/ Spanish name for **SPAIN**.

esparto /ɛˈspɑːtəʊ, ɪ-/ (also **esparto grass**) ▶ **noun** (pl. **espartos**) a coarse grass with tough narrow leaves, native to Spain and North Africa. It is used to make ropes, wickerwork, and good-quality paper. ● *Stipa tenacissima*, family Gramineae.
– ORIGIN mid 19th cent.: from Spanish, via Latin from Greek *sparton* 'rope'.

especial /ɪˈspɛʃ(ə)l, ɛ-/ ▶ **adjective** [attrib.] **1** better or greater than usual; special: *these traditions are of especial interest to feminists*.
2 for or belonging chiefly to one person or thing: *her outburst was for my especial benefit*.
– ORIGIN late Middle English: via Old French from Latin *specialis* 'special', from *species* (see **SPECIES**).

especially ▶ **adverb 1** used to single out one person or thing over all others: *he despised them all, especially Sylvester* | *a new song, written* ***especially for*** *Jonathan*.
2 to a great extent; very much: *he didn't especially like dancing* | [as submodifier] *sleep is especially important in growing children*.

> **USAGE** There is some overlap in the uses of **especially** and **specially**. In the broadest terms, both words mean 'particularly' and the preference for one word over the other is linked with particular conventions of use rather than with any deep difference in meaning. For example, there is little to choose between *written **especially** for Jonathan* and *written **specially** for Jonathan* and neither is more correct than the other. On the other hand, in sentences such as *he despised them all, **especially** Sylvester*, substitution of **specially** is found in informal uses but should not be used in written English, while in *the car was **specially** made for the occasion* substitution of **especially** is somewhat unusual. Overall, **especially** is by far the commoner of the two, occurring twenty times as frequently as **specially** in the Oxford English Corpus.

Esperanto /ˌɛspəˈrantəʊ/ ▶ **noun** [mass noun] an artificial language devised in 1887 as an international medium of communication, based on roots from the chief European languages. It retains the structure of these languages and has the advantage of grammatical regularity and ease of pronunciation.

– DERIVATIVES **Esperantist** noun.
– ORIGIN from the name *Dr Esperanto*, used as a pen name by the inventor of the language, Ludwik L. Zamenhof (1858–1917), Polish physician; the literal sense is 'one who hopes' (based on Latin *sperare* 'to hope').

espial /ɪˈspʌɪ(ə)l, ɛ-/ ▶ noun [mass noun] archaic the action of watching or catching sight of something or someone: *he withdrew from his point of espial.*
– ORIGIN late Middle English (in the sense 'spying'): from Old French *espiaille*, from *espier* 'espy'.

espionage /ˈɛspɪənɑːʒ, -ɪdʒ/ ▶ noun [mass noun] the practice of spying or of using spies, typically by governments to obtain political and military information.
– ORIGIN late 18th cent.: from French *espionnage*, from *espionner* 'to spy', from *espion* 'a spy'.

E

Espírito Santo /ɛˌspɪrɪtuː ˈsantuː/ a state of eastern Brazil, on the Atlantic coast; capital, Vitória.

esplanade /ˌɛspləˈneɪd, -ˈnɑːd/ ▶ noun a long, open, level area, typically beside the sea, along which people may walk for pleasure. ■ an open, level space separating a fortress from a town.
– ORIGIN late 16th cent. (denoting an area of flat ground on top of a rampart): from French, from Italian *spianata*, from Latin *explanatus* 'flattened, levelled', from *explanare* (see EXPLAIN).

espousal /ɪˈspaʊz(ə)l, ɛ-/ ▶ noun **1** [in sing.] an act of adopting or supporting a cause, belief, or way of life: *his espousal of Western ideas.*
2 archaic a marriage or engagement.
– ORIGIN late Middle English: from Old French *espousaille*, from Latin *sponsalia* 'betrothal', neuter plural of *sponsalis* (adjective), from *sponsare* 'espouse, betroth' (see ESPOUSE).

espouse /ɪˈspaʊz, ɛ-/ ▶ verb [with obj.] **1** adopt or support (a cause, belief, or way of life): *the left has espoused the causes of sexual and racial equality.*
2 archaic marry. ■ (**be espoused to**) (of a woman) be engaged to (a particular man).
– DERIVATIVES **espouser** noun.
– ORIGIN late Middle English (in the sense 'take as a spouse'): from Old French *espouser*, from Latin *sponsare*, from *sponsus* 'betrothed', past participle of *spondere*.

espressivo /ˌɛsprɛˈsiːvəʊ/ ▶ adverb & adjective Music (especially as a direction) with expression of feeling.
– ORIGIN Italian, from Latin *expressus* 'distinctly presented'.

espresso /ɛˈsprɛsəʊ/ ▶ noun (pl. **espressos**) a type of strong black coffee made by forcing steam through ground coffee beans.

> **USAGE** The spelling **expresso** is not used in the original Italian and is strictly incorrect, although it is common.

– ORIGIN from Italian (*caffè*) *espresso*, literally 'pressed out (coffee)'.

esprit /ɛˈspriː/, French /ɛspʀi/ ▶ noun [mass noun] the quality of being lively, vivacious, or witty.
– ORIGIN French, from Latin *spiritus* 'spirit'.

esprit de corps /ɛˌspriː də ˈkɔː/, French /ɛspʀi də kɔʀ/ ▶ noun [mass noun] a feeling of pride and mutual loyalty shared by the members of a group.
– ORIGIN French, literally 'spirit of the body'.

esprit de l'escalier /ɛˌspriː də lɛˈskaljeɪ/, French /ɛspʀi də lɛskalje/ ▶ noun [mass noun] used to refer to the fact that a witty remark or retort often comes to mind after the opportunity to make it has passed.
– ORIGIN French, literally 'wit of the staircase' (i.e. a witty remark coming to mind on the stairs leading away from a gathering).

espy /ɪˈspʌɪ, ɛ-/ ▶ verb (**espies**, **espying**, **espied**) [with obj.] literary catch sight of: *she espied her daughter rounding the corner.*
– ORIGIN Middle English: from Old French *espier*, ultimately of Germanic origin and related to Dutch *spieden* and German *spähen*. Compare with SPY.

Esq. ▶ abbreviation Esquire.

-esque ▶ suffix (forming adjectives) in the style of; resembling: *carnivalesque* | *Dantesque*.
– ORIGIN from French, via Italian *-esco* from medieval Latin *-iscus*.

Esquimau ▶ noun (pl. **Esquimaux**) archaic spelling of ESKIMO.

Esquipulas /ˌɛskiːˈpuːlas/ a town in SE Guatemala, near the border with Honduras; pop. 25,000 (est. 2009). Noted for the image of the 'Black Christ of Esquipulas' in its church, the town is a centre of pilgrimage.

esquire /ɪˈskwʌɪə, ɛ-/ (abbrev.: **esq.**) ▶ noun **1** (**Esquire**) Brit. a polite title appended to a man's name when no other title is used, typically in the address of a letter or other documents: *J. C. Pearson Esquire.* ■ N. Amer. a title appended to the surname of a lawyer (of either sex).
2 historical a young nobleman who, in training for knighthood, acted as an attendant to a knight. ■ an officer in the service of a king or nobleman. ■ [as title] a landed proprietor or country squire.
– PHRASES **esquire of the (king's) body** historical an officer in charge of dressing and undressing the king.
– ORIGIN late Middle English: from Old French *esquier*, from Latin *scutarius* 'shield-bearer', from *scutum* 'shield'; compare with SQUIRE. Sense 2 was the original denotation, sense 1 being at first a courtesy title given to such a person.

ESR ▶ abbreviation Physics electron spin resonance.

ESRC ▶ abbreviation (in the UK) Economic and Social Research Council.

-ess[1] ▶ suffix forming nouns denoting female gender: *abbess* | *adulteress* | *tigress*.
– ORIGIN from French *-esse*, via late Latin from Greek *-issa*.

> **USAGE** The suffix **-ess** has been used since the Middle Ages to form nouns denoting female persons, using a neutral or a male form as the base (as **hostess** and **actress** from **host** and **actor**, for example). Despite the apparent equivalence between the male and female pairs of forms, they are rarely equivalent in terms of actual use and connotation in modern English (consider the differences in meaning and use between **manager** and **manageress** or **poet** and **poetess**). In the late 20th century, as the role of women in society changed, some of these feminine forms became problematic and were seen as old-fashioned, sexist, and patronizing (e.g. **poetess, authoress, editress**). The 'male' form is increasingly being used as the 'neutral' form, where the gender of the person concerned is simply unspecified.

-ess[2] ▶ suffix forming abstract nouns from adjectives, such as *largess*.
– ORIGIN Middle English via French *-esse* from Latin *-itia*.

essay ▶ noun /ˈɛseɪ/ **1** a short piece of writing on a particular subject.
2 formal an attempt or effort: *a misjudged essay in job preservation.* ■ a trial design of a postage stamp yet to be accepted.
▶ verb /ɛˈseɪ/ [with obj.] formal attempt or try: *Donald essayed a smile.*
– ORIGIN late 15th cent. (as a verb in the sense 'test the quality of'): alteration of ASSAY, by association with Old French *essayer*, based on late Latin *exagium* 'weighing', from the base of *exigere* 'ascertain, weigh'; the noun (late 16th cent.) is from Old French *essai* 'trial'.

essayist ▶ noun a person who writes essays, especially as a literary genre.

essayistic ▶ adjective characteristic of or used in essays.

esse /ˈɛsi/ ▶ noun [mass noun] Philosophy essential nature or essence. See also IN ESSE.
– ORIGIN Latin, 'to be' (used as a noun).

Essen /ˈɛs(ə)n/ an industrial city in the Ruhr valley, in NW Germany; pop. 583,200 (est. 2006).

essence ▶ noun [mass noun] **1** the intrinsic nature or indispensable quality of something, especially something abstract, which determines its character: *conflict is the essence of drama.* ■ [count noun] Philosophy a property or group of properties of something without which it would not exist or be what it is.
2 an extract or concentrate obtained from a plant or other matter and used for flavouring or scent: *vanilla essence.*
– PHRASES **in essence** basically and without regard for peripheral details; fundamentally: *in detail the class system is complex but in essence it is simple.* **of the essence** critically important: *time will be of the essence during negotiations.*
– ORIGIN late Middle English: via Old French from Latin *essentia*, from *esse* 'be'.

Essene /ˈɛsiːn/ ▶ noun a member of an ancient Jewish ascetic sect of the period from the 2nd century BC to the 2nd century AD in Palestine, who lived in highly organized groups and held property in common. The Essenes are widely regarded as the authors of the Dead Sea Scrolls.
– ORIGIN from Latin *Esseni* (plural), from Greek *Essēnoi*, perhaps from Aramaic.

essential /ɪˈsɛnʃ(ə)l/ ▶ adjective **1** absolutely necessary; extremely important: [with infinitive] *it is essential to keep up-to-date records* | *fibre is an essential ingredient of our diet.* ■ [attrib.] fundamental or central to the nature of something or someone: *the essential weakness of the plaintiff's case.*
2 (of an amino acid or fatty acid) required for normal growth but not synthesized in the body and therefore necessary in the diet.
3 Medicine (of a disease) with no known external stimulus or cause; idiopathic: *essential hypertension.*
▶ noun (usu. **essentials**) a thing that is absolutely necessary: *we only had the bare essentials in the way of equipment.* ■ (**essentials**) the fundamental elements or characteristics of something: *he was quick to grasp the essentials of an opponent's argument.*
– DERIVATIVES **essentiality** noun, **essentialness** noun.
– ORIGIN Middle English (in the sense 'in the highest degree'): from late Latin *essentialis*, from Latin *essentia* (see ESSENCE).

essentialism ▶ noun [mass noun] Philosophy a belief that things have a set of characteristics which make them what they are, and that the task of science and philosophy is their discovery and expression; the doctrine that essence is prior to existence. Compare with EXISTENTIALISM. ■ the view that all children should be taught on traditional lines the ideas and methods regarded as essential to the prevalent culture. ■ the view that categories of people, such as women and men, or heterosexuals and homosexuals, or members of ethnic groups, have intrinsically different and characteristic natures or dispositions.
– DERIVATIVES **essentialist** noun & adjective.

essentially ▶ adverb used to emphasize the basic, fundamental, or intrinsic nature of a person or thing: [sentence adverb] *essentially, they are amateurs.*

essential oil ▶ noun a natural oil typically obtained by distillation and having the characteristic odour of the plant or other source from which it is extracted.

Essequibo /ˌɛsɪˈkiːbəʊ/ a river in Guyana, rising in the Guiana Highlands and flowing about 965 km (600 miles) northwards to the Atlantic.

Essex a county of eastern England; county town, Chelmsford.

EST ▶ abbreviation Eastern Standard Time (see EASTERN TIME).

est /ɛst/ ▶ noun [mass noun] a system for self-improvement aimed at developing a person's potential through intensive group awareness and training sessions.
– ORIGIN 1970s (originally US): acronym from *Erhard Seminars Training*, from the name of Werner *Erhard* (born 1935), the American businessman who devised the technique.

est. ▶ abbreviation ■ established. ■ estimated.

-est[1] ▶ suffix forming the superlative of adjectives (such as *shortest*, *widest*), and of adverbs (such as *soonest*).
– ORIGIN Old English *-ost-*, *-ust-*, *-ast-*.

-est[2] (also **-st**) ▶ suffix archaic forming the second person singular of verbs: *canst* | *goest*.
– ORIGIN Old English *-est*, *-ast*, *-st*.

establish ▶ verb [with obj.] **1** set up on a firm or permanent basis: *the scheme was established in 1975.* ■ initiate or bring about (contact or communication): *the two countries established diplomatic relations in 1992.*
2 achieve permanent acceptance or recognition for: *the principle of the supremacy of national parliaments needs to be firmly established* | *he had* ***established himself as*** *a film star.* ■ introduce (a character, set, or location) into a film or play and allow its identification: *establish the location with a wide shot.*
3 show (something) to be true or certain by determining the facts: [with clause] *the police established that the two passports were forgeries.*
4 Bridge ensure that one's remaining cards in (a suit) will be winners (if not trumped) by playing off the high cards in that suit.
– DERIVATIVES **establisher** noun.
– ORIGIN late Middle English (recorded earlier as *stablish*): from Old French *establiss-*, lengthened stem of *establir*, from Latin *stabilire* 'make firm', from *stabilis* (adjective) 'stable'.

established ▶ adjective **1** having existed or done something for a long time and therefore recognized and generally accepted: *the ceremony was an established event in the annual calendar* | *an established artist.* ■ (of a plant) having taken root; growing well.

2 (of a Church or religion) recognized by the state as the national Church or religion.
– PHRASES **the Established Church** the Church of England or of Scotland.

establishment ▸ **noun 1** [mass noun] the action of establishing something or being established: *the establishment of an independent government.* ■ [count noun] archaic a marriage.
2 a business organization, public institution, or household: *hotels or catering establishments.*
3 (usu. **the Establishment**) a group in a society exercising power and influence over matters of policy, opinion, or taste, and seen as resisting change. ■ [with adj. or noun modifier] an influential group within a specified profession or area of activity: *rumblings of discontent among the medical establishment.*
4 (**the Establishment** or **the Church Establishment**) the ecclesiastical system organized by law. ■ the Church of England or of Scotland.

establishmentarian /ɪˌstablɪʃm(ə)nˈtɛːrɪən/ ▸ **adjective** adhering to, advocating, or relating to the principle of an established Church.
▸ **noun** a person adhering to or advocating the principle of an established Church.
– DERIVATIVES **establishmentarianism** noun.

estaminet /ɛˈstamɪneɪ/, French /ɛstamine/ ▸ **noun** a small cafe selling alcoholic drinks.
– ORIGIN French, from Walloon *staminé* 'byre', from *stamo* 'a pole for tethering a cow', probably from German *Stamm* 'stem'.

estancia /ɛˈstansɪə/ ▸ **noun** a cattle ranch in Latin America or the southern US.
– ORIGIN mid 17th cent.: from Spanish, literally 'station', from medieval Latin *stantia*, based on Latin *stare* 'to stand'.

estate ▸ **noun 1** an area or amount of land or property, in particular: ■ Brit. an area of land and modern buildings developed for residential, industrial, or commercial purposes. ■ an extensive area of land in the country, usually with a large house, owned by one person, family, or organization. ■ all the money and property owned by a particular person, especially at death: *in his will, he divided his estate between his wife and daughter.* ■ a property where coffee, rubber, grapes, or other crops are cultivated.
2 (also **estate of the realm**) a class or order regarded as forming part of the body politic, in particular (in Britain), one of the three groups constituting Parliament, now the Lords spiritual (the heads of the Church), the Lords temporal (the peerage), and the Commons. They are also known as **the three estates**. ■ dated a particular class or category of people in society: *the spiritual welfare of all estates of men.*
3 archaic or literary a particular state, period, or condition in life: *programmes for the improvement of man's estate* | *the holy estate of matrimony.*
4 Brit. short for ESTATE CAR.
– ORIGIN Middle English (in the sense 'state or condition'): from Old French *estat*, from Latin *status* 'state, condition', from *stare* 'to stand'.

estate agency ▸ **noun** Brit. a company or business that sells and rents out buildings and land for clients. ■ [mass noun] the activity or profession of selling and renting out buildings and land for clients.

estate agent ▸ **noun** Brit. a person whose job involves selling and renting out buildings and land for clients.

estate car ▸ **noun** Brit. a car with a large carrying area behind the seats, accessed by a door at the rear.

estate duty ▸ **noun** [mass noun] Brit. historical a former death duty levied on property from 1889. It was replaced in 1975 by capital transfer tax and in 1986 by inheritance tax.

estate of the realm ▸ **noun** see ESTATE (sense 2).

Estates General another term for STATES GENERAL.

estate tax ▸ **noun** US another term for INHERITANCE TAX.

esteem ▸ **noun** [mass noun] respect and admiration: *he was held in high esteem by colleagues.*
▸ **verb** [with obj.] **1** respect and admire: *many of these qualities are esteemed by managers* | (as adj., with submodifier **esteemed**) *a highly esteemed scholar.*
2 formal consider; deem: [with two objs] *I should esteem it a favour if you could speak to them.*
– ORIGIN Middle English (as a noun in the sense 'worth, reputation'): from Old French *estime* (noun), *estimer* (verb), from Latin *aestimare* 'to estimate'. The verb was originally in the Latin sense, also 'appraise' (compare with ESTIMATE), used figuratively to mean 'assess the merit of'. Current senses date from the 16th cent.

ester /ˈɛstə/ ▸ **noun** Chemistry an organic compound made by replacing the hydrogen of an acid by an alkyl or other organic group. Many naturally occurring fats and essential oils are esters of fatty acids.
– DERIVATIVES **esterify** /ɛˈstɛrɪfʌɪ/ verb (**esterifies, esterifying, esterified**).
– ORIGIN mid 19th cent.: from German, probably from a blend of *Essig* 'vinegar' and *Äther* 'ether'.

esterase /ˈɛstəreɪz/ ▸ **noun** Biochemistry an enzyme which hydrolyses particular esters into acids and alcohols or phenols.

Esth. ▸ **abbreviation** Esther (in biblical references).

Esther /ˈɛstə/ (in the Bible) a woman chosen on account of her beauty by the Persian king Ahasuerus (generally supposed to be Xerxes I) to be his queen. She used her influence with him to save the Israelites in captivity from persecution. ■ a book of the Bible containing an account of these events; a part survives only in Greek and is included in the Apocrypha.

esthetic etc. ▸ **adjective** US spelling of AESTHETIC etc.

Estima /ɛˈstiːmə/ ▸ **noun** a Dutch potato of a yellow-fleshed variety.

estimable /ˈɛstɪməb(ə)l/ ▸ **adjective** worthy of great respect.
– DERIVATIVES **estimably** adverb.
– ORIGIN late 15th cent. (in the sense 'able to be estimated or appraised'; earlier in *inestimable*): via Old French from Latin *aestimabilis*, from *aestimare* 'to estimate'.

estimate ▸ **verb** /ˈɛstɪmeɪt/ [with obj.] roughly calculate or judge the value, number, quantity, or extent of: *the aim is to estimate the effects of macroeconomic policy on the economy* | [with clause] *it is estimated that smoking causes 100,000 premature deaths every year* | (as adj. **estimated**) *an estimated cost of $1,000 million.*
▸ **noun** /ˈɛstɪmət/ an approximate calculation or judgement of the value, number, quantity, or extent of something: *at a rough estimate, staff are recycling a quarter of paper used.* ■ a written statement indicating the likely price that will be charged for specified work or repairs. ■ a judgement of the worth or character of someone or something: *his high estimate of the poem.*
– DERIVATIVES **estimative** /-mətɪv/ adjective.
– ORIGIN late Middle English: from Latin *aestimat-* 'determined, appraised', from the verb *aestimare*. The noun originally meant 'intellectual ability, comprehension' (only in late Middle English), later 'valuing, a valuation' (compare with ESTIMATION). The verb originally meant 'to think well or badly of someone or something' (late 15th cent.), later 'regard as being, consider to be' (compare with ESTEEM).

estimation ▸ **noun 1** a rough calculation of the value, number, quantity, or extent of something: *estimations of protein concentrations.*
2 [usu. in sing.] a judgement of the worth or character of someone or something: *the pop star rose in my estimation.*
– ORIGIN late Middle English (originally in the sense 'comprehension, intuition', also 'valuing, a valuation'): from Latin *aestimatio(n-)*, from *aestimare* 'determine, appraise' (see ESTIMATE).

estimator ▸ **noun** Statistics a rule, method, or criterion for arriving at an estimate of the value of a parameter. ■ a quantity used or evaluated as an estimate of the value of a parameter. ■ a person who estimates the price, value, number, quantity, or extent of something.

estival ▸ **adjective** US spelling of AESTIVAL.

estivate ▸ **verb** US spelling of AESTIVATE.

estivation ▸ **noun** US spelling of AESTIVATION.

estoile /ɪˈstɔɪl, ɛ-/ ▸ **noun** Heraldry a star with wavy points or rays, usually six in number.
– ORIGIN late 16th cent.: via Old French from Latin *stella* 'star'.

Estonia /ɪˈstəʊnɪə/ a Baltic country on the south coast of the Gulf of Finland; pop. 1,299,400 (est. 2009); languages, Estonian (official), Russian; capital, Tallinn.

> Previously ruled by the Teutonic Knights and then by Sweden, Estonia was ceded to Russia in 1721. It was proclaimed an independent republic in 1918 but was annexed by the USSR in 1940 as a constituent republic, the Estonian SSR. With the break-up of the Soviet Union Estonia regained its independence in 1991.

Estonian ▸ **adjective** relating to Estonia or its people or their language.
▸ **noun 1** a native or inhabitant of Estonia, or a person of Estonian descent.
2 [mass noun] the Finno-Ugric language of Estonia, which is closely related to Finnish and is spoken by about a million people.

estop /ɪˈstɒp/ ▸ **verb** (**estops, estopping, estopped**) [with obj.] (usu. **be estopped from**) Law bar or preclude by estoppel.
– ORIGIN late Middle English (in the sense 'stop up, dam, plug'): from Old French *estopper* 'stop up, impede', from late Latin *stuppare*, from Latin *stuppa* 'tow, oakum'. Compare with STOP and STUFF.

estoppel /ɪˈstɒp(ə)l/ ▸ **noun** [mass noun] Law the principle which precludes a person from asserting something contrary to what is implied by a previous action or statement of that person or by a previous pertinent judicial determination.
– ORIGIN mid 16th cent.: from Old French *estouppail* 'bung', from *estopper* (see ESTOP).

Estoril /ˌɛʃtəˈrɪl/ a resort on the Atlantic coast of Portugal; pop. 24,000 (est. 2009).

estovers /ɪˈstəʊvəz, ɛ-/ ▸ **plural noun** (usu. **common/right of estovers**) Brit., chiefly historical the right to take wood from land one does not own, especially land of which one is the tenant or lessee.
– ORIGIN late 15th cent.: plural of Anglo-Norman French *estover*, noun use of a verb meaning 'be necessary', based on Latin *est opus* 'it is necessary'.

estradiol ▸ **noun** US spelling of OESTRADIOL.

estrange /ɪˈstreɪn(d)ʒ, ɛ-/ ▸ **verb** [with obj.] cause (someone) to be no longer on friendly terms with someone: *he became* **estranged from** *his father.* ■ (as adj. **estranged**) (of a wife or husband) no longer living with their spouse: *his estranged wife.*
– ORIGIN late 15th cent.: from Old French *estranger*, from Latin *extraneare* 'treat as a stranger', from *extraneus* 'not belonging to the family', used as a noun to mean 'stranger'. Compare with STRANGE.

estrangement /ɪˈstreɪn(d)ʒm(ə)nt, ɛ-/ ▸ **noun** [mass noun] the fact of no longer being on friendly terms or part of a social group: *the growing estrangement of the police from their communities.* ■ the fact of no longer living with one's spouse or partner; separation.

estreat /ɪˈstriːt, ɛ-/ Law, chiefly historical ▸ **verb** [with obj.] enforce the forfeit of (a surety for bail or other recognizance).
▸ **noun** a copy of a court record for use in the enforcement of a fine or forfeiture of a recognizance.
– DERIVATIVES **estreatment** noun.
– ORIGIN Middle English: from Old French *estraite*, feminine past participle of *estraire*, from Latin *extrahere* 'draw out' (see EXTRACT).

Estremadura /ˌɛʃtrəməˈdʊərə/ a coastal region and former province of west central Portugal.

estrogen etc. ▸ **noun** US spelling of OESTROGEN etc.

estrus etc. ▸ **noun** US spelling of OESTRUS etc.

estuary /ˈɛstjʊ(ə)ri/ ▸ **noun** (pl. **estuaries**) the tidal mouth of a large river, where the tide meets the stream.
– DERIVATIVES **estuarial** adjective, **estuarine** /-rʌɪn/ adjective.
– ORIGIN mid 16th cent. (denoting a tidal inlet of any size): from Latin *aestuarium* 'tidal part of a shore', from *aestus* 'tide'.

Estuary English ▸ **noun** [mass noun] (in the UK) a type of accent identified as spreading outwards from London and containing features of both received pronunciation and London speech.

estufa /ɛˈstuːfə/ ▸ **noun 1** a heated chamber in which Madeira wine is stored and matured.
2 US an underground chamber in which a fire is kept permanently alight, used as a place of assembly by Pueblo Indians.
– ORIGIN mid 19th cent.: from Spanish, probably based on Greek *tuphos* 'steam or smoke'.

e.s.u. ▸ **abbreviation** electrostatic unit(s).

esurient /ɪˈsjʊərɪənt, ɛ-/ ▸ **adjective** archaic or humorous hungry or greedy.
– ORIGIN late 17th cent.: from Latin *esurient-* 'being hungry', from the verb *esurire*, from *esse* 'eat'.

Esztergom /ˈɛstəgɒm/ a town and river port on the Danube in Hungary; pop. 30,928 (2009).

ET ▸ **abbreviation** ■ (in North America) Eastern time. ■ Egypt (international vehicle registration). ■ extra-terrestrial.

-et[1] ▸ **suffix** forming nouns which were originally diminutives: *baronet* | *hatchet* | *tablet.*
– ORIGIN from Old French *-et, -ete.*

E

-et² (also **-ete**) ▶ **suffix** forming nouns such as *comet*, and often denoting people: *athlete | poet*.
– ORIGIN from Greek *-ētēs*.

ETA¹ /ˌiːtiːˈeɪ/ ▶ **abbreviation** estimated time of arrival, in particular the time at which an aircraft or ship is expected to arrive at its destination.

ETA² /ˈɛtə/ a Basque separatist movement in Spain, founded in 1959, which is waging a terrorist campaign for an independent Basque state.
– ORIGIN Basque acronym, from *Euzkadi ta Azkatasuna* 'Basque homeland and liberty'.

eta /ˈiːtə/ ▶ **noun** the seventh letter of the Greek alphabet (Η, η), transliterated as 'e' or 'ē'. ■ (**Eta**) [followed by Latin genitive] Astronomy the seventh star in a constellation: *Eta Carinae*.
– ORIGIN from Greek *ēta*.

E

etagere /ˌɛtəˈʒɛː/ (also **étagère** /ɛtəˈʒɛː/) ▶ **noun** (pl. **same** or **etageres**) a piece of furniture with open shelves for displaying ornaments.
– ORIGIN French *étagère*, from *étage* 'shelf'.

e-tailer ▶ **noun** a retailer selling goods via electronic transactions on the Internet.
– ORIGIN 1990s: blend of E-² and RETAILER (see RETAIL).

et al. /ɛt ˈal/ ▶ **abbreviation** and others (used especially in referring to academic books or articles that have more than one author): *the conclusions of Gardner et al.*
– ORIGIN from Latin *et alii*.

etalon /ˈɛtəlɒn/ ▶ **noun** Physics a device consisting of two reflecting plates, for producing interfering light beams.
– ORIGIN early 20th cent.: from French *étalon*, literally 'standard of measurement'.

etc. ▶ **abbreviation** et cetera.

et cetera /ɛtˈsɛt(ə)rə, ɪt-/ (also **etcetera**) ▶ **adverb** used at the end of a list to indicate that further, similar items are included: *we're trying to resolve problems of obtaining equipment, drugs, et cetera.* ■ indicating that a list is too tedious or clichéd to give in full: *we've all got to do our duty, pull our weight, et cetera, et cetera.*
– ORIGIN Latin, from *et* 'and' and *cetera* 'the rest' (neuter plural of *ceterus* 'left over').

> **USAGE** A common mispronunciation of **et cetera** involves replacing the **t** in **et** with a **k**. This follows a process known as *assimilation* by which sounds become easier for the speaker to articulate.

etceteras ▶ **plural noun** unspecified or typical extra items: *she began to pack her compact, comb, and other etceteras.*

etch ▶ **verb** [with obj.] **1** engrave (metal, glass, or stone) by coating it with a protective layer, drawing on it with a needle, and then covering it with acid to attack the parts the needle has exposed, especially in order to produce prints from it: (as adj. **etched**) *etched glass windows.* ■ use the etching process to produce (a print or design).
2 (of an acid or other solvent) corrode or eat away the surface of (something). ■ selectively dissolve the surface of (a semiconductor or printed circuit) with a solvent, laser, or stream of electrons.
3 cut or carve (a text or design) on a surface: *her initials were **etched on** the table flap.* ■ mark (a surface) with a carved text or design: *a Pictish stone **etched with** mysterious designs* | figurative *her face was **etched with** tiredness.* ■ cause to stand out or be clearly defined or visible: *the outline of the town was **etched against** the sky.* ■ (**be etched**) (of an experience, image, etc.) be permanently fixed in someone's memory: *the events remain etched in the minds of all who witnessed them.*
▶ **noun** [mass noun] the action or process of etching something.
– DERIVATIVES **etcher** noun.
– ORIGIN mid 17th cent.: from Dutch *etsen*, from German *ätzen*, from a base meaning 'cause to eat'; related to EAT.

etchant /ˈɛtʃ(ə)nt/ ▶ **noun** an acid or corrosive chemical used in etching; a mordant.

etching ▶ **noun** a print produced by the process of etching: *etchings of animals and wildflowers.* ■ [mass noun] the art or process of producing etched plates or objects.

-ete ▶ **suffix** variant spelling of -ET² (as in *athlete*).

eternal /ɪˈtəːn(ə)l, iː-/ ▶ **adjective 1** lasting or existing forever; without end: *the secret of eternal youth | fear of eternal damnation.* ■ (of truths, values, or questions) valid for all time; essentially unchanging: *eternal truths of art and life.* ■ informal seeming to last or persist forever, especially on account of being tedious or annoying: *eternal nagging demands | she is an eternal optimist.*
2 used to emphasize expressions of admiration, gratitude, etc.: *to his eternal credit, he maintained his dignity throughout.*
3 (**the Eternal**) used to refer to an everlasting or universal spirit, as represented by God.
– PHRASES **the Eternal City** a name for the city of Rome. **eternal life** Christian Theology spiritual existence after death of the body. **eternal triangle** see TRIANGLE (sense 2).
– DERIVATIVES **eternality** /ɪˌtəːˈnalɪti, iː-/ noun, **eternalize** (also **eternalise**) verb, **eternalness** noun.
– ORIGIN late Middle English: via Old French from late Latin *aeternalis*, from Latin *aeternus*, from *aevum* 'age'.

eternally /ɪˈtəːn(ə)li, i-/ ▶ **adverb 1** in a way that continues or lasts forever; permanently: [as submodifier] *his eternally optimistic attitude.* ■ informal in an annoying or tedious way that seems to last forever; constantly: *he was prattling on eternally.*
2 [as submodifier] used to emphasize expressions of admiration, gratitude, etc.: *I shall be eternally grateful.*

eternity ▶ **noun** (pl. **eternities**) [mass noun] infinite or unending time: *their love was sealed for eternity | this state of affairs has lasted **for all eternity**.* ■ a state to which time has no application; timelessness. ■ Theology endless life after death: *immortal souls destined for eternity.* ■ used euphemistically to refer to death: *he could have crashed the car and taken them both to eternity.* ■ (**an eternity**) informal a period of time that seems very long, especially on account of being tedious or annoying: *a silence that lasted an eternity.*
– ORIGIN late Middle English: from Old French *eternite*, from Latin *aeternitas*, from *aeternus* 'without beginning or end' (see ETERNAL).

eternity ring ▶ **noun** a ring given as a symbol of lasting affection, typically set with an unbroken circle of gems.

eternize /ɪˈtəːnʌɪz, iː-/ (also **eternise**) ▶ **verb** [with obj.] literary make eternal; cause to live or last forever.

Etesian wind /ɪˈtiːʒɪən, ɪˈtiːz-, ɪˈtiːʒ(ə)n/ ▶ **noun** another term for MELTEMI.
– ORIGIN early 17th cent.: *Etesian* from Latin *etesius* 'annual' (from Greek *etēsios*, from *etos* 'year') + -AN.

ETH ▶ **abbreviation** Ethiopia (international vehicle registration).

eth /ɛð/ (also **edh**) ▶ **noun** an Old English letter, ð or Đ, representing the dental fricatives /ð/ and /θ/. It was superseded by the digraph *th*, but is now used as a phonetic symbol for the voiced dental fricative /ð/. Compare with THORN (sense 3).
– ORIGIN from Danish *edh*, perhaps representing the sound of the letter.

-eth¹ ▶ **suffix** variant spelling of -TH¹ (as in *fiftieth*).

-eth² (also **-th**) ▶ **suffix** archaic forming the third person singular of the present tense of verbs: *doeth | saith.*
– ORIGIN Old English *-eth, -ath, -th*.

ethacrynic acid /ˌɛθəˈkrɪnɪk/ ▶ **noun** [mass noun] Medicine a powerful diuretic drug used in the treatment of fluid retention, especially that associated with heart, liver, and kidney disorders. ● Alternative name: **2,3-dichloro-4-(2-ethylacryloyl)phenoxy)acetic acid**; chem. formula: $C_{13}H_{12}Cl_2O_4$.
– ORIGIN 1960s: *ethacrynic* from elements of the systematic name (see above).

ethambutol /ɛˈθambjʊtɒl/ ▶ **noun** [mass noun] Medicine a synthetic compound with bacteriostatic properties, used in combination with other drugs in the treatment of tuberculosis. ● A derivative of ethylenediamine; chem. formula: $C_{10}H_{24}N_2O_2$.
– ORIGIN 1960s: from *eth(yl)* + *am(ine)* + *but(an)ol*.

ethanal /ˈɛθ(ə)nal/ ▶ **noun** systematic chemical name for ACETALDEHYDE.
– ORIGIN late 19th cent.: blend of ETHANE and ALDEHYDE.

ethanamide /ɪˈθanəmʌɪd/ ▶ **noun** systematic chemical name for ACETAMIDE.

ethane /ˈiːθeɪn, ˈɛθ-/ ▶ **noun** [mass noun] Chemistry a colourless, odourless, flammable gas which is a constituent of petroleum and natural gas. It is the second member of the alkane series. ● Chem. formula: C_2H_6.
– ORIGIN late 19th cent.: from ETHER + -ANE².

ethanediol /ˈiːθeɪnˌdʌɪɒl, ˈɛθ-/ ▶ **noun** systematic chemical name for ETHYLENE GLYCOL.

ethanoic acid /ˌɛθəˈnəʊɪk/ ▶ **noun** systematic chemical name for ACETIC ACID.

ethanol /ˈɛθənɒl/ ▶ **noun** systematic chemical name for ETHYL ALCOHOL (see ALCOHOL).
– ORIGIN early 20th cent.: blend of ETHANE and ALCOHOL.

Ethelred /ˈɛθəlrɛd/ the name of two English kings:
■ **Ethelred I** (d.871), king of Wessex and Kent 865–71, elder brother of Alfred. His reign was marked by the continuing struggle against the invading Danes. Alfred joined Ethelred's campaigns and succeeded him on his death. ■ **Ethelred II** (*c.*969–1016), king of England 978–1016; known as **Ethelred the Unready**. Ethelred's inability to confront the Danes after he succeeded his murdered half-brother St Edward the Martyr led to his payment of tribute to prevent their attacks. In 1013 he briefly lost his throne to the Danish king Sweyn I. [*Unready*, later form of obsolete *unredy* 'badly advised'.]

ethene /ˈɛθiːn/ ▶ **noun** systematic chemical name for ETHYLENE.
– ORIGIN mid 19th cent.: from ETHER + -ENE.

ether /ˈiːθə/ ▶ **noun** [mass noun] **1** Chemistry a pleasant-smelling colourless volatile liquid that is highly flammable. It is used as an anaesthetic and as a solvent or intermediate in industrial processes.
● Alternative names: **diethyl ether**, ethoxyethane; chem. formula: $C_2H_5OC_2H_5$.
■ [count noun] any organic compound with a similar structure to ether, having an oxygen atom linking two alkyl or other organic groups: *methyl t-butyl ether.*
2 (also **aether**) chiefly literary the clear sky; the upper regions of air beyond the clouds: *nasty gases and smoke disperse into the ether.* ■ (**the ether**) informal air regarded as a medium for radio: *choral evensong still wafts across the ether.*
3 (also **aether**) Physics, archaic a very rarefied and highly elastic substance formerly believed to permeate all space, including the interstices between the particles of matter, and to be the medium whose vibrations constituted light and other electromagnetic radiation.
– DERIVATIVES **etheric** /iːˈθɛrɪk, ˈiːθ(ə)rɪk/ adjective.
– ORIGIN late Middle English: from Old French, or via Latin from Greek *aithēr* 'upper air', from the base of *aithein* 'burn, shine'. Originally the word denoted a substance believed to occupy space beyond the sphere of the moon. Sense 3 arose in the mid 17th cent. and sense 1 in the mid 18th cent.

ethereal /ɪˈθɪərɪəl/ (also **etherial**) ▶ **adjective 1** extremely delicate and light in a way that seems not to be of this world: *her ethereal beauty.* ■ heavenly or spiritual: *ethereal, otherworldly visions.*
2 Chemistry (of a solution) having diethyl ether as a solvent.
– DERIVATIVES **ethereality** noun, **ethereally** adverb.
– ORIGIN early 16th cent.: via Latin from Greek *aitherios* (from *aithēr* 'ether') + -AL.

etherize (also **etherise**) ▶ **verb** [with obj.] chiefly historical anaesthetize (a person or animal) with ether.
– DERIVATIVES **etherization** noun.

Ethernet /ˈiːθənɛt/ ▶ **noun** Computing a system for connecting a number of computer systems to form a local area network, with protocols to control the passing of information and to avoid simultaneous transmission by two or more systems.
– ORIGIN 1970s: blend of ETHER and NETWORK.

ethic /ˈɛθɪk/ ▶ **noun** [in sing.] a set of moral principles, especially ones relating to or affirming a specified group, field, or form of conduct: *the puritan ethic was being replaced by the hedonist ethic.*
▶ **adjective** rare relating to moral principles or the branch of knowledge dealing with these.
– ORIGIN late Middle English (denoting ethics or moral philosophy; also used attributively): from Old French *éthique*, from Latin *ethice*, from Greek (*hē*) *ēthikē* (*tekhnē*) '(the science of) morals', based on *ēthos* (see ETHOS).

ethical ▶ **adjective 1** relating to moral principles or the branch of knowledge dealing with these: *ethical issues in nursing | ethical standards.* ■ morally good or correct: *can a profitable business ever be ethical?* ■ avoiding activities or organizations that do harm to people or the environment: *an expert on ethical investment | switching to more ethical products | ethical holidays.*
2 [attrib.] (of a medicine) legally available only on a doctor's prescription and usually not advertised to the general public.
– DERIVATIVES **ethicality** noun, **ethically** adverb *is capitalism ethically justifiable?*

ethics ▶ **plural noun 1** [usu. treated as pl.] moral principles that govern a person's behaviour or the conducting of an activity: *medical ethics also enter into the question.*

2 [usu. treated as sing.] the branch of knowledge that deals with moral principles.

Schools of ethics in Western philosophy can be divided, very roughly, into three sorts. The first, drawing on the work of Aristotle, holds that the virtues (such as justice, charity, and generosity) are dispositions to act in ways that benefit both the person possessing them and that person's society. The second, defended particularly by Kant, makes the concept of duty central to morality: humans are bound, from a knowledge of their duty as rational beings, to obey the categorical imperative to respect other rational beings. Thirdly, utilitarianism asserts that the guiding principle of conduct should be the greatest happiness or benefit of the greatest number.

– DERIVATIVES **ethicist** noun.

ethidium bromide /ɛˈθɪdɪəm/ ▸ noun [mass noun] Chemistry a purple synthetic dye used in the treatment of trypanosome blood infection, to stain DNA, and to destroy the superhelical structure of DNA. It is a derivative of phenanthridine.

Ethiopia /ˌiːθɪˈəʊpɪə/ a country in NE Africa, on the Red Sea; pop. 85,237,300 (est. 2009); languages, Amharic (official), several other Afro-Asiatic languages; capital, Addis Ababa. Former name **ABYSSINIA**.

Ethiopia is the oldest independent country in Africa, having a recorded civilization that dates from the 2nd millennium BC. Little known to Europeans until the late 19th century, it was invaded and conquered by Italy in 1935. The emperor Haile Selassie was restored by the British in 1941 and ruled until overthrown in a Marxist coup in 1974. The subsequent period was marked by civil war, fighting against separatist guerrillas in Eritrea and Tigray, and by repeated famines; after the fall of the government in 1991 a multiparty system was adopted.

– ORIGIN via Latin from Greek *Aethiops*, from *aithein* 'to burn' + *ōps* 'the face'.

Ethiopian ▸ noun **1** a native or inhabitant of Ethiopia, or a person of Ethiopian descent.
2 archaic a black person.
▸ adjective **1** relating to Ethiopia or its people.
2 Zoology relating to or denoting a zoogeographical region comprising Africa south of the Sahara, together with the tropical part of the Arabian peninsula and (usually) Madagascar. Distinctive animals include the giraffes, hippopotamuses, aardvark, elephant shrews, tenrecs, and lemurs. Also called **AFROTROPICAL**.

Ethiopic /ˌiːθɪˈɒpɪk/ ▸ noun another term for **GE'EZ**.
▸ adjective in or relating to Ge'ez.
– ORIGIN mid 17th cent. (as an adjective): via Latin from Greek *aithiopikos*, from *Aethiops* (see **ETHIOPIA**).

ethmoid /ˈɛθmɔɪd/ (also **ethmoid bone**) ▸ noun Anatomy a square bone at the root of the nose, forming part of the cranium, and having many perforations through which the olfactory nerves pass to the nose.
– DERIVATIVES **ethmoidal** adjective.
– ORIGIN mid 18th cent.: from Greek *ēthmoeidēs*, from *ēthmos* 'a sieve'.

ethnic ▸ adjective **1** relating to a population subgroup (within a larger or dominant national or cultural group) with a common national or cultural tradition: *ethnic and cultural rights and traditions | leaders of ethnic communities.* ■ relating to national and cultural origins: *pupils from a wide variety of ethnic origins.* ■ denoting origin by birth or descent rather than by present nationality: *ethnic Indian populations.* ■ characteristic of or belonging to a non-Western cultural tradition: *ethnic jewellery | folk and ethnic music.*
2 archaic neither Christian nor Jewish; pagan or heathen.
▸ noun chiefly N. Amer. a member of an ethnic minority.
– DERIVATIVES **ethnically** adverb.
– ORIGIN late Middle English (denoting a person not of the Christian or Jewish faith): via ecclesiastical Latin from Greek *ethnikos* 'heathen', from *ethnos* 'nation'. Current senses date from the 19th cent.

USAGE In recent years **ethnic** has begun to be used in a euphemistic way to refer to non-white people as a whole, as in *a radio station which broadcasts to the ethnic community in Birmingham*. Although this usage is quite common, especially in journalism, it is better expressed by more accurate terms such as 'black', 'Asian', etc.

ethnic cleansing ▸ noun [mass noun] the mass expulsion or killing of members of one ethnic or religious group in an area by those of another.

ethnicity ▸ noun (pl. **ethnicities**) [mass noun] the fact or state of belonging to a social group that has a common national or cultural tradition: *the interrelationship between gender, ethnicity, and class* | [count noun] *the diverse experience of women of different ethnicities.*

ethnic minority ▸ noun a group within a community which has different national or cultural traditions from the main population.

ethno- /ˈɛθnəʊ/ ▸ combining form ethnic; ethnological: *ethnocentric | ethnology.*
– ORIGIN from Greek *ethnos* 'nation'.

ethnoarchaeology ▸ noun [mass noun] the study of the social organization and other ethnological features of present-day societies on the basis of their material culture, in order to draw conclusions about past societies from their material remains.
– DERIVATIVES **ethnoarchaeological** adjective.

ethnobotany ▸ noun [mass noun] the scientific study of the traditional knowledge and customs of a people concerning plants and their medical, religious, and other uses.
– DERIVATIVES **ethnobotanic** adjective, **ethnobotanical** adjective, **ethnobotanist** noun.

ethnocentric ▸ adjective evaluating other cultures according to preconceptions originating in the standards and customs of one's own culture.
– DERIVATIVES **ethnocentrically** adverb, **ethnocentricity** noun, **ethnocentrism** noun.

ethnocide /ˈɛθnə(ʊ)sʌɪd/ ▸ noun [mass noun] the deliberate and systematic destruction of the culture of an ethnic group.

ethnocultural ▸ adjective relating to or denoting a particular ethnic group.

ethnogenesis /ˌɛθnə(ʊ)ˈdʒɛnɪsɪs/ ▸ noun the formation or emergence of an ethnic group.

ethnography /ɛθˈnɒɡrəfi/ ▸ noun [mass noun] the scientific description of peoples and cultures with their customs, habits, and mutual differences.
– DERIVATIVES **ethnographer** noun, **ethnographic** adjective, **ethnographical** adjective, **ethnographically** adverb.

ethnohistory ▸ noun [mass noun] the branch of anthropology concerned with the history of peoples and cultures, especially non-Western ones.
– DERIVATIVES **ethnohistorian** noun, **ethnohistoric** adjective, **ethnohistorical** adjective.

ethnolinguistics /ˌɛθnəʊlɪŋˈɡwɪstɪks/ ▸ plural noun [treated as sing.] the branch of linguistics concerned with the relations between linguistic and cultural behaviour.
– DERIVATIVES **ethnolinguist** noun.

ethnology /ɛθˈnɒlədʒi/ ▸ noun [mass noun] the study of the characteristics of different peoples and the differences and relationships between them.
– DERIVATIVES **ethnologic** /-nəˈlɒdʒɪk/ adjective, **ethnological** adjective, **ethnologically** adverb, **ethnologist** noun.

ethnomethodology /ˌɛθnəʊˌmɛθəˈdɒlədʒi/ ▸ noun [mass noun] a method of sociological analysis that examines how individuals use everyday conversation to construct a common-sense view of the world.
– DERIVATIVES **ethnomethodological** adjective.

ethnomusicology ▸ noun [mass noun] the study of the music of different cultures, especially non-Western ones.
– DERIVATIVES **ethnomusicological** adjective, **ethnomusicologist** noun.

ethnoscience ▸ noun [mass noun] the study of the different ways the world is perceived and categorized in different cultures.

ethogram /ˈiːθəɡram/ ▸ noun Zoology a catalogue or table of all the different kinds of behaviour or activity observed in an animal.
– ORIGIN 1930s: from Greek *ēthos* 'nature, disposition' + **-GRAM**[1].

ethology /iːˈθɒlədʒi/ ▸ noun [mass noun] the science of animal behaviour. ■ the study of human behaviour and social organization from a biological perspective.
– DERIVATIVES **ethological** adjective, **ethologist** noun.
– ORIGIN late 19th cent.: via Latin from Greek *ēthologia*, from *ēthos* (see **ETHOS**).

ethos /ˈiːθɒs/ ▸ noun the characteristic spirit of a culture, era, or community as manifested in its attitudes and aspirations: *a challenge to the ethos of the 1960s.*
– ORIGIN mid 19th cent.: from modern Latin, from Greek *ēthos* 'nature, disposition', (plural) 'customs'.

ethoxyethane /iːˌθɒksɪˈiːθeɪn/ ▸ noun systematic chemical name for **DIETHYL ETHER** (see **ETHER** (sense 1)).

ethyl /ˈɛθʌɪl, -θɪl, ˈiː-/ ▸ noun [usu. as modifier] Chemistry of or denoting the hydrocarbon radical $-C_2H_5$, derived from ethane and present in many organic compounds: *ethyl acetate | an ethyl group.*
– ORIGIN mid 19th cent.: from German, from *Äther* 'ether' + **-YL**.

ethyl acetate ▸ noun [mass noun] Chemistry a colourless volatile liquid with a fruity smell, used as a plastics solvent and in flavourings and perfumes. ● Chem. formula: $CH_3COOC_2H_5$.

ethyl alcohol ▸ noun see **ALCOHOL**.

ethylbenzene ▸ noun [mass noun] Chemistry a colourless flammable liquid hydrocarbon, used in the manufacture of styrene. ● Chem. formula: $C_6H_5C_2H_5$.

ethylene /ˈɛθɪliːn, -θ(ə)l-/ ▸ noun [mass noun] Chemistry a flammable hydrocarbon gas of the alkene series, occurring in natural gas, coal gas, and crude oil and given off by ripening fruit. It is used in chemical synthesis, especially in the manufacture of polythene. ● Alternative name: **ethene**; chem. formula: C_2H_4.

ethylenediamine /ˌɛθɪliːndʌɪˈeɪmiːn, -θ(ə)l-, -dʌɪˈam-, -ˈdʌɪəmiːn/ ▸ noun [mass noun] Chemistry a viscous liquid used in making detergents and emulsifying agents. ● Chem. formula: $NH_2CH_2CH_2NH_2$.

ethylene glycol ▸ noun [mass noun] Chemistry a colourless viscous hygroscopic liquid used as an antifreeze, in the manufacture of polyesters, and in the preservation of ancient waterlogged timbers. ● Alternative name: **ethanediol**; chem. formula: $CH_2(OH)CH_2OH$.

ethylene oxide ▸ noun [mass noun] Chemistry a flammable toxic gas used as an intermediate and fumigant. ● An epoxide; chem. formula: $(CH_2)_2O$.

ethyne /ˈiːθʌɪn, ˈɛθ-/ ▸ noun systematic chemical name for **ACETYLENE**.

etic /ˈɛtɪk/ ▸ adjective Anthropology studying or describing a particular language or culture in a way that is general, non-structural, and objective in its perspective. Often contrasted with **EMIC**.
– ORIGIN 1950s: abstracted from **PHONETIC**.

-etic ▸ suffix forming adjectives and nouns such as *pathetic, peripatetic.*
– ORIGIN from Greek *-ētikos* or *-ētikos*.

etiolated /ˈiːtɪəˌleɪtɪd/ ▸ adjective **1** (of a plant) pale and drawn out due to a lack of light.
2 having lost vigour or substance; feeble: *a tone of etiolated nostalgia.*
– DERIVATIVES **etiolation** noun.
– ORIGIN late 18th cent.: from the verb *etiolate* (from French *étioler*, from Norman French *étieuler* 'grow into haulm') + **-ED**[2].

etiology ▸ noun US spelling of **AETIOLOGY**.

etiquette /ˈɛtɪkɛt, ɛtɪˈkɛt/ ▸ noun [mass noun] the customary code of polite behaviour in society or among members of a particular profession or group.
– ORIGIN mid 18th cent.: from French *étiquette* 'list of ceremonial observances of a court', also 'label, etiquette', from Old French *estiquette* (see **TICKET**).

Etna, Mount /ˈɛtnə/ a volcano in eastern Sicily, rising to 3,323 m (10,902 ft). It is the highest and most active volcano in Europe.

Eton collar ▸ noun a broad, stiff white collar worn outside the coat collar, especially with an Eton jacket.

Eton College /ˈiːt(ə)n/ a boys' public school in southern England, on the River Thames opposite Windsor, founded in 1440 by Henry VI to prepare scholars for King's College, Cambridge.

Eton crop ▸ noun a short hairstyle worn by women in the 1920s.

Etonian /iːˈtəʊnɪən/ ▸ noun a past or present member of Eton College: *an Old Etonian.*
▸ adjective relating to or typical of Eton College.

Eton jacket ▸ noun a short jacket reaching only to the waist, typically black and having a point at the back, formerly worn by pupils of Eton College.

Eton wall game ▸ noun see **WALL GAME**.

Etosha Pan /ɪˈtɒʃə/ a depression in the plateau of northern Namibia, filled with salt water and having no outlets, extending over an area of 4,800 sq. km (1,854 sq. miles).

étouffée /ˌeɪtuːˈfeɪ/ ▸ noun US a spicy Cajun stew made with vegetables and seafood.

etrier /ˈeɪtrɪeɪ/ ▸ noun Climbing a short rope ladder with a few rungs of wood or metal.
– ORIGIN 1950s: from French *étrier* 'stirrup'.

Etruria /ɪˈtrʊərɪə/ an ancient state of central Italy, situated between the Rivers Arno and Tiber and

E

corresponding approximately to modern Tuscany and parts of Umbria. It was the centre of the Etruscan civilization.
– DERIVATIVES **Etrurian** noun & adjective.

Etruscan /ɪˈtrʌsk(ə)n/ ▶ **adjective** relating to ancient Etruria, its people, or their language. The Etruscan civilization was at its height *c.*500 BC and was an important influence on the Romans, who had subdued the Etruscans by the end of the 3rd century BC.
▶ **noun 1** a native of ancient Etruria.
2 [mass noun] the language of ancient Etruria, which was written in an alphabet derived from Greek but is not related to any known language.
– ORIGIN from Latin *Etruscus* + **-AN**.

E

et seq. (also **et seqq.**) ▶ **adverb** and what follows (used in page references): *see volume 35, p. 329 et seq.*
– ORIGIN from Latin *et sequens* 'and the following', or from *et sequentes, et sequentia* 'and the following things'.

-ette ▶ **suffix** forming nouns: **1** denoting relatively small size: *kitchenette*.
2 denoting an imitation or substitute: *flannelette*.
3 denoting female gender: *suffragette*.
– ORIGIN from Old French *-ette*, feminine of **-ET**[1].

USAGE The use of **-ette** as a feminine suffix for forming new words is relatively recent: it was first recorded in the word **suffragette** at the beginning of the 20th century and has since been used to form only a handful of well-established words, including **usherette** and **drum majorette**, for example. In the modern context, where the tendency is to use words which are neutral in gender, the suffix **-ette** is not very productive and new words formed using it tend to be restricted to the deliberately flippant or humorous, as, for example, **ladette** and **punkette**.

étude /ˈeɪtjuːd, eɪˈtjuːd/ ▶ **noun** a short musical composition, typically for one instrument, designed as an exercise to improve the technique or demonstrate the skill of the player.
– ORIGIN mid 19th cent.: from French, literally 'study'.

etui /ɛˈtwiː/ ▶ **noun** (pl. **etuis**) dated a small ornamental case for holding needles, cosmetics, and other articles.
– ORIGIN early 17th cent.: from French *étui*, from Old French *estui* 'prison', from *estuier* 'shut up, keep'. Compare with **TWEEZERS**.

-etum ▶ **suffix** (forming nouns) denoting a collection or plantation of trees or other plants: *arboretum | pinetum*.
– ORIGIN from Latin.

etymologize (also **etymologise**) ▶ **verb** [with obj.] give or trace the etymology of (a word).
– ORIGIN mid 16th cent.: from medieval Latin *etymologizare*, from Latin *etymologia* (see **ETYMOLOGY**).

etymology /ˌɛtɪˈmɒlədʒi/ ▶ **noun** (pl. **etymologies**) [mass noun] the study of the origin of words and the way in which their meanings have changed throughout history. ■ [count noun] the origin of a word and the historical development of its meaning.
– DERIVATIVES **etymological** adjective, **etymologically** adverb, **etymologist** noun.
– ORIGIN late Middle English: from Old French *ethimologie*, via Latin from Greek *etumologia*, from *etumologos* 'student of etymology', from *etumon*, neuter singular of *etumos* 'true'.

etymon /ˈɛtɪmɒn/ ▶ **noun** (pl. **etymons** or **etyma**) a word or morpheme from which a later word is derived.
– ORIGIN late 16th cent. (denoting the original form of a word): via Latin from Greek *etumon* 'true thing' (see **ETYMOLOGY**).

EU ▶ **abbreviation** European Union.

Eu ▶ **symbol** the chemical element europium.

eu- ▶ **combining form** well; easily: *eupeptic | euphony*.
– ORIGIN from Greek *eu* 'well', from *eus* 'good'.

eubacterium /juːbakˈtɪərɪəm/ ▶ **noun** (pl. **eubacteria** /-rɪə/) **1** a bacterium of a large group typically having simple cells with rigid cell walls and often flagella for movement. The group comprises the 'true' bacteria and cyanobacteria, as distinct from archaea. ● Division (or subkingdom) Eubacteria, kingdom Monera; this group is sometimes taken to exclude non-rigid forms such as spirochaetes and mycoplasmas.
2 a bacterium found mainly in the intestines of vertebrates and in the soil. ● Genus *Eubacterium*; Gram-positive, anaerobic, rod-shaped bacteria.
– DERIVATIVES **eubacterial** adjective.

Euboea /juːˈbiːə/ an island of Greece in the western Aegean Sea, separated from the mainland by only a narrow channel at its capital, Chalcis. Greek name **ÉVVOIA**.

eucalyptus /juːkəˈlɪptəs/ (also **eucalypt**) ▶ **noun** (pl. **eucalyptuses** or **eucalypti** /-tʌɪ/) a fast-growing evergreen Australasian tree that has been widely introduced elsewhere. It is valued for its timber, oil, gum, resin, and as an ornamental tree. Also called **GUM**[1], **GUM TREE**. ● Genus *Eucalyptus*, family Myrtaceae: numerous species.
■ (also **eucalyptus oil**) [mass noun] the oil from eucalyptus leaves, chiefly used for its medicinal properties.
– ORIGIN modern Latin, from Greek *eu* 'well' + *kaluptos* 'covered' (from *kaluptein* 'to cover'), because the unopened flower is protected by a cap.

eucaryote ▶ **noun** variant spelling of **EUKARYOTE**.

eucatastrophe /juːkəˈtastrəfi/ ▶ **noun** rare a sudden and favourable resolution of events in a story; a happy ending.
– ORIGIN mid 20th cent.: said to have been coined by Tolkien.

Eucharist /ˈjuːk(ə)rɪst/ ▶ **noun** the Christian service, ceremony, or sacrament commemorating the Last Supper, in which bread and wine are consecrated and consumed. ■ the consecrated elements, especially the bread.

The bread and wine are referred to as the body and blood of Christ, though much theological controversy has focused on how substantially or symbolically this is to be interpreted. The service of worship is also called **Holy Communion** or (chiefly in the Protestant tradition) **the Lord's Supper** or (chiefly in the Catholic tradition) **the Mass**. See also **CONSUBSTANTIATION, TRANSUBSTANTIATION**.

– DERIVATIVES **Eucharistic** adjective.
– ORIGIN late Middle English: from Old French *eucariste*, based on ecclesiastical Greek *eukharistia* 'thanksgiving', from Greek *eukharistos* 'grateful', from *eu* 'well' + *kharizesthai* 'offer graciously' (from *kharis* 'grace').

euchre /ˈjuːkə/ ▶ **noun** [mass noun] a North American card game for two to four players, played with the thirty-two highest cards, the aim being to win at least three of the five tricks played.
▶ **verb** [with obj.] (in euchre) gain the advantage over (another player) by preventing them from taking three tricks. ■ N. Amer. informal deceive, outwit, or cheat (someone): *they **euchred** Congress **out of** $50 billion*. ■ (**be euchred**) Austral. informal be exhausted or ruined.
– ORIGIN early 19th cent.: from German dialect *Jucker(spiel)*.

euchromatin /juːˈkrəʊmətɪn/ ▶ **noun** [mass noun] Genetics chromosome material which does not stain strongly except during cell division. It represents the major genes and is involved in transcription. Compare with **HETEROCHROMATIN**.
– DERIVATIVES **euchromatic** adjective.

Euclid /ˈjuːklɪd/ (*c.*300 BC), Greek mathematician. His great work *Elements of Geometry*, which covered plane geometry, the theory of numbers, irrationals, and solid geometry, was the standard work until other kinds of geometry were discovered in the 19th century.

Euclidean /juːˈklɪdɪən/ ▶ **adjective** relating to or denoting the system of geometry based on the work of Euclid and corresponding to the geometry of ordinary experience. ■ of such a nature that the postulates of this system of geometry are valid. Compare with **NON-EUCLIDEAN**.

eucrite /ˈjuːkrʌɪt/ ▶ **noun** [mass noun] Geology a highly basic form of gabbro containing anorthite or bytownite with augite. ■ [count noun] a stony meteorite which contains no chondrules and consists mainly of anorthite and augite.
– ORIGIN mid 19th cent.: from Greek *eukritos* 'easily discerned', from *eu-* 'well' + *kritos* 'separated' (from *krinein* 'to separate').

eucryphia /juːˈkrɪfɪə/ ▶ **noun** a shrub or small tree with glossy dark green leaves and large white flowers, native to Australia and South America. ● Genus *Eucryphia*, family Eucryphiaceae.
– ORIGIN modern Latin, from Greek *eu* 'well' + *-kruphos* 'hidden' (with reference to its joined sepals).

eudaemonic /juːdɪˈmɒnɪk/ (also **eudemonic**) ▶ **adjective** rare conducive to happiness.
– ORIGIN mid 19th cent.: from Greek *eudaimonikos*, from *eudaimōn* 'happy' (see **EUDAEMONISM**).

eudaemonism /juːˈdiːmənɪz(ə)m/ (also **eudemonism**) ▶ **noun** [mass noun] a system of ethics that bases moral value on the likelihood of actions producing happiness.
– DERIVATIVES **eudaemonist** noun, **eudaemonistic** adjective.
– ORIGIN early 19th cent.: from Greek *eudaimonismos* 'system of happiness', from *eudaimōn* 'happy', from *eu* 'well' + *daimōn* 'guardian spirit'.

eudiometer /juːdɪˈɒmɪtə/ ▶ **noun** Chemistry a graduated glass tube in which mixtures of gases can be made to react by an electric spark, used to measure changes in volume during chemical reactions.
– DERIVATIVES **eudiometry** noun.
– ORIGIN late 18th cent. (denoting an instrument used to measure amounts of oxygen, thought to be greater in fine weather): from Greek *eudios* 'clear, fine' (weather), from *eu* 'well' + *dios* 'heavenly'.

eugenics /juːˈdʒɛnɪks/ ▶ **plural noun** [treated as sing.] the science of improving a population by controlled breeding to increase the occurrence of desirable heritable characteristics.
– DERIVATIVES **eugenic** adjective, **eugenically** adverb, **eugenicist** noun & adjective, **eugenist** noun & adjective.

eugenol /ˈjuːdʒɪnɒl/ ▶ **noun** [mass noun] Chemistry a colourless or pale yellow liquid compound present in oil of cloves and other essential oils and used in perfumery. ● Alternative name: **4-allyl-2-methoxyphenol**; chem. formula: $C_{10}H_{12}O_2$.
– ORIGIN late 19th cent.: from *eugenia* (genus name of the tree from which oil of cloves is obtained, named in honour of Prince *Eugene* of Savoy (1663–1736)) + **-OL**.

euglena /juːˈgliːnə/ ▶ **noun** Biology a green single-celled freshwater organism with a flagellum, sometimes forming a green scum on stagnant water. ● Genus *Euglena*, division Euglenophyta (or phylum Euglenophyta, kingdom Protista).
– ORIGIN modern Latin, from **EU-** 'well' + Greek *glēnē* 'eyeball, socket of joint'.

euglenoid /juːˈgliːnɔɪd/ Biology ▶ **noun** a flagellated single-celled organism of a group that comprises euglena and its relatives. ● Division (or phylum) Euglenophyta.
▶ **adjective** relating to organisms of this group. ■ (of cell locomotion) achieved by peristaltic waves that pass along the cell, characteristic of the euglenoids.

euhedral /juːˈhiːdr(ə)l/ ▶ **adjective** Geology (of a mineral crystal in a rock) bounded by faces corresponding to its regular crystal form, not constrained by adjacent minerals.

eukaryote /juːˈkarɪəʊt/ (also **eucaryote**) ▶ **noun** Biology an organism consisting of a cell or cells in which the genetic material is DNA in the form of chromosomes contained within a distinct nucleus. Eukaryotes include all living organisms other than the eubacteria and archaea. Compare with **PROKARYOTE**.
– DERIVATIVES **eukaryotic** adjective.
– ORIGIN 1960s: from **EU-** 'easily (formed)' + **KARYO-** 'kernel' + *-ote* as in *zygote*.

eulachon /ˈjuːləkɒn/ ▶ **noun** (pl. **same**) another term for **CANDLEFISH**.
– ORIGIN mid 19th cent.: from Lower Chinook.

Euler[1] /ˈɔɪlə/, Leonhard (1707–83), Swiss mathematician. Euler attempted to elucidate the nature of functions, and his study of infinite series led his successors, notably Abel and Cauchy, to introduce ideas of convergence and rigorous argument into mathematics.

Euler[2] /ˈɔɪlə/, Ulf Svante von (1905–83), Swedish physiologist, the son of Hans Euler-Chelpin. He was the first to discover a prostaglandin, which he isolated from semen. Euler also identified noradrenaline as the principal chemical neurotransmitter of the sympathetic nervous system. Nobel Prize for Physiology or Medicine (1970).

Euler-Chelpin /ˌɔɪləˈkɛlpɪn/, Hans Karl August Simon von (1873–1964), German-born Swedish biochemist. He worked mainly on enzymes and vitamins, and explained the role of enzymes in the alcoholic fermentation of sugar. Nobel Prize for Chemistry (1929).

Euler's constant ▶ **noun** Mathematics a constant used in numerical analysis, approximately equal to 0.577216. It represents the limit of the series $1 + {}^1/_2 + {}^1/_3 + {}^1/_4 \ldots {}^1/_n - \ln n$ as n tends to infinity. It is not known whether this is a rational number or not.
– ORIGIN mid 19th cent.: named after L. *Euler* (see **EULER**[1]).

Euler's formula ▶ **noun** the geometrical formula $V - E + F = 2$, where V, E, and F are the numbers of vertices, edges, and faces of any simple convex polyhedron or of an equivalent topological graph.

eulogium /juːˈləʊdʒɪəm/ ▶ **noun** (pl. **eulogia** /-dʒɪə/ or **eulogiums**) another term for **EULOGY**.
– ORIGIN early 17th cent.: from medieval Latin, 'praise'.

eulogize /ˈjuːlədʒʌɪz/ (also **eulogise**) ▶ **verb** [with obj.] praise highly in speech or writing: *he was eulogized as a rock star | a plaque that eulogizes the workers.*
– DERIVATIVES **eulogist** noun, **eulogistic** adjective, **eulogistically** adverb.

eulogy /ˈjuːlədʒi/ ▶ **noun** (pl. **eulogies**) a speech or piece of writing that praises someone or something highly, especially a tribute to someone who has just died: *a eulogy to the Queen Mother.*
– ORIGIN late Middle English (in the sense 'high praise'): from medieval Latin *eulogium, eulogia* (from Greek *eulogia* 'praise'), apparently influenced by Latin *elogium* 'inscription on a tomb' (from Greek *elegia* 'elegy'). The current sense dates from the late 16th cent.

Eumenides /juːˈmɛnɪdiːz/ Greek Mythology a name given to the Furies. The Eumenides probably originated as well-disposed deities of fertility, whose name was given to the Furies either by confusion or euphemistically.
– ORIGIN via Latin from Greek, from *eumenēs* 'well disposed', from *eu* 'well' + *menos* 'spirit'.

eunuch /ˈjuːnək/ ▶ **noun** a man who has been castrated, especially (in the past) one employed to guard the women's living areas at an oriental court. ■ an ineffectual person: *a nation of political eunuchs.*
– ORIGIN Old English, via Latin from Greek *eunoukhos*, literally 'bedroom guard', from *eunē* 'bed' + a second element related to *ekhein* 'to hold'.

euonymus /juːˈɒnɪməs/ ▶ **noun** a shrub or small tree that is widely cultivated for its autumn colours and bright fruit. ● Genus *Euonymus*, family Celastraceae: numerous species, including the spindle tree.
– ORIGIN modern Latin (named by Linnaeus), from Latin *euonymos*, from Greek *euōnumos* 'having an auspicious or honoured name', from *eus* 'good' + *onoma* 'name'.

eupeptic /juːˈpɛptɪk/ ▶ **adjective** relating to or having good digestion or a consequent air of healthy good spirits.
– ORIGIN late 17th cent. (in the sense 'helping digestion'): from Greek *eupeptos*, from *eu* 'well, easily' + *peptein* 'to digest'.

euphausiid /juːˈfɔːzɪɪd/ ▶ **noun** Zoology a shrimp-like planktonic marine crustacean of an order which includes krill. ● Order Euphausiaceae, subclass Malacostraca.
– ORIGIN late 19th cent.: from modern Latin *Euphausia* (genus name from Greek *eu* 'well' + *phainein* 'to show' + *ousia* 'substance') + **-ID**[2].

euphemism /ˈjuːfəmɪz(ə)m/ ▶ **noun** a mild or indirect word or expression substituted for one considered to be too harsh or blunt when referring to something unpleasant or embarrassing: *the jargon has given us 'downsizing' as a* ***euphemism for*** *cuts.* The opposite of **DYSPHEMISM**.
– ORIGIN late 16th cent.: from Greek *euphēmismos*, from *euphēmizein* 'use auspicious words', from *eu* 'well' + *phēmē* 'speaking'.

euphemistic ▶ **adjective** using or of the nature of a euphemism: *the euphemistic terms she uses to describe her relationships.*
– DERIVATIVES **euphemistically** adverb.

euphemize (also **euphemise**) ▶ **verb** [with obj.] refer to (something unpleasant or embarrassing) by means of a euphemism.
– ORIGIN mid 19th cent.: from Greek *euphēmizein* 'use auspicious words' (see **EUPHEMISM**).

euphonious /juːˈfəʊnɪəs/ ▶ **adjective** (of sound, especially speech) pleasing to the ear: *a stream of fine, euphonious phrases.*
– DERIVATIVES **euphoniously** adverb.

euphonium /juːˈfəʊnɪəm/ ▶ **noun** a valved brass musical instrument of tenor pitch, resembling a small tuba.
– ORIGIN mid 19th cent.: from Greek *euphōnos* 'having a pleasing sound' + **-IUM**.

euphony /ˈjuːf(ə)ni/ ▶ **noun** (pl. **euphonies**) [mass noun] the quality of being pleasing to the ear. ■ the tendency to make phonetic change for ease of pronunciation.
– DERIVATIVES **euphonic** adjective.
– ORIGIN late Middle English: from French *euphonie*, via late Latin from Greek *euphōnia*, from *euphōnos* 'well sounding' (based on *phōnē* 'sound').

euphorbia /juːˈfɔːbɪə/ ▶ **noun** a plant of a genus that comprises the spurges. ● Genus *Euphorbia*, family Euphorbiaceae.
– ORIGIN late Middle English: from Latin *euphorbea*, named after *Euphorbus*, Greek physician to the reputed discoverer of the plant, Juba II of Mauretania (1st cent. BC).

euphoria /juːˈfɔːrɪə/ ▶ **noun** [mass noun] a feeling or state of intense excitement and happiness: *in his euphoria, he had become convinced he could defeat them.*
– ORIGIN late 17th cent. (denoting well-being produced in a sick person by the use of drugs): modern Latin, from Greek, from *euphoros* 'borne well, healthy', from *eu* 'well' + *pherein* 'to bear'.

euphoriant ▶ **adjective** (chiefly of a drug) producing a feeling of euphoria.
▶ **noun** a euphoriant drug.

euphoric ▶ **adjective** characterized by or feeling intense excitement and happiness: *a euphoric sense of freedom.*
– DERIVATIVES **euphorically** adverb.

euphrasia /juːˈfreɪzɪə/ ▶ **noun** a plant of the genus *Euphrasia* in the figwort family, especially eyebright. ■ [mass noun] a preparation of eyebright used in herbal medicine and homeopathy, especially for treating eye problems.
– ORIGIN early 18th cent.: via medieval Latin from Greek, literally 'cheerfulness', from *euphrainein* 'gladden the mind'.

Euphrates /juːˈfreɪtiːz/ a river of SW Asia which rises in the mountains of eastern Turkey and flows through Syria and Iraq to join the Tigris, forming the Shatt al-Arab waterway.

euphuism /ˈjuːfjuːɪz(ə)m/ ▶ **noun** [mass noun] formal an artificial, highly elaborate way of writing or speaking.
– DERIVATIVES **euphuist** noun, **euphuistic** adjective, **euphuistically** adverb.
– ORIGIN late 16th cent.: from *Euphues*, the name of a character in John Lyly's prose romance of the same name (1578–80), from Greek *euphuēs* 'well endowed by nature', from *eu* 'well' + the base of *phuē* 'growth'.

euploid /ˈjuːplɔɪd/ ▶ **adjective** Genetics having an equal number of all the chromosomes of the haploid set.
– DERIVATIVES **euploidy** noun.
– ORIGIN early 20th cent.: from **EU-** + **-OID** as in **DIPLOID**, **HAPLOID**.

Eurasia /jʊ(ə)ˈreɪʒ(ə), -ʃ(ə)/ a term used to describe the total continental land mass of Europe and Asia combined.

Eurasian ▶ **adjective 1** of mixed European (or European-American) and Asian parentage.
2 relating to Eurasia.
▶ **noun** a person of mixed European (or European-American) and Asian parentage.

> **USAGE** In the 19th century the word **Eurasian** was normally used to refer to a person of mixed British and Indian parentage. In its modern uses, however, the term is more often used to refer to a person of mixed white American and SE Asian parentage.

Euratom /jʊ(ə)ˈratəm/ ▶ **abbreviation** European Atomic Energy Community.

eureka /jʊ(ə)ˈriːkə/ ▶ **exclamation** a cry of joy or satisfaction when one finds or discovers something.
▶ **noun** [mass noun] an alloy of copper and nickel used for electrical filaments and resistance wire.
– ORIGIN early 17th cent.: from Greek *heurēka* 'I have found it' (from *heuriskein* 'find'), said to have been uttered by Archimedes when he hit upon a method of determining the purity of gold. The noun dates from the early 20th cent.

eurhythmic /jʊ(ə)ˈrɪðmɪk/ ▶ **adjective** rare (especially of architecture or art) in or relating to harmonious proportion.
– ORIGIN mid 19th cent.: based on Greek *eurhuthmia* 'proportion' + **-IC**.

eurhythmics (also **eurhythmy**; US also **eurythmics**, **eurythmy**) ▶ **plural noun** [treated as sing.] a system of rhythmical physical movements to music used to teach musical understanding (especially in Steiner schools) or for therapeutic purposes, evolved by Émile Jaques-Dalcroze.
– ORIGIN early 20th cent.: from **EU-** 'well' + **RHYTHM** + **-ICS**.

Euripides /jʊ(ə)ˈrɪpɪdiːz/ (480–*c.*406 BC), Greek dramatist. His nineteen surviving plays show important innovations in the handling of traditional myths, such as the introduction of realism, an interest in feminine psychology, and the portrayal of abnormal and irrational states of mind. Notable works: *Medea, Hippolytus, Electra, Trojan Women*, and *Bacchae*.

Euro /ˈjʊərəʊ/ ▶ **adjective** informal relating to Europe or the European Union: *a Euro court.*

euro[1] ▶ **noun** (pl. **euros** or **euro**) the single European currency, which replaced the national currencies of France, Germany, Spain, Italy, Greece, Portugal, Luxembourg, Austria, Finland, the Republic of Ireland, Belgium, and the Netherlands in 2002. Sixteen member states of the European Union now use the euro.

euro[2] ▶ **noun** (pl. **euros**) the common wallaroo (see **WALLAROO**).
– ORIGIN mid 19th cent.: from Adnyamathanha *yuru*.

Euro- ▶ **combining form** European; European and ...: *Euro-American.* ■ relating to Europe or the European Union: *a Euro-MP.*

Eurobond ▶ **noun** an international bond issued in Europe or elsewhere outside the country in whose currency its value is stated (usually the US or Japan).

Eurocentric ▶ **adjective** focusing on European culture or history to the exclusion of a wider view of the world; implicitly regarding European culture as pre-eminent.
– DERIVATIVES **Eurocentricity** noun, **Eurocentrism** noun.

Eurocommunism ▶ **noun** [mass noun] a political system advocated by some communist parties in western European countries, which stresses independence from the former Soviet Communist Party and advocates the preservation of many elements of Western liberal democracy.
– DERIVATIVES **Eurocommunist** adjective & noun.

Eurocrat ▶ **noun** informal, chiefly derogatory a bureaucrat in the administration of the European Union.

eurocreep ▶ **noun** [mass noun] informal the gradual acceptance of the euro in European Union countries that have not yet officially adopted it as their national currency.

Eurocurrency ▶ **noun 1** a form of money held or traded outside the country in whose currency its value is stated (originally US dollars held in Europe).
2 a single currency for use by the member states of the European Union.

Eurodollar ▶ **noun** a US dollar held in Europe or elsewhere outside the US.

euroland /ˈjʊərə(ʊ)land/ ▶ **noun** another term for **EUROZONE**.

Euromarket ▶ **noun 1** a financial market which deals with Eurocurrencies.
2 the European Union regarded as a single commercial or financial market.

Euro-MP ▶ **noun** a member of the European Parliament.

Europa /jʊ(ə)ˈrəʊpə/ **1** Greek Mythology a princess of Tyre who was courted by Zeus in the form of a bull. She was carried off by him to Crete, where she bore him three sons (Minos, Rhadamanthus, and Sarpedon).
2 Astronomy one of the Galilean moons of Jupiter, the sixth-closest satellite to the planet, having a network of dark lines on a bright icy surface (diameter 3,138 km).

Europe a continent of the northern hemisphere, separated from Africa to the south by the Mediterranean Sea and from Asia to the east roughly by the Bosporus, the Caucasus Mountains, and the Ural Mountains. Europe contains approximately 20 per cent of the world's population. ■ the European Union: *the Prime Minister who took Britain into Europe.* ■ Brit. the mainland of continental Europe as distinct from the British Isles: *A Guide to the Birds of Britain and Europe.*

Europe, Council of an association of European states founded in 1949 to safeguard the political and cultural heritage of Europe and promote economic and social cooperation. One of the Council's principal achievements is the European Convention on Human Rights.

European ▶ **adjective** relating to or characteristic of Europe or its inhabitants. ■ relating to the European Union: *a single European currency.*
▶ **noun** a native or inhabitant of Europe. ■ a national of a state belonging to the European Union. ■ a person who is committed to the European Union: *they claimed to be the party of good Europeans.* ■ a person of European parentage.
– DERIVATIVES **Europeanism** noun.
– ORIGIN from French *européen*, from Latin *europaeus*, based on Greek *Eurōpē* 'Europe'.

European Atomic Energy Community (abbrev.: **Euratom**) an institution established in 1957 to aid the exploitation of nuclear discoveries in Europe.

European Bank for Reconstruction and Development a bank established in London in 1991 to help the former communist countries of eastern Europe and the former Soviet Union make the transition to the free-market system.

European Coal and Steel Community (abbrev.: **ECSC**) an organization established in 1952 to regulate pricing, transport, and tariffs for the coal and steel industries of the member countries.

European Commission a group, appointed by agreement among the governments of the European Union, which initiates Union action and safeguards its treaties. It meets in Brussels.

E

European Commission for Human Rights an institution of the Council of Europe, set up under the European Convention on Human Rights to examine complaints of alleged breaches of the Convention. It is based in Strasbourg.

European Community (abbrev.: **EC**) an economic and political association of certain European countries, incorporated since 1993 in the European Union.

> The European Community was formed in 1967 from the European Coal and Steel Community (ECSC), the European Economic Community (EEC), and the European Atomic Energy Community (Euratom); it comprises also the European Commission, the European Parliament, and the European Court of Justice. Until 1987 it was still commonly known as the EEC. The name 'European Communities' is still used in legal contexts where the three distinct organizations are recognized. See also **European Union**.

European Convention on Human Rights an international agreement set up by the Council of Europe in 1950 to protect human rights. Under the Convention were established the European Commission for Human Rights and the European Court of Human Rights.

European Council a grouping of the heads of government of the European Union countries, inaugurated in 1975, which meets two or three times a year.

European Court of Human Rights an institution of the Council of Europe, set up to protect human rights in conjunction with the European Commission for Human Rights. The Court, based in Strasbourg, is called to give judgement in cases where the Commission has failed to secure a settlement.

European Court of Justice an institution of the European Union, with thirteen judges appointed by its member governments, meeting in Luxembourg. Established in 1958, it exists to safeguard the law in the interpretation and application of Community treaties.

European currency unit ▶ noun see **ecu**.

European Economic Community (abbrev.: **EEC**) an institution of the European Union, an economic association of western European countries set up by the Treaty of Rome (1957). The original members were France, West Germany, Italy, Belgium, the Netherlands, and Luxembourg. See also **European Community** and **European Union**.

European Free Trade Association (abbrev.: **EFTA**) a customs union of western European countries, established in 1960 as a trade grouping without the political implications of the European Economic Community. The original members were Austria, Denmark, Norway, Portugal, Sweden, Switzerland, and the UK.

European Investment Bank a bank set up in 1958 by the Treaty of Rome to finance capital investment projects promoting the balanced development of members of the European Community. It is based in Luxembourg.

Europeanize (also **Europeanise**) ▶ verb [with obj.] (often as adj. **Europeanized**) give (someone or something) a European character or scope: *a highly Europeanized city*. ■ transfer to the control or responsibility of the European Union.
– DERIVATIVES **Europeanization** noun.

European Monetary System (abbrev.: **EMS**) a monetary system inaugurated by the European Community in 1979 to coordinate and stabilize the exchange rates of the currencies of member countries, as a prelude to monetary union. It is based on the use of the Exchange Rate Mechanism.

European Monetary Union (abbrev.: **EMU**) a European Union programme intended to work towards full economic unity in Europe based on the phased introduction of a common currency (the euro). The programme was announced in 1989; the second stage came into effect on 1 January 1994 under the terms of the Maastricht Treaty, and in 2002 the euro replaced the currencies of twelve European Union countries (see **euro**[1]).

European Parliament the Parliament of the European Union, originally established in 1952. From 1958 to 1979 it was composed of representatives drawn from the parliaments of member countries, but since 1979 direct elections have taken place every five years. Through the Single European Act (1987) it assumed a degree of sovereignty over national parliaments. It meets in Strasbourg, and its committee is in Brussels.

European plan ▶ noun N. Amer. a system of charging for a hotel room only, without meals. Often contrasted with **American plan**.

European Recovery Program official name for the **Marshall Plan**.

European Space Agency (abbrev.: **ESA**) an organization set up in 1975 to coordinate the national space programmes of the collaborating countries. It is based in Paris.

European Union (abbrev.: **EU**) an economic and political association of certain European countries as a unit with internal free trade and common external tariffs.

> The European Union was created on 1 November 1993, with the coming into force of the Maastricht Treaty. It encompasses the old European Community (EC) together with two intergovernmental 'pillars' for dealing with foreign affairs and with immigration and justice. The terms **European Economic Community** (EEC) and **European Community** (EC) continue to be used loosely to refer to what is now the European Union. The European Union consists of 27 member states, 16 of which use the common currency unit, the euro.

Europhile ▶ noun a person who admires Europe or is in favour of participation in the European Union.

Europhobe ▶ noun a person having a strong dislike of Europe or opposing participation in the European Union.

europium /jʊ(ə)rˈəʊpɪəm/ ▶ noun [mass noun] the chemical element of atomic number 63, a soft silvery-white metal of the lanthanide series. Europium oxide is used with yttrium oxide as a red phosphor in colour television screens. (Symbol: **Eu**)
– ORIGIN early 20th cent.: modern Latin, based on **Europe**.

Europoort /ˈjʊərəʊpɔːt/ a major European port in the Netherlands, near Rotterdam.

Europop ▶ noun [mass noun] pop music from continental Europe with simple melodies and lyrics, often sung in English.

Eurosceptic ▶ noun a person who is opposed to increasing the powers of the European Union.
– DERIVATIVES **Eurosceptical** adjective, **Euroscepticism** noun.

Eurostar ▶ noun trademark the high-speed passenger rail service that links London with various European cities via the Channel Tunnel.

Eurotrash ▶ noun [mass noun] informal rich European socialites, especially those living or working in the United States.

Eurovision a network of European television production administered by the European Broadcasting Union.

eurozone /ˈjʊərə(ʊ)zəʊn/ ▶ noun the economic region formed by those member countries of the European Union that have adopted the euro.

eury- ▶ combining form denoting a wide variety or range of something specified: *eurytopic*.
– ORIGIN from Greek *eurus* 'wide'.

euryapsid /jʊərɪˈapsɪd/ ▶ noun a Mesozoic marine reptile of a group characterized by a single upper temporal opening in the skull, including the nothosaurs, plesiosaurs, and ichthyosaurs. ● Sometimes placed in a subclass Euryapsida, though this taxon is no longer widely recognized.
– ORIGIN from Greek *eurus* 'wide' + *apsis, apsid-* 'arch'.

Eurydice /jʊəˈrɪdɪsi/ Greek Mythology the wife of Orpheus. After she was killed by a snake Orpheus secured her release from the underworld on the condition that he did not look back at her on their way back to the world of the living. But Orpheus did look back, whereupon Eurydice disappeared.

euryhaline /jʊərɪˈheɪlʌɪn, -ˈheɪliːn/ ▶ adjective Ecology (of an aquatic organism) able to tolerate a wide range of salinity. Often contrasted with **stenohaline**.
– ORIGIN late 19th cent.: from Greek *eurus* 'wide' + *halinos* 'of salt'.

eurypterid /jʊ(ə)ˈrɪptərɪd/ ▶ noun a giant fossil marine arthropod of a group occurring in the Palaeozoic era. They are related to horseshoe crabs, and resemble large scorpions with a terminal pair of paddle-shaped swimming appendages. ● Subclass Eurypterida, class Merostomata, subphylum Chelicerata.
– ORIGIN late 19th cent.: from modern Latin *Eurypterus* (genus name), from **eury-** + Greek *pteron* 'wing' + **-id**[2].

eurythermal /jʊərɪˈθəːm(ə)l/ ▶ adjective Ecology (of an organism) able to tolerate a wide range of temperatures. Often contrasted with **stenothermal**.

eurythmics ▶ plural noun US spelling of **eurhythmics**.

eurythmy ▶ noun US spelling of **eurhythmy** (see **eurhythmics**).

eurytopic /jʊərɪˈtɒpɪk/ ▶ adjective Ecology (of an organism) able to tolerate a wide range of habitats or ecological conditions. Often contrasted with **stenotopic**.

Eusebio /juːˈseɪbɪəʊ/ (b.1942), Mozambican-born Portuguese footballer; born *Ferraira da Silva Eusebio*. He was a forward who played largely for the Portuguese club Benfica.

Eusebius /juːˈsiːbɪəs/ (*c.*264–*c.*340 AD), bishop and Church historian; known as **Eusebius of Caesarea**. His *Ecclesiastical History* is the principal source for the history of Christianity (especially in the Eastern Church) from the age of the Apostles until 324.

Euskara /ˈjuːskərə/ ▶ noun [mass noun] the Basque language.
– ORIGIN the name in Basque.

eusocial /juːˈsəʊʃ(ə)l/ ▶ adjective Zoology denoting social organisms (e.g. the honeybee) in which a single female or caste produces the offspring and non-reproductive individuals cooperate in caring for the young.
– DERIVATIVES **eusociality** noun.

eusol /ˈjuːsɒl/ ▶ noun [mass noun] an antiseptic solution of chlorinated lime and boric acid.
– ORIGIN early 20th cent.: from *E(dinburgh) U(niversity) sol(ution)*, with reference to the university's Pathology Department, where it was developed.

Eustachian tube /juːˈsteɪʃ(ə)n/ ▶ noun Anatomy a narrow passage leading from the pharynx to the cavity of the middle ear, permitting the equalization of pressure on each side of the eardrum.
– ORIGIN mid 18th cent.: named after Bartolomeo *Eustachio* (died 1574), the Italian anatomist who identified and described it.

eustasy /ˈjuːstəsi/ ▶ noun [mass noun] a change of sea level throughout the world, caused typically by movements of parts of the earth's crust or melting of glaciers.
– DERIVATIVES **eustatic** adjective.
– ORIGIN 1940s: back-formation from *eustatic*, coined in German from Greek *eu* 'well' + *statikos* 'static'.

Euston Road /ˈjuːstən/ ▶ noun [as modifier] relating to or denoting a group of English post-Impressionist realistic painters of the 1930s, whose members included **William Coldstream** (1908–87) and **Victor Pasmore** (1908–98).
– ORIGIN from the name of a road in London, site of a former School of Drawing and Painting (1938–9).

eutectic /juːˈtɛktɪk/ Chemistry ▶ adjective relating to or denoting a mixture of substances (in fixed proportions) that melts and freezes at a single temperature that is lower than the melting points of the separate constituents or of any other mixture of them.
▶ noun a eutectic mixture. ■ short for **eutectic point**.
– ORIGIN late 19th cent.: from Greek *eutēktos* 'easily melting', from *eu* 'well, easily' + *tēkein* 'melt'.

eutectic point (also **eutectic temperature**) ▶ noun Chemistry the temperature at which a particular eutectic mixture freezes or melts.

eutectoid /juːˈtɛktɔɪd/ Metallurgy ▶ adjective relating to or denoting an alloy which has a minimum transformation temperature between a solid solution and a simple mixture of metals.
▶ noun a eutectoid mixture or alloy.

Euterpe /juːˈtəːpi/ Greek & Roman Mythology the Muse of flutes.
– ORIGIN Greek, literally 'well pleasing'.

euthanasia /juːθəˈneɪzɪə/ ▸ **noun** [mass noun] the painless killing of a patient suffering from an incurable and painful disease or in an irreversible coma.
– ORIGIN early 17th cent. (in the sense 'easy death'): from Greek, from *eu* 'well' + *thanatos* 'death'.

euthanize /ˈjuːθənʌɪz/ (also **euthanise**) ▸ **verb** [with obj.] N. Amer. put (an animal) to death humanely.
– ORIGIN 1970s: formed irregularly from EUTHANASIA + -IZE.

Eutheria /juːˈθɪərɪə/ ▸ **plural noun** Zoology a major group of mammals that comprises the placentals. Compare with METATHERIA. ● Infraclass Eutheria, subclass Theria.
– ORIGIN modern Latin (plural), from EU- 'well, prospering' + Greek *thērion* 'wild beast'.

eutherian Zoology ▸ **noun** a mammal of the major group Eutheria, which excludes the marsupials and monotremes.
▸ **adjective** relating to or denoting eutherians.

euthyroid /juːˈθʌɪrɔɪd/ ▸ **adjective** Medicine having a normally functioning thyroid gland.

eutrophic /juːˈtrəʊfɪk, -ˈtrɒfɪk/ ▸ **adjective** Ecology (of a lake or other body of water) rich in nutrients and so supporting a dense plant population, the decomposition of which kills animal life by depriving it of oxygen. Compare with DYSTROPHIC and OLIGOTROPHIC.
– ORIGIN early 18th cent. (denoting a medicine promoting good nutrition): from Greek *eutrophia*, from *eu* 'well' + *trephein* 'nourish'. The current sense dates from the 1930s.

eutrophication /ˌjuːtrəfɪˈkeɪʃ(ə)n/ ▸ **noun** [mass noun] excessive richness of nutrients in a lake or other body of water, frequently due to run-off from the land, which causes a dense growth of plant life.

eV ▸ **abbreviation** electronvolt(s).

EVA ▸ **abbreviation** ■ ethyl vinyl acetate, a material used as cushioning in running shoes, consisting of a rubbery copolymer of ethylene and vinyl acetate. ■ (in space) extravehicular activity.

evacuant /ɪˈvakjʊənt/ ▸ **adjective** (of a medicine or treatment) acting to induce some kind of bodily discharge.
▸ **noun** an evacuant medicine, such as a laxative, an emetic, or a sudorific.
– ORIGIN mid 18th cent.: from Latin *evacuant-* 'emptying (the bowels')', from the verb *evacuare*, later in the more general sense 'remove (contents)'.

evacuate /ɪˈvakjʊeɪt/ ▸ **verb** [with obj.] **1** remove (someone) from a place of danger to a safer place: *several families were evacuated from their homes.* ■ leave or cause the occupants to leave (a place of danger): *fire alarms forced staff to evacuate the building* | [no obj.] *nearly five million had to evacuate because of air terror.* ■ (of troops) withdraw from (a place): *the last British troops evacuated the Canal Zone.*
2 technical remove air, water, or other contents from (a container): *when it springs a leak, evacuate the pond.* ■ empty (the bowels or another bodily organ). ■ discharge (faeces or other matter) from the body.
– ORIGIN late Middle English (in the sense 'clear the contents of'): from Latin *evacuat-* '(of the bowels) emptied', from the verb *evacuare*, from *e-* (variant of *ex-*) 'out of' + *vacuus* 'empty'.

evacuation ▸ **noun** [mass noun] **1** the action of evacuating a person or a place: *there were waves of evacuation during the blitz* | [count noun] *a full-scale evacuation of the city centre.*
2 the action of emptying the bowels or another bodily organ. ■ [count noun] a quantity of matter discharged from the bowels or another bodily organ. ■ technical the action of emptying a container of air, water, or other contents.

evacuative ▸ **adjective & noun** another term for EVACUANT.

evacuee ▸ **noun** a person evacuated from a place of danger.
– ORIGIN early 20th cent. (originally in the French form): from French *évacué*, past participle of *évacuer*, from Latin *evacuare* (see EVACUATE).

evade ▸ **verb** [with obj.] escape or avoid (someone or something), especially by guile or trickery: *friends helped him to evade capture for a time.* ■ (of an abstract thing) elude (someone): *sleep still evaded her.* ■ avoid giving a direct answer to (a question): *he denied evading the question.* ■ avoid dealing with or accepting (something unpleasant or morally or legally required): *he never sought to evade responsibility for his actions.* ■ escape paying (tax or duty), especially by illegitimate presentation of one's finances. ■ act contrary to the intention of (a law or rule), especially while complying with its letter.
– DERIVATIVES **evadable** adjective, **evader** noun.
– ORIGIN late 15th cent.: from French *évader*, from Latin *evadere* from *e-* (variant of *ex-*) 'out of' + *vadere* 'go'.

evaginate /ɪˈvadʒɪneɪt/ ▸ **verb** Biology & Physiology (with reference to a tubular or pouch-shaped organ or structure) turn or be turned inside out.
– DERIVATIVES **evagination** noun.
– ORIGIN mid 17th cent.: from Latin *evaginat-* 'unsheathed', from the verb *evaginare*, from *e-* (variant of *ex-*) 'out of' + *vagina* 'sheath'.

evaluate ▸ **verb** [with obj.] **1** form an idea of the amount, number, or value of; assess: *the study will assist in evaluating the impact of recent changes* | [with clause] *a system for evaluating how well the firm is performing.*
2 Mathematics find a numerical expression or equivalent for (an equation, formula, or function).
– DERIVATIVES **evaluative** adjective, **evaluator** noun.
– ORIGIN mid 19th cent. (earlier (mid 18th cent.) as *evaluation*): from French *évaluer*, from *es-* (from Latin *ex-*) 'out, from' + Old French *value* 'value'.

evaluation ▸ **noun** [mass noun] the making of a judgement about the amount, number, or value of something; assessment: *the evaluation of each method* | [count noun] *an initial evaluation of the programme.*

evanesce /ˌiːvəˈnɛs, ɛv-/ ▸ **verb** [no obj.] literary pass out of sight, memory, or existence.
– ORIGIN mid 19th cent.: from Latin *evanescere*, from *e-* (variant of *ex-*) 'out of' + *vanus* 'empty'.

evanescent ▸ **adjective 1** chiefly literary soon passing out of sight, memory, or existence; quickly fading or disappearing: *the evanescent Arctic summer.*
2 Physics denoting a field or wave which extends into a region where it cannot propagate and whose amplitude therefore decreases with distance.
– DERIVATIVES **evanescence** noun, **evanescently** adverb.
– ORIGIN early 18th cent. (in the sense 'almost imperceptible'): from Latin *evanescent-* 'disappearing', from the verb *evanescere* (see EVANESCE).

evangel /ɪˈvan(d)ʒɛl, -(d)ʒ(ə)l/ ▸ **noun 1** archaic the Christian gospel. ■ any of the four Gospels.
2 North American term for EVANGELIST.
– ORIGIN Middle English (in the sense 'gospel'): from Old French *evangile*, via ecclesiastical Latin from Greek *euangelion* 'good news', from *euangelos* 'bringing good news', from *eu-* 'well' + *angelein* 'announce'.

evangelical ▸ **adjective** of or according to the teaching of the gospel or the Christian religion. ■ of or denoting a tradition within Protestant Christianity emphasizing the authority of the Bible, personal conversion, and the doctrine of salvation by faith in the Atonement. ■ zealous in advocating or supporting a particular cause: *she was evangelical about organic farming.*
▸ **noun** a member of the evangelical tradition in the Christian Church.
– DERIVATIVES **evangelic** adjective, **evangelicalism** noun, **evangelically** adverb.
– ORIGIN mid 16th cent.: via ecclesiastical Latin from ecclesiastical Greek *euangelikos*, from *euangelos* (see EVANGEL).

evangelism ▸ **noun** [mass noun] the spreading of the Christian gospel by public preaching or personal witness. ■ zealous advocacy or support of a particular cause.

evangelist ▸ **noun 1** a person who seeks to convert others to the Christian faith, especially by public preaching. ■ a layperson engaged in Christian missionary work. ■ a zealous advocate of a particular cause: *he has become an evangelist for the European Union.*
2 the writer of one of the four Gospels (Matthew, Mark, Luke, or John): *St John the Evangelist.*
– ORIGIN Middle English (in sense 2): from Old French *évangéliste*, via ecclesiastical Latin from ecclesiastical Greek *euangelistēs*, from *euangelizesthai* 'evangelize'.

evangelistic ▸ **adjective** seeking to convert others to the Christian faith; missionary: *an evangelistic preacher.* ■ zealously advocating a particular cause; campaigning: *an almost evangelistic zeal for the product.*

evangelize (also **evangelise**) ▸ **verb** [with obj.] convert or seek to convert (someone) to Christianity. ■ [no obj.] preach the gospel.
– DERIVATIVES **evangelization** noun, **evangelizer** noun.
– ORIGIN late Middle English: from ecclesiastical Latin *evangelizare*, from Greek *euangelizesthai*, from *euangelos* (see EVANGEL).

Evans[1], Sir Arthur (John) (1851–1941), English archaeologist. His excavations at Knossos (1899–1935) resulted in the discovery of the Bronze Age civilization of Crete, which he named Minoan after the legendary Cretan king Minos.

Evans[2], Gil (1912–88), Canadian jazz pianist, composer, and arranger; born *Ian Ernest Gilmore Green.* In 1947 he began a long association with Miles Davis, producing albums such as *Porgy and Bess* (1958) and *Sketches of Spain* (1959).

evaporate /ɪˈvapəreɪt/ ▸ **verb** turn from liquid into vapour: [no obj.] *cook until most of the liquid has evaporated* | [with obj.] *this gets the oil hot enough to evaporate any moisture.* ■ lose or cause to lose moisture or solvent as vapour: [with obj.] *the solution was evaporated to dryness.* ■ [no obj.] (of something abstract) cease to exist: *the militancy of earlier years had evaporated in the wake of defeat.*
– DERIVATIVES **evaporation** noun, **evaporator** noun.
– ORIGIN late Middle English: from Latin *evaporat-* 'changed into vapour', from the verb *evaporare*, from *e-* (variant of *ex-*) 'out of' + *vapor* 'steam, vapour'.

evaporated milk ▸ **noun** [mass noun] a processed form of milk that has had some of the liquid removed by evaporation.

evaporating dish ▸ **noun** Chemistry a small ceramic dish in which liquids are heated over a flame so that they evaporate, leaving a solid residue.

evaporative /ɪˈvap(ə)rətɪv/ ▸ **adjective** relating to or involving evaporation: *evaporative water loss.*
– ORIGIN late Middle English: from late Latin *evaporativus*, from *evaporare* 'change into vapour' (see EVAPORATE).

evaporative cooling ▸ **noun** [mass noun] reduction in temperature resulting from the evaporation of a liquid, which removes latent heat from the surface from which evaporation takes place. This process is employed in industrial and domestic cooling systems, and is also the physical basis of sweating.

evaporite /ɪˈvapərʌɪt/ ▸ **noun** Geology a natural salt or mineral deposit left after the evaporation of a body of water.
– ORIGIN 1920s: alteration of EVAPORATE (see also -ITE[1]).

evapotranspiration /ɪˌvapəʊtranspɪˈreɪʃ(ə)n/ ▸ **noun** [mass noun] the process by which water is transferred from the land to the atmosphere by evaporation from the soil and other surfaces and by transpiration from plants.

evasion ▸ **noun** [mass noun] the action of evading something: *their adroit evasion of almost all questions.* ■ [count noun] an indirect answer; a prevaricating excuse: *the protestations and evasions of a witness.*
– ORIGIN late Middle English (in the sense 'prevaricating excuse'): via Old French from Latin *evasio(n-)*, from *evadere* (see EVADE).

evasive ▸ **adjective** tending to avoid commitment or self-revelation, especially by responding only indirectly: *she was evasive about her phone number.* ■ directed towards avoidance or escape: *they decided to take evasive action.*
– DERIVATIVES **evasively** adverb, **evasiveness** noun.
– ORIGIN early 18th cent.: from Latin *evas-* 'evaded' (from the verb *evadere*) + -IVE.

Eve (in the Bible) the first woman, companion of Adam and mother of Cain and Abel.

eve ▸ **noun** the day or period of time immediately before an event or occasion: ***on the eve of*** *her departure he gave her a little parcel.* ■ the evening or day before a religious festival: *the service for Passover eve.* ■ chiefly literary evening: *a bitter winter's eve.*
– ORIGIN late Middle English (in the sense 'close of day'): short form of EVEN[2].

evection /ɪˈvɛkʃ(ə)n/ ▸ **noun** [mass noun] Astronomy regular variation in the eccentricity of the moon's orbit around the earth, caused mainly by the sun's attraction.
– ORIGIN mid 17th cent. (in the sense 'elevation, exaltation'): from Latin *evectio(n-)*, from *evehere* 'carry out or up', from *e-* (variant of *ex-*) 'out' + *vehere* 'carry'.

Eve hypothesis (also **African Eve hypothesis**) ▸ **noun** the hypothesis (based on study of mitochondrial DNA) that modern humans have a common female ancestor who lived in Africa around 200,000 years ago.

E

E

Evelyn /ˈiːvlɪn/, John (1620–1706), English diarist and writer. He is remembered chiefly for his *Diary* (published posthumously in 1818), which describes such important historical events as the Great Plague and the Great Fire of London.

Even /eɪˈvɛn/ ▶ **noun** (pl. **same**) **1** a member of an indigenous people living in the Kamchatka peninsula of eastern Siberia.
2 [mass noun] the language of the Even, a Tungusic language with about 6,000 speakers, closely related to Evenki.
▶ **adjective** relating to the Even or their language.

even[1] ▶ **adjective** (**evener, evenest**) **1** flat and smooth: *prepare the site, then lay an even bed of mortar.* ■ in the same plane or line; level: *run a file along the saw to make all of the teeth* ***even with*** *each other.*
2 equal in number, amount, or value: *an even gender balance among staff and students.* ■ equally balanced: *the first half of the match was fairly even.* ■ having little variation in quality; regular: *they travelled at an even and leisurely pace.* ■ (of a person's temper or disposition) equable; calm: *she was known to have an even temper and to be difficult to rile.*
3 (of a number, such as 2, 6, or 108) divisible by two without a remainder. ■ bearing a number that is divisible by two without a remainder: *headers can be placed on odd or even pages or both.*
▶ **verb** make or become even: [with obj.] *she cut the hair again to* ***even up*** *the ends.*
▶ **adverb** used to emphasize something surprising or extreme: *they have never even heard of the United States | they wore fur hats, even in summer.* ■ used in comparisons for emphasis: *he knows even less about it than I do.*
– PHRASES **even as** at the very same time as: *even as he spoke their baggage was being unloaded.* **an even break** informal a fair chance: *the fact is suckers never get an even break.* **an even chance** an equal likelihood of success or failure: *the team has an even chance of winning.* **even if** despite the possibility that; no matter whether: *always try everything even if it turns out to be a dud.* ■ despite the fact that: *he is a great President, even if he has many enemies.* **even now** (or **then**) **1** now (or then) as well as before: *even now, after all these years, it upsets me.* **2** in spite of what has (or had) happened: *even then he never raised his voice to me.* **3** at this (or that) very moment: *very likely you are even now picking up the telephone to ring.* **even so** in spite of that; nevertheless: *not the most exciting of places, but even so I was having a good time.* **even though** despite the fact that: *even though he was bigger, he never looked down on me.* **get** (or **be**) **even** informal inflict similar trouble or harm on someone to that which they have inflicted on oneself: *I'll get* ***even with*** *you for this.* **of even date** Law or formal of the same date. **on an even keel** (of a ship or aircraft) not listing or tilting to one side. ■ (of a person or situation) functioning normally after a period of difficulty: *getting her life back on to an even keel after their break-up had been difficult.*
– DERIVATIVES **evenly** adverb, **evenness** noun.
– ORIGIN Old English *efen* (adjective), *efne* (adverb), of Germanic origin; related to Dutch *even, effen* and German *eben.*

even[2] ▶ **noun** archaic or literary the end of the day; evening: *bring it to my house this even.*
– ORIGIN Old English *ǣfen*, of Germanic origin; related to Dutch *avont* and German *Abend.*

even-aged ▶ **adjective** Forestry (of woodland) composed of trees of approximately the same age.

even-handed ▶ **adjective** fair and impartial in treatment or judgement: *an even-handed approach to industrial relations.*
– DERIVATIVES **even-handedly** adverb, **even-handedness** noun.

evening ▶ **noun** the period of time at the end of the day, usually from about 6 p.m. to bedtime: *it was seven o'clock* ***in the evening*** | [as modifier] *the evening meal.* ■ an evening characterized by a particular event or activity: *some pubs hold Irish music evenings.* ■ [as modifier] prescribed by fashion as suitable for relatively formal social events held in the evening: *a couple in evening dress.*
▶ **adverb** (**evenings**) informal in the evening; every evening: *Saturday evenings he invariably fell asleep.*
▶ **exclamation** informal short for GOOD EVENING.
– ORIGIN Old English *ǣfnung* 'dusk falling, the time around sunset', from *ǣfnian* 'approach evening', from *ǣfen* (see EVEN[2]).

evening class ▶ **noun** a class held in the evening, forming part of a course for adults.

eveninger /ˈiːv(ə)nɪŋə/ ▶ **noun** Indian informal an evening newspaper: *interviews in a Mumbai eveninger.*

evening prayer ▶ **noun** (usu. **evening prayers**) a formal act of worship held in the evening. ■ (in the Anglican Church) the service of evensong.

evening primrose ▶ **noun** a plant with pale yellow flowers that open in the evening and yielding seeds from which a medicinal oil is extracted. ● Genus *Oenothera*, family Onagraceae: numerous species.

evening star ▶ **noun** (**the evening star**) the planet Venus, seen shining in the western sky after sunset.

Evenki /eɪˈvɛnki/ ▶ **noun** (pl. **same** or **Evenkis**) **1** a member of an indigenous people living scattered through the wastes of northern Siberia. Also called TUNGUS.
2 [mass noun] the Tungusic language of the Evenki, which has about 15,000 speakers.
▶ **adjective** relating to the Evenki or their language.

even money ▶ **noun** [mass noun] (in betting) odds offering an equal chance of winning or losing, with the amount won being the same as the stake: *players bet on each throw for even money* | [as modifier] *Romany King swept past the even-money favourite Paco's Boy.* ■ [as modifier] (of a chance) equally likely to happen or not; fifty-fifty: *above those engines there was an even-money chance of being heard.*

evens ▶ **plural noun** Brit. another term for EVEN MONEY: *the colt was 4-6 favourite after opening* ***at evens.***

evensong ▶ **noun** (in the Christian Church) a service of evening prayers, psalms, and canticles, conducted according to a set form, especially that of the Anglican Church: *choral evensong.*
– ORIGIN Old English *ǣfensang*, originally applied to the pre-Reformation service of vespers (see EVEN[2], SONG).

even-steven (also **even-stevens**) ▶ **adjective & adverb** informal used in reference to fair and equal competition or distribution of resources: [as adv.] *I split the money with my wife even-steven.*
– ORIGIN mid 19th cent.: rhyming phrase, used as an intensive.

event ▶ **noun** a thing that happens or takes place, especially one of importance: *the momentous political events of the late 1980s.* ■ a planned public or social occasion: *staff have been holding a number of events to raise money for charity.* ■ each of several particular contests making up a sports competition: *he repeated the success in the four-lap, 600 cc event.* ■ Physics a single occurrence of a process, e.g. the ionization of one atom.
– PHRASES **in any event** (or **at all events**) whatever happens or may have happened: *in any event, I was not in a position to undertake such a task.* **in the event** as it turns (or turned) out: *he was sent on this important and, in the event, quite fruitless mission.* **in the event of ——** if —— happens: *this will reduce the chance of serious injury in the event of an accident.* **in the event that** if; should it happen that: *he planned to start a business, in the event that he lost his job.* **in that event** if that happens: *in that event, the US would incline toward a lifting of the arms embargo.*
– DERIVATIVES **eventless** adjective, **eventlessness** noun.
– ORIGIN late 16th cent.: from Latin *eventus*, from *evenire* 'result, happen', from *e-* (variant of *ex-*) 'out of' + *venire* 'come'.

even-tempered ▶ **adjective** not easily annoyed or made angry: *he was a gentle and even-tempered man.*

eventer ▶ **noun** Brit. a horse or rider that takes part in eventing.
– ORIGIN 1970s: from EVENT, in *three-day event* (see EVENTING).

eventful ▶ **adjective** marked by interesting or exciting events: *his long and eventful life.*
– DERIVATIVES **eventfully** adverb, **eventfulness** noun.

event horizon ▶ **noun** Astronomy a notional boundary around a black hole beyond which no light or other radiation can escape. ■ a point of no return: *we're nearing the event horizon of the presidential election.*

eventide ▶ **noun** archaic or literary the end of the day; evening: *the moonflower opens its white, trumpet-like flowers at eventide.*
– ORIGIN Old English *ǣfentīd* (see EVEN[2], TIDE).

eventing ▶ **noun** [mass noun] an equestrian sport in which competitors must take part in each of several contests, usually cross-country, dressage, and showjumping.
– ORIGIN 1960s: from EVENT, in *three-day event*, horse trials held on three consecutive days.

eventive /ɪˈvɛntɪv/ ▶ **adjective** Linguistics (of the subject or object of a sentence) denoting an event.

even-toed ungulate ▶ **noun** a hoofed mammal of an order which includes the ruminants, camels, pigs, and hippopotamuses. Mammals of this group have either two or four toes on each foot. Compare with ODD-TOED UNGULATE. ● Order Artiodactyla: three suborders. See also RUMINANT, TYLOPOD.

eventual /ɪˈvɛn(t)ʃʊəl/ ▶ **adjective** [attrib.] occurring or existing at the end of or as a result of a process or period of time: *it's impossible to predict the eventual outcome of the competition.*
– ORIGIN early 17th cent. (in the sense 'relating to an event or events'): from Latin *eventus* (see EVENT), on the pattern of *actual.*

eventuality ▶ **noun** (pl. **eventualities**) a possible event or outcome: *be prepared for all eventualities.*

eventually ▶ **adverb** [sentence adverb] in the end, especially after a long delay, dispute, or series of problems: *eventually, after midnight, I arrived at the hotel.*

eventuate /ɪˈvɛn(t)ʃʊeɪt, -tjʊ-/ ▶ **verb** [no obj.] formal occur as a result: *you never know what might eventuate.* ■ (**eventuate in**) lead to as a result: *circumstances that eventuate in crime.*
– DERIVATIVES **eventuation** noun.
– ORIGIN late 18th cent. (originally US): from EVENT, on the pattern of *actuate.*

ever ▶ **adverb 1** [usu. with negative or in questions] at any time: *nothing ever seemed to ruffle her | don't you ever regret giving up all that money?* ■ used in comparisons for emphasis: *they felt better than ever before | our biggest ever range.*
2 at all times; always: *ever the man of action, he was impatient with intellectuals | caravan holidays remain* ***as popular as ever*** *| they lived* ***happily ever after*** | [in combination] *he toyed with his ever-present cigar.*
3 [with comparative] increasingly; constantly: *having to borrow ever larger sums.*
4 used for emphasis in questions expressing astonishment or outrage: *who ever heard of a grown man being frightened of the dark? | why ever did you do it?*
– PHRASES **ever again** [usu. with negative] at any time in the future: *I never have to set foot inside a classroom ever again | I honestly cannot imagine ever again working in an office for someone else.* **ever and anon** archaic occasionally: *ever and anon the stillness is rent by the scream of a gibbon.* [from Shakespeare's *Love's Labour's Lost* (v. ii. 101).] **ever since** throughout the period since: *she had lived alone ever since her husband died.* **ever so/such** Brit. informal very; very much: *I am ever so grateful | she's ever such a pretty cat | thanks ever so.* **for ever** see FOREVER. **yours ever** (also **ever yours**) a formula used to end an informal letter, before the signature.
– ORIGIN Old English *ǣfre*, of unknown origin.

Everest, Mount /ˈɛvərɪst/ a mountain in the Himalayas, on the border between Nepal and Tibet. Rising to 8,848 m (29,028 ft), it is the highest mountain in the world; it was first climbed in 1953 by Sir Edmund Hillary and Tenzing Norgay. Tibetan name QOMOLUNGMA.
– ORIGIN named after Sir George *Everest* (1790–1866), British surveyor general of India.

Everglades a vast area of marshland and coastal mangrove in southern Florida, part of which is protected as a national park.

evergreen ▶ **adjective** relating to or denoting a plant that retains green leaves throughout the year: *the glossy laurel is fully hardy and evergreen | evergreen shrubs.* Often contrasted with DECIDUOUS. ■ having an enduring freshness, success, or popularity: *this symphony is an evergreen favourite.*
▶ **noun** a plant that retains green leaves throughout the year: *evergreens planted to cut off the east wind.* ■ a person or thing of enduring freshness, success, or popularity.

evergreen oak ▶ **noun** the holm oak.

Evergreen State informal name for the state of WASHINGTON[1].

everlasting ▶ **adjective** lasting forever or a very long time: *the damned would suffer everlasting torment | an everlasting reminder of this evening.*
▶ **noun 1** (**the everlasting**) literary eternity.
2 (also **everlasting flower**) a flower of the daisy family with a papery texture, retaining its shape and colour after being dried, especially a helichrysum. Also called IMMORTELLE.

– DERIVATIVES **everlastingly** adverb, **everlastingness** noun.

evermore ▶ adverb (chiefly used for rhetorical effect or in ecclesiastical contexts) always: *we pray that we may evermore dwell in him and he in us.*

evert /ɪˈvəːt/ ▶ verb [with obj.] Biology & Physiology turn (a structure or organ) outwards or inside out.
– DERIVATIVES **eversible** adjective, **eversion** noun.
– ORIGIN mid 16th cent. (in the sense 'upset, overthrow'): from Latin *evertere*, from *e-* (variant of *ex-*) 'out' + *vertere* 'to turn'. The current sense dates from the late 18th cent.

every ▶ determiner used before a singular noun to refer to all the individual members of a set without exception: *the hotel assures every guest of personal attention* | [with possessive determiner] *the children hung on his every word.* ■ used before an amount to indicate how often something happens: *tours are every thirty minutes* | *they had every third week off.* ■ (used for emphasis) all possible; the utmost: *you have every reason to be disappointed.*
– PHRASES **every bit as** (in comparisons) quite as: *the planning should be every bit as enjoyable as the event itself.* **every inch** see INCH[1]. **every last** (or **every single**) used to emphasize that every member of a group is included: *unbelievers, every last one of them.* **every man has his price** proverb everyone is open to bribery if the inducement offered is large enough. **every now and again** (or **now and then**) from time to time; occasionally. **every other** (or **every second**) each alternate in a series: *I train with weights every other day* | *the auctions are held every second week.* **every so often** from time to time; occasionally. **every time** without exception: *Maris Piper potatoes cook beautifully every time.* **every which way** informal in all directions: *my feet went every which way.* ■ by all available means: *since then he has tried every which way to avoid contact with his ex.*
– ORIGIN Old English *ǣfre ǣlc* (see EVER, EACH).

everybody ▶ pronoun every person: *everybody agrees with his views.*

everyday ▶ adjective [attrib.] happening or used every day; daily: *everyday chores like shopping and housework.* ■ commonplace: *everyday drugs like aspirin.*
▶ adverb (**every day**) each day; daily: *I get up at six every day.*

> **USAGE** The adjective **everyday**, meaning 'happening or used every day' or 'commonplace' (*everyday chores*), is written as one word, whereas the adverb meaning 'each day, daily' (*I get up at six every day*) is written as two.

Everyman (also **Everywoman**) ▶ noun [in sing.] an ordinary or typical human being: *at £1.80 a dozen, the oysters are Everyman's treat.*
– ORIGIN early 20th cent.: the name of the principal character in a 15th-cent. morality play.

everyone ▶ pronoun every person: *everyone needs time to unwind.*

every one ▶ pronoun each one.

> **USAGE** The pronoun **everyone**, meaning 'every person,' is spelled as one word: *everyone had a great time at the party*. The pronoun **every one**, meaning 'each one,' is spelled as two words: *he visited every one of those countries many times.*

everyplace ▶ adverb N. Amer. informal everywhere.

everything ▶ pronoun **1** all things: *they did everything together.* ■ all things of importance: *I lost everything in the crash.* ■ the most important thing or aspect: *money isn't everything.*
2 the current situation; life in general: *how's everything?* | *everything is going okay.*
– PHRASES **and everything** informal used to refer vaguely to other things associated with what has been mentioned: *you'll still get paid and everything.* **have everything** informal possess every attraction or advantage: *she was articulate, she was fun—it seemed to me she had everything.*

everywhere ▶ adverb in or to all places: *I've looked everywhere* | *everywhere she went she was feted.* ■ common or widely distributed: *sandwich bars are everywhere.*
▶ noun [mass noun] all places or directions: *everywhere was in darkness.*
– PHRASES **everywhere else** in all other places.
– ORIGIN Middle English: formerly also as two words.

Everywoman ▶ noun [in sing.] an ordinary or typical woman: *Lorna is rich and privileged, hardly Everywoman.*
– ORIGIN early 20th cent: on the pattern of EVERYMAN.

eve-teasing ▶ noun [mass noun] Indian the making of unwanted sexual remarks or advances by a man to a woman in a public place.
– DERIVATIVES **eve-teaser** noun.
– ORIGIN 1960s: from EVE + TEASE.

evict ▶ verb [with obj.] expel (someone) from a property, especially with the support of the law: *a single mother and her children have been evicted from their home.*
– DERIVATIVES **evictor** noun.
– ORIGIN late Middle English (in the sense 'recover property by legal process'): from Latin *evict-* 'overcome, defeated', from the verb *evincere*, from *e-* (variant of *ex-*) 'out' + *vincere* 'conquer'.

eviction ▶ noun [mass noun] the action of expelling someone from a property; expulsion: *the forced eviction of residents.*

evidence ▶ noun [mass noun] the available body of facts or information indicating whether a belief or proposition is true or valid: *the study finds little evidence of overt discrimination.* ■ Law information drawn from personal testimony, a document, or a material object, used to establish facts in a legal investigation or admissible as testimony in a law court: *without evidence, they can't bring a charge.* ■ signs or indications of something: *there was no obvious evidence of a break-in.*
▶ verb [with obj.] be or show evidence of: *the quality of the bracelet, as evidenced by the workmanship, is exceptional.*
– PHRASES **give evidence** Law give information and answer questions formally and in person in a law court or at an inquiry. **in evidence** noticeable; conspicuous: *his dramatic flair is still very much in evidence.* **turn King's** (or **Queen's** or US **state's**) **evidence** Law (of a criminal) give information in court against one's partners in order to receive a less severe punishment.
– ORIGIN Middle English: via Old French from Latin *evidentia*, from *evident-* 'obvious to the eye or mind' (see EVIDENT).

evident ▶ adjective clearly seen or understood; obvious: *she ate the biscuits with evident enjoyment.*
– ORIGIN late Middle English: from Old French, or from Latin *evidens*, *evident-* 'obvious to the eye or mind', from *e-* (variant of *ex-*) 'out' + *videre* 'to see'.

evidential /ˌɛvɪˈdɛnʃ(ə)l/ ▶ adjective formal of or providing evidence: *the evidential bases for her argument.*
– DERIVATIVES **evidentiality** noun, **evidentially** adverb.
– ORIGIN early 17th cent.: from medieval Latin *evidentialis*, from Latin *evidentia* (see EVIDENCE).

evidentiary /ˌɛvɪˈdɛnʃ(ə)ri/ ▶ adjective chiefly US Law another term for EVIDENTIAL.

evidently ▶ adverb **1** in a way that is clearly seen or understood; obviously: *a work so evidently laden with significance.*
2 [sentence adverb] it would seem that: *evidently Mrs Smith thought differently.* ■ used as an affirmative response: *'Were they old pals or something?' 'Evidently.'*

evil ▶ adjective **1** profoundly immoral and wicked: *his evil deeds* | *no man is so evil as to be beyond redemption.* ■ (of a force or spirit) embodying or associated with the forces of the devil. ■ harmful or tending to harm: *the evil effects of high taxes.*
2 (of a smell or sight) extremely unpleasant: *a bathroom with an ineradicably evil smell.*
▶ noun [mass noun] profound immorality and wickedness, especially when regarded as a supernatural force: *his struggle against the forces of evil.* ■ [count noun] a manifestation of this, especially in people's actions: *the evil that took place last Thursday.* ■ [count noun] something which is harmful or undesirable: *sexism, racism, and all other unpleasant social evils.*
– PHRASES **the evil eye** a gaze or stare superstitiously believed to cause harm. **the Evil One** archaic the Devil. **put off the evil day** (or **hour**) postpone something unpleasant for as long as possible. **speak evil of** slander: *it is a sin to speak evil of the king.*
– DERIVATIVES **evilly** adverb, **evilness** noun.
– ORIGIN Old English *yfel*, of Germanic origin; related to Dutch *euvel* and German *Übel*.

evildoer ▶ noun a person who commits profoundly immoral and wicked deeds.
– DERIVATIVES **evildoing** noun.

evince /ɪˈvɪns/ ▶ verb [with obj.] formal reveal the presence of (a quality or feeling); indicate: *the news stories evinced the usual mixture of sympathy and satisfaction.*
– ORIGIN late 16th cent. (in the sense 'prove by argument or evidence'): from Latin *evincere* 'overcome, defeat' (see EVICT).

eviscerate /ɪˈvɪsəreɪt/ ▶ verb [with obj.] formal disembowel (a person or animal): *the goat had been skinned and neatly eviscerated.* ■ deprive (something) of its essential content: *myriad little concessions that would eviscerate the project.* ■ Surgery remove the contents of (the eyeball).
– DERIVATIVES **evisceration** noun.
– ORIGIN late 16th cent.: from Latin *eviscerat-* 'disembowelled', from the verb *eviscerare*, from *e-* (variant of *ex-*) 'out' + *viscera* 'internal organs'.

eviternity /ˌiːvɪˈtəːnɪti/ ▶ noun [mass noun] literary eternal existence.
– DERIVATIVES **eviternal** adjective.
– ORIGIN late 16th cent.: from Latin *aeviternus* 'eternal' + -ITY.

evocative /ɪˈvɒkətɪv/ ▶ adjective bringing strong images, memories, or feelings to mind: *powerfully evocative lyrics* | *the building's cramped interiors are highly evocative of past centuries.*
– DERIVATIVES **evocatively** adverb, **evocativeness** noun.
– ORIGIN mid 17th cent.: from Latin *evocativus*, from *evocat-* 'called forth', from the verb *evocare* (see EVOKE).

evoke /ɪˈvəʊk/ ▶ verb [with obj.] **1** bring or recall (a feeling, memory, or image) to the conscious mind: *the sight evoked pleasant memories of his childhood.* ■ elicit (a response): *the Green Paper evoked critical reactions from various bodies.*
2 invoke (a spirit or deity).
– DERIVATIVES **evocation** noun, **evoker** noun.
– ORIGIN early 17th cent. (in sense 2): from Latin *evocare*, from *e-* (variant of *ex-*) 'out of, from' + *vocare* 'to call'.

evolute /ˈiːvəl(j)uːt, ˈɛv-/ ▶ noun (also **evolute curve**) Mathematics a curve which is the locus of the centres of curvature of another curve (its involute).
▶ adjective Zoology & Botany rolled outwards at the edges: *an evolute shell.*
– ORIGIN mid 18th cent.: from Latin *evolutus*, past participle of *evolvere* 'roll out' (see EVOLVE).

evolution /ˌiːvəˈluːʃ(ə)n, ˈɛv-/ ▶ noun [mass noun] **1** the process by which different kinds of living organism are believed to have developed from earlier forms during the history of the earth.

> The idea of organic evolution was proposed by some ancient Greek thinkers but was long rejected in Europe as contrary to the literal interpretation of the Bible. Lamarck proposed a theory that organisms became transformed by their efforts to respond to the demands of their environment. Lyell demonstrated that geological deposits were the cumulative product of slow processes over vast ages. This helped Darwin towards a theory of gradual evolution over a long period by the natural selection of those varieties of an organism slightly better adapted to the environment and hence more likely to produce descendants. Combined with the later discoveries of the cellular and molecular basis of genetics, Darwin's theory of evolution has, with some modification, become the dominant unifying concept of modern biology.

2 the gradual development of something: *the forms of written languages undergo constant evolution.*
3 Chemistry the giving off of a gaseous product, or of heat.
4 [count noun] a pattern of movements or manoeuvres: *flocks of waders often perform aerial evolutions.*
5 Mathematics, dated the extraction of a root from a given quantity.
– DERIVATIVES **evolutional** adjective, **evolutionally** adverb, **evolutionarily** adverb, **evolutionary** adjective, **evolutive** adjective.
– ORIGIN early 17th cent.: from Latin *evolutio(n-)* 'unrolling', from the verb *evolvere* (see EVOLVE). Early senses related to movement, first recorded in describing a 'wheeling' manoeuvre in the realignment of troops or ships. Current senses stem from a notion of 'opening out', giving rise to the sense 'development'.

evolutionist ▶ noun a person who believes in the theories of evolution and natural selection.
▶ adjective relating to the theories of evolution and natural selection: *an evolutionist model.*
– DERIVATIVES **evolutionism** noun.

evolve ▶ verb **1** develop gradually: [no obj.] *the company has evolved into a major chemical manufacturer* | *the Gothic style evolved from the Romanesque* | [with obj.] *each school must evolve its own way of working.* ■ (with reference to an organism or biological

E

feature) develop over successive generations as a result of natural selection: [no obj.] *the domestic dog is thought to have **evolved from** the wolf*.
2 [with obj.] Chemistry give off (gas or heat).
– DERIVATIVES **evolvable** adjective, **evolvement** noun.
– ORIGIN early 17th cent. (in the general sense 'make more complex, develop'): from Latin *evolvere*, from *e-* (variant of *ex-*) 'out of' + *volvere* 'to roll'.

Évros /ˈɛvrɒs/ Greek name for the MARITSA.

Évvoia /ˈɛvia/ Greek name for EUBOEA.

evzone /ˈɛvzəʊn/ ▶ noun a kilted soldier belonging to a select Greek infantry regiment.
– ORIGIN late 19th cent.: from modern Greek *euzōnos*, from Greek, 'dressed for exercise' (from *eu-* 'fine' + *zōnē* 'belt'), because of their uniform, which includes a fustanella.

E

e-waste ▶ noun [mass noun] discarded electronic appliances such as mobile phones, computers, and televisions.

Ewe /ˈeɪweɪ/ ▶ noun (pl. **same**) **1** a member of a West African people of Ghana, Togo, and Benin.
2 [mass noun] the language of the Ewe, belonging to the Kwa group. It has about 3 million speakers.
▶ adjective relating to or denoting the Ewe or their language.
– ORIGIN the name in Ewe.

ewe /juː/ ▶ noun a female sheep.
– ORIGIN Old English *eowu*, of Germanic origin; related to Dutch *ooi* and German *Aue*.

ewe neck ▶ noun a horse's neck of which the upper outline curves inwards instead of outwards.
– DERIVATIVES **ewe-necked** adjective.

ewer /ˈjuːə/ ▶ noun a large jug with a wide mouth, formerly used for carrying water.
– ORIGIN late Middle English: from Anglo-Norman French, variant of Old French *aiguiere*, based on Latin *aquarius* 'of water', from *aqua* 'water'.

eww /ˈɪəuː, ˈiːuː/ ▶ exclamation informal used to express disgust or distaste: *eww, how can you eat that?*
– ORIGIN 1970s: imitative.

ex[1] ▶ preposition **1** Brit. (of goods) sold direct from: *carpet tiles offered at a special price, ex stock*. ■ N. Amer. (of goods) without charges to the purchaser until removed from: *ex warehouse*.
2 Brit. not including: *the cost is £5,000 ex VAT*.
– ORIGIN mid 19th cent. (in sense 2): from Latin, 'out of'.

ex[2] ▶ noun informal a former husband, wife, or other partner in a relationship: *I don't want my ex to spoil what I have now*.
– ORIGIN early 19th cent.: independent usage of EX-[1].

Ex. ▶ abbreviation Exodus (in biblical references).

ex-[1] (also **e-**) ▶ prefix **1** out: *exclude* | *excite*.
2 upward: *extol*.
3 thoroughly: *excruciate*.
4 denoting removal or release: *excommunicate* | *exculpate*.
5 forming verbs which denote inducement of a state: *exasperate*.
6 forming nouns which denote a former state: *ex-husband* | *ex-convict*.
– ORIGIN from Latin *ex* 'out of'.

ex-[2] ▶ prefix out: *exodus* | *exorcism*.
– ORIGIN from Greek *ex* 'out of'.

exa- ▶ combining form (used in units of measurement) denoting a factor of 10^{18}: *exajoule*.
– ORIGIN from *(h)exa-* (see HEXA-), based on the supposed analogy of *tera-* and *tetra-*.

exabyte (abbrev.: **Eb** or **EB**) ▶ noun Computing a unit of information equal to one quintillion (10^{18}) bytes, or one billion gigabytes.

exacerbate /ɪgˈzasəbeɪt, ɛkˈsas-/ ▶ verb [with obj.] make (a problem, bad situation, or negative feeling) worse: *rising inflation was exacerbated by the collapse of oil prices*.
– DERIVATIVES **exacerbation** noun.
– ORIGIN mid 17th cent.: from Latin *exacerbat-* 'made harsh', from the verb *exacerbare*, from *ex-* (expressing inducement of a state) + *acerbus* 'harsh, bitter'. The noun *exacerbation* (late Middle English) originally meant 'provocation to anger'.

exact ▶ adjective not approximated in any way; precise: *the exact details were still being worked out*. ■ accurate or correct in all details: *an exact replica, two feet tall, was constructed*. ■ (of a person) accurate and careful about minor details: *she was an exact, clever manager*. ■ (of a subject of study) permitting precise measurements as a basis for rigorously testable theories: *psychomedicine isn't an exact science yet*.
▶ verb [with obj.] demand and obtain (something) from someone: *he exacted promises that another Watergate would never be allowed to happen*. ■ inflict (revenge) on someone.
– DERIVATIVES **exactitude** noun, **exactor** noun.
– ORIGIN late Middle English (as a verb): from Latin *exact-* 'completed, ascertained, enforced', from the verb *exigere*, from *ex-* 'thoroughly' + *agere* 'perform'. The adjective dates from the mid 16th cent. and reflects the Latin *exactus* 'precise'.

exacta /ɪgˈzaktə/ ▶ noun N. Amer. another term for PERFECTA.
– ORIGIN 1960s: from American Spanish *quiniela exacta* 'exact quinella'.

exacting ▶ adjective making great demands on one's skill, attention, or other resources: *the exacting standards laid down by the organic food industry*.
– DERIVATIVES **exactingly** adverb, **exactingness** noun.

exaction ▶ noun [mass noun] formal the action of demanding and obtaining something from someone, especially a payment: *he supervised the exaction of tolls at various ports*. ■ [count noun] a sum of money demanded in such a way.
– ORIGIN late Middle English: from Latin *exactio(n-)*, from *exigere* 'ascertain, perfect, enforce' (see EXACT).

exactly ▶ adverb **1** used to emphasize the accuracy of a figure or description: *they met in 1989 and got married exactly two years later*. ■ in exact terms; without vagueness: *what exactly are you looking for?*
2 used as a reply to confirm or agree with what has just been said: *'You mean that you're going to tell me the truth?' 'Exactly.'*
– PHRASES **not exactly** informal **1** not at all: *that too was not exactly convincing*. **2** not quite but close to being: *not exactly agitated, but disturbed*.

exactness ▶ noun [mass noun] the quality of being accurate or correct; precision: *it is impossible to calculate with mathematical exactness*.

exaggerate /ɪgˈzadʒəreɪt, ɛg-/ ▶ verb [with obj.] represent (something) as being larger, better, or worse than it really is: *she was apt to exaggerate any aches and pains* | [no obj.] *I couldn't sleep for three days—I'm not exaggerating*. ■ (as adj. **exaggerated**) enlarged or altered beyond normal proportions: *exaggerated features such as a massive head and beetling brows*.
– DERIVATIVES **exaggeratedly** adverb, **exaggerative** adjective, **exaggerator** noun.
– ORIGIN mid 16th cent.: from Latin *exaggerat-* 'heaped up', from the verb *exaggerare*, from *ex-* 'thoroughly' + *aggerare* 'heap up' (from *agger* 'heap'). The word originally meant 'pile up, accumulate', later 'intensify praise or blame', giving rise to current senses.

exaggeration ▶ noun a statement that represents something as better or worse than it really is: *it would be an exaggeration to say I had morning sickness, but I did feel queasy*. ■ [mass noun] the action of making such statements: *he was prone to exaggeration*.

exalt /ɪgˈzɔːlt, ɛg-/ ▶ verb [with obj.] **1** think or speak very highly of (someone or something): *the party will continue to exalt their hero*.
2 raise to a higher rank or position: *this naturally exalts the peasant above his brethren in the same rank of society*. ■ make noble in character; dignify: *romanticism liberated the imagination and exalted the emotions*.
– ORIGIN late Middle English: from Latin *exaltare*, from *ex-* 'out, upward' + *altus* 'high'.

exaltation ▶ noun [mass noun] **1** a feeling or state of extreme happiness: *she was in a frenzy of exaltation and terror*.
2 the action of elevating someone in rank or power: *the exaltation of Jesus to the Father's right hand*.
3 the action of praising someone or something highly: *the exaltation of the army as a place for brotherhood*.
– ORIGIN late Middle English (in the sense 'the action of raising high'): from late Latin *exaltatio(n-)*, from Latin *exaltare* 'raise aloft' (see EXALT).

exalté /ɪgˈzɔːlteɪ/ literary ▶ noun a person who is elated or impassioned.
▶ adjective inspiring or stimulating.
– ORIGIN mid 19th cent.: French, 'lifted up', past participle of *exalter*.

exalted ▶ adjective **1** (of a person or their rank or status) at a high or powerful level: *it had taken her years of infighting to reach her present exalted rank*.
2 of a noble, elevated, or lofty nature: *his exalted hopes of human progress*.
3 in a state of extreme happiness: *I felt exalted and newly alive*.
– DERIVATIVES **exaltedly** adverb, **exaltedness** noun.

exam ▶ noun **1** short for EXAMINATION (sense 2).
2 [with adj. or noun modifier] N. Amer. a medical test of a specified kind: *routine eye exams*.

examination ▶ noun **1** a detailed inspection or study: *an examination of marketing behaviour* | *a medical examination is conducted without delay*. ■ [mass noun] the action or process of conducting such an inspection or study: *the role of the planning system has come under increasing critical examination*.
2 a formal test of a person's knowledge or proficiency in a subject or skill: *he scraped through the examinations at the end of his first year*.
3 Law the formal questioning of a defendant or witness in court.
– ORIGIN late Middle English (also in the sense 'testing (one's conscience) by a standard'): via Old French from Latin *examinatio(n-)*, from *examinare* 'weigh, test' (see EXAMINE).

examination-in-chief ▶ noun [mass noun] Law the questioning of a witness by the party which has called that witness to give evidence, in support of the case being made. Compare with CROSS-EXAMINE.

examination paper ▶ noun a set of printed questions used as a test of proficiency or knowledge.

examine ▶ verb [with obj.] **1** inspect (someone or something) thoroughly in order to determine their nature or condition: *a doctor examined me and said I might need a caesarean* | *this forced us to examine every facet of our business*.
2 test the knowledge or proficiency of (someone) by requiring them to answer questions or perform tasks: *the colleges set standards by examining candidates*.
3 Law formally question (a defendant or witness) in court. Compare with CROSS-EXAMINE.
– DERIVATIVES **examinable** adjective, **examinee** noun.
– ORIGIN Middle English: from Old French *examiner*, from Latin *examinare* 'weigh, test', from *examen* 'examination'.

examiner ▶ noun **1** a person whose job is to inspect something; an inspector: *a police vehicle examiner*.
2 a person who sets and marks examinations to test people's knowledge or proficiency: *exams are marked by external examiners*.

example ▶ noun **1** a thing characteristic of its kind or illustrating a general rule: *advertising provides a good example of an industry where dreams have faded*. ■ a written problem or exercise designed to illustrate a rule.
2 a person or thing regarded in terms of their fitness to be imitated: *it is important that parents should **set an example*** | *he **followed** his brother's **example** and deserted his family*.
▶ verb (**be exampled**) be illustrated or exemplified: *the extent of Allied naval support is exampled by the navigational specialists provided*.
– PHRASES **for example** used to introduce something chosen as a typical case: *many, like Hilda, for example, come from very poor backgrounds*. **make an example of** punish as a warning or deterrent to others.
– ORIGIN late Middle English: from Old French, from Latin *exemplum*, from *eximere* 'take out', from *ex-* 'out' + *emere* 'take'. Compare with SAMPLE.

ex ante /ɛks ˈanti/ ▶ adjective & adverb based on forecasts rather than actual results: [as adj.] *an ex ante estimate*.
– ORIGIN modern Latin, from Latin *ex* 'from, out of' + *ante* 'before'.

exanthema /ɪkˈsanθɪmə, ˌɛksanˈθiːmə/ ▶ noun (pl. **exanthemata**) Medicine a skin rash accompanying a disease or fever.
– DERIVATIVES **exanthematic** adjective, **exanthematous** adjective.
– ORIGIN mid 17th cent.: via late Latin from Greek *exanthēma* 'eruption', from *ex-* 'out' + *antheein* 'to blossom' (from *anthos* 'flower').

exaptation /ˌɛksapˈteɪʃ(ə)n/ ▶ noun [mass noun] Biology the process by which features acquire functions for which they were not originally adapted or selected. ■ [count noun] a character or feature which evolved in this way.
– ORIGIN 1980s: from EX-[1] + *aptation* as in ADAPTATION.

exarch /ˈɛksɑːk/ ▶ noun **1** (in the Orthodox Church) a bishop lower in rank than a patriarch and having jurisdiction wider than the metropolitan of a diocese.

2 historical a governor of a distant province under the Byzantine emperors.
– ORIGIN late 16th cent.: via ecclesiastical Latin from Greek *exarkhos*, from *ex-* 'out of' + *arkhos* 'ruler'.

exarchate /ˈɛksɑːkeɪt/ ▶ **noun** historical a Byzantine province governed by an exarch.
– ORIGIN mid 16th cent.: from medieval Latin *exarchatus*, from ecclesiastical Latin *exarchus*, from Greek (see EXARCH).

exasperate /ɪɡˈzasp(ə)reɪt, ɛɡ-/ ▶ **verb** [with obj.] irritate intensely; infuriate: *this futile process exasperates prison officers.*
– DERIVATIVES **exasperatedly** adverb.
– ORIGIN mid 16th cent.: from Latin *exasperat-* 'irritated to anger', from the verb *exasperare* (based on *asper* 'rough').

exasperating /ɪɡˈzɑːsp(ə)reɪtɪŋ, ɛɡ-/ ▶ **adjective** intensely irritating; infuriating: *they suffered a number of exasperating setbacks.*
– DERIVATIVES **exasperatingly** adverb.

exasperation /ɪɡˌzɑːspəˈreɪʃ(ə)n, ɛɡ-/ ▶ **noun** [mass noun] a feeling of intense irritation or annoyance: *she rolled her eyes **in exasperation**.*

Excalibur /ɛksˈkalɪbə/ (in Arthurian legend) King Arthur's magic sword.

ex cathedra /ˌɛks kəˈθiːdrə/ ▶ **adverb & adjective** with the full authority of office (especially that of the Pope, implying infallibility as defined in Roman Catholic doctrine).
ORIGIN Latin, 'from the (teacher's) chair', from *ex* 'from' and *cathedra* 'seat' (from Greek *kathedra*).

excavate /ˈɛkskəveɪt/ ▶ **verb** [with obj.] **1** make (a hole or channel) by digging. ■ dig out material from (the ground). ■ extract (material) from the ground by digging: *a large amount of gravel would be excavated to form the channel.*
2 remove earth carefully from (an area) in order to find buried remains: *the site was excavated in 1975.* ■ reveal or extract (buried remains) in this way: *clothing and weapons were excavated from the burial site.*
– ORIGIN late 16th cent.: from Latin *excavat-* 'hollowed out', from the verb *excavare*, from *ex-* 'out' + *cavare* 'make or become hollow' (from *cavus* 'hollow').

excavation ▶ **noun** [mass noun] the action of excavating something, especially an archaeological site: *the methods of excavation have to be extremely rigorous.* ■ [count noun] a site that is being or has been excavated.

excavator ▶ **noun 1** a person who excavates an archaeological site.
2 a large machine for digging and moving earth.

exceed ▶ **verb** [with obj.] be greater in number or size than (a quantity, number, or other measurable thing): *production costs have exceeded £60,000.* ■ go beyond what is allowed or stipulated by (a set limit): *the Tribunal's decision clearly exceeds its powers under the statute.* ■ be better than; surpass: *economic growth exceeded expectations this year.*
– DERIVATIVES **exceedance** noun.
– ORIGIN late Middle English (in the sense 'go over a boundary or specified point'): from Old French *exceder*, from Latin *excedere*, from *ex-* 'out' + *cedere* 'go'.

exceeding archaic ▶ **adjective** very great: *she spoke warmly of his exceeding kindness.*
▶ **adverb** [as submodifier] extremely; exceedingly: *an ale of exceeding poor quality.*

exceedingly ▶ **adverb 1** [as submodifier] extremely: *the team played exceedingly well.*
2 archaic to a great extent: *the supply multiplied exceedingly.*

excel /ɪkˈsɛl, ɛk-/ ▶ **verb** (**excels**, **excelling**, **excelled**) [no obj.] be exceptionally good at or proficient in an activity or subject: *she **excelled at** landscape painting.* ■ (**excel oneself**) Brit. perform exceptionally well: *the keeper excelled himself to keep out an Elliott header.*
– ORIGIN late Middle English: from Latin *excellere*, from *ex-* 'out, beyond' + *celsus* 'lofty'.

excellence ▶ **noun** [mass noun] the quality of being outstanding or extremely good: *awards for excellence* | *a centre of academic excellence.* ■ [count noun] archaic an outstanding feature or quality.
– ORIGIN late Middle English: from Latin *excellentia*, from the verb *excellere* 'surpass' (see EXCEL).

excellency ▶ **noun** (pl. **excellencies**) **1** (**His**, **Your**, etc. **Excellency**) a title or form of address given to certain high officials of state, especially ambassadors, or of the Roman Catholic Church: *His Excellency the Indian Consul General.*
2 archaic an outstanding feature or quality.
– ORIGIN Middle English (in the sense 'excellence'): from Latin *excellentia*, from *excellere* 'surpass' (see EXCEL). Sense 1 dates from the mid 16th cent.

excellent ▶ **adjective** extremely good; outstanding: *the lorry was in excellent condition* | *their results are excellent.*
▶ **exclamation** used to indicate approval or pleasure: *'What a lovely idea! Excellent!'.*
– DERIVATIVES **excellently** adverb.
– ORIGIN late Middle English (in the general sense 'outstanding' in either a good or bad way): from Old French, from Latin *excellent-* 'being pre-eminent', from *excellere* (see EXCEL). The current appreciatory sense dates from the early 17th cent.

excelsior /ɛkˈsɛlsɪɔː/ ▶ **noun 1** used in the names of hotels and products to indicate superior quality: *they stayed at the Excelsior.*
2 [mass noun] N. Amer. softwood shavings used for packing fragile goods or stuffing furniture.
– ORIGIN late 18th cent. (as an exclamation): from Latin, comparative of *excelsus*, from *ex-* 'out, beyond' + *celsus* 'lofty'.

excentric /ɪkˈsɛntrɪk, ɛk-/ ▶ **adjective** chiefly Biology not placed centrally or arranged symmetrically about a centre: *a distinct excentric nucleus.*
– DERIVATIVES **excentrically** adverb.

except ▶ **preposition** not including; other than: *I was naked **except for** my socks* | *they work every day except Sunday.*
▶ **conjunction** used before a statement that forms an exception to one just made: *I didn't tell him anything, **except that** I needed the money* | *our berets were the same except mine was blue.* ■ archaic unless: *she never offered advice, except it were asked of her.*
▶ **verb** [with obj.] formal specify as excluded from a category or group: *five classes of advertisement are excepted from control.*
– ORIGIN late Middle English: from Latin *except-* 'taken out', from the verb *excipere*, from *ex-* 'out of' + *capere* 'take'.

excepted ▶ **adjective** [postpositive] excluded from the category or group specified: *most museums (the Getty excepted) have small acquisitions budgets.*

excepting ▶ **preposition** formal except for; apart from: *excepting a scratched door, the car was in good condition.*

exception ▶ **noun** a person or thing that is excluded from a general statement or does not follow a rule: *he always plays top tunes, and tonight was **no exception*** | *the administrator **made an exception** in the Colonel's case and waived the normal visiting hours.*
– PHRASES **the exception proves the rule** proverb the fact that some cases do not follow a rule proves that the rule applies in all other cases. **take exception to** object strongly to: *many viewers took great exception to the programme's content.* **with the exception of** except; not including. **without exception** with no one or nothing excluded.
– ORIGIN late Middle English: via Old French from Latin *exceptio(n-)*, from *excipere* 'take out' (see EXCEPT).

exceptionable ▶ **adjective** formal open to objection; causing disapproval or offence: *his drawings are almost the only exceptionable part of his work.*

exceptional ▶ **adjective** unusual; not typical: *late claims will only be accepted in exceptional circumstances.* ■ unusually good, outstanding: *a child of exceptional ability.*
▶ **noun** (usu. **exceptionals**) an item in a company's accounts arising from its normal activity but much larger or smaller than usual. Compare with EXTRAORDINARY.
– DERIVATIVES **exceptionality** noun.

exceptionalism ▶ **noun** [mass noun] the belief that something is exceptional, especially the theory that the peaceful capitalism of the US constitutes an exception to the general economic laws governing national historical development.

exceptionally ▶ **adverb** to a greater degree than normal; unusually: [as submodifier] *the weather was exceptionally mild for the time of the year.* ■ only in unusual circumstances: *the court allows half an hour in most cases, one hour exceptionally for a very important case.*

excerpt ▶ **noun** /ˈɛksəːpt/ a short extract from a film, broadcast, or piece of music or writing.
▶ **verb** /ɪkˈsəːpt, ɛk-/ [with obj.] take (a short extract) from a text: *the notes are excerpted from his forthcoming biography.* ■ take an excerpt or excerpts from (a text): *a book excerpted in this week's Time magazine.*
– DERIVATIVES **excerption** noun.
– ORIGIN mid 16th cent. (as a verb): from Latin *excerpt-* 'plucked out', from the verb *excerpere*, from *ex-* 'out of' + *carpere* 'to pluck'.

excess /ɪkˈsɛs, ɛk-, ˈɛksɛs/ ▶ **noun 1** an amount of something that is more than necessary, permitted, or desirable: *are you suffering from **an excess of** stress in your life?* ■ the amount by which one quantity or number exceeds another. ■ [mass noun] the action of exceeding a permitted or acceptable limit: *there is no issue as to excess of jurisdiction.*
2 [mass noun] lack of moderation, especially in eating or drinking: *bouts of alcoholic excess.* ■ (**excesses**) outrageous or immoderate behaviour: *the worst excesses of the French Revolution.*
3 Brit. a part of an insurance claim to be paid by the insured.
▶ **adjective** [attrib.] usually /ˈɛksɛs/ **1** exceeding a prescribed or desirable amount: *trim any excess fat off the meat.*
2 Brit. required as extra payment: *the full excess fare had to be paid.*
– PHRASES **in** (or **to**) **excess** exceeding the proper amount or degree: *she insisted that he did not drink to excess.* **in excess of** more than: *a top speed in excess of 20 knots.*
– ORIGIN late Middle English: via Old French from Latin *excessus*, from *excedere* 'go out, surpass' (see EXCEED).

excess baggage ▶ **noun** [mass noun] luggage weighing more than the limit allowed on an aircraft and liable to an extra charge.

excessive ▶ **adjective** more than is necessary, normal, or desirable; immoderate: *he was drinking excessive amounts of brandy.*
– DERIVATIVES **excessiveness** noun.
– ORIGIN late Middle English: from Old French *excessif, -ive*, from medieval Latin *excessivus*, from Latin *excedere* 'surpass' (see EXCEED).

excessively ▶ **adverb** to a greater degree or in greater amounts than is necessary, normal, or desirable; inordinately: *they don't drink excessively* | [as submodifier] *excessively high taxes.*

exchange ▶ **noun 1** an act of giving one thing and receiving another (especially of the same kind) in return: *negotiations should lead to an **exchange of** land **for** peace* | [mass noun] *opportunities for the exchange of information.* ■ a visit or visits in which two people or groups from different countries stay with each other or do each other's jobs: [as modifier] *an exchange visit to Germany.*
2 [mass noun] the changing of money to its equivalent in the currency of another country. ■ [count noun] a system or market in which commercial transactions involving currency, shares, etc. can be carried out within or between countries. ■ [count noun] a building or institution used for the trading of a particular commodity or commodities: *the old Corn Exchange.*
3 a short conversation or an argument: *there was a heated exchange.*
4 short for TELEPHONE EXCHANGE.
5 Chess a move or short sequence of moves in which both players capture material of comparable value, or particularly (**the exchange**) in which one captures a rook in return for a knight or bishop.
▶ **verb** [with obj.] give something and receive something of the same kind in return: *we exchanged addresses* | *he **exchanged** a concerned glance **with** Stephen.* ■ give or receive one thing in place of another: *we regret that tickets cannot be exchanged* | *he **exchanges** his cigarette ends **for** food.* ■ [no obj.] exchange contracts.
– PHRASES **exchange contracts** Brit. (of a buyer) sign a legal contract with the vendor of a property or piece of land, making the purchase legally binding and enforceable. **in exchange** as a thing exchanged: *he carried bags of groceries in exchange for a nickel.*
– DERIVATIVES **exchangeability** noun, **exchangeable** adjective, **exchanger** noun.
– ORIGIN late Middle English: from Old French *eschange* (noun), *eschangier* (verb), based on *changer* (see CHANGE). The spelling was influenced by Latin *ex-* 'out, utterly' (see EX-[1]).

exchange control ▶ **noun** a governmental restriction on the movement of currency between countries.

exchange rate (also **rate of exchange**) ▶ **noun** the value of one currency for the purpose of conversion to another.

Exchange Rate Mechanism (abbrev.: **ERM**) an arrangement within the European Monetary System that allows the value of participating currencies to fluctuate to a defined degree in relation to each other so as to control exchange rates. Each currency

E

is given a rate of exchange with the euro, from which it is allowed to fluctuate by no more than a specified amount; if it moves beyond this the government in question must alter its economic policies or reset the currency's rate with the euro.

exchange transfusion ▶ **noun** [mass noun] Medicine the simultaneous removal of a patient's blood and replacement by donated blood, used in treating serious conditions such as haemolytic disease of the newborn.

exchequer /ɪks'tʃɛkə, ɛks-/ ▶ **noun** a royal or national treasury. ■ (**Exchequer**) Brit. the account at the Bank of England in which is held the Consolidated Fund, into which tax receipts and other public monies are paid. ■ (**Exchequer**) Brit. historical the former government office responsible for collecting revenue and making payments on behalf of the sovereign, auditing official accounts, and trying legal cases relating to revenue.
– ORIGIN Middle English: from Old French *eschequier*, from medieval Latin *scaccarium* 'chessboard', from *scaccus* (see **CHECK**[1]). The original sense was 'chessboard'. Current senses derive from the Norman department of state dealing with the royal revenues, named *Exchequer* from the chequered tablecloth on which accounts were kept by means of counters. The spelling was influenced by Latin *ex-* 'out' (see **EX**[1]). Compare with **CHEQUER**.

E

excimer /'ɛksɪmə/ ▶ **noun** Chemistry an unstable excited molecule which is formed by the combination of two smaller molecules and rapidly dissociates with emission of radiation, utilized in some kinds of laser.
– ORIGIN 1960s: blend of **EXCITED** and **DIMER**.

excipient /ɛk'sɪpɪənt/ ▶ **noun** an inactive substance that serves as the vehicle or medium for a drug or other active substance.
– ORIGIN early 18th cent. (as an adjective in the sense 'that takes exception'): from Latin *excipient-* 'taking out', from the verb *excipere*.

excise[1] /'ɛksʌɪz/ ▶ **noun** [mass noun] [usu. as modifier] a tax levied on certain goods and commodities produced or sold within a country and on licences granted for certain activities: *the rate of excise duty on spirits*.
▶ **verb** [with obj.] (usu. as adj. **excised**) charge excise on (goods): *excised goods*.
– ORIGIN late 15th cent. (in the general sense 'a tax or toll'): from Middle Dutch *excijs*, *accijs*, perhaps based on Latin *accensare* 'to tax', from *ad-* 'to' + *census* 'tax' (see **CENSUS**).

excise[2] /ɪk'sʌɪz, ɛk-/ ▶ **verb** [with obj.] cut out surgically: *the precision with which surgeons can excise brain tumours* | (as adj. **excised**) *excised tissue*. ■ remove (a section) from a text or piece of music: *the clauses were excised from the treaty*.
– ORIGIN late 16th cent. (in the sense 'notch or hollow out'): from Latin *excis-* 'cut out', from the verb *excidere*, from *ex-* 'out of' + *caedere* 'to cut'.

exciseman ▶ **noun** (pl. **excisemen**) Brit. historical an official responsible for collecting excise duty and preventing infringement of the excise laws (especially by smuggling).

excision /ɪk'sɪʒ(ə)n, ɛk-/ ▶ **noun** [mass noun] the action of excising something: *the excision of the carcinoma*.
– DERIVATIVES **excisional** adjective.

excitable ▶ **adjective** **1** responding too readily to something new or stimulating; easily excited: *a rather excitable young man*.
2 (of tissue or a cell) responsive to stimulation.
– DERIVATIVES **excitability** noun, **excitably** adverb.

excitant /'ɛksɪt(ə)nt, ɪk'sʌɪt(ə)nt, ɛk-/ ▶ **noun** Biology a substance which elicits an active physiological or behavioural response.

excitation /,ɛksɪ'teɪʃ(ə)n/ ▶ **noun** [mass noun] **1** technical the application of energy to something, in particular: ■ Physics the process in which an atom or other particle adopts a higher energy state when energy is supplied: *thermal excitation*. ■ Physiology the state of enhanced activity of a cell, organism, or tissue which results from its stimulation. ■ the application of current to the winding of an electromagnet to produce a magnetic field. ■ the application of a signal voltage to the control electrode of an electron tube or the base of a transistor.
2 the action of exciting or the state of being excited; excitement: *a state of sexual excitation*.
– ORIGIN late Middle English: from Old French, from late Latin *excitatio(n-)*, from *excitare* 'rouse, call forth' (see **EXCITE**).

excitative /ɪk'sʌɪtətɪv/ ▶ **adjective** rare causing excitation.

excitatory /ɪk'sʌɪtət(ə)ri, ɛk-/ ▶ **adjective** chiefly Physiology characterized by, causing, or constituting excitation: *the excitatory action of these impulses*.

excite ▶ **verb** [with obj.] **1** cause (someone) to feel very enthusiastic and eager: *flying still excites me* | *Gould was excited by these discoveries*. ■ arouse (someone) sexually: *his Mediterranean vibrancy excited and stimulated her*.
2 give rise to (a feeling or reaction): *the ability to excite interest in others*.
3 produce a state of increased energy or activity in (a physical or biological system): *the energy of an electron is sufficient to excite the atom*.
– ORIGIN Middle English (in the sense 'incite someone to do something'): from Old French *exciter* or Latin *excitare*, frequentative of *exciere* 'call out or forth'. Sense 1 dates from the mid 19th cent.

excited ▶ **adjective** **1** very enthusiastic and eager: *they were excited about the prospect* | *the excited children*. ■ sexually aroused.
2 Physics of or in an energy state higher than the normal or ground state.
– DERIVATIVES **excitedly** adverb.

excitement ▶ **noun** [mass noun] a feeling of great enthusiasm and eagerness: *her cheeks were flushed with excitement*. ■ [count noun] something that arouses such a feeling: *the excitements of the previous night*. ■ sexual arousal.

exciter ▶ **noun** a thing that produces excitation, in particular a device that provides a magnetizing current for the electromagnets in a motor or generator.

exciting ▶ **adjective** causing great enthusiasm and eagerness: *one of the most exciting matches I've ever seen*.
– DERIVATIVES **excitingly** adverb, **excitingness** noun.

exciton /'ɛksɪtɒn, ɪk'sʌɪ-, ɛk-/ ▶ **noun** Physics a mobile concentration of energy in a crystal formed by an excited electron and an associated hole.
– ORIGIN 1930s: from **EXCITATION** + **-ON**.

exclaim ▶ **verb** [no obj.] cry out suddenly in surprise, strong emotion, or pain: [with direct speech] *'Well I never,' she exclaimed* | *she looked in the mirror, exclaiming in dismay at her appearance*.
– ORIGIN late 16th cent.: from French *exclamer* or Latin *exclamare*, from *ex-* 'out' + *clamare* 'to shout'.

exclamation ▶ **noun** a sudden cry or remark expressing surprise, strong emotion, or pain: *an exclamation of amazement*.
– ORIGIN late Middle English: from Latin *exclamatio(n-)*, from *exclamare* 'shout out' (see **EXCLAIM**).

exclamation mark (N. Amer. **exclamation point**) ▶ **noun** a punctuation mark (!) indicating an exclamation.

exclamatory /ɪk'sklamət(ə)ri, ɛk-/ ▶ **adjective** (of a cry or remark) expressing surprise, strong emotion, or pain.

exclave /'ɛkskleɪv/ ▶ **noun** a portion of territory of one state completely surrounded by territory of another or others, as viewed by the home territory. Compare with **ENCLAVE**.
– ORIGIN late 19th cent.: from **EX-**[1] 'out' + a shortened form of **ENCLAVE**.

exclosure /ɪk'skləʊʒə, ɛk-/ ▶ **noun** Forestry an area from which unwanted animals are excluded.
– ORIGIN 1920s: from **EX-**[1] 'out' + **CLOSURE**, on the pattern of *enclosure*.

exclude ▶ **verb** [with obj.] **1** deny (someone) access to a place, group, or privilege: *the public were excluded from the board meeting*. ■ keep (something) out of a place: *apply flux to exclude oxygen*. ■ expel (a pupil) from school.
2 remove from consideration: *one cannot exclude the possibility of a fall in house prices*. ■ prevent the occurrence of: *clauses seeking to exclude liability for loss or damage*.
– PHRASES **law** (or **principle**) **of the excluded middle** Logic the principle that one (and one only) of two contradictory propositions must be true.
– DERIVATIVES **excludable** adjective, **excluder** noun.
– ORIGIN late Middle English: from Latin *excludere*, from *ex-* 'out' + *claudere* 'to shut'.

excluding ▶ **preposition** not taking someone or something into account; except: *the holiday cost £180, excluding accommodation*.

exclusion ▶ **noun** [mass noun] the process of excluding or the state of being excluded: *he had a hand in my exclusion from the committee*. ■ [count noun] an item or eventuality specifically not covered by an insurance policy or other contract: *exclusions can be added to your policy*.
– PHRASES **to the exclusion of** so as to exclude something specified: *don't revise a few topics to the exclusion of all others*.
– DERIVATIVES **exclusionary** adjective.
– ORIGIN late Middle English: from Latin *exclusio(n-)*, from *excludere* 'shut out' (see **EXCLUDE**).

exclusionary rule ▶ **noun** US Law a law that prohibits the use of illegally obtained evidence in a criminal trial.

exclusion clause ▶ **noun** a contractual provision disclaiming liability for a particular eventuality.

exclusionist ▶ **adjective** acting to bar someone or something from a place, group, or privilege: *an exclusionist foreign policy*.
▶ **noun** a person favouring the exclusion of someone or something from a place, group, or privilege.

exclusion order ▶ **noun** Brit. an official order excluding a person from a particular place, especially to prevent a crime being committed.

exclusion principle ▶ **noun** another term for **PAULI EXCLUSION PRINCIPLE**.

exclusion zone ▶ **noun** an area into which entry is forbidden, especially by ships or aircraft of particular nationalities.

exclusive ▶ **adjective** **1** excluding or not admitting other things: *an exclusive focus on success and making money* | *the list is not exclusive*. ■ unable to exist or be true if something else exists or is true: *mutually exclusive options*. ■ (of terms) excluding all but what is specified.
2 restricted to the person, group, or area concerned: *the couple had exclusive possession of the flat* | *the problem isn't exclusive to Dublin*. ■ (of an item or story) not published or broadcast elsewhere: *an exclusive interview*.
3 catering for or available to only a few, select customers; high class and expensive: *one of Britain's most exclusive clubs*.
4 (**exclusive of**) not including: *prices are exclusive of VAT*.
▶ **noun** an item or story published or broadcast by only one source.
– DERIVATIVES **exclusiveness** noun, **exclusivity** noun.
– ORIGIN late 15th cent. (as a noun denoting something that excludes): from medieval Latin *exclusivus*, from Latin *excludere* 'shut out' (see **EXCLUDE**).

Exclusive Brethren ▶ **plural noun** the more rigorous of two principal divisions of the Plymouth Brethren (the other is the Open Brethren). The Exclusive Brethren greatly restrict their contact with outsiders and modern technology.

exclusive economic zone ▶ **noun** an area of coastal water and seabed within a certain distance of a country's coastline, to which the country claims exclusive rights for fishing, drilling, and other economic activities.

exclusively ▶ **adverb** to the exclusion of others; only: *paints produced exclusively for independent retailers* | [as submodifier] *exclusively female concerns*. ■ as the only source: *I can exclusively reveal that Gail shares a birthday with Rod Stewart*.

exclusive OR ▶ **noun** Electronics a Boolean operator working on two variables that has the value one if one but not both of the variables is one. Also called **XOR**. ■ (also **exclusive OR gate**) a circuit which produces an output signal when a signal is received through one and only one of its two inputs.

exclusivism ▶ **noun** [mass noun] the action or policy of excluding a person or group from a place, group, or privilege.
– DERIVATIVES **exclusivist** adjective & noun.

excogitate /ɪks'kɒdʒɪteɪt, ɛks-/ ▶ **verb** [with obj.] formal think out, plan, or devise: *all the rubrics, forms, and functions remained to be excogitated*.
– DERIVATIVES **excogitation** noun.
– ORIGIN early 16th cent.: from Latin *excogitat-* 'found by process of thought', from the verb *excogitare*, from *ex-* 'out' + *cogitare* 'think'.

excommunicant /,ɛkskə'mju:nɪk(ə)nt/ ▶ **noun** an excommunicated person.
– ORIGIN late 16th cent.: based on ecclesiastical Latin *excommunicare* (see **EXCOMMUNICATE**), with irregular use of the suffix **-ANT**.

excommunicate ▶ **verb** /,ɛkskə'mju:nɪkeɪt/ [with obj.] officially exclude (someone) from participation in the sacraments and services of the Christian Church.
▶ **adjective** /,ɛkskə'mju:nɪkət/ excommunicated.
▶ **noun** /,ɛkskə'mju:nɪkət/ an excommunicated person.

– DERIVATIVES **excommunication** noun, **excommunicatory** adjective.
– ORIGIN late Middle English: from ecclesiastical Latin *excommunicat-* 'excluded from communication with the faithful', from the verb *excommunicare*, from *ex-* 'out' + Latin *communis* 'common to all', on the pattern of Latin *communicare* (see COMMUNICATE).

ex-con ▶ noun informal an ex-convict.
– ORIGIN early 20th cent.: abbreviation.

excoriate /ɪkˈskɔːrɪeɪt, ɛks-/ ▶ verb [with obj.] **1** Medicine damage or remove part of the surface of (the skin).
2 formal criticize (someone) severely: *he excoriated the government for censorship.*
– DERIVATIVES **excoriation** noun.
– ORIGIN late Middle English: from Latin *excoriat-* 'skinned', from the verb *excoriare*, from *ex-* 'out, from' + *corium* 'skin, hide'.

excrement /ˈɛkskrɪm(ə)nt/ ▶ noun [mass noun] waste matter discharged from the bowels; faeces.
– DERIVATIVES **excremental** /ˌɛkskrɪˈmɛnt(ə)l/ adjective.
– ORIGIN mid 16th cent.: from French *excrément* or Latin *excrementum*, from *excernere* 'to sift out' (see EXCRETE).

excrescence /ɪkˈskrɛs(ə)ns, ɛks-/ ▶ noun a distinct outgrowth on a body or plant, resulting from disease or abnormality. ■ an unattractive or superfluous object or feature: *the building is a sixties excrescence foisted on an otherwise flawless street.*
– ORIGIN late Middle English: from Latin *excrescentia*, from *excrescere* 'grow out', from *ex-* 'out' + *crescere* 'grow'.

excrescent /ɪkˈskrɛs(ə)nt, ɛks-/ ▶ adjective **1** forming or constituting an excrescence.
2 (of a speech sound) added without etymological justification (e.g. the *-t* at the end of the surname *Bryant*).

excreta /ɪkˈskriːtə, ɛk-/ ▶ noun [treated as sing. or pl.] waste matter discharged from the body, especially faeces and urine.
– ORIGIN mid 19th cent.: from Latin, 'things sifted out', neuter plural of *excretus*, past participle of *excernere* (see EXCRETE).

excrete /ɪkˈskriːt, ɛk-/ ▶ verb [with obj.] (of a living organism or cell) separate and expel as waste (a substance, especially a product of metabolism): *excess bicarbonate is excreted by the kidney.*
– DERIVATIVES **excreter** noun, **excretive** adjective.
– ORIGIN early 17th cent.: from Latin *excret-* 'sifted out', from the verb *excernere*, from *ex-* 'out' + *cernere* 'sift'.

excretion ▶ noun [mass noun] (in living organisms and cells) the process of eliminating or expelling waste matter. ■ [count noun] a product of this process: *bodily excretions.*
– ORIGIN early 17th cent.: from French *excrétion* or Latin *excretio(n-)*, from *excernere* 'sift out' (see EXCRETE).

excretory ▶ adjective relating to or concerned with excretion: *the excretory organs.*

excruciate /ɪkˈskruːʃɪeɪt, ɛk-/ ▶ verb [with obj.] rare torment (someone) physically or mentally: *I stand back, excruciated by the possibility.*
– DERIVATIVES **excruciation** noun.
– ORIGIN late 16th cent.: from Latin *excruciat-* 'tormented', from the verb *excruciare* (based on *crux, cruc-* 'a cross').

excruciating ▶ adjective intensely painful: *excruciating back pain.* ■ very embarrassing, awkward, or tedious: *he explained the procedure in excruciating detail.*
– DERIVATIVES **excruciatingly** adverb [as submodifier] *the sting was excruciatingly painful.*

exculpate /ˈɛkskʌlpeɪt/ ▶ verb [with obj.] formal show or declare that (someone) is not guilty of wrongdoing: *the article exculpated the mayor.*
– DERIVATIVES **exculpation** noun, **exculpatory** adjective.
– ORIGIN mid 17th cent.: from medieval Latin *exculpat-* 'freed from blame', from the verb *exculpare*, from *ex-* 'out, from' + Latin *culpa* 'blame'.

excurrent ▶ adjective chiefly Zoology (of a vessel or opening) conveying fluid outwards. The opposite of INCURRENT.
– ORIGIN early 17th cent.: from Latin *excurrent-* 'running out', from the verb *excurrere*.

excursion ▶ noun **1** a short journey or trip, especially one taken as a leisure activity: *an excursion to London Zoo.*
2 technical a movement of something along a path or through an angle.
3 a deviation from a regular activity or course: *the firm's disastrous* **excursion into** *the US electrical market.*
– DERIVATIVES **excursionist** noun.
– ORIGIN late 16th cent. (in the sense 'act of running out', also 'sortie' in the phrase *alarums and excursions* (see ALARUM)): from Latin *excursio(n-)*, from the verb *excurrere* 'run out', from *ex-* 'out' + *currere* 'to run'.

excursive ▶ adjective formal tending to deviate from a course or activity; digressive.
– ORIGIN late 17th cent.: from Latin *excurs-* 'digressed, run out' (from the verb *excurrere*) + -IVE, perhaps influenced by *discursive*.

excursus /ɪkˈskəːsəs, ɛk-/ ▶ noun (pl. **same** or **excursuses**) a detailed discussion of a particular point in a book, usually in an appendix. ■ a digression in a written text.
– ORIGIN early 19th cent.: from Latin, 'excursion', from *excurrere* 'run out'.

excusable /ɪkˈsjuːzəb(ə)l, ɛk-/ ▶ adjective able to be justified or forgiven; forgivable: *the error is excusable.*
– DERIVATIVES **excusably** adverb.

excusal ▶ noun [mass noun] the action or fact of excusing or being excused, typically from an official duty or requirement: *if any members of the jury felt unable to serve that long, they would be considered for excusal.*

excuse ▶ verb /ɪkˈskjuːz, ɛk-/ [with obj.] **1** seek to lessen the blame attaching to (a fault or offence); try to justify: *he did nothing to hide or excuse Jacob's cruelty.* ■ forgive (someone) for a fault or offence: *you must excuse my brother | he* **could be excused for** *feeling that he was born at the wrong time.* ■ overlook or make allowances for: *sit down—excuse the mess.* ■ (of a fact) serve to mitigate (a person or act): *his ability excuses most of his faults.*
2 release (someone) from a duty or requirement: *it will not be possible to* **excuse** *you* **from** *attendance |* [with two objs] *may I be excused hockey?* ■ (used in polite formulas) allow (someone) to leave a room or gathering: *and now, if you'll excuse us, duty calls.* ■ (**excuse oneself**) say politely that one is leaving. ■ (**be excused**) (used by school pupils) be allowed to leave the room, especially to go to the toilet.
▶ noun /ɪkˈskjuːs, ɛk-/ **1** a reason or explanation given to justify a fault or offence: *there can be* **no excuse for** *any further delay | the excuse that half the team failed to turn up.* ■ a reason put forward to conceal the real reason for an action; a pretext: *as an excuse to get out of the house she went to post a letter.* ■ US a note written by a doctor or parent excusing a pupil from school.
2 (**an excuse for**) informal a poor or inadequate example of: *that pathetic excuse for a man!*
– PHRASES **excuse me** used as a polite apology in various contexts, such as when attempting to get someone's attention, asking someone to move so that one may pass, or interrupting a speaker. ■ N. Amer. used to ask someone to repeat what they have just said. **make one's excuses** say politely that one is leaving or cannot be present.
– DERIVATIVES **excusatory** adjective.
– ORIGIN Middle English: from Old French *escuser* (verb), from Latin *excusare* 'to free from blame', from *ex-* 'out' + *causa* 'accusation, cause'.

excuse-me ▶ noun informal a social dance in which participants may interrupt other pairs in order to change partners.

ex-directory ▶ adjective Brit. (of a person or telephone number) not listed in a telephone directory or available through directory enquiries, at the wish of the subscriber.

ex div. ▶ abbreviation ex dividend.

ex dividend ▶ adjective & adverb (of stocks or shares) not including the next dividend.

exeat /ˈɛksɪat/ ▶ noun Brit. a permission from a college, boarding school, or other institution for temporary absence.
– ORIGIN early 18th cent.: from Latin, 'let him or her go out', third person singular present subjunctive of *exire* (see EXIT).

exec /ɪɡˈzɛk, ɛɡ-/ ▶ noun informal an executive: *top Hollywood execs.*
– ORIGIN late 19th cent.: abbreviation.

execrable /ˈɛksɪkrəb(ə)l/ ▶ adjective extremely bad or unpleasant: *execrable cheap wine.*
– DERIVATIVES **execrably** adverb.
– ORIGIN late Middle English (in the sense 'expressing or involving a curse'): via Old French from Latin *execrabilis*, from *exsecrari* 'to curse' (see EXECRATE).

execrate /ˈɛksɪkreɪt/ ▶ verb **1** [with obj.] feel or express great loathing for: *they were execrated as dangerous and corrupt.*
2 [no obj.] archaic curse; swear.
– DERIVATIVES **execration** noun.
– ORIGIN mid 16th cent.: from Latin *exsecrat-* 'cursed', from the verb *exsecrari*, based on *sacrare* 'dedicate' (from *sacer* 'sacred').

executable /ɪɡˈzɛkjʊtəb(ə)l, ɪɡ-/ Computing ▶ adjective (of a file or program) able to be run by a computer.
▶ noun an executable file or program.

executant /ɪɡˈzɛkjʊt(ə)nt, ɛɡ-/ formal ▶ noun a person who puts something into effect: *executants of the royal will.* ■ an artist or musician.
▶ adjective relating to artistic creation or the performance of music: *music is both an art and an executant skill.*
– ORIGIN mid 19th cent.: from French *exécutant* 'carrying out', present participle of *exécuter* (see EXECUTE).

execute /ˈɛksɪkjuːt/ ▶ verb [with obj.] **1** put (a plan, order, or course of action) into effect: *the corporation executed a series of financial deals.* ■ produce (a work of art). ■ perform (a skilful action or manoeuvre): *they had to execute their dance steps with the greatest precision.* ■ Law make (a legal instrument) valid by signing or sealing it. ■ Law carry out (a judicial sentence, the terms of a will, or other order): *police executed a search warrant.* ■ Computing carry out an instruction or program.
2 carry out a sentence of death on (a legally condemned person): *he was convicted of treason and executed.* ■ kill (someone) as a political act.
– ORIGIN late Middle English: from Old French *executer*, from medieval Latin *executare*, from Latin *exsequi* 'follow up, punish', from *ex-* 'out' + *sequi* 'follow'.

execution ▶ noun [mass noun] **1** the carrying out of a plan, order, or course of action: *he was fascinated by the entire operation and its execution.* ■ the technique or style with which an artistic work is produced or carried out: *the film is entirely professional in its execution.* ■ Law the putting into effect of a legal instrument or order. ■ Law seizure of the property or person of a debtor in default of payment. ■ Computing the performance of an instruction or program.
2 the carrying out of a sentence of death on a condemned person: *the execution of juveniles is prohibited by international law |* [count noun] *there were mass arrests and executions.* ■ the killing of someone as a political act.

executioner ▶ noun an official who carries out a sentence of death on a condemned person.

executive /ɪɡˈzɛkjʊtɪv, ɛɡ-/ ▶ adjective [attrib.] relating to or having the power to put plans or actions into effect: *an executive chairman | executive authority.* ■ denoting or relating to the part of a political administration with responsibility for putting into effect laws drawn up by the legislature: *the executive branch of government.* Often contrasted with LEGISLATIVE.
▶ noun **1** a person with senior managerial responsibility in a business. ■ [as modifier] suitable for a senior business executive: *an executive house.* ■ an executive committee or other body within an organization: *the union executive.*
2 (**the executive**) the branch of a government responsible for putting decisions or laws into effect.
– DERIVATIVES **executively** adverb.
– ORIGIN late Middle English: from medieval Latin *executivus*, from *exsequi* (see EXECUTE).

executive council ▶ noun a council with executive power. ■ (**Executive Council**) (in Australia) a body presided over by the Governor General or Governor and consisting of ministers of the Crown, which gives legal form to cabinet decisions.

executive officer ▶ noun an officer with executive power. ■ (in naval vessels and some other military contexts) the officer who is second in command to the captain or commanding officer.

executive order ▶ noun US Law a rule or order issued by the President to an executive branch of the government and having the force of law.

executive privilege ▶ noun [mass noun] the privilege, claimed by the President for the executive branch of the US government, of withholding information in the public interest.

executive session ▶ noun US a closed meeting of a governing body.

E

executor /ɪɡˈzɛkjʊtə, ɛɡ-/ ▶ **noun 1** Law a person or institution appointed by a testator to carry out the terms of their will.
2 a person who produces something or puts something into effect: *the makers and executors of policy.*
– DERIVATIVES **executorial** /-ˈtɔːrɪəl/ **adjective** (rare), **executorship noun**, **executory adjective**.
– ORIGIN Middle English: via Anglo-Norman French from Latin *execut-* 'carried out', from *exsequi* (see EXECUTE).

executrix /ɪɡˈzɛkjuːtrɪks, ɛɡ-/ ▶ **noun** (pl. **executrices** /-trɪsiːz/ or **executrixes**) Law a female executor of a will.
– ORIGIN late Middle English: from late Latin, from Latin *executor* (see EXECUTOR).

E

exedra /ˈɛksɪdrə, ɪkˈsiːdrə, ɛk-/ ▶ **noun** (pl. **exedrae** /-driː/) Architecture a room, portico, or arcade with a bench or seats where people may converse, especially in ancient Roman and Greek buildings.
– ORIGIN Latin, from Greek *ex-* 'out of' + *hedra* 'seat'.

exegesis /ˌɛksɪˈdʒiːsɪs/ ▶ **noun** (pl. **exegeses** /-siːz/) [mass noun] critical explanation or interpretation of a text, especially of scripture: *the task of biblical exegesis.*
– DERIVATIVES **exegetic** /-ˈdʒɛtɪk/ **adjective**, **exegetical adjective**.
– ORIGIN early 17th cent.: from Greek *exēgēsis*, from *exēgeisthai* 'interpret', from *ex-* 'out of' + *hēgeisthai* 'to guide, lead'.

exegete /ˈɛksɪdʒiːt/ ▶ **noun** a person who interprets text, especially scripture.
– ORIGIN mid 18th cent.: from Greek *exēgētēs*, from *exēgeisthai* 'interpret'.

exemplar /ɪɡˈzɛmplə, ɛɡ-/ ▶ **noun** a person or thing serving as a typical example or appropriate model: *the place is an exemplar of multicultural Britain.*
– ORIGIN late Middle English: from Old French *exemplaire*, from late Latin *exemplarium*, from Latin *exemplum* 'sample, imitation' (see EXAMPLE).

exemplary ▶ **adjective 1** serving as a desirable model; very good: *exemplary behaviour.*
2 (of a punishment) serving as a warning or deterrent: *exemplary sentencing may discourage the violent minority.* ■ Law (of damages) exceeding the amount needed for simple compensation.
– DERIVATIVES **exemplarily adverb**, **exemplariness noun**, **exemplarity noun**.
– ORIGIN late 16th cent.: from late Latin *exemplaris*, from Latin *exemplum* 'sample, imitation' (see EXAMPLE).

exemplify /ɪɡˈzɛmplɪfʌɪ, ɛɡ-/ ▶ **verb** (**exemplifies, exemplifying, exemplified**) [with obj.] **1** be a typical example of: *the best dry sherry is exemplified by the fino of Jerez.*
2 illustrate or clarify by giving an example.
– DERIVATIVES **exemplification** /-fɪˈkeɪʃ(ə)n/ **noun**.
– ORIGIN late Middle English: from medieval Latin *exemplificare*, from Latin *exemplum* 'sample' (see EXAMPLE).

exemplum /ɪɡˈzɛmpləm, ɛɡ-/ ▶ **noun** (pl. **exempla**) an example or model, especially a story told to illustrate a moral point.
– ORIGIN Latin.

exempt /ɪɡˈzɛm(p)t, ɛɡ-/ ▶ **adjective** free from an obligation or liability imposed on others: *these patients are **exempt from** all charges* | [in combination] *a tax-exempt savings plan.*
▶ **verb** [with obj.] free (a person or organization) from an obligation or liability imposed on others: *they were **exempted from** paying the tax.*
▶ **noun** a person who is exempt from something, especially the payment of tax.
– ORIGIN late Middle English: from Latin *exemptus* 'taken out, freed', past participle of *eximere*.

exemption ▶ **noun** [mass noun] the action of freeing or state of being free from an obligation or liability imposed on others: *vehicles that may qualify for **exemption from** tax.*
– ORIGIN late Middle English: from Old French, or from Latin *exemptio(n-)*, from *eximere* 'take out, free'.

exenteration /ɪkˌsɛntəˈreɪʃ(ə)n, ɛk-/ ▶ **noun** [mass noun] Medicine complete surgical removal of the eyeball and other contents of the eye socket, usually in cases of malignant cancer.
– ORIGIN mid 17th cent. (originally in the sense 'disembowelment'): from Latin *exenterat-* 'removed', from the verb *exenterare* (suggested by Greek *exenterizein*), from *ex-* 'out of' + *enteron* 'intestine'.

exequatur /ˌɛksɪˈkweɪtə/ ▶ **noun** an official recognition by a government of a consul or other representative of a foreign state, authorizing them to exercise office.
– ORIGIN Latin, literally 'let him or her perform'.

exequy /ˈɛksɪkwi/ ▶ **noun** (**exequies**) formal funeral rites: *he attended the exequies for the dead pope.*
■ (**exequy**) literary a funeral ode.
– ORIGIN late Middle English: via Old French from Latin *exsequias*, accusative of *exsequiae* 'funeral ceremonies', from *exsequi* 'follow after'.

exercise ▶ **noun 1** [mass noun] activity requiring physical effort, carried out to sustain or improve health and fitness: *exercise improves your heart and lung power* | [count noun] *loosening-up exercises.*
2 an activity carried out for a specific purpose: *an exercise in public relations.* ■ [count noun] a task set to practise or test a skill: *there are exercises at the end of each book to check comprehension.* ■ (often **exercises**) a military drill or training manoeuvre. ■ (**exercises**) N. Amer. ceremonies: *Bar Mitzvah exercises.*
3 [mass noun] the use or application of a faculty, right, or process: *the exercise of authority.*
▶ **verb** [with obj.] **1** use or apply (a faculty, right, or process): ***control is exercised by the Board*** | *anyone receiving a suspect package should exercise extreme caution.*
2 [no obj.] engage in physical activity to sustain or improve health and fitness: *she still exercised every day.* ■ [with obj.] exert (part of the body) to promote or improve muscular strength: *raise your knee to exercise the upper leg muscles.* ■ [with obj.] cause (an animal) to take exercise: *she exercised her dogs before breakfast.*
3 occupy the thoughts of; worry or perplex: *Macdougall was greatly **exercised about** the exchange rate.*
– DERIVATIVES **exercisable adjective**, **exerciser noun**.
– ORIGIN Middle English (in the sense 'application of a right'): via Old French from Latin *exercitium*, from *exercere* 'keep busy, practise', from *ex-* 'thoroughly' + *arcere* 'keep in or away'.

exercise bike ▶ **noun** a stationary piece of exercise equipment resembling an ordinary bicycle.

exercise book ▶ **noun 1** Brit. a booklet with blank pages for students to write schoolwork in.
2 N. Amer. a book containing printed exercises for the use of students.

exercise price ▶ **noun** Stock Exchange the price per share at which the owner of a traded option is entitled to buy or sell the underlying security.

exercise yard ▶ **noun** an enclosed area used for physical exercise in a prison.

exercycle ▶ **noun** trademark an exercise bike.
– ORIGIN 1930s: blend of EXERCISE and BICYCLE.

exergonic /ˌɛksəːˈɡɒnɪk/ ▶ **adjective** Biochemistry (of a metabolic or chemical process) accompanied by the release of energy. The opposite of ENDERGONIC.
– ORIGIN mid 20th cent.: from EX-[2] 'out of' + Greek *ergon* 'work' + -IC.

exergue /ɪkˈsəːɡ, ɛkˈsəːɡ, ˈɛksəːɡ/ ▶ **noun** a small space or inscription below the principal emblem on a coin or medal, usually on the reverse side.
– ORIGIN late 17th cent.: from French, from medieval Latin *exergum*, from *ex-* 'out' + Greek *ergon* 'work' (probably as a rendering of French *hors d'oeuvre* 'something lying outside the work').

exert /ɪɡˈzəːt, ɛɡ-/ ▶ **verb 1** [with obj.] apply or bring to bear (a force, influence, or quality): *the moon **exerts** a force **on** the Earth* | *how much control can he **exert over** his own life?*
2 (**exert oneself**) make a physical or mental effort: *he needs to exert himself to try to find an answer.*
– ORIGIN mid 17th cent. (in the sense 'perform, practise'): from Latin *exserere* 'put forth', from *ex-* 'out' + *serere* 'bind'.

exertion ▶ **noun** [mass noun] **1** physical or mental effort: *she was panting with the exertion* | [count noun] *a well-earned rest after their exertions.*
2 the application of a force, influence, or quality: *the exertion of authority.*

Exeter /ˈɛksɪtə/ the county town of Devon, on the River Exe; pop. 109,200 (est. 2009). Exeter was founded by the Romans, who called it Isca.

exeunt /ˈɛksɪʌnt/ ▶ **verb** used as a stage direction in a play to indicate that a group of actors leave the stage: *exeunt Hamlet and Polonius.*
– PHRASES **exeunt omnes** used to indicate that all the actors leave the stage.
– ORIGIN late 15th cent.: Latin, literally 'they go out', third person plural present tense of *exire*.

exfiltrate ▶ **verb** [with obj.] withdraw (troops or spies) surreptitiously, especially from a dangerous situation.
– DERIVATIVES **exfiltration noun**.
– ORIGIN late 20th cent. (earlier (late 19th cent.) as *exfiltration*): perhaps suggested by *infiltration, infiltrate.*

exfoliant ▶ **noun** a cosmetic product designed to remove dead cells from the surface of the skin.
– ORIGIN 1980s: from EXFOLIATE + -ANT.

exfoliate /ɪksˈfəʊlɪeɪt, ɛks-/ ▶ **verb** [no obj.] (of a material) be shed from a surface in scales or layers: *the bark exfoliates in papery flakes.* ■ [with obj.] cause to do this: *salt solutions exfoliate rocks on evaporating.* ■ [with obj.] wash or rub (a part of the body) with a granular substance to remove dead skin cells: *exfoliate your legs to get rid of dead skin.* ■ [with obj.] shed (material) in scales or layers: *diagnosing cancer from cells exfoliated into the intestine.*
– DERIVATIVES **exfoliation noun**, **exfoliative adjective**, **exfoliator noun**.
– ORIGIN mid 17th cent.: from late Latin *exfoliat-* 'stripped of leaves', from the verb *exfoliare*, from *ex-* 'out, from' + *folium* 'leaf'.

ex gratia /ɛks ˈɡreɪʃə/ ▶ **adverb & adjective** (with reference to payment) done from a sense of moral obligation rather than because of any legal requirement: [as adj.] *an ex gratia payment.*
– ORIGIN Latin, literally 'from favour', from *ex* 'from' and *gratia* (see GRACE).

exhalation ▶ **noun** [mass noun] the process or action of exhaling. ■ [count noun] an expiration of air from the lungs: *he let his breath out in a long exhalation of relief.* ■ [count noun] an amount of vapour or fumes given off by something.

exhale /ɪksˈheɪl, ɛks-/ ▶ **verb** breathe out: [no obj.] *she sat back and exhaled deeply* | [with obj.] *he exhaled the smoke towards the ceiling.* ■ [with obj.] give off (vapour or fumes): *the jungle exhaled mists of early morning.*
– ORIGIN late Middle English (in the sense 'be given off as vapour'): from Old French *exhaler*, from Latin *exhalare*, from *ex-* 'out' + *halare* 'breathe'.

exhaust /ɪɡˈzɔːst, ɛɡ-/ ▶ **verb** [with obj.] **1** make (someone) feel very tired: *her day out had exhausted her.*
2 use up (resources or reserves) completely: *the country has exhausted its treasury reserves.*
■ expound on or explore (a subject or options) so fully that there is nothing further to be said or discovered: *she seemed to have exhausted all permissible topics of conversation.*
3 expel (gas or steam) from or into a particular place.
▶ **noun** [mass noun] waste gases or air expelled from an engine, turbine, or other machine in the course of its operation: *buses spewing out black clouds of exhaust* | [as modifier] *exhaust fumes.* ■ [count noun] the system through which such gases are expelled: [as modifier] *an exhaust pipe.*
– DERIVATIVES **exhauster noun**, **exhaustibility** /-ˈbɪlɪti/ **noun**, **exhaustible adjective**.
– ORIGIN mid 16th cent. (in the sense 'draw off or out'): from Latin *exhaust-* 'drained out', from the verb *exhaurire*, from *ex-* 'out' + *haurire* 'draw (water), drain'.

exhausted ▶ **adjective 1** very tired: *she returned home, **exhausted from** work.*
2 (of resources or reserves) completely used up: *Kirov spat, his patience suddenly exhausted.* ■ (of a place) no longer productive as a result of being drained of resources: *exhausted peat workings.*
– DERIVATIVES **exhaustedly adverb**.

exhausting /ɪɡˈzɔːstɪŋ, ɛɡ-/ ▶ **adjective** making one feel very tired; very tiring: *a long and exhausting journey.*
– DERIVATIVES **exhaustingly adverb**.

exhaustion ▶ **noun** [mass noun] **1** a state of extreme physical or mental tiredness: *he was pale with exhaustion.*
2 the action of using something up or the state of being used up: *the rapid exhaustion of fossil fuel reserves.*
3 Logic the process of establishing a conclusion by eliminating all the alternatives.
– ORIGIN early 17th cent.: from late Latin *exhaustio(n-)*, from Latin *exhaurire* 'drain out' (see EXHAUST).

exhaustive ▶ **adjective** including or considering all elements or aspects; fully comprehensive: *the guide outlines every bus route in exhaustive detail.*
– DERIVATIVES **exhaustively adverb**, **exhaustiveness noun**.

exhibit /ɪɡˈzɪbɪt, ɛɡ-/ ▸ **verb** [with obj.] **1** publicly display (a work of art or item of interest) in an art gallery or museum or at a trade fair: *only one sculpture was exhibited in the artist's lifetime.* ■ [no obj.] (of an artist) display one's work to the public in an art gallery or museum: *she was invited to exhibit at several French museums.* ■ publicly display the work of (an artist) in an art gallery or museum: *no foreign painters were exhibited.*
2 manifest clearly (a quality or a type of behaviour): *he could exhibit a saintlike submissiveness.* ■ show as a sign or symptom: *patients with alcoholic liver disease exhibit many biochemical abnormalities.*
▸ **noun** an object or collection of objects on public display in an art gallery or museum or at a trade fair: *the museum is rich in exhibits.* ■ N. Amer. an exhibition. ■ Law a document or other object produced in a court as evidence.
– ORIGIN late Middle English (in the sense 'submit for consideration', also 'present a document as evidence in court'): from Latin *exhibit-* 'held out', from the verb *exhibere*, from *ex-* 'out' + *habere* 'hold'.

exhibition ▸ **noun 1** a public display of works of art or items of interest, held in an art gallery or museum or at a trade fair: *an exhibition of French sculpture* | [mass noun] *he never lent his treasures out for exhibition.*
2 a display or demonstration of a skill: *fields which have been ploughed with a supreme exhibition of the farm worker's skills.* ■ a display of a quality or emotion: *a false exhibition of concern for smaller nations.*
3 [usu. as modifier] chiefly N. Amer. (in sport) a game whose outcome does not affect a team's standing, typically one played before the start of a regular season: *an exhibition match.*
4 Brit. a scholarship awarded to a student at a school or university, usually after a competitive examination.
– PHRASES **make an exhibition of oneself** behave in a very foolish or ill-judged way in public.
– ORIGIN late Middle English (in the sense 'maintenance, support'; hence sense 4, mid 17th cent.): via Old French from late Latin *exhibitio(n-)*, from Latin *exhibere* 'hold out' (see EXHIBIT).

exhibitioner ▸ **noun** Brit. a student who has been awarded an exhibition (scholarship).

exhibitionism ▸ **noun** [mass noun] extravagant behaviour that is intended to attract attention to oneself. ■ Psychiatry a mental condition characterized by the compulsion to display one's genitals in public.

exhibitionist ▸ **noun** a person who behaves in an extravagant way in order to attract attention: *I am something of an exhibitionist.*
▸ **adjective** behaving extravagantly in order to attract attention.
– DERIVATIVES **exhibitionistic** adjective, **exhibitionistically** adverb.

exhibitor ▸ **noun** a person who displays works of art or other items of interest at an exhibition.

exhilarate /ɪɡˈzɪləreɪt, ɛɡ-/ ▸ **verb** [with obj.] make (someone) feel very happy, animated, or elated: *she was exhilarated by the day's events* | (as adj. **exhilarated**) *all this hustle and bustle makes me feel exhilarated.*
– ORIGIN mid 16th cent.: from Latin *exhilarat-* 'made cheerful', from the verb *exhilarare*, from *ex-* (expressing inducement of a state) + *hilaris* 'cheerful'.

exhilarating /ɪɡˈzɪləreɪtɪŋ, ɛɡ-/ ▸ **adjective** making one feel very happy, animated, or elated; thrilling: *an exhilarating two-hour rafting experience.*
– DERIVATIVES **exhilaratingly** adverb.

exhilaration /ɪɡzɪləˈreɪʃ(ə)n, ɛɡ-/ ▸ **noun** [mass noun] a feeling of excitement, happiness, or elation: *they felt the exhilaration of victory.*

exhort /ɪɡˈzɔːt, ɛɡ-/ ▸ **verb** [with obj. and infinitive] strongly encourage or urge (someone) to do something: *I exhorted her to be a good child* | [with direct speech] *'Come on, you guys,' exhorted Linda.*
– DERIVATIVES **exhortative** adjective, **exhortatory** /-tət(ə)ri/ adjective, **exhorter** noun.
– ORIGIN late Middle English: from Old French *exhorter* or Latin *exhortari*, from *ex-* 'thoroughly' + *hortari* 'encourage'.

exhortation ▸ **noun** an address or communication emphatically urging someone to do something: *exhortations to consumers to switch off electrical appliances* | [mass noun] *no amount of exhortation had any effect.*

exhume /ɛksˈ(h)juːm, ɪɡˈzjuːm/ ▸ **verb** [with obj.] dig out (something buried, especially a corpse) from the ground: *the bodies were exhumed on the orders of a judge.* ■ Geology expose (a land surface) that was formerly buried: *various landforms have been exhumed from beneath a covering of Triassic sediments.*
– DERIVATIVES **exhumation** noun.
– ORIGIN late Middle English: from medieval Latin *exhumare*, from *ex-* 'out of' + *humus* 'ground'.

ex hypothesi /ˌɛks hʌɪˈpɒθəsʌɪ/ ▸ **adverb** according to the hypothesis proposed.
– ORIGIN modern Latin, from *ex* 'from' and *hypothesi*, ablative of late Latin *hypothesis* (see HYPOTHESIS).

exigence /ˈɛksɪdʒ(ə)ns, ˈɛɡzɪ-/ ▸ **noun** another term for EXIGENCY.

exigency /ˈɛksɪdʒ(ə)nsi, ˈɛɡzɪ-, ɪɡˈzɪ-, ɛɡˈzɪ-/ ▸ **noun** (pl. **exigencies**) an urgent need or demand: *women worked long hours when the exigencies of the family economy demanded it* | [mass noun] *he put financial exigency before personal sentiment.*
– ORIGIN late 16th cent.: from late Latin *exigentia*, from Latin *exigere* 'enforce' (see EXACT).

exigent /ˈɛksɪdʒ(ə)nt, ˈɛɡzɪ-/ ▸ **adjective** formal pressing; demanding.
– ORIGIN early 17th cent.: from Latin *exigent-* 'completing, ascertaining', from the verb *exigere* (see EXACT).

exigible /ˈɛksɪdʒɪb(ə)l, ˈɛɡzɪ-/ ▸ **adjective** (of a tax, duty, or other payment) able to be charged or levied.
– ORIGIN early 17th cent.: from French, from *exiger* 'demand, exact', from Latin *exigere* (see EXACT).

exiguous /ɪɡˈzɪɡjʊəs, ɛɡ-/ ▸ **adjective** formal very small in size or amount: *my exiguous musical resources.*
– DERIVATIVES **exiguity** /-ˈɡjuːɪti/ noun.
– ORIGIN mid 17th cent.: from Latin *exiguus* 'scanty' (from *exigere* 'weigh exactly') + -OUS.

exile ▸ **noun** [mass noun] the state of being barred from one's native country, typically for political or punitive reasons: *he knew now that he would die in exile.* ■ [count noun] a person who lives away from their native country, either from choice or compulsion: *the return of political exiles.*
▸ **verb** [with obj.] expel and bar (someone) from their native country, typically for political or punitive reasons: *a corrupt dictator who had been* ***exiled from*** *his country* | (as adj. **exiled**) *supporters of the exiled King.*
– ORIGIN Middle English: the noun partly from Old French *exil* 'banishment' and partly from Old French *exile* 'banished person'; the verb from Old French *exiler*; all based on Latin *exilium* 'banishment', from *exul* 'banished person'.

exilic /ɪɡˈzɪlɪk, ɪk-, ɛɡ-, ɛk-/ ▸ **adjective** relating to a period of exile, especially that of the Jews in Babylon in the 6th century BC.

exine /ˈɛksɪn, -ʌɪn/ ▸ **noun** Botany the decay-resistant outer coating of a pollen grain or spore.
– ORIGIN late 19th cent.: perhaps from EX-[2] 'out' + Greek *is, in-* 'fibre'.

exist ▸ **verb** [no obj.] **1** have objective reality or being: *dossiers existed on almost everyone of prominence* | *there existed no organization to cope with espionage.* ■ occur or be found, especially in a particular place or situation: *two conflicting stereotypes of housework exist in popular thinking.*
2 live, especially under adverse conditions: *a minority of people* ***exist on*** *unemployment benefit alone* | *how am I going to exist without you?*
– ORIGIN early 17th cent.: probably a back formation from EXISTENCE.

existence ▸ **noun** [mass noun] the fact or state of living or having objective reality: *the organization has been* ***in existence*** *for fifteen years.* ■ continued survival: *she kept the company alive when its very existence was threatened.* ■ [count noun] a way of living: *our stressed-out urban existence.* ■ [count noun] (in certain beliefs) any of a person's successive earthly lives. ■ all that exists: *he believed in the essential unity of all existence.* ■ [count noun] archaic something that exists; a being.
– ORIGIN late Middle English: from Old French, or from late Latin *existentia*, from Latin *exsistere* 'come into being', from *ex-* 'out' + *sistere* 'take a stand'.

existent ▸ **adjective** formal having reality or existence: *the technique has been existent for some years.*

existential /ˌɛɡzɪˈstɛnʃ(ə)l/ ▸ **adjective** relating to existence. ■ Philosophy concerned with existentialism. ■ Logic (of a proposition) affirming or implying the existence of a thing.
– DERIVATIVES **existentially** adverb.
– ORIGIN late 17th cent.: from late Latin *existentialis*, from *existentia* (see EXISTENCE).

existentialism ▸ **noun** [mass noun] a philosophical theory or approach which emphasizes the existence of the individual person as a free and responsible agent determining their own development through acts of the will.
– DERIVATIVES **existentialist** noun & adjective.
– ORIGIN translating Danish *existents-forhold* 'condition of existence' (frequently used by Kierkegaard), from EXISTENTIAL.

existential quantifier ▸ **noun** Logic a formal expression used in asserting that something exists of which a stated general proposition can be said to be true.

existing ▸ **adjective** [attrib.] in existence or operation at the current time: *opponents of the existing political system.*

exit ▸ **noun 1** a way out of a building, room, or passenger vehicle: *she slipped out by the rear exit* | *a fire exit.* ■ a place for traffic to leave a major road or roundabout.
2 an act of leaving a place: *he made a hasty* ***exit from*** *the room.* ■ a departure from a particular situation: *Australia's early* ***exit from*** *the World Cup.* ■ literary a person's death.
▸ **verb** (**exits, exiting, exited**) [no obj.] go out of or leave a place: *he* ***exited from*** *the changing rooms* | *the bullet entered her back and exited through her chest* | [with obj.] *queues of vehicles tried to exit the airfield.* ■ (**exit**) used as a stage direction in a play to indicate that an actor leaves the stage: *exit Pamela.* ■ leave a particular situation: *organizations which do not have freedom to exit from unprofitable markets.* ■ literary die. ■ Computing terminate a process or program: *this key enables you to temporarily exit from a LIFESPAN option.* ■ Bridge relinquish the lead.
– ORIGIN mid 16th cent. (as a stage direction): from Latin *exit* 'he or she goes out', third person singular present tense of *exire*, from *ex-* 'out' + *ire* 'go'. The noun (late 16th cent.) is from Latin *exitus* 'going out', from the verb *exire*, and the other verb uses (early 17th cent.) derive from it.

exit line ▸ **noun** a line spoken by an actor immediately before leaving the stage. ■ a parting remark.

exit poll ▸ **noun** an opinion poll of people leaving a polling station, asking how they voted.

exit strategy ▸ **noun** a pre-planned means of extricating oneself from a situation that is likely to become difficult or unpleasant.

exit visa (also **exit permit**) ▸ **noun** a document giving authorization to leave a particular country.

exit wound ▸ **noun** a wound made by a bullet or other missile passing out of the body.

ex libris /ɛks ˈlɪbrɪs, ˈliːb-, ˈlʌɪb-, ˈliːbriːs/ ▸ **adverb** used as an inscription on a bookplate to show the name of the book's owner: *ex libris Edith Wharton.*
▸ **noun** (pl. **same**) a bookplate inscribed in such a way.
– ORIGIN Latin, literally 'out of the books or library (of someone)'.

Exmoor /ˈɛksmɔː, -mʊə/ an area of moorland in north Devon and west Somerset, SW England, rising to 520 m (1,706 ft) at Dunkery Beacon. The area is designated a national park.

Exmoor pony ▸ **noun** a pony of a small hardy breed, typically bay, brown, or dun in colour with a light muzzle.

ex nihilo /ɛks ˈnʌɪhɪləʊ/ ▸ **adverb** formal out of nothing: *he went on to create a paradise ex nihilo.*
– ORIGIN Latin.

exo- ▸ **prefix** external; from outside: *exodermis.*
– ORIGIN from Greek *exō* 'outside'.

exoatmospheric ▸ **adjective** operating or taking place outside the atmosphere.

exobiology ▸ **noun** [mass noun] the branch of science that deals with the possibility and likely nature of life on other planets or in space.
– DERIVATIVES **exobiological** adjective, **exobiologist** noun.

exocarp /ˈɛksəʊkɑːp/ ▸ **noun** Botany the outer layer of the pericarp of a fruit.

exocentric /ˌɛksəʊˈsɛntrɪk/ ▸ **adjective** Linguistics denoting or being a construction which has no explicit head, for example *John slept.* Contrasted with ENDOCENTRIC.

Exocet /ˈɛksə(ʊ)sɛt/ ▸ **noun** trademark a French-made guided anti-ship missile.
– ORIGIN 1970s: from French, literally 'flying fish', via Latin from Greek *ekōkoitos* 'fish that comes up on the beach' (literally 'out of bed').

exocrine /ˈɛksə(ʊ)krʌɪn, -krɪn/ ▸ **adjective** Physiology relating to or denoting glands which secrete their products through ducts opening on to an epithelium rather than directly into the blood.

E

– ORIGIN early 20th cent.: from **exo-** 'outside' + Greek *krinein* 'sift'.

exocytosis /ˌɛksəʊsʌɪˈtəʊsɪs/ ▸ **noun** [mass noun] Biology a process by which the contents of a cell vacuole are released to the exterior through fusion of the vacuole membrane with the cell membrane.
– DERIVATIVES **exocytotic** adjective.

Exod. ▸ abbreviation Exodus (in biblical references).

exodermis /ˌɛksə(ʊ)ˈdəːmɪs/ ▸ **noun** [mass noun] Botany a specialized layer in a root beneath the epidermis or velamen.
– ORIGIN early 20th cent.: from **exo-** 'outside', on the pattern of *endodermis*, *epidermis*.

E

Exodus /ˈɛksədəs/ (abbrev.: **Exod.**) the second book of the Bible, which recounts the departure of the Israelites from slavery in Egypt, their journey across the Red Sea and through the wilderness led by Moses, and the giving of the Ten Commandments. The events have been variously dated by scholars between about 1580 and 1200 BC.
– ORIGIN Old English, via ecclesiastical Latin from Greek *exodos*, from *ex-* 'out of' + *hodos* 'way'.

exodus /ˈɛksədəs/ ▸ **noun** a mass departure of people: *the annual exodus of sun-seeking Canadians to Florida.* ■ (**the Exodus**) the departure of the Israelites from Egypt.
– ORIGIN early 17th cent.: from Greek (see **Exodus**).

exoenzyme ▸ **noun** Biochemistry an enzyme which acts outside the cell that produces it.

ex officio /ˌɛks əˈfɪʃɪəʊ/ ▸ **adverb & adjective** by virtue of one's position or status: [as adj.] *an ex officio member of the committee.*
– ORIGIN Latin, from *ex* 'out of, from' + *officium* 'duty'.

exogamy /ɪkˈsɒgəmi, ɛk-/ ▸ **noun** [mass noun]
1 Anthropology the custom of marrying outside a community, clan, or tribe. Compare with **endogamy**.
2 Biology the fusion of reproductive cells from distantly related or unrelated individuals; cross-pollination.
– DERIVATIVES **exogamous** adjective.

exogenic /ˌɛksə(ʊ)ˈdʒɛnɪk/ ▸ **adjective** Geology formed or occurring on the surface of the earth. Often contrasted with **endogenic**.

exogenous /ɪkˈsɒdʒɪnəs, ɛk-/ ▸ **adjective** having an external cause or origin. Often contrasted with **endogenous**. ■ Biology growing or originating from outside an organism: *an exogenous hormone.* ■ chiefly Psychiatry (of a disease or symptom) attributable to an agent or organism outside the body: *exogenous depression.* ■ relating to an external group or society: *exogenous marriage.*
– DERIVATIVES **exogenously** adverb.
– ORIGIN mid 19th cent.: from modern Latin *exogena* (denoting an exogenous plant, suggested by classical Latin *indigena* 'native') + **-ous**.

exoglossic /ˌɛksə(ʊ)ˈglɒsɪk/ ▸ **adjective** Linguistics denoting or relating to a non-indigenous language that is used as an official or second language in a particular country or community. Compare with **endoglossic**.
– ORIGIN 1980s: from **exo-**, Greek *glōssa* 'language, tongue', and **-ic**.

exon[1] /ˈɛksɒn/ ▸ **noun** Biochemistry a segment of a DNA or RNA molecule containing information coding for a protein or peptide sequence. Compare with **intron**.
– ORIGIN 1970s: from *expressed* (see **express**[1]) + **-on**.

exon[2] /ˈɛksɒn/ ▸ **noun** Brit. each of the four officers acting as commanders of the Yeomen of the Guard.
– ORIGIN mid 18th cent.: representing the pronunciation of French *exempt* 'free from', from Latin *exempt-* 'taken out', from the verb *eximere*, so named because these officers were exempt from normal duties.

exonerate /ɪgˈzɒnəreɪt, ɛg-/ ▸ **verb** [with obj.] **1** (of an official body) absolve (someone) from blame for a fault or wrongdoing: *an inquiry exonerated those involved* | *they should* ***exonerate*** *these men* ***from*** *this crime.*
2 (**exonerate someone from**) release someone from (a duty or obligation).
– ORIGIN late Middle English: from Latin *exonerat-* 'freed from a burden', from the verb *exonerare*, from *ex-* 'from' + *onus*, *oner-* 'a burden'.

exoneration /ɪgzɒnəˈreɪʃ(ə)n, ɛg-/ ▸ **noun** [mass noun]
1 the action of officially absolving someone from blame; vindication: *the defendants' eventual exoneration.*
2 the release of someone from a duty or obligation.

exonuclease /ˌɛksəʊˈnjuːklɪeɪz/ ▸ **noun** Biochemistry an enzyme which removes successive nucleotides from the end of a polynucleotide molecule.

exopeptidase /ˌɛksəʊˈpɛptɪdeɪz/ ▸ **noun** Biochemistry an enzyme which breaks the terminal peptide bond in a peptide chain.

exophora /ɪkˈsɒf(ə)rə/ ▸ **noun** [mass noun] Linguistics reference in a text to something external to it, which is only fully intelligible in terms of information about the extralinguistic situation. Compare with **endophora**.
– DERIVATIVES **exophoric** /ˌɛksə(ʊ)ˈfɒrɪk/ **adjective**.

exophthalmic /ˌɛksɒfˈθalmɪk/ ▸ **adjective** Medicine having or characterized by protruding eyes.

exophthalmic goitre ▸ **noun** another term for **Graves' disease**.

exophthalmos /ˌɛksɒfˈθalmɒs/ (also **exophthalmus** or **exophthalmia** /-mɪə/) ▸ **noun** [mass noun] Medicine abnormal protrusion of the eyeball or eyeballs.
– ORIGIN early 17th cent.: from modern Latin *exophthalmus*, from Greek *exophthalmos* 'having prominent eyes', from *ex-* 'out' + *ophthalmos* 'eye'.

exoplanet /ˈɛksəʊplanɪt/ ▸ **noun** a planet which orbits a star outside the solar system.

exopodite /ɛkˈsɒpədʌɪt/ (also **exopod** /ˈɛksə(ʊ)pɒd/) ▸ **noun** Zoology the outer branch of the biramous limb or appendage of a crustacean. Compare with **endopodite, protopodite**.
– ORIGIN late 19th cent.: from **exo-** 'outside' + Greek *pous*, *pod-* 'foot' + **-ite**[1].

exor ▸ abbreviation an executor (of a will).

exorbitant /ɪgˈzɔːbɪt(ə)nt/ ▸ **adjective** (of a price or amount charged) unreasonably high: *some hotels charge exorbitant rates for phone calls.*
– DERIVATIVES **exorbitance** noun, **exorbitantly** adverb.
– ORIGIN late Middle English (originally describing a legal case that is outside the scope of a law): from late Latin *exorbitant-* 'going off the track', from *exorbitare*, from *ex-* 'out from' + *orbita* 'course, track'.

exorcise /ˈɛksɔːsʌɪz/ (also **exorcize**) ▸ **verb** [with obj.] drive out or attempt to drive out (a supposed evil spirit) from a person or place: *an attempt to exorcise an unquiet spirit.* ■ rid (a person or place) of a supposed evil spirit: *infants were exorcised prior to baptism.* ■ completely remove (something unpleasant) from one's mind or memory: *she wanted to exorcise some of the pain.*
– ORIGIN late Middle English: from French *exorciser* or ecclesiastical Latin *exorcizare*, from Greek *exorkizein*, from *ex-* 'out' + *horkos* 'oath'. The word originally meant 'conjure up an evil spirit'; the current sense dates from the mid 16th cent.

exorcism ▸ **noun** [mass noun] the expulsion or attempted expulsion of a supposed evil spirit from a person or place.
– DERIVATIVES **exorcist** noun.
– ORIGIN late Middle English: via ecclesiastical Latin from ecclesiastical Greek *exorkismos*, from *exorkizein* 'exorcize'.

exordium /ɪgˈzɔːdɪəm, ɛg-/ ▸ **noun** (pl. **exordiums** or **exordia**) formal the beginning or introductory part, especially of a discourse or treatise.
– DERIVATIVES **exordial** adjective.
– ORIGIN late 16th cent.: from Latin, from *exordiri* 'begin', from *ex-* 'out, from' + *ordiri* 'begin'.

exoskeleton ▸ **noun** Zoology a rigid external covering for the body in some invertebrate animals, especially arthropods. Compare with **endoskeleton**.
– DERIVATIVES **exoskeletal** adjective.

exosphere /ˈɛksə(ʊ)sfɪə/ ▸ **noun** Astronomy the outermost region of a planet's atmosphere.
– DERIVATIVES **exospheric** adjective.

exostosis /ˌɛksɒsˈtəʊsɪs/ ▸ **noun** (pl. **exostoses** /-siːz/) Medicine a benign outgrowth of cartilaginous tissue on a bone.
– ORIGIN late 16th cent.: from Greek, from *ex-* 'out' + *osteon* 'bone'.

exoteric /ˌɛksə(ʊ)ˈtɛrɪk/ ▸ **adjective** formal intended for or likely to be understood by the general public.
– ORIGIN mid 17th cent.: via Latin from Greek *exōterikos*, from *exōterō* 'outer', comparative of *exō* 'outside'.

exothermic /ˌɛksə(ʊ)ˈθəːmɪk/ ▸ **adjective** Chemistry (of a reaction or process) accompanied by the release of heat. The opposite of **endothermic** (sense 1). ■ (of a compound) formed from its constituent elements with a net release of heat.
– DERIVATIVES **exothermically** adverb.
– ORIGIN late 19th cent.: from French *exothermique*.

exotic /ɪgˈzɒtɪk, ɛg-/ ▸ **adjective** originating in or characteristic of a distant foreign country: *exotic birds* | *they loved to visit exotic places.* ■ attractive or striking because colourful or out of the ordinary: *youths with exotic haircuts* | (as noun **the exotic**) *there was a touch of the exotic in her appearance.* ■ (especially of metals or fuels) of a kind not ordinarily encountered; specially produced.
▸ **noun** an exotic plant or animal: *he planted exotics in the sheltered garden.*
– DERIVATIVES **exotically** adverb, **exoticism** noun.
– ORIGIN late 16th cent.: via Latin from Greek *exōtikos* 'foreign', from *exō* 'outside'.

exotica /ɪgˈzɒtɪkə, ɛg-/ ▸ **plural noun** objects considered interesting because they are out of the ordinary, especially because they originated in a distant foreign country.
– ORIGIN late 19th cent.: from Latin, neuter plural of *exoticus* 'foreign' (see **exotic**).

exotic dancer ▸ **noun** a striptease dancer.

exotoxin ▸ **noun** Microbiology a toxin released by a living bacterial cell into its surroundings. Compare with **endotoxin**.

exp ▸ abbreviation ■ experience (usually in the context of job advertisements): *previous exp an advantage.* ■ (**Exp.**) experimental (in titles of periodicals). ■ expiry: *exp date.* ■ Mathematics the exponential function raising *e* to the power of the given quantity: *it is reduced by exp (−U).* ■ Photography exposures.

expand /ɪkˈspand, ɛk-/ ▸ **verb** become or make larger or more extensive: [no obj.] *their business* ***expanded into*** *other hotels* | [with obj.] *the work began as a short story and was later* ***expanded into*** *a novel.* ■ [no obj.] Physics (of the universe) undergo a continuous change whereby, according to theory based on observed red shifts, all the galaxies recede from one another. ■ [no obj.] (**expand on**) give a fuller version or account of: *the minister expanded on the government's proposals.* ■ [no obj.] become less reserved in character or behaviour: *Alice opened and expanded in this normality.*
– DERIVATIVES **expandability** noun, **expandable** adjective, **expander** noun, **expansibility** noun, **expansible** adjective.
– ORIGIN late Middle English: from Latin *expandere* 'to spread out', from *ex-* 'out' + *pandere* 'to spread'.

expanded ▸ **adjective** being or having been enlarged or extended, in particular: ■ denoting materials which have a light cellular structure: *expanded polystyrene.* ■ denoting sheet metal slit and stretched into a mesh, used to reinforce concrete and other brittle materials. ■ relatively broad in shape: *the expanded fins of the ray.*

expanse ▸ **noun** a wide continuous area of something: *the green expanse of the forest.* ■ the distance to which something expands or can be expanded: *the moth has a wing expanse of 20 to 24 mm.*
– ORIGIN mid 17th cent.: from modern Latin *expansum* 'something expanded', neuter past participle of *expandere* (see **expand**).

expansile ▸ **adjective** Physics relating to or capable of expansion.

expansion ▸ **noun** [mass noun] the action of becoming larger or more extensive: *the rapid expansion of suburban London* | [count noun] *a small expansion of industry.* ■ the political strategy of extending a state's territory by encroaching on that of other nations: *German expansion in the 1930s.* ■ [count noun] a thing formed by the enlargement or broadening of something: *the book is an expansion of a lecture given last year.* ■ the increase in the volume of fuel on combustion in the cylinder of an engine, or the piston stroke in which this occurs.
– ORIGIN early 17th cent.: from late Latin *expansio(n-)*, from Latin *expandere* (see **expand**).

expansionary ▸ **adjective** (of a policy or action) intended to result in economic or political expansion: *an expansionary budget.*

expansion bolt ▸ **noun** a bolt that expands when inserted, no thread being required in the surrounding material.

expansion card (also **expansion board**) ▸ **noun** Computing a circuit board that can be inserted in a computer to give extra facilities or memory.

expansionism ▸ **noun** [mass noun] the policy of territorial or economic expansion.
– DERIVATIVES **expansionist** noun & adjective, **expansionistic** adjective.

expansion joint ▸ **noun** a joint that makes allowance for thermal expansion of the parts joined without distortion.

expansion slot ▸ **noun** Computing a place in a computer where an expansion card can be inserted.

expansive ▸ adjective **1** covering a wide area in terms of space or scope; extensive: *expansive beaches*.
2 (of a person or their manner) relaxed and genially frank and communicative: *he was in an expansive mood*.
3 tending towards economic or political expansion: *expansive domestic economic policies*.
– DERIVATIVES **expansively** adverb, **expansiveness** noun.

expansivity ▸ noun Physics the amount a material expands or contracts per unit length due to a one-degree change in temperature.

ex parte /ɛks ˈpɑːteɪ/ ▸ adjective & adverb Law with respect to or in the interests of one side only or of an interested outside party.
– ORIGIN Latin, 'from a side'.

expat ▸ noun & adjective informal short for **EXPATRIATE**.

expatiate /ɪkˈspeɪʃɪeɪt, ɛk-/ ▸ verb [no obj.] (**expatiate on**) speak or write in detail about: *she expatiated on working-class novelists*.
– DERIVATIVES **expatiation** noun.
– ORIGIN mid 16th cent. (in the sense 'roam freely'): from Latin *exspatiari* 'move beyond one's usual bounds', from *ex-* 'out, from' + *spatiari* 'to walk' (from *spatium* 'space').

expatriate ▸ noun /ɪksˈpatrɪət, -ˈpeɪtrɪət, ɛks-/ a person who lives outside their native country: *American expatriates in London*. ■ archaic an exile.
▸ adjective /ɪksˈpatrɪət, -ˈpeɪtrɪət, ɛks-/ denoting or relating to a person living outside their native country: *expatriate workers*.
▸ verb /ɪksˈpatrɪeɪt, -ˈpeɪtrɪeɪt, ɛks-/ [with obj.] send (a person or money) abroad: *we expatriated the prisoners of war immediately after the end of the war* | *people that have illegally expatriated funds*.
– DERIVATIVES **expatriation** noun.
– ORIGIN mid 18th cent. (as a verb): from medieval Latin *expatriat-* 'gone out from one's country', from the verb *expatriare*, from *ex-* 'out' + *patria* 'native country'.

expect ▸ verb [with obj.] regard (something) as likely to happen: *it's as well to expect the worst* | [with obj. and infinitive] *the hearing is expected to last a week* | [with clause] *one might expect that Hollywood would adjust its approach*. ■ regard (someone) as likely to do or be something: [with obj. and infinitive] *they were not expecting him to continue*. ■ believe that (someone or something) will arrive soon: *Celia was expecting a visitor*. ■ require (something) as rightfully due or appropriate in the circumstances: *we expect great things of you*. ■ require (someone) to fulfil an obligation: [with obj. and infinitive] *we expect employers to pay a reasonable salary*. ■ (**I expect**) informal used to indicate that one supposes something to be so but has no firm evidence: *they're just friends of his, I expect* | [with clause] *I expect you know them?*
– PHRASES **be expecting (a baby)** informal be pregnant. (**only**) **to be expected** completely normal: *he had a few lines about the eyes, but at forty-seven that was only to be expected*. **what can** (or **do**) **you expect?** used to emphasize that there was nothing unexpected about a person or event, however disappointed one might be.
– DERIVATIVES **expectable** adjective, **expectably** adverb, **expectedly** adverb.
– ORIGIN mid 16th cent. (in the sense 'defer action, wait'): from Latin *exspectare* 'look out for', from *ex-* 'out' + *spectare* 'to look' (frequentative of *specere* 'see').

expectancy ▸ noun (pl. **expectancies**) [mass noun] the state of thinking or hoping that something, especially something good, will happen: *they waited with an **air of expectancy*** | [count noun] *our expectancies about the future*.
– ORIGIN early 17th cent.: from Latin *exspectantia*, from *exspectare* 'look out for' (see **EXPECT**).

expectant ▸ adjective having or showing an excited feeling that something is about to happen, especially something good: *expectant crowds arrived early*. ■ [attrib.] used to describe a pregnant woman or a man who is about to become a father: *an expectant mother*.
▸ noun archaic a person who anticipates receiving something, especially high office.
– DERIVATIVES **expectantly** adverb.
– ORIGIN late Middle English: from Latin *exspectant-* 'expecting', from the verb *exspectare* (see **EXPECT**).

expectation ▸ noun **1** a strong belief that something will happen or be the case: *reality had not lived up to expectations* | [mass noun] *I sat down in expectation of a feast of nostalgia*. ■ a belief that someone will or should achieve something: *students had high expectations for their future*. ■ (**expectations**) archaic one's prospects of inheritance.
2 Mathematics another term for **EXPECTED VALUE**.

expected utility ▸ noun Mathematics & Economics a predicted utility value for one of several options, calculated as the sum of the utility of every possible outcome each multiplied by the probability of its occurrence.

expected value ▸ noun Mathematics a predicted value of a variable, calculated as the sum of all possible values each multiplied by the probability of its occurrence.

expectorant ▸ noun a medicine which promotes the secretion of sputum by the air passages, used to treat coughs.
– ORIGIN mid 18th cent.: from Latin *expectorant-* 'expelling from the chest', from the verb *expectorare* (see **EXPECTORATE**).

expectorate /ɪkˈspɛktəreɪt, ɛk-/ ▸ verb [with obj.] cough or spit out (phlegm) from the throat or lungs.
– DERIVATIVES **expectoration** noun.
– ORIGIN early 17th cent. (in the sense 'enable sputum to be coughed up', referring to medicine): from Latin *expectorat-* 'expelled from the chest', from the verb *expectorare*, from *ex-* 'out' + *pectus, pector-* 'breast'.

expediency /ɪkˈspiːdɪənsi, ɛk-/ ▸ noun [mass noun] the quality of being convenient and practical despite possibly being improper or immoral; convenience: *an act of political expediency*.

expedient /ɪkˈspiːdɪənt, ɛk-/ ▸ adjective (of an action) convenient and practical although possibly improper or immoral: *either side could break the agreement if it were expedient to do so*. ■ (of an action) suitable or appropriate: *holding a public enquiry into the scheme was not expedient*.
▸ noun a means of attaining an end, especially one that is convenient but possibly improper or immoral: *the current policy is a political expedient*.
– DERIVATIVES **expedience** noun, **expediently** adverb.
– ORIGIN late Middle English: from Latin *expedient-* 'extricating, putting in order', from the verb *expedire* (see **EXPEDITE**).

expedite /ˈɛkspɪdʌɪt/ ▸ verb [with obj.] make (an action or process) happen sooner or be accomplished more quickly: *he promised to expedite economic reforms*.
– DERIVATIVES **expediter** (also **expeditor**) noun.
– ORIGIN late 15th cent. (in the sense 'perform quickly'): from Latin *expedire* 'extricate (originally by freeing the feet), put in order', from *ex-* 'out' + *pes, ped-* 'foot'.

expedition ▸ noun **1** a journey undertaken by a group of people with a particular purpose, especially that of exploration, research, or war: *an expedition to the jungles of the Orinoco* | informal *a shopping expedition*. ■ the people involved in such a journey: *many of the expedition have passed rigorous courses*.
2 [mass noun] formal promptness or speed in doing something: *the landlord shall remedy the defects with all possible expedition*.
– ORIGIN late Middle English: via Old French from Latin *expeditio(n-)*, from *expedire* 'extricate' (see **EXPEDITE**). Early senses included 'prompt supply of something' and 'setting out with aggressive intent'. The notions of 'speed' and 'purpose' are retained in current senses. Sense 1 dates from the late 16th cent.

expeditionary ▸ adjective [attrib.] of or forming an expedition, especially a military expedition: *an expeditionary force*.

expeditious /ˌɛkspɪˈdɪʃəs/ ▸ adjective done with speed and efficiency: *an expeditious investigation*.
– DERIVATIVES **expeditiously** adverb, **expeditiousness** noun.
– ORIGIN late 15th cent.: from **EXPEDITION** + **-OUS**.

expel ▸ verb (**expels, expelling, expelled**) [with obj.] officially make (someone) leave a school or other organization: *she was **expelled from** school*. ■ force (someone) to leave a place: *eight diplomats were expelled from Norway for espionage*. ■ force out (something), especially from the body: *she expelled a shuddering breath*.
– DERIVATIVES **expellable** adjective, **expellee** noun, **expeller** noun.
– ORIGIN late Middle English: from Latin *expellere*, from *ex-* 'out' + *pellere* 'to drive'.

expend ▸ verb [with obj.] spend or use up (a resource such as money or energy): *the energy expended in sport could be directed into other areas*.
– ORIGIN late Middle English: from Latin *expendere*, from *ex-* 'out' + *pendere* 'weigh, pay'. Compare with **SPEND**.

expendable ▸ adjective of relatively little significance, and therefore able to be abandoned or destroyed: *the region is expendable in the wider context of national politics*. ■ (of an object) designed to be used only once and then abandoned or destroyed: *unmanned and expendable launch vehicles*.
– DERIVATIVES **expendability** noun.

expenditure /ɪkˈspɛndɪtʃə, ɛk-/ ▸ noun [mass noun] the action of spending funds: *the expenditure of taxpayers' money*. ■ an amount of money spent: *cuts in public expenditure*. ■ the use of energy, time, or other resources: *work is the expenditure of energy*.
– ORIGIN mid 18th cent.: from **EXPEND**, suggested by obsolete *expenditor* 'officer in charge of expenditure', from medieval Latin, from *expenditus*, irregular past participle of Latin *expendere* (see **EXPEND**).

E

expense ▸ noun [mass noun] the cost incurred in or required for something: *conference rooms were equipped **at great expense*** | *book into the best hotel you can find and hang the expense*. ■ (**expenses**) the costs incurred in the performance of one's job or a specific task: *his hotel and travel expenses*. ■ [count noun] a thing on which one is required to spend money: *tolls are a daily expense*.
▸ verb [with obj.] offset (an item of expenditure) as an expense against taxable income. ■ informal charge (something) to an expense account: *I can expense the refreshments*.
– PHRASES **at someone's expense** paid for by someone. ■ with someone as the victim, especially of a joke: *my friends all had a good laugh at my expense*. **at the expense of** so as to cause harm to or neglect of: *the pursuit of profit at the expense of the environment*.
– ORIGIN late Middle English: from Anglo-Norman French, alteration of Old French *espense*, from late Latin *expensa (pecunia)* '(money) spent', from Latin *expendere* 'pay out' (see **EXPEND**).

expense account ▸ noun an arrangement under which money spent in the course of business is later reimbursed by one's employer.

expensive ▸ adjective costing a lot of money: *keeping a horse is expensive* | *an expensive bottle of wine*.
– DERIVATIVES **expensively** adverb, **expensiveness** noun.
– ORIGIN early 17th cent. (in the sense 'lavish, extravagant'): from Latin *expens-* 'paid out', from the verb *expendere* (see **EXPEND**), + **-IVE**.

experience ▸ noun **1** [mass noun] practical contact with and observation of facts or events: *he had learned his lesson by painful experience* | *she spoke from experience*. ■ the knowledge or skill acquired by such means over time, especially that gained in a particular profession: *you should have the necessary experience in health management*.
2 an event or occurrence which leaves an impression on someone: *audition day is an enjoyable experience for any seven-year old*.
▸ verb [with obj.] encounter or undergo (an event or occurrence): *the company is experiencing difficulties*. ■ feel (an emotion or sensation): *an opportunity to experience the excitement of New York*.
– DERIVATIVES **experienceable** adjective, **experiencer** noun.
– ORIGIN late Middle English: via Old French from Latin *experientia*, from *experiri* 'try'. Compare with **EXPERIMENT** and **EXPERT**.

experienced ▸ adjective having gained knowledge or skill in a particular field over time: *an experienced social worker* | *she was **experienced in** marketing*.

experiential /ɪkˌspɪərɪˈɛntʃ(ə)l, ɛk-/ ▸ adjective involving or based on experience and observation: *the experiential learning associated with employment*.
– DERIVATIVES **experientially** adverb.
– ORIGIN early 19th cent.: from **EXPERIENCE**, on the pattern of words such as *inferential*.

experiment ▸ noun a scientific procedure undertaken to make a discovery, test a hypothesis, or demonstrate a known fact: *a laboratory which carried out **experiments on** pigs* | [mass noun] *I have tested this by experiment*. ■ a course of action tentatively adopted without being sure of the outcome: *the previous **experiment in** liberal democracy had ended in disaster*.
▸ verb [no obj.] perform a scientific procedure, especially in a laboratory, to determine something: *experimenting **on** animals causes suffering*. ■ try out new ideas or methods: *the designers **experimented with** new ideas in lighting*.
– DERIVATIVES **experimentation** noun, **experimenter** noun.

– ORIGIN Middle English: from Old French, or from Latin *experimentum*, from *experiri* 'try'. Compare with EXPERIENCE and EXPERT.

experimental ▶ **adjective 1** (of a new invention or product) based on untested ideas or techniques and not yet established or finalized: *an experimental drug*. ■ relating to scientific experiments: *experimental results*.
2 (of art or an artistic technique) involving a radically new and innovative style: *experimental music*.
3 archaic based on experience as opposed to authority or conjecture: *an experimental knowledge of God*.
– DERIVATIVES **experimentalism** noun, **experimentalist** noun, **experimentally** adverb.
– ORIGIN late 15th cent. (in the sense 'having personal experience', also 'experienced, observed'): from medieval Latin *experimentalis*, from Latin *experimentum* (see EXPERIMENT).

E

experimental psychology ▶ **noun** [mass noun] the branch of psychology concerned with the scientific investigation of the responses of individuals to stimuli in controlled situations.

experimenter effect ▶ **noun** an influence exerted by the experimenter's expectations or other characteristics on the results of an experiment, especially in psychology.

expert ▶ **noun** a person who is very knowledgeable about or skilful in a particular area: *an expert in health care | a financial expert*.
▶ **adjective** having or involving such knowledge or skill: *he had received expert academic advice | I have a friend who is very **expert at** the language*.
– DERIVATIVES **expertly** adverb, **expertness** noun.
– ORIGIN Middle English (as an adjective): from French, from Latin *expertus*, past participle of *experiri* 'try'. The noun use dates from the early 19th cent. Compare with EXPERIENCE and EXPERIMENT.

expertise /ˌɛkspəːˈtiːz/ ▶ **noun** [mass noun] expert skill or knowledge in a particular field: *technical expertise*.
– ORIGIN mid 19th cent.: from French, from *expert* (see EXPERT).

expertize /ˈɛkspətʌɪz/ (also **expertise**) ▶ **verb** [no obj.] give an expert opinion on something.

expert system ▶ **noun** Computing a piece of software which uses databases of expert knowledge to offer advice or make decisions in such areas as medical diagnosis.

expert witness ▶ **noun** Law a person whose level of specialized knowledge or skill in a particular field qualifies them to present their opinion about the facts of a case during legal proceedings.

expiate /ˈɛkspɪeɪt/ ▶ **verb** [with obj.] make amends or reparation for (guilt or wrongdoing): *their sins must be expiated by sacrifice*.
– DERIVATIVES **expiable** adjective, **expiator** noun, **expiatory** /ˈɛkspɪət(ə)ri, ˌɛkspɪˈeɪt(ə)ri/ adjective.
– ORIGIN late 16th cent. (in the sense 'end (rage, sorrow, etc.) by suffering it to the full'): from Latin *expiat-* 'appeased by sacrifice', from the verb *expiare*, from *ex-* 'out' + *piare* (from *pius* 'pious').

expiation /ɛkspɪˈeɪʃ(ə)n/ ▶ **noun** [mass noun] the act of making amends or reparation for guilt or wrongdoing; atonement: *an act of public expiation*.

expiration /ˌɛkspɪˈreɪʃ(ə)n/ ▶ **noun** [mass noun] **1** N. Amer. the ending of the fixed period for which a contract is valid: *the expiration of the lease*. ■ the end of a period of time: *the expiration of three years*.
2 technical the exhalation of breath from the lungs.
– ORIGIN late Middle English (denoting a vapour or exhalation): from Latin *exspiratio(n-)*, from the verb *exspirare* (see EXPIRE).

expiratory /ɛksˈpʌɪrət(ə)ri/ ▶ **adjective** relating to the exhalation of air from the lungs.

expire /ɪkˈspʌɪə, ɛk-/ ▶ **verb 1** [no obj.] (of a document, authorization, or agreement) come to the end of the period of validity: *his driving licence expired*. ■ (of a period of time) come to an end: *the three-year period has expired*.
2 (of a person) die.
3 [with obj.] technical exhale (air) from the lungs.
– ORIGIN late Middle English: from Old French *expirer*, from Latin *exspirare* 'breathe out', from *ex-* 'out' + *spirare* 'breathe'.

expiry ▶ **noun** [mass noun] **1** Brit. the end of the period for which something is valid: *the expiry of the patent* | [as modifier] *an expiry date*. ■ the end of a fixed period of time.
2 archaic death.

explain ▶ **verb** [reporting verb] make (an idea or situation) clear to someone by describing it in more detail or revealing relevant facts: [with clause] *they explained that their lives centred on the religious rituals* | [with direct speech] *'It's a device of great age,' the professor explained* | [with obj.] *he explained the situation*. ■ [with obj.] give a reason so as to justify or excuse (an action or event): *Cassie found it necessary to explain her blackened eye* | [with clause] *he makes athletes explain why they made a mistake* | [no obj.] ***I explained about** Maureen calling round*. ■ (**explain something away**) minimize the significance of an embarrassing fact or action by giving an excuse or justification.
– PHRASES **explain oneself** expand on what one has said in order to make oneself clear. ■ excuse or justify one's motives or conduct: *he was too panicked to stay and explain himself to the policeman*.
– DERIVATIVES **explainable** adjective, **explainer** noun.
– ORIGIN late Middle English: from Latin *explanare*, based on *planus* 'plain'.

explanandum /ˌɛkspləˈnandəm/ ▶ **noun** (pl. **explananda** /-ˈnandə/) Philosophy another term for EXPLICANDUM.
– ORIGIN late 19th cent.: from Latin, 'something to be explained', neuter gerundive of *explanare*.

explanans /ˌɛkspləˈnanz/ ▶ **noun** (pl. **explanantia** /-ˈnantɪə/) Philosophy another term for EXPLICANS.
– ORIGIN 1940s: Latin, 'explaining', from the verb *explanare*.

explanation ▶ **noun** a statement or account that makes something clear: *the birth rate is central to any explanation of population trends*. ■ a reason or justification given for an action or belief: *Freud tried to make sex the explanation for everything* | [mass noun] *my application was rejected without explanation*.
– ORIGIN late Middle English: from Latin *explanatio(n-)*, from the verb *explanare* (see EXPLAIN).

explanatory /ɪkˈsplanəˌt(ə)ri, ɛk-/ ▶ **adjective** serving to explain something: *explanatory notes*.
– DERIVATIVES **explanatorily** adverb.

explant Biology ▶ **verb** /ɪksˈplɑːnt, ɛks-/ [with obj.] (usu. as adj. **explanted**) transfer (living cells, tissues, or organs) from animals or plants to a nutrient medium.
▶ **noun** /ˈɛksplɑːnt/ a cell, organ, or piece of tissue which has been transferred in this way.
– DERIVATIVES **explantation** noun.
– ORIGIN early 20th cent.: from modern Latin *explantare*, from *ex-* 'out' + *plantare* 'to plant'.

expletive /ɪkˈspliːtɪv, ɛk-/ ▶ **noun 1** an oath or swear word.
2 Grammar a word or phrase used to fill out a sentence or a line of verse without adding to the sense.
▶ **adjective** Grammar (of a word or phrase) serving to fill out a sentence or line of verse.
– ORIGIN late Middle English (as an adjective): from late Latin *expletivus*, from *explere* 'fill out', from *ex-* 'out' + *plere* 'fill'. The noun sense 'word used merely to fill out a sentence' (early 17th cent.) was applied specifically to a swear word in the early 19th cent.

explicable /ɪkˈsplɪkəb(ə)l, ɛk-, ˈɛksplɪˌkəb(ə)l/ ▶ **adjective** able to be accounted for or understood: *differences in schools were not explicable in terms of differences in intake*.
– ORIGIN mid 16th cent.: from French, or from Latin *explicabilis*, from *explicare* (see EXPLICATE).

explicandum /ˌɛksplɪˈkandəm/ ▶ **noun** (pl. **explicanda** /-ˈkandə/) Philosophy the fact, thing, or expression which is to be explained or explicated. Compare with EXPLICANS.
– ORIGIN mid 19th cent.: Latin, 'something to be explained', neuter gerundive of *explicare*.

explicans /ˌɛksplɪˈkanz/ ▶ **noun** (pl. **explicantia** /ˌɛksplɪˈkantɪə/) Philosophy the explanation or explication given for a fact, thing, or expression. Compare with EXPLICANDUM.
– ORIGIN late 19th cent.: Latin, present participle of *explicare* 'explain'.

explicate /ˈɛksplɪkeɪt/ ▶ **verb** [with obj.] analyse and develop (an idea or principle) in detail: *an attempt to explicate the relationship between crime and economic forces*. ■ analyse (a literary work) in order to reveal its meaning.
– DERIVATIVES **explication** noun, **explicative** /ɛkˈsplɪkətɪv, ˈɛksplɪkeɪtɪv/ adjective, **explicator** noun, **explicatory** /ɛkˈsplɪkət(ə)ri, ˈɛksplɪkeɪt(ə)ri/ adjective.
– ORIGIN mid 16th cent.: from Latin *explicat-* 'unfolded', from the verb *explicare*, from *ex-* 'out' + *plicare* 'to fold'.

explicit /ɪkˈsplɪsɪt, ɛk-/ ▶ **adjective** stated clearly and in detail, leaving no room for confusion or doubt: *the arrangement had not been made explicit*. ■ (of a person) stating something in such a way: *let me be explicit*. ■ describing or representing sexual activity in a graphic fashion: *a sexually explicit blockbuster*.
▶ **noun** the closing words of a manuscript, early printed book, or chanted liturgical text. Compare with INCIPIT. [Middle English: late Latin, 'here ends', or abbreviation of *explicitus est liber* 'the scroll is unrolled'.]
– DERIVATIVES **explicitly** adverb, **explicitness** noun.
– ORIGIN early 17th cent. (as an adjective): from French *explicite* or Latin *explicitus*, past participle of *explicare* 'unfold' (see EXPLICATE).

explode ▶ **verb** [no obj.] **1** burst or shatter violently and noisily as a result of rapid combustion, excessive internal pressure, or other process: *an ammunition lorry exploded with a roar* | [with obj.] *Britain had not yet exploded her first nuclear weapon*. ■ technical undergo a violent expansion in which much energy is released as a shock wave: *lead ensures that petrol burns rather than explodes*. ■ (as adj. **exploded**) (of a diagram) showing the components of a mechanism in the normal relative positions but slightly separated from each other.
2 (of a violent emotion or a situation) arise or develop suddenly: *tension which could explode into violence at any time*. ■ (of a person) suddenly give expression to violent emotion, especially anger: *he **exploded with** rage* | [with direct speech] *'This is ludicrous!' she exploded*. ■ (**explode into**) suddenly begin to move or start a new activity: *workers exploded into action as trade revived*.
3 increase suddenly in size, number, or extent: *the use of this drug exploded in the nineties*.
4 [with obj.] show (a belief or theory) to be false or unfounded: *the myths that link smoking with glamour need to be exploded*.
– DERIVATIVES **exploder** noun.
– ORIGIN mid 16th cent. (in the sense 'reject scornfully'): from Latin *explodere* 'drive out by clapping, hiss off the stage', from *ex-* 'out' + *plaudere* 'to clap'. Sense 4 is derived from the original sense of the word. Sense 1 (late 18th cent.) evolved via an old sense 'expel with violence and sudden noise', perhaps influenced by obsolete *displode* 'burst with a noise'.

exploit ▶ **verb** /ɪkˈsplɔɪt, ɛk-/ [with obj.] **1** make full use of and derive benefit from (a resource): *500 companies sprang up to exploit this new technology*.
2 make use of (a situation) in a way considered unfair or underhand: *the company was exploiting a legal loophole*. ■ benefit unfairly from the work of (someone), typically by overworking or underpaying them: *women are exploited in the workplace*.
▶ **noun** /ˈɛksplɔɪt/ a bold or daring feat.
– DERIVATIVES **exploitable** adjective, **exploiter** noun.
– ORIGIN Middle English: from Old French *esploit* (noun), based on Latin *explicare* 'unfold' (see EXPLICATE). The early notion of 'success, progress' gave rise to the sense 'attempt to capture', 'military expedition', hence the current sense of the noun. Verb senses (mid 19th cent.) are from modern French *exploiter*.

exploitation /ɛksplɔɪˈteɪʃ(ə)n/ ▶ **noun 1** [mass noun] the action or fact of treating someone unfairly in order to benefit from their work: *the exploitation of migrant workers*.
2 the action of making use of and benefiting from resources: *the Bronze Age saw exploitation of gold deposits*. ■ the fact of making use of a situation to gain unfair advantage for oneself: *the Government's exploitation of the fear of crime*.

exploitative (also **exploitive**) ▶ **adjective** making use of a situation or treating others unfairly in order to gain an advantage or benefit: *an exploitative form of labour*.

exploration ▶ **noun** [mass noun] **1** the action of exploring an unfamiliar area: *space exploration* | [count noun] *an exploration of the African interior*. ■ the action of searching an area for natural resources: *onshore oil and gas exploration*.
2 thorough examination of a subject: *some changes in the care-giving situation may need exploration* | [count noun] *an exploration of society and human nature*.
– DERIVATIVES **explorational** adjective.

exploratory /ɪkˈsplɒrət(ə)ri, ɛk-/ ▶ **adjective** relating to or involving exploration or investigation: *surgeons performed an exploratory operation | exploratory talks*.
– ORIGIN late Middle English: from Latin *exploratorius*, from Latin *explorare* (see EXPLORE).

explore ▶ **verb** [with obj.] **1** travel through (an unfamiliar area) in order to learn about it: *he explored the Fontainebleau forest* | figurative *the project encourages children to explore the world of photography*. ■ [no obj.]

(**explore for**) search for resources such as mineral deposits.
2 inquire into or discuss (a subject) in detail: *he sets out to explore fundamental questions.* ■ examine or evaluate (an option or possibility): *the firm will explore joint development projects.*
3 examine by touch: *her fingers explored his hair.*
4 Medicine surgically examine (a wound or part of the body) in detail.
– DERIVATIVES **explorative** adjective.
– ORIGIN mid 16th cent. (in the sense 'investigate (why)'): from French *explorer*, from Latin *explorare* 'search out', from *ex-* 'out' + *plorare* 'utter a cry'.

explorer ▸ noun a person who explores a new or unfamiliar area: *a polar explorer.*

explosion ▸ noun **1** a violent shattering or blowing apart of something, as is caused by a bomb. ■ technical a violent expansion in which energy is transmitted outwards as a shock wave.
2 a sudden outburst of something such as violent emotion, especially anger: *an explosion of anger inside the factory.*
3 a sudden increase in amount or extent: *an explosion in the adder population.*
– ORIGIN early 17th cent.: from Latin *explosio(n-)* 'scornful rejection', from the verb *explodere* (see EXPLODE).

explosive ▸ adjective **1** able or likely to shatter violently or burst apart: *an explosive device.* ■ (of a vocal sound) produced with a sharp release of air.
2 likely to cause an outburst of anger or controversy: *Marco's explosive temper | the idea was politically explosive.*
3 (of an increase) sudden and dramatic: *the explosive growth of personal computers in the 1980s.*
▸ noun (often **explosives**) a substance which can be made to explode, especially any of those used in bombs or shells.
– DERIVATIVES **explosively** adverb, **explosiveness** noun.

explosive bolt ▸ noun a bolt that can be released by being blown out of position by an integral explosive charge.

expo /ˈɛkspəʊ/ ▸ noun (pl. **expos**) a large international exhibition.
– ORIGIN 1960s (referring to the World Fair held in Montreal in 1967): abbreviation of EXPOSITION.

exponent /ɪkˈspəʊnənt, ɛk-/ ▸ noun **1** a person who supports an idea or theory and tries to persuade people of its truth or benefits: *an early* **exponent of** *the teachings of Thomas Aquinas.* ■ a person who demonstrates a particular skill to a high standard: *he's the world's leading exponent of country rock guitar.*
2 Mathematics a quantity representing the power to which a given number or expression is to be raised, usually expressed as a raised symbol beside the number or expression (e.g. 3 in $2^3 = 2 \times 2 \times 2$).
3 Linguistics a linguistic unit that realizes another, more abstract unit.
– ORIGIN late 16th cent. (as an adjective in the sense 'expounding'): from Latin *exponent-* 'putting out', from the verb *exponere* (see EXPOUND).

exponential /ˌɛkspəˈnɛnʃ(ə)l/ ▸ adjective **1** (of an increase) becoming more and more rapid: *the social security budget was rising at an exponential rate.*
2 Mathematics of or expressed by a mathematical exponent: *an exponential curve.*
– DERIVATIVES **exponentially** adverb.
– ORIGIN early 18th cent.: from French *exponentiel*, from Latin *exponere* 'put out' (see EXPOUND).

exponential function ▸ noun Mathematics a function whose value is a constant raised to the power of the argument, especially the function where the constant is *e*.

exponential growth ▸ noun [mass noun] growth whose rate becomes ever more rapid in proportion to the growing total number or size.

exponentiation /ˌɛkspənɛnʃɪˈeɪʃ(ə)n/ ▸ noun [mass noun] Mathematics the operation of raising one quantity to the power of another.
– DERIVATIVES **exponentiate** verb.

export ▸ verb /ɪkˈspɔːt, ɛk-, ˈɛk-/ [with obj.] send (goods or services) to another country for sale: *nearly all the bananas produced were exported to Britain.* ■ spread or introduce (ideas and beliefs) to another country: *the Greeks exported Hellenic culture around the Mediterranean basin.* ■ Computing transfer (data) in a format that can be used by other programs.
▸ noun /ˈɛkspɔːt/ (usu. **exports**) a product or service sold abroad: *wool and mohair were the principal exports.* ■ (**exports**) sales of goods or services abroad, or the revenue from such sales: *meat exports.* ■ [mass noun] the selling and sending out of goods or services to other countries: *the export of Western technology.* ■ [as modifier] of a high standard suitable for export: *export ales.*
– DERIVATIVES **exportability** noun, **exportable** adjective, **exportation** noun, **exporter** noun.
– ORIGIN late 15th cent. (in the sense 'take away'): from Latin *exportare*, from *ex-* 'out' + *portare* 'carry'. Current senses date from the 17th cent.

export surplus ▸ noun the amount by which the value of a country's exports exceeds that of its imports.

expose ▸ verb [with obj.] **1** make (something) visible by uncovering it: *at low tide the sands are exposed.* ■ (as adj. **exposed**) unprotected, especially from the weather: *the coast is very exposed to the south-west.* ■ (often **expose someone to**) cause someone to be vulnerable or at risk: *many newcomers are exposing themselves to injury.* ■ (**expose someone to**) introduce someone to (a subject or area of knowledge): *students were exposed to statistics in high school.* ■ (**expose oneself**) publicly and indecently display one's genitals. ■ leave (a child) in the open to die.
2 reveal the true, objectionable nature of (someone or something): *he has been* **exposed as** *a liar and a traitor.* ■ make (something embarrassing or damaging) public: *the situation exposed a conflict within the government.*
3 subject (photographic film) to light when operating a camera.
– DERIVATIVES **exposer** noun.
– ORIGIN late Middle English: from Old French *exposer*, from Latin *exponere* (see EXPOUND), but influenced by Latin *expositus* 'put or set out' and Old French *poser* 'to place'.

exposé /ɪkˈspəʊzeɪ, ɛk-/ ▸ noun a report in the media that reveals something discreditable: *a shocking exposé of a medical cover-up.*
– ORIGIN early 19th cent.: from French, 'shown, set out', past participle of *exposer* (see EXPOSE).

exposition ▸ noun **1** a comprehensive description and explanation of an idea or theory: *a systematic exposition of the idea of biodiversity.*
2 a large public exhibition of art or trade goods.
3 Music the part of a movement, especially in sonata form, in which the principal themes are first presented.
4 [mass noun] archaic the action of making something public.
– DERIVATIVES **expositional** adjective.
– ORIGIN Middle English: from Latin *expositio(n-)*, from the verb *exponere* 'expose, publish, explain'.

expositor /ɪkˈspɒzɪtə, ɛk-/ ▸ noun a person that explains complicated ideas or theories.
– ORIGIN Middle English: via Old French or late Latin, from Latin *exposit-* 'exposed, explained', from *exponere* (see EXPOUND).

expository ▸ adjective intended to explain or describe something: *an expository prologue.*

ex post /ɛks ˈpəʊst/ ▸ adjective & adverb based on actual results rather than forecasts: [as adj.] *the ex post trade balance.*
– ORIGIN modern Latin, from *ex* 'from' and *post* 'after'.

ex post facto /ˌɛks pəʊst ˈfaktəʊ/ ▸ adjective & adverb with retrospective action or force: [as adj.] *ex post facto laws.*
– ORIGIN erroneous division of Latin *ex postfacto* 'in the light of subsequent events'.

expostulate /ɪkˈspɒstjʊleɪt, ɛk-/ ▸ verb [no obj.] express strong disapproval or disagreement: *he found Fox* **expostulating with** *a young man.*
– DERIVATIVES **expostulation** noun, **expostulatory** /-lət(ə)ri/ adjective.
– ORIGIN mid 16th cent. (in the sense 'demand how or why, state a complaint'): from Latin *expostulat-* 'demanded', from the verb *expostulare*, from *ex-* 'out' + *postulare* 'demand'.

exposure ▸ noun [mass noun] **1** the state of having no protection from something harmful: *the dangers posed by* **exposure to** *asbestos.* ■ a physical condition resulting from being outside in severe weather without adequate protection: *they were suffering from exposure.* ■ experience of something: *his* **exposure to** *the banking system.* ■ the action of placing oneself at risk of financial losses, e.g. through making loans or underwriting insurance.
2 the revelation of something secret, especially something embarrassing or damaging: *she took her life for fear of exposure as a spy.* ■ the publicizing of information or an event: *scientific findings receive regular exposure in the media.*
3 the action of exposing a photographic film to light: *a camera which would give a picture immediately after exposure* | [count noun] *trial exposures made with a UV filter.* ■ [count noun] the quantity of light reaching a photographic film, as determined by shutter speed and lens aperture.
4 [count noun] the direction in which a building faces; an outlook: *the exposure is perfect—a gentle slope to the south-west.*
– ORIGIN early 17th cent.: from EXPOSE, on the pattern of words such as *enclosure*.

exposure meter ▸ noun Photography a light meter.

expound ▸ verb [with obj.] present and explain (a theory or idea) in detail: *he was expounding a powerful argument* | [no obj.] *he declined to* **expound on** *his decision.* ■ explain the meaning of (a literary or doctrinal work): *the abbess expounded the scriptures to her nuns.*
– DERIVATIVES **expounder** noun.
– ORIGIN Middle English *expoune* (in the sense 'explain (what is difficult)'): from Old French *espon-*, present tense stem of *espondre*, from Latin *exponere* 'expose, publish, explain', from *ex-* 'out' + *ponere* 'put'. The origin of the final *-d* (recorded from the Middle English period) is uncertain.

E

express[1] /ɪkˈsprɛs, ɛk-/ ▸ verb [with obj.] **1** convey (a thought or feeling) in words or by gestures and conduct: *he expressed complete satisfaction.* ■ (**express oneself**) say what one thinks or means: *with a diplomatic smile, she expressed herself more subtly.* ■ Mathematics represent (a number, relation, or property) by a figure, symbol, or formula: *constants can be* **expressed in terms of** *the Fourier transform.*
2 press out (liquid or air).
3 Genetics cause (an inherited characteristic or gene) to appear in a phenotype: *the genes are expressed in a variety of cell lines.*
– DERIVATIVES **expresser** noun, **expressible** adjective.
– ORIGIN late Middle English (also in the sense 'press out, obtain by squeezing', used figuratively to mean 'extort'): from Old French *expresser*, based on Latin *ex-* 'out' + *pressare* 'to press'.

express[2] /ɪkˈsprɛs, ɛk-/ ▸ adjective operating at high speed, in particular: ■ (of a train or other form of public transport) making few intermediate stops and reaching its destination quickly: *an express train bound for Innsbruck | an express bus service.* ■ denoting a service in which letters or packages are delivered by a special service to ensure speed or security: *an express letter.*
▸ adverb by express train or delivery service: *I got my wife to send my gloves express to the hotel.*
▸ noun **1** (also **express train**) a train that stops at few stations and travels quickly.
2 a special delivery service: *the books arrived by express.*
3 an express rifle.
▸ verb [with obj.] send by express messenger or delivery: *I expressed my clothes to my destination.*
– ORIGIN early 18th cent. (as a verb): extension of EXPRESS[3]; sense 1 of the noun from *express train*, so named because it served a particular destination without intermediate stops, reflecting an earlier sense of *express* 'done or made for a special purpose', later interpreted in the sense 'rapid'. Senses relating to *express delivery* date from the institution of this postal service in 1891.

express[3] /ɪkˈsprɛs, ɛk-, ˈɛksprɛs/ ▸ adjective stated explicitly, not merely implied: *it was his express wish that the celebration should continue.* ■ specifically identified to the exclusion of anything else: *the schools were founded for the express purpose of teaching deaf children.* ■ archaic (of a likeness) exact.
– ORIGIN late Middle English: from Old French *expres*, from Latin *expressus* 'distinctly presented', past participle of *exprimere* 'press out', from *ex-* 'out' + *primere* 'press'.

expression ▸ noun [mass noun] **1** the action of making known one's thoughts or feelings: *the prisoners developed a dialect as an everyday means of expression* | [count noun] *she accepted his expressions of sympathy.* ■ the conveying of feeling in a work of art or in the performance of a piece of music.
2 [count noun] a look on someone's face that conveys a particular emotion: *a sad expression.*
3 [count noun] a word or phrase, especially an idiomatic one, used to convey an idea: *we have an expression, 'You don't get owt for nowt.'* ■ Mathematics a collection of symbols that jointly express a quantity: *the expression for the circumference of a circle is $2\pi r$.*

4 the production of something by pressing it out: *essential oils obtained by distillation or expression.* **5** Genetics the appearance in a phenotype of a characteristic or effect attributed to a particular gene.
– DERIVATIVES **expressional** adjective.
– ORIGIN late Middle English: from Latin *expressio(n-)*, from *exprimere* 'press out, express'. Compare with EXPRESS[1].

expressionism ▶ noun [mass noun] a style of painting, music, or drama in which the artist or writer seeks to express the inner world of emotion rather than external reality.

> Expressionists characteristically reject traditional ideas of beauty or harmony and use distortion, exaggeration, and other non-naturalistic devices in order to express emotional states. The paintings of El Greco and Grünewald exemplify expressionism in this broad sense, but the term is also used of a late 19th and 20th century European and specifically German movement tracing its origins to Van Gogh, Edvard Munch, and James Ensor, which insisted on the primacy of the artist's feelings and mood, often incorporating violence and the grotesque.

E

– DERIVATIVES **expressionist** noun & adjective, **expressionistic** adjective, **expressionistically** adverb.

expressionless ▶ adjective (of a person's face or voice) not conveying any emotion; unemotional: *her face was expressionless.*
– DERIVATIVES **expressionlessly** adverb, **expressionlessness** noun.

expression mark ▶ noun Music a word or phrase on a musical score which indicates the expression required of a performer.

expressive ▶ adjective effectively conveying thought or feeling: *she has big expressive eyes.* ■ **(expressive of)** conveying (a specified quality or idea): *the spires are expressive of religious aspiration.*
– DERIVATIVES **expressively** adverb, **expressiveness** noun, **expressivity** noun.
– ORIGIN late Middle English (in the sense 'tending to press out'): from French *expressif, -ive* or medieval Latin *expressivus*, from *exprimere* 'press out' (see EXPRESS[3]). Compare with EXPRESS[1].

express lift ▶ noun a fast-moving lift which does not stop at every floor.

expressly /ɪk'sprɛsli, ɛk-/ ▶ adverb explicitly; clearly: *she was expressly forbidden to use the stove.* ■ for a specific purpose; solely: *the house was expressly built for entertaining.*

expresso /ɛk'sprɛsəʊ/ ▶ noun (pl. **expressos**) see ESPRESSO.

express rifle ▶ noun a rifle that discharges a bullet at high speed, used in big-game hunting.

expressway ▶ noun N. Amer. an urban motorway.

expropriate /ɪks'prəʊprɪeɪt, ɛks-/ ▶ verb [with obj.] (of the state or an authority) take (property) from its owner for public use or benefit: *their assets were expropriated by the government.* ■ dispossess (someone) of property: *the measures expropriated the landlords.*
– DERIVATIVES **expropriation** noun, **expropriator** noun.
– ORIGIN late 16th cent.: from medieval Latin *expropriat-* 'taken from the owner', from the verb *expropriare*, from *ex-* 'out, from' + *proprium* 'property', neuter singular of *proprius* 'own'.

expulsion ▶ noun [mass noun] the action of forcing someone to leave an organization: *his* ***expulsion from*** *the union* | [count noun] *a rise in the number of pupil expulsions.* ■ the action or process of forcing someone to leave a place: *the expulsion of two diplomats from the embassy.* ■ the action of forcing something out of the body.
– DERIVATIVES **expulsive** adjective.
– ORIGIN late Middle English: from Latin *expulsio(n-)*, from *expellere* 'drive out' (see EXPEL).

expunge /ɪk'spʌn(d)ʒ, ɛk-/ ▶ verb [with obj.] obliterate or remove completely (something unwanted or unpleasant): *the kind of man that could expunge an unsatisfactory incident from his memory.*
– DERIVATIVES **expunction** noun, **expungement** noun, **expunger** noun.
– ORIGIN early 17th cent.: from Latin *expungere* 'mark for deletion by means of points', from *ex-* 'out' + *pungere* 'to prick'.

expurgate /'ɛkspəːgeɪt/ ▶ verb [with obj.] (usu. as adj. **expurgated**) remove matter thought to be objectionable or unsuitable from (a text or account): *an expurgated English translation.*
– DERIVATIVES **expurgation** noun, **expurgator** noun, **expurgatory** /ɛk'spəːgət(ə)ri/ adjective.
– ORIGIN early 17th cent. (in the sense 'purge of excrement'): from Latin *expurgat-* 'thoroughly cleansed', from the verb *expurgare*, from *ex-* 'out' + *purgare* 'cleanse'.

exquisite /'ɛkskwɪzɪt, ɪk'skwɪzɪt, ɛk-/ ▶ adjective **1** extremely beautiful and delicate: *exquisite, jewel-like portraits.* **2** intensely felt: *the most exquisite kind of agony.* ■ highly sensitive or discriminating: *her exquisite taste in painting.*
▶ noun literary a man who is affectedly concerned with his clothes and appearance; a dandy.
– DERIVATIVES **exquisitely** adverb, **exquisiteness** noun.
– ORIGIN late Middle English (in the sense 'precise'): from Latin *exquisit-* 'sought out', from the verb *exquirere*, from *ex-* 'out' + *quaerere* 'seek'.

exsanguination /ɪk,saŋgwɪ'neɪʃ(ə)n, ɛk-/ ▶ noun [mass noun] Medicine the action of draining a person, animal, or organ of blood. ■ severe loss of blood.
– DERIVATIVES **exsanguinate** verb.
– ORIGIN early 20th cent.: from Latin *exsanguinatus* 'drained of blood' (from *ex-* 'out' + *sanguis, sanguin-* 'blood') + -ION.

exsanguine /ɪk'saŋgwɪn, ɛk-/ ▶ adjective literary bloodless; anaemic.
– ORIGIN mid 17th cent.: from EX-[1] 'out' + Latin *sanguis, sanguin-* 'blood'.

exsert /ɪk'səːt, ɛk-/ ▶ verb [with obj.] (usu. as adj. **exserted**) Biology cause to protrude: *an exserted stigma.*
– ORIGIN mid 17th cent.: from Latin *exsert-* 'put forth', from the verb *exserere* (see EXERT).

ex-service ▶ adjective Brit. denoting or relating to former members of the armed forces: *ex-service personnel.*

ex-serviceman (or **ex-servicewoman**) ▶ noun (pl. **ex-servicemen** or **ex-servicewomen**) Brit. a person who was formerly a member of the armed forces.

ex silentio /,ɛks sɪ'lɛnʃɪəʊ/ ▶ adjective & adverb (with reference to an argument or theory) based on lack of contrary evidence.
– ORIGIN Latin, 'from silence'.

exsolve /ɪk'sɒlv, ɛk-/ ▶ verb [no obj.] Geology (of a mineral) separate out from solid solution in a rock. ■ [with obj.] (usu. as adj. **exsolved**) form (a mineral) in this way.
– DERIVATIVES **exsolution** noun.
– ORIGIN mid 20th cent.: (originally as *exsolution*) from EX-[1] + SOLUTION.

ext. ▶ abbreviation ■ extension (in a telephone number). ■ exterior. ■ external.

extant /ɪk'stant, ɛk-, 'ɛkst(ə)nt/ ▶ adjective still in existence; surviving: *an extant letter.*
– ORIGIN mid 16th cent. (in the sense 'able to be publicly seen or reached'): from Latin *exstant-* 'being visible or prominent, existing', from the verb *exstare*, from *ex-* 'out' + *stare* 'to stand'.

extemporaneous /ɪk,stɛmpə'reɪnɪəs, ɛk-/ ▶ adjective another term for EXTEMPORARY.
– DERIVATIVES **extemporaneously** adverb, **extemporaneousness** noun.

extemporary /ɪk'stɛmp(ə)(rə)ri, ɛk-/ ▶ adjective spoken or done without preparation: *an extemporary prayer.*
– DERIVATIVES **extemporarily** adverb.
– ORIGIN late 16th cent.: from EXTEMPORE, on the pattern of *temporary.*

extempore /ɪk'stɛmp(ə)ri, ɛk-/ ▶ adjective & adverb spoken or done without preparation: [as adj.] *extempore public speaking* | [as adv.] *he recited the poem extempore.*
– ORIGIN mid 16th cent.: from Latin *ex tempore* 'on the spur of the moment' (literally 'out of the time').

extemporize /ɪk'stɛmpərʌɪz, ɛk-/ (also **extemporise**) ▶ verb [no obj.] compose or perform something such as music or a speech without preparation; improvise: *he extemporized at the piano* | [with obj.] *she was extemporizing touching melodies.*
– DERIVATIVES **extemporization** noun.

extend ▶ verb [with obj.] **1** cause to cover a wider area; make larger: *the car park has been extended.* ■ cause to last longer: *they asked the government to extend its period of deliberation.* ■ straighten or spread out (the body or a limb or device) at full length: *hold the index finger down with the thumb extended* | (as adj. **extending**) *a case with wheels and an extending handle.* ■ [no obj.] spread from a central point to cover a wider area: *the damage extended 400 yards either side of the shop.* ■ [no obj.] occupy a specified area: *the mountains extend over the western end of the island.* ■ [no obj.] **(extend to)** be applicable to: *her generosity did not extend to all adults.* **2** hold (something) out towards someone: *I nod and extend my hand.* ■ offer or make available: *she extended an invitation to her to stay.* **3** cause (someone or something) to exert the utmost effort: *horses have the strength of character to* ***extend themselves*** *to their utmost limit.*
– DERIVATIVES **extendability** noun, **extendable** adjective, **extendibility** noun, **extendible** adjective.
– ORIGIN late Middle English: from Latin *extendere* 'stretch out', from *ex-* 'out' + *tendere* 'stretch'.

extended ▶ adjective made larger; enlarged: *an extended kitchen and new balcony.* ■ lasting longer than is usual or expected; prolonged: *an extended period of time.*

extended family ▶ noun a family which extends beyond the nuclear family to include grandparents and other relatives.

extended-play ▶ adjective (of a record) that plays for longer than most singles.

extender ▶ noun a person or thing that extends something. ■ a substance added to a product such as paint or glue, to dilute its colour or increase its bulk. ■ Photography another term for EXTENSION TUBE.

extensible ▶ adjective able to be extended; extendable: *an extensible architecture designed to accommodate changes.*
– DERIVATIVES **extensibility** noun.

extensile /ɪk'stɛnsʌɪl, ɛk-/ ▶ adjective capable of being stretched out or protruded.
– ORIGIN mid 18th cent.: from Latin *extens-* 'stretched out' (from the verb *extendere*) + -ILE.

extension ▶ noun **1** a part that is added to something to enlarge or prolong it: *the railway's southern extension.* ■ a room or rooms added to an existing building. ■ **(extensions)** lengths of artificial hair woven into a person's own hair to create a very long hairstyle. ■ [mass noun] the action or process of enlarging or extending something: *the extension of the President's powers.* ■ an application of an existing system or activity to a new area: *direct marketing is an extension of telephone selling.* ■ an additional period of time given to someone to hold office or fulfil an obligation. ■ Brit. permission granted to licensed premises for the sale of alcoholic drinks until later than usual. ■ Computing an optional suffix to a filename, typically consisting of a full stop followed by several characters, indicating the file's content or function. **2** (Brit. also **extension lead** or **cable**; US also **extension cord**) a length of electric cable which permits the use of appliances at some distance from a fixed socket. **3** a subsidiary telephone on the same line as the main one. ■ a subsidiary telephone in a large building, on a line leading from the main switchboard but having its own additional number. **4** [mass noun] the action of moving a limb from a bent to a straight position: *seizures with sudden rigid extension of the limbs.* ■ Ballet the ability of a dancer to raise one leg above their waist, especially to the side: *she has amazing extension.* ■ Medicine the application of traction to a fractured or dislocated limb or to an injured spinal column to restore it to its normal position. ■ the lengthening of a horse's stride at a particular pace. **5** [as modifier] denoting instruction by a university or college arranged for people who are not full-time students: *a postgraduate extension course.* **6** Logic the range of a term or concept as measured by the objects which it denotes or contains. Often contrasted with INTENSION. **7** Physics & Philosophy the property of occupying space: *nature, for Descartes, was pure extension in space.*
– PHRASES **by extension** taking the same line of argument further: *the study shows how television and, by extension, the media, alter political relationships.*
– DERIVATIVES **extensional** adjective.
– ORIGIN late Middle English: from late Latin *extensio(n-)*, from *extendere* 'stretch out' (see EXTEND).

extension tube ▶ noun Photography a tube fitted to a camera between the body and lens to shorten the distance of closest focus of an object so that close-up pictures can be taken.

extensive ▶ adjective **1** covering or affecting a large area: *an extensive garden.* ■ large in amount or scale: *an extensive collection of silver.*

2 (of agriculture) obtaining a relatively small crop from a large area with a minimum of capital and labour: *extensive farming techniques*. Often contrasted with INTENSIVE (sense 1 of the adjective).
– DERIVATIVES **extensively** adverb, **extensiveness** noun.
– ORIGIN late Middle English: from French *extensif, -ive* or late Latin *extensivus*, from *extens-* 'stretched out', from the verb *extendere* (see EXTEND).

extensometer /ˌɛkstɛnˈsɒmɪtə/ ▶ noun an instrument for measuring the deformation of a material under stress.
– ORIGIN late 19th cent.: from Latin *extens-* 'extended' (from the verb *extendere*) + -METER.

extensor /ɪkˈstɛnsə, ɛk-/ (also **extensor muscle**) ▶ noun Anatomy a muscle whose contraction extends or straightens a limb or other part of the body. Often contrasted with FLEXOR.
– ORIGIN early 18th cent.: from late Latin, from *extens-* 'stretched out', from the verb *extendere* (see EXTEND).

extent ▶ noun [in sing.] 1 the area covered by something: *an enclosure ten acres in extent*. ■ the size or scale of something: *the extent of global warming*.
2 the particular degree to which something is or is believed to be the case: *everyone will have to compromise to some extent | decision-making was **to a large extent** outside his control*.
– ORIGIN Middle English (in the sense 'valuation of property, especially for taxation'): from Anglo-Norman French *extente*, from medieval Latin *extenta*, feminine past participle of Latin *extendere* 'stretch out' (see EXTEND).

extenuate /ɪkˈstɛnjʊeɪt, ɛk-/ ▶ verb [with obj.] 1 (as adj. **extenuating**) (of a factor or situation) acting in mitigation to lessen the seriousness of guilt or an offence: *hunger and poverty are not treated by the courts as **extenuating circumstances***.
2 (usu. as adj. **extenuated**) literary make (someone) thin: *drawings of extenuated figures*.
– DERIVATIVES **extenuation** noun.
– ORIGIN late Middle English (in the sense 'make thin'): from Latin *extenuat-* 'made thin', from the verb *extenuare* (based on *tenuis* 'thin').

exterior ▶ adjective forming, situated on, or relating to the outside of something: *exterior and interior walls*. ■ coming from outside: *exterior noise*. ■ (in filming) outdoor: *exterior locations*.
▶ noun the outer surface or structure of something: *a jar with floral designs on the exterior*. ■ the outer structure of a building: *the museum has a modern exterior*. ■ a person's behaviour and demeanour, especially when at variance with their true character: *beneath that assured exterior, she's vulnerable*. ■ (in filming) an outdoor scene.
– DERIVATIVES **exteriority** noun, **exteriorly** adverb.
– ORIGIN early 16th cent.: from Latin, comparative of *exter* 'outer'.

exterior angle ▶ noun Geometry the angle between a side of a rectilinear figure and an adjacent side extended outward.

exteriorize (also **exteriorise**) ▶ verb make exterior; give exterior form to.
– DERIVATIVES **exteriorization** (also **exteriorisation**) noun.

exterminate /ɪkˈstəːmɪneɪt, ɛk-/ ▶ verb [with obj.] destroy completely: *leftist ideals had not been totally exterminated*. ■ kill (a pest): *they use poison to exterminate moles*.
– DERIVATIVES **exterminator** noun, **exterminatory** /-nət(ə)ri/ adjective.
– ORIGIN late Middle English (in the sense 'drive out'): from Latin *exterminat-* 'driven out', from the verb *exterminare*, from *ex-* 'out' + *terminus* 'boundary'. The sense 'destroy' (mid 16th cent.) comes from the Latin of the Vulgate.

extermination /ɪkˌstəːmɪˈneɪʃ(ə)n, ɛk-/ ▶ noun [mass noun] killing, especially of a whole group of people or animals: *the near extermination of the buffalo herds*. ■ complete destruction.

extern /ɪkˈstəːn, ɛk-/ ▶ noun 1 N. Amer. a non-resident doctor or other worker in a hospital.
2 (in a strictly enclosed order of nuns) a sister who does not live exclusively within the enclosure and goes on outside errands.
▶ verb [with obj.] SE Asian banish (someone considered politically undesirable) from a region or district: *he was externed for inciting communal tension in the city*.
– DERIVATIVES **externment** noun.
– ORIGIN mid 16th cent. (as an adjective in the sense 'external'): from French *externe* or Latin *externus*, from *exter* 'outer'. The word was used by Shakespeare to mean 'outward appearance'; current noun senses date from the early 17th cent.

external ▶ adjective 1 belonging to or forming the outer surface or structure of something: *the external walls*. ■ relating to or denoting a medicine or similar substance for use on the outside of the body: *for external application only*.
2 coming or derived from a source outside the subject affected: *for many the Church was a symbol of external authority | the child learns to form conceptions of the external world*. ■ coming from or relating to a country or institution other than the main subject: *a department of external affairs*. ■ for or concerning students registered with and taking the examinations of a university but not resident there: *external degrees*.
3 Computing (of hardware) not contained in the main computer; peripheral. ■ (of storage) using a disk or tape drive rather than the main memory.
▶ noun (**externals**) the outward features of something: *the place has all the appropriate externals, such as chimneys choked with ivy*. ■ inessential or superficial features.
– DERIVATIVES **externally** adverb.
– ORIGIN late Middle English: from medieval Latin, from Latin *exter* 'outer'.

external auditory meatus ▶ noun see MEATUS.

external ear ▶ noun the parts of the ear outside the eardrum, especially the pinna.

externalism ▶ noun [mass noun] 1 excessive regard for outward form in religion.
2 Philosophy the view that mental events and acts are essentially dependent on the world external to the mind, in opposition to the Cartesian separation of mental and physical worlds.
– DERIVATIVES **externalist** noun & adjective.

externality /ˌɛkstəːˈnalɪti/ ▶ noun (pl. **externalities**) 1 Economics a consequence of an industrial or commercial activity which affects other parties without this being reflected in market prices, such as the pollination of surrounding crops by bees kept for honey.
2 [mass noun] Philosophy the fact of existing outside the perceiving subject.

externalize (also **externalise**) ▶ verb [with obj.] 1 give external existence or form to: *elements of the internal construction were externalized on to the facade*. ■ express (a thought or feeling) in words or actions: *an urgent need to externalize the experience*. ■ Psychology project (a mental image or process) on to a figure outside oneself: *such neuroses are externalized as interpersonal conflicts*.
2 Economics fail or choose not to incorporate (costs) as part of a pricing structure, especially social and environmental costs resulting from a product's manufacture and use.
– DERIVATIVES **externalization** noun.

exteroceptive /ˌɛkstərə(ʊ)ˈsɛptɪv/ ▶ adjective Physiology relating to stimuli that are external to an organism. Compare with INTEROCEPTIVE.
– DERIVATIVES **exteroception** noun.
– ORIGIN early 20th cent.: probably a blend of EXTERIOR or EXTERNAL and RECEPTIVE.

exteroceptor /ˈɛkstərə(ʊ)ˌsɛptə/ ▶ noun Physiology a sensory receptor which receives external stimuli. Compare with INTEROCEPTOR.

extinct ▶ adjective 1 (of a species, family, or other larger group) having no living members: *trilobites and dinosaurs are extinct*. ■ no longer in existence: *an extinct language | the sort of girls' school that is now extinct*. ■ (of a title of nobility) having no valid claimant.
2 (of a volcano) not having erupted in recorded history. ■ no longer alight: *his now extinct pipe*.
– ORIGIN late Middle English (in the sense 'no longer alight'): from Latin *exstinct-* 'extinguished', from the verb *exstinguere* (see EXTINGUISH).

extinction ▶ noun [mass noun] 1 the state or process of being or becoming extinct: *the extinction of the great auk* | [count noun] *mass extinctions*. ■ the wiping out of a debt.
2 Physics reduction to zero in the intensity of light or other radiation as it passes through a medium, due to absorption, reflection, or scattering.
– ORIGIN late Middle English: from Latin *exstinctio(n-)*, from *exstinguere* 'quench' (see EXTINGUISH).

extinguish ▶ verb [with obj.] cause (a fire or light) to cease to burn or shine: *firemen were soaking everything to extinguish the blaze*. ■ put an end to; destroy: *hope is extinguished little by little*. ■ subdue or reduce (someone) to silence: *a look which would have extinguished any man*. ■ cancel (a debt) by full payment: *the debt was absolutely extinguished*. ■ Law render (a right or obligation) void.
– DERIVATIVES **extinguishable** adjective, **extinguishment** noun (Law).
– ORIGIN mid 16th cent.: from Latin *exstinguere*, from *ex-* 'out' + *stinguere* 'quench'. Compare with DISTINGUISH.

extinguisher ▶ noun short for FIRE EXTINGUISHER.

extirpate /ˈɛkstəːpeɪt/ ▶ verb [with obj.] eradicate or destroy completely: *timber wolves were extirpated from New England more than a century ago*.
– DERIVATIVES **extirpation** noun, **extirpator** noun.
– ORIGIN late Middle English (as *extirpation*): from Latin *exstirpare*, from *ex-* 'out' + *stirps* 'a stem'.

extol /ɪkˈstəʊl, ɛk-/ ▶ verb (**extols, extolling, extolled**) [with obj.] praise enthusiastically: *he extolled the virtues of the Russian peoples*.
– ORIGIN late Middle English: from Latin *extollere*, from *ex-* 'out, upward' + *tollere* 'raise'.

extort /ɪkˈstɔːt, ɛk-/ ▶ verb [with obj.] obtain (something) by force, threats, or other unfair means: *he attempted to extort money from the company*.
– DERIVATIVES **extortive** adjective.
– ORIGIN early 16th cent.: from Latin *extort-* 'wrested', from the verb *extorquere*, from *ex-* 'out' + *torquere* 'to twist'.

extortion ▶ noun [mass noun] the practice of obtaining something, especially money, through force or threats.
– DERIVATIVES **extortioner** noun.
– ORIGIN Middle English: from late Latin *extortio(n-)*, from Latin *extorquere* 'wrest' (see EXTORT).

extortionate /ɪkˈstɔːʃ(ə)nət, ɛk-/ ▶ adjective 1 (of a price) much too high; exorbitant: *£2,700 for that guitar is extortionate*.
2 using or given to extortion: *the extortionate power of the unions*.
– DERIVATIVES **extortionately** adverb.

extortionist ▶ noun a person who tries to obtain something through force or violence; a racketeer: *he is a blackmailer and an extortionist*.

extra ▶ adjective added to an existing or usual amount or number: *they offered him an extra thirty-five cents an hour | a lot of extra work is involved*.
▶ adverb 1 [as submodifier] to a greater extent than usual; especially: *he is trying to be extra good*.
2 in addition: *installation will cost about £60 extra*.
▶ noun an item in addition to what is usual or strictly necessary: *I had an education with all the extras*. ■ an item for which an additional charge is made: *the price includes all major charges—there are no hidden extras*. ■ a person engaged temporarily to fill out a crowd scene in a film or play. ■ Cricket a run scored other than from a hit with the bat, credited to the batting side rather than to a batsman. ■ dated a special issue of a newspaper.
– ORIGIN mid 17th cent. (as an adjective): probably a shortening of EXTRAORDINARY, suggested by similar forms in French and German.

extra- ▶ prefix outside; beyond: *extracellular | extraterritorial*. ■ beyond the scope of: *extracurricular*.
– ORIGIN via medieval Latin from Latin *extra* 'outside'.

extracellular ▶ adjective Biology situated or taking place outside a cell or cells: *extracellular space in the cortex*.
– DERIVATIVES **extracellularly** adverb.

extrachromosomal element ▶ noun Genetics the DNA of a cytoplasmic organelle, such as a mitochondrion or chloroplast, responsible for cytoplasmic inheritance.

extracorporeal /ˌɛkstrəkɔːˈpɔːrɪəl/ ▶ adjective chiefly Surgery situated or occurring outside the body. ■ denoting a technique of lithotripsy using shock waves generated externally.

extra cover ▶ noun Cricket a fielding position between cover point and mid-off but further from the wicket. ■ a fielder at this position.

extract ▶ verb /ɪkˈstrakt, ɛk-/ [with obj.] 1 remove or take out, especially by effort or force: *the fossils are **extracted from** the chalk*. ■ obtain (a substance or resource) from something by a special method: *lead was **extracted from** the copper*. ■ obtain (something such as money or information) from someone unwilling to give it: *I won't let you go without trying to extract a promise **from** you*. ■ select (a passage from a text, film, or piece of music) for quotation,

E

performance, or reproduction: *the table is extracted from the report.* ■ derive (an idea) from a body of information: *there are few attempts to extract generalities about the nature of the disciplines.*
2 Mathematics calculate (a root of a number).
▶ **noun** /ˈɛkstrakt/ **1** a short passage taken from a text, film, or piece of music: *an extract from a historical film.*
2 a preparation containing the active ingredient of a substance in concentrated form: *natural plant extracts* | [mass noun] *a shampoo with extract of camomile.*
– DERIVATIVES **extractability** noun, **extractable** adjective.
– ORIGIN late Middle English: from Latin *extract-* 'drawn out', from the verb *extrahere*, from *ex-* 'out' + *trahere* 'draw'.

E

extraction ▶ **noun** [mass noun] **1** the action of extracting something, especially using effort or force: *mineral extraction* | [count noun] *a dental extraction.*
2 [with adj.] the ethnic origin of someone's family: *a worker of Polish extraction.*
– ORIGIN late Middle English: via Old French from late Latin *extractio(n-)*, from Latin *extrahere* 'draw out' (see EXTRACT).

extractive ▶ **adjective** of or involving extraction, especially the extensive extraction of natural resources without provision for their renewal: *extractive industry.*

extractor ▶ **noun** [often with modifier] a machine or device used to extract something: *a juice extractor.* ■ [as modifier] denoting a device used to extract odours and stale air from an area: *the engine room's* ***extractor*** *fans.*

extracurricular ▶ **adjective** (of an activity at a school or college) pursued in addition to the normal course of study: *extracurricular activities include sports, music, and gym clubs.* ■ often humorous outside the normal routine, especially that provided by a job or marriage: *Harriet's extracurricular sweetheart.*
– DERIVATIVES **extracurricularly** adverb.

extraditable /ˈɛkstrəˌdʌɪtəb(ə)l/ ▶ **adjective** (of a crime) making an accused or convicted person liable to extradition: *possession of explosives will be an extraditable offence.* ■ (of an accused or convicted person) liable to extradition.

extradite /ˈɛkstrədʌɪt/ ▶ **verb** [with obj.] hand over (a person accused or convicted of a crime) to the jurisdiction of the foreign state in which the crime was committed: *Brazil refused to* ***extradite*** *him* ***to*** *Britain.*
– ORIGIN mid 19th cent.: back-formation from EXTRADITION.

extradition ▶ **noun** [mass noun] the action of extraditing a person accused or convicted of a crime: *they fought to prevent his extradition to the US* | [count noun] *emergency extraditions.*
– ORIGIN mid 19th cent.: from French, from *ex-* 'out, from' + *tradition* 'delivery'.

extrados /ɪkˈstreɪdɒs, ɛk-/ ▶ **noun** Architecture the upper or outer curve of an arch. Often contrasted with INTRADOS.
– ORIGIN late 18th cent.: from French, from Latin *extra* 'outside' + French *dos* 'back' (from Latin *dorsum*).

extradural /ˌɛkstrəˈdjʊər(ə)l/ ▶ **adjective** Medicine another term for EPIDURAL.

extrafamilial /ˌɛkstrəfəˈmɪljəl/ ▶ **adjective** outside the family.

extrafloral ▶ **adjective** Botany (of a nectary) situated outside a flower, especially on a leaf or stem.

extragalactic /ˌɛkstrəgəˈlaktɪk/ ▶ **adjective** Astronomy situated, occurring, or originating outside the Milky Way galaxy: *extragalactic radio sources.*

extrajudicial ▶ **adjective** Law (of a sentence) not legally authorized: *there have been reports of extrajudicial executions.* ■ (of a settlement, statement, or confession) not made in court.
– DERIVATIVES **extrajudicially** adverb.

extralegal ▶ **adjective** (of an action or situation) beyond the province of the law.

extralimital /ˌɛkstrəˈlɪmɪt(ə)l/ ▶ **adjective** chiefly Biology situated, occurring, or derived from outside a particular area.

extralinguistic /ˌɛkstrəlɪŋˈgwɪstɪk/ ▶ **adjective** not involving or beyond the bounds of language: *extralinguistic reality.*

extramarital /ˌɛkstrəˈmarɪt(ə)l/ ▶ **adjective** (especially of sexual relations) occurring outside marriage: *an extramarital affair.*
– DERIVATIVES **extramaritally** adverb.

extramundane /ɛkstrəˈmʌndeɪn/ ▶ **adjective** rare outside or beyond the physical world.

extramural /ˌɛkstrəˈmjʊər(ə)l/ ▶ **adjective 1** Brit. (of a course of study) arranged for people who are not full-time members of a university or other educational establishment: *extramural education.* ■ additional to one's work or course of study: *extramural activities.*
2 outside the walls or boundaries of a town or city: *the extramural cemetery in Brighton.*
– DERIVATIVES **extramurally** adverb.
– ORIGIN mid 19th cent. (in sense 2): from Latin *extra muros* 'outside the walls' + -AL.

extramusical ▶ **adjective** extrinsic to a piece of music or outside the field of music.

extraneous /ɪkˈstreɪnɪəs, ɛk-/ ▶ **adjective 1** irrelevant or unrelated to the subject being dealt with: *one is obliged to wade through many pages of extraneous material.*
2 of external origin: *when the transmitter pack is turned off no extraneous noise is heard.* ■ separate from the object to which it is attached: *other insects attach extraneous objects or material to themselves.*
– DERIVATIVES **extraneously** adverb, **extraneousness** noun.
– ORIGIN mid 17th cent.: from Latin *extraneus* + -OUS.

extranet ▶ **noun** an intranet that can be partially accessed by authorized outside users, enabling businesses to exchange information over the Internet in a secure way.
– ORIGIN 1990s: from EXTRA- + NET[1] by analogy with INTRANET.

extraordinaire /ɪkˌstrɔːdɪˈnɛː/ ▶ **adjective** [postpositive] informal outstanding in a particular capacity: *the noted Hollywood middleman extraordinaire.*
– ORIGIN 1940s: French, 'extraordinary'.

extraordinary /ɪkˈstrɔːd(ə)n(ə)ri, ɛk-, ˌɛkstrəˈɔːdɪn(ə)ri/ ▶ **adjective 1** very unusual or remarkable: *the extraordinary plumage of the male* | [with clause] *it is extraordinary that no consultation took place.* ■ unusually great: *young children need extraordinary amounts of attention.*
2 [attrib.] (of a meeting) specially convened: *an extraordinary session of the Congress.* ■ [postpositive] (of an official) specially employed in addition to the usual staff: *an Ambassador Extraordinary.*
▶ **noun** (usu. **extraordinaries**) an item in a company's accounts not arising from its normal activities. Compare with EXCEPTIONAL.
– DERIVATIVES **extraordinarily** adverb [as submodifier] *an extraordinarily beautiful girl*, **extraordinariness** noun.
– ORIGIN late Middle English: from Latin *extraordinarius*, from *extra ordinem* 'outside the normal course of events'.

extraordinary general meeting (abbrev.: **EGM**) ▶ **noun** Brit. a meeting of the members or shareholders of a club, company, or other organization, held at short notice, especially in order to consider a particular matter.

extraordinary ray ▶ **noun** Optics (in double refraction) the light ray that does not obey the ordinary laws of refraction. Compare with ORDINARY RAY.

extraordinary rendition ▶ **noun** see RENDITION (sense 2).

extrapolate /ɪkˈstrapəleɪt, ɛk-/ ▶ **verb** [with obj.] extend the application of (a method or conclusion) to an unknown situation by assuming that existing trends will continue or similar methods will be applicable: *the results cannot be* ***extrapolated to*** *other patient groups* | [no obj.] *it is always dangerous to* ***extrapolate from*** *a sample.* ■ estimate or conclude (something) in this way: *the figures were extrapolated from past trends.* ■ Mathematics extend (a graph, curve, or range of values) by inferring unknown values from trends in the known data.
– DERIVATIVES **extrapolation** noun, **extrapolative** adjective, **extrapolator** noun.
– ORIGIN late 19th cent.: from EXTRA- 'outside' + a shortened form of INTERPOLATE.

extraposition /ˌɛkstrəpəˈzɪʃ(ə)n/ ▶ **noun** [mass noun] Grammar the placing of a word or group of words outside or at the end of a clause, while retaining the sense. The subject is often postponed and replaced by *it* at the start, as in *it's no use crying over spilt milk* rather than *crying over spilt milk is no use.*

extrapyramidal /ˌɛkstrəpɪˈramɪd(ə)l/ ▶ **adjective** Anatomy & Medicine relating to or denoting motor nerves that descend from the cortex to the spine but are not part of the pyramidal system: *extrapyramidal symptoms.*

extrasensory perception /ɛkstrəˈsɛns(ə)ri/ (abbrev.: **ESP**) ▶ **noun** [mass noun] the supposed faculty of perceiving things by means other than the known senses, e.g. by telepathy.

extrasolar /ˌɛkstrəˈsəʊlə/ ▶ **adjective** outside the solar system: *extrasolar planets.*

extrasystole /ˌɛkstrəˈsɪst(ə)li/ ▶ **noun** Medicine a heartbeat outside the normal rhythm, as often occurs in normal individuals.

extraterrestrial /ˌɛkstrətəˈrɛstrɪəl/ ▶ **adjective** of or from outside the earth or its atmosphere: *searches for extraterrestrial intelligence.*
▶ **noun** a hypothetical or fictional being from outer space.

extraterritorial /ˌɛkstrətɛrɪˈtɔːrɪəl/ ▶ **adjective** (of a law or decree) valid outside a country's territory. ■ denoting the freedom of embassy staff from the jurisdiction of the territory of residence. ■ situated outside a country's territory: *extraterritorial industrial zones.*
– DERIVATIVES **extraterritoriality** noun.
– ORIGIN mid 19th cent.: from Latin *extra territorium* 'outside the territory' + -AL.

extra time ▶ **noun** [mass noun] Brit. a further period of play added on to a game if the scores are equal.

extratropical ▶ **adjective** Meteorology situated or occurring outside the tropics.

extrauterine /ˌɛkstrəˈjuːtərʌɪn/ ▶ **adjective** Medicine existing, formed, or occurring outside the uterus: *the first hour of extrauterine life.*

extravagance ▶ **noun** [mass noun] lack of restraint in spending money or using resources: *his reckless extravagance with other people's money.* ■ [count noun] a thing on which too much money has been spent or which has used up too many resources: *salmon trout is an unnecessary extravagance.* ■ excessive elaboration: *the extravagance of the decor.*
– DERIVATIVES **extravagancy** noun.
– ORIGIN mid 17th cent.: from French, from medieval Latin *extravagant-* 'diverging greatly', from the verb *extravagari* (see EXTRAVAGANT).

extravagant /ɪkˈstravəg(ə)nt, ɛk-/ ▶ **adjective** lacking restraint in spending money or using resources: *it was rather extravagant to buy both.* ■ resulting from or showing such a lack of restraint: *extravagant gifts like computer games.* ■ exceeding what is reasonable or appropriate; excessive or elaborate: *extravagant claims about the merchandise.*
– DERIVATIVES **extravagantly** adverb.
– ORIGIN late Middle English (in the sense 'unusual, unsuitable'): from medieval Latin *extravagant-* 'diverging greatly', from the verb *extravagari*, from Latin *extra-* 'outside' + *vagari* 'wander'.

extravaganza /ɪkˌstravəˈganzə, ɛk-/ ▶ **noun** an elaborate and spectacular entertainment or production: *an extravaganza of dance in many forms.*
– ORIGIN mid 18th cent. (in the sense 'extravagance in language or behaviour'): from Italian *estravaganza* 'extravagance'. The change was due to association with words beginning with EXTRA-.

extravasate /ɪkˈstravəseɪt, ɛk-/ ▶ **verb** [with obj.] (usu. as adj. **extravasated**) chiefly Medicine let or force out (a fluid, especially blood) from the vessel that contains it into the surrounding area.
– DERIVATIVES **extravasation** noun.
– ORIGIN mid 17th cent.: from EXTRA- 'outside' + Latin *vas* 'vessel' + -ATE[3].

extravascular /ˌɛkstrəˈvaskjʊlə/ ▶ **adjective** Medicine situated or occurring outside the vascular system: *extravascular fluid.*

extravehicular /ˌɛkstrəvɪˈhɪkjʊlə/ ▶ **adjective** relating to work performed in space outside a spacecraft.

extravert ▶ **noun** variant spelling of EXTROVERT.

extra virgin ▶ **adjective** denoting a particularly fine grade of olive oil made from the first pressing of the olives and containing a maximum of one per cent oleic acid.

extrema plural form of EXTREMUM.

Extremadura /ˌɛkstrəmə'd(j)ʊərə/ an autonomous region of western Spain, on the border with Portugal; capital, Mérida. Spanish name **Estremadura** /estrema'ðura/.

extreme ▶ adjective **1** reaching a high or the highest degree; very great: *extreme cold.* ■ not usual; exceptional: *in extreme cases the soldier may be discharged.* ■ very severe or serious: *expulsion is an extreme sanction.* ■ (of a person or their opinions) far from moderate, especially politically: *groups of his more extreme supporters rioted in front of parliament.* ■ denoting or relating to a sport performed in a hazardous environment and involving great risk, such as white-water rafting.
2 [attrib.] furthest from the centre or a given point: *the extreme north-west of Scotland.*
▶ noun **1** either of two abstract things that are as different from each other as possible: *we represented opposite extremes of college society—he a member of the Old Guard, I one of the radicals.* ■ the highest or most extreme degree of something: *extremes of temperature.* ■ a very severe or serious measure: *the extreme of applying for poor relief.*
2 Logic the subject or predicate in a proposition, or the major or minor term in a syllogism (as contrasted with the middle term).
– PHRASES **go** (or **take something**) **to extremes** take an extreme course of action; do something to an extreme degree: *they took a commendable anti-ageist policy to extremes.* **in the extreme** to an extreme degree.
– DERIVATIVES **extremeness** noun.
– ORIGIN late Middle English: via Old French from Latin *extremus* 'outermost, utmost', superlative of *exterus* 'outer'.

extremely ▶ adverb [as submodifier] to a very great degree; very: *this is an extremely difficult thing to do.*

extreme unction ▶ noun [mass noun] (in the Roman Catholic Church) a former name for the sacrament of anointing of the sick, especially when administered to the dying.

extremism ▶ noun [mass noun] the holding of extreme political or religious views; fanaticism: *the dangers of religious extremism.*

extremist ▶ noun chiefly derogatory a person who holds extreme political or religious views, especially one who advocates illegal, violent, or other extreme action: *right-wing extremists* | [as modifier] *extremist groups.*

extremity /ɪk'strɛmɪti, ɛk-/ ▶ noun (pl. **extremities**) **1** the furthest point or limit of something: *the peninsula's western extremity.* ■ (**extremities**) the hands and feet: *tingling and numbness in the extremities.*
2 [mass noun] the degree to which something is extreme: *the extremity of the violence concerns us.* ■ a condition of extreme adversity: *the terror of an animal in extremity.*
– ORIGIN late Middle English: from Old French *extremite* or Latin *extremitas*, from *extremus* 'utmost' (see **extreme**).

extremophile /ɛks'trɛməfʌɪl/ ▶ noun Biology a microorganism, especially an archaean, that lives in conditions of extreme temperature, acidity, alkalinity, or chemical concentration.

extremum /ɪk'striːməm, ɛk-/ ▶ noun (pl. **extremums** or **extrema**) [usu. as modifier] Mathematics the maximum or minimum value of a function.
– ORIGIN early 20th cent.: from Latin, neuter of *extremus* 'utmost' (see **extreme**).

extricate /'ɛkstrɪkeɪt/ ▶ verb [with obj.] free (someone or something) from a constraint or difficulty: *he was trying to extricate himself from official duties.*
– DERIVATIVES **extricable** adjective, **extrication** noun.
– ORIGIN early 17th cent. (in the sense 'unravel, untangle'): from Latin *extricat-* 'unravelled', from the verb *extricare*, from *ex-* 'out' + *tricae* 'perplexities'.

extrinsic /ɪk'strɪnsɪk, ɛk-/ ▶ adjective **1** not part of the essential nature of someone or something; coming or operating from outside: *a complex interplay of extrinsic and intrinsic factors* | *reasons extrinsic to the music itself.*
2 (of a muscle, such as an eye muscle) having its origin some distance from the part which it moves.
– DERIVATIVES **extrinsically** adverb.
– ORIGIN mid 16th cent. (in the sense 'outward'): from late Latin *extrinsecus* 'outward', from Latin *extrinsecus* 'outwardly', based on *exter* 'outer'; the ending was altered under the influence of **-ic**.

extropy /'ɛkstrəpi/ ▶ noun [mass noun] the pseudoscientific principle that life will expand indefinitely and in an orderly, progressive way throughout the entire universe by the means of human intelligence and technology.
– DERIVATIVES **extropian** adjective & noun.
– ORIGIN 1980s: from **ex-**[1] 'out' + a shortened form of **entropy**.

extrorse /ɛks'trɔːs/ ▶ adjective Botany & Zoology turned outwards. The opposite of **introrse**. ■ (of anthers) releasing their pollen on the outside of the flower.
– ORIGIN mid 19th cent.: from late Latin *extrorsus* 'outwards' (adverb).

extrovert /'ɛkstrəvəːt/ (also **extravert**) ▶ noun an outgoing, socially confident person. ■ Psychology a person predominantly concerned with external things or objective considerations. Compare with **introvert**.
▶ adjective relating to, denoting, or typical of an extrovert: *his extrovert personality made him the ideal host.*
– DERIVATIVES **extroversion** noun, **extroverted** adjective.
– ORIGIN early 20th cent.: from *extro-* (variant of **extra-**, on the pattern of *intro-*) + Latin *vertere* 'to turn'.

> **USAGE** The original spelling **extravert** is now rare in general use but is found in technical use in psychology.

extrude /ɪk'struːd, ɛk-/ ▶ verb [with obj.] thrust or force out: *lava was being extruded from the volcano.* ■ shape (a material such as metal or plastic) by forcing it through a die.
– DERIVATIVES **extrudable** adjective, **extrusion** noun.
– ORIGIN mid 16th cent.: from Latin *extrudere*, from *ex-* 'out' + *trudere* 'to thrust'.

extrusive ▶ adjective Geology relating to or denoting rock that has been extruded at the earth's surface as lava or other volcanic deposits.

exuberance /ɪg'z(j)uːb(ə)r(ə)ns, ɛg-/ ▶ noun [mass noun] the quality of being full of energy, excitement, and cheerfulness; ebullience: *a sense of youthful exuberance.* ■ the quality of growing profusely; luxuriance: *plants growing with wild exuberance.*

exuberant /ɪg'z(j)uːb(ə)r(ə)nt, ɛg-/ ▶ adjective full of energy, excitement, and cheerfulness: *a noisy bunch of exuberant youngsters.* ■ characterized by a vigorously imaginative artistic style: *exuberant, over-the-top sculptures.* ■ literary growing luxuriantly or profusely: *exuberant foliage.*
– DERIVATIVES **exuberantly** adverb.
– ORIGIN late Middle English (in the sense 'overflowing, abounding'): from French *exubérant*, from Latin *exuberant-* 'being abundantly fruitful', from the verb *exuberare* (based on *uber* 'fertile').

exudate /'ɛgzjʊdeɪt/ ▶ noun **1** Medicine a mass of cells and fluid that has seeped out of blood vessels or an organ, especially in inflammation.
2 Botany & Entomology a substance secreted by a plant or insect.
– ORIGIN late 19th cent.: from Latin *exsudat-* 'exuded', from the verb *exsudare*.

exude /ɪg'zjuːd, ɛg-/ ▶ verb **1** (with reference to moisture or a smell) discharge or be discharged slowly and steadily: [with obj.] *the beetle exudes a caustic liquid* | [no obj.] *slime **exudes from** the fungus.*
2 [with obj.] (of a person) display (an emotion or quality) strongly and openly: *Sir Thomas exuded goodwill.* ■ (of a place) have a strong atmosphere of: *the building exudes an air of tranquillity.*
– DERIVATIVES **exudation** noun, **exudative** /ɪg'zjuːdətɪv, ɛg-/ adjective.
– ORIGIN late 16th cent.: from Latin *exsudare*, from *ex-* 'out' + *sudare* 'to sweat'.

exult ▶ verb [no obj.] show or feel triumphant elation or jubilation: ***exulting in** her escape, Lisa closed the door behind her.*
– DERIVATIVES **exultingly** adverb.
– ORIGIN late 16th cent.: from Latin *exsultare*, frequentative of *exsilire* 'leap up', from *ex-* 'out, upward' + *salire* 'to leap'.

exultant ▶ adjective triumphantly happy: *he waved to the exultant crowds.*
– DERIVATIVES **exultancy** noun, **exultantly** adverb.

exultation ▶ noun [mass noun] a feeling of triumphant elation or jubilation; rejoicing: *she laughs in exultation.*

Exuma Cays /ɪk'suːmə/ a group of some 350 small islands in the Bahamas.

exurb /'ɛksəːb/ ▶ noun N. Amer. a prosperous area beyond a city's suburbs.
– DERIVATIVES **exurban** adjective, **exurbanite** noun & adjective.
– ORIGIN 1955: coined by A. C. Spectorsky (1919–72), American author, either from Latin *ex* 'out of' + *urbs* 'city', or as a back-formation from the earlier adjective *exurban*.

exurbia /ɛk'səːbɪə/ ▶ noun [mass noun] the exurbs collectively; the area beyond the suburbs.
– ORIGIN 1955 (originally US, see **exurb**) 'out of' + *-urbia*, on the pattern of *suburbia*.

exuviae /ɪg'zjuːvɪiː, ɛg-/ ▶ plural noun [also treated as sing.] Zoology the cast or sloughed skin of an animal, especially of an insect larva.
– ORIGIN mid 17th cent.: from Latin, literally 'animal skins, spoils of the enemy', from *exuere* 'divest oneself of'.

exuviate /ɪg'zjuːvɪeɪt, ɛg-/ ▶ verb [with obj.] technical shed (a skin or shell).
– DERIVATIVES **exuviation** noun.
– ORIGIN mid 19th cent.: from **exuviae** + **-ate**[3].

ex-voto /ɛks 'vəʊtəʊ/ ▶ noun (pl. **ex-votos**) an offering given in order to fulfil a vow.
– ORIGIN late 18th cent.: from Latin *ex voto* 'from a vow'.

ex-works ▶ adjective & adverb Brit. direct from the factory or place of manufacture.

-ey ▶ suffix variant spelling of **-y**[2] (as in *Charley*, *Limey*).

eyas /'ʌɪəs/ ▶ noun (pl. **eyasses**) a young hawk, especially (in falconry) an unfledged nestling taken from the nest for training.
– ORIGIN late 15th cent. (originally *nyas*): from French *niais*, based on Latin *nidus* 'nest'. The initial *n* was lost by wrong division of *a nyas*; compare with **adder**[1].

eye ▶ noun **1** each of a pair of globular organs of sight in the head of humans and vertebrate animals: *my cat is blind in one eye* | *closing her eyes, she tried to relax.* ■ the corresponding visual or light-detecting organ of many invertebrate animals. ■ the region of the face surrounding the eyes: *her eyes were swollen with crying.* ■ used to refer to someone's power of vision and in descriptions of the direction of someone's gaze: *his sharp eyes had missed nothing.* ■ used to refer to someone's opinion or attitude towards something: ***in the eyes of** his younger colleagues, Mr Arnett was an eccentric* | ***to** European **eyes**, it may seem that the city is overcrowded.*

> The basic components of the vertebrate eye are a transparent cornea, an adjustable iris, a lens for focusing, a sensitive retina lining the back of the eye, and a clear fluid- or jelly-filled centre. The most primitive animals only have one or two eyespots, while many other invertebrates have several simple eyes or a pair of compound eyes.

2 a thing resembling an eye in appearance, shape, or relative position, in particular: ■ a rounded eye-like marking on an animal, such as those on the tail of a peacock; an eyespot. ■ a round, dark spot on a potato from which a new shoot can grow. ■ the centre of a flower, especially when distinctively coloured. ■ (also **eye of the storm** or **eye of the hurricane**) the calm region at the centre of a storm or hurricane. ■ (**eyes**) Nautical the extreme forward part of a ship.
3 the small hole in a needle through which the thread is passed. ■ a small metal loop into which a hook is fitted as a fastener on a garment. ■ Nautical a loop at the end of a rope, especially one at the top end of a shroud or stay.
4 S. African the source of a spring or river.
▶ verb (**eyes**, **eyeing** or **eying**, **eyed**) [with obj.] look at closely or with interest: *Rose eyed him warily.* ■ (**eye someone up**) informal look at someone in a way that reveals a particular, especially sexual, interest: *Margot saw the women eyeing up her boyfriend.*
– PHRASES **all eyes are on ——** used to convey that a particular person or thing is currently the focus of public interest: *over the next few weeks **all eyes will be on** the pound.* **be all eyes** be watching eagerly and attentively. **before** (or **in front of** or **under**) **one's** (**very**) **eyes** right in front of one (used for emphasis): *he saw his life's work destroyed before his very eyes.* **cannot take one's eyes off** be unable to stop looking at someone or something because they are so interesting, attractive, etc.: *I'm telling you, I couldn't take my eyes off of him.* **clap** (or **lay** or **set**) **eyes on** informal see: *I'd never clapped eyes on the guy before.* **close** (or **shut**) **one's eyes to** refuse to acknowledge (something unpleasant): *he couldn't close his eyes to the truth—he had cancer.* **an eye for an eye and a tooth for a tooth** used to refer to

the belief that retaliation in kind is the appropriate way to deal with an offence or crime. [with biblical allusion to Exod. 21: 24.] **the eye of the wind** (also **the wind's eye**) the direction from which the wind is blowing. **eyes front** (or **left** or **right**) a military command to turn the head in the direction stated. **eyes out on stalks** used to emphasize the extreme degree of someone's eager curiosity. **a ——'s-eye view** a view from the position or standpoint of a ——: *seeing a story from a child's-eye view.* See also BIRD'S-EYE VIEW, WORM'S-EYE VIEW. **get** (or **keep**) **one's eye in** Brit. become (or remain) able to make good judgements about a task or activity in which one is engaged: *I've got my eye in now; I'm landing them just where I want them.* **give someone the eye** informal look at someone with clear sexual interest. **half an eye** used in reference to a slight degree of perception or attention: *he kept **half an eye on** the house as he worked.* **have an eye for** be able to recognize, appreciate, and make good judgements about: *applicants should have an eye for detail.* **have** (or **keep**) **one's eye on** keep under careful observation. ■ (**have one's eye on**) hope or plan to acquire: *there was a vacant bishopric which the Dean had his eye on.* **have** (or **with**) **an eye to** have (or having) as one's objective: *with an eye to transatlantic business, he made a deal in New York.* ■ consider (or be considering) prudently: *the charity must have an eye to the future.* **have** (or **with**) **an eye to** (or **for** or **on**) **the main chance** look or be looking for an opportunity to take advantage of a situation for personal gain: *a developer with an eye on the main chance.* **have eyes bigger than one's stomach** (or **belly**) have asked for or taken more food than one can actually eat. (**only**) **have eyes for** be (exclusively) interested in or attracted to: *he has eyes for no one but you.* **have eyes in the back of one's head** know what is going on around one even when one cannot see it. **hit someone in the eye** (or **between the eyes**) informal be very obvious or impressive: *he wouldn't notice talent if it hit him right between the eyes.* **keep an eye on** keep under careful observation. **keep an eye out** (or **open**) look out for something with particular attention. **keep one's eyes open** (or **peeled** or Brit. **skinned**) be on the alert; watch carefully or vigilantly for something. **make eyes at someone** look at someone with clear sexual interest. **more to someone/thing than meets the eye** see MEET[1]. **my eye** (or **all my eye and Betty Martin**) Brit. informal, dated used to indicate surprise or disbelief. [said to be originally nautical slang.] **one in the eye for** a disappointment or setback for (someone or something): *this success for Manchester is one in the eye for London.* **open someone's eyes** cause someone to realize or discover something: *the letter finally **opened my eyes to** the truth.* **pull the wool over someone's eyes** see WOOL. **see eye to eye** be in full agreement: *the boss and I do not always see eye to eye.* **turn a blind eye** see BLIND. **a twinkle** (or **gleam**) **in someone's eye** something that is as yet no more than an idea or dream: *the scheme is only a gleam in the developer's eye.* **up to the** (or **one's**) **eyes** (**in**) informal extremely busy. ■ used to emphasize the extreme degree of an unpleasant situation: *the council is up to its eyes in debt.* **what the eye doesn't see, the heart doesn't grieve over** proverb if you're unaware of an unpleasant fact or situation you can't be troubled by it. **with one's eyes open** fully aware of the possible difficulties or consequences: *I went into this job with my eyes open.* **with one's eyes shut** (or **closed**) **1** without having to make much effort; easily. **2** without considering the possible difficulties or consequences: *she didn't go to Hollywood with her eyes closed.* **with one eye on** giving some but not all one's attention to: *I sat with one eye on the clock, waiting for my turn.*
– DERIVATIVES **eyed** adjective [in combination] *a brown-eyed girl*, **eyeless** adjective.
– ORIGIN Old English *ēage*, of Germanic origin; related to Dutch *oog* and German *Auge*.

eyeball ▶ noun the round part of the eye of a vertebrate, within the eyelids and socket.
▶ verb [with obj.] informal look or stare at closely: *we eyeballed one another.*
– PHRASES **eyeball to eyeball** face to face with someone, especially in an aggressive way. **give someone the hairy eyeball** N. Amer. informal stare at someone in a disapproving or angry way, especially with one's eyelids partially lowered. **up to the** (or **one's**) **eyeballs** informal used to emphasize the extreme degree of an undesirable situation: *he's up to his eyeballs in debt.*

eyebath ▶ noun Brit. a small container used for applying cleansing solutions to the eye.

eyeblack ▶ noun old-fashioned term for MASCARA.

eye bolt ▶ noun a bolt or bar with an eye at the end for attaching a hook or ring to.

eyebright ▶ noun [mass noun] a small white-flowered plant of dry fields and heaths, traditionally used as a remedy for eye problems. ● Genus *Euphrasia*, family Scrophulariaceae: several species.

eyebrow ▶ noun the strip of hair growing on the ridge above a person's eye socket.
– PHRASES **raise one's eyebrows** (or **an eyebrow**) show surprise or mild disapproval.

eyebrow pencil ▶ noun a cosmetic pencil for defining or accentuating the eyebrows.

eye candy ▶ noun [mass noun] informal visual images that are superficially attractive and entertaining but intellectually undemanding: *this movie looks like tasty eye candy.*

eye-catching ▶ adjective immediately appealing or noticeable; striking: *an eye-catching poster.*
– DERIVATIVES **eye-catcher** noun, **eye-catchingly** adverb.

eye contact ▶ noun [mass noun] the state in which two people are aware of looking directly into one another's eyes: ***make eye contact** with your interviewers.*

eyecup ▶ noun **1** a piece of an optical device such as a microscope, camera, or pair of binoculars which is contoured to provide a comfortable rest against the user's eye.
2 another term for OPTIC CUP.
3 North American term for EYEBATH.

eyeful ▶ noun [in sing.] informal **1** a long steady look at something. ■ an eye-catching person or thing: *she was quite an eyeful.*
2 a quantity or piece of something thrown or blown into the eye: ***an eyeful of** woodworm fluid.*

eyeglass ▶ noun a single lens for correcting or assisting defective eyesight, especially a monocle. ■ (**eyeglasses**) N. Amer. another term for GLASSES. ■ another term for EYEPIECE.

eyehole ▶ noun a hole to look through.

eyelash ▶ noun each of the short curved hairs growing on the edges of the eyelids, serving to protect the eyes from dust.

eyelet ▶ noun **1** a small round hole in leather or cloth for threading a lace, string, or rope through. ■ a metal ring used to reinforce such a hole. ■ a small hole ornamented with stitching around its edge, used as a form of decoration in embroidery.
2 a small hole or slit in a wall for looking through.
▶ verb (**eyelets**, **eyeleting**, **eyeleted**) [with obj.] make eyelets in (fabric).
– ORIGIN late Middle English *oilet*, from Old French *oillet*, diminutive of *oil* 'eye', from Latin *oculus*. The change in the first syllable in the 17th cent. was due to association with EYE.

eye level ▶ noun [mass noun] the level of the eyes looking straight ahead: *pictures hung at eye level.*

eyelid ▶ noun each of the upper and lower folds of skin which cover the eye when closed.

eyeline ▶ noun a person's line of sight.

eyeliner ▶ noun [mass noun] a cosmetic applied as a line round the eyes to accentuate them.

eye-opener ▶ noun informal **1** an event or situation that proves to be unexpectedly enlightening: *a visit to the docks can be a fascinating eye-opener.*
2 N. Amer. an alcoholic drink taken early in the day.
– DERIVATIVES **eye-opening** adjective.

eyepatch ▶ noun a patch worn to protect an injured eye.

eye pencil ▶ noun a cosmetic pencil for defining or accentuating the eyes.

eyepiece ▶ noun the lens or group of lenses that is closest to the eye in a microscope, telescope, or other optical instrument. Also called OCULAR.

eye-popping ▶ adjective informal astonishingly large, impressive, or blatant: *the company has doubled its assets to an eye-popping $113 billion.*

eye rhyme ▶ noun a similarity between words in spelling but not in pronunciation, for example *love* and *move*.

eyeshade ▶ noun a translucent visor used to protect the eyes from strong light.

eyeshadow ▶ noun [mass noun] a coloured cosmetic applied to the eyelids or to the skin around the eyes to accentuate them.

eyeshot ▶ noun [mass noun] the distance for which one can see: *he is **within eyeshot**.*

eyesight ▶ noun [mass noun] a person's ability to see: *poor eyesight ended his plans for a naval career.*

eye socket ▶ noun the cavity in the skull which encloses an eyeball with its surrounding muscles. Also called ORBIT.

eyesore ▶ noun a thing that is very ugly, especially a building.

eye splice ▶ noun a splice made by turning the end of a rope back on itself and interlacing the strands, thereby forming a loop.

eyespot ▶ noun **1** Zoology a light-sensitive pigmented spot on the bodies of invertebrates such as flatworms, starfishes, and microscopic crustaceans, and also in some unicellular organisms.
2 a rounded eye-like marking on an animal, especially on the wing of a butterfly or moth.
3 [mass noun] a fungal disease of cereals and other cultivated grasses, characterized by yellowish oval spots on the leaves and stems. ● The fungus is typically *Pseudocercosporella herpotrichoides*, subdivision Deuteromycotina.

eyestalk ▶ noun Zoology a movable stalk that bears an eye near its tip, especially in crabs, shrimps, and related crustaceans, and in some molluscs.

eye strain ▶ noun [mass noun] fatigue of the eyes, such as that caused by reading or looking at a computer screen for too long.

eyestripe ▶ noun a stripe on a bird's head which encloses or appears to run through the eye.

Eyetie /ˈʌɪtʌɪ/ ▶ adjective & noun (pl. **Eyeties**) Brit. informal, offensive Italian or an Italian.
– ORIGIN 1920s: abbreviation of 19th-cent. *Eyetalian*, representing a humorous pronunciation of *Italian*.

eye tooth ▶ noun a canine tooth, especially one in the upper jaw.
– PHRASES **give one's eye teeth for** (or **to be**) do anything in order to have or be something: *many women would give their eye teeth to be married to him.*

eyewash ▶ noun [mass noun] **1** cleansing lotion for a person's eye.
2 informal insincere talk; nonsense: *all that stuff about blood being thicker than water was a lot of eyewash.*

eyewater ▶ noun [mass noun] literary or W. Indian water secreted by the eyes; tears.

eyewear ▶ noun [mass noun] things worn on the eyes, such as spectacles and contact lenses.

eyewitness ▶ noun a person who has seen something happen and can give a first-hand description of it: [as modifier] ***eyewitness accounts** of the London blitz.*

eye worm ▶ noun either of two parasitic nematode worms which affect the eyes of mammals: ● a filarial worm of equatorial Africa, infesting humans and other primates, causing loiasis and sometimes passing across the cornea (*Loa loa*, class Phasmida). ● a nematode that occurs in the region of the eyelid and tear duct, found chiefly in hoofed mammals (genus *Thelazia*, class Phasmida).

eyot /ˈeɪət/ ▶ noun another term for AIT.

eyra /ˈeɪrə/ ▶ noun a reddish-brown form of the jaguarundi (cat).
– ORIGIN early 17th cent.: from Spanish, from Tupi *eirara, irara*.

Eyre /ɛː/, Edward John (1815–1901), British-born Australian explorer and colonial statesman. He undertook explorations in the interior deserts of Australia (1840–1) and later served as Lieutenant Governor of New Zealand and Governor of Jamaica.

eyre /ɛː/ ▶ noun historical a circuit court held in medieval England by a judge (a **justice in eyre**) who rode from county to county.
– ORIGIN Middle English: from Old French *eire*, from Latin *iter* 'journey'.

Eyre, Lake a lake in South Australia, Australia's largest salt lake.
– ORIGIN named after the explorer E. J. EYRE.

eyrie /ˈɪəri, ˈʌɪri, ˈɛːri/ (N. Amer. also **aerie**) ▶ noun a large nest of an eagle or other bird of prey, built high in a tree or on a cliff.

– ORIGIN late 15th cent.: from medieval Latin *aeria*, *aerea*, *eyria*, probably from Old French *aire*, from Latin *area* 'level piece of ground', in late Latin 'nest of a bird of prey'.

eyrir /ˈeɪriːr/ ▶ **noun** (pl. **aurar** /ˈøɪrar/) a monetary unit of Iceland, equal to one hundredth of a krona.

– ORIGIN Icelandic, from Old Norse, literally 'ounce (of silver etc.), money', probably from Latin *aureus* 'golden, a golden coin'.

Eysenck /ˈʌɪsɛŋk/, Hans (Jürgen) (1916–97), German-born British psychologist. He was noted for his strong criticism of Freudian psychoanalysis and for his ideas concerning the assessment of intelligence and personality (published in *Race, Intelligence, and Education*, 1971).

Ezek. ▶ **abbreviation** Ezekiel (in biblical references).

Ezekiel /ɪˈziːkɪəl/ a Hebrew prophet of the 6th century BC who prophesied the forthcoming destruction of Jerusalem and the Jewish nation and inspired hope for the future well-being of a restored state. ■ a book of the Bible containing his prophecies.

e-zine ▶ **noun** a magazine only published in electronic form on a computer network.

Ezra /ˈɛzrə/ a Jewish priest and scribe who played a central part in the reform of Judaism in the 5th or 4th century BC, continuing the work of Nehemiah and forbidding mixed marriages. ■ a book of the Bible telling of Ezra, the return of the Jews from Babylon, and the rebuilding of the Temple.

E

Ff

F

F[1] (also **f**) ▶ **noun** (pl. **Fs** or **F's**) **1** the sixth letter of the alphabet. ▪ denoting the next after E in a set of items, categories, etc. ▪ the sixth highest or lowest class of academic marks (also used to represent 'Fail'). ▪ (**f**) Chess denoting the sixth file from the left, as viewed from White's side of the board.
2 (usu. **F**) Music the fourth note of the diatonic scale of C major. ▪ a key based on a scale with F as its keynote.

F[2] ▶ **abbreviation** ▪ Fahrenheit: *60°F.* ▪ farad(s). ▪ Chemistry faraday(s). ▪ (in racing results) favourite. ▪ female. ▪ fighter (in designations of US aircraft types): *the F117 Stealth fighter.* ▪ Biology filial generation. ▪ Brit. fine (used in describing grades of pencil lead): *an F pencil.* ▪ (in motor racing) formula: *an F1 driver.* ▪ franc(s). ▪ France (international vehicle registration). ▪ (in tables of sports results) goals or points for.
▶ **symbol** ▪ the chemical element fluorine. ▪ Physics force: *F=ma.*

f ▶ **abbreviation** ▪ Grammar feminine. ▪ [in combination] (in units of measurement) femto- (10^{-15}). ▪ (in textual references) folio. ▪ Music forte. ▪ (in racing results) furlong(s). ▪ Chemistry denoting electrons and orbitals possessing three units of angular momentum: *f-orbitals.* [*f* from *fundamental*, originally applied to lines in atomic spectra.]
▶ **symbol** ▪ focal length: *apertures of f/5.6 to f/11.* See also **F-NUMBER**. ▪ Mathematics a function of a specified variable: *the value of f(x).* ▪ Electronics frequency.

F_1 (also **F1**) ▶ **abbreviation** Biology the first filial generation, i.e. the generation of hybrids arising from a first cross. The second filial generation is designated F_2 (or **F2**), and so on.

FA ▶ **abbreviation** ▪ **FANNY ADAMS** (sense 1): *sweet FA seems to have been done.* ▪ (in the UK) Football Association.

fa ▶ **noun** variant spelling of **FAH**.

FAA ▶ **abbreviation** ▪ (in the US) Federal Aviation Administration. ▪ (in the UK) Fleet Air Arm.

fab[1] ▶ **adjective** informal fabulous; wonderful.
– PHRASES **the Fab Four** the Beatles.
– DERIVATIVES **fabbo adjective**, **fabby adjective**.
– ORIGIN 1960s: abbreviation.

fab[2] Electronics ▶ **noun** a microchip manufacturing plant. ▪ a process in a microchip manufacturing plant.
▶ **verb** (**fabs**, **fabbing**, **fabbed**) [with obj.] produce (a microchip).

faba bean /ˈfɑːbə/ ▶ **noun** variant spelling of **FAVA BEAN**.

Fabergé /ˈfabəʒeɪ/, Peter Carl (1846–1920), Russian goldsmith and jeweller, of French descent. He is famous for the intricate Easter eggs that he made for Tsar Alexander III and other royal households.

Fabian /ˈfeɪbɪən/ ▶ **noun** a member or supporter of the Fabian Society, an organization of socialists aiming to achieve socialism by gradual rather than revolutionary means.
▶ **adjective** relating to or characteristic of the Fabians: *the Fabian movement.* ▪ employing a cautiously persistent and dilatory strategy to wear out an enemy: *Fabian tactics.*
– DERIVATIVES **Fabianism noun**.
– ORIGIN late 18th cent.: from the name of *Quintus Fabius Maximus Verrucosus* (see **FABIUS**).

Fabius /ˈfeɪbɪəs/ (d.203 BC), Roman general and statesman; full name *Quintus Fabius Maximus Verrucosus*; known as **Fabius Cunctator**. After Hannibal's defeat of the Roman army at Cannae in 216 BC, Fabius successfully pursued a strategy of caution and delay in order to wear down the Carthaginian invaders. This earned him his nickname, which means 'delayer'.

fable /ˈfeɪb(ə)l/ ▶ **noun** a short story, typically with animals as characters, conveying a moral. ▪ a supernatural story incorporating elements of myth and legend. ▪ [mass noun] myth and legend: *the unnatural monsters of fable.* ▪ a false statement or belief.
▶ **verb** [no obj.] archaic tell fictitious tales: *I do not dream nor fable.* ▪ [with obj.] invent (an incident, person, or story).
– DERIVATIVES **fabler noun**.
– ORIGIN Middle English: from Old French *fable* (noun), from Latin *fabula* 'story', from *fari* 'speak'.

fabled ▶ **adjective** [attrib.] **1** famous, especially by reputation: *a fabled art collection.*
2 mythical; imaginary: *the fabled kingdom.*

fabless ▶ **adjective** denoting or relating to a company which designs microchips but contracts out their production rather than owning its own factory.
– ORIGIN 1980s: from **FAB**[2] + **-LESS**.

fabliau /ˈfablɪəʊ/ ▶ **noun** (pl. **fabliaux** /-əʊz/) a metrical tale, typically a bawdily humorous one, of a type found chiefly in early French poetry.
– ORIGIN from Old French (Picard dialect) *fabliaux*, plural of *fablel* 'short fable', diminutive of *fable*.

Fablon ▶ **noun** [mass noun] trademark flexible self-adhesive plastic sheeting used for covering table tops and working surfaces.

Fabriano, Gentile da, see **GENTILE DA FABRIANO**.

fabric ▶ **noun** [mass noun] **1** cloth produced by weaving or knitting textile fibres: *heavy cream fabric* | [count noun] *stretch fabrics.*
2 the walls, floor, and roof of a building. ▪ the body of a car or aircraft. ▪ the basic structure of a society, culture, activity, etc.: *the multicultural fabric of Canadian society.*
– ORIGIN late 15th cent.: from French *fabrique*, from Latin *fabrica* 'something skilfully produced', from *faber* 'worker in metal, stone, etc.' The word originally denoted a building, later a machine, the general sense being 'something made', hence sense 1 (mid 18th cent., originally denoting any manufactured material). Sense 2 dates from the mid 17th cent.

fabricate ▶ **verb** [with obj.] **1** invent (something) in order to deceive: *officers fabricated evidence.*
2 construct or manufacture (an industrial product), especially from prepared components: *you will have to fabricate an exhaust system.*
– DERIVATIVES **fabricator noun**.
– ORIGIN late Middle English: from Latin *fabricat-* 'manufactured', from the verb *fabricare*, from *fabrica* 'something skilfully produced' (see **FABRIC**).

fabrication ▶ **noun** [mass noun] the action or process of manufacturing or inventing something: *the assembly and fabrication of electronic products.* ▪ [count noun] an invention; a lie: *the story was a complete fabrication.*

fabric conditioner ▶ **noun** [mass noun] a liquid used to soften clothes after they have been washed.

Fabry–Pérot interferometer /ˌfabrɪˈpɛrəʊ/ ▶ **noun** an interferometer that incorporates an etalon, used chiefly in astronomy.
– ORIGIN early 20th cent.: named after Charles *Fabry* (1867–1945) and Alfred *Pérot* (1863–1925), French physicists.

fabulate /ˈfabjʊleɪt/ ▶ **verb** [no obj.] relate invented stories.
– DERIVATIVES **fabulation noun**, **fabulator noun**.
– ORIGIN early 17th cent.: from Latin *fabulat-* 'narrated as a fable', from the verb *fabulari*, from *fabula* (see **FABLE**).

fabulist ▶ **noun** a person who composes or relates fables. ▪ a liar, especially one who invents elaborately dishonest stories.
– ORIGIN late 16th cent.: from French *fabuliste*, from Latin *fabula* (see **FABLE**).

fabulous ▶ **adjective** **1** extraordinary, especially extraordinarily large: *fabulous riches.* ▪ informal very good; wonderful: *a fabulous two-week holiday.*
2 having no basis in reality; mythical: *fabulous creatures.*
– DERIVATIVES **fabulosity noun**, **fabulously adverb** [as submodifier] *a fabulously wealthy man*, **fabulousness noun**.
– ORIGIN late Middle English (in the sense 'known through fable'): from French *fabuleux* or Latin *fabulosus* 'celebrated in fable', from *fabula* (see **FABLE**).

facade /fəˈsɑːd/ (also **façade**) ▶ **noun** **1** the principal front of a building, that faces on to a street or open space.
2 a deceptive outward appearance: *her flawless public facade masked private despair.*
– ORIGIN mid 17th cent.: from French *façade*, from *face* 'face', on the pattern of Italian *facciata*.

face ▶ **noun** **1** the front part of a person's head from the forehead to the chin, or the corresponding part in an animal. ▪ an expression shown on the face: *the happy faces of these children.* ▪ an aspect of something: *the unacceptable face of social drinking.*
2 the surface of a thing, especially one that is presented to the view or has a particular function, in particular: ▪ Geometry each of the surfaces of a solid. ▪ a vertical or sloping side of a mountain or cliff: *the north face of the Eiger.* ▪ the side of a planet or moon facing the observer. ▪ the front of a building. ▪ the plate of a clock or watch bearing the digits or hands. ▪ the distinctive side of a playing card. ▪ the obverse of a coin.
3 [with adj.] a person of a particular type: *this season's squad has a lot of old faces in it.*
4 short for **TYPEFACE**.
▶ **verb** [with obj.] **1** be positioned with the face or front towards (someone or something): *he turned to face her.* ▪ [no obj., with adverbial of direction] have the face or front pointing in a specified direction: *the house faces due east.* ▪ [no obj., with adverbial of direction] (of a soldier) turn in a particular direction: *the men had faced about to the front.*
2 confront and deal with or accept: *honesty forced her to face facts* | [no obj.] *he was too old to face up to the responsibilities of his position.* ▪ have (a difficult situation) in prospect: *each defendant faced a maximum sentence of 10 years.* ▪ (of a problem or difficult situation) present itself to and require action from (someone): *the difficulties facing British farming.* ▪ (**face someone/thing down**) overcome someone

or something by a show of determination: *he climbed atop a tank to face down a coup.*
3 cover the surface of (something) with a layer of a different material: *the external basement walls were faced with granite slabs.*
– PHRASES **face down** (or **downwards**) with the face or surface turned towards the ground: *he lay face down on his bed.* **someone's face fits** Brit. someone has the necessary qualities for something: *if your face didn't fit they could get rid of you within twelve months.* **face the music** be confronted with the unpleasant consequences of one's actions. **the face of the earth** used for emphasis, to refer to the existence or disappearance of someone or something: *he's just disappeared **off the face of the earth**.* **face up** (or **upwards**) with the face or surface turned upwards to view: *place the panel face up before cutting.* **get out of someone's face** [usu. as imperative] N. Amer. informal stop harassing or annoying someone. **have the face to do something** Brit. dated have the effrontery to do something. **in one's face** directly at or against one; as one approaches: *she slammed the door in my face.* **in face** (or **the face**) **of** when confronted with: *her resolution in the face of the enemy.* ■ despite: *reform had been introduced in the face of considerable opposition.* **in-your-face** informal blatantly aggressive or provocative; impossible to ignore or avoid: *an in-your-face advertising campaign.* **lose face** be humiliated. **loss of face** humiliation. **make** (or **pull**) **a face** (or **faces**) produce a facial expression that shows dislike or some other negative emotion, or that is intended to be amusing: *Anna pulled a funny face at the girl.* **off one's face** informal very drunk or under the influence of illegal drugs. **on the face of it** without knowing all of the relevant facts; apparently: *on the face of it, these improvements look to be insignificant.* **put a brave** (or **bold**) **face on something** act as if something unpleasant is not as bad as it really is: *he was putting a brave face on it but she knew he was shattered.* **put one's face on** informal apply make-up to one's face. **save face** avoid humiliation. **save someone's face** enable someone to avoid humiliation. **set one's face against** resist with determination: *he had set his face against the idea.* **throw something back in someone's face** reject something in a brusque or ungracious manner: *she'd given him her trust and he'd thrown it back in her face.* **to one's face** openly in one's presence: *if you've got something to say to me, say it to my face.*
– PHRASAL VERBS **face off** chiefly N. Amer. take up an attitude of confrontation, especially at the start of a fight or game: *close to a million soldiers face off in the desert.*
DERIVATIVES **faced** adjective [in combination] *red-faced.*
– ORIGIN Middle English: from Old French, based on Latin *facies* 'form, appearance, face'.

faceache ▶ noun Brit. informal an ugly or miserable-looking person.

face card ▶ noun chiefly N. Amer. another term for COURT CARD.

face-centred ▶ adjective denoting a crystal structure in which there is an atom at each vertex and at the centre of each face of the unit cell.

facecloth ▶ noun a small towelling cloth for washing one's face. ■ [mass noun] Brit. smooth-surfaced woollen cloth.

face cream ▶ noun [mass noun] cosmetic cream applied to the face to improve the complexion.

face flannel ▶ noun Brit. a facecloth.

faceless ▶ adjective (of a person) remote and impersonal; anonymous: *the faceless bureaucrats who made the rules.* ■ (of a building or place) characterless and dull.
– DERIVATIVES **facelessness** noun.

facelift ▶ noun a cosmetic surgical operation to remove unwanted wrinkles by tightening the skin of the face. ■ a procedure carried out to improve the appearance of something: *the station has undergone a multimillion pound facelift.*

face mask ▶ noun 1 a protective mask covering the nose and mouth or nose and eyes.
2 another term for FACE PACK.

face-off ▶ noun chiefly N. Amer. a direct confrontation between two people or groups: *last night's vice presidential face-off.* ■ Ice Hockey the start of play, in which the puck is dropped by the referee between two opposing players.

face pack ▶ noun Brit. a cosmetic preparation spread over the face and left for some time to cleanse and improve the condition of the skin.

face paint ▶ noun [mass noun] bold-coloured paint used to decorate the face.
– DERIVATIVES **face-painter** noun, **face-painting** noun.

faceplate ▶ noun 1 an enlarged end or attachment on the end of the mandrel on a lathe, with slots and holes on which work can be mounted.
2 the transparent window of a diver's or astronaut's helmet.
3 the part of a cathode ray tube that carries the phosphor screen.
4 a plate protecting a piece of machinery.

face powder ▶ noun [mass noun] flesh-tinted cosmetic powder used to improve the appearance of the face by reducing shine and concealing blemishes.

facer ▶ noun informal, chiefly Brit. a blow to the face. ■ a sudden difficulty.

face-saving ▶ noun [mass noun] the preserving of one's reputation, credibility, or dignity.
– DERIVATIVES **face-saver** noun.

facet /'fasɪt, -ɛt/ ▶ noun 1 one side of something many-sided, especially of a cut gem.
2 a particular aspect or feature of something: *a philosophy that extends to all facets of the business.*
3 Zoology any of the individual units (ommatidia) that make up the compound eye of an insect or crustacean.
– DERIVATIVES **faceted** adjective [in combination] *a multi-faceted approach.*
– ORIGIN early 17th cent.: from French *facette*, diminutive of *face* 'face, side' (see FACE).

facetiae /fə'siːʃiː/ ▶ plural noun 1 dated pornographic literature.
2 archaic humorous or witty sayings.
– ORIGIN early 16th cent.: from Latin, plural of *facetia* 'jest', from *facetus* 'witty'.

face time ▶ noun [mass noun] N. Amer. informal time spent in face-to-face contact with someone. ■ time spent being filmed or photographed by the media.

facetious /fə'siːʃəs/ ▶ adjective treating serious issues with deliberately inappropriate humour; flippant: *a facetious remark.*
– DERIVATIVES **facetiously** adverb, **facetiousness** noun.
– ORIGIN late 16th cent. (in the general sense 'witty, amusing'): from French *facétieux*, from *facétie*, from Latin *facetia* 'jest', from *facetus* 'witty'.

face-to-face ▶ adjective & adverb (of two people) close together and facing each other: [as adj.] *a face-to-face conversation* | [as adv.] *the two men stood face-to-face.* ■ [as adv.] in direct confrontation: *he brings his readers face-to-face with situations they would rather not confront.*

facety /'feɪsti/ ▶ adjective W. Indian rude, arrogant, or excessively bold.
– ORIGIN probably from obsolete English *facey*, perhaps influenced by FEISTY.

face value ▶ noun the value printed or depicted on a coin, banknote, postage stamp, ticket, etc., especially when less than the actual value. ■ the apparent worth or implication of something: *her lie was unconvincing, but he **took it at face value**.*

faceworker ▶ noun a miner who works at the coalface.

facia ▶ noun see FASCIA.

facial /'feɪʃ(ə)l/ ▶ adjective of or affecting the face: *facial expressions.*
▶ noun a beauty treatment for the face.
– DERIVATIVES **facially** adverb.
– ORIGIN early 17th cent. (as a theological term meaning 'face to face, open'): from medieval Latin *facialis*, from *facies* (see FACE). The current sense of the adjective dates from the early 19th cent.

facialist /'feɪʃ(ə)lɪst/ ▶ noun a person who gives facials and other beauty treatments for the face.

facial nerve ▶ noun Anatomy each of the seventh pair of cranial nerves, supplying the facial muscles and the tongue.

-facient ▶ combining form producing a specified action or state: *abortifacient.*
– ORIGIN from Latin *facient-* 'doing, making'.

facies /'feɪʃiiːz/ ▶ noun (pl. **same**) 1 Medicine the facial expression of an individual that is typical of a particular disease or condition.
2 Geology the character of a rock expressed by its formation, composition, and fossil content.
– ORIGIN early 17th cent. (denoting the face): from Latin, 'form, appearance, face'.

facile /'fasʌɪl, -sɪl/ ▶ adjective 1 ignoring the true complexities of an issue; superficial: *facile generalizations.* ■ (of a person) having a superficial or simplistic knowledge or approach: *a man of facile and shallow intellect.*
2 (of success, especially in sport) easily achieved: *a facile seven-lengths victory.*
– DERIVATIVES **facilely** adverb, **facileness** noun.
– ORIGIN late 15th cent. (in the sense 'easily accomplished'): from French, or from Latin *facilis* 'easy', from *facere* 'do, make'.

facilitate /fə'sɪlɪteɪt/ ▶ verb [with obj.] make (an action or process) easy or easier: *schools were located in the same campus to facilitate the sharing of resources.*
– DERIVATIVES **facilitative** adjective, **facilitator** noun, **facilitatory** adjective.
– ORIGIN early 17th cent.: from French *faciliter*, from Italian *facilitare*, from *facile* 'easy', from Latin *facilis* (see FACILE).

facilitation ▶ noun [mass noun] the action of facilitating something. ■ Physiology the enhancement of the response of a neuron to a stimulus following prior stimulation.

facility ▶ noun (pl. **facilities**) 1 a place, amenity, or piece of equipment provided for a particular purpose: *cooking facilities* | *facilities for car parking* | *a manufacturing facility.* ■ a special feature of a service or machine, which offers the opportunity to do or benefit from something: *an overdraft facility.*
2 [usu. in sing.] a natural ability to do or learn something well and easily: *he had **a facility for** languages.* ■ [mass noun] absence of difficulty or effort: *the pianist played with great facility.*
– ORIGIN early 16th cent. (denoting the means or unimpeded opportunity for doing something): from French *facilité* or Latin *facilitas*, from *facilis* 'easy' (see FACILE).

facing ▶ noun 1 a piece of material sewn on the inside of a garment, especially at the neck and armholes, to strengthen it. ■ (**facings**) the cuffs, collar, and lapels of a military jacket, contrasting in colour with the rest of the garment.
2 an outer layer covering the surface of a wall.
▶ adjective [attrib.] positioned so as to face: *two facing pages* | [in combination] *a south-facing garden.*

facsimile /fak'sɪmɪli/ ▶ noun an exact copy, especially of written or printed material. ■ another term for FAX[1].
▶ verb (**facsimiles**, **facsimileing**, **facsimiled**) [with obj.] make a copy of.
– PHRASES **in facsimile** as an exact copy.
– ORIGIN late 16th cent. (originally as *fac simile*, denoting the making of an exact copy, especially of writing): modern Latin, from Latin *fac!* (imperative of *facere* 'make') and *simile* (neuter of *similis* 'like').

fact ▶ noun a thing that is known or proved to be true: *the most commonly known fact about hedgehogs is that they have fleas* | [mass noun] *a body of fact.* ■ (**facts**) information used as evidence or as part of a report or news article. ■ (**the fact that**) used to refer to a particular situation under discussion: *despite the fact that I'm so tired, sleep is elusive.* ■ [mass noun] chiefly Law the truth about events as opposed to interpretation: *there was a question of fact as to whether they had received the letter.*
– PHRASES **before** (or **after**) **the fact** before (or after) the committing of a crime: *an accessory before the fact.* **facts and figures** precise details. **a fact of life** something that must be accepted and cannot be changed, however unpalatable: *baldness is a fact of life for a lot of men.* **the facts of life** information about sexual functions and practices, especially as given to children. **the fact of the matter** the truth. **in** (**point of**) **fact** used to emphasize the truth of an assertion, especially one opposite to what might be expected or what has been asserted: *the brook trout is in fact a char.*
– ORIGIN late 15th cent.: from Latin *factum*, neuter past participle of *facere* 'do'. The original sense was 'an act', later 'a crime', surviving in the phrase *before (or after) the fact*. The earliest of the current senses ('truth, reality') dates from the late 16th cent.

fact-finding ▶ adjective [attrib.] (especially of a committee or its activity) having the purpose of establishing the facts of an issue: *a fact-finding mission.*
▶ noun the discovery and establishment of the facts of an issue.
– DERIVATIVES **factfinder** noun.

facticity /fak'tɪsɪti/ ▶ noun [mass noun] the quality or condition of being fact: *the facticity of death.*

faction[1] ▶ noun a small organized dissenting group within a larger one, especially in politics: *the*

left-wing faction of the party. ■ [mass noun] dissension within an organization.
– ORIGIN late 15th cent. (denoting the action of doing or making something): via French from Latin *factio(n-)*, from *facere* 'do, make'.

faction² ▶ **noun** [mass noun] a literary and cinematic genre in which real events are used as a basis for a fictional narrative or dramatization.
– ORIGIN 1960s: blend of **FACT** and **FICTION**.

-faction ▶ **combining form** in nouns of action derived from verbs ending in *-fy* (such as *liquefaction* from *liquefy*).
– ORIGIN from Latin *factio(n)-*, from *facere* 'do, make'.

factional ▶ **adjective** relating or belonging to a faction: *factional leaders.* ■ characterized by dissent: *factional conflicts.*
– DERIVATIVES **factionalism noun, factionally adverb.**

factionalize (also **factionalise**) ▶ **verb** [no obj.] (especially of a political party or other organized group) split or divide into factions: *there was a tendency for students to factionalize.*

F

factious /ˈfakʃəs/ ▶ **adjective** relating or inclined to dissension: *a factious country.*
– DERIVATIVES **factiously adverb, factiousness noun.**
– ORIGIN mid 16th cent.: from French *factieux* or Latin *factiosus*, from *factio* (see **FACTION¹**).

factitious /fakˈtɪʃəs/ ▶ **adjective** artificially created or developed: *a largely factitious national identity.*
– DERIVATIVES **factitiously adverb, factitiousness noun.**
– ORIGIN mid 17th cent. (in the general sense 'made by human skill or effort'): from Latin *facticius* 'made by art', from *facere* 'do, make'.

factitive /ˈfaktɪtɪv/ ▶ **adjective** Linguistics (of a verb) having a sense of causing a result and taking a complement as well as an object, as in *he appointed me captain.*
– ORIGIN mid 19th cent.: from modern Latin *factitivus*, formed irregularly from Latin *factitare*, frequentative of *facere* 'do, make'.

factive ▶ **adjective** Linguistics denoting a verb that assigns the status of an established fact to its object (normally a clausal object), e.g. *know, regret, resent.* Contrasted with **CONTRAFACTIVE, NON-FACTIVE.**

factoid ▶ **noun** an item of unreliable information that is reported and repeated so often that it becomes accepted as fact. ■ N. Amer. a brief or trivial item of news or information.

factor ▶ **noun 1** a circumstance, fact, or influence that contributes to a result: *his skill was a factor in ensuring that so much was achieved* | *she worked fast, conscious of the time factor.* ■ Biology a gene that determines a hereditary characteristic: *the Rhesus factor.*
2 a number or quantity that when multiplied with another produces a given number or expression. ■ Mathematics a number or algebraic expression by which another is exactly divisible.
3 a level on a scale of measurement. ■ (with numeral) a sunscreen of the sun protection factor specified: *factor 30 sun cream.*
4 Physiology any of a number of substances in the blood, mostly identified by numerals, which are involved in coagulation. See **FACTOR VIII.**
5 an agent who buys and sells goods on commission. ■ a company that buys a manufacturer's invoices at a discount and takes responsibility for collecting the payments due on them. ■ Scottish a land agent or steward.
▶ **verb** [with obj.] **1** Mathematics another term for **FACTORIZE.**
2 (of a company) sell (its invoices) to a factor.
– PHRASAL VERBS **factor something in** (or **out**) include (or exclude) something as a relevant element when making a decision: *when the psychological costs are factored in, a different picture will emerge.*
– DERIVATIVES **factorable adjective.**
– ORIGIN late Middle English (meaning 'doer', also in the Scots sense 'agent'): from French *facteur* or Latin *factor*, from *fact-* 'done', from the verb *facere*.

factor VIII (also **factor eight**) ▶ **noun** [mass noun] Physiology a blood protein (a beta globulin) involved in clotting. A deficiency of this causes one of the main forms of haemophilia.

factorage ▶ **noun** [mass noun] the commission or charges payable to a factor.

factor analysis ▶ **noun** [mass noun] Statistics a process in which the values of observed data are expressed as functions of a number of possible causes in order to find which are the most important.

factor cost ▶ **noun** the cost of an item of goods or a service in terms of the various factors which have played a part in its production or availability, and exclusive of tax costs.

factorial ▶ **noun** Mathematics the product of an integer and all the integers below it; e.g. factorial four (*4!*) is equal to 24. (Symbol: **!**) ■ the product of a series of factors in an arithmetical progression.
▶ **adjective** chiefly Mathematics relating to a factor or factorial.
– DERIVATIVES **factorially adverb.**

factorize (also **factorise**) ▶ **verb** Mathematics (with reference to a number) resolve or be resolvable into factors.
– DERIVATIVES **factorization noun.**

factory ▶ **noun** (pl. **factories**) **1** a building or group of buildings where goods are manufactured or assembled chiefly by machine. ■ [with modifier] a person or organization that continually produces a great quantity of something specified: *the group have become a rock-and-roll hit factory.*
2 historical an establishment for traders carrying on business in a foreign country.
– ORIGIN late 16th cent. (in sense 2): via Portuguese *feitoria* from medieval Latin *factoria*, from Latin *factor* (see **FACTOR**). Sense 1 based on late Latin *factorium*, literally 'oil press'.

Factory Acts (in the UK) a series of laws regulating the operation of factories, designed to improve the working conditions of employees, especially women and children.

factory farming ▶ **noun** [mass noun] a system of rearing livestock using highly intensive methods, by which poultry, pigs, or cattle are confined indoors under strictly controlled conditions.
– DERIVATIVES **factory farm noun.**

factory floor ▶ **noun** the workers in a company or industry, rather than the management.

factory ship ▶ **noun** a fishing or whaling ship, or a ship accompanying a fishing or whaling fleet, with facilities for immediate processing of the catch.

factory shop (chiefly N. Amer. also **factory outlet**) ▶ **noun** a shop in which goods, especially surplus stock, are sold directly by the manufacturers at a discount.

factotum /fakˈtəʊtəm/ ▶ **noun** (pl. **factotums**) an employee who does all kinds of work: *he was employed as the general factotum.*
– ORIGIN mid 16th cent. (originally in the phrases *dominum* (or *magister factotum*), translating roughly as 'master of everything', and *Johannes factotem* 'John do-it-all' or 'Jack of all trades'): from medieval Latin, from Latin *fac!* 'do!' (imperative of *facere*) + *totum* 'the whole thing' (neuter of *totus*).

fact sheet ▶ **noun** a paper giving useful information about a particular issue, especially one discussed on a television or radio programme.

factual /ˈfaktʃʊəl, -tjʊəl/ ▶ **adjective** concerned with what is actually the case: *a mixture of comment and factual information.* ■ actually occurring: *cases mentioned are factual.*
– DERIVATIVES **factuality noun, factually adverb, factualness noun.**

factum /ˈfaktəm/ ▶ **noun** (pl. **factums** or **facta**) Law, chiefly Canadian a statement of the facts of a case.
– ORIGIN late 18th cent.: from Latin, literally 'something done or made'.

facture /ˈfaktʃə/ ▶ **noun** [mass noun] the quality of the execution of a painting; an artist's characteristic handling of the paint: *Manet's sensuous facture.*
– ORIGIN late Middle English (in the general sense 'construction, workmanship'): via Old French from Latin *factura* 'formation, manufacture', from *facere* 'do, make'. The current sense dates from the late 19th cent.

facula /ˈfakjʊlə/ ▶ **noun** (pl. **faculae** /-liː/) a bright region on the surface of the sun, linked to the subsequent appearance of sunspots in the same area. ■ a bright spot on the surface of a planet.
– ORIGIN early 18th cent.: from Latin, diminutive of *fax, fac-* 'torch'.

facultative /ˈfak(ə)l,tətɪv/ ▶ **adjective** occurring optionally in response to circumstances rather than by nature. ■ Biology capable of but not restricted to a particular function or mode of life: *a facultative parasite.* Often contrasted with **OBLIGATE.**
– DERIVATIVES **facultatively adverb.**
– ORIGIN early 19th cent.: from French *facultatif, -ive*, from *faculté* (see **FACULTY**).

faculty ▶ **noun** (pl. **faculties**) **1** an inherent mental or physical power: *her critical faculties* | *the faculty of sight.* ■ an aptitude for doing something: *his faculty for taking the initiative.*
2 a group of university departments concerned with a major division of knowledge: *the Faculty of Arts* | *the law faculty.* ■ [in sing.] the teaching or research staff of a group of university departments, or (N. Amer.) of a university or college, viewed as a body. ■ dated the members of a particular profession, especially medicine, considered collectively.
3 a licence or authorization from a Church authority.
– ORIGIN late Middle English: from Old French *faculte*, from Latin *facultas*, from *facilis* 'easy', from *facere* 'make, do'.

Faculty of Advocates (in the UK) the society constituting the Scottish Bar.

FA Cup the major annual knockout competition for soccer clubs in England, first held in 1872.

FAD ▶ **abbreviation** Biochemistry flavin adenine dinucleotide, a coenzyme derived from riboflavin and important in various metabolic reactions.

fad ▶ **noun** an intense and widely shared enthusiasm for something, especially one that is short-lived; a craze: *some regard green politics as no more than the latest fad.* ■ an arbitrary like or dislike: *his fads about the type of coffee he must have.*
– DERIVATIVES **faddish adjective, faddishly adverb, faddishness noun, faddism noun, faddist noun.**
– ORIGIN mid 19th cent. (originally dialect): probably the second element of *fidfad*, contraction of **FIDDLE-FADDLE.** Compare with **FADDY.**

faddy ▶ **adjective** (**faddier, faddiest**) Brit. having many arbitrary and often unusual likes and dislikes about food: *a faddy eater.*
– DERIVATIVES **faddiness noun.**

fade ▶ **verb** [no obj.] **1** gradually grow faint and disappear: *the light had faded and dusk was advancing* | *the noise faded away* | figurative *hopes of peace had faded.* ■ lose or cause to lose colour or brightness: [no obj.] *his fair hair had faded to a dusty grey* | [with obj.] (usu. as adj. **faded**) *faded jeans.* ■ (of a flower) lose freshness and wither. ■ (**fade away**) (of a person) gradually become thin and weak, especially to the point of death: *without help, those of us who are ill will surely fade away and die.* ■ (of a racehorse, runner, etc.) lose strength and cease to perform well: *she faded near the finish.* ■ (of a vehicle brake) become temporarily less efficient as a result of frictional heating.
2 [with adverbial] (with reference to film and television images) come or cause to come gradually into or out of view, or to merge into another shot: [no obj.] *fade into scenes of rooms strewn with festive remains* | [with obj.] *some shots have to be faded in.* ■ (with reference to recorded sound) increase or decrease in volume or merge into another recording: [no obj.] *they let you edit the digital data, making it fade in and out* | [with obj.] *he skilfully fades the guitar lines up and down.*
3 Golf (of the ball) deviate to the right (or, for a left-handed golfer, the left), typically as a result of spin given to the ball. ■ [with obj.] (of a golfer) cause (the ball) to deviate.
4 [with obj.] N. Amer. informal (in craps) match the bet of (another player): *Lovejoy faded him for twenty-five cents.*
▶ **noun 1** [mass noun] the process of becoming less bright: *the sun can cause colour fade.* ■ [count noun] an act of causing a film or television image to darken and disappear gradually: *a fade to black would bring the sequence to a close.*
2 Golf a shot causing the ball to deviate to the right (or, for a left-handed golfer, the left).
– DERIVATIVES **fadeless adjective.**
– ORIGIN Middle English (in the sense 'grow weak'): from Old French *fader*, from *fade* 'dull, insipid', probably based on a blend of Latin *fatuus* 'silly, insipid' and *vapidus* 'vapid'.

fade-in ▶ **noun** a film-making and broadcasting technique whereby an image is made to appear gradually or the volume of sound is gradually increased from zero.

fade-out ▶ **noun** a film-making and broadcasting technique whereby an image is made to disappear gradually or the sound volume is gradually decreased to zero.

fader ▶ **noun** a device for varying the volume of sound, the intensity of light, or the gain on a video or audio signal.

fade-up ▶ **noun** an instance of increasing the brightness of an image or the volume of a sound.

fado /ˈfɑːdəʊ/ ▶ **noun** (pl. **fados**) a type of popular Portuguese song, usually with a melancholy theme and accompanied by mandolins or guitars. ■ [mass noun] the music for a fado.
– ORIGIN Portuguese, literally 'fate'.

faeces /ˈfiːsiːz/ (US **feces**) ▶ **plural noun** waste matter remaining after food has been digested, discharged from the bowels; excrement.
– DERIVATIVES **faecal** /ˈfiːk(ə)l/ **adjective**.
– ORIGIN late Middle English: from Latin, plural of *faex* 'dregs'.

Faenza /fɑːˈɛntsə/ a town in Emilia-Romagna in northern Italy; pop. 56,922 (2008). The town gave its name to the type of pottery known as faience.

faerie /ˈfeɪəri, ˈfɛːri/ (also **faery**) ▶ **noun** [mass noun] archaic or literary fairyland: *the world of faerie*. ■ [count noun] a fairy.
– ORIGIN late 16th cent. (introduced by Spenser): pseudo-archaic variant of **FAIRY**.

Faeroe Islands (also **the Faeroes**) variant spelling of **FAROE ISLANDS**.

Faeroese ▶ **adjective & noun** variant spelling of **FAROESE**.

faff Brit. informal ▶ **verb** [no obj.] spend time in ineffectual activity: *we can't **faff around** forever*.
▶ **noun** [in sing.] a great deal of ineffectual activity: *there was the usual faff of getting back to the plane*.
– ORIGIN late 18th cent. (originally dialect in the sense 'blow in puffs', describing the wind): imitative. The current sense may have been influenced by dialect *faffle* 'stammer, stutter', later 'flap in the wind', which came to mean 'fuss, dither' at about the same time as *faff* (late 19th cent.).

fag[1] Brit. ▶ **noun 1** [in sing.] informal a tiring or unwelcome task: *it's too much of a fag to drive all the way there and back again*.
2 a junior pupil at a public school who does minor chores for a senior pupil.
▶ **verb** (**fags, fagging, fagged**) [no obj.] informal work hard, especially at a tedious task: *he didn't have to fag away in a lab to get the right answer*. ■ (of a public-school pupil) do minor chores for a senior pupil: *the lower boys in each house **fagged for** members of the Library*.
– ORIGIN mid 16th cent. (as a verb in the sense 'grow weary'): of unknown origin. Compare with **FLAG**[4].

fag[2] ▶ **noun** N. Amer. informal, derogatory a male homosexual.
– DERIVATIVES **faggy adjective**.
– ORIGIN 1920s: short for **FAGGOT** (sense 3 of the noun).

fag[3] ▶ **noun** Brit. informal a cigarette.
– ORIGIN late 19th cent.: elliptically from **FAG END**.

fag end ▶ **noun** Brit. informal a cigarette end. ■ the last part of something, especially when regarded as less important or interesting: ***the fag end of** the Indian cricket season*.
– ORIGIN early 17th cent. (in the sense 'remnant'): from 15th-cent. *fag* 'a flap', of unknown origin. The current sense dates from the early 20th cent.

fagged ▶ **adjective** [predic.] chiefly Brit. extremely tired; exhausted: *we were all absolutely **fagged out***.

faggot /ˈfagət/ ▶ **noun 1** (usu. **faggots**) Brit. a ball or roll of seasoned chopped liver, baked or fried.
2 (US **fagot**) a bundle of sticks bound together as fuel. ■ a bundle of iron rods bound together for reheating, welding, and hammering into bars.
3 N. Amer. informal, derogatory a male homosexual.
4 Brit. informal, dated an unpleasant or contemptible woman.
▶ **verb** (**faggots, faggoting, faggoted**; US **fagots, fagoting, fagoted**) [with obj.] **1** archaic bind in or make into faggots.
2 (in embroidery) join by faggoting.
– DERIVATIVES **faggoty adjective**.
– ORIGIN Middle English (in the sense 'bundle of sticks for fuel'): from Old French *fagot*, from Italian *fagotto*, based on Greek *phakelos* 'bundle'.

faggoting (US **fagoting**) ▶ **noun** [mass noun] embroidery in which threads are fastened together in bundles: *a black silk dress with tiers of faggoting*.

fag hag ▶ **noun** informal, derogatory a heterosexual woman who spends much of her time with homosexual men.

fah (also **fa**) ▶ **noun** Music (in tonic sol-fa) the fourth note of a major scale. ■ the note F in the fixed-doh system.
– ORIGIN Middle English: representing (as an arbitrary name for the note) the first syllable of *famuli*, taken from a Latin hymn (see **SOLMIZATION**).

fahlerz /ˈfɑːlɛːts/ ▶ **noun** [mass noun] a grey crystalline copper-containing mineral, of which tetrahedrite and tennantite are the typical forms.
– ORIGIN late 18th cent.: from German, from *fahl* 'ash-coloured' + *Erz* 'ore'.

Fahr. ▶ **abbreviation** Fahrenheit.

Fahrenheit /ˈfar(ə)nhʌɪt, ˈfɑː-/ (abbrev.: **F**) ▶ **adjective** [postpositive when used with a numeral] of or denoting a scale of temperature on which water freezes at 32° and boils at 212° under standard conditions.
▶ **noun** (also **Fahrenheit scale**) this scale of temperature.
– ORIGIN mid 18th cent.: named after Gabriel Daniel *Fahrenheit* (1686–1736), German physicist.

faience /fʌɪˈɒs, -ˈɒs/ ▶ **noun** [mass noun] glazed ceramic ware, in particular decorated tin-glazed earthenware of the type which includes delftware and maiolica. ■ Architecture moulded glazed or unglazed terracotta blocks used structurally or as cladding.
– ORIGIN late 17th cent. (originally denoting pottery made at Faenza): from French *faïence*, from *Faïence*, the French name for **FAENZA**.

fail ▶ **verb** [no obj.] **1** be unsuccessful in achieving one's goal: *he **failed in** his attempt to secure election* | [with infinitive] *they failed to be ranked in the top ten*. ■ [with obj.] be unsuccessful in (an examination or interview): *she failed her finals*. ■ [with obj.] (of a person or a commodity) be unable to meet the standards set by (a test of quality or eligibility): *a player has failed a drugs test*. ■ [with obj.] judge (a candidate in an examination or test) not to have passed.
2 neglect to do something: [with infinitive] *the firm failed to give adequate risk warnings*. ■ [with infinitive] behave in a way contrary to expectations by not doing something: *commuter chaos has again failed to materialize*. ■ [with obj.] desert or let down (someone): *at the last moment her nerve failed her*.
3 cease to work properly; break down: *a lorry whose brakes had failed*. ■ become weaker or of poorer quality: *the light began to fail* | (as adj. **failing**) *his failing health*. ■ (of rain or a crop or supply) be insufficient when needed or expected. ■ (of a business or a person) cease trading because of lack of funds.
▶ **noun 1** a mark which is not high enough to pass an examination or test.
2 informal a mistake, failure, or instance of poor performance: *their customer service is a massive fail* | [mass noun] *his first product demo was full of fail*.
– PHRASES **without fail** with no exception; always: *he writes every week without fail*.
– ORIGIN Middle English: from Old French *faillir* (verb), *faille* (noun), based on Latin *fallere* 'deceive'.

> **WORD TRENDS** **Fail** is an example of an Internet-created word craze. While it has been used as a noun for some time, mainly to describe an instance of failing a test or in the phrase 'without fail', the meaning of 'a mistake, failure, or poor performance' is a 21st-century coinage. Probably derived from a computer game which declared 'You fail it' when a player lost, **fail** grew in popularity as an Internet meme, with people attaching the word to pictures showing acts of stupidity. In wider use it is often paired with intensifying adjectives such as *massive, total*, and *epic*: *my first attempt at ice racing turned out to be an absolutely epic fail*. **Fail** can also be used as a general exclamation of disgust, as the ultimate dismissal at the end of a critical statement: *God, she's such a loser. FAIL*.

failed ▶ **adjective** [attrib.] **1** (of an undertaking or a relationship) not achieving its end or not lasting; unsuccessful: *a failed coup attempt*. ■ (of a person) unsuccessful in a particular activity: *a failed writer*. ■ (of a business) unable to continue owing to financial difficulties.
2 (of a mechanism) not functioning properly: *an aircraft with a failed engine*.

failing ▶ **noun** a weakness, especially in a person's character; a shortcoming: *pride is a terrible failing*.
▶ **preposition** in the absence of; if not: *she longed to be with him and, **failing that**, to be alone*.

faille /feɪl/ ▶ **noun** [mass noun] a soft, light-woven fabric having a ribbed texture, originally of silk.
– ORIGIN mid 16th cent. (denoting a kind of hood or veil worn by women): from Old French. The current sense dates from the mid 19th cent.

failover ▶ **noun** [mass noun] Computing a procedure by which a system automatically transfers control to a duplicate system when it detects a fault or failure.

fail-safe ▶ **adjective 1** causing a piece of machinery to revert to a safe condition in the event of a breakdown or malfunction: *a forklift truck with a fail-safe device*.
2 unlikely or unable to fail: *there is no guaranteed fail-safe procedure*.
▶ **noun** [usu. in sing.] a system or plan that comes into operation in the event of something going wrong or that is in place to prevent such an occurrence.

fáilte /ˈfɑːltə/, Irish /ˈfɑːlʲtʲə/ Scottish & Irish ▶ **exclamation** welcome.
▶ **noun** an act or instance of welcoming someone.
– ORIGIN Irish.

failure ▶ **noun** [mass noun] **1** lack of success: *an economic policy that is doomed to failure*. ■ [count noun] an unsuccessful person or thing: *bad weather had resulted in crop failures*.
2 the neglect or omission of expected or required action: *their failure to comply with the basic rules*. ■ [count noun] a lack or deficiency of a desirable quality: *a failure of imagination*.
3 the action or state of not functioning: *symptoms of heart failure* | [count noun] *a chance engine failure*. ■ [count noun] a sudden cessation of power. ■ [count noun] the collapse of a business.
– ORIGIN mid 17th cent. (originally as *failer*, in the senses 'non-occurrence' and 'cessation of supply'): from Anglo-Norman French *failer* for Old French *faillir* (see **FAIL**).

fain archaic ▶ **adjective** [with infinitive] **1** pleased or willing under the circumstances: *the traveller was fain to proceed*.
2 compelled by the circumstances; obliged: *he was fain to acknowledge that the agreement was sacrosanct*.
▶ **adverb** gladly: *I am weary and **would fain** get a little rest*.
– ORIGIN Old English *fægen* 'happy, well pleased', of Germanic origin, from a base meaning 'rejoice'; related to **FAWN**[2].

fainéant /ˈfeɪneɪɒ̃/ ▶ **noun** archaic an idle or ineffective person.
– ORIGIN early 17th cent.: from French, from *fait* 'does' + *néant* 'nothing'.

faint ▶ **adjective 1** (of a sight, smell, or sound) barely perceptible: *the faint murmur of voices*. ■ (of a hope or chance) possible but unlikely; slight: *there is a faint chance that the enemy may flee*. ■ lacking conviction or enthusiasm; feeble: *she sent him a faint answering smile*.
2 [predic.] feeling weak and dizzy and close to losing consciousness: *the heat made him feel faint*.
▶ **verb** [no obj.] lose consciousness for a short time because of a temporarily insufficient supply of oxygen to the brain. ■ archaic grow weak or feeble; decline.
▶ **noun** [in sing.] a sudden loss of consciousness: *she hit the floor **in a dead faint***.
– PHRASES **not have the faintest** informal have no idea: *I haven't the faintest what it means*.
– DERIVATIVES **faintness noun**.
– ORIGIN Middle English (in the sense 'feigned', also 'feeble, cowardly', surviving in **FAINT HEART**): from Old French *faint*, past participle of *faindre* (see **FEIGN**). Compare with **FEINT**[1].

faint heart ▶ **noun** a person who lacks courage or conviction.
– PHRASES **faint heart never won fair lady** proverb timidity will prevent you from achieving your objective.

faint-hearted ▶ **adjective** lacking courage; timid: *they were feeling faint-hearted at the prospect of war* | (as plural noun **the faint-hearted**) *litigation **is not for the faint-hearted***.
– DERIVATIVES **faint-heartedly adverb**.

faintly ▶ **adverb** in a faint manner; indistinctly: *she smiled faintly*. ■ [as submodifier] slightly: *his faintly ridiculous air*.

fair[1] ▶ **adjective 1** treating people equally without favouritism or discrimination: *the group has achieved fair and equal representation for all its members* | *a fairer distribution of wealth*. ■ just or appropriate in the circumstances: ***to be fair**, this subject poses special problems* | *it's not fair to take it out on her*. ■ archaic (of a means or procedure) not violent.
2 (of hair or complexion) light; blonde: *a pretty girl with long fair hair*. ■ (of a person) having a light complexion or hair: *he's very fair with blue eyes*.
3 considerable though not outstanding in size or amount: *he did a fair bit of coaching*. ■ moderately good: *he believes he has a fair chance of success*. ■ Austral./NZ informal complete; utter: *this cow is a fair swine*.
4 (of weather) fine and dry: *a fair autumn day*. ■ (of the wind) favourable: *they set sail with a fair wind*.
5 archaic beautiful: *the fairest of her daughters*. ■ (of words) specious despite being initially attractive.

F

▸ **adverb 1** without cheating or trying to achieve unjust advantage: *no one could say he played fair.*
2 [as submodifier] dialect to a high degree: *she'll be fair delighted to see you.*
▸ **noun** archaic a beautiful woman.
▸ **verb** [no obj.] dialect (of the weather) become fine: *looks like it's fairing off some.*
– PHRASES **all's fair in love and war** proverb in certain highly charged situations, any method of achieving your objective is justifiable. **by fair means or foul** using whatever means are necessary. **fair and square 1** Brit. with absolute accuracy: *he got you fair and square in his gunsight.* **2** honestly and straightforwardly: *we won the match fair and square.* **a fair deal** equitable treatment. **fair dinkum** see **DINKUM**. **fair dos** Brit. informal used to request just treatment or accept that it has been given: *Fair dos—you don't believe I've been idle all this time?* **fair enough** informal used to admit that something is reasonable or acceptable. **fair game** a person or thing that is considered a reasonable target for criticism, exploitation, or attack. **fair go** Austral./NZ informal used for emphasis or to request someone to be reasonable or fair: *Fair go! How can I ask a thing like that?* **fair name** dated a good reputation. **the fair** (or **fairer**) **sex** dated or humorous women. **fair's fair** informal used to request just treatment or assert that a situation is just: *Fair's fair—we were here first.* **for fair** US informal completely and finally: *I hope we'll be rid of him for fair.* **in a fair way to do something** likely to achieve something: *you are in a fair way to have cured yourself.* **it's a fair cop** Brit. informal an admission that the speaker has been caught doing wrong and deserves punishment. **no fair** N. Amer. informal unfair (often used in or as a petulant protestation). **be set fair** Brit. (of the weather) be fine and likely to stay fine for a time.
– DERIVATIVES **fairish** adjective, **fairness** noun.
– ORIGIN Old English *fæger* 'pleasing, attractive', of Germanic origin; related to Old High German *fagar*.

F

fair² ▸ **noun 1** a gathering of stalls and amusements for public entertainment.
2 a periodic gathering for the sale of goods. ■ an exhibition to promote particular products: *the European Fine Art Fair.* ■ N. Amer. an annual competitive exhibition of livestock, agricultural products, etc., held by a town, county, or state.
– ORIGIN Middle English (in the sense 'periodic gathering for the sale of goods'): from Old French *feire*, from late Latin *feria*, singular of Latin *feriae* 'holy days' (on which such fairs were often held).

fair³ ▸ **verb** [with obj.] (usu. as adj. **faired**) streamline (a vehicle, boat, or aircraft) by adding fairings.
– ORIGIN Old English in the senses 'beautify' and 'appear or become clean'. The current sense dates from the mid 19th cent.

Fairbanks the name of two American actors. **Douglas (Elton)** (1883–1939, born *Julius Ullman*) cofounded United Artists in 1919 and became famous for his swashbuckling film roles. His son **Douglas** (1909–2000, known as **Douglas Fairbanks Jr**) played similar roles.

fair copy ▸ **noun** written or printed matter transcribed or reproduced after final correction.

Fairfax, Thomas, 3rd Baron Fairfax of Cameron (1612–71), English Parliamentary general. He was appointed commander of the New Model Army in 1645 and won the Battle of Naseby. Fairfax later helped to secure the restoration of Charles II.

fairground ▸ **noun** an outdoor area where a fair is held.

fair-haired ▸ **adjective 1** having light-coloured hair.
2 N. Amer. (of a person) favourite; cherished: *the critics' fair-haired boy of the moment.*

fairies' bonnets ▸ **plural noun** a small toadstool with a grooved, yellowish-brown, thimble-shaped cap, growing in large clusters on rotten wood or in soil. ● *Coprinus disseminatus*, family Coprinaceae, class Hymenomycetes.

fairing¹ ▸ **noun** an external metal or plastic structure added to increase streamlining on a high-performance car, motorcycle, boat, or aircraft.

fairing² ▸ **noun** archaic a small present bought at a fair.

Fair Isle one of the Shetland Islands, lying about halfway between Orkney and the main Shetland group. ■ a shipping forecast area in the NE Atlantic off the north coast of Scotland, including Orkney and Shetland. ■ [as noun] [usu. as modifier] denoting traditional multicoloured geometric designs used in woollen knitwear: *Fair Isle sweaters.*

fairlead /ˈfɛːliːd/ ▸ **noun** a ring mounted on a boat to guide a rope, keeping it clear of obstructions and preventing it from cutting or chafing.

fairly ▸ **adverb 1** with justice: *he could not fairly be accused of wasting police time.*
2 [usu. as submodifier] to a moderately high degree: *I was fairly certain she had nothing to do with the affair.* ■ actually (used to emphasize something surprising or extreme): *he fairly snarled at her.*
– PHRASES **fairly and squarely** another term for **FAIR AND SQUARE** (see **FAIR¹**).

fair-minded ▸ **adjective** impartial in judgement; just: *a fair-minded employer.*
– DERIVATIVES **fair-mindedly** adverb, **fair-mindedness** noun.

fair play ▸ **noun** [mass noun] respect for the rules or equal treatment of all concerned.
– PHRASES **fair play to someone** Brit. used as an expression of approval when someone has done something praiseworthy or the right thing under the circumstances: *he must have decided to bring the children up himself—fair play to him.*

fair trade ▸ **noun** [mass noun] trade between companies in developed countries and producers in developing countries in which fair prices are paid to the producers: [as modifier] *fair trade coffee.*

fair use ▸ **noun** [mass noun] (in US copyright law) the doctrine that brief excerpts of copyright material may, under certain circumstances, be quoted verbatim for purposes such as criticism, teaching, and research without the need for permission from or payment to the copyright holder.

fairwater ▸ **noun** a structure that improves the streamlining of a ship to assist its smooth passage through water.

fairway ▸ **noun 1** the part of a golf course between a tee and the corresponding green, where the grass is kept short.
2 a navigable channel in a river or harbour. ■ a regular course or track followed by ships.

fair-weather friend ▸ **noun** a person whose friendship cannot be relied on in times of difficulty.

fairy ▸ **noun** (pl. **fairies**) **1** a small imaginary being of human form that has magical powers, especially a female one.
2 a Central and South American hummingbird with a green back and long tail. ● Genus *Heliothryx*, family Trochilidae: two species.
3 informal, derogatory a male homosexual.
– PHRASES **away with the fairies** Brit. informal giving the impression of being mad, distracted, or in a dreamworld.
– DERIVATIVES **fairylike** adjective.
– ORIGIN Middle English (denoting fairyland, or fairies collectively): from Old French *faerie*, from *fae*, 'a fairy', from Latin *fata* 'the Fates', plural of *fatum* (see **FATE**). Compare with **FAY**.

fairy cake ▸ **noun** Brit. a small individual sponge cake, usually with icing or other decoration.

fairy dust ▸ **noun** [mass noun] used to refer to a hypothetical substance with magical properties that brings great success, good luck, or happiness: *their whole life has been **sprinkled with fairy dust**.*

fairy floss ▸ **noun** Australian term for **CANDYFLOSS**.

fairy fly ▸ **noun** a minute parasitic wasp which lays its eggs in the eggs of other insects. ● Family Mymaridae, order Hymenoptera: numerous genera.

fairy godmother ▸ **noun** a female character in some fairy stories who has magical powers and brings good fortune to the hero or heroine. ■ a person who comes to the aid of someone in difficulty.

fairyland ▸ **noun** the imaginary home of fairies. ■ a beautiful place. ■ an imagined ideal place.

fairy lights ▸ **plural noun** Brit. small coloured electric lights used for decoration, especially at festivals such as Christmas.

fairy ring ▸ **noun** a circular area of grass that is darker in colour than the surrounding grass due to the growth of certain fungi. They were popularly believed to have been caused by fairies dancing.

fairy ring champignon ▸ **noun** see **CHAMPIGNON**.

fairy shrimp ▸ **noun** a small transparent crustacean which typically swims on its back, using its legs to filter food particles from the water. ● Order Anostraca, class Branchiopoda: many species, including brine shrimps.

fairy story ▸ **noun** a children's tale about magical and imaginary beings and lands. ■ an untrue account.

fairy tale ▸ **noun** a fairy story. ■ [often as modifier] something resembling a fairy story in being magical, idealized, or extremely happy: *a fairy-tale romance.* ■ a fabricated story, especially one intended to deceive.

fairy tern ▸ **noun** a small white tropical tern which lays its single egg on a narrow ledge or on the bare branch of a tree. When flying against a bright sky the wings appear somewhat translucent, allowing the bone structure to be seen. ● *Gygis alba*, family Sternidae.

fairy wren ▸ **noun** a small Australian songbird with a long cocked tail, the male of which has partly or mainly blue plumage. ● Genus *Malurus*, family Maluridae: several species, in particular the common **superb fairy wren** or blue wren (*M. cyaneus*).

Faisal /ˈfʌɪs(ə)l/ the name of two kings of Iraq:
■ **Faisal I** (1885–1933), reigned 1921–33. A British-sponsored ruler, he was also supported by fervent Arab nationalists. Under his rule Iraq achieved full independence in 1932. ■ **Faisal II** (1935–58), grandson of Faisal I, reigned 1939–58. He was assassinated in a military coup, after which a republic was established.

Faisalabad /ˈfʌɪsələˌbad/ an industrial city in Punjab, Pakistan; pop. 2,793,700 (est. 2009). Until 1979 it was known as Lyallpur.

faisandé /ˈfɛzɒ̃deɪ/ ▸ **adjective** literary affected; artificial.
– ORIGIN French, literally '(of game) hung until high'.

fait accompli /ˌfɛɪt əˈkɒmpli/, French /fɛt akɔ̃pli/ ▸ **noun** [in sing.] a thing that has already happened or been decided before those affected hear about it, leaving them with no option but to accept it: *the results were presented to shareholders as a fait accompli.*
– ORIGIN mid 19th cent.: from French, literally 'accomplished fact'.

faith ▸ **noun** [mass noun] **1** complete trust or confidence in someone or something: *this restores one's faith in politicians.*
2 strong belief in the doctrines of a religion, based on spiritual conviction rather than proof. ■ [count noun] a particular religion: *the Christian faith.* ■ [count noun] a strongly held belief: *men with strong political faiths.*
▸ **exclamation** chiefly Irish said to express surprise or emphasis: *faith, I was shown the door myself and came home.*
– PHRASES **break** (or **keep**) **faith** be disloyal (or loyal): *an attempt to make us **break faith with** our customers.*
– ORIGIN Middle English: from Old French *feid*, from Latin *fides*.

faithful ▸ **adjective 1** remaining loyal and steadfast: *the city has always been **faithful to** the Conservative party | employees who had notched up decades of faithful service.* ■ (of a spouse or partner) never having a sexual relationship with anyone else: *her husband was faithful to her.* ■ (of an object) reliable: *my faithful compass.*
2 true to the facts or the original: *the film was faithful to the book.*
▸ **noun** (as plural noun **the faithful**) those who are faithful to a particular religion or political party: *a muezzin called the faithful to prayer.*

faithfully ▸ **adverb 1** in a loyal manner.
2 in a manner that is true to the facts or the original: *she translated the novel as faithfully as possible.*
– PHRASES **yours faithfully** Brit. a formula for ending a formal letter in which the recipient is not addressed by name.

faithfulness ▸ **noun** [mass noun] the quality of being faithful; fidelity: *faithfulness in marriage.*

faith healing ▸ **noun** [mass noun] healing achieved by religious belief and prayer, rather than by medical treatment.
– DERIVATIVES **faith healer** noun.

faithless ▸ **adjective 1** disloyal, especially to a spouse or partner: *her faithless lover.*
2 without religious faith.
– DERIVATIVES **faithlessly** adverb, **faithlessness** noun.

faith school ▸ **noun** a school intended for students of a particular religious faith.

fajitas /fəˈhiːtəz, fəˈdʒiːtəz/ ▸ **plural noun** a dish of Mexican origin consisting of strips of spiced beef or chicken, chopped vegetables, and grated cheese, wrapped in a soft tortilla and often served with sour cream.

– ORIGIN Mexican Spanish, literally 'little strips'.

fake[1] ▶ **adjective** not genuine; imitation or counterfeit: *she got on the plane with a fake passport | a fake Cockney accent.* ■ (of a person) claiming to be something that one is not: *a fake doctor.*
▶ **noun** a thing that is not genuine; a forgery or sham: *fakes of Old Masters.* ■ a person who falsely claims to be something.
▶ **verb** [with obj.] forge or counterfeit (something): *she faked her spouse's signature.* ■ pretend to feel or have (an emotion, illness, or injury): *Rob faked suspicion, a jealous concern.* ■ make (an event) appear to happen: *he faked his own death.* ■ (**fake someone out**) N. Amer. informal trick or deceive someone.
– DERIVATIVES **faker** noun, **fakery** noun.
– ORIGIN late 18th cent. (originally slang): origin uncertain; perhaps ultimately related to German *fegen* 'sweep, thrash'. Compare with FIG[2].

fake[2] ▶ **noun & verb** variant spelling of FLAKE[4].
– ORIGIN late Middle English (as a verb): of unknown origin.

fakie /ˈfeɪki/ ▶ **noun** (pl. **fakies**) (in skateboarding or snowboarding) a movement in which the board is ridden backwards.
▶ **adverb** with a movement in which the board is ridden backwards.

fakir /ˈfeɪkɪə, ˈfa-/ (also **faquir**) ▶ **noun** a Muslim (or, loosely, a Hindu) religious ascetic who lives solely on alms.
– ORIGIN early 17th cent.: via French from Arabic *faqīr* 'needy man'.

Falabella /ˌfaləˈbɛlə/ ▶ **noun** a horse of a miniature breed, the adult of which does not usually exceed 75 cm in height.
– ORIGIN late 20th cent.: named after Julio *Falabella* (died 1981), an Argentinian breeder.

falafel /fəˈlaf(ə)l, -ˈlɑː-/ (also **felafel**) ▶ **noun** [mass noun] a Middle Eastern dish of spiced mashed chickpeas or other pulses formed into balls or fritters and deep-fried, usually eaten with or in pitta bread.
– ORIGIN from colloquial Egyptian Arabic *falāfil*, plural of Arabic *fulful, filfil* 'pepper'.

Falange /fəˈlan(d)ʒ/, Spanish /faˈlaŋxe/ the Spanish Fascist movement that merged with traditional right-wing elements in 1937 to form the ruling party, the Falange Española Tradicionalista, under General Franco. It was formally abolished in 1977.
– DERIVATIVES **Falangism** noun, **Falangist** noun & adjective.
– ORIGIN Spanish, from Latin *phalanx, phalang-* (see PHALANX).

Falasha /fəˈlɑːʃə/ ▶ **noun** (pl. **same** or **Falashas**) a member of a group of people in Ethiopia who hold the Jewish faith but use Ge'ez rather than Hebrew as a liturgical language. The Falashas were not formally recognized as Jews until 1975, and many of them were airlifted to Israel in 1984–5 and after.
– ORIGIN Amharic, literally 'exile, immigrant'.

falcate /ˈfalkeɪt/ ▶ **adjective** Botany & Zoology curved like a sickle; hooked: *the mandibles are falcate.*
– ORIGIN early 19th cent.: from Latin *falcatus*, from *falx, falc-* 'sickle'.

falcated teal ▶ **noun** a small duck that is native to China and NE Asia. ● *Anas falcata*, family Anatidae.
– ORIGIN early 18th cent.: named from the long sickle-shaped inner secondary feathers of the male.

falchion /ˈfɔːl(t)ʃ(ə)n/ ▶ **noun** historical a broad, slightly curved sword with the cutting edge on the convex side.
– ORIGIN Middle English *fauchon*, from Old French, based on Latin *falx, falc-* 'sickle'. The *-l-* was added in the 16th cent. to conform with the Latin spelling.

falciform /ˈfalsɪfɔːm/ ▶ **adjective** Anatomy & Zoology curved like a sickle; hooked: *the falciform ligament.*
– ORIGIN mid 18th cent.: from Latin *falx, falc-* 'sickle' + -IFORM.

falciparum /falˈsɪpərəm/ (also **falciparum malaria**) ▶ **noun** [mass noun] the most severe form of malaria: [as modifier] *the falciparum parasite.* ● This is caused by infection with *Plasmodium falciparum*.
– ORIGIN 1930s: modern Latin, from Latin *falx, falc-* 'sickle' + *-parum* (from *-parus* 'bearing').

falcon /ˈfɔː(l)k(ə)n, ˈfɒlk(ə)n/ ▶ **noun** a diurnal bird of prey with long pointed wings and a notched beak, typically catching prey by diving on it from above. Compare with HAWK[1] (sense 1 of the noun). ● Family Falconidae, in particular the genus *Falco*: many species, including the peregrine, hobby, merlin, and kestrel.
■ Falconry a female falcon, especially a peregrine. Compare with TERCEL.
– ORIGIN Middle English *faucon* (originally denoting any diurnal bird of prey used in falconry): from Old French, from late Latin *falco*, from Latin *falx, falc-* 'sickle', or of Germanic origin and related to Dutch *valk* and German *Falke*. The *-l-* was added in the 15th cent. to conform with the Latin spelling.

falconer ▶ **noun** a person who keeps, trains, or hunts with falcons, hawks, or other birds of prey.
– ORIGIN late Middle English: from Old French *fauconier*, from *faucon* (see FALCON).

falconet /ˈfɔː(l)k(ə)nɪt/ ▶ **noun 1** historical a light cannon.
2 a very small falcon of Asia and South America, typically having bold black-and-white plumage.
● Genus *Microhierax* (and *Spiziapteryx*), family Falconidae: six species.
– ORIGIN mid 16th cent.: from Italian *falconetto*, diminutive of *falcone* 'falcon', from Latin *falco* (see FALCON). Sense 2 is from FALCON + -ET[1].

falconry ▶ **noun** [mass noun] the keeping and training of falcons or other birds of prey; the sport of hunting with such birds.
– ORIGIN late 16th cent.: from French *fauconnerie*, from *faucon* (see FALCON).

falderal /ˈfaldəral/ ▶ **noun** variant spelling of FOLDEROL.

faldstool /ˈfɔːldstuːl/ ▶ **noun 1** a folding chair used by a bishop when not occupying the throne or when officiating in a church other than his own.
2 a small movable folding desk or stool for kneeling at prayer.
– ORIGIN late Old English *fældestōl*, of Germanic origin, from the base of FOLD[1] and STOOL, influenced by medieval Latin *faldistolium*, from Germanic.

fale /ˈfɑːleɪ/ ▶ **noun** a Samoan house with open sides and a thatched roof.

Falkirk /ˈfɔːlkəːk, ˈfɒl-/ a town in central Scotland, administrative centre of Falkirk council area; pop. 33,900 (est. 2009). Edward I defeated the Scots here in 1298.

Falkland Islands /ˈfɔːlklənd, ˈfɒlk-/ (also **the Falklands**) a group of islands in the South Atlantic, forming a British overseas territory; pop. 3,100 (est. 2008); capital, Stanley (on East Falkland).

> The group consists of two main islands and over a hundred smaller ones, about 500 km (300 miles) east of the Strait of Magellan. The Falklands were occupied and colonized by Britain in 1832–3, following the expulsion of an Argentinian garrison. Argentina refused to recognize British sovereignty and continues to refer to the islands by their old Spanish name, the Malvinas.

Falkland Islands Dependencies an overseas territory of the UK in the South Atlantic, consisting of the South Sandwich Islands and South Georgia, which is administered from the Falkland Islands.

Falklands War an armed conflict between Britain and Argentina in 1982.

> On the orders of General Galtieri's military junta, Argentinian forces invaded the Falkland Islands in support of their claim to sovereignty. In response Britain sent a task force of ships and aircraft, which forced the Argentinians to surrender six weeks after its arrival.

fall ▶ **verb** (past **fell**; past participle **fallen**) [no obj., with adverbial] **1** move from a higher to a lower level, typically rapidly and without control: *bombs could be seen falling from the planes | my purse fell out of my bag* | (as adj. **falling**) *she was injured by a falling tree.* ■ (**fall off**) become detached and drop to the ground: *my sunglasses fell off and broke on the pavement.* ■ hang down: *hair that was allowed to fall to the shoulders.* ■ (of land) slope downwards: *the land fell away in a steep bank.* ■ [no obj.] (of someone's eyes or glance) be directed downwards. ■ [no obj.] (of someone's face) show dismay or disappointment by appearing to droop: *her face fell as she thought about her life with George.*
2 (of a person) lose one's balance and collapse: *she fell down at school today.* ■ throw oneself to the ground: *she fell to her knees and began to weep.* ■ (of a tree or structure) collapse to the ground: *after the earthquake, part of the city fell down.* ■ (**fall over**) informal (of computer hardware or software) stop working suddenly; crash.
3 decrease in number, amount, intensity, or quality: *imports fell by 12 per cent | we're worried that standards are falling.* ■ (of a measuring instrument) show a lower reading: *the barometer had fallen a further ten points.* ■ (**fall away**) (in sport) play less well.
4 be captured or defeated: *their mountain strongholds fell to enemy attack.* ■ Cricket (of a wicket) be taken by the bowling side. ■ die in battle: *an English leader who had fallen at the hands of the Danes.* ■ [no obj.] (of a government or leader) lose office or be overthrown. ■ [no obj.] archaic yield to temptation: *it is their husbands' fault if wives do fall.*
5 pass into a specified state, situation, or position: *many of the buildings fell into disrepair* | [with complement] *she fell pregnant.* ■ occur or take place: *when night fell we crawled back to our lines | her birthday fell on May Day.* ■ (**fall to doing something**) begin to do something: *he fell to musing about how it had happened.* ■ be drawn accidentally into: *you must not fall into this common error.*
6 be classified in the way specified: *canals fall within the Minister's brief.*
▶ **noun 1** an act of falling or collapsing: *his mother had a fall as she alighted from a train.* ■ Wrestling a move which pins the opponent's shoulders on the ground for a count of three. ■ a downward difference in height between parts of a surface.
2 a thing which falls or has fallen: *in October came the first fall of snow | a rock fall.* ■ a sudden onset or arrival: *the fall of darkness.* ■ (usu. **falls**) a waterfall or cascade. ■ literary a downward turn in a melody: *that strain again, it had a dying fall.* ■ the way in which something falls or hangs: *the fall of her hair.* ■ (**falls**) the parts or petals of a flower which bend downwards, especially the outer perianth segments of an iris.
3 a decrease in size, number, rate, or level: *a big fall in unemployment.*
4 a defeat or downfall: *the fall of the government.* ■ a person's moral decline. ■ (**the Fall** or **the Fall of Man**) the lapse of humankind into a state of sin, ascribed in traditional Jewish and Christian theology to the disobedience of Adam and Eve as described in Genesis.
5 (also **Fall**) N. Amer. autumn.
– PHRASES **be riding** (or **heading**) **for a fall** informal be acting in a reckless way that is likely to end in trouble or disaster. **fall between two stools** see STOOL. **fall foul** (or N. Amer. **afoul**) **of** come into conflict with: *one of his songs has fallen foul of censorship regulations.* **fall in** (or **into**) **line** conform with others. [with reference to military formation.] **fall in** (or **out of**) **love** (**with someone**) see LOVE. **fall into place** (of a series of events or facts) begin to make sense: *once he knew what to look for, the theory fell quickly into place.* **fall on stony ground** see STONY. **fall over oneself to do something** informal be excessively eager to do something: *critics fell over themselves to compliment him.* **fall prey to** see PREY. **fall short** (**of**) (of a missile) fail to reach its target. ■ be deficient or inadequate: *the total vote fell short of the required two-thirds majority.* **fall to pieces** see FALL APART below. **fall victim to** see VICTIM. **take the fall** N. Amer. informal incur blame or punishment in the place of another person.
– PHRASAL VERBS **fall about** Brit. informal laugh uncontrollably. **fall apart** (or **to pieces**) break up, come apart, or disintegrate: *their marriage is likely to fall apart.* ■ (of a person) lose one's capacity to cope: *Angie fell to pieces because she had lost everything.* **fall back** move or turn back; retreat. **fall back on** have recourse to when in difficulty: *they normally fell back on one of three arguments.* **fall behind** fail to keep up with one's competitors. ■ fail to meet a commitment to make a regular payment: *borrowers falling behind with their mortgage repayments.* **fall down** be inadequate or unsuccessful; fail: *the deal fell down because there were a lot of unanswered questions.* **fall for** informal **1** fall in love with. **2** be deceived by (something): *he didn't expect Duncan to fall for a cheap trick like that.* **fall in** take one's place in a military formation: *the soldiers fell in by the side of the road.* **fall in with 1** meet by chance and become involved with: *he fell in with thieves.* **2** agree to: *Rob was happy to fall in with her plans.* **fall on** (or **upon**) **1** attack fiercely or unexpectedly: *the army fell on the besiegers.* ■ seize enthusiastically: *she fell on the sandwiches as though she had not eaten in weeks.* **2** (of someone's eyes or gaze) be directed towards: *her gaze fell on the mud-stained coverlet.* **3** be the responsibility of: *the cost of tuition should not fall on the student.* **fall out 1** (of the hair, teeth, etc.) become detached and drop out. **2** have an argument: *he had fallen out with his family.* **3** leave one's place in a military formation, or on parade. **4** happen; turn out: *matters fell out as Stephen arranged.* **fall through** come to nothing; fail: *the project fell through due to lack of money.* **fall to** (of a task) become the duty or responsibility of: *it*

fell to me to write to Shephard. ■ (of property) revert to the ownership of.
– ORIGIN Old English *fallan, feallan*, of Germanic origin; related to Dutch *vallen* and German *fallen*; the noun is partly from the verb, partly from Old Norse *fall* 'downfall, sin'.

Falla /ˈfʌɪjə/, Manuel de (1876–1946), Spanish composer and pianist. He composed the ballets *Love, the Magician* (1915) and *The Three-Cornered Hat* (1919); the latter was produced by Diaghilev, with designs by Picasso.

fallacious /fəˈleɪʃəs/ ▸ **adjective** based on a mistaken belief: *fallacious arguments.*
– DERIVATIVES **fallaciously** adverb, **fallaciousness** noun.
– ORIGIN early 16th cent.: from Old French *fallacieux*, from Latin *fallaciosus*, from *fallacia* (see FALLACY).

fallacy /ˈfaləsi/ ▸ **noun** (pl. **fallacies**) a mistaken belief, especially one based on unsound arguments: *the notion that the camera never lies is a fallacy.* ■ Logic a failure in reasoning which renders an argument invalid. ■ [mass noun] faulty reasoning: *the potential for fallacy which lies behind the notion of self-esteem.*
– ORIGIN late 15th cent. (in the sense 'deception, guile'; gradually superseding Middle English *fallace*): from Latin *fallacia*, from *fallax, fallac-* 'deceiving', from *fallere* 'deceive'.

fallaway ▸ **noun** [usu. as modifier] Basketball a shot made while the shooter jumps or falls away from the basket.

fallback ▸ **noun 1** an alternative plan that may be used in an emergency.
2 a reduction or decrease.

fallen past participle of FALL. ▸ **adjective 1** Theology having sinned: *fallen human nature.* ■ dated (of a woman) regarded as having lost her honour through engaging in a sexual relationship outside marriage.
2 (of a soldier) killed in battle: *fallen heroes.*
– DERIVATIVES **fallenness** noun.

fallen angel ▸ **noun** (in Christian, Jewish, and Muslim tradition) an angel who rebelled against God and was cast out of heaven.

faller ▸ **noun 1** Brit. a person or thing that falls, in particular: ■ a horse that falls during a race, especially at a fence in a steeplechase. ■ a company whose shares have lost value on the stock market.
2 N. Amer. a person who fells trees for a living.

fallfish ▸ **noun** (pl. **same** or **fallfishes**) a North American freshwater fish resembling the chub. ● *Semotilus corporalis*, family Cyprinidae.

fall guy ▸ **noun** informal, chiefly N. Amer. a scapegoat.

fallibilism /ˈfalɪbɪˌlɪz(ə)m/ ▸ **noun** [mass noun] Philosophy the principle that propositions concerning empirical knowledge can be accepted even though they cannot be proved with certainty.
– DERIVATIVES **fallibilist** noun & adjective.

fallible /ˈfalɪb(ə)l/ ▸ **adjective** capable of making mistakes or being wrong: *experts can be fallible.*
– DERIVATIVES **fallibility** noun, **fallibly** adverb.
– ORIGIN late Middle English: from medieval Latin *fallibilis*, from Latin *fallere* 'deceive'.

falling-out ▸ **noun** (pl. **fallings-out**) a quarrel or disagreement: *the two of them had a falling-out.*

falling sickness ▸ **noun** [mass noun] archaic term for EPILEPSY.

falling star ▸ **noun** a meteor or shooting star.

fall line ▸ **noun 1** (**the fall line**) Skiing the route leading straight down any particular part of a slope.
2 a narrow zone that marks the geological boundary between an upland region and a plain, distinguished by the occurrence of falls and rapids where rivers and streams cross it.

fall-off (also **falling-off**) ▸ **noun** (pl. **fall-offs** or **fallings-off**) a decrease in something: *a fall-off in work caused by the recession.*

fallopian tube /fəˈləʊpɪən/ ▸ **noun** (in a female mammal) either of a pair of tubes along which eggs travel from the ovaries to the uterus.
– ORIGIN early 18th cent.: from *Fallopius*, Latinized form of the name of Gabriello *Fallopio* (1523–62), the Italian anatomist who first described them.

fallout ▸ **noun** [mass noun] **1** radioactive particles that are carried into the atmosphere after a nuclear explosion and gradually fall back as dust or in precipitation. ■ [usu. with modifier] airborne substances resulting from an industrial process or accident: *acid fallout from power stations.*
2 the adverse results of a situation or action: *he's prepared to take calculated risks regardless of political fallout.*

fallow[1] ▸ **adjective 1** (of farmland) ploughed and harrowed but left for a period without being sown in order to restore its fertility or to avoid surplus production: *incentives for farmers to let land lie fallow.* ■ (of a period of time) characterized by inaction; unproductive: *long fallow periods when nothing seems to happen.*
2 (of a sow) not pregnant.
▸ **noun** a piece of fallow land.
▸ **verb** [with obj.] leave (land) fallow for a period.
– DERIVATIVES **fallowness** noun.
– ORIGIN Old English *fealgian* 'to break up land for sowing', of Germanic origin; related to Low German *falgen*.

fallow[2] ▸ **noun** [mass noun] a pale brown or reddish yellow colour.
– ORIGIN Old English *falu, fealu*, of Germanic origin; related to Dutch *vaal* and German *fahl, falb*.

fallow deer ▸ **noun** a Eurasian deer with branched palmate antlers, typically having a white-spotted reddish-brown coat in summer. ● *Cervus dama*, family Cervidae.

false ▸ **adjective 1** not according with truth or fact; incorrect: *he was feeding false information to his customers | the allegations were false.* ■ not according with rules or law: *false imprisonment.*
2 made to imitate something in order to deceive: *the trunk had a false bottom | a false passport.* ■ artificial: *false eyelashes.* ■ not sincere: *a horribly false smile.*
3 illusory; not actually so: *sunscreens give users a false sense of security.* ■ [attrib.] used in names of plants, animals, and gems that superficially resemble the thing properly so called, e.g. **false oat**.
4 disloyal; unfaithful: *a false lover.*
– PHRASES **false position** a situation in which one is compelled to act in a manner inconsistent with one's true nature or principles. **play someone false** deceive or cheat someone.
– DERIVATIVES **falsely** adverb, **falseness** noun.
– ORIGIN Old English *fals* 'fraud, deceit', from Latin *falsum* 'fraud', neuter past participle of *fallere* 'deceive'; reinforced or re-formed in Middle English from Old French *fals, faus* 'false'.

false acacia ▸ **noun** a North American tree with compound leaves and dense hanging clusters of fragrant white flowers, widely grown as an ornamental. ● *Robinia pseudoacacia*, family Leguminosae.

false alarm ▸ **noun** a warning given about something that fails to happen.

false bedding ▸ **noun** Geology another term for CROSS-BEDDING.

false card Bridge ▸ **noun** a card played in order to give one's opponents a misleading impression of one's strength in the suit led.
▸ **verb** (**false-card**) [with obj.] play (a card) in such a way.

false colour ▸ **noun** [mass noun] colour added during the processing of a photographic or computer image to aid interpretation of the subject.

false consciousness ▸ **noun** [mass noun] (especially in Marxist theory) a way of thinking that prevents a person from perceiving the true nature of their social or economic situation.

false cypress ▸ **noun** a conifer of a genus that includes Lawson's cypress. ● Genus *Chamaecyparis*, family Cupressaceae.

false dawn ▸ **noun 1** a promising situation which comes to nothing: *after so many false dawns, Britain was finally enjoying an export-led boom.*
2 a transient light which precedes the rising of the sun by about an hour, commonly seen in Eastern countries.

false economy ▸ **noun** an apparent financial saving that in fact leads to greater expenditure.

false face ▸ **noun** a mask, especially as traditionally worn ceremonially by some North American Indian peoples.

false friend ▸ **noun** a word or expression that has a similar form to one in a person's native language, but a different meaning (for example English *magazine* and French *magasin* 'shop').
– ORIGIN translating French *faux ami*.

false fruit ▸ **noun** a fruit formed from other parts of the plant as well as the ovary, especially the receptacle, such as the strawberry or fig. Also called PSEUDOCARP.

false helleborine (also **false hellebore**) ▸ **noun** a herbaceous plant of the lily family which resembles a helleborine, with pleated leaves and a tall dense spike of small flowers, found in north temperate regions. ● Genus *Veratrum*, family Liliaceae: many species.

falsehood ▸ **noun** [mass noun] the state of being untrue: *the truth or falsehood of the many legends which surround her.* ■ [count noun] a lie. ■ lying: *the right to sue for malicious falsehood.*

false memory ▸ **noun** Psychology an apparent recollection of an event which did not actually occur, especially one of childhood sexual abuse arising from suggestion during psychoanalysis: [as modifier] *false memory syndrome.*

false move ▸ **noun** an unwise or careless action that could have dangerous consequences: *one false move would lead to nuclear war.*

false oxlip ▸ **noun** see OXLIP.

false pretences ▸ **plural noun** behaviour intended to deceive others: *he obtained money by false pretences.*

false rib ▸ **noun** another term for FLOATING RIB.

false scorpion ▸ **noun** a minute arachnid which has pincers but no long abdomen or sting, occurring abundantly in leaf litter. Also called PSEUDOSCORPION. ● Order Pseudoscorpiones.

false start ▸ **noun** an invalid start to a race, usually due to a competitor beginning before the official signal has been given. ■ an unsuccessful attempt to begin something.

false step ▸ **noun** a slip or stumble: *one false step and we would have fallen in the sea.* ■ a careless or unwise act; a mistake.

false teeth ▸ **plural noun** another term for DENTURES (see DENTURE).

false topaz ▸ **noun** another term for CITRINE.

falsetto /fɔːlˈsɛtəʊ, fɒl-/ ▸ **noun** (pl. **falsettos**) Music a method of voice production used by male singers, especially tenors, to sing notes higher than their normal range: *he sang in a piercing falsetto.* ■ a singer using this method. ■ a voice or sound that is unusually high.
– ORIGIN late 18th cent.: from Italian, diminutive of *falso* 'false', from Latin *falsus* (see FALSE).

false vampire ▸ **noun** a large carnivorous bat that includes rodents, reptiles, and other small vertebrates among its prey: ● an Old World bat (three species in the family Megadermatidae, including the large Australian ghost bat, *Macroderma gigas*). ● a tropical New World bat (*Vampyrum spectrum*, family Phyllostomidae).

falsework ▸ **noun** [mass noun] temporary framework structures used to support a building during its construction.

falsies ▸ **plural noun** informal pads of material in women's clothing used to increase the apparent size of the breasts. ■ false eyelashes.

falsification /ˌfɔːlsɪfɪˈkeɪʃ(ə)n, ˌfɒls-/ ▸ **noun** [mass noun] the action of falsifying information or a theory: *an investigation into fraud and the falsification of records.*

falsify /ˈfɔːlsɪfʌɪ, ˈfɒls-/ ▸ **verb** (**falsifies, falsifying, falsified**) [with obj.] **1** alter (information, a document, or evidence) so as to mislead: *a laboratory which was alleged to have falsified test results.*
2 prove (a statement or theory) to be false: *the hypothesis is falsified by the evidence.* ■ fail to fulfil (a hope, fear, or expectation): *changes falsify individual expectations.*
– DERIVATIVES **falsifiability** noun, **falsifiable** adjective.
– ORIGIN late Middle English (in sense 2): from French *falsifier* or medieval Latin *falsificare*, from Latin *falsificus* 'making false', from *falsus* 'false'.

falsity ▸ **noun** [mass noun] the fact of being untrue, incorrect, or insincere: *he exposed the falsity of the claim.*

Falstaffian /fɔːlˈstɑːfɪən, fɒl-/ ▸ **adjective** relating to or resembling Shakespeare's character Sir John Falstaff in being fat, jolly, and debauched: *a Falstaffian gusto for life.*

Falster /ˈfɑːlstə/ a Danish island in the Baltic Sea, south of Zealand.

falter /ˈfɔːltə, ˈfɒl-/ ▸ **verb** [no obj.] lose strength or momentum: *the music faltered, stopped, and started up again* | (as adj. **faltering**) *his faltering career.* ■ speak hesitantly: [with direct speech] *'A-Adam?' he faltered.* ■ move unsteadily or hesitantly: *he faltered and finally stopped in mid-stride.*

– DERIVATIVES **falteringly** adverb.
– ORIGIN late Middle English (in the senses 'stammer' and 'stagger'): perhaps from the verb **FOLD[1]** (which was occasionally used of the faltering of the legs or tongue) + *-ter* as in *totter*.

Falun Gong /ˌfalən ˈɡɒŋ/ (also **Falun Dafa** /ˈdafə/) ▶ noun [mass noun] a spiritual exercise and meditation regime with similarities to t'ai chi ch'uan, practised predominantly in China. ▪ a Taoist-Buddhist sect practising Falun Gong.
– ORIGIN 1990s: Chinese, literally 'wheel of law', from *fǎ* 'law' + *lún* 'wheel' (+ *gōng* 'skill' or *dàfǎ* 'great method').

fame ▶ noun [mass noun] the state of being known by many people: *the song's success rocketed him to stardom and fame.*
– PHRASES **of —— fame** having a particular famous association; famous for having or being ——: *the village is the birthplace of Mrs Beeton, of cookery fame.*
– ORIGIN Middle English (also in the sense 'reputation', which survives in **HOUSE OF ILL FAME**): via Old French from Latin *fama*.

famed ▶ adjective known about by many people; renowned: *he is* **famed for** *his eccentricities.* ▪ archaic widely reported or rumoured.
– ORIGIN Middle English: past participle of archaic *fame* (verb), from Old French *famer*, from Latin *fama*.

familia /fəˈmɪlɪə/ ▶ noun (pl. **familiae** /-lɪiː/) historical a household or religious community under one head, regarded as a unit.
– ORIGIN Latin.

familial /fəˈmɪljəl/ ▶ adjective relating to or occurring in a family or its members: *the familial Christmas dinner.*
– ORIGIN early 20th cent.: from French, from Latin *familia* 'family'.

familiar ▶ adjective **1** well known from long or close association: *their faces will be* **familiar to** *many of you | a familiar voice.* ▪ often encountered or experienced; common: *the situation was all too familiar.* ▪ (**familiar with**) having a good knowledge of: *ensure that you are familiar with the heating controls.*
2 in close friendship; intimate: *she had not realized they were on such familiar terms.* ▪ informal or intimate to an inappropriate degree.
▶ noun **1** (also **familiar spirit**) a demon supposedly attending and obeying a witch, often said to assume the form of an animal.
2 a close friend or associate.
3 (in the Roman Catholic Church) a person rendering certain services in a pope's or bishop's household.
– DERIVATIVES **familiarly** adverb.
– ORIGIN Middle English (in the sense 'intimate', 'on a family footing'): from Old French *familier*, from Latin *familiaris*, from *familia* 'household servants, family', from *famulus* 'servant'.

familiarity ▶ noun (pl. **familiarities**) [mass noun] **1** close acquaintance with or knowledge of something: *his* **familiarity with** *the works of Thomas Hardy.* ▪ the quality of being well known from long or close association: *the reassuring familiarity of his parents' home.*
2 relaxed friendliness or intimacy between people: *familiarity allows us to give each other nicknames.* ▪ inappropriate informality or intimacy: *the unnecessary familiarity made me dislike him at once.*
– PHRASES **familiarity breeds contempt** proverb extensive knowledge of or close association with someone or something leads to a loss of respect for them or it.
– ORIGIN Middle English (in the senses 'close relationship' and 'sexual intimacy'): via Old French from Latin *familiaritas*, from *familiaris* 'familiar, intimate' (see **FAMILIAR**).

familiarize (also **familiarise**) ▶ verb [with obj.] give (someone) knowledge or understanding of something: *the need to* **familiarize** *pupils* **with** *dictionaries and their structures.* ▪ make (something) better known or more easily grasped: *exercises which will help to familiarize the terms used.*
– DERIVATIVES **familiarization** noun.

Familist /ˈfamɪlɪst/ ▶ noun a member of the Christian sect of the 16th and 17th centuries called the Family of Love, which asserted the importance of love and the necessity for absolute obedience to any government.

familist /ˈfamɪlɪst/ ▶ adjective relating to or advocating a social framework centred on family relationships.
– DERIVATIVES **familistic** adjective.

famille /faˈmiː/ ▶ noun [mass noun] Chinese enamelled porcelain of particular periods in the 17th and 18th centuries with a specified predominant colour: **famille jaune** /ʒəʊn/ (yellow), **famille noire** /nwɑː/ (black), **famille rose** /rəʊz/ (red), or **famille verte** /vɛːt/ (green).
– ORIGIN French, literally 'family'.

family ▶ noun (pl. **families**) **1** [treated as sing. or pl.] a group consisting of two parents and their children living together as a unit. ▪ a group of people related by blood or marriage: *friends and family can provide support | I could not turn him away, for he was family.* ▪ the children of a person or couple being discussed: *she has the sole responsibility for a large family.* ▪ informal a local organizational unit of the Mafia or other large criminal group.
2 all the descendants of a common ancestor: *the house has been owned by the same family for 300 years.* ▪ a group of peoples from a common stock.
3 a group of related things. ▪ Biology a principal taxonomic category that ranks above genus and below order, usually ending in *-idae* (in zoology) or *-aceae* (in botany). ▪ all the languages ultimately derived from a particular early language, regarded as a group: *the Austronesian language family.* ▪ Mathematics a group of curves or surfaces obtained by varying the value of a constant in the equation generating them.
▶ adjective [attrib.] designed to be suitable for children as well as adults: *a family newspaper.*
– PHRASES **the** (or **one's**) **family jewels** informal a man's genitals. **in the family way** informal pregnant. **sell** (or **sell off**) **the family silver** part with a valuable resource for immediate advantage.
– ORIGIN late Middle English (in sense 2 of the noun; also denoting the servants of a household or the retinue of a nobleman): from Latin *familia* 'household servants, family', from *famulus* 'servant'.

family allowance ▶ noun Brit. former term for **CHILD BENEFIT**.

family bible ▶ noun a bible designed to be used at family prayers, typically one with space on its flyleaves for recording important family events.

family credit ▶ noun [mass noun] (in the UK) a regular payment by the state to a family with an income below a certain level.

Family Division (in the UK) the division of the High Court dealing with adoption, divorce, and other family matters.

family man ▶ noun a man with a wife (or long-term partner) and children, especially one who enjoys home life.

family name ▶ noun a surname. ▪ a family's good reputation: *he won't disgrace the family name.*

family planning ▶ noun [mass noun] the practice of controlling the number of children one has and the intervals between their births, particularly by means of contraception or voluntary sterilization: [as modifier] *family-planning clinics.* ▪ contraception.

family tree ▶ noun a diagram showing the relationship between people in several generations of a family.

family values ▶ plural noun values supposedly learned within a traditional family unit, typically those of high moral standards and discipline.

famine /ˈfamɪn/ ▶ noun [mass noun] extreme scarcity of food: *drought resulted in famine throughout the region* | [count noun] *the famine of 1921–2.* ▪ [count noun] a shortage: *the cotton famine of the 1860s.* ▪ archaic hunger.
– ORIGIN late Middle English: from Old French, from *faim* 'hunger', from Latin *fames*.

famish ▶ verb [with obj.] archaic reduce (someone) to extreme hunger: *they had famished the city into surrender.* ▪ [no obj.] be extremely hungry.
– ORIGIN Middle English: from obsolete *fame* 'starve, famish', from Old French *afamer*, based on Latin *fames* 'hunger'.

famished /ˈfamɪʃt/ ▶ adjective informal extremely hungry.
– ORIGIN late Middle English: past participle of the verb *famish*, from Middle English *fame* 'starve', from Old French *afamer*, based on Latin *fames* 'hunger'.

famous ▶ adjective **1** known about by many people: *a famous star | the country is* **famous for** *its natural beauty.*
2 informal excellent: *Galway stormed to a famous victory.*
– PHRASES **famous for being famous** having no recognizable reason for one's fame other than high media exposure. **famous for fifteen minutes** see **FIFTEEN MINUTES OF FAME** at **FIFTEEN**. **famous last words** said as an ironic comment on an overconfident assertion that may later be proved wrong.
– DERIVATIVES **famousness** noun.
– ORIGIN late Middle English: from Old French *fameus*, from Latin *famosus* 'famed', from *fama* (see **FAME**).

famously ▶ adverb **1** informal excellently: *we got on famously.*
2 in a way that is widely known: *they have famously reclusive lifestyles.*

famulus /ˈfamjʊləs/ ▶ noun (pl. **famuli** /-lʌɪ, -liː/) historical an assistant or servant, especially one working for a magician or scholar.
– ORIGIN mid 19th cent.: from Latin, 'servant'.

Fan /fan/ ▶ noun & adjective variant spelling of **FANG**.

fan[1] ▶ noun **1** an apparatus with rotating blades that creates a current of air for cooling or ventilation. ▪ a small sail for keeping the head of a windmill towards the wind.
2 a handheld device, typically folding and shaped like a segment of a circle when spread out, that is waved so as to cool the person holding it. ▪ a thing resembling an open fan. ▪ a fan-shaped alluvial or talus deposit at the foot of a slope.
▶ verb (**fans, fanning, fanned**) **1** [with obj.] cool (someone or something) by waving an object to create a current of air: *he fanned himself with his hat.* ▪ (of breath or a breeze) blow gently on: *his breath fanned her skin as he leant towards her.* ▪ [with obj. and adverbial of direction] brush or drive away with a waving movement: *a veil of smoke which she* **fanned away** *with a jewelled hand.* ▪ [no obj.] Baseball & Ice Hockey swing unsuccessfully at the ball or puck. ▪ Baseball strike out (a batter).
2 [with obj.] increase the strength of (a fire) by blowing on it or stirring up the air near it: *fanned by an easterly wind, the fire spread rapidly.* ▪ cause (a belief or emotion) to become stronger or more widespread: *a fury fanned by press coverage.*
3 [no obj.] (**fan out**) disperse or radiate from a central point to cover a wide area: *the arriving passengers began to fan out through the town in search of lodgings.* ▪ spread out or cause to spread out into a semicircular shape: [no obj.] *a dress made of tiny pleats that fanned out as she walked* | [with obj.] *a wind fanned her hair out behind her.*
– PHRASES **fan the flames (of something)** cause an emotion, such as anger or hatred, to become stronger: *instead of being a calming force you fanned the flames of hostility.*
– DERIVATIVES **fan-like** adjective, **fanner** noun.
– ORIGIN Old English *fann* (as a noun denoting a device for winnowing grain), *fannian* (verb), from Latin *vannus* 'winnowing fan'. Compare with **VANE**.

fan[2] ▶ noun a person who has a strong interest in or admiration for a particular sport, art form, or famous person: *football fans | I'm a fan of this author.*
– DERIVATIVES **fandom** noun.
– ORIGIN late 19th cent. (originally US): abbreviation of **FANATIC**.

Fanakalo /ˌfanagaˈlɒ, ˈfanagalɒ/ (also **Fanagalo**) ▶ noun [mass noun] S. African a lingua franca developed and used by the southern African mining companies, composed of frequently corrupted elements of the Nguni languages, English, and Afrikaans.
– ORIGIN 1940s: from Nguni *fana ka lo*, from *fana* 'be like' + the possessive suffix *-ka* + *lo* 'this'.

fanatic /fəˈnatɪk/ ▶ noun a person filled with excessive and single-minded zeal, especially for an extreme religious or political cause. ▪ informal a person with an obsessive interest in and enthusiasm for a particular activity: *a fitness fanatic.*
▶ adjective filled with or expressing excessive zeal: *his eyes had a fanatic iciness.*
– DERIVATIVES **fanaticize** (also **fanaticise**) verb.
– ORIGIN mid 16th cent. (as an adjective): from French *fanatique* or Latin *fanaticus* 'of a temple, inspired by a god', from *fanum* 'temple'. The adjective originally described behaviour that might result from possession by a god or demon, hence the earliest sense of the noun 'a religious maniac' (mid 17th cent.).

fanatical ▶ adjective filled with excessive and single-minded zeal: *fanatical revolutionaries.* ▪ obsessively concerned with something: *her husband was fanatical about tidiness.*
– DERIVATIVES **fanatically** adverb.

fanaticism /fəˈnatɪsɪz(ə)m/ ▶ noun [mass noun] the quality of being fanatical: *the dangers of religious fanaticism.*

fan base ▸ **noun** [mass noun] the fans of a sports team, pop group, etc. considered as a distinct social grouping.

fan belt ▸ **noun** (in a motor-vehicle engine) a belt that transmits motion from the driveshaft to the radiator fan and the dynamo or alternator.

fanboy ▸ **noun** informal a male fan, especially one who is obsessive about comics, music, film, or science fiction.

fanciable ▸ **adjective** Brit. informal sexually attractive.

fancier ▸ **noun** [with modifier] a connoisseur or enthusiast of something, especially someone who has a special interest in or breeds a particular animal: *a pigeon fancier*.

fanciful ▸ **adjective** **1** over-imaginative and unrealistic: *ever more fanciful proposals were raised*. ■ existing only in the imagination: *fanciful lunar inhabitants*.
2 highly ornamental or imaginative in design: *a fanciful Art Nouveau bar*.
– DERIVATIVES **fancifully** adverb, **fancifulness** noun.

F

fan club ▸ **noun** an organized group of fans of a famous person or team.

fancy ▸ **verb** (**fancies, fancying, fancied**) [with obj.]
1 Brit. informal feel a desire or liking for: *do you fancy a drink?* ■ find sexually attractive. ■ (**fancy oneself**) informal have an unduly high opinion of oneself, or of one's ability in a particular area: *he **fancied himself** as an amateur psychologist*.
2 Brit. regard (a horse, team, or player) as a likely winner: [with obj. and infinitive] *I fancy him to win the tournament*.
3 [with clause] imagine; think: *he fancied he could smell the perfume of roses*. ■ [in imperative] chiefly Brit. used to express surprise at something: *fancy meeting all those television actors!*
▸ **adjective** (**fancier, fanciest**) **1** elaborate in structure or decoration: *the furniture was very fancy | a fancy computerized system*. ■ sophisticated or expensive in a way that is intended to impress: *fancy hotels and restaurants*. ■ chiefly N. Amer. (especially of foodstuffs) of high quality: *fancy molasses*. ■ (of a flower) of two or more colours. ■ (of an animal) bred to develop particular points of appearance: *fancy goldfish*.
2 archaic (of a drawing, painting, or sculpture) created from the imagination rather than from life.
▸ **noun** (pl. **fancies**) **1** a superficial or transient feeling of liking or attraction: *this was no **passing fancy**, but a feeling he would live by*. ■ dated a person or thing that one finds attractive: *people jostled to ride alongside their fancy*. ■ a favourite in a race or other sporting contest: *the filly is already a leading fancy for next year's races*. ■ (**the fancy**) dated enthusiasts for a sport, especially boxing or racing, considered collectively.
2 [mass noun] the faculty of imagination: *he is prone to **flights of fancy***. ■ [count noun] an unfounded or tentative belief or idea: *I've a fancy they want to be alone*.
3 (also **fancy cake**) Brit. a small iced cake.
4 (in 16th and 17th century music) a composition for keyboard or strings in free or variation form.
– PHRASES **as** (or **when** or **where**) **the fancy takes one** according to one's inclination: *you could move about as the fancy took you*. **fancy one's** (or **someone's**) **chances** believe that one (or someone else) is likely to be successful: *we fancy our chances in the replay*. **take** (or **catch**) **someone's fancy** appeal to someone. **take a fancy to** become fond of, especially without an obvious reason.
– DERIVATIVES **fancily** adverb, **fanciness** noun.
– ORIGIN late Middle English: contraction of **FANTASY**.

fancy dress ▸ **noun** [mass noun] an unusual or amusing costume worn to a social event to make someone look like, for example, a famous person or well-known fictional character.

fancy-free ▸ **adjective** not emotionally involved with or committed to anyone: *her recent divorce meant that she was footloose and fancy-free*.

fancy goods ▸ **plural noun** items for sale that are purely or chiefly ornamental.

fancy man ▸ **noun** informal, often derogatory a woman's lover. ■ archaic a pimp.

fancy-pants ▸ **adjective** informal superior or high-class in a pretentious way: *a fancy-pants restaurant*.

fancy woman (Brit. also **fancy piece**) ▸ **noun** informal, often derogatory a married man's mistress.

fancywork ▸ **noun** [mass noun] ornamental needlework, crochet, or knitting, as opposed to plain or purely functional stitches.

fan dance ▸ **noun** a dance in which the female performer is apparently nude and remains partly concealed throughout by large fans.

fandangle /fanˈdaŋg(ə)l/ ▸ **noun** archaic a useless or purely ornamental thing: *a solo with no end of shakes and trills and fandangles*.
– ORIGIN mid 19th cent.: perhaps from **FANDANGO**, influenced by *newfangle*.

fandango /fanˈdaŋgəʊ/ ▸ **noun** (pl. **fandangoes** or **fandangos**) **1** a lively Spanish dance for two people, typically accompanied by castanets or tambourine.
2 an elaborate or complicated process or activity: *the Washington inaugural fandango*.
– ORIGIN mid 18th cent.: Spanish, of unknown origin.

fane ▸ **noun** archaic a temple or shrine.
– ORIGIN late Middle English: from Latin *fanum*.

fanfare ▸ **noun** a short ceremonial tune or flourish played on brass instruments, typically to introduce something or someone important. ■ [mass noun] media attention or elaborate ceremony: *the studio released this film with great fanfare but no commercial success*.
– ORIGIN mid 18th cent.: from French, ultimately of imitative origin.

fanfaronade /ˌfanfarəˈneɪd, -ˈnɑːd/ ▸ **noun** **1** [mass noun] arrogant or boastful talk.
2 a fanfare.
– ORIGIN mid 17th cent.: from French *fanfaronnade*, from *fanfaron* 'braggart', from *fanfare* (see **FANFARE**).

fan fiction (also informal **fanfic**) ▸ **noun** [mass noun] fiction written by a fan of, and featuring characters from, a particular TV series, film, etc.

Fang /faŋ/ (also **Fan**) ▸ **noun** (pl. **same** or **Fangs**) **1** a member of a people inhabiting parts of Cameroon, Equatorial Guinea, and Gabon.
2 [mass noun] the Bantu language of the Fang, with over 500,000 speakers.
▸ **adjective** relating to the Fang or their language.
– ORIGIN French, probably from Fang *Pangwe*.

fang¹ ▸ **noun** a large sharp tooth, especially a canine tooth of a dog or wolf. ■ the tooth of a venomous snake, by which poison is injected. ■ the biting mouthpart of a spider.
– DERIVATIVES **fanged** adjective, **fangless** adjective.
– ORIGIN late Old English (denoting booty or spoils), from Old Norse *fang* 'capture, grasp'; compare with **VANG**. A sense 'trap, snare' is recorded from the mid 16th cent.; both this and the original sense survive in Scots. The current sense (also mid 16th cent.) reflects the same notion of 'something that catches and holds'.

fang² Austral. informal ▸ **verb** drive at high speed: [no obj.] *let's fang up to the beach!*
▸ **noun** a high-speed drive in a car.
– ORIGIN 1960s: from the name of J. M. **FANGIO**.

Fangio /ˈfandʒɪəʊ/, Juan Manuel (1911–95), Argentinian motor-racing driver. He first won the world championship in 1951 and then held the title from 1954 until 1957.

fango /ˈfaŋgəʊ/ ▸ **noun** [mass noun] [usu. as modifier] mud from thermal springs in Italy, used in curative treatment at spas and health farms: *fango mud baths*.
– ORIGIN early 20th cent.: Italian, literally 'mud'.

fan heater ▸ **noun** an electric heater in which a fan drives air over a hot element and back into the room.

fan jet ▸ **noun** another term for **TURBOFAN**.

fankle /ˈfaŋk(ə)l/ ▸ **verb** [with obj.] Scottish entangle: *the tape got fankled in the motorbike's front wheels*.
– ORIGIN late Middle English: from Scots *fank* 'coil of rope' + **-LE⁴**.

fanlight ▸ **noun** a small semicircular or rectangular window over a door or another window. ■ another term for **SKYLIGHT**.

fan mail letters sent to a famous person from his or her fans.

Fannie Mae /fani ˈmeɪ/ informal the Federal National Mortgage Association, a US corporation that trades in mortgages.
– ORIGIN 1940s: elaboration of the acronym *FNMA*, suggested by the given names *Fanny* and *Mae*. Compare with **FREDDIE MAC**.

fanny ▸ **noun** (pl. **fannies**) **1** Brit. vulgar slang a woman's genitals.
2 N. Amer. informal a person's buttocks.
▸ **verb** (**fannies, fannying, fannied**) [no obj.] (**fanny about** (or **around**)) Brit. informal mess around and waste time.
– ORIGIN late 19th cent.: of unknown origin.

Fanny Adams ▸ **noun** Brit. informal **1** (also **sweet Fanny Adams**) nothing at all: *I know sweet Fanny Adams about mining*.
2 a nautical term for tinned meat or stew.
– ORIGIN late 19th cent. (in sense 2): black humour, from the name of a murder victim c.1870. Sense 1 dates from the early 20th cent., and is sometimes understood as a euphemism for *fuck all*.

fanny pack ▸ **noun** North American term for **BUMBAG**.

fan palm ▸ **noun** a palm with large lobed fan-shaped leaves. ● *Chamaerops* and other genera, family Palmae: many species, including the **dwarf** (or **European**) **fan palm** (*C. humilis*), which is the only palm native to Europe.

fantabulous /fanˈtabjʊləs/ ▸ **adjective** informal excellent; wonderful: *a fantabulous prize*.
– ORIGIN 1950s: blend of **FANTASTIC** and **FABULOUS**.

fantail ▸ **noun** **1** a fan-shaped tail or end. ■ chiefly N. Amer. the overhanging part of the stern of a boat, especially a warship.
2 (also **fantail pigeon**) a domestic pigeon of a broad-tailed variety.
3 (also **fantail flycatcher**) a flycatcher with a long tapering tail that is often fanned out, found mainly in SE Asia and Australasia. ● Genus *Rhipidura*, family Monarchidae: numerous species.
– DERIVATIVES **fan-tailed** adjective.

fan-tailed warbler (also **fantail warbler**) ▸ **noun** a small Old World warbler with streaked plumage and a stubby boldly marked tail. ● Genus *Cisticola*, family Sylviidae: several species, in particular *C. juncidis*, found from western Europe to Australia. See also **CISTICOLA**.

fan-tan /ˈfantan/ ▸ **noun** [mass noun] **1** a Chinese gambling game in which players try to guess the remainder after the banker has divided a number of hidden objects into four groups.
2 a card game in which players build on sequences of sevens.
– ORIGIN late 19th cent.: from Chinese *fān tān*, literally 'repeated divisions'.

fantasia /fanˈteɪzɪə, ˌfantəˈziːə/ ▸ **noun** a musical composition with a free form and often an improvisatory style. ■ a musical composition based on several familiar tunes. ■ a thing composed of a mixture of different forms or styles: *the theatre is a kind of Moorish and Egyptian fantasia*.
– ORIGIN early 18th cent.: from Italian, 'fantasy', from Latin *phantasia* (see **FANTASY**).

fantasize (also **fantasise**) ▸ **verb** [no obj.] indulge in daydreaming about something desired: *he sometimes **fantasized about** emigrating*. ■ [with obj.] imagine (something that one wants to happen): *one might fantasize the death of someone seen as a threat*.
– DERIVATIVES **fantasist** noun.

fantast /ˈfantast/ (also **phantast**) ▸ **noun** archaic or N. Amer. an impractical, impulsive person; a dreamer.
– ORIGIN late 16th cent. (formerly also as *phantast*): originally via medieval Latin from Greek *phantastēs* 'boaster', from *phantazein* or *phantazesthai* (see **FANTASTIC**); in modern use from German *Phantast*.

fantastic ▸ **adjective** **1** imaginative or fanciful; remote from reality: *fantastic hybrid creatures*. ■ (of an object) seeming more appropriate to the imagination than to reality; strange or exotic: *a fantastic, maze-like building*.
2 informal extraordinarily good or attractive: *she's got a fantastic body*. ■ of an extraordinary size or degree: *she had spent a fantastic amount of cash*.
– DERIVATIVES **fantastical** adjective (sense 1), **fantasticality** noun (sense 1), **fantastically** adverb.
– ORIGIN late Middle English (in the sense 'unreal'): from Old French *fantastique*, via medieval Latin from Greek *phantastikos*, from *phantazein* 'make visible', *phantazesthai* 'have visions, imagine', from *phantos* 'visible' (related to *phainein* 'to show'). From the 16th to the 19th cents the Latinized spelling *phantastic* was also used.

fantasticate ▸ **verb** [with obj.] rare make (something) seem fanciful or fantastic.

fantasy ▸ **noun** (pl. **fantasies**) **1** [mass noun] the faculty or activity of imagining impossible or improbable things: *his researches had moved into the **realms of fantasy***. ■ [count noun] a fanciful mental image, typically one on which a person often dwells and which reflects their conscious or unconscious wishes: *the notion of being independent is a child's ultimate fantasy*. ■ [count noun] an idea with no basis in reality: *it is a misleading fantasy to suggest that the bill can be implemented*. ■ a genre of imaginative fiction involving magic and adventure, especially in a setting other than the real world.
2 Music a fantasia.

▸ verb (**fantasies, fantasying, fantasied**) [with obj.] literary imagine the occurrence of; fantasize about.
– ORIGIN late Middle English: from Old French *fantasie*, from Latin *phantasia*, from Greek 'imagination, appearance', later 'phantom', from *phantazein* 'make visible'. From the 16th to the 19th cents the Latinized spelling *phantasy* was also used.

fantasy football ▸ noun [mass noun] a competition in which participants select imaginary teams from among the players in a league and score points according to the actual performance of their players.

fantasy land ▸ noun [mass noun] a place that is unreal or imaginary or that excites wonder: *I live in the real world, not fantasy land* | [in sing.] *you step out of the realm of reality and enter a fantasy land.*

Fante /ˈfanti/ (also **Fanti**) ▸ noun (pl. **same** or **Fantis**) **1** a member of a people of southern Ghana.
2 [mass noun] the dialect of Akan spoken by the Fante.
▸ adjective relating to the Fante or their language.
– ORIGIN the name in Akan.

fantod /ˈfantɒd/ ▸ noun N. Amer. informal a state or attack of uneasiness or unreasonableness: *people calling me Ray just gives me* ***the fantods.***
– ORIGIN mid 19th cent.: of unknown origin.

fan worm ▸ noun a tube-dwelling marine bristle worm which bears a fan-like crown of filaments that are typically brightly coloured and project from the top of the tube, filtering the water for food particles.
• Families Sabellidae and Serpulidae, class Polychaeta: numerous species, including the peacock worm.

fanzine /ˈfanziːn/ ▸ noun a magazine, usually produced by amateurs, for fans of a particular performer, group, or form of entertainment.
– ORIGIN 1940s (originally US): blend of FAN[2] and MAGAZINE.

FAO ▸ abbreviation ■ Food and Agriculture Organization. ■ for the attention of.

FAQ ▸ noun Computing a list of questions and answers relating to a particular subject, especially one giving basic information for users of a website.
– ORIGIN 1990s: acronym from *frequently asked questions.*

faquir ▸ noun variant spelling of FAKIR.

far ▸ adverb (**further, furthest** or **farther, farthest**)
1 [often with adverbial] at, to, or by a great distance (used to indicate the extent to which one thing is distant from another): *the house was not too* ***far away*** | *the mountains far in the distance glowed in the sun.*
2 over a large expanse of space or time: *he had not travelled far* | figurative *that's why we have come so far and done as well as we have.*
3 by a great deal: *he is able to function far better than usual.*
▸ adjective [attrib.] situated at a great distance in space or time: *the far reaches of the universe.* ■ more distant than another object of the same kind: *he was standing in the far corner.* ■ distant from a point seen as central; extreme: *the far north of Scotland* | *the success of the far Right.*
– PHRASES **as far as** for as great a distance as: *the river stretched away as far as he could see.* ■ for a great enough distance to reach: *I decided to walk as far as the village.* ■ to the extent that: *as far as I am concerned it is no big deal.* **be a far cry from** be very different to: *he is a far cry from the telegenic legislators who increasingly prowl Capitol Hill.* **by far** by a great amount: *this was by far the largest city in the area.* **far and away** by a very large amount: *he is far and away the most accomplished player.* **far and near** everywhere. **far and wide** over a large area. **far be it from** (or **for**) **me to** used to express reluctance to do something which one thinks may be resented: *far be it from me to speculate on his reasons.* **far from** tending to the opposite of what is expected: *conditions were far from satisfactory.* **far gone 1** in a bad or worsening state: *a few frames from the original film were too far gone to salvage.* ■ informal very intoxicated or ill. **2** advanced in time: *when he awoke the day was far gone.* **far off** remote in time or space: *a far-off country.* **go far 1** achieve a great deal: *everyone was sure he would go far.* **2** be worth or amount to much: *the money would not go far at this year's prices.* **go so far as to do something** do something regarded as extreme: *surely they wouldn't go so far as to break in?* **go too far** exceed the limits of what is reasonable or acceptable. **how far 1** used to ask how great a distance is: *they wanted to know how far he could travel.* **2** to what extent: *he was not sure how far she was committed.* **so far 1** to a certain limited extent: *jabs and pills can protect you only so far.* **2** (of a trend that seems likely to continue) up to this time: *diplomatic activity so far has failed.* (**in**) **so far as** (or **that**) to the extent that: *the play was a great success so far as attendance was concerned.* **so far so good** progress has been satisfactory up to now. **a —— too far** a —— regarded as being one step or stage beyond what is safe, sensible, or desirable: *the statement appears to be a claim too far.*
– ORIGIN Old English *feorr*, of Germanic origin; related to Dutch *ver*, from an Indo-European root shared by Sanskrit *para* and Greek *pera* 'further'.

farad /ˈfarad/ (abbrev.: **F**) ▸ noun the SI unit of electrical capacitance, equal to the capacitance of a capacitor in which one coulomb of charge causes a potential difference of one volt.
– ORIGIN mid 19th cent.: shortening of FARADAY. The term was originally proposed as a unit of electrical charge.

faradaic /ˌfarəˈdeɪɪk/ (also **faradic**) ▸ adjective produced by or associated with electrical induction.
– ORIGIN late 19th cent.: from the name of Michael FARADAY + -IC.

Faraday /ˈfarədeɪ/, Michael (1791–1867), English physicist and chemist. He contributed significantly to the field of electromagnetism, discovering electromagnetic induction and demonstrating electromagnetic rotation (the key to the electric dynamo and motor). Faraday also discovered the laws of electrolysis and set the foundations for the classical field theory of electromagnetic behaviour.

faraday /ˈfarədeɪ/ (abbrev.: *F*) ▸ noun Chemistry a unit of electric charge equal to Faraday's constant.
– ORIGIN early 20th cent.: coined in German from the name of Michael FARADAY.

Faraday cage ▸ noun Physics an earthed metal screen surrounding a piece of equipment to exclude electrostatic and electromagnetic influences.

Faraday effect ▸ noun Physics the rotation of the plane of polarization of electromagnetic waves in certain substances in a magnetic field.

Faraday's constant ▸ noun Chemistry the quantity of electric charge carried by one mole of electrons (equal to roughly 96,490 coulombs). Compare with FARADAY.

Faraday's law ▸ noun **1** Physics a law stating that when the magnetic flux linking a circuit changes, an electromotive force is induced in the circuit proportional to the rate of change of the flux linkage.
2 Chemistry a law stating that the amount of any substance deposited or liberated during electrolysis is proportional to the quantity of electric charge passed and to the equivalent weight of the substance.

faradic /fəˈradɪk/ ▸ adjective another term for FARADAIC.

farandole /ˌfar(ə)nˈdəʊl, ˈfar(ə)ndəʊl/ ▸ noun historical a lively Provençal dance in which the dancers join hands and wind in and out in a chain.
– ORIGIN mid 19th cent.: French, from modern Provençal *farandoulo.*

farang /fəˈraŋ/ ▸ noun (among Thais) a European or other foreigner.
– ORIGIN Thai, from FRANK[2].

faraway ▸ adjective distant in space or time: *exotic and faraway locations.* ■ seeming remote from one's immediate surroundings: *she had a faraway look in her eyes.*

farce ▸ noun a comic dramatic work using buffoonery and horseplay and typically including crude characterization and ludicrously improbable situations. ■ [mass noun] the genre of such works. ■ a event or situation that is absurd or disorganized: *the debate turned into a drunken farce.*
– ORIGIN early 16th cent.: from French, literally 'stuffing', from *farcir* 'to stuff', from Latin *farcire.* An earlier sense of 'forcemeat stuffing' became used metaphorically for comic interludes 'stuffed' into the texts of religious plays, which led to the current usage.

farceur /fɑːˈsəː/ ▸ noun a writer of or performer in farces. ■ a comedian.
– ORIGIN late 17th cent.: French, from obsolete *farcer* 'act farces'.

farcical ▸ adjective relating to or resembling farce, especially because of absurd or ridiculous aspects: *he considered the whole idea farcical* | *a farcical situation.*
– DERIVATIVES **farcicality** noun, **farcically** adverb.

farcy /ˈfɑːsi/ ▸ noun [mass noun] glanders in horses (or a similar disease in cattle) in which there is inflammation of the lymph vessels, causing nodules (**farcy buds** or **buttons**).
– ORIGIN late Middle English: from Old French *farcin*, from late Latin *farciminum*, from *farcire* 'to stuff' (because of the appearance of the swollen nodules).

fardel /ˈfɑːd(ə)l/ ▸ noun archaic a bundle or collection: *a fardel of stories, personages, emotions.*
– ORIGIN Middle English: from Old French.

fare ▸ noun **1** the money paid for a journey on public transport. ■ a passenger paying to travel in a taxi.
2 [mass noun] a range of food of a particular type: *traditional Scottish fare.* ■ something offered to the public, typically as a form of entertainment: *those expecting conventional Hollywood fare will be disappointed.*
▸ verb [no obj.] **1** [with adverbial] perform in a specified way in a particular situation or over a particular period: *the party fared badly in the elections.* ■ archaic happen; turn out: *beware that it fare not with you as with your predecessor.*
2 [with adverbial of direction] archaic travel: *a knight fares forth.*
– ORIGIN Old English *fær, faru* 'travelling, a journey or expedition', *faran* 'to travel', also 'get on (well or badly)', of Germanic origin; related to Dutch *varen* and German *fahren* 'to travel', Old Norse *ferja* 'ferry boat', also to FORD. Sense 1 of the noun stems from an earlier meaning 'a journey for which a price is paid'. Noun sense 2 was originally used with reference to the quality or quantity of food provided, probably from the idea of faring well or badly.

Far East China, Japan, and other countries of east Asia.
– DERIVATIVES **Far Eastern** adjective.

fare stage ▸ noun Brit. a section of a bus or tram route for which a fixed price is charged.

fare-thee-well (also **fare-you-well**) ▸ noun (in phrase **to a fare-thee-well**) US to perfection; thoroughly: *coated in aspic and decorated to a fare-thee-well.*

farewell ▸ exclamation used to express good wishes on parting.
▸ noun an act of parting or of marking someone's departure: *the dinner had been arranged as a farewell.* ■ [mass noun] parting good wishes: *he had come on the pretext of* ***bidding her farewell.***
▸ verb [with obj.] Austral./NZ mark the departure or retirement of (someone) with a ceremony or party.
– ORIGIN late Middle English: from the imperative of FARE + the adverb WELL[1].

Farewell, Cape 1 the southernmost point of Greenland. Danish name KAP FARVEL.
2 the northernmost point of the South Island, New Zealand. The cape was named by Captain James Cook as the last land sighted before he left for Australia in March 1770.

farfalle /fɑːˈfaleɪ, -li/ ▸ plural noun small pieces of pasta shaped like bows or butterflies' wings.
– ORIGIN Italian, plural of *farfalla* 'butterfly'.

far-fetched ▸ adjective unlikely and unconvincing; implausible: *the theory sounded bizarre and far-fetched.*

far-flung ▸ adjective distant or remote: *the far-flung corners of the world.* ■ widely distributed: *newsletters provided an important link to a far-flung membership.*

Fargo, William, see WELLS, FARGO & CO.

Faridabad /fəˈriːdəbad/ an industrial city in northern India, south of Delhi, in the state of Haryana; pop. 1,464,100 (est. 2009).

farina /fəˈrʌɪnə, fəˈriːnə/ ▸ noun [mass noun] flour or meal made of cereal grains, nuts, or starchy roots. ■ [count noun] archaic a powdery substance.
– ORIGIN late Middle English: from Latin, from *far* 'corn'.

farinaceous /ˌfarɪˈneɪʃəs/ ▸ adjective consisting of or containing starch.
– ORIGIN mid 17th cent.: from late Latin *farinaceus*, from FARINA.

farkleberry /ˈfɑːk(ə)lˌb(ə)ri, -ˌbɛri/ ▸ noun (pl. **farkleberries**) a shrub or small tree with thick leathery leaves and inedible black berries, native to the south-eastern US. • *Vaccinium arboreum*, family Ericaceae.
– ORIGIN mid 18th cent.: probably an alteration of WHORTLEBERRY.

farl /fɑːl/ ▸ noun a bread roll of Scottish origin made of oatmeal or flour, typically triangular in shape.
– ORIGIN late 17th cent.: from obsolete *fardel* 'quarter', contraction of *fourth deal* (i.e. DEAL[1] in the earlier sense 'portion, share').

farm ▸ noun an area of land and its buildings, used for growing crops and rearing animals. ■ a farmhouse: *a half-timbered farm.* ■ [with modifier] a place for breeding a particular type of animal or producing a specified crop: *a fish farm.* ■ [with modifier] a place devoted to producing or promoting something: *an energy farm.*
▸ verb **1** [no obj.] make one's living by growing crops or keeping livestock: *he has farmed organically for years.* ■ [with obj.] use (land) for growing crops and rearing animals. ■ [with obj.] breed or grow (a type of livestock or crop) commercially: *ostriches are farmed in South Africa and Australia* | (as adj. **farmed**) *farmed salmon.*
2 [with obj.] (**farm someone/thing out**) send out or subcontract work to others: *it saves time and money to farm out some writing work to specialized companies.* ■ arrange for a child to be looked after by someone, usually for payment. ■ dated send a sports player temporarily to another team in return for a fee.
3 [with obj.] historical allow someone to collect and keep the revenues from (a tax) on payment of a fee.
– DERIVATIVES **farmable** adjective.
– ORIGIN Middle English: from Old French *ferme*, from medieval Latin *firma* 'fixed payment', from Latin *firmare* 'fix, settle' (in medieval Latin 'contract for'), from *firmus* 'constant, firm'; compare with FIRM². The noun originally denoted a fixed annual amount payable as rent or tax; this is reflected in sense 3 of the verb, which later gave rise to 'to subcontract' (sense 2 of the verb). The noun came to denote a lease, and, in the early 16th cent., land leased for farming. The verb sense 'grow crops or keep livestock' dates from the early 19th cent.

farman ▸ noun another term for FIRMAN.

farmer ▸ noun **1** a person who owns or manages a farm.
2 historical a person to whom the collection of taxes was contracted for a fee.
– ORIGIN late Middle English: from Old French *fermier*, from medieval Latin *firmarius*, *firmator*, from *firma* (see FARM). Sense 1 originally denoted a bailiff or steward who farmed land on the owner's behalf, or a tenant farmer.

farmer's lung ▸ noun [mass noun] a type of pneumonitis caused by an allergic reaction to spores in mouldy hay.

farmers' market ▸ noun a market where local farmers and growers sell their produce directly to the public.

farmhand ▸ noun a worker on a farm.

farmhouse ▸ noun a house attached to a farm, especially the main house in which the farmer lives.

farmhouse loaf ▸ noun a loaf of white bread, oval or rectangular in shape, with a rounded top.

farming ▸ noun [mass noun] the activity or business of growing crops and raising livestock.

farmland ▸ noun [mass noun] (also **farmlands**) land used for farming.

farmstead ▸ noun a farm and its buildings.

farm team ▸ noun N. Amer. a minor-league baseball team that provides players as needed to an affiliated major-league team.

farmworker ▸ noun a person employed to work on a farm.

farmyard ▸ noun a yard surrounded by farm buildings. ■ [as modifier] denoting coarse speech or behaviour: *he insulted them in farmyard language.*

Farnborough /ˈfɑːnbərə/ a town in southern England, in Hampshire; pop. 56,800 (est. 2009). Noted as a centre of aviation, it is the site of an air show held every other year.

Farne Islands /fɑːn/ a group of seventeen small islands off the coast of Northumberland, noted for their wildlife.

Farnese¹ /fɑːˈneɪzeɪ, -zi/, Italian /farˈnese/, Alessandro, see PAUL III.

Farnese² /fɑːˈneɪzeɪ, -zi/, Alessandro, Duke of Parma (1545–92), Italian general and statesman. While in the service of Philip II of Spain he acted as Governor General of the Netherlands (1578–92). He captured Antwerp in 1585, securing the southern Netherlands for Spain.

Faro /ˈfɑːrəʊ/ a seaport on the south coast of Portugal, capital of the Algarve; pop. 58,739 (2007).

faro /ˈfɛːrəʊ/ ▸ noun [mass noun] a gambling card game in which players bet on the order in which the cards will appear.
– ORIGIN early 18th cent. (originally as *pharaoh* or *pharo*): from French *pharaon* (see PHARAOH), said to have been the name of the king of hearts.

Faroe Islands /ˈfɛːrəʊ/ (also **Faeroe Islands** or **the Faroes**) a group of islands in the North Atlantic between Iceland and the Shetland Islands, belonging to Denmark but partly autonomous; pop. 48,900 (est. 2009); languages, Faroese (official), Danish; capital, Tórshavn. The shipping forecast area **Faroes** covers this area of the Atlantic.

Faroese /ˌfɛːrəʊˈiːz/ (also **Faeroese**) ▸ adjective relating to the Faroe Islands or their people or language.
▸ noun (pl. **same**) **1** a native or inhabitant of the Faroes, or a person of Faroese descent.
2 [mass noun] the official language of the Faroes, a Scandinavian language closely related to Icelandic.

farouche /fəˈruːʃ/ ▸ adjective sullen or shy in company.
– ORIGIN mid 18th cent.: from French, alteration of Old French *forache*, based on Latin *foras* 'out of doors'.

Farouk /fəˈruːk/ (1920–65), king of Egypt, reigned 1936–52. Farouk's defeat in the Arab–Israeli conflict of 1948, together with the general corruption of his reign, led to a military coup in 1952, masterminded by Nasser. Farouk was forced to abdicate in favour of his infant son, Fuad.

far out ▸ adjective unconventional or avant-garde: *a far-out psychic technique.* ■ [often as exclamation] informal excellent: *it's really far out!*

Farquhar /ˈfɑːkə/, George (1678–1707), Irish dramatist. He was a principal figure in Restoration comedy. Notable works: *The Recruiting Officer* (1706) and *The Beaux' Stratagem* (1707).

farrago /fəˈrɑːgəʊ/ ▸ noun (pl. **farragos** or US **farragoes**) a confused mixture: *a farrago of fact and myth about Abraham Lincoln.*
– DERIVATIVES **farraginous** /fəˈrɑːdʒɪnəs/ adjective.
– ORIGIN mid 17th cent.: from Latin, literally 'mixed fodder', from *far* 'corn'.

far-reaching ▸ adjective having important and widely applicable effects or implications: *a series of far-reaching political reforms.*

farrier /ˈfarɪə/ ▸ noun a smith who shoes horses.
– DERIVATIVES **farriery** noun.
– ORIGIN mid 16th cent.: from Old French *ferrier*, from Latin *ferrarius*, from *ferrum* 'iron, horseshoe'.

farrow ▸ noun a litter of pigs. ■ an act of giving birth to a litter of pigs.
▸ verb [with obj.] (of a sow) give birth to (piglets): *the pig is one of a litter of nine farrowed in July.*
– ORIGIN Old English *fearh*, *færh* 'young pig', of West Germanic origin, from an Indo-European root shared by Greek *porkos* and Latin *porcus* 'pig'.

farruca /fəˈruːkə/ ▸ noun a type of flamenco dance.
– ORIGIN 1930s: Spanish, feminine of *farruco* 'of Galicia or Asturias', from *Farruco*, pet form of the given name *Francisco*.

farse ▸ adjective W. Indian another term for FAST¹ (sense 7 of the adjective).

far-seeing ▸ adjective having shrewd judgement and an ability to predict and plan for future eventualities.

Farsi /ˈfɑːsiː/ ▸ noun [mass noun] the modern Persian language, the official language of Iran, with over 20 million speakers.
– ORIGIN from Arabic *fārsī*, from *Fārs*, from Persian *Pārs* 'Persia'. Compare with PARSEE.

far-sighted ▸ adjective **1** showing a prudent awareness of future possibilities: *far-sighted ideas on education.*
2 N. Amer. long-sighted.
– DERIVATIVES **far-sightedly** adverb, **far-sightedness** noun.

fart informal ▸ verb [no obj.] **1** emit wind from the anus.
2 (**fart around** (or Brit. also **fart about**)) waste time on silly or trivial things.
▸ noun **1** an emission of wind from the anus.
2 a boring or contemptible person: *he was such an old fart.*
– ORIGIN Old English (recorded in the verbal noun *feorting* 'farting') of Germanic origin; related to German *farzen*, *furzen*.

farther ▸ adverb & adjective variant form of FURTHER.

> **USAGE** On the difference in use of **farther** and **further**, see **USAGE** at **FURTHER**.

farthermost ▸ adjective variant form of FURTHERMOST.

farthest ▸ adjective & adverb variant form of FURTHEST.

farthing ▸ noun a former monetary unit and coin of the UK, withdrawn in 1961, equal to a quarter of an old penny. ■ [usu. with negative] the least possible amount: *she didn't care a farthing for the woman.*
– ORIGIN Old English *fēorthing*, from *fēortha* 'fourth', perhaps on the pattern of Old Norse *fjórthungr* 'quarter'.

farthingale /ˈfɑːðɪŋgeɪl/ ▸ noun historical a hooped petticoat or circular pad of fabric around the hips, formerly worn under women's skirts to extend and shape them.
– ORIGIN early 16th cent. (formerly also as *vardingale*): from French *verdugale*, alteration of Spanish *verdugado*, from *verdugo* 'rod, stick', from *verde* 'green'.

fartlek /ˈfɑːtlɛk/ ▸ noun [mass noun] Athletics a system of training for distance runners in which the terrain and pace are continually varied.
– ORIGIN 1940s: from Swedish, from *fart* 'speed' + *lek* 'play'.

Far West the regions of North America in the Rocky Mountains and along the Pacific coast. ■ former term for MIDWEST.

FAS ▸ abbreviation fetal alcohol syndrome.

fasces /ˈfasiːz/ ▸ plural noun historical a bundle of rods with a projecting axe blade, carried by a lictor in ancient Rome as a symbol of a magistrate's power, and used as an emblem of authority in Fascist Italy.
– ORIGIN Latin, plural of *fascis* 'bundle'.

fascia /ˈfeɪʃɪə, -ʃə/ (also chiefly Brit. **facia** except in sense 3) ▸ noun **1** a board or other flat piece of material covering the ends of rafters or other fittings. ■ Brit. a signboard on the upper part of a shopfront showing the name of the shop. ■ (in classical architecture) a long flat surface between mouldings on an architrave.
2 Brit. the dashboard of a motor vehicle. ■ a board or panel of controls on any piece of equipment.
3 /ˈfaʃə/ (pl. **fasciae** /-ʃiː/) Anatomy a thin sheath of fibrous tissue enclosing a muscle or other organ.
4 a covering, typically a detachable one, for the front part of a mobile phone.
– DERIVATIVES **fascial** adjective (sense 3).
– ORIGIN mid 16th cent.: from Latin, 'band, door frame', related to FASCES. Compare with FESS¹.

fasciated /ˈfaʃɪeɪtɪd, -ɪətɪd/ ▸ adjective Botany showing abnormal fusion of parts or organs, resulting in a flattened ribbon-like structure.
– DERIVATIVES **fasciation** noun.
– ORIGIN mid 18th cent. (in the sense 'banded'): from Latin *fasciatus* (past participle of *fasciare* 'swathe', from *fascia* 'band') + -ED¹.

fascicle /ˈfasɪk(ə)l/ ▸ noun **1** (also **fascicule** /-kjuːl/) a separately published instalment of a book or other printed work.
2 (also **fasciculus** /faˈsɪkjʊləs/) (pl. **fasciculi**) Anatomy & Biology a bundle of structures, such as nerve or muscle fibres or conducting vessels in plants.
– DERIVATIVES **fascicled** adjective, **fascicular** adjective, **fasciculate** /-ˈsɪkjʊlət/ adjective.
– ORIGIN late 15th cent. (in sense 2): from Latin *fasciculus*, diminutive of *fascis* 'bundle'.

fasciculation /faˌsɪkjʊˈleɪʃ(ə)n/ ▸ noun **1** Medicine a brief spontaneous contraction affecting a small number of muscle fibres, often causing a flicker of movement under the skin.
2 [mass noun] chiefly Biology arrangement in bundles.

fasciitis /ˌfasɪˈʌɪtɪs, ˌfaʃɪ-/ ▸ noun [mass noun] Medicine inflammation of the fascia of a muscle or organ.

fascinate ▸ verb [with obj.] attract the strong attention and interest of (someone): *I've always been fascinated by computers* | (as adj. **fascinated**) *a crowd of fascinated onlookers.* ■ archaic (especially of a snake) deprive (prey) of the ability to resist or escape by the power of a gaze.
– ORIGIN late 16th cent. (in the sense 'bewitch'): from Latin *fascinat-* 'bewitched', from the verb *fascinare*, from *fascinum* 'spell, witchcraft'.

fascinating ▸ adjective extremely interesting: *a fascinating book.*
– DERIVATIVES **fascinatingly** adverb.

fascination ▸ noun [mass noun] the power to fascinate someone; the quality of being fascinating: *television has always held a fascination for me.* ■ the state of being fascinated: *he had a lifelong fascination with science.*

> **USAGE** The two senses of **fascination** each take a different preposition. A person has a **fascination with** something they are very interested in (*her fascination with the royal family*), whereas something interesting

holds a **fascination for** a person (*words have always held a fascination for me*). The Oxford English Corpus shows that the distinction is often blurred today, but it should be maintained in careful writing.

fascinator ▶ noun **1** a woman's light, decorative headpiece consisting of feathers, flowers, beads, etc. attached to a comb or hair clip.
2 a fascinating person.

fascine /fa'si:n/ ▶ noun a bundle of rods or plastic pipes bound together, used in construction or military operations for filling in marshy ground or other obstacles and for strengthening the sides of embankments, ditches, or trenches.
– ORIGIN late 17th cent.: via French from Latin *fascina*, from *fascis* 'bundle'.

fascioliasis /ˌfasɪə'lʌɪəsɪs/ ▶ noun [mass noun] Medicine infestation of a human or an animal with the liver fluke.
– ORIGIN late 19th cent.: from modern Latin *Fasciola hepatica*, the name of the liver fluke (from Latin *fasciola* 'small bandage') + **-IASIS**.

fascism /'faʃɪz(ə)m, -sɪz(ə)m/ ▶ noun [mass noun] an authoritarian and nationalistic right-wing system of government and social organization. ■ (in general use) extreme right-wing, authoritarian, or intolerant views or practices.

The term Fascism was first used of the totalitarian right-wing nationalist regime of Mussolini in Italy (1922–43); the regimes of the Nazis in Germany and Franco in Spain were also Fascist. Fascism tends to include a belief in the supremacy of one national or ethnic group, a contempt for democracy, an insistence on obedience to a powerful leader, and a strong demagogic approach.

– DERIVATIVES **fascistic** adjective.
– ORIGIN from Italian *fascismo*, from *fascio* 'bundle, political group', from Latin *fascis* (see **FASCES**).

fascist /'faʃɪst/ ▶ noun an advocate or follower of fascism.
▶ adjective of or relating to fascism: *a military coup threw out the old fascist regime.*

fash ▶ verb (**fash oneself**) Scottish feel upset or worried: *she'll be coming soon, don't fash yourself.*
– ORIGIN mid 16th cent.: from early modern French *fascher*, based on Latin *fastus* 'disdain, scornful contempt'.

fashion ▶ noun **1** a popular or the latest style of clothing, hair, decoration, or behaviour: *the latest Parisian fashions.* ■ [mass noun] the production and marketing of new styles of clothing and cosmetics: [as modifier] *a fashion magazine.*
2 a manner of doing something: *the work is done in a rather casual fashion.*
▶ verb [with obj.] make into a particular form: *the bottles were* **fashioned from** *green glass.* ■ (**fashion something into**) use materials to produce (something): *the skins were fashioned into boots and shoes.*
– PHRASES **after a fashion** to a certain extent but not perfectly: *he could read after a fashion.* **after** (or **in**) **the fashion of** in a manner similar to: *she took servants for granted after the fashion of wealthy girls.* **in** (or **out of**) **fashion** popular (or unpopular) and considered (or not considered) to be smart at the time in question.
– DERIVATIVES **fashioner** noun.
– ORIGIN Middle English (in the sense 'make, shape, appearance', also 'a particular make or style'): from Old French *façon*, from Latin *factio(n-)*, from *facere* 'do, make'.

-fashion ▶ combining form in the manner of something specified: *the masts extend concertina-fashion.* ■ in the style associated with a specified place or people: *American-fashion.*

fashionable ▶ adjective characteristic of, influenced by, or representing a current popular style: *fashionable clothes.* ■ (of a person) dressing or behaving according to the current trend. ■ (of a place) frequented by fashionable people: *a fashionable Manhattan restaurant.*
– DERIVATIVES **fashionability** noun, **fashionableness** noun, **fashionably** adverb.

fashion-forward ▶ adjective (of a person or style of clothing) very fashionable: *the clothing line of choice for fashion-forward women.*

fashionista /ˌfaʃən'iːstə/ ▶ noun informal **1** a designer of haute couture.
2 a devoted follower of fashion.
– ORIGIN 1990s: from **FASHION** + **-ISTA**.

fashion plate ▶ noun **1** a person who dresses very fashionably.
2 a picture, typically in a magazine, illustrating a new or current fashion in clothes.

fashion victim ▶ noun informal a person who follows popular fashions slavishly.

Fassbinder /'fasbɪndə/, German /'fasbɪndɐ/, Rainer Werner (1946–82), German film director. His films dealt largely with Germany during the Second World War and post-war West German society. Notable films: *The Bitter Tears of Petra von Kant* (1972) and *The Marriage of Maria Braun* (1979).

fast[1] ▶ adjective **1** moving or capable of moving at high speed: *a fast and powerful car.* ■ taking place at high speed; taking a short time: *the journey was fast and enjoyable.* ■ performing or able to perform a particular action quickly: *a fast reader.* ■ (of a surface) allowing or producing high-speed movement: *a wide, fast road.* ■ Sports (of a playing field) likely to make the ball bounce or run quickly or to allow competitors to reach a high speed.
2 [predic. or as complement] (of a clock or watch) showing a time ahead of the correct time: *I keep my watch fifteen minutes fast.*
3 firmly fixed or attached: *he* **made** *a rope* **fast** *to each corner.* ■ (of friends) close and loyal.
4 Photography (of a film) needing only a short exposure. ■ (of a lens) having a large aperture and therefore suitable for use with short exposure times.
5 (of a dye) not fading in light or when washed.
6 (of a person or their lifestyle) engaging in or involving exciting or shocking activities: *the fast life she led in London.*
7 (also **farse**) W. Indian (of a person) prone to act in an unacceptably familiar way: *Mammy said, 'Stop asking questions, you too damn farse.'*
▶ adverb **1** at high speed: *he was driving too fast.* ■ within a short time: *we're going to have to get to the bottom of this fast.*
2 so as to be hard to move; securely: *the ship was held fast by the anchor chain.*
3 so as to be hard to wake: *they were too fast asleep to reply.*
– PHRASES **fast and furious** lively and exciting. **fast worker** informal a person who makes rapid progress or achieves results quickly, especially in love affairs. **pull a fast one** informal trick someone: *he had been trying to* **pull a fast one on** *his producer.*
– ORIGIN Old English *fæst* 'firmly fixed, steadfast' and *fæste* 'firmly', of Germanic origin; related to Dutch *vast* and German *fest* 'firm, solid' and *fast* 'almost'. In Middle English the adverb developed the senses 'strongly, vigorously' (compare with *run hard*), and 'close, immediate' (just surviving in the archaic *fast by*; compare with *hard by*), hence 'closely, immediately' and 'quickly'; the idea of rapid movement was then reflected in adjectival use.

fast[2] ▶ verb [no obj.] abstain from all or some kinds of food or drink, especially as a religious observance. ■ (**be fasted**) technical be deprived of all or some kinds of food, especially for medical or experimental reasons.
▶ noun an act or period of fasting: *a five-day fast.*
– ORIGIN Old English *fæstan* (verb), of Germanic origin; related to Dutch *vasten* and German *fasten*, also to Old Norse *fasta*, the source of the noun.

fastback ▶ noun a car with a rear that slopes continuously down to the bumper.

fastball ▶ noun a baseball pitch thrown at or near a pitcher's maximum speed. ■ another term for **FAST-PITCH SOFTBALL**.

fast break ▶ noun a swift attack from a defensive position in basketball, soccer, and other ball games.

fast breeder (also **fast breeder reactor**) ▶ noun a breeder reactor in which the neutrons causing fission are not slowed by any moderator.

fast buck ▶ noun see **BUCK**[2].

fasten ▶ verb **1** [with obj.] close or do up securely: *the tunic was fastened with a row of gilt buttons.* ■ [no obj., with adverbial] be closed or done up in a particular manner: *a blue nightie that fastens down the back.* ■ [with obj. and adverbial] fix or hold in place: *she fastened her locket round her neck.* ■ (**fasten something off**) secure the end of a thread with stitches or a knot.
2 [no obj.] (**fasten on/upon**) single out (someone or something) and concentrate on them or it obsessively: *the critics fastened upon two sections of the report.* ■ [with obj.] (**fasten something on/upon**) direct one's eyes, thoughts, etc. intently at: *his gaze was fastened on his daughter* | [no obj.] *his eyes seemed to fasten on her.*
– DERIVATIVES **fastener** noun.
– ORIGIN Old English *fæstnian* 'make sure', also 'immobilize', of West Germanic origin; related to **FAST**[1].

fastening ▶ noun a device that closes or secures something: *a fly-front fastening.*

Fastext /'fɑːstɛkst/ ▶ noun [mass noun] a facility in certain televisions to store some teletext pages in advance, displaying them instantly when requested by the user.
– ORIGIN late 20th cent.: contraction of *fast teletext.*

fast food ▶ noun [mass noun] easily prepared processed food served in snack bars and restaurants as a quick meal or to be taken away: [as modifier] *a fast-food restaurant.*

fast forward ▶ noun a control on a tape or video recorder for winding the tape forward rapidly. ■ a facility for cueing audio equipment by allowing the tape to be played at high speed during fast-forward wind and stopped at the desired place.
▶ verb (**fast-forward**) [with obj.] wind (a tape) forward rapidly. ■ [no obj.] move speedily forward in time: *the text fast-forwards to 1990.*

fast ice ▶ noun [mass noun] ice that covers seawater but is attached to land.

fastidious /fa'stɪdɪəs/ ▶ adjective very attentive to and concerned about accuracy and detail: *she dressed with fastidious care.* ■ very concerned about matters of cleanliness: *the child seemed fastidious about getting her fingers dirty.*
– DERIVATIVES **fastidiously** adverb, **fastidiousness** noun.
– ORIGIN late Middle English: from Latin *fastidiosus*, from *fastidium* 'loathing'. The word originally meant 'disagreeable', later 'disgusted'. Current senses date from the 17th cent.

fastigiate /fa'stɪdʒɪət, -eɪt/ ▶ adjective Botany (of a tree or shrub) having the branches more or less parallel to the main stem.
– ORIGIN mid 17th cent.: from Latin *fastigium* 'tapering point, gable' + **-ATE**[2].

fast lane ▶ noun a lane of a motorway or dual carriageway for use by traffic that is overtaking or moving more quickly than the rest.
– PHRASES **in the fast lane** where life is exciting or highly pressured: *his face showed the strain of a life lived in the fast lane.*

fastness ▶ noun **1** a secure place well protected by natural features: *a remote Himalayan mountain fastness.*
2 [mass noun] the ability of a material or dye to maintain its colour without fading or washing away: *the dyes differ in their fastness to light.*
– ORIGIN Old English *fæstnes* (see **FAST**[1], **-NESS**).

Fastnet /'fɑːs(t)nɛt/ a rocky islet off the SW coast of Ireland. ■ a shipping forecast area covering the Celtic Sea off the south coast of Ireland as far as the latitude of the Scilly Isles.

fast neutron ▶ noun a neutron with high kinetic energy, especially one released by nuclear fission and not slowed by any moderator.

fast-pitch softball (also **fast-pitch**) ▶ noun [mass noun] a variety of the game of softball, featuring fast underhand pitching.

fast reactor ▶ noun a nuclear reactor in which fission is caused mainly by fast neutrons.

fast-talk ▶ verb [with obj.] informal, chiefly N. Amer. pressurize (someone) into doing something using rapid or misleading speech: *heroin dealers tried to* **fast-talk** *him* **into** *a quick sale* | (as adj. **fast-talking**) *a fast-talking confidence trickster.*

fast track ▶ noun [in sing.] a route or method which provides for more rapid results than usual: *a career in the fast track of the Civil Service.*
▶ verb (**fast-track**) [with obj.] accelerate the progress of (a person or project): *the board voted to fast-track the stadium plan.*

fast-twitch ▶ adjective [attrib.] Physiology (of a muscle fibre) contracting rapidly, thus providing strength rather than endurance.

fat ▶ noun **1** [mass noun] a natural oily substance occurring in animal bodies, especially when deposited as a layer under the skin or around certain organs: *whales and seals insulate themselves with layers of fat.* ■ a fatty substance made from animal or plant products, used in cooking: *sizzling fat* | [count noun] *a diet high in animal fats.* ■ the presence of excess fat in a person or animal: *he was a tall man,* **running to fat.**
2 Chemistry any of a group of natural esters of glycerol and various fatty acids, which are solid at room

F

temperature and are the main constituents of animal and vegetable fat. Compare with OIL.
▶ adjective (**fatter**, **fattest**) **1** (of a person or animal) having a large amount of excess flesh: *the driver was a fat wheezing man.* ■ (of an animal bred for food) made plump for slaughter. ■ containing much fat: *fat bacon.* ■ (of coal) containing a high proportion of volatile oils.
2 large in bulk or circumference: *a fat cigarette.* ■ informal (especially in the context of financial reward) substantial: *a fat profit* | *a fat cheque.* ■ informal used ironically to express the belief that something is unlikely or does not exist: *fat chance she had of influencing Guy's decisions.*
▶ verb (**fats**, **fatting**, **fatted**) archaic make or become fat: (as adj. **fatted**) *a fatted duck.*
– PHRASES **the fat is in the fire** something has happened that will inevitably cause trouble. **kill the fatted calf** produce one's best food to celebrate, especially at a prodigal's return. [with biblical allusion to Luke 15.] **live off** (or **on**) **the fat of the land** have the best of everything.
– DERIVATIVES **fatless** adjective, **fatly** adverb, **fatness** noun, **fattish** adjective.
– ORIGIN Old English *fǣtt* 'well fed, plump', also 'fatty, oily', of West Germanic origin; related to Dutch *vet* and German *feist*.

F

Fatah /ˈfatə/ (also **al-Fatah**) a Palestinian political and military organization founded in 1958 by Yasser Arafat and others to bring about the establishment of a Palestinian state. It dominated the Palestine Liberation Organization from the 1960s, but more recently has been challenged by more extreme groups, and in 2006 was defeated by Hamas in the elections for the Palestinian National Authority.
– ORIGIN Arabic, literally 'victory'.

fatal /ˈfeɪt(ə)l/ ▶ adjective causing death: *a fatal accident.* ■ leading to failure or disaster: *there were three fatal flaws in the strategy.*
– DERIVATIVES **fatally** adverb.
– ORIGIN late Middle English (in the senses 'destined by fate' and 'ominous'): from Old French, or from Latin *fatalis*, from *fatum* (see FATE).

fatalism ▶ noun [mass noun] the belief that all events are predetermined and therefore inevitable. ■ a submissive attitude to events, resulting from such a belief.
– DERIVATIVES **fatalist** noun, **fatalistic** adjective, **fatalistically** adverb.

fatality /fəˈtalɪti, feɪ-/ ▶ noun (pl. **fatalities**) **1** an occurrence of death by accident, in war, or from disease: *80 per cent of pedestrian fatalities occur in built-up areas.*
2 [mass noun] helplessness in the face of fate: *a sense of fatality gripped her.*
– ORIGIN late 15th cent. (denoting the quality of causing death or disaster): from French *fatalité* or late Latin *fatalitas*, from Latin *fatalis* 'decreed by fate', from *fatum* (see FATE). Sense 1 dates from the mid 19th cent.

Fata Morgana /ˌfɑːtə mɔːˈɡɑːnə/ ▶ noun a mirage.
– ORIGIN Italian, literally 'fairy Morgan'; originally referring to a mirage seen in the Strait of Messina between Italy and Sicily and attributed to MORGAN LE FAY, whose legend and reputation were carried to Sicily by Norman settlers.

fatback ▶ noun **1** [mass noun] N. Amer. fat from the upper part of a side of pork, especially when dried and salted in strips.
2 US informal term for MENHADEN.

fat body ▶ noun Zoology each of a number of small white structures in the body of an animal, especially an insect, which act as a store of fats and glycogen.

fat camp ▶ noun a residential course for overweight children, promoting exercise and healthy eating to facilitate weight loss.

fat cat ▶ noun informal, derogatory a wealthy and powerful person, especially a businessman or politician: [as modifier] *a fat-cat developer.*

fat dormouse ▶ noun a squirrel-like burrowing dormouse found in Europe and Asia Minor, sometimes farmed or hunted for food. Also called EDIBLE DORMOUSE. ● *Myoxus glis*, family Myoxidae.

fate ▶ noun **1** [mass noun] the development of events outside a person's control, regarded as predetermined by a supernatural power: *fate decided his course for him* | *his injury is a cruel twist of fate.* ■ [count noun] the course of someone's life, or the outcome of a situation for someone or something, seen as outside their control: *he stared at the faces of the committee, trying to guess his fate.* ■ [in sing.] the inescapable death of a person: *the guards led her to her fate.*
2 (**the Fates**) Greek & Roman Mythology the three goddesses who preside over the birth and life of humans. Each person was thought of as a spindle, around which the three Fates (Clotho, Lachesis, and Atropos) would spin the thread of human destiny. ■ (**Fates**) another term for NORNS.
▶ verb (**be fated**) be destined to happen, turn out, or act in a particular way: [with infinitive] *the regime was fated to end badly.*
– PHRASES **a fate worse than death** see DEATH. **seal someone's fate** make it inevitable that something unpleasant will happen to someone.
– ORIGIN late Middle English: from Italian *fato* or (later) from its source, Latin *fatum* 'that which has been spoken', from *fari* 'speak'.

fateful ▶ adjective having far-reaching and often disastrous consequences or implications: *a fateful oversight.*
– DERIVATIVES **fatefully** adverb, **fatefulness** noun.

fat farm ▶ noun informal, chiefly N. Amer. a health farm for people who are overweight.

fat-free ▶ adjective (of a food) not containing animal or vegetable fats: *virtually fat-free yogurt.*

fathead ▶ noun informal a stupid person.
– DERIVATIVES **fat-headed** adjective.

fat hen ▶ noun [mass noun] a herbaceous plant with mealy edible leaves, often considered to be a weed. ● *Chenopodium alba*, family Chenopodiaceae.
– ORIGIN late 18th cent.: said to be so named because the seeds were eaten by poultry.

father ▶ noun **1** a man in relation to his child or children. ■ a male animal in relation to its offspring. ■ (**fathers**) literary ancestors. ■ an important male figure in the origin and early history of something: *he's held to be the father of abstract art.* ■ a man who provides care and protection: *the prince is widely regarded as the father of the nation.* ■ the oldest member or doyen of a society or other body. ■ (**the Father**) (in Christian belief) the first person of the Trinity; God. ■ (**Father**) used as a title of respect for an old and venerable man or for something personified as such a man: *Father Thames.*
2 (also **Father**) (often as a title or form of address) a priest: *pray for me, father.*
3 (**Fathers** or **Fathers of the Church**) early Christian theologians (in particular of the first five centuries) whose writings are regarded as especially authoritative.
▶ verb [with obj.] be the father of: *he fathered three children.* ■ (usu. as noun **fathering**) treat with the protective care associated with a father: *the two males share the fathering of the cubs.* ■ be the source or originator of: *a culture which has fathered half the popular music in the world.* ■ (**father someone/thing on**) assign the paternity of a child or responsibility for a book, idea, or action to: *a collection of Irish stories was fathered on him.*
– PHRASES **how's your father** Brit. informal used euphemistically to refer to sexual intercourse. ■ used euphemistically to refer to a penis. **like father, like son** proverb a son's character or behaviour can be expected to resemble that of his father.
– DERIVATIVES **fatherhood** noun, **fatherless** adjective, **fatherlessness** noun, **fatherlike** adjective & adverb.
– ORIGIN Old English *fæder*, of Germanic origin; related to Dutch *vader* and German *Vater*, from an Indo-European root shared by Latin *pater* and Greek *patēr*.

Father Christmas Brit. an imaginary figure said to bring presents for children on the night before Christmas Day, conventionally pictured as a jolly old man with a long white beard and red clothes. Also called SANTA CLAUS.

father figure ▶ noun an older man who is respected for his paternal qualities and may be an emotional substitute for a father.

father-in-law ▶ noun (pl. **fathers-in-law**) the father of one's husband or wife.

fatherland ▶ noun a person's native country, especially when referred to in patriotic terms. ■ (**the Fatherland**) historical Germany during the period of Hitler's control.

fatherly ▶ adjective relating to, resembling, or characteristic of a father, especially in being protective and affectionate: *he gave me such a kind and fatherly look.*
– DERIVATIVES **fatherliness** noun.

father of the chapel ▶ noun Brit. the shop steward of a printers' trade union.

Father of the House ▶ noun (in the UK) the member of the House of Commons with the longest continuous service.

Father's Day ▶ noun a day of the year on which fathers are particularly honoured by their children. It was first observed in the state of Washington in 1910; in the US, South Africa, and Britain, it is usually the third Sunday in June, in Australia, the first Sunday in September.

Father Time ▶ noun see TIME (sense 1 of the noun).

fathom ▶ noun a unit of length equal to six feet (1.8 metres), chiefly used in reference to the depth of water: *sonar says that we're in eighteen fathoms.*
▶ verb [with obj.] **1** [usu. with negative] understand (a difficult problem or an enigmatic person) after much thought: *the locals could not fathom out the reason behind his new-found prosperity* | [with clause] *he couldn't fathom why she was being so anxious.*
2 measure the depth of (water): *an attempt to fathom the ocean.*
– DERIVATIVES **fathomable** adjective.
– ORIGIN Old English *fæthm*, of Germanic origin; related to Dutch *vadem*, *vaam* and German *Faden* 'six feet'. The original sense was 'something which embraces', (plural) 'the outstretched arms'; hence, a unit of measurement based on the span of the outstretched arms, later standardized to six feet.

Fathometer /faˈðɒmɪtə/ ▶ noun US trademark a type of echo sounder.

fathomless ▶ adjective unable to be measured or understood; extremely deep: *staring into a pair of cold, fathomless grey eyes* | *the fathomless depths of the novel.*

fatigue ▶ noun **1** [mass noun] extreme tiredness resulting from mental or physical exertion or illness: *he was nearly dead with fatigue.* ■ a reduction in the efficiency of a muscle or organ after prolonged activity. ■ [with modifier] a lessening in one's response to or enthusiasm for something, caused by overexposure: *votes were showing signs of election fatigue.*
2 weakness in metal or other materials caused by repeated variations of stress: *metal fatigue.*
3 (**fatigues**) menial non-military tasks performed by a soldier, sometimes as a punishment: *we're on cookhouse fatigues, sir.* ■ (also **fatigue party**) [count noun] a group of soldiers ordered to do menial tasks.
4 (**fatigues**) loose clothing, typically khaki, olive drab, or camouflaged, of a sort worn by soldiers on active duty: *battle fatigues.*
▶ verb (**fatigues**, **fatiguing**, **fatigued**) [with obj.] cause (someone) to feel exhausted: *they were fatigued by their journey.* ■ reduce the efficiency of (a muscle or organ) by prolonged activity. ■ weaken (a metal or other material) by repeated variations of stress.
– DERIVATIVES **fatiguability** (also **fatigability**) noun, **fatiguable** (also **fatigable**) adjective.
– ORIGIN mid 17th cent. (in the sense 'task that causes weariness'): from French *fatigue* (noun), *fatiguer* (verb), from Latin *fatigare* 'tire out', from *ad fatim, affatim* 'to satiety or surfeit'.

Fatiha /ˈfɑːtɪə, ˈfat-/ (also **Fatihah**) ▶ noun the short first sura of the Koran, used by Muslims as an essential element of ritual prayer.
– ORIGIN from Arabic *al-Fātiḥah* 'the opening (sura)', from *fātiḥa* 'opening', from *fataḥa* 'to open'.

Fatima /ˈfatɪmə/ (*c.*606–32 AD), youngest daughter of the prophet Muhammad and wife of the fourth caliph, Ali. The descendants of Muhammad trace their lineage through her; she is revered especially by Shiite Muslims as the mother of the imams Hasan and Husayn.

Fátima /ˈfatɪmə/ a village in west central Portugal, north-east of Lisbon; pop. 8,500 (est. 2008). It became a centre of Roman Catholic pilgrimage after the reported sighting in the village in 1917 of the Virgin Mary.

Fatimid /ˈfatɪmɪd/ ▶ noun a member of a dynasty which ruled in parts of northern Africa, Egypt, and Syria from 909 to 1171, and founded Cairo as its capital in 969.
▶ adjective relating to the Fatimids.
– DERIVATIVES **Fatimite** noun & adjective.
– ORIGIN from Arabic *Fāṭima* (see FATIMA, from whom the dynasty is said to descend) + -ID³.

fatling ▶ noun a young animal that has been fattened in readiness for slaughter.

fatso ▶ noun (pl. **fatsos**) informal, derogatory a fat person.

fatstock ▶ noun [mass noun] Brit. livestock that has been fattened for slaughter.

fatten ▶ verb make or become fat or fatter: [with obj.] *he could do with some good food to **fatten him up*** | [no obj.] *Irish cattle **fatten up** quickly.*

fattening ▶ adjective (of a foodstuff) liable to make a person overweight.

fattism ▶ noun [mass noun] prejudice or discrimination against people who are fat.
– DERIVATIVES **fattist** noun & adjective.

fattoush /fa'tu:ʃ/ (also **fatoush**) ▶ noun a Middle Eastern salad dish consisting of tomatoes, cucumber, and other vegetables together with croutons made from toasted pitta bread.
– ORIGIN Arabic *fattūš*.

fatty ▶ adjective (**fattier**, **fattiest**) containing a large amount of fat: *go easy on fatty foods* | *fatty tissue.* ■ Medicine (of a disease or lesion) marked by abnormal deposition of fat in cells: *fatty degeneration of the liver.*
▶ noun (pl. **fatties**) informal a fat person (often as a nickname).
– DERIVATIVES **fattiness** noun.

fatty acid ▶ noun Chemistry a carboxylic acid consisting of a hydrocarbon chain and a terminal carboxyl group, especially any of those occurring as esters in fats and oils.

fatty oil ▶ noun another term for **FIXED OIL**.

fatuous /'fatjʊəs/ ▶ adjective silly and pointless: *a fatuous comment.*
– DERIVATIVES **fatuity** noun (pl. **fatuities**), **fatuously** adverb, **fatuousness** noun.
– ORIGIN early 17th cent.: from Latin *fatuus* 'foolish' + **-OUS**.

fatwa /'fatwɑ:/ ▶ noun a ruling on a point of Islamic law given by a recognized authority.
– ORIGIN early 17th cent.: from Arabic *fatwā*, from *'aftā* 'decide a point of law'. Compare with **MUFTI**[1].

faubourg /'fəʊbʊəɡ/, French /fobuʀ/ ▶ noun [usu. in place names] a suburb, especially one in Paris: *the Faubourg Saint-Germain.*
– ORIGIN French (earlier *faux-bourg* 'false borough'), perhaps an alteration of *forsborc*, literally 'outside the town', but perhaps based on Middle High German *phâlburgere* 'burghers of the pale', i.e. people living outside the city wall but still inside the palisade.

fauces /'fɔ:si:z/ ▶ plural noun Anatomy the arched opening at the back of the mouth leading to the pharynx.
– DERIVATIVES **faucial** /'fɔ:ʃ(ə)l/ adjective.
– ORIGIN late Middle English: from Latin, 'throat'.

faucet /'fɔ:sɪt/ ▶ noun N. Amer. a tap.
– ORIGIN late Middle English (denoting a bung for the vent hole of a cask, or a tap for drawing liquid from a container): from Old French *fausset*, from Provençal *falset*, from *falsar* 'to bore'. The current sense dates from the mid 19th cent.

faugh /fɔ:/ ▶ exclamation expressing disgust: *'Faugh! This place stinks!'.*
– ORIGIN natural exclamation: first recorded in English in the mid 16th cent.

faujdar /'fɔ:dʒɪdɑ:/ (also **faujidar**) ▶ noun Indian a police officer.
– ORIGIN late 17th cent. (in the sense 'Mogul state official in charge of the police'): from Persian *fawjdār* 'military commander', from Arabic *fawj* 'troop' + Persian *-dār* 'holding, holder'.

Faulkner /'fɔ:knə/, William (1897–1962), American novelist. His works deal with the history and legends of the American South and have a strong sense of a society in decline. Notable works: *The Sound and the Fury* (1929), *As I Lay Dying* (1930), and *Absalom! Absalom!* (1936). Nobel Prize for Literature (1949).

fault /fɔ:lt, fɒlt/ ▶ noun **1** an unattractive or unsatisfactory feature, especially in a piece of work or in a person's character: *my worst fault is impatience.* ■ a break or other defect in an electric circuit or piece of machinery: *a fire caused by an electrical fault.* ■ a misguided action or habit: *the fault of the keen therapist is to start to intervene during the assessment phase.* ■ (in tennis and similar games) a service of the ball not in accordance with the rules. ■ (usu. **faults**) (in showjumping) a penalty point imposed for an error.
2 [mass noun] responsibility for an accident or misfortune: *if books were not selling, it wasn't **the fault of** the publishers* | *it was his fault she had died.*
3 Geology an extended break in a rock formation, marked by the relative displacement and discontinuity of strata on either side of a particular plane.
▶ verb **1** [with obj.] [usu. with negative] criticize for inadequacy or mistakes: *her superiors could not fault her dedication to the job* | *you cannot **fault him for** the professionalism of his approach.* ■ [no obj.] archaic do wrong: *the people of Caesarea faulted greatly when they called King Herod a god.*
2 (**be faulted**) Geology (of a rock formation) be broken by a fault or faults: *the continental crust has been thinned and faulted as a result of geological processes* | (as noun **faulting**) *a complex pattern of faulting.*
– PHRASES **at fault 1** responsible for an undesirable situation; in the wrong: *we recover compensation from the person at fault.* **2** defective: *he suspected that his calculator was at fault.* **find fault** make an adverse criticism or objection, sometimes unfairly: *he **finds fault with** everything I do.* **—— to a fault** displaying the specified commendable quality to an almost excessive extent: *you're kind and generous to a fault.*
– ORIGIN Middle English *faut(e)* 'lack, failing', from Old French, based on Latin *fallere* 'deceive'. The *-l-* was added (in French and English) in the 15th cent. to conform with the Latin word, but did not become standard in English until the 17th cent., remaining silent in pronunciation until well into the 18th.

fault-finding ▶ noun [mass noun] **1** continual criticism, typically concerning trivial things.
2 the investigation of the cause of malfunction in machinery, especially electronic equipment.
– DERIVATIVES **fault-finder** noun.

faultless ▶ adjective free from defect or error: *your logic is faultless.*
– DERIVATIVES **faultlessly** adverb, **faultlessness** noun.

fault line ▶ noun a line on a rock surface or the ground that traces a geological fault. ■ a divisive issue or difference of opinion that is likely to have serious consequences: *religion is now the great fault line of American politics.*

faulty ▶ adjective (**faultier**, **faultiest**) not working or made correctly; having defects: *a faulty brake.* ■ (of reasoning and other mental processes) mistaken or misleading because of flaws: *faulty logic.* ■ having or displaying weaknesses: *her character was faulty.*
– DERIVATIVES **faultily** adverb, **faultiness** noun.

faun /fɔ:n/ ▶ noun Roman Mythology one of a class of lustful rural gods, represented as a man with a goat's horns, ears, legs, and tail.
– ORIGIN late Middle English: from the name of the pastoral god **FAUNUS**.

fauna /'fɔ:nə/ ▶ noun (pl. **faunas**) [mass noun] the animals of a particular region, habitat, or geological period: *the **flora and fauna** of Siberia* | [count noun] *the local Mesozoic rocks and their faunas.* ■ [count noun] a book or other work detailing the animal life of a region.
– DERIVATIVES **faunal** adjective, **faunistic** /-'nɪstɪk/ adjective.
– ORIGIN late 18th cent.: modern Latin application of *Fauna*, the name of a rural goddess, sister of **FAUNUS**.

faunal region ▶ noun another term for **ZOOGEOGRAPHICAL REGION**.

Fauntleroy /'fɔ:ntlərɔɪ/ (also **Little Lord Fauntleroy**) ▶ noun an excessively well-mannered or elaborately dressed young boy.
– ORIGIN from the name of the boy hero of Frances Hodgson Burnett's novel *Little Lord Fauntleroy* (1886).

Faunus /'fɔ:nəs/ Roman Mythology an ancient Italian pastoral god, grandson of Saturn, associated with wooded places.

Fauré /'fɔ:reɪ/, French /fɔʀe/, Gabriel (Urbain) (1845–1924), French composer and organist. His best-known work is the *Requiem* (1887) for solo voices, choir, and orchestra; he also wrote songs, piano pieces, chamber music, and incidental music for the theatre.

Faust /faʊst/ (also **Faustus** /-təs/) (died c.1540), German astronomer and necromancer. Reputed to have sold his soul to the Devil, he became the subject of a drama by Goethe, an opera by Gounod, and a novel by Thomas Mann.
– DERIVATIVES **Faustian** adjective.

faute de mieux /fəʊt də 'mjə:/, French /fot də mjø/ ▶ adverb for want of a better alternative.
– ORIGIN French.

fauteuil /fəʊ'tə:i/ ▶ noun a wooden seat in the form of an armchair with open sides and upholstered arms.
– ORIGIN French, from Old French *faudestuel*, from medieval Latin *faldistolium* (see **FALDSTOOL**).

Fauve /fəʊv/, French /fɔv/ ▶ noun a member of a group of French painters who favoured Fauvism: [as modifier] *the Fauve movement.*

Fauvism /'fəʊvɪz(ə)m/ ▶ noun [mass noun] a style of painting with vivid expressionistic and non-naturalistic use of colour that flourished in Paris from 1905 and, although short-lived, had an important influence on subsequent artists, especially the German expressionists. Matisse was regarded as the movement's leading figure.
– DERIVATIVES **Fauvist** noun & adjective.
– ORIGIN French *fauvisme*, from *fauve* 'wild beast'. The name originated from a remark of the French art critic Louis Vauxcelles at the Salon of 1905; coming across a quattrocento-style statue in the midst of works by Matisse and his associates, he is reputed to have said, 'Donatello au milieu des fauves!' ('Donatello among the wild beasts').

faux /fəʊ/ ▶ adjective made in imitation; artificial: *a rope of faux pearls.* ■ not genuine; fake or false: *their faux concern for the well-being of the voters didn't fool many* | [as submodifier] *his faux-macho banter caused offence.*
– ORIGIN French, 'false'.

faux naïf /,fəʊ nʌɪ'i:f/, French /fo naif/ ▶ adjective artificially or affectedly simple or naive: *faux-naif pastoralism.*
▶ noun a person who pretends to be ingenuous.
– ORIGIN from French *faux* 'false' + *naïf* 'naive'.

faux pas /fəʊ 'pɑ:/, French /fo pa/ ▶ noun (pl. **same**) an embarrassing or tactless act or remark in a social situation.
– ORIGIN French, literally 'false step'.

fava bean /'fɑ:və/ (also **faba bean**) ▶ noun North American term for **BROAD BEAN**.
– ORIGIN Italian *fava*, from Latin *faba* 'bean'.

fave ▶ noun & adjective informal short for **FAVOURITE**.

favela /fa'vɛlə/ ▶ noun a Brazilian shack or shanty town; a slum.
– ORIGIN Portuguese.

favicon /'favɪkɒn, 'feɪvɪkɒn/ ▶ noun an icon associated with a particular website, typically displayed in the address bar of a browser accessing the site or next to the site name in a user's list of bookmarks.
– ORIGIN blend of *favourites* and **ICON**.

favour (US **favor**) ▶ noun **1** [mass noun] approval, support, or liking for someone or something: *training is looked upon with favour by many employers.* ■ overgenerous preferential treatment: *he was accused of showing favour to one of the players.* ■ [count noun] archaic a thing such as a badge or knot of ribbons that is given or worn as a mark of liking or support.
2 an act of kindness beyond what is due or usual: *I've come to ask you a favour.* ■ (**one's favours**) dated used with reference to a woman allowing a man to have sexual intercourse with her: *she had granted her favours to him.*
3 (also **party favor**) N. Amer. a small inexpensive gift given to guests at a party.
▶ verb [with obj.] **1** feel or show approval or preference for: *slashing public spending is a policy that few politicians favour.* ■ give unfairly preferential treatment to: *critics argued that the policy favoured the private sector.* ■ work to the advantage of: *natural selection has favoured bats.*
2 (**favour someone with**) (often used in polite requests) give someone (something desired): *please favour me with an answer.*
3 dated or N. Amer. resemble (a parent or other relative) in facial features: *she's pretty, and she favours you.*
4 treat (an injured limb) gently, not putting one's full weight on it: *he favours his sore leg.*
– PHRASES **do someone a favour** [in imperative] Brit. informal used to express brusque dismissal of a remark: *'Are you some kind of social worker?' 'Do me a favour!'* **do someone no favours** informal do something that is unhelpful to someone: *you won't do yourself any favours by getting worked up.* **in** (or **out of**) **favour** meeting with (or having lost) approval: *they were not in favour with the party.* **in one's favour** to one's advantage: *events were moving in his favour.* **in favour of 1** to be replaced by: *he stepped down as leader in favour of his rival.* **2** in support or to the advantage of: *members have voted in favour of strike action* | *the judge decided in favour of the defendant.*
– DERIVATIVES **favourer** noun.
– ORIGIN Middle English (in the noun sense 'liking, preference'): via Old French from Latin *favor*, from *favere* 'show kindness to' (related to *fovere* 'cherish').

favourable (US **favorable**) ▶ adjective **1** expressing approval: *the exhibitions received favourable reviews.*

F

■ giving consent: *their demands rarely received a favourable response.*
2 to the advantage of someone or something: *favourable conditions for vegetation growth | the settlement was* ***favourable to*** *the unions.* ■ (of a wind) blowing in the direction of travel. ■ suggesting a good outcome: *a favourable prognosis.*
– DERIVATIVES **favourableness** noun.
– ORIGIN Middle English: via Old French from Latin *favorabilis*, from *favor* (see FAVOUR).

favourably (US **favorably**) ▸ **adverb 1** with approval: *the audience responded very favourably.*
2 to the advantage of someone or something: *the deal will work out favourably for the company.*

favoured (US **favored**) ▸ **adjective** preferred or recommended: *she was his favoured candidate | the most favoured destination of visitors to Canada.*

F

favourite (US **favorite**) ▸ **adjective** [attrib.] preferred to all others of the same kind: *their favourite Italian restaurant.*
▸ **noun** a person or thing that is preferred to all others of the same kind or is especially well liked: *my favourite is tandoori chicken | the song is still a favourite after 20 years.* ■ the competitor thought most likely to win a game or contest, especially by people betting on the outcome: *the team are strong favourites.* ■ a record of the address of a website or other data made to enable quick access; a bookmark.
▸ **verb** [with obj.] record the address of (a website or other data) to enable quick access in future: *you can see who else favourited the same pictures.*
– PHRASES **favourite son** a famous man who is particularly popular in his native area: *Essex's favourite son will open at Lord's to launch the cricket season.* ■ US a person supported as a presidential candidate by delegates from the candidate's home state.
– ORIGIN late 16th cent. (as a noun): from obsolete French *favorit*, from Italian *favorito*, past participle of *favorire* 'to favour', from Latin *favor* (see FAVOUR).

WORD TRENDS As with *friend*, the transformation of **favourite** into a verb is an Internet phenomenon. On the Web you can record the address of a particular site using an online bookmark, to allow you to find it quickly in the future. On Internet Explorer the bookmarks are called **favorites**, and the browser's dominance has led to the term being adopted as a synonym for **bookmark** (itself used in computing contexts since the 1980s) as both noun and verb: *voting is open for another 17 days, so favourite the page and do it daily.* The term can also refer to the process of tagging and collecting together your favourite online pictures, videos, or messages: *I spent forever on Flickr searching out, and favouriting, examples of my newest passion.*

favouritism (US **favoritism**) ▸ **noun** [mass noun] **1** the practice of giving unfair preferential treatment to one person or group at the expense of another.
2 the state or condition of being the competitor thought most likely to win a sporting contest: *the horse shares favouritism with her French-trained rival at 6-1.*

favrile glass /fəˈvriːl/ ▸ **noun** [mass noun] a richly coloured iridescent glass, developed by L. C. Tiffany.
– ORIGIN late 19th cent.: formed as a trademark from the obsolete adjective *fabrile* 'of a craftsman'.

Fawkes /fɔːks/, Guy (1570–1606), English conspirator. He was hanged for his part in the Gunpowder Plot of 5 November 1605. The occasion is commemorated annually on Bonfire Night with fireworks, bonfires, and the burning of a guy.

fawn[1] ▸ **noun 1** a young deer in its first year.
2 [mass noun] a light brown colour.
▸ **verb** [no obj.] (of a deer) produce young.
– PHRASES **in fawn** (of a deer) pregnant.
– ORIGIN late Middle English: from Old French *faon*, based on Latin *fetus* 'offspring'; compare with FETUS.

fawn[2] ▸ **verb** [no obj.] (of a person) give a servile display of exaggerated flattery or affection, typically in order to gain favour: *congressmen* ***fawn over*** *the President.* ■ (of a dog) show slavish devotion, especially by rubbing against someone: *the dogs started fawning on me.*
– ORIGIN Old English *fagnian* 'make or be glad', of Germanic origin; related to FAIN.

fawning ▸ **adjective** displaying exaggerated flattery or affection; obsequious: *fawning adoration | fawning interviews with Hollywood celebs.*
– DERIVATIVES **fawningly** adverb.

fax[1] ▸ **noun** an exact copy of a document made by electronic scanning and transmitted as data by telecommunications links. ■ [mass noun] the production or transmission of documents in this way: *he received the report by fax.* ■ (also **fax machine**) a machine for transmitting and receiving such documents.
▸ **verb** [with obj.] send (a document) by fax. ■ contact (someone) by fax: *to obtain a brochure fax the agent.*
– ORIGIN 1940s: abbreviation of FACSIMILE.

fax[2] ▸ **plural noun** non-standard spelling of 'facts': *food fax.*

fay ▸ **noun** literary a fairy.
– ORIGIN late Middle English: from Old French *fae, faie*, from Latin *fata* 'the Fates', plural of *fatum* (see FATE). Compare with FAIRY.

fayalite /ˈfeɪəlʌɪt/ ▸ **noun** [mass noun] a black or brown mineral which is an iron-rich form of olivine and occurs in many igneous rocks.
– ORIGIN mid 19th cent.: from *Fayal* (the name of an island in the Azores) + -ITE[1].

fayre ▸ **noun** pseudo-archaic spelling of FAIR[2] and FARE (sense 2 of the noun).

faze ▸ **verb** [with obj.] informal disturb or disconcert (someone): *she was not fazed by his show of anger.*
– ORIGIN mid 19th cent. (originally US): variant of dialect *feeze* 'drive or frighten off', from Old English *fēsian*, of unknown origin.

USAGE **Faze** has no connection with the word **phase** and should not be spelled with a *ph-*, although this is a common error: almost a quarter of citations for the word in the Oxford English Corpus are for the incorrect spelling.

fazenda /fəˈzɛndə/ ▸ **noun** an estate or large farm in Portugal, Brazil, and other Portuguese-speaking countries.
– ORIGIN Portuguese; compare with Spanish *hacienda*.

fazendeiro /ˌfazɛnˈdɛːrəʊ/ ▸ **noun** (pl. **fazendeiros**) a person who owns or occupies a fazenda.
– ORIGIN Portuguese.

FBA ▸ **abbreviation** Fellow of the British Academy.

FBI ▸ **abbreviation** (in the US) Federal Bureau of Investigation.

FC ▸ **abbreviation** ■ Brit. Football Club: *Liverpool FC.* ■ (in the UK) Forestry Commission.

FCC ▸ **abbreviation** (in the US) Federal Communications Commission.

FCO ▸ **abbreviation** (in the UK) Foreign and Commonwealth Office.

FD ▸ **abbreviation** Defender of the Faith.
– ORIGIN from Latin *Fidei Defensor*.

FDA ▸ **abbreviation** (in the US) Food and Drug Administration.

FDC ▸ **abbreviation** first-day cover.

FDDI ▸ **abbreviation** fibre distributed data interface, a communications, cabling, and hardware standard for high-speed optical-fibre networks.

FDI ▸ **abbreviation** foreign direct investment.

FDIC ▸ **abbreviation** Federal Deposit Insurance Corporation, a body which underwrites most private bank deposits in the US.

FDR the nickname of President Franklin Delano Roosevelt (see ROOSEVELT[2]).

FE ▸ **abbreviation** (in the UK) further education.

Fe ▸ **symbol** the chemical element iron.
– ORIGIN from Latin *ferrum*.

fealty /ˈfiːəlti/ ▸ **noun** [mass noun] historical a feudal tenant's or vassal's sworn loyalty to a lord: *they owed* ***fealty to*** *the Earl rather than the King.* ■ formal acknowledgement of loyalty to a lord.
– ORIGIN Middle English: from Old French *feau(l)te, fealte*, from Latin *fidelitas* (see FIDELITY).

fear ▸ **noun** [mass noun] an unpleasant emotion caused by the threat of danger, pain, or harm: *I cowered in fear as bullets whizzed past | fear of unemployment is paralysing the economy* | [count noun] *he is prey to irrational fears.* ■ [count noun] (**fear for**) a feeling of anxiety concerning the outcome of something or the safety of someone: *police launched a hunt for the family amid fears for their safety.* ■ the likelihood of something unwelcome happening: *she observed the other guests without fear of attracting attention.* ■ archaic a mixed feeling of dread and reverence: *the love and fear of God.*
▸ **verb** [with obj.] be afraid of (someone or something) as likely to be dangerous, painful, or harmful: *I hated him but didn't fear him any more* | [with clause] *farmers fear that they will lose business.* ■ [no obj.] (**fear for**) feel anxiety on behalf of: *I fear for the city with this madman let loose in it.* ■ [with infinitive] avoid doing something because one is afraid: *she eventually feared to go out at all.* ■ used to express regret or apology: *I shall buy her book, though not, I fear, the hardback version.* ■ archaic regard (God) with reverence and awe.
– PHRASES **for fear of** (or **that**) to avoid the risk of (or that): *no one dared refuse the order for fear of losing their job.* **never fear** used to reassure someone: *we shall meet again, never fear.* **no fear** Brit. informal used as an emphatic expression of denial or refusal: *'Are you coming with me?' 'No fear—it's too exciting here.'* **put the fear of God in** (or **into**) **someone** make someone very frightened. **without fear or favour** impartially.
– ORIGIN Old English *fǣr* 'calamity, danger', *fǣran* 'frighten', also 'revere', of Germanic origin; related to Dutch *gevaar* and German *Gefahr* 'danger'.

fearful ▸ **adjective 1** feeling or showing fear or anxiety: *they are fearful of the threat of nuclear war* | [with clause] *he's fearful that his career is over.* ■ causing or likely to cause people to be afraid; horrifying: *a fearful accident.*
2 informal very great: *he was in a fearful hurry.*
– DERIVATIVES **fearfulness** noun.

fearfully ▸ **adverb 1** in an anxious manner; apprehensively: *he glanced over his shoulder fearfully.*
2 [as submodifier] dreadfully; extremely: *she was fearfully worried for the welfare of her family.*

fearless ▸ **adjective** showing a lack of fear: *a fearless crusader for animal rights.*
– DERIVATIVES **fearlessly** adverb, **fearlessness** noun.

fearmongering ▸ **noun** [mass noun] the action of deliberately arousing public fear or alarm about a particular issue: *his campaign for re-election was based on fearmongering and deception.*
– DERIVATIVES **fearmonger** noun.

fearsome ▸ **adjective** frightening, especially in appearance: *the cat mewed, displaying a fearsome set of teeth.*
– DERIVATIVES **fearsomely** adverb, **fearsomeness** noun.

feart /fɪət/ (also **feared**) ▸ **adjective** Scottish afraid: *ye're feart to stand out from the crowd.*

feasibility ▸ **noun** [mass noun] the state or degree of being easily or conveniently done: *the feasibility of screening athletes for cardiac disease.*

feasibility study ▸ **noun** an assessment of the practicality of a proposed plan or method.

feasible /ˈfiːzɪb(ə)l/ ▸ **adjective 1** possible and practical to do easily or conveniently: *the Dutch have demonstrated that it is perfectly feasible to live below sea level.*
2 likely; probable: *the most feasible explanation.*
– DERIVATIVES **feasibly** adverb.
– ORIGIN late Middle English: from Old French *faisible*, from *fais-*, stem of *faire* 'do, make', from Latin *facere*.

feast ▸ **noun 1** a large meal, typically a celebratory one: *a wedding feast.* ■ a plentiful supply of something enjoyable: *the concert season offers* ***a feast of*** *classical music.*
2 an annual religious celebration. ■ a day dedicated to a particular saint: *the feast of St John.* ■ Brit. an annual village festival.
▸ **verb** [no obj.] eat and drink sumptuously: *the men would congregate and feast after hunting.* ■ (**feast on**) eat large quantities of: *we sat feasting on barbecued chicken and beer.* ■ [with obj.] give (someone) a plentiful and delicious meal: *they feasted the deputation.*
– PHRASES **ghost** (or **skeleton**) **at the feast** a person or thing that brings gloom to an otherwise pleasant occasion. **feast one's eyes on** gaze at with pleasure. **feast or famine** either too much of something or too little.
– DERIVATIVES **feaster** noun.
– ORIGIN Middle English: from Old French *feste* (noun), *fester* (verb), from Latin *festa*, neuter plural of *festus* 'joyous'. Compare with FETE and FIESTA.

feast day ▸ **noun** a day on which a celebration, especially an annual Christian one, is held.

Feast of Dedication ▸ **noun** another name for HANUKKAH.

Feast of Tabernacles ▸ **noun** another name for SUCCOTH.

Feast of Weeks ▸ **noun** another name for SHAVUOTH.

feat ▸ **noun** an achievement that requires great courage, skill, or strength: *the new printing presses were considerable feats of engineering.*
– ORIGIN late Middle English (in the general sense 'action or deed'): from Old French *fait*, from Latin *factum* (see FACT).

feather ▸ noun any of the flat appendages growing from a bird's skin and forming its plumage, consisting of a partly hollow horny shaft fringed with vanes of barbs. ■ (**feathers**) a fringe of long hair on the legs of a dog, horse, or other animal.
▸ verb **1** [with obj.] rotate the blades of (a propeller) about their own axes in such a way as to lessen the air or water resistance. ■ vary the angle of attack of (rotor blades). ■ Rowing turn (an oar) so that it passes through the air edgeways: *he turned, feathering one oar slowly.*
2 [no obj., with adverbial] float or move like a feather: *the green fronds feathered against a blue sky.*
3 [with obj.] blend or smooth delicately: *feather the paint in, in a series of light strokes.*
4 [no obj.] (of ink, lipstick, etc.) separate into tiny lines after application: (as noun **feathering**) *a long-lasting formula that resists feathering and protects the lips.*
5 short for FEATHER-CUT.
– PHRASES **a feather in one's cap** an achievement to be proud of. **feather one's (own) nest** make money for oneself in an opportunistic or selfish way. **(as) light as a feather** extremely light and insubstantial.
– DERIVATIVES **featherless** adjective.
– ORIGIN Old English *fether*, of Germanic origin; related to Dutch *veer* and German *Feder*, from an Indo-European root shared by Sanskrit *patra* 'wing', Latin *penna* 'feather', and Greek *pteron*, *pterux* 'wing'.

featherback ▸ noun a tropical freshwater fish native to southern Asia and Africa, with a strongly humped back, a small feather-like dorsal fin, and a long anal fin that runs from the belly to the tail. Also called KNIFEFISH. ● Family Notopteridae: four genera and several species, in particular the large edible *Notopterus chitala* of Asia.

feather bed ▸ noun a bed that has a mattress stuffed with feathers.
▸ verb (**feather-bed**) [with obj.] chiefly Brit. provide (someone) with excessively favourable economic or working conditions.

feather-brain ▸ noun a silly or absent-minded person.
– DERIVATIVES **feather-brained** adjective.

feather-cut ▸ verb [with obj.] cut (hair) into wispy feather-like points: [as adj.] *black feather-cut hair.*
▸ noun (**feathercut**) a hairstyle produced by such cutting.

feather duster ▸ noun **1** a long-handled brush with a head made of feathers, used for dusting.
2 (also **feather duster worm**) US another term for FAN WORM.

feathered ▸ adjective (of a bird) covered with feathers: [in combination] *black-feathered ostriches.* ■ decorated with feathers: *a feathered hat.*

feathered friend ▸ noun informal (usu. **feathered friends**) a bird.

feather edge ▸ noun a fine edge produced by tapering a board, plank, or other object.

feathering ▸ noun [mass noun] **1** the plumage of a bird or part of a bird. ■ the feathers of an arrow. ■ fringes of hairs on the appendages or body of a dog. ■ feather-like markings or structure: *traditional finishes such as marbling and feathering.* ■ Architecture cusping in tracery.
2 the action of varying the angle of propellers, rotor blades, or oars so as to reduce air or water resistance.

feather-light ▸ adjective extremely light: *a feather-light touch.*

feather star ▸ noun an echinoderm (marine invertebrate) with a small disc-like body, long feathery arms for feeding and movement, and short appendages for grasping the surface. ● Order Comatulida, class Crinoidea.

feather stitch ▸ noun [mass noun] ornamental zigzag sewing.
▸ verb (**feather-stitch**) [with obj.] (usu. as noun **feather-stitching**) sew (something) using feather stitch.

feathertail glider ▸ noun an Australian pygmy possum with a flap of skin between the fore- and hindlimbs for gliding, and a feathery tail. ● *Acrobates pygmaeus*, family Burramyidae. Alternative name: **flying mouse**.

featherweight ▸ noun **1** [mass noun] a weight in boxing and other sports intermediate between bantamweight and lightweight. In the amateur boxing scale it ranges from 54 to 57 kg. ■ [count noun] a boxer or other competitor of this weight.
2 a very light person or thing. ■ a person or thing not worth serious consideration: *he is an intellectual featherweight.*

feathery ▸ adjective having, covered with, or resembling feathers: *wisps of feathery blonde hair.*

feature ▸ noun **1** a distinctive attribute or aspect of something: *a well-appointed house with interesting decorative features | one salient feature of the case has been overlooked.* ■ (usu. **features**) a part of the face, such as the mouth or eyes, making a significant contribution to its overall appearance: *a dark-haired man with strong, regular features.* ■ Linguistics a distinctive characteristic of a linguistic unit, especially a speech sound or vocabulary item, that serves to distinguish it from others of the same type.
2 a newspaper or magazine article or a broadcast programme devoted to the treatment of a particular topic, typically at length: *a special feature on children's reference books.* ■ (also **feature film**) a full-length film intended as the main item in a cinema programme.
▸ verb [with obj.] have as a prominent attribute or aspect: *the hotel features a large lounge, a sauna, and a coin-operated solarium.* ■ have as an important actor or participant: *the film featured Glenn Miller and his Orchestra.* ■ [no obj.] (**feature in**) be a significant characteristic of or take an important part in: *his later paintings feature prominently in the exhibition.*
– DERIVATIVES **featured** adjective [in combination] *fine-featured women*, **featureless** adjective.
– ORIGIN late Middle English (originally denoting the form or proportions of the body, or a physical feature): from Old French *faiture* 'form', from Latin *factura* (see FACTURE).

feature-length ▸ adjective of the length of a typical feature film or programme: *a feature-length documentary.*

featurette /fiːtʃəˈrɛt/ ▸ noun a short feature film or programme.

Feb. ▸ abbreviation February.

febrifuge /ˈfɛbrɪfjuːdʒ/ ▸ noun a medicine used to reduce fever.
– DERIVATIVES **febrifugal** /fɪˈbrɪfjʊg(ə)l, ˌfɛbrɪˈfjuːg(ə)l/ adjective.
– ORIGIN late 17th cent.: from French *fébrifuge*, from Latin *febris* 'fever' + *fugare* 'drive away'. Compare with FEVERFEW.

febrile /ˈfiːbrʌɪl/ ▸ adjective **1** having or showing the symptoms of a fever: *a febrile illness.*
2 characterized by a great deal of nervous excitement or energy: *the febrile atmosphere of the city.*
– DERIVATIVES **febrility** noun.
– ORIGIN mid 17th cent.: from French *fébrile* or medieval Latin *febrilis*, from Latin *febris* 'fever'.

February /ˈfɛbrʊəri, ˈfɛbjʊəri/ ▸ noun (pl. **Februaries**) the second month of the year, in the northern hemisphere usually considered the last month of winter: *even in February the place is busy | the coldest February in 40 years.*
– ORIGIN Middle English *feverer*, from Old French *feverier*, based on Latin *februarius*, from *februa*, the name of a purification feast held in this month. The spelling change in the 15th cent. was due to association with the Latin word.

> **USAGE** Note that **February** is spelled with an **r** following the **Feb-**. Precise speakers insist that this **r** should be pronounced, but this is not easy, and most people replace the **r** following **Feb** with a y sound: **Feb-yoo-** rather than **Feb-roo-**. This is now becoming the accepted standard.

February Revolution see RUSSIAN REVOLUTION.

feces ▸ noun US spelling of FAECES.

Fechner /ˈfɛxnə/, German /ˈfɛçnɐ/, Gustav Theodor (1801–87), German physicist and psychologist. Fechner hoped to make psychology a truly objective science and coined the termed *psychophysics* to define his study of the quantitative relationship between degrees of physical stimulation and the resulting sensations.

feck ▸ verb Irish vulgar slang used as a euphemism for 'fuck'.
– DERIVATIVES **fecking** adjective & adverb.

feckless ▸ adjective lacking initiative or strength of character; irresponsible: *her feckless younger brother.*
– DERIVATIVES **fecklessly** adverb, **fecklessness** noun.
– ORIGIN late 16th cent.: from Scots and northern English dialect *feck* (from *effeck*, variant of EFFECT) + -LESS.

feculent /ˈfɛkjʊl(ə)nt/ ▸ adjective of or containing dirt, sediment, or waste matter: *their feet were forever slipping on feculent bog.*
– DERIVATIVES **feculence** noun.
– ORIGIN late 15th cent.: from French *féculent* or Latin *faeculentus*, from *faex*, *faec-* 'dregs'.

fecund /ˈfɛk(ə)nd, ˈfiːk-/ ▸ adjective producing or capable of producing an abundance of offspring or new growth; highly fertile: *a lush and fecund garden.* ■ producing many new ideas: *her fecund imagination.* ■ technical capable of bearing children.
– DERIVATIVES **fecundity** /fɪˈkʌndɪti/ noun.
– ORIGIN late Middle English: from French *fécond* or Latin *fecundus*.

fecundability /fɪˌkʌndəˈbɪlɪti/ ▸ noun [mass noun] Medicine & Zoology the probability of a woman or female animal conceiving within a given period of time, especially during a specific month or menstrual cycle.

fecundate /ˈfɛk(ə)ndeɪt, ˈfiːk-/ ▸ verb [with obj.] archaic fertilize. ■ literary make fruitful.
– DERIVATIVES **fecundation** noun.
– ORIGIN mid 17th cent.: from Latin *fecundat-* 'made fruitful', from the verb *fecundare*, from *fecundus* 'fruitful'.

Fed ▸ noun US informal **1** a federal agent or official, especially a member of the FBI.
2 (usu. **the Fed**) short for FEDERAL RESERVE.
– ORIGIN early 20th cent.: abbreviation of FEDERAL. The abbreviation *fed* had previously been used in the late 18th cent. to denote a member of the Federalist Party, who advocated a union of American colonies after the War of Independence.

fed past and past participle of FEED.

fedayeen /ˌfɛdəˈjiːn, fəˈdɑːjiːn/ (also **fidayeen**) ▸ plural noun Arab guerrillas operating especially against Israel.
– ORIGIN 1950s: from colloquial Arabic *fidā'iyīn*, plural of classical Arabic *fidā'ī* 'one who gives his life for another or for a cause', from *fadā* 'to ransom someone'. The singular *fedai* (from Arabic and Persian *fidā'ī*) had previously been used (late 19th cent.) to denote an Ismaili Muslim assassin.

federal ▸ adjective **1** having or relating to a system of government in which several states form a unity but remain independent in internal affairs: *a federal Europe.*
2 relating to or denoting the central government as distinguished from the separate units constituting a federation: *the health ministry has sole federal responsibility for health care.* ■ (**Federal**) US historical of the Northern states in the Civil War.
– DERIVATIVES **federalization** noun, **federalize** (also **federalise**) verb, **federally** adverb.
– ORIGIN mid 17th cent.: from Latin *foedus*, *foeder-* 'league, covenant' + -AL.

Federal Bureau of Investigation (abbrev.: **FBI**) an agency of the US federal government that deals principally with internal security and counter-intelligence and that also conducts investigations in federal law enforcement. It was established in 1908 as a branch of the Department of Justice, but was substantially reorganized under the controversial directorship (1924–72) of J. Edgar Hoover.

federal case ▸ noun US Law a criminal case that falls under the jurisdiction of a federal court. ■ informal a matter of great concern: *I'm not trying to **make a federal case out of** this, Christine, but you've got to do something.*

federalism ▸ noun [mass noun] the federal principle or system of government.
– DERIVATIVES **federalist** noun & adjective.

Federalist Party an early political party in the US, joined by George Washington during his presidency (1789–97) and in power until 1801. The party's emphasis on strong central government was extremely important in the early years after independence, but by the 1820s it had been superseded by the Democratic Republican Party.

Federal Republic of Germany 1 former name for West Germany.
2 the official name of Germany.

Federal Reserve (in the US) the banking authority that performs the functions of a central bank and is used to implement the country's monetary policy, providing a national system of reserve cash available to banks.

Federal Union see UNION (sense 3).

federate ▸ verb /ˈfɛdəreɪt/ [no obj.] (of a number of states or organizations) form a single centralized unit, within which each keeps some internal autonomy. ■ [with obj.] (usu. as adj. **federated**) form (states or organizations) into such a centralized unit: *a federated state consisting of 15 union republics.*

▸ adjective /ˈfɛd(ə)rət/ relating to such an arrangement: *federate armies*.
– DERIVATIVES **federative** adjective.
– ORIGIN early 18th cent. (as an adjective): from late Latin *foederatus*, based on *foedus*, *foeder-* 'league, covenant'.

Federated States of Micronesia full name for MICRONESIA (sense 2).

federation ▸ noun **1** a group of states with a central government but independence in internal affairs: [in names] *the Russian Federation*. ■ an organization or group within which smaller divisions have some degree of internal autonomy: [in names] *the World Chess Federation*.
2 [mass noun] the action of forming states or organizations into a single group with centralized control: *a first step in the federation of Europe*.
– DERIVATIVES **federationist** noun.
– ORIGIN early 18th cent.: from French *fédération*, from late Latin *foederatio(n-)*, from the verb *foederare* 'to ally', from *foedus* 'league'.

F

fedora /fɪˈdɔːrə/ ▸ noun a low, soft felt hat with a curled brim and the crown creased lengthways.
– ORIGIN late 19th cent. (originally US): from *Fédora*, the title of a drama (1882) written by the French dramatist Victorien Sardou (1831–1908).

fed up ▸ adjective informal annoyed, unhappy, or bored, especially with a situation that has existed for a long time: *I am **fed up** with being put down and made to feel stupid*.
– PHRASES **fed up to the teeth** (or **back teeth**) extremely annoyed: *I'm **fed up to the teeth** with the mess he's landed us in*.

fee ▸ noun **1** a payment made to a professional person or to a professional or public body in exchange for advice or services: *they were faced with legal fees of £3000*. ■ money paid as part of a special transaction, for example for a privilege or for admission to something: *an annual membership fee*. ■ (usu. **fees**) money regularly paid to a school or similar institution for continuing services: *tuition fees have now reached $9000 a year*.
2 Law, historical an estate of land, especially one held on condition of feudal service.
▸ verb (**fees**, **feeing**, **fee'd** or **feed**) [with obj.] rare make a payment to (someone) in return for services.
– PHRASES **hold something in fee** Law, historical hold an estate in return for feudal service to a superior.
– ORIGIN Middle English: from an Anglo-Norman French variant of Old French *feu*, *fief*, from medieval Latin *feodum*, *feudum*, ultimately of Germanic origin. Compare with FEU, FEUD, and FIEF.

feeb ▸ noun N. Amer. informal a feeble-minded person.
– ORIGIN early 20th cent.: abbreviation of FEEBLE.

feebate ▸ noun a system of charges and rebates whereby energy-efficient or environmentally friendly practices are rewarded while failure to adhere to such practices is penalized.
– ORIGIN 1990s: blend of FEE and REBATE[1].

feeble ▸ adjective (**feebler**, **feeblest**) lacking physical strength, especially as a result of age or illness: *by now, he was too feeble to leave his room*. ■ (of a sound) faint: *her feeble cries of pain*. ■ lacking strength of character: *I know it's feeble but I've never been one to stand up for myself*. ■ failing to convince or impress: *a feeble excuse*.
– DERIVATIVES **feebleness** noun, **feebly** adverb.
– ORIGIN Middle English: from Old French *fieble*, earlier *fleible*, from Latin *flebilis* 'lamentable', from *flere* 'weep'.

feeble-minded ▸ adjective unable to make intelligent decisions or judgements; foolish or stupid. ■ dated (of a person) having less than average intelligence.
– DERIVATIVES **feeble-mindedly** adverb, **feeble-mindedness** noun.

feed ▸ verb (past and past participle **fed** /fɛd/) [with obj.] **1** give food to: *did you remember to feed the cat?* | [with two objs] *she fed him bits of biscuit*. ■ [no obj.] (especially of an animal or baby) take food; eat something: *the baby will feed according to her needs*. ■ (**feed someone/thing up**) Brit. give a person or animal large amounts of food: *you look as though you need feeding up*. ■ provide an adequate supply of food for: *the island's simple agriculture could hardly feed its inhabitants*. ■ [no obj.] (**feed on/off**) derive regular nourishment from (a particular substance): *the bird feeds on cliff-top vegetation* | figurative *his powerful mind fed off political discussion*. ■ give fertilizer to (a plant). ■ put fuel on (a fire). ■ encourage the growth of: *I could feed my melancholy by reading Romantic poetry*. ■ informal satisfy (a drug habit): *users who commit crime to feed their habit*.
2 supply with material or power: *a radial circuit fed by a 20 amp fuse* | *the pond is fed by a small stream*. ■ put into a machine: *the programs are **fed into** the computer* | *Kevin fed coins into the jukebox*. ■ insert further coins into (a meter) to extend the time for which it operates. ■ [with two objs] supply (someone) with (information, ideas, etc.): *I think he is feeding his old employer commercial secrets*. ■ [with two objs] prompt (an actor) with (a line): *you were still in the wings feeding Micky his lines*. ■ (in ball games) pass (the ball) to a player.
3 [with obj. and adverbial of direction] cause to pass gradually and steadily, typically through a confined space: *make holes through which to feed the cables*. ■ [no obj.] (**feed through**) (of a new factor or development) begin to be effective or influential; have an impact on someone or something: *it could take time for higher earnings and dividends to **feed through** to investors*.
▸ noun **1** an act of giving food, especially to animals or a baby, or of having food given to one: *the baby's morning feed*. ■ informal a meal: *I gave him a big feed of rashers and eggs and mashed potatoes*. ■ [mass noun] food for domestic animals: *the crops are grown for animal feed* | *cow feed*.
2 a device or pipe for supplying material to a machine: *a paper feed*. ■ the supply of raw material to a machine or device: [as modifier] *a feed pipe*. ■ a broadcast distributed by a satellite or network from a central source to a large number of radio or television stations: *a satellite feed from Washington*. ■ Computing a facility for notifying the user of a blog or other frequently updated website that new content has been added: *most blogs and news sites offer RSS feeds of their latest content*.
3 a line or prompt given to an actor on stage. ■ an actor who gives a feed to a fellow performer.
– PHRASES **off one's feed** informal having no appetite.
– PHRASAL VERBS **feed back** (of an electrical or other system) produce feedback.
– ORIGIN Old English *fēdan* (verb), of Germanic origin; related to Dutch *voeden* and FOOD.

feedback ▸ noun [mass noun] **1** information about reactions to a product, a person's performance of a task, etc. which is used as a basis for improvement.
2 the modification or control of a process or system by its results or effects, for example in a biochemical pathway or behavioural response. See also NEGATIVE FEEDBACK, POSITIVE FEEDBACK.
3 the return of a fraction of the output signal from an amplifier, microphone, or other device to the input of the same device; sound distortion produced by this.

feed dog ▸ noun the mechanism in a sewing machine which feeds the material under the needle.

feeder ▸ noun **1** a person or animal that eats a particular food or in a particular manner: *a plankton feeder*.
2 a container filled with food for birds or mammals. ■ Brit. a child's feeding bottle. ■ Brit. a bib for an infant. ■ Fishing short for SWIMFEEDER.
3 a person or thing that supplies something, in particular: ■ a device supplying material to a machine: *the automatic sheet feeder holds up to 10 sheets of paper*. ■ a tributary stream. ■ [usu. as modifier] a branch road or railway line linking outlying districts with a main communication system. ■ a main carrying electricity to a distribution point. ■ [usu. as modifier] a school, sports team, etc. from which members move on to one more advanced: *a sixth-form college and its feeder schools*.

feedforward ▸ noun [mass noun] the modification or control of a process using its anticipated results or effects.

feeding bottle ▸ noun Brit. a bottle fitted with a teat for giving milk or other drinks to babies and very young children.

feeding frenzy ▸ noun an aggressive and competitive group attack on prey by a number of sharks or piranhas. ■ an episode of frantic competition or rivalry for something: *the remark caused a media feeding frenzy*.

feedlot ▸ noun an area or building where livestock are fed or fattened up.

feedstock ▸ noun [mass noun] raw material to supply or fuel a machine or industrial process.

feedstuff ▸ noun (usu. **feedstuffs**) a food provided for cattle and other livestock.

feedthrough ▸ noun [mass noun] **1** the passage or transfer of something through or beyond a specified point or stage: *the feedthrough to further education*.
2 an electrical connector used to join two parts of a circuit on opposite sides of something, such as a circuit board or an earthing screen.

fee farm ▸ noun Law, chiefly historical an estate or land held in fee simple subject to a perpetual fixed rent. ■ [mass noun] the tenure of land by such means. ■ [mass noun] the rent paid for such land.

feel ▸ verb (past and past participle **felt**) [with obj.] **1** be aware of (a person or object) through touching or being touched: *she felt someone touch her shoulder* | *you can feel the soft grass beneath your feet*. ■ be aware of (something happening) through physical sensation: *she felt the ground give way beneath her*. ■ examine or search by touch: *he touched her head and felt her hair* | [no obj.] *he **felt around** for the matches*. ■ [no obj.] be capable of sensation: *the dead cannot feel*. ■ [no obj., with complement] give a sensation of a particular physical quality when touched: *the wool feels soft*. ■ (**feel something out**) informal investigate something cautiously: *they want to feel out the situation*. ■ (**feel someone up**) informal fondle someone surreptitiously and without their consent, for one's own sexual stimulation.
2 experience (an emotion or sensation): *I felt a sense of excitement* | [no obj., with complement] *she started to feel really sick* | ***it felt** odd to be alone again* | [no obj.] *we feel very strongly **about** freedom of expression*. ■ [no obj., with complement] consider oneself to be in a particular state or exhibiting particular qualities: *he doesn't feel obliged to visit every weekend* | *she felt such a fool*. ■ [no obj.] (**feel up to**) have the strength and energy to do or deal with: *after the accident she didn't feel up to driving*. ■ [usu. with negative] (**feel oneself**) be healthy and well: *Ruth was not quite feeling herself*. ■ be strongly affected by: *he didn't feel the loss of his mother so keenly* | *investors who have felt the effects of the recession*. ■ [no obj.] (**feel for**) have compassion for: *poor woman—I do feel for her*.
3 [with clause] have a belief or impression, especially without an identifiable reason: *she felt that the woman positively disliked her*. ■ hold an opinion: *I felt I could make a useful contribution*.
▸ noun [usu. in sing.] **1** an act of touching something to examine it. ■ [mass noun] the sense of touch: *he worked by feel rather than using his eyes*.
2 a sensation given by an object or material when touched: *nylon cloth with a cotton feel*. ■ the impression given by something: *a cafe with a cosmopolitan feel*.
– PHRASES **feel one's age** become aware that one is growing older and less energetic. **feel free (to do something)** have no hesitation or shyness (often used as an invitation or for reassurance): *feel free to say what you like*. **feel like (doing) something** be inclined to have or do: *I feel like celebrating*. **feel one's oats** see OAT. **feel the pinch** see PINCH. **feel the pulse of** see PULSE[1]. **feel small** see SMALL. **feel one's way** find one's way by touch rather than sight: *he felt his way back to the stairs*. ■ proceed cautiously, especially in a situation that is unfamiliar: *she was new in the job, still feeling her way*. **get a** (or **the**) **feel for** (or **of**) become accustomed to: *you can explore to get a feel of the place*. **have a feel for** have a sensitive appreciation or an intuitive understanding of: *you have to have a feel for animals*. **make oneself** (or **one's presence**) **felt** have a noticeable effect: *the economic crisis began to make itself felt*.
– ORIGIN Old English *fēlan*, of West Germanic origin; related to Dutch *voelen* and German *fühlen*.

feeler ▸ noun an animal organ such as an antenna or palp that is used for testing things by touch or for searching for food. ■ a tentative proposal intended to ascertain someone's attitude or opinion: *he has already **put out feelers** to local employers*.

feeler gauge ▸ noun a gauge consisting of a number of thin blades for measuring narrow gaps or clearances.

feel-good ▸ adjective [attrib.] causing a feeling of happiness and well-being: *a feel-good movie*.
– PHRASES **feel-good factor** Brit. a widespread feeling of well-being and financial security, especially viewed as a factor in increased consumer spending.
– DERIVATIVES **feel-goodism** noun.

feeling ▸ noun **1** an emotional state or reaction: *a feeling of joy*. ■ (**feelings**) the emotional side of someone's character; emotional responses or tendencies to respond: *I don't want to hurt her feelings*. ■ [mass noun] strong emotion: *'God bless you!' she said with feeling*.

2 an idea or belief, especially a vague or irrational one: [with clause] *he had the feeling that he was being watched.* ■ an attitude or opinion: *a feeling grew that justice had not been done | if you have strong feelings about the proposal, you should contact the Office at once.*
3 [mass noun] the capacity to experience the sense of touch: *a loss of feeling in the hands.* ■ the sensation of touching or being touched by a particular thing: *the feeling of the water against your skin.*
4 (**feeling for**) a sensitivity to or intuitive understanding of: *she says I have a feeling for medicine.*
▸ **adjective** showing emotion or sensitivity: *she was a feeling child.*
– PHRASES **one's better feelings** one's conscience.
– DERIVATIVES **feelingless** adjective.

feelingly ▸ **adverb** (of the expression of a feeling or opinion) in a heartfelt way: *'Thank goodness,' she said feelingly.*

fee simple ▸ **noun** (pl. **fees simple**) Law a permanent and absolute tenure in land with freedom to dispose of it at will, especially (in full **fee simple absolute in possession**) a freehold tenure, which is the main type of land ownership.

feet plural form of FOOT.

fee tail ▸ **noun** (pl. **fees tail**) Law, chiefly historical a type of tenure in land with restrictions (entailments) regarding the line of heirs to whom it may be willed.
– ORIGIN late Middle English: from Anglo-Norman French *fee tailé* (see FEE, TAIL[2]).

feh /fɛ/ ▸ **exclamation** (in Jewish use) conveying disapproval, displeasure, or disgust: *The greatest writer in the English language? Feh!*

Fehling's solution /ˈfeɪlɪŋz/ (also **Fehling's reagent**) ▸ **noun** [mass noun] an alkaline solution of copper(II) sulphate and a tartrate, used in a laboratory test for sugars.
– ORIGIN late 19th cent.: named after the German chemist Hermann von *Fehling* (1812–85).

feign ▸ **verb** [with obj.] pretend to be affected by (a feeling, state, or injury): *she feigned nervousness.*
– ORIGIN Middle English: from Old French *feign-*, stem of *feindre*, from Latin *fingere* 'mould, contrive'. Senses in Middle English (taken from Latin) included 'make something', 'invent a story, excuse, or allegation', hence 'make a pretence of a feeling or response'. Compare with FICTION and FIGMENT.

feigned ▸ **adjective** simulated or pretended; insincere: *her eyes widened with feigned shock.*

feijoa /feɪˈ(d)ʒəʊə, fɛ-, fiː-, -ˈjəʊə/ ▸ **noun** an evergreen shrub or small tree that bears edible green fruit resembling guavas. It is native to tropical South America and cultivated in New Zealand for its fruit.
● Genus *Feijoa*, family Myrtaceae: two species.
■ the fruit of the feijoa.
– ORIGIN late 19th cent.: modern Latin, named after J. da Silva *Feijó* (1760–1824), Brazilian naturalist.

feijoada /feɪˈ(d)ʒwaðə, -də/ ▸ **noun** [mass noun] a Brazilian or Portuguese stew of black beans with pork or other meat and vegetables, served with rice.
– ORIGIN Portuguese, from *feijão*, from Latin *phaseolus* 'bean'.

feint[1] /feɪnt/ ▸ **noun** a deceptive or pretended blow, thrust, or other movement, especially in boxing or fencing: *a brief feint at the opponent's face.* ■ a mock attack or movement in warfare, made in order to distract or deceive an enemy.
▸ **verb** [no obj.] make a deceptive or distracting movement, especially during a fight: *Adam feinted with his right and then swung a left.*
– ORIGIN late 17th cent.: from French *feinte*, past participle (used as a noun) of *feindre* 'feign'.

feint[2] /feɪnt/ ▸ **adjective** denoting paper printed with faint lines as a guide for handwriting.
– ORIGIN mid 19th cent.: variant of FAINT.

feis /fɛʃ/ ▸ **noun** (pl. **feiseanna** /ˈfɛʃənə/) an Irish or Scottish festival of music and dancing.
– ORIGIN Irish *feis*, *fess* 'meeting, assembly'.

feisty /ˈfʌɪsti/ ▸ **adjective** (**feistier**, **feistiest**) informal (of a person, typically one who is relatively small) lively, determined, and courageous: *a love story with a feisty heroine who's more than a pretty face.*
– DERIVATIVES **feistily** adverb, **feistiness** noun.
– ORIGIN late 19th cent.: from earlier *feist*, *fist* 'small dog', from *fisting cur* or *hound*, a derogatory term for a lapdog, from Middle English *fist* 'break wind', of West Germanic origin. Compare with FIZZLE.

felafel /fəˈlaf(ə)l, -ˈlɑː-/ ▸ **noun** variant spelling of FALAFEL.

Feldenkrais method /ˈfɛld(ə)nkrʌɪs/ ▸ **noun** a system designed to promote bodily and mental efficiency and well-being by conscious analysis of neuromuscular activity via exercises which improve flexibility and coordination and increase ease and range of motion.
– ORIGIN 1930s: named after Moshe *Feldenkrais* (1904–84), Russian-born physicist and mechanical engineer.

feldspar /ˈfɛl(d)spɑː/ (also **felspar**) ▸ **noun** [mass noun] an abundant rock-forming mineral typically occurring as colourless or pale-coloured crystals and consisting of aluminosilicates of potassium, sodium, and calcium.
– ORIGIN mid 18th cent.: alteration of German *Feldspat*, *Feldspath*, from *Feld* 'field' + *Spat*, *Spath* 'spar' (see SPAR[3]). The form *felspar* is by mistaken association with German *Fels* 'rock'.

feldspathic /fɛldˈspaθɪk/ ▸ **adjective** Geology (of a mineral or rock) of the nature of or containing feldspar.

feldspathoid /ˈfɛl(d)spəˌθɔɪd/ ▸ **noun** Geology any of a group of minerals chemically similar to feldspar but containing less silica, such as nepheline and leucite.

felicific /ˌfiːlɪˈsɪfɪk/ ▸ **adjective** Philosophy relating to or promoting increased happiness: *the institution of a rule against murder is in general felicific.*
– ORIGIN mid 19th cent.: from Latin *felicificus*, from *felix*, *felic-* 'happy'.

felicitate /fɪˈlɪsɪteɪt/ ▸ **verb** [with obj.] congratulate: *the award winner was felicitated by the cultural association.*
– ORIGIN early 17th cent. (in the sense 'regard as or pronounce happy or fortunate'): from late Latin *felicitat-* 'made happy', from the verb *felicitare*, from Latin *felix*, *felic-* 'happy'.

felicitations ▸ **plural noun** words expressing praise for an achievement or good wishes on a special occasion.

felicitous /fɪˈlɪsɪtəs/ ▸ **adjective** well chosen or suited to the circumstances: *a felicitous phrase.* ■ pleasing and fortunate: *the view was the room's only felicitous feature.*
– DERIVATIVES **felicitously** adverb, **felicitousness** noun.

felicity ▸ **noun** (pl. **felicities**) [mass noun] **1** intense happiness: *domestic felicity.*
2 the ability to find appropriate expression for one's thoughts: *he exposed the kernel of the matter with his customary elegance and felicity.* ■ [count noun] a particularly effective feature of a work of literature or art: *a book full of minor felicities.*
– ORIGIN late Middle English: from Old French *felicite*, from Latin *felicitas*, from *felix*, *felic-* 'happy'.

felid /ˈfiːlɪd/ ▸ **noun** Zoology a mammal of the cat family (Felidae); a wild cat.
– ORIGIN late 19th cent.: from modern Latin *Felidae* (plural), from Latin *feles* 'cat'.

feline /ˈfiːlʌɪn/ ▸ **adjective** relating to or affecting cats or other members of the cat family: *feline leukaemia.* ■ resembling or suggestive of a cat: *he moved with feline grace.*
▸ **noun** a cat or other member of the cat family.
– DERIVATIVES **felinity** noun.
– ORIGIN late 17th cent.: from Latin *felinus*, from *feles* 'cat'.

felix culpa /ˌfiːlɪkɛ ˈkʌlpə, ˌfeɪlɪks, ˈkʊlpɑː/ ▸ **noun** (in Christian theology) the sin of Adam viewed as fortunate, because it brought about the blessedness of the Redemption. ■ an apparent error or disaster with happy consequences.
– ORIGIN Latin, literally 'happy fault'.

Felixstowe /ˈfiːlɪkstəʊ/ a port on the east coast of England, in Suffolk; pop. 31,400 (est. 2009).

fell[1] past of FALL.

fell[2] ▸ **verb** [with obj.] **1** cut down (a tree). ■ knock down: *Whitlock felled him with one punch.*
2 (also **flat-fell**) stitch down (the edge of a seam) to lie flat.
▸ **noun** an amount of timber cut.
– ORIGIN Old English *fellan*, of Germanic origin; related to Dutch *vellen* and German *fällen*, also to FALL.

fell[3] ▸ **noun** a hill or stretch of high moorland, especially in northern England: [in place names] *Cross Fell.*
– ORIGIN Middle English: from Old Norse *fjall*, *fell* 'hill'; probably related to German *Fels* 'rock'.

fell[4] ▸ **adjective** literary of terrible evil or ferocity; deadly: *the fell disease that was threatening her sister.*
– PHRASES **in** (or **at**) **one fell swoop** all in one go: *in one fell swoop they exceeded the total number of tries scored last year.* [from Shakespeare's *Macbeth* (IV. iii. 219).]
– ORIGIN Middle English: from Old French *fel*, nominative of *felon* 'wicked (person)' (see FELON[1]).

fell[5] ▸ **noun** archaic an animal's hide or skin with its hair.
– ORIGIN Old English *fel*, *fell*, of Germanic origin; related to Dutch *vel* and German *Fell*, from an Indo-European root shared by Latin *pellis* and Greek *pella* 'skin'.

fella (also **fellah**) ▸ **noun 1** non-standard spelling of FELLOW, used in representing speech in various dialects: *you can't blame the wee fella.*
2 informal a person's boyfriend or lover: *she took a fancy to her best friend's fella.*

fellah /ˈfɛlə/ ▸ **noun** (pl. **fellahin** /-ˈhiːn/) an Egyptian peasant.
– ORIGIN from Arabic *fallāḥ* 'tiller of the soil', from *falaḥa* 'till the soil'.

fellate /fɛˈleɪt/ ▸ **verb** [with obj.] perform fellatio on (a man).
– ORIGIN late 19th cent.: from Latin *fellat-* 'sucked', from the verb *fellare*.

fellatio /fɛˈleɪʃɪəʊ, -ˈlɑːt-/ ▸ **noun** [mass noun] oral stimulation of a man's penis.
– DERIVATIVES **fellator** /fɛˈleɪtə/ noun.
– ORIGIN late 19th cent.: modern Latin, from Latin *fellare* 'to suck'.

feller[1] ▸ **noun** non-standard spelling of FELLOW, used in representing speech in various dialects.

feller[2] ▸ **noun** a person who cuts down trees.

Fellini /fəˈliːni/, Federico (1920–93), Italian film director. He rose to international fame with *La Strada* (1954), which won an Oscar for best foreign film. Other major films include *La Dolce vita* (1960), a satire on Rome's high society and winner of the Grand Prix at Cannes.

felloes /ˈfɛləʊz/ (also **fellies** /ˈfɛliz/) ▸ **plural noun** the outer rim of a wheel, to which the spokes are fixed.
– ORIGIN Old English *felg* (singular); related to Dutch *velg* and German *Felge*; of unknown ultimate origin.

fellow ▸ **noun 1** informal a man or boy: *he was an extremely obliging fellow.*
2 (usu. **fellows**) a person in the same position, involved in the same activity, or otherwise associated with another: *he was learning with a rapidity unique among his fellows.* ■ a thing of the same kind as or otherwise associated with another: *the page has been torn away from its fellows.*
3 a member of a learned society. ■ Brit. an incorporated senior member of a college: *a tutorial fellow.* ■ (also **research fellow**) an elected graduate receiving a stipend for a period of research. ■ a member of the governing body in some universities.
▸ **adjective** [attrib.] sharing a particular activity, quality, or condition with someone or something: *they urged the troops not to fire on their fellow citizens.*
– ORIGIN late Old English *fēolaga* 'a partner or colleague' (literally 'one who lays down money in a joint enterprise'), from Old Norse *félagi*, from *fé* 'cattle, property, money' + the Germanic base of LAY[1].

fellow feeling ▸ **noun** [mass noun] sympathy and fellowship existing between people based on shared experiences or feelings.

fellowship ▸ **noun 1** [mass noun] friendly association, especially with people who share one's interests: *they valued fun and good fellowship as the cement of the community.* ■ [count noun] a group of people meeting to pursue a shared interest or aim. ■ [count noun] a guild or corporation.
2 the status of a fellow of a college or society: *a fellowship in mathematics.*

fellow-traveller ▸ **noun** a person who travels with another. ■ a person who is not a member of a particular group or political party (especially the Communist Party), but who sympathizes with the group's aims and policies.
– DERIVATIVES **fellow-travelling** adjective.

Fell pony ▸ **noun** a large pony, typically black, of a breed with a long wavy mane and tail.

fell-walking ▸ **noun** [mass noun] the activity of walking or rambling on the fells.
– DERIVATIVES **fell-walker** noun.

felo de se /ˌfiːləʊ deɪ ˈseɪ, ˌfɛ-/ ▸ **noun** (pl. **felos de se**) [mass noun] suicide.
– ORIGIN from Anglo-Latin, literally 'felon of himself'; formerly a criminal act in the UK.

felon[1] /ˈfɛlən/ ▸ **noun** a person who has committed a felony.
▸ **adjective** [attrib.] archaic cruel; wicked.

F

– ORIGIN Middle English: from Old French, literally 'wicked, a wicked person' (oblique case of *fel* 'evil'), from medieval Latin *fello, fellon-*, of unknown origin. Compare with FELON².

felon² /ˈfɛlən/ ▸ **noun** archaic term for WHITLOW.
– ORIGIN Middle English: perhaps a specific use of FELON¹; medieval Latin *fello, fellon-* had the same sense.

felonious /fɛˈləʊnɪəs, fɪ-/ ▸ **adjective** relating to or involved in crime: *they turned their felonious talents to the smuggling trade.* ■ Law relating to or of the nature of felony.
– DERIVATIVES **feloniously** adverb.

felony ▸ **noun** (pl. **felonies**) a crime regarded in the US and many other judicial systems as more serious than a misdemeanour: *he pleaded guilty to six felonies* | [mass noun] *an accusation of felony.*

F

In the US the distinction between felonies and misdemeanours usually depends on the penalties or consequences attaching to the crime. In English law felony originally comprised those offences (murder, wounding, arson, rape, and robbery) for which the penalty included forfeiture of land and goods. Forfeiture was abolished in 1870, and in 1967 felonies and misdemeanours were replaced by indictable and non-indictable offences.

– ORIGIN Middle English: from Old French *felonie*, from *felon* (see FELON¹).

felsic /ˈfɛlsɪk/ ▸ **adjective** Geology relating to or denoting a group of light-coloured minerals including feldspar, feldspathoids, quartz, and muscovite. Often contrasted with MAFIC.
– ORIGIN early 20th cent.: from FELDSPAR + a contraction of SILICA.

felspar /ˈfɛlspɑː/ ▸ **noun** variant spelling of FELDSPAR.

felt¹ ▸ **noun** [mass noun] a kind of cloth made by rolling and pressing wool or another suitable textile accompanied by the application of moisture or heat, which causes the constituent fibres to mat together to create a smooth surface.
▸ **verb** [with obj.] **1** make into felt; mat together. ■ [no obj.] become matted: *care must be taken in washing, or the wool will shrink and felt.*
2 cover with felt: (as adj. **felted**) *a felted roof.*
– DERIVATIVES **felty** adjective.
– ORIGIN Old English, of West Germanic origin; related to Dutch *vilt*, also to FILTER.

felt² past and past participle of FEEL.

felt-tip pen (also **felt-tipped pen** or **felt tip**) ▸ **noun** a pen with a writing point made of felt or other tightly packed fibres.

felucca /fɛˈlʌkə/ ▸ **noun** a small boat propelled by oars or lateen sails or both, used on the Nile and formerly more widely in the Mediterranean region.
– ORIGIN early 17th cent.: from Italian *feluc(c)a*, probably from obsolete Spanish *faluca*, of Arabic origin.

felwort /ˈfɛlwəːt/ ▸ **noun** a European gentian of dry grassland, which produces mauve flowers in the autumn. ● *Gentianella amarella*, family Gentianaceae.
– ORIGIN Old English *feldwyrt* (see FIELD, WORT).

fem ▸ **noun** variant spelling of FEMME.

FEMA ▸ **abbreviation** (in the US) Federal Emergency Management Agency.

female ▸ **adjective** of or denoting the sex that can bear offspring or produce eggs, distinguished biologically by the production of gametes (ova) which can be fertilized by male gametes: *a herd of female deer.* ■ relating to or characteristic of women or female animals: *a female audience* | *female names.* ■ (of a plant or flower) having a pistil but no stamens. ■ (of parts of machinery, fittings, etc.) manufactured hollow so that a corresponding male part can be inserted.
▸ **noun** a female person, animal, or plant.
– PHRASES **the female of the species** humorous women or a woman: *it was one of those subtle hints that the female of the species sometimes use.*
– DERIVATIVES **femaleness** noun.
– ORIGIN Middle English: from Old French *femelle*, from Latin *femella*, diminutive of *femina* 'a woman'. The change in the ending was due to association with MALE, but the words *male* and *female* are not linked etymologically.

female circumcision ▸ **noun** see CIRCUMCISION.

female condom ▸ **noun** a contraceptive device made of thin rubber, inserted into a woman's vagina before sexual intercourse.

feme covert /fiːm ˈkʌvət/ ▸ **noun** Law, historical a married woman.
– ORIGIN early 16th cent.: from Anglo-Norman French, literally 'a woman covered (i.e. protected by marriage)'.

feme sole /fiːm ˈsəʊl/ (also **femme sole**) ▸ **noun** Law, historical a woman without a husband, especially one that is divorced.
– ORIGIN early 16th cent.: from Anglo-Norman French *feme soule* 'a woman alone'.

feminal /ˈfɛmɪn(ə)l/ ▸ **adjective** archaic relating to a woman.
– DERIVATIVES **feminality** noun.
– ORIGIN late Middle English: from medieval Latin *feminalis*, from Latin *femina* 'woman'.

feminazi /ˈfɛmɪnɑːtʃi/ ▸ **noun** (pl. **feminazis**) derogatory a radical feminist.
– ORIGIN 1990s: blend of FEMINIST and NAZI.

femineity /ˌfɛmɪˈniːɪti, -ˈneɪɪti/ ▸ **noun** [mass noun] archaic the quality of being feminine.
– ORIGIN early 19th cent.: from Latin *femineus* 'womanish' (from *femina* 'woman') + -ITY.

feminine ▸ **adjective 1** having qualities or an appearance traditionally associated with women, especially delicacy and prettiness: *the snowdrops gave a feminine touch to the table.* ■ relating to women; female: *he enjoys feminine company.*
2 Grammar of or denoting a gender of nouns and adjectives, conventionally regarded as female.
▸ **noun** (**the feminine**) **1** the female sex or gender: *the association of the arts with the feminine.*
2 Grammar a feminine word or form.
– DERIVATIVES **femininely** adverb.
– ORIGIN late Middle English: from Latin *femininus*, from *femina* 'woman'.

feminine rhyme ▸ **noun** Prosody a rhyme between stressed syllables followed by one or more unstressed syllables (e.g. *stocking/shocking, glamorous/amorous*). Compare with MASCULINE RHYME.

femininity ▸ **noun** [mass noun] the quality of being female; womanliness: *she celebrates her femininity by wearing make-up and high heels.*

feminism ▸ **noun** [mass noun] the advocacy of women's rights on the ground of the equality of the sexes.

The issue of rights for women first became prominent during the French and American revolutions in the late 18th century. In Britain it was not until the emergence of the suffragette movement in the late 19th century that there was significant political change. A 'second wave' of feminism arose in the 1960s, with an emphasis on unity and sisterhood; seminal figures included Betty Friedan and Germaine Greer.

– ORIGIN late 19th cent.: from French *féminisme*.

feminist ▸ **noun** a person who supports feminism.
▸ **adjective** relating to or supporting feminism: *feminist literature.*
– ORIGIN late 19th cent.: from French *féministe*, from Latin *femina* 'woman'.

feminity ▸ **noun** rare femininity.
– ORIGIN late Middle English: from Old French *feminite*, from medieval Latin *feminitas*, from Latin *femina* 'woman'.

feminize (also **feminise**) ▸ **verb** [with obj.] make (something) more characteristic of or associated with women: *as office roles changed, clerical work was increasingly feminized.* ■ induce female sexual characteristics in (a male).
– DERIVATIVES **feminization** noun.

femme /fɛm/ (also **fem**) ▸ **noun** informal a lesbian who takes a traditionally feminine sexual role. Often contrasted with BUTCH.
– ORIGIN 1960s: French, 'woman'.

femme fatale /ˌfam fəˈtɑːl/ ▸ **noun** (pl. **femmes fatales** pronunc. **same**) an attractive and seductive woman, especially one who will ultimately cause distress to a man who becomes involved with her.
– ORIGIN early 20th cent.: French, literally 'disastrous woman'.

femme sole ▸ **noun** variant spelling of FEME SOLE.

femto- /ˈfɛmtəʊ/ ▸ **combining form** (used in units of measurement) denoting a factor of 10^{-15}: *femtosecond.*
– ORIGIN from Danish or Norwegian *femten* 'fifteen'.

femur /ˈfiːmə/ ▸ **noun** (pl. **femurs** or **femora** /ˈfɛm(ə)rə/) **1** Anatomy the bone of the thigh or upper hindlimb, articulating at the hip and the knee.
2 Zoology the third segment of the leg in insects and some other arthropods, typically the longest and thickest segment.
– DERIVATIVES **femoral** /ˈfɛm(ə)r(ə)l/ adjective.
– ORIGIN late 15th cent.: from Latin *femur, femor-* 'thigh'.

fen¹ ▸ **noun** a low and marshy or frequently flooded area of land: *a native species of fens and damp meadows* | [mass noun] *55 acres of fen.* ■ (**the Fens**) the flat low-lying areas of eastern England, mainly in Lincolnshire, Cambridgeshire, and Norfolk, formerly marshland but largely drained for agriculture since the 17th century. ■ [mass noun] Ecology wetland with alkaline, neutral, or only slightly acid peaty soil. Compare with BOG.
– DERIVATIVES **fenny** adjective.
– ORIGIN Old English *fen(n)*, of Germanic origin; related to Dutch *veen* and German *Fenn*.

fen² ▸ **noun** (pl. **same**) a monetary unit of China, equal to one hundredth of a yuan.
– ORIGIN from Chinese *fēn* 'a hundredth part'.

fenberry ▸ **noun** (pl. **fenberries**) another term for CRANBERRY.

fence ▸ **noun 1** a barrier, railing, or other upright structure, typically of wood or wire, enclosing an area of ground to prevent or control access or escape. ■ a large upright obstacle in steeplechasing, showjumping, or cross-country.
2 a guard or guide on a plane, saw, or other tool.
3 informal a person who deals in stolen goods.
▸ **verb** [with obj.] **1** surround or protect with a fence: *our garden was not fully fenced.* ■ (**fence something in/off**) enclose or separate an area with a fence: *a small plantation of young trees had been fenced off.* ■ (**fence someone/thing out**) use a barrier to exclude someone or something: *walkers may find themselves fenced out of the moor.*
2 informal buy or sell (stolen goods).
3 [no obj.] engage in the sport of fencing. ■ conduct a discussion or argument in an evasive way: *twelve months of fencing with McLaren had taken a toll his nerves.*
– PHRASES **mend (one's) fences** see MEND. **over the fence** Austral./NZ informal unreasonable or unacceptable. **side of the fence** used to refer to either of the opposing positions or interests involved in a particular situation: *whatever side of the fence you are on, the debate on conventional versus organic farming is not going to disappear.* **sit on the fence** avoid making a decision or choice.
– DERIVATIVES **fenceless** adjective, **fencer** noun.
– ORIGIN Middle English (in the sense 'defending, defence'): shortening of DEFENCE. Compare with FENCIBLE and FEND.

fence post ▸ **noun** a timber or metal post set in the ground as a supporting part of a fence.

fencerow /ˈfɛnsrəʊ/ ▸ **noun** N. Amer. an uncultivated strip of land on each side of and below a fence.

fencible /ˈfɛnsɪb(ə)l/ ▸ **noun** (usu. **fencibles**) historical a soldier belonging to a British militia which could be called up only for service on home soil.
– ORIGIN Middle English (in the sense 'fit or suitable for defence'): shortening of DEFENSIBLE. Compare with FENCE, FEND.

fencing ▸ **noun** [mass noun] **1** the sport of fighting with swords, especially foils, épées, or sabres, according to a set of rules, in order to score points against an opponent. ■ the action of conducting a discussion or argument in an evasive way.
2 a series of fences: *security fencing.* ■ material used for the construction of fences: *chestnut is still in demand for fencing.* ■ the erection of fences. ■ the jumping of fences by a racehorse.

fend ▸ **verb 1** [no obj.] (**fend for oneself**) look after and provide for oneself, without any help from others: *she left her 14-year-old daughter to fend for herself.*
2 [with obj.] (**fend someone/thing off**) defend oneself from a blow, attack, or attacker: *Meredith tried frantically to fend him off* | figurative *he fended off the awkward questions.*
– ORIGIN Middle English (in the sense 'defend'): shortening of DEFEND. Compare with FENCE and FENCIBLE.

Fender /ˈfɛndə/, Leo (1907–91), American guitar-maker. He pioneered the production of electric guitars, designing the first solid-body electric guitar to be widely available.

fender ▸ **noun 1** a low frame bordering a fireplace to prevent burning coals from falling out.
2 a plastic cylinder, tyre, piece of old rope or matting, etc., hung over a ship's side to protect it against impact.
3 N. Amer. the mudguard or area around the wheel well of a vehicle.

fender bender ▸ **noun** N. Amer. informal a minor collision between motor vehicles.

fenestella /ˌfɛnɪˈstɛlə/ ▶ **noun** Architecture a niche in a wall south of a church's altar, holding the piscina and often the credence.
– ORIGIN late Middle English: from Latin, diminutive of *fenestra* 'window'.

fenestra /fɪˈnɛstrə/ ▶ **noun** (pl. **fenestrae** /-triː/)
1 Anatomy & Zoology a small natural hole or opening, especially in a bone. The mammalian middle ear is linked by the **fenestra ovalis** to the vestibule of the inner ear, and by the **fenestra rotunda** to the cochlea.
2 Medicine an artificial opening. ■ an opening in a bandage or cast. ■ a perforation in a forceps blade. ■ a hole made by surgical fenestration.
– ORIGIN early 19th cent. (as a botanical term denoting a small scar left by the separation of the seed from the ovary): from Latin, literally 'window'.

fenestrate /ˈfɛnəstrət, fɪˈnɛstrət/ ▶ **adjective** Botany & Zoology having small window-like perforations or transparent areas.
– ORIGIN mid 19th cent.: from Latin *fenestratus* 'provided with openings', from the verb *fenestrare*.

fenestrated /ˈfɛnəˌstreɪtɪd, fɪˈnɛstreɪtɪd/ ▶ **adjective**
1 provided with a window or windows: *the fenestrated heights of nearby buildings*.
2 chiefly Anatomy having perforations, apertures, or transparent areas: *the capillaries have a fenestrated epithelium*.
– ORIGIN early 19th cent.: from Latin *fenestrare* (see **FENESTRATE**) + **-ED1**.

fenestration /ˌfɛnɪˈstreɪʃ(ə)n/ ▶ **noun** [mass noun]
1 Architecture the arrangement of windows in a building.
2 Botany & Zoology the condition of being fenestrate.
3 Medicine a surgical operation in which a new opening is formed, especially in the bony labyrinth of the inner ear to treat certain types of deafness.

fen-fire ▶ **noun** a will-o'-the-wisp.

feng shui /ˌfɛŋ ˈʃuːi, ˌfʌŋ ˈʃweɪ/ ▶ **noun** [mass noun] (in Chinese thought) a system of laws considered to govern spatial arrangement and orientation in relation to the flow of energy (*chi*), and whose favourable or unfavourable effects are taken into account when siting and designing buildings.
– ORIGIN Chinese, from *fēng* 'wind' and *shuǐ* 'water'.

Fenian /ˈfiːnɪən/ ▶ **noun** **1** a member of the Irish Republican Brotherhood, a 19th-century revolutionary nationalist organization among the Irish in the US and Ireland. The Fenians staged an unsuccessful revolt in Ireland in 1867 and were responsible for isolated revolutionary acts against the British until the early 20th century, when they were gradually eclipsed by the IRA.
2 informal, offensive (chiefly in Northern Ireland) a Protestant name for a Catholic.
– DERIVATIVES **Fenianism** noun.
– ORIGIN from Old Irish *féne*, the name of an ancient Irish people, confused with *fiann, fianna* (see **FIANNA FÁIL**).

fening /ˈfɛnɪŋ/ ▶ **noun** (pl. **same**, **fenings**, or **feninga** /ˈfɛnɪŋə/) a monetary unit of Bosnia and Herzegovina, equal to one hundredth of a marka.
– ORIGIN Bosnian *feninga*, from **PFENNIG**.

fenland ▶ **noun** [mass noun] (also **fenlands**) land consisting of fens: *thousands of acres of fenland*. ■ (usu. **the Fenland**) the Fens of eastern England.

fennec /ˈfɛnɛk/ (also **fennec fox**) ▶ **noun** a small pale fox with large pointed ears, native to the deserts of North Africa and Arabia. ● *Vulpes zerda*, family Canidae.
– ORIGIN late 18th cent.: via Arabic from Persian *fanak, fanaj*.

fennel /ˈfɛn(ə)l/ ▶ **noun** [mass noun] an aromatic yellow-flowered European plant of the parsley family, with feathery leaves. ● *Foeniculum vulgare*, family Umbelliferae: two subspecies, a hardy perennial (*dulce*), the seeds and leaves of which are used as culinary herbs, and the annual **Florence** (or **sweet**) **fennel** (*azoricum*), with swollen leaf bases which are eaten as a vegetable.
– ORIGIN Old English *finule, fenol*, from Latin *faeniculum*, diminutive of *faenum* 'hay'.

Fennoscandia /ˌfɛnəʊˈskandɪə/ a land mass in NW Europe comprising Scandinavia, Finland, and the adjacent area of NE Russia.

fentanyl /ˈfɛntənʌɪl, -nɪl/ ▶ **noun** [mass noun] Medicine a synthetic opiate drug which is a powerful painkiller and tranquillizer.
– ORIGIN 1960s: apparently from *fen-* (representing **PHEN-**) + *-t-* + *an-* + **-YL**.

fenugreek /ˈfɛnjʊɡriːk/ ▶ **noun** [mass noun] a white-flowered herbaceous plant of the pea family, with aromatic seeds that are used for flavouring, especially ground and used in curry powder. ● *Trigonella foenum-graecum*, family Leguminosae.
– ORIGIN Old English *fenogrecum* (superseded in Middle English by forms from Old French *fenugrec*), from Latin *faenugraecum*, from *faenum graecum* 'Greek hay' (the Romans used the dried plant as fodder).

feodary /ˈfjuːdəri/ ▶ **noun** (pl. **feodaries**) historical a feudal tenant.

feoffee /fɛˈfiː, fiː-/ ▶ **noun** a trustee invested with a freehold estate to hold in possession for a purpose, typically a charitable one. ■ historical (in feudal law) a person to whom a grant of freehold property is made.
– ORIGIN late Middle English: from Anglo-Norman French *feoffe* 'enfeoffed', past participle of *feoffer*, variant of Old French *fieffer* (see **FEOFFMENT**).

feoffment /ˈfiːfm(ə)nt, ˈfɛf-/ ▶ **noun** historical (in feudal law) a grant of ownership of freehold property to someone.
– DERIVATIVES **feoffor** /ˈfɛfə/ **noun**.
– ORIGIN Middle English: from an Anglo-Norman French variant of Old French *fieffer* 'put in legal possession', from *fief* (see **FEE** and **FIEF**).

feral /ˈfɛr(ə)l, ˈfɪə-/ ▶ **adjective** (especially of an animal) in a wild state, especially after escape from captivity or domestication: *a feral cat*. ■ resembling or characteristic of a wild animal: *a feral snarl* | *feral youths*.
– ORIGIN early 17th cent.: from Latin *fera* 'wild animal' (from *ferus* 'wild') + **-AL**.

feral pigeon ▶ **noun** see **PIGEON1** (sense 1).

ferberite /ˈfəːbərʌɪt/ ▶ **noun** [mass noun] a black mineral consisting of ferrous tungstate, typically occurring as elongated prisms.
– ORIGIN early 19th cent.: named after Rudolph *Ferber* (1743–90), Swedish mineralogist, + **-ITE1**.

fer de lance /ˌfɛː də ˈlɑːns/ ▶ **noun** (pl. **fers de lance** pronunc. **same** or **fer de lances**) a large and dangerous pit viper native to Central and South America. ● Genus *Bothrops*, family Viperidae: several species, in particular *B. atrox*.
– ORIGIN late 19th cent.: from French, literally 'iron (head) of a lance'.

Ferdinand /ˈfəːdɪnənd/ of Aragon (1452–1516), king of Castile 1474–1516 and of Aragon 1479–1516; known as **Ferdinand the Catholic**. His marriage to Isabella of Castile in 1469 ensured his accession (as Ferdinand V) to the throne of Castile with her. Ferdinand subsequently succeeded to the throne of Aragon (as Ferdinand II) and was joined as monarch by Isabella. They instituted the Spanish Inquisition in 1478 and supported Columbus's expedition in 1492. Their capture of Granada from the Moors in the same year effectively united Spain as one country.

feretory /ˈfɛrət(ə)ri/ ▶ **noun** (pl. **feretories**) rare a portable shrine containing the relics of a saint. ■ a chapel containing such a shrine.
– ORIGIN Middle English: from Old French *fiertre*, via Latin from Greek *pheretron* 'bier', from *pherein* 'bear, carry'.

Ferguson /ˈfəːɡəs(ə)n/, Sir Alex (b.1941), Scottish football manager and footballer; full name *Alexander Chapman Ferguson*. He became manager of Manchester United in 1986: he took them to a seventh Premier League Championship in 2001, and in 1999 won it as part of a treble with the FA Cup and the European Champions League.

feria /ˈfɛrɪə/ ▶ **noun** (in Spain and Spanish-speaking America) a fair.
– ORIGIN Spanish, from Latin, literally 'holiday'.

ferial /ˈfɪərɪəl, ˈfɛ-/ ▶ **adjective** Christian Church denoting an ordinary weekday, as opposed to one appointed for a festival or fast.
– ORIGIN late Middle English: from medieval Latin *ferialis*, from Latin *feria* 'holiday'. In late Latin *feria* was used with a prefixed ordinal number to mean 'day of the week' (e.g. *secunda feria* 'second day, Monday'), but Sunday (Dominicus) and Saturday (Sabbatum) were usually referred to by their names; hence *feria* came to mean 'ordinary weekday'.

feringhee /fəˈrɪŋɡi/ (also **feringhi**) ▶ **noun** **1** chiefly derogatory (in India and other parts of Asia) a foreigner, especially one with white skin.
2 archaic a person of Indian–Portuguese parentage.
– ORIGIN via Urdu from Persian *firangī*, from the base of **FRANK2**.

Ferlinghetti /ˌfəːlɪŋˈɡɛti/, Lawrence (Monsanto) (b.1919), American poet and publisher; born *Lawrence Ferling*. Identified with San Francisco's beat movement, he founded the publishing house City Lights, which produced works such as Allen Ginsberg's *Howl* (1957). Notable works: *A Coney Island of the Mind* (1958).

Ferm. ▶ **abbreviation** Fermanagh.

Fermanagh /fəˈmanə/ one of the Six Counties of Northern Ireland, since 1973 an administrative district; chief town, Enniskillen.

Fermat /ˈfəːmɑː/, French /fɛʀma/, Pierre de (1601–65), French mathematician. His work on curves led directly to the general methods of calculus introduced by Newton and Leibniz. He is also recognized as the founder of the theory of numbers.

fermata /fəːˈmɑːtə/ ▶ **noun** Music a pause of unspecified length on a note or rest. ■ a sign indicating a prolonged note or rest.
– ORIGIN Italian, from *fermare* 'to stop'.

Fermat's last theorem ▶ **noun** Mathematics a conjecture by Fermat that if *n* is an integer greater than 2, the equation *xn* + *yn* = *zn* has no positive integral solutions. Fermat noted that he had 'a truly wonderful proof' of the conjecture, but never wrote it down. In 1995 a general proof was published by the Princeton-based British mathematician Andrew Wiles.

ferment ▶ **verb** /fəˈmɛnt/ **1** [no obj.] (of a substance) undergo fermentation: *the drink had fermented, turning some of the juice into alcohol*. ■ [with obj.] cause the fermentation of (a substance).
2 [with obj.] incite or stir up (trouble or disorder): *the politicians and warlords who are fermenting this chaos*.
▶ **noun** /ˈfəːmɛnt/ **1** [mass noun] agitation and excitement among a group of people, typically concerning major change and leading to trouble or violence: *a period of political and religious ferment*.
2 archaic a fermenting agent or enzyme.
– DERIVATIVES **fermentable** adjective.
– ORIGIN late Middle English: from Old French *ferment* (noun), *fermenter* (verb), based on Latin *fermentum* 'yeast', from *fervere* 'to boil'.

fermentation ▶ **noun** [mass noun] **1** the chemical breakdown of a substance by bacteria, yeasts, or other microorganisms, typically involving effervescence and the giving off of heat. ■ the process of this kind involved in the making of beers, wines, and spirits, in which sugars are converted to ethyl alcohol.
2 archaic agitation; excitement: *I had found Paris in high fermentation*.
– DERIVATIVES **fermentative** adjective.
– ORIGIN late Middle English: from late Latin *fermentatio(n-)*, from Latin *fermentare* 'to ferment' (see **FERMENT**).

fermenter (US also **fermentor**) ▶ **noun** a container in which fermentation takes place. ■ an organism which causes fermentation.

Fermi /ˈfəːmi, ˈfɛːmi/, Italian /ˈfermi/, Enrico (1901–54), Italian-born American atomic physicist, who directed the first controlled nuclear chain reaction in 1942. Nobel Prize for Physics (1938).

fermi /ˈfəːmi/ ▶ **noun** (pl. **same**) a unit of length equal to 10^{-15} metre (one femtometre), used in nuclear physics. It is similar to the diameter of a proton.
– ORIGIN early 20th cent.: named after E. **FERMI**.

Fermi–Dirac statistics ▶ **plural noun** [treated as sing.] Physics a type of quantum statistics used to describe systems of fermions.
– ORIGIN 1920s: named after E. **FERMI** and P. A. M. **DIRAC**.

fermion /ˈfəːmɪɒn/ ▶ **noun** Physics a subatomic particle, such as a nucleon, which has half-integral spin and follows the statistical description given by Fermi and Dirac.
– ORIGIN 1940s: from the name of E. **FERMI** + **-ON**.

fermium /ˈfəːmɪəm/ ▶ **noun** [mass noun] the chemical element of atomic number 100, a radioactive metal of the actinide series. Fermium does not occur naturally and was discovered in 1953 in the debris of the first hydrogen bomb explosion. (Symbol: **Fm**)
– ORIGIN 1950s: from the name of E. **FERMI** + **-IUM**.

fern ▶ **noun** (pl. **same** or **ferns**) a flowerless plant which has feathery or leafy fronds and reproduces by spores released from the undersides of the fronds. Ferns have a vascular system for the transport of water and nutrients. ● Class Filicopsida, division Pteridophyta.
– DERIVATIVES **fernery** noun (pl. **ferneries**), **ferny** adjective.
– ORIGIN Old English *fearn*, of West Germanic origin; related to Dutch *varen* and German *Farn*.

Fernando Póo /fəˌnandəʊ ˈpəʊ/ former name (until 1973) for **Bioko**.

fernbird ▶ noun a secretive warbler found only in New Zealand, with dark streaked plumage. ● *Megalurus punctatus*, family Sylviidae.

fernbrake ▶ noun a bed or thicket of ferns.
– ORIGIN Old English *fearnbraca* (plural): see **FERN**, **BRAKE**[4].

ferocious ▶ adjective savagely fierce, cruel, or violent: *a ferocious beast* | *a ferocious battle*. ■ informal very great; extreme: *a ferocious headache*.
– DERIVATIVES **ferociously** adverb, **ferociousness** noun.
– ORIGIN mid 17th cent.: from Latin *ferox*, *feroc-* 'fierce' + **-IOUS**.

ferocity ▶ noun (pl. **ferocities**) [mass noun] the state or quality of being ferocious: *the ferocity of the storm caught them by surprise* | [count noun] *she hated him with a ferocity that astonished her*.
– ORIGIN mid 16th cent.: from French, or from Latin *ferocitas*, from *ferox*, *feroc-* 'fierce'.

-ferous (usu. **-iferous**) ▶ combining form having, bearing, or containing (a specified thing): *Carboniferous* | *pestiferous*.
– DERIVATIVES **-ferously** combining form in corresponding adverbs, **-ferousness** combining form in corresponding nouns.
– ORIGIN from French *-fère* or Latin *-fer* 'producing', from *ferre* 'to bear'.

ferox /ˈfɛrɒks/ (also **ferox trout**) ▶ noun a brown trout of a very large variety, occurring in large deep lakes in NW Europe.
– ORIGIN mid 19th cent.: from modern Latin *Salmo ferox*, literally 'fierce salmon', former name of the variety.

Ferranti /fəˈranti/, Sebastian Ziani de (1864–1930), English electrical engineer. He was one of the pioneers of electricity generation and distribution in Britain, his chief contribution being the use of high voltages for economical transmission over a distance.

Ferrara /fəˈrɑːrə/, Italian /ferˈrara/ a city in northern Italy, capital of a province of the same name; pop. 130,486 (est. 2009). Ferrara grew to prominence in the 13th century under the rule of the powerful Este family.

Ferrari /fəˈrɑːri/, Italian /ferˈrari/, Enzo (1898–1988), Italian car designer and manufacturer. In 1929 he founded the company named after him, producing a range of high-quality sports and racing cars. Since the early 1950s Ferraris have won more world championship Grands Prix than any other car.

ferrate /ˈfɛreɪt/ ▶ noun Chemistry a salt in which the anion contains both iron (typically ferric iron) and oxygen.
– ORIGIN mid 19th cent.: from Latin *ferrum* 'iron' + **-ATE**[1].

Ferrel's law /ˈfɛrəlz/ ▶ noun Meteorology a law stating that Coriolis forces deflect winds and freely moving objects to the right in the northern hemisphere and to the left in the southern hemisphere.
– ORIGIN early 20th cent.: named after William *Ferrel* (1817–91), American meteorologist.

ferret /ˈfɛrɪt/ ▶ noun **1** a domesticated polecat used chiefly for catching rabbits. It is typically albino in coloration, but sometimes brown. See **POLECAT-FERRET**. ● *Mustela furo*, family Mustelidae; descended mainly from the European polecat.
2 an assiduous search for something: *he had a quick ferret around*.
▶ verb (**ferrets**, **ferreting**, **ferreted**) **1** [no obj.] (of a person) hunt with ferrets, typically for rabbits: (as noun **ferreting**) *ferreting is increasing in popularity*. ■ [with obj.] clear (a hole or area of ground) of rabbits with ferrets.
2 [no obj.] rummage about in a place or container in search of something: *he shambled over to the desk and ferreted around*. ■ [with obj.] (**ferret something out**) discover information by means of an assiduous search or investigation: *she had the ability to ferret out the facts*.
– DERIVATIVES **ferreter** noun, **ferrety** adjective.
– ORIGIN late Middle English: from Old French *fuiret*, alteration of *fuiron*, based on late Latin *furo* 'thief, ferret', from Latin *fur* 'thief'.

ferret-badger ▶ noun a small tree-climbing badger found in SE Asia, having a long tail and a brownish coat with conspicuous facial markings. ● Genus *Melogale*, family Mustelidae: three species.

ferri- /ˈfɛri/ ▶ combining form Chemistry of iron with a valency of three; ferric. Compare with **FERRO-**.
– ORIGIN from Latin *ferrum* 'iron'.

ferriage /ˈfɛrɪɪdʒ/ ▶ noun [mass noun] archaic the action of transporting someone or something by ferry. ■ the fare paid for a journey by ferry.

ferric /ˈfɛrɪk/ ▶ adjective relating to iron. ■ Chemistry of iron with a valency of three; of iron(III). Compare with **FERROUS**.
– ORIGIN late 18th cent.: from Latin *ferrum* 'iron' + **-IC**.

ferricyanide ▶ noun Chemistry a salt containing the anion $Fe(CN)_6^{3-}$.

ferrimagnetic ▶ adjective Physics (of a substance) displaying a weak form of ferromagnetism associated with parallel but opposite alignment of neighbouring atoms. In contrast with antiferromagnetic materials, these alignments do not cancel out and there is a net magnetic moment.
– DERIVATIVES **ferrimagnetism** noun.

Ferris wheel /ˈfɛrɪs/ ▶ noun a fairground ride consisting of a giant vertical revolving wheel with passenger cars suspended on its outer edge.
– ORIGIN late 19th cent.: named after George *Ferris* (1859–96), the American engineer who invented it.

ferrite /ˈfɛrʌɪt/ ▶ noun [mass noun] **1** a ceramic compound consisting of a mixed oxide of iron and one or more other metals which has ferrimagnetic properties and is used in high-frequency electrical components such as aerials.
2 Metallurgy a form of pure iron with a body-centred cubic crystal structure, occurring in low-carbon steel.
– DERIVATIVES **ferritic** /fɛˈrɪtɪk/ adjective (sense 2).
– ORIGIN mid 19th cent.: from Latin *ferrum* 'iron' + **-ITE**[1].

ferritin /ˈfɛrɪtɪn/ ▶ noun [mass noun] Biochemistry a protein produced in mammalian metabolism which serves to store iron in the tissues.
– ORIGIN 1930s: from **FERRI-** + *-t-* (for ease of pronunciation) + **-IN**[1].

ferro- /ˈfɛrəʊ/ ▶ combining form containing iron: *ferroconcrete*. ■ Chemistry of iron with a valency of two; ferrous. Compare with **FERRI-**.
– ORIGIN from Latin *ferrum* 'iron'.

ferrocene /ˈfɛrəsiːn/ ▶ noun Chemistry an orange crystalline compound whose molecule has a sandwich structure in which two planar cyclic hydrocarbon ligands enclose an iron atom. ● Chem. formula: $Fe(C_5H_5)_2$.
– ORIGIN 1950s: from **FERRO-** 'containing iron' + *-cene* from *c(yclopentadi)ene*.

ferroconcrete ▶ noun [mass noun] [often as modifier] concrete reinforced with steel: *a ferroconcrete storage tank*.

ferrocyanide ▶ noun Chemistry a salt containing the anion $Fe(CN)_6^{4-}$.

ferroelectric Physics ▶ adjective (of a substance) exhibiting permanent electric polarization which varies in strength with the applied electric field.
▶ noun a ferroelectric substance.
– DERIVATIVES **ferroelectricity** noun.

ferrofluid ▶ noun [often as modifier] a fluid containing a magnetic suspension: *ferrofluid cooling*.

ferromagnesian /ˌfɛrə(ʊ)magˈniːʒ(ə)n, -zɪən/ ▶ adjective Geology (of a rock or mineral) containing iron and magnesium as major components.

ferromagnetic ▶ adjective Physics (of a body or substance) having a high susceptibility to magnetization, the strength of which depends on that of the applied magnetizing field, and which may persist after removal of the applied field. This is the kind of magnetism displayed by iron, and is associated with parallel magnetic alignment of neighbouring atoms.
– DERIVATIVES **ferromagnetism** noun.

ferrous /ˈfɛrəs/ ▶ adjective **1** (chiefly of metals) containing or consisting of iron.
2 Chemistry of iron with a valency of two; of iron(II). Compare with **FERRIC**.
– ORIGIN mid 19th cent.: from Latin *ferrum* 'iron' + **-OUS**.

ferrous sulphate ▶ noun [mass noun] a pale green iron salt used in inks, tanning, water purification, and treating anaemia. ● Alternative name: **iron(II) sulphate**; chem. formula (crystals): $FeSO_4.7H_2O$.

ferruginous /fɛˈruːdʒɪnəs/ ▶ adjective containing iron oxides or rust: *a band of ferruginous limestone*. ■ reddish brown; rust-coloured: *the ferruginous earth of southern Brazil*.
– ORIGIN mid 17th cent.: from Latin *ferrugo*, *ferrugin-* 'rust, dark red' (from *ferrum* 'iron') + **-OUS**.

ferruginous duck ▶ noun a Eurasian diving duck related to the pochard, the male of which has mainly dark red-brown breeding plumage. ● *Aythya nyroca*, family Anatidae.

ferrule /ˈfɛruːl, ˈfɛr(ə)l/ ▶ noun a ring or cap, typically a metal one, which strengthens the end of a handle, stick, or tube and prevents it from splitting or wearing. ■ a metal band strengthening or forming a joint.
– ORIGIN early 17th cent.: alteration (probably by association with Latin *ferrum* 'iron') of obsolete *verrel*, from Old French *virelle*, from Latin *viriola*, diminutive of *viriae* 'bracelets'.

ferry ▶ noun (pl. **ferries**) (also **ferry boat**) a boat or ship for conveying passengers and goods, especially over a relatively short distance and as a regular service. ■ a service using another mode of transport, especially aircraft, to convey passengers or goods.
▶ verb (**ferries**, **ferrying**, **ferried**) [with obj. and adverbial of direction] convey by ferry or other mode of transport, especially on short or regular trips: *the British Expeditionary Force was safely ferried across the Channel* | *ambulances ferried the injured to hospital*.
– DERIVATIVES **ferryman** noun (pl. **ferrymen**).
– ORIGIN Middle English: from Old Norse *ferja* 'ferry boat', of Germanic origin and related to **FARE**.

fertile /ˈfəːtʌɪl/ ▶ adjective **1** (of soil or land) producing or capable of producing abundant vegetation or crops: *the fertile coastal plain*. ■ producing many new and inventive ideas: *her fertile imagination*. ■ (of a situation) encouraging a particular activity or feeling: *conditions at the time provided **fertile ground** for revolutionary movements*.
2 (of a person, animal, or plant) able to conceive young or produce seed. ■ (of a seed or egg) capable of becoming a new individual. ■ Physics (of nuclear material) able to become fissile by the capture of neutrons.
– ORIGIN late Middle English: via French from Latin *fertilis*, from *ferre* 'to bear'.

Fertile Crescent a crescent-shaped area of fertile land in the Middle East extending from the eastern Mediterranean coast through the valley of the Tigris and Euphrates Rivers to the Persian Gulf. It was the centre of the Neolithic development of agriculture (from 7000 BC), and the cradle of the Assyrian, Sumerian, and Babylonian civilizations.

fertility ▶ noun [mass noun] the quality of being fertile; productiveness: *improve the soil fertility by adding compost*. ■ the ability to conceive children or young: *anxiety and stress affect fertility in both men and women*.

fertility cult ▶ noun a pagan religious system of some agricultural societies in which seasonal rites are performed with the aim of ensuring good harvests and the future well-being of the community.

fertilization (also **fertilisation**) ▶ noun [mass noun] **1** the action or process of fertilizing an egg or a female animal or plant, involving the fusion of male and female gametes to form a zygote.
2 the action or process of applying a fertilizer to soil or land.

fertilize (also **fertilise**) ▶ verb [with obj.] **1** cause (an egg, female animal, or plant) to develop a new individual by introducing male reproductive material.
2 make (soil or land) more fertile or productive by adding suitable substances to it.
– DERIVATIVES **fertilizable** adjective.

fertilizer (also **fertiliser**) ▶ noun a chemical or natural substance added to soil or land to increase its fertility.

Fertő Tó /ˌfɛrtø ˈtəɔː/ Hungarian name for **Neusiedler See**.

ferula /ˈfɛrjʊlə/ ▶ noun **1** a tall large-leaved Eurasian plant of a genus that includes asafoetida and its relatives. ● Genus *Ferula*, family Umbelliferae.
2 rare term for **FERULE**.
– ORIGIN late Middle English: from Latin, 'giant fennel, rod'.

ferule /ˈfɛruːl/ ▶ noun historical a flat ruler with a widened end, formerly used for beating children.
– ORIGIN late Middle English (denoting the giant fennel): from Latin *ferula* (see **FERULA**).

fervent /ˈfəːv(ə)nt/ ▶ adjective **1** having or displaying a passionate intensity: *a fervent supporter of the revolution*.
2 archaic hot, burning, or glowing.
– DERIVATIVES **fervency** noun, **fervently** adverb.
– ORIGIN Middle English: via Old French from Latin *fervent-* 'boiling', from the verb *fervere*. Compare with **FERVID** and **FERVOUR**.

fervid /ˈfəːvɪd/ ▶ **adjective 1** intensely enthusiastic or passionate, especially to an excessive degree: *his fervid protestations of love.*
2 literary hot, burning, or glowing.
– DERIVATIVES **fervidly** adverb.
– ORIGIN late 16th cent. (in the sense 'glowing, hot'): from Latin *fervidus*, from *fervere* 'to boil'. Compare with **FERVENT** and **FERVOUR**.

fervour /ˈfəːvə/ (US **fervor**) ▶ **noun 1** [mass noun] intense and passionate feeling: *he talked with all the fervour of a new convert.*
2 archaic intense heat.
– ORIGIN Middle English: via Old French from Latin *fervor*, from *fervere* 'to boil'. Compare with **FERVENT** and **FERVID**.

Fès variant spelling of **FEZ**.

fescue /ˈfɛskjuː/ ▶ **noun** any of a number of narrow-leaved grasses: ● a perennial grass that is a valuable pasture and fodder species (genus *Festuca*, family Gramineae). ● an annual grass that typically occurs on drier soils such as on dunes and heathland (genus *Vulpia*, family Gramineae).
– ORIGIN Middle English *festu*, *festue* 'straw, twig', from Old French *festu*, based on Latin *festuca* 'stalk, straw'. The change of *-t-* to *-c-* occurred in the 16th cent.; the current sense dates from the mid 18th cent.

fess[1] /fɛs/ (also **fesse**) ▶ **noun** Heraldry an ordinary in the form of a broad horizontal stripe across the middle of the shield.
– PHRASES **in fess** across the middle third of the field.
– ORIGIN late 15th cent.: from Old French *fesse*, alteration of *faisse*, from Latin *fascia* 'band'. Compare with **FASCIA**.

fess[2] /fɛs/ ▶ **verb** [no obj.] (**fess up**) informal confess; own up: *'Fess up,' she demanded. 'What were you doing in Peter's private office?'*
– ORIGIN early 19th cent.: shortening of **CONFESS**.

fess point ▶ **noun** Heraldry a point at the centre of a shield.

-fest ▶ **combining form** in nouns denoting a festival or gathering of a specified kind: *a media-fest | a gabfest.*
– ORIGIN from German *Fest* 'festival'.

festa /ˈfɛstə/ ▶ **noun** (in Italy and other Mediterranean countries) a religious or other festival.
– ORIGIN early 19th cent.: from Italian, 'festival', from Latin.

festal ▶ **adjective** chiefly archaic relating to or characteristic of a celebration or festival: *plum pudding was originally served on festal days as a main course.*
– ORIGIN late 15th cent.: via Old French from late Latin *festalis*, from Latin *festum*, (plural) *festa* 'feast'.

fester ▶ **verb** [no obj.] (of a wound or sore) become septic; suppurate: (as adj. **festering**) *a festering abscess.* ■ (of food or rubbish) become rotten and offensive to the senses: *piles of mouldy grey paper festered by the sink.* ■ (of a negative feeling or a problem) become worse or more intense, especially through long-term neglect or indifference: *below the surface, the old antagonisms festered.* ■ (of a person) deteriorate physically and mentally in isolated inactivity: *remand prisoners are left to fester in our jails while they wait for trial.*
– ORIGIN late Middle English: from the rare word *fester* 'fistula', later 'festering sore', or Old French *festrir* (verb), both from Old French *festre* (noun), from Latin *fistula* 'pipe, reed, fistula'.

festival ▶ **noun 1** a day or period of celebration, typically for religious reasons: *traditional Jewish festivals.*
2 an organized series of concerts, plays, or films, typically one held annually in the same place: *a major international festival of song.*
– ORIGIN Middle English (as an adjective): via Old French from medieval Latin *festivalis*, from Latin *festivus*, from *festum*, (plural) *festa* 'feast'.

Festival of Britain a festival celebrated with lavish exhibitions and shows throughout Britain in May 1951 to mark the centenary of the Great Exhibition of 1851.

festival of lights ▶ **noun 1** another term for **HANUKKAH**.
2 another term for **DIWALI**.

Festival of the Dead ▶ **noun** another term for **BON**.

festive ▶ **adjective** relating to a festival, especially Christmas: *the festive season is fast approaching.* ■ cheerful and jovially celebratory: *the sombre atmosphere has given way to a festive mood.*
– DERIVATIVES **festively** adverb, **festiveness** noun.
– ORIGIN mid 17th cent.: from Latin *festivus*, from *festum*, (plural) *festa* 'feast'.

festivity ▶ **noun** (pl. **festivities**) [mass noun] the celebration of something in a joyful and exuberant way: *a time of great rejoicing and festivity.* ■ (**festivities**) activities or events celebrating a special occasion: *the traditional Christmas and New Year festivities.*
– ORIGIN late Middle English: from Old French *festivite* or Latin *festivitas*, from *festivus* 'festive', from *festum*, (plural) *festa* 'feast'.

festoon /fɛˈstuːn/ ▶ **noun 1** a chain or garland of flowers, leaves, or ribbons, hung in a curve as a decoration. ■ a carved or moulded ornament representing a festoon.
2 a Eurasian butterfly or moth patterned with dark arcs on a lighter background: ● a large yellowish butterfly with black and red markings (*Zerynthia* and other genera, family Papilionidae). ● a small brown moth (*Apoda avellana*, family Limacodidae).
▶ **verb** [with obj.] (often **be festooned with**) adorn (a place) with chains, garlands, or other decorations: *the staffroom was festooned with balloons and streamers.*
– ORIGIN mid 17th cent.: from French *feston*, from Italian *festone* 'festal ornament', from *festum*, (plural) *festa* 'feast'.

festoon blind ▶ **noun** a window blind consisting of vertical rows of horizontally gathered fabric that may be drawn up into a series of ruches.

Festschrift /ˈfɛstˌʃrɪft/ ▶ **noun** (pl. **Festschriften** or **Festschrifts**) a collection of writings published in honour of a scholar.
– ORIGIN late 19th cent.: from German, from *Fest* 'celebration' + *Schrift* 'writing'.

FET ▶ **abbreviation** field-effect transistor.

feta /ˈfɛtə/ (also **feta cheese** or **fetta**) ▶ **noun** [mass noun] a white salty Greek cheese made from the milk of ewes or goats.
– ORIGIN from modern Greek *pheta*.

fetal /ˈfiːt(ə)l/ ▶ **adjective** relating to a fetus: *nutrients essential for normal fetal growth.* ■ denoting a posture characteristic of a fetus, with the back curved forwards and the limbs folded in front of the body.

fetal alcohol syndrome ▶ **noun** [mass noun] Medicine a congenital syndrome associated with excessive consumption of alcohol by the mother during pregnancy, and characterized by retardation of mental development and of physical growth, particularly of the skull and face.

fetch[1] ▶ **verb** [with obj.] **1** go for and then bring back (someone or something) for someone: *he ran to fetch help* | [with two objs] *she fetched me a cup of tea.* ■ archaic bring forth (blood or tears): *kind offers fetched tears from me.* ■ archaic take a (breath); heave (a sigh).
2 achieve (a particular price) when sold: *the land could fetch over a million pounds.*
3 [with two objs] informal inflict (a blow or slap) on (someone): *that brute Cullam fetched him a wallop.*
4 informal, dated cause great interest or delight in (someone): *that air of his always fetches women.*
▶ **noun 1** the distance travelled by wind or waves across open water. ■ the distance a vessel must sail to reach open water.
2 archaic a stratagem or trick.
– PHRASES **fetch and carry** perform a succession of menial tasks for someone as if one was their servant.
– PHRASAL VERBS **fetch up** informal arrive or come to rest somewhere, typically by accident or unintentionally: *all four of them fetched up in the saloon bar of the Rose and Crown.*
– DERIVATIVES **fetcher** noun.
– ORIGIN Old English *fecc(e)an*, variant of *fetian*, probably related to *fatian* 'grasp', of Germanic origin and related to German *fassen*.

fetch[2] ▶ **noun** the apparition or double of a living person, formerly believed to be a warning of that person's impending death.
– ORIGIN late 17th cent.: of unknown origin.

fetching ▶ **adjective** attractive: *a fetching little garment of pink satin.*
– DERIVATIVES **fetchingly** adverb.

fete /feɪt/ (also **fête**) ▶ **noun** Brit. a public function, typically held outdoors and organized to raise funds for a charity, including entertainment and the sale of goods and refreshments: *a church fete.* ■ chiefly N. Amer. a celebration or festival.
▶ **verb** [with obj.] honour or entertain (someone) lavishly: *she was an instant celebrity, feted by the media.*
– ORIGIN late Middle English (in the sense 'festival, fair'): from French, from Old French *feste* (see **FEAST**).

fête champêtre /ˌfɛt ʃɒ̃ˈpɛtr(ə)/, French /fɛt ʃɑ̃pɛtʀ/ ▶ **noun** (pl. **fêtes champêtres** pronunc. **same**) an outdoor entertainment such as a garden party.
– ORIGIN French, literally 'rural festival'.

fête galante /ˌfɛt gaˈlɒ̃t/, French /fɛt galɑ̃t/ ▶ **noun** (pl. **fêtes galantes** pronunc. **same**) an outdoor entertainment or rural festival, especially as depicted in 18th-century French painting. ■ a painting in this genre.
– ORIGIN French, literally 'elegant festival'.

fetich ▶ **noun** archaic spelling of **FETISH**.

feticide /ˈfiːtɪsʌɪd/ ▶ **noun** [mass noun] destruction or abortion of a fetus.

fetid /ˈfɛtɪd, ˈfiːt-/ (also **foetid**) ▶ **adjective** smelling extremely unpleasant: *the fetid water of the marsh.*
– DERIVATIVES **fetidly** adverb, **fetidness** noun.
– ORIGIN late Middle English: from Latin *fetidus* (often erroneously spelled *foetidus*), from *fetere* 'to stink'. Compare with **FETOR**.

fetish /ˈfɛtɪʃ/ ▶ **noun 1** a form of sexual desire in which gratification is linked to an abnormal degree to a particular object, item of clothing, part of the body, etc.: *a man with a fetish for surgical masks | a foot fetish.* ■ an excessive and irrational devotion or commitment to a particular thing: *men will never understand a woman's fetish for shoes and handbags | the western fetish for all things North African.*
2 an inanimate object worshipped for its supposed magical powers or because it is considered to be inhabited by a spirit.
– DERIVATIVES **fetishism** noun, **fetishist** noun, **fetishistic** adjective.
– ORIGIN early 17th cent. (originally denoting an object used by the peoples of West Africa as an amulet or charm): from French *fétiche*, from Portuguese *feitiço* 'charm, sorcery' (originally an adjective meaning 'made by art'), from Latin *facticius* (see **FACTITIOUS**).

fetishize (also **fetishise**) ▶ **verb** [with obj.] make (something) the object of a sexual fetish: *women's bodies are so intensely fetishized.* ■ have an excessive and irrational commitment to (something): *an author who fetishizes privacy.*
– DERIVATIVES **fetishization** noun.

fetlock /ˈfɛtlɒk/ (also **fetlock joint**) ▶ **noun** the joint of a horse's or other quadruped's leg between the cannon bone and the pastern.
– ORIGIN Middle English: ultimately of Germanic origin; related to German *Fessel* 'fetlock', also to **FOOT**.

feto- ▶ **combining form** representing **FETUS**.

fetor /ˈfiːtə/ (also **foetor**) ▶ **noun** a strong, foul smell: *the fetor of decay.*
– ORIGIN late 15th cent.: from Latin, from *fetere* 'to stink'. Compare with **FETID**.

fetta ▶ **noun** variant spelling of **FETA**.

fetter ▶ **noun** (usu. **fetters**) a chain or manacle used to restrain a prisoner, typically placed around the ankles: *he lay bound with fetters of iron.* ■ a restraint or check on someone's freedom to act: *the fetters of convention.*
▶ **verb** [with obj.] restrain with chains or manacles, typically around the ankles: (as adj. **fettered**) *a ragged and fettered prisoner.* ■ confine or restrict (someone): *he was not fettered by tradition.*
– ORIGIN Old English *feter*, of Germanic origin; related to Dutch *veter* 'a lace', from an Indo-European root shared by **FOOT**.

fetterlock ▶ **noun** a D-shaped fetter for tethering a horse by the leg, now only as represented as a heraldic charge.

fettle ▶ **noun** [mass noun] condition: *Marguerite was in fine fettle.*
▶ **verb** [with obj.] trim or clean the rough edges of (a metal casting or a piece of pottery) before firing. ■ N. English make or repair (something).
– ORIGIN late Middle English (as a verb in the general sense 'get ready, prepare', specifically 'prepare oneself for battle, gird up'): from dialect *fettle* 'strip of material, girdle', from Old English *fetel*, of Germanic origin; related to German *Fessel* 'chain, band'.

fettler ▶ **noun 1** Brit. a person who does repair or maintenance work on a railway.
2 a person who fettles metal castings or pottery.

fettuccine /ˌfɛtʊˈtʃiːni/ ▶ **plural noun** pasta made in ribbons.
– ORIGIN from Italian, plural of *fettuccina*, diminutive of *fetta* 'slice, ribbon'.

fetus /ˈfiːtəs/ (Brit. (in non-technical use) also **foetus**) ▶ **noun** (pl. **fetuses**) an unborn or unhatched offspring of a mammal, in particular, an unborn human more than eight weeks after conception.

– ORIGIN late Middle English: from Latin *fetus* 'pregnancy, childbirth, offspring'.

USAGE The spelling **foetus** has no etymological basis but is recorded from the 16th century and until recently was the standard British spelling in both technical and non-technical use. In technical usage **fetus** is now the standard spelling throughout the English-speaking world, but **foetus** is still found in British English outside technical contexts.

feu /fjuː/ Scots Law ▸ **noun** a perpetual lease at a fixed rent. ■ a piece of land held by such a lease.
▸ **verb** (**feus, feuing, feued**) [with obj.] grant (land) on such a lease.
– ORIGIN late 15th cent. (originally denoting a feudal tenure in which an annual payment was made in lieu of military service): from Old French (see **FEE**).

feud ▸ **noun** a prolonged and bitter quarrel or dispute: *his long-standing feud with Universal Pictures.* ■ a state of prolonged mutual hostility, typically between two families or communities, characterized by murderous assaults in revenge for previous injuries: *a savage feud over drugs money.*
▸ **verb** [no obj.] take part in such a quarrel or violent conflict: *Hoover **feuded with** the CIA for decades.*
– ORIGIN Middle English *fede* 'hostility, ill will', from Old French *feide*, from Middle Dutch, Middle Low German *vēde*, of Germanic origin; related to **FOE**.

feudal /ˈfjuːd(ə)l/ ▸ **adjective** according to, resembling, or denoting the system of feudalism. ■ absurdly outdated or old-fashioned: *his view of patriotism was more than old-fashioned—it was positively feudal.*
– DERIVATIVES **feudalization** /-ˈzeɪʃ(ə)n/ **noun**, **feudally adverb**.
– ORIGIN early 17th cent.: from medieval Latin *feudalis*, from *feudum* (see **FEE**).

feudalism ▸ **noun** [mass noun] the dominant social system in medieval Europe, in which the nobility held lands from the Crown in exchange for military service, and vassals were in turn tenants of the nobles, while the peasants (villeins or serfs) were obliged to live on their lord's land and give him homage, labour, and a share of the produce, notionally in exchange for military protection.
– DERIVATIVES **feudalist noun**, **feudalistic adjective**.

feudality ▸ **noun** [mass noun] archaic the principles and practice of the feudal system.
– ORIGIN late 18th cent.: from French *féodalité*, from *féodal*, from medieval Latin *feudalis* 'feudal', from *feudum* (see **FEE**).

feudatory /ˈfjuːdət(ə)ri/ historical ▸ **adjective** owing feudal allegiance to another: *a feudatory state.*
▸ **noun** (pl. **feudatories**) a person who holds land under the conditions of the feudal system.
– ORIGIN late 16th cent.: from medieval Latin *feudatorius*, from *feudare* 'enfeoff', from *feudum* (see **FEE**).

feu de joie /ˌfəː də ˈʒwɑː/ ▸ **noun** (pl. **feux de joie** pronunc. **same**) a rifle salute fired by soldiers on a ceremonial occasion, each soldier firing in succession along the ranks to make a continuous sound.
– ORIGIN French, literally 'fire of joy'.

Feuerbach /ˈfɔɪəˌbɑːx/, German /ˈfɔyɐˌbax/, Ludwig (Andreas) (1804–72), German materialist philosopher. In his best-known work, *The Essence of Christianity* (1841), he argued that the dogmas and beliefs of Christianity are figments of human imagination, fulfilling a need inherent in human nature.

feuilleté /fəːjəˈteɪ/ ▸ **noun** a puff pastry case with a sweet or savoury filling.
– ORIGIN French, 'flaky'.

feuilleton /ˈfəːɪtɒ̃/ ▸ **noun** a part of a newspaper or magazine devoted to fiction, criticism, or light literature. ■ an article printed in a feuilleton.
– ORIGIN mid 19th cent.: French, from *feuillet*, diminutive of *feuille* 'leaf'.

fever ▸ **noun** an abnormally high body temperature, usually accompanied by shivering, headache, and in severe instances, delirium: *she had a slight fever* | [mass noun] *quinine was used to reduce malarial fever.* ■ a state of nervous excitement or agitation: *I was mystified, and in a fever of expectation.* ■ [mass noun] [with modifier] the excitement felt by a group of people about a particular public event: *election fever reaches its climax tomorrow.*
▸ **verb** [with obj.] archaic bring about a high body temperature or a state of nervous excitement in: *a heart which sin has fevered.*
– ORIGIN Old English *fēfor*, from Latin *febris*; reinforced in Middle English by Old French *fievre*, also from *febris*.

fevered ▸ **adjective** having or showing the symptoms associated with a dangerously high temperature: *they mopped his fevered brow.* ■ feeling or displaying an excessive degree of nervous excitement, agitation, or energy: *my fevered adolescent imagination.*

feverfew /ˈfiːvəfjuː/ ▸ **noun** a small bushy aromatic Eurasian plant of the daisy family, with feathery leaves and daisy-like flowers, used in herbal medicine to treat headaches. ● *Tanacetum parthenium*, family Compositae.
– ORIGIN Old English *feferfuge*, from Latin *febrifuga*, from *febris* 'fever' + *fugare* 'drive away'. Compare with **FEBRIFUGE**.

fever grass ▸ **noun** West Indian term for **LEMON GRASS**.

feverish ▸ **adjective** having or showing the symptoms of a fever: *she felt sick and feverish* | *a feverish cold.* ■ characterized by or displaying a frenetic excitement or energy: *the next couple of weeks were spent in a whirl of feverish activity.*
– DERIVATIVES **feverishly adverb**, **feverishness noun**.

feverous ▸ **adjective** archaic tending to cause fever. ■ feverish.

fever pitch ▸ **noun** [mass noun] a state of extreme excitement: *the football crowd was **at fever pitch*** | [in sing.] *a fever pitch of nervous excitement.*

fever tree ▸ **noun** any of a number of trees which are believed to either cause or cure fever, in particular: ● a North American tree used in the treatment of malaria during the civil war (*Pinckneya pubens*, family Rubiaceae). ● a southern African tree which was formerly believed to cause malaria (*Acacia xanthophloea*, family Leguminosae).

few ▸ **determiner, pronoun, & adjective 1** (**a few**) a small number of: [as determiner] *may I ask a few questions?* | [as pronoun] *I will recount **a few of** the stories told me* | *there are hundreds of applicants but only a few are selected.*
2 used to emphasize how small a number of people or things is: [as determiner] *he had few friends* | [as pronoun] *few thought to challenge these assumptions* | ***very few of** the titles have any literary merit* | *a club with **as few as** 20 members* | [comparative] *a population of fewer than two million* | [as adj.] *sewing was one of her few pleasures* | [superlative] *ask which products have the fewest complaints.*
▸ **noun** (as plural noun **the few**) the minority of people; the elect: *art is not just for the few.* ■ (**the Few**) Brit. the RAF pilots who took part in the Battle of Britain. [alluding to a speech of Sir Winston Churchill (20 August, 1940).]
– PHRASES **every few** once in every small group of (typically units of time): *she visits every few weeks.* **few and far between** scarce; infrequent: *my inspired moments are few and far between.* **a good few** Brit. a fairly large number of: *we sat there for a good few minutes.* **have a few** informal drink enough alcohol to be slightly drunk. **no fewer than** used to emphasize a surprisingly large number: *there are no fewer than seventy different brand names.* **not a few** a considerable number: *virtually every soul star, and not a few blues singers, learned to sing in church.* **quite a few** a fairly large number: *quite a few people got the wrong impression.* **some few** some but not many.
– ORIGIN Old English *fēawe*, *fēawa*, of Germanic origin; related to Old High German *fao*, from an Indo-European root shared by Latin *paucus* and Greek *pauros* 'small'.

USAGE Fewer versus less: strictly speaking, the rule is that **fewer**, the comparative form of **few**, is used with words denoting people or countable things (***fewer** members*; ***fewer** books*). **Less**, on the other hand, is used with mass nouns, denoting things which cannot be counted (***less** money*; ***less** bother*). It is regarded as incorrect in standard English to use **less** with count nouns, as in ***less** people* or ***less** words*, although this is one of the most widespread errors made by native speakers. It is not so obvious which word should be used with **than**. **Less** is normally used with numerals (*a score of **less** than 100*) and with expressions of measurement or time (***less** than two weeks*; ***less** than four miles away*), but **fewer** is used if the things denoted by the number are seen as individual items or units (*there were **fewer** than ten contestants*).

fey /feɪ/ ▸ **adjective** (**feyer, feyest**) **1** giving an impression of vague unworldliness or mystery: *a rather fey romantic novelist.*
2 having supernatural powers of clairvoyance.
3 archaic, chiefly Scottish fated to die or at the point of death.
– DERIVATIVES **feyly adverb**, **feyness noun**.
– ORIGIN Old English *fǣge* (in the sense 'fated to die soon'), of Germanic origin; related to Dutch *veeg* and to German *feige* 'cowardly'.

Feydeau /ˈfeɪdəʊ/, French /fɛdo/, Georges (1862–1921), French dramatist. His name has become a byword for French bedroom farce. He wrote some forty plays, including *Hotel Paradiso* (1894) and *Le Dindon* (1896).

Feynman /ˈfʌɪnmən/, Richard Phillips (1918–88), American theoretical physicist, noted for his work on quantum electrodynamics. Nobel Prize for Physics (1965).

Feynman diagram ▸ **noun** Physics a diagram showing electromagnetic interactions between subatomic particles.

Fez /fɛz/ (also **Fès**) a city in northern Morocco, founded in 808; pop. 977,946 (2004).

fez /fɛz/ ▸ **noun** (pl. **fezzes**) a flat-topped conical red hat with a black tassel on top, worn by men in some Muslim countries (formerly the Turkish national headdress).
– DERIVATIVES **fezzed adjective**.
– ORIGIN early 19th cent.: from Turkish *fes* (perhaps via French *fez*), named after **FEZ**, once the chief place of manufacture.

ff ▸ **abbreviation** Music fortissimo.

ff. ▸ **abbreviation** ■ folios. ■ following pages.

Fg Off ▸ **abbreviation** (in the UK) Flying Officer.

f-hole ▸ **noun** either of a pair of soundholes resembling an ʃ and a reversed ʃ in shape, cut in the front of musical instruments of the violin family, and some other stringed instruments such as semi-acoustic electric guitars or mandolins.

FHSA ▸ **abbreviation** (in the UK) Family Health Services Authority, a body responsible for running general health services, such as those provided by general practitioners, dentists, and opticians, for a particular area.

FIA the international governing body for motor-racing events.
– ORIGIN acronym from French *Fédération Internationale de l'Automobile*.

fiacre /fɪˈɑːkrə, -kə/ ▸ **noun** historical a small four-wheeled carriage for public hire.
– ORIGIN late 17th cent.: from French, named after the Hôtel de St *Fiacre* in Paris, where such vehicles were first hired out.

fiancé /fɪˈɒnseɪ, -ˈɑːns-, -ˈɒ̃s-/ ▸ **noun** a man to whom a woman is engaged to be married.
– ORIGIN mid 19th cent.: from French, past participle of *fiancer* 'betroth', from Old French *fiance* 'a promise', based on Latin *fidere* 'to trust'.

fiancée /fɪˈɒnseɪ, -ˈɑːns-, -ˈɒ̃s-/ ▸ **noun** a woman to whom a man is engaged to be married.

fianchetto /ˌfɪənˈtʃɛtəʊ, -ˈkɛtəʊ/ Chess ▸ **noun** (pl. **fianchettoes**) the development of a bishop by moving it one square to a long diagonal of the board.
▸ **verb** (**fianchettoes, fianchettoing, fianchettoed**) [with obj.] develop (a bishop) in such a way.
– ORIGIN mid 19th cent.: from Italian, diminutive of *fianco* 'flank', ultimately of Germanic origin.

Fianna Fáil /fɪˌanə ˈfɔɪl/, Irish /ˌfʲiənə ˈfaːlʲ/ one of the two main political parties of the Republic of Ireland. Larger and traditionally more republican than its rival Fine Gael, it was formed in 1926 in opposition to the Anglo-Irish Treaty of 1921 by Eamon de Valera together with some of the moderate members of Sinn Fein.
– ORIGIN Irish, from *fianna* 'band of warriors' (applied to the soldiers of Finn MacCool; compare with **FENIAN**) and *Fáil*, genitive of *Fál*, an ancient name for Ireland. The phrase *Fianna Fáil* was used in 15th-cent. poetry in the neutral sense 'people of Ireland', but the founders of the political party interpreted it to mean 'soldiers of destiny'.

fiasco /fɪˈaskəʊ/ ▸ **noun** (pl. **fiascos**) a complete failure, especially a ludicrous or humiliating one: *his plans turned into a fiasco.*
– ORIGIN mid 19th cent.: from Italian, literally 'bottle, flask', in the phrase *far fiasco*, literally 'make a bottle', figuratively 'fail in a performance': the reason for the figurative sense is unexplained.

fiat /ˈfiːat, ˈfʌɪat/ ▸ **noun** a formal authorization or proposition; a decree: *the reforms left most prices fixed by government fiat.* ■ an arbitrary order.
– ORIGIN late Middle English: from Latin, 'let it be done', from *fieri* 'be done or made'.

fiat money ▸ **noun** [mass noun] inconvertible paper money made legal tender by a government decree.

fib ▸ noun a lie, typically an unimportant one: *why did you tell him such a dreadful fib?*
▸ verb (**fibs, fibbing, fibbed**) [no obj.] tell a fib.
– DERIVATIVES **fibber** noun.
– ORIGIN mid 16th cent.: perhaps a shortening of obsolete *fible-fable* 'nonsense', reduplication of FABLE.

fiber etc. ▸ noun US spelling of FIBRE etc.

Fibonacci /ˌfɪbəˈnɑːtʃi/, Leonardo (*c*.1170–*c*.1250), Italian mathematician; known as **Fibonacci of Pisa**. Fibonacci popularized the use of the 'new' Arabic numerals in Europe. He made many original contributions in complex calculations, algebra, and geometry, and pioneered number theory and indeterminate analysis, discovering the Fibonacci series.

Fibonacci series ▸ noun Mathematics a series of numbers in which each number (**Fibonacci number**) is the sum of the two preceding numbers. The simplest is the series 1, 1, 2, 3, 5, 8, etc.

fibre (US **fiber**) ▸ noun **1** a thread or filament from which a vegetable tissue, mineral substance, or textile is formed: *the basket comes lined with natural coco fibres.* ■ a substance formed of fibres: *ordinary synthetics don't breathe as well as natural fibres* | [mass noun] *high strength carbon fibre.* ■ a thread-like structure forming part of the muscular, nervous, connective, or other tissue in the human or animal body: *there were degenerative changes in muscle fibres* | figurative *she wanted him with every fibre of her being.* ■ (also **moral fibre**) [mass noun] strength of character: *a weak person with no moral fibre.*
2 [mass noun] dietary material containing substances such as cellulose, lignin, and pectin, that are resistant to the action of digestive enzymes.
– DERIVATIVES **fibred** adjective [in combination] *long-fibred wools*, **fibreless** adjective.
– ORIGIN late Middle English (in the sense 'lobe of the liver', (plural) 'entrails'): via French from Latin *fibra* 'fibre, filament, entrails'.

fibreboard (US **fiberboard**) ▸ noun [mass noun] a building material made of wood or other plant fibres compressed into boards.

fibrefill ▸ noun [mass noun] synthetic material used for padding and insulation in garments and soft furnishings such as cushions and duvets.

fibreglass (US **fiberglass**) ▸ noun [mass noun] **1** a reinforced plastic material composed of glass fibres embedded in a resin matrix.
2 a textile fabric made from woven glass filaments.

fibre optics ▸ plural noun [treated as sing.] the use of thin flexible fibres of glass or other transparent solids to transmit light signals, chiefly for telecommunications or for internal inspection of the body. ■ [treated as pl.] the fibres and associated devices so used.
– DERIVATIVES **fibre-optic** adjective.

fibrescope (US **fiberscope**) ▸ noun a fibre-optic device for viewing inaccessible internal structures, especially in the human body.

fibre tip ▸ noun a pen with a writing point made of tightly packed fibres which hold the ink.

fibril /ˈfʌɪbrɪl/ ▸ noun technical a small or slender fibre: *each muscle fibre is subdivided into smaller fibrils.*
– DERIVATIVES **fibrillar** adjective, **fibrillary** adjective.
– ORIGIN mid 17th cent.: from modern Latin *fibrilla*, diminutive of Latin *fibra* (see FIBRE).

fibrillate /ˈfʌɪbrɪleɪt, ˈfɪb-/ ▸ verb [no obj.] **1** (of a muscle, especially in the heart) make a quivering movement due to uncoordinated contraction of the individual fibrils.
2 (of a fibre) split up into fibrils. ■ [with obj.] break (a fibre) into fibrils.
– DERIVATIVES **fibrillation** noun.

fibrin /ˈfʌɪbrɪn, ˈfɪb-/ ▸ noun [mass noun] Biochemistry an insoluble protein formed from fibrinogen during the clotting of blood. It forms a fibrous mesh that impedes the flow of blood.
– DERIVATIVES **fibrinoid** adjective, **fibrinous** adjective.
– ORIGIN early 19th cent.: from FIBRE + -IN[1].

fibrinogen /fʌɪˈbrɪnədʒ(ə)n, fɪ-/ ▸ noun [mass noun] Biochemistry a soluble protein present in blood plasma, from which fibrin is produced by the action of the enzyme thrombin.

fibrinolysis /ˌfʌɪbrɪˈnɒlɪsɪs, ˌfɪb-/ ▸ noun [mass noun] Physiology the enzymatic breakdown of the fibrin in blood clots.
– DERIVATIVES **fibrinolytic** adjective.

fibro /ˈfʌɪbrəʊ/ ▸ noun (pl. **fibros**) [mass noun] Austral. a mixture of sand, cement, and cellulose fibre, used in sheets for building. ■ [count noun] a house constructed mainly of such sheets.
– ORIGIN 1950s: abbreviation of *fibro-cement*.

fibro- /ˈfʌɪbrəʊ/ ▸ combining form relating to or characterized by fibres: *fibroblast* | *fibroma.*
– ORIGIN from Latin *fibra* 'fibre'.

fibroadenoma /ˌfʌɪbrəʊadɪˈnəʊmə/ ▸ noun (pl. **fibroadenomas** or **fibroadenomata** /-mətə/) Medicine a tumour formed of mixed fibrous and glandular tissue, typically occurring as a benign growth in the breast.

fibroblast /ˈfʌɪbrə(ʊ)blast/ ▸ noun Physiology a cell in connective tissue which produces collagen and other fibres.

fibrocystic /ˌfʌɪbrə(ʊ)ˈsɪstɪk/ ▸ adjective Medicine (of a disease) characterized by the development of fibrous tissue and cystic spaces, typically in the pancreas or the breast.

fibroid /ˈfʌɪbrɔɪd/ ▸ adjective of or characterized by fibres or fibrous tissue.
▸ noun Medicine a benign tumour of muscular and fibrous tissues, typically developing in the wall of the womb.

fibroin /ˈfʌɪbrəʊɪn/ ▸ noun [mass noun] a protein which is the chief constituent of silk.
– ORIGIN mid 19th cent.: from FIBRO- + -IN[1].

fibrolite /ˈfʌɪbrə(ʊ)lʌɪt/ ▸ noun another term for SILLIMANITE.

fibroma /fʌɪˈbrəʊmə/ ▸ noun (pl. **fibromas** or **fibromata** /-mətə/) Medicine a benign fibrous tumour of connective tissue.
– DERIVATIVES **fibromatous** adjective.
– ORIGIN mid 19th cent.: from Latin *fibra* (see FIBRE) + -OMA.

fibromyalgia /ˌfʌɪbrəʊmʌɪˈaldʒɪə/ ▸ noun [mass noun] a rheumatic condition characterized by muscular or musculoskeletal pain with stiffness and localized tenderness at specific points on the body.

fibrosarcoma /ˌfʌɪbrəʊsɑːˈkəʊmə/ ▸ noun (pl. **fibrosarcomas** or **fibrosarcomata** /-mətə/) Medicine a sarcoma in which the predominant cell type is a malignant fibroblast.
– DERIVATIVES **fibrosarcomatous** adjective.

fibrosis /fʌɪˈbrəʊsɪs/ ▸ noun [mass noun] Medicine the thickening and scarring of connective tissue, usually as a result of injury.
– DERIVATIVES **fibrotic** adjective.
– ORIGIN late 19th cent.: from Latin *fibra* (see FIBRE) + -OSIS.

fibrositis /ˌfʌɪbrəˈsʌɪtɪs/ ▸ noun [mass noun] Medicine inflammation of fibrous connective tissue, typically affecting the back and causing stiffness and pain.

fibrous ▸ adjective consisting of or characterized by fibres: *a good fibrous root system.*
– DERIVATIVES **fibrousness** noun.

fibula /ˈfɪbjʊlə/ ▸ noun (pl. **fibulae** /-liː/ or **fibulas**) **1** Anatomy the outer and usually smaller of the two bones between the knee and the ankle (or the equivalent joints in other terrestrial vertebrates), parallel with the tibia.
2 Archaeology a brooch or clasp.
– DERIVATIVES **fibular** adjective.
– ORIGIN late 16th cent.: from Latin, 'brooch', perhaps related to *figere* 'to fix'. The bone is so named because the shape it makes with the tibia resembles a clasp, the fibula being the pin.

-fic (usu. as **-ific**) ▸ suffix (forming adjectives) producing; making: *prolific* | *soporific.*
– DERIVATIVES **-fically** suffix forming corresponding adverbs.
– ORIGIN from French *-fique* or Latin *-ficus* from *facere* 'do, make'.

-fication (usu. as **-ification**) ▸ suffix forming nouns of action from verbs ending in *-fy* (such as *simplification* from *simplify*).
– ORIGIN from French, or from Latin *-fication-* (from verbs ending in *-ficare*).

fiche ▸ noun short for MICROFICHE.

Fichte /ˈfɪxtə/, German /ˈfɪçtə/, Johann Gottlieb (1762–1814), German philosopher. A pupil of Kant, he postulated that the ego is the basic reality and that the world outside it is posited by the ego in defining and delimiting itself. His political addresses had some influence on the development of German nationalism and the overthrow of Napoleon.

fichu /ˈfiːʃuː/ ▸ noun a small triangular shawl, worn round a woman's shoulders and neck.
– ORIGIN mid 18th cent.: from French, from *ficher* 'to fix, pin'.

fickle ▸ adjective changing frequently, especially as regards one's loyalties or affections: *celebs trying to appeal to an increasingly fickle public.*
– DERIVATIVES **fickly** adverb.
– ORIGIN Old English *ficol* 'deceitful', of Germanic origin.

fickleness ▸ noun [mass noun] changeability, especially as regards one's loyalties or affections: *the fickleness of youth.*

fictile /ˈfɪktʌɪl, -tɪl/ ▸ adjective technical made of earth or clay by a potter. ■ relating to pottery or its manufacture.
– ORIGIN early 17th cent.: from Latin *fictilis*, from *fict-* 'formed, contrived', from the verb *fingere*.

fiction ▸ noun **1** [mass noun] literature in the form of prose, especially novels, that describes imaginary events and people.
2 something that is invented or untrue: *they were supposed to be keeping up the fiction that they were happily married.* ■ a belief or statement which is false, but is often held to be true because it is expedient to do so: *the notion of the country being a democracy is a polite fiction.*
– DERIVATIVES **fictionist** noun.
– ORIGIN late Middle English (in the sense 'invented statement'): via Old French from Latin *fictio(n-)*, from *fingere* 'form, contrive'. Compare with FEIGN and FIGMENT.

fictional ▸ adjective relating to or occurring in fiction; invented for the purposes of fiction: *fictional texts* | *a fictional character.*
– DERIVATIVES **fictionality** noun, **fictionalization** noun, **fictionalize** (also **fictionalise**) verb, **fictionally** adverb.

fictitious /fɪkˈtɪʃəs/ ▸ adjective **1** not real or true; imaginary or fabricated: *reports of a deal were dismissed as fictitious by the Minister.*
2 occurring in or invented for fiction.
– DERIVATIVES **fictitiously** adverb, **fictitiousness** noun.
– ORIGIN early 17th cent.: from Latin *ficticius* (from *fingere* 'contrive, form') + -OUS (see also -ITIOUS[2]).

fictive ▸ adjective created by the imagination: *the novel's fictive universe.* ■ relating to the writing of fiction: *the obviously fictive genres, poetry, drama and the novel.*
– DERIVATIVES **fictiveness** noun.
– ORIGIN early 17th cent. (but rare before the 19th cent.): from French *fictif, -ive* or medieval Latin *fictivus*, from Latin *fingere* 'contrive, form'.

ficus /ˈfiːkəs, ˈfʌɪkəs/ ▸ noun (pl. **same**) a tree, shrub, or climber of a large genus that includes the figs and the rubber plant, growing in tropical and warm climates. ● Genus *Ficus*, family Moraceae.
– ORIGIN mid 19th cent.: from Latin, 'fig, fig tree'.

fid ▸ noun Nautical **1** a square wooden or iron bar which takes the weight of a topmast stepped to a lower mast by being passed through holes in both masts.
2 a conical pin or spike used in splicing rope.
ORIGIN early 17th cent.: of unknown origin.

fidayeen ▸ plural noun variant of FEDAYEEN.

Fid. Def. ▸ abbreviation Fidei Defensor. See DEFENDER OF THE FAITH.

fiddle ▸ noun **1** informal a violin.
2 informal, chiefly Brit. an act of defrauding, cheating, or falsifying: *a major mortgage fiddle.*
3 Brit. informal a small task that seems awkward and unnecessarily complex: *inserting a tape is a bit of a fiddle.*
4 Nautical a ledge or raised rim that prevents things from rolling or sliding off a table in rough seas.
▸ verb **1** [no obj.] touch or fidget with something in a restless or nervous way: *Lena **fiddled with** her cup.* ■ tinker with something in an attempt to make minor adjustments or improvements: *he fiddled with the blind, trying to prevent the sun from shining in her eyes.* ■ (**fiddle around**) pass time aimlessly, without doing or achieving anything of substance.
2 [with obj.] informal, chiefly Brit. falsify (figures, data, or records), typically in order to gain money: *everyone is fiddling their expenses.*
3 [no obj.] informal play the violin.
– PHRASES **fiddle while Rome burns** be concerned with relatively trivial matters while ignoring the serious or disastrous events going on around one. **(as) fit as a fiddle** in very good health. **on the fiddle** informal, chiefly Brit. engaged in cheating or swindling. **play second fiddle** have a subordinate role to someone or something; be treated as less important than someone or something: *he resented **playing second fiddle** to his younger brother.*
– ORIGIN Old English *fithele*, denoting a violin or similar instrument (originally not an informal or depreciatory term), related to Dutch *vedel* and German *Fiedel*, based on Latin *vitulari* 'celebrate a festival,

F

be joyful', perhaps from *Vitula*, the name of a Roman goddess of joy and victory. Compare with VIOL.

fiddleback ▶ noun **1** [usu. as modifier] a thing shaped like the back of a violin, with the sides deeply curved inwards, especially the back of a chair or the front of a chasuble.
2 [mass noun] a rippled effect in the grain of fine wood, often exploited when making the backs of violins: [as modifier] *fiddleback mahogany*.

fiddle-de-dee ▶ noun [mass noun] [often as exclamation] dated nonsense.
– ORIGIN late 18th cent.: from FIDDLE + a reduplication without meaning.

fiddle-faddle ▶ noun [mass noun] trivial matters; nonsense.
▶ verb [no obj.] mess about; fuss.
– ORIGIN late 16th cent.: reduplication of FIDDLE.

fiddlehead ▶ noun **1** (also **fiddlehead fern** or **fiddlehead green**) N. Amer. the young, curled, edible frond of certain ferns.
2 a scroll-like carving at a ship's bows.

fiddle pattern ▶ noun [mass noun] a design of spoons and forks, with handles shaped like the body of a violin.

fiddler ▶ noun **1** informal a person who plays the violin, especially one who plays folk music.
2 Brit. informal a person who cheats or swindles, especially one indulging in petty theft.
– ORIGIN Old English *fithelere*, from *fithele* (see FIDDLE).

fiddler crab ▶ noun a small amphibious crab, the males of which have one greatly enlarged claw which they wave in territorial display and courtship. ● Genus *Uca*, family Ocypodidae.

Fiddler's Green an imaginary paradise to which sailors are conveyed after death, traditionally a place of wine, women, and song.

fiddlestick informal ▶ exclamation (**fiddlesticks**) nonsense.
▶ noun a violin bow.

fiddling ▶ adjective annoyingly trivial or petty: *fiddling little details*.

fiddly ▶ adjective (**fiddlier**, **fiddliest**) Brit. informal complicated or detailed and awkward to do or use: *replacing the battery is fiddly*.

Fidei Defensor /ˌfʌɪdɪʌɪ dɪˈfɛnsɔː, ˌfiːdeɪiː/ ▶ noun Latin term for DEFENDER OF THE FAITH.
– ORIGIN Latin.

fideism /ˈfʌɪdɪɪz(ə)m/ ▶ noun [mass noun] the doctrine that knowledge depends on faith or revelation.
– DERIVATIVES **fideist** noun, **fideistic** adjective.
– ORIGIN late 19th cent.: from Latin *fides* 'faith' + -ISM.

fidelity /fɪˈdɛlɪti/ ▶ noun [mass noun] **1** faithfulness to a person, cause, or belief, demonstrated by continuing loyalty and support: *his fidelity to liberal ideals*. ■ sexual faithfulness to a spouse or partner.
2 the degree of exactness with which something is copied or reproduced: *the 1949 recording provides reasonable fidelity*.
– ORIGIN late Middle English: from Old French *fidelite* or Latin *fidelitas*, from *fidelis* 'faithful', from *fides* 'faith'. Compare with FEALTY.

fidelity insurance ▶ noun [mass noun] insurance taken out by an employer against losses incurred through dishonesty by employees.

fidget /ˈfɪdʒɪt/ ▶ verb (**fidgets**, **fidgeting**, **fidgeted**) [no obj.] make small movements, especially of the hands and feet, through nervousness or impatience: *the audience began to fidget and whisper*. ■ be impatient or uneasy: [with infinitive] *he was fidgeting to get back to his shop*.
▶ noun a person who fidgets. ■ (usu. **fidgets**) a state of mental or physical restlessness or unease: *Captain Osborne had the fidgets*.
– DERIVATIVES **fidgeter** noun.
– ORIGIN late 17th cent.: from obsolete or dialect *fidge* 'to twitch'; perhaps related to Old Norse *fikja* 'move briskly, be restless or eager'.

fidget pie ▶ noun Brit. a savoury pie containing onions, apples, bacon, and sometimes potatoes.
– ORIGIN late 18th cent. (as *fitchet-pie*): perhaps from *fitchet*, a dialect word for 'polecat', because of the strong, unpleasant odour of the pie during cooking. The change in spelling of the first word was due to association with FIDGET.

fidgety ▶ adjective inclined to fidget; restless or uneasy: *I get nervous and fidgety at the dentist*.
– DERIVATIVES **fidgetiness** noun.

Fido[1] /ˈfʌɪdəʊ/ ▶ noun informal a generic name for a pet dog.
– ORIGIN from Latin *fido* 'I trust'.

Fido[2] /ˈfʌɪdəʊ/ historical ▶ noun a system for enabling aircraft to land, involving the dispersal of fog by means of petrol burners on the ground. It was developed by the Allies during the Second World War.
– ORIGIN acronym from *Fog Intensive Dispersal Operation*.

fiducial /fɪˈdjuːʃ(ə)l/ ▶ adjective technical (especially of a point or line) assumed as a fixed basis of comparison.
– ORIGIN late 16th cent.: from late Latin *fiducialis*, from *fiducia* 'trust', from *fidere* 'to trust'.

fiduciary /fɪˈdjuːʃ(ə)ri/ ▶ adjective **1** Law involving trust, especially with regard to the relationship between a trustee and a beneficiary: *the company has a fiduciary duty to shareholders*. ■ archaic held or given in trust: *fiduciary estates*.
2 Finance (of a paper currency) depending for its value on securities (as opposed to gold) or the reputation of the issuer.
▶ noun (pl. **fiduciaries**) a trustee.
– ORIGIN late 16th cent. (in the sense 'something inspiring trust; credentials'): from Latin *fiduciarius*, from *fiducia* 'trust', from *fidere* 'to trust'.

fidus Achates /ˌfʌɪdəs əˈkeɪtiːz/ ▶ noun a faithful friend or devoted follower.
– ORIGIN Latin, literally 'faithful Achates' (see ACHATES).

fie /fʌɪ/ ▶ exclamation archaic or humorous used to express disgust or outrage.
– ORIGIN Middle English: via Old French from Latin *fi*, an exclamation of disgust at a stench.

fief /fiːf/ ▶ noun **1** Law, historical an estate of land, especially one held on condition of feudal service; a fee.
2 a person's sphere of operation or control.
– ORIGIN early 17th cent.: from French (see FEE).

fiefdom ▶ noun **1** Law, historical a fief.
2 a territory or sphere of operation controlled by a particular person or group: *a mafia boss who has turned the town into his private fiefdom*.

Field, John (1782–1837), Irish composer and pianist. He is noted for the invention of the nocturne and for his twenty compositions in this form.

field ▶ noun **1** an area of open land, especially one planted with crops or pasture, typically bounded by hedges or fences: *a wheat field | a field of corn*. ■ a piece of land used for a particular purpose, especially an area marked out for a game or sport: *a football field*. ■ a large area of land or water completely covered in a particular substance, especially snow or ice. ■ an area rich in a natural product, typically oil or gas. ■ a place where a subject of scientific study or of artistic representation can be observed in its natural location or context. ■ (usu. **the field**) an area which is or is to become the scene of a battle or campaign. ■ archaic a battle: *many a bloody field was to be fought*.
2 a particular branch of study or sphere of activity or interest: *we talked to professionals in various fields*. ■ Computing a part of a record, representing an item of data. ■ Linguistics & Psychology a general area of meaning within which individual words make particular distinctions.
3 a space or range within which objects are visible from a particular viewpoint or through a piece of apparatus. See also FIELD OF VISION.
4 (usu. **the field**) all the participants in a contest or sport: *he destroyed the rest of the field with a devastating injection of speed*. ■ Cricket fielders collectively, or the manner in which they are spread over the pitch: *he sees the ball early and strokes it through the gap in the field*. ■ a fielder.
5 Physics the region in which a particular condition prevails, especially one in which a force or influence is effective regardless of the presence or absence of a material medium. ■ the force exerted or potentially exerted in such an area.
6 Mathematics a system subject to two binary operations analogous to those for the multiplication and addition of real numbers, and having similar commutative and distributive laws.
7 Heraldry the surface of an escutcheon or of one of its divisions. ■ an area on a flag with a single background colour: *fifty white stars on a blue field*.
▶ verb **1** [no obj.] chiefly Cricket & Baseball attempt to catch or stop the ball and return it after it has been hit by the batsman or batter, thereby preventing runs being scored or base runners advancing. ■ [with obj.] catch or stop (the ball) and return it.
2 [with obj.] send out (a team or individual) to play in a game: *Leeds fielded a team of youngsters*. ■ (of a political party) put up (a candidate) to stand in an election: *the Ecology party fielded 109 candidates*. ■ deploy (an army): *Russia was committed to fielding 800,000 men*.
3 [with obj.] deal with (a difficult question, telephone call, etc.).
▶ adjective [attrib.] carried out or working in the natural environment, rather than in a laboratory or office: *field observations and interviews*. ■ (of military equipment) light and mobile for use on campaign: *field artillery*. ■ used in names of animals or plants found in the open country, rather than among buildings or as cultivated varieties, e.g.: **field mouse**. ■ denoting a game played outdoors on a marked field.
– PHRASES **hold the field** remain the most important. **in the field** on campaign; (while) engaged in combat or manoeuvres: *troops in the field*. ■ away from the laboratory, office, or studio; engaged in practical work in a natural environment. **keep the field** archaic continue a military campaign. **lead the field** be the leader in a race. ■ be the best or most popular: *the brand leads the field in vegetarian ready meals*. **play the field** informal indulge in a series of sexual relationships without committing oneself to anyone. **take the field** (of a sports team) go on to a field to begin a game. ■ start a military campaign.
– ORIGIN Old English *feld* (also denoting a large tract of open country; compare with VELD), of West Germanic origin; related to Dutch *veld* and German *Feld*.

field bean ▶ noun a bean plant closely related to the broad bean but with smaller seeds, grown to improve soil fertility and for stockfeed. ● *Vicia faba*, family Leguminosae.

field book ▶ noun a book in which a surveyor writes down measurements and other technical notes taken in the field.

field boot ▶ noun a close-fitting, knee-length military boot.

field cornet ▶ noun S. African historical **1** a civilian official invested with the rank and responsibilities of a military officer and with judicial powers enabling him to act as a local administrator and magistrate.
2 a rank in the army equivalent to that of lieutenant.
– ORIGIN translating South African Dutch *veld kornet*, from *veld* 'field' + *kornet*, specifying a military rank.

fieldcraft ▶ noun [mass noun] the techniques involved in living, travelling, or making military or scientific observations in the field, especially while remaining undetected.

field cricket ▶ noun a European cricket that lives in a burrow in grassland and has a musical bird-like chirp. ● *Gryllus campestris*, family Gryllidae.

field day ▶ noun **1** [in sing.] an opportunity for action or success, especially at the expense of others: *the newspapers **had a field day** as the case came to court*.
2 Military a review or an exercise, especially in manoeuvring.
3 N. Amer. a day devoted to athletics or other sporting events and contests.
4 Austral./NZ a day set aside for the display of agricultural machinery.

field-effect transistor ▶ noun Electronics a transistor in which most current is carried along a channel whose effective resistance can be controlled by a transverse electric field.

field emission ▶ noun [mass noun] Physics the emission of electrons from the surface of a conductor under the influence of a strong electrostatic field, as a result of the tunnel effect.

fielder ▶ noun chiefly Cricket & Baseball a player on the fielding team, especially one other than the bowler or pitcher.

field events ▶ plural noun athletic sports other than races, such as throwing and jumping events. Compare with TRACK EVENTS.

fieldfare ▶ noun a large migratory thrush with a grey head, breeding in northern Eurasia. ● *Turdus pilaris*, family Turdidae.
– ORIGIN late Old English *feldefare*, perhaps from *feld* 'field' + the base of *faran* 'to travel' (see FARE).

field glasses ▶ plural noun binoculars for outdoor use.

field goal ▶ noun **1** American Football a goal scored by a place kick, scoring three points.
2 Basketball a goal scored while the clock is running and the ball is in play.

field grey ▶ noun [mass noun] a dark shade of grey, the regulation colour of the uniform of a German infantryman.

field guide ▸ noun a book for the identification of animals, birds, flowers, or other things in their natural environment.

field hand ▸ noun chiefly historical a person, especially a US slave, employed as a farm labourer.

field hockey ▸ noun see HOCKEY[1].

field holler ▸ noun see HOLLER.

field hospital ▸ noun a temporary hospital set up near a battlefield to provide emergency care for the wounded.

Fielding, Henry (1707–54), English novelist. He provoked the introduction of censorship in theatres with his political satire *The Historical Register for 1736*. He then turned to writing picaresque novels, notably *Joseph Andrews* (1742) and *Tom Jones* (1749). Fielding was also responsible for the formation of the Bow Street Runners in 1749.

field mark ▸ noun a visible mark or characteristic that can be used in identifying a bird or other animal in the field.

field marshal ▸ noun the highest rank of officer in the British army.

field mouse (also **long-tailed field mouse**) ▸ noun another term for WOOD MOUSE.

field mushroom ▸ noun the common edible mushroom, which is widely grown commercially. ● *Agaricus campestris*, family Agaricaceae, class Hymenomycetes.

field mustard ▸ noun another term for CHARLOCK.

field notes ▸ plural noun notes made by a person who is engaged in fieldwork.

field officer ▸ noun **1** a person in an organization with a position of responsibility involving practical activities in a particular area or region.
2 Military a major, lieutenant colonel, or colonel.

field of honour ▸ noun the place where a duel or battle is fought.

Field of the Cloth of Gold the scene of a meeting between Henry VIII of England and Francis I of France near Calais in 1520, for which both monarchs erected elaborate temporary palaces, including a sumptuous display of golden cloth. Little of importance was achieved, although the meeting symbolized Henry's determination to play a full part in European dynastic politics.

field of vision ▸ noun the entire area that a person or animal is able to see when their eyes are fixed in one position.

field pea ▸ noun a pea plant of a variety grown chiefly for stockfeed or as green manure.

field rank ▸ noun [mass noun] the rank attained by a military field officer.

Fields[1], Dame Gracie (1898–1979), English singer and comedienne; born *Grace Stansfield*. During the 1930s she enjoyed great success with English music-hall audiences, and went on to star in a series of popular films.

Fields[2], W. C. (1880–1946), American comedian; born *William Claude Dukenfield*. Having made his name as a comedy juggler he became a vaudeville star, appearing in the *Ziegfeld Follies* revues between 1915 and 1921. Notable films: *The Bank Dick* (1940).

fieldsman ▸ noun (pl. **fieldsmen**) **1** Cricket, Brit. a fielder.
2 an agent or salesman working for a company.

field sports ▸ plural noun outdoor sports, especially hunting, shooting, and fishing.

fieldstone ▸ noun [mass noun] [often as modifier] stone used in its natural form: *a fieldstone fireplace*.

field telegraph ▸ noun historical a movable telegraph for use on campaign.

field test ▸ noun a test carried out in the environment in which a product or device is to be used.
▸ verb (**field-test**) [with obj.] test (a product or device) in the environment in which it is to be used.

field theory ▸ noun Physics a theory that explains physical phenomena in terms of a field and the manner in which it interacts with matter or with other fields.

field trial ▸ noun **1** a field test.
2 a competition for gun dogs to test their levels of skill and training in retrieving or pointing.

field trip ▸ noun a trip made by students or research workers to study something at first hand.

field vole ▸ noun a vole with a dark shaggy coat and short tail, found abundantly in the grasslands of northern Eurasia. Also called SHORT-TAILED VOLE. ● *Microtus arvalis*, family Muridae.

field walking ▸ noun [mass noun] a technique for finding or studying archaeological sites by walking systematically across a ploughed field collecting artefacts on the surface.

fieldwork ▸ noun **1** [mass noun] practical work conducted by a researcher in the natural environment, rather than in a laboratory or office.
2 rare a temporary fortification.
– DERIVATIVES **fieldworker** noun.

fiend /fiːnd/ ▸ noun **1** an evil spirit or demon. ■ (**the fiend**) archaic the Devil. ■ a very wicked or cruel person: *Britain's most notorious sex fiend*.
2 informal an enthusiast or devotee of a particular thing: *a football fiend*.
– DERIVATIVES **fiendlike** adjective.
– ORIGIN Old English *fēond* 'an enemy, the devil, a demon', of Germanic origin; related to Dutch *vijand* and German *Feind* 'enemy'.

fiendish ▸ adjective extremely cruel or unpleasant: *fiendish methods of torture*. ■ informal extremely awkward or complex: *a fiendish problem*.
– DERIVATIVES **fiendishly** adverb [as submodifier] *a fiendishly clever plan*, **fiendishness** noun.

fierce ▸ adjective (**fiercer**, **fiercest**) having or displaying a violent or ferocious aggressiveness: *fierce fighting continued throughout the day*. ■ (of the weather or temperature) powerful and destructive: *fierce storms lashed the country*. ■ showing a heartfelt and powerful intensity: *his fierce loyalty | there was fierce local opposition to the plans*. ■ (of a mechanism) having a jolting and powerful abruptness of action: *the fire door had a fierce pneumatic return*.
▸ adverb Irish informal very; extremely: *he was fierce proud*.
– PHRASES **something fierce** N. Amer. informal to a great and almost overwhelming extent: *I missed the country something fierce*.
– DERIVATIVES **fiercely** adverb, **fierceness** noun.
– ORIGIN Middle English: from Old French *fiers* 'fierce, brave, proud', from Latin *ferus* 'untamed'.

fieri facias /ˌfʌɪərʌɪ ˈfeɪʃɪas/ ▸ noun [mass noun] Law a writ to a sheriff for executing a judgement.
– ORIGIN Latin, 'cause to be made or done'.

fiery ▸ adjective (**fierier**, **fieriest**) consisting of fire or burning strongly and brightly: *the sun was a fiery ball low on the hills* | figurative *a fiery pepper sauce*. ■ having the bright colour of fire: *the car was painted a fiery red*. ■ having a passionate and quick-tempered nature: *a fiery, imaginative Aries*. ■ showing strong emotion, typically anger: *a fiery speech*.
– DERIVATIVES **fierily** adverb, **fieriness** noun.

fiery cross ▸ noun a burning wooden cross carried as a symbol by the Ku Klux Klan. ■ historical a wooden cross, charred and dipped in blood, used among Scottish clans to summon men to battle.

fiesta /fɪˈɛstə/ ▸ noun (in Spanish-speaking countries) a religious festival: *the yearly fiesta of San Juan*. ■ an event marked by festivities or celebration: [in names] *the Bristol International Balloon Fiesta*.
– ORIGIN Spanish, from Latin *festum*, (plural) *festa* (see FEAST).

FIFA /ˈfiːfə/ the international governing body of soccer, formed in 1904 and based in Zurich, Switzerland.
– ORIGIN acronym from French *Fédération Internationale de Football Association*.

fi. fa. ▸ abbreviation fieri facias.

Fife a council area and former county of east central Scotland; administrative centre, Glenrothes.

fife ▸ noun a kind of small shrill flute used with the drum in military bands.
▸ verb [no obj.] archaic play the fife.
– DERIVATIVES **fifer** noun.
– ORIGIN mid 16th cent.: from German *Pfeife* 'pipe', or from French *fifre* from Swiss German *Pfifer* 'piper'.

fife rail ▸ noun chiefly historical a rail round the mainmast of a sailing ship, holding belaying pins. ■ the rail on top of the bulwark at the edge of a sailing ship's poop or forecastle.
– ORIGIN early 18th cent.: of unknown origin.

FIFO /ˈfʌɪfəʊ/ ▸ abbreviation first in, first out (chiefly with reference to methods of stock valuation and data storage). Compare with **LIFO**.

fifteen ▸ cardinal number **1** equivalent to the product of three and five; one more than fourteen, or five more than ten; 15: *all fifteen bedrooms have private facilities | fifteen feet high | fifteen of Howard's troops were killed*. (Roman numeral: **xv** or **XV**) ■ a size of garment or other merchandise denoted by fifteen. ■ fifteen years old: *she must be fifteen by now*. ■ a team of fifteen players, especially in rugby. ■ (**15**) Brit. (of a film) classified as suitable for people of 15 years and over.
2 (**the Fifteen**) historical the Jacobite rebellion of 1715.
– PHRASES **fifteen minutes of fame** (or **famous for fifteen minutes**) used with reference to a brief period of fame enjoyed by an ordinary person. [from a remark made by Andy Warhol in 1968, predicting that in the future, everyone would be 'world famous for fifteen minutes'.]
– ORIGIN Old English *fīftēne*, *fīftiene* (see FIVE, -TEEN).

fifteenth ▸ ordinal number **1** constituting number fifteen in a sequence; 15th: *August the fifteenth | the fifteenth century | on the fifteenth floor*. ■ an organ stop sounding a register of pipes two octaves (fifteen notes) above the diapason.
2 each of fifteen equal parts into which something is or may be divided.

F

fifth ▸ ordinal number **1** constituting number five in a sequence; 5th: *the fifth century* BC *| her mother had just given birth to another child, her fifth | the world's fifth-largest oil exporter | the fifth of November*. ■ the fifth finisher or position in a race or competition: *he finished fifth*. ■ (in some vehicles) the fifth (and typically highest) in a sequence of gears. ■ chiefly Brit. the fifth form of a school or college. ■ fifthly (used to introduce a fifth point or reason): *fourth, it can aid the process of life review, and fifth, it is an enjoyable and stimulating experience*. ■ Music an interval spanning five consecutive notes in a diatonic scale, in particular (also **perfect fifth**) an interval of three tones and a semitone (e.g. C to G): *strings tuned a fifth apart*. ■ Music the note which is higher by such an interval than the root of a diatonic scale. ■ US informal a fifth of a gallon, as a measure of alcoholic drink, or a bottle of this capacity: *a fifth of whisky*.
2 each of five equal parts into which something is or may be divided.
– PHRASES **take the fifth** (in the US) exercise the right guaranteed by the Fifth Amendment to the Constitution of refusing to answer questions in order to avoid incriminating oneself.
– DERIVATIVES **fifthly** adverb.

fifth column ▸ noun a group within a country at war who are sympathetic to or working for its enemies.
– DERIVATIVES **fifth columnist** noun.
– ORIGIN The term dates from the Spanish Civil War, when General Mola, leading four columns of troops towards Madrid, declared that he had a fifth column inside the city.

fifth-generation ▸ adjective denoting a proposed new class of computer or programming language employing artificial intelligence.

Fifth-monarchy-man ▸ noun historical a member of a 17th-century sect expecting the immediate Second Coming of Christ and repudiating all other government.
– ORIGIN from *Fifth Monarchy*, denoting the last of the five great empires prophesied by Daniel (Dan. 2:44).

fifth position ▸ noun **1** Ballet a posture in which the feet are placed turned outwards, one immediately in front of but touching the other so that the toe of the back foot just protrudes beyond the heel of the front foot. ■ a position of the arms in which they are held curved in front of the body, at hip level, waist level, or above the head, with the palms facing the body.
2 Music a position of the left hand on the fingerboard of a stringed instrument nearer to the bridge than the fourth position, enabling a higher set of notes to be played.

Fifth Republic the republican regime established in France with de Gaulle's introduction of a new constitution in 1958.

fifth wheel ▸ noun chiefly N. Amer. **1** an extra wheel for a four-wheeled vehicle. ■ informal a superfluous person or thing.
2 a coupling between a vehicle used for towing and a trailer. ■ (also **fifth-wheel trailer**) a trailer with accommodation for camping out.
3 historical a horizontal turntable over the front axle of a carriage as an extra support to prevent its tipping.

fifty ▸ cardinal number (pl. **fifties**) the number equivalent to the product of five and ten; half of one hundred; 50: *only fifty per cent of the aircraft were serviceable | about fifty of us filed in | a fifty-pound salmon*. (Roman numeral: **l** or **L**) ■ (**fifties**) the numbers from 50 to 59, especially the years of a century or of a person's life: *Elvis is the icon of the Fifties*. ■ fifty years old: *she looked about fifty*. ■ fifty

miles an hour: *I was doing about fifty.* ■ a size of garment or other merchandise denoted by fifty. ■ a fifty-pound note or fifty-dollar bill.
– DERIVATIVES **fiftieth** ordinal number, **fiftyfold** adjective & adverb.
– ORIGIN Old English *fiftig* (see FIVE, -TY²).

fifty-fifty ▸ adjective the same in share or proportion; equal: *fifty-fifty partners.* ■ used to refer to one of two possibilities that are equally likely to happen: *he has a fifty-fifty chance of surviving the operation.*
▸ adverb in two amounts or parts that are the same in size; equally: *they divided the spoil fifty-fifty.*

fifty-year rule ▸ noun Brit. historical a rule that public records may be open to inspection after a lapse of fifty years. Superseded in the UK in 1968 by the thirty-year rule.

F

fig¹ ▸ noun **1** a soft pear-shaped fruit with sweet dark flesh and many small seeds, eaten fresh or dried.
2 (also **fig tree**) the deciduous Old World tree or shrub which bears figs. ● *Ficus carica*, family Moraceae. ■ used in names of other plants of this genus, e.g. **strangling fig**, **weeping fig**.
– PHRASES **not give** (or **care**) **a fig** not have the slightest concern about: *Elaine didn't give a fig for Joe's comfort or his state of mind.*
– ORIGIN Middle English: from Old French *figue*, from Provençal *fig(u)a*, based on Latin *ficus*.

fig² informal ▸ noun (in phrase **full fig**) smart clothes, especially those appropriate to a particular occasion or profession: *a soldier walking up the street **in full fig**.*
▸ verb (**figs**, **figging**, **figged**) [with obj.] archaic dress up (someone) to look smart: *he was **figged out** as fine as fivepence, with white trousers and rings and chains.*
– ORIGIN late 17th cent. (as a verb): variant of obsolete *feague* 'liven up' (earlier 'whip'); perhaps related to German *fegen* 'sweep, thrash'; compare with FAKE¹. An early sense of the verb was 'fill the head with nonsense'; later (early 19th cent.) 'cause (a horse) to be lively and carry its tail well (by applying ginger to its anus)'; hence 'smarten up'.

fig. ▸ abbreviation figure: *see fig.34.*

figbird ▸ noun a gregarious fruit-eating Australasian bird of the oriole family, the male of which has a green back and a yellow or green breast. ● *Sphecotheres viridis*, family Oriolidae; formerly treated as several species.

fight ▸ verb (past and past participle **fought**) **1** [no obj.] take part in a violent struggle involving the exchange of physical blows or the use of weapons: *the men were fighting | protesters fought with police | Cameron **fought back** as hard as he could.* ■ engage in a war or battle: *those who had fought for King and country |* [with obj.] *the country is still fighting a civil war.* ■ [with obj.] archaic command, manage, or manoeuvre (troops, a ship, or military equipment) in battle: *General Hill fights his troops well.* ■ quarrel or argue: *they were **fighting over** who pays the bill.* ■ [with obj.] take part in a boxing match against (an opponent): *McCracken will fight Sheffield's Martin Smith.*
2 [with obj.] struggle to overcome, eliminate, or prevent: *a churchman who has dedicated his life to fighting racism | the company intends to fight the decision.* ■ [no obj.] strive to achieve or do something: *I will **fight for** a fairer society | for several days, doctors fought to save his life.* ■ endeavour vigorously to win (an election or other contest). ■ attempt to repress (a feeling or its expression): *she had to **fight back** tears of frustration.* ■ (**fight one's way**) move forward with difficulty, especially by pushing through a crowd: *she watched him fight his way across the room.*
▸ noun a violent confrontation or struggle: *he'd **got into a fight** with some bouncers outside a club.* ■ a boxing match. ■ a battle or war: *Britain might have given up her fight against Germany.* ■ a vigorous struggle or campaign for or against something: *their **fight for** control of the company | a long fight against cancer.* ■ an argument or quarrel: *he'd had another fight with Katie.* ■ [mass noun] the inclination or ability to fight or struggle: *Ginny felt the fight trickle out of her.*
– PHRASES **fight fire with fire** use the weapons or tactics of one's enemy or opponent, even if one finds them distasteful. **fight like cat and dog** (of two people) be continually arguing with one another. **fight a losing battle** be fated to fail in one's efforts: *the police are fighting a losing battle against a rising tide of crime.* **fight shy of** be unwilling to undertake or become involved with: *MacMillan has never fought shy of controversy.* **make a fight of it** put up a spirited show of resistance in a fight or contest. **fight or flight** the instinctive physiological response to a threatening situation, which readies one either to resist forcibly or to run away. **put up a fight** offer resistance to an attack.
– PHRASAL VERBS **fight someone/thing off** defend oneself against an attack by someone or something: *Candice fought her assailant off |* figurative *well-fed people are better able to fight off infectious disease.*
– ORIGIN Old English *feohtan* (verb), *feoht(e)*, *gefeoht* (noun), of West Germanic origin; related to Dutch *vechten*, *gevecht* and German *fechten*, *Gefecht*.

fightback ▸ noun Brit. a great effort to gain a position of strength made by a person or group who seem likely to lose a contest: *a storming second-half fightback from Chelsea.*

fighter ▸ noun **1** a person or animal that fights: *the distinction between civilian populations and fighters.* ■ a person who does not easily admit defeat in spite of difficulties or opposition: *there'll be months of physiotherapy but medical staff say she's a fighter.*
2 a fast military aircraft designed for attacking other aircraft: [as modifier] *fighter pilots.*

> **WORD TRENDS** Labels are powerful things, carrying with them a great raft of associations and assumptions, and **terrorist** is one of the most inflammatory. Since the War on Terror was proclaimed in 2001 and wars were initiated in Iraq and Afghanistan, frequency of the word **terrorist** in the Oxford English Corpus peaked sharply but has now declined, whereas evidence for **fighter**, **insurgent**, and **militant**, more neutral labels for non-governmental forces opposing Western troops, has steadily increased. However, the neutrality of **fighter** is a matter of debate: in the Corpus it is typically associated with such positive tags as *liberation*, *heroic*, and *courageous*. Such words are not attached to **terrorist**, which is far more likely to be linked to *fanatical*, *dangerous*, or *deadly*.

fighter-bomber ▸ noun an aircraft serving as both a fighter and bomber.

fighting ▸ noun [mass noun] the action of fighting; violence or conflict: *terrible fighting broke out in the streets.*
▸ adjective displaying or engaging in violence, combat, or aggression: *he was a fighting man | he put up his fists and took a fighting stance.*

fighting chair ▸ noun N. Amer. a fixed chair on a boat used by a person trying to catch large fish.

fighting chance ▸ noun a possibility of success if great effort is made: *they still have a fighting chance of clinching the title.*

fighting fish (also **Siamese fighting fish**) ▸ noun a small labyrinth fish native to Thailand, the males of which fight vigorously. It has been bred in a variety of colours for aquaria. ● *Betta splendens*, family Belontiidae.

fighting fit ▸ adjective in excellent health: *Mary had responded to treatment and seemed fighting fit.*

fighting fund ▸ noun Brit. money raised to finance a campaign, especially one supporting a political or social cause.

fighting top ▸ noun historical a platform high on a warship's mast on which guns or marksmen can be stationed.

fighting words ▸ plural noun (also **fighting talk**) informal **1** words indicating a willingness to fight or challenge a person or thing.
2 US insulting or provocative words, especially of an ethnic, racial, or sexist nature, considered unacceptable or illegal by certain institutions and afforded less protection than free speech.

fig leaf ▸ noun a leaf of a fig tree, often used for concealing the genitals in paintings and sculpture. ■ a thing intended to conceal a difficulty or embarrassment: *the amendment was just a fig leaf intended to cover the cracks in the party.*
– ORIGIN early 16th cent.: with reference to the story of Adam and Eve (Gen. 3:7).

figment /ˈfɪgm(ə)nt/ ▸ noun a thing that someone believes to be real but that exists only in their imagination: *it really was Ross and not **a figment of her overheated imagination**.*
– ORIGIN late Middle English (denoting an invented statement or story): from Latin *figmentum*, related to *fingere* 'form, contrive'. Compare with FEIGN and FICTION. The current sense dates from the early 17th cent.

fig parrot ▸ noun a very small short-tailed Australasian parrot, with mainly green plumage and a coloured head, feeding on soft fruit. Also called LORILET. ● Genera *Opopsitta* and *Psittaculirostris*, family Psittacidae: five species.

figura /fɪˈgjʊərə/ ▸ noun (pl. **figurae** /-riː/) (in literary theory) a person or thing representing or symbolizing a fact or ideal.
– ORIGIN Latin, literally 'figure' (representing an early use of *figure* to denote an emblem or type).

figural /ˈfɪgjʊr(ə)l/ ▸ adjective another term for FIGURATIVE. ■ (in postmodernist writing) relating to or denoting a form of signification which relies on imagery and association rather than on rational and linguistic concepts.
– ORIGIN late Middle English: from Old French, or from late Latin *figuralis*, from *figura* 'form, shape' (see FIGURE).

figurant /ˈfɪgjʊr(ə)nt/ ▸ noun (fem. **figurante** /ˌfɪgjʊˈrɒ̃t/) a supernumerary actor who has little or nothing to say.
– ORIGIN French, present participle of *figurer* 'to figure'.

figuration /ˌfɪgəˈreɪʃ(ə)n, -gjʊ-/ ▸ noun [mass noun] **1** ornamentation by means of figures or designs. ■ Music the use of florid counterpoint.
2 allegorical representation: *the figuration of 'The Possessed' is much more complex.*
– ORIGIN Middle English (in the senses 'outline' and 'making of arithmetical figures'): from Latin *figuratio(n-)*, from *figurare* 'to form or fashion', from *figura* (see FIGURE).

figurative ▸ adjective **1** departing from a literal use of words; metaphorical: *a figurative expression.*
2 (of an artist or work of art) representing forms that are recognizably derived from life.
– DERIVATIVES **figuratively** adverb, **figurativeness** noun.
– ORIGIN Middle English: from late Latin *figurativus*, from *figurare* 'to form or fashion', from *figura* (see FIGURE).

figure /ˈfɪgə/ ▸ noun **1** a number, especially one which forms part of official statistics or relates to the financial performance of a company: *the trade figures | by 1998, this figure had risen to 14 million.* ■ a numerical symbol, especially any of the ten in Arabic notation: *the figure 7.* ■ one of a specified number of digits making up a larger number, used to give a rough idea of the order of magnitude: [in combination] *a six-figure sum of money.* ■ an amount of money: *a figure of two thousand pounds.* ■ (**figures**) arithmetical calculations: *she has no **head for figures**.*
2 a person's bodily shape, especially that of a woman and when considered to be attractive: *she had always been so proud of her figure.* ■ a person seen indistinctly or from a distance: *a dark figure emerged from the shadows.* ■ a representation of a human or animal form in drawing or sculpture: *starkly painted figures.*
3 a person of a particular kind, especially one who is important or distinctive in some way: *Williams became something of a cult figure.*
4 a shape which is defined by one or more lines in two dimensions (such as a circle or a triangle), or one or more surfaces in three dimensions (such as a sphere or a cuboid), either considered mathematically in geometry or used as a decorative design: *a red ground with white and blue geometrical figures.* ■ a diagram or illustrative drawing, especially in a book or magazine: *figure 1 shows an ignition circuit.* ■ (in skating) a movement or series of movements following a prescribed pattern and often beginning and ending at the same point. ■ a pattern formed by the movements of a group of people, for example in country dancing, as part of a longer dance or display. ■ archaic the external form or shape of something.
5 Music a short succession of notes producing a single impression; a brief melodic or rhythmic formula out of which longer passages are developed.
6 Logic the form of a syllogism, classified according to the position of the middle term.
▸ verb [no obj.] **1** have a significant part or role in a situation or process: *the issue of nuclear policy **figured** prominently **in** the talks | human rights do not figure high on their agenda.*
2 [with obj.] N. Amer. calculate or work out (an amount or value) arithmetically: *my accountant figured my tax wrong.*
3 [with clause] informal, chiefly N. Amer. think, consider, or expect to be the case: *I figured that I didn't have much of a chance |* [with obj.] *for years, teachers had figured him for a dullard.* ■ (of a recent event or newly discovered fact) be perfectly understandable and only to be expected: *well, she supposed **that figured**.*
4 [with obj.] represent in a diagram or picture. ■ (usu. as adj. **figured**) embellish (something) with a pattern: *the floors were covered with figured linoleum.*
– PHRASES **figure of fun** a person who is considered ridiculous. **lose** (or **keep**) **one's figure** lose (or retain) a slim and attractive bodily shape. **put a figure on** give a price or exact number for.

– PHRASAL VERBS **figure on** N. Amer. informal expect (something) to happen or be the case: *anyone thinking of salmon fishing should figure on paying $200 a day.* **figure something out** informal solve or discover the cause of a problem: *he was trying to figure out why the camera wasn't working.* **figure someone out** reach an understanding of a person's actions, motives, or personality.
– DERIVATIVES **figureless** adjective.
– ORIGIN Middle English (in the senses 'distinctive shape of a person or thing', 'representation of something material or immaterial', and 'numerical symbol', among others): from Old French *figure* (noun), *figurer* (verb), from Latin *figura* 'shape, figure, form'; related to *fingere* 'form, contrive'.

figured bass ▶ noun Music a bass line with the intended harmonies indicated by figures rather than written out as chords, typical of continuo parts in baroque music.

figure-ground ▶ adjective [attrib.] Psychology & Art relating to or denoting the perception of images by the distinction of objects from a background from which they appear to stand out, especially in contexts where this distinction is ambiguous.

figurehead ▶ noun **1** a carving, typically a bust or a full-length figure, set at the prow of an old-fashioned sailing ship.
2 a nominal leader or head without real power.

figure-hugging ▶ adjective (of a garment) fitting closely to the contours of a woman's body: *a low-cut, figure-hugging dress.*

figure of eight (N. Amer. **figure eight**) ▶ noun an object or movement having the shape of the number eight.

figure of merit ▶ noun a numerical expression taken as representing the performance or efficiency of a given device, material, or procedure.

figure of speech ▶ noun a word or phrase used in a non-literal sense for rhetorical or vivid effect.

figure skating ▶ noun [mass noun] the sport of skating in prescribed patterns from a stationary position.
– DERIVATIVES **figure skater** noun.

figurine /ˈfɪɡəriːn, -ɡjʊ-/ ▶ noun a statuette, especially one of a human form.
– ORIGIN mid 19th cent.: from French, from Italian *figurina*, diminutive of *figura*, from Latin *figura* (see FIGURE).

fig wasp ▶ noun a minute Old World wasp which lays its eggs inside the flower of the wild fig. It was introduced into the New World to effect cross-fertilization of the cultivated fig. ● *Blastophaga psenes*, family Agaonidae, superfamily Chalcidoidea.

figwort ▶ noun a widely distributed herbaceous plant with purplish brown two-lobed flowers. It was formerly considered to be effective in the treatment of scrofula. ● Genus *Scrophularia*, family Scrophulariaceae (the **figwort family**): several species. Plants of this family have distinctive two-lobed flowers and include the snapdragons, toadflaxes, foxgloves, mulleins, monkey flowers, and speedwells.
– ORIGIN mid 16th cent.: from obsolete *fig* 'piles' + WORT. The word originally denoted the pilewort or lesser celandine, which was used as a treatment for piles; the current sense dates from the late 16th cent.

Fiji /ˈfiːdʒiː/ a country in the South Pacific consisting of a group of some 840 islands, of which about a hundred are inhabited; pop. 944,700 (est. 2009); languages, English (official), Fijian, Hindi; capital, Suva.

> First visited by Abel Tasman in 1643, the Fiji Islands became a British Crown Colony in 1874 and an independent Commonwealth state in 1970. In 1987, following a coup, Fiji became a republic and withdrew from the Commonwealth, rejoining in 1997.

Fijian /fiːˈdʒiːən/ ▶ adjective relating to Fiji, its people, or their language.
▶ noun **1** a native or inhabitant of Fiji, or a person of Fijian descent.
2 [mass noun] the Austronesian language of the indigenous people of Fiji.

filagree /ˈfɪləɡriː/ ▶ noun variant spelling of FILIGREE.

filagreed ▶ adjective variant spelling of FILIGREED.

filament /ˈfɪləm(ə)nt/ ▶ noun **1** a slender thread-like object or fibre, especially one found in animal or plant structures: *each myosin filament is usually surrounded by 12 actin filaments.* ■ Botany the slender part of a stamen that supports the anther. ■ Astronomy a narrow streamer from the sun's chromosphere or in its corona.
2 a conducting wire or thread with a high melting point, forming part of an electric bulb or thermionic valve and heated or made incandescent by an electric current.
– DERIVATIVES **filamentary** adjective, **filamented** adjective, **filamentous** adjective.
– ORIGIN late 16th cent.: from French, or from modern Latin *filamentum*, from late Latin *filare* 'to spin', from Latin *filum* 'thread'.

filaria /fɪˈlɛːrɪə/ ▶ noun (pl. **filariae** /-rɪiː/) a thread-like parasitic nematode worm which is transmitted by biting flies and mosquitoes, causing filariasis and related diseases. ● Superfamily Filarioidea, class Phasmida.
– DERIVATIVES **filarial** adjective.
– ORIGIN mid 19th cent.: from modern Latin *Filaria* (former genus name), from Latin *filum* 'thread'.

filariasis /fɪˌlɛːrɪˈeɪsɪs, ˌfɪləˈrʌɪəsɪs/ ▶ noun [mass noun] Medicine a tropical disease caused by the presence of filarial worms, especially in the lymph vessels where heavy infestation can result in elephantiasis.

filature /ˈfɪlətʃə, -tjə/ ▶ noun a place where silk is obtained from silkworm cocoons. ■ [mass noun] the process of obtaining silk from the cocoons of silkworms.
– ORIGIN mid 18th cent.: from French, from Italian *filatura*, from *filare* 'to spin'.

filbert ▶ noun **1** a cultivated hazel tree that bears edible oval nuts. ● Genus *Corylus*, family Betulaceae: several species, in particular the Kentish cob (*Corylus maxima*). ■ the nut of the filbert tree. Also called COB[1].
2 (also **filbert brush**) a brush with bristles forming a flattened oval head, used in oil painting.
– ORIGIN Middle English *fylberd*, from Anglo-Norman French *philbert*, dialect French *noix de filbert* (so named because it is ripe about 20 August, the feast day of *St Philibert*).

filch /fɪltʃ/ ▶ verb [with obj.] informal pilfer or steal (something, especially an item of small value) in a casual way: *they filched milk off morning doorsteps.*
– DERIVATIVES **filcher** noun.
– ORIGIN Middle English: of unknown origin.

file[1] ▶ noun **1** a folder or box for holding loose papers together and in order for easy reference: *a file of correspondence.* ■ a collection of information about a particular person or thing: *MI5 were keeping a file on him.* ■ Computing a collection of data, programs, etc. stored in a computer's memory or on a storage device under a single identifying name: *you can save the file to your hard disk.*
2 Canadian a number of issues and responsibilities relating to a particular policy area: *what progress has the Prime Minister made on the unity file?*
▶ verb [with obj.] place (a document) in a cabinet, box, or folder in a particular order: *the contract, when signed, is filed* | figurative *he still had the moment filed away in his memory.* ■ submit (a legal document, application, or charge) to be placed on record by the appropriate authority: *criminal charges were filed against the firm* | [no obj.] *the company had filed for bankruptcy.* ■ (of a reporter) send (a story) to a newspaper or news organization.
– PHRASES **on file** in a file or filing system.
– DERIVATIVES **filer** noun.
– ORIGIN late Middle English (as a verb meaning 'string documents on a thread or wire to keep them in order'): from French *filer* 'to string', *fil* 'a thread', both from Latin *filum* 'a thread'. Compare with FILE[2].

file[2] ▶ noun a line of people or things one behind another: *files of tourists stream up the narrow lanes of Mont St Michel.* ■ Military a small detachment of troops: *a file of English soldiers had ridden out from Perth.* ■ Chess each of the eight rows of eight squares on a chessboard running away from the player towards the opponent. Compare with RANK[1] (sense 2 of the noun).
▶ verb [no obj., with adverbial of direction] (of a group of people) walk one behind the other, typically in an orderly and solemn manner: *the mourners filed into the church.*
– ORIGIN late 16th cent.: from French *file*, from *filer* 'to string'.

file[3] ▶ noun a tool with a roughened surface or surfaces, typically of steel, used for smoothing or shaping a hard material.
▶ verb [with obj.] smooth or shape with a file: *never file your nails from the centre to the sides.* ■ (**file something away/off**) remove something by grinding it off with a file.
– DERIVATIVES **filer** noun.
– ORIGIN Old English *fīl*, of West Germanic origin; related to Dutch *vijl* and German *Feile*.

filé /ˈfiːleɪ/ ▶ noun [mass noun] N. Amer. pounded or powdered sassafras leaves used to flavour and thicken soup, especially gumbo.
– ORIGIN mid 19th cent.: from French, past participle of *filer* 'to twist'.

file cabinet ▶ noun N. Amer. another term for FILING CABINET.

file extension ▶ noun Computing a string of characters attached to a filename, usually preceded by a full stop and indicating the format of the file.

filefish ▶ noun (pl. **same** or **filefishes**) a fish with a dorsal spine and rough scales, related to the triggerfishes and occurring in tropical and sometimes temperate seas. ● Numerous genera and species, family Balistidae (or Monacanthidae).
– ORIGIN late 18th cent.: from FILE[3] (because of its rough skin, suggesting the surface of a file).

filename ▶ noun an identifying name given to a computer file.

file server ▶ noun Computing a device which controls access to separately stored files, as part of a multi-user system.

file shell ▶ noun a free-swimming bivalve mollusc, the shell of which is typically white and has a rough, ribbed external surface. ● Family Limidae.

file snake ▶ noun **1** a widespread but rarely seen nocturnal African constricting snake which is triangular in cross section with rough scales, giving it the appearance of a three-cornered file. ● Genus *Mehelya*, family Colubridae: several species.
2 another term for WART SNAKE.

filet /ˈfiːleɪ, ˈfɪlɪt/ ▶ noun **1** French spelling of FILLET, used especially in the names of French or French-sounding dishes: *filet de boeuf.*
2 [mass noun] a kind of net or lace with a square mesh. [late 19th cent.: from French, 'net'.]

filet mignon /ˌfiːleɪ ˈmiːnjɒ̃/ ▶ noun [mass noun] a small tender piece of beef from the end of the undercut.
– ORIGIN French, literally 'dainty fillet'.

filial /ˈfɪlɪəl/ ▶ adjective **1** relating to or due from a son or daughter: *a display of filial affection.*
2 Biology denoting the offspring of a cross. See also F[1] (sense 1).
– DERIVATIVES **filially** adverb.
– ORIGIN late Middle English: from Old French, or from ecclesiastical Latin *filialis*, from *filius* 'son', *filia* 'daughter'.

filiation /ˌfɪlɪˈeɪʃ(ə)n/ ▶ noun [mass noun] the fact of being the child of a particular parent or parents: *relationships based on ties of filiation as opposed to marriage.* ■ the fact of being descended or derived from something: *the filiation of many of his ideas from those developed by Carpenter.* ■ the relation of one thing to another from which it is derived or descended in some respect: *the filiation of Old Norse manuscripts.*
– ORIGIN late Middle English: from French, from ecclesiastical and medieval Latin *filiatio(n-)*, from Latin *filius* 'son', *filia* 'daughter'.

filibeg /ˈfɪlɪbɛɡ/ (also **philibeg**) ▶ noun Scottish, chiefly historical a kilt.
– ORIGIN mid 18th cent.: from Scottish Gaelic *feileadh-beag* 'little kilt', from *feileadh* 'plaid' and *beag* 'little'.

filibuster /ˈfɪlɪbʌstə/ ▶ noun **1** an action such as prolonged speaking which obstructs progress in a legislative assembly in a way that does not technically contravene the required procedures.
2 historical a person engaging in unauthorized warfare against a foreign state.
▶ verb [no obj.] (often as noun **filibustering**) act in an obstructive manner in a legislative assembly, especially by speaking at inordinate length: *several measures were killed by Republican filibustering.* ■ [with obj.] obstruct (proposed legislation) with a filibuster.
– ORIGIN late 18th cent.: from French *flibustier*, first applied to pirates who pillaged the Spanish colonies in the West Indies. In the mid 19th cent. (via Spanish *filibustero*), the term denoted American adventurers who incited revolution in several Latin American states, whence sense 2 of the noun. The verb was used to describe tactics intended to sabotage US congressional proceedings, whence sense 1 of the noun.

filicide /ˈfɪlɪsʌɪd/ ▶ noun [mass noun] the killing of one's son or daughter: *maternal filicide.* ■ [count noun] a person who kills their son or daughter.
– ORIGIN mid 17th cent. from Latin *filius* 'son', *filia* 'daughter' + -CIDE.

Filicopsida /ˌfɪlɪˈkɒpsɪdə/ ▶ plural noun Botany a class of pteridophyte plants that comprises the ferns.
– ORIGIN modern Latin (plural), from Latin *filix*, *filic-* 'fern' + *opsis* 'appearance'.

F

filiform /ˈfʌɪlɪfɔːm/ ▶ **adjective** Biology thread-like: *the antennae are filiform.*
– ORIGIN mid 18th cent.: from Latin *filum* 'thread' + **-IFORM**.

filigree /ˈfɪlɪɡriː/ (also **filagree**) ▶ **noun** [mass noun] ornamental work of fine (typically gold or silver) wire formed into delicate tracery: [as modifier] *filigree earrings* | figurative *pine needles draped with a delicate filigree of mist.*
– ORIGIN late 17th cent. (earlier as *filigreen, filigrane*): from French *filigrane*, from Italian *filigrana* (from Latin *filum* 'thread' + *granum* 'seed').

filigreed (also **filagreed**) ▶ **adjective** ornamented with or resembling filigree work: *white filigreed stockings.*

filing ▶ **noun** (usu. **filings**) a small particle rubbed off by a file when smoothing or shaping something: *iron filings.*

F

filing cabinet ▶ **noun** a large piece of office furniture, typically made of metal, with deep drawers for storing documents.

Filioque /ˌfiːlɪˈəʊkwi/ the word inserted in the Western version of the Nicene Creed to assert the doctrine of the procession of the Holy Ghost from the Son as well as from the Father, which is not admitted by the Eastern Church. It was one of the central issues in the Great Schism of 1054.
– ORIGIN Latin, literally 'and from the Son'.

Filipina /ˌfɪlɪˈpiːnə/ ▶ **noun** a female Filipino.
– ORIGIN Spanish.

Filipino /ˌfɪlɪˈpiːnəʊ/ (also **Pilipino**) ▶ **adjective** relating to the Philippines, the Filipinos, or their language.
▶ **noun** (pl. **Filipinos**) **1** a native or inhabitant of the Philippines, or a person of Filipino descent.
2 [mass noun] the national language of the Philippines, a standardized form of Tagalog.
– ORIGIN Spanish, from *las Islas Filipinas* 'the Philippine Islands'.

Filippoi /ˈfilipi/ Greek name for **PHILIPPI**.

fill ▶ **verb 1** [with obj.] cause (a space or container) to become full or almost full: *I **filled up** the bottle with water* | *the office was **filled with** reporters.* ▪ block up (a cavity in a tooth) with cement, amalgam, or gold. ▪ [no obj.] become full: *Elinor's eyes **filled with** tears* | *the dining car filled up.* ▪ [no obj.] (**fill up**) fill the fuel tank of a car. ▪ become an overwhelming presence in; pervade: *a pungent smell of garlic filled the air.* ▪ cause (someone) to experience a strong emotion or feeling: *his presence **filled** us **with** foreboding.* ▪ [no obj.] (of a sail) curve out tautly from its supports as the wind blows into it. ▪ (of the wind) blow into (a sail), causing it to curve outwards.
2 appoint a person to hold (a vacant post): *the board contacted him to say they had already filled the position.* ▪ hold and perform the expected duties of (a post or role): *he had filled the post in an acting capacity for some time.* ▪ satisfy or fulfil (a want or need): *community land trusts are a way to fill the pressing need for housing.*
3 occupy or take up (a period of time): *the next few days were **filled with** meetings.*
4 chiefly N. Amer. be supplied with the items described in (a prescription or order).
5 (in poker) complete (a good hand) by drawing the necessary cards.
▶ **noun 1** (**one's fill**) an amount of something which is as much as one wants or can bear: *we have eaten our fill* | *I've **had my fill of** surprises for one day.*
2 an amount of something which will occupy all the space in a container: ***a fill of** tobacco.* ▪ [mass noun] material, typically loose or compacted, which fills a space, especially in building or engineering work: *loose polystyrene fill.* ▪ [mass noun] the action of filling something, especially of shading in a region of a computer graphics display. ▪ (in popular music) a short interjected phrase on a particular instrument.
– PHRASES **fill the bill** see **BILL**[1]. **fill one's boots** informal have as much of something as one wants; do something to the full: *fill your boots with spicy Szechuan food for under five bucks a plate.* **fill someone's shoes** (or **boots**) informal take over someone's function or duties and fulfil them satisfactorily.
– PHRASAL VERBS **fill in** act as a substitute for someone when they are unable to do their job: *my producer will have to have someone standing by to **fill in for** me.* **fill someone in 1** inform someone more fully of a matter: *they filled me in on all the latest news from Cambridge.* **2** Brit. informal, dated hit or punch someone: *I filled in a chap and took his money.* **fill something in 1** chiefly Brit. add information to complete a form or other official document: *simply fill in the application form and return it to your local branch.* **2** complete a drawing by adding colour or shade to the spaces within an outline: *incised letters, filled in with gold.* **3** occupy one's spare time, typically while waiting for something else to happen: *with all the shops to keep you occupied, you'll have no problem filling in a couple of hours.* **fill out** (of a person) put on weight to a noticeable extent. **fill something out** chiefly N. Amer. add information to complete an official form or document. ▪ give more details about something: *further research will fill out these early findings.*
– ORIGIN Old English *fyllan* (verb), *fyllu* (noun) of Germanic origin; related to Dutch *vullen* and German *füllen* (verbs), *Fülle* (noun), also to **FULL**[1].

fille de joie /ˌfiː də ˈʒwɑː/ ▶ **noun** (pl. **filles de joie**) euphemistic a prostitute.
– ORIGIN French, literally 'girl of pleasure'.

filler[1] /ˈfɪlə/ ▶ **noun 1** [usu. in combination] a thing put in a space or container to fill it: *these plants are attractive gap-fillers or ground cover.* ▪ [mass noun] a substance used for filling cracks or holes in a surface, especially before painting it: *wood filler.* ▪ [mass noun] material used to fill a cavity or increase bulk: *foam filler.* ▪ an item serving only to fill space or time in a newspaper, broadcast, or recording. ▪ a word or sound filling a pause in an utterance or conversation (e.g. *er, well, you know*). ▪ a linguistic unit that fills a particular slot in syntactic structure.
2 [in combination] a person or thing that fills a space or container: *supermarket shelf-fillers.*
3 [mass noun] US the tobacco blend used in a cigar.

filler[2] /ˈfɪlɜː/ ▶ **noun** (pl. **same**) a monetary unit of Hungary, equal to one hundredth of a forint.
– ORIGIN from Hungarian *fillér*.

filler cap ▶ **noun** a cap closing the pipe leading to the petrol tank of a motor vehicle.

fillet ▶ **noun 1** a fleshy boneless piece of meat from near the loins or the ribs of an animal: *a chicken breast fillet* | [mass noun] *roast **fillet of** lamb.* ▪ (also **fillet steak**) a beef steak cut from the lower part of a sirloin. ▪ a boned side of a fish.
2 a band or ribbon worn round the head, especially for binding the hair. ▪ Architecture a narrow flat band separating two mouldings. ▪ Architecture a small band between the flutes of a column.
3 a roughly triangular strip of material which rounds off an interior angle between two surfaces.
4 (in bookbinding) a plain line impressed on the cover of a book. ▪ a roller used to impress a fillet on the cover of a book.
▶ **verb** (**fillets, filleting, filleted**) [with obj.] remove the bones from (a fish). ▪ cut (fish or meat) into boneless strips.
– DERIVATIVES **filleter** noun.
– ORIGIN Middle English (denoting a band worn round the head): from Old French *filet* 'thread', based on Latin *filum* 'thread'.

filling ▶ **noun** a quantity of soft material that fills or is used to fill something: *duvets with synthetic fillings.* ▪ a piece of metal or other material used to fill a cavity in a tooth: *a gold filling.* ▪ an edible substance placed between the layers of a sandwich, cake, or other foodstuff: *a Swiss roll with a chocolate filling.* ▪ N. Amer. another term for **WEFT**[1].
▶ **adjective** (of food) leaving one with a pleasantly satiated feeling: *the full English breakfast was delicious and also very filling.*

filling station ▶ **noun** a petrol station.

fillip /ˈfɪlɪp/ ▶ **noun 1** something which acts as a stimulus or boost to an activity: *the halving of car tax would provide **a fillip to** sales.*
2 archaic a movement made by bending the last joint of the finger against the thumb and suddenly releasing it; a flick of the finger. ▪ a slight smart stroke or tap inflicted with a flick of the finger.
▶ **verb** (**fillips, filliping, filliped**) [with obj.] archaic propel (a small object) with a flick of the fingers. ▪ strike slightly and smartly.
– ORIGIN late Middle English (in the sense 'make a fillip with the fingers'): symbolic; compare with **FLICK**, **FLIP**[1].

fillister /ˈfɪlɪstə/ ▶ **noun** a rebate for holding a sash window. ▪ (also **fillister plane**) a rebate plane.
– ORIGIN early 19th cent.: perhaps from French *feuilleret*.

fill light ▶ **noun** a supplementary light used in photography or filming that does not change the character of the main light and is used chiefly to lighten shadows.

Fillmore, Millard (1800–74), American Whig statesman, 13th President of the US 1850–3. He was an advocate of compromise on the slavery issue, but his unpopular enforcement of the 1850 Fugitive Slave Act hastened the end of the Whig Party.

fill-up ▶ **noun** an instance of filling something, especially the fuel tank of a car.

filly ▶ **noun** (pl. **fillies**) a young female horse, especially one less than four years old. ▪ humorous a lively girl or young woman.
– ORIGIN late Middle English: from Old Norse *fylja*, of Germanic origin; related to **FOAL**.

film ▶ **noun 1** [mass noun] a thin flexible strip of plastic or other material coated with light-sensitive emulsion for exposure in a camera, used to produce photographs or motion pictures: *he had already shot a whole roll of film* | [count noun] *a new range of films and cameras.* ▪ material in the form of a very thin flexible sheet: *clear plastic film between the layers of glass.* ▪ [count noun] a thin layer covering a surface: *she quickly wiped away the light film of sweat.* ▪ archaic a fine thread or filament: *films of silk.*
2 a story or event recorded by a camera as a set of moving images and shown in a cinema or on television: *a horror film* | [as modifier] *a film director.* ▪ [mass noun] cinema considered as an art or industry: *a critical overview of feminist writing on film.*
▶ **verb 1** [with obj.] capture on film as part of a series of moving images; make a film of (a story, event, or book): *she glowered at the television crew who were filming them.*
2 [no obj.] become or appear to become covered with a thin layer of something: *his eyes had filmed over.*
– DERIVATIVES **filmdom** noun (sense 2 of the noun).
– ORIGIN Old English *filmen* 'membrane', of West Germanic origin; related to **FELL**[5].

film badge ▶ **noun** a device containing photographic film which registers the wearer's exposure to radiation.

filmgoer ▶ **noun** a person who goes to the cinema, especially regularly.
– DERIVATIVES **film-going** noun & adjective.

filmi /ˈfɪlmi/ ▶ **adjective** Indian related to or characteristic of the Mumbai (Bombay) film industry: *a filmi magazine.*

filmic ▶ **adjective** relating to films or cinematography: *he has reconceived the stage production in filmic terms.*

film-maker ▶ **noun** a person who directs or produces films for the cinema or television.
– DERIVATIVES **film-making** noun.

film noir /fɪlm ˈnwɑː/, French /film nwaʀ/ ▶ **noun** [mass noun] a style or genre of cinematographic film marked by a mood of pessimism, fatalism, and menace. The term was originally applied (by a group of French critics) to American thriller or detective films made in the period 1944–54 and to the work of directors such as Orson Welles, Fritz Lang, and Billy Wilder. ▪ [count noun] a film of this genre.
– ORIGIN French, literally 'black film'.

filmography ▶ **noun** (pl. **filmographies**) a list of films by one director or actor, or on one subject.
– ORIGIN 1960s: from **FILM** + **-GRAPHY**, on the pattern of *bibliography*.

filmsetting ▶ **noun** [mass noun] Printing the setting of material to be printed by projecting it on to photographic film from which the printing surface is prepared.
– DERIVATIVES **filmset** verb, **filmsetter** noun.

film star ▶ **noun** an actor or actress who is famous for playing leading roles in films.

film stock ▶ **noun** see **STOCK** (sense 1 of the noun).

filmstrip ▶ **noun** a series of transparencies in a strip for projection, used especially as a teaching aid.

filmy ▶ **adjective** (**filmier, filmiest**) **1** (especially of fabric) thin and translucent: *filmy white voile.*
2 covered with or as with a thin layer of something: *her eyes were dull and filmy.*
– DERIVATIVES **filmily** adverb, **filminess** noun.

filmy fern ▶ **noun** a small fern of damp shady places, with wiry creeping stems and delicate forked fronds which are only one cell thick. They occur chiefly in tropical and subtropical regions. • Family Hymenophyllaceae: *Hymenophyllum* and other genera.

filo /ˈfiːləʊ/ (also **phyllo**) ▶ **noun** [mass noun] a kind of dough that can be stretched into very thin sheets, used in layers to make both sweet and savoury pas-

tries, especially in eastern Mediterranean cookery: [as modifier] *filo pastry*.
– ORIGIN 1950s: from modern Greek *phullo* 'leaf'.

Filofax /ˈfʌɪlə(ʊ)faks/ ▸ **noun** trademark a loose-leaf notebook for recording appointments, addresses, and notes.
– ORIGIN 1930s: representing a colloquial pronunciation of *file of facts*.

filopodium /ˌfʌɪlə(ʊ)ˈpəʊdɪəm/ ▸ **noun** (pl. **filopodia**) Biology a long, slender, tapering pseudopodium, as found in some protozoans and in embryonic cells.
– DERIVATIVES **filopodial** adjective.
– ORIGIN early 20th cent.: from Latin *filium* 'thread' + **PODIUM**.

filoselle /ˈfɪlə(ʊ)sɛl/ ▸ **noun** [mass noun] floss silk, or silk thread resembling this, used in embroidery.
– ORIGIN mid 16th cent.: from French, from Italian *filosello*, of uncertain ultimate origin.

filovirus /ˈfiːləʊˌvʌɪrəs/ ▸ **noun** a filamentous RNA virus of a genus which causes severe haemorrhagic fevers in humans and primates, and which includes the Ebola and Marburg viruses.

fils¹ /fɪls/ ▸ **noun** (pl. **same**) a monetary unit of Iraq, Bahrain, Jordan, Kuwait, and Yemen, equal to one hundredth of a riyal in Yemen and one thousandth of a dinar elsewhere.
– ORIGIN from a colloquial pronunciation of Arabic *fals*, denoting a small copper coin.

fils² /fiːs/, French /fis/ ▸ **noun** used after a surname to distinguish a son from a father of the same name: *Alexandre Dumas fils*. Compare with **PÈRE**.
– ORIGIN French, 'son'.

filter ▸ **noun 1** a porous device for removing impurities or solid particles from a liquid or gas passed through it: *an oil filter*. ■ a filter tip: [as modifier] *a cheap filter cigarette*. ■ a screen, plate, or layer of a substance which absorbs light or other radiation or selectively absorbs some of its components: *filters can be used in photography to reduce haze*. ■ a device for suppressing electrical or sound waves of frequencies not required. ■ Computing a piece of software that processes data before passing it to another application, for example to reformat characters or to remove unwanted types of material.
2 Brit. an arrangement whereby vehicles may turn left (or right) while other traffic waiting to go straight ahead or turn right (or left) is stopped by a red light: [as modifier] *a filter lane*. ■ a traffic light signalling a filter arrangement.
▸ **verb 1** [with obj.] pass (a liquid, gas, light, or sound) through a device to remove unwanted material: *the eye filters out ultraviolet radiation*. ■ process or assess (items) in order to reject those that are unwanted: *you'll be put through to a secretary whose job it is to filter calls* | *the brain has the ability to filter out information it considers non-essential*. ■ Computing process or treat with a filter.
2 [no obj., with adverbial of direction] move slowly in a specified direction: *the players filtered out on to the pitch*. ■ (of light or sound) enter a place slowly or in small quantities: *sunlight filtered in through the thin curtains*. ■ (of information) gradually become known: *the news began to filter in from the hospital*. ■ Brit. (of traffic) be allowed to pass to the left or right at a junction while traffic going straight ahead is halted.
– ORIGIN late Middle English (denoting a piece of felt): from French *filtre*, from medieval Latin *filtrum* 'felt used as a filter', of West Germanic origin and related to **FELT¹**.

filterable (also **filtrable**) ▸ **adjective 1** capable of passing through a filter.
2 capable of being separated out by a filter: *filterable solids*.

filter bed ▸ **noun** a tank or pond containing a layer of sand or gravel, used for filtering large quantities of liquid.

filter cake ▸ **noun** a deposit of insoluble material left on a filter.

filter-feeding ▸ **adjective** Zoology (of an aquatic animal) feeding by filtering out plankton or nutrients suspended in the water.
– DERIVATIVES **filter-feeder** noun.

filter paper ▸ **noun** a piece of porous paper for filtering liquids, used especially in chemical processes and coffee-making.

filter press ▸ **noun** a device consisting of a series of cloth filters fixed to frames, used for the large-scale filtration of liquid under pressure.

filter tip ▸ **noun** a filter attached to a cigarette for removing impurities from the inhaled smoke. ■ a cigarette with a filter tip.
– DERIVATIVES **filter-tipped** adjective.

filth ▸ **noun** [mass noun] disgusting dirt: *stagnant pools of filth*. ■ obscene and offensive language or printed material: *some calls were vitriolic, accusing us of publishing pornography and filth*. ■ corrupt behaviour; decadence. ■ used as a term of abuse for a person or people one greatly despises: *you and all the others like you are filth*. ■ (as plural noun **the filth**) Brit. informal, derogatory the police.
– ORIGIN Old English *fȳlth* 'rotting matter, rottenness', also 'corruption, obscenity', of Germanic origin; related to Dutch *vuilte*, also to **FOUL**.

filthy ▸ **adjective** (**filthier**, **filthiest**) disgustingly dirty: *a filthy hospital with no sanitation*. ■ obscene and offensive: *filthy language*. ■ Brit. informal (of weather) very unpleasant: *it looked like being a filthy night*. ■ informal angry and bad-tempered: *he arrived at the meeting half an hour late and in a filthy temper*. ■ informal contemptible (used for emphasis): *you filthy liar*.
▸ **adverb** [as submodifier] informal to an extreme extent: *he has become filthy rich*.
– DERIVATIVES **filthily** adverb, **filthiness** noun.

filtrable ▸ **adjective** variant spelling of **FILTERABLE**.

filtrate /ˈfɪltreɪt/ ▸ **noun** a liquid which has passed through a filter.
▸ **verb** [with obj.] rare filter.
– ORIGIN early 17th cent.: from modern Latin *filtrat-* 'filtered', from the verb *filtrare*, from medieval Latin *filtrum* (see **FILTER**).

filtration ▸ **noun** [mass noun] the action or process of filtering something: *small particles are difficult to remove without filtration*.

fimbria /ˈfɪmbrɪə/ ▸ **noun** (pl. **fimbriae** /-rɪiː/) chiefly Anatomy a series of threads or other projections resembling a fringe. ■ (usu. **fimbriae**) an individual thread in such a structure, especially a finger-like projection at the end of the fallopian tube near the ovary.
– DERIVATIVES **fimbrial** adjective.
– ORIGIN mid 18th cent.: from late Latin, 'border, fringe'.

fimbriated /ˈfɪmbrɪeɪtɪd/ (also **fimbriate**) ▸ **adjective 1** Biology having a fringe or border of hair-like or finger-like projections.
2 Heraldry having a narrow border, typically of a specified tincture.
– ORIGIN late 15th cent. (in sense 2): from Latin *fimbriatus* (from *fimbria* 'fringe') + **-ED¹**.

fin ▸ **noun** a flattened appendage on various parts of the body of many aquatic vertebrates, including fish and cetaceans, and some invertebrates, used for propelling, steering, and balancing. ■ an underwater swimmer's flipper. ■ a small flattened projecting surface or attachment on an aircraft, rocket, or car, for providing aerodynamic stability. ■ a flattened projection on a device, used for increasing heat transfer.
▸ **verb** (**fins**, **finning**, **finned**) [no obj., with adverbial of direction] swim under water by means of flippers: *we finned along the side of the wreck*.
– DERIVATIVES **finless** adjective, **finned** adjective [in combination] *long-finned pike*.
– ORIGIN Old English *finn*, *fin*, of Germanic origin; related to Dutch *vin* and probably ultimately to Latin *pinna* 'feather, wing'.

finagle /fɪˈneɪɡ(ə)l/ ▸ **verb** [with obj.] informal, chiefly US obtain by dishonest or devious means: *Ted attended all the football games he could finagle tickets for*. ■ [no obj.] act in a dishonest or devious manner: *they wrangled and finagled over the fine points*.
– DERIVATIVES **finagler** noun.
– ORIGIN 1920s (originally US): from dialect *fainaigue* 'cheat'; perhaps from Old French *fornier* 'deny'.

final ▸ **adjective** coming at the end of a series: *the final version of the report was presented*. ■ reached or designed to be reached as the outcome of a process or a series of actions and events: *the final cost will easily run into six figures*. ■ allowing no further doubt or dispute: *the decision of the judging panel is final*.
▸ **noun 1** the last game in a sports tournament or other competition, which will decide the winner of the tournament. ■ (**finals**) a series of games constituting the final stage of a competition: *the World Cup finals*.
2 (**finals**) Brit. a series of examinations at the end of a degree course: *she was doing her history finals*. ■ (**final**) N. Amer. an examination at the end of a term, school year, or particular class.
3 Music the principal note in a mode.
4 (**finals**) the final approach of an aircraft to the runway it will be landing on.
– PHRASES **the final straw** see **STRAW**.
– ORIGIN Middle English (in the adjectival sense 'conclusive'): from Old French, or from Latin *finalis*, from *finis* 'end'. Compare with **FINISH**.

final cause ▸ **noun** Philosophy the purpose or aim of an action or the end towards which a thing naturally develops.

final clause ▸ **noun** Grammar a clause expressing purpose or intention (e.g. one introduced by *in order that* or *lest*).

final demand ▸ **noun** a creditor's last request for payment of money owed, before taking punitive measures.

final drive ▸ **noun** the last part of the transmission system in a motor vehicle.

finale /fɪˈnɑːli, -leɪ/ ▸ **noun** the last part of a piece of music, an entertainment, or a public event, especially when particularly dramatic or exciting: *the festival ends with a grand finale*.
– ORIGIN mid 18th cent.: from Italian, from Latin *finalis* (see **FINAL**).

finalism ▸ **noun** [mass noun] the doctrine that natural processes, for example evolution, are directed towards some goal.
– DERIVATIVES **finalistic** adjective.

finalist ▸ **noun 1** a competitor or team in the final or finals of a competition.
2 a student taking finals.

finality /fʌɪˈnalɪti/ ▸ **noun** (pl. **finalities**) [mass noun] the fact or impression of being final and irreversible: *the abrupt finality of death*. ■ a tone or manner which indicates that no further comment or argument is possible: *'No,' she said with finality*. ■ [count noun] an action or event that ends something irreversibly: *death is the ultimate finality*.
– ORIGIN mid 19th cent.: from French *finalité*, from late Latin *finalitas*, from Latin *finalis* (see **FINAL**).

finalize (also **finalise**) ▸ **verb** [with obj.] complete or agree on a finished and definitive version of: *efforts intensified to finalize plans for post-war reconstruction*.
– DERIVATIVES **finalization** noun.

finally ▸ **adverb** after a long time, typically when there has been difficulty or delay: *he finally arrived to join us*. ■ as the last in a series of related events or items: *a referendum followed by local, legislative and, finally, presidential elections*. ■ [sentence adverb] used to introduce a final point or reason: *finally, it is common knowledge that travel broadens the horizons*. ■ in such a way as to put an end to doubt and dispute: *the need to dispel finally the belief that auditors were clients of the company*.

final salary scheme ▸ **noun** a company pension scheme in which employees' pension payments are calculated according to their length of service and their salary at the time of retirement.

final solution ▸ **noun** the Nazi policy of exterminating European Jews. Introduced by Heinrich Himmler and administered by Adolf Eichmann, the policy resulted in the murder of 6 million Jews in concentration camps between 1941 and 1945.
– ORIGIN translation of German *Endlösung*.

finance /fʌɪˈnans, fɪ-, ˈfʌɪnans/ ▸ **noun** [mass noun] the management of large amounts of money, especially by governments or large companies: [as modifier] *the firm's finance department*. ■ monetary support for an enterprise: *the clearing banks are important sources of finance*. ■ (**finances**) the monetary resources and affairs of a state, organization, or person: *the club's finances are stretched to the limit*.
▸ **verb** [with obj.] provide funding for (a person or enterprise): *the health service is financed almost entirely by the taxpayer*.
– ORIGIN late Middle English: from Old French, from *finer* 'make an end, settle a debt', from *fin* 'end' (see **FINE²**). The original sense was 'payment of a debt, compensation, or ransom'; later 'taxation, revenue'. Current senses date from the 18th cent., and reflect sense development in French.

finance company (also Brit. **finance house**) ▸ **noun** a company concerned primarily with providing money, e.g. for hire-purchase transactions.

financial /fʌɪˈnanʃ(ə)l, fɪ-/ ▸ **adjective** relating to finance: *an independent financial adviser*. ■ Austral./NZ informal possessing money. ■ W. Indian & Austral./NZ (of a member of a club or society) paid-up.
▸ **noun** (**financials**) the finances or financial situation of an organization or individual: *he needs to pay*

F

serious attention to his financials, particularly cash flow. ■ shares in financial companies.
– DERIVATIVES **financially** adverb [as submodifier] *she was financially dependent on her husband.*

financial intermediary ▶ noun an institution, such as a bank, building society, or unit-trust company, that holds funds from lenders in order to make loans to borrowers.

Financial Times index another term for **FTSE INDEX**.

financial year ▶ noun Brit. a year as reckoned for taxing or accounting purposes, for example the British tax year, reckoned from 6 April.

financier /fʌɪˈnansɪə, fɪ-/ ▶ noun a person concerned in the management of large amounts of money on behalf of governments or other large organizations.
– ORIGIN early 17th cent.: from French, from *finance* (see **FINANCE**).

finback (also **finback whale**) ▶ noun another term for **FIN WHALE**.

finca /ˈfɪŋkə/ ▶ noun (in Spain and Spanish-speaking countries) a country estate; a ranch.
– ORIGIN early 20th cent.: from Spanish, from *fincar* ‘cultivate’, perhaps from Latin *figere* ‘fix, fasten, plant’.

finch ▶ noun a seed-eating songbird that typically has a stout bill and colourful plumage. ● The true finches belong to the family Fringillidae (the **finch family**), which includes chaffinches, canaries, linnets, crossbills, etc. Many other finches belong to the bunting, waxbill, or sparrow families.
– ORIGIN Old English *finc*, of West Germanic origin; related to Dutch *vink* and German *Fink*.

find ▶ verb (past and past participle **found**) [with obj.] **1** discover or perceive by chance or unexpectedly: *Lindsey looked up to find Niall watching her | the remains of a headless body had been found.* ■ discover after a deliberate search: *I can't find my keys | the sailor and his crew were found safe and well last night.* ■ (**find oneself**) discover oneself to be in a particular situation: *phobia sufferers often find themselves virtual prisoners in their own home.* ■ succeed in obtaining (something): *he's still struggling to find the money for the trip.* ■ summon up (a quality, especially courage) with an effort: *I found the courage to speak.* ■ [no obj.] (of hunters or hounds) discover game, especially a fox.
2 identify (something) as being present: *vitamin B12 is found in dairy products | a rare species found only in the Italian Alps.* ■ discover or experience to be the case: [with obj. and infinitive] *the majority of staff find the magazine to be informative and useful* | [with clause] *she found that none of the local nursery schools had an available slot.* ■ ascertain by study, calculation, or inquiry: *the class are encouraged to find their own solutions to problems.* ■ (**find oneself**) discover the fundamental truths about one's own character and identity. ■ [with obj. and complement] experience or regard (something) in a specified way: *both men found it difficult to put ideas into words.* ■ Law (of a court) officially declare to be the case: [with obj. and complement] *he was found guilty of speeding* | [with clause] *the court found that a police lab expert had fabricated evidence.*
3 reach or arrive at by a natural or normal process: *water finds its own level.* ■ (**find one's way**) reach one's destination, typically without first knowing how to get there: *she'll never find her way to the house on her own.* ■ (of a letter) reach (someone).
▶ noun a discovery of something valuable, typically something of archaeological interest: *he made his most spectacular finds in the Valley of the Kings.* ■ a person who is discovered to be useful or interesting in some way: *Ted had turned out to be a real find.* ■ Hunting the finding of a fox.
– PHRASES **all found** Brit. dated (of an employee's wages) with board and lodging provided free. **find fault** see **FAULT**. **find favour** be liked or prove acceptable: *the ballets did not find favour with the public.* **find one's feet** stand up and become able to walk. ■ establish oneself in a particular field: *he never really found his feet in the House of Lords.* **find God** experience a religious conversion or awakening. **find in favour of** see **FIND FOR** below. **find it in one's heart to do something** allow or force oneself to do something: *Seb could not find it in his heart to dislike Plunkett.*
– PHRASAL VERBS **find against** Law (of a court) make a decision against or judge to be guilty. **find for** (or **find in favour of**) Law (of a court) make a decision in favour of, or judge to be innocent: *the Court of Exchequer found for the plaintiffs.* **find someone out** detect a person's immoral or offensive actions: *she would always find him out if he tried to lie.* **find something out** (or **find out about something**) discover a fact: *he hadn't time to find out what was bothering her.*
– DERIVATIVES **findable** adjective.
– ORIGIN Old English *findan*, of Germanic origin; related to Dutch *vinden* and German *finden*.

finder ▶ noun a person that finds someone or something. ■ a small telescope attached to a large one to locate an object for observation. ■ the viewfinder of a camera.
– PHRASES **finders keepers (losers weepers)** informal used to assert that whoever finds something by chance is entitled to keep it.

fin de siècle /ˌfã də ˈsjɛkl(ə)/ ▶ adjective relating to or characteristic of the end of a century, especially the 19th century: *fin-de-siècle art.* ■ decadent: *there was a fin-de-siècle air in London's clubland last night.*
▶ noun the end of a century, especially the 19th century.
– ORIGIN French, ‘end of century’.

finding ▶ noun **1** [mass noun] the action of finding someone or something: *a local doctor reported the finding of numerous dead rats.*
2 (often **findings**) information discovered as the result of an inquiry or investigation: *the researchers' findings were published in Nature.* ■ Law a verdict or decision made by a judge or jury.
3 (**findings**) N. Amer. small articles or tools used in making garments, shoes, or jewellery.

find-spot ▶ noun Archaeology the place where an object is found.

fine[1] /fʌɪn/ ▶ adjective **1** of very high quality; very good of its kind: *this was a fine piece of film-making | fine wines.* ■ worthy of or eliciting admiration: *what a fine human being he is | a fine musician.* ■ good; satisfactory: *relations in the group were fine.* ■ used to express one's agreement with or acquiescence to something: *anything you want is **fine by me**, Linda | he said such a solution would be fine.* ■ in good health and feeling well: *'I'm fine, just fine. And you?'* ■ (of the weather) bright and clear: *it was another fine winter day.* ■ imposing or impressive in appearance: *Donleavy was **a fine figure of a man**.* ■ (of speech or writing) sounding impressive and grand but ultimately insincere: *fine words seemed to produce few practical benefits.* ■ denoting or displaying a state of good, though not excellent, preservation in stamps, books, coins, etc. ■ (of gold or silver) containing a specified high proportion of pure metal: *the coin is struck in .986 fine gold.*
2 very thin or narrow: *a fine nylon thread | fine flyaway hair.* ■ (of a point) sharp. ■ made or consisting of small particles: *the soils were all fine silt.* ■ of delicate or intricate workmanship or structure: *fine bone china.* ■ (of something abstract) subtle and therefore perceived only with difficulty and care: *there is a fine distinction between misrepresenting the truth and lying.* ■ (of a physical faculty) sensitive and discriminating: *he has a fine eye for the detail and texture of social scenery.*
3 Cricket directed or stationed behind the wicket and close to the line of flight of the ball when it is bowled.
▶ noun (**fines**) very small particles found in mining, milling, etc.
▶ adverb **1** informal in a satisfactory or pleasing manner; very well: *'And how's the job-hunting going?' 'Oh, fine.' | mother and baby are both doing fine.*
2 Cricket behind the wicket and close to the line of flight of the ball when it is bowled.
▶ verb **1** [with obj.] clarify (beer or wine) by causing the precipitation of sediment during production. ■ [no obj.] (of liquid) become clear.
2 make or become thinner: [no obj.] *she'd certainly **fined down**—her face was thinner.*
3 [no obj.] (**fine up**) N. English & Austral./NZ informal (of the weather) become bright and clear.
– PHRASES **cut it** (or **things**) **fine** allow a very small margin of something, especially time: *boys who have cut it rather fine are scuttling into chapel.* **do someone fine** suit or be enough for someone. **fine feathers make fine birds** proverb beautiful or expensive clothes may make the wearer seem more impressive than is really the case. **a fine line** a subtle distinction between two concepts or situations: *there's **a fine line between** humour and inappropriateness | the president has been **treading a fine line** on immigration.* **the finer points of** the more complex or detailed aspects of: *he went on to discuss the finer points of his work.* **——'s finest** N. Amer. informal the police of a particular city: *Moscow's finest.* **one's finer feelings** one's feelings of honour, loyalty, or duty; one's conscience or sense of morality. **one's finest hour** the time of one's greatest success. **fine words butter no parsnips** proverb nothing is achieved by empty promises or flattery. **not to put too fine a point on it** to speak bluntly: *not to put too fine a point on it, your Emily is a liar.* [figuratively, with reference to the sharpening of a weapon, tool, etc.] **one fine day** at some unspecified or unknown time: *one fine day he decided to take an apartment in Rome.*
– DERIVATIVES **finely** adverb, **fineness** noun.
– ORIGIN Middle English: from Old French *fin*, based on Latin *finire* ‘to finish’ (see **FINISH**).

fine[2] /fʌɪn/ ▶ noun a sum of money exacted as a penalty by a court of law or other authority: *a parking fine.*
▶ verb [with obj.] punish (someone) for an illegal or illicit act by making them pay a sum of money: *she was **fined** £1500 **for** driving offences.*
– DERIVATIVES **fineable** adjective.
– ORIGIN Middle English: from Old French *fin* ‘end, payment’, from Latin *finis* ‘end’ (in medieval Latin denoting a sum paid on settling a lawsuit). The original sense was ‘conclusion’ (surviving in the phrase **IN FINE**); also used in the medieval Latin sense, the word came to denote a penalty of any kind, later specifically a monetary penalty.

fine[3] /fiːn/ ▶ noun [mass noun] French brandy of high quality made from distilled wine rather than from pomace. ■ short for **FINE CHAMPAGNE**.

fine[4] /ˈfiːneɪ/ ▶ noun (in musical directions) the place where a piece of music finishes (when this is not at the end of the score but at the end of an earlier section which is repeated at the end of the piece).
– ORIGIN Italian, from Latin *finis* ‘end’.

fine art ▶ noun **1** [mass noun] (also **fine arts**) creative art, especially visual art whose products are to be appreciated primarily or solely for their imaginative, aesthetic, or intellectual content: *the convergence of popular culture and fine art.*
2 an activity requiring great skill or accomplishment: ***the fine art of** drinking tequila.*
– PHRASES **have** (or **get**) **something down to a fine art** achieve a high level of skill or accomplishment in a particular activity through experience: *Mike had got the breakfast routine down to a fine art.*

fine champagne /ˌfiːn ʃɒ̃ˈpɑːnj(ə)/ ▶ noun [mass noun] brandy from the Champagne district of the Cognac region of which half or more of the content comes from the central Grande Champagne.
– ORIGIN French, ‘fine (brandy from) Champagne’.

fine chemicals ▶ plural noun chemical substances prepared to a very high degree of purity for use in research and industry.

fine-draw ▶ verb [with obj.] sew together (two pieces of cloth or edges of a tear) so that the join is imperceptible: *a table cover composed of cloth fine-drawn together.*

Fine Gael /ˌfiːnə ˈɡeɪl/, Irish /ˌfʲinʲə ˈɡeːl/ one of the two major political parties of the Republic of Ireland (the other being Fianna Fáil). Founded in 1923 as Cumann na nGaedheal, it changed its name in 1933. It has advocated the concept of a united Ireland achieved by peaceful means.
– ORIGIN Irish, literally ‘tribe of Gaels’.

fine-grained ▶ adjective **1** (chiefly of wood) having a fine or delicate arrangement of fibres. ■ (chiefly of rock) consisting of small particles.
2 involving great attention to detail: *fine-grained analysis.*

fine leg ▶ noun Cricket a fielding position behind the batsman on the leg side, between long leg and square leg. ■ a fielder at fine leg.

fine needle aspiration ▶ noun [mass noun] Medicine a procedure in which a thin needle is used to draw cells or fluid from a lump or mass under the skin.

fine print ▶ noun another term for **SMALL PRINT**.

finery[1] /ˈfʌɪn(ə)ri/ ▶ noun [mass noun] expensive or ostentatious clothes or decoration: *officers in their blue, gold, and scarlet finery.*
– ORIGIN late 17th cent.: from **FINE[1]**, on the pattern of *bravery*.

finery[2] /ˈfʌɪnəri/ ▶ noun (pl. **fineries**) historical a hearth where pig iron was converted into wrought iron.
– ORIGIN late 16th cent.: from French *finerie*, from Old French *finer* ‘refine’.

fines herbes /fiːnz ˈɛːb/ ▶ plural noun mixed herbs used in cooking, especially fresh herbs chopped as a flavouring for omelettes.
– ORIGIN French, literally ‘fine herbs’.

fine-spun ▶ adjective (especially of fabric) fine or delicate in texture.

finesse ▸ **noun 1** [mass noun] impressive delicacy and skill: *orchestral playing of great finesse.* ▪ great subtlety and tact in handling or manipulating people or difficult situations: *clients want advice and action that calls for considerable finesse.*
2 (in bridge and whist) an attempt to win a trick with a card that is not a certain winner, typically by playing it as the third card in a trick in the hope that any card that could beat it is in the hand of the opponent who has already played.
▸ **verb** [with obj.] **1** bring about or deal with (something) by using great delicacy and skill: *Karen spent ten months finessing the financing for the property.* ▪ chiefly N. Amer. slyly attempt to avoid blame or censure when dealing with (a situation or problem): *despite the administration's attempts to finesse its mishaps, the public remained wary.*
2 (in bridge and whist) play (a card) in the hope of winning a trick with it because any card that could beat it is in the hand of the opponent who has already played.
– ORIGIN late Middle English (in the sense 'purity, delicacy'): from French, related to **FINE**^{1}.

fine structure ▸ **noun** [mass noun] the composition of an object, substance, or energy phenomenon as viewed on a small scale and in considerable detail. ▪ Physics the presence of groups of closely spaced lines in spectra corresponding to slightly different energy levels.

fine-structure constant ▸ **noun** Physics a fundamental and dimensionless physical constant, equal to approximately $^{1}/_{137}$, which occurs in expressions describing the fine structure of atomic spectra.

fine-tooth comb (also **fine-toothed comb**) ▸ **noun** a comb with narrow teeth that are close together. ▪ [in sing.] used with reference to a very thorough search or analysis of something: *they went through the house **with a fine-tooth comb**.* See also **TOOTHCOMB**.

fine-tune ▸ **verb** [with obj.] make small adjustments to (something) in order to achieve the best or a desired performance: *they can fine-tune the computer programs to focus on a small region of space.*

finfoot ▸ **noun** (pl. **finfoots**) a grebe-like waterbird with a long bill, neck, and tail, and lobed feet.
● Family Heliornithidae: three genera and species, one each in Africa, Asia, and America. See also **SUNGREBE**.

Fingal /ˈfɪŋɡ(ə)l/ a character in an epic poem by the Scottish poet James Macpherson (1736–96), based on the legendary Irish hero Finn MacCool but fictionally transformed and depicted as fighting both the Norse invaders and the Romans from an invented kingdom in NW Scotland.

Fingal's Cave a cave on the island of Staffa in the Inner Hebrides, noted for the clustered basaltic pillars that form its cliffs. It is said to have been the inspiration of Mendelssohn's overture *The Hebrides* (also known as *Fingal's Cave*).

finger ▸ **noun** each of the four slender jointed parts attached to either hand (or five, if the thumb is included). ▪ a part of a glove intended to cover a finger. ▪ a measure of spirits in a glass, based on the breadth of a finger: *two **fingers** of brandy.* ▪ an object that has roughly the long, narrow shape of a finger: *a shortbread finger.*
▸ **verb** [with obj.] **1** touch or feel with the fingers: *the thin man fingered his moustache.* ▪ play (a musical instrument) with the fingers, especially in a tentative or casual manner: *a woman fingered a lute.*
2 informal, chiefly N. Amer. inform on (someone) to the police: *he was fingered by a supergrass and charged with murder.* ▪ identify or select: *the additive had **been fingered as** a possible human health risk.*
3 Music play (a passage) with a particular sequence of positions of the fingers. See also **FINGERING**^{1}. ▪ mark (music) with signs showing which fingers are to be used.
– PHRASES **be all fingers and thumbs** Brit. informal be clumsy or awkward in one's actions. **get** (or **pull**) **one's finger out** Brit. informal cease prevaricating and start to act. **get one's fingers burned/burnt** (or **burn one's fingers**) (especially in a financial context) suffer unpleasant consequences as a result of one's actions, discouraging one from trying a similar action again. **give someone the finger** N. Amer. informal make a gesture with the middle finger raised as an obscene sign of contempt. **have a finger in every pie** be involved in a large and varied number of activities or enterprises. **have a finger in the pie** be involved in a matter, especially in an annoyingly interfering way. **have** (or **keep**) **one's finger on the pulse** be aware of all the latest news or developments: *he keeps his finger on the pulse of world music.* **lay a finger on someone** touch someone, especially with the intention of harming them. **put the finger on** informal inform against (someone) to the authorities. **put something on the long finger** Irish postpone consideration of something; put something off: *don't put retirement planning on the long finger.* **put one's finger on something** identify something exactly: *he cannot put his finger on what has gone wrong.* **snap** (or **click**) **one's fingers** make a sharp clicking sound by bending the last joint of the middle finger against the thumb and suddenly releasing it, typically in order to attract attention in a peremptory way or to accompany the beat of music. **twist** (or **wind** or **wrap**) **someone around one's little finger** see **LITTLE FINGER**. **work one's fingers to the bone** see **BONE**.
– DERIVATIVES **fingered adjective** [in combination] *a two-fingered whistle*, **fingerless adjective**.
– ORIGIN Old English, of Germanic origin; related to Dutch *vinger* and German *Finger*.

finger alphabet ▸ **noun** a form of sign language using the fingers to spell out words.

fingerboard ▸ **noun** a flat or roughly flat strip on the neck of a stringed instrument, against which the strings are pressed to shorten the vibrating length and produce notes of higher pitches.

finger bowl ▸ **noun** a small bowl containing water for rinsing the fingers during or after a meal.

finger buffet ▸ **noun** a buffet consisting of food of a kind that may be easily eaten with the fingers.

finger chip ▸ **noun** Indian term for **CHIP** (sense 2 of the noun).

finger-dry ▸ **verb** [with obj.] dry and style (hair) by repeatedly running one's fingers through it.

fingerfish ▸ **noun** (pl. **same** or **fingerfishes**) a small silvery fish with a deep laterally compressed body, occurring in warm inshore and estuarine waters and popular in aquaria. Also called **MOONFISH**. ● Family Monodactylidae and genus *Monodactylus*: several species.
– ORIGIN late 18th cent.: from the genus name *monodactylus*, literally 'single finger'.

finger food ▸ **noun** [mass noun] food served in such a form and style that it can conveniently be eaten with the fingers.

fingering^{1} ▸ **noun** [mass noun] a manner or technique of using the fingers, especially to play a musical instrument. ▪ [count noun] an indication of fingering in a musical score.

fingering^{2} ▸ **noun** [mass noun] dated fine wool for hand knitting.
– ORIGIN early 17th cent. (as *fingram*): perhaps from French *fin grain* 'fine grain'. Compare with **GROGRAM** and **GROSGRAIN**.

finger jam (also **finger lock**) ▸ **noun** Climbing a handhold formed by wedging a finger in a crack in the rock.

finger language ▸ **noun** [mass noun] language expressed by means of the finger alphabet.

finger-licking ▸ **adjective** chiefly N. Amer. very tasty; delicious: [as submodifier] *finger-licking good.*

fingerling ▸ **noun** a salmon parr.
– ORIGIN early 18th cent.: from **FINGER** (with reference to its transverse dusky bars) + **-LING**.

fingermark ▸ **noun** a mark left on a surface by a dirty or greasy finger.

fingernail ▸ **noun** the flattish horny part on the upper surface of the tip of each finger.

finger paint ▸ **noun** [mass noun] thick paint designed to be applied with the fingers, used especially by young children.
▸ **verb** (**finger-paint**) [no obj.] (usu. as noun **finger-painting**) (especially of children) apply paint with the fingers.

fingerpick ▸ **verb** [with obj.] play (a guitar or banjo) using the fingernails or small plectrums worn on the fingertips to pluck the strings: *he was fingerpicking an acoustic guitar* | (as noun **fingerpicking**) *fingerpicking accentuates the tone of guitars.* ▪ play (a tune) on a guitar or banjo by using the fingernails or small plectrums on the fingertips to pluck the strings.
▸ **noun** a plectrum worn on a fingertip.
– DERIVATIVES **fingerpicker noun**.

fingerplate ▸ **noun** a piece of metal or porcelain fixed to a door above the handle to prevent fingermarks on the surface of the door itself.

fingerpost ▸ **noun** a post at a road junction from which signs project in the direction of the place or route indicated.

fingerprint ▸ **noun** an impression or mark made on a surface by a person's fingertip, able to be used for identifying individuals from the unique pattern of whorls and lines on the fingertips. ▪ a distinctive identifying characteristic: *the faint chemical fingerprint of plastic explosives.*
▸ **verb** [with obj.] record the fingerprints of: *I was booked, fingerprinted, and locked up for the night.*

fingerstall ▸ **noun** a cover to protect a finger, used in some handicrafts or when a finger is injured.

fingertip ▸ **noun** the tip of a finger. ▪ [as modifier] using or operated by the fingers: *police made a fingertip search of the area.*
– PHRASES **at one's fingertips** (especially of information) readily available; accessible: *until we have more facts at our fingertips, there is no use in speculating.* **by one's fingertips** only with difficulty: *the prime minister clung on to power by his fingertips.* **to one's fingertips** Brit. completely: *he is a professional to his fingertips.*

finger-wagging ▸ **noun** [mass noun] the action of reprimanding or warning someone: [as modifier] *a finger-wagging speech.*

finger wave ▸ **noun** a wave set in wet hair using the fingers.

fingle ▸ **verb** [with obj.] W. Indian handle or finger (something); touch all over.
– ORIGIN blend of obsolete *fangle* 'to trifle' and the verb **FINGER**.

finial /ˈfɪnɪəl, ˈfʌɪn-/ ▸ **noun** a distinctive section or ornament at the apex of a roof, canopy, etc. on a building. ▪ an ornament at the top, end, or corner of an object: *ornate curtain poles with decorative finials.*
– ORIGIN late Middle English: from Old French *fin* or Latin *finis* 'end'.

finical /ˈfɪnɪk(ə)l/ ▸ **adjective** another term for **FINICKY**.
– DERIVATIVES **finically adverb**, **finicalness noun**.
– ORIGIN late 16th cent. (probably originally university slang): probably from **FINE**^{1} + **-ICAL**, perhaps suggested by Middle Dutch *fijnkens* 'accurately, neatly, prettily'.

finicking ▸ **adjective** another term for **FINICKY**.
– ORIGIN mid 17th cent.: from **FINICAL** + **-ING**^{2}.

finicky ▸ **adjective** (of a person) fussy about their needs or requirements: *a finicky eater.* ▪ showing or requiring great attention to detail: *his finicky copperplate hand.*

fining ▸ **noun** (usu. **finings**) a substance used for clarifying liquid, especially beer or wine. ▪ [mass noun] the process of clarifying wine or beer.

finis /ˈfiːnɪs, ˈfɪnɪs, ˈfʌɪnɪs/ ▸ **noun** the end (printed at the end of a book or shown at the end of a film).
– ORIGIN late Middle English: from Latin.

finish ▸ **verb** [with obj.] **1** bring (a task or activity) to an end; complete: *they were straining to finish the job* | [with present participle] *we finished eating our meal.* ▪ consume or get through the final amount or portion of (something, especially food or drink): *Seagram **finished off** a margarita as he waited.* ▪ [no obj.] (of a period or activity) come to an end: *the war has finished but nothing has changed.* ▪ [no obj.] end a period of time or course of action by doing something or being in a particular position: *he **finished up** as one of Britain's greatest architects.* ▪ [no obj.] reach the end of a race or other competition: *the first four horses to finish* | [with complement] *Falkirk finished fifth in the Scottish Premier League.* ▪ [no obj.] Brit. (in soccer) score a goal or goals: *Dean finished well to put his team ahead.* ▪ kill, destroy, or comprehensively defeat: *the English men-at-arms **finished** them **off** in hand-to-hand combat.* ▪ reduce to utter exhaustion or helplessness.
2 complete the manufacture or decoration of (an article) by giving it an attractive surface appearance: *the interior was finished with American oak.* ▪ complete the fattening of (livestock) before slaughter.
3 dated prepare (a girl) for entry into fashionable society.
▸ **noun 1** [usu. in sing.] an end or final part or stage of something: *a bowl of raspberries was the perfect finish to the meal* | *I really enjoyed the film **from start to finish**.* ▪ a point or place at which a race or competition ends: *he surged into a winning lead 200 metres from the finish.*
2 [mass noun] the manner in which the manufacture of an article is completed in detail: *the car's popularity is helped by its high-quality finish and strong diesel engine.* ▪ [count noun] the surface appearance of a manufactured material or object, or the material used to produce this: *lightweight nylon with a shiny*

F

finish. ■ the final taste impression of a wine or beer: *the wine has a lemony tang on the finish*.
– PHRASES **to the finish** until the complete defeat of one of the parties involved: *Linfield clinched their first championship in a thrilling **fight to the finish***.
– PHRASAL VERBS **finish with** Brit. have no more need for or nothing more to do with: *they give me the newspaper when they've finished with it*. ■ informal end an emotional relationship with: *'I've finished with Tom,' Gloria said*.
– ORIGIN Middle English: from Old French *feniss-*, lengthened stem of *fenir*, from Latin *finire*, from *finis* 'end'.

finished ▸ **adjective** **1** (of a task or activity) brought to an end; completed: *a preparatory drawing for the finished painting*. ■ (of a person) no longer useful or valued; ruined: *he was told he was finished at the club*.
2 (of a person's work) expert or accomplished: *his highly finished craftsmanship | she gave a fine finished performance*.

F

finisher ▸ **noun** **1** a person or thing that finishes something, in particular: ■ a person who reaches the end of a race or other competition. ■ Brit. (in soccer) a goalscorer: *he is one of the best finishers at the club*. ■ a worker or machine performing the last operation in a manufacturing process.
2 an animal that has been fattened ready for slaughter: [as modifier] *finisher pigs*.

finishing line (chiefly N. Amer. also **finish line**) ▸ **noun** a line marking the end of a race.

finishing school ▸ **noun** a private college where girls are prepared for entry into fashionable society.

finishing touch (also **finishing stroke**) ▸ **noun** (usu. **finishing touches**) a final detail or action completing and enhancing a piece of work: *now they're **putting the finishing touches to** a new album*.

Finisterre, Cape /ˌfɪnɪˈstɛː/ a promontory of NW Spain, forming the westernmost point of the mainland. The shipping forecast area formerly known as **Finisterre** was renamed **FITZROY** in 2002.

finite /ˈfʌɪnʌɪt/ ▸ **adjective** **1** limited in size or extent: *every computer has a finite amount of memory*.
2 Grammar (of a verb form) having a specific tense, number, and person.
– DERIVATIVES **finitely** adverb, **finiteness** noun.
– ORIGIN late Middle English: from Latin *finitus* 'finished', past participle of *finire* (see FINISH).

finite state grammar ▸ **noun** [mass noun] Linguistics a deliberately oversimplified form of generative grammar, which generates sentences by working through word by word in a strictly linear fashion. It was used by Chomsky to illustrate the need for more complex features, such as transformations, to account adequately for real language.

finitism /ˈfʌɪnʌɪtɪz(ə)m/ ▸ **noun** [mass noun] Philosophy & Mathematics rejection of the belief that anything can actually be infinite.
– DERIVATIVES **finitist** noun & adjective.

finito /fɪˈniːtəʊ/ ▸ **adjective** [predic.] informal finished: *it's all done—finito*.
– ORIGIN Italian.

finitude /ˈfɪnɪtjuːd/ ▸ **noun** [mass noun] formal the state of having limits or bounds: *one quickly senses the finitude of his patience*.

fink N. Amer. informal ▸ **noun** an unpleasant or contemptible person. ■ a person who informs on people to the authorities: *he was assumed by some to be the management's fink*. ■ dated a strike-breaker.
▸ **verb** [no obj.] **1** (**fink on**) inform on (someone) to the authorities: *there was no shortage of people willing to fink on their neighbours*.
2 (**fink out**) fail to do something promised or expected. ■ cease to function: *your immune system begins finking out and you get sick*.
– ORIGIN late 19th cent.: of unknown origin; perhaps from German, literally 'finch', but also a pejorative term. Students started to refer to non-members of fraternities as *finks*, probably by association with the freedom of wild birds as opposed to caged ones. The term was later generalized to denote those not belonging to organizations such as trade unions.

fin keel ▸ **noun** a boat's keel shaped like an inverted dorsal fin.

Finland /ˈfɪnlənd/ a country on the Baltic Sea, between Sweden and Russia; pop. 5,250,300 (est. 2009); official languages, Finnish and Swedish; capital, Helsinki. Finnish name **SUOMI**.

> The northern third of the country lies within the Arctic Circle. Long an area of Swedish–Russian rivalry, Finland was ceded to Russia in 1809, becoming an independent republic after the Russian Revolution. Wars with the Soviet Union were fought in 1939–40. Finland joined the European Union in 1995.

Finland, Gulf of an arm of the Baltic Sea between Finland and Estonia, extending eastwards to St Petersburg in Russia.

Finlandization /ˌfɪnləndʌɪˈzeɪʃ(ə)n/ (also **Finlandisation**) ▸ **noun** [mass noun] historical the process or result of being obliged for economic reasons to favour, or at least not oppose, the interests of the former Soviet Union despite not being politically allied to it.
– ORIGIN 1960s: translation of German *Finnlandisierung*, referring to the case of Finland after 1944.

Finn ▸ **noun** a native or inhabitant of Finland or a person of Finnish descent.
– ORIGIN Old English *Finnas* (plural), originally applied more widely to denote a people of Scandinavia and NE Europe speaking a Finno-Ugric language.

finnan /ˈfɪnən/ (also **finnan haddock**) ▸ **noun** [mass noun] haddock cured with the smoke of green wood, turf, or peat.
– ORIGIN early 18th cent.: alteration of *Findon*, the name of a fishing village near Aberdeen in Scotland, but sometimes confused with the Scottish river and village of *Findhorn*.

finnesko /ˈfɪnəskəʊ/ ▸ **noun** (pl. **same**) a boot of tanned reindeer skin with the hair on the outside.
– ORIGIN late 19th cent.: from Norwegian *finnsko*, from *Finn* (see FINN) + *sko* (see SHOE).

Finney /ˈfɪni/, Sir Tom (b.1929), English footballer; full name *Thomas Finney*. He played for Preston North End as a winger and won 76 caps for England between 1946 and 1958.

Finnic ▸ **adjective** **1** relating to or denoting a group of Finno-Ugric languages including Finnish and Estonian.
2 relating to or denoting the group of peoples which includes the Finns.

Finnish ▸ **adjective** relating to the Finns or their language.
▸ **noun** [mass noun] the language of the Finns, spoken by about 4.6 million people in Finland, and also in parts of Russia and Sweden. It is a Finno-Ugric language related to Estonian, and more distantly to Hungarian, and is noted for its morphological complexity.

Finn MacCool /ˌfɪn məˈkuːl/ (also **Finn Mac Cumhaill**) Irish Mythology the warrior hero of a cycle of legends about a band of warriors defending Ireland. Father of the legendary Irish warrior and bard Ossian, he is supposed to have lived in the 3rd century AD. See also **FINGAL**.

Finno-Ugric /ˌfɪnəʊˈuːgrɪk, -ˈjuːgrɪk/ (also **Finno-Ugrian** /-ˈuːgrɪən, -ˈjuːgrɪən/) ▸ **adjective** relating to the major group of Uralic languages, which includes Finnish, Estonian, Hungarian (Magyar), and several north central Asian languages.
▸ **noun** [mass noun] the Finno-Ugric group of languages.

finny ▸ **adjective** literary relating to or resembling a fish: *members of the finny tribe*.

fino /ˈfiːnəʊ/ ▸ **noun** (pl. **finos**) [mass noun] a light-coloured dry sherry. ■ sherry on which a covering of flor (yeast) is developed during production, used to make commercial fino and manzanilla sherries. Compare with OLOROSO.
– ORIGIN Spanish, literally 'fine', based on Latin *finire* 'to finish' (see FINISH).

finocchio /fɪˈnɒkɪəʊ/ ▸ **noun** another term for FLORENCE FENNEL (see FENNEL).
– ORIGIN early 18th cent.: from Italian, from a popular Latin variant of Latin *faeniculum* (see FENNEL).

fin ray ▸ **noun** see RAY[1] (sense 3 of the noun).

fin whale ▸ **noun** a large rorqual with a small dorsal fin, a dark grey back, and white underparts. Also called FINBACK, COMMON RORQUAL. ● *Balaenoptera physalus*, family Balaenopteridae.

fiord ▸ **noun** variant spelling of FJORD.

fioritura /fɪˌɔːrɪˈt(j)ʊərə/ ▸ **noun** (pl. **fioriture** /fɪˌɔːrɪˈt(j)ʊəri, -reɪ/) Music an embellishment of a melody, especially as improvised by an operatic singer.
– ORIGIN Italian, literally 'flowering', from *fiorire* 'to flower'.

fipple /ˈfɪp(ə)l/ ▸ **noun** the mouthpiece of a recorder or similar wind instrument which is blown endwise, in which a thin channel cut through a block directs a stream of air against a sharp edge. The term has been applied to various parts of this, including the block and the channel.
– ORIGIN early 17th cent.: perhaps related to Icelandic *flipi* 'horse's lip'.

fipple flute ▸ **noun** a flute, such as a recorder, played by blowing endwise.

fiqh /fiːk/ ▸ **noun** [mass noun] the theory or philosophy of Islamic law, based on the teachings of the Koran and the traditions of the Prophet.
– ORIGIN Arabic, literally 'understanding'.

fir ▸ **noun** (also **fir tree**) an evergreen coniferous tree with upright cones and flat needle-shaped leaves, typically arranged in two rows. Firs are an important source of timber and resins. Compare with PINE[1] (sense 1). ● Genus *Abies*, family Pinaceae: many species.
– DERIVATIVES **firry** adjective.
– ORIGIN late Middle English: probably from Old Norse *fyri-* (recorded in *fyriskógr* 'fir wood').

fir cone ▸ **noun** Brit. the dry fruit of a fir tree or other conifer.

fire ▸ **noun** [mass noun] **1** a process in which substances combine chemically with oxygen from the air and typically give out bright light, heat, and smoke; combustion or burning: *his house was destroyed by fire*. ■ [count noun] a destructive burning of something: *a fire at a hotel*. ■ [count noun] a collection of fuel, especially coal or wood, burnt in a controlled way to provide heat or a means for cooking: *we had a bath in a tin tub by the fire*. ■ [count noun] (also **electric fire** or **gas fire**) chiefly Brit. a domestic heating appliance that uses electricity or gas as fuel. ■ one of the four elements in ancient and medieval philosophy and in astrology (considered essential to the nature of the signs Aries, Leo, and Sagittarius): [as modifier] *a fire sign*.
2 a burning sensation: [count noun] *the whisky lit a fire in the back of his throat*. ■ fervent or passionate emotion or enthusiasm: *the fire of their religious conviction*. ■ literary a glowing or luminous quality: *their soft smiles light the air like a star's fire*.
3 the shooting of projectiles from weapons, especially bullets from guns: *a burst of machine-gun fire*. ■ strong criticism or antagonism: *he directed his fire against policies promoting American capital flight*.
▸ **verb** [with obj.] **1** discharge a gun or other weapon in order to propel (a bullet or projectile): *he fired a shot at the retreating prisoners | they **fired off** a few rounds*. ■ discharge (a gun or other weapon): *another gang fired a pistol through the window of a hostel* | [no obj.] *troops **fired on** crowds*. ■ [no obj.] (of a gun) be discharged. ■ direct (questions or statements, especially unwelcome ones) towards someone in rapid succession: *they **fired** questions **at** me for what seemed like ages*. ■ (**fire something off**) send a message aggressively: *he fired off a letter informing her that he regarded the matter with the utmost seriousness*.
2 informal dismiss (an employee) from a job: *I had to fire men who've been with me for years | you're fired!*
3 supply (a furnace, engine, etc.) with fuel. ■ [no obj.] (of an internal-combustion engine) undergo ignition of its fuel when started: *the engine fired and she pushed her foot down on the accelerator*. ■ archaic set fire to: *I fired the straw*.
4 stimulate or excite (the imagination or an emotion): *India fired my imagination*. ■ fill (someone) with enthusiasm: *he was **fired up** for last season's FA Cup final*. ■ [no obj.] (**fire up**) archaic show sudden anger: *If I were to hear anyone speak slightingly of you, I should fire up in a moment*.
5 bake or dry (pottery, bricks, etc.) in a kiln.
– PHRASES **breathe fire** be extremely angry: *I don't want an indignant boyfriend on my doorstep breathing fire*. **catch fire** begin to burn. ■ become interesting or exciting: *the show never caught fire*. **fire and brimstone** the supposed torments of hell: *his father was preaching fire and brimstone sermons*. **fire away** informal used to give someone permission to begin speaking, typically to ask questions: *'I want to clear up some questions which have been puzzling me.' 'Fire away.'* **fire in the** (or **one's**) **belly** a powerful sense of ambition or determination. **firing on all cylinders** working or functioning at a peak level. **go on fire** Scottish & Irish begin to burn; catch fire. **go through fire** (**and water**) face any peril. **light a fire under** N. Amer. stimulate (someone) to work or act more quickly or enthusiastically. **on fire** in flames; burning. ■ in a state of excitement: *Wright is now on fire with confidence*. **set fire to** (or **set something on fire**) cause to burn; ignite. **set the world on fire** do something remarkable or sensational: *the film hasn't exactly set the world on fire*. **take fire** start to burn. **under fire** being shot at: *observers sent to look for the men came under heavy fire*. ■ being rigorously criticized: *the president was under fire from all sides*.

where's the fire? informal used to ask someone why they are in such a hurry or state of excitement.
– DERIVATIVES **fireless** adjective, **firer** noun.
– ORIGIN Old English *fȳr* (noun), *fȳrian* 'supply with material for a fire', of West Germanic origin; related to Dutch *vuur* and German *Feuer*.

fire alarm ▸ noun a device making a loud noise that gives warning of a fire.

fire-and-forget ▸ adjective [attrib.] (of a missile) able to guide itself to its target once fired.

fire ant ▸ noun a tropical American ant that has a painful and sometimes dangerous sting. ● Genus *Solenopsis*, family Formicidae: several species, in particular the South American *S. invicta*, which has become a serious pest in the south-eastern US.

firearm ▸ noun a rifle, pistol, or other portable gun.

fireback ▸ noun **1** the back wall of a fireplace. ■ a metal plate covering the back wall of a fireplace.
2 (also **fireback pheasant**) a SE Asian pheasant, the male of which has mainly grey or blue plumage with a reddish rump. ● Genus *Lophura*, family Phasianidae: three species.

fireball ▸ noun a ball of flame or fire: *a crashed petrol tanker exploded in a fireball*. ■ a large bright meteor. ■ historical a ball filled with combustibles or explosives, fired at an enemy or enemy fortifications. ■ a person with a fiery temper or a great deal of energy.

fireballer ▸ noun Baseball a pitcher who throws a very good fastball.
– DERIVATIVES **fireballing** adjective.

fire balloon ▸ noun a balloon made buoyant by the heat of a fire burning at its mouth.

fire-bellied toad ▸ noun a warty European aquatic toad, the underside of which is vividly marked in red, orange, yellow, black, and white. ● Genus *Bombina*, family Discoglossidae: in particular *B. bombina*.

fire blanket ▸ noun a sheet of flexible material, typically woven fibreglass, used to smother a fire in an emergency.

fireblight ▸ noun [mass noun] a serious bacterial disease of plants of the rose family, especially fruit trees, giving the leaves a scorched appearance. ● The bacterium is the Gram-negative *Erwinia amylovora*.

firebomb ▸ noun a bomb designed to cause a fire.
▸ verb [with obj.] attack or destroy with a firebomb: *two bookshops and a newspaper office have been firebombed*.

firebox ▸ noun the chamber of a steam engine or boiler in which the fuel is burnt.

firebrand ▸ noun **1** a piece of burning wood.
2 a person who is very passionate about a particular cause: *a political firebrand*.

firebrat ▸ noun a fast-moving brownish bristletail (wingless insect) that frequents warm places indoors. ● *Thermobia domestica*, family Lepismatidae, order Thysanura.

firebreak ▸ noun an obstacle to the spread of fire, such as a strip of open space in a forest.

firebrick ▸ noun a brick capable of withstanding intense heat, used especially to line furnaces and fireplaces.

fire brigade ▸ noun Brit. an organized body of people trained and employed to extinguish fires.

firebug ▸ noun informal an arsonist.

fire certificate ▸ noun a certificate confirming that statutory fire regulations have been complied with in a building.

fireclay ▸ noun [mass noun] clay capable of withstanding high temperatures, chiefly used for making firebricks.

fire company ▸ noun North American term for **FIRE BRIGADE**.

fire control ▸ noun [mass noun] **1** the process of aiming and firing heavy weapons.
2 the prevention and monitoring of accidental fires.

fire coral ▸ noun a colonial coral-like hydrozoan, the heavy external skeleton of which forms reefs. The polyps bear nematocysts which can inflict painful stings. ● Genus *Millepora*, order Hydroida (or Milleporina), class Hydrozoa.

firecracker ▸ noun a loud, explosive firework; a banger. ■ an outstanding, exciting, or attractive person or thing: *the book was solidly excellent but hardly a literary firecracker*.

firecrest ▸ noun a very small warbler related to the goldcrest, having a red and orange crest and occurring mainly in Europe. ● *Regulus ignicapillus*, family Sylviidae.

firedamp ▸ noun [mass noun] methane, especially as forming an explosive mixture with air in coal mines.

fire department ▸ noun N. Amer. the department of a local or municipal authority in charge of preventing and fighting fires.

firedog ▸ noun one of a pair of decorative metal supports for wood burning in a fireplace.

fire door ▸ noun a fire-resistant door to prevent the spread of fire. ■ a door to the outside of a building used only as an emergency exit.

firedrake ▸ noun Germanic Mythology a dragon.
– ORIGIN Old English *fȳr-draca*, from *fȳr* (see **FIRE**) + *draca* 'dragon', from Latin *draco*.

fire drill ▸ noun **1** a practice of the emergency procedures to be used in case of fire.
2 a primitive device for kindling fire, consisting of a pointed stick which is twirled in a hole in a flat piece of soft wood.

fire-eater ▸ noun **1** an entertainer who appears to eat fire.
2 dated a person prone to quarrelling or fighting.

fire engine ▸ noun a vehicle carrying firefighters and equipment for fighting large fires.

fire escape ▸ noun a staircase or other apparatus used for escaping from a building on fire.

fire extinguisher ▸ noun a portable device that discharges a jet of water, foam, gas, or other material to extinguish a fire.

firefight ▸ noun Military a battle using guns rather than bombs or other weapons.

firefighter ▸ noun a person whose job is to extinguish fires.

firefighting ▸ noun [mass noun] **1** the action or process of extinguishing fires, as a person's job.
2 (in business) the practice of dealing with problems as they arise rather than planning strategically to avoid them.

firefinch ▸ noun a small African songbird of the waxbill family, the male of which has mainly pink or reddish plumage. ● Genus *Lagonosticta*, family Estrildidae: several species.

firefish ▸ noun (pl. **same** or **firefishes**) **1** a scorpionfish with venomous spines. ● Genera *Pterois* and *Dendrochirus*, family Scorpaenidae.
2 a pink- or red-coloured fish related to the wormfishes. ● Subfamily Ptereleotrinae, family Microdesmidae.

firefly ▸ noun (pl. **fireflies**) a soft-bodied beetle related to the glow-worm, the winged male and flightless female of which both have luminescent organs. The light is chiefly produced in flashes and typically functions as a signal between the sexes.
● Family Lampyridae: many species, especially in the tropics, and including the European *Luciola lusitanica*.

fireguard ▸ noun **1** a protective screen or grid placed in front of an open fire.
2 N. Amer. a firebreak in a forest.

fire hose ▸ noun a broad hosepipe used in extinguishing fires.

firehouse (also **firehall**) ▸ noun N. Amer. a fire station.

fire irons ▸ plural noun implements for tending a domestic fire, typically tongs, a poker, and a shovel.

fireless cooker ▸ noun historical an insulated container capable of maintaining a temperature at which food can be cooked.

firelight ▸ noun [mass noun] light from a fire in a fireplace.
– DERIVATIVES **firelit** adjective.
– ORIGIN Old English *fȳr-lēoht* (see **FIRE**, **LIGHT**[1]).

firelighter ▸ noun Brit. a piece of flammable material used to help start a fire.

fire line ▸ noun N. Amer. a firebreak in a forest.

firelock ▸ noun historical a musket in which the priming is ignited by sparks.

fireman ▸ noun (pl. **firemen**) **1** a male firefighter.
2 a person who tends a furnace or the fire of a steam engine or steamship.

firemaster ▸ noun Scottish the chief officer of a fire brigade.

Firenze /fiˈrɛntse/ Italian name for **FLORENCE**.

Fire of London the huge and devastating fire which destroyed some 13,000 houses over 400 acres of London between 2 and 6 September 1666, having started in a bakery in Pudding Lane. Also called **GREAT FIRE**.

fire opal ▸ noun another term for **GIRASOL** (sense 1).

firepit ▸ noun a pit dug into the ground or made from stones, in which a fire for cooking food is made.

fireplace ▸ noun a place for a domestic fire, especially a grate or hearth at the base of a chimney. ■ a structure surrounding a fireplace.

fireplug ▸ noun US a hydrant for a fire hose. ■ N. Amer. informal a short, stocky person, especially an athlete.

firepower ▸ noun [mass noun] the destructive capacity of guns, missiles, or a military force (used with reference to the number and size of guns available): *the enormous disparity in firepower between the two sides* | figurative *he combines intellectual firepower with persuasive charm*.

fire practice ▸ noun Brit. a fire drill.

fireproof ▸ adjective able to withstand fire or great heat: *a fireproof dish*.
▸ verb [with obj.] make (something) fireproof: *nearby museum buildings will be fireproofed*.

fire-raiser ▸ noun Brit. an arsonist.
– DERIVATIVES **fire-raising** noun.

fire salamander ▸ noun a robust short-tailed nocturnal salamander that has black skin with bright red, orange, and yellow markings, native to upland forests of Europe, NW Africa, and SW Asia.
● *Salamandra salamandra*, family Salamandridae.

fire sale ▸ noun a sale of goods remaining after the destruction of commercial premises by fire. ■ a sale of goods or assets at a very low price, typically when the seller is facing bankruptcy.

fire screen ▸ noun a protective screen placed in front of an open fire.

fire service ▸ noun Brit. an organization in charge of preventing and fighting fires.

fireship ▸ noun historical a ship loaded with burning material and explosives and set adrift to ignite and blow up an enemy's ships.

fireside ▸ noun the area round a fireplace (used especially with reference to a person's home or family life).

fireside chat ▸ noun an informal conversation.

fire starter ▸ noun North American term for **FIRELIGHTER**.

fire station ▸ noun the headquarters of a fire brigade, where fire engines and other equipment are housed.

fire step ▸ noun a step or ledge on which soldiers in a trench stand to fire.

fire stone ▸ noun [mass noun] stone that can withstand fire and great heat, used especially for lining furnaces and ovens.

firestorm ▸ noun a very intense and destructive fire (typically one caused by bombing) in which strong currents of air are drawn into the blaze from the surrounding area making it burn more fiercely: *firestorms after a nuclear exchange* | figurative *the incident ignited a firestorm of controversy*.

firethorn ▸ noun another term for **PYRACANTHA**.

fire tongs ▸ plural noun tongs for handling pieces of coal and wood when tending a fire.

fire trail ▸ noun N. Amer. & Austral. a track through forest or bush for use in fighting fires.

fire trap ▸ noun a building which would be extremely dangerous if a fire should start due to a lack of precautions such as fire exits.

fire truck ▸ noun US term for **FIRE ENGINE**.

fire-walking ▸ noun [mass noun] the practice of walking barefoot over a substance such as hot stones or wood ashes, often as part of a traditional ceremony.
– DERIVATIVES **fire-walker** noun.

firewall ▸ noun a wall or partition designed to inhibit or prevent the spread of fire. ■ Computing a part of a computer system or network which is designed to block unauthorized access while permitting outward communication. ■ another term for **CHINESE WALL**.
▸ verb [with obj.] Computing protect (a network or system) from unauthorized access with a firewall.

fire warden ▸ noun N. Amer. a person employed to prevent or extinguish fires, especially in a town, camp, or forest.

fire-watcher ▸ noun a person keeping watch for fires, especially forest fires or those caused by bombs.
– DERIVATIVES **fire-watching** noun.

firewater ▸ noun [mass noun] informal strong alcoholic drink.

F

F

fireweed ▶ noun [mass noun] a plant that springs up on burnt land, especially the rosebay willowherb.

FireWire ▶ noun [mass noun] trademark a standard high-performance serial bus for connecting digital devices together or to a computer: [as modifier] *a FireWire port.*

firewood ▶ noun [mass noun] wood that is burnt as fuel.

firework ▶ noun a device containing gunpowder and other combustible chemicals which causes spectacular effects and explosions when ignited, used for display or in celebrations: *they were oohing and aahing as if they were watching the fireworks* | [as modifier] *a firework display.* ■ (**fireworks**) an outburst of anger, or a display of great skill or energy: *when you put these men together you're bound to get fireworks.*

firing ▶ noun [mass noun] **1** the action of setting fire to something: *the deliberate firing of 600 oil wells.*
2 the discharging of a gun or other weapon: *the prolonged firing caused heavy losses* | [count noun] *no missile firings were planned.*
3 the baking or drying of pottery or bricks in a kiln.
4 the dismissal of an employee from a job: *the recent firing of the head of the department* | [count noun] *a series of firings and resignations.*
– PHRASES **the firing line 1** the front line of troops in a battle. **2** a situation where one is subject to criticism or blame because of one's responsibilities or position: *the referee* ***in the firing line*** *is an experienced official.*

firing party ▶ noun **1** a group of soldiers detailed to fire the salute at a military funeral.
2 another term for FIRING SQUAD.

firing squad ▶ noun a group of soldiers detailed to shoot a condemned person.

firing step ▶ noun another term for FIRE STEP.

firkin /ˈfəːkɪn/ ▶ noun a small cask formerly used for liquids, butter, or fish. ■ a unit of liquid volume equal to half a kilderkin (usually 9 imperial gallons or about 41 litres).
– ORIGIN Middle English *ferdekyn*, probably from the Middle Dutch diminutive of *vierde* 'fourth' (a firkin originally contained a quarter of a barrel).

firm[1] ▶ adjective **1** having a solid, almost unyielding surface or structure: *the bed should be reasonably firm, but not too hard.* ■ solidly in place and stable: *no building can stand without firm foundations* | figurative *he was unable to establish the shop on a firm financial footing.* ■ having steady but not excessive power or strength: *you need a firm grip on the steering.* ■ showing resolute determination and strength of character: *parents should be* ***firm with*** *children and not give in to their demands.*
2 strongly felt and unlikely to change: *he retains a firm belief in the efficacy of prayer.* ■ steadfast and constant: *we became firm friends.* ■ decided upon and fixed or definite: *she had no firm plans for the next day.* ■ (of a currency, shares, etc.) having a steady value or price which is more likely to rise than fall: *the pound was* ***firm against*** *the dollar.*
▶ verb [with obj.] make more solid or resilient: *how can I* ***firm up*** *a sagging bustline?* ■ fix (a plant) securely in the soil. ■ make (an agreement or plan) explicit and definite: *the agreements still have to be* ***firmed up.*** ■ [no obj.] (of a price) rise slightly to reach a level considered secure: *he believed house prices would firm by the end of the year* | [with complement] *the shares firmed 15p to 620p.*
▶ adverb in a resolute and determined manner: *the Chancellor has* ***held firm*** *to tough economic policies* | *she will* ***stand firm*** *against the government's proposal.*
– PHRASES **be on firm ground** be sure of one's facts or secure in one's position. **a firm hand** strict discipline or control.
– DERIVATIVES **firmly** adverb, **firmness** noun.
– ORIGIN Middle English: from Old French *ferme*, from Latin *firmus*.

firm[2] ▶ noun a business concern, especially one involving a partnership of two or more people: *state support for small firms* | *a law firm.* ■ a group of hospital doctors working as a team, headed by a consultant. ■ Brit. informal an organized group of football supporters known for their aggressive attitudes towards rival fans.
– ORIGIN late 16th cent.: from Spanish and Italian *firma*, from medieval Latin, from Latin *firmare* 'fix, settle' (in late Latin 'confirm by signature'), from *firmus* 'firm'; compare with FARM. The word originally denoted one's autograph or signature; later (mid 18th cent.) the name under which the business of a firm was transacted, hence the firm itself (late 18th cent.).

firmament /ˈfəːməm(ə)nt/ ▶ noun literary the heavens or sky: *thunder shakes the firmament* | figurative *one of the great stars in the American golfing firmament.*
– DERIVATIVES **firmamental** adjective.
– ORIGIN Middle English: via Old French from Latin *firmamentum*, from *firmare* 'fix, settle'.

firman /ˈfəːmən, fəːˈmɑːn/ (also **farman**) ▶ noun (pl. **firmans** or **farmans**) **1** an oriental sovereign's edict.
2 a grant or permit.
– ORIGIN early 17th cent.: from Persian *firmān*, Sanskrit *pramāṇa* 'right measure, standard, authority'.

firmware ▶ noun [mass noun] Computing permanent software programmed into a read-only memory.

firn /ˈfɪən/ ▶ noun [mass noun] crystalline or granular snow, especially on the upper part of a glacier, where it has not yet been compressed into ice.
– ORIGIN mid 19th cent.: from German, from Old High German *firni* 'old'; related to Swedish *forn* 'former'.

firni /ˈfɪəni/ ▶ noun [mass noun] a sweet Indian dish of thickened milk, dried fruit, and ground rice.
– ORIGIN from Hindi *firnī*, from Persian.

first ▶ ordinal number **1** coming before all others in time or order; earliest; 1st: *his first wife* | *the first of five daughters* | *many valuable drugs have been recognized first as poisons.* ■ never previously done or occurring: *her first day at school.* ■ coming or encountered next after a specified or implied time, event, etc.: *the first house I came to.* ■ before doing something else specified or implied: *Do you mind if I take a shower first?* ■ for the first time: *she first picked up a guitar out of sheer boredom.* ■ informal the first occurrence of something notable: *we travelled by air, a first for both of us.* ■ the first in a sequence of a vehicle's gears: *he stuck the car in first and revved.* ■ Baseball first base: *he made it all the way home from first.* ■ chiefly Brit. the first form of a school or college.
2 foremost in position, rank, or importance: *the doctor's first duty is to respect this right* | *a first prize of £250* | *career women who* ***put work first*** | *football must* ***come first.*** ■ firstly; in the first place (used to introduce a main point or reason): *first, it is wrong that the victims should have no remedy.* ■ in preference; rather (used when strongly rejecting a suggestion or possibility): *she longed to go abroad, but not at this man's expense—she'd die first!* ■ the first finisher or position in a race or competition. ■ [in titles] having precedence over all others of a similar kind: *First Lord of the Admiralty.* ■ Brit. a place in the top grade in an examination, especially that for a degree: *chaps with firsts from Oxbridge.* ■ Brit. a person who has received the top grade in an examination for a degree. ■ (**the firsts**) the best or main team of a sports club. ■ (**firsts**) goods of the best quality: *factory firsts, seconds, and discontinued styles.*
3 with a specified part or person in a leading position: *the car plunged nose first into the river.*
4 [often with infinitive] the most pressing, likely, or suitable: *his first problem is where to live* | *he is the first to admit he was not the best of patients.*
5 Music performing the highest or chief of two or more parts for the same instrument or voice: *the first violins.*
– PHRASES **at first** at the beginning; in the initial stage or stages: *at first Hugo tried to be patient.* **at first glance** see GLANCE[1]. **at first hand** see FIRST-HAND. **at first instance** see INSTANCE. **at first sight** see SIGHT. **(the) first among equals** see EQUAL. **first blood** see BLOOD. **first come, first served** used to indicate that people will be dealt with strictly in the order in which they arrive or apply: *tickets are available on a first come, first served basis.* **first and foremost** most importantly; more than anything else: *he considered himself first and foremost a writer .* **first and last** fundamentally; on the whole: *museums are first and last about curatorship.* **first of all** before doing anything else: *first of all, let me ask you something.* ■ most importantly: *German unity depends first of all on the German people.* **first off** informal, chiefly N. Amer. as a first point; firstly: *first off, I owe you a heck of an apology.* **first past the post** (of a contestant, especially a horse) winning a race by being the first to reach the finishing line. ■ [attrib.] Brit. denoting an electoral system in which a candidate or party is selected by achievement of a simple majority: *our first-past-the-post electoral system.* **first thing** early in the morning; before anything else: *I have to meet Josh first thing tomorrow.* **first things first** important matters should be dealt with before other things. **first up** Brit. first of all. ■ Austral./NZ at the first attempt. **from the (very) first** from the beginning: *he should have realized it from the first.* **from first to last** from beginning to end; throughout: *it's a fine performance that commands attention from first to last.* **get to first base** see BASE[1]. **in the first place** as the first consideration or point: *political reality was not quite that simple—in the first place, divisions existed within the parties.* ■ at the beginning; to begin with: *I should have told you in the first place.* **of the first order** (or **magnitude**) excellent or considerable of its kind: *it is a media event of the first order.* **of the first water** see WATER.
– ORIGIN Old English *fyr(e)st*; of Germanic origin, related to Old Norse *fyrstr* and German *Fürst* 'prince', from an Indo-European root shared by Sanskrit *prathama*, Latin *primus*, and Greek *prōtos*.

First Adar see ADAR.

first aid ▶ noun [mass noun] help given to a sick or injured person until full medical treatment is available: [as modifier] *a first-aid kit.*
– DERIVATIVES **first-aider** noun.

First Boer War see BOER WARS.

firstborn ▶ adjective denoting the first child born to a particular person: *the firstborn child of the queen.*
▶ noun a person's first child: *their firstborn arrived.*

First Cause ▶ noun Philosophy a supposed ultimate cause of all events, which does not itself have a cause, identified with God.

first class ▶ noun [in sing.] a set of people or things grouped together as the best: *the first class of the orders of chivalry.* ■ [mass noun] the best accommodation in a train, ship, or aircraft: *a seat in first class.*
▶ adjective & adverb of the best quality or in the highest division: [as adj.] *the hotel offers first-class accommodation.* ■ relating to the best accommodation in a train, ship, or aircraft: [as adj.] *a first-class carriage* | [as adv.] *you can travel first class on any train.* ■ relating to a class of mail given priority: [as adj.] *first-class mail* | [as adv.] *send it first class.* ■ Brit. relating to the highest division in the results of a university examination: *a first-class honours degree.* ■ [as adj.] (of cricket) played between sides of recognized stature and with matches of two innings per side.

First Consul the title held by Napoleon Bonaparte from 1799 to 1804, when he became Emperor of France.

first cost ▶ noun another term for PRIME COST.

first cousin ▶ noun see COUSIN.

first-day cover ▶ noun an envelope bearing a stamp or set of stamps postmarked on their day of issue.

first-degree ▶ adjective [attrib.] **1** Medicine denoting burns that affect only the surface of the skin and cause reddening.
2 Law, chiefly N. Amer. denoting the most serious category of a crime, especially murder.
– PHRASES **first-degree relative** a person's parent, sibling, or child.

first down ▶ noun American Football the score achieved by a team who have kept possession of the ball by advancing at least ten yards in a series of four downs.

First Empire the period of the reign of Napoleon I as emperor of the French (1804–15).

first finger ▶ noun the finger next to the thumb; the forefinger; the index finger.

first floor ▶ noun Brit. the floor of a building above the ground floor. ■ N. Amer. the ground floor of a building.

first-foot ▶ verb [with obj.] be the first person to cross the threshold of the house of (someone) in the New Year, in accordance with a Scottish custom.
▶ noun the first person to cross a householder's threshold in the New Year.
– DERIVATIVES **first-footer** noun.

first fruits ▶ plural noun the first agricultural produce of a season, especially when given as an offering to God. ■ the initial results of an enterprise or endeavour: *the first fruits of the companies' collaboration.*

first gear ▶ noun the lowest in a set of gears on a vehicle, used when travelling very slowly. ■ used in reference to a failure to make progress: *in a scrappy first half neither team seemed to* ***get out of first gear.***

first-hand ▶ adjective & adverb (of information or experience) from the original source or personal experience; direct: [as adj.] *first-hand accounts of activities behind the enemy lines* | [as adv.] *data which is obtained first-hand from customers.*
– PHRASES **at first hand** directly or from personal experience: *scientists observed the process at first hand.*

first intention ▶ noun [mass noun] Medicine the healing of a wound by natural contact of the parts involved: ***healing by first intention.***

First International see INTERNATIONAL (sense 2 of the noun).

First Lady ▸ noun the wife of the President of the US or other head of state. ▪ (usu. **first lady**) the leading woman in a particular activity or profession: *the first lady of rock.*

first language ▸ noun a person's native language.

first lieutenant ▸ noun a naval officer with executive responsibility for a ship or other command. ▪ a rank of officer in the US army or air force, above second lieutenant and below captain.

first light ▸ noun the time when light first appears in the morning; dawn: *you are to set off at first light.*

firstling ▸ noun (usu. **firstlings**) archaic the first agricultural produce or animal offspring of a season.

firstly ▸ adverb used to introduce a first point or reason: *firstly it is wrong and secondly it is extremely difficult to implement.*

first mate ▸ noun the officer second in command to the master of a merchant ship.

first minister ▸ noun the leader of the ruling political party in some regions or countries.

first name ▸ noun a personal name given to someone at birth or baptism and used before a family name.
– PHRASES **on first-name terms** having a friendly and informal relationship: *staff and pupils were on first-name terms.*

First Nation ▸ noun (in Canada) an indigenous American Indian community officially recognized as an administrative unit by the federal government or functioning as such without official status.

first night ▸ noun the first public performance of a play or show: [as modifier] *first-night nerves.*

first-nighter ▸ noun a person who attends a first night.

first offender ▸ noun a person who is convicted of a criminal offence for the first time.

first officer ▸ noun the first mate on a merchant ship. ▪ the second in command to the captain on an aircraft.

first-order ▸ adjective relating to the simplest or most fundamental level of organization, experience, or analysis; primary or immediate: *for a teacher, of course, drama must be a first-order experience.* ▪ technical having an order of one, especially denoting mathematical equations involving only the first power of the independent variable or only the first derivative of a function.

first person ▸ noun see PERSON (sense 2). ▪ (**the first person**) a type of narrative in which the protagonist relates their story using the first person, i.e. using the pronoun 'I'.

first position ▸ noun **1** Ballet a posture in which the feet are placed turned outwards with the heels touching. ▪ a position of the arms in which both are held curved in front of the body at waist level, with the palms facing the body.
2 Music the position of the hand on the fingerboard of a stringed instrument furthest from the bridge.

first post ▸ noun (in the British armed forces) the first of two bugle calls giving notice of the hour of retiring at night.

first principles ▸ plural noun the fundamental concepts or assumptions on which a theory, system, or method is based: *I think we have to start again and go right back to first principles.*

first-rate ▸ adjective of the best class or quality; excellent: *first-rate musicians.* ▪ in good health or condition; very well: *I think you look first-rate.*

first reading ▸ noun the first presentation of a bill to a legislative assembly, to permit its introduction.

first refusal ▸ noun [mass noun] the privilege of deciding whether to accept or reject something before it is offered to others: *group employees have first refusal on the tickets.*

First Reich see REICH[1].

First Republic the republican regime in France from the abolition of the monarchy in 1792 until Napoleon's accession as emperor in 1804.

first responder ▸ noun N. Amer. a person whose job entails being the first on the scene of an emergency, such as a firefighter or police officer.

first school ▸ noun Brit. a school for children from five to nine years old.

first sergeant ▸ noun (in the US army) the highest-ranking non-commissioned officer in a company or equivalent unit.

First State informal name for DELAWARE[1].

first strike ▸ noun an attack with nuclear weapons designed to destroy the enemy's nuclear weapons before use.

First World ▸ noun the industrialized capitalist countries of western Europe, North America, Japan, Australia, and New Zealand. Compare with SECOND WORLD and THIRD WORLD.

First World War a war (1914–18) in which the Central Powers (Germany and Austria–Hungary, joined later by Turkey and Bulgaria) were defeated by an alliance of Britain and its dominions, France, Russia, and others, joined later by Italy and the US.

> Political tensions over the rise of the German Empire were the war's principal cause, although it was set off by the assassination of Archduke Franz Ferdinand of Austria by a Bosnian Serb nationalist in Sarajevo, an event used as a pretext by Austria for declaring war on Serbia. Most of the fighting took place on land in Europe and was generally characterized by long periods of bloody stalemate; the balance eventually shifted in the Allies' favour in 1917 when the US joined the war. Total casualties of the war are estimated at 10 million killed. One of the consequences of the war was the collapse of the German, Austro-Hungarian, Russian, and Ottoman empires.

Firth, J. R. (1890–1960), English linguist; full name *John Rupert Firth.* Firth was noted for his contributions to linguistic semantics and prosodic phonology and for his insistence on studying both speech sounds and words in context. He was a major influence on the development of systemic grammar.

firth ▸ noun a narrow inlet of the sea; an estuary: [in place names] *the Moray Firth.*
– ORIGIN Middle English (originally Scots), from Old Norse *fjǫrthr* (see FJORD).

fir tree ▸ noun see FIR.

fisc /fɪsk/ ▸ noun Roman History the public treasury of Rome or the emperor's privy purse. ▪ archaic & N. Amer. a public treasury or exchequer. ▪ (also **fisk**) Scottish archaic the public treasury to which estates lapse by escheat.
– ORIGIN late 16th cent.: from French, or from Latin *fiscus* 'rush basket, purse, treasury'.

fiscal /ˈfɪsk(ə)l/ ▸ adjective relating to government revenue, especially taxes: *monetary and fiscal policy.* ▪ chiefly N. Amer. relating to financial matters: *the domestic fiscal crisis.* ▪ N. Amer. denoting a financial year: *the budget deficit for fiscal 1996.*
▸ noun **1** archaic a legal or treasury official in some countries. ▪ Scottish archaic short for PROCURATOR FISCAL.
2 (also **fiscal shrike**) an African shrike (songbird) with black-and-white plumage. ● Genus *Lanius*, family Laniidae: several species.
– DERIVATIVES **fiscally** adverb.
– ORIGIN mid 16th cent.: from French, or from Latin *fiscalis*, from *fiscus* 'purse, treasury' (see FISC).

fiscal drag ▸ noun [mass noun] Economics the deflationary effect of a progressive taxation system on a country's economy. As wages rise, a higher proportion of income is paid in tax.

fiscality ▸ noun fiscal policy or considerations.

fiscal year ▸ noun North American term for FINANCIAL YEAR.

Fischer[1] /ˈfɪʃə/, Bobby (1943–2008), American chess player; full name *Robert James Fischer.* He defeated Boris Spassky in 1972 to take the world championship, which he held until 1975.

Fischer[2] /ˈfɪʃə/, Emil Hermann (1852–1919), German organic chemist. He studied the structure of sugars, other carbohydrates, and purines, and synthesized many of them. He also confirmed that peptides and proteins consist of chains of amino acids. Nobel Prize for Chemistry (1902).

Fischer[3] /ˈfɪʃə/, German /ˈfɪʃɐ/, Hans (1881–1945), German organic chemist. He determined the structure of the porphyrin group of many natural pigments, including the red oxygen-carrying part of haemoglobin, the green chlorophyll pigments found in plants, and the orange bile pigment bilirubin. Nobel Prize for Chemistry (1930).

Fischer-Dieskau /ˌfɪʃəˈdiːskaʊ/, Dietrich (b.1925), German baritone. He is noted for his interpretations of German lieder, in particular Schubert's song cycles.

fish[1] ▸ noun (pl. **same** or **fishes**) **1** a limbless cold-blooded vertebrate animal with gills and fins living wholly in water: *the huge lakes are now devoid of fish.* ▪ [mass noun] the flesh of fish as food. ▪ (**the Fish** or **Fishes**) the zodiacal sign or constellation Pisces. ▪ used in names of invertebrate animals living wholly in water, e.g. **cuttlefish**, **shellfish**, **jellyfish**. ▪ informal a torpedo.
2 [with adj.] Brit. informal a person who is strange in a specified way: *he is generally thought to be a bit of a cold fish.*
▸ verb [no obj.] **1** catch or try to catch fish, typically by using a net or hook and line: *he was fishing for pike | I've told the girls we've gone fishing.* ▪ [with obj.] catch or try to catch fish in (a particular body of water): *many of the lochs we used to fish are now affected by forestry.*
2 search by groping or feeling for something concealed: *he fished for his registration certificate and held it up to the policeman's torch.* ▪ try subtly or deviously to elicit a response or some information from someone: *I was not fishing for compliments.* ▪ [with obj.] (**fish something out**) pull or take something out of water or a receptacle: *the body of a woman had been fished out of the river.*
– PHRASES **all's fish that comes to the net** proverb you can or should take advantage of anything that comes your way. **a big fish** an important or influential person: *he became a big fish in the world of politics.* **a big fish in a small pond** a person who is important only within the limited scope of a small field or group. **drink like a fish** drink excessive amounts of alcohol. **a fish out of water** a person in a completely unsuitable environment or situation. **have other** (or **bigger**) **fish to fry** have other (or more important) matters to attend to. **like shooting fish in a barrel** very easy: *picking cultivated berries is like shooting fish in a barrel.* **neither fish nor fowl** (**nor good red herring**) of indefinite character and difficult to identify or classify. **there are plenty more fish in the sea** used to console someone whose romantic relationship has ended by pointing out that there are many other people with whom they may have a successful relationship in the future.
– DERIVATIVES **fishable** adjective, **fishlike** adjective.
– ORIGIN Old English *fisc* (as a noun denoting any animal living exclusively in water), *fiscian* (verb), of Germanic origin; related to Dutch *vis*, *vissen* and German *Fisch*, *fischen*.

> **USAGE** The normal plural of fish is fish (*a shoal of fish; he caught two huge fish*). The older form **fishes** is still used, when referring to different kinds of fish (*freshwater fishes of the British Isles*).

fish[2] ▸ noun a flat plate that is fixed on a beam or across a joint in order to give additional strength. ▪ a long, slightly curved piece of wood that is lashed to a ship's damaged mast or spar as a temporary repair.
▸ verb [with obj.] **1** mend or strengthen with a fish.
2 join (rails in a railway track) with a fishplate.
– ORIGIN early 16th cent.: probably from French *fiche*, from *ficher* 'to fix', based on Latin *figere.*

fishbowl ▸ noun a round glass bowl for keeping pet fish in.

fishcake ▸ noun a patty of shredded fish and mashed potato, typically coated in batter or breadcrumbs and fried.

fish eagle ▸ noun an eagle that catches and feeds on fish. ● Genus *Haliaetus*, family Accipitridae: two or three species, in particular the white-headed **African fish eagle** (*H. vocifer*).

Fisher a shipping forecast area in the North Sea off northern Jutland and the mouth of the Skagerrak.

fisher ▸ noun **1** a large brown marten valued for its fur, found in North American woodland where it frequently preys on porcupines. ● *Martes pennanti*, family Mustelidae.
2 archaic a fisherman.
– ORIGIN Old English *fiscere* 'fisherman', of Germanic origin; related to Dutch *visser* and German *Fischer*, also to FISH[1].

Fisher, St John (1469–1535), English churchman. In 1504 he became bishop of Rochester and earned the disfavour of Henry VIII by opposing his divorce from Catherine of Aragon. When he refused to accept the king as supreme head of the Church, he was condemned to death. Feast day, 22 June.

fisherfolk ▸ plural noun people who catch fish for a living.

fisherman ▸ noun (pl. **fishermen**) a person who catches fish for a living or for sport.

fisherman bat ▸ noun another term for BULLDOG BAT.

fisherman's bend ▸ noun a knot tied by making a full turn round something (typically the ring of an

F

F

anchor), a half hitch through the turn, and a half hitch round the standing part of the rope.

fisherman's knot ▶ **noun** a knot used to join two small ropes by tying an overhand knot in the end of each around the opposite standing part.

fisherman's rib (also **fisherman knit**) ▶ **noun** [mass noun] a type of thick ribbed knitting.

fisherwoman ▶ **noun** (pl. **fisherwomen**) a woman who catches fish, especially for a living.

fishery ▶ **noun** (pl. **fisheries**) a place where fish are reared for commercial purposes. ■ a fishing ground or area where fish are caught. ■ [mass noun] the occupation or industry of catching or rearing fish.

fisheye ▶ **noun 1** (also **fisheye lens**) a very wide-angle lens with a field of vision covering up to 180°, the scale being reduced towards the edges.
2 US informal a suspicious or unfriendly look: *Wally gave him the fisheye.*
3 a defect in metal causing a spot to stand out brightly against its surroundings.

fish farm ▶ **noun** a place where fish are bred for commercial purposes.
– DERIVATIVES **fish farmer** noun, **fish farming** noun.

fish finger (N. Amer. **fish stick**) ▶ **noun** Brit. a small oblong piece of flaked or minced fish coated in batter or breadcrumbs and fried or grilled.

fish hawk ▶ **noun** another term for OSPREY.

fish hook ▶ **noun** see HOOK (sense 1 of the noun).

fishing ▶ **noun** [mass noun] the activity of catching fish, either for food or as a sport.
– PHRASES **fishing expedition** a search or investigation undertaken with the hope, though not the stated purpose, of discovering information: *they worried about an FBI fishing expedition.*

fishing cat ▶ **noun** a small wild cat found in wetland habitats in India and SE Asia, having a light brown coat with dark spots, a ringed tail, and slightly webbed paws. ● *Felis viverrina*, family Felidae.

fishing fly ▶ **noun** a natural or artificial flying insect used as bait in fishing.

fishing line ▶ **noun** a long thread of silk or nylon attached to a baited hook, with a sinker or float, and used for catching fish.

fishing pole ▶ **noun** N. Amer. a fishing rod, especially a simple one with no reel.

fishing rod ▶ **noun** a long, tapering rod to which a fishing line is attached, typically on a reel.

fish kettle ▶ **noun** an oval pan for cooking a whole fish.

fish knife ▶ **noun** a blunt knife with a broad blade for eating or serving fish.

fish ladder ▶ **noun** a series of pools built like steps to enable fish to ascend a dam or waterfall.

fish louse ▶ **noun** an aquatic crustacean which is a parasite of fish, typically attached to the skin or gills: ● a free-swimming crustacean with a shield-like carapace and a pair of suckers (class Branchiura: several genera, in particular *Argulus*). ● an elongated crustacean that becomes permanently attached to the host and typically highly modified (class Copepoda: several orders and numerous species).

fishmeal ▶ **noun** [mass noun] ground dried fish used as fertilizer or animal feed.

fishmonger ▶ **noun** a person or shop that sells fish for food.

fishnet ▶ **noun** [mass noun] a fabric with an open mesh resembling a fishing net: [as modifier] *black fishnet stockings.*

fishplate ▶ **noun** a flat piece of metal used to connect adjacent rails in a railway track. ■ a flat piece of metal with ends like a fish's tail, used to position masonry.

fish pond ▶ **noun** a pond in which live fish are kept.

fish slice ▶ **noun** Brit. a kitchen utensil with a broad flat blade for lifting fish and fried foods.

fishtail ▶ **noun 1** [usu. as modifier] an object which is forked like a fish's tail: *fishtail battlements.*
2 an uncontrolled sideways movement of the back of a motor vehicle: *he hit the brake, sending the car into a fishtail that carried him across the street.*
▶ **verb** [no obj.] [usu. with adverbial of direction] (of a vehicle) make an uncontrolled sideways movement: *the vehicle fishtailed from one side of the road to the other.*

fishway ▶ **noun** another term for FISH LADDER.

fishwife ▶ **noun** (pl. **fishwives**) **1** a coarse-mannered woman who is prone to shouting.
2 archaic a woman who sells fish.

fishy ▶ **adjective** (**fishier**, **fishiest**) **1** relating to or resembling fish or a fish: *a fishy smell.*
2 informal arousing feelings of doubt or suspicion: *I'm convinced there is something fishy going on.*
– DERIVATIVES **fishily** adverb, **fishiness** noun.

fisk ▶ **noun** Scottish archaic variant spelling of FISC.

fissile /ˈfɪsʌɪl/ ▶ **adjective 1** (of an atom or element) able to undergo nuclear fission: *a fissile isotope.*
2 (chiefly of rock) easily split.
– DERIVATIVES **fissility** /-ˈsɪlɪti/ noun.
– ORIGIN mid 17th cent. (in the sense 'easily split'): from Latin *fissilis*, from *fiss-* 'split, cracked', from the verb *findere*.

fission /ˈfɪʃ(ə)n/ ▶ **noun** [mass noun] division or splitting into two or more parts: *the party dissolved into fission and acrimony.* ■ Biology reproduction by means of a cell or organism dividing into two or more new cells or organisms: *bacteria divide by transverse **binary fission**.* ■ short for NUCLEAR FISSION.
▶ **verb** [no obj.] (chiefly of atoms) undergo fission: *these heavy nuclei can also fission.*
– ORIGIN early 17th cent.: from Latin *fissio(n-)*, from *findere* 'to split'.

fissionable ▶ **adjective** another term for FISSILE.

fission bomb ▶ **noun** another term for ATOM BOMB.

fission-track dating ▶ **noun** [mass noun] Geology a technique for establishing the age of a mineral sample from its uranium content. It involves microscopically counting tracks produced by uranium fission fragments and then establishing the existing concentration of uranium by counting again after irradiating the sample with neutrons.

fissiparous /fɪˈsɪp(ə)rəs/ ▶ **adjective** inclined to cause or undergo division into separate parts or groups. ■ Biology (of an organism) reproducing by fission: *small fissiparous worms.*
– ORIGIN mid 19th cent.: from Latin *fissus*, past participle of *findere* 'split', on the pattern of *viviparous*.

fissure /ˈfɪʃə/ ▶ **noun 1** a long, narrow opening or line of breakage made by cracking or splitting, especially in rock or earth. ■ Anatomy a long, narrow opening, e.g. any of the spaces separating convolutions of the brain.
2 a state of incompatibility or disagreement: *a fissure between philosophy and reality.*
▶ **verb** [with obj.] (usu. as adj. **fissured**) split or crack (something) to form a long, narrow opening: *low cliffs of fissured Silurian rock.*
– ORIGIN late Middle English: from Old French, or from Latin *fissura*, from *findere* 'to split'.

fissure of Sylvius /ˈsɪlvɪəs/ ▶ **noun** another term for SYLVIAN FISSURE.

fist ▶ **noun** a person's hand when the fingers are bent in towards the palm and held there tightly, typically in order to strike a blow or grasp something.
▶ **verb 1** [with obj. and adverbial of direction] strike with the fist: *he fisted a goal-bound shot over the bar.*
2 [with obj.] clench (the hand or fingers) into a fist: *she fisted her hands on her hips.*
3 (also **fist-fuck**) [with obj.] vulgar slang penetrate (a person's anus or vagina) with one's fist.
– PHRASES **make a —— fist of** informal do something to the specified degree of success: *they're all solid citizens, all capable of making a good fist of being an MP.* **shake one's fist** gesture angrily with one's clenched fist: *'Stupid fool!' he shouted, shaking his fist.*
– DERIVATIVES **fisted** adjective [in combination] *a bare-fisted combat*, **fistful** noun.
– ORIGIN Old English *fȳst*, of West Germanic origin; related to Dutch *vuist* and German *Faust*.

fist fight ▶ **noun** a fight with the fists.
– DERIVATIVES **fist fighting** noun.

fistic /ˈfɪstɪk/ ▶ **adjective** humorous relating to boxing.

fisticuffs ▶ **plural noun** fighting with the fists.
– ORIGIN early 17th cent.: probably from obsolete *fisty* 'relating to the fists or to fist fighting' + CUFF[2].

fistula /ˈfɪstjʊlə/ ▶ **noun** (pl. **fistulas** or **fistulae** /-liː/) Medicine an abnormal or surgically made passage between a hollow or tubular organ and the body surface, or between two hollow or tubular organs.
– DERIVATIVES **fistular** adjective, **fistulous** adjective.
– ORIGIN late Middle English: from Latin, 'pipe, flute, fistula'. Compare with FESTER.

fit[1] ▶ **adjective** (**fitter**, **fittest**) **1** [predic.] of a suitable quality, standard, or type to meet the required purpose: *the house was not fit for human habitation* | [with infinitive] *is the water clean and fit to drink?* ■ having the requisite qualities or skills to undertake something competently: [with infinitive] *the party was fit to govern.* ■ suitable and correct according to accepted social standards: *a fit subject on which to correspond.* ■ [with infinitive] informal having reached such an extreme condition as to be on the point of doing the thing specified: *he baited even his close companions until they were fit to kill him.* ■ informal ready: *well, are you fit?*
2 in good health, especially because of regular physical exercise: *my family keep fit by walking and cycling* | figurative *the measures would ensure a leaner, fitter company.* ■ Brit. informal sexually attractive; good-looking.
▶ **verb** (**fits**, **fitting**, **fitted** or US also **fit**) [with obj.] **1** be of the right shape and size for: *those jeans still fit me* | [no obj.] *the shoes fitted better after being stretched.* ■ (usu. **be fitted for**) try clothing on (someone) in order to make or alter it to the correct size: *she was about to be fitted for her costume.* ■ [no obj., with adverbial of place] be of the right size, shape, or number to occupy a particular place: *Fiona says we can all fit in her car.*
2 install or fix (something) into place: *they fitted smoke alarms to their home.* ■ (often **be fitted with**) provide (something) with a particular component or article: *most tools can be fitted with a new handle.* ■ join or cause to join together to form a whole: [no obj.] *their bodies **fitted together** perfectly* | [with obj.] *many physicists tried to **fit together** the various pieces of the puzzle.*
3 be compatible or in agreement with; match: *the landlord had not seen anyone fitting that description.* ■ be suitable or appropriate for: *the punishment should fit the crime.* ■ (of an attribute, qualification, or skill) make (someone) suitable to fulfil a particular role or undertake a particular task: *an MSc **fits** the student **for** a professional career.*
▶ **noun** the particular way in which something, especially a garment or component, fits: *the dress was a perfect fit.* ■ the particular way in which things match: *a close fit between teachers' qualifications and their teaching responsibilities.* ■ Statistics the correspondence between observed data and the values expected by theory.
– PHRASES **(as) fit as a fiddle** see FIDDLE. **fit for purpose** (of an institution, facility, etc.) well equipped or well suited for its designated role or purpose. **fit like a glove** see GLOVE. **fit the bill** see BILL[1]. **fit to be tied** informal very angry. **fit to bust** informal with great energy: *they laughed fit to bust.* **see** (or **think**) **fit** consider it correct or acceptable to do something: *why did the company **see fit to** give you the job?*
– PHRASAL VERBS **fit in** be socially compatible with other members of a group: *he feels he should become tough to **fit in with** his friends.* ■ be in harmony with other elements in a situation: *her project **fitted in with** the organization's general aims.* ■ (also **fit into**) constitute part of a situation or larger structure: *I don't think I fit into his plans for next season.* **fit someone/thing in** (or **into**) find room or have sufficient space for someone or something: *can you fit any more water into the jug?* ■ succeed in finding time in a busy schedule to see someone or do something: *I could fit you in at 3.45 this afternoon.* **fit someone/thing out** (or **up**) provide someone or something with the necessary equipment, clothes, or other items for a particular situation: *the cabin had been fitted out to a high standard.* **fit someone up** Brit. informal incriminate someone by falsifying evidence against them.
– DERIVATIVES **fitly** adverb.
– ORIGIN late Middle English: of unknown origin.

fit[2] ▶ **noun 1** a sudden attack of convulsions and/or loss of consciousness, typical of epilepsy and some other medical conditions: *the child had frequent fits.*
2 a sudden short period of uncontrollable coughing, laughter, etc. ■ a sudden burst of intense emotion: *he had killed her **in a fit of** jealous rage.*
▶ **verb** [no obj.] have an epileptic fit: *he started fitting uncontrollably.*
– PHRASES **give someone a fit** informal greatly shock or anger someone. **have** (or **throw**) **a fit** informal be very shocked or angry. **in fits** (**of laughter**) informal highly amused: *he had us all in fits.* **in** (or **by**) **fits and starts** with irregular bursts of activity: *the economy was recovering in fits and starts.*
– ORIGIN Old English *fitt* 'conflict', in Middle English 'position of danger or excitement', also 'short period'; the sense 'sudden attack of illness' dates from the mid 16th cent.

fit[3] (also **fytte**) ▶ **noun** archaic a section of a poem.
– ORIGIN Old English *fitt*, perhaps the same word as FIT[2], or related to German *Fitze* 'skein of yarn', in the obsolete sense 'thread with which weavers mark off a day's work'.

fitch ▶ noun old-fashioned term for POLECAT. ■ [mass noun] the fur of a polecat.
– ORIGIN late Middle English (denoting the fur of a polecat): from Middle Dutch *visse* 'polecat'. Compare with FITCHEW.

fitché /ˈfɪtʃeɪ/ (also **fitchy** or **fitched**) ▶ adjective Heraldry (of a cross) having the foot extended into a point.
– ORIGIN late 16th cent.: from French *fiché*, past participle of *ficher* 'to fix'.

fitchew /ˈfɪtʃuː/ ▶ noun archaic term for POLECAT.
– ORIGIN late Middle English: from Old French *ficheau*, *fissel*, diminutive related to Middle Dutch *visse*. Compare with FITCH.

fitful ▶ adjective active or occurring spasmodically or intermittently; not regular or steady: *a few hours' fitful sleep* | *business was fitful*.
– DERIVATIVES **fitfulness** noun.

fitfully ▶ adverb not regularly or continuously; intermittently: *he slept fitfully*.

fitment ▶ noun (usu. **fitments**) Brit. a fixed item of furniture or piece of equipment, especially in a house.

fitna /ˈfɪtnə/ (also **fitnah**) ▶ noun [mass noun] Islam unrest or rebellion, especially against a rightful ruler.
– ORIGIN Arabic *fitnah* 'rebellion, strife'.

fitness ▶ noun [mass noun] **1** the condition of being physically fit and healthy: *disease and lack of fitness are closely related* | [as modifier] *a fitness test*. ■ Biology an organism's ability to survive and reproduce in a particular environment.
2 (**fitness for/to do**) the quality of being suitable to fulfil a particular role or task: *the medical board assessed his fitness for active service*.

fit-out ▶ noun an act of providing the necessary equipment for a house or flat, especially the final decoration and fitments.

fitted ▶ adjective **1** made or shaped to fill a space or to cover something closely or exactly: *the blouse has a fitted bodice* | *navy-blue fitted sheets*. ■ Brit. (of a carpet) cut and laid to cover a floor completely. ■ chiefly Brit. (of furniture) built to be fixed into a particular space: *a fitted wardrobe*. ■ chiefly Brit. (of a room) equipped with matching units of fitted furniture: *a fitted kitchen*.
2 attached to or provided with a particular component or article: *a piping bag **fitted with** a star nozzle*.
3 (**fitted for/to do**) having the appropriate qualities or skills to do something: *I don't think he was fitted for the job*.

fitter ▶ noun **1** a person who puts together or installs machinery, engine parts, or other equipment: *a qualified gas fitter* | *kitchen fitters*.
2 a person who supervises the cutting, fitting, or alteration of garments or shoes.

fitting ▶ noun **1** (often **fittings**) a small part on or attached to a piece of furniture or equipment: *the wooden fittings were made of walnut*. ■ (**fittings**) chiefly Brit. items, such as a cooker or shelves, which are fixed in a building but can be removed when the owner moves: *little remains of the house's Victorian fittings*. Compare with FIXTURE (sense 1).
2 [mass noun] the action of fitting something: *the fitting of new engines by the shipyard*. ■ [count noun] an occasion when one tries on a garment that is being made or altered for one: *she's coming tomorrow for a fitting*.
▶ adjective **1** suitable or appropriate under the circumstances; right or proper: *a fitting reward* | [with clause] ***it was fitting that** his last innings for Middlesex should bring him his highest first-class score*.
2 [in combination] fitted around or to something or someone in a specified way: *loose-fitting trousers*.
– DERIVATIVES **fittingly** adverb, **fittingness** noun.

fitting room ▶ noun a room in a shop in which one can try on clothes before deciding whether to purchase them.

fitting shop ▶ noun a part of a factory where machine parts are put together.

fit-up ▶ noun Brit. informal **1** an instance of incriminating someone by falsifying evidence against them.
2 dated a temporary stage or other piece of theatrical equipment.

Fitzgerald[1] /fɪtsˈdʒɛr(ə)ld/, Edward (1809–83), English scholar and poet. Notable works: *The Rubáiyát of Omar Khayyám* (translation, 1859).

Fitzgerald[2] /fɪtsˈdʒɛr(ə)ld/, Ella (1917–96), American jazz singer, known for her distinctive style of scat singing.

Fitzgerald[3] /fɪtsˈdʒɛr(ə)ld/, F. Scott (1896–1940), American novelist; full name *Francis Scott Key Fitzgerald*. His novels, in particular *The Great Gatsby* (1925), provide a vivid portrait of the US during the jazz era of the 1920s.

FitzGerald contraction (also **FitzGerald–Lorentz contraction**) ▶ noun Physics the shortening of a moving body in the direction of its motion, especially at speeds close to that of light.
– ORIGIN named after George. F. FitzGerald (1851–1901), Irish physicist, and H. A. LORENTZ, who independently postulated the theory in 1892.

Fitzroy /ˈfɪtsrɔɪ/ a shipping forecast area covering part of the Atlantic off NW Spain, west of the Bay of Biscay. Formerly (until 2002) called FINISTERRE (see FINISTERRE, CAPE).

Fiume /ˈfjuːme/ Italian name for RIJEKA.

five ▶ cardinal number equivalent to the sum of two and three; one more than four, or half of ten; 5: *five minutes later she came back* | *five of Sweden's top financial experts*. (Roman numeral: **v**, **V**) ■ a group or unit of five people or things: *the bulbs are planted in threes or fives*. ■ five years old: *Vic moved to Darlington when he was five*. ■ five o'clock: *we left at half past five*. ■ a size of garment or other merchandise denoted by five. ■ a playing card or domino with five pips.
– ORIGIN Old English *fīf*, of Germanic origin; related to Dutch *vijf* and German *fünf*, from an Indo-European root shared by Latin *quinque* and Greek *pente*.

five-alarm ▶ adjective [attrib.] US informal (of a fire) very large or fierce. ■ (of food, such as chillies) extremely pungent or hot.

five-and-dime (also **five-and-dime store** or **five-and-ten**) ▶ noun N. Amer. a shop selling a wide variety of inexpensive household and personal goods.
■ historical a shop where all the articles were priced at five or ten cents.

five-a-side ▶ noun [mass noun] Brit. a form of soccer with five players in each team, typically played on an indoor pitch: [as modifier] *a five-a-side tournament*.

five-corner (also **five-corners**) ▶ noun an Australian shrub that has stiff pointed leaves, tubular flowers, and five-cornered fruit. ● Genus *Styphelia*, family Epacridaceae: several species.
■ the pentagonal fruit of the five-corner shrub.

five-eighth ▶ noun Rugby, chiefly Austral./NZ a player positioned between the scrum half and the three-quarters.

five finger (also **five fingers**) ▶ noun any of a number of plants with leaves that are divided into five leaflets or with flowers that have five petals, such as cinquefoil.

five-finger discount ▶ noun N. Amer. informal an act of shoplifting.

five-finger exercise ▶ noun an exercise on the piano for all the fingers on both hands. ■ an easy task.

fivefold ▶ adjective five times as great or as numerous: *a fivefold increase in funding*. ■ having five parts or elements: *fivefold rotational symmetry*.
▶ adverb by five times; to five times the number or amount: *the unemployment rate rose almost fivefold*.

five hundred ▶ noun [mass noun] a form of euchre (card game) in which making 500 points wins a game.

five Ks ▶ plural noun (**the five Ks**) see KHALSA.

Five Nations ▶ plural noun **1** [treated as sing.] former name for SIX NATIONS (sense 1).
2 the Iroquois confederacy as originally formed, including the Mohawk, Oneida, Seneca, Onondaga, and Cayuga peoples. Compare with SIX NATIONS (sense 2).

five o'clock shadow ▶ noun a dark appearance on a man's chin and face caused by the slight growth of beard that has occurred since he shaved in the morning.

Five Pillars of Islam the five duties expected of every Muslim: profession of the faith in a prescribed form, observance of ritual prayer, giving alms to the poor, fasting during the month of Ramadan, and performing a pilgrimage to Mecca. See HAJJ, SALAT, SAWM, SHAHADA, and ZAKAT.

fiver ▶ noun Brit. informal a five-pound note. ■ N. Amer. a five-dollar bill.

fives ▶ plural noun [treated as sing.] a game, played especially in the UK, in which a ball is hit with a gloved hand or a bat against the walls of a court with three walls (**Eton fives**) or four walls (**Rugby fives**).
– ORIGIN mid 17th cent.: plural of FIVE used as a singular noun; the significance is unknown.

five senses ▶ plural noun the faculties of sight, smell, hearing, taste, and touch.

five-spice (also **five-spice powder**) ▶ noun [mass noun] a blend of five powdered spices, typically fennel seeds, cinnamon, cloves, star anise, and peppercorns, used in Chinese cuisine.

five-star ▶ adjective having five stars in a grading system in which this denotes the highest standard: *a five-star restaurant*. [early 20th cent.: from a system used to grade hotels, the highest grade being indicated by five asterisks or stars.] ■ having or denoting the highest military rank, distinguished in the US armed forces by five stars on the uniform: *a five-star general*.

fivestones ▶ noun Brit. a game of jacks played with five pieces of metal or stone and usually no ball.

five-year plan ▶ noun (especially in the former Soviet Union) a government plan for economic development over five years. The first such plan in the Soviet Union was inaugurated in 1928.

fix ▶ verb [with obj.] **1** [with obj. and adverbial of place] fasten (something) securely in a particular place or position: *they had candles fixed to their helmets* | figurative *her words have remained fixed in my memory*. ■ (**fix something on/upon**) direct one's eyes, mind, or attention steadily or unwaveringly towards: *Ben nodded, his eyes fixed on the ground*. ■ [no obj.] (**fix on/upon**) (of a person's eyes, attention, or mind) be directed steadily or unwaveringly towards: *her gaze fixed on Jess*. ■ (**fix someone with**) look at someone unwaveringly: *Cowley fixed him with a cold stare*.
2 decide or settle on (a specific price, date, course of action, etc.): *no date has yet been fixed for a hearing*. ■ arrange (something) on a permanent basis: *the rate of interest is fixed for the life of the loan*. ■ establish the exact location of (something) by using radar or visual bearings or astronomical observation: *having made landfall, he fixed his position*. ■ settle the form of (a language). ■ assign or determine (a person's liability or responsibility) for legal purposes: *there are no facts which **fix** the defendant **with** liability*.
3 mend or repair: *you've forgotten to fix that shelf*. ■ put (a bad or unwelcome situation) right: *the international community should not rely on the UN to fix the world's problems*. ■ (**fix something up**) do the necessary work to improve or adapt something: *we were trying to fix up the house so that it became vaguely comfortable*. ■ informal, chiefly N. Amer. tidy or neaten (something, especially one's hair, clothes, or make-up).
4 make arrangements for (something); organize: *Harry's **fixed up** a meeting* | [no obj.] *I've **fixed for** you to see him on Thursday*. ■ (**fix someone up**) informal arrange for someone to have something; provide someone with something: *I'll **fix** you **up** with a room*. ■ informal, chiefly N. Amer. prepare or arrange for the provision of (food or drink): [with two objs] *Ruth fixed herself a cold drink*. ■ (**be fixing to do something**) N. Amer. informal be intending or planning to do something: *I'm fixing to call the state patrol*.
5 make (a dye, photographic image, or drawing) permanent. ■ Biology preserve or stabilize (a specimen) with a chemical substance prior to microscopic or other examination: *specimens were fixed in buffered formalin*. ■ (of a plant or microorganism) assimilate (nitrogen or carbon dioxide) by forming a non-gaseous compound: *lupins fix gaseous nitrogen in their root nodules*.
6 informal influence the outcome of (something, especially a race, match, or election) by illegal or underhand means: *the club attempted to fix last Thursday's league match*. ■ take revenge on or punish (someone): *that little swine—I'll fix him next time*.
7 [no obj.] informal take an injection of a narcotic drug.
8 N. Amer. castrate or spay (an animal).
▶ noun **1** [in sing.] informal a difficult or awkward situation from which it is hard to extricate oneself; a predicament: *how on earth did you get into such a fix?*
2 informal a dose of a narcotic drug to which one is addicted: *he hadn't had his fix*. ■ an experience of something from which one derives great pleasure or stimulation: *get your coffee fix at home with this state-of-the-art espresso-maker*.
3 informal a solution to a problem, especially one that is hastily devised or makeshift: *there is going to be no **quick fix** to the recession*.
4 a position determined by visual or radio bearings or astronomical observations.
5 [in sing.] informal a dishonest or underhand arrangement: *obviously, his appointment was a fix*.

– PHRASES **get a fix on** determine the position of (something) by visual or radio bearings or astronomical observation. ■ informal assess or determine the nature or facts of: *it is hard to get a fix on their ages.*
– DERIVATIVES **fixable** adjective.
– ORIGIN late Middle English: partly from Old French *fix* 'fixed', partly from medieval Latin *fixare* 'to fix', both from Latin *fixus*, past participle of *figere* 'fix, fasten'. The noun dates from the early 19th cent.

fixate /fɪk'seɪt/ ▸ **verb** [with obj.] **1** (often **be fixated on/upon**) cause (someone) to develop an obsessive attachment to someone or something: *he became fixated on the idea of a Third World War.* ■ [no obj.] (**fixate on/upon**) develop a fixation with: *erotomaniacs are convinced that the person they have fixated on loves them in return.* ■ (in Freudian theory) arrest (a person or their libidinal energy) at an immature stage, causing an obsessive attachment.
2 technical direct one's eyes towards: *subjects fixated a central point.*
– ORIGIN late 19th cent.: from Latin *fixus*, past participle of *figere* (see **FIX**) + **-ATE**[3].

fixation ▸ **noun** [mass noun] **1** an obsessive interest in or feeling about someone or something: *our fixation with diet and fitness.* ■ Psychoanalysis (in Freudian theory) the arresting of part of the libido at an immature stage, causing an obsessive attachment: *fixation at the oral phase might result in dependence on others.*
2 the action or process of fixing or being fixed: *sand-dune fixation.* ■ the process by which some plants and microorganisms assimilate nitrogen or carbon dioxide.
– ORIGIN late Middle English (originally as an alchemical term denoting the process of reducing a volatile spirit or essence to a permanent bodily form): from medieval Latin *fixatio(n-)*, from *fixare* (see **FIX**).

fixative /'fɪksətɪv/ ▸ **noun 1** a chemical substance used to preserve or stabilize biological material prior to microscopy or other examination. ■ a substance used to stabilize the volatile components of perfume. ■ a liquid sprayed on to a pastel or charcoal drawing to fix colours or prevent smudging.
2 a substance used to keep things in position or stick them together: *the swift glues these thin twigs to a wall using its own saliva as a fixative.*
▸ **adjective** (of a substance) used to fix or stabilize something.

fixed ▸ **adjective 1** fastened securely in position: *a fixed iron ladder down the port side.* ■ (of a person's expression) held for a long time without changing, especially to conceal other feelings: *a fixed smile.*
2 (especially of a price, rate, or time) predetermined and not able to be changed: *loans are provided for a fixed period.* ■ (of a view or idea) firm or inflexible: *the fixed assumptions of the Cold War.*
3 (of a sports contest) having the outcome dishonestly predetermined: *the fight's fixed—the ref has your card marked.*
4 (**fixed for**) informal situated with regard to: *how's the club fixed for money now?*
– DERIVATIVES **fixedly** adverb, **fixedness** noun.

fixed assets ▸ **plural noun** assets which are purchased for long-term use and are not likely to be converted quickly into cash, such as land, buildings, and equipment. Compare with **CURRENT ASSETS**.

fixed capital ▸ **noun** [mass noun] capital invested in fixed assets.

fixed charge ▸ **noun** a liability to a creditor which relates to specific assets of a company. Compare with **FLOATING CHARGE**.

fixed costs ▸ **plural noun** business costs, such as rent, that are constant whatever the amount of goods produced.

fixed-doh (also **fixed-do**) ▸ **adjective** denoting a system of solmization in which C is called 'doh', D is called 'ray', etc., irrespective of the key in which they occur. Compare with **MOVABLE-DOH**.

fixed focus ▸ **noun** a camera focus that cannot be adjusted, typically used with a small-aperture lens having a large depth of field.

fixed idea ▸ **noun** another term for **IDÉE FIXE**.

fixed income ▸ **noun** an income from a pension or investment that is set at a particular figure and does not vary like a dividend or rise with the rate of inflation.

fixed-line ▸ **adjective** denoting or relating to telecommunications systems using cables laid across land, as opposed to cellular radio systems.

fixed odds ▸ **plural noun** odds in betting (especially on soccer results) that are predetermined, as opposed to a pool system or a starting price.

fixed oil ▸ **noun** a non-volatile oil of animal or plant origin.

fixed point ▸ **noun 1** Physics a well-defined reproducible temperature which can be used as a reference point, e.g. one defined by a change of phase.
2 [as modifier] Computing denoting a mode of representing a number by a single sequence of digits whose values depend on their location relative to a predetermined radix point. Often contrasted with **FLOATING-POINT**.

fixed star ▸ **noun** see **STAR** (sense 1 of the noun).

fixed-wing ▸ **adjective** denoting aircraft of the conventional type as opposed to those with rotating wings, such as helicopters.

fixer ▸ **noun 1** a person who makes arrangements for other people, especially of an illicit or devious kind.
2 [mass noun] a substance used for fixing a photographic image.

fixer-upper ▸ **noun** N. Amer. informal a house in need of repairs (used chiefly in connection with the purchase of such a house).

fixing ▸ **noun 1** [mass noun] the action of fixing something: *artificial price fixing.*
2 (**fixings**) Brit. screws, bolts, or other items used to fix or assemble building material, furniture, or equipment: *masonry fixings.*
3 N. Amer. the ingredients necessary to make a dish or meal: *have all the fixings ready before starting.* ■ apparatus or equipment for a particular purpose: *picnic fixings.*

fixit ▸ **noun** [usu. as modifier] informal an act of repairing or putting something right: *a fixit shop.* ■ a person known for repairing things or putting things in order: *he pictured himself as a Mr Fixit.*
– ORIGIN early 20th cent.: from *Little Miss Fixit*, the title of a musical show.

fixity ▸ **noun** [mass noun] the state of being unchanging or permanent: *the fixity of his stare.*
– ORIGIN mid 17th cent. (denoting the property of a substance of not evaporating or losing weight when heated): partly from obsolete *fix* 'fixed', partly from French *fixité*.

fixture /'fɪkstʃə, -tjə/ ▸ **noun 1** a piece of equipment or furniture which is fixed in position in a building or vehicle: *plumbing fixtures.* ■ (**fixtures**) articles attached to a house or land and considered legally part of it so that they normally remain in place when an owner moves: *the hotel retains many original **fixtures and fittings**.* Compare with **FITTING** (sense 1 of the noun). ■ informal a person or thing that is well established in a particular place or situation: *the midfielder is set to become **a permanent fixture in** the England line-up.*
2 Brit. a sporting event arranged to take place on a particular date: *the team's last away fixture of the season.*
– ORIGIN late 16th cent. (in the sense 'fixing, becoming fixed'): alteration (first found in Shakespeare) of obsolete *fixure* (from late Latin *fixura*, from Latin *figere* 'to fix'), with *t* inserted on the pattern of *mixture*.

fizgig /'fɪzgɪg/ ▸ **noun 1** archaic a silly or flirtatious young woman.
2 archaic a kind of small firework.
3 Austral. informal a police informer.
– ORIGIN early 16th cent.: probably from **FIZZ** + obsolete *gig* 'flighty girl'. Compare with **GIG**[1] and **WHIRLIGIG**.

fizz ▸ **verb** [no obj.] (of a liquid) produce bubbles of gas and make a hissing sound: *his lemonade was still fizzing at the top of the glass.* ■ make a buzzing or crackling sound: *carbide lamps fizzed in the darkness.* ■ [with adverbial] move with or display excitement, exuberance, or liveliness: *anticipation began to fizz through his veins.*
▸ **noun** [mass noun] the quality of being fizzy; effervescence: *the champagne had lost its fizz.* ■ informal an effervescent drink, especially sparkling wine: *a glass of your favourite fizz.* ■ exuberance or liveliness: *she saw I had lost some of my fizz.*
– ORIGIN mid 17th cent.: imitative.

fizzer ▸ **noun** informal **1** Brit. an outstandingly lively, energetic, or excellent thing: *that fizzer of a letter.*
2 Austral./NZ a failure or fiasco: *the greatest fizzer in the history of Australian politics.*

fizzle ▸ **verb** [no obj.] make a feeble hissing or spluttering sound: *the strobe lights fizzled and flickered.* ■ end or fail in a weak or disappointing way: *their threatened revolt **fizzled out** at yesterday's meeting.*
▸ **noun** a feeble hissing or spluttering sound. ■ a failure.
– ORIGIN late Middle English (in the sense 'break wind quietly'): probably imitative (compare with **FIZZ**), but perhaps related to Middle English *fist* (see **FEISTY**). Current senses date from the 19th cent.

fizzog ▸ **noun** variant spelling of **PHIZ**.

fizzy ▸ **adjective** (**fizzier**, **fizziest**) (of a drink) containing bubbles of gas; effervescent: *fizzy mineral water.* ■ full of energy or exuberance; lively: *fizzy new wave pop.*
– DERIVATIVES **fizzily** adverb, **fizziness** noun.

fjord /fjɔːd, 'fiːɔːd/ (also **fiord**) ▸ **noun** a long, narrow, deep inlet of the sea between high cliffs, as in Norway, typically formed by submergence of a glaciated valley.
– ORIGIN late 17th cent.: Norwegian, from Old Norse *fjǫrthr*. Compare with **FIRTH**.

FL ▸ **abbreviation** ■ Florida (in official postal use). ■ Liechtenstein (international vehicle registration). [from German *Fürstentum Liechtenstein* 'Principality of Liechtenstein'.]

fl. ▸ **abbreviation** ■ floor. ■ floruit. ■ fluid.

Fla ▸ **abbreviation** Florida.

flab ▸ **noun** [mass noun] informal soft loose flesh on a person's body; fat.
– ORIGIN 1950s: back-formation from **FLABBY**.

flabbergast /'flabəgɑːst/ ▸ **verb** [with obj.] (usu. as adj. **flabbergasted**) informal surprise (someone) greatly; astonish: *this news has left me totally flabbergasted.*
– ORIGIN late 18th cent.: of unknown origin.

flabby ▸ **adjective** (**flabbier**, **flabbiest**) (of a part of a person's body) soft, loose, and fleshy: *this exercise helps to flatten a flabby stomach.* ■ having soft, loose flesh; overweight. ■ lacking strength, vitality, or effectiveness: *flabby, colourless prose.*
– DERIVATIVES **flabbily** adverb, **flabbiness** noun.
– ORIGIN late 17th cent.: alteration of earlier *flappy*.

flaccid /'flasɪd, 'flaksɪd/ ▸ **adjective** (of part of the body) soft and hanging loosely or limply, especially so as to look or feel unpleasant: *she took his flaccid hand in hers.* ■ (of plant tissue) drooping or inelastic through lack of water. ■ lacking vigour or effectiveness: *the flaccid leadership campaign was causing concern.*
– DERIVATIVES **flaccidity** /flək'sɪdɪti, flə'sɪd-/ noun, **flaccidly** adverb.
– ORIGIN early 17th cent.: from French *flaccide* or Latin *flaccidus*, from *flaccus* 'flabby'.

flack[1] N. Amer. informal ▸ **noun** a publicity agent.
▸ **verb** [with obj.] publicize or promote: *each author is flacking his 'exclusive' account of the whole mess.*
– DERIVATIVES **flackery** noun.
– ORIGIN 1940s: of unknown origin.

flack[2] ▸ **noun** variant spelling of **FLAK**.

flacon /'flakɔ̃, 'flak(ə)n/ ▸ **noun** (pl. pronunc. **same**) a small stoppered bottle, especially one for perfume.
– ORIGIN early 19th cent.: French, 'flask'.

flag[1] ▸ **noun 1** a piece of cloth or similar material, typically oblong or square, attachable by one edge to a pole or rope and used as the symbol or emblem of a country or institution or as a decoration during public festivities: *the American flag.* ■ used in reference to one's home country or its system of beliefs and values: *he pledged allegiance to the flag.* ■ the ensign carried by a flagship as an emblem of an admiral's rank: *Hawke first hoisted his flag at Spithead.*
2 a small piece of cloth attached at one edge to a pole and used as a marker or signal in various sports: *the flag's up.* ■ a drawing or symbol resembling a flag, used as a marker: *golf courses are indicated by a numbered flag on the map.* ■ a small paper badge given to people who donate to a charity appeal in the street. ■ a mechanism that can be raised to indicate that a taxi is for hire.
3 Computing a variable used to indicate a particular property of the data in a record.
▸ **verb** (**flags**, **flagging**, **flagged**) [with obj.] **1** mark (an item) for attention or treatment in a specified way: *the spellcheck program flags any words that are not in its dictionary.* ■ draw attention to: *cancer was **flagged up** as a priority area for research.*
2 (**flag someone/thing down**) signal to a vehicle or driver to stop, especially by waving one's arm: *she flagged down a police patrol car.* ■ (**flag someone/thing off**) wave a flag at someone or something as a starting signal: *the vintage car fiesta will be flagged off by the minister for tourism.* ■ [no obj.] (of an

official) raise a flag to draw the referee's attention to a breach of the rules in soccer, rugby, and other sports: *the goalkeeper brought down Hendrie and a linesman immediately flagged.*
3 provide or decorate with a flag or flags. ■ register (a vessel) in a particular country, under whose flag it then sails.
– PHRASES **fly the flag** (of a ship) be registered in a particular country and sail under its flag. ■ (also **show** or **carry** or **wave the flag**) represent or demonstrate support for one's country, political party, or organization, especially when one is abroad: *he will be flying the flag for British fashion on the Paris catwalks.* **put the flags** (or **flag**) **out** celebrate: *temperatures are increasing again—that's why we're putting out the flags.* **show the flag** (of a naval vessel) make an official visit to a foreign port, especially as a show of strength. **wrap oneself in the flag** chiefly N. Amer. make an excessive show of one's patriotism, especially for political ends.
– DERIVATIVES **flagger** noun.
– ORIGIN mid 16th cent.: perhaps from obsolete *flag* 'drooping', of unknown ultimate origin.

flag² ▶ noun a flat stone slab, typically rectangular or square, used for paving.
– DERIVATIVES **flagged** adjective [often in combination] *stone-flagged steps.*
– ORIGIN late Middle English (also in the sense 'turf, sod'): probably of Scandinavian origin and related to Icelandic *flag* 'spot from which a sod has been cut' and Old Norse *flaga* 'slab of stone'.

flag³ ▶ noun a plant with sword-shaped leaves that grow from a rhizome: ● a plant of the iris family (genus *Iris*, family Iridaceae). See **YELLOW FLAG** (sense 2) ● see **SWEET FLAG.**
■ the long slender leaf of a flag.
– ORIGIN late Middle English: related to Middle Dutch *flag* and Danish *flæg*; of unknown ultimate origin.

flag⁴ ▶ verb (**flags, flagging, flagged**) [no obj.] become tired or less enthusiastic or dynamic: *if you begin to flag, there is an excellent cafe to revive you* | (as adj. **flagging**) *an attempt to resurrect his flagging career.*
– ORIGIN mid 16th cent. (in the sense 'flap about loosely, hang down'): related to obsolete *flag* 'hanging down'.

flag boat ▶ noun a boat serving as a mark in sailing matches.

flag captain ▶ noun the captain of a flagship.

flag day ▶ noun **1** Brit. a day on which money is collected for a charity in the street and donors are given small paper badges to show they have contributed.
2 (**Flag Day**) (in the US) 14 June, the anniversary of the adoption of the Stars and Stripes in 1777.

flagellant /ˈfladʒ(ə)l(ə)nt, fləˈdʒɛl(ə)nt/ ▶ noun a person who subjects themselves or others to flogging, either as a religious discipline or for sexual gratification.
– ORIGIN late 16th cent.: from Latin *flagellant-* 'whipping', from the verb *flagellare*, from *flagellum* 'whip' (see **FLAGELLUM**).

flagellate¹ /ˈfladʒ(ə)leɪt/ ▶ verb [with obj.] flog (someone), either as a religious discipline or for sexual gratification: *he flagellated himself with branches.*
– DERIVATIVES **flagellator** noun, **flagellatory** /-lət(ə)ri/ adjective.
– ORIGIN early 17th cent.: from Latin *flagellat-* 'whipped', from *flagellare.*

flagellate² /ˈfladʒ(ə)lət, -eɪt/ Zoology ▶ noun a protozoan that has one or more flagella used for swimming.
● Several phyla in the kingdom Protista (formerly subphylum Mastigophora, phylum Protozoa), including forms such as euglena that are sometimes regarded as algae.
▶ adjective (of a cell or single-celled organism) bearing one or more flagella.
– ORIGIN mid 19th cent.: from **FLAGELLUM** + **-ATE²**.

flagellation /fladʒəˈleɪʃ(ə)n/ ▶ noun flogging or beating, either as a religious discipline or for sexual gratification: *pursuing the path of penance and flagellation.*

flagellum /fləˈdʒɛləm/ ▶ noun (pl. **flagella**) Biology a slender thread-like structure, especially a microscopic whip-like appendage which enables many protozoa, bacteria, spermatozoa, etc. to swim.
– DERIVATIVES **flagellar** adjective.
– ORIGIN early 19th cent. (denoting a whip or scourge): from Latin, diminutive of *flagrum* 'scourge'.

flageolet¹ /ˌfladʒəˈlɛt, ˈfladʒəlɪt, ˈfla(d)ʒəleɪ/ ▶ noun (also **French flageolet**) a very small flute-like instrument resembling a recorder but with four finger holes on top and two thumb holes below.
■ another term for **TIN WHISTLE**.
– ORIGIN mid 17th cent.: from French, diminutive of Old French *flageol*, from Provençal *flaujol*, of unknown origin.

flageolet² /ˈfla(d)ʒəleɪ, ˌfladʒəˈlɛt/ ▶ noun a French kidney bean of a small variety used in cooking.
– ORIGIN late 19th cent.: from French, based on Latin *phaseolus* 'bean'.

flagfish ▶ noun (pl. **same** or **flagfishes**) any of a number of small fish with prominent or boldly marked fins, in particular: ● a colourful freshwater fish with spots and iridescent scales, native to Florida (*Jordanella floridae*, family Cyprinodontidae). ● a marine fish with a dark-barred tail, of shallow Indo-Pacific waters (*Kuhlia taeniurus*, family Kuhliidae).

flagitious /fləˈdʒɪʃəs/ ▶ adjective formal (of a person or their actions) criminal; villainous.
– ORIGIN late Middle English: from Latin *flagitiosus*, from *flagitium* 'importunity, shameful crime', from *flagitare* 'demand earnestly'.

flag lieutenant ▶ noun a lieutenant acting as an admiral's aide-de-camp.

flagman ▶ noun (pl. **flagmen**) a person who gives signals with a flag, especially at horse races or on railway lines.

flag of convenience ▶ noun a flag of a country under which a ship is registered in order to avoid financial charges or restrictive regulations in the owner's country.

flag officer ▶ noun an admiral, vice admiral, or rear admiral, or the commodore of a yacht club.

flag of truce ▶ noun a white flag indicating a desire for a truce.

flagon /ˈflag(ə)n/ ▶ noun a large container in which drink is served, typically with a handle and spout: *a silver flagon.* ■ the amount of liquid held in a flagon: *a flagon of beer.* ■ a container similar to a flagon used to hold the wine for the Eucharist. ■ a large bottle in which wine or cider is sold, typically holding 1.13 litres (about 2 pints).
– ORIGIN late Middle English: from Old French *flacon*, based on late Latin *flasco, flascon-*, of unknown origin. Compare with **FLASK**.

flagpole ▶ noun a pole used for flying a flag.
– PHRASES **run something up the flagpole** (**to see who salutes**) test the popularity of a new idea or proposal: *the idea was first run up the flagpole in 1997.*

flag rank ▶ noun [mass noun] the rank attained by flag officers.

flagrant /ˈfleɪgr(ə)nt/ ▶ adjective (of an action considered wrong or immoral) conspicuously or obviously offensive: *a flagrant violation of the law.*
– DERIVATIVES **flagrancy** noun, **flagrantly** adverb.
– ORIGIN late 15th cent. (in the sense 'blazing, resplendent'): from French, or from Latin *flagrant-* 'blazing', from the verb *flagrare.*

flagship ▶ noun the ship in a fleet which carries the commanding admiral. ■ the best or most important thing owned or produced by a particular organization: *this bill is the flagship of the government's legislative programme.*

flagstaff /ˈflagstɑːf/ ▶ noun another term for **FLAGPOLE**.

flagstone ▶ noun a flat stone slab, typically rectangular or square, used for paving.
– DERIVATIVES **flagstoned** adjective.

flag-waving ▶ noun [mass noun] the expression of patriotism in a populist and emotional way: [as modifier] *flag-waving conservatism.*
– DERIVATIVES **flag-waver** noun.

flail /fleɪl/ ▶ noun a threshing tool consisting of a wooden staff with a short heavy stick swinging from it. ■ a similar device used as a weapon or for flogging. ■ a machine having a similar action, used for threshing or slashing: [as modifier] *a flail hedge trimmer.*
▶ verb **1** wave or swing wildly: [no obj.] *his arms flailed as he sought to maintain his balance.* ■ [no obj.] flounder; struggle uselessly: *I was flailing about in the water.*
2 [with obj.] beat or flog (someone). ■ Brit. cut (vegetation) with a flail: *the modern practice of flailing hedges every year with mechanical cutters.*
– ORIGIN Old English, of West Germanic origin, based on Latin *flagellum* 'whip' (see **FLAGELLUM**); probably influenced in Middle English by Old French *flaiel* or Dutch *vlegel.*

flair ▶ noun **1** [in sing.] a special or instinctive aptitude or ability for doing something well: *she had a flair for languages* | [mass noun] *none of us had much artistic flair.*
2 [mass noun] stylishness and originality: *she dressed with flair.*
– ORIGIN late 19th cent.: from French, from *flairer* 'to smell', based on Latin *fragrare* 'smell sweet'. Compare with **FRAGRANT**.

flak (also **flack**) ▶ noun [mass noun] anti-aircraft fire. ■ strong criticism: *you must be strong enough to take the flak if things go wrong.*
– ORIGIN 1930s: from German, abbreviation of *Fliegerabwehrkanone*, literally 'aviator-defence gun'.

flake¹ ▶ noun **1** a small, flat, very thin piece of something, typically one which has broken away or been peeled off from a larger piece: *he licked the flakes of croissant off his finger.* ■ a snowflake. ■ Archaeology a piece of hard stone chipped off for use as a tool by prehistoric humans. ■ [mass noun] thin pieces of crushed, dried food or bait for fish.
2 N. Amer. informal a crazy or eccentric person.
▶ verb **1** [no obj.] come or fall away from a surface in flakes: *the paint had been flaking off for years.* ■ lose small fragments from the surface: *my nails have started to flake at the ends.*
2 [with obj.] separate (food) into flakes or thin pieces: (as adj. **flaked**) *flaked almonds.* ■ [no obj.] (of food) come apart in flakes or thin pieces: *cook until the fish flakes easily.*
– ORIGIN Middle English: the immediate source is unknown, the senses perhaps deriving from different words; probably of Germanic origin and related to **FLAG²** and **FLAW¹**.

flake² ▶ noun a rack or shelf for storing or drying food such as fish.
– ORIGIN Middle English (denoting a wicker hurdle): perhaps of Scandinavian origin and related to Old Norse *flaki, fleki* 'wicker shield' and Danish *flage* 'hurdle'.

flake³ ▶ verb [no obj.] (**flake out**) informal fall asleep; drop from exhaustion.
– ORIGIN late 15th cent. (in the senses 'become languid' and (of a garment) 'fall in folds'): variant of obsolete *flack* and the verb **FLAG⁴**. The current sense dates from the 1940s.

flake⁴ (also **fake**) Nautical ▶ noun a single turn of a coiled rope or hawser.
▶ verb [with obj.] lay (a rope) in loose coils in order to prevent it tangling: *a cable had to be flaked out.* ■ lay (a sail) down in folds either side of the boom.
– ORIGIN early 17th cent. (as a noun): of unknown origin; compare with German *Flechte* in the same sense.

flake white ▶ noun [mass noun] a pure white pigment made from flakes of white lead.

flak jacket ▶ noun a sleeveless jacket made of heavy fabric reinforced with metal, worn as protection against bullets and shrapnel.

flaky ▶ adjective (**flakier, flakiest**) **1** breaking or separating easily into flakes: *she ate flaky rolls spread with cherry jam.*
2 informal liable to act in an unconventional or eccentric way: *a game-show host with a penchant for flaky blondes.* ■ (of a device or software) prone to break down; unreliable.
– DERIVATIVES **flakiness** noun, **flakily** adverb.

flaky pastry ▶ noun [mass noun] pastry consisting of thin light layers when baked.

flam ▶ noun Music one of the basic patterns (rudiments) of drumming, consisting of a stroke preceded by a grace note.
– ORIGIN late 18th cent.: probably imitative.

flambé /ˈflɒmbeɪ/ ▶ adjective **1** [postpositive] (of food) covered with spirits and set alight briefly: *crêpes flambé.*
2 denoting or characterized by a lustrous red copper-based porcelain glaze with purple streaks.
▶ verb (**flambés, flambéed, flambéing**) [with obj.] cover (food) with spirits and set it alight briefly.
– ORIGIN late 19th cent.: French, literally 'singed', past participle of *flamber*, from *flambe* 'a flame'.

flambeau /ˈflambəʊ/ ▶ noun (pl. **flambeaus** or **flambeaux** /-əʊz/) historical a flaming torch, especially one made of several thick wicks dipped in wax. ■ a large candlestick with several branches.
– ORIGIN mid 17th cent.: from French, from *flambe* 'a flame'.

Flamborough Head /ˈflamb(ə)rə/ a rocky promontory on the east coast of England, in the East Riding of Yorkshire.

F

flamboyant¹ /flamˈbɔɪənt/ ▶ **adjective 1** (of a person or their behaviour) tending to attract attention because of their exuberance, confidence, and stylishness: *the band's flamboyant lead singer.* ■ bright, colourful, and very noticeable: *a flamboyant bow tie.* **2** Architecture of or denoting a style of French Gothic architecture marked by wavy flame-like tracery and ornate decoration. Compare with RAYONNANT.
– DERIVATIVES **flamboyance noun, flamboyancy noun, flamboyantly adverb.**
– ORIGIN mid 19th cent.: from French, literally 'flaming, blazing', present participle of *flamboyer*, from *flambe* 'a flame'.

flamboyant² /flamˈbɔɪənt/ ▶ **noun** a Madagascan tree with bright red flowers and leaves composed of numerous leaflets, planted as a street tree in the tropics. ● *Delonix regia*, family Leguminosae.
– ORIGIN late 19th cent.: probably a noun use of the French adjective *flamboyant* 'blazing' (see FLAMBOYANT¹).

flame ▶ **noun 1** a hot glowing body of ignited gas that is generated by something on fire: *the car was engulfed in flames* | [mass noun] *a sheet of flame blocked my escape.* ■ a thing compared to a flame's ability to burn fiercely or be extinguished: *the flame of hope flickered and died* | *there's nothing like a holiday to rekindle the flames of passion.* ■ [mass noun] a brilliant orange-red colour like that of flames: [in combination] *a flame-red Alfa Romeo.*
2 Computing, informal a vitriolic or abusive message posted on an Internet message board or newsgroup, typically in quick response to another message.
▶ **verb 1** [no obj.] burn and give off flames: *a great fire flamed in an open fireplace* | figurative *hope flamed in her.* ■ [with obj.] set (something) alight: *warm the whisky slightly, pour over the lobster, and flame it.* ■ shine or glow like a flame: *her thick hair flamed against the light.* ■ (of a person's face) suddenly become red with intense emotion, especially anger or embarrassment: *Jess's cheeks flamed.*
2 [with obj.] Computing, informal direct an abusive or vitriolic posting at (someone) on an Internet message board or newsgroup.
– PHRASES **burst into flame** (or **flames**) suddenly begin to burn fiercely: *the car crashed into a tree and burst into flames.* **go up in flames** be destroyed by fire: *last night two factories went up in flames.* **old flame** informal a former lover.
– PHRASAL VERBS **flame out** (of a jet engine) lose power through the extinction of the flame in the combustion chamber. ■ informal, chiefly N. Amer. fail badly or conspicuously: *he and the rest of the team flamed out in the last three minutes.*
– DERIVATIVES **flameless adjective, flame-like adjective, flamer noun** (Computing), **flamy** (also **flamey**) **adjective** (**flamier, flamiest**).
– ORIGIN Middle English: from Old French *flame* (noun), *flamer* (verb), from Latin *flamma* 'a flame'.

flame gun ▶ **noun** a device for producing a jet of flame, used especially for destroying weeds.

flamen /ˈfleɪmɛn, ˈflɑː-/ ▶ **noun** (pl. **flamens** or **flamines**) Roman History a priest serving a particular deity.
– ORIGIN Latin.

flamenco /fləˈmɛŋkəʊ/ ▶ **noun** [mass noun] a style of Spanish music, played especially on the guitar and accompanied by singing and dancing. ■ a style of spirited, rhythmical dance performed to flamenco music, often with castanets.
– ORIGIN late 19th cent.: Spanish, 'like a Gypsy', literally 'Fleming', from Middle Dutch *Vlaminc.*

flame of the forest ▶ **noun** a tropical tree which bears showy bright red flowers, in particular: ● an Asian tree of the pea family (*Butea monosperma*, family Leguminosae). ● another term for FLAMBOYANT².

flameout ▶ **noun** an instance of the flame in the combustion chamber of a jet engine being extinguished, with a resultant loss of power. ■ informal, chiefly N. Amer. a complete or conspicuous failure: *his first-round flameout at the US Open.*

flameproof ▶ **adjective** (especially of a fabric) treated so as to be non-flammable. ■ (of cookware) able to be used either in an oven or on a hob: *a flameproof casserole.*
▶ **verb** [with obj.] make (something) flameproof.

flamethrower ▶ **noun** a weapon that sprays out burning fuel.

flame tree ▶ **noun** any of a number of trees with brilliant red flowers, in particular: ● an Australian bottle tree (*Brachychiton acerifolius*, family Sterculiaceae). ● another term for FLAMBOYANT².

flaming ▶ **adjective** [attrib.] **1** burning fiercely and emitting flames: *they dragged her away from the flaming car.* ■ very hot: *flaming June.* ■ of a bright orange or red colour: *her flaming hair.* ■ (especially of an argument) violent: *a flaming row.*
2 Brit. informal used for emphasis to express annoyance: *where's that flaming taxi?*

flamingo /fləˈmɪŋgəʊ/ ▶ **noun** (pl. **flamingos** or **flamingoes**) a tall wading bird with mainly pink or scarlet plumage and long legs and neck. It has a heavy bent bill that is held upside down in the water in order to filter-feed on small organisms. ● Family Phoenicopteridae: three genera and four species, in particular the **greater flamingo** (*Phoenicopterus ruber*).
– ORIGIN mid 16th cent.: from Spanish *flamengo*, earlier form of *flamenco* (see FLAMENCO); associated, because of its colour, with Latin *flamma* 'a flame'.

flammable /ˈflaməb(ə)l/ ▶ **adjective** easily set on fire: *the use of highly flammable materials.*
– DERIVATIVES **flammability noun.**
– ORIGIN early 19th cent.: from Latin *flammare*, from *flamma* 'a flame'.

> **USAGE** The words **flammable** and **inflammable** actually mean the same thing: see **USAGE** at **INFLAMMABLE**.

flammulated owl /ˈflamjʊleɪtɪd/ ▶ **noun** a small reddish-grey migratory American owl which sometimes occurs in loose colonies. ● *Otus flammeolus*, family Strigidae.

Flamsteed /ˈflamstiːd/, John (1646–1719), English astronomer. He was the first Astronomer Royal at the Royal Greenwich Observatory and produced the first star catalogue (for use in navigation).

flan ▶ **noun 1** a baked dish consisting of an open-topped pastry case with a savoury or sweet filling. **2** a disc of metal such as one from which a coin is made.
– ORIGIN mid 19th cent.: from French (originally denoting a round cake) from Old French *flaon*, from medieval Latin *flado, fladon-*, of West Germanic origin; related to Dutch *vlade* 'custard'.

Flanders /ˈflɑːndəz/ a region in the south-western part of the Low Countries, now divided between Belgium (where it forms the provinces of East and West Flanders), France, and the Netherlands. It was a powerful medieval principality and the scene of prolonged fighting during the First World War.

Flanders poppy ▶ **noun** a red poppy used as an emblem of the Allied soldiers who fell in the First World War.

Flandrian /ˈflɑːndrɪən/ ▶ **adjective** Geology relating to or denoting the current (Holocene or Recent) stage in northern Europe, especially when treated as an interglacial period. ■ (as noun **the Flandrian**) the Flandrian interglacial or the system of deposits laid down during it.
– ORIGIN mid 17th cent.: from FLANDERS + -IAN.

flânerie /flanˈriː/, French /flanʀi/ ▶ **noun** [mass noun] aimless idle behaviour.
– ORIGIN French, from *flâner* 'saunter, lounge'.

flâneur /flaˈnəː/, French /flanœʀ/ ▶ **noun** (pl. **flâneurs** pronunc. **same**) a man who saunters around observing society.
– ORIGIN French, from *flâner* 'saunter, lounge'.

flange /flan(d)ʒ/ ▶ **noun** a projecting flat rim, collar, or rib on an object, serving for strengthening or attachment or (on a wheel) for maintaining position on a rail.
– DERIVATIVES **flanged adjective, flangeless adjective.**
– ORIGIN late 17th cent.: perhaps based on Old French *flanchir* 'to bend'.

flanger /ˈflan(d)ʒə/ ▶ **noun** an electronic device which alters a sound signal by introducing a cyclically varying phase shift into one of two identical copies of the signal and recombining them, used especially in popular music to alter the sound of an instrument.

flanging /ˈflandʒɪŋ/ ▶ **noun** [mass noun] **1** the provision of a flange or flanges on an object.
2 the alteration of sound using a flanger.

flank ▶ **noun 1** the side of a person's or animal's body between the ribs and the hip: *leaning against his horse's flanks.* ■ a cut of meat from the flank of an animal: *a thick flank of beef.* ■ the side of a large object or structure: *the northern flank of the Rockies.*
2 the right or left side of a body of people such as an army, a naval force, or a soccer team: *the left flank of the Russian Third Army.* ■ the right or left side of a gaming area such as a chessboard. ■ (also **flank forward**) Rugby another term for WING FORWARD.
▶ **verb** [with obj.] be on each or on one side of: *the three defendants stood in the dock, flanked by police officers* | *cherry-red sofas flanked the enormous fireplace.* ■ (usu. as adj. **flanking**) guard or strengthen (a military force or position) from the side: *massive walls, defended by four flanking towers.* ■ (usu. as adj. **flanking**) attack down or from the sides, or rake with gunfire from the sides: *a flanking attack from the north-east.*
– PHRASES **in flank** Military at the side: *they were to hit the tail of the column in flank.*
– ORIGIN late Old English, from Old French *flanc*, of Germanic origin.

flanker ▶ **noun 1** a person or thing situated on the flank of something, in particular: ■ Rugby another term for WING FORWARD. ■ American Football an offensive back who is positioned to the outside of an end. ■ Military a fortification guarding or menacing the side of a force or position.
2 Brit. informal, dated a trick or swindle: *he's certainly* ***pulled a flanker*** *on the army.*

flannel ▶ **noun 1** [mass noun] a kind of soft woven fabric, typically made of wool or cotton and slightly milled and raised: [as modifier] *a check flannel shirt.* ■ (**flannels**) men's trousers made of flannel. ■ short for FLANNELETTE.
2 Brit. a small piece of towelling used for washing oneself.
3 [mass noun] Brit. informal bland fluent talk indulged in to avoid addressing a difficult subject or situation directly: *a simple admittance of ignorance was much to be preferred to any amount of flannel.*
▶ **verb** (**flannels, flannelling, flannelled**) [no obj.] (often as noun **flannelling**) Brit. informal use bland fluent talk to avoid addressing a difficult subject or situation directly.
– ORIGIN Middle English: probably from Welsh *gwlanen* 'woollen article', from *gwlân* 'wool'.

flannelboard ▶ **noun** a board covered with flannel to which paper or cloth cut-outs will stick, used as a toy or a teaching aid.

flannelette /ˌflanəˈlɛt/ ▶ **noun** [mass noun] a napped cotton fabric resembling flannel: [as modifier] *a flannelette nightdress.*

flannelgraph ▶ **noun** another term for FLANNELBOARD.

flannelled (US also **flanneled**) ▶ **adjective** [usu. in combination] wearing flannel trousers: *a rather stout boy, grey-flannelled, pulling off a school cap.*

flannelmouth ▶ **noun** N. Amer. informal a person who talks too much, especially in a boastful or deceitful way.

flap ▶ **verb** (**flaps, flapping, flapped**) **1** [with obj.] (of a bird) move (its wings) up and down when flying or preparing to fly: *a pheasant flapped its wings* | [no obj.] *gulls flapped around uttering their strange cries.* ■ [no obj.] (of something loosely fastened) flutter or wave around: *lines of washing flapped in the wind.* ■ move (something) up and down or to and fro: *he flapped the envelope in front of my face.* ■ [with obj. and adverbial of direction] strike at (something) loosely, especially to drive it away: *she flapped my hands away as she sat up.*
2 [no obj.] Brit. informal be agitated or panicky: *it's all right, Mother, don't flap.*
▶ **noun 1** a thin, flat piece of cloth, paper, metal, etc. that is hinged or attached on one side only and covers an opening or hangs down from something: *the flap of the envelope* | *he pushed through the tent flap.* ■ a hinged or sliding section of an aircraft wing used to control lift: *flaps are normally moved by the hydraulics.*
2 an act of flapping something, typically a wing or arm, up and down or from side to side: *the surviving bird made a few final despairing flaps.*
3 [in sing.] informal a state of agitation; a panic: *your Gran was* ***in a flap****, worrying she'd put her foot in it.*
4 a large broad mushroom.
5 Phonetics a type of consonant produced by allowing the tip of the tongue to strike the palate very briefly.
– PHRASES **someone's ears are flapping** Brit. informal someone is trying to a listen to a conversation between other people.
– DERIVATIVES **flappy adjective** (**flappier, flappiest**).
– ORIGIN Middle English: probably imitative.

flapdoodle ▶ **noun** informal, chiefly US **1** [mass noun] nonsense: *four hundred pages of mystical flapdoodle.*
2 a foolish person.
– ORIGIN mid 19th cent.: an arbitrary formation.

flapjack ▶ **noun 1** Brit. a sweet dense cake made from oats, golden syrup, and melted butter, served in rectangles.

2 N. Amer. a pancake.
– ORIGIN early 17th cent. (in sense 2): from **FLAP** (in the dialect sense 'toss a pancake') + **JACK**[1]; sense 1 dates from the 1930s and is probably a regional coinage.

flapper ▸ **noun** informal (in the 1920s) a fashionable young woman intent on enjoying herself and flouting conventional standards of behaviour.

flapshell (also **flap-shelled turtle**) ▸ **noun** a soft-shelled turtle, native to India and Africa, with flaps of skin on the lower shell that fold to protect the hindlimbs and tail, and flexible margins to the upper shell that protect the head and limbs. • Genera *Lissemys* and other genera, family Trionychidae: several species, in particular the **Indian flapshell** (*L. punctata*).

flap valve (also **flapper valve**) ▸ **noun** a valve opened and closed by a plate hinged at one side.

flare ▸ **noun 1** a sudden brief burst of bright flame or light: *the flare of the match lit up his face.* ■ a device producing a very bright flame, used especially as a signal or marker: *a distress flare* | [as modifier] *a flare gun.* ■ [in sing.] a sudden burst of intense emotion: *she felt a flare of anger within her.* ■ a sudden recurrence of an inflammation or other medical condition: *corticosteroid treatment for colitis flares.* ■ Astronomy a sudden explosion in the chromosphere and corona of the sun or another star, resulting in an intense burst of radiation. See also **SOLAR FLARE.** ■ [mass noun] Photography extraneous illumination on film caused by internal reflection in the camera.
2 a gradual widening in shape, especially towards the hem of a garment. ■ (**flares**) trousers whose legs get progressively wider from the knees down. ■ [mass noun] an upward and outward curve of a ship's bows, designed to throw the water outwards when in motion.
▸ **verb** [no obj.] **1** burn or shine with a sudden intensity: *the bonfire crackled and **flared up** | behind him, lightning flared.* ■ (of a situation or emotion) suddenly become intense or violent: *tempers flared as supporters scuffled with other passengers | the controversy **flared up** again in 2003.* ■ (**flare up**) (of a person) suddenly become angry: *she flared up, shouting at Geoffrey.*
2 (often as adj. **flared**) gradually become wider at one end: *a flared skirt | the dress flared out into a huge train.* ■ (of a person's nostrils) dilate. ■ [with obj.] (of a person) cause (the nostrils) to dilate.
– ORIGIN mid 16th cent. (in the sense 'spread out one's hair'): of unknown origin. Current senses date from the 17th cent.

flarepath ▸ **noun** an area illuminated to enable an aircraft to land or take off.

flare star ▸ **noun** Astronomy a dwarf star which displays spasmodic outbursts of radiation, believed to be due to extremely intense flares.

flare-up ▸ **noun** a sudden outburst of something, especially violence or hostility: *a flare-up between the two countries.*

flash[1] ▸ **verb 1** [no obj.] shine in a bright but brief, sudden, or intermittent way: *lightning flashed overhead | an irritating neon sign flashed on and off* | (as adj. **flashing**) *a police car with a flashing light.* ■ [with obj.] cause to shine briefly or suddenly: *the oncoming car flashed its lights.* ■ [with obj.] shine or show a light to send (a signal): *red lights started to flash a warning.* ■ [with obj.] give (a swift look): *Carrie flashed a glance in his direction* | [with two objs] *she flashed him a withering look.* ■ (of a person's eyes) indicate sudden emotion, especially anger: *she glared at him, her eyes flashing.*
2 [no obj., with adverbial of direction] move or pass very quickly: *a look of terror flashed across Kirov's face* | figurative *a sudden thought flashed through his mind.* ■ [with obj. and adverbial of direction] send (news or information) swiftly by means of telegraphy or telecommunications: *the story **was flashed around** the world.*
3 [with obj.] display (information or an image) suddenly on a television or computer screen or electronic sign, typically briefly or repeatedly: *the screen **flashed up** a menu.* ■ [no obj.] (of information or an image) be displayed briefly or repeatedly on a screen: *the election results flashed on the screen.* ■ informal hold up or show (something, often proof of one's identity) quickly before replacing it: *she opened her purse and flashed her ID card.* ■ informal make a conspicuous display of (something) so as to impress or attract attention: *they flashed huge wads of money about.* ■ [no obj.] informal (of a man) show one's genitals briefly in public.
▸ **noun 1** a sudden brief burst of bright light: *a flash of lightning.* ■ a patch or sudden display of a bright colour: *the woodpecker swooped from tree to tree with a flash of yellow, green, and red.* ■ Brit. a coloured patch of cloth on a uniform used as the distinguishing emblem of a regiment, formation, or country. ■ a coloured band on the packaging of a product used to catch the consumer's eye: *on-pack flashes offer a free 'Taste of the Caribbean'.* ■ a pre-drawn design for a tattoo.
2 a sudden or brief manifestation or occurrence of something: *she had **a flash of inspiration**.* ■ a newsflash.
3 a camera attachment that produces a brief very bright light, used for taking photographs in poor light: *an electronic flash* | [mass noun] *if in any doubt use flash.*
4 (**Flash**) [mass noun] Computing (trademark in the US) a platform for producing and displaying animation and video in Web browsers.
5 [mass noun] informal ostentatious stylishness or display of wealth: *workwear represents a move away from Eighties designer flash.*
6 [mass noun] excess plastic or metal forced between facing surfaces as two halves of a mould close up, forming a thin projection on the finished object.
7 a rush of water, especially down a weir to take a boat over shallows.
▸ **adjective** informal, chiefly Brit. **1** ostentatiously stylish or expensive: *a flash new car.* ■ ostentatiously displaying one's wealth: *he's a bit flash and refers to his gold card a few times too many.*
2 archaic relating to the language used by criminals or prostitutes.
– PHRASES **flash in the pan** a thing or person whose sudden but brief success is not repeated or repeatable: *our start to the season was just a flash in the pan.* [with allusion to priming of a firearm, the flash arising from an explosion of gunpowder within the lock.] **in** (or **like**) **a flash** very quickly; immediately: *she was out of the back door in a flash.* **(as) quick as a flash** (especially of a person's response or reaction) very quickly: *quick as a flash he was at her side.*
– PHRASAL VERBS **flash over** make an electric circuit by sparking across a gap. ■ (of a fire) spread instantly across a gap because of intense heat.
– ORIGIN Middle English (in the sense 'splash water about'): probably imitative; compare with **FLUSH**[1] and **SPLASH.**

flash[2] ▸ **noun** Brit. a water-filled hollow formed by subsidence, especially any of those due to rock salt extraction in or near Cheshire.
– ORIGIN Middle English (in the sense 'a marshy place'): from Old French *flache*, variant of Picard and Norman dialect *flaque*, from Middle Dutch *vlacke*. The current sense dates from the late 19th cent.

flashback ▸ **noun 1** a scene in a film, novel, etc. set in a time earlier than the main story: *in a series of flashbacks, we follow the pair through their teenage years* | [mass noun] *the movie tells the story **in flashback**.* ■ a disturbing sudden vivid memory of an event in the past, typically as the result of psychological trauma or taking LSD.
2 a flame moving rapidly back through a combustible vapour: *cooling the area prevented a flashback.*

flashboard ▸ **noun** a board used for sending more water from a mill dam into a mill race.

flashbulb ▸ **noun** a bulb for a flashgun, of a type that is used only once.

flash burn ▸ **noun** a burn caused by sudden intense heat, e.g. from a nuclear explosion.

flash card ▸ **noun** a card containing a small amount of information, held up for pupils to see, as an aid to learning.

flash drive ▸ **noun** a small electronic device containing flash memory that is used for storing data or transferring it to or from a computer, digital camera, etc.

flasher ▸ **noun 1** an automatic device causing a light to flash on and off rapidly. ■ a signal using a flashing device, for example a car's indicator.
2 informal a man who exposes his genitals in public.

flash flood ▸ **noun** a sudden local flood, typically due to heavy rain.

flash-freeze ▸ **verb** [with obj.] freeze (food or other material) very rapidly so as to prevent the formation of ice crystals.

flash-fry ▸ **verb** [with obj.] fry (food) briefly and at a very high temperature.

flashgun ▸ **noun** a device which gives a brief flash of intense light, used for taking photographs indoors or in poor light.

flashing ▸ **noun** a strip of metal used to stop water penetrating the junction of a roof with another surface: *flashings around chimneys* | [mass noun] *the lead flashing on the roof.*
– ORIGIN late 18th cent.: from the earlier synonym *flash* (of unknown origin) + **-ING**[1].

flashlight ▸ **noun 1** chiefly N. Amer. an electric torch.
2 a flashing light used for signals and in lighthouses.
3 another term for **FLASHGUN.**

flash memory ▸ **noun** [mass noun] Computing a kind of memory that retains data in the absence of a power supply.

flash mob ▸ **noun** a public gathering of complete strangers, organized via the Internet or mobile phone, who perform a pointless act and then disperse again.
– DERIVATIVES **flash mobber** noun, **flash mobbing** noun.

flashover ▸ **noun 1** a high-voltage electric short circuit made through the air between exposed conductors.
2 an instance of a fire spreading very rapidly through the air because of intense heat.

flash photolysis ▸ **noun** [mass noun] Chemistry the use of a very intense flash of light to bring about decomposition or dissociation in a heated gas, usually as a means of generating and studying short-lived molecules.

flashpoint ▸ **noun 1** a place, event, or time at which violence or hostility flares up: *the conflict reached a flashpoint last year.*
2 Chemistry the temperature at which a particular organic compound gives off sufficient vapour to ignite in air.

flash tube ▸ **noun** a gas-discharge tube used, especially in photography, to provide an electronic flash when a current is suddenly passed through it.

flashy ▸ **adjective** (**flashier, flashiest**) ostentatiously attractive or impressive: *he always had a flashy car.*
– DERIVATIVES **flashily** adverb, **flashiness** noun.

flask ▸ **noun 1** a container for liquids, in particular: ■ a narrow-necked glass container, typically conical or spherical, used in a laboratory to hold reagents or samples. ■ a narrow-necked bulbous glass container, typically with a covering of wickerwork, for storing wine or oil. ■ Brit. a vacuum flask. ■ a hip flask. ■ the contents of a flask: ***a flask of** coffee.*
2 an extremely strong lead-lined container for transporting or storing radioactive nuclear waste.
3 historical short for **POWDER FLASK.**
– ORIGIN Middle English (in the sense 'cask'): from medieval Latin *flasca*. From the mid 16th cent. the word denoted a case of horn, leather, or metal for carrying gunpowder. The sense 'glass container' (late 17th cent.) was influenced by Italian *fiasco*, from medieval Latin *flasco*. Compare with **FLAGON.**

flat[1] ▸ **adjective** (**flatter, flattest**) **1** having a level surface; without raised areas or indentations: *he sat down on a flat rock | trim the surface of the cake to make it completely flat.* ■ (of land) without hills: *thirty-five acres of flat countryside.* ■ (of an expanse of water) calm and without waves. ■ not sloping: *the flat roof of a garage.* ■ having a broad level surface but little height or depth; shallow: *a flat rectangular box | a flat cap.* ■ (of shoes) without heels or with very low heels.
2 lacking emotion; dull and lifeless: *'I'm sorry,' he said, in a flat voice.* ■ (of a person) without energy or enthusiasm: *his sense of intoxication wore off until he felt flat and weary.* ■ (of trade, prices, etc.) not showing much activity; sluggish: *the UK housing market was flat.* ■ (of a colour) uniform: *a flat shade of grey.* ■ (of a photograph or negative) lacking contrast.
3 (of a sparkling drink) having lost its effervescence. ■ (of something kept inflated, especially a tyre) having lost some or all of its air, typically because of a puncture. ■ Brit. (of a battery) having exhausted its charge.
4 [attrib.] (of a fee, wage, or price) the same in all cases, not varying with changed conditions or in particular cases: *a flat fare of £2.50.* See also **FLAT RATE.** ■ (of a denial, contradiction, or refusal) completely definite and firm; absolute: *the request was met with a flat refusal.*
5 (of musical sound) below true or normal pitch. ■ [postpositive] (of a key) having a flat or flats in the signature. ■ [postpositive] (of a note) a semitone lower than a specified note: *E flat.*
6 (**Flat**) relating to flat racing: *the Flat season.*
▸ **adverb 1** in or to a horizontal position: *he was lying flat on his back | she had been knocked flat by the blast.*

■ lying in close juxtaposition, especially against another surface: *his black curly hair was blown flat across his skull.* ■ so as to become smooth and even: *I hammered the metal flat.*
2 informal completely; absolutely: *I thought you'd turn me down flat* | [as submodifier] *Myers was flat broke.* ■ used with an expression of time to emphasize how quickly something can be done or has been done: *you can prepare a healthy meal in ten minutes flat.*
3 below the true or normal pitch of musical sound.
▶ **noun 1** [in sing.] the flat part of something: *she placed the flat of her hand over her glass.* ■ (usu. **flats**) an area of low level ground, especially near water: *the shingle flats of the lake.* ■ N. Amer. a shallow container in which seedlings are grown and sold. ■ (often **flats**) chiefly US a shoe with a very low heel or no heel. ■ a railway wagon with a flat floor and no sides or roof; a flatcar.
2 (often **flats**) an upright section of stage scenery mounted on a movable frame.
3 informal, chiefly N. Amer. a flat tyre.
4 (**the Flat**) Brit. flat racing.
5 a musical note lowered a semitone below natural pitch. ■ the sign (♭) indicating this.
▶ **verb** (**flats, flatting, flatted**) [with obj.] **1** (usu. as adj. **flatted**) Music, N. Amer. lower (a note) by a semitone: *'blue' harmony emphasizing the flatted third and seventh.*
2 archaic make flat; flatten: *flat the loaves down.*
– PHRASES **fall flat** fail completely to produce the intended or expected effect: *his jokes fell flat.* **fall flat on one's face** fail in an embarrassingly obvious way: *we might fall flat on our faces and end up bankrupt.* **(as) flat as a pancake** see PANCAKE. **flat out 1** as fast or as hard as possible: *the whole team is working flat out to satisfy demand.* **2** informal, chiefly N. Amer. without hesitation or reservation: *she flat out said she didn't trust her fellow board members* | (as adj. **flat-out**) *flat-out perjury.* **3** lying stretched out, especially asleep or in a state of exhaustion. **on the flat** Brit. on level ground as opposed to uphill: *the car wouldn't go uphill or overtake on the flat.* ■ (**on the Flat**) (of a horse race) on an open course as opposed to one with jumps. **that's flat** informal used to indicate that one has reached a decision and will not be persuaded to change one's mind: *he won't leave and that's flat.*
– DERIVATIVES **flatness** noun, **flattish** adjective.
– ORIGIN Middle English: from Old Norse *flatr*.

flat² ▶ **noun** chiefly Brit. a set of rooms forming an individual residence, typically on one floor and within a larger building containing a number of such residences: *a block of flats.*
▶ **verb** (**flats, flatting, flatted**) [no obj., with adverbial of place] Austral./NZ live in or share a flat: *Zoë flats in Auckland.*
– PHRASES **go flatting** Austral./NZ leave one's family home to live in a flat: *in my third year I left home and went flatting with David.*
– DERIVATIVES **flatlet** noun.
– ORIGIN early 19th cent. (denoting a floor or storey): alteration of obsolete *flet* 'floor, dwelling', of Germanic origin and related to FLAT¹.

flatbed ▶ **noun** a long flat area or structure: *the flatbed of a truck.* ■ a vehicle with a flat load-carrying area: [as modifier] *a flatbed truck.* ■ [as modifier] denoting a letterpress printing machine in which the forme is carried on a horizontal surface: *a flatbed press.* ■ Computing a scanner, plotter, or other device which keeps paper flat during use.

flatbill ▶ **noun** a tropical American bird of the tyrant flycatcher family, with a wide flat bill and mainly olive-green plumage. ● Genera *Ramphotrigon* and *Rhynchocyclus*, family Tyrannidae: several species.

flatbill flycatcher ▶ **noun** another term for BOATBILL (sense 2).

flatboat ▶ **noun** a boat with a flat bottom for transport in shallow water.

flatbread ▶ **noun** [mass noun] N. Amer. flat, thin bread that is often unleavened.

flatbug ▶ **noun** a broad very flat bug that typically lives on or under loose bark. ● Family Aradidae, suborder Heteroptera: several species.

flatcar ▶ **noun** N. Amer. a railway freight wagon without a roof or sides.

flat-chested ▶ **adjective** (of a woman) having small breasts.

flat-fell ▶ **verb** see FELL² (sense 2 of the verb).

flat file ▶ **noun** Computing a file having no internal hierarchy.

flatfish ▶ **noun** (pl. **same** or **flatfishes**) a flattened marine fish that swims on its side with both eyes on the upper side. They live typically on the seabed and are coloured to resemble it. ● Order Pleuronectiformes: several families, in particular Bothidae (left-eye flounders), Pleuronectidae (right-eye flounders), and Soleidae (soles).

flatfoot ▶ **noun** a condition in which the foot has an arch that is lower than usual. ■ (pl. **flatfoots** or **flatfeet**) informal, dated a police officer.

flat foot ▶ **noun** a foot with an arch that is lower than usual. Also called PES PLANUS.

flat-footed ▶ **adjective** having flat feet: *a flat-footed, overweight colonel.* ■ informal unprepared: *many local companies were caught flat-footed by international competition.* ■ informal inelegant, awkward, or uninspired: *a flat-footed prose style.*
– DERIVATIVES **flat-footedly** adverb, **flat-footedness** noun.

flat-four ▶ **adjective** (of an engine) having four horizontal cylinders, two on each side of the crankshaft.
▶ **noun** a flat-four engine.

flathead ▶ **noun 1** an edible tropical marine fish that has a pointed flattened head with the eyes positioned on the top, typically burrowing in the seabed with just the eyes showing. ● Family Platycephalidae: several genera and species.
2 (**Flathead**) a member of certain North American Indian peoples such as the Chinook, Choctaw, and Salish, named from their supposed practice of flattening their children's heads artificially.
3 [as modifier] US (of an engine) having the valves and spark plugs in the cylinder block rather than the cylinder head, which is essentially a flat plate. ■ (of a vehicle) having a flathead engine.
4 [as modifier] US (of a screw) countersunk.

flat iron ▶ **noun** historical an iron used for pressing clothes which was heated on a hotplate or fire.

flatland ▶ **noun** [mass noun] (also **flatlands**) land with no hills, valleys, or mountains.

flat-leaved parsley (also **flat** or **flat-leaf parsley**) ▶ **noun** [mass noun] parsley of a variety with large flat leaves, popular in southern Europe. Also called ITALIAN PARSLEY.

flatline ▶ **verb** [no obj.] **1** informal (of a person) die. ■ (of a project or undertaking) fail: *her career has flatlined about three times already.*
2 fail to increase; remain static: *their share of the vote has flatlined at about 3%.*
– DERIVATIVES **flatliner** noun.
– ORIGIN 1980s: from FLAT¹ + LINE¹ (with reference to the continuous straight line displayed on a heart monitor, indicating death).

flatly ▶ **adverb 1** showing little interest or emotion: *'You'd better go' she said flatly.*
2 in a firm and unequivocal manner; absolutely: *they flatly refused to play.*
3 in a smooth and even way: *I applied the paint flatly.* ■ Photography without marked contrast of light and dark: *the photographs were lit very flatly.*

flatmate ▶ **noun** Brit. a person who shares a flat with others: *my flatmate moved out a month ago.*

flat-pack ▶ **noun 1** [often as modifier] Brit. a piece of furniture or other equipment that is sold in pieces packed flat in a box for easy transport and is assembled by the buyer: *a flat-pack bookcase.*
2 Electronics a package for an integrated circuit consisting of a rectangular sealed unit with a number of horizontal metal pins protruding from its sides.
▶ **verb** [with obj.] (usu. as adj. **flat-packed**) pack (a self-assembly item) flat in a box: *this workstation is provided flat-packed.*

flat parsley ▶ **noun** another term for FLAT-LEAVED PARSLEY.

flat race ▶ **noun** a horse race over a course with no jumps, as opposed to a steeplechase or hurdles.
– DERIVATIVES **flat racing** noun.

flat rate ▶ **noun** a charge or level of payment that is the same in all cases: *clients are charged a flat rate of £250 annually* | [as modifier] *the flat-rate state pension.* ■ a rate of taxation that is not progressive, but remains at the same proportion on all amounts.

flat screen ▶ **noun** [usu. as modifier] a television or computer screen that is perfectly flat rather than slightly curved and that has a slim casing: *a flat-screen TV.*

flat sheet ▶ **noun** an ordinary sheet for a bed as distinct from a fitted one.

flat spin ▶ **noun** Aeronautics a spin in which an aircraft descends in tight circles while remaining almost horizontal. ■ [in sing.] Brit. informal a state of agitation or panic: *a scandal has put the university into a flat spin.*

flatten ▶ **verb 1** make or become flat or flatter: [with obj.] *her hair had been flattened by the storm* | [no obj.] *after Kendal, the countryside begins to flatten out.* ■ [with obj. and adverbial of place] press (oneself or one's body) against a surface: *Guy flattened himself against the wall.*
2 [with obj.] raze (a building or settlement) to the ground: *the entire town centre was flattened by the 500 lb bomb.* ■ informal strike (someone) so as to make them fall down: *Flynn flattened him with a single punch.* ■ informal defeat heavily in a contest: *they flattened Bridgend by forty-two points to fifteen.* ■ informal humiliate or depress (someone): *the controversy has flattened everybody here.*
3 [with obj.] Music lower (a note) in pitch by a semitone.
– PHRASAL VERBS **flatten out 1** (of an increasing quantity or rate) show a less marked rise; slow down. **2** make an aircraft fly horizontally after a dive or climb: *he flattened out and made a fine three-point landing.*
– DERIVATIVES **flattener** noun.

flatter ▶ **verb** [with obj.] lavish praise and compliments on (someone), often insincerely and with the aim of furthering one's own interests: *she was flattering him in order to avoid doing what he wanted.* ■ cause (someone) to feel honoured and pleased: [with obj. and infinitive] *I was very flattered to be given the commission* | [with obj. and clause] *she felt flattered that he was confiding in her.* ■ (**flatter oneself**) choose to believe something favourable about oneself, typically when this belief is unfounded: *'Don't flatter yourself! I wasn't doing it for your benefit!'* ■ give an unrealistically favourable impression of: *the final scoreline flattered England.* ■ (of a colour or a style of clothing) cause (someone) to appear to the best advantage: *the fuchsia shade flattered her pale skin.* ■ archaic please (the ear or eye): *the beauty of the stone flattered the clergyman's eyes.*
– PHRASES **flatter to deceive** appear promising but ultimately disappoint.
– ORIGIN Middle English: perhaps a back-formation from FLATTERY.

flatterer ▶ **noun** a person who lavishes praise, often insincerely; a sycophant: *he is not allowing flatterers to deceive him.*

flattering ▶ **adjective** full of praise and compliments: *the article began with some flattering words about us.* ■ pleasing or gratifying: [with infinitive] *it was flattering to have a pretty girl like Fiona so obviously fond of him.* ■ enhancing someone's appearance: *I don't think anything sleeveless is very flattering.*
– DERIVATIVES **flatteringly** adverb.

flattery ▶ **noun** (pl. **flatteries**) [mass noun] excessive and insincere praise, given especially to further one's own interests: *she allowed no hint of flattery to enter her voice.*
– ORIGIN Middle English: from Old French *flaterie*, from *flater* 'stroke, flatter', probably of Germanic origin and related to FLAT¹.

flattie (also **flatty**) ▶ **noun** (pl. **flatties**) informal **1** a flat-heeled shoe.
2 a flatfish.
3 a flatboat.
4 dated a police officer. [late 19th cent.: informal abbreviation of FLATFOOT.]

flat-top ▶ **noun 1** a man's hairstyle in which the hair is cropped short so that it bristles up into a flat surface.
2 an acoustic guitar that has a flat rather than a curved front.
3 US informal an aircraft carrier.

flatulence /ˈflatjʊl(ə)ns/ ▶ **noun** [mass noun] the accumulation of gas in the alimentary canal: *foods that may cause flatulence.* ■ inflated or pretentious speech or writing; pomposity: *the flatulence characterizing his writings.*
– DERIVATIVES **flatulency** noun.

flatulent /ˈflatjʊl(ə)nt/ ▶ **adjective** suffering from or marked by an accumulation of gas in the alimentary canal. ■ related to or causing an accumulation of gas in the alimentary canal: *the flatulent effect of beans.* ■ inflated or pretentious in speech or writing: *his flatulent oratory.*
– DERIVATIVES **flatulently** adverb.
– ORIGIN late 16th cent.: via French from modern Latin *flatulentus*, from Latin *flatus* 'blowing' (see FLATUS).

flatus /ˈfleɪtəs/ ▶ **noun** [mass noun] technical gas in or from the stomach or intestines, produced by swallowing air or by bacterial fermentation.
– ORIGIN mid 17th cent.: from Latin, literally 'blowing', from *flare* 'to blow'.

flatware ▶ **noun** [mass noun] relatively flat items of crockery such as plates and saucers. ■ N. Amer. domestic cutlery.

flatwater ▶ **noun** [mass noun] N. Amer. slowly moving water in a river, as opposed to rapids.

flatworm ▶ **noun** a worm of a phylum which includes the planarians together with the parasitic flukes and tapeworms. They are distinguished by having a simple flattened body which lacks blood vessels, and a digestive tract which, if present, has a single opening. ● Phylum Platyhelminthes: several classes.

flat-woven ▶ **adjective** (of a carpet or rug) woven so as not to form a projecting pile.
– DERIVATIVES **flat-weave** noun.

Flaubert /ˈfləʊbɛː/, French /floobɛʀ/, Gustave (1821–80), French novelist and short-story writer. A dominant figure in the French realist school, he achieved fame with his first published novel, *Madame Bovary* (1857). Its portrayal of the adulteries and suicide of a provincial doctor's wife caused Flaubert to be tried for immorality (and acquitted).

flaunching /ˈflɔːntʃɪŋ/ ▶ **noun** [mass noun] the sloping fillet of cement or mortar embedding the base of a chimney pot.
– ORIGIN mid 19th cent.: from *flaunch* meaning 'flange', (as verb) 'slope towards the top': perhaps based on Old French *flanchir* 'to bend', from *flanc(he)* 'flank'.

flaunt ▶ **verb** [with obj.] display (something) ostentatiously, especially in order to provoke envy or admiration or to show defiance: *newly rich consumers eager to flaunt their prosperity.* ■ (**flaunt oneself**) dress or behave in a sexually provocative way.
– DERIVATIVES **flaunter** noun, **flaunty** adjective.
– ORIGIN mid 16th cent.: of unknown origin.

> **USAGE** **Flaunt** and **flout** may sound similar but they have different meanings. **Flaunt** means 'display ostentatiously', as in *visitors who liked to **flaunt** their wealth*, while **flout** means 'openly disregard a rule or convention', as in *new recruits growing their hair and **flouting** convention.* It is a common error, recorded since around the 1940s, to use **flaunt** when **flout** is intended, as in *the young woman had been **flaunting** the rules and regulations.* In the Oxford English Corpus the second and third commonest objects of **flaunt**, after **wealth**, are **law** and **rules**.

flautist /ˈflɔːtɪst/ ▶ **noun** a flute player.
– ORIGIN mid 19th cent. (superseding 17th-cent. *flutist* in British English use): from Italian *flautista*, from *flauto* 'flute'.

Flavian /ˈfleɪvɪən/ ▶ **adjective** relating to a dynasty (AD 69–96) of Roman emperors including Vespasian and his sons Titus and Domitian.
▶ **noun** a member of the Flavian dynasty.
– ORIGIN from Latin *Flavianus*, from *Flavius*, a given name used by this dynasty.

flavin /ˈfleɪvɪn/ ▶ **noun** Biochemistry any of a group of naturally occurring pigments including riboflavin. They have a tricyclic aromatic molecular structure.
– ORIGIN mid 19th cent.: from Latin *flavus* 'yellow' + -IN[1].

flavone /ˈfleɪvəʊn/ ▶ **noun** [mass noun] Chemistry a colourless crystalline compound which is the basis of a number of white or yellow plant pigments. ● A tricyclic aromatic compound; chem. formula: $C_{15}H_{10}O_2$. ■ [count noun] any of these pigments.
– ORIGIN late 19th cent.: from Latin *flavus* 'yellow' + -ONE.

flavonoid /ˈfleɪvənɔɪd/ ▶ **noun** Chemistry any of a large class of plant pigments having a structure based on or similar to that of flavone.

flavoprotein /ˌfleɪvə(ʊ)ˈprəʊtiːn/ ▶ **noun** Biochemistry any of a class of conjugated proteins that contain flavins and are involved in oxidation reactions in cells.
– ORIGIN 1930s: blend of FLAVIN and PROTEIN.

flavorous ▶ **adjective** dated having a pleasant or pungent flavour.

flavour (US **flavor**) ▶ **noun 1** the distinctive taste of a food or drink: *the yoghurt comes in eight fruit flavours* | [mass noun] *adding sun-dried tomatoes gives the sauce extra flavour.* ■ chiefly US a substance used to alter or enhance the taste of food or drink; a flavouring.
2 [in sing.] an indication of the essential character of something: *the extracts give **a flavour of** the content and tone of the conversation.* ■ [in sing.] a distinctive quality or atmosphere: *whitewashed walls and red pantiles gave the resort a Mediterranean flavour.*
3 a kind, variety, or sort: *various flavours of firewall are evolving.*
4 Physics a quantized property of quarks which differentiates them into at least six varieties (up, down, charmed, strange, top, bottom). Compare with COLOUR.
▶ **verb** [with obj.] alter or enhance the taste of (food or drink) by adding a particular ingredient: *chunks of chicken flavoured with herbs.*
– PHRASES **flavour of the month** a person or thing that enjoys a short period of great popularity: *American sitcoms are currently flavour of the month.*
– DERIVATIVES **flavourful** adjective, **flavourless** adjective, **flavoursome** adjective.
– ORIGIN late Middle English (in the sense 'fragrance, aroma'): from Old French *flaor*, perhaps based on a blend of Latin *flatus* 'blowing' and *foetor* 'stench'; the *-v-* appears to have been introduced in Middle English by association with SAVOUR. Sense 1 of the noun dates from the late 17th cent.

flavoured (US **flavored**) ▶ **adjective** (of food or drink) having a particular flavour: [in combination] *the peanut oil is light but fairly full-flavoured.* ■ (of food or drink) having been given a particular taste by the addition of a flavouring: [in combination] *chicken breasts poached in lemon-flavoured stock.* ■ [in combination] having a particular distinctive quality: *the band knocked out some fine rock 'n' roll-flavoured singles.*

flavouring (US **flavoring**) ▶ **noun** [mass noun] a substance used to give a different, stronger, or more agreeable taste to food or drink: *vanilla flavouring* | [count noun] *only natural flavourings are allowed.*

flaw[1] ▶ **noun** a mark, blemish, or other imperfection which mars a substance or object: *a flaw in the glass.* ■ a fault or weakness in a person's character: *he had his flaws, but he was still a great teacher.* ■ a mistake or shortcoming in a plan, theory, etc. which causes it to fail or reduces its effectiveness: *there were fundamental **flaws in** the case for reforming local government.*
▶ **verb** [with obj.] mar, weaken, or invalidate (something): *the computer game was flawed by poor programming.*
– ORIGIN Middle English: perhaps from Old Norse *flaga* 'slab'. The original sense was 'a flake of snow', later, 'a fragment or splinter', hence 'a defect or imperfection' (late 15th cent.).

flaw[2] ▶ **noun** literary a squall of wind; a short storm.
– ORIGIN early 16th cent.: probably from Middle Dutch *vlāghe*, Middle Low German *vlāge*.

flawed ▶ **adjective** having or characterized by a fundamental weakness or imperfection: *a fatally flawed strategy.* ■ (of a person) having a weakness in character: *a flawed hero.*

flawless ▶ **adjective** without any imperfections or defects; perfect: *her smooth flawless skin* | *a British accent that was almost flawless.*
– DERIVATIVES **flawlessly** adverb, **flawlessness** noun.

flax ▶ **noun** [mass noun] a blue-flowered herbaceous plant that is cultivated for its seed (linseed) and for textile fibre made from its stalks. ● *Linum usitatissimum*, family Linaceae.
■ textile fibre obtained from the flax plant: *a mill for the preparation and spinning of flax.* ■ used in names of other plants of the flax family (e.g. **purging flax**) or plants that yield similar fibre (e.g. **false flax**). ■ another term for NEW ZEALAND FLAX.
– ORIGIN Old English *flæx*, of West Germanic origin; related to Dutch *vlas* and German *Flachs*, from an Indo-European root shared by Latin *plectere* and Greek *plekein* 'to plait, twist'.

flaxen ▶ **adjective** made of flax. ■ literary (especially of hair) of the pale yellow colour of dressed flax.

flax lily ▶ **noun** a New Zealand plant that yields valuable fibre and is also grown as an ornamental. Also called NEW ZEALAND FLAX. ● *Phormium tenax*, family Agavaceae.

Flaxman /ˈflaksmən/, John (1755–1826), English sculptor and draughtsman, noted for his church monuments and his engraved illustrations to Homer (1793).

flaxseed ▶ **noun** another term for LINSEED.

flay ▶ **verb** [with obj.] strip the skin off (a corpse or carcass): *the captured general was flayed alive.* ■ strip (the skin) off a corpse or carcass: *she flayed the white skin from the flesh.* ■ whip or beat (someone) so harshly as to remove their skin: *he flayed them viciously with a branch.* ■ criticize severely and brutally: *he flayed the government for not moving fast enough on economic reform.*
– DERIVATIVES **flayer** noun.
– ORIGIN Old English *flēan*, of Germanic origin; related to Middle Dutch *vlaen*.

F-layer ▶ **noun** the highest and most strongly ionized region of the ionosphere.
– ORIGIN 1920s: arbitrary use of *F* + LAYER.

flea ▶ **noun** a small wingless jumping insect which feeds on the blood of mammals and birds. It sometimes transmits diseases through its bite, including plague and myxomatosis. ● Order Siphonaptera: several families and many species, including the **human flea** (*Pulex irritans*).
– PHRASES **(as) fit as a flea** in very good health. **a flea in one's ear** a sharp reproof: *she expected to be sent away with a flea in her ear.*
– ORIGIN Old English *flēa*, *flēah*, of Germanic origin; related to Dutch *vlo* and German *Floh*.

F

fleabag ▶ **noun** informal a dirty or shabby person or animal, typically one infested with fleas. ■ N. Amer. a seedy or dilapidated hotel.

fleabane ▶ **noun** a herbaceous plant of the daisy family, reputed to drive away fleas. ● *Pulicaria*, *Erigeron*, and other genera, family Compositae: in particular the yellow-flowered **common fleabane** (*P. dysenterica*).

flea beetle ▶ **noun** a small jumping leaf beetle that can be a pest of plants such as crucifers. ● *Phyllotreta* and other genera, family Chrysomelidae.

flea bite ▶ **noun** a small red mark caused by the bite of a flea. ■ an insignificant inconvenience or cost: *the proposed energy tax amounted to little more than a flea bite.*

flea-bitten ▶ **adjective** bitten by or infested with fleas. ■ shabby, dilapidated, or disreputable: *a flea-bitten Miami Beach hotel.*

flea circus ▶ **noun** a novelty show of performing fleas.

flea collar ▶ **noun** a collar for a cat or dog that is impregnated with insecticide to kill or deter fleas.

fleadh /flɑː/ ▶ **noun** a festival of Irish or Celtic music, dancing, and culture.
– ORIGIN from Irish *fleadh ceoil* 'music festival'.

flea market ▶ **noun** a street market selling second-hand goods.

fleapit ▶ **noun** Brit. informal a dingy, dirty place, especially a run-down cinema.

fleawort ▶ **noun** a Eurasian plant related to ragwort, reputed to drive away fleas. ● Genus *Senecio*, family Compositae: several species, in particular *S. integrifolius*.

flèche /fleɪʃ, flɛʃ/ ▶ **noun** a slender spire, typically over the intersection of the nave and the transept of a church.
– ORIGIN mid 19th cent.: French, literally 'arrow'.

flechette /fleɪˈʃɛt, flɛ-/ ▶ **noun** a type of ammunition resembling a small dart, shot from a gun.
– ORIGIN early 20th cent.: from French *fléchette*, diminutive of *flèche* 'arrow'.

fleck ▶ **noun** a very small patch of colour or light: *his blue eyes had grey flecks in them* | ***flecks of** sunshine.* ■ a small particle or speck of something: *brushing a few **flecks of** dandruff from his suit.*
▶ **verb** [with obj.] mark or dot with small patches of colour or particles of something: *the minarets are flecked with gold leaf.*
– ORIGIN late Middle English (as a verb): perhaps from Old Norse *flekkr* (noun), *flekka* (verb), or from Middle Low German, Middle Dutch *vlecke*.

fled past and past participle of FLEE.

fledge /flɛdʒ/ ▶ **verb** [no obj.] (of a young bird) develop wing feathers that are large enough for flight. ■ [with obj.] bring up (a young bird) until its wing feathers are developed enough for flight.
– ORIGIN mid 16th cent.: from the obsolete adjective *fledge* 'ready to fly', from Old English, of Germanic origin; related to Dutch *vlug* 'quick, agile', also to FLY[1].

fledged ▶ **adjective** (of a young bird) having wing feathers that are large enough for flight; able to fly. ■ [in combination] (of a person or thing) having just taken on the role specified: *a newly fledged Detective Inspector.* ■ chiefly literary (of an arrow) fitted with feathers.

fledgling (also **fledgeling**) ▶ **noun** a young bird that has just fledged. ■ [usu. as modifier] a person or organization that is immature, inexperienced, or underdeveloped: *the country's fledgling democracy.*
– ORIGIN mid 19th cent.: from the obsolete adjective *fledge* (see FLEDGE), on the pattern of *nestling*.

flee ▶ verb (**flees**, **fleeing**; past and past participle **fled**) [no obj.] run away from a place or situation of danger: *to escape the fighting, his family fled from their village.* ■ [with obj.] run away from (someone or something): *he was forced to **flee the country**.*
– ORIGIN Old English *flēon*, of Germanic origin; related to Dutch *vlieden* and German *fliehen*.

fleece ▶ noun **1** the woolly covering of a sheep or goat. ■ the wool shorn from a sheep in a single piece at one time. ■ Heraldry a representation of a fleece suspended from a ring.
2 [mass noun] a soft warm fabric with a texture similar to sheep's wool, used as a lining material. ■ a jacket or other garment made from a fleece fabric.
▶ verb [with obj.] **1** informal obtain a great deal of money from (someone), typically by overcharging or swindling them: *the city's cab drivers are notorious for fixing fares and fleecing tourists.*
2 literary cover as if with a fleece: *the sky was half blue, half fleeced with white clouds.*
– DERIVATIVES **fleeced** adjective.
– ORIGIN Old English *flēos*, *flēs*, of West Germanic origin; related to Dutch *vlies* and German *Vlies*.

F

fleecy ▶ adjective (**fleecier**, **fleeciest**) **1** made of or lined with a soft, warm fabric: *a fleecy sweatshirt.*
2 white and fluffy-looking: *little fleecy clouds.*

fleer /flɪə/ ▶ verb [no obj.] literary laugh impudently or jeeringly.
▶ noun archaic an impudent or jeering look or speech.
– ORIGIN late Middle English: probably of Scandinavian origin and related to Norwegian and Swedish dialect *flira* 'to grin'.

fleet[1] ▶ noun a group of ships sailing together, engaged in the same activity, or under the same ownership: *the small port supports a fishing fleet | **a fleet of** battleships.* ■ (**the fleet**) a country's navy: *the US fleet.* ■ a number of vehicles or aircraft operating together or under the same ownership: ***a fleet of** ambulances took the injured to hospital.*
– ORIGIN Old English *flēot* 'ship, shipping', from *flēotan* 'float, swim' (see FLEET[5]).

fleet[2] ▶ adjective chiefly literary fast and nimble in movement: *a man of advancing years, but **fleet of foot**.*
– DERIVATIVES **fleetly** adverb, **fleetness** noun.
– ORIGIN early 16th cent.: probably from Old Norse *fljótr*, of Germanic origin and related to FLEET[5].

fleet[3] ▶ noun **1** dialect a marshland creek, channel, or ditch.
2 (**the Fleet**) a stream, now wholly underground, running into the Thames east of Fleet Street. ■ historical a prison that stood near this stream.
– ORIGIN Old English *flēot*, of Germanic origin; related to Dutch *vliet*, also to FLEET[5].

fleet[4] dialect ▶ adjective (of water) shallow.
▶ adverb at or to a small depth.
– ORIGIN early 17th cent.: perhaps based on an Old English cognate of Dutch *vloot* 'shallow' and related to FLEET[5].

fleet[5] ▶ verb [no obj.] literary move or pass quickly: *a variety of expressions fleeted across his face.* ■ [with obj.] pass (time) rapidly. ■ fade away; be transitory: *the cares of boyhood **fleet away**.*
– ORIGIN Old English *flēotan* 'float, swim', of Germanic origin; related to Dutch *vlieten* and German *fliessen*, also to FLIT and FLOAT.

Fleet Admiral ▶ noun the highest rank of admiral in the US navy.

Fleet Air Arm historical the aviation service of the Royal Navy.

fleet-footed ▶ adjective nimble and fast on one's feet: *the fleet-footed sprinter ran full out.*

fleeting ▶ adjective lasting for a very short time: *for a fleeting moment I saw the face of a boy.*
– DERIVATIVES **fleetingly** adverb, **fleetingness** noun.

Fleet Street a street in central London in which the offices of national newspapers were located until the mid 1980s (often used to refer to the British Press): *the hottest story in Fleet Street.*

flehmen /ˈfleɪmən/ ▶ noun [mass noun] a behavioural response found in many male mammals when they detect particular smells from females, characterized by a curling of the upper lip and a raising of the head.
– ORIGIN German (verb), '(of a horse) curl the lip in sexual excitement'.

Fleming[1] /ˈflɛmɪŋ/, Sir Alexander (1881–1955), Scottish bacteriologist. In 1928, Fleming discovered the effect of penicillin on bacteria. Twelve years later Howard Florey and Ernst Chain established its therapeutic use as an antibiotic. Nobel Prize for Physiology or Medicine (1945, shared with Florey and Chain).

Fleming[2] /ˈflɛmɪŋ/, Ian (Lancaster) (1908–64), English novelist. He is known for his spy novels whose hero is the secret agent James Bond.

Fleming[3] /ˈflɛmɪŋ/ ▶ noun **1** a native of Flanders.
2 a member of the Flemish-speaking people inhabiting northern and western Belgium. Compare with WALLOON.
– ORIGIN late Old English *Flæmingi*, from Old Norse, reinforced by Middle Dutch *Vlāming*, related to *Vlaanderen* 'Flanders'.

Fleming's left-hand rule ▶ noun Physics a mnemonic concerning the behaviour of a current-carrying conductor in a magnetic field, according to which the directions of the magnetic field, the current, and the force exerted on the conductor are indicated respectively by the first finger, second finger, and thumb of the left hand when these are held out perpendicular to each other.
– ORIGIN 1920s: proposed by the British electrical engineer J. A. Fleming.

Fleming's right-hand rule ▶ noun Physics a mnemonic concerning the behaviour of a conductor moving in a magnetic field, according to which the directions of the magnetic field, the induced current, and the motion of the conductor are indicated respectively by the first finger, second finger, and thumb of the right hand when these are held out perpendicular to each other.

Flemish /ˈflɛmɪʃ/ ▶ adjective relating to Flanders, its people, or their language.
▶ noun **1** [mass noun] the Dutch language as spoken in Flanders. It is one of the two official languages of Belgium.
2 (**the Flemish**) [as plural noun] the people of Flanders.
– ORIGIN Middle English: from Middle Dutch *Vlāmisch*, related to *Vlaanderen* 'Flanders'.

Flemish bond ▶ noun Building a pattern of bricks in a wall in which each course consists of alternate headers and stretchers.

flense /flɛns/ (also **flench** /flɛn(t)ʃ/) ▶ verb [with obj.] slice the skin or fat from (a carcass, especially that of a whale). ■ strip (skin or fat) from a carcass: *the skin had been **flensed off**.*
– ORIGIN early 19th cent.: from Danish *flensa*.

flesh ▶ noun [mass noun] the soft substance consisting of muscle and fat that is found between the skin and bones of a human or an animal: *she grabbed Anna's arm, her fingers sinking into the flesh.* ■ the flesh of an animal or fish, regarded as food: *the food an animal eats will affect the taste and texture of its flesh.* ■ the edible pulpy part of a fruit or vegetable: *halve the avocados and scrape out the flesh.* ■ the skin or surface of the human body with reference to its appearance or sensory properties: *she gasped as the cold water hit her flesh.* ■ (**the flesh**) the human body and its physical needs and desires, especially as contrasted with the mind or the soul: *I have never been one to deny the **pleasures of the flesh**.* ■ flesh colour.
▶ verb **1** [no obj.] (**flesh out**) put weight on: *he had fleshed out to a solid 220 pounds.* ■ [with obj.] (**flesh something out**) add more details to something which only exists in a draft or outline form: *the arguments were fleshed out by the minister.*
2 [with obj.] stimulate (a hound or hawk) to hunt by feeding it a piece of flesh from a recently killed animal. ■ literary accustom to bloodshed or warfare: *he fleshed his troops with enterprises against the enemy's posts.*
3 [with obj.] (often as noun **fleshing**) remove the flesh adhering to (a skin or hide).
– PHRASES **all flesh** all human and animal life. **go the way of all flesh** die or come to an end. **flesh and blood** used to refer to a person's physical body and their needs and frailties, often as opposed to their mind or soul: *the strain on his self-control had been more than flesh and blood could endure.* ■ (**one's flesh and blood**) a near relative or one's close family: *he felt as much for that girl as if she had been **his own flesh and blood**.* **in the flesh** in person or (of a thing) in its actual state: *they decided that they should meet Alexander in the flesh.* **lose flesh** archaic become thinner. **make someone's flesh creep** (or **crawl**) cause someone to feel fear, horror, or disgust. **one flesh** used to refer to the spiritual and physical union of two people in a relationship, especially marriage: *my body is his, his is mine: one flesh.* [with biblical allusion to Gen. 2:24.] **put flesh on (the bones of) something** add more details to something: *he has yet to put flesh on his 'big idea'.* **put on flesh** put on weight. **sins of the flesh** archaic or humorous sins related to physical indulgence, especially sexual gratification.
– DERIVATIVES **fleshed** adjective [usu. in combination] *a white-fleshed fish*, **fleshless** adjective.
– ORIGIN Old English *flǣsc*, of Germanic origin; related to Dutch *vlees* and German *Fleisch*.

flesh colour ▶ noun [mass noun] a light brownish pink.
– DERIVATIVES **flesh-coloured** adjective.

flesher ▶ noun **1** chiefly Scottish a butcher.
2 N. Amer. a knife for fleshing hides.

flesh fly ▶ noun a fly that breeds in carrion, typically producing live young which are deposited on a carcass. ● Family Sarcophagidae: *Sarcophaga* and other genera.

fleshings ▶ plural noun flesh-coloured tights worn by actors.

fleshly ▶ adjective (**fleshlier**, **fleshliest**) **1** relating to human desire or bodily appetites; sensual: *fleshly pleasures.*
2 having an actual physical presence.
– ORIGIN Old English *flǣsclic* (see FLESH, -LY[1]).

fleshpots ▶ plural noun places providing luxurious or hedonistic living: *he had lived the life of a roué in the fleshpots of London and Paris.*
– ORIGIN early 16th cent.: with biblical allusion to the *fleshpots of Egypt* (Exod. 16:3).

flesh side ▶ noun the side of a hide that adjoined the flesh.

flesh wound ▶ noun a wound that breaks the skin but does not damage bones or vital organs.

fleshy ▶ adjective (**fleshier**, **fleshiest**) **1** (of a person or part of the body) having a substantial amount of flesh; plump: *her fleshy arms.* ■ (of plant or fruit tissue) soft and thick: *fleshy, greeny-grey leaves.*
2 resembling flesh in appearance or texture: *normally, the tissue is fleshy pink.*
– DERIVATIVES **fleshiness** noun.

fletch /flɛtʃ/ ▶ verb [with obj.] provide (an arrow) with feathers for flight.
▶ noun each of the feathered vanes of an arrow: [in combination] *a four-fletch arrow.*
– ORIGIN mid 17th cent.: alteration of FLEDGE, probably influenced by *fletcher*.

Fletcher, John (1579–1625), English dramatist. A writer of Jacobean tragicomedies, he wrote some fifteen plays with Francis Beaumont, including *The Maid's Tragedy* (1610–11).

fletcher ▶ noun chiefly historical a person who makes and sells arrows.
– ORIGIN Middle English: from Old French *flechier*, from *fleche* 'arrow'.

fletching ▶ noun [mass noun] the feathers of an arrow.

fleur-de-lis /ˌfləːdəˈliː/ (also **fleur-de-lys**) ▶ noun (pl. **fleurs-de-lis** pronunc. **same**) **1** Art & Heraldry a stylized lily composed of three petals bound together near their bases. It is especially known from the former royal arms of France, in which it appears in gold on a blue field.
2 a European iris. ● Genus *Iris*, family Iridaceae, in particular *I.* × *germanica* 'Florentina' (with bluish-white flowers) or *I. pseudacorus* (the yellow flag).
– ORIGIN Middle English: from Old French *flour de lys* 'flower of the lily'.

fleuron /ˈflʊərɒn, ˈfləː-/ ▶ noun **1** a flower-shaped ornament or motif, used especially on buildings, coins, and books.
2 a small piece of puff pastry used for garnishing.
– ORIGIN late Middle English: from Old French *floron*, from *flour* 'flower'.

fleury /ˈflʊəri/ ▶ adjective variant spelling of FLORY

Flevoland /ˈfleɪvəʊland/ a province of the Netherlands, created in 1986 and reclaimed from the Zuider Zee during the 1950s and 1960s.

flew past of FLY[1].

flews /fluːz/ ▶ plural noun the thick hanging lips of a bloodhound or similar dog.
– ORIGIN late 16th cent.: of unknown origin.

flex[1] ▶ verb **1** (with reference to a limb or joint) bend or become bent: [with obj.] *she saw him flex his ankle and wince* | [no obj.] *it's important to prevent the damaged wrist from flexing.* ■ [with obj.] cause (a muscle) to stand out by contracting or tensing it: *a group of bodybuilders flexed their muscles.* ■ [no obj.] (of a muscle) contract or be tensed: *a muscle flexed in his jaw.* ■ [no obj.] (of a material) be capable of warping or bending and then reverting to shape: *set windows in rubber so they flex during an earthquake.*

2 (as adj. **flexed**) Archaeology relating to or denoting a practice of burying a corpse with the legs drawn up under the chin.
– PHRASES **flex one's muscles** see MUSCLE.
– ORIGIN early 16th cent.: from Latin *flex-* 'bent', from the verb *flectere*.

flex[2] ▶ **noun** Brit. a flexible insulated cable used for carrying electric current to an appliance.
– ORIGIN early 20th cent.: abbreviation of FLEXIBLE.

flexibility ▶ **noun** [mass noun] the quality of bending easily without breaking: *players gained improved flexibility in their ankles.* ■ the ability to be easily modified: *I enjoyed the flexibility of the schedule.* ■ willingness to change or compromise: *the government has shown flexibility in applying its policy.*

flexible ▶ **adjective** capable of bending easily without breaking: *flexible rubber seals.* ■ able to be easily modified to respond to altered circumstances: *small businesses which are dependent on flexible working hours.* ■ (of a person) ready and able to change so as to adapt to different circumstances: *you can save money if you're flexible about where your room is located.*
– DERIVATIVES **flexibly** adverb.
– ORIGIN late Middle English: from Old French, or from Latin *flexibilis*, from *flectere* 'to bend'.

flexile /ˈflɛksʌɪl/ ▶ **adjective** archaic pliant and flexible: *the serpent's flexile body.*
– ORIGIN mid 17th cent.: from Latin *flexilis*, from *flectere* 'to bend'.

flexion /ˈflɛkʃ(ə)n/ (also **flection**) ▶ **noun** [mass noun] the action of bending or the condition of being bent, especially the bending of a limb or joint: *flexion of the fingers.*
– ORIGIN early 17th cent.: from Latin *flexio(n-)*, from *flectere* 'to bend'.

flexitime (N. Amer. also **flextime**) ▶ **noun** [mass noun] a system of working a set number of hours with the starting and finishing times chosen within agreed limits by the employee: *a 35-hour week with flexitime.*
– ORIGIN 1970s: blend of FLEXIBLE and TIME.

flexo ▶ **noun** short for FLEXOGRAPHY.
▶ **adjective** short for FLEXOGRAPHIC (see FLEXOGRAPHY).

flexography /flɛkˈsɒɡrəfi/ ▶ **noun** [mass noun] a rotary relief printing method using rubber or plastic plates and fluid inks or dyes for printing on fabrics and impervious materials such as plastics, as well as on paper.
– DERIVATIVES **flexographic** adjective.
– ORIGIN 1950s: from Latin *flexus* 'a bending' (from the verb *flectere*) + -GRAPHY.

flexor /ˈflɛksə/ (also **flexor muscle**) ▶ **noun** Anatomy a muscle whose contraction bends a limb or other part of the body. Often contrasted with EXTENSOR. ■ any of a number of specific muscles in the arm, hand, leg, or foot.

flexuous /ˈflɛksjʊəs/ ▶ **adjective** chiefly literary full of bends and curves: *he put an arm around her flexuous waist.*
– ORIGIN early 17th cent.: from Latin *flexuosus*, from *flexus* 'a bending', from the verb *flectere*.

flexure /ˈflɛkʃə/ ▶ **noun** [mass noun] technical, chiefly Anatomy & Geology the action of bending or curving, or the condition of being bent or curved. ■ [count noun] a bent or curved part: *these lesser hills were flexures of the San Andreas system.*
– DERIVATIVES **flexural** adjective.
– ORIGIN late 16th cent.: from Latin *flexura*, from *flectere* 'to bend'.

flexwing ▶ **noun** a collapsible fabric delta wing, as used in hang-gliders: [as modifier] *a flexwing microlight.*

flibbertigibbet /ˌflɪbətɪˈdʒɪbɪt/ ▶ **noun** a frivolous, flighty, or excessively talkative person.
– ORIGIN late Middle English: probably imitative of idle chatter.

flic[1] ▶ **noun** Computing a data file containing computer animations.
– ORIGIN usage of the cinematographic sense of FLICK.

flic[2] ▶ **noun** informal a French policeman.
– ORIGIN French.

flick ▶ **verb** [with obj.] strike or propel (something) with a sudden quick movement of the fingers: *Max flicked his bow tie | Ursula flicked some ash off her sleeve.* ■ make or cause to make a sudden quick movement: [with obj.] *the horse flicked its tail* | [no obj.] *the tip of his tongue flicked out.* ■ turn (an electrical device) on or off: *he flicked on the air conditioning | Urquart flicked the switch and she blinked in the harsh light.* ■ [with obj.] move (an object) rapidly up and down so as to strike something or someone: *the driver flicked his whip and the cab moved off.*
▶ **noun 1** a sudden quick movement: *the flick of a switch | a flick of the wrist.* ■ the sudden release of a bent finger or thumb, especially to propel a small object: *he sent his cigarette spinning away with a flick of his fingers.* ■ a light, sharp, quickly retracted blow, especially with a whip. ■ (**a flick through**) a quick look through (a book, magazine, etc.): *a quick flick through the family album.*
2 informal a cinema film: *a Hollywood action flick.* ■ (**the flicks**) Brit. the cinema: *fancy a night at the flicks?*
– PHRASES **give someone the flick** (or **get the flick**) informal, chiefly Austral. reject someone (or be rejected) in a casual or offhand way.
– PHRASAL VERBS **flick through** look quickly through a book, magazine, etc.: *she was flicking through a copy of Vogue.*
– DERIVATIVES **flicky** adjective.
– ORIGIN late Middle English: symbolic, *fl-* frequently beginning words denoting sudden movement.

flicker[1] ▶ **verb** [no obj.] **1** (of light or a source of light) shine unsteadily; vary rapidly in brightness: *the interior lights flickered, and came on.* ■ (of a flame) burn fitfully, alternately flaring up and dying down: *the candle flickered again* | (as adj. **flickering**) *the flickering flames cast long shadows.* ■ (of an emotion) be felt or shown briefly or faintly: *amusement flickered briefly in his eyes.*
2 make small, quick movements: *her eyelids flickered* | [with complement] *Forster's eyes flickered open.*
▶ **noun 1** an unsteady movement of a flame or light causing rapid variations in brightness: *the flicker of a candle flame caught our eyes.* ■ [mass noun] fluctuations in the brightness of a film or television image such as occur when the number of frames per second is too small for persistence of vision.
2 a tiny movement: *the flicker of an eyelid.* ■ a brief feeling or indication of emotion: *a flicker of a smile passed across her face.*
– ORIGIN Old English *flicorian*, *flycerian* 'to flutter', probably of Germanic origin and related to Low German *flickern* and Dutch *flikkeren*.

flicker[2] ▶ **noun** an American woodpecker that often feeds on ants on the ground. ● Genus *Colaptes*, family Picidae: several species, in particular the **common** (or **northern**) **flicker** (*C. auratus*).
– ORIGIN early 19th cent.: imitative of its call.

flick knife ▶ **noun** Brit. a knife with a blade that springs out from the handle when a button is pressed.

flick roll ▶ **noun** another term for SNAP ROLL.

flier ▶ **noun** variant spelling of FLYER.

flight ▶ **noun 1** [mass noun] the action or process of flying through the air: *an eagle in flight | the history of space flight.* ■ [count noun] an act of flying; a journey made through the air or in space, especially a timetabled journey made by an airline: *a return flight from Gatwick to Berlin.* ■ the movement or trajectory of a projectile or ball through the air. ■ [as modifier] relating to or denoting archery in which the main concern is shooting long distances: *short, light flight arrows.*
2 a flock or large body of birds or insects in the air, especially when migrating: *flights of whooper swans.* ■ a group of aircraft operating together, especially an RAF or USAF unit of about six aircraft: *he dispatched the Hurricanes in three flights.*
3 [mass noun] the action of fleeing: *the enemy were now in flight* | [in sing.] *a headlong flight from reality.* ■ the selling of currency or shares by many investors: *an anti-inflationary move aimed at stemming the flight of capital.* ■ literary the swift passage of time: *the never-ending flight of future days.*
4 a series of steps between floors or levels: *I climbed the three flights of stairs which led to his office.* ■ a series of hurdles across a racetrack. ■ a sequence of locks by which a canal ascends an incline.
5 an extravagant or far-fetched idea or thought process: *his research assistant was prone to flights of fancy.*
6 the tail of a dart.
▶ **verb** [with obj.] **1** Brit. (in soccer, cricket, etc.) deliver (a ball) with well-judged trajectory and pace: *he flighted a free kick into the box.*
2 provide (an arrow or dart) with feathers or vanes: *shafts of wood flighted with a handful of feathers.*
3 shoot (wildfowl) in flight.
– PHRASES **in full flight** escaping as fast as possible. ■ having gained momentum in a run or activity: *Yorke was brought down in full flight.* **put someone/thing to flight** cause someone or something to flee. **take flight 1** take off and fly. **2** (also **take to flight**) flee: *many Huguenots took flight from France.*
– ORIGIN Old English *flyht* 'action or manner of flying', of Germanic origin; related to Dutch *vlucht* and FLY[1]. This was probably merged in Middle English with an unrecorded Old English word related to German *Flucht* and to FLEE, which is represented by sense 3 of the noun.

flight attendant ▶ **noun** a steward or stewardess on an aircraft.

flight bag ▶ **noun** a small zipped shoulder bag carried by air travellers.

flight capital ▶ **noun** [mass noun] money transferred abroad to avoid taxes or inflation or provide for possible emigration.

flight case ▶ **noun** a sturdy case used for transporting equipment.

flight control ▶ **noun** [mass noun] the activity of directing the movement of aircraft. ■ [count noun] a flap or other control surface on an aircraft.

F

flight crew ▶ **noun** [treated as sing. or pl.] the personnel who are responsible for the operation of an aircraft during flight.

flight deck ▶ **noun 1** the cockpit of a large aircraft.
2 the deck of an aircraft carrier, used for take-off and landing.

flight engineer ▶ **noun** a member of a flight crew responsible for the aircraft's engines and other systems during flight.

flight envelope ▶ **noun** the range of combinations of speed, altitude, angle of attack, etc., within which a flying object is aerodynamically stable.

flight feather ▶ **noun** any of the large primary or secondary feathers in a bird's wing, supporting it in flight. Also called REMEX.

flightless ▶ **adjective** (of a bird or an insect) naturally unable to fly.
– DERIVATIVES **flightlessness** noun.

flight lieutenant ▶ **noun** a rank of officer in the RAF, above flying officer and below squadron leader.

flight line ▶ **noun 1** the part of an airport around the hangars where aircraft can be parked and serviced.
2 a line of flight: *the birds move in well-defined flight lines to the feeding grounds.*

flight path ▶ **noun** the actual or planned course of an aircraft or spacecraft.

flight plan ▶ **noun** Aeronautics a written account of the details of a particular proposed flight.

flight recorder ▶ **noun** a device in an aircraft that records technical details during a flight, used in the event of an accident to discover its cause.

flightseeing ▶ **noun** [mass noun] N. Amer. the activity of viewing places of interest from an aircraft.

flight sergeant ▶ **noun** a rank of non-commissioned officer in the RAF, above sergeant and below warrant officer.

flight simulator ▶ **noun** a machine designed to resemble an aircraft's cockpit, with computer-generated images that mimic the pilot's view and the aircraft's motion, used for training pilots.

flight test ▶ **noun** a flight of an aircraft, rocket, or equipment to see how well it functions.
▶ **verb** (**flight-test**) [with obj.] test (an aircraft or rocket) by flying it.

flighty ▶ **adjective** (**flightier**, **flightiest**) fickle and irresponsible: *her mother was a flighty Southern belle.*
– DERIVATIVES **flightily** adverb, **flightiness** noun.
– ORIGIN mid 16th cent.: from FLIGHT + -Y[1].

flimflam informal ▶ **noun 1** [mass noun] nonsensical or insincere talk: *pseudo-intellectual flimflam.*
2 a confidence trick: *flimflams perpetrated against us by our elected officials.*
▶ **verb** (**flimflams**, **flimflamming**, **flimflammed**) [with obj.] swindle (someone) with a confidence trick: *the tribe was flimflammed out of its land.*
– DERIVATIVES **flimflammer** noun, **flimflammery** noun.
– ORIGIN mid 16th cent.: symbolic reduplication.

flimsy ▶ **adjective** (**flimsier**, **flimsiest**) insubstantial and easily damaged: *a flimsy barrier.* ■ (of clothing) very light and thin: *the flimsy garment fell from her.* ■ (of a pretext or account) weak and unconvincing: *a pretty flimsy excuse.*
▶ **noun** (pl. **flimsies**) Brit. a document, especially a copy, made on very thin paper: *credit-card flimsies.* ■ [mass noun] very thin paper: *sheets of yellow flimsy.*
– DERIVATIVES **flimsily** adverb, **flimsiness** noun.
– ORIGIN early 18th cent.: probably from FLIMFLAM.

flinch ▸ verb [no obj.] make a quick, nervous movement of the face or body as an instinctive reaction to fear or pain: *she **flinched at** the acidity in his voice* | *he had faced death **without flinching**.* ■ (**flinch from**) avoid doing or becoming involved in (something) through fear or anxiety: *I rarely flinch from a fight when I'm sure of myself.*
▸ noun [in sing.] an act of flinching.
– DERIVATIVES **flinching** adjective, **flinchingly** adverb.
– ORIGIN mid 16th cent. (in the sense 'slink or sneak off'): from Old French *flenchir* 'turn aside', of West Germanic origin and related to German *lenken* 'to guide, steer'.

Flinders, Matthew (1774–1814), English explorer. He explored the coast of New South Wales (1795–1800) and circumnavigated Australia (1801–3) for the Royal Navy, charting much of the west coast of the continent for the first time.

flinders ▸ plural noun small fragments or splinters: *the panel has been smashed to flinders.*
– ORIGIN late Middle English: probably of Scandinavian origin and related to Norwegian *flindra* 'chip, splinter'.

Flinders bar ▸ noun a bar of soft iron placed vertically in or near the housing of a ship's compass to correct deviation caused by the local magnetic field of the ship.
– ORIGIN late 19th cent.: name after Captain Matthew FLINDERS.

Flinders Island the largest island in the Furneaux group, situated in the Bass Strait between Tasmania and mainland Australia.

fling ▸ verb (past and past participle **flung**) [with obj. and adverbial of direction] throw or hurl forcefully: *he picked up the debris and flung it away* | *she **flung herself** down on his bed* | figurative *I was flung into jail.* ■ move or push (something) suddenly or violently: *he flung back the bedclothes* | [with obj. and complement] *Jennifer flung open a door.* ■ (**fling oneself into**) start or engage in (an activity or enterprise) with great energy and enthusiasm: *he flung himself into his athletics.* ■ [no obj., with adverbial of direction] go quickly and angrily: *Lisa had flung out of the house without so much as a glance at him.*
▸ noun **1** a short period of enjoyment or wild behaviour: *one final fling before a tranquil retirement.* ■ a short, spontaneous sexual relationship: *I had a fling with someone when I was at college.*
2 short for HIGHLAND FLING.
– DERIVATIVES **flinger** noun.
– ORIGIN Middle English (in the sense 'go violently'): perhaps related to Old Norse *flengja* 'flog'. The main verb sense is based on an earlier sense 'reckless movement of the body' and dates from the early 19th cent.

flint ▸ noun [mass noun] a hard grey rock consisting of nearly pure silica (chert), occurring chiefly as nodules in chalk. ■ [count noun] a piece of flint, especially as flaked or ground in ancient times to form a tool or weapon. ■ [count noun] a piece of flint used with steel to produce an igniting spark, e.g. in a flintlock gun, or (in modern use) a piece of an alloy used similarly, especially in a cigarette lighter.
– ORIGIN Old English; related to Middle Dutch *vlint* and Old High German *flins*.

flint corn ▸ noun [mass noun] maize of a variety that has hard slightly translucent grains.

flint glass ▸ noun [mass noun] a pure lustrous kind of glass originally made with flint.

flintlock ▸ noun an old-fashioned type of gun fired by a spark from a flint. ■ the lock on such a gun.

Flintshire /ˈflɪntʃɪə, -ʃə/ a county of NE Wales; administrative centre, Mold. It was part of Clwyd from 1974 to 1996.

flinty ▸ adjective (**flintier**, **flintiest**) of, containing, or reminiscent of flint: *flinty soil* | *a flinty wine.* ■ (of a person or their expression) very hard and unyielding: *a flinty stare.*
– DERIVATIVES **flintily** adverb, **flintiness** noun.

flip[1] ▸ verb (**flips**, **flipping**, **flipped**) **1** turn over or cause to turn over with a sudden quick movement: [no obj.] *the plane **flipped over** and then exploded* | [with obj.] *the six-foot wave **flipped** the dinghy **over**.*
2 [with obj. and adverbial] move, push, or throw (something) with a sudden quick movement: *she flipped off her dark glasses* | *she flipped a few coins on to the bar.* ■ [with obj.] turn (an electrical appliance or switch) on or off: *he flipped a switch and the front door opened.* ■ [with obj.] toss (a coin) to decide an issue: *given those odds one might as well flip a coin.*
3 [no obj.] informal suddenly lose control or become very angry: *he had clearly flipped under the pressure.* ■ suddenly become very enthusiastic: *I walked into a store, saw the guitar on the wall, and just flipped.*
4 [with obj.] buy and sell (something, especially shares or property) quickly in order to make a profit: *individual investors often flip the shares they buy within days, even hours.*
▸ noun **1** a sudden quick movement: *the fish made little leaps and flips.* ■ (**a flip through**) a quick look through a book, magazine, etc.: *a quick flip through my cookery books.*
2 Brit. informal, dated a quick tour or pleasure trip: *I did a flip round the post-show party.* [derived from an earlier sense 'short flight in an aircraft'.]
▸ adjective glib or flippant: *he couldn't get away with flip, funny conversation.*
▸ exclamation informal used to express mild annoyance.
– PHRASES **flip burgers** N. Amer. informal work as a cook in a fast-food restaurant. **flip one's lid** (or chiefly N. Amer. **one's wig**) informal suddenly lose control or become very angry.
– PHRASAL VERBS **flip through** look quickly through (a book, magazine, etc.): *McLeish flipped through his notes.*
– ORIGIN mid 16th cent. (as a verb in the sense 'make a flick with the finger and thumb'): probably a contraction of FILLIP.

flip[2] ▸ noun [mass noun] a drink of heated, sweetened beer and spirit. ■ another term for EGGNOG.
– ORIGIN late 17th cent.: perhaps from FLIP[1] in the sense 'whip up'.

flip chart ▸ noun a large pad of paper bound so that each page can be turned over at the top to reveal the next, used on a stand at presentations.

flip chip ▸ noun Computing a chip on one side of which all the connections are in the form of contacts which can be made simultaneously by pressing the chip against the matching substrate and applying heat or pressure.

flip-flop ▸ noun **1** a light sandal, typically of plastic or rubber, with a thong between the big and second toe.
2 N. Amer. a backward handspring. ■ informal an abrupt reversal of policy: *his **flip-flop** on taxes.*
3 Electronics a switching circuit which works by changing from one stable state to another, or through an unstable state back to its stable state, in response to a triggering pulse.
▸ verb [no obj.] **1** [with adverbial of direction] move with a flapping sound or motion: *she flip-flopped off the porch in battered trainers.*
2 N. Amer. informal make an abrupt reversal of policy: *the candidate **flip-flopped** on a number of issues.*
– ORIGIN mid 17th cent. (in the general sense 'something that flaps or flops'): imitative reduplication of FLOP.

flippancy ▸ noun [mass noun] lack of respect or seriousness; frivolousness: *she was infuriated by his careless flippancy.*

flippant ▸ adjective not showing a serious or respectful attitude: *a flippant remark.*
– DERIVATIVES **flippantly** adverb.
– ORIGIN early 17th cent.: from FLIP[1] + -ANT, perhaps on the pattern of heraldic terms such as *couchant* and *rampant*. Early senses included 'nimble' and 'talkative', hence 'playful', giving rise to the current use 'lacking seriousness'.

flipper ▸ noun a broad flat limb without fingers, used for swimming by various sea animals such as seals, whales, and turtles. ■ a flat rubber attachment worn on the foot for underwater swimming. ■ a pivoted arm in a pinball machine, controlled by the player and used for sending the ball back up the table.

flipping ▸ adjective [attrib.] Brit. informal used for emphasis or to express mild annoyance: *are you out of your flipping mind?* | [as submodifier] *it's flipping cold today.*
– ORIGIN early 20th cent.: from FLIP[1] + -ING[2].

flippy ▸ adjective (of a skirt) flared and relatively short, so as to flick up as the wearer walks.

flip side ▸ noun informal the less important side of a pop single; the B-side. ■ another aspect or version of something, especially its reverse or its unwanted concomitant: *our recent pessimism is the flip side of an exaggerated optimism.*

flip-top ▸ adjective having or denoting a lid or cover that can be easily flipped open.
▸ noun a flip-top lid or cover.

flirt ▸ verb **1** [no obj.] behave as though sexually attracted to someone, but playfully rather than with serious intentions: *she began to tease him, **flirting with** other men in front of him.* ■ (**flirt with**) experiment with or show a superficial interest in (an idea, activity, or movement) without committing oneself to it seriously: *a painter who had flirted briefly with Cubism.* ■ (**flirt with**) deliberately expose oneself to (danger or difficulty): *the need of some individuals to flirt with death.*
2 [with obj.] (of a bird) wave or open and shut (its wings or tail) with a quick flicking motion. ■ [no obj., with adverbial of direction] move quickly to and fro with a fluttering motion: *the lark was flirting around the site.*
▸ noun a person who habitually flirts: *Jim was an outrageous flirt.*
– DERIVATIVES **flirty** adjective (**flirtier**, **flirtiest**).
– ORIGIN mid 16th cent.: apparently symbolic, the elements *fl-* and *-irt* both suggesting sudden movement; compare with FLICK and SPURT. The original verb senses were 'give someone a sharp blow' and 'sneer at'; the earliest noun senses were 'joke, jibe' and 'flighty girl' (defined by Dr Johnson as 'a pert young hussey'), with a notion originally of cheeky behaviour, later of playfully amorous behaviour.

flirtation ▸ noun [mass noun] behaviour that demonstrates a playful sexual attraction to someone: *Fabia was in no mood for his light-hearted flirtation.* ■ [count noun] a short or casual relationship: *she had had plenty of flirtations—now she had fallen in love.* ■ a short period of casual experimentation with or interest in a particular idea or activity: *his brief flirtation with the avant-garde in the 1920s.*

flirtatious ▸ adjective behaving in such a way as to suggest a playful sexual attraction to someone: *she was beautiful and very flirtatious.* ■ expressing a playful sexual attraction: *a flirtatious smile.*
– DERIVATIVES **flirtatiously** adverb, **flirtatiousness** noun.

flit ▸ verb (**flits**, **flitting**, **flitted**) [no obj., with adverbial of direction] move swiftly and lightly: *small birds flitted about in the branches* | figurative *the idea had flitted through his mind.* ■ [no obj.] chiefly Scottish & N. English move house or leave one's home, typically secretly so as to escape creditors or obligations.
▸ noun Brit. informal an act of moving house or leaving one's home, typically secretly so as to escape creditors or obligations: ***moonlight flits** from one insalubrious dwelling to another.*
– ORIGIN Middle English (in the Scots and northern English sense): from Old Norse *flytja*; related to FLEET[5].

flitch /flɪtʃ/ ▸ noun **1** a slab of timber cut from a tree trunk, usually from the outside.
2 (also **flitch plate**) the strengthening plate in a flitch beam.
3 chiefly dialect a side of bacon.
– ORIGIN Old English *flicce*, originally denoting the salted and cured side of any meat, of Germanic origin; related to Middle Low German *vlicke*.

flitch beam ▸ noun a compound beam made of an iron plate between two slabs of wood.

flitter ▸ verb [no obj., with adverbial of direction] move quickly in an apparently random or purposeless manner: *her fingers flittered over the sheets.*
▸ noun a fluttering movement: *the flash and flitter of coloured wings.*
– ORIGIN late Middle English: frequentative of FLIT.

flittermouse ▸ noun (pl. **flittermice**) old-fashioned term for BAT[2] (sense 1).
– ORIGIN mid 16th cent.: on the pattern of Dutch *vledermuis* or German *Fledermaus*.

flivver /ˈflɪvə/ ▸ noun N. Amer. informal a cheap car or aircraft, especially one in bad condition.
– ORIGIN early 20th cent.: of unknown origin.

flixweed /ˈflɪkswiːd/ ▸ noun [mass noun] a Eurasian plant with small yellow flowers and finely divided leaves, which was formerly thought to cure dysentery. ● *Descurainia sophia*, family Cruciferae.
– ORIGIN late 16th cent.: from obsolete *flix* (variant of FLUX) + WEED.

FLN ▸ abbreviation Front de Libération Nationale.

float ▸ verb [no obj.] **1** rest or move on or near the surface of a liquid without sinking: *she relaxed, floating gently in the water.* ■ [with obj. and adverbial] cause (a buoyant object) to rest or move on or near the surface of a liquid: *trees were felled and floated downstream.* ■ be suspended freely in a liquid or gas: *fragments of chipped cartilage floated in the joint.*
2 [with adverbial of direction] move or hover slowly and lightly in a liquid or the air; drift: *clouds floated across a brilliant blue sky.* ■ (**float about/around**) (of a rumour, idea, etc.) circulate: *the notion was floating around Capitol Hill.* ■ move in a casual or

leisurely way: *Araminta floated down the stairs.* ■ [with obj. and adverbial of direction] (in sport) make (the ball) travel lightly and effortlessly through the air: *he floated the kick into the net.*
3 [with obj.] put forward (an idea) as a suggestion or test of reactions. ■ offer the shares of (a company) for sale on the stock market for the first time.
4 (of a currency) fluctuate freely in value in accordance with supply and demand in the financial markets: *a policy of letting the pound float.* ■ [with obj.] allow (a currency) to fluctuate in such a way.
▸ **noun 1** a thing that is buoyant in water, in particular: ■ a small object attached to a fishing line to indicate by moving when a fish bites. ■ a cork or buoy supporting the edge of a fishing net. ■ a light object held for support by a person learning to swim. ■ a hollow or inflated organ enabling an organism (such as the Portuguese man-of-war) to float in the water. ■ a hollow structure fixed underneath an aircraft enabling it to take off and land on water. ■ a floating device on the surface of a liquid which forms part of a valve apparatus controlling flow in and out of the enclosing container, e.g. in a water cistern or a carburettor.
2 Brit. a small vehicle or cart, especially one powered by electricity. ■ a platform mounted on a truck and carrying a display in a procession: *a carnival float.*
3 Brit. a sum of money used for change at the beginning of a period of trading in a shop or stall etc., or for minor expenditures.
4 a hand tool with a rectangular blade used for smoothing plaster.
5 chiefly N. Amer. a soft drink with a scoop of ice cream floating in it: *ice-cream floats.*
6 (in critical path analysis) the period of time by which the duration of an activity may be extended without affecting the overall time for the process.
– PHRASES **float someone's boat** informal appeal to or excite someone, especially sexually.
– ORIGIN Old English *flotian* (verb), of Germanic origin and related to FLEET[5], reinforced in Middle English by Old French *floter*, also from Germanic.

floatable ▸ **adjective** capable of floating. ■ chiefly US (of water) able to support floating objects; deep enough to float in.

float arm ▸ **noun** the hinged arm attached to the ball float in the ballcock of a water cistern.

floatation ▸ **noun** variant spelling of FLOTATION.

float chamber ▸ **noun** the cavity in a carburettor containing a device which floats on the surface of the fuel and seals off the flow as the level rises.

floatel /fləʊˈtɛl/ (also **flotel**) ▸ **noun** a floating hotel, especially a boat used as a hotel. ■ an accommodation vessel for workers on an offshore oil rig.
– ORIGIN 1950s: blend of FLOAT and HOTEL; compare with BOATEL.

floater ▸ **noun 1** a person or thing that floats. ■ a loose particle within the eyeball which is apparent in one's field of vision.
2 a floating voter. ■ informal, chiefly N. Amer. a person who frequently changes occupation or residence. ■ N. Amer. a worker who is required to do a variety of tasks as the need for each arises.
3 Brit. informal, dated a mistake; a gaffe.
4 US an insurance policy covering loss of articles without specifying a location.

float glass ▸ **noun** [mass noun] plate glass made by allowing it to solidify on a layer of molten metal.

floating ▸ **adjective 1** buoyant or suspended in water or air: *a floating platform.*
2 not settled permanently; fluctuating or variable: *floating exchange rates.*

floating charge ▸ **noun** a liability to a creditor which relates to the company's assets as a whole and may become fixed in particular circumstances (such as liquidation). Compare with FIXED CHARGE.

floating cloche ▸ **noun** a lightweight material (such as polypropylene film) placed over growing plants to protect them, unsupported except by the plants themselves.

floating debt ▸ **noun** a debt which is repayable in the short term. Compare with FUNDED DEBT.

floating dock ▸ **noun** a floating structure used as a dry dock.

floating kidney ▸ **noun** [mass noun] a condition in which the kidneys are abnormally movable.

floating-point ▸ **noun** [as modifier] Computing denoting a mode of representing numbers as two sequences of bits, one representing the digits in the number and the other an exponent which determines the position of the radix point. Often contrasted with FIXED POINT (sense 2).

floating rib ▸ **noun** any of the lower ribs which are not attached directly to the breastbone. Also called FALSE RIB.

floating voter ▸ **noun** Brit. a person who has not decided which way to vote in an election, or one who does not consistently vote for the same political party.

floatplane ▸ **noun** an aircraft equipped with floats for landing on water; a seaplane.

float valve ▸ **noun** a ball valve.

floaty ▸ **adjective** (**floatier**, **floatiest**) (especially of a woman's garment or a fabric) light and flimsy: *elegant floaty dresses.*

floc /flɒk/ ▸ **noun** technical a loosely clumped mass of fine particles.
– ORIGIN 1920s: abbreviation of FLOCCULUS.

floccinaucinihilipilification /ˌflɒksɪˌnɔːsɪˌnɪhɪlɪˌpɪlɪfɪˈkeɪʃ(ə)n/ ▸ **noun** [mass noun] rare the action or habit of estimating something as worthless.
– ORIGIN mid 18th cent.: from Latin *flocci, nauci, nihili, pili* (words meaning 'at little value') + -FICATION. The Latin elements were listed in a well-known rule of the Eton Latin Grammar.

> **USAGE** **Floccinaucinihilipilification** is one of a number of very long words that occur very rarely in genuine use. For more details see **USAGE** at **ANTIDISESTABLISHMENTARIANISM.**

floccose /ˈflɒkəʊs/ ▸ **adjective** chiefly Botany covered with or consisting of woolly tufts.
– ORIGIN mid 18th cent.: from late Latin *floccosus*, from Latin *floccus* 'flock'.

flocculant /ˈflɒkjʊl(ə)nt/ ▸ **noun** a substance which promotes the clumping of particles, especially one used in treating waste water.

flocculate /ˈflɒkjʊleɪt/ ▸ **verb** technical form or cause to form into small clumps or masses: [no obj.] *it tends to flocculate in high salinities* | [with obj.] *both units contain magnets that are claimed to flocculate algae.*
– DERIVATIVES **flocculation** noun.
– ORIGIN late 19th cent.: from modern Latin *flocculus* 'floccule' + -ATE[3].

floccule /ˈflɒkjuːl/ ▸ **noun** a small clump of material that resembles a tuft of wool.
– ORIGIN mid 19th cent.: from modern Latin *flocculus*, diminutive of *floccus* 'flock'.

flocculent /ˈflɒkjʊl(ə)nt/ ▸ **adjective** having or resembling tufts of wool: *the first snows of winter lay thick and flocculent.* ■ having a loosely clumped texture: *a brown flocculent precipitate.*
– DERIVATIVES **flocculence** noun.
– ORIGIN early 19th cent.: from Latin *floccus* 'tuft of wool' + -ULENT.

flocculus /ˈflɒkjʊləs/ ▸ **noun** (pl. **flocculi** /-lʌɪ, -liː/)
1 Anatomy a small egg-shaped lobe on the undersurface of the cerebellum.
2 Astronomy a small cloudy wisp on the surface of the sun.
3 a floccule.
– ORIGIN late 18th cent.: modern Latin, diminutive of Latin *floccus* (see FLOCCUS).

floccus /ˈflɒkəs/ ▸ **noun** (pl. **flocci** /ˈflɒksʌɪ/) a tuft of wool or similar clump of fibres or filaments.
– ORIGIN mid 19th cent.: from Latin, 'lock or tuft of wool'. Compare with FLOCK[2].

flock[1] ▸ **noun** a number of birds of one kind feeding, resting, or travelling together: ***a flock of** gulls.* ■ a number of domestic animals, especially sheep, goats, or geese, that are kept together: ***a flock of** sheep.* ■ a large number or crowd of people: ***a flock of** paparazzi tailed them all over London.* ■ a group of children or pupils in someone's charge. ■ a Christian congregation or body of believers, especially one under the charge of a particular minister: *Thomas addressed his flock.* [alluding to the metaphor of Christ or a Christian pastor as a shepherd.]
▸ **verb** [no obj.] (of birds) congregate in a flock: *sandgrouse are liable to flock with other species.* ■ [with adverbial] move or go together in a crowd: *tourists flock to Oxford in their thousands.*
– ORIGIN Old English *flocc*, of unknown origin. The original sense was 'a band or body of people': this became obsolete, but has been reintroduced as a transferred use of the sense 'a number of animals kept together'.

flock[2] ▸ **noun** [mass noun] [often as modifier] a soft material for stuffing cushions, quilts, and other soft furnishings, made of wool refuse or torn-up cloth: *flock mattresses.* ■ powdered wool or cloth, used in making flock wallpaper. ■ [count noun] a lock or tuft of wool or cotton.
– DERIVATIVES **flocky** adjective.
– ORIGIN Middle English: from Old French *floc*, from Latin *floccus* (see FLOCCUS).

flockmaster ▸ **noun** a sheep farmer.

flock wallpaper ▸ **noun** [mass noun] wallpaper sized and sprinkled with powdered wool to make a raised pattern.

Flodden, Battle of /ˈflɒd(ə)n/ (also **Flodden Field**) a decisive battle of the Anglo-Scottish war of 1513, at Flodden, a hill near the Northumbrian village of Branxton. A Scottish army under James IV was defeated by a smaller but better-led English force and suffered heavy losses, including the king and most of his nobles.

floe /fləʊ/ (also **ice floe**) ▸ **noun** a sheet of floating ice.
– ORIGIN early 19th cent. (superseding FLAKE[1] in this sense): probably from Norwegian *flo*, from Old Norse *fló* 'layer'.

F

flog ▸ **verb** (**flogs**, **flogging**, **flogged**) [with obj.] **1** beat (someone) with a whip or stick as a punishment: *the men had been flogged and branded on the forehead* | (as noun **flogging**) *public floggings.* ■ informal promote or talk about (something) repetitively or at excessive length: *the issue has been flogged to death already.*
2 Brit. informal sell or offer for sale: *he made a fortune flogging beads to hippies.*
3 [no obj., with adverbial of direction] Brit. informal make one's way with strenuous effort: *by 10 pm we had flogged up the slopes to Grey Crag.*
▸ **noun** [in sing.] Brit. informal an arduous climb or struggle: *a long flog up the mountainside.*
– PHRASES **flog a dead horse** Brit. waste energy on a lost cause or unalterable situation.
– DERIVATIVES **flogger** noun.
– ORIGIN late 17th cent. (originally slang): perhaps imitative, or from Latin *flagellare* 'to whip', from *flagellum* 'whip'.

flogger (also **flogging brush**) ▸ **noun** a brush used in interior decorating to give a marbled or woodgrain effect.

flokati /flɒˈkɑːti/ (also **flokati rug**) ▸ **noun** (pl. **flokatis**) a Greek woven woollen rug with a thick loose pile.
– ORIGIN mid 20th cent.: from modern Greek *phlokatē* 'peasant's blanket'.

flood ▸ **noun 1** an overflow of a large amount of water beyond its normal limits, especially over what is normally dry land: *the villagers had been cut off by floods and landslides* | [as modifier] *a flood barrier.* ■ (**the Flood**) the biblical flood brought by God upon the earth because of the wickedness of the human race (Gen. 6 ff.). ■ the inflow of the tide. ■ literary a river, stream, or sea.
2 an outpouring of tears: *she burst into **floods of** tears.* ■ an overwhelming quantity of things or people happening or appearing at the same time: *his column provoked **a flood of** complaints* | ***floods of** tourists come each year to marvel at the sights.*
3 short for FLOODLIGHT.
▸ **verb** [with obj.] **1** cover or submerge (an area) with water in a flood: *the dam burst, flooding a small town* | (as noun **flooding**) *a serious risk of flooding.* ■ [no obj.] become covered or submerged by a flood: *part of the vessel flooded* | figurative *Sarah's eyes **flooded with** tears.* ■ (usu. **be flooded out**) (of a flood) force (someone) to leave their home. ■ (of a river) become swollen and overflow (its banks).
2 fill or suffuse completely: *she flooded the room with light* | [no obj., with adverbial of direction] *sunlight flooded in at the windows.* ■ overfill the carburettor of (an engine) with petrol, causing the engine to fail to start.
3 [no obj., with adverbial of direction] arrive in overwhelming amounts or quantities: *congratulatory messages flooded in* | figurative *his old fears came flooding back.* ■ [with obj.] overwhelm with large amounts or quantities: *our switchboard was **flooded with** calls.*
4 [no obj.] (of a woman) experience a uterine haemorrhage.
– PHRASES **be in (full) flood** (of a river) be overflowing its banks. ■ (**be in full flood**) be progressing vigorously: *discussion was already in full flood and refused to be dammed.*
– ORIGIN Old English *flōd*, of Germanic origin; related to Dutch *vloed* and German *Flut*, also to FLOW.

floodgate ▸ **noun** a gate that can be opened or closed to admit or exclude water, especially the lower gate of a lock. ■ (**the floodgates**) a last restraint holding back an outpouring of something powerful or substantial: *his lawsuit could* ***open the floodgates*** *for thousands of similar claims.*

floodlight ▶ noun a large, powerful light, typically one of several used to illuminate a sports ground, a stage, or the exterior of a building. ■ [mass noun] the illumination provided by a floodlight: *a tennis court where you can play by floodlight.*
▶ verb (past and past participle **floodlit**) [with obj.] (usu. as adj. **floodlit**) illuminate (a building or outdoor area) with floodlights: *floodlit football pitches.*

floodplain ▶ noun an area of low-lying ground adjacent to a river, formed mainly of river sediments and subject to flooding.

flood tide ▶ noun an incoming tide. ■ an overwhelming quantity or amount of people or things: *the trickle of tourists has become a flood tide.*

floodwater (also **floodwaters**) ▶ noun [mass noun] water left by flooding.

F

floor ▶ noun **1** the lower surface of a room, on which one may walk: *a wooden floor.* ■ the bottom of the sea, a cave, or an area of land: *the ocean floor | the forest floor.* ■ informal the ground: *the best way to play is to pass the ball on the floor.* ■ a minimum level of prices or wages: *share prices have* ***gone through the floor.***
2 all the rooms or areas on the same level of a building; a storey: [as modifier, in combination] *a third-floor flat.*
3 (**the floor**) (in a legislative assembly) the part of the house in which members sit and from which they speak. ■ the right or opportunity to speak next in debate: *other speakers* ***have the floor.*** ■ (in the Stock Exchange) the large central hall where trading takes place: [as modifier] *a floor trader.*
▶ verb [with obj.] **1** provide (a room or area) with a floor: *a room floored in yellow wood* | (as adj., in combination **-floored**) *a stone-floored building.*
2 informal knock (someone) to the ground, especially with a punch. ■ baffle (someone) completely: *that question floored him.*
– PHRASES **from the floor** (of a speech or question) delivered by an individual member at a meeting, not by a representative on the platform: *questions from the floor will be invited.* **take the floor 1** begin to dance on a dance floor. **2** speak in a debate or assembly.
– ORIGIN Old English *flōr*, of Germanic origin; related to Dutch *vloer* and German *Flur.*

floorboard ▶ noun a long plank making up part of a wooden floor in a building. ■ N. Amer. the floor of a motor vehicle.

floorcloth ▶ noun **1** Brit. a cloth used for washing a floor.
2 N. Amer. a thin canvas rug or similar light floor covering.

floor exercise ▶ noun (usu. **floor exercises**) a routine of gymnastic exercises performed without the use of apparatus.

flooring ▶ noun [mass noun] the boards or other material of which a floor is made.

floor lamp ▶ noun chiefly N. Amer. a standard lamp.

floor leader ▶ noun US the leader of a party in a legislative assembly.

floor-length ▶ adjective (especially of clothing) reaching down to the floor: *a floor-length skirt.*

floorman ▶ noun (pl. **floormen**) a person who supervises the gaming tables in a casino.

floor manager ▶ noun **1** the stage manager of a television production.
2 a member of staff in a large store who supervises other shop assistants.

floorpan ▶ noun the lower part of the body of a motor vehicle, forming the floor of the passenger compartment.

floor plan ▶ noun a scale diagram of the arrangement of rooms in one storey of a building.

floor show ▶ noun an entertainment presented on the floor (as opposed to the stage) of a nightclub, restaurant, or similar venue.

floorwalker ▶ noun N. Amer. a shopwalker.

floozy (also **floosie**, **floozie**) ▶ noun (pl. **floozies**) informal a girl or a woman who has many casual sexual partners.
– ORIGIN early 20th cent.: perhaps related to FLOSSY or to dialect *floosy* 'fluffy'.

flop ▶ verb (**flops**, **flopping**, **flopped**) [no obj.] **1** [with adverbial] fall, move, or hang in a loose and ungainly way: *his blond hair flopped over his eyes.* ■ sit or lie down heavily and suddenly, especially when very tired: *Liz flopped down into the armchair.* ■ informal rest or sleep in a specified place: *I'm going to flop here for the night.*
2 informal (of a performer or show) be completely unsuccessful; fail totally: *the show flopped in London.*
▶ noun **1** a heavy, loose, and ungainly movement, or a sound made by it: *they hit the ground with a flop.*
2 informal a total failure: *the play had been a flop.*
3 informal, chiefly US a cheap place to sleep.
– ORIGIN early 17th cent.: variant of FLAP.

-flop ▶ combining form Computing floating-point operations per second (used as a measure of computing power): *a gigaflop computer.*
– ORIGIN acronym; originally spelled *-flops* (*s* = second) but shortened to avoid misinterpretation as plural.

flophouse ▶ noun informal, chiefly US a dosshouse.

flopperoo ▶ noun informal a complete failure, especially with theatre, cinema, or TV audiences or critics.
– ORIGIN 1930s: from the verb FLOP + *-eroo*, suffix in the sense 'large, unexpected'.

floppy ▶ adjective (**floppier**, **floppiest**) tending to flop or hang loosely: *his dark floppy hair.*
▶ noun (pl. **floppies**) (also **floppy disk**) Computing a flexible removable magnetic disk (typically encased in a hard plastic shell) used for storing data.
– DERIVATIVES **floppily** adverb, **floppiness** noun.

flor ▶ noun [mass noun] yeast allowed to develop in a whitish film on the surface of dry (fino) sherries and similar wines during fermentation.
– ORIGIN late 19th cent.: from Spanish, literally 'flower'.

flor. ▶ abbreviation floruit.

Flora Roman Mythology the goddess of flowering plants.

flora ▶ noun (pl. **floras**) [mass noun] the plants of a particular region, habitat, or geological period: *Britain's native flora.* Compare with FAUNA. ■ [count noun] a treatise on or list of such plant life.
– ORIGIN late 18th cent.: from Latin *flos, flor-* 'flower'.

floral /ˈflɔːr(ə)l, ˈflɒ-/ ▶ adjective of flowers: *floral tributes.* ■ decorated with or depicting flowers: *a floral pattern.* ■ Botany of flora or floras: *faunal and floral evolution.*
▶ noun a fabric with a floral design.
– DERIVATIVES **florally** adverb.
– ORIGIN mid 18th cent.: from Latin *flos, flor-* 'flower' + -AL.

floral kingdom ▶ noun another term for PHYTOGEOGRAPHICAL KINGDOM.

Floréal /ˈflɔːrɪəl/, French /flɔreal/ ▶ noun the eighth month of the French Republican calendar (1793–1805), originally running from 20 April to 19 May.
– ORIGIN French, from Latin *floreus* 'flowery', from *flos, flor-* 'flower'.

floreat /ˈflɒrɪat/ ▶ exclamation used before a name to express one's desire that the specified institution or person will flourish.
– ORIGIN Latin, 'let flourish ...', originally used in *floreat Etona*, the motto of Eton College.

Florence a city in west central Italy, the capital of Tuscany, on the River Arno; pop. 365,659 (2008). Florence was a leading centre of the Italian Renaissance from the 14th to the 16th century, especially under the rule of the Medici family during the 15th century. Italian name FIRENZE.

Florentine /ˈflɒr(ə)ntʌɪn/ ▶ adjective **1** relating to Florence.
2 (**florentine** /-tiːn/) [postpositive] (of a dish) served on a bed of spinach: *eggs florentine.*
▶ noun **1** a native or citizen of Florence.
2 a biscuit consisting mainly of nuts and preserved fruit, coated on one side with chocolate.
– ORIGIN Middle English (as a noun): from French *Florentin(e)* or Latin *Florentinus*, from *Florentia* 'Florence'.

flore pleno /ˌflɔːreɪ ˈpleɪnəʊ, ˌflɔːri/ ▶ adjective (of a plant variety) double-flowered.
– ORIGIN Latin, literally 'with a full flower'.

Flores /ˈflɔːrɛs/ the largest of the Lesser Sunda Islands in Indonesia.

florescence /flɔːˈrɛs(ə)ns, flə-/ ▶ noun [mass noun] the process of flowering. ■ the process of developing richly and fully: *the great florescence of Classical poetry, music, and drama.*
– ORIGIN late 18th cent.: from modern Latin *florescentia*, from Latin *florescere* 'begin to flower', based on *flos, flor-* 'flower'.

floret /ˈflɒrɪt, ˈflɔː-/ ▶ noun Botany **1** one of the small flowers making up a composite flower head. ■ a small flower.
2 one of the flowering stems making up a head of cauliflower or broccoli.
– ORIGIN late 17th cent.: from Latin *flos, flor-* 'flower' + -ET[1].

Florey /ˈflɔːri/, Howard Walter, Baron (1898–1968), Australian pathologist. With Ernst Chain he isolated and purified penicillin; in 1945 they shared a Nobel Prize with Alexander Fleming.

Florianópolis /ˌflɔːrɪəˈnɒpəlɪs/ a city in southern Brazil, on the Atlantic coast, capital of the state of Santa Catarina; pop. 396,723 (2007).

floriated /ˈflɔːrɪeɪtɪd/ ▶ adjective decorated with floral designs.

floribunda /ˌflɒrɪˈbʌndə, ˌflɔː-/ ▶ noun a plant, especially a rose, which bears dense clusters of flowers.
– ORIGIN late 19th cent.: modern Latin, feminine (used as a noun) of *floribundus* 'freely flowering', from Latin *flos, flor-* 'flower', influenced by Latin *abundus* 'copious'.

florican /ˈflɔːrɪkan/ ▶ noun a small Asian bustard (bird), the male of which has mainly black plumage with white wings. ● Family Otidae: the **Bengal florican** (*Houbaropsis begalensis*) and the **lesser florican** (*Sypheotides indica*).
– ORIGIN late 18th cent.: of unknown origin.

floriculture /ˈflɒrɪˌkʌltʃə, ˈflɔː-/ ▶ noun [mass noun] the cultivation of flowers.
– DERIVATIVES **floricultural** adjective, **floriculturist** noun.
– ORIGIN early 19th cent.: from Latin *flos, flor-* 'flower' + CULTURE, on the pattern of *horticulture.*

florid /ˈflɒrɪd/ ▶ adjective **1** having a red or flushed complexion: *a stout man with a florid face.*
2 excessively intricate or elaborate: *a florid, baroque building.* ■ (of language) using unusual words or complicated rhetorical devices: *his florid and exciting prose.*
3 Medicine (of a disease or its manifestations) occurring in a fully developed form: *florid symptoms of psychiatric disorder.*
– DERIVATIVES **floridity** noun, **floridly** adverb, **floridness** noun.
– ORIGIN mid 17th cent.: from Latin *floridus*, from *flos, flor-* 'flower'.

Florida /ˈflɒrɪdə/ a state forming a peninsula of the south-eastern US; pop. 18,328,340 (est. 2008); capital, Tallahassee. Explored by Ponce de León in 1513, it was purchased from Spain by the US in 1819; it became the 27th state of the Union in 1845.
– DERIVATIVES **Floridian** adjective & noun.

Florida Keys a chain of small islands off the tip of the Florida peninsula. Linked to each other and to the mainland by a series of causeways and bridges forming the Overseas Highway, the islands extend south-westwards over a distance of 160 km (100 miles).

Florida room ▶ noun N. Amer. a room built at the back of a house and partly or wholly glazed, typically with a brick or tile floor and a drinks bar.

floriferous /flɒˈrɪf(ə)rəs, flɔː-/ ▶ adjective (of a plant) producing many flowers.
– ORIGIN mid 17th cent.: from Latin *florifer* (from *flos, flor-* 'flower', + *-fer* 'producing') + -OUS.

florilegium /ˌflɒrɪˈliːdʒɪəm, flɔː-/ ▶ noun (pl. **florilegia** /-ˈliːdʒɪə/ or **florilegiums**) a collection of literary extracts; an anthology.
– ORIGIN early 17th cent.: modern Latin, literally 'bouquet' (from Latin *flos, flor-* 'flower' + *legere* 'gather'), translation of Greek *anthologion* (see ANTHOLOGY).

florin /ˈflɒrɪn/ ▶ noun **1** a former British coin and monetary unit worth two shillings. ■ an English gold coin of the 14th c., worth six shillings and eight old pence.
2 a foreign coin of gold or silver, especially a Dutch guilder.
3 the basic monetary unit of Aruba, equal to 100 cents.
– ORIGIN via Old French from Italian *fiorino*, diminutive of *fiore* 'flower', from Latin *flos, flor-*. The word originally denoted a gold coin issued in Florence, bearing a fleur-de-lis (the city's emblem) on the reverse.

Florio /ˈflɔːrɪəʊ/, John (*c.*1553–1625), English lexicographer, of Italian descent. He produced an Italian–English dictionary entitled *A Worlde of Wordes* (1598) and translated Montaigne's essays into English (1603).

florist ▶ noun a person who sells and arranges cut flowers.
– DERIVATIVES **floristry** noun.

– ORIGIN early 17th cent.: from Latin *flos, flor-* 'flower', on the pattern of French *fleuriste* or Italian *florista*.

floristic /flə'rɪstɪk/ ▸ **adjective** Botany relating to the study of the distribution of plants.
– DERIVATIVES **floristically** adverb.

floristics ▸ **plural noun** [treated as sing.] Botany the branch of phytogeography concerned with the study of plant species present in an area.

floruit /'flɒrʊɪt, 'flɔː-/ (abbrev.: **fl.** or **flor.**) ▸ **verb** used in conjunction with a specified period or set of dates to indicate when a particular historical figure lived, worked, or was most active.
▸ **noun** the period during which a historical figure lived or worked.
– ORIGIN Latin, literally 'he or she flourished', from *florere* 'to flourish'.

flory /'flɔːri/ (also **fleury**) ▸ **adjective** [predic. or postpositive] Heraldry decorated with fleurs-de-lis. ■ (of a cross) having the end of each limb splayed out into three pointed lobes.
– PHRASES **flory counter-flory** decorated with fleurs-de-lis set in alternating directions.
– ORIGIN late Middle English: from Old French *floure*, from *flour* 'flower'.

floss ▸ **noun** [mass noun] **1** the rough silk enveloping a silkworm's cocoon. ■ (also **floss silk**) untwisted silk fibres used in embroidery. ■ the silky down in maize and other plants.
2 short for DENTAL FLOSS.
▸ **verb 1** [with obj.] clean between (one's teeth) with dental floss.
2 [no obj.] black slang behave in a flamboyant manner; show off.
– ORIGIN mid 18th cent.: from French *(soie) floche* 'floss (silk)', from Old French *flosche* 'down, nap of velvet', of unknown origin.

flossy ▸ **adjective** (**flossier, flossiest**) **1** of or like floss: *short flossy curls*.
2 N. Amer. informal excessively showy: *she cultivated flossy friends*.

flotation /fləʊ'teɪʃ(ə)n/ (also **floatation**) ▸ **noun** [mass noun] **1** the action of floating in a liquid or gas: *the body form is modified to assist in flotation*. ■ the separation of small particles of a solid by their different capacities to float. ■ the capacity to float; buoyancy.
2 the process of offering a company's shares for sale on the stock market for the first time.
– ORIGIN early 19th cent.: alteration of *floatation* (from FLOAT) on the pattern of French *flottaison*. The spelling *flot-* was influenced by FLOTILLA.

flotation tank ▸ **noun** a lightproof, soundproof tank of salt water in which a person floats as a form of deep relaxation.

flotel ▸ **noun** variant spelling of FLOATEL.

flotilla /flə'tɪlə/ ▸ **noun** a small fleet of ships or boats: *a flotilla of cargo boats*.
– ORIGIN early 18th cent.: from Spanish, diminutive of *flota* 'fleet'.

flotsam /'flɒts(ə)m/ ▸ **noun** [mass noun] the wreckage of a ship or its cargo found floating on or washed up by the sea. Compare with JETSAM. ■ people or things that have been rejected or discarded as worthless: *the room was cleared of boxes and other flotsam*.
– PHRASES **flotsam and jetsam** useless or discarded objects.
– ORIGIN early 17th cent.: from Anglo-Norman French *floteson*, from *floter* 'to float'.

flounce[1] ▸ **verb** [no obj., with adverbial of direction] go or move in an exaggeratedly impatient or angry manner: *he stood up in a fury and flounced out*.
▸ **noun** [in sing.] an exaggerated action intended to express annoyance or impatience: *she left the room with a flounce*.
– ORIGIN mid 16th cent.: perhaps of Scandinavian origin and related to Norwegian *flunsa* 'hurry', or perhaps symbolic, like *bounce* or *pounce*.

flounce[2] ▸ **noun** a wide ornamental strip of material gathered and sewn to a skirt or dress; a frill.
▸ **verb** (as adj. **flounced**) trimmed with a flounce or flounces: *a flounced skirt*.
– DERIVATIVES **flouncy** adjective (**flouncier, flounciest**).
– ORIGIN early 18th cent.: from an alteration of obsolete *frounce* 'a fold or pleat', from Old French *fronce*, of Germanic origin; related to RUCK[2].

flounder[1] ▸ **verb** [no obj.] struggle or stagger clumsily in mud or water: *he was floundering about in the shallow offshore waters*. ■ struggle mentally; show or feel great confusion: *she floundered, not knowing quite what to say*. ■ be in serious difficulty: *many firms are floundering*.
– DERIVATIVES **flounderer** noun.
– ORIGIN late 16th cent.: perhaps a blend of FOUNDER[3] and BLUNDER, or perhaps symbolic, *fl-* frequently beginning words connected with swift or sudden movement.

flounder[2] ▸ **noun** a small flatfish that typically occurs in shallow coastal water. ● Families Pleuronectidae and Bothidae: several species, in particular the edible *Platichthys flesus* of European waters.
■ (**flounders**) a collective term for flatfishes other than soles. See FLATFISH.
– ORIGIN Middle English: from Old French *flondre*, probably of Scandinavian origin and related to Danish *flynder*.

flour ▸ **noun** [mass noun] a powder obtained by grinding grain, typically wheat, and used to make bread, cakes, and pastry. ■ fine, soft powder obtained by grinding the seeds or roots of starchy vegetables: *manioc flour*.
▸ **verb** [with obj.] **1** sprinkle (something, especially a work surface or cooking utensil) with a thin layer of flour.
2 US grind (grain) into flour.
– ORIGIN Middle English: a specific use of FLOWER in the sense 'the best part', used originally to mean 'the finest quality of ground wheat'. The spelling *flower* remained in use alongside *flour* until the early 19th cent.

flour beetle ▸ **noun** a small brown darkling beetle that is a widespread pest of flour and other cereal products. ● Genera *Tribolium*, *Gnathocerus*, and others, family Tenebrionidae: several species.

flourish ▸ **verb 1** [no obj.] (of a living organism) grow or develop in a healthy or vigorous way, especially as the result of a particularly congenial environment: *wild plants flourish on the banks of the lake*. ■ develop rapidly and successfully: *the organization has continued to flourish*. ■ [with adverbial] be working or at the height of one's career during a specified period: *the caricaturist and wit who flourished in the early years of this century*.
2 [with obj.] wave (something) about to attract attention: *'Happy New Year!' he yelled, flourishing a bottle of whisky*.
▸ **noun 1** a bold or extravagant gesture or action, made especially to attract attention: ***with a flourish****, she ushered them inside*. ■ an elaborate rhetorical or literary expression. ■ an ornamental flowing curve in handwriting or scrollwork: *letters with an emphatic flourish beneath them*.
2 an impressive and successful act or period: *United produced a late second-half flourish*.
3 Music a fanfare played by brass instruments: *a flourish of trumpets*. ■ an ornate musical passage. ■ an extemporized addition played especially at the beginning or end of a composition.
– ORIGIN Middle English: from Old French *floriss-*, lengthened stem of *florir*, based on Latin *florere*, from *flos, flor-* 'a flower'. The noun senses 'ornamental curve' and 'florid expression' come from an obsolete sense of the verb, 'adorn' (originally with flowers).

flourishing ▸ **adjective** developing rapidly and successfully; thriving: *a flourishing career*.

floury ▸ **adjective** (**flourier, flouriest**) **1** of, resembling, or covered with flour: *Maggie wiped her floury hands on her apron*.
2 (of a potato) having a soft, fluffy texture when cooked.

flout /flaʊt/ ▸ **verb 1** [with obj.] openly disregard (a rule, law, or convention): *the advertising code is being flouted*.
2 [no obj.] archaic mock; scoff: *the women pointed and* ***flouted at*** *her*.
– ORIGIN mid 16th cent.: perhaps from Dutch *fluiten* 'whistle, play the flute, hiss (in derision)'; German dialect *pfeifen auf*, literally 'pipe at', has a similar extended meaning.

> **USAGE** Flout and flaunt do not have the same meaning: see USAGE at FLAUNT.

flow ▸ **verb** [no obj.] **1** (of a liquid, gas, or electricity) move steadily and continuously in a current or stream: *from here the river flows north | ventilation channels keep the air flowing*. ■ (of the sea or a tidal river) move towards the land; rise. Compare with EBB.
2 [with adverbial of direction] go from one place to another in a steady stream, typically in large numbers: *people* ***flowed into*** *the huge courtyard*. ■ proceed or be produced continuously and effortlessly: *talk flowed freely around the table*. ■ (of clothing or hair) hang loosely in an easy and graceful manner: *her red hair flowed over her shoulders*. ■ be available in copious quantities: *their talk and laughter grew louder as the excellent brandy flowed*. ■ (**flow from**) be caused by: *there are certain advantages that may flow from that decision*.
3 (of a solid) undergo a permanent change of shape under stress, without melting.
▸ **noun 1** [in sing.] the action or fact of moving along in a steady, continuous stream: *the flow of water into the pond*. ■ the rate or speed at which something flows: *under the ford the river backs up, giving a deep sluggish flow*. ■ the rise of a tide or a river. Compare with EBB.
2 a steady, continuous stream or supply of something: *a constant flow of people | the flow of words was interrupted by painful sobs*.
3 Scottish a watery swamp; a morass.
4 the gradual permanent deformation of a solid under stress, without melting.
– PHRASES **go with the flow** informal be relaxed and accept a situation, rather than trying to alter or control it. **in full flow** talking fluently and showing no sign of stopping. ■ performing vigorously and enthusiastically.
– ORIGIN Old English *flōwan*, of Germanic origin; related to Dutch *vloeien*, also to FLOOD.

flow chart (also **flow diagram**) ▸ **noun** a diagram of the sequence of movements or actions of people or things involved in a complex system or activity. ■ a graphical representation of a computer program in relation to its sequence of functions (as distinct from the data it processes).

flower ▸ **noun 1** the seed-bearing part of a plant, consisting of reproductive organs (stamens and carpels) that are typically surrounded by a brightly coloured corolla (petals) and a green calyx (sepals). ■ a flower together with its stalk, picked for use as a decoration: *a bunch of flowers*. ■ [mass noun] the state or period in which a plant's flowers have developed and opened: *the roses were just coming* ***into flower***.
2 (**the flower of**) the finest individuals out of a number of people or things: *he wasted the flower of French youth on his dreams of empire*.
▸ **verb** [no obj.] **1** (of a plant) produce flowers; bloom: *Michaelmas daisies can flower as late as October*. ■ [with obj.] induce (a plant) to produce flowers.
2 be in or reach an optimum stage of development; develop fully and richly: *she* ***flowered into*** *as striking a beauty as her mother* | (as noun **flowering**) *the flowering of Viennese intellectual life*.
– DERIVATIVES **flowerless** adjective, **flower-like** adjective.
– ORIGIN Middle English *flour*, from Old French *flour, flor*, from Latin *flos, flor-*. The original spelling was no longer in use by the late 17th cent. except in its specialized sense 'ground grain' (see FLOUR).

flower bed ▸ **noun** a garden plot in which flowers are grown.

flower beetle ▸ **noun** any of a number of beetles that frequent flowers, in particular: ● an elongated beetle with soft wing cases (chiefly of the family Melyridae). ● a day-flying chafer (family Scarabaeidae). ● a small dark beetle that frequently occurs in large numbers (family Nitidulidae).

flower children ▸ **plural noun** historical hippies who wore flowers as symbols of peace and love.

flowered ▸ **adjective 1** having a floral design: *flowered curtains*.
2 [in combination] (of a plant) bearing flowers of a specified kind or number: *yellow-flowered japonica*.

flowerer ▸ **noun** a plant that flowers at a specified time or in a specified manner: *bedding plants and other summer flowerers*.

floweret /'flaʊərɪt/ ▸ **noun** a floret, especially of cauliflower or broccoli.

flower girl ▸ **noun 1** Brit. dated a woman or girl who sells flowers, especially in the street.
2 a young girl who carries flowers or scatters them in front of the bride at a wedding.

flower head ▸ **noun** a compact mass of flowers at the top of a stem, especially a capitulum.

flowering ▸ **adjective** (of a plant) in bloom: *a window box of flowering geraniums*. ■ capable of producing flowers, especially in contrast to a similar plant with the flowers inconspicuous or absent: *flowering dogwood*. ■ [in combination] producing flowers at a specified time or of a specified type: *winter-flowering heathers*.

flowering cherry ▸ **noun** an ornamental tree grown for its spring blossom, the fruit not being considered edible. ● Genus *Prunus*, family Rosaceae: several species, in particular *P. serrulata* and its hybrids.

flowering currant ▶ noun an ornamental shrub grown for its clusters of small pinkish-red flowers. ● Genus *Ribes*, family Grossulariaceae: several species, in particular *R. sanguineum*.

flowering plant ▶ noun a plant that produces flowers; an angiosperm.

flowering rush ▶ noun a tall rush-like plant with long, narrow leaves and pinkish flowers, living in shallow slow-moving water and native to Eurasia. ● *Butomus umbellatus*, the only member of the family Butomaceae.

flowerpecker ▶ noun a very small songbird with a short bill and tail, feeding chiefly on insects in flowers and found in Australasia and SE Asia. ● Family Dicaeidae (the **flowerpecker family**): two genera, especially *Dicaeum*. The flowerpecker family also includes the pardalotes and the mistletoe bird.

F

flowerpot ▶ noun a small container, typically with sloping sides and made from plastic or earthenware, used for growing a plant in.

flower power ▶ noun [mass noun] historical the ideas of the flower children, especially the promotion of peace and love as means of changing the world.

flowers of sulphur ▶ plural noun [treated as sing.] Chemistry a fine yellow powdered form of sulphur produced by sublimation.

flowers of zinc ▶ plural noun [treated as sing.] finely powdered zinc oxide.

flowery ▶ adjective covered with flowers or having a floral design: *a flowery meadow | flowery wallpaper.* ■ smelling of flowers: *her flowery perfume.* ■ (of speech or writing) full of elaborate or literary words and phrases.
– DERIVATIVES **floweriness** noun.

flowing ▶ adjective (especially of long hair or clothing) hanging or draping loosely and gracefully: *a long flowing gown of lavender silk.* ■ (of a line or contour) smoothly continuous: *the flowing curves of the lawn.* ■ graceful and fluent: *a flowing prose style.*
– DERIVATIVES **flowingly** adverb.

flowing sheet ▶ noun Sailing a sheet (rope) that has been eased to allow free movement in the wind.

flow line ▶ noun a route followed by a product through successive stages of manufacture or treatment.

flowmeter ▶ noun an instrument for measuring the rate of flow of water, gas, or fuel, especially through a pipe.

flown past participle of **FLY**[1].

flow-on ▶ noun Austral./NZ a wage adjustment or an improvement in working conditions made as a consequence of one already made in a similar or related occupation.

flowsheet ▶ noun another term for **FLOW CHART**.

flowstone ▶ noun [mass noun] Geology rock deposited as a thin sheet by precipitation from flowing water.

FLQ ▶ abbreviation (in Canada) Front de Libération du Québec, a Quebec separatist terrorist organization, especially active in the 1960s and early 1970s.
– ORIGIN French.

Flt Lt ▶ abbreviation Flight Lieutenant.

Flt Sgt ▶ abbreviation Flight Sergeant.

flu ▶ noun [mass noun] influenza: *she was in bed with flu.*
– DERIVATIVES **flu-like** adjective.
– ORIGIN mid 19th cent.: abbreviation.

flub N. Amer. informal ▶ verb (**flubs, flubbing, flubbed**) [with obj.] botch or bungle (something): *she glanced at her notes and flubbed her lines.*
▶ noun a thing badly or clumsily done; a blunder.
– ORIGIN 1920s: of unknown origin.

fluctuant ▶ adjective literary or technical fluctuating; unstable.
– ORIGIN mid 16th cent.: from Old French 'undulating', from Latin *fluctuare* 'undulate'.

fluctuate /ˈflʌktʃʊeɪt, -tjʊ-/ ▶ verb [no obj.] rise and fall irregularly in number or amount: *trade with other countries tends to fluctuate from year to year* | (as adj. **fluctuating**) *a fluctuating level of demand.*
– ORIGIN mid 17th cent. (earlier (late Middle English) as *fluctuation*): from Latin *fluctuat-* 'undulated', from the verb *fluctuare*, from *fluctus* 'flow, current, wave', from *fluere* 'to flow'.

fluctuation /ˌflʌktʃʊˈeɪʃ(ə)n, -tjʊ-/ ▶ noun an irregular rising and falling in number or amount; a variation: *fluctuations in the yearly values could be caused by a variety of factors.*

flue /fluː/ ▶ noun a duct for smoke and waste gases produced by a fire, a gas heater, a power station, or other fuel-burning installation. ■ a channel for conveying heat.
– ORIGIN late Middle English (denoting the mouthpiece of a hunting horn): of unknown origin. Current senses date from the late 16th cent.

flue-cure ▶ verb [with obj.] (often as adj. **flue-cured**) cure (tobacco) using heat from pipes or flues connected to a furnace.

fluellen /flʊˈɛlɪn/ ▶ noun a small creeping Eurasian plant with yellow and purple flowers, widely occurring in cornfields. ● Genus *Kickxia*, family Scrophulariaceae: two species.
– ORIGIN mid 16th cent.: alteration of Welsh *llysiau Llywelyn* 'Llewelyn's herbs'; compare with *Fluellen*, used by Shakespeare to represent the Welsh name *Llywelyn*.

fluence[1] /ˈfluːəns/ ▶ noun [mass noun] Brit. informal mysterious, magical, or hypnotic power: *you've put the fluence on me, haven't you?*
– ORIGIN early 20th cent.: shortening of **INFLUENCE**.

fluence[2] /ˈfluːəns/ ▶ noun Physics a stream of particles crossing a unit area, usually expressed as the number of particles per second.
– ORIGIN early 17th cent. (in the sense 'a flowing, a stream'): from French, from Latin *fluentia*, from *fluere* 'to flow'.

fluency ▶ noun [mass noun] the quality or condition of being fluent, in particular: ■ the ability to speak or write a particular foreign language easily and accurately: *fluency in Spanish is essential.* ■ the ability to express oneself easily and articulately.
– ORIGIN early 17th cent.: from Latin *fluentia*, from *fluere* 'to flow'.

fluent /ˈfluːənt/ ▶ adjective **1** able to express oneself easily and articulately: *a fluent speaker and writer on technical subjects.* ■ able to speak or write a particular foreign language easily and accurately: *she became fluent in French and German.* ■ (of a foreign language) spoken accurately and with facility: *he spoke fluent Spanish.*
2 smoothly graceful and effortless: *his style of play was fast and fluent.*
3 able to flow freely; fluid: *a fluent discharge from the nose.*
– DERIVATIVES **fluently** adverb.
– ORIGIN late 16th cent.: from Latin *fluent-* 'flowing', from the verb *fluere*.

flue pipe ▶ noun **1** a pipe acting as a flue.
2 an organ pipe into which the air enters directly without striking a reed.

fluey /ˈfluːi/ ▶ adjective Brit. informal suffering from flu: *when I woke up I felt really fluey.*

fluff ▶ noun **1** [mass noun] soft fibres from fabrics such as wool or cotton which accumulate in small light clumps: *he brushed his sleeve to remove the fluff.* ■ any soft downy substance, especially the fur or feathers of a young mammal or bird.
2 entertainment or writing perceived as trivial or superficial: *the film is a piece of typical Hollywood fluff.*
3 informal a mistake made in speaking or playing music, or by an actor in delivering their lines.
▶ verb [with obj.] **1** make (something) appear fuller and softer by shaking or brushing it: *I fluffed up the pillows.*
2 informal fail to perform or accomplish (something) successfully or well: *the extra fluffed his only line.*
– ORIGIN late 18th cent.: probably a dialect alteration of 16th-cent. *flue* 'down, nap, fluff', apparently from Flemish *vluwe*.

fluffy ▶ adjective (**fluffier, fluffiest**) **1** of, like, or covered with fluff: *a fluffy kitten | fluffy white clouds.*
2 (of food) light in texture and containing air: *cream the butter and sugar until pale and fluffy.*
3 informal frivolous or silly; lacking depth or seriousness: *a fluffy blonde in leopard-skin pedal-pushers.*
– DERIVATIVES **fluffily** adverb, **fluffiness** noun.

flugelhorn /ˈfluːg(ə)lhɔːn/ ▶ noun a valved brass musical instrument like a cornet but with a fuller tone.
– ORIGIN mid 19th cent.: from German *Flügelhorn*, from *Flügel* 'wing' + *Horn* 'horn'.

fluid ▶ noun a substance that has no fixed shape and yields easily to external pressure; a gas or (especially) a liquid: *body fluids* | [mass noun] *a bottle of cleaning fluid.*
▶ adjective **1** (of a substance) able to flow easily: *the paint is more fluid than tube watercolours.* ■ smoothly elegant or graceful: *her movements were fluid and beautiful to watch.* ■ not settled or stable; likely or able to change: *our plans are still fluid | the fluid political situation of the 1930s.*
2 (of a clutch or coupling) using a liquid to transmit power.
– DERIVATIVES **fluidity** noun, **fluidly** adverb.
– ORIGIN late Middle English (as an adjective): from French *fluide* or Latin *fluidus*, from *fluere* 'to flow'.

fluid drachm ▶ noun see **DRACHM**.

fluidics /fluːˈɪdɪks/ ▶ plural noun [often treated as sing.] the study and technique of using small interacting flows and fluid jets for functions usually performed by electronic devices.
– DERIVATIVES **fluidic** adjective.

fluidize /ˈfluːɪdʌɪz/ (also **fluidise**) ▶ verb [with obj.] technical give (a finely divided solid) the characteristics of a fluid by passing a gas upwards through it.
– DERIVATIVES **fluidization** noun.

fluidized bed ▶ noun a layer of a fluidized solid, used in chemical processes and in the efficient burning of coal for power generation.

fluid mechanics ▶ plural noun [treated as sing.] the study of forces and flow within fluids.

fluid ounce ▶ noun **1** Brit. a unit of capacity equal to one twentieth of a pint (approximately 0.028 litre).
2 (also **fluidounce**) US a unit of capacity equal to one sixteenth of a US pint (approximately 0.03 litre).

fluidram /ˈfluːɪdram/ ▶ noun US a fluid drachm. See **DRACHM**.

fluke[1] ▶ noun an unlikely chance occurrence, especially a surprising piece of luck: *their victory was a bit of a fluke.*
▶ verb [with obj.] achieve (something) by luck rather than skill.
– ORIGIN mid 19th cent. (originally a term in games such as billiards denoting a lucky stroke): perhaps a dialect word.

fluke[2] ▶ noun **1** a parasitic flatworm which typically has suckers and hooks for attachment to the host. Some species are of veterinary or medical importance. ● Classes Trematoda and Monogenea, phylum Platyhelminthes. See **DIGENEAN** and **MONOGENEAN**.
2 chiefly dialect or N. Amer. a flatfish, especially a flounder.
– ORIGIN Old English *flōc* (in sense 2), of Germanic origin; related to German *flach* 'flat'.

fluke[3] ▶ noun **1** a broad triangular plate on the arm of an anchor.
2 either of the lobes of a whale's tail.
– ORIGIN mid 16th cent.: perhaps from **FLUKE**[2] (because of the shape).

fluky (also **flukey**) ▶ adjective (**flukier, flukiest**) obtained or achieved more by chance than skill: *a fluky goal.*
– DERIVATIVES **flukily** adverb, **flukiness** noun.

flume /fluːm/ ▶ noun an artificial channel conveying water, typically used for transporting logs or timber. ■ a winding tubular water slide or chute at a swimming pool or amusement park.
– ORIGIN Middle English (denoting a river or stream): from Old French *flum*, from Latin *flumen* 'river', from *fluere* 'to flow'. The sense 'artificial channel' dates from the mid 18th cent.; 'water chute for amusement' is a late 20th-cent. usage.

flummery /ˈflʌm(ə)ri/ ▶ noun (pl. **flummeries**) [mass noun] **1** meaningless or insincere flattery or conventions: *she hated the flummery of public relations.*
2 a sweet dish made with beaten eggs, sugar, and flavourings.
– ORIGIN early 17th cent. (denoting a dish made with oatmeal or wheatmeal boiled to a jelly): from Welsh *llymru*; perhaps related to *llymrig* 'soft, slippery'.

flummox /ˈflʌməks/ ▶ verb [with obj.] informal perplex (someone) greatly; bewilder: *I was completely flummoxed by the whole thing.*
– ORIGIN mid 19th cent.: probably of dialect origin; *flummock* 'to make untidy, confuse' is recorded in western counties and the north Midlands.

flummoxed ▶ adjective bewildered or perplexed: *he became flummoxed and speechless.*

flump ▶ verb [no obj., with adverbial of direction] fall or sit down heavily: *I flumped back into bed.*
▶ noun [in sing.] the action or sound of a heavy fall.
– ORIGIN early 17th cent.: imitative.

flung past and past participle of **FLING**.

flunk ▶ verb [with obj.] informal, chiefly N. Amer. fail to reach the required standard in (an examination, test, or

course of study): *I flunked biology in the tenth grade.* ■ judge (an examination candidate) to have failed to reach the required standard. ■ [no obj.] (**flunk out**) (of a student) leave or be dismissed from school or college as a result of failing to reach the required standard: *Tip flunked out of Caltech and moved back home.*
– ORIGIN early 19th cent. (in the general sense 'back down, fail utterly'; originally US): perhaps related to FUNK[1] or to US *flink* 'be a coward', perhaps a variant of FLINCH.

flunkey (also **flunky**) ▶ noun (pl. **flunkeys** or **flunkies**) chiefly derogatory a liveried manservant or footman. ■ a person who performs relatively menial tasks for someone else, especially obsequiously.
– DERIVATIVES **flunkeyism** noun.
– ORIGIN mid 18th cent. (originally Scots): perhaps from FLANK in the sense 'a person who stands at one's flank'.

fluoresce /flʊəˈrɛs, flɔː-/ ▶ verb [no obj.] shine or glow brightly due to fluorescence: *the molecules fluoresce when excited by ultraviolet radiation.*
– ORIGIN late 19th cent.: back-formation from FLUORESCENCE.

fluorescein /ˈflʊərəsiːn, -sɪn, ˈflɔː-/ ▶ noun [mass noun] Chemistry an orange dye with a yellowish-green fluorescence, used as an indicator and tracer. ● A derivative of resorcinol and phthalic anhydride; chem. formula: $C_{20}H_{12}O_5$.
– ORIGIN late 19th cent.: from FLUORESCENCE + -IN[1].

fluorescence /flʊəˈrɛs(ə)ns, flɔː-/ ▶ noun [mass noun] the visible or invisible radiation produced from certain substances as a result of incident radiation of a shorter wavelength such as X-rays or ultraviolet light. ■ the property of absorbing light of short wavelength and emitting light of longer wavelength.
– ORIGIN mid 19th cent.: from FLUORSPAR (which fluoresces), on the pattern of *opalescence*.

fluorescent ▶ adjective **1** (of a substance) having or showing fluorescence: *a fluorescent dye.* ■ containing a fluorescent tube: *fluorescent lighting.*
2 vividly colourful: *a fluorescent T-shirt.*
▶ noun a fluorescent tube or lamp.

fluorescent screen ▶ noun a transparent screen coated with fluorescent material to show images from X-rays.

fluorescent tube (also **fluorescent bulb**) ▶ noun a glass tube which radiates light when phosphor on its inside surface is made to fluoresce by ultraviolet radiation from mercury vapour.

fluoridate /ˈflʊərɪdeɪt, ˈflɔː-/ ▶ verb [with obj.] add traces of fluorides to (something): (as adj. **fluoridated**) *fluoridated toothpaste.*
– DERIVATIVES **fluoridation** noun.
– ORIGIN 1940s: back-formation from earlier *fluoridation*.

fluoride /ˈflʊərʌɪd, flɔː-/ ▶ noun **1** Chemistry a compound of fluorine with another element or group, especially salt of the anion F^- or an organic compound with fluorine bonded to an alkyl group.
2 [mass noun] sodium fluoride or another fluorine-containing salt added to water supplies or toothpaste in order to reduce tooth decay.
– ORIGIN early 19th cent.: from FLUORINE + -IDE.

fluorinate /ˈflʊərɪneɪt, ˈflɔː-/ ▶ verb [with obj.] **1** Chemistry introduce fluorine into (a compound).
2 another term for FLUORIDATE.
– DERIVATIVES **fluorination** noun.

fluorine /ˈflʊəriːn, ˈflɔː-/ ▶ noun [mass noun] the chemical element of atomic number 9, a poisonous pale yellow gas of the halogen series. It is the most reactive of all the elements, causing very severe burns on contact with skin. (Symbol: **F**)
– ORIGIN early 19th cent.: from *fluor* (see FLUORSPAR) + -INE[4].

fluorite /ˈflʊərʌɪt, ˈflɔː-/ ▶ noun [mass noun] a mineral consisting of calcium fluoride which typically occurs as cubic crystals, colourless when pure but often coloured by impurities.
– ORIGIN mid 19th cent.: from *fluor* (see FLUORSPAR) + -ITE[1].

fluoro- /ˈflʊərəʊ, ˈflɔː-/ ▶ combining form **1** representing FLUORINE.
2 representing FLUORESCENCE.

fluorocarbon ▶ noun Chemistry a compound formed by replacing one or more of the hydrogen atoms in a hydrocarbon with fluorine atoms.

fluorochrome ▶ noun a chemical that fluoresces, especially one used as a label in biological research.

fluorography /flʊəˈrɒɡrəfi, flɔː-/ ▶ noun [mass noun] photography in which the image is formed by fluorescence, used chiefly in biomedical research.
– DERIVATIVES **fluorograph** noun.

fluorometer /flʊəˈrɒmɪtə, flɔː-/ (also **fluorimeter**) ▶ noun an instrument for measuring the intensity of fluorescence, used chiefly in biochemical analysis.
– DERIVATIVES **fluorometric** adjective, **fluorometrically** adverb, **fluorometry** noun.

fluoropolymer /ˈflʊərəʊˌpɒlɪmə, ˈflɔː-/ ▶ noun an organic polymer containing fluorine atoms, such as PTFE.

fluoroquinolone /ˌflʊərəʊˈkwɪnələʊn, ˌflɔː-/ ▶ noun [mass noun] an antibiotic used especially in the treatment of systemic infections.

fluoroscope ▶ noun an instrument with a fluorescent screen used for viewing X-ray images without taking and developing X-ray photographs.
– DERIVATIVES **fluoroscopic** adjective, **fluoroscopy** noun.

fluorosis /flʊəˈrəʊsɪs, flɔː-/ ▶ noun [mass noun] Medicine a chronic condition caused by excessive intake of fluorine compounds, marked by mottling of the teeth and, if severe, calcification of the ligaments.

fluorspar /ˈflʊəspɑː, ˈflɔː-/ ▶ noun another term for FLUORITE.
– ORIGIN late 18th cent.: from *fluor* 'a flow, a mineral used as a flux, fluorspar' (from Latin *fluor*, from *fluere* 'to flow') + SPAR[3].

fluoxetine /fluːˈɒksətiːn/ ▶ noun [mass noun] Medicine a synthetic compound which inhibits the uptake of serotonin in the brain and is taken to treat depression. Also called **PROZAC** (trademark).
– ORIGIN 1970s: from *fluo(rine)* + *ox(y)* + *-etine* (perhaps from *e* + a blend of TOLUENE and AMINE).

flurried ▶ adjective agitated, nervous, or anxious: *Jack was never flurried.*

flurry ▶ noun (pl. **flurries**) a small swirling mass of something, especially snow or leaves, moved by sudden gusts of wind: *a **flurry of** snow.* ■ a sudden short period of activity or excitement: *there was a brief **flurry of** activity in the hall.* ■ a number of things arriving or happening suddenly and during the same period: *a **flurry of** editorials hostile to the government.*
▶ verb (**flurries**, **flurrying**, **flurried**) [no obj., with adverbial of direction] (especially of snow or leaves) be moved in small swirling masses by sudden gusts of wind: *gusts of snow flurried through the door.* ■ (of a person) move quickly in a busy or agitated way: *the waiter flurried between them.*
– ORIGIN late 17th cent.: from obsolete *flurr* 'fly up, flutter, whirr' (imitative), probably influenced by HURRY.

flush[1] ▶ verb **1** [no obj.] (of a person's skin, face, etc.) become red and hot, typically as the result of illness or strong emotion: *Rachel flushed angrily.* ■ [with obj.] make red and hot: *a wave of colour flushed his cheeks.* ■ glow or cause to glow with warm colour or light: [with obj.] *the sky was flushed with the gold of dawn.*
2 [with obj.] cleanse (something, especially a toilet) by causing large quantities of water to pass through it: *she flushed the loo | the nurse **flushed out** the catheter.* ■ [no obj.] (of a toilet) be cleansed by flushing. ■ [with obj. and adverbial of direction] remove or dispose of (an object or substance) by flushing: *I **flushed** the pills **down the lavatory** | the kidneys require more water to **flush out** waste products.* ■ [with obj. and adverbial of direction] cause (a liquid) to flow through something: *0.3 ml of saline is gently flushed through the tube.*
3 [with obj. and adverbial of direction] drive (a bird, especially a game bird, or an animal) from its cover: *the grouse were flushed from the woods.* ■ cause to be revealed; force into the open: *they're trying to flush him out of hiding.*
4 [no obj.] (of a plant) send out fresh shoots: *the plant had started to flush by late March.*
▶ noun **1** a reddening of the face, skin, etc., typically caused by illness or strong emotion: *a flush of embarrassment rose to her cheeks.* ■ an area of warm colour or light: *the bird has a pinkish flush on the breast.*
2 [in sing.] a sudden rush of intense emotion: *I was carried away in a **flush of** enthusiasm.* ■ a period when something is new or particularly fresh and vigorous: *he is no longer **in the first flush of** youth.* ■ a sudden abundance or spate of something: *the frogs feast on the great **flush of** insects.* ■ a fresh growth of leaves, flowers, or fruit.
3 an act of cleansing something, especially a toilet, with a sudden flow of water. ■ the device used for flushing a toilet. ■ [as modifier] denoting a type of toilet that has a flushing device. ■ a sudden flow: *the melting snow provides a flush of water.*
4 the action of driving an animal or game bird from its cover: *labradors retrieve the birds after the flush.*
– DERIVATIVES **flushable** adjective, **flusher** noun.
– ORIGIN Middle English (in the sense 'move rapidly, spring up', especially of a bird 'fly up suddenly'): symbolic, *fl-* frequently beginning words connected with sudden movement; perhaps influenced by FLASH[1] and BLUSH.

flush[2] ▶ adjective **1** completely level or even with another surface: *the gates are **flush with** the adjoining fencing.* ■ (of printed text) not indented or protruding: *each line is **flush with** the left-hand margin.* ■ (of a door) having a smooth surface, without indented or protruding panels or mouldings.
2 [predic.] informal having plenty of something, especially money: *the banks are flush with funds.* ■ (of money) plentiful: *the years when cash was flush.*
▶ adverb **1** so as to be level or even: *the screw must fit **flush with** the surface.*
2 so as to be directly centred; squarely: *Hodson caught him flush on the jaw with a straight right.*
▶ verb [with obj.] fill in (a joint) level with a surface.
– DERIVATIVES **flushness** noun.
– ORIGIN mid 16th cent. (in the sense 'perfect, lacking nothing'): probably related to FLUSH[1].

flush[3] ▶ noun (in poker or brag) a hand of cards all of the same suit.
– ORIGIN early 16th cent.: from French *flux* (formerly *flus*), from Latin *fluxus* 'a flow' (see FLUX: the use in cards can be compared with English *run*).

flush[4] ▶ noun Ecology a piece of wet ground over which water flows without being confined to a definite channel.
– ORIGIN late Middle English (in the sense 'marshy place'): variant of FLASH[2].

flushed ▶ adjective **1** (of a person's skin) red and hot, typically as the result of illness or strong emotion: *her flushed cheeks.*
2 (of a person) excited or elated by something: ***flushed with** success, I was getting into my stride.*

Flushing /ˈflʌʃɪŋ/ a port in the SW Netherlands; pop. 44,798 (2008). Dutch name **VLISSINGEN**.

fluster ▶ verb [with obj.] (often as adj. **flustered**) make (someone) agitated or confused: *Rosamund seemed rather flustered this morning.*
▶ noun [in sing.] an agitated or confused state: *the main thing is not to get all in a fluster.*
– ORIGIN early 17th cent. (in the sense 'make slightly drunk'): perhaps of Scandinavian origin and related to Icelandic *flaustra* 'hurry, bustle'.

flute ▶ noun **1** a wind instrument made from a tube with holes that are stopped by the fingers or keys, held vertically or horizontally (**transverse flute**) so that the player's breath strikes a narrow edge. ■ a modern orchestral instrument of this type, typically of metal, held horizontally, with the mouthpiece near one end, which is closed. ■ an organ stop with wooden or metal flue pipes producing a tone similar to that of a flute.
2 Architecture an ornamental vertical groove in a column. ■ a trumpet-shaped frill on a dress or other garment.
3 a tall, narrow wine glass: *a flute of champagne.*
▶ verb **1** [no obj.] literary play a flute or pipe. ■ speak in a melodious way: *'What do you do?' she fluted.*
2 [with obj.] make flutes or grooves in.
– DERIVATIVES **flute-like** adjective.
– ORIGIN Middle English: from Old French *flahute*, probably from Provençal *flaüt*, perhaps a blend of *flaujol* 'flageolet' + *laüt* 'lute'.

fluted ▶ adjective having flutes or grooves; ridged: *fluted pillars.*

fluting ▶ noun **1** [mass noun] sound reminiscent of that of a flute: *the silvery fluting of a blackbird.*
2 a groove or set of grooves forming a surface decoration: *a hollow stem with vertical flutings.*
▶ adjective reminiscent of the sound of a flute: *the golden, fluting voice filled the room.*

flutist ▶ noun US term for FLAUTIST.

flutter ▶ verb [no obj.] (of a bird or other winged creature) fly unsteadily or hover by flapping the wings quickly and lightly: *a couple of butterflies fluttered around the garden.* ■ [with obj.] (of a bird or other winged creature) flap (its wings) quickly and lightly. ■ move with a light irregular or trembling motion: *flags of different countries fluttered in the breeze* | (as adj. **fluttering**) *a fluttering banner.* ■ [with adverbial of direction] (of a person) move restlessly or uncertainly:

F

Mavis fluttered about nervously. ■ (of a pulse or heartbeat) beat feebly or irregularly.
▶ **noun 1** an act of fluttering: *there was a flutter of wings at the window.* ■ a state or sensation of tremulous excitement: *her insides were in a flutter.* ■ [mass noun] Medicine disturbance of the rhythm of the heart that is less severe than fibrillation. ■ [mass noun] Aeronautics undesired oscillation in a part of an aircraft under stress. ■ [mass noun] Electronics rapid variation in the pitch or amplitude of a signal, especially of recorded sound. Compare with **wow**[2].
2 Brit. informal a small bet: *a **flutter on the horses**.*
– PHRASES **flutter one's eyelashes** open and close one's eyes rapidly in a coy, flirtatious manner.
– DERIVATIVES **flutterer** noun, **flutteringly** adverb, **fluttery** adjective.
– ORIGIN Old English *floterian, flotorian*, a frequentative form related to **FLEET**[5].

flutter-tonguing ▶ **noun** [mass noun] the action of vibrating the tongue (as if rolling an *r*) in playing a wind instrument to produce a whirring effect.

fluty (also **flutey**) ▶ **adjective** (**flutier, flutiest**) reminiscent of the sound of a flute: *a drawn-out fluty whistle.*

fluvial /ˈfluːvɪəl/ ▶ **adjective** chiefly Geology of or found in a river.
– ORIGIN Middle English: from Latin *fluvialis*, from *fluvius* 'river', from *fluere* 'to flow'.

fluviatile /ˈfluːvɪəˌtʌɪl/ ▶ **adjective** technical of, found in, or produced by a river: *fluviatile sediments.*
– ORIGIN late 16th cent.: from French, from Latin *fluviatilis*, from *fluviatus* 'moistened', from *fluvius* 'river'.

fluvio- /ˈfluːvɪəʊ/ ▶ **combining form** river; relating to rivers: *fluvioglacial.*
– ORIGIN from Latin *fluvius* 'river'.

fluvioglacial ▶ **adjective** Geology relating to or denoting erosion or deposition caused by flowing meltwater from glaciers or ice sheets.

fluviolacustrine /ˌfluːvɪə(ʊ)ləˈkʌstrʌɪn, -trɪn/ ▶ **adjective** Geology (of sediments) produced by both rivers and lakes.

fluviometer /ˌfluːvɪˈɒmɪtə/ ▶ **noun** an instrument for measuring the rise and fall of rivers.

fluvoxamine /fluːˈvɒxəmiːn/ ▶ **noun** [mass noun] Medicine a synthetic antidepressant drug which acts by prolonging the effect of the neurotransmitter serotonin on the brain.

flux /flʌks/ ▶ **noun 1** [mass noun] the action or process of flowing or flowing out: *the flux of ions across the membrane.* ■ Physics the rate of flow of a fluid, radiant energy, or particles across a given area. ■ the amount of radiation or particles incident on an area in a given time. ■ the total electric or magnetic field passing through a surface.
2 Medicine an abnormal discharge of blood or other matter from or within the body. ■ (usu. **the flux**) archaic diarrhoea or dysentery.
3 [mass noun] continuous change: *the whole political system is in a state of flux.*
4 a substance mixed with a solid to lower its melting point, used especially in soldering and brazing metals or to promote vitrification in glass or ceramics. ■ a substance added to a furnace during metal-smelting or glass-making which combines with impurities to form slag.
▶ **verb** [with obj.] treat (a metal object) with a flux to promote melting.
– ORIGIN late Middle English: from Latin *fluxus*, from *fluere* 'to flow'.

flux density ▶ **noun** the amount of magnetic, electric, or other flux passing through a unit area.

fluxgate ▶ **noun** Physics a device consisting of one or more soft iron cores each surrounded by primary and secondary windings, used for determining the characteristics of an external magnetic field from the signals produced in the secondary windings.

fluxion /ˈflʌkʃ(ə)n/ ▶ **noun** Mathematics, dated a function corresponding to the rate of change of a variable quantity; a derivative.
– ORIGIN late 17th cent.: from French, or from Latin *flux-* 'flowed', from the verb *fluere*.

fluxional ▶ **adjective 1** subject to flux.
2 Mathematics, dated relating to fluxions.

fly[1] ▶ **verb** (**flies, flying**; past **flew**; past participle **flown**) [no obj.] **1** (of a bird, bat, or insect) move through the air using wings: *close the door or the moths will fly in | the bird can fly enormous distances.* ■ (of an aircraft or its occupants) travel through the air: *I fly back to London this evening.* ■ [with obj.] control the flight of (an aircraft): *he flew Hurricanes in the war.* ■ [with obj. and adverbial of direction] transport in an aircraft: *helicopters flew the injured to hospital.* ■ [with obj.] accomplish (a purpose) in an aircraft: *pilots trained to fly combat missions.* ■ [with obj.] release (a bird) to fly, especially a hawk for hunting or a pigeon for racing.
2 [usu. with adverbial of direction] move or be hurled quickly through the air: *balls kept flying over her hedge | he **was sent flying** by the tackle.* ■ (past **flied**) Baseball hit a ball high into the air: *he flied out to the left field.*
3 [with adverbial] wave or flutter in the wind: *she ran after him, her hair flying behind her.* ■ (with reference to a flag) display or be displayed on a flagpole: [with obj.] *vessels which flew the Spanish flag* | [no obj.] *flags were flying at half mast.*
4 [usu. with adverbial of direction] go or move quickly: *she flew along the path | his fingertips flew across the keyboard.* ■ informal depart hastily: *I must fly!* ■ (of time) pass swiftly: *the evening had just flown by.* ■ (of accusations or insults) be exchanged swiftly and heatedly: *the accusations flew thick and fast.* ■ (of a report) be circulated swiftly and widely: *rumours were **flying around** Manchester.* ■ archaic run away. ■ [with obj.] archaic escape from in haste: *you must fly the country for a while.*
5 N. Amer. informal be successful: *that idea didn't fly with most other council members.*
▶ **noun** (pl. **flies**) **1** (Brit. often **flies**) an opening at the crotch of a pair of trousers, closed with a zip or buttons and typically covered with a flap. ■ a flap of material covering the opening or fastening of a garment or of a tent.
2 (**the flies**) the space over the stage in a theatre.
3 Baseball short for **FLY BALL**.
4 (pl. usu. **flys**) Brit. historical a one-horse hackney carriage.
5 Austral./NZ informal an attempt: *we decided to give it a fly.*
– PHRASES **fly the coop** informal make one's escape. **fly the flag** see **FLAG**[1]. **fly high** be very successful; prosper. **fly in the face of** be openly at variance with (what is usual or expected): *a need to fly in the face of convention.* **fly into a rage** (or **temper**) become suddenly or violently angry. **fly a kite** informal try something out to test public opinion. **fly the nest** (of a young bird) leave its nest on becoming able to fly. ■ informal (of a young person) leave their parents' home to set up home elsewhere. **fly off the handle** informal lose one's temper suddenly and unexpectedly. [figuratively, with reference to the loose head of an axe.] **go fly a kite** [in imperative] N. Amer. informal go away. **on the fly** while in motion or progress: *producers were able to schedule the day's Olympic coverage on the fly.* ■ Computing during the running of a computer program without interrupting the run.
– PHRASAL VERBS **fly at 1** attack verbally or physically: *Robbie flew at him, fists clenched.* **2** (of a hawk) pursue and attack, or habitually pursue (prey).
– DERIVATIVES **flyable** adjective.
– ORIGIN Old English *flēogan*, of Germanic origin; related to Dutch *vliegen* and German *fliegen*, also to **FLY**[2].

fly[2] ▶ **noun** (pl. **flies**) a flying insect of a large order characterized by a single pair of transparent wings and sucking (and often also piercing) mouthparts. Flies are of great importance as vectors of disease. See also **DIPTERA**. ● Order Diptera: numerous families.
■ [usu. in combination] used in names of flying insects of other orders, e.g. **butterfly, dragonfly, firefly**. ■ [mass noun] an infestation of flying insects on a plant or animal: *cattle to be treated for warble fly.* ■ a natural or artificial flying insect used as bait in fishing, especially a mayfly.
– PHRASES **die** (or **drop**) **like flies** die or collapse in large numbers. **drink with the flies** Austral./NZ drink alone. **a fly in the ointment** a minor irritation that spoils the success or enjoyment of something. **fly on the wall** an unnoticed observer of a particular situation. ■ [as modifier] denoting a film-making technique whereby events are recorded realistically with minimum interference rather than acted out under direction: *a fly-on-the-wall documentary.* **like a blue-arsed fly** Brit. vulgar slang in an extremely hectic or frantic way. (**there are**) **no flies on ——** used to emphasize a person's cleverness and astuteness: *no flies on Phyllis—she paid six months in advance.* **wouldn't hurt** (or **harm**) **a fly** used to emphasize how inoffensive and harmless a person or animal is.
– ORIGIN Old English *flȳge, flēoge*, denoting any winged insect, of West Germanic origin; related to Dutch *vlieg* and German *Fliege*, also to **FLY**[1].

fly[3] ▶ **adjective** (**flyer, flyest**) informal **1** Brit. knowing and clever: *she's fly enough not to get tricked out of it.*
2 N. Amer. fashionably attractive and impressive: *a fly dude.*
– ORIGIN early 19th cent.: of unknown origin.

fly agaric ▶ **noun** a poisonous toadstool which has a red cap with fluffy white spots, growing particularly among birch trees. It contains hallucinogenic alkaloids and has long been used by the indigenous peoples of NE Siberia. ● *Amanita muscaria*, family Amanitaceae, class Hymenomycetes.

fly ash ▶ **noun** [mass noun] ash produced in small dark flecks by the burning of powdered coal or other materials and carried into the air.

flyaway ▶ **adjective** (of a person's hair) fine and difficult to control.

flyback ▶ **noun** [mass noun] the return of the scanning spot in a cathode ray tube to the starting point.

fly ball ▶ **noun** Baseball a ball batted high into the air.

flyblow ▶ **noun** [mass noun] flies' eggs contaminating food, especially meat.

flyblown ▶ **adjective** contaminated through contact with flies and their eggs and larvae: *flyblown meat.* ■ infested with flies; dirty and unpleasant: *the flyblown pool halls of his youth.*

fly boy ▶ **noun** N. Amer. informal a pilot, especially one in the air force.

flybridge ▶ **noun** an open deck above the main bridge of a vessel such as a yacht or cabin cruiser, typically equipped with duplicate controls.

fly-by ▶ **noun** (pl. **fly-bys**) a flight past a point, especially the close approach of a spacecraft to a planet or moon for observation. ■ another term for **FLY-PAST**.

fly-by-night ▶ **adjective** [attrib.] unreliable or untrustworthy, especially in business or financial matters: *cheap suits made by fly-by-night operators.*
▶ **noun** (also **fly-by-nighter**) an unreliable or untrustworthy person.

fly-by-wire ▶ **noun** [often as modifier] a semi-automatic and typically computer-regulated system for controlling the flight of an aircraft or spacecraft: *sophisticated fly-by-wire technology.*

flycatcher ▶ **noun** a perching bird that catches flying insects, especially in short flights from a perch.
● Typical Old World flycatchers belong to the family Muscicapidae. Many others belong to the Old World family Monarchidae (**monarch** and **paradise flycatchers**) and the New World family Tyrannidae (**tyrant flycatchers**), while some belong to families Eopsaltridae (Australasia), Platysteiridae (Africa), and Bombycillidae (America).

fly-drive ▶ **adjective** denoting a package holiday which includes a flight and car rental at the destination.
▶ **noun** a fly-drive holiday.

flyer (also **flier**) ▶ **noun 1** a person or thing that flies, especially in a particular way: *frequent flyers.* ■ a person who flies something, especially an aircraft. ■ informal a fast-moving person or thing: *his free kick was a real flyer.*
2 a small handbill advertising an event or product.
3 short for **FLYING START**.
4 chiefly N. Amer. a speculative investment.
– PHRASES **take a flyer** chiefly N. Amer. take a chance.

fly fishing ▶ **noun** [mass noun] the sport of fishing using a rod and an artificial fly as bait.
– DERIVATIVES **fly-fish** verb.

fly half ▶ **noun** Rugby another term for **STAND-OFF HALF**.

fly-in ▶ **noun** a meeting or other event attended by people who arrive by air: *a helicopter fly-in.* ■ an act of transporting people or goods by air: *one or two fly-ins to remote lakes.*

flying ▶ **adjective** moving or able to move through the air with wings: *a flying ant.* ■ moving rapidly, especially through the air: *one passenger was cut by flying glass.* ■ done while launching oneself at someone: *he took a flying kick at a policeman.* ■ hasty; brief: *a flying visit.* ■ used in names of animals that can glide by using wing-like membranes or other structures, e.g. **flying squirrel**.
▶ **noun** [mass noun] flight, especially in an aircraft: *she hates flying.*
– PHRASES **go flying** informal, chiefly Brit. fall or be knocked over: *Rob tripped over a branch and went flying.* **with flying colours** with distinction: *Sylvia had passed her exams with flying colours.*

flying boat ▶ **noun** a large seaplane that lands with its fuselage in the water.

flying bomb ▶ **noun** a small pilotless aircraft with an explosive warhead, especially a V-1.

flying bridge ▶ **noun** another term for **FLYBRIDGE**.

flying buttress ▸ noun Architecture a buttress slanting from a separate column, typically forming an arch with the wall it supports.

flying change ▸ noun a movement in riding in which the leading leg in the canter position is changed without loss of speed while the horse is in the air.

flying doctor ▸ noun (in Australia) a doctor who uses radio communication and travels by aircraft to visit patients in remote areas of the country.

flying dragon ▸ noun another term for FLYING LIZARD.

Flying Dutchman a legendary ghostly ship supposedly seen in the region of the Cape of Good Hope and presaging disaster. ■ the captain of this ship.

flying fish ▸ noun a fish of warm seas which leaps out of the water and uses its wing-like pectoral fins to glide over the surface for some distance. ● Family Exocoetidae: several genera and species, in particular *Exocoetus volitans*.

flying fox ▸ noun **1** a large fruit bat with a foxlike face, found in Madagascar, SE Asia, and northern Australia. ● *Pteropus* and two other genera, family Pteropodidae: numerous species.
2 Austral./NZ an overhead cable and apparatus for transporting materials over difficult terrain.

flying frog ▸ noun a nocturnal arboreal Asian frog which is able to glide between trees using the large webs between its extended toes. ● *Polypedates leucomystax*, family Rhacophoridae.

flying gurnard ▸ noun a bottom-dwelling marine fish that has bony armour on the skull and large brightly coloured pectoral fins. It moves through the water with a gliding or flying motion. ● Family Dactylopteridae: two genera and several species.

flying jacket ▸ noun a short jacket similar to a bomber jacket, typically of leather and with a warm lining or collar and several pockets.

flying lemur ▸ noun a nocturnal tree-dwelling SE Asian mammal resembling a lemur, with a membrane between the fore- and hindlimbs for gliding from tree to tree. Also called COLUGO. ● Family Cynocephalidae and genus *Cynocephalus*, order Dermoptera: two species.

flying lizard ▸ noun an arboreal SE Asian lizard which has expanding membranes along the sides of the body, used for gliding between trees. Also called DRAGON, FLYING DRAGON. ● Genus *Draco*, family Agamidae: several species.

flying machine ▸ noun an aircraft, especially an early or unconventional one.

flying mouse ▸ noun another term for FEATHERTAIL GLIDER.

flying officer ▸ noun a rank of commissioned officer in the RAF, above pilot officer and below flight lieutenant.

flying phalanger ▸ noun a small Australasian marsupial with a membrane between the fore- and hindlimbs for gliding. Also called GLIDER. ● Genera *Petaurus* and *Petauroides*, family Petauridae: five species.

flying picket ▸ noun Brit. a person who, with others, travels to picket any workplace where there is an industrial dispute.

flying saucer ▸ noun a disc-shaped flying craft supposedly piloted by aliens; a UFO.

flying snake ▸ noun a greenish semi-arboreal SE Asian snake which can glide down from a tree in a stiff horizontal position, with the belly hollowed to slow its descent. ● *Chrysopelea ornata*, family Colubridae.

flying squad ▸ noun Brit. a division of a police force or other organization which is capable of reaching an incident quickly.

flying squirrel ▸ noun a small squirrel that has skin joining the fore- and hindlimbs for gliding from tree to tree. ● Subfamily Pteromyinae, family Sciuridae (many species in SE Asia, northern Eurasia, and North America), and family Anomaluridae (several species in Africa; see also SCALY-TAILED SQUIRREL).

flying start ▸ noun a start of a race or time trial in which the starting point is passed at speed. ■ a good beginning, especially one giving an advantage over competitors: *the team **got off to a flying start** in last year's rally*.

flying suit ▸ noun a one-piece garment worn by the pilot and crew of a military or light aircraft.

flying trapeze ▸ noun another term for TRAPEZE (sense 1).

flying wing ▸ noun an aircraft with little or no fuselage and no tailplane.

fly kick chiefly Rugby ▸ noun a kick made while running.
▸ verb (**fly-kick**) [with obj.] kick (the ball) while running.

flyleaf ▸ noun (pl. **flyleaves**) a blank page at the beginning or end of a book.

flyman ▸ noun (pl. **flymen**) Theatre a person positioned in the flies to raise and lower scenery.

Flynn[1], Errol (1909–59), Australian-born American actor; born *Leslie Thomas Flynn*. He was best known for his roles as the swashbuckling hero of romantic costume dramas in films such as *Captain Blood* (1935) and *The Adventures of Robin Hood* (1938).

Flynn[2] ▸ noun (in phrase **be in like Flynn**) informal, chiefly N. Amer. & Austral. act quickly and impetuously; seize an opportunity.
– ORIGIN 1940s: probably from Errol *Flynn* (see FLYNN[1]), known for his wild behaviour.

fly orchid ▸ noun a European woodland orchid with flowers that resemble flies. ● *Ophrys insectifera*, family Orchidaceae.

flyover ▸ noun **1** chiefly Brit. a bridge carrying one railway line or road over another.
2 N. Amer. a low flight by one or more aircraft over a specific location. ■ another term for FLY-PAST.
3 [as modifier] US informal, derogatory denoting central regions of the US regarded as less significant than the East or West coasts: *his appeal extends way beyond the Bible Belt and the flyover states*.

flypaper ▸ noun [mass noun] sticky, poison-treated strips of paper that are hung indoors to catch and kill flies.

fly-past ▸ noun Brit. a ceremonial flight of aircraft past a person or a place.

fly-pitcher ▸ noun Brit. informal a street trader.
– DERIVATIVES **fly-pitching** noun.

fly-post ▸ verb [with obj.] Brit. put up (advertising posters) in unauthorized places.
– ORIGIN early 20th cent.: from ON THE FLY at FLY[1].

fly-poster ▸ noun Brit. **1** an advertising poster put up in an unauthorized place.
2 a person who fly-posts.

flysch /flɪʃ/ ▸ noun [mass noun] Geology a sedimentary deposit consisting of thin beds of shale or marl alternating with coarser strata such as sandstone or conglomerate.
– ORIGIN mid 19th cent.: from Swiss German dialect.

flysheet ▸ noun **1** Brit. a fabric cover pitched outside and over a tent to give extra protection against bad weather.
2 a tract or circular of two or four pages.

flyspeck ▸ noun a tiny stain made by the excrement of an insect. ■ a thing which is contemptibly small or insignificant: *a sleepy flyspeck of a town*.
– DERIVATIVES **flyspecked** adjective.

fly spray ▸ noun a substance sprayed from an aerosol that kills flying insects.

fly strike ▸ noun [mass noun] infestation of an animal with blowfly maggots.

fly swatter (also **fly swat**) ▸ noun an implement used for swatting insects.

fly-tip ▸ verb [no obj.] Brit. illegally dump waste.
– DERIVATIVES **fly-tipper** noun.
– ORIGIN 1960s: from ON THE FLY at FLY[1].

flytrap ▸ noun see VENUS FLYTRAP.

flyway ▸ noun Ornithology a route regularly used by large numbers of migrating birds.

flyweight ▸ noun [mass noun] a weight in boxing and other sports intermediate between light flyweight and bantamweight. In the amateur boxing scale it ranges from 48 to 51 kg. ■ [count noun] a flyweight boxer or other competitor.

flywheel ▸ noun a heavy revolving wheel in a machine which is used to increase the machine's momentum and thereby provide greater stability or a reserve of available power.

fly whisk ▸ noun see WHISK (sense 2 of the noun).

FM ▸ abbreviation ■ Field Marshal. ■ frequency modulation: [as modifier] *an FM radio station*.

Fm ▸ symbol the chemical element fermium.

fm ▸ abbreviation fathom(s).

FMCG ▸ abbreviation fast-moving consumer goods: [as modifier] *the FMCG sector*.

FMV ▸ abbreviation full-motion video.

f-number ▸ noun Photography the ratio of the focal length of a camera lens to the diameter of the aperture being used for a particular shot (e.g. *f8*, indicating that the focal length is eight times the diameter).
– ORIGIN early 20th cent.: from *f* (denoting the focal length) and NUMBER.

FO ▸ abbreviation ■ Flying Officer. ■ Foreign Office.

fo. ▸ abbreviation folio.

FOAF (also **FOF**) ▸ abbreviation friend of a friend, denoting a story or rumour which has no definite source and cannot be authenticated: *investigations never do succeed in finding the FOAF who started any of these yarns*.

foal ▸ noun a young horse or related animal.
▸ verb [no obj.] (of a mare) give birth to a foal. ■ (**be foaled**) (of a foal) be born.
– PHRASES **in** (or **with**) **foal** (of a mare) pregnant.
– ORIGIN Old English *fola*, of Germanic origin; related to Dutch *veulen* and German *Fohlen*, also to FILLY.

foam ▸ noun [mass noun] a mass of small bubbles formed on or in liquid, typically by agitation or fermentation: *a beer with a thick head of foam*. ■ a mass of small bubbles formed from saliva or sweat. ■ a liquid preparation containing many small bubbles: *shaving foam*. ■ a lightweight form of rubber or plastic made by solidifying such a liquid: [as modifier] *foam rubber*. ■ (**the foam**) literary the sea: *Venus rising from the foam*.
▸ verb [no obj.] form or produce a mass of small bubbles, froth: *the sea foamed beneath them* | (as adj. **foaming**) *pints of foaming bitter*.
– PHRASES **foam at the mouth** informal be very angry.
– DERIVATIVES **foamless** adjective.
– ORIGIN Old English *fām* (noun), *fǣman* (verb), of West Germanic origin; related to Old High German *feim* (noun), *feimen* (verb).

foam board ▸ noun [mass noun] a type of thin, pliable polystyrene board used for insulation and in arts and crafts.

foamy ▸ adjective (**foamier**, **foamiest**) producing or consisting of foam; frothy: *a beach with foamy waves* | *a mug of foamy beer*.

fob[1] ▸ noun (also **fob chain**) a chain attached to a watch for carrying in a waistcoat or waistband pocket. ■ a small ornament attached to a watch chain. ■ (also **fob pocket**) a small pocket for carrying a watch. ■ a tab on a key ring.
– ORIGIN mid 17th cent. (denoting a fob pocket in a waistband): origin uncertain; probably related to German dialect *Fuppe* 'pocket'.

fob[2] ▸ verb (**fobs**, **fobbing**, **fobbed**) [with obj.] (**fob someone off**) deceitfully attempt to satisfy someone by making excuses or giving them something inferior: *I was **fobbed off** with bland reassurances*. ■ (**fob something off on**) give (someone) something inferior to or different from what they want: *the second-rate products fobbed off on many beer-drinkers*.
– ORIGIN late Middle English (in the sense 'cheat out of'): origin uncertain; perhaps related to German *foppen* 'deceive, cheat, banter', or to FOP.

f.o.b. ▸ abbreviation free on board. See FREE.

fob watch ▸ noun a pocket watch.

focaccia /fəˈkatʃə/ ▸ noun [mass noun] a type of flat Italian bread made with yeast and olive oil and flavoured with herbs.
– ORIGIN Italian.

focal /ˈfəʊk(ə)l/ ▸ adjective **1** relating to the centre or most important part: *the focal symbol of sovereignty is the crown*.
2 Optics relating to the focus of a lens.
3 (of a disease or medical condition) occurring in one particular site in the body.
– DERIVATIVES **focally** adverb.
– ORIGIN late 17th cent.: from modern Latin *focalis*, from Latin *focus*, or directly from FOCUS.

focalize (also **focalise**) ▸ verb [with obj.] technical focus (something), in particular: ■ (in literary theory) provide an internal focus for (a text). ■ Medicine confine (a disease or infection) to a particular site in the body.
– DERIVATIVES **focalization** noun.

focal length ▸ noun the distance between the centre of a lens or curved mirror and its focus. ■ the equivalent distance in a compound lens or telescope.

focal plane ▸ noun the plane through the focus perpendicular to the axis of a mirror or lens.

focal point ▸ noun the point at which rays or waves meet after reflection or refraction, or the point from which diverging rays or waves appear to proceed.

F

■ the centre of interest or activity: *the community shop is the focal point of the village.*

Foch /fɒʃ/, Ferdinand (1851–1929), French general. He supported the use of offensive warfare which resulted in many of his 20th Corps being killed in August 1914. He was later the senior French representative at the Armistice negotiations.

fo'c'sle /ˈfəʊks(ə)l/ ▶ noun variant spelling of FORECASTLE.

focus ▶ noun (pl. **focuses** or **foci** /ˈfəʊsʌɪ/) **1** the centre of interest or activity: *this generation has made the environment a focus of attention.* ■ an act of concentrating interest or activity on something: *our focus on the customer's requirements.* ■ Geology the point of origin of an earthquake. Compare with EPICENTRE. ■ Medicine the principal site of an infection or other disease.
2 [mass noun] the state or quality of having or producing clear visual definition: *his face is rather out of focus* | figurative *the incident brought her feelings for Alexander sharply into focus.* ■ another term for FOCAL POINT. ■ [count noun] the point at which an object must be situated with respect to a lens or mirror for an image of it to be well defined. ■ [count noun] a device on a lens which can be adjusted to produce a clear image.
3 Geometry one of the fixed points from which the distances to any point of a given curve, such as an ellipse or parabola, are connected by a linear relation.
4 Linguistics an element of a sentence that is given prominence by intonational or other means.
▶ verb (**focuses, focusing, focused** or **focusses, focussing, focussed**) [no obj.] **1** adapt to the prevailing level of light and become able to see clearly: *try to focus on a stationary object.* ■ [with obj.] cause (one's eyes) to do this: *she focused her eyes on his face.* ■ [with obj.] adjust the focus of (a telescope, camera, or other instrument): *they were focusing a telescope on a star.* ■ (of rays or waves) meet at a single point. ■ [with obj.] (of a lens) make (rays or waves) meet at a single point. ■ [no obj.] (of light, radio waves, or other energy) become concentrated into a sharp beam. ■ [with obj.] (of a lens) concentrate (light, radio waves, or energy) into a sharp beam.
2 (**focus on**) pay particular attention to: *the study will focus on a number of areas in Wales.* ■ [with obj.] concentrate: *an opportunity to focus research on the health needs of the population.* ■ [with obj.] Linguistics place the focus on (an element of a sentence).
– DERIVATIVES **focuser** noun.
– ORIGIN mid 17th cent. (as a term in geometry and physics): from Latin, literally 'domestic hearth'.

focused (also **focussed**) ▶ adjective directing a great deal of attention, interest, or activity towards a particular aim: *Darren knows what he wants and he's very focused.*

focus group ▶ noun a group of people assembled to participate in a discussion about a product before it is launched, or to provide feedback on a political campaign, television series, etc.

focus puller ▶ noun an assistant to a film or television cameraman, who is responsible for keeping the lens focused during filming.

fodder ▶ noun [mass noun] food, especially dried hay or straw, for cattle and other livestock. ■ a person or thing regarded only as material for a specific use: *young people ending up as factory fodder.*
▶ verb [with obj.] give fodder to (cattle or other livestock).
– ORIGIN Old English *fōdor*, of Germanic origin; related to Dutch *voeder* and German *Futter*, also to FOOD.

fody /ˈfəʊdi/ ▶ noun (pl. **fodies**) a songbird of the weaver family occurring in Madagascar and islands in the Indian Ocean, the male of which typically has mainly red plumage. ● Genus *Foudia*, family Ploceidae: several species.
– ORIGIN a local word.

FoE ▶ abbreviation Friends of the Earth.

foe ▶ noun literary or formal an enemy or opponent: *his work was praised by friends and foes alike.*
– ORIGIN Old English *fāh* 'hostile' and *gefā* 'enemy', of West Germanic origin; related to FEUD.

foefie slide /ˈfʊfi/ ▶ noun S. African a rope or cable with a suspended handle or pulley by means of which one may slide between two points.
– ORIGIN from Afrikaans *foefie* 'stunt, trick' + SLIDE.

foehn ▶ noun variant spelling of FÖHN.

foetid ▶ adjective variant spelling of FETID.

foetor ▶ noun variant spelling of FETOR.

foetus ▶ noun variant spelling of FETUS (chiefly in British non-technical use).
– DERIVATIVES **foetal** adjective, **foeticide** noun.

FOF ▶ abbreviation variant of **FOAF**.

fog[1] ▶ noun **1** [mass noun] a thick cloud of tiny water droplets suspended in the atmosphere at or near the earth's surface which obscures or restricts visibility (to a greater extent than mist; strictly, reducing visibility to below 1 km): *the collision occurred in thick fog.* ■ [in sing.] an opaque mass of particles in the air: *a whirling fog of dust.* ■ Photography cloudiness which obscures the image on a developed negative or print.
2 [in sing.] a state or cause of perplexity or confusion: *the coffee helped clear the fog in my brain.*
▶ verb (**fogs, fogging, fogged**) [with obj.] **1** (with reference to a glass surface) cover or become covered with steam: [with obj.] *hot steam drifted about her, fogging up the window* | [no obj.] *the windscreen was starting to fog up.* ■ Photography make (a film, negative, or print) obscure or cloudy.
2 bewilder or puzzle: *she stared at him, confusion fogging her brain.* ■ make (an idea or situation) difficult to understand: *the government has been fogging the issue.*
3 spray with an insecticide.
– PHRASES **the fog of war** confusion caused by the chaos of war or battle: *he argues that the fog of war clouded everyone's judgement.*
– ORIGIN mid 16th cent.: perhaps a back-formation from FOGGY.

fog[2] ▶ noun [mass noun] the grass which grows in a field after a crop of hay has been taken. ■ long grass left standing in a pasture and used as winter grazing.
– ORIGIN late Middle English: origin uncertain; perhaps related to Norwegian *fogg*.

fog bank ▶ noun a dense mass of fog, especially at sea.

fogbound ▶ adjective unable to travel normally because of thick fog: *day after day we sat fogbound in East Anglia.* ■ enveloped or obscured by fog: *a fogbound motorway.*

fogbow ▶ noun a phenomenon similar to a rainbow, produced by sunlight shining on fog.

fogey /ˈfəʊgi/ (also **fogy**) ▶ noun (pl. **fogeys** or **fogies**) a very old-fashioned or conservative person: *a bunch of old fogeys.*
– DERIVATIVES **fogeydom** noun, **fogeyish** adjective, **fogeyism** noun.
– ORIGIN late 18th cent.: related to earlier slang *fogram*, of unknown origin.

Foggia /ˈfɒdʒə/ a town in SE Italy, in Apulia; pop. 153,239 (2008).

foggy ▶ adjective (**foggier, foggiest**) **1** full of or characterized by fog: *a dark and foggy night.*
2 unable to think clearly; confused: *she was foggy with sleep.* ■ indistinctly expressed or remembered; obscure: *my memories of the event are foggy.*
– PHRASES **not have the foggiest** (**idea** or **notion**) informal, chiefly Brit. have no idea at all.
– DERIVATIVES **foggily** adverb, **fogginess** noun.
– ORIGIN late 15th cent.: perhaps from FOG[2].

Foggy Bottom US informal the US State Department.
– ORIGIN the name of a riverside area of Washington DC where the department is based.

foghorn ▶ noun a device making a loud, deep sound as a warning to ships in fog.

fog lamp (also **fog light**) ▶ noun a bright light on a motor vehicle, used in foggy conditions to improve road visibility or warn other drivers of one's presence.

fogou /ˈfəʊguː, -gəʊ/ ▶ noun (pl. **fogous**) Archaeology a form of artificial underground passage or chamber found in Cornwall.
– ORIGIN from Cornish *fogo, fougo*.

fog signal ▶ noun a small explosive charge which can be placed on a railway line in fog to be set off by the train as a signal to the driver.

fogy ▶ noun variant spelling of FOGEY.

föhn /fəːn/ (also **foehn**) ▶ noun (often **the föhn**) a hot southerly wind on the northern slopes of the Alps. ■ (also **föhn wind**) Meteorology a warm dry wind of this type developing in the lee of any mountain range.
– ORIGIN mid 19th cent.: from German, based on Latin (*ventus*) *Favonius* 'mild west wind', *Favonius* being the Roman personification of the west or west wind.

foible /ˈfɔɪb(ə)l/ ▶ noun **1** a minor weakness or eccentricity in someone's character: *they have to tolerate each other's little foibles.*
2 Fencing the part of a sword blade from the middle to the point. Compare with FORTE[1].
– ORIGIN late 16th cent. (as an adjective in the sense 'feeble'): from obsolete French, in Old French *fieble* (see FEEBLE). Both noun senses also formerly occurred as senses of the word *feeble* and all date from the 17th cent.

foie gras /fwɑː ˈgrɑː/ ▶ noun the liver of a specially fattened goose or duck prepared as food. ■ short for PÂTÉ DE FOIE GRAS.
– ORIGIN French, 'fat liver'.

foil[1] ▶ verb [with obj.] prevent (something considered wrong or undesirable) from succeeding: *a brave policewoman foiled the armed robbery.* ■ frustrate the efforts or plans of: *their rivals were foiled by the weather.* ■ Hunting (of a hunted animal) run over or cross (ground or a scent or track) in such a way as to confuse the hounds.
▶ noun **1** Hunting the track or scent of a hunted animal.
2 archaic a setback in an enterprise; a defeat.
– ORIGIN Middle English (in the sense 'trample down'): perhaps from Old French *fouler* 'to full cloth, trample', based on Latin *fullo* 'fuller'. Compare with FULL[2].

foil[2] ▶ noun **1** [mass noun] metal hammered or rolled into a thin flexible sheet, used chiefly for covering or wrapping food: *aluminium foil.*
2 a person or thing that contrasts with and so emphasizes and enhances the qualities of another: *his white cravat was a perfect foil for his bronzed features.* ■ a thin leaf of metal placed under a precious stone to increase its brilliance.
3 Architecture a leaf-shaped curve formed by the cusping of an arch or circle.
– ORIGIN Middle English: via Old French from Latin *folium* 'leaf'.

foil[3] ▶ noun a light, blunt-edged fencing sword with a button on its point.
– DERIVATIVES **foilist** noun.
– ORIGIN late 16th cent.: of unknown origin.

foil[4] ▶ noun each of the structures fitted to a hydrofoil's hull to lift it clear of the water at speed.
– ORIGIN abbreviation of HYDROFOIL.

foist /fɔɪst/ ▶ verb [with obj.] (**foist someone/thing on**) impose an unwelcome or unnecessary person or thing on: *she had no desire to have an elderly relative foisted on her.*
– ORIGIN mid 16th cent. (in the sense 'palm a false die, so as to produce it at the right moment'): from Dutch dialect *vuisten* 'take in the hand', from *vuist* (see FIST).

Fokine /ˈfəʊkiːn/, Michel (1880–1942), Russian-born American dancer and choreographer; born *Mikhail Mikhailovich Fokin*. He was a reformer of modern ballet: as Diaghilev's chief choreographer he staged the premieres of Chopin's *Les Sylphides* (1909) and Stravinsky's *The Firebird* (1910).

Fokker /ˈfɒkə/, Anthony Herman Gerard (1890–1939), Dutch-born American aircraft designer and pilot. Having built his first aircraft in 1908, he designed fighters used by the Germans in the First World War and founded the Fokker company.

fol. ▶ abbreviation folio.

folacin /ˈfəʊləsɪn/ ▶ noun another term for FOLIC ACID.

folate /ˈfəʊleɪt/ ▶ noun Biochemistry a salt or ester of folic acid.

fold[1] ▶ verb [with obj.] **1** bend (something flexible and relatively flat) over on itself so that one part of it covers another: *Sam folded up the map.* ■ (**fold something in/into**) mix an ingredient gently with (another ingredient), especially by lifting a mixture with a spoon so as to enclose it without stirring or beating: *fold the egg whites into the chocolate mixture.* ■ [no obj.] (of a piece of furniture or equipment) be able to be bent or rearranged into a flatter or more compact shape, typically in order to make it easier to store or carry: [with complement] *the deckchair folds flat* | (as adj. **folding**) *a folding chair.* ■ bend or rearrange (a piece of furniture or equipment) into a flatter or more compact shape: *the small card table was folded up and put away.* ■ [no obj.] (**fold out**) be able to be opened out; unfold: *the sofa folds out.* ■ Geology cause (rock strata) to undergo bending or curvature. ■ Biochemistry (of a polypeptide or polynucleotide chain) adopt a specific three-dimensional structure.
2 [with adverbial] cover or wrap something in (a soft or flexible material): *a bag was folded around the book.* ■ hold or clasp (someone) in one's arms affectionately or passionately: *Bob folded her in his arms.*
3 [no obj.] informal (of an enterprise or organization) cease trading or operating as a result of financial

problems: *the club folded earlier this year.* ■ (especially of a sports player or team) suddenly stop performing well or effectively. ■ (in poker and other card games) drop out of a hand.
▶ noun **1** (usu. **folds**) a form or shape produced by the gentle draping of a loose, full garment or piece of cloth: *the fabric fell in soft folds.* ■ an area of skin that sags or hangs loosely.
2 chiefly Brit. a slight hill or hollow in the ground: *the house lay in a fold of the hills.* ■ Geology a bend or curvature of strata.
3 a line or crease produced in paper or cloth as the result of folding it. ■ a piece of paper or cloth that has been folded: *a fold of paper slipped out of the diary.*
– PHRASES **fold one's arms** bring one's arms together and cross them over one's chest. **fold one's hands** bring or hold one's hands together.
– DERIVATIVES **foldable** adjective.
– ORIGIN Old English *falden, fealden*, of Germanic origin; related to Dutch *vouwen* and German *falten.*

fold[2] ▶ noun a pen or enclosure in a field where livestock, especially sheep, can be kept. ■ (**the fold**) a group or community, especially when perceived as having shared aims and values: *government whips tried to persuade the waverers back into the fold.*
▶ verb [with obj.] shut (livestock) in a fold.
– ORIGIN Old English *fald*, of Germanic origin; related to Dutch *vaalt.*

-fold ▶ suffix forming adjectives and adverbs from cardinal numbers: **1** in an amount multiplied by: *threefold.*
2 consisting of so many parts or facets: *twofold.*
– ORIGIN Old English *-fald, -feald*; related to FOLD[1].

foldaway ▶ adjective [attrib.] adapted or designed to be folded up for ease of storage or transport: *a foldaway table.*

folder ▶ noun **1** a folding cover or holder, typically made of stiff paper or card, for storing loose papers. ■ Computing a directory containing related files or documents.
2 N. Amer. a folded leaflet or a booklet made of folded sheets of paper.

folderol /ˈfɒldərɒl/ (also **falderal**) ▶ noun [mass noun] **1** trivial or nonsensical fuss: *all the folderol of the athletic contests and the cheerleaders.*
2 dated a showy but useless item.
– ORIGIN early 18th cent.: first used as a meaningless refrain in popular songs.

folding door ▶ noun a door with vertical jointed sections that can be folded together to one side to allow access to a room or building.

folding money ▶ noun [mass noun] informal money in the form of notes.

fold-out ▶ adjective [attrib.] (of a page in a book or magazine or a piece of furniture) designed to be opened out for use and folded away for convenient storage: *a fold-out map.*
▶ noun a fold-out page or piece of furniture.

foley /ˈfəʊli/ ▶ noun [as modifier] relating to or concerned with the addition of recorded sound effects after the shooting of a film: *a foley artist.*
– ORIGIN named after the US film technician Jack Foley (1891–1967), the inventor of the process.

folia plural form of FOLIUM.

foliaceous /ˌfəʊlɪˈeɪʃəs/ ▶ adjective **1** of or resembling a leaf or leaves.
2 chiefly Geology consisting of thin sheets or laminae.
– ORIGIN mid 17th cent.: from Latin *foliaceus* 'leafy' (from *folium* 'leaf') + -OUS.

foliage /ˈfəʊlɪɪdʒ/ ▶ noun [mass noun] plant leaves collectively: *healthy green foliage.*
– ORIGIN late Middle English *foilage* (in the sense 'design resembling leaves'): from Old French *feuillage*, from *feuille* 'leaf', from Latin *folium*. The change in the first syllable was due to association with Latin *folium.*

foliage leaf ▶ noun Botany a normal leaf, as opposed to petals and other modified leaves.

foliar /ˈfəʊlɪə/ ▶ adjective [attrib.] technical relating to leaves: *foliar colour and shape.*
– ORIGIN late 19th cent.: from modern Latin *foliaris*, from Latin *folium* 'leaf'.

foliar feed ▶ noun [mass noun] nutrients supplied to the leaves of a plant.
– DERIVATIVES **foliar feeding** noun.

foliate ▶ adjective /ˈfəʊlɪət, -eɪt/ decorated with leaves or leaf-like motifs: *foliate scrolls.*
▶ verb /ˈfəʊlɪeɪt/ [with obj.] **1** decorate with leaves or leaf-like motifs.
2 number the leaves of (a book) rather than the pages.
– ORIGIN mid 17th cent.: from Latin *foliatus* 'leaved', from *folium* 'leaf'.

foliated ▶ adjective **1** decorated with leaves or leaf-like motifs. ■ Architecture decorated with foils.
2 chiefly Geology consisting of thin sheets or laminae.

foliation /ˌfəʊlɪˈeɪʃ(ə)n/ ▶ noun [mass noun] chiefly Geology the process of splitting into thin sheets or laminae.

folic acid /ˈfəʊlɪk, ˈfɒl-/ ▶ noun [mass noun] Biochemistry a vitamin of the B complex found especially in leafy green vegetables, liver, and kidney. Also called PTEROYLGLUTAMIC ACID, VITAMIN M.
– ORIGIN 1940s: *folic* from Latin *folium* 'leaf' + -IC.

folie à deux /ˌfɒlɪ a ˈdəː/ ▶ noun (pl. **folies à deux**) [mass noun] delusion or mental illness shared by two people in close association.
– ORIGIN French, literally 'shared madness'.

folie de grandeur /ˌfɒlɪ də ɡrɒ̃ˈdəː/ ▶ noun [mass noun] delusions of grandeur.
– ORIGIN French.

Folies-Bergère /ˌfɒlɪbɛːˈʒɛː/, French /fɔli bɛʀʒɛʀ/ a variety theatre in Paris, opened in 1869, known for its lavish productions featuring nude and semi-nude female performers.

folio /ˈfəʊlɪəʊ/ ▶ noun (pl. **folios**) **1** an individual leaf of paper or parchment, either loose as one of a series or forming part of a bound volume, which is numbered on the recto or front side only. ■ the page number in a printed book.
2 a sheet of paper folded once to form two leaves (four pages) of a book. ■ a size of book made up of such sheets. ■ a book or manuscript made up of sheets of paper folded in such a way; a volume of the largest standard size.
– ORIGIN late Middle English: from Latin, ablative of *folium* 'leaf', in medieval Latin used in references to mean 'on leaf so-and-so'. The original sense of *in folio* (from Italian *in foglio*) was 'in the form of a full-sized sheet or leaf folded once' (designating the largest size of book).

foliose /ˈfəʊlɪəʊs, -z/ ▶ adjective Botany (of a lichen) having a lobed, leaf-like shape.
– ORIGIN early 18th cent.: from Latin *foliosus*, from *folium* 'leaf'.

folium /ˈfəʊlɪəm/ ▶ noun (pl. **folia**) technical a thin leaf-like structure, e.g. in some rocks or in the cerebellum of the brain.
– ORIGIN mid 18th cent.: from Latin, literally 'leaf'.

folivore /ˈfəʊlɪvɔː/ ▶ noun Zoology an animal that feeds on leaves.
– DERIVATIVES **folivorous** adjective.

folk /fəʊk/ ▶ plural noun **1** (also **folks**) informal people in general: *her parents were country folk | an old folks' home.* ■ (**folks**) used as a friendly form of address to a group of people: *meanwhile folks, why not relax and enjoy the atmosphere?* ■ (**one's folks**) chiefly N. Amer. the members of one's family, especially one's parents: *his folks still live here.*
2 [mass noun] folk music: *a mixture of folk and reggae* | [as modifier] *a folk singer.*
▶ adjective [attrib.] relating to the traditional art or culture of a community or nation: *a folk museum.* ■ relating to or originating from the beliefs and opinions of ordinary people: *a folk hero | folk wisdom.*
– ORIGIN Old English *folc*, of Germanic origin; related to Dutch *volk* and German *Volk.*

folk dance ▶ noun a popular dance considered as part of the tradition of a particular people or area.
– DERIVATIVES **folk dancer** noun, **folk dancing** noun.

folk devil ▶ noun a person or thing held to be a bad influence on society: *the strikers had been identified and pilloried as the new folk devils.*

Folkestone /ˈfəʊkstən/ a seaport and resort in Kent, on the SE coast of England; pop. 45,400 (est. 2009).

folk etymology ▶ noun a popular but mistaken account of the origin of a word or phrase. ■ [mass noun] the process by which the form of an unfamiliar or foreign word is adapted to a more familiar form through popular usage.

folkie ▶ noun informal a singer, player, or fan of folk music.

folkish ▶ adjective **1** characteristic of ordinary people or traditional culture: *folkish humour.*
2 relating to or resembling folk music: *the most conventionally folkish number on the album.*

folklife ▶ noun [mass noun] the way of life of a rural or traditional community.

folklore ▶ noun [mass noun] the traditional beliefs, customs, and stories of a community, passed through the generations by word of mouth. ■ a body of popular myths or beliefs relating to a particular place, activity, or group of people: *Hollywood folklore.*
– DERIVATIVES **folkloric** adjective, **folklorist** noun, **folkloristic** adjective.

folk memory ▶ noun a recollection or body of recollections of the past that persists among a particular group of people.

folk music ▶ noun [mass noun] music that originates in traditional popular culture or that is written in such a style. Folk music is typically of unknown authorship and is transmitted orally from generation to generation.

folk rock ▶ noun [mass noun] popular music resembling or derived from folk music but incorporating the stronger beat of rock music and using electric instruments.

folk song ▶ noun a song that originates in traditional popular culture or that is written in such a style.
– DERIVATIVES **folk singer** noun.

folksonomy /fəʊkˈsɒnəmi/ ▶ noun a user-generated system of classifying and organizing online content into different categories by the use of metadata such as electronic tags.
– ORIGIN early 21st cent.: blend of *folks* (see FOLK) and TAXONOMY.

folksy ▶ adjective (**folksier, folksiest**) **1** having the characteristics of traditional culture and customs, especially in a contrived or artificial way: *the shop's folksy, small-town image.*
2 informal and unpretentious: *his folksy, direct style.*
– DERIVATIVES **folksiness** noun.

folk tale ▶ noun a story originating in popular culture, typically passed on by word of mouth.

folkways ▶ plural noun the traditional behaviour or way of life of a particular community or group of people: *a study of Cherokee folklore and folkways.*

folky ▶ adjective (**folkier, folkiest**) another term for FOLKSY or FOLKISH.
– DERIVATIVES **folkiness** noun.

follicle /ˈfɒlɪk(ə)l/ ▶ noun **1** Anatomy a small secretory cavity, sac, or gland, in particular: ■ (also **hair follicle**) the sheath of cells and connective tissue which surrounds the root of a hair. ■ short for GRAAFIAN FOLLICLE.
2 Botany a dry fruit that is derived from a single carpel and opens on one side only to release its seeds.
– DERIVATIVES **follicular** /fɒˈlɪkjʊlə/ adjective, **follicularly** adverb, **folliculate** /-lət/ adjective, **folliculated** adjective.
– ORIGIN late Middle English: from Latin *folliculus* 'little bag', diminutive of *follis* 'bellows'.

follicle mite ▶ noun a parasitic mite which burrows into the hair follicles, causing demodectic mange.
● Genus *Demodex*, family Demodicidae.

follicle-stimulating hormone (abbrev.: **FSH**) ▶ noun Biochemistry a hormone secreted by the anterior pituitary gland which promotes the formation of ova or sperm.

folliculitis /fəˌlɪkjʊˈlʌɪtɪs/ ▶ noun [mass noun] Medicine inflammation of the hair follicles.

follis /ˈfɒlɪs/ ▶ noun (pl. **folles**) a bronze or copper coin of a type introduced by the Roman emperor Diocletian in AD 296 and also used later in Byzantine currency.
– ORIGIN Latin.

follow ▶ verb [with obj.] **1** go or come after (a person or thing proceeding ahead); move or travel behind: *she went back into the house, and Ben followed her* | [no obj.] *the men followed in another car.* ■ go after (someone) in order to observe or monitor them: *the KGB man followed her everywhere.* ■ archaic strive after; aim at: *I follow fame.* ■ go along (a route or path). ■ (of a route or path) go in the same direction as or parallel to (another): *the road follows the track of the railway line.* ■ trace the movement or direction of: *she followed his gaze, peering into the gloom.*
2 come after in time or order: *the six years that followed his restoration* | [no obj.] *the rates are* **as follows**. ■ happen after (something else) as a consequence: *raucous laughter followed the ribald remark | the announcement* **followed on from** *the collapse of the merchant bank* | [no obj.] *retribution soon followed.* ■ [no obj.] be a logical consequence of something: *it thus* **follows from** *this equation that the value must be negative.* ■ [with obj. and adverbial] (of a person) do something after (something else): *they* **follow** *their March show* **with** *four UK dates next month.* ■ have

(a dish or course) after another or others during a meal: *turkey was followed by dessert.*
3 act according to (an instruction or precept): *he has difficulty in following written instructions.* ■ conform to: *the film faithfully follows Shakespeare's plot.* ■ act according to the lead or example of (someone): *he follows Aristotle in believing this.* ■ treat as a teacher or guide: *those who seek to follow Jesus Christ.*
4 pay close attention to: *I've been following this discussion closely.* ■ take an active interest in or be a supporter of: *supporters who have followed the club through thick and thin.* ■ (of a book, film, programme, etc.) be concerned with the development of: *the book follows the life and career of Henry Clay.* ■ understand the meaning or tendency of (a speaker or argument): *I still don't follow you.*
5 practise (a trade or profession). ■ undertake or carry out (a course of action or study): *she followed a strict diet.*
– PHRASES **follow in someone's footsteps** see FOOTSTEP. **follow one's nose 1** trust to one's instincts. **2** move along guided by one's sense of smell. **3** go straight ahead. **follow suit** (in bridge, whist, and other card games) play a card of the suit led. ■ conform to another's actions: *Spain cut its rates by half a per cent but no other country has followed suit.*
– PHRASAL VERBS **follow on** (of a cricket team) be required to bat again immediately after failing in their first innings to reach a score within a set number of runs of the score made by their opponents. **follow through** (in golf, cricket, and other sports) continue the movement of a stroke after the ball has been struck. **follow something through** continue an action or task to its conclusion. **follow something up** pursue or investigate something further: *I decided to follow up the letters with phone calls.*
– ORIGIN Old English *folgian*, of Germanic origin; related to Dutch *volgen* and German *folgen*.

follower ▶ noun **1** a person who supports and admires a particular person or set of ideas: *followers of Nietzsche.* ■ a person who takes an active interest in a particular activity: *he is a keen follower of football.*
2 a person who moves or travels behind someone or something.
– DERIVATIVES **followership** noun.

following ▶ preposition coming after or as a result of: *police are hunting for two men following a spate of robberies in the area.*
▶ noun **1** a body of supporters or admirers: *he attracted a worldwide following.*
2 (**the following**) [treated as sing. or pl.] what follows or comes next: *the following are both grammatically correct sentences.*
▶ adjective [attrib.] **1** next in time: *the following day there was a ceremony in St Peter's Square.* ■ about to be mentioned: *you are required to provide us with the following information.*
2 (of a wind) blowing in the same direction as the course of a vessel etc.

follow-on ▶ noun a thing which follows on from another: *it will act as the follow-on to the current version of the software.* ■ Cricket a second innings played immediately after their first by a team that failed to reach a score within a set number of runs of that made by their opponents.

follow-the-leader (also **follow-my-leader**) ▶ noun a children's game in which the participants must copy the actions and words of a person who has been chosen as leader. ■ the copying of the actions of others, often without consideration of their suitability for oneself: *consumers* ***play follow-the-leader*** *when it comes to buying fashion.*

follow-through ▶ noun [mass noun] continuation of the movement of a bat, racket, or club after striking a ball. ■ the continuing of an action or task to its conclusion: *the firm assures follow-through on all aspects of the contract.*

follow-up ▶ noun a continuation or repetition of something that has already been started or done: [as modifier] *a follow-up study of the same interviewees after retirement.* ■ a further examination or observation of a patient in order to monitor the success of earlier treatment. ■ a piece of work that builds on or exploits the success of earlier work: *she is writing a follow-up to Jane Austen's Pride and Prejudice.*

folly ▶ noun (pl. **follies**) **1** [mass noun] lack of good sense; foolishness: *an act of sheer folly.* ■ [count noun] a foolish act, idea, or practice: *the follies of youth.*
2 a costly ornamental building with no practical purpose, especially a tower or mock-Gothic ruin built in a large garden or park.
3 (**Follies**) a theatrical revue with glamorous female performers: [in names] *the Ziegfeld Follies.*
– ORIGIN Middle English: from Old French *folie* 'madness', in modern French also 'delight, favourite dwelling' (compare with sense 2), from *fol* 'fool, foolish'.

Folsom /ˈfəʊlsəm/ ▶ noun [usu. as modifier] Archaeology a Palaeo-Indian culture of Central and North America, dated to about 10,500–8,000 years ago. The culture is distinguished by fluted stone projectile points or spearheads (**Folsom points**). Compare with CLOVIS[2].
– ORIGIN early 20th cent.: from *Folsom*, NE New Mexico, the area where remains were first found.

Fomalhaut /ˈfəʊm(ə)l,hɔːt, -mə,ləʊt/ Astronomy the brightest star in the constellation Piscis Austrinus.
– ORIGIN Arabic, 'mouth of the fish'.

foment /fə(ʊ)ˈmɛnt/ ▶ verb [with obj.] **1** instigate or stir up (an undesirable or violent sentiment or course of action): *they accused him of fomenting political unrest.*
2 archaic bathe (a part of the body) with warm or medicated lotions.
– DERIVATIVES **fomenter** noun.
– ORIGIN late Middle English (in sense 2): from French *fomenter*, from late Latin *fomentare*, from Latin *fomentum* 'poultice, lotion', from *fovere* 'to heat, cherish'.

fomentation /,fəʊmɛnˈteɪʃ(ə)n/ ▶ noun **1** [mass noun] the action of instigating or stirring up undesirable sentiment or actions: *the fomentation of discontent.*
2 archaic a poultice.
– ORIGIN late Middle English: from late Latin *fomentatio(n-)*, from the verb *fomentare* (see FOMENT).

fomites /ˈfəʊmɪtiːz/ ▶ plural noun Medicine objects or materials which are likely to carry infection, such as clothes, utensils, and furniture.
– ORIGIN early 19th cent.: from Latin, plural of *fomes*, literally 'touchwood, tinder'.

Fon /fɒn/ ▶ noun (pl. **same** or **Fons**) **1** a member of a people inhabiting the southern part of Benin.
2 [mass noun] the language of the Fon, belonging to the Kwa group, with about 1 million speakers.
▶ adjective relating to the Fon or their language.
– ORIGIN the name in Fon.

fond ▶ adjective **1** (**fond of**) having an affection or liking for: *I'm very fond of Mel | he was not too fond of dancing.* ■ [attrib.] affectionate; loving: *I have very fond memories of Oxford | a fond farewell.*
2 [attrib.] (of a hope or belief) foolishly optimistic; naive.
– DERIVATIVES **fondly** adverb.
– ORIGIN late Middle English (in the sense 'infatuated, foolish'): from obsolete *fon* 'a fool, be foolish', of unknown origin. Compare with FUN.

Fonda /ˈfɒndə/ a family of American actors. **Henry Fonda** (1905–82) was noted for his roles in such films as *The Grapes of Wrath* (1939) and *Twelve Angry Men* (1957). He won his only Oscar for his role in his final film, *On Golden Pond* (1981). His daughter **Jane** (b.1937) is known for films including *Klute* (1971), for which she won an Oscar, and *The China Syndrome* (1979); she also acted alongside her father in *On Golden Pond*.

fondant /ˈfɒnd(ə)nt/ ▶ noun [mass noun] a thick paste made of sugar and water and often flavoured or coloured, used in the making of sweets and the icing and decoration of cakes. ■ [count noun] a sweet made of fondant.
– ORIGIN late 19th cent.: from French, literally 'melting', present participle of *fondre*.

fondle ▶ verb [with obj.] stroke or caress lovingly or erotically: *he kissed and fondled her.*
▶ noun an act of fondling.
– DERIVATIVES **fondler** noun.
– ORIGIN late 17th cent. (in the sense 'pamper'): back-formation from obsolete *fondling* 'much-loved or petted person', from FOND + -LING.

fondness ▶ noun [mass noun] affection or liking for someone or something: *I remember him with great fondness | I have a* ***fondness for*** *spicy food.*

fondu /fɒ̃ˈd(j)uː/ ▶ adjective [postpositive] Ballet (of a position) involving a lowering of the body by bending the knee of the supporting leg: *an arabesque fondu.*
– ORIGIN French, literally 'melted'.

fondue /ˈfɒnd(j)uː/ ▶ noun a dish in which small pieces of food are dipped into a hot sauce or a hot cooking medium such as oil or broth.
– ORIGIN French, feminine past participle of *fondre* 'to melt'.

fons et origo /,fɒnz ɛt ˈɒrɪgəʊ, ɒˈrʌɪgəʊ/ ▶ noun the source and origin of something: *they recognized the sixties as the fons et origo of music as they knew it.*
– ORIGIN Latin, originally as *fons et origo mali* 'the source and origin of evil'.

font[1] ▶ noun **1** a receptacle in a church for the water used in baptism, typically a free-standing stone structure.
2 a reservoir for oil in an oil lamp.
– DERIVATIVES **fontal** adjective.
– ORIGIN late Old English: from Latin *fons, font-* 'spring, fountain', occurring in the ecclesiastical Latin phrase *fons* or *fontes baptismi* 'baptismal water(s)'.

font[2] (Brit. also **fount**) ▶ noun Printing a set of type of one particular face and size.
– ORIGIN late 16th cent. (denoting the action or process of casting or founding): from French *fonte*, from *fondre* 'to melt'.

fontanelle /,fɒntəˈnɛl/ (US **fontanel**) ▶ noun a space between the bones of the skull in an infant or fetus, where ossification is not complete and the sutures not fully formed. The main one is between the frontal and parietal bones.
– ORIGIN mid 16th cent. (denoting a hollow of the skin between muscles): from French, from modern Latin *fontanella*, from an Old French diminutive of *fontaine* (see FOUNTAIN). The current sense dates from the mid 18th cent.

Fonteyn /fɒnˈteɪn/, Dame Margot (1919–91), English ballet dancer; born *Margaret Hookham*. In 1962 she began a celebrated partnership with Rudolf Nureyev, dancing with him in *Giselle* and *Romeo and Juliet*. In 1979 she was named ***prima ballerina assoluta***, a title given only three times in the history of ballet.

fontina /fɒnˈtiːnə/ ▶ noun [mass noun] a kind of pale yellow Italian cheese.
– ORIGIN from Italian.

Foochow /fuːˈtʃaʊ/ variant of FUZHOU.

food ▶ noun [mass noun] any nutritious substance that people or animals eat or drink or that plants absorb in order to maintain life and growth: *tins of cat food* | [count noun] *baby foods.*
– PHRASES **food for thought** something that warrants serious consideration.
– ORIGIN late Old English *fōda*, of Germanic origin; related to FODDER.

Food and Agriculture Organization (abbrev.: **FAO**) an agency of the United Nations established in 1945 to secure improvements in the production and distribution of all food and agricultural products and to raise levels of nutrition. Its headquarters are in Rome.

food bank ▶ noun N. Amer. a place supplying food to poor or destitute people.

food body ▶ noun Botany a small nutrient-rich structure developed on the leaves, flowers, or petioles of some tropical plants to attract ants.

food chain ▶ noun a series of organisms each dependent on the next as a source of food.

food court ▶ noun N. Amer. an area in a shopping mall where fast-food outlets are located.

food fish ▶ noun a species of fish which is used as food by humans, or forms a major part of the diet of a particular predator.

foodgrain ▶ noun any of a variety of grains that are grown for human consumption, such as wheat, oats, etc.

food hall ▶ noun Brit. a large section of a department store, where food is sold.

foodie (also **foody**) ▶ noun (pl. **foodies**) informal a person with a particular interest in food; a gourmet.

food mile ▶ noun Brit. a mile over which a food item is transported during the journey from producer to consumer, as a unit of measurement of the fuel used to transport it.

food poisoning ▶ noun [mass noun] illness caused by bacteria or other toxins in food, typically with vomiting and diarrhoea.

food processor ▶ noun an electric kitchen appliance used for chopping, mixing, or puréeing foods.

food stamp ▶ noun (in the US) a voucher issued cheaply by the state to those on low income and exchangeable for food.

foodstuff ▶ noun a substance suitable for consumption as food.

food value ▶ noun [mass noun] the nutritional value of a foodstuff.

food web ▶ noun Ecology a system of interlocking and interdependent food chains.

foody ▶ noun (pl. **foodies**) variant spelling of FOODIE.

foo fighter ▶ noun an unidentified flying object, originally one of a kind reported by US pilots during the Second World War, usually described as a bright light or ball of fire.
– ORIGIN 1940s: from 'Where there's foo there's fire', a nonsense catchphrase from the US *Smoky Stover* cartoon strip.

foo-foo ▶ noun variant spelling of FUFU.

fool[1] ▶ noun **1** a person who acts unwisely or imprudently; a silly person: *I felt a bit of a fool.* ■ archaic a person who is duped or imposed on: *he is the fool of circumstances.*
2 historical a jester or clown, especially one retained in a royal or noble household.
▶ verb **1** [with obj.] trick or deceive (someone); dupe: *don't be* **fooled into** *paying out any more of your hard-earned cash* | *she tried to* **fool herself** *that she had stopped loving him.*
2 [no obj.] act in a joking, frivolous, or teasing way: *some lads in the pool were* **fooling around**. ■ [no obj.] (**fool around**) chiefly N. Amer. engage in casual or extramarital sexual activity.
▶ adjective [attrib.] informal foolish; silly: *that damn fool waiter.*
– PHRASES **be no** (or **nobody's**) **fool** be a shrewd or prudent person. **a fool and his money are soon parted** proverb a foolish person spends money carelessly and will soon be penniless. **fools rush in where angels fear to tread** proverb people without good sense or judgement will have no hesitation in tackling a situation that even the wisest would avoid. **make a fool of** trick or deceive (someone) so that they look foolish. ■ (**make a fool of oneself**) behave in an incompetent or inappropriate way that makes one appear foolish. **more fool ——** used to convey that a specified person is behaving unwisely: *if suckers will actually pay to do the work, more fool them.* **play** (or **act**) **the fool** behave in a playful or silly way. **there's no fool like an old fool** proverb the foolish behaviour of an older person seems especially foolish as they are expected to think and act more sensibly than a younger one. **you could have fooled me!** used to express cynicism or doubt about an assertion: *'Fun, was it? Well, you could have fooled me!'*
– ORIGIN Middle English: from Old French *fol* 'fool, foolish', from Latin *follis* 'bellows, windbag', by extension 'empty-headed person'.

fool[2] ▶ noun [mass noun] [usu. with modifier] chiefly Brit. a cold dessert made of puréed fruit mixed or served with cream or custard: *raspberry fool with cream.*
– ORIGIN late 16th cent.: perhaps from FOOL[1].

foolery ▶ noun [mass noun] silly or foolish behaviour.

foolhardy ▶ adjective (**foolhardier**, **foolhardiest**) recklessly bold or rash: *it would be foolhardy to go into the scheme without support.*
– DERIVATIVES **foolhardily** adverb, **foolhardiness** noun.
– ORIGIN Middle English: from Old French *folhardi*, from *fol* 'foolish' + *hardi* 'bold' (see HARDY).

foolish ▶ adjective lacking good sense or judgement; unwise: *he was foolish enough to confide in her* | *a foolish decision.*

foolishly ▶ adverb in an unwise manner; stupidly: *they were condemned for acting foolishly* | *foolishly, I decided to give it a go.*

foolishness ▶ noun [mass noun] lack of good sense or judgement; stupidity: *she was realizing the foolishness of her actions.*

foolproof ▶ adjective incapable of going wrong or being misused: *a foolproof security system.*

foolscap /ˈfuːlzkap, ˈfuːls-/ ▶ noun [mass noun] Brit. a size of paper, about 330 × 200 (or 400) mm. ■ paper of this size: *several sheets of foolscap.*
– ORIGIN late 17th cent.: said to be named from a former watermark representing a fool's cap.

fool's errand ▶ noun a task or activity that has no hope of success.

fool's gold ▶ noun [mass noun] a brassy yellow mineral that can be mistaken for gold, especially pyrites.

fool's mate ▶ noun see MATE[2].

fool's paradise ▶ noun a state of happiness based on a person's not knowing about or denying the existence of potential trouble: *they were living in a fool's paradise, refusing to accept that they were in debt.*

fool's parsley ▶ noun a poisonous white-flowered plant of the parsley family, with fern-like leaves and an unpleasant smell, native to Eurasia and North Africa. ● *Aethusa cynapium*, family Umbelliferae.

fooster /ˈfuːstə/ ▶ verb [no obj.] Irish busy oneself in a restless or agitated way: *he was foostering around his caravan.*
– ORIGIN late 19th cent.: from Irish *fústar* 'bustle, fussy behaviour'.

foot ▶ noun (pl. **feet** /fiːt/) **1** the lower extremity of the leg below the ankle, on which a person stands or walks. ■ a corresponding part of the leg in vertebrate animals. ■ the part of a sock, stocking, etc. that covers the foot. ■ W. Indian a person's body below the torso, including the entire leg and the foot. ■ [mass noun] literary a person's manner or speed of walking or running: *fleet of foot.* ■ [treated as pl.] Brit. historical or formal infantry; foot soldiers: *a captain of foot.*
2 something resembling a foot in form or function, in particular: ■ a projecting part on which a piece of furniture or each of its legs stands. ■ a device on a sewing machine for holding the material steady as it is sewn. ■ Zoology a locomotory or adhesive organ of an invertebrate. ■ Botany the part by which a petal is attached.
3 the lower or lowest part of something; the base or bottom: *the foot of the stairs* | *complete the form at the foot of the page.* ■ the end of a table that is furthest from where the host sits. ■ the end of a bed, couch, or grave where the occupant's feet normally rest. ■ the lower edge of a sail.
4 a unit of linear measure equal to 12 inches (30.48 cm): *shallow water no more than a foot deep* | *he's about six feet tall.* ■ [usu. as modifier] Music a unit used in describing a set of organ pipes according to its pitch, the designation being the length of one particular pipe: *an 8-foot reed stop.* ■ [usu. as modifier] Music a unit used in describing a set of harpsichord strings playing at the same pitch as a set of organ pipes of the same designation: *the 16-foot register.*
5 Prosody a group of syllables constituting a metrical unit. In English poetry it consists of stressed and unstressed syllables, while in ancient classical poetry it consists of long and short syllables.
▶ verb [with obj.] informal **1** (**foot it**) cover a distance, especially a long one, on foot: *the rider was left to foot it ten or twelve miles back to camp.* ■ [no obj.] archaic dance.
2 pay (the bill) for something, typically when the amount is considered large or unreasonable.
– PHRASES **at someone's feet** as someone's disciple or subject. **be rushed** (or **run**) **off one's feet** be very busy. **feet first** with the feet in front. ■ dead, as in a coffin: *they hoped to be carried feet first out of the house they lived in for twenty-five years.* **feet of clay** a fundamental flaw or weakness in a person otherwise revered. [with biblical allusion (Dan. 2:33) to the dream of Nebuchadnezzar, in which a magnificent idol has feet 'part of iron and part of clay'; Daniel interprets this to signify a future kingdom that will be 'partly strong, and partly broken', and will eventually fall.] **get one's feet under the table** chiefly Brit. establish oneself securely in a new situation. **get one's feet wet** begin to participate in an activity. **get** (or **start**) **off on the right** (or **wrong**) **foot** make a good (or bad) start at something. **have something at one's feet** have something in one's power or command: *a perfect couple with the world at their feet.* **have** (or **keep**) **one's** (or **both**) **feet on the ground** be (or remain) practical and sensible. **have a foot in both camps** have an interest or stake concurrently in two parties or sides: *I can have a foot in both the creative and business camps.* **have** (or **get**) **a foot in the door** have (or gain) a first introduction to a profession or organization. **have one foot in the grave** informal, often humorous be near death through old age or illness. **my foot!** informal said to express strong contradiction: *'He's clever at his business,' Matilda said. 'Clever my foot!'* **off one's feet** so as to be no longer standing: *she was blown off her feet by the shock wave from the explosion.* **on one's feet** standing: *she's in the shop on her feet all day.* ■ well enough after an illness or injury to walk about: *we'll have you back on your feet in no time.* **on** (or **by**) **foot** walking rather than travelling by car or using other transport. **on foot of** Irish because of; by reason of: *the decision was taken on foot of advice from the Attorney General.* **put one's best foot forward** embark on an undertaking with as much effort and determination as possible. **put one's feet up** informal take a rest, especially when reclining with one's feet raised and supported. **put foot** S. African informal hurry up; make a prompt start. [originally in the sense 'press on the accelerator of a car'.] **put one's foot down** informal **1** adopt a firm policy when faced with opposition or disobedience. **2** Brit. accelerate a motor vehicle by pressing the accelerator pedal. **put one's foot in it** (or **put one's foot in one's mouth**) informal say or do something tactless or embarrassing. **put a foot wrong** [usu. with negative] make a mistake in performing an action: *he hardly put a foot wrong in the first round.* **set foot on** (or **in**) [often with negative] enter; go into: *he hasn't set foot in the place since the war.* **set something on foot** archaic set an action or process in motion. **sweep someone off their feet** quickly and overpoweringly charm someone. **think on one's feet** react to events decisively, effectively, and without prior thought. **to one's feet** to a standing position: *he leaped to his feet.* **under one's feet** in one's way: *when you're at home you just get under my feet.* **under foot** on the ground: *it is very wet under foot in places.*
– DERIVATIVES **footless** adjective.
– ORIGIN Old English *fōt*, of Germanic origin; related to Dutch *voet* and German *Fuss*, from an Indo-European root shared by Sanskrit *pad, pāda*, Greek *pous, pod-*, and Latin *pes, ped-* 'foot'.

footage ▶ noun [mass noun] **1** part of a cinema or television film recording a particular event: *film footage of the riot.*
2 size or length measured in feet: *the square footage of the room.*

foot-and-mouth disease ▶ noun [mass noun] a contagious viral disease of cattle and sheep, causing ulceration of the hoofs and around the mouth.

football ▶ noun **1** [mass noun] any of various forms of team game involving kicking (and in some cases also handling) a ball, in particular (in the UK) soccer or (in the US) American football. ■ the playing of such a game, especially in a stylish and entertaining way: *his team played some impressive football.*
2 a ball used in football, either round (as in soccer) or oval (as in rugby and American football) and typically made of leather or plastic and filled with compressed air. ■ a topical issue that is the subject of continued argument or controversy: *the use of education as a* **political football**.
– DERIVATIVES **footballer** noun, **footballing** adjective.

football pool ▶ noun (usu. **the football pools**) a form of gambling on the results of football matches, the winners receiving large sums accumulated from entry money.

footbath ▶ noun an act of washing one's feet. ■ a small shallow bowl used for washing one's feet.

footbed ▶ noun an insole in a boot or shoe, used for cushioning or to provide a better fit.

footboard ▶ noun **1** an upright panel forming the foot of a bed.
2 a board serving as a step up to a vehicle such as a carriage or train.

footbrake ▶ noun a brake lever in a motor vehicle, which the driver operates by pressing down with their foot.

footbridge ▶ noun a bridge designed to be used by pedestrians.

foot-candle ▶ noun a unit of illumination (now little used) equal to that given by a source of one candela at a distance of one foot (equivalent to one lumen per square foot or 10.764 lux).

foot-dragging ▶ noun [mass noun] reluctance or deliberate delay concerning a decision or action: *bureaucratic foot-dragging has continued to delay the project.*
– DERIVATIVES **foot-dragger** noun.

footed ▶ adjective **1** having a foot or feet: *a footed bowl.*
2 [in combination] having a foot or feet of a specified type or number: *a quick-footed American chappie.*

footer[1] /ˈfʊtə/ ▶ noun **1** [in combination] a person or thing of a specified number of feet in length or height: *a tall, sturdy six-footer.* ■ a kick of a football performed with a specified foot: *he hammered a low left-footer past the keeper.*
2 variant of FOOTY.
3 a line or block of text appearing at the foot of each page of a book or document. Compare with HEADER (sense 5).

footer[2] /ˈfuːtə/ ▶ verb [no obj.] Scottish fiddle about: *he nodded and started to footer with his watch.*

F

– ORIGIN mid 18th cent.: variant of obsolete *foutre* 'valueless thing, contemptible person', from Old French.

footfall ▶ noun **1** the sound of a footstep or footsteps: *you will recognize his footfall on the stairs.*
2 [mass noun] the number of people entering a shop or shopping area in a given time.

foot fault ▶ noun (in tennis, squash, and similar games) an infringement of the rules made by over-stepping the baseline when serving.
▶ verb (**foot-fault**) [no obj.] (of a player) make a foot fault. ■ [with obj.] award a foot fault against (a player).

footgear ▶ noun another term for **FOOTWEAR**.

foot guards ▶ noun infantrymen with a specific guarding role. ■ (**Foot Guards**) (in the British army) the regiments of the Brigade of Guards: the Grenadier, Coldstream, Scots, Irish, and Welsh Guards.

foothill ▶ noun (usu. **foothills**) a low hill at the base of a mountain or mountain range: *the camp lies in the foothills of the Andes.*

foothold ▶ noun a place where a person's foot can be lodged to support them securely, especially while climbing. ■ [usu. in sing.] a secure position from which further progress may be made: *the company is attempting to gain **a foothold in** the Russian market.*

footie ▶ noun variant spelling of **FOOTY**.

footing ▶ noun **1** (**one's footing**) a secure grip with one's feet: *he suddenly lost his footing.*
2 [in sing.] the basis on which something is established or operates: *attempts to establish the shop on a firm financial footing.* ■ the position or status of a person in relation to others: *the suppliers are **on an equal footing with** the buyers.*
3 (usu. **footings**) the foundations of a wall, usually with a course of brickwork wider than the base of the wall.

footle /ˈfuːt(ə)l/ ▶ verb [no obj.] chiefly Brit. engage in fruitless activity; mess about: *where's that pesky creature that was **footling about** outside?*
– ORIGIN late 19th cent.: perhaps from dialect *footer* 'idle, potter about', from 16th-cent. *foutre* 'worthless thing', from Old French, literally 'have sexual intercourse with'.

footlights ▶ plural noun (usu. **the footlights**) a row of spotlights along the front of a stage at the level of the actors' feet.

footling /ˈfuːtlɪŋ/ ▶ adjective trivial and irritating: *year after year you come with the same footling complaint.*

footlocker ▶ noun N. Amer. a small trunk or storage chest.

foot log ▶ noun N. Amer. a log used as a simple footbridge.

footloose ▶ adjective able to travel freely and do as one pleases due to a lack of responsibilities or commitments: *I am **footloose and fancy-free**—I can follow my job wherever it takes me.* ■ (of a commercial, industrial, or financial operation) unrestricted in its location or field of operations and able to respond to fluctuations in the market.

footman ▶ noun (pl. **footmen**) **1** a liveried servant whose duties include admitting visitors and waiting at table.
2 historical a soldier in the infantry.
3 archaic a trivet to hang on the bars of a grate.
4 a slender moth that is typically of a subdued colour, the caterpillar feeding almost exclusively on lichens. ● Several genera in the family Arctiidae: many species, including the common European *Eilem lurideola*.

footmark ▶ noun a footprint.

footnote ▶ noun an additional piece of information printed at the bottom of a page. ■ a thing that is additional or less important: *this incident seemed destined to become a mere footnote in history.*
▶ verb [with obj.] add a footnote or footnotes to (a piece of writing).

foot overbridge ▶ noun Indian a footbridge.

foot pace ▶ noun **1** [mass noun] walking speed.
2 a raised piece of flooring.

footpad ▶ noun historical a highwayman operating on foot rather than riding a horse.

foot passenger ▶ noun a person travelling on foot rather than by car, especially one taking a ferry.

footpath ▶ noun a path for people to walk along, especially a right of way in the countryside. ■ Brit. a path for pedestrians in a built-up area; a pavement.

footplate ▶ noun chiefly Brit. the platform for the crew in the cab of a locomotive. ■ [as modifier] denoting railway staff responsible for operating trains, as opposed to other employees.

foot-pound ▶ noun **1** a unit of energy equal to the amount required to raise 1 lb a distance of 1 foot.
2 a unit of torque equal to the force of 1 lb acting perpendicularly to an axis of rotation at a distance of 1 foot.

foot-pound-second system ▶ noun a system of measurement with the foot, pound, and second as basic units.

footprint ▶ noun **1** the impression left by a foot or shoe on the ground or a surface. ■ the impact on the environment of human activity in terms of pollution, damage to ecosystems, and the depletion of natural resources: *these countries are so populous that they can have a very big footprint.* ■ Computing the amount of memory or disk space required by a program.
2 the area covered by something, in particular: ■ the area beneath an aircraft or a land vehicle which is affected by its noise or pressure. ■ the area in which a broadcast signal from a particular source can be received. ■ the space taken up on a surface by a piece of computer hardware.

WORD TRENDS Explorers of the great outdoors have long been urged to 'leave only footprints'. Now we are all being advised to keep an eye on the size of our **footprints**, since the word has become a common metaphor for the impact of human activities on the environment. The first extended use emerged in the 1960s, in reference to the area beneath a vehicle or aircraft that is affected by its noise or pressure, and a few years later the word came to denote the area within which a broadcast signal can be received. **Environmental footprint** is first recorded in the late 1970s, and the word is now very often seen in **carbon footprint**, which refers specifically to the amount of carbon dioxide produced through a person's everyday activities.

footrest ▶ noun a support for the feet or a foot, used when sitting.

foot rope ▶ noun Sailing **1** a rope to which the lower edge of a sail is sewn.
2 a rope below a yard on which a sailor can stand while furling or reefing a sail.

foot rot ▶ noun [mass noun] a bacterial disease of the feet in hoofed animals, especially sheep. ● The bacteria belong to the Gram-negative genera *Bacteroides* and *Fusobacterium*.
■ any of a number of fungal diseases of plants in which the base of the stem rots.

foot rule ▶ noun historical a foot-long measuring instrument.

Footsie /ˈfʊtsi/ ▶ noun Brit. trademark informal term for **FTSE INDEX**.
– ORIGIN 1980s: fanciful elaboration of *FTSE*, influenced by *footsie*.

footsie /ˈfʊtsi/ ▶ noun [mass noun] informal the action of touching someone's feet lightly with one's own feet, especially under a table, as a playful expression of romantic interest: *he was **playing footsie** under the table with Mara.*
– PHRASES **play footsie** work with someone in a close but covert way: *the minister was rebuked for **playing footsie with** the nationalists.*
– ORIGIN 1940s: humorous diminutive of **FOOT**.

footslog ▶ verb (**footslogs**, **footslogging**, **footslogged**) [no obj.] (especially of a soldier) walk or march for a long distance, typically wearily or with effort.
▶ noun a long and exhausting walk or march.
– DERIVATIVES **footslogger** noun.

foot soldier ▶ noun a soldier who fights on foot. ■ a person who carries out important work but does not have a role of authority in an organization or field: *programmers are the foot soldiers of the computer revolution.*

footsore ▶ adjective (of a person or animal) having raw and painful feet from much walking.

footstalk ▶ noun the short supporting stalk of a leaf or flower.

footstep ▶ noun a step taken by a person in walking, especially as heard by another person.
– PHRASES **follow** (or **tread**) **in someone's footsteps** do as another person did before, especially in making a journey or following a particular career.

footstool ▶ noun a low stool for resting the feet on when sitting.

footsure ▶ adjective another term for **SURE-FOOTED**.

foot-tapping ▶ adjective having or creating a strong rhythmical musical beat: *foot-tapping gospel hymns.*

foot valve ▶ noun a one-way valve at the inlet of a pipe or the base of a suction pump.

footwall ▶ noun Geology the block of rock which lies on the underside of an inclined fault or of a vein of mineral.

footway ▶ noun Brit. a path or track for pedestrians.

footwear ▶ noun [mass noun] outer coverings for the feet, such as shoes, boots, and sandals.

footwell ▶ noun a space for the feet in front of a seat in a vehicle or aircraft.
– ORIGIN 1980s: from **FOOT** + **WELL**[2] (in the sense 'a depression in the floor').

footwork ▶ noun [mass noun] the manner in which one moves one's feet in various sports, especially in dancing, boxing, and football: *a deft piece of footwork.* ■ adroit response to sudden danger or new opportunities: *the company had to do a lot of nimble footwork to stay alive.*

footy (also **footie** or **footer**) ▶ noun Brit. informal term for **FOOTBALL** (sense 1). ■ Austral./NZ informal term for **RUGBY** or **AUSTRALIAN RULES**.

foo yong /fuː ˈjɒŋ/ ▶ noun [mass noun] a Chinese dish or sauce made with egg as a main ingredient.
– ORIGIN from Chinese (Cantonese dialect) *foō yung*, literally 'hibiscus'.

foozle /ˈfuːz(ə)l/ informal ▶ noun a clumsy or botched attempt at something, especially a shot in golf.
▶ verb [with obj.] botch; bungle.
– ORIGIN mid 19th cent.: from German dialect *fuseln* 'work badly'; compare with **FUSEL OIL**.

fop ▶ noun a man who is concerned with his clothes and appearance in an affected and excessive way.
– DERIVATIVES **foppery** noun.
– ORIGIN late Middle English (in the sense 'fool'): perhaps related to **FOB**[2].

foppish ▶ adjective (of a man) concerned with his clothes and appearance in an affected and excessive way: *he is foppish and vain | a foppish dandy.*
– DERIVATIVES **foppishly** adverb, **foppishness** noun.

for ▶ preposition **1** in support of or in favour of (a person or policy): *troops who had fought for Napoleon | they voted for independence in a referendum.*
2 affecting, with regard to, or in respect of: *she is responsible for the efficient running of their department | the demand for money.*
3 on behalf of or to the benefit of: *I got a present for you | these parents aren't speaking for everyone.* ■ employed by: *she is a tutor for the Open University.*
4 having (the thing mentioned) as a purpose or function: *networks for the exchange of information | the necessary tools for making a picture frame.*
5 having (the thing mentioned) as a reason or cause: *Aileen is proud of her family for their support | I could dance and sing for joy.*
6 having (the place mentioned) as a destination: *they are leaving for London tomorrow.*
7 representing (the thing mentioned): *the 'F' is for Fascinating.*
8 in place of or in exchange for: *will you swap these two bottles for that one?* ■ charged as (a price): *copies are available for £1.20.*
9 in relation to the expected norm of: *she was tall for her age | it's quite warm for this time of year.*
10 indicating the length of (a period of time): *he was jailed for 12 years | I haven't seen him for some time.*
11 indicating the extent of (a distance): *he crawled for 300 yards.*
12 indicating an occasion in a series: *the camcorder failed for the third time.*
▶ conjunction literary because; since: *he felt guilty, for he knew that he bore a share of responsibility for Fanny's death.*
– PHRASES **be for it** Brit. informal be in imminent danger of punishment or other trouble. **do something for one's country** (or **England** etc.) Brit. informal used to indicate that someone does or can do the specified activity with great enthusiasm or tirelessness: *you eating for England, Barry?* **for Africa** S. African informal in huge numbers or quantities; galore: *I've got homework for Africa.* **for all ——** see **ALL**. **for ever** see **FOREVER**. **for why** informal for what reason: *you're going to and I'll tell you for why.* **oh for ——** I long for ——: *oh for a strong black coffee!* **there's** (or **that's**) **—— for you** used ironically to indicate a particularly poor example of (a quality mentioned): *there's gratitude for you.*
– ORIGIN Old English, probably a reduction of a Germanic preposition meaning 'before' (in place or time); related to German *für*, also to **FORE**.

for- ▶ prefix **1** denoting prohibition: *forbid.*

2 denoting abstention, neglect, or renunciation: *forgive | forget | forgo.*
3 used as an intensifier: *forlorn.*
– ORIGIN Old English.

f.o.r. ▸ **abbreviation** free on rail. See FREE.

fora plural form of FORUM (sense 3).

forage /ˈfɒrɪdʒ/ ▸ **verb** [no obj.] (of a person or animal) search widely for food or provisions: *the birds forage for aquatic invertebrates, insects, and seeds.* ■ [with obj.] obtain (food or provisions) by searching: *a girl foraging grass for oxen.* ■ [with obj.] search (a place) so as to obtain food. ■ [with obj.] archaic supply with food.
▸ **noun 1** [mass noun] food such as grass or hay for horses and cattle; fodder.
2 [in sing.] a wide search over an area in order to obtain something, especially food or provisions.
– DERIVATIVES **forager** noun.
– ORIGIN Middle English: from Old French *fourrage* (noun), *fourrager* (verb), from *fuerre* 'straw', of Germanic origin and related to FODDER.

forage cap ▸ **noun** a cloth undress cap, usually with a peak, worn as part of a soldier's uniform.

forage fish ▸ **noun** a species of fish which is the prey of more valuable game fish.

forage harvester ▸ **noun** a large agricultural machine for harvesting forage crops.

foramen /fəˈreɪmɛn/ ▸ **noun** (pl. **foramina** /-ˈramɪnə/) Anatomy an opening, hole, or passage, especially in a bone.
– ORIGIN late 17th cent.: from Latin, from *forare* 'bore a hole'.

foramen magnum /ˈmagnəm/ ▸ **noun** Anatomy the hole in the base of the skull through which the spinal cord passes.
– ORIGIN Latin, 'large opening'.

foraminifer /ˌfɒrəˈmɪnɪfə/ ▸ **noun** (pl. **foraminifers** or **foraminifera** /ˌfɒrəmɪˈnɪf(ə)rə/) Zoology a single-celled planktonic animal with a perforated chalky shell through which slender protrusions of protoplasm extend. Most kinds are marine, and when they die thick ocean-floor sediments are formed from their shells. See also GLOBIGERINA. ● Order Foraminiferida, phylum Rhizopoda, kingdom Protista.
– DERIVATIVES **foraminiferal** /ˌfɒrəmɪˈnɪf(ə)rəl/ **adjective**, **foraminiferan** noun & adjective, **foraminiferous** adjective.
– ORIGIN mid 19th cent.: from Latin *foramen*, *foramin-* (see FORAMEN) + *-fer* 'bearing' (from *ferre* 'to bear').

for'ard /ˈfɒrəd/ ▸ **adjective & adverb** non-standard spelling of FORWARD, used to represent a nautical pronunciation.

forasmuch as ▸ **conjunction** archaic because; since.
– ORIGIN Middle English *for as much*, translating Old French *por tant que* 'for so much as'.

forastero /ˌfɒrəˈstɛːrəʊ/ (also **forastero tree**) ▸ **noun** (pl. **forasteros**) a widely grown cacao tree of a variety which provides the bulk of the world's cocoa beans.
– ORIGIN mid 19th cent.: from Spanish, literally 'foreign', because the tree was a 'foreign' import to Venezuela from the West Indies, as distinct from the CRIOLLO or native variety.

foray /ˈfɒreɪ/ ▸ **noun** a sudden attack or incursion into enemy territory, especially to obtain something; a raid: *the garrison made a foray against Richard's camp.* ■ a brief but spirited attempt to become involved in a new activity or sphere: *my first foray into journalism.*
▸ **verb** [no obj., with adverbial of direction] make or go on a foray.
– ORIGIN Middle English: back-formation from *forayer* 'a person who forays', from Old French *forrier* 'forager', from *fuerre* 'straw' (see FORAGE).

forb /fɔːb/ ▸ **noun** Botany a herbaceous flowering plant other than a grass.
– ORIGIN 1920s: from Greek *phorbē* 'fodder', from *phorbein* 'to feed'.

forbade (also **forbad**) past of FORBID.

forbear[1] /fɔːˈbɛː/ ▸ **verb** (past **forbore**; past participle **forborne**) [no obj.] politely or patiently restrain an impulse to do something; refrain: [with infinitive] *he modestly forbears to include his own work.*
– ORIGIN Old English *forberan* (see FOR-, BEAR[1]). The original senses were 'endure, bear with', hence 'endure the absence of, do without', also 'control oneself', hence 'refrain from' (Middle English).

forbear[2] /ˈfɔːbɛː/ ▸ **noun** variant spelling of FOREBEAR.

forbearance ▸ **noun** [mass noun] patient self-control; restraint and tolerance: *his unfailing courtesy and forbearance under great provocation.* ■ Law the action of refraining from exercising a legal right, especially enforcing the payment of a debt.

forbearing ▸ **adjective** patient and restrained: *he proved to be remarkably forbearing whenever I was impatient or angry.*

forbid ▸ **verb** (**forbids**, **forbidding**; past **forbade** /-ˈbad, -ˈbeɪd/ or **forbad**; past participle **forbidden**) [with obj.] refuse to allow (something): *mixed marriages were forbidden.* ■ order (someone) not to do something: *I was* ***forbidden from*** *seeing him again* | [with obj. and infinitive] *my doctor has forbidden me to eat sugar.* ■ refuse entry to a place or area: *all vehicles are forbidden.* ■ (of a circumstance or quality) make (something) impossible; prevent: *the cliffs forbid any easy turning movement.*
– PHRASES **God** (or **Heaven**) **forbid** used to express a fervent wish that something does not happen: *if, God forbid, a close family member of yours were killed.*
– ORIGIN Old English *forbēodan* (see FOR-, BID[2]).

forbidden ▸ **adjective 1** not allowed; banned: *a list of forbidden books.*
2 Physics denoting or involving a transition between two quantum-mechanical states that does not conform to some selection rule, especially for electric dipole radiation.
– PHRASES **the forbidden degrees** the number of steps of descent from the same ancestor that bar two related people from marrying. **forbidden fruit** a thing that is desired all the more because it is not allowed. [with biblical allusion to Gen. 2:17.]

Forbidden City 1 an area of Beijing containing the former imperial palaces, to which entry was forbidden to all except the members of the imperial family and their servants.
2 a name given to Lhasa in Tibet.

forbidding ▸ **adjective** unfriendly or threatening in appearance: *a grim and forbidding building.*
– DERIVATIVES **forbiddingly** adverb.

forbore past of FORBEAR[1].

forborne past participle of FORBEAR[1].

forbye /fəˈbʌɪ, fɔː-/ (also **forby**) ▸ **adverb & preposition** archaic or Scottish in addition; besides: [as prep.] *no doubt he had many a sin on his soul, forbye murder.*

force[1] ▸ **noun** [mass noun] **1** strength or energy as an attribute of physical action or movement: *he was thrown backwards by the force of the explosion.* ■ Physics an influence tending to change the motion of a body or produce motion or stress in a stationary body. The magnitude of such an influence is often calculated by multiplying the mass of the body and its acceleration. ■ [in combination] used with a number as a measure of wind strength on the Beaufort scale: *a force-nine gale.*
2 coercion or compulsion, especially with the use or threat of violence: *they ruled by law and not* ***by force.***
3 mental or moral strength or power: *the force of popular opinion.* ■ [count noun] a person or thing regarded as exerting power or influence: *he might still be* ***a force for*** *peace and unity.* ■ the powerful effect of something: *the Committee accepted the force of this argument.*
4 [count noun] an organized body of military personnel or police: *a British peacekeeping force.* ■ (**forces**) troops and weaponry: *left-wing guerrilla forces* | figurative *a battle between the forces of good and evil.* ■ (**the forces**) Brit. informal the army, navy, and air force of a country. ■ (**the force**) Brit. informal the police. ■ a group of people brought together and organized for a particular activity: *a sales force.*
▸ **verb** [with obj.] **1** make a way through or into by physical strength; break open by force: *the back door of the bank was forced.* ■ [with obj. and adverbial] drive or push into a specified position or state using physical strength or against resistance: *thieves tried to force open the cash register | Mark forced her arms back above her head.* ■ achieve or bring about (something) by effort: *Sabine forced a smile | they* ***forced a way*** *through the crowd.* ■ artificially hasten the development or maturity of (a plant).
2 make (someone) do something against their will: *she was* ***forced into*** *early retirement* | [with obj. and infinitive] *the universities were forced to cut staff.* ■ Baseball put out (a runner) by necessitating an advance to the next base when it is not possible to do so safely.
– PHRASES **by force of** by means of: *disputes were sometimes settled by force of arms.* **force the bidding** (at an auction) make bids to raise the price rapidly. **force someone's hand** make someone do something. **force the issue** compel the making of an immediate decision. **force the pace** adopt a fast pace in a race in order to tire out one's opponents quickly. **in force** in great strength or numbers: *birdwatchers were out in force.* **in** (or **into**) **force** in or into effect: *the law came into force in January.*
– PHRASAL VERBS **force something down 1** manage to swallow food or drink when one does not want to. **2** compel an aircraft to land: *the plane might have been forced down by fighters.* **force oneself on/upon** rape (a woman). **force something on/upon** impose or press something on: *economic cutbacks were forced on the government.* **force someone out** compel someone to leave a job or position, especially by indirect means: *Fields was forced out as director.*
– DERIVATIVES **forceable** adjective, **forcer** noun.
– ORIGIN Middle English: from Old French *force* (noun), *forcer* (verb), based on Latin *fortis* 'strong'.

force[2] ▸ **noun** N. English a waterfall.
– ORIGIN late Middle English: from Old Norse *fors*.

forced ▸ **adjective 1** obtained or imposed by coercion or physical power: *there was no sign of a forced entry.* ■ (of a plant) having its development or maturity artificially hastened.
2 (of a gesture or expression) produced or maintained with effort; affected or unnatural: *a forced smile.*
– PHRASES **forced march** a fast march by soldiers, typically over a long distance.

forced landing ▸ **noun** an act of abruptly bringing an aircraft to the ground or the surface of water in an emergency.
– DERIVATIVES **force-land** verb.

force-feed ▸ **verb** [with obj.] force (a person or animal) to eat food. ■ impose or force (information or ideology) on someone: [with two objs] *those teaching our kids should not be force-feeding them political ideas.*

force feedback ▸ **noun** [mass noun] Computing the simulating of physical attributes such as weight in computer gaming and virtual reality, allowing the user to interact directly with virtual objects using touch.

force field ▸ **noun** (chiefly in science fiction) an invisible barrier of force.

forceful ▸ **adjective** strong and assertive; vigorous and powerful: *she was a forceful personality.*
– DERIVATIVES **forcefully** adverb, **forcefulness** noun.

force majeure /ˌfɔːs maˈʒəː/ ▸ **noun** [mass noun] **1** Law unforeseeable circumstances that prevent someone from fulfilling a contract.
2 irresistible compulsion or superior strength.
– ORIGIN French, literally 'superior strength'.

forcemeat ▸ **noun** [mass noun] a mixture of meat or vegetables chopped and seasoned for use as a stuffing or garnish.
– ORIGIN late 17th cent.: from obsolete *force* 'to stuff', alteration (influenced by the FORCE[1] (verb)) of *farce*, from French *farcir* (see FARCE).

force out ▸ **noun** Baseball a putting out of a base runner who is forced to advance to a base at which a fielder is holding the ball.

forceps /ˈfɔːsɛps, -sɪps/ (also **a pair of forceps**) ▸ **plural noun** a pair of pincers or tweezers used in surgery or in a laboratory. ■ a large instrument of such a type with broad blades, used to encircle a baby's head and assist in birth: [as modifier] *a forceps delivery.* ■ Zoology an organ or structure resembling forceps, especially the cerci of an earwig.
– ORIGIN late 16th cent.: from Latin, 'tongs, pincers'.

force pump ▸ **noun** a pump used to move water or other liquid under greater than ambient pressure.

force-ripe ▸ **adjective** W. Indian (of a person) old or mature in certain respects without having developed fully in others.
– ORIGIN by association with a fruit that has ripened by forcing.

forcible ▸ **adjective** done by force: *signs of forcible entry.* ■ vigorous and strong; forceful: *they could only be deterred by forcible appeals.*
– ORIGIN late Middle English: from Old French, from *force* (see FORCE[1]).

forcibly ▸ **adverb** using force or violence: *no one will be forcibly evicted.* ■ in a forceful way; convincingly: *they argued forcibly against the proposal.*

forcing ▸ **adjective** Bridge (of a bid) requiring by convention a response from one's partner, no matter how weak their hand may be.

forcing house ▸ **noun** a place in which the growth or development of something (especially plants) is artificially hastened.

F

Ford[1], Ford Madox (1873–1939), English novelist and editor; born *Ford Hermann Hueffer*. He is chiefly remembered as the author of the novel *The Good Soldier* (1915).

Ford[2], Gerald (Rudolph) (1913–2006), American Republican statesman, 38th President of the US 1974–7. He became President on the resignation of Richard Nixon in the wake of the Watergate affair.

Ford[3], Henry (1863–1947), American motor manufacturer. A pioneer of large-scale mass production, he founded the Ford Motor Company, which in 1909 produced his famous Model T. Control of the company passed to his grandson, **Henry Ford II** (1917–1987) in 1945.

Ford[4], John (1586–*c.*1639), English dramatist. His plays, which include *'Tis Pity She's a Whore* (1633) and *The Broken Heart* (1633), explore human delusion, melancholy, and horror.

Ford[5], John (1895–1973), American film director; born *Sean Aloysius O'Feeney*. He is chiefly known for his westerns of which many, including *Stagecoach* (1939) and *She Wore a Yellow Ribbon* (1949), starred John Wayne.

ford ▶ **noun** a shallow place in a river or stream allowing one to walk or drive across.
▶ **verb** [with obj.] (of a person or vehicle) cross (a river or stream) at a shallow place.
– DERIVATIVES **fordable** adjective.
– ORIGIN Old English, of West Germanic origin; related to Dutch *voorde*, also to **FARE**.

Fordism ▶ **noun** [mass noun] the use in manufacturing industry of the methods pioneered by Henry Ford, typified by large-scale mechanized mass production.
– DERIVATIVES **Fordist** noun & adjective.

fordo /fɔːˈduː/ (also **foredo**) ▶ **verb** (**fordoes**, **fordoing**, **fordid**; past participle **fordone**) [with obj.] archaic kill; destroy: *by the sword's edge his life shall be foredone.*
– ORIGIN Old English *fordōn*; related to Dutch *verdoen* and German *vertun*, and ultimately to **FOR** and **DO**[1].

fore ▶ **adjective** [attrib.] situated or placed in front: *the fore and hind pairs of wings.*
▶ **noun** the front part of something, especially a ship.
▶ **exclamation** called out as a warning to people in the path of a golf ball.
▶ **preposition** (also **'fore**) non-standard form of **BEFORE**: *'fore you know it, you're in trouble.*
– PHRASES **to the fore** in or to a conspicuous or leading position: *the succession issue **came to the fore**.*
– ORIGIN Old English (as a preposition, also in the sense 'before in time, previously'): of Germanic origin; related to Dutch *voor* and German *vor*. The adjective and noun represent the prefix **FORE-** used independently (late 15th cent.).

fore- ▶ **combining form 1** (added to verbs) in front: *foreshorten.* ■ beforehand; in advance: *forebode | foreshadow.*
2 (added to nouns) situated in front of: *forecourt.* ■ the front part of: *forebrain.* ■ of or near the bow of a ship: *forecastle.* ■ preceding; going before: *forefather.*
– ORIGIN Old English (see **FORE**).

fore and aft ▶ **adverb** at the front and rear (often used with reference to a ship or plane): *we're moored fore and aft.* ■ backwards and forwards: *a sperm whale cannot see directly fore and aft.*
▶ **adjective** [attrib.] **1** backwards and forwards: *the fore-and-aft motion of the handles.*
2 (of a sail or rigging) set lengthwise, not on the yards.
3 N. Amer. (of a road) constructed of logs laid end to end.
4 historical (of a man's hat) having three corners and a peak at the front and back.
– ORIGIN early 17th cent.: perhaps translating a phrase of Low German origin; compare with Dutch *van voren en van achteren.*

forearm[1] /ˈfɔːrɑːm/ ▶ **noun** the part of a person's arm extending from the elbow to the wrist or the fingertips.

forearm[2] /fɔːrˈɑːm/ ▶ **verb** [with obj.] prepare (someone) in advance for danger, attack, or another undesirable future event: *within ourselves, we are forearmed against unpleasant possibilities.*

forebear (also **forbear**) ▶ **noun** (usu. **one's forebears**) an ancestor.
– ORIGIN late 15th cent.: from **FORE** + *bear*, variant of obsolete *beer* 'someone who exists' (from **BE** + **-ER**[1]).

forebode ▶ **verb** [with obj.] archaic (of a situation or occurrence) act as an advance warning of (something bad): *this lull foreboded some new assault upon him.* ■ have a presentiment of (something bad): *I foreboded mischief the moment I heard.*

foreboding ▶ **noun** [mass noun] a feeling that something bad will happen; fearful apprehension: *with a sense of foreboding she read the note.*
▶ **adjective** implying that something bad is going to happen: *when the Doctor spoke, his voice was dark and foreboding.*
– DERIVATIVES **forebodingly** adverb.

forebrain ▶ **noun** Anatomy the anterior part of the brain, including the cerebral hemispheres, the thalamus, and the hypothalamus. Also called **PROSENCEPHALON**.

forecabin ▶ **noun** a cabin in the forward part of a vessel.

forecaddie ▶ **noun** (pl. **forecaddies**) a caddie who goes ahead of golfers to see where the balls fall.

forecast ▶ **verb** (past and past participle **forecast** or **forecasted**) [with obj.] predict or estimate (a future event or trend): *rain is forecast for Scotland* | [with obj. and infinitive] *coal consumption in Europe is forecast to increase.*
▶ **noun** a calculation or estimate of future events, especially coming weather or a financial trend.
– DERIVATIVES **forecaster** noun.

forecastle /ˈfəʊks(ə)l/ (also **fo'c'sle**) ▶ **noun** the forward part of a ship below the deck, traditionally used as the crew's living quarters. ■ historical a raised deck at the front of a ship.

forecheck ▶ **verb** [no obj.] Ice Hockey play an aggressive style of defence, checking opponents before they can organize an attack.
– DERIVATIVES **forechecker** noun.

foreclose ▶ **verb 1** [no obj.] take possession of a mortgaged property when the mortgagor fails to keep up their mortgage payments: *the bank was threatening to **foreclose on** his mortgage.* ■ [with obj.] take away someone's power to redeem (a mortgage) and take possession of the mortgaged property.
2 [with obj.] rule out or prevent (a course of action): *the decision effectively foreclosed any possibility of his early rehabilitation.*
– DERIVATIVES **foreclosure** noun.
– ORIGIN Middle English: from Old French *forclos*, past participle of *forclore*, from *for-* 'out' (from Latin *foras* 'outside') + *clore* 'to close'. The original sense was 'bar from escaping', in late Middle English 'shut out', and 'bar from doing something' (sense 2), hence specifically 'bar someone from redeeming a mortgage' (sense 1, early 18th cent.).

forecourt ▶ **noun 1** an open area in front of a large building or petrol station.
2 Tennis the part of the court between the service line and the net.

foredawn ▶ **noun** literary the time before dawn.

foredeck ▶ **noun** the deck at the forward part of a ship.

foredo ▶ **verb** variant spelling of **FORDO**.

foredoom ▶ **verb** [with obj.] condemn beforehand to certain failure or destruction: *the policy is foredoomed to failure.*

foredune ▶ **noun** Ecology a part of a system of sand dunes on the side nearest to the sea.

fore-edge ▶ **noun** technical the outer vertical edge of the pages of a book.

forefather ▶ **noun** (usu. **one's forefathers**) a member of the past generations of one's family or people; an ancestor. ■ a precursor of a particular movement: *the forefathers of modern British socialism.*

forefend ▶ **verb** variant spelling of **FORFEND** (sense 2).

forefinger ▶ **noun** the finger next to the thumb; the first or index finger.

forefoot ▶ **noun** (pl. **forefeet**) **1** each of the front feet of a four-footed animal.
2 the foremost section of a ship's keel. ■ the foremost section of a shoe.

forefront ▶ **noun** (**the forefront**) the leading or most important position or place: *the issue has moved to the forefront of the political agenda.*

foregather (also **forgather**) ▶ **verb** [no obj.] formal assemble or gather together.
– ORIGIN late 15th cent. (originally Scots as *forgadder*): from Dutch *vergaderen*.

forego[1] ▶ **verb** variant spelling of **FORGO**.

forego[2] ▶ **verb** (**foregoes**, **foregoing**, **forewent**; past participle **foregone**) [with obj.] archaic precede in place or time.
– DERIVATIVES **foregoer** noun.

foregoing formal ▶ **adjective** [attrib.] just mentioned or stated; preceding: *the foregoing analysis of the economic class structure.*
▶ **noun** (**the foregoing**) [treated as sing. or pl.] the things just mentioned or stated.

foregone past participle of **FOREGO**[2]. ▶ **adjective** [often postpositive] archaic past: *poets dream of lives foregone in worlds fantastical.*
– PHRASES **a foregone conclusion** a result that can be predicted with certainty.

foreground ▶ **noun** (**the foreground**) the part of a view that is nearest to the observer, especially in a picture or photograph: *the intricate garden depicted in the foreground.* ■ the most prominent or important position or situation: *issues which have occupied the political foreground in recent years.*
▶ **verb** [with obj.] make (something) the most prominent or important feature: *sexual relationships are foregrounded and idealized.*
– ORIGIN late 17th cent.: from **FORE-** + **GROUND**[1], on the pattern of Dutch *voorgrond*.

foregut ▶ **noun** Anatomy & Zoology the anterior part of the gut, towards the mouth.

forehand ▶ **noun 1** (in tennis and other racket sports) a stroke played with the palm of the hand facing in the direction of the stroke: [as modifier] *a good forehand drive.*
2 the part of a horse in front of the saddle.

forehanded ▶ **adverb** (in tennis and other racket sports) with a forehand stroke.
▶ **adjective** US looking to the future; prudent or thrifty: *his faculty for forehanded thought about problems to be resolved in the future.*

forehead /ˈfɔːhɛd, ˈfɒrɪd/ ▶ **noun** the part of the face above the eyebrows.
– ORIGIN Old English *forhēafod* (see **FORE-**, **HEAD**).

forehock /ˈfɔːhɒk/ ▶ **noun** Brit. a foreleg cut of pork or bacon.

foreign /ˈfɒrɪn/ ▶ **adjective 1** of, from, in, or characteristic of a country or language other than one's own: *foreign currency | a man with a foreign accent.* ■ dealing with or relating to other countries: *foreign policy.* ■ of or belonging to another district or area: *a visit to a foreign clan.* ■ coming or introduced from outside: *the quotation is a foreign element imported into the work.*
2 strange and unfamiliar: *I suppose this all feels pretty **foreign to** you.* ■ (**foreign to**) not belonging to or characteristic of: *crime and brutality are foreign to our nature.*
– DERIVATIVES **foreignness** /ˈfɒr(ə)nnɪs/ noun.
– ORIGIN Middle English *foren*, *forein*, from Old French *forein*, *forain*, based on Latin *foras*, *foris* 'outside', from *fores* 'door'. The current spelling arose in the 16th cent., by association with **SOVEREIGN**.

foreign aid ▶ **noun** [mass noun] money, food, or other resources given or lent by one country to another.

Foreign and Commonwealth Office the British government department dealing with foreign affairs.

foreign body ▶ **noun** an object or piece of extraneous matter that has entered the body by accident or design.

foreigner ▶ **noun 1** a person born in or coming from a country other than one's own. ■ informal a person not belonging to a particular place or group; a stranger or outsider.
2 Brit. informal a piece of work done for private gain without an employer's permission or without declaration to the relevant authorities.

foreign exchange ▶ **noun** an institution or system for dealing in the currencies of other countries. ■ [mass noun] the currencies of other countries.

Foreign Legion a military formation of the French army founded in the 1830s to fight France's colonial wars. Composed, except for the higher ranks, of non-Frenchmen, the Legion was famed for its audacity and endurance. Its most famous campaigns were in French North Africa in the late 19th and early 20th centuries.

foreign minister ▶ **noun** a government minister in charge of their country's relations with other countries.

Foreign Office short for **FOREIGN AND COMMONWEALTH OFFICE**.

foreign-returned ▶ **adjective** Indian (of a person) educated or trained abroad and now living again in India.

Foreign Secretary ▸ noun (in the UK) the government minister who heads the Foreign and Commonwealth Office.

foreign service ▸ noun another term for DIPLOMATIC SERVICE.

foreknow ▸ verb (past **foreknew**; past participle **foreknown**) [with obj.] literary be aware of (an event) before it happens: *he foreknows his death like a saint.*

foreknowledge ▸ noun [mass noun] awareness of something before it happens or exists.

forelady ▸ noun (pl. **foreladies**) N. Amer. dated a forewoman.

foreland ▸ noun **1** an area of land bordering on another or lying in front of a particular feature.
2 a cape or promontory.
3 Geology a stable unyielding block of the earth's crust, against which compression produces a folded mountain range.

foreleg ▸ noun either of the front legs of a four-footed animal.

forelimb ▸ noun either of the front limbs of an animal; a foreleg, wing, flipper, etc.

forelock ▸ noun a lock of hair growing just above the forehead. ■ the part of the mane of a horse or similar animal, which grows from the poll and hangs down over the forehead.
– PHRASES **take time by the forelock** literary seize an opportunity. **touch** (or **tug**) **one's forelock** Brit. raise a hand to one's forehead in deference when meeting a person of higher social rank.

foreman ▸ noun (pl. **foremen**) **1** a male worker who supervises and directs other workers.
2 (in a law court) a person who presides over a jury and speaks on its behalf.
– ORIGIN Middle English: perhaps suggested by Dutch *voorman* (compare with German *Vormann*).

foremast ▸ noun the mast of a ship nearest the bow.

foremost ▸ adjective most prominent in rank, importance, or position: *one of the foremost art collectors of his day.*
▸ adverb before anything else in rank, importance, or position; in the first place.
– ORIGIN Old English *formest*, *fyrmest*, from *forma* 'first' (ultimately a superlative formed from the Germanic base of FORE) + -EST[1]. Compare with FIRST and FORMER[1]. The current spelling arose by association with FORE and MOST.

foremother ▸ noun (usu. **one's foremothers**) a female ancestor or precursor of something.

forename ▸ noun another term for FIRST NAME.

forenoon ▸ noun N. Amer. or Nautical the morning.

forensic /fəˈrɛnsɪk/ ▸ adjective **1** relating to or denoting the application of scientific methods and techniques to the investigation of crime: *forensic evidence.*
2 relating to courts of law.
▸ noun (**forensics**) scientific tests or techniques used in connection with the detection of crime. ■ (also **forensic**) [treated as sing. or pl.] informal a laboratory or department responsible for forensic tests.
– DERIVATIVES **forensically** adverb.
– ORIGIN mid 17th cent.: from Latin *forensis* 'in open court, public', from *forum* (see FORUM).

forensic accounting ▸ noun [mass noun] the use of accounting skills to investigate fraud or embezzlement and to analyse financial information for use in legal proceedings.

forensic medicine ▸ noun [mass noun] the application of medical knowledge to the investigation of crime, particularly in establishing the causes of injury or death.

foreordain /ˌfɔːrɔːˈdeɪn/ ▸ verb [with obj.] (of God or fate) appoint or decree (something) beforehand: *progress is not foreordained.*
– DERIVATIVES **foreordination** noun.

forepart ▸ noun the part situated at the front of something; the foremost part: *the forepart of the brain.*

forepaw ▸ noun either of the front paws of a four-footed animal.

forepeak ▸ noun the front end of the hold in the angle of the bows of a ship.

foreperson ▸ noun (pl. **forepersons**) a foreman or forewoman (used as a neutral alternative).

foreplay ▸ noun [mass noun] sexual activity that precedes intercourse.

forequarters ▸ plural noun the front legs and adjoining parts of a quadruped.

forerib ▸ noun a cut of beef for roasting, containing the rib from just in front of the sirloin.

forerun ▸ verb (**foreruns**, **forerunning**, **foreran**; past participle **forerun**) [with obj.] literary go before or indicate the coming of: *the vast inquietude that foreruns the storm.*

forerunner ▸ noun **1** a person or thing that precedes the coming or development of someone or something else: *the ice safe was a forerunner of today's refrigerator.*
2 a sign or warning of something to come: *overcast mornings are the sure forerunners of steady rain.* ■ archaic an advance messenger.

foresail /ˈfɔːseɪl, -s(ə)l/ ▸ noun the principal sail on a foremast.

foresee ▸ verb (**foresees**, **foreseeing**, **foresaw**; past participle **foreseen**) [with obj.] be aware of beforehand; predict: *we did not foresee any difficulties* | [with clause] *it is impossible to foresee how life will work out.*
– DERIVATIVES **foreseer** /-ˈsiːə/ noun.
– ORIGIN Old English *foresēon* (see FORE-, SEE[1]).

foreseeable ▸ adjective able to be foreseen or predicted: *the situation is unlikely to change* ***in the foreseeable future.***
– DERIVATIVES **foreseeability** noun, **foreseeably** adverb.

foreshadow ▸ verb [with obj.] be a warning or indication of (a future event): *other new measures are foreshadowed in the White Paper.*

foresheet ▸ noun **1** a rope by which the lee corner of a foresail is kept in place.
2 (**foresheets**) the inner part of the bows of a boat.

foreshock ▸ noun a mild tremor preceding the violent shaking movement of an earthquake.

foreshore ▸ noun the part of a shore between high- and low-water marks, or between the water and cultivated or developed land.

foreshorten ▸ verb [with obj.] portray or show (an object or view) as closer than it really is or as having less depth or distance, as an effect of perspective or the angle of vision: *seen from the road, the mountain is greatly foreshortened.* ■ (often as adj. **foreshortened**) prematurely or dramatically shorten or reduce (something) in time or scale: *Leicestershire won by 133 runs in a foreshortened contest.*

foreshow ▸ verb (past participle **foreshown**) [with obj.] archaic give warning or promise of; foretell.

foresight ▸ noun **1** [mass noun] the ability to predict what will happen or be needed in the future: *he had the foresight to check that his escape route was clear.*
2 the front sight of a gun.
3 Surveying a sight taken forwards.
– ORIGIN Middle English: from FORE- + SIGHT, probably suggested by Old Norse *forsjá*, *forsjó*.

foresighted ▸ adjective having or using foresight: *he had the backing of the more foresighted part of the council.*
– DERIVATIVES **foresightedly** adverb, **foresightedness** noun.

foreskin ▸ noun the retractable roll of skin covering the end of the penis. Also called PREPUCE.

forest ▸ noun **1** a large area covered chiefly with trees and undergrowth: *a pine forest* | [mass noun] *a large tract of forest.* ■ historical an area, typically owned by the sovereign and partly wooded, kept for hunting and having its own laws. ■ [in place names] denoting an area that was formerly a royal forest: *Waltham Forest.*
2 a large number or dense mass of vertical or tangled objects: *a forest of high-rise apartments.*
▸ verb [with obj.] (usu. as adj. **forested**) cover (land) with forest; plant with trees: *a forested hillside.*
– DERIVATIVES **forestation** noun.
– ORIGIN Middle English (in the sense 'wooded area kept for hunting', also denoting any uncultivated land): via Old French from late Latin *forestis* (*silva*), literally '(wood) outside', from Latin *foris* 'outside' (see FOREIGN).

forestall /fɔːˈstɔːl/ ▸ verb [with obj.] prevent or obstruct (an anticipated event or action) by taking advance action: *they will present their resignations to forestall a vote of no confidence.* ■ act in advance of (someone) in order to prevent them from doing something: *he would have spoken but David forestalled him.* ■ historical buy up (goods) in order to profit by an enhanced price.
– DERIVATIVES **forestaller** noun.
– ORIGIN Old English *foresteall* 'an ambush' (see FORE- and STALL). As a verb the earliest sense (Middle English) was 'intercept and buy up goods before they reach the market, so as to raise the price' (formerly an offence).

forestay /ˈfɔːsteɪ/ ▸ noun a rope to support a ship's foremast, running from its top to the deck at the bow.

Forester, C. S. (1899–1966), English novelist; pseudonym of *Cecil Lewis Troughton Smith*. He is remembered for his seafaring novels set during the Napoleonic Wars, featuring Captain Horatio Hornblower.

forester ▸ noun **1** a person in charge of a forest or skilled in planting, managing, or caring for trees.
2 chiefly archaic a person or animal living in a forest.
3 a small day-flying moth with metallic green forewings and a greenish-bronze body. ● Genus *Adscita*, family Zygaenidae: several species.
4 Austral. the eastern grey kangaroo. See GREY KANGAROO.
5 (**Forester**) Brit. a member of the Ancient Order of Foresters, a friendly society.
– ORIGIN Middle English: from Old French *forestier*, from *forest* (see FOREST).

forest fly ▸ noun a bloodsucking European louse fly of wooded areas, attacking horses and other animals. ● *Hippobosca equina*, family Hippoboscidae.

forestry ▸ noun [mass noun] the science or practice of planting, managing, and caring for forests. ■ country covered by forests.

Forestry Commission the government department responsible for forestry policy in the UK, established in 1919.

forest tree ▸ noun a large tree growing in or typical of those growing in a forest.

foretaste ▸ noun [in sing.] a sample or suggestion of something that lies ahead: *his behemoth task force is just a foretaste of what is to come.*

foretell ▸ verb (past and past participle **foretold**) [with obj.] predict (the future or a future event): [with clause] *a seer had foretold that the earl would assume the throne.*
– DERIVATIVES **foreteller** noun.

forethought ▸ noun [mass noun] careful consideration of what will be necessary or may happen in the future: *Jim had the forethought to book in advance.*

foretoken /fɔːˈtəʊk(ə)n/ ▸ verb [with obj.] literary be a sign of (a future event): *a shiver in the night air foretokening December.*
– ORIGIN Old English *foretācn* (noun: see FORE-, TOKEN).

foretold past and past participle of FORETELL.

foretop /ˈfɔːtɒp, -təp/ ▸ noun a platform around the head of the lower section of a sailing ship's foremast.

fore-topgallant mast ▸ noun the third section of a sailing ship's foremast, above the foretopmast.

fore-topgallant sail ▸ noun the sail above a sailing ship's foretopsail.

foretopmast /fɔːˈtɒpmɑːst, -məst/ ▸ noun the second section of a sailing ship's foremast.

foretopsail /fɔːˈtɒps(ə)l, -seɪl/ ▸ noun the sail above a sailing ship's foresail.

foretriangle ▸ noun the triangular space between the deck, foremast, and forestay of a sailing vessel. ■ the area of sail within the foretriangle.

forever ▸ adverb **1** (also **for ever**) for all future time; for always: *she would love him forever.* ■ a very long time (used hyperbolically): *it took forever to get a passport.* ■ used in slogans of support after the name of something or someone: *Scotland Forever!*
2 continually: *they are forever on the move.*

for evermore (also **forever more** and N. Amer. **forevermore**) ▸ adverb Brit. forever (used for rhetorical effect): *time has been and shall be for evermore.*

forewarn ▸ verb [with obj.] inform (someone) of a possible future danger or problem: *he had been forewarned of a coup plot.*
– PHRASES **forewarned is forearmed** proverb prior knowledge of possible dangers or problems gives one a tactical advantage.

forewarning ▸ noun an advance warning: *officials had no forewarning of the attacks.*

forewent past of FOREGO[1], FOREGO[2].

forewing ▸ noun either of the two front wings of a four-winged insect.

forewoman ▸ noun (pl. **forewomen**) a female worker who supervises and directs other workers. ■ N. Amer. (in a law court) a woman who presides over a jury and speaks on its behalf.

foreword ▸ noun a short introduction to a book, typically by a person other than the author.
– ORIGIN mid 19th cent.: from **FORE-** + **WORD**, on the pattern of German *Vorwort*.

forex ▸ abbreviation foreign exchange.

foreyard ▸ noun the lowest yard on a sailing ship's foremast.

Forfar /ˈfɔːfə/ a town in eastern Scotland, administrative centre of Angus region. It is noted for its castle, the meeting place in 1057 of an early Scottish Parliament and the home of several Scottish kings.

Forfarshire former name (from the 16th century until 1928) for **ANGUS**[1].

forfeit /ˈfɔːfɪt/ ▸ verb (**forfeits**, **forfeiting**, **forfeited**) [with obj.] lose or be deprived of (property or a right or privilege) as a penalty for wrongdoing: *those unable to meet their taxes were liable to forfeit their estates.* ■ lose or give up (something) as a necessary consequence of something else: *she didn't mind forfeiting an hour in bed to muck out the horses.*
▸ noun a fine or penalty for wrongdoing. ■ Law an item of property or a right or privilege lost as a legal penalty. ■ (**forfeits**) a game in which trivial penalties are exacted for minor misdemeanours. ■ [mass noun] the action of forfeiting something.
▸ adjective [predic.] lost or surrendered as a penalty for wrongdoing: *his possessions were declared forfeit.*
– DERIVATIVES **forfeitable** adjective, **forfeiter** noun.
– ORIGIN Middle English (originally denoting a crime or transgression, hence a fine): from Old French *forfet*, *forfait*, past participle of *forfaire* 'transgress', from *for-* 'out' (from Latin *foris* 'outside') + *faire* 'do' (from Latin *facere*).

forfeiture ▸ noun [mass noun] the loss or giving up of something as a penalty for wrongdoing: *magistrates ordered the forfeiture of his computer.*

forfend /fɔːˈfɛnd/ ▸ verb [with obj.] **1** archaic avert or prevent (something evil or unpleasant).
2 (also **forefend**) US protect (something) by precautionary measures.
– PHRASES **Heaven** (or **God**) **forfend** archaic or humorous used to express dismay or horror at the thought of something happening: *Heaven forfend I should wound her susceptibilities.*

forgather ▸ verb variant spelling of **FOREGATHER**.

forgave past of **FORGIVE**.

forge[1] /fɔːdʒ/ ▸ verb [with obj.] **1** make or shape (a metal object) by heating it in a fire or furnace and hammering it.
2 create (something) strong, enduring, or successful: *the two women forged a close bond* | *the country is forging a bright new future.*
3 produce a fraudulent copy or imitation of (a document, signature, banknote, or work of art).
▸ noun a blacksmith's workshop; a smithy. ■ a furnace for melting or refining metal. ■ a workshop or factory containing a furnace for melting metal.
– DERIVATIVES **forgeable** adjective.
– ORIGIN Middle English (also in the general sense 'make, construct'): from Old French *forger*, from Latin *fabricare* 'fabricate', from *fabrica* 'manufactured object, workshop'. The noun is via Old French from Latin *fabrica*.

forge[2] /fɔːdʒ/ ▸ verb [no obj., with adverbial of direction] move forward gradually or steadily: *he forged through the crowded streets.*
– PHRASAL VERBS **forge ahead** take the lead or make good progress: *it may be that exports are forging ahead whilst home sales sag.*
– ORIGIN mid 18th cent.: perhaps an aberrant pronunciation of **FORCE**[1].

forged ▸ adjective copied fraudulently; fake: *they have illegally entered the UK using forged travel documents.*

forger ▸ noun a person who produces fraudulent copies or imitations: *one of Europe's most notorious art forgers.*

forgery ▸ noun (pl. **forgeries**) [mass noun] the action of forging a copy or imitation of a document, signature, banknote, or work of art. ■ [count noun] a forged document, signature, banknote, or work of art.

forget ▸ verb (**forgets**, **forgetting**, **forgot** ; past participle **forgotten** or chiefly US **forgot**) [with obj.] fail to remember: *he had forgotten his lines* | [with clause] *she had completely forgotten how hungry she was.* ■ inadvertently neglect to do or mention something: [with infinitive] *she forgot to lock her door.* ■ deliberately cease to think of: *forget all this romantic stuff* | [no obj.] *for years she had struggled to **forget about** him.* ■ (**forget it**) informal said when insisting to someone that there is no need for apology or thanks. ■ (**forget oneself**) neglect to behave in an appropriate way.
– PHRASES **not forgetting ——** (at the end of a list) and also ——: *there are wild goats and deer, not forgetting the famous Lundy ponies.*
– DERIVATIVES **forgetter** noun.
– ORIGIN Old English *forgietan*, of West Germanic origin; related to Dutch *vergeten* and German *vergessen*, and ultimately to **FOR-** and **GET**.

forgetful ▸ adjective apt or likely not to remember: *I'm a bit forgetful these days* | *she was soon **forgetful of** the time.*
– DERIVATIVES **forgetfully** adverb.

forgetfulness ▸ noun [mass noun] lapse of memory: *she teased him for his forgetfulness.*

forget-me-not ▸ noun a low-growing plant of the borage family, which typically has blue flowers and is a popular ornamental. ● *Myosotis* and other genera, family Boraginaceae: several species, in particular the common European *M. scorpioides*, whose bright blue flowers have a yellow centre.
– ORIGIN mid 16th cent.: translating the Old French name *ne m'oubliez mye*; said to have the virtue of ensuring that the wearer of the flower would never be forgotten by a lover.

forgettable ▸ adjective easily forgotten, especially through being uninteresting or mediocre: *eminently forgettable horror movies.*

forgivable ▸ adjective able to be forgiven or tolerated; excusable: *the flaws are forgivable.*
– DERIVATIVES **forgivably** adverb.

forgive ▸ verb (past **forgave**; past participle **forgiven**) [with obj.] stop feeling angry or resentful towards (someone) for an offence, flaw, or mistake: *I'll never **forgive** David **for** the way he treated her.* ■ no longer feel angry about or wish to punish (an offence, flaw, or mistake): *I was willing to forgive all her faults for the sake of our friendship* | [no obj.] *he had never found it easy to **forgive and forget**.* ■ cancel (a debt): *he proposed that their debts should be forgiven.* ■ used in polite expressions as a request to excuse one's foibles, ignorance, or impoliteness: *you will have to forgive my suspicious mind.*
– PHRASES **one could** (or **may**) **be forgiven for doing something** it would be understandable if one mistakenly did a particular thing: *with the plaster palm trees, you could be forgiven for thinking you were on Hollywood Boulevard.*
– DERIVATIVES **forgiver** noun.
– ORIGIN Old English *forgiefan*, of Germanic origin, related to Dutch *vergeven* and German *vergeben*, and ultimately to **FOR-** and **GIVE**.

forgiveness ▸ noun [mass noun] the action or process of forgiving or being forgiven: *she is quick to ask forgiveness when she has overstepped the line.*
– ORIGIN Old English *forgiefenes*, from *forgiefen* (past participle of *forgiefan* 'forgive') + the noun suffix *-nes*.

forgiving ▸ adjective ready and willing to forgive: *Taylor was in a forgiving mood* | *Perry is surprisingly **forgiving of** his stepfather.* ■ (of a thing) easy or safe to deal with: *snow is a forgiving surface on which to fall.*
– DERIVATIVES **forgivingly** adverb.

forgo (also **forego**) ▸ verb (**forgoes**, **forgoing**, **forwent**; past participle **forgone**) [with obj.] go without (something desirable): *she wanted to forgo the tea and leave while they could.* ■ refrain from: *we forgo any comparison between the two men.*
– ORIGIN Old English *forgān* (see **FOR-**, **GO**[1]).

forgone past participle of **FORGO**.

forgot past of **FORGET**.

forgotten past participle of **FORGET**.

forint /ˈfɒrɪnt/ ▸ noun the basic monetary unit of Hungary, equal to 100 filler.
– ORIGIN Hungarian, from Italian *fiorino* (see **FLORIN**).

fork ▸ noun **1** an implement with two or more prongs used for lifting food to the mouth or holding it when cutting. ■ a farm or garden tool with three or four prongs, used for digging or lifting. ■ [as modifier] denoting a light meal or buffet that may be eaten solely with a fork, while standing: *a fork supper.*
2 the point where something, especially a road or (N. Amer.) river, divides into two parts: *turn right at the next fork.* ■ either of two forked parts.
3 (usu. **forks**) each of a pair of supports in which a bicycle or motorcycle wheel revolves.
4 a flash of forked lightning.
5 Chess a simultaneous attack on two or more pieces by one.
▸ verb **1** [no obj.] (especially of a route) divide into two parts: *the place where the road forks.* ■ [no obj., with adverbial of direction] take or constitute one route or the other at the point where a route divides: *we forked north-west for Rannoch.* ■ Computing split (a process) into two or more independent processes.
2 [with obj.] dig or move (something) with a fork: *fork in some compost.*
3 [with obj.] Chess attack (two pieces) simultaneously with one.
– PHRASAL VERBS **fork something out/up** informal pay money for something, especially reluctantly: *my car had been towed away and I had to fork out 70 quid.*
– DERIVATIVES **forkful** noun (pl. **forkfuls**).
– ORIGIN Old English *forca*, *force* (denoting a farm implement), based on Latin *furca* 'pitchfork, forked stick'; reinforced in Middle English by Anglo-Norman French *furke* (also from Latin *furca*).

forkball ▸ noun Baseball a pitch released from between the widely spread index finger and middle finger.

Forkbeard, Sweyn, see **SWEYN I**.

forked ▸ adjective having a divided or pronged end or branches; bifurcated: *a deeply forked tail.*
– PHRASES **with forked tongue** humorous untruthfully; deceitfully.

forked lightning ▸ noun [mass noun] lightning that is visible in the form of a zigzag or branching line across the sky.

forklift ▸ noun (also **forklift truck**) a vehicle with a pronged device in front for lifting and carrying heavy loads.
▸ verb [with obj. and adverbial of place] lift and carry (a load) with a forklift truck.

forktail ▸ noun an Asian songbird of the thrush family, with a long forked tail and typically with black-and-white plumage. ● Genus *Enicurus*, family Turdidae: several species.

forlorn /fəˈlɔːn/ ▸ adjective **1** pitifully sad and abandoned or lonely: *forlorn figures at bus stops.*
2 (of an aim or endeavour) unlikely to succeed or be fulfilled: *a forlorn attempt to escape.*
– PHRASES **forlorn hope** a persistent or desperate hope that is unlikely to be fulfilled. [mid 16th cent.: from Dutch *verloren hoop* 'lost troop', from *verloren* (past participle of *verliezen* 'lose') and *hoop* 'company'. The phrase originally denoted a band of soldiers picked to begin an attack, many of whom would not survive; the current sense (mid 17th cent.), derives from a misunderstanding of the etymology.]
– DERIVATIVES **forlornly** adverb, **forlornness** noun.
– ORIGIN Old English *forloren* 'depraved, morally abandoned', past participle of *forlēosan* 'lose', of Germanic origin; related to Dutch *verliezen* and German *verlieren*, and ultimately to **FOR-** and **LOSE**. Sense 1 dates from the 16th cent.

form ▸ noun **1** the visible shape or configuration of something: *the form, colour, and texture of the tree* | [mass noun] *the flowers of this shrub are remarkable both in form and colour.* ■ the body or shape of a person or animal: *his eyes scanned her slender form.* ■ [mass noun] style, design, and arrangement in an artistic work as distinct from its content: *these videos are a triumph of form over content.*
2 a particular way in which a thing exists or appears: *essays in book form* | *energy **in the form of** light.* ■ any of the ways in which a word may be spelled, pronounced, or inflected: *an adjectival form.* ■ Philosophy the essential nature of a species or thing, especially (in Plato's thought) regarded as an abstract ideal which real things imitate or participate in.
3 a type or variety of something: *sponsorship is a form of advertising.* ■ an artistic or literary genre. ■ Botany a taxonomic category that ranks below variety, which contains organisms differing from the typical kind in some trivial, frequently impermanent, character, e.g. a colour variant. Also called **FORMA**.
4 [mass noun] the customary or correct method or procedure: *an excessive concern for legal form and precedent.* ■ [count noun] a ritual or convention: *the outward forms of religion.* ■ [count noun] a set order of words; a formula.
5 a printed document with blank spaces for information to be inserted: *an application form.*
6 chiefly Brit. a class or year in a school, usually given a specifying number: *the fifth form.*

7 [mass noun] the state of a sports player or team with regard to their current standard of play: *they are one of the best teams around on current form.* ■ details of previous performances by a racehorse or greyhound: *an interested bystander studying the form.* ■ a person's mood and state of health: *she seemed to be **on good form**.* ■ Brit. informal a criminal record: *they both had form.*
8 Brit. a long bench without a back.
9 Printing, chiefly US variant spelling of FORME.
10 Brit. a hare's lair.
11 another term for SHUTTERING.
▶ **verb** [with obj.] **1** bring together parts or combine to create (something): *the company was formed in 1982* | *peasants and miners were **formed into** a militia.* ■ go to make up or constitute: *the precepts which form the basis of the book.* ■ [no obj.] gradually appear or develop: *a thick mist was forming all around.* ■ conceive (an idea) in one's mind. ■ establish (a relationship): *the women would form supportive friendships.* ■ articulate (a word or other linguistic unit). ■ construct (a new word) by derivation or inflection.
2 make or be made into a specific shape or form: [with obj.] ***form the dough into balls*** | [no obj.] *his features **formed into** a smile of pleasure.* ■ (**be formed**) have a specified shape: *her body was slight and flawlessly formed.* ■ (**form people/things up** or **form up**) chiefly Military bring or be brought into a certain formation: *Mortimer formed up his troops for the march.* ■ influence (something abstract): *the role of the news media in forming public opinion.*
– PHRASES **in** (or chiefly Brit. **on**) **form** (of a sports player or team) playing or performing well. **off** (or **out of**) **form** (of a sports player or team) not playing or performing well.
– DERIVATIVES **formability** noun, **formable** adjective.
– ORIGIN Middle English: from Old French *forme* (noun), *fo(u)rmer* (verb, from Latin *formare* 'to form'), both based on Latin *forma* 'a mould or form'.

-form (usu. as **-iform**) ▶ **combining form 1** having the form of: *cruciform.*
2 having a particular number of: *multiform.*
– ORIGIN from French *-forme*, from Latin *-formis*, from *forma* 'form'.

forma /ˈfɔːmə/ ▶ **noun** (pl. **formas** or **formae** /-miː/) Botany another term for FORM (sense 3 of the noun).

formal ▶ **adjective 1** done in accordance with convention or etiquette; suitable for or constituting an official or important occasion: *a formal dinner party.* ■ (of a person or their manner) strictly conventional. ■ having a conventionally recognized form, structure, or set of rules: *he had little formal education.* ■ of or denoting a style of writing or public speaking characterized by more elaborate grammatical structures and more conservative and technical vocabulary.
2 officially sanctioned or recognized: *a formal complaint.*
3 of or concerned with outward form or appearance as distinct from content: *I don't know enough about art to appreciate the purely formal qualities.* ■ having the form or appearance without the spirit: *the committee stage would be purely formal.* ■ relating to linguistic or logical form as opposed to function or meaning.
▶ **noun** N. Amer. an evening dress. ■ an occasion on which evening dress is worn.
– ORIGIN late Middle English: from Latin *formalis*, from *forma* 'shape, mould' (see FORM).

formal cause ▶ **noun** Philosophy (in Aristotelian thought) the pattern which determines the form taken by something.

formaldehyde /fɔːˈmaldɪhʌɪd/ ▶ **noun** [mass noun] Chemistry a colourless pungent gas in solution made by oxidizing methanol. ● Alternative name: **methanal**; chem. formula: CH_2O.
– ORIGIN late 19th cent.: blend of FORMIC ACID and ALDEHYDE.

formalin /ˈfɔːm(ə)lɪn/ ▶ **noun** [mass noun] a colourless solution of formaldehyde in water, used chiefly as a preservative for biological specimens.
– ORIGIN late 19th cent.: from FORMALDEHYDE + -IN[1].

formalism ▶ **noun 1** [mass noun] excessive adherence to prescribed forms: *academic dryness and formalism.* ■ the basing of ethics on the form of the moral law without regard to intention or consequences. ■ concern or excessive concern with form and technique rather than content in artistic creation. ■ (in the theatre) a symbolic and stylized manner of production. ■ the treatment of mathematics as a manipulation of meaningless symbols.
2 a description of something in formal mathematical or logical terms.
– DERIVATIVES **formalist** noun, **formalistic** adjective.

formality ▶ **noun** (pl. **formalities**) [mass noun] the rigid observance of convention or etiquette: *the formality of life in an English public school.* ■ strictly conventional behaviour: *with disconcerting formality the brothers shook hands.* ■ [count noun] (usu. **formalities**) a thing that is done simply to comply with convention, regulations, or custom: *legal formalities.* ■ (**a formality**) something done or happening as a matter of course and without question: *promotion looks a formality.*
– ORIGIN mid 16th cent. (in the sense 'accordance with legal rules or conventions'): from French *formalité* or medieval Latin *formalitas*, from *formalis* (see FORMAL).

formalize (also **formalise**) ▶ **verb** [with obj.] **1** give (something) legal or formal status: *a year has elapsed since the marriage was formalized.*
2 give a definite structure or shape to: *we became able to formalize our thoughts.*
– DERIVATIVES **formalization** noun.

formally ▶ **adverb 1** in accordance with convention or etiquette: *he was formally attired.*
2 officially: *the Mayor will formally open the new Railway Centre.*
3 [sentence adverb] in outward form or appearance: *formally, ministers are responsible to the monarch.* ■ in terms of form or structure: *formally complex types of text.*

Forman /ˈfɔːmən/, Milos (b.1932), Czech-born American film director. He made *One Flew Over the Cuckoo's Nest* (1975), which won five Oscars, and *Amadeus* (1983), which won eight Oscars, including that for best director.

formant /ˈfɔːm(ə)nt/ ▶ **noun** Phonetics any of the three characteristic pitch constituents of a vowel. In a high front vowel such as /iː/ the formants are bunched closely together, whereas in a low back vowel such as /ɑː/ they are further apart.
– ORIGIN early 20th cent.: coined in German from Latin *formant-* 'forming', from the verb *formare*.

format ▶ **noun** the way in which something is arranged or set out: *the conventional format of TV situation comedies.* ■ the shape, size, and presentation of a book or periodical. ■ the medium in which a sound recording is made available: *he has just re-issued the collection in CD format.* ■ Computing a defined structure for the processing, storage, or display of data: *a data file in binary format.*
▶ **verb** (**formats, formatting, formatted**) [with obj.] (especially in computing) arrange or put into a format. ■ prepare (a storage medium) to receive data.
– ORIGIN mid 19th cent.: via French and German from Latin *formatus (liber)* 'shaped (book)', past participle of *formare* 'to form'.

formate ▶ **noun** a salt or ester of formic acid.

formation ▶ **noun 1** [mass noun] the action of forming or process of being formed: *the formation of the Great Rift Valley.*
2 a thing that has been formed: *strange black rock formations.* ■ a group of people or things in a particular arrangement or pattern: *they sat in orderly ranks in a circular formation* | [mass noun] *the jets took off **in formation**.*
– DERIVATIVES **formational** adjective.
– ORIGIN late Middle English: from Latin *formatio(n-)*, from *formare* 'to form' (see FORM).

formation dancing ▶ **noun** [mass noun] a variety of competitive ballroom dancing in which a team of couples dance a prepared routine.

formative ▶ **adjective** serving to form something, especially having a profound influence on a person's development: *his formative years.* ■ relating to a person's development: *a formative assessment.* ■ Linguistics denoting or relating to any of the smallest meaningful units that are used to form words in a language, typically combining forms and inflections.
▶ **noun** Linguistics a formative element.
– DERIVATIVES **formatively** adverb.
– ORIGIN late 15th cent.: from Old French *formatif, -ive* or medieval Latin *formativus*, from Latin *formare* 'to form' (see FORM).

Formby /ˈfɔːmbi/, George (1904–61), English comedian; born *George Booth*. He became famous for his numerous musical films in the 1930s in which he played a Lancashire working lad and accompanied his songs on the ukulele.

form class ▶ **noun** Linguistics a class of linguistic forms with grammatical or syntactic features in common; a part of speech or subset of a part of speech.

form criticism ▶ **noun** [mass noun] analysis of the Bible by tracing the history of its content of parables, psalms, and other literary forms.

form drag ▶ **noun** [mass noun] Aeronautics that part of the drag on an aerofoil which arises from its shape. It varies according to the angle of attack and can be decreased by streamlining.

forme /fɔːm/ (also **form**) ▶ **noun** Printing a body of type secured in a chase for printing. ■ a quantity of film arranged for making a plate.
– ORIGIN late 15th cent.: variant of FORM.

Formentera /ˌfɔːmənˈtɛːrə/ a small island in the Mediterranean, south of Ibiza. It is the southernmost of the Balearic Islands.

former[1] ▶ **adjective** [attrib.] **1** having previously been a particular thing: *her former boyfriend.* ■ of or occurring in the past: *the seafarers of former times.*
2 (**the former**) denoting the first or first mentioned of two people or things: *I take the former view* | [as noun] *the powers of the former are more comprehensive than those of the latter.*
– ORIGIN Middle English: from Old English *forma* (see FOREMOST) + -ER[2].

> **USAGE** Traditionally, **former** and **latter** are used in relation to pairs of items: either the first of two items (**former**) or the second of two items (**latter**). The reason for this is that **former** and **latter** were formed as comparatives, and comparatives are correctly used with reference to just two things, while a superlative is used where there are more than two things. So, for example, strictly speaking one should say *the **longest** of the **three** books* but *the **longer** of the **two** books*. In practice, **former** and **latter** are now sometimes used just as synonyms for **first** and **last** and are routinely used to refer to a contrast involving more than two items. Such uses, however, are not acceptable in good English style.

former[2] ▶ **noun 1** a person or thing that forms something: [in combination] *an opinion-former.* ■ a tool, mould, or other device used to form articles or shape materials: *an arch former.* ■ a transverse strengthening part in an aircraft wing or fuselage. ■ a frame or core around which an electrical coil can be wound.
2 [in combination] Brit. a person in a particular school year: *fifth-formers.*

formerly ▶ **adverb** in the past; in earlier times: *Mumbai, formerly Bombay* | *the building formerly housed the National Assembly.*

form factor ▶ **noun 1** a mathematical factor which compensates for irregularity in the shape of an object, usually the ratio between its volume and that of a regular object of the same breadth and height.
2 the physical size and shape of a piece of computer hardware.

form-fitting ▶ **adjective** (of clothing) fitting someone's body closely: *a pair of form-fitting jeans.*

form genus ▶ **noun** Palaeontology a classificatory category used for fossils which are similar in appearance but cannot be reliably assigned to an established animal or plant genus, such as fossil parts of organisms and trace fossils.

Formica /fɔːˈmʌɪkə/ ▶ **noun** [mass noun] trademark a hard durable plastic laminate used for worktops, cupboard doors, and other surfaces.
– ORIGIN 1920s (originally US): of unknown origin.

formic acid /ˈfɔːmɪk/ ▶ **noun** [mass noun] Chemistry a colourless irritant volatile acid made catalytically from carbon monoxide and steam. It is present in the fluid emitted by some ants. ● Alternative name: **methanoic acid**; chem. formula: HCOOH.
– ORIGIN late 18th cent.: *formic* from Latin *formica* 'ant'.

formicarium /ˌfɔːmɪˈkɛːrɪəm/ ▶ **noun** (pl. **formicaria**) an ant's nest, especially one in an artificial container for purposes of study.
– ORIGIN early 19th cent.: from medieval Latin, from Latin *formica* 'ant'.

formication /ˌfɔːmɪˈkeɪʃ(ə)n/ ▶ **noun** [mass noun] a sensation like insects crawling over the skin.
– ORIGIN early 18th cent.: from Latin *formicatio(n-)*, from *formicare* 'crawl like an ant' (said of the pulse or skin), from *formica* 'ant'.

formidable /ˈfɔːmɪdəb(ə)l, fɔːˈmɪd-/ ▶ **adjective** inspiring fear or respect through being impressively large, powerful, intense, or capable: *a formidable opponent.*
– DERIVATIVES **formidableness** noun, **formidably** adverb.

F

– ORIGIN late Middle English: from French, or from Latin *formidabilis*, from *formidare* 'to fear'.

> **USAGE** There are two possible pronunciations of **formidable**: one with the stress on the **for-** and the other with the stress on the **-mid-**. The second pronunciation is now common in British English, but the traditional pronunciation places the stress on the first syllable. Both pronunciations are acceptable in modern standard English.

formless ▶ **adjective** without a clear or definite shape or structure: *a dark and formless idea.*
– DERIVATIVES **formlessly** adverb, **formlessness** noun.

form letter ▶ **noun** a standardized letter to deal with frequently occurring matters.

formol /ˈfɔːmɒl/ ▶ **noun** another term for FORMALIN.

Formosa /fɔːˈməʊsə/ former name for TAIWAN.
– ORIGIN Portuguese, literally 'beautiful'.

F

formula /ˈfɔːmjʊlə/ ▶ **noun 1** (pl. **formulae** /-liː/) a mathematical relationship or rule expressed in symbols. ■ (also **chemical formula**) a set of chemical symbols showing the elements present in a compound and their relative proportions.
2 (pl. **formulas**) a method or procedure for achieving something: *the forlorn hope of finding a peace formula.* ■ a list of ingredients with which something is made: *a blend of fifteen whiskies compiled to a secret formula.* ■ a formulation: *an original coal tar formula that helps prevent dandruff.* ■ [mass noun] (also **formula milk**) a baby's liquid food based on cow's milk or soya protein, given as a substitute for breast milk.
3 (pl. **formulas**) a set form of words, especially one used in particular contexts or as a conventional usage: *polite formulas and stock phrases | a legal formula.* ■ a rule or style followed mechanically: [as modifier] *one of those formula tunes.* ■ a stock epithet, phrase, or line repeated for various effects, especially in epic poetry.
4 (usually followed by a numeral) a classification of racing car, especially by the engine capacity.
– ORIGIN early 17th cent. (in the sense 'fixed form of words'): from Latin, diminutive of *forma* 'shape, mould'.

formulable ▶ **adjective** capable of being formulated: *easily formulable propositions.*

formulaic /ˌfɔːmjʊˈleɪɪk/ ▶ **adjective** constituting or containing a set form of words: *formulaic expressions such as 'Once upon a time'.* ■ produced in accordance with a mechanically followed rule or style: *formulaic, disposable pop.*
– DERIVATIVES **formulaically** adverb.

Formula One ▶ **noun** [mass noun] trademark an international form of motor racing, whose races are called Grands Prix.

formularize (also **formularise**) ▶ **verb** [with obj.] make formulaic or predictable: *their stage shows have become a little formularized.*

formulary /ˈfɔːmjʊləri/ ▶ **noun** (pl. **formularies**) **1** a collection of set forms, especially for use in religious ceremonies.
2 an official list giving details of prescribable medicines.
▶ **adjective** relating to or using officially prescribed formulas.
– ORIGIN mid 16th cent.: the noun from French *formulaire* or medieval Latin *formularius (liber)* '(book) of formulae', from Latin *formula* (see FORMULA); the adjective (early 18th cent.) is directly from FORMULA.

formulate /ˈfɔːmjʊleɪt/ ▶ **verb** [with obj.] create or prepare methodically: *the government has formulated a policy on waste management | use special-effects paints that are formulated for the task.* ■ express (an idea) in a concise or systematic way: *the argument is sufficiently clear that it can be formulated mathematically.*
– DERIVATIVES **formulator** noun.
– ORIGIN mid 19th cent.: from FORMULA + -ATE³, on the pattern of French *formuler*, from medieval Latin *formulare*.

formulation ▶ **noun 1** [mass noun] the action of creating or preparing something: *the formulation of foreign policy.* ■ [count noun] a particular expression of an idea, thought, or theory.
2 a material or mixture prepared according to a formula.

formwork ▶ **noun** another term for SHUTTERING.

formyl /ˈfɔːmʌɪl, -mɪl/ ▶ **noun** [as modifier] Chemistry of or denoting the acyl radical –CHO, derived from formic acid: *N-formyl methionine.*

Fornax /ˈfɔːnaks/ Astronomy an inconspicuous southern constellation (the Furnace), near Eridanus.
– ORIGIN Latin.

fornent /fɔːˈnɛnt, fə-/ (also **fornenst**) ▶ **preposition** dialect, chiefly Scottish alongside, opposite, or close by.
– ORIGIN late Middle English: blend of the adverb FORE and ANENT.

fornicate ▶ **verb** [no obj.] formal or humorous have sexual intercourse with someone one is not married to.
– DERIVATIVES **fornicator** noun.
– ORIGIN Middle English (as *fornication*): from ecclesiastical Latin *fornicat-* 'arched', from *fornicari*, from Latin *fornix, fornic-* 'vaulted chamber', later 'brothel'.

fornication ▶ **noun** [mass noun] formal or humorous sexual intercourse between people not married to each other: *laws forbidding adultery and fornication.*

fornix /ˈfɔːnɪks/ ▶ **noun** (pl. **fornices** /ˈfɔːnɪsiːz/) Anatomy a vaulted or arched structure in the body, in particular: ■ (also **fornix cerebri** /ˈsɛrɪbrʌɪ/) a triangular area of white matter in the mammalian brain between the hippocampus and the hypothalamus.
– ORIGIN late 17th cent.: from Latin, literally 'arch, vaulted chamber'.

for-profit ▶ **adjective** denoting an organization operated to make a profit.

forrader /ˈfɒrədə/ ▶ **adjective & adverb** non-standard spelling of FORWARDER², used humorously or to represent dialect pronunciation: [as adv.] *well, that didn't get me much forrader, but it was something.*

forrard /ˈfɒrəd/ ▶ **adjective & adverb** non-standard spelling of FORWARD, used to represent a nautical or dialect pronunciation.

Forrest, John, 1st Baron (1847–1918), Australian explorer and statesman, first Premier of Western Australia 1890–1901.

forsake ▶ **verb** (past **forsook**; past participle **forsaken**) [with obj.] chiefly literary abandon or leave: *he would never forsake Tara.* ■ renounce or give up (something valued or pleasant): *I won't forsake my vegetarian principles.*
– DERIVATIVES **forsaker** noun.
– ORIGIN Old English *forsacan* 'renounce, refuse', of West Germanic origin; related to Dutch *verzaken*, and ultimately to FOR- and SAKE¹.

forsaken ▶ **adjective** abandoned or deserted: *a journey into forgotten and forsaken places.*
– DERIVATIVES **forsakenness** noun.

forsooth /fəˈsuːθ/ ▶ **adverb** [sentence adverb] archaic or humorous indeed (often used ironically): *it's a kind of wine bar for royals, forsooth.*
– ORIGIN Old English *forsōth* (see FOR, SOOTH).

Forster /ˈfɔːstə/, E. M. (1879–1970), English novelist and literary critic; full name *Edward Morgan Forster*. His novels, several of which have been made into films, include *A Room with a View* (1908) and *A Passage to India* (1924).

forsterite /ˈfɔːstərʌɪt/ ▶ **noun** [mass noun] a magnesium-rich variety of olivine, occurring as white, yellow, or green crystals.
– ORIGIN early 19th cent.: from the name of J. R. *Forster* (1729–98), German naturalist, + -ITE¹.

forswear ▶ **verb** (past **forswore**; past participle **forsworn**) [with obj.] **1** formal agree to give up or do without: *the country has not forsworn nuclear weapons.*
2 (**forswear oneself/be forsworn**) archaic commit perjury; swear falsely.
– ORIGIN Old English *forswerian* (see FOR-, SWEAR).

forsythia /fɔːˈsʌɪθɪə, fə-/ ▶ **noun** an ornamental Eurasian shrub whose bright yellow flowers appear in early spring before the leaves. ● Genus *Forsythia*, family Oleaceae: several species.
– ORIGIN modern Latin, named after William *Forsyth* (1737–1804), Scottish botanist and horticulturalist, said to have introduced the shrub into Britain from China.

fort ▶ **noun** a fortified building or strategic position. ■ historical a trading station. [so named because such stations were originally fortified.]
– DERIVATIVES **fortlet** noun.
– ORIGIN late Middle English: from Old French *fort* or Italian *forte*, from Latin *fortis* 'strong'.

Fortaleza /ˌfɔːtəˈleɪzə/ a port in NE Brazil, on the Atlantic coast, capital of the state of Ceará; pop. 2,431,415 (2007).

fortalice /ˈfɔːtəlɪs/ ▶ **noun** a small fort, fortified house, or outwork of fortification.
– ORIGIN late Middle English: from medieval Latin *fortalitia, -itium*, from Latin *fortis* 'strong'.

Fort-de-France /ˌfɔːdəˈfrɑːns/, French /fɔʀ də fʀɑ̃s/ the capital of Martinique; pop. 93,000 (est. 2007).

forte¹ /ˈfɔːteɪ, ˈfɔːti, fɔːt/ ▶ **noun 1** (**one's forte**) a thing at which someone excels: *small talk was not his forte.*
2 Fencing the part of a sword blade from the hilt to the middle. Compare with FOIBLE.
– ORIGIN mid 17th cent. (in sense 2; originally as *fort*): from French *fort* (masculine), *forte* (feminine) 'strong', from Latin *fortis*.

forte² /ˈfɔːteɪ/ Music ▶ **adverb & adjective** (especially as a direction) loud or loudly.
▶ **noun** a passage performed or marked to be performed loudly.
– ORIGIN Italian, literally 'strong, loud', from Latin *fortis*.

Fortean /ˈfɔːtɪən/ ▶ **adjective** relating to or denoting paranormal phenomena.
– DERIVATIVES **Forteana** plural noun.
– ORIGIN 1970s: from the name of Charles H. *Fort* (1874–1932), American student of paranormal phenomena.

fortepiano /ˌfɔːteɪˈpjɑːnəʊ, -ˈpjanəʊ/ ▶ **noun** (pl. **fortepianos**) Music a piano, especially of the kind made in the 18th and early 19th centuries.
– ORIGIN mid 18th cent.: from FORTE² + PIANO².

forte piano /ˌfɔːteɪ ˈpjɑːnəʊ/ ▶ **adverb & adjective** Music (especially as a direction) loud and then immediately soft.
– ORIGIN Italian.

Forth a river of central Scotland, rising on Ben Lomond and flowing eastwards through Stirling into the North Sea. ■ a shipping forecast area covering Scottish coastal waters roughly from Berwick in the south to Aberdeen in the north, including the Firth of Forth.

forth ▶ **adverb** formal or literary **1** out and away from a starting point: *we rose at dawn and sallied forth.* ■ so as to be known or revealed; out: *a paper setting forth their grievances.*
2 onwards in time: ***from that day forth** he gave me endless friendship.*
– PHRASES **and so forth** and so on: *particular services like education, housing, and so forth.*
– ORIGIN Old English, of Germanic origin; related to Dutch *voort* and German *fort*, from an Indo-European root shared by FORE-.

Forth, Firth of the estuary of the River Forth, spanned by a cantilever railway bridge (opened 1890) and a road suspension bridge (1964).
– PHRASES **paint the Forth Bridge** used to indicate that a task is never-ending: *it's all over for another year except that we must immediately set about seeking next year's sponsor—it's a bit like painting the Forth Bridge.* [with reference to the fact that the railway bridge is so long that once its painters had reached one end, they would have to begin again at the other.]

forthcoming ▶ **adjective 1** about to happen or appear: *the forthcoming cricket season.*
2 [predic.] [often with negative] ready or made available when wanted or needed: *financial support was not forthcoming.* ■ willing to divulge information: *she had never been forthcoming about her time in the States.*
– DERIVATIVES **forthcomingness** noun.

forthright ▶ **adjective 1** (of a person or their manner or speech) direct and outspoken: *his most forthright attack yet on the reforms.*
2 archaic proceeding directly forwards.
▶ **adverb** archaic directly forwards. ■ immediately.
– DERIVATIVES **forthrightly** adverb, **forthrightness** noun.
– ORIGIN Old English *forthriht* 'straight forward, directly' (see FORTH, RIGHT).

forthwith /fɔːθˈwɪθ, -ð/ ▶ **adverb** (especially in official use) immediately; without delay: *we undertake to pay forthwith the money required.*
– ORIGIN Middle English (in the sense 'along with, at the same time'): partly from earlier *forthwithal*, partly representing *forth with* used alone without a following noun.

fortification /ˌfɔːtɪfɪˈkeɪʃ(ə)n/ ▶ **noun** a defensive wall or other reinforcement built to strengthen a place against attack. ■ [mass noun] the action of fortifying or process of being fortified: *the fortification of the frontiers.*
– ORIGIN late Middle English: via French from late Latin *fortificatio(n-)*, from *fortificare* (see FORTIFY).

fortify /ˈfɔːtɪfʌɪ/ ▶ **verb** (**fortifies**, **fortifying**, **fortified**) [with obj.] **1** provide (a place) with defensive

works as protection against attack: *the whole town was heavily fortified* | (as adj. **fortified**) *a fortified manor house.* ■ strengthen (someone) mentally or physically: *the girl was fortified by her religious faith.* **2** (often as adj. **fortified**) add spirits to (wine) to make port, sherry, etc.: *fortified wine.* ■ increase the nutritive value of (food) by adding vitamins.
– DERIVATIVES **fortifiable** adjective, **fortifier** noun.
– ORIGIN late Middle English: from French *fortifier*, from late Latin *fortificare*, from Latin *fortis* 'strong'.

fortis /ˈfɔːtɪs/ ▶ **adjective** Phonetics (of a consonant, in particular a voiceless consonant) strongly articulated, especially more so than another consonant articulated in the same place. The opposite of **LENIS**.
– ORIGIN early 20th cent.: from Latin, literally 'strong'.

fortissimo /fɔːˈtɪsɪməʊ/ Music ▶ **adverb & adjective** (especially as a direction) very loud or loudly.
▶ **noun** (pl. **fortissimos** or **fortissimi** /-mi/) a passage performed or marked to be performed very loudly.
– ORIGIN Italian, from Latin *fortissimus* 'very strong'.

fortitude /ˈfɔːtɪtjuːd/ ▶ **noun** [mass noun] courage in pain or adversity: *she endured her illness with great fortitude.*
– ORIGIN Middle English: via French from Latin *fortitudo*, from *fortis* 'strong'.

Fort Knox /fɔːt ˈnɒks/ a US military reservation in Kentucky, famous as the site of the depository (built in 1936) which holds the bulk of the nation's gold bullion in its vaults.

Fort Lamy /ˈlɑːmi/ former name (until 1973) for **N'DJAMENA**.

fortnight ▶ **noun** Brit. a period of two weeks. ■ informal (preceded by a specified day) used to indicate that something will take place two weeks after that day.
– ORIGIN Old English *fēowertīene niht* 'fourteen nights'.

fortnightly Brit. ▶ **adjective** happening or produced every two weeks: *a fortnightly bulletin.*
▶ **adverb** every two weeks: *evening classes will run fortnightly.*
▶ **noun** (pl. **fortnightlies**) a magazine or other periodical issued every two weeks.

Fortran /ˈfɔːtran/ ▶ **noun** [mass noun] a high-level computer programming language used especially for scientific calculations.
– ORIGIN 1950s: contraction of *formula translation*.

fortress ▶ **noun** a military stronghold, especially a strongly fortified town. ■ a person or thing not susceptible to outside influence or disturbance: *he had proved himself to be a fortress of moral rectitude.*
– ORIGIN Middle English: from Old French *forteresse* 'strong place', based on Latin *fortis* 'strong'.

fortuitous /fɔːˈtjuːɪtəs/ ▶ **adjective** happening by chance rather than intention: *the similarity between the paintings may not be simply fortuitous.* ■ happening by a lucky chance; fortunate: *the ball went into the goal by a fortuitous ricochet.*
– DERIVATIVES **fortuitously** adverb, **fortuitousness** noun.
– ORIGIN mid 17th cent.: from Latin *fortuitus*, from *forte* 'by chance', from *fors* 'chance, luck'.

> **USAGE** The traditional, etymological meaning of fortuitous is 'happening by chance': a *fortuitous meeting* is a chance meeting, which might turn out to be either a good thing or a bad thing. Today, however, **fortuitous** tends to be often used to refer only to fortunate outcomes and the word has become more or less a synonym for 'lucky' or 'fortunate' (*the ball went into the goal by a fortuitous ricochet*). Although this usage is now widespread, it is still regarded by some people as incorrect.

fortuity /fɔːˈtjuːɪti/ ▶ **noun** (pl. **fortuities**) a chance occurrence. ■ [mass noun] the state of being controlled by chance.

fortunate ▶ **adjective** favoured by or involving good luck; lucky: [with infinitive] *she'd been fortunate to escape serious injury* | *it was fortunate that the weather was good.* ■ auspicious or favourable: *a most fortunate match for our daughter.* ■ materially well off; prosperous: *a federal programme aimed at helping less fortunate families.*
– ORIGIN late Middle English: from Latin *fortunatus*, from *fortuna* (see **FORTUNE**).

fortunately ▶ **adverb** [sentence adverb] it is fortunate that: *fortunately, no shots were fired and no one was hurt.*

fortune ▶ **noun 1** [mass noun] chance or luck as an arbitrary force affecting human affairs: *some malicious act of fortune keeps them separate.* ■ luck, especially good luck: *only good fortune has prevented British casualties.* ■ (**fortunes**) the success or failure of a person or enterprise over a period of time: *he is credited with turning round the company's fortunes.*
2 a large amount of money or assets: *he inherited a substantial fortune.* ■ (**a fortune**) informal a surprisingly high price or amount of money: *I spent a fortune on drink.*
– PHRASES **fortune favours the brave** proverb a successful person is often one who is willing to take risks. **the fortunes of war** the unpredictable events of war. **make a** (or **one's**) **fortune** acquire great wealth by one's own efforts. **a small fortune** informal a large amount of money. **tell someone's fortune** make predictions about a person's future by palmistry, using a crystal ball, or similar methods.
– ORIGIN Middle English: via Old French from Latin *Fortuna*, the name of a goddess personifying luck or chance.

Fortune 500 ▶ **noun** (trademark in the US) an annual list of the five hundred largest US industrial corporations, as measured by gross income.

fortune cookie ▶ **noun** N. Amer. a small biscuit containing a slip of paper with a prediction or motto written on it, served in Chinese restaurants.

fortune hunter ▶ **noun** a person who seeks to become rich through marrying someone wealthy.
– DERIVATIVES **fortune hunting** noun.

fortune teller ▶ **noun** a person who tells people's fortunes.
– DERIVATIVES **fortune telling** noun.

Fort William a town in western Scotland, on Loch Linnhe near Ben Nevis; pop 9,000 (est. 2009).

Fort Worth a city in northern Texas; pop. 703,073 (est. 2008).

forty ▶ **cardinal number** (pl. **forties**) **1** the number equivalent to the product of four and ten; ten less than fifty; 40: *York was only forty miles away* | *forty were arrested* | *there were about thirty or forty of them.* (Roman numeral: **xl** or **XL**) ■ (**forties**) the numbers from forty to forty-nine, especially the years of a century or of a person's life: *Terry was in his early forties.* ■ forty years old: *a tall woman of about forty.* ■ forty miles an hour: *they were doing about forty.* ■ a size of garment or other merchandise denoted by forty.
2 (**the Forties**) the central North Sea between Scotland and southern Norway, so called from its prevailing depth of forty fathoms or more. See also **THE ROARING FORTIES** at **ROARING**. ■ (**Forties**) a shipping forecast area covering the central North Sea east of Scotland.
– PHRASES **forty winks** informal a short sleep, especially during the day.
– DERIVATIVES **fortieth** ordinal number, **fortyfold** adjective & adverb.
– ORIGIN Old English *fēowertig* (see **FOUR**, **-TY²**).

forty-five ▶ **noun** a record played at 45 rpm; a single.
– PHRASES **the Forty-five** an informal name for the Jacobite rebellion of 1745.

forty-niner ▶ **noun** a seeker for gold in the California gold rush of 1849.

forty-ninth parallel the parallel of latitude 49° north of the equator, especially as forming the boundary between Canada and the US west of the Lake of the Woods.

forum /ˈfɔːrəm/ ▶ **noun** (pl. **forums**) **1** a meeting or medium where ideas and views on a particular issue can be exchanged: *we hope these pages act as a forum for debate.* ■ an Internet message board.
2 chiefly N. Amer. a court or tribunal.
3 (pl. **fora**) (in an ancient Roman city) a public square or marketplace used for judicial and other business.
– ORIGIN late Middle English (in sense 3): from Latin, literally 'what is out of doors', originally denoting an enclosure surrounding a house; related to *fores* '(outside) door'. Sense 1 dates from the mid 18th cent.

forward ▶ **adverb** (also **forwards**) **1** in the direction that one is facing or travelling; towards the front: *he started up the engine and the car moved forward* | *Rory leaned forward over the table.* ■ in or towards the bow or nose of a ship or aircraft. ■ in the normal order or sequence: *the number was the same backwards as forwards.*
2 onward so as to make progress: *the signing of the treaty is a big step forward.*
3 towards the future: *looking forward, earnings are expected to hit £7.2 billion.* ■ to an earlier time: *the special issue has been moved forward to November.*
▶ **adjective 1** directed or facing towards the front or the direction that one is facing or travelling: *forward flight* | *the pilot's forward view.* ■ positioned near the enemy lines: *troops moved to the forward areas.* ■ situated in or towards the bow or nose of a ship or aircraft. ■ Electronics (of a voltage applied to a semiconductor junction) in the direction which allows significant current to flow.
2 [attrib.] relating to the future: *forward planning.*
3 progressing towards a successful conclusion: *the decision is a forward step.* ■ further advanced than expected or required: *an alarmingly forward yet painfully vulnerable child.*
4 (of a person) bold or overfamiliar in manner.
▶ **noun 1** an attacking player in football, hockey, or other sports.
2 (**forwards**) agreements to trade specified assets, typically currency, at a specified price at a certain future date. Compare with **FUTURE** (sense 2 of the noun).
▶ **verb** [with obj.] **1** send (a letter or email) on to a further destination: *my emails were forwarded to a friend* |(as adj. **forwarding**) *a forwarding address.* ■ dispatch or send (a document or goods): *apply by forwarding a CV.*
2 help to advance (something); promote: *the scientists are forwarding the development of biotechnology.*
– PHRASES **forward of** in front of: *the units are located forward of the flight deck control and display panels.*
– DERIVATIVES **forwardly** adverb.
– ORIGIN Old English *forweard* (in the sense 'towards the future', as in *from this day forward*), variant of *forthweard* (see **FORTH**, **-WARD**).

forwarder¹ /ˈfɔːwədə/ ▶ **noun** a person or organization that dispatches or delivers goods.

forwarder² /ˈfɒrədə/ ▶ **adjective & adverb** informal further forward; more advanced: *time was drawing on and we were no forwarder.*

forward-looking (also **forward-thinking**) ▶ **adjective** favouring innovation and development; progressive: *a forward-looking company.*

forwardness ▶ **noun** [mass noun] boldness or overfamiliarity in manner: *he was taken aback by the girl's forwardness.*

forwards ▶ **adverb** variant spelling of **FORWARD**.

forward scattering ▶ **noun** [mass noun] Physics the scattering of radiation involving a change of direction of less than 90 degrees, in particular the propagation of high-frequency radio waves beyond the horizon by scattering or reflection from the ionosphere.

forwent past of **FORGO**.

Fosbury /ˈfɒzb(ə)ri/, Richard (b.1947), American high jumper. He originated the now standard style of jumping known as the 'Fosbury flop', in which the jumper clears the bar head first and backwards. In 1968 he won the Olympic gold medal using this technique.

fossa¹ /ˈfɒsə/ ▶ **noun** (pl. **fossae** /-siː/) Anatomy a shallow depression or hollow.
– ORIGIN mid 17th cent.: from Latin, literally 'ditch', feminine past participle of *fodere* 'to dig'.

fossa² /ˈfɒsə/ ▶ **noun** a large nocturnal reddish-brown catlike mammal of the civet family, found in the rainforests of Madagascar. ● *Cryptoprocta ferox*, family Viverridae.
– ORIGIN mid 19th cent.: from Malagasy *fosa*.

fosse /fɒs/ ▶ **noun** Archaeology a long, narrow trench or excavation, especially in a fortification.
– ORIGIN late Old English, via Old French from Latin *fossa* (see **FOSSA¹**).

Fosse Way an ancient road in Britain. It ran from Axminster to Lincoln, via Bath and Leicester (about 300 km, 200 miles), and marked the limit of the first stage of the Roman occupation (mid 1st century AD).

fossick /ˈfɒsɪk/ ▶ **verb** [no obj.] Austral./NZ informal rummage; search: *he spent years fossicking through documents.* ■ search for gold in abandoned workings.
– DERIVATIVES **fossicker** noun.
– ORIGIN mid 19th cent. (referring to mining): probably from the English dialect sense 'obtain by asking' (i.e. 'ferret out').

fossil /ˈfɒs(ə)l, -sɪl/ ▶ **noun** the remains or impression of a prehistoric plant or animal embedded in rock and preserved in petrified form. ■ derogatory or humorous a person or thing that is outdated or resistant to change: *he can be a cantankerous old fossil at times.* ■ a word or phrase that has become obsolete except in set phrases or forms, e.g. *hue* in *hue and cry*.
– ORIGIN mid 16th cent. (denoting a fossilized fish found, and believed to have lived, underground):

F

from French *fossile*, from Latin *fossilis* 'dug up', from *fodere* 'dig'.

fossil fuel ▶ noun a natural fuel such as coal or gas, formed in the geological past from the remains of living organisms.

fossiliferous /ˌfɒsɪˈlɪf(ə)rəs/ ▶ adjective Geology (of a rock or stratum) containing fossils or organic remains.

fossil ivory ▶ noun [mass noun] ivory from the tusks of a mammoth.

fossilize (also **fossilise**) ▶ verb [with obj.] preserve (an animal or plant) so that it becomes a fossil: *the hard parts of the body are readily fossilized.* ■ [no obj.] become a fossil. ■ become or cause to become fixed and incapable of change or development: [with obj.] *we want to see a working countryside—we don't want to see it fossilized.*
– DERIVATIVES **fossilization** noun.

F

fossilized (also **fossilised**) ▶ adjective preserved to become a fossil: *a fossilized bone* | *fossilized human remains.* ■ archaic and incapable of change: *a faltering economy and a fossilized political system.*

fossil record ▶ noun the record of the occurrence and evolution of living organisms through geological time as inferred from fossils.

fossorial /fɒˈsɔːrɪəl/ ▶ adjective Zoology (of an animal) burrowing. ■ (of limbs) adapted for use in burrowing.
– ORIGIN mid 19th cent.: from medieval Latin *fossorius* (from Latin *fossor* 'digger', from *fodere* 'to dig') + **-AL**.

Foster[1], Sir Norman (Robert), Baron Foster of Thames Bank (b.1935), English architect. His work is notable for its sophisticated engineering approach and technological style. Examples include the Terminal Zone at Stansted Airport (1991) and the German Reichstag building in Berlin (1998).

Foster[2], Stephen (Collins) (1826–64), American composer. He wrote more than 200 songs and, though a Northerner, was best known for songs which captured the Southern plantation spirit, such as 'Oh! Susannah' (1848) and 'Camptown Races' (1850).

foster ▶ verb [with obj.] **1** encourage the development of (something, especially something desirable): *the teacher's task is to foster learning.* ■ develop (a feeling or idea) in oneself: *appropriate praise helps a child foster a sense of self-worth.*
2 bring up (a child that is not one's own by birth). ■ Brit. (of a parent or authority) assign (a child) to be brought up by someone other than its parents: *when **fostering out** a child, placement workers will be looking for a home similar to their own.*
– DERIVATIVES **fosterage** noun, **fosterer** noun.
– ORIGIN Old English *fōstrian* 'feed, nourish', from *fōster* 'food, nourishment', of Germanic origin; related to **FOOD**. The sense 'bring up another's (originally also one's own) child' dates from Middle English. See also **FOSTER-**.

foster- ▶ combining form denoting someone that has a specified family connection through fostering: *foster-parent* | *foster-child.* ■ involving or concerned with fostering a child: *foster care.*
– ORIGIN *foster-father*, *foster-mother*, *foster-child*, and *foster-brother* all date from Old English. *Foster-mother* has also been used to mean a wet nurse, her husband being *foster-father* to the child she fed, and a *foster-brother* or *-sister* one reared at the same breast.

fosterling ▶ noun chiefly archaic a child who is fostered or adopted.
– ORIGIN Old English *fōstorling* (see **FOSTER**, **-LING**).

fou /fuː/ ▶ adjective Scottish inebriated; drunk.
– ORIGIN mid 16th cent.: variant of **FULL**[1].

Foucault[1] /ˈfuːkəʊ/, French /fuko/, Jean Bernard Léon (1819–68), French physicist. He is chiefly remembered for the huge pendulum which he hung from the roof of the Panthéon in Paris in 1851 to demonstrate the rotation of the earth. He also invented the gyroscope and was the first to determine the velocity of light reasonably accurately.

Foucault[2] /ˈfuːkəʊ/, French /fukəo/, Michel (Paul) (1926–84), French philosopher. A student of Louis Althusser, he was mainly concerned with exploring how society defines categories of abnormality such as insanity, sexuality, and criminality, and the manipulation of social attitudes towards such things by those in power.
– DERIVATIVES **Foucauldian** /fuːˈkəʊdɪən/ adjective, **Foucaultian** /-ˈkəʊɪən/ adjective.

fouetté /ˈfwɛteɪ/ ▶ noun Ballet a pirouette performed with a circular whipping movement of the raised leg to the side. ■ a quick shift of direction of the upper body, performed with one leg extended.
– ORIGIN French, past participle of *fouetter* 'to whip'.

fought past and past participle of **FIGHT**.

Fou-hsin variant spelling of **FUXIN**.

foul ▶ adjective **1** offensive to the senses, especially through having a disgusting smell or taste or being dirty: *a foul odour* | *his foul breath.* ■ informal very disagreeable or unpleasant: *the news had put Michelle in a foul mood.*
2 wicked or immoral: *murder most foul.* ■ (of language) obscene. ■ done contrary to the rules of a sport: *a foul tackle.*
3 containing or full of noxious matter; polluted: *foul, swampy water.* ■ (**foul with**) clogged or choked with: *the land was foul with weeds.* ■ Nautical (of a rope or anchor) entangled. ■ (of a ship's bottom) overgrown with weed, barnacles, or similar matter.
4 (of the weather) wet and stormy. ■ Sailing (of wind or tide) opposed to one's desired course.
▶ noun (in sport) an unfair or invalid stroke or piece of play, especially one involving interference with an opponent. ■ a collision or entanglement in riding, rowing, or running.
▶ adverb contrary to the rules; unfairly.
▶ verb [with obj.] **1** make foul or dirty; pollute: *factories which fouled the atmosphere.* ■ (of an animal) make (something) dirty with excrement: *make sure that your pet never fouls paths.* ■ (**foul oneself**) (of a person) defecate involuntarily.
2 (in sport) commit a foul against (an opponent).
3 (of a ship) collide with or interfere with the passage of (another). ■ cause (a cable, anchor, or other object) to become entangled or jammed: *watch out for driftwood which might **foul up** the engine.*
– PHRASES **foul one's (own) nest** do something damaging or harmful to oneself or one's own interests.
– PHRASAL VERBS **foul something up** (or **foul up**) make a mistake with or spoil something: *leaders should admit when they foul things up.*
– DERIVATIVES **foully** adverb, **foulness** noun.
– ORIGIN Old English *fūl*, of Germanic origin; related to Old Norse *fúll* 'foul', Dutch *vuil* 'dirty', and German *faul* 'rotten, lazy', from an Indo-European root shared by Latin *pus*, Greek *puos* 'pus', and Latin *putere* 'to stink'.

Foulah /ˈfuːlə/ ▶ noun (pl. **same** or **Foulahs**) & adjective variant spelling of **FULA**.

foulard /ˈfuːlɑː(d)/ ▶ noun [mass noun] a thin, soft material of silk or silk and cotton, typically having a printed pattern. ■ [count noun] a tie or handkerchief made of foulard.
– ORIGIN mid 19th cent.: from French, of unknown origin.

foul ball ▶ noun Baseball a ball struck so that it falls outside the lines drawn from home plate down to the first and third bases.

foul brood ▶ noun [mass noun] a fatal bacterial disease of larval honeybees. ● This disease is caused by the bacteria *Bacillus larvae* or *Melissococcus pluton*.

foul line ▶ noun Baseball either of the straight lines extending from home plate down to the first and third bases and marking the limit of the playing area, within which a hit is deemed to be fair.

foul mouth ▶ noun a tendency to use bad language: *he had a foul mouth and an even fouler disposition.*

foul-mouthed ▶ adjective using or characterized by a great deal of bad language: *a foul-mouthed cop.*

foul play ▶ noun [mass noun] **1** unfair play in a game or sport.
2 criminal or violent behaviour, in particular when resulting in another's death.

foul-up ▶ noun a problem caused by a stupid mistake.

foumart /ˈfuːmət, -mɑːt/ ▶ noun old-fashioned term for **POLECAT**.
– ORIGIN Middle English: from **FOUL** + Old English *mearth* 'marten'; of Germanic origin and related to **MARTEN**.

found[1] past and past participle of **FIND**. ▶ adjective **1** having been discovered by chance or unexpectedly. ■ (of an object or sound) collected in its natural state and presented in a new context as part of a work of art or piece of music: *collages of found photos.* ■ (of art) comprising or making use of found objects.
2 [with submodifier] (of a ship) equipped: *the ship was well found and seaworthy.*

found[2] ▶ verb [with obj.] **1** establish or originate (an institution or organization): *the monastery was founded in 1665* | (as adj. **founding**) *the three founding partners.* ■ plan and begin the building of (a settlement).
2 (usu. **be founded on/upon**) base (something) on a particular principle, idea, or feeling: *a society founded on the highest principles of religion and education.* ■ serve as a basis for: *the company's fortunes are founded on its minerals business.*
– ORIGIN Middle English: from Old French *fonder*, from Latin *fundare*, from *fundus* 'bottom, base'.

found[3] ▶ verb [with obj.] melt and mould (metal). ■ fuse (materials) to make glass. ■ make (an article) by melting and moulding metal.
– ORIGIN early 16th cent.: from French *fondre*, from Latin *fundere* 'melt, pour'.

foundation ▶ noun **1** (often **foundations**) the lowest load-bearing part of a building, typically below ground level. ■ [mass noun] a cream or powder used as a base to even out facial skin tone before applying other cosmetics.
2 an underlying basis or principle: *this study provides **a foundation for** for further research.* ■ [mass noun] [often with negative] justification or reason: *misleading accusations with no foundation.*
3 [mass noun] the action of establishing an institution or organization. ■ [count noun] an institution established with an endowment, for example a research body or charity.
– DERIVATIVES **foundational** adjective.
– ORIGIN late Middle English: from Old French *fondation*, from Latin *fundatio(n-)*, from *fundare* 'to lay a base for' (see **FOUND**[2]).

foundation course ▶ noun Brit. a course taken at some colleges and universities, either in a wide range of subjects or in one subject at a basic level, preparing students for more advanced study.

foundation garment ▶ noun a woman's supportive undergarment, such as a corset.

foundation stone ▶ noun a stone laid at a ceremony to celebrate the beginning of construction of a building. ■ a basic or essential element of something: *family life is one of the foundation stones of a good society.*

foundation subjects ▶ plural noun Brit. the subjects which form the basis of the National Curriculum, including (or loosely, those other than) the compulsory core subjects.

founder[1] ▶ noun a person who establishes an institution or settlement. ■ Zoology an animal, especially a fertilized female insect, that founds a new colony.

founder[2] ▶ noun a person who manufactures articles of cast metal; the owner or operator of a foundry: *an iron founder.*
– ORIGIN Middle English: probably from Old French *fondeur*, from *fondre* (see **FOUND**[3]).

founder[3] ▶ verb **1** [no obj., with adverbial] (of a ship) fill with water and sink: *six drowned when the yacht foundered off the Cornish coast.* ■ (of a plan or undertaking) fail or break down as a result of a particular problem: *the talks **foundered on** the issue of reform.*
2 [no obj.] (of a horse or its rider) stumble or fall from exhaustion, lameness, etc. ■ chiefly N. Amer. (of a hoofed animal, especially a horse or pony) succumb to laminitis.
▶ noun [mass noun] chiefly N. Amer. laminitis in horses, ponies, or other hoofed animals.
– ORIGIN Middle English (in the sense 'knock to the ground'): from Old French *fondrer*, *esfondrer* 'submerge, collapse', based on Latin *fundus* 'bottom, base'.

founder effect ▶ noun Biology the reduced genetic diversity which results when a population is descended from a small number of colonizing ancestors.

founding father ▶ noun a person who starts or helps to start a movement or institution. ■ (**Founding Father**) a member of the convention that drew up the constitution of the US in 1787.

foundling ▶ noun an infant that has been abandoned by its parents and is discovered and cared for by others.
– ORIGIN Middle English: from **FOUND**[1] (past participle) + **-LING**, perhaps on the pattern of Dutch *vondeling*.

foundress ▶ noun a female founder, especially a fertile female animal that founds a colony.

foundry ▶ noun (pl. **foundries**) a workshop or factory for casting metal.
– ORIGIN early 17th cent. (earlier as *foundery*): from **FOUND**[3] + **-RY**, perhaps suggested by French *fonderie*.

fount[1] ▸ noun a source of a desirable quality or commodity: *our courier was a fount of knowledge.* ■ literary a spring or fountain.
– ORIGIN late 16th cent.: back-formation from FOUNTAIN, on the pattern of the pair *mountain, mount*.

fount[2] ▸ noun Brit. variant spelling of FONT[2].

fountain ▸ noun 1 an ornamental structure in a pool or lake from which one or more jets of water are pumped into the air. ■ a thing that spurts or cascades into the air: *little fountains of dust*.
2 chiefly literary a natural spring of water. ■ a source of a desirable quality: *the government always quote this report as the fountain of truth*.
3 Heraldry a roundel barry wavy argent and azure (i.e. a circle with wavy horizontal stripes of white and blue).
▸ verb [no obj.] spurt or cascade like a fountain: *a river of cold air fountained into the hold*.
– PHRASES **the fountain of youth** a legendary fountain supposed to guarantee eternal youth to anyone who drinks from it: *while yogurt may not be the fountain of youth, it is exceptionally good for you*.
– DERIVATIVES **fountained** adjective (literary).
– ORIGIN Middle English (in sense 2 of the noun): from Old French *fontaine*, from late Latin *fontana*, feminine of Latin *fontanus*, adjective from *fons, font-* 'a spring'.

fountainhead ▸ noun an original source of something: *he was the sole fountainhead of advice*.

fountain pen ▸ noun a pen with a reservoir or cartridge from which ink flows continuously to the nib.

four ▸ cardinal number equivalent to the product of two and two; one more than three, or six less than ten; 4: *Francesca's got four brothers | it took four of them to lift it | a four-bedroom house*. (Roman numeral: **iv** or **IV**, archaic **iiii** or **IIII**) ■ a group or unit of four people or things: *the girls walked in pairs or fours*. ■ four years old: *I began to read at four*. ■ four o'clock: *it's half past four*. ■ Cricket a hit that reaches the boundary after first striking the ground, scoring four runs. ■ a size of garment or other merchandise denoted by four. ■ a playing card or domino with four pips. ■ a four-oared rowing boat or its crew: *the British women's coxed four*.
– PHRASES **the four freedoms** the four essential human freedoms as proclaimed in a speech to Congress by Franklin D. Roosevelt in 1941: freedom of speech and expression, freedom of worship, freedom from want, and freedom from fear. **four noble truths** the four central beliefs containing the essence of Buddhist teaching. See BUDDHISM.
– ORIGIN Old English *fēower*, of Germanic origin; related to Dutch and German *vier*, from an Indo-European root shared by Latin *quattuor* and Greek *tessares*.

four-by-four (also **4 × 4**) ▸ noun a vehicle with four-wheel drive.

Four Cantons, Lake of the another name for Lake Lucerne (see LUCERNE, LAKE).

fourchette /fʊəˈʃɛt/ ▸ noun Anatomy a thin fold of skin at the back of the vulva.
– ORIGIN mid 18th cent.: from French, diminutive of *fourche* 'fork'.

four-dimensional ▸ adjective having four dimensions, typically the three dimensions of space (length, breadth, and depth) plus time.

four-eyed fish ▸ noun a small live-bearing freshwater fish of tropical America. Each eye is divided into two, allowing the fish to see both above and below the water while swimming at the surface. ● Family Anablepidae and genus *Anableps*: several species.

four-eyes ▸ noun informal, derogatory a person who wears glasses.
– DERIVATIVES **four-eyed** adjective.

four flush N. Amer. ▸ noun a poker hand of little value, having four cards of the same suit and one of another.
▸ verb (**four-flush**) [no obj.] informal keep up a pretence; bluff: *your mother will get wise that you're four-flushing*.
– DERIVATIVES **four-flusher** noun.

fourfold ▸ adjective four times as great or as numerous: *a fourfold increase in break-ins*. ■ having four parts or elements: *fourfold symmetry*.
▸ adverb by four times; to four times the number or amount: *the price of electricity rose fourfold*.

four hundred ▸ noun US the social elite of a community.
– ORIGIN mid 19th cent.: from Ward McAllister's remark 'There are only 400 people in New York that one really knows', later popularized in society reports by the New York *Sun*. The notion 'elite' is said to be from the selection of high-society guests by the socialite Mrs William B. Astor Jr, whose ballroom could hold 400.

Fourier /ˈfʊərɪeɪ/, French /furje/, Jean Baptiste Joseph (1768–1830), French mathematician. His studies involved him in the solution of partial differential equations by the method of separation of variables and superposition; this led him to analyse the series and integrals that are now known by his name.

Fourier analysis /ˈfʊrɪə, -rɪeɪ/ ▸ noun Mathematics the analysis of a complex waveform expressed as a series of sinusoidal functions, the frequencies of which form a harmonic series.

Fourierism /ˈfʊrɪərɪz(ə)m/ ▸ noun [mass noun] a system for the reorganization of society into self-sufficient cooperatives, in accordance with the principles of the French socialist Charles Fourier (1772–1837).
– DERIVATIVES **Fourierist** noun & adjective.

Fourier series ▸ noun Mathematics an infinite series of trigonometric functions which represents an expansion or approximation of a periodic function, used in Fourier analysis.

Fourier transform ▸ noun Mathematics a function derived from a given function and representing it by a series of sinusoidal functions.

four-in-hand ▸ noun 1 a vehicle with four horses driven by one person.
2 N. Amer. a necktie tied in a loose knot with two hanging ends, popular in the late 19th and early 20th centuries. [said to be by association with the sport of driving four-in-hand carriages.]

four-leaf clover (also **four-leaved clover**) ▸ noun a clover leaf with four lobes, thought to bring good luck.

four-letter word ▸ noun any of several short words referring to sexual or excretory functions, regarded as coarse or offensive.

four o'clock plant ▸ noun another term for MARVEL OF PERU.

fourpenny ▸ adjective [attrib.] Brit. costing or worth four pence, especially before decimalization (1971).

fourpenny one ▸ noun Brit. informal a blow: *I hit her such a fourpenny one that I sent her flying*.

four-ply ▸ adjective (of a material) having four strands or layers: *four-ply yarn*.
▸ noun [mass noun] knitting wool made of four strands.

four-poster (also **four-poster bed**) ▸ noun a bed with a post at each corner supporting a canopy.

fours ▸ plural noun 1 a race for four-oared rowing boats.
2 a competition for teams of four players, especially in bowls.

fourscore ▸ cardinal number archaic eighty.

foursome ▸ noun a group of four people. ■ a golf match between two pairs of players, with partners playing the same ball.

four-square ▸ adjective (of a building or structure) having a square shape and solid appearance. ■ (of a person or quality) firm and resolute: *a four-square and formidable hero*.
▸ adverb squarely and solidly: *a castle **standing four-square** on a peninsula*. ■ firmly and resolutely in support of someone or something: *they **stand four-square behind** integration*.

four-star ▸ adjective (especially of accommodation) given four stars in a grading system, typically one in which this denotes the highest standard or the next standard to the highest. ■ having or denoting the second-highest military rank, distinguished in the US armed forces by four stars on the uniform.
▸ noun [mass noun] leaded petrol with a grading of four stars, indicating a relatively high octane number.

four-stroke ▸ adjective denoting an internal-combustion engine having a cycle of four strokes (intake, compression, combustion, and exhaust). ■ denoting a vehicle having a four-stroke engine.
▸ noun a four-stroke engine or vehicle.

fourteen ▸ cardinal number equivalent to the product of seven and two; one more than thirteen, or six less than twenty; 14: *they had spent fourteen days in solitary confinement | all fourteen of us were seated*. (Roman numeral: **xiv** or **XIV**) ■ a size of garment or other merchandise denoted by fourteen. ■ fourteen years old: *he left school at fourteen*.
– DERIVATIVES **fourteenth** ordinal number.
– ORIGIN Old English *fēowertīene* (see FOUR, -TEEN).

fourth ▸ ordinal number 1 constituting number four in a sequence; 4th: *the fourth and fifth centuries | there were three bedrooms, with potential for a fourth*. ■ the fourth finisher or position in a race or competition: *he could do no better than finish fourth*. ■ the fourth (and often highest) in a sequence of a vehicle's gears: *he took the corner in fourth*. ■ chiefly Brit. the fourth form of a school or college. ■ fourthly (used to introduce a fourth point): *third, visit popular attractions during lunch; fourth, stay late*. ■ Music an interval spanning four consecutive notes in a diatonic scale, in particular (also **perfect fourth**) an interval of two tones and a semitone (e.g. C to F). ■ Music the note which is higher by a fourth than the tonic of a diatonic scale or root of a chord.
2 chiefly N. Amer. a quarter: *nearly three fourths of that money is now gone*.
– PHRASES **the fourth estate** the press; the profession of journalism. [originally used humorously in various contexts; its first usage with reference to the press has been attributed to Edmund Burke but this remains unconfirmed.] **the fourth wall** the space which separates a performer or performance from an audience. ■ the conceptual barrier between any fictional work and its viewers or readers: *he **breaks the fourth wall** by having Sam refer to the script and the play he's acting in*.

fourth dimension ▸ noun 1 a postulated spatial dimension additional to those determining length, area, and volume.
2 time regarded as analogous to linear dimensions.

Fourth International see INTERNATIONAL (sense 2 of the noun).

fourthly ▸ adverb in the fourth place (used to introduce a fourth point): *fourthly, and last, there are variations in context that influence the process*.

Fourth of July ▸ noun (in the US) a national holiday celebrating the anniversary of the adoption of the Declaration of Independence in 1776. Also called INDEPENDENCE DAY.

fourth position ▸ noun 1 Ballet a posture in which the feet are placed turned outwards one in front of the other, separated by the distance of one step. ■ a position of the arms in which one is held curved over the head and the other curved in front of the body at waist level.
2 Music a position of the left hand on the fingerboard of a stringed instrument nearer to the bridge than the third position, enabling a higher set of notes to be played.

Fourth Republic the republican regime in France between the end of the Second World War (1945) and the introduction of a new constitution by Charles de Gaulle in 1958.

Fourth World ▸ noun those countries and communities considered to be the poorest and most underdeveloped of the Third World.

four-wheel drive ▸ noun [mass noun] a transmission system which provides power directly to all four wheels of a vehicle. ■ a vehicle with four-wheel drive, typically designed for off-road driving.

fovea /ˈfəʊvɪə/ (also **fovea centralis**) ▸ noun (pl. **foveae** /-vɪiː/) Anatomy a small depression in the retina of the eye where visual acuity is highest. The centre of the field of vision is focused in this region, where retinal cones are particularly concentrated.
– DERIVATIVES **foveal** adjective.
– ORIGIN late 17th cent.: from Latin, literally 'small pit'.

fowl ▸ noun (pl. **same** or **fowls**) (also **domestic fowl**) a gallinaceous bird kept for its eggs and flesh; a domestic cock or hen. ● The domestic fowl is derived from the wild **red junglefowl** of SE Asia (see JUNGLEFOWL). ■ any other domesticated bird kept for its eggs or flesh, e.g. a turkey or goose. ■ [mass noun] the flesh of domesticated birds as food; poultry. ■ used in names of birds that resemble the domestic fowl: *spurfowl*. ■ birds collectively, especially as the quarry of hunters. ■ archaic a bird.
– ORIGIN Old English *fugol* 'bird', of Germanic origin; related to Dutch *vogel* and German *Vogel*, also to FLY[1].

Fowler, H. W. (1858–1933), English lexicographer and grammarian; full name *Henry Watson Fowler*. He compiled the first *Concise Oxford Dictionary* (1911) with his brother F. G. Fowler, and wrote the moderately prescriptive guide to style and idiom, *Modern English Usage*, first published in 1926.

fowling ▸ noun [mass noun] the hunting, shooting, or trapping of wildfowl.
– DERIVATIVES **fowler** noun.

fowl pest ▸ **noun** Newcastle disease or fowl plague.

fowl plague ▸ **noun** [mass noun] an acute and often fatal infectious disease of birds, especially poultry, caused by certain strains of influenza virus.

Fox[1], Charles James (1749–1806), British statesman. He became a Whig MP in 1768, supporting American independence and the French Revolution, and collaborated with Lord North to form a coalition government (1783–4).

Fox[2], George (1624–91), English preacher and founder of the Society of Friends (Quakers).

Fox[3] ▸ **noun** (pl. **same**) **1** a member of an American Indian people formerly living in southern Wisconsin, and now mainly in Iowa, Nebraska, and Kansas.
2 [mass noun] the Algonquian language of the Fox, now almost extinct.
▸ **adjective** relating to the Fox or their language.

fox ▸ **noun 1** a carnivorous mammal of the dog family with a pointed muzzle and bushy tail, proverbial for its cunning. ● *Vulpes* and three other genera, family Canidae: several species, including the red fox and the arctic fox. ■ [mass noun] the fur of a fox.
2 a cunning or sly person: *a wily old fox.*
3 N. Amer. informal a sexually attractive woman.
▸ **verb** [with obj.] informal baffle or deceive (someone): *the abbreviation foxed me completely.* ■ [no obj.] dated behave in a cunning or sly way.
– DERIVATIVES **foxlike** adjective.
– ORIGIN Old English, of Germanic origin; related to Dutch *vos* and German *Fuchs*.

Foxe, John (1516–87), English religious writer. He is famous for his *Actes and Monuments* popularly known as *The Book of Martyrs*, which appeared in England in 1563. This passionate account of the persecution of English Protestants fuelled hostility to Catholicism for generations.

foxed ▸ **adjective 1** (of the paper of old books or prints) discoloured with brown spots.
2 archaic, informal drunk.
– DERIVATIVES **foxing** noun (sense 1).

foxfire ▸ **noun** [mass noun] N. Amer. the phosphorescent light emitted by certain fungi on decaying timber.

foxglove ▸ **noun** a tall Eurasian plant with erect spikes of pinkish-purple (or white) flowers shaped like the fingers of gloves. It is a source of the drug digitalis. ● Genus *Digitalis*, family Scrophulariaceae: many species, in particular *D. purpurea*.

foxhole ▸ **noun** a hole in the ground used by troops as a shelter against enemy fire or as a firing point. ■ a place of refuge or concealment.

foxhound ▸ **noun** a dog of a smooth-haired breed with drooping ears, often trained to hunt foxes in packs over long distances.

fox hunting ▸ **noun** [mass noun] the sport of hunting a fox across country with a pack of hounds by a group of people on foot and horseback, a traditional sport of the English landed gentry.
– DERIVATIVES **fox hunter** noun.

foxie ▸ **noun** (pl. **foxies**) Austral./NZ a fox terrier.
– ORIGIN early 20th cent.: abbreviation.

fox moth ▸ **noun** a reddish-brown moth with a velvety black and orange caterpillar. ● *Macrothylacia rubi*, family Lasiocampidae.

foxtail ▸ **noun** a common meadow grass that has soft brush-like flowering spikes. ● Genus *Alopecurus*, family Gramineae: several species, in particular *A. pratensis*.

Fox Talbot, William Henry, see TALBOT.

fox terrier ▸ **noun** a terrier of a short-haired or wire-haired breed originally used for unearthing foxes.

foxtrot ▸ **noun 1** a ballroom dance having an uneven rhythm with alternation of slow and quick steps. ■ a piece of music written for a foxtrot.
2 a code word representing the letter F, used in radio communication.
▸ **verb** (**foxtrots, foxtrotting, foxtrotted**) [no obj.] perform a foxtrot.

foxy ▸ **adjective** (**foxier, foxiest**) **1** resembling or likened to a fox: *a terrier with prick ears and a foxy expression.* ■ cunning or sly: *a foxy method to miss conscription.* ■ reddish brown in colour.
2 informal (of a woman) sexually attractive.
3 (of wine) having a musky flavour.
– DERIVATIVES **foxily** adverb, **foxiness** noun.

foyer /ˈfɔɪeɪ/ ▸ **noun** an entrance hall or other open area in a building used by the public, especially a hotel or theatre. ■ N. Amer. an entrance hall in a house or flat.
– ORIGIN late 18th cent. (denoting the centre of attention or activity): from French, 'hearth, home', based on Latin *focus* 'domestic hearth'.

FP ▸ **abbreviation** former pupils (especially in the name of some rugby teams).

fp ▸ **abbreviation** ■ forte piano. ■ (**f.p.**) freezing point.

FPA ▸ **abbreviation** (in the UK) Family Planning Association.

FPS ▸ **abbreviation** Fellow of the Pharmaceutical Society of Great Britain.

fps (also **f.p.s.**) ▸ **abbreviation** ■ feet per second. ■ foot-pound-second. ■ frames per second.

FPU ▸ **abbreviation** Computing floating-point unit, a processor that performs arithmetic operations.

Fr ▸ **abbreviation** Father (as a courtesy title of priests): *Fr Buckley.* [from French *frère*, literally 'brother'.]
▸ **symbol** the chemical element francium.

fr. ▸ **abbreviation** franc(s).

Fra /frɑː/ ▸ **noun** a prefixed title given to an Italian monk or friar: *Fra Angelico.*
– ORIGIN Italian, abbreviation of *frate* 'brother', from Latin *frater*.

frabjous /ˈfrabdʒəs/ ▸ **adjective** humorous delightful; joyous: *'Oh frabjous day!' she giggled.*
– DERIVATIVES **frabjously** adverb.
– ORIGIN 1871: coined by Lewis Carroll in *Through the Looking Glass*, apparently to suggest *fair* and *joyous*.

fracas /ˈfrakɑː/ ▸ **noun** (pl. **same** /-kɑːz/ or US **fracases**) a noisy disturbance or quarrel.
– ORIGIN early 18th cent.: French, from *fracasser*, from Italian *fracassare* 'make an uproar'.

fractal /ˈfrakt(ə)l/ Mathematics ▸ **noun** a curve or geometrical figure, each part of which has the same statistical character as the whole. They are useful in modelling structures (such as snowflakes) in which similar patterns recur at progressively smaller scales, and in describing partly random or chaotic phenomena such as crystal growth and galaxy formation.
▸ **adjective** relating to or of the nature of a fractal or fractals: *fractal geometry.*
– ORIGIN 1970s: from French, from Latin *fract-* 'broken', from the verb *frangere*.

fraction /ˈfrakʃ(ə)n/ ▸ **noun 1** a numerical quantity that is not a whole number (e.g. $^{1}/_{2}$, 0.5).
2 a small or tiny part, amount, or proportion of something: *he hesitated for **a fraction of** a second* | *her eyes widened a fraction.* ■ a dissenting group within a larger one.
3 Chemistry each of the portions into which a mixture may be separated according to a physical property such as boiling point or solubility.
4 [mass noun] (usu. **the Fraction**) (in the Christian Church) the breaking of the Eucharistic bread.
– ORIGIN late Middle English: via Old French from ecclesiastical Latin *fractio(n-)* 'breaking (bread)', from Latin *frangere* 'to break'.

fractional ▸ **adjective 1** relating to or expressed as a fraction, especially a fraction less than one.
2 small or tiny in amount: *there was a fractional hesitation before he said yes.*
3 Chemistry relating to or denoting the separation of a mixture into fractions: *fractional crystallization.*
– DERIVATIVES **fractionally** adverb.

fractional distillation ▸ **noun** [mass noun] Chemistry separation of a liquid mixture into fractions differing in boiling point (and hence chemical composition) by means of distillation, typically using a fractionating column.

fractionalize (also **fractionalise**) ▸ **verb** [with obj.] (usu. as adj. **fractionalized**) divide (someone or something) into separate groups or parts: *fractionalized consumer markets.*
– DERIVATIVES **fractionalization** noun.

fractionate /ˈfrakʃ(ə)neɪt/ ▸ **verb** [with obj.] chiefly Chemistry divide into fractions or components. ■ separate (a mixture) by fractional distillation.
– DERIVATIVES **fractionation** noun.

fractionating column ▸ **noun** Chemistry a tall, horizontally subdivided container for fractional distillation in which vapour passes upwards and condensing liquid flows downwards. The vapour becomes progressively enriched in more volatile components as it ascends, and the less volatile components become concentrated in the descending liquid, which can be drawn off.

fractious /ˈfrakʃəs/ ▸ **adjective** (typically of children) irritable and quarrelsome: *they fight and squabble like fractious children.* ■ (of a group or organization) difficult to control; unruly: *King Malcolm struggled to unite his fractious kingdom.*
– DERIVATIVES **fractiously** adverb, **fractiousness** noun.
– ORIGIN late 17th cent.: from FRACTION, probably on the pattern of the pair *faction, factious*.

fracture ▸ **noun** [mass noun] **1** the cracking or breaking of a hard object or material: *ground movements could cause fracture of the pipe.* ■ [count noun] a crack or break in a hard object or material, typically a bone or a rock stratum: *a fracture of the left leg.* ■ the physical appearance of a freshly broken rock or mineral, especially as regards the shape of the surface formed.
2 Phonetics the replacement of a simple vowel by a diphthong owing to the influence of a following sound, typically a consonant. ■ [count noun] a diphthong substituted by fracture.
▸ **verb** break or cause to break: [no obj.] *the stone has fractured* | [with obj.] *ancient magmas fractured by the forces of wind and ice.* ■ [with obj.] sustain a fracture of (a bone): (as adj. **fractured**) *a fractured skull.* ■ (with reference to a group or organization) split or fragment and become unable to function or exist: [no obj.] *the movement had fractured without his leadership.* ■ (as adj. **fractured**) (of speech or a language) faltering and full of mistakes; broken.
– ORIGIN late Middle English: from French, or from Latin *fractura*, from *frangere* 'to break'.

frae /freɪ/ ▸ **preposition** Scottish from: *you better collect the tab frae the office.*

fraenulum ▸ **noun** variant spelling of FRENULUM.

fraenum ▸ **noun** variant spelling of FRENUM.

frag N. Amer. military slang ▸ **noun** a hand grenade.
▸ **verb** (**frags, fragging, fragged**) [with obj.] deliberately kill (an unpopular senior officer) with a hand grenade.
– ORIGIN 1970s: from FRAGMENTATION GRENADE.

fragile /ˈfradʒʌɪl/ ▸ **adjective** (of an object) easily broken or damaged: *fragile items such as glass and china.* ■ easily destroyed or threatened: *you have a fragile grip on reality.* ■ (of a person) not strong or sturdy; delicate and vulnerable.
– DERIVATIVES **fragilely** adverb.
– ORIGIN late 15th cent. (in the sense 'morally weak'): from Latin *fragilis*, from *frangere* 'to break'. The sense 'liable to break' dates from the mid 16th cent.

fragile X syndrome ▸ **noun** [mass noun] Medicine an inherited condition characterized by an X chromosome that is abnormally susceptible to damage, especially by folic acid deficiency. Affected individuals tend to have limited intellectual functions.

fragility /frəˈdʒɪlɪti/ ▸ **noun** [mass noun] the quality of being easily broken or damaged: *osteoporosis is characterized by bone fragility.* ■ the quality of being delicate or vulnerable: *a film about the fragility of relationships* | *his emotional fragility.*

fragment ▸ **noun** /ˈfragm(ə)nt/ a small part broken off or separated from something: *small fragments of pottery.* ■ an isolated or incomplete part of something: *Nathan remembered fragments of the conversation.*
▸ **verb** /fragˈmɛnt/ break or cause to break into fragments: [no obj.] *Lough Erne **fragmented into** a series of lakes* | [with obj.] *management has tighter control through fragmenting the tasks.*
– DERIVATIVES **fragmental** adjective (chiefly Geology).
– ORIGIN late Middle English: from French, or from Latin *fragmentum*, from *frangere* 'to break'.

fragmentary ▸ **adjective** consisting of small disconnected or incomplete parts: *excavations have revealed fragmentary remains of masonry.*
– DERIVATIVES **fragmentarily** adverb.

fragmentation ▸ **noun** [mass noun] the process or state of breaking or being broken into fragments: *the **fragmentation of** society **into** a collection of interest groups.* ■ Computing the storing of a file in several separate areas of memory scattered throughout a hard disk.

fragmentation grenade (also **fragmentation bomb**) ▸ **noun** a grenade (or bomb) designed to break into small fragments as it explodes.

Fragonard /ˈfragənɑː/, French /fʀagɔnaʀ/, Jean-Honoré (1732–1806), French painter in the rococo style. He is famous for landscapes and for erotic canvases such as *The Progress of Love* (1771).

fragrance /ˈfreɪgr(ə)ns/ ▸ **noun** a pleasant, sweet smell: *the fragrance of fresh-ground coffee* | [mass noun] *the bushes fill the air with fragrance.* ■ a perfume or aftershave.

– DERIVATIVES **fragranced** adjective.
– ORIGIN mid 17th cent.: from French, or from Latin *fragrantia*, from *fragrare* 'smell sweet'.

fragrancy ▸ noun (pl. **fragrancies**) dated fragrance.

fragrant ▸ adjective having a pleasant or sweet smell: *she gathered the fragrant blooms.*
– DERIVATIVES **fragrantly** adverb.
– ORIGIN late Middle English: from French, or from Latin *fragrant-* 'smelling sweet', from the verb *fragrare*.

'fraid ▸ verb informal non-standard contraction of 'afraid' or 'I'm afraid', expressing regret: *'fraid not, doll.*

frail ▸ adjective (of a person) weak and delicate: *his small, frail body | she looked frail and vulnerable.* ■ easily damaged or broken; weak: *the balcony is frail | the country's frail economy.* ■ archaic weak in character or morals.
▸ noun US informal, dated a woman.
– DERIVATIVES **frailly** adverb, **frailness** noun.
– ORIGIN Middle English: from Old French *fraile*, from Latin *fragilis* (see **FRAGILE**).

frailty ▸ noun (pl. **frailties**) [mass noun] the condition of being weak and delicate: *the increasing frailty of old age.* ■ weakness in character or morals: *all drama begins with human frailty* | [count noun] *you're too self-righteous to see your own frailties.*
– ORIGIN Middle English (in the sense 'weakness in morals'): from Old French *frailete*, from Latin *fragilitas*, from *fragilis* (see **FRAGILE**).

fraise /frɛz, freɪz/ ▸ noun (pl. pronunc. **same**) (in cookery) a strawberry. ■ [mass noun] a white brandy distilled from strawberries.
– ORIGIN French.

Fraktur /ˈfraktʊə/, German /frakˈtuːɐ/ ▸ noun [mass noun] a German style of black-letter type.
– ORIGIN late 19th cent.: German, from Latin *fractura* 'fracture' (because of its angularity).

framboesia /framˈbiːzɪə/ (US **frambesia**) ▸ noun another term for **YAWS**.
– ORIGIN early 19th cent.: modern Latin, from French *framboise* 'raspberry', so named because of the red swellings caused by the disease, likened to raspberries.

framboise /frɒmˈbwɑːz/ ▸ noun (in cookery) a raspberry. ■ [mass noun] a white brandy distilled from raspberries.
– ORIGIN French, 'raspberry', from a conflation of Latin *fraga ambrosia* 'ambrosial strawberry'.

Frame, Janet (Paterson) (1924–2004), New Zealand novelist. Her novels draw on her experiences of psychiatric hospitals after she suffered a severe mental breakdown. Her three-volume autobiography (1982–5) was made into the film *An Angel at my Table* (1990).

frame ▸ noun **1** a rigid structure that surrounds something such as a picture, door, or windowpane. ■ (**frames**) a metal or plastic structure holding the lenses of a pair of glasses. ■ the rigid supporting structure of an object such as a vehicle, building, or piece of furniture. ■ a box-like structure of glass or plastic in which seeds or young plants are grown. ■ an apparatus with a surrounding structure, especially one used in weaving, knitting, or embroidery. ■ [in sing.] archaic the universe, or part of it, regarded as an embracing structure.
2 a person's body with reference to its size or build: *a shiver shook her slim frame.*
3 [usu. in sing.] a basic structure that underlies or supports a system, concept, or text: *the establishment of conditions provides a frame for interpretation.* ■ technical short for **FRAME OF REFERENCE** below. ■ [in sing.] archaic the structure, constitution, or nature of someone or something: *we have in our inward frame various affections.*
4 Linguistics a structural environment within which a class of words or other linguistic units can be correctly used. For example *I —— him* is a frame for a large class of transitive verbs. ■ a feature which marks a transition from one section of discourse to another: *frames are realized by linguistic items such as 'well', 'right', and 'OK'.* ■ a section of a discourse separated by a frame. ■ (in semantics) an underlying conceptual structure into which the meanings of a number of related words fit: *the frame of verbs of perception.* ■ a social context determining the interpretation of an utterance: *an utterance may mean the opposite of what it says if used within a frame of teasing.*
5 a single complete picture in a series forming a cinema, television, or video film. ■ a single picture in a comic strip. ■ Computing a graphic panel in a display window, especially in an Internet browser, which encloses a self-contained section of data and permits multiple independent document viewing.
6 the triangular structure for positioning the red balls in snooker. ■ a single game of snooker.
▸ verb [with obj.] **1** place (a picture or photograph) in a frame. ■ surround so as to create a striking or attractive image: *a short style cut to frame the face.*
2 formulate (a concept, plan, or system): *staff have proved invaluable in framing the proposals.* ■ form or articulate (words): *he walked out before she could frame a reply.* ■ archaic make or construct (something) by fitting parts together or in accordance with a plan: *what immortal hand or eye could frame thy fearful symmetry?*
3 informal produce false evidence against (an innocent person) so that they appear guilty: *he claims he was framed.*
– PHRASES **be in** (or **out of**) **the frame** be (or not be) eligible. ■ be wanted (or not wanted) by the police: *he was always in the frame for the killing.* **frame of mind** a particular mood that influences one's attitude or behaviour. **frame of reference** a set of criteria in relation to which judgements can be made: *the observer interprets what he sees in terms of his own cultural frame of reference.* ■ a system of geometrical axes in relation to which size, position, or motion can be defined.
– DERIVATIVES **frameable** adjective, **frameless** adjective, **framer** noun.
– ORIGIN Old English *framian* 'be useful', of Germanic origin and related to **FROM**. The general sense in Middle English, 'make ready for use', probably led to sense 2 of the verb; it also gave rise to the specific meaning 'prepare timber for use in building', later 'make the wooden parts (framework) of a building', hence the noun sense 'structure' (late Middle English).

framed ▸ adjective **1** (of a picture, photograph, etc.) held in a frame: *a framed photograph of her father.*
2 [in combination] (of a building) having a frame of a specified material: *a traditional **oak-framed** house.*

frame house ▸ noun chiefly N. Amer. a house constructed from a wooden skeleton, typically covered with timber boards.

frame saw ▸ noun a saw with a thin blade kept rigid by being stretched in a frame.

frameset ▸ noun the frame and front fork of a bicycle.

frameshift mutation ▸ noun Genetics a mutation caused by the addition or deletion of a base pair or base pairs in the DNA of a gene resulting in the translation of the genetic code in an unnatural reading frame from the position of the mutation to the end of the gene.

frame tent ▸ noun chiefly Brit. a tent supported by a tall frame, giving it nearly perpendicular sides and standing headroom throughout.

frame-up ▸ noun [in sing.] informal a conspiracy to incriminate someone falsely.

framework ▸ noun an essential supporting structure of a building, vehicle, or object: *a conservatory in a delicate framework of iron.* ■ a basic structure underlying a system, concept, or text: *the theoretical framework of political sociology.*

framing ▸ noun [mass noun] the action of framing something. ■ frames collectively.

franc /fraŋk/ ▸ noun the basic monetary unit of France, Belgium, Switzerland, Luxembourg, and several other countries, equal to 100 centimes (replaced in France, Belgium, and Luxembourg by the euro in 2002).
– ORIGIN from Old French, from Latin *Francorum Rex* 'king of the Franks', the legend on gold coins struck in the 14th cent. in the reign of Jean le Bon.

France[1] /frɑːns/ a country in western Europe; pop. 64,420,100 (est. 2009); official language, French; capital, Paris.

> France became a major power under the Valois and Bourbon dynasties in the 16th–18th centuries, and, after the overthrow of the monarchy in the French Revolution (1789), briefly dominated Europe under Napoleon. Defeated in the Franco-Prussian war (1870–1), the country suffered much destruction and loss of life in the First World War and during the Second World War was occupied by the Germans. France was a founder member of the EEC in 1957.

France[2] /frɑːns/, French /frɑ̃s/, Anatole (1844–1924), French writer; pseudonym of *Jacques-Anatole-François Thibault*. Works include the novel *Le Crime de Sylvestre Bonnard* (1881) and his ironic version of the Dreyfus case, *L'Ile des pingouins* (1908). Nobel Prize for Literature (1921).

Franche-Comté /ˌfrɒ̃ʃkɒ̃ˈteɪ/, French /frɑ̃ʃkɔ̃te/ a region of eastern France, in the northern foothills of the Jura mountains.

franchise /ˈfran(t)ʃʌɪz/ ▸ noun **1** an authorization granted by a government or company to an individual or group enabling them to carry out specified commercial activities, for example acting as an agent for a company's products. ■ a business or service given a franchise to operate. ■ a general title or concept used for creating or marketing a series of products, typically films or television shows: *the Harry Potter franchise.* ■ N. Amer. an authorization given by a league to own a sports team. ■ N. Amer. informal a professional sports team. ■ (also **franchise player**) N. Amer. informal a star player in a team.
2 [mass noun] (usu. **the franchise**) the right to vote in public elections. ■ the rights of citizenship.
▸ verb [with obj.] grant a franchise to (an individual or group). ■ grant a franchise for the sale of (goods) or the operation of (a service): *all the catering was franchised out.*
– DERIVATIVES **franchisee** noun, **franchiser** (also **franchisor**) noun.
– ORIGIN Middle English (denoting a grant of legal immunity): from Old French, based on *franc, franche* 'free' (see **FRANK**[1]). Sense 2 of the noun dates from the late 18th cent. and sense 1 of the noun from the 20th cent.

> **WORD TRENDS** Nowadays a successful film is rarely just a film—studios hope their productions will spawn lucrative spin-offs in the form of toys, games, books, DVDs, and, of course, sequels. Such film series are known as **franchises**, borrowing and extending the term used for a proven business model licensed for use by others, such as fast-food restaurants. The Oxford English Corpus shows that **franchise** is increasingly used in the cinematic sense, with common collocates representing familiar Hollywood brands such as *James Bond, Star Trek, Batman,* and *Harry Potter*. A hint of cynicism is creeping in, however, with the sense that franchises are often little more than manufactured moneymaking schemes: *a greedy franchise that doesn't care to develop its characters beyond their punchlines | he managed to milk the franchise on screen for nearly a decade.*

Francis I (1494–1547), king of France 1515–47. Much of his reign (1521–44) was spent at war with Charles V of Spain. He supported the arts and commissioned new buildings, including the Louvre.

Franciscan /franˈsɪsk(ə)n/ ▸ noun a friar, sister, or lay member of a Christian religious order founded in 1209 by St Francis of Assisi or based on its rule, and noted for its preachers and missionaries.

> Divergences of practice led to the separation of the Friars Minor of the Observance (the Observants) and the Friars Minor Conventual (the Conventuals) in 1517, and to the foundation of the stricter Friars Minor Capuchin (the Capuchins) in 1529. The order of Franciscan nuns was founded by St Clare (*c.*1212) under the direction of St Francis; they are known as 'Poor Clares'.

▸ adjective relating to or denoting St Francis or the Franciscans.
– ORIGIN from French *franciscain*, from modern Latin *Franciscanus*, from *Franciscus* 'Francis'.

francise ▸ verb variant spelling of **FRANCIZE**.

Francis of Assisi, St (*c.*1181–1226), Italian monk, founder of the Franciscan order; born *Giovanni di Bernardone*. He founded the Franciscan order in 1209 and drew up its original rule (based on complete poverty). He is revered for his generosity, simple faith, humility, and love of nature. Feast day, 4 October.

Francis of Sales, St /sɑːl/ (1567–1622), French bishop. One of the leaders of the Counter-Reformation, he was bishop of Geneva 1602–22. The Salesian order (founded in 1859) is named after him. Feast day, 24 January.

Francis Xavier, St, see **XAVIER, ST FRANCIS**.

francium /ˈfransɪəm/ ▸ noun [mass noun] the chemical element of atomic number 87, a radioactive member of the alkali metal group. Francium occurs naturally as a decay product in uranium and thorium ores. (Symbol: **Fr**)
– ORIGIN 1940s: from **FRANCE**[1] (the discoverer's native country) + **-IUM**.

francize /ˈfransʌɪz/ (also **francise**) ▸ verb [with obj.] Canadian (in Quebec) cause (a person or business) to adopt French as an official or working language.
– DERIVATIVES **francization** noun.

F

Franck[1] /fraŋk/, French /fʀɑ̃k/, César (Auguste) (1822–90), Belgian-born French composer and organist. His reputation as a composer rests on the *Symphonic Variations* for piano and orchestra (1885), the D minor Symphony (1886–8), and the *String Quartet* (1889).

Franck[2] /fraŋk/, James (1882–1964), German-born American physicist. He worked on the bombardment of atoms by electrons and became involved in the US atom bomb project; he advocated the explosion of the bomb in an uninhabited area to demonstrate its power to Japan.

Franco, Francisco (1892–1975), Spanish general and dictator, head of state 1939–75. Leader of the Nationalists in the Civil War, in 1937 Franco became head of the Falange Party and proclaimed himself *Caudillo* ('leader') of Spain. With the defeat of the republic in 1939, he took control of the government and established a dictatorship that ruled Spain until his death.
– DERIVATIVES **Francoism** noun, **Francoist** noun & adjective.

Franco- (also **franco-**) ▶ **combining form** French; French and ...: *francophone* | *Franco-German*. ■ relating to France: *Francophile*.
– ORIGIN from medieval Latin *Francus* 'Frank'.

francolin /ˈfraŋkə(ʊ)lɪn/ ▶ **noun** a large game bird resembling a partridge, with bare skin on the head or neck, found in Africa and southern Asia. ● Genus *Francolinus*, family Phasianidae: many species.
– ORIGIN mid 17th cent.: from French, from Italian *francolino*, of unknown origin.

Franconia /fraŋˈkəʊnɪə/ a medieval duchy of southern Germany, inhabited by the Franks.

Franconian ▶ **noun 1** a native or inhabitant of Franconia.
2 [mass noun] a group of medieval West Germanic dialects, combining features of Low and High German. ■ the group of modern German dialects of Franconia.
▶ **adjective** relating to Franconia or its inhabitants.

Francophile ▶ **noun** a person who is fond of or greatly admires France or the French.

francophone /ˈfraŋkə(ʊ)fəʊn/ ▶ **adjective** French-speaking: *a summit of francophone countries*.
▶ **noun** a person who speaks French.
– ORIGIN early 20th cent.: from **Franco-** 'French' + Greek *phōnē* 'voice'.

Franco-Prussian War the war of 1870–1 between France (under Napoleon III) and Prussia, in which Prussian troops advanced into France and decisively defeated the French at Sedan. The defeat marked the end of the French Second Empire. For Prussia, the proclamation of the new German Empire at Versailles was the climax of Bismarck's ambitions to unite Germany.

frangible /ˈfran(d)ʒɪb(ə)l/ ▶ **adjective** able to be broken into fragments; brittle or fragile: *the frangible skull of an infant* | figurative *she had kept his frangible mind together through many troubled years*. ■ denoting ammunition designed to disintegrate into very small particles on impact: *frangible bullets*.
– ORIGIN late Middle English: from Old French, or from medieval Latin *frangibilis*, from Latin *frangere* 'to break'.

frangipane /ˈfran(d)ʒɪpeɪn/ ▶ **noun** [mass noun] an almond-flavoured cream or paste.
– ORIGIN late 17th cent.: from French, named after the Marquis Muzio *Frangipani* (see **frangipani**). The term originally denoted the frangipani shrub or tree, the perfume of which is said to have been used to flavour the almond cream.

frangipani /ˌfran(d)ʒɪˈpɑːni/ ▶ **noun** (pl. **frangipanis**) a tropical American tree or shrub with clusters of fragrant white, pink, or yellow flowers. ● Genus *Plumeria*, family Apocynaceae: several species, in particular *P. rubra*.
■ [mass noun] perfume obtained from the frangipani plant.
– ORIGIN mid 19th cent.: named after the Marquis Muzio *Frangipani*, a 16th-cent. Italian nobleman who invented a perfume for scenting gloves.

franglais /ˈfrɒ̃gleɪ/ ▶ **noun** [mass noun] a blend of French and English, either French speech that makes excessive use of English expressions, or unidiomatic French spoken by an English person.
– ORIGIN 1960s: coined in French, from a blend of *français* 'French' and *anglais* 'English'.

Frank[1], Anne (1929–45), German Jewish girl known for her diary, which records the experiences of her family living for two years in hiding from the Nazis in occupied Amsterdam. They were eventually betrayed and sent to concentration camps; Anne died in Belsen.

Frank[2] ▶ **noun** a member of a Germanic people that conquered Gaul in the 6th century and controlled much of western Europe for several centuries afterwards. ■ dated (in the eastern Mediterranean region) a person of western European nationality or descent.
– ORIGIN Old English *Franca*, of Germanic origin; perhaps from the name of a weapon and related to Old English *franca* 'javelin' (compare with **Saxon**); reinforced in Middle English by medieval Latin *Francus* and Old French *Franc*, of the same origin and related to **French**.

frank[1] ▶ **adjective** open, honest, and direct in speech or writing, especially when dealing with unpalatable matters: *a long and frank discussion* | ***to be perfectly frank**, I don't know*. ■ open, sincere, or undisguised: *Kate looked at Sam with frank admiration*. ■ Medicine unmistakable; obvious: *frank ulceration*.
– DERIVATIVES **frankness** noun.
– ORIGIN Middle English (in the sense 'free'): from Old French *franc*, from medieval Latin *francus* 'free', from *Francus* (see **Frank[2]**: only Franks had full freedom in Frankish Gaul). Another Middle English sense was 'generous', which led to the current sense.

frank[2] ▶ **verb** [with obj.] **1** stamp an official mark on (a letter or parcel) to indicate that postage has been paid or does not need to be paid. ■ historical sign (a letter or parcel) to ensure delivery free of charge. ■ archaic facilitate or pay the passage of (someone): *English will **frank** the traveller **through** most of North America*.
2 (as adj. **franked**) Brit. denoting dividends and other payments carrying a tax credit which can be offset against advance corporation tax by the company which receives them.
▶ **noun** an official mark or signature on a letter or parcel, indicating that postage has been paid or does not need to be paid. [formerly as a superscribed signature of an eminent person entitled to send letters free of charge.]
– DERIVATIVES **franker** noun.
– ORIGIN early 18th cent.: from **frank[1]**, an early sense being 'free of obligation'.

frank[3] ▶ **noun** N. Amer. short for **frankfurter**.

franked investment income ▶ **noun** [mass noun] (in the UK) income in the form of dividends paid to a company from earnings on which corporation tax has already been paid by the originating company.

Frankenfood /ˈfraŋk(ə)nfuːd/ ▶ **noun** [mass noun] informal, derogatory genetically modified food.
– ORIGIN 1990s: from **Frankenstein** + **food**.

Frankenstein /ˈfraŋk(ə)nstʌɪn/ a character in the novel *Frankenstein, or the Modern Prometheus* (1818) by Mary Shelley. Frankenstein is a scientist who creates and brings to life a manlike monster which eventually turns on him and destroys him; Frankenstein is not the name of the monster itself, as is often assumed. ■ (also **Frankenstein's monster**) [as noun] a thing that becomes terrifying or destructive to its maker.

Frankfort /ˈfraŋkfət/ the state capital of Kentucky; pop. 27,322 (est. 2008).

Frankfurt /ˈfraŋkfəːt/, German /ˈfraŋkfʊrt/ a commercial city in western Germany, in Hesse; pop. 652,600 (est. 2006). The headquarters of the Bundesbank are located there. Full name **Frankfurt am Main** /am ˈmʌɪn/.

frankfurter ▶ **noun** a seasoned smoked sausage made of beef and pork.
– ORIGIN from German *Frankfurter Wurst* 'Frankfurt sausage'.

Frankfurt School a school of philosophy of the 1920s whose adherents were involved in a reappraisal of Marxism, particularly in terms of the cultural and aesthetic dimension of modern industrial society. Principal figures include Theodor Adorno, Max Horkheimer, and Herbert Marcuse.

frankincense /ˈfraŋkɪnsɛns/ ▶ **noun** [mass noun] an aromatic gum resin obtained from an African tree and burnt as incense. Also called **olibanum**, **gum olibanum**. ● This resin is obtained from the tree *Boswellia sacra*, family Burseraceae, native to Somalia.
– ORIGIN late Middle English: from Old French *franc encens*, literally 'high-quality incense', from *franc* (see **frank[1]**) in an obsolete sense 'superior, of high quality' (which also existed in English) + *encens* 'incense'.

franking ▶ **noun** [mass noun] the action of franking a letter or parcel: [as modifier] *a franking machine*. ■ [count noun] an official mark or signature on a letter or parcel to indicate that postage has been paid or does not need to be paid.

Frankish ▶ **adjective** relating to the ancient Franks or their language.
▶ **noun** [mass noun] the Germanic language of the ancient Franks.

Franklin[1], Aretha (b.1942), American soul and gospel singer. Her best-known songs include 'I Say a Little Prayer' (1967).

Franklin[2], Benjamin (1706–90), American statesman, inventor, and scientist. He was one of the signatories to the peace between the US and Great Britain after the War of American Independence. His main scientific achievements were the formulation of a theory of electricity, which introduced positive and negative electricity, and a demonstration of the electrical nature of lightning, which led to the invention of the lightning conductor.

Franklin[3], (Stella Maria Sarah) Miles (1879–1954), Australian novelist. She wrote the first true Australian novel, *My Brilliant Career* (1901). She also produced a series of chronicle novels under her pseudonym 'Brent of Bin Bin' (1928–56).

Franklin[4], Rosalind Elsie (1920–58), English physical chemist and molecular biologist. Together with Maurice Wilkins she investigated the structure of DNA by means of X-ray crystallography, and contributed to the discovery of its helical structure.

franklin ▶ **noun** a landowner of free but not noble birth in the 14th and 15th centuries in England.
– ORIGIN Middle English: from Anglo-Latin *francalanus*, from *francalis* 'held without dues', from *francus* 'free' (see **frank[1]**).

Franklin stove ▶ **noun** N. Amer. a large cast-iron stove for heating a room, resembling an open fireplace in shape.
– ORIGIN late 18th cent.: named after B. *Franklin* (see **Franklin[2]**).

frankly ▶ **adverb** in an open, honest, and direct manner: *she talks very frankly about herself*. ■ [sentence adverb] used to emphasize the truth of a statement, however unpalatable this may be: *frankly, I was pleased to leave*.

frantic ▶ **adjective** distraught with fear, anxiety, or other emotion: *she was **frantic with** worry*. ■ conducted in a hurried, excited, and disorganized way: *frantic attempts to resuscitate the girl*.
– DERIVATIVES **frantically** adverb, **franticness** noun.
– ORIGIN late Middle English *frentik*, 'insane, violently mad', from Old French *frenetique* (see **frenetic**).

Franz Josef /ˌfrants ˈjəʊzɛf/ (1830–1916), emperor of Austria 1848–1916 and king of Hungary 1867–1916. He gave Hungary equal status with Austria in 1867. His annexation of Bosnia and Herzegovina (1908) contributed to European political tensions, and the assassination in Sarajevo of his heir apparent, Archduke Franz Ferdinand, precipitated the First World War.

Franz Josef Land a group of islands in the Arctic Ocean, discovered in 1873 by an Austrian expedition and annexed by the USSR in 1928.

frap ▶ **verb** (**fraps**, **frapping**, **frapped**) [with obj.] Nautical bind (something) tightly.
– ORIGIN Middle English (in the sense 'strike, beat', now only dialect): from Old French *fraper* 'to bind, strike', of unknown origin. The current sense dates from the mid 16th cent.

frappé[1] /ˈfrapeɪ/ ▶ **adjective** [postpositive] (of a drink) iced or chilled: *a crème de menthe frappé*.
▶ **noun** a drink served with ice or frozen to a slushy consistency.
– ORIGIN French.

frappé[2] /ˈfrapeɪ/ ▶ **adjective** [postpositive] Ballet (of a position) involving a beating action of the toe of one foot against the ankle of the supporting leg: *a battement frappé*.
– ORIGIN French, literally 'struck'.

Frascati /fraˈskɑːti/ ▶ **noun** [mass noun] a wine, typically white, produced in the region of Frascati, Italy.

Fraser[1] /ˈfreɪzə/ a river of British Columbia. It rises in the Rocky Mountains and flows in a wide curve 1,360 km (850 miles) into the Strait of Georgia, just south of Vancouver.

Fraser[2] /ˈfreɪzə/, Dawn (b.1937), Australian swimmer. She won the Olympic gold medal for the 100-metres freestyle in 1956, 1960, and 1964, the first competitor to win the same title at three successive Olympics.

Fraser³ /ˈfreɪzə/, (John) Malcolm (b.1930), Australian Liberal statesman, Prime Minister 1975–83. He was the youngest-ever Australian MP when elected in 1955.

frass /fras/ ▶ **noun** [mass noun] **1** fine powdery refuse or fragile perforated wood produced by the activity of boring insects.
2 the excrement of insect larvae.
– ORIGIN mid 19th cent.: from German *Frass*, from *fressen* 'devour'.

frat ▶ **noun** [usu. as modifier] N. Amer. informal a students' fraternity: *a frat party*.
– ORIGIN late 19th cent.: abbreviation.

frat boy ▶ **noun** N. Amer. informal a young man who behaves in a boisterous or foolish manner considered typical of members of some college fraternities.

frater /ˈfreɪtə/ ▶ **noun** historical the dining room or refectory of a monastery.
– ORIGIN Middle English: from Old French *fraitur*, shortening of *refreitor*, from late Latin *refectorium* 'refectory'.

fraternal /frəˈtəːn(ə)l/ ▶ **adjective 1** of or like a brother or brothers: *his lack of fraternal feeling shocked me*. ■ of or denoting an organization for people, especially men, that have common interests or beliefs.
2 (of twins) developed from separate ova and therefore genetically distinct and not necessarily of the same sex or more similar than other siblings. Compare with IDENTICAL (sense 1).
– DERIVATIVES **fraternalism** noun, **fraternally** adverb.
– ORIGIN late Middle English: from medieval Latin *fraternalis*, from Latin *fraternus*, from *frater* 'brother'.

fraternity /frəˈtəːnɪti/ ▶ **noun** (pl. **fraternities**)
1 [treated as sing. or pl.] a group of people sharing a common profession or interests: *members of the hunting fraternity*. ■ N. Amer. a male students' society in a university or college. ■ a religious or Masonic society or guild.
2 [mass noun] friendship and mutual support within a group: *the ideals of liberty, equality, and fraternity*.
– ORIGIN Middle English: from Old French *fraternite*, from Latin *fraternitas*, from *fraternus* (see FRATERNAL).

fraternize /ˈfratənʌɪz/ (also **fraternise**) ▶ **verb** [no obj.] associate or form a friendship with someone, especially when one is not supposed to: *she ignored Elisabeth's warning glare against* **fraternizing with** *the enemy*.
– DERIVATIVES **fraternization** noun.
– ORIGIN early 17th cent.: from French *fraterniser*, from medieval Latin *fraternizare*, from Latin *fraternus* 'brotherly' (see FRATERNAL).

fratricidal /ˌfratrɪˈsʌɪd(ə)l/ ▶ **adjective** relating to or denoting conflict within a single family or organization: *the fratricidal strife within the Party*.

fratricide /ˈfratrɪsʌɪd/ ▶ **noun** [mass noun] the killing of one's brother or sister. ■ [count noun] a person who kills their brother or sister. ■ the accidental killing of one's own forces in war.
– ORIGIN late 15th cent. (denoting a person who kills their brother or sister, derived from Latin *fratricida*): the primary current sense comes via French from late Latin *fratricidium*, from *frater* 'brother' + *-cidium* (see -CIDE).

Frau /fraʊ/ ▶ **noun** (pl. **Frauen** /ˈfraʊən/) a title or form of address for a married or widowed German-speaking woman: *Frau Nordern*.
– ORIGIN German.

fraud /frɔːd/ ▶ **noun** [mass noun] wrongful or criminal deception intended to result in financial or personal gain: *he was convicted of fraud* | [count noun] *prosecutions for social security frauds*. ■ [count noun] a person or thing intended to deceive others, typically by unjustifiably claiming or being credited with accomplishments or qualities: *mediums exposed as tricksters and frauds*.
– ORIGIN Middle English: from Old French *fraude*, from Latin *fraus, fraud-* 'deceit, injury'.

fraud squad ▶ **noun** [treated as sing. or pl.] Brit. a division of a police force appointed to investigate fraud.

fraudster ▶ **noun** Brit. a person who commits fraud, especially in business dealings.

fraudulent /ˈfrɔːdjʊl(ə)nt/ ▶ **adjective** obtained, done by, or involving deception, especially criminal deception: *fraudulent share dealing*. ■ unjustifiably claiming or being credited with particular accomplishments or qualities: *fraudulent psychics*.
– DERIVATIVES **fraudulence** noun, **fraudulently** adverb.
– ORIGIN late Middle English: from Old French, or from Latin *fraudulentus*, from *fraus, fraud-* 'deceit, injury'.

fraught /frɔːt/ ▶ **adjective 1** (**fraught with**) (of a situation or course of action) filled with (something undesirable): *marketing any new product is fraught with danger*.
2 causing or affected by anxiety or stress: *there was a fraught silence* | *she sounded a bit fraught*.
– ORIGIN late Middle English, 'laden, equipped', past participle of obsolete *fraught* 'load with cargo', from Middle Dutch *vrachten*, from *vracht* 'ship's cargo'. Compare with FREIGHT.

Fräulein /ˈfrɔɪlʌɪn/, German /ˈfrɔylaɪn/ ▶ **noun** a title or form of address for an unmarried German-speaking woman, especially a young woman: *Fräulein Winkelmann*.
– ORIGIN German, diminutive of FRAU.

Fraunhofer /ˈfraʊnˌhəʊfə/, German /ˈfraʊnˌhoːfɐ/, Joseph von (1787–1826), German optician and pioneer in spectroscopy. He observed and mapped the dark lines in the solar spectrum (**Fraunhofer lines**) which result from the absorption of particular frequencies of light by elements present in the outer layers; these are now used to determine the chemical composition of the sun and stars.

fraxinella /ˌfraksɪˈnɛlə/ ▶ **noun** another term for GAS PLANT.
– ORIGIN mid 17th cent.: modern Latin (former specific epithet), diminutive of Latin *fraxinus* 'ash tree' (because of its leaves, thought to resemble those of the ash).

fray¹ ▶ **verb 1** [no obj.] (of a fabric, rope, or cord) unravel or become worn at the edge, typically through constant rubbing: *cheap fabric soon frays*. ■ (of a person's nerves or temper) show the effects of strain: *as the temperature rose, tempers frayed*.
2 [with obj.] (of a male deer) rub (a bush or small tree) with the head in order to remove the velvet from newly formed antlers, or to mark territory during the rut.
– ORIGIN late Middle English: from Old French *freiier*, from Latin *fricare* 'to rub'.

fray² ▶ **noun** (**the fray**) a situation of intense competitive activity: *ten companies intend to bid for the contract, with three more expected to* **enter the fray**. ■ a battle or fight.
– ORIGIN late Middle English: from archaic *fray* 'to quarrel', from *affray* 'startle', from Anglo-Norman French *afrayer* (see AFFRAY).

Fray Bentos /ˌfreɪ ˈbɛntɒs/ a port and meat-packing centre in western Uruguay; pop. 23,100 (est. 2004).

frayed ▶ **adjective** (of a fabric, rope, or cord) unravelled or worn at the edge: *the frayed collar of her old coat*. ■ (of a person's nerves or temper) showing the effects of strain: *an effort to soothe frayed nerves*.

Frazer, Sir James George (1854–1941), Scottish anthropologist. In *The Golden Bough* (1890–1915) he proposed an evolutionary theory of the development of human thought, from the magical and religious to the scientific.

frazil /ˈfreɪz(ɒ)l/ (also **frazil ice**) ▶ **noun** [mass noun] N. Amer. soft or amorphous ice formed by the accumulation of ice crystals in water that is too turbulent to freeze solid.
– ORIGIN late 19th cent.: from Canadian French *frasil* 'snow floating in the water', from French *fraisil* 'cinders'.

frazzle informal ▶ **verb** [with obj.] **1** (as adj. **frazzled**) completely exhausted: *a frazzled parent*.
2 cause to shrivel up with burning: *we frazzle our hair with heated appliances*.
▶ **noun** (**a frazzle**) **1** the state of being completely exhausted: *I'm tired,* **worn to a frazzle**.
2 the state of being completely burnt: *the grass was regrowing within days of being* **burnt to a frazzle**.
– ORIGIN early 19th cent.: perhaps a blend of FRAY¹ and obsolete *fazle* 'ravel out', of Germanic origin. The word was originally East Anglian dialect; it came into standard British English via the US.

freak ▶ **noun 1** a very unusual and unexpected event or situation: *the teacher says the accident was a total freak* | [as modifier] *a freak storm*.
2 (also **freak of nature**) a person, animal, or plant with an unusual physical abnormality. ■ informal a person regarded as strange because of their unusual appearance or behaviour.
3 [with modifier] informal a person who is obsessed with a particular activity or interest: *a fitness freak*. ■ [usu. with modifier] a person addicted to a particular drug: *the twins were cocaine freaks*.
4 archaic a sudden arbitrary change of mind; a whim: *follow this way or that, as the freak takes you*.
▶ **verb 1** informal behave or cause to behave in a wild and irrational way, typically because of the effects of extreme emotion or drugs: [no obj.] ***he freaked out*** *and smashed the place up* | [with obj.] *what he'd said had really* ***freaked her out***.
2 [with obj.] archaic fleck or streak randomly: *the white pink and the pansy freaked with jet*.
– ORIGIN mid 16th cent. (in sense 4 of the noun): probably from a dialect word.

freaking ▶ **adjective** US informal used as a euphemism for 'fucking': *I'm going out of my freaking mind!*

freakish ▶ **adjective** very unusual, strange, or unexpected: *freakish weather*.
– DERIVATIVES **freakishly** adverb, **freakishness** noun.

freak-out ▶ **noun** informal a wildly irrational reaction or spell of behaviour.

freak show ▶ **noun** a sideshow at a fair, featuring abnormally developed people or animals. ■ an unusual or grotesque event viewed for pleasure, especially when in bad taste.

freaky ▶ **adjective** (**freakier, freakiest**) informal very odd, strange, or eccentric: *a freaky coincidence*.
– DERIVATIVES **freakily** adverb, **freakiness** noun.

freckle ▶ **noun** a small patch of light brown colour on the skin, often becoming more pronounced through exposure to the sun.
▶ **verb** cover or become covered with freckles: [no obj.] *skin which freckles easily* | (as adj. **freckled**) *a freckled face*.
– DERIVATIVES **freckly** adjective (**frecklier, freckliest**).
– ORIGIN late Middle English: alteration of dialect *frecken*, from Old Norse *freknur* (plural).

freckle-faced ▶ **adjective** having freckles on the face.

Freddie Mac /fredi ˈmak/ informal the Federal Home Loan Mortgage Corporation, a US corporation that trades in mortgages.
– ORIGIN 1970s: loosely from the initial letters of *Federal Home Loan Mortgage Corporation*, on the model of FANNIE MAE.

Frederick I (*c*.1123–90), king of Germany and Holy Roman emperor 1152–90; known as **Frederick Barbarossa** ('Redbeard'). He made a sustained attempt to subdue Italy and the papacy, but was eventually defeated at the battle of Legnano in 1176.

Frederick II (1712–86), king of Prussia 1740–86; known as **Frederick the Great**. His campaigns in the War of the Austrian Succession (1740–8) and the Seven Years War (1756–63) succeeded in considerably strengthening Prussia's position; by the end of his reign he had doubled the area of his country.

Frederick William (1620–88), Elector of Brandenburg 1640–88; known as **the Great Elector**. His programme of reconstruction and reorganization following the Thirty Years War brought stability to his country and laid the basis for the expansion of Prussian power in the 18th century.

Fredericton /ˈfrɛdrɪktən/ the capital of New Brunswick, Canada; pop. 50,535 (2006).
– ORIGIN named after *Frederick* Augustus, second son of George III.

free ▶ **adjective** (**freer**, **freest**) **1** able to act or be done as one wishes; not under the control of another: *I have no ambitions other than to have a happy life and be free* | *a free choice*. ■ [with infinitive] able or permitted to take a specified action: *you are free to leave*. ■ (of a state or its citizens or institutions) subject neither to foreign domination nor to despotic government: *a free press*. ■ historical not a slave. ■ [in names] denoting an ethnic or political group actively opposing an occupying or invading force, in particular the groups that continued resisting the Germans in the Second World War after the fall of their countries. See also FREE FRENCH.
2 [often as complement] not or no longer confined or imprisoned: *the researchers set the birds free*. ■ not physically obstructed or fixed: *he tried to kick his legs free*. ■ Physics (of power or energy) disengaged or available. See also FREE ENERGY. ■ Physics & Chemistry not bound in an atom, a molecule, or a compound: *the atmosphere of that time contained virtually no free oxygen*. See also FREE RADICAL. ■ Linguistics denoting a linguistic form that can be used in isolation.
3 not subject to engagements or obligations: *she spent her free time shopping*. ■ (of a facility or piece of equipment) not occupied or in use: *the bathroom was free*.

F

4 (**free of/from**) not subject to or affected by (something undesirable): *our salsas are free of preservatives.*
5 given or available without charge: *free health care.*
6 using or expending something without restraint; lavish: *she was always free with her money.* ■ frank or unrestrained in speech, expression, or action: *he was free in his talk of revolution.* ■ archaic overfamiliar or forward.
7 (of literature or music) not observing the normal conventions of style or form. ■ (of a translation) conveying only the broad sense; not literal.
8 Sailing (of the wind) blowing from a favourable direction to the side or aft of a vessel.
▶ **adverb 1** without cost or payment: *ladies were admitted free.*
2 Sailing with the sheets eased.
▶ **verb** (**frees, freeing, freed**) [with obj.] **1** release from confinement or slavery: *they were freed from jail.* ■ release from physical obstruction or restraint: *I had to tug hard and at last freed him* | *she struggled to free herself from the tenacious mud.*
2 remove something undesirable or restrictive from: *his inheritance freed him from financial constraints* | *free your body of excess tension.*
3 make available for a particular purpose: *we are freeing management time for alternative work.*
– PHRASES **for free** informal without cost or payment. **free and easy** informal and relaxed: *enjoy the free and easy lifestyle.* **a free hand** freedom to act completely at one's own discretion. **free on board** (or **rail**) (abbrev.: **f.o.b.** or **f.o.r.**) including or assuming delivery without charge to a ship (or railway wagon). (**a**) **free rein** see **REIN**. **a free ride** used in reference to a situation in which someone benefits without having to make a fair contribution: *it is time for the scientific community to stop giving alternative medicine a free ride.* **the free world** the non-communist countries of the world, as formerly opposed to the Soviet bloc. **it's a free country** said when justifying a course of action. **make free with** treat without proper respect: *he'll have something to say about your making free with his belongings.*
– DERIVATIVES **freeness** noun.
– ORIGIN Old English *frēo* (adjective), *frēon* (verb), of Germanic origin; related to Dutch *vrij* and German *frei*, from an Indo-European root meaning 'to love', shared by **FRIEND**.

-free ▶ **combining form** free of or from: *smoke-free* | *tax-free.*

free agent ▶ **noun** a person who does not have any commitments that restrict their actions.

free association ▶ **noun** [mass noun] **1** Psychology the mental process by which one word or image may spontaneously suggest another without any necessary logical connection. ■ a psychoanalytic technique for investigation of the unconscious mind, in which a relaxed subject reports all passing thoughts without reservation.
2 the forming of a group, political alliance, or other organization without any external restriction.
– DERIVATIVES **free-associate** verb (sense 1).

free ball ▶ **noun** Snooker the option to nominate any ball as the object ball when snookered as a result of a foul stroke.

freebase ▶ **noun** (also **freebase cocaine**) [mass noun] cocaine that has been purified by heating with ether, taken by inhaling the fumes or smoking the residue.
▶ **verb** [with obj.] take (freebase cocaine).

freebie ▶ **noun** informal a thing that is provided or given free of charge: *a freebie to the Himalayas.*
– ORIGIN 1940s (originally US): an arbitrary formation from **FREE**.

freeboard ▶ **noun** the height of a ship's side between the waterline and the deck.

freebooter ▶ **noun** a pirate or lawless adventurer.
– ORIGIN late 16th cent.: from Dutch *vrijbuiter*, from *vrij* 'free' + *buit* 'booty', + the noun suffix *-er*. Compare with **FILIBUSTER**.

freeborn ▶ **adjective** not born in slavery: *an encroachment on the rights of the freeborn Englishman.*

Free Church ▶ **noun** a Christian Church which has dissented or seceded from an established Church.

Free Church of Scotland a strict Presbyterian Church organized by dissenting members of the established Church of Scotland in 1843. In 1900 its majority amalgamated with the United Presbyterian Church to form the United Free Church; its name was retained by the minority group, nicknamed the **Wee Free Kirk** (see **WEE FREE**).

free climbing ▶ **noun** [mass noun] rock climbing without the assistance of devices such as pegs placed in the rock, but occasionally using ropes and belays. Compare with **AID CLIMBING**.

freedman ▶ **noun** (pl. **freedmen**) historical an emancipated slave.

freedom ▶ **noun** [mass noun] **1** the power or right to act, speak, or think as one wants: *we do have some freedom of choice* | [count noun] *he talked of revoking some of the freedoms.* ■ absence of subjection to foreign domination or despotic government: *he was a champion of Irish freedom.* ■ the power of self-determination attributed to the will; the quality of being independent of fate or necessity.
2 the state of not being imprisoned or enslaved: *the shark thrashed its way to freedom.* ■ the state of being unrestricted and able to move easily: *the shorts have a side split for freedom of movement.* ■ unrestricted use of something: *the dog has the freedom of the house when we are out.*
3 (**freedom from**) the state of not being subject to or affected by (something undesirable): *government policies to achieve freedom from want.*
4 (**the freedom of ——**) Brit. a special privilege or right of access, especially that of full citizenship of a city granted to a public figure as an honour: *he accepted the freedom of the City of Glasgow.*
5 archaic familiarity or openness in speech or behaviour.
– ORIGIN Old English *frēodōm* (see **FREE**, **-DOM**).

freedom fighter ▶ **noun** a person who takes part in a revolutionary struggle to achieve a political goal, especially in order to overthrow their government.

freedom of conscience ▶ **noun** [mass noun] the right to follow one's own beliefs in matters of religion and morality.

freedom of religion ▶ **noun** [mass noun] the right to practise whatever religion one chooses.

freedom rider ▶ **noun** US a person who challenged racial laws in the American South during in the 1960s, originally by refusing to abide by the laws governing the segregation of seating in buses.

free energy ▶ **noun** [mass noun] Physics a thermodynamic quantity equivalent to the capacity of a system to do work. See also **GIBBS FREE ENERGY**.

free enterprise ▶ **noun** [mass noun] an economic system in which private business operates in competition and largely free of state control.

free fall ▶ **noun** [mass noun] downward movement under the force of gravity only: *the path of a body in free fall.* ■ a rapid decline that cannot be stopped: *her career seemed about to go into free fall.* ■ the movement of a spacecraft in space without thrust from the engines.
▶ **verb** (**free-fall**) [no obj.] move under the force of gravity only; fall rapidly.

free flight ▶ **noun** [mass noun] the flight of a spacecraft, rocket, or missile when the engine is not producing thrust.

free-floating ▶ **adjective 1** not attached to anything and able to move freely: *free-floating aquatic plants.* ■ not assigned to a particular category or level: *free-floating exchange rates.*
2 Psychiatry (of anxiety) chronic and generalized, without an obvious cause.
– DERIVATIVES **free-float** verb.

Freefone ▶ **noun** variant spelling of **FREEPHONE**.

free-for-all ▶ **noun** a disorganized or unrestricted situation or event in which everyone may take part, especially a fight, discussion, or trading market.

free-form ▶ **adjective** not conforming to a regular or formal structure or shape: *a free-form jazz improvisation.*

Free French an organization of French troops and volunteers in exile formed under General de Gaulle in 1940. Based in London, the movement organized forces that opposed the Axis powers in French Equatorial Africa, Lebanon, and elsewhere, and cooperated with the French Resistance.

freehand ▶ **adjective & adverb** (especially with reference to drawing) done manually without the aid of instruments such as rulers: [as adj.] *a freehand sketch* | [as adv.] *the pictures should be drawn freehand.*

free-handed ▶ **adjective** generous, especially with money.

freehold chiefly Brit. ▶ **noun** [mass noun] permanent and absolute tenure of land or property with freedom to dispose of it at will. Often contrasted with **LEASEHOLD**. ■ [count noun] a piece of land or property held by freehold.
▶ **adjective** held by or having the status of freehold.
– DERIVATIVES **freeholder** noun.

free house ▶ **noun** Brit. a pub not controlled by a brewery and therefore not restricted to selling particular brands of beer or spirits.

free jazz ▶ **noun** [mass noun] an improvised style of jazz characterized by the absence of set chord patterns or time patterns.

free kick ▶ **noun** (in soccer and rugby) an unimpeded kick of the stationary ball awarded to one side as a penalty for a foul or infringement by the other side.

freelance /ˈfriːlɑːns/ ▶ **adjective** self-employed and hired to work for different companies on particular assignments: *a freelance journalist.*
▶ **adverb** earning one's living as a freelance: *I work freelance from home.*
▶ **noun 1** a freelance worker.
2 historical a medieval mercenary.
▶ **verb** [no obj.] earn one's living as a freelance.
– ORIGIN early 19th cent. (denoting a mercenary): originally as two words.

freelancer ▶ **noun** a person who works freelance.

free-living ▶ **adjective** Biology living freely and independently, not as a parasite or attached to a substrate.

freeloader ▶ **noun** informal a person who takes advantage of others' generosity without giving anything in return.
– DERIVATIVES **freeload** verb.

free love ▶ **noun** [mass noun] the idea or practice of having sexual relations according to choice, without being restricted by marriage or long-term relationships.

freely ▶ **adverb 1** not under the control of another; as one wishes: *I roamed freely.* ■ without restriction or interference: *air can freely circulate.* ■ openly and honestly: *you may speak freely.* ■ willingly and readily: *I freely confess to this failing.*
2 in copious or generous amounts: *she drank freely to keep up her courage.*

Freeman, Cathy (b.1973), Australian athlete. She became the first Aboriginal to represent Australia at the Olympic Games in 1992, and won the Olympic gold medal in the 400 metres in 2000.

freeman ▶ **noun** (pl. **freemen**) **1** Brit. a person who has been given the freedom of a city or borough.
2 historical a person who is not a slave or serf.

free market ▶ **noun** an economic system in which prices are determined by unrestricted competition between privately owned businesses.
– DERIVATIVES **free marketeer** noun, **free marketeering** noun.

freemartin /ˈfriːmɑːtɪn/ ▶ **noun** a hermaphrodite or imperfect sterile female calf which is the twin of a male calf whose hormones affected its development.
– ORIGIN late 17th cent.: of unknown origin.

Freemason ▶ **noun** a member of an international order established for mutual help and fellowship, which holds elaborate secret ceremonies.

> The original **free masons** were itinerant skilled stonemasons of the 14th century, who are said to have recognized fellow craftsmen by secret signs. Modern freemasonry is usually traced to the formation of the Grand Lodge in London in 1717; members are typically professionals and businessmen.

Freemasonry ▶ **noun** [mass noun] **1** the system and institutions of the Freemasons.
2 (**freemasonry**) instinctive sympathy or fellow feeling between people with something in common: *the unshakeable freemasonry of actors in a crisis.*

freemium /ˈfriːmɪəm/ ▶ **noun** [usu. as modifier] a business model, especially on the Internet, whereby basic services are provided free of charge while more advanced features must be paid for.
– ORIGIN early 21st cent.: blend of **FREE** and **PREMIUM**.

free pardon ▶ **noun** Brit. an unconditional remission of the legal consequences of an offence or conviction.

Freephone (also trademark **Freefone**) ▶ **noun** a telephone service whereby a subscribing organization can pay for incoming calls made by its clients or customers.

free port ▶ **noun** a port open to all traders. ■ a port area where goods in transit are exempt from customs duty.

Freepost ▸ noun [mass noun] Brit. (chiefly as an element of an address) a postal service whereby the cost of postage is paid by the business that receives the letter.

free radical ▸ noun Chemistry an uncharged molecule (typically highly reactive and short-lived) having an unpaired valency electron.

free-range ▸ adjective (of livestock, especially poultry) kept in natural conditions, with freedom of movement. ■ (of eggs) produced by free-range poultry.

freeride ▸ noun (also **freeride board**) a type of snowboard designed for all-round use on and off piste.
▸ verb [no obj.] ride on a freeride snowboard.

free safety ▸ noun American Football a defensive back who is usually free from an assignment to cover a particular player on the opposing team.

free school ▸ noun historical a school for which no fees are charged, typically run at public expense.

free sheet ▸ noun a free newspaper.

freesia /ˈfriːzɪə/ ▸ noun a small southern African plant with fragrant, colourful, tubular flowers, many varieties of which are cultivated for the cut-flower trade. ● Genus *Freesia*, family Iridaceae.
– ORIGIN modern Latin, named after Friedrich H. T. *Freese* (died 1876), German physician.

free skating ▸ noun [mass noun] the sport of performing variable skating figures to music.

free space ▸ noun [mass noun] Physics space unoccupied by matter or, more particularly, containing no electromagnetic or gravitational field and used as a reference.

free speech ▸ noun [mass noun] the right to express any opinions without censorship or restraint.

free spirit ▸ noun an independent or uninhibited person.

free-spoken ▸ adjective archaic speaking candidly and openly.

free-standing ▸ adjective not attached to or supported by another structure: *a free-standing cooker.* ■ not relying on or linked to anything else; independent: *most nursing homes and free-standing therapeutic facilities are investor-owned.*

Free State ▸ noun **1** historical a state of the US in which slavery did not exist. ■ (**the Free State**) informal name for MARYLAND.
2 a province in central South Africa, situated to the north of the Orange River; capital, Bloemfontein. Formerly called (until 1995) ORANGE FREE STATE.

Free Stater ▸ noun historical a member of the Irish Free State army.

freestone ▸ noun **1** [mass noun] a fine-grained stone which can be cut easily in any direction, in particular a type of sandstone or limestone.
2 a stone fruit in which the stone is easily separated from the flesh when the fruit is ripe: [as modifier] *freestone peaches.* Contrasted with CLINGSTONE.

freestyle ▸ adjective denoting a contest, race, or version of a sport in which there are few restrictions on the moves or techniques that competitors employ: *freestyle wrestling.*
▸ noun a freestyle contest, in particular a swimming race in which competitors may use any stroke.
▸ verb [no obj.] dance, perform, or compete in an improvised or unrestricted fashion: *he just came in and freestyled over the music.*
– DERIVATIVES **freestyler** noun.

free-swimming ▸ adjective Zoology (of an aquatic animal) not attached to an object or substrate and able to swim freely.

free-tailed bat ▸ noun a streamlined fast-flying insectivorous bat with a projecting tail, found in tropical and subtropical countries. ● Family Molossidae: several genera and numerous species, including the mastiff bats and hairless bats.

freethinker ▸ noun a person who rejects accepted opinions, especially those concerning religious belief.
– DERIVATIVES **freethinking** noun & adjective.

free throw ▸ noun Basketball an unimpeded attempt at a goal awarded to a player following a foul or other infringement.

free-to-air ▸ adjective denoting or relating to television programmes broadcast on standard public or commercial networks, as opposed to satellite, cable, or digital programmes available only to fee-paying viewers.

Freetown the capital and chief port of Sierra Leone; pop. 827,000 (est. 2007).

free trade ▸ noun [mass noun] international trade left to its natural course without tariffs, quotas, or other restrictions.

free vector ▸ noun Mathematics a vector of which only the magnitude and direction are specified, not the position or line of action.

free verse ▸ noun [mass noun] poetry that does not rhyme or have a regular rhythm. Also called VERS LIBRE.

free vote ▸ noun chiefly Brit. a parliamentary division in which members vote according to their own beliefs rather than following a party policy.

freeware ▸ noun [mass noun] Computing software that is available free of charge.

freeway ▸ noun N. Amer. a dual-carriageway main road, especially one with controlled access. ■ a toll-free highway.

freewheel ▸ verb [no obj.] **1** ride a bicycle with the pedals at rest, especially downhill: *the postman came freewheeling down the track.*
2 (as adj. **freewheeling**) not concerned with rules, conventions, or the consequences of one's actions: *the freewheeling drug scene of the sixties.*
▸ noun (**free wheel**) a bicycle wheel which is able to revolve freely when no power is being applied to the pedals. ■ a device in a motor vehicle transmission allowing the drive shaft to spin faster than the engine.

free will ▸ noun [mass noun] the power of acting without the constraint of necessity or fate; the ability to act at one's own discretion.
▸ adjective [attrib.] (especially of a donation) voluntary: *free-will offerings.*

freeze ▸ verb (past **froze**; past participle **frozen**) **1** (with reference to a liquid) turn or be turned into ice or another solid as a result of extreme cold: [no obj.] *in the winter the milk froze* | [with obj.] *frost freezes water that has seeped into joints.* ■ become or cause to become blocked, covered, or rigid with ice: [no obj.] *the pipes had frozen* | [with complement] *the ground was frozen hard.* ■ be so cold that one feels near death (often used hyperbolically): *you'll freeze to death standing there.* ■ [with obj.] deprive (a part of the body) of feeling, especially by the application of a chilled anaesthetic substance.
2 [with obj.] store (something) at a very low temperature in order to preserve it: *the cake can be frozen.* ■ [no obj., with complement] (of food) be able to be preserved at a very low temperature: *this soup freezes well.*
3 [no obj.] become suddenly motionless or paralysed with fear or shock: *she froze in horror.* ■ stop moving when ordered.
4 [with obj.] hold (something) at a fixed level or in a fixed state for a period of time: *new spending on defence was to be frozen.* ■ prevent (assets) from being used for a period of time: *the charity's bank account has been frozen.* ■ stop (a moving image) at a particular frame when filming or viewing: *the camera will set fast shutter speeds to freeze the action.* ■ [no obj.] (of a computer screen) become temporarily locked because of system problems.
5 [with obj.] stare coldly at (someone); treat coldly: *she would freeze him with a look when he tried to talk to her.*
▸ noun **1** an act of holding or being held at a fixed level or in a fixed state: *workers faced a pay freeze.* ■ short for FREEZE-FRAME.
2 a period of frost or very cold weather: *the big freeze surprised the weathermen.*
– PHRASES **freeze one's blood** (or **one's blood freezes**) fill (or be filled) with a sudden feeling of great fear or horror.
– PHRASAL VERBS **freeze someone out** informal behave in a hostile or obstructive way so as to exclude someone: *during a banquet, she completely froze out her husband.*
– DERIVATIVES **freezable** adjective.
– ORIGIN Old English *frēosan* (in the phrase *hit frēoseth* 'it is freezing'), of Germanic origin; related to Dutch *vriezen* and German *frieren*, from an Indo-European root shared by Latin *pruina* 'hoar frost' and FROST.

freeze-dry ▸ verb [with obj.] (usu. as adj. **freeze-dried**) preserve (something) by rapidly freezing it and then subjecting it to a high vacuum which removes ice by sublimation: *freeze-dried beef stew.*

freeze-frame ▸ noun a single frame forming a motionless image from a film or videotape. ■ [mass noun] the facility or process of stopping a film or videotape to obtain a freeze-frame.
▸ verb [with obj.] use a freeze-frame facility on (an image or a recording).

freeze-out ▸ noun informal an exclusion of a person or organization from something, by boycotting or ignoring them.

freezer ▸ noun a refrigerated cabinet or room for preserving food at very low temperatures.

freeze-up ▸ noun a period of extreme cold.

freezing ▸ adjective below 0°C: *strong winds and freezing temperatures.* ■ (used hyperbolically) very cold: *he was freezing and miserable* | [as submodifier] *it was freezing cold outside.* ■ (of fog or rain) consisting of droplets which freeze rapidly on contact with a surface to form ice crystals.
▸ noun the freezing point of water (0°C): *the temperature was well above freezing.*

freezing mixture ▸ noun a mixture of two or more substances (e.g. ice water and salt, or dry ice and alcohol) which can be used to produce temperatures below the freezing point of water.

freezing point ▸ noun the temperature at which a liquid turns into a solid when cooled.

freezing works ▸ plural noun [treated as sing.] Austral./NZ a place where animals are slaughtered and carcasses frozen, usually for export.

Frege /ˈfreɪgə/, Gottlob (1848–1925), German philosopher and mathematician, founder of modern logic. He developed a logical system for the expression of mathematics. He also worked on general questions of philosophical logic and semantics and devised his influential theory of meaning, based on his use of a distinction between what a linguistic term refers to and what it expresses.

Freiburg /ˈfrʌɪbəːg/, German /ˈfraɪbʊrk/ a city in SW Germany, in Baden-Württemberg, on the edge of the Black Forest; pop. 220,600 (est. 2009). Full name **Freiburg im Breisgau** /ɪm ˈbrʌɪsgaʊ/, German /ɪm ˈbraɪsgaʊ/.

freight /freɪt/ ▸ noun [mass noun] goods transported in bulk by truck, train, ship, or aircraft. ■ the transport of bulk goods by truck, train, ship, or aircraft. ■ a charge for transport by freight.
▸ verb [with obj.] **1** transport (goods) in bulk by truck, train, ship, or aircraft: *the metals had been freighted from the city.*
2 (**be freighted with**) be laden or burdened with: *each word was freighted with anger.*
– ORIGIN late Middle English (in the sense 'hire of a ship for transporting goods'): from Middle Dutch, Middle Low German *vrecht*, variant of *vracht* 'ship's cargo'. Compare with FRAUGHT.

freightage ▸ noun [mass noun] the carrying of goods in bulk. ■ goods carried in bulk; freight.

freight car ▸ noun N. Amer. a railway wagon for carrying freight.

freighter ▸ noun a large ship or aircraft designed to carry goods in bulk. ■ a person who loads, receives, or forwards goods for transport.

freighting ▸ noun [mass noun] the action of transporting goods in bulk by truck, train, ship, or aircraft.

Freightliner ▸ noun Brit. trademark a train carrying freight in containers.

freight ton ▸ noun see TON[1] (sense 1 of the noun).

Frelimo /frɛˈliːməʊ/ the nationalist liberation party of Mozambique, founded in 1962. After independence in 1975, Frelimo governed Mozambique as a one-party state until 1990, when a multiparty system was introduced.
– ORIGIN Portuguese, contraction of *Frente de Libertação de Moçambique*, the name of the party.

Fremantle /ˈfriːmant(ə)l/ the principal port of Western Australia, part of the Perth metropolitan area; pop. 27,453 (2008).

Frémont /ˈfriːmɒnt/, John Charles (1813–90), American explorer and politician. He was responsible for exploring several viable routes to the Pacific across the Rockies in the 1840s.

French ▸ adjective relating to France or its people or language.
▸ noun **1** [mass noun] the language of France, also used in parts of Belgium, Switzerland, and Canada, in several countries of northern and western Africa and the Caribbean, and elsewhere.
2 (as plural noun **the French**) the people of France collectively.
3 short for FRENCH VERMOUTH.

F

French is the first or official language of over 200 million people and is widely used as a second language. It is a Romance language which developed from the Latin spoken in Gaul; it had a very great influence on English as the language of the Norman ruling class.

– PHRASES **(if you'll) excuse** (or **pardon**) **my French** informal used to apologize for swearing.
– DERIVATIVES **Frenchness** noun.
– ORIGIN Old English *Frencisc*, of Germanic origin, from the base of FRANK².

French bean ▸ noun Brit. a tropical American bean plant of which many varieties are commercially cultivated. ● *Phaseolus vulgaris*, family Leguminosae: many varieties, including the haricot bean and the kidney bean. ■ the seed of the French bean plant used as food.

French bread ▸ noun [mass noun] white bread in a long, crisp loaf.

F

French Canadian ▸ noun **1** a Canadian whose principal language is French.
2 [mass noun] the form of French spoken in Canada.
▸ adjective relating to French-speaking Canadians or their language.

French chalk ▸ noun [mass noun] a kind of steatite used for marking cloth and removing grease and, in powder form, as a dry lubricant.

French Congo former name (until 1910) for FRENCH EQUATORIAL AFRICA.

French cricket ▸ noun [mass noun] an informal game resembling cricket but played with a soft ball which is bowled at the batter's legs.

French cuff ▸ noun a shirt cuff that is folded back before fastening, creating a double-layered cuff.

French curve ▸ noun a template used for drawing curved lines.

French-cut ▸ adjective (of women's knickers) cut high in the leg.

French door ▸ noun chiefly N. Amer. a French window.

French dressing ▸ noun [mass noun] a salad dressing of vinegar, oil, and seasonings. ■ N. Amer. a sweet, creamy salad dressing commercially prepared from oil, tomato purée, and spices.

French Equatorial Africa a former federation of French territories in west central Africa (1910–58). Previously called French Congo, its constituent territories were Chad, Ubanghi Shari (now the Central African Republic), Gabon, and Middle Congo (now Congo).

French flageolet ▸ noun see FLAGEOLET¹.

French fries ▸ plural noun chiefly N. Amer. potatoes deep-fried in thin strips; chips.

French Guiana an overseas department of France, in northern South America; pop. 202,000 (est. 2007); capital, Cayenne.

French horn ▸ noun a brass instrument with a coiled tube, valves, and a wide bell, developed from the simple hunting horn in the 17th century. It is played with the right hand in the bell to soften the tone and increase the range of available harmonics.

Frenchie ▸ noun (pl. **Frenchies**) variant spelling of FRENCHY.

Frenchify ▸ verb (**Frenchifies**, **Frenchifying**, **Frenchified**) [with obj.] (usu. as adj. **Frenchified**) often derogatory make French in form, character, or manners: *Frenchified academicians.*

French kiss ▸ noun a kiss with contact between tongues.
– DERIVATIVES **French kissing** noun.

French knickers ▸ plural noun loose-fitting, wide-legged knickers, typically of silk or satin.

French knot ▸ noun (in embroidery) a stitch in which the thread is wound around the needle, which is then passed back through the fabric at almost the same point to form a small dot.

French leave ▸ noun [mass noun] informal, dated absence from work or duty without permission.
– ORIGIN mid 18th cent.: said to derive from the French custom of leaving a dinner or ball without saying goodbye to the host or hostess. The phrase was first recorded shortly after the Seven Years War; the equivalent French expression is *filer à l'Anglaise*, literally 'to escape in the style of the English'.

French letter ▸ noun Brit. informal, dated a condom.

French loaf ▸ noun a loaf of French bread.

Frenchman ▸ noun (pl. **Frenchmen**) **1** a man who is French by birth or descent.
2 a knife with a right-angled bend in its blade, used in bricklaying.

French manicure ▸ noun a style of manicure in which the fingernails are painted pale pink with a white band at the tip.

French mustard ▸ noun [mass noun] Brit. mild mustard mixed with vinegar.

French plait ▸ noun Brit. a woman's hairstyle in which all the hair is gathered tightly and pulled back from the forehead into one large plait down the back of the head.

French pleat ▸ noun **1** a French roll.
2 a pleat at the top of a curtain consisting of three smaller pleats.

French polish Brit. ▸ noun [mass noun] shellac polish that produces a high gloss on wood.
▸ verb (**french-polish**) [with obj.] treat (wood) with French polish.

French Polynesia an overseas territory of France in the South Pacific; pop. 287,000 (est. 2009); capital, Papeete (on Tahiti). French Polynesia comprises the Society Islands, the Gambier Islands, the Tuamotu Archipelago, the Tubuai Islands, and the Marquesas. It became an overseas territory of France in 1946, and was granted partial autonomy in 1977.

French Republican calendar ▸ noun a reformed calendar officially introduced by the French Republican government on 5 October 1793, having twelve months of thirty days each, with five days of festivals at the year's end (six in leap years). It was abandoned under the Napoleonic regime and the Gregorian calendar was formally reinstated on 1 January 1806.

French Revolution the overthrow of the Bourbon monarchy in France (1789–99).

The Revolution began with the meeting of the legislative assembly (the States General) in May 1789, when the French government was already in crisis; the Bastille was stormed in July of the same year. The Revolution became steadily more radical and ruthless with power increasingly in the hands of the Jacobins and Robespierre; Louis XVI's execution in January 1793 was followed by Robespierre's Reign of Terror. The Revolution failed to produce a stable form of republican government and after several different forms of administration the last, the Directory, was overthrown by Napoleon in 1799.

French roll ▸ noun a hairstyle in which the hair is tucked into a vertical roll down the back of the head.

French roof ▸ noun a mansard roof.

French seam ▸ noun a seam with the raw edges enclosed.

French Somaliland /sə'mɑːlɪˌland/ former name (until 1967) for DJIBOUTI.

French Southern and Antarctic Territories an overseas territory of France, comprising Adélie Land in Antarctica, and the Kerguelen and Crozet archipelagos and the islands of Amsterdam and St Paul in the southern Indian Ocean.

French stick ▸ noun a French loaf.

French Sudan former name for MALI.

French tickler ▸ noun informal a ribbed condom.

French toast ▸ noun [mass noun] bread coated in egg and milk and fried. ■ Brit. bread buttered on one side and toasted on the other.

French twist ▸ noun N. Amer. a French roll.

French vermouth ▸ noun [mass noun] Brit. dry vermouth.

French Wars of Religion a series of religious and political conflicts in France (1562–98) involving the Protestant Huguenots on one side and Catholic groups on the other. The wars were complicated by interventions from Spain, Rome, England, the Netherlands, and elsewhere, and were not brought to an end until the settlement of the Edict of Nantes.

French West Africa a former federation of French territories in NW Africa (1895–1959). Its constituent territories were Senegal, Mauritania, French Sudan (now Mali), Upper Volta (now Burkina Faso), Niger, French Guinea (now Guinea), Côte d'Ivoire (Ivory Coast), and Dahomey (now Benin).

French window ▸ noun (usu. **French windows**) each of a pair of glazed doors in an outside wall, serving as a window and door, typically opening on to a garden or balcony.

Frenchwoman ▸ noun (pl. **Frenchwomen**) a female native or inhabitant of France, or a woman of French descent.

Frenchy (also **Frenchie**) ▸ adjective (**Frenchier**, **Frenchiest**) informal, chiefly derogatory typically French in character: *progressive Frenchy art.*
▸ noun (pl. **Frenchies**) **1** informal, chiefly derogatory a French person. ■ Canadian a French Canadian.
2 Brit. informal, dated short for FRENCH LETTER.

frenemy /'frɛnəmi/ ▸ noun (pl. **frenemies**) informal a person with whom one is friendly despite a fundamental dislike or rivalry.
– ORIGIN 1950s: blend of FRIEND and ENEMY.

frenetic /frə'nɛtɪk/ ▸ adjective fast and energetic in a rather wild and uncontrolled way: *a frenetic pace of activity.*
– DERIVATIVES **frenetically** adverb, **freneticism** noun.
– ORIGIN late Middle English (in the sense 'insane'): from Old French *frenetique*, via Latin from Greek *phrenitikos*, from *phrenitis* 'delirium', from *phrēn* 'mind'. Compare with FRANTIC.

frenulum /'friːnjʊləm/ (also **fraenulum**) ▸ noun **1** Anatomy a small fold or ridge of tissue which supports or checks the motion of the part to which it is attached, in particular a fold of skin beneath the tongue, or between the lip and the gum.
2 Entomology (in some moths and butterflies) a bristle or row of bristles on the edge of the hindwing which keeps it in contact with the forewing.
– ORIGIN early 18th cent.: modern Latin, diminutive of Latin *frenum* 'bridle'.

frenum /'friːnəm/ (also **fraenum**) ▸ noun another term for FRENULUM.
– ORIGIN mid 18th cent.: from Latin, literally 'bridle'.

frenzied ▸ adjective wildly excited or uncontrolled: *a frenzied attack.*
– DERIVATIVES **frenziedly** adverb.

frenzy ▸ noun (pl. **frenzies**) [usu. in sing.] a state or period of uncontrolled excitement or wild behaviour: *Doreen worked herself into a frenzy of rage.*
– ORIGIN Middle English: from Old French *frenesie*, from medieval Latin *phrenesia*, from Latin *phrenesis*, from Greek *phrēn* 'mind'.

freon /'friːɒn/ ▸ noun [mass noun] trademark an aerosol propellant, refrigerant, or organic solvent consisting of one or more of a group of chlorofluorocarbons and related compounds.
– ORIGIN 1930s: of unknown origin.

frequency ▸ noun (pl. **frequencies**) **1** [mass noun] the rate at which something occurs over a particular period of time or in a given sample: *an increase in the frequency of accidents due to increased overtime.* ■ the fact or state of being frequent or happening often.
2 the rate per second of a vibration constituting a wave, either in a material (as in sound waves), or in an electromagnetic field (as in radio waves and light): *different thicknesses of glass will absorb different frequencies of sound.* (Symbol: **f** or ν) ■ the particular waveband at which radio signals are broadcast or transmitted.
– ORIGIN mid 16th cent. (gradually superseding late Middle English *frequence*; originally denoting a gathering of people): from Latin *frequentia*, from *frequens, frequent-* 'crowded, frequent'.

frequency distribution ▸ noun Statistics a mathematical function showing the number of instances in which a variable takes each of its possible values.

frequency division multiplex ▸ noun [mass noun] Telecommunications a technique for sending two or more signals over the same telephone line, radio channel, or other medium. Each signal is transmitted as a unique range of frequencies within the bandwidth of the channel as a whole, enabling several signals to be transmitted simultaneously. Compare with TIME DIVISION MULTIPLEX.

frequency modulation (abbrev.: **FM**) ▸ noun [mass noun] the modulation of a radio or other wave by variation of its frequency, especially to carry an audio signal. Often contrasted with AMPLITUDE MODULATION.

frequency response ▸ noun [mass noun] Electronics the dependence on signal frequency of the output–input ratio of an amplifier or other device.

frequent ▸ adjective /'friːkw(ə)nt/ occurring or done many times at short intervals: *frequent changes in policy | the showers will become heavier and more frequent.* ■ [attrib.] (of a person) doing something often; habitual: *a frequent visitor to Scotland.* ■ archaic found at short distances apart: *walls flanked by frequent square towers.*

▸ **verb** /frɪˈkwɛnt/ [with obj.] visit (a place) often: *pubs frequented by soldiers* | (as adj., with submodifier **frequented**) *one of the most frequented sites*.
– DERIVATIVES **frequentation** noun.
– ORIGIN late Middle English (in the sense 'profuse, ample'): from French, or from Latin *frequens, frequent-* 'crowded, frequent', of unknown ultimate origin.

frequentative /frɪˈkwɛntətɪv/ Grammar ▸ **adjective** (of a verb or verbal form) expressing frequent repetition or intensity of action.
▸ **noun** a frequentative verb or verbal form (for example *chatter* in English).
– ORIGIN mid 16th cent.: from French *fréquentatif, -ive* or Latin *frequentativus*, from *frequens, frequent-* 'crowded, frequent'.

frequenter ▸ **noun** a person who visits a place often: *he is an avid frequenter of discount supermarkets*.

frequently ▸ **adverb** regularly or habitually; often: *they go abroad frequently*.

fresco /ˈfrɛskəʊ/ ▸ **noun** (pl. **frescoes** or **frescos**) a painting done rapidly in watercolour on wet plaster on a wall or ceiling, so that the colours penetrate the plaster and become fixed as it dries. ■ [mass noun] this method of painting, used in Roman times and by the great masters of the Italian Renaissance including Giotto, Raphael, and Michelangelo.
– DERIVATIVES **frescoed** adjective.
– ORIGIN late 16th cent.: Italian, literally 'cool, fresh'. The word was first recorded in English in the phrase *in fresco*, representing Italian *affresco, al fresco* 'on the fresh (plaster)'.

fresco secco ▸ **noun** see SECCO.

fresh ▸ **adjective 1** not previously known or used; new or different: *the court had heard fresh evidence*. ■ recently created or experienced and not faded or impaired: *the memory was still fresh in their minds*. ■ (of a person) attractively youthful and unspoilt.
2 (of food) recently made or obtained; not tinned, frozen, or otherwise preserved: *fresh fruit*.
3 [predic.] (of a person) full of energy and vigour: *they are feeling fresh after a good night's sleep*. ■ (of a colour or a person's complexion) bright or healthy in appearance.
4 (of water) not salty.
5 (of the wind) cool and fairly strong. ■ Brit. informal (of the weather) rather cold and windy. ■ pleasantly clean and cool: *a bit of fresh air does her good*.
6 (**fresh from/out of**) (of a person) having just had (a particular experience) or come from (a particular place): *we were fresh out of art school*.
7 informal presumptuous towards someone, especially in a sexual way: *some of the men tried to get fresh with the girls*.
8 W. Indian having an unpleasant, slightly rotten smell: *this place was covered in water and smelled fresh like hell*.
▸ **adverb** [usu. in combination] newly; recently: *fresh-baked bread* | *fresh-cut grass*.
– PHRASES **be fresh out of** informal have just sold or run out of a supply of (something). **be (as) fresh as a daisy** see DAISY. **fresh blood** see BLOOD.
– DERIVATIVES **freshness** noun.
– ORIGIN Old English *fersc* 'not salt, fit for drinking', superseded in Middle English by forms from Old French *freis, fresche*; both ultimately of Germanic origin and related to Dutch *vers* and German *frisch*.

fresh breeze ▸ **noun** a wind of force 5 on the Beaufort scale (17–21 knots or 31–9 kph).

freshen ▸ **verb 1** [with obj.] make (something) newer, cleaner, or more attractive: *it didn't take long to freshen her make-up*.
2 [no obj.] (of wind) become stronger and colder.
3 chiefly N. Amer. add more liquid to (a drink); top up.
4 [no obj.] N. Amer. (of a cow) give birth and come into milk.
– PHRASAL VERBS **freshen up** refresh oneself by washing or changing into clean clothes.
– DERIVATIVES **freshener** noun [usu. in combination] *an air-freshener*.

fresher ▸ **noun** Brit. informal term for FRESHMAN.

freshet /ˈfrɛʃɪt/ ▸ **noun** the flood of a river from heavy rain or melted snow. ■ a rush of fresh water flowing into the sea.
– ORIGIN late 16th cent.: probably from Old French *freschete*, diminutive of *freis* 'fresh'.

fresh-faced ▸ **adjective** having a clear and young-looking complexion: *he looked like a fresh-faced schoolboy*.

fresh gale ▸ **noun** see GALE.

freshie (also **freshy**) ▸ **noun** Austral. a freshwater crocodile native to northern Australia. ● *Crocodylus johnstoni*, family Crocodylidae.

freshly ▸ **adverb** [usu. as submodifier] newly; recently: *freshly ground black pepper*.

freshman ▸ **noun** (pl. **freshmen**) a first-year student at university. ■ N. Amer. a first-year student at high school.

fresh-run ▸ **adjective** (of a migratory fish, especially a salmon) newly arrived in fresh water from the sea in order to spawn.

freshwater ▸ **adjective 1** of or found in fresh water; not of the sea: *freshwater and marine fish*.
2 US informal (especially of a school or college) situated in a remote or obscure area; provincial.

freshwater flea ▸ **noun** another term for DAPHNIA.

freshwoman ▸ **noun** (pl. **freshwomen**) a female first-year student.

freshy ▸ **noun** variant spelling of FRESHIE.

Fresnel /ˈfreɪn(ə)l/, French /frɛnɛl/, Augustin Jean (1788–1827), French physicist and civil engineer. He correctly postulated that light has a wave-like motion transverse to the direction of propagation, contrary to the longitudinal direction suggested by Christiaan Huygens and Thomas Young.

fresnel /freɪˈnɛl/ (also **fresnel lens**) ▸ **noun** Photography a flat lens made of a number of concentric rings, to reduce spherical aberration.
– ORIGIN mid 19th cent.: named after A. J. FRESNEL.

Fresno /ˈfrɛznəʊ/ a city in central California, in the San Joaquin valley; pop. 476,050 (est. 2008).

fret[1] ▸ **verb** (**frets, fretting, fretted**) **1** [no obj.] be constantly or visibly anxious: *she fretted about the cost of groceries*. ■ [with obj.] cause anxiety to: *his absence during her times awake began to fret her*.
2 [with obj.] gradually wear away (something) by rubbing or gnawing: *the bay's black waves fret the seafront*. ■ form (a channel or passage) by rubbing or wearing away.
3 [no obj.] flow or move in small waves: *squelchy clay that fretted between his toes*.
▸ **noun** [in sing.] chiefly Brit. a state of anxiety.
– ORIGIN Old English *fretan* 'devour, consume', of Germanic origin; related to Dutch *vreten* and German *fressen*, and ultimately to FOR- and EAT.

fret[2] ▸ **noun 1** Art & Architecture a repeating ornamental design of vertical and horizontal lines, such as the Greek key pattern.
2 Heraldry a device of narrow diagonal bands interlaced through a diamond.
▸ **verb** (**frets, fretting, fretted**) [with obj.] (usu. as adj. **fretted**) decorate with fretwork: *intricately carved and fretted balustrades*.
– ORIGIN late Middle English: from Old French *frete* 'trelliswork' and *freter* (verb), of unknown origin.

fret[3] ▸ **noun** each of a sequence of ridges on the fingerboard of some stringed musical instruments (such as the guitar), used for fixing the positions of the fingers to produce the desired notes.
▸ **verb** (**frets, fretting, fretted**) [with obj.] (often as adj. **fretted**) **1** provide (a stringed instrument) with frets.
2 play (a note) while pressing the string down against a fret: *fretted notes*.
– DERIVATIVES **fretless** adjective.
– ORIGIN early 16th cent.: of unknown origin.

fret[4] (also **sea fret**) ▸ **noun** N. English a mist coming in off the sea; a sea fog.
– ORIGIN mid 19th cent.: of unknown origin.

fretboard ▸ **noun** a fretted fingerboard on a guitar or other musical instrument.

fretful ▸ **adjective** feeling or expressing distress or irritation: *the baby was crying with a fretful whimper*.
– DERIVATIVES **fretfully** adverb, **fretfulness** noun.

fretsaw ▸ **noun** a saw with a narrow blade stretched vertically on a frame, for cutting thin wood in patterns.

fretwork ▸ **noun** [mass noun] ornamental design in wood, typically openwork, done with a fretsaw.

Freud[1] /frɔɪd/, Anna (1895–1982), Austrian-born British psychoanalyst, the youngest child of Sigmund Freud. She introduced important innovations in method and theory to her father's work, notably with regard to disturbed children, and set up a child therapy course and clinic in London.

Freud[2] /frɔɪd/, Lucian (b.1922), German-born British painter, grandson of Sigmund Freud. His subjects, typically portraits and nudes, are painted in a powerful naturalistic style.

Freud[3] /frɔɪd/, Sigmund (1856–1939), Austrian neurologist and psychotherapist.

> He was the first to emphasize the significance of unconscious processes in normal and neurotic behaviour, and was the founder of psychoanalysis as both a theory of personality and a therapeutic practice. He proposed the existence of an unconscious element in the mind which influences consciousness, and of conflicts in it between various sets of forces. Freud also stated the importance of a child's semi-consciousness of sex as a factor in mental development; his theory of the sexual origin of neuroses aroused great controversy.

Freudian Psychology ▸ **adjective** relating to or influenced by Sigmund Freud and his methods of psychoanalysis, especially with reference to the importance of sexuality in human behaviour. ■ susceptible to analysis in terms of unconscious desires: *he wasn't sure whether his passion for water power had some deep Freudian significance*.
▸ **noun** a follower of Freud or his methods.
– DERIVATIVES **Freudianism** noun.

Freudian slip ▸ **noun** an unintentional error regarded as revealing subconscious feelings.

Frey /freɪ/ (also **Freyr** /ˈfreɪə/) Scandinavian Mythology the god of fertility and dispenser of rain and sunshine.

Freya /ˈfreɪə/ Scandinavian Mythology the goddess of love and of the night, sister of Frey. She is often identified with Frigga.

Fri. ▸ **abbreviation** Friday.

friable /ˈfrʌɪəb(ə)l/ ▸ **adjective** easily crumbled: *the soil was friable between her fingers*.
– DERIVATIVES **friability** noun.
– ORIGIN mid 16th cent.: from French, or from Latin *friabilis*, from *friare* 'to crumble'.

friar ▸ **noun** a member of any of certain religious orders of men, especially the four mendicant orders (Augustinians, Carmelites, Dominicans, and Franciscans).
– ORIGIN Middle English: from Old French *frere*, from Latin *frater* 'brother'.

friarbird ▸ **noun** a large Australasian honeyeater with a dark, partly naked head and a long curved bill. ● Genus *Philemon*, family Meliphagidae: many species.

Friar Minor ▸ **noun** a Franciscan friar.
– ORIGIN so named because the Franciscans regarded themselves of humbler rank than members of other orders.

friar's balsam ▸ **noun** [mass noun] a solution containing benzoin in alcohol, used chiefly as an inhalant.

friary ▸ **noun** (pl. **friaries**) a building or community occupied by or consisting of friars.

fribble ▸ **noun** informal a frivolous or foolish person. ■ a thing of no great importance.
– ORIGIN mid 17th cent.: symbolic, from the earlier (now obsolete) verb meaning 'stammer', also 'act aimlessly or frivolously'.

fricandeau /ˈfrɪkandəʊ/ ▸ **noun** (pl. **fricandeaux** /-dəʊz/) a slice of meat, especially veal, cut from the leg. ■ a dish consisting of a veal fillet stewed or fried and served with a sauce.
– ORIGIN French, probably related to *fricassée* 'stew', from the verb *fricasser* (see FRICASSEE).

fricassee /ˈfrɪkəsiː, ˌfrɪkəˈsiː/ ▸ **noun** a dish of stewed or fried pieces of meat served in a thick white sauce.
▸ **verb** (**fricassees, fricasseeing, fricasseed**) [with obj.] make a fricassee of (meat).
– ORIGIN French *fricassée*, feminine past participle of *fricasser* 'cut up and cook in sauce' (probably a blend of *frire* 'to fry' and *casser* 'to break').

fricative /ˈfrɪkətɪv/ Phonetics ▸ **adjective** denoting a type of consonant made by the friction of breath in a narrow opening, producing a turbulent air flow.
▸ **noun** a consonant made in this way, e.g. *f* and *th*.
– ORIGIN mid 19th cent.: from modern Latin *fricativus*, from Latin *fricare* 'to rub'.

fricking (also chiefly Austral./NZ **fricken**) ▸ **adjective** [attrib.] & **adverb** [as submodifier] another term for FRIGGING.

friction ▸ **noun** [mass noun] the resistance that one surface or object encounters when moving over another: *a lubrication system which reduces friction*. ■ the action of one surface or object rubbing against another: *the friction of braking*. ■ conflict or animosity caused by a clash of wills, temperaments, or opinions: *a considerable amount of friction between father and son*.
– DERIVATIVES **frictionless** adjective.
– ORIGIN mid 16th cent. (denoting chafing or rubbing of the body or limbs, formerly much used in medical

treatment): via French from Latin *frictio(n-)*, from *fricare* 'to rub'.

frictional ▶ adjective of or produced by the action of one surface or object rubbing against or moving over another: *frictional drag*.

frictional unemployment ▶ noun [mass noun] Economics the unemployment which exists in any economy due to people being in the process of moving from one job to another.

friction tape ▶ noun another term for INSULATING TAPE.

friction welding ▶ noun [mass noun] welding in which the heat is produced by rotating one component against the other under compression.

Friday ▶ noun the day of the week before Saturday and following Thursday: *he was arrested **on Friday** | the cleaning woman came on Fridays* | [as modifier] *Friday evening*.

F

▶ adverb chiefly N. Amer. on Friday: *we'll try again Friday*. ■ (**Fridays**) on Fridays; each Friday: *he goes there Fridays*.

– ORIGIN Old English *Frīgedæg*, named after the Germanic goddess FRIGGA; translation of late Latin *Veneris dies* 'day of the planet Venus'; compare with Dutch *vrijdag* and German *Freitag*.

fridge ▶ noun chiefly Brit. a refrigerator: *she put the carton of milk back in the fridge*.

– ORIGIN 1920s: abbreviation, probably influenced by the proprietary name *Frigidaire*.

fridge-freezer ▶ noun an upright unit comprising a refrigerator and a freezer, each self-contained.

fried past and past participle of FRY[1]. ▶ adjective **1** (of food) cooked in hot fat or oil: *a breakfast of fried eggs and bacon*.

2 [predic.] N. Amer. informal exhausted or worn out: *I had just come from doing a shoot and I was really fried*. ■ under the influence of alcohol or drugs.

Friedan /ˈfriːd(ə)n/, Betty (1921–2006), American feminist and writer, known for *The Feminine Mystique* (1963), which presented femininity as an artificial construct and traced the ways in which American women are socialized to become mothers and housewives.

Friedman /ˈfriːdmən/, Milton (1912–2006), American economist. A principal exponent of monetarism, he acted as a policy adviser to President Reagan from 1981 to 1989. Nobel Prize for Economics (1976).

Friedrich /ˈfriːdrɪk/, German /ˈfriːdrɪç/, Caspar David (1774–1840), German painter, noted for his romantic landscapes. He caused controversy with his altarpiece *The Cross in the Mountains* (1808), which lacked a specifically religious subject.

friend ▶ noun **1** a person with whom one has a bond of mutual affection, typically one exclusive of sexual or family relations. ■ (used as a polite form of address or in ironic reference) an acquaintance or a stranger one comes across: *my friends, let me introduce myself*. ■ (**one's friends**) archaic one's close relatives. ■ a person who supports a cause, organization, or country by giving financial or other help: *the Friends of the Welsh National Opera*. ■ a person who is not an enemy or opponent; an ally: *she was unsure whether he was **friend or foe***. ■ a familiar or helpful thing: *he settled for that old friend the compensation grant*. ■ a contact on a social networking website: *all of a sudden you've got 50 friends online who need to stay connected*.

2 (**Friend**) a member of the Religious Society of Friends; a Quaker.

▶ verb [with obj.] **1** informal add (someone) to a list of friends or contacts on a social networking website: *I am friended by 29 people who I have not friended back*. **2** archaic befriend (someone). ■ [no obj.] (**friend with**) black English have a sexual relationship with: *the woman got married and you still used to friend with she?*

– PHRASES **be** (or **make**) **friends with** be (or become) on good or affectionate terms with. **be no friend of** (or **to**) show no support or sympathy for. **a friend at court** a person in a position to use their influence on one's behalf. **a friend in need is a friend indeed** proverb a person who helps at a difficult time is a person who you can really rely on. **friends in high places** people in senior positions who are able and willing to use their influence on one's behalf. **my honourable friend** Brit. used to address or refer to another member of one's own party in the House of Commons. **my learned friend** used by a barrister or solicitor in court to address or refer to another barrister or solicitor. **my noble friend** Brit. used to address or refer to another member of one's own party in the House of Lords. **my Right Honourable friend** Brit. used to address or refer to another member of one's own party in the House of Commons who is also a privy counsellor.

– ORIGIN Old English *frēond*, of Germanic origin; related to Dutch *vriend* and German *Freund*, from an Indo-European root meaning 'to love', shared by FREE.

> **WORD TRENDS** Until very recently the notion of **friending** someone was archaic, confined to dusty tomes or poetic musings. Now, thanks to the growth of social networking sites, the use of **friend** as a verb has been revived, in reference to the process of adding someone to a list of online contacts (*I haven't friended my mother on Facebook and I don't intend to*). This has, of course, opened up whole new realms of social anxiety, from finding those you have **friended** won't **friend** you in return, to discovering that someone has **unfriended** or **defriended** you—removed you from their list of friends (*rather than being an adult about it and telling me how he felt, he unfriended me*).

friendless ▶ adjective having no friends; alone: *they have been left virtually friendless*.

friendliness ▶ noun [mass noun] the quality of being friendly; affability: *I was overwhelmed by the friendliness of the people here*.

friendly ▶ adjective (**friendlier**, **friendliest**) **1** kind and pleasant: *they were **friendly to** me | she gave me a friendly smile*. ■ [predic.] (of a person) on good or affectionate terms: *I was **friendly with** one of the local farmers*. ■ (of relations) not in conflict: *we want friendly relations with all countries*. ■ not seriously competitive or divisive: *friendly rivalry between the two schools*. ■ Brit. (of a game or match) not forming part of a serious competition.

2 [in combination] denoting something that is adapted for or is not harmful to a specified thing: *an environment-friendly agronomic practice | child-friendly policies*.

3 favourable or serviceable: *no one noticed her as she slipped out—it was a friendly night*.

4 Military (of troops or equipment) of, belonging to, or allied with one's own forces.

▶ noun (pl. **friendlies**) Brit. a game or match that does not form part of a serious competition.

– DERIVATIVES **friendlily** adverb.

friendly fire ▶ noun [mass noun] Military weapon fire coming from one's own side that causes accidental injury or death to one's own forces.

Friendly Islands another name for TONGA[1].

friendly society ▶ noun (in the UK) a mutual association providing sickness benefits, life assurance, and pensions.

– ORIGIN originally the name of a particular fire-insurance company operating *c.*1700.

friend of Dorothy ▶ noun informal a homosexual man.

– ORIGIN from the name of *Dorothy*, a character played by the actress Judy Garland (a gay icon) in the film *The Wizard of Oz* (1939).

friendship ▶ noun [mass noun] the emotions or conduct of friends; the state of being friends. ■ [count noun] a relationship between friends: *she formed close friendships with women*. ■ a state of mutual trust and support between allied nations.

– ORIGIN Old English *frēondscipe* (see FRIEND, -SHIP).

Friends of the Earth (abbrev.: **FoE**) an international pressure group established in 1971 to campaign for a better awareness of and response to environmental problems.

Friesian /ˈfriːʒ(ə)n/ ▶ noun Brit. an animal of a black-and-white breed of chiefly dairy cattle originally from Friesland.

– ORIGIN 1920s: alteration of FRISIAN.

Friesland[1] /ˈfriːzlənd/ the western part of the ancient region of Frisia. ■ a northern province of the Netherlands, bounded to the west and north by the IJsselmeer and the North Sea; capital, Leeuwarden.

Friesland[2] /ˈfriːzlənd/ ▶ noun South African term for FRIESIAN.

frieze[1] /friːz/ ▶ noun a broad horizontal band of sculpted or painted decoration, especially on a wall near the ceiling. ■ a horizontal paper strip mounted on a wall to give an effect similar to that of a sculpted or painted frieze. ■ Architecture the part of an entablature between the architrave and the cornice.

– ORIGIN mid 16th cent.: from French *frise*, from medieval Latin *frisium*, variant of *frigium*, from Latin *Phrygium* (*opus*) '(work) of Phrygia'.

frieze[2] /friːz/ ▶ noun [mass noun] heavy, coarse woollen cloth with a nap, usually on one side only.

– ORIGIN late Middle English: from French *frise*, from medieval Latin *frisia*, 'Frisian wool'.

frig[1] vulgar slang ▶ verb (**frigs**, **frigging**, **frigged**) [with obj.] have sexual intercourse with. ■ masturbate.

▶ noun an act of sexual intercourse or masturbation.

▶ exclamation expressing anger, annoyance, or contempt.

– PHRASAL VERBS **frig about/around** spend time doing unimportant or trivial things.

– ORIGIN late Middle English: of unknown origin. The original sense was 'move restlessly, wriggle', later 'rub, chafe', hence 'masturbate' (late 17th cent.).

frig[2] ▶ noun informal, chiefly Brit. old-fashioned spelling of FRIDGE.

frigate /ˈfrɪgət/ ▶ noun a warship with a mixed armament, generally lighter than a destroyer (in the US navy, heavier) and of a kind originally introduced for convoy escort work. ■ historical a sailing warship of a size and armament just below that of a ship of the line.

– ORIGIN late 16th cent. (denoting a light, fast boat which was rowed or sailed): from French *frégate*, from Italian *fregata*, of unknown origin.

frigate bird ▶ noun a predatory tropical seabird with dark plumage, long narrow wings, a deeply forked tail, and a long hooked bill. Also called MAN-OF-WAR BIRD. ● Family Fregatidae and genus *Fregata*: five species.

Frigga /ˈfrɪgə/ Scandinavian Mythology the wife of Odin and goddess of married love and of the hearth, often identified with Freya. Friday is named after her.

frigging ▶ adjective [attrib.] & adverb vulgar slang used as a euphemism for 'fucking', especially for emphasis or to express anger, annoyance, contempt, or surprise.

fright ▶ noun [mass noun] a sudden intense feeling of fear: *I jumped up in fright*. ■ [count noun] an experience that causes one to feel sudden intense fear: *she's had a nasty fright*.

▶ verb [with obj.] archaic frighten.

– PHRASES **look a fright** informal have a dishevelled or ridiculous appearance. **take fright** suddenly become frightened or panicked.

– ORIGIN Old English *fryhto*, *fyrhto* (noun), of Germanic origin; related to Dutch *furcht* and German *furcht*.

frighten ▶ verb [with obj.] make (someone) afraid or anxious: *the savagery of his thoughts frightened him | farmers are being **frightened into** scaling down their breeding plans*. ■ (**frighten someone/thing off**) deter someone or something from involvement or action by making them afraid.

– PHRASES **frighten the horses** see HORSE.

frightened ▶ adjective afraid or anxious: *a frightened child | I'm not **frightened of** him*.

frightener ▶ noun a person or thing that frightens someone. ■ Brit. informal a member of a criminal gang who intimidates its victims.

– PHRASES **put the frighteners on** Brit. informal threaten or intimidate (someone).

frightening ▶ adjective making someone afraid or anxious; terrifying: *a frightening experience*.

– DERIVATIVES **frighteningly** adverb [as submodifier] *the standard air fare proved to be frighteningly expensive*.

frightful ▶ adjective chiefly Brit. very unpleasant, serious, or shocking: *there's been a most frightful accident*. ■ informal used for emphasis, especially of something bad: *her hair was a frightful mess*.

– DERIVATIVES **frightfulness** noun.

frightfully ▶ adverb [as submodifier] dated very (used for emphasis): *it was frightfully hot | I'm frightfully sorry*.

fright wig ▶ noun a wig with the hair arranged standing up or sticking out, as worn by a clown or similar performer.

frigid /ˈfrɪdʒɪd/ ▶ adjective very cold in temperature: *frigid water*. ■ (of a woman) unable to be sexually aroused and responsive. ■ stiff or formal in behaviour or style: *the frigid elegance of the new Opera Bastille*.

– DERIVATIVES **frigidity** noun, **frigidly** adverb, **frigidness** noun.

– ORIGIN late Middle English: from Latin *frigidus*, from *frigere* 'be cold', from *frigus* (noun) 'cold'.

frigidarium /ˌfrɪdʒɪˈdɛːrɪəm/ ▶ noun (pl. **frigidaria** /-rɪə/) historical a cold room in an ancient Roman bath.

– ORIGIN Latin.

frigid zone ▶ noun each of the two areas of the earth respectively north of the Arctic Circle and south of the Antarctic Circle.

frijoles /frɪˈhəʊlɛs/ ▶ **plural noun** (in Mexican cookery) beans.
– ORIGIN Spanish, plural of *frijol* 'bean'.

frikkadel /ˌfrɪkəˈdɛl/ ▶ **noun** (pl. **frikkadels** or **frikkadelle**) S. African a fried or baked meatball; a rissole.
– ORIGIN Afrikaans, from French *fricadelle*.

frill ▶ **noun 1** a strip of gathered or pleated material sewn on to a garment or larger piece of material as a decorative edging or ornament. ■ a thing resembling a frill in appearance or function: *tiny frills of foam glistened white on the sea.* ■ a natural fringe of feathers or hair on a bird or other animal. ■ Palaeontology an upward-curving bony plate extending behind the skull of many ceratopsian dinosaurs.
2 (usu. **frills**) an unnecessary extra feature or embellishment: *it was just a comfortable flat with no frills.*
– DERIVATIVES **frilled** adjective.
– ORIGIN late 16th cent.: from or related to Flemish *frul*.

frilled lizard (also **frill-necked lizard**) ▶ **noun** a large north Australian lizard with a membrane round the neck which can be erected to form a ruff for defensive display. When disturbed it runs away on its hind legs. ● *Chlamydosaurus kingii*, family Agamidae.

frilling ▶ **noun** [mass noun] material for frills; frills collectively.

frilly ▶ **adjective** (**frillier**, **frilliest**) decorated with frills: *a frilly apron.* ■ over-elaborate or showy in character or style: *seafood dishes that avoid being too frilly or rich.*
▶ **plural noun** (**frillies**) informal women's underwear.
– DERIVATIVES **frilliness** noun.

Frimaire /frɪˈmɛː/, French /fʀimɛʀ/ ▶ **noun** the third month of the French Republican calendar (1793–1805), originally running from 21 November to 20 December.
– ORIGIN French, from *frimas* 'hoar frost'.

fringe ▶ **noun 1** an ornamental border of threads left loose or formed into tassels or twists, used to edge clothing or material.
2 chiefly Brit. the front part of someone's hair, cut so as to hang over the forehead. ■ a natural border of hair or fibres in an animal or plant.
3 (often **the fringes**) the outer, marginal, or extreme part of an area, group, or sphere of activity: *his uncles were on the fringes of crooked activity.* ■ (**the Fringe**) a secondary festival on the periphery of the Edinburgh Festival.
4 a band of contrasting brightness or darkness produced by diffraction or interference of light. ■ a strip of false colour in an optical image.
5 N. Amer. short for FRINGE BENEFIT.
▶ **verb** (**fringes**, **fringing**, **fringed**) [with obj.] decorate (clothing or material) with a fringe: *a rich robe of gold, fringed with black velvet.* ■ form a border around (something): *the sea is fringed by palm trees.* ■ (as adj. **fringed**) (of a plant or animal) having a border of hair or fibre.
– DERIVATIVES **fringeless** adjective, **fringy** adjective.
– ORIGIN Middle English: from Old French *frenge*, based on late Latin *fimbria*, earlier a plural noun meaning 'fibres, shreds'.

fringe benefit ▶ **noun** an extra benefit supplementing an employee's money wage or salary, for example a company car, private health care, etc.

fringe medicine ▶ **noun** another term for ALTERNATIVE MEDICINE.

fringing ▶ **noun** [mass noun] material used to make a fringe.

fringing reef ▶ **noun** a coral reef that lies close to the shore.

Frink /frɪŋk/, Dame Elisabeth (1930–93), English sculptor and graphic artist. She made her name with angular bronzes, often of birds. During the 1960s her figures became smoother, although she retained a feeling for the bizarre.

frippery /ˈfrɪp(ə)ri/ ▶ **noun** (pl. **fripperies**) [mass noun] showy or unnecessary ornament in architecture, dress, or language. ■ [count noun] a tawdry or frivolous thing.
▶ **adjective** archaic frivolous and tawdry.
– ORIGIN mid 16th cent. (denoting old or second-hand clothes): from French *friperie*, from Old French *freperie*, from *frepe* 'rag', of unknown ultimate origin.

frippet /ˈfrɪpɪt/ ▶ **noun** Brit. informal, dated a frivolous or showy young woman.
– ORIGIN early 20th cent.: of unknown origin.

frisbee /ˈfrɪzbi/ ▶ **noun** trademark a concave plastic disc designed for skimming through the air as an outdoor game or amusement. ■ [mass noun] the activity of skimming such a disc.
– ORIGIN 1950s: said to be named after the *Frisbie* bakery (Bridgeport, Connecticut), whose pie tins could be used similarly.

Frisch[1] /frɪʃ/, Karl von (1886–1982), Austrian zoologist. He worked mainly on honeybees and showed that they perform an elaborate dance in the hive to indicate the direction and distance of food.

Frisch[2] /frɪʃ/, Otto Robert (1904–79), Austrian-born British physicist. With his aunt, Lise Meitner, he recognized that Otto Hahn's experiments with uranium had produced a new type of nuclear reaction. Frisch named it nuclear fission, and indicated the explosive potential of its chain reaction.

Frisch[3] /frɪʃ/, Ragnar (Anton Kittil) (1895–1973), Norwegian economist. A pioneer of econometrics, he shared the first Nobel Prize for Economics with Jan Tinbergen (1969).

frisée /ˈfriːzeɪ/ ▶ **noun** [mass noun] the curly endive (see ENDIVE (sense 1)).
– ORIGIN French, from *chicorée frisée* 'curly endive'.

Frisia /ˈfrɪzɪə, ˈfriːʒə/ an ancient region of NW Europe. It consisted of the Frisian Islands and parts of the mainland corresponding to the modern provinces of Friesland and Groningen in the Netherlands and the regions of Ostfriesland and Nordfriesland in NW Germany.

Frisian /ˈfriːzɪən, ˈfriːʒ(ə)n, ˈfrɪ-/ ▶ **adjective** relating to Frisia or Friesland, its people, or language.
▶ **noun 1** a native or inhabitant of Frisia or Friesland.
2 [mass noun] the Germanic language of Frisia or Friesland, most closely related to English and Dutch, now with fewer than 400,000 speakers.
– ORIGIN late 16th cent.: from Latin *Frisii* 'Frisians' (from Old Frisian *Frīsa*, *Frēsa*) + -IAN.

Frisian Islands a chain of islands lying off the coast of NW Europe, extending from the IJsselmeer in the Netherlands to Jutland. The islands consist of three groups: the **West Frisian Islands** form part of the Netherlands, the **East Frisian Islands** form part of Germany, and the **North Frisian Islands** are divided between Germany and Denmark.

frisk ▶ **verb 1** [with obj.] (of a police officer or other official) pass the hands over (someone) in a search for hidden weapons, drugs, or other items.
2 [no obj., with adverbial of direction] skip or leap playfully; frolic: *spaniels frisked around me.*
▶ **noun 1** [in sing.] an act of frisking someone.
2 a playful skip or leap.
– DERIVATIVES **frisker** noun.
– ORIGIN early 16th cent. (in sense 2 of the noun): from obsolete *frisk* 'lively, frisky', from Old French *frisque* 'alert, lively, merry', perhaps of Germanic origin. Sense 1 of the noun, originally a slang term, dates from the late 18th cent.

frisket /ˈfrɪskɪt/ ▶ **noun** Printing a thin metal frame keeping the paper in position during printing on a hand press. ■ [mass noun] US fluid or adhesive paper used in painting or crafts to cover areas of a surface on which paint is not wanted.
– ORIGIN late 17th cent.: from French *frisquette*, from Provençal *frisqueto*, from Spanish *frasqueta*.

frisky ▶ **adjective** (**friskier**, **friskiest**) playful and full of energy: *he bounds about like a frisky pup.*
– DERIVATIVES **friskily** adverb, **friskiness** noun.

frisson /ˈfriːsɔ̃, ˈfrɪsɒn/ ▶ **noun** a sudden strong feeling of excitement or fear; a thrill: *a frisson of excitement.*
– ORIGIN late 18th cent.: French, 'a shiver or thrill'.

frit[1] ▶ **noun** [mass noun] the mixture of silica and fluxes which is fused at high temperature to make glass. ■ a similar calcined and pulverized mixture used to make soft-paste porcelain or ceramic glazes.
▶ **verb** (**frits**, **fritting**, **fritted**) [with obj.] make into frit.
– ORIGIN mid 17th cent.: from Italian *fritta*, feminine past participle of *friggere* 'to fry'.

frit[2] ▶ **adjective** [predic.] dialect frightened.
– ORIGIN early 19th cent.: dialect past participle of FRIGHT.

frites /friːt(s)/ ▶ **plural noun** short for POMMES FRITES.

frit fly ▶ **noun** a very small black fly whose larvae are a serious pest of cereal crops and maize. ● *Oscinella frit*, family Chloropidae.
– ORIGIN late 19th cent.: from Latin *frit* 'particle on an ear of corn'.

frith ▶ **noun** archaic spelling of FIRTH.

fritillary /frɪˈtɪləri/ ▶ **noun** (pl. **fritillaries**) **1** a Eurasian plant of the lily family, with hanging bell like flowers. ● Genus *Fritillaria*, family Liliaceae: numerous species, in particular the snake's head.
2 a butterfly with orange-brown wings that are chequered with black. ● Subfamilies Argynninae and Melitaeinae, family Nymphalidae: *Argynnis* and other genera, and numerous species.
– ORIGIN mid 17th cent.: from modern Latin *fritillaria*, from Latin *fritillus* 'dice box' (probably with reference to the chequered corolla of the snake's head fritillary).

frittata /frɪˈtɑːtə/ ▶ **noun** an Italian dish made with fried beaten eggs, resembling a Spanish omelette.
– ORIGIN Italian, from *fritto*, past participle of *friggere* 'to fry'. Compare with FRITTER[2].

fritter[1] ▶ **verb** [with obj.] **1** (**fritter something away**) waste time, money, or energy on trifling matters: *I wish we hadn't frittered the money away so easily.*
2 archaic divide (something) into small pieces.
– ORIGIN early 18th cent.: based on obsolete *fitter* 'break into fragments, shred'; perhaps related to German *Fetzen* 'rag, scrap'.

F

fritter[2] ▶ **noun** a piece of fruit, vegetable, or meat that is coated in batter and deep-fried.
– ORIGIN late Middle English: from Old French *friture*, based on Latin *frigere* (see FRY[1]). Compare with FRITTATA.

fritto misto /ˌfrɪtəʊ ˈmɪstəʊ/ ▶ **noun** [mass noun] a dish of various foods, typically seafood, deep-fried in batter.
– ORIGIN Italian, 'mixed fry'.

Fritz ▶ **noun** Brit. informal, dated a German, especially a soldier in the First World War (often used as a nickname). ■ [in sing.] the Germans collectively.
– ORIGIN abbreviation of the German given name *Friedrich*.

fritz ▶ **noun** (in phrase **go** or **be on the fritz**) N. Amer. informal (of a machine) stop working properly.
– ORIGIN early 20th cent.: said to be a use of FRITZ, with allusion to cheap German imports into the US before the First World War.

Friuli /friːˈuːli/ a historic region of SE Europe now divided between Slovenia and the Italian region of Friuli-Venezia Giulia. A Rhaeto-Romance dialect is spoken locally in the region.
– DERIVATIVES **Friulian** adjective & noun.

Friuli-Venezia Giulia /frɪˌuːlɪvɛˌnɛtsɪə ˈdʒuːlɪə/ a region in NE Italy, on the border with Slovenia and Austria; capital, Trieste.

frivol /ˈfrɪv(ə)l/ ▶ **verb** (**frivols**, **frivolling**, **frivolled**; US **frivols**, **frivoling**, **frivoled**) [no obj.] behave in a frivolous way.
– ORIGIN mid 19th cent.: back-formation from FRIVOLOUS.

frivolity ▶ **noun** [mass noun] lack of seriousness; light-heartedness: *a night of fun and frivolity.*

frivolous ▶ **adjective** not having any serious purpose or value: *frivolous ribbons and lacy frills | rules to stop frivolous lawsuits.* ■ (of a person) carefree and superficial: *the frivolous, fun-loving flappers of the twenties.*
– DERIVATIVES **frivolously** adverb, **frivolousness** noun.
– ORIGIN late Middle English: from Latin *frivolus* 'silly, trifling' + -OUS.

frizz /frɪz/ ▶ **verb** [with obj.] **1** form (hair) into a mass of small, tight curls: *her hair was crimped and frizzed into a leonine mane.* ■ [no obj.] (of hair) form itself into a mass of small, tight curls: *his hair had frizzed out symmetrically.*
2 dress (chamois or a similar leather) with pumice or a scraping knife.
▶ **noun** [mass noun] the state of being formed into a mass of small, tight curls: *a perm system designed to add curl without frizz.*
– ORIGIN late Middle English (in sense 2 of the verb): from French *friser*. Sense 1 of the verb dates from the late 16th cent.

frizzante /frɪtˈzanteɪ, -ti/ ▶ **adjective** (of wine) semi-sparkling.
– ORIGIN Italian.

frizzle[1] ▶ **verb** [no obj.] fry or grill with a sizzling noise: *Elsie had the fat frizzling in the chip pan.* ■ [with obj.] fry until crisp, shrivelled, or burnt: (as adj. **frizzled**) *add diced frizzled salt pork to taste.*
▶ **noun** [in sing.] the sound or act of frying: *the frizzle of the pan.*
– ORIGIN mid 18th cent.: from FRY[1], probably influenced by SIZZLE.

frizzle[2] ▶ **verb** [with obj.] form (hair) into tight curls.
▶ **noun** a tight curl in hair.

– DERIVATIVES **frizzly** adjective.
– ORIGIN mid 16th cent.: from FRIZZ + -LE[4].

frizzy ▶ adjective (**frizzier, frizziest**) formed of a mass of small, tight curls: *frizzy red hair*.
– DERIVATIVES **frizziness** noun.

Frl. ▶ abbreviation Fräulein.

fro ▶ adverb see TO AND FRO.
– ORIGIN Middle English: from Old Norse *frá* (see FROM).

'fro /frəʊ/ ▶ noun (pl. **'fros**) an Afro hairstyle or a frizzy or bushy hairstyle resembling one.
– ORIGIN 1970s: abbreviation of AFRO.

Frobisher /ˈfrəʊbɪʃə/, Sir Martin (*c.*1535–94), English explorer. In 1576 he led an unsuccessful expedition in search of the North-West Passage. Frobisher served in Sir Francis Drake's Caribbean expedition of 1585–6 and played a prominent part in the defeat of the Spanish Armada.

frock ▶ noun chiefly Brit. **1** a woman's or girl's dress.
2 a loose outer garment, in particular: ▪ a long gown with flowing sleeves worn by monks, priests, or clergy. ▪ historical an agricultural worker's smock; a smock-frock. ▪ short for FROCK COAT. ▪ archaic a woollen jersey worn by sailors.
3 archaic the work and position of a priest: *such words as these cost the preacher his frock*.
– DERIVATIVES **frocked** adjective [in combination] *a black-frocked Englishman*.
– ORIGIN late Middle English: from Old French *froc*, of Germanic origin. The sense 'priest's or monk's gown' is preserved in *defrock*.

frock coat ▶ noun a man's double-breasted, long-skirted coat, now worn chiefly on formal occasions.

froe /frəʊ/ ▶ noun a cleaving tool with a handle at right angles to the blade.
– ORIGIN late 16th cent.: abbreviation of obsolete *frower*, from FROWARD in the sense 'turned away'.

Froebel /ˈfrəʊb(ə)l, ˈfrɜːb-/, German /ˈfrøːbl/, Friedrich (Wilhelm August) (1782–1852), German educationist and founder of the kindergarten system. Believing that play materials, practical occupations, and songs are needed to develop a child's real nature, he opened a school for young children in 1837.
– DERIVATIVES **Froebelian** /frəʊˈbiːlɪən, frɜːˈbiː-/ adjective.

frog[1] ▶ noun **1** a tailless amphibian with a short squat body, moist smooth skin, and very long hind legs for leaping. ● Frogs are found in most families of the order Anura, but the 'true frogs' are confined to the large family Ranidae, which includes the **European common frog** (*Rana temporaria*).
2 (**Frog**) informal, derogatory a French person.
– PHRASES **have a frog in one's throat** informal lose one's voice or find it hard to speak because of hoarseness.
– ORIGIN Old English *frogga*, of Germanic origin; related to Dutch *vors* and German *Frosch*. Used as a general term of abuse in Middle English, the term was applied specifically to the Dutch in the 17th cent.; its application to the French (late 18th cent.) is partly alliterative, partly from the reputation of the French for eating frogs' legs.

frog[2] ▶ noun a thing used to hold or fasten something, in particular: ▪ an ornamental coat fastener or braid consisting of a spindle-shaped button and a loop through which it passes. ▪ an attachment to a belt for holding a sword, bayonet, or similar weapon. ▪ a perforated or spiked device for holding the stems of flowers in an arrangement. ▪ the piece into which the hair is fitted at the lower end of the bow of a stringed instrument. ▪ a grooved metal plate for guiding the wheels of a railway vehicle at an intersection.
– DERIVATIVES **frogging** noun.
– ORIGIN early 18th cent.: perhaps a use of FROG[1], influenced by synonymous Italian *forchetta* or French *fourchette* 'small fork', because of the shape.

frog[3] ▶ noun an elastic horny pad growing in the sole of a horse's hoof, helping to absorb the shock when the hoof hits the ground. ▪ a raised or swollen area on a surface.
– ORIGIN early 17th cent.: perhaps from FROG[1]; perhaps also influenced by Italian *forchetta* or French *fourchette* (see FROG[2]).

frogbit ▶ noun a floating freshwater plant with creeping stems which bear clusters of small rounded leaves. ● Two species in the family Hydrocharitaceae: **Eurasian frogbit** (*Hydrocharis morsus-ranae*) and **American frogbit** (*Hydromystria laevigatum*).

frogfish ▶ noun (pl. **same** or **frogfishes**) an anglerfish that typically lives on the seabed, where its warty skin and colour provide camouflage. ● Families Antennariidae (numerous species, including *Antennaria hispidus* of the Indo-Pacific), and Brachionichthyidae (four Australian species).

frogged ▶ adjective (of a coat) having an ornamental braid or fastening consisting of a spindle-shaped button and a loop.

froggy ▶ adjective **1** of or like a frog or frogs.
2 informal, derogatory French.
▶ noun (**Froggy**) (pl. **Froggies**) informal, derogatory a French person.

froghopper ▶ noun a jumping, plant-sucking bug, the larva of which produces cuckoo spit. Also called SPITTLEBUG. ● Family Cercopidae, suborder Homoptera: several genera.

frog kick ▶ noun a movement used in swimming, especially in breaststroke, in which the legs are brought towards the body with the knees bent and the feet together and then kicked outwards before being brought together again, all in one continuous movement.

froglet ▶ noun **1** a small kind of frog. ● Several genera, including *Crinia* of Australia (family Myobatrachidae), and *Philautus* of Malaysia (family Rhacophoridae).
2 a tiny frog that has recently developed from a tadpole.

frogman ▶ noun (pl. **frogmen**) a person who swims under water wearing a rubber suit, flippers, and an oxygen supply.

frogmarch ▶ verb [with obj. and adverbial of direction] force (someone) to walk forward by holding and pinning their arms from behind: *the cop frogmarched him down the steep stairs*.

frogmouth ▶ noun a nocturnal bird resembling a nightjar, occurring in SE Asia and Australasia. ● Family Podargidae: two genera and several species.

frogspawn ▶ noun [mass noun] the eggs of a frog, which are surrounded by transparent jelly.

froideur /frwʌˈdəː/, French /fʀwadœʀ/ ▶ noun [mass noun] coolness or reserve between people.
– ORIGIN French, from *froid* 'cold'.

frolic ▶ verb (**frolics, frolicking, frolicked**) [no obj., usu. with adverbial] play or move about in a cheerful and lively way: *Edward **frolicked on** the sand*.
▶ noun (often **frolics**) a playful and lively movement or activity: *film of her poolside frolics*.
▶ adjective archaic cheerful, merry, or playful.
– DERIVATIVES **frolicker** noun.
– ORIGIN early 16th cent. (as an adjective): from Dutch *vrolijk* 'merry, cheerful'.

frolicsome ▶ adjective lively and playful.
– DERIVATIVES **frolicsomely** adverb, **frolicsomeness** noun.

from ▶ preposition **1** indicating the point in space at which a journey, motion, or action starts: *she began to walk away from him* | *I leapt from my bed* | figurative *he was turning the Chamberlain government away from appeasement*. ▪ indicating the distance between a particular place and another place used as a point of reference: *the ambush occurred 50 metres from a checkpoint*.
2 indicating the point in time at which a particular process, event, or activity starts: *the show will run from 10 a.m. to 2 p.m.*
3 indicating the source or provenance of someone or something: *I'm from Hackney* | *she rang him from the hotel* | *she demanded the keys from her husband*. ▪ indicating the date at which something was created: *a document dating from the thirteenth century*.
4 indicating the starting point of a specified range on a scale: *men who ranged in age **from** seventeen **to** eighty-four*. ▪ indicating one extreme in a range of conceptual variations: *anything **from** geography **to** literature*.
5 indicating the point at which an observer is placed: *you can see the island from here* | figurative *the ability to see things from another's point of view*.
6 indicating the raw material out of which something is manufactured: *a paint made from a natural resin*.
7 indicating separation or removal: *the party was ousted from power after sixteen years*.
8 indicating prevention: *the story of how he was saved from death*.
9 indicating a cause: *a child suffering from asthma*.
10 indicating a source of knowledge or the basis for one's judgement: *information obtained from papers, books, and presentations*.
11 indicating a distinction: *these fees are quite distinct from expenses*.
– PHRASES **as from** see AS[1]. **from day to day** (or **hour to hour** etc.) daily (or hourly etc.); as the days (or hours etc.) pass. **from now** (or **then** etc.) **on** now (or then etc.) and in the future: *they were friends from that day on*. **from time to time** occasionally.
– ORIGIN Old English *fram, from*, of Germanic origin; related to Old Norse *frá* (see FRO).

fromage blanc /ˌfrɒmɑːʒ ˈblɒ̃/ ▶ noun [mass noun] a type of soft French cheese made from cow's milk and having a creamy sour taste.
– ORIGIN French, literally 'white cheese'.

fromage frais /ˈfreɪ/ ▶ noun [mass noun] a type of smooth soft fresh cheese, with the consistency of thick yogurt.
– ORIGIN French, literally 'fresh cheese'.

Fromm /frɒm/, Erich (1900–80), German-born American psychoanalyst and social philosopher. His works, which include *Escape from Freedom* (1941), *Man for Himself* (1947), and *The Sane Society* (1955), emphasize the role of culture in neurosis and strongly criticize materialist values.

frond ▶ noun the leaf or leaf-like part of a palm, fern, or similar plant: *fronds of bracken*.
– DERIVATIVES **fronded** adjective, **frondose** adjective.
– ORIGIN late 18th cent.: from Latin *frons, frond-* 'leaf'.

Fronde /frɒnd/, French /fʀɔ̃d/ a series of civil wars in France 1648–53, in which the nobles rose in rebellion against Mazarin and the court during the minority of Louis XIV. ▪ the party which rose in rebellion against Mazarin and the court at this time.
– ORIGIN French, from the name for a type of sling used in a children's game played in the streets of Paris at this time.

frondeur /frɒnˈdəː/, French /fʀɔ̃dœʀ/ ▶ noun rare a political rebel.
– ORIGIN French, literally 'slinger', used to denote a rebel taking part in the FRONDE.

frons /frɒnz/ ▶ noun (pl. **frontes**) Zoology the forehead or equivalent part of an animal, especially the middle part of an insect's face between the eyes and above the clypeus.
– ORIGIN mid 19th cent.: from Latin, 'front, forehead'.

front ▶ noun **1** the side or part of an object that presents itself to view or that is normally seen or used first; the most forward part of something: *a page at the front of the book had been torn out* | *he sealed the envelope and wrote on the front*. ▪ [in sing.] the position directly ahead of someone or something; the most forward position or place: *she quickly turned her head to face the front*. ▪ the forward-facing part of a person's body, on the opposite side to their back: *she rolled over on to her front*. ▪ the part of a garment covering a person's front: *porridge slopped from the tray on to his shirt front*. ▪ informal a woman's bust or cleavage. ▪ any face of a building, especially that of the main entrance: *the west front of the Cathedral*. ▪ chiefly Brit. short for SEAFRONT or WATERFRONT.
2 the foremost line or part of an armed force; the furthest position that an army has reached and where the enemy is or may be engaged: *his regiment was immediately sent to the front*. ▪ the direction towards which a line of troops faces when formed. ▪ a particular formation of troops for battle. ▪ a particular situation or sphere of operation: *there was some good news on the jobs front*. ▪ [often in names] an organized political group: *the National Progressive Patriotic Front*. ▪ Meteorology the forward edge of an advancing mass of air. See COLD FRONT, WARM FRONT.
3 [in sing.] an appearance or form of behaviour assumed by a person to conceal their genuine feelings: *she put on a brave front*. ▪ a person or organization serving as a cover for subversive or illegal activities: *the CIA identified the company as a **front for** a terrorist group*.
4 [mass noun] boldness and confidence of manner: *he's got a bit of talent and a lot of front*.
5 archaic a person's face or forehead.
▶ adjective [attrib.] **1** of or at the front: *the front cover of the magazine* | *she was in the front garden*.
2 Phonetics (of a vowel sound) formed by raising the tongue, excluding the blade and tip, towards the hard palate.
▶ verb [with obj.] **1** (of a building or piece of land) have the front facing or directed towards: *the flats which fronted Crow Road* | [no obj.] *both properties fronted on to the beach*. ▪ be or stand in front of: *they reached the hedge fronting the garden*. ▪ archaic stand face to face with; confront.

2 provide (something) with a front or facing of a particular type or material: *a metal box fronted by an alloy panel* | (as adj., in combination **-fronted**) *a glass-fronted bookcase.*
3 lead or be the most prominent member in (an organization, group, or activity): *the group is fronted by two girl singers.* ■ present or host (a television or radio programme).
4 [no obj.] act as a front or cover for illegal or secret activity: *he fronted for them in illegal property deals.*
5 [no obj.] (often **front up**) Austral./NZ make an appearance; turn up: *parents get a bit worried if you don't front up now and then.* ■ [with obj.] archaic or Austral./NZ stand face to face with; confront.
6 Phonetics articulate (a vowel sound) with the tongue further forward.
7 Linguistics place (a sentence element) at the beginning of a sentence instead of in its usual position, typically for emphasis or as a feature of some dialects, as in *horrible it was.*
– PHRASES **front of house** Brit. the parts of a theatre in front of the proscenium arch. ■ the business of a theatre that concerns the audience, such as ticket sales. **in front 1** in a position just ahead of or further forward than someone or something else: *the car in front stopped suddenly.* ■ in the lead in a game or contest: *United went back in front thanks to a penalty.* **2** on the part or side that normally first presents itself to view: *a house with a wide porch in front.* **in front of 1** in a position just ahead or at the front part of someone or something else: *the lawn in front of the house.* ■ in a position facing someone or something: *she sat in front of the mirror.* **2** in the presence of: *the teacher didn't want his authority challenged in front of the class.* **out front** chiefly N. Amer. at or to the front; in front: *two station wagons stopped out front.* ■ in the auditorium of a theatre.
– DERIVATIVES **frontless** adjective, **frontmost** adjective, **frontward** adjective & adverb, **frontwards** adverb.
– ORIGIN Middle English (denoting the forehead): from Old French *front* (noun), *fronter* (verb), from Latin *frons, front-* 'forehead, front'.

frontage ▸ noun the facade of a building. ■ a strip or extent of land abutting on a street or water: *the houses have a narrow frontage to the street* | [mass noun] *the house is set in parkland with river frontage.*

frontager /ˈfrʌntɪdʒə/ ▸ noun an owner of land or property adjoining a street or water.

frontage road ▸ noun N. Amer. a service road.

frontal[1] ▸ adjective of, at, or directed at the front: *a frontal assault on the Maginot line* | *the frontal view misses the octagonal tower.* ■ relating to the forehead or front part of the skull: *the frontal sinuses.*
– DERIVATIVES **frontally** adverb.
– ORIGIN mid 17th cent. (in the sense 'relating to the forehead'): from modern Latin *frontalis*, from Latin *frons, front-* 'front, forehead'.

frontal[2] ▸ noun a decorative cloth for covering the front of an altar.
– ORIGIN Middle English (denoting a band or ornament worn on the forehead): from Old French *frontel*, from Latin *frontale*, from *frons, front-* 'front, forehead'.

frontal bone ▸ noun the bone which forms the front part of the skull and the upper part of the eye sockets. ■ either of the pair of bones from which this is formed by fusion in infancy.

frontal lobe ▸ noun each of the paired lobes of the brain lying immediately behind the forehead, including areas concerned with behaviour, learning, personality, and voluntary movement.

front bench ▸ noun (in the UK) the foremost seats in the House of Commons, occupied by the members of the cabinet and shadow cabinet.
– DERIVATIVES **frontbencher** noun.

front bottom ▸ noun Brit. informal a child's term for the female genitals.

Front de Libération Nationale /ˌfrɒ̃ də ˌlɪbəˌrasjɒ̃ ˌnasjəˈnɑːl/, French /frɔ̃ də libeʁasjɔ̃ nasjɔnal/ (abbrev.: **FLN**) a revolutionary political party in Algeria that supported the war of independence against France 1954–62.
– ORIGIN French, 'National Liberation Front'.

front desk ▸ noun the registration and reception desk in a hotel or large organization.

front door ▸ noun the main entrance to a house.

front end ▸ noun **1** the front of a car or other vehicle.
2 the part of a radio or television receiver to which the aerial signal goes first.
3 Computing a part of a computer or program that allows access to other parts.
▸ adjective [attrib.] **1** (of money) paid or charged at the beginning of a transaction: *a front-end fee.*
2 Computing (of a device or program) directly accessed by the user and allowing access to further devices or programs.

front-end loader ▸ noun N. Amer. a machine with a scoop or bucket on an articulated arm at the front for digging and loading earth. ■ a hydraulic bucket or scoop that fits on to the front of a tractor.

front-fanged ▸ adjective (of a snake such as a cobra or viper) having the front pair of teeth modified as fangs, with grooves or canals to conduct the venom. Compare with **BACK-FANGED**.

frontier /ˈfrʌntɪə, frʌnˈtɪə/ ▸ noun a line or border separating two countries. ■ the extreme limit of settled land beyond which lies wilderness, especially in reference to the western US before Pacific settlement: *his novel of the American frontier.* ■ the extreme limit of understanding or achievement in a particular area: *the success of science in extending the frontiers of knowledge.*
– DERIVATIVES **frontierless** adjective.
– ORIGIN late Middle English: from Old French *frontiere*, based on Latin *frons, front-* 'front'.

frontiersman (or **frontierswoman**) ▸ noun (pl. **frontiersmen** or **frontierswomen**) a person living in the region of a frontier, especially that between settled and unsettled country.

frontispiece /ˈfrʌntɪspiːs/ ▸ noun **1** an illustration facing the title page of a book.
2 Architecture the principal face of a building. ■ a decorated entrance. ■ a pediment over a door or window.
– ORIGIN late 16th cent. (in sense 2): from French *frontispice* or late Latin *frontispicium* 'facade', from Latin *frons, front-* 'front' + *specere* 'to look'. The change in the ending (early in the word's history) was by association with **PIECE**.

frontlet ▸ noun **1** an ornamental piece of cloth hanging over the upper part of an altar frontal.
2 dated a decorative band or ornament worn on the forehead. ■ another term for **PHYLACTERY**. ■ a piece of armour or harness for an animal's forehead.
– ORIGIN late 15th cent. (in sense 2): from Old French *frontelet*, diminutive of *frontel* (see **FRONTAL**[2]).

front line ▸ noun (usu. **the front line**) the military line or part of an army that is closest to the enemy: [as modifier] *the front-line troops.* ■ the most important or influential position in a debate or movement: *it is doctors who are on the front line of the euthanasia debate.*

front-line states ▸ plural noun those countries bordering on an area troubled by a war or other crisis.

front-load ▸ verb [with obj.] distribute or allocate (costs, effort, etc.) unevenly, with the greater proportion at the beginning of the enterprise or process.

frontman ▸ noun (pl. **frontmen**) **1** (also **frontwoman**) the lead singer of a pop or rock group.
2 a person who represents an illegal or disreputable organization to give it an air of legitimacy.

front office ▸ noun chiefly N. Amer. the main administrative office of a business or other organization.

fronton /ˈfrʌnt(ə)n/ ▸ noun **1** a building where pelota or jai alai is played.
2 another term for **PEDIMENT**.
– ORIGIN late 17th cent.: from French, from Italian *frontone*, from *fronte* 'forehead', from Latin *frons, front-* 'front, forehead'.

front page ▸ noun the first page of a newspaper, containing the most important or remarkable news of the day: [as modifier] *the story is still front-page news.*
– PHRASES **hold the front page** chiefly ironic used to draw attention to an important or noteworthy fact or occurrence: *Pop star tries new look. Blimey, hold the front page.*

front row ▸ noun Rugby the forwards who make up the first row in a scrum.

front runner ▸ noun the contestant that is leading in a race or other competition. ■ an athlete or horse that runs best when in the front of the field.

front-running ▸ adjective ahead in a race or other competition. ■ (of an athlete or horse) running best when in front of the field.
▸ noun [mass noun] **1** Stock Exchange the practice by market-makers of dealing on advance information provided by their brokers and investment analysts, before their clients have been given the information.
2 US the practice of giving one's support to a competitor because they are in front.

frontside ▸ adjective denoting a manoeuvre in surfing and other board sports which is done anticlockwise for a regular rider and clockwise for a goofy rider.

front-wheel drive ▸ noun [mass noun] a transmission system that provides power to the front wheels of a motor vehicle.

frore /frɔː/ ▸ adjective literary frozen; frosty.
– ORIGIN Middle English: archaic past participle of **FREEZE**.

frosh /frɒʃ/ ▸ noun (pl. **same** or **froshes**) N. Amer. informal a college freshman: [as modifier] *frosh week.*
– ORIGIN early 20th cent.: alteration of **FRESHMAN**, perhaps influenced by German *Frosch* 'frog' (in dialect use 'grammar-school student').

Frost, Robert (Lee) (1874–1963), American poet, noted for his ironic tone and simple language. Much of his poetry reflects his affinity with New England, including the collections *North of Boston* (1914) and *New Hampshire* (1923). He won the Pulitzer Prize on three occasions (1924; 1931; 1937).

frost ▸ noun [mass noun] a deposit of small white ice crystals formed on the ground or other surfaces when the temperature falls below freezing. ■ [count noun] a period of cold weather when deposits of frost form: *there have been several sharp frosts recently.* ■ a person's cold or unfriendly manner: *Caroline was shocked to hear the frost in her brother's voice .* ■ [in sing.] Brit. informal, dated a failure.
▸ verb [with obj.] **1** cover (something) with or as if with frost; freeze: *shop windows were still frosted over.* ■ [no obj.] become covered with small ice crystals: *no one has managed to stop outdoor heat exchangers frosting up during winter.* ■ damage or otherwise affect as a result of frost.
2 N. Amer. decorate (a cake or biscuit) with icing.
– PHRASES **degrees of frost** Brit. degrees below freezing point.
– DERIVATIVES **frostless** adjective.
– ORIGIN Old English *frost, forst*, of Germanic origin; related to Dutch *vorst* and German *Frost*, also to **FREEZE**.

frostbite ▸ noun [mass noun] injury to body tissues caused by exposure to extreme cold, typically affecting the nose, fingers, or toes and often resulting in gangrene.
– DERIVATIVES **frostbitten** adjective.

frosted ▸ adjective **1** covered with or as if with frost: *I stood looking out on the frosted garden.* ■ (of glass or a window) having a translucent textured surface so that it is difficult to see through.
2 chiefly N. Amer. (of food) decorated or dusted with icing or sugar.

frost heave ▸ noun [mass noun] the uplift of soil or other surface deposits due to expansion of groundwater on freezing. ■ [count noun] a mound formed in this way.
– DERIVATIVES **frost heaving** noun.

frost hollow ▸ noun a valley bottom or other hollow which is prone to frost.

frosting ▸ noun [mass noun] **1** N. Amer. icing.
2 a roughened matt finish on otherwise shiny material such as glass or steel.

frost line ▸ noun N. Amer. the maximum depth of ground below which the soil does not freeze in winter.

frost stat ▸ noun a thermostat used to turn on a heating system automatically when the ambient temperature drops below a set threshold.

frosty ▸ adjective (**frostier, frostiest**) **1** (of the weather) very cold, with frost forming on surfaces: *a cold and frosty morning.* ■ covered with or as if with frost: *the dog crouched in the frosty grass.*
2 cold and unfriendly in manner: *Sebastian gave her a frosty look.*
– DERIVATIVES **frostily** adverb, **frostiness** noun.

froth ▸ noun [mass noun] **1** a mass of small bubbles in liquid caused by agitation, fermentation, or salivating: *leave the yeast until there is a good head of froth.* ■ impure matter that rises to the surface of liquid: *skim off any surface froth.* ■ something that rises in a soft, light mass: *her skirt swirled in a froth of black lace.*
2 worthless or insubstantial talk, ideas, or activities: *the froth of party politics.*
▸ verb [no obj.] form or contain a rising or overflowing mass of small bubbles: *the red blood frothed at his lips.* ■ rise in a soft, light mass: *she wore an ivory silk blouse, frothing at neck and cuffs.* ■ [with obj.] agitate (a liquid) so as to produce a mass of small bubbles.

■ behave or talk angrily: *the cinema lobby frothed with indignation.*
– PHRASES **froth at the mouth** emit a large amount of saliva from the mouth in a bodily seizure. ■ informal be very angry.
– ORIGIN late Middle English: from Old Norse *frotha, frauth.*

frothy ▶ adjective (**frothier**, **frothiest**) **1** full of or covered with a mass of small bubbles: *steaming mugs of frothy coffee.*
2 light and entertaining but of little substance: *lots of frothy interviews.*
– DERIVATIVES **frothily** adverb, **frothiness** noun.

frottage /ˈfrɒtɑːʒ/ ▶ noun [mass noun] **1** Art the technique or process of taking a rubbing from an uneven surface to form the basis of a work of art. ■ [count noun] a work of art produced by taking a rubbing from an uneven surface.
2 the practice of touching or rubbing against the clothed body of another person in a crowd as a means of obtaining sexual gratification.
– ORIGIN 1930s: French, 'rubbing, friction', from *frotter* 'to rub', of unknown origin.

frotteur /frɒˈtəː/ ▶ noun a person who obtains sexual gratification by touching or rubbing against the clothed body of another person in a crowd.
– DERIVATIVES **frotteurism** noun.

frottola /ˈfrɒtələ/ ▶ noun (pl. **frottole** /-leɪ/) Music a form of Italian comic or amorous song, especially from the 15th and 16th centuries.
– ORIGIN Italian, literally 'fib, tall story'.

Froude number /fruːd/ ▶ noun a dimensionless number used in hydrodynamics to indicate how well a particular model works in relation to a real system.
– ORIGIN mid 19th cent.: named after William *Froude* (1810–79), English civil engineer.

frou-frou /ˈfruːfruː/ ▶ noun [mass noun] frills or other ornamentation, particularly of women's clothes: [as modifier] *a little frou-frou skirt.*
– ORIGIN late 19th cent.: from French, imitative of the sound of a woman walking in a dress.

frounce /fraʊns/ ▶ noun [mass noun] Falconry a form of trichomoniasis affecting hawks, resulting in a sore with a cheesy secretion in the mouth or throat.
– ORIGIN late Middle English: of unknown origin.

frow /fraʊ/ ▶ noun archaic a Dutchwoman.
– ORIGIN late Middle English: from Dutch *vrouw* 'woman'.

froward /ˈfrəʊəd/ ▶ adjective archaic (of a person) difficult to deal with; contrary.
– DERIVATIVES **frowardly** adverb, **frowardness** noun.
– ORIGIN late Old English *frāward* 'leading away from, away', based on Old Norse *frá* (see **FRO, FROM**).

frown ▶ verb [no obj.] furrow one's brows in an expression indicating disapproval, displeasure, or concentration: *he frowned as he reread the letter.*
■ (**frown on/upon**) disapprove of: *promiscuity was frowned upon.*
▶ noun a facial expression or look characterized by a furrowing of one's brows: *a frown of disapproval.*
– ORIGIN late Middle English: from Old French *froignier*, from *froigne* 'surly look', of Celtic origin.

frowst /fraʊst/ Brit. informal ▶ noun [in sing.] a warm, stuffy atmosphere in a room.
▶ verb [no obj.] lounge about in a warm, stuffy atmosphere: *don't frowst by the fire all day.*
– ORIGIN late 19th cent.: back-formation from **FROWSTY**.

frowsty ▶ adjective (**frowstier**, **frowstiest**) Brit. having a stale, warm, and stuffy atmosphere: *a small, frowsty office.*
– ORIGIN mid 19th cent. (originally dialect): variant of **FROWZY**.

frowzy /ˈfraʊzi/ (also **frowsy**) ▶ adjective (**frowzier**, **frowziest**; **frowsier**, **frowsiest**) scruffy and neglected in appearance. ■ dingy and stuffy: *a frowzy drinking-club.*
– ORIGIN late 17th cent. (originally dialect): of unknown origin.

froze past of **FREEZE**.

frozen past participle of **FREEZE**.
▶ adjective (of a liquid) having turned into ice as a result of extreme cold. ■ covered or rigid with ice: *frozen wastes.* ■ (of food) stored at a very low temperature in order to preserve it: *frozen fish.* ■ (used hyperbolically) very cold: *the wind whistled in my hair, and I was absolutely frozen.*

frozen shoulder ▶ noun [mass noun] Medicine chronic painful stiffness of the shoulder joint.

FRS ▶ abbreviation ■ (in the UK) Fellow of the Royal Society. ■ (in the UK) Financial Reporting Standard.

FRSE ▶ abbreviation Fellow of the Royal Society of Edinburgh.

Fructidor /ˈfrʊktɪdɔː/, French /fʀyktidɔʀ/ ▶ noun the twelfth month of the French Republican calendar (1793–1805), originally running from 18 August to 16 September.
– ORIGIN French, from Latin *fructus* 'fruit' + Greek *dōron* 'gift'.

fructification /ˌfrʌktɪfɪˈkeɪʃ(ə)n/ ▶ noun [mass noun] the process of fructifying. ■ [count noun] Botany a spore-bearing or fruiting structure, especially in a fungus.
– ORIGIN late 15th cent.: from late Latin *fructificatio(n-)*, from Latin *fructificare* 'fructify', from *fructus* 'fruit'.

fructify /ˈfrʌktɪfʌɪ/ ▶ verb (**fructifies**, **fructifying**, **fructified**) [with obj.] formal make (something) fruitful or productive: *they were sacrificed in order that their blood might fructify the crops.* ■ [no obj.] bear fruit or become productive.
– ORIGIN Middle English: from Old French *fructifier*, from Latin *fructificare*, from *fructus* 'fruit'.

fructose /ˈfrʌktəʊz, -s/ ▶ noun [mass noun] Chemistry a sugar of the hexose class found especially in honey and fruit.
– ORIGIN mid 19th cent.: from Latin *fructus* 'fruit' + **-OSE**².

fructuous /ˈfrʌktjʊəs/ ▶ adjective formal full of or producing a great deal of fruit.
– ORIGIN late Middle English: from Latin *fructuosus*, from *fructus* 'fruit'.

frug ▶ noun a vigorous dance to pop music, popular in the mid 1960s.
▶ verb (**frugs**, **frugging**, **frugged**) [no obj.] perform the frug.
– ORIGIN 1960s: of unknown origin.

frugal /ˈfruːg(ə)l/ ▶ adjective sparing or economical as regards money or food: *I'm a bit too frugal to splash out on designer clothes.* ■ simple and plain and costing little: *a frugal meal.*
– DERIVATIVES **frugally** adverb.
– ORIGIN mid 16th cent.: from Latin *frugalis*, from *frugi* 'economical, thrifty', from *frux, frug-* 'fruit'.

frugality ▶ noun [mass noun] the quality of being economical with money or food; thriftiness: *he scorned the finer things in life and valued frugality and simplicity.*

frugivore /ˈfruːdʒɪvɔː/ ▶ noun Zoology an animal that feeds on fruit.
– DERIVATIVES **frugivorous** adjective.
– ORIGIN mid 20th cent.: from Latin *frux, frug-* 'fruit' + *-vore* (see **-VOROUS**).

fruit ▶ noun **1** the sweet and fleshy product of a tree or other plant that contains seed and can be eaten as food: *tropical fruits such as mangoes and papaya* | [mass noun] *eat plenty of fresh fruit and vegetables.*
■ Botany the seed-bearing structure of a plant, e.g. an acorn. ■ archaic or literary natural produce that can be used for food: *we give thanks for the fruits of the earth.* ■ (**the fruits** or **the fruit**) the result or reward of work or activity: *the pupils began to appreciate the fruits of their labours.* ■ archaic offspring.
2 N. Amer. informal, derogatory a male homosexual.
▶ verb [no obj.] (of a tree or other plant) produce fruit: *the trees fruit very early* | (as noun **fruiting**) *cover strawberries with cloches to encourage early fruiting.*
– PHRASES **bear fruit** have good results: *their long-term business plan is beginning to bear fruit.* **in fruit** (of a tree or plant) at the stage of producing fruit.
– ORIGIN Middle English: from Old French, from Latin *fructus* 'enjoyment of produce, harvest', from *frui* 'enjoy', related to *fruges* 'fruits of the earth', plural (and most common form) of *frux, frug-* 'fruit'.

fruit acid ▶ noun another term for **ALPHA-HYDROXY ACID**.

fruitage ▶ noun [mass noun] archaic or literary fruit collectively.

fruitarian ▶ noun a person who eats only fruit.
– DERIVATIVES **fruitarianism** noun.
– ORIGIN late 19th cent.: from **FRUIT**, on the pattern of *vegetarian.*

fruit bat ▶ noun a bat with a long snout and large eyes, feeding chiefly on fruit or nectar and found mainly in the Old World tropics. ● Family Pteropodidae: many genera and numerous species. See also **FLYING FOX**.

fruit body ▶ noun another term for **FRUITING BODY**.

fruit cake ▶ noun **1** a cake containing dried fruit and nuts.
2 (**fruitcake**) informal an eccentric or mad person. [compare with *nutty as a fruitcake* (see **NUTTY**).]

fruit cocktail ▶ noun [mass noun] a finely chopped fruit salad, often commercially produced in tins.

fruitcrow ▶ noun a large tropical American cotinga with mainly black or red and black plumage. ● Family Cotingidae: four genera and species.

fruit cup ▶ noun **1** Brit. a drink consisting of a mixture of fruit juices, typically with pieces of fruit in it.
2 N. Amer. a fruit salad.

fruit dove ▶ noun a tropical fruit-eating dove that typically has brightly coloured plumage, usually with a green back, and occurs mainly in Indonesia and Australasia. Compare with **FRUIT PIGEON**. ● Genus *Ptilonopus* (and *Phapitreron*), family Columbidae: many species.

fruit drop ▶ noun [mass noun] the shedding of unripe fruit from a tree.

fruited ▶ adjective [usu. in combination] (of a tree or plant) producing fruit, especially of a specified kind: *heavy-fruited plants like tomatoes.*

fruiter ▶ noun a tree producing fruit at a specified time or in a specified manner: *a prolific fruiter.*
– ORIGIN Middle English (in the sense 'fruit grower'): from Old French *fruitier*, from *fruit* 'fruit'; in later use from **FRUIT** + **-ER**¹. The current sense dates from the 19th cent.

fruiterer ▶ noun chiefly Brit. a retailer of fruit.
– ORIGIN late Middle English: from **FRUITER** + **-ER**¹; the reason for the addition of the suffix is unclear.

fruit fly ▶ noun a small fly which feeds on fruit in both its adult and larval stages. ● Families Drosophilidae and Tephritidae: many genera. See also **DROSOPHILA**.

fruitful ▶ adjective (of a tree, plant, or land) producing much fruit; fertile. ■ producing good or helpful results; productive: *memoirs can be a fruitful source of information.* ■ (of a person) producing many offspring.
– DERIVATIVES **fruitfully** adverb, **fruitfulness** noun.

fruit gum ▶ noun a firm, jelly-like, fruit-flavoured sweet made with gelatin or gum arabic.

fruiting body ▶ noun Botany the spore-producing organ of a fungus, often seen as a toadstool.

fruition /fruˈɪʃ(ə)n/ ▶ noun [mass noun] **1** the realization or fulfilment of a plan or project: *the plans have come to fruition rather sooner than expected.*
2 literary the state or action of producing fruit.
– ORIGIN late Middle English (in the sense 'enjoyment'): via Old French from late Latin *fruitio(n-)*, from *frui* 'enjoy' (see **FRUIT**); the current senses (dating from the late 19th cent.) arose by association with **FRUIT**.

fruitless ▶ adjective **1** failing to achieve the desired results; unproductive or useless: *his fruitless attempts to publish poetry.*
2 (of a tree or plant) not producing fruit.
– DERIVATIVES **fruitlessly** adverb, **fruitlessness** noun.

fruitlet ▶ noun an immature or small fruit. ■ Botany another term for **DRUPEL**.

fruit loop ▶ noun N. Amer. informal a mad or crazy person.
– ORIGIN 1970s: from *Froot Loops*, the name of a breakfast cereal.

fruit machine ▶ noun Brit. a coin-operated gaming machine that generates random combinations of symbols (typically representing fruit) on a dial, certain combinations winning varying amounts of money for the player.

fruit pigeon ▶ noun a fruit-eating pigeon occurring in the Old World tropics. Compare with **FRUIT DOVE**.
● a relative of the imperial pigeons occurring in New Guinea (genus *Ducula*, family Columbidae). ● a green pigeon occurring in Africa (genus *Treron*, family Columbidae).

fruit salad ▶ noun [mass noun] a mixture of different types of chopped fruit served in syrup or juice.

fruit sugar ▶ noun [mass noun] **1** another term for **FRUCTOSE**.
2 Canadian a very fine type of granulated sugar suitable for sprinkling on fruit.

fruit tree ▶ noun a tree grown for its edible fruit.

fruitwood ▶ noun [mass noun] [often with negative] the wood of a fruit tree, especially when used in furniture: *a fruitwood dressing table.*

fruity ▶ adjective (**fruitier**, **fruitiest**) **1** (of food or drink) containing fruit: *fruity jams.* ■ resembling the flavour of fruit: *a light and fruity Beaujolais.*
2 (of a voice or sound) mellow, deep, and rich: *Jeffery had a wonderfully fruity voice.* ■ Brit. informal sexually suggestive in content or style.

3 N. Amer. informal, derogatory relating to or associated with homosexuals.
4 informal, chiefly US eccentric or crazy: *a kind of fruity professor*.
– DERIVATIVES **fruitily** adverb, **fruitiness** noun.

frumenty /ˈfruːm(ə)nti/ (also **furmety**) ▸ noun [mass noun] Brit. an old-fashioned dish consisting of hulled wheat boiled in milk and seasoned with cinnamon and sugar.
– ORIGIN late Middle English: from Old French *frumentee*, from *frument*, from Latin *frumentum* 'corn'.

frump ▸ noun an unattractive woman who wears dowdy old-fashioned clothes.
– DERIVATIVES **frumpish** adjective.
– ORIGIN mid 16th cent.: probably a contraction of late Middle English *frumple* 'wrinkle', from Middle Dutch *verrompelen*. The word originally denoted a mocking speech or action; later (in the plural) ill humour, the sulks; hence a bad-tempered, (later) dowdy woman (early 19th cent.).

frumpy ▸ adjective (**frumpier**, **frumpiest**) (of a woman or her clothes) dowdy and old-fashioned: *a frumpy housewife | her frumpy, shapeless dresses*.
– DERIVATIVES **frumpily** adverb, **frumpiness** noun.

Frunze /ˈfruːnzi/ former name (1926–91) for BISHKEK.

frusemide /ˈfruːsəmʌɪd/ (chiefly US also **furosemide**) ▸ noun [mass noun] Medicine a synthetic compound with a strong diuretic action, used especially in the treatment of oedema. ● Chem. formula: $C_{12}H_{11}ClN_2O_5S$.
– ORIGIN 1960s: from *fru-* (alteration of *fur(yl)*, denoting a radical derived from furan) + *sem-* (of unknown origin) + -IDE.

frustrate ▸ verb [with obj.] 1 prevent (a plan or attempted action) from progressing, succeeding, or being fulfilled: *the rescue attempt was frustrated by bad weather*. ■ prevent (someone) from doing or achieving something: *in numerous policy areas, central government has been frustrated by local authorities*.
2 cause (someone) to feel upset or annoyed as a result of being unable to change or achieve something: (as adj. **frustrating**) *it can be very frustrating to find that the size you want isn't there*.
▸ adjective archaic frustrated.
– DERIVATIVES **frustratingly** adverb [as submodifier] *progress turned out to be frustratingly slow*.
– ORIGIN late Middle English: from Latin *frustrat-* 'disappointed', from the verb *frustrare*, from *frustra* 'in vain'.

frustrated ▸ adjective 1 feeling or expressing distress and annoyance resulting from an inability to change or achieve something: *young people get frustrated with the system*. ■ unfulfilled sexually: *jealousies and frustrated passions*.
2 [attrib.] (of a person) unable to follow or be successful in a particular career: *a frustrated actor*. ■ prevented from progressing, succeeding, or being fulfilled: *years of frustrated attempts to regain control of the site*.
– DERIVATIVES **frustratedly** adverb.

frustration ▸ noun [mass noun] 1 the feeling of being upset or annoyed as a result of being unable to change or achieve something: *tears of frustration rolled down her cheeks*. ■ [count noun] an event or circumstance that causes one to feel frustrated: *the inherent frustrations of assembly line work*.
2 the prevention of the progress, success, or fulfilment of something: *the frustration of their wishes*.
– ORIGIN mid 16th cent.: from Latin *frustratio(n-)*, from *frustrare* 'disappoint' (see FRUSTRATE).

frustule /ˈfrʌstjuːl/ ▸ noun Botany the silicified cell wall of a diatom, consisting of two valves or overlapping halves.
– ORIGIN mid 19th cent.: from Latin *frustulum*, diminutive of *frustum* (see FRUSTUM).

frustum /ˈfrʌstəm/ ▸ noun (pl. **frusta** /-tə/ or **frustums**) Geometry the portion of a cone or pyramid which remains after its upper part has been cut off by a plane parallel to its base, or which is intercepted between two such planes.
– ORIGIN mid 17th cent.: from Latin, 'piece cut off'.

fruticose /ˈfruːtɪkəʊz, -s/ ▸ adjective Botany (of a lichen) having upright or pendulous branches.
– ORIGIN mid 17th cent.: from Latin *fruticosus*, from *frutex, frutic-* 'bush, shrub'.

Fry[1], Christopher (Harris) (1907–2005), English dramatist. He was known chiefly for his comic verse dramas, especially *The Lady's not for Burning* (1948) and *Venus Observed* (1950).

Fry[2], Elizabeth (1780–1845), English Quaker prison reformer, a leading figure in the early 19th-century campaign for penal reform.

Fry[3], Roger (Eliot) (1866–1934), English art critic and painter. He argued for an aesthetics of pure form, regarding content as incidental.

fry[1] ▸ verb (**fries**, **frying**, **fried**) [with obj.] 1 cook (food) in hot fat or oil, typically in a shallow pan. ■ [no obj.] (of food) be cooked in hot fat or oil: *put half a dozen steaks to fry in a pan*. ■ [no obj.] informal (of a person) burn or overheat: *with the sea and sun and wind you'll fry if you don't take care*.
2 informal destroy: *drugs fry the brain*. ■ US execute or be executed by electrocution.
▸ noun (pl. **fries**) 1 (**fries**) French fries; chips.
2 [in sing.] a fried dish or meal. ■ [mass noun] chiefly Brit. any of various types of offal, usually eaten fried. ■ N. Amer. a social gathering where fried food is served: *you'll explore islands and stop for a fish fry*.
– ORIGIN Middle English: from Old French *frire*, from Latin *frigere*.

fry[2] ▸ plural noun young fish, especially when newly hatched. ■ the young of other animals produced in large numbers, such as frogs.
– ORIGIN Middle English: from Old Norse *frjó*.

Frye, (Herman) Northrop (1912–91), Canadian literary critic. His work explores the use of myth and symbolism. Notable works: *Fearful Symmetry* (1947) and *The Great Code: The Bible and Literature* (1982).

fryer ▸ noun 1 a large, deep container for frying food.
2 N. Amer. a small young chicken suitable for frying.

frying pan (N. Amer. also **frypan**) ▸ noun a shallow pan with a long handle, used for cooking food in hot fat or oil.
– PHRASES **out of the frying pan into the fire** from a bad situation to one that is worse.

fry-up ▸ noun Brit. informal a dish of various types of fried food.

FS ▸ abbreviation (in the UK) Flight Sergeant.

FSA ▸ abbreviation 1 (in the UK) Fellow of the Society of Antiquaries.
2 Financial Services Act (or Authority).

FSH ▸ abbreviation follicle-stimulating hormone.

FST ▸ abbreviation flat screen television.

f-stop ▸ noun Photography a camera setting corresponding to a particular f-number.

FT ▸ abbreviation (in the UK) Financial Times.

Ft ▸ abbreviation Fort: *Ft Lauderdale*.

ft ▸ abbreviation foot; feet.

FTA ▸ abbreviation N. Amer. Free Trade Agreement, used to refer to that signed in 1988 between the US and Canada.

FTC ▸ abbreviation (in the US) Federal Trade Commission.

FT index another term for FTSE INDEX.

F2F ▸ abbreviation informal face-to-face: *F2F communication*.

FTP Computing ▸ abbreviation file transfer protocol, a standard for the exchange of program and data files across a network.
▸ verb (**FTPs**, **FTPing** or **FTP'ing**, **FTPed** or **FTP'ed**) [with obj.] informal transfer (a file) from one computer or system to another, especially on the Internet.

FTSE index a figure indicating the relative prices of shares on the London Stock Exchange, especially (also **FTSE 100 index**) one calculated on the basis of Britain's one hundred largest public companies.
– ORIGIN *FTSE*, abbreviation of *Financial Times Stock Exchange*.

Fuad /ˈfuːad/ the name of two kings of Egypt:
■ **Fuad I** (1868–1936), reigned 1922–36. Formerly sultan of Egypt (1917–1922), he became Egypt's first king after independence. ■ **Fuad II** (b.1952), grandson of Fuad I, reigned 1952–3. Named king as an infant on the forced abdication of his father, Farouk, he was deposed when Egypt became a republic.

fubsy /ˈfʌbzi/ ▸ adjective (**fubsier**, **fubsiest**) Brit. informal fat and squat.
– ORIGIN late 18th cent.: from dialect *fubs* 'small fat person', perhaps a blend of FAT and CHUB.

Fuchs[1] /fʊks/, (Emil) Klaus (Julius) (1911–88), German-born British physicist. He was a communist who fled Nazi persecution. During the 1940s he passed to the USSR secret information acquired while working on the development of the atom bomb in the US, and while engaged in research in Britain.

Fuchs[2] /fʊks/, Sir Vivian (Ernest) (1908–99), English geologist and explorer. He led the Commonwealth Trans-Antarctic Expedition (1955–8), making the first overland crossing of the Antarctic.

fuchsia /ˈfjuːʃə/ ▸ noun a shrub with pendulous tubular flowers that are typically of two contrasting colours. They are native to America and New Zealand and are commonly grown as ornamentals. ● Genus *Fuchsia*, family Onagraceae: many cultivars. ■ Austral. used in names of plants of other families with flowers similar to the fuchsia, e.g. **native fuchsia**. ■ [mass noun] a vivid purplish-red colour like that of the sepals of a typical fuchsia flower.
– ORIGIN modern Latin, named in honour of Leonhard *Fuchs* (1501–66), German botanist.

fuchsin /ˈfuːksiːn/ (also **fuchsine**) ▸ noun [mass noun] a deep red synthetic dye used as a biological stain and disinfectant. ● A chloride of rosaniline; chem. formula: $C_{20}H_{20}N_3Cl$.
– ORIGIN mid 19th cent.: from German *Fuchs* 'fox', translating French *Renard* (the name of the chemical company which first produced fuchsin commercially) + -IN[1].

F

fuck vulgar slang ▸ verb [with obj.] 1 have sexual intercourse with (someone). ■ [no obj.] (of two people) have sexual intercourse.
2 damage or ruin (something).
▸ noun an act of sexual intercourse. ■ [with adj.] a sexual partner of a specified ability.
▸ exclamation used alone or as a noun or verb in various phrases to express annoyance, contempt, or impatience.
– PHRASES **fuck all** Brit. absolutely nothing.
– DERIVATIVES **fuckable** adjective.
– PHRASAL VERBS **fuck about** (or **around**) spend time doing unimportant or trivial things. **fuck someone around** (or **about**) waste someone's time. **fuck off** 1 [usu. in imperative] (of a person) go away. 2 chiefly US another way of saying FUCK ABOUT. **fuck someone off** make someone angry. **fuck someone over** US treat someone in an unfair or humiliating way. **fuck someone up** damage or confuse someone emotionally. **fuck something up** (or **fuck up**) do something badly or ineptly.
– ORIGIN early 16th cent.: of Germanic origin (compare Swedish dialect *focka* and Dutch dialect *fokkelen*); possibly from an Indo-European root meaning 'strike', shared by Latin *pugnus* 'fist'.

> **USAGE** Despite the wideness and proliferation of its use in many sections of society, the word **fuck** remains (and has been for centuries) one of the most taboo words in English. Until relatively recently it rarely appeared in print; even today, there are a number of euphemistic ways of referring to it in speech and writing, e.g. **the F-word**, **f*****, or **f—k**.

fucker ▸ noun vulgar slang a contemptible or stupid person (often used as a general term of abuse).

fuckhead ▸ noun vulgar slang a stupid or contemptible person (often used as a general term of abuse).

fucking ▸ adjective [attrib.] & adverb [as submodifier] vulgar slang used for emphasis or to express anger, annoyance, contempt, or surprise.

fuck-up ▸ noun vulgar slang a mess or muddle.

fuckwit ▸ noun vulgar slang a stupid or contemptible person (often used as a general term of abuse).

fucoid /ˈfjuːkɔɪd/ Botany ▸ noun a brown seaweed or fossil plant of a group to which bladderwrack belongs. ● Order Fucales, class Phaeophyceae, including genus *Fucus*.
▸ adjective relating to or resembling a brown seaweed, especially a fucoid.
– ORIGIN mid 19th cent.: from FUCUS + -OID.

fucoxanthin /ˌfjuːkəˈzanθɪn/ ▸ noun [mass noun] Chemistry a brown carotenoid pigment occurring in and generally characteristic of the brown algae.
– ORIGIN late 19th cent.: from FUCUS + *xanthin*, variant of XANTHINE.

fucus /ˈfjuːkəs/ ▸ noun (pl. **fuci** /ˈfjuːsʌɪ/) a seaweed of a large genus of brown algae having flat leathery fronds. ● Genus *Fucus*, class Phaeophyceae.
– ORIGIN early 17th cent. (denoting a cosmetic): from Latin, 'rock lichen, red dye, rouge', from Greek *phukos* 'seaweed', of Semitic origin.

fuddle /ˈfʌd(ə)l/ ▸ verb [with obj.] (usu. as adj. **fuddled**) confuse or stupefy (someone), especially with alcohol. ■ [no obj.] archaic go on a drinking bout.
▸ noun [in sing.] a state of confusion or intoxication: *through the fuddle of wine he heard some of the conversation*. ■ archaic a drinking bout.
– ORIGIN late 16th cent. (in the sense 'go on a drinking bout'): of unknown origin.

fuddled ▸ adjective confused or stupefied, especially as a result of drinking alcohol: [in combination] *Benjamin was trying to clear his drink-fuddled brain*.

fuddy-duddy ▸ **noun** (pl. **fuddy-duddies**) informal a person who is very old-fashioned and pompous: *he probably thinks I'm an old fuddy-duddy.*
– ORIGIN early 20th cent. (originally dialect): of unknown origin.

fudge ▸ **noun 1** [mass noun] a soft crumbly or chewy sweet made from sugar, butter, and milk or cream. ■ [as modifier] chiefly N. Amer rich chocolate, used as a sauce or a filling for cakes.
2 an attempt to fudge an issue: *the new settlement is a fudge rushed out to win cheers at the conference.* ■ [mass noun] archaic nonsense.
3 a piece of late news inserted in a newspaper page.
▸ **verb** [with obj.] present or deal with (something) in a vague or inadequate way, especially so as to conceal the truth or mislead: *the authorities have **fudged the issue**.* ■ adjust or manipulate (facts or figures) so as to present a desired picture.
▸ **exclamation** dated nonsense! (expressing disbelief or annoyance).
– ORIGIN early 17th cent.: probably an alteration of obsolete *fadge* 'to fit'. Early usage was as a verb in the sense 'turn out as expected', also 'merge together': this probably gave rise to its use in confectionery. In the late 17th cent. the verb came to mean 'fit together in a clumsy or underhand manner', which included facts or figures being cobbled together in a superficially convincing way: this led to the exclamation 'fudge!' and to noun sense 3 of the noun.

F

fudge factor ▸ **noun** informal a figure included in a calculation to account for some unquantified but significant phenomenon or to ensure a desired result.

fuehrer ▸ **noun** variant spelling of **FÜHRER**.

fuel ▸ **noun** [mass noun] material such as coal, gas, or oil that is burned to produce heat or power. ■ short for **NUCLEAR FUEL**. ■ food, drink, or drugs as a source of energy: *any protein intake can also be used as fuel.* ■ a thing that sustains or inflames passion, argument, or other intense emotion: *the remuneration packages will add fuel to the debate about top-level rewards.*
▸ **verb** (**fuels, fuelling, fuelled**; US **fuels, fueling, fueled**) [with obj.] **1** supply or power (an industrial plant, vehicle, or machine) with fuel: *power stations fuelled by low-grade coal.*
2 cause (a fire) to burn more intensely. ■ sustain or inflame (an intense feeling): *his resignation fuelled speculation of an imminent cabinet reshuffle.*
– PHRASES **add fuel to the fire** (or **flames**) cause a situation or conflict to become more intense.
– ORIGIN Middle English: from Old French *fouaille*, based on Latin *focus* 'hearth' (in late Latin 'fire').

fuel cell ▸ **noun** a cell producing an electric current direct from a chemical reaction.

fuel element ▸ **noun** an element consisting of nuclear fuel and other materials for use in a reactor.

fuel injection ▸ **noun** [mass noun] the direct introduction of fuel under pressure into the combustion units of an internal-combustion engine.
– DERIVATIVES **fuel-injected** adjective.

fuel oil ▸ **noun** [mass noun] oil used as fuel in an engine or furnace.

fuel rod ▸ **noun** a rod-shaped fuel element in a nuclear reactor.

fuelwood ▸ **noun** [mass noun] wood used as fuel.

Fuentes /'fwɛntɛz/, Carlos (b.1928), Mexican novelist and writer. Notable works: *Where the Air is Clear* (1958), *Terra nostra* (1975), and *The Old Gringo* (1984).

fufu /'fu:fu:/ (also **foo-foo**) ▸ **noun** [mass noun] dough made from boiled and ground plantain or cassava, used as a staple food in parts of West and central Africa.
– ORIGIN from Akan *fufuu*.

fug ▸ **noun** [in sing.] Brit. informal a warm, stuffy or smoky atmosphere in a room: *the cosy fug of the music halls.*
– ORIGIN late 19th cent. (originally dialect and schoolchildren's slang): of unknown origin.

fugacious /fjʊ'geɪʃəs/ ▸ **adjective** literary tending to disappear; fleeting: *she was acutely conscious of her fugacious youth.*
– ORIGIN mid 17th cent.: from Latin *fugax, fugac-* (from *fugere* 'flee') + **-IOUS**.

fugacity /fjʊ'gasɪti/ ▸ **noun** [mass noun] **1** literary the quality of being fleeting or evanescent.
2 Chemistry a thermodynamic property of a real gas which if substituted for the pressure or partial pressure in the equations for an ideal gas gives equations applicable to the real gas.

fugal /'fju:g(ə)l/ ▸ **adjective** of the nature of a fugue: *the virtuosity of the fugal finale.*
– DERIVATIVES **fugally** adverb.

Fugard /'fu:gɑ:d/, Athol (b.1932), South African dramatist. His plays, including *Blood Knot* (1963) and *The Road to Mecca* (1985), deal mostly with social deprivation and other aspects of life under apartheid.

fugato /fju:'gɑ:təʊ, fu:-/ Music ▸ **adjective & adverb** in the style of a fugue, but not in strict or complete fugal form.
▸ **noun** (pl. **fugatos**) a passage in fugato style.
– ORIGIN Italian.

-fuge ▸ **combining form** expelling or dispelling either a specified thing or in a specified way: *vermifuge | centrifuge.*
– ORIGIN from modern Latin *-fugus*, from Latin *fugare* 'cause to flee'.

Fuggle ▸ **noun** (usu. **Fuggles**) hops of a variety used in beer-making.
– ORIGIN late 19th cent.: of unknown origin.

fuggy ▸ **adjective** (**fuggier, fuggiest**) (of a room or atmosphere) warm, stuffy, or smoky: *it was fuggy in the cabin | a fuggy pub.*

fugitive ▸ **noun** a person who has escaped from captivity or is in hiding: *fugitives from justice.*
▸ **adjective** quick to disappear; fleeting: *the fugitive effects of light | a fugitive dye.*
– ORIGIN late Middle English: from Old French *fugitif, -ive*, from Latin *fugitivus*, from *fugere* 'flee'.

fugleman /'fju:g(ə)lmən/ ▸ **noun** (pl. **fuglemen**) historical a soldier who stands in front of a regiment or company to demonstrate and maintain time in drilling exercises. ■ a leader, organizer, or spokesman: *fuglemen of the ideological right.*
– ORIGIN early 19th cent.: from German *Flügelmann* 'leader of the file', from *Flügel* 'wing' + *Mann* 'man'.

fugly /'fʌgli/ ▸ **adjective** (**fuglier, fugliest**) informal very ugly or unattractive: *we all thought he was fugly.*
– ORIGIN 1970s: blend of **FUCKING** and **UGLY**.

fugu /'fu:gu:/ ▸ **noun** [mass noun] a pufferfish that is eaten as a Japanese delicacy, after some highly poisonous parts have been removed.
– ORIGIN from Japanese.

fugue /fju:g/ ▸ **noun 1** Music a contrapuntal composition in which a short melody or phrase (the subject) is introduced by one part and successively taken up by others and developed by interweaving the parts.
2 Psychiatry a loss of awareness of one's identity, often coupled with flight from one's usual environment, associated with certain forms of hysteria and epilepsy.
– ORIGIN late 16th cent.: from French, or from Italian *fuga*, from Latin *fuga* 'flight', related to *fugere* 'flee'.

führer /'fjʊərə/ (also **fuehrer**) ▸ **noun** a tyrannical leader.
– ORIGIN from German *Führer* 'leader', part of the title *Führer und Reichskanzler* 'Leader and Chancellor of the Empire' assumed in 1934 by Adolf **HITLER**.

Fujairah /fu:'dʒʌɪərə/ (also **al-Fujayrah**) one of the seven member states of the United Arab Emirates; pop. 107,900 (est. 2009).

Fuji /'fu:dʒi/ ▸ **noun** a Japanese dessert apple of a variety with crisp sweet flesh and an orange flush to the skin.

Fuji, Mount /'fu:dʒi/ a dormant volcano in the Chubu region of Japan. Rising to 3,776 m (12,385 ft), it is Japan's highest mountain and is regarded by the Japanese as sacred. Also called **Fujiyama** /ˌfu:dʒɪ'jɑ:mə/.

Fujian /ˌfu:dʒɪ'an/ (also **Fukien** /fu:'kjɛn/) a province of SE China, on the China Sea; capital, Fuzhou.

Fukuoka /ˌfu:ku:'əʊkə/ an industrial city and port in southern Japan, capital of Kyushu island; pop. 1,363,841 (2007).

-ful ▸ **suffix 1** (forming adjectives from nouns) full of: *sorrowful.* ■ having the qualities of: *masterful.*
2 forming adjectives from adjectives or from Latin stems with little change of sense: *grateful.*
3 (forming adjectives from verbs) apt to; able to; accustomed to: *forgetful | watchful.*
4 (pl. **-fuls**) forming nouns denoting the amount needed to fill the specified container, holder, etc.: *bucketful | handful.*
– ORIGIN from **FULL**[1].

Fula /'fu:lə/ (also **Foulah, Ful**) ▸ **noun** [mass noun] the language of the Fulani people, spoken as a first language by about 10 million people and widely used in West Africa as a lingua franca. It belongs to the Benue-Congo language family. Also called **FULANI**, **FULFULDE**.

Fulani /fu:'lɑ:ni/ ▸ **noun** (pl. **same**) **1** a member of a people living in a region of West Africa from Senegal to northern Nigeria and Cameroon. They are traditionally nomadic cattle herders of Muslim faith.
2 another term for **FULA**.
– ORIGIN the name in Hausa.

Fulbe /'fʊlbeɪ/ ▸ **plural noun** (**the Fulbe**) another term for the **FULANI** people.

Fulbright, (James) William (1905–95), American senator. His name designates grants awarded under the Fulbright Act of 1946, which authorized funds from the sale of surplus war materials overseas to be used to finance exchange programmes of students and teachers between the US and other countries. The scheme was later supported by grants from the US government.

fulcrum /'fʊlkrəm, 'fʌl-/ ▸ **noun** (pl. **fulcrums** or **fulcra** /-rə/) the point against which a lever is placed to get a purchase, or on which it turns or is supported. ■ a thing that plays a central or essential role in an activity, event, or situation: *research is the fulcrum of the academic community.*
– ORIGIN late 17th cent. (originally in the general sense 'a prop or support'): from Latin, literally 'post of a couch', from *fulcire* 'to prop up'.

fulfil (US **fulfill**) ▸ **verb** (**fulfils, fulfilling, fulfilled**)
1 achieve or realize (something desired, promised, or predicted): *he wouldn't be able to fulfil his ambition to visit Naples.* ■ (**fulfil oneself**) gain happiness or satisfaction by achieving one's potential. ■ archaic complete (a period of time or piece of work).
2 carry out (a duty or role) as required, promised, or expected. ■ satisfy or meet (a requirement, condition, or need): *goods must fulfil three basic conditions.*
– DERIVATIVES **fulfillable** adjective, **fulfiller** noun.
– ORIGIN late Old English *fullfyllan* 'fill up, make full' (see **FULL**[1], **FILL**).

fulfilled ▸ **adjective** satisfied or happy because of fully developing one's abilities or character.

fulfilling ▸ **adjective** making someone satisfied or happy through allowing their character or abilities to develop fully: *a fulfilling and rewarding career.*

fulfilment (US **fulfillment**) ▸ **noun** [mass noun] **1** the achievement of something desired, promised, or predicted: *winning the championship was the fulfilment of a childhood dream.* ■ satisfaction or happiness as a result of fully developing one's potential: *she did not believe that marriage was the key to happiness and fulfilment.*
2 the meeting of a requirement, condition, or need: *the fulfilment of statutory requirements.* ■ the performance of a duty or role as required, pledged, or expected.

Fulfulde /fʊl'fʊldeɪ/ ▸ **noun** another term for **FULA**.

fulgent /'fʌldʒ(ə)nt/ ▸ **adjective** literary shining brightly.
– ORIGIN late Middle English: from Latin *fulgent-* 'shining', from the verb *fulgere*.

fulguration /ˌfʌlgjʊ'reɪʃ(ə)n/ ▸ **noun 1** [mass noun] Medicine the destruction of small growths or areas of tissue using diathermy.
2 literary a flash like that of lightning.
– DERIVATIVES **fulgurate** verb (sense 2).
– ORIGIN mid 17th cent. (usually plural in the sense 'flashes of lightning'): from Latin *fulguratio(n-)* 'sheet lightning', from *fulgur* 'lightning'. Sense 1 dates from the early 20th cent.

fulgurite /'fʌlgjʊrʌɪt/ ▸ **noun** [mass noun] Geology vitreous material formed of sand or other sediment fused by lightning. ■ [count noun] a piece of fulgurite.
– ORIGIN mid 19th cent.: from Latin *fulgur* 'lightning' + **-ITE**[1].

fuliginous /fju:'lɪdʒɪnəs/ ▸ **adjective** literary sooty; dusky.
– ORIGIN late 16th cent. (originally describing a vapour as 'thick and noxious'): from late Latin *fuliginosus*, from *fuligo, fuligin-* 'soot'.

full[1] ▸ **adjective 1** containing or holding as much or as many as possible; having no empty space: *waste bins **full of** rubbish | she could only nod, for her mouth was full | the hotel is **full up**.* ■ having eaten to one's limits or satisfaction: *she just ate till she was **full up**.* ■ (**full of**) containing or holding much or many; having a large number of: *his diary is full of entries about her.* ■ (**full of**) having a lot of (a particular quality): *she was full of confidence.* ■ (**full of**) unable to stop talking or thinking about: *they had their photographs taken and he was full of it.* ■ (**full of**) filled with intense emotion: *his heart was full of hate.* ■ involving many activities: *he lived a full life.* ■ Austral./NZ & Scottish informal drunk.

2 [attrib.] not lacking or omitting anything; complete: *a full range of sports facilities.* ■ (often used for emphasis) reaching the utmost limit; maximum: *he reached for the engine control and turned it up to full power | John made full use of all the tuition provided.* ■ having all the privileges and status attached to a particular position: *the country applied for full membership of the European Community.* ■ (of a report or account) containing as much detail or information as possible. ■ used to emphasize an amount or quantity: *he kept his fast pace going for the full 14-mile distance.* ■ (of a covering material in bookbinding) used for the entire cover: *bound in full cloth.*
3 (of a person's figure or part of the body) plump or rounded: *she had full lips | the fuller figure.* ■ (of the hair) having body. ■ (of a garment) cut generously with gathers or folds or so as to fit loosely: *the dress has a square neck and a full skirt.* ■ (of a sound) strong and resonant. ■ (of a flavour or colour) rich or intense.
▶ **adverb 1** straight; directly: *she turned her head and looked full into his face.*
2 very: *he* ***knew full well*** *she was too polite to barge in.* ■ archaic entirely (used to emphasize an amount or quantity): *they talked for full half an hour.*
▶ **noun** (**the full**) archaic the period, point, or state of the greatest fullness or strength. ■ the state or time of full moon. ■ archaic or Irish the whole.
▶ **verb 1** [with obj.] black English make (something) full; fill up: *he* ***full up*** *the house with bawling.*
2 [with obj.] gather or pleat (fabric) so as to make a garment full.
3 [no obj.] dialect or US (of the moon or tide) become full.
– PHRASES **full and by** Sailing close-hauled but with sails filling. **full colour** the full range of colours: *lively illustrations* ***in full colour***. **full English breakfast** see ENGLISH BREAKFAST. **full of beans** see BEAN. **full of oneself** very self-satisfied and with an exaggerated sense of self-worth. **full of years** archaic having lived to a considerable age. **full on 1** running at or providing maximum power or capacity: *he had the heater full on.* **2** so as to make a direct or significant impact: *the recession has hit us full on.* ■ (**full-on**) informal not diluted in nature or effect: *this is full-on ballroom boogie.* **full out 1** as much or as far as possible; with maximum effort or power: *he held his foot to the floor until the car raced full out.* **2** Printing flush with the margin. **full steam** (or **speed**) **ahead** with as much speed or energy as possible. **full to the brim** see BRIM. **in full** with nothing omitted: *I shall expect your life story in full.* ■ to the full amount due: *their relocation costs would be paid in full.* ■ to the utmost; completely: *the textbooks have failed to exploit in full the opportunities offered.* **to the full** to the greatest possible extent: *enjoy your free trip to Europe to the full.*
– ORIGIN Old English, of Germanic origin; related to Dutch *vol* and German *voll*.

full[2] ▶ **verb** [with obj.] (often as noun **fulling**) clean, shrink, and felt (cloth) by heat, pressure, and moisture.
– ORIGIN Middle English: probably a back-formation from FULLER[1], influenced by Old French *fouler* 'press hard upon' or medieval Latin *fullare*, based on Latin *fullo* 'fuller'.

full age ▶ **noun** [mass noun] Brit. adult status (especially with reference to legal rights and duties).

full back (US **fullback**) ▶ **noun** (in certain team games) a player in a defensive position, playing at the side of the field in soccer and hockey and behind the other backs in rugby.

full beam ▶ **noun** [mass noun] Brit. the brightest setting of a vehicle's headlights.

full-blooded ▶ **adjective 1** of unmixed race: *a full-blooded Cherokee.*
2 vigorous, enthusiastic, and without compromise: *a full-blooded performance.*
– DERIVATIVES **full-blood noun** (sense 1), **full-bloodedly adverb**, **full-bloodedness noun**.

full-blown ▶ **adjective 1** fully developed: *the onset of full-blown AIDS in persons infected with HIV.*
2 (of a flower) in full bloom.

full board ▶ **noun 1** [mass noun] Brit. provision of accommodation and all meals at a hotel or guest house.
2 Austral./NZ a full complement of shearers. [*board*, denoting part of the floor of a shearing shed (see BOARD).]

full-bodied ▶ **adjective** rich and satisfying in flavour or sound: *a spicy, full-bodied white wine.*

full bore ▶ **noun** full speed or maximum capacity: *the real excitement comes from driving it* ***at full bore*** | [as adv.] *the boat came full bore towards us.*
▶ **adjective** [attrib.] denoting firearms of relatively large calibre: *full-bore hand guns.* ■ complete; thoroughgoing: *a full-bore leftist.*

full-bottomed ▶ **adjective** (of a wig) long at the back (as worn formerly and still by some judges).

full brother ▶ **noun** a brother born of the same mother and father.

full-court press ▶ **noun** Basketball an aggressive tactic in which members of a team cover their opponents throughout the court and not just in the region near their own basket.

full-cream ▶ **adjective** Brit. (of milk) unskimmed.

full dress ▶ **noun** [mass noun] clothes worn on ceremonial or very formal occasions. ■ [as modifier] treated with complete seriousness or possessing all the characteristics of a genuine example of the type: *the lender will usually want a full-dress environmental audit.*

full dress uniform ▶ **noun** [mass noun] military uniform worn on ceremonial occasions.

Fuller[1], R. Buckminster (1895–1983), American designer and architect; full name *Richard Buckminster Fuller*. He is best known for his invention of the geodesic dome and for his ideals of using the world's resources with maximum purpose and least waste.

Fuller[2], Thomas (1608–61), English cleric and historian. He is chiefly remembered for *The History of the Worthies of England* (1662), a description of the counties with short biographies of local personages.

fuller[1] ▶ **noun** a person whose occupation is fulling cloth.
– ORIGIN Old English *fullere*, from Latin *fullo*, of unknown origin.

fuller[2] ▶ **noun** a grooved or rounded tool on which iron is shaped. ■ a groove made by a fuller, especially in a horseshoe.
▶ **verb** [with obj.] stamp (iron) with a fuller.
– ORIGIN early 19th cent. (as a verb): of unknown origin.

fullerene /ˈfʊləriːn/ ▶ **noun** Chemistry a form of carbon having a large spheroidal molecule consisting of a hollow cage of sixty or more atoms, of which buckminsterfullerene was the first known example. Fullerenes are produced chiefly by the action of an arc discharge between carbon electrodes in an inert atmosphere.
– ORIGIN 1980s: contraction of BUCKMINSTERFULLERENE.

fuller's earth ▶ **noun** [mass noun] a type of clay used in fulling cloth and as an adsorbent.

fuller's teasel ▶ **noun** a teasel with stiff bracts which curve backwards from the prickly flower head.
● *Dipsacus sativus*, family Dipsacaceae.
– ORIGIN so named because it was formerly dried and used for raising the nap on woven cloth.

full face ▶ **adverb** (also **in full face**) with all the face visible; facing directly at someone or something: *she looked full face at the mirror.*
▶ **adjective** [attrib.] **1** showing all of the face: *a full-face mugshot.*
2 covering all of the face: *a full-face motorcycle helmet.*

full-fledged ▶ **adjective** North American term for FULLY FLEDGED.

full flood ▶ **noun** [mass noun] the tide at its highest.
– PHRASES **in full flood** speaking enthusiastically and volubly: *she was in full flood about the glories of bicycling.*

full forward ▶ **noun** Australian Rules the centrally positioned player in front of the goal on the forward line of the attacking team.

full-frontal ▶ **adjective** (of nudity or a nude figure) with full exposure of the front of the body. ■ with nothing concealed or held back: *they put a full-frontal guitar assault to clever lyrics.*

full-grown ▶ **adjective** having reached maturity.

full growth ▶ **noun** [mass noun] the greatest size that a plant or animal naturally attains; maturity.

full-hearted ▶ **adjective** with great enthusiasm and commitment; full of sincere feeling: *a full-hearted commitment to proportional representation.*
– DERIVATIVES **full-heartedly adverb**, **full-heartedness noun**.

full house ▶ **noun 1** an audience that fills the venue for an event to capacity: *he seemed a trifle unnerved playing to a full house.*
2 a poker hand with three of a kind and a pair, which beats a flush and loses to four of a kind. ■ a winning card at bingo in which all the numbers have been successfully marked off.

full-length ▶ **adjective** of the standard length: *a full-length Disney cartoon.* ■ (of a garment or curtain) extending to, or almost to, the ground. ■ (of a mirror or portrait) showing the whole human figure.
▶ **adverb** (usu. **full length**) (of a person) with the body lying stretched out and flat: *Lucy flung herself full length on the floor.*

full lock ▶ **noun** see LOCK[1] (sense 3 of the noun).

full marks ▶ **plural noun** chiefly Brit. the maximum award in an examination or assessment. ■ used to show praise for someone's intelligence, hard work, or other quality: *she had to give him full marks for originality.*

full measure ▶ **noun** [mass noun] the total amount or extent: *the full measure of their worth.* ■ [count noun] an amount not less than that professed: *only one out of 208 pints served came up to a full measure.*

F

full moon ▶ **noun** the phase of the moon in which its whole disc is illuminated. ■ the time when this occurs: *it was several days after full moon.*

full-motion video ▶ **noun** [mass noun] digital video data that is transmitted or stored on video discs for real-time reproduction on a computer (or other multimedia system) at a rate of not less than 25 frames per second.

full-mouthed ▶ **adjective 1** (of cattle, sheep, etc.) having a full set of adult teeth.
2 spoken loudly or vigorously.

full nelson ▶ **noun** see NELSON.

fullness (also **fulness**) ▶ **noun** [mass noun] **1** the state of being filled to capacity: *scores of tins in different states of fullness.* ■ the state of having eaten enough or more than enough and feeling full up. ■ the state of being complete or whole: *the honesty and fullness of the information they provide.*
2 the state of being filled out so as to produce a rounded shape: *the childish fullness of his cheeks.* ■ the condition of having been cut or designed to give a full shape: *hair was cut with a high crown and fullness.* ■ richness or intensity of flavour, sound, or colour: *the champagne is a fine example of mature fullness and ripeness.*
– PHRASES **in the fullness of time** after a due length of time has elapsed; eventually: *he'll tell us in the fullness of time.*

full point ▶ **noun** another term for FULL STOP (as a punctuation mark).

full professor ▶ **noun** N. Amer. a professor of the highest grade in a university.
– DERIVATIVES **full professorship noun**.

full-rigged ▶ **adjective** (of a sailing ship) having three or more masts that all carry square sails.

full-scale ▶ **adjective** of the same size as the thing represented: *a full-scale model of the Golden Hind.* ■ unrestricted in size, extent, or intensity; complete and thorough: *a full-scale invasion of the mainland.*

full score ▶ **noun** a score of a musical composition giving the parts for all performers on separate staves.

full sister ▶ **noun** a sister born of the same mother and father.

full stop ▶ **noun** Brit. a punctuation mark (.) used at the end of a sentence or an abbreviation. ■ [as exclamation] used to suggest that there is nothing more to say on a topic: *women are just generally better people full stop.* ■ a complete cessation: *her life had simply come to a full stop.*

full term ▶ **noun 1** see TERM (sense 2 of the noun).
2 (at Oxford and Cambridge) the main part of the university term, during which lectures are given.

full tilt ▶ **adverb** see TILT.

full-time ▶ **adjective** occupying or using the whole of someone's available working time: *a full-time job.*
▶ **adverb** on a full-time basis: *both parents were employed full-time.*
▶ **noun** (**full time**) Brit. the end of a game, especially a football match.

full-timer ▶ **noun** a person who does a full-time job.

full toss Cricket ▶ **noun** a ball pitched right up to the batsman.
▶ **adverb** without the ball having touched the ground.

fully ▶ **adverb 1** completely or entirely; to the fullest extent: *I fully understand the fears of the workers.*
2 no less or fewer than (used to emphasize an amount): *fully 65 per cent of all funerals are by cremation.*
– ORIGIN Old English *fullīce* (see FULL[1], -LY[2]).

-fully ▶ suffix forming adverbs corresponding to adjectives ending in *-ful* (such as *sorrowfully* corresponding to *sorrowful*).

fully fashioned (also **full-fashioned**) ▶ adjective (of women's clothing, especially hosiery) shaped and seamed to fit the body. ■ (of a knitted garment) shaped by increasing or decreasing the number of loops made along the fabric length without alteration of the stitch.

fully fledged ▶ adjective Brit. **1** completely developed or established; of full status: *David had become a fully fledged pilot.*
2 (of a bird) having developed all its feathers and able to fly.

fulmar /ˈfʊlmə/ ▶ noun a gull-sized grey and white seabird of the petrel family, with a stocky body and tubular nostrils. ● Genus *Fulmarus*, family Procellariidae: two species, in particular the **northern fulmar** (*F. glacialis*) of the arctic area and British Isles.
– ORIGIN late 17th cent.: from Hebridean Norn dialect, from Old Norse *fúll* 'stinking, foul' (because of its habit of regurgitating its stomach contents when disturbed) + *már* 'gull'.

F

fulminant /ˈfʊlmɪnənt, ˈfʌl-/ ▶ adjective Medicine (of a disease or symptom) severe and sudden in onset.
– ORIGIN early 17th cent.: from French, or from Latin *fulminant-* 'striking with lightning', from the verb *fulminare* (see FULMINATE).

fulminate /ˈfʊlmɪneɪt, ˈfʌl-/ ▶ verb [no obj.] **1** express vehement protest: *all **fulminated against** the new curriculum.*
2 literary explode violently or flash like lightning: *thunder fulminated around the house.*
3 (usu. as adj. **fulminating**) Medicine (of a disease or symptom) develop suddenly and severely: *fulminating appendicitis.*
▶ noun Chemistry a salt or ester of fulminic acid.
– ORIGIN late Middle English: from Latin *fulminat-* 'struck by lightning', from *fulmen, fulmin-* 'lightning'. The earliest sense (derived from medieval Latin *fulminare*) was 'denounce formally', later 'issue formal censures' (originally said of the Pope). A sense 'emit thunder and lightning', based on the original Latin meaning, arose in the early 17th cent., and hence 'explode violently' (late 17th cent.).

fulmination ▶ noun **1** an expression of vehement protest: *the fulminations of media moralists.*
2 a violent explosion or a flash like lightning.

fulminic acid /fʌlˈmɪnɪk, fʊl-/ ▶ noun [mass noun] Chemistry a very unstable acid isomeric with cyanic acid. ● Chem. formula: HONC.
– ORIGIN early 19th cent.: *fulminic* from Latin *fulmen, fulmin-* 'lightning' + -IC.

fulness ▶ noun variant spelling of FULLNESS.

fulsome ▶ adjective **1** complimentary or flattering to an excessive degree: *the press are embarrassingly fulsome in their appreciation.*
2 of large size or quantity; generous or abundant: *the fulsome details of the later legend.*
– DERIVATIVES **fulsomely** adverb, **fulsomeness** noun.
– ORIGIN Middle English (in the sense 'abundant'): from FULL[1] + -SOME[1].

USAGE Although the earliest use of **fulsome** (first recorded in the 13th century) was 'generous or abundant', this meaning is now regarded by some people as wrong. The correct meaning today is held to be 'excessively complimentary or flattering'. However, the word is still often used in its original sense of 'abundant', especially in sentences such as *she was fulsome in her praise for the people who organized it*, and this use can give rise to ambiguity: for one speaker, **fulsome praise** may be a genuine compliment, whereas for others it will be interpreted as an insult.

Fulton, Robert (1765–1815), American pioneer of the steamship. He constructed a steam-propelled 'diving-boat' in 1800, which submerged to a depth of 7.6 m (25 ft), and in 1806 he built the first successful paddle steamer, the *Clermont*.

fulvous /ˈfʌlvəs, ˈfʊl-/ ▶ adjective reddish yellow; tawny.
– ORIGIN mid 17th cent.: from Latin *fulvus* + -OUS.

fumarate /ˈfjuːməreɪt/ ▶ noun Chemistry a salt or ester of fumaric acid.

fumaric acid /fjuːˈmarɪk/ ▶ noun [mass noun] Chemistry a crystalline acid, isomeric with maleic acid, present in fumitory and many other plants. ● Alternative name: *trans*-**butenedioic acid**; chem. formula: HOOCCH=CHCOOH.
– ORIGIN mid 19th cent.: *fumaric* from modern Latin *Fumaria* 'fumitory' + -IC.

fumarole /ˈfjuːmərəʊl/ ▶ noun an opening in or near a volcano, through which hot sulphurous gases emerge.
– DERIVATIVES **fumarolic** adjective.
– ORIGIN early 19th cent.: from obsolete Italian *fumaruolo*, from late Latin *fumariolum* 'vent, hole for smoke', a diminutive based on Latin *fumus* 'smoke'.

fumble ▶ verb [no obj., with adverbial] do or handle something clumsily: *she fumbled with the lock.* ■ (**fumble about/around**) move clumsily in various directions using the hands to find one's way: *he fumbled about in the dark but could not find her.* ■ [with obj. and adverbial] use the hands clumsily to move (something) as specified: *she fumbled a cigarette from her bag.* ■ [with obj.] (in ball games) fail to catch or field (the ball) cleanly. ■ express oneself or deal with something clumsily or nervously: *Michael had fumbled for words.*
▶ noun [usu. in sing.] an act of doing or handling something clumsily: *just one fumble during a tyre change could separate the winners from the losers.* ■ informal an act of fondling someone for sexual pleasure. ■ (in ball games) an act of failing to catch or field the ball cleanly. ■ an act of managing or dealing with something clumsily: *we are not talking about subtle errors of judgement, but major fumbles.*
– DERIVATIVES **fumbler** noun.
– ORIGIN late Middle English: from Low German *fommeln* or Dutch *fommelen*.

fumbling ▶ noun [mass noun] the action of fumbling. ■ (also **fumblings**) informal the action of fondling someone for sexual pleasure: *a few furtive fumblings and unfulfilled flirtations.*
▶ adjective doing or handling something clumsily: *she bolted the door with fumbling fingers.*
– DERIVATIVES **fumblingly** adverb.

fume ▶ noun (usu. **fumes**) an amount of gas or vapour that smells strongly or is dangerous to inhale: *clouds of exhaust fumes spewed by cars.* ■ a pungent odour of a particular thing: *he breathed **fumes of** wine into her face.*
▶ verb [no obj.] **1** emit gas or vapour: *fragments of lava hit the ground, fuming and sizzling.* ■ [with obj.] (usu. as adj. **fumed**) expose (especially wood) to ammonia fumes in order to produce dark tints.
2 feel, show, or express great anger: *he is fuming over the interference in his work.*
– DERIVATIVES **fumy** adjective (**fumier**, **fumiest**).
– ORIGIN late Middle English: from Old French *fumer* (verb), from Latin *fumare* 'to smoke'.

fume cupboard ▶ noun Brit. a ventilated enclosure in a chemistry laboratory, in which harmful volatile chemicals can be used or kept.

fume hood ▶ noun US a fume cupboard.

fumet[1] /fjuːˈmɛt/ ▶ noun [mass noun] a concentrated stock, especially of game or fish, used as flavouring.
– ORIGIN early 18th cent. (in the senses 'smell of game' and 'game flavour'): from French, from *fumer* 'to smoke'. The current sense dates from the early 20th cent.

fumet[2] /fjuːˈmɛt/ ▶ noun (usu. **fumets**) archaic the excrement of a deer.
– ORIGIN late Middle English: from an Anglo-Norman French variant of Old French *fumees* 'droppings'.

fumigate ▶ verb [with obj.] disinfect or purify (an area) with the fumes of certain chemicals.
– DERIVATIVES **fumigant** noun, **fumigation** noun, **fumigator** noun.
– ORIGIN mid 16th cent. (earlier (late Middle English) as *fumigation*, in the sense 'the action of perfuming'): from Latin *fumigat-* 'fumigated', from the verb *fumigare*, from *fumus* 'smoke'.

fumitory /ˈfjuːmɪt(ə)ri/ ▶ noun an Old World plant with spikes of small tubular pink or white flowers and finely divided greyish leaves, often considered a weed. ● Genus *Fumaria*, family Fumariaceae.
– ORIGIN late Middle English: from Old French *fumeterre*, from medieval Latin *fumus terrae* 'smoke of the earth' (because of its greyish leaves).

fun ▶ noun [mass noun] enjoyment, amusement, or lighthearted pleasure: *the children were having fun in the play area.* ■ a source of fun: *people-watching is great fun.* ■ playfulness or good humour: *she's full of fun.* ■ behaviour or an activity that is intended purely for amusement and should not be interpreted as having any serious or malicious purpose: *the column's just a bit of fun.*
▶ adjective (**funner**, **funnest**) informal amusing, entertaining, or enjoyable: *it was a fun evening.*
▶ verb (**funs**, **funning**, **funned**) N. Amer. informal joke or tease: [no obj.] *no need to get sore—I was only funning* | [with obj.] *they are just funning you.*
– PHRASES **for fun** (or **for the fun of it**) in order to amuse oneself and not for any more serious purpose. **fun and games** amusing and enjoyable activities: *teaching isn't all fun and games.* **in fun** not intended seriously; as a joke: *remember when you meet the press to say that your speech was all in fun.* **make fun of** tease, laugh at, or joke about (someone) in a mocking or unkind way. **not much** (or **a lot of**) **fun** used to indicate that something strikes one as extremely unpleasant and depressing: *it can't be much fun living next door to him.* **not one's idea of fun** used to emphasize one's dislike for an activity or to mock someone else's liking for it: *being stuck behind a desk all day isn't my idea of fun.*
– ORIGIN late 17th cent. (denoting a trick or hoax): from obsolete *fun* 'to cheat or hoax', dialect variant of late Middle English *fon* 'make a fool of, be a fool', related to *fon* 'a fool', of unknown origin. Compare with FOND.

USAGE The use of fun as an adjective meaning 'enjoyable,' as in *we had a fun evening*, is now established in informal use, although not accepted in standard English. The adjective now has comparative and superlative forms **funner** and **funnest**, formed as if **fun** were a standard adjective.

Funafuti /ˌfuːnəˈfuːti/ the capital of Tuvalu, situated on an island of the same name; pop. 5,000 (est. 2007).

funambulist /fjuːˈnambjʊlɪst/ ▶ noun a tightrope walker.
– ORIGIN late 18th cent.: from French *funambule* or Latin *funambulus* (from *funis* 'rope' + *ambulare* 'to walk') + -IST.

funboard ▶ noun a type of windsurfing board that is less stable but faster than a standard board.

Funchal /fʊnˈʃɑːl/ the capital and chief port of Madeira, on the south coast of the island; pop. 99,759 (2006).

function ▶ noun **1** an activity that is natural to or the purpose of a person or thing: *bridges perform the function of providing access across water | bodily functions.* ■ [mass noun] practical use or purpose in design: *building designs that prioritize style over function.* ■ a basic task of a computer, especially one that corresponds to a single instruction from the user.
2 Mathematics a relation or expression involving one or more variables: *the function* ($bx + c$). ■ a variable quantity regarded in relation to one or more other variables in terms of which it may be expressed or on which its value depends. ■ Chemistry a functional group.
3 a thing dependent on another factor or factors: *class shame is a function of social power.*
4 a large or formal social event or ceremony.
▶ verb [no obj.] work or operate in a proper or particular way: *her liver is functioning normally.* ■ (**function as**) fulfil the purpose or task of (a specified thing): *the museum intends to function as an educational and study centre.*
– DERIVATIVES **functionless** adjective.
– ORIGIN mid 16th cent.: from French *fonction*, from Latin *functio(n-)*, from *fungi* 'perform'.

functional ▶ adjective **1** of or having a special activity, purpose, or task: *a functional role.* ■ relating to the way in which something works or operates: *there are important functional differences between left and right brain.* ■ (of a disease) affecting the operation, rather than the structure, of an organ. ■ (of a mental illness) having no discernible organic cause: *functional psychosis.*
2 designed to be practical and useful, rather than attractive: *a small, functional bathroom.*
3 in operation; working: *the museum will be fully functional from the opening of the festival.*
4 Mathematics relating to a variable quantity whose value depends upon one or more other variables.
– DERIVATIVES **functionally** adverb [sentence adverb] *functionally, the role of the library service is clearly educational.*

functional food ▶ noun a food containing health-giving additives.

functional grammar ▶ noun [mass noun] a theory of grammar concerned with the social and pragmatic functions of language, relating these to both formal syntactic properties and prosodic properties.

functional group ▶ noun Chemistry a group of atoms responsible for the characteristic reactions of a particular compound.

functionalism ▶ noun [mass noun] **1** the theory that the design of an object should be determined by its function rather than by aesthetic considerations, and that anything practically designed will be inherently beautiful.
2 the theory that all aspects of a society serve a function and are necessary for the survival of that society.
3 (in the philosophy of mind) the theory that mental states can be sufficiently defined by their cause, their effect on other mental states, and their effect on behaviour.
– DERIVATIVES **functionalist** noun & adjective.

functionality ▶ noun [mass noun] **1** the quality of being suited to serve a purpose well; practicality: *I like the feel and functionality of this bakeware.* ■ the purpose that something is designed or expected to fulfil: *manufacturing processes may be affected by the functionality of the product.*
2 the range of operations that can be run on a computer or other electronic system: *new software with additional functionality.*

functionary /ˈfʌŋ(k)ʃ(ə)n(ə)ri/ ▶ noun (pl. **functionaries**) a person who has to perform official functions or duties; an official.

function key ▶ noun Computing a button on a computer keyboard, distinct from the main alphanumeric keys, to which software can assign a particular function.

function word ▶ noun Linguistics a word whose purpose is to contribute to the syntax rather than the meaning of a sentence, for example *do* in *we do not live here.*

functor /ˈfʌŋktə/ ▶ noun **1** Logic & Mathematics a function; an operator.
2 Linguistics another term for FUNCTION WORD.
– ORIGIN 1930s: from FUNCTION, on the pattern of words such as *factor*.

fund ▶ noun a sum of money saved or made available for a particular purpose: *he had set up a fund to coordinate economic investment.* ■ (**funds**) financial resources: *a concert to raise funds for the church.* ■ a large stock or supply of something: *a vast **fund of** information.*
▶ verb [with obj.] provide with money for a particular purpose: *the World Bank refused to fund the project.*
– PHRASES **in funds** Brit. having money to spend.
– DERIVATIVES **funder** noun.
– ORIGIN mid 17th cent.: from Latin *fundus* 'bottom, piece of landed property'. The earliest sense was 'the bottom or lowest part', later 'foundation or basis'; the association with money has perhaps arisen from the idea of landed property being a source of wealth.

funda ▶ noun (pl. **fundas**) Indian a basic or fundamental principle underlying something: *her fundas in life are crystal clear.*

fundal /ˈfʌnd(ə)l/ ▶ adjective Medicine relating to the fundus of an organ, especially of the stomach, uterus, or eyeball.

fundament /ˈfʌndəm(ə)nt/ ▶ noun **1** the foundation or basis of something.
2 formal or humorous a person's buttocks or anus.
– ORIGIN Middle English (also denoting the base of a building, or the founding of a building or institution): from Old French *fondement*, from Latin *fundamentum*, from *fundare* 'to found'.

fundamental /fʌndəˈmɛnt(ə)l/ ▶ adjective forming a necessary base or core; of central importance: *the protection of fundamental human rights | interpretation of evidence is **fundamental to** the historian's craft.* ■ affecting or relating to the essential nature of something or the crucial point about an issue: *the fundamental problem remains that of the housing shortage.* ■ so basic as to be hard to alter, resolve, or overcome: *the theories are based on a fundamental error.*
▶ noun **1** (usu. **fundamentals**) a central or primary rule or principle on which something is based: *two courses cover the fundamentals of microbiology.*
2 Music a fundamental note, tone, or frequency.
– DERIVATIVES **fundamentality** noun.
– ORIGIN late Middle English: from French *fondamental*, or late Latin *fundamentalis*, from Latin *fundamentum*, from *fundare* 'to found'.

fundamental frequency ▶ noun Physics the lowest frequency which is produced by the oscillation of the whole of an object, as distinct from the harmonics of higher frequency.

fundamentalism ▶ noun [mass noun] a form of Protestant Christianity which upholds belief in the strict and literal interpretation of the Bible. ■ strict maintenance of the doctrines of any religion, notably Islam, according to a strict, literal interpretation of scripture.

> Modern Christian fundamentalism arose from American millenarian sects of the 19th century, and has become associated with reaction against social and political liberalism and rejection of the theory of evolution. Islamic fundamentalism appeared in the 18th and 19th centuries as a reaction to the disintegration of Islamic political and economic power, asserting that Islam is central to both state and society and advocating strict adherence to the Koran (*Qur'an*) and to Islamic law (*sharia*).

– DERIVATIVES **fundamentalist** noun & adjective.

fundamentally ▶ adverb [often as submodifier] in central or primary respects: *two fundamentally different concepts of democracy.* ■ [sentence adverb] used to make an emphatic statement about the basic truth of something: *fundamentally, this is a matter for doctors.*

fundamental note ▶ noun Music the lowest note of a chord in its original form.

fundamental particle ▶ noun another term for ELEMENTARY PARTICLE.

fundamental tone ▶ noun Music the tone which represents the fundamental frequency of a vibrating object such as a string or bell.

fundamental unit ▶ noun each of a set of unrelated units of measurement, which are arbitrarily defined and from which other units are derived. For example, in the SI system the fundamental units are the metre, kilogram, and second.

funded debt ▶ noun a debt in the form of securities with long-term or indefinite redemption. Compare with FLOATING DEBT.

fundholding ▶ noun [mass noun] (in the UK) a former system of state funding for general practitioners, in which a GP was allocated a budget with which they could buy a limited range of hospital services.
– DERIVATIVES **fundholder** noun.

fundi[1] plural form of FUNDUS.

fundi[2] ▶ noun (pl. **fundis**) see FUNDIE.

fundi[3] /ˈfʊndi/ ▶ noun (pl. **fundis**) S. African informal an expert in a particular area: *a turtle fundi.* ■ an enthusiast for a subject or activity: *she provides classes for the fitness fundis.*
– ORIGIN perhaps originally Rhodesian (Zimbabwean) English, from Nguni *umfundi* 'learner'.

fundie /ˈfʌndi/ ▶ noun (pl. **fundies**) informal a fundamentalist, especially a Christian fundamentalist. ■ (also **fundi**) (pl. also **fundis**) a member of the radical, as opposed to the pragmatic, wing of the Green movement. Often contrasted with REALO.
– ORIGIN 1980s: from German, abbreviation of *Fundamentalist* 'fundamentalist'.

funding ▶ noun [mass noun] money provided, especially by an organization or government, for a particular purpose. ■ the action or practice of providing funding.

fund manager ▶ noun an employee of a large institution (such as a pension fund or an insurance company) who manages the investment of money on its behalf.

fundraiser ▶ noun a person whose job or task is to seek financial support for a charity, cause, or other enterprise. ■ an event held to generate financial support for such an enterprise.
– DERIVATIVES **fundraising** noun & adjective.

fundus /ˈfʌndəs/ ▶ noun (pl. **fundi** /-dʌɪ/) Anatomy the part of a hollow organ (such as the uterus or the gall bladder) that is furthest from the opening. ■ the upper part of the stomach, which forms a bulge above the level of the opening of the oesophagus (furthest from the pylorus). ■ the part of the eyeball opposite the pupil.
– ORIGIN mid 18th cent.: from Latin, literally 'bottom'.

Fundy, Bay of /ˈfʌndi/ an arm of the Atlantic Ocean extending between the Canadian provinces of New Brunswick and Nova Scotia. It is subject to fast-running tides, the highest in the world, which reach 12–15 m (40–8 ft) and are used to generate electricity.

funeral ▶ noun a ceremony or service held shortly after a person's death, usually including the person's burial or cremation. ■ US rare a sermon delivered at a funeral. ■ archaic or literary a procession of mourners at a burial.
– PHRASES **it's your funeral** informal used to warn someone that an unwise act or decision is their responsibility: *'I won't discuss it.' 'Don't then—it's your funeral.'*
– ORIGIN late Middle English: from Old French *funeraille*, from medieval Latin *funeralia*, neuter plural of late Latin *funeralis*, from Latin *funus, funer-* 'funeral, death, corpse'.

funeral director ▶ noun an undertaker.

funeral parlour (also **funeral home**, **funeral chapel**) ▶ noun an establishment where the dead are prepared for burial or cremation.

funeral pyre (also **funeral pile**) ▶ noun a pile of wood on which a corpse is burnt as part of a funeral ceremony.

funeral urn ▶ noun an urn holding the ashes of a cremated body.

funerary /ˈfjuːn(ə)(rə)ri/ ▶ adjective relating to a funeral or the commemoration of the dead: *funerary ceremonies.*
– ORIGIN late 17th cent.: from late Latin *funerarius*, from *funus, funer-* 'funeral'.

funereal /fjuːˈnɪərɪəl/ ▶ adjective having the mournful, sombre character appropriate to a funeral: *Erika was moving at a funereal pace.*
– DERIVATIVES **funereally** adverb.
– ORIGIN early 18th cent.: from Latin *funereus* (from *funus, funer-* 'funeral') + -AL.

funfair ▶ noun chiefly Brit. a fair consisting of rides, sideshows, and other amusements.

fun fur ▶ noun [mass noun] an artificial fabric with a texture resembling fur, typically in bright colours.

fungal /ˈfʌŋg(ə)l/ ▶ adjective of or caused by a fungus or fungi: *fungal diseases such as mildew.*

fungi plural form of FUNGUS.

fungible /ˈfʌn(d)ʒɪb(ə)l/ ▶ adjective Law (of goods contracted for without an individual specimen being specified) replaceable by another identical item; mutually interchangeable.
– DERIVATIVES **fungibility** noun.
– ORIGIN late 17th cent.: from medieval Latin *fungibilis*, from *fungi* 'perform, enjoy', with the same sense as *fungi vice* 'serve in place of'.

fungicide /ˈfʌn(d)ʒɪsʌɪd, ˈfʌŋgɪ-/ ▶ noun a chemical that destroys fungus.
– DERIVATIVES **fungicidal** adjective.

fungiform /ˈfʌŋ(d)ʒɪfɔːm/ ▶ adjective having the shape of or resembling a fungus or mushroom.

fungistatic /ˌfʌn(d)ʒɪˈstatɪk/ ▶ adjective inhibiting the growth of fungi.

fungivorous /fʌŋˈdʒɪv(ə)rəs/ ▶ adjective feeding on fungi or mushrooms.

fungo /ˈfʌŋgəʊ/ ▶ noun (pl. **fungoes** or **fungos**) (also **fungo fly**) Baseball a fly ball hit for practice. ■ (also **fungo bat** or **stick**) a long lightweight bat for hitting practice balls to fielders.
– ORIGIN mid 19th cent.: of unknown origin.

fungoid /ˈfʌŋgɔɪd/ ▶ adjective of or caused by a fungus or fungi: *she suffered from a fungoid disease of her feet.* ■ resembling a fungus in shape, texture, or speed of growth.
▶ noun a fungus or a growth resembling a fungus.

fungous /ˈfʌŋgəs/ ▶ adjective resembling, caused by, or having the nature of a fungus.
– ORIGIN late Middle English: from Latin *fungosus*, from *fungus* (see FUNGUS).

fungus /ˈfʌŋgəs/ ▶ noun (pl. **fungi** /-gʌɪ, -(d)ʒʌɪ/ or **funguses**) any of a group of unicellular, multicellular, or syncytial spore-producing organisms feeding on organic matter, including moulds, yeast, mushrooms, and toadstools. ■ [mass noun] fungal infection (especially on fish). ■ [in sing.] used to describe something that has appeared or grown rapidly and is considered unpleasant or unattractive: *there was a fungus of outbuildings behind the house.*

> Fungi lack chlorophyll and are therefore incapable of photosynthesis. Many play an ecologically vital role in breaking down dead organic matter, some are an important source of antibiotics or are used in fermentation, and others cause disease. The familiar mushrooms and toadstools are merely the fruiting bodies of organisms that exist mainly as a thread-like mycelium in the soil. Some fungi form associations with other plants, growing with algae to form lichens, or in the roots of higher plants to form mycorrhizas. Fungi are now often classified as a separate kingdom distinct from the green plants.

– ORIGIN late Middle English: from Latin, perhaps from Greek *spongos* (see SPONGE).

F

fungus garden ▶ noun Entomology a growth of fungus cultivated by certain ants or termites as a source of food.

fungus gnat ▶ noun a small, delicate fly whose larvae feed chiefly on fungi. ● Family Mycetophilidae: numerous species.

funhouse ▶ noun chiefly N. Amer. (in an amusement park) a building equipped with trick mirrors, shifting floors, and other devices designed to scare or amuse people as they walk through.

funicle /ˈfjuːnɪk(ə)l/ ▶ noun Botany a filamentous stalk attaching a seed or ovule to the placenta. Also called FUNICULUS. ■ Entomology a filamentous section of an insect's antenna, supporting the club.
– ORIGIN mid 17th cent.: anglicized form of Latin *funiculus* (see FUNICULUS).

funicular /fjʊˈnɪkjʊlə, fəˈnɪk-/ ▶ adjective **1** (of a railway, especially one on a mountainside) operating by cable with ascending and descending cars counterbalanced.
2 relating to a rope or its tension.
▶ noun a funicular railway.
– ORIGIN mid 17th cent. (in the sense 'of or like a cord or thread'): from Latin *funiculus* (diminutive of *funis* 'rope') + -AR1.

funiculus /fjʊˈnɪkjʊləs/ ▶ noun (pl. **funiculi** /-lʌɪ, -liː/) Anatomy a bundle of nerve fibres enclosed in a sheath of connective tissue, or forming one of the main tracts of white matter in the spinal cord. ■ another term for FUNICLE.
– ORIGIN mid 17th cent.: from Latin, diminutive of *funis* 'rope'.

Funk /fʌŋk/, Casimir (1884–1967), Polish-born American biochemist. He showed that a number of diseases, including scurvy, rickets, beriberi, and pellagra, were each caused by the deficiency of a particular dietary component, and coined the term *vitamins* for the chemicals concerned.

funk1 informal ▶ noun **1** (also **blue funk**) chiefly Brit. a state of great fear or panic: *are you in a blue funk about running out of things to say?* ■ chiefly N. Amer. a state of depression: *I sat absorbed in my own blue funk.*
2 dated, chiefly Brit. a coward.
▶ verb [with obj.] chiefly Brit. avoid (something) out of fear: *I could have seen him this morning but I funked it.*
– ORIGIN mid 18th cent. (first recorded as Oxford University slang): perhaps from FUNK2 in the slang sense 'tobacco smoke', or from obsolete Flemish *fonck* 'disturbance, agitation'.

funk2 ▶ noun **1** [mass noun] a style of popular dance music of US black origin, based on elements of blues and soul and having a strong rhythm that typically accentuates the first beat in the bar.
2 [in sing.] N. Amer. informal, dated a strong musty smell of sweat or tobacco.
▶ verb [with obj.] (**funk something up**) give music elements of funk.
– ORIGIN early 17th cent. (in the sense 'musty smell'): perhaps from French dialect *funkier* 'blow smoke on', based on Latin *fumus* 'smoke'.

funkia /ˈfʌŋkɪə/ ▶ noun another term for HOSTA.
– ORIGIN mid 19th cent.: modern Latin (former genus name), named after Heinrich Christian *Funck* (1771–1839), Prussian botanist.

funkster ▶ noun informal a performer or fan of funky music.

funky1 ▶ adjective (**funkier**, **funkiest**) informal **1** (of music) having or using a strong dance rhythm, in particular that of funk: *some excellent funky beats.* ■ modern and stylish in an unconventional or striking way: *she likes wearing funky clothes.*
2 N. Amer. strongly musty: *cooked greens make the kitchen smell really funky.*
– DERIVATIVES **funkily** adverb, **funkiness** noun.
– ORIGIN late 18th cent. (in the sense 'smelling strong or bad'): from FUNK2.

funky2 ▶ adjective (**funkier**, **funkiest**) Brit. dated, informal frightened, panicky, or cowardly.
– ORIGIN mid 19th cent.: from FUNK1.

funnel ▶ noun **1** a tube or pipe that is wide at the top and narrow at the bottom, used for guiding liquid or powder into a small opening.
2 a metal chimney on a ship or steam engine.
▶ verb (**funnels**, **funnelling**, **funnelled**; US **funnels**, **funneling**, **funneled**) [with obj. and adverbial of direction] guide or channel (something) through or as if through a funnel: *some $12.8 billion was funnelled through the Marshall Plan.* ■ [no obj., with adverbial of direction] move or be guided through or as if through a funnel: *the wind funnelled down through the valley.* ■ [no obj.] assume the shape of a funnel by widening or narrowing at the end: *the crevice funnelled out.*
– ORIGIN late Middle English: apparently via Old French from Provençal *fonilh*, from late Latin *fundibulum*, from Latin *infundibulum*, from *infundere*, from *in-* 'into' + *fundere* 'pour'.

funnel cake ▶ noun US a cake made of batter that is poured through a funnel into hot fat or oil, deep-fried until crisp, and served sprinkled with sugar.

funnel cap ▶ noun a common edible European mushroom with a funnel-shaped cap, growing in open grassy places and woodland clearings. ● *Clitocybe infundibuliformis*, family Tricholomataceae, class Hymenomycetes.

funnel cloud ▶ noun a rotating funnel-shaped cloud forming the core of a tornado or waterspout.

funnel neck ▶ noun a high, wide neck on a garment such as a sweater.

funnel-web spider ▶ noun any of a number of spiders that build a funnel-shaped web, in particular: ● a large and dangerously venomous Australian spider (genera *Atrax* and *Hadronyche*, family Dipluridae, suborder Mygalomorphae). Also called TRAPDOOR SPIDER in Australia. ● US a spider of the family Agelenidae.

funnily ▶ adverb in a strange or amusing way: *you do talk funnily.* ■ [sentence adverb] (**funnily enough**) used to admit that a situation or fact is surprising or curious: *funnily enough, I was starting to like the idea.*

funniosity /ˌfʌnɪˈɒsɪti/ ▶ noun (pl. **funniosities**) Brit. humorous a comical person, object, act, or remark: *Grandma looked a bit of a funniosity.*

funny ▶ adjective (**funnier**, **funniest**) **1** causing laughter or amusement; humorous: *a funny story | the play is hilariously funny.* ■ [predic.] [with negative] informal used to emphasize that something is unpleasant or wrong and should be regarded seriously or avoided: *stealing other people's work isn't funny.*
2 difficult to explain or understand; strange or curious: *I had a funny feeling you'd be around.* ■ unusual, especially in such a way as to arouse suspicion: *there was something funny going on.* ■ informal (of a person or part of the body) not in wholly good health or order; slightly ill: *my eyes go all funny after a bit.* ■ Brit. informal slightly deranged or eccentric: *I heard she'd gone a bit funny.*
▶ noun (**funnies**) informal amusing jokes. ■ N. Amer. the comic strips in newspapers.
– PHRASES **funny ha-ha** (or **funny peculiar**) informal amusing (or strange): used to distinguish the two main senses of 'funny'. [coined by Ian Hay in his novel *Housemaster* (1936).] **see the funny side (of something)** appreciate the humorous aspect of a situation or experience.
– DERIVATIVES **funniness** noun.

funny bone ▶ noun informal the part of the elbow over which passes the ulnar nerve, which may cause numbness and pain along the forearm and hand if knocked.

funny business ▶ noun [mass noun] deceptive, disobedient, or lecherous behaviour: *they sent a big strong farmer's lad to make sure there was no funny business.*

funny-face ▶ noun informal an affectionate form of address.

funny farm ▶ noun (often **the funny farm**) informal, offensive a psychiatric hospital.

funny man ▶ noun a professional clown or comedian.

funny money ▶ noun [mass noun] informal currency that is forged or otherwise worthless.

funny papers ▶ plural noun N. Amer. a section of a newspaper containing cartoons and humorous matter.

fun run ▶ noun informal an uncompetitive run, especially for sponsored runners in support of a charity.

fun-size (also **fun-sized**) ▶ adjective (of a product) smaller than the standard or usual size: *fun-size chocolate bars.*

funster ▶ noun informal a person who makes fun; a joker.

Fur /fʊə, fəː/ ▶ noun (pl. **same**) **1** a member of a Muslim people of the mountainous and desert regions of SW Sudan.
2 [mass noun] the language of the Fur, an isolated member of the Nilo-Saharan family, with about 500,000 speakers.
▶ adjective relating to the Fur or their language.

fur ▶ noun **1** [mass noun] the short, fine, soft hair of certain animals: *a long, lean, muscular cat with sleek fur.* ■ [count noun] the skin of an animal with fur on it: *the trapper can sell his furs to the highest bidder.* ■ animal skin with fur on it, or fabric resembling this, used in making or trimming garments: *a Parka with nylon fur round the hood* | [as modifier] *a fur coat.* ■ [count noun] a coat, cape, or similar garment made of fur: *I'd just seen her sitting in her furs.* ■ Heraldry any of several heraldic tinctures representing animal skins in stylized form (e.g. ermine, vair).
2 Brit. a coating formed by hard water on the inside surface of a pipe, kettle, or other container. ■ a coating formed on the tongue, typically as a symptom of sickness.
▶ verb (**furs**, **furring**, **furred**) [with obj.] **1** Brit. coat or clog with a deposit: *the stuff that furs up coronary arteries.*
2 (as adj., often in combination **furred**) covered with or made from a particular type of fur: *the black-furred rabbit.*
3 level (floor or wall timbers) by inserting strips of wood.
– PHRASES **be all fur coat and no knickers** Brit. informal have an impressive or sophisticated appearance which belies the fact that there is nothing to substantiate it. **fur and feather** game mammals and birds. **the fur will fly** informal there will be serious or violent trouble.
– DERIVATIVES **furless** adjective.
– ORIGIN Middle English (as a verb): from Old French *forrer* 'to line, sheathe', from *forre* 'sheath', of Germanic origin.

fur. ▶ abbreviation furlong(s).

furan /ˈfjʊəran/ ▶ noun [mass noun] Chemistry a colourless volatile liquid with a planar unsaturated five-membered ring in its molecule. ● Chem. formula: C_4H_4O. ■ [count noun] any substituted derivative of this.
– ORIGIN late 19th cent.: from synonymous *furfuran*.

furball ▶ noun **1** another term for HAIRBALL.
2 informal a furry pet animal: *I opened the door and a little grey furball walked in.*

furbelow /ˈfəːbɪləʊ/ ▶ noun a gathered strip or pleated border of a skirt or petticoat. ■ (**furbelows**) showy ornaments or trimmings: *frills and furbelows just made her look stupid.*
▶ verb [with obj.] (usu. as adj. **furbelowed**) literary adorn with trimmings.
– ORIGIN late 17th cent.: from French *falbala* 'trimming, flounce', of unknown ultimate origin.

furbish /ˈfəːbɪʃ/ ▶ verb [with obj.] (usu. as adj. **furbished**) give a fresh look to (something old or shabby); renovate: *the newly furbished church.* ■ archaic brighten up (a weapon) by polishing it.
– ORIGIN late Middle English: from Old French *forbiss-*, lengthened stem of *forbir*, of Germanic origin.

fur brigade ▶ noun Canadian historical a convoy that transported furs to and from trading posts by land and river.

furca /ˈfəːkə/ ▶ noun (pl. **furcae** /-siː, -kiː/) Zoology **1** an ingrowth of the thorax of many insects.
2 the furcula of a springtail.
– DERIVATIVES **furcal** adjective.
– ORIGIN early 17th cent.: from Latin, literally 'fork'.

furcate technical ▶ verb /ˈfəːkeɪt, fəːˈkeɪt/ [no obj.] divide into two or more branches; fork: *lines of descent furcating from a common source.*
▶ adjective /ˈfəːkeɪt, -kət/ divided into two or more branches; forked.
– DERIVATIVES **furcation** noun.
– ORIGIN early 19th cent.: from late Latin *furcatus* 'cloven', from Latin *furca* 'fork'.

furcula /ˈfəːkjʊlə/ ▶ noun (pl. **furculae** /-liː/) Zoology **1** the wishbone of a bird.
2 the forked appendage at the end of the abdomen in a springtail, by which the insect jumps.
– DERIVATIVES **furcular** adjective.
– ORIGIN mid 19th cent.: from Latin, diminutive of *furca* 'fork'.

furfuraceous /ˌfəːf(j)əˈreɪʃəs/ ▶ adjective Botany & Medicine covered with or characterized by bran-like scales.
– ORIGIN mid 17th cent.: from late Latin *furfuraceus* (from Latin *furfur* 'bran') + -OUS.

furfural /ˈfəːf(j)əral/ ▶ noun [mass noun] Chemistry a colourless liquid used in synthetic resin manufacture, originally obtained by distilling bran. ● An aldehyde derived from furan; chem. formula: C_4H_3OCHO.
– ORIGIN late 19th cent.: from obsolete *furfurol* (in the same sense) + -AL.

furfuraldehyde /ˌfəːf(j)əˈraldɪhʌɪd/ ▶ noun Chemistry another term for FURFURAL.

furioso /ˌfjʊərɪˈəʊzəʊ, -səʊ/ ▶ adverb & adjective Music (especially as a direction) furiously and wildly.
– ORIGIN Italian.

furious ▶ adjective **1** extremely angry: *he was furious when he learned about it.*
2 full of anger or energy; violent or intense: *he drove at a furious speed.*
– DERIVATIVES **furiously** adverb, **furiousness** noun.
– ORIGIN late Middle English: from Old French *furieus*, from Latin *furiosus*, from *furia* 'fury'.

furl ▶ verb [with obj.] roll or fold up (something) neatly and securely: *the flag was tightly furled* | (as adj. **furled**) *the plant sends up cones of furled leaves.*
– ORIGIN late 16th cent.: from French *ferler*, from Old French *fer, ferm* 'firm' + *lier* 'bind' (from Latin *ligare*).

furling ▶ noun [mass noun] equipment for rolling up sails securely and neatly around their yards or booms.

furlong ▶ noun an eighth of a mile, 220 yards.
– ORIGIN Old English *furlang*, from *furh* 'furrow' + *lang* 'long'. The word originally denoted the length of a furrow in a common field (formally regarded as a square of ten acres). It was also used as the equivalent of the Roman *stadium*, one eighth of a Roman mile, whence the current sense. Compare with **STADIUM**.

furlough /ˈfəːləʊ/ ▶ noun [mass noun] leave of absence, especially that granted to a member of the services or a missionary: *a civil servant home on furlough* | [count noun] *a six-week furlough in Australia.*
▶ verb [with obj.] (usu. as adj. **furloughed**) US grant leave of absence to: *furloughed workers.*
– ORIGIN early 17th cent.: from Dutch *verlof*, modelled on German *Verlaub*, of West Germanic origin and related to **LEAVE**[2].

furmety /ˈfəːmɪti/ ▶ noun variant spelling of **FRUMENTY**.

furnace ▶ noun an enclosed structure in which material can be heated to very high temperatures, e.g. for smelting metals. ■ N. Amer. an appliance fired by gas or oil in which air or water is heated to be circulated throughout a building in a heating system. ■ a very hot place: *her car was a furnace.*
– ORIGIN Middle English: from Old French *fornais(e)*, from Latin *fornax, fornac-*, from *fornus* 'oven'.

Furneaux Islands /ˈfəːnəʊ/ a group of islands off the coast of NE Tasmania, in the Bass Strait. The largest island is Flinders Island.

furnish ▶ verb [with obj.] **1** provide (a house or room) with furniture and fittings: *the proprietor has furnished the bedrooms in a variety of styles.*
2 be a source of; provide: *fish furnish an important source of protein.* ■ (**furnish someone with**) supply someone with (something); give (something) to someone: *she was able to furnish me with details of the incident.*
– ORIGIN late Middle English (in the general sense 'provide or equip with what is necessary or desirable'): from Old French *furniss-*, lengthened stem of *furnir*, ultimately of West Germanic origin.

furnished ▶ adjective (of accommodation) available to be rented with furniture.

furnisher ▶ noun a person who supplies furniture.

furnishing ▶ noun (usu. **furnishings**) furniture, fittings, and other decorative accessories such as curtains and carpets, for a house or room. ■ [as modifier] denoting fabrics used for curtains or upholstery.

furniture ▶ noun [mass noun] **1** the movable articles that are used to make a room or building suitable for living or working in, such as tables, chairs, or desks.
2 [usu. with adj. or noun modifier] the small accessories or fittings that are required for a particular task or function. ■ the mountings of a rifle. ■ Printing pieces of wood or metal placed round or between metal type to make blank spaces and fasten the type in the chase.
– PHRASES **part of the furniture** informal a person or thing that has been somewhere so long as to seem a permanent, unquestioned, or invisible feature of the landscape.
– ORIGIN early 16th cent. (denoting the action of furnishing): from French *fourniture*, from *fournir*, from Old French *furnir* 'to furnish'.

furniture beetle ▶ noun a small brown beetle, the larva of which (the woodworm) bores holes in dead wood and causes considerable damage to old furniture and building timbers. ● *Anobium punctatum*, family Anobiidae.

furore /fjʊ(ə)ˈrɔːri, ˌfjʊ(ə)ˈrɔː/ (US **furor** /ˈfjʊərɔː/) ▶ noun [in sing.] an outbreak of public anger or excitement: *the verdict raised a furore over the role of courtroom psychiatry.* ■ archaic a wave of enthusiastic admiration; a craze.
– ORIGIN late 18th cent.: from Italian, from Latin *furor*, from *furere* 'be mad, rage'.

furosemide /fjʊəˈrɒsəmʌɪd/ ▶ noun variant spelling of **FRUSEMIDE**.

furphy /ˈfəːfi/ ▶ noun (pl. **furphies**) Austral. informal a rumour or story, especially one that is untrue or absurd.
– ORIGIN First World War: from the name painted on water and sanitary carts manufactured by the *Furphy* family of Shepparton, Victoria.

furrier /ˈfʌrɪə/ ▶ noun a person who prepares or deals in furs.
– ORIGIN Middle English: from Old French *forreor*, from *forrer* 'to line, sheathe' (see **FUR**). The change in the ending in the 16th cent. was due to association with **-IER**.

furriery /ˈfʌrɪəri/ ▶ noun [mass noun] the art or trade of dressing and preparing furs.

furring strip ▶ noun a length of wood tapering to nothing, used in roofing and other construction work.

furrow ▶ noun **1** a long, narrow trench made in the ground by a plough, especially for planting seeds or irrigation. ■ a rut, groove, or trail in the ground or another surface: *lorry wheels had dug furrows in the sand.*
2 a line or wrinkle on a person's face: *there were deep furrows in his brow.*
▶ verb **1** [with obj.] make a rut, groove, or trail in (the ground or the surface of something): *gorges furrowing the deep-sea floor* | *John's face was furrowed with tears.* ■ (usu. as adj. **furrowed**) use a plough to make a long, narrow trench in (land or earth): *furrowed fields.*
2 (with reference to the forehead or face) mark or be marked with lines or wrinkles caused by frowning, anxiety, or concentration: [with obj.] *a look of concern furrowed his brow* | [no obj.] *his brows furrowed in concentration* | (as adj. **furrowed**) *he stroked his furrowed brow.*
– ORIGIN Old English *furh*, of Germanic origin; related to Dutch *voor* and German *Furche*, from an Indo-European root shared by Latin *porca* 'ridge between furrows'.

furrow slice ▶ noun a slice of earth turned up by the mouldboard of a plough.

furry ▶ adjective (**furrier**, **furriest**) covered with fur: *furry creatures in fields.* ■ having a soft surface like fur: *a layer of furry soot.*
– DERIVATIVES **furriness** noun.

fur seal ▶ noun a gregarious eared seal that frequents the coasts of the Pacific and southern oceans, the male of which is substantially larger than the female. The thick fur on the underside is used commercially as sealskin. ● Two genera in the family Otariidae: the **northern fur seal** (*Callorhinus ursinus*) and the **southern fur seal** (genus *Arctocephalus*)

further used as comparative of **FAR**. ▶ adverb (also **farther**) **1** at, to, or by a greater distance (used to indicate the extent to which one thing or person is or becomes distant from another): *for some time I had wanted to move further from London* | figurative *the EU seems to have moved further away from the original aims.* ■ [with negative] used to emphasize the difference between a supposed or suggested fact or state of mind and the truth: *as for her being a liar, nothing could be further from the truth* | *nothing could be further from his mind than marrying.*
2 over a greater expanse of space or time; for a longer way: *we had walked further than I realized* | figurative *wages have been driven down even further.* ■ beyond the point already reached or the distance already covered: *Amelie decided to drive further up the coast* | *before going any further we need to define our terms.* ■ beyond or in addition to what has already been done: *this theme will be developed further in Chapter 6.* ■ [sentence adverb] used to introduce a new point relating to or reinforcing a previous statement: *On the Internet, the size and scope of the market is several orders of magnitude higher. Further, it is available 24 hours per day, 7 days per week.* ■ at or to a more advanced, successful, or desirable stage: *determination could not get her any further* | *at the end of three years they were no further on.*
▶ adjective **1** (also **farther**) more distant in space than another item of the same kind: *two men were standing at the further end of the clearing.* ■ more remote from a central point: *the museum is in the further reaches of the town.*
2 additional to what already exists or has already taken place, been done, or been accounted for: *cook for a further ten minutes.*
▶ verb [with obj.] help the progress or development of (something); promote: *he had depended on using them to further his own career.*
– PHRASES **further to your** (or **our**) —— formal used at the beginning of a letter or in speech as a way of raising a matter discussed in an earlier letter, article, or conversation: ***further to our letter** of 12th October, we confirm that our client will give full vacant possession on completion.* **not go any further** (of a secret) not be told to anyone else. **until further notice** used to indicate that a situation will not change until another announcement is made: *the museum is closed to the public until further notice.* **until further orders** used to indicate that a situation is only to change when another command is received: *they were to be kept in prison until further orders.*
– DERIVATIVES **furtherer** noun.
– ORIGIN Old English *furthor* (adverb), *furthra* (adjective), *fyrthrian* (verb), of Germanic origin; related to **FORTH**.

> **USAGE** Is there any difference between **further** and **farther** in *she moved **further** down the train* and *she moved **farther** down the train*? Both words share the same roots: in the sentences given above, where the sense is 'at, to, or by a greater distance', there is no difference in meaning, and both are equally correct. **Further** is a much commoner word, though, and is in addition used in various abstract and metaphorical contexts, for example referring to time, in which **farther** is unusual, e.g. *without **further** delay; have you anything **further** to say?; we intend to stay a **further** two weeks.* The same distinction is made between **farthest** and **furthest**: *the **farthest** point from the sun* versus *this first team has gone **furthest** in its analysis.*

furtherance ▶ noun [mass noun] the advancement of a scheme or interest: *the court held that the union's acts were not **in furtherance of** a trade dispute.*

further education ▶ noun [mass noun] Brit. education below degree level for people above school age.

furthermore ▶ adverb [sentence adverb] in addition; besides (used to introduce a fresh consideration in an argument): *It was also a highly desirable political end. Furthermore, it gave the English a door into France.*

furthermost (also **farthermost**) ▶ adjective (of an edge or extreme) at the greatest distance from a central point or implicit standpoint: *the furthermost end of the street.*

furthest (also **farthest**) used as superlative of **FAR**.
▶ adjective [attrib.] situated at the greatest distance from a specified or understood point: *the furthest door led to a kitchen* | figurative *it was the furthest thing from my mind.* ■ covering the greatest area or distance: *the aim is to travel the furthest distance.* ■ extremely remote: *the furthest ends of the earth.*
▶ adverb **1** at or by the greatest distance (used to indicate how far one thing or person is or becomes distant from another): *the bed furthest from the window* | figurative *the people who are furthest removed from the political process.*
2 over the greatest distance or area: *his group probably had furthest to ride.* ■ used to indicate the most distant point reached in a specified direction. *it was the furthest north I had ever travelled.* ■ to the most extreme or advanced point: *countries where industrialization had gone furthest.*
– PHRASES **at the furthest** at the greatest distance; at most: *the Allied line had been pushed forward, at the furthest, about 1.6 km.*
– ORIGIN late Middle English: formed as a superlative of **FURTHER**.

> **USAGE** For a discussion of the differences between **farther** and **further**, **farthest** and **furthest**, see **USAGE** at **FURTHER**.

furtive /ˈfəːtɪv/ ▶ adjective attempting to avoid notice or attention, typically because of guilt or a belief that discovery would lead to trouble; secretive: *they spent a furtive day together* | *he stole a furtive glance at her.* ■ suggestive of guilty nervousness: *the look in his eyes became furtive.*
– DERIVATIVES **furtively** adverb, **furtiveness** noun.
– ORIGIN early 17th cent.: from French *furtif, -ive* or Latin *furtivus*, from *furtum* 'theft'.

Furtwängler /ˈfʊət,vɛŋglə/, German /ˈfʊrt,vɛŋlɐ/, Wilhelm (1886–1954), German conductor, chief conductor of the Berlin Philharmonic Orchestra from 1922. He is noted particularly for his interpretations of Beethoven and Wagner.

F

furuncle /ˈfjʊərʌŋk(ə)l/ ▶ **noun** technical term for **BOIL²**.
– ORIGIN late Middle English: from Latin *furunculus*, literally 'petty thief', also 'knob on a vine' (regarded as stealing the sap), from *fur* 'thief'.

furunculosis /fjʊˌrʌŋkjʊˈləʊsɪs/ ▶ **noun** [mass noun] **1** Medicine the simultaneous or repeated occurrence of boils on the skin.
2 a bacterial disease of salmon and trout.
– ORIGIN late 19th cent.: from **FURUNCLE** + **-OSIS**.

fury ▶ **noun** (pl. **furies**) **1** [mass noun] wild or violent anger: *tears of fury and frustration* | *Rachel shouted, beside herself with fury.* ▪ (**a fury**) a surge of violent anger or other strong feeling: *in a fury, he lashed the horse on.*
2 extreme strength or violence in an action or a natural phenomenon: *the fury of a gathering storm* | *she was paddling with a new fury.*
3 (**Fury**) Greek Mythology a spirit of punishment, often represented as one of three goddesses who pronounced curses on the guilty and inflicted famines and pestilences. The Furies were identified at an early date with the Eumenides.
– PHRASES **like fury** informal with great energy or effort: *she fought like fury in his arms.*
– ORIGIN late Middle English: from Old French *furie*, from Latin *furia*, from *furiosus* 'furious', from *furere* 'be mad, rage'.

furze /fəːz/ ▶ **noun** another term for **GORSE**.
– DERIVATIVES **furzy adjective**.
– ORIGIN Old English *fyrs*, of unknown origin.

fusain /ˈfjuːzeɪn/ ▶ **noun** [mass noun] Geology a lustreless, crumbly, porous type of coal resembling wood charcoal.
– ORIGIN late 19th cent.: from French, literally 'spindle tree', also 'fine charcoal' (made from the spindle tree).

fusarium /fjʊˈzɛːrɪəm/ ▶ **noun** (pl. **fusaria** or **fusariums**) a mould of a large genus which includes a number that cause plant diseases, especially wilting. ● Genus *Fusarium*, subdivision Deuteromycotina. ▪ [mass noun] infestation with any of the fusaria or related moulds.
– ORIGIN early 20th cent.: modern Latin, from Latin *fusus* 'spindle'.

fuscous /ˈfʌskəs/ ▶ **adjective** technical or literary dark and sombre in colour.
– ORIGIN mid 17th cent.: from Latin *fuscus* 'dusky' + **-OUS**.

fuse¹ ▶ **verb 1** [with obj.] join or blend to form a single entity: *intermarriage had fused the families into a large unit.* ▪ [no obj.] (of groups of atoms or cellular structures) join or coalesce. ▪ melt (a material or object) with intense heat so as to join it with something else: *powdered glass was fused to a metal base* | [no obj.] *when fired in a special kiln, the metals fused on to the pot.*
2 [no obj.] Brit. (of an electrical appliance) stop working when a fuse melts: *the crew were left in darkness after the lights fused.* ▪ [with obj.] cause (an electrical appliance) to stop working when a fuse melts.
3 [with obj.] provide (a circuit or electrical appliance) with a fuse: (as adj. **fused**) *a fused plug.*
▶ **noun** a safety device consisting of a strip of wire that melts and breaks an electric circuit if the current exceeds a safe level.
– ORIGIN late 16th cent.: from Latin *fus-* 'poured, melted', from the verb *fundere*.

fuse² (N. Amer. also **fuze**) ▶ **noun** a length of material along which a small flame moves to explode a bomb or firework, meanwhile allowing time for those who light it to move to a safe distance. ▪ a device in a bomb that controls the timing of the explosion.
▶ **verb** [with obj.] fit a fuse to (a bomb, shell, or mine): *the bomb was fused to go off during a charity performance.*
– PHRASES **light the** (or **a**) **fuse** do something that creates a tense or exciting situation: *his goal midway through the first half lit the fuse.* **have** (or **be on**) **a short fuse** have a tendency to lose one's temper quickly.
– ORIGIN mid 17th cent.: from Italian *fuso*, from Latin *fusus* 'spindle'.

fuse box (also **fuse board**) ▶ **noun** a box housing the fuses for circuits in a building.

fusee /fjuːˈziː/ (US **fuzee**) ▶ **noun 1** a conical pulley or wheel, especially in a watch or clock.
2 a large-headed match capable of staying alight in strong wind.
3 N. Amer. a railway signal flare.
– ORIGIN late 16th cent. (denoting a spindle-shaped figure): from French *fusée* 'spindle-ful', based on Latin *fusus* 'spindle'.

fuselage /ˈfjuːzəlɑːʒ, -lɪdʒ/ ▶ **noun** the main body of an aircraft.
– ORIGIN early 20th cent.: from French, from *fuseler* 'shape into a spindle', from *fuseau* 'spindle'.

Fuseli /ˈfjuːz(ə)li, fjuːˈzɛli/, Henry (1741–1825), Swiss-born British painter and art critic; born *Johann Heinrich Füssli*. A prominent figure of the romantic movement, he tended towards the horrifying and the fantastic, as in *The Nightmare* (1781).

fusel oil /ˈfjuːz(ə)l/ ▶ **noun** [mass noun] a mixture of several alcohols (chiefly amyl alcohol) produced as a by-product of alcoholic fermentation.
– ORIGIN mid 19th cent.: from German *Fusel* 'bad liquor', probably related to *fuseln* 'to bungle'.

fuse wire ▶ **noun** [mass noun] thin wire used in an electric fuse.

Fushun /fuːˈʃʊn/ a coal-mining city in NE China, in the province of Liaoning; pop. 1,264,700 (est. 2006).

fusible /ˈfjuːzɪb(ə)l/ ▶ **adjective** able to be fused or melted easily.
– DERIVATIVES **fusibility noun**.
– ORIGIN late Middle English: from Old French, or from medieval Latin *fusibilis*, from *fundere* 'pour, melt'.

fusiform /ˈfjuːzɪfɔːm/ ▶ **adjective** Botany & Zoology tapering at both ends; spindle-shaped.
– ORIGIN mid 18th cent.: from Latin *fusus* 'spindle' + **-IFORM**.

fusil¹ /ˈfjuːzɪl/ ▶ **noun** historical a light musket.
– ORIGIN late 16th cent. (denoting a flint in a tinderbox): from French, based on Latin *focus* 'hearth, fire'.

fusil² /ˈfjuːzɪl/ ▶ **noun** Heraldry an elongated lozenge.
– ORIGIN late Middle English: from Old French *fusel*, from a diminutive of Latin *fusus* 'spindle'.

fusilier /ˌfjuːzɪˈlɪə/ (N. Amer. also **fusileer**) ▶ **noun** (usu. **Fusiliers**) a member of any of several British regiments formerly armed with fusils: *the Royal Scots Fusiliers.* ▪ historical a soldier armed with a fusil.
– ORIGIN late 17th cent.: from French, from *fusil* (see **FUSIL¹**).

fusillade /ˌfjuːzɪˈleɪd, -ˈlɑːd/ ▶ **noun** a series of shots fired or missiles thrown all at the same time or in quick succession: *marchers had to dodge a fusillade of missiles.*
▶ **verb** [with obj.] archaic fire a fusillade at (a place or person).
– ORIGIN early 19th cent.: from French, from *fusiller* 'to shoot', from *fusil* (see **FUSIL¹**).

fusilli /f(j)ʊˈziːli/ ▶ **plural noun** pasta pieces in the form of short spirals.
– ORIGIN Italian, literally 'little spindles', diminutive of *fuso*.

fusimotor /ˈfjuːzɪməʊtə/ ▶ **adjective** Anatomy relating to or denoting the motor neurons with slender fibres which innervate muscle spindles.

fusion ▶ **noun** [mass noun] the process or result of joining two or more things together to form a single entity: *the election results produced pressure for fusion of the parties* | [in sing.] *the film showed a perfect fusion of image and sound.* ▪ Physics short for **NUCLEAR FUSION**. ▪ the process of causing a material or object to melt with intense heat so as to join with another: *the fusion of resin and glass fibre in the moulding process.* ▪ music that is a mixture of different styles, especially jazz and rock: *jazz fusion.* ▪ [as modifier] referring to food or cooking which incorporates elements of both Eastern and Western cuisine: *fusion cuisine.*
– DERIVATIVES **fusional adjective**.
– ORIGIN mid 16th cent.: from Latin *fusio(n-)*, from *fundere* 'pour, melt'.

fusion bomb ▶ **noun** a bomb deriving its energy from nuclear fusion, especially a hydrogen bomb.

fusionist ▶ **noun 1** a person who strives for coalition between political parties or factions.
2 a player or fan of music that is mixture of two modern styles.
– DERIVATIVES **fusionism noun**.

fuss ▶ **noun** [mass noun] a display of unnecessary or excessive excitement, activity, or interest: *I don't know what all the fuss is about.* ▪ [in sing.] a protest or dispute of a specified degree or kind: *he didn't put up too much of a fuss.* ▪ elaborate or complex procedures; trouble or difficulty: *they settled in with very little fuss.*
▶ **verb** [no obj.] show unnecessary or excessive concern about something: *she's always fussing about her food.* ▪ busy oneself restlessly: *beside him Kegan was fussing with sheets of paper.* ▪ [with obj.] Brit. disturb or bother (someone): *when she cries in her sleep, try not to fuss her.* ▪ [with obj.] treat (someone) with excessive attention or affection: *she flattered and fussed her.*
– PHRASES **make a fuss** become angry and complain. **make a fuss over** (or Brit. **of**) treat (a person or animal) with excessive attention or affection.
– DERIVATIVES **fusser noun**.
– ORIGIN early 18th cent.: perhaps Anglo-Irish.

fussbudget ▶ **noun** N. Amer. informal a fussy person.

fussed ▶ **adjective** [predic.] Brit. informal (of a person) feeling concern, distress, or annoyance; having strong feelings about something: *it'd be great to be there but I'm not that fussed.*

fusspot ▶ **noun** informal a fussy person.

fussy ▶ **adjective** (**fussier**, **fussiest**) fastidious about one's needs or requirements; hard to please: *he is very fussy about what he eats.* ▪ showing excessive or anxious concern about detail: *Eleanor patted her hair with quick, fussy movements.* ▪ full of unnecessary detail or decoration: *I hate fussy clothes.*
– PHRASES **not be fussy** informal not be very concerned about something, especially a decision that is to be made: *he's quite welcome to do that because the rest of us are not fussy.*
– DERIVATIVES **fussily adverb**, **fussiness noun**.

fustanella /ˌfʌstəˈnɛlə/ ▶ **noun** a stiff white kilt, worn by men in Albania and Greece.
– ORIGIN mid 19th cent.: from Italian, from modern Greek *phoustani*, *phoustanela*, probably from Italian *fustagno*, from medieval Latin *fustaneum* (see **FUSTIAN**).

fustian /ˈfʌstɪən/ ▶ **noun** [mass noun] **1** thick, hard-wearing twilled cloth with a short nap, usually dyed in dark colours.
2 pompous or pretentious speech or writing: *a smokescreen of fustian and fantasy.*
– ORIGIN Middle English: from Old French *fustaigne*, from medieval Latin *fustaneum*, from (*pannus*) *fustaneus* 'cloth from *Fostat*', a suburb of Cairo; sense 2 perhaps from the fact that fustian was sometimes used to cover pillows and cushions, implying that the language was 'padded'; compare with **BOMBAST**.

fustic /ˈfʌstɪk/ ▶ **noun 1** [mass noun] archaic a yellow dye obtained from either of two kinds of timber, especially that of old fustic.
2 (also **old fustic**) a tropical American tree with heartwood that yields dyes and other products. See also **YOUNG FUSTIC**. ● *Maclura* (or *Chlorophora*) *tinctoria*, family Moraceae.
– ORIGIN late Middle English: via French from Spanish *fustoc*, from Arabic *fustuq*, from Greek *pistakē* 'pistachio tree'.

fusty ▶ **adjective** (**fustier**, **fustiest**) smelling stale, damp, or stuffy: *the fusty odour of decay.* ▪ old-fashioned in attitude or style: *grammar in the classroom became a fusty notion.*
– DERIVATIVES **fustily adverb**, **fustiness noun**.
– ORIGIN late 15th cent.: from Old French *fuste* 'smelling of the cask', from *fust* 'cask, tree trunk', from Latin *fustis* 'cudgel'.

futhark /ˈfuːθɑːk/ (also **futhorc** /ˈfuːθɔːk/, **futhork**) ▶ **noun** the runic alphabet.
– ORIGIN mid 19th cent.: from its first six letters: *f*, *u*, *th*, *a* (or *o*), *r*, *k*.

futile ▶ **adjective** incapable of producing any useful result; pointless: *a futile attempt to keep fans from mounting the stage* | *it is futile to allocate blame for this.*
– DERIVATIVES **futilely adverb**.
– ORIGIN mid 16th cent.: from Latin *futilis* 'leaky, futile', apparently from *fundere* 'pour'.

futilitarian /fjuːˌtɪlɪˈtɛːrɪən/ ▶ **adjective** devoted to futile pursuits.
▶ **noun** a person devoted to futile pursuits.

futility ▶ **noun** [mass noun] pointlessness or uselessness: *the horror and futility of war.*

futon /ˈfuːtɒn/ ▶ **noun** a padded unsprung mattress originating in Japan, that can be rolled up or folded in two.
– ORIGIN late 19th cent.: Japanese.

futsal /ˈfʊtsal/ ▶ **noun** [mass noun] a modified form of soccer played with five players per side on a smaller, typically indoor, pitch.
– ORIGIN 1980s: partly from Brazilian Portuguese, shortened from *futebol du salão*, and partly from Spanish, shortened from *fútbol sala* or *fútbol de salón*.

futtock /ˈfʌtək/ ▶ **noun** each of the middle timbers of a ship's frame, between the floor and the top timbers.
– ORIGIN Middle English: perhaps from Middle Low German, or from FOOT + HOOK.

future ▶ **noun 1** (usu. **the future**) a period of time following the moment of speaking or writing; time regarded as still to come: *we plan on getting married in the near future | work on the building will be shelved for the foreseeable future.* ■ events that will or are likely to happen in time to come: *nobody can predict the future.* ■ the likely prospects for or fate of someone or something in time to come: *MPs will debate the future of the railways.* ■ a prospect of success or happiness: *he'd decided that there was no future in the gang | I began to believe I might have a future as an artist.* ■ Grammar a tense of verbs expressing events that have not yet happened.
2 (**futures**) contracts for assets (especially commodities or shares) bought at agreed prices but delivered and paid for later. Compare with FORWARD (sense 2 of the noun).
▶ **adjective** [attrib.] at a later time; going or likely to happen or exist: *the needs of future generations.* ■ (of a person) planned or destined to hold a specified position: *his future wife.* ■ existing after death: *heaven and the future life with Christ.* ■ Grammar (of a tense) expressing an event yet to happen.
– PHRASES **for future reference** see REFERENCE. **in future** from now onwards: *she would be more careful in future.*
– ORIGIN late Middle English: via Old French from Latin *futurus*, future participle of *esse* 'be' (from the stem *fu-*, ultimately from a base meaning 'grow, become').

future history ▶ **noun** (in science fiction) a narration of imagined future events.

future perfect ▶ **noun** Grammar a tense of verbs expressing expected completion in the future, in English exemplified by *will have done.*

future-proof ▶ **adjective** (of a product or system) unlikely to become obsolete.
▶ **verb** [with obj.] make (a product or system) future-proof: *this approach allows you to future-proof your applications.*

future shock ▶ **noun** [mass noun] a state of distress or disorientation due to rapid social or technological change.

futurism ▶ **noun** [mass noun] concern with events and trends of the future, or which anticipate the future. ■ (**Futurism**) an artistic movement begun in Italy in 1909, which strongly rejected traditional forms and embraced the energy and dynamism of modern technology. Launched by Filippo Marinetti, it had effectively ended by 1918 but was widely influential, particularly in Russia on figures such as Malevich and Mayakovsky.
– ORIGIN from FUTURE + -ISM, translating Italian *futurismo*, French *futurisme*.

futurist ▶ **noun 1** (**Futurist**) an adherent of Futurism **2** a person who studies the future and makes predictions about it based on current trends.
3 Theology a person who believes that eschatological prophecies are still to be fulfilled.
▶ **adjective 1** (**Futurist**) relating to Futurism or the Futurists.
2 relating to a vision of the future.

futuristic ▶ **adjective 1** having or involving very modern technology or design: *a swimming pool and futuristic dome.* ■ (of a film or book) set in the future, typically in a world of advanced or menacing technology.
2 (**Futuristic**) dated of or characteristic of Futurism.
– DERIVATIVES **futuristically** adverb.

futurity /fjuːˈtjʊərɪti, -tʃ-/ ▶ **noun** (pl. **futurities**)
1 [mass noun] the future time: *the tremendous shadows which futurity casts upon the present.* ■ [count noun] a future event. ■ renewed or continuing existence: *the snowdrops were a promise of futurity.*
2 US short for FUTURITY RACE.

futurity race (also **futurity stakes**) ▶ **noun** US a horse race for young horses for which entries are made long in advance, sometimes before the horses are born.

futurology /ˌfjuːtʃəˈrɒlədʒi/ ▶ **noun** [mass noun] systematic forecasting of the future, especially from present trends in society.
– DERIVATIVES **futurological** adjective, **futurologist** noun.

futz /fʌts/ ▶ **verb** [no obj.] N. Amer. informal waste time; idle or busy oneself aimlessly: *mother futzed around in the kitchen.*
– ORIGIN 1930s: perhaps an alteration of Yiddish *arumfartzen* 'fart about'.

Fuxin /fuːˈʃɪn/ (also **Fou-hsin**) an industrial city in NE China, in Liaoning province; pop. 691,800 (est. 2006).

fuze ▶ **noun** variant spelling of FUSE[2].

fuzee ▶ **noun** US spelling of FUSEE.

Fuzhou /fuːˈdʒəʊ/ (also **Foochow**) a port in SE China, capital of Fujian province; pop. 1,457,600 (est. 2006).

fuzz[1] ▶ **noun 1** a frizzy mass of hair or fibre: *a fuzz of black hair* | [mass noun] *his face was covered with white fuzz.* ■ a blurred image: *she saw Jess surrounded by a fuzz of sunlight.*
2 a buzzing or distorted sound, especially one deliberately produced as an effect on an electric guitar.
▶ **verb 1** make or become blurred or indistinct: [with obj.] *snow fuzzes the outlines of the signs* | [no obj.] *her head fuzzed and the classroom swam.*
2 [no obj.] (of hair) become frizzy: *her hair fuzzed out uncontrollably in the heat.*
– ORIGIN late 16th cent.: probably of Low German or Dutch origin; compare with Dutch *voos*, Low German *fussig* 'spongy'.

fuzz[2] ▶ **noun** (**the fuzz**) informal the police.
– ORIGIN 1920s (originally US): of unknown origin.

fuzzbox ▶ **noun** a device which adds a distorted buzzing quality to the sound of an electric guitar or other instrument.

fuzzed ▶ **adjective** (of popular music or electric instruments) having or producing a distorted buzzing tone: *fuzzed guitars.*

fuzzy ▶ **adjective** (**fuzzier**, **fuzziest**) **1** having a frizzy texture or appearance: *a girl with fuzzy dark hair.*
2 difficult to perceive; indistinct or vague: *the picture is very fuzzy | that fuzzy line between right and wrong.* ■ (of a person or the mind) unable to think clearly; confused: *my mind felt fuzzy.*
3 another term for FUZZED.
4 Computing & Logic relating to a form of set theory and logic in which predicates may have degrees of applicability, rather than simply being true or false. It has important uses in artificial intelligence and the design of control systems.
– DERIVATIVES **fuzzily** adverb, **fuzziness** noun.

fuzzy-wuzzy ▶ **noun** (pl. **fuzzy-wuzzies**) Brit. informal, offensive a black person, especially one with tightly curled hair. ■ historical a Sudanese soldier.
– ORIGIN late 19th cent.: reduplication of FUZZY.

fwd ▶ **abbreviation** forward.

f.w.d. ▶ **abbreviation** ■ four-wheel drive. ■ front-wheel drive.

FWIW ▶ **abbreviation** informal for what it's worth: *FWIW, my ex-wife kept her maiden name when we married.*

F-word ▶ **noun** informal used instead of or in reference to the word 'fuck' because of its taboo nature.

FX ▶ **abbreviation** (visual or sound) effects: *films which require actors rather than special FX.*
– ORIGIN from the pronunciation of the two letters forming the two syllables of *effects*.

FY ▶ **abbreviation** ■ Brit. financial year. ■ N. Amer. fiscal year.

-fy ▶ **suffix 1** (added to nouns) forming verbs denoting making or producing: *speechify.* ■ denoting transformation or the process of making into: *deify | petrify.*
2 forming verbs denoting the making of a state defined by an adjective: *amplify | falsify.*
3 forming verbs expressing a causative sense: *horrify.*
– ORIGIN from French *-fier*, from Latin *-ficare*, *-facere*, from *facere* 'do, make'.

FYI ▶ **abbreviation** for your information.

fyke /fʌɪk/ (also **fyke net**) ▶ **noun** chiefly US a bag net for catching fish.
– ORIGIN mid 19th cent.: from Dutch *fuik* 'fish trap'.

fylfot /ˈfɪlfɒt/ ▶ **noun** a swastika.
– ORIGIN late 15th cent.: perhaps from *fill-foot* 'pattern filling the foot of a painted window'.

fynbos /ˈfeɪnbɒs/ ▶ **noun** [mass noun] a distinctive type of vegetation found only on the southern tip of Africa. It includes a very wide range of plant species, particularly small heather-like trees and shrubs.
– ORIGIN Afrikaans, literally 'fine bush'.

fyrd /fəːd, fɪəd/ ▶ **noun** the English militia before 1066.
– ORIGIN Old English, of Germanic origin; related to German *Fahrt*, also to FARE.

FYROM ▶ **abbreviation** Former Yugoslav Republic of Macedonia.

fytte ▶ **noun** variant spelling of FIT[3].

F

Gg

G[1] (also **g**) ▶ **noun** (pl. **Gs** or **G's**) **1** the seventh letter of the alphabet. ■ denoting the next after F in a set of items, categories, etc. ■ **(g)** Chess denoting the seventh file from the left, as viewed from White's side of the board.
2 Music the fifth note in the diatonic scale of C major. ■ a key based on a scale with G as its keynote.

G[2] ▶ **abbreviation** ■ Physics gauss. ■ [in combination] (in units of measurement) giga- (10^9). ■ N. Amer. informal grand (a thousand dollars). ■ a unit of acceleration equal to that produced by the earth's gravitational field.
▶ **symbol** ■ N. Amer. general audiences, a rating for a film that is suitable for all ages. ■ Chemistry Gibbs free energy. ■ Physics the gravitational constant, equal to 6.67×10^{-11} N m² kg^{-2}.

g ▶ **abbreviation** ■ Chemistry gas. ■ gelding. ■ gram(s). ■ Physics denoting quantum states or wave functions which do not change sign on inversion through the origin. The opposite of **u**. [from German *gerade* 'even'.]
▶ **symbol** Physics the acceleration due to gravity, equal to 9.81 m s^{-2}.

G7 ▶ **abbreviation** Group of Seven.

G8 ▶ **abbreviation** Group of Eight.

G20 ▶ **abbreviation** Group of Twenty.

G77 ▶ **abbreviation** Group of Seventy-Seven.

GA ▶ **abbreviation** ■ general aviation. ■ Georgia (in official postal use).

Ga ▶ **symbol** the chemical element gallium.

Ga. ▶ **abbreviation** Georgia (US).

GAA ▶ **abbreviation** Gaelic Athletic Association.

gab informal ▶ **verb (gabs, gabbing, gabbed)** [no obj.] talk at length: *Celeste was **gabbing about** the country before the war.*
▶ **noun** [mass noun] talk; chatter.
– PHRASES **the gift of the gab** (N. Amer. **gift of gab**) the ability to speak with eloquence and fluency.
– ORIGIN early 18th cent.: variant of **GOB**[1].

GABA ▶ **abbreviation** gamma-aminobutyric acid.

gabardine ▶ **noun** see **GABERDINE**.

gabble ▶ **verb** [no obj.] talk rapidly and unintelligibly: *he gabbled on in a panicky way until he was dismissed.*
▶ **noun** [mass noun] rapid unintelligible talk.
– DERIVATIVES **gabbler** noun.
– ORIGIN late 16th cent.: from Dutch *gabbelen*, of imitative origin.

gabbro /ˈɡabrəʊ/ ▶ **noun** (pl. **gabbros**) [mass noun] Geology a dark, coarse-grained plutonic rock of crystalline texture, consisting mainly of pyroxene, plagioclase feldspar, and often olivine.
– DERIVATIVES **gabbroic** adjective.
– ORIGIN mid 19th cent.: from Italian, from Latin *glaber, glabr-* 'smooth'.

gabby ▶ **adjective (gabbier, gabbiest)** informal excessively or annoyingly talkative.

gaberdine /ˌɡabəˈdiːn, ˈɡabədiːn/ (also chiefly N. Amer. **gabardine**) ▶ **noun 1** [mass noun] a smooth, durable twill-woven worsted or cotton cloth. ■ [count noun] Brit. a raincoat made of gaberdine.
2 historical a long, loose upper garment, worn particularly by Jews.
– ORIGIN early 16th cent.: from Old French *gauvardine*, earlier *gallevardine*, perhaps from Middle High German *wallevart* 'pilgrimage' and originally 'a garment worn by a pilgrim'. The textile sense is first recorded in the early 20th cent.

Gabès /ˈɡɑːbɪs/ (also **Qabis**) an industrial seaport in eastern Tunisia; pop. 116,300 (est. 2004).

gabfest ▶ **noun** informal, chiefly N. Amer. a prolonged conference or other gathering with much talking.

gabion /ˈɡeɪbɪən/ ▶ **noun** a cylindrical basket or container filled with earth, stones, or other material and used in civil engineering works or (formerly) fortifications.
– ORIGIN mid 16th cent.: via French from Italian *gabbione*, from *gabbia* 'cage', from Latin *cavea*.

Gable, (William) Clark (1901–60), American actor, famous for films such as *It Happened One Night* (1934), for which he won an Oscar, and *Gone with the Wind* (1939).

gable ▶ **noun** the triangular upper part of a wall at the end of a ridged roof. ■ (also **gable end**) a wall topped with a gable. ■ a gable-shaped canopy over a window or door.
– DERIVATIVES **gabled** adjective.
– ORIGIN Middle English: via Old French from Old Norse *gafl*, of Germanic origin; related to Dutch *gaffel* and German *Gabel* 'fork' (the point of the gable originally being the fork of two crossed timbers supporting the end of the roof-tree).

gablet /ˈɡeɪblɪt/ ▶ **noun** Architecture a small ornamental gable over a buttress or similar feature.
– ORIGIN late Middle English: from **GABLE** + **-ET**[1].

Gabo /ˈɡɑːbəʊ/, Naum (1890–1977), Russian-born American sculptor, brother of Antoine Pevsner; born *Naum Neemia Pevsner*. A founder of Russian constructivism, Gabo experimented with kinetic art and transparent materials.

Gabon /ɡəˈbɒn/ an equatorial country in West Africa, on the Atlantic coast; pop. 1,515,000 (est. 2009); languages, French (official), West African languages; capital, Libreville. Gabon became a French territory in 1888. Part of French Equatorial Africa from 1910 to 1958, it became an independent republic in 1960.
– DERIVATIVES **Gabonese** /ˌɡabəˈniːz/ adjective & noun.

gaboon /ɡəˈbuːn/ (also **gaboon mahogany**) ▶ **noun** a tropical West African hardwood tree which is valued for its timber. ● *Aucoumea klaineana*, family Burseraceae.
– ORIGIN early 20th cent.: from *Gaboon* (now **GABON**).

Gaboon viper /ɡəˈbuːn/ ▶ **noun** a large, thick-bodied venomous African snake with a pair of horn-like scales on the snout, having a body richly patterned with brown, purple, and cream. ● *Bitis gabonica*, family Viperidae.
– ORIGIN early 20th cent.: named after *Gaboon* (now **GABON**).

Gabor /ˈɡɑːbɔː, ɡəˈbɔː/, Dennis (1900–79), Hungarian-born British electrical engineer, who conceived the idea of holography. Nobel Prize for Physics (1971).

Gaborone /ˌɡabəˈrəʊni/ the capital of Botswana, in the south of the country near the border with South Africa; pop. 223,200 (est. 2009).

Gabriel /ˈɡeɪbrɪəl/ (in the Bible) the archangel who foretold the birth of Jesus to the Virgin Mary (Luke 1:26–38), and who also appeared to Zacharias, father of John the Baptist, and to Daniel; (in Islam) the archangel who revealed the Koran to the Prophet Muhammad.

Gabrieli /ˌɡabrɪˈɛli, -ˈeɪli/, Giovanni (*c.*1556–1612), Italian composer and organist. He was a leading Venetian musician who wrote a large number of motets with instrumental accompaniments for St Mark's Cathedral.

Gad /ɡad/ (in the Bible) a Hebrew patriarch, son of Jacob and Zilpah. ■ the tribe of Israel traditionally descended from him.

gad[1] ▶ **verb (gads, gadding, gadded)** [no obj.] informal go from place to place in the pursuit of pleasure: *he had heard that I was **gadding about** with an airline stewardess.*
– PHRASES **on** (or **upon**) **the gad** archaic on the move.
– ORIGIN late Middle English: back-formation from obsolete *gadling* 'wanderer, vagabond', (earlier) 'companion', of Germanic origin.

gad[2] ▶ **exclamation** archaic an expression of surprise or emphatic assertion: *By gad! You look young for a doctor!*
– ORIGIN late 15th cent.: euphemistic alteration of **GOD**.

gadabout ▶ **noun** informal a habitual pleasure-seeker: *Walter was a restless charmer and a gadabout.*

Gadarene /ˈɡadəriːn/ ▶ **adjective** involving or engaged in a headlong or potentially disastrous rush to do something.
– ORIGIN early 19th cent.: from New Testament Greek *Gadarēnos* 'inhabitant of *Gadara*', with reference to the story of the swine that rushed down a steep cliff into the sea (Matt. 8:28–32).

Gaddafi /ɡəˈdɑːfi/ (also **Qaddafi**), Mu'ammer Muhammad al- (b.1942), Libyan colonel, head of state since 1970. After leading the coup which overthrew King Idris in 1969, he established the Libyan Arab Republic. He pursues an anti-colonial policy and has been accused of supporting international terrorism.

gadfly ▶ **noun** (pl. **gadflies**) a fly that bites livestock, especially a horsefly, warble fly, or botfly. ■ a person who annoys or criticizes others in order to provoke them into action.
– ORIGIN late 16th cent.: from **GAD**[1], or obsolete *gad* 'goad, spike', from Old Norse *gaddr*, of Germanic origin; related to **YARD**[1].

gadget ▶ **noun** a small mechanical device or tool, especially an ingenious or novel one.
– DERIVATIVES **gadgeteer** noun, **gadgetry** noun, **gadgety** adjective.
– ORIGIN late 19th cent. (originally in nautical use): probably from French *gâchette* 'lock mechanism' or from the French dialect word *gagée* 'tool'.

gadid /ˈɡeɪdɪd/ ▶ **noun** Zoology a fish of the cod family (Gadidae).
– ORIGIN late 19th cent.: from modern Latin *Gadidae* (plural), from *gadus* 'cod'.

gadoid /ˈɡeɪdɔɪd, ˈɡa-/ ▶ **noun** Zoology a bony fish of an order (Gadiformes) that comprises the cods, hakes, and their relatives.
▶ **adjective** relating to or denoting fish of this group.
– ORIGIN mid 19th cent.: from modern Latin *gadus* (from Greek *gados* 'cod') + **-OID**.

gadolinite /ˈɡad(ə)lɪnʌɪt, ɡəˈdəʊlɪnʌɪt/ ▶ **noun** [mass noun] a rare dark brown or black mineral, consisting of a silicate of iron, beryllium, and rare earths.
– ORIGIN early 19th cent.: named after Johan *Gadolin* (1760–1852), the Finnish mineralogist who first identified it.

gadolinium /ˌgadəˈlɪnɪəm/ ▸ **noun** [mass noun] the chemical element of atomic number 64, a soft silvery-white metal of the lanthanide series. (Symbol: **Gd**)
– ORIGIN late 19th cent.: from GADOLINITE.

gadroon /gəˈdruːn/ ▸ **noun** a decorative edging on metal or wood formed by parallel rounded strips (reeding) like inverted fluting.
– DERIVATIVES **gadrooned** adjective, **gadrooning** noun.
– ORIGIN late 17th cent.: from French *godron*, probably related to *goder* 'to pucker', also to GODET.

gadwall /ˈgadwɔːl/ ▸ **noun** (pl. **same** or **gadwalls**) a brownish-grey freshwater duck found across Eurasia and North America. ● *Anas strepera*, family Anatidae.
– ORIGIN mid 17th cent.: of unknown origin.

gadzooks /gadˈzuːks/ ▸ **exclamation** archaic an exclamation of surprise or annoyance.
– ORIGIN late 17th cent.: alteration of *God's hooks*, i.e. the nails by which Christ was fastened to the cross; see GAD².

Gaea /ˈdʒiːə/ variant spelling of GAIA (sense 1).

Gael /geɪl/ ▸ **noun** a Gaelic-speaking person.
– DERIVATIVES **Gaeldom** noun.
– ORIGIN from Scottish Gaelic *Gaidheal*.

Gaelic /ˈgeɪlɪk, ˈgalɪk/ ▸ **adjective** relating to the Goidelic group of Celtic languages, particularly Scottish Gaelic, and the speakers of these languages and their culture.
▸ **noun** (also **Scottish Gaelic**) [mass noun] a Celtic language spoken in the highlands and islands of western Scotland. It was brought from Ireland in the 5th and 6th centuries AD and is now spoken by about 40,000 people. ■ (also **Irish Gaelic**) another term for IRISH (the language).

Gaelic coffee ▸ **noun** [mass noun] coffee served with cream and whisky.

Gaelic football ▸ **noun** [mass noun] a type of football played mainly in Ireland between teams of fifteen players, with a goal resembling that used in rugby but having a net attached. The object is to kick or punch the round ball into the net (scoring three points) or over the crossbar (one point).

Gaelic League a movement founded in 1893 to revive Irish language and culture.

Gaeltacht /ˈgeɪltəxt/, Irish /ˈgeːltəxt/ (**the Gaeltacht**) a region of Ireland in which the vernacular language is Irish.
– ORIGIN Irish, earlier *Gaedhealtacht*, from *Gaedheal* 'Gael' + *tacht* 'talk, speech'.

gaff¹ ▸ **noun 1** a stick with a hook or barbed spear, for landing large fish.
2 Sailing a spar to which the head of a fore-and-aft sail is bent.
▸ **verb** [with obj.] seize or impale with a gaff.
– ORIGIN Middle English: from Provençal *gaf* 'hook'; related to GAFFE.

gaff² ▸ **noun** (in phrase **blow the gaff**) Brit. informal reveal a plot or secret.
– ORIGIN early 19th cent.: of unknown origin.

gaff³ ▸ **noun** Brit. informal a house, flat, or other building, especially as being a person's home: *Gav's new gaff is in McDonald Road*.
– ORIGIN 1930s: of unknown origin.

gaffe /gaf/ ▸ **noun** an unintentional act or remark causing embarrassment to its originator; a blunder.
– ORIGIN early 20th cent.: from French, literally 'boathook' (from Provençal *gaf*: see GAFF¹), used colloquially to mean 'blunder'.

gaffer ▸ **noun 1** Brit. informal a person in charge of others; a boss.
2 the chief electrician in a film or television production unit.
3 informal an old man.
– ORIGIN late 16th cent. (in sense 3): probably a contraction of GODFATHER; compare with GAMMER.

gaffer tape ▸ **noun** [mass noun] strong cloth-backed waterproof adhesive tape.

gag¹ ▸ **noun 1** a piece of cloth put in or over a person's mouth to prevent them from speaking. ■ a restriction on dissemination of information: *every contract contains a self-signed gag*.
2 a device for keeping the patient's mouth open during a dental or surgical operation.
▸ **verb** (**gags, gagging, gagged**) **1** [with obj.] put a gag on (someone). ■ prevent (someone) from speaking freely or disseminating information: *the government is trying to gag its critics* | (as adj. **gagging**) *a gagging order*.
2 [no obj.] choke or retch: *he gagged on the wine*.
– ORIGIN Middle English: perhaps related to Old Norse *gaghâls* 'with the neck thrown back', or imitative of a person choking.

gag² ▸ **noun** a joke or an amusing story, especially one forming part of a comedian's act or in a film.
▸ **verb** [no obj.] tell jokes.
– ORIGIN mid 19th cent. (originally theatrical slang): of unknown origin.

gaga /ˈgɑːgɑː, ˈgagə/ ▸ **adjective** informal slightly mad, typically as a result of old age, infatuation, or excessive enthusiasm.
– ORIGIN early 20th cent.: from French, 'senile, a senile person', reduplication based on *gâteux*, variant of *gâteur*, hospital slang in the sense 'bed-wetter'.

Gagarin /gəˈgɑːrɪn/, Yuri (Alekseevich) (1934–68), Russian cosmonaut. In 1961 he made the first manned space flight, completing a single orbit of the earth in 108 minutes.

Gagauz /gəˈgaʊz/ ▸ **noun** (pl. **same**) **1** a member of a people living mainly in southern Moldova and speaking a Turkic language.
2 [mass noun] the language of the Gagauz, closely related to Turkish and having about 150,000 speakers.
▸ **adjective** relating to the Gagauz or their language.
– ORIGIN probably from Persian *Kaykaus*, perhaps from the name of Sultan Izzedin *Kaykaus* (reigned 1242–57).

gage¹ /geɪdʒ/ archaic ▸ **noun** a valued object deposited as a guarantee of good faith. ■ a pledge, especially a glove, thrown down as a symbol of a challenge to fight.
▸ **verb** [with obj.] offer (an object or one's life) as a guarantee of good faith.
– ORIGIN Middle English: from Old French *gage* (noun), *gager* (verb), of Germanic origin; related to WAGE and WED.

gage² ▸ **noun & verb** variant spelling of GAUGE.

gage³ /geɪdʒ/ ▸ **noun** another term for GREENGAGE.
– ORIGIN mid 19th cent.: from the name of Sir William *Gage* (1657–1727), the English botanist who introduced it to England.

gaggle ▸ **noun 1** a flock of geese.
2 informal a disorderly group of people: *the gaggle of photographers that dogged his every step*.
– ORIGIN Middle English (as a verb): imitative of the noise that a goose makes; compare with Dutch *gaggelen* and German *gackern*.

gagster ▸ **noun** a writer or performer of gags.

gah /gɑː/ ▸ **exclamation** used to express exasperation or dismay: *had to go the dentist this morning (arrived late—gah!)*.
– ORIGIN early 20th cent.: natural exclamation.

Gaia /ˈgʌɪə/ **1** (also **Gaea, Ge**) Greek Mythology the Earth personified as a goddess, daughter of Chaos. She was the mother and wife of Uranus (Heaven); their offspring included the Titans and the Cyclops.
2 the earth viewed as a vast self-regulating organism (see GAIA HYPOTHESIS).
– DERIVATIVES **Gaian** noun & adjective.
– ORIGIN Greek, 'Earth'. Sense 2 was coined by James Lovelock, at the suggestion of the writer William Golding.

Gaia hypothesis ▸ **noun** the theory, put forward by James Lovelock, that living matter on the earth collectively defines and regulates the material conditions necessary for the continuance of life. The planet, or rather the biosphere, is thus likened to a vast self-regulating organism.

gaiety (US also **gayety**) ▸ **noun** (pl. **gaieties**) [mass noun] the state or quality of being light-hearted or cheerful: *the sudden gaiety of children's laughter*. ■ lively celebration or festivities: *he seemed to be a part of the gaiety, having a wonderful time*. ■ (**gaieties**) dated entertainments or amusements.
– PHRASES **the gaiety of nations** Brit., often ironic general cheerfulness or amusement: *editors added to the gaiety of nations by suing each other*.
– ORIGIN mid 17th cent.: from French *gaieté*, from *gai* (see GAY).

gaijin /gʌɪˈdʒɪn/ ▸ **noun** (pl. **same**) (in Japan) a foreigner.
– ORIGIN Japanese, contraction of *gaikoku-jin*, from *gaikoku* 'foreign country' + *jin* 'person'.

gaillardia /geɪˈlɑːdɪə/ ▸ **noun** an American plant of the daisy family, which is cultivated for its bright red and yellow flowers. ● Genus *Gaillardia*, family Compositae.
– ORIGIN modern Latin, named after *Gaillard* de Marentonneau, 18th-cent. French amateur botanist.

gaily ▸ **adverb 1** in a cheerful or light-hearted way. ■ without thinking of the consequences: *she plunged gaily into speculation on the stock market*.
2 [as submodifier] with a bright or attractive appearance: *gaily coloured sailing boats*.

gain ▸ **verb** [with obj.] **1** obtain or secure (something wanted or desirable): *we gained entry to the car in five seconds* | [with two objs] *their blend of acoustic pop gained them several chart hits*. ■ [no obj.] benefit: *managers would* **gain from** *greater openness*. ■ archaic win over to one's interest or views: *to gratify the queen, and gain the court*.
2 reach or arrive at (a destination): *we gained the ridge*. ■ [no obj.] (**gain on**) come closer to (a person or thing pursued): *a huge bear was gaining on him with every stride*.
3 increase the amount or rate of (something, typically weight or speed): *she had gained weight since her wedding*. ■ [no obj.] increase in value: *shares gained for the third day in a row*. ■ [no obj.] (**gain in**) improve or advance in (some respect): *canoeing is gaining in popularity*. ■ (of a clock or watch) become fast by (a specific amount of time): *this atomic clock will neither gain nor lose a second in the next 1 million years*.
▸ **noun** [mass noun] **1** an increase in wealth or resources: *the pursuit of personal gain* | [count noun] *shares showed gains of up to 21 per cent*. ■ a thing that is achieved or acquired: *the potential gain from rail privatization would be a more commercial railway*.
2 the factor by which power or voltage is increased in an amplifier or other electronic device, usually expressed as a logarithm.
– PHRASES **gain time** obtain extra time to achieve something by deliberate delaying tactics: *the government was using the negotiations to gain time*.
– DERIVATIVES **gainer** noun.
– ORIGIN late 15th cent. (as a noun, originally in the sense 'booty'): from Old French *gaigne* (noun), *gaignier* (verb), of Germanic origin.

gainful ▸ **adjective** [attrib.] serving to increase wealth or resources: *he soon found gainful employment*.
– DERIVATIVES **gainfully** adverb, **gainfulness** noun.

gainsay /geɪnˈseɪ/ ▸ **verb** (past and past participle **gainsaid**) [with obj.] [with negative] formal deny or contradict (a fact or statement): *the impact of the railways cannot be gainsaid*. ■ speak against or oppose (someone).
– DERIVATIVES **gainsayer** noun.
– ORIGIN Middle English: from obsolete *gain-* 'against' + SAY.

Gainsborough /ˈgeɪnzbərə/, Thomas (1727–88), English painter. He was famous for his society portraits, including *Mr and Mrs Andrews* (1748) and *The Blue Boy* (*c.*1770), and for landscapes such as *The Watering Place* (1777).

'gainst ▸ **preposition** literary short for AGAINST.

gait /geɪt/ ▸ **noun** a person's manner of walking: *the easy gait of an athlete*. ■ the pattern of steps of a horse or dog at a particular speed.
– ORIGIN late Middle English (originally Scots): variant of GATE².

gaita /ˈgʌɪtə/ ▸ **noun** a kind of bagpipe played in northern Spain and Portugal.
– ORIGIN Spanish and Portuguese.

gaiter ▸ **noun** (usu. **gaiters**) a protective covering of cloth or leather for the ankle and lower leg. ■ chiefly US a shoe or overshoe extending to the ankle or above. ■ a flexible covering for the base of a gear lever or other mechanical part.
– DERIVATIVES **gaitered** adjective.
– ORIGIN early 18th cent.: from French *guêtre*, probably of Germanic origin and related to WRIST.

Gaitskell /ˈgeɪtskɪl/, Hugh (Todd Naylor) (1906–63), British Labour statesman, Chancellor of the Exchequer 1950–1 and leader of the Labour Party 1955–63. He opposed the government over the Suez crisis and resisted calls within his own party for unilateral disarmament.

gal¹ ▸ **noun** informal, chiefly N. Amer. a girl or young woman.
– ORIGIN late 18th cent.: representing a pronunciation.

gal² ▸ **noun** Physics a unit of gravitational acceleration equal to one centimetre per second per second.
– ORIGIN early 20th cent.: named after GALILEO GALILEI.

Gal. ▸ **abbreviation** Epistle to the Galatians (in biblical references).

gal. ▸ **abbreviation** gallon(s).

gala /ˈgɑːlə, ˈgeɪlə/ ▸ **noun** a social occasion with special entertainments or performances: [as modifier] *a gala performance by the Royal Ballet*. ■ Brit. a special sports meeting, especially a swimming competition.

– ORIGIN early 17th cent. (in the sense 'showy dress'): via Italian and Spanish from Old French *gale* 'rejoicing'.

galactagogue /gəˈlaktəgɒg/ ▶ **noun** Medicine a food or drug that promotes or increases the flow of a mother's milk.
– ORIGIN mid 19th cent.: from Greek *gala, galakt-* 'milk' + *agōgos* 'leading'.

galactic /gəˈlaktɪk/ ▶ **adjective** relating to a galaxy or galaxies, especially the galaxy containing the solar system. ■ Astronomy measured relative to the galactic equator.
– DERIVATIVES **galactically** adverb.
– ORIGIN mid 19th cent.: from Greek *galaktias* (variant of *galaxias* 'galaxy') + **-IC**.

galactic equator ▶ **noun** Astronomy the great circle of the celestial sphere passing as closely as possible through the densest parts of the Milky Way.

galactico /gəˈlaktɪkəʊ/ ▶ **noun** (pl. **galacticos**) informal an exceptionally skilled and celebrated soccer player.
– ORIGIN early 21st cent.: Spanish *galáctico*, literally 'galactic person' (i.e. bigger than a 'star').

G

galactorrhoea /gəˌlaktəˈriːə/ ▶ **noun** [mass noun] Medicine excessive or inappropriate production of milk.
– ORIGIN mid 19th cent.: from Greek *gala, galakt-* 'milk' + *rhoia* 'flux, flow'.

galactosamine /ˌgalakˈtəʊsəmiːn/ ▶ **noun** Biochemistry a crystalline amino sugar, of which chondroitin is a derivative. ● Chem. formula: $C_6H_{13}NO_5$.
– ORIGIN early 20th cent.: from **GALACTOSE** + **AMINE**.

galactose /gəˈlaktəʊz, -s/ ▶ **noun** [mass noun] Chemistry a sugar of the hexose class which is a constituent of lactose and many polysaccharides.
– ORIGIN mid 19th cent.: from Greek *gala, galaktos* 'milk' + **-OSE²**.

galago /gəˈleɪgəʊ/ ▶ **noun** (pl. **galagos**) another term for **BUSHBABY**.
– ORIGIN modern Latin (genus name).

galah /gəˈlɑː/ ▶ **noun 1** a small Australian cockatoo with a grey back and rosy pink head and underparts. ● *Eulophus roseicapillus*, family Cacatuidae (or Psittacidae).
2 Austral. informal a stupid person.
– ORIGIN mid 19th cent.: from Yuwaalaraay (an Aboriginal language of New South Wales).

Galahad /ˈgaləhad/ (also **Sir Galahad**) the noblest of King Arthur's knights, renowned for immaculate purity and destined to find the Holy Grail. ■ (as noun **a (Sir) Galahad**) a person characterized by nobility, integrity, or courtesy.

galangal /ˈgal(ə)ŋgal/ (also **galingale**) ▶ **noun** [mass noun] an Asian plant of the ginger family, the aromatic rhizome of which is widely used in cookery and herbal medicine. ● Genera *Alpinia* and *Kaempferia*, family Zingiberaceae.
– ORIGIN Middle English *galingale*, via Old French from Arabic *ḵalanjān*, perhaps from Chinese *gāoliángjiāng*, from *gāoliáng* (the name of a district in Guangdong Province, China) + *jiāng* 'ginger'.

galant /gaˈlant, gaˈlɒ̃/ ▶ **adjective** relating to or denoting a light and elegant style of 18th-century music.
– ORIGIN French and German (see **GALLANT**).

galantine /ˈgal(ə)ntiːn/ ▶ **noun** [mass noun] a dish of white meat or fish boned, cooked, pressed, and served cold in aspic.
– ORIGIN Middle English (in the sense 'sauce for fish'): from Old French, alteration of *galatine*, from medieval Latin *galatina*; the current sense dates from the early 18th cent.

Galapagos finches ▶ **plural noun** another term for **DARWIN'S FINCHES**.

Galapagos Islands /gəˈlapəgəs/ a Pacific archipelago on the equator, about 1,045 km (650 miles) west of Ecuador, to which it belongs; pop. 28,000 (est. 2009). Spanish name **ARCHIPIÉLAGO DE COLÓN**.

> The islands are noted for their abundant wildlife, including giant tortoises and many other endemic species. They were the site of Charles Darwin's observations of 1835, which helped him to form his theory of natural selection.

Galatea /ˌgaləˈtɪə/ Greek Mythology **1** a sea nymph courted by the Cyclops Polyphemus, who in jealousy killed his rival Acis.
2 the name given to the statue fashioned by Pygmalion and brought to life.

Galaţi /gaˈlats/ an industrial city in eastern Romania, a river port on the lower Danube; pop. 296,697 (2006).

Galatia /gəˈleɪʃə/ an ancient region in central Asia Minor, settled by invading Gauls (the Galatians) in the 3rd century BC. It later became a province of the Roman Empire.
– DERIVATIVES **Galatian** adjective & noun.

Galatians, Epistle to the /gəˈleɪʃ(ə)nz/ a book of the New Testament, an epistle of St Paul to the Church in Galatia.

galaxy ▶ **noun** (pl. **galaxies**) a system of millions or billions of stars, together with gas and dust, held together by gravitational attraction. ■ **(the Galaxy)** the galaxy of which the solar system is a part; the Milky Way. ■ a large group of impressive people or things: *the four musicians have played with a galaxy of stars*.
– ORIGIN late Middle English (originally referring to the Milky Way): via Old French from medieval Latin *galaxia*, from Greek *galaxias* (*kuklos*) 'milky (vault)', from *gala, galakt-* 'milk'.

Galba /ˈgalbə/ (*c.*3 BC–AD 69), Roman emperor AD 68–9; full name *Servius Sulpicius Galba*. The successor to Nero, he aroused hostility by his severity and parsimony and was murdered in a conspiracy organized by Otho.

galbanum /ˈgalbənəm/ ▶ **noun** [mass noun] a bitter aromatic resin produced from kinds of ferula.
– ORIGIN Middle English: via Latin from Greek *khalbanē*, probably of Semitic origin.

Galbraith /galˈbreɪθ/, John Kenneth (1908–2006), Canadian-born American economist. He was well known for his criticism of consumerism and of the power of large multinational corporations.

gale ▶ **noun 1** a very strong wind: [as modifier] *gale-force winds*. ■ (also **fresh gale**) (on the Beaufort scale) a wind of force 8 (34–40 knots or 63–74 kph). ■ a storm at sea.
2 (**a gale of/gales of**) an outburst of laughter: *she collapsed into gales of laughter*.
– ORIGIN mid 16th cent.: perhaps related to Old Norse *galinn* 'mad, frantic'.

galea /ˈgeɪlɪə/ ▶ **noun** (pl. **galeae** /-lɪiː/ or **galeas**) Botany & Zoology a structure shaped like a helmet.
– ORIGIN mid 19th cent.: from Latin, literally 'helmet'.

Galen /ˈgeɪlən/ (129–99), Greek physician; full name *Claudios Galenos*; Latin name *Claudius Galenus*. He attempted to systematize the whole of medicine, making important discoveries in anatomy and physiology. His works became influential in Europe when retranslated from Arabic in the 12th century.

galena /gəˈliːnə/ ▶ **noun** [mass noun] a bluish, grey, or black mineral of metallic appearance, consisting of lead sulphide. It is the chief ore of lead.
– ORIGIN late 17th cent.: from Latin, 'lead ore' (in a partly purified state).

galenic /gəˈlɛnɪk/ ▶ **adjective 1** (**Galenic**) Medicine relating to Galen or his methods.
2 (of a medicine) galenical.

galenical Medicine ▶ **adjective 1** (of a medicine) made of natural rather than synthetic components.
2 (**Galenical**) relating to Galen.
▶ **noun** a medicine made of natural rather than synthetic components.

galère /gaˈlɛː/, French /galɛʀ/ ▶ **noun** an undesirable group or coterie: *the repulsive galère of Lolita's admirers*.
– ORIGIN French, literally 'galley'. The term was used in Molière's play *Scapin* meaning 'coterie'.

galette /gəˈlɛt/ ▶ **noun** a flat round cake of pastry or bread. ■ a savoury pancake made from potatoes or buckwheat.
– ORIGIN French, from Old French *galet* 'pebble'.

gali /ˈgʌli/ ▶ **noun** (pl. **galis**) Indian variant spelling of **GULLY** (sense 3 of the noun).

galia melon /ˈgɑːlɪə/ ▶ **noun** a small rounded melon of a variety with rough skin and fragrant orange flesh.
– ORIGIN from the Hebrew given name *Galia*.

Galibi /gəˈliːbi/ ▶ **noun** another term for **CARIB** (sense 2 of the noun).
– ORIGIN Carib, literally 'strong man'.

Galicia /gəˈlɪsɪə, -ˈlɪʃə/, Spanish /gaˈliθja, -sja/ **1** an autonomous region and former kingdom of NW Spain; capital, Santiago de Compostela.
2 a region of east central Europe, north of the Carpathian Mountains. A former province of Austria, it now forms part of SE Poland and western Ukraine.

Galician ▶ **adjective 1** relating to Galicia in NW Spain, its people, or their language.
2 relating to Galicia in east central Europe.
▶ **noun 1** a native or inhabitant of Galicia in NW Spain. ■ [mass noun] the language of Galicia in NW Spain, a Romance language closely related to Portuguese. It is spoken by about 3 million people, most of whom also speak Spanish.
2 a native or inhabitant of Galicia in east central Europe.

Galilean¹ /ˌgalɪˈleɪən/ ▶ **adjective** relating to Galileo or his methods.

Galilean² /ˌgalɪˈliːən/ ▶ **adjective** relating to Galilee. ■ archaic, derogatory Christian.
▶ **noun** a native or inhabitant of Galilee. ■ archaic, derogatory a Christian.

Galilean moons Astronomy the four largest satellites of Jupiter (Callisto, Europa, Ganymede, and Io), discovered by Galileo in 1610 and independently by the German astronomer Simon Marius (1573–1624).

Galilean telescope ▶ **noun** an astronomical telescope of the earliest type, with a biconvex objective and biconcave eyepiece.

Galilee /ˈgalɪliː/ a northern region of ancient Palestine, west of the River Jordan, associated with the ministry of Jesus. It is now part of Israel.

galilee /ˈgalɪliː/ ▶ **noun** a chapel or porch at the entrance of a church.
– ORIGIN Middle English: from Old French, from medieval Latin *galilea* 'Galilee'. Compare with **GALLERY**.

Galilee, Sea of a lake in northern Israel. The River Jordan flows through it from north to south. Also called **TIBERIAS, LAKE, KINNERET, LAKE**.

Galileo /ˌgalɪˈleɪəʊ/ an American space probe to Jupiter, launched in 1989. It reached the vicinity of Jupiter in 1995 and released a probe which descended into Jupiter's atmosphere.

Galileo Galilei /ˌgalɪˈleɪəʊ ˌgalɪˈleɪi/ (1564–1642), Italian astronomer and physicist. He discovered the constancy of a pendulum's swing, formulated the law of uniform acceleration of falling bodies, and described the parabolic trajectory of projectiles. He applied the telescope to astronomy and observed craters on the moon, sunspots, Jupiter's moons, and the phases of Venus.

galingale /ˈgalɪŋgeɪl/ ▶ **noun 1** (also **English galingale** or **sweet galingale**) a Eurasian sedge with an aromatic rhizome, formerly used in perfumes. ● *Cyperus longus*, family Cyperaceae.
2 variant spelling of **GALANGAL**.
– ORIGIN late 16th cent.: variant of **GALANGAL**.

galiot ▶ **noun** variant spelling of **GALLIOT**.

galipot /ˈgalɪpɒt/ ▶ **noun** [mass noun] hardened resin deposits formed on the stem of the maritime pine.
– ORIGIN late 18th cent.: from French, of unknown origin.

galjoen /xalˈjʊn/ ▶ **noun** (pl. **same**) a deep-bodied marine fish with a spiny dorsal fin, occurring in shallow waters around South Africa. Also called **BLACKFISH**. ● *Coracinus capensis*, family Coracinidae.
– ORIGIN mid 19th cent.: from Afrikaans and Dutch, literally 'galleon'.

gall¹ /gɔːl/ ▶ **noun** [mass noun] **1** bold and impudent behaviour: *the bank had the gall to demand a fee*.
2 the contents of the gall bladder; bile (proverbial for its bitterness). ■ [count noun] an animal's gall bladder. ■ used to refer to something bitter or cruel: *accept life's gall without blaming somebody else*.
– ORIGIN Old English *gealla* (denoting bile), of Germanic origin; related to Dutch *gal*, German *Galle* 'gall', from an Indo-European root shared by Greek *kholē* and Latin *fel* 'bile'.

gall² /gɔːl/ ▶ **noun 1** [mass noun] annoyance or resentment: *he imagined Linda's gall as she found herself still married and not rich*.
2 a sore on the skin made by chafing.
▶ **verb** [with obj.] **1** make (someone) feel annoyed or resentful: *it galled him to have to sit impotently in silence*.
2 make sore by rubbing.
– ORIGIN Old English *gealle* 'sore on a horse', perhaps related to **GALL¹**; superseded in Middle English by forms from Middle Low German or Middle Dutch.

gall³ /gɔːl/ ▶ **noun** an abnormal growth formed in response to the presence of insect larvae, mites, or fungi on plants and trees, especially oaks. ■ [as modifier] denoting insects or mites that produce galls: *gall flies*.
– ORIGIN Middle English: via Old French from Latin *galla*.

gall. ▶ **abbreviation** gallon(s).

Galla /ˈgalə/ ▶ **noun & adjective** another term for **OROMO**.
– ORIGIN of unknown origin.

gallant ▶ adjective **1** /ˈgal(ə)nt/ (of a person or their behaviour) brave; heroic: *she had made gallant efforts to pull herself together.* ■ archaic grand or impressive: *they made a gallant array as they marched off.*
2 /ˈgal(ə)nt, gəˈlant/ (of a man) charmingly attentive and chivalrous to women.
▶ noun /ˈgal(ə)nt, gəˈlant/ archaic a man who is charmingly attentive to women. ■ a dashing and fashionable gentleman.
▶ verb /gəˈlant, ˈgal(ə)nt/ [with obj.] archaic (of a man) flirt with (a woman).
– DERIVATIVES **gallantly** adverb.
– ORIGIN Middle English (in the sense 'finely dressed'): from Old French *galant*, from *galer* 'have fun, make a show', from *gale* 'pleasure, rejoicing'.

gallantry ▶ noun (pl. **gallantries**) [mass noun] **1** courageous behaviour, especially in battle: *a medal awarded for outstanding gallantry during the raid.*
2 polite attention or respect given by men to women. ■ [count noun] (**gallantries**) gallant actions or words. ■ archaic sexual intrigue.
– ORIGIN late 16th cent. (in the sense 'splendour, ornamentation'): from French *galanterie*, from *galant* (see **GALLANT**).

gallate /ˈgaleɪt/ ▶ noun Chemistry a salt or ester of gallic acid.

gallberry /ˈgɔːlb(ə)ri, -bɛri/ ▶ noun (pl. **gallberries**) another term for **INKBERRY**.

gall bladder ▶ noun the small sac-shaped organ beneath the liver, in which bile is stored after secretion by the liver and before release into the intestine.

Galle /ˈgɑːlə/ a seaport on the SW coast of Sri Lanka; pop. 95,000 (est. 2007).

galleon ▶ noun a sailing ship in use (especially by Spain) from the 15th to the 18th centuries, originally as a warship, later for trade. Galleons were typically square-rigged and had three or more decks and masts.
– ORIGIN early 16th cent.: either via Middle Dutch from French *galion*, from *galie* 'galley', or from Spanish *galeón*.

galleria /ˌgaləˈriːə/ ▶ noun a collection of small shops under a single roof; an arcade.
– ORIGIN Italian (see **GALLERY**).

gallery ▶ noun (pl. **galleries**) **1** a room or building for the display or sale of works of art. ■ a collection of pictures.
2 a balcony or upper floor projecting from an interior back or side wall of a hall or church, providing space for an audience or musicians. ■ (**the gallery**) the highest balcony in a theatre, containing the cheapest seats. ■ a group of spectators, especially those at a golf tournament.
3 a long room or passage, typically one that is partly open at the side to form a portico or colonnade. ■ a horizontal underground passage, especially in a mine.
– PHRASES **play to the gallery** act in an exaggerated way in order to appeal to popular taste.
– DERIVATIVES **galleried** adjective.
– ORIGIN late Middle English (in sense 3): via Old French from Italian *galleria* 'gallery', formerly also 'church porch', from medieval Latin *galeria*, perhaps an alteration of *galilea* (see **GALILEE**).

gallery forest ▶ noun a forest restricted to the banks of a river or stream.

gallery grave ▶ noun Archaeology an underground megalithic burial chamber which may be divided into sections but has no separate entrance passage.

gallet /ˈgalɪt/ ▶ noun a chip or splinter of stone inserted into wet mortar.
– ORIGIN early 18th cent.: from French *galet* 'rounded beach pebble', from Old French *gal* 'pebble, stone'.

galley ▶ noun (pl. **galleys**) **1** historical a low, flat ship with one or more sails and up to three banks of oars, chiefly used for warfare or piracy and often manned by slaves or criminals. ■ a large open rowing boat kept on a warship for use by the captain.
2 the kitchen in a ship or aircraft.
3 (also **galley proof**) a printer's proof in the form of long single-column strips, not in sheets or pages. [*galley* from French *galée* denoting an oblong tray for holding set-up type.]
– ORIGIN Middle English: via Old French from medieval Latin *galea*, from medieval Greek *galaia*, of unknown origin.

galley slave ▶ noun historical a person condemned to man the oars in a galley. ■ a person who works very hard, typically performing menial or thankless tasks: *call-centre workers are the galley slaves of the twenty-first century.*

galliambic /ˌgalɪˈambɪk/ Prosody ▶ adjective relating to or written in a metre consisting of two catalectic iambic dimeters.
▶ noun (usu. **galliambics**) galliambic verse.
– ORIGIN mid 19th cent.: from Latin *galliambus*, a song of the *Galli* (name given to priests of Cybele) + **-IC**.

Gallia Narbonensis /ˌgalɪə ˌnɑːbəˈnɛnsɪs/ the southern province of Transalpine Gaul.

Galliano /ˌgalɪˈɑːnəʊ/ ▶ noun [mass noun] a golden-yellow Italian liqueur flavoured with herbs.
– ORIGIN named after Major Giuseppe *Galliáno*, noted for halting Ethiopian forces in the war of 1895–6.

galliard /ˈgalɪɑːd, -ɪəd/ ▶ noun historical a lively dance in triple time for two people, including complicated turns and steps.
– ORIGIN late Middle English (as an adjective meaning 'valiant, sturdy' and 'lively, brisk'): from Old French *gaillard* 'valiant', of Celtic origin. The current sense dates from the mid 16th cent.

galliass /ˈgalɪəs/ ▶ noun a large type of galley, chiefly used during the 16th and 17th centuries.
– ORIGIN mid 16th cent.: from Old French *galleasse*, from Italian *galeaza* 'large galley', from *galea* (see **GALLEY**).

Gallic /ˈgalɪk/ ▶ adjective **1** of or characteristic of France or the French: *a Gallic shrug.*
2 relating to the Gauls.
– ORIGIN late 17th cent.: from Latin *Gallicus*, from *Gallus* 'a Gaul'.

gallic acid ▶ noun [mass noun] Chemistry an acid extracted from oak galls and other vegetable products, formerly used in making ink. ● Alternative name: **3,4,5-trihydroxybenzoic acid**; chem. formula: $C_6H_2(OH)_3COOH$.
– ORIGIN late 18th cent.: *gallic* from Latin *galla* 'oak gall' (see **GALL[3]**) + **-IC**.

Gallican /ˈgalɪk(ə)n/ ▶ adjective **1** relating to the ancient Church of Gaul or France.
2 of or holding a doctrine (reaching its peak in the 17th century) which asserted the freedom of the Roman Catholic Church in France and elsewhere from the ecclesiastical authority of the papacy. Compare with **ULTRAMONTANE**.
▶ noun an adherent of the Gallican doctrine.
– DERIVATIVES **Gallicanism** noun.
– ORIGIN late Middle English: from Old French *gallican*, or from Latin *Gallicanus*, from *Gallicus* (see **GALLIC**).

gallice /ˈgalɪsi/ ▶ adverb archaic in French.
– ORIGIN Latin, 'in Gaulish'.

Gallicism /ˈgalɪˌsɪz(ə)m/ ▶ noun a French idiom, especially one adopted by speakers of another language.
– ORIGIN mid 17th cent.: from French *gallicisme*, from Latin *Gallicus* (see **GALLIC**).

Gallic Wars Julius Caesar's campaigns 58–51 BC, which established Roman control over Gaul north of the Alps and west of the River Rhine (Transalpine Gaul). During this period Caesar twice invaded Britain (55 and 54 BC).

galligaskins /ˌgalɪˈgaskɪnz/ ▶ plural noun Brit. historical breeches, trousers, or gaiters.
– ORIGIN late 16th cent.: perhaps an alteration (influenced by *galley* and *Gascon*) of obsolete French *gargesque*, from Italian *grechesca*, feminine of *grechesco* 'Greek'.

gallimaufry /ˌgalɪˈmɔːfri/ ▶ noun [in sing.] a confused jumble or medley of things.
– ORIGIN mid 16th cent.: from archaic French *galimafrée* 'unappetizing dish', perhaps from Old French *galer* 'have fun' + Picard *mafrer* 'eat copious quantities'.

gallimimus /ˌgalɪˈmʌɪməs/ ▶ noun an ostrich dinosaur of the late Cretaceous period. ● Genus *Gallimimus*, infraorder Ornithomimosauria, suborder Theropoda.
– ORIGIN modern Latin, from Latin *galli* 'of a cockerel' (genitive of *gallus*) + *mimus* 'mime, pretence'.

gallinaceous /ˌgalɪˈneɪʃəs/ ▶ adjective dated relating to birds of an order (Galliformes) which includes domestic poultry and game birds.
– ORIGIN late 18th cent.: from Latin *gallinaceus* (from *gallina* 'hen', from *gallus* 'cock') + **-OUS**.

galling /ˈgɔːlɪŋ/ ▶ adjective causing annoyance or resentment; annoying: *it would be galling to lose your job because of a dispute with a customer.*
– DERIVATIVES **gallingly** adverb.

gallinule /ˈgalɪnjuːl/ ▶ noun a marshbird of the rail family, with mainly black, purplish-blue, or dark green plumage and a red bill. ● Genera *Porphyrio* and *Porphyrula* (or *Gallinula*), family Rallidae: several species.
– ORIGIN late 18th cent.: from modern Latin *Gallinula* (genus term), diminutive of Latin *gallina* 'hen', from *gallus* 'cock'.

galliot /ˈgalɪət/ (also **galiot**) ▶ noun historical a single-masted Dutch cargo boat or fishing vessel. ■ a small, fast galley used in the Mediterranean.
– ORIGIN Middle English: from Old French *galiote* or Dutch *galjoot*, from a diminutive of medieval Latin *galea* 'galley'.

Gallipoli /gəˈlɪpəli/ a major campaign of the First World War which took place on the Gallipoli peninsula, on the European side of the Dardanelles, in 1915–16. The Allies (with heavy involvement of troops from Australia and New Zealand) hoped to gain control of the strait, but the campaign reached stalemate after each side suffered heavy casualties.

gallipot /ˈgalɪpɒt/ ▶ noun historical a small pot made from glazed earthenware or metal, used by pharmacists to hold medicines or ointments.
– ORIGIN late Middle English: probably from **GALLEY** + **POT[1]** (because gallipots were brought from the Mediterranean in galleys).

gallium /ˈgalɪəm/ ▶ noun [mass noun] the chemical element of atomic number 31, a soft silvery-white metal which melts at about 30°C, just above room temperature. (Symbol: **Ga**)
– ORIGIN late 19th cent.: modern Latin, from Latin *Gallia* 'France' or *gallus* 'cock'; named (either patriotically or as a translation of his own name) by Paul-Émile *Lecoq de Boisbaudran* (1838–1912), the French chemist who discovered it in 1875.

gallivant /ˈgalɪvant, ˌgalɪˈvant/ ▶ verb [no obj., with adverbial] informal go around from one place to another in the pursuit of pleasure or entertainment: *she quit her job to go gallivanting around the globe.*
– ORIGIN early 19th cent.: perhaps an alteration of **GALLANT**.

galliwasp /ˈgalɪwɒsp/ ▶ noun a marsh lizard found in Central America and the Caribbean. ● Genus *Diploglossus*, family Anguidae: many species, in particular *D. monotropis* of the West Indies.
– ORIGIN late 17th cent.: of unknown origin.

gall midge ▶ noun a small, delicate fly which induces gall formation in plants or may cause other damage to crops. ● Family Cecidomyiidae: numerous genera and species, including the **saddle gall midge** (*Haplodiplosis marginata*), which is a pest of cereals.

gall mite ▶ noun a minute mite which is parasitic on plants, typically living inside buds and causing them to form hard galls. ● Family Eriophyidae, order Prostigmata: numerous species, in particular *Cecidophyopsis ribis*, which affects blackcurrant bushes, causing big bud and transmitting the reversion virus.

Gallo- /ˈgaləʊ/ ▶ combining form French; French and ...: *Gallo-German.* ■ relating to France.
– ORIGIN from Latin *Gallus* 'a Gaul'.

galloglass /ˈgalə(ʊ)glɑːs/ (also **gallowglass**) ▶ noun historical (in Ireland) a mercenary or member of a special class of soldiers in the service of a chieftain.
– ORIGIN late 15th cent.: from Irish *gallóglach*, from *gall* 'foreigner' and *óglach* 'youth, servant, warrior'.

gallon /ˈgalən/ ▶ noun **1** a unit of volume for liquid measure equal to eight pints, in particular: ■ (also **imperial gallon**) Brit. (also used for dry measure) a unit of volume equivalent to 4.55 litres. ■ US a unit of volume equivalent to 3.79 litres.
2 (**gallons of**) informal a large volume of something: *gallons of fake blood.*
– DERIVATIVES **gallonage** noun.
– ORIGIN Middle English: from Anglo-Norman French *galon*, from the base of medieval Latin *galleta*, *galletum* 'pail, liquid measure', perhaps of Celtic origin.

galloon /gəˈluːn/ ▶ noun a narrow ornamental strip of fabric, typically a silk braid or piece of lace, used to trim clothing or finish upholstery.
– ORIGIN early 17th cent.: from French *galon*, from *galonner* 'to trim with braid', of unknown ultimate origin.

gallop ▶ noun [in sing.] the fastest pace of a horse or other quadruped, with all the feet off the ground together in each stride: *the horse broke into a furious gallop* | [mass noun] *a mounted police charge at full gallop.* ■ a ride on a horse at a gallop: *Wilfred went for a gallop on the sands.* ■ a very fast pace of running by a person. ■ Brit. a track or ground where horses are exercised at a gallop.
▶ verb (**gallops, galloping, galloped**) [no obj., with adverbial of direction] **1** (of a horse) go at the pace of a gallop.

G

■ [with obj. and adverbial of direction] make (a horse) gallop. ■ (of a person) run fast.
2 proceed at great speed: *don't gallop through your speech*. ■ (of a process or event) progress in a rapid and seemingly uncontrollable manner: *his life gallops headlong towards disaster* | (as adj. **galloping**) *galloping inflation*.
– DERIVATIVES **galloper** noun.
– ORIGIN early 16th cent.: from Old French *galop* (noun), *galoper*, variants of Old Northern French *walop*, *waloper* (see WALLOP).

gallous ▶ adjective variant spelling of GALLUS.

Galloway /ˈgaləweɪ/ an area of SW Scotland consisting of the two former counties of Kirkcudbrightshire and Wigtownshire, and now part of Dumfries and Galloway region.

galloway /ˈgaləweɪ/ ▶ noun an animal of a black hornless breed of beef cattle which originated in Galloway. ■ (also **belted galloway**) a variety of galloway cattle marked with a broad white band.

gallows ▶ plural noun [usu. treated as sing.] a structure, typically of two uprights and a crosspiece, for the hanging of criminals. ■ (**the gallows**) execution by hanging: *he was saved from the gallows by a last-minute reprieve*.
– ORIGIN Old English *galga*, *gealga*, of Germanic origin; related to Dutch *galg* and German *Galgen*; reinforced in Middle English by Old Norse *gálgi*.

gallows humour ▶ noun [mass noun] grim and ironical humour in a desperate or hopeless situation.

gallows tree ▶ noun another term for GALLOWS.

gallstone /ˈgɔːlstəʊn/ ▶ noun a small, hard crystalline mass formed abnormally in the gall bladder or bile ducts from bile pigments, cholesterol, and calcium salts. Gallstones can cause severe pain and blockage of the bile duct.

Gallup poll /ˈgaləp/ ▶ noun trademark an assessment of public opinion by the questioning of a representative sample, typically as a basis for forecasting votes in an election.
– ORIGIN 1940s: named after George H. *Gallup* (1901–84), the American statistician who devised the method.

gallus /ˈgaləs/ (also **gallous**) ▶ adjective chiefly Scottish bold, cheeky, or flashy.
– ORIGIN late Middle English (in the sense 'fit to be hanged'): variant of GALLOWS used attributively.

galluses /ˈgaləsɪz/ ▶ plural noun chiefly Scottish & N. Amer. braces for a person's trousers.
– ORIGIN mid 19th cent.: plural of *gallus*, variant of GALLOWS.

gall wasp ▶ noun a small winged insect of ant-like appearance. The female lays its egg in the food plant and when the larva hatches the surrounding plant tissue swells up around it to form a gall. ● Superfamily Cynipoidea, order Hymenoptera: several genera.

Galois /ˈgalwʌ/, French /galwɑ/, Évariste (1811–32), French mathematician. His memoir on the conditions for solubility of polynomial equations was highly innovative but was not published until 1846, after his death.

Galois theory ▶ noun Mathematics a method of applying group theory to the solution of algebraic equations.

galoot /gəˈluːt/ ▶ noun N. Amer. & Scottish informal a clumsy or stupid person (often as a term of abuse).
– ORIGIN early 19th cent. (originally in nautical use meaning 'an inexperienced marine'): of unknown origin.

galop /ˈgaləp, gəˈlɒp/ ▶ noun a lively ballroom dance in duple time, popular in the late 18th century.
– ORIGIN French, literally 'gallop'.

galore ▶ adjective [postpositive] in abundance: *there were prizes galore for everything*.
– ORIGIN early 17th cent.: from Irish *go leor*, literally 'to sufficiency'.

galosh /gəˈlɒʃ/ ▶ noun (usu. **galoshes**) a waterproof overshoe, typically made of rubber.
– ORIGIN Middle English (denoting a type of clog): via Old French from late Latin *gallicula*, diminutive of Latin *gallica (solea)* 'Gallic (shoe)'. The current sense dates from the mid 19th cent.

Galsworthy /ˈgɔːlzwəːði/, John (1867–1933), English novelist and dramatist. He is remembered chiefly for *The Forsyte Saga* (1906–28), a series of novels which was adapted for television in 1967. Nobel Prize for Literature (1932).

Galtieri /ˌgaltɪˈɛːri/, Leopoldo Fortunato (1926–2003), Argentinian general and statesman, President 1981–2. Galtieri's military junta ordered the invasion of the Falkland Islands in 1982, precipitating the Falklands War.

Galton /ˈgɔːlt(ə)n/, Sir Francis (1822–1911), English scientist. He founded eugenics and introduced methods of measuring human mental and physical abilities. He also pioneered the use of fingerprints as a means of identification.

galumph /gəˈlʌmf/ ▶ verb [no obj., with adverbial of direction] informal move in a clumsy, ponderous, or noisy manner: *she galumphed along beside him* | (as adj. **galumphing**) *a galumphing giant*.
– ORIGIN 1871 (in the sense 'prance in triumph'): coined by Lewis Carroll in *Through the Looking Glass*; perhaps a blend of GALLOP and TRIUMPH.

Galvani /galˈvɑːni/, Luigi (1737–98), Italian anatomist. He studied the structure of organs and the physiology of tissues, but he is best known for his discovery of the twitching of frogs' legs in an electric field.

galvanic /galˈvanɪk/ ▶ adjective **1** relating to or involving electric currents produced by chemical action.
2 sudden and dramatic: *a searing, galvanic experience*.
– DERIVATIVES **galvanically** adverb.
– ORIGIN late 18th cent.: from French *galvanique*, from GALVANI.

galvanic skin response (also **galvanic skin reflex**) ▶ noun a change in the electrical resistance of the skin caused by emotional stress, measurable with a sensitive galvanometer, e.g. in lie-detector tests.

galvanism ▶ noun [mass noun] historical **1** electricity produced by chemical action.
2 the therapeutic use of electric currents.
– ORIGIN late 18th cent.: from French *galvanisme*, from GALVANI.

galvanize /ˈgalvənʌɪz/ (also **galvanise**) ▶ verb [with obj.] **1** shock or excite (someone) into taking action: *the urgency of his voice* ***galvanized*** *them* ***into*** *action*.
2 (often as adj. **galvanized**) coat (iron or steel) with a protective layer of zinc: *an old galvanized bucket*.
▶ noun [mass noun] W. Indian or dialect galvanized tin sheeting, typically as used for roofing or fencing.
– DERIVATIVES **galvanization** noun, **galvanizer** noun.
– ORIGIN early 19th cent. (in the sense 'stimulate by electricity'): from French *galvaniser* (see GALVANI).

galvanometer /ˌgalvəˈnɒmɪtə/ ▶ noun an instrument for detecting and measuring small electric currents.
– DERIVATIVES **galvanometric** adjective.

galvanoscope /ˈgalv(ə)nəˌskəʊp/ ▶ noun a galvanometer that works by measuring the deflection of a needle in the magnetic field induced by the electric current.

Galveston /ˈgalvɪst(ə)n/ a port in Texas, south-east of Houston; pop. 57,086 (est. 2008). It is situated on Galveston Bay, an inlet of the Gulf of Mexico.

galvo /ˈgalvəʊ/ ▶ noun [mass noun] Austral. informal galvanized iron.

Galway /ˈgɔːlweɪ/ a county of the Republic of Ireland, on the west coast in the province of Connacht. ■ its county town, a seaport at the head of Galway Bay; pop. 72,414 (2006).

Galway Bay an inlet of the Atlantic Ocean on the west coast of Ireland.

gam ▶ noun informal a leg, especially a woman's.
– ORIGIN late 18th cent.: probably a variant of the heraldic term *gamb*, which denotes a charge representing an animal's leg, from Old Northern French *gambe* 'leg'.

Gama, Vasco da see DA GAMA.

Gamay /ˈgameɪ/ ▶ noun [mass noun] a variety of black wine grape native to the Beaujolais district of France. ■ a fruity red wine made from the Gamay grape.
– ORIGIN from the name of a hamlet in Burgundy, eastern France.

gamba /ˈgambə/ ▶ noun short for VIOLA DA GAMBA.

gambado[1] /gamˈbeɪdəʊ, -ˈbɑːdəʊ/ (also **gambade** /-ˈbeɪd, -ˈbɑːd/) ▶ noun (pl. **gambados** or **gambadoes**) a leap or bound, especially an exaggerated one.
– ORIGIN early 19th cent.: from Spanish *gambada*, from *gamba* 'leg'.

gambado[2] /gamˈbeɪdəʊ/ ▶ noun (pl. **gambados** or **gambadoes**) a gaiter, typically one attached to a saddle to protect a rider's leg from the weather.
– ORIGIN mid 17th cent.: from Italian *gamba* 'leg' + -ADO.

Gambia /ˈgambɪə/ **1** (also **the Gambia**) a country on the coast of West Africa; pop. 1,778,100 (est. 2009); languages, English (official), Malinke and other indigenous languages, Creole; capital, Banjul.

> Gambia consists of a narrow strip of territory on either side of the Gambia River that forms an enclave in Senegal. It was created a British colony in 1843, becoming an independent member of the Commonwealth in 1965 and a republic in 1970.

2 a river of West Africa, which rises near Labé in Guinea and flows 800 km (500 miles) through Senegal and Gambia to meet the Atlantic at Banjul.
– DERIVATIVES **Gambian** adjective & noun.

gambier /ˈgambɪə/ ▶ noun [mass noun] an astringent extract of a tropical Asiatic plant, used in tanning. Also called CATECHU. ● The chief source of gambier is the climber *Uncaria gambier*, family Rubiaceae.
– ORIGIN early 19th cent.: from Malay *gambir*, the name of the plant.

Gambier Islands /ˈgambɪə/ a group of coral islands in the South Pacific, forming part of French Polynesia; pop. 1,641 (2007).

gambit ▶ noun **1** an act or remark that is calculated to gain an advantage, especially at the outset of a situation: *his resignation was a tactical gambit*.
2 (in chess) an opening move in which a player makes a sacrifice, typically of a pawn, for the sake of a compensating advantage.
– ORIGIN mid 17th cent.: originally *gambett*, from Italian *gambetto*, literally 'tripping up', from *gamba* 'leg'.

gamble ▶ verb [no obj.] **1** play games of chance for money; bet: *he* ***gambles on*** *football*. ■ [with obj.] bet (a sum of money): *they gambled their money on cards*.
2 take risky action in the hope of a desired result: *he was* ***gambling on*** *the success of his satellite TV channel*.
▶ noun [usu. in sing.] **1** an act of gambling.
2 a risky action undertaken with the hope of success: *we decided to* ***take a gamble*** *and offer him a place on our staff*.
– ORIGIN early 18th cent.: from obsolete *gamel* 'play games', or from the verb GAME[1].

gambler ▶ noun a person who gambles: *a compulsive gambler*.

gamboge /gamˈbəʊʒ, -ˈbuːʒ/ ▶ noun [mass noun] a gum resin produced by various East Asian trees, used as a yellow pigment and in medicine as a purgative. ● The trees belong to the genus *Garcinia* (family Guttiferae), in particular *G. xanthochymus*.
– ORIGIN early 18th cent. (earlier in the Latin form): from modern Latin *gambaugium*, from CAMBODIA.

gambol ▶ verb (**gambols**, **gambolling**, **gambolled**; US **gambols**, **gamboling**, **gamboled**) [no obj., usu. with adverbial] run or jump about playfully: *the mare gambolled towards Constance*.
▶ noun an act of running or jumping about playfully.
– ORIGIN early 16th cent.: alteration of *gambade* (see GAMBADO[1]), via French from Italian *gambata* 'trip up', from *gamba* 'leg'.

gambrel /ˈgambr(ə)l/ (also **gambrel roof**) ▶ noun a roof with two sides, each of which has a shallower slope above a steeper one. ■ Brit. a hipped roof with a small gable forming the upper part of each end.
– ORIGIN mid 16th cent. (in the sense 'bent piece of wood or iron to hang carcasses on'): from Old Northern French *gamberel*, from *gambier* 'forked stick', from *gambe* 'leg'. The sense 'hipped roof' (mid 19th cent.) is based on an earlier meaning 'joint in the upper part of a horse's hind leg', the shape of which the roof resembles.

gambusia /gamˈb(j)uːsɪə/ ▶ noun a small live-bearing fish found in mangrove creeks and brackish waters of the southern US and northern Mexico. ● Genus *Gambusia*, family Poeciliidae: several species, in particular *G. affinis*, widely introduced for mosquito control (also called MOSQUITO FISH).
– ORIGIN modern Latin, alteration of American Spanish *gambusino*.

game[1] ▶ noun **1** a form of competitive activity or sport played according to rules. ■ (**games**) a meeting for sporting contests: *the Olympic Games*. ■ (**games**) Brit. athletics or sports as a lesson or activity at school. ■ a person's performance in a game; a person's standard of play: *Rooks attempted to raise his game to another level*.
2 an activity that one engages in for amusement: *a computer game*. ■ the equipment for a game, especially a board game or a computer game.
3 a complete episode or period of play, ending in a final result: *a baseball game*. ■ a single portion of play forming a scoring unit in a match, especially in tennis. ■ Bridge a score of 100 points for tricks bid

and made (the best of three games constituting a rubber).
4 informal a type of activity or business regarded as a game: *he was in the restaurant game for the glamour.* ■ a secret and clever plan or trick: *I was on to his little game.*
5 [mass noun] wild mammals or birds hunted for sport or food. ■ the flesh of wild mammals or birds, used as food: [as modifier] *a game pie.*
▶ **adjective** eager or willing to do something new or challenging: *they were **game for** anything.*
▶ **verb 1** [no obj.] (usu. as noun modifier **gaming**) play at games of chance for money: *a gaming machine.* ■ play video or computer games: *the next generation of gaming consoles.*
2 [with obj.] manipulate (a situation), typically in a way that is unfair or unscrupulous: *it was very easy for a few big companies to **game the system** | politicians blamed electricity generators for gaming the market.*
– PHRASES **ahead of** (or **behind**) **the game** ahead of (or lagging behind) one's competitors or peers in the same sphere of activity. **beat someone at their own game** use someone's own methods to outdo them in their chosen activity. **the game is up** the deception or crime is revealed or foiled. **game on** a signal for play to begin in a game or match. ■ Brit. informal said when one feels that a situation is about to develop in one's favour: *She soon invited me back to her place. Game on!* **game over** informal said when a situation is regarded as hopeless or irreversible. [probably from the use of the phrase at the conclusion of a computer game.] **game, set, and match** used to indicate a decisive victory: *the trade unions have won—game, set, and match to the workers.* [said at the end of a tennis match, indicating that a player has won a game that also wins them the set and the match.] **the Great Game 1** spying. **2** the rivalry between Britain and Russia in central Asia during the 19th century. [first used by Rudyard Kipling in *Kim* (1901).] **make (a) game of** archaic mock; taunt. **off** (or **on**) **one's game** playing badly (or well). **on the game** Brit. informal working as a prostitute. **the only game in town** informal the only thing worth concerning oneself with. **play someone's game** advance another's plans, whether intentionally or not: *to what extent are they playing the government's game?* **play the game** behave in a fair or honourable way; abide by the rules. **play games** deal with someone or something in a way that lacks due seriousness or respect. **what's your** (or **the**) **game?** Brit. informal what's going on?
– DERIVATIVES **gamely** adverb, **gameness** noun, **gamester** noun.
– ORIGIN Old English *gamen* 'amusement, fun', *gamenian* 'play, amuse oneself', of Germanic origin.

game² ▶ **adjective** dated (of a person's leg) permanently injured; lame.
– ORIGIN late 18th cent.: originally dialect, of unknown origin.

game bird ▶ **noun 1** a bird shot for sport or food. **2** a bird of a large group that includes pheasants, grouse, quails, guinea fowl, etc. ● Order Galliformes: several families.

gamecock (also **gamefowl**) ▶ **noun** a cock bred and trained for cockfighting.

game engine ▶ **noun** the basic software of a computer game or video game.

game face ▶ **noun** N. Amer. a sports player's neutral or serious facial expression, displaying determination and concentration.

game farm ▶ **noun** a farm where a variety of wild animals are kept or bred, often with facilities for visitors to observe or hunt the animals.

game fish ▶ **noun** (pl. **same**) a fish caught by anglers for sport, especially (in fresh water) salmon and trout and (in the sea) billfishes, sharks, bass, and many members of the mackerel family. Compare with **COARSE FISH**.

gamekeeper ▶ **noun** a person employed to breed and protect game, typically for a large estate.
– DERIVATIVES **gamekeeping** noun.

gamelan /ˈgaməlan/ ▶ **noun** a traditional instrumental ensemble in Java and Bali, including many bronze percussion instruments.
– ORIGIN early 19th cent.: from Javanese.

game misconduct ▶ **noun** Ice Hockey a punitive suspension of a player for the remainder of a game, with a substitution permitted.

gamepad ▶ **noun** a handheld controller for video games.

game plan ▶ **noun** a strategy worked out in advance, especially in sport, politics, or business.

gameplay ▶ **noun** [mass noun] the features of a computer game, such as its plot and the way it is played, as distinct from the graphics and sound effects.

game point ▶ **noun** (in tennis and other sports) a point which if won by one of the players or sides will also win them a game.

gamer ▶ **noun** a person who plays a game or games, typically a participant in a computer or role-playing game. ■ N. Amer. a person known for consistently making a strong effort, especially in sport.

games console ▶ **noun** see **CONSOLE²** (sense 1).

game show ▶ **noun** a television programme in which people compete to win prizes.

gamesmanship ▶ **noun** [mass noun] the art of winning games by using various ploys and tactics to gain a psychological advantage.
– DERIVATIVES **gamesman** noun (pl. **gamesmen**).

gamesome ▶ **adjective** playful and merry.
– DERIVATIVES **gamesomeness** noun.

gametangium /ˌgamɪˈtan(d)ʒɪəm/ ▶ **noun** (pl. **gametangia**) Botany a specialized organ or cell in which gametes are formed in algae, ferns, and some other plants.
– ORIGIN late 19th cent.: from modern Latin *gameta* (see **GAMETE**) + Greek *angeion* 'vessel' + **-IUM**.

gamete /ˈgamiːt/ ▶ **noun** Biology a mature haploid male or female germ cell which is able to unite with another of the opposite sex in sexual reproduction to form a zygote.
– DERIVATIVES **gametic** /gəˈmɛtɪk/ adjective.
– ORIGIN late 19th cent.: from modern Latin *gameta*, from Greek *gametē* 'wife', *gametēs* 'husband', from *gamos* 'marriage'.

game theory (also **games theory**) ▶ **noun** [mass noun] the branch of mathematics concerned with the analysis of strategies for dealing with competitive situations where the outcome of a participant's choice of action depends critically on the actions of other participants. Game theory has been applied to contexts in war, business, and biology. Compare with **DECISION THEORY**.

gameto- /gəˈmiːtəʊ/ ▶ **combining form** Biology representing **GAMETE**.

gametocyte /gəˈmiːtə(ʊ)sʌɪt/ ▶ **noun** Biology a cell that divides (by meiosis) to form gametes.

gametogenesis /gəˌmiːtə(ʊ)ˈdʒɛnɪsɪs/ ▶ **noun** [mass noun] Biology the process in which cells undergo meiosis to form gametes.
– DERIVATIVES **gametogenic** adjective,.

gametophyte /gəˈmiːtə(ʊ)fʌɪt/ ▶ **noun** Botany (in the life cycle of plants with alternating generations) the gamete-producing and usually haploid phase, producing the zygote from which the sporophyte arises. It is the dominant form in bryophytes.
– DERIVATIVES **gametophytic** adjective.

game warden ▶ **noun** a person who is employed to supervise game and hunting in a particular area.

gamey ▶ **adjective** variant spelling of **GAMY**.

gamgee /ˈgamdʒi/ ▶ **noun** [mass noun] surgical dressing consisting of a thickness of cotton wool between two layers of gauze.
– ORIGIN late 19th cent.: named after Joseph S. Gamgee (1828–86), English surgeon.

gamin /ˈgamɪn, -mã/ ▶ **noun** dated a street urchin.
– ORIGIN mid 19th cent.: French, originally an eastern dialect word, of unknown origin.

gamine /gaˈmiːn/ ▶ **noun 1** a girl with a mischievous, boyish charm.
2 dated a female street urchin.
▶ **adjective** (of a girl) attractively boyish.
– ORIGIN late 19th cent.: French, feminine of *gamin* (see **GAMIN**).

gaming house ▶ **noun** dated a public building where gambling games are played; a casino.

gamma /ˈgamə/ ▶ **noun 1** the third letter of the Greek alphabet (Γ, γ), transliterated as 'g'. ● The combinations γγ, γκ, and γχ are usually transliterated as 'ng', 'nk', and 'nkh' or 'nch'. ■ [as modifier] denoting the third in a series of items, categories, etc. ■ Brit. a third-class mark given for an essay or other piece of work. ■ (**Gamma**) [followed by Latin genitive] Astronomy the third (usually third-brightest) star in a constellation: *Gamma Orionis.*
2 [as modifier] relating to gamma rays: *gamma detector.*
3 Physics (pl. **same**) a unit of magnetic field strength equal to 10^{-5} oersted.
– ORIGIN via Latin from Greek.

gamma-aminobutyric acid /ˌgaməəˌmiːnəʊbjuːˈtɪrɪk, -əˌmʌɪnəʊ-, -ˈamɪnəʊ-/ ▶ **noun** [mass noun] Biochemistry an amino acid which acts to inhibit the transmission of nerve impulses in the central nervous system. ● Chem. formula: $H_2NCH_2CH_2CH_2COOH$.
– ORIGIN early 20th cent.: *gamma* indicating the relative position of amino on the third carbon away from the acid group.

gamma globulin ▶ **noun** [mass noun] Biochemistry a mixture of blood plasma proteins, mainly immunoglobulins, which have relatively low electrophoretic mobility.

gamma-HCH ▶ **noun** another term for **LINDANE**.
– ORIGIN *HCH* from *hexachlorocyclohexane*.

gamma-linolenic acid ▶ **noun** Biochemistry see **LINOLENIC ACID**.

gamma radiation ▶ **noun** [mass noun] gamma rays.

gamma rays ▶ **plural noun** penetrating electromagnetic radiation of shorter wavelength than X-rays.

gammer ▶ **noun** archaic an old countrywoman.
– ORIGIN late 16th cent.: probably a contraction of **GODMOTHER**; see also **GAFFER**.

gammon¹ ▶ **noun** [mass noun] Brit. ham which has been cured or smoked like bacon. ■ [count noun] the bottom piece of a side of bacon, including a hind leg.
– ORIGIN late 15th cent. (denoting the haunch of a pig): from Old Northern French *gambon*, from *gambe* 'leg'.

gammon² ▶ **noun** a victory in backgammon (carrying a double score) in which the winner removes all their pieces before the loser has removed any.
▶ **verb** [with obj.] defeat (an opponent) with a gammon.
– ORIGIN mid 18th cent.: apparently from Old English *gamen* or *gamenian* (see **GAME¹**), with survival of the *-n* ending.

gammon³ informal, dated ▶ **noun** nonsense; rubbish.
▶ **verb** [with obj.] hoax or deceive (someone).
– ORIGIN early 18th cent.: origin uncertain; the term was first used as criminals' slang in *give gammon to* 'give cover to a pickpocket' and *keep in gammon* 'distract a victim for a pickpocket'.

gammy ▶ **adjective** (**gammier**, **gammiest**) Brit. informal (especially of a leg) unable to function normally because of injury or chronic pain.
– ORIGIN mid 19th cent. (in the sense 'bad, false'): dialect form of **GAME²**.

Gamow /ˈgeɪmaʊ/, George (1904–68), Russian-born American physicist. He was a proponent of the Big Bang theory and also suggested the triplet code of bases in DNA, which governs the synthesis of amino acids.

gamp ▶ **noun** Brit. informal, dated an umbrella, especially a large unwieldy one.
– ORIGIN mid 19th cent.: named after Mrs *Gamp* in Charles Dickens's *Martin Chuzzlewit*, who carried such an umbrella.

gamut /ˈgamət/ ▶ **noun** (**the gamut**) **1** the complete range or scope of something: *the whole gamut of human emotion.*
2 Music a complete scale of musical notes; the range of a voice or instrument. ■ historical a scale consisting of seven overlapping hexachords, containing all the recognized notes used in medieval music, covering almost three octaves from bass G to treble E. ■ historical the lowest note in this scale.
– PHRASES **run the gamut** experience, display, or perform the complete range of something: *Owen **runs the gamut of** emotions in the space of the film.*
– ORIGIN late Middle English: from medieval Latin *gamma ut*, originally the name of the lowest note in the medieval scale (bass G an octave and a half below middle C), then applied to the whole range of notes used in medieval music. The Greek letter Γ (gamma) was used for bass G, with *ut* indicating that it was the first note in the lowest of the hexachords or six-note scales (see **SOLMIZATION**).

gamy (also **gamey**) ▶ **adjective** (**gamier**, **gamiest**) **1** (of meat) having the strong flavour or smell of game, especially when it is high.
2 chiefly N. Amer. racy or disreputable: *gamy language.*
– DERIVATIVES **gamily** adverb, **gaminess** noun.

Gan /gan/ ▶ **noun** [mass noun] a dialect of Chinese spoken by about 20 million people, mainly in Jiangxi province.
– ORIGIN from Chinese *Gàn*, another name for **JIANGXI**.

G

ganache /gəˈnaʃ/ ▶ **noun** [mass noun] a whipped filling of chocolate and cream, used in confectioneries such as cakes and truffles.
– ORIGIN French.

Ganapati /ˌgʌnəˈpʌti/ another name for **GANESH**.

Gäncä /ˈgəndʒə/ an industrial city in Azerbaijan; pop. 307,900 (est. 2008). The city was formerly called Yelizavetpol (1804–1918) and Kirovabad (1935–89). Russian name **GYANDZHE**.

Gance /gɒ̃s/, Abel (1889–1981), French film director. He was an early pioneer of technical experimentation in film. Notable films: *La Roue* (1921) and *Napoléon* (1926).

Gand /gɑ̃/ French name for **GHENT**.

Ganda ▶ **noun & adjective** see **LUGANDA**.

Gander /ˈgandə/ a town on the island of Newfoundland, on Lake Gander; pop. 9,951 (2006). Its airport served the first regular transatlantic flights during the Second World War.

gander /ˈgandə/ ▶ **noun 1** a male goose.
2 [in sing.] informal a look or glance: *take a gander at the luggage, will ya?* [from criminals' slang.]
▶ **verb** [no obj.] US informal look or glance at something.
– ORIGIN Old English *gandra*, of Germanic origin; related to Dutch *gander*, also to **GANNET**.

G

Gandhi[1] /ˈgandi, ˈgɑːndi/, Mrs Indira (1917–84), Indian stateswoman, Prime Minister 1966–77 and 1980–4. The daughter of Jawaharlal Nehru, she sought to establish a secular state and to lead India out of poverty. She was assassinated by her own Sikh bodyguards following prolonged religious disturbance.

Gandhi[2] /ˈgandi, ˈgɑːndi/, Mahatma (1869–1948), Indian nationalist and spiritual leader; full name *Mohandas Karamchand Gandhi*. He became prominent in the opposition to British rule in India, pursuing a policy of non-violent civil disobedience. He never held government office, but was regarded as the country's supreme political and spiritual leader; he was assassinated by a Hindu following his agreement to the creation of the state of Pakistan.
– DERIVATIVES **Gandhian** adjective.

Gandhi[3] /ˈgandi, ˈgɑːndi/, Rajiv (1944–91), Indian statesman, Prime Minister 1984–9. The eldest son of Indira Gandhi, he became Prime Minister after his mother's assassination. His premiership was marked by continuing unrest and he was assassinated during an election campaign.

Gandhinagar /ˌgandɪˈnʌgə/ a city in western India, capital of the state of Gujarat; pop. 271,300 (est. 2009).

G and T (also **G & T**) ▶ **noun** a drink of gin and tonic.

gandy dancer ▶ **noun** N. Amer. informal a track maintenance worker on a railway.
– ORIGIN early 20th cent.: of unknown origin.

ganef /ˈganɛf/ ▶ **noun** US informal a dishonest or unscrupulous person.
– ORIGIN 1990s: Yiddish, from Hebrew, literally 'thief'.

Ganesh /gəˈneɪʃ/ (also **Ganesha** /gəˈneɪʃə/) Hinduism an elephant-headed deity, son of Shiva and Parvati. He is usually depicted coloured red, with a pot belly and one broken tusk, riding a rat. Also called **GANAPATI**.
– ORIGIN from Sanskrit *Gaṇeśa* 'lord of the ganas' (Shiva's attendants).

gang[1] ▶ **noun 1** an organized group of criminals. ■ a group of young people involved in petty crime or violence. ■ informal a group of people, especially young people, who regularly associate together. ■ an organized group of people doing manual work: *a government road gang*.
2 a set of switches, sockets, or other electrical or mechanical devices grouped together.
▶ **verb 1** [no obj.] **(gang together)** (of a number of people) form a group or gang: *three banks ganged together to form a 'virtual bank'*. ■ **(gang up)** join together in order to intimidate or oppose someone: *they ganged up on me and nicked my pocket money*.
2 [with obj.] arrange (electrical devices or machines) together to work in coordination.
– ORIGIN Old English, from Old Norse *gangr*, *ganga* 'gait, course, going', of Germanic origin; related to **GANG[2]**. The original meaning was 'going, a journey', later in Middle English 'a way', also 'set of things or people which go together'.

gang[2] ▶ **verb** [no obj.] Scottish go; proceed: *gang to your bed, lass*.
– PHRASES **gang agley** (of a plan) go wrong. [1786: from Robert Burns's 'The best laid schemes o' Mice an' Men, Gang aft agley' (*Poems and Songs*).]
– ORIGIN Old English *gangan*, of Germanic origin; related to **GO[1]**.

Ganga /ˈgʌŋgə/ Hindi name for **GANGES**.

gang bang ▶ **noun** informal **1** the successive rape of one person by a group of people. ■ a sexual orgy involving changes of partner.
2 N. Amer. an instance of violence involving members of a criminal gang.
▶ **verb (gang-bang) 1** [with obj.] (of a group of people) rape (someone).
2 (as noun **gang-banging**) N. Amer. the violent activities of a criminal gang.
– DERIVATIVES **gang-banger** noun.

gangboard ▶ **noun** another term for **GANGPLANK**.

gangbuster ▶ **noun** N. Amer. informal **1** an officer of a law-enforcement agency who takes part in breaking up criminal gangs.
2 [as modifier] very successful: *the restaurant did gangbuster business*.
– PHRASES **go** (or **like**) **gangbusters** N. Amer. used to refer to great vigour, speed, or success: *the real estate market was going gangbusters*.

ganger ▶ **noun** Brit. the foreman of a gang of labourers.

Ganges /ˈgandʒiːz/ a river of northern India and Bangladesh, which rises in the Himalayas and flows some 2,700 km (1,678 miles) south-east to the Bay of Bengal, where it forms the world's largest delta. The river is regarded by Hindus as sacred. Hindi name **GANGA**.
– DERIVATIVES **Gangetic** adjective.

gangland ▶ **noun** [mass noun] the world of criminal gangs: [as modifier] *he was the victim of a gangland killing*.

gangling ▶ **adjective** (of a person) tall, thin, and awkward in movements or bearing.
– DERIVATIVES **gangle** verb.
– ORIGIN early 19th cent.: from the verb **GANG[2]** + **-LE[4]** + **-ING[2]**.

ganglion /ˈgaŋglɪən/ ▶ **noun** (pl. **ganglia** or **ganglions**) **1** Anatomy a structure containing a number of nerve cell bodies, typically linked by synapses, and often forming a swelling on a nerve fibre. ■ a network of cells forming a nerve centre in the nervous system of an invertebrate. ■ a well-defined mass of grey matter within the central nervous system. See also **BASAL GANGLIA**.
2 Medicine an abnormal benign swelling on a tendon sheath.
– DERIVATIVES **ganglionic** adjective.
– ORIGIN late 17th cent.: from Greek *ganglion* 'tumour on or near sinews or tendons', used by Galen to denote the complex nerve centres.

ganglioside /ˈgaŋglɪə(ʊ)sʌɪd/ ▶ **noun** Biochemistry any of a group of complex lipids which are present in the grey matter of the human brain.
– ORIGIN 1940s: from **GANGLION** + *-oside* (see **-OSE[2]**, **-IDE**).

gangly ▶ **adjective (ganglier, gangliest)** another term for **GANGLING**.

gangmaster ▶ **noun** Brit. a person who organizes and oversees the work of casual manual labourers.

Gang of Four (in China) a group of four associates, including Mao Zedong's wife, involved in implementing the Cultural Revolution. They were among the groups competing for power on Mao's death in 1976, but were arrested and imprisoned.

gangplank ▶ **noun** a movable plank, typically with cleats nailed on it, used by passengers to board or disembark from a ship or boat.

gang rape ▶ **noun** the rape of one person by a group of other people.
– DERIVATIVES **gang-rape** verb.

gangrene /ˈgaŋgriːn/ ▶ **noun** [mass noun] localized death and decomposition of body tissue, resulting from obstructed circulation or bacterial infection.
▶ **verb** [no obj.] become affected with gangrene.
– DERIVATIVES **gangrenous** /ˈgaŋgrɪnəs/ adjective.
– ORIGIN mid 16th cent.: via French from Latin *gangraena*, from Greek *gangraina*.

gang show ▶ **noun** Brit. a locally produced variety show performed annually by members of the Scout and Guide Association.

gangsta ▶ **noun 1** black slang a gang member.
2 (also **gangsta rap**) [mass noun] a type of rap music featuring aggressive macho lyrics, often with reference to gang violence.
– ORIGIN 1980s: alteration of **GANGSTER**.

gangster ▶ **noun** a member of a gang of violent criminals.
– DERIVATIVES **gangsterism** noun.

Gangtok /gaŋˈtɒk/ a city in northern India, in the foothills of the Kanchenjunga mountain range, capital of the state of Sikkim; pop. 32,500 (est. 2009).

gangue /gaŋ/ ▶ **noun** [mass noun] the commercially valueless material in which ore is found.
– ORIGIN early 19th cent.: from French, from German *Gang* 'course, lode'; related to **GANG[1]**.

gangway ▶ **noun 1** a raised platform or walkway providing a passage. ■ a movable bridge linking a ship to the shore. ■ an opening in the bulwarks by which a ship is entered or left.
2 Brit. a passage between rows of seats, especially in a theatre or aircraft.
▶ **exclamation** make way!

ganister /ˈganɪstə/ ▶ **noun** [mass noun] a close-grained, hard siliceous rock found in the coal measures of northern England, and used for furnace linings.
– ORIGIN early 19th cent.: of unknown origin.

ganja /ˈgan(d)ʒə, ˈgɑː-/ ▶ **noun** [mass noun] cannabis.
– ORIGIN early 19th cent.: from Hindi *gā̃jā*.

gannet /ˈganɪt/ ▶ **noun 1** a large seabird with mainly white plumage, which catches fish by plunging into the water. ● Genus *Morus* (or *Sula*), family Sulidae: three species, in particular the **northern gannet** (*M. bassanus*) of the North Atlantic (also called **SOLAN GOOSE**).
2 Brit. informal a greedy person.
– ORIGIN Old English *ganot*, of Germanic origin; related to Dutch *gent* 'gander', also to **GANDER**.

gannetry ▶ **noun** (pl. **gannetries**) a breeding colony of gannets, usually on an isolated rock.

ganoid /ˈganɔɪd/ Zoology ▶ **adjective** (of fish scales) hard and bony with a shiny enamelled surface. Compare with **CTENOID** and **PLACOID**. ■ (of a fish) having ganoid scales.
▶ **noun** a primitive fish that has ganoid scales, e.g. a sturgeon or freshwater garfish.
– ORIGIN mid 19th cent.: from French *ganoïde*, from Greek *ganos* 'brightness'.

gansey /ˈganzi/ ▶ **noun** dialect & W. Indian a sweater or T-shirt.
– ORIGIN late 19th cent.: representing a pronunciation of **GUERNSEY[2]**.

Gansu /ganˈsuː/ (also **Kansu**) a province of NW central China; capital, Lanzhou. This narrow, mountainous province forms a corridor through which the Silk Road passed.

gantlet /ˈgantlɪt/ ▶ **noun** US spelling of **GAUNTLET[2]**.

gantline /ˈgantlʌɪn/ ▶ **noun** Sailing a line passed through a block near the masthead and used to hoist sails or rigging.
– ORIGIN mid 18th cent. (originally *girtline*): of unknown origin.

gantry ▶ **noun** (pl. **gantries**) **1** a bridge-like overhead structure with a platform supporting equipment such as a crane, signals, or cameras. ■ a tall framework supporting a space rocket prior to launching.
2 (in a bar) a structure containing inverted bottles and fitted with optics for serving measures.
– ORIGIN late Middle English (denoting a wooden stand for barrels): probably from dialect *gawn* (contraction of **GALLON**) + **TREE**.

Gantt chart /gant/ ▶ **noun** a chart in which a series of horizontal lines shows the amount of work done or production completed in certain periods of time in relation to the amount planned for those periods.
– ORIGIN early 20th cent.: named after Henry L. *Gantt* (1861–1919), American management consultant.

Ganymede /ˈganɪmiːd/ **1** Greek Mythology a Trojan youth who was so beautiful that he was carried off to be Zeus' cup-bearer.
2 Astronomy one of the Galilean moons of Jupiter, the seventh-closest satellite to the planet and the largest satellite in the solar system (diameter 5,262 km).

ganzfeld /ˈganzfɛld/ ▶ **noun** [often as modifier] a technique of controlled sensory input used with the aim of improving results in tests of telepathy and other paranormal phenomena: *ganzfeld tests*.
– ORIGIN 1980s: from German, literally 'whole field'.

GAO ▶ **abbreviation** General Accounting Office, a body that undertakes investigations for the US Congress.

gaol ▶ **noun** Brit. variant spelling of **JAIL**.

gaoler ▶ **noun** Brit. variant spelling of **JAILER**.

gap ▶ **noun 1** a break or hole in an object or between two objects: *he peeped through the gap in the curtains*. ■ a pass or way through a range of hills.

2 a space or interval; a break in continuity: *there are many gaps in our understanding of what happened.* ■ a difference, especially an undesirable one, between two views or situations: *the media were **bridging the gap** between government and people.*
– DERIVATIVES **gapped** adjective, **gappy** adjective (**gappier**, **gappiest**).
– ORIGIN Middle English: from Old Norse, 'chasm'; related to GAPE.

gape ▶ verb [no obj.] be or become wide open: [with complement] *a carpet bag gaped open by her feet.* ■ stare with one's mouth open wide in amazement or wonder: *he **gaped at** Sharp in silence.*
▶ noun a wide opening: *a wide gape of the jaws.* ■ an open-mouthed stare: *she climbed into her sports car to the gapes of passers-by.* ■ a widely open mouth or beak: *juvenile birds with yellow gapes.* ■ (**the gapes**) a disease of birds with gaping of the mouth as a symptom, caused by infestation with gapeworm.
– ORIGIN Middle English: from Old Norse *gapa*; related to GAP.

gaper ▶ noun **1** a burrowing bivalve mollusc, the shell valves of which have an opening at one or both ends. ● Genus *Mya*, family Myidae.
2 another term for COMBER[2].
3 a deep-sea anglerfish that is able to inflate itself with water. ● Family Chaunacidae and genus *Chaunax*.
4 a person who stares in amazement or wonder.

gapeworm ▶ noun a parasitic nematode worm that infests the trachea and bronchi of birds, causing the gapes. ● *Syngamus trachea*, class Phasmida.

gaping ▶ adjective (of a hole, wound, etc.) wide open: *there was a gaping hole in the wall.*
– DERIVATIVES **gapingly** adverb.

gapper ▶ noun Brit. informal a student who is on a gap year.

gapping ▶ noun [mass noun] Grammar the omission of a verb in the second of two coordinated clauses, as in *I went by bus and Mary by car.*

gap-toothed ▶ adjective having or showing gaps between the teeth.

gap year ▶ noun chiefly Brit. a period, typically an academic year, taken by a student as a break between school and university or college education.

gar ▶ noun the freshwater garfish of North America.
– ORIGIN mid 18th cent.: abbreviation.

garage /ˈgarɑː(d)ʒ, -ɪdʒ, gəˈrɑːʒ/ ▶ noun **1** a building for housing a motor vehicle or vehicles. ■ an establishment which sells fuel or which repairs and sells motor vehicles.
2 (also **garage rock**) [mass noun] a style of unpolished, energetic rock music associated with suburban amateur bands. [from the idea of amateur bands practising in garages.]
3 (also **UK garage**) [mass noun] a form of dance music incorporating elements of drum and bass, house music, and soul, characterized by a rhythm in which the second and fourth beats of the bar are omitted. [from *Paradise Garage*, the name of a Manhattan dance club.]
▶ verb [with obj.] put or keep (a motor vehicle) in a garage.
– DERIVATIVES **garaging** noun.
– ORIGIN early 20th cent.: from French, from *garer* 'to shelter'.

garage sale ▶ noun chiefly N. Amer. a sale of unwanted household goods held in the garage or front garden of someone's house.

garam masala /ˌgʌrəm məˈsɑːlə/ ▶ noun [mass noun] a spice mixture used in Indian cookery.
– ORIGIN from Urdu *garam maṣālaḥ*, from *garam* 'hot, pungent' + *maṣālaḥ* 'spice'.

garb[1] ▶ noun [mass noun] clothing, especially of a distinctive or special kind: *kids in combat garb.*
▶ verb [with obj.] dress in distinctive clothes: *she was garbed in Indian shawls.*
– ORIGIN late 16th cent.: via French from Italian *garbo* 'elegance', of Germanic origin; related to GEAR.

garb[2] ▶ noun Heraldry a sheaf of wheat.
– ORIGIN early 16th cent.: from Old Northern French *garbe*; compare with French *gerbe*.

garba /ˈgɑːbə/ ▶ noun a traditional Gujarati folk dance and song, originally performed as a fertility ritual.
– ORIGIN from Sanskrit *Garbadeep*, literally 'lamp inside a pot'.

garbage ▶ noun [mass noun] chiefly N. Amer. rubbish or waste, especially domestic refuse. ■ worthless or meaningless material or ideas; rubbish: *a store full of overpriced garbage.* ■ Computing unwanted data in a computer's memory.
– PHRASES **garbage in, garbage out** used to express the idea that in computing and other fields, incorrect or poor-quality input will produce faulty output.
– ORIGIN late Middle English (in the sense 'offal'): from Anglo-Norman French, of unknown ultimate origin.

garbage can (also **garbage bin**) ▶ noun N. Amer. a dustbin.

garbage collector ▶ noun **1** N. Amer. a dustman.
2 Computing a program that automatically removes unwanted data held temporarily in memory during processing.

garbanzo /gɑːˈbanzəʊ/ (also **garbanzo bean**) ▶ noun (pl. **garbanzos**) N. Amer. a chickpea.
– ORIGIN mid 18th cent.: from Spanish.

garble ▶ verb [with obj.] reproduce (a message, sound, or transmission) in a confused and distorted way: (as adj. **garbled**) *garbled directions.*
▶ noun a garbled account or transmission.
– DERIVATIVES **garbler** noun.
– ORIGIN late Middle English (in the sense 'sift out, cleanse'): from Anglo-Latin and Italian *garbellare*, from Arabic *ġarbala* 'sift', perhaps from late Latin *cribellare* 'to sieve', from Latin *cribrum* 'sieve'.

Garbo, Greta (1905–90), Swedish-born American actress; born *Greta Gustafsson*. She is remembered for films such as *Anna Christie* (1930), *Mata Hari* (1931), and *Anna Karenina* (1935). After her retirement in 1941 she lived as a recluse.

garbo ▶ noun (pl. **garbos**) Austral. informal a garbage collector.

garboard /ˈgɑːbɔːd/ (also **garboard strake**) ▶ noun the first range of planks or plates laid on a ship's bottom next to the keel.
– ORIGIN early 17th cent.: from Dutch *gaarboord*, perhaps from *garen* 'gather' + *boord* 'board'.

garbology /gɑːˈbɒlədʒi/ ▶ noun [mass noun] the study of a community or culture by analysing its waste.
– DERIVATIVES **garbologist** noun.
– ORIGIN 1960s: from GARBAGE + -LOGY.

García Lorca see LORCA.

García Márquez /gɑːˌsɪə ˈmɑːkɛz, mɑːˈkɛz/, Spanish /garˌθia marˈkeθ, -ˌsia, -ˈkes/, Gabriel (b.1927), Colombian novelist. His works include *One Hundred Years of Solitude* (1967), a classic example of magic realism, and *Chronicle of a Death Foretold* (1981). Nobel Prize for Literature (1982).

garçon /ˈgɑːsɒn, ˈgɑːsɔ̃/, French /garsɔ̃/ ▶ noun a waiter in a French restaurant or hotel.
– ORIGIN French, literally 'boy'.

garçonnière /ˌgɑːsɒnˈjɛː/ ▶ noun a bachelor's flat or set of rooms.
– ORIGIN French, from *garçon* 'boy'.

Garda /ˈgɑːdə/, Irish /ˈgaːrdə/ ▶ noun [treated as sing. or pl.] the state police force of the Republic of Ireland. ■ (pl. **Gardai** /-diː/, Irish /gaːrˈdiː/) a member of the Irish police force.
– ORIGIN from Irish *Garda Síochána* 'Civic Guard'.

Garda, Lake /ˈgɑːdə/, Italian /ˈgarda/ a lake in NE Italy, lying between Lombardy and Venetia.

garden ▶ noun **1** chiefly Brit. a piece of ground adjoining a house, used for growing flowers, fruit, or vegetables. ■ (**gardens**) ornamental grounds laid out for public enjoyment and recreation: *botanical gardens.* ■ [in names] Brit. a street or square: *Burlington Gardens.*
2 [in names] N. Amer. a large public hall: *Madison Square Garden.*
▶ verb [no obj.] cultivate or work in a garden.
– PHRASES **everything in the garden is rosy** Brit. everything is satisfactory. **the garden of England** a very fertile region of England, in particular Kent or the Vale of Evesham.
– DERIVATIVES **gardener** noun.
– ORIGIN Middle English: from Old Northern French *gardin*, variant of Old French *jardin*, of Germanic origin; related to YARD[2].

garden centre ▶ noun Brit. an establishment where plants and gardening equipment are sold.

garden chafer ▶ noun a small brown and metallic-green chafer which sometimes swarms in sunshine and may damage pasture and fruit crops. Also called JUNE BUG. ● *Phyllopertha horticola*, family Scarabaeidae.

garden city ▶ noun Brit. a new town designed as a whole with much open space and greenery.

garden cress ▶ noun [mass noun] a type of cress that is usually grown as a sprouting vegetable, often mixed with sprouting mustard, and used in salads. ● *Lepidium sativum*, family Cruciferae.

gardener bowerbird ▶ noun a drab New Guinea bowerbird that builds its bower over a mat of moss decorated with colourful flowers and fruits. ● Genus *Amblyornis*, family Ptilonorhynchidae: four species.

garden flat ▶ noun a basement or ground floor flat which opens on to a garden.

gardenia /gɑːˈdiːnɪə/ ▶ noun a tree or shrub of warm climates, with large, fragrant white or yellow flowers. ● Genus *Gardenia*, family Rubiaceae: several species, in particular the Cape jasmine.
– ORIGIN modern Latin, named in honour of Dr Alexander *Garden* (1730–91), Scottish naturalist.

gardening ▶ noun [mass noun] the activity of tending and cultivating a garden, especially as a pastime.

gardening leave ▶ noun [mass noun] Brit. an employee's suspension from work on full pay for the duration of a notice period, typically to prevent them from having any further influence on the organization or from accessing confidential information.

Garden of Eden see EDEN[2].

Garden of Gethsemane see GETHSEMANE, GARDEN OF.

G

garden party ▶ noun a social event held on a lawn in a garden.

garden pea ▶ noun a variety of pea grown for food. ■ a pea canned or frozen when freshly picked.

garden snail ▶ noun a large European snail with a brownish shell, often abundant in gardens. ● *Helix aspersa*, family Helicidae.

garden spider ▶ noun a common European orb-web spider with pale markings on the large rounded abdomen. ● *Araneus diadematus*, family Araneidae.

Garden State informal name for NEW JERSEY.

garden suburb ▶ noun Brit. a suburb set in rural surroundings or incorporating much landscaping.

garden tiger ▶ noun a large European tiger moth with boldly marked, chiefly brown and white forewings and orange and black hindwings. ● *Arctia caja*, family Arctiidae.

garden-variety ▶ adjective [attrib.] N. Amer. of the usual or ordinary type; commonplace.

garden warbler ▶ noun a migratory Eurasian songbird with drab plumage, frequenting woodland. ● *Sylvia borin*, family Sylviidae.

garderobe /ˈgɑːdrəʊb/ ▶ noun a toilet in a medieval building. ■ a wardrobe or small storeroom in a medieval building.
– ORIGIN late Middle English: French, from *garder* 'to keep' + *robe* 'robe, dress'; compare with WARDROBE.

Gardner, Ava (Lavinia) (1922–90), American actress. Notable films: *The Killers* (1946), *Bhowani Junction* (1956), and *The Night of the Iguana* (1964).

Garfield, James Abram (1831–81), American Republican statesman, 20th President of the US March–September 1881. He was assassinated within months of becoming President.

garfish ▶ noun (pl. **same** or **garfishes**) any of a number of long, slender fish with elongated beak-like jaws containing sharply pointed teeth: ● a marine fish (family Belonidae, in particular the common European *Belone belone*). Also called GARPIKE or (N. Amer.) NEEDLEFISH ● N. Amer. a freshwater fish (family Lepisosteidae and genus *Lepisosteus*). Also called GAR or GARPIKE ● Australian and New Zealand term for HALFBEAK.
– ORIGIN Middle English: apparently from Old English *gār* 'spear' + FISH[1].

garganey /ˈgɑːg(ə)ni/ ▶ noun (pl. **same** or **garganeys**) a small Eurasian duck, the male of which has a dark brown head with a white stripe from the eye to the neck. ● *Anas querquedula*, family Anatidae.
– ORIGIN mid 17th cent.: from Italian dialect *garganei*, of imitative origin.

gargantuan /gɑːˈgantjʊən/ ▶ adjective enormous: *a gargantuan appetite.*
– ORIGIN late 16th cent.: from *Gargantua*, the name of a voracious giant in Rabelais' book of the same name (1534), + -AN.

garget /ˈgɑːgɪt/ ▶ noun [mass noun] inflammation of a cow's or ewe's udder.
– ORIGIN early 18th cent.: perhaps a special use of Old French *gargate* 'throat'; related to GARGOYLE. The term was used earlier to denote inflammation of the throat in cattle.

gargle ▶ verb [no obj.] wash one's mouth and throat with a liquid that is kept in motion by breathing through it with a gurgling sound: *he gargled with alcohol for toothache.*

▶ **noun** an act or the sound of gargling: *a swig and gargle of mouthwash.* ■ [usu. in sing.] a liquid used for gargling. ■ Brit. informal an alcoholic drink.
– ORIGIN early 16th cent.: from French *gargouiller* 'gurgle, bubble', from *gargouille* 'throat' (see GARGOYLE).

gargoyle /ˈɡɑːɡɔɪl/ ▶ **noun** a grotesque carved human or animal face or figure projecting from the gutter of a building, typically acting as a spout to carry water clear of a wall.
– ORIGIN Middle English: from Old French *gargouille* 'throat', also 'gargoyle' (because of the water passing through the throat and mouth of the figure); related to Greek *gargarizein* 'to gargle' (imitating the sounds made in the throat).

gargoylism ▶ **noun** another term for **HURLER'S SYNDROME**.
– ORIGIN early 20th cent.: from GARGOYLE (because the deformities which characterize the syndrome were thought to resemble Gothic gargoyles) + **-ISM**.

Garibaldi /ˌɡarɪˈbɔːldi/, Italian /ɡariˈbaldi/, Giuseppe (1807–82), Italian patriot and military leader of the Risorgimento. With his volunteer force of 'Red Shirts' he captured Sicily and southern Italy from the Bourbons in 1860–1, thereby playing a key role in the establishment of a united kingdom of Italy.

garibaldi /ˌɡarɪˈbɔːldi, -ˈbaldi/ ▶ **noun** (pl. **garibaldis**) **1** Brit. a biscuit containing a layer of compressed currants.
2 a small bright orange marine fish found off California. ● *Hypsypops rubicundus*, family Pomacentridae.
3 historical a woman's or child's loose blouse, originally bright red in imitation of the shirts worn by Garibaldi and his followers.
– ORIGIN mid 19th cent.: named after G. **GARIBALDI**.

garimpeiro /ˌɡarimˈpeɪruː/ ▶ **noun** (pl. **garimpeiros**) (in Brazil) an independent prospector for minerals.
– ORIGIN Portuguese.

garish /ˈɡɛːrɪʃ/ ▶ **adjective** obtrusively bright and showy; lurid: *garish shirts in all sorts of colours.*
– DERIVATIVES **garishly** adverb, **garishness** noun.
– ORIGIN mid 16th cent.: of unknown origin.

Garland, Judy (1922–69), American singer and actress; born *Frances Gumm*. Her most famous early film role was in *The Wizard of Oz* (1939), in which she played Dorothy and sang 'Over the Rainbow'. Other notable films include *Meet Me in St Louis* (1944) and *A Star is Born* (1954).

garland ▶ **noun 1** a wreath of flowers and leaves, worn on the head or hung as a decoration.
2 dated a prize or distinction.
3 archaic a literary anthology or miscellany.
▶ **verb** [with obj.] decorate with a garland: *they were garlanded with flowers.*
– ORIGIN Middle English: from Old French *garlande*, of unknown origin.

garlic ▶ **noun** [mass noun] **1** a strong-smelling pungent-tasting bulb, used as a flavouring in cookery and in herbal medicine.
2 the central Asian plant, closely related to the onion, which produces garlic. ● *Allium sativum*, family Liliaceae (or Alliaceae).
■ used in names of plants with a similar smell or flavour, e.g. **wild garlic**.
– DERIVATIVES **garlicky** adjective.
– ORIGIN Old English *gārlēac*, from *gār* 'spear' (because the shape of a clove resembles the head of a spear) + *lēac* 'leek'.

garlic bread ▶ **noun** [mass noun] bread spread with butter and crushed garlic and heated in the oven, often served as a side dish.

garment ▶ **noun** an item of clothing: *a windproof outer garment | fashion garments.*
– ORIGIN Middle English: from Old French *garnement* 'equipment', from *garnir* 'equip' (see GARNISH).

Garmo, Mount /ˈɡɑːməʊ/ former name (until 1933) for **ISMAIL SAMANI PEAK**.

garms ▶ **plural noun** informal clothes; garments.

Garnacha /ɡɑːˈnatʃə/ ▶ **noun** [mass noun] a variety of wine grape grown in Spain. ■ a red or rosé wine made from Garnacha grapes.
– ORIGIN Spanish, from Italian *vernaccia* (see **VERNACCIA**). The grape is known in France and elsewhere as **GRENACHE**.

garner ▶ **verb** [with obj.] gather or collect (something, especially information or approval): *the police struggled to garner sufficient evidence.* ■ archaic store; deposit: *the crop was ready to be reaped and garnered.*
▶ **noun** archaic a granary.
– ORIGIN Middle English (originally as a noun): from Old French *gernier*, from Latin *granarium* 'granary', from *granum* 'grain'.

garnet /ˈɡɑːnɪt/ ▶ **noun** a precious stone consisting of a deep red vitreous silicate mineral. ■ [mass noun] Mineralogy any of a class of silicate minerals including this, which belong to the cubic system and have the general chemical formula $A_3B_2(SiO_4)_3$ (A and B being respectively divalent and trivalent metals).
– ORIGIN Middle English: probably via Middle Dutch from Old French *grenat*, from medieval Latin *granatus*, perhaps from *granatum* (see **POMEGRANATE**), because the garnet is similar in colour to the pulp of the fruit.

garnierite /ˈɡɑːnɪərʌɪt, ɡɑːˈnɪərʌɪt/ ▶ **noun** [mass noun] a bright green amorphous mineral consisting of a hydrated silicate of nickel and magnesium.
– ORIGIN 1875: named after Jules *Garnier* (1839–1904), French geologist.

garnish ▶ **verb** [with obj.] **1** decorate or embellish (something, especially food): *garnish each serving with a dollop of sour cream.*
2 Law serve notice on (a third party) for the purpose of legally seizing money belonging to a debtor or defendant. ■ seize (money, especially part of a person's salary) to settle a debt or claim: *the IRS garnished his earnings.*
▶ **noun** a small amount of food used to decorate other food.
– DERIVATIVES **garnishment** noun.
– ORIGIN Middle English (in the sense 'equip, arm'): from Old French *garnir*, probably of Germanic origin and related to **WARN**. Sense 1 of the verb dates from the late 17th cent.

garnishee /ˌɡɑːnɪˈʃiː/ Law ▶ **noun** a third party who is instructed by way of legal notice to surrender money to settle a debt or claim.
▶ **verb** (**garnishees, garnisheeing, garnisheed**) another term for **GARNISH** (sense 2 of the verb).

garniture /ˈɡɑːnɪtʃə/ ▶ **noun** a set of decorative accessories, in particular vases.
– ORIGIN late 15th cent.: from French, from *garnir* 'to garnish'.

Garonne /ɡaˈrɒn/, French /ɡarɔn/ a river of SW France, which rises in the Pyrenees and flows 645 km (400 miles) north-west through Toulouse and Bordeaux to join the Dordogne at the Gironde estuary.

garotte ▶ **verb & noun** variant spelling of **GARROTTE**.

Garoua /ɡaˈruːə/ a river port in northern Cameroon, on the River Bénoué; pop. 409,000 (est. 2007).

garpike ▶ **noun** another term for **GARFISH**.
– ORIGIN late 18th cent.: from **GAR** + **PIKE**[1].

garret ▶ **noun** a top-floor or attic room, especially a small dismal one.
– ORIGIN Middle English (in the sense 'watchtower'): from Old French *garite*, from *garir* (see **GARRISON**).

Garrick, David (1717–79), English actor and dramatist. He was a notably versatile actor and the manager of the Drury Lane Theatre.

garrick ▶ **noun** South African term for **LEERVIS**.
– ORIGIN of unknown origin.

garrison ▶ **noun** a group of troops stationed in a fortress or town to defend it. ■ the building occupied by a garrison.
▶ **verb** [with obj.] provide (a place) with a group of troops: *air reconnaissance showed the Germans had not garrisoned the island.* ■ [with obj. and adverbial of place] station (troops) in a particular place: *French troops were garrisoned at Phillipsburg.*
– ORIGIN Middle English (in the sense 'safety, means of protection'): from Old French *garison*, from *garir* 'defend, provide', of Germanic origin.

garrison cap ▶ **noun** US a peakless cap, especially one worn as part of a military uniform.

garrison town ▶ **noun** a town that has troops permanently stationed in it.

garron /ˈɡarən/ ▶ **noun** another term for **HIGHLAND PONY**.
– ORIGIN mid 16th cent.: from Scottish Gaelic *gearran*, Irish *gearrán*.

garrotte /ɡəˈrɒt/ (also **garotte**; US **garrote**) ▶ **verb** [with obj.] kill (someone) by strangulation, especially with a length of wire or cord.
▶ **noun** a wire, cord, or other implement used for garrotting.
– ORIGIN early 17th cent.: via French from Spanish *garrote* 'a cudgel, a garrotte', perhaps of Celtic origin.

garrulity /ɡəˈruːlɪti/ ▶ **noun** [mass noun] excessive talkativeness, especially on trivial matters: *the character's comic garrulity.*

garrulous /ˈɡar(j)ʊləs/ ▶ **adjective** excessively talkative, especially on trivial matters: *a garrulous cab driver.*
– DERIVATIVES **garrulously** adverb, **garrulousness** noun.
– ORIGIN early 17th cent.: from Latin *garrulus* (from *garrire* 'to chatter, prattle') + **-OUS**.

garryowen /ˌɡarɪˈəʊɪn/ ▶ **noun** Rugby an up-and-under.
– ORIGIN 1960s: named after a rugby club in Limerick, Republic of Ireland.

garter ▶ **noun 1** a band worn around the leg to keep a stocking or sock up. ■ a band worn on the arm to keep a shirtsleeve up. ■ N. Amer. a suspender for a sock or stocking.
2 (**the Garter**) short for **ORDER OF THE GARTER**. ■ membership of the Order of the Garter.
– PHRASES **have someone's guts for garters** see **GUT**.
– DERIVATIVES **gartered** adjective.
– ORIGIN Middle English: from Old French *gartier*, from *garet* 'bend of the knee, calf of the leg', probably of Celtic origin.

garter belt ▶ **noun** N. Amer. a suspender belt.

Garter King of Arms ▶ **noun** Heraldry (in the UK) the principal King of Arms of the English College of Arms.

garter snake ▶ **noun 1** a common, harmless North American snake that typically has well-defined longitudinal stripes and favours damp habitats. ● Genus *Thamnophis*, family Colubridae: several species, in particular *T. sirtalis*.
2 a venomous burrowing African snake that is typically dark with lighter bands. ● Genus *Elapsoidea*, family Elapidae: several species.

garter stitch ▶ **noun** [mass noun] knitting in which all of the rows are knitted in plain stitch, rather than alternating with purl rows.

garth ▶ **noun** Brit. an open space surrounded by cloisters. ■ archaic a yard or garden.
– ORIGIN Middle English (also, in early use, denoting a hollow): from Old Norse *garthr*; related to **YARD**[2].

Garuda /ˈɡarʊdə/ Hinduism an eagle-like being that serves as the mount of Vishnu.
– ORIGIN from Sanskrit *garuḍa*.

Garvey /ˈɡɑːvi/, Marcus (Mosiah) (1887–1940), Jamaican political activist and black nationalist leader. He advocated the establishment of an African homeland for black Americans and his thinking was later an important influence on Rastafarianism.

Gary /ˈɡari/ an industrial city in NW Indiana, on Lake Michigan south-east of Chicago; pop. 95,920 (est. 2008).

gas ▶ **noun** (pl. **gases** or chiefly US **gasses**) [mass noun] **1** an air-like fluid substance which expands freely to fill any space available, irrespective of its quantity: *hot balls of gas that become stars* | [count noun] *poisonous gases.* ■ Physics a gaseous substance that cannot be liquefied by the application of pressure alone. Compare with **VAPOUR**. ■ a flammable gas used as a fuel. ■ a gaseous anaesthetic such as nitrous oxide, used in dentistry. ■ gas or vapour used as a poisonous agent in warfare. ■ N. Amer. gas generated in the alimentary canal; flatulence. ■ Mining an explosive mixture of firedamp with air.
2 N. Amer. informal short for **GASOLINE**. ■ used in reference to power or the accelerator of a car: *I ordered my friend to step on the gas.*
3 (**a gas**) informal an entertaining or amusing person or situation: *the party would be a gas.* ■ [mass noun] Irish enjoyment, amusement, or fun: *it was great gas in the club last night.*
▶ **verb** (**gases, gassing, gassed**) [with obj.] **1** kill or harm by exposure to gas: *my son was gassed at Verdun.* ■ [no obj.] (of a storage battery or dry cell) give off gas.
2 [no obj.] informal talk excessively about trivial matters: *I thought you'd never stop gassing.*
3 N. Amer. informal fill the tank of (a motor vehicle) with petrol: *after gassing up the car, he went into the restaurant.*
▶ **adjective** Irish informal very amusing or entertaining: *Ruthie, that's gas—you're a gem.*
– PHRASES **run out of gas** N. Amer. informal run out of energy; lose momentum.
– ORIGIN mid 17th cent.: invented by J. B. van Helmont (1577–1644), Belgian chemist, to denote an occult principle which he believed to exist in all matter; suggested by Greek *khaos* 'chaos', with Dutch *g* representing Greek *kh*.

gasbag ▸ noun **1** informal a person who talks excessively about trivial things.
2 the container holding the gas in a balloon or airship.

gas chamber ▸ noun an airtight room that can be filled with poisonous gas to kill people or animals.

gas chromatography ▸ noun [mass noun] chromatography employing a gas as the moving carrier medium. Compare with **GAS–LIQUID CHROMATOGRAPHY**.

Gascogne /gaskɔɲ/ French name for **GASCONY**.

Gascon /ˈgask(ə)n/ ▸ noun **1** a native or inhabitant of Gascony.
2 (**gascon**) archaic a boastful person. [with allusion to the perceived character of natives of Gascony.]
▸ adjective relating to Gascony or its people.
– ORIGIN via Old French from Latin *Vasco, Vascon-*; related to **BASQUE**.

gasconade /ˌgaskəˈneɪd/ ▸ noun [mass noun] literary extravagant boasting.
– ORIGIN mid 17th cent.: from French *gasconnade*, from *gasconner* 'talk like a Gascon, brag'.

gas constant (Symbol: **R**) ▸ noun Chemistry the constant of proportionality in the gas equation. It is equal to 8.314 joule kelvin^{-1} mole^{-1}.

Gascony /ˈgaskəni/ a region and former province of SW France, in the northern foothills of the Pyrenees. It was held by England between 1154 and 1453. French name **GASCOGNE**.

gaseous /ˈgasɪəs, ˈgeɪsɪəs/ ▸ adjective relating to or having the characteristics of a gas: *gaseous emissions from motor vehicles | gaseous oxygen*.
– DERIVATIVES **gaseousness** noun.

gas equation ▸ noun Chemistry the equation of state of an ideal gas, $PV = nRT$, where P = pressure, V = volume, T = absolute temperature, R = the gas constant, and n = the number of moles of gas.

gas fire ▸ noun a domestic heating appliance which uses gas as its fuel.

gas-fired ▸ adjective using gas as its fuel: *gas-fired central heating*.

gas fitter ▸ noun Brit. a person trained to connect, disconnect, and service gas fittings and appliances.

gas gangrene ▸ noun [mass noun] rapidly spreading gangrene affecting injured tissue infected by a soil bacterium and accompanied by the evolution of foul-smelling gas. ● This disease is usually caused by anaerobic bacteria of the genus *Clostridium*.

gas giant ▸ noun Astronomy a large planet of relatively low density consisting predominantly of hydrogen and helium, such as Jupiter, Saturn, Uranus, or Neptune.

gas guzzler ▸ noun informal a large car with a high fuel consumption.
– DERIVATIVES **gas-guzzling** adjective.

gash¹ ▸ noun **1** a long, deep cut or wound: *a bad gash in one leg became infected*. ■ a cleft made as if by a slashing cut: *the blast ripped a 25-foot gash in the hull*.
2 vulgar slang a woman's vulva. ■ [mass noun] offensive women collectively regarded in sexual terms.
▸ verb [with obj.] make a long, deep cut in: *the jagged edges gashed their fingers*.
– ORIGIN Middle English *garse*, from Old French *garcer* 'to chap, crack', perhaps based on Greek *kharassein* 'sharpen, scratch, engrave'. The current spelling is recorded from the mid 16th cent.

gash² ▸ noun [mass noun] Brit. informal rubbish or waste: [as modifier] *the gash bucket*.
– ORIGIN 1920s (originally in nautical use): of unknown origin.

gasholder ▸ noun another term for **GASOMETER**.

gasify /ˈgasɪfʌɪ/ ▸ verb (**gasifies, gasifying, gasified**) [with obj.] convert (a solid or liquid, especially coal) into gas. ■ [no obj.] become a gas: *if PVC is overheated it will gasify*.
– DERIVATIVES **gasification** noun.

Gaskell /ˈgask(ə)l/, Mrs Elizabeth (Cleghorn) (1810–65), English novelist. Notable works: *Mary Barton* (1848), *Cranford* (1853), and *North and South* (1855). She also wrote a biography (1857) of her friend Charlotte Brontë.

gasket /ˈgaskɪt/ ▸ noun **1** a shaped sheet or ring of rubber or other material sealing the junction between two surfaces in an engine or other device.
2 archaic a cord securing a furled sail to the yard of a sailing ship.
– PHRASES **blow a gasket 1** suffer a leak in a gasket of an engine. **2** informal lose one's temper.
– ORIGIN early 17th cent. (in sense 2): perhaps from French *garcette* 'thin rope' (originally 'little girl'), diminutive of *garce*, feminine of *gars* 'boy'.

gaskin /ˈgaskɪn/ ▸ noun the muscular part of the hind leg of a horse between the stifle and the hock.
– ORIGIN late 16th cent.: perhaps from **GALLIGASKINS** (the original sense).

gas laws ▸ plural noun Chemistry the physical laws that describe the properties of gases, including Boyle's and Charles's laws.

gaslight ▸ noun a type of lamp in which an incandescent mantle is heated by a jet of burning gas. ■ [mass noun] the light produced by a gaslight: *in the gaslight she looked paler than ever*.
– DERIVATIVES **gaslit** adjective.

gas–liquid chromatography ▸ noun [mass noun] chromatography employing a gas as the moving carrier medium and a liquid as the stationary medium.

gasman ▸ noun (pl. **gasmen**) a man who installs or services gas appliances or reads gas meters.

gas mantle ▸ noun see **MANTLE¹** (sense 3 of the noun).

gas mask ▸ noun a protective mask used to cover a person's face as a defence against poison gas.

gasohol /ˈgasəhɒl/ ▸ noun [mass noun] N. Amer. a mixture of petrol and ethanol used as fuel in internal-combustion engines.
– ORIGIN 1970s: blend of **GAS** and **ALCOHOL**.

gas oil ▸ noun [mass noun] a type of fuel oil distilled from petroleum and heavier than paraffin oil.

gasoline (also **gasolene**) ▸ noun North American term for **PETROL**.
– ORIGIN mid 19th cent.: from **GAS** + **-OL** + **-INE⁴** (or **-ENE**).

gasometer ▸ noun a large metal tank, typically cylindrical, in which gas for use as fuel is stored before being distributed through pipes to consumers.
– ORIGIN late 18th cent. (in the sense 'container for holding or measuring a gas'): from French *gazomètre*, from *gaz* 'gas' + *-mètre* '(instrument) measuring'.

gasp ▸ verb [no obj.] catch one's breath with an open mouth, owing to pain or astonishment: *a woman gasped in horror at the sight of him*. ■ [with obj.] say (something) while catching one's breath: *Jeremy gasped out an apology* | [with direct speech] *'It's beautiful!' she gasped, much impressed*. ■ (**gasp for**) strain to obtain (air) by gasping: *she surfaced and gasped for air*. ■ (**be gasping for**) Brit. informal be desperate to obtain or consume; crave: *I'm gasping for a drink!*
▸ noun a convulsive catching of breath: *his breath was coming in gasps*.
– PHRASES **one's** (or **the**) **last gasp** the point of exhaustion, death, or completion: *the last gasp of the Cold War*.
– ORIGIN late Middle English: from Old Norse *geispa* 'to yawn'.

gasper ▸ noun Brit. informal, dated a cigarette.

gas-permeable ▸ adjective (of a contact lens) allowing the diffusion of gases into and out of the cornea.

gas plant ▸ noun an aromatic Eurasian plant of the rue family, with showy white flowers and fragrant leaves that emit a flammable vapour. This can sometimes be ignited without harming the plant. Also called **BURNING BUSH, DITTANY, FRAXINELLA**. ● *Dictamnus* (formerly *Fraxinella*) *albus*, family Rutaceae.

Gassendi /gaˈsɛndi/, French /gasɑ̃di/, Pierre (1592–1655), French astronomer and philosopher. He is best known for his atomic theory of matter, which was based on his interpretation of the works of Epicurus.

gasser ▸ noun informal **1** a chatterer.
2 US a very attractive or impressive person or thing.

gas station ▸ noun N. Amer. a petrol station.

gassy ▸ adjective (**gassier, gassiest**) **1** resembling or full of gas: *the beer was served too gassy and too cold*. ■ N. Amer. (of a person) flatulent.
2 informal (of a person or language) inclined to be verbose: *a long and gassy book*.
– DERIVATIVES **gassiness** noun.

Gastarbeiter /ˈgastˌɑːbʌɪtə/, German /ˈgastˌarbaɪtɐ/ ▸ noun (pl. **same** or **Gastarbeiters**) a person with temporary permission to work in another country, especially in Germany.
– ORIGIN German, from *Gast* 'guest' + *Arbeiter* 'worker'.

gasteropod ▸ noun old-fashioned spelling of **GASTROPOD**.

Gasthaus /ˈgasthaʊs/ ▸ noun (pl. **Gasthäuser** /-ˌhɔɪzə/) a small inn or hotel in a German-speaking country.
– ORIGIN from German, from *Gast* 'guest' + *Haus* 'house'.

Gasthof /ˈgasthɒf/, German /ˈgasthoːf/ ▸ noun (pl. **Gasthöfe** or **Gasthofs** /-ˌhəːfə/, German /-ˌhøːfə/) a hotel in a German-speaking country, typically larger than a Gasthaus.
– ORIGIN from German, from *Gast* 'guest' + *Hof* 'hotel, large house'.

Gastornis /gaˈstɔːnɪs/ ▸ noun a very large flightless bird of the Eocene epoch.
– ORIGIN modern Latin, from the name of the French scientist *Gaston* Planté (1834–89), who found the first specimen, + Greek *ornis* 'bird'.

gastr- ▸ combining form variant spelling of **GASTRO-** shortened before a vowel (as in *gastrectomy*).

gastrectomy /gaˈstrɛktəmi/ ▸ noun (pl. **gastrectomies**) [mass noun] surgical removal of a part or the whole of the stomach.

gastric ▸ adjective of the stomach.
– ORIGIN mid 17th cent.: from modern Latin *gastricus*, from Greek *gastēr, gastr-* 'stomach'.

G

gastric flu ▸ noun [mass noun] a short-lived stomach disorder of unknown cause, popularly attributed to a virus.

gastric juice ▸ noun [mass noun] a thin, clear, virtually colourless acid fluid secreted by the stomach glands and active in promoting digestion.

gastrin ▸ noun [mass noun] Biochemistry a hormone which stimulates secretion of gastric juice and is secreted into the bloodstream by the stomach wall in response to the presence of food.
– ORIGIN early 20th cent.: from **GASTRIC** + **-IN¹**.

gastritis /gaˈstrʌɪtɪs/ ▸ noun [mass noun] Medicine inflammation of the lining of the stomach.

gastro- /ˈgastrəʊ/ (also **gastr-** before a vowel) ▸ combining form relating to the stomach: *gastrectomy | gastroenteritis*.
– ORIGIN from Greek *gastēr, gastr-* 'stomach'.

gastrocnemius /ˌgastrə(ʊ)ˈkniːmɪəs/ (also **gastrocnemius muscle**) ▸ noun (pl. **gastrocnemii** /-mɪʌɪ/) Anatomy the chief muscle of the calf of the leg, which flexes the knee and foot. It runs to the Achilles tendon from two heads attached to the femur.
– ORIGIN late 17th cent.: modern Latin, from Greek *gastroknēmia* 'calf of the leg', from *gaster, gastr-* 'stomach' + *knēmē* 'leg' (from the bulging shape of the calf).

gastrocolic /ˌgastrə(ʊ)ˈkɒlɪk/ ▸ adjective relating to the stomach and the colon.

gastroenteric ▸ adjective Medicine & Physiology relating to the stomach and intestines.

gastroenteritis ▸ noun [mass noun] inflammation of the stomach and intestines, typically resulting from bacterial toxins or viral infection and causing vomiting and diarrhoea.

gastroenterology /ˌgastrəʊɛntəˈrɒlədʒi/ ▸ noun [mass noun] the branch of medicine which deals with disorders of the stomach and intestines.
– DERIVATIVES **gastroenterological** adjective, **gastroenterologist** noun.

gastrointestinal /ˌgastrəʊɪnˈtɛstɪn(ə)l, -ɪntɛsˈtʌɪn(ə)l/ ▸ adjective relating to the stomach and the intestines.

gastrolith /ˈgastrə(ʊ)lɪθ/ ▸ noun **1** Zoology a small stone swallowed by a bird, reptile, or fish to aid digestion in the gizzard.
2 Medicine a hard concretion in the stomach.

gastronome /ˈgastrənəʊm/ ▸ noun a gourmet.
– ORIGIN early 19th cent.: from French, from *gastronomic* (see **GASTRONOMY**).

gastronomy /gaˈstrɒnəmi/ ▸ noun [mass noun] the practice or art of choosing, cooking, and eating good food. ■ the cookery of a particular area: *traditional American gastronomy*.
– DERIVATIVES **gastronomic** adjective, **gastronomical** adjective, **gastronomically** adverb.
– ORIGIN early 19th cent.: from French *gastronomie*, from Greek *gastronomia*, alteration of *gastrologia* (see **GASTRO-, -LOGY**).

gastropod ▸ noun Zoology a mollusc of the large class Gastropoda, such as a snail, slug, or whelk.

Gastropoda /ˌgastrəˈpəʊdə, gasˈtrɒpədə/ ▸ plural noun Zoology a large class of molluscs which includes snails, slugs, whelks, and all terrestrial kinds. They have a large muscular foot for movement and (in many kinds) a single asymmetrical spiral shell.
– ORIGIN modern Latin (plural), from Greek *gastēr, gastr-* 'stomach' + *pous, pod-* 'foot'.

gastropub ▸ noun Brit. a pub that specializes in serving high-quality food.
– ORIGIN 1990s: from *gastro-* in GASTRONOMY + PUB.

gastroscope ▸ noun an optical instrument used for inspecting the interior of the stomach.
– DERIVATIVES **gastroscopic** adjective, **gastroscopy** noun.

gastrostomy /ga'strɒstəmi/ ▸ noun (pl. **gastrostomies**) an opening into the stomach from the abdominal wall, made surgically for the introduction of food. ▪ a surgical operation for making a gastrostomy.

Gastrotricha /,gastrə'trʌɪkə/ ▸ plural noun Zoology a small phylum of minute aquatic worm-like animals which bear bristles and cilia. They are thought to be related to the nematode worms and rotifers.
– DERIVATIVES **gastrotrich** /'gastrətrɪk/ noun.
– ORIGIN modern Latin (plural), from Greek *gastēr*, *gastr-* 'stomach' + *thrix*, *trikh-* 'hair'.

gastrula /'gastrʊlə/ ▸ noun (pl. **gastrulae** /-li:/) Embryology an embryo at the stage following the blastula, when it is a hollow cup-shaped structure having three layers of cells.
– DERIVATIVES **gastrulation** noun.
– ORIGIN late 19th cent.: modern Latin, from Greek *gastēr*, *gastr-* 'stomach' + the Latin diminutive ending *-ula*.

gas turbine ▸ noun a turbine driven by expanding hot gases produced by burning fuel, as in a jet engine.

gasworks ▸ plural noun [treated as sing.] a place where gas is manufactured and processed.

gat[1] ▸ noun informal a revolver or pistol.
– ORIGIN early 20th cent.: abbreviation of GATLING GUN.

gat[2] archaic past of GET.

gate[1] ▸ noun **1** a hinged barrier used to close an opening in a wall, fence, or hedge. ▪ a gateway: *she went out through the gate.* ▪ an exit from an airport building to an aircraft: *a departure gate.* ▪ [in names] a mountain pass or other natural passage: *the Golden Gate.*
2 the number of people who pay to enter a sports ground for an event: *an average home gate of more than 12,000.* ▪ the money taken for admission.
3 a device resembling a gate in structure or function, in particular: ▪ a hinged or sliding barrier for controlling the flow of water: *a sluice gate.* ▪ an arrangement of slots into which the gear lever of a motor vehicle moves to engage each gear. ▪ a device for holding each frame of a film in position behind the lens of a camera or projector.
4 an electric circuit with an output which depends on the combination of several inputs: *a logic gate.* ▪ the part of a field-effect transistor to which a signal is applied to control the resistance of the conductive channel of the device.
▸ verb [with obj.] Brit. confine (a pupil or student) to school or college: *he was gated for the rest of term.*
– PHRASES **get** (or **be given**) **the gate** N. Amer. informal be dismissed from a job.
– ORIGIN Old English *gæt*, *geat*, plural *gatu*, of Germanic origin; related to Dutch *gat* 'gap, hole, breach'.

gate[2] ▸ noun Brit. (in place names) a street: *Kirkgate.*
– ORIGIN Middle English (also meaning 'way' in general): from Old Norse *gata*; related to German *Gasse* 'street, lane'.

-gate ▸ combining form in nouns denoting an actual or alleged scandal, especially one involving a cover-up: *Irangate.*
– ORIGIN early 1970s: suggested by the *Watergate* scandal in the US, 1972.

gate array ▸ noun Computing a regular arrangement of logic gates. ▪ an electronic chip consisting of a regular arrangement of logic gates.

gateau /'gatəʊ/ ▸ noun (pl. **gateaus** or **gateaux** /-əʊz/) chiefly Brit. a rich cake, typically one containing layers of cream or fruit.
– ORIGIN mid 19th cent.: from French *gâteau* 'cake'.

gatecrash ▸ verb [with obj.] enter (a party or other gathering) without an invitation or ticket.
– DERIVATIVES **gatecrasher** noun.

gated ▸ adjective **1** having gates to control the movement of traffic, people, or animals: *a gated road.* ▪ denoting a residential development in which access is allowed only through a secured gate, often protected by additional security measures: *a gated community.*
2 technical denoting a channel or pathway through a system that can be opened and closed depending on set conditions.

gatefold ▸ noun an oversized page in a book or magazine folded to the same size as the other pages but intended to be opened out for reading.

gatehouse ▸ noun **1** a house standing by a gateway, especially on a country estate.
2 historical a room over a city or palace gate, often used as a prison.

gatekeeper ▸ noun **1** (also **gateman**) an attendant employed to control who goes through a gate. ▪ a person or thing that controls access to something: *GPs can act as gatekeepers, filtering demands made on hospital services.*
2 an orange and brown European butterfly with small eyespots on the wings, frequenting hedgerows and woods. Also called HEDGE BROWN. ● *Pyronia tithonus*, subfamily Satyrinae, family Nymphalidae.
– DERIVATIVES **gatekeeping** noun.

gateleg table ▸ noun a table with hinged legs that are swung out from the centre to support folding leaves and make the table larger.
– DERIVATIVES **gatelegged** adjective.

gatepost ▸ noun a post on which a gate is hinged, or against which it shuts.
– PHRASES **between you and me and the gatepost** see BEDPOST.

Gates, Bill (b.1955), American computer entrepreneur; full name *William Henry Gates.* He co-founded the computer software company Microsoft and became the youngest multibillionaire in American history.

Gateshead an industrial town in NE England, on the south bank of the River Tyne opposite Newcastle; pop. 73,400 (est. 2009).

gate valve ▸ noun a valve with a sliding part that controls the extent of the aperture.

gateway ▸ noun **1** an opening that can be closed by a gate: *we turned into a gateway leading to a cottage.* ▪ a frame or arch built around or over a gate: *a big house with a wrought-iron gateway.* ▪ a place regarded as giving access to another place: *Mombasa, the gateway to East Africa.* ▪ a means of achieving a state or condition: *to me a home in the country was a gateway to happiness.*
2 Computing a device used to connect two different networks, especially a connection to the Internet.

gateway drug ▸ noun a drug which supposedly leads the user on to more addictive or dangerous drugs.

Gatha /'gɑ:θɑ:/ ▸ noun any of seventeen poems attributed to Zoroaster which are the most ancient texts of the Avesta.
– ORIGIN from Avestan *gāthā*.

gather ▸ verb **1** [no obj.] come together; assemble or accumulate: *as soon as a crowd gathered, the police came.*
2 [with obj.] bring together and take in from scattered places or sources: *information that we have gathered about people.* ▪ (**gather something up**) pick something up: *I gathered up the prescription and went to the door.* ▪ (**gather something in**) harvest grain or other crops. ▪ [no obj.] collect plants, fruits, etc., for food: *the Bushmen live by hunting and gathering.*
3 [with obj.] increase in (speed, force, etc.): *the destroyer gathered speed.*
4 [with obj.] infer; understand: [with clause] *I gathered that they were old friends.*
5 [with obj.] summon up (a mental or physical attribute) for a purpose: *she lay gathering her thoughts together* | *he* ***gathered himself*** *for a tremendous leap.* ▪ gain or recover (one's breath).
6 [with obj.] pull (someone) into one's arms: *she gathered the child in her arms.* ▪ pull (clothing) more tightly around one's body.
7 [with obj.] draw and hold together (fabric or a part of a garment) by running thread through it: *the front is gathered at the waist.*
▸ noun (**gathers**) a part of a garment that is gathered.
– PHRASES **gather way** (of a ship) begin to move.
– DERIVATIVES **gatherer** noun.
– ORIGIN Old English *gaderian*, of West Germanic origin; related to Dutch *gaderen*, also to TOGETHER.

gathering ▸ noun **1** an assembly or meeting, especially one held for a specific purpose: *a family gathering.*
2 a group of leaves taken together, one inside another, in binding a book.

Gatling gun (also **Gatling**) ▸ noun a rapid-fire, crank-driven gun with clustered barrels. The first practical machine gun, it was officially adopted by the US army in 1866.
– ORIGIN named after Richard J. *Gatling* (1818–1903), its American inventor.

gator ▸ noun informal, chiefly N. Amer. an alligator.
– ORIGIN mid 19th cent.: shortened form.

Gatso /'gatsəʊ/ (also **Gatso camera**) ▸ noun (pl. **Gatsos**) a camera which automatically takes a photograph of road vehicles travelling over a certain speed (as measured by radar).
– ORIGIN 1970s: from the name of Maurice *Gats*onides, Dutch racing driver (1911–98).

GATT General Agreement on Tariffs and Trade, an international treaty (1948–94) to promote trade and economic development by reducing tariffs and other restrictions. It was superseded by the establishment of the World Trade Organization in 1995.

Gatwick an international airport in SE England, to the south of London.

gauche /gəʊʃ/ ▸ adjective unsophisticated and socially awkward: *a shy and gauche teenager.*
– DERIVATIVES **gauchely** adverb, **gaucheness** noun.
– ORIGIN mid 18th cent.: French, literally 'left'.

gaucherie /'gəʊʃ(ə)ri/ ▸ noun [mass noun] awkward or unsophisticated ways: *I was ridiculed for my sartorial gaucherie* | [count noun] *she had long since got over gaucheries such as blushing.*
– ORIGIN late 18th cent.: French, from *gauche* (see GAUCHE).

Gaucher's disease /'gəʊʃeɪz, gəʊ'ʃeɪz/ ▸ noun [mass noun] a hereditary disease in which the metabolism and storage of fats is abnormal. It results in bone fragility, neurological disturbance, anaemia, and enlargement of the liver and spleen.
– ORIGIN mid 20th cent.: named after Phillippe C. E. *Gaucher* (1854–1918), French physician.

gaucho /'gaʊtʃəʊ, 'gɔ:-/ ▸ noun (pl. **gauchos**) a cowboy from the South American pampas.
– ORIGIN Latin American Spanish, probably from Araucanian *kauču* 'friend'.

gaud /gɔ:d/ ▸ noun archaic a showy and purely ornamental thing: *displays of overpriced gauds.*
– ORIGIN Middle English (denoting a trick or pretence): perhaps via Anglo-Norman French from Old French *gaudir* 'rejoice', from Latin *gaudere*; perhaps influenced by obsolete *gaud* 'ornamental bead in a rosary'.

Gaudí /gaʊ'di/, Antonio (1853–1926), Spanish architect; full name *Antonio Gaudí y Cornet.* He was a leading but idiosyncratic exponent of art nouveau, known mainly for his ornate and extravagant church of the Sagrada Familia in Barcelona (begun 1884).

Gaudier-Brzeska /,gəʊdɪeɪ'bʒeskə/, Henri (1891–1915), French sculptor, a leading member of the Vorticist movement. Notable works: the faceted bust of Horace Brodzky (1912) and *Bird Swallowing a Fish* (1913).

gaudy[1] ▸ adjective (**gaudier**, **gaudiest**) extravagantly bright or showy, typically so as to be tasteless: *silver bows and gaudy ribbons.*
– DERIVATIVES **gaudily** adverb, **gaudiness** noun.
– ORIGIN late 15th cent.: probably from GAUD + -Y[1].

gaudy[2] ▸ noun (pl. **gaudies**) Brit. a celebratory dinner or entertainment held by a college for old members.
– ORIGIN mid 16th cent. (in the sense 'rejoicing, a celebration'): from Latin *gaudium* 'joy', or from *gaude* 'rejoice!', imperative of *gaudere*.

gauge /geɪdʒ/ (chiefly US also **gage**) ▸ noun **1** an instrument that measures and gives a visual display of the amount, level, or contents of something: *a fuel gauge.* ▪ a tool for checking whether something conforms to a desired dimension. ▪ a means of estimating something: *emigration is perhaps the best gauge of public unease.*
2 the thickness, size, or capacity of something, especially as a standard measure, in particular: ▪ the diameter of a wire, fibre, tube, etc.: [as modifier] *a fine 0.018-inch gauge wire.* ▪ [in combination] a measure of the diameter of a gun barrel, or of its ammunition, expressed as the number of spherical pieces of shot of the same diameter as the barrel that can be made from 1 lb (454 g) of lead: [as modifier] *a 12-gauge shotgun.* ▪ [in combination] the thickness of sheet metal or plastic: [as modifier] *500-gauge polythene.* ▪ the distance between the rails of a line of railway track: *the line was laid to a gauge of 2 ft 9 ins.*

3 Nautical, archaic the position of a sailing ship to windward (**the weather gage**) or leeward (**the lee gage**) of another.

▶ **verb** [with obj.] **1** estimate or determine the amount, level, or volume of: *astronomers can gauge the star's intrinsic brightness.* ■ judge or assess (a situation, mood, etc.): *she was unable to gauge his mood.*
2 measure the dimensions of (an object) with a gauge: *when dry the assemblies can be gauged exactly.* ■ (as adj. **gauged**) made in standard dimensions: *gauged sets of strings.*
– DERIVATIVES **gauger** noun.
– ORIGIN Middle English (denoting a standard measure): from Old French *gauge* (noun), *gauger* (verb), variant of Old Northern French *jauge* (noun), *jauger* (verb), of unknown origin.

gauge pressure ▶ **noun** Engineering the amount by which the pressure measured in a fluid exceeds that of the atmosphere.

gauge theory ▶ **noun** Physics a quantum theory using mathematical functions to describe subatomic interactions in terms of particles that are not directly detectable.

Gauguin /ˈɡəʊɡã/, French /ɡoɡɛ̃/, (Eugène Henri) Paul (1848–1903), French painter. From 1891 he lived mainly in Tahiti, painting in a post-Impressionist style that was influenced by primitive art. Notable works: *The Vision after the Sermon* (1888) and *Faa Iheihe* (1898).

Gauhati /ɡaʊˈhɑːti/ former name for **GUWAHATI**.

Gaul[1] /ɡɔːl/ an ancient region of Europe, corresponding to modern France, Belgium, the south Netherlands, SW Germany, and northern Italy. The area south of the Alps was conquered in 222 BC by the Romans, who called it **Cisalpine Gaul**. The area north of the Alps, known as **Transalpine Gaul**, was taken by Julius Caesar between 58 and 51 BC.

Gaul[2] /ɡɔːl/ ▶ **noun** a native or inhabitant of ancient Gaul.
– ORIGIN from Latin *Gallus*, probably of Celtic origin.

Gauleiter /ˈɡaʊlʌɪtə/, German /ˈɡaʊlaɪtɐ/ ▶ **noun**
1 historical a political official governing a district under Nazi rule.
2 an overbearing official.
– ORIGIN 1930s: German, from *Gau* 'administrative district' + *Leiter* 'leader'.

Gaulish ▶ **adjective** relating to or denoting the ancient Gauls.
▶ **noun** [mass noun] the Celtic language of the ancient Gauls.

Gaulle, Charles de, see **DE GAULLE**.

Gaullism /ˈɡəʊlɪz(ə)m/ ▶ **noun** [mass noun] the principles and policies of Charles de Gaulle, characterized by conservatism, nationalism, and advocacy of centralized government.
– DERIVATIVES **Gaullist** noun & adjective.
– ORIGIN 1940s: from French *Gaullisme*.

gault /ɡɔːlt/ ▶ **noun** [mass noun] (also **gault clay**) a thick, heavy clay. ■ (**Gault**) Geology a series of Cretaceous clays and marls forming strata in southern England.
– ORIGIN late 16th cent.: possibly related to Old Swedish *galt*, neuter of *galder* 'barren'.

Gaunt[1] former name for **GHENT**.

Gaunt[2], John of, see **JOHN OF GAUNT**.

gaunt ▶ **adjective** (of a person) lean and haggard, especially because of suffering, hunger, or age. ■ (of a building or place) grim or desolate in appearance.
– DERIVATIVES **gauntly** adverb, **gauntness** noun.
– ORIGIN late Middle English: of unknown origin.

gauntlet[1] ▶ **noun** a strong glove with a long, loose wrist. ■ historical an armoured glove. ■ the part of a glove covering the wrist.
– PHRASES **take up** (or **throw down**) **the gauntlet** accept (or issue) a challenge. [from the medieval custom of issuing a challenge by throwing one's gauntlet to the ground; whoever picked it up was deemed to have accepted the challenge.]
– ORIGIN late Middle English: from Old French *gantelet*, diminutive of *gant* 'glove', of Germanic origin.

gauntlet[2] (US also **gantlet**) ▶ **noun** (in phrase **run the gauntlet**) **1** go through an intimidating or dangerous crowd or experience in order to reach a goal: *she had to run the gauntlet of male autograph seekers.*
2 historical undergo the military punishment of receiving blows while running between two rows of men with sticks.
– ORIGIN mid 17th cent.: alteration of *gantlope* (from Swedish *gatlopp*, from *gata* 'lane' + *lopp* 'course') by association with **GAUNTLET**[1].

gaur /ˈɡaʊə/ ▶ **noun** a wild ox having a large head, a dark brown or black coat with white stockings, and a hump, native to India and Malaysia. Also called **INDIAN BISON, SELADANG**. ● *Bos gaurus*, family Bovidae; it is the ancestor of the domestic gayal.
– ORIGIN early 19th cent.: from Sanskrit *gaura*; related to **COW**[1].

Gauss /ɡaʊs/, Karl Friedrich (1777–1855), German mathematician, astronomer, and physicist. Gauss laid the foundations of number theory, and applied rigorous mathematical analysis to geometry, geodesy, electrostatics, and electromagnetism.

gauss /ɡaʊs/ (abbrev.: **G**) ▶ **noun** (pl. **same** or **gausses**) a unit of magnetic induction, equal to one ten-thousandth of a tesla.
– ORIGIN late 19th cent.: named after Karl **GAUSS**.

Gaussian distribution /ˈɡaʊsɪən/ ▶ **noun** Statistics another term for **NORMAL DISTRIBUTION**.
– ORIGIN early 20th cent.: named after Karl **GAUSS**, who described it.

Gautama /ˈɡaʊtəmə/, Siddhartha, see **BUDDHA**.

Gauteng /xaʊˈtɛŋ, xaʊəˈtɛŋ/ a province of north-eastern South Africa, formerly part of Transvaal; capital, Johannesburg. Former name (until 1995) **PRETORIA-WITWATERSRAND-VEREENIGING**.

gauze /ɡɔːz/ ▶ **noun** [mass noun] **1** a thin transparent fabric of silk, linen, or cotton. ■ Medicine thin, loosely woven cloth used for dressings and swabs. ■ [in sing.] a transparent haze or film: *they saw the grasslands through a gauze of golden dust.*
2 (also **wire gauze**) a very fine wire mesh.
– ORIGIN mid 16th cent.: from French *gaze*, perhaps from *Gaza*, the name of a town in Palestine.

gauzy ▶ **adjective** (**gauzier, gauziest**) resembling gauze; thin and translucent: *a gauzy dress.*
– DERIVATIVES **gauzily** adverb, **gauziness** noun.

gavage /ɡaˈvɑːʒ/ ▶ **noun** [mass noun] the administration of food or drugs by force, especially to an animal, typically through a tube leading down the throat to the stomach.
– ORIGIN late 19th cent.: French, from *gaver* 'force-feed', from a base meaning 'throat'.

Gavaskar /ˈɡavəskə, -kɑː/, Sunil Manohar (b.1949), Indian cricketer. He made his Test debut in the West Indies in 1970, later captained India, and in 1987 became the first batsman to score 10,000 runs in Test cricket.

gave past of **GIVE**.

gavel /ˈɡav(ə)l/ ▶ **noun** a small hammer with which an auctioneer, a judge, or the chair of a meeting hits a surface to call for attention or order.
▶ **verb** (**gavels, gavelling, gavelled**; US **gavels, gaveling, gaveled**) [with obj. and adverbial] bring (a hearing or person) to order by use of a gavel: *he gavelled the convention to order.*
– ORIGIN early 19th cent. (originally US in the sense 'stonemason's mallet'): of unknown origin.

gavelkind /ˈɡav(ə)lkʌɪnd/ ▶ **noun** [mass noun] historical a system of inheritance in which a deceased person's land is divided equally among all male heirs.
– ORIGIN Middle English: from obsolete *gavel* 'payment, rent' + **KIND**[1].

gavial /ˈɡeɪvɪəl/ ▶ **noun** variant spelling of **GHARIAL**.
– ORIGIN from French, the *-v-* probably being substituted for *-r-* by scribal error.

gavotte /ɡəˈvɒt/ ▶ **noun** a medium-paced French dance, popular in the 18th century. ■ a piece of music accompanying or in the rhythm of a gavotte, composed in common time beginning on the third beat of the bar.
– ORIGIN French, from Provençal *gavoto* 'dance of the mountain people', from *Gavot* 'native of the Alps'.

Gawain /ˈɡɑːweɪn, ɡəˈweɪn/ (in Arthurian legend) one of the knights of the Round Table who quested after the Holy Grail. He is the hero of the medieval poem *Sir Gawain and the Green Knight.*

Gawd ▶ **exclamation** informal God (used for emphasis or to express surprise, anger, etc.): *Oh Gawd! I'd completely forgotten about it.*

gawk ▶ **verb** [no obj.] stare openly and stupidly: *they were gawking at some pin-up.*
▶ **noun** an awkward or shy person.
– DERIVATIVES **gawker** noun, **gawkish** adjective.
– ORIGIN late 17th cent. (as a noun): perhaps related to obsolete *gaw* 'to gaze', from Old Norse *gá* 'heed'.

gawky ▶ **adjective** (**gawkier, gawkiest**) nervously awkward and ungainly: *a gawky teenager.*
– DERIVATIVES **gawkily** adverb, **gawkiness** noun.

gawp ▶ **verb** [no obj.] Brit. informal stare openly in a stupid or rude manner: *what are you gawping at?*
– DERIVATIVES **gawper** noun.
– ORIGIN late 17th cent.: perhaps an alteration of **GAPE**.

Gay, John (1685–1732), English poet and dramatist. He is chiefly known for *The Beggar's Opera* (1728), a low-life ballad opera combining burlesque and political satire.

gay ▶ **adjective** (**gayer, gayest**) **1** (of a person, especially a man) homosexual. ■ relating to or used by homosexuals: *a gay bar.*
2 dated light-hearted and carefree: *Nan had a gay disposition and a very pretty face.*
3 dated brightly coloured; showy: *a gay profusion of purple and pink sweet peas.*
▶ **noun** a homosexual, especially a man.
– DERIVATIVES **gayness** noun.
– ORIGIN Middle English (in sense 2 of the adjective): from Old French *gai*, of unknown origin.

> **USAGE** **Gay** meaning 'homosexual' became established in the 1960s as the term preferred by homosexual men to describe themselves. It is now the standard accepted term throughout the English-speaking world. As a result, the centuries-old other senses of **gay** meaning either 'carefree' or 'bright and showy' have more or less dropped out of natural use. The word **gay** cannot be readily used today in these older senses without arousing a sense of double entendre, despite concerted attempts by some to keep them alive.
> **Gay** in its modern sense typically refers to men (**lesbian** being the standard term for homosexual women) but in some contexts it can be used of both men and women.

Gaya /ˈɡɑːjə/ a city in NE India, in the state of Bihar south of Patna; pop. 470,400 (est. 2009). It is a place of Hindu pilgrimage.

gayal /ɡʌɪˈjɑːl, -ˈjal/ ▶ **noun** a domesticated ox used in South Asia. ● *Bos frontalis*, family Bovidae, descended from the wild gaur.
– ORIGIN late 18th cent.: from Bengali.

gaydar /ˈɡeɪdɑː/ ▶ **noun** [mass noun] informal the supposed ability of homosexuals to recognize one another by means of very slight indications.
– ORIGIN 1980s: blend of **GAY** and **RADAR**.

Gaye, Marvin (1939–84), American soul singer, composer, and musician. Best known for 'I Heard It Through the Grapevine' (1968), he later recorded the albums *Let's Get It On* (1973) and *Midnight Love* (1982). He was shot dead by his father in a quarrel.

gayelle /ˈɡajɛl, ˈɡajal/ ▶ **noun** W. Indian an arena or ring for cockfighting or stick-fighting.
– ORIGIN from Spanish *gallera* 'cockpit'.

gayety ▶ **noun** US variant spelling of **GAIETY**.

gay liberation ▶ **noun** [mass noun] the freeing of homosexuals from social and legal discrimination.

Gay-Lussac's law /ɡeɪˈluːsaks/ ▶ **noun** Chemistry a law stating that the volumes of gases undergoing a reaction at constant pressure and temperature are in a simple ratio to each other and to that of the product.
– ORIGIN early 19th cent.: named after Joseph L. *Gay-Lussac* (1778–1850), French chemist and physicist.

gay marriage ▶ **noun** informal the legally recognized union between partners of the same sex.

gay pride ▶ **noun** [mass noun] a sense of strong self-esteem associated with a person's public acknowledgement of their homosexuality.

gay rights ▶ **plural noun** the legal and civil rights of homosexuals, especially the right to be treated without discrimination.

gazania /ɡəˈzeɪnɪə/ ▶ **noun** a tropical herbaceous plant of the daisy family, with showy flowers that are typically orange or yellow. ● Genus *Gazania*, family Compositae.
– ORIGIN modern Latin, named after Theodore of *Gaza* (1398–1478), Greek scholar.

Gazankulu /ˌɡazəŋˈkuːluː/ a former homeland established in South Africa for the Tsonga people, now part of the provinces of Limpopo and Mpumalanga.

gazar /ɡəˈzɑː/ ▶ **noun** [mass noun] a stiff gauzy kind of silk fabric.
– ORIGIN from French, from *gaze* (see **GAUZE**).

Gaza Strip /ˈɡɑːzə/ a strip of territory in Palestine, on the SE Mediterranean coast, including the town of Gaza; pop. 1,551,900 (est. 2009). Administered by Egypt from 1949, and occupied by Israel from 1967, it became a self-governing enclave under the PLO–Israeli accord of 1994 and elected its own legislative council in 1996.

gaze ▸ **verb** [no obj., with adverbial of direction] look steadily and intently, especially in admiration, surprise, or thought: *he could only gaze at her in astonishment*.
▸ **noun** a steady intent look: *he turned, following her gaze | offices screened from the public gaze*. ■ (in literary theory) a particular perspective considered as embodying certain aspects of the relationship between observer and observed: *the male gaze*.
– DERIVATIVES **gazer** noun.
– ORIGIN late Middle English: perhaps related to obsolete *gaw* (see GAWK).

gazebo /gəˈziːbəʊ/ ▸ **noun** (pl. **gazebos**) a small building, especially one in the garden of a house, that gives a wide view of the surrounding area.
– ORIGIN mid 18th cent.: perhaps humorously from GAZE, in imitation of Latin future tenses ending in *-ebo*: compare with LAVABO.

gazelle ▸ **noun** a small, slender antelope that typically has curved horns and a fawn-coloured coat with white underparts, found in open country in Africa and Asia. ● *Gazella* and other genera, family Bovidae: several species.
– ORIGIN early 17th cent.: from French, probably via Spanish from Arabic *ghazāl*.

gazette ▸ **noun** a journal or newspaper, especially the official one of an organization or institution. ■ historical a news-sheet.
▸ **verb** [with obj.] Brit. announce or publish (something) in an official gazette. ■ [with obj. and adverbial] publish the appointment of (someone) to a military or other official post: *he was **gazetted to** the Somerset Light Infantry*.
– ORIGIN early 17th cent.: via French from Italian *gazzetta*, originally Venetian *gazeta de la novità* 'a halfpennyworth of news' (because the news-sheet sold for a *gazeta*, a Venetian coin of small value).

gazetteer /ˌgazəˈtɪə/ ▸ **noun** a geographical index or dictionary.
– ORIGIN early 17th cent. (in the sense 'journalist'): via French from Italian *gazzettiere*, from *gazzetta* (see GAZETTE). The current sense comes from a late 17th-cent. gazetteer called *The Gazetteer's: or, Newsman's Interpreter: Being a Geographical Index*.

Gaziantep /ˌgazɪənˈtɛp/ a city in southern Turkey, near the border with Syria; pop. 1,175,000 (est. 2007). Former name (until 1921) **AINTAB**.

gazillion /gəˈzɪljən/ (also **kazillion**) ▸ **cardinal number** N. Amer. informal a very large number or quantity (used for emphasis): ***gazillions of books***.
– ORIGIN 1970s: fanciful formation on the pattern of *billion* and *million*.

gazpacho /gəsˈpatʃəʊ/ ▸ **noun** (pl. **gazpachos**) [mass noun] a cold Spanish soup made from tomatoes, peppers, and other salad vegetables.
– ORIGIN Spanish.

gazump /gəˈzʌmp/ ▸ **verb** [with obj.] Brit. informal **1** make a higher offer for a house than (someone whose offer has already been accepted by the seller) and thus succeed in acquiring the property.
2 dated swindle (someone).
– DERIVATIVES **gazumper** noun.
– ORIGIN 1920s (in sense 2): from Yiddish *gezumph* 'overcharge'. Sense 1 dates from the 1970s.

gazunder /gəˈzʌndə/ ▸ **verb** [with obj.] Brit. informal lower the amount of an offer that one has made to (the seller of a property), typically just before the exchange of contracts.
– ORIGIN late 1980s: humorous blend of GAZUMP and UNDER.

GB ▸ **abbreviation** ■ (also **Gb**) Computing gigabit(s) or gigabyte(s). ■ Great Britain.

GBA ▸ **abbreviation** Alderney (international vehicle registration).

GBE ▸ **abbreviation** (in the UK) Knight or Dame Grand Cross of the Order of the British Empire.

GBG ▸ **abbreviation** Guernsey (international vehicle registration).

GBH ▸ **abbreviation** Brit. grievous bodily harm.

GBJ ▸ **abbreviation** Jersey (international vehicle registration).

GBM ▸ **abbreviation** Isle of Man (international vehicle registration).

Gbyte ▸ **abbreviation** gigabyte(s).

GBZ ▸ **abbreviation** Gibraltar (international vehicle registration).

GC ▸ **abbreviation** (in the UK and Commonwealth countries) George Cross.

GCA ▸ **abbreviation** Guatemala (international vehicle registration).

GCB ▸ **abbreviation** (in the UK) Knight or Dame Grand Cross of the Order of the Bath.

GCE ▸ **abbreviation** (in the UK) General Certificate of Education.

GCHQ ▸ **abbreviation** (in the UK) Government Communications Headquarters.

GCMG ▸ **abbreviation** (in the UK) Knight or Dame Grand Cross of the Order of St Michael and St George.

GCSE ▸ **abbreviation** General Certificate of Secondary Education: *grade A in GCSE English*.

GCVO ▸ **abbreviation** (in the UK) Knight or Dame Grand Cross of the Royal Victorian Order.

Gd ▸ **symbol** the chemical element gadolinium.

Gdańsk /g(ə)ˈdansk/ an industrial port and shipbuilding centre in northern Poland, on an inlet of the Baltic Sea; pop. 456,103 (2007). Disputed between Prussia and Poland during the 19th century, it was a free city under a League of Nations mandate from 1919 until 1939, when it was annexed by Nazi Germany, precipitating hostilities with Poland and the outbreak of the Second World War. German name **DANZIG**.

g'day ▸ **exclamation** Austral./NZ good day.

gdn ▸ **abbreviation** garden.

Gdns ▸ **abbreviation** Brit. Gardens: *Milbrook Gdns*.

GDP ▸ **abbreviation** gross domestic product.

GDR ▸ **abbreviation** historical German Democratic Republic (East Germany).

Gdynia /ˈgdɪnjə/ a port and naval base in northern Poland, on the Baltic Sea north-west of Gdańsk; pop. 251,183 (2007).

Ge[1] ▸ **symbol** the chemical element germanium.

Ge[2] /geɪ/ Greek Mythology another name for **GAIA**.

gean /giːn/ ▸ **noun** the wild or sweet cherry, which is native to both Eurasia and North America. ● *Prunus avium*, family Rosaceae.
– ORIGIN mid 16th cent.: from Old French *guine*, of unknown origin.

geanticline /dʒiːˈantɪklʌɪn/ ▸ **noun** Geology a large-scale upwardly flexed structure in the earth's crust.
– ORIGIN late 19th cent.: from Greek *gē* 'earth' + ANTICLINE.

gear ▸ **noun 1** (often **gears**) a toothed wheel that works with others to alter the relation between the speed of a driving mechanism (such as the engine of a vehicle) and the speed of the driven parts (the wheels). ■ a particular setting of engaged gears: *he was belting along in fifth gear*. ■ used in reference to the level of effort or intensity expended in an activity or undertaking: *from this weekend, the campaign is expected to **step up a gear** | now the champions **moved up a gear***.
2 [mass noun] [usu. with modifier] equipment or apparatus that is used for a particular purpose: *camping gear*. ■ informal clothing, especially of a specified kind: *designer gear*. ■ informal personal possessions and clothes. ■ Brit. informal illegal drugs.
▸ **verb** [with obj.] design or adjust the gears in a machine to give a specified speed or power output: *the vehicle's geared too high for serious off-road use*.
– PHRASES **change** (or **switch** or **shift**) **gear** adopt a different approach to a situation or task: *from February 1942, British air strategy changed gear*. **in** (or **into**) **gear** with a gear engaged: *he revved the engines and put them in gear*. ■ proceeding with energy, determination, or speed: *I couldn't get myself into gear early enough on Saturday morning*. **out of gear** with no gear engaged: *she took the engine out of gear* | figurative *sometimes his brain seems to slip out of gear*.
– PHRASAL VERBS **gear down** change to a lower gear. **gear someone/thing for** make ready; prepare: *a nation geared for war*. **gear something for/to/towards** adapt something to make it suitable for (someone or something). **gear up 1** equip or prepare oneself: *the region **geared up for** the tourist season*. **2** change to a higher gear. ■ (of a company) increase its borrowings. **gear someone/thing up** adapt or equip someone or something for a purpose: *a city not **geared up to** an outdoor lifestyle*.
– ORIGIN Middle English: of Scandinavian origin; compare with Old Norse *gervi*. Early senses expressed the general meaning 'equipment or apparatus', later 'mechanism': hence sense 1 of the noun (early 19th cent.).

gearbox ▸ **noun** a set of gears with its casing, especially in a motor vehicle; the transmission.

gear change ▸ **noun** a mechanism which changes gear on a motor vehicle.

geared ▸ **adjective 1** fitted with gears.
2 [with adv.] (of a company) having a specified ratio of loan capital (debt) to the value of its ordinary shares (equity): *highly geared companies*.

gearhead ▸ **noun** informal **1** a person who is very enthusiastic about new gadgets.
2 a person who is very interested in cars.

gearing ▸ **noun 1** the set or arrangement of gears in a machine.
2 Brit. the ratio of a company's loan capital (debt) to the value of its ordinary shares (equity).

gear lever (also **gearstick**) ▸ **noun** Brit. a lever used to engage or change gear in a motor vehicle.

gear shift ▸ **noun** N. Amer. a gear lever.

gear train ▸ **noun** a system of gears which transmits motion from one shaft to another.

gearwheel ▸ **noun** a toothed wheel in a set of gears. ■ (on a bicycle) a cogwheel driven directly by the chain.

geas /gas/ ▸ **noun** (pl. **geasa**) (in Irish folklore) an obligation or prohibition magically imposed on a person.
– ORIGIN Irish.

gecko /ˈgɛkəʊ/ ▸ **noun** (pl. **geckos** or **geckoes**) a nocturnal and often highly vocal lizard which has adhesive pads on the feet to assist in climbing on smooth surfaces. It is widespread in warm regions. ● Gekkonidae and related families: numerous genera and species.
– ORIGIN late 18th cent.: from Malay dialect *geko*, *gekok*, imitative of its cry.

GED ▸ **abbreviation** N. Amer. General Educational Development, a certificate attesting that the holder has passed examinations considered as equivalent to completion of high school.

gee[1] (also **gee whiz**) ▸ **exclamation** informal, chiefly N. Amer. a mild expression, typically of surprise, enthusiasm, or sympathy: *Gee, Linda looks great at fifty!*
– ORIGIN mid 19th cent.: perhaps an abbreviation of **JESUS**.

gee[2] ▸ **exclamation** (**gee up**) a command to a horse to go faster.
▸ **verb** (**gees, geeing, geed**) [with obj.] (**gee someone/thing up**) Brit. command (a horse) to go faster. ■ encourage (someone) to put more effort into an activity: *I was running around geeing people up*.
– ORIGIN early 17th cent.: of unknown origin.

gee[3] ▸ **noun** US informal a thousand dollars.
– ORIGIN 1930s: representing the initial letter of GRAND.

geebung /ˈdʒiːbʌŋ/ ▸ **noun** an Australian shrub or small tree which bears creamy-yellow flowers and small green fruit. ● Genus *Persoonia*, family Proteaceae.
– ORIGIN early 19th cent.: from Dharuk.

Geechee /ˈgiːtʃiː/ ▸ **noun 1** [mass noun] an English creole spoken by blacks in parts of South Carolina and Georgia. Compare with **GULLAH**.
2 a speaker of Geechee.
– ORIGIN from the name of the Ogeechee River, in Georgia, US.

geegaw /ˈdʒiːgɔː/ ▸ **noun** chiefly N. Amer. variant spelling of **GEWGAW**.

gee-gee ▸ **noun** Brit. informal (in children's use or in racehorse betting) a horse.
– ORIGIN mid 19th cent. (originally a child's word): reduplication of **GEE**[2].

geek[1] /giːk/ ▸ **noun** informal an unfashionable or socially inept person. ■ [usu. with modifier] a knowledgeable and obsessive enthusiast: *a computer geek*.
– DERIVATIVES **geekdom** noun, **geekiness** noun, **geeky** adjective (**geekier**, **geekiest**).
– ORIGIN late 19th cent.: from the related English dialect word *geck* 'fool', of Germanic origin; related to Dutch *gek* 'mad, silly'.

WORD TRENDS Is being a **geek** something to be proud of? A few decades ago the answer would almost certainly have been no: the word was a cruel and critical label attached to clever, but socially awkward, people: *train-spotters, computer geeks, and unpopular college students*. Then in the 1990s everything changed. The computer industry helped many **geeks** to achieve great success, and the wider perception of **geeks** began to shift. Being a **geek** was suddenly a positive thing, suggesting an admirable level of knowledge, expertise, and passion: **geeks** could do 'cool stuff'. It's now common for people to be *self-proclaimed* or *self-confessed* **geeks**, with **geekiness** no longer confined to the world of science and technology (*a music geek with an awesome vinyl collection | the kind of film that every true movie* *geek would give five stars).* **Nerds** have undergone a similar change of image but to a lesser extent, with some negative terms such as *boring* and *pathetic* still commonly attached to the word.

geek[2] /giːk/ ▸ **noun** Austral./NZ informal a look: *there was a lot I wanted to have a geek at.*
– ORIGIN early 20th cent.: from Scots and northern English dialect *geck* 'toss the head scornfully'.

Geelong /dʒiːˈlɒŋ/ a port and oil-refining centre on the south coast of Australia, in the state of Victoria; pop. 134,100 (est. 2008).

geese plural form of GOOSE.

gee-string ▸ **noun** variant spelling of G-STRING.

gee whiz informal, chiefly N. Amer. ▸ **exclamation** another term for GEE[1].
▸ **adjective** (**gee-whiz**) [attrib.] characterized by or causing naive astonishment or wonder: *this era of gee-whiz gadgetry.*

geez ▸ **exclamation** variant spelling of JEEZ.

Ge'ez /ˈgiːɛz/ ▸ **noun** [mass noun] an ancient Semitic language of Ethiopia, which survives as the liturgical language of the Ethiopian Orthodox Church. It is the ancestor of the modern Ethiopian languages such as Amharic. Also called ETHIOPIC.
– ORIGIN of Ethiopic origin.

geezer /ˈgiːzə/ ▸ **noun** Brit. informal a man: *he strikes me as a decent geezer.* ■ N. Amer. informal, derogatory an old man.
– ORIGIN late 19th cent.: representing a dialect pronunciation of earlier *guiser* 'mummer'.

GEF ▸ **abbreviation** Global Environment Facility.

gefilte fish /gəˈfɪltə/ ▸ **noun** [mass noun] a dish of stewed or baked stuffed fish, or of fish cakes boiled in a fish or vegetable broth.
– ORIGIN Yiddish, 'stuffed fish', from *filn* 'to fill' + FISH[1].

gegenschein /ˈgeɪgən,ʃʌɪn/ ▸ **noun** [mass noun] Astronomy a patch of very faint nebulous light sometimes seen in the night sky opposite the position of the sun. It is thought to be the image of the sun reflected from gas and dust outside the atmosphere.
– ORIGIN late 19th cent.: German *Gegenschein*, from *gegen* 'opposite' + *Schein* 'glow, shine'.

Gehenna /gəˈhɛnə/ (in Judaism and the New Testament) hell.
– ORIGIN via ecclesiastical Latin from Greek *geenna*, from Hebrew *gē' hinnōm* 'hell', literally 'valley of Hinnom', a place near Jerusalem where children were sacrificed to Baal (Jer. 19:5,6).

Gehrig /ˈgɛrɪg/, Lou (1903–41), American baseball player; full name *Henry Louis Gehrig*; known as **the Iron Horse**. He played a record 2,130 major-league games for the New York Yankees from 1925 to 1939. He died from a form of motor neurone disease now often called Lou Gehrig's disease.

Gehry /ˈgɛːri/, Frank (Owen) (b.1929), Canadian-born American architect. His buildings include the titanium-clad Guggenheim Museum in Bilbao (1997).

Geiger /ˈgʌɪgə/, Hans (Johann) Wilhelm (1882–1945), German nuclear physicist. In 1908 he developed his prototype radiation counter for detecting alpha particles, later improved in collaboration with Walther Müller.

Geiger counter (also **Geiger-Müller counter**) ▸ **noun** a device for measuring radioactivity by detecting and counting ionizing particles.

geisha /ˈgeɪʃə/ (also **geisha girl**) ▸ **noun** (pl. **same** or **geishas**) a Japanese hostess trained to entertain men with conversation, dance, and song.
– ORIGIN Japanese, 'entertainer', from *gei* 'performing arts' + *sha* 'person'.

Geissler tube /ˈgʌɪslə/ ▸ **noun** a sealed tube of glass or quartz with a central constriction, filled with vapour for the production of a luminous electrical discharge.
– ORIGIN mid 19th cent.: named after Heinrich *Geissler* (1814–79), the German mechanic and glass-blower who invented it.

Geist /gʌɪst/ ▸ **noun** the spirit of an individual or group.
– ORIGIN German; related to GHOST.

geitonogamy /ˌgʌɪtəˈnɒgəmi/ ▸ **noun** [mass noun] Botany the fertilization of a flower by pollen from another flower on the same (or a genetically identical) plant. Compare with XENOGAMY.
– DERIVATIVES **geitonogamous** adjective.
– ORIGIN late 19th cent.: from Greek *geitōn, geitono-* 'neighbour' + *-gamos* 'marrying'.

Gejiu /gɛˈdʒuː/ (also **Geju**) a tin-mining city in southern China, near the border with Vietnam; pop. 216,500 (est. 2006).

gel[1] /dʒɛl/ ▸ **noun 1** [mass noun] a jelly-like substance, especially one used in cosmetic or medicinal products: *hair gel.* ■ Chemistry a semi-solid colloidal suspension of a solid dispersed in a liquid.
2 Biochemistry a semi-rigid slab or cylinder of an organic polymer used as a medium for the separation of macromolecules.
▸ **verb** (**gels, gelling, gelled**) **1** [no obj.] Chemistry form into a gel: *the mixture gelled at 7 degrees Celsius.*
2 [with obj.] apply gel to (the hair).
– ORIGIN late 19th cent.: abbreviation of GELATIN.

gel[2] /dʒɛl/ (also **jell**) ▸ **verb** (**gels, gelling, gelled**) [no obj.] chiefly Brit. (of a liquid) set or become more solid: *the stew is gelling.* ■ (of a project or idea) take a definite form or begin to work well: *everything seemed to gel for the magazine.* ■ (of people) work well together: *during the tour they continued to gel as a band.*
– ORIGIN late 19th cent.: *gel* from GEL[1]; the variant *jell* is a back-formation from JELLY.

gel[3] /gɛl/ ▸ **noun** Brit. informal an upper-class or well-bred girl or young woman: *fastidiously reared Home Counties gels.*
– ORIGIN late 19th cent.: representing a pronunciation.

gelada /dʒəˈlɑːdə/ (also **gelada baboon**) ▸ **noun** (pl. **same** or **geladas**) a brownish baboon with a long mane and naked red rump, native to Ethiopia.
● *Theropithecus gelada*, family Cercopithecidae.
– ORIGIN mid 19th cent.: from Amharic *č'ällada.*

gelati plural form of GELATO.

gelatin /ˈdʒɛlətɪn/ (also **gelatine** /-tiːn/) ▸ **noun** [mass noun] **1** a virtually colourless and tasteless water-soluble protein prepared from collagen and used in food preparation, in photographic processes, and in glue.
2 (usu. **blasting gelatin**) a high explosive consisting chiefly of a gel of nitroglycerine with added cellulose nitrate.
– ORIGIN early 19th cent.: from French *gélatine*, from Italian *gelatina*, from *gelata*, from Latin (see JELLY).

gelatinize /dʒɪˈlatɪnʌɪz/ (also **gelatinise**) ▸ **verb** make or become gelatinous or jelly-like. ■ [with obj.] (usu. as adj. **gelatinized**) coat with gelatin: *gelatinized glass microscope slides.*
– DERIVATIVES **gelatinization** noun.

gelatinous ▸ **adjective** having a jelly-like consistency: *a sweet, gelatinous drink.* ■ of or like the protein gelatin.
– DERIVATIVES **gelatinously** adverb.

gelatin paper ▸ **noun** [mass noun] Brit. paper coated with sensitized gelatin for photographic use.

gelation[1] ▸ **noun** [mass noun] technical solidification by freezing.
– ORIGIN mid 19th cent.: from Latin *gelatio(n-)*, from *gelare* 'freeze'.

gelation[2] ▸ **noun** [mass noun] Chemistry the process of forming a gel.

gelato /dʒəˈlɑːtəʊ/ ▸ **noun** (pl. **gelati** /dʒəˈlɑːti/) an Italian or Italian-style ice cream.
– ORIGIN Italian.

gelcoat /ˈdʒɛlkəʊt/ ▸ **noun** the smooth, hard polyester resin surface coating of a fibreglass structure.

geld ▸ **verb** [with obj.] castrate (a male animal).
■ deprive of vitality or vigour: *the English version of the book has been gelded.*
– ORIGIN Middle English: from Old Norse *gelda*, from *geldr* 'barren'.

Gelderland /ˈgɛldəland/ a province of the Netherlands, on the border with Germany; capital, Arnhem. Formerly a duchy, the province was variously occupied by the Spanish, the French, and the Prussians until 1815.

gelding ▸ **noun** a castrated animal, especially a male horse.
– ORIGIN late Middle English: from Old Norse *geldingr*, from *geldr* 'barren'.

gelid /ˈdʒɛlɪd/ ▸ **adjective** icy; extremely cold: *the gelid pond | she gave a gelid reply.*
– ORIGIN early 17th cent.: from Latin *gelidus*, from *gelu* 'frost, intense cold'.

gelignite /ˈdʒɛlɪgnʌɪt/ ▸ **noun** [mass noun] a high explosive made from a gel of nitroglycerine and nitrocellulose in a base of wood pulp and sodium or potassium nitrate, used particularly for rock-blasting.
– ORIGIN late 19th cent.: probably from GELATIN + Latin *(l)ignis* 'wood' + -ITE[1].

Gell-Mann /gɛlˈman/, Murray (b.1929), American theoretical physicist. He coined the word *quark* and proposed the concept of strangeness in quarks. Nobel Prize for Physics (1969).

gelly ▸ **noun** [mass noun] Brit. informal gelignite.
– ORIGIN 1940s: abbreviation.

gelsemium /dʒɛlˈsiːmɪəm/ ▸ **noun 1** [mass noun] a preparation of the rhizome of yellow jasmine, used in homeopathy to treat flu-like symptoms.
2 a plant of a genus that includes the yellow jasmine.
● Genus *Gelsemium*, family Loganiaceae.
– ORIGIN late 19th cent.: modern Latin, from Italian *gelsomino* 'jasmine'.

Gelsenkirchen /ˈgɛlz(ə)n,kɪəx(ə)n/, German /ˌgɛlzn̩ˈkɪrçn/ an industrial city in western Germany, in North Rhine-Westphalia north-east of Essen; pop. 266,800 (est. 2006).

gelt /gɛlt/ ▸ **noun** [mass noun] informal money.
– ORIGIN early 16th cent. (originally often used to refer to the pay of a German army): from German *Geld* 'money'.

gem ▸ **noun 1** a precious or semi-precious stone, especially when cut and polished or engraved. ■ used in names of some brilliantly coloured hummingbirds, e.g. **mountain gem**.
2 an outstanding person or thing: *this architectural gem of a palace.*
▸ **verb** (**gems, gemming, gemmed**) [with obj.] (usu. as adj. **gemmed**) literary decorate with or as with gems.
– DERIVATIVES **gem-like** adjective, **gemmy** adjective.
– ORIGIN Old English *gim*, from Latin *gemma* 'bud, jewel'; influenced in Middle English by Old French *gemme*.

Gemara /gəˈmɑːrə/ ▸ **noun** (**the Gemara**) a rabbinical commentary on the Mishnah, forming the second part of the Talmud.
– ORIGIN from Aramaic *gĕmārā* 'completion'.

gematria /gɪˈmeɪtrɪə/ ▸ **noun** [mass noun] a Kabbalistic method of interpreting the Hebrew scriptures by computing the numerical value of words, based on the values of their constituent letters.
– ORIGIN mid 17th cent.: from Aramaic *gīmaṭrēyā*, from Greek *geōmetria* (see GEOMETRY).

Gemayel /dʒəˈmʌɪəl/, Pierre (1905–84), Lebanese political leader. A Maronite Christian, he founded the right-wing Phalange Party in 1936 and served as a Member of Parliament 1960–84. His youngest son, **Bashir** (1947–82), was assassinated while President-elect; his eldest son, **Amin** (b.1942), served as President 1982–8.

Gemeinschaft /gəˈmʌɪnʃaft/ ▸ **noun** [mass noun] social relations between individuals, based on close personal and family ties; community. Contrasted with GESELLSCHAFT.
– ORIGIN German, from *gemein* 'common' + *schaft* (see -SHIP).

geminal /ˈdʒɛmɪn(ə)l/ ▸ **adjective** Chemistry denoting substituent atoms or groups, especially protons, attached to the same atom in a molecule.
– DERIVATIVES **geminally** adverb.
– ORIGIN 1960s: from Latin *geminus* 'twin' + -AL.

geminate Phonetics ▸ **adjective** /ˈdʒɛmɪneɪt, -nət/ consisting of identical adjacent speech sounds; doubled.
▸ **verb** /ˈdʒɛmɪneɪt/ [with obj.] double or repeat (a speech sound).
– DERIVATIVES **gemination** noun.
– ORIGIN late Middle English: from Latin *geminatus*, past participle of *geminare* 'double, pair with', from *geminus* 'twin'.

Gemini 1 Astronomy a northern constellation (the Twins), said to represent the twins Castor and Pollux, whose names are given to its two brightest stars. See DIOSCURI.
2 Astrology the third sign of the zodiac, which the sun enters about 21 May. ■ (**a Gemini**) (pl. **Geminis**) a person born when the sun is in this sign.
3 a series of twelve manned American orbiting spacecraft, launched in the 1960s in preparation for the Apollo programme.
– DERIVATIVES **Geminian** /dʒɛmɪˈniːən/ **noun & adjective** (sense 2).
– ORIGIN Latin, plural of *geminus* 'twin'.

Geminids Astronomy an annual meteor shower with a radiant in the constellation Gemini, reaching a peak about 13 December.

gemma /ˈdʒɛmə/ ▸ **noun** (pl. **gemmae** /-miː/) Biology a small cellular body or bud that can separate to form a new organism. ■ another term for CHLAMYDOSPORE.
– ORIGIN late 18th cent. (denoting a leaf bud): from Latin, literally 'bud, jewel'.

G

gemmation /dʒɛˈmeɪʃ(ə)n/ ▸ **noun** [mass noun] Biology asexual reproduction by the production of gemmae; budding.
– ORIGIN mid 18th cent.: from French, from *gemmer* 'to bud', from *gemme* 'bud', from Latin *gemma*.

gemmiparous /dʒɛˈmɪp(ə)rəs/ ▸ **adjective** Biology (of a plant or animal) reproducing by gemmation.
– ORIGIN late 18th cent.: from modern Latin *gemmiparus*, from Latin *gemma* 'bud, jewel' + *parere* 'produce, give birth to'.

gemmology (also **gemology**) ▸ **noun** [mass noun] the study of precious stones.
– DERIVATIVES **gemmological** adjective, **gemmologist** noun.
– ORIGIN early 19th cent.: from Latin *gemma* 'bud, jewel' + **-LOGY**.

gemmule /ˈdʒɛmjuːl/ ▸ **noun** Zoology a tough-coated dormant cluster of embryonic cells produced by a freshwater sponge for development in more favourable conditions.
– DERIVATIVES **gemmulation** noun.
– ORIGIN mid 19th cent.: from French, from Latin *gemmula*, diminutive of *gemma* 'bud, jewel'.

gemsbok /ˈxɛmzbɒk, ˈxɛms-/ ▸ **noun** a large antelope that has a grey coat, distinctive black-and-white head markings, and long straight horns, native to SW and East Africa. ● *Oryx gazella*, family Bovidae. See also **BEISA**.
– ORIGIN late 18th cent.: via Afrikaans from Dutch, literally 'chamois', from *gems* 'chamois' + *bok* 'buck'.

Gem State informal name for **IDAHO**.

gemstone ▸ **noun** a precious or semi-precious stone, especially one cut, polished, and used in a piece of jewellery.

gemütlich /gəˈmuːtlɪx/, German /gəˈmyːtlɪç/ ▸ **adjective** pleasant and cheerful.
– ORIGIN German.

Gemütlichkeit /gəˈmuːtlɪxkʌɪt/, German /gəˈmyːtlɪçkaɪt/ ▸ **noun** [mass noun] geniality; friendliness.
– ORIGIN German.

gen /dʒɛn/ Brit. informal ▸ **noun** [mass noun] information: ***you've got more gen on him than we have.***
▸ **verb** (**gens, genning, genned**) [with obj.] (**gen someone up**) provide (someone) with information. ■ [no obj.] (**gen up on**) find out about: *I gen up on any developments with my manageress.*
– ORIGIN Second World War (originally used in the armed services): perhaps from the first syllable of *general information*.

Gen. ▸ **abbreviation** ■ General: *Gen. Eisenhower*. ■ Genesis (in biblical references).

-gen ▸ **combining form 1** Chemistry denoting a substance that produces something: *oxygen | allergen*.
2 Botany denoting a substance or plant that is produced: *cultigen*.
– ORIGIN via French *-gène* from Greek *-genēs* '-born, of a specified kind', from *gen-* (root of *gignomai* 'be born, become', *genos* 'a kind').

gena /ˈdʒiːnə/ ▸ **noun** (pl. **genae** /ˈdʒiːniː/) Zoology the lateral part of the head of an insect or other arthropod below the level of the eyes.
– DERIVATIVES **genal** adjective.
– ORIGIN early 19th cent.: Latin, literally 'cheek'.

gendarme /ˈʒɒndɑːm/, French /ʒɑ̃daʀm/ ▸ **noun 1** a paramilitary police officer in France and other French-speaking countries.
2 a rock pinnacle on a mountain, occupying and blocking an arête.
– ORIGIN mid 16th cent. (originally denoting a mounted officer in the French army): French, from *gens d'armes* 'men of arms'. Sense 1 dates from the late 18th cent.

gendarmerie /ʒɒnˈdɑːməri/, French /ʒɑ̃daʀm(ə)ʀi/ ▸ **noun** a force of gendarmes. ■ the headquarters of such a force.
– ORIGIN mid 16th cent.: French (see **GENDARME**).

gender ▸ **noun 1** Grammar (in languages such as Latin, French, and German) each of the classes (typically masculine, feminine, common, neuter) of nouns and pronouns distinguished by the different inflections which they have and which they require in words syntactically associated with them. Grammatical gender is only very loosely associated with natural distinctions of sex. ■ [mass noun] the property (in nouns and related words) of belonging to such a class: *determiners and adjectives usually agree with the noun in gender and number*.
2 [mass noun] the state of being male or female (typically used with reference to social and cultural differences rather than biological ones): *traditional concepts of gender*. ■ [count noun] the members of one or other sex: *differences between the genders are encouraged from an early age*.
– DERIVATIVES **genderless** adjective.
– ORIGIN late Middle English: from Old French *gendre* (modern *genre*), based on Latin *genus* 'birth, family, nation'. The earliest meanings were 'kind, sort, genus' and 'type or class of noun, etc.' (which was also a sense of Latin *genus*).

> **USAGE** The word **gender** has been used since the 14th century as a grammatical term, referring to classes of noun designated as *masculine*, *feminine*, or *neuter* in some languages. The sense 'the state of being male or female' has also been used since the 14th century, but this did not become common until the mid 20th century. Although the words **gender** and **sex** both have the sense 'the state of being male or female', they are typically used in slightly different ways: **sex** tends to refer to biological differences, while **gender** refers to cultural or social ones.

gender bender ▸ **noun** informal a person who dresses and behaves in a way characteristic of the opposite sex.
– DERIVATIVES **gender-bending** adjective.

gender changer ▸ **noun** an electrical adaptor which allows two male or two female connectors to be connected to each other.

gender dysphoria ▸ **noun** [mass noun] Medicine the condition of feeling one's emotional and psychological identity as male or female to be opposite to one's biological sex.
– DERIVATIVES **gender dysphoric** adjective & noun.

gendered ▸ **adjective** of, specific to, or biased towards the male or female sex: *gendered occupations*.

gene /dʒiːn/ ▸ **noun** Biology (in informal use) a unit of heredity which is transferred from a parent to offspring and is held to determine some characteristic of the offspring: *playing tennis is in my genes*. ■ (in technical use) a distinct sequence of nucleotides forming part of a chromosome, the order of which determines the order of monomers in a polypeptide or nucleic acid molecule which a cell (or virus) may synthesize.
– ORIGIN early 20th cent.: from German *Gen*, from *Pangen*, a supposed ultimate unit of heredity (from Greek *pan-* 'all' + *genos* 'race, kind, offspring').

genealogical /ˌdʒiːnɪəˈlɒdʒɪk(ə)l, ˌdʒɛn-/ ▸ **adjective** relating to the study or tracing of lines of family descent: *genealogical research*.
– DERIVATIVES **genealogically** adverb.
– ORIGIN late 16th cent.: from French *généalogique*, via medieval Latin from Greek *genealogikos*, from *genealogia* (see **GENEALOGY**).

genealogical tree ▸ **noun** a chart like an inverted branching tree showing the lines of descent of a family or of an animal species.

genealogy /dʒiːnɪˈalədʒi, dʒɛn-/ ▸ **noun** (pl. **genealogies**) a line of descent traced continuously from an ancestor. ■ [mass noun] the study and tracing of lines of descent. ■ a plant's or animal's line of evolutionary development from earlier forms.
– DERIVATIVES **genealogist** noun, **genealogize** (also **genealogise**) verb.
– ORIGIN Middle English: via Old French and late Latin from Greek *genealogia*, from *genea* 'race, generation' + *-logia* (see **-LOGY**).

gene conversion ▸ **noun** [mass noun] the process whereby, during meiosis, one allele in a heterozygote is converted to the other by a process of mismatch repair.

gene pool ▸ **noun** the stock of different genes in an interbreeding population.

genera plural form of **GENUS**.

general ▸ **adjective 1** affecting or concerning all or most people or things; widespread: *books of general interest | the general opinion was that prices would fall*. ■ not specialized or limited in range of subject, application, activity, etc.: *brush up on your general knowledge*. ■ (of a rule, principle, etc.) true for all or most cases. ■ normal or usual: *it is not general practice to confirm or deny such reports*.
2 considering or including only the main features or elements of something; not exact or detailed: *the arrangements were outlined in very general terms | a general introduction to the subject*.
3 [often in titles] chief or principal: *the Director General of the BBC | the general manager*.
▸ **noun 1** a commander of an army, or an army officer of very high rank. ■ a high rank of officer in the army and in the US air force, above lieutenant general and below field marshal, general of the army, or general of the air force. ■ informal short for **LIEUTENANT GENERAL** or **MAJOR GENERAL**. ■ the head of a religious order organized on quasi-military lines, e.g. the Jesuits, the Dominicans, or the Salvation Army.
2 (**the general**) archaic the general public.
– PHRASES **as a general rule** in most cases. **in general 1** usually; mainly: *in general, Alexander was a peaceful, loving man*. **2** as a whole: *our understanding of culture in general and of literature in particular*.
– ORIGIN Middle English: via Old French from Latin *generalis*, from *genus*, *gener-* 'class, race, kind'. The noun primarily denotes a person having overall authority: the sense 'army commander' is an abbreviation of *captain general*, from French *capitaine général* 'commander-in-chief'.

General American ▸ **noun** [mass noun] (in non-technical use) the variety of English spoken in the greater part of the US, particularly with reference to the lack of regional characteristics.

general anaesthetic ▸ **noun** [mass noun] an anaesthetic that affects the whole body and usually causes a loss of consciousness: *he had the operation under general anaesthetic*. Compare with **LOCAL ANAESTHETIC**.

general average ▸ **noun** [mass noun] (in maritime law) the apportionment of financial liability for the loss arising from the jettisoning of cargo by dividing the costs among all those whose property (ship or cargo) was preserved by the action.

general aviation ▸ **noun** [mass noun] civil aviation other than large-scale passenger or freight operations.

General Certificate of Education (abbrev.: **GCE**) ▸ **noun** an examination set especially for secondary-school pupils in England, Wales, and Northern Ireland at Advanced level (at about age 18) and, formerly, at Ordinary level (at about age 16).

General Certificate of Secondary Education (abbrev.: **GCSE**) ▸ **noun** an examination set especially for secondary-school pupils of about age 16 in England, Wales, and Northern Ireland.

general counsel ▸ **noun** (in the US) the main lawyer who gives legal advice to a company.

general dealer ▸ **noun** (in South Africa) the keeper of a rural or township store.

general delivery ▸ **noun** North American term for **POSTE RESTANTE**.

general election ▸ **noun** the election of representatives to a legislature (in the UK, to the House of Commons) from constituencies throughout the country.

general headquarters ▸ **noun** [treated as sing. or pl.] the headquarters of a military commander.

generalissimo /ˌdʒɛn(ə)rəˈlɪsɪməʊ/ ▸ **noun** (pl. **generalissimos**) the commander of a combined military force consisting of army, navy, and air force units.
– ORIGIN early 17th cent.: Italian, 'having greatest authority', superlative of *generale* (see **GENERAL**).

generalist ▸ **noun** a person competent in several different fields or activities.
– DERIVATIVES **generalism** noun.

generality ▸ **noun** (pl. **generalities**) **1** a statement or principle having general rather than specific validity or force: *he confined his remarks to generalities*. ■ [mass noun] the quality or state of being general: *policy should be formulated at an appropriate level of generality*.
2 (**the generality**) the majority: *his service was better than that offered by **the generality of** doctors*.
– ORIGIN late Middle English: from Old French *generalite*, from late Latin *generalitas*, from *generalis* (see **GENERAL**).

generalization (also **generalisation**) ▸ **noun** a general statement or concept obtained by inference from specific cases: *he was making sweeping generalizations*. ■ [mass noun] the action of generalizing: *such anecdotes cannot be a basis for generalization*.

generalize (also **generalise**) ▸ **verb 1** [no obj.] make a general or broad statement by inferring from specific cases: *it is not easy to **generalize about** the poor*.
2 [with obj.] make (something) more widespread or widely applicable: *attempts to generalize an elite education*. ■ (as adj. **generalized**) Medicine (of a disease) affecting much or all of the body: *generalized myalgia*.
– DERIVATIVES **generalizability** noun, **generalizable** adjective, **generalizer** noun.
– ORIGIN Middle English (in the sense 'reduce to a general statement'): from **GENERAL** + **-IZE**.

generally ▸ adverb **1** [sentence adverb] in most cases; usually: *the term of a lease is generally 99 years.*
2 in general terms; without regard to particulars or exceptions: *a decade when France was moving generally to the left* | [as sentence adverb] *generally speaking, things have been getting better.*
3 by or to most people; widely: *the best scheme is generally reckoned to be the Canadian one.*

general meeting ▸ noun a meeting open to all members of an organization.

general of the air force ▸ noun the highest rank of officer in the US air force, above general.

general of the army ▸ noun the highest rank of officer in the US army, above general.

general paralysis of the insane ▸ noun see **GPI**.

general practitioner (abbrev.: **GP**) ▸ noun a doctor based in the community who treats patients with minor or chronic illnesses and refers those with serious conditions to a hospital.
– DERIVATIVES **general practice** noun (Brit.).

general-purpose ▸ adjective having a range of potential uses or functions; not specialized in design: *a general-purpose detergent.*

generalship ▸ noun [mass noun] the skill or practice of exercising military command.

general staff ▸ noun [treated as sing. or pl.] the staff assisting a military commander in planning and executing operations.

general store (also **general stores**) ▸ noun a shop that sells a wide variety of goods, typically one in a small town or village.

general strike ▸ noun a strike of workers in all or most industries. ■ (**the General Strike**) the strike of May 1926 in the UK, called by the Trades Union Congress in support of the mineworkers.

General Synod ▸ noun the highest governing body of the Church of England, an elected assembly of three houses (bishops, clergy, and laity).

General Thanksgiving ▸ noun a form of thanksgiving in the Book of Common Prayer or the Alternative Service Book.

general theory of relativity ▸ noun see **RELATIVITY** (sense 2).

generate ▸ verb [with obj.] produce or create: *changes which are likely to generate controversy* | *the income generated by the sale of council houses.* ■ produce (energy, especially electricity). ■ Mathematics & Linguistics produce (a set or sequence of items) by performing specified mathematical or logical operations on an initial set. ■ Linguistics produce (a sentence or other unit, especially a well-formed one) by the application of a finite set of rules to lexical or other linguistic input. ■ Mathematics form (a line, surface, or solid) by notionally moving a point, line, or surface.
– DERIVATIVES **generable** adjective.
– ORIGIN early 16th cent. (in the sense 'beget, procreate'): from Latin *generat-* 'created', from the verb *generare*, from *genus*, *gener-* 'stock, race'.

generation ▸ noun **1** all of the people born and living at about the same time, regarded collectively: *one of his generation's finest songwriters.* ■ the average period, generally considered to be about thirty years, in which children grow up, become adults, and have children of their own: *the same families have lived here for generations.* ■ a set of members of a family regarded as a single step or stage in descent: [as modifier, in combination] *a third-generation Canadian.* ■ a group of people of similar age involved in a particular activity: *a new generation of actors and directors.* ■ a single stage in the development of a type of product: *a new generation of rear-engined sports cars.*
2 [mass noun] the production or creation of something: *methods of electricity generation* | *the generation of wealth.* ■ the propagation of living organisms; procreation.
– DERIVATIVES **generational** adjective, **generationally** adverb.
– ORIGIN Middle English: via Old French from Latin *generatio(n-)*, from the verb *generare* (see **GENERATE**).

generation gap ▸ noun (usu. **the generation gap**) a difference of attitudes between people of different generations, leading to a lack of understanding.

Generation X ▸ noun the generation born after that of the baby boomers (roughly from the early 1960s to mid 1970s), typically perceived to be disaffected and directionless.
– DERIVATIVES **Generation Xer** noun.
– ORIGIN 1950s: in recent use popularized by Douglas Coupland in his novel *Generation X* (1991).

Generation Y ▸ noun the generation born in the 1980s and 1990s, comprising primarily the children of the baby boomers and typically perceived as increasingly familiar with digital and electronic technology.
– DERIVATIVES **Generation Yer** noun.
– ORIGIN 1990s: after **GENERATION X**.

generative /ˈdʒɛn(ə)rətɪv/ ▸ adjective **1** relating to or capable of production or reproduction.
2 denoting an approach to any field of linguistics that involves applying a finite set of rules to linguistic input in order to produce all and only the well-formed items of a language: *generative phonology.*
– DERIVATIVES **generativity** noun.
– ORIGIN late Middle English: from late Latin *generativus*, from *generare* 'beget' (see **GENERATE**).

generative grammar ▸ noun [mass noun] a type of grammar which describes a language in terms of a set of logical rules formulated so as to be capable of generating the infinite number of possible sentences of that language and providing them with the correct structural description.

generator ▸ noun **1** a person or thing that generates something. ■ [with modifier] Computing a routine that constructs other routines or subroutines using given parameters, for specific applications. ■ Mathematics a point, line, or surface regarded as moving and so notionally forming a line, surface, or solid.
2 a dynamo or similar machine for converting mechanical energy into electricity. ■ an apparatus for producing gas, steam, or another substance.

generatrix /ˌdʒɛnəˈreɪtrɪks/ ▸ noun (pl. **generatrices** /-trɪsiːz/) Mathematics another term for **GENERATOR**.
– ORIGIN mid 19th cent.: from Latin (feminine).

generic /dʒɪˈnɛrɪk/ ▸ adjective **1** characteristic of or relating to a class or group of things; not specific: *chèvre is a generic term for all goats' milk cheese.* ■ (of goods, especially medicinal drugs) having no brand name; not protected by a registered trademark.
2 Biology relating to a genus.
▸ noun a consumer product having no brand name or registered trademark: *substituting generics for brand-name drugs.*
– DERIVATIVES **generically** adverb.
– ORIGIN late 17th cent.: from French *générique*, from Latin *genus*, *gener-* 'stock, race'.

generosity ▸ noun [mass noun] **1** the quality of being kind and generous: *I was overwhelmed by the generosity of friends and neighbours.*
2 the quality or fact of being plentiful or large: *diners certainly cannot complain about the generosity of portions.*
– ORIGIN late Middle English (denoting nobility of birth): from Latin *generositas*, from *generosus* 'magnanimous' (see **GENEROUS**). Current senses date from the 17th cent.

generous ▸ adjective **1** showing a readiness to give more of something, especially money, than is strictly necessary or expected: *a generous benefactor to the University.* ■ showing kindness towards others: *a generous assessment of his work.*
2 (of a thing) larger or more plentiful than is usual or necessary: *a generous helping of pasta.*
– DERIVATIVES **generously** adverb, **generousness** noun.
– ORIGIN late 16th cent.: via Old French from Latin *generosus* 'noble, magnanimous', from *genus*, *gener-* 'stock, race'. The original sense was 'of noble birth', hence 'characteristic of noble birth, courageous, magnanimous, not mean'.

gene silencing ▸ noun [mass noun] the switching off of the expression of a gene, for example by the introduction of an antisense RNA that blocks translation of the messenger RNA.

Genesis /ˈdʒɛnɪsɪs/ the first book of the Bible, which includes the stories of the creation of the world, Noah's Ark, the Tower of Babel, and the patriarchs Abraham, Isaac, Jacob, and Joseph.
– ORIGIN late Old English, via Latin from Greek, 'generation, creation, nativity, horoscope', from the base of *gignesthai* 'be born or produced'. The name was given to the first book of the Old Testament in the Greek translation (the Septuagint), hence in the Latin translation (the Vulgate).

genesis /ˈdʒɛnɪsɪs/ ▸ noun [in sing.] the origin or mode of formation of something: *this tale had its genesis in fireside stories.*
– ORIGIN early 17th cent.: from Greek (see **GENESIS**).

Genet /ʒəˈneɪ/, French /ʒənɛ/, Jean (1910–86), French novelist, poet, and dramatist. Much of his work portrayed life in the criminal and homosexual underworlds, of which he was a part. Notable works: *Our Lady of the Flowers* (novel, 1944), *The Thief's Journal* (autobiography, 1949), and *The Maids* (play, 1947).

genet /ˈdʒɛnɪt/ ▸ noun a catlike nocturnal mammal of the civet family with short legs, spotted fur, and a long bushy ringed tail, found in Africa, SW Europe, and Arabia. ● Genus *Genetta*, family Viverridae: several species, in particular the **common** (or **small-spotted**) **genet** (*G. genetta*).
■ [mass noun] the fur of the genet.
– ORIGIN Middle English (used in the plural meaning 'genet skins'): from Old French *genete*, probably via Catalan, Portuguese, or Spanish from Arabic *jarnaiṭ*.

gene therapy ▸ noun [mass noun] the introduction of normal genes into cells in place of missing or defective ones in order to correct genetic disorders.

genetic /dʒɪˈnɛtɪk/ ▸ adjective **1** relating to genes or heredity: *genetic abnormalities.* ■ relating to genetics: *there are fears that genetic techniques could be abused.*
2 relating to origin, or arising from a common origin: *the genetic relations between languages.*
– DERIVATIVES **genetical** adjective, **genetically** adverb.
– ORIGIN mid 19th cent. (in sense 2): from **GENESIS**, on the pattern of pairs such as *antithesis*, *antithetic*.

G

genetically modified ▸ adjective (of an organism) containing genetic material that has been artificially altered so as to produce a desired characteristic.

genetic code ▸ noun [mass noun] the means by which DNA and RNA molecules carry genetic information in living cells. See **TRIPLET CODE**.

genetic counselling ▸ noun [mass noun] the giving of advice to prospective parents concerning the risks of genetic disorders in a future child.

genetic drift ▸ noun [mass noun] Biology variation in the relative frequency of different genotypes in a small population, owing to the chance disappearance of particular genes as individuals die or do not reproduce.

genetic engineering ▸ noun [mass noun] the deliberate modification of the characteristics of an organism by manipulating its genetic material.

genetic fingerprinting (also **genetic profiling**) ▸ noun [mass noun] the analysis of DNA from samples of body tissues or fluids in order to identify individuals.

genetic imprinting ▸ noun [mass noun] the differential expression of genetic traits depending on the parent from which they were inherited.

genetic information ▸ noun [mass noun] the genetic potential of an organism carried in the base sequence of its DNA (or, in some viruses, RNA) according to the genetic code.

genetic load ▸ noun [mass noun] Biology the presence of unfavourable genetic material in the genes of a population.

genetic pollution ▸ noun [mass noun] the spread of altered genes from genetically engineered organisms to other, non-engineered organisms, especially by cross-pollination.

genetics ▸ plural noun [treated as sing.] the study of heredity and the variation of inherited characteristics. ■ [treated as sing. or pl.] the genetic properties or features of an organism, characteristic, etc.: *the effects of family genetics on the choice of career.*
– DERIVATIVES **geneticist** noun.

genetic testing (also **genetic screening**) ▸ noun [mass noun] the study of a person's DNA in order to identify genetic differences or susceptibility to particular diseases or abnormalities.

Geneva /dʒɪˈniːvə/ a city in SW Switzerland, on Lake Geneva; pop. 179,971 (2007). It is the headquarters of international bodies such as the Red Cross, various organizations of the United Nations, and the World Health Organization. French name **GENÈVE**.

Geneva, Lake a lake in SW central Europe, between the Jura mountains and the Alps. Its southern shore forms part of the border between France and Switzerland. French name **LAC LÉMAN**.

Geneva bands ▸ plural noun two white cloth strips attached to the collar of some Protestants' clerical dress.
– ORIGIN late 19th cent.: from the place name **GENEVA**, where they were originally worn by Calvinists.

Geneva Bible ▸ noun an English translation of the Bible published in 1560 by Protestant scholars working in Europe.

Geneva Convention an international agreement first made at Geneva in 1864 and later revised, governing the status and treatment of captured and wounded military personnel and civilians in wartime.

Geneva Protocol any of various protocols drawn up in Geneva, especially that of 1925 limiting chemical and bacteriological warfare.

Genève /ʒənɛv/ French name for **Geneva**.

genever /dʒɪ'niːvə/ (also literary **geneva**) ▸ **noun** [mass noun] Dutch gin.
– ORIGIN early 18th cent.: from Dutch, from Old French *genevre*, from an alteration of Latin *juniperus* (gin being flavoured with juniper berries). The variant spelling is due to association with **Geneva**.

Genghis Khan /ˌɡɛŋɡɪs 'kɑːn, ˌdʒɛŋ-/ (1162–1227), founder of the Mongol empire; born *Temujin*. He took the name Genghis Khan ('ruler of all') in 1206 after uniting the nomadic Mongol tribes, and by the time of his death his empire extended from China to the Black Sea.

genial¹ /'dʒiːnɪəl/ ▸ **adjective** friendly and cheerful: *our genial host*. ■ literary (especially of air or climate) pleasantly mild and warm.
– DERIVATIVES **genially** adverb.
– ORIGIN mid 16th cent.: from Latin *genialis* 'nuptial, productive', from *genius* (see **genius**). The Latin sense was adopted into English; hence the senses 'mild and conducive to growth' (mid 17th cent.), later 'cheerful, kindly' (mid 18th cent.).

genial² /dʒɪ'niːəl/ ▸ **adjective** Anatomy, rare relating to the chin.
– ORIGIN mid 19th cent.: from Greek *geneion* 'chin' (from *genus* 'jaw') + **-al**.

geniality ▸ **noun** [mass noun] the quality of having a friendly and cheerful manner; affability: *he was endowed with geniality and good humour*.

genic /'dʒiːnɪk, 'dʒɛn-/ ▸ **adjective** Biology relating to genes: *a genic mutation*.

-genic ▸ **combining form 1** producing: *carcinogenic*. ■ produced by: *iatrogenic*.
2 well suited to: *mediagenic*. [on the pattern of words such as *(photo)genic*.]
– DERIVATIVES **-genically** suffix forming corresponding adverbs.
– ORIGIN from **-gen** + **-ic**.

geniculate /dʒɪ'nɪkjʊlət/ ▸ **adjective** Anatomy bent at a sharp angle.
– ORIGIN mid 17th cent.: from Latin *geniculatus*, from *geniculum* 'small knee, joint (of a plant)'.

geniculate body (also **geniculate nucleus**) ▸ **noun** Anatomy each of two protuberances on the inferior surface of the thalamus which relay auditory and visual impulses respectively to the cerebral cortex.

genie ▸ **noun** (pl. **genies** or **genii** /'dʒiːnɪʌɪ/) a spirit of Arabian folklore, as depicted traditionally imprisoned within a bottle or oil lamp, and capable of granting wishes when summoned. Compare with **jinn**.
– ORIGIN mid 17th cent. (denoting a guardian or protective spirit): from French *génie*, from Latin *genius* (see **genius**). *Génie* was adopted in the current sense by the 18th-cent. French translators of *The Arabian Nights' Entertainments*, because of its resemblance in form and sense to Arabic *jinnī* 'jinnee'.

genii plural form of **genie**, **genius**.

genip /ɡɛ'nɪp/ ▸ **noun 1** the edible fruit of a tropical American tree.
2 (also **genipap tree**) either of two tropical American trees which yield this fruit: ● (also **guinep**) a large spreading tree (*Melicoccus bijugatus*, family Sapindaceae). ● another term for **genipapo**.
– ORIGIN mid 18th cent.: from American Spanish *quenepo* 'guinep tree', *quenepa*, denoting the fruit.

genipapo /ˌdʒɛnɪ'papəʊ/ (also **genipap** /'dʒɛnɪpap/) ▸ **noun** (pl. **genipapos**) a tropical American tree whose fruit has a jelly-like pulp which is used for flavouring drinks and to make a black dye. Also called **genip**. ● *Genipa americana*, family Rubiaceae.
■ [mass noun] a drink, flavouring, or dye made from the fruit of the genipapo.
– ORIGIN early 17th cent.: from Portuguese *jenipapo*, from Tupi.

genista /dʒɪ'nɪstə, dʒɛ-/ ▸ **noun** an almost leafless Eurasian shrub of the pea family, which bears a profusion of yellow flowers. ● Genus *Genista*, family Leguminosae: many species, including dyer's greenweed and several kinds of broom.
– ORIGIN modern Latin, from Latin, 'broom plant'.

genital ▸ **adjective** relating to the human or animal reproductive organs: *the genital area*. ■ Psychoanalysis (in Freudian theory) relating to or denoting the final stage of psychosexual development reached in adulthood.
▸ **noun (genitals)** a person's or animal's external organs of reproduction.
– DERIVATIVES **genitally** adverb.
– ORIGIN late Middle English: from Old French, or from Latin *genitalis*, from *genitus*, past participle of *gignere* 'beget'.

genitalia /ˌdʒɛnɪ'teɪlɪə/ ▸ **plural noun** formal or technical the genitals.
– ORIGIN late 19th cent.: from Latin, neuter plural of *genitalis* (see **genital**).

genitive /'dʒɛnɪtɪv/ Grammar ▸ **adjective** relating to or denoting a case of nouns and pronouns (and words in grammatical agreement with them) indicating possession or close association.
▸ **noun** a word in the genitive case. ■ **(the genitive)** the genitive case.
– DERIVATIVES **genitival** /-'tʌɪv(ə)l/ **adjective**.
– ORIGIN late Middle English: from Old French *genitif, -ive* or Latin *genitivus (casus)* '(case) of production or origin', from *gignere* 'beget'.

genito- /'dʒɛnɪtəʊ/ ▸ **combining form** representing **genital**.

genitor /'dʒɛnɪtə/ ▸ **noun** Anthropology a person's biological father. Often contrasted with **pater**.
– ORIGIN late Middle English (in the sense 'father'): from Old French *geniteur* or Latin *genitor*, from the root of *gignere* 'beget'. The current sense dates from the mid 20th cent.

genito-urinary /ˌdʒɛnɪtəʊ'jʊərɪn(ə)ri/ ▸ **adjective** chiefly Medicine relating to the genital and urinary organs.

geniture /'dʒɛnɪtʃə/ ▸ **noun** archaic a person's birth or parentage.
– ORIGIN late Middle English: from Old French *geniture* or Latin *genitura*, from the root of *gignere* 'beget'.

genius ▸ **noun** (pl. **geniuses**) **1** [mass noun] exceptional intellectual or creative power or other natural ability: *she was a teacher of genius* | [in sing.] *that woman has a genius for organization*.
2 an exceptionally intelligent person or one with exceptional skill in a particular area of activity: *a mathematical genius*.
3 (pl. **genii** /-nɪʌɪ/) (in some mythologies) a spirit associated with a particular person, place, or institution. ■ a person regarded as exerting a powerful influence over another for good or evil: *he sees Adams as the man's evil genius*.
4 the prevailing character or spirit of something: *Boucher's paintings did not suit the austere genius of neoclassicism*.
– ORIGIN late Middle English: from Latin, 'attendant spirit present from one's birth, innate ability or inclination', from the root of *gignere* 'beget'. The original sense 'spirit attendant on a person' gave rise to a sense 'a person's characteristic disposition' (late 16th cent.), which led to a sense 'a person's natural ability', and finally 'exceptional natural ability' (mid 17th cent.).

genius loci /'ləʊsʌɪ, 'lɒkiː/ ▸ **noun** the prevailing character or atmosphere of a place. ■ the presiding god or spirit of a place.
– ORIGIN Latin, literally 'spirit of the place'.

genizah /ɡɛ'niːzə/ ▸ **noun** a room attached to a synagogue and housing damaged, discarded, or heretical texts and sacred relics.
– ORIGIN from Hebrew *gĕnīzāh*, literally 'hiding place', from *gānaz* 'hide, set aside'.

genlock /'dʒɛnlɒk/ ▸ **noun** a device for maintaining synchronization between two different video signals, or between a video signal and a computer or audio signal, enabling video images and computer graphics to be mixed.
▸ **verb** [no obj.] maintain synchronization between two signals using the genlock technique.
– ORIGIN 1960s: from **generator** + the verb **lock¹**.

Genoa /'dʒɛnəʊə/ a seaport on the NW coast of Italy, capital of Liguria region; pop. 611,171 (2008). It was the birthplace of Christopher Columbus. Italian name **Genova**.
– DERIVATIVES **Genoese** /ˌdʒɛnəʊ'iːz/ **adjective & noun**.

genoa /'dʒɛnəʊə, dʒɛ'nəʊə/ ▸ **noun 1** (also **genoa jib**) Sailing a large jib or foresail whose foot extends aft of the mast, used especially on racing yachts.
2 (also **Genoa cake**) a rich fruit cake with almonds on top.

genocide /'dʒɛnəsʌɪd/ ▸ **noun** [mass noun] the deliberate killing of a large group of people, especially those of a particular nation or ethnic group.
– DERIVATIVES **genocidal** adjective.
– ORIGIN 1940s: from Greek *genos* 'race' + **-cide**.

genome /'dʒiːnəʊm/ ▸ **noun** [mass noun] Biology the haploid set of chromosomes in a gamete or microorganism, or in each cell of a multicellular organism. ■ the complete set of genes or genetic material present in a cell or organism.
– DERIVATIVES **genomic** adjective.
– ORIGIN 1930s: blend of **gene** and **chromosome**.

genomics /dʒɪ'nəʊmɪks, dʒɪ'nɒmɪks/ ▸ **plural noun** [treated as sing.] the branch of molecular biology concerned with the structure, function, evolution, and mapping of genomes.

genotype /'dʒɛnətʌɪp, 'dʒiːn-/ Biology ▸ **noun** the genetic constitution of an individual organism. Often contrasted with **phenotype**.
▸ **verb** [with obj.] investigate the genotype of.
– DERIVATIVES **genotypic** /-'tɪpɪk/ **adjective**.
– ORIGIN early 20th cent.: from German *Genotypus*, from Greek *genos* 'race, offspring' + *-tupos* 'type'.

-genous ▸ **combining form 1** producing; inducing: *erogenous*.
2 originating in: *endogenous*.
– ORIGIN from **-gen** + **-ous**.

Genova /'dʒɛnəova/ Italian name for **Genoa**.

genre /'ʒɒ̃rə, '(d)ʒɒnrə/ ▸ **noun 1** a style or category of art, music, or literature: *the spy thriller is a very masculine genre* | *the science fiction genre*.
2 [as modifier] denoting or relating to a style of painting depicting scenes from ordinary life, typically domestic situations, associated particularly with 17th-century Dutch and Flemish artists: *genre scenes*.
– ORIGIN early 19th cent.: French, literally 'a kind' (see **gender**).

gens /dʒɛnz/ ▸ **noun** (pl. **gentes** /-tiːz, -teɪz/) **1** a group of families in ancient Rome who shared a name and claimed a common origin.
2 Anthropology a group of people who are related through their male ancestors.
– ORIGIN Latin, from the root of *gignere* 'beget'.

Gent /xɛnt/ Flemish name for **Ghent**.

gent ▸ **noun** informal a gentleman. ■ **(gents)** Brit. (in shop titles) men's: *a gents hairdressing shop*. ■ **(the Gents)** Brit. a men's public toilet.
– ORIGIN mid 16th cent.: originally a standard written abbreviation; a colloquial usage since the early 19th cent.

gentamicin /ˌdʒɛntə'mʌɪsɪn/ ▸ **noun** [mass noun] a broad-spectrum antibiotic used chiefly for severe systemic infections. ● This antibiotic is derived from bacteria of the genus *Micromonospora*.
– ORIGIN 1960s: from *genta-* (of unknown origin) + *-micin* (alteration of **-mycin**).

genteel ▸ **adjective** characterized by exaggerated or affected politeness, refinement, or respectability: *her genteel upbringing*.
– DERIVATIVES **genteelly** adverb, **genteelness** noun.
– ORIGIN late 16th cent. (in the sense 'fashionable, stylish'): from French *gentil* 'well-born'. From the 17th cent. to the 19th cent. the word was used in such senses as 'of good social position', 'having the manners of a well-born person', 'well bred'. The ironic or derogatory implication dates from the 19th cent.

genteelism ▸ **noun** a word or expression used because it is thought to be socially more acceptable than the everyday word.

gentes plural form of **gens**.

gentian /'dʒɛnʃ(ə)n/ ▸ **noun** a plant of temperate and mountainous regions, which typically has violet or vivid blue trumpet-shaped flowers. Many kinds are cultivated as ornamentals, especially as arctic alpines, and some are of medicinal use. ● Family Gentianaceae: genera *Gentiana* and *Gentianella*.
■ [mass noun] a tonic liquid substance formerly extracted from the root of the gentian.
– ORIGIN late Middle English: from Latin *gentiana*, according to Pliny named after *Gentius*, king of Illyria, who is said to have discovered the medicinal properties of a common species.

gentian violet ▸ **noun** [mass noun] a synthetic violet dye derived from rosaniline, used as an antiseptic.

gentile /'dʒɛntʌɪl/ ▸ **adjective 1 (Gentile)** not Jewish: *a predominantly Gentile audience*. ■ (of a person) not belonging to one's own religious community. ■ historical non-Mormon.

2 chiefly Anthropology relating to or indicating a nation or clan, especially a gens.
▶ **noun (Gentile)** a person who is not Jewish.
– ORIGIN late Middle English: from Latin *gentilis* 'of a family or nation, of the same clan' (used in the Vulgate to refer to non-Jews), from *gens, gent-* 'family, race', from the root of *gignere* 'beget'.

Gentile da Fabriano /dʒɛnˌtiːleɪ da ˌfabrɪˈɑːnəʊ/ (*c*.1370–1427), Italian painter. His major surviving work is the altarpiece *The Adoration of the Magi* (1423), most others having been destroyed.

gentility /dʒɛnˈtɪlɪti/ ▶ **noun** [mass noun] social superiority as demonstrated by polite and respectable manners, behaviour, or appearances: *her grandmother's pretensions to gentility*.
– ORIGIN Middle English (in the sense 'honourable birth'): from Old French *gentilite*, from *gentil* (see GENTLE[1]).

gentle[1] ▶ **adjective (gentler, gentlest) 1** having or showing a mild, kind, or tender temperament or character: *a gentle, sensitive man | her gentle voice*.
2 moderate in action, effect, or degree; not strong or violent: *take some gentle exercise | a gentle breeze*. ■ (of a slope) gradual: *a gentle embankment*.
3 archaic (of a person) noble or having the qualities attributed to noble birth; courteous and chivalrous.
▶ **verb** make or become gentle: [no obj.] *Cobb's tone gentled a little*. ■ [with obj.] touch (a person or animal) gently, typically in order to make them calmer or more docile.
– DERIVATIVES **gentleness** noun, **gently** adverb.
– ORIGIN Middle English: from Old French *gentil* 'high-born, noble', from Latin *gentilis* 'of the same clan' (see GENTILE). The original sense was 'nobly born', hence 'courteous, chivalrous', later 'mild, moderate in action or disposition' (mid 16th cent.).

gentle[2] ▶ **noun** Fishing a maggot, especially the larva of a blowfly, used as bait.
– ORIGIN late 16th cent.: probably from an obsolete sense of the adjective, 'soft, pliant'.

gentle breeze ▶ **noun** a light wind of force 3 on the Beaufort scale (7–10 knots or 13–19 kph).

gentlefolk ▶ **plural noun** archaic people of noble birth or good social position.

gentleman ▶ **noun** (pl. **gentlemen**) **1** a chivalrous, courteous, or honourable man: *he behaved throughout like a perfect gentleman*. ■ a man of good social position, especially one of wealth and leisure. ■ a man of noble birth attached to a royal household: *a Gentleman of the Bedchamber*.
2 a polite or formal way of referring to a man: *opposite her an old gentleman sat reading | can I help you, gentlemen?* ■ used as a courteous title for a male fellow member of the House of Commons or the House of Representatives: *the Right Honourable Gentleman opposite*.
– ORIGIN Middle English (in the sense 'man of noble birth'): from GENTLE[1] + MAN, translating Old French *gentilz hom*. In later use the term denoted a man of a good family (especially one entitled to a coat of arms) but not of the nobility.

gentleman-at-arms ▶ **noun** one of the bodyguards of the British monarch on ceremonial occasions.

gentleman farmer ▶ **noun** (pl. **gentlemen farmers**) a country gentleman who has a farm as part of his estate.

gentlemanly ▶ **adjective** chivalrous, courteous, or honourable: *his gentlemanly behaviour*. ■ befitting a gentleman: *a gentlemanly profession*.
– DERIVATIVES **gentlemanliness** noun.

gentleman's agreement (also **gentlemen's agreement**) ▶ **noun** an arrangement or understanding which is based upon the trust of both or all parties, rather than being legally binding.

gentleman's gentleman ▶ **noun** a valet.

Gentleman's Relish ▶ **noun** [mass noun] Brit. trademark a highly seasoned anchovy paste.

Gentleman Usher of the Black Rod ▶ **noun** see BLACK ROD.

gentlewoman ▶ **noun** (pl. **gentlewomen**) archaic a woman of noble birth or good social standing.

gentoo /dʒɛnˈtuː/ (also **gentoo penguin**) ▶ **noun** a tall penguin with a white triangular patch above the eye, breeding on subantarctic islands. ● *Pygoscelis papua*, family Spheniscidae.
– ORIGIN mid 19th cent.: perhaps from Anglo-Indian *Gentoo* 'a Hindu', from Portuguese *gentio* 'gentile'.

gentrify ▶ **verb (gentrifies, gentrifying, gentrified)** [with obj.] renovate and improve (a house or district) so that it conforms to middle-class taste. ■ (usu. as adj. **gentrified**) make (someone or their way of life) more genteel: *a gentrified Irish American*.
– DERIVATIVES **gentrification** noun, **gentrifier** noun.

gentry /ˈdʒɛntri/ ▶ **noun** [mass noun] (often **the gentry**) people of good social position, specifically the class of people next below the nobility in position and birth: *a member of the landed gentry*.
– ORIGIN late Middle English (in the sense 'superiority of birth or rank'): from Anglo-Norman French *genterie*, based on *gentil* (see GENTLE[1]).

genu /ˈdʒɛnjuː/ ▶ **noun** (pl. **genua**) Anatomy the knee. ■ Anatomy & Biology a part of certain structures resembling a knee, in particular a bend in the corpus callosum of mammals.
– ORIGIN mid 19th cent.: from Latin.

genuflect /ˈdʒɛnjʊflɛkt/ ▶ **verb** [no obj.] lower one's body briefly by bending one knee to the ground, typically in worship or as a sign of respect. ■ show deference or servility: *politicians had to genuflect to the far left to advance their careers*.
– DERIVATIVES **genuflection** (also **genuflexion**) noun, **genuflector** noun.
– ORIGIN mid 17th cent. (in the sense 'bend (the knee)'): from ecclesiastical Latin *genuflectere*, from Latin *genu* 'knee' + *flectere* 'to bend'.

genuine ▶ **adjective** truly what something is said to be; authentic: *genuine 24-carat gold*. ■ (of a person, emotion, or action) sincere: *a genuine attempt to put things right | there was genuine affection in his voice*.
– DERIVATIVES **genuinely** adverb, **genuineness** noun.
– ORIGIN late 16th cent. (in the sense 'natural or proper'): from Latin *genuinus*, from *genu* 'knee' (with reference to the Roman custom of a father acknowledging paternity of a newborn child by placing it on his knee); later associated with *genus* 'birth, race, stock'.

genus /ˈdʒiːnəs, ˈdʒɛnəs/ ▶ **noun** (pl. **genera** /ˈdʒɛn(ə)rə/) Biology a principal taxonomic category that ranks above species and below family, and is denoted by a capitalized Latin name, e.g. *Leo*. ■ (in philosophical and general use) a class of things which have com-mon characteristics and which can be divided into subordinate kinds.
– ORIGIN mid 16th cent.: from Latin, 'birth, race, stock'.

-geny ▶ **combining form** denoting the mode by which something develops or is produced: *orogeny | organogeny*.
– ORIGIN related to French *-génie*; both forms derive from Greek *-geneia*, from *gen-* (root of *gignomai* 'be born, become' and *genos* 'a kind').

geo /gjəʊ, ˈdʒiːəʊ/ ▶ **noun** (pl. **geos**) a long, narrow, steep-sided cleft formed by erosion in coastal cliffs.
– ORIGIN early 17th cent. (originally Orkney and Shetland dialect): from Old Norse *gjá*.

Geo. ▶ **abbreviation** dated George.

geo- /ˈdʒiːəʊ/ ▶ **combining form** relating to the earth: *geocentric | geochemistry*.
– ORIGIN from Greek *gē* 'earth'.

geobotany ▶ **noun** another term for PHYTOGEOGRAPHY.
– DERIVATIVES **geobotanical** adjective,.

geocaching /ˈdʒiːə(ʊ)kaʃɪŋ/ ▶ **noun** [mass noun] a form of treasure hunt using GPS, in which an item is hidden somewhere in the world and its coordinates posted on the Internet, so that GPS users can locate it.
– DERIVATIVES **geocacher** noun.
– ORIGIN early 21st cent.: from GEO- + CACHE.

geocentric ▶ **adjective 1** having or representing the earth as the centre, as in former astronomical systems. Compare with HELIOCENTRIC.
2 Astronomy measured from or considered in relation to the centre of the earth.
– DERIVATIVES **geocentrically** adverb, **geocentrism** noun.

geocentric latitude ▶ **noun** the latitude at which a planet would appear if viewed from the centre of the earth.

geochemistry ▶ **noun** [mass noun] the study of the chemical composition of the earth and its rocks and minerals.
– DERIVATIVES **geochemical** adjective, **geochemist** noun.

geochronology ▶ **noun** [mass noun] the branch of geology concerned with the dating of rock formations and geological events.
– DERIVATIVES **geochronological** adjective, **geochronologist** noun.

geochronometric /ˌdʒiːə(ʊ)ˌkrɒnəˈmɛtrɪk/ ▶ **adjective** relating to geochronological measurement.
– DERIVATIVES **geochronometry** noun.

geode /ˈdʒiːəʊd/ ▶ **noun** a small cavity in rock lined with crystals or other mineral matter. ■ a rock containing such a cavity.
– DERIVATIVES **geodic** /dʒiːˈɒdɪk/ adjective.
– ORIGIN late 17th cent.: via Latin from Greek *geōdēs* 'earthy', from *gē* 'earth'.

geodesic /ˌdʒiːə(ʊ)ˈdɛsɪk, -ˈdiːsɪk/ ▶ **adjective 1** relating to or denoting the shortest possible line between two points on a sphere or other curved surface. ■ (of a dome or other structure) constructed from struts which follow geodesic lines and typically form an open framework of triangles and polygons.
2 another term for GEODETIC.
▶ **noun** a geodesic line or structure.
– ORIGIN early 19th cent.: from GEODESY + -IC.

geodesy /dʒɪˈɒdɪsi/ ▶ **noun** [mass noun] the branch of mathematics dealing with the shape and area of the earth or large portions of it.
– DERIVATIVES **geodesist** noun.
– ORIGIN late 16th cent.: from modern Latin *geodaesia*, from Greek *geōdaisia*, from *gē* 'earth' + *daiein* 'divide'.

G

geodetic /ˌdʒiːə(ʊ)ˈdɛtɪk/ ▶ **adjective** relating to geodesy, especially as applied to land surveying.
– ORIGIN late 17th cent.: from Greek *geōdaitēs* 'land surveyor', from *geōdaisia* (see GEODESY).

geoduck /ˈdʒiːəʊdʌk/ ▶ **noun** a giant mud-burrowing bivalve mollusc occurring on the west coast of North America, where it is collected for food. Its shell valves are not large enough to enclose its body and very long siphon. ● *Panopea generosa*, family Hyatellidae.
– ORIGIN late 19th cent.: from Chinook Jargon.

geoengineering /ˌdʒiːəʊɛndʒɪˈnɪərɪŋ/ ▶ **noun** [mass noun] the deliberate large-scale manipulation of an environmental process that affects the earth's climate, in an attempt to counteract the effects of global warming.

Geoffrey of Monmouth (*c*.1100–*c*.1154), Welsh chronicler. His *Historia Regum Britanniae* (*c*.1139; first printed in 1508), an account of the kings of Britain, was a major source for English literature but is now thought to contain little historical fact.

geographical ▶ **adjective** relating to geography.
– DERIVATIVES **geographic** adjective, **geographically** adverb.

geographical latitude ▶ **noun** the angle made with the plane of the equator by a perpendicular to the earth's surface at any point.

geographical mile ▶ **noun** a distance equal to one minute of longitude or latitude at the equator (about 1,850 metres).

geography ▶ **noun** [mass noun] the study of the physical features of the earth and its atmosphere, and of human activity as it affects and is affected by these, including the distribution of populations and resources and political and economic activities. ■ [usu. in sing.] the nature and relative arrangement of places and physical features: *the geography of post-war London*. ■ (pl. **geographies**) (especially in business) a geographical area; a region.
– DERIVATIVES **geographer** noun.
– ORIGIN late 15th cent.: from French *géographie* or Latin *geographia*, from Greek *geōgraphia*, from *gē* 'earth' + *-graphia* 'writing'.

geoid /ˈdʒiːɔɪd/ ▶ **noun (the geoid)** a hypothetical solid figure whose surface corresponds to mean sea level and its imagined extension under (or over) land areas.
– ORIGIN late 19th cent.: from Greek *geoeidēs*, from *gē* 'earth' + *-oeidēs* (see -OID).

geology ▶ **noun** [mass noun] the science which deals with the physical structure and substance of the earth, their history, and the processes which act on them. ■ the geological features of a district: *the geology of the Outer Hebrides*. ■ the geological features of a planetary body: *an article on the Moon's geology*.
– DERIVATIVES **geologic** adjective, **geological** adjective, **geologically** adverb, **geologist** noun, **geologize** (also **geologise**) verb.
– ORIGIN late 18th cent.: from modern Latin *geologia*, from Greek *gē* 'earth' + *-logia* (see -LOGY).

geomagnetism ▶ **noun** [mass noun] the branch of geology concerned with the magnetic properties of the earth.
– DERIVATIVES **geomagnetic** adjective, **geomagnetically** adverb.

geomancy /ˈdʒiːə(ʊ)mansi/ ▶ **noun** [mass noun] **1** the art of placing or arranging buildings or other sites auspiciously.

2 divination from the configuration of a handful of earth or random dots.
– DERIVATIVES **geomancer** noun, **geomantic** adjective.

geomatics /ˌdʒiːə(ʊ)ˈmatɪks/ ▶ plural noun [treated as sing.] the application of computerization to information in geography and related fields.
– DERIVATIVES **geomatic** adjective.
– ORIGIN 1980s: from GEOGRAPHY and INFORMATICS.

geometer /dʒɪˈɒmɪtə/ ▶ noun 1 a person skilled in geometry.
2 (also **geometer moth**) Entomology a geometrid moth or its caterpillar.
– ORIGIN late Middle English: from late Latin *geometra*, based on Greek *geōmetrēs*, from *gē* 'earth' + *metrēs* 'measurer'.

geometric /ˌdʒɪəˈmɛtrɪk/ ▶ adjective 1 relating to geometry, or according to its methods.
2 characterized by or decorated with regular lines and shapes: *a geometric pattern*. ■ (**Geometric**) Archaeology relating to or denoting a period of Greek culture (around 900–700 BC) characterized by geometrically decorated pottery. ■ (**Geometric** or **Geometrical**) Architecture relating to or denoting a style of Early English tracery based on the geometry of circles.
▶ noun a geometric pattern.
– DERIVATIVES **geometrical** adjective, **geometrically** adverb.
– ORIGIN mid 17th cent.: via French from Latin *geometricus*, from Greek *geōmetrikos*, from *geōmetrēs* (see GEOMETER).

geometrical isomer (also **geometric isomer**) ▶ noun Chemistry each of two or more compounds which differ from each other in the arrangement of groups with respect to a double bond, ring, or other rigid structure.
– DERIVATIVES **geometrical isomerism** noun.

geometrical series ▶ noun a series of numbers or quantities in geometric progression.

geometric mean ▶ noun the central number in a geometric progression (e.g. 9 in 3, 9, 27), also calculable as the nth root of a product of n numbers.

geometric progression ▶ noun a progression of numbers with a constant ratio between each number and the one before (e.g. 1, 3, 9, 27, 81).

geometrid /dʒɪˈɒmɪtrɪd/ ▶ noun Entomology a moth of a large family (Geometridae), distinguished by having twig-like caterpillars (**loopers**) that move by looping and straightening the body. Also called GEOMETER.
– ORIGIN late 19th cent.: from modern Latin *Geometridae* (plural), from the genus name *Geometra*, from Greek *geōmetrēs* (see GEOMETER).

geometry /dʒɪˈɒmɪtri/ ▶ noun (pl. **geometries**) [mass noun] the branch of mathematics concerned with the properties and relations of points, lines, surfaces, solids, and higher dimensional analogues. ■ [count noun] a particular mathematical system describing such properties: *non-Euclidean geometries*. ■ [in sing.] the shape and relative arrangement of the parts of something: *the geometry of spiders' webs*.
– DERIVATIVES **geometrician** /ˌdʒiːəmɪˈtrɪʃ(ə)n/ noun.
– ORIGIN Middle English: via Old French from Latin *geometria*, from Greek, from *gē* 'earth' + *metria* (see -METRY).

geomorphic /ˌdʒiːə(ʊ)ˈmɔːfɪk/ ▶ adjective relating to the form of the landscape and other natural features of the earth's surface; geomorphological.

geomorphology /ˌdʒiːə(ʊ)mɔːˈfɒlədʒi/ ▶ noun [mass noun] the study of the physical features of the surface of the earth and their relation to its geological structures.
– DERIVATIVES **geomorphological** adjective, **geomorphologist** noun.

geopark ▶ noun a UNESCO-designated area containing one or more sites of particular geological importance, intended to conserve the geological heritage and promote public awareness of it, typically through tourism.

geophagy /dʒɪˈɒfədʒi/ ▶ noun [mass noun] the practice in some tribal societies of eating earth.
– ORIGIN mid 19th cent.: from GEO- 'earth' + Greek *phagia* 'eating, feeding' (from *phagein* 'eat').

geophysics ▶ plural noun [treated as sing.] the physics of the earth.
– DERIVATIVES **geophysical** adjective, **geophysicist** noun.

geopolitical ▶ adjective relating to politics, especially international relations, as influenced by geographical factors.
– DERIVATIVES **geopolitically** adverb, **geopolitician** noun, **geopolitics** noun [treated as sing. or pl.].

Geordie Brit. informal ▶ noun a person from Tyneside. ■ [mass noun] the English dialect or accent typical of people from Tyneside.
▶ adjective relating to Tyneside, its people, or their accent or dialect: *Geordie humour*.
– ORIGIN mid 19th cent.: diminutive of the given name *George*.

George the name of four kings of Great Britain and Ireland, one of Great Britain and Ireland (from 1920 of the United Kingdom), and one of the United Kingdom: ■ **George I** (1660–1727), great-grandson of James I, reigned 1714–27, Elector of Hanover 1698–1727. He succeeded to the British throne as a result of the Act of Settlement (1701). Unpopular in England as a foreigner who never learned English, he left administration to his ministers. ■ **George II** (1683–1760), son of George I, reigned 1727–60, Elector of Hanover 1727–60. He depended heavily on his ministers, although he took an active part in the War of the Austrian Succession (1740–8). His later withdrawal from active politics allowed the development of constitutional monarchy. ■ **George III** (1738–1820), grandson of George II, reigned 1760–1820, Elector of Hanover 1760–1815 and king of Hanover 1815–20. He exercised considerable political influence, but it declined from 1788 after bouts of mental illness, as a result of which his son was made regent in 1811. ■ **George IV** (1762–1830), son of George III, reigned 1820–30. Known as a patron of the arts and *bon viveur*, he gained a bad reputation which was further damaged by his attempt to divorce his estranged wife, Caroline of Brunswick, just after coming to the throne. ■ **George V** (1865–1936), son of Edward VII, reigned 1910–36. He exercised restrained but important influence over British politics, playing an especially significant role in the formation of the government in 1931. ■ **George VI** (1895–1952), son of George V, reigned 1936–52. He came to the throne on the abdication of his elder brother Edward VIII. Despite a retiring disposition he became a popular monarch, gaining respect for the staunch example he and his family set during the London Blitz.

George, St patron saint of England. He is reputed in legend to have slain a dragon, and may have been martyred near Lydda in Palestine some time before the reign of Constantine. His cult did not become popular until the 6th century, and he probably became patron saint of England in the 14th century. Feast day, 23 April.

George Cross (abbrev.: **GC**) ▶ noun (in the UK and Commonwealth countries) a decoration for bravery awarded especially to civilians, instituted in 1940 by King George VI and taking precedence over all other medals and decorations except the Victoria Cross.

George Medal (abbrev.: **GM**) ▶ noun (in the UK and Commonwealth countries) a medal for bravery awarded especially to civilians, instituted with the George Cross in 1940.

Georgetown the capital of Guyana, a port at the mouth of the Demerara River; pop. 133,000 (est. 2007).

George Town 1 the capital of the Cayman Islands, on the island of Grand Cayman; pop. 28,000 (est. 2007).
2 the chief port of Malaysia and capital of the state of Penang, on Penang island; pop. 158,800 (est. 2009). It was founded in 1786 by the British East India Company. Also called PENANG.

georgette /dʒɔːˈdʒɛt/ ▶ noun [mass noun] a thin silk or crêpe dress material.
– ORIGIN early 20th cent.: named after *Georgette* de la Plante (*c.*1900), French dressmaker.

Georgia 1 a country in the Caucasus of SW Asia, on the eastern shore of the Black Sea; pop. 4,615,800 (est. 2009); languages, Georgian (official), Russian, and Armenian; capital, Tbilisi.

> An independent kingdom in medieval times, Georgia became part of the Russian empire in the 19th century and then was absorbed into the Soviet Union. On the break-up of the USSR in 1991, Georgia became an independent republic outside the Commonwealth of Independent States.

2 a state of the south-eastern US, on the Atlantic coast; pop. 9,685,744 (est. 2008); capital, Atlanta. Founded as an English colony in 1732 and named after George II, it became one of the original thirteen states of the Union (1788).

Georgian[1] ▶ adjective 1 of or characteristic of the reigns of the British Kings George I–IV (1714–1830). ■ relating to British architecture of this period, characterized by restrained elegance and the use of neoclassical styles.
2 of or characteristic of the reigns of the British Kings George V and VI (1910–52). ■ relating to British literature of 1910–20, in particular pastoral poetry of a type strongly attacked by the early modernists.

Georgian[2] ▶ adjective relating to the country of Georgia, its people, or their language.
▶ noun 1 a native or inhabitant of Georgia, or a person of Georgian descent.
2 [mass noun] the official language of Georgia, spoken by around 4 million people. It is the main member of the small South Caucasian (or Kartvelian) language family, and has its own alphabet.

Georgian[3] ▶ adjective relating to the state of Georgia in the US.
▶ noun a native or inhabitant of Georgia.

georgic /ˈdʒɔːdʒɪk/ ▶ noun a poem or book dealing with agriculture or rural topics. ■ (**Georgics**) the title of a poetic treatise by Virgil.
▶ adjective literary rustic; pastoral.
– ORIGIN early 16th cent.: via Latin from Greek *geōrgikos*, from *geōrgos* 'farmer'.

geoscience ▶ noun [mass noun] (also **geosciences**) earth sciences, especially geology.
– DERIVATIVES **geoscientist** noun.

geospatial /ˌdʒiːəʊˈspeɪʃ(ə)l/ ▶ adjective Geography relating to or denoting data that is associated with a particular location.

geosphere /ˈdʒiːə(ʊ)sfɪə/ ▶ noun any of the almost spherical concentric regions of the earth and its atmosphere, especially the lithosphere.

geostationary ▶ adjective (of an artificial satellite of the earth) moving in a circular geosynchronous orbit in the plane of the equator, so that it appears to be stationary in the sky above a fixed point on the surface.

geostrategic ▶ adjective relating to the strategy required in dealing with geopolitical problems.
– DERIVATIVES **geostrategy** noun.

geostrophic /ˌdʒiːə(ʊ)ˈstrɒfɪk, -ˈstrəʊf-/ ▶ adjective Meteorology & Oceanography relating to or denoting the component of a wind or current that arises from a balance between pressure gradients and coriolis forces.
– ORIGIN early 20th cent.: from GEO- 'of the earth' + Greek *strophē* 'a turning' (from *strephein* 'to turn').

geosynchronous /ˌdʒiːə(ʊ)ˈsɪŋkrənəs/ ▶ adjective another term for SYNCHRONOUS (sense 2). Compare with GEOSTATIONARY.

geosyncline /dʒiːəʊˈsɪŋklʌɪn/ ▶ noun Geology a large-scale depression in the earth's crust containing very thick deposits.

geotagging /ˈdʒiːə(ʊ)tagɪŋ/ ▶ noun [mass noun] the practice of adding geographical information to digital photographs, typically the latitude and longitude of the location.

geotaxis /ˌdʒiːə(ʊ)ˈtaksɪs/ ▶ noun [mass noun] Biology the motion of a motile organism or cell in response to the force of gravity.
– DERIVATIVES **geotactic** adjective.

geotechnics ▶ plural noun [treated as sing.] the branch of civil engineering concerned with the study and modification of soil and rocks.
– DERIVATIVES **geotechnic** adjective, **geotechnical** adjective.

geothermal ▶ adjective relating to or produced by the internal heat of the earth: *some 70 per cent of Iceland's energy needs are met from geothermal sources*.
– DERIVATIVES **geothermally** adverb.

geotropism /ˌdʒiːə(ʊ)ˈtrəʊpɪz(ə)m/ ▶ noun [mass noun] Botany the growth of the parts of plants in response to the force of gravity. The upward growth of plant shoots is an instance of **negative geotropism**; the downward growth of roots is **positive geotropism**.
– DERIVATIVES **geotropic** adjective.
– ORIGIN late 19th cent.: from GEO- 'earth' + Greek *tropē* 'turning' + -ISM.

Gera /ˈgeːrə/ an industrial city in east central Germany, in Thuringia; pop. 102,700 (est. 2006).

Geraldton /ˈdʒɛrəldt(ə)n/ a seaport and resort on the west coast of Australia; pop. 26,200 (est. 2009).

geranial /dʒɪˈreɪnɪəl/ ▶ noun [mass noun] Chemistry a fragrant oil present in lemon grass oil and used in perfumery. ● An isomer of citral; chem. formula: $C_{10}H_{16}O$.

– ORIGIN late 19th cent.: from German, contraction of *Geraniumaldehyde*.

geraniol /dʒɪˈreɪnɪɒl/ ▶ **noun** [mass noun] Chemistry a fragrant liquid present in some floral oils and used in perfumery. ● A terpenoid alcohol; chem. formula: $C_{10}H_{18}O$.
– ORIGIN late 19th cent.: from German, from GERANIUM + -OL.

geranium /dʒɪˈreɪnɪəm/ ▶ **noun** a herbaceous plant or small shrub of a genus that comprises the cranesbills and their relatives. Geraniums bear a long, narrow fruit that is said to be shaped like the bill of a crane. ● Genus *Geranium*, family Geraniaceae.
■ (in general or informal use) a cultivated pelargonium.
■ [mass noun] the scarlet colour of many cultivated pelargoniums.
– ORIGIN modern Latin, from Greek *geranion*, from *geranos* 'crane'.

gerbera /ˈdʒəːb(ə)rə, ˈɡəː-/ ▶ **noun** a tropical Old World plant of the daisy family, with large brightly coloured flowers, cultivated under glass in cooler regions. ● Genus *Gerbera*, family Compositae: many species, in particular the Transvaal daisy.
– ORIGIN modern Latin, named after Traugott *Gerber* (died 1743), German naturalist.

gerbil /ˈdʒəːbɪl/ ▶ **noun** a burrowing mouse-like rodent that is specially adapted to living in arid conditions, found in Africa and Asia. ● Subfamily Gerbillinae, family Muridae: several genera, in particular *Gerbillus*; the **Mongolian gerbil** (*Meriones unguiculatus*) is popular as a pet.
– ORIGIN mid 19th cent.: from French *gerbille*, from modern Latin *gerbillus*, diminutive of *gerboa* (see JERBOA).

gerenuk /ˈɡɛrənʊk/ ▶ **noun** a slender East African antelope with a long neck, often browsing on tall bushes by standing on its hind legs. ● *Litocranius walleri*, family Bovidae.
– ORIGIN late 19th cent.: from Somali.

geriatric /ˌdʒɛrɪˈatrɪk/ ▶ **adjective** relating to old people, especially with regard to their health care: *a geriatric hospital*. ■ informal decrepit; very old or outdated: *replacements for a geriatric locomotive fleet*.
▶ **noun** an old person, especially one receiving special care: *a rest home for geriatrics*.
– ORIGIN 1920s: from Greek *gēras* 'old age' + *iatros* 'doctor', on the pattern of *paediatric*.

> **USAGE** **Geriatric** is the normal, semi-official term used in Britain and the US when referring to the health care of old people (*a geriatric ward*; *geriatric patients*). When used outside such contexts, it typically carries overtones of being worn out and decrepit and can therefore be offensive if used with reference to people.

geriatrics ▶ **plural noun** [treated as sing. or pl.] the branch of medicine or social science dealing with the health and care of old people.
– DERIVATIVES **geriatrician** noun.

Géricault /ˈʒɛrɪkəʊ/, French /ʒeʀiko/, (Jean Louis André) Théodore (1791–1824), French painter, criticized for his rejection of classicism in favour of a more realistic style. His most famous work, *The Raft of the Medusa* (1819), depicts the survivors of a famous shipwreck of 1816.

germ ▶ **noun 1** a microorganism, especially one which causes disease.
2 a portion of an organism capable of developing into a new one or part of one. ■ the embryo in a cereal grain or other plant seed. ■ an initial stage from which something may develop: ***the germ of a brilliant idea***.
– DERIVATIVES **germy** adjective (**germier**, **germiest**) informal, GERM (sense 1)).
– ORIGIN late Middle English (in sense 2): via Old French from Latin *germen* 'seed, sprout'. Sense 1 dates from the late 19th cent.

German ▶ **noun 1** a native or inhabitant of Germany, or a person of German descent.
2 [mass noun] a West Germanic language used in Germany, Austria, and parts of Switzerland, and by communities in the US and elsewhere. It is spoken by some 100 million people. See also HIGH GERMAN, LOW GERMAN.
▶ **adjective** relating to Germany, its people, or their language.
– DERIVATIVES **Germanist** noun.
– ORIGIN from Latin *Germanus*, used to designate related peoples of central and northern Europe, a name perhaps given by Celts to their neighbours; compare with Old Irish *gair* 'neighbour'.

german ▶ **adjective** archaic germane. See also BROTHER-GERMAN, COUSIN-GERMAN, SISTER-GERMAN.
– ORIGIN Middle English: from Old French *germain*, from Latin *germanus* 'genuine, of the same parents'.

German Bight a shipping forecast area covering the eastern North Sea off the northern Netherlands, Germany, and southern Denmark.

German Democratic Republic (abbrev.: **GDR**, **DDR**) official name for the former state of East Germany.

germander /dʒəˈmandə/ ▶ **noun** a widely distributed plant of the mint family. Some kinds are cultivated as ornamentals and some are used in herbal medicine. ● Genus *Teucrium*, family Labiatae: many species, including the European **wall germander** (*T. chamaedrys*).
– ORIGIN late Middle English: from medieval Latin *germandra*, based on Greek *khamaidrus*, literally 'ground oak', from *khamai* 'on the ground' + *drus* 'oak' (because the leaves of some species were thought to resemble those of the oak).

germander speedwell ▶ **noun** a speedwell with bright blue flowers and leaves resembling those of the germander, native to Eurasia. ● *Veronica chamaedrys*, family Scrophulariaceae.

germane /dʒəːˈmeɪn/ ▶ **adjective** relevant to a subject under consideration: *that is not germane to our theme*.
– DERIVATIVES **germanely** adverb, **germaneness** noun.
– ORIGIN early 17th cent.: variant of GERMAN, with which it was synonymous from Middle English. The current sense has arisen from a usage in Shakespeare's *Hamlet*.

German East Africa a former German protectorate in East Africa (1891–1918), corresponding to present-day Tanzania, Rwanda, and Burundi.

German Empire an empire in German-speaking central Europe, created by Bismarck in 1871 after the Franco-Prussian War by the union of twenty-five German states under the Hohenzollern king of Prussia. Also called SECOND REICH.

> Forming an alliance with Austria-Hungary, the German Empire became the greatest industrial power in Europe and engaged in colonial expansion in Africa, China, and the Far East. Tensions arising with other colonial powers led to the First World War, after which the German Empire collapsed and the Weimar Republic was created.

Germanic ▶ **adjective 1** relating to or denoting the branch of the Indo-European language family that includes English, German, Dutch, Frisian, and the Scandinavian languages. ■ relating to or denoting the peoples of ancient northern and western Europe speaking such languages.
2 having characteristics of or attributed to Germans or Germany: *she had an almost Germanic regard for order*.
▶ **noun** [mass noun] the Germanic languages collectively. See also EAST GERMANIC, NORTH GERMANIC, WEST GERMANIC. ■ the unrecorded ancient language from which these developed, thought to have been spoken on the shores of the Baltic Sea in the 3rd millennium BC. Also called PROTO-GERMANIC.
– ORIGIN mid 17th cent.: from Latin *Germanicus*, from *Germanus* (see GERMAN).

germanium /dʒəːˈmeɪnɪəm/ ▶ **noun** [mass noun] the chemical element of atomic number 32, a shiny grey semimetal. Germanium was important in the making of transistors and other semiconductor devices, but has been largely replaced by silicon. (Symbol: **Ge**)
– ORIGIN late 19th cent.: modern Latin, from Latin *Germanus* (see GERMAN).

Germanize (also **Germanise**) ▶ **verb** [with obj.] make German; cause to adopt German language and customs: *the Poles had Germanized their family names*.
– DERIVATIVES **Germanization** noun,.

German measles ▶ **plural noun** [usu. treated as sing.] a contagious viral disease, with symptoms like mild measles. It can cause fetal malformation if caught in early pregnancy. Also called RUBELLA.

Germano- /dʒəːˈmanəʊ, ˈdʒəːmənəʊ/ ▶ **combining form** German; German and ...: *Germanophile*. ■ relating to Germany: *Germanocentric*.

German shepherd ▶ **noun** an Alsatian.

German silver ▶ **noun** [mass noun] a white alloy of nickel, zinc, and copper.

German South West Africa a former German protectorate in SW Africa (1884–1918), corresponding to present-day Namibia.

Germany a country in central Europe; pop. 82,329,800 (est. 2009); official language, German; capital, Berlin. German name DEUTSCHLAND.

> The multiplicity of small German states achieved real unity only with the rise of Prussia and the formation of the German Empire in the mid 19th century. After being defeated in the First World War, Germany was taken over in the 1930s by the Nazi dictatorship, which led to a policy of expansionism and eventually to complete defeat in the Second World War. Germany was occupied for a time by the victorious Allies and was partitioned. The western part (including West Berlin), which was occupied by the US, Britain, and France, became the Federal Republic of Germany or **West Germany**, with its capital at Bonn. The eastern part, occupied by the Soviet Union, became the German Democratic Republic or **East Germany**, with its capital in East Berlin. West Germany emerged as a major European industrial power and was a founder member of the EEC while the East remained under Soviet domination. After the general collapse of communism in eastern Europe, East and West Germany reunited on 3 October 1990.

germ cell ▶ **noun** Biology a cell containing half the number of chromosomes of a somatic cell and able to unite with one from the opposite sex to form a new individual; a gamete. ■ an embryonic cell with the potential of developing into a gamete.

G

germicide ▶ **noun** a substance or other agent which destroys harmful microorganisms.
– DERIVATIVES **germicidal** adjective.

Germinal /ˈdʒəːmɪn(ə)l/, French /ʒɛʀminal/ ▶ **noun** the seventh month of the French Republican calendar (1793–1805), originally running from 21 March to 19 April.

germinal ▶ **adjective** [attrib.] relating to or of the nature of a germ cell or embryo. ■ in the earliest stage of development: *a germinal idea*. ■ providing material for future development: *de Beauvoir's germinal book The Second Sex*.
– DERIVATIVES **germinally** adverb.
– ORIGIN early 19th cent.: from Latin *germen*, *germin-* 'sprout, seed' + -AL.

germinate /ˈdʒəːmɪneɪt/ ▶ **verb** [no obj.] (of a seed or spore) begin to grow and put out shoots after a period of dormancy. ■ [with obj.] cause (a seed or spore) to sprout in such a way. ■ come into existence and develop: *the idea germinated and slowly grew into an obsession*.
– DERIVATIVES **germination** noun, **germinative** adjective, **germinator** noun.
– ORIGIN late 16th cent.: from Latin *germinat-* 'sprouted forth, budded', from the verb *germinare*, from *germen*, *germin-* 'sprout, seed'.

Germiston /ˈdʒəːmɪst(ə)n/ a city in South Africa, in the province of Gauteng, south-east of Johannesburg; pop. 139,700 (est. 2001). It is the site of a large gold refinery, which serves the Witwatersrand gold-mining region.

germ layer ▶ **noun** Embryology each of the three layers of cells (ectoderm, mesoderm, and endoderm) that are formed in the early embryo.

germ line ▶ **noun** Biology a series of germ cells each descended or developed from earlier cells in the series, regarded as continuing through successive generations of an organism.

germ plasm ▶ **noun** [mass noun] Biology germ cells collectively. ■ the genetic material of such cells.

germ warfare ▶ **noun** [mass noun] the use of disease-spreading microorganisms as a military weapon.

Geronimo[1] /dʒəˈrɒnɪməʊ/ (*c*.1829–1909), Apache chief. He led his people in raids on settlers and US troops before surrendering in 1886.

Geronimo[2] /dʒəˈrɒnɪməʊ/ ▶ **exclamation** used to express exhilaration, especially when leaping from a great height or moving at speed.
– ORIGIN Second World War: by association with GERONIMO[1], adopted as a slogan by American paratroopers.

gerontic /dʒɛˈrɒntɪk/ ▶ **adjective** relating to old age, elderly people, or senescent animals or plants.
– ORIGIN late 19th cent.: from Greek *gerōn*, *geront-* 'old man' + -IC.

gerontocracy /ˌdʒɛrənˈtɒkrəsi/ ▶ **noun** a state, society, or group governed by old people. ■ [mass noun] government based on rule by old people.
– DERIVATIVES **gerontocrat** noun, **gerontocratic** adjective.
– ORIGIN mid 19th cent.: from Greek *gerōn*, *geront-* 'old man' + -CRACY.

gerontology /ˌdʒɛrənˈtɒlədʒi/ ▶ **noun** [mass noun] the scientific study of old age, the process of ageing, and the particular problems of old people.

– DERIVATIVES **gerontological** adjective, **gerontologist** noun.
– ORIGIN early 20th cent.: from Greek *gerōn*, *geront-* 'old man' + **-LOGY**.

-gerous ▶ combining form bearing (a specified thing): *armigerous*.
– ORIGIN from Latin *-ger* 'bearing' (from the root of *gerere* 'to bear, carry') + **-OUS**.

gerrymander /ˈdʒɛrɪˌmandə/ (Brit. also **jerrymander**) ▶ verb [with obj.] (often as noun **gerrymandering**) manipulate the boundaries of (an electoral constituency) so as to favour one party or class. ■ achieve (a result) by such manipulation: *an attempt to gerrymander the election result*.
▶ noun an instance of gerrymandering.
– DERIVATIVES **gerrymanderer** noun.
– ORIGIN early 19th cent.: from the name of Governor Elbridge *Gerry* of Massachusetts + **SALAMANDER**, from the supposed similarity between a salamander and the shape of a new voting district on a map drawn when he was in office (1812), the creation of which was felt to favour his party; the map (with claws, wings, and fangs added) was published in the Boston *Weekly Messenger*, with the title *The Gerry-Mander*.

Gershwin, George (1898–1937), American composer and pianist, of Russian-Jewish descent; born *Jacob Gershovitz*. He composed many successful songs and musicals, the orchestral work *Rhapsody in Blue* (1924), and the opera *Porgy and Bess* (1935). The lyrics for many of these were written by his brother **Ira Gershwin** (1896–1983).

Gerson therapy /ˈgɛːs(ə)n/ ▶ noun [mass noun] (in complementary medicine) a detoxifying and nutritional programme designed to stimulate the immune system.
– ORIGIN named after Max *Gerson*, the German physician who developed the therapy in the 1920s.

gerund /ˈdʒɛrʌnd/ ▶ noun Grammar a verb form which functions as a noun, in Latin ending in *-ndum* (declinable), in English ending in *-ing* (e.g. *asking* in *do you mind my asking you?*).
– ORIGIN early 16th cent.: from late Latin *gerundium*, from *gerundum*, variant of *gerendum*, the gerund of Latin *gerere* 'do'.

gerundive /dʒəˈrʌndɪv/ ▶ noun Grammar a form of a Latin verb, ending in *-ndus* (declinable) and functioning as an adjective meaning 'that should or must be done'.
– ORIGIN Middle English (in the sense 'gerund'): from late Latin *gerundivus* (*modus*) 'gerundive (mood)', from *gerundium* (see **GERUND**).

Gesellschaft /gəˈzɛlʃaft/ ▶ noun [mass noun] social relations based on impersonal ties, such as duty to a society or organization. Contrasted with **GEMEINSCHAFT**.
– ORIGIN German, from *Gesell(e)* 'companion' + *-schaft* (see **-SHIP**).

gesneriad /gɛsˈnɪərɪad, dʒɛs-/ ▶ noun a tropical plant of a family that includes African violets, gloxinias, and their relatives. ● Family Gesneriaceae.
– ORIGIN mid 19th cent.: from modern Latin *Gesneria* (genus name), from the name of Conrad von *Gesner* (1516–65), Swiss naturalist, + **-AD**[1].

gesso /ˈdʒɛsəʊ/ ▶ noun (pl. **gessoes**) [mass noun] a hard compound of plaster of Paris or whiting in glue, used in sculpture or as a base for gilding or painting on wood.
– ORIGIN late 16th cent.: Italian, from Latin *gypsum* (see **GYPSUM**).

gestalt /gəˈʃtɑːlt, -ˈʃtalt/ ▶ noun Psychology an organized whole that is perceived as more than the sum of its parts.
– DERIVATIVES **gestaltist** noun.
– ORIGIN 1920s: from German *Gestalt*, literally 'form, shape'.

gestalt psychology ▶ noun [mass noun] a movement in psychology founded in Germany in 1912, seeking to explain perceptions in terms of gestalts rather than by analysing their constituents.

gestalt therapy ▶ noun [mass noun] a psychotherapeutic approach developed by Fritz Perls (1893–1970). It focuses on insight into gestalts in patients and their relations to the world, and often uses role playing to aid the resolution of past conflicts.

Gestapo /gəˈstɑːpəʊ/ the German secret police under Nazi rule. It ruthlessly suppressed opposition to the Nazis in Germany and occupied Europe, and sent Jews and others to concentration camps. From 1936 it was headed by Heinrich Himmler.
– ORIGIN German, from *Geheime Staatspolizei* 'secret state police'.

gestate /dʒɛˈsteɪt/ ▶ verb [no obj.] carry a fetus in the womb from conception to birth: *rabbits gestate for approximately twenty-eight days*. ■ (of a fetus) undergo gestation. ■ develop over a long period: *a series that has been gestating for three years*.
– ORIGIN mid 19th cent.: from Latin *gestat-* 'carried in the womb', from the verb *gestare*.

gestation ▶ noun [mass noun] the process or period of developing inside the womb between conception and birth. ■ the development of something over a period of time: *a thorough and painstaking work which was a long time in gestation*.
– DERIVATIVES **gestational** adjective.
– ORIGIN mid 16th cent. (denoting an excursion on horseback, in a carriage, etc., considered as exercise): from Latin *gestatio(n-)*, from *gestare* 'carry, carry in the womb', frequentative of *gerere* 'carry'.

gesticulate /dʒɛˈstɪkjʊleɪt/ ▶ verb [no obj.] use gestures, especially dramatic ones, instead of speaking or to emphasize one's words: *they were shouting and gesticulating frantically at drivers who did not slow down*.
– DERIVATIVES **gesticulative** adjective, **gesticulator** noun, **gesticulatory** adjective.
– ORIGIN early 17th cent.: from Latin *gesticulat-* 'gesticulated', from the verb *gesticulari*, from *gesticulus*, diminutive of *gestus* 'action'.

gesticulation ▶ noun a gesture, especially a dramatic one, used instead of speaking or to emphasize one's words: *he punctuated his speech with wild gesticulations* | [mass noun] *there was a lot of gesticulation*.

gesture ▶ noun a movement of part of the body, especially a hand or the head, to express an idea or meaning: *Alex made a gesture of apology* | [mass noun] *so much is conveyed by gesture*. ■ an action performed to convey a feeling or intention: *Maggie was touched by the kind gesture* | *a gesture of goodwill*. ■ an action performed for show in the knowledge that it will have no effect: *I hope the amendment will not be just a gesture*.
▶ verb [no obj.] make a gesture: *she gestured meaningfully with the pistol*. ■ [with obj. and adverbial or infinitive] direct (someone) somewhere by means of a gesture: *he gestured her towards a chair*.
– DERIVATIVES **gestural** adjective.
– ORIGIN late Middle English: from medieval Latin *gestura*, from Latin *gerere* 'bear, wield, perform'. The original sense was 'bearing, deportment', hence 'the use of posture and bodily movements for effect in oratory'.

gesundheit /gɛˈzʊndhʌɪt/, German /gɛˈzʊnthaɪt/ ▶ exclamation used to wish good health to a person who has just sneezed.
– ORIGIN from German *Gesundheit* 'health'.

get ▶ verb (**gets**, **getting**; past **got**; past participle **got**, N. Amer. or archaic **gotten**) **1** [with obj.] come to have (something); receive: *I got a letter from him the other day* | *what kind of reception did you get?* ■ experience, suffer, or be afflicted with (something bad): *I got a sudden pain in my left eye*. ■ receive as a punishment or penalty: *I'll get the sack if things go wrong*. ■ contract (a disease or ailment): *I might be getting the flu*.
2 [with obj.] succeed in attaining, achieving, or experiencing; obtain: *I need all the sleep I can get* | *he got a teaching job in California*. ■ move in order to pick up or bring (something); fetch: *get another chair* | [with two objs] *I'll get you a drink*. ■ prepare (a meal): *Celia went to the kitchen to start getting their dinner*. ■ [with obj. and adverbial] tend to meet with or find in a specified place or situation: *for someone used to the tiny creatures we get in England it was something of a shock*. ■ travel by or catch (a bus, train, or other form of transport): *I got a taxi across to Baker Street*. ■ obtain (a figure or answer) as a result of calculation. ■ make contact with, especially by telephone: *you can get me at home if you need me*. ■ respond to a ring of (a telephone or doorbell): *I'll get the door!* ■ [in imperative] informal used to draw attention to someone whom one regards as pretentious or vain: *get her!*
3 reach or cause to reach a specified state or condition: [no obj., with complement] *he'd got thinner* | *it's getting late* | [with past participle] *you'll get used to it* | [with obj. and complement] *I need to get my hair cut*. ■ [as auxiliary verb] used with past participle to form the passive mood: *the cat got drowned*. ■ [with obj. and past participle] cause to be treated in a specified way: *get the form signed by a doctor*. ■ [with obj. and infinitive] induce or prevail upon (someone) to do something: *they got her to sign the consent form*. ■ [no obj., with infinitive] have the opportunity to do: *he got to try out a few of these nice new cars*. ■ [no obj., with present participle or infinitive] begin to be or do something, especially gradually or by chance: *we got talking one evening*.
4 [no obj., with adverbial of direction] come, go, or make progress eventually or with some difficulty: *Nigel got home very late* | *he hadn't got very far with the book yet*. ■ [no obj., with adverbial] move or come into a specified position, situation, or state: *she got into the car* | *Henry got to his feet* | *you don't want to get into debt*. ■ [with obj. and adverbial] succeed in making (someone or something) come, go, or move somewhere: *she had to get them away from the rocks* | *let's get you home*. ■ [no obj., with clause] informal, chiefly N. Amer. reach a specified point or stage: ***it's getting so** I can't even think*.
5 (**have got**) see **HAVE**.
6 [with obj.] catch or apprehend (someone): *the police have got him*. ■ strike or wound (someone) with a blow or missile: *you got me in the eye!* ■ informal punish, injure, or kill (someone), especially as retribution: *I'll get you for this!* ■ (**get it**) informal be punished, injured, or killed: *wait until dad comes home, then you'll get it!* ■ (**get mine, his**, etc.) informal be appropriately punished or rewarded: *I'll get mine, you'll get yours, we'll all get wealthy*. ■ informal annoy (someone) greatly: *cleaning the same things all the time, that's what gets me*. ■ baffle (someone): *she had got me there: I could not answer*.
7 [with obj.] informal understand (an argument or the person making it): *What do you mean? I don't get it*.
8 [with obj.] archaic acquire (knowledge) by study; learn: *that knowledge which is gotten at school*.
▶ noun **1** dated an animal's offspring.
2 Brit. informal or dialect a person whom the speaker dislikes or despises.
– PHRASES (**as**) —— **as all get out** N. Amer. informal to a great or extreme extent: *he was stubborn as all get out*. **get it on** N. Amer. informal embark on an activity; get going. ■ informal have sexual intercourse. **get it up** vulgar slang (of a man) achieve an erection. **get one's own back** informal have one's revenge; retaliate. **get over oneself** informal stop being conceited or pretentious. **get-rich-quick** derogatory designed or concerned to make a lot of money fast. **getting on for** chiefly Brit. approaching (a specified time, age, or amount); almost: *there are getting on for 700 staff*. **get-up-and-go** informal energy, enthusiasm, and initiative. **get someone with child** archaic make a woman pregnant.
– PHRASAL VERBS **get something across** manage to communicate an idea clearly. **get ahead** become successful in one's life or career. **get along 1** another way of saying **GET ON** (sense 2). **2** manage to live or survive: *don't worry, we'll get along without you*. ■ [in imperative] Brit. informal used to express scepticism or disbelief or to tell someone to go away: *oh, get along with you!* **get around** see **GET ROUND**. **get at 1** reach or gain access to (something): *it's difficult to get at the screws*. ■ bribe or unfairly influence (someone): *he had been got at by government officials*. **2** informal imply (something): *I can see what you're getting at*. **3** Brit. informal criticize (someone) subtly and repeatedly: *I hope you didn't think I was getting at you*. **get away 1** escape: *the robbers got away with £6,000*. **2** [in imperative] informal said to express disbelief or scepticism. **get away with** escape blame, punishment, or undesirable consequences for (an act that is wrong or mistaken): *if he thinks he can get away with cheating me, he's very much mistaken*. **get back at** take revenge on (someone). **get back to** contact (someone) later to give a reply or return a message. **get by** manage with difficulty to live or accomplish something: *he had just enough money to get by*. **get down** N. Amer. informal dance energetically: *get down and party!* **get someone down** depress or demoralize someone. **get something down 1** write something down. **2** swallow food or drink, especially with difficulty. **get down to** begin to do or give serious attention to: *let's get down to business*. **get in 1** (of a train, aircraft, or other transport) arrive at its destination. **2** (of a political party or candidate) be elected. **get in on** become involved in (a profitable or exciting activity). **get in with** become friendly with (someone), especially in order to gain an advantage: *I hope he doesn't get in with the wrong crowd*. **get off 1** informal escape a punishment; be acquitted: *you'll get off with a caution*. **2** Brit. go to sleep, especially after some difficulty. **3** Brit. informal have a sexual encounter: *Linda got off with the ski instructor*. **4** N. Amer. vulgar slang have an orgasm. **get off on** informal be excited or aroused by (something): *he was obviously getting off on the adrenalin of performing before the crowd*. **get on 1** perform or make progress in a specified way: *how are you getting on?* ■ continue doing something, especially after an interruption: *I've got to get on with this job*. ■ chiefly Brit. be successful in one's life or career. **2** chiefly Brit. have a harmonious or friendly

relationship: *they seem to get on pretty well.* **3** (**be getting on**) informal be old or comparatively old. **get on to** chiefly Brit. make contact with (someone) about a particular topic. **get out 1** (of something previously secret) become known: *news got out that we were coming.* **2** (also **get out of here**) [in imperative] informal, chiefly N. Amer. used to express disbelief: *get out, you're a liar.* **get something out 1** succeed in uttering, publishing, or releasing something: *we're keen to get a record out.* **2** Brit. succeed in solving or finishing a puzzle or mathematical problem. **get out of** contrive to avoid or escape (a duty or responsibility): *they wanted to get out of paying.* **get something out of** achieve benefit from (an undertaking or exercise): *everyone who took part in the course got a lot out of it.* **get outside** (**of**) Brit. informal eat or drink (something) heartily: *we'll get outside of some bacon and eggs.* **get over 1** recover from (an ailment or an upsetting or startling experience): *the trip will help him get over Sal's death.* **2** overcome (a difficulty). **get something over 1** manage to communicate an idea or theory. **2** complete an unpleasant or tedious but necessary task promptly: *come on, let's get it over with.* **get round** (or N. Amer. **around**) **1** coax or persuade (someone) to do or allow something that they initially do not want to. **2** deal successfully with (a problem). ■ evade (a regulation or restriction) without contravening it: *the company changed its name to get round the law.* **get round to** (or N. Amer. **around to**) deal with (a task) in due course: *I might get round to organizing another trip in the spring.* **get through 1** (also **get someone through**) pass or assist someone in passing (a difficult or testing experience or period): *I need these lessons to get me through my exam.* ■ (also **get something through**) (with reference to a piece of legislation) make or become law. **2** chiefly Brit. finish or use up (a large amount or number of something), especially within a short time: *we got through four whole jars of mustard.* **3** make contact by telephone. ■ succeed in communicating with someone in a meaningful way: *I just don't think anyone can* **get through** *to these kids.* **get to** informal annoy or upset (someone) by persistent action: *he started crying—we were getting to him.* **get together** gather or assemble socially or to cooperate. **get up 1** (also **get someone up**) rise or cause to rise from bed after sleeping. **2** (of wind or the sea) become strong or agitated. **get someone up** dress someone in a specified smart, elaborate, or unusual way: *he was got up in striped trousers and a dinner jacket.* **get something up 1** prepare or organize a project or piece of work: *we used to get up little plays.* **2** enhance or refine one's knowledge of a subject. **get up to** Brit. informal be involved in (typically something illicit or surprising): *what did you get up to last weekend?*
– DERIVATIVES **gettable** adjective.
– ORIGIN Middle English: from Old Norse *geta* 'obtain, beget, guess'; related to Old English *gietan* (in *begietan* 'beget', *forgietan* 'forget'), from an Indo-European root shared by Latin *praeda* 'booty, prey', *praehendere* 'get hold of, seize', and Greek *khandanein* 'hold, contain, be able'.

> **USAGE** The verb **get** is in the top five of the most common verbs in the English language. Nevertheless, there is still a feeling that almost any use containing **get** is somewhat informal. No general informal label has been applied to this dictionary entry, but in formal writing it is worth bearing this reservation in mind.

get-at-able ▶ adjective informal accessible.

getaway ▶ noun **1** an escape or quick departure, especially after committing a crime: *the thugs made their getaway* | [as modifier] *a getaway car.*
2 informal a short holiday: *a weekend getaway.* ■ a holiday destination: *the island getaway of Penang.*

get-go ▶ noun informal, chiefly N. Amer. the very beginning: *the quintet experienced difficulties* **from the get-go**.

Gethsemane, Garden of /gɛθˈsɛməni/ a garden between Jerusalem and the Mount of Olives, where Jesus went with his disciples after the Last Supper and was betrayed (Matt. 26:36–46).

get-out ▶ noun Brit. a means of avoiding something; an excuse: [as modifier] *a get-out clause.*
– PHRASES **as —— as all get-out** N. Amer. informal as —— as is possible; to the highest degree: *the rituals of the racing world are as macho as all get-out.*

getter ▶ noun **1** [in combination] a person or thing that gets a specified desirable thing: *an attention-getter* | *a vote-getter.*
2 Electronics & Physics a substance used to remove residual gas from a vacuum tube, or impurities or defects from a semiconductor crystal.

gettering ▶ noun [mass noun] Electronics & Physics the removal of impurities or defects with a getter.

get-together ▶ noun an informal gathering.

Getty /ˈgɛti/, Jean Paul (1892–1976), American industrialist. He made a large fortune in the oil industry and was also a noted art collector. He founded the J. Paul Getty Museum in Los Angeles.

Gettysburg, Battle of /ˈgɛtɪzbəːg/ a decisive battle of the American Civil War, fought near the town of Gettysburg in Pennsylvania in July 1863. A Union army under General Meade repulsed the Confederate army of General Lee and forced him to abandon his invasion of the north.

Gettysburg Address a speech delivered on 19 November 1863 by President Abraham Lincoln at the dedication of the national cemetery on the site of the Battle of Gettysburg.

get-up ▶ noun informal a style or arrangement of dress, especially an elaborate or unusual one: *her ridiculous Cossack's get-up.*

geum /ˈdʒiːəm/ ▶ noun a plant of a genus which comprises the avens. ● Genus *Geum*, family Rosaceae.
– ORIGIN modern Latin, variant of Latin *gaeum*.

GeV ▶ abbreviation gigaelectronvolt, equivalent to 10^9 electronvolts.

gewgaw /ˈgjuːgɔː/ (also chiefly N. Amer. **geegaw**) ▶ noun (usu. **gewgaws**) a showy thing, especially one that is useless or worthless.
– ORIGIN Middle English: of unknown origin.

Gewürztraminer /gəˈvʊətstrəˌmiːnə/, German /gəˈvyrtstraˌmiːnɐ/ ▶ noun [mass noun] a variety of white grape grown mainly in the Alsace, Austria, and the Rhine valley. ■ a wine made from this grape.
– ORIGIN German, from *Gewürz* 'spice' + TRAMINER.

gey /gʌɪ/ ▶ adverb Scottish very; considerably: *he was gey fond of you.*
– ORIGIN early 18th cent.: variant of GAY.

geyser /ˈgiːzə, ˈgʌɪ-/ ▶ noun **1** a hot spring in which water intermittently boils, sending a tall column of water and steam into the air. ■ a jet or stream of liquid: *the pipe sent up* **a geyser of** *sewer water into the street.*
2 /ˈgiːzə/ Brit. a gas-fired water heater through which water flows as it is rapidly heated. ■ S. African a hot-water storage tank with an electric heating element.
▶ verb [no obj., with adverbial of direction] (especially of water or steam) gush or burst out with great force: *a fissure opened and yellow smoke geysered upward.*
– ORIGIN late 18th cent.: from Icelandic *Geysir*, the name of a particular spring in Iceland; related to *geysa* 'to gush'.

geyserite ▶ noun [mass noun] a hard opaline siliceous deposit occurring around geysers and hot springs.
– ORIGIN early 19th cent.: from GEYSER + -ITE[1].

GF (also **gf**) ▶ noun (pl. **GFs**) informal a person's girlfriend: *when his GF isn't around, he always flirts with me.*

GG ▶ abbreviation Brit. Governor General.

GH ▶ abbreviation Ghana (international vehicle registration).

ghaghra /ˈgagrə, ˈgɑːgrɑː/ (also **ghagra**) ▶ noun (in South Asia) a long full skirt, often decorated with embroidery, mirrors, or bells.
– ORIGIN Hindi *ghāghrā*, from Sanskrit *gharghara* 'gurgle, rattle'.

Ghana /ˈgɑːnə/ a country of West Africa, with its southern coastline bordering on the Atlantic Ocean; pop. 23,887,800 (est. 2009); languages, English (official), West African languages; capital, Accra. Former name (until 1957) GOLD COAST.

> Formerly a centre of the slave trade, the area became the British colony of Gold Coast in 1874. In 1957 it was the first British colony to gain independence as a member of the Commonwealth, under the leadership of Kwame Nkrumah.

– DERIVATIVES **Ghanaian** /gɑːˈneɪən/ adjective & noun.

gharana /gʌˈrɑːnə/ ▶ noun (in South Asia) any of the various specialist schools or methods of classical music or dance.
– ORIGIN from Hindi *gharānā* 'family'.

gharara /gʌˈrɑːrə/ ▶ noun a pair of loose trousers with pleats below the knee, worn by women from South Asia, typically with a kameez.
– ORIGIN from Persian *garāra* 'trousers, large sack'.

gharial /ˈgarɪɑːl, ˌgʌrɪˈɑːl, ˈgɛːrɪəl/ (also **gavial**) ▶ noun a large fish-eating crocodile with a long, narrow snout that widens at the nostrils, native to the Indian subcontinent. ● *Gavialis gangeticus*, the only member of the family Gavialidae.
– ORIGIN early 19th cent.: from Hindi *ghariyāl*. The spelling *gavial* (from French) is an alteration probably due to scribal error.

gharry /ˈgɑːri/ ▶ noun (pl. **gharries**) (in South Asia) a horse-drawn carriage available for hire.
– ORIGIN from Hindi *gāṛī*.

ghastly ▶ adjective (**ghastlier**, **ghastliest**) **1** causing great horror or fear: *one of the most ghastly crimes ever committed.*
2 extremely unwell: *she had sobered up but she felt ghastly.* ■ deathly white: *a ghastly pallor.*
3 informal very objectionable, bad, or unpleasant: *the weather was ghastly.*
– DERIVATIVES **ghastliness** noun.
– ORIGIN Middle English: from obsolete *gast* 'terrify', from Old English *gǣstan*, of Germanic origin; related to GHOST. The *gh* spelling is by association with GHOST. The sense 'objectionable' dates from the mid 19th cent.

ghat /gɑːt/ ▶ noun **1** (in South Asia) a flight of steps leading down to a river. ■ (also **burning ghat**) a level place on the edge of a river where Hindus cremate their dead.
2 (in South Asia) a mountain pass.
– ORIGIN from Hindi *ghāṭ*.

ghatam /ˈgɑːtʌm/ ▶ noun a circular pot beaten with the hands as a percussion instrument in south Indian music.
– ORIGIN from Sanskrit via Tamil or Telugu.

Ghats /gɑːts/ two mountain ranges in central and southern India. Known as **the Eastern Ghats** and **the Western Ghats**, they run parallel to the coast on either side of the Deccan plateau.

ghazal /ˈgʌʒʌl/ ▶ noun (in Middle Eastern and Indian literature and music) a lyric poem with a fixed number of verses and a repeated rhyme, typically on the theme of love, and normally set to music.
– ORIGIN via Persian from Arabic *ġazal*.

ghazi /ˈgɑːzi/ ▶ noun (pl. **ghazis**) (often as an honorific title) a Muslim fighter against non-Muslims.
– ORIGIN from Arabic *al-ġāzī*, participle of *ġazā* 'invade, raid'.

Ghaziabad /ˈgɑːzɪəbad/ a city in northern India, in Uttar Pradesh east of Delhi; pop. 1,437,900 (est. 2009).

Ghaznavid /gazˈnɑːvɪd/ ▶ noun a member of a Turkish Muslim dynasty founded in Ghazna, Afghanistan, in AD 977. The dynasty extended its power into Persia and the Punjab and lasted until 1186.

GHB ▶ abbreviation (sodium) gamma-hydroxybutyrate, a designer drug with anaesthetic properties. ● Chem. formula: $CH_2OH(CH_2)_2COONa$.

ghee /giː/ ▶ noun [mass noun] clarified butter made from the milk of a buffalo or cow, used in Indian cooking.
– ORIGIN from Hindi *ghī*, from Sanskrit *ghṛtá* 'sprinkled'.

Gheg /gɛg/ ▶ noun (pl. **same** or **Ghegs**) **1** a member of one of the two main ethnic groups of Albania, living mainly in the north of the country.
2 [mass noun] the dialect of Albanian spoken by this people, with about 2 million speakers. Compare with TOSK.
▶ adjective relating to the Gheg or their dialect.
– ORIGIN from Albanian *Geg*.

Ghent /gɛnt/ a city in Belgium, capital of the province of East Flanders; pop. 237,250 (2008). Founded in the 10th century, it became the capital of the medieval principality of Flanders. It was formerly known in English as Gaunt (surviving in names, e.g. John of Gaunt). French name GAND, Flemish name GENT.

gherao /gɛˈraʊ/ ▶ noun (pl. **gheraos**) Indian a protest in which workers prevent employers leaving a place of work until certain demands are met.
– ORIGIN from Hindi *gherāo* 'surround, besiege'.

gherkin /ˈgəːkɪn/ ▶ noun a small variety of cucumber, or a young green cucumber used for pickling.
– ORIGIN early 17th cent.: from Dutch *augurkje*, *gurkje*, diminutive of *augurk*, *gurk*, from Slavic, based on medieval Greek *angourion* 'cucumber'.

ghetto /ˈgɛtəʊ/ ▶ noun (pl. **ghettos** or **ghettoes**) a part of a city, especially a slum area, occupied by a minority group or groups. ■ historical the Jewish quarter in a city: *the Warsaw Ghetto.* ■ an isolated or segregated group or area: *the relative security of the gay ghetto.*

▶ verb (**ghettoes, ghettoing, ghettoed**) [with obj.] put in or restrict to an isolated or segregated area or group.
– ORIGIN early 17th cent.: perhaps from Italian *getto* 'foundry' (because the first ghetto was established in 1516 on the site of a foundry in Venice), or from Italian *borghetto*, diminutive of *borgo* 'borough'.

ghetto blaster ▶ noun informal a large portable radio and cassette or CD player.

ghetto-fabulous ▶ adjective informal denoting or exemplyifing an ostentatious or flamboyant lifestyle or style of clothing of a type associated with the hip-hop subculture: *ghetto-fabulous rappers*.

ghettoize (also **ghettoise**) ▶ verb [with obj.] put in or restrict to an isolated or segregated place, group, or situation: *they called for a policy that seeks to integrate foreign labourers rather than ghettoize them*.
– DERIVATIVES **ghettoization** noun.

Ghibelline /ˈɡɪbɪlʌɪn/ ▶ noun a member of one of the two great political factions in Italian medieval politics, traditionally supporting the Holy Roman emperor against the Pope and his supporters, the Guelphs.
– ORIGIN from Italian *Ghibellino*, perhaps from German *Waiblingen*, an estate belonging to Hohenstaufen emperors.

Ghiberti /ɡɪˈbɛːti/, Italian /ɡiˈbɛrti/, Lorenzo (1378–1455), Italian sculptor and goldsmith. His career was dominated by his work on two successive pairs of bronze doors for the baptistery in Florence.

ghibli /ˈɡɪbli/ ▶ noun [mass noun] a hot, dry southerly wind of North Africa.
– ORIGIN early 19th cent.: from Arabic *qiblī* 'southern'.

ghillie ▶ noun variant spelling of GILLIE.

Ghirlandaio /ˌɡɪəlanˈdʌɪəʊ/, Italian /ɡirlanˈdajəo/ (*c.*1448–94), Italian painter; born *Domenico di Tommaso Bigordi*. He is noted for his religious frescoes, particularly *Christ Calling Peter and Andrew* (1482–4) in the Sistine Chapel, Rome.

ghost ▶ noun an apparition of a dead person which is believed to appear or become manifest to the living, typically as a nebulous image: *the building is haunted by the ghost of a monk* | [as modifier] *a ghost ship*. ■ a slight trace or vestige of something: *she gave the ghost of a smile*. ■ a faint secondary image produced by a fault in an optical system or on a cathode ray screen, e.g. by faulty television reception or internal reflection in a mirror or camera.
▶ verb **1** [with obj.] act as ghostwriter of (a work): *his memoirs were smoothly ghosted by a journalist*.
2 [no obj., with adverbial of direction] glide smoothly and effortlessly: *they ghosted up the river*.
– PHRASES **the ghost in the machine** Philosophy the mind viewed as distinct from the body (usually used in a derogatory fashion by critics of dualism). [coined by the philosopher Gilbert Ryle (1949).] **give up the ghost** die. ■ (of a machine) stop working. **look as if one has seen a ghost** look very pale and shocked. **not stand the ghost of a chance** have no chance at all.
– DERIVATIVES **ghostlike** adjective.
– ORIGIN Old English *gāst* (in the sense 'spirit, soul'), of Germanic origin; related to Dutch *geest* and German *Geist*. The *gh-* spelling occurs first in Caxton, probably influenced by Flemish *gheest*.

ghost bat ▶ noun any of a number of bats with mainly white or grey fur, in particular: ■ N. Amer. see WHITE BAT. ■ Austral. another term for FALSE VAMPIRE.

ghostbuster ▶ noun informal **1** a person who claims to be able to banish ghosts and poltergeists.
2 an official whose job is to investigate tax fraud.

ghost crab ▶ noun a pale yellowish crab that lives in a burrow in the sand above the high-water mark and goes down to the sea at night to feed. ● Genus *Ocypode*, family Ocypodidae.

Ghost Dance ▶ noun an American Indian religious cult of the second half of the 19th century, based on the performance of a ritual dance, which, it was believed, would drive away white people and restore the traditional lands and way of life.

ghosting ▶ noun [mass noun] the appearance of a ghost or secondary image on a television or other display screen.

ghostly ▶ adjective (**ghostlier, ghostliest**) of or like a ghost in appearance or sound; eerie and unnatural: *a frightening, ghostly figure with a hood*.
– DERIVATIVES **ghostliness** noun.
– ORIGIN Old English *gāstlic*, from *gāst* 'ghost'.

ghost moth (also **ghost swift**) ▶ noun a large European swift moth, the male of which has white wings. ● *Hepialus humuli*, family Hepialidae. See SWIFT (sense 2 of the noun).

ghost story ▶ noun a story about ghosts, intended to be frightening.

ghost town ▶ noun a deserted town with few or no remaining inhabitants.

ghost train ▶ noun Brit. a miniature train at a funfair designed to scare its passengers with eerie sights and sounds.

ghost word ▶ noun a word recorded in a dictionary or other reference work which is not actually used.

ghostwriter ▶ noun a person whose job it is to write material for someone else who is the named author.
– DERIVATIVES **ghostwrite** verb.

ghoul /ɡuːl/ ▶ noun **1** an evil spirit or phantom, especially one supposed to rob graves and feed on dead bodies.
2 a person morbidly interested in death or disaster.
– ORIGIN late 18th cent.: from Arabic *ġūl*, a desert demon believed to rob graves and devour corpses.

ghoulish ▶ adjective **1** resembling or characteristic of a ghoul: *a ghoulish mask*.
2 morbidly interested in death or disaster: *she told the story with ghoulish relish*.
– DERIVATIVES **ghoulishly** adverb, **ghoulishness** noun.

GHQ ▶ abbreviation General Headquarters.

Ghulghuleh /ɡʊlˈɡʊlə/ a ruined ancient city near Bamian in central Afghanistan. It was destroyed by Genghis Khan *c.*1221.

ghusl /ˈɡuːs(ə)l/ ▶ noun [mass noun] ritual washing of the whole body, as prescribed by Islamic law to be performed in preparation for prayer and worship, and after sexual activity, childbirth, menstruation, etc. Compare with WUDU.
– ORIGIN Arabic *ġusl* 'washing', from *ġasala* 'to wash'.

ghyll ▶ noun variant spelling of GILL[3].

GHz ▶ abbreviation gigahertz.

GI[1] ▶ noun (pl. **GIs**) a private soldier in the US army.
– ORIGIN 1930s (originally denoting equipment supplied to US forces): abbreviation of *government* (or *general*) *issue*.

GI[2] ▶ abbreviation glycaemic index.

gi /ɡiː/ ▶ noun the loose white jacket worn in judo.
– ORIGIN Japanese.

Giacometti /ˌdʒakəˈmɛti/, Alberto (1901–66), Swiss sculptor and painter. His most typical works are emaciated and extremely elongated human forms, such as *Pointing Man* (1947).

giant ▶ noun **1** an imaginary or mythical being of human form but superhuman size. ■ an abnormally or extremely tall or large person, animal, or plant. ■ a very large company or organization. ■ a person of exceptional talent or qualities: *a giant among sportsmen*.
2 Astronomy a star of relatively great size and luminosity compared to ordinary stars of the main sequence, and 10–100 times the diameter of the sun.
▶ adjective [attrib.] of very great size or force; gigantic: *giant multinational corporations* | *a giant meteorite*. ■ used in names of very large animals and plants, e.g. **giant hogweed, giant tortoise**.
– DERIVATIVES **giantlike** adjective.
– ORIGIN Middle English *geant* (with the first syllable later influenced by Latin *gigant-*), from Old French, via Latin from Greek *gigas, gigant-*.

giant anteater ▶ noun a large insectivorous mammal with long, coarse fur, large claws, an elongated snout, and a long tongue for catching ants. It is native to Central and South America. ● *Myrmecophaga tridactyla*, family Myrmecophagidae, order Xenartha (or Edentata).

giant clam ▶ noun a very large bivalve mollusc that occurs in the tropical Indo-Pacific. ● Family Tridacnidae: several species, including *Tridacna gigas*, which is the largest living shelled mollusc.

giant deer ▶ noun another term for IRISH ELK.

giantess ▶ noun a female giant.

giant gourami ▶ noun a large edible freshwater fish that is native to Asia. It is widely farmed there and has been introduced elsewhere. ● Family Osphronemidae and genus *Osphronemus*, in particular *O. goramy*.

giantism ▶ noun [mass noun] a tendency towards abnormally large size; gigantism.

giant-killer ▶ noun a person or team that defeats a seemingly much more powerful opponent.
– DERIVATIVES **giant-killing** noun.

giant panda ▶ noun see PANDA[1].

giant petrel ▶ noun the largest petrel, which is found around southern oceans, has a massive bill, and scavenges from carcasses. ● Genus *Macronectes*, family Procellariidae: two species.

giant puffball ▶ noun a European fungus which produces a spherical white fruiting body with a diameter of up to 80 cm, edible when young. ● *Langermannia gigantea*, family Lycoperdaceae, class Gasteromycetes.

giant salamander ▶ noun a very large salamander that is native to North America and eastern Asia, in particular: ● a permanently aquatic salamander (three species in the family Cryptobranchidae), e.g. the American hellbender. ● a terrestrial salamander (three species in the family Dicamptodontidae), of western North America.

Giant's Causeway a geological formation of basalt columns, dating from the Tertiary period, on the north coast of Northern Ireland. It was once believed to be the end of a road made by a legendary giant to Staffa in the Inner Hebrides, where there is a similar formation.

giant sequoia ▶ noun the giant redwood. See REDWOOD.

giant silk moth ▶ noun see SILK MOTH.

giant slalom ▶ noun Skiing a long-distance slalom with fast, wide turns.

giant squid ▶ noun a deep-sea squid which is the largest known invertebrate, reaching a length of 18 m (59 ft) or more. ● Genus *Architeuthis*, order Teuthoidea.

giant toad ▶ noun another term for CANE TOAD.

giant tortoise ▶ noun a very large tortoise with a long lifespan, occurring on several tropical oceanic islands. ● Genus *Geochelone*, family Testudinidae: *G. nigra* (Galapagos Islands) and *G. gigantea* (Aldabra and the Seychelles).

giant zonure ▶ noun another term for SUNGAZER.

giaour /ˈdʒaʊə/ ▶ noun archaic, derogatory a non-Muslim, especially a Christian.
– ORIGIN from Turkish *gâvur*, from Persian *gaur*, probably from Arabic *kāfir* (see KAFFIR).

giardiasis /ˌdʒiːɑːˈdʌɪəsɪs/ ▶ noun [mass noun] infection of the intestine with a flagellate protozoan, which causes diarrhoea and other symptoms. ● The protozoan is *Giardia lamblia*, phylum Metamonada, kingdom Protista.
– ORIGIN early 20th cent.: from modern Latin *Giardia* (from the name of Alfred M. *Giard* (1846–1908), French biologist) + -ASIS.

Gib ▶ noun Brit. short for GIBRALTAR.

gibber[1] /ˈdʒɪbə, ˈɡɪbə/ ▶ verb [no obj.] speak rapidly and unintelligibly, typically through fear or shock: *they shrieked and gibbered as flames surrounded them* | (as adj. **gibbering**) *a gibbering idiot*.
– ORIGIN early 17th cent.: imitative.

gibber[2] /ˈɡɪbə/ (also **gibber stone**) ▶ noun Austral. a stone or boulder forming part of a boulder plain. ■ any small stone.
– ORIGIN from Dharuk *giba* 'stone'.

gibberbird /ˈɡɪbəbəːd/ ▶ noun Austral. the desert chat, a bird inhabiting the plains of central Australia. ● *Ashbyia lovensis*, family Ephthianuridae.
– ORIGIN *gibber* from GIBBER[2].

gibberellic acid /ˌdʒɪbəˈrɛlɪk/ ▶ noun [mass noun] a gibberellin which is used commercially, notably in germinating barley for malt.
– ORIGIN 1950s: *gibberellic* from modern Latin *Gibberella* (see GIBBERELLIN) + -IC.

gibberellin /ˌdʒɪbəˈrɛlɪn/ ▶ noun [mass noun] any of a group of plant hormones that stimulate stem elongation, germination, and flowering.
– ORIGIN 1930s: from modern Latin *Gibberella* (from *Gibberella fujikuroi*, the fungus from which one of the gibberellins was first extracted), diminutive of the genus name *Gibbera*, from Latin *gibber* 'hump', + -IN[1].

gibberish /ˈdʒɪb(ə)rɪʃ, ˈɡɪb-/ ▶ noun [mass noun] unintelligible or meaningless speech or writing; nonsense: *he talks gibberish*.
– ORIGIN early 16th cent.: perhaps from GIBBER[1] (but recorded earlier) + the suffix -ISH[1] (denoting a language as in *Spanish, Swedish*, etc.).

gibbet historical ▶ noun a gallows. ■ an upright post with an arm on which the bodies of executed criminals were left hanging as a warning or deterrent to others. ■ (**the gibbet**) execution by hanging: *the four ringleaders were sentenced to the gibbet*.

▸ verb (**gibbets, gibbeting, gibbeted**) [with obj.] hang up (a body) on a gibbet. ▪ execute (someone) by hanging. ▪ archaic subject to ridicule and derision: *poor Melbourne is gibbeted in The Times.*
– ORIGIN Middle English: from Old French *gibet* 'staff, cudgel, gallows', diminutive of *gibe* 'club, staff', probably of Germanic origin.

Gibbon[1], Edward (1737–94), English historian. He is best known for his multi-volume work *The History of the Decline and Fall of the Roman Empire* (1776–88), chapters of which aroused controversy for their critical account of the spread of Christianity.

Gibbon[2], Lewis Grassic (1901–35), Scottish writer; pseudonym of *James Leslie Mitchell*. His short stories were regularly published in the *Cornhill Magazine*, and his novels include the trilogy *A Scots Quair* (1932–4).

gibbon ▸ noun a small, slender tree-dwelling ape with long powerful arms and loud hooting calls, native to the forests of SE Asia. ● Family Hylobatidae and genus *Hylobates*: several species.
– ORIGIN late 18th cent.: from French, from an Indian dialect word.

Gibbons[1], Grinling (1648–1721), Dutch-born English sculptor. He is famous for his decorative carvings, chiefly in wood, as in the choir stalls of St Paul's Cathedral, London.

Gibbons[2], Orlando (1583–1625), English composer and musician. He was the organist of Westminster Abbey from 1623 and composed mainly sacred music, although he is also known for madrigals such as *The Silver Swan* (1612).

gibbous /ˈɡɪbəs/ ▸ adjective (of the moon) having the illuminated part greater than a semicircle and less than a circle. ▪ convex or protuberant: *his gibbous eyes.*
– DERIVATIVES **gibbosity** /-ˈbɒsɪti/ noun,.
– ORIGIN late Middle English: from late Latin *gibbosus*, from Latin *gibbus* 'hump'.

Gibbs, James (1682–1754), Scottish architect. He developed Wren's ideas for London's city churches, notably at St Martin's-in-the-Fields (1722–6); his best-known secular building is the Radcliffe Camera in Oxford (completed 1737–48), which he developed from earlier designs by Hawksmoor.

Gibbs free energy ▸ noun Chemistry a thermodynamic quantity equal to the enthalpy (of a system or process) minus the product of the entropy and the absolute temperature. (Symbol: **G**)
– ORIGIN named after J. W. *Gibbs* (see **Gibbs**[2]).

gibbsite /ˈɡɪbzʌɪt/ ▸ noun [mass noun] a colourless mineral consisting of hydrated aluminium hydroxide, occurring chiefly as a constituent of bauxite or in encrustations.
– ORIGIN early 19th cent.: named after George *Gibbs* (1776–1833), American mineralogist, + **-ite**[1].

gibe /dʒʌɪb/ ▸ noun & verb variant spelling of **jibe**[1].

giblets /ˈdʒɪblɪts/ ▸ plural noun the liver, heart, gizzard, and neck of a chicken or other fowl, usually removed before the bird is cooked, and often used to make gravy, stuffing, or soup.
– ORIGIN Middle English (in the sense 'an inessential appendage', later 'garbage, offal'): from Old French *gibelet* 'game bird stew', probably from *gibier* 'birds or mammals hunted for sport'.

Gibraltar /dʒɪˈbrɔːltə/ a British overseas territory near the southern tip of the Iberian peninsula, at the eastern end of the Strait of Gibraltar; pop. 28,800 (est. 2009); languages, English (official), Spanish.

> Occupying a site of great strategic importance, Gibraltar consists of a fortified town and military base at the foot of a rocky headland, the **Rock of Gibraltar**. Britain captured it during the War of the Spanish Succession in 1704 and is responsible for its defence, external affairs, and internal security.

– DERIVATIVES **Gibraltarian** /ˌdʒɪbrɔːlˈtɛːrɪən/ adjective & noun.

Gibraltar, Strait of a channel between the southern tip of the Iberian peninsula and North Africa, forming the only outlet of the Mediterranean Sea to the Atlantic. It is some 60 km (38 miles) long and varies in width from 24 km (15 miles) to 40 km (25 miles) at its western extremity.

Gibran /dʒɪˈbrɑːn/ (also **Jubran**), Khalil (1883–1931), Lebanese-born American writer and artist. His writings in both Arabic and English are deeply romantic, displaying his religious and mystical nature.

Gibson[1], Althea (1927–2003), American tennis player. She was the first black player to succeed at the highest level of tennis, winning all the major world women's singles titles in the late 1950s.

Gibson[2], Mel (b.1956), Australian actor and director, born in the US. Notable film appearances: *Mad Max* (1979), the *Lethal Weapon* series (1987, 1989, 1992, 1998), and *Braveheart* (1995), which he also directed and which won five Oscars.

Gibson Desert a desert region in Western Australia, to the south-east of the Great Sandy Desert. The first European to cross it (1876) was Ernest Giles, who named it after his companion Alfred Gibson, who went missing on an earlier expedition.

Gibson girl ▸ noun a girl typifying the fashionable ideal of the late 19th and early 20th centuries.
– ORIGIN represented in the work of Charles D. *Gibson* (1867–1944), American artist and illustrator.

gibus /ˈdʒʌɪbəs/ (also **gibus hat**) ▸ noun a kind of collapsible top hat.
– ORIGIN mid 19th cent.: named after *Gibus*, the French inventor of this type of hat.

gid /ɡɪd/ ▸ noun [mass noun] (often **the gid**) a fatal disease of sheep and goats, marked by loss of balance. It is caused by larvae of the dog tapeworm encysted in the brain.
– ORIGIN early 17th cent.: back-formation from **giddy**.

giddap /ˈɡɪdap, ɡɪˈdap/ ▸ exclamation N. Amer. another term for **giddy-up**.

giddiness ▸ noun [mass noun] **1** a sensation of whirling and a tendency to fall or stagger; dizziness: *symptoms include nausea, vomiting, and giddiness.*
2 a state of excitable frivolity.

giddy ▸ adjective (**giddier, giddiest**) having a sensation of whirling and a tendency to fall or stagger; dizzy: *Luke felt almost giddy with relief.* ▪ disorientating and alarming, but exciting: *her giddy rise to power.* ▪ excitable and frivolous: *Isobel's giddy young sister-in-law.*
▸ verb (**giddies, giddying, giddied**) [with obj.] make (someone) feel excited to the point of disorientation.
– PHRASES **my giddy aunt!** dated used to express astonishment. **play the giddy goat** dated behave in an irresponsible, silly, or playful way.
– DERIVATIVES **giddily** adverb.
– ORIGIN Old English *gidig* 'insane', literally 'possessed by a god', from the base of **God**. Current senses date from late Middle English.

giddy-up ▸ exclamation said to make a horse start moving or go faster.
– ORIGIN 1920s (originally US as *giddap*): reproducing a pronunciation of *get up*.

Gide /ʒiːd/, André (Paul Guillaume) (1869–1951), French novelist, essayist, and critic, regarded as the father of modern French literature. Notable works: *The Immoralist* (1902), *La Porte étroite* (1909, *Strait is the Gate*), *The Counterfeiters* (1927), and his *Journal* (1939–50). Nobel Prize for Literature (1947).

Gideon /ˈɡɪdɪən/ **1** (in the Bible) an Israelite leader, described in Judges 6:11 ff.
2 a member of Gideons International.

Gideon Bible ▸ noun a bible placed in a hotel room or hospital ward by Gideons International with the aim of spreading the Christian faith.

Gideons International an international Christian organization of business and professional people, founded in 1899 in the US.

gidgee /ˈɡɪdʒiː/ ▸ noun Austral. any of a number of acacia trees of inland Australia. ● Genus *Acacia*, family Labiatae: several species, in particular *A. cambagei*, whose foliage emits an unpleasant odour at times.
– ORIGIN mid 19th cent.: from Wiradhuri *gijir*.

gie /ɡiː/ ▸ verb Scottish form of **give**.

Gielgud /ˈɡiːlɡʊd/, Sir (Arthur) John (1904–2000), English actor and director. A notable Shakespearean actor, particularly remembered for his interpretation of the role of Hamlet, he also appeared in contemporary plays and films and won an Oscar for his role as a butler in *Arthur* (1980).

GIF ▸ noun [mass noun] Computing a lossless format for compressing image files: [as modifier] *a GIF image.* ▪ [count noun] a file in this format.
– ORIGIN 1980s: acronym from *graphic interchange format*.

GIFT ▸ noun [mass noun] Medicine gamete intrafallopian transfer, a technique for assisting conception by introducing mixed ova and sperm into a fallopian tube.
– ORIGIN 1980s: acronym.

gift ▸ noun **1** a thing given willingly to someone without payment; a present: *wedding gifts.* ▪ an act of giving something as a present: *his mother's gift of a pen.* ▪ informal a very easy task or unmissable opportunity: *that goal was an absolute gift.*
2 a natural ability or talent: *he has a gift for comedy.*
▸ verb [with obj.] give (something) as a gift, especially formally or as a donation or bequest: *the company gifted 2,999 shares to a charity.* ▪ present (someone) with a gift or gifts: *the queen gifted him with a heart-shaped brooch.* ▪ (**gift someone with**) endow with (something): *man is gifted with a moral sense.* ▪ informal inadvertently allow (an opponent) to have something: [with two objs] *the goalkeeper gifted Liverpool their last-minute winner.*
– PHRASES **the gift of the gab** see **gab**. **the gift of tongues** see **tongue**. **in the gift of** (of a Church living or official appointment) in the power of (someone) to award: *nine seats in parliament were now in his gift.* **don't look a gift horse in the mouth** proverb don't find fault with something that you have discovered or been given. [prospective purchasers would often inspect the condition of a horse's teeth.]
– ORIGIN Middle English: from Old Norse *gipt*; related to **give**.

gift certificate ▸ noun N. Amer. a gift token.

gifted ▸ adjective having exceptional talent or natural ability: *a gifted amateur musician.*
– DERIVATIVES **giftedness** noun.

gift token (also **gift voucher**) ▸ noun Brit. a voucher given as a present which is exchangeable for goods.

giftware ▸ noun [mass noun] goods sold as being suitable as gifts.

gift wrap ▸ noun [mass noun] decorative paper for wrapping presents.
▸ verb (**gift-wrap**) [with obj.] (usu. as adj. **gift-wrapped**) wrap (a present) in decorative paper. ▪ informal inadvertently allow someone to have (something): *the first England goal came gift-wrapped.*

Gifu /ˈɡiːfuː/ a city in central Japan, on the island of Honshu; pop. 413,099 (2007).

gig[1] /ɡɪɡ/ ▸ noun **1** chiefly historical a light two-wheeled carriage pulled by one horse.
2 a light, fast, narrow boat adapted for rowing or sailing.
– ORIGIN late 18th cent.: apparently a transferred sense of obsolete *gig* 'a flighty girl', which was also applied to various objects or devices that whirled.

gig[2] /ɡɪɡ/ informal ▸ noun a live performance by a musician or group playing popular or jazz music. ▪ a task or assignment: *working on the sea and spotting whales seemed like a great gig.*
▸ verb (**gigs, gigging, gigged**) [no obj.] perform a gig or gigs. ▪ [with obj.] use (a piece of musical equipment) at a gig.
– ORIGIN 1920s: of unknown origin.

gig[3] /ɡɪɡ/ ▸ noun a harpoon-like weapon used for catching fish.
▸ verb (**gigs, gigging, gigged**) [no obj.] fish using a gig.
– ORIGIN early 18th cent.: shortening of earlier (rarely used) *fizgig*, probably from Spanish *fisga* 'harpoon'.

gig[4] /ɡɪɡ, dʒɪɡ/ ▸ noun Computing, informal short for **gigabyte**.

giga- /ˈɡɪɡə, ˈdʒɪɡə/ ▸ combining form used in units of measurement: **1** denoting a factor of 10^9: *gigahertz.*
2 Computing denoting a factor of 2^{30}.
– ORIGIN from Greek *gigas* 'giant'.

gigabit /ˈɡɪɡəbɪt, ˈdʒ-/ (abbrev.: **Gb** or **GB**) ▸ noun Computing a unit of information equal to one thousand million (10^9) or (strictly) 2^{30} bits.

gigabyte /ˈɡɪɡəbʌɪt, ˈdʒ-/ (abbrev.: **Gb** or **GB**) ▸ noun Computing a unit of information equal to one thousand million (10^9) or, strictly, 2^{30} bytes.

gigaflop /ˈɡɪɡəflɒp, ˈdʒ-/ ▸ noun Computing a unit of computing speed equal to one thousand million floating-point operations per second.
– ORIGIN 1970s: back-formation from *gigaflops* (see **giga-**, **-flop**).

gigahertz (abbrev.: **GHz** or **gHz**) ▸ noun a measure of frequency equivalent to one thousand million (10^9) cycles per second.

giganotosaurus /dʒʌɪɡaˌnəʊtəˈsɔːrəs/ ▸ noun an enormous carnivorous dinosaur of the late Cretaceous period, resembling the tyrannosaurs. ● Genus *Giganotosaurus*, suborder Theropoda, order Saurischia.
– ORIGIN modern Latin, from Greek *gigas* 'giant' + *nōton* 'back' + *sauros* 'lizard'.

gigantic ▸ adjective of very great size or extent; huge or enormous: *a gigantic concrete tower.*
– DERIVATIVES **gigantically** adverb.

G

– ORIGIN early 17th cent. (in the sense 'like or suited to a giant'): from Latin *gigas, gigant-* (see GIANT) + -IC.

gigantism /ˈdʒʌɪɡantɪz(ə)m, dʒʌɪˈɡantɪz(ə)m/ ▶ noun [mass noun] chiefly Biology unusual or abnormal largeness. ■ Medicine excessive growth due to hormonal imbalance. ■ Botany excessive size in plants due to polyploidy.

gigantomachy /ˌdʒʌɪɡanˈtɒməki/ ▶ noun (in Greek mythology) the struggle between the gods and the giants.
– ORIGIN late 16th cent.: from Greek *gigantomakhia*, from *gigas, gigant-* (see GIANT) + *-makhia* 'fighting'.

Gigantopithecus /dʒʌɪˌɡantəˈpɪθɪkəs/ ▶ noun a very large fossil Asian ape of the Upper Miocene to Lower Pleistocene epochs. ● Genus *Gigantopithecus*, family Pongidae.
– ORIGIN modern Latin, from Greek *gigas, gigant-* (see GIANT) + *pithēkos* 'ape'.

gigawatt (abbrev.: **Gw**) ▶ noun a unit of power equal to one thousand million (10^9) watts.

giggle ▶ verb [no obj.] laugh lightly in a nervous, affected, or silly manner: *they giggled at some private joke* | (as adj. **giggling**) *three young, giggling girls*.
▶ noun a laugh of such a kind. ■ (**the giggles**) continuous uncontrollable giggling: *I got a fit of the giggles*. ■ Brit. informal an amusing person or thing; a joke: *it should be a right giggle*.
– DERIVATIVES **giggler** noun, **giggly** adjective.
ORIGIN early 16th cent.: imitative.

G

GIGO /ˈɡʌɪɡəʊ/ ▶ abbreviation chiefly Computing garbage in, garbage out.

gigolo /ˈ(d)ʒɪɡələʊ/ ▶ noun (pl. **gigolos**) a young man paid or financially supported by a woman, typically an older woman, to be her escort or lover.
– ORIGIN 1920s (in the sense 'dancing partner'): from French, formed as the masculine of *gigole* 'dance hall woman', from colloquial *gigue* 'leg'.

gigot /ˈdʒɪɡət/ ▶ noun a leg of mutton or lamb.
– ORIGIN French, diminutive of colloquial *gigue* 'leg', from *giguer* 'to hop, jump', of unknown origin.

gigot sleeve ▶ noun a leg-of-mutton sleeve.

gigue /ʒiːɡ/ ▶ noun Music a lively piece of music in the style of a dance, typically of the Renaissance or baroque period, and usually in compound time.
– ORIGIN late 17th cent.: French, literally 'jig'.

Gijón /ɡɪˈhɒn/, Spanish /xiˈxɔn/ a port and industrial city in northern Spain, on the Bay of Biscay; pop. 275,699 (2008).

Gila monster /ˈhiːlə/ ▶ noun a venomous beaded lizard native to the south-western US and Mexico. ● *Heloderma suspectum*, family Helodermatidae.
– ORIGIN late 19th cent.: named after *Gila*, a river in New Mexico and Arizona.

Gilbert¹, Sir Humphrey (*c.*1539–83), English explorer. He claimed Newfoundland for Elizabeth I in 1583, but was lost when his ship foundered in a storm on the way home.

Gilbert², William (1544–1603), English physician and physicist. He discovered how to make magnets, and coined the term *magnetic pole*. His book *De Magnete* (1600) is an important early work on physics.

Gilbert³, Sir W. S. (1836–1911), English dramatist; full name *William Schwenck Gilbert*. He is best known as a librettist who collaborated on light operas with the composer Sir Arthur Sullivan. Notable works: *HMS Pinafore* (1878), *The Pirates of Penzance* (1879), and *The Mikado* (1885).
– DERIVATIVES **Gilbertian** adjective.

Gilbert and Ellice Islands a former British colony (1915–75) in the central Pacific, consisting of two groups of islands: the Gilbert Islands, now a part of Kiribati, and the Ellice Islands, now Tuvalu.

Gilbertese ▶ noun **1** a native or inhabitant of the Gilbert Islands.
2 [mass noun] the Micronesian language spoken in the Gilbert Islands (see KIRIBATI).
▶ adjective relating to the Gilbert Islands.

Gilbert Islands a group of islands in the central Pacific, forming part of Kiribati. The islands straddle the equator and lie immediately west of the International Date Line. They were formerly part of the British colony of the Gilbert and Ellice Islands.
– ORIGIN named by the British after Thomas *Gilbert*, an English adventurer who arrived there in 1788.

gild¹ ▶ verb [with obj.] (often as adj. **gilded**) cover thinly with gold: *Camelot's gilded towers* | figurative *the first rays of the sun were gilding the grassy hillside*. ■ (as adj. **gilded**) wealthy and privileged: *the gilded fools who surrounded the Prince*.
– PHRASES **gild the lily** try to improve what is already beautiful or excellent. [misquotation, from 'To gild refined gold, to paint the lily; to throw perfume on the violet, ... is wasteful, and ridiculous excess' (Shakespeare's *King John* VI. ii. 11.).]
– DERIVATIVES **gilder** noun.
– ORIGIN Old English *gyldan*, of Germanic origin; related to GOLD.

gild² ▶ noun archaic spelling of GUILD.

gilded cage ▶ noun a luxurious but restrictive environment.

gilded youth ▶ noun [treated as sing. or pl.] young people of wealth, fashion, and flair.
– ORIGIN late 19th cent.: translating JEUNESSE DORÉE.

gilding ▶ noun [mass noun] the process of applying gold leaf or gold paint. ■ the material used in, or the surface produced by, gilding.

gilet /ˈʒɪleɪ, ˈʒiːleɪ/ ▶ noun (pl. **gilets** pronunc. **same**) a light sleeveless padded jacket.
– ORIGIN late 19th cent.: French, 'waistcoat', from Spanish *jileco*, from Turkish *yelek*.

gilgai /ˈɡɪlɡʌɪ/ (also **gilgai hole**) ▶ noun Austral. a hollow where rainwater collects; a waterhole.
– ORIGIN from Wiradhuri and Kamilaroi *gilgaay*.

Gilgamesh /ˈɡɪlɡəmɛʃ/ a legendary king of the Sumerian city-state of Uruk who is supposed to have ruled sometime during the first half of the 3rd millennium BC. He is the hero of the Babylonian epic of Gilgamesh, which recounts his exploits in an ultimately unsuccessful quest for immortality.

Gill /ɡɪl/, (Arthur) Eric (Rowton) (1882–1940), English sculptor, engraver, and typographer. His best-known sculptures are the relief carvings *Stations of the Cross* (1914–18) at Westminster Cathedral and *Prospero and Ariel* (1931) on Broadcasting House in London. He designed the popular sans serif typeface, Gill Sans.

gill¹ /ɡɪl/ ▶ noun (often **gills**) **1** the paired respiratory organ of fish and some amphibians, by which oxygen is extracted from water flowing over surfaces within or attached to the walls of the pharynx. ■ an organ of similar function in an invertebrate animal.
2 the vertical plates arranged radially on the underside of mushrooms and many toadstools.
3 the wattles or dewlap of a domestic fowl.
▶ verb [with obj.] **1** gut or clean (a fish).
2 catch (a fish) in a gill net.
– PHRASES **green about** (or **around** or **at**) **the gills** (of a person) looking or feeling ill or nauseous. **to the gills** until completely full.
– DERIVATIVES **gilled** adjective [in combination] *a six-gilled shark*.
– ORIGIN Middle English: from Old Norse.

gill² /dʒɪl/ ▶ noun a unit of liquid measure, equal to a quarter of a pint.
– ORIGIN Middle English: from Old French *gille* 'measure or container for wine', from late Latin *gillo* 'water pot'.

gill³ /ɡɪl/ (also **ghyll**) ▶ noun chiefly N. English **1** a deep ravine, especially a wooded one.
2 a narrow mountain stream.
– ORIGIN Middle English: from Old Norse *gil* 'deep glen'. The spelling *ghyll* was introduced by Wordsworth.

gill⁴ /dʒɪl/ (also **jill**) ▶ noun **1** a female ferret. Compare with HOB² (sense 1).
2 derogatory a young woman.
– ORIGIN late Middle English: abbreviation of the given name *Gillian*.

Gillard /ˈɡɪlɑːd/, Julia (b.1961), Australian Labor stateswoman, Prime Minister since 2010; full name *Julia Eileen Gillard*.

gill cover ▶ noun a flap of skin protecting a fish's gills, typically stiffened by bony plates. Also called OPERCULUM.

Gillespie /ɡɪˈlɛspi/, Dizzy (1917–93), American jazz trumpet player and bandleader; born *John Birks Gillespie*. He was a virtuoso trumpet player and a leading exponent of the bebop style.

gillie /ˈɡɪli/ (also **ghillie**) ▶ noun **1** (in Scotland) a man or boy who attends someone on a hunting or fishing expedition. ■ historical a Highland chief's attendant.
2 (usu. **ghillie**) a type of shoe with laces along the instep and no tongue, used especially for Scottish country dancing.
– ORIGIN late 16th cent.: from Scottish Gaelic *gille* 'lad, servant'. The word was also found in the term *gilliewetfoot*, denoting a servant who carried the chief over a stream, used as a contemptuous name by Lowlanders for the follower of a Highland chief. Sense 2 dates from the 1930s.

Gillingham /ˈdʒɪlɪŋəm/ a town in Kent, SE England, on the Medway estuary; pop. 96,300 (est. 2009).

gill net ▶ noun a fishing net which is hung vertically so that fish get trapped in it by their gills.
– DERIVATIVES **gill-netter** noun.

gillyflower /ˈdʒɪlɪˌflaʊə/ (also **gilliflower**) ▶ noun any of a number of fragrant flowers, such as the wallflower or white stock. ■ (also **clove gillyflower**) archaic a clove-scented pink or carnation. See CLOVE¹ (sense 3).
– ORIGIN Middle English *gilofre* (in the sense 'clove'), from Old French *gilofre, girofle*, via medieval Latin from Greek *karuophullon* (from *karuon* 'nut' + *phullon* 'leaf'). The ending was altered by association with FLOWER, but *gilliver* survived in dialect.

Gilsonite /ˈɡɪlsənʌɪt/ ▶ noun [mass noun] trademark a very pure, shiny, brittle black form of asphalt, used in making inks, paints, and varnishes.
– ORIGIN late 19th cent.: named after Samuel H. *Gilson*, 19th-cent. American mineralogist, + -ITE¹.

gilt¹ ▶ adjective covered thinly with gold leaf or gold paint.
▶ noun **1** [mass noun] gold leaf or gold paint applied in a thin layer to a surface.
2 (**gilts**) fixed-interest loan securities issued by the UK government.
– PHRASES **take the gilt off the gingerbread** see GINGERBREAD.
– ORIGIN Middle English: archaic past participle of GILD¹.

gilt² ▶ noun a young sow.
– ORIGIN Middle English: from Old Norse *gyltr*.

gilt-edged ▶ adjective (especially of paper or a book) having a gilded edge or edges. ■ relating to or denoting stocks or securities (such as gilts) that are regarded as extremely reliable investments.

giltwood ▶ adjective [attrib.] made of wood and gilded: *an 18th-century carved giltwood chair*.

gimbal /ˈdʒɪmb(ə)l/ (also **gimbals**) ▶ noun a device for keeping an instrument such as a compass or chronometer horizontal in a moving vessel or aircraft, typically consisting of rings pivoted at right angles.
– DERIVATIVES **gimballed** adjective.
– ORIGIN late 16th cent. (used in the plural denoting connecting parts in machinery): variant of earlier *gimmal*, itself a variant of late Middle English *gemel* 'twin, hinge, finger ring which can be divided into two rings', from Old French *gemel* 'twin', from Latin *gemellus*, diminutive of *geminus*.

gimcrack /ˈdʒɪmkrak/ ▶ adjective showy but cheap or badly made.
▶ noun a cheap and showy ornament; a knick-knack.
– DERIVATIVES **gimcrackery** noun.
– ORIGIN Middle English *gibecrake*, of unknown origin. Originally a noun, the term denoted some kind of inlaid work in wood, later a fanciful notion or mechanical contrivance, hence a knick-knack.

gimlet /ˈɡɪmlɪt/ ▶ noun **1** a small T-shaped tool with a screw tip for boring holes.
2 a cocktail of gin (or sometimes vodka) and lime juice.
– ORIGIN Middle English: from Old French *guimbelet*, diminutive of *guimble* 'drill', ultimately of Germanic origin.

gimlet eye ▶ noun an eye with a piercing stare.
– DERIVATIVES **gimlet-eyed** adjective.

gimme informal ▶ contraction give me (not acceptable in standard use): *just gimme the damn thing*.
▶ noun N. Amer. a thing that is very easy to perform or obtain, especially in a game or sport: *the kick would hardly be a gimme in that wind*.

gimmer /ˈɡɪmə/ ▶ noun Scottish & N. English a ewe between its first and second shearing.
– ORIGIN late Middle English: from Old Norse *gymbr*, of unknown ultimate origin.

gimmick ▶ noun a trick or device intended to attract attention, publicity, or trade.
– DERIVATIVES **gimmicky** adjective.
– ORIGIN 1920s (originally US): of unknown origin but possibly an approximate anagram of *magic*, the original sense being 'a piece of magicians' apparatus'.

gimmickry ▶ noun [mass noun] gimmicks collectively; the use of gimmicks: *it does what it says it does, with no design gimmickry*.

gimp¹ /ɡɪmp/ (also **guimp** or **gymp**) ▶ noun **1** [mass noun] twisted silk, worsted, or cotton with cord or

wire running through it, used chiefly as upholstery trimming. ■ (in lacemaking) coarser thread which forms the outline of the design in some techniques.
2 fishing line made of silk bound with wire.
– ORIGIN mid 17th cent.: from Dutch, of unknown ultimate origin.

gimp[2] /gɪmp/ N. Amer. informal, derogatory ▶ **noun 1** a physically disabled or lame person. ■ a limp.
2 a feeble or contemptible person.
▶ **verb** [no obj., with adverbial of direction] limp; hobble: *I gimped over to the door.*
– DERIVATIVES **gimpy** adjective.
– ORIGIN 1920s: of unknown origin.

gin[1] ▶ **noun 1** [mass noun] a clear alcoholic spirit distilled from grain or malt and flavoured with juniper berries.
2 (also **gin rummy**) a form of the card game rummy in which a player holding cards totalling ten or less may terminate play.
– ORIGIN early 18th cent.: abbreviation of GENEVER.

gin[2] ▶ **noun 1** a machine for separating cotton from its seeds.
2 a machine for raising and moving heavy weights.
3 (also **gin trap**) a trap for catching birds or small mammals.
▶ **verb** (**gins, ginning, ginned**) [with obj.] treat (cotton) in a gin.
– DERIVATIVES **ginner** noun, **ginnery** noun.
– ORIGIN Middle English (in the sense 'a tool or device, a trick'): from Old French *engin* (see ENGINE).

gin[3] ▶ **noun** Austral. offensive an Aboriginal woman.
– ORIGIN from Dharuk *diyin* 'woman, wife'.

ginger ▶ **noun** [mass noun] **1** a hot, fragrant spice made from the rhizome of a plant, which may be chopped or powdered for cooking, preserved in syrup, or candied. ■ short for GINGER ALE.
2 a SE Asian plant, which resembles bamboo in appearance, from which ginger is taken. ● *Zingiber officinale*, family Zingiberaceae.
3 a light reddish-yellow colour.
4 a quality of energy or spiritedness: *the ginger had gone out of the men.*
▶ **adjective** (chiefly of hair or fur) of a light reddish-yellow colour. ■ (of a person or animal) having ginger hair or fur.
▶ **verb** [with obj.] **1** (usu. as adj. **gingered**) flavour with ginger: *gingered sweet-potato salad.*
2 (**ginger someone/thing up**) make someone or something more lively: *she slapped his hand lightly to ginger him up.*
– DERIVATIVES **gingery** adjective.
– ORIGIN late Old English *gingifer*, conflated in Middle English with Old French *gingimbre*, from medieval Latin *gingiber*, from Greek *zingiberis*, from Pali *siṅgivera*, of Dravidian origin.

ginger ale ▶ **noun** [mass noun] a clear effervescent non-alcoholic drink flavoured with ginger extract.

ginger beer ▶ **noun** [mass noun] a cloudy effervescent drink made from a mixture of root or ground ginger and syrup.

gingerbread ▶ **noun** [mass noun] **1** cake made with treacle or syrup and flavoured with ginger.
2 [often as modifier] elaborate or ornate decoration, especially on the eaves or porch of a building.
– PHRASES **take the gilt off the gingerbread** Brit. make something no longer attractive or desirable.
– ORIGIN Middle English (originally denoting preserved ginger), from Old French *gingembrat*, from medieval Latin *gingibratum*, from *gingiber* (see GINGER). The change in the ending in the 15th cent. was due to association with BREAD.

gingerbread man ▶ **noun** a flat ginger biscuit shaped like a person.

ginger group ▶ **noun** Brit. a highly active faction within a party or movement that presses for stronger action on a particular issue.

ginger jar ▶ **noun** a small ceramic jar with a high rim over which a lid fits.

gingerly ▶ **adverb** in a careful or cautious manner: *Jackson sat down very gingerly.*
▶ **adjective** showing great care or caution: *a gingerly pace.*
– DERIVATIVES **gingerliness** noun.
– ORIGIN early 16th cent. (in the sense 'daintily, mincingly'): perhaps from Old French *gensor* 'delicate', comparative of *gent* 'graceful', from Latin *genitus* '(well-) born'.

ginger nut (also **ginger snap**) ▶ **noun** Brit. a hard ginger-flavoured biscuit.

ginger wine ▶ **noun** [mass noun] an alcoholic drink made from fermented sugar, water, and bruised ginger.

gingham /ˈgɪŋəm/ ▶ **noun** [mass noun] lightweight plain-woven cotton cloth, typically checked in white and a bold colour: [as modifier] *gingham curtains.*
– ORIGIN early 17th cent.: from Dutch *gingang*, from Malay *genggang* (originally an adjective meaning 'striped').

gingival /dʒɪnˈdʒʌɪv(ə)l/ ▶ **adjective** Medicine concerned with the gums: *the gingival tissues.*
– ORIGIN mid 17th cent.: from Latin *gingiva* 'gum' + -AL.

gingivitis /ˌdʒɪndʒɪˈvʌɪtɪs/ ▶ **noun** [mass noun] Medicine inflammation of the gums.

ginglymus /ˈgɪŋglɪməs/ ▶ **noun** (pl. **ginglymi** /-mʌɪ/) Anatomy a hinge-like joint such as the elbow or knee, which allows movement in only one plane.
– ORIGIN late 16th cent.: modern Latin, from Greek *ginglumos* 'hinge'.

gink /gɪŋk/ ▶ **noun** informal, chiefly N. Amer. a foolish or contemptible person.
– ORIGIN early 20th cent. (originally US): of unknown origin.

ginkgo /ˈgɪŋkgəʊ, ˈgɪŋkəʊ/ (also **gingko**) ▶ **noun** (pl. **ginkgos** or **ginkgoes**) a deciduous Chinese tree related to the conifers, with fan-shaped leaves and yellow flowers. It has a number of primitive features and is similar to some Jurassic fossils. Also called MAIDENHAIR TREE. ● *Ginkgo biloba*, the only living member of the family Ginkgoaceae and order Ginkgoales, class Coniferopsida.
– ORIGIN late 18th cent.: from Japanese *ginkyō*, from Chinese *yinxing*.

gin mill ▶ **noun** N. Amer. informal a run-down or seedy nightclub or bar.

ginnel /ˈgɪn(ə)l/ ▶ **noun** N. English a narrow passage between buildings; an alley.
– ORIGIN early 17th cent.: perhaps from French *chenel* 'channel'.

ginormous ▶ **adjective** Brit. informal extremely large: *ginormous piles of rubbish.*
– ORIGIN 1940s (originally military slang): blend of GIANT and ENORMOUS.

gin rummy ▶ **noun** see GIN[1].

Ginsberg /ˈgɪnzbəːg/, Allen (1926–97), American poet. A leading poet of the beat generation, and later influential in the hippy movement of the 1960s, he is notable for *Howl and Other Poems* (1956), in which he attacked American society for its materialism and complacency.

ginseng /ˈdʒɪnsɛŋ/ ▶ **noun 1** [mass noun] a plant tuber credited with various tonic and medicinal properties.
2 the plant from which this tuber is obtained, native to eastern Asia and North America. ● Genus *Panax*, family Araliaceae: several species, in particular the Asian *P. pseudoginseng* and the North American *P. quinquefolius*.
– ORIGIN mid 17th cent.: from Chinese *rénshēn*, from *rén* 'man' + *shēn*, a kind of herb (because of the supposed resemblance of the forked root to a person).

gin sling ▶ **noun** a drink of gin and water, sweetened and flavoured with lemon or lime juice.

ginzo /ˈgɪnzəʊ/ US informal, derogatory ▶ **noun** (pl. **ginzos**) an Italian person.
▶ **adjective** Italian.
– ORIGIN 1930s: perhaps from US slang *Guinea*, denoting an Italian or Spanish immigrant.

Giorgione /ˌdʒɔːdʒɪˈəʊneɪ, -nɪ/, Italian /dʒorˈdʒoːne/ (*c.*1478–1510), Italian painter; also called **Giorgio Barbarelli** or **Giorgio da Castelfranco**. An influential figure in Renaissance art, he introduced the small easel picture in oils intended for private collectors. Notable works: *The Tempest* (*c.*1505) and *Sleeping Venus* (*c.*1510).

Giotto[1] /ˈdʒɒtəʊ/ (*c.*1267–1337), Italian painter; full name *Giotto di Bondone*. He introduced a naturalistic style showing human expression. Notable works include the frescoes in the Arena Chapel, Padua (1305–8), and the church of Santa Croce in Florence (*c.*1320).

Giotto[2] /ˈdʒɒtəʊ/ a European space probe which photographed the nucleus of Halley's comet in March 1986.

Giovanni de' Medici the name of Pope Leo X (see LEO[1]).

gip ▶ **noun** variant spelling of GYP[1].

gippo ▶ **noun** variant spelling of GYPPO.

gippy tummy /ˈdʒɪpi/ (also **gyppy tummy**) ▶ **noun** [mass noun] Brit. informal diarrhoea affecting visitors to hot countries.
– ORIGIN 1940s: *gippy*, abbreviation of EGYPTIAN.

gipsy ▶ **noun** variant spelling of GYPSY.

gipsywort ▶ **noun** variant spelling of GYPSYWORT.

giraffe ▶ **noun** (pl. **same** or **giraffes**) a large African mammal with a very long neck and forelegs, having a coat patterned with brown patches separated by lighter lines. It is the tallest living animal. ● *Giraffa camelopardalis*, family Giraffidae.
– ORIGIN late 16th cent.: from French *girafe*, Italian *giraffa*, or Spanish and Portuguese *girafa*, based on Arabic *zarāfa*. The animal was known in Europe in the medieval period, and isolated instances of names for it based on the Arabic are recorded in Middle English, when it was commonly called the CAMELOPARD.

girandole /ˈdʒɪr(ə)ndəʊl/ ▶ **noun** a branched support for candles or other lights, which either stands on a surface or projects from a wall.
– ORIGIN mid 17th cent. (denoting a revolving cluster of fireworks): from French, from Italian *girandola*, from *girare* 'gyrate, turn', from Latin *gyrare* (see GYRATE).

G

girasol /ˈdʒɪrəsɒl, -səʊl/ (also **girasole** /-səʊl/) ▶ **noun 1** a kind of opal reflecting a reddish glow.
2 North American term for JERUSALEM ARTICHOKE.
– ORIGIN late 16th cent. (in the sense 'sunflower'): from French, or from Italian *girasole*, from *girare* 'to turn' + *sole* 'sun' (because the sunflower turns to follow the path of the sun).

gird[1] ▶ **verb** (past and past participle **girded** or **girt**) [with obj.] literary encircle (a person or part of the body) with a belt or band: *a young man was to be **girded** with the belt of knighthood.* ■ secure (a garment or sword) on the body with a belt or band: *a white robe girded with a magenta sash.* ■ surround; encircle: *the ruins are girded by two deep gorges.*
– PHRASES **gird (up) one's loins** (or **gird oneself for something**) prepare and strengthen oneself for future actions, typically ones that may be dangerous or difficult.
– ORIGIN Old English *gyrdan*, of Germanic origin; related to Dutch *gorden* and German *gürten*, also to GIRDLE[1] and GIRTH.

gird[2] archaic ▶ **verb** [no obj.] make cutting or critical remarks: *the clubmen **girded** at the Committee.*
▶ **noun** a cutting or critical remark.
– ORIGIN Middle English (in the sense 'strike, stab'): of unknown origin.

girder ▶ **noun** a large iron or steel beam or compound structure used for building bridges and the framework of large buildings.
– ORIGIN early 17th cent.: from GIRD[1] in the archaic sense 'brace, strengthen'.

girdle[1] ▶ **noun 1** a belt or cord worn round the waist. ■ a thing that encircles something like a girdle: *a communications girdle around the world.* ■ Anatomy either of two sets of bones encircling the body, to which the limbs are attached. See PECTORAL GIRDLE, PELVIC GIRDLE.
2 a woman's elasticated corset extending from waist to thigh.
3 the part of a cut gem dividing the crown from the base and embraced by the setting.
4 a ring made around a tree by removing bark.
▶ **verb** [with obj.] **1** encircle (the body) with a girdle: *the Friar loosened the rope that girdled his waist.* ■ surround; encircle: *the chain of volcanoes which girdles the Pacific.*
2 cut through the bark all the way round (a tree or branch), typically in order to kill it.
– ORIGIN Old English *gyrdel*, of Germanic origin; related to Dutch *gordel* and German *Gürtel*, also to GIRD[1] and GIRTH.

girdle[2] ▶ **noun** Scottish and northern English term for GRIDDLE (sense 1 of the noun).
– ORIGIN late Middle English: variant of GRIDDLE.

girdled lizard (also **girdle-tailed lizard**) ▶ **noun** an African lizard with rough or spiny scales which give a banded appearance to the body and tail. Also called ZONURE. ● Genus *Cordylus*, family Cordylidae: several species, in particular the **common** (or **Cape**) **girdled lizard** (*C. cordylus*).

girdler ▶ **noun 1** archaic a maker of girdles.
2 an insect which removes rings of bark from trees.

girl ▶ **noun 1** a female child. ■ a person's daughter: *he was devoted to his little girl.*

2 a young or relatively young woman. ■ [with modifier] a young woman of a specified kind or having a specified job: *a career girl.* ■ (**girls**) informal women who mix socially: *I look forward to having a night with the girls.* ■ a person's girlfriend: *his girl eloped with an accountant.* ■ dated a female servant.
– ORIGIN Middle English (denoting a child or young person of either sex): perhaps related to Low German *gör* 'child'.

girl Friday ▶ **noun** a female assistant, especially a junior office worker.
– ORIGIN 1940s: on the pattern of *man Friday*.

girlfriend ▶ **noun** a person's regular female companion with whom they have a romantic or sexual relationship. ■ a woman's female friend.

Girl Guide ▶ **noun** Brit. a member of the Guide Association.

Girl Guides Association former name for **GUIDE ASSOCIATION**.

girlhood ▶ **noun** [mass noun] the state or time of being a girl: *they had been friends since girlhood.*

G

girlie (also **girly**) ▶ **adjective 1** often derogatory characteristic of or appropriate to a girl: *girlie pink paper.*
2 [attrib.] depicting or featuring nude or partially nude young women in erotic poses: *girlie magazines.*
▶ **noun** (pl. **girlies**) informal a girl or young woman (often used as a term of address).

girlish ▶ **adjective** of or characteristic of a girl: *girlish giggles.*
– DERIVATIVES **girlishly adverb**, **girlishness noun**.

Girl Scout ▶ **noun** a girl belonging to the Scout Association.

girn ▶ **verb** variant spelling of **GURN**.

giro /ˈdʒʌɪrəʊ/ ▶ **noun** (pl. **giros**) [mass noun] a system of electronic credit transfer used in Europe and Japan, involving banks, post offices, and public utilities. ■ [count noun] Brit. a cheque or payment by giro, especially a social security payment: *any chance of a pound till the giro comes?*
– ORIGIN late 19th cent.: via German from Italian, 'circulation (of money)'.

Gironde /ʒɪˈrɒnd/, French /ʒiʀɔ̃d/ a river estuary in SW France, formed at the junction of the Garonne and Dordogne Rivers, north of Bordeaux, and flowing north-west for 72 km (45 miles) into the Bay of Biscay. ■ a department in Aquitaine, SW France.

Girondist /dʒɪˈrɒndɪst/ (also **Girondin** /dʒɪˈrɒndɪn/, French /ʒiʀɔ̃dɛ̃/) ▶ **noun** a member of the French moderate republican Party in power during the Revolution 1791–3, so called because the party leaders were the deputies from the department of the Gironde.
– ORIGIN from archaic French *Girondiste* (now *Girondin*).

girt[1] past participle of **GIRD**[1].

girt[2] ▶ **noun** old-fashioned term for **GIRTH**.

girth ▶ **noun 1** [mass noun] the measurement around the middle of something, especially a person's waist. ■ a person's waist or stomach, especially when large.
2 a band attached to a saddle and fastened around a horse's belly to keep the saddle in place.
▶ **verb** [with obj.] archaic surround; encircle: *the four seas that girth Britain.*
– ORIGIN Middle English (in sense 2 of the noun): from Old Norse *gjǫrth*.

GIS ▶ **abbreviation** geographic information system, a system for storing and manipulating geographical information on computer.

Gisborne /ˈɡɪzbən/ a port and resort on the east coast of the North Island, New Zealand; pop. 32,500 (est. 2006).

Giscard d'Estaing /ˌʒiːskɑː dɛˈstã/, French /ʒiskaʀ dɛstɛ̃/, Valéry (b.1926), French statesman, President 1974–81. He was a member of the European Parliament (1989–93) and was leader of the centre-right *Union pour la démocratie française* 1988–96.

Gish /ɡɪʃ/, Lillian (1896–1993), American actress. She and her sister **Dorothy** (1898–1968) appeared in a number of D. W. Griffith's films, including *Hearts of the World* (1918) and *Orphans of the Storm* (1922).

gismo ▶ **noun** variant spelling of **GIZMO**.

Gissing /ˈɡɪsɪŋ/, George (Robert) (1857–1903), English novelist. Notable works: *New Grub Street* (1891), *Born in Exile* (1892), and *The Private Papers of Henry Ryecroft* (1903).

gist /dʒɪst/ ▶ **noun** [in sing.] **1** the substance or general meaning of a speech or text: *it was hard to get the gist of Pedro's talk.*
2 Law the real point of an action.
– ORIGIN early 18th cent.: from Old French, third person singular present tense of *gesir* 'to lie', from Latin *jacere*. The Anglo-French legal phrase *cest action gist* 'this action lies' denoted that there were sufficient grounds to proceed; *gist* was adopted into English denoting the grounds themselves (sense 2).

git ▶ **noun** Brit. informal an unpleasant or contemptible person.
– ORIGIN 1940s: variant of **GET** (sense 2 of the noun).

Gita /ˈɡiːtə/ ▶ **noun** short for **BHAGAVADGITA**.

gîte /ʒiːt/, French /ʒit/ ▶ **noun** a furnished holiday house in France, typically in a rural district.
– ORIGIN French, from Old French *giste*; related to *gésir* 'to lie'.

gittern /ˈɡɪtəːn/ ▶ **noun** historical a lute-like medieval stringed instrument, forerunner of the guitar.
– ORIGIN late Middle English: from Old French *guiterne*; perhaps related to **CITTERN** and **GUITAR**.

give ▶ **verb** (past **gave**; past participle **given**) **1** [with two objs] freely transfer the possession of (something) to (someone): *she gave him presents and clothes* | *the cheque given to the jeweller proved worthless* | [with obj.] *he gave the papers back.* ■ [with obj.] hand over (an amount) in payment; pay: *how much did you give for that?* ■ [with obj.] used hyperbolically to express how greatly one wants to have or do something: *I'd give anything for a cup of tea.* ■ [with obj.] commit or entrust: *a baby given into their care by the accident of her birth.* ■ [with obj.] freely set aside or devote for a purpose: *all who have given thought to the matter agree* | [no obj.] *committees who give so generously of their time and effort.* ■ [with obj.] dated (of a man) sanction the marriage of (his daughter) to someone: *he gave her in marriage to a noble.* ■ (**give oneself to**) dated (of a woman) consent to have sexual intercourse with (a man).
2 [with two objs] cause or allow (someone or something) to have or experience (something); provide with: *you gave me such a fright* | [with obj.] *this leaflet gives our opening times.* ■ provide (love or other emotional support) to: *his parents gave him the encouragement he needed* | (as adj. **giving**) *he was very giving and supportive.* ■ allow (someone) to have (a specified amount of time) for an activity or undertaking: *give me a second to bring the car around* | [with obj.] *I'll give you until tomorrow morning.* ■ pass on (an illness or infection) to (someone): *I hope I don't give you my cold.* ■ pass (a message) to (someone): *give my love to all the girls.* ■ [usu. in imperative] make a connection to allow (someone) to speak to (someone else) on the telephone: *give me the police.*
3 [with obj.] carry out or perform (a specified action): *I gave a bow* | [with two objs] *he gave the counter a polish.* ■ produce (a sound): *he gave a gasp.* ■ present (an appearance or impression): *he gave no sign of life.* ■ provide (a party or social meal) as host or hostess: *a dinner given in honour of an American diplomat* | [with two objs] *Kate gave him a leaving party.*
4 [with obj.] yield as a product or result: *milk is sometimes added to give a richer cheese.* ■ (**give something off/out/forth**) emit odour, vapour, or similar substances: *some solvents give off toxic fumes.*
5 [with obj.] concede (something) as valid or deserved in respect of (someone): *give him his due.* ■ allot (a score) to: *I gave it five out of ten.* ■ (**give something for**) place a specified value on (something): *he never gave anything for French painting.* ■ sentence (someone) to (a specified penalty): *for the first offence I was given a fine.* ■ [with obj. and complement] (of an umpire or referee) declare whether or not (a player) is out or offside: *Gooch was given out, caught behind.* ■ adjudicate that (a goal) has been legitimately scored.
6 [with obj.] state or put forward (information or argument): *he did not give his name.* ■ pledge or offer as a guarantee: [with two objs] *I give you my word.* ■ [with two objs, usu. with negative] say to (someone) as an excuse or inappropriate answer: *don't give me any of your backchat.* ■ deliver (a judgement) authoritatively: *I gave my verdict.* ■ informal predict that (an activity or relationship) will last no longer than (a specified time): *this is a place that will not improve with time—I give it three weeks.* ■ [no obj.] informal tell what one knows: *okay, give—what's that all about?*
7 [no obj.] alter in shape under pressure rather than resist or break: *that chair doesn't give.* ■ yield or give way to pressure: *the heavy door didn't give until the fifth push* | figurative *when two people who don't get on are thrust together, something's got to give.* ■ [no obj.] N. Amer. informal concede defeat; surrender: *I give!*
▶ **noun** [mass noun] capacity to bend or alter in shape under pressure: *plastic pots that have enough give to accommodate the vigorous roots.* ■ ability to adapt; flexibility: *there is no give at all in the British position.*
– PHRASES **give oneself airs** act pretentiously or snobbishly. **give and take** mutual concessions and compromises. **give as good as one gets** respond with equal force when attacked. **give the game** (or **show**) **away** inadvertently reveal something secret. **give it to someone** informal scold or punish someone. **give me ——** I prefer or admire ——: *give me the mainland any day!* **give me a break** informal used to express exasperation, protest, or disbelief. **give someone one** Brit. vulgar slang (of a man) have sexual intercourse with a woman. **give or take ——** informal to within a specified amount: *three hundred and fifty years ago, give or take a few.* ■ apart from: *it's a process that runs fairly smoothly, give or take the occasional glitch.* **give rise to** cause to happen: *decisions which give rise to arguments.* **give someone to understand** (or **believe** or **know**) inform someone in a rather indirect way: *I was given to understand that I had been invited.* **give up the ghost** see **GHOST**. **give someone what for** informal, chiefly Brit. punish or scold someone severely. **I give you ——** used to present a speaker or entertainer or when making a toast: *for your entertainment this evening I give you ... Mister Albert DeNero!* **not give a damn** (or **hoot** etc.) informal not care at all: *people who don't give a damn about the environment.* **what gives?** informal what's the news?; what's happening? (often used as a friendly greeting).
– PHRASAL VERBS **give someone away 1** reveal the true identity of someone: *his strangely shaped feet gave him away.* ■ reveal information which incriminates someone. **2** hand over a bride ceremonially to her bridegroom as part of a wedding ceremony. **give something away 1** reveal something secret. **2** (in sport) concede a goal or advantage to the opposition, especially through careless play. **3** Austral./NZ stop doing something: *he'd given away some of the things he got up to.* **give in** cease fighting or arguing; admit defeat: *he reluctantly gave in to the pressure.* **give something in** Brit. hand in a completed document to an official or a piece of work to a supervisor. **give on to** (or **into**) Brit. (of a window, door, corridor, etc.) overlook or lead into: *a plate glass window gave on to the roof.* **give out 1** be completely used up: *their allowances soon gave out.* ■ stop functioning: *he curses and swears till his voice gives out.* **2** Irish speak in an angry way: *the woman began giving out to poor Paddy.* **give something out** distribute or broadcast something: *I've been giving out leaflets.* **give over** [often in imperative] Brit. informal stop doing something. ■ used to express vehement disagreement: *I suggested her salary might be £100,000. 'Give over!'.* **give up** cease making an effort; admit defeat. **give it up** [usu. in imperative] US informal applaud a performer or entertainer. **give oneself up** (or **over**) **to** allow oneself to be taken over by (an emotion or addiction): *he gave himself up to pleasure.* **give someone up 1** deliver a wanted person to authority: *a voice told him to come out and give himself up.* **2** stop hoping that someone is still going to arrive. **give something up** part with something that one would prefer to keep: *she would have given up everything for love.* ■ stop doing or consuming something: *I've decided to give up drinking.* **give up on** stop having faith or belief in: *they weren't about to give up on their heroes so easily.*
– ORIGIN Old English *giefan*, *gefan*, of Germanic origin; related to Dutch *geven* and German *geben*.

giveaway informal ▶ **noun 1** a thing that is given free, often for promotional purposes: *every issue is packed with competitions and great giveaways.*
2 a thing that makes an inadvertent revelation: *the shape of the parcel was a dead giveaway.*
▶ **adjective** [attrib.] **1** free of charge: *giveaway CDs.* ■ (of prices) very low.
2 inadvertently revealing something: *small giveaway mannerisms.*

giveback ▶ **noun** N. Amer. an agreement by workers to surrender benefits and conditions previously agreed in return for new concessions or awards.

given past participle of **GIVE**. ▶ **adjective 1** specified or stated: *they gathered at a given time.*
2 (**given to**) inclined or disposed to: *she was not often given to anger.*
3 Law, archaic (of a document) signed and dated.
▶ **preposition** taking into account: *given the complexity of the task, they did a good job.*
▶ **noun** a known or established fact or situation: *at a couture house, attentive service is a given.*

given name ▶ **noun** another term for **FIRST NAME**.

giver ▶ noun a person who gives something: *a giver of advice* | [in combination] *care-givers*.

Giza /ˈgiːzə/ a city south-west of Cairo in northern Egypt, on the west bank of the Nile, site of the Pyramids and the Sphinx; pop. 2,891,300 (est. 2006). Also called **EL-GIZA**; Arabic name **AL-JIZAH**.

gizmo /ˈgɪzməʊ/ (also **gismo**) ▶ noun (pl. **gizmos**) informal a gadget, especially one whose name the speaker does not know or cannot recall: *the latest multimedia gizmo*.
– ORIGIN 1940s (originally US): of unknown origin.

gizzard /ˈgɪzəd/ ▶ noun a muscular, thick-walled part of a bird's stomach for grinding food, typically with grit. ■ a muscular stomach of some fish, insects, molluscs, and other invertebrates.
– ORIGIN late Middle English *giser*: from Old French, based on Latin *gigeria* 'cooked entrails of fowl'. The final *-d* was added in the 16th cent.

Gjetost /ˈjɛtɒst/ ▶ noun [mass noun] a very sweet, firm golden-brown Norwegian cheese, traditionally made with goat's milk.
– ORIGIN Norwegian, from *gjet, geit* 'goat' + *ost* 'cheese'.

GLA ▶ abbreviation ■ (in the UK) Greater London Authority, established in 2000. ■ gamma linolenic acid.

glabella /gləˈbɛlə/ ▶ noun (pl. **glabellae** /-liː/) Anatomy the smooth part of the forehead above and between the eyebrows.
– DERIVATIVES **glabellar** adjective.
– ORIGIN early 19th cent.: modern Latin, from Latin *glabellus* (adjective), diminutive of *glaber* 'smooth'.

glabrous /ˈgleɪbrəs/ ▶ adjective technical (chiefly of the skin or a leaf) free from hair or down; smooth.
– ORIGIN mid 17th cent.: from Latin *glaber, glabr-* 'hairless, smooth' + **-OUS**.

glacé /ˈglaseɪ/ ▶ adjective **1** (of fruit) preserved in sugar: *a glacé cherry*.
2 (of cloth or leather) smooth and highly polished.
– ORIGIN mid 19th cent.: French, literally 'iced', past participle of *glacer*, from *glace* 'ice'.

glacé icing ▶ noun [mass noun] icing made with icing sugar and water.

glacial /ˈgleɪsɪəl, -ʃ(ə)l/ ▶ adjective **1** relating to or denoting the presence or agency of ice, especially in the form of glaciers: *thick glacial deposits* | *a glacial lake*. ■ very cold; icy: *glacial temperatures* | figurative *his glacial blue eyes*. ■ extremely slow (like the movement of a glacier): *an official described progress in the talks as glacial*.
2 Chemistry denoting pure organic acids (especially acetic acid) which form ice-like crystals on freezing.
▶ noun Geology a glacial period.
– DERIVATIVES **glacially** adverb.
– ORIGIN mid 17th cent.: from French, or from Latin *glacialis* 'icy', from *glacies* 'ice'.

glacial period ▶ noun a period in the earth's history when polar and mountain ice sheets were unusually extensive across the earth's surface.

glaciated /ˈgleɪsɪeɪtɪd/ ▶ adjective covered or having been covered by glaciers or ice sheets: *a glaciated valley*.
– ORIGIN mid 19th cent.: past participle of obsolete *glaciate*, from Latin *glaciare* 'freeze', from *glacies* 'ice'.

glaciation /ˌgleɪsɪˈeɪʃ(ə)n/ ▶ noun [mass noun] Geology the process or state of being covered by glaciers or ice sheets. ■ [count noun] a glacial period.

glacier /ˈglasɪə, ˈgleɪsɪə/ ▶ noun a slowly moving mass or river of ice formed by the accumulation and compaction of snow on mountains or near the poles.
– ORIGIN mid 18th cent.: from French, from *glace* 'ice', based on Latin *glacies*.

Glacier Bay National Park a national park in SE Alaska, on the Pacific coast. Extending over an area of 12,880 sq. km (4,975 sq. miles), it contains the terminus of the Grand Pacific Glacier.

glaciology /ˌgleɪsɪˈɒlədʒi/ ▶ noun [mass noun] the study of the internal dynamics and effects of glaciers.
– DERIVATIVES **glaciological** adjective, **glaciologist** noun.
– ORIGIN late 19th cent.: from Latin *glacies* 'ice' + **-LOGY**.

glacis /ˈglasɪs, -si/ ▶ noun (pl. **same** /-sɪz, -siːz/) **1** a bank sloping down from a fort which exposes attackers to the defenders' missiles.
2 (also **glacis plate**) a sloping piece of armour plate protecting part of a vehicle.
– ORIGIN late 17th cent.: from French, from Old French *glacier* 'to slip', from *glace* 'ice', based on Latin *glacies*.

glad ▶ adjective (**gladder, gladdest**) [predic.] feeling pleasure or happiness: [with infinitive] *I'm really glad to hear that* | [with clause] *he was glad that Phyllis was gone*. ■ [attrib.] causing happiness: *glad tidings*. ■ grateful: *she was* **glad of** *Hank's lively company*. ■ [with infinitive] willing and eager (to do something): *he will be glad to carry your bags*.
▶ verb (**glads, gladding, gladded**) [with obj.] literary make happy; please: *Albion's lessening shore could grieve or glad mine eye*.
– PHRASES **give someone the glad eye** informal, dated look at someone in a flirtatious way.
– DERIVATIVES **gladness** noun.
– ORIGIN Old English *glæd* (originally in the sense 'bright, shining'), of Germanic origin; related to Old Norse *glathr* 'bright, joyous' and German *glatt* 'smooth', also to Latin *glaber* 'smooth, hairless'.

gladden ▶ verb [with obj.] make glad: *the high, childish laugh was a sound that gladdened her heart*.

gladdon /ˈglad(ə)n/ ▶ noun a purple-flowered iris native to Eurasia and North Africa, which produces an unpleasant odour, especially when bruised. Also called **STINKING IRIS**. ● *Iris foetidissima*, family Iridaceae.
– ORIGIN Old English *glædene*, based on Latin *gladiolus* (see **GLADIOLUS**).

glade ▶ noun an open space in a wood or forest.
– ORIGIN late Middle English: of unknown origin; perhaps related to **GLAD** or **GLEAM**, with reference to the comparative brightness of a clearing (obsolete senses of *glade* include 'a gleam of light' and 'a bright space between clouds').

glad-hand ▶ verb [with obj.] (especially of a politician) greet or welcome warmly: *they had been taking every free minute to glad-hand loyal supporters*.
▶ noun (**glad hand**) [in sing.] a warm and hearty greeting or welcome.
– DERIVATIVES **glad-hander** noun.

gladiator /ˈgladɪeɪtə/ ▶ noun (in ancient Rome) a man trained to fight with weapons against other men or wild animals in an arena.
– DERIVATIVES **gladiatorial** /ˌgladɪəˈtɔːrɪəl/ adjective.
– ORIGIN late Middle English: from Latin, from *gladius* 'sword'.

gladiolus /ˌgladɪˈəʊləs/ ▶ noun (pl. **gladioli** /-lʌɪ/) an Old World plant of the iris family, with sword-shaped leaves and spikes of brightly coloured flowers, popular in gardens and as a cut flower. ● Genus *Gladiolus*, family Iridaceae: many species.
– ORIGIN Old English (originally denoting the gladdon), from Latin, diminutive of *gladius* 'sword' (used as a plant name by Pliny).

gladly ▶ adverb willingly or eagerly: *I would have gladly paid for it*. ■ with pleasure or gratitude; happily: *she offered me a lift and I gladly accepted*.

glad rags ▶ plural noun informal clothes for a special occasion; smart or showy clothes.

gladsome ▶ adjective literary (of a person) having a cheerful disposition. ■ filled with, marked by, or causing pleasure.

Gladstone, William Ewart (1809–98), British Liberal statesman, Prime Minister 1868–74, 1880–5, 1886, and 1892–4. At first a Conservative minister, he later joined the Liberal Party, becoming its leader in 1867. His ministries saw the introduction of elementary education, the passing of the Irish Land Acts and the third Reform Act, and his campaign in favour of Home Rule for Ireland.
– DERIVATIVES **Gladstonian** adjective.

Gladstone bag ▶ noun a bag like a briefcase having two equal compartments joined by a hinge.
– ORIGIN late 19th cent.: named after W. E. **GLADSTONE**, who was noted for the amount of travelling he undertook when electioneering.

Glagolitic /ˌglagəˈlɪtɪk/ ▶ adjective denoting or relating to an alphabet based on Greek minuscules, formerly used in writing some Slavic languages.
▶ noun [mass noun] the Glagolitic alphabet.

> The alphabet is of uncertain origin, and was introduced in the 9th century, at about the same time as the Cyrillic alphabet, which has superseded it except in some Orthodox Church liturgies.

– ORIGIN from modern Latin *glagoliticus*, from *glagòljica*, the name in Croatian of the Glagolitic alphabet, from Old Church Slavonic *glagolŭ* 'word'.

glaikit /ˈgleɪkɪt/ ▶ adjective Scottish & N. English stupid, foolish, or thoughtless.
– ORIGIN late Middle English: related to Scots *glaiks* 'tricks, pranks'.

glair /glɛː/ ▶ noun [mass noun] a preparation made from egg white, especially as an adhesive for bookbinding and gilding.
– DERIVATIVES **glairy** adjective
– ORIGIN Middle English: from Old French *glaire*, based on Latin *clara*, feminine of *clarus* 'clear'.

glaive /gleɪv/ ▶ noun literary a sword.
– ORIGIN Middle English (denoting a lance or halberd): from Old French, apparently from Latin *gladius* 'sword'.

glam informal ▶ adjective glamorous: *a dapper magician and his glam assistant*. ■ relating to or denoting glam rock.
▶ noun [mass noun] glamour: *Nigel, for all his glam, was Karen's sort*. ■ glam rock.
▶ verb (**glams, glamming, glammed**) (**glam up** or **glam someone up**) make oneself or someone else look glamorous: [with obj.] *the girls get glammed up for a night on the town*.
– ORIGIN 1930s: abbreviation.

Glam. ▶ abbreviation Glamorgan.

glamazon /ˈglaməz(ə)n/ ▶ noun informal a glamorous, powerfully assertive woman.
– ORIGIN 1960s: from **GLAM** + **AMAZON**[2].

Glamorgan /gləˈmɔːg(ə)n/ a former county of South Wales. Welsh name **MORGANNWG**.

glamorize (also **glamourize** or **glamorise**) ▶ verb [with obj.] make (something) seem glamorous or desirable, especially spuriously so: *the lyrics glamorize drugs*.
– DERIVATIVES **glamorization** noun.

glamorous ▶ adjective having glamour: *one of the world's most glamorous women*.
– DERIVATIVES **glamorously** adverb.

> **USAGE** Note that although **glamor** is an American spelling of **glamour**, **glamorous** is not an American form. This word is spelled the same way in both British and American English, and **glamourous** is regarded as an error.

glamour (US also **glamor**) ▶ noun [mass noun] **1** an attractive or exciting quality that makes certain people or things seem appealing: *the glamour of Monte Carlo*. ■ beauty or charm that is sexually attractive: *pile hair up for evening glamour*. ■ [as modifier] denoting or relating to sexually suggestive or mildly pornographic photography or publications: *a glamour model*.
2 archaic enchantment; magic: *that maiden, made by glamour out of flowers*.
– ORIGIN early 18th cent. (originally Scots in the sense 'enchantment, magic'): alteration of **GRAMMAR**. Although *grammar* itself was not used in this sense, the Latin word *grammatica* (from which it derives) was often used in the Middle Ages to mean 'scholarship, learning', including the occult practices popularly associated with learning.

glamour girl ▶ noun a fashionable, attractive young woman, especially a model or film star.

glamour puss ▶ noun informal a glamorous person, typically a woman.

glam rock ▶ noun [mass noun] a style of rock music first popular in the early 1970s, characterized by male performers wearing exaggeratedly flamboyant clothes and make-up.

glance[1] ▶ verb [no obj., with adverbial of direction] **1** take a brief or hurried look: *Ginny* **glanced at** *her watch*. ■ (**glance at/through**) read quickly or cursorily: *I glanced through your personnel file last night*.
2 hit something at an angle and bounce off obliquely: *the stone* **glanced off** *a crag and hit Tom on the head*. ■ (of light) reflect off something with a brief flash: *sunlight* **glanced off** *the curved body of a dolphin*. ■ [with obj. and adverbial of direction] (in ball games) deflect (the ball) slightly with a delicate contact. ■ [with obj.] Cricket deflect (the ball) with the bat held slantwise; play such a stroke against (the bowler).
▶ noun **1** a brief or hurried look: *I stole* **a glance at** *John*.
2 archaic a flash or gleam of light.
3 Cricket a stroke with the bat's face turned slantwise to deflect the ball slightly.
– PHRASES **at a glance** immediately upon looking: *she saw at a glance what had happened*. **at first glance** when seen or considered briefly and for the first time: *good news, at first glance, for frequent travellers*. **glance one's eye** archaic look briefly.
– ORIGIN late Middle English (in the sense 'rebound obliquely'): probably a nasalized form of obsolete

glace in the same sense, from Old French *glacier* 'to slip', from *glace* 'ice', based on Latin *glacies*.

glance[2] ▶ **noun** [mass noun] a shiny black or grey sulphide ore of lead, copper, or other metal.
– ORIGIN late Middle English: from German *Glanz* 'brightness, lustre'; compare with Dutch *glanserts* 'glance ore'.

glancing ▶ **adjective** striking someone or something at an angle rather than directly and with full force: *he was struck a glancing blow*.
– DERIVATIVES **glancingly adverb**.

gland[1] ▶ **noun** an organ in the human or animal body which secretes particular chemical substances for use in the body or for discharge into the surroundings. ■ a structure resembling a gland, especially a lymph node. ■ Botany a secreting cell or group of cells on or within a plant structure.
– ORIGIN late 17th cent.: from French *glande*, alteration of Old French *glandre*, from Latin *glandulae* 'throat glands'.

gland[2] ▶ **noun** a sleeve used to produce a seal round a piston rod or other shaft.
– ORIGIN early 19th cent.: probably a variant of Scots *glam* 'a vice or clamp'; related to CLAMP[1].

G

glanders /ˈglandəz/ ▶ **plural noun** [usu. treated as sing.] a rare contagious disease that mainly affects horses, characterized by swellings below the jaw and mucous discharge from the nostrils. ● Glanders is caused by the bacterium *Pseudomonas mallei*.
– ORIGIN late 15th cent.: from Old French *glandre* (see GLAND[1]).

glandular /ˈglandjʊlə, ˈglan(d)ʒʊlə/ ▶ **adjective** relating to or affecting a gland or glands.
– ORIGIN mid 18th cent.: from French *glandulaire*, from *glandule* 'gland', from Latin *glandulae* (see GLAND[1]).

glandular fever ▶ **noun** [mass noun] Brit. an infectious viral disease characterized by swelling of the lymph glands and prolonged lassitude. Also called **infectious mononucleosis**.

glans /glanz/ ▶ **noun** (pl. **glandes** /ˈglandiːz/) Anatomy the rounded part forming the end of the penis or clitoris.
– ORIGIN mid 17th cent.: from Latin, literally 'acorn'.

glare ▶ **verb** [no obj.] **1** stare in an angry or fierce way: *she glared at him, her cheeks flushing*. ■ [with obj.] express (a feeling) by staring fiercely: *he glared defiance at the pistols pointing at him*.
2 [with adverbial] (of the sun or an electric light) shine with a strong or dazzling light: *the sun glared out of a clear blue sky*.
▶ **noun 1** a fierce or angry stare: *she gave Harley a glare of contempt*.
2 [mass noun] strong and dazzling light: *Murray narrowed his eyes against the glare of the sun*. ■ oppressive public attention: *he carried on his life in the full glare of publicity*.
3 [mass noun] archaic dazzling or showy appearance: *the pomp and glare of rhetoric*.
– DERIVATIVES **glary adjective**.
– ORIGIN Middle English (in the sense 'shine strongly'): from Middle Dutch and Middle Low German *glaren* 'to gleam, glare': perhaps related to GLASS. The sense 'stare' occurred first in the adjective *glaring* (late Middle English).

glare ice ▶ **noun** [mass noun] N. Amer. smooth, glassy ice.
– ORIGIN mid 19th cent.: probably from obsolete *glare* 'frost'; perhaps related to GLARE.

glareshield ▶ **noun** a screen attached to the cockpit canopy of an aircraft to reduce the effects of glare.

glaring ▶ **adjective 1** giving out or reflecting a strong or dazzling light.
2 staring fiercely or fixedly: *their glaring eyes*.
3 highly obvious or conspicuous: *there is a glaring omission in the data*.
– DERIVATIVES **glaringly adverb**.

Glasgow a city in Scotland on the River Clyde; pop. 578,700 (est. 2009). Formerly a major shipbuilding centre, it is the largest city in Scotland.

Glashow /ˈglaʃaʊ/, Sheldon Lee (b.1932), American theoretical physicist. He independently developed a unified theory to explain electromagnetic interactions and the weak nuclear force, and extended the quark theory of Murray Gell-Mann. Nobel Prize for Physics (1979, shared with Abdus Salam and Steven Weinberg).

glasnost /ˈglaznɒst, ˈglɑːs-/ ▶ **noun** [mass noun] (in the former Soviet Union) the policy or practice of more open consultative government and wider dissemination of information, initiated by leader Mikhail Gorbachev from 1985. See also PERESTROIKA.
– ORIGIN from Russian *glasnost'*, literally 'the fact of being public', from *glasnyy* 'public, open' + *-nost'* '-ness'.

Glass, Philip (b.1937), American composer, a leading minimalist. Notable works: *Einstein on the Beach* (opera, 1976), *Glass Pieces* (ballet, 1982), and *Low Symphony* (1993).

glass ▶ **noun 1** [mass noun] a hard, brittle substance, typically transparent or translucent, made by fusing sand with soda and lime and cooling rapidly. It is used to make windows, drinking containers, and other articles. ■ a substance similar to glass which has solidified from a molten state without crystallizing. ■ glassware. ■ greenhouses or cold frames considered collectively: *lettuces grown under glass*.
2 a drinking container made from glass: *a beer glass*. ■ the contents of a glass: *have a glass of wine*.
3 a lens, or an optical instrument containing a lens or lenses, in particular a monocle or a magnifying lens.
4 chiefly Brit. a mirror. ■ dated a weather glass. ■ archaic an hourglass.
▶ **verb** [with obj.] **1** cover or enclose with glass: *the inn has a long gallery, now glassed in*.
2 (especially in hunting) scan (one's surroundings) with binoculars: *the first day was spent glassing the rolling hills*.
3 Brit. informal hit (someone) in the face with a beer glass.
– PHRASES **the glass is half-full** (or **half-empty**) used to refer to an optimistic (or pessimistic) outlook on life: *she remains a person for whom the glass is always half-full, not half-empty* | *I like to think of myself as a glass half-full kind of guy*. **people** (**who live**) **in glass houses shouldn't throw stones** proverb you shouldn't criticize others when you have similar faults of your own.
– DERIVATIVES **glassful noun** (pl. **glassfuls**), **glassless adjective**, **glass-like adjective**.
– ORIGIN Old English *glæs*, of Germanic origin; related to Dutch *glas* and German *Glas*.

glass-blowing ▶ **noun** [mass noun] the craft of making glassware by blowing air into semi-molten glass through a long tube.
– DERIVATIVES **glass-blower noun**.

glass ceiling ▶ **noun** an unacknowledged barrier to advancement in a profession, especially affecting women and members of minorities.

glass cloth ▶ **noun 1** Brit. a cloth covered with powdered glass or other abrasive, used for smoothing and polishing.
2 [mass noun] woven fabric of fine-spun glass thread.

glass cutter ▶ **noun** a tool which scores a line on a piece of glass, allowing the glass to be snapped along the line.

glassed-in ▶ **adjective** (of a building or part of a building) covered or enclosed with glass.

glass eel ▶ **noun** an elver at the time that it first enters brackish or fresh water, when it is translucent.

glasses ▶ **plural noun** a pair of lenses set in a frame resting on the nose and ears, used to correct or assist defective eyesight. ■ a pair of binoculars.

glass eye ▶ **noun** a false eye made from glass.

glass fibre ▶ **noun** [mass noun] chiefly Brit. a strong plastic, textile, or other material containing embedded glass filaments for reinforcement.

glassfish ▶ **noun** (pl. **same** or **glassfishes**) a small fish with an almost transparent body, in particular: ● a marine or freshwater fish which is popular in aquaria (genus *Chanda*, family Centropomidae), including the **Indian glassfish** (*C. ranga*). ● an elongated marine fish of the West Pacific (*Salangichthys microdon*, family Salangidae), eaten as a delicacy in Japan.

glass harmonica ▶ **noun** a musical instrument in which the sound is made by a row of rotating, concentric glass bowls, kept moist and pressed with the fingers or with keys. It was invented in 1761 by Benjamin Franklin and was popular until about 1830.

glasshouse ▶ **noun** Brit. **1** a greenhouse.
2 military slang a prison.

glassine /ˈglɑːsiːn/ ▶ **noun** [mass noun] [usu. as modifier] a glossy transparent paper.
– ORIGIN early 20th cent.: from GLASS + -INE[4].

glass lizard ▶ **noun** a legless burrowing lizard of snake-like appearance, with smooth, shiny skin and an easily detached tail, native to Eurasia, Africa, and America. Also called GLASS SNAKE. ● Genus *Ophisaurus*, family Anguidae: several species.

glassmaking ▶ **noun** [mass noun] the manufacture of glass.
– DERIVATIVES **glassmaker noun**.

glasspaper ▶ **noun** [mass noun] paper covered with powdered glass, used for smoothing and polishing.

glass snake ▶ **noun** another term for GLASS LIZARD.

glass sponge ▶ **noun** a deep-water sponge which has a skeleton of intricately shaped spines of silica that may fuse to form a filmy lattice with a glass-like appearance. See also VENUS'S FLOWER BASKET. ● Class Hexactinellida.

glassware ▶ **noun** [mass noun] ornaments and articles made from glass.

glass wool ▶ **noun** [mass noun] glass in the form of fine fibres used for packing and insulation.

glassworks ▶ **noun** [treated as sing. or pl.] a factory where glass and glass articles are made.

glasswort ▶ **noun** a widely distributed salt-marsh plant with fleshy scale-like leaves. The ashes of the burnt plant were formerly used in glass-making. ● Genus *Salicornia*, family Chenopodiaceae: several species.

glassy ▶ **adjective** (**glassier**, **glassiest**) **1** of or resembling glass. ■ having the physical properties of glass; vitreous: *glassy lavas*. ■ (of water) having a smooth surface. ■ (of sound) resembling the sharp noise made when glass is struck: *a glassy clink*.
2 (of a person's eyes or expression) showing no interest or animation.
▶ **noun** (also **glassie**) dialect a glass marble.
– DERIVATIVES **glassily adverb**, **glassiness noun**.

Glastonbury /ˈglastənb(ə)ri/ a town in Somerset; pop. 9,000 (est. 2009). It is the legendary burial place of King Arthur and Queen Guinevere and the site of a ruined abbey held by legend to have been founded by Joseph of Arimathea.

Glaswegian /glazˈwiːdʒ(ə)n, glɑːz-/ ▶ **adjective** relating to Glasgow.
▶ **noun** a native of Glasgow. ■ [mass noun] the dialect or accent of people from Glasgow.
– ORIGIN from GLASGOW, on the pattern of words such as *Norwegian*.

glatt (also **glatt kosher**) ▶ **adjective** Judaism (of food) completely kosher; prepared according to a strict interpretation of Jewish dietary law.
– ORIGIN Yiddish, from German *glatt* 'smooth' + Hebrew *kāšēr* 'proper'.

Glatzer Neisse /ˈglatsə ˌnaɪsə/ German name for NEISSE (sense 2).

Glauber's salt /ˈglaʊbəz, ˈglɔː-/ ▶ **noun** (also **Glauber's salts**) a crystalline hydrated form of sodium sulphate, used chiefly as a laxative.
– ORIGIN mid 18th cent.: named after Johann R. *Glauber* (1604–1668), the German chemist who first produced the substance artificially.

glaucoma /glɔːˈkəʊmə/ ▶ **noun** [mass noun] Medicine a condition of increased pressure within the eyeball, causing gradual loss of sight.
– DERIVATIVES **glaucomatous adjective**.
– ORIGIN mid 17th cent.: via Latin from Greek *glaukōma*, based on *glaukos* 'bluish-green, bluish-grey' (because of the grey-green haze in the pupil).

glauconite /ˈglɔːkənʌɪt/ ▶ **noun** [mass noun] a greenish clay mineral of the illite group, found chiefly in marine sands.
– ORIGIN mid 19th cent.: from German *Glaukonit*, from Greek *glaukon* (neuter of *glaukos* 'bluish-green') + -ITE[1].

glaucophane /ˈglɔːkəfeɪn/ ▶ **noun** [mass noun] a bluish sodium-containing mineral of the amphibole group, found chiefly in schists and other metamorphic rocks.
– ORIGIN mid 19th cent.: from German *Glaukophan*, from Greek *glaukos* 'bluish-green' + *-phanēs* 'shining'.

glaucous /ˈglɔːkəs/ ▶ **adjective** technical or literary **1** of a dull greyish-green or blue colour.
2 covered with a powdery bloom like that on grapes.
– ORIGIN late 17th cent.: via Latin from Greek *glaukos* + -OUS.

glaucous gull ▶ **noun** a large white and pale grey gull breeding on Arctic coasts. ● *Larus hyperboreus*, family Laridae.

glaze ▶ **verb** [with obj.] **1** fit panes of glass into (a window or door frame or similar structure): *windows can be glazed using laminated glass*. ■ enclose or cover with glass: *the verandas were glazed in*.
2 overlay or cover (food, fabric, etc.) with a smooth, shiny coating or finish: *new potatoes which had been glazed in mint-flavoured butter*.

3 [no obj.] lose brightness and animation: *the prospect makes my eyes **glaze over** with boredom* | (as adj. **glazed**) *she had a glazed look in her eyes.*
▶ noun 1 a vitreous substance fused on to the surface of pottery to form an impervious decorative coating. ■ a smooth, shiny surface formed on pottery by glazing: *the glaze of the white cups.* ■ Art a thin topcoat of transparent paint used to modify the tone of an underlying colour.
2 a liquid such as milk or beaten egg used to form a smooth, shiny coating on food.
3 N. Amer. a thin, glassy coating of ice on the ground or water.
– DERIVATIVES **glazer** noun, **glazy** adjective.
– ORIGIN late Middle English *glase*, from GLASS.

glazed frost ▶ noun [mass noun] a glassy coating of ice, typically caused by rain freezing on impact.

glazier /ˈgleɪzɪə/ ▶ noun a person whose trade is fitting glass into windows and doors.

glazing ▶ noun 1 [mass noun] the action of installing windows. ■ glass windows: *sealed protective glazing.*
2 a glaze.

glazing bar ▶ noun a bar or rigid supporting strip between adjacent panes of glass.

GLBT (also **GLB**) ▶ abbreviation gay, lesbian, bisexual, or transgendered.

GLC ▶ abbreviation ■ Chemistry gas–liquid chromatography. ■ (in the UK) Greater London Council, abolished in 1986.

gleam ▶ verb [no obj.] shine brightly, especially with reflected light: *light gleamed on the china cats* | *her eyes gleamed with satisfaction.* ■ (of a smooth surface or object) reflect light because well polished: *Victor buffed the glass until it gleamed* | (as adj. **gleaming**) *gleaming black limousines.* ■ (of an emotion or quality) be expressed through the brightness of a person's eyes: *affection gleamed in her large green eyes.*
▶ noun a faint or brief light, especially one reflected from something: *the gleam of a silver tray.* ■ a brief or faint instance of a quality or emotion: *the **gleam of** hope vanished.* ■ an expression of an emotion or quality in a person's eyes: *she saw a **gleam of** triumph in his eyes.*
– PHRASES **a gleam in someone's eye** see EYE.
– DERIVATIVES **gleamingly** adverb, **gleamy** adjective (archaic).
– ORIGIN Old English *glǣm* 'brilliant light', of Germanic origin.

glean /gliːn/ ▶ verb [with obj.] 1 obtain (information) from various sources, often with difficulty: *the information is **gleaned from** press cuttings.* ■ collect gradually: *objects gleaned from local markets.*
2 historical gather (leftover grain) after a harvest.
– DERIVATIVES **gleaner** noun.
– ORIGIN late Middle English: from Old French *glener*, from late Latin *glennare*, probably of Celtic origin.

gleanings ▶ plural noun things, especially facts, that are gathered or collected from various sources rather than acquired as a whole.

glebe /gliːb/ ▶ noun 1 historical a piece of land serving as part of a clergyman's benefice and providing income.
2 [mass noun] archaic land; fields.
– ORIGIN late Middle English: from Latin *gleba, glaeba* 'clod, land, soil'.

glee ▶ noun 1 [mass noun] great delight, especially from one's own good fortune or another's misfortune: *his face lit up with impish glee.*
2 a song for men's voices in three or more parts, usually unaccompanied, of a type popular especially c.1750–1830.
– ORIGIN Old English *glēo* 'entertainment, music, fun', of Germanic origin.

glee club ▶ noun a society for singing part-songs.

gleeful ▶ adjective exuberantly or triumphantly joyful: *she gave a gleeful chuckle.*
– DERIVATIVES **gleefully** adverb, **gleefulness** noun.

gleeman ▶ noun (pl. **gleemen**) historical a professional entertainer, especially a singer.

gleesome ▶ adjective archaic gleeful.

gleet /gliːt/ ▶ noun [mass noun] Medicine a watery discharge from the urethra caused by gonorrhoeal infection.
– ORIGIN Middle English (denoting mucus formed in the stomach): from Old French *glette* 'slime, secretion', of unknown origin.

Gleichschaltung /ˈglʌɪxˌʃaltʊŋ/, German /ˈglaɪçˌʃaltʊŋ/ ▶ noun [mass noun] the standardization of political, economic, and social institutions as carried out in authoritarian states.
– ORIGIN German, from *gleich* 'same' + *schalten* 'force or bring into line'.

glen ▶ noun a narrow valley, especially in Scotland or Ireland.
– ORIGIN late Middle English: from Scottish Gaelic and Irish *gleann* (earlier *glenn*).

Glencoe, Massacre of /glɛnˈkəʊ/ a massacre in 1692 of members of the Jacobite MacDonald clan by Campbell soldiers, which took place near Glencoe in the Scottish Highlands.

Glendower /glɛnˈdaʊə/ (also **Glyndwr**), Owen (c.1354–c.1417), Welsh chief. He proclaimed himself Prince of Wales and led a national uprising against Henry IV.

Gleneagles /glɛnˈiːg(ə)lz/ a valley in eastern Scotland, south-west of Perth, site of a noted hotel and golfing centre.

glengarry ▶ noun (pl. **glengarries**) a brimless boat-shaped hat with a cleft down the centre, typically having two ribbons hanging at the back, worn as part of Highland dress.
– ORIGIN mid 19th cent.: from *Glengarry*, the name of a valley in the Highlands of Scotland.

Glen More another name for GREAT GLEN.

glenoid cavity /ˈgliːnɔɪd/ (also **glenoid fossa**) ▶ noun Anatomy a shallow depression on a bone into which another bone fits to form a joint, especially that on the scapula into which the head of the humerus fits.
– ORIGIN early 18th cent.: *glenoid* from French *glénoïde*, from Greek *glēnoeidēs*, from *glēnē* 'socket'.

Glenrothes /glɛnˈrɒθɪs/ a town in eastern Scotland, administrative centre of Fife region; pop. 38,900 (est. 2009).

gley /gleɪ/ ▶ noun Soil Science a sticky waterlogged soil lacking in oxygen, typically grey to blue in colour.
– ORIGIN 1920s: from Ukrainian, 'sticky blue clay'; related to CLAY.

glia /ˈglʌɪə, ˈgliːə/ ▶ noun [mass noun] Anatomy the connective tissue of the nervous system, consisting of several different types of cell associated with neurons. Also called NEUROGLIA.
– DERIVATIVES **glial** adjective.
– ORIGIN late 19th cent.: from Greek, literally 'glue'.

glib ▶ adjective (**glibber**, **glibbest**) (of words or a speaker) fluent but insincere and shallow: *the glib phrases soon roll off the tongue.*
– DERIVATIVES **glibly** adverb, **glibness** noun.
– ORIGIN late 16th cent. (also in the sense 'smooth, unimpeded'): ultimately of Germanic origin; related to Dutch 'slippery' and German *glibberig* 'slimy'.

glide ▶ verb 1 [no obj., with adverbial of direction] move with a smooth, quiet continuous motion: *a few gondolas glided past.* ■ [with obj. and adverbial of direction] move (something) with a smooth continuous motion.
2 [no obj.] make an unpowered flight, either in a glider or in an aircraft with engine failure. ■ (of a bird) fly with very little movement of the wings.
▶ noun [in sing.] 1 a gliding movement. ■ a smooth continuous step in ballroom dancing. ■ a flight in a glider or unpowered aircraft.
2 Phonetics a sound produced as the vocal organs move towards or away from articulation of a vowel or consonant, for example /j/ in *duke* /djuːk/.
3 Cricket a glancing stroke which slightly deflects the ball, especially towards the leg side.
– ORIGIN Old English *glīdan*, of Germanic origin; related to Dutch *glijden* and German *gleiten*.

glide path ▶ noun an aircraft's line of descent to land, especially as indicated by ground radar. ■ a series of events or actions leading smoothly to a particular outcome: *we are on a glide path to success.*

glider ▶ noun 1 a light aircraft that is designed to fly without using an engine.
2 a person or thing that glides. ■ another term for FLYING PHALANGER.
3 US a long swinging seat suspended from a frame in a porch.

glide reflection ▶ noun Mathematics a transformation consisting of a translation combined with a reflection about a plane parallel to the direction of the translation.

gliding ▶ noun [mass noun] the sport of flying in a glider.

glim ▶ noun archaic, informal a candle or lantern.
– ORIGIN late Middle English (denoting brightness): perhaps an abbreviation of GLIMMER. The current sense dates from the late 17th cent.

glimmer ▶ verb [no obj.] shine faintly with a wavering light: *the moonlight glimmered on the lawn* | (as adj. **glimmering**) *pools of glimmering light.*
▶ noun 1 a faint or wavering light.
2 a faint sign of a feeling or quality, especially a desirable one: *there is one glimmer of hope for Becky.*
– DERIVATIVES **glimmeringly** adverb.
– ORIGIN late Middle English: probably of Scandinavian origin; related to Swedish *glimra* and Danish *glimre*.

glimmering ▶ noun a glimmer.

glimpse ▶ noun a momentary or partial view: *she caught a glimpse of the ocean.* ■ a brief insight or indication: *during the interview he offered a behind-the-scenes glimpse of television.*
▶ verb [with obj.] see or perceive briefly or partially: *he glimpsed a figure standing in the shade.* ■ [no obj.] archaic shine or appear faintly or intermittently: *glow-worms glimpsing in the dark.*
– ORIGIN Middle English (in the sense 'shine faintly'): probably of Germanic origin; related to Middle High German *glimsen*, also to GLIMMER.

Glinka /ˈglɪŋkə/, Mikhail (Ivanovich) (1804–57), Russian composer. Regarded as the father of the Russian national school of music, he is best known for his operas *A Life for the Tsar* (1836) and *Russlan and Ludmilla* (1842).

glint ▶ verb [no obj.] give out or reflect small flashes of light: *her glasses glinted in the firelight.* ■ (of a person's eyes) shine with a particular emotion: *his eyes glinted angrily.*
▶ noun a small flash of light, especially a reflected one: *the glint of gold in his teeth.* ■ [in sing.] an expression of an emotion in a person's eyes: *she saw the glint of excitement in his eyes.*
– ORIGIN Middle English (in the sense 'move quickly or obliquely'): variant of dialect *glent*, probably of Scandinavian origin and related to Swedish dialect *glänta, glinta* 'to slip, slide, gleam'.

glioblastoma /ˌglʌɪə(ʊ)blaˈstəʊmə/ ▶ noun (pl. **glioblastomas** or **glioblastomata** /-mətə/) Medicine a highly invasive glioma in the brain.

glioma /glʌɪˈəʊmə/ ▶ noun (pl. **gliomas** or **gliomata** /-mətə/) Medicine a malignant tumour of the glial tissue of the nervous system.
– ORIGIN late 19th cent.: from Greek *glia* 'glue' + -OMA.

glissade /glɪˈsɑːd, -ˈseɪd/ ▶ noun 1 a way of sliding down a steep slope of snow or ice, typically on the feet with the support of an ice axe.
2 Ballet a movement, typically used as a joining step, in which one leg is brushed outwards from the body, which then takes the weight while the second leg is brushed in to meet it.
▶ verb [no obj.] slide down a steep slope of snow or ice with the support of an ice axe.
– ORIGIN mid 19th cent.: French, from *glisser* 'to slip, slide'.

glissando /glɪˈsandəʊ/ ▶ noun (pl. **glissandi** /-di/ or **glissandos**) Music a continuous slide upwards or downwards between two notes.
– ORIGIN Italian, from French *glissant*, present participle of *glisser* 'to slip, slide'.

glissé /gliːˈseɪ/ ▶ noun (pl. pronunc. **same**) Ballet a movement in which weight is transferred from one foot, which is slid outward from the body and briefly extended off the ground, to the other, which is then brought to meet it.
– ORIGIN French, literally 'slipped, glided', past participle of *glisser*.

glisten ▶ verb [no obj.] (of something wet or greasy) shine with a sparkling light: *his cheeks glistened with tears* | (as adj. **glistening**) *the glistening pavements.*
▶ noun [in sing.] a sparkling light reflected from something wet.
– ORIGIN Old English *glisnian*, of Germanic origin; related to Middle Low German *glisen*. The noun dates from the mid 19th cent.

glister /ˈglɪstə/ literary ▶ verb [no obj.] sparkle; glitter.
▶ noun a sparkle.
– ORIGIN late Middle English: probably from Middle Low German *glistern* or Middle Dutch *glisteren*.

glitch informal ▶ noun a sudden, usually temporary malfunction or fault of equipment: *a draft version was lost in a computer glitch.* ■ an unexpected setback: *the only glitch in his year is failing to qualify for the Masters.* ■ Astronomy a brief irregularity in the rotation of a pulsar.
▶ verb [no obj.] chiefly US suffer a sudden malfunction or fault: *the elevators glitched.*

G

– ORIGIN 1960s (originally US): of unknown origin. The original sense was 'a sudden surge of current', hence 'malfunction, hitch' in astronautical slang.

glitchy ▶ **adjective** informal prone to glitches.

glitter ▶ **verb** [no obj.] shine with a bright, shimmering reflected light: *the grass glittered with dew.* ■ (of eyes) shine with a particular emotion: *her eyes glittered with excitement.*
▶ **noun 1** [in sing.] a bright, shimmering reflected light: *the blue glitter of the sea.* ■ an expression of an emotion in a person's eyes: *the scathing glitter in his eyes.*
2 [mass noun] tiny pieces of sparkling material used for decoration: *sneakers trimmed with sequins and glitter.*
3 [mass noun] an attractive and exciting but superficial quality: *he avoids the glitter of show business.*
– PHRASES **all that glitters is not gold** proverb the attractive external appearance of something is not a reliable indication of its true nature.
– DERIVATIVES **glittery** adjective.
– ORIGIN late Middle English: from Old Norse *glitra*.

G

glitterati /ˌglɪtəˈrɑːti/ ▶ **plural noun** informal the fashionable set of people engaged in show business or some other glamorous activity.
– ORIGIN 1950s (originally US): blend of GLITTER and LITERATI.

glittering ▶ **adjective** shining with a shimmering or sparkling light: *glittering chandeliers.* ■ impressively successful or elaborate: *a glittering military career.*
– DERIVATIVES **glitteringly** adverb.

Glittertind /ˈglɪtətɪn/ a mountain in Norway, in the Jotunheim range. Rising to 2,470 m (8,104 ft), it is the highest mountain in the country.

glitz informal ▶ **noun** [mass noun] extravagant but superficial display: *the glitz and sophisticated night life of Ibiza.*
▶ **verb** [with obj.] N. Amer. make (something) glamorous or showy.
– ORIGIN 1970s (originally a North American usage): back-formation from GLITZY.

glitzy ▶ **adjective** (**glitzier**, **glitziest**) informal attractive in a showy and often superficial way: *glitzy hotel restaurants.*
– DERIVATIVES **glitzily** adverb, **glitziness** noun.
– ORIGIN 1960s (originally a North American usage): from GLITTER, suggested by RITZY, and perhaps also by German *glitzerig* 'glittering'.

Gliwice /gliːˈviːtsə/ a mining and industrial city in southern Poland, near the border with the Czech Republic; pop. 197,874 (2007).

gloaming ▶ **noun** (**the gloaming**) literary twilight; dusk.
– ORIGIN Old English *glōmung*, from *glōm* 'twilight', of Germanic origin; related to GLOW.

gloat ▶ **verb** [no obj.] dwell on one's own success or another's misfortune with smugness or malignant pleasure: *his enemies **gloated over** his death* | (as adj. **gloating**) *gloating accounts of his triumphs.*
▶ **noun** [in sing.] informal an act of gloating.
– DERIVATIVES **gloater** noun, **gloatingly** adverb.
– ORIGIN late 16th cent.: of unknown origin; perhaps related to Old Norse *glotta* 'to grin' and Middle High German *glotzen* 'to stare'. The original sense was 'give a sideways or furtive look', hence 'cast amorous or admiring glances'; the current sense dates from the mid 18th cent.

glob ▶ **noun** informal a lump of a semi-liquid substance: *thick **globs of** mozzarella cheese.*
– ORIGIN early 20th cent.: perhaps a blend of BLOB and GOB².

global /ˈgləʊb(ə)l/ ▶ **adjective 1** relating to the whole world; worldwide: *the downturn in the global economy.*
2 relating to or encompassing the whole of something, or of a group of things: *give students a global picture of what is involved in the task.* ■ Computing operating or applying through the whole of a file, program, etc.: *global searches.*
– DERIVATIVES **globally** adverb.

global distillation ▶ **noun** [mass noun] a process whereby certain volatile substances vaporize in warm climates and condense in cooler areas, causing the accumulation of pollutants.

globalism ▶ **noun** [mass noun] the operation or planning of economic and foreign policy on a global basis.
– DERIVATIVES **globalist** noun & adjective.

globalization (also **globalisation**) ▶ **noun** [mass noun] the process by which businesses or other organizations develop international influence or start operating on an international scale: *fears about the increasing globalization of the world economy.*
– DERIVATIVES **globalize** verb, **globalizer** noun.

Global Surveyor (in full **Mars Global Surveyor**) an unmanned American spacecraft which went into orbit around Mars in 1997 to begin detailed photography and mapping of the surface. Contact with the spacecraft was lost in 2006.

global village ▶ **noun** the world considered as a single community linked by telecommunications.

global warming ▶ **noun** [mass noun] a gradual increase in the overall temperature of the earth's atmosphere generally attributed to the greenhouse effect caused by increased levels of carbon dioxide, CFCs, and other pollutants.

WORD TRENDS See CLIMATE CHANGE.

globe ▶ **noun 1** (**the globe**) the earth: *goods from all over the globe.* ■ a spherical representation of the earth or of the constellations with a map on the surface.
2 a spherical or rounded object: *orange trees clipped into giant globes.* ■ a golden orb as an emblem of sovereignty.
3 Austral./NZ a lightbulb.
▶ **verb** [with obj.] literary form (something) into a globe.
– DERIVATIVES **globe-like** adjective, **globoid** adjective & noun, **globose** adjective.
– ORIGIN late Middle English (in the sense 'spherical object'): from Old French, or from Latin *globus*.

globe artichoke ▶ **noun** see ARTICHOKE (sense 1).

globefish ▶ **noun** (pl. **same** or **globefishes**) a pufferfish or porcupine fish.

globeflower ▶ **noun** a plant of the buttercup family with globular yellow or orange flowers, native to north temperate regions. ● Genus *Trollius*, family Ranunculaceae.

Globe Theatre a theatre in Southwark, London, erected in 1599, where many of Shakespeare's plays were first publicly performed. The theatre's site was rediscovered in 1989 and a reconstruction of the original theatre was opened in 1997.

globe thistle ▶ **noun** an Old World thistle with globe-shaped heads of metallic blue-grey flowers. ● Genus *Echinops*, family Compositae.

globetrotter ▶ **noun** informal a person who travels widely.
– DERIVATIVES **globetrot** verb, **globetrotting** noun & adjective.

globigerina /ˌgləʊbɪdʒəˈrʌɪnə/ ▶ **noun** (pl. **globigerinas** or **globigerinae** /-niː/) a planktonic marine protozoan with a calcareous shell. The shells collect as a deposit (**globigerina ooze**) over much of the ocean floor. ● Genus *Globigerina*, order Foraminiferida, kingdom Protista.
– ORIGIN modern Latin, from Latin *globus* 'spherical object, globe' (because of the globular chambers in its shell) + *-ger* 'carrying' + -INA.

globular /ˈglɒbjʊlə/ ▶ **adjective 1** globe-shaped; spherical.
2 composed of globules.
▶ **noun** Astronomy short for GLOBULAR CLUSTER.
– DERIVATIVES **globularity** noun.

globular cluster ▶ **noun** Astronomy a large compact spherical star cluster, typically of old stars in the outer regions of a galaxy.

globule /ˈglɒbjuːl/ ▶ **noun 1** a small round particle of a substance; a drop: ***globules of** fat.*
2 Astronomy a small dark cloud of gas and dust seen against a brighter background such as a luminous nebula.
– DERIVATIVES **globulous** adjective.
– ORIGIN mid 17th cent.: from French, or from Latin *globulus*, diminutive of *globus* 'spherical object, globe'.

globulin /ˈglɒbjʊlɪn/ ▶ **noun** Biochemistry any of a group of simple proteins soluble in salt solutions and forming a large fraction of blood serum protein.
– ORIGIN mid 19th cent.: from GLOBULE (in the archaic sense 'blood corpuscle') + -IN¹.

globus hystericus /ˌgləʊbəs hɪˈstɛrɪkəs/ ▶ **noun** [mass noun] Medicine the sensation of a lump in the throat, as a symptom of anxiety or hysteria.
– ORIGIN late 18th cent.: from Latin.

globus pallidus /ˈpalɪdəs/ ▶ **noun** Anatomy the median part of the lentiform nucleus in the brain.
– ORIGIN late 18th cent.: from Latin, 'pale globus'.

glocalization (also **glocalisation**) ▶ **noun** [mass noun] the practice of conducting business according to both local and global considerations.
– ORIGIN 1990s: blend of GLOBAL + LOCALIZATION.

glochid /ˈgləʊkɪd/ ▶ **noun** Botany a barbed bristle on the areole of some cacti.
– ORIGIN late 19th cent.: from Greek *glōkhis*, *glōkhid-* 'arrowhead'.

glochidium /gləʊˈkɪdɪəm/ ▶ **noun** (pl. **glochidia**) Zoology a parasitic larva of certain freshwater bivalve molluscs, which attaches itself by hooks and suckers to the fins or gills of fish.
– ORIGIN late 19th cent.: modern Latin, based on Greek *glōkhis*, *glōkhid-* 'arrowhead'.

glockenspiel /ˈglɒk(ə)nspiːl, -ʃpiːl/ ▶ **noun** a musical percussion instrument having a set of tuned metal pieces mounted in a frame and struck with small hammers.
– ORIGIN early 19th cent. (denoting an organ stop imitating the sound of bells): from German *Glockenspiel*, literally 'bell play'.

glögg /gləːg/ (also **glugg** /glʌg/) ▶ **noun** [mass noun] a type of Scandinavian mulled wine made with brandy, almonds, raisins, and spices.
– ORIGIN Swedish.

glom /glɒm/ ▶ **verb** (**gloms**, **glomming**, **glommed**) N. Amer. informal **1** [with obj.] steal: *I thought he was about to glom my wallet.*
2 [no obj.] (**glom on to**) become stuck or attached to.
– ORIGIN early 20th cent.: variant of Scots *glaum*, of unknown origin.

glomerulonephritis /glɒˌmɛrjʊləʊnɪˈfrʌɪtɪs/ ▶ **noun** [mass noun] Medicine acute inflammation of the kidney, typically caused by an immune response.

glomerulus /glɒˈmɛr(j)ʊləs/ ▶ **noun** (pl. **glomeruli** /-lʌɪ, -liː/) Anatomy & Biology a cluster of nerve endings, spores, or small blood vessels, especially a cluster of capillaries around the end of a kidney tubule.
– DERIVATIVES **glomerular** adjective.
– ORIGIN mid 19th cent.: modern Latin, diminutive of Latin *glomus*, *glomer-* 'ball of thread'.

gloom ▶ **noun** [mass noun] **1** partial or total darkness: *he strained his eyes peering into the gloom.* ■ [count noun] literary a dark or shady place.
2 a state of depression or despondency: *a year of economic gloom for the car industry* | *his gloom deepened.*
▶ **verb** [no obj.] **1** literary have a dark or sombre appearance: *the black gibbet glooms beside the way.* ■ [with obj.] make dark or dismal.
2 be or look depressed or despondent: *Charles was always glooming about money.*
– PHRASES **gloom and doom** see DOOM.
– ORIGIN late Middle English (as a verb): of unknown origin.

gloomy ▶ **adjective** (**gloomier**, **gloomiest**) **1** dark or poorly lit, especially so as to appear depressing or frightening: *a gloomy corridor badly lit by oil lamps.*
2 causing or feeling depression or despondency: *gloomy forecasts about the economy.*
– DERIVATIVES **gloomily** adverb, **gloominess** noun.

gloop ▶ **noun** [mass noun] informal sloppy or sticky semi-fluid matter, typically something unpleasant.
– DERIVATIVES **gloopy** adjective.
– ORIGIN 1960s: the letters *gl*, *o*, and *p* are said to be symbolic of semi-liquid matter (compare with GLOP).

glop informal, chiefly N. Amer. ▶ **noun** [mass noun] sticky and amorphous matter, typically something unpleasant: *a cup of vile green glop.* ■ [count noun] a soft, shapeless lump of something: *a **glop of** creamy dressing.* ■ worthless writing, music, or other material.
▶ **verb** (**glops**, **glopping**, **glopped**) [with obj. and adverbial of direction] transfer (a sloppy or sticky substance) to a container: *glop 2 gallons of premixed compound into a bucket.*
– DERIVATIVES **gloppy** adjective (**gloppier**, **gloppiest**).
– ORIGIN 1940s: symbolic (see GLOOP).

Gloria ▶ **noun** a Christian liturgical hymn or formula beginning (in the Latin text) with *Gloria*, in particular: ■ the hymn beginning *Gloria in excelsis Deo* (Glory be to God in the highest), forming a set part of the Mass. ■ the doxology beginning *Gloria Patris* (Glory be to the Father), used after psalms and in formal prayer (e.g. in the rosary).
– ORIGIN Latin, 'glory'.

Gloriana /ˌglɔːrɪˈɑːnə/ the nickname of Queen Elizabeth I.

glorified ▶ **adjective 1** [attrib.] (of something or someone ordinary or unexceptional) represented as or appearing more elevated or special than is the

case: *I did the paperwork and was basically a glorified secretary.*
2 (in religious contexts) made glorious: *the transformed and glorified Jesus.*

glorify ▶ verb (**glorifies, glorifying, glorified**) [with obj.] **1** praise and worship (God). ■ reveal the glory of (God) by one's actions: *God can be glorified through a life of scholarship.*
2 describe or represent as admirable, especially unjustifiably: *a football video glorifying violence.*
– DERIVATIVES **glorification** noun, **glorifier** noun.
– ORIGIN Middle English: from Old French *glorifier*, from ecclesiastical Latin *glorificare*, from late Latin *glorificus*, from Latin *gloria* 'glory'.

gloriole /ˈglɔːrɪəʊl/ ▶ noun literary a halo or aureole.
– ORIGIN mid 19th cent.: French, from Latin *gloriola*, diminutive of *gloria* 'glory'.

glorious ▶ adjective **1** having, worthy of, or bringing fame or admiration: *the most glorious victory of all time.*
2 having a striking beauty or splendour: *a glorious autumn day.* ■ informal very enjoyable: *glorious platters of succulent crabs.*
– DERIVATIVES **gloriously** adverb, **gloriousness** noun.
– ORIGIN Middle English: from Old French *glorieus*, from Latin *gloriosus*, from *gloria* 'glory'.

Glorious Revolution the events (1688–9) that led to the replacement, in 1689, of James II by his daughter Mary II and her husband William of Orange (who became William III) as joint monarchs. The bloodless 'revolution' greatly enhanced the constitutional powers of Parliament, with William and Mary's acceptance of the conditions laid down in the Bill of Rights.

glory ▶ noun (pl. **glories**) [mass noun] **1** high renown or honour won by notable achievements: *to fight and die for the glory of one's nation.*
2 magnificence or great beauty: *the train has been restored to all its former glory.* ■ [count noun] (often **glories**) a thing that is beautiful, impressive, or worthy of praise: *the glories of Paris.* ■ the splendour and bliss of heaven: *images of Christ in glory.*
3 praise, worship, and thanksgiving offered to God.
4 [count noun] a luminous ring or halo, especially as depicted around the head of Christ or a saint.
▶ verb [no obj.] (**glory in**) take great pride or pleasure in: *they gloried in their independence.* ■ exult in unpleasantly or boastfully: *readers tended to defend their paper or even to glory in its bias.*
– PHRASES **glory be!** expressing enthusiastic piety. ■ informal used as an exclamation of surprise or delight. **to glory** to death or destruction. **in one's glory** informal in a state of extreme joy or exaltation.
– ORIGIN Middle English: from Old French *glorie*, from Latin *gloria*.

glory box ▶ noun Austral./NZ a box for a woman's clothes and household items, stored in preparation for marriage.

glory days ▶ plural noun a time in the past regarded as being better than the present: *the glory days of Silicon Valley.*

glory hole ▶ noun **1** informal an untidy room or cupboard used for storage.
2 N. Amer. an open quarry.
3 a small furnace used to keep glass malleable so that it can be worked.
4 US informal a hole in a wall through which fellatio or masturbation is conducted incognito between male homosexuals.
– ORIGIN early 19th cent.: of unknown origin.

glory-of-the-snow ▶ noun another term for CHIONODOXA.

glory pea ▶ noun another term for CLIANTHUS.

Glos. ▶ abbreviation Gloucestershire.

gloss[1] ▶ noun [mass noun] **1** shine or lustre on a smooth surface: *hair with a healthy gloss.* ■ (also **gloss paint**) a type of paint which dries to a bright shiny surface.
2 [in sing.] a superficially attractive appearance or impression: *beneath the gloss of success was a tragic private life.*
▶ verb [with obj.] **1** apply a glossy substance to.
2 (**gloss over**) try to conceal or disguise (something unfavourable) by treating it briefly or representing it misleadingly: *the social costs of this growth are glossed over.*
– DERIVATIVES **glosser** noun.
– ORIGIN mid 16th cent.: of unknown origin.

gloss[2] ▶ noun a translation or explanation of a word or phrase. ■ an explanation, interpretation, or paraphrase of a text: *the chapter acts as a helpful gloss on Pynchon's general method.*
▶ verb [with obj.] provide an explanation, interpretation, or paraphrase for (a text, word, etc.). ■ [no obj.] (**gloss on/upon**) archaic make comments, especially unfavourable ones, about (something).
– ORIGIN mid 16th cent.: alteration of the noun *gloze*, from Old French *glose* (see GLOZE), suggested by medieval Latin *glossa* 'explanation of a difficult word', from Greek *glōssa* 'word needing explanation, language, tongue'.

glossal /ˈglɒs(ə)l/ ▶ adjective Anatomy, rare of the tongue; lingual.
– ORIGIN early 19th cent.: from Greek *glōssa* 'tongue' + -AL.

glossary ▶ noun (pl. **glossaries**) an alphabetical list of words relating to a specific subject, text, or dialect, with explanations; a brief dictionary.
– DERIVATIVES **glossarial** adjective,.
– ORIGIN late Middle English: from Latin *glossarium*, from *glossa* (see GLOSS[2]).

glossator /glɒˈseɪtə/ ▶ noun chiefly historical a person who writes glosses, especially a scholarly commentator on the texts of classical, civil, or canon law.
– ORIGIN late Middle English: from medieval Latin, from *glossare*, from Latin *glossa* (see GLOSS[2]).

glossitis /glɒˈsʌɪtɪs/ ▶ noun [mass noun] Medicine inflammation of the tongue.
– ORIGIN early 19th cent.: from Greek *glōssa* 'tongue' + -ITIS.

glossographer /glɒˈsɒgrəfə/ ▶ noun a writer of glosses or commentaries.

glossolalia /ˌglɒsəˈleɪlɪə/ ▶ noun [mass noun] the phenomenon of (apparently) speaking in an unknown language, especially in religious worship. It is practised especially by Pentecostal and charismatic Christians.
– DERIVATIVES **glossolalic** adjective.
– ORIGIN late 19th cent.: from Greek *glōssa* 'language, tongue' + *lalia* 'speech'.

glossopharyngeal /ˌglɒsəʊfəˈrɪn(d)ʒɪəl, -ˌfar(ə)nˈdʒiːəl/ ▶ adjective relating to the tongue and pharynx.
– ORIGIN early 19th cent.: from Greek *glōssa* 'tongue' + *pharyngeal* (from modern Latin *pharynx*, *pharyng-* 'pharynx').

glossopharyngeal nerve ▶ noun Anatomy each of the ninth pair of cranial nerves, supplying the tongue and pharynx.

glossy ▶ adjective (**glossier, glossiest**) **1** shiny and smooth: *thick, glossy, manageable hair.* ■ (of a magazine or photograph) printed on high-quality smooth shiny paper.
2 superficially attractive, stylish, and suggesting wealth: *a glossy TV miniseries.*
▶ noun (pl. **glossies**) informal a magazine printed on glossy paper with many colour photographs. ■ a photograph printed on glossy paper.
– DERIVATIVES **glossily** adverb, **glossiness** noun.

glossy starling ▶ noun an African starling with dark glossy plumage that has metallic blue, green, and purple reflections. ● Genus *Lamprotornis*, family Sturnidae: several species.

glost ▶ noun the second firing of ceramic ware, in which the glaze is fused: [as modifier] *a glost kiln.*
– ORIGIN late 19th cent.: apparently a dialect alteration of GLOSS[1].

glottal ▶ adjective of or produced by the glottis.

glottal stop ▶ noun a consonant formed by the audible release of the airstream after complete closure of the glottis. It is widespread in some non-standard English accents and in some other languages, such as Arabic, it is a standard consonant.

glottis /ˈglɒtɪs/ ▶ noun the part of the larynx consisting of the vocal cords and the slit-like opening between them. It affects voice modulation through expansion or contraction.
– DERIVATIVES **glottic** adjective.
– ORIGIN late 16th cent.: modern Latin, from Greek *glōttis*, from *glōtta*, variant of *glōssa* 'tongue'.

glottochronology /ˌglɒtəʊkrəˈnɒlədʒi/ ▶ noun [mass noun] the use of statistical data to date the divergence of languages from their common sources.
– DERIVATIVES **glottochronological** adjective.

Gloucester /ˈglɒstə/ a city in SW England, the county town of Gloucestershire; pop. 127,100 (est. 2009). It was founded by the Romans, who called it Glevum, in AD 96.

Gloucester Old Spot ▶ noun a pig of a white breed with black spots, now rarely kept commercially.

Gloucestershire a county of SW England; county town, Gloucester.

glove ▶ noun a covering for the hand worn for protection against cold or dirt and typically having separate parts for each finger and the thumb. ■ a padded protective covering for the hand used in boxing, cricket, baseball, and other sports.
▶ verb [with obj.] informal (of a wicketkeeper, baseball catcher, etc.) catch, deflect, or touch (the ball) with a gloved hand.
– PHRASES **fit someone like a glove** (of clothes) fit someone exactly. **the gloves are off** (or **with the gloves off** or **take the gloves off**) used to express the notion that something will be done in an uncompromising or ruthless way: *for the banks chasing this growing business, the gloves are now definitely off.*
– DERIVATIVES **gloved** adjective, **gloveless** adjective.
– ORIGIN Old English *glōf*, of Germanic origin.

glovebox ▶ noun **1** a glove compartment in a vehicle.
2 a closed chamber with sealed-in gloves for handling radioactive or other hazardous material.

glove compartment ▶ noun a recess with a flap in the dashboard of a motor vehicle, used for storing small items.

glove puppet ▶ noun Brit. a cloth puppet fitted on the hand and worked by the fingers.

glover ▶ noun a maker of gloves.

glow ▶ verb [no obj.] give out steady light without flame: *the tips of their cigarettes glowed in the dark.* ■ have an intense colour and a slight shine: [with complement] *a fluorescent screen glowed a faint green colour.* ■ (of a person's face) appear pink or red as a result of warmth, health, embarrassment, etc.: *he was glowing with health.* ■ convey deep pleasure through one's expression or bearing: *Katy always glowed when he praised her.*
▶ noun [in sing.] a steady radiance of light or heat: *the setting sun cast a deep red glow over the city.* ■ a feeling of warmth in the face or body: *he could feel the brandy filling him with a warm glow.* ■ a redness of the cheeks. ■ a strong feeling of pleasure or well-being: *with a glow of pride, Mildred walked away.*
– ORIGIN Old English *glōwan*, of Germanic origin; related to Dutch *gloeien* and German *glühen*.

glow discharge ▶ noun a luminous sparkless electrical discharge from a pointed conductor in a gas at low pressure.

glower /ˈglaʊə/ ▶ verb [no obj.] have an angry or sullen look on one's face; scowl: *she glowered at him suspiciously* | [as adjective] (**glowering**) *his father's glowering face.*
▶ noun [in sing.] an angry or sullen look.
– DERIVATIVES **gloweringly** adverb.
– ORIGIN late 15th cent.: perhaps a Scots variant of synonymous dialect *glore*, or from obsolete *glow* 'to stare', both possibly of Scandinavian origin.

glowing ▶ adjective expressing great praise: *he received a glowing report from his teachers.*
– DERIVATIVES **glowingly** adverb.

glow stick ▶ noun a novelty item consisting of a plastic tube containing two chemicals which combine when the tube is bent, so producing a luminescent glow.

glow-worm ▶ noun a soft-bodied beetle with luminescent organs in the abdomen, especially the larvalike wingless female which emits light to attract the flying male. ● Families Lampyridae (in particular the European *Lampyris noctiluca*) and Phengodidae (in particular the American *Zarhipis integripennis*).

gloxinia /glɒkˈsɪnɪə/ ▶ noun a tropical American plant with large, velvety, bell-shaped flowers. ● Genera *Gloxinia* and *Sinningia*, family Gesneriaceae: several species, in particular the florists' gloxinia (*S. speciosa*), which is a popular houseplant.
– ORIGIN modern Latin, named after Benjamin P. *Gloxin*, the 18th-cent. German botanist who first described it.

gloze /gləʊz/ ▶ verb **1** [with obj.] literary make excuses for: *the demeanour of Mathews is rather glozed over.*
2 [no obj.] archaic use ingratiating language.
3 [no obj.] archaic make a comment or comments.
– ORIGIN Middle English: from Old French *gloser*, from *glose* 'a gloss, comment', based on Latin *glossa* (see GLOSS[2]).

glucagon /ˈgluːkəg(ə)n, -gɒn/ ▶ noun [mass noun] Biochemistry a hormone formed in the pancreas which promotes the breakdown of glycogen to glucose in the liver.

G

– ORIGIN 1920s: from Greek *glukus* 'sweet' + *agōn* 'leading, bringing'.

glucan /ˈgluːkan/ ▶ **noun** Biochemistry a polysaccharide consisting of glucose units.
– ORIGIN 1940s: from GLUCOSE + -AN.

Gluck /glʊk/, Christoph Willibald von (1714–87), German composer. Gluck is noted for operas in which he sought a balance of music and drama and reduced the emphasis on the star singer. Examples are *Orfeo ed Euridice* (1762) and *Iphigénie en Aulide* (1774).

glucocorticoid /ˌgluːkə(ʊ)ˈkɔːtɪkɔɪd/ ▶ **noun** Biochemistry any of a group of corticosteroids (e.g. hydrocortisone) which are involved in the metabolism of carbohydrates, proteins, and fats and have anti-inflammatory activity.

glucosamine /gluːˈkəʊsəmiːn/ ▶ **noun** Biochemistry a crystalline compound which occurs widely in connective tissue, especially as a component of chitin.
● A glucose derivative containing an amino group; chem. formula: $C_6H_{13}NO_5$.
■ a synthesized form of this, taken to relieve arthritis pain.

G

glucose /ˈgluːkəʊs, -z/ ▶ **noun** [mass noun] a simple sugar which is an important energy source in living organisms and is a component of many carbohydrates. ● A hexose; chem. formula: $C_6H_{12}O_6$.
■ a syrup containing glucose and other sugars, made by hydrolysis of starch and used in the food industry.
– ORIGIN mid 19th cent.: from French, from Greek *gleukos* 'sweet wine', related to *glukus* 'sweet'.

glucoside /ˈgluːkəsʌɪd/ ▶ **noun** Biochemistry a glycoside derived from glucose.
– DERIVATIVES **glucosidic** adjective.

glucuronate /gluːˈkjʊərəneɪt/ ▶ **noun** Biochemistry a salt or ester of glucuronic acid.

glucuronic acid /ˌgluːkjʊˈrɒnɪk/ ▶ **noun** [mass noun] Biochemistry an acid derived from glucose which occurs naturally as a constituent of hyaluronic acid and other mucopolysaccharides. ● A uronic acid; chem. formula: $HOOC(CHOH)_4CHO$.

glue ▶ **noun** [mass noun] an adhesive substance used for sticking objects or materials together.
▶ **verb** (**glues, gluing** or **glueing, glued**) [with obj. and adverbial] fasten or join with or as if with glue: *the wood is cut into pieces which are then glued together.*
■ (**be glued to**) informal be paying very close attention to (something, especially a television): *I was glued to the telly when the Olympics were on.*
– DERIVATIVES **glue-like** adjective, **gluey** adjective, **glueyness** noun.
– ORIGIN Middle English: from Old French *glu* (noun), *gluer* (verb), from late Latin *glus, glut-*, from Latin *gluten*.

glue ear ▶ **noun** [mass noun] Brit. blocking of the Eustachian tube by mucus (occurring especially in children).

glue pot ▶ **noun** a pot with an outer container holding water, used to heat glue that sets when it cools.

glue-sniffing ▶ **noun** [mass noun] the practice of inhaling intoxicating fumes from the solvents in adhesives.
– DERIVATIVES **glue-sniffer** noun.

glug informal ▶ **verb** (**glugs, glugging, glugged**) [with obj. and adverbial of direction] pour or drink (liquid) with a hollow gurgling sound: *Jeff glugged whisky into glasses.* ■ [no obj., with adverbial of direction] (of liquid) make a hollow gurgling sound when being poured or drunk.
▶ **noun** a hollow gurgling sound or sounds as of liquid being poured from a bottle. ■ an amount of liquid poured from a bottle: *a couple of good glugs of gin.*
– DERIVATIVES **gluggable** adjective (informal).
– ORIGIN late 17th cent.: imitative.

glugg ▶ **noun** variant spelling of GLÖGG.

glühwein /ˈgluːvʌɪn/, German /ˈglyːvaɪn/ ▶ **noun** [mass noun] mulled wine.
– ORIGIN German, from *glühen* 'to mull' + *Wein* 'wine'.

glum ▶ **adjective** (**glummer, glummest**) looking or feeling dejected; morose: *the princess looked glum but later cheered up.*
– DERIVATIVES **glumly** adverb, **glumness** noun.
– ORIGIN mid 16th cent.: related to dialect *glum* 'to frown', variant of GLOOM.

glume /gluːm/ ▶ **noun** Botany each of two membranous bracts surrounding the spikelet of a grass (forming the husk of a cereal grain) or one surrounding the florets of a sedge.
– ORIGIN late 18th cent.: from Latin *gluma* 'husk'.

gluon /ˈgluːɒn/ ▶ **noun** Physics a hypothetical massless subatomic particle believed to transmit the force binding quarks together in a hadron.
– ORIGIN 1970s: from GLUE + -ON.

glut ▶ **noun** an excessively abundant supply of something: *there is a glut of cars on the market.*
▶ **verb** (**gluts, glutting, glutted**) [with obj.] supply or fill to excess: *the roads are glutted with cars.* ■ archaic satisfy fully: *he planned a treacherous murder to glut his desire for revenge.*
– ORIGIN Middle English: probably via Old French from Latin *gluttire* 'to swallow'; related to GLUTTON.

glutamate /ˈgluːtəmeɪt/ ▶ **noun** Biochemistry a salt or ester of glutamic acid. ■ [mass noun] glutamic acid, its salts, or its anion. ■ short for MONOSODIUM GLUTAMATE.

glutamic acid /gluːˈtamɪk/ ▶ **noun** [mass noun] Biochemistry an acidic amino acid which is a constituent of many proteins. ● Chem. formula: $HOOC(CH_2)_2(NH_2)COOH$.
– ORIGIN late 19th cent.: from GLUTEN + AMINE + -IC.

glutamine /ˈgluːtəmiːn/ ▶ **noun** [mass noun] Biochemistry a hydrophilic amino acid which is a constituent of most proteins. ● An amide of glutamic acid; chem. formula: $H_2NCOCH_2CH_2(NH_2)COOH$.
– ORIGIN late 19th cent.: blend of GLUTAMIC ACID and AMINE.

glutathione /ˌgluːtəˈθʌɪəʊn/ ▶ **noun** [mass noun] Biochemistry a compound involved as a coenzyme in oxidation–reduction reactions in cells. It is a tripeptide derived from glutamic acid, cysteine, and glycine.

glute ▶ **noun** (usu. **glutes**) informal a gluteus muscle.

gluteal ▶ **adjective** relating to the gluteus muscles: *the gluteal region.*
▶ **noun** (usu. **gluteals**) a gluteus muscle.

gluten /ˈgluːt(ə)n/ ▶ **noun** [mass noun] a mixture of two proteins present in cereal grains, especially wheat, which is responsible for the elastic texture of dough.
– ORIGIN late 16th cent. (originally denoting protein from animal tissue): via French from Latin, literally 'glue'.

gluteus /ˈgluːtɪəs/ (also **gluteus muscle**) ▶ **noun** (pl. **glutei** /-tɪʌɪ/) any of three muscles in each buttock which move the thigh, the largest of which is the **gluteus maximus**.
– ORIGIN late 17th cent.: modern Latin, from Greek *gloutos* 'buttock'.

glutinous /ˈgluːtɪnəs/ ▶ **adjective** like glue in texture; sticky: *glutinous mud.*
– DERIVATIVES **glutinously** adverb, **glutinousness** noun.
– ORIGIN late Middle English: from Old French *glutineux* or Latin *glutinosus*, from *gluten* 'glue'.

glutton ▶ **noun 1** an excessively greedy eater. ■ a person who is excessively fond of something: *he's a glutton for adventure.*
2 old-fashioned term for WOLVERINE.
– PHRASES **a glutton for punishment** a person who is always eager to undertake hard or unpleasant tasks.
– DERIVATIVES **gluttonize** (also **gluttonise**) verb.
– ORIGIN Middle English: from Old French *gluton*, from Latin *glutto(n-)* related to *gluttire* 'to swallow', *gluttus* 'greedy', and *gula* 'throat'.

gluttonous ▶ **adjective** excessively greedy: *a gluttonous, cigar-smoking capitalist.*
– DERIVATIVES **gluttonously** adverb.

gluttony ▶ **noun** [mass noun] habitual greed or excess in eating.
– ORIGIN Middle English: from Old French *glutonie*, from *gluton* 'glutton'.

glycaemia /glʌɪˈsiːmɪə/ (US also **glycemia**) ▶ **noun** [mass noun] the presence of glucose in the blood.
– DERIVATIVES **glycaemic** adjective.
– ORIGIN early 20th cent.: from GLYCO- + -AEMIA.

glycaemic index /glʌɪˈsiːmɪk/ (US also **glycemic index**) ▶ **noun** a figure representing the relative ability of a carbohydrate food to increase the level of glucose in the blood.

glyceride /ˈglɪs(ə)rʌɪd/ ▶ **noun** a fatty acid ester of glycerol.

glycerine /ˈglɪs(ə)riːn, -ɪn/ (US **glycerin**) ▶ **noun** another term for GLYCEROL.
– ORIGIN mid 19th cent.: from French *glycerin*, from Greek *glukeros* 'sweet'.

glycerol /ˈglɪs(ə)rɒl/ ▶ **noun** [mass noun] a colourless, sweet, viscous liquid formed as a by-product in soap manufacture. It is used as an emollient and laxative, and for making explosives and antifreeze. ● A trihydric alcohol; chem. formula: $CH_2(OH)CH(OH)CH_2(OH)$.
– ORIGIN late 19th cent.: from GLYCERINE + -OL.

glyceryl /ˈglɪs(ə)rʌɪl, -rɪl/ ▶ **noun** [as modifier] Chemistry of or denoting a radical derived from glycerol by replacement of one or more hydrogen atoms: *glyceryl trinitrate.*
– ORIGIN mid 19th cent.: from GLYCERINE + -YL.

glycine /ˈglʌɪsiːn/ ▶ **noun** [mass noun] Biochemistry the simplest naturally occurring amino acid, which is a constituent of most proteins. ● Chem. formula: H_2NCH_2COOH.
– ORIGIN mid 19th cent.: from Greek *glukus* 'sweet' + -INE[4].

glyco- ▶ **combining form** relating to or producing sugar: *glycogenesis | glycoside.*
– ORIGIN from Greek *glukus* 'sweet'.

glycogen /ˈglʌɪkədʒ(ə)n/ ▶ **noun** [mass noun] Biochemistry a substance deposited in bodily tissues as a store of carbohydrates. It is a polysaccharide which forms glucose on hydrolysis.
– DERIVATIVES **glycogenic** /-ˈdʒɛnɪk/ adjective.

glycogenesis /ˌglʌɪkə(ʊ)ˈdʒɛnɪsɪs/ ▶ **noun** [mass noun] Biochemistry the formation of glycogen from sugar.

glycol /ˈglʌɪkɒl/ ▶ **noun** short for ETHYLENE GLYCOL. ■ Chemistry another term for DIOL.
– DERIVATIVES **glycolic** /-ˈkɒlɪk/ adjective, **glycollic** /-ˈkɒlɪk/ adjective.
– ORIGIN mid 19th cent. (applied to ethylene glycol): from GLYCERINE + -OL (originally intended to designate a substance intermediate between glycerine and alcohol).

glycolysis /glʌɪˈkɒlɪsɪs/ ▶ **noun** [mass noun] Biochemistry the breakdown of glucose by enzymes, releasing energy and pyruvic acid.
– DERIVATIVES **glycolytic** adjective /ˌglʌɪkəˈlɪtɪk/.

glycoprotein /ˌglʌɪkə(ʊ)ˈprəʊtiːn/ ▶ **noun** Biochemistry any of a class of proteins which have carbohydrate groups attached to the polypeptide chain.

glycosaminoglycan /ˌglʌɪkəʊsˌəmiːnə(ʊ)ˈglʌɪkan/ ▶ **noun** another term for MUCOPOLYSACCHARIDE.

glycoside /ˈglʌɪkə(ʊ)sʌɪd/ ▶ **noun** Biochemistry a compound formed from a simple sugar and another compound by replacement of a hydroxyl group in the sugar molecule. Many drugs and poisons derived from plants are glycosides.
– DERIVATIVES **glycosidic** adjective.
– ORIGIN late 19th cent.: from GLYCO- 'relating to sugar', on the pattern of *glucoside*.

glycosuria /ˌglʌɪkə(ʊ)ˈsjʊərɪə/ ▶ **noun** [mass noun] Medicine a condition characterized by an excess of sugar in the urine, typically associated with diabetes or kidney disease.
– ORIGIN mid 19th cent.: from French *glycosurie*, from *glucos* 'glucose'.

Glyndebourne Festival /ˈglʌɪndbɔːn/ an annual festival of opera, held at the estate of Glyndebourne near Lewes, East Sussex.

Glyndwr /glɪnˈdʊr/ Welsh form of GLENDOWER.

glyph /glɪf/ ▶ **noun 1** a hieroglyphic character or symbol. ■ a sculptured symbol (e.g. as forming the ancient Mayan writing system). ■ Computing a small graphic symbol.
2 Architecture an ornamental carved groove or channel, as on a Greek frieze.
– DERIVATIVES **glyphic** adjective.
– ORIGIN late 18th cent. (in sense 2): from French *glyphe*, from Greek *gluphē* 'carving'.

glyphosate /ˈglʌɪfə(ʊ)seɪt/ ▶ **noun** [mass noun] a synthetic compound which is a non-selective systemic herbicide, particularly effective against perennial weeds. ● Alternative name: ***N*-(phosphonomethyl) glycine**; chem. formula: $C_3H_8NO_5P$.

glyptic /ˈglɪptɪk/ ▶ **adjective** of or concerning carving or engraving.
– ORIGIN early 19th cent.: from French *glyptique* or Greek *gluptikos*, from *gluptēs* 'carver', from *gluphein* 'carve'.

glyptodont /ˈglɪptə(ʊ)dɒnt/ ▶ **noun** a fossil South American edentate mammal of the Cenozoic era, related to armadillos but much larger. Glyptodonts had fluted teeth and a body covered in a thick bony carapace. ● Family Glyptodontidae, order Xenarthra (or Edentata): several genera, including *Glyptodon*.
– ORIGIN mid 19th cent.: from Greek *gluptos* 'carved' (from *gluphein* 'carve') + *odous, odont-* 'tooth'.

glyptography /glɪpˈtɒgrəfi/ ▶ **noun** [mass noun] the art or scientific study of gem engraving.
– ORIGIN late 18th cent.: from Greek *gluptos* 'carved' (from *gluphein* 'carve') + -GRAPHY.

GM ▶ abbreviation ■ general manager. ■ (in the US) General Motors. ■ (in the UK) George Medal. ■ Chess grand master. ■ (of a school in the UK) grant-maintained. ■ genetically modified.

gm ▶ abbreviation gram(s).

G-man ▶ noun **1** US informal an FBI agent. [1930s: probably an abbreviation of *Government man*.]
2 Irish a political detective. [early 20th cent.: perhaps an arbitrary use of *G*.]

GMB ▶ noun (in the UK) a general trade union, with members from many employment sectors.
– ORIGIN from *General, Municipal, Boilermakers and Allied Trade Union*, a former name of the union.

GMS ▶ abbreviation grant-maintained status (with reference to schools in the UK).

GMT ▶ abbreviation Greenwich Mean Time.

gn ▶ abbreviation guinea(s).

gnamma /ˈnamə/ (also **namma**) ▶ noun Austral. a natural hole in a rock in which rainwater collects.
– ORIGIN from Nyungar.

gnarl /nɑːl/ ▶ noun a rough, knotty protuberance, especially on a tree.
– ORIGIN early 19th cent.: back-formation from GNARLED.

gnarled ▶ adjective knobbly, rough, and twisted, especially with age: *the gnarled old oak tree*.
– ORIGIN early 17th cent.: variant of *knarled*, from KNAR.

gnarly ▶ adjective (**gnarlier**, **gnarliest**) **1** gnarled.
2 N. Amer. informal difficult, dangerous, or challenging: *he'd taken a fall during a particularly gnarly practice session*. [originally surfers' slang, perhaps from the appearance of rough sea.] ■ unpleasant or unattractive: *stations can be pretty gnarly places*. ■ very good; excellent: *you're going to make some lucky guy a pretty gnarly wife*.

gnash /naʃ/ ▶ verb [with obj.] grind (one's teeth) together as a sign of anger (often used hyperbolically): *no doubt he is gnashing his teeth in rage*. ■ [no obj.] (of teeth) strike together; grind.
– ORIGIN late Middle English: perhaps related to Old Norse *gnastan* 'a gnashing'.

gnashers ▶ plural noun Brit. informal teeth.

gnat /nat/ ▶ noun a small two-winged fly that resembles a mosquito. Gnats include both biting and non-biting forms, and they typically form large swarms. ● Several families, especially Culicidae (the biting gnats), which includes the **common gnat** (*Culex pipiens*). ■ a person regarded as tiny or insignificant: *she'd be marking O'Brien—a gnat trying to curb an elephant*.
– ORIGIN Old English *gnætt*, of Germanic origin; related to German *Gnitze*.

gnatcatcher ▶ noun a tiny grey-backed New World songbird, with a long tail that is often cocked. ● Genus *Polioptila*, family Polioptilidae (or Sylviidae): several species.

gnathic /ˈnaθɪk, ˈneɪ-/ ▶ adjective rare relating to the jaws.
– ORIGIN late 19th cent.: from Greek *gnathos* 'jaw' + -IC.

Gnathostomulida /ˌneɪθə(ʊ)stəʊˈmjuːlɪdə/ ▶ plural noun Zoology a minor phylum of minute marine worms which appear to be intermediate between coelenterates and flatworms.
– DERIVATIVES **gnathostomulid** /ˌneɪθə(ʊ)ˈstəʊmjʊlɪd/ noun & adjective.
– ORIGIN modern Latin (plural), from Greek *gnathos* 'jaw' + *stoma* 'mouth'.

gnaw /nɔː/ ▶ verb [no obj.] **1** bite at or nibble something persistently: *watching a dog gnaw at a big bone*. ■ [with obj. and adverbial] bite at or nibble (something) so as to wear it away: *the grubs tunnel into the wood and gnaw it away*.
2 cause persistent distress or anxiety: *the doubts continued to gnaw at me*.
– ORIGIN Old English *gnagen*, of Germanic origin; related to German *nagen*, ultimately imitative.

gnawing /ˈnɔː(r)ɪŋ/ ▶ adjective persistently worrying or distressing: *that gnawing pain in her stomach* | *gnawing doubts*.
– DERIVATIVES **gnawingly** adverb.

gneiss /nʌɪs/ ▶ noun [mass noun] a metamorphic rock with a banded or foliated structure, typically coarse-grained and consisting mainly of feldspar, quartz, and mica.
– DERIVATIVES **gneissic** adjective, **gneissose** adjective.
– ORIGIN mid 18th cent.: from German, from Old High German *gneisto* 'spark' (because of the rock's sheen).

gnocchi /ˈn(j)ɒki/ ▶ plural noun (in Italian cooking) small dumplings made from potato, semolina, or flour, usually served with a sauce.
– ORIGIN Italian, plural of *gnocco*, alteration of *nocchio* 'knot in wood'.

gnome¹ /nəʊm/ ▶ noun a legendary dwarfish creature supposed to guard the earth's treasures underground. ■ a small garden ornament in the form of a bearded man with a pointed hat. ■ informal a small ugly person. ■ informal a person regarded as having secret or sinister influence in financial matters: *the gnomes of Zurich*.
– DERIVATIVES **gnomish** adjective.
– ORIGIN mid 17th cent.: from French, from modern Latin *gnomus*, a word used by Paracelsus as a synonym of *Pygmaeus*, denoting a mythical race of very small people said to inhabit parts of Ethiopia and India (compare with PYGMY).

gnome² /nəʊm, ˈnəʊmi/ ▶ noun a short statement encapsulating a general truth; a maxim.
– ORIGIN late 16th cent.: from Greek *gnōmē* 'thought, opinion' (related to *gignōskein* 'know').

gnomic /ˈnəʊmɪk/ ▶ adjective expressed in or of the nature of short, pithy maxims or aphorisms. ■ difficult to understand because enigmatic or ambiguous: *I had to have the gnomic response interpreted for me*.
– DERIVATIVES **gnomically** adverb.
– ORIGIN early 19th cent.: from Greek *gnōmikos* (perhaps via French *gnomique*), from *gnōmē* 'thought, judgement', (plural) *gnōmai* 'sayings, maxims', related to *gignōskein* 'know'.

gnomon /ˈnəʊmɒn/ ▶ noun **1** the projecting piece on a sundial that shows the time by the position of its shadow. ■ Astronomy a structure, especially a column, used in observing the sun's meridian altitude.
2 Geometry the part of a parallelogram left when a similar parallelogram has been taken from its corner.
– DERIVATIVES **gnomonic** /-ˈmɒnɪk/ adjective.
– ORIGIN mid 16th cent.: via Latin from Greek *gnōmōn* 'indicator, carpenter's square' (related to *gignōskein* 'know').

gnosis /ˈnəʊsɪs/ ▶ noun [mass noun] knowledge of spiritual mysteries.
– ORIGIN late 16th cent.: from Greek *gnōsis* 'knowledge' (related to *gignōskein* 'know').

gnostic /ˈnɒstɪk/ ▶ adjective relating to knowledge, especially esoteric mystical knowledge. ■ (**Gnostic**) relating to Gnosticism.
▶ noun (**Gnostic**) an adherent of Gnosticism.
– ORIGIN late 16th cent. (as a noun): via ecclesiastical Latin from Greek *gnōstikos*, from *gnōstos* 'known' (related to *gignōskein* 'know').

Gnosticism /ˈnɒstɪˌsɪz(ə)m/ ▶ noun [mass noun] a prominent heretical movement of the 2nd-century Christian Church, partly of pre-Christian origin. Gnostic doctrine taught that the world was created and ruled by a lesser divinity, the demiurge, and that Christ was an emissary of the remote supreme divine being, esoteric knowledge (gnosis) of whom enabled the redemption of the human spirit.

gnotobiotic /ˌnəʊtə(ʊ)bʌɪˈɒtɪk/ ▶ adjective Biology relating to or denoting an environment for rearing or culturing organisms in which all the microorganisms are either known or excluded.
– ORIGIN 1940s: from Greek *gnōtos* 'known' + BIOTIC.

GNP ▶ abbreviation gross national product.

Gnr ▶ abbreviation Gunner (in the British army).

gns ▶ abbreviation guineas.

gnu /(g)nuː, (g)njuː/ ▶ noun a large dark antelope with a long head, a beard and mane, and a sloping back. Also called WILDEBEEST. ● Genus *Connochaetes*, family Bovidae: two species, in particular the abundant **brindled gnu** or blue wildebeest (*C. taurinus*).
– ORIGIN late 18th cent.: from Khoikhoi and San, perhaps imitative of the sound made by the animal when alarmed.

GNVQ ▶ abbreviation General National Vocational Qualification, a general qualification offered by schools and colleges in the UK to prepare students for specific training or higher education, set at various levels of which Intermediate and Advanced correspond in standard to GCSE and GCE A level.

go¹ ▶ verb (**goes**, **going**; past **went**; past participle **gone**)
1 [no obj., usu. with adverbial of direction] move from one place to another; travel: *he **went out** to the shops* | *she longs to **go back** home* | *we've a long way to go*. ■ travel a specified distance: *you just have to go a few miles to get to the road*. ■ travel or move in order to engage in a specified activity: *let's **go and** have a pint* | [with infinitive] *we went to see her* | [with present participle] *she used to go hunting*. ■ (**go to**) attend or visit for a particular purpose: *we went to the cinema* | *he went to Cambridge University*. ■ (of a thing) lie or extend in a certain direction: *the scar went all the way up her leg*. ■ change in level, amount, or rank: *prices **went up** by 15 per cent*. ■ [in imperative] begin motion (used in a starter's order to begin a race): *ready, steady, go!* ■ informal said in various expressions when angrily or contemptuously dismissing someone: ***go and** get stuffed*.
2 [no obj.] leave; depart: *I really must go*. ■ (of time) pass or elapse: *the hours **went by*** | *three years **went past***. ■ pass a specified amount of time in a particular way: *they **went for** two weeks without talking*. ■ come to an end; cease to exist: *a golden age that has now gone for good* | *11,500 jobs are due to go by next year*. ■ cease operating or functioning: *the power went in our road last week*. ■ die (used euphemistically): *I'd like to see my grandchildren before I go*. ■ be lost or stolen: *when he returned minutes later his equipment had gone*. ■ (**go to**) be sold or awarded to: *the top prize went to a twenty-four-year-old sculptor*. ■ (of money) be spent, especially in a specified way: *the rest of his money **went on** medical expenses*.
3 (**be going to be/do something**) intend or be likely or intended to be or do something (used to express a future tense): *I'm going to be late for work* | *she's going to have a baby*.
4 [no obj., with complement] pass into or be in a specified state, especially an undesirable one: *the food is going bad* | *no one went hungry in our house* | *he's gone crazy*. ■ (**go to/into**) enter into a specified state or course of action: *she went back to sleep* | *the car went into a spin*. ■ make a sound of a specified kind: *the engine went bang*.
5 [no obj.] proceed or turn out in a specified way: *how did the weekend go?* | *at first all went well*. ■ be acceptable or permitted: *underground events where anything goes*.
6 [no obj.] be harmonious, complementary, or matching: *rosemary **goes with** roast lamb* | *the earrings and the scarf don't really go*. ■ be found in the same place or situation; be associated: *cooking and eating **go together***.
7 [no obj.] (of a machine or device) function: *my car won't go*. ■ continue in operation or existence: *the committee was **kept going** even when its existence could no longer be justified*.
8 [no obj.] (**go into/to/towards**) contribute to or be put into (a whole): *considerable effort went into making the operation successful*. ■ used to indicate how many people a supply of a resource is sufficient for or how much can be achieved using it: *the sale will **go a long way towards** easing the huge debt burden* | *a little luck can **go a long way***.
9 [no obj.] (of an article) be regularly kept or put in a particular place: *remember which card goes in which slot*. ■ fit into a particular place or space: *you're trying to squeeze a quart into a pint pot, and it just won't go*.
10 [no obj.] (of a song or account) have a specified content or wording: *if you haven't heard it, the story goes like this*. ■ (**go by/under**) be known or called by (a specified name): *he now goes under the name Charles Perez*. ■ [with direct speech] informal say: *the kids go, 'Yeah, sure.'*.
11 [no obj.] informal use a toilet; urinate or defecate.
12 [no obj.] informal used to emphasize the speaker's annoyance at someone's action: *then he **goes and** spoils it all* | [with present participle] *don't go poking your nose where you shouldn't*.
▶ noun (pl. **goes**) informal **1** chiefly Brit. an attempt or trial at something: ***have a go at** answering the questions yourself*.
2 Brit. a person's turn to use or do something: *I **had a go on** Nigel's racing bike* | *come on Tony, it's your go*. ■ used in reference to a single item, action, or spell of activity: *he drank a pint in one go*.
3 [mass noun] Brit. spirit, animation, or energy: *there's no go in me at all these days*. ■ vigorous activity: *it's **all go** around here*.
4 dated a state of affairs: *this seems a rum sort of go*. ■ an attack of illness: *he's had this nasty go of dysentery*.
5 N. Amer. an enterprise which has been approved: *tell them the project is a go*.
▶ adjective [predic.] informal functioning properly: *all systems go*.
– PHRASES **all the go** Brit. informal, dated in fashion. **as** (or **so**) **far as it goes** bearing in mind its limitations (said when qualifying praise of something): *the book is a useful catalogue as far as it goes*. **as —— go** compared to the average or typical one of the specified kind: *as castles go it is small and old*. **from the**

G

G

word go informal from the very beginning. **get going** 1 leave a place in order to go somewhere else: *it's been wonderful seeing you again, but I think it's time we got going.* 2 start happening or taking place: *the campaign got going in 1983.* **get someone going** Brit. informal make someone angry or sexually aroused: *I want a girl who's sexy, but in a subtle way—that's what gets me going.* **get something going** succeed in starting a machine, vehicle, process, etc.: *we got the car going again after much trying.* **go figure!** N. Amer. informal said to express the belief that something is amazing or incredible. **go halves** (or **shares**) share something equally. **going!, gone!** an auctioneer's announcement that bidding is closing or closed. **go off on one** Brit. informal become very angry or excited. **going on ——** (Brit. also **going on for ——**) approaching a specified time, age, or amount: *I was going on fourteen when I went to my first gig.* **go (to) it** Brit. informal act in an energetic or dissipated way: *Go it, Dad! Give him what for!* **go to show** (or **prove**) (of an occurrence) serve as evidence or proof of something. **have a go at** chiefly Brit. attack or criticize (someone). **have —— going for one** informal used to indicate how much someone has in their favour or to their advantage: *Why did she do it? She had so much going for her.* **make a go of** informal be successful in (something): *he's determined to make a go of his marriage.* **on the go** informal very active or busy. **to be going on with** Brit. to start with; for the time being: *this is not a full critical appraisal but it will do to be going on with.* **to go** N. Amer. (of food or drink from a restaurant or cafe) to be eaten or drunk off the premises: *one large cheese-and-peppers pizza, to go.* **what goes around comes around** proverb the consequences of one's actions will have to be dealt with eventually. **who goes there?** said by a sentry as a challenge.

– PHRASAL VERBS **go about** 1 begin or carry on with (an activity): *you are going about this in the wrong way.* 2 Sailing change to an opposite tack. **go against** oppose or resist: *he refused to go against the unions.* ■ be contrary to (a feeling or principle): *these tactics go against many of our instincts.* ■ (of a decision or result) be unfavourable for. **go ahead** proceed or be carried out: *the project will go ahead.* **go along with** consent or agree to (a person or proposal). **go around** see GO ROUND. **go around with** be regularly in the company of: *he goes around with some of the local lads.* **go at** energetically attack or tackle: *he went at things with a daunting eagerness.* **go back** 1 (of a clock) be set to an earlier standard time, especially at the end of summertime. 2 (of two people) have known each other for a length of time: *Victor and I go back a long way.* **go back on** fail to keep (a promise): *he wouldn't go back on his word.* **go down** 1 (of a ship or aircraft) sink or crash. ■ be defeated in a contest: *they went down 2–1.* 2 be recorded or remembered in a particular way: *his name will **go down in history**.* 3 be swallowed: *solids can sometimes go down much easier than liquids.* 4 elicit a specified reaction: *my slide shows **went down** reasonably well.* 5 N. Amer. informal happen: *you really don't know what's going down?* 6 Brit. informal leave a university, especially Oxford or Cambridge, after finishing one's studies. 7 Brit. informal be sent to prison. **go down on** vulgar slang perform oral sex on. **go down with** begin to suffer from (an illness): *I went down with an attack of bronchitis.* **go for** 1 decide on; choose: *I went for grilled halibut.* ■ tend to find (a particular type of person) attractive: *Dionne went for the outlaw type.* 2 attempt to gain or attain: *he went for a job as a delivery driver.* ■ (**go for it**) strive to the utmost to gain or achieve something (frequently said as an exhortation): *sounds like a good idea—go for it!* 3 launch oneself at (someone); attack: *she went for him with clawed hands.* 4 finally have a specified negative result: *my good intentions **went for nothing**.* 5 apply to; have relevance for: *the same goes for money-grabbing lawyers.* **go forward** (of a clock) be set to a later standard time, especially summertime. **go in for** 1 Brit. enter (a competition) or sit (an examination). 2 like or habitually take part in (an activity): *I don't go in for the social whirl.* **go into** 1 investigate or enquire into (something): *there's no need to go into it now.* 2 (of a whole number) be capable of dividing another, typically without a remainder: *six into five won't go.* **go off** 1 (of a gun, bomb, or similar device) explode or fire. ■ (of an alarm) begin to sound. 2 Brit. (of food or drink) begin to decompose and become inedible. 3 Brit. informal begin to dislike: *I went off men after my husband left me.* 4 go to sleep. 5 gradually cease to be felt: *I had a bad headache but it's going off now.* **go on** 1 [often with present participle] continue or persevere: *I can't go on protecting you.* ■ talk at great length, especially tediously or angrily: *the twins were always **going on about** him.* ■ continue speaking or doing something after a short pause: [with direct speech] *'I don't understand,' she went on.* ■ informal said when encouraging someone or expressing disbelief: *go on, tell him!* 2 happen: *we still don't know what went on there.* 3 [often with infinitive] proceed to do: *she went on to do postgraduate work.* 4 [usu. with negative] informal have a specified amount of care or liking for (something): *I heard this album last month and didn't go much on it.* **go out** 1 (of a fire or light) be extinguished. 2 (of the tide) ebb. 3 leave one's home to go to a social event: *I'm going out for dinner.* 4 carry on a regular romantic or sexual relationship: *he was **going out with** her best friend.* 5 used to convey someone's deep sympathy or similar feeling: *her heart went out to the pitiful figure.* 6 Golf play the first nine holes in a round of eighteen holes. Compare with COME HOME (see HOME). 7 (in some card games) be the first to dispose of all the cards in one's hand. **go over** 1 consider, examine, or check (something): *I want to go over these plans with you again.* 2 change one's allegiance or religion: *he **went over to** the pro-English party.* 3 be received in a specified way: *his earnestness would go over well in a courtroom.* **go round** (chiefly US also **go around**) 1 spin; revolve: *the wheels were going round.* 2 (especially of food) be sufficient to supply everybody present: *there was barely enough food to go round.* **go through** 1 undergo (a difficult period or experience): *the country is going through a period of economic instability.* 2 search through or examine methodically: *she started to go through the bundle of letters.* 3 (of a proposal or contract) be officially approved or completed: *the sale of the building is set to go through.* 4 informal use up or spend (available money or other resources). 5 (of a book) be successively published in (a specified number of editions). 6 Austral. informal leave hastily to avoid an obligation; abscond. **go through with** perform (an action) to completion despite difficulty or unwillingness. **go to!** archaic said to express disbelief, impatience, or admonition. **go under** 1 (of a business) become bankrupt. 2 (of a person) die or suffer an emotional collapse. **go up** 1 (of a building or other structure) be built: *housing developments went up.* 2 explode or suddenly burst into flames: *two factories **went up in flames**.* 3 Brit. informal begin one's studies at a university, especially Oxford or Cambridge. **go with** 1 give one's consent or agreement to (a person or proposal). 2 have a romantic or sexual relationship with. **go without** suffer lack or deprivation: *I like to give my children what they want, even if I have to go without.*

– ORIGIN Old English *gān*, of Germanic origin; related to Dutch *gaan* and German *gehen*; the form *went* was originally the past tense of WEND.

> **USAGE** The use of **go** followed by **and**, as in *I must go and change* (rather than *I must go to change*), is extremely common but is regarded by some grammarians as an oddity. For more details, see **USAGE** at **AND**.

go² ▶ **noun** [mass noun] a Japanese board game of territorial possession and capture.

– ORIGIN late 19th cent.: Japanese, literally 'small stone', also the name of the game.

Goa /ˈɡəʊə/ a state on the west coast of India; capital, Panaji. Formerly a Portuguese territory, it was seized by India in 1961. It formed a Union Territory with Daman and Diu until 1987, when it was made a state.

– DERIVATIVES **Goan** adjective & noun, **Goanese** /ˌɡəʊəˈniːz/ adjective & noun.

goad /ɡəʊd/ ▶ **verb** 1 [with obj.] provoke or annoy (someone) so as to stimulate an action or reaction: *he was trying to **goad her into** a fight.*
2 [with obj. and adverbial of direction] drive (an animal) with a spiked stick.

▶ **noun** a spiked stick used for driving cattle. ■ a thing that stimulates someone into action: *for him the visit was a goad to renewed effort.*

– ORIGIN Old English *gād*, of Germanic origin.

go-ahead informal ▶ **noun** [in sing.] permission to proceed: *the government had given the go-ahead for the power station.*

▶ **adjective** 1 willing to consider new ideas; enterprising: *a young and go-ahead managing director.*
2 [attrib.] N. Amer. denoting the run or score which gives a team the lead in a game.

goal ▶ **noun** 1 (in football, rugby, hockey, and some other games) a pair of posts linked by a crossbar and typically with a net between, forming a space into or over which the ball has to be sent in order to score. ■ an instance of sending the ball into or over the goal, especially as a unit of scoring in a game: *the decisive opening goal | we won by three goals to two.* ■ a cage or basket used as a goal in other sports.
2 the object of a person's ambition or effort; an aim or desired result: *he achieved his goal of becoming King of England.* ■ the destination of a journey: *the aircraft bumped towards our goal some 400 miles to the west.* ■ literary a point marking the end of a race.

– PHRASES **in goal** in the position of goalkeeper.

– DERIVATIVES **goalless** adjective, **goalwards** adverb.

– ORIGIN Middle English (in the sense 'limit, boundary'): of unknown origin.

goal area ▶ **noun** Soccer a rectangular area in front of the goal from within which goal kicks must be taken.

goal average ▶ **noun** [mass noun] Soccer the ratio of the numbers of goals scored for and against a team in a series of matches, sometimes used in deciding the team's position in a table.

goalball ▶ **noun** [mass noun] a ball game for blind and visually impaired players, played by teams of three. The object is to roll a large ball containing bells over a line at the end of the court.

goal difference ▶ **noun** [mass noun] Soccer the difference between the number of goals scored for and against a team in a series of matches, sometimes used in deciding the team's position in a table.

goalhanger ▶ **noun** Soccer, derogatory a player who spends much of the game near the opposing team's goal in the hope of scoring easy goals.

goalie ▶ **noun** informal term for GOALKEEPER or GOALTENDER.

goalkeeper ▶ **noun** a player in soccer or field hockey whose special role is to stop the ball from entering the goal.

– DERIVATIVES **goalkeeping** noun.

goal kick ▶ **noun** 1 Soccer a free kick taken by the defending side from within their goal area after attackers send the ball over the byline.
2 Rugby an attempt to kick a goal.

– DERIVATIVES **goal-kicker** noun (Rugby), **goal-kicking** noun (Rugby).

goal line ▶ **noun** a line across a football or hockey field at or near its end, on which the goal is placed or which acts as the boundary beyond which a try or touchdown is scored.

goalmouth ▶ **noun** the area just in front of a goal in soccer or hockey.

goalpost ▶ **noun** either of the two upright posts of a goal.

– PHRASES **move the goalposts** (US also **move the goalpost**) unfairly alter the conditions or rules of a procedure during its course.

goalscorer ▶ **noun** a player who scores a goal: *Sunderland's prolific goalscorer.*

– DERIVATIVES **goalscoring** adjective & noun.

goaltender ▶ **noun** N. Amer. a goalkeeper, especially in ice hockey.

– DERIVATIVES **goaltending** noun.

goanna /ɡəʊˈanə/ ▶ **noun** Australian term for MONITOR (sense 4 of the noun).

– ORIGIN mid 19th cent.: alteration of IGUANA.

go-around (also **go-round**) ▶ **noun** 1 a flight path taken by an aircraft after an aborted approach to landing.
2 N. Amer. informal a confrontation or argument.
3 N. Amer. informal each of several recurring opportunities.

goat ▶ **noun** 1 a hardy domesticated ruminant mammal that has backward-curving horns and (in the male) a beard. It is kept for its milk and meat, and noted for its lively behaviour. ● *Capra hircus*, family Bovidae, descended from the wild bezoar.
■ a wild mammal related to the goat, such as the ibex. See also MOUNTAIN GOAT. ■ (**the Goat**) the zodiacal sign Capricorn or the constellation Capricornus.
2 a lecherous man.
3 Brit. informal a stupid person; a fool: *just for once, stop **acting the goat**.*
4 US a scapegoat.

– PHRASES **get someone's goat** informal irritate someone.

– DERIVATIVES **goatish** adjective, **goaty** adjective.

– ORIGIN Old English *gāt* 'nanny goat', of Germanic origin; related to Dutch *geit* and German *Geiss*, also to Latin *haedus* 'kid'.

goat-antelope ▶ **noun** a ruminant mammal of a group that combines the characteristics of both goats and antelopes. ● Subfamily Caprinae, family Bovidae: tribes

Rupicaprini (the chamois, goral, serow, and mountain goat) and Ovibonini (the musk ox and takin).

goatee /gəʊˈtiː/ (also **goatee beard**) ▶ noun a small pointed beard like that of a goat.
– DERIVATIVES **goateed** adjective.

goatfish ▶ noun (pl. **same** or **goatfishes**) North American term for RED MULLET.

goatherd ▶ noun a person who tends goats.
– ORIGIN Old English, from GOAT + obsolete *herd* 'herdsman'.

goat moth ▶ noun a large greyish moth, the caterpillar of which bores into wood and has a goat-like smell. ● *Cossus cossus*, family Cossidae.

goat's beard ▶ noun **1** a Eurasian plant of the daisy family, with slender grass-like leaves, yellow flowers that close at about midday, and downy fruits which resemble those of a dandelion. ● *Tragopogon pratensis*, family Compositae.
2 a plant of the rose family, with long plumes of white flowers, found in both Eurasia and North America. ● *Aruncus dioicus*, family Rosaceae.
– ORIGIN mid 16th cent.: translating Greek *tragopōgon* or Latin *Barba Capri*.

goatskin ▶ noun the skin of a goat. ■ [mass noun] leather made from the skin of a goat. ■ a garment or object made out of goatskin.

goat's rue ▶ noun a herbaceous plant of the pea family, which was formerly used in medicine, especially as a vermifuge. ● Two species in the family Leguminosae: a bushy Eurasian plant which is cultivated as an ornamental (*Galega officinalis*), and a North American plant with pink and yellow flowers and which smells of goats (*Tephrosia virginiana*).

goatsucker ▶ noun another term for NIGHTJAR.
– ORIGIN early 17th cent.: so named because the bird was thought to suck goats' udders.

goat willow ▶ noun a common European willow with broad leaves and soft fluffy catkins. Also called SALLOW[1] or PUSSY WILLOW. ● *Salix caprea*, family Salicaceae.

go-away bird ▶ noun a crested long-tailed African bird of the turaco family, with mainly grey plumage and a call that resembles the words 'go away'. Also called LOERIE or LOURIE in South Africa. ● Family Musophagidae: two genera and three species.

gob[1] ▶ noun Brit. informal a person's mouth: *Jean told him to shut his big gob.*
– ORIGIN mid 16th cent.: perhaps from Scottish Gaelic *gob* 'beak, mouth'.

gob[2] informal ▶ noun **1** a lump of a viscous or slimy substance: *a gob of phlegm.* ■ N. Amer. a small lump.
2 (**gobs of**) N. Amer. a large amount of: *they pumped gobs of money into the candidates' election coffers.*
▶ verb (**gobs, gobbing, gobbed**) [no obj.] Brit. spit.
– ORIGIN late Middle English: from Old French *gobe* 'mouthful, lump', from *gober* 'to swallow, gulp', perhaps of Celtic origin.

gob[3] ▶ noun informal, dated an American sailor.
– ORIGIN early 20th cent.: of unknown origin.

go-bag ▶ noun chiefly N. Amer. a bag packed with essential items, kept ready for use in the event of an emergency evacuation of one's home.

gobar /ˈgɒbə(r)/ ▶ noun [mass noun] Indian cattle dung.
– ORIGIN Hindi.

gobbet /ˈgɒbɪt/ ▶ noun **1** a piece or lump of flesh, food, or viscous matter.
2 an extract from a text, especially one set for translation or comment in an examination.
– ORIGIN Middle English: from Old French *gobet*, diminutive of *gobe* (see GOB[2]).

gobble[1] ▶ verb [with obj.] (often **gobble something up**) eat (something) hurriedly and noisily: *he gobbled up the rest of his sandwich.* ■ use a large amount of (something) very quickly: *these old houses just gobble up money.* ■ (of a large organization) incorporate or take over (a smaller one): *this small department was gobbled up by the Ministry of Transport.*
– ORIGIN early 17th cent.: probably from GOB[2].

gobble[2] ▶ verb [no obj.] (of a turkeycock) make a characteristic swallowing sound in the throat.
– ORIGIN late 17th cent.: imitative, perhaps influenced by GOBBLE[1].

gobbledegook /ˈgɒb(ə)lɪdɪˌguːk, -ˌgʊk/ (also **gobbledygook**) ▶ noun [mass noun] informal language that is meaningless or is made unintelligible by excessive use of technical terms: *reams of financial gobbledegook.*
– ORIGIN 1940s (originally US): probably imitating a turkey's gobble.

gobbler[1] ▶ noun a person who eats greedily and noisily.

gobbler[2] ▶ noun N. Amer. informal a turkeycock.

gobby ▶ adjective (**gobbier, gobbiest**) Brit. informal (of a person) tending to talk too loudly and in a blunt or opinionated way: *a gobby Glaswegian.*

gobdaw /ˈgɒbdɔː/ ▶ noun informal, chiefly Irish a foolish or pretentious person.
– ORIGIN 1960s: of unknown origin; compare with Irish *gabhdán* 'gullible person'.

Gobelin /ˈgɒb(ə)lã, ˈgəʊb-, -lɪn/ (also **Gobelin tapestry**) ▶ noun a tapestry made at the Gobelins factory in Paris, or in imitation of one.

Gobelins /ˈgɒb(ə)lãz, ˈgəʊb-, -lɪnz/, French /gɔblɛ̃/ a tapestry and textile factory in Paris, established by the Gobelin family *c.*1440 and taken over by the French Crown in 1662. It was highly successful in the late 17th and 18th centuries, when designs by leading French painters were used, and tapestry panels became used as alternatives to oil paintings.

go-between ▶ noun an intermediary or negotiator.

gobi /ˈgəʊbi/ ▶ noun Indian term for CAULIFLOWER or CABBAGE.
– ORIGIN Punjabi.

Gobi Desert /ˈgəʊbi/ a barren plateau of southern Mongolia and northern China.

Gobineau /ˈgɒbɪnəʊ/, French /gɔbinəo/, Joseph Arthur, Comte de (1816–82), French writer and anthropologist. His stated view that the races are innately unequal and that the white Aryan race is superior to all others later influenced the ideology and policies of the Nazis.

goblet ▶ noun **1** a drinking glass with a foot and a stem. ■ archaic a metal or glass bowl-shaped drinking cup, sometimes with a foot and a cover.
2 Brit. a receptacle forming part of a liquidizer.
– ORIGIN late Middle English: from Old French *gobelet*, diminutive of *gobel* 'cup', of unknown origin.

goblet cell ▶ noun Anatomy a column-shaped cell found in the respiratory and intestinal tracts, which secretes the main component of mucus.

goblin ▶ noun a mischievous, ugly, dwarf-like creature of folklore.
– ORIGIN Middle English: from Old French *gobelin*, possibly related to German *Kobold* (see KOBOLD) or to Greek *kobalos* 'mischievous goblin'. In medieval Latin *Gobelinus* occurs as the name of a mischievous spirit, said to haunt Évreux in northern France in the 12th cent.

gobo[1] /ˈgəʊbəʊ/ ▶ noun (pl. **gobos**) a dark plate or screen used to shield a lens from light. ■ Theatre a partial screen used in front of a spotlight to project a shape. ■ a shield used to mask a microphone from extraneous noise.
– ORIGIN 1930s: of unknown origin, perhaps from *go between.*

gobo[2] /ˈgəʊbəʊ/ ▶ noun [mass noun] a vegetable root used in Japanese and other oriental cookery.
– ORIGIN Japanese.

gobony /gɒˈbəʊni/ ▶ adjective Heraldry another term for COMPONY.
– ORIGIN late Middle English: from obsolete *gobbon* 'piece, gobbet' + -Y[3].

gobshite /ˈgɒbʃʌɪt/ ▶ noun vulgar slang, chiefly Irish a stupid, foolish, or incompetent person.

gobsmacked ▶ adjective Brit. informal utterly astonished; astounded.
– DERIVATIVES **gobsmacking** adjective.
– ORIGIN 1980s: from GOB[1] + SMACK[1], with reference to being shocked by a blow to the mouth, or to clapping a hand to one's mouth in astonishment.

gobstopper ▶ noun chiefly Brit. a large, hard spherical sweet.

goby /ˈgəʊbi/ ▶ noun (pl. **gobies**) a small, usually marine fish that typically has a sucker on the underside. ● Family Gobiidae: numerous genera and species.
– ORIGIN mid 18th cent.: from Latin *gobius*, from Greek *kōbios*, denoting some kind of small fish.

go-by ▶ noun informal (in phrase **give someone the go-by**) avoid or snub someone. ■ end a romantic relationship with someone.

GOC ▶ abbreviation Brit. General Officer Commanding.

go-cart ▶ noun **1** variant spelling of GO-KART.
2 a handcart.
3 dated a pushchair. ■ archaic a baby walker.
– ORIGIN late 17th cent. (denoting a baby walker): from GO[1] (in the obsolete sense 'walk') + CART.

God ▶ noun **1** (in Christianity and other monotheistic religions) the creator and ruler of the universe and source of all moral authority; the supreme being.
2 (**god**) (in certain other religions) a superhuman being or spirit worshipped as having power over nature or human fortunes; a deity: *a moon god | the Hindu god Vishnu.* ■ an image, animal, or other object worshipped as divine or symbolizing a god. ■ used as a conventional personification of fate: *he dialled the number and, the gods relenting, got through at once.*
3 (**god**) a greatly admired or influential person: *he has little time for the fashion victims for whom he is a god.* ■ a thing accorded the supreme importance appropriate to a god: *don't make money your god.*
4 (**the gods**) informal the gallery in a theatre.
▶ exclamation used for emphasis or to express emotions such as surprise, anger, or distress: *God, what did I do to deserve this? | God, how I hate that woman!*
– PHRASES **God's acre** archaic a churchyard. **for God's sake!** see SAKE[1] (sense 3). **God bless** an expression of good wishes on parting. **God damn** (**you, him,** etc.) used to express anger or annoyance with someone. **God the Father** (in Christian doctrine) the first person of the Trinity, God as creator and supreme authority. **God forbid** see FORBID. **God grant** used to express a wish that something should happen: *God grant he will soon regain his freedom.* **God help** (**you, him,** etc.) used to express the belief that someone is in a difficult or dangerous situation: *God help anyone who tried to jolly me out of my bad mood.* **God's gift** chiefly Brit. the ideal or best possible person or thing for someone or something (used chiefly ironically or in negative statements): *he appeared to think he was God's gift to women.* **God's truth** the absolute truth (often used for emphasis): *I loved him, that's God's truth.* **God the Son** (in Christian doctrine) Christ regarded as the second person of the Trinity; God as incarnate and resurrected saviour. **God willing** used to express a wish or hope: *one day, God willing, she and John might have a daughter.* **in God's name** used in questions to emphasize anger or surprise: *what in God's name are you doing?* **in the lap of the gods** see LAP[1]. **play God** behave as if all-powerful. **please God** used to emphasize a strong wish or hope: *please God the money will help us find a cure.* **thank God** see THANK. **to God** used after a verb to emphasize a strong wish or hope: *I hope to God you've got something else to put on.* **with God** dead and in heaven.
– DERIVATIVES **godhood** noun, **godship** noun, **godward** adjective & adverb.
– ORIGIN Old English, of Germanic origin; related to Dutch *god* and German *Gott*.

Godard /ˈgɒdɑː/, French /gɔdaʀ/, Jean-Luc (b.1930), French film director. He was one of the leading figures of the *nouvelle vague*. His films include *Breathless* (1960) and *Alphaville* (1965).

Godavari /gəʊˈdɑːvəri/ a river in central India which rises in the state of Maharashtra and flows about 1,440 km (900 miles) south-east across the Deccan plateau to the Bay of Bengal.

God-awful ▶ adjective informal extremely bad or unpleasant: *the most God-awful row.*

God-botherer ▶ noun informal, derogatory a deeply religious person.

godchild ▶ noun (pl. **godchildren**) a person in relation to a godparent.

goddam (also **goddamn, goddamned**) ▶ adjective & adverb informal, chiefly N. Amer. used for emphasis, especially to express anger or frustration.
– ORIGIN mid 17th cent.: abbreviation of *God damn (me)*.

Goddard /ˈgɒdɑːd/, Robert Hutchings (1882–1945), American physicist. He carried out pioneering work in rocketry, and designed and built the first successful liquid-fuelled rocket. NASA's Goddard Space Flight Center is named after him.

god-daughter ▶ noun a female godchild.

goddess ▶ noun a female deity: *Athena Nike, goddess of victory.* ■ a woman who is greatly admired, especially for her beauty: *he had an affair with a screen goddess.*

Gödel /ˈgəːd(ə)l/, Kurt (1906–78), Austrian-born American mathematician. He made several important contributions to mathematical logic, especially the incompleteness theorem.

Gödel's incompleteness theorem ▶ noun see INCOMPLETENESS THEOREM.

godet /gəʊˈdɛt, ˈgəʊdeɪ/ ▶ noun a triangular piece of material inserted in a dress, shirt, or glove to make it flared or for ornamentation.
– ORIGIN late 19th cent.: from French.

G

godetia /ɡə(ʊ)ˈdiːʃə/ ▸ **noun** a North American plant with showy lilac to red flowers. ● Genus *Clarkia* (or *Godetia*), family Onagraceae.
– ORIGIN modern Latin, named after Charles H. *Godet* (1797–1879), Swiss botanist.

go-devil ▸ **noun** N. Amer., chiefly historical **1** a crude sled, used chiefly for dragging logs.
2 a jointed apparatus for cleaning pipelines.

godfather ▸ **noun 1** a male godparent.
2 a man who is influential or pioneering in a movement or organization: *the godfather of alternative comedy.* ■ a person directing a criminal organization, especially a leader of the American Mafia.

God-fearing ▸ **adjective** earnestly religious: *an honest, God-fearing woman.*

godforsaken ▸ **adjective** lacking any merit or attraction: *what are you doing in this godforsaken place?*

God-given ▸ **adjective** received from God. ■ possessed by unquestionable right, as if by divine authority: *being my stepsister doesn't give you a God-given right to know all my business.*

G

Godhavn /ˈɡɒdˌhɑːv(ə)n/ a town in western Greenland, on the south coast of the island of Disko.

godhead ▸ **noun 1** (usu. **the Godhead**) God. ■ [mass noun] divine nature.
2 informal a greatly admired or influential person.

Godiva /ɡəˈdʌɪvə/, Lady (d.1080), English noblewoman, wife of Leofric, Earl of Mercia. According to a 13th-century legend, she agreed to her husband's proposition that he would reduce unpopular taxes only if she rode naked on horseback through the marketplace of Coventry. According to later versions of the story, all the townspeople refrained from watching, except for peeping Tom, who was struck blind as a punishment.

godless ▸ **adjective** not believing in God: *a sceptical, godless society.* ■ without a god. ■ profane; wicked.
– DERIVATIVES **godlessness** noun.

godlike ▸ **adjective** resembling God or a god in qualities such as power, beauty, or benevolence: *our parents are godlike figures to our childish eyes.* ■ befitting a god: *he is a noble figure of godlike magnanimity.*

godly ▸ **adjective** (**godlier**, **godliest**) devoutly religious; pious: *how to live the godly life.*
– DERIVATIVES **godliness** noun.

god-man ▸ **noun 1** Indian, often derogatory a holy man; a guru.
2 an incarnation of a god in human form.

godmother ▸ **noun 1** a female godparent.
2 a woman who is influential or pioneering in a movement or organization: *the godmother of the regiment.*

godown /ˈɡəʊdaʊn, ɡəʊˈdaʊn/ ▸ **noun** (in eastern Asia, especially India) a warehouse.
– ORIGIN late 16th cent.: from Portuguese *gudão*, from Tamil *kiṭaṅku*, Malayalam *kiṭaṅṅu*, or Kannada *gadaṅgu* 'store, warehouse'.

godparent ▸ **noun** a person who presents a child at baptism and promises to take responsibility for their religious education.

God Save the Queen (or **King**) ▸ **noun** the British national anthem.
– ORIGIN evidence suggests a 17th-cent. origin for the complete words and tune of the anthem. The ultimate origin is obscure: the phrase 'God save the King' occurs in various passages in the Old Testament, while as early as 1545 it was a watchword in the navy, with 'long to reign over us' as a countersign.

God's country (also **God's own country**) ▸ **noun** an area or region supposedly favoured by God, especially the United States regarded in this way.

godsend ▸ **noun** a very helpful or valuable event, person, or article: *these information packs are* ***a godsend to*** *schools.*
– ORIGIN early 19th cent.: from *God's send* 'what God has sent'.

God slot ▸ **noun** informal a period in a broadcasting schedule regularly reserved for religious programmes.

godson ▸ **noun** a male godchild.

God's own ▸ **noun** Australian and NZ term for **God's country**.

Godspeed ▸ **exclamation** dated an expression of good wishes to a person starting a journey.
– ORIGIN Middle English: from *God speed you* 'may God help you prosper'.

God squad ▸ **noun** informal, derogatory used to refer to evangelical Christians.

Godthåb /ˈɡɒdhɔːb/ former name (until 1979) for **Nuuk**.

Godunov /ˈɡɒdʊnɒf/, Boris (1550–1605), tsar of Russia 1598–1605. A counsellor of Ivan the Terrible, he succeeded Ivan's son as tsar. His reign was marked by famine, doubts over his involvement in the earlier death of Ivan's eldest son, and the appearance of a pretender, the so-called False Dmitri.

Godwin, William (1756–1836), English social philosopher and novelist. He advocated a system of anarchism based on a belief in the goodness of human reason and on his doctrine of extreme individualism.

Godwin-Austen, Mount former name for **K2**.

godwit ▸ **noun** a large, long-legged wader with a long, slightly upturned or straight bill, and typically a reddish-brown head and breast in the breeding male. ● Genus *Limosa*, family Scolopacidae: four species.
– ORIGIN mid 16th cent.: of unknown origin.

Godwottery /ɡɒdˈwɒt(ə)ri/ ▸ **noun** [mass noun] Brit. humorous an affected quality of archaism, excessive fussiness, and sentimentality.
– ORIGIN 1930s: from the line 'A garden is a lovesome thing, God wot!', in T. E. Brown's poem *My Garden* (1876).

Godzilla /ɡɒdˈzɪlə/ ▸ **noun** informal a particularly enormous example of something: *a Godzilla of a condominium tower.*
– ORIGIN from the name of a huge prehistoric monster featuring in a series of Japanese films from 1954.

Godzone ▸ **noun** New Zealand term for **God's country**.

Goebbels /ˈɡəːb(ə)lz/ (also **Göbbels**), (Paul) Joseph (1897–1945), German Nazi leader and politician. From 1933 Goebbels was Hitler's Minister of Propaganda, with control of the press, radio, and all aspects of culture. He committed suicide rather than surrender to the Allies.

goer ▸ **noun 1** [in combination] a person who attends a specified place or event, especially regularly: *churchgoers | a filmgoer.*
2 [with adj.] informal a person or thing that goes in a specified way: *horse no. 7 is a fast goer.* ■ a project likely to succeed: *if the business is a goer, the entrepreneur moves on.*
3 Brit. informal a sexually unrestrained woman.

Goering /ˈɡəːrɪŋ/ (also **Göring**), Hermann Wilhelm (1893–1946), German Nazi leader and politician. Goering was responsible for the German rearmament programme, founded the Gestapo, and from 1936 until 1943 directed the German economy. Sentenced to death at the Nuremberg war trials, he committed suicide in his cell.

Goes /ɡuːs/, Hugo van der (*fl. c.*1467–82), Flemish painter, born in Ghent. His best-known work is the large-scale *Portinari Altarpiece* (1475), commissioned for a church in Florence.

goes third person singular present of **go**¹.

goest /ˈɡəʊɪst/ archaic second person singular present of **go**¹.

goeth /ˈɡəʊɪθ/ archaic third person singular present of **go**¹.

Goethe /ˈɡəːtə/, Johann Wolfgang von (1749–1832), German poet, dramatist, and scholar. Involved at first with the *Sturm und Drang* movement, Goethe changed to a more measured and classical style, as in the 'Wilhelm Meister' novels (1796–1829). Notable dramas: *Götz von Berlichingen* (1773), *Tasso* (1790), and *Faust* (1808–32).
– DERIVATIVES **Goethean** (also **Goethian**) adjective.

goethite /ˈɡəːtʌɪt/ ▸ **noun** [mass noun] a dark or yellowish-brown mineral consisting of hydrated iron oxide, occurring typically as masses of fibrous crystals.
– ORIGIN early 19th cent.: from the name of J.W. von **Goethe** + **-ite**¹.

go-faster stripes ▸ **plural noun** Brit. informal striped stickers on the bodywork of a car, intended to make it look more sporty.

gofer /ˈɡəʊfə/ (also **gopher**) ▸ **noun** informal a person who runs errands, especially on a film set or in an office; a dogsbody.
– ORIGIN 1960s: from *go for* (i.e. go and fetch).

goffer /ˈɡɒfə/ ▸ **verb** [with obj.] (usu. as adj. **goffered**) crimp or flute (a lace edge or frill) with heated irons: *a goffered frill.* ■ (as adj. **goffered**) (of the gilt edges of a book) embossed with a repeating design.
▸ **noun** an iron used to crimp or flute lace.
– ORIGIN late 16th cent.: from French *gaufrer* 'stamp with a patterned tool', from *gaufre* 'honeycomb', from Middle Low German *wāfel* (see **waffle**²).

Gog and Magog /ɡɒɡ, ˈmeɪɡɒɡ/ **1** (in the Bible) the names of enemies of God's people. In Ezek. 38–9, Gog is apparently a ruler from the land of Magog, while in Rev. 20:8, Gog and Magog are nations under the dominion of Satan.
2 (in medieval legend) opponents of Alexander the Great, living north of the Caucasus.
3 two giant statues standing in Guildhall, London, representing either the last two survivors of a race of giants supposed to have inhabited Britain before Roman times, or Gogmagog, chief of the giants, and Corineus, a Roman invader.

go-getter ▸ **noun** informal an aggressively enterprising person.
– DERIVATIVES **go-getting** adjective.

gogga /ˈxɔxə, ˈxɔxɔ/ ▸ **noun** S. African informal an insect or creepy-crawly.
– ORIGIN Afrikaans, from Khoikhoi *xo-xon*, a collective term for slithering and creeping creatures.

goggle ▸ **verb** [no obj.] look with wide open eyes, typically in amazement: *I goggled at them in total disbelief.* ■ (of the eyes) open wide or protrude.
▸ **adjective** [attrib.] (of the eyes) protuberant or rolling.
▸ **noun 1** (**goggles**) close-fitting glasses with side shields, for protecting the eyes from glare, dust, water, etc. ■ informal glasses.
2 [in sing.] a stare with protruding eyes.
3 (**goggles**) the staggers (a disease of sheep).
– DERIVATIVES **goggled** adjective.
– ORIGIN Middle English (in the sense 'look to one side, squint'): probably from a base symbolic of oscillating movement.

goggle-box ▸ **noun** (**the goggle-box**) Brit. informal a television set.

goggle-eye ▸ **noun** any of a number of edible fishes with large eyes that occur widely on reefs in tropical and subtropical seas: ● a nocturnal fish related to the bigeye (*Priacanthus hamrur*, family Priacanthidae). ● (also **goggle-eye jack**) a fish often found in shoals (*Selar crumenophthalmus*, family Carangidae).

goggle-eyed ▸ **adjective** having staring or protuberant eyes, especially through astonishment.

go-go ▸ **adjective** [attrib.] **1** relating to or denoting an unrestrained and erotic style of dancing to popular music: *a go-go bar | go-go dancers.*
2 N. Amer. assertively dynamic: *the go-go bravado of the 1980s.*
▸ **noun** [mass noun] a style of soul music originating in the black communities of Washington DC and characterized by an incessant funk beat.
– ORIGIN 1960s: reduplication of **go**¹, perhaps influenced by **a gogo**.

Gogol /ˈɡəʊɡɒl, ˈɡɒɡ(ə)l/, Nikolai (Vasilevich) (1809–52), Russian novelist, dramatist, and short-story writer, born in Ukraine. His writings are satirical, often exploring themes of fantasy and the supernatural. Notable works: *The Government Inspector* (play, 1836), *Notes of a Madman* (short fiction, 1835), and *Dead Souls* (novel, 1842).

Goiânia /ɡɔɪˈɑːnɪə/ a city in south central Brazil, capital of the state of Goiás; pop. 1,244,645 (2007). Founded as a new city in 1933, it replaced the town of Goiás as state capital in 1942.

Goiás /ɡɔɪˈɑːs/ a state in south central Brazil; capital, Goiânia.

Goidelic /ɡɔɪˈdɛlɪk/ ▸ **adjective** relating to or denoting the northern group of Celtic languages, including Irish, Scottish Gaelic, and Manx. Speakers of the Celtic precursor of the Goidelic languages are thought to have invaded Ireland from Europe *c.*1000 BC, spreading into Scotland and the Isle of Man from the 5th century AD onwards. Compare with **Brythonic**. Also called **Q-Celtic**.
▸ **noun** [mass noun] the Goidelic languages collectively.

going ▸ **noun 1** an act of leaving a place; a departure: *don't lose track of your child's* ***comings and goings****.*
2 [in sing.] the condition of the ground viewed in terms of suitability for horse racing, riding, or walking: *the going was ideal here, with short turf and a level surface.* ■ progress affected by the condition of the ground: *the paths were covered with drifting snow and the going was difficult.* ■ conditions for, or progress in, an endeavour: *an opportunity to get out while the going is good.*
▸ **adjective 1** [predic.] chiefly Brit. existing or available; to be had: *he asked if there were any other jobs going.*
2 [attrib.] (of a price) accepted or usual at the current time: *people willing to work for* ***the going rate****.*

going concern ▸ noun a business that is operating and making a profit.

going-over ▸ noun [in sing.] informal a thorough cleaning or inspection: *give the place a going-over with the Hoover.* ■ a physical or verbal attack. ■ a heavy defeat: *Pontypool gave them a 35–6 going-over.*

goings-on ▸ plural noun events or behaviour, especially of an unusual or suspect nature.

goitre /ˈɡɔɪtə/ (US **goiter**) ▸ noun a swelling of the neck resulting from enlargement of the thyroid gland: *a woman with a goitre* | [mass noun] *the belief that amber necklaces were good for curing goitre.*
– DERIVATIVES **goitred** adjective, **goitrous** adjective.
– ORIGIN early 17th cent.: from French, a back-formation from *goitreux* 'having a goitre', or from Old French *goitron* 'gullet', both based on Latin *guttur* 'throat'.

goji berry /ˈɡəʊdʒi/ ▸ noun **1** a bright red edible berry widely cultivated in China, supposed to contain high levels of certain vitamins.
2 either of two shrubs on which goji berries grow, *Lycium barbarum* and *Lycium chinense*. See also **WOLFBERRY**.
– ORIGIN from Chinese *gouqi*.

go-kart (also **go-cart**) ▸ noun a small racing car with a lightweight or skeleton body.
– DERIVATIVES **go-karting** noun.
– ORIGIN 1950s: *kart*, alteration of **CART**.

Gokhale /ˈɡəʊkəleɪ/, Gopal Krishna (1866–1915), Indian political leader and social reformer, president of the Indian National Congress from 1905. He was a leading advocate of Indian self-government through constitutional or moderate means.

Golan Heights /ɡəʊˈlɑːn, ˈɡəʊlən/ a range of hills on the border between Syria and Israel, north-east of the Sea of Galilee. Formerly under Syrian control, the area was occupied by Israel in 1967 and annexed in 1981. Negotiations for the withdrawal of Israeli troops from the region began in 1992.

Golconda /ɡɒlˈkɒndə/ ▸ noun a source of wealth, advantages, or happiness: *the posters calling emigrants from Europe to the Golconda of the American West.*
– ORIGIN late 19th cent.: from the name of a city near Hyderabad, India, famous for its diamonds.

gold ▸ noun [mass noun] **1** a yellow precious metal, the chemical element of atomic number 79, used in jewellery and decoration and to guarantee the value of currencies. (Symbol: **Au**) ■ [with modifier] an alloy of gold: *9-carat gold.*
2 a deep lustrous yellow or yellow-brown colour: *her eyes were light green and flecked with gold.*
3 coins or other articles made of gold: *her ankles and wrists were glinting with gold.* ■ money in large sums; wealth: *he proved to be a rabid seeker for gold and power.* ■ a thing that is precious or beautiful: *they scout continents in search of the new green gold.*
4 [count noun] short for **GOLD MEDAL**.
5 [count noun] the bullseye of an archery target.
– PHRASES **go gold** (of a recording) achieve sales meriting a gold disc. **pot** (or **crock**) **of gold** a large but distant or imaginary reward. [with allusion to the story of a crock of gold supposedly to be found at the end of a rainbow.]
– ORIGIN Old English, of Germanic origin; related to Dutch *goud* and German *Gold*, from an Indo-European root shared by **YELLOW**.

gold-beater ▸ noun a person who beats gold out into gold leaf.

gold-beater's skin ▸ noun a membrane used to separate leaves of gold during beating.

gold beetle (also **goldbug**) ▸ noun N. Amer. a leaf beetle with metallic gold coloration. ● Several species in the family Chrysomelidae, in particular *Metriona bicolor*.

gold brick US informal ▸ noun **1** a thing that looks valuable, but is in fact worthless. ■ (also **goldbricker**) a confidence trickster.
2 a lazy person.
▸ verb (**goldbrick**) **1** [no obj.] invent excuses to avoid a task; shirk: *he wasn't goldbricking; he was really sick.*
2 [with obj.] swindle (someone).

goldbug ▸ noun chiefly US **1** informal an advocate of a single gold standard for currency. ■ a person favouring gold as an investment.
2 another term for **GOLD BEETLE**.

gold card ▸ noun a charge card or credit card issued to people with a high credit rating and giving benefits not available with the standard card.

Gold Coast 1 former name (until 1957) for **GHANA**.
2 a resort region on the east coast of Australia, to the south of Brisbane.

goldcrest ▸ noun a very small Eurasian warbler with a black-bordered yellow or orange crest. ● *Regulus regulus*, family Sylviidae.

gold-digger ▸ noun informal a woman who forms relationships with men purely to obtain money or gifts from them.
– DERIVATIVES **gold-digging** adjective.

gold disc ▸ noun a framed golden disc awarded to a recording artist or group for sales of a recording exceeding a specified high figure.

gold dust ▸ noun [mass noun] **1** fine particles of gold. ■ Brit. a thing that is difficult to find or obtain: *council nursery places are like gold dust.*
2 a cultivated evergreen alyssum, with grey-green leaves and numerous small yellow flowers. ● *Alyssum saxatile*, family Cruciferae.

golden ▸ adjective **1** coloured or shining like gold: *curls of glossy golden hair* | *miles of golden sand.*
2 made or consisting of gold: *a golden crown.*
3 (of a period) very happy and prosperous: *those golden days before World War I.* ■ (of an opportunity) very favourable: *a golden opportunity to boost foreign trade.*
4 (of a singing voice) rich and smooth: *a choir of young golden voices.*
– DERIVATIVES **goldenly** adverb.

golden age ▸ noun an idyllic, often imaginary past time of peace, prosperity, and happiness. ■ the period when a specified art or activity is at its peak: *the golden age of cinema.*
– ORIGIN mid 16th cent.: the Greek and Roman poets' name for the first period of history, when the human race lived in an ideal state.

golden ager ▸ noun N. Amer., euphemistic an old person.

golden boy ▸ noun informal a very popular or successful man: *the golden boy of British golf.*

golden calf ▸ noun (in the Bible) an image of gold in the shape of a calf, made by Aaron in response to the Israelites' plea for a god while they awaited Moses' return from Mount Sinai, where he was receiving the Ten Commandments (Exod. 32). ■ an unworthy or inappropriate object of worship, typically wealth.

golden cat ▸ noun a small forest-dwelling cat found in Africa and Asia. ● Genus *Felis*, family Felidae: the African *F. aurata*, with a chestnut to silver-grey coat, and the Asiatic *F. temmincki*, with a golden-brown coat and striped head.

golden chain ▸ noun the common laburnum.

Golden Delicious ▸ noun a widely grown dessert apple of a greenish-yellow, soft-fleshed variety.

golden eagle ▸ noun a large Eurasian and North American eagle with yellow-tipped head feathers in the mature adult. ● *Aquila chrysaetos*, family Accipitridae.

goldeneye ▸ noun (pl. **same** or **goldeneyes**) a migratory northern diving duck, the male of which has a dark head with a white cheek patch and yellow eyes. ● Genus *Bucephala*, family Anatidae: two species, in particular the **common goldeneye** (*B. clangula*).

Golden Fleece Greek Mythology the fleece of a golden ram, guarded by an unsleeping dragon, and sought and won by Jason with the help of Medea. ■ a goal that is highly desirable but difficult to achieve.

Golden Gate a deep channel connecting San Francisco Bay with the Pacific Ocean, spanned by the Golden Gate suspension bridge (completed 1937).

golden girl ▸ noun informal a very popular or successful young woman.

golden glow ▸ noun N. Amer. a tall rudbeckia with globular yellow flower heads. ● *Rudbeckia laciniata*, family Compositae.

golden goal ▸ noun (in some soccer and hockey competitions) the first goal scored during extra time which ends the match and gives victory to the scoring side.

golden goose ▸ noun a continuing source of wealth or profit that may be exhausted if it is misused: *they were killing the golden goose of tourism.* See also **KILL THE GOOSE THAT LAYS THE GOLDEN EGGS** at **EGG**[1].

golden hamster ▸ noun see **HAMSTER**.

golden handcuffs ▸ plural noun informal benefits, typically deferred payments, provided by an employer to discourage an employee from taking employment elsewhere.

golden handshake ▸ noun informal a payment given to someone who is made redundant or retires early.

golden hello ▸ noun Brit. informal a substantial payment made by an employer to a keenly sought recruit.

Golden Hind the ship in which Francis Drake circumnavigated the globe in 1577–80.
– ORIGIN named by Drake in honour of his patron, Sir Christopher Hatton (1540–91), whose crest was a golden hind.

Golden Horde the Tartar and Mongol army, led by descendants of Genghis Khan, that overran Asia and parts of eastern Europe in the 13th century and maintained an empire until around 1500 (so called from the richness of the leader's camp).

Golden Horn a curved inlet of the Bosporus forming the harbour of Istanbul. Turkish name **HALIÇ**.

golden hour ▸ noun Medicine the first hour after a traumatic injury, when emergency treatment is most likely to be successful.

golden jubilee ▸ noun the fiftieth anniversary of a significant event.

golden mean ▸ noun **1** the ideal moderate position between two extremes.
2 another term for **GOLDEN SECTION**.

golden mole ▸ noun a blind mole with an iridescent sheen to its coat, native to southern Africa. ● Family Chrysochloridae: several genera and species.

golden number ▸ noun the number showing a year's place in the Metonic lunar cycle, used to fix the date of Easter for that year.

golden oldie ▸ noun informal an old song or film that is still well known and popular.

golden orfe ▸ noun an orfe (fish) of an ornamental yellow variety, widely kept in aquaria and ponds.

golden oriole ▸ noun a Eurasian oriole with a melodious call, the male being bright yellow and black and the female mainly green. ● *Oriolus oriolus*, family Oriolidae.

golden parachute ▸ noun informal a large payment or other financial compensation guaranteed to a company executive if they should be dismissed as a result of a merger or takeover.

golden perch ▸ noun another term for **CALLOP**.

golden plover ▸ noun a North Eurasian and North American plover, with a gold-speckled back and black face and underparts in the breeding season. ● Genus *Pluvialis*, family Charadriidae: three species, in particular *P. apricaria* of Europe and *P. dominica* of Canada.

golden raisin ▸ noun N. Amer. a sultana.

golden retriever ▸ noun a retriever of a breed with a thick golden-coloured coat.

golden rice ▸ noun [mass noun] a genetically modified variety of rice rich in the orange or red plant pigment beta-carotene, a substance important in the human diet as a precursor of vitamin A.

goldenrod ▸ noun a plant of the daisy family, which bears tall spikes of small bright yellow flowers. ● Genus *Solidago*, family Compositae.

golden rule ▸ noun a basic principle which should always be followed to ensure success in general or in a particular activity. ■ the biblical rule of 'do as you would be done by' (Matt. 7:12).

goldenseal ▸ noun a North American woodland plant of the buttercup family, with a bright yellow root that is used in herbal medicine. ● *Hydrastis canadensis*, family Ranunculaceae.

golden section ▸ noun the division of a line so that the whole is to the greater part as that part is to the smaller part (i.e. in a ratio of 1 to $\frac{1}{2}(\sqrt{5}+1)$), a proportion which is considered to be particularly pleasing to the eye.

golden share ▸ noun Brit. a share in a company that gives control of at least 51 per cent of the voting rights, especially when held by the government.

Golden State informal name for **CALIFORNIA**.

golden syrup ▸ noun [mass noun] Brit. a pale treacle.

golden wattle ▸ noun an Australian acacia with golden flowers. ● Genus *Acacia*, family Leguminosae: *A. pycnatha*, whose flowers are used as Australia's national emblem, and *A. longifolia*.

golden wedding ▸ noun Brit. the fiftieth anniversary of a wedding.

goldfield ▸ noun a district in which gold is found as a mineral.

goldfinch ▸ noun a brightly coloured finch with yellow feathers in the plumage. ● Genus *Carduelis*, family

G

Fringillidae: four species, especially the **Eurasian goldfinch** (*C. carduelis*) and the **American goldfinch** (*C. tristis*).
– ORIGIN late Old English *goldfinc* (see GOLD, FINCH).

goldfish ▶ noun (pl. **same** or **goldfishes**) a small reddish-golden Eurasian carp, popular in ponds and aquaria. A long history of breeding in China and Japan has resulted in many varieties of form and colour. ● *Carassius auratus*, family Cyprinidae.

goldfish bowl ▶ noun a spherical glass container for goldfish. ■ a place or situation lacking privacy: *she was tired of the travel and tired of living in a goldfish bowl*.

goldilocks ▶ noun **1** informal a person with golden hair.
2 a Eurasian woodland buttercup. ● *Ranunculus auricomus*, family Ranunculaceae.
3 a yellow-flowered European plant of the daisy family, resembling the Michaelmas daisy. ● *Aster linosyris*, family Compositae.

Golding, Sir William (Gerald) (1911–93), English novelist. He achieved literary success with his first novel, *Lord of the Flies* (1954), about boys stranded on a desert island who revert to savagery. Other notable works: *Rites of Passage* (Booker Prize, 1980). Nobel Prize for Literature (1983).

G

gold leaf ▶ noun [mass noun] gold that has been beaten into a very thin sheet, used in gilding.
▶ verb (**gold-leaf**) [with obj.] apply a layer of gold leaf to.

Goldman, Emma (1869–1940), Lithuanian-born American political activist, involved in New York's anarchist movement and an opponent of US conscription. Notable works: *Anarchism and Other Essays* (1910) and *My Disillusionment in Russia* (1923).

Goldmark, Peter Carl (1906–77), Hungarian-born American inventor and engineer. He made the first colour television broadcast in 1940, invented the long-playing record in 1948, and pioneered video cassette recording.

gold medal ▶ noun a medal made of or coloured gold, customarily awarded for first place in a race or competition.

gold mine ▶ noun a place where gold is mined. ■ a source of wealth, valuable information, or resources: *the book is a gold mine of sporting trivia*.
– DERIVATIVES **gold miner** noun, **gold-mining** noun & adjective.

gold of pleasure ▶ noun [mass noun] a yellow-flowered Mediterranean plant of the cabbage family, which yields fibre, oilseed, and seed for cage birds. ● *Camelina sativa*, family Cruciferae.

gold plate ▶ noun [mass noun] a thin layer of gold, electroplated or otherwise applied as a coating to another metal. ■ plates, dishes, or other objects made of or plated with gold.
▶ verb (**gold-plate**) [with obj.] cover (something) with a thin layer of gold.

gold-plated ▶ adjective covered with a thin layer of gold: *a gold-plated tiepin*. ■ likely to prove profitable; secure: *houses are no longer the gold-plated investment they were*.

gold record ▶ noun North American term for GOLD DISC.

gold reserve ▶ noun a quantity of gold held by a central bank to support the issue of currency.

gold rush ▶ noun a rapid movement of people to a newly discovered goldfield. The first major gold rush, to California in 1848, was followed by others in the US, Australia (1851–3), South Africa (1884), and Canada (Klondike, 1897–8).

Goldsmith, Oliver (1728–74), Irish novelist, poet, essayist, and dramatist. Notable works: *The Vicar of Wakefield* (novel, 1766), *The Deserted Village* (poem, 1770), and *She Stoops to Conquer* (play, 1773).

goldsmith ▶ noun a person who makes gold articles.
– ORIGIN late Old English (see GOLD, SMITH).

gold standard ▶ noun the system, abandoned in the Depression of the 1930s, by which the value of a currency was defined in terms of gold, for which the currency could be exchanged. ■ a thing of superior quality which serves as a point of reference against which other things of its type may be compared: *breast milk provides the gold standard by which infant feeds are measured*.

Gold Stick ▶ noun (in the UK) a ceremonial officer in the Sovereign's household, entitled to carry a gilt rod on state occasions.

gold thread ▶ noun [mass noun] a plant of the buttercup family, which yields a yellow dye and is used in herbal medicine as a treatment for mouth ulcers. It grows in North America and NE Asia. ● *Coptis trifolia*, family Ranunculaceae.

goldwasser /ˈɡəʊldvasə, ˈɡɒl-/ ▶ noun [mass noun] a liqueur containing particles of gold leaf, originally made at Gdańsk in Poland.
– ORIGIN from German, literally 'gold water'.

goldwork ▶ noun [mass noun] gold objects collectively.
– DERIVATIVES **goldworking** noun.

Goldwyn, Samuel (1882–1974), Polish-born American film producer; born *Schmuel Gelbfisz*; changed to *Samuel Goldfish* then *Goldwyn*. With Louis B. Mayer, he founded the film company Metro-Goldwyn-Mayer (MGM) in 1924.

golem /ˈɡəʊləm, ˈɡɔɪl-/ ▶ noun (in Jewish legend) a clay figure brought to life by magic. ■ an automaton or robot.
– ORIGIN late 19th cent.: from Yiddish *goylem*, from Hebrew *gōlem* 'shapeless mass'.

golf ▶ noun **1** [mass noun] a game played on a large open-air course, in which a small hard ball is struck with a club into a series of small holes in the ground, the object being to use the fewest possible strokes to complete the course.

> A golf course usually has 18 holes, each set in a smooth lawn (a green) separated from the others by stretches of smooth grass (fairways), rough ground, sand-filled bunkers, and other hazards. Various clubs are used to hit the ball from a tee towards the green, up to 450 m away, and then putt it into the hole.

2 a code word representing the letter G, used in radio communication.
▶ verb [no obj.] (often as noun **golfing**) play golf.
– ORIGIN late Middle English (originally Scots): perhaps related to Dutch *kolf* 'club, bat', used as a term in several Dutch games; *golf*, however, is recorded before these games.

golf ball ▶ noun a small hard ball used in the game of golf, typically made of dimpled white latex. ■ (**golf-ball**) a small metal globe used in some electric typewriters to carry the type.

golf cart ▶ noun a small motorized vehicle for golfers and their equipment.

golf club ▶ noun **1** a club used to hit the ball in golf, with a heavy wooden or metal head on a slender shaft.
2 an organization of members for playing golf. ■ the premises used by such an organization.

golf course ▶ noun a course on which golf is played.

golfer ▶ noun **1** a person who plays golf.
2 Brit. dated a cardigan.

golf links ▶ plural noun see LINKS.

golf shirt ▶ noun N. Amer. a light, short-sleeved shirt with a collar, typically of a knitted fabric and with buttons at the neck only.

golgappa /ɡəʊlˈɡʌpə/ ▶ noun another term for PANI PURI.
– ORIGIN from Hindi *golgappā*.

Golgi /ˈɡɒldʒi/, Camillo (1844–1926), Italian histologist and anatomist. He devised a staining technique to investigate nerve tissue, classified types of nerve cell, and described the structure in the cytoplasm of most cells, now named after him. Nobel Prize for Physiology or Medicine (1906).

Golgi body /ˈɡɒldʒi, -ɡi/ (also **Golgi apparatus**) ▶ noun Biology a complex of vesicles and folded membranes within the cytoplasm of most eukaryotic cells, involved in secretion and intracellular transport.

Golgotha /ˈɡɒlɡəθə/ the site of the crucifixion of Jesus; Calvary.
– ORIGIN from late Latin, via Greek from an Aramaic form of Hebrew *gulgoleth* 'skull' (see Matt. 27:33).

Goliath /ɡəˈlʌɪəθ/ (in the Bible) a Philistine giant, according to one tradition slain by David (1 Sam. 17), but according to another slain by Elhanan (2 Sam. 21:19). ■ (as noun also **goliath**) a person or thing of enormous size or strength: *the two unassuming hippies took on a corporate Goliath*.

goliath beetle ▶ noun a very large, boldly marked tropical beetle related to the chafers, the male of which has a forked horn on the head. ● Genus *Goliathus*, family Scarabaeidae: several species, in particular *G. giganteus* of Africa, which is the largest known beetle.

goliath frog ▶ noun a giant frog of West Central Africa. ● *Rana goliath*, family Ranidae.

Gollancz /ˈɡɒlants/, Sir Victor (1893–1967), British publisher and philanthropist. A committed socialist, he founded the charity War on Want.

golliwog ▶ noun a soft doll with bright clothes, a black face, and fuzzy hair.
– ORIGIN late 19th cent.: from *Golliwogg*, the name of a doll character in books by Bertha Upton (died 1912), American writer; perhaps suggested by GOLLY[1] and POLLIWOG.

gollop /ˈɡɒləp/ Brit. informal ▶ verb (**gollops, golloping, golloped**) [with obj.] swallow (food) hastily or greedily.
▶ noun a hasty gulp.
– ORIGIN early 19th cent.: perhaps from GULP, influenced by GOBBLE[1].

golly[1] ▶ exclamation informal used to express surprise or delight: *Golly! Is that the time?*
– ORIGIN late 18th cent.: euphemism for GOD.

golly[2] ▶ noun (pl. **gollies**) Brit. informal short for GOLLIWOG.

GOM ▶ abbreviation Brit. Grand Old Man, a name originally applied to Gladstone.

gombeen /ɡɒmˈbiːn/ ▶ noun [mass noun] [as modifier] Irish involved in the lending of money at unreasonably high interest rates: *a gombeen man*.
– ORIGIN mid 19th cent.: from Irish *gaimbín*, perhaps from the same Celtic source as medieval Latin *cambire* 'to change'.

Gomel /ˈɡəʊmʲilʲ/ Russian name for HOMEL.

gomer /ˈɡəʊmə/ ▶ noun US **1** military slang an inept or stupid colleague, especially a trainee.
2 informal (used by doctors) a troublesome patient, especially an elderly one.
– ORIGIN 1960s: origin uncertain; sense 1 perhaps from *Gomer* Pyle, a US television character portrayed as an ignorant hillbilly; sense 2 perhaps an acronym from *get out of my emergency room*.

Gomorrah /ɡəˈmɒrə/ a town in ancient Palestine, probably south of the Dead Sea. According to Gen. 19:24, it was destroyed by fire from heaven, along with Sodom, for the wickedness of its inhabitants.

-gon ▶ combining form in nouns denoting plane figures with a specified number of angles and sides: *hexagon | pentagon*.
– ORIGIN from Greek *-gōnos* '-angled'.

gonad /ˈɡəʊnad/ ▶ noun Physiology & Zoology an organ that produces gametes; a testis or ovary.
– DERIVATIVES **gonadal** /ɡə(ʊ)ˈneɪd(ə)l/ adjective.
– ORIGIN late 19th cent.: from modern Latin *gonades*, plural of *gonas*, from Greek *gonē* 'generation, seed'.

gonadotrophic hormone /ˌɡəʊnədə(ʊ)ˈtrəʊfɪk, -ˈtrɒfɪk/ (also **gonadotropic hormone** /-ˈtrəʊpɪk, -ˈtrɒpɪk/) ▶ noun another term for GONADOTROPHIN.

gonadotrophin /ˌɡəʊnədə(ʊ)ˈtrəʊfɪn/ (also **gonadotropin** /-ˈtrəʊpɪn, -ˈtrɒpɪn/) ▶ noun Biochemistry any of a group of hormones secreted by the pituitary which stimulate the activity of the gonads.

Goncharov /ˈɡɒntʃərɒf/, Ivan (Aleksandrovich) (1812–91), Russian novelist. His novel *Oblomov* (1857) is regarded as one of the greatest works of Russian realism.

Goncourt /ɡɒnˈkʊə/, French /ɡɔ̃kuʀ/, Edmond de (1822–96) and Jules de (1830–70), French novelists and critics. Working together, the brothers wrote art criticism, realist novels and social history. In his will Edmond provided for the establishment of the Académie Goncourt, which awards the annual Prix Goncourt.

Gond /ɡɒnd, ɡaʊnd/ ▶ noun (pl. **same**) **1** a member of an indigenous people living in the hill forests of central India.
2 [mass noun] the Dravidian language of the Gond, with several highly differentiated dialects and about 2 million speakers.
▶ adjective relating to the Gond or their language.
– DERIVATIVES **Gondi** noun & adjective.
– ORIGIN from Sanskrit *goṇḍa*.

gondola /ˈɡɒndələ/ ▶ noun **1** a light flat-bottomed boat used on Venetian canals, having a high point at each end and worked by one oar at the stern.
2 the seating compartment in a ski lift. ■ an enclosed compartment suspended from an airship or balloon.
3 (also **gondola car**) N. Amer. an open railway freight wagon.
4 Brit. a free-standing block of shelves used to display goods in a supermarket.
– ORIGIN mid 16th cent.: from Venetian Italian, from Rhaeto-Romance *gondolà* 'to rock, roll'.

gondolier /ˌɡɒndəˈlɪə/ ▶ noun a person who propels and steers a gondola.
– ORIGIN early 17th cent.: via French from Italian *gondoliere*, from *gondola* (see GONDOLA).

Gondwana /gɒnˈdwɑːnə/ (also **Gondwanaland**) a vast continental area believed to have existed in the southern hemisphere and to have resulted from the break-up of Pangaea in Mesozoic times. It comprised present-day Arabia, Africa, South America, Antarctica, Australia, and the peninsula of India.
– ORIGIN late 19th cent. (originally denoting any of a series of rocks in India, especially fluviatile shales and sandstones): from the name of a region in central northern India, from Sanskrit *goṇḍavana* 'forest of Gond'.

gone past participle of **GO**[1]. ▶ **adjective** [predic.] **1** no longer present; departed: *you were gone a long time* | *the bad old days are gone.* ■ no longer in existence; dead or extinct: *an aunt of mine, long since gone.* ■ no longer available; consumed or used up: *the food's all gone, I'm afraid.* ■ informal in a trance or stupor, especially through exhaustion, drink, or drugs: *she sat, half-gone, on a folding chair.* ■ [attrib.] informal, chiefly US beyond help; in a hopeless state: *spending time and effort on a gone sucker like Galindez.* ■ US informal, dated excellent; inspired: *a bunch of real gone cats.*
2 informal having reached a specified time in a pregnancy: *she is now four months gone.*
▶ **preposition** Brit. (of time) past: *it's gone half past eleven.* ■ (of age) older than: *she was gone sixty by then.*
– PHRASES **be gone on** informal be infatuated with: *I knew he was awfully gone on you.* **gone away!** a huntsman's cry, indicating that a fox has been started.

gone goose ▶ **noun** informal, dated a person or thing that is beyond hope.

goner /ˈgɒnə/ ▶ **noun** informal a person or thing that is doomed or cannot be saved.

gonfalon /ˈgɒnf(ə)lən/ ▶ **noun** a banner or pennant, especially one with streamers, hung from a crossbar.
– DERIVATIVES **gonfalonier** /ˌgɒnfələˈnɪə/ **noun.**
– ORIGIN late 16th cent.: from Italian *gonfalone*, from a Germanic compound whose second element is related to **VANE**.

gong ▶ **noun 1** a metal disc with a turned rim, giving a resonant note when struck.
2 Brit. informal a medal or award.
▶ **verb** [no obj.] sound a gong or make a sound like that of a gong being struck.
– ORIGIN early 17th cent.: from Malay *gong, gung*, of imitative origin.

gongoozler /gɒŋˈguːzlə/ ▶ **noun** informal an idle spectator.
– ORIGIN early 20th cent. (originally denoting a person who idly watched activity on a canal); rare before 1970: perhaps from Lincolnshire dialect *gawn* and *gooze* 'stare, gape'.

goniatite /ˈgəʊnɪətʌɪt/ ▶ **noun** an ammonoid fossil of an early type found chiefly in the Devonian and Carboniferous periods, typically with simple angular suture lines. Compare with **AMMONITE** and **CERATITE**.
● Typified by the genus *Goniatites*, order Goniatitida.
– ORIGIN mid 19th cent.: from modern Latin *Goniatites*, from Greek *gōnia* 'angle'.

gonif /ˈgɒnɪf/ (also **goniff**) ▶ **noun** N. Amer. informal a disreputable or dishonest person (often used as a general term of abuse).
– ORIGIN mid 19th cent.: from Yiddish *ganev*, from Hebrew *gannāḇ* 'thief'.

goniometer /ˌgəʊnɪˈɒmɪtə/ ▶ **noun** an instrument for the precise measurement of angles, especially one used to measure the angles between the faces of crystals.
– DERIVATIVES **goniometric** adjective, **goniometrical** adjective, **goniometry** noun.
– ORIGIN mid 18th cent.: from French *goniomètre*, from Greek *gōnia* 'angle' + French *-mètre* '(instrument) measuring'.

Gonk ▶ **noun** trademark a spherical or egg-shaped doll with frizzy hair.

gonna informal ▶ **contraction** going to: *so what you gonna do now?*

gonococcus /ˌgɒnəˈkɒkəs/ ▶ **noun** (pl. **gonococci** /-k(s)ʌɪ, -k(s)iː/) a bacterium which causes gonorrhoea. ● *Neisseria gonorrhoeae*, a Gram-negative diplococcus.
– DERIVATIVES **gonococcal** adjective.
– ORIGIN late 19th cent.: blend of **GONORRHOEA** and **COCCUS**.

gonolek /ˈgɒnəlɛk/ ▶ **noun** an African shrike (songbird) with a mainly black back and red underparts.
● Genus *Laniarius*, family Laniidae: three species, in particular the **common gonolek** (*L. barbarus*).

gonorrhoea /ˌgɒnəˈrɪə/ (US **gonorrhea**) ▶ **noun** [mass noun] a venereal disease involving inflammatory discharge from the urethra or vagina.
– DERIVATIVES **gonorrhoeal** adjective.
– ORIGIN early 16th cent.: via late Latin from Greek *gonorrhoia*, from *gonos* 'semen' + *rhoia* 'flux'.

gonzo ▶ **adjective** informal, chiefly N. Amer. **1** relating to or denoting journalism of an exaggerated, subjective, and fictionalized style.
2 bizarre or crazy: *the woman was either gonzo or stoned.*
– ORIGIN 1970s: perhaps from Italian *gonzo* 'foolish' or Spanish *ganso* 'goose, fool'.

goo ▶ **noun** [mass noun] informal **1** a sticky or slimy substance.
2 excessive sentimentality.
– ORIGIN early 20th cent. (originally US): perhaps from *burgoo*, a nautical slang term for porridge, based on Persian *bulġūr* 'bruised grain'.

goober /ˈguːbə/ ▶ **noun** N. Amer. informal a person from the south-eastern US, especially Georgia or Arkansas. ■ derogatory an unsophisticated person.
– ORIGIN late 19th cent.: from an earlier sense 'peanut', from Kikongo *nguba*.

good ▶ **adjective** (**better, best**) **1** to be desired or approved of: *it's good that he's back to his old self* | *a good quality of life.* ■ pleasing and welcome: *we've had some good news* | *it's good to see you again.* ■ showing approval: *the play had good reviews.*
2 having the required qualities; of a high standard: *a good restaurant* | *his marks are just not good enough.* ■ skilled at doing or dealing with a specified thing: *I'm* ***good at*** *crosswords* | *he was* ***good with*** *children.* ■ healthy, strong, or well: *she's not feeling too good.* ■ useful, advantageous, or beneficial in effect: *too much sun is not* ***good for*** *you.* ■ appropriate to a particular purpose: *this is a* ***good*** *month* ***for*** *planting seeds.* ■ (of language) with correct grammar and pronunciation: *she speaks good English.* ■ strictly adhering to or fulfilling all the principles of a particular religion or cause: *a good Catholic girl.*
3 possessing or displaying moral virtue: *her father was a good man.* ■ showing kindness: *it was* ***good of*** *you to come.* ■ obedient to rules or conventions: *accustom the child to being rewarded for good behaviour.* ■ used to address or refer to people in a courteous, patronizing, or ironic way: *a man very like your good self, in fact* | *the good lady of the house.* ■ commanding respect: *he was concerned with establishing and maintaining his good name.* ■ belonging or relating to a high social class: *he comes from a good family.*
4 giving pleasure; enjoyable or satisfying: *the streets fill up with people looking for a good time.* ■ pleasant to look at; attractive: *you're looking pretty good.* ■ (of clothes) smart and suitable for formal wear: *he went upstairs to change out of his good suit.*
5 [attrib.] thorough: *now is the time to have a really good clear-up* | *have a good look around.* ■ used to emphasize that a number is at least as great as one claims: *they're a good twenty years younger.* ■ used to emphasize a following adjective or adverb: *we had a good long hug* | *it'll be good and dark by then.* ■ fairly large in number, amount, or size: *the match attracted a good crowd* | *there's a good chance that we may be able to help.*
6 (usu. **good for**) valid: *the ticket is good for travel from May to September.* ■ likely to provide: *she's always good for a laugh.* ■ sufficient to pay for: *his money was good for a bottle of whisky.*
7 used in conjunction with the name of God or a related expression as an exclamation of extreme surprise or anger: *good heavens!*
▶ **noun 1** [mass noun] that which is morally right; righteousness: *a mysterious balance of good and evil.*
2 [mass noun] benefit or advantage to someone or something: *he is* ***too clever for his own good.***
3 (**goods**) merchandise or possessions: *imports of luxury goods* | *stolen goods.* ■ Brit. things to be transported, as distinct from passengers: *a means of transporting passengers as well as goods* | [as modifier] *a goods train.* ■ (**the goods**) informal the genuine article.
▶ **adverb** informal well: *my mother could never cook this good.*
– PHRASES **all to the good** to be welcomed without qualification. **as good as ——** very nearly ——: *the editor as good as told him he was lucky to get £50 a week.* ■ used of a result which will inevitably follow: *if we pass on the information, he's as good as dead.* **be any** (or **no** or **much**) **good** have some (or none or a lot of) merit: *tell me whether that picture is any good.* ■ be of some (or none or a lot of) help in dealing with a situation: *it's no good arguing with him.* **be so good as** (or **be good enough**) **to do something** used to make a polite request: *would you be so good as to answer me.* **be —— to the good** have a specified net profit or advantage: *I came out £7 to the good.* **come up with** (or **deliver**) **the goods** informal do what is expected or required of one. **do good 1** act virtuously, especially by helping others. **2** make a helpful contribution to a situation: *could the discussion do any good?* **do someone good** be beneficial to someone, especially to their health: *the walk will do you good.* **for good** (**and all**) forever; definitively: *the experience almost frightened me away for good.* **get** (or **have**) **the goods on** informal obtain (or possess) information about (someone) which may be used to their detriment. (**as**) **good as gold** (of a child) extremely well behaved. (**as**) **good as new** in a very good condition or state; close to the original state again after damage, injury, or illness. **the Good Book** the Bible. **good for** (or **on**) **you** (or **him, her**, etc.)**!** used as an exclamation of praise or approval: *'I'm having driving lessons and taking my test next month.' 'Good for you!'.* **good money** money that could usefully be spent elsewhere; hard-earned money: *I paid good money for that computer.* **the Good Shepherd** Jesus. [with biblical allusion to John 10:1–16.] **good wine needs no bush** see **WINE**[1]. **a good word** words in recommendation or defence of a person: *I hoped you might* ***put in a good word for*** *me with your friends.* **in good time 1** with no risk of being late: *I arrived in good time.* **2** (also **all in good time**) in due course but without haste: *'I want to see him.' 'You will. All in good time.'.* **make good** be successful: *a college friend who made good in Hollywood.* **make something good 1** compensate for loss, damage, or expense: *if I scratched the table I'd make good the damage.* ■ repair or restore after damage: *make good the wall where you have buried the cable.* **2** fulfil a promise or claim: *I challenged him to make good his boast.* **take something in good part** not be offended by something: *he took her abruptness in good part.* **up to no good** doing something wrong.
– ORIGIN Old English *gōd*, of Germanic origin; related to Dutch *goed* and German *gut*.

good afternoon ▶ **exclamation** expressing good wishes on meeting or parting in the afternoon.

Goodall, Jane (b.1934), English zoologist. After working with Louis Leakey in Tanzania from 1957, she made prolonged and intimate studies of chimpanzees at the Gombe Stream Reserve by Lake Tanganyika from 1970.

goodbye (US also **goodby**) ▶ **exclamation** used to express good wishes when parting or at the end of a conversation.
▶ **noun** (pl. **goodbyes**; US also **goodbys**) an instance of saying 'goodbye'; a parting: *we said our goodbyes and set off.*
– ORIGIN late 16th cent.: contraction of *God be with you!*, with *good* substituted on the pattern of phrases such as *good morning*.

good day ▶ **exclamation** expressing good wishes on meeting or parting during the day.

good doer ▶ **noun** Brit. informal a thing, especially a cultivated plant or domesticated animal, that thrives or performs well without special attention.

good evening ▶ **exclamation** expressing good wishes on meeting or parting during the evening.

good fairy ▶ **noun** a fairy godmother.

good faith ▶ **noun** [mass noun] honesty or sincerity of intention: *the details contained in this brochure have been published* ***in good faith.***

goodfella ▶ **noun** informal, chiefly N. Amer. a gangster, especially a member of a Mafia family.

good form ▶ **noun** [mass noun] behaviour that complies with current social conventions: *it wasn't considered good form to show too much enthusiasm.*

good-for-nothing ▶ **adjective** (of a person) lazy and feckless: *his good-for-nothing son.*
▶ **noun** a lazy, feckless person.

Good Friday ▶ **noun** the Friday before Easter Sunday, on which the Crucifixion of Christ is commemorated in the Christian Church. It is traditionally a day of fasting and penance.
– ORIGIN from **GOOD**, in the sense 'holy, observed as a holy day'.

good-hearted ▶ **adjective** kind and well meaning.
– DERIVATIVES **good-heartedness** noun.

Good Hope, Cape of a mountainous promontory south of Cape Town, South Africa, near the southern extremity of Africa.

G

good humour ▶ noun [mass noun] a genial disposition or mood: *I admire your dignity and good humour*.

good-humoured ▶ adjective naturally cheerful and friendly; genial: *a good-humoured and tolerant man*.
– DERIVATIVES **good-humouredly** adverb.

goodie ▶ noun variant spelling of **GOODY**[1].

goodish ▶ adjective fairly good: *a goodish performance*. ■ fairly large: *a goodish portion*.

Good King Henry ▶ noun an edible plant of the goosefoot family, with large dark green leaves and insignificant clusters of flowers, native to Europe.
● *Chenopodium bonus-henricus*, family Chenopodiaceae.
– ORIGIN late 16th cent.: of unknown origin.

good-looking ▶ adjective (of a person) physically attractive: *a good-looking woman in her late thirties*.
– DERIVATIVES **good-looker** noun.

goodly ▶ adjective (**goodlier**, **goodliest**) **1** considerable in size or quantity: *a goodly number of our countrymen*.
2 archaic attractive, excellent, or admirable.
– DERIVATIVES **goodliness** noun.
– ORIGIN Old English *gōdlic* (see **GOOD**, **-LY**[1]).

G

Goodman, Benny (1909–86), American jazz clarinettist and bandleader; full name *Benjamin David Goodman*; known as **the King of Swing**. In 1934 he formed his own big band, which was the first to include both black and white musicians.

goodman ▶ noun (pl. **goodmen**) archaic, chiefly Scottish the male head of a household.

good manners ▶ plural noun polite or well-bred social behaviour: *it's nice to meet a young man with such good manners*.

good morning ▶ exclamation expressing good wishes on meeting or parting during the morning.

good nature ▶ noun a kind and unselfish disposition: *your boy has a good nature*.

good-natured ▶ adjective kind, friendly, and patient: *everyone was very good-natured about it*.
– DERIVATIVES **good-naturedly** adverb.

goodness ▶ noun **1** the quality of being good: *a belief in the basic goodness of mankind*.
2 the beneficial or nourishing element of food.
▶ exclamation (as a substitution for 'God') expressing surprise, anger, etc.: ***goodness knows** why she didn't go herself* | ***my goodness**, you gave me quite a fright!*
– PHRASES **for goodness' sake** see **SAKE**[1]. **goodness of fit** Statistics the extent to which observed data matches the values expected by theory. **have the goodness to do something** used in exaggeratedly polite requests: *have the goodness to look at me when I'm speaking to you*.
– ORIGIN Old English *gōdnes* (see **GOOD**, **-NESS**).

Good News Bible ▶ noun a translation of the Bible in simple everyday English, published 1966–76 by the United Bible Societies.

goodnight ▶ exclamation expressing good wishes on parting at night or before going to bed.

goodo /ˈɡʊdəʊ/ ▶ adjective Austral./NZ informal good.

good-oh /ˈɡʊdəʊ, ɡʊdˈəʊ/ ▶ exclamation dated used to express pleasure or approval.

goods and chattels ▶ plural noun chiefly Law all kinds of personal possessions.

good-tempered ▶ adjective not easily irritated or made angry.
– DERIVATIVES **good-temperedly** adverb.

good-time ▶ adjective [attrib.] (of a person) having the pursuit of pleasure as one's chief aim: *a good-time girl*. ■ (of music) intended purely to entertain.

goodwife ▶ noun (pl. **goodwives**) archaic, chiefly Scottish the female head of a household.

goodwill ▶ noun [mass noun] **1** friendly, helpful, or cooperative feelings or attitude: *the scheme is dependent on goodwill between the two sides* | [as modifier] *a goodwill gesture*.
2 the established reputation of a business regarded as a quantifiable asset and calculated as part of its value when it is sold.

Goodwin Sands an area of sandbanks in the Strait of Dover. Often exposed at low tide, the sandbanks are a hazard to shipping.

Goodwood a racecourse in West Sussex, near Chichester. It is the scene of an annual summer race meeting.

good works ▶ plural noun charitable acts.

goody[1] ▶ noun (also **goodie**) (pl. **goodies**) informal
1 Brit. a good or favoured person, especially a hero in a book, film, etc.
2 (usu. **goodies**) something attractive or desirable, especially something tasty to eat.
▶ exclamation expressing childish delight: *goody, we can have a party*.

goody[2] ▶ noun (pl. **goodies**) archaic (often as a title prefixed to a surname) an elderly woman of humble station: *the tale of Goody Blake and Harry Gill*.
– ORIGIN mid 16th cent.: pet form of **GOODWIFE**; compare with **HUSSY**.

goody bag ▶ noun a bag containing a selection of desirable products, especially one given away as a promotional offer.

Goodyear, Charles (1800–60), American inventor. He developed the process of the vulcanization of rubber, after accidentally dropping some rubber mixed with sulphur and white lead on to a hot stove.

goody-goody informal ▶ noun a smug or ostentatiously virtuous person.
▶ adjective smug or ostentatiously virtuous.

gooey ▶ adjective (**gooier**, **gooiest**) informal **1** soft and sticky: *a gooey chocolate dessert*.
2 mawkishly sentimental: *she gets all gooey over babies*.
– DERIVATIVES **gooeyness** noun.

goof informal, chiefly N. Amer. ▶ noun **1** a mistake: *one of the most embarrassing goofs of his tenure*.
2 a foolish or stupid person.
▶ verb [no obj.] **1** behave in a silly way or playful way: *they started **goofing around** in front of the cameras*. ■ (**goof off**) be lazy; avoid one's work or duties: *too many students are goofing off*. ■ (**goof on**) make fun of; ridicule: *Lew and I started goofing on Alison's friend*.
2 make a mistake: *someone at the bank had goofed*.
– ORIGIN early 20th cent.: of unknown origin; compare with **GOOP**[1].

goofball ▶ noun informal, chiefly N. Amer. **1** a naive or stupid person.
2 a narcotic drug in the form of a pill, especially a barbiturate.

goof-off ▶ noun N. Amer. informal a person who is habitually lazy or does less than their fair share of work.

goof-up ▶ noun informal, chiefly N. Amer. a stupid mistake.

goofus /ˈɡuːfəs/ ▶ noun US informal a foolish or stupid person (often used as a general term of abuse).
– ORIGIN 1920s: based on **GOOF**.

goofy ▶ adjective (**goofier**, **goofiest**) informal **1** chiefly N. Amer. foolish; harmlessly eccentric.
2 having or displaying protruding or crooked front teeth: *a goofy grin*.
3 (in surfing and other board sports) with the right leg in front of the left on the board.
– DERIVATIVES **goofily** adverb, **goofiness** noun.

goog ▶ noun Austral./NZ informal an egg.
– PHRASES **(as) full as a goog** very drunk.
– ORIGIN early 20th cent.: abbreviation of *googie*, from Scots dialect *goggie*, child's word for an egg.

google ▶ verb [with obj.] informal search for information about (someone or something) on the Internet.
– ORIGIN 1990s: from *Google*, the proprietary name of a popular Internet search engine.

google bombing ▶ noun [mass noun] the designing of Internet links that will bias search engine results so as to create an inaccurate (often humorous) impression of the search target.

googly ▶ noun (pl. **googlies**) Cricket an off break bowled with an apparent leg-break action.
– ORIGIN early 20th cent.: of unknown origin.

googol /ˈɡuːɡɒl/ ▶ cardinal number equivalent to ten raised to the power of a hundred (10^{100}).
– ORIGIN 1940s: said to have been coined by the nine-year-old nephew of E. Kasner (1878–1955), American mathematician, at Kasner's request.

googolplex /ˈɡuːɡ(ə)lplɛks/ ▶ cardinal number equivalent to ten raised to the power of a googol.
– ORIGIN 1940s: from **GOOGOL** + *-plex* as in *multiplex*.

goo-goo informal ▶ adjective **1** amorously adoring: *they made goo-goo eyes at each other*.
2 (of speech or vocal sounds) childish or meaningless: *soothing goo-goo noises*.
– ORIGIN early 20th cent.: possibly related to **GOGGLE**.

gook[1] /ɡuːk, ɡʊk/ ▶ noun offensive, chiefly N. Amer. a foreigner, especially a person of SE Asian descent.
– ORIGIN 1930s: of unknown origin.

gook[2] /ɡuːk, ɡʊk/ ▶ noun [mass noun] informal a sloppy wet or viscous substance: *all that gook she kept putting on her face*.
– ORIGIN 1970s: variant of **GUCK**.

Goolagong /ˈɡuːləɡɒŋ/, Evonne, see **CAWLEY**.

goolie /ˈɡuːli/ (also **gooly**) ▶ noun (pl. **goolies**)
1 (usu. **goolies**) Brit. vulgar slang a testicle.
2 Austral./NZ informal a stone or pebble.
– ORIGIN 1930s (in sense 1): apparently of Indian origin; compare with Hindi *golī* 'bullet, ball, pill'. Sense 2 is possibly from an Aboriginal language of New South Wales.

goombah /ɡuːmˈbɑː/ ▶ noun N. Amer. informal an associate or accomplice, especially a senior member of a criminal gang.
– ORIGIN 1960s: probably a dialect alteration of Italian *compare* 'godfather, friend, accomplice'.

goombay /ˈɡuːmbeɪ/ ▶ noun W. Indian a goatskin drum with a round or squared top, played with the hands. ■ [mass noun] the calypso-style music associated with the playing of goombay drums. ■ a dance to goombay music. ■ (chiefly in the Bahamas) a festival or season of goombay music and dance.
– ORIGIN perhaps from Kikongo *ngoma*, denoting a type of drum.

goon ▶ noun informal **1** a silly, foolish, or eccentric person.
2 chiefly N. Amer. a bully or thug, especially a member of an armed or security force.
3 Brit. a guard in a German prisoner-of-war camp during the Second World War.
– ORIGIN mid 19th cent.: perhaps from dialect *gooney* 'booby'; influenced by the subhuman cartoon character 'Alice the *Goon*', created by E. C. Segar (1894–1938), American cartoonist.

goonda /ˈɡuːndə/ ▶ noun Indian a hired thug or bully.
– ORIGIN from Hindi *guṇḍā* 'rascal'.

gooney bird (also **goony bird**) ▶ noun chiefly US another term for an albatross of the North Pacific.
● Genus *Diomedea*, family Diomedeidae: the Laysan albatross (*D. immutabilis*) and the black-footed albatross (*D. nigripes*).
– ORIGIN mid 19th cent.: of unknown origin.

goop[1] ▶ noun informal a stupid person.
– DERIVATIVES **goopiness** noun, **goopy** adjective (**goopier**, **goopiest**).
– ORIGIN early 20th cent. (originally US): of unknown origin; compare with **GOOF**.

goop[2] ▶ noun informal, chiefly N. Amer. another term for **GLOOP**.
– DERIVATIVES **goopiness** noun, **goopy** adjective (**goopier**, **goopiest**).

Goorkha ▶ noun old-fashioned spelling of **GURKHA**.

goosander /ɡuːˈsandə/ ▶ noun (pl. **same** or **goosanders**) a large Eurasian and North American merganser (diving duck), the male of which has a dark green head and whitish underside. ● *Mergus merganser*, family Anatidae. North American name: **common merganser**.
– ORIGIN early 17th cent.: probably from **GOOSE** + *-ander* as in dialect *bergander* 'shelduck' (the colouring of the male goosander resembling that of the shelduck).

goose /ɡuːs/ ▶ noun (pl. **geese** /ɡiːs/) **1** a large waterbird with a long neck, short legs, webbed feet, and a short broad bill. Generally geese are larger than ducks and have longer necks and shorter bills.
● Several genera in the family Anatidae; most domesticated geese are descended from the greylag.
■ a female goose. ■ [mass noun] the flesh of a goose as food.
2 informal a foolish person.
3 (pl. **gooses**) a tailor's smoothing iron.
▶ verb [with obj.] informal **1** poke (someone) in the bottom.
2 N. Amer. give (something) a boost; invigorate: *the government's desire to goose the tired housing market*.
– ORIGIN Old English *gōs*, of Germanic origin; related to Dutch *gans* and German *Gans*, from an Indo-European root shared by Latin *anser* and Greek *khēn*.

goose barnacle ▶ noun a stalked barnacle which hangs down from driftwood or other slow-moving floating objects, catching passing prey with its feathery legs. ● Genus *Lepas*, class Cirripedia.

gooseberry ▶ noun (pl. **gooseberries**) **1** a round edible yellowish-green or reddish berry with a thin translucent hairy skin.
2 the thorny European shrub which bears gooseberries. ● *Ribes grossularia*, family Grossulariaceae.
3 Brit. informal a third person in the company of two people, especially lovers, who would prefer to be alone: *they didn't want me **playing gooseberry** on their first date*. [from *gooseberry-picker*, referring to an activity used as a pretext for the lovers to be together.]
– ORIGIN mid 16th cent.: the first element perhaps from **GOOSE**, or perhaps based on Old French *groseille*,

altered because of an unexplained association with the bird.

goosebumps ▶ plural noun chiefly N. Amer. another term for GOOSE PIMPLES.

goose egg ▶ noun N. Amer. informal a zero score in a game.
– ORIGIN late 19th cent.: with reference to the shape of the zero; compare with DUCK[3].

goosefish ▶ noun (pl. same or goosefishes) N. Amer. a bottom-dwelling anglerfish. ● Family Lophiidae: several species, in particular *Lophius americanus* of North American waters.

gooseflesh ▶ noun [mass noun] a pimply state of the skin with the hairs erect, produced by cold or fright.
– ORIGIN early 19th cent.: so named because the skin resembles that of a plucked goose.

goosefoot ▶ noun (pl. goosefoots) a plant of temperate regions with divided leaves which are said to resemble the foot of a goose. Some kinds are edible and many are common weeds. ● Genus *Chenopodium*, family Chenopodiaceae.

goosegog /ˈɡʊzɡɒɡ, ˈɡuːsɡɒɡ/ ▶ noun Brit. informal a gooseberry.
– ORIGIN early 19th cent.: humorous alteration, *gog* being an altered form of GOB[2].

goosegrass ▶ noun [mass noun] a widely distributed scrambling plant related to bedstraws, with hooked bristles on the stem, leaves, and seeds which cling to fur and clothing. Also called CLEAVERS. ● *Galium aparine*, family Rubiaceae.

gooseneck ▶ noun 1 a support or pipe curved like a goose's neck.
2 Sailing a metal fitting at the end of a boom, connecting it to a pivot or ring at the base of the mast.

goose pimples ▶ plural noun the pimples that form gooseflesh.

gooseskin ▶ noun another term for GOOSEFLESH.

goose-step ▶ noun a military marching step in which the legs are not bent at the knee.
▶ verb [no obj., with adverbial] march with a goose-step.

goosey (also **goosy**) ▶ adjective 1 having or showing a quality considered to be characteristic of a goose, especially foolishness or nervousness.
2 informal exhibiting gooseflesh: *I've gone all goosey.*

Goossens /ˈɡuːs(ə)nz/, Sir (Aynsley) Eugene (1893–1962), English conductor, violinist, and composer, of Belgian descent.

GOP ▶ abbreviation Grand Old Party (the Republican Party in the US).

gopak /ˈɡəʊpak/ (also **hopak**) ▶ noun an energetic Ukrainian dance in duple time, traditionally performed by men.
– ORIGIN 1920s: via Russian, from Ukrainian *hopak*.

gopher /ˈɡəʊfə/ ▶ noun 1 (also **pocket gopher**) a burrowing rodent with fur-lined pouches on the outside of the cheeks, found in North and Central America. ● Family Geomyidae: several genera and species.
■ North American term for GROUND SQUIRREL.
2 (also **gopher tortoise**) a tortoise of dry sandy regions that excavates tunnels as shelter from the sun, native to the southern US. ● *Gopherus polyphemus*, family Testudinidae.
■ [usu. as modifier] N. Amer. any of a number of burrowing reptiles and amphibians.
3 (also **Gopher**) Computing a menu-based system for Internet searching and document retrieval, largely superseded by the World Wide Web. [1990s: named after the gopher mascot of the University of Minnesota, US, where the system was invented.]
4 variant spelling of GOFER.
– ORIGIN late 18th cent.: perhaps from Canadian French *gaufre* 'honeycomb' (because the gopher 'honeycombs' the ground with its burrows).

gopher snake ▶ noun a large harmless yellowish-cream snake with darker markings, native to western North America. ● *Pituophis catenifer*, family Colubridae.
■ (also **blue gopher snake**) another term for INDIGO SNAKE.

Gopher State informal name for MINNESOTA.

gopher wood ▶ noun 1 [mass noun] (in biblical use) the timber from which Noah's ark was made, from an unidentified tree (Gen. 6:14).
2 (**gopherwood**) either of two North American trees: ● stinking cedar. ● yellow-wood.
– ORIGIN early 17th cent.: *gopher* from Hebrew *gōper*.

gopik /ˈɡəʊpɪk/ ▶ noun (pl. same or gopiks) a monetary unit of Azerbaijan, equal to one hundredth of a manat.
– ORIGIN Azerbaijani, 'kopek'.

gopura /ˈɡəʊpʊrə/ (also **gopuram** /ˈɡəʊpʊrəm/) ▶ noun (in southern India) a large pyramidal tower over the entrance gate to a temple precinct.
– ORIGIN mid 19th cent.: Sanskrit *gōpura* 'city gate', from *gō* 'eye' and *pura* 'city'.

gora /ˈɡɔːrə/ ▶ noun (fem. **gori** pl. **goras** /ˈɡɔːrəz/ or **goray** /ˈɡɔːreɪ/) (in the Indian subcontinent, and among British Asians) a white person.
– ORIGIN from Hindi *gorā* 'fair, white'.

Gorakhpur /ˈɡɔːrək,pʊə/ an industrial city in NE India, in Uttar Pradesh near the border with Nepal; pop. 719,100 (est. 2009).

goral /ˈɡɔːr(ə)l/ ▶ noun a long-haired goat-antelope with backward curving horns, found in mountainous regions of eastern Asia. ● Genus *Nemorhaedus*, family Bovidae: two species.
– ORIGIN mid 19th cent.: a local word in the Himalayas.

Gorbachev /ˈɡɔːbətʃɒf, ˌɡɔːbəˈtʃɒf/, Mikhail (Sergeevich) (b.1931), Soviet statesman, General Secretary of the Communist Party of the USSR 1985–91 and President 1988–91. His foreign policy brought about an end to the Cold War, while within the USSR he introduced major reforms known as glasnost and perestroika. Opposition to his policies led to an attempted coup in 1991, after which he resigned. Nobel Peace Prize (1990).

Gorbals /ˈɡɔːb(ə)lz/ a district of Glasgow on the south bank of the River Clyde, formerly noted for its slums and tenement buildings.

gorblimey Brit. informal ▶ exclamation an expression of surprise or indignation.
▶ adjective [attrib.] vulgarly lower-class.
– ORIGIN late 19th cent.: alteration of *God blind me*; also in use as a noun in the early 20th cent. to denote various kinds of unusual clothing.

gorcock /ˈɡɔːkɒk/ ▶ noun Scottish & N. English the male of the red grouse.
– ORIGIN early 17th cent.: from *gor-* (of unknown origin) + COCK[1].

Gordian knot /ˈɡɔːdɪən/ ▶ noun an extremely difficult or involved problem.
– PHRASES **cut the Gordian knot** solve or remove a problem in a direct or forceful way, rejecting gentler or more indirect methods.
– ORIGIN mid 16th cent.: from the legend that *Gordius*, king of Gordium, tied an intricate knot and prophesied that whoever untied it would become the ruler of Asia. It was cut through with a sword by Alexander the Great.

gordian worm ▶ noun another term for HORSEHAIR WORM.

Gordimer /ˈɡɔːdɪmə/, Nadine (b.1923), South African novelist and short-story writer. Her experience of the effects of apartheid underlies much of her work. Notable novels: *The Conservationist* (Booker Prize, 1974). Nobel Prize for Literature (1991).

Gordium /ˈɡɔːdɪəm/ an ancient city of Asia Minor (now NW Turkey), the capital of Phrygia in the 8th and 9th centuries BC.

gordo /ˈɡɔːdəʊ/ ▶ noun (pl. gordos) Austral. a popular variety of grape.
– ORIGIN abbreviation of Spanish *gordo blanco*, literally 'fat white'.

Gordon, Charles George (1833–85), British general and colonial administrator. He made his name by crushing the Taiping Rebellion (1863–4) in China. In 1884 he fought Mahdist forces in Sudan led by Muhammad Ahmad (see MAHDI), but was trapped at Khartoum and killed.

Gordon Bennett ▶ exclamation Brit. expressing surprise, incredulity, or exasperation.
– ORIGIN 1890s: probably an alteration of GORBLIMEY, after James *Gordon Bennett* (1841–1918), American publisher and sports sponsor.

Gordon Riots a series of anti-Catholic riots in London in June 1780 in which about 300 people were killed. The riots were provoked by a petition presented to Parliament by Lord George Gordon (1751–93) against the relaxation of restrictions on the holding of landed property by Roman Catholics.

Gordon setter ▶ noun a setter of a black-and-tan breed, used as a gun dog.
– ORIGIN mid 19th cent.: named after the 4th Duke of *Gordon* (1743–1827), who promoted the breed.

Gordy /ˈɡɔːdi/, Berry, Jr (b.1929), American record producer. He founded the Motown record company in 1959.

gore[1] ▶ noun [mass noun] blood that has been shed, especially as a result of violence: ***the film omitted the blood and gore in order to avoid controversy.***
– ORIGIN Old English *gor* 'dung, dirt', of Germanic origin; related to Dutch *goor*, Swedish *gorr* 'muck, filth'. The current sense dates from the mid 16th cent.

gore[2] ▶ verb [with obj.] (of an animal such as a bull) pierce or stab (a person or other animal) with a horn or tusk.
– ORIGIN late Middle English (in the sense 'stab, pierce'): of unknown origin.

gore[3] ▶ noun a triangular or tapering piece of material used in making a garment, sail, or umbrella.
▶ verb [with obj.] shape with a gore or gores: (as adj. **gored**) *a gored skirt*.
– ORIGIN Old English *gāra* 'triangular piece of land', of Germanic origin; related to Dutch *geer* and German *Gehre*, also probably to Old English *gār* 'spear' (a spearhead being triangular).

Górecki /ɡəˈrɛtski/, Henryk (Mikołaj) (b.1933), Polish composer. His works, influenced by religious music, include the Third Symphony (1976), known as the *Symphony of Sorrowful Songs*.

Göreme /ɡəːriːmi/ a valley in Cappadocia in central Turkey, noted for its cave dwellings hollowed out of the soft tufa rock. In the Byzantine era these contained hermits' cells, monasteries, and more than 400 churches.

Gore-Tex /ˈɡɔːtɛks/ ▶ noun [mass noun] trademark a synthetic waterproof fabric permeable to air and water vapour, used in outdoor and sports clothing.

gorge ▶ noun 1 a narrow valley between hills or mountains, typically with steep rocky walls and a stream running through it.
2 archaic the throat. ■ Falconry the crop of a hawk.
3 a narrow rear entrance to a bastion, outwork, or other fortification.
4 a mass of ice obstructing a narrow passage, especially a river.
▶ verb [no obj.] eat a large amount greedily; fill oneself with food: ***they gorged themselves on** Cornish cream teas.*
– PHRASES **one's gorge rises** one is sickened or disgusted: *the pork smelt rancid and his gorge rose.*
– DERIVATIVES **gorger** noun.
– ORIGIN Middle English (as a verb): from Old French *gorger*, from *gorge* 'throat', based on Latin *gurges* 'whirlpool'. The noun originally meant 'throat' and is from Old French *gorge*; sense 1 of the noun dates from the mid 18th cent.

gorged ▶ adjective [postpositive] Heraldry having the neck encircled by a coronet or collar, especially one of a specified tincture.
– ORIGIN early 17th cent.: from French *gorge* 'throat' + -ED[1].

gorgeous ▶ adjective beautiful; very attractive: *gorgeous colours and exquisite decoration.* ■ informal very pleasant or enjoyable: *the weather was gorgeous.*
– DERIVATIVES **gorgeously** adverb, **gorgeousness** noun.
– ORIGIN late 15th cent. (describing sumptuous clothing): from Old French *gorgias* 'fine, elegant', of unknown origin.

gorget /ˈɡɔːdʒɪt/ ▶ noun 1 historical an article of clothing that covered the throat. ■ a piece of armour for the throat. ■ a wimple.
2 a patch of colour on the throat of a bird or other animal, especially a hummingbird.
– ORIGIN late Middle English (denoting a piece of armour protecting the throat): from Old French *gorgete*, from *gorge* 'throat' (see GORGE).

gorgio /ˈɡɔːdʒɪəʊ/ ▶ noun (pl. gorgios) the Gypsy name for a non-Gypsy.
– ORIGIN from Romany *gorjo*.

gorgon /ˈɡɔːɡ(ə)n/ ▶ noun Greek Mythology each of three sisters, Stheno, Euryale, and Medusa, with snakes for hair, who had the power to turn anyone who looked at them to stone. Medusa was killed by Perseus. ■ a fierce, frightening, or repulsive woman.
– ORIGIN via Latin from Greek *Gorgō*, from *gorgos* 'terrible'.

gorgoneion /ˌɡɔːɡəˈnʌɪən/ ▶ noun (pl. gorgoneia /-ˈnʌɪə/) a representation of a gorgon's head.
– ORIGIN Greek, neuter of *gorgoneios* 'of or relating to a gorgon' (see GORGON).

gorgonian /ɡɔːˈɡəʊnɪən/ Zoology ▶ noun a colonial coral of an order distinguished by having a horny tree-like skeleton, including the sea fans and precious red coral. ● Order Gorgonacea, class Anthozoa.
▶ adjective relating to gorgons or gorgonians.

– ORIGIN mid 19th cent.: from modern Latin *Gorgonia*, from Latin *Gorgo* (see **GORGON**), with reference to its petrifaction, + **-AN**.

Gorgonzola /ˌɡɔːɡ(ə)nˈzəʊlə/ ▶ **noun** [mass noun] a type of rich, strong-flavoured Italian cheese with bluish-green veins.
– ORIGIN named after *Gorgonzola*, a village in northern Italy, where it was originally made.

gorilla ▶ **noun** a powerfully built great ape with a large head and short neck, found in the forests of central Africa. It is the largest living primate. ● *Gorilla gorilla*, family Pongidae: three races (two **lowland gorillas** and the **mountain gorilla**).
■ informal a heavily built aggressive-looking man.
■ [with modifier] a dominant contender within a particular sphere of operation or activity: *the 800-lb gorilla of the home mortgage industry*.
– ORIGIN from an alleged African word for a wild or hairy person, found in the Greek account of the voyage of the Carthaginian explorer Hanno in the 5th or 6th cent. BC; adopted in 1847 as the specific name of the ape.

G

Gorkhali /ɡɔːˈkɑːli/ ▶ **noun** variant spelling of **GURKHALI**.

Gorky[1] /ˈɡɔːki/ former name (1932–91) for **NIZHNI NOVGOROD**.

Gorky[2] /ˈɡɔːki/, Arshile (1904–48), Turkish-born American painter. An exponent of abstract expressionism, he is best known for his work of the early 1940s, for example *Waterfall* (1943).

Gorky[3] /ˈɡɔːki/, Maxim (1868–1936), Russian writer and revolutionary; pseudonym of *Aleksei Maksimovich Peshkov*. His best-known works include the play *The Lower Depths* (1901) and his autobiographical trilogy (1915–23).

Gorlovka /ˈɡəɔrləfkə/ Russian name for **HORLIVKA**.

gormandize /ˈɡɔːm(ə)ndʌɪz/ (also **gormandise**) ▶ **verb** variant spelling of **GOURMANDIZE**.

gormless ▶ **adjective** Brit. informal lacking sense or initiative; foolish.
– DERIVATIVES **gormlessly** adverb, **gormlessness** noun.
– ORIGIN mid 18th cent. (originally as *gaumless*): from dialect *gaum* 'understanding' (from Old Norse *gaumr* 'care, heed') + **-LESS**.

Gorno-Altai /ˌɡɔːnəʊalˈtʌɪ/ an autonomous republic in south central Russia, on the border with Mongolia; pop. 205,900 (est. 2009); capital, Gorno-Altaisk.

Gorno-Altaisk /ˌɡɔːnəʊalˈtʌɪsk/ a city in south central Russia, capital of the republic of Gorno-Altai; pop. 53,100 (est. 2009). It was known as Ulala until 1932 and as Oirot-Tura from 1932 until 1948.

gorp ▶ **noun** [mass noun] N. Amer. informal another term for **TRAIL MIX**.
– ORIGIN 1970s: perhaps an acronym from *good old raisins and peanuts*.

gorse ▶ **noun** [mass noun] a yellow-flowered shrub of the pea family, the leaves of which are modified to form spines, native to western Europe and North Africa. ● Genus *Ulex*, family Leguminosae: several species, in particular the common European *U. europaeus*, which grows widely in heathy places.
– ORIGIN Old English *gors, gorst*, from an Indo-European root meaning 'rough, prickly', shared by German *Gerste* and Latin *hordeum* 'barley'.

Gorsedd /ˈɡɔːsɛð/ ▶ **noun** a council of Welsh or other Celtic bards and Druids, especially as meeting before the eisteddfod.
– ORIGIN Welsh, 'mound, throne, assembly'.

gory ▶ **adjective** (**gorier**, **goriest**) involving or showing violence and bloodshed: *a gory horror film*.
■ covered in blood.
– PHRASES **the gory details** humorous the explicit details of something: *she told him the gory details of her past*.
– DERIVATIVES **gorily** adverb, **goriness** noun.

gosh ▶ **exclamation** informal used to express surprise or give emphasis: *gosh, it's freezing!* ■ chiefly N. Amer. used as a euphemism for 'God': *a gosh-awful team*.
– ORIGIN mid 18th cent.: euphemism for **GOD**.

goshawk /ˈɡɒshɔːk/ ▶ **noun** a large short-winged hawk, resembling a large sparrowhawk. ● Genus *Accipiter*, family Accipitridae: several species, in particular the **northern goshawk** (*A. gentilis*) of Eurasia and North America.
– ORIGIN Old English *gōshafoc*, from *gōs* 'goose' + *hafoc* 'hawk'.

gosht /ɡəʊʃt/ ▶ **noun** [mass noun] Indian red meat (beef, lamb, or mutton): [as modifier] *gosht biryani*.
– ORIGIN from Urdu *gośt*.

gosling /ˈɡɒzlɪŋ/ ▶ **noun** a young goose.
– ORIGIN Middle English (originally *gesling*): from Old Norse *gæslingr*, from *gás* 'goose' + **-LING**, later altered by association with **GOOSE**.

go-slow ▶ **noun** chiefly Brit. a form of industrial action in which work or progress is deliberately delayed or slowed down.

gospel ▶ **noun 1** [in sing.] the teaching or revelation of Christ: *it is the Church's mission to preach the gospel*. ■ (also **gospel truth**) [mass noun] a thing that is absolutely true: *they say it's sold out, but don't take that as gospel*. ■ a set of principles or beliefs: *the gospel of market economics*.
2 (**Gospel**) the record of Christ's life and teaching in the first four books of the New Testament. ■ each of these books. ■ a portion from one of these read at a church service.

> The four Gospels ascribed to St Matthew, St Mark, St Luke, and St John all give an account of the ministry, crucifixion, and resurrection of Christ, though the Gospel of John differs greatly from the other three. There are also several apocryphal gospels of later date.

3 (also **gospel music**) [mass noun] a fervent style of black American evangelical religious singing, developed from spirituals sung in Southern Baptist and Pentecostal Churches.
– ORIGIN Old English *gōdspel*, from *gōd* 'good' + *spel* 'news, a story' (see **SPELL**[2]), translating ecclesiastical Latin *bona annuntiatio* or *bonus nuntius*, used to gloss ecclesiastical Latin *evangelium*, from Greek *euangelion* 'good news' (see **EVANGEL**); after the vowel was shortened in Old English, the first syllable was mistaken for *god* 'God'.

gospeller (US **gospeler**) ▶ **noun** a person who zealously teaches or professes faith in the gospel. ■ (in church use) the reader of the Gospel in a Communion service.

Gospel side ▶ **noun** (in a church) the north side of the altar, at which the Gospel is read.

goss ▶ **noun** Brit. informal gossip: *a bit of background goss*.
– ORIGIN late 20th cent.: abbreviation.

gossamer ▶ **noun** [mass noun] a fine, filmy substance consisting of cobwebs spun by small spiders, seen especially in autumn. ■ a light, thin, and insubstantial or delicate material or substance: [as modifier] *a fine gossamer fabric that clung to her skin*.
– ORIGIN Middle English: apparently from **GOOSE** + **SUMMER**[1], perhaps from the time of year around St Martin's summer, i.e. early November, when geese were eaten (gossamer being common then).

gossan /ˈɡɒz(ə)n/ ▶ **noun** [mass noun] Geology & Mining an iron-containing secondary deposit, largely consisting of oxides and typically yellowish or reddish, occurring above a deposit of a metallic ore.
– ORIGIN late 18th cent.: of unknown origin.

gossip ▶ **noun** [mass noun] casual or unconstrained conversation or reports about other people, typically involving details which are not confirmed as true: *he became the subject of much local gossip*. ■ [count noun] a conversation about such matters: *she just comes round here for a gossip*. ■ [count noun] chiefly derogatory a person who likes talking about other people's private lives.
▶ **verb** (**gossips**, **gossiping**, **gossiped**) [no obj.] engage in gossip: *they would start **gossiping about** her as soon as she left*.
– DERIVATIVES **gossiper** noun, **gossipy** adjective.
– ORIGIN late Old English *godsibb*, 'godfather, godmother, baptismal sponsor', literally 'a person related to one in God', from *god* 'God' + *sibb* 'a relative' (see **SIB**). In Middle English the sense was 'a close friend, a person with whom one gossips', hence 'a person who gossips', later (early 19th cent.) 'idle talk' (from the verb, which dates from the early 17th cent.).

gossip column ▶ **noun** a section of a newspaper devoted to gossip about well-known people.
– DERIVATIVES **gossip columnist** noun.

gossoon /ɡɒˈsuːn/ ▶ **noun** Irish a lad.
– ORIGIN late 17th cent.: from French *garçon* 'boy'.

gossypol /ˈɡɒsɪpɒl/ ▶ **noun** [mass noun] Chemistry a toxic crystalline compound present in cotton-seed oil. ● A polycyclic phenol; chem. formula: $C_{30}H_{30}O_8$.
– ORIGIN late 19th cent.: from modern Latin *Gossypium* (genus name), from Latin *gossypinum, -pion* 'cotton plant' (of unknown origin) + **-OL**.

got past and past participle of **GET**.

gotcha (also **gotcher**) informal ▶ **exclamation** I have got you (used to express satisfaction at having captured or defeated someone or uncovered their faults).
▶ **noun 1** N. Amer. an instance of catching someone out or exposing them to ridicule.
2 N. Amer. a sudden unforeseen problem.
– ORIGIN 1930s: representing a pronunciation.

Göteborg /ˌjœtəˈbɔrj/ Swedish name for **GOTHENBURG**.

Goth /ɡɒθ/ ▶ **noun 1** a member of a Germanic people that invaded the Roman Empire from the east between the 3rd and 5th centuries. The eastern division, the Ostrogoths, founded a kingdom in Italy, while the Visigoths went on to found one in Spain.
2 (**goth**) [mass noun] a style of rock music derived from punk, typically with apocalyptic or mystical lyrics. ■ [count noun] a member of a subculture favouring black clothing, white and black make-up, and goth music.
– ORIGIN Old English *Gota*, superseded in Middle English by the adoption of late Latin *Gothi* (plural), from Greek *Gothoi*, from Gothic *Gutthiuda* 'the Gothic people'.

Gotha /ˈɡəʊtə, ˈɡəʊθə/, German /ˈɡoːta/ a city in central Germany, in Thuringia; pop. 46,500 (est. 2006). From 1640 until 1918 it was the residence of the dukes of Saxe-Gotha and Saxe-Coburg-Gotha.

Gotham 1 /ˈɡɒθəm/ a nickname for New York City, used originally by Washington Irving and now associated with the Batman stories.
2 /ˈɡəʊtəm/ a village in Nottinghamshire whose inhabitants were proverbial for their stupidity, or (in the folk tale *The Wise Men of Gotham*) who demonstrated cunning by feigning stupidity.

Gothenburg /ˈɡɒθənbəːɡ/ a seaport in SW Sweden, on the Kattegat strait; pop. 500,197 (2008). It is the second-largest city in Sweden. Swedish name **GÖTEBORG**.

Gothic ▶ **adjective 1** relating to the Goths or their extinct language, which belongs to the East Germanic branch of the Indo-European language family. It provides the earliest manuscript evidence of any Germanic language (4th–6th centuries AD).
2 of or in the style of architecture prevalent in western Europe in the 12th–16th centuries (and revived in the mid 18th to early 20th centuries), characterized by pointed arches, rib vaults, and flying buttresses, together with large windows and elaborate tracery. English Gothic architecture is divided into Early English, Decorated, and Perpendicular.
3 (also pseudo-archaic **Gothick**) belonging to or redolent of the Dark Ages; portentously gloomy or horrifying: *19th-century Gothic horror*.
4 (of lettering) of or derived from the angular style of handwriting with broad vertical downstrokes used in western Europe from the 13th century, including Fraktur and black-letter typefaces.
5 (**gothic**) relating to goths or goth music.
▶ **noun** [mass noun] **1** the extinct language of the Goths.
2 the Gothic style of architecture.
3 Gothic type.
– DERIVATIVES **Gothically** adverb, **Gothicism** noun, **Gothicize** /-sʌɪz/ (also **Gothicise**) verb.
– ORIGIN from French *gothique* or late Latin *gothicus*, from *Gothi* (see **GOTH**). It was used in the 17th and 18th cents to mean 'not classical' (i.e. not Greek or Roman), and hence to refer to medieval architecture which did not follow classical models (sense 2 of the adjective) and a typeface based on medieval handwriting (sense 4 of the adjective).

Gothic novel ▶ **noun** an English genre of fiction popular in the 18th to early 19th centuries, characterized by an atmosphere of mystery and horror and having a pseudo-medieval setting.

Gotland /ˈɡɒtlənd/ an island and province of Sweden, in the Baltic Sea; pop. 57,004 (2008); capital, Visby.

go-to guy ▶ **noun** N. Amer. informal a person who can be relied upon for help or support.

go-to-meeting ▶ **adjective** (also **Sunday-go-to-meeting**) dated (of clothes) suitable for wearing to church.

gotta ▶ **contraction** informal have got a: *I gotta licence*. ■ have got to: *you gotta be careful*.

gotten N. Amer. past participle of **GET**.

> **USAGE** As past participles of **get**, **got** and **gotten** both date back to Middle English. The form **gotten** is not used in British English but is very common in North American English, though even there it is often regarded as non-standard. In North American English, **got** and **gotten** are not identical in use. **Gotten** usually implies the process of obtaining something, as in *he had **gotten** us tickets for the show*, while **got** implies the state of possession or ownership, as in *I haven't **got** any money*.

Götterdämmerung /ˌɡəːtəˈdɛmərʊŋ/ (in Germanic mythology) the downfall of the gods.
– ORIGIN German, literally 'twilight of the gods', popularized by Wagner's use of the word as the title of the last opera of the Ring cycle.

Göttingen /ˈɡəːtɪŋən/, German /ˈɡœtɪŋən/ a town in north central Germany, on the River Leine; pop. 121,600 (est. 2006). It is noted for its university.

gouache /ɡuːˈɑːʃ, ɡwɑːʃ/ ▸ **noun** [mass noun] a method of painting using opaque pigments ground in water and thickened with a glue-like substance. ▪ paint of this kind; opaque watercolour. ▪ [count noun] a picture painted in this way.
– ORIGIN late 19th cent.: French, from Italian *guazzo*.

Gouda[1] /ˈɡaʊdə/ a market town in the Netherlands, just north-east of Rotterdam; pop. 70,857 (2008).

Gouda[2] /ˈɡaʊdə/ ▸ **noun** [mass noun] a flat round cheese with a yellow rind, originally made in Gouda.

gouge /ɡaʊdʒ, ɡuːdʒ/ ▸ **noun 1** a chisel with a concave blade, used in carpentry, sculpture, and surgery.
2 an indentation or groove made by gouging.
▸ **verb** [with obj.] **1** make (a groove, hole, or indentation) with or as if with a gouge: *the channel had been gouged out by the ebbing water.* ▪ make a rough hole or indentation in (a surface), especially so as to mar or disfigure it: *he had wielded the blade inexpertly, gouging the grass in several places.*
▪ (**gouge something out**) cut or force something out roughly or brutally: *one of the young man's eyes had been gouged out.* ▪ [no obj.] Austral. dig for minerals, especially opal.
2 N. Amer. informal overcharge or swindle (someone): *drugs sold by the same manufacturers who are gouging patients in this country.* ▪ (**gouge something out**) obtain money by swindling or extortion: *he'd gouged wads out of Morty.*
– DERIVATIVES **gouger** noun.
– ORIGIN late Middle English: from Old French, from late Latin *gubia, gulbia*, perhaps of Celtic origin; compare with Old Irish *gulba* 'beak' and Welsh *gylf* 'beak, pointed instrument'.

Gough Island /ɡɒf/ an island in the South Atlantic, south of Tristan da Cunha. In 1938 it became a dependency of the British Crown Colony of St Helena.

goujons /ˈɡuː(d)ʒənz/ ▸ **plural noun** Brit. deep-fried strips of chicken or fish.
– ORIGIN from French *goujon* 'gudgeon' (see GUDGEON[1]).

goulash /ˈɡuːlaʃ/ ▸ **noun 1** [mass noun] a highly seasoned Hungarian soup or stew of meat and vegetables, flavoured with paprika.
2 (in informal bridge) a further deal of the four hands after no player has bid.
– ORIGIN from Hungarian *gulyás-hús*, from *gulyás* 'herdsman' + *hús* 'meat'; sense 2 (dating from the 1920s) is an extended use.

Gould[1] /ɡuːld/, Glenn (Herbert) (1932–82), Canadian pianist and composer. Best known for his performances of works by Bach, he retired from the concert platform in 1964 to concentrate on recording and broadcasting.

Gould[2] /ɡuːld/, John (1804–81), English bird artist. He produced many large illustrated volumes, though it is believed that many of the finest plates were actually drawn by Gould's wife and other employed artists.

Gould[3] /ɡuːld/, Stephen Jay (1941–2002), American palaeontologist. A noted popularizer of science, he studied modifications of Darwinian evolutionary theory, proposed the concept of punctuated equilibrium, and wrote on the social context of scientific theory.

Gounod /ˈɡuːnəʊ/, French /ɡuno/, Charles François (1818–93), French composer, conductor, and organist. He is best known for his opera *Faust* (1859).

goura /ˈɡʊərə/ ▸ **noun** another term for CROWNED PIGEON.
– ORIGIN mid 19th cent.: modern Latin genus name, from a local word in New Guinea.

gourami /ɡʊ(ə)ˈrɑːmi, ˈɡʊərəmi/ ▸ **noun** (pl. **same** or **gouramis**) a small brightly coloured Asian labyrinth fish, popular in aquaria. ● Belontiidae and related families: several species.
– ORIGIN late 19th cent.: from Malay *gurami*.

gourd /ɡʊəd, ɡɔːd/ ▸ **noun 1** a fleshy, typically large fruit with a hard skin, some varieties of which are edible. ▪ a drinking or water container made from the hollowed and dried skin of a gourd.
2 a climbing or trailing plant which bears gourds. ● Family Cucurbitaceae (the **gourd family**): several genera and species, including the coloured **ornamental gourds** (*Cucurbita pepo* var. *ovifera*). The gourd family also includes the marrows, squashes, pumpkins, melons, and cucumbers.
– PHRASES **out of one's gourd** N. Amer. informal out of one's mind; crazy. ▪ under the influence of alcohol or drugs.
– DERIVATIVES **gourdful** noun (pl. **gourdfuls**).
– ORIGIN Middle English: from Old French *gourde*, based on Latin *cucurbita*.

gourde /ɡʊəd/ ▸ **noun** the basic monetary unit of Haiti, equal to 100 centimes.
– ORIGIN the Franco-American name for a dollar.

gourmand /ˈɡʊəmənd, ˈɡɔː-/ ▸ **noun** a person who enjoys eating and often eats too much. ▪ a connoisseur of good food; a gourmet.
– DERIVATIVES **gourmandism** noun.
– ORIGIN late Middle English: from Old French, of unknown origin.

> **USAGE** The words **gourmand** and **gourmet** overlap in meaning but are not identical. Both can be used to mean 'a connoisseur of good food' but **gourmand** is more usually used to mean 'a person who enjoys eating and often eats too much'.

gourmandize /ˌɡʊəm(ə)nˈdiːz, ˈɡɔː-/ (also **gormandize, gourmandise**) ▸ **verb** [no obj.] eat good food, especially to excess.
▸ **noun** [mass noun] the appreciation or consumption of good food.
– DERIVATIVES **gourmandizer** noun.
– ORIGIN late Middle English (as a noun): from French *gourmandise*, from *gourmand*; the verb dates from the mid 16th cent.

gourmet /ˈɡʊəmeɪ, ˈɡɔː-/ ▸ **noun** a connoisseur of good food; a person with a discerning palate. ▪ [as modifier] of a kind or standard suitable for a gourmet: *a gourmet meal.*
– ORIGIN early 19th cent.: French, originally meaning 'wine taster', influenced by GOURMAND.

> **USAGE** On the distinction between **gourmet** and **gourmand**, see USAGE at GOURMAND.

gout /ɡaʊt/ ▸ **noun 1** [mass noun] a disease in which defective metabolism of uric acid causes arthritis, especially in the smaller bones of the feet, deposition of chalk-stones, and episodes of acute pain.
2 literary a drop or spot of something: *gouts of blood erupted from the wound.*
– DERIVATIVES **gouty** adjective (**goutier, goutiest**).
– ORIGIN Middle English: from Old French *goute*, from medieval Latin *gutta*, literally 'drop' (because gout was believed to be caused by the dropping of diseased matter from the blood into the joints).

goutweed ▸ **noun** [mass noun] ground elder, which was formerly used to treat gout. Compare with HERB GERARD.

gov. ▸ **abbreviation** ▪ government. ▪ governor.

govern /ˈɡʌv(ə)n/ ▸ **verb** [with obj.] **1** conduct the policy, actions, and affairs of (a state, organization, or people) with authority: *he was incapable of governing the country* | (as adj. **governing**) *the governing coalition.* ▪ control, influence, or regulate (a person, action, or course of events): *the future of Jamaica will be governed by geography not history.* ▪ (**govern oneself**) conduct oneself, especially with regard to controlling one's emotions: *he does not have the ability to govern himself or others successfully.* ▪ serve to decide (a legal case).
2 Grammar (of a word) require that (another word or group of words) be in a particular case.
– DERIVATIVES **governability** noun, **governable** adjective.
– ORIGIN Middle English: from Old French *governer*, from Latin *gubernare* 'to steer, rule', from Greek *kubernan* 'to steer'.

governance ▸ **noun** [mass noun] the action or manner of governing a state, organization, etc.: *a more responsive system of governance will be required.*
▪ archaic rule; control: *what, shall King Henry be a pupil still, under the surly Gloucester's governance?*
– ORIGIN Middle English: from Old French, from *governer* (see GOVERN).

governess ▸ **noun** (especially in former times) a woman employed to teach children in a private household.
– ORIGIN Middle English (originally *governeress*, denoting a female ruler): from Old French *governeresse*, feminine of *governeour* 'governor', from Latin *gubernator*, from *gubernare* (see GOVERN).

governessy ▸ **adjective** having or showing characteristics considered to be characteristic of a governess, especially primness or strictness: *her governessy tone.*

governing body ▸ **noun** a group of people who formulate the policy and direct the affairs of an institution in partnership with the managers, especially on a voluntary or part-time basis: *the school's governing body.*

government /ˈɡʌv(ə)nˌm(ə)nt, ˈɡʌvəm(ə)nt/ ▸ **noun 1** [treated as sing. or pl.] the group of people with the authority to govern a country or state; a particular ministry in office: *the government's economic record* | *successive Labour governments.* ▪ [mass noun] the system by which a state or community is governed: *a democratic form of government.* ▪ [mass noun] the action or manner of controlling or regulating a state, organization, or people: *rules for the government of the infirmary.*
2 Grammar the relation between a governed and a governing word.
– DERIVATIVES **governmental** adjective, **governmentally** adverb.
– ORIGIN Middle English: from Old French *governement*, from *governer* (see GOVERN).

Government House ▸ **noun** Brit. the official residence of a governor, especially in a colony or Commonwealth state that regards the British monarch as head of state.

government issue ▸ **adjective** (of equipment) provided by the government.

government paper ▸ **noun** [mass noun] bonds or other promissory certificates issued by the government.

government securities ▸ **plural noun** another term for GOVERNMENT PAPER.

government surplus ▸ **noun** [mass noun] unused equipment sold by the government.

governor ▸ **noun 1** an official appointed to govern a town or region. ▪ the elected executive head of a state of the US. ▪ the representative of the British Crown in a colony or in a Commonwealth state that regards the monarch as head of state.
2 the head of a public institution: *the governor of the Bank of England.* ▪ a member of a governing body.
3 Brit. informal the person in authority; one's employer.
4 a device automatically regulating the supply of fuel, steam, or water to a machine, ensuring uniform motion or limiting speed.
– DERIVATIVES **governorate** noun, **governorship** noun.
– ORIGIN Middle English: from Old French *governeour*, from Latin *gubernator*, from *gubernare* (see GOVERN).

governor general ▸ **noun** (pl. **governors general**) the chief representative of the Crown in a Commonwealth country of which the British monarch is head of state.

govt ▸ **abbreviation** government: *local govt.*

gowan /ˈɡaʊən/ ▸ **noun** Scottish & N. English a wild white or yellow flower, especially a daisy.
– ORIGIN mid 16th cent.: probably a variant of dialect *gollan*, denoting various yellow-flowered plants, perhaps related to Old English *golde* 'marigold'.

gowk /ɡaʊk/ ▸ **noun** dialect **1** an awkward or foolish person (often used as a general term of abuse).
2 a cuckoo.
– ORIGIN Middle English (in sense 2): from Old Norse *gaukr*.

gown ▸ **noun** a long elegant dress worn on formal occasions: *a silk ball gown.* ▪ a dressing gown. ▪ a protective garment worn in hospital, either by a staff member during surgery or by a patient. ▪ a loose cloak indicating one's profession or status, worn by a lawyer, teacher, academic, or university student.
▪ [mass noun] the members of a university as distinct from the permanent residents of the university town. Often contrasted with TOWN.
▸ **verb** (**be gowned**) be dressed in a gown: *she was gowned in luminous silk.* ▪ [no obj.] (**gown up**) put on a surgical gown: *the lab is supposed to be sterile, so you have to gown up.*
– ORIGIN Middle English: from Old French *goune*, from late Latin *gunna* 'fur garment'; probably related to Byzantine Greek *gouna* 'fur, fur-lined garment'.

Gowon /ˈɡəʊwɒn/, Yakubu (b.1934), Nigerian general and statesman, head of state 1966–75. Following the Biafran civil war (1967–70) he maintained a policy of 'no victor, no vanquished' which helped to reconcile the warring factions.

goy /ɡɔɪ/ ▸ **noun** (pl. **goyim** /ˈɡɔɪɪm/ or **goys**) informal, derogatory a Jewish name for a non-Jew.
– DERIVATIVES **goyish** adjective.
– ORIGIN from Hebrew *gōy* 'people, nation'.

Goya /ˈgɔɪə/ (1746–1828), Spanish painter and etcher; full name *Francisco José de Goya y Lucientes*. He is famous for his works treating the French occupation of Spain (1808–14), including *The Shootings of May 3rd 1808* (painting, 1814) and *The Disasters of War* (etchings, 1810–14), depicting the cruelty and horror of war.

Gozo /ˈgəʊzəʊ/ a Maltese island, to the north-west of the main island of Malta.

GP ▶ abbreviation ■ Brit. general practitioner. ■ Grand Prix.

GPA ▶ abbreviation N. Amer. grade point average, an indication of a student's academic achievement at a school or college.

Gp Capt ▶ abbreviation Group Captain.

gph ▶ abbreviation gallons per hour.

GPI ▶ abbreviation general paralysis of the insane, a condition associated with the late stages of syphilis which is characterized by a combination of dementia, weakness of the limbs, speech and hearing difficulties, and various other symptoms.

G

gpm ▶ abbreviation gallons per minute.

GPO ▶ abbreviation ■ historical (in the UK) General Post Office. ■ (in the US) Government Printing Office.

GPRS ▶ abbreviation general packet radio services, a technology for radio transmission of small packets of data, especially between mobile phones and the Internet.

GPS ▶ abbreviation Global Positioning System, an accurate worldwide navigational and surveying facility based on the reception of signals from an array of orbiting satellites.

GPU a Soviet secret police agency from 1922 to 1923. See also **OGPU**.
– ORIGIN abbreviation of Russian *Gosudarstvennoe politicheskoe upravlenie* 'State Political Directorate'.

GR ▶ abbreviation ■ Greece (international vehicle registration). ■ King George. [from Latin *Georgius Rex*.]

gr. ▶ abbreviation ■ grain(s). ■ gram(s). ■ grey. ■ gross.

Graafian follicle /ˈgrɑːfɪən/ ▶ noun Physiology a fluid-filled structure in the mammalian ovary within which an ovum develops prior to ovulation.
– ORIGIN mid 19th cent.: named after R. de *Graaf* (1641–73), Dutch anatomist.

grab ▶ verb (**grabs, grabbing, grabbed**) [with obj.]
1 grasp or seize suddenly and roughly: *she grabbed him by the shirt collar* | *she grabbed her keys and rushed out*. ■ informal obtain or get (something) quickly or opportunistically: *I'll grab another drink while there's still time*. ■ [no obj.] (of a brake on a vehicle) grip the wheel harshly or jerkily: *the brakes grabbed very badly*.
2 [usu. with negative or in questions] informal attract the attention of; make an impression on: *how does that grab you?*
▶ noun **1** a quick sudden clutch or attempt to seize: *he made a grab at the pistol*. ■ [usu. with modifier] Computing a frame of video or television footage, digitized and stored as a still image in a computer memory for subsequent display, printing, or editing: *a screen grab from Wednesday's programme*.
2 a mechanical device for clutching, lifting, and moving things, especially materials in bulk. ■ [as modifier] denoting a bar or strap for people to hold on to for support or in a moving vehicle: *a grab rail*.
– PHRASES **up for grabs** informal available: *a £1 million jackpot is up for grabs*.
– DERIVATIVES **grabber** noun.
– ORIGIN late 16th cent.: from Middle Low German and Middle Dutch *grabben*; perhaps related to GRIP, GRIPE, and GROPE.

grab bag ▶ noun N. Amer. a lucky dip in which wrapped items are chosen by people at random. ■ an assortment of items in a sealed bag which one buys or is given without knowing what the contents are.

grabble ▶ verb [no obj.] archaic **1** feel or search with the hands; grope about.
2 sprawl or tumble on all fours.
– ORIGIN late 16th cent.: probably from Dutch *grabbelen* 'scramble for a thing', from Middle Dutch *grabben* (see GRAB).

grabby ▶ adjective (**grabbier, grabbiest**) informal, chiefly N. Amer. **1** having or showing a selfish desire for something; greedy: *don't be so grabby—I was here before you*.
2 attracting attention; arousing people's interest: *a really grabby end to the series*.

graben /ˈgrɑːb(ə)n/ ▶ noun (pl. **same** or **grabens**) Geology an elongated block of the earth's crust lying between two faults and displaced downwards relative to the blocks on either side, as in a rift valley.
– ORIGIN late 19th cent.: from German *Graben* 'a ditch'.

Gracchus /ˈgrakəs/, Tiberius Sempronius (c.163–133 BC) and his brother Gaius Sempronius (c.153–121 BC), Roman tribunes; known as **the Gracchi**. They were responsible for radical social and economic legislation, especially concerning the redistribution of land to the poor.

Grace, W. G. (1848–1915), English cricketer; full name *William Gilbert Grace*. In a first-class career that lasted until 1908, he made 126 centuries, scored 54,896 runs, and took 2,864 wickets. He twice captained England in Test matches against Australia (1880 and 1882).

grace ▶ noun [mass noun] **1** smoothness and elegance of movement: *she moved through the water with effortless grace*.
2 courteous good will: *he had the good grace to apologize to her afterwards*. ■ (**graces**) an attractively polite manner of behaving: *she has all the social graces*.
3 (in Christian belief) the free and unmerited favour of God, as manifested in the salvation of sinners and the bestowal of blessings. ■ [count noun] a divinely given talent or blessing. ■ the condition or fact of being favoured by someone: *he fell from grace with the tabloids after he was sent off for swearing*.
4 a period officially allowed for payment of a sum due or for compliance with a law or condition, especially an extended period granted as a special favour: *we'll give them 30 days' grace and then we'll be doing checks*.
5 a short prayer of thanks said before or after a meal.
6 (**His, Her,** or **Your Grace**) used as forms of description or address for a duke, duchess, or archbishop: *His Grace, the Duke of Atholl*.
7 (**the Graces** or **the Three Graces**) (in Greek mythology) three beautiful goddesses (Aglaia, Thalia, and Euphrosyne) believed to personify and bestow charm, grace, and beauty.
▶ verb [with obj. and adverbial] bring honour or credit to (someone or something) by one's attendance or participation: *he is one of the best players ever to have graced the game* | ironic *she had deigned to grace the city of New York with her presence*. ■ [with obj.] (of a person or thing) be an attractive presence in or on; adorn: *Ms Pasco has graced the front pages of magazines like Elle and Vogue*.
– PHRASES **be in someone's good** (or **bad**) **graces** be regarded by someone with favour (or disfavour). **there but for the grace of God** (**go I**) used to acknowledge one's good fortune in avoiding another's mistake or misfortune. **with good** (or **bad**) **grace** in a willing and happy (or resentful and reluctant) manner.
– ORIGIN Middle English: via Old French from Latin *gratia*, from *gratus* 'pleasing, thankful'; related to GRATEFUL.

grace and favour ▶ adjective [attrib.] Brit. denoting accommodation occupied free or at a low rent by permission of a sovereign or government.

graceful ▶ adjective having or showing grace or elegance: *she was a tall girl, slender and graceful*.
– DERIVATIVES **gracefully** adverb, **gracefulness** noun.

graceless ▶ adjective lacking grace, elegance, or charm.
– DERIVATIVES **gracelessly** adverb, **gracelessness** noun.

grace note ▶ noun Music an extra note added as an embellishment and not essential to the harmony or melody.

Gracias a Dios, Cape /ˌgrasɪas a ˈdiːɒs/ a cape forming the easternmost extremity of the Mosquito Coast in Central America, on the border between Nicaragua and Honduras.
– ORIGIN Spanish, literally 'thanks (be) to God', so named by Columbus, who, becalmed off the coast in 1502, was able to continue his voyage with the arrival of a following wind.

gracile /ˈgrasɪl, ˈgrasʌɪl/ ▶ adjective Anthropology (of a hominid species) of slender build. ■ (of a person) attractively slender or thin.
– ORIGIN early 17th cent.: from Latin *gracilis* 'slender'.

gracilis /ˈgrasɪlɪs/ (also **gracilis muscle**) ▶ noun Anatomy a slender superficial muscle of the inner thigh.
– ORIGIN early 17th cent.: from Latin, literally 'slender'.

gracility /grəˈsɪlɪti/ ▶ noun [mass noun] formal **1** the state of being gracefully slender.
2 plain simplicity of literary style.

gracious ▶ adjective **1** courteous, kind, and pleasant, especially towards someone of lower social status: *a gracious hostess* | *Greig was gracious in defeat*. ■ showing the elegance and comfort brought by wealth or high social status: *gracious living*.
2 (in Christian belief) showing divine grace: *I am saved by God's gracious intervention on my behalf*.
3 Brit. a polite epithet used of royalty or their acts: *the accession of Her present gracious Majesty*.
▶ exclamation used to express polite surprise: *good gracious, that was close!*
– DERIVATIVES **graciously** adverb, **graciousness** noun.
– ORIGIN Middle English: via Old French from Latin *gratiosus*, from *gratia* 'esteem, favour' (see GRACE).

grackle ▶ noun **1** a songbird of the American blackbird family, the male of which has shiny black plumage with a blue-green sheen. ● Several genera and species, family Icteridae, in particular the **common grackle** (*Quiscalus quiscula*).
2 another term for an Asian mynah or starling, with mainly black plumage. ● *Gracula* and other genera, family Sturnidae; **southern grackle** is another term for the hill mynah.
– ORIGIN late 18th cent.: from modern Latin *Gracula*, from Latin *graculus* 'jackdaw'.

grad[1] ▶ noun informal term for GRADUATE.

grad[2] ▶ abbreviation gradient.

gradable ▶ adjective Grammar denoting an adjective that can be used in the comparative and superlative and take a submodifier. Contrasted with CLASSIFYING.
– DERIVATIVES **gradability** noun.

gradate ▶ verb pass or cause to pass by gradations from one shade of colour to another: [no obj.] *the black background gradated towards a dark purple*. ■ [with obj.] arrange in steps or grades of size, amount, or quality: (as adj. **gradated**) *the Temple compound became a series of concentric circles of gradated purity*.
– ORIGIN mid 18th cent.: back-formation from GRADATION.

gradation ▶ noun **1** a scale or a series of successive changes, stages, or degrees: *the Act fails to provide both a clear and defensible gradation of offences*. ■ a stage in such a scale or series: *gradations of size*. ■ a minute variation in shade, tone, or colour: *amorphous shapes in subtle gradations of green and blue*.
2 (in historical linguistics) another term for ABLAUT.
– DERIVATIVES **gradational** adjective, **gradationally** adverb.
– ORIGIN mid 16th cent.: from Latin *gradatio(n-)*, based on *gradus* 'step'.

Grade, Lew, Baron Grade of Elstree (1906–98), British television producer and executive, born in Russia; born *Louis Winogradsky*. A pioneer of British commercial television, he served as president of ATV (Associated Television) from 1977 to 1982.

grade ▶ noun **1** a particular level of rank, quality, proficiency, or value: *sea salt is usually available in coarse or fine grades* | [in combination] *high-grade steel*. ■ a level in a salary or employment structure: *clerical and secretarial grades*. ■ Brit. a level of importance allocated to a listed building: [as modifier] *a Grade I listed building*. ■ (in historical linguistics) a relative position in a series of forms involving ablaut. ■ Zoology a group of animals at a similar evolutionary level.
2 chiefly N. Amer. a mark indicating the quality of a student's work: *I got good grades last semester*. ■ (with specifying ordinal number) those pupils in a school or school system who are grouped by age or ability for teaching at a particular level for a year: *she teaches first grade*. ■ Brit. an examination, especially in music: *I took grade five and got a distinction*.
3 chiefly N. Amer. a gradient or slope: *just over the crest of a long seven per cent grade*.
4 [usu. as modifier] a variety of cattle produced by crossing with a superior breed: *grade stock*.
▶ verb [with obj.] **1** arrange in or allocate to grades; classify or sort: *the timber is graded according to its thickness*.
2 chiefly N. Amer. give a mark to (a student or a piece of work).
3 [no obj.] pass gradually from one level, especially a shade of colour, into another: *the sky graded from blue at the top of the shot to white on the horizon*.
4 reduce (a road) to an easy gradient.
5 cross (livestock) with a superior breed.
– PHRASES **at grade** N. Amer. on the same level: *the crossing at grade of two streets*. **make the grade** informal succeed; reach the desired standard.
– ORIGIN early 16th cent.: from French, or from Latin *gradus* 'step'. Originally used as a unit of

measurement of angles (a degree of arc), the term later referred to degrees of merit or quality.

grade crossing ▶ **noun** North American term for LEVEL CROSSING.

gradely ▶ **adjective** N. English fine, decent, or respectable: *she were a gradely lass.*
– ORIGIN Middle English (originally in the sense 'excellent, noble'): from Old Norse *greithligr*, from *greithr* 'ready'.

grader ▶ **noun 1** a person or thing that grades.
2 a wheeled machine for levelling the ground, especially in making roads.
3 [in combination] N. Amer. a pupil of a specified grade in a school: *a first-grader.*

grade school ▶ **noun** N. Amer. an elementary school.
– DERIVATIVES **grade schooler** noun.

gradience ▶ **noun** [mass noun] Linguistics the absence of a clear-cut boundary between one category and another, for example between *cup* and *mug* in semantics.

gradient /ˈɡreɪdɪənt/ ▶ **noun 1** an inclined part of a road or railway; a slope: *fail-safe brakes for use on steep gradients.* ■ the degree of such a slope: *the path becomes very rough as the gradient increases.* ■ Mathematics the degree of steepness of a graph at any point.
2 Physics an increase or decrease in the magnitude of a property (e.g. temperature, pressure, or concentration) observed in passing from one point or moment to another. ■ the rate of such a change. ■ Mathematics the vector formed by the operator ∇ acting on a scalar function at a given point in a scalar field.
– ORIGIN mid 19th cent.: from GRADE, on the pattern of *salient*.

gradine /ɡrəˈdiːn/ (also **gradin** /ˈɡreɪdɪn/) ▶ **noun** archaic a low step or ledge, especially one at the back of an altar.
– ORIGIN mid 19th cent.: from Italian *gradino*, diminutive of *grado* 'step'.

gradiometer /ˌɡreɪdɪˈɒmɪtə/ ▶ **noun** a surveying instrument used for setting out or measuring the gradient of a slope. ■ Physics an instrument for measuring the gradient of an energy field, especially the horizontal gradient of the earth's gravitational or magnetic field.

gradual /ˈɡradʒʊəl/ ▶ **adjective 1** taking place or progressing slowly or by degrees: *the gradual introduction of new methods.*
2 (of a slope) not steep or abrupt.
▶ **noun** (**Gradual**) (in the Western Christian Church) a response sung or recited between the Epistle and Gospel in the Mass. ■ a book of plainsong for the Mass.
– DERIVATIVES **gradualness** noun.
– ORIGIN late Middle English: from medieval Latin *gradualis*, from Latin *gradus* 'step'. The original sense of the adjective was 'arranged in degrees'; the noun refers to the altar steps in a church, from which the antiphons were sung.

gradualism ▶ **noun** [mass noun] a policy of gradual reform rather than sudden change or revolution. ■ Biology the hypothesis that evolution proceeds chiefly by the accumulation of gradual changes (in contrast to the punctuationist model).
– DERIVATIVES **gradualist** noun, **gradualistic** adjective.

gradually ▶ **adverb** in a gradual way; slowly; by degrees: *the situation gradually improved.*

graduand /ˈɡradʒʊand, -dj-, -ənd/ ▶ **noun** Brit. a person who is about to receive an academic degree.
– ORIGIN late 19th cent.: from medieval Latin *graduandus*, gerundive of *graduare* 'take a degree' (see GRADUATE).

graduate ▶ **noun** /ˈɡradʒʊət, -djʊət/ a person who has successfully completed a course of study or training, especially a person who has been awarded an undergraduate or first academic degree. ■ N. Amer. a person who has received a high-school diploma.
▶ **verb** /ˈɡradʒʊeɪt, -djʊeɪt/ **1** [no obj.] successfully complete an academic degree, course of training, or (N. Amer.) high school: *he **graduated from** Glasgow University in 1990.* ■ [with obj.] N. Amer. confer a degree or other academic qualification on: *the school graduated more than one hundred arts majors in its first year.* ■ (**graduate to**) move up to (a more advanced level or position): *he started with motorbikes but now he's graduated to his first car.*
2 [with obj.] arrange in a series or according to a scale: (as adj. **graduated**) *a graduated tax.* ■ mark out (an instrument or container) in degrees or other proportionate gradations: *the stem was graduated with marks for each hour.*
3 [with obj.] change (something, typically colour or shade) gradually or step by step: *the colour is graduated from the middle of the frame to the top.*
– ORIGIN late Middle English: from medieval Latin *graduat-* 'graduated', from *graduare* 'take a degree', from Latin *gradus* 'degree, step'.

graduated pension ▶ **noun** (in the UK) a state pension paid under a system (in operation 1961–75) in which both contributions and payments were in proportion to wages or salary.

graduate school ▶ **noun** N. Amer. a department of a university for advanced work by graduates.

graduation ▶ **noun** [mass noun] **1** the receiving or conferring of an academic degree or diploma. ■ [count noun] the ceremony at which degrees are conferred.
2 the action of dividing into degrees or other proportionate divisions on a graduated scale. ■ [count noun] a mark on a container or instrument indicating a degree of quantity.

gradus /ˈɡreɪdəs/ ▶ **noun** (pl. **graduses**) historical a manual of classical prosody formerly used in schools to help in writing Greek and Latin verse.
– ORIGIN mid 18th cent.: Latin, from *Gradus ad Parnassum* 'Step(s) to Parnassus', the title of one such manual.

Graecism /ˈɡriːsɪz(ə)m, ˈɡrʌɪ-/ (also **Grecism**) ▶ **noun** a Greek idiom or grammatical feature, especially as imitated in another language. ■ [mass noun] the Greek spirit, style, or mode of expression, especially as imitated in a work of art.
– DERIVATIVES **Graecize** (also **Graecise**) verb.
– ORIGIN late 16th cent.: from French *grécisme* or medieval Latin *Graecismus*, from *Graecus* (see GREEK).

Graeco- /ˈɡriːkəʊ, ˈɡrʌɪ-/ (also **Greco-**) ▶ **combining form** Greek; Greek and ...: *Graecophile* | *Graeco-Turkish.*
– ORIGIN from Latin *Graecus* (see GREEK).

Graeco-Roman (also **Greco-Roman**) ▶ **adjective**
1 relating to the ancient Greeks and Romans.
2 denoting a style of wrestling in which holds below the waist are prohibited.

Graf /ɡrɑːf/, Steffi (b.1969), German tennis player; full name *Stefanie Maria Graf*. She was ranked top women's player at the age of 16 and won her seventh Wimbledon singles title in 1996.

graffiti /ɡrəˈfiːti/ ▶ **plural noun** (sing. **graffito** /-təʊ/) [treated as sing. or pl.] writing or drawings scribbled, scratched, or sprayed illicitly on a wall or other surface in a public place: *the station was covered in graffiti.*
▶ **verb** [with obj.] (usu. as adj. **graffitied**) write or draw graffiti on (something): *the graffitied walls.* ■ write (words or drawings) as graffiti: *graffitied names sprayed on bus shelters.*
– DERIVATIVES **graffitist** noun.
– ORIGIN mid 19th cent.: from Italian (plural), from *graffio* 'a scratch'.

USAGE In Italian the word **graffiti** is a plural noun and its singular form is **graffito**. Traditionally, the same distinction has been maintained in English, so that **graffiti**, being plural, would require a plural verb: *the **graffiti were** all over the wall.* By the same token, the singular would require a singular verb: *there **was** a **graffito** on the wall.* Today, these distinctions survive in some specialist fields such as archaeology but sound odd to most native speakers. The most common modern use is to treat **graffiti** as if it were a mass noun, similar to a word like **writing**, and not to use **graffito** at all. In this case, **graffiti** takes a singular verb, as in *the **graffiti was** all over the wall.* Such uses are now widely accepted as standard. A similar process is going on with other words such as **agenda**, **data**, and **media**.

graft[1] ▶ **noun 1** a shoot or twig inserted into a slit on the trunk or stem of a living plant, from which it receives sap. ■ an instance of inserting a shoot or twig in this way.
2 Medicine a piece of living tissue that is transplanted surgically. ■ a surgical operation in which tissue is transplanted.
▶ **verb** [with obj. and adverbial] **1** insert (a shoot or twig) as a graft: *it was common to graft different varieties on to a single tree trunk.* ■ insert a graft on (a trunk or stem).
2 Medicine transplant (living tissue) as a graft: *they can graft a new hand on to the nerve ends.*
3 combine or integrate (an idea, system, etc.) with another, typically in a way considered inappropriate: *old values have been **grafted on to** a new economic class.*
– ORIGIN late Middle English *graff*, from Old French *grafe*, via Latin from Greek *graphion* 'stylus, writing implement' (with reference to the tapered tip of the scion), from *graphein* 'write'. The final *-t* is typical of phonetic confusion between *-f* and *-ft* at the end of words; compare with TUFT.

graft[2] Brit. informal ▶ **noun** [mass noun] hard work: *success came after years of hard graft.*
▶ **verb** [no obj.] work hard: *I need people prepared to go out and graft.*
– DERIVATIVES **grafter** noun.
– ORIGIN mid 19th cent.: perhaps related to the phrase *spade's graft* 'the amount of earth that one stroke of a spade will move', based on Old Norse *grǫftr* 'digging'.

graft[3] ▶ **noun** [mass noun] bribery and other corrupt practices used to secure illicit advantages or gains in politics or business: *sweeping measures to curb official graft.* ■ such advantages or gains.
▶ **verb** [no obj.] make money by shady or dishonest means.
– DERIVATIVES **grafter** noun.
– ORIGIN mid 19th cent.: of unknown origin.

Grafton /ˈɡrɑːftən/, Augustus Henry Fitzroy, 3rd Duke of (1735–1811), British Whig statesman, Prime Minister 1768–70.

graft union ▶ **noun** the point on a plant where the graft is joined to the rootstock.

Graham[1], Martha (1893–1991), American dancer, teacher, and choreographer. She evolved a new dance language using more flexible movements intended to express psychological complexities and emotional power.

Graham[2], Billy (b.1918), American evangelical preacher; full name *William Franklin Graham*. He is world famous as a mass evangelist.

graham ▶ **adjective** N. Amer. denoting or made from wholewheat flour that has not been sifted: *a box of graham crackers.*
– ORIGIN mid 19th cent.: named after Sylvester *Graham* (1794–1851), an American advocate of dietary reform.

Grahame, Kenneth (1859–1932), Scottish-born writer of children's stories, resident in England from 1864. He is remembered for the children's classic *The Wind in the Willows* (1908).

Graham Land the northern part of the Antarctic Peninsula, the only part of Antarctica lying outside the Antarctic Circle. Discovered in 1831–2 by the English navigator John Biscoe (1794–1843), it now forms part of British Antarctic Territory, but is claimed also by Chile and Argentina.

Graham's law ▶ **noun** Chemistry a law stating that the rates of diffusion and effusion of a gas are inversely proportional to the square root of the density of the gas.
– ORIGIN mid 19th cent.: named after T. *Graham* (see GRAHAM[2]).

grail ▶ **noun 1** (**the Grail** or **the Holy Grail**) (in medieval legend) the cup or platter used by Christ at the Last Supper, and in which Joseph of Arimathea received Christ's blood at the Cross. Quests for it undertaken by medieval knights are described in versions of the Arthurian legends written from the early 13th century onward.
2 a thing which is eagerly pursued or sought after: *the enterprise society where profit at any cost has become the holy grail.*
– ORIGIN from Old French *graal*, from medieval Latin *gradalis* 'dish'.

grain ▶ **noun 1** [mass noun] wheat or any other cultivated cereal used as food. ■ the seeds of such cereals.
2 a single fruit or seed of a cereal: *a few **grains of** corn.* ■ a small hard particle of a substance such as salt or sand: ***a grain of** salt.* ■ the smallest possible quantity or amount of a quality: *there wasn't **a grain of** truth in what he said.* ■ a discrete particle or crystal in a metal, igneous rock, etc., typically visible only when a surface is magnified. ■ a piece of solid propellant for use in a rocket engine.
3 (abbrev.: **gr.**) the smallest unit of weight in the troy and avoirdupois systems, equal to $^1/_{5760}$ of a pound troy and $^1/_{7000}$ of a pound avoirdupois (approximately 0.0648 gram). [because originally the weight was equivalent to that of a grain of corn.]
4 [mass noun] the longitudinal arrangement or pattern of fibres in wood, paper, etc.: *he scored along the grain of the table with the knife.* ■ the texture of wood, stone, etc., as determined by the arrangement and size of constituent particles: *the lighter, finer grain of the wood is attractive.* ■ the rough or wrinkled outer surface of leather, or of a similar artificial

material. ■ Mining lamination or planes of cleavage in materials such as stone and coal. ■ Photography a grainy appearance of a photograph or negative, which is in proportion to the size of the emulsion particles composing it.
5 archaic a person's character or natural tendency.
6 [mass noun] historical kermes or cochineal, or dye made from either of these.
▶ **verb** [with obj.] **1** give a rough surface or texture to: *her fingers were **grained** with chalk dust.* ■ [no obj.] form into grains.
2 (usu. as noun **graining**) paint (especially furniture or interior surfaces) in imitation of the grain of wood or marble.
3 remove hair from (a hide).
4 N. Amer. feed (a horse) on grain.
– PHRASES **against the grain** contrary to the natural inclination or feeling of someone or something: *it goes **against the grain** to tell outright lies.* [from the fact that wood is easier to cut along the line of the grain.]
– DERIVATIVES **grained adjective** [usu. in combination] *coarse-grained sandstone*, **grainer noun**, **grainless adjective**.
– ORIGIN Middle English (originally in the sense 'seed, grain of corn'): from Old French *grain*, from Latin *granum*.

grain beetle ▶ **noun** a small beetle which infests grain stores and warehouses. ● Cucujidae and other families: several species, in particular the tropical **saw-toothed grain beetle** (*Oryzaephilus surinamensis*), now found worldwide.

grain borer ▶ **noun** a beetle that feeds on grain and rice and is a common pest of granaries and flour mills. ● Family Bostrichidae: several species, including the tropical **lesser grain borer** (*Rhizopertha dominica*), now found worldwide.

Grainger /ˈɡreɪndʒə/, (George) Percy (Aldridge) (1882–1961), Australian-born American composer and pianist. From 1901 he lived in London, where he collected, edited, and arranged English folk songs. Notable works: *Shepherd's Hey* (1911).

grain leather ▶ **noun** [mass noun] leather dressed with the grain side outwards.

grain side ▶ **noun** the side of a hide on which the hair was.

grains of Paradise ▶ **plural noun** the seeds of a West African plant of the ginger family, resembling those of cardamom and used as a spice and in herbal medicine. Also called MALAGUETTA. ● The plant is *Aframomum melegueta*, family Zingiberaceae.

grain weevil ▶ **noun** a weevil that is a common pest of stored grain, which is eaten by the larvae. ● *Sitophilus granarius*, family Curculionidae.

grain whisky ▶ **noun** [mass noun] whisky made mainly from wheat or maize.

grainy ▶ **adjective** (**grainier**, **grainiest**) **1** granular: *soft cheese with a slightly grainy texture.* ■ Photography showing visible grains of emulsion, as characteristic of old photographs or modern high-speed film. ■ (of sound, especially recorded music) having a rough or gravelly quality: *the grainy sound of bootleg cassettes.*
2 (of wood) having prominent grain.
– DERIVATIVES **graininess noun**.

gralloch /ˈɡralək/ ▶ **noun** [mass noun] the viscera of a dead deer.
▶ **verb** [with obj.] disembowel (a deer that has been shot).
– ORIGIN mid 19th cent.: from Scottish Gaelic *grealach* 'entrails'.

gram[1] (Brit. also **gramme**) (abbrev.: **g**) ▶ **noun** a metric unit of mass equal to one thousandth of a kilogram.
– ORIGIN late 18th cent.: from French *gramme*, from late Latin *gramma* 'a small weight', from Greek.

gram[2] ▶ **noun** [mass noun] chickpeas or other pulses used as food.
– ORIGIN early 18th cent.: from Portuguese *grão*, from Latin *granum* 'grain'.

gram[3] ▶ **noun** variant of GRAMMA.

-gram[1] ▶ **combining form** in nouns denoting something written or recorded (especially in a certain way): *cryptogram* | *heliogram*.
– DERIVATIVES **-grammatic combining form** in corresponding adjectives.
– ORIGIN from Greek *gramma* 'thing written, letter of the alphabet', from *graphein* 'write'.

-gram[2] ▶ **combining form** in nouns denoting a person paid to deliver a novelty greeting or message as a humorous surprise for the recipient: *kissogram*.
– ORIGIN on the pattern of *telegram*.

gramadoelas /ˈxramadʊləz, -las/ ▶ **plural noun** [treated as sing.] S. African informal wild, remote country: *they were stuck in the parched gramadoelas, kilometres from anywhere.*
– ORIGIN Afrikaans, of unknown origin.

gramicidin /ˌɡramɪˈsʌɪdɪn/ ▶ **noun** [mass noun] Medicine an antibiotic with a wide range of activity, used in many medicinal preparations. ● This antibiotic is obtained from the bacterium *Bacillus brevis*.

graminaceous /ˌɡramɪˈneɪʃəs/ ▶ **adjective** Botany relating to or denoting plants of the grass family (Gramineae).
– ORIGIN mid 19th cent.: from Latin *gramen*, *gramin-* 'grass' + -ACEOUS.

graminivorous /ˌɡramɪˈnɪv(ə)rəs/ ▶ **adjective** Zoology (of an animal) feeding on grass.
– ORIGIN mid 18th cent.: from Latin *gramen*, *gramin-* 'grass' + -VOROUS.

gramma (also **gram**) ▶ **noun** N. Amer. informal one's grandmother.

grammar ▶ **noun** **1** [mass noun] the whole system and structure of a language or of languages in general, usually taken as consisting of syntax and morphology (including inflections) and sometimes also phonology and semantics. ■ [usu. with modifier] a particular analysis of the system and structure of language or of a specific language: *Chomskyan grammar.* ■ [count noun] a book on grammar: *my old Latin grammar.* ■ a set of actual or presumed prescriptive notions about correct use of a language: *it was not bad grammar, just dialect.* ■ the basic elements of an area of knowledge or skill: *the grammar of wine.* ■ Computing a set of rules governing what strings are valid or allowable in a language or text.
2 Brit. informal a grammar school.
– ORIGIN late Middle English: from Old French *gramaire*, via Latin from Greek *grammatikē* (*tekhnē*) '(art) of letters', from *gramma*, *grammat-* 'letter of the alphabet, thing written'.

grammarian /ɡrəˈmɛːrɪən/ ▶ **noun** a person who studies and writes about grammar.
– ORIGIN Middle English: from Old French *gramarien*, from *gramaire* (see GRAMMAR).

grammar school ▶ **noun** **1** (in the UK) a state secondary school to which pupils are admitted on the basis of ability. Since 1965 most have been absorbed into the comprehensive school system. ■ historical a school founded in or before the 16th century for teaching Latin, later becoming a secondary school teaching academic subjects.
2 US another term for ELEMENTARY SCHOOL.

grammatical /ɡrəˈmatɪk(ə)l/ ▶ **adjective** relating to grammar: *the grammatical function of a verb.* ■ well formed; in accordance with the rules of the grammar of a language: *a grammatical sentence.*
– DERIVATIVES **grammaticality noun**, **grammatically adverb**, **grammaticalness noun**.
– ORIGIN early 16th cent.: from late Latin *grammaticalis*, via Latin from Greek *grammatikos*, from *gramma*, *grammatos* 'letter of the alphabet, thing written'.

grammaticalize (also **grammaticalise**) ▶ **verb** [with obj.] Linguistics change (an element) from being one having lexical meaning into one having a largely grammatical function.
– DERIVATIVES **grammaticalization noun**.

gramme ▶ **noun** variant spelling of GRAM[1].

Grammy ▶ **noun** (pl. **Grammys** or **Grammies**) each of a number of annual awards given by the American National Academy of Recording Arts and Sciences for achievement in the record industry.
– ORIGIN 1950s: blend of GRAMOPHONE and EMMY.

Gram-negative ▶ **adjective** see GRAM STAIN.

gramophone ▶ **noun** old-fashioned term for RECORD PLAYER.
– DERIVATIVES **gramophonic adjective**.
– ORIGIN late 19th cent.: formed by inversion of elements of *phonogram* 'sound recording'.

gramophone record ▶ **noun** fuller form of RECORD (sense 4 of the noun).

gramp (also **gramps**, **grampy**) ▶ **noun** dialect or informal one's grandfather.
– ORIGIN late 19th cent.: contraction of GRANDPAPA.

Grampian /ˈɡrampɪən/ a former local government region in NE Scotland, dissolved in 1996.

Grampian Mountains (also **the Grampians**) **1** a mountain range in north central Scotland. Its southern edge forms a natural boundary between the Highlands and the Lowlands.
2 a mountain range in SE Australia, in Victoria. It forms a spur of the Great Dividing Range at its western extremity.

Gram-positive ▶ **adjective** see GRAM STAIN.

grampus /ˈɡrampəs/ ▶ **noun** (pl. **grampuses**) a cetacean of the dolphin family, in particular: ■ another term for RISSO'S DOLPHIN. ■ another term for KILLER WHALE.
– ORIGIN early 16th cent.: alteration (by association with GRAND 'big') of Old French *grapois*, from medieval Latin *craspiscis*, from Latin *crassus piscis* 'fat fish'.

Gramsci /ˈɡramʃi/, Antonio (1891–1937), Italian political theorist and activist, co-founder and leader of the Italian Communist Party. Imprisoned in 1926 when the Fascists banned the Communist Party, he died shortly after his release. *Letters from Prison* (1947) remains an important work.

Gram stain ▶ **noun** [mass noun] Medicine a staining technique for the preliminary identification of bacteria, in which a violet dye is applied, followed by a decolorizing agent and then a red dye. The cell walls of certain bacteria (denoted **Gram-positive**) retain the first dye and appear violet, while those that lose it (denoted **Gram-negative**) appear red.
– ORIGIN late 19th cent.: named after Hans C. J. *Gram* (1853–1938), the Danish physician who devised the method.

gran ▶ **noun** Brit. informal one's grandmother.
– ORIGIN mid 19th cent.: abbreviation.

grana /ˈɡrɑːnə, ˈɡreɪnə/ ▶ **plural noun** (sing. **granum**) Botany the stacks of thylakoids embedded in the stroma of a chloroplast.
– ORIGIN late 19th cent.: plural of Latin *granum* 'grain'.

Granada /ɡrəˈnɑːdə/, Spanish /ɡraˈnaða/ **1** a city in Andalusia in southern Spain; pop. 236,988 (2008). Founded in the 8th century, it became the capital of the Moorish kingdom of Granada in 1238. It is the site of the Alhambra palace.
2 a city in Nicaragua, on the NW shore of Lake Nicaragua; pop. 105,171 (2006). Founded by the Spanish in 1523, it is the oldest city in the country.

granadilla /ɡranəˈdɪlə/ (also **grenadilla**) ▶ **noun** a passion fruit, or the fruit of a related plant. ● This fruit comes from plants of the genus *Passiflora*, family Passifloraceae, including the **giant granadilla** (*P. quadrangularis*), which has large pale fruits.
– ORIGIN late 16th cent.: Spanish, diminutive of *granada* 'pomegranate'.

granary ▶ **noun** (pl. **granaries**) **1** a storehouse for threshed grain. ■ a region producing large quantities of corn.
2 Brit. short for GRANARY BREAD.
– ORIGIN late 16th cent.: from Latin *granarium*, from *granum* 'grain'.

granary bread ▶ **noun** [mass noun] Brit. trademark a type of brown bread containing whole grains of wheat.

Gran Canaria /ˌɡran kəˈnɛːrɪə/, Spanish /ɡraŋ kaˈnarja/ a volcanic island off the NW coast of Africa, one of the Canary Islands. Its chief town, Las Palmas, is the capital of the Canary Islands.

Gran Chaco /ɡran ˈtʃakəʊ/ (also **Chaco**) a lowland plain in central South America, extending from southern Bolivia through Paraguay to northern Argentina.

grand ▶ **adjective** **1** magnificent and imposing in appearance, size, or style: *a grand country house* | *the dinner party was very grand.* ■ large, ambitious, or impressive in scope or scale: *his grand design for the future of Europe* | *this was opera on a grand scale.* ■ (of a person) of high rank and behaving in an appropriately proud or dignified way: *she was such a grand lady.* ■ used in names of places or buildings to suggest size or splendour: *the Grand Canyon* | *the Grand Hotel.*
2 [attrib.] denoting the largest or most important item of its kind: *the grand entrance.* ■ of the highest rank (used especially in official titles): *the Grand Vizier.* ■ Law (of a crime) serious: *grand theft.* Compare with PETTY (sense 2).
3 informal very good or enjoyable; excellent: *we had a grand day.*
4 [in combination] (in names of family relationships) denoting one generation removed in ascent or descent: *a grand-niece.*
▶ **noun** **1** (pl. **same**) informal a thousand dollars or pounds: *he gets thirty-five grand a year.*
2 a grand piano.

– PHRASES **a** (or **the**) **grand old man of** a man long and highly respected in (a particular field): *the grand old man of the Labour Left.*
– DERIVATIVES **grandly** adverb, **grandness** noun.
– ORIGIN Middle English: from Old French *grant, grand*, from Latin *grandis* 'full-grown, big, great'. The original uses were to denote family relationships (sense 4 of the adjective, following Old French usage) and as a title (*the Grand*, translating Old French *le Grand*); hence the senses 'of the highest rank', 'of great importance'.

grandad (also **granddad**) ▸ noun **1** informal one's grandfather. ■ used as a form of address to an elderly man: *cheer up, grandad, it may never happen.*
2 [as modifier] denoting a style of shirt or shirt neckline with a collar in the form of a narrow upright band fastened with buttons.

grandaddy (also **granddaddy**) ▸ noun (pl. **grandaddies**) N. Amer. informal one's grandfather. ■ the largest or most notable example or instance of a particular thing: *that young fellow is going to have **the grandaddy of** all headaches.*

grandam /ˈgrandam/ (also **grandame**) ▸ noun archaic term for GRANDMOTHER. ■ an old woman. ■ a female ancestor.
– ORIGIN Middle English: from Anglo-Norman French *graund dame* (see GRAND, DAME). Of the English terms of relationship formed with *grand*, this is the oldest.

grand apartheid ▸ noun [mass noun] historical (in South Africa) a form of apartheid, prevalent in the 1960s and 1970s, which involved comprehensive racial segregation and measures such as the removal of black people from white areas and the creation of black homelands.

grand-aunt ▸ noun another term for GREAT-AUNT.

Grand Banks a submarine plateau of the continental shelf off the SE coast of Newfoundland, Canada. It is a meeting place of the warm Gulf Stream and the cold Labrador Current; this promotes the growth of plankton, making the waters an important feeding area for fish.

grand battement /grɒ̃/ ▸ noun Ballet a movement in which both legs are kept straight and one leg is kicked outwards from the body and in again.

Grand Canal 1 a series of waterways in eastern China, extending from Beijing southwards to Hangzhou, a distance of 1,700 km (1,060 miles). Its original purpose was to transport rice from the river valleys to the cities. Its construction proceeded in stages between 486 BC and AD 1327.
2 the main waterway of Venice in Italy, lined on each side by fine palazzos and spanned by the Rialto Bridge.

Grand Canyon a deep gorge in Arizona, formed by the Colorado River. It is about 440 km (277 miles) long, 8 to 24 km (5 to 15 miles) wide, and, in places, 1,800 m (6,000 ft) deep. The area was designated a national park in 1919.

Grand Canyon State informal name for ARIZONA.

grandchild ▸ noun (pl. **grandchildren**) a child of one's son or daughter.

grand cross ▸ noun Astrology an arrangement of four planets in which each is in opposition to one other planet and square to the other two, forming a cross.

grand cru /grɒ̃ ˈkruː/, French /grɑ̃ kʀy/ ▸ noun (pl. **grands crus** pronunc. **same**) (chiefly in French official classifications) a wine of the most superior grade, or the vineyard which produces it. Compare with PREMIER CRU.
– ORIGIN French, literally 'great growth'.

granddad ▸ noun variant spelling of GRANDAD.

granddaughter ▸ noun a daughter of one's son or daughter.

grand duchess ▸ noun **1** the wife or widow of a grand duke. ■ a woman holding the rank of grand duke in her own right.
2 historical a daughter (or granddaughter) of a Russian tsar.

grand duchy ▸ noun a state or territory ruled by a grand duke or duchess.

grand duke ▸ noun **1** a prince or nobleman ruling over a territory in certain European countries.
2 historical a son (or grandson) of a Russian tsar.

Grande Comore /ˌgrɒd kəˈmɔː/ the largest of the islands of the Comoros, off the NW coast of Madagascar; pop. 316,600 (est. 2006); chief town (and capital of the Comoros), Moroni.

grande dame /grɒd ˈdam/ ▸ noun a woman holding an influential position within a particular sphere: *the grande dame of British sculpture.*
– ORIGIN French, literally 'grand lady'.

grandee /granˈdiː/ ▸ noun a Spanish or Portuguese nobleman of the highest rank. ■ a person of high rank or eminence: *several City grandees and eminent lawyers.*
– ORIGIN late 16th cent.: from Spanish and Portuguese *grande* 'grand', used as a noun. The change of ending was due to association with -EE.

grande horizontale /ˌgrɒd ˌɒrizɒ̃ˈtɑːl/ ▸ noun (pl. **grandes horizontales** pronunc. **same**) humorous a prostitute.
– ORIGIN late 19th cent.: French, literally 'great horizontal'.

grandeur /ˈgrandjə, -(d)ʒə/ ▸ noun [mass noun] splendour and impressiveness, especially of appearance or style: *the majestic grandeur and simplicity of Roman architecture.* ■ high rank or social importance: *his facade of grandeur.*
– ORIGIN late 16th cent. (denoting tall stature): from French, from *grand* 'great, grand' (see GRAND).

grandfather ▸ noun the father of one's father or mother. ■ the person who founded or originated something: *Freud is often called **the grandfather of** psychoanalysis.*
▸ verb [with obj.] N. Amer. informal exempt (someone or something) from a new law or regulation: *smokers who worked here before the ban have been grandfathered.*
– DERIVATIVES **grandfatherly** adjective.

grandfather clause ▸ noun N. Amer. informal a clause exempting certain pre-existing classes of people or things from the requirements of a piece of legislation.
– ORIGIN early 20th cent.: from a clause in the constitutions of some Southern states, exempting from voting restrictions the descendants of men who voted before the Civil War.

grandfather clock ▸ noun a clock in a tall free-standing wooden case, driven by weights.

Grand Fleet historical the main British naval fleet, either that based at Spithead in the 18th century or that based at Scapa Flow in the First World War.

Grand Guignol /ˌgrɒ̃ giːˈnjɒl/, French /gʀɑ̃ giɲɔl/ ▸ noun a dramatic entertainment of a sensational or horrific nature, originally a sequence of short pieces as performed at the Grand Guignol theatre in Paris.
– ORIGIN French, literally 'Great Punch'.

grandiflora /ˌgrandɪˈflɔːrə/ ▸ adjective [attrib.] (of a cultivated plant) bearing large flowers.
▸ noun a grandiflora plant.
– ORIGIN early 20th cent.: modern Latin (often used in specific names of large-flowered plants), from Latin *grandis* 'great' + *flos, flor-* 'flower'.

grandiloquent /granˈdɪləkwənt/ ▸ adjective pompous or extravagant in language, style, or manner, especially in a way that is intended to impress: *a grandiloquent celebration of Spanish glory.*
– DERIVATIVES **grandiloquence** noun, **grandiloquently** adverb.
– ORIGIN late 16th cent.: from Latin *grandiloquus*, literally 'grand-speaking', from *grandis* 'grand' + *loqui* 'speak'. The ending was altered in English by association with ELOQUENT.

Grand Inquisitor ▸ noun historical the director of the court of Inquisition, especially in Spain and Portugal.

grandiose /ˈgrandɪəʊs/ ▸ adjective extravagantly or pretentiously imposing in appearance or style: *the court's grandiose facade.* ■ conceived on a very grand or ambitious scale: *grandiose plans to reform the world.*
– DERIVATIVES **grandiosely** adverb, **grandiosity** noun.
– ORIGIN mid 19th cent.: from French, from Italian *grandioso*, from *grande* 'grand'.

grand jeté /grɒ̃ ʒɛˈteɪ, ʒəˈteɪ/ ▸ noun Ballet a jump in which a dancer springs from one foot to land on the other with one leg forward of their body and the other stretched backwards while in the air.

grand jury ▸ noun US Law a jury, normally of twenty-three jurors, selected to examine the validity of an accusation prior to trial.

grandkid ▸ noun N. Amer. informal a grandchild.

grand larceny ▸ noun [mass noun] Law (in many US states and formerly in Britain) theft of personal property having a value above a legally specified amount.

grandma ▸ noun informal one's grandmother.

grand mal /grɒ̃ ˈmal/ ▸ noun [mass noun] a serious form of epilepsy with muscle spasms and prolonged loss of consciousness. Compare with PETIT MAL. ■ [count noun] an epileptic fit of this kind.
– ORIGIN late 19th cent.: from French, literally 'great sickness'.

grandmama (also **grandmamma**) ▸ noun archaic form of GRANDMA.

Grandma Moses see MOSES[2].

grand manner ▸ noun (**the grand manner**) a style considered appropriate for noble and stately matters: *formal dining in the grand manner.* ■ (**the Grand Manner**) the lofty and rhetorical manner of historical painting exemplified by Raphael and Poussin.

Grand Marnier /grɒ̃ ˈmɑːnɪeɪ/ ▸ noun [mass noun] trademark an orange-flavoured cognac-based liqueur.
– ORIGIN from the name of the French manufacturer *Marnier*-Lapostolle.

grand master ▸ noun **1** (usu. **grandmaster**) a chess player of the highest class, especially one who has won an international tournament.
2 (**Grand Master**) the head of an order of chivalry or of Freemasons.

grandmother ▸ noun the mother of one's father or mother.
– PHRASES **teach one's grandmother to suck eggs** presume to advise a more experienced person.
– DERIVATIVES **grandmotherly** adjective.

grandmother clock ▸ noun a clock similar to a grandfather clock but about two thirds the size.

grandmother's footsteps ▸ plural noun [treated as sing.] Brit. a children's game in which one player turns round often and without warning with the aim of catching the other players stealthily creeping up to touch him or her on the back.

Grand National an annual horse race established in 1839, a steeplechase run over a course of 4 miles 856 yards (about 7,200 metres) with thirty jumps, at Aintree, Liverpool, in late March or early April.

grand-nephew ▸ noun another term for GREAT-NEPHEW.

grand-niece ▸ noun another term for GREAT-NIECE.

grand opera ▸ noun an opera on a serious theme in which the entire libretto (including dialogue) is sung. ■ [mass noun] the genre of grand opera.

grandpa ▸ noun informal one's grandfather.

grandpapa ▸ noun old-fashioned term for GRANDFATHER.

grandpappy ▸ noun (pl. **grandpappies**) North American term for GRANDFATHER.

grandparent ▸ noun a parent of one's father or mother; a grandmother or grandfather.
– DERIVATIVES **grandparental** adjective, **grandparenthood** noun.

Grand Penitentiary ▸ noun (in the Roman Catholic Church) a cardinal presiding over the penitentiary.

grand piano ▸ noun a large, full-toned piano which has the body, strings, and soundboard arranged horizontally and in line with the keys and is supported by three legs.

Grand Prix /grɒ̃ ˈpriː/ ▸ noun (pl. **Grands Prix** pronunc. **same**) any of a series of motor-racing or motorcycling contests forming part of a world championship series, held in various countries under international rules. ■ (in full **Grand Prix de Paris**) an international horse race for three-year-olds, founded in 1863 and run annually in June at Longchamps, Paris. ■ an important competitive event in various other sports.
– ORIGIN mid 19th cent.: French, literally 'great or chief prize'.

grand seigneur /ˌgrɒ̃ seɪˈnjəː/ ▸ noun a man whose rank or position allows him to command others.
– ORIGIN French, literally 'great lord'.

grand serjeanty ▸ noun see SERJEANTY.

grand siècle /ˌgrɒ̃ sɪˈɛkl(ə)/, French /gʀɑ̃ sjɛkl/ ▸ noun the reign of Louis XIV, seen as France's period of political and cultural pre-eminence.
– ORIGIN French, literally 'great century or age'.

grandsire ▸ noun **1** archaic term for GRANDFATHER.
2 Bell-ringing a particular method of change-ringing involving an odd number of bells.

grand slam ▸ noun trademark in the UK the winning of each of a group of major championships or matches in a particular sport in the same year, in particular in tennis, golf, or rugby union. ■ Bridge the bidding and winning of all thirteen tricks. ■ Baseball a home

G

run hit when each of the three bases is occupied by a runner, thus scoring four runs.
– ORIGIN early 19th cent. (as a term in cards, especially bridge): from **SLAM**[2].

grandson ▶ **noun** the son of one's son or daughter.

grandstand ▶ **noun** the main stand, usually roofed, commanding the best view for spectators at racecourses or sports grounds. ■ [as modifier] (of a view) seen from an advantageous position, as if from a grandstand: *a balcony which gave us a grandstand view of Loch Fyne.*
▶ **verb** [no obj.] (usu. as noun **grandstanding**) derogatory seek to attract applause or favourable attention from spectators or the media: *they accused him of political grandstanding.*

grandstand finish ▶ **noun** (in sport) a close or exciting finish to a race or competition.

grand total ▶ **noun** the final amount after everything is added up; the sum of other totals.

grand tour ▶ **noun** a cultural tour of Europe formerly undertaken, especially in the 18th century, by a young man of the upper classes as a part of his education. ■ informal a guided tour or inspection of a building, exhibition, etc.: *he gave me the grand tour of his ranch and studio.*

G

grand tourer ▶ **noun** dated a car designed for comfortable long-distance touring.

grand trine ▶ **noun** Astrology an arrangement of three planets in which each planet is in trine with the other two, forming an equilateral triangle.

grand-uncle ▶ **noun** another term for **GREAT-UNCLE**.

grand unified theory ▶ **noun** Physics a theory attempting to give a single explanation of the strong, weak, and electromagnetic interactions between subatomic particles.

grange ▶ **noun** [usu. in names] Brit. a country house with farm buildings attached: *Biddulph Grange.* ■ historical an outlying farm with tithe barns belonging to a monastery or feudal lord. ■ archaic a barn.
– ORIGIN Middle English (in the sense 'granary, barn'): from Old French, from medieval Latin *granica* (*villa*) 'grain house or farm', based on Latin *granum* 'grain'.

grangerize /ˈgreɪn(d)ʒərʌɪz/ (also **grangerise**) ▶ **verb** [with obj.] (usu. as adj. **grangerized**) illustrate (a book) by later insertion of material, especially prints cut from other works.
– ORIGIN late 19th cent.: from the name of James *Granger* (1723–76), English biographer.

graniferous /graˈnɪf(ə)rəs/ ▶ **adjective** Botany (of a plant) producing grain or a grain-like seed.
– ORIGIN mid 17th cent.: from Latin *granum* 'grain' + **-FEROUS**.

granita /graˈniːtə/ ▶ **noun** (pl. **granitas** or **granite** /-ˈniːteɪ/) an Italian-style water ice with a granular texture. ■ a drink made with crushed ice.
– ORIGIN Italian.

granite /ˈgranɪt/ ▶ **noun** [mass noun] a very hard, granular, crystalline, igneous rock consisting mainly of quartz, mica, and feldspar and often used as a building stone: [as modifier] *granite columns* | figurative *a man with granite determination.*
– DERIVATIVES **granitic** adjective, **granitoid** adjective & noun.
– ORIGIN mid 17th cent.: from Italian *granito*, literally 'grained', from *grano* 'grain', from Latin *granum*.

Granite State informal name for **NEW HAMPSHIRE**.

graniteware ▶ **noun** [mass noun] **1** a speckled form of earthenware imitating the appearance of granite.
2 a kind of enamelled ironware.

granitize (also **granitise**) ▶ **verb** [with obj.] (usu. as adj. **granitized**) Geology give (rock) a granitic character.
– DERIVATIVES **granitization** noun.

granivorous /graˈnɪv(ə)rəs/ ▶ **adjective** Zoology (of an animal) feeding on grain.
– DERIVATIVES **granivore** noun.
– ORIGIN mid 17th cent.: from Latin *granum* 'grain' + **-VOROUS**.

granny (also **grannie**) ▶ **noun** (pl. **grannies**) informal one's grandmother.
– ORIGIN mid 17th cent.: from *grannam* (representing a colloquial pronunciation of **GRANDAM**) + **-Y**[2].

granny bond ▶ **noun** Brit. informal a form of index-linked National Savings certificate, originally available only to pensioners.

granny flat ▶ **noun** informal, chiefly Brit. a part of a house made into self-contained accommodation suitable for an elderly relative.

granny gear ▶ **noun** informal the lowest gear on a bicycle.

granny glasses ▶ **plural noun** informal round steel-rimmed or gold-rimmed glasses.

granny knot ▶ **noun** a reef knot with the ends crossed the wrong way and therefore liable to slip.

Granny Smith ▶ **noun** a dessert apple of a bright green variety with crisp sharp-flavoured flesh, originating in Australia.
– ORIGIN late 19th cent.: named after Maria Ann (*Granny*) *Smith* (c.1801–1870), who first produced such apples.

granodiorite /ˌgranə(ʊ)ˈdʌɪərʌɪt/ ▶ **noun** [mass noun] Geology a coarse-grained plutonic rock containing quartz and plagioclase, between granite and diorite in composition.
– ORIGIN late 19th cent.: from **GRANITE** + **DIORITE**.

granola /graˈnəʊlə/ ▶ **noun** [mass noun] N. Amer. a kind of breakfast cereal resembling muesli. ■ [as modifier] chiefly derogatory denoting people with liberal or Green political views, typified as eating health foods: *Fran wasn't a grow-your-own granola type.*
– ORIGIN late 19th cent. (as a trademark): from *gran-* (representing **GRANULAR** or **GRAIN**) + *-ola* (suffix chiefly in US usage). The current term dates from the 1970s.

granolithic /ˌgranə(ʊ)ˈlɪθɪk/ ▶ **adjective** (of concrete) containing fine granite chippings or crushed granite, used to render floors and surfaces. ■ (of a floor or surface) rendered with granolithic concrete.
▶ **noun** [mass noun] granolithic concrete or rendering.
– ORIGIN late 19th cent.: from *grano-* (irregular combining form from Latin *granum* 'grain') + Greek *lithos* 'stone' + **-IC**.

granophyre /ˈgranə(ʊ)ˌfʌɪə/ ▶ **noun** [mass noun] Geology a granitic rock consisting of intergrown feldspar and quartz crystals in a medium- to fine-grained groundmass.
– DERIVATIVES **granophyric** /ˌgranə(ʊ)ˈfɪrɪk/ adjective.
– ORIGIN late 19th cent.: from German *Granophyr*, from *Granit* 'granite' + *Porphyr* (see **PORPHYRY**).

Grant[1], Cary (1904–86), British-born American actor; born *Alexander Archibald Leach*. He acted in more than seventy films, including *Holiday* (1938) and *The Philadelphia Story* (1940).

Grant[2], Duncan (James Corrow) (1885–1978), Scottish painter and designer, a pioneer of abstract art in Britain. He was a cousin of Lytton Strachey and a member of the Bloomsbury Group.

Grant[3], Ulysses S. (1822–85), American general and 18th President of the US 1869–77; born *Hiram Ulysses Grant*; full name *Ulysses Simpson Grant*. As supreme commander of the Union armies, he defeated the Confederate army in 1865 with a policy of attrition.

grant ▶ **verb** [usu. with two objs] **1** agree to give or allow (something requested) to: *they were granted a meeting* | *her request was granted.* ■ give (a right, power, property, etc.) formally or legally to: *they will grant you asylum.*
2 agree or admit to (someone) that (something) is true: *he hasn't made much progress, I'll grant you that.*
▶ **noun** a sum of money given by a government or other organization for a particular purpose: *a research grant.* ■ [mass noun] formal the action of granting something: *we had to recommend the grant or refusal of broadcasting licences.* ■ Law a legal conveyance or formal conferment: *a grant of probate.*
– PHRASES **take for granted 1** fail to properly appreciate (someone or something), especially as a result of overfamiliarity: *the comforts that people take for granted.* **2** (**take something for granted**) assume that something is true without questioning it: *George had taken it for granted that they'd get married.*
– DERIVATIVES **grantable** adjective, **granter** noun.
– ORIGIN Middle English: from Old French *granter* 'consent to support', variant of *creanter* 'to guarantee', based on Latin *credere* 'entrust'.

grant aid Brit. ▶ **noun** [mass noun] financial assistance, especially money that is granted by central government to local government or an institution.
▶ **verb** (**grant-aid**) [with obj.] give grant aid to.

granted ▶ **adverb** [sentence adverb] admittedly; it is true (used to introduce a factor which is opposed to the main line of argument but is not regarded as so strong as to invalidate it): *granted, Marie was two years older than her, but it wasn't a question of age.*
▶ **conjunction** (**granted that**) even assuming that: *granted that officers were used to making decisions, they still couldn't be expected to understand.*

grantee ▶ **noun** chiefly Law a person to whom a grant or conveyance is made.

Granth /grʌnt/ short for **GURU GRANTH SAHIB**.

Grantha /ˈgrʌntə/ ▶ **noun** [mass noun] a southern Indian alphabet dating from the 5th century AD, used by Tamil brahmans for the Sanskrit transcriptions of their sacred books.
– ORIGIN from Sanskrit *grantha* (see **ADI GRANTH**).

Granthi /ˈgrʌntiː/ ▶ **noun** a priest who acts as custodian of the Guru Granth Sahib, the sacred scripture of the Sikhs.

Granth Sahib another term for **GURU GRANTH SAHIB**.

grant-in-aid ▶ **noun** (pl. **grants-in-aid**) an amount of money given to local government, an institution, or a particular scholar.

grant-maintained ▶ **adjective** Brit. (of a school) funded by central rather than local government, and self-governing.

grantor ▶ **noun** chiefly Law a person or institution that makes a grant or conveyance.

gran turismo /ˌgran tʊˈrɪzməʊ/ (abbrev.: **GT**) ▶ **noun** (pl. **gran turismos**) a high-performance car.
– ORIGIN 1960s: Italian, literally 'great touring'.

granular ▶ **adjective 1** resembling or consisting of small grains or particles. ■ having a roughened surface or structure.
2 technical characterized by a high level of granularity: *a granular database.*
– ORIGIN late 18th cent.: from late Latin *granulum* (see **GRANULE**) + **-AR**[1].

granularity ▶ **noun** [mass noun] **1** the quality or condition of being granular.
2 technical the scale or level of detail in a set of data.

granulate ▶ **verb 1** [with obj.] (usu. as adj. **granulated**) form (something) into grains or particles: *granulated sugar.* ■ [no obj.] (of a substance) take the form of grains or particles.
2 [no obj.] (often as adj. **granulating**) Medicine (of a wound or lesion) form multiple small prominences as part of the healing process. ■ (as adj. **granulated**) chiefly Biology having a roughened surface: *the skin is densely granulated.*
– DERIVATIVES **granulation** noun, **granulator** noun.

granule /ˈgranjuːl/ ▶ **noun** a small compact particle of a substance: *coffee granules.*
– ORIGIN mid 17th cent.: from late Latin *granulum*, diminutive of Latin *granum* 'grain'.

granulite ▶ **noun** [mass noun] Geology a fine-grained granular metamorphic rock in which the main component minerals are typically feldspars and quartz.
– DERIVATIVES **granulitic** adjective.
– ORIGIN mid 19th cent.: from **GRANULE** + **-ITE**[1].

granulocyte /ˈgranjʊlə(ʊ)ˌsʌɪt/ ▶ **noun** Physiology a white blood cell with secretory granules in its cytoplasm, e.g. an eosinophil or a basophil.
– DERIVATIVES **granulocytic** adjective.
– ORIGIN early 20th cent.: from late Latin *granulum* 'granule' + **-CYTE**.

granuloma /ˌgranjʊˈləʊmə/ ▶ **noun** (pl. **granulomas** or **granulomata** /-mətə/) Medicine a mass of granulation tissue, typically produced in response to infection, inflammation, or the presence of a foreign substance.
– DERIVATIVES **granulomatous** adjective.

granulometric /ˌgranjʊlə(ʊ)ˈmɛtrɪk/ ▶ **adjective** relating to the distribution or measurement of grain sizes in sand, rock, or other deposits.

granum /ˈgrɑːnəm, ˈgreɪnəm/ singular form of **GRANA**.

Granville-Barker, Harley (1877–1946), English dramatist, critic, theatre director, and actor. His *Prefaces to Shakespeare* (1927–46) influenced subsequent interpretation of Shakespeare's work. Notable plays: *The Voysey Inheritance* (1905).

grape ▶ **noun 1** a berry (typically green, purple, or black) growing in clusters on a grapevine, eaten as fruit and used in making wine. ■ (**the grape**) informal wine.
2 short for **GRAPESHOT**.
– DERIVATIVES **grapey** (also **grapy**) adjective (**grapier**, **grapiest**).
– ORIGIN Middle English (also in the Old French sense): from Old French, 'bunch of grapes', probably from *graper* 'gather grapes', from *grap* 'hook' (denoting an implement used in harvesting grapes), of Germanic origin.

grapefruit ▶ **noun** (pl. **same**) **1** a large round yellow citrus fruit with an acid juicy pulp.
2 the tree which bears grapefruit. ● *Citrus paradisi*, family Rutaceae.

– ORIGIN early 19th cent.: from GRAPE + FRUIT (probably because the fruits grow in clusters).

grape hyacinth ▶ noun a small Eurasian plant of the lily family, with clusters of small globular blue flowers, cultivated as an ornamental or for use in perfume. ● Genus *Muscari*, family Liliaceae.

grape ivy ▶ noun an evergreen climbing plant of the vine family which is grown as a houseplant. ● Genera *Cissus* and *Rhoicissus*, family Vitaceae: several species, in particular *C. rhombifolia* (or *R. rhomboidea*).

grapeseed oil ▶ noun [mass noun] oil extracted from the residue of grapes which have been juiced.

grapeshot ▶ noun [mass noun] historical ammunition consisting of a number of small iron balls fired together from a cannon.

grape sugar ▶ noun [mass noun] dextrose present in or derived from grapes.

grapevine ▶ noun 1 a vine native to both Eurasia and North America, especially one bearing grapes used for eating or winemaking. ● Genus *Vitis*, family Vitaceae: many species, in particular *V. vinifera* and the American *V. labrusca*.
2 informal used to refer to the circulation of rumours and unofficial information: *I'd heard on the grapevine that the business was nearly settled.*

graph[1] /grɑːf, graf/ ▶ noun a diagram showing the relation between variable quantities, typically of two variables, each measured along one of a pair of axes at right angles. ■ Mathematics a collection of points whose coordinates satisfy a given relation.
▶ verb [with obj.] plot or trace on a graph.
– ORIGIN late 19th cent.: abbreviation of *graphic formula*.

graph[2] /grɑːf, graf/ ▶ noun Linguistics a visual symbol representing a unit of sound or other feature of speech. Graphs include not only letters of the alphabet but also punctuation marks.
– ORIGIN 1930s: from Greek *graphē* 'writing'.

-graph ▶ combining form 1 in nouns denoting something written or drawn in a specified way: *autograph*.
2 in nouns denoting an instrument that records: *seismograph*.
– ORIGIN from French *-graphe*, based on Greek *graphos* 'written, writing'.

grapheme /ˈgrafiːm/ ▶ noun Linguistics the smallest meaningful contrastive unit in a writing system. Compare with PHONEME.
– DERIVATIVES **graphemic** adjective,.
– ORIGIN 1930s: from GRAPH[2] + -EME.

-grapher ▶ combining form indicating a person concerned with a subject denoted by a noun ending in *-graphy* (such as *geographer* corresponding to *geography*).
– ORIGIN from Greek *graphos* 'writer' + -ER[1].

graphic ▶ adjective 1 relating to visual art, especially involving drawing, engraving, or lettering: *his mature graphic work.* ■ Computing relating to or denoting a visual image: *graphic information such as charts and diagrams.*
2 giving clear and vividly explicit details: *a graphic account of the riots.*
3 of or in the form of a graph.
4 [attrib.] Geology of or denoting rocks having a surface texture resembling cuneiform writing.
▶ noun Computing a graphical item displayed on a screen or stored as data.
– DERIVATIVES **graphically** adverb, **graphicness** noun.
– ORIGIN mid 17th cent.: via Latin from Greek *graphikos*, from *graphē* 'writing, drawing'.

-graphic ▶ combining form in adjectives corresponding to nouns ending in *-graphy* (such as *demographic* corresponding to *demography*).
– DERIVATIVES **-graphically** combining form in corresponding adverbs.
– ORIGIN from or suggested by Greek *-graphikos*, from *graphē* 'writing, drawing'; partly from -GRAPHY or -GRAPH + -IC.

graphicacy /ˈgrafɪkəsi/ ▶ noun [mass noun] the ability to understand and use a map or graph.
– ORIGIN 1960s: from GRAPHIC, on the pattern of *literacy* and *numeracy*.

graphical ▶ adjective 1 relating to or in the form of a graph.
2 relating to visual art or computer graphics.

-graphical ▶ combining form equivalent to -GRAPHIC.

graphical user interface (abbrev.: **GUI**) ▶ noun Computing a visual way of interacting with a computer using items such as windows, icons, and menus, used by most modern operating systems.

graphic arts ▶ plural noun the visual arts based on the use of line and tone rather than three-dimensional work or the use of colour. ■ [mass noun] (**graphic art**) the practice of graphic arts, especially as a subject of study.
– DERIVATIVES **graphic artist** noun.

graphic design ▶ noun [mass noun] the art or skill of combining text and pictures in advertisements, magazines, or books.
– DERIVATIVES **graphic designer** noun.

graphic equalizer ▶ noun an electronic device or computer program which allows the separate control of the strength and quality of selected frequency bands.

graphic novel ▶ noun a novel in comic-strip format.

graphics ▶ plural noun [usu. treated as sing.] 1 the products of the graphic arts, especially commercial design or illustration.
2 the use of diagrams in calculation and design.
3 (also **computer graphics**) [treated as pl.] visual images produced by computer processing. ■ [treated as sing.] the use of computers linked to display screens to generate and manipulate visual images.

graphics card ▶ noun Computing a printed circuit board that controls the output to a display screen.

graphics tablet ▶ noun Computing an input device consisting of a flat, pressure-sensitive pad which the user draws on or points at with a special stylus, to guide a pointer displayed on the screen.

graphite ▶ noun [mass noun] a grey crystalline allotropic form of carbon which occurs as a mineral in some rocks and can be made from coke. It is used as a solid lubricant, in pencils, and as a moderator in nuclear reactors.
– DERIVATIVES **graphitic** adjective.
– ORIGIN late 18th cent.: coined in German (*Graphit*), from Greek *graphein* 'write' (because of its use as pencil 'lead').

graphitize /ˈgrafɪtʌɪz/ (also **graphitise**) ▶ verb technical convert or be converted into graphite.
– DERIVATIVES **graphitization** noun.

graphology ▶ noun [mass noun] 1 the study of handwriting, for example as used to infer a person's character.
2 Linguistics the study of written and printed symbols and of writing systems.
– DERIVATIVES **graphological** adjective, **graphologist** noun.
– ORIGIN mid 19th cent.: from Greek *graphē* 'writing' + -LOGY.

graph paper ▶ noun [mass noun] paper printed with a network of small squares to assist the drawing of graphs or other diagrams.

graph theory ▶ noun [mass noun] the mathematical theory of the properties and applications of graphs.

-graphy ▶ combining form in nouns denoting: 1 a descriptive science: *geography*.
2 a technique of producing images: *radiography*.
3 a style or method of writing or drawing: *calligraphy*. ■ writing about (a specified subject): *hagiography*. ■ a written or printed list: *filmography*.
– ORIGIN from or suggested by Greek *-graphia* 'writing'.

grapnel /ˈgrapn(ə)l/ ▶ noun 1 a grappling hook.
2 a small anchor with several flukes.
– ORIGIN late Middle English: from an Anglo-Norman French diminutive of Old French *grapon*, of Germanic origin.

grappa /ˈgrapə/ ▶ noun [mass noun] a brandy distilled from the fermented residue of grapes after they have been pressed in winemaking.
– ORIGIN Italian, literally 'grape stalk', of Germanic origin.

Grappelli /grəˈpɛli/, Stephane (1908–97), French jazz violinist. With Django Reinhardt, he founded the group the Quintette du Hot Club de France in 1934.

grapple ▶ verb 1 [no obj.] engage in a close fight or struggle without weapons; wrestle: *passers-by grappled with the man after the knife attack.* ■ [with obj.] seize hold of (someone): *he grappled the young man around the throat.* ■ (**grapple with**) struggle to deal with or overcome (a difficulty or challenge): *other towns are still grappling with the problem.*
2 [with obj.] archaic seize or hold with a grappling hook.
▶ noun 1 an act of grappling. ■ informal a wrestling match.
2 an instrument for seizing hold of something; a grappling hook.
– DERIVATIVES **grappler** noun.
– ORIGIN Middle English (as a noun denoting a grappling hook): from Old French *grapil*, from Provençal, diminutive of *grapa* 'hook', of Germanic origin; related to GRAPE. The verb dates from the mid 16th cent.

grappling hook (also **grappling iron**) ▶ noun a device with iron claws, attached to a rope and used for dragging or grasping.

graptolite /ˈgraptəlʌɪt/ ▶ noun a fossil marine invertebrate animal of the Palaeozoic era, forming mainly planktonic colonies and believed to be related to the pterobranchs. ● Class Graptolithina, phylum Hemichordata.
– ORIGIN mid 19th cent.: from Greek *graptos* 'marked with letters' + -LITE: so named because of the impressions left on hard shales, resembling markings with a slate pencil.

Grasmere /ˈgrɑːsmɪə/ a village in Cumbria, beside a small lake of the same name; pop. 1,000 (est. 2009). William and Dorothy Wordsworth lived there from 1799.

grasp /grɑːsp/ ▶ verb [with obj.] seize and hold firmly: *she grasped the bottle | Edward grasped her by the wrist.* ■ take (an opportunity) eagerly: *many companies grasped the opportunity to expand.* ■ comprehend fully: *the press failed to grasp the significance of what had happened.*
▶ noun [in sing.] a firm hold or grip: *the child slipped from her grasp.* ■ a person's power or capacity to attain something: *he knew success was within his grasp.* ■ a person's understanding: *meanings that are beyond my grasp | his grasp of detail.*
– PHRASES **grasp at straws** see STRAW. **grasp the nettle** Brit. tackle a difficulty boldly. [because a nettle stings when touched lightly, but not when grasped firmly.]
– DERIVATIVES **graspable** adjective, **grasper** noun.
– ORIGIN late Middle English: perhaps related to GROPE.

grasping ▶ adjective avaricious; greedy: *they were regarded as grasping landlords.*
– DERIVATIVES **graspingly** adverb, **graspingness** noun.

Grass /grɑːs, gras/, Günter (Wilhelm) (b.1927), German novelist, poet, and dramatist. Notable works: *The Tin Drum* (novel, 1959) and *The Flounder* (novel, 1977). He was awarded the 1999 Nobel Prize for Literature.

grass ▶ noun 1 [mass noun] vegetation consisting of typically short plants with long, narrow leaves, growing wild or cultivated on lawns and pasture, and as a fodder crop. ■ ground covered with grass. ■ pasture land: *the farms were mostly given over to grass.*
2 a mainly herbaceous plant with jointed stems and spikes of small wind-pollinated flowers, predominant in grass.

> Grasses belong to the large family Gramineae (or Poaceae; the **grass family**), and form the dominant vegetation of many areas of the world. The possession of a growing point that is mainly at ground level makes grasses suitable as the food of many grazing animals, and for use in lawns and playing fields.

3 [mass noun] informal cannabis.
4 Brit. informal a police informer. [perhaps related to the 19th-cent. rhyming slang *grasshopper* 'copper'.]
▶ verb [with obj.] 1 cover (an area of ground) with grass: *the railway tracks were mostly grassed over.* ■ US feed (livestock) on grass.
2 Brit. informal inform the police of someone's criminal activities or plans: [no obj.] *someone had grassed on the thieves* | [with obj.] *she threatened to grass me up.*
3 catch and bring (a fish) to the riverbank.
4 chiefly Rugby & Australian Rules knock (someone) down.
– PHRASES **at grass** grazing. **the grass is always greener on the other side (of the fence)** proverb other people's lives or situations always seem better than your own. **not let the grass grow under one's feet** not delay in acting or taking an opportunity. **put out to grass** put (an animal) out to graze. ■ informal force (someone) to retire.
– DERIVATIVES **grassless** adjective, **grass-like** adjective.
– ORIGIN Old English *græs*, of Germanic origin; related to Dutch *gras*, German *Gras*, also ultimately to GREEN and GROW.

grassbird ▶ noun a brown streaked warbler frequenting long grass and reed beds. ● Family Sylviidae: genus *Megalurus* of Australasia and Asia (also called MARSHBIRD), and *Sphenoeacus afer* of southern Africa.

grassbox ▶ noun a rigid receptacle on a lawnmower for collecting the cut grass.

G

grass carp ▶ noun a large Chinese freshwater fish, farmed for food in SE Asia and introduced elsewhere to control the growth of vegetation in waterways. ● *Ctenopharyngodon idella*, family Cyprinidae.

grasscloth ▶ noun [mass noun] a fine, light cloth resembling linen, woven from the fibres of the inner bark of the ramie plant.

Grasse /grɑːs/, French /gʀas/ a town near Cannes in SE France, centre of the French perfume industry; pop. 49,770 (2006).

grasshopper ▶ noun a plant-eating insect with long hind legs which are used for jumping and for producing a chirping sound, frequenting grassy places and low vegetation. ● Family Acrididae, order Orthoptera: many genera.

grasshopper warbler ▶ noun a secretive Eurasian warbler whose song is a high-pitched mechanical-sounding trill. ● Genus *Locustella*, family Sylviidae: several species, in particular the widespread *L. naevia*.

grassland ▶ noun [mass noun] (also **grasslands**) a large open area of country covered with grass, especially one used for grazing: *acres of rough grassland.*

grass of Parnassus ▶ noun a herbaceous plant of north temperate regions, which bears a solitary white flower. ● Genus *Parnassia*, family Saxifragaceae: several species, in particular *P. palustris*.

grass parrot (also **grass parakeet**) ▶ noun Austral. a small parrot frequenting grassy country. ● Family Psittacidae: several genera, in particular *Psephotus* and *Neophema*.

grass pea ▶ noun a plant of the pea family which is cultivated as food for animals and humans, though excessive consumption can lead to lathyrism. Also called **CHICKLING PEA**. ● *Lathyrus sativus*, family Leguminosae.

grassquit /ˈgrɑːskwɪt/ ▶ noun a small Caribbean and tropical American songbird related to the buntings, the male being partly or mainly black. ● Family Emberizidae (subfamily Emberizinae): three genera, in particular *Tiaris*, and several species.

grass roots ▶ plural noun the most basic level of an activity or organization: [as modifier] *improving the game at grass-roots level.* ■ ordinary people regarded as the main body of an organization's membership: *you have lost touch with the grass roots of the party.*

grass sickness ▶ noun [mass noun] a disease of horses which affects the workings of the bowel and is usually fatal.

grass ski ▶ noun each of a pair of devices resembling caterpillar tracks, worn on the feet for going down grass-covered slopes as if on skis.
– DERIVATIVES **grass skiing** noun.

grass skirt ▶ noun a skirt made of long grass and leaves fastened to a waistband, associated especially with female dancers from some Pacific islands.

grass snake ▶ noun a common harmless Eurasian snake that typically has a yellowish band around the neck and is often found in or near water. ● *Natrix natrix*, family Colubridae.
■ North American term for **GREEN SNAKE**.

grass tetany (also **grass staggers**) ▶ noun [mass noun] a disease of livestock caused by magnesium deficiency, occurring especially when there is a change from indoor feeding to outdoor grazing.

grass tree ▶ noun another term for **BLACKBOY**.

grassveld /ˈgrɑːsfɛlt/ ▶ noun [mass noun] S. African uncultivated land on which the dominant vegetation type is indigenous grass.
– ORIGIN partly translating Afrikaans *grasveld* 'prairie'.

grass widow ▶ noun a woman whose husband is away often or for a prolonged period.
– ORIGIN early 16th cent. (denoting an unmarried woman with a child): from **GRASS** + **WIDOW**, perhaps from the idea of the couple having lain on the grass instead of in bed. The current sense dates from the mid 19th cent; compare with Dutch *grasweduwe* and German *Strohwitwe* 'straw widow'.

grassy ▶ adjective (**grassier**, **grassiest**) covered with grass: *grassy slopes.* ■ characteristic of or resembling grass: *an intense grassy green | try the pleasant, grassy Chablis.*
– DERIVATIVES **grassiness** noun.

grate¹ ▶ verb **1** [with obj.] reduce (food) to small shreds by rubbing it on a grater: (as adj. **grated**) *grated cheese.*
2 [no obj.] make an unpleasant rasping sound: *the hinges of the door grated.* ■ [with direct speech] say something in a harsh tone: *'How dare you!' he grated.*
3 [no obj.] have an irritating effect: *the buzzing sound grated on her nerves.*
– ORIGIN late Middle English: from Old French *grater*, of Germanic origin; related to German *kratzen* 'to scratch'.

grate² ▶ noun **1** the recess of a fireplace or furnace. ■ a metal frame for holding fuel in a fireplace or furnace.
2 a grating.
– ORIGIN Middle English (meaning 'a grating'): from Old French, based on Latin *cratis* 'hurdle'.

grateful ▶ adjective feeling or showing an appreciation for something done or received: *I'm grateful to you for all your help | she gave him a grateful smile.* ■ archaic received or experienced with gratitude; welcome: *the grateful shade.*
– DERIVATIVES **gratefully** adverb, **gratefulness** noun.
– ORIGIN mid 16th cent.: from obsolete *grate* 'pleasing, thankful' (from Latin *gratus*) + **-FUL**.

grater ▶ noun a device having a surface covered with holes edged by slightly raised cutting edges, used for grating cheese and other foods.

graticule /ˈgratɪkjuːl/ ▶ noun technical a network of lines representing meridians and parallels, on which a map or plan can be represented. ■ a series of fine lines or fibres in the eyepiece of an optical device, such as a microscope, or on the screen of an oscilloscope, used as a measuring scale or an aid in locating objects.
– ORIGIN late 19th cent.: from French, from medieval Latin *graticula* 'a little grating', from Latin *craticula* 'gridiron', diminutive of *cratis* 'hurdle'.

gratification ▶ noun [mass noun] pleasure, especially when gained from the satisfaction of a desire: *a thirst for sexual gratification.* ■ [count noun] a source of pleasure.

gratify ▶ verb (**gratifies**, **gratifying**, **gratified**) [with obj.] give (someone) pleasure or satisfaction: *she was gratified to see the shock in Jim's eyes* | (as adj. **gratifying**) *the results were gratifying.* ■ indulge or satisfy (a desire): *not all the sexual impulses can be gratified.*
– DERIVATIVES **gratifyingly** adverb.
– ORIGIN late Middle English (in the sense 'make pleasing'): from French *gratifier* or Latin *gratificari* 'give or do as a favour', from *gratus* 'pleasing, thankful'.

gratin /ˈgratã, ˈgratan/ ▶ noun a dish with a lightly browned crust of breadcrumbs or melted cheese.
– ORIGIN French, from *gratter*, earlier *grater* 'to grate'.

gratiné /ˌgratɪˈneɪ/ (also **gratinée**) ▶ adjective [postpositive] another term for **AU GRATIN**.
– DERIVATIVES **gratinéed** adjective.
– ORIGIN French, past participle of *gratiner* 'cook au gratin'.

grating¹ ▶ adjective sounding harsh and unpleasant: *her high, grating voice.* ■ irritating: *his grating confrontational personality.*
– DERIVATIVES **gratingly** adverb.

grating² ▶ noun a framework of parallel or crossed bars, typically preventing access through an opening while permitting communication or ventilation. ■ (also **diffraction grating**) Optics a set of equally spaced parallel wires, or a surface ruled with equally spaced parallel lines, used to produce spectra by diffraction.

gratis /ˈgratɪs, ˈgrɑː-, ˈgreɪ-/ ▶ adverb without charge; free: *a monthly programme was issued gratis.*
▶ adjective given or done for nothing; free: *gratis books.*
– ORIGIN late Middle English: from Latin, contraction of *gratiis* 'as a kindness', from *gratia* 'grace, kindness'.

gratitude ▶ noun [mass noun] the quality of being thankful; readiness to show appreciation for and to return kindness: *she expressed her gratitude to the committee for their support.*
– ORIGIN late Middle English: from Old French, or from medieval Latin *gratitudo*, from Latin *gratus* 'pleasing, thankful'.

gratuitous /grəˈtjuːɪtəs/ ▶ adjective **1** done without good reason; uncalled for: *gratuitous violence.*
2 given or done free of charge.
– DERIVATIVES **gratuitously** adverb, **gratuitousness** noun.
– ORIGIN mid 17th cent.: from Latin *gratuitus* 'given freely, spontaneous' + **-OUS**.

gratuity /grəˈtjuːɪti/ ▶ noun (pl. **gratuities**) **1** formal a tip given to a waiter, taxi driver, etc.
2 Brit. a sum of money paid to an employee at the end of a period of employment.
– ORIGIN late 15th cent. (denoting graciousness or favour): from Old French *gratuité* or medieval Latin *gratuitas* 'gift', from Latin *gratus* 'pleasing, thankful'.

graunch /grɔːn(t)ʃ/ informal, chiefly Brit. ▶ verb [no obj.] make a crunching or grinding noise: *the wheels graunched against a stone wall.* ■ [with obj.] NZ damage (something): *she sat massaging a shoulder she'd graunched last week.*
▶ noun a crunching or grinding noise.
– ORIGIN late 19th cent. (originally Leicestershire dialect): imitative.

graupel /ˈgraʊp(ə)l/ ▶ noun [mass noun] small particles of snow with a fragile crust of ice; soft hail.
– ORIGIN late 19th cent.: German *Graupel*, back-formation from *graupeln* 'to hail with soft hailstones', from *Graupe* 'cereal grain'.

gravadlax /ˈgravədˌlaks/ ▶ noun variant spelling of **GRAVLAX**.

gravamen /grəˈveɪmɛn/ ▶ noun (pl. **gravamina** /-mɪnə/) chiefly Law the essence or most serious part of a complaint or accusation. ■ a grievance.
– ORIGIN early 17th cent. (as an ecclesiastical term denoting formal presentation of a grievance): from late Latin, literally 'physical inconvenience', from Latin *gravare* 'to load', from *gravis* 'heavy'.

grave¹ /greɪv/ ▶ noun a hole dug in the ground to receive a coffin or corpse, typically marked by a stone or mound. ■ (often **the grave**) used as an allusive term for death: *life beyond the grave.* ■ a place where a broken or discarded object lies: *they lifted the aircraft from its watery grave.*
– PHRASES **dig one's own grave** do something foolish which causes one's downfall. **(as) silent** (or **quiet**) **as the grave** extremely quiet. **take the** (or **one's** etc.) **secret to the grave** die without revealing a secret. **turn** (N. Amer. also **roll over** or **turn over**) **in one's grave** used to express the opinion that something would have caused anger or distress in someone who is now dead: *if my father saw the weeds he would turn in his grave.*
– ORIGIN Old English *græf*, of Germanic origin; related to Dutch *graf* and German *Grab*.

grave² /greɪv/ ▶ adjective **1** giving cause for alarm; serious: *a matter of grave concern.*
2 serious or solemn in manner or appearance: *his face was grave.*
▶ noun /grɑːv/ another term for **GRAVE ACCENT**.
– DERIVATIVES **gravely** adverb, **graveness** noun.
– ORIGIN late 15th cent. (originally of a wound in the sense 'severe, serious'): from Old French *grave* or Latin *gravis* 'heavy, serious'.

grave³ /greɪv/ ▶ verb (past participle **graven** or **graved**) [with obj.] archaic engrave (an inscription or image) on a surface. ■ literary fix (something) indelibly in the mind: *the times are graven on my memory.*
– ORIGIN Old English *grafan* 'dig', of Germanic origin; related to German *graben*, Dutch *graven* 'dig' and German *begraben* 'bury', also to **GRAVE¹** and **GROOVE**.

grave⁴ /greɪv/ ▶ verb [with obj.] historical clean (a ship's bottom) by burning off the accretions and then tarring it.
– ORIGIN late Middle English: perhaps from French dialect *grave*, variant of Old French *greve* 'shore' (because originally the ship would have been run aground).

grave⁵ /grɑːˈveɪ/ ▶ adverb & adjective Music (as a direction) slowly; with solemnity.
– ORIGIN Italian, 'slow'.

grave accent /grɑːv/ ▶ noun a mark (`) placed over a vowel in some languages to indicate a feature such as altered sound quality, vowel length, or intonation.
– ORIGIN early 17th cent.: French *grave* (see **GRAVE²**).

gravedigger ▶ noun a person who digs graves.

grave goods ▶ plural noun Archaeology utilitarian and valuable objects deposited with bodies in prehistoric and ancient graves, probably intended for use in the afterlife.

gravel ▶ noun [mass noun] **1** a loose aggregation of small water-worn or pounded stones. ■ a mixture of gravel with coarse sand, used for paths and roads and as an aggregate. ■ a stratum or deposit of gravel.
2 Medicine aggregations of crystals formed in the urinary tract.
▶ verb (**gravels**, **gravelling**, **gravelled**; US **gravels**, **graveling**, **graveled**) [with obj.] **1** cover (an area) with gravel.
2 US informal make (someone) angry or annoyed: *the strike was badly organized and it gravelled him to involve himself in it.* ■ archaic confuse or puzzle (someone).
– ORIGIN Middle English: from Old French, diminutive of *grave* (see **GRAVE⁴**).

gravel-blind ▸ adjective archaic almost completely blind.
– ORIGIN early 17th cent.: originally as *high-gravel-blind*, a humorous usage meaning 'more than sand-blind (= half-blind)', with reference to Shakespeare's *Merchant of Venice*.

gravelly ▸ adjective **1** resembling, containing, or consisting of gravel: *a dry gravelly soil*.
2 (of a voice) deep and rough-sounding.

graven past participle of GRAVE³.

graven image ▸ noun a carved idol or representation of a god used as an object of worship.
– ORIGIN with biblical allusion to Exod. 20:4.

Gravenstein /ˈgrɑːv(ə)nˌstʌɪn/ ▸ noun an apple of a large variety having yellow, red-streaked skin. It is widely grown in North America, where it is used for cooking and as a dessert apple.
– ORIGIN early 19th cent.: the German form of *Graasten*, a village in Denmark formerly in Schleswig-Holstein, Germany.

graver ▸ noun a burin or other engraving tool. ■ archaic an engraver.

Graves¹ /greɪvz/, Robert (Ranke) (1895–1985), English poet, novelist, and critic, known for his interest in classics and mythology. Notable prose works: *Goodbye to All That* (autobiography, 1929), *I, Claudius* (historical fiction, 1934), and *The White Goddess* (non-fiction, 1948).

Graves² /grɑːv/, French /grav/ ▸ noun [mass noun] a red or white wine from the district of Graves, to the south of Bordeaux in France.

Graves' disease /greɪvz/ ▸ noun [mass noun] a swelling of the neck and protrusion of the eyes resulting from an overactive thyroid gland. Also called EXOPHTHALMIC GOITRE.
– ORIGIN mid 19th cent.: named after Robert J. *Graves* (1796–1853), the Irish physician who first identified it.

graveside ▸ noun the ground around the edge of a grave.

gravestone ▸ noun an inscribed headstone marking a grave.

Gravettian /grəˈvɛtɪən/ ▸ adjective Archaeology relating to or denoting an Upper Palaeolithic culture in Europe following the Aurignacian, dated to about 28,000–19,000 years ago. ■ (as noun **the Gravettian**) the Gravettian culture or period.
– ORIGIN 1930s: from *la Gravette*, an archaeological site in SW France, where objects from this culture were found.

graveyard ▸ noun a burial ground, especially one beside a church.

graveyard shift ▸ noun a work shift that runs through the early morning hours, typically covering the period between midnight and 8 a.m.

gravid /ˈgravɪd/ ▸ adjective **1** technical carrying eggs or young; pregnant.
2 full of meaning or a specified quality: *the scene is gravid with unease*.
– ORIGIN late 16th cent.: from Latin *gravidus* 'laden, pregnant', from *gravis* 'heavy'.

gravimeter /grəˈvɪmɪtə/ ▸ noun an instrument for measuring the difference in the force of gravity from one place to another.
– ORIGIN late 18th cent.: from French *gravimètre*, from *grave* 'heavy' (from Latin *gravis*) + *-mètre* '(instrument) measuring'.

gravimetric /ˌgravɪˈmɛtrɪk/ ▸ adjective **1** relating to the measurement of weight.
2 relating to the measurement of gravity.
– DERIVATIVES **gravimetry** /grəˈvɪmɪtri/ noun.

graving dock ▸ noun another term for DRY DOCK.
– ORIGIN early 19th cent.: *graving* from GRAVE⁴.

gravitas /ˈgravɪtas, -tɑːs/ ▸ noun [mass noun] dignity, seriousness, or solemnity of manner: *a post for which he has the expertise and the gravitas*.
– ORIGIN Latin, from *gravis* 'serious'.

gravitate /ˈgravɪteɪt/ ▸ verb [no obj., with adverbial]
1 move towards or be attracted to a person or thing: *young western Europeans will gravitate to Berlin*.
2 Physics move, or tend to move, towards a centre of gravity or other attractive force. ■ archaic descend or sink by the force of gravity.
– ORIGIN mid 17th cent.: from modern Latin *gravitat-*, from the verb *gravitare*, from Latin *gravitas* 'weight'.

gravitation ▸ noun [mass noun] **1** movement, or a tendency to move, towards a centre of gravity, as in the falling of bodies to the earth. ■ Physics the force responsible for gravitation; gravity.
2 movement towards or attraction to something: *this recent gravitation towards the Continent*.
– DERIVATIVES **gravitational** adjective, **gravitationally** adverb.
– ORIGIN mid 17th cent.: from modern Latin *gravitatio(n-)*, from the verb *gravitare* (see GRAVITATE).

gravitational constant (abbrev.: **G**) ▸ noun Physics the constant in Newton's law of gravitation relating gravity to the masses and separation of particles, equal to 6.67×10^{-11} N m² kg⁻².

gravitational field ▸ noun Physics the region of space surrounding a body in which another body experiences a force of gravitational attraction.

gravitational lens ▸ noun Astronomy a region of space containing a massive object whose gravitational field distorts electromagnetic radiation passing through it in a similar way to a lens, sometimes producing a multiple image of a remote object.

graviton /ˈgravɪtɒn/ ▸ noun Physics a hypothetical quantum of gravitational energy, regarded as a particle.
– ORIGIN 1940s: from GRAVITATION + -ON.

gravity ▸ noun [mass noun] **1** Physics the force that attracts a body towards the centre of the earth, or towards any other physical body having mass. ■ the degree of intensity of gravity, measured by acceleration.
2 extreme importance; seriousness: *crimes of the utmost gravity*.
3 solemnity of manner: *has the poet ever spoken with greater eloquence or gravity?*
– ORIGIN late 15th cent. (in sense 2): from Old French, or from Latin *gravitas* 'weight, seriousness', from *gravis* 'heavy'. Sense 1 dates from the 17th cent.

gravity feed ▸ noun [mass noun] a supply system making use of gravity to maintain the flow of material.
– DERIVATIVES **gravity-fed** adjective.

gravity wave ▸ noun Physics **1** a hypothetical wave carrying gravitational energy, postulated by Einstein to be emitted when a massive body is accelerated.
2 a wave propagated on a liquid surface or in a fluid through the effects of gravity.

gravlax /ˈgravlaks/ (also **gravadlax**) ▸ noun [mass noun] a Scandinavian dish of dry-cured salmon marinated in herbs.
– ORIGIN Swedish, from *grav* 'trench' + *lax* 'salmon' (from the former practice of burying the salmon in salt in a hole in the ground).

gravure /grəˈvjʊə, grəˈvjɔː/ ▸ noun short for PHOTOGRAVURE.

gravy ▸ noun (pl. **gravies**) [mass noun] **1** the fat and juices exuding from meat during cooking. ■ a sauce made from these juices together with stock and other ingredients.
2 informal, chiefly N. Amer. unearned or unexpected money.
– PHRASES **gravy train** informal used to refer to a situation in which someone can make a lot of money for very little effort: *come to Hollywood and get on to the gravy train*.
– ORIGIN Middle English (denoting a spicy sauce): perhaps from a misreading (as *gravé*) of Old French *grané*, probably from *grain* 'spice', from Latin *granum* 'grain'.

gravy boat ▸ noun a long, narrow jug used for serving gravy.

Gray¹, Asa (1810–88), American botanist, author of many textbooks which greatly popularized botany. He supported Darwin's theories at a time when they were anathema to many.

Gray², Thomas (1716–71), English poet, best known for 'Elegy Written in a Country Church-Yard' (1751).

gray¹ (abbrev.: **Gy**) ▸ noun Physics the SI unit of the absorbed dose of ionizing radiation, corresponding to one joule per kilogram.
– ORIGIN 1970s: named after Louis H. *Gray* (1905–65), English radiobiologist.

gray² ▸ adjective US spelling of GREY.

graybeard ▸ noun US spelling of GREYBEARD.

Gray code ▸ noun a numerical code used in computing in which consecutive integers are represented by binary numbers differing in only one digit.
– ORIGIN mid 20th cent.: named after Frank *Gray* (1887–1969), American physicist.

graylag ▸ noun US spelling of GREYLAG.

grayling ▸ noun **1** an edible freshwater fish which is silvery-grey with horizontal violet stripes and has a long high dorsal fin, of both Eurasia and North America. ● Genus *Thymallus*, family Salmonidae: several species.
2 a mainly brown European butterfly which has wings with bright eyespots and greyish undersides. ● *Hipparchia semele*, subfamily Satyrinae, family Nymphalidae.
– ORIGIN Middle English: from *gray* (variant of GREY) + -LING.

grayscale ▸ noun US spelling of GREYSCALE.

graywacke ▸ noun US spelling of GREYWACKE.

Graz /grɑːts/ a city in southern Austria, on the River Mur, capital of the state of Styria; pop. 247,515 (2006). It is the second-largest city in Austria.

graze¹ ▸ verb [no obj.] (of cattle, sheep, etc.) eat grass in a field: *cattle graze on the open meadows*. ■ [with obj.] (of an animal) feed on (grass or grassland): *downland areas grazed by sheep*. ■ [with obj.] put (cattle, sheep, etc.) to feed on grassland. ■ informal (of a person) eat frequent snacks at irregular intervals: *advertisers should not encourage children to graze on snacks or sweets*. ■ informal, chiefly N. Amer. casually sample something: *we grazed up and down the TV channels*.
– DERIVATIVES **grazer** noun.
– ORIGIN Old English *grasian*, from *græs* 'grass'.

graze² ▸ verb [with obj.] scrape and break the surface of the skin of (a part of the body): *she fell down and grazed her knees*. ■ touch or scrape lightly in passing: *his hands just grazed hers*.
▸ noun a slight injury where the skin is scraped.
– ORIGIN late 16th cent.: perhaps a specific use of GRAZE¹.

grazier /ˈgreɪzɪə/ ▸ noun a person who rears or fattens cattle or sheep for market. ■ Austral./NZ a large-scale sheep or cattle farmer.
– ORIGIN Middle English: from GRASS + -IER.

grazing ▸ noun [mass noun] grassland suitable for pasturage: *large areas of rough grazing*.

grease ▸ noun [mass noun] **1** a thick oily substance, especially as used as a lubricant: *axle grease*.
2 animal fat used or produced in cooking.
▸ verb [with obj.] smear or lubricate with grease.
– PHRASES **grease the palm of** informal bribe (someone). [*grease* expressing the sense 'cause to run smoothly' and *palm*, by association with the taking of money.] **grease the wheels** (or **skids**) informal, chiefly N. Amer. help matters run smoothly: *he used his budgetary skills to grease the skids for new projects*. **like greased lightning** informal extremely fast.
– DERIVATIVES **greaseless** adjective.
– ORIGIN Middle English: from Old French *graisse*, based on Latin *crassus* 'thick, fat'.

greaseball ▸ noun N. Amer. informal, offensive a foreigner, especially one of Mediterranean or Latin American origin.

grease gun ▸ noun a device for pumping grease under pressure to a particular point.

grease monkey ▸ noun informal a mechanic.

greasepaint ▸ noun [mass noun] a waxy substance used as make-up by actors.

greaseproof ▸ adjective Brit. (especially of paper used in cooking) impermeable to oil or grease.

greaser ▸ noun **1** a motor mechanic or unskilled engineer on a ship.
2 informal a young man with long hair belonging to a motorcycle gang.
3 US informal, offensive a Hispanic American, especially a Mexican.
4 informal a smooth or gentle aircraft landing.

greasewood ▸ noun a resinous dwarf shrub of the goosefoot family, which yields hard yellow wood used chiefly for fuel. It grows in dry areas of the western US and is toxic to stock if eaten in large quantities. ● *Sarcobatus vermiculatus*, family Chenopodiaceae.

greasy ▸ adjective (**greasier**, **greasiest**) **1** covered with, resembling, or produced by grease or oil: *he wiped his greasy fingers* | *a greasy mark*. ■ producing excessive body oil: *greasy skin*. ■ containing or cooked with too much oil or fat: *greasy food*. ■ slippery: *the rain's making the roads greasy*.
2 (of a person or their manner) unpleasantly or insincerely polite or ingratiating: *the greasy little man from the newspaper*.
– DERIVATIVES **greasily** adverb, **greasiness** noun.

greasy pole ▸ noun informal a pole covered with grease to make it more difficult to climb or walk along, used especially as a form of entertainment. ■ used to refer to the difficult route to the top of a profession: *he steadily climbed the greasy pole towards the job he coveted most*.

G

greasy spoon ▶ noun informal a cheap, run-down cafe or restaurant serving fried foods.

great ▶ adjective **1** of an extent, amount, or intensity considerably above average: *the article was of great interest* | *she showed great potential as an actor.* ■ [attrib.] used to reinforce another adjective of size or extent: *a great big grin.* ■ (also **greater**) [attrib.] used in names of animals or plants which are larger than similar kinds, e.g. **great tit**, **greater celandine**. ■ (**Great**) [attrib.] [in place names] denoting the larger or largest part of a place: *Great Malvern.* ■ (**Greater**) [attrib.] (of a city) including adjacent urban areas: *Greater Manchester.*
2 of ability, quality, or eminence considerably above average: *the great Italian conductor* | *great art has the power to change lives.* ■ [attrib.] important or most important: *the great day arrived* | *the great thing is the challenge.* ■ (**the Great**) used as a title to denote the most important person of the name: *Alexander the Great.* ■ impressive or grand: *the great Victorian house.* ■ informal very good; excellent: *another great goal from Alan* | *wouldn't it be great to have him back?* | [as exclamation] *'Great!' said Tom.* ■ informal (of a person) very skilled in a particular area: *she's great at French.*
3 [attrib.] used before a noun to emphasize a particular description of someone or something: *I was a great fan of Hank's* | *her great friend Joe.* ■ used to express surprise, admiration, or contempt, especially in exclamations: *you great oaf!*
4 [in combination] (in names of family relationships) denoting one degree further removed upwards or downwards: *great-aunt* | *great-great-grandfather.*
5 [predic.] Irish (of two people) on very close or intimate terms: *one of the boys was very great with her.*
▶ noun **1** an important or distinguished person: *the Beatles, Bob Dylan, all the greats* | (as plural noun **the great**) *the lives of the great, including Churchill and Newton.*
2 (**Greats**) another term for LITERAE HUMANIORES.
▶ adverb informal very well; excellently: *we played awful, they played great.*
– PHRASES **the great and the good** often ironic distinguished and worthy people collectively: *an impressive gathering of the great and the good.* **great and small** of all sizes, classes, or types: *all creatures great and small.* **a great deal** see DEAL[1]. **a great many** see MANY. **a great one for** a habitual doer of; an enthusiast for: *my father was a great one for buying gadgets.* **Great Scott!** dated expressing surprise or amazement. [arbitrary euphemism for *Great God!*]
– ORIGIN Old English *grēat* 'big', of West Germanic origin; related to Dutch *groot* and German *gross*.

great ape ▶ noun a large ape of a family closely related to humans, including the gorilla, orang-utan, and chimpanzees, but excluding the gibbons; an anthropoid ape. ● Family Pongidae, order Primates.

Great Attractor Astronomy a massive grouping of galaxies in the direction of the constellations Hydra and Centaurus, whose gravitational pull is thought to be responsible for deviations in the velocity of other galaxies.

great auk ▶ noun a large extinct flightless auk (seabird) of the North Atlantic, resembling a giant razorbill. The great auk was the original 'penguin'; many were taken for food, and the last individuals were killed on an islet off Iceland in 1844. ● *Alca* (or *Pinguinus*) *impennis*, family Alcidae.

great-aunt ▶ noun an aunt of one's father or mother.

Great Australian Bight a wide bay on the south coast of Australia, part of the southern Indian Ocean.

Great Barrier Reef a coral reef in the western Pacific, off the coast of Queensland, Australia. It extends for about 2,000 km (1,250 miles), roughly parallel to the coast, and is the largest coral reef in the world.

Great Basin an arid region of the western US between the Sierra Nevada and the Rocky Mountains, including most of Nevada and parts of the adjacent states.

Great Bear Astronomy the constellation Ursa Major.

Great Bear Lake a large lake in the Northwest Territories, Canada. It drains into the Mackenzie River via the Great Bear River.

Great Bible ▶ noun the edition of the English Bible which Thomas Cromwell ordered to be set up in every parish church. It was the work of Miles Coverdale, and was first issued in 1539.

Great Britain England, Wales, and Scotland considered as a unit. The name is also often used loosely to refer to the United Kingdom.

> **USAGE** Great Britain is the name for the island that comprises England, Scotland, and Wales, although the term is also used loosely to refer to the United Kingdom. The **United Kingdom** is a political unit that includes these countries and Northern Ireland. The **British Isles** is a geographical term that refers to the United Kingdom, Ireland, and surrounding smaller islands such as the Hebrides and the Channel Islands.

Great Charter another name for MAGNA CARTA.

great circle ▶ noun a circle on the surface of a sphere which lies in a plane passing through the sphere's centre. As it represents the shortest distance between any two points on a sphere, a great circle of the earth is the preferred route taken by a ship or aircraft.

greatcoat ▶ noun a long heavy overcoat.

great crested grebe ▶ noun a large grebe with a crest and ear ruffs in the breeding season, found from Europe to New Zealand. ● *Podiceps cristatus*, family Podicipedidae.

great crested newt ▶ noun another term for CRESTED NEWT.

Great Dane ▶ noun a dog of a very large, powerful, short-haired breed.

Great Depression see DEPRESSION.

Great Dismal Swamp (also **Dismal Swamp**) an area of swampland in SE Virginia and NE North Carolina.

Great Divide another name for CONTINENTAL DIVIDE or GREAT DIVIDING RANGE.

great divide ▶ noun a boundary between two contrasting groups, cultures, etc. that is regarded as very difficult to ignore or overcome: *the great divide between workers and management.* ■ the boundary between life and death: *she is still on the human side of the great divide.*

Great Dividing Range a mountain system in eastern Australia. Curving roughly parallel to the coast, it extends from eastern Victoria to northern Queensland. Also called GREAT DIVIDE.

Greater Antilles see ANTILLES.

Greater Bairam ▶ noun another term for EID UL-ADHA (see EID).

greater celandine ▶ noun a yellow-flowered Eurasian plant of the poppy family. Its toxic orange sap has long been used in herbal medicine, especially for disorders of the eyes and skin. ● *Chelidonium majus*, family Papaveraceae.

Greater London a metropolitan area comprising central London and the surrounding regions. It is divided administratively into the City of London, thirteen inner London boroughs, and twenty outer London boroughs.

Greater Manchester a former metropolitan county of NW England including the city of Manchester and adjacent areas.

Greater Sunda Islands see SUNDA ISLANDS.

Great Exhibition the first international exhibition of the products of industry, promoted by Prince Albert and held in the Crystal Palace in London in 1851.

Great Fire another name for FIRE OF LONDON.

Great Glen a large fault valley in Scotland, extending from the Moray Firth south-west for 96 km (approx. 60 miles) to Loch Linnhe, and containing Loch Ness. Also called GLEN MORE.

great-grandchild ▶ noun a son or daughter of one's grandchild.

great-granddaughter ▶ noun a daughter of one's grandchild.

great-grandfather ▶ noun the father of one's grandmother or grandfather.

great-grandmother ▶ noun the mother of one's grandmother or grandfather.

great-grandparent ▶ noun the mother or father of one's grandparent.

great-grandson ▶ noun a son of one's grandchild.

Great Grimsby official name for GRIMSBY.

great-hearted ▶ adjective dated having a noble, generous, and courageous spirit.
– DERIVATIVES **great-heartedness** noun.

Great Indian Desert another name for THAR DESERT.

Great Lakes a group of five large interconnected lakes in central North America, consisting of Lakes Superior, Michigan, Huron, Erie, and Ontario, and constituting the largest area of fresh water in the world. Lake Michigan is wholly within the US, and the others lie on the Canada–US border. Connected to the Atlantic Ocean by the St Lawrence Seaway, the Great Lakes form an important commercial waterway.

Great Lake State informal name for MICHIGAN.

Great Land informal name for ALASKA.

Great Leap Forward an unsuccessful attempt made under Mao Zedong in China 1958–60 to hasten the process of industrialization and improve agricultural production by reorganizing the population into large rural collectives and adopting labour-intensive industrial methods.

greatly ▶ adverb by a considerable amount; very much: *I admire him greatly* | [as submodifier] *they now have greatly increased powers.*

Great Mother ▶ noun another name for MOTHER GODDESS.

Great Nebula Astronomy **1** (also **Great Nebula in Andromeda**) the Andromeda Galaxy.
2 (also **Great Nebula in Orion**) a bright emission nebula in Orion, visible to the naked eye.

great-nephew ▶ noun a son of one's nephew or niece.

greatness ▶ noun [mass noun] the quality of being great; eminence or distinction: *Elgar's greatness as a composer.*

great-niece ▶ noun a daughter of one's nephew or niece.

great northern diver ▶ noun a diving waterbird with a black streamlined head, breeding in northern North America, Greenland, and Iceland. ● *Gavia immer*, family Gaviidae. North American name: **common loon**.

Great Northern War a conflict 1700–21 in which Russia, Denmark, Poland, and Saxony opposed Sweden. The war resulted in Sweden losing her imperial possessions in central Europe, and Russia under Peter the Great becoming a major power in the Baltic.

great organ ▶ noun the chief keyboard in a large organ and its related pipes and mechanism.

Great Ouse another name for OUSE (sense 1).

Great Plague a serious outbreak of bubonic plague in England in 1665–6, in which about one fifth of the population of London died. It was the last major outbreak in Britain.

Great Plains a vast area of plains to the east of the Rocky Mountains in North America, extending from the valleys of the Mackenzie River in Canada to southern Texas.

Great Rebellion the Royalist name for the English Civil War of 1642–51.

Great Red Spot Astronomy a weather system on the planet Jupiter which measures over 10,000 km across and has persisted at least since the beginning of telescopic observations.

Great Rift Valley a large system of rift valleys in eastern Africa and the Middle East, forming the most extensive such system in the world and running for some 4,285 km (3,000 miles) from the Jordan valley in Syria into Mozambique. It is marked by a chain of lakes and a series of volcanoes, including Mount Kilimanjaro.

Great Russian ▶ adjective & noun former term for RUSSIAN (language and people), as distinguished from other peoples and languages of the old Russian Empire.

Great St Bernard Pass see ST BERNARD PASS.

Great Salt Lake a salt lake in northern Utah, near Salt Lake City. With an area of some 2,590 sq. km (1,000 sq. miles), it is the largest salt lake in North America.

Great Sand Sea an area of desert in NE Africa, on the border between Libya and Egypt.

Great Sandy Desert 1 a large tract of desert in north central Western Australia.
2 another name for RUB' AL-KHALI.

Great Schism 1 the breach between the Eastern and the Western Churches, traditionally dated to 1054 and becoming final in 1472.
2 the period 1378–1417, when the Western Church was divided by the creation of antipopes.

Great Seal ▶ noun a seal used for the authentication of state documents of the highest importance. That of the UK is held by the Lord Chancellor and that of the US by the Secretary of State.

great skua ▶ noun a large North Atlantic skua with mainly brown plumage, feeding by robbing other seabirds. Also called BONXIE. ● *Catharacta skua*, family Stercorariidae.

Great Slave Lake a large lake in the Northwest Territories in Canada. The deepest lake in North America, it reaches a depth of 615 m (2,015 ft). The Mackenzie River flows out of it.

great tit ▶ noun a tit (songbird) with a black head and white cheeks, occurring in many different races from western Europe to eastern Asia. ● *Parus major*, family Paridae.

Great Trek the northward migration 1835–7 of large numbers of Boers discontented with British rule in the Cape, to the areas where they eventually founded the Transvaal Republic and Orange Free State.

great-uncle ▶ noun an uncle of one's mother or father.

Great Victoria Desert a desert region of Australia, which straddles the boundary between Western Australia and South Australia.

Great Wall of China a fortified wall in northern China, extending some 2,400 km (1,500 miles) from Gansu province to the Yellow Sea north of Beijing. It was first built *c.*210 BC, as a protection against nomad invaders. The present wall dates from the Ming dynasty.

Great War another name for FIRST WORLD WAR.

Great Wen an archaic nickname for London.

great white shark ▶ noun a large aggressive shark of warm seas, with a brownish or grey back, white underparts, and large triangular teeth. Also called WHITE POINTER, MANEATER. ● *Carcharodon carcharias*, family Lamnidae.

Great White Way nickname for BROADWAY.

greave ▶ noun historical a piece of armour used to protect the shin.
– ORIGIN Middle English: from Old French *greve* 'shin, greave', of unknown origin.

grebe /griːb/ ▶ noun a diving waterbird with a long neck, lobed toes, and almost no tail, typically having bright breeding plumage used in display. ● Family Podicipedidae: several genera.
– ORIGIN mid 18th cent.: from French *grèbe* (term used in the Savoie region), of unknown origin.

grebo /ˈgriːbəʊ/ ▶ noun (pl. **grebos**) Brit. informal a youth favouring heavy metal or punk rock music, and having long hair.
– ORIGIN 1980s: perhaps from GREASER, on the pattern of words such as *dumbo*.

Grecian ▶ adjective relating to ancient Greece, especially its architecture.
– ORIGIN late Middle English: from Old French *grecien*, from Latin *Graecia* 'Greece'.

Grecian nose ▶ noun a straight nose that continues the line of the forehead without a dip.

Grecism ▶ noun variant spelling of GRAECISM.

Greco- ▶ combining form variant spelling of GRAECO-.

Greco, El see EL GRECO.

Greco-Roman ▶ adjective variant spelling of GRAECO-ROMAN.

Greece a country in SE Europe; pop. 10,737,428 (est. 2009); official language, Greek; capital, Athens.

> The age of the classical city-states, of which the most prominent were Athens and Sparta, reached its peak in the 5th century BC, after which Greece fell to Macedon and then became part of the Roman and Byzantine Empires. It was conquered by the Ottoman Turks in 1466 and remained under Turkish rule until the war of independence (1821–30), after which it became a kingdom. The monarchy was overthrown in a military coup in 1967; a civilian republic was established in 1974. Greece joined the EC in 1981.

greed ▶ noun [mass noun] intense and selfish desire for something, especially wealth, power, or food.
– ORIGIN late 16th cent.: back-formation from GREEDY.

greedy ▶ adjective (**greedier**, **greediest**) having an excessive desire or appetite for food: *he's scoffed the lot, the greedy pig.* ■ having or showing an intense and selfish desire for wealth or power: *people driven from their land by greedy developers.*
– DERIVATIVES **greedily** adverb, **greediness** noun.
– ORIGIN Old English *grǣdig*, of Germanic origin.

greegree ▶ noun variant spelling of GRIS-GRIS.

Greek ▶ adjective relating to Greece, its people, or their language. Compare with HELLENIC.
▶ noun **1** a native or inhabitant of modern Greece, or a person of Greek descent. ■ a Greek-speaking person in the ancient world, especially a native of one of the city-states of Greece and the eastern Mediterranean.
2 [mass noun] the ancient or modern language of Greece, the only representative of the Hellenic branch of the Indo-European family.

> The ancient form of Greek was spoken in the southern Balkan peninsula from the 2nd millennium BC. The Greek alphabet, used from the 1st millennium BC onwards, was adapted from the Phoenician alphabet. The dialect of classical Athens formed the basis of the standard dialect (*koinē*) from the 3rd century BC onwards, and this remained as a literary language during the periods of the Byzantine Empire and Turkish rule (see KATHAREVOUSA). The colloquial language, however, continued to evolve independently (see DEMOTIC).

3 US a member of a fraternity or sorority having a Greek-letter name.
– PHRASES **beware** (or **fear**) **the Greeks bearing gifts** proverb if a rival or enemy shows one generosity or kindness, one should be suspicious of their motives. [with allusion to Virgil's *Aeneid* (ii. 49).] **it's** (**all**) **Greek to me** informal I can't understand it at all.
– DERIVATIVES **Greekness** noun.
– ORIGIN Old English *Grēcas* 'the Greeks', from Latin *Graeci*, the name given by the Romans to the people who called themselves the Hellenes, from Greek *Graikoi*, which according to Aristotle was the prehistoric name of the Hellenes.

Greek Church another term for GREEK ORTHODOX CHURCH.

Greek coffee ▶ noun [mass noun] very strong black coffee served with the fine grounds in it.

Greek cross ▶ noun a cross of which all four arms are of equal length.

Greek fire ▶ noun [mass noun] historical a combustible compound emitted by a flame-throwing weapon, used to set light to enemy ships. It was first used by the Greeks besieged in Constantinople (673–8). It ignited on contact with water, and was probably based on naphtha and quicklime.

Greek god ▶ noun informal an extremely handsome man.

Greek key ▶ noun a pattern of interlocking right-angled spirals.

Greek Orthodox Church (also **Greek Church**) the Eastern Orthodox Church which uses the Byzantine rite in Greek, in particular the national Church of Greece. See ORTHODOX CHURCH.

Greek salad ▶ noun a salad consisting of tomatoes, olives, and feta cheese.

green ▶ adjective **1** of the colour between blue and yellow in the spectrum; coloured like grass or emeralds: *her flashing green eyes | the leaves are bright green.* ■ consisting of fresh green vegetables: *a green salad.* ■ denoting a green light or flag used as a signal to proceed. ■ (of a ski run) of the lowest level of difficulty, as indicated by green markers on the run. ■ Physics denoting one of three colours of quark.
2 covered with grass or other vegetation: *proposals that would smother green fields with development.* ■ (usu. **Green**) concerned with or supporting protection of the environment as a political principle: *official Green candidates.* ■ (of a product or service) not harmful to the environment.
3 (of a plant or fruit) young or unripe: *green shoots.* ■ (of wood, food, or leather) in its original or untreated state; not seasoned, tanned, cured, or dried. ■ still strong or vigorous: *clubs devoted to keeping green the memory of Sherlock Holmes.* ■ archaic (of a wound) fresh; not healed.
4 (of a person) inexperienced or naive: *a green recruit fresh from college.*
5 (of a person or their complexion) pale and sickly-looking.
▶ noun **1** [mass noun] green colour or pigment: *major roads are marked **in green**.* ■ green clothes or material: *two girls in red and green.* ■ green foliage or vegetation: *that lovely canopy of green over Stratford Road.* ■ informal, dated low-grade cannabis.
2 a green thing, in particular: ■ (**greens**) green vegetables: *eat up your greens.* ■ a green light. ■ the green ball in snooker. ■ informal, dated money: *that's a lot of green.*
3 a piece of public grassy land, especially in the centre of a village: *a house overlooking the green.* ■ an area of smooth, very short grass immediately surrounding a hole on a golf course.
4 (usu. **Green**) a member or supporter of an environmentalist group or party.
▶ verb **1** make or become green in colour: [no obj.] *the roof was greening with lichen.*
2 [with obj.] make (an urban or desert area) more verdant by planting trees or other vegetation: *they will continue greening the many treeless and dusty suburbs.*
3 [with obj.] make less harmful to the environment: *tips on how to green your home.*
– PHRASES **the green-eyed monster** informal, humorous jealousy personified. [from Shakespeare's *Othello* (III. iii. 166).] **green shoots** (**of recovery**) signs of growth or renewal, especially of economic recovery. **green with envy** very envious or jealous.
– DERIVATIVES **greenish** adjective, **greenly** adverb, **greenness** noun.
– ORIGIN Old English *grēne* (adjective), *grēnian* (verb), of Germanic origin; related to Dutch *groen*, German *grün*, also to GRASS and GROW.

green algae ▶ plural noun photosynthetic algae which contain chlorophyll and store starch in discrete chloroplasts. They are eukaryotic and most live in fresh water, ranging from unicellular flagellates to more complex multicellular forms. ● Treated either as plants (division Chlorophyta) or as protozoans (phylum Chlorophyta, kingdom Protista). The classification of green algae is complex and under review.

green audit ▶ noun an assessment of a business in terms of its impact on the environment.

Greenaway, Kate (1846–1901), English artist; full name *Catherine Greenaway*. She is known especially for her illustrations of children's books such as *Mother Goose* (1881).

greenback ▶ noun US informal a dollar bill; a dollar: *he's worth a boatload of greenbacks.*

green belt ▶ noun **1** chiefly Brit. an area of open land around a city, on which building is restricted.
2 a green belt marking a level of proficiency in judo, karate, or other martial arts below that of a brown belt. ■ a person qualified to wear a green belt.

Green Beret ▶ noun informal a British commando or a member of the US Army Special Forces.

greenbottle ▶ noun a metallic green fly which sometimes lays eggs in wounds on sheep or other animals. ● Genus *Lucilia*, family Calliphoridae: several species, in particular the common *L. caesar*.

green box ▶ noun a set of farming subsidies in the EU that do not affect production levels or prices.

greenbul /ˈgriːnbʊl/ ▶ noun an African bulbul (songbird) with an olive-green back. ● Family Pycnonotidae: several genera, in particular *Phyllastrephus* and *Pycnonotus*, and numerous species.

green card ▶ noun **1** (in the US) a permit allowing a foreign national to live and work permanently in the US.
2 (in the UK) an international insurance document for motorists.

green channel ▶ noun (at a customs area in an airport or port) the passage which should be taken by arriving passengers who have no goods to declare.

Green Cloth (in full **Board of Green Cloth**) ▶ noun (in the UK) the Lord Steward's department of the royal household.

green-collar ▶ adjective denoting or relating to employment concerned with products and services designed to improve the quality of the environment: *green-collar jobs.*
– ORIGIN on the pattern of WHITE-COLLAR and BLUE-COLLAR.

green crop ▶ noun Brit. a crop used in a green or unripe state as fodder.

green dragon ▶ noun a North American arum with a large divided leaf, a greenish-cream spathe, and a very long white spadix. Also called DRAGON ARUM. ● *Arisaema dracontium*, family Araceae.

green drake ▶ noun Brit. the green subadult of certain mayflies. ● Genus *Ephemera*, family Ephemeridae. ■ an artificial fishing fly that imitates a green drake.

Greene, (Henry) Graham (1904–91), English novelist. The moral paradoxes he saw in his Roman Catholic faith underlie much of his work. Notable works: *Brighton Rock* (1938), *The Power and the Glory* (1940), and *The Third Man* (written as a screenplay, and filmed in 1949; novel 1950).

green earth ▶ noun another term for TERRE VERTE.

Greener ▶ noun a type of shotgun.

G

– ORIGIN late 19th cent.: named after William *Greener* (1806–69) or his son William W. *Greener*, gunsmiths and authors.

greenery ▸ noun [mass noun] green foliage, growing plants, or vegetation.

greenery-yallery /ˌgriːnərɪˈjaləri/ ▸ adjective informal green and yellow. ■ of or in the style of the 19th-century Aesthetic Movement (used to convey the idea of affectation): *a greenery-yallery fin-de-siècle lyricism*.
– ORIGIN late 19th cent.: from GREEN + *yaller* (variant of YELLOW), with reduplication of the suffix -Y¹.

greeneye ▸ noun a small slender-bodied fish with iridescent pale green eyes, occurring in deep waters of the western Atlantic. ● Family Chlorophthalmidae: two genera and several species.

green fat ▸ noun [mass noun] the green gelatinous part of a turtle, highly regarded by gourmets.

green fee (US also **greens fee**) ▸ noun a charge for playing one round or session on a golf course.

greenfeed ▸ noun [mass noun] Austral./NZ forage grown to be fed fresh to livestock.

G

greenfield ▸ adjective Brit. denoting or relating to previously undeveloped sites for commercial development or exploitation.

greenfinch ▸ noun a Eurasian finch with green and yellow plumage. ● Genus *Carduelis*, family Fringillidae: three species, in particular the common *C. chloris* of Europe and the Middle East.

green fingers ▸ plural noun Brit. informal natural ability in growing plants.
– DERIVATIVES **green-fingered** adjective.

greenfly ▸ noun (pl. **same** or **greenflies**) a green aphid which is a common pest of crops and garden plants. ● Several species in the family Aphididae.

greengage ▸ noun **1** a sweet greenish fruit resembling a small plum. Also called GAGE³.
2 the tree bearing greengages. ● *Prunus domestica* subsp. *italica* (or *P. italica*), family Rosaceae.
– ORIGIN early 18th cent.: named after Sir William *Gage* (1657–1727), the English botanist who introduced it to England.

green goose ▸ noun a goose that is killed when under four months old and eaten without stuffing.

greengrocer ▸ noun Brit. a retailer of fruit and vegetables.
– DERIVATIVES **greengrocery** noun.

greenhead (also **greenhead fly**) ▸ noun chiefly US a biting horsefly with green eyes. ● Genus *Chrysops*, family Tabanidae.

greenheart ▸ noun a South American evergreen tree of the laurel family, yielding hard greenish timber which is used for marine work because of its resistance to marine borers. ● *Ocotea rodiaei*, family Lauraceae. ■ [mass noun] the timber of the greenheart, or similar timber from various other tropical trees.

greenhide ▸ noun Austral. the untanned hide of an animal.

greenhorn ▸ noun informal, chiefly N. Amer. a person who is new to or inexperienced at a particular activity.

greenhouse ▸ noun a glass building in which plants that need protection from cold weather are grown.

greenhouse effect ▸ noun the trapping of the sun's warmth in a planet's lower atmosphere, due to the greater transparency of the atmosphere to visible radiation from the sun than to infrared radiation emitted from the planet's surface.

> On earth the increasing quantity of atmospheric carbon dioxide from the burning of fossil fuels, together with the release of other gases, is causing an increased greenhouse effect and leading to global warming. A greenhouse effect involving CO_2 is also responsible for the very high surface temperature of Venus. See also GLOBAL WARMING.

greenhouse gas ▸ noun a gas that contributes to the greenhouse effect by absorbing infrared radiation. Carbon dioxide and chlorofluorocarbons are examples of greenhouse gases.

greenie ▸ noun informal, often derogatory a person who campaigns for protection of the environment.

greening ▸ noun an apple of a variety that is green when ripe.
– ORIGIN early 17th cent. (originally denoting a kind of pear): probably from Middle Dutch *groeninc*, a kind of apple, from *groen* 'green'.

green jersey ▸ noun (in a cycling race involving stages) a green jersey worn each day by the rider accumulating the highest number of points, and presented at the end of the race to the rider with the highest overall points total.

greenkeeper (N. Amer. also **greenskeeper**) ▸ noun a person employed to look after a golf course.
– DERIVATIVES **greenkeeping** noun.

Greenland a large island lying to the north-east of North America and mostly within the Arctic Circle; pop. 57,600 (est. 2009); capital, Nuuk (Godthåb). Danish name GRØNLAND; called in Inuit KALAALLIT NUNAAT.

> Only 5 per cent of Greenland is habitable; the population is largely Inuit. Formerly a Norse and a Danish settlement, Greenland became a dependency of Denmark in 1953 with internal autonomy from 1979. It withdrew from the EC in 1985.

– DERIVATIVES **Greenlander** noun.

Greenland halibut ▸ noun an edible halibut with a black or dark brown upper side, which is found in cold deep waters of the north. ● *Reinhardtius hippoglossoides*, family Pleuronectidae.

Greenlandic /griːnˈlandɪk/ ▸ noun [mass noun] a dialect of the Inuit (Eskimo) language which is one of the official languages of Greenland (the other being Danish).

Greenland right whale (also **Greenland whale**) ▸ noun another term for BOWHEAD.

Greenland Sea a sea which lies between the east coast of Greenland and the Svalbard archipelago, forming part of the Arctic Ocean.

green leek ▸ noun Austral. a green-faced or mainly green parrot. ● Family Psittacidae: several species, e.g. the superb parrot (*Polytelis swainsonii*).

greenlet /ˈgriːnlɪt/ ▸ noun a small warbler-like vireo (songbird) with drab plumage, found in Central and South America. ● Genus *Hylophilus*, family Vireonidae: several species.

green light ▸ noun a green traffic light giving permission to proceed. ■ permission to go ahead with a project: *the council has given the green light for a housing development*.
▸ verb (**green-light**) [with obj.] chiefly N. Amer. give permission to go ahead with (a project).

greenling ▸ noun a spiny-finned edible fish of the North Pacific. ● Family Hexagrammidae: two genera and several species, including the lingcod.

green lizard ▸ noun a lizard that is typically green with (especially in the male) a blue throat, native to Europe and SW Asia. ● *Lacerta viridis*, family Lacertidae.

greenmail ▸ noun [mass noun] Stock Exchange the practice of buying enough shares in a company to threaten a takeover, forcing the owners to buy them back at a higher price in order to retain control.
– DERIVATIVES **greenmailer** noun.
– ORIGIN 1980s: blend of GREEN and BLACKMAIL.

green man ▸ noun **1** (in the UK) a symbol of an illuminated green human figure at a pedestrian crossing, indicating that it is safe to cross the road.
2 historical a man dressed up in greenery to represent a wild man of the woods or seasonal fertility. ■ a carved image of a green man, often seen in medieval English churches as a human face with branches and foliage growing out of the mouth.

green manure ▸ noun [mass noun] a fertilizer consisting of growing plants that are ploughed back into the soil.

green monkey ▸ noun a common African guenon with greenish-brown upper parts and a black face. Compare with GRIVET and VERVET. ● *Cercopithecus aethiops*, family Cercopithecidae, in particular the race *C. a. sabaeus* of West Africa, which is often tamed.

Green Mountain State informal name for VERMONT.

Greenock /ˈgriːnək/ a port in west central Scotland, on the Firth of Clyde; pop. 42,400 (est. 2009).

greenockite /ˈgriːnəkʌɪt/ ▸ noun [mass noun] a mineral consisting of cadmium sulphide which typically occurs as a yellow crust on zinc ores.
– ORIGIN mid 19th cent.: from the name of Lord *Greenock*, who later became Earl Cathcart (1783–1859), + -ITE¹.

green onion ▸ noun N. Amer. a spring onion.

Green Paper ▸ noun (in the UK) a preliminary report of government proposals that is published in order to provoke discussion.

Green Party ▸ noun an environmentalist political party.

Greenpeace an international organization that campaigns actively but non-violently for conservation of the environment and the preservation of endangered species.

green pepper ▸ noun the mild-flavoured unripe fruit of a sweet pepper, which may be eaten raw or cooked. ■ the plant which yields green peppers. See CAPSICUM.

green pigeon ▸ noun a fruit-eating pigeon with mainly green plumage occurring in the Old World tropics. ● Genus *Treron*, family Columbidae: many species. See also FRUIT PIGEON.

green plover ▸ noun Brit. the northern lapwing.

green pound ▸ noun the exchange rate for the pound applied to payments for agricultural produce in the EU.

green revolution ▸ noun **1** a large increase in crop production in developing countries achieved by the use of artificial fertilizers, pesticides, and high-yield crop varieties.
2 a dramatic rise in concern about the environment in industrialized countries.

green room ▸ noun a room in a theatre or studio in which performers can relax when they are not performing.

greensand ▸ noun [mass noun] Geology a greenish kind of sandstone, often loosely consolidated. ■ (usu. **the Greensand**) a stratum largely composed of greensand, deposited during the Cretaceous period and often underlying chalk.

green screen ▸ noun see BLUE SCREEN.

greens fee ▸ noun US term for GREEN FEE.

greenshank ▸ noun a large sandpiper with long greenish legs and grey plumage, breeding in northern Eurasia and North America. ● Genus *Tringa*, family Scolopacidae: two species, in particular *T. nebularia*.

greenskeeper ▸ noun North American term for GREENKEEPER.

green snake ▸ noun a harmless American snake with a green back and white or yellowish underparts. ● Genus *Opheodrys*, family Colubridae: two species.

green space ▸ noun an area of grass, trees, or other vegetation set apart for recreational or aesthetic purposes in an otherwise urban environment.

greenstick fracture ▸ noun a fracture of the bone, occurring typically in children, in which one side of the bone is broken and the other only bent.

greenstone ▸ noun [mass noun] Geology a greenish igneous rock containing feldspar and hornblende. ■ chiefly NZ a variety of jade.

greenstuff ▸ noun [mass noun] vegetation. ■ green vegetables.

greensward /ˈgriːnˌswɔːd/ ▸ noun [mass noun] literary grass-covered ground.

green tea ▸ noun [mass noun] tea made from unfermented leaves that is pale in colour and slightly bitter in flavour, produced mainly in China and Japan. Compare with BLACK TEA.

green thumb ▸ noun North American term for GREEN FINGERS.
– DERIVATIVES **green-thumbed** adjective.

green turtle ▸ noun a sea turtle with an olive-brown shell, often living close to the coast and extensively hunted for food. ● *Chelonia mydas*, family Cheloniidae.

green vitriol ▸ noun [mass noun] archaic crystalline ferrous sulphate.

greenware ▸ noun [mass noun] unfired pottery.

greenwash ▸ noun [mass noun] disinformation disseminated by an organization so as to present an environmentally responsible public image.
– DERIVATIVES **greenwashing** noun.
– ORIGIN 1980s: from GREEN, on the pattern of *whitewash*.

greenway ▸ noun N. Amer. a strip of undeveloped land near an urban area, set aside for recreational use or environmental protection.

Greenwich /ˈgrɛnɪtʃ, ˈgrɪnɪdʒ/ a London borough on the south bank of the Thames, the original site of the Royal Greenwich Observatory.

Greenwich Mean Time (abbrev.: **GMT**) (also **Greenwich time**) the mean solar time at the Greenwich meridian, adopted as the standard time in a zone that includes the British Isles.

Greenwich meridian ▸ noun the prime meridian, which passes through the former Royal Observatory at Greenwich. It was adopted internationally as the zero of longitude in 1884.

Greenwich Village a district of New York City on the lower west side of Manhattan, traditionally associated with writers, artists, and musicians.

greenwood ▶ **noun** archaic a wood or forest in leaf (regarded as the typical scene of medieval outlaw life).

green woodpecker ▶ **noun** a large green and yellow woodpecker with a red crown and a laughing call, found from Europe to central Asia. ● *Picus viridis*, family Picidae.

greeny ▶ **adjective** [often in combination] slightly green: *the greeny-brown surface of the stone.*

Greer, Germaine (b.1939), Australian feminist and writer. She first achieved recognition with *The Female Eunuch* (1970), an analysis of women's subordination in a male-dominated society.

greet[1] ▶ **verb** [with obj.] give a polite word of recognition or sign of welcome when meeting (someone): *some of the customers greeted the barman in Gaelic.* ■ [with obj. and adverbial] receive or acknowledge (something) in a specified way: *everyone greeted this idea warmly.* ■ (especially of a sight or sound) become apparent to (a person arriving somewhere): *Sam threw open the door and was greeted by a cacophony of noise.*
– ORIGIN Old English *grētan* 'approach, attack, or salute', of West Germanic origin; related to Dutch *groeten* and German *grüssen* 'greet'.

greet[2] ▶ **verb** [no obj.] Scottish weep; cry: *he sat down on the armchair and started to greet.*
– ORIGIN Old English, partly from *grētan* 'cry out, rage', partly from *grēotan* 'lament', both of Germanic origin.

greeter ▶ **noun** a person employed to greet customers at a shop, restaurant, or other business.

greeting ▶ **noun** a polite word or sign of welcome or recognition: *Mandy shouted a greeting.* ■ [mass noun] the action of giving a sign of welcome: *she raised her hand in greeting.* ■ (usu. **greetings**) a formal expression of goodwill, said on meeting or in a written message: *warm greetings to you all.*

greetings card (N. Amer. **greeting card**) ▶ **noun** a decorative card sent to convey good wishes.

gregarine /ˈgrɛgərʌɪn/ Zoology ▶ **adjective** relating to a group of microscopic worm-like protozoans that are internal parasites of insects, annelids, and other invertebrates. ■ (of movement) slow and gliding, as seen in gregarines.
▶ **noun** a gregarine protozoan. ● Class Gregarina (or subclass Gregarinidia), phylum Sporozoa, kingdom Protista.
– ORIGIN mid 19th cent.: from modern Latin *Gregarina*, from Latin *gregarius* (see **GREGARIOUS**).

gregarious /grɪˈgɛːrɪəs/ ▶ **adjective** (of a person) fond of company; sociable: *he was a popular and gregarious man.* ■ (of animals) living in flocks or loosely organized communities: *gregarious species forage in flocks from colonies or roosts.* ■ (of plants) growing in open clusters or in pure associations.
– DERIVATIVES **gregariously** adverb, **gregariousness** noun.
– ORIGIN mid 17th cent.: from Latin *gregarius* (from *grex, greg-* 'a flock') + **-OUS**.

Gregorian calendar /grɪˈgɔːrɪən/ ▶ **noun** the calendar introduced in 1582 by Pope Gregory XIII, as a modification of the Julian calendar.

> To bring the calendar back into line with the solar year, 10 days were suppressed, and centenary years were only made leap years if they were divisible by 400. Scotland adopted the Gregorian calendar in 1600, but England and Wales did not follow suit until 1752 (by which time 11 days had to be suppressed). At the same time New Year's Day was changed from 25 March to 1 January, and dates using the new calendar were designated 'New Style'.

Gregorian chant ▶ **noun** [mass noun] church music sung as a single vocal line in free rhythm and a restricted scale (plainsong), in a style developed for the medieval Latin liturgy.
– ORIGIN mid 18th cent.: named after St Gregory the Great (in Latin *Gregorius*), who is said to have standardized it.

Gregorian telescope ▶ **noun** an early reflecting telescope in which light reflected from a concave elliptical secondary mirror passes through a hole in the primary mirror. It was rendered obsolete by the introduction of Newtonian and Cassegrain telescopes.
– ORIGIN mid 18th cent.: named after James *Gregory* (1638–75), the Scottish mathematician who invented it.

Gregory, St (*c.*540–604), pope (as Gregory I) 590–604 and Doctor of the Church; known as **St Gregory the Great**. An important reformer, he did much to establish the temporal power of the papacy. He sent St Augustine to England to lead the country's conversion to Christianity, and is also credited with the introduction of Gregorian chant. Feast day, 12 March.

Gregory XIII (1502–85), pope 1572–85. The Gregorian calendar, still in use, was introduced in 1582 as a result of his efforts to correct the errors in the Julian calendar.

Gregory of Nazianzus, St /ˌnazɪˈanzəs/ (329–89), Doctor of the Church, bishop of Constantinople. With St Basil and St Gregory of Nyssa he was an upholder of Orthodoxy against the Arian and Apollinarian heresies, and influential in restoring adherence to the Nicene Creed. Feast day, (in the Eastern Church) 25 and 30 January; (in the Western Church) 2 January (formerly 9 May).

Gregory of Nyssa, St /ˈnɪsə/ (*c.*330–*c.*395), Doctor of the Eastern Church, bishop of Nyssa in Cappadocia. The brother of St Basil, he was an Orthodox follower of Origen and joined with St Basil and St Gregory of Nazianzus in opposing Arianism. Feast day, 9 March.

Gregory of Tours, St /tʊə/ (*c.*540–94), Frankish bishop and historian. He was elected bishop of Tours in 573; his writings provide the chief authority for the early Merovingian period of French history. Feast day, 17 November.

greige /greɪʒ/ ▶ **noun** [mass noun] a colour between beige and grey.
– ORIGIN blend of **GREY** and **BEIGE**, perhaps influenced by French *grège* 'raw (silk)'.

greisen /ˈgrʌɪz(ə)n/ ▶ **noun** [mass noun] Geology a light-coloured rock containing quartz, mica, and fluorine-rich minerals, resulting from the alteration of granite by hot vapour from magma.
– ORIGIN late 19th cent.: from German, probably a dialect word, from *greis* 'grey with age'.

gremlin ▶ **noun** informal an imaginary mischievous sprite regarded as responsible for an unexplained mechanical or electronic problem or fault: *a gremlin in my computer omitted a line.* ■ an unexplained problem or fault.
– ORIGIN 1940s: perhaps suggested by **GOBLIN**.

Grenache /grəˈnaʃ/ ▶ **noun** [mass noun] a variety of black wine grape native to the Languedoc-Roussillon region of France. ■ a red or rosé wine made from the Grenache grape.
– ORIGIN French. The grape is known in Spain as **GARNACHA**.

Grenada /grəˈneɪdə/ a country in the Caribbean, consisting of the island of Grenada (the southernmost of the Windward Islands) and the southern Grenadine Islands; pop. 90,700 (est. 2009), languages, English (official), English Creole; capital, St George's.

> The island of Grenada was sighted in 1498 by Columbus. Colonized by the French, it was ceded to Britain in 1763, recaptured by the French, and restored to Britain in 1783. It became an independent Commonwealth state in 1974. Seizure of power by a left-wing military group in 1983 prompted an invasion by the US and some Caribbean countries; they withdrew in 1985.

– DERIVATIVES **Grenadian** adjective & noun.

grenade /grəˈneɪd/ ▶ **noun** a small bomb thrown by hand or launched mechanically. ■ a glass receptacle containing chemicals which are released when the receptacle is thrown and broken, used for testing drains and extinguishing fires.
– ORIGIN mid 16th cent. (in the sense 'pomegranate'): from French, alteration of Old French (*pome*) *grenate* (see **POMEGRANATE**), on the pattern of Spanish *granada*. The bomb was so named because it supposedly resembled a pomegranate in shape.

grenadier /ˌgrɛnəˈdɪə/ ▶ **noun 1** historical a soldier armed with grenades. ■ (**Grenadiers** or **Grenadier Guards**) (in the UK) the first regiment of the royal household infantry.
2 a common bottom-dwelling fish with a large head, a long tapering tail, and typically a luminous gland on the belly. Also called **RAT-TAIL**. ● Family Macrouridae: numerous genera and species.
3 a reddish-brown African waxbill with a red bill and a bright blue rump. ● Genus *Uraeginthus*, family Estrildidae: the **common grenadier** (*U. granatina*), with violet cheeks, and the **purple grenadier** (*U. ianthinogaster*), with a blue belly.
– ORIGIN late 17th cent.: from French, from *grenade* (see **GRENADE**).

grenadilla /ˌgrɛnəˈdɪlə/ ▶ **noun** variant spelling of **GRANADILLA**.

grenadine[1] /ˈgrɛnədiːn/ ▶ **noun** [mass noun] a sweet cordial made in France from pomegranates.
– ORIGIN French, from *grenade* 'pomegranate' (see **GRENADE**).

grenadine[2] /ˈgrɛnədiːn/ ▶ **noun** [mass noun] dress fabric of loosely woven silk or silk and wool.
– ORIGIN mid 19th cent.: from French (earlier *grenade*), 'grained silk', from *grenu* 'grained', from *grain* 'grain'.

Grenadine Islands /ˈgrɛnədiːn/ (also **the Grenadines**) a chain of small islands in the Caribbean, part of the Windward Islands. They are divided administratively between St Vincent and Grenada.

Grendel /ˈgrɛnd(ə)l/ the water monster killed by Beowulf in the Old English epic poem *Beowulf*.

Grenoble /grəˈnəʊb(ə)l/, French /grənɔbl/ an industrial city in SE France; pop. 158,746 (2006).

Grenville /ˈgrɛnvɪl/, George (1712–70), British Whig statesman, Prime Minister 1763–5.

Gresham /ˈgrɛʃəm/, Sir Thomas (*c.*1519–79), English financier. He founded the Royal Exchange in 1566 and served as the chief financial adviser to the Elizabethan government.

Gresham's law ▶ **noun** Economics the tendency for money of lower intrinsic value to circulate more freely than money of higher intrinsic and equal nominal value (often expressed as 'Bad money drives out good').

Gresley /ˈgrɛzli/, Sir (Herbert) Nigel (1876–1941), British railway engineer. He is most famous for designing express steam locomotives, such as the A4 class exemplified by the *Mallard*.

Gretna Green a village in Dumfries and Galloway, Scotland, just north of the English border near Carlisle, formerly a popular place for runaway couples from England to be married without the parental consent required in England for people under a certain age.

Gretzky /ˈgrɛtski/, Wayne (b.1961), Canadian ice-hockey player. He was voted Most Valuable Player nine times, before retiring from the sport in 1999.

Greuze /grəːz/, French /grøz/, Jean-Baptiste (1725–1805), French painter, noted for his genre paintings and portraits.

grevillea /grɪˈvɪlɪə/ ▶ **noun** an evergreen tree or shrub which bears conspicuous flowers that lack petals, most kinds of which are native to Australia. ● Genus *Grevillea*, family Proteaceae.
– ORIGIN modern Latin, named after Charles F. *Greville* (1749–1809), Scottish horticulturalist.

grew past of **GROW**.

Grey[1], Charles, 2nd Earl (1764–1845), British statesman, Prime Minister 1830–4. His government passed the first Reform Act (1832) as well as important factory legislation and the Act abolishing slavery throughout the British Empire.

Grey[2], Lady Jane (1537–54), great-niece of Henry VIII, queen of England 9–19 July 1553. In 1553, to ensure a Protestant succession, John Dudley, the Duke of Northumberland, forced Jane to marry his son and persuaded the dying Edward VI to name Jane as his successor. She was quickly deposed by forces loyal to Edward's (Catholic) sister Mary, who had popular support, and executed the following year.

Grey[3], Zane (1872–1939), American writer; born *Pearl Grey*. He wrote fifty-four westerns in a somewhat romanticized and formulaic style, which sold over 13 million copies during his lifetime.

grey (US **gray**) ▶ **adjective** (**greyer, greyest; grayer, grayest**) **1** of a colour intermediate between black and white, as of ashes or lead: *grey flannel trousers | his hair was grey and wispy.* ■ (of the weather) cloudy and dull: *a cold, grey November day.* ■ (of a person) having grey hair: [as complement] *she's getting on a bit, and going grey.* ■ informal relating to old people collectively: *grey power | the grey market.* ■ (of a person's face) pale, as through tiredness, age, or illness: *his face looked grey and drawn.*
2 without interest or character; dull and nondescript: *grey, faceless men | the grey daily routine.*
3 (of financial or trading activity) not accounted for in official statistics: *the grey economy.*
4 S. African historical relating to an ethnically mixed residential area.
▶ **noun 1** [mass noun] grey colour or pigment: *dirty intermediate tones of grey.* ■ grey clothes or material:

the gentleman in grey. ■ grey hair: *he sighed at the amount of grey at his temple.*
2 a grey thing or animal, in particular a grey or white horse.
▸ **verb** [no obj.] (especially of hair) become grey with age: *he had put on weight and greyed somewhat* | (as adj. **greying**) *a man with greying hair.* ■ (of a person) become older: (as adj. **greying**) *a greying workforce.*
– PHRASAL VERBS **grey something out** Computing display a menu option in a light font to indicate that it is not available.
– DERIVATIVES **greyish** adjective, **greyly** adverb, **greyness** noun.
– ORIGIN Old English *grǣg*, of Germanic origin; related to Dutch *grauw* and German *grau*.

grey area ▸ **noun** an ill-defined situation or area of activity not readily conforming to a category or set of rules: *grey areas in the legislation have still to be clarified.*

greybeard (US **graybeard**) ▸ **noun 1** humorous or derogatory an old man.
2 archaic a large stoneware jug for holding spirits.

G

grey drake ▸ **noun** Brit. the greyish gravid female of certain mayflies. ● Genus *Ephemera*, family Ephemeridae.
■ an artificial fishing fly that imitates the grey drake.

grey eminence ▸ **noun** another term for **ÉMINENCE GRISE**.

Grey Friar ▸ **noun** a Franciscan friar.
– ORIGIN Middle English: so named because of the colour of the order's habit.

grey goods ▸ **plural noun** computing equipment. Compare with **BROWN GOODS**, **WHITE GOODS**.

grey goose ▸ **noun** a goose of a group distinguished by having mainly grey plumage. ● Genus *Anser*, family Anatidae: several species, e.g. greylag and white-fronted geese.

greyhen ▸ **noun** the female of the black grouse.

greyhound ▸ **noun** a dog of a tall, slender breed having keen sight and capable of high speed, used since ancient times for hunting small game and now chiefly in racing and coursing.
– ORIGIN Old English *grighund*; the first element, related to Old Norse *grey* 'bitch', is of unknown origin.

greyhound racing ▸ **noun** [mass noun] a sport in which greyhounds race around a circular or oval track in pursuit of a moving dummy hare and spectators bet on the outcome.

grey jay ▸ **noun** a fluffy long-tailed jay with dark grey upper parts and a whitish face, found in Canada and the north-western US. ● *Perisoreus canadensis*, family Corvidae.

grey kangaroo ▸ **noun** a large forest-dwelling kangaroo native to Australia. ● Genus *Macropus*, family Macropodidae: the eastern *M. giganteus* (also called **FORESTER**), with silvery-grey fur, and the western *M. fuliginosus*, with brownish fur.

grey knight ▸ **noun** Stock Exchange a person or company making a possibly hostile counter offer for a company already facing a hostile takeover bid.
– ORIGIN by association with **BLACK KNIGHT** and **WHITE KNIGHT**.

greylag (also **greylag goose**) ▸ **noun** a large goose with mainly grey plumage, which is native to Eurasia and is the ancestor of the domestic goose. ● *Anser anser*, family Anatidae.
– ORIGIN early 18th cent.: probably from **GREY** + dialect *lag* 'goose', of unknown origin.

grey matter ▸ **noun** [mass noun] the darker tissue of the brain and spinal cord, consisting mainly of nerve cell bodies and branching dendrites. Compare with **WHITE MATTER**. ■ informal intelligence: *I wish I had a little of her grey matter.*

grey mullet ▸ **noun** a thick-bodied, blunt-headed fish that typically lives in inshore or estuarine waters and is a valued food fish. ● Family Mugilidae: several genera and species.

grey nurse ▸ **noun** see **NURSE[2]**.

grey parrot (also **African grey parrot**) ▸ **noun** a parrot of western equatorial Africa, with grey plumage and a red tail, often kept as a pet for its mimicking abilities. ● *Psittacus erithacus*, family Psittacidae.

greyscale ▸ **noun** Computing a range of grey shades from white to black, as used in a monochrome display or printout: [as modifier] *a greyscale scanner.*

grey seal ▸ **noun** a large seal with a spotted greyish coat and a convex profile, found commonly in the North Atlantic. Also called **ATLANTIC SEAL**. ● *Halichoerus grypus*, family Phocidae.

grey squirrel ▸ **noun** an American tree squirrel with mainly grey fur. ● Genus *Sciurus*, family Sciuridae: four species, in particular *S. carolinensis*, native to eastern North America and introduced to Britain and elsewhere.

greywacke /ˈɡreɪwakə/ (US **graywacke**) ▸ **noun** [mass noun] Geology a dark coarse-grained sandstone containing more than 15 per cent clay.
– ORIGIN late 18th cent. (as *grauwacke*): from German *Grauwacke*, from *grau* 'grey' + **WACKE**. The anglicized form dates from the early 19th cent.

grey water ▸ **noun** [mass noun] technical the relatively clean waste water from baths, sinks, washing machines, and other kitchen appliances. Compare with **BLACK WATER**.

grey whale ▸ **noun** a mottled grey baleen whale that typically has heavy encrustations of barnacles on the skin, commonly seen in coastal waters of the NE Pacific. ● *Eschrichtius robustus*, the only member of the family Eschrichtiidae.

grey wolf ▸ **noun** another term for **TIMBER WOLF**.

gribble ▸ **noun** a small marine isopod crustacean that bores into submerged wooden structures, often causing damage to pier timbers. ● *Limnoria lignorum*, order Isopoda.
– ORIGIN late 18th cent.: perhaps related to the verb **GRUB**.

gricer /ˈɡrʌɪsə/ ▸ **noun** Brit. informal a fanatical railway enthusiast.
– DERIVATIVES **gricing** noun.
– ORIGIN 1960s: origin uncertain; perhaps a humorous representation of an upper-class pronunciation of *grouser* 'grouse-shooter'.

grid ▸ **noun 1** a framework of spaced bars that are parallel to or cross each other; a grating.
2 a network of lines that cross each other to form a series of squares or rectangles: *a grid of tree-lined streets.* ■ a grid of regular squares on a map that are marked with numbers or letters to enable a place to be precisely located. ■ a pattern of lines marking the starting places on a motor-racing track: *the 20-year-old didn't get the best of starts off the grid.* ■ a field for American football; a gridiron.
3 a network of cables or pipes for distributing power, especially high-voltage transmission lines for electricity: *the reactor was connected to the grid in 1985.*
■ Computing a number of computers linked together via the Internet so that their combined power may be harnessed to work on difficult problems.
4 Electronics an electrode placed between the cathode and anode of a thermionic valve or cathode ray tube, serving to control or modulate the flow of electrons.
▸ **verb** [with obj.] (usu. as adj. **gridded**) put into or set out as a grid: *a core of gridded streets.*
– PHRASES **off the grid** chiefly US not connected to the basic services, especially electricity.
– ORIGIN mid 19th cent.: back-formation from **GRIDIRON**.

grid bias ▸ **noun** Electronics a fixed voltage applied between the cathode and the control grid of a thermionic valve which determines its operating conditions.

gridder ▸ **noun** US an American football player.

griddle ▸ **noun 1** a heavy, flat iron plate that is heated and used for cooking food: [as modifier] *griddle cakes.*
2 historical a miner's wire-bottomed sieve.
▸ **verb** [with obj.] **1** cook on a griddle: (as adj. **griddled**) *griddled corn cakes.*
2 historical screen (ore) with a griddle.
– ORIGIN Middle English (denoting a gridiron): from Old French *gredil*, from Latin *craticula*, diminutive of *cratis* 'hurdle'; related to **CRATE**, **GRATE[2]**, and **GRILL[1]**.

G-ride ▸ **noun** N. Amer. informal a stolen car.
– ORIGIN probably related to **G-MAN** (sense 1).

gridiron /ˈɡrɪdʌɪən/ ▸ **noun 1** a frame of parallel bars or beams, typically in two sets forming a grid, in particular: ■ a frame of parallel metal bars used for grilling meat or fish over an open fire. ■ a frame of parallel beams for supporting a ship in dock. ■ (in the theatre) a framework over a stage supporting scenery and lighting.
2 a field for American football, marked with regularly spaced parallel lines. ■ [mass noun] N. Amer. the sport of American football: [as modifier] *the national gridiron season.*
3 a grid pattern, especially of streets.
– ORIGIN Middle English *gredire*, alteration of *gredile* 'griddle' by association with **IRON**.

gridlock ▸ **noun 1** [mass noun] a situation of very severe traffic congestion: *the city reaches gridlock during peak hours.*
2 another term for **DEADLOCK** (sense 1 of the noun).
– DERIVATIVES **gridlocked** adjective.
– ORIGIN 1980s (originally US): from **GRID** (in sense 2) + **LOCK[1]**.

grid reference ▸ **noun** a map reference indicating a location in terms of a series of vertical and horizontal grid lines identified by numbers or letters.

grief ▸ **noun** [mass noun] **1** intense sorrow, especially caused by someone's death: *she was overcome with grief.* ■ [count noun] an instance or cause of intense sorrow: *time heals griefs and quarrels.*
2 informal trouble or annoyance: *the police gave us constant grief at the match.*
– PHRASES **come to grief** have an accident; meet with disaster: *many a ship has come to grief along this shore.* **good grief!** an exclamation of surprise or alarm.
– ORIGIN Middle English: from Old French *grief*, from *grever* 'to burden' (see **GRIEVE[1]**).

grief-stricken ▸ **adjective** overcome with deep or intense sorrow.

Grieg /ɡriːɡ/, Edvard (1843–1907), Norwegian composer, conductor, and violinist. Famous works include the Piano Concerto in A minor (1869) and the incidental music to Ibsen's play *Peer Gynt* (1876).

Grierson /ˈɡrɪəs(ə)n/, John (1898–1972), Scottish film director and producer, pioneer in British documentary film-making. He directed or produced films such as *Drifters* (1928) and *Night Mail* (1936) that broke new ground in showing the lives of working people. He headed the GPO Film Unit (1933–9) and established the National Film Board of Canada (1939).

grievance ▸ **noun** a real or imagined cause for complaint, especially unfair treatment: *a website which enabled staff to air their grievances.* ■ an official statement of a complaint over something believed to be wrong or unfair: *three pilots have filed grievances against the company.* ■ a feeling of resentment over something believed to be wrong or unfair: *he was nursing a grievance.*
– ORIGIN Middle English (also in the sense 'injury'): from Old French *grevance*, from *grever* 'to burden' (see **GRIEVE[1]**).

grieve[1] ▸ **verb** [no obj.] feel intense sorrow: *she grieved for her father.* ■ [with obj.] feel intense sorrow about: *he is still grieving his mother's death.* ■ [with obj.] cause great distress to (someone): [with obj. and infinitive] *it grieves me to think of you in that house alone.*
– DERIVATIVES **griever** noun.
– ORIGIN Middle English (also in the sense 'harm, oppress'): from Old French *grever* 'burden, encumber', based on Latin *gravare*, from *gravis* 'heavy, grave' (see **GRAVE[2]**).

grieve[2] ▸ **noun** Scottish an overseer, manager, or bailiff on a farm.
– ORIGIN late 15th cent.: related to **REEVE[1]**.

grievous /ˈɡriːvəs/ ▸ **adjective** formal (of something bad) very severe or serious: *his death was a grievous blow* | *the American fleet suffered grievous losses.*
– DERIVATIVES **grievously** adverb, **grievousness** noun.
– ORIGIN Middle English: from Old French *greveus*, from *grever* (see **GRIEVE[1]**).

> **USAGE** **Grievous** ends with **-ous** and has two syllables: it should not be pronounced as if it ended **-ious** and had an extra syllable.

grievous bodily harm (abbrev.: **GBH**) ▸ **noun** [mass noun] Law serious physical injury inflicted on a person by the deliberate action of another. Compare with **ACTUAL BODILY HARM**.

griff ▸ **noun** [mass noun] informal, dated news or reliable information.
– ORIGIN late 19th cent.: abbreviation of the slang term *griffin* 'a betting tip', of unknown origin.

griffin (also **gryphon**) ▸ **noun** a mythical creature with the head and wings of an eagle and the body of a lion, typically depicted with pointed ears and with the eagle's legs taking the place of the forelegs.
– ORIGIN Middle English: from Old French *grifoun*, based on late Latin *gryphus*, via Latin from Greek *grups*, *grup-*.

Griffith[1], Arthur (1872–1922), Irish nationalist leader and statesman, President of the Irish Free State 1922. In 1905 he founded and became president of Sinn Fein. He became Vice-President of the newly declared Irish Republic in 1919 and negotiated the Anglo-Irish Treaty (1921).

Griffith[2], D. W. (1875–1948), American film director; full name *David Lewelyn Wark Griffith*. A pioneer in film, he is responsible for introducing many cinematic techniques, including flashback and fade-out. Notable films: *The Birth of a Nation* (1915), *Intolerance* (1916), and *Broken Blossoms* (1919).

griffon /ˈgrɪf(ə)n/ ▶ **noun 1** a dog of any of several terrier-like breeds originating in NW Europe. ■ (also **Brussels griffon**) a dog of a toy breed with a flat face and upturned chin.
2 (also **griffon vulture**) a large Old World vulture with predominantly pale brown plumage. ● Genus *Gyps*, family Accipitridae: four species, in particular the Eurasian *G. fulvus* and the African **Ruppell's griffon** (*G. ruepelli*).
– ORIGIN Middle English (in sense 2): variant of **GRIFFIN**; sense 1 was adopted from French in the 18th cent.

grift N. Amer. informal ▶ **verb** [no obj.] engage in petty or small-scale swindling.
▶ **noun** a petty or small-scale swindle.
– DERIVATIVES **grifter** noun.
– ORIGIN early 20th cent.: alteration of **GRAFT[2]**.

grig ▶ **noun** dialect **1** a small eel.
2 a grasshopper or cricket.
– PHRASES **(as) merry** (or **lively**) **as a grig** full of fun; very lively.
– ORIGIN Middle English (in the sense 'dwarf'): of unknown origin.

gri-gri ▶ **noun** variant spelling of **GRIS-GRIS**.

grike /grʌɪk/ (also **gryke**) ▶ **noun** a fissure separating blocks or clints in a limestone pavement.
– ORIGIN late 18th cent. (originally northern English dialect): of unknown origin.

grill[1] ▶ **noun** Brit. a device on a cooker that radiates heat downwards for cooking food. ■ a gridiron used for cooking food on an open fire. ■ a dish of grilled food, especially meat. ■ (also **grill room**) a restaurant serving grilled food.
▶ **verb** [with obj.] **1** cook (food) using a grill: *grill the trout for five minutes*.
2 informal subject (someone) to intense questioning or interrogation: *my father grilled us about what we had been doing* | (as noun **grilling**) *they faced a grilling over the latest results*.
– DERIVATIVES **griller** noun.
– ORIGIN mid 17th cent.: from French *gril* (noun), *griller* (verb), from Old French *graille* 'grille'.

grill[2] ▶ **noun** variant spelling of **GRILLE**.

grillade /grɪˈleɪd, -ˈjɑːd, ˈgriːɑːd/ ▶ **noun** a kind of meat stew usually made with beef steak, typical of French regional and Cajun cookery.
– ORIGIN French.

grillage /ˈgrɪlɪdʒ/ ▶ **noun** a heavy framework of cross-timbering or metal beams forming a foundation for building on difficult ground.
– ORIGIN late 18th cent.: from French (see **GRILLE**, **-AGE**).

grille (also **grill**) ▶ **noun** a grating or screen of metal bars or wires, placed in front of something as protection or to allow ventilation or discreet observation.
– ORIGIN mid 17th cent.: from French, from medieval Latin, *craticula*, diminutive of *cratis* 'hurdle'; related to **CRATE**, **GRATE[2]**, and **GRIDDLE**.

grill room ▶ **noun** see **GRILL[1]**.

grilse /grɪls/ ▶ **noun** a salmon that has returned to fresh water after a single winter at sea.
– ORIGIN late Middle English: of unknown origin.

grim ▶ **adjective** (**grimmer**, **grimmest**) **1** very serious or gloomy: *his grim expression*. ■ depressing or worrying to consider: *the grim news of the murder*. ■ (of humour) lacking genuine levity; black.
2 (especially of a place) unattractive or forbidding: *rows of grim, dark housing developments*. ■ unrelentingly harsh: *few creatures thrive in this grim and hostile land*.
– PHRASES **the Grim Reaper** a personification of death in the form of a cloaked skeleton wielding a large scythe. **like** (or **for**) **grim death** Brit. with great determination: *we had to hold on like grim death*.
– DERIVATIVES **grimly** adverb, **grimness** noun.
– ORIGIN Old English, of Germanic origin; related to Dutch *grim* and German *grimm*.

grimace /ˈgrɪməs, grɪˈmeɪs/ ▶ **noun** an ugly, twisted expression on a person's face, typically expressing disgust, pain, or wry amusement: *she gave a grimace of pain*.
▶ **verb** [no obj.] make a grimace: *I sipped the coffee and grimaced*.
– DERIVATIVES **grimacer** noun.
– ORIGIN mid 17th cent.: from French, from Spanish *grimazo* 'caricature', from *grima* 'fright'.

Grimaldi[1] /grɪˈmaldi/, Francesco Maria (1618–63), Italian physicist and astronomer, who discovered the diffraction of light and verified Galileo's law of the uniform acceleration of falling bodies.

Grimaldi[2] /grɪˈmaldi/, Joseph (1779–1837), English circus entertainer, who created the role of the circus clown. He performed at Covent Garden, where he became famous for his acrobatic skills.

grimalkin /grɪˈmalkɪn, -ˈmɔːl-/ ▶ **noun** archaic a cat. ■ a spiteful old woman.
– ORIGIN late 16th cent.: from **GREY** + *Malkin* (pet form of the given name *Matilda*).

grime ▶ **noun** [mass noun] **1** dirt ingrained on the surface of something: *the windows were thick with grime*.
2 a form of dance music influenced by UK garage, characterized by machine-like sounds.
▶ **verb** [with obj.] blacken or make dirty with grime: *the windows were grimed like a coal miner's goggles*.
– ORIGIN Middle English: from Middle Low German and Middle Dutch.

Grimm /grɪm/, Jacob (Ludwig Carl) (1785–1863) and Wilhelm (Carl) (1786–1859), German philologists and folklorists. In 1852 the brothers jointly inaugurated a dictionary of German on historical principles, which was eventually completed by other scholars in 1960. They also compiled an anthology of German fairy tales, which appeared in three volumes between 1812 and 1822.

Grimm's law ▶ **noun** Linguistics the observation that certain Indo-European consonants (mainly stops) undergo regular changes in the Germanic languages which are not seen in others such as Greek or Latin. Examples include *p* becoming *f* so that Latin *pedem* corresponds to English *foot* and German *Fuss*. The principle was set out by Jacob Grimm in his German grammar (2nd edition, 1822).

grimoire /grɪmˈwɑː/ ▶ **noun** a book of magic spells and invocations.
– ORIGIN mid 19th cent.: French, alteration of *grammaire* 'grammar'.

Grimsby /ˈgrɪmzbi/ a port on the south shore of the Humber estuary, administrative centre of North East Lincolnshire; pop. 84,100 (est. 2009). Official name **GREAT GRIMSBY**.

grimy ▶ **adjective** (**grimier**, **grimiest**) covered with or characterized by grime: *the grimy industrial city*.
– DERIVATIVES **grimily** adverb, **griminess** noun.

grin ▶ **verb** (**grins**, **grinning**, **grinned**) [no obj.] smile broadly: *Dennis appeared, grinning cheerfully*. ■ grimace grotesquely so as to reveal the teeth: (as adj. **grinning**) *a grinning skull*.
▶ **noun** a broad smile: *a silly grin*.
– PHRASES **grin and bear it** suffer pain or misfortune in a stoical manner.
– DERIVATIVES **grinner** noun, **grinningly** adverb.
– ORIGIN Old English *grennian* 'bare the teeth in pain or anger', of Germanic origin; probably related to **GROAN**.

Grinch /grɪntʃ/ ▶ **noun** N. Amer. informal a spoilsport or killjoy.
– ORIGIN 1970s: the name of a character in the children's story *How the Grinch Stole Christmas* (1957) by Dr Seuss.

grind ▶ **verb** (past and past participle **ground**) **1** [with obj.] reduce (something) to small particles or powder by crushing it: *grind some black pepper over the salad* | *she ground up the rice prior to boiling*. ■ sharpen, smooth, or produce (something) by crushing or by friction: *power from a waterwheel was used to grind cutlery*. ■ operate (a mill or machine) by turning the handle: *she was grinding a coffee mill*. ■ [no obj.] (of a mill or machine) work with a crushing action.
2 rub or cause to rub together gratingly: [no obj.] *tectonic plates that inexorably grind against each other* | [with obj.] *he keeps me awake at night, grinding his teeth*. ■ [with obj.] press or rub (something) into a surface: *she ground a half-smoked cigarette into the ashtray*. ■ [no obj., with adverbial] move noisily and laboriously: *the truck was grinding slowly up the hill*.
3 [no obj.] informal (of a dancer) gyrate the hips erotically: *go-go girls grinding to blaring disco*. ■ Brit. vulgar slang, dated have sexual intercourse.
▶ **noun 1** a crushing or grating sound or motion: *the crunch and grind of bulldozers* | figurative *the slow grind of the US legal system*. ■ the size of ground particles: *only the right grind gives you all the fine flavour*.
2 hard dull work: *relief from the daily grind*. ■ US informal an excessively hard-working student. ■ Irish a private tuition class: *experienced teacher offers grinds in Maths and Irish, to all levels*.
3 informal a dancer's erotic gyration of the hips. ■ Brit. vulgar slang, dated an act of sexual intercourse.
– PHRASES **grind to a halt** (or **come to a grinding halt**) slow down gradually and then stop completely.
– PHRASAL VERBS **grind away** work or study hard. **grind someone down** wear someone down with continuous harsh treatment: *mundane everyday things which just grind people down*. **grind on** continue for a long time in a wearying or tedious way: *the rail talks grind on*. **grind something out** produce something dull or tedious slowly and laboriously: *the band was grinding out the inevitable summer songs*.
– ORIGIN Old English *grindan*, probably of Germanic origin. Although no cognates are known, it may be distantly related to Latin *frendere* 'rub away, gnash'.

grinder ▶ **noun 1** a machine used for grinding something: *a coffee grinder*. ■ a person employed to grind cutlery, tools, or cereals.
2 a molar tooth.
3 US informal another name for **HOAGIE**.

grinding ▶ **adjective** [attrib.] **1** (of a difficult situation) oppressive and seemingly without end: *grinding poverty*.
2 (of a sound or movement) harsh and grating.
– DERIVATIVES **grindingly** adverb.

grinding wheel ▶ **noun** a wheel used for cutting, grinding, or finishing metal or other objects, and typically made of abrasive particles bonded together.

grindstone ▶ **noun** a thick disc of stone or other abrasive material mounted so as to revolve, used for grinding, sharpening, or polishing metal objects. ■ rare another term for **MILLSTONE**.
– PHRASES **keep one's nose to the grindstone** work hard and continuously.

gringo /ˈgrɪŋgəʊ/ ▶ **noun** (pl. **gringos**) informal a white person from an English-speaking country (used in Spanish-speaking countries, chiefly Central and South America).
– ORIGIN Spanish, literally 'foreign, foreigner, or gibberish'.

griot /ˈgriːəʊ/ ▶ **noun** a member of a class of travelling poets, musicians, and storytellers who maintain a tradition of oral history in parts of West Africa.
– ORIGIN French, earlier *guiriot*, perhaps from Portuguese *criado*.

grip ▶ **verb** (**grips**, **gripping**, **gripped**) [with obj.] **1** take and keep a firm hold of; grasp tightly: *his knuckles were white as he gripped the steering wheel*. ■ [no obj.] maintain a firm contact, especially by friction: *a sole that really grips well on wet rock*.
2 (of an emotion or situation) have a strong or adverse effect on: *she was gripped by a feeling of excitement* | *the country was gripped by recession*. ■ firmly hold the attention or interest of: *we were gripped by the drama*.
▶ **noun 1** [in sing.] a firm hold; a tight grasp: *his arm was held in a vice-like grip* | figurative *the icy grip of winter*. ■ a manner of holding something: *I've changed my grip and my backswing*. ■ [mass noun] the ability of something, especially a wheel or shoe, to maintain a firm contact with a surface: *these shoes have got no grip*.
2 [in sing.] effective control over something: *he had to take a grip on his nerves*. ■ an understanding of something: *you've got a good* **grip on** *what's going on*.
3 a part or attachment by which something is held in the hand: *handlebar grips*. ■ Brit. a hairgrip.
4 a travelling bag: *a grip crammed with new clothes*.
5 a stagehand in a theatre. ■ a member of a camera crew responsible for moving and setting up equipment.
– PHRASES **come** (or **get**) **to grips with** engage in combat with. ■ begin to deal with or understand: *a real tough problem to come to grips with*. **get a grip** [usu. in imperative] informal keep or recover one's self-control: *get a grip, guys!* **in the grip of** dominated or affected by something undesirable or adverse: *Britain was in the grip of a crime wave*. **lose one's grip** become unable to understand or control one's situation.
– DERIVATIVES **gripper** noun.
– ORIGIN Old English *grippa* (verb), *gripe* 'grasp, clutch' (noun), *gripa* 'handful, sheath'; related to **GRIPE**.

gripe ▶ **verb 1** [no obj.] informal complain about something in a persistent, irritating way: *it's no use griping about your boss or your pay* | [with direct speech] *'Holidays make no difference to Simon,' Pat griped*.
2 [with obj.] (usu. as adj. **griping**) affect with gastric or intestinal pain: *spasmodic griping pains*.
3 [with obj.] archaic grasp tightly; clutch: *Hilyard griped his dagger*.

G

4 [with obj.] Nautical secure (a boat) with gripes.
5 [no obj.] Sailing (of a ship) turn to face the wind despite the efforts of the helmsman.
▶ noun 1 informal a minor complaint: *my only gripe is the size of the page numbers.*
2 [mass noun] gastric or intestinal pain; colic.
3 archaic an act of grasping something tightly.
4 (**gripes**) Nautical lashings securing a boat in its place on deck or in davits.
– DERIVATIVES **griper** noun.
– ORIGIN Old English *grīpan* 'grasp, clutch', of Germanic origin; related to Dutch *grijpen*, German *greifen* 'seize', also to GRIP and GROPE. Sense 2 of the verb dates from the 17th cent.; sense 1 of the verb, of US origin, dates from the 1930s.

gripe water ▶ noun [mass noun] Brit. trademark a solution given to babies for the relief of colic, wind, and indigestion.

grippe /ɡrɪp/ ▶ noun old-fashioned term for INFLUENZA.
– ORIGIN late 18th cent.: French, from *gripper* 'seize'.

gripping ▶ adjective firmly holding the attention or interest; exciting: *a gripping TV thriller.*
– DERIVATIVES **grippingly** adverb.

G

grippy ▶ adjective (**grippier**, **grippiest**) (of a wheel or shoe) able to grip a surface well: *a comfortable boot with a grippy rubber sole.*

Griqua /ˈɡriːkwə/ ▶ noun (pl. **same** or **Griquas**) a member of a people of mixed European and Khoikhoi origin, living mainly in the Eastern and Western Cape provinces of South Africa.
– ORIGIN the name in Nama.

Gris /ɡriːs/, Juan (1887–1927), Spanish painter; born *José Victoriano Gonzales*. His main contribution was to the development of the later phase of synthetic cubism. His work features the use of collage and paint in simple fragmented shapes.

grisaille /ɡrɪˈzʌɪ(l), -zeɪl/ ▶ noun [mass noun] Art a method of painting in grey monochrome, typically to imitate sculpture. ■ [count noun] a grisaille painting or stained-glass window.
– ORIGIN mid 19th cent.: French, from *gris* 'grey'.

griseofulvin /ˌɡrɪzɪə(ʊ)ˈfʊlvɪn/ ▶ noun [mass noun] Medicine an antibiotic used against fungal infections of the hair and skin. ● This antibiotic is obtained from the mould *Penicillium griseofulvum*.
– ORIGIN 1930s: from the modern Latin binomial, from medieval Latin *griseus* 'greyish' + Latin *fulvus* 'reddish yellow'.

grisette /ɡrɪˈzɛt/ ▶ noun 1 a common edible woodland mushroom with a brown or grey cap, a slender stem, and white gills. ● *Amanita vaginata* and *A. fulva*, family Amanitaceae, class Hymenomycetes.
2 archaic a young working-class Frenchwoman.
– ORIGIN French, from *gris* 'grey' + the diminutive suffix *-ette*; in sense 2 the term derives from the grey dress material typically worn by such women; sense 1 is an extended use.

gris-gris /ˈɡriːɡriː/ (also **gri-gri**, **greegree**) ▶ noun (pl. **same**) an African or Caribbean charm or amulet. ■ [mass noun] the use of such charms, especially in voodoo.
– ORIGIN late 17th cent.: from French *grisgris*, of West African origin.

griskin /ˈɡrɪskɪn/ ▶ noun [mass noun] Brit. the lean part of a loin of pork.
– ORIGIN late 17th cent.: perhaps from archaic *grice* 'pig' + -KIN.

grisly /ˈɡrɪzli/ ▶ adjective (**grislier**, **grisliest**) causing horror or disgust: *the town was shaken by a series of grisly crimes.*
– DERIVATIVES **grisliness** noun.
– ORIGIN Old English *grislic* 'terrifying', of Germanic origin; related to Dutch *griezelig*.

USAGE The words **grisly** and **grizzly** are quite different in meaning, though often confused. **Grisly** means 'causing horror or disgust', as in *grisly crimes*, whereas **grizzly** is chiefly used with reference to a kind of large American bear, and can also mean 'grey or grey-haired'.

grison /ˈɡrɪz(ə)n, ˈɡrʌɪs(ə)n/ ▶ noun a weasel-like mammal with dark fur and a white stripe across the forehead, found in Central and South America. ● Genus *Galictis*, family Mustelidae: two species.
– ORIGIN late 18th cent.: from French, from *gris* 'grey'.

grissini /ɡrɪˈsiːni/ ▶ plural noun thin, crisp Italian breadsticks.
– ORIGIN Italian.

grist ▶ noun [mass noun] 1 corn that is ground to make flour. ■ malt crushed to make mash for brewing.
2 useful material, especially to support an argument: *the research provided the most sensational grist for opponents of tobacco.*
– PHRASES **grist to the** (or **one's**) **mill** useful experience, material, or knowledge: *all this free publicity was grist to his mill.*
– ORIGIN Old English 'grinding', of Germanic origin; related to GRIND.

gristle /ˈɡrɪs(ə)l/ ▶ noun [mass noun] cartilage, especially when found as tough inedible tissue in meat.
– ORIGIN Old English, of unknown origin.

gristly ▶ adjective (**gristlier**, **gristliest**) consisting of or full of gristle: *gristly bits of beef.*

gristmill ▶ noun a mill for grinding corn.

grit ▶ noun [mass noun] 1 small loose particles of stone or sand: *she had a bit of grit in her eye.* ■ [as modifier] (with numeral) indicating the grade of fineness of an abrasive: *400 grit paper.* ■ (also **gritstone**) a coarse sandstone.
2 courage and resolve; strength of character: *I've known few men who could match Maude's grit.*
▶ verb (**grits**, **gritting**, **gritted**) 1 [with obj.] spread grit and often salt on (an icy road).
2 [no obj.] grate: *fine red dust that gritted between the teeth.*
– PHRASES **grit one's teeth** clench one's teeth, especially when faced with something unpleasant: *grit your teeth and splash yourself with cold water!* ■ resolve to do something difficult or unpleasant: *Parliament must grit its teeth and take action.*
– ORIGIN Old English *grēot* 'sand, gravel', of Germanic origin; related to German *Griess*, also to GROATS.

grits ▶ plural noun [also treated as sing.] US a dish of coarsely ground maize kernels boiled with water or milk. ■ coarsely ground maize kernels from which this dish is made.
– ORIGIN Old English *grytt*, *grytte* 'bran, mill dust', of Germanic origin: related to Dutch *grutten*, German *Grütze*, also to GROATS.

gritter ▶ noun Brit. a vehicle or machine for spreading grit and often salt on roads in icy or potentially icy weather.

gritty ▶ adjective (**grittier**, **grittiest**) 1 containing or covered with grit.
2 showing courage and resolve: *a typically gritty performance by the British player.* ■ showing something unpleasant as it really is; uncompromising: *a gritty look at urban life.*
– DERIVATIVES **grittily** adverb, **grittiness** noun.

Grivas /ˈɡriːvəs/, George (Theodorou) (1898–1974), Greek Cypriot patriot and soldier. A supporter of the union of Cyprus with Greece, he led the guerrilla campaign against British rule which culminated in the country's independence in 1959.

grivet /ˈɡrɪvɪt/ (also **grivet monkey**) ▶ noun a common African guenon with greenish-brown upper parts and a black face. Compare with GREEN MONKEY and VERVET. ● *Cercopithecus aethiops*, family Cercopithecidae, in particular the race *C. a. aethiops* of Ethiopia and Sudan, with long white cheek tufts.
– ORIGIN mid 19th cent.: from French, of unknown origin.

grizzle[1] ▶ verb [no obj.] Brit. informal (of a child) cry fretfully: *sometimes children grizzled, sometimes they wailed* | (as noun **grizzling**) *no grizzling, now!* ■ sulk or grumble.
– DERIVATIVES **grizzler** noun.
– ORIGIN mid 18th cent. (in the sense 'show the teeth, grin'): of unknown origin.

grizzle[2] ▶ adjective [often in combination] (of hair or fur) having dark and white hairs mixed: *grizzle-haired.*
▶ noun [mass noun] a mixture of dark and white hairs.
– ORIGIN Middle English: from Old French *grisel*, from *gris* 'grey'.

grizzled ▶ adjective having or streaked with grey hair: *grizzled hair.*
– ORIGIN late Middle English: from the adjective GRIZZLE[2] + -ED[1].

grizzly[1] ▶ noun (also **grizzly bear**) (pl. **grizzlies**) an animal of a large race of the brown bear native to North America. ● *Ursus arctos horribilis*, family Ursidae.
▶ adjective (**grizzlier**, **grizzliest**) grey or grey-haired: *a grizzly beard.*
– ORIGIN mid 16th cent. (as adjective): from GRIZZLE[2]. The noun dates from the early 19th century.

USAGE On the confusion of **grizzly** and **grisly**, see USAGE at GRISLY.

grizzly[2] ▶ adjective (**grizzlier**, **grizzliest**) (of a child) inclined to cry fretfully: *a grizzly baby.*

groan ▶ verb [no obj.] 1 make a deep inarticulate sound conveying pain, despair, pleasure, etc.: *Marty groaned and pulled the blanket over his head.* ■ [with direct speech] say something in a despairing or miserable tone: *'Oh no!' I groaned.* ■ complain; grumble: *they were moaning and groaning about management.*
2 (of an object) make a low creaking sound when pressure or weight is applied: *James slumped back into his chair, making it groan.* ■ (**groan with**/**under**) be heavily loaded with: *tables groan with joints of venison.* ■ (**groan beneath**/**under**) be oppressed by: *families groaning under mortgage increases.*
▶ noun 1 a deep inarticulate sound conveying pain, despair, pleasure, etc. ■ a complaint: *listen to everyone's moans and groans.*
2 a low creaking sound made by an object under pressure: *the protesting groan of timbers.*
– PHRASES **groan inwardly** feel dismayed by something but remain silent: *everything has a tepid inevitability, and even as you smile you may be groaning inwardly.*
– DERIVATIVES **groaner** noun, **groaning** adjective, **groaningly** adverb.
– ORIGIN Old English *grānian*, of Germanic origin; related to German *greinen* 'grizzle, whine', *grinsen* 'grin', also probably to GRIN.

groat ▶ noun historical any of various medieval European coins, in particular an English silver coin worth four old pence, issued between 1351 and 1662. ■ [in sing.] [with negative] archaic a small amount: *I do not care a groat.*
– ORIGIN from Middle Dutch *groot* or Middle Low German *grōte* 'great, thick', hence 'thick penny'; compare with GROSCHEN.

groats ▶ plural noun hulled or crushed grain, especially oats.
– ORIGIN late Old English *grotan* (plural): related to GRIT and GRITS.

Gro-bag ▶ noun trademark for GROWBAG.

grocer ▶ noun a person who sells food and small household goods.
– ORIGIN Middle English (originally 'a person who sold things in the gross' (i.e. in large quantities)): from Old French *grossier*, from medieval Latin *grossarius*, from late Latin *grossus* 'gross'.

grocery ▶ noun (pl. **groceries**) a grocer's shop or business. ■ (**groceries**) items of food sold in a grocery or supermarket.

groceteria /ˌɡrəʊsəˈtiːrɪə/ ▶ noun N. Amer. a small grocery.

grockle ▶ noun Brit. informal, often derogatory a holidaymaker, especially one visiting a resort in Devon or Cornwall.
– ORIGIN an invented word, originally a fantastic creature in a children's comic, adopted arbitrarily and popularized by the film *The System* (1962).

Grodno /ˈɡrəʊdnə/ Russian name for HRODNA.

grog ▶ noun [mass noun] 1 spirits (originally rum) mixed with water. ■ informal or Austral./NZ alcoholic drink.
2 crushed unglazed pottery or brick used as an additive in plaster or clay.
– ORIGIN mid 18th cent.: said to be from *Old Grog*, the reputed nickname (because of his grogram cloak) of Admiral Vernon (1684–1757), who in 1740 first ordered diluted (instead of neat) rum to be served out to sailors.

groggy ▶ adjective (**groggier**, **groggiest**) dazed, weak, or unsteady, especially from illness, intoxication, sleep, or a blow: *the sleeping pills had left her feeling groggy.*
– DERIVATIVES **groggily** adverb, **grogginess** noun.

grogram /ˈɡrɒɡrəm/ ▶ noun [mass noun] a coarse fabric made of silk, often combined with mohair or wool and stiffened with gum.
– ORIGIN mid 16th cent.: from French *gros grain* 'coarse grain' (see also GROSGRAIN).

groin[1] ▶ noun 1 the area between the abdomen and the upper thigh on either side of the body. ■ informal the region of the genitals: *she kicked him in the groin.*
2 Architecture a curved edge formed by two intersecting vaults.
– ORIGIN late Middle English *grynde*, perhaps from Old English *grynde* 'depression, abyss'.

groin[2] ▶ noun US spelling of GROYNE.

groined ▶ adjective Architecture (of a vault) formed by the intersection of two barrel vaults, usually with plain groins without ribs.

grok ▶ verb (**groks**, **grokking**, **grokked**) [with obj.] US informal understand (something) intuitively or by

empathy: *corporate leaders seemed to grok this concept fairly quickly.* ■ [no obj.] establish a rapport.
– ORIGIN 1960s: a word invented by Robert Heinlein (1907–88), American author.

grommet /ˈgrɒmɪt/ ▶ **noun 1** an eyelet placed in a hole to protect or insulate a rope or cable passed through it or to reinforce the hole.
2 Brit. a tube surgically implanted in the eardrum to drain fluid from the middle ear.
3 informal, chiefly Austral. a young or inexperienced surfer or skateboarder.
– ORIGIN early 17th cent. (in nautical use in the sense 'a circle of rope used as a fastening'): from obsolete French *grommette*, from *gourmer* 'to curb', of unknown ultimate origin. Current senses date from the mid 20th cent.

gromwell ▶ **noun** a widely distributed plant of the borage family, typically having white or blue flowers which are followed by smooth hard nutlets. ● Genus *Lithospermum*, family Boraginaceae: several species, in particular the common Eurasian *L. officinale*.
– ORIGIN Middle English: from Old French *gromil*, probably from a medieval Latin phrase meaning 'crane's millet'.

Gromyko /grəˈmiːkəʊ/, Andrei (Andreevich) (1909–89), Soviet statesman, Foreign minister 1957–1985, President of the USSR 1985–8. His appointment to the presidency (largely a formal position) by Gorbachev was widely interpreted as a manoeuvre to reduce Gromyko's influence and make possible an ending of the Cold War.

Groningen /ˈgrəʊnɪŋən, ˈgrɒn-/ a city in the northern Netherlands, capital of a province of the same name; pop. 182,484 (2008).

Grønland /ˈgrœnlan/ Danish name for **GREENLAND**.

groom ▶ **verb** [with obj.] **1** brush and clean the coat of (a horse, dog, or other animal): *the horses were groomed and taken to shows.* ■ (of an animal) clean the fur or skin of (itself or another animal). ■ (often as adj. **groomed**) give a neat and tidy appearance to (someone): [with submodifier] *a beautifully groomed woman* | (as noun **grooming**) *she pays great attention to grooming and clothes.* ■ look after (a lawn, ski slope, or other surface).
2 prepare or train (someone) for a particular purpose or activity: *star pupils who are **groomed for** higher things.* ■ (of a paedophile) prepare (a child) for a meeting, especially via an Internet chat room, with the intention of committing a sexual offence.
▶ **noun 1** a person employed to take care of horses.
2 a bridegroom.
3 Brit. any of various officials of the royal household.
– DERIVATIVES **groomer** noun.
– ORIGIN Middle English (in the sense 'boy', later 'man, male servant'): of unknown origin.

groomsman ▶ **noun** (pl. **groomsmen**) N. Amer. a male friend officially attending the bridegroom at a wedding.

groove ▶ **noun 1** a long, narrow cut or depression in a hard material. ■ a spiral track cut in a record, into which the stylus fits. ■ Climbing an indentation where two planes of rock meet at an angle of more than 120°.
2 an established routine or habit: *his thoughts were slipping **into a familiar groove**.*
3 informal a particular rhythm in popular or jazz music: *her vocals drift delicately across a soaring soul groove.*
▶ **verb 1** [with obj.] make a groove or grooves in: *deep lines grooved her face.*
2 [no obj.] informal dance to or play popular or jazz music: *they were **grooving to** Motown.* ■ dated play popular or jazz music in an accomplished manner: *the rhythm section grooves in the true Basic manner.* ■ enjoy oneself: *Harley relaxed and began to groove.*
3 [with obj.] Baseball, informal pitch (a ball) in the centre of the strike zone. ■ N. Amer. (in the context of other sports) kick or throw (the ball) successfully; score (a goal) with stylish ease: *the San Diego kicker grooved the winning field goal.*
– PHRASES **in** (or **into**) **the groove** informal performing consistently well or confidently: *it might take me a couple of races to get back into the groove.* ■ enjoying oneself, especially by dancing: *get into the groove!*
– DERIVATIVES **groover** noun.
– ORIGIN Middle English (denoting a mine or shaft): from Dutch *groeve* 'furrow, pit'; related to **GRAVE**[1].

grooved ▶ **adjective** having a groove or grooves: *grooved tyres.*

grooved ware ▶ **noun** [mass noun] Archaeology prehistoric pottery of the mid to late Neolithic in Britain (*c.*3300–2100 BC), characterized by a flat base and decorated chiefly with grooves and straight lines.

grooving saw ▶ **noun** a circular saw used for cutting grooves.

groovy ▶ **adjective** (**groovier**, **grooviest**) informal, dated or humorous fashionable and exciting: *a groovy new haircut.* ■ excellent: *a groovy, smooth-sounding album.*
– DERIVATIVES **groovily** adverb, **grooviness** noun.

grope ▶ **verb 1** [no obj., with adverbial] search blindly or uncertainly by feeling with the hands: *she **groped for** her spectacles.* ■ move along uncertainly by feeling objects as one goes: *she blew out the candle and **groped her way** to the door.* ■ (**grope for**) search uncertainly for (a word or answer) in one's mind: *she was groping for the words which would express what she thought.*
2 [with obj.] informal fondle (someone) for sexual pleasure roughly or clumsily, or without the person's consent: *he was accused of groping office girls.*
▶ **noun** an act of fondling someone for sexual pleasure: *she and Steve sneaked off for a quick grope.*
– DERIVATIVES **gropingly** adverb.
– ORIGIN Old English *grāpian*, of West Germanic origin; related to **GRIPE**.

groper[1] ▶ **noun 1** chiefly Austral./NZ variant spelling of **GROUPER**.
2 (also **blue groper**) a large Australian wrasse which is a popular sporting fish. ● *Achoerodus gouldii*, family Labridae.

groper[2] ▶ **noun** a person who fondles someone for sexual pleasure, especially without the person's consent.

Gropius /ˈgrəʊpɪəs/, Walter (1883–1969), German-born American architect. He was the first director of the Bauhaus School of Design (1919–28) and a pioneer of the International Style. He settled in the US in 1938, where he was professor of architecture at Harvard University until 1952.

grosbeak /ˈgrəʊsbiːk/ ▶ **noun** a finch or related songbird with a stout conical bill and typically brightly coloured plumage. ● Several genera in the family Fringillidae and subfamily Cardinalinae (family Emberizidae); the **white-fronted grosbeak** or **grosbeak weaver** (*Amblyospiza albifrons*) belongs to the family Ploceidae.
– ORIGIN late 17th cent.: from French *grosbec*, from *gros* 'big, fat' + *bec* 'beak'.

groschen /ˈgrəʊʃ(ə)n, ˈgrɒʃ(ə)n/ ▶ **noun** (pl. **same**) (until the introduction of the euro in 2002) a monetary unit in Austria, equal to one hundredth of a schilling. ■ historical a small German silver coin. ■ informal (until the introduction of the euro in 2002) a German ten-pfennig piece.
– ORIGIN German, from Middle High German *grosse*, from medieval Latin (*denarius*) *grossus* 'thick (penny)'; compare with **GROAT**.

grosgrain /ˈgrəʊgreɪn/ ▶ **noun** a heavy ribbed fabric, typically of silk or rayon.
– ORIGIN mid 19th cent.: French, 'coarse grain' (see also **GROGRAM**).

gros point /grəʊ ˈpwã/ ▶ **noun** [mass noun] a type of needlepoint embroidery consisting of stitches crossing two or more threads of the canvas in each direction.
– ORIGIN mid 19th cent.: French, literally 'large stitch', from *gros point de Venise*, a type of lace originally from Venice, worked in bold relief. The current sense dates from the 1930s.

gross ▶ **adjective 1** unattractively fat or bloated: *I feel fat, gross—even my legs feel flabby.* ■ informal very unpleasant; repulsive: *'Then I threw up,' said Russ. 'How gross,' Ellie muttered.*
2 very rude or coarse; vulgar: *a gross, slap-and-tickle version of 'The Taming of the Shrew'.*
3 (especially of wrongdoing) very obvious and unacceptable: *gross human rights abuses.*
4 (of income, profit, or interest) without deduction of tax or other contributions; total: *the gross amount of the gift was £1,000.* Often contrasted with **NET**[2] (sense 1 of the adjective). ■ (of weight) including contents, wrappings, or other variable items; overall: *a projected gross take-off weight of 500,000 pounds.* ■ (of a score in golf) as actually played, without taking handicap into account.
5 general or large-scale; not detailed: *at the gross anatomical level.*
▶ **adverb** without tax or other contributions having been deducted.
▶ **verb** [with obj.] produce or earn (an amount of money) as gross profit or income: *the film went on to gross $8 million.* ■ (**gross something up**) add deductions such as tax to a net amount: *all commuting costs were grossed up for tax and National Insurance deductions.*
▶ **noun 1** (pl. **same**) an amount equal to twelve dozen; 144: *fifty-five gross of tins of processed milk.* [from French *grosse douzaine*, literally 'large dozen'.]
2 (pl. **grosses**) a gross profit or income: *the box office grosses mounted.*
– PHRASES **by the gross** in large numbers or amounts: *on D-Day men drowned by the gross.*
– PHRASAL VERBS **gross someone out** N. Amer. informal disgust someone.
– DERIVATIVES **grossly** adverb [as submodifier] *Freda was grossly overweight*, **grossness** noun.
– ORIGIN Middle English (in the sense 'thick, massive, bulky'): from Old French *gros, grosse* 'large', from late Latin *grossus*.

gross domestic product (abbrev.: **GDP**) ▶ **noun** the total value of goods produced and services provided in a country during one year. Compare with **GROSS NATIONAL PRODUCT**.

grosser ▶ **noun** [with adj. or noun modifier] a film that earns a specified level of gross profit or income: *the 1965 film version was an even bigger grosser* | *a $50 million-plus grosser.*

Grossglockner /ˈgrəʊsˌglɒknə/ the highest mountain in Austria, in the eastern Tyrolean Alps, rising to a height of 3,797 m (12,457 ft).

gross national product (abbrev.: **GNP**) ▶ **noun** the total value of goods produced and services provided by a country during one year, equal to the gross domestic product plus the net income from foreign investments.

gross-out ▶ **noun** informal, chiefly N. Amer. something disgusting or repellent: [as modifier] *the movie features several gross-out scenes.*

gross ton ▶ **noun** see **TON**[1] (sense 2 of the noun).

grossular /ˈgrɒsjʊlə/ (also **grossularite**) ▶ **noun** [mass noun] a mineral of the garnet group, consisting essentially of calcium aluminium silicate.
– ORIGIN early 19th cent.: from modern Latin *grossularia* 'gooseberry'. The yellow-green variety is sometimes known as *gooseberry garnet*.

Gros Ventre /grəʊ ˈvɒntrə/ ▶ **noun** (pl. **Gros Ventres**) another term for **HIDATSA**.
– ORIGIN French, literally 'big belly'.

Grosz /grəʊs/, German /grɔs/, George (1893–1959), German painter and draughtsman. His satirical drawings and paintings characteristically depict a decadent society in which gluttony and depraved sensuality are juxtaposed with poverty and disease.

grosz /grɔːʃ/ ▶ **noun** (pl. **groszy** or **grosze** /ˈgrɔːʃi/) a monetary unit in Poland, equal to one hundredth of a zloty.
– ORIGIN Polish; compare with **GROSCHEN**.

grot[1] ▶ **noun** [mass noun] Brit. informal something unpleasant, dirty, or of poor quality.
– ORIGIN 1960s: back-formation from **GROTTY**.

grot[2] ▶ **noun** literary a grotto.
– ORIGIN early 16th cent.: from French *grotte*, from Italian *grotta*, via Latin from Greek *kruptē* 'vault, crypt'.

grotesque /grə(ʊ)ˈtɛsk/ ▶ **adjective** comically or repulsively ugly or distorted: *a figure wearing a grotesque mask.* ■ incongruous or inappropriate to a shocking degree: *a lifestyle of grotesque luxury.*
▶ **noun 1** a very ugly or comically distorted figure or image: *the rods are carved in the form of a series of gargoyle faces and grotesques.* ■ [mass noun] a style of decorative painting or sculpture consisting of the interweaving of human and animal forms with flowers and foliage.
2 [mass noun] Printing a family of 19th-century sans serif typefaces.
– DERIVATIVES **grotesquely** adverb, **grotesqueness** noun.
– ORIGIN mid 16th cent. (as noun): from French *crotesque* (the earliest form in English), from Italian *grottesca*, from *opera* or *pittura grottesca* 'work or painting resembling that found in a grotto'; 'grotto' here probably denoted the rooms of ancient buildings in Rome which had been revealed by excavations, and which contained murals in the grotesque style.

grotesquerie /grəʊˈtɛskəri/ ▶ **noun** (pl. **grotesqueries**) [mass noun] grotesque quality or grotesque things collectively: *current tastes for horror and grotesquerie.* ■ [count noun] a grotesque thing or action.
– ORIGIN late 17th cent.: French (see **GROTESQUE**).

Grotius /ˈgrəʊtɪəs/, Hugo (1583–1645), Dutch jurist and diplomat; Latinized name of *Huig de Groot*. His legal treatise *De Jure Belli et Pacis* (1625) established the basis of modern international law.

G

grotto ▸ noun (pl. **grottoes** or **grottos**) a small picturesque cave, especially an artificial one in a park or garden. ■ an indoor structure resembling a cave: *visits to Father Christmas's grotto*.
– DERIVATIVES **grottoed** adjective.
– ORIGIN early 17th cent.: from Italian *grotta*, via Latin from Greek *kruptē* (see CRYPT).

grotty ▸ adjective (**grottier**, **grottiest**) Brit. informal
1 unpleasant and of poor quality: *a grotty little hotel*.
2 [as complement] unwell: *I felt grotty and had to leave early*.
– DERIVATIVES **grottiness** noun.
– ORIGIN 1960s: from GROTESQUE + -Y[1].

grouch /graʊtʃ/ ▸ noun a habitually grumpy person: *rock's foremost poet and ill-mannered grouch*. ■ a trivial complaint. ■ a sulky or discontented mood: *he's in a thundering grouch*.
▸ verb [no obj.] voice one's discontent ill-temperedly; grumble: *there's not a lot to grouch about*.
– ORIGIN late 19th cent.: variant of obsolete *grutch*, from Old French *grouchier* 'to grumble, murmur', of unknown origin. Compare with GRUDGE.

G

grouchy ▸ adjective (**grouchier**, **grouchiest**) irritable and bad-tempered; grumpy; complaining: *the old man grew sulky and grouchy*.
– DERIVATIVES **grouchily** adverb, **grouchiness** noun.

ground[1] ▸ noun 1 [in sing.] the solid surface of the earth: *he lay on the ground*. ■ [mass noun] a limited extent of the earth's surface; land: *an adjoining area of ground had been purchased*. ■ [mass noun] land of a specified kind: *my feet squelched over marshy ground*. ■ Brit. the floor of a room.
2 (also **grounds**) an area of land or sea used for a specified purpose: *shore dumping can pollute fishing grounds*. ■ (**grounds**) an area of enclosed land surrounding a large house or other building: *the house stands in seven acres of grounds | the university grounds*. ■ an area of land, often with associated buildings, used for a particular sport: *a football ground | Liverpool's new ground is nearing completion*.
3 [mass noun] an area of knowledge or subject of discussion or thought: *third-year courses **cover** less **ground** and go into more depth* | [count noun] *he shifted the argument on to theoretical grounds of his own choosing*.
4 (**grounds**) factors forming a basis for action or the justification for a belief: *there are some **grounds for** optimism | they called for a retrial **on the grounds of** the new evidence*.
5 chiefly Art a prepared surface to which paint is applied. ■ a substance used to prepare a surface for painting. ■ (in embroidery or ceramics) a plain surface to which decoration is applied. ■ a piece of wood fixed to a wall as a base for boards, plaster, or joinery.
6 (**grounds**) solid particles, especially of coffee, which form a residue; sediment.
7 N. Amer. electrical connection to the earth.
8 Music short for GROUND BASS.
▸ verb [with obj.] 1 prohibit or prevent (a pilot or an aircraft) from flying: *a bitter wind blew from the north-east and the bombers were grounded*. ■ informal (of a parent) refuse to allow (a child) to go out socially as a punishment.
2 (with reference to a ship) run or go aground: [with obj.] *rather than be blown up, Muller grounded his ship on a coral reef*.
3 (usu. **be grounded in**) give (something abstract) a firm theoretical or practical basis: *the study of history must be grounded in a thorough knowledge of the past*. ■ instruct (someone) thoroughly in a subject: *Eva's governess grounded her in Latin and Greek*. ■ (as adj. **grounded**) well balanced and sensible: *for someone so young, Chris is extremely grounded*.
4 place (something) on the ground or touch the ground with (something): *he was penalized two strokes for grounding his club in a bunker*.
5 N. Amer. connect (an electrical device) with the ground.
6 [no obj.] (**ground out**) Baseball (of a batter) be put out because of hitting a ground ball to a fielder who throws it to first base before the batter touches that base: *he **grounded out to** shortstop*.
▸ adjective [attrib.] 1 (of an animal) living on or in the ground. ■ (of a fish) bottom-dwelling. ■ (of a plant) low-growing.
2 (in aviation) relating to the ground rather than the air (with particular reference to the maintenance and servicing of aircraft: *ground crew*.
– PHRASES **be thick** (or **thin**) **on the ground** exist in large (or small) numbers or amounts: *good men are thin on the ground*. **break ground** N. Amer. 1 do preparatory digging or other work prior to building or planting something. 2 another term for BREAK NEW GROUND below. **break new** (or **fresh**) **ground** do something innovative and beneficial. **cut the ground from under someone's feet** do something which leaves someone without a reason for their actions or opinions. **from the ground up** informal completely or complete: *they needed a rethink of their doctrine from the ground up*. **gain ground** become more popular or accepted: *new moral attitudes are gaining ground*. **gain ground on** get closer to someone or something that is ahead in a pursuit or competitive situation: *the dollar gained ground on all other major currencies*. **get off the ground** (or **get something off the ground**) start or cause to start happening successfully: *there'd have to be a public inquiry before the project got off the ground*. **give** (or **lose**) **ground** retreat or lose one's advantage during a conflict or competition: *he refused to give ground on this issue*. **go to ground** (of a fox or other animal) enter its earth or burrow. ■ (of a person) hide or become inaccessible, especially for a long time: *he went to ground following the presidential coup*. **hold** (or **stand**) **one's ground** not retreat or lose one's advantage during a conflict or competition. **make up ground** get closer to someone ahead in a race or competition. **on the ground** in a place where real, practical work is done: *the troops on the ground are cynical*. **on one's own ground** in one's own territory or area of knowledge or experience: *I feel relaxed if I'm interviewed on my own ground*. **prepare the ground** make it easier for something to occur or be developed: *these measures prepared the ground for further reform*. **run someone/thing to ground** see RUN. **work** (or **run**) **oneself into the ground** exhaust oneself by working or running very hard.
– ORIGIN Old English *grund*, of Germanic origin; related to Dutch *grond* and German *Grund*.

ground[2] past and past participle of GRIND. ▸ adjective [attrib.] reduced to fine particles by crushing or mincing: *ground cumin*. ■ shaped, roughened, or polished by grinding: *the thick opaque ground perimeter of the lenses*.
– PHRASES **ground down** exhausted or worn down.

groundbait ▸ noun [mass noun] Brit. bait thrown into the water while fishing (as distinct from hookbait).
– DERIVATIVES **groundbaiting** noun.

ground ball ▸ noun Baseball a ball hit along the ground.

ground bass ▸ noun Music a short theme, usually in the bass, which is constantly repeated as the other parts of the music vary.

ground beef ▸ noun [mass noun] N. Amer. minced beef.

ground beetle ▸ noun any of a number of beetles that live mainly on or near the ground, in particular: ● a fast-running predatory beetle, typically black in colour (family Carabidae). ● (**nocturnal ground beetle**) another term for DARKLING BEETLE.

groundbreaking ▸ adjective innovative; pioneering: *groundbreaking research into fertility problems*.
– DERIVATIVES **groundbreaker** noun.

ground cherry ▸ noun an American plant of the nightshade family which resembles the Cape gooseberry. ● Genus *Physalis*, family Solanaceae: several species, in particular *P. pruinosa*, which yields edible fruit.

ground control ▸ noun [treated as sing. or pl.] the personnel and equipment that monitor and direct the flight and landing of aircraft or spacecraft.
– DERIVATIVES **ground controller** noun.

ground cover ▸ noun [mass noun] low-growing, spreading plants that help to stop weeds growing.

ground dove ▸ noun a small dove that spends much of its time on the ground, feeding and frequently nesting there. ● *Columbina*, *Gallicolumba*, and related genera, family Columbidae: several species, including the **common ground dove** (*C. passerina*) of North and Central America.

ground effect ▸ noun the effect of added aerodynamic buoyancy produced by a cushion of air below a vehicle moving close to the ground.

ground elder ▸ noun a common weed of the parsley family, with leaves that resemble those of the elder and spreading underground stems, native to Europe. ● *Aegopodium podagraria*, family Umbelliferae: a variegated cultivar is sometimes grown as ground cover.

grounder ▸ noun Baseball a ground ball.

ground floor ▸ noun Brit. the floor of a building at ground level.
– PHRASES **get in on the ground floor** informal join an enterprise in its early stages.

ground frost ▸ noun [mass noun] Brit. frost formed on the surface of the ground or in the top layer of soil.

ground game ▸ noun [mass noun] 1 game animals such as rabbits and hares that live in the ground.
2 American Football play consisting of running to advance the ball.

ground glass ▸ noun [mass noun] 1 glass with a smooth ground surface that renders it non-transparent while retaining its translucency.
2 glass ground into an abrasive powder.

groundhog ▸ noun North American term for WOODCHUCK.

Groundhog Day ▸ noun (in North America) 2 February, when the groundhog is said to come out of its hole at the end of hibernation. If the animal sees its shadow—i.e. if the weather is sunny—it is said to portend six weeks more of winter weather.

groundhopper ▸ noun a small predominantly brown insect that resembles a grasshopper and has well-developed wings. ● Family Tetrigidae, order Orthoptera: several species, including the European **common groundhopper** (*Tetrix undulata*).

grounding ▸ noun [in sing.] basic training or instruction in a subject: *every child needs **a good grounding in** science and technology*.

ground ivy ▸ noun a creeping plant of the mint family, with bluish-purple flowers, native to Europe where it commonly grows on hedge banks and in woodland. ● *Glechoma hederacea*, family Labiatae.

groundless ▸ adjective not based on any good reason: *your fears are quite groundless*.
– DERIVATIVES **groundlessly** adverb, **groundlessness** noun.
– ORIGIN Old English *grundlēas* (see GROUND[1], -LESS).

ground level ▸ noun [mass noun] 1 the level of the ground. ■ the ground floor of a building.
2 Physics another term for GROUND STATE.

groundling /ˈgraʊn(d)lɪŋ/ ▸ noun 1 an unsophisticated or uncritical spectator or reader (originally a member of the part of a theatre audience that stood in the pit below the stage): *Dante is not for groundlings*. [with reference to Shakespeare's *Hamlet* III. ii. 11.]
2 a person on the ground as opposed to one in a spacecraft or aircraft.
3 a fish that lives at the bottom of lakes and streams, especially a gudgeon or loach.
4 a creeping or dwarf plant.
– ORIGIN early 17th cent. (denoting a fish): from GROUND[1] + -LING; compare with Dutch *grondeling*, German *Gründling* 'gudgeon'.

ground loop ▸ noun 1 a violent, uncontrolled horizontal rotation of an aircraft while landing, taking off, or taxiing.
2 North American term for EARTH LOOP.
▸ verb (**ground-loop**) [no obj.] (of an aircraft) make a ground loop.

groundmass ▸ noun [in sing.] Geology the compact, finer-grained material in which the crystals are embedded in a porphyritic rock.

groundnut ▸ noun 1 another term for PEANUT.
2 a North American plant of the pea family, which yields a sweet edible tuber. ● Genus *Apios*, family Leguminosae: several species, in particular *A. tuberosa*.

groundout ▸ noun Baseball a play in which a batter is put out by hitting a ground ball to a fielder who throws it to first base before the batter touches that base.

ground pine ▸ noun 1 a small yellow-flowered Eurasian plant of the mint family, which resembles a pine seedling in appearance and smell. ● *Ajuga chamaepitys*, family Labiatae.
2 a North American clubmoss with small shiny leaves, resembling a miniature conifer and growing typically in coniferous woodland. ● Genus *Lycopodium*, family Lycopodiaceae: several species, in particular *L. obscurum* and *L. tristachyum*.

ground plan ▸ noun the plan of a building at ground level. ■ the general outline or basis of a scheme.

ground rent ▸ noun [mass noun] Brit. rent paid under the terms of a lease by the owner of a building to the owner of the land on which it is built.

ground rule ▸ noun 1 (usu. **ground rules**) a basic principle: *some ground rules for assessing new machines*.
2 Baseball a rule relating to the limits of play on a particular field.

groundsel /ˈgraʊn(d)s(ə)l/ ▸ noun a widely distributed plant of the daisy family, with yellow rayless flowers. ● Genus *Senecio*, family Compositae: several species,

in particular the **common groundsel** (*S. vulgaris*), which is a common weed.
– ORIGIN Old English *gundæswelgiæ* (later *grundeswylige*), probably from *gund* 'pus' + *swelgan* 'to swallow' (with reference to its use in poultices). The later form may be by association with GROUND¹, and refer to the plant's rapid growth.

groundsheet ▸ noun Brit. a waterproof sheet spread on the ground inside a tent.

groundskeeper ▸ noun North American term for GROUNDSMAN.

ground sloth ▸ noun an extinct terrestrial edentate mammal of the Cenozoic era in America, typically of very large size. ● Order Xenarthra (or Edentata). See MEGATHERIUM, MYLODON.

groundsman ▸ noun (pl. **groundsmen**) Brit. a person who maintains a sports ground, a park, or the grounds of a school or other institution.

ground speed ▸ noun an aircraft's speed relative to the ground. Compare with AIRSPEED.

ground squirrel ▸ noun a burrowing squirrel that is typically highly social, found chiefly in North America and northern Eurasia, where it usually hibernates in winter. Also called GOPHER in North America. ● *Spermophilus* and other genera, family Sciuridae: many species, including the sousliks and chipmunks.

ground state ▸ noun Physics the lowest energy state of an atom or other particle.

groundstroke ▸ noun Tennis a stroke played after the ball has bounced, as opposed to a volley.

groundswell /ˈɡraʊn(d)ˌswɛl/ ▸ noun **1** an increase in a particular opinion among a large section of the population: ***a groundswell of** opposition developed*. **2** a large or extensive swell in the sea.

ground tackle ▸ noun [mass noun] the equipment used to anchor or moor a boat or ship.

groundwater ▸ noun [mass noun] water held underground in the soil or in pores and crevices in rock.

ground wave ▸ noun a radio wave which reaches a receiver from a transmitter directly, without reflection from the ionosphere.

groundwork ▸ noun [mass noun] preliminary or basic work: *the inquiry's findings are expected to **lay the groundwork for** a complete overhaul of the system.*

ground zero ▸ noun **1** the point on the earth's surface directly above or below an exploding nuclear bomb. ■ (**Ground Zero**) the site of the World Trade Center in New York, destroyed by terrorists on 11 September 2001.
2 a starting point or base for an activity: *if you're starting at ground zero in terms of knowledge, go to the library.*

group ▸ noun [treated as sing. or pl.] **1** a number of people or things that are located, gathered, or classed together: *a group of boys approached | the bulbs should be planted in groups.* ■ a number of people that work together or share certain beliefs: *I now belong to my local drama group.* ■ a commercial organization consisting of several companies under common ownership: *the largest newspaper group in the UK.* ■ a number of musicians who play popular music together. ■ Military a division of an air force, usually consisting of two or more stations.
2 Chemistry a set of elements occupying a column in the periodic table and having broadly similar properties arising from their similar electronic structure. ■ a combination of atoms having a recognizable identity in a number of compounds.
3 Mathematics a set of elements, together with an associative binary operation, which contains an inverse for each element and an identity element.
4 Linguistics (in systemic grammar) a level of structure between clause and word, broadly corresponding to phrase in other grammars.
▸ verb [with obj. and adverbial] put in a group or groups: *three chairs were grouped around a table.* ■ put into categories; classify: *molluscs are grouped into seven different classes.* ■ [no obj., with adverbial] form a group or groups: *growers began to group together to form cooperatives.*
– DERIVATIVES **groupage** noun.
– ORIGIN late 17th cent.: from French *groupe*, from Italian *gruppo*, of Germanic origin; related to CROP.

group captain ▸ noun a rank of officer in the RAF, above wing commander and below air commodore.

group dynamics ▸ plural noun [also treated as sing.] Psychology the study or use of the processes involved when people in a group interact.

grouper (chiefly Austral./NZ also **groper**) ▸ noun a large or very large heavy-bodied fish of the sea bass family, with a big head and wide mouth, found in warm seas. ● Family Serranidae: several genera, in particular *Epinephelus* and *Mycteroperca*.
– ORIGIN early 17th cent.: from Portuguese *garoupa*, probably from a local term in South America.

group home ▸ noun a home where a small number of unrelated people in need of care, support, or supervision can live together.

groupie ▸ noun informal a young woman who regularly follows a pop group or other celebrity, especially in the hope of having a sexual relationship with them. ■ [with modifier] often derogatory an enthusiastic or uncritical follower: *he's a political groupie and fantasist.*

grouping ▸ noun a set of associated people acting together, especially within a larger organization: *a grouping of left-wing trade union leaders.* ■ [mass noun] the action of putting people or things in a group or groups: *the grouping of pupils by overall aptitude.*

Group of Eight (abbrev.: **G8**) the eight leading industrial nations (the US, Japan, Germany, France, the UK, Italy, Canada, and Russia), whose heads of government meet regularly.

Group of Seven 1 (abbr.: **G7**) a group of seven leading industrial nations, consisting of the US, Japan, Germany, France, the UK, Italy, and Canada. **2** a group of Canadian landscape painters, officially established in 1920, who formed the first major national movement in Canadian art. Their work exhibited a bold and colourful expressionistic style.

Group of Seventy-Seven (abbr.: **G77**) a grouping of the developing countries of the world established after the first United Nations Conference on Trade and Development in 1964 (originally consisting of 77 members but now with 130 member countries).

Group of Three the three largest industrialized economies (the US, Germany, and Japan).

Group of Twenty (abbr.: **G20**) a group of finance ministers and central bank governors from 19 countries and the European Union who meet to discuss global economic issues.

group practice ▸ noun a medical practice run by several doctors.

groupset ▸ noun the brakes and gears for a bicycle.

group therapy ▸ noun [mass noun] a form of psychotherapy in which patients meet to describe and discuss their problems.

groupthink ▸ noun [mass noun] chiefly N. Amer. the practice of thinking or making decisions as a group, resulting typically in unchallenged, poor-quality decision-making: *there's always a danger of groupthink when two leaders are so alike.*
– ORIGIN late 20th cent.: on the pattern of *doublethink*.

groupuscule /ˈɡruːpəˌskjuːl/ ▸ noun a political or religious splinter group.
– ORIGIN 1960s: from French, diminutive of *groupe* 'group'.

group velocity ▸ noun Physics the speed at which the energy of a wave travels.

groupware ▸ noun [mass noun] Computing software designed to facilitate collective working by a number of different users.

grouse¹ ▸ noun (pl. **same**) a medium to large game bird with a plump body and feathered legs, the male being larger and more brightly coloured than the female. ● Family Tetraonidae (or Phasianidae): several genera, especially *Lagopus* and *Tetrao*.
■ [mass noun] the flesh of the grouse as food.
– ORIGIN early 16th cent.: perhaps related to medieval Latin *gruta* or to Old French *grue* 'crane'.

grouse² ▸ verb [no obj.] complain about something trivial; grumble: *she heard him grousing about his assistant.*
▸ noun a complaint or grumble: *our biggest grouse was about the noise of construction work.*
– DERIVATIVES **grouser** noun.
– ORIGIN early 19th cent.: of unknown origin; compare with GROUCH.

grouse³ ▸ adjective Austral./NZ informal very good (used as a general term of approval): *the car was a grouse tomato red which everyone liked.*
– ORIGIN 1920s: of unknown origin.

grouse moor ▸ noun an area of managed moorland for the shooting of red grouse.

grout /ɡraʊt/ ▸ noun [mass noun] a mortar or paste for filling crevices, especially the gaps between wall or floor tiles.
▸ verb [with obj.] fill in with grout.
– ORIGIN mid 17th cent.: perhaps from GROUTS, or related to French dialect *grouter* 'grout a wall'.

grouter¹ ▸ noun a tool used for grouting tiles.

grouter² ▸ noun Austral. informal a lucky but unfair advantage: *he has managed to **come in on the grouter** with a borrowed pound.*
– ORIGIN early 20th cent.: of unknown origin.

grouts /ɡraʊts/ ▸ plural noun archaic sediment, dregs, or grounds: *old women told fortunes in grouts of tea.*
– ORIGIN Old English *grūt*, of Germanic origin; related to Dutch *gruit* 'dregs', German *Grauss* 'grain, weak beer', also to GRITS and GROATS. The original meaning was 'coarse meal, groats', also denoting the infusion of malt which was fermented to make beer, hence, in Middle English, 'sediment'.

Grove, Sir George (1820–1900), English musicologist. He was the founder and first editor of the multi volume *Dictionary of Music and Musicians* (1879–89) and served as the first director of the Royal College of Music (1883–94).

grove ▸ noun a small wood or other group of trees: *an olive grove* | [in place names] *Ladbroke Grove.*
– PHRASES **the groves of Academe** the academic world. [translating Horace's *silvas Academi*.]
– ORIGIN Old English *grāf*, of Germanic origin.

grovel ▸ verb (**grovels, grovelling, grovelled**; US **grovels, groveling, groveled**) [no obj.] lie or crawl abjectly on the ground with one's face downwards: *he grovelled at George's feet.* ■ act obsequiously in order to obtain forgiveness or favour: *they criticized leaders who grovelled to foreign patrons* | (as adj. **grovelling**) *his grovelling references to 'great' historians.*
– DERIVATIVES **groveller** noun, **grovellingly** adverb.
– ORIGIN Middle English: back-formation from the obsolete adverb *grovelling*, from obsolete *groof, grufe* 'the face or front' (in the phrase *on grufe*, from Old Norse *á grúfu* 'face downwards') + the suffix *-ling*.

grow /ɡrəʊ/ ▸ verb (past **grew** /ɡruː/; past participle **grown** /ɡrəʊn/) [no obj.] **1** (of a living thing) undergo natural development by increasing in size and changing physically: *he would watch Nick grow to manhood* | (as adj. **growing**) *the needs of the growing child* | (as adj. **grown**) *grown men don't act so stupidly.* ■ (of a plant) germinate and develop: *morels grow in a variety of places.* ■ [with obj.] cause (plants) to germinate and develop: *more land was needed to grow crops for export.* ■ [with obj.] allow or cause (a part of the body) to grow or develop: *if a newt's leg is amputated, it will grow a new one* | [with obj. and complement] *she grew her hair long.*
2 come into existence and develop: *the play **grew out of** a drama school project* | *a school of painting **grew up** in Cuzco.* ■ [with infinitive] (of a person) come to feel or think something over time: *supposing we had grown to know and love nuclear power.*
3 become larger or greater over a period of time; increase: *turnover grew to more than $100,000 within three years* | (as adj. **growing**) *the growing concern over ozone levels.* ■ [with obj.] develop or expand (something, especially a business): *entrepreneurs who are struggling to grow their businesses.* ■ [with complement] become gradually or increasingly: *sharing our experiences we grew braver.*
– PHRASES **grow on trees** [usu. with negative] informal be plentiful or easily obtained: *jobs don't grow on trees.*
– PHRASAL VERBS **grow apart** (of two or more people) become gradually estranged. **grow away from** become gradually separated from (one's family, friends, or background): *emotionally his family had grown away from him.* **grow into 1** become as a result of natural development or gradual increase: *Rome began as a city and grew into a huge empire.* **2** become large enough to wear (a garment) comfortably. **grow on** become gradually more appealing to (someone): *the tune grows on you.* **grow out** disappear because of normal growth: *Colette's old perm had almost grown out.* **grow out of** become too large to wear (a garment). ■ become too mature to retain (a childish habit): *most children grow out of tantrums by the time they're three.* **grow up** become an adult: *a young girl who grew up in Texas.* ■ [often in imperative] begin to behave or think sensibly: *grow up, sister, and come into the real world.*
– DERIVATIVES **growable** adjective.
– ORIGIN Old English *grōwan* (originally referring chiefly to plants), of Germanic origin; related to Dutch *groeien*, also to GRASS and GREEN.

growbag (also trademark **Gro-bag**) ▸ noun Brit. a bag containing potting compost for growing plants such as tomatoes in.

grower ▸ noun **1** a person who grows a particular type of crop: *a fruit grower.*

2 [with adj.] a plant that grows in a specified way: *a fast grower*.

growing bag ▸ noun Brit. another term for GROWBAG.

growing pains ▸ plural noun neuralgic pains which occur in the limbs of some young children. ■ the difficulties experienced in the early stages of an enterprise: *the growing pains of a young republic*.

growing point ▸ noun Botany the meristem region at the apex of a plant shoot at which continuous cell division and differentiation occur.

growing season ▸ noun the part of the year during which rainfall and temperature allow plants to grow.

growl ▸ verb [no obj.] (of an animal, especially a dog) make a low guttural sound of hostility in the throat: *the dogs yapped and growled at his heels*. ■ [with direct speech] (of a person) say something in a low harsh voice, typically in a threatening manner: *'Keep out of this,' he growled*. ■ make a low or harsh rumbling sound: *thunder growls without warning from a summer sky*.
▸ noun a growling sound made by a hostile animal. ■ a low, harsh sound or utterance: *with a growl of fury, he tightened his grip*.
– DERIVATIVES **growlingly** adverb, **growly** adjective.
– ORIGIN mid 17th cent.: probably imitative.

G

growler ▸ noun 1 a person or thing that growls.
2 a small iceberg.
3 historical a four-wheeled hansom cab.
4 US informal a pail or other container used for carrying drink, especially draught beer.

growmore ▸ noun [mass noun] Brit. a balanced inorganic fertilizer of a standard kind.

grown past participle of GROW.

grown-up ▸ adjective adult: *Joe has two grown-up children*. ■ suitable for or characteristic of an adult: *it was my first grown-up party*.
▸ noun (especially in children's use) an adult: *I don't like it when grown-ups get all serious*.

growth ▸ noun 1 [mass noun] the process of increasing in size: *the upward growth of plants | the growth of the city affects the local climate*. ■ the process of developing physically, mentally, or spiritually: *keeping a journal can be a vital step in our personal growth*. ■ the process of increasing in amount, value, or importance: *the rates of population growth are lowest in the north*. ■ increase in economic activity or value: *the government aims to get growth back into the economy*.
2 something that has grown or is growing: *a day's growth of unshaven stubble on his chin*. ■ Medicine & Biology a tumour or other abnormal formation.
3 a vineyard or crop of grapes of a specified classification of quality, or a wine from it.

growth factor ▸ noun Biology a substance, such as a vitamin or hormone, which is required for the stimulation of growth in living cells.

growth hormone ▸ noun a hormone which stimulates growth in animal or plant cells, especially (in animals) that secreted by the pituitary gland.

growth industry ▸ noun an industry that is developing particularly rapidly.

growth ring ▸ noun a concentric layer of wood, shell, or bone developed during an annual or other regular period of growth.

growth stock ▸ noun a company stock that tends to increase in capital value rather than yield high income.

groyne (US **groin**) ▸ noun a low wall or sturdy timber barrier built out into the sea from a beach to check erosion and drifting.
– ORIGIN late 16th cent.: from dialect *groin* 'snout', from Old French *groign*, from late Latin *grunium* 'pig's snout', from Latin *grunnire* 'to grunt'.

grozing iron /ˈgrəʊzɪŋ/ ▸ noun chiefly historical a pair of pliers for clipping the edges of pieces of glass. ■ historical a tool for smoothing soldered joints in lead pipes.
– ORIGIN Middle English: *grozing* from Middle Dutch, from the stem of *gruizen* 'crush, trim glass', from *gruis* 'fragments'.

Grozny /ˈgrɒzni/ a city in SW Russia, near the border with Georgia, capital of Chechnya; pop. 226,100 (est. 2008).

GRP ▸ abbreviation glass-reinforced plastic.

grrrl /grrl/ (also **grrl**) ▸ noun a young woman regarded as independent and strong or aggressive, especially in her attitude to men or in her sexuality.
– ORIGIN 1990s: blend of *grrr*, representing the sound of an animal growling (and thus human anger) and GIRL, originally a variant of *girl* in RIOT GIRL.

grt ▸ abbreviation gross registered tonnage, a measure of a ship's size found by dividing the volume of the space enclosed by its hull (measured in cubic feet) by one hundred.

grub ▸ noun 1 the larva of an insect, especially a beetle. ■ a maggot or small caterpillar.
2 [mass noun] informal food: *a popular bar serving excellent pub grub*.
▸ verb (**grubs, grubbing, grubbed**) [no obj., with adverbial]
1 dig or poke about in soil: *the damage done to pastures by badgers **grubbing for** worms*. ■ [with obj.] (**grub something up/out**) remove something from the earth by digging it up: *many miles of hedgerows were grubbed up*.
2 search in a clumsy and unmethodical manner: *I began grubbing about in the waste-paper basket to find the envelope*.
3 work hard, especially at a dull or demeaning task: *she has achieved independence without having to **grub for** it*. ■ [with obj.] achieve or acquire (something) by doing demeaning work: *they were grubbing a living from garbage pails*.
– ORIGIN Middle English: perhaps related to Dutch *grobbelen*, also to GRAVE[1].

grubber ▸ noun 1 [usu. in combination] a person who is determined to acquire or amass something, especially in an unscrupulous manner: *a money-grubber | a vote-grubber*.
2 [usu. in combination] an implement for digging up plants: *a daisy-grubber*.
3 Cricket a ball that is bowled along the ground. ■ (also **grubber kick**) Rugby a forward kick of the ball along the ground.

grubby ▸ adjective (**grubbier, grubbiest**) covered with dirt; grimy: *the grubby face of a young boy*. ■ involving dishonest or disreputable activity; sordid: *the grubby business of selling arms*.
– DERIVATIVES **grubbily** adverb, **grubbiness** noun.

grub screw ▸ noun Brit. a small headless screw, used typically to attach a handle or cam to a spindle.

grubstake N. Amer. informal ▸ noun an amount of material, provisions, or money supplied to an enterprise (originally a prospector for ore) in return for a share in the resulting profits.
▸ verb [with obj.] provide with a grubstake.

Grub Street ▸ noun used in reference to a world or class of impoverished journalists and writers.
– ORIGIN the name of a street (later Milton Street) in Moorgate, London, inhabited by such authors in the 17th cent.

grudge ▸ noun a persistent feeling of ill will or resentment resulting from a past insult or injury: *those who have reason to **bear you a grudge** | Miss Ironside seems to have had some **grudge against** her*.
▸ verb [with obj.] be resentfully unwilling to give or allow (something): *he grudged the work and time that the meeting involved*. ■ [with two objs] [usu. with negative] feel resentful that (someone) has achieved (something): *I don't grudge him his moment of triumph*.
– ORIGIN late Middle English: variant of obsolete *grutch* 'complain, murmur, grumble', from Old French *grouchier*, of unknown origin. Compare with GROUCH.

grudge match ▸ noun a contest or other competitive situation based on personal antipathy between the participants.

grudging ▸ adjective given or allowed only reluctantly or resentfully: *a grudging apology*.
DERIVATIVES **grudgingly** adverb.

gruel ▸ noun [mass noun] a thin liquid food of oatmeal or other meal boiled in milk or water.
– ORIGIN Middle English: from Old French, of Germanic origin.

gruelling (US **grueling**) ▸ adjective extremely tiring and demanding: *a gruelling schedule*.
– DERIVATIVES **gruellingly** adverb.
– ORIGIN mid 19th cent.: from the verb *gruel* 'exhaust, punish', from an old phrase *get one's gruel* 'receive one's punishment'.

gruesome ▸ adjective causing repulsion or horror; grisly: *the most gruesome murder*. ■ informal extremely unpleasant: *gruesome catering*.
– DERIVATIVES **gruesomely** adverb, **gruesomeness** noun.
– ORIGIN late 16th cent.: from Scots *grue* 'to feel horror, shudder' (of Scandinavian origin) + -SOME[1]. Rare before the late 18th cent., the word was popularized by Sir Walter Scott.

gruff ▸ adjective (of a voice) rough and low in pitch: *she spoke with a gruff, masculine voice*. ■ abrupt or taciturn in manner: *Robert's gruff, no-nonsense approach*.
– DERIVATIVES **gruffly** adverb, **gruffness** noun.
– ORIGIN late 15th cent. (in the sense 'coarse-grained'): from Flemish and Dutch *grof* 'coarse, rude', of West Germanic origin.

grumble ▸ verb 1 [reporting verb] complain about something in a bad-tempered way: [with direct speech] *'I'm getting old,' she grumbled* | [no obj.] *the cashier **grumbled about** changing Swiss money* | [with clause] *his father was grumbling that he hadn't heard from him*.
2 [no obj.] make a low rumbling sound: *thunder was grumbling somewhere in the distance*.
3 [no obj.] (usu. as adj. **grumbling**) (of an internal organ) give intermittent discomfort: *a grumbling appendix*.
▸ noun 1 a complaint: *the main grumble is that he spends too much time away*.
2 a low rumbling sound.
– DERIVATIVES **grumbler** noun, **grumblingly** adverb, **grumbly** adjective.
– ORIGIN late 16th cent.: from obsolete *grumme* (probably of Germanic origin and related to Dutch *grommen*) + -LE[4].

grumbling ▸ noun (usu. **grumblings**) a complaint or protest: *there were grumblings from the trustees*.

grump informal ▸ noun a grumpy person. ■ a fit of sulking: *the priest was in such a grump about the contributions to a new altar*.
▸ verb [no obj.] act in a sulky, grumbling manner: *he grumped at me when I moved the papers*.
– ORIGIN early 18th cent.: imitating inarticulate sounds expressing displeasure.

grumpy ▸ adjective (**grumpier, grumpiest**) bad-tempered and sulky.
– DERIVATIVES **grumpily** adverb, **grumpiness** noun.

Grundy ▸ noun see MRS GRUNDY.

Grünewald /ˈgruːnəˌvald/, German /ˈgryːnəvalt/, Mathias (*c*.1460–1528), German painter; born *Mathis Nithardt*; also called **Mathis Gothardt**. His most famous work is the nine-panel *Isenheim Altar* (completed 1516).

grunge ▸ noun [mass noun] 1 informal grime; dirt.
2 (also **grunge rock**) a style of rock music characterized by a raucous guitar sound and lazy vocal delivery. ■ the fashion associated with grunge rock, including loose, layered clothing and ripped jeans.
– DERIVATIVES **grunginess** noun, **grungy** adjective (**grungier, grungiest**).
– ORIGIN 1960s: back-formation from *grungy*, perhaps suggested by GRUBBY and DINGY.

grunion /ˈgrʌnjən/ ▸ noun a small, slender Californian fish that swarms on to beaches at night to spawn. The eggs are buried in the sand and the young fish are swept out to sea on the following spring tide. ● *Leuresthes tenuis*, family Atherinidae.
– ORIGIN early 20th cent.: probably from Spanish *gruñón* 'grunter'.

grunt ▸ verb [no obj.] (of an animal, especially a pig) make a low, short guttural sound. ■ (of a person) make a low inarticulate sound, typically to express effort or indicate assent: *the men cursed and grunted as they lassoed the steer* | [with direct speech] *'What is it?' he grunted irritably*.
▸ noun 1 a low, short guttural sound made by an animal or a person.
2 N. Amer. informal a low-ranking soldier or unskilled worker: *he went from grunt to senior executive vice-president in five years*. [alteration of *ground*, from *ground man* (with reference to unskilled railway work before progressing to lineman).]
3 [mass noun] Brit. informal mechanical power, especially in a motor vehicle: *what the big wagon needs is grunt, and the turbo does the business*.
4 an edible shoaling fish of tropical coasts and coral reefs, able to make a loud noise by grinding its teeth and amplifying the sound in the swim bladder.
● Family Pomadasyidae: numerous genera and species.
– ORIGIN Old English *grunnettan*, of Germanic origin and related to German *grunzen*; probably originally imitative.

grunter ▸ noun a fish that makes a grunting noise, especially when caught, in particular: ● a mainly marine fish of warm waters (family Theraponidae: several genera). ● another term for GRUNT (sense 4 of the noun).

gruntled ▸ adjective humorous pleased, satisfied, and contented.
– ORIGIN 1930s: back-formation from DISGRUNTLED.

G

Grus /grʌs/ Astronomy a small southern constellation (the Crane), south of Piscis Austrinus.
– ORIGIN Latin.

Gruyère /ˈgruːjɛː/ ▶ **noun** [mass noun] a firm, tangy cheese.
– ORIGIN named after *Gruyère*, a district in Switzerland, where it was first made.

gryke ▶ **noun** variant spelling of **GRIKE**.

gryphon ▶ **noun** variant spelling of **GRIFFIN**.

grysbok /ˈgrʌɪsbɒk, ˈxreɪs-/ ▶ **noun** a small mainly nocturnal antelope with small vertical horns and a slightly arched back, found in SW Africa. ● Genus *Raphicerus*, family Bovidae: two species.
– ORIGIN late 18th cent.: from Afrikaans, from Dutch *grijs* 'grey' + *bok* 'buck'.

Grytviken /ˈgrɪt,viːk(ə)n/ the chief settlement on the island of South Georgia, in the South Atlantic, a former whaling station.

gs ▶ **abbreviation** historical guineas.

GSM ▶ **abbreviation** Global System (or Standard) for Mobile, a standardized international system for digital mobile telecommunication.

gsm ▶ **abbreviation** grams per square metre, a measure of weight for paper: *100 gsm paper*.

GSOH ▶ **abbreviation** good sense of humour (used in personal advertisements).

G spot ▶ **noun** a sensitive area of the anterior wall of the vagina believed by some to be highly erogenous and capable of ejaculation.
– ORIGIN 1944: *G* from *Gräfenberg*, because first described by the gynaecologist Ernst Gräfenberg (1881–1957) and R. L. Dickinson in the *Western Journal of Surgery*.

GSR ▶ **abbreviation** galvanic skin response.

GST ▶ **abbreviation** (in Australia, New Zealand, and Canada) Goods and Services Tax, a broadly applied value added tax.

Gstaad /gəˈʃtɑːt/, German /kʃtaːt/ a winter-sports resort in western Switzerland.

G-string (also **gee-string**) ▶ **noun** a garment consisting of a narrow strip of cloth attached to a waistband that covers only the genital area, worn as underwear or by striptease performers.

G-suit ▶ **noun** a garment with pressurized pouches that are inflatable with air or fluid, worn by fighter pilots and astronauts to enable them to withstand high gravitational forces.
– ORIGIN 1940s: from *g* (symbol of *gravity*) + **SUIT**.

GT ▶ **adjective** denoting a high-performance car.
▶ **noun** a high-performance car.
– ORIGIN 1960s: abbreviation of Italian **GRAN TURISMO**.

Gt ▶ **abbreviation** Great: *Gt Britain*.

GTi ▶ **adjective** denoting a high-performance car with a fuel-injected engine.
▶ **noun** a high-performance car with a fuel-injected engine.
– ORIGIN late 20th cent.: from **GT** + *i* for *injection*.

G2B ▶ **abbreviation** government-to-business, referring to the conducting of transactions between government bodies and business via the Internet.

guacamole /,gwɑːkəˈməʊleɪ, -lɪ/ ▶ **noun** [mass noun] a dish of mashed avocado mixed with chopped onion, tomatoes, chilli peppers, and seasoning.
– ORIGIN Latin American Spanish, from Nahuatl *ahuacamolli*, from *ahuacatl* 'avocado' + *molli* 'sauce'.

guacharo /ˈgwɑːtʃərəʊ/ ▶ **noun** (pl. **guacharos**) North American term for **OILBIRD**.
– ORIGIN early 19th cent.: from Spanish *guáchero*, of South American origin.

Guadalajara /,gwɑːdələˈhɑːrə/ **1** a city in central Spain, to the north-east of Madrid; pop. 81,221 (2008).
2 a city in west central Mexico, capital of the state of Jalisco; pop. 1,600,940 (2005).

Guadalcanal /,gwɑːdəlkəˈnal/ an island in the SW Pacific, the largest of the Solomon Islands (the country); pop. 73,000 (2007). During the Second World War it was the scene of the first major US offensive against the Japanese (August 1942).

Guadalquivir /,gwɑːdəlkɪˈvɪə/, Spanish /gwaðalkiˈβir/ a river of Andalusia in southern Spain. It flows for 657 km (410 miles) through Cordoba and Seville to reach the Atlantic north-west of Cadiz.

Guadeloupe /,gwɑːdəˈluːp/, French /gwadlup/ a group of islands in the Lesser Antilles, forming an overseas department of France; pop. 445,000 (est. 2009); languages, French (official), French Creole; capital, Basse-Terre.
– DERIVATIVES **Guadeloupian** **adjective & noun**.

Guadiana /,gwɑːdɪˈɑːnə/ a river of Spain and Portugal. Rising in a plateau region south-east of Madrid, it flows south-westwards for some 580 km (360 miles), entering the Atlantic at the Gulf of Cadiz. For the last part of its course it forms the border between Spain and Portugal.

guaiac /ˈgwʌɪak/ ▶ **noun** [mass noun] brown resin obtained from guaiacum trees, used as a flavouring and in varnishes.

guaiacol /ˈgwʌɪəkɒl/ ▶ **noun** [mass noun] Chemistry an oily yellow liquid with a penetrating odour, obtained by distilling wood tar or guaiac, used as a flavouring and an expectorant. ● Alternative name: ***o*-methoxyphenol**; chem. formula: $HOC_6H_4OCH_3$.
– ORIGIN mid 19th cent.: from **GUAIACUM** + **-OL**.

guaiacum /ˈgwʌɪəkəm/ ▶ **noun** an evergreen tree of the Caribbean and tropical America, formerly important for its hard, heavy, oily timber but now scarce. Also called **LIGNUM VITAE**. ● *Guaiacum officinale* and *G. sanctum*, family Zygophyllaceae.
■ another term for **GUAIAC**.
– ORIGIN mid 16th cent.: modern Latin, via Spanish from Taino *guayacan*.

Guam /gwɑːm/ the largest and southernmost of the Mariana Islands, administered as an unincorporated territory of the US; pop. 178,400 (est. 2009); languages, English (official), Austronesian languages; capital, Agaña. Guam was ceded to the US by Spain in 1898.
– DERIVATIVES **Guamanian** /gwɑːˈmeɪnɪən/ **adjective & noun**.

guan /gwɑːn/ ▶ **noun** a large pheasant-like tree-dwelling bird of tropical American rainforests. ● Family Cracidae (the **guan family**): several genera, especially *Penelope*. The guan family also includes curassows and chachalacas.
– ORIGIN late 17th cent.: via American Spanish from Miskito *kwamu*.

guanaco /gwəˈnɑːkəʊ/ ▶ **noun** (pl. **guanacos**) a wild Andean mammal similar to the domestic llama, which is probably derived from it. It has a valuable pale brown pelt. ● *Lama guanicoe*, family Camelidae.
– ORIGIN early 17th cent.: via Spanish from Quechua *huanacu*.

Guanajuato /,gwɑːnəˈhwɑːtəʊ/ a state of central Mexico. ■ its capital city; pop. 70,798 (2005). The city developed as a silver-mining centre after a rich vein of silver was discovered there in 1558.

Guanche /ˈgwɑːntʃɪ/ ▶ **noun** (pl. **same** or **Guanches**) a member of an aboriginal people speaking a Berber language who formerly inhabited the Canary Islands.
– ORIGIN Spanish.

Guangdong /gwaŋˈdʊŋ/ (also **Kwangtung**) a province of southern China, on the South China Sea; capital, Guangzhou (Canton).

Guangxi Zhuang /,gwaŋʃiː ˈʒwaŋ/ (also **Kwangsi Chuang**) an autonomous region of southern China, on the Gulf of Tonkin; capital, Nanning.

Guangzhou /gwaŋˈdʒəʊ/ (also **Kwangchow**) a city in southern China, the capital of Guangdong province; pop. 6,172,800 (est. 2006). It is the leading industrial and commercial centre of southern China. Also called **CANTON**.

guanidine /ˈgwɑːnɪdiːn/ ▶ **noun** [mass noun] Chemistry a strongly basic crystalline compound, used in organic synthesis. ● An imide derived from urea; chem. formula: $HNC(NH_2)_2$.
– ORIGIN mid 19th cent.: from **GUANO** + **-IDE** + **-INE**[4].

guanine /ˈgwɑːniːn/ ▶ **noun** [mass noun] Biochemistry a compound that occurs in guano and fish scales, and is one of the four constituent bases of nucleic acids. A purine derivative, it is paired with cytosine in double-stranded DNA. ● Alternative name: **6-oxy-2-aminopurine**; chem. formula: $C_5H_5N_5O$.
– ORIGIN mid 19th cent.: from **GUANO** + **-INE**[4].

guano /ˈgwɑːnəʊ/ ▶ **noun** (pl. **guanos**) [mass noun] the excrement of seabirds, occurring in thick deposits notably on the islands off Peru and Chile, and used as fertilizer. ■ an artificial fertilizer resembling natural guano, especially one made from fish.
– ORIGIN early 17th cent.: from Spanish, or from Latin American Spanish *huano*, from Quechua *huanu* 'dung'.

guanosine /ˈgwɑːnəsiːn/ ▶ **noun** [mass noun] Biochemistry a compound consisting of guanine combined with ribose, present in all living tissue in combined form as nucleotides.
– ORIGIN early 20th cent.: from **GUANINE**, with the insertion of **-OSE**[2].

Guantánamo Bay /gwanˈtanəməʊ/ a bay on the SE coast of Cuba. It is the site of a US naval base established in 1903, where suspected members of al-Qaeda and the Taliban were held from 2002.

guanxi /gwanˈʃiː/ ▶ **noun** [mass noun] (in China) the system of social networks and influential relationships which facilitate business and other dealings.
– ORIGIN Mandarin, literally 'connection'.

guar /gwɑː/ ▶ **noun** a drought-resistant plant of the pea family, which is grown as a vegetable and fodder crop and as a source of guar gum, native to dry regions of Africa and Asia. Also called **CLUSTER BEAN**. ● *Cyamopsis tetragonoloba*, family Leguminosae.
■ (also **guar flour** or **guar gum**) [mass noun] a fine powder obtained by grinding guar seeds, which is used chiefly in the food and paper industries.
– ORIGIN late 19th cent.: from Hindi *guār*.

guarache /gwəˈrɑːtʃɪ/ ▶ **noun** variant spelling of **HUARACHE**.

guarana /gwəˈrɑːnə/ ▶ **noun** **1** [mass noun] a substance prepared from the seeds of a Brazilian shrub, used as a tonic or stimulant.
2 the shrub that yields guarana. ● *Paullinia cupana*, family Sapindaceae.
– ORIGIN mid 19th cent.: from Tupi.

Guarani /,gwɑːrəˈniː/ ▶ **noun** (pl. **same**) **1** a member of an American Indian people of Paraguay and adjacent regions.
2 [mass noun] the language of the Guarani, which has over 3 million speakers. It is one of the main divisions of the Tupi-Guarani language family and is a national language of Paraguay.
3 (**guarani**) (pl. **guaranis**) the basic monetary unit of Paraguay, equal to 100 centimos.
▶ **adjective** relating to the Guarani or their language.
– ORIGIN Spanish.

guarantee ▶ **noun** **1** a formal assurance (typically in writing) that certain conditions will be fulfilled, especially that a product will be repaired or replaced if not of a specified quality: *we offer a 10-year **guarantee against** rusting | the treaty provides a **guarantee of** free trade*. ■ something that ensures a particular outcome: *a degree is no **guarantee of** a fast-track career*.
2 (also **guaranty**) Law an undertaking to answer for the payment or performance of another person's debt or obligation in the event of a default by the person primarily responsible for it. ■ a thing serving as security for such a pledge. ■ less common term for **GUARANTOR**.
▶ **verb** (**guarantees, guaranteeing, guaranteed**)
1 [no obj.] provide a formal assurance, especially that certain conditions will be fulfilled relating to a product, service, or transaction: [with infinitive] *the company guarantees to refund your money*. ■ [with obj.] provide a guarantee for: *the cooker is guaranteed for five years* | (as adj. **guaranteed**) *the guaranteed bonus is not very high*. ■ [with obj.] provide financial security for; underwrite.
2 [with obj.] promise with certainty: *no one can guarantee a profit on stocks and shares*.
– ORIGIN late 17th cent. (in the sense 'guarantor'): perhaps from Spanish *garante*, corresponding to French *garant* (see **WARRANT**), later influenced by French *garantie* 'guaranty'.

guarantee fund ▶ **noun** a sum of money pledged as a contingent indemnity for loss.

guarantor /,gar(ə)nˈtɔː/ ▶ **noun** a person or thing that gives or acts as a guarantee: *the role of the police as guarantors of public order*. ■ Law a person or organization that provides a guaranty.

guaranty /ˈgar(ə)ntɪ/ ▶ **noun** (pl. **guaranties**) variant form of **GUARANTEE** (sense 2 of the noun).

guard ▶ **verb** [with obj.] **1** watch over in order to protect or control: *two men were left to guard the stockade | the gates were guarded by soldiers*. ■ watch over (someone) to prevent them from escaping: *his task was to help guard Japanese prisoners*. ■ Basketball stay close to (an opponent) in order to prevent them getting or passing the ball.
2 protect against damage or harm: *the company fiercely guarded its independence*. ■ [no obj.] (**guard against**) take precautions against: *farmers must guard against sudden changes in the market*.
▶ **noun** **1** a person who keeps watch, especially a soldier or other person assigned to protect a person or to control access to a place: *a security guard* | [as modifier] *soldiers on guard duty*. ■ [treated as sing. or pl.] a body of soldiers serving to protect a place or person: *he's the*

captain of the palace guard. ■ (**Guards**) the household troops of the British army. ■ Irish a member of the Irish police force; a Garda. ■ N. Amer. a prison warder.
2 a device worn or fitted to prevent injury or damage: *a retractable blade guard.*
3 [in sing.] a defensive posture that is adopted in a boxing or martial arts contest or in a fight: *before Seb could raise his guard Boz swung a wild punch.* ■ a state of vigilance or preparedness against adverse circumstances: *he let his guard slip enough to make some unwise comments.*
4 Brit. an official who rides on and is in general charge of a train.
5 American Football each of two players either side of the centre. ■ Basketball each of two players chiefly responsible for marking opposing players.
– PHRASES **guard of honour** a group of soldiers detailed to ceremonially welcome an important visitor. **keep** (or **stand**) **guard** act as a guard. **off guard** unprepared for a surprise or difficulty: *the government was caught off guard by the unexpected announcement.* **on guard** on duty to protect or defend something. ■ (also **on one's guard**) prepared for any contingency: *wine producers are constantly on guard against cheap imitations.* **take guard** Cricket (of a batsman) stand in position ready to receive the ball, especially having asked the umpire to check the position of one's bat with respect to the stumps. **under guard** being guarded.
– ORIGIN late Middle English (in the sense 'care, custody'): from Old French *garde* (noun), *garder* (verb), of West Germanic origin. Compare with **WARD**.

guardant /ˈgɑːd(ə)nt/ ▶ **adjective** [usu. postpositive] Heraldry (especially of an animal) depicted with the body sideways and the face towards the viewer: *three lions passant guardant.*
– ORIGIN late 16th cent.: from French *gardant* 'guarding', from *garder* 'to guard'.

guard cell ▶ **noun** Botany each of a pair of curved cells that surround a stoma, becoming larger or smaller according to the pressure within the cells.

guarded ▶ **adjective** cautious and having possible reservations: *he has given a guarded welcome to the idea.*
– DERIVATIVES **guardedly** adverb, **guardedness** noun.

guardee ▶ **noun** Brit. informal a guardsman, especially one seen as representing smartness or elegance.

guard hair ▶ **noun** [mass noun] long, coarse hair forming an animal's outer fur.

guardhouse ▶ **noun** a building used to accommodate a military guard or to detain military prisoners.

Guardi /ˈgwɑːdi/, Italian /ˈgwardi/, Francesco (1712–93), Italian painter. A pupil of Canaletto, he produced paintings of Venice notable for their free handling of light and atmosphere.

guardian ▶ **noun 1** a person who protects or defends something: *self-appointed guardians of public morality.* ■ a person who is legally responsible for the care of someone who is unable to manage their own affairs, especially a child whose parents have died.
2 the superior of a Franciscan convent.
– DERIVATIVES **guardianship** noun.
– ORIGIN late Middle English: from Old French *garden*, of Germanic origin; compare with **WARD** and **WARDEN**. The ending was altered by association with **-IAN**.

guardian angel ▶ **noun** a spirit that is thought to watch over and protect a person or place.

guard rail ▶ **noun** a rail at the edge of something such as a cliff or the deck of a boat that prevents people from falling off. ■ North American term for **CRASH BARRIER**.

guard ring ▶ **noun** a ring-shaped electrode used to limit the extent of an electric field, especially in a capacitor.

guardroom ▶ **noun** a room in a military base used to accommodate a guard or detain prisoners.

guardsman ▶ **noun** (pl. **guardsmen**) (in the UK) a soldier of a regiment of Guards. ■ (in the US) a member of the National Guard.

guard's van ▶ **noun** Brit. a carriage or wagon occupied by the guard on a train.

Guarneri /gwɑːˈnɛːri/, Giuseppe (1687–1744), Italian violin-maker; known as **del Gesù**. He is the most famous of a family of three generations of violin-makers based in Cremona.

Guatemala /ˌgwɑːtəˈmɑːlə/ a country in Central America, bordering on the Pacific Ocean and with a short coastline on the Caribbean Sea; pop. 13,276,500 (est. 2009); official language, Spanish; capital, Guatemala City.

> A former centre of Mayan civilization, Guatemala was conquered by the Spanish in 1523–4. After independence it formed the core of the short-lived United Provinces of Central America (1828–38) before becoming an independent republic in its own right.

– DERIVATIVES **Guatemalan** adjective & noun.

Guatemala City the capital of Guatemala; pop. 1,090,000 (est. 2009). Situated at an altitude of 1,500 m (4,920 ft) in the central highlands, the city was founded in 1776 to replace the former capital, Antigua Guatemala, which was destroyed by an earthquake in 1773.

guava /ˈgwɑːvə/ ▶ **noun 1** an edible, pale orange tropical fruit with pink juicy flesh and a strong sweet aroma.
2 the small tropical American tree which bears guavas. ● Genus *Psidium*, family Myrtaceae: several species, in particular *P. guajava*.
– ORIGIN mid 16th cent.: from Spanish *guayaba*, probably from Taino.

guayabera /ˌgwʌɪəˈbɛːrə/ ▶ **noun** a lightweight open-necked Cuban or Mexican shirt with two breast pockets and two pockets over the hips, typically having short sleeves and worn untucked.
– ORIGIN 1970s: Cuban Spanish, apparently originally from the name of the *Yayabo* river, influenced by Spanish *guayaba* 'guava'.

Guayaquil /ˌgwɑːjəˈkiːl/ a seaport in Ecuador, the country's principal port and second-largest city; pop. 2,223,200 (est. 2008).

guayule /gwʌɪˈuːli/ ▶ **noun** a silver-leaved Mexican shrub of the daisy family which yields large amounts of latex. ● *Parthenium argentatum*, family Compositae. ■ [mass noun] a rubber substitute made from the guayule.
– ORIGIN early 20th cent.: via Latin American Spanish from Nahuatl *cuauhuli*.

gub (also **gubba** or **gubber** /ˈgʌbə/) ▶ **noun** chiefly derogatory (among Australian Aborigines) a white person.
– ORIGIN 1940s: of uncertain origin.

gubbins ▶ **plural noun** [treated as sing. or pl.] Brit. informal miscellaneous items; paraphernalia: *all the latest films, books, and electronic gubbins.* ■ [treated as sing.] a gadget: *a little gubbins he had made as a boy.*
– ORIGIN mid 16th cent. (in the sense 'fragments'): from obsolete *gobbon* 'piece, slice, gob', from Old French; probably related to **GOBBET**. Current senses date from the early 20th cent.

gubernatorial /ˌg(j)uːbənəˈtɔːrɪəl/ ▶ **adjective** relating to a governor, particularly that of a state in the US: *a gubernatorial election.*
– ORIGIN mid 18th cent.: from Latin *gubernator* 'governor' (from *gubernare* 'steer, govern', from Greek *kubernan* 'to steer') + **-IAL**.

guck ▶ **noun** [mass noun] N. Amer. informal a slimy, dirty, or otherwise unpleasant substance: *he got mud and cow guck all over his white jersey.*
– ORIGIN mid 20th cent.: possibly a blend of **GOO** and **MUCK**.

guddle Scottish ▶ **verb** [no obj.] fish with the hands by groping under the stones or banks of a stream. ■ [with obj.] catch (a fish) in such a way.
– ORIGIN mid 17th cent.: of unknown origin.

gudgeon[1] /ˈgʌdʒ(ə)n/ ▶ **noun 1** a small edible European freshwater fish, often used as bait by anglers. ● *Gobio gobio*, family Cyprinidae.
2 archaic a credulous or easily fooled person.
– ORIGIN late Middle English: from Old French *goujon*, from Latin *gobio(n-)*, from *gobius* 'goby'.

gudgeon[2] /ˈgʌdʒ(ə)n/ ▶ **noun** a pivot or spindle on which a bell or other object swings or rotates. ■ the tubular part of a hinge into which the pin fits to unite the joint. ■ a socket at the stern of a boat, into which a rudder is fitted. ■ a pin holding two blocks of stone together.
– ORIGIN Middle English: from Old French *goujon*, diminutive of *gouge* (see **GOUGE**).

gudgeon pin ▶ **noun** a pin holding a piston rod and a connecting rod together.

Gudrun /ˈgʊdruːn/ (in Norse legend) the Norse equivalent of Kriemhild, wife of Sigurd and later of Atli (Attila the Hun).

guelder rose /ˈgɛldə/ ▶ **noun** a deciduous Eurasian shrub with flattened heads of fragrant creamy-white flowers, followed by clusters of translucent red berries. ● *Viburnum opulus*, family Caprifoliaceae. See also **SNOWBALL TREE**.
– ORIGIN late 16th cent.: from Dutch *geldersche roos* 'rose of *Gelderland*' (see **GELDERLAND**).

Guelph /gwɛlf/ ▶ **noun 1** a member of one of two great factions in Italian medieval politics, traditionally supporting the Pope against the Holy Roman emperor. Compare with **GHIBELLINE**.
2 a member of a princely family of Swabian origin from which the British royal house is descended through George I.
– DERIVATIVES **Guelphic** adjective.
– ORIGIN from Italian *Guelfo*, from Middle High German *Welf*, the name of the founder of one of the two great rival dynasties in the Holy Roman Empire.

guenon /gəˈnɒn/ ▶ **noun** an African monkey found mainly in forests, with a long tail and typically a brightly coloured coat. The male is much larger than the female. ● Genus *Cercopithecus*, family Cercopithecidae: several species, including the vervet, mona, and Diana monkeys.
– ORIGIN mid 19th cent.: from French, of unknown origin.

guerdon /ˈgəːd(ə)n/ chiefly archaic ▶ **noun** a reward or recompense.
▶ **verb** [with obj.] give a reward to (someone).
– ORIGIN late Middle English: from Old French, from medieval Latin *widerdonum*, alteration (by association with Latin *donum* 'gift') of a West Germanic compound represented by Old High German *widarlōn* 'repayment'.

Guericke /ˈgɛːrɪkə/, Otto von (1602–86), German engineer and physicist. He was the first to investigate the properties of a vacuum, and he devised the Magdeburg hemispheres to demonstrate atmospheric pressure.

Guernica /gəːˈniːkə, ˈgəːnɪkə/ a town in the Basque Provinces of northern Spain, to the east of Bilbao; pop. 16,255 (2008). Formerly the seat of a Basque parliament, it was bombed in 1937, during the Spanish Civil War, by German planes in support of Franco, an event depicted in a famous painting by Picasso. Full name **Guernica y Luno** /iː ˈluːnəʊ/.

Guernsey[1] /ˈgəːnzi/ an island in the English Channel, to the north-west of Jersey; pop. 62,650 (2001); capital, St Peter Port. It is the second-largest of the Channel Islands.

Guernsey[2] /ˈgəːnzi/ ▶ **noun** (pl. **Guernseys**) **1** an animal of a breed of dairy cattle from Guernsey, noted for producing rich, creamy milk.
2 (**guernsey**) a thick sweater made with oiled navy-blue wool and originally worn by fishermen. ■ Austral. a football jumper, especially one of the sleeveless kind worn by Australian Rules players.
– PHRASES **get** (or **be given**) **a guernsey** Austral. informal be selected for a football team. ■ gain recognition or approval.

Guernsey lily ▶ **noun** a nerine with large heads of pink lily-like flowers. Native to South Africa, but widely cultivated, it was first described in Guernsey. ● *Nerine sarniensis*, family Liliaceae (or Amaryllidaceae).

Guerrero /gɛˈrɛːrəʊ/ a state of SW central Mexico, on the Pacific coast; capital, Chilpancingo.

guerrilla /gəˈrɪlə/ (also **guerilla**) ▶ **noun** a member of a small independent group taking part in irregular fighting, typically against larger regular forces: *this town fell to the guerrillas* | [as modifier] *guerrilla warfare.* ■ [as modifier] referring to actions or activities performed in an impromptu way, often without authorization: *guerrilla gigs.*
– ORIGIN early 19th cent. (introduced during the Peninsular War): from Spanish, diminutive of *guerra* 'war'.

> **WORD TRENDS** A new kind of **guerrilla** action is emerging. Like the soldiers of the same name, its proponents are pitted against authority, using ambush and surprise as their primary weapons. Their interests, however, are far from violent: gardening, music, and film-making, to be exact. **Guerrilla** is now used to refer to activities performed in an impromptu way, often without permission. **Guerrilla gardening** involves activists planting seeds on abandoned or public land, usually in secret. Then there are the independent film-makers on low budgets, who shoot their scenes quickly in real locations. Or how about **guerrilla rockers**, who perform unexpectedly in unlikely places: *their live shows have become legendary, including guerrilla gigs on a tube train and in the BBC's foyer.*

guess ▶ **verb** [with obj.] estimate or conclude (something) without sufficient information to be sure

of being correct: *she guessed the child's age at 14 or 15* | [with clause] *he took her aside and I guessed that he was offering her a job* | [no obj.] *we can only guess at Alan's motives.* ▪ form a correct conclusion about (something) by guessing: [with clause] *she's guessed where we're going.* ▪ (**I guess**) informal used to indicate that although one thinks or supposes something, it is without any great conviction or strength of feeling: [with clause] *I guess I'd better tell you everything.*
▸ **noun** an estimate or conclusion formed by guessing: *my guess is that within a year we will have a referendum.*
– PHRASES **anybody's** (or **anyone's**) **guess** very difficult or impossible to determine: *how well the system will work is anybody's guess.* **keep someone guessing** informal leave someone uncertain or in doubt as to one's intentions or plans.
– DERIVATIVES **guessable** adjective, **guesser** noun.
– ORIGIN Middle English: origin uncertain; perhaps from Dutch *gissen*, and probably related to **GET**.

guesstimate (also **guestimate**) informal ▸ **noun** /ˈgɛstɪmət/ an estimate based on a mixture of guesswork and calculation.
▸ **verb** /ˈgɛstɪmeɪt/ [with obj.] form such an estimate of.
– ORIGIN 1930s: blend of **GUESS** and **ESTIMATE**.

guesswork ▸ **noun** [mass noun] the process or results of guessing.

guest ▸ **noun 1** a person who is invited to visit someone's home or attend a particular social occasion: *I have two guests coming to dinner tonight* | [as modifier] *the guest list.* ▪ a person invited to participate in an official event: *he was in Warsaw as a guest of the Polish government* | [as modifier] *a guest speaker.* ▪ a person invited to take part in a radio or television programme or other entertainment: *a regular guest on the morning show.*
2 a person staying at a hotel or guest house: *a reduction for guests staying seven nights or more.* ▪ chiefly US a customer at a restaurant.
3 Entomology a small invertebrate that lives unharmed within an ants' nest.
▸ **verb** [no obj.] informal appear as a temporary or visiting performer or participant in a television or radio programme or other entertainment: *he guested on the show two weeks ago.*
– PHRASES **be my guest** informal please do: *May I choose the restaurant? Be my guest!* **guest of honour** the most important guest at an occasion.
– ORIGIN Middle English: from Old Norse *gestr*, of Germanic origin; related to Dutch *gast* and German *Gast*, from an Indo-European root shared by Latin *hostis* 'enemy' (originally 'stranger').

guest beer ▸ **noun** Brit. (in a tied pub) a beer offered in addition to those produced by the parent brewery. ▪ (in a free house) a beer available only temporarily.

guestbook ▸ **noun** Computing a facility on a website on which visitors to the site may record their comments.

guest house ▸ **noun** a private house offering accommodation to paying guests.

guestimate ▸ **noun & verb** variant spelling of **GUESSTIMATE**.

guest list ▸ **noun** a list of the people invited to a particular event. ▪ a list of people who are to be admitted to a concert or similar event without payment.

guest rope ▸ **noun** a second rope fastened to a boat in tow to keep it steady. ▪ a rope slung outside a ship to give a hold for boats coming alongside.
– ORIGIN early 17th cent.: of unknown origin.

guest worker ▸ **noun** English term for **GASTARBEITER**.
– ORIGIN 1960s: translation of the German.

gueuze /gəːz/ ▸ **noun** [mass noun] a type of sour, strong, sparkling Belgian beer made by blending new and aged Lambic beers before a secondary fermentation.
– ORIGIN Flemish: origin uncertain.

Guevara /gəˈvɑːrə/, Spanish /geˈβara/, Che /tʃeɪ/ (1928–67), Argentinian revolutionary and guerrilla leader; full name *Ernesto Guevara de la Serna.* He played a significant part in the Cuban revolution (1956–9) and became a government minister under Castro. He was captured and executed by the Bolivian army while training guerrillas for a planned uprising in Bolivia.

guff ▸ **noun 1** [mass noun] informal foolish talk or ideas.
2 Scottish an unpleasant smell.
– ORIGIN early 19th cent. (in the sense 'puff, whiff of a bad smell'): imitative.

guffaw /gəˈfɔː/ ▸ **noun** a loud and hearty laugh.
▸ **verb** [no obj.] laugh loudly and heartily: *both men guffawed at the remark.*
– ORIGIN early 18th cent. (originally Scots): imitative.

Guggenheim /ˈgʊgənhʌɪm/, Meyer (1828–1905), Swiss-born American industrialist. With his seven sons he established companies involved in mining and metal processing. His son **Solomon** (1861–1949) set up several foundations providing support for the arts, including the Guggenheim Museum in New York.

GUI ▸ **abbreviation** Computing graphical user interface.

Guiana /gɪˈɑːnə, gʌɪˈanə/ a region in northern South America, bounded by the Orinoco, Negro, and Amazon Rivers and the Atlantic Ocean. It now comprises Guyana, Suriname, French Guiana, and the Guiana Highlands.

Guiana Highlands a mountainous plateau region of northern South America, lying between the Orinoco and Amazon River basins, largely in SE Venezuela and northern Brazil. Its highest peak is Roraima (2,774 m; 9,094 ft).

guid /gɪd/ ▸ **noun** Scottish form of **GOOD**.

guidance ▸ **noun** [mass noun] **1** advice or information aimed at resolving a problem or difficulty, especially as given by someone in authority: *he looked to his father for inspiration and guidance.*
2 the directing of the motion or position of something, especially an aircraft, spacecraft, or missile: [as modifier] *a laser guidance system.*

guide ▸ **noun 1** a person who shows the way to others, especially one employed to show tourists around places of interest: *a tour guide.* ▪ a professional mountain climber in charge of a group.
2 a person who advises others, especially in matters of behaviour or belief: *his spiritual guide.* ▪ a thing that helps someone to form an opinion or make a decision or calculation: *your resting pulse rate is a rough guide to your general physical condition.* ▪ a book, document, or display providing information on a subject or about a place: *a comprehensive guide to British hotels and restaurants.*
3 a structure or marking which directs the motion or positioning of something: *the guides for the bolt needed straightening.*
4 (**Guide**) a member of the Guide Association.
▸ **verb 1** [with obj. and adverbial of direction] show or indicate the way to (someone): *he guided her to the front row and sat beside her* | figurative *information is available to guide you through the planning and development process.* ▪ [with obj.] direct the motion or positioning of (something): *the groove in the needle guides the thread.*
2 [with obj.] direct or influence the behaviour or development of: *his life was guided by his religious beliefs.*
– DERIVATIVES **guidable** adjective, **guider** noun.
– ORIGIN late Middle English: from Old French *guide* (noun), *guider* (verb), of Germanic origin; related to **WIT**[2].

Guide Association (in the UK) an organization for girls, corresponding to the Scout Association. Formerly (until 1992) called **GIRL GUIDES ASSOCIATION**.

> It was established in 1910 by Lord Baden-Powell with his wife and sister. The three sections into which it is divided, originally Brownies, Guides, and Rangers, are now called Brownie Guides (7–11 years), Guides (10–16 years), and Ranger Guides (14–19 years). Similar organizations exist in many countries worldwide under the aegis of the World Association of Girl Guides and Girl Scouts, formed in 1928.

guidebook ▸ **noun** a book of information about a place, designed for the use of visitors or tourists.

guided ▸ **adjective 1** conducted by a guide: *a guided tour of the castle.*
2 directed by remote control or by internal equipment: *a guided missile.*

guided imagery ▸ **noun** [mass noun] a method of relaxation which concentrates the mind on positive images in an attempt to reduce pain, stress, etc.

guide dog ▸ **noun** a dog that has been trained to lead a blind person.

guideline ▸ **noun** a general rule, principle, or piece of advice: *the organization has issued guidelines for people working with prisoners.*

guide number ▸ **noun** Photography a measure of the power of a flashgun expressed in metres or feet.

guidepost ▸ **noun** archaic term for **SIGNPOST**.

Guider (also **Guide Guider**) ▸ **noun** Brit. an adult leader in the Guide Association.

guide rope ▸ **noun** a rope used to guide the movement of the load of a crane.

guideway ▸ **noun** a groove or track along which something moves.

guidon /ˈgʌɪd(ə)n/ ▸ **noun** a pennant that narrows to a point or fork at the free end, especially one used as the standard of a light cavalry regiment.
– ORIGIN mid 16th cent.: from French, from Italian *guidone*, from *guida* 'a guide'.

Guienne variant spelling of **GUYENNE**.

Guignol /giːˈnjɒl/, French /giɲɔl/ the bloodthirsty chief character in a French puppet show of the same name which is similar to Punch and Judy. See also **GRAND GUIGNOL**.

guild (also **gild**) ▸ **noun** a medieval association of craftsmen or merchants, often having considerable power. ▪ an association of people for mutual aid or the pursuit of a common goal. ▪ Ecology a group of species that have similar requirements and play a similar role within a community.
– DERIVATIVES **guildsman** noun (pl. **guildsmen**).
– ORIGIN late Old English: probably from Middle Low German and Middle Dutch *gilde*, of Germanic origin; related to **YIELD**.

guilder /ˈgɪldə/ ▸ **noun** (pl. **same** or **guilders**) (until the introduction of the euro in 2002) the basic monetary unit of the Netherlands, equal to 100 cents. ▪ historical a gold or silver coin formerly used in the Netherlands, Germany, and Austria.
– ORIGIN alteration of Dutch *gulden* (see **GULDEN**).

Guildford /ˈgɪlfəd/ a town in Surrey, southern England; pop. 68,600 (est. 2009).

guildhall ▸ **noun** a building used as the meeting place of a guild or corporation. ▪ Brit. a town hall. ▪ (**Guildhall**) the hall of the Corporation of the City of London, used for ceremonial occasions.

guile /gʌɪl/ ▸ **noun** [mass noun] sly or cunning intelligence: *he used all his guile and guts to free himself from the muddle he was in.*
– DERIVATIVES **guileful** adjective, **guilefully** adverb.
– ORIGIN Middle English: from Old French, probably from Old Norse; compare with **WILE**.

guileless ▸ **adjective** devoid of guile; innocent and without deception: *his face, once so open and guileless.*
– DERIVATIVES **guilelessly** adverb, **guilelessness** noun.

Guilin /gweɪˈlɪn/ (also **Kweilin**) a city in southern China, on the Li River, in the autonomous region of Guangxi Zhuang; pop. 573,800 (est. 2006).

Guillain–Barré syndrome /ˌgiјãˈbareɪ/ ▸ **noun** [mass noun] Medicine an acute disorder of the peripheral nerves, often preceded by a respiratory infection, causing weakness and often paralysis of the limbs.
– ORIGIN 1916: named after Georges *Guillain* (1876–1961) and Jean *Barré* (1880–1967), two of those who first described the syndrome.

guillemet /ˈgiːmeɪ/, French /gijmɛ/ ▸ **noun** each of a pair of punctuation marks (« ») used as quotation marks in French and other European languages.
– ORIGIN French, of uncertain origin; probably derived from the male forename *Guillaume* or the surname *Guillemet*.

guillemot /ˈgɪlɪmɒt/ ▸ **noun** an auk (seabird) with a narrow pointed bill, typically nesting on cliff ledges. ● Family Alcidae, genera *Uria* (white-breasted) and *Cepphus* (black-breasted): five species. Compare with **MURRE**.
– ORIGIN late 17th cent.: from French, diminutive of *Guillaume* 'William'.

guilloche /gɪˈləʊʃ, -ˈlɒʃ/ ▸ **noun** [mass noun] ornamentation resembling braided or interlaced ribbons.
– ORIGIN mid 19th cent.: from French *guillochis*, denoting the ornamentation, or *guilloche*, a carving tool.

guillotine /ˈgɪlətiːn, ˌgɪləˈtiːn/ ▸ **noun** a machine with a heavy blade sliding vertically in grooves, used for beheading people. ▪ a device for cutting that incorporates a descending or sliding blade, used typically for cutting paper, card, or sheet metal. ▪ a surgical instrument with a sliding blade used typically for the removal of the tonsils. ▪ Brit. (in parliament) a procedure used to prevent delay in the discussion of a legislative bill by fixing times at which various parts of it must be voted on.
▸ **verb** [with obj.] execute (someone) by guillotine. ▪ cut (paper, card, etc.) with a guillotine. ▪ Brit. (in parliament) end discussion by applying a guillotine to (a bill or debate).
– ORIGIN late 18th cent.: from French, named after Joseph-Ignace *Guillotin* (1738–1814), the French physician who recommended its use for executions in 1789.

guilt ▸ **noun** [mass noun] the fact of having committed a specified or implied offence or crime: *it is the duty*

G

G

of the prosecution to prove the prisoner's guilt. ■ a feeling of having committed wrong or failed in an obligation: *he remembered with sudden guilt the letter from his mother that he had not yet read.*
▶ **verb** [with obj.] informal short for GUILT-TRIP: *Celeste had been guilted into going by her parents.*
– PHRASES **guilt by association** guilt ascribed to someone not because of any evidence but because of their association with an offender.
– ORIGIN Old English *gylt*, of unknown origin.

guilt complex ▶ **noun** an obsession with the idea of having done wrong.

guilt culture ▶ **noun** Anthropology a culture in which conformity of behaviour is maintained through the individual's internalization of a moral code. Compare with SHAME CULTURE.

guiltless ▶ **adjective** having no guilt; innocent.
– DERIVATIVES **guiltlessly** adverb, **guiltlessness** noun.

guilt trip informal ▶ **noun** an experience of feeling guilty about something, especially when such guilt is self-indulgent or unjustified.
▶ **verb** (**guilt-trip**) [with obj.] make (someone) feel guilty, especially in order to induce them to do something: *a pay increase will not guilt-trip them into improvements.*

guilty ▶ **adjective** (**guiltier**, **guiltiest**) culpable of or responsible for a specified wrongdoing: *he was found guilty of manslaughter | Williams **pleaded guilty to** three separate offences.* ■ justly chargeable with a particular fault or error: *she was guilty of a serious error of judgement.* ■ conscious of, affected by, or revealing a feeling of guilt: *he felt guilty about the way he had treated her | a guilty conscience.* ■ causing a feeling of guilt: *a guilty secret.*
– PHRASES **not guilty** innocent, especially of a formal charge.
– DERIVATIVES **guiltily** adverb, **guiltiness** noun.
– ORIGIN Old English *gyltig* (see GUILT, -Y[1]).

guimp ▶ **noun** variant spelling of GIMP[1] and GUIMPE.

guimpe /gɪmp/ (also **guimp**) ▶ **noun** historical a high-necked blouse or undergarment worn showing beneath a low-necked dress.
– ORIGIN mid 19th cent.: from French; related to German *Wimpel*, Dutch *wimpel* 'pennant, streamer', also to WIMPLE and *gimp* 'nun's neckerchief'.

Guinea /ˈɡɪni/ a country on the west coast of Africa; pop. 10,058,000 (est. 2009); languages, French (official), Fulani, Susu, Malinke, and others; capital, Conakry.

> Part of a feudal Fulani empire from the 16th century, Guinea was colonized by France, becoming part of French West Africa. It became an independent republic in 1958.

– DERIVATIVES **Guinean** adjective & noun.

guinea /ˈɡɪni/ (abbrev.: **gn.**) ▶ **noun** Brit. the sum of £1.05 (21 shillings in pre-decimal currency), now used mainly for determining professional fees and auction prices. ■ historical a former British gold coin that was first minted in 1663 from gold imported from West Africa, with a value that was later fixed at 21 shillings. It was replaced by the sovereign from 1817.
– ORIGIN named after GUINEA in West Africa.

Guinea, Gulf of a large inlet of the Atlantic Ocean bordering on the southern coast of West Africa.

Guinea-Bissau /ˌɡɪnɪbɪˈsaʊ/ a country on the west coast of Africa, between Senegal and Guinea; pop. 1,534,000 (est. 2009); languages, Portuguese (official), West African languages, Creoles; capital, Bissau.

> The area was explored by the Portuguese in the 15th century and was a centre of the slave trade. Formerly called Portuguese Guinea, it became a colony in 1879, and the independent republic of Guinea-Bissau in 1974.

guinea fowl ▶ **noun** (pl. **same**) a large African game bird with slate-coloured, white-spotted plumage and a loud call. It is sometimes domesticated. ● Family Numididae (or Phasianidae): several genera and species, e.g. the **helmeted guinea fowl** (*Numida meleagris*).

guinea pig ▶ **noun** a domesticated tailless South American cavy, originally raised for food. It no longer occurs in the wild and is now typically kept as a pet or for laboratory research. ● *Cavia porcellus*, family Caviidae.
■ a person or thing used as a subject for experiment.

guinea worm ▶ **noun** a very long parasitic nematode worm which lives under the skin of infected humans and other mammals in rural Africa and Asia. ● *Dracunculus medinensis*, class Phasmida.

Guinevere /ˈɡwɪnɪvɪə/ (in Arthurian legend) the wife of King Arthur and mistress of Lancelot.

Guinness /ˈɡɪnɪs/, Sir Alec (1914–2000), English actor. He gave memorable performances in films such as *Bridge on the River Kwai* (1957) and *Star Wars* (1977).

guipure /ɡɪˈpjʊə/ ▶ **noun** [mass noun] a heavy lace consisting of embroidered motifs held together by large connecting stitches.
– ORIGIN mid 19th cent.: from French, from *guiper* 'cover with silk', of Germanic origin.

guiro /ˈɡwɪərəʊ/ ▶ **noun** (pl. **guiros**) a musical instrument with a serrated surface which gives a rasping sound when scraped with a stick, originally made from a gourd and used in Latin American music.
– ORIGIN Spanish, 'gourd'.

guise /ɡʌɪz/ ▶ **noun** an external form, appearance, or manner of presentation, typically concealing the true nature of something: *he visited **in the guise of** an inspector | sums paid **under the guise of** consultancy fees.*
– ORIGIN Middle English: from Old French, of Germanic origin; related to WISE[2].

guiser /ˈɡʌɪzə/ ▶ **noun** archaic a mummer in a folk play performed especially at Christmas or Halloween.
– ORIGIN late 15th cent.: from the archaic verb *guise* 'dress fantastically', from the noun GUISE.

guitar ▶ **noun** a stringed musical instrument, with a fretted fingerboard, typically incurved sides, and six or twelve strings, played by plucking or strumming with the fingers or a plectrum. See also ELECTRIC GUITAR.
– DERIVATIVES **guitarist** noun.
– ORIGIN early 17th cent.: from Spanish *guitarra* (partly via French), from Greek *kithara*, denoting an instrument similar to the lyre.

guitarfish ▶ **noun** (pl. **same** or **guitarfishes**) a fish of shallow warm seas, related to the rays and having a guitar-like body shape. ● Several species in the family Rhinobatidae, including *Rhinobatus rhinobatus*, common in European waters, and the **Chinese guitarfish** (*Platyrhina sinensis*, family Platyrhinidae).

Guiyang /ɡweɪˈjaŋ/ (also **Kweiyang**) an industrial city in southern China, capital of Guizhou province; pop. 1,475,900 (est. 2006).

Guizhou /ɡweɪˈdʒəʊ/ (also **Kweichow**) a province of southern China; capital, Guiyang.

Gujarat /ˌɡʊdʒəˈrɑːt/ (also **Gujerat**) a state in western India, with an extensive coastline on the Arabian Sea; capital, Gandhinagar. Formed in 1960 from the northern and western parts of the former state of Bombay, it is one of the most industrialized parts of the country.

Gujarati /ˌɡuːdʒəˈrɑːti, ˌɡʊ-/ (also **Gujerati**) ▶ **noun** (pl. **Gujaratis**) **1** a native or inhabitant of Gujarat.
2 [mass noun] the Indic language of Gujarat, spoken by about 40 million people.
▶ **adjective** relating to Gujarat, its people, or its language.

Gujranwala /ˌɡʊdʒrənˈwɑːlə/ a city in Pakistan, in Punjab province, north-west of Lahore; pop. 1,526,200 (est. 2009). It was the birthplace of the Sikh ruler Ranjit Singh, and was an important centre of Sikh influence in the early 19th century.

Gujrat /ɡʊdʒˈrɑːt/ a city in Pakistan, in Punjab province, north of Lahore; pop. 328,500 (est. 2009).

gulab jamun /ɡʊˌlɑːb ˈjɑːmʌn/ ▶ **noun** an Indian sweet consisting of a ball of deep-fried paneer boiled in a sugar syrup.
– ORIGIN from Hindi *gulāb* 'rose water' and *jāmun* 'fruit'.

Gulag /ˈɡuːlaɡ/ ▶ **noun** a system of labour camps maintained in the Soviet Union from 1930 to 1955 in which many people died. ■ (**gulag**) a camp in the Gulag system, or any political labour camp.
– ORIGIN Russian, from *G(lavnoe) u(pravlenie ispravitel'no-trudovykh) lag(ereĭ)* 'Chief Administration for Corrective Labour Camps'.

gular /ˈɡjuːlə/ Zoology ▶ **adjective** relating to or situated on the throat of an animal, especially a reptile, fish, or bird.
▶ **noun** a plate or scale on the throat of a reptile or fish.
– ORIGIN early 19th cent.: from Latin *gula* 'throat' + -AR[1].

Gulbarga /ɡʊlˈbɑːɡə/ a city in south central India, in the state of Karnataka; pop. 532,000 (est. 2009). Formerly the seat of the Bahmani kings of the Deccan (1347–c.1424), it is now a centre of the cotton trade.

Gulbenkian /ɡʊlˈbɛŋkɪən/, Calouste Sarkis (1869–1955), Turkish-born British oil magnate and philanthropist, of Armenian descent. He founded the Gulbenkian Foundation, to which he left his large fortune and art collection.

gulch /ɡʌltʃ/ ▶ **noun** N. Amer. a narrow and steep-sided ravine marking the course of a fast stream.
– ORIGIN mid 19th cent.: perhaps from dialect *gulch* 'to swallow'.

gulden /ˈɡʊld(ə)n/ ▶ **noun** (pl. **same** or **guldens**) another term for GUILDER.
– ORIGIN Dutch and German, literally 'golden'.

gules /ɡjuːlz/ ▶ **noun** [mass noun] red, as a heraldic tincture: [postpositive] *sword and long cross gules.*
– ORIGIN Middle English: from Old French *goles* (plural of *gole* 'throat', from Latin *gula*), used to denote pieces of red-dyed fur used as a neck ornament.

gulet /ˈɡuːlɛt/ ▶ **noun** a traditional Turkish wooden sailing boat, now often used for holiday cruises.
– ORIGIN Turkish, via Italian *goletta* from French *goélette*.

gulf ▶ **noun** **1** a deep inlet of the sea almost surrounded by land, with a narrow mouth. ■ (**the Gulf**) informal name for PERSIAN GULF.
2 a deep ravine, chasm, or abyss.
3 a large difference or division between two people or groups, or between viewpoints, concepts, or situations: *the widening gulf between the rich and the poor.*
– ORIGIN late Middle English: from Old French *golfe*, from Italian *golfo*, based on Greek *kolpos* 'bosom, gulf'.

Gulf of Aden, Gulf of Boothia, etc. see ADEN, GULF OF; BOOTHIA, GULF OF, etc.

Gulf States **1** the states bordering on the Persian Gulf (Iran, Iraq, Kuwait, Saudi Arabia, Bahrain, Qatar, the United Arab Emirates, and Oman).
2 the states of the US bordering on the Gulf of Mexico (Florida, Alabama, Mississippi, Louisiana, and Texas).

Gulf Stream a warm ocean current which flows from the Gulf of Mexico parallel with the American coast towards Newfoundland, continuing across the Atlantic Ocean towards NW Europe as the North Atlantic Drift.

Gulf War **1** another name for IRAN–IRAQ WAR.
2 the war of January and February 1991 in which an international coalition of forces assembled in Saudi Arabia under the auspices of the United Nations forced the withdrawal of Saddam Hussein's Iraqi forces from Kuwait, which they had invaded and occupied in August 1990.

Gulf War syndrome ▶ **noun** [mass noun] a medical condition affecting many veterans of the 1991 Gulf War, characterized by fatigue, chronic headaches, and skin and respiratory disorders. Its origin is uncertain, though it has been attributed to exposure to a combination of pesticides, vaccines, and other chemicals.

gulfweed ▶ **noun** another term for SARGASSUM.

gull[1] ▶ **noun** a long-winged web-footed seabird with a raucous call, typically having white plumage with a grey or black mantle. ● Family Laridae: several genera, in particular *Larus*, and numerous species.
– ORIGIN late Middle English: of Celtic origin; related to Welsh *gwylan* and Breton *gwelan*.

gull[2] ▶ **verb** [with obj.] fool or deceive (someone): *he had been **gulled into** believing that the documents were authentic.*
▶ **noun** a person who is fooled or deceived.
– ORIGIN late 16th cent.: of unknown origin.

Gullah /ˈɡʌlə/ ▶ **noun** (pl. **same** or **Gullahs**) **1** a member of a black people living on the coast of South Carolina and nearby islands.
2 [mass noun] the Creole language of the Gullah, having an English base with elements from various West African languages. It has about 125,000 speakers.
▶ **adjective** relating to the Gullah or their language.
– ORIGIN perhaps a shortening of *Angola*, or from *Gola*, the name of an agricultural people of Liberia and Sierra Leone.

gullery ▶ **noun** (pl. **gulleries**) a breeding colony, breeding place, or roost of gulls.

gullet ▶ **noun** the passage by which food passes from the mouth to the stomach; the oesophagus.
– ORIGIN late Middle English: from Old French *goulet*, diminutive of *goule* 'throat', from Latin *gula*.

gulley ▶ **noun** (pl. **gulleys**) variant spelling of GULLY.

gullible ▶ adjective easily persuaded to believe something; credulous: *an attempt to persuade a gullible public to spend their money.*
– DERIVATIVES **gullibility** noun, **gullibly** adverb.
– ORIGIN early 19th cent.: from GULL² + -IBLE.

gull wing ▶ noun [as modifier] (of a door on a car or aircraft) opening upwards: *gull-wing doors.*
– DERIVATIVES **gull-winged** adjective.

gully ▶ noun (pl. **gullies**) **1** (also **gulley**) a ravine formed by the action of water. ■ Austral./NZ a river valley. ■ a deep artificial channel serving as a gutter or drain.
2 Cricket a fielding position on the off side between point and the slips. ■ a fielder at this position.
3 (also **gali**) Indian an alley. [from Hindi *galī*.]
▶ verb (also **gulley**) [with obj.] (usu. as adj. **gullied**) (of water) make gullies or deep channels in (land).
– ORIGIN mid 16th cent. (in the sense 'gullet'): from French *goulet* (see GULLET).

gulp ▶ verb [with obj.] swallow (drink or food) quickly or in large mouthfuls, often audibly: ***he gulped down*** *the last of his coffee.* ■ breathe in (air) deeply and quickly. ■ [no obj.] breathe or swallow with difficulty, typically in response to strong emotion: *she* ***gulped back*** *the tears | Laura gulped nervously.*
▶ noun an act of gulping food or drink: *she finished her drink in one gulp.* ■ a large mouthful of liquid hastily drunk: *I took* ***a gulp of*** *beer.* ■ a large quantity of air breathed in. ■ a swallowing movement of the throat: *the chairman gave an audible gulp.*
– PHRASES **at a gulp** with one gulp: *having emptied his glass at a gulp, Roger pulled out a cigar.*
– DERIVATIVES **gulpy** adjective.
– ORIGIN Middle English: probably from Middle Dutch *gulpen*, of imitative origin.

gulper (also **gulper eel**) ▶ noun a deep-sea eel with very large jaws that open to give an enormous gape and with eyes near the tip of the snout. ● Order Saccopharyngiformes: several families.

GUM ▶ abbreviation genito-urinary medicine.

gum¹ ▶ noun **1** [mass noun] a viscous secretion of some trees and shrubs that hardens on drying but is soluble in water, and from which adhesives and other products are made. Compare with RESIN. ■ glue that is used for sticking paper or other light materials together. ■ a sticky secretion collecting in the corner of the eye.
2 short for CHEWING GUM or BUBBLEGUM.
3 a gum tree, especially a eucalyptus. See also SWEET GUM.
4 North American term for GUMBOOT.
▶ verb (**gums, gumming, gummed**) [with obj.] cover with gum or glue: (as adj. **gummed**) *gummed paper.* ■ [with obj. and adverbial] fasten with gum or glue: *the receipts are gummed into a special book.* ■ (**gum something up**) clog up a mechanism and prevent it from working properly: *open and close the valves to make sure they don't get gummed up.*
– ORIGIN Middle English: from Old French *gomme*, based on Latin *gummi*, from Greek *kommi*, from Egyptian *kemai*.

gum² ▶ noun the firm area of flesh around the roots of the teeth in the upper or lower jaw.
▶ verb (**gums, gumming, gummed**) [with obj.] chew (something) with toothless gums.
– ORIGIN Old English *gōma* 'inside of the mouth or throat', of Germanic origin; related to German *Gaumen* 'roof of the mouth'.

gum³ ▶ noun (in phrase **by gum!**) chiefly N. English an exclamation used for emphasis.
– ORIGIN early 19th cent.: euphemistic alteration of *God*.

gum arabic ▶ noun [mass noun] a gum exuded by some kinds of acacia, used in the food industry and in glue and incense.

gumball ▶ noun N. Amer. a ball of chewing gum, typically with a coloured sugar coating.

gum benzoin (also **gum benjamin**) ▶ noun another term for BENZOIN (sense 1).

gumbo ▶ noun (pl. **gumbos**) [mass noun] **1** N. Amer. okra, especially the gelatinous pods used in cooking. ■ (in Cajun cooking) a spicy chicken or seafood soup thickened typically with okra or rice.
2 (**Gumbo**) a French-based patois spoken by some blacks and Creoles in Louisiana.
3 N. Amer. a fine clayey soil that becomes sticky and impervious when wet.
4 a type of Cajun music consisting of a lively blend of styles and sounds.
– ORIGIN early 19th cent.: from the Angolan word *kingombo* 'okra'.

gumboil ▶ noun a small swelling formed on the gum over an abscess at the root of a tooth.

gumboot ▶ noun (usu. **gumboots**) dated, chiefly Brit. a long rubber boot; a wellington.

gumboot dance ▶ noun (in South Africa) a dance developed and performed by mineworkers, mimicking military marching.

gumdrop ▶ noun a firm, jelly-like translucent sweet made with gelatin or gum arabic.

gumma /ˈɡʌmə/ ▶ noun (pl. **gummas** or **gummata** /-mətə/) Medicine a small soft swelling which is characteristic of the late stages of syphilis and occurs in the connective tissue of the liver, brain, testes, and heart.
– DERIVATIVES **gummatous** adjective.
– ORIGIN early 18th cent.: modern Latin, from Latin *gummi* (see GUM¹).

gummosis /ɡəˈməʊsɪs/ ▶ noun [mass noun] the copious production and exudation of gum by a diseased or damaged tree, especially as a symptom of a disease of fruit trees.

gummy¹ ▶ adjective (**gummier, gummiest**) having a viscous or sticky consistency: *a gummy discharge.* ■ covered with or exuding a viscous substance: *his gummy eyes.*
– DERIVATIVES **gumminess** noun.

gummy² ▶ adjective (**gummier, gummiest**) toothless: *a gummy grin.*
▶ noun (pl. **gummies**) **1** (also **gummy shark**) a small edible shark of Australasian coastal waters, with rounded teeth that it uses to crush hard-shelled prey. ● *Mustelus antarcticus*, family Triakidae.
2 Austral./NZ a sheep that has lost or is losing its teeth.
– DERIVATIVES **gummily** adverb.

gum olibanum ▶ noun another term for FRANKINCENSE.

gum opopanax ▶ noun see OPOPANAX (sense 2).

gumption /ˈɡʌm(p)ʃ(ə)n/ ▶ noun [mass noun] informal shrewd or spirited initiative and resourcefulness: *the president would hire almost any young man who* ***had the gumption to*** *ask for a job.*
– ORIGIN early 18th cent. (originally Scots): of unknown origin.

gum resin ▶ noun [mass noun] a plant secretion consisting of resin mixed with gum.

gum sandarac ▶ noun see SANDARAC.

gumshield ▶ noun a pad or plate held in the mouth by a sports player to protect the teeth and gums.

gumshoe ▶ noun N. Amer. informal a detective.
– ORIGIN early 20th cent.: from *gumshoes* in the sense 'sneakers', suggesting stealth.

gum tragacanth ▶ noun see TRAGACANTH.

gum tree ▶ noun a tree that exudes gum, especially a eucalyptus.
– PHRASES **up a gum tree** Brit. informal in or into a predicament: *offers of devolution will lead ministers straight up a gum tree.*

gum turpentine ▶ noun see TURPENTINE.

gun ▶ noun a weapon incorporating a metal tube from which bullets, shells, or other missiles are propelled by explosive force, typically making a characteristic loud, sharp noise. ■ a device for discharging a particular object or substance in a required direction: *a grease gun.* ■ a starting pistol used in athletics. ■ the firing of a piece of artillery as a salute or signal: *the boom of the one o'clock gun echoed across the river.* ■ chiefly N. Amer. a gunman: *a hired gun.* ■ Brit. a member of a shooting party. ■ (**guns**) Nautical slang, dated used as a nickname for a ship's gunnery officer.
▶ verb (**guns, gunning, gunned**) [with obj.] **1** (**gun someone down**) shoot someone with a gun: *they were gunned down by masked snipers.*
2 informal cause (an engine) to race: *as Neil gunned the engine the boat jumped forward.* ■ [with obj. and adverbial of direction] accelerate (a vehicle): *he gunned the car away from the kerb.*
– PHRASES **be gunning for** be seeking an opportunity to blame or attack (someone): *the Republican candidate was gunning for his rival over campaign payments.* ■ be striving for (something) in a determined way: *he had been gunning for a place in the squad.* **big gun** informal an important or powerful person. **go great guns** informal proceed forcefully, vigorously, or successfully: *the film industry has been going great guns recently.* **jump the gun** informal act before the proper or appropriate time. **stick to one's guns** informal refuse to compromise or change, despite criticism. **top gun** informal the most important or powerful person in a particular sphere. **under the gun** N. Amer. informal under great pressure: *manufacturers are under the gun to offer alternatives.*
– DERIVATIVES **gunless** adjective, **gunned** adjective [in combination] *a heavy-gunned ship.*
– ORIGIN Middle English *gunne, gonne*, perhaps from a pet form of the Scandinavian name *Gunnhildr*, from *gunnr* + *hildr*, both meaning 'war'.

gunboat ▶ noun a small fast ship with guns mounted on it, for use in shallow coastal waters and rivers.

gunboat diplomacy ▶ noun [mass noun] foreign policy that is supported by the use or threat of military force.

gun carriage ▶ noun a wheeled support for a piece of artillery.

guncotton ▶ noun [mass noun] a highly nitrated form of nitrocellulose, used as an explosive.

gun deck ▶ noun a deck on a ship on which guns are placed. ■ historical the lowest such deck on a ship of the line.

gundi /ˈɡʌndi/ ▶ noun (pl. **gundis**) a small gregarious rodent living on rocky outcrops in the deserts of North and East Africa. ● Family Ctenodactylidae: four genera and several species.
– ORIGIN late 18th cent.: from North African Arabic.

gun dog ▶ noun a dog trained to retrieve game for a gamekeeper or the members of a shoot.

gunfight ▶ noun a fight involving an exchange of fire with guns.
– DERIVATIVES **gunfighter** noun.

gunfire ▶ noun [mass noun] the repeated firing of a gun or guns.

gunge Brit. informal ▶ noun [mass noun] an unpleasantly sticky or viscous substance.
▶ verb (**gunges, gungeing, gunged**) [with obj.] (**gunge something up**) clog or obstruct something with gunge.
– DERIVATIVES **gungy** adjective (**gungier, gungiest**).
– ORIGIN 1960s: perhaps suggested by GOO and GUNK.

gung-ho /ɡʌŋˈhəʊ/ ▶ adjective unthinkingly enthusiastic and eager, especially about taking part in fighting or warfare: *the gung-ho tabloids have wrapped themselves in the Union Jack.*
– ORIGIN Second World War: from Chinese *gōnghé*, taken to mean 'work together' and adopted as a slogan by US Marines.

gunite /ˈɡʌnʌɪt/ ▶ noun [mass noun] a mixture of cement, sand, and water applied through a pressure hose, producing a dense hard layer of concrete used in building for lining tunnels and structural repairs.
– ORIGIN early 20th cent.: from GUN + -ITE¹.

gunk ▶ noun [mass noun] informal an unpleasantly sticky or messy substance.
– ORIGIN 1930s (originally US): the proprietary name of a detergent.

gunkhole N. Amer. informal ▶ noun a shallow inlet or cove that is difficult or dangerous to navigate.
▶ verb [no obj., with adverbial of direction] cruise in and out of gunkholes.
– ORIGIN early 20th cent.: of unknown origin.

gunlock ▶ noun a mechanism by which the charge of a gun is exploded.

gunmaker ▶ noun a manufacturer of guns.

gunman ▶ noun (pl. **gunmen**) a man who uses a gun to commit a crime or terrorist act: *a gang of masked gunmen.*

gunmetal ▶ noun [mass noun] a grey corrosion-resistant form of bronze containing zinc. ■ a dull bluish-grey colour.

gun microphone ▶ noun a highly directional microphone with an elongated barrel which can be directed from a distance at a localized sound source.

gun moll ▶ noun informal a gangster's mistress or girlfriend.

Gunn, Thom (1929–2004), English poet, resident in California from 1954 until his death; full name *Thomson William Gunn*. His works, written in a predominantly low-key, laconic, and colloquial style, include *Fighting Terms* (1954), *My Sad Captains* (1961), and *The Passages of Joy* (1982).

gunnel¹ /ˈɡʌn(ə)l/ ▶ noun an elongated laterally compressed fish with a dorsal fin that runs along most of the back and reduced or absent pelvic fins. It occurs in cool inshore waters of the northern hemisphere. ● Family Pholidae: two genera and several species.
– ORIGIN late 17th cent.: of unknown origin.

gunnel² ▶ noun variant spelling of GUNWALE.

gunner ▶ noun **1** a serviceman who operates or specializes in guns, in particular: ■ (in the British army)

an artillery soldier (used especially as an official term for a private). ■ a member of an aircraft crew who operates a gun, especially (formerly) in a gun turret on a bomber. ■ historical a naval warrant officer in charge of a ship's guns, gun crews, and ordnance stores.
2 a person who hunts game with a gun.

gunnera /ˈɡʌn(ə)rə, ɡʌˈnɪərə/ ▸ **noun** a South American plant with extremely large leaves that resemble rhubarb and which is grown as a waterside ornamental. ● Genus *Gunnera*, family Gunneraceae: several species, in particular *G. manicata* and *G. tinctoria*.
– ORIGIN modern Latin, named after Johann E. *Gunnerus* (1718–73), Norwegian botanist.

gunnery ▸ **noun** [mass noun] the design, manufacture, or firing of heavy guns: *a pioneer of naval gunnery*.

gunnery sergeant ▸ **noun** a rank of non-commissioned officer in the US Marines, above staff sergeant and below master sergeant.

gunny /ˈɡʌni/ ▸ **noun** (pl. **gunnies**) [mass noun] chiefly N. Amer. coarse sacking, typically made of jute fibre. ■ [count noun] (also **gunnysack**) a sack made of gunny.
– ORIGIN early 18th cent.: from Marathi *gōnī*, from Sanskrit *goṇī* 'sack'.

gunplay ▸ **noun** [mass noun] chiefly N. Amer. the use of guns: *movies which are full of gunplay and sex*.

gunpoint ▸ **noun** (in phrase **at gunpoint**) while threatening someone or being threatened with a gun: *two robbers **held** a family **at gunpoint** while they searched their house*.

gun port ▸ **noun** see PORT⁴.

gunpowder ▸ **noun** [mass noun] **1** an explosive consisting of a powdered mixture of saltpetre, sulphur, and charcoal, now chiefly used for quarry blasting and in fuses and fireworks.
2 a fine green China tea of granular appearance.

Gunpowder Plot a conspiracy by a small group of Catholic extremists to blow up James I and his Parliament on 5 November 1605.

> The plot is commemorated by the traditional searching of the vaults before the opening of each session of Parliament, and by bonfires and fireworks, with the burning of an effigy of Guy Fawkes, one of the conspirators, annually on 5 November.

gunroom ▸ **noun 1** a room used for storing sporting guns in a house.
2 Brit. dated a set of quarters for midshipmen or other junior officers in a warship.

gunrunner ▸ **noun** a person engaged in the illegal sale or importing of firearms.
– DERIVATIVES **gunrunning** noun.

gunsel /ˈɡʌns(ə)l/ ▸ **noun** US informal a criminal carrying a gun.
– ORIGIN early 20th cent. (denoting a tramp's young companion): from Yiddish *gendzel* 'little goose', influenced in sense by GUN.

gunship ▸ **noun** a heavily armed helicopter.

gunshot ▸ **noun** a shot fired from a gun. ■ [mass noun] archaic the range of a gun: *we bore down and came nearly **within gunshot***.

gun-shy ▸ **adjective** (especially of a hunting dog) alarmed at the firing of a gun. ■ (of a person) nervous and apprehensive: *she's still gun-shy about new relationships*.

gunsight ▸ **noun** a device on a gun that enables it to be aimed accurately.

gunslinger ▸ **noun** informal (especially in the context of the American Wild West) a man who carries and readily uses a gun: *a frontier gunslinger who was quick on the draw*. ■ a forceful and adventurous participant in a particular sphere of activity: *political gunslingers like Rick never apologize*.
– DERIVATIVES **gunslinging** noun & adjective.

gunsmith ▸ **noun** a person who makes, sells, and repairs small firearms.

gunstock ▸ **noun** the wooden stock or support to which the barrel of a gun is attached.

gunter ▸ **noun** Sailing **1** a fore-and-aft sail whose spar is nearly vertical, so that the sail is nearly triangular.
2 (also **gunter rig**) historical a type of rig in which the topmast slides up and down the lower mast on rings.
– ORIGIN late 18th cent.: named after E. *Gunter* (see GUNTER'S CHAIN).

Gunter's chain /ˈɡʌntəz/ ▸ **noun** Surveying a former measuring instrument 66 ft (20.1 m) long, subdivided into 100 links, each of which is a short section of wire connected to the next link by a loop. ■ this length as a unit, equal to $^1/_{10}$ furlong or $^1/_{80}$ mile. Also called CHAIN.
– ORIGIN late 17th cent.: named after Edmund *Gunter* (1581–1626), the English mathematician who devised it.

Gunther /ˈɡʊntə/ (in the Nibelungenlied) the husband of Brunhild and brother of Kriemhild, by whom he was beheaded in revenge for Siegfried's murder.

Guntur /ɡʊnˈtʊə/ a city in eastern India, in Andhra Pradesh; pop. 542,500 (est. 2009).

gunwale /ˈɡʌn(ə)l/ (also **gunnel**) ▸ **noun** (often **gunwales**) the upper edge or planking of the side of a boat or ship.
– PHRASES **to the gunwales** informal so as to be almost overflowing: *the car is stuffed to the gunwales with camera equipment*.
– ORIGIN late Middle English: from GUN + WALE (because it was formerly used to support guns).

gunyah /ˈɡʌnjə/ ▸ **noun** Austral. an Aboriginal bush hut, typically made of sheets of bark and branches.
– ORIGIN from Dharuk *ganya* 'house, hut'.

Günz /ɡʊnts/ ▸ **noun** [usu. as modifier] Geology a Middle Pleistocene glaciation in the Alps, preceding the Mindel and possibly corresponding to the Menapian of northern Europe. ■ the system of deposits laid down at this time.
– ORIGIN early 20th cent.: named after a river near the Alps in southern Germany.

Guomindang /ˌɡwəʊmɪnˈdaŋ/ variant spelling of KUOMINTANG.

guppy /ˈɡʌpi/ ▸ **noun** (pl. **guppies**) a small live-bearing freshwater fish widely kept in aquaria. Native to tropical America, it has been introduced elsewhere to control mosquito larvae. ● *Poecilia reticulata*, family Poeciliidae.
– ORIGIN 1920s: named after R. J. Lechmere *Guppy* (1836–1916), a Trinidadian who sent the first specimen to the British Museum.

Gupta /ˈɡʊptə/ a Hindu dynasty established in AD 320 by Chandragupta I in Bihar. At one stage it ruled most of the north of the Indian subcontinent, but it began to disintegrate towards the end of the 5th century.
– DERIVATIVES **Guptan** adjective.

Gur /ɡəː/ ▸ **noun** [mass noun] a branch of the Niger–Congo family of languages, spoken in parts of West Africa. It includes More and Senufo. Also called VOLTAIC.
▸ **adjective** relating to or denoting the Gur group of languages.

gur /ɡʊə/ ▸ **noun** [mass noun] (in South Asia) a type of unrefined, solid brown sugar made from boiling sugar cane juice until dry.
– ORIGIN from Hindi *guṛ* and Marathi *gūr*, from Sanskrit *guḍa*.

Gurdjieff /ˈɡəːdjɛf/, George (Ivanovich) (1877–1949), Russian spiritual leader and occultist. He founded the Institute for the Harmonious Development of Man in Paris (1922).

gurdwara /ɡʊəˈdwɑːrə, ɡəːˈdwɑːrə/ ▸ **noun** a Sikh place of worship.
– ORIGIN from Punjabi *gurduārā*, from Sanskrit *guru* 'teacher' + *dvāra* 'door'.

gurgle ▸ **verb** [no obj.] make a hollow bubbling sound like that made by water running out of a bottle: *my stomach gurgled* | (as adj. **gurgling**) *a faint gurgling noise*. ■ [with adverbial of direction] (of a liquid) run or flow with a gurgling sound: *the rain gurgled along the gutters*. ■ (of a baby) make a contented sound: *the baby snuggled closer to Julie and gurgled*.
▸ **noun** a gurgling sound: *Catherine gave a gurgle of laughter*.
– ORIGIN late Middle English: imitative, or directly from Dutch *gorgelen*, German *gurgeln*, or medieval Latin *gurgulare*, all from Latin *gurgulio* 'gullet'.

gurgler ▸ **noun** Austral./NZ informal a drain.
– PHRASES **go down the gurgler** be wasted or lost: *before we know it, another $2 million will have gone down the gurgler*.

Gurkha /ˈɡəːkə, ˈɡʊəkə/ ▸ **noun** a member of any of several peoples of Nepal noted for their military prowess. ■ a member of a regiment in the British army established specifically for Nepalese recruits in the mid 19th century.
– ORIGIN name of a locality, from Sanskrit *gorakṣa* 'cowherd' (from *go* 'cow' + *rakṣ-* 'protect'), used as an epithet of their patron deity.

Gurkhali /ɡəːˈkɑːli/ (also **Gorkhali**) ▸ **noun** another term for NEPALI (the language).

Gurmukhi /ˈɡʊəmʊki/ ▸ **noun** [mass noun] the script used by Sikhs for writing Punjabi. ■ the Punjabi language as written in this script.
– ORIGIN Punjabi, from Sanskrit *guru* (see GURU) + *mukha* 'mouth'.

gurn /ɡəːn/ (also **girn**) ▸ **verb** [no obj.] **1** Brit. pull a grotesque face.
2 (usu. **girn**) chiefly Scottish & Irish complain peevishly.
– DERIVATIVES **gurner** noun.
– ORIGIN early 20th cent.: dialect variant of GRIN.

gurnard /ˈɡəːnəd/ ▸ **noun** a bottom-dwelling fish of coastal waters, with a heavily boned head and three finger-like pectoral rays which it uses for searching for food and for walking on the seabed. ● Family Triglidae: several genera and many species, including the common European *Eutrigla gurnardus*.
– ORIGIN Middle English: from Old French *gornart*, from *grondir* 'to grunt', from Latin *grundire, grunnire*.

Gurney /ˈɡəːni/, Ivor (Bertie) (1890–1937), English poet and composer. He fought on the Western Front during the First World War, and wrote the verse collections *Severn and Somme* (1917) and *War's Embers* (1919).

gurney /ˈɡəːni/ ▸ **noun** (pl. **gurneys**) chiefly N. Amer. a wheeled stretcher used for transporting hospital patients.
– ORIGIN late 19th cent.: apparently named after J. T. *Gurney* of Boston, Massachusetts, patentee of a new cab design in 1883.

gurrier /ˈɡʌrɪə/ ▸ **noun** Irish a tough or unruly young man.
– ORIGIN 1950s: perhaps from French *guerrier* 'warrior', or *gur cake*, an Irish English term for a mincemeat-filled pastry slice formerly associated with street urchins.

gurry /ˈɡʌri/ ▸ **noun** [mass noun] chiefly N. Amer. the entrails of fish or whales.
– ORIGIN late 18th cent.: of unknown origin.

guru /ˈɡʊruː/ ▸ **noun 1** a Hindu spiritual teacher. ■ each of the ten first leaders of the Sikh religion.
2 an influential teacher or popular expert: *a management guru*.
– ORIGIN from Hindi and Punjabi, from Sanskrit *guru* 'weighty, grave' (compare with Latin *gravis*), hence 'elder, teacher'.

Guru Granth Sahib the principal sacred scripture of Sikhism. Originally compiled under the direction of Arjan Dev (1563–1606), the fifth Sikh guru, it contains hymns and religious poetry as well as the teachings of the first five gurus. Also called **Adi Granth**, **Granth**, **Granth Sahib**.

gush ▸ **verb** [no obj.] **1** [with adverbial of direction] (of a liquid) flow out of something in a rapid and plentiful stream: *water **gushed out** of the washing machine*. ■ [with obj. and adverbial of direction] discharge (liquid) in this way: *the tanker began to gush oil from its damaged hull*.
2 speak or write effusively or with exaggerated enthusiasm: *everyone came up to me and gushed about how lucky I was*.
▸ **noun 1** a rapid and plentiful stream or burst of something: *a gush of blood*.
2 [mass noun] effusiveness or exaggerated enthusiasm.
– ORIGIN late Middle English: probably imitative.

gusher ▸ **noun 1** an oil well from which oil flows profusely without being pumped.
2 an effusive person.

gushing ▸ **adjective** (of speech or writing) effusive or exaggeratedly enthusiastic: *gushing praise*.
– DERIVATIVES **gushingly** adverb.

gushy ▸ **adjective** (**gushier**, **gushiest**) excessively effusive: *her gushy manner*.
– DERIVATIVES **gushily** adverb, **gushiness** noun.

gusset /ˈɡʌsɪt/ ▸ **noun 1** a piece of material sewn into a garment to strengthen or enlarge a part of it.
2 a bracket strengthening an angle of a structure.
– DERIVATIVES **gusseted** adjective.
– ORIGIN late Middle English: from Old French *gousset*, diminutive of *gousse* 'pod, shell', of unknown origin.

gussy ▸ **verb** (**gussies**, **gussying**, **gussied**) [with obj.] (**gussy someone/thing up**) N. Amer. informal make someone or something more attractive, especially in a showy or gimmicky way: *shopkeepers gussied up their window displays*.
– ORIGIN 1940s: perhaps from *Gussie*, pet form of the given name *Augustus*.

gust ▸ **noun** a sudden strong rush of wind. ■ a sudden burst of something such as rain, sound, or emotion: *gusts of rain and snow flurried through the open door*.

▶ **verb** [no obj.] (of the wind) blow in gusts: *the wind was gusting through the branches of the tree.*
– ORIGIN late 16th cent.: from Old Norse *gustr*, related to *gjósa* 'to gush'.

gustation ▶ **noun** [mass noun] formal the action or faculty of tasting.
– DERIVATIVES **gustative adjective.**
– ORIGIN late 16th cent.: from Latin *gustatio(n-)*, from *gustare* 'to taste', from *gustus* 'taste'.

gustatory /gʌˈsteɪt(ə)ri, ˈgʌstət(ə)ri/ ▶ **adjective** formal concerned with tasting or the sense of taste: *gustatory delights.*

Gustavus Adolphus /gʊˌstɑːvəs əˈdɒlfəs/ (1594–1632), king of Sweden 1611–32. His repeated victories in battle made Sweden a European power, and in 1630 he intervened on the Protestant side in the Thirty Years War. His domestic reforms laid the foundation of the modern state.

gusto ▶ **noun** [mass noun] **1** enjoyment and enthusiasm in doing something: *Hawkins tucked into his breakfast with gusto.* ■ [in sing.] archaic a relish or liking: *he had a particular **gusto for** those sort of performances.*
2 archaic the style in which a work of art is executed.
– ORIGIN early 17th cent.: from Italian, from Latin *gustus* 'taste'.

gusty ▶ **adjective (gustier, gustiest) 1** characterized by or blowing in gusts: *gusty winds.*
2 having or showing gusto: *gusty female vocals.*
– DERIVATIVES **gustily adverb, gustiness noun.**

gut ▶ **noun 1** (also **guts**) the stomach or belly: *the terrible pain in his gut.* ■ Medicine & Biology the lower alimentary canal or a part of this; the intestine: *microbes which naturally live in the human gut.* ■ **(guts)** entrails that have been removed or exposed in violence or by a butcher. ■ informal a fat stomach. ■ **(guts)** the inner parts or essence of something: *the guts of a modern computer.* ■ **(guts)** [with modifier] used to form names attributing negative characteristics to people: *what's the matter with you, misery guts?* | *greedy guts.*
2 [often as modifier] informal used in reference to a feeling or reaction based on an instinctive emotional response rather than considered thought: *I had a gut feeling that something was wrong* | *I could feel it in my guts – he was out there, watching me.*
3 (guts) informal personal courage and determination; toughness of character: *he didn't have the guts to tell the truth.*
4 [mass noun] fibre made from the intestines of animals, used especially for violin or racket strings or for surgical use.
5 a narrow passage or strait.
▶ **verb (guts, gutting, gutted)** [with obj.] remove the intestines and other internal organs from (a fish or other animal) before cooking it. ■ remove or destroy completely the internal parts of (a building or other structure): *the fire gutted most of the factory.*
– PHRASES **bust a gut** informal **1** make a strenuous effort. **2** laugh very heartily: *his facial expressions and ad libs were enough to get audiences to bust a gut.* **—— one's guts out** informal used to indicate that the specified action is done or performed as hard as possible: *I've worked my guts out to get where I am today.* **hate someone's guts** informal feel a strong hatred for someone. **have someone's guts for garters** Brit. humorous punish someone severely: *if you breathe a word to anyone, I'll have your guts for garters.*
– ORIGIN Old English *guttas* (plural), probably related to *gēotan* 'pour'.

gutbucket informal ▶ **noun 1** Brit. a glutton.
2 [as modifier] chiefly N. Amer. (of jazz or blues) raw and spirited in style: *his gutbucket guitar solos.* [early 20th cent.: perhaps from the earlier meaning of a one-stringed plucked instrument, with reference to its construction, or referring to the bucket which caught *gutterings* (streams of liquid) from beer barrels in low-class saloons where such music was played.]

Gutenberg /ˈguːt(ə)nbəːg/, German /ˈguːtnbɛrk/, Johannes (*c.*1400–68), German printer. He was the first in the West to print using movable type and was the first to use a press. By *c.*1455 he had produced what later became known as the Gutenberg Bible.

Gutenberg Bible ▶ **noun** the edition of the Bible (Vulgate version) completed by Johannes Gutenberg in about 1455 in Mainz, Germany. It is the first complete book extant in the West and is also the earliest to be printed from movable type.

gut flora ▶ **plural noun** another term for **INTESTINAL FLORA.**

gutful ▶ **noun** (pl. **gutfuls**) another term for **BELLYFUL.**

Guthrie /ˈgʌθri/, Woody (1912–1967), American folk singer and songwriter; full name *Woodrow Wilson Guthrie*. His radical politics and the rural hardships of the Depression inspired many of his songs.

Guthrie test ▶ **noun** Medicine a routine blood test carried out on babies a few days after birth to detect the condition phenylketonuria.
– ORIGIN named after Robert Guthrie (1916–95), American microbiologist.

Gutiérrez /ˌgʊtɪˈɛːrəz/, Spanish /guˈtjerres, -rreθ/, Gustavo (b.1928), Peruvian theologian. He was an important figure in the emergence of liberation theology in Latin America, outlining its principles in *A Theology of Liberation* (1971).

gutkha /ˈguːtkə/ ▶ **noun** [mass noun] a sweetened mixture of chewing tobacco, betel nut, and palm nut, originating in India as a breath freshener.
– ORIGIN Hindi, 'a shred, small piece'.

gutless ▶ **adjective** informal lacking courage or determination.
– DERIVATIVES **gutlessly adverb, gutlessness noun.**

gut-rot ▶ **noun** [mass noun] Brit. informal **1** another term for **ROTGUT.**
2 a stomach upset.

gutser /ˈgʌtsə/ (also **gutzer**) ▶ **noun** Austral./NZ informal a heavy fall or collision.
– PHRASES **come a gutser** suffer a failure or defeat.
– ORIGIN early 20th cent.: from the noun **GUT.**

gutsy ▶ **adjective (gutsier, gutsiest)** informal **1** having or showing courage, determination, and spirit: *her gutsy 80-year-old grandmother.* ■ (of food or drink) strongly flavoured: *a smooth Bordeaux that is gutsy enough to accompany steak.*
2 greedy.
– DERIVATIVES **gutsily adverb, gutsiness noun.**

gutta-percha /ˌgʌtəˈpəːtʃə/ ▶ **noun** [mass noun] a hard tough thermoplastic substance which is the coagulated latex of certain Malaysian trees. It consists chiefly of a hydrocarbon isomeric with rubber and is now used chiefly in dentistry and for electrical insulation. ● This substance is obtained from trees of the genus *Palaquium*, family Sapotaceae, in particular *P. gutta*.
– ORIGIN mid 19th cent.: from Malay *getah perca*, from *getah* 'gum' + *perca* 'strips of cloth' (which it resembles), altered by association with obsolete *gutta* 'gum', from Latin *gutta* 'a drop'.

guttate /ˈgʌteɪt/ ▶ **adjective** chiefly Biology resembling drops; having drop-like markings.
– ORIGIN early 19th cent.: from Latin *guttatus* 'speckled', from *gutta* 'a drop'.

guttation /gʌˈteɪʃ(ə)n/ ▶ **noun** [mass noun] the secretion of droplets of water from the pores of plants.
– ORIGIN late 19th cent.: from Latin *gutta* 'drop' + **-ATION.**

gutted ▶ **adjective** Brit. informal bitterly disappointed or upset: *I know how gutted the players must feel.*

gutter ▶ **noun 1** a shallow trough fixed beneath the edge of a roof for carrying off rainwater. ■ a channel at the side of a street for carrying off rainwater. ■ **(the gutter)** used to refer to a poor or squalid existence or environment: *men who had fought their way out of the gutter.* ■ technical a groove or channel for flowing liquid. ■ a channel on either side of a lane in a bowling alley.
2 the blank space between facing pages of a book or between adjacent columns of type or stamps in a sheet.
▶ **verb 1** [no obj.] (of a candle or flame) flicker and burn unsteadily.
2 [with obj.] archaic make channels or furrows in (something): *my cheeks are guttered with tears.* ■ [no obj.] **(gutter down)** flow in streams: *the raindrops gutter down her visage.*
– ORIGIN Middle English: from Old French *gotiere*, from Latin *gutta* 'a drop'; the verb dates from late Middle English, originally meaning 'cut grooves in' and later (early 18th cent.) used of a candle which melts rapidly because it has become channelled on one side.

guttered ▶ **adjective** Scottish informal very drunk.

guttering ▶ **noun** [mass noun] chiefly Brit. the gutters of a building. ■ material used to make gutters.

gutter press ▶ **noun (the gutter press)** chiefly Brit. reporters or newspapers engaging in sensational journalism, especially accounts of the private lives of public figures.

guttersnipe ▶ **noun** derogatory a scruffy and badly behaved child who spends most of their time on the street.

guttural /ˈgʌt(ə)r(ə)l/ ▶ **adjective** (of a speech sound) produced in the throat; harsh-sounding. ■ (of a manner of speech) characterized by the use of guttural sounds: *his parents' guttural central European accent.*
▶ **noun** a guttural consonant (e.g. *k*, *g*) or other speech sound.
– DERIVATIVES **gutturally adverb.**
– ORIGIN late 16th cent.: from French, or from medieval Latin *gutturalis*, from Latin *guttur* 'throat'.

gutty[1] ▶ **noun** (pl. **gutties**) Irish & Scottish informal a plimsoll.
– ORIGIN from **GUTTA-PERCHA**, because the soles of the shoes are made of rubber.

gutty[2] ▶ **adjective (guttier, guttiest)** N. Amer. informal gutsy.

gut-wrenching ▶ **adjective** informal extremely unpleasant or upsetting: *the film is a gut-wrenching portrait of domestic violence.*

gutzer ▶ **noun** variant spelling of **GUTSER.**

guv ▶ **noun** Brit. informal (as a form of address) sir: *'Excuse me, guv,' he began.*
– ORIGIN late 19th cent.: abbreviation of **GUV'NOR.**

guv'nor ▶ **noun** Brit. informal a man in a position of authority such as one's employer or father (often used as a term of address): *I had a lecture from the guv'nor* | *can I help you, guv'nor?*
– ORIGIN mid 19th cent.: representing a non-standard or colloquial pronunciation.

Guwahati /gaʊˈhɑːti/ an industrial city in NE India, in Assam, a river port on the Brahmaputra; pop. 997,700 (est. 2009). Formerly called **GAUHATI.**

GUY ▶ **abbreviation** Guyana (international vehicle registration).

guy[1] ▶ **noun 1** informal a man: *he's a nice guy.* ■ **(guys)** people of either sex: *you guys want some coffee?*
2 Brit. a figure representing Guy Fawkes, burnt on a bonfire on Guy Fawkes Night, and often displayed by children begging for money for fireworks.
▶ **verb** [with obj.] make fun of; ridicule: *she never stopped guying him about his weight.*
– ORIGIN early 19th cent. (in sense 2 of the noun): named after *Guy* Fawkes (see **GUNPOWDER PLOT**).

guy[2] ▶ **noun** (also **guy rope**) a rope or line fixed to the ground to secure a tent or other structure.
▶ **verb** [with obj.] secure with a guy or guys.
– ORIGIN late Middle English: probably of Low German origin; related to Dutch *gei* 'brail' and German *Geitaue* 'brails'.

Guyana /gʌɪˈanə/ a country on the NE coast of South America; pop. 752,900 (est. 2009); languages, English (official), English Creole, Hindi; capital, Georgetown. Official name **COOPERATIVE REPUBLIC OF GUYANA.**

> The Spaniards explored the area in 1499, and the Dutch settled there in the 17th century. It was occupied by the British from 1796 and established, with adjacent areas, as the colony of British Guiana in 1831. In 1966 it became an independent Commonwealth state.

– DERIVATIVES **Guyanese** /ˌgʌɪəˈniːz/ **adjective & noun.**
– ORIGIN from an American Indian word meaning 'land of waters'.

Guyenne /giːˈɛn/ (also **Guienne**) a region and former province of southern France, stretching from the Bay of Biscay to the SW edge of the Massif Central.

Guy Fawkes Night ▶ **noun** another term for **BONFIRE NIGHT.**

guyot /ˈgiːəʊ/ ▶ **noun** Geology an undersea mountain with a flat top.
– ORIGIN 1940s: named after Arnold H. *Guyot* (1807–84), Swiss geographer.

guzzle ▶ **verb** [with obj.] eat or drink (something) greedily: *he would guzzle his ale* | figurative *this car guzzles petrol.*
– DERIVATIVES **guzzler noun.**
– ORIGIN late 16th cent.: perhaps from Old French *gosillier* 'chatter, vomit', from *gosier* 'throat', from late Latin *geusiae* 'cheeks'.

Gvozdena Vrata /ˌgvɒzdɛnə ˈvrɑːtə/ Serbian name for **IRON GATE.**

GVW ▶ **abbreviation** US gross vehicle weight.

GW ▶ **abbreviation** gigawatt(s).

Gwalior /ˈgwɑːlɪɔː/ a city in a district of the same name in Madhya Pradesh, central India; pop. 931,800 (est. 2009), noted for its 6th-century fortress.

gweilo /ˈgweɪləʊ/ ▶ **noun** (pl. **gweilos**) SE Asian a foreigner, especially a westerner.
– ORIGIN Cantonese, literally 'ghost man'.

G

Gwent /gwɛnt/ a former county of SE Wales, formed in 1974 from most of Monmouthshire, part of Breconshire, and Newport, and dissolved in 1996.

GWR ▶ abbreviation historical (in the UK) Great Western Railway.

Gwyn, Nell (1650–87), English actress; full name *Eleanor Gwyn*. Originally an orange seller, she became famous as a comedienne at the Theatre Royal, Drury Lane, London. She was a mistress of Charles II.

Gwynedd /ˈgwɪnɛð/ a county of NW Wales, formed in 1974 from Anglesey, Caernarfonshire, part of Denbighshire, and most of Merionethshire and re-formed in 1996 with a smaller area; administrative centre, Caernarfon. ■ a former principality of North Wales. Powerful in the mid 13th century under Llewelyn, it was finally subjugated by the English forces of Edward I in 1282, following Llewelyn's death.

gwyniad /ˈgwɪnɪad/ ▶ noun a powan (fish) of a variety occurring only in Bala Lake in North Wales.
– ORIGIN early 17th cent.: Welsh, from *gwyn* 'white'.

G

Gy ▶ abbreviation Physics gray(s).

gyan /gjɑːn/ ▶ noun [mass noun] Indian knowledge, especially spiritual or religious knowledge.
– ORIGIN from Hindi *jñān*.

Gyandzhe /ˈgʲandʒə/ Russian name for **GÄNCÄ**.

gybe /dʒʌɪb/ (US **jibe**) Sailing ▶ verb [no obj.] change course by swinging the sail across a following wind. ■ [with obj.] swing (a sail or boom) across the wind in such a way. ■ (of a sail or boom) swing or be swung across the wind.
▶ noun an act or instance of gybing.
– ORIGIN late 17th cent.: from obsolete Dutch *gijben*.

gym ▶ noun **1** a gymnasium. ■ a place, typically a private club, providing a range of facilities designed to improve and maintain physical fitness and health.
2 [mass noun] gymnastics: *I can't do gym today*.
– ORIGIN late 19th cent.: abbreviation.

gymkhana /dʒɪmˈkɑːnə/ ▶ noun **1** an equestrian day event comprising races and other competitions on horseback, typically for children.
2 Indian a public place with facilities for sports.
– ORIGIN mid 19th cent.: from Urdu *gendkānah* 'racket court', from Hindi *gem̐d* 'ball' + Persian *kānah* 'house', altered by association with **GYMNASTIC**.

gymnasium /dʒɪmˈneɪzɪəm/ ▶ noun (pl. **gymnasiums** or **gymnasia** /-zɪə/) **1** a room or building equipped for gymnastics, games, and other physical exercise.
2 also /gɪmˈnɑːzɪəm/ a school in Germany, Scandinavia, or central Europe that prepares pupils for university entrance.
– ORIGIN late 16th cent.: via Latin from Greek *gumnasion*, from *gumnazein* 'exercise naked', from *gumnos* 'naked'.

gymnast ▶ noun a person trained or skilled in gymnastics.
– ORIGIN late 16th cent.: from French *gymnaste* or Greek *gumnastēs* 'trainer of athletes', from *gumnazein* 'exercise naked' (see **GYMNASIUM**).

gymnastic ▶ adjective relating to gymnastics: *a gymnastic display*.
– DERIVATIVES **gymnastically** adverb.

gymnastics ▶ plural noun [also treated as sing.] exercises developing or displaying physical agility and coordination. The modern sport of gymnastics typically involves exercises on bars, beam, floor, and vaulting horse. ■ [with adj.] other physical or mental agility of a specified kind: *these vocal gymnastics make the music unforgettable*.

gymno- /ˈdʒɪmnəʊ/ ▶ combining form bare; naked: *gymnosophist* | *gymnosperm*.
– ORIGIN from Greek *gumnos* 'naked'.

gymnogene /ˈdʒɪmnə(ʊ)dʒiːn/ ▶ noun a name used in Africa for the harrier hawk.
– ORIGIN late 19th cent.: from modern Latin *Gymnogenys* (former genus name), literally 'bare-chinned'.

gymnosophist /dʒɪmˈnɒsəfɪst/ ▶ noun a member of an ancient Hindu sect who wore very little clothing and were given to asceticism and contemplation.
– DERIVATIVES **gymnosophy** noun.
– ORIGIN late Middle English: from French *gymnosophiste*, via Latin from Greek *gumnosophistai* (plural), from *gumnos* 'naked' + *sophistēs* 'teacher of philosophy, sophist' (see **SOPHIST**).

gymnosperm /ˈdʒɪmnə(ʊ)spəːm/ ▶ noun Botany a plant of a group that comprises those that have seeds unprotected by an ovary or fruit, including the conifers, cycads, and ginkgo. Compare with **ANGIOSPERM**.
● Subdivision Gymnospermae, division Spermatophyta.
– DERIVATIVES **gymnospermous** /-ˈspəːməs/ adjective.

gymnure /ˈgɪmnjʊə/ ▶ noun another term for **MOONRAT**.
– ORIGIN late 19th cent.: from modern Latin *Gymnura* (former genus name), from Greek *gumnos* 'naked' + *oura* 'tail'.

gymslip ▶ noun Brit. a sleeveless belted tunic reaching from the shoulder to the knee, formerly worn by schoolgirls.

gynaeceum /dʒʌɪˈniːsɪəm, g-/ ▶ noun (pl. **gynaecea**) a part of a building set apart for women in an ancient Greek or Roman house.
– ORIGIN Latin, from Greek *gunaikeion* (see **GYNOECIUM**).

gynaeco- /ˈgʌɪnɪkɒ, gʌɪˈniːkəʊ, dʒ-/ (US **gyneco-**) ▶ combining form relating to women; female: *gynaecocracy* | *gynaecophobia*.
– ORIGIN from Greek *gunē*, *gunaik-* 'woman, female'.

gynaecocracy /ˌgʌɪnɪˈkɒkrəsi, dʒ-/ (US **gynecocracy**) ▶ noun another term for **GYNARCHY**.

gynaecology /ˌgʌɪnɪˈkɒlədʒi, dʒ-/ (US **gynecology**) ▶ noun [mass noun] the branch of physiology and medicine which deals with the functions and diseases specific to women and girls, especially those affecting the reproductive system.
– DERIVATIVES **gynaecologic** adjective, **gynaecological** adjective, **gynaecologically** adverb, **gynaecologist** noun.

gynaecomastia /ˌgʌɪnɪkə(ʊ)ˈmastɪə, gʌɪˈniːkə(ʊ)-, dʒ-/ (US **gynecomastia**) ▶ noun [mass noun] Medicine enlargement of a man's breasts, usually due to hormone imbalance or hormone therapy.

gynandromorph /dʒɪˈnandrəmɔːf, gʌɪ-/ ▶ noun Zoology & Medicine an abnormal individual, especially an insect, having some male and some female characteristics.
– DERIVATIVES **gynandromorphic** adjective, **gynandromorphy** noun.
– ORIGIN late 19th cent.: from Greek *gunandros* 'of doubtful sex' (see **GYNANDROUS**) + *morphē* 'form'.

gynandrous /dʒɪˈnandrəs, gʌɪ-/ ▶ adjective **1** Botany (of a flower) having stamens and pistil united in one column, as in orchids.
2 (of a person or animal) hermaphrodite.
– ORIGIN early 19th cent.: from Greek *gunandros* 'of doubtful sex' (from *gunē* 'woman' + *anēr*, *andr-* 'man, male') + **-OUS**.

gynarchy /ˈgʌɪnɑːki, ˈdʒʌɪ-/ ▶ noun (pl. **gynarchies**) [mass noun] rule by women or a woman.

gyneco- ▶ combining form US spelling of **GYNAECO-**.

gynocentric /ˌgʌɪnə(ʊ)ˈsɛntrɪk, ˌdʒʌɪ-/ ▶ adjective centred on or concerned exclusively with women; taking a female (or specifically a feminist) point of view.

gynoecium /gʌɪˈniːsɪəm, dʒ-/ ▶ noun (pl. **gynoecia** /-sɪə/) Botany the female part of a flower, consisting of one or more carpels.
– ORIGIN mid 19th cent.: modern Latin, from Greek *gunaikeion* 'women's apartments', from *gunē*, *gunaik-* 'woman, female' + *oikos* 'house'.

gynophobia /ˌgʌɪnə(ʊ)ˈfəʊbɪə, ˌdʒʌɪ-/ ▶ noun extreme or irrational fear of women.
– DERIVATIVES **gynophobic** adjective.

-gynous ▶ combining form Botany having female organs or pistils of a specified kind or number: *epigynous*.
– ORIGIN based on modern Latin *-gynus* (from Greek *-gunos*, from *gunē* 'woman') + **-OUS**.

gyp[1] /dʒɪp/ (also **gip**) ▶ noun [mass noun] Brit. informal pain or discomfort: *one of her Achilles tendons had begun giving her gyp*.
– ORIGIN late 19th cent.: perhaps from *gee-up* (see **GEE**[2]).

gyp[2] /dʒɪp/ ▶ noun Brit. a college servant at the Universities of Cambridge and Durham.
– ORIGIN mid 18th cent.: perhaps from obsolete *gippo* 'menial kitchen servant', originally denoting a man's short tunic, from obsolete French *jupeau*.

gyp[3] /dʒɪp/ informal ▶ verb (**gyps**, **gypping**, **gypped**) [with obj.] cheat or swindle (someone): *a young inventor gypped by greedy financiers*.
▶ noun an act of cheating someone; a swindle.
– ORIGIN late 19th cent.: of unknown origin.

gyppo /ˈdʒɪpəʊ/ (also **gippo**) ▶ noun (pl. **gyppos**) informal, offensive a Gypsy.

gyppy tummy ▶ noun variant spelling of **GIPPY TUMMY**.

gypsophila /dʒɪpˈsɒfɪlə/ ▶ noun a plant of the genus *Gypsophila* in the pink family, especially (in gardening) baby's breath.
– ORIGIN modern Latin, from Greek *gupsos* 'chalk, gypsum' + *philos* 'loving'.

gypsum /ˈdʒɪpsəm/ ▶ noun [mass noun] a soft white or grey mineral consisting of hydrated calcium sulphate. It occurs chiefly in sedimentary deposits and is used to make plaster of Paris and fertilizers, and in the building industry.
– DERIVATIVES **gypsiferous** /-ˈsɪf(ə)rəs/ adjective.
– ORIGIN late Middle English: from Latin, from Greek *gupsos*.

gypsum board ▶ noun North American term for **PLASTERBOARD**.

gypsy (also **gipsy**) ▶ noun (pl. **gypsies**) **1** (usu. **Gypsy**) a member of a travelling people with dark skin and hair, traditionally living by itinerant trade and fortune telling. Gypsies speak a language (Romany) that is related to Hindi and are believed to have originated in South Asia.
2 informal a nomadic or free-spirited person: *why should she choose to wander the world with a penniless gypsy like me?*
– DERIVATIVES **gypsyish** adjective.
– ORIGIN mid 16th cent.: originally *gipcyan*, short for **EGYPTIAN** (because Gypsies were popularly supposed to have come from Egypt).

gypsy moth ▶ noun a tussock moth having a brown male and larger white female, the latter being fully winged but flightless. The caterpillar can be a serious pest of orchards and woodland. ● *Lymantria dispar*, family Lymantriidae.

gypsywort (also **gipsywort**) ▶ noun a white-flowered Eurasian plant of the mint family, which grows in damp habitats. ● *Lycopus europaeus*, family Labiatae.
– ORIGIN late 18th cent.: so named because it was reputed to have been used by Gypsies to stain the skin brown.

gyral /ˈdʒʌɪr(ə)l/ ▶ adjective Anatomy relating to a gyrus or gyri.

gyrate /dʒʌɪˈreɪt/ ▶ verb move or cause to move rapidly in a circle or spiral: [with obj.] *the dog yelped frenetically, wildly gyrating her tail*. ■ dance in a wild or suggestive manner: *strippers gyrated to rock music on a low stage*.
– ORIGIN early 19th cent.: earlier (early 17th cent.) as *gyration*, from Latin *gyrat-* 'revolved', from the verb *gyrare*, from Greek *guros* 'a ring'.

gyration /dʒʌɪˈreɪʃ(ə)n/ ▶ noun (usu. **gyrations**) a rapid movement in a circle or spiral; a whirling motion: *the gyrations of the dancers' arms and legs*.

gyratory /dʒʌɪˈreɪt(ə)ri, ˈdʒʌɪrət-/ ▶ adjective denoting or involving circular or spiral motion.
▶ noun (pl. **gyratories**) a road junction or traffic system requiring the circular movement of traffic, larger or more complex than an ordinary roundabout.

gyre /ˈdʒʌɪə, ˈgʌɪə/ ▶ verb [no obj.] literary whirl or gyrate: *a swarm of ghosts gyred around him*.
▶ noun a spiral or vortex. ■ Geography a circular pattern of currents in an ocean basin: *the central North Pacific gyre*.
– ORIGIN late Middle English (in the sense 'whirl someone or something round'): from late Latin *gyrare*, from Latin *gyrus* 'a ring', from Greek *guros*. The noun is from Latin *gyrus*.

gyrfalcon /ˈdʒəːˌfɔː(l)k(ə)n, -ˌfɒlk(ə)n/ ▶ noun the largest falcon, found in arctic regions and occurring in several colour forms, one of which is mainly white.
● *Falco rusticolus*, family Falconidae.
– ORIGIN Middle English: from Old French *gerfaucon*, of Germanic origin. The first element is probably related to Old High German *gēr* 'spear'; the spelling *gyr-* arose from a mistaken idea that the bird's name came from Latin *gyrare* 'revolve'.

gyri plural form of **GYRUS**.

gyro[1] /ˈdʒʌɪrəʊ/ ▶ noun (pl. **gyros**) short for **GYROSCOPE** or **GYROCOMPASS**.

gyro[2] /ˈdʒʌɪrəʊ/ ▶ noun (pl. **gyros**) N. Amer. a sandwich made with slices of spiced meat cooked on a spit, served with salad in pitta bread.
– ORIGIN 1970s: from modern Greek *guros* 'turning'.

gyro- /ˈdʒʌɪrəʊ/ ▶ combining form **1** relating to rotation: *gyromagnetic*.
2 gyroscopic: *gyrostabilizer*.
– ORIGIN from Greek *guros* 'a ring'.

gyrocompass ▶ noun a non-magnetic compass in which the direction of true north is maintained by a continuously driven gyroscope whose axis is parallel to the earth's axis of rotation.

gyrocopter ▶ noun a small, light single-seater autogiro.
– ORIGIN from **GYRO-** 'relating to rotation', on the pattern of *helicopter*.

gyromagnetic ▶ **adjective** **1** Physics relating to the magnetic and mechanical properties of a rotating charged particle.
2 (of a compass) combining a gyroscope and a normal magnetic compass.

gyron /ˈdʒʌɪr(ə)n/ ▶ **noun** Heraldry a triangular ordinary formed by two lines from the edge of the shield meeting at the fess point at 45 degrees.
– ORIGIN late 16th cent.: from Old French *giron* 'gusset'.

gyronny /dʒʌɪˈrɒni/ ▶ **adjective** Heraldry (of a shield) divided into eight gyrons by straight lines all crossing at the fess point.
– ORIGIN late Middle English: from French *gironné*, from *giron* (see **GYRON**).

gyropilot ▶ **noun** a gyrocompass used to provide automatic steering for a ship or aircraft.

gyroplane ▶ **noun** an autogiro or similar aircraft.

gyroscope ▶ **noun** a device consisting of a wheel or disc mounted so that it can spin rapidly about an axis which is itself free to alter in direction. The orientation of the axis is not affected by tilting of the mounting, so gyroscopes can be used to provide stability or maintain a reference direction in navigation systems, automatic pilots, and stabilizers.
– DERIVATIVES **gyroscopic** adjective, **gyroscopically** adverb.
– ORIGIN mid 19th cent.: from French, from Greek *guros* 'a ring' + modern Latin *scopium* (see **-SCOPE**).

gyrostabilizer (also **gyrostabiliser**) ▶ **noun** a gyroscopic device for maintaining the equilibrium of something such as a ship, aircraft, or platform.
– DERIVATIVES **gyrostabilized** adjective.

gyrus /ˈdʒʌɪrəs/ ▶ **noun** (pl. **gyri** /-rʌɪ/) Anatomy a ridge or fold between two clefts on the cerebral surface in the brain.
– ORIGIN mid 19th cent.: from Latin, from Greek *guros* 'a ring'.

GySgt ▶ **abbreviation** Gunnery Sergeant.

gyttja /ˈjɪtʃə/ ▶ **noun** [mass noun] Geology sediment rich in organic matter deposited at the bottom of a eutrophic lake.
– ORIGIN late 19th cent.: Swedish, literally 'mud, ooze'.

Gyumri /ˈgjʊmri/ an industrial city in NW Armenia, close to the border with Turkey; pop. 147,000 (est. 2008). Founded as a fortress in 1837, the city was destroyed by an earthquake in 1926 and again in 1988. It was formerly called Aleksandropol (1840–1924) and Leninakan (1924–91). Russian name **KUMAYRI**.

gyve /dʒʌɪv, gʌɪv/ ▶ **noun** (usu. **gyves**) archaic a fetter or shackle.
– ORIGIN Middle English: of unknown origin.

G

Hh

H¹ (also **h**) ▶ **noun** (pl. **Hs** or **H's**) **1** the eighth letter of the alphabet. ■ denoting the next after G in a set of items, categories, etc. ■ **(h)** Chess denoting the file on the right-hand edge of the board, as viewed from White's side.
2 a shape like that of a capital H.
3 Music (in the German system) the note B natural.

H² ▶ **abbreviation** ■ hard (used in describing grades of pencil lead): *a 2H pencil.* ■ height (in giving the dimensions of an object). ■ Physics henry(s). ■ informal heroin. ■ Hungary (international vehicle registration). ■ Brit. (on signs in the street) hydrant.
▶ **symbol** ■ Chemistry enthalpy. ■ the chemical element hydrogen. ■ Physics magnetic field strength.

h ▶ **abbreviation** ■ (in measuring the height of horses) hand(s). ■ [in combination] (in units of measurement) hecto-: *wine production reached 624,000 hl last year.* ■ Brit. (with reference to sporting fixtures) home. ■ horse. ■ (especially with reference to water) hot: *nine rooms, all with h & c.* ■ hour(s): *breakfast at 0700 h.*
▶ **symbol** ■ Physics Planck's constant. ■ (ħ) Physics Planck's constant divided by 2π.

h & c ▶ **abbreviation** Brit. hot and cold (used in describing the water supply to a hotel bedroom or a room in a house): *all rooms have h & c.*

Ha ▶ **symbol** the chemical element hahnium.

ha¹ (also **hah**) ▶ **exclamation** used to express surprise, suspicion, triumph, etc.: *Ha! That'll teach you!*
– PHRASES **hum and ha** see HUM AND HAW at HUM¹.
– ORIGIN natural utterance: first recorded in Middle English.

ha² ▶ **abbreviation** hectare(s).

haaf /hɑːf, haf/ ▶ **noun** (**the haaf**) (in Orkney and Shetland) the area of sea used for deep-sea fishing.
– ORIGIN late 18th cent.: from Old Norse *haf* 'high sea, ocean'; related to Danish *hav* and Swedish *haf*.

haar /hɑː/ ▶ **noun** a cold sea fog on the east coast of England or Scotland.
– ORIGIN late 17th cent.: perhaps from Old Norse *hárr* 'hoar, hoary'.

Haarlem /ˈhɑːləm/ a city in the Netherlands, near Amsterdam; pop. 147,640 (2008). It is the capital of the province of North Holland and the commercial centre of the Dutch bulb industry.

HAART ▶ **abbreviation** Medicine highly active antiretroviral therapy, a form of drug treatment for HIV infection consisting of a course of at least three antiretroviral drugs.

haat /hɑːt/ ▶ **noun** Indian a market, especially one held on a regular basis in a rural area.
– ORIGIN Hindi.

Hab. ▶ **abbreviation** Habakkuk (in biblical references).

Habakkuk /ˈhabəkək, həˈbak-/ a Hebrew minor prophet, probably of the 7th century BC. ■ a book of the Bible containing his prophecies.

habanera /ˌhabəˈnɛːrə, ˌɑːbə-/ ▶ **noun** a Cuban dance in slow duple time.
– ORIGIN late 19th cent.: Spanish, short for *danza habanera* 'dance of Havana'.

Habanero /ˌabəˈnɛːrəʊ/ ▶ **noun** (pl. **Habaneros**) N. Amer. another term for SCOTCH BONNET.
– ORIGIN Spanish, literally 'of Havana'.

habdabs ▶ **plural noun** variant spelling of ABDABS.

Habdalah /havˈdɑːlə/ (also **Havdalah**) ▶ **noun** a Jewish religious ceremony or formal prayer marking the end of the Sabbath.
– ORIGIN from Hebrew *habdālāh* 'separation, division'.

habeas corpus /ˌheɪbɪəs ˈkɔːpəs/ ▶ **noun** [mass noun] Law a writ requiring a person under arrest to be brought before a judge or into court, especially to secure the person's release unless lawful grounds are shown for their detention. ■ the legal right to apply for such a writ.
– ORIGIN late Middle English: Latin, literally 'you shall have the body (in court)'.

habendum /həˈbɛndəm/ ▶ **noun** Law the part of a deed or conveyance which states the estate or quantity of interest to be granted, e.g. the term of a lease.
– ORIGIN Latin, literally 'that is to be had', gerundive of *habere* 'have'.

haberdasher /ˈhabəˌdaʃə/ ▶ **noun 1** Brit. a dealer in small items used in sewing, such as buttons, zips, and thread.
2 N. Amer. a dealer in men's clothing.
– ORIGIN Middle English: probably based on Anglo-Norman French *hapertas*, perhaps the name of a fabric, of unknown origin. In early use the term denoted a dealer in a variety of household goods, later also specifically a hatter. Current senses date from the early 17th cent.

haberdashery ▶ **noun** (pl. **haberdasheries**) [mass noun]
1 Brit. small items used in sewing, such as buttons, zips, and thread.
2 N. Amer. men's clothing and other items sold by a haberdasher.
3 a shop or a department within a larger store that sells haberdashery.

habergeon /ˈhabədʒ(ə)n, həˈbəːdʒ(ə)n/ ▶ **noun** historical a sleeveless coat of mail or scale armour.
– ORIGIN Middle English: from Old French *haubergeon*, from *hauberc* (see HAUBERK), originally denoting a garment protecting the neck; compare with Dutch *halsberg*.

Habermas /ˈhɑːbəmas/, Jürgen (b.1929), German social philosopher. A leading figure of the Frankfurt School, he developed its cultural reappraisal of Marxism and is especially noted for his work on communication theory.

Haber process /ˈhɑːbə/ (also **Haber–Bosch process**) ▶ **noun** [mass noun] an industrial process for producing ammonia from nitrogen and hydrogen, using an iron catalyst at high temperature and pressure.
– ORIGIN named after Fritz *Haber* (1868–1934) and Carl *Bosch* (1874–1940), German chemists.

habiliment /həˈbɪlɪm(ə)nt/ ▶ **noun** (usu. **habiliments**) archaic clothing.
– ORIGIN late Middle English (in the general sense 'outfit, attire'): from Old French *habillement*, from *habiller* 'fit out', from Latin *habilis* (see ABLE).

habilitate /həˈbɪlɪteɪt/ ▶ **verb** [no obj.] qualify for office, especially as a teacher in a German university.
– DERIVATIVES **habilitation** noun.
– ORIGIN early 17th cent.: from medieval Latin *habilitat-* 'made able', from the verb *habilitare*, from *habilitas* (see ABILITY).

habit ▶ **noun 1** a settled or regular tendency or practice, especially one that is hard to give up: *he has an annoying habit of interrupting me | good eating habits |* [mass noun] *we stayed together out of habit.* ■ informal an addictive practice, especially one of taking drugs: *a cocaine habit.* ■ Psychology an automatic reaction to a specific situation. ■ [mass noun] general shape or mode of growth, especially of a plant or a mineral: *a shrub of spreading habit.*
2 a long, loose garment worn by a member of a religious order. ■ short for RIDING HABIT. ■ [mass noun] archaic clothes.
3 archaic a person's health or constitution.
▶ **verb** (**be habited**) archaic be dressed or clothed: *a boy habited as a serving lad.*
– PHRASES **break** (or informal **kick**) **the habit** stop engaging in a habitual practice.
– ORIGIN Middle English: from Old French *abit*, *habit*, from Latin *habitus* 'condition, appearance', from *habere* 'have, consist of'. The term originally meant 'dress, attire', later coming to denote physical or mental constitution.

habitable ▶ **adjective** suitable or good enough to live in: *the house should be habitable by Christmas.*
– DERIVATIVES **habitability** noun.
– ORIGIN late Middle English: via Old French from Latin *habitabilis*, from *habitare* 'possess, inhabit'.

habitant ▶ **noun 1** /ˈhabɪt(ə)nt/ archaic an inhabitant.
2 /abiːˈtɒ̃/ [often as modifier] an early French settler in Canada (especially Quebec) or Louisiana: *the habitant farmhouses of old Quebec.*
– ORIGIN late Middle English (in sense 1): from Old French, from *habiter*, from Latin *habitare* 'inhabit'.

habitat ▶ **noun** the natural home or environment of an animal, plant, or other organism: *wild chimps in their natural habitat.*
– ORIGIN late 18th cent.: from Latin, literally 'it dwells', from *habitare* (see HABITABLE).

habitation ▶ **noun** [mass noun] the fact of living in a particular place: *signs of human habitation.* ■ [count noun] formal a house or home.
– ORIGIN late Middle English: via Old French from Latin *habitatio(n-)*, from *habitare* 'inhabit'.

habit-forming ▶ **adjective** (of a drug or activity) addictive.

habitual /həˈbɪtʃʊəl, -tjʊəl/ ▶ **adjective** done constantly or as a habit: *his habitual use of heroin | this pattern of behaviour can become habitual.* ■ doing something constantly or regularly: *a habitual late sleeper.* ■ regular; usual: *his habitual dress.*
– DERIVATIVES **habitually** adverb.
– ORIGIN late Middle English (in the sense 'part of one's character'): from medieval Latin *habitualis*, from *habitus* 'condition, appearance' (see HABIT).

habituate ▶ **verb** make or become accustomed or used to something: [with obj.] *bears can become habituated to people very easily.*
– ORIGIN late 15th cent.: from late Latin *habituat-* 'accustomed', from the verb *habituare*, from *habitus* (see HABIT).

habituation ▶ **noun** [mass noun] the action or process of becoming habituated. ■ Psychology the diminishing of an innate response to a frequently repeated stimulus.
– ORIGIN late Middle English (in the sense 'formation of habit'): from French or from Latin *habitatio(n)-*, from late Latin *habituare* (see HABITUATE).

habitude ▶ **noun** rare a habitual tendency or way of behaving.

– ORIGIN late Middle English: via Old French from Latin *habitudo*, from *habere* 'have' (compare with HABIT).

habitué /(h)əˈbɪtjʊeɪ/ ▶ **noun** a resident of or frequent visitor to a particular place: *a habitué of the West End.*
– ORIGIN early 19th cent.: French, literally 'accustomed', past participle of *habituer*.

habitus /ˈhabɪtəs/ ▶ **noun** [mass noun] chiefly Medicine & Psychology general constitution, especially physical build.
– ORIGIN late 19th cent.: from Latin.

haboob /həˈbuːb/ ▶ **noun** a violent and oppressive wind blowing in summer in Sudan and elsewhere, bringing sand from the desert.
– ORIGIN late 19th cent.: from Arabic *habūb* 'blowing furiously'.

Habsburg /ˈhapsbəːg/ (also **Hapsburg**) one of the principal dynasties of central Europe from medieval to modern times.

> The family established a hereditary monarchy in Austria in 1282 and secured the title of Holy Roman emperor from 1452. Austrian and Spanish branches were created when Charles divided the territories between his son Philip II and his brother Ferdinand; the Habsburgs ruled Spain 1504–1700, while Habsburg rule in Austria ended with the collapse of Austria-Hungary in 1918.

háček /ˈhɑːtʃɛk, ˈha-/ ▶ **noun** a diacritic mark (ˇ) placed over a letter to indicate modification of the sound in Slavic and other languages.
– ORIGIN Czech, diminutive of *hák* 'hook'.

hacendado /ˌasɛnˈdɑːdəʊ/, Spanish /aθenˈdaðəɔ, asen-/ (also **haciendado** /ˌasjɛn-/, Spanish /aθjen-, asjen-/) ▶ **noun** (pl. **hacendados**) the owner of a hacienda.
– ORIGIN Spanish.

hachures /haˈʃjʊəz/ ▶ **plural noun** parallel lines used in hill-shading on maps, their closeness indicating steepness of gradient.
– ORIGIN mid 19th cent.: from French, from *hacher* (see HATCH[3]).

hacienda /ˌhasɪˈɛndə/, Spanish /aˈθjenda, aˈsjenda/ ▶ **noun** (in Spanish-speaking countries or regions) a large estate or plantation with a dwelling house.
– ORIGIN Spanish, from Latin *facienda* 'things to be done', from *facere* 'make, do'.

hack[1] ▶ **verb 1** [with obj.] cut with rough or heavy blows: *I watched them hack the branches* | [no obj.] *men **hack** at the coalface.* ■ kick wildly or roughly: *he had to race from his line to hack the ball into the stand.*
2 [no obj.] gain unauthorized access to data in a system or computer: *they **hacked into** the bank's computer* | [with obj.] *someone hacked his computer from another location.* ■ program quickly and roughly.
3 [no obj.] cough persistently: *I was waking up in the middle of the night and coughing and hacking for hours.*
4 [usu. with negative] (**hack it**) informal manage; cope: *lots of people leave because they **can't hack it**.*
▶ **noun 1** a rough cut, blow, or stroke: *he was sure one of us was going to take a hack at him.* ■ (in sport) a kick or a stroke with a stick inflicted on another player. ■ a notch cut in the ice, or a peg inserted, to steady the foot when delivering a stone in curling. ■ a tool for rough striking or cutting, e.g. a mattock or a miner's pick. ■ archaic a gash or wound.
2 informal an act of computer hacking. ■ a piece of computer code which performs some function, especially an unofficial alternative or addition to a commercial program: *freeware and shareware hacks.*
– PHRASAL VERBS **hack around** N. Amer. informal pass one's time idly or with no definite purpose. **hack someone off** informal annoy or infuriate someone: *it really hacks me off when they whine about what a poor job we're doing.*
– ORIGIN Old English *haccian* 'cut in pieces', of West Germanic origin; related to Dutch *hakken* and German *hacken*.

hack[2] ▶ **noun 1** a writer or journalist producing dull, unoriginal work. ■ a person who does dull routine work.
2 a horse for ordinary riding. ■ a good-quality lightweight riding horse, especially one used in the show ring. ■ a ride on a horse. ■ a horse let out for hire. ■ an inferior or worn-out horse.
3 N. Amer. a taxi.
▶ **verb** [no obj.] (usu. as noun **hacking**) ride a horse for pleasure or exercise.
– DERIVATIVES **hackery** noun.
– ORIGIN Middle English (in sense 2 of the noun): abbreviation of HACKNEY. Sense 1 of the noun dates from the late 17th cent.

hack[3] ▶ **noun 1** Falconry a board on which a hawk's meat is laid.
2 a wooden frame for drying bricks, cheeses, etc. ■ a pile of bricks stacked up to dry before firing.
– PHRASES **at hack** (of a young hawk) given partial liberty but not yet allowed to hunt for itself.
– ORIGIN late Middle English (denoting the lower half of a divided door): variant of HATCH[1].

hackamore /ˈhakəmɔː/ ▶ **noun** a bridle without a bit, operating by exerting pressure on the horse's nose.
– ORIGIN mid 19th cent.: perhaps from Spanish *jaquima*, earlier *xaquima* 'halter'.

hackberry ▶ **noun** (pl. **hackberries**) a tree of the elm family which has leaves that resemble those of nettles, found in both tropical and temperate regions. See also NETTLE TREE. ● Genus *Celtis*, family Ulmaceae: several species, in particular the **North American hackberry** (*C. occidentalis*), which bears purple edible berries.
■ the berry of the hackberry tree.
– ORIGIN mid 18th cent.: variant of northern English dialect *hagberry*, of Scandinavian origin.

hacker ▶ **noun 1** a person who uses computers to gain unauthorized access to data. ■ informal an enthusiastic and skilful computer programmer or user.
2 a person or thing that hacks or cuts roughly.

hackette ▶ **noun** Brit. informal, chiefly derogatory a female journalist.

hacking cough ▶ **noun** a short, dry, frequent cough.

hacking jacket ▶ **noun** a riding jacket with slits at the side or back.

hackle ▶ **noun 1** (**hackles**) erectile hairs along an animal's back, which rise when it is angry or alarmed.
2 a long, narrow feather on the neck or saddle of a domestic cock or other bird. ■ Fishing a feather wound around a fishing fly so that its filaments are splayed out. ■ [mass noun] fly-fishing feathers collectively. ■ a bunch of feathers in a military headdress, for example of a regiment of fusiliers or the Black Watch.
3 a steel comb for dressing flax.
▶ **verb** [with obj.] dress or comb (flax) with a hackle.
– PHRASES **make someone's hackles rise** make someone angry or indignant.
– ORIGIN late Middle English (in sense 2 of the noun): variant of HATCHEL.

hackmatack /ˈhakmətak/ ▶ **noun** any of a number of North American coniferous trees, in particular the tamarack.
– ORIGIN late 18th cent.: perhaps from Western Abnaki.

hackney ▶ **noun** (pl. **hackneys**) chiefly historical a horse or pony of a light breed with a high-stepping trot, used in harness. ■ [usu. as modifier] a horse-drawn vehicle kept for hire: *a hackney coach.*
– ORIGIN Middle English: probably from *Hackney* in East London, where horses were pastured. The term originally denoted an ordinary riding horse (as opposed to a war horse or draught horse), especially one available for hire: hence *hackney carriage* or *coach*, and the verb *hackney* meaning 'use (a horse) for general purposes', later 'make commonplace by overuse' (see HACKNEYED).

hackney carriage ▶ **noun** Brit. the official term for a taxi.

hackneyed ▶ **adjective** (of a phrase or idea) having been overused; unoriginal and trite: *hackneyed old sayings.*

hacksaw ▶ **noun** a saw with a narrow fine-toothed blade set in a frame, used especially for cutting metal.
▶ **verb** (past participle **hacksawn** or **hacksawed**) [with obj.] cut (something) using a hacksaw.

hacktivist ▶ **noun** a person who uses computer crimes to further social or political ends.
– DERIVATIVES **hacktivism** noun.
– ORIGIN 1990s: blend of HACK[1] and *activist*.

had past and past participle of HAVE.

hadada /ˈhɑːdədɑː/ (also **hadeda**, **hadada ibis**) ▶ **noun** a large grey-brown African ibis with iridescent patches on the wings and a loud, harsh call.
● *Bostrychia* (or *Hagedashia*) *hagedash*, family Threskiornithidae.
– ORIGIN late 18th cent.: imitative of its call.

hadal /ˈheɪdəl/ ▶ **adjective** relating to the zone of the sea greater than 6000 m in depth (chiefly oceanic trenches).
– ORIGIN mid 20th cent.: from HADES + -AL.

haddock ▶ **noun** (pl. **same**) a silvery-grey bottom-dwelling fish of North Atlantic coastal waters, related to the cod. It is popular as a food fish and is of great commercial value. ● *Melanogrammus aeglefinus*, family Gadidae.
– ORIGIN Middle English: from Anglo-Norman French *hadoc*, from Old French *hadot*, of unknown origin.

hade /heɪd/ Geology ▶ **noun** the inclination of a mineral vein or fault from the vertical.
▶ **verb** [no obj.] (of a shaft, vein, or fault) incline from the vertical.
– ORIGIN late 17th cent.: perhaps a dialect form of the verb HEAD.

hadeda /ˈhɑːdɪdɑː/ ▶ **noun** variant spelling of HADADA.

Hades /ˈheɪdiːz/ Greek Mythology the underworld; the land of the spirits of the dead. ■ the god of the underworld, one of the sons of Cronus. Also called PLUTO. ■ informal hell.
– DERIVATIVES **Hadean** adjective.
– ORIGIN from Greek *Haidēs*, of unknown origin.

Hadhramaut /ˌhɑːdrəˈmaʊt, -ˈmɔːt/ a narrow region on the southern coast of Yemen, separating the Gulf of Aden from the desert land of the southern Arabian peninsula.

Hadith /haˈdiːθ/ ▶ **noun** (pl. **same** or **Hadiths**) a collection of traditions containing sayings of the prophet Muhammad which, with accounts of his daily practice (the Sunna), constitute the major source of guidance for Muslims apart from the Koran. ■ any of the sayings from the Hadith.
– ORIGIN from Arabic *ḥadīt* 'tradition'.

Hadlee /ˈhadli/, Sir Richard (John) (b.1951), New Zealand cricketer. An all-rounder, he took a record of 431 Test wickets during his career.

Hadley cell ▶ **noun** Meteorology a large-scale atmospheric convection cell in which air rises at the equator and sinks at medium latitudes, typically about 30° north or south.
– ORIGIN 1950s: named after George *Hadley* (1685–1768), English scientific writer.

hadn't ▶ **contraction** had not.

Hadrian /ˈheɪdrɪən/ (AD 76–138), Roman emperor 117–138; full name *Publius Aelius Hadrianus*. The adopted successor of Trajan, he toured the provinces of the Empire and secured the frontiers.

Hadrian's Wall a Roman defensive wall across northern England, stretching from the Solway Firth in the west to the mouth of the River Tyne in the east (about 120 km, 74 miles). It was begun in AD 122, after the emperor Hadrian's visit, to defend the province of Britain against invasions by tribes from the north.

hadron /ˈhadrɒn/ ▶ **noun** Physics a subatomic particle of a type including the baryons and mesons, which can take part in the strong interaction.
– DERIVATIVES **hadronic** adjective.
– ORIGIN 1960s: from Greek *hadros* 'bulky' + -ON.

hadrosaur /ˈhadrəsɔː/ ▶ **noun** a large herbivorous mainly bipedal dinosaur of the late Cretaceous period, with jaws flattened like the bill of a duck. Also called DUCK-BILLED DINOSAUR. ● Family Hadrosauridae, infraorder Ornithopoda, order Ornithischia.
– ORIGIN late 19th cent.: from modern Latin *Hadrosaurus* (genus name), from Greek *hadros* 'thick, stout' + *sauros* 'lizard'.

hadst archaic second person singular past of HAVE.

haecceity /hɛkˈsiːɪti, hiːk-/ ▶ **noun** [mass noun] Philosophy that property or quality of a thing by virtue of which it is unique or describable as 'this (one)'. ■ the property of being a unique and individual thing.
– ORIGIN mid 17th cent.: from medieval Latin *haecceitas*, from Latin *haec*, feminine of *hic* 'this'.

Haeckel /ˈhɛk(ə)l/, Ernst Heinrich (1834–1919), German biologist and philosopher. He popularized Darwin's theories and saw evolution as providing a framework for describing the world, with the German Empire representing the highest evolved form of a civilized nation.

haem /hiːm/ (US **heme**) ▶ **noun** [mass noun] Biochemistry an iron-containing compound of the porphyrin class which forms the non-protein part of haemoglobin and some other biological molecules.
– ORIGIN 1920s: back-formation from HAEMOGLOBIN.

haem- /hiːm/ (US **hem-**) ▶ **combining form** variant spelling of HAEMO- shortened before a vowel (as in *haemangioma*).

haemagglutination /ˌhiːməgluːtɪˈneɪʃ(ə)n/ (US **hemagglutination**) ▶ **noun** [mass noun] Medicine & Biology the clumping together of red blood cells.

haemagglutinin /ˌhiːməˈgluːtɪnɪn/ (US **hemagglutinin**) ▶ **noun** Medicine & Biology a substance, such as a viral protein, which causes haemagglutination.

H

H

haemal /ˈhiːm(ə)l/ (US **hemal**) ▶ **adjective** Physiology of or concerning the blood. ▪ Zoology situated on the same side of the body as the heart and major blood vessels (i.e. in chordates, ventral).
– ORIGIN mid 19th cent.: from Greek *haima* 'blood' + **-AL**.

haemangioma /ˌhiːmandʒɪˈəʊmə/ (US **hemangioma**) ▶ **noun** (pl. **haemangiomas** or **haemangiomata** /-mətə/) Medicine a benign tumour of blood vessels, often forming a red birthmark.

haematemesis /ˌhiːməˈtɛmɪsɪs/ (US **hematemesis**) ▶ **noun** [mass noun] Medicine the vomiting of blood.
– ORIGIN early 19th cent.: from **HAEMATO-** 'of blood' + Greek *emesis* 'vomiting'.

haematic /hiːˈmatɪk/ (US **hematic**) ▶ **adjective** Medicine, dated relating to or affecting the blood.
– ORIGIN mid 19th cent.: from Greek *haimatikos*, from *haima, haimat-* 'blood'.

haematin /ˈhiːmətɪn/ (US **hematin**) ▶ **noun** [mass noun] Biochemistry a bluish-black compound derived from haemoglobin by removal of the protein part and oxidation of the iron atom.
– ORIGIN mid 19th cent.: from Greek *haima, haimat-* 'blood' + **-IN**[1].

haematite /ˈhiːmətʌɪt/ (US **hematite**) ▶ **noun** a reddish-black mineral consisting of ferric oxide. It is an important ore of iron.
– ORIGIN late Middle English: via Latin from Greek *haimatitēs (lithos)* 'blood-like (stone)', from *haima, haimat-* 'blood'.

haemato- (US **hemato-**) ▶ **combining form** relating to the blood: *haematoma*.
– ORIGIN from Greek *haima, haimat-* 'blood'.

haematocele /ˈhiːmətə(ʊ)siːl/ (US **hematocele**) ▶ **noun** Medicine a swelling caused by blood collecting in a body cavity.

haematocrit /ˈhiːmətə(ʊ)krɪt/ (US **hematocrit**) ▶ **noun** Physiology the ratio of the volume of red blood cells to the total volume of blood. ▪ an instrument for measuring the ratio of the volume of red blood cells to the total volume of blood, typically by centrifugation.
– ORIGIN late 19th cent.: from **HAEMATO-** 'of blood' + Greek *kritēs* 'judge'.

haematogenous /ˌhiːməˈtɒdʒɪnəs/ (US **hematogenous**) ▶ **adjective** Medicine originating in or carried by the blood.

haematology /ˌhiːməˈtɒlədʒi/ (US **hematology**) ▶ **noun** [mass noun] the branch of medicine involving study and treatment of the blood.
– DERIVATIVES **haematologic** adjective, **haematological** adjective, **haematologist** noun.

haematoma /ˌhiːməˈtəʊmə/ (US **hematoma**) ▶ **noun** (pl. **haematomas** or **haematomata** /-mətə/) Medicine a solid swelling of clotted blood within the tissues.

haematophagous /ˌhiːməˈtɒfəgəs/ (US **hematophagous**) ▶ **adjective** (of an animal, especially an insect or tick) feeding on blood.

haematopoiesis /ˌhiːmatə(ʊ)pɔɪˈiːsɪs/ (US **hematopoiesis**) ▶ **noun** another term for **HAEMOPOIESIS**.
– DERIVATIVES **haematopoietic** adjective.

haematoxylin /ˌhiːməˈtɒksɪlɪn/ (US **hematoxylin**) ▶ **noun** [mass noun] Chemistry a colourless compound present in logwood, which is easily converted into blue, red, or purple dyes and is used as a biological stain.
● A phenol; chem. formula: $C_{16}H_{14}O_6$.
– ORIGIN mid 19th cent.: from modern Latin *Haematoxylum* (genus name), from **HAEMATO-** 'of blood' + Greek *xulon* 'wood'.

haematuria /ˌhiːməˈtjʊərɪə/ (US **hematuria**) ▶ **noun** [mass noun] Medicine the presence of blood in urine.

-haemia ▶ **combining form** variant spelling of **-AEMIA**.

haemo- (US **hemo-**) ▶ **combining form** equivalent to **HAEMATO-**.
– ORIGIN from Greek *haima* 'blood'.

haemochromatosis /ˌhiːmə(ʊ)ˌkrəʊməˈtəʊsɪs/ (US **hemochromatosis**) ▶ **noun** [mass noun] Medicine a hereditary disorder in which iron salts are deposited in the tissues, leading to liver damage, diabetes mellitus, and bronze discoloration of the skin.

haemocoel /ˈhiːməsiːl/ (US **hemocoel**) ▶ **noun** Zoology the primary body cavity of most invertebrates, containing circulatory fluid.
– ORIGIN late 19th cent.: from **HAEMO-** 'of blood' + Greek *koilos* 'hollow, cavity'.

haemocyanin /ˌhiːmə(ʊ)ˈsʌɪənɪn/ (US **hemocyanin**) ▶ **noun** [mass noun] Biochemistry a protein containing copper, responsible for transporting oxygen in the blood plasma of arthropods and molluscs.
– ORIGIN mid 19th cent.: from **HAEMO-** 'of blood' + **CYAN** + **-IN**[1].

haemocyte /ˈhiːmə(ʊ)sʌɪt/ (US **hemocyte**) ▶ **noun** a cell of the haemolymph of various invertebrates, especially arthropods.

haemocytometer /ˌhiːmə(ʊ)sʌɪˈtɒmɪtə/ (US **hemocytometer**) ▶ **noun** an instrument for visual counting of the number of cells in a blood sample or other fluid under a microscope.

haemodialysis /ˌhiːmə(ʊ)dʌɪˈalɪsɪs/ (US **hemodialysis**) ▶ **noun** (pl. **haemodialyses** /-siːz/) Medicine kidney dialysis.

haemodynamic (US **hemodynamic**) ▶ **adjective** Physiology relating to the flow of blood within the organs and tissues of the body.
– DERIVATIVES **haemodynamically** adverb, **haemodynamics** noun.

haemoglobin /ˌhiːməˈgləʊbɪn/ (US **hemoglobin**) ▶ **noun** [mass noun] Biochemistry a red protein responsible for transporting oxygen in the blood of vertebrates. Its molecule comprises four subunits, each containing an iron atom bound to a haem group.
– ORIGIN mid 19th cent.: a contracted form of *haematoglobulin*, in the same sense.

haemoglobinopathy /ˌhiːməˌgləʊbɪˈnɒpəθi/ (US **hemoglobinopathy**) ▶ **noun** Medicine a hereditary condition involving an abnormality in the structure of haemoglobin.

haemoglobinuria /ˌhiːməˌgləʊbɪˈnjʊərɪə/ (US **hemoglobinuria**) ▶ **noun** [mass noun] Medicine excretion of free haemoglobin in the urine.

haemolymph /ˈhiːmə(ʊ)lɪmf/ (US **hemolymph**) ▶ **noun** [mass noun] a fluid equivalent to blood in most invertebrates, occupying the haemocoel.

haemolysis /hiːˈmɒlɪsɪs/ (US **hemolysis**) ▶ **noun** [mass noun] the rupture or destruction of red blood cells.

haemolytic /ˌhiːməˈlɪtɪk/ (US **hemolytic**) ▶ **adjective** Medicine relating to or involving the rupture or destruction of red blood cells: *haemolytic anaemia*.

haemolytic disease of the newborn ▶ **noun** [mass noun] Medicine a severe form of anaemia caused in a fetus or newborn infant by incompatibility with the mother's blood type, typically when the mother is rhesus negative and produces antibodies which attack rhesus positive fetal blood through the placenta. Also called **ERYTHROBLASTOSIS**.

haemophilia /ˌhiːməˈfɪlɪə/ (US **hemophilia**) ▶ **noun** [mass noun] a medical condition in which the ability of the blood to clot is severely reduced, causing the sufferer to bleed severely from even a slight injury. The condition is typically caused by a hereditary lack of a coagulation factor, most often factor VIII.
– DERIVATIVES **haemophiliac** noun, **haemophilic** adjective.

haemopoiesis /ˌhiːmə(ʊ)pɔɪˈiːsɪs/ (US **hemopoiesis**) ▶ **noun** [mass noun] the production of blood cells and platelets, which occurs in the bone marrow.
– DERIVATIVES **haemopoietic** adjective.
– ORIGIN early 20th cent.: from **HAEMO-** 'of blood' + Greek *poiēsis* 'making'.

haemoptysis /hiːˈmɒptɪsɪs/ (US **hemoptysis**) ▶ **noun** [mass noun] the coughing up of blood.
– ORIGIN mid 17th cent.: from modern Latin *hemoptysis*, from **HAEMO-** 'of blood' + Greek *ptusis* 'spitting'.

haemorrhage /ˈhɛmərɪdʒ/ (US **hemorrhage**) ▶ **noun** an escape of blood from a ruptured blood vessel. ▪ a damaging loss of valuable people or resources: *a haemorrhage of highly qualified teachers*.
▶ **verb** [no obj.] (of a person) suffer a haemorrhage: *he had begun haemorrhaging in the night*. ▪ [with obj.] lose or expend large amounts of (something valuable) in a seemingly uncontrollable way: *the business was haemorrhaging cash*.
– ORIGIN late 17th cent. (as a noun): alteration of obsolete *haemorrhagy*, via Latin from Greek *haimorrhagia*, from *haima* 'blood' + the stem of *rhēgnunai* 'burst'.

haemorrhagic /ˌhɛməˈradʒɪk/ (US **hemorrhagic**) ▶ **adjective** accompanied by or produced by haemorrhage: *a viral haemorrhagic fever | haemorrhagic colitis*.

haemorrhoid /ˈhɛmərɔɪd/ (US **hemorrhoid**) ▶ **noun** (usu. **haemorrhoids**) a swollen vein or group of veins in the region of the anus. Also (collectively) called **PILES**.
– DERIVATIVES **haemorrhoidal** adjective.
– ORIGIN late Middle English: via Old French and Latin from Greek *haimorrhoides (phlebes)* 'bleeding (veins)', from *haima* 'blood' + an element related to *rhein* 'to flow'.

haemostasis /ˌhiːmə(ʊ)ˈsteɪsɪs/ (US **hemostasis**) ▶ **noun** [mass noun] Medicine the stopping of a flow of blood.
– DERIVATIVES **haemostatic** adjective.

haemostat /ˈhiːməstat/ (US **hemostat**) ▶ **noun** Medicine an instrument for preventing blood flow by compression of a blood vessel.
– DERIVATIVES **haemostatic** adjective.

haere mai /ˌhʌɪrə ˈmʌɪ/ ▶ **exclamation** used as a Maori greeting.
– ORIGIN Maori, literally 'come hither'.

hafiz /ˈhɑːfɪz/ ▶ **noun** a Muslim who knows the Koran by heart.
– ORIGIN Persian, from Arabic *ḥāfiẓ* 'guardian', from *ḥāfiẓa* 'guard, know by heart'.

Haflinger /ˈhaflɪŋə/ ▶ **noun** a draught pony of a sturdy chestnut breed with a flaxen mane and tail.
– ORIGIN late 19th cent.: German, from *Hafling*, the name of a Tyrolean village where the breed originated.

hafnium /ˈhafnɪəm/ ▶ **noun** [mass noun] the chemical element of atomic number 72, a hard silver-grey metal of the transition series, resembling and often occurring with zirconium. (Symbol: **Hf**)
– ORIGIN 1920s: modern Latin, from *Hafnia*, Latinized form of Danish *Havn*, former name of Copenhagen.

haft /hɑːft/ ▶ **noun** the handle of a knife, axe, or spear.
▶ **verb** [with obj.] (often as adj. **hafted**) provide (a blade, axe head, or spearhead) with a haft: *the motifs included animals and hafted axes*.
– ORIGIN Old English *hæft*, of Germanic origin: related to Dutch *heft, hecht* and German *Heft*, also to **HEAVE**.

Haftorah /hɑːfˈtəʊrɑː/ (also **Haphtarah** or **Haphtorah**) ▶ **noun** (pl. **Haftoroth** /-rəʊt/) Judaism a short reading from the Prophets which follows the reading from the Law in a Jewish synagogue.
– ORIGIN from Hebrew *hapṭārāh* 'dismissal'.

hag[1] ▶ **noun** **1** a witch. ▪ an ugly old woman: *a fat old hag in a dirty apron*.
2 short for **HAGFISH**.
– DERIVATIVES **haggish** adjective.
– ORIGIN Middle English: perhaps from Old English *hægtesse, hegtes*, related to Dutch *heks* and German *Hexe* 'witch', of unknown ultimate origin.

hag[2] ▶ **noun** Scottish & N. English **1** (also **peat hag**) an overhang of peat.
2 a soft place on a moor or a firm place in a bog.
– ORIGIN Middle English (denoting a gap in a cliff): from Old Norse *hǫgg* 'gap', from *hǫggva* 'hack, hew'.

Hag. ▶ **abbreviation** Haggai (in biblical references).

Hagar /ˈheɪgɑː/ (in the Bible and in Islamic tradition) the mother of Ishmael (Ismail), son of Abraham.

Hagen /ˈhɑːg(ə)n/ an industrial city in NW Germany, in North Rhine-Westphalia; pop. 195,700 (est. 2006).

hagfish ▶ **noun** (pl. **same** or **hagfishes**) a primitive jawless marine vertebrate distantly related to the lampreys, with a slimy eel-like body, a slit-like mouth surrounded by barbels, and a rasping tongue used for feeding on dead or dying fish. ● Class Myxini and family Myxinidae: several genera, in particular *Myxine*, and numerous species.
– ORIGIN early 17th cent.: from **HAG**[1] + **FISH**[1].

Haggadah /həˈgɑːdə, hagaˈdɑː/ (also **Aggadah**) ▶ **noun** (pl. **Haggadoth** or **Haggadot** /-dəʊt/) Judaism
1 the text recited at the Seder on the first two nights of the Jewish Passover, including a narrative of the Exodus.
2 a legend, parable, or anecdote used to illustrate a point of the Law in the Talmud. ▪ [mass noun] the non-legal, narrative element of the Talmud. Compare with **HALACHA**.
– ORIGIN from Hebrew *Haggāḏāh*, 'tale, parable', from *higgîḏ* 'tell, expound'.

Haggai /ˈhageɪˌʌɪ/ a Hebrew minor prophet of the 6th century BC. ▪ a book of the Bible containing his prophecies of a glorious future in the Messianic age.

Haggard, Sir (Henry) Rider (1856–1925), English novelist. He is famous for adventure novels such as *King Solomon's Mines* (1885) and *She* (1889).

haggard ▶ **adjective** **1** looking exhausted and unwell, especially from fatigue, worry, or suffering: *she was pale and haggard | Alex's haggard face*.

2 (of a hawk) caught for training as a wild adult of more than twelve months. Compare with **PASSAGE HAWK**.
▸ **noun** a haggard hawk.
– DERIVATIVES **haggardly adverb**, **haggardness noun**.
– ORIGIN mid 16th cent. (used in falconry): from French *hagard*; perhaps related to **HEDGE**; later influenced by **HAG**[1].

haggis ▸ **noun** (pl. **same** or **haggises**) a Scottish dish consisting of a sheep's or calf's offal mixed with suet, oatmeal, and seasoning and boiled in a bag, traditionally one made from the animal's stomach.
– ORIGIN late Middle English: probably from earlier *hag* 'hack, hew', from Old Norse *hǫggva*.

haggle ▸ **verb** [no obj.] dispute or bargain persistently, especially over the cost of something: *the two sides are haggling over television rights*.
▸ **noun** a period of haggling.
– DERIVATIVES **haggler noun**.
– ORIGIN late 16th cent. (in the sense 'hack, mangle'): from Old Norse *hǫggva* 'hew'.

Hagia Sophia /ˌhagɪə səˈfiːə/ another name for **ST SOPHIA**.
– ORIGIN Greek, literally 'holy wisdom'.

hagio- ▸ **combining form** relating to saints or holiness: *hagiographer*.
– ORIGIN from Greek *hagios* 'holy'.

Hagiographa /ˌhagɪˈɒɡrəfə/ ▸ **plural noun** the books of the Bible comprising the last of the three major divisions of the Hebrew scriptures, other than the Law and the Prophets. The books of the Hagiographa are: Ruth, Psalms, Job, Proverbs, Ecclesiastes, Song of Solomon, Lamentations, Daniel, Esther, Ezra–Nehemiah, and Chronicles. Also called **THE WRITINGS**.
– ORIGIN via late Latin from Greek.

hagiographer /ˌhagɪˈɒɡrəfə/ ▸ **noun** 1 a writer of the lives of the saints. ■ a biographer who treats their subject with undue reverence.
2 Theology a writer of any of the Hagiographa.

hagiography /ˌhagɪˈɒɡrəfi/ ▸ **noun** [mass noun] the writing of the lives of saints. ■ [count noun] a biography that treats its subject with undue reverence.
– DERIVATIVES **hagiographic adjective**, **hagiographical adjective**.

hagiolatry /ˌhagɪˈɒlətri/ ▸ **noun** [mass noun] the worship of saints. ■ undue veneration of a famous person.

hagiology /ˌhagɪˈɒlədʒi/ ▸ **noun** [mass noun] literature dealing with the lives and legends of saints.
– DERIVATIVES **hagiological adjective**, **hagiologist noun**.

hagioscope /ˈhagɪəskəʊp/ ▸ **noun** another term for **SQUINT** (sense 3 of the noun).

hag-ridden ▸ **adjective** afflicted by nightmares or anxieties: *he was hag-ridden by his early success*.

Hague /heɪɡ/ (**The Hague**) the seat of government and administrative centre of the Netherlands, on the North Sea coast, capital of the province of South Holland; pop. 475,681 (2008). The International Court of Justice is based there. Dutch name **DEN HAAG**; also called **'S-GRAVENHAGE**.

hah ▸ **exclamation** variant spelling of **HA**[1].

ha ha ▸ **exclamation** used to represent laughter.
– ORIGIN natural utterance: first recorded in Old English (compare with **HA**[1]).

ha-ha ▸ **noun** a ditch with a wall on its inner side below ground level, forming a boundary to a park or garden without interrupting the view.
– ORIGIN early 18th cent.: from French, said to be from the cry of surprise on suddenly encountering such an obstacle.

haham /ˈhɑːhəm/ (also **chacham**) ▸ **noun** a spiritual leader among Sephardic Jews, or, more generally, a person learned in Jewish law.
– ORIGIN from Hebrew *ḥāḵām* 'wise'.

Hahn /hɑːn/, Otto (1879–1968), German chemist, co-discoverer of nuclear fission. Together with Lise Meitner he discovered the new element protactinium in 1917. The pair discovered nuclear fission in 1938 with **Fritz Strassmann** (1902–80). Nobel Prize for Chemistry (1944).

hahnium /ˈhɑːnɪəm/ ▸ **noun** [mass noun] the name formerly proposed by the American Chemical Society for the chemical element of atomic number 105 (**dubnium**), and by IUPAC for element 108 (**hassium**).
– ORIGIN 1970s: named in honour of Otto **HAHN**.

hai /hʌɪ/ ▸ **exclamation** Indian used to express grief, horror, regret, etc.: *hai, hai, this boy is nothing but trouble and misfortune*.
– ORIGIN Hindi *hāy* 'woe'.

Haida /ˈhʌɪdə/ ▸ **noun** (pl. **same** or **Haidas**) **1** a member of an American Indian people living on the Pacific coast of Canada.
2 [mass noun] the language of the Haida, now almost extinct.
▸ **adjective** relating to the Haida or their language.
– ORIGIN the name in Haida, literally 'people'.

Haifa /ˈhʌɪfə/ the chief port of Israel, in the northwest of the country on the Mediterranean coast; pop. 264,800 (est. 2008).

Haig, Douglas, 1st Earl Haig of Bemersyde (1861–1928), British Field Marshal. During the First World War he served as Commander-in-Chief of British forces in France, maintaining a strategy of attrition throughout his command.

haik /heɪk, hɑːɪk/ (also **haick**) ▸ **noun** a large wrap, typically white, worn by people from North Africa.
– ORIGIN early 18th cent.: from Arabic *ḥā'ik*.

Haikou /hʌɪˈkəʊ/ the capital of Hainan autonomous region, a port on the NE coast of Hainan island; pop. 410,000 (1990).

haiku /ˈhʌɪkuː/ ▸ **noun** (pl. **same** or **haikus**) a Japanese poem of seventeen syllables, in three lines of five, seven, and five, traditionally evoking images of the natural world. ■ a poem in English written in the form of a haiku.
– ORIGIN Japanese, contracted form of *haikai no ku* 'light verse'.

hail[1] ▸ **noun** [mass noun] pellets of frozen rain which fall in showers from cumulonimbus clouds. ■ [in sing.] a large number of things hurled forcefully through the air: ***a hail of bullets***.
▸ **verb** [no obj.] **1** (**it hails, it is hailing**, etc.) hail falls: *it hailed so hard we had to stop*.
2 [with adverbial of direction] (of a large number of objects) fall or be hurled forcefully: *missiles and bombs **hail down** from the sky*.
– ORIGIN Old English *hagol, hægl* (noun), *hagalian* (verb), of Germanic origin; related to Dutch *hagel* and German *Hagel*.

hail[2] ▸ **verb 1** [with obj.] call out to (someone) to attract attention: *I hailed her in English*. ■ signal (an approaching taxi) to stop.
2 [with obj.] praise (someone or something) enthusiastically: *he has been **hailed as** the new James Dean*.
3 [no obj.] (**hail from**) have one's home or origins in (a place): *they hail from Turkey*.
▸ **exclamation** archaic expressing greeting or acclaim: *hail, Caesar!*
▸ **noun** a shout or call used to attract attention.
– PHRASES **all hail** archaic or humorous a cry of greeting or welcome: *all hail the new kids on the block*. **within hail** dated at a distance within which someone may be called to; within earshot.
– DERIVATIVES **haller noun**.
– ORIGIN Middle English: from the obsolete adjective *hail* 'healthy' (occurring in greetings and toasts, such as *wæs hæil*: see **WASSAIL**), from Old Norse *heill*, related to **HALE**[1] and **WHOLE**.

Haile Selassie /ˌhʌɪlɪ səˈlasi/ (1892–1975), emperor of Ethiopia 1930–74; born *Tafari Makonnen*. In exile in Britain during the Italian occupation of Ethiopia (1936–41), he was restored to the throne by the Allies and ruled until deposed by a military coup. He is revered by the Rastafarian religious sect.

hail-fellow-well-met ▸ **adjective** showing excessive familiarity or friendliness: *Arnold was very cheerful in a hail-fellow-well-met sort of way*.

Hail Mary ▸ **noun** (pl. **Hail Marys**) **1** a prayer to the Virgin Mary used chiefly by Roman Catholics, beginning with part of Luke 1:28. Also called **AVE MARIA**.
2 [usu. as modifier] US (in American football) a long, typically unsuccessful pass made in an attempt to score late in the game. ■ a plan or project with little chance of success.

hailstone ▸ **noun** a pellet of hail.

hailstorm ▸ **noun** a storm of heavy hail.

Hainan /hʌɪˈnan/ an island in the South China Sea, forming an autonomous region of China; pop. 8,450,000 (est. 2007); capital, Haikou.

Hainaut /eɪˈnəʊ, ˈ(h)eɪnəʊ/ a province of southern Belgium; capital, Mons.

Haiphong /hʌɪˈfɒŋ/ a port in northern Vietnam, on the delta of the Red River in the Gulf of Tonkin; pop. 485,300 (est. 2009).

hair ▸ **noun 1** any of the fine thread-like strands growing from the skin of humans, mammals, and some other animals. ■ a fine thread-like strand growing from the epidermis of a plant, or forming part of a living cell.
2 [mass noun] hairs collectively, especially those growing on a person's head: *her shoulder-length fair hair*.
3 (**a hair**) a very small quantity or extent: *his magic takes him a hair above the competition*.
– PHRASES **hair of the dog** informal an alcoholic drink taken to cure a hangover. [from *hair of the dog that bit you*, formerly recommended as an efficacious remedy for the bite of a mad dog.] **a hair's breadth** a very small amount or margin: ***you escaped death by a hair's breadth***. **in** (or **out of**) **someone's hair** informal annoying (or ceasing to annoy) someone: *they sent him to America, just to **get him out of their hair***. **keep your hair on!** Brit. informal used to urge someone not to panic or lose their temper. **let one's hair down** informal behave uninhibitedly. **make someone's hair stand on end** alarm or horrify someone. **not turn a hair** remain apparently unmoved or unaffected. **split hairs** make small and overfine distinctions.
– DERIVATIVES **haired adjective** [in combination] *a curly-haired boy*, **hair-like adjective**.
– ORIGIN Old English *hær*, of Germanic origin; related to Dutch *haar* and German *Haar*.

hairball ▸ **noun** a ball of hair which collects in the stomach of a cat or similar animal as a result of the animal licking its coat.

hairband ▸ **noun** a band for securing or tying back one's hair.

hairbrush ▸ **noun** a brush for smoothing a person's hair.

haircare ▸ **noun** [mass noun] the care of one's hair: [as modifier] *haircare products*.

haircloth ▸ **noun** [mass noun] stiff cloth woven with a cotton or linen warp and horsehair weft.

haircut ▸ **noun 1** the style in which a person's hair is cut. ■ an act of cutting a person's hair.
2 US informal a reduction in the stated value of an asset: *the banks would probably be willing to take a haircut on the rest*.

hairdo ▸ **noun** (pl. **hairdos**) informal the style of a woman's hair.

hairdresser ▸ **noun** a person who cuts and styles hair as an occupation.
– DERIVATIVES **hairdressing noun**.

hairdryer (also **hairdrier**) ▸ **noun** an electrical device for drying a person's hair by blowing warm air over it.

hair grass ▸ **noun** [mass noun] a slender-stemmed grass of temperate and cool regions. ● *Deschampsia*, *Aira*, and other genera, family Gramineae.

hairgrip ▸ **noun** Brit. a flat hairpin with the ends close together.

hairless ▸ **adjective** lacking hair; bare or bald: *his hairless chest*.

hairless bat ▸ **noun** an almost hairless black free-tailed bat found in SE Asia. ● Genus *Cheiromeles*, family Molossidae: two species, in particular *C. torquatus*.

hairline ▸ **noun 1** the edge of a person's hair, especially on the forehead.
2 [as modifier] very thin or fine: *a hairline fracture*.

hairnet ▸ **noun** a piece of fine mesh worn to keep the hair in place.

hairpiece ▸ **noun** a patch or bunch of false hair used to augment a person's natural hair.

hairpin ▸ **noun** a U-shaped pin for fastening the hair.

hairpin bend (N. Amer. **hairpin turn**) ▸ **noun** a sharp U-shaped bend in a road.

hair-raising ▸ **adjective** extremely alarming, astonishing, or frightening: *hair-raising adventures*.

hair shirt ▸ **noun** a shirt of haircloth, formerly worn by penitents and ascetics.
▸ **adjective** (**hair-shirt** or **hair-shirted**) austere and self-sacrificing.

hairslide ▸ **noun** Brit. a clip for keeping a woman's hair in position.

hair-splitting ▸ **adjective** characterized by or fond of small and overfine distinctions: *the legal experts have a particularly hair-splitting mentality*.
▸ **noun** [mass noun] the action of making small and overfine distinctions; quibbling.
– DERIVATIVES **hair-splitter noun**.

hairspray ▸ **noun** [mass noun] a solution sprayed on to a person's hair to keep it in place.

hairspring ▸ **noun** a slender flat coiled spring regulating the movement of the balance wheel in a watch.

H

hairstreak ▶ **noun** a butterfly with a narrow streak or row of dots on the underside of the hindwing and a small tail-like projection on the hindwing. ● Many genera in the family Lycaenidae.

hairstyle ▶ **noun** a particular way in which a person's hair is cut or arranged.

hairstylist ▶ **noun** a person who cuts and styles people's hair professionally.
– DERIVATIVES **hairstyling** noun.

hair trigger ▶ **noun** a trigger of a firearm set for release at the slightest pressure. ■ [as modifier] denoting something that is quickly and easily activated or provoked: *his hair-trigger temperament.*

hair worm ▶ **noun** another term for HORSEHAIR WORM.

hairy ▶ **adjective** (**hairier**, **hairiest**) **1** covered with hair: *a hairy chest.* ■ having a rough feel or appearance suggestive of coarse hair: *a hairy tweed coat and skirt.*
2 informal alarming and difficult: *we drove up yet another hairy mountain road.*
– PHRASES **give someone the hairy eyeball** see EYEBALL.
– DERIVATIVES **hairily** adverb, **hairiness** noun.

Haiti /ˈheɪti/ a country in the Caribbean, occupying the western third of the island of Hispaniola; pop. 9,035,500 (est. 2009); official languages, Haitian Creole, French; capital, Port-au-Prince.

> The area was ceded to France by Spain in 1697, and many slaves were imported from West Africa to work on sugar plantations. In 1791 the slaves rose in rebellion under Toussaint L'Ouverture, and in 1804 the colony was proclaimed an independent state under the name of Haiti. It was administered by the US 1915–34 after a succession of corrupt dictatorships. From 1957 to 1986 the country was under the oppressive dictatorship of the Duvalier family. Haiti's first democratically chosen President was elected in 1990 but overthrown by the military the following year; democracy was restored by US and UN intervention in 1994. In 2010 the area around the capital was devastated by an earthquake.

Haitian /ˈheɪʃɪən, -ʃ(ə)n/ ▶ **adjective** relating to Haiti, its inhabitants, or their language.
▶ **noun 1** a native or inhabitant of Haiti.
2 (also **Haitian Creole**) [mass noun] the French-based Creole language spoken in Haiti.

Haitink /ˈhʌɪtɪŋk/, Bernard (Johann Herman) (b.1929), Dutch conductor, principal conductor of the London Philharmonic Orchestra 1967–79 and musical director of Glyndebourne (1977–87) and Covent Garden (from 1987).

haji /ˈhadʒiː/ (also **hajji**) ▶ **noun** (pl. **hajis**) a Muslim who has been to Mecca as a pilgrim: [as title] *Haji Hadi.*
– ORIGIN from Persian and Turkish *ḥājjī*, *ḥājī*, from Arabic *ḥajj* (see HAJJ).

hajj /hadʒ/ (also **haj**) ▶ **noun** the greater Muslim pilgrimage to Mecca, which takes place in the last month of the year and which all Muslims are expected to make at least once during their lifetime if they can afford to do so. It is one of the Five Pillars of Islam. Compare with UMRAH.
– ORIGIN from Arabic (*al-*) *ḥajj* '(the Great) Pilgrimage'.

haka /ˈhɑːkə/ ▶ **noun** a Maori ceremonial war dance involving chanting, an imitation of which is performed by New Zealand rugby teams before a match.
– ORIGIN Maori.

hakama /ˈhakəmə, ˈhɑː-/ ▶ **noun** [treated as sing. or pl.] loose trousers with many pleats in the front, forming part of Japanese formal dress.
– ORIGIN mid 19th cent.: Japanese.

hake ▶ **noun 1** a large-headed elongated fish with long jaws and strong teeth. It is a valuable commercial food fish. ● Family Merlucciidae and genus *Merluccius*: several species, including the **European hake** (*M. merluccius*).
2 any of a number of fishes related to the true hakes. ● Species in several families, especially in the NW Atlantic genus *Urophycis* (family Phycidae).
– ORIGIN Middle English: perhaps from Old English *haca* 'hook'.

Hakenkreuz /ˈhɑːk(ə)n,krɔɪts/, German /ˈhaːkən,krɔyts/ ▶ **noun** a swastika, especially in its clockwise form as a Nazi symbol.
– ORIGIN German, from *Haken* 'hook' + *Kreuz* 'cross'.

hakim /haˈkiːm/ ▶ **noun 1** a physician using traditional remedies in India and Muslim countries.
2 (in Muslim countries and formerly in India) a judge, ruler, or governor.
– ORIGIN Arabic: sense 1 from *ḥakīm* 'wise man, physician'; sense 2 from *ḥākim* 'ruler'.

Hakka /ˈhakə/ ▶ **noun** (pl. **same** or **Hakkas**) **1** a member of a people of SE China who migrated from the north during the 12th century.
2 [mass noun] the dialect of Chinese spoken by the Hakka, with about 27 million speakers. Also called KEJIA.
▶ **adjective** relating to the Hakka or their language.
– ORIGIN from Chinese (Cantonese dialect) *haāk ka* 'stranger'.

Hakluyt /ˈhakluːt/, Richard (*c.*1552–1616), English geographer and historian. He compiled *Principal Navigations, Voyages, and Discoveries of the English Nation* (1598), a collection of accounts of great voyages of discovery.

Hakodate /ˌhɑːkəʊˈdɑːteɪ/ a port in northern Japan, on the southern tip of the island of Hokkaido; pop. 290,873 (2007).

Halab /hɑːˈlɑːb/ Arabic name for ALEPPO.

Halacha /ˌhalɑːˈxɑː, həˈlɑːkə/ (also **Halakha**, **Halakah**) ▶ **noun** [mass noun] Jewish law and jurisprudence, based on the Talmud.
– DERIVATIVES **Halachic** adjective.
– ORIGIN from Hebrew *hălāḵāh* 'law'.

Halafian /həˈlɑːfɪən/ ▶ **adjective** Archaeology relating to or denoting a prehistoric culture extending from Syria to the Mediterranean coast and eastern Turkey (late 6th and early 5th millennium BC). This culture is identified primarily by the use of polychrome pottery (**Halaf ware**). ■ (as noun **the Halafian**) the Halafian culture or period.
– ORIGIN 1930s: from the place name Tell *Halaf* (in NE Syria, where the pottery was first discovered) + -IAN.

halal /həˈlɑːl/ ▶ **adjective** denoting or relating to meat prepared as prescribed by Muslim law: *halal butchers.* ■ religiously acceptable according to Muslim law: *halal banking.*
▶ **noun** [mass noun] halal meat.
– ORIGIN mid 19th cent.: from Arabic *ḥalāl* 'according to religious law'.

halala /həˈlɑːlə/ ▶ **noun** (pl. **same** or **halalas**) a monetary unit of Saudi Arabia, equal to one hundredth of a rial.
– ORIGIN Arabic.

halation /həˈleɪʃ(ə)n/ ▶ **noun** [mass noun] the spreading of light beyond its proper boundaries to form a fog round the edges of a bright image in a photograph or on a television screen.
– ORIGIN mid 19th cent.: formed irregularly from HALO + -ATION.

halberd /ˈhalbəːd/ (also **halbert**) ▶ **noun** historical a combined spear and battleaxe.
– ORIGIN late 15th cent.: from French *hallebarde*, from Italian *alabarda*, from Middle High German *helmbarde* (from *helm* 'handle' + *barde* 'hatchet').

halberdier /ˌhalbəˈdɪə/ ▶ **noun** historical a man armed with a halberd.
– ORIGIN early 16th cent.: from French *hallebardier*, from *hallebarde* (see HALBERD).

halcyon /ˈhalsɪən, -ʃ(ə)n/ ▶ **adjective** denoting a period of time in the past that was idyllically happy and peaceful: *the halcyon days of the mid 1980s, when profits were soaring.*
▶ **noun 1** a mythical bird said by ancient writers to breed in a nest floating at sea at the winter solstice, charming the wind and waves into calm.
2 a tropical Asian and African kingfisher with brightly coloured plumage. ● Genus *Halcyon*, family Alcedinidae: many species.
– ORIGIN late Middle English (in the mythological sense): via Latin from Greek *alkuōn* 'kingfisher' (also *halkuōn*, by association with *hals* 'sea' and *kuōn* 'conceiving').

haldi /ˈhʌldi/ ▶ **noun** Indian term for TURMERIC.
– ORIGIN via Hindi from Sanskrit *haridrā*.

Hale, George Ellery (1868–1938), American astronomer. He discovered that sunspots are associated with strong magnetic fields and invented the spectroheliograph. He also initiated the construction of several large telescopes.

hale[1] ▶ **adjective** (of an old person) strong and healthy: *he's only just sixty, very **hale and hearty**.*
– ORIGIN Old English, northern variant of *hāl* 'whole'.

hale[2] ▶ **verb** [with obj. and adverbial of direction] archaic drag or draw forcibly: *he haled an old man out of the audience.*
– ORIGIN Middle English: from Old French *haler*, from Old Norse *hala*.

Hale–Bopp a periodic comet which passed close to the sun in the spring of 1997 and was one of the brightest of the 20th century.
– ORIGIN named after Alan *Hale* and Thomas *Bopp*, the American astronomers who discovered it (independently of each other).

haler /ˈhɑːlə/ ▶ **noun** (pl. **same** or **halers**) a monetary unit of the Czech Republic, equal to one hundredth of a koruna.
– ORIGIN from Czech *haléř*, from Middle High German *haller*, from *Schwäbisch Hall*, a town in Germany where coins were minted.

halesome ▶ **adjective** chiefly Scottish wholesome: *the friendly pub and halesome fare.*

Halesowen /heɪlzˈəʊɪn/ an engineering town in the west Midlands; pop. 54,400 (est. 2009).

Haley /ˈheɪli/, Bill (1925–81), American rock-and-roll singer; full name *William John Clifton Haley*. His song 'Rock Around the Clock' (1954) was the first to popularize rock and roll.

half ▶ **noun** (pl. **halves**) either of two equal or corresponding parts into which something is or can be divided: *two and a half years | the northern half of the island | divide the cake **in half** | spending was reduced **by half**.* ■ either of two equal periods of time into which a sports game or a performance is divided. ■ Brit. informal half a pint of beer or a similar drink: ***a half of** bitter.* ■ informal a half-price fare or ticket, especially for a child. ■ Golf a score for an individual hole that is the same as one's opponent's. ■ short for HALF BACK.
▶ **predeterminer, pronoun, & adjective** an amount equal to a half: [as predeterminer] *half an hour | almost half the children turned up* | [as pronoun] *half of the lectures are delivered by him* | [as adj.] *the last half century.* ■ an amount thought of as roughly a half: [as predeterminer] *half the audience were blubbing away* | [as pronoun] *half of them are gatecrashers.*
▶ **adverb** to the extent of half: *the glass was half full.* ■ [often in combination] to a certain extent; partly: *the chicken is half-cooked | I am half inclined to believe you.*
– PHRASES **a —— and a half** informal used to indicate that one considers a particular person or thing to be an impressive example of their kind: *Aunt Edie was a woman and a half.* **half the battle** see BATTLE. **half a chance** informal the slightest opportunity: *given half a chance he can make anything work.* **half an eye** see EYE. **the half of it** [usu. with negative] informal the most important part or aspect of something: *you don't know the half of it.* **half one** (or **two** etc.) informal way of saying HALF PAST ONE. **half past one** (or **two** etc.) thirty minutes after one (two, etc.) o'clock. **half the time** see TIME. **not do things by halves** do things thoroughly or extravagantly. **not half 1** not nearly: *he is not half such a fool as they thought.* **2** informal not at all: *the players are not half bad.* **3** Brit. informal to an extreme degree; very much so: *she didn't half flare up!* **too —— by half** Brit. used to emphasize something considered bad: *the idea seems too superstitious by half.*
– ORIGIN Old English *half*, *healf*, of Germanic origin; related to Dutch *half* and German *halb* (adjectives). The earliest meaning of the Germanic base was 'side', also a noun sense in Old English.

half a crown ▶ **noun** another term for HALF-CROWN.

half a dozen ▶ **noun** another term for HALF-DOZEN.

half-and-half ▶ **adverb & adjective** in equal parts: [as adv.] *views were split almost exactly half-and-half* | [as adj.] *a half-and-half mixture.*
▶ **noun** [mass noun] N. Amer. a mixture of milk and cream.

half-arsed (US **half-assed**, **half-ass**) ▶ **adjective** vulgar slang incompetent; inadequate.

half back (US **halfback**) ▶ **noun** a player in a ball game such as soccer, rugby, or field hockey whose position is between the forwards and full backs.

half-baked ▶ **adjective** not fully thought through; lacking a sound basis: *a half-baked conspiracy theory.* ■ foolish: *a half-baked hippie chick.*

half-ball ▶ **noun** Billiards & Snooker a stroke in which the centre of the cue ball is aimed at the edge of the object ball: [as modifier] *a half-ball shot.*

halfbeak ▶ **noun** a slender shoaling fish of coastal areas, with small pectoral fins and the lower jaw lengthened into a beak. It is related to the flying fishes and often skitters along the surface. Also called GARFISH in Australia and New Zealand. ● Several genera and species in the family Exocoetidae, including the widely distributed *Euleptorhamphus viridis*.

half binding ▶ **noun** [mass noun] a type of bookbinding in which the spine and corners are bound in one material (typically leather) and the rest of the cover in another.
– DERIVATIVES **half-bound** adjective.

half blood ▶ **noun 1** [mass noun] the relationship between people having one parent in common: *brothers and sisters of the half blood.* ■ [count noun] a person related to another through having one parent in common.
2 offensive another term for **HALF-BREED**.
– DERIVATIVES **half-blooded** adjective (sense 2).

half-blue ▶ **noun** Brit. a person who has represented Oxford or Cambridge University in a minor sport or as a second choice in any sport. ■ the distinction gained as a half-blue.

half board ▶ **noun** [mass noun] Brit. provision of bed, breakfast, and one main meal at a hotel or guest house.

half-boot ▶ **noun** a boot that reaches up to the calf.

half-bottle ▶ **noun** a bottle that is half the standard size.

half-breed ▶ **noun** offensive a person whose parents are of different races, especially the offspring of an American Indian and a person of white European ancestry.

half-brother ▶ **noun** a brother with whom one has only one parent in common.

half-butt ▶ **noun** a long billiard cue about 2.4 m (8 feet) in length.

half-caste ▶ **noun** offensive a person whose parents are of different races.

half-century ▶ **noun** a period of fifty years. ■ a score of fifty in a sporting event, especially a batsman's score of fifty in cricket.

half-cock ▶ **noun** the partly raised position of the cock of a gun.
– PHRASES **at half-cock** (of a gun) with the cock partly raised. ■ when only partly ready: *the postponement saved the army from setting off another attack at half-cock.*
– DERIVATIVES **half-cocked** adjective.

half-crown (also **half a crown**) ▶ **noun** a former British coin and monetary unit equal to two shillings and sixpence (12$^1/_2$p).

half-cut ▶ **adjective** Brit. informal drunk.

half-deck ▶ **noun** a deck reaching half the length of a ship or boat, fore or aft.
– DERIVATIVES **half-decked** adjective.

half-dozen (also **half a dozen**) ▶ **noun** a set or group of six: *a half-dozen slices of smoked salmon.*

half-duplex ▶ **adjective** (of a communications system or computer circuit) allowing the transmission of signals in both directions but not simultaneously.

half-hardy ▶ **adjective** (of a plant) able to grow outdoors at all times except in severe frost: *a half-hardy annual.*

half-hearted ▶ **adjective** without enthusiasm or energy: *a half-hearted attempt.*
– DERIVATIVES **half-heartedly** adverb, **half-heartedness** noun.

half hitch ▶ **noun** a knot formed by passing the end of a rope round its standing part and then through the loop.

half holiday ▶ **noun** a day of which either the morning or (usually) the afternoon is taken as a holiday.

half-hose ▶ **noun** [mass noun] archaic socks.

half hour ▶ **noun** (also **half an hour**) a period of thirty minutes: *buses run every half hour.* ■ a point in time thirty minutes after any full hour of the clock: *the library clock struck the half hour.*
– DERIVATIVES **half-hourly** adjective & adverb.

half-hunter ▶ **noun** a pocket watch with a hinged cover in the middle of which a small opening or window allows one to read the approximate time.

half-inch ▶ **noun** a unit of length half as long as an inch.
▶ **verb** [with obj.] Brit. informal steal: *she had her handbag half-inched.* [1920s: rhyming slang for 'pinch'.]

half-integer ▶ **noun** a number obtained by dividing an odd integer by two ($^1/_2$, 1$^1/_2$, 2$^1/_2$, etc.).
– DERIVATIVES **half-integral** adjective.

half landing ▶ **noun** Brit. an area of floor where a flight of stairs turns through 180 degrees.

half-lap ▶ **noun** another term for **LAP JOINT**.

half-length ▶ **adjective** of approximately half the normal length. ■ (of a painting or sculpture) showing a person down to their waist.
▶ **noun** a painting or sculpture of a person down to their waist.

half-life ▶ **noun** the time taken for the radioactivity of a specified isotope to fall to half its original value. ■ the time required for any specified property (e.g. the concentration of a substance in the body) to decrease by half.

half-light ▶ **noun** [mass noun] dim light such as at dusk or dawn: *the trees had a slightly spooky look in the half-light.*

half-marathon ▶ **noun** a long-distance running race, strictly one of 13 miles 352 yards (21.243 km).

half mast ▶ **noun** the position of a flag which is being flown some way below the top of its staff as a mark of respect for a person who has died: *each club flew its flag at half mast.* ■ chiefly humorous a position lower than normal or acceptable, especially for clothes: *his tie was at half mast.*

half measure ▶ **noun** (usu. **half measures**) an action or policy that is not forceful or decisive enough: *there are **no half measures** with this company.*

half-moon ▶ **noun** the moon when only half its illuminated surface is visible from the earth; the first or last quarter. ■ the time when this occurs. ■ a semicircular or crescent-shaped object: [as modifier] *half-moon spectacles.*

half-move ▶ **noun** Chess a move made by one player (especially in the context of the analysis of play made by a chess-playing computer program).

half nelson ▶ **noun** see **NELSON**.

half note ▶ **noun** Music, chiefly N. Amer. a minim.

half-pants ▶ **noun** Indian a pair of shorts.

half pay ▶ **noun** [mass noun] half of a person's normal or previous salary or wages: *he and other senior execs will be **on half pay** for the next six months.*

halfpenny /ˈheɪpni/ (also **ha'penny**) ▶ **noun** (pl. for separate coins **halfpennies**, for a sum of money **halfpence** /ˈheɪp(ə)ns/) a former British coin equal to half an old or new penny. The last halfpenny was withdrawn in 1984.

halfpennyworth /ˈheɪpəθ, ˈheɪpnɪˌwəθ/ (also **ha'p'orth**) ▶ **noun** Brit. as much as could be bought for a halfpenny. ■ [usu. with negative] (**ha'p'orth**) informal a negligible amount: *he's never been a ha'p'orth of bother.*
– PHRASES **don't spoil the ship for a ha'p'orth of tar** proverb don't risk the failure of a large project by trying to economize on trivial things. [referring to the use of tar to keep flies off sores on sheep (from dialect pronunciation of *sheep* as *ship*).]

half-pie ▶ **adjective** NZ informal imperfect; mediocre.
– ORIGIN *pie* perhaps from Maori *pai* 'good'.

half-pipe ▶ **noun** a channel made of concrete or cut into the snow with a U-shaped cross section, used by skateboarders, rollerbladers, or snowboarders to perform jumps and other manoeuvres.

half plate ▶ **noun** Brit. a photographic plate measuring 4$^3/_4$ × 6$^1/_2$ inches (*c.* 10.8 × 16.5 cm).

half-price ▶ **adjective & adverb** costing half the normal price: [as adj.] *half-price admission* | [as adv.] *a brooch I bought half-price in the sale.*
▶ **noun** half the usual price: *selected lines are **at half price**.*

half relief ▶ **noun** [mass noun] a method of moulding, carving, or stamping in relief a design in which figures project to half their true proportions. ■ [count noun] a sculpture or carving in half relief.

half seas over ▶ **adjective** [predic.] Brit. informal, dated fairly drunk.

half-sister ▶ **noun** a sister with whom one has only one parent in common.

half sovereign ▶ **noun** a former British gold coin worth ten shillings (50p).

half-standard ▶ **noun** a tree or shrub that grows on an erect stem of half height and stands alone without support.

half step ▶ **noun** Music, N. Amer. a semitone.

half-term ▶ **noun** Brit. a short holiday about halfway through a school term.

half-tester ▶ **noun** historical a canopy extending over half the length of a bed. ■ a bed with a half-tester.

half-timbered ▶ **adjective** having walls with a timber frame and a brick or plaster filling.
– DERIVATIVES **half-timbering** noun.

half-time ▶ **noun** the time at which half of a game or contest is completed, especially when marked by an interval: *Spain led 9-7 at half-time.*

half-title ▶ **noun** the title of a book, printed on the right-hand page before the title page. ■ the title of a section of a book printed on the right-hand page before it. ■ a page on which a title of either of these kinds is printed.

halftone ▶ **noun 1** a reproduction of a photograph or other image in which the various tones of grey or colour are produced by variously sized dots of ink: [as modifier] *halftone illustrations.*
2 Music, chiefly N. Amer. a semitone.

half-track ▶ **noun** a military or other vehicle with wheels at the front and caterpillar tracks at the rear.

half-truth ▶ **noun** a statement that conveys only part of the truth, especially one used deliberately in order to mislead someone.

half-uncial ▶ **adjective** denoting a style of medieval letter showing features of both uncial and cursive script.
▶ **noun** a half-uncial letter.

half-volley ▶ **noun** (chiefly in tennis or soccer) a strike or kick of the ball made immediately after it bounces off the ground.

H

halfway ▶ **adverb & adjective** at or to a point equidistant between two others: [as adv.] *he stopped halfway down the passage* | [as adj.] *during the night we passed Kingoonya, the halfway mark.* ■ in the middle of a period of time: [as adv.] *halfway through the night.* ■ [as adv.] to some extent: *I'm incapable of doing anything even halfway decent.*

halfway house ▶ **noun 1** the halfway point in a progression. ■ Brit. a compromise between two different or opposing views or courses of action: *the formula seems a good halfway house and avoids another row.*
2 a centre for rehabilitating former prisoners, psychiatric patients, or others unused to non-institutional life.
3 historical an inn midway between two towns.

halfway line ▶ **noun** a line across a sports field midway between the ends.

halfwit ▶ **noun** informal a foolish or stupid person.

half-witted ▶ **adjective** informal foolish or stupid: *a half-witted proposal.*
– DERIVATIVES **half-wittedly** adverb, **half-wittedness** noun.

half-yearly ▶ **adjective & adverb** at intervals of six months: [as adj.] *the loan was to be repaid by 80 half-yearly instalments* | [as adv.] *the interest will be paid half-yearly in June and December.* ■ [as adj.] relating to half a financial year: *half-yearly sales.*

halibut /ˈhalɪbət/ ▶ **noun** (pl. **same**) a northern marine fish which is the largest of the flatfishes and important as a food fish. ● Genus *Hippoglossus*, family Pleuronectidae: *H. hippoglossus* of the Atlantic and *H. stenolepis* of the Pacific.
■ used in names of large edible flatfishes of families other than the true halibut, e.g. **Greenland halibut**.
– ORIGIN late Middle English: from *haly* 'holy' + obsolete *butt* 'flatfish' (because it was often eaten on holy days).

Haliç /haˈliːtʃ/ Turkish name for **GOLDEN HORN**.

Halicarnassus /ˌhalɪkɑːˈnasəs/ an ancient Greek city on the SW coast of Asia Minor, at what is now the Turkish city of Bodrum. It is the site of the Mausoleum of Halicarnassus, one of the Seven Wonders of the World.

halide /ˈheɪlʌɪd/ ▶ **noun** Chemistry a binary compound of a halogen with another element or group.

halier /ˈhaljɛː/ ▶ **noun** (pl. **same** or **haliers**) a monetary unit of Slovakia, equal to one hundredth of a koruna.
– ORIGIN Slovak; compare with **HALER**.

halieutic /ˌhalɪˈjuːtɪk/ ▶ **adjective** formal relating to fishing.
– ORIGIN mid 19th cent.: via Latin from Greek *halieutikos*, from *halieutēs* 'fisherman'.

Halifax /ˈhalɪfaks/ **1** the capital of Nova Scotia, Canada; pop. 372,679 (2006). It is Canada's principal ice-free port on the Atlantic coast. [named after George Montagu Dunk (1716–71), the second earl of *Halifax*.]
2 a town in West Yorkshire, northern England, on the River Calder; pop. 76,000 (est. 2009).

halite /ˈhalʌɪt/ ▶ **noun** [mass noun] sodium chloride as a mineral, typically occurring as colourless cubic crystals; rock salt.

– ORIGIN mid 19th cent.: from Greek *hals* 'salt' + **-ITE**[1].

halitosis /ˌhalɪˈtəʊsɪs/ ▶ **noun** technical term for **BAD BREATH**.
– DERIVATIVES **halitotic** adjective.
– ORIGIN late 19th cent.: from Latin *halitus* 'breath' + **-OSIS**.

Hall, (Marguerite) Radclyffe (1883–1943), English novelist and poet. She is chiefly remembered for her novel *The Well of Loneliness* (1928), an exploration of a lesbian relationship, which caused outrage and was banned in Britain for many years.

hall ▶ **noun 1** the room or space just inside the front entrance of a house or flat. ■ N. Amer. a corridor or area on to which rooms open.
2 a building or large room used for meetings, concerts, or other events: *the village hall*. ■ historical the building in which a guild was housed.
3 a large room in a mansion or palace used for receptions and banquets. ■ [in names] Brit. a large country house, especially one with a landed estate: *Darlington Hall*. ■ the principal living room of a medieval house.
4 (also **hall of residence**) Brit. a university building containing rooms for students to live in. ■ the room used for meals in a college, university, or school: *he dined in hall*.
– ORIGIN Old English *hall*, *heall* (originally denoting a roofed space, located centrally, for the communal use of a tribal chief and his people); of Germanic origin and related to German *Halle*, Dutch *hall*, also to Norwegian and Swedish *hall*.

H

Halle /ˈhalə/ a city in east central Germany, on the River Saale, in Saxony-Anhalt; pop. 235,700 (est. 2006).

Hallé /ˈhaleɪ/, Sir Charles (1819–95), German-born pianist and conductor; born *Karl Halle*. He left Paris in 1848 and settled in Manchester, where he founded the Hallé Orchestra (1858).

Hall effect ▶ **noun** Physics the production of a potential difference across an electrical conductor when a magnetic field is applied in a direction perpendicular to that of the flow of current.
– ORIGIN early 20th cent.: named after Edwin H. *Hall* (1855–1938), American physicist.

Hallel /ˈhalɛl, haˈleɪl/ ▶ **noun** (usu. **the Hallel**) a portion of the service for certain Jewish festivals, consisting of Psalms 113–118.
– ORIGIN from Hebrew *hallēl* 'praise'.

hallelujah /ˌhalɪˈluːjə/ (also **alleluia**) ▶ **exclamation** God be praised (uttered in worship or as an expression of rejoicing).
▶ **noun** an utterance of the word 'hallelujah' as an expression of worship or rejoicing. ■ (usu. **Alleluia**) a piece of music or church liturgy containing this: *the Gospel comes after the Alleluia verse*.
– ORIGIN Old English, via ecclesiastical Latin *alleluia* from Greek *allēlouia* (in the Septuagint), or (from the 16th century) directly from Hebrew *hallĕlûyāh* 'praise ye the Lord'.

Haller /ˈhalə/, Albrecht von (1708–77), Swiss anatomist and physiologist. He pioneered the study of neurology and experimental physiology and wrote the first textbook of physiology.

Halley /ˈhali, ˈhɔːli/, Edmond (1656–1742), English astronomer and mathematician. He is best known for identifying a bright comet (later named after him), and for successfully predicting its return.

Halley's comet a periodical comet with an orbital period of about 76 years, its reappearance in 1758–9 having been predicted by Edmond Halley. It was first recorded in 240 BC and last appeared, rather faintly, in 1985–6.

Halliday /ˈhalɪdeɪ/, Michael (Alexander Kirkwood) (b.1925), English linguist. He built on the work of J. R. Firth in pursuit of a psychologically and sociologically realistic overall theory of language and its functions.

hallmark ▶ **noun** a mark stamped on articles of gold, silver, or platinum by the British assay offices, certifying their standard of purity. ■ a distinctive feature: *the tiny bubbles are **the hallmark of** fine champagnes*.
▶ **verb** [with obj.] stamp with a hallmark. ■ mark as distinctive: *this attitude hallmarks many a Briton's behaviour abroad*.
– ORIGIN early 18th cent. (as a noun): from *Goldsmiths' Hall* in London, where articles were tested and stamped with such a mark.

hallo ▶ **exclamation, noun, & verb** variant spelling of **HELLO**.

Hall of Fame a national memorial in New York City containing busts and memorials honouring the achievements of famous Americans. ■ [as noun] chiefly N. Amer. the class or category of those who have excelled in a particular activity: *the Hockey Hall of Fame*.
– DERIVATIVES **Hall of Famer** noun.

hall of residence ▶ **noun** see **HALL** (sense 4).

halloo ▶ **exclamation** used to incite dogs to the chase during a hunt. ■ used to attract someone's attention.
▶ **noun** a cry of 'halloo'.
▶ **verb** (**halloos**, **hallooing**, **hallooed**) [no obj.] cry or shout 'halloo' to attract attention or to give encouragement to dogs in hunting. ■ [with obj.] shout to (someone) to attract their attention.
– ORIGIN mid 16th cent.: probably from the rare verb *hallow* 'pursue or urge on with shouts', from imitative Old French *haloer*.

halloumi /həˈluːmi/ ▶ **noun** [mass noun] a mild, firm white Cypriot cheese made from goat's or ewe's milk, used especially in cooked dishes.
– ORIGIN from Egyptian Arabic *ḥalūm*, probably from Arabic *ḥaluma* 'to be mild'.

hallow /ˈhaləʊ/ ▶ **verb** [with obj.] honour as holy: *the Ganges is hallowed as a sacred, cleansing river*. ■ make holy; consecrate: (as adj. **hallowed**) *hallowed ground*. ■ (usu. as adj. **hallowed**) greatly revere and honour: *the hallowed turf of Wimbledon*.
▶ **noun** archaic a saint or holy person.
– ORIGIN Old English *hālgian* (verb), *hālga* (noun), of Germanic origin; related to Dutch and German *heiligen*, also to **HOLY**.

Halloween (also **Hallowe'en**) ▶ **noun** the night of 31 October, the eve of All Saints' Day, often celebrated by children dressing up in frightening masks and costumes. Halloween is thought to be associated with the Celtic festival Samhain, when ghosts and spirits were believed to be abroad.
– ORIGIN late 18th cent.: contraction of *All Hallow Even* (see **HALLOW**, **EVEN**[2]).

Hallowes /ˈhaləʊz/, Odette (1912–95), French heroine of the Second World War; born *Marie Céline*. She worked as a British secret agent in occupied France from 1942 until captured in 1943. Imprisoned for two years, she refused to betray her associates in spite of torture and was awarded the George Cross in 1946.

hall porter ▶ **noun** Brit. a concierge or a person who carries guests' luggage in a hotel.

hallstand (US **hall tree**) ▶ **noun** a coat stand in the hall of a house.

Hallstatt /ˈhalʃtat/ ▶ **noun** [usu. as modifier] Archaeology a cultural phase of the late Bronze Age and early Iron Age in Europe (*c.*1200–600 BC in temperate continental areas), preceding the La Tène period. It is generally equated with the Urnfield complex and is associated with the early Celts.
– ORIGIN mid 19th cent.: the name of a village in Austria, site of a burial ground of this period.

halluces plural form of **HALLUX**.

hallucinate /həˈluːsɪneɪt/ ▶ **verb** [no obj.] experience a seemingly real perception of something not actually present, typically as a result of a mental disorder or of taking drugs: *Ben began hallucinating and having fits*. ■ [with obj.] experience a hallucination of (something).
– DERIVATIVES **hallucinant** adjective & noun, **hallucinator** noun.
– ORIGIN mid 17th cent. (in the sense 'be deceived, have illusions'): from Latin *hallucinat-* 'gone astray in thought', from the verb *hallucinari*, from Greek *alussein* 'be uneasy or distraught'.

hallucination ▶ **noun** an experience involving the apparent perception of something not present: *he continued to suffer from horrific hallucinations*.

hallucinatory /həˈluːsɪnəˌt(ə)ri/ ▶ **adjective** of or resembling a hallucination: *a hallucinatory fantasy*. ■ inducing hallucinations: *a hallucinatory drug*.

hallucinogen /həˈluːsɪnədʒ(ə)n/ ▶ **noun** a drug that causes hallucinations, such as LSD.
– DERIVATIVES **hallucinogenic** adjective.

hallux /ˈhaləks/ ▶ **noun** (pl. **halluces** /-jʊsiːz, -ləsiːz/) Anatomy a person's big toe. ■ Zoology the innermost digit of the hind foot of vertebrates.
– ORIGIN mid 19th cent.: modern Latin alteration of medieval Latin *allex*, Latin *hallus*.

hallway ▶ **noun** another term for **HALL** (sense 1).

halma /ˈhalmə/ ▶ **noun** [mass noun] a game played by two or four people using a board of 256 squares, with pieces advancing from one corner to the opposite corner by being moved over other pieces into vacant squares.
– ORIGIN late 19th cent.: from Greek, literally 'leap'.

Halmahera /ˌhalməˈhɪərə/ the largest of the Molucca Islands.

halo /ˈheɪləʊ/ ▶ **noun** (pl. **haloes** or **halos**) **1** a circle of light shown around or above the head of a saint or holy person to represent their holiness. ■ the glory associated with an esteemed person: *he has lost his halo for many ordinary Russians*.
2 a circle of white or coloured light around the sun, moon, or other luminous body caused by refraction through ice crystals in the atmosphere.
▶ **verb** (**haloes**, **haloing**, **haloed**) [with obj.] surround with or as if with a halo.
– ORIGIN mid 16th cent. (denoting a circle of light round the sun etc.): from medieval Latin, from Latin *halos*, from Greek *halōs* 'disc of the sun or moon'.

halo- /ˈheɪləʊ/ ▶ **combining form 1** relating to salinity: *halophile*. [from Greek *hals*, *halo-* 'salt'.]
2 representing **HALOGEN**.

halocarbon ▶ **noun** Chemistry a CFC or other compound in which the hydrogen of a hydrocarbon is replaced by halogens.

halo effect ▶ **noun** the tendency for an impression created in one area to influence opinion in another area.

haloform ▶ **noun** Chemistry a compound derived from methane by substituting three hydrogen atoms by halogen atoms, e.g. chloroform.
– ORIGIN 1930s: from **HALOGEN**, on the pattern of *chloroform*.

halogen /ˈhalədʒ(ə)n, ˈheɪl-/ ▶ **noun** Chemistry any of the elements fluorine, chlorine, bromine, iodine, and astatine, occupying group VIIA (17) of the periodic table. They are reactive non-metallic elements which form strongly acidic compounds with hydrogen from which simple salts can be made. ■ [as modifier] denoting lamps and radiant heat sources using a filament surrounded by the vapour of iodine or another halogen: *a halogen bulb*.
– DERIVATIVES **halogenic** adjective.
– ORIGIN mid 19th cent.: from Greek *hals*, *halo-* 'salt' + **-GEN**.

halogenate /həˈlɒdʒɪneɪt/ ▶ **verb** [with obj.] (usu. as adj. **halogenated**) Chemistry introduce one or more halogen atoms into (a compound or molecule), usually in place of hydrogen.
– DERIVATIVES **halogenation** noun.

halon /ˈheɪlɒn/ ▶ **noun** any of a number of unreactive gaseous compounds of carbon with bromine and other halogens, used in fire extinguishers, but now known to damage the ozone layer.
– ORIGIN 1960s: from **HALOGEN** + **-ON**.

haloperidol /ˌhaləʊˈpɛrɪdɒl, ˌheɪlə(ʊ)-/ ▶ **noun** [mass noun] Medicine a synthetic antidepressant drug used chiefly in the treatment of psychotic conditions.
– ORIGIN 1960s: blend of **HALOGEN** and **PIPERIDINE** + **-OL**.

halophile /ˈhalə(ʊ)fʌɪl, ˈheɪl-/ ▶ **noun** Ecology an organism, especially a microorganism, that grows in or can tolerate saline conditions.
– DERIVATIVES **halophilic** adjective.

halophyte /ˈhaləfʌɪt, ˈheɪlə-/ ▶ **noun** Botany a plant adapted to growing in saline conditions, as in a salt marsh.

halothane /ˈhalə(ʊ)θeɪn/ ▶ **noun** [mass noun] Medicine a volatile synthetic organic compound used as a general anaesthetic. ● Chem. formula: $CF_3CHBrCl$.
– ORIGIN 1950s: blend of **HALOGEN** and **ETHANE**.

Hals /hals/, Frans (*c.*1580–1666), Dutch portrait and genre painter. He endowed his portraits with vitality, departing from conventional portraiture with works such as *The Banquet of the Officers of the St George Militia Company* (1616) and *The Laughing Cavalier* (1624).

Hälsingborg /ˌhɛlsɪŋˈbɔrj/ Swedish name for **HELSINGBORG**.

halt[1] ▶ **verb** bring or come to an abrupt stop: [with obj.] *there is growing pressure to halt the bloodshed* | [no obj.] *she halted in mid sentence*. ■ [in imperative] used as a military command to bring marching soldiers to a stop: *company, halt!*
▶ **noun** a suspension of movement or activity, typically a temporary one: *a halt in production* | *a bus screeched to a halt*. ■ Brit. a minor stopping place on a local railway line.
– PHRASES **call a halt** demand or order a stop: *he decided to call a halt to all further discussion*.

– ORIGIN late 16th cent.: originally in the phrase *make halt*, from German *haltmachen*, from *halten* 'to hold'.

halt[2] archaic ▶ **adjective** lame.
▶ **verb** [no obj.] walk with a limp.
– ORIGIN Old English *healtian* (verb), *halt, healt* (adjective), of Germanic origin.

halter ▶ **noun 1** a strap or rope placed around the head of a horse or other animal, used for leading or tethering it. ■ archaic a rope with a noose for hanging a person.
2 [usu. as modifier] a strap around the neck that holds a dress or top in place, leaving the shoulders and back bare: *tourists in halter tops and shorts*.
▶ **verb** [with obj.] put a halter on (an animal). ■ archaic hang (someone).
– ORIGIN Old English *hælftre*, of Germanic origin, meaning 'something to hold things by'; related to German *Halfter*, also to HELVE.

halter-break ▶ **verb** [with obj.] accustom (a young horse) to wearing and being handled in a halter.

haltere /hal'tɪə/ ▶ **noun** (usu. **halteres**) Entomology the balancing organ of a two-winged fly, seen as either of a pair of knobbed filaments that take the place of the hindwings, vibrating during flight.
– ORIGIN mid 16th cent. (originally plural, denoting a pair of weights like dumb-bells held in the hands to give impetus when jumping): from Greek *haltēres* (plural), from *hallesthai* 'to leap'.

halter-neck ▶ **adjective** [attrib.] (of a woman's garment) held up by a strap around the neck.
▶ **noun** a halter-neck garment.

halting ▶ **adjective** slow and hesitant, especially through lack of confidence; faltering: *she speaks halting English with a heavy accent*.
– DERIVATIVES **haltingly** adverb.

halva /'halvə, -vɑː/ (also **halvah**) ▶ **noun** [mass noun] a Middle Eastern sweet made of sesame flour and honey.
– ORIGIN Yiddish, or from Turkish *helva*, from Arabic and Persian *ḥalwā* 'sweetmeat'.

halve ▶ **verb** [with obj.] **1** divide into two parts of equal or roughly equal size: *halve the aubergine lengthways*. ■ reduce or be reduced by half: [no obj.] *pre-tax profits nearly halved to £5 m* | [with obj.] *his pledge to halve the deficit over the next four years*. ■ share (something) equally with another person: *she insisted on halving the bill*. ■ Golf use the same number of strokes as one's opponent and thus draw (a hole or match).
2 (usu. as noun **halving**) fit (crossing timbers) together by cutting out half the thickness of each.
– ORIGIN Middle English: from HALF.

halvers /'hɑːvəz/ ▶ **plural noun** (in phrase **go halvers**) informal, chiefly Scottish, N. English, & N. Amer. agree to have a half share each.

halves plural form of HALF.

halwa /'halwɑː/ (also **halwah**) ▶ **noun** [mass noun] a sweet Indian dish consisting of carrots or semolina boiled with milk, almonds, sugar, butter, and cardamom.
– ORIGIN from Arabic, literally 'sweetmeat'.

halyard /'haljəd/ ▶ **noun** a rope used for raising and lowering a sail, yard, or flag on a sailing ship.
– ORIGIN late Middle English *halier*, from HALE[2] + -IER. The change in the ending in the 18th cent. was due to association with YARD[1].

Ham /ham/ (in the Bible) a son of Noah (Gen. 10:1), traditional ancestor of the Hamites.

ham[1] ▶ **noun 1** [mass noun] salted or smoked meat from the upper part of a pig's leg: *thin slices of ham* | [count noun] *a honey-baked ham*.
2 (**hams**) the back of the thigh or the thighs and buttocks: *he squatted down on his hams*.
– ORIGIN Old English *ham, hom* (originally denoting the back of the knee), from a Germanic base meaning 'be crooked'. In the late 15th cent. the term came to denote the back of the thigh, hence the thigh or hock of an animal.

ham[2] ▶ **noun 1** [usu. as modifier] an excessively theatrical actor: *ham actors*. ■ [mass noun] excessively theatrical acting.
2 (also **radio ham**) informal an amateur radio operator.
▶ **verb** (**hams, hamming, hammed**) [no obj.] informal overact: *she hammed it up for the cameras*.
– ORIGIN late 19th cent. (originally US): perhaps from the first syllable of AMATEUR; compare with the US slang term *hamfatter* 'inexpert performer'. Sense 2 of the noun dates from the early 20th cent.

Hama /'hɑːmɑː/ (also **Hamah**) an industrial city in western Syria, on the River Orontes; pop. 531,000 (est. 2009). It was the centre of an Aramaean kingdom in the 11th century BC. Much of the modern city was destroyed during an unsuccessful uprising against the government in 1982.

hamachi /ha'matʃi/ ▶ **noun** [mass noun] the young of the Japanese amberjack or yellowtail, which is fished and bred in Japan as a food fish.
– ORIGIN Japanese.

hamadryad /ˌhamə'drʌɪəd, -ad/ ▶ **noun 1** Greek & Roman Mythology a nymph who lives in a tree and dies when the tree dies.
2 another term for KING COBRA.
– ORIGIN via Latin from Greek *Hamadruas*, from *hama* 'together' + *drus* 'tree'.

hamadryas /ˌhamə'drʌɪəs, -as/ (also **hamadryas baboon**) ▶ **noun** a large Arabian and NE African baboon, the male of which has a silvery-grey cape of hair and a naked red face and rump. It was held sacred in ancient Egypt. ● *Papio hamadryas*, family Cercopithecidae.
– ORIGIN 1930s: modern Latin (see HAMADRYAD).

Hamah variant spelling of HAMA.

Hamamatsu /ˌhamə'matsuː/ an industrial city on the southern coast of the island of Honshu, Japan; pop. 788,078 (2007).

hamamelis /ˌhamə'miːlɪs/ ▶ **noun** the witch hazel.
– ORIGIN mid 18th cent.: modern Latin (genus name), from Greek *hamamēlis* 'medlar'.

ham-and-egger ▶ **noun** US informal an ordinary man.

hamartia /hə'mɑːtɪə/ ▶ **noun** a fatal flaw leading to the downfall of a tragic hero or heroine.
– ORIGIN late 18th cent.: Greek, 'fault, failure, guilt'; the term was used in Aristotle's *Poetics* with reference to ancient Greek tragedy.

Hamas /ha'mas, 'hamas/ a Palestinian Islamic movement founded in 1987 with the aim of establishing a Palestinian state incorporating present-day Israel and the West Bank. In 2006 Hamas defeated the more moderate Fatah in the elections for the Palestinian National Authority.
– ORIGIN Arabic, acronym from the official name of the organization, *Ḥarakat al-Muqāwama al-Islāmiyya* 'Islamic Resistance Movement'.

hamate /'heɪmət/ (also **hamate bone**) ▶ **noun** Anatomy a carpal bone situated on the lower outside edge of the hand. It has a hook-shaped projection on the palmar side to which muscles of the little finger are attached.
– ORIGIN early 18th cent.: from Latin *hamatus* 'hooked', from *hamus* 'hook'.

hambone /'hambəʊn/ ▶ **noun** N. Amer. informal an inferior actor or performer, especially one who uses a spurious black accent.

Hamburg[1] /'hambəːg/, German /'hambʊrk/ a port in northern Germany, on the River Elbe; pop. 1,754,200 (est. 2006). Founded by Charlemagne in the 9th century, it is now the largest port in Germany, with extensive shipyards.

Hamburg[2] /'hambəːg/ ▶ **noun 1** (also **Hamburg steak**) N. Amer. another term for HAMBURGER.
2 (also **Black** or **Muscat Hamburg**) a black variety of grape of German origin, specially adapted to hothouse cultivation.
– ORIGIN from HAMBURG[1].

hamburger ▶ **noun** a patty of minced beef, fried or grilled and typically served in a bread roll. ■ N. Amer. minced beef.
– ORIGIN late 19th cent. (originally US): from German, from HAMBURG[1].

hamel /'haməl, 'hɑːməl/ ▶ **noun** S. African a castrated ram.
– ORIGIN Afrikaans.

Hameln /'hɑːm(ə)ln/ (also **Hamelin** /'hamlɪn/) a town in NW Germany, in Lower Saxony, on the River Weser; pop. 58,500 (est. 2006). A medieval market town, it is the setting of the legend of the Pied Piper of Hamelin.

hamerkop /'hɑːməkɒp, 'haməkɒp/ (also **hammerkop** /'haməkɒp/) ▶ **noun** a brown African marshbird related to the storks, which has a crest that looks like a backward projection of the head, and constructs an enormous nest. ● *Scopus umbretta*, the only member of the family Scopidae.
– ORIGIN mid 19th cent.: Afrikaans, from *hamer* 'hammer' + *kop* 'head'.

hames /heɪmz/ ▶ **plural noun** two curved pieces of iron or wood forming or attached to the collar of a draught horse, to which the traces are attached.
– PHRASES **make a hames of** Irish informal do (something) very badly or ineptly; make a mess of: *Galway made a hames of their chance of a goal*.
– ORIGIN Middle English: from Middle Dutch.

ham-fisted ▶ **adjective** Brit. informal clumsy; bungling: *a ham-fisted attempt*.
– DERIVATIVES **ham-fistedly** adverb, **ham-fistedness** noun.

ham-handed ▶ **adjective** North American term for HAM-FISTED.
– DERIVATIVES **ham-handedly** adverb, **ham-handedness** noun.

Hamhung /ham'hʌŋ/ an industrial city in eastern North Korea; pop. 773,000 (est. 2007). It was the centre of government of NE Korea during the Yi dynasty of 1392–1910.

Hamilcar /ha'mɪlkɑː, 'hamɪlˌkɑː/ (*c.*270–229 BC), Carthaginian general, father of Hannibal. He fought Rome in the first Punic War and negotiated the terms of peace after Carthaginian defeat.

Hamilton[1] **1** a town in South Lanarkshire, southern Scotland, near Glasgow; pop. 48,000 (est. 2009).
2 a port and industrial city in southern Canada, at the western end of Lake Ontario; pop. 504,559 (2006).
3 a city in the North Island, New Zealand; pop. 129,249 (2006).
4 the capital of Bermuda; pop. 11,000 (est. 2009).

Hamilton[2], Alexander (*c.*1757–1804), American Federalist politician. He established the US central banking system, and advocated strong central government. He was killed in a duel with Aaron Burr.

Hamilton[3], Lady Emma (*c.*1765–1815), English beauty and mistress of Lord Nelson; born *Amy Lyon*. She met Lord Nelson while married to Sir William Hamilton, the British ambassador to Naples. She had a daughter by Nelson in 1801 and lived with him after her husband's death in 1803.

Hamilton[4], Lewis (Carl Davidson) (b.1985), English motor-racing driver. He won the Formula One world championship in 2008.

Hamilton[5], Sir William Rowan (1806–65), Irish mathematician and theoretical physicist. Hamilton made influential contributions to optics and to the foundations of algebra and quantum mechanics.

Hamiltonian /ˌham(ə)l'təʊnɪən/ ▶ **adjective 1** Physics & Mathematics of or relating to the mathematician Sir William Rowan Hamilton, especially denoting concepts employed in the wave-mechanical description of particles.
2 relating to the American statesman Alexander Hamilton or his doctrines.
▶ **noun 1** (also **hamiltonian**) Physics & Mathematics a Hamiltonian operator or function.
2 a follower or adherent of Alexander Hamilton or his doctrines.
– DERIVATIVES **Hamiltonianism** noun (sense 2 of the adjective).

Hamite /'hamʌɪt/ ▶ **noun** a member of a group of North African peoples, including the ancient Egyptians and Berbers, supposedly descended from Ham, son of Noah.

Hamitic /hə'mɪtɪk/ ▶ **adjective** historical of or denoting a hypothetical language family formerly proposed to comprise Berber, ancient Egyptian, the Cushitic languages, and the Chadic languages. These are now recognized as independent branches of the Afro-Asiatic family.
– ORIGIN from HAMITE + -IC.

Hamito-Semitic /ˌhamɪtəʊsɪ'mɪtɪk/ ▶ **adjective** former term for AFRO-ASIATIC.

Hamlet a legendary prince of Denmark, hero of a tragedy by Shakespeare.
– PHRASES **Hamlet without the Prince** a performance or event taking place without the principal actor or central figure.

hamlet ▶ **noun** a small settlement, generally one smaller than a village, and strictly (in Britain) one without a church.
– ORIGIN Middle English: from Old French *hamelet*, diminutive of *hamel* 'little village'; related to HOME (*hám* in Old English).

Hamm /ham/ an industrial city in NW Germany, in North Rhine-Westphalia, on the Lippe River; pop. 183,700 (est. 2006).

hammam /ha'mam, hə'mɑːm/ ▶ **noun** a Turkish bath.

H

– ORIGIN from Turkish or Arabic *ḥammām* 'bath', from *ḥamma* 'to heat'.

Hammarskjöld /ˈhaməˌʃʊld/, Dag (Hjalmar Agne Carl) (1905–61), Swedish diplomat and politician. As Secretary General of the United Nations (1953–61) he was influential in the establishment of the UN emergency force in Sinai and Gaza (1956), and also initiated peace moves in the Middle East (1957–8). He was posthumously awarded the 1961 Nobel Peace Prize.

Hammer (in full **Hammer Film Productions**) a British film company founded in 1948, known especially for its horror films. ■ [usu. as modifier] a film produced by this company: *a **Hammer** horror movie*.

hammer ▶ noun **1** a tool with a heavy metal head mounted at right angles at the end of a handle, used for jobs such as breaking things and driving in nails. ■ a machine with a metal block for giving a heavy blow to something. ■ an auctioneer's gavel, tapped to indicate a sale. ■ a part of a mechanism that hits another part to make it work, such as one exploding the charge in a gun or one striking the strings of a piano.
2 a metal ball of about 7 kg attached to a wire for throwing in an athletic contest. ■ (**the hammer**) the sport of throwing such a ball.
3 another term for MALLEUS.
▶ verb [with obj.] **1** hit or beat (something) repeatedly with a hammer or similar object: *he hammered the tack in*. ■ [no obj.] strike or knock at or on something violently with one's hand or with a hammer or other object: *she **hammered on** his door* | [with obj.] *he hammered the ball wildly over the crossbar*. ■ [no obj.] (**hammer away**) work hard and persistently: *they must hammer away at these twin themes day after day*. ■ (**hammer something in/into**) inculcate something forcefully or repeatedly: *a commercial image that was hammered into English consciousness*.
2 informal attack or criticize forcefully and relentlessly: *he got **hammered** for an honest mistake*. ■ utterly defeat in a game or contest: *they hammered St Mirren 4–0*.
3 Stock Exchange, informal beat down the price of (a stock).
4 Stock Exchange declare (a person or company) a defaulter. [from the practice of striking three strokes with a mallet on the side of a rostrum in the Stock Exchange before a formal declaration of default.]
– PHRASES **come** (or **go**) **under the hammer** be sold at an auction. **hammer and tongs** informal energetically, enthusiastically, or with great vehemence: *racehorses **going at it hammer and tongs***. **hammer something home** see HOME.
– PHRASAL VERBS **hammer something out**
1 laboriously work out the details of a plan or agreement. **2** play something on a piano loudly and unskilfully.
– DERIVATIVES **hammerless** adjective.
– ORIGIN Old English *hamor*, *hamer*, of Germanic origin: related to Dutch *hamer*, German *Hammer*, and Old Norse *hamarr* 'rock'. The original sense was probably 'stone tool'.

hammer and sickle ▶ noun the symbols of the industrial worker and the peasant used as the emblem of the former Soviet Union and of international communism.

hammer beam ▶ noun a short wooden beam (typically carved) projecting from a wall to support either a principal rafter or one end of an arch.

hammer drill ▶ noun a power drill that works by delivering a rapid succession of blows, used chiefly for drilling in masonry or rock.

hammered ▶ adjective informal very drunk.

Hammerfest /ˈhaməfɛst/ a port in northern Norway, on North Kvaløy island; pop. 9,407 (2008). It is the northernmost town in Europe.

hammerhead ▶ noun **1** (also **hammerhead shark**) a shark of tropical and temperate oceans that has flattened blade-like extensions on either side of the head, with the eyes and nostrils placed at or near the ends. ● Family Sphyrnidae and genus *Sphyrna*: several species.
2 another term for HAMERKOP.

hammering ▶ noun **1** [mass noun] the action or sound of hammering something.
2 informal a heavy defeat: *a 7–0 hammering by the league leaders*.
– PHRASES **take a hammering** informal be subjected to a heavy defeat or harsh treatment.

hammerkop /ˈhaməkɒp/ ▶ noun variant spelling of HAMERKOP.

hammerlock ▶ noun an armlock in which a person's arm is bent up behind their back.

hammer price ▶ noun the price realized by an item sold at auction.

Hammerstein /ˈhaməstʌɪn/, Oscar (1895–1960), American librettist; full name *Oscar Hammerstein II*. He collaborated with various composers, most notably Richard Rodgers, with whom he wrote *Oklahoma!* (1943), *South Pacific* (1949), and *The Sound of Music* (1959).

hammer toe ▶ noun a toe that is bent permanently downwards, typically as a result of pressure from footwear.

Hammett /ˈhamɪt/, (Samuel) Dashiell (1894–1961), American novelist. His hard-boiled style of detective fiction is exemplified in works such as *The Maltese Falcon* (1930) and *The Thin Man* (1932).

hammock ▶ noun a bed made of canvas or rope mesh suspended from two supports by cords at both ends.
– ORIGIN mid 16th cent. (in the Spanish form *hamaca*): via Spanish from Taino *hamaka*; the ending was altered in the 16th cent. by association with **-OCK**.

Hammond, Dame Joan (1912–96), Australian operatic soprano, born in New Zealand.

Hammond organ ▶ noun trademark a type of electronic organ.
– ORIGIN 1930s: named after Laurens *Hammond* (1895–1973), American mechanical engineer.

Hammurabi /ˌhamʊˈrɑːbi/ (d.1750 BC), the sixth king of the first dynasty of Babylonia, reigned 1792–1750 BC. He extended the Babylonian empire and instituted one of the earliest known collections of laws.

hammy ▶ adjective (**hammier**, **hammiest**) **1** informal (of acting or an actor) exaggerated or over-theatrical.
2 (of a hand or thigh) thick and solid.
– DERIVATIVES **hammily** adverb, **hamminess** noun.

hamper[1] ▶ noun a basket with a carrying handle and a hinged lid, used for food, cutlery, and plates on a picnic. ■ Brit. a basket or box containing food for a special occasion: *a Christmas food hamper*. ■ N. Amer. a large basket with a lid, used for laundry.
– ORIGIN Middle English (denoting any large case or casket): from Anglo-Norman French *hanaper* 'case for a goblet', from Old French *hanap* 'goblet', of Germanic origin.

hamper[2] ▶ verb [with obj.] hinder or impede the movement or progress of: *their work is hampered by lack of funds*.
▶ noun [mass noun] Nautical necessary but cumbersome equipment on a ship.
– ORIGIN late Middle English (in the sense 'shackle, entangle, catch'): perhaps related to German *hemmen* 'restrain'.

Hampshire[1] a county on the coast of southern England; county town, Winchester.

Hampshire[2] ▶ noun a pig of a black breed with a white saddle and erect ears.

Hampstead a residential suburb of NW London.

Hampton a city in SE Virginia, on the harbour of Hampton Roads, on Chesapeake Bay; pop. 145,494 (est. 2008).

Hampton Court a palace on the north bank of the Thames in the borough of Richmond-upon-Thames, London, a favourite royal residence until the reign of George II. Its gardens contain a well-known maze.

Hampton Roads a deep-water estuary 6 km (4 miles) long, formed by the James River where it joins Chesapeake Bay, on the Atlantic coast in SE Virginia.

hamster ▶ noun a solitary burrowing rodent with a short tail and large cheek pouches for carrying food, native to Europe and North Asia. ● Subfamily Cricetinae, family Muridae: several genera and species, in particular the **golden hamster** (*Mesocricetus auratus*), often kept as a pet or laboratory animal, and the **common hamster** (*Cricetus cricetus*).
– ORIGIN early 17th cent.: from German, from Old High German *hamustro* 'corn weevil'.

hamstring ▶ noun any of five tendons at the back of a person's knee: *he pulled a hamstring*. ■ the great tendon at the back of a quadruped's hock.
▶ verb (past and past participle **hamstrung**) [with obj.] cripple (a person or animal) by cutting their hamstrings. ■ severely restrict the efficiency or effectiveness of: *we were hamstrung by a total lack of knowledge*.
– ORIGIN 16th cent.: from HAM[1] + STRING.

Hamsun /ˈhamsʊn/, Knut (1859–1952), Norwegian novelist; pseudonym of *Knut Pedersen*. Notable works: *Hunger* (1890) and *Growth of the Soil* (1917). Nobel Prize for Literature (1920).

hamulus /ˈhamjʊləs/ ▶ noun (pl. **hamuli** /-lʌɪ, -liː/) Anatomy & Zoology a small hook or hook-like projection, especially one of a number linking the fore- and hindwings of a bee or wasp.
– ORIGIN early 18th cent.: from Latin, diminutive of *hamus* 'hook'.

hamza /ˈhamzə/ ▶ noun (in Arabic script) a symbol representing a glottal stop. ■ a glottal stop.
– ORIGIN Arabic, literally 'compression'.

Han /han/ **1** the Chinese dynasty that ruled from 206 BC until AD 220 with only a brief interruption. During this period Chinese rule was extended over Mongolia, Confucianism was recognized as the state philosophy, and detailed historical records were kept.
2 the dominant ethnic group in China.

Hancock, Tony (1924–68), English comedian; full name *Anthony John Hancock*. He made his name in 1954 with the radio series *Hancock's Half Hour*, which was later adapted to television (1956–61).

hand ▶ noun **1** the end part of a person's arm beyond the wrist, including the palm, fingers, and thumb: *the palm of her hand* | *he was leading her by the hand*. ■ a prehensile organ resembling the hand and forming the end part of a limb of various mammals, such as that on all four limbs of a monkey. ■ W. Indian a person's arm, including the hand. ■ [as modifier] operated by or held in the hand: *hand luggage*. ■ [as modifier or in combination] done or made manually rather than by machine: *hand signals* | *a hand-stitched quilt*. ■ [in sing.] informal a round of applause: *his fans gave him a **big hand***. ■ a person's handwriting: *he inscribed the statement in a bold hand*. ■ dated a pledge of marriage by a woman: *he wrote to request the hand of her daughter in marriage*.
2 something resembling a hand in form, in particular: ■ a bunch of bananas. ■ Brit. a forehock of pork.
3 a pointer on a clock or watch indicating the passing of units of time: *the second hand*.
4 (**hands**) used in reference to the power to direct something: *the day-to-day running of the house was in her hands* | *they are taking the law into their own hands*. ■ (usu. **a hand**) an active role in achieving or influencing something: *he **had a big hand in** organizing the event*. ■ (usu. **a hand**) help in doing something: *do you need a hand?*
5 a person's workmanship, especially in artistic work: *his idiosyncratic hand*. ■ [with adj.] a person who does something to a specified standard: *I'm a great **hand at** inventing*.
6 a person who engages in manual labour, especially in a factory, on a farm, or on board a ship: *a factory hand* | *the ship was lost with all hands*.
7 the set of cards dealt to a player in a card game. ■ a round or short spell of play in a card game: *they played **a hand of** whist*. ■ Bridge the cards held by a declarer as opposed to those in the dummy.
8 a unit of measurement of a horse's height, equal to 4 inches (10.16 cm). [denoting the breadth of a hand, formerly used as a more general lineal measure and taken to equal three inches.]
▶ verb **1** [with two objs] pick (something) up and give it to (someone): *he handed each man a glass* | *I handed the trowel back to him*.
2 [with obj. and adverbial of direction] hold the hand of (someone) in order to guide them in a specified direction: *he handed them into the carriage*.
3 [with obj.] Sailing take in or furl (a sail): ***hand in** the main!*
– PHRASES **all hands on deck** a cry or signal used on board ship, typically in an emergency, to indicate that all crew members are to go on deck. ■ used to indicate that the involvement of all members of a team is required: *it was all hands on deck getting breakfast ready*. **at hand** close by: *a mortar burst close at hand*. ■ readily accessible when needed. ■ close in time; about to happen: *a breakthrough in combating the disease may be at hand*. **at** (or **by**) **the hands** (or **hand**) **of** through the agency of: *he will undergo tests at the hands of a senior neurologist*. **bind** (or **tie**) **someone hand and foot** tie someone's hands and feet together. **by hand** by a person and not a machine: *the crop has to be harvested by hand*. ■ (of mail) delivered in person rather than posted. **get** (or **keep**) **one's hand in** become (or remain) practised in something. **get** (or **lay**) **one's hands on** find or get something: *I haven't got my hands on a copy yet*. **give** (or **lend**) **a hand** assist in an action or enterprise. **hand in glove** in close collusion or association: *they were working hand in glove with our enemies*. **hand in hand** (of

two people) with hands joined, especially as a mark of affection. ■ closely associated or connected: *she had the confidence that usually **goes hand in hand** with experience.* **hand someone something on a plate** informal make something very easily obtainable for someone: *it was a win handed to him on a plate.* **(from) hand to mouth** satisfying only one's immediate needs because of lack of money fo future plans and investments: *they were flat broke and living hand to mouth* | [as modifier] *a hand-to-mouth existence.* **hands down** easily and decisively: *Swindon won hands down.* **hands off** used as a warning not to touch or interfere with something: *hands off that cake tin!* ■ (as adj. **hands-off**) not involving or requiring direct control or intervention: *a hands-off management style.* **hands-on** involving or offering active participation rather than theory: *hands-on in-service training.* ■ Computing involving or requiring personal operation at a keyboard. **hands up!** used as an instruction to raise one's hands in surrender or to signify assent or participation: *hands up who saw the programme!* **have a hand in something** be involved in doing something: *the girls had a hand in writing the lyrics.* **have one's hands full** have as much work as one can do. **have one's hands tied** informal be unable to act freely. **have to hand it to someone** informal used to acknowledge the merit or achievement of someone: *I've got to hand it to you—you've got the magic touch.* **in hand 1** receiving or requiring immediate attention: *he threw himself into the work in hand.* ■ in progress: *negotiations are now well in hand.* **2** ready for use if required; in reserve: *he had £1,000 of borrowed cash in hand.* **3** under one's control: *the police had the situation well in hand.* ■ (of land) farmed directly by its owner and not let to tenants. **in safe hands** protected by or in the care of someone trustworthy: *the future of the cathedral is in safe hands.* **make** (or **lose** or **spend**) **money hand over fist** informal make (or lose or spend) money very rapidly. **many hands make light work** proverb a task is soon accomplished if several people help. **not** (or **never**) **do a hand's turn** informal do no work at all: *they sit there without doing a hand's turn.* **off someone's hands** not having to be dealt with or looked after by the person specified: *they just want the problem off their hands.* **on every hand** all around: *new technologies were springing up on every hand.* **on hand 1** present, especially for a specified purpose: *her trainer was on hand to give advice.* ■ readily available. **2** needing to be dealt with: *they had many urgent and pressing matters on hand.* **on someone's hands 1** used to indicate that someone is responsible for dealing with someone or something: *he has a difficult job on his hands.* ■ used to indicate that someone is to blame for something: *he has my son's blood on his hands.* **2** at someone's disposal: *since I retired I've had more time on my hands.* **on the one** (or **the other**) **hand** used to present factors which are opposed or which support opposing opinions: *a conflict between their rationally held views on the one hand and their emotions and desires on the other.* **out of hand 1** not under control. **2** without taking time to think: *they rejected negotiations out of hand.* **the right hand doesn't know what the left hand's doing** used to convey that there is a state of confusion within a group or organization. **a safe pair of hands** (in a sporting context) used to refer to someone who is reliable when catching a ball. ■ used to denote someone who is capable, reliable, or trustworthy in the management of a situation. **set** (or **put**) **one's hand to** start work on. **stay someone's hand** restrain someone from acting. **take a hand** become influential in determining something; intervene: *fate was about to take a hand in the outcome of the championship.* **take some-one/something in hand** deal with or take control of someone or something: *their parents are incapable of taking their children in hand.* **to hand** within easy reach: *have a pen and paper to hand.* **turn one's hand to** undertake (an activity different from one's usual occupation). **wait on someone hand and foot** attend to all someone's needs or requests, especially when this is regarded as unreasonable. **with one hand (tied) behind one's back** with serious limitations or restrictions: *at the moment, the police are tackling record crime rates with one hand tied behind their back.*

– PHRASAL VERBS **hand something down 1** pass something on to a younger person or a successor: *songs are handed down from mother to daughter.* **2** announce something, especially a judgement or sentence, formally or publicly. **hand something in** give something to a person in authority for their attention. **hand someone off** Rugby push away a tackling opponent with one's hand. **hand something on** pass something to the next person in a series or succession: *he had handed on the family farm to his son.* ■ pass responsibility for something to someone else; delegate. **hand something out 1** give a share of something or one of a set of things to each of a number of people; distribute: *Ralph handed out cigars.* **2** impose or inflict a penalty or misfortune on someone. **hand over** pass responsibility to someone else: *he will soon hand over to a new director.* **hand someone/thing over** give someone or something, or the responsibility for someone or something, to someone else. **hand something round** (or **around**) offer something to each of a number of people in turn: *a big box of chocolates was handed round.*

– DERIVATIVES **handless** adjective.

– ORIGIN Old English *hand, hond*, of Germanic origin; related to Dutch *hand* and German *Hand*.

handbag ▶ noun **1** Brit. a small bag used by a woman to carry everyday personal items.
2 (**handbags**) humorous a confrontation that does not lead to serious fighting, especially among soccer players. [from the idea of women fighting with their handbags.]
▶ verb (**handbags, handbagging, handbagged**) [with obj.] informal, humorous (of a woman) verbally attack or crush (a person or idea) ruthlessly and forcefully: *I saw her last week and got handbagged for 15 minutes.* [1980s: coined by Julian Critchley, Conservative MP, with reference to Margaret Thatcher's ministerial style in cabinet meetings.]

handball ▶ noun [mass noun] **1** a game similar to fives, in which the ball is hit with the hand in a walled court. ■ a team game similar to soccer in which the ball is thrown or hit with the hands rather than kicked. ■ the ball used in these games.
2 Soccer touching of the ball with the hand or arm, constituting a foul.

handbasin ▶ noun Brit. a washbasin.

handbell ▶ noun a small bell with a handle or strap, especially one of a set tuned to a range of notes and played by a group of people.

handbill ▶ noun a small printed advertisement or other notice distributed by hand.

handbook ▶ noun a book giving information such as facts on a particular subject or instructions for operating a machine.

handbrake ▶ noun chiefly Brit. a brake operated by hand, used to hold an already stationary vehicle.

handbrake turn ▶ noun a skidding turn in a fast-moving car, typically through 180°, effected by a sudden application of the handbrake.

handcar ▶ noun N. Amer. a light railway vehicle propelled by cranks or levers and used by workers for inspecting the track.

handcart ▶ noun a small cart pushed or drawn by hand, used for delivering merchandise or luggage.

handclap ▶ noun a clap of the hands.
– DERIVATIVES **handclapping** noun.

handcraft ▶ verb [with obj.] (usu. as adj. **handcrafted**) make skilfully by hand: *a handcrafted rocking chair.*
▶ noun another term for HANDICRAFT.

hand crank ▶ noun a crank that is turned by hand.
▶ verb (**hand-crank**) [with obj.] operate (a device) by turning a crank by hand.

hand cream ▶ noun a moisturizing cream for the hands.

handcuff ▶ noun (**handcuffs**) a pair of lockable linked metal rings for securing a prisoner's wrists.
▶ verb [with obj.] put handcuffs on (someone): *he was led into court **handcuffed to** a policeman.*

-handed ▶ combining form **1** for or involving a specified number of hands: *four-handed piano pieces.*
2 chiefly using or designed for use by the hand specified: *a right-handed batsman* | *a left-handed guitar.*
3 having hands of a specified kind: *strong-handed.*
– DERIVATIVES **-handedly** adverb, **-handedness** noun.

handedness ▶ noun [mass noun] the tendency to use either the right or the left hand more naturally than the other.

Handel /ˈhand(ə)l/, George Frideric (1685–1759), German-born composer and organist, resident in England from 1712; born *Georg Friedrich Händel*. A prolific composer, he is chiefly remembered for his choral works, especially the oratorio *Messiah* (1742), and, for orchestra, his *Water Music* suite (*c*.1717) and *Music for the Royal Fireworks* (1749).

handful ▶ noun (pl. **handfuls**) **1** a quantity that fills the hand: *a small handful of fresh coriander.* ■ a small number or amount: *only **a handful of** people were in the pub.*
2 informal a person or group that is very difficult to deal with or control: *the kids could be such a handful.*

hand gallop ▶ noun an easily controlled gallop.

handglass ▶ noun **1** a magnifying glass held in the hand.
2 a small mirror with a handle.

hand grenade ▶ noun a hand-thrown grenade.

handgrip ▶ noun **1** a handle for holding something by.
2 a grasp with the hand, especially considered in terms of its strength, as in a handshake.
3 a soft bag with handles for carrying belongings in on a journey.

handgun ▶ noun a gun designed for use by one hand, chiefly either a pistol or a revolver.

handheld ▶ adjective designed to be held in the hand: *a handheld camera.*
▶ noun a small computer that can be used in the hand.

handhold ▶ noun something for a hand to grip on.

hand-holding ▶ noun [mass noun] the provision of support, reassurance, or guidance: *he hires experienced managers who don't need hand-holding.*

hand-hot ▶ adjective (of water) hot, but not too hot to put one's hands into.

handi ▶ noun (pl. **handis**) an earthenware or metal pot used in Indian cooking.
– ORIGIN Hindi *hāṇḍī*, from Sanskrit *bhāṇḍa* 'pot'.

handicap ▶ noun **1** a condition that markedly restricts a person's ability to function physically, mentally, or socially: *he was born with a significant visual handicap.* ■ a circumstance that makes progress or success difficult: *not being able to drive was something of a handicap.*
2 a disadvantage imposed on a superior competitor in sports such as golf, horse racing, and competitive sailing in order to make the chances more equal. ■ a race or contest in which a handicap is imposed: [in names] *the National Hunt Handicap Chase.* ■ the extra weight allocated to be carried in a race by a racehorse on the basis of its previous form to make its chances of winning the same as those of the other horses. ■ the number of strokes by which a golfer normally exceeds par for a course (used as a method of enabling players of unequal ability to compete with each other): *he plays off a handicap of 10.*
▶ verb (**handicaps, handicapping, handicapped**) [with obj.] act as an impediment to: *lack of funding has handicapped the development of research.* ■ place (someone) at a disadvantage: *her lack of formal training handicapped her.*
– PHRASES **out of the handicap** Horse Racing having a handicap rating that would merit carrying a weight below the minimum specified for a race.
– ORIGIN mid 17th cent.: from the phrase *hand in cap*; originally a pastime in which one person claimed an article belonging to another and offered something in exchange, any difference in value being decided by an umpire. All three deposited forfeit money in a cap; the two opponents showed their agreement or disagreement with the valuation by bringing out their hands either full or empty. If both were the same, the umpire took the forfeit money; if not it went to the person who accepted the valuation. The term *handicap race* was applied (late 18th cent.) to a horse race in which an umpire decided the weight to be carried by each horse, the owners showing acceptance or dissent in a similar way: hence in the late 19th cent. *handicap* came to mean the extra weight given to the superior horse.

handicap mark ▶ noun see MARK[1] (sense 3 of the noun).

handicapped ▶ adjective (of a person) having a condition that markedly restricts their ability to function physically, mentally, or socially.

> **USAGE** The word **handicapped** is first recorded in the early 20th century in the sense referring to a person's mental or physical disabilities. In British English it was the standard term until relatively recently but, like many terms in this sensitive field, its prominence has been shortlived. It has been superseded by more recent terms such as **disabled**, or, in reference to mental disability, **having learning difficulties** or **learning-disabled**. In American English, however, **handicapped** remains acceptable.

handicapper ▶ noun a person appointed to fix or assess a competitor's handicap, especially in golf or horse racing. ■ [usu. in combination] a person or horse having a specified handicap: *a three-handicapper.*

H

handicraft ▶ noun [mass noun] (also **handicrafts**) activity involving the making of decorative domestic or other objects by hand: *the traditional handicrafts of this region.* ■ decorative domestic objects made by hand.
– ORIGIN Middle English: alteration of HANDCRAFT, on the pattern of *handiwork*.

handiwork ▶ noun [mass noun] **1** (**one's handiwork**) something that one has made or done: *the dressmakers stood back to survey their handiwork.*
2 making things by hand, considered as a subject of instruction.
– ORIGIN Old English *handgeweorc*, from HAND + *geweorc* 'something made', interpreted in the 16th cent. as *handy* + *work*.

handjob ▶ noun vulgar slang an act of male masturbation, especially as performed on a man by someone else.

handkerchief /ˈhaŋkətʃɪf/ ▶ noun (pl. **handkerchiefs** or **handkerchieves** /-tʃiːvz/) a square of cotton or other finely woven material intended for wiping one's nose.
– ORIGIN mid 16th cent.: from HAND + KERCHIEF.

handkerchief tree ▶ noun another term for DOVE TREE.

H

handle ▶ verb [with obj.] **1** feel or manipulate with the hands: *heavy paving slabs can be difficult to handle* | *people who handle food.* ■ (chiefly in soccer) touch (the ball) with the hand or lower arm in contravention of the rules.
2 manage (a situation or problem): *a lawyer's ability to handle a case properly.* ■ have commercial responsibility for: *the advertising company that is handling the account.* ■ receive or deal in (stolen goods): *he admitted handling the stolen chequebook.* ■ informal cope or deal with (someone or something): *I don't think I could handle it if they turned me down.* ■ [with adverbial] (**handle oneself**) conduct oneself in a specified manner: *he handled himself with considerable aplomb.* ■ (**handle oneself**) informal defend oneself physically or verbally: *I can handle myself in a fight.*
3 drive or control (a vehicle): *he was going too fast and couldn't handle the car.* ■ [no obj., with adverbial] (of a vehicle) respond in a specified manner when being driven or controlled: *the new model does not handle nearly so well.*
▶ noun **1** the part by which a thing is held, carried, or controlled: *a holdall with two carrying handles.* ■ (**a handle on**) a means of understanding, controlling, or approaching (a person or situation): *this analogy will help readers to **get a handle on** the concept.*
2 informal the name of a person or place: *that's some handle for a baby.*
3 [in sing.] the feel of goods, especially textiles, when handled: *fabrics with a softer handle.*
4 [in sing.] US informal the total amount of money bet over a particular time or at a particular event: *the monthly handle of a couple of casinos in Las Vegas.*
– DERIVATIVES **handleable** adjective, **handled** adjective [in combination] *a side-handled baton*, **handleless** adjective.
– ORIGIN Old English *handle* (noun), *handlian* (verb), from HAND.

handlebar ▶ noun (usu. **handlebars**) the steering bar of a bicycle, motorbike, scooter, or other vehicle, with a handgrip at each end.

handlebar moustache ▶ noun a wide, thick moustache with the ends curving slightly upwards.

handler ▶ noun **1** [usu. with modifier] a person who handles or deals with certain articles or commodities: *a baggage handler* | *a food handler.*
2 a person who trains or has charge of an animal, in particular a police officer in charge of a dog.
3 a person who trains or manages another person, in particular: ■ a person who trains and acts as second to a boxer. ■ a publicity agent. ■ a person who directs the activities of a spy or other freelance agent.

Handley Page, Frederick, see PAGE.

handlist ▶ noun a short list of something such as items on display at a sale or exhibition or essential reading for a course of study.

handloom ▶ noun chiefly Indian a manually operated loom.

handmade ▶ adjective made by hand, not by machine, and typically therefore of superior quality: *his expensive handmade leather shoes.*

handmaid ▶ noun archaic a female servant. ■ a subservient partner or element: *this is not to say that the researcher simply becomes the handmaid of the practitioner.*

handmaiden ▶ noun another term for HANDMAID.

hand-me-down ▶ noun (usu. **hand-me-downs**) a garment or other item that has been passed on from another person.

handoff ▶ noun American Football an exchange made by handing the ball to a teammate.

handout ▶ noun **1** a quantity of financial or other material aid given to a person or organization: *dependence on central government handouts.*
2 a piece of printed information provided free of charge, especially to accompany a lecture or advertise something.

handover ▶ noun chiefly Brit. an act or instance of handing something over.

handphone ▶ noun SE Asian a mobile phone.

hand-pick ▶ verb [with obj.] (usu. as adj. **hand-picked**) select carefully with a particular purpose in mind: *a small hand-picked group of MPs.*

hand plant ▶ noun a jump or other manoeuvre in skateboarding and snowboarding involving the use of a hand to push away from a surface.

handprint ▶ noun the mark left by the impression of a hand.

handpump ▶ noun a pump operated by hand, especially for drawing well water or draught beer.

handrail ▶ noun a rail fixed to posts or a wall for people to hold on to for support.

handroll ▶ noun a type of sushi consisting of a cone of dried seaweed filled with rice, fish, vegetables, etc.

handsaw ▶ noun a wood saw worked by one hand.

handsel ▶ noun & verb variant spelling of HANSEL.

handset ▶ noun the part of a telephone that is held up to speak into and listen to. ■ a handheld controller for a piece of electronic equipment, such as a television or video recorder.

hands-free ▶ adjective (especially of a telephone) designed to be operated without using the hands.

handshake ▶ noun an act of shaking a person's hand with one's own as a greeting. ■ Computing an exchange of standardized signals between devices in a computer network regulating the transfer of data.

handshaking ▶ noun [mass noun] the action of shaking hands with a person. ■ Computing the action of exchanging standardized signals between devices in a computer network to regulate the transfer of data. ■ Computing a system of standardized signals used in handshaking.

handsome ▶ adjective (**handsomer**, **handsomest**) **1** (of a man) good-looking. ■ (of a woman) striking and imposing rather than conventionally pretty. ■ (of a thing) well made, imposing, and of obvious quality: *handsome cookery books.*
2 (of a number, sum of money, or margin) substantial: *he was elected by a handsome majority.*
– PHRASES **handsome is as handsome does** proverb character and behaviour are more important than appearance.
– DERIVATIVES **handsomely** adverb, **handsomeness** noun.
– ORIGIN Middle English: from HAND + -SOME[1]. The original sense was 'easy to handle or use', hence 'suitable' and 'apt, clever' (mid 16th cent.), giving rise to the current appreciatory senses (late 16th cent.).

handspan ▶ noun see SPAN[1] (sense 1 of the noun).

handspike ▶ noun historical a wooden rod with an iron tip, used as a lever on board ship and by artillery soldiers.

handspring ▶ noun a jump through the air on to one's hands followed by another on to one's feet.

handstand ▶ noun an act of balancing on one's hands with one's feet in the air or against a wall.

handstroke ▶ noun Bell-ringing a pull of the sally of the rope so as to swing the bell through a full circle. Compare with BACKSTROKE.

hand-to-hand ▶ adjective (of fighting) at close quarters: *hand-to-hand combat.*

hand tool ▶ noun a tool held in the hand and operated without electricity or other power.

handwork ▶ noun [mass noun] work done with the hands: *the transition from handwork to machine production.*
– DERIVATIVES **handworked** adjective.

handwoven ▶ adjective (of fabric) woven by hand or on an unpowered loom.

hand-wringing ▶ noun [mass noun] the excessive display of concern or distress: *this is no time for more hand-wringing about bias in the media.*

handwriting ▶ noun [mass noun] writing with a pen or pencil. ■ a person's particular style of writing: *her handwriting was small and neat.*

handwritten ▶ adjective written with a pen, pencil, or other handheld implement.

Handy, W. C. (1873–1958), American blues musician; full name *William Christopher Handy*. He set up a music-publishing house in 1914, and his transcriptions of traditional blues helped establish the pattern of the modern twelve-bar blues.

handy ▶ adjective (**handier**, **handiest**) **1** convenient to handle or use; useful: *a handy desktop encyclopedia* | *the brush is handy for vacuuming stubborn dust and dirt.*
2 ready to hand: *keep credit cards handy.* ■ placed or occurring conveniently: *a hotel in a handy central location.*
3 skilful: *he's handy with a needle.*
▶ noun (pl. **handies**) (in Europe) a mobile phone.
– PHRASES **come in handy** informal turn out to be useful: *the sort of junk that might come in handy one day.*
– DERIVATIVES **handily** adverb, **handiness** noun.

handyman ▶ noun (pl. **handymen**) a person able or employed to do occasional domestic repairs and minor renovations.

hanepoot /ˈhɑːnəˌpʊət/ ▶ noun [mass noun] a variety of muscat grape, Muscat d'Alexandrie, grown in South Africa. ■ a sweet wine made from the hanepoot grape, unfortified for table use, and fortified as a muscatel dessert wine.
– ORIGIN Afrikaans, from Dutch *haan* 'cock' + *poot* 'foot'.

hang ▶ verb (past and past participle **hung** except in sense 2) **1** suspend or be suspended from above with the lower part dangling free: [with obj.] *that's where people are supposed to hang their washing* | [no obj.] *he stood swaying, his arms hanging limply by his sides.* ■ attach or be attached to a hook on a wall: [with obj.] *we could just hang the pictures on the walls* | [no obj.] *the room in which the pictures will hang.* ■ (**be hung with**) be adorned with (pictures or other decorations): *the walls of her hall were hung with examples of her work.* ■ attach or be attached so as to allow free movement about the point of attachment: [with obj.] *a long time was spent hanging a couple of doors* | [no obj., with complement] *she just sat with her mouth hanging open.* ■ [with obj.] attach (meat or game) to a hook and leave it until dry, tender, or high. ■ [no obj., with adverbial] (of fabric or a garment) fall or drape from a fixed point in a specified way: *this blend of silk and wool hangs well and resists creases.* ■ [with obj.] paste (wallpaper) to a wall.
2 (past and past participle **hanged**) [with obj.] kill (someone) by tying a rope attached from above around their neck and removing the support from beneath them (often used as a form of capital punishment): *he was hanged for murder* | *she hanged herself in her cell.* ■ [no obj.] be killed by hanging: *both men were sentenced to hang.* ■ dated used in expressions as a mild oath: [no obj.] *they could all go hang* | [with obj.] *I'm hanged if I know.*
3 [no obj., with adverbial of place] remain static in the air: *a black pall of smoke hung over Valletta.* ■ be present or imminent, especially oppressively or threateningly: *a sense of dread hung over him for days.*
4 Computing come or cause to come unexpectedly to a state in which no further operations can be carried out.
5 [with obj.] Baseball deliver (a pitch) which does not change direction and is easily hit by a batter.
6 N. Amer. informal way of saying HANG AROUND (sense 2) or HANG OUT (sense 3).
▶ noun [in sing.] a downward droop or bend: *the bullish hang of his head.* ■ the way in which something hangs: *the hang of the garments.* ■ the way in which pictures are displayed in an exhibition.
▶ exclamation S. African & NZ dated used to express a range of strong emotions from enthusiasm to anger: *hang, but I loved those soldiers!*
– PHRASES **get the hang of** informal learn how to operate or do (something): *I never got the hang of roller-skating.* **hang by a thread** see THREAD. **hang fire** delay or be delayed in taking action or progressing. **hang one's hat** N. Amer. informal be resident. **hang heavily** (or **heavy**) (of time) pass slowly. **hang in the air** remain unresolved: *the success of the Green movement has left that rather uncomfortable question hanging in the air.* **hang a left** (or **right**) informal, N. Amer. make a left (or right) turn. **hang loose** see LOOSE. **(a) hang of (a)** S. African & Austral./NZ informal used

to emphasize something very bad or great: *we had to walk a hang of a long way*. [*hang*, a euphemism for *hell*, apparently from New Zealand English.] **hang someone out to dry** informal leave someone in a difficult or vulnerable situation. **hang ten** Surfing ride a surfboard with all ten toes curled over the board's front edge. **hang tough** N. Amer. informal be or remain inflexible or firmly resolved. **let it all hang out** informal be very relaxed or uninhibited. **not care** (or **give**) **a hang** informal not care at all. **you may** (or **might**) **as well be hanged for a sheep as for a lamb** proverb if the penalty for two offences is the same, you might as well commit the more serious one, especially if it brings more benefit.

– PHRASAL VERBS **hang around** (or **round** or Brit. **about**) **1** loiter; wait around: *undercover officers spent most of their time hanging around bars*. ■ informal wait: [in imperative] *hang about, you see what it says here?* **2** (**hang around with**) associate with (someone): *I hung around with the thugs*. **hang back** remain behind: *Stephen hung back for fear of being seen*. ■ show reluctance to act or move: *I do not believe that our European neighbours will hang back from this*. **hang in** informal remain persistent and determined in difficult circumstances: *in the second half, we just had to **hang in there***. **hang on 1** hold tightly: *he hung on to the back of her coat*. ■ informal remain firm or persevere, especially in difficult circumstances: *United hung on for victory*. ■ (**hang on to**) keep; retain: *he is determined to hang on to his job*. **2** informal wait for a short time: *hang on a minute—do you think I might have left anything out?* ■ (on the telephone) remain connected until one is able to talk to a particular person. **3** be contingent or dependent on: *everything hangs on the forthcoming by-elections*. **4** listen closely to: *she hung on his every word*. **hang something on** informal attach the blame for something to (someone). **hang out 1** (of washing) hang from a clothes line to dry. **2** protrude and hang loosely downwards: *chaps in jeans with their shirts hanging out*. ■ (**hang out of**) lean out of: *he was found after the collision hanging out of the defendant's car*. **3** informal spend time relaxing or enjoying oneself: *musicians hang out with their own kind*. **4** Austral./NZ resist or survive in difficult circumstances; hold out. ■ (**hang out for**) desire strongly; crave. **hang something out** hang something on a line or pole or from a window. **hang together 1** make sense; be consistent: *it helps the speech to hang together*. **2** (of people) remain associated; help or support each other. **hang up 1** hang from a hook: *your dressing gown's hanging up behind the door*. **2** end a telephone conversation by cutting the connection. ■ (**hang up on**) end a telephone conversation with (someone) by abruptly and unexpectedly cutting the connection. **hang something up** hang something on a hook: *Jamie hung up our jackets*. ■ informal cease or retire from the activity associated with the garment or object specified: *the midfielder has finally decided to hang up his boots*.

– ORIGIN Old English *hangian* (intransitive verb), of West Germanic origin, related to Dutch and German *hangen*, reinforced by the Old Norse transitive verb *hanga*.

> **USAGE** In modern English **hang** has two past tense and past participle forms: **hanged** and **hung. Hung** is the normal form in most general uses, e.g. *they **hung** out the washing; she **hung** around for a few minutes; he had **hung** the picture over the fireplace*, but **hanged** is the form normally used in reference to execution by hanging: *the prisoner was **hanged***. The reason for this distinction is a complex historical one: **hanged**, the earlier form, was superseded by **hung** sometime after the 16th century; it is likely that the retention of **hanged** for the execution sense may have to do with the tendency of archaic forms to remain in the legal language of the courts.

hangar /ˈhaŋə/ ▶ **noun** a large building with an extensive floor area, typically for housing aircraft.
▶ **verb** [with obj.] house (an aircraft) in a hangar.
– DERIVATIVES **hangarage** noun.
– ORIGIN late 17th cent. (in the sense 'shelter'): from French; probably from Germanic bases meaning 'hamlet' and 'enclosure'.

Hangchow /haŋˈtʃaʊ/ variant of **HANGZHOU**.

hangdog ▶ **adjective** having a dejected or guilty appearance; shamefaced: *the hangdog look of a condemned man*.

hanger¹ ▶ **noun 1** [in combination] a person who hangs something: *a wallpaper-hanger*.
2 (also **coat hanger**) a shaped piece of wood, plastic, or metal with a hook at the top, from which clothes may be hung in order to keep them in shape.

hanger² ▶ **noun** Brit. a wood on the side of a steep hill.
– ORIGIN Old English *hangra*, from *hangian* 'hang'.

hanger-on ▶ **noun** (pl. **hangers-on**) a person who associates with another person or a group in a sycophantic manner or for the purpose of gaining some personal advantage.

hang-glider ▶ **noun** an unpowered flying apparatus for a single person, consisting of a frame with a fabric aerofoil stretched over it. The operator is suspended from a harness below and controls flight by body movement. ■ a person flying a hang-glider.
– DERIVATIVES **hang-glide** verb, **hang-gliding** noun.

hangi /ˈhaŋi, ˈhɑːŋi/ ▶ **noun** NZ a pit in which food is cooked on heated stones. ■ [mass noun] the food cooked in such a pit. ■ a meal or gathering at which such food is cooked and served.
– ORIGIN Maori.

hanging ▶ **noun 1** [mass noun] the practice of hanging condemned people as a form of capital punishment.
2 a decorative piece of fabric or curtain hung on the wall of a room or around a bed.
▶ **adjective** [attrib.] suspended in the air: *hanging palls of smoke*. ■ situated or designed so as to appear to hang down: *hanging gardens*.

hanging basket ▶ **noun** a basket or similar container which can be suspended from a building by a small rope or chain and in which decorative flowering plants are grown.

Hanging Gardens of Babylon legendary terraced gardens at Babylon, watered by pumps from the Euphrates, whose construction was ascribed to Nebuchadnezzar (*c*.600 BC). They were one of the Seven Wonders of the World.

hanging valley ▶ **noun** a valley which is cut across by a deeper valley or a cliff.

hangman ▶ **noun** (pl. **hangmen**) an executioner who hangs condemned people. ■ [mass noun] a game for two in which one player tries to guess the letters of a word, the other player recording failed attempts by drawing a gallows and someone hanging on it, line by line.

hangnail ▶ **noun** a piece of torn skin at the root of a fingernail.
– ORIGIN late 17th cent.: alteration of *agnail* 'painful swelling around a nail' (from Old English *angnægl*, denoting a corn on the toe), influenced by **HANG**.

hang-out ▶ **noun** informal a place one lives in or frequently visits.

hangover ▶ **noun 1** a severe headache or other aftereffects caused by drinking an excess of alcohol.
2 a custom, habit, feeling, etc. that survives from the past: *this feeling of insecurity was in part **a hangover from** her schooldays*.

Hang Seng index /haŋ ˈsɛŋ/ a figure indicating the relative price of shares on the Hong Kong Stock Exchange.
– ORIGIN named after the *Hang Seng Bank* in Hong Kong, where it was devised.

hang-up ▶ **noun** informal an emotional problem or inhibition: *people with hang-ups about their age*.

Hangzhou /haŋˈdʒəʊ/ (also **Hangchow**) the capital of Zhejiang province in eastern China, situated on Hangzhou Bay, an inlet of the Yellow Sea, at the southern end of the Grand Canal; pop. 2,455,600 (est. 2006).

hank ▶ **noun 1** a coil or skein of wool, hair, or other material: ***a thick hank of** her blonde hair*.
2 a measurement of the length per unit mass of cloth or yarn, which varies according to the type being measured. For example it is equal to 840 yards for cotton yarn and 560 yards for worsted.
3 Sailing a ring for securing a staysail to the stay.
– ORIGIN Middle English: from Old Norse *hǫnk*; compare with Swedish *hank* 'string' and Danish *hank* 'handle'.

hanker ▶ **verb** [no obj.] (**hanker after/for/to do something**) feel a strong desire for or to do something: *he hankered after a lost golden age* | *she hankered to go back*.
– DERIVATIVES **hankerer** noun.
– ORIGIN early 17th cent.: probably related to **HANG**; compare with Dutch *hunkeren*.

hankering ▶ **noun** a strong desire to have or do something: *a hankering for family life*.

hanky (also **hankie**) ▶ **noun** (pl. **hankies**) informal a handkerchief.
– ORIGIN late 19th cent.: abbreviation.

hanky-panky ▶ **noun** [mass noun] informal, humorous behaviour, in particular sexual or legally dubious behaviour, considered improper but not seriously so: *suspicions of financial hanky-panky*.
– ORIGIN mid 19th cent.: perhaps an alteration of **HOKEY-POKEY**.

Hannibal /ˈhanɪb(ə)l/ (247–182 BC), Carthaginian general. In the second Punic War he attacked Italy via the Alps, repeatedly defeating the Romans, but failed to take Rome itself.

Hanoi /haˈnɔɪ/ the capital of Vietnam, situated on the Red River in the north of the country; pop. 2,632,100 (est. 2009). It was the capital of French Indo-China from 1887 to 1946 and of North Vietnam before the reunification of North and South Vietnam.

Hanover /ˈhanə(ʊ)və/ an industrial city in NW Germany, on the Mittelland Canal; pop. 516,300 (est. 2006). It is the capital of Lower Saxony. German name **Hannover** /haˈnoːfɐ/. ■ a former state and province in northern Germany. In 1714 the Elector of Hanover succeeded to the British throne as George I, and from then until the accession of Victoria (1837) the same monarch ruled both Britain and Hanover. ■ the British royal house from 1714 to the death of Queen Victoria in 1901.

Hanoverian /ˌhanə(ʊ)ˈvɪərɪən/ ▶ **adjective** relating to the royal house of Hanover.
▶ **noun 1** (usu. **the Hanoverians**) any of the British sovereigns from George I to Victoria.
2 a medium-built horse of a German breed, developed for use both as a riding horse and in harness.

Hansard /ˈhansɑːd, -səd/ ▶ **noun** the official verbatim record of debates in the British, Canadian, Australian, New Zealand, or South African parliament.
– ORIGIN late 19th cent.: named after Thomas C. *Hansard* (1776–1833), an English printer whose company originally printed it.

Hanse /ˈhansə/ ▶ **noun** a medieval guild of merchants. ■ (**the Hanse**) the Hanseatic League. ■ a fee payable to a guild of merchants.
– ORIGIN Middle English: from Old French *hanse* 'guild, company', from Old High German *hansa* 'company, troop'.

Hanseatic League /ˌhansɪˈatɪk/ a medieval association of north German cities, formed in 1241 and surviving until the 19th century. In the later Middle Ages it included over 100 towns and functioned as an independent political power.
– ORIGIN *Hanseatic* from medieval Latin *Hanseaticus*, from *hansa* (see **HANSE**).

hansel /ˈhans(ə)l/ (also **handsel**) archaic or US ▶ **noun** a gift given at the beginning of the year or to mark an acquisition or the start of an enterprise, supposedly to bring good luck. ■ the first instalment of a payment.
▶ **verb** (**hansels, hanselling, hanselled**; US **hansels, hanseling, hanseled**) [with obj.] give a hansel to: *the practice of hanselling the master still flourished in Scotland*. ■ inaugurate (something), especially by being the first to try it: *a floodlit fixture to officially hansel the completed stadium*.
– ORIGIN Middle English (denoting luck): apparently related to late Old English *handselen* 'giving into a person's hands', and Old Norse *handsal* 'giving of the hand to seal a promise', from **HAND** + an element related to **SELL**; the notion of 'luck', however, is not present in these words.

Hansen's disease /ˈhans(ə)nz/ ▶ **noun** another term for **LEPROSY**.
– ORIGIN 1930s: named after Gerhard H. A. *Hansen* (1841–1912), the Norwegian physician who discovered the causative agent of the disease.

hansom /ˈhans(ə)m/ (also **hansom cab**) ▶ **noun** historical a two-wheeled horse-drawn cab accommodating two inside, with the driver seated behind.
– ORIGIN mid 19th cent.: named after Joseph A. *Hansom* (1803–82), English architect, patentee of such a cab in 1834.

hantavirus /ˈhantəˌvʌɪrəs/ ▶ **noun** a virus of a genus carried by rodents and causing various febrile haemorrhagic diseases, often with kidney damage or failure.
– ORIGIN 1980s: from *Hantaan* (the name of a river in Korea where the virus was first isolated) + **VIRUS**.

Hants ▶ **abbreviation** Hampshire.

Hanukkah /ˈhanʊkə, ˈx-/ (also **Chanukkah**) ▶ **noun** a lesser Jewish festival, lasting eight days from the 25th day of Kislev (in December) and commemorating the rededication of the Temple in 165 BC by the

H

Maccabees after its desecration by the Syrians. It is marked by the successive kindling of eight lights.
– ORIGIN from Hebrew *ḥănukkāh* 'consecration'.

Hanuman /ˌhʌnʊˈmɑːn/ Hinduism a semi-divine being of monkey-like form, whose exploits are described in the Ramayana.
– ORIGIN from Sanskrit *hanumant* 'large-jawed'.

hanuman /ˌhʌnʊˈmɑːn/ (also **hanuman langur**) ▶ **noun** a pale-coloured langur monkey of southern Asia, venerated by Hindus. ● *Presbytis entellus*, family Cercopithecidae.

Haora variant spelling of **HOWRAH**.

hap archaic ▶ **noun** [mass noun] luck; fortune. ■ [count noun] a chance occurrence, especially an event that is considered unlucky.
▶ **verb** (**haps, happing, happed**) [no obj.] come about by chance. ■ [with infinitive] have the fortune or luck to do something: *where'er I happ'd to roam.*
– ORIGIN Middle English: from Old Norse *happ*.

hapax legomenon /ˌhapaks lɪˈgɒmɪnɒn/ ▶ **noun** (pl. **hapax legomena** /-mɪnə/) a term of which only one instance of use is recorded.
– ORIGIN mid 17th cent.: Greek, 'a thing said once', from *hapax* 'once' and the passive participle of *legein* 'to say'.

H

ha'penny ▶ **noun** variant spelling of **HALFPENNY**.

haphazard /hapˈhazəd/ ▶ **adjective** lacking any obvious principle of organization: *the music business works in a haphazard fashion.*
– DERIVATIVES **haphazardly** adverb, **haphazardness** noun.
– ORIGIN late 16th cent.: from **HAP** + **HAZARD**.

Haphtarah /ˌhɑːftɑːˈrɑː/ (also **Haphtorah**) ▶ **noun** (pl. **Haphtaroth, Haphtoroth** /-rəʊt/) variant spelling of **HAFTORAH**.

hapkido /ˌhapkiːˈdəʊ/ ▶ **noun** [mass noun] a Korean martial art characterized by kicking and circular movements.
– ORIGIN Korean, literally 'way of coordinated energy'.

hapless ▶ **adjective** (especially of a person) unfortunate: *the hapless victims of the disaster.*
– DERIVATIVES **haplessly** adverb, **haplessness** noun.
– ORIGIN late Middle English: from **HAP** (in the early sense 'good fortune') + **-LESS**.

haplo- ▶ **combining form** single; simple: *haplography* | *haploid.*
– ORIGIN from Greek *haploos* 'single'.

haplochromine /ˌhapləʊˈkrəʊmʌɪn/ Zoology ▶ **adjective** relating to or denoting cichlid fishes of a large and diverse group that are particularly abundant in the large lakes of East Africa.
▶ **noun** a haplochromine fish. ● *Haplochromis* and related genera, family Cichlidae.
– ORIGIN from the modern Latin genus name.

haplodiploid /ˌhapləʊˈdɪplɔɪd/ ▶ **adjective** Biology denoting or possessing a genetic system in which females develop from fertilized (diploid) eggs and males from unfertilized (haploid) ones.

haplography /hapˈlɒgrəfi/ ▶ **noun** [mass noun] the inadvertent omission of a repeated letter or letters in writing (e.g. writing *philogy* for *philology*).
– ORIGIN late 19th cent.: from Greek *haploos* 'single' + **-GRAPHY**.

haploid /ˈhaplɔɪd/ Genetics ▶ **adjective** (of a cell or nucleus) having a single set of unpaired chromosomes. Compare with **DIPLOID**. ■ (of an organism or part) composed of haploid cells.
▶ **noun** a haploid organism or cell.
– DERIVATIVES **haploidy** noun.
– ORIGIN early 20th cent.: from Greek *haploos* 'single' + **-OID**.

haplology /hapˈlɒlədʒi/ ▶ **noun** the omission of one occurrence of a sound or syllable which is repeated within a word (e.g. in *February* pronounced as /ˈfɛbri/).
– ORIGIN late 19th cent.: from Greek *haploos* 'single' + **-LOGY**.

haplotype /ˈhapləʊtʌɪp/ ▶ **noun** Genetics a set of genetic determinants located on a single chromosome.

ha'p'orth ▶ **noun** variant spelling of **HALFPENNYWORTH**.

happen ▶ **verb** [no obj.] **1** take place; occur: *two hours had passed and still nothing had happened* | *the accident happened at 7.40 a.m.* ■ ensue as an effect or result of an action or event: *this is what happens when the mechanism goes wrong.* ■ [with infinitive] chance to do something or come about: *we just happened to meet Paul* | *there happens to be a clash of personalities.* ■ [with clause] come about by chance: *it just so happened that she turned up that afternoon.* ■ (**happen on**) find or come across by chance: *I happened on a street with a few modest restaurants.* ■ [with infinitive] used as a polite formula in questions: *do you happen to know who her doctor is?*
2 (**happen to**) be experienced by (someone); befall: *the same thing happened to me.* ■ become of: *I don't care what happens to the money.*
▶ **adverb** [sentence adverb] N. English perhaps; maybe: *happen I'll go back just for a while.*
– PHRASES **as it happens** actually; as a matter of fact: *we've got a room vacant, as it happens.*
– ORIGIN late Middle English (superseding the verb *hap*): from the noun **HAP** + **-EN**[1].

happening ▶ **noun 1** an event or occurrence: *altogether it was an eerie happening.*
2 a partly improvised or spontaneous piece of theatrical or other artistic performance, typically involving audience participation.
▶ **adjective** informal fashionable; trendy: *a happening neighbourhood.*

happenstance /ˈhap(ə)nˌstans/ ▶ **noun** [mass noun] chiefly N. Amer. coincidence: *it was just happenstance that I happened to be there* | [count noun] *an untoward happenstance for Trudy.*
– ORIGIN late 19th cent.: blend of **HAPPEN** and **CIRCUMSTANCE**.

happi /ˈhapi/ (also **happi coat**) ▶ **noun** (pl. **happis**) a loose informal Japanese coat.
– ORIGIN late 19th cent.: Japanese.

happily ▶ **adverb** in a happy way. ■ [sentence adverb] it is fortunate that: *happily, today's situation is very different.*

happiness ▶ **noun** [mass noun] the state of being happy: *she struggled to find happiness in her life.*

happy ▶ **adjective** (**happier, happiest**) **1** feeling or showing pleasure or contentment: *Melissa came in looking happy and excited* | [with clause] *we're just happy that he's still alive* | [with infinitive] *they are happy to see me doing well.* ■ (**happy about**) having a sense of trust and confidence in (a person, arrangement, or situation): *he was not happy about the proposals.* ■ (**happy with**) satisfied with the quality or standard of: *I'm happy with his performance.* ■ [with infinitive] willing to do something: *we will be happy to advise you.* ■ [attrib.] used in greetings: *happy Christmas.*
2 [attrib.] fortunate and convenient: *he had the happy knack of making people like him.*
3 [in combination] informal inclined to use a specified thing excessively or at random: *they tended to be grenade-happy.*
– PHRASES (**as**) **happy as a sandboy** (or Brit. **Larry** or N. Amer. **a clam** or vulgar slang **a pig in shit**) extremely happy. **happy hunting ground** a place where success or enjoyment is obtained. [originally referring to the optimistic hope of American Indians for good hunting grounds in the afterlife.]
– ORIGIN Middle English (in the sense 'lucky'): from the noun **HAP** + **-Y**[1].

happy-clappy Brit. informal ▶ **adjective** belonging to or characteristic of a Christian group whose worship is marked by enthusiastic participation.
▶ **noun** (pl. **happy-clappies**) a member of a Christian group whose worship is marked by enthusiastic participation.

happy families ▶ **noun** [mass noun] Brit. a children's card game played with special cards in sets of four, each depicting members of a 'family', the object being to acquire as many sets as possible.

happy-go-lucky ▶ **adjective** cheerfully unconcerned about the future: *a happy-go-lucky attitude.*

happy hour ▶ **noun** a period of the day when drinks are sold at reduced prices in a bar or other licensed establishment.

happy medium ▶ **noun** a satisfactory compromise: *you have to* ***strike a happy medium between*** *looking like royalty and looking like a housewife.*

Hapsburg /ˈhapsbəːg/ variant spelling of **HABSBURG**.

hapten /ˈhaptən/ ▶ **noun** Physiology a small molecule which, when combined with a larger carrier such as a protein, can elicit the production of antibodies which bind specifically to it (in the free or combined state).
– ORIGIN early 20th cent.: from Greek *haptein* 'fasten'.

haptic /ˈhaptɪk/ ▶ **adjective** technical relating to the sense of touch, in particular relating to the perception and manipulation of objects using the senses of touch and proprioception.
– ORIGIN late 19th cent.: from Greek *haptikos* 'able to touch or grasp', from *haptein* 'fasten'.

haptoglobin /ˌhaptə(ʊ)ˈgləʊbɪn/ ▶ **noun** [mass noun] Biochemistry a protein present in blood serum which binds to and removes free haemoglobin from the bloodstream.
– ORIGIN 1940s: from Greek *haptein* 'fasten' + (*haemo*) *globin.*

hapu /ˈhɑːpuː/ ▶ **noun** NZ a division of a Maori people or community.
– ORIGIN Maori.

hara-kiri /ˌharəˈkɪri/ ▶ **noun** [mass noun] ritual suicide by disembowelment with a sword, formerly practised in Japan by samurai as an honourable alternative to disgrace or execution.
– ORIGIN mid 19th cent.: colloquial Japanese, from *hara* 'belly' + *kiri* 'cutting'.

haram /hɑːˈrɑːm/ ▶ **adjective** forbidden or proscribed by Islamic law.
– ORIGIN from Arabic *ḥarām* 'forbidden'.

harambee /həˈrambiː/ ▶ **noun** (in East Africa) an event held to raise funds for a charitable purpose: [as modifier] *harambee functions.*
– ORIGIN Swahili, literally 'pulling or working together' (a slogan of the first independent government of Kenya).

harangue /həˈraŋ/ ▶ **noun** a lengthy and aggressive speech.
▶ **verb** [with obj.] lecture (someone) at length in an aggressive and critical manner: *he harangued the public on their ignorance.*
– DERIVATIVES **haranguer** noun.
– ORIGIN late Middle English: from Old French *arenge*, from medieval Latin *harenga*, perhaps of Germanic origin. The spelling was later altered to conform with French *harangue* (noun), *haranguer* (verb).

Harappa /həˈrapə/ an ancient city of the Indus valley civilization (*c.*2600–1700 BC), in northern Pakistan. The site of the ruins was discovered in 1920.

Harare /həˈrɑːri/ the capital of Zimbabwe; pop. 1,696,000 (est. 2009). Former name (until 1982) **SALISBURY**[1].

harass /ˈharəs, həˈras/ ▶ **verb** [with obj.] subject to aggressive pressure or intimidation: *if someone is being harassed at work because of their sexuality they should contact the police.* ■ make repeated small-scale attacks on (an enemy): *the squadron's task was to harass the retreating enemy forces.*
– DERIVATIVES **harasser** noun, **harassingly** adverb.
– ORIGIN early 17th cent.: from French *harasser*, from *harer* 'set a dog on', from Germanic *hare*, a cry urging a dog to attack.

USAGE There are two possible pronunciations of the word **harass**: one with the stress on the **har-** and the other with the stress on the **-ass**. The former pronunciation is the older one and is regarded by some people as the only correct one, especially in British English. However, the pronunciation with the stress on the second syllable **-rass** is very common and is now accepted as a standard alternative.

harassed /ˈharəst, həˈrast/ ▶ **adjective** feeling or looking strained as a result of having too many demands made on one: *it is a godsend for harassed parents.*

USAGE See **USAGE** at **HARASS**.

harassment /ˈharəsm(ə)nt, həˈrasm(ə)nt/ ▶ **noun** [mass noun] aggressive pressure or intimidation: *they face daily harassment by the police.*

Harbin /hɑːˈbiːn, -ˈbɪn/ the capital of Heilongjiang province in NE China, on the Songhua River; pop. 3,075,300 (est. 2006).

harbinger /ˈhɑːbɪn(d)ʒə/ ▶ **noun** a person or thing that announces or signals the approach of another: *witch hazels are the harbingers of spring.* ■ a forerunner of something.
– ORIGIN Middle English: from Old French *herbergere*, from *herbergier* 'provide lodging for', from *herberge* 'lodging', from Old Saxon *heriberga* 'shelter for an army, lodging' (from *heri* 'army' + a Germanic base meaning 'fortified place'), related to **HARBOUR**. The term originally denoted a person who provided lodging, later one who went ahead to find lodgings for an army or for a nobleman and his retinue, hence, a herald (mid 16th cent.).

harbour (US **harbor**) ▶ **noun** a place on the coast where ships may moor in shelter, especially one protected from rough water by piers, jetties, and other artificial structures. ■ a place of refuge: *a safe harbour for children in distress.*

▶ **verb** [with obj.] **1** keep (a thought or feeling, typically a negative one) in one's mind, especially secretly: *she started to harbour doubts about the wisdom of their journey.*
2 give a home or shelter to: *woodlands that once harboured a colony of red deer.* ■ shelter or hide (a criminal or wanted person): *he was suspected of harbouring an escaped prisoner.* ■ carry the germs of (a disease).
3 [no obj.] archaic (of a ship or its crew) moor in a harbour: *he might have harboured in Falmouth.*
– DERIVATIVES **harbourless** adjective.
– ORIGIN late Old English *herebeorg* 'shelter, refuge', *herebeorgian* 'occupy shelter', of Germanic origin; related to Dutch *herberge* and German *Herberge*, also to French *auberge* 'inn'; see also HARBINGER.

harbourage (US **harborage**) ▶ **noun** a harbour or other place of shelter.

harbour master (US **harbormaster**) ▶ **noun** an official in charge of a harbour.

harbour seal ▶ **noun** North American term for COMMON SEAL[1].

harbourside ▶ **noun** the area immediately adjacent to a harbour.

hard ▶ **adjective 1** solid, firm, and rigid; not easily broken, bent, or pierced: *the slate broke on the hard floor* | *rub the varnish down when it's hard.* ■ (of a person) not showing any signs of weakness; tough: *only a handful are hard enough to join the SAS.* ■ (of prices of shares, commodities, etc.) high and stable; firm.
2 done with a great deal of force or strength: *a hard whack.*
3 requiring a great deal of endurance or effort: *airship-flying was pretty hard work* | *it's hard for drummers these days* | [with infinitive] *she found it hard to believe that he could be involved.* ■ putting a lot of energy into an activity: *he'd been a hard worker all his life* | *everyone has been hard at work.* ■ difficult to bear; causing suffering: *times were hard at the end of the war* | *he'd had a hard life.* ■ difficult to understand or solve: *this is a really hard question.* ■ not showing sympathy or affection; strict: *he can be such a hard taskmaster.* ■ denoting an extreme or dogmatic faction within a political party: *the hard left.* ■ (of a season or the weather) severe: *it's been a long, hard winter.* ■ harsh or unpleasant to the senses: *the hard light of morning.* ■ (of wine) harsh or sharp to the taste, especially because of tannin.
4 (of information) reliable, especially because based on something true or substantiated: *hard facts about the underclass are maddeningly elusive.* ■ (of a subject of study) dealing with precise and verifiable facts: *efforts to turn psychology into hard science.* ■ (of science fiction) scientifically accurate rather than purely fantastic or whimsical: *a hard SF novel.*
5 very potent, powerful, or intense, in particular: ■ strongly alcoholic; denoting a spirit rather than beer or wine. ■ (of a drug) potent and addictive. ■ (of radiation) highly penetrating. ■ (of pornography) highly obscene and explicit.
6 (of water) containing mineral salts that make lathering difficult.
7 (of a consonant) pronounced as a velar plosive (as *c* in *cat*, *g* in *go*).
▶ **adverb 1** with a great deal of effort: *they work hard at school.* ■ with a great deal of force; violently: *it was raining hard.*
2 so as to be solid or firm: *the mortar has set hard.*
3 to the fullest extent possible: *put the wheel* **hard** *over to starboard.*
▶ **noun** Brit. a road leading down across a foreshore.
– PHRASES **be hard on 1** treat or criticize (someone) severely: *you're being too hard on her.* **2** be difficult for or unfair to: *it was hard on her, because she had to walk nearly a mile out of her way.* **3** be likely to hurt or damage: *the monitor flickers, which is hard on the eyes.* **be hard put (to it)** [usu. with infinitive] find it very difficult: *you'll be hard put to find a better compromise.* **give someone a hard time** informal deliberately make a situation difficult for someone. **go hard with** dated turn out to (someone's) disadvantage: *it would go hard with the poor.* **hard and fast** (of a rule or a distinction made) fixed and definitive: *there are no hard and fast rules about that.* **hard as nails** see NAIL. **hard at it** informal busily working or occupied: *they were hard at it with brooms and mops.* **hard by** close to: *he lived hard by the cathedral.* **hard done by** Brit. harshly or unfairly treated: *she would be justified in feeling hard done by.* **hard feelings** [usu. with negative] feelings of resentment: *there are no hard feelings and we wish him well.* **hard going** difficult to understand or enjoy: *the studying is at times hard going.* **hard hit** badly affected: *Trinidad had been hard hit by falling oil prices.* **hard luck** (or **lines**) Brit. informal used to express sympathy or commiserations: ironic *if you don't like it then hard luck.* **a hard nut to crack** informal a person or thing that is difficult to understand or influence. **hard of hearing** not able to hear well. **hard on** (or **upon**) close to; following soon after: *hard on the heels of Wimbledon comes the Henley Regatta.* **hard up** informal short of money: *I'm too hard up to buy fancy clothes.* **the hard way** through suffering or learning from the unpleasant consequences of mistakes: *you're going to learn the hard way who you're up against.* **play hard to get** informal deliberately adopt an aloof or uninterested attitude, typically in order to make oneself more attractive or interesting. **put the hard word on** Austral./NZ informal ask a favour of (someone), especially a sexual or financial one. ■ put pressure on (someone).
– DERIVATIVES **hardish** adjective.
– ORIGIN Old English *hard*, *heard*, of Germanic origin; related to Dutch *hard* and German *hart*.

hardback ▶ **noun** a book bound in stiff covers.
– PHRASES **in hardback** in an edition bound in stiff covers: *the novel was first published in hardback in 1981.*

hardball ▶ **noun** [mass noun] N. Amer. baseball, especially as contrasted with softball. ■ informal uncompromising and ruthless methods or dealings: *the leadership played hardball to win the vote.*

hard-bitten ▶ **adjective** tough and cynical: *a hard-bitten war reporter.*

hardboard ▶ **noun** [mass noun] stiff board made of compressed and treated wood pulp.

hardbody ▶ **noun** informal a person with very toned or well-developed muscles.
– DERIVATIVES **hardbodied** adjective.

hard-boiled ▶ **adjective 1** (of an egg) boiled until the white and the yolk are solid.
2 (of a person) tough and cynical. ■ denoting a tough, realistic style of detective fiction: *a hard-boiled thriller.*

hard case ▶ **noun** informal **1** a tough or intractable person.
2 Austral./NZ an amusing or eccentric person.

hard cash ▶ **noun** [mass noun] negotiable coins and banknotes as opposed to other forms of payment.

hard cheese ▶ **noun** see CHEESE[1].

hard clam ▶ **noun** another term for QUAHOG.

hard coal ▶ **noun** another term for ANTHRACITE.

hard-code ▶ **verb** [with obj.] Computing fix (data or parameters) in a program in such a way that they cannot be altered without modifying the program.

hard copy ▶ **noun** a printed version on paper of data held in a computer.

hard core ▶ **noun 1** the most active, committed, or doctrinaire members of a group or movement: *there is always a hard core of trusty stalwarts* | [as modifier] *a hard-core following.*
2 (usu. **hardcore**) [mass noun] popular music that is experimental in nature and typically characterized by high volume and aggressive presentation. ■ pornography of a very explicit kind: [as modifier] *hard-core porn*
3 [mass noun] Brit. broken bricks, rubble, or similar solid material used as a filling or foundation in building.

hardcover ▶ **adjective & noun** chiefly N. Amer. another term for HARDBACK.

hard currency ▶ **noun** [mass noun] currency that is not likely to depreciate suddenly or to fluctuate greatly in value.

hard disk ▶ **noun** Computing a rigid non-removable magnetic disk with a large data storage capacity.

hard doer ▶ **noun** see DOER.

hard drive ▶ **noun** a disk drive used to read from and write to a hard disk.

hard-earned ▶ **adjective** having taken a great deal of effort to earn or acquire: *her hard-earned money.*

Hardecanute /ˈhɑːdɪkənjuːt/ (*c.*1019–1042), Danish king of Denmark 1028–42 and England 1040–42, son of King Canute and Emma, daughter of Richard I, Duke of Normandy. Hardecanute's absence in Denmark allowed Canute's illegitimate son Harold, who had been made Regent on Canute's death in 1035, to take the English throne in 1037. Hardecanute became king on Harold's death in 1040.

harden ▶ **verb** make or become hard or harder: [no obj.] *wait for the glue to harden* | [with obj.] *bricks which seem to have been hardened by firing.* ■ make or become more severe and less sympathetic: [with obj.] *she hardened her heart.* ■ make or become tougher and more clearly defined: [no obj.] *suspicion* **hardened into** *certainty* | [with obj.] *this served only to harden the resolve of the island nations.* ■ [no obj.] (of prices of shares, commodities, etc.) rise and remain steady at a higher level.
– PHRASES **hardening of the arteries** another term for ARTERIOSCLEROSIS.
– PHRASAL VERBS **harden something off** inure a plant to cold by gradually increasing its exposure to it.
– DERIVATIVES **hardener** noun.

hardened ▶ **adjective 1** having become or been made hard or harder: *hardened steel.* ■ strengthened or made secure against attack, especially by nuclear weapons: *the silos are hardened against air attack.*
2 [attrib.] very experienced in a particular job or activity and therefore not easily upset by its more unpleasant aspects: *hardened police officers* | [in combination] *a battle-hardened veteran.* ■ utterly fixed in a habit or way of life seen as bad: *hardened criminals* | *a hardened liar.*

hard error ▶ **noun** Computing an error or hardware fault causing failure of a program or operating system, especially one that gives no option of recovery.

hard fern ▶ **noun** a European fern of heathy places, which has long, narrow leathery fronds consisting of a row of thin lobes on each side of the stem.
• *Blechnum spicant*, family Blechnaceae.

hardgainer ▶ **noun** (in bodybuilding) a person who does not find it easy to gain muscle through exercise.

hard hat ▶ **noun** a rigid protective helmet, as worn by factory and building workers. ■ informal a worker who wears a hard hat. ■ N. Amer. informal a reactionary or conservative person.

hard-headed ▶ **adjective** practical and realistic; not sentimental: *a hard-headed businessman.*
– DERIVATIVES **hard-headedly** adverb, **hard-headedness** noun.

hardheads (also **hardhead**) ▶ **plural noun** [treated as sing.] Brit. another term for KNAPWEED.

hard-hearted ▶ **adjective** incapable of being moved to pity or tenderness; unfeeling.
– DERIVATIVES **hard-heartedly** adverb, **hard-heartedness** noun.

hard-hitting ▶ **adjective** uncompromisingly direct and honest, especially in revealing unpalatable facts: *a hard-hitting anti-fox-hunting poster.*

Hardie, (James) Keir (1856–1915), Scottish Labour politician. A miner before becoming an MP in 1892, he became the first leader of both the Independent Labour Party (1893) and the Labour Party (1906).

hardihood ▶ **noun** [mass noun] dated boldness; daring.

hardiness ▶ **noun** [mass noun] the ability to endure difficult conditions: *I applaud you on your hardiness.* ■ the ability of a plant to survive outside during winter.

Harding, Warren (Gamaliel) (1865–1923), American Republican statesman, 29th President of the US 1921–3.

hard labour ▶ **noun** [mass noun] heavy manual work as a punishment.

hard landing ▶ **noun 1** an uncontrolled landing in which a spacecraft crashes on to the surface of a planet or moon and is destroyed.
2 the slowing down of economic growth at an unacceptable degree relative to inflation and unemployment.

hard line ▶ **noun** an uncompromising adherence to a firm policy: *he is known to* **take a hard line on** *sentencing policy for murder.*
▶ **adjective** uncompromising; strict: *a hard-line party activist.*

hardliner ▶ **noun** a member of a group, typically a political group, who adheres uncompromisingly to a set of ideas or policies.

hard-luck story ▶ **noun** an account of one's problems intended to gain someone else's sympathy or help.

hardly ▶ **adverb 1** scarcely (used to qualify a statement by saying that it is true to an insignificant degree): *the little house in which he lived was hardly bigger than a hut* | *we hardly know each other.* ■ only a very short time before: *the party had hardly started when the police arrived.* ■ only with great difficulty: *she could* **hardly** *sit up* | *I nodded,* **hardly able to** *breath.* ■ no or not (suggesting surprise at or disagreement with a statement): *I hardly think so.*
2 archaic harshly: *the rule worked hardly.*

H

– PHRASES **hardly any** almost no: *they sold hardly any books.* ■ almost none: *hardly any had previous convictions.* **hardly ever** very rarely: *we hardly ever see them.*

USAGE Words like **hardly**, **scarcely**, and **rarely** should not be used with negative constructions. Thus, it is correct to say *I can hardly wait* but incorrect to say *I can't hardly wait.* This is because adverbs like **hardly** are treated as if they were negatives, and it is a well-known grammatical rule of standard English that double negatives (i.e. in this case having **hardly** and **not** in the same clause) are not acceptable. Words like **hardly** behave as negatives in other respects as well, as for example in combining with words like **any** or **at all**, which normally only occur where a negative is present (thus, standard usage is *I've got hardly any money* but not *I've got any money*). See also **USAGE** at **DOUBLE NEGATIVE.**

hardman ▶ noun (pl. **hardmen**) informal a tough, aggressive, or ruthless man.

hardness ▶ noun [mass noun] the quality or condition of being hard: *people complained about the hardness of the chairs | a lack of mental hardness.*

hard-nosed ▶ adjective informal realistic and determined; tough-minded: *a hard-nosed businessman.*

H

hard nut ▶ noun Brit. informal a tough, aggressive, or insensitive person.

hard-on ▶ noun vulgar slang an erection of the penis.

hard pad ▶ noun [mass noun] hardening of the pads of the feet, a symptom of distemper in dogs and other animals.

hard palate ▶ noun the bony front part of the palate.

hardpan ▶ noun [mass noun] Geology a hardened impervious layer, typically of clay, occurring in or below the soil and impairing drainage and plant growth.

hard-paste ▶ adjective denoting true porcelain made of fusible and infusible materials (usually kaolin and china stone) fired at a high temperature. Developed in early medieval China, it was not made in Europe until the early 18th century.

hard power ▶ noun [mass noun] a coercive approach to international political relations, especially one that involves the use of military power. Compare with **SOFT POWER.**

hard-pressed ▶ adjective 1 closely pursued: *the hard-pressed French infantry.*
2 burdened with urgent business: *training centres are hard-pressed and insufficient in numbers.* ■ in difficulties: [with infinitive] *the staff were hard-pressed to give even basic care.*

hard rock ▶ noun [mass noun] highly amplified rock music with a heavy beat.

hard roe ▶ noun see **ROE**[1].

hard sauce ▶ noun [mass noun] a sauce of butter and sugar, typically with brandy, rum, or vanilla added.

hardscape ▶ noun [mass noun] chiefly US the man-made features used in landscape architecture, e.g. paths or walls, as contrasted with vegetation.
– DERIVATIVES **hardscaping** noun.

hardscrabble ▶ adjective N. Amer. involving hard work and struggle: *a brutally hardscrabble life.*
– ORIGIN early 19th cent.: originally as a noun in the sense 'place thought of as the epitome of barrenness'.

hard sell ▶ noun (often **the hard sell**) a policy or technique of aggressive salesmanship or advertising: *they invited 1,000 participants and gave them the hard sell.*

hard-shell ▶ adjective [attrib.] 1 having a hard shell or outer casing: *a hard-shell suitcase.*
2 chiefly N. Amer. rigid or uncompromising.

hardshell clam ▶ noun another term for **QUAHOG.**

hardship ▶ noun [mass noun] severe suffering or privation: *intolerable levels of hardship* | [count noun] *the shared hardships of wartime.*

hard shoulder ▶ noun Brit. a hardened strip alongside a motorway for stopping on in an emergency.

hardstanding ▶ noun [mass noun] Brit. ground surfaced with a hard material for parking vehicles on.

hardstone ▶ noun [mass noun] precious or semi-precious stone used for intaglio, mosaic work, etc.

hard stuff ▶ noun (**the hard stuff**) informal strong alcoholic drink.

hard tack ▶ noun [mass noun] archaic hard dry bread or biscuit, especially as rations for sailors or soldiers.

hardtop ▶ noun 1 a motor vehicle with a rigid roof which in some cases is detachable. ■ a roof of this type.
2 (also **hardtop road**) Canadian a metalled road.

Hardwar variant spelling of **HARIDWAR.**

hardware ▶ noun [mass noun] 1 tools, machinery, and other durable equipment: *high-tech military hardware.* ■ tools, implements, and other items used in home life and activities such as gardening.
2 the machines, wiring, and other physical components of a computer or other electronic system. Compare with **SOFTWARE.**

hard-wearing ▶ adjective able to stand much wear: *a hard-wearing fabric.*

hard wheat ▶ noun [mass noun] wheat of a variety having a hard grain rich in gluten.

hardwired ▶ adjective Electronics involving or achieved by permanently connected circuits rather than software. ■ informal genetically determined or compelled: *fear is hardwired in our brain.*
– DERIVATIVES **hardwire** verb, **hardwiring** noun.

hardwood ▶ noun [mass noun] 1 the wood from a broadleaved tree (such as oak, ash, or beech) as distinguished from that of conifers. ■ [count noun] a broadleaved tree that produces hardwood.
2 (in gardening) mature growth on shrubs and other plants.

hard-working ▶ adjective (of a person) tending to work with energy and commitment; diligent.

Hardy[1], Oliver, see **LAUREL AND HARDY.**

Hardy[2], Thomas (1840–1928), English novelist and poet. Much of his work deals with the struggle against the indifferent force that inflicts the sufferings and ironies of life. Notable novels: *The Mayor of Casterbridge* (1886), *Tess of the D'Urbervilles* (1891), and *Jude the Obscure* (1896).

hardy ▶ adjective (**hardier**, **hardiest**) capable of enduring difficult conditions; robust: *a hardy breed of cattle.* ■ (of a plant) able to survive outside during winter.
– DERIVATIVES **hardily** adverb.
– ORIGIN Middle English (in the sense 'bold, daring'): from Old French *hardi*, past participle of *hardir* 'become bold', of Germanic origin; related to **HARD.**

hardy annual ▶ noun an annual plant that may be sown in the open ground.

hardy perennial ▶ noun 1 a perennial plant which can survive in the open all year.
2 Brit. informal a thing that recurs continually or at regular intervals: *quiz shows, those hardy perennials of TV and radio.*

Hare, William, see **BURKE**[4].

hare ▶ noun a fast-running, long-eared mammal that resembles a large rabbit, having very long hind legs and typically found in grassland or open woodland. ● *Lepus* and other genera, family Leporidae: several species. ■ (also **electric hare**) a dummy hare propelled around the track in greyhound racing.
▶ verb [no obj., with adverbial of direction] Brit. run with great speed: *he hared off between the trees.*
– PHRASES **run with the hare and hunt with the hounds** Brit. try to remain on good terms with both sides in a conflict or dispute. **start a hare** Brit. dated raise a topic of conversation.
– ORIGIN Old English *hara*, of Germanic origin: related to Dutch *haas* and German *Hase.*

hare and hounds ▶ noun [mass noun] a game, especially a paperchase, in which a group of people chase another person or group across the countryside.

harebell ▶ noun a widely distributed bellflower with slender stems and pale blue flowers in late summer. Also called **BLUEBELL**, especially in Scotland. ● *Campanula rotundifolia*, family Campanulaceae.
– ORIGIN Middle English: probably so named because it is found growing in places frequented by hares.

hare-brained ▶ adjective rash; ill-judged: *a hare-brained scheme.*

Haredi /ha'rɛdi/ ▶ noun (pl. **Haredim** /-dɪm/) a member of any of various Orthodox Jewish sects characterized by strict adherence to the traditional form of Jewish law and rejection of modern secular culture, many of whom do not recognize the modern state of Israel as a spiritual authority.
– ORIGIN Hebrew, literally 'one who trembles (in awe at the word of God)'.

Harefoot, Harold, see **HAROLD.**

Hare Krishna /ˌharɪ 'krɪʃnə, ˌhɑːreɪ/ ▶ noun a member of the International Society for Krishna Consciousness, a religious sect based mainly in the US and other Western countries. Its devotees typically wear saffron robes, favour celibacy, practise vegetarianism, and chant mantras based on the name of the Hindu god Krishna. ■ [mass noun] the sect to which Hare Krishnas belong; the International Society for Krishna Consciousness.
– ORIGIN 1960s: Sanskrit, literally 'O Vishnu Krishna', the words of a devotional chant.

harelip ▶ noun another term for **CLEFT LIP.**
– DERIVATIVES **harelipped** adjective.
– ORIGIN mid 16th cent.: from a perceived resemblance to the mouth of a hare.

USAGE Use of the word **harelip** can cause offence and should be avoided; use **cleft lip** instead.

harem /'hɑːriːm, hɑː'riːm, 'hɛːrəm/ ▶ noun 1 the separate part of a Muslim household reserved for wives, concubines, and female servants.
2 the wives (or concubines) of a polygamous man.
3 a group of female animals sharing a single mate.
– ORIGIN mid 17th cent. (in sense 1): from Arabic *ḥaram, ḥarīm*, literally 'prohibited, prohibited place' (hence 'sanctuary, women's quarters, women'), from *ḥarama* 'be prohibited'.

hare's-foot (also **hare's-foot clover**) ▶ noun a slender clover which has soft hairs around the flowers. ● *Trifolium arvense*, family Leguminosae.

hare's-tail (also **hare's-tail grass**) ▶ noun a Mediterranean grass with white silky flowering heads and woolly grey-green leaves. ● *Lagurus ovatus*, family Gramineae.

hare wallaby ▶ noun a small, agile, fast-moving Australian wallaby with orange rings of fur around the eyes. ● Genera *Lagorchestes* and *Lagostrophus*, family Macropodidae: several species.

harewood ▶ noun [mass noun] stained sycamore wood used for making furniture.
– ORIGIN late 17th cent.: from German dialect *Ehre* (from Latin *acer* 'maple') + **WOOD.**

Hargeisa /hɑː'geɪsə/ (also **Hargeysa**) a city in NW Somalia; pop. 407,200 (est. 2004).

Hargreaves, James (1720–78), English inventor. A pioneer of the Lancashire cotton industry, he invented the spinning jenny (*c.*1764).

haricot /'harɪkəʊ/ (also **haricot bean**) ▶ noun chiefly Brit. a French bean of a variety with small white seeds. ■ the dried seed of haricot bean plants used as a vegetable.
– ORIGIN mid 17th cent.: French, perhaps from Aztec *ayacotli.*

Haridwar /hɑː'dwɑː/ (also **Hardwar**) a city in Uttar Pradesh, northern India, on the River Ganges; pop. 197,300 (est. 2009). It is a place of Hindu pilgrimage.

Harijan /'hʌrɪdʒ(ə)n, 'harɪdʒan/ ▶ noun a member of a hereditary Hindu group of the lowest social and ritual status. See **UNTOUCHABLE.**
– ORIGIN from Sanskrit *harijana*, literally 'a person dedicated to Vishnu', from *Hari* 'Vishnu' + *jana* 'person'. The term was adopted and popularized by Gandhi.

harissa /'arɪsə/ ▶ noun [mass noun] a hot sauce or paste used in North African cuisine, made from chilli peppers, paprika, and olive oil.
– ORIGIN from Arabic.

hark ▶ verb [no obj.] [usu. in imperative] literary listen: *Hark! He knocks.* ■ (**hark at**) Brit. informal used to draw attention to someone who has said or done something considered to be foolish or silly: *just hark at you, speaking all lah-de-dah!*
– PHRASAL VERBS **hark back to** mention or remember (something from the past): *if it was such a rotten holiday, why hark back to it?* [originally a hunting term, used of hounds retracing their steps to find a lost scent.] ■ evoke (an older style or genre): *paintings that hark back to Constable and Turner.*
– ORIGIN Middle English: of Germanic origin; related to German *horchen*, also to **HEARKEN.**

harken ▶ verb variant spelling of **HEARKEN.**

Harlech /'hɑːlɛk, -ləx/ a village on the west coast of Wales, in Gwynedd; pop. 1,300 (est. 2009). It is noted for the ruins of its 13th-century castle.

Harlem /'hɑːləm/ a district of New York City, situated to the north of 96th Street in NE Manhattan. It has a large black population and in the 1920s and 1930s was noted for its nightclubs and jazz bands.

Harlem Renaissance a movement in US literature in the 1920s which centred on Harlem and was an early manifestation of black consciousness in the US.

The movement included writers such as Langston Hughes and Zora Neale Hurston.

harlequin /ˈhɑːlɪkwɪn/ ▸ **noun 1** (**Harlequin**) a mute character in traditional pantomime, typically masked and dressed in a diamond-patterned costume. ▪ historical a stock comic character in Italian commedia dell'arte.
2 (also **harlequin duck**) a small duck of fast-flowing streams around the Arctic and North Pacific, the male having mainly grey-blue plumage with bold white markings. ● *Histrionicus histrionicus*, family Anatidae.
▸ **adjective** in varied colours; variegated.
– ORIGIN late 16th cent.: from obsolete French, from earlier *Herlequin* (or *Hellequin*), the name of the leader of a legendary troop of demon horsemen; perhaps ultimately related to Old English *Herla cyning* 'King Herla', a mythical figure sometimes identified with Woden.

harlequinade /ˌhɑːlɪkwɪˈneɪd/ ▸ **noun 1** historical the section of a traditional pantomime in which Harlequin played a leading role.
2 dated a piece of foolish or ridiculous behaviour.
– ORIGIN late 18th cent.: from French *arlequinade*, from *(h)arlequin* (see HARLEQUIN).

harlequin fish ▸ **noun** a small brightly coloured freshwater fish of SE Asia, popular in aquaria. ● *Rasbora heteromorpha*, family Cyprinidae.

Harley Street a street in central London where many eminent physicians and surgeons have consulting rooms.

harlot /ˈhɑːlət/ ▸ **noun** archaic a prostitute or promiscuous woman.
– DERIVATIVES **harlotry** noun.
– ORIGIN Middle English (denoting a vagabond or beggar, later a lecherous man or woman): from Old French *harlot, herlot* 'young man, knave, vagabond'.

Harlow[1] a town in Essex, SE England; pop. 81,500 (est. 2009). It was designated as a new town in 1947.

Harlow[2], Jean (1911–37), American film actress; born *Harlean Carpenter*. Her six films with Clark Gable included *Red Dust* (1932) and *Saratoga* (1937).

harm ▸ **noun** [mass noun] physical injury, especially that which is deliberately inflicted: *I didn't mean to cause him any harm.* ▪ material damage: *it's unlikely to do much harm to the engine.* ▪ actual or potential ill effects or danger: *there's no harm in asking her.*
▸ **verb** [with obj.] physically injure: *the villains didn't harm him.* ▪ damage the health of: *smoking when pregnant can harm your baby.* ▪ have an adverse effect on: *this could harm his World Cup prospects.*
– PHRASES **come to no harm** be unhurt or undamaged. **do more harm than good** inadvertently make a situation worse rather than better. **no harm done** used to reassure someone that what they have done has caused no real damage or problems. **out of harm's way** in a safe place. **there is no harm in ——** the specified course of action may not be guaranteed success but is at least unlikely to have unwelcome repercussions: *other stores may be offering similar deals—there's no harm in asking.*
– ORIGIN Old English *hearm* (noun), *hearmian* (verb), of Germanic origin; related to German *Harm* and Old Norse *harmr* 'grief, sorrow'.

harmattan /hɑːˈmat(ə)n/ ▸ **noun** a very dry, dusty easterly or north-easterly wind on the West African coast, occurring from December to February.
– ORIGIN late 17th cent.: from Akan *haramata*.

harmful ▸ **adjective** causing or likely to cause harm: *the ozone layer blocks the harmful rays from the sun* | *sugars which can be* ***harmful to*** *the teeth.*
– DERIVATIVES **harmfully** adverb, **harmfulness** noun.

harmless ▸ **adjective** not able or likely to cause harm: *the venom of most spiders is* ***harmless to*** *humans.* ▪ inoffensive: *as an entertainer, he's pretty harmless.*
– DERIVATIVES **harmlessly** adverb, **harmlessness** noun.

harmolodics /ˌhɑːməˈlɒdɪks/ ▸ **plural noun** [treated as sing.] a form of free jazz in which musicians improvise simultaneously on a melodic line at various pitches.
– DERIVATIVES **harmolodic** adjective.
– ORIGIN 1970s: coined by the American saxophonist Ornette Coleman (born 1930) and said to be a blend of *harmony, movement,* and *melodic*.

harmonic /hɑːˈmɒnɪk/ ▸ **adjective 1** Music relating to or characterized by harmony: *a basic four-chord harmonic sequence.* ▪ relating to or denoting a harmonic or harmonics.
2 Mathematics relating to a harmonic progression. ▪ Physics relating to component frequencies of a complex oscillation or wave.
3 Astrology using or produced by the application of a harmonic: *harmonic charts.*
▸ **noun 1** Music an overtone accompanying a fundamental tone at a fixed interval, produced by vibration of a string, column of air, etc. in an exact fraction of its length. ▪ a note produced on a musical instrument as an overtone, e.g. by lightly touching a string while sounding it.
2 Physics a component frequency of an oscillation or wave.
3 Astrology a division of the zodiacal circle by a specified number, used in the interpretation of a birth chart.
– DERIVATIVES **harmonically** adverb.
– ORIGIN late 16th cent. (in the sense 'relating to music, musical'): via Latin from Greek *harmonikos*, from *harmonia* (see HARMONY).

harmonica /hɑːˈmɒnɪkə/ ▸ **noun** a small rectangular wind instrument with a row of metal reeds along its length, held against the lips and moved from side to side to produce different notes by blowing or sucking. Also called MOUTH ORGAN.
– ORIGIN mid 18th cent.: from Latin, feminine singular or neuter plural of *harmonicus* 'musical' (see HARMONIC).

harmonic minor (also **harmonic minor scale**) ▸ **noun** Music a scale containing a minor third, minor sixth, and major seventh, forming the basis of conventional harmony in minor keys.

harmonic motion ▸ **noun** another term for SIMPLE HARMONIC MOTION.

harmonic progression ▸ **noun 1** Music a series of chord changes forming the underlying harmony of a piece of music.
2 Mathematics a sequence of quantities whose reciprocals are in arithmetical progression (e.g. 1, $^1/_3$, $^1/_5$, $^1/_7$, etc.).

harmonic series ▸ **noun 1** Music a set of frequencies consisting of a fundamental and the harmonics related to it by an exact fraction.
2 Mathematics a harmonic progression.

harmonious ▸ **adjective** tuneful; not discordant: *harmonious music.* ▪ forming a pleasing or consistent whole: *the decor is a harmonious blend of traditional and modern.* ▪ free from disagreement or dissent: *harmonious relationships.*
– DERIVATIVES **harmoniously** adverb, **harmoniousness** noun.

harmonist ▸ **noun** a person skilled in musical harmony.

harmonium /hɑːˈməʊnɪəm/ ▸ **noun** a keyboard instrument in which the notes are produced by air driven through metal reeds by foot operated bellows.
– ORIGIN mid 19th cent.: from French, from Latin *harmonia* (see HARMONY) or Greek *harmonios* 'harmonious'.

harmonize (also **harmonise**) ▸ **verb** [with obj.] **1** add notes to (a melody) to produce harmony. ▪ [no obj.] sing or play in harmony.
2 [no obj.] produce a pleasing visual combination: *steeply pitched roofs which* ***harmonize with*** *the form of the main roof.*
3 make consistent or compatible: *plans to harmonize the railways of Europe* | *the need to* ***harmonize*** *British practice* ***with*** *the new European standards.*
– DERIVATIVES **harmonization** noun, **harmonizer** noun.
– ORIGIN late 15th cent. (in the sense 'sing or play in harmony'): from French *harmoniser*, from *harmonie* (see HARMONY).

harmony ▸ **noun** (pl. **harmonies**) **1** [mass noun] the combination of simultaneously sounded musical notes to produce a pleasing effect: *the piece owes its air of tranquillity largely to the harmony* | [count noun] *an exciting variety of improvised harmonies.* ▪ the quality of forming a pleasing and consistent whole: *delightful cities where old and new blend in harmony.* ▪ the state of being in agreement or concord: *man and machine in perfect harmony.*
2 an arrangement of the four Gospels, or of any parallel narratives, which presents a single continuous narrative text.
– PHRASES **harmony of the spheres** see SPHERE.
– ORIGIN late Middle English: via Old French from Latin *harmonia* 'joining, concord', from Greek, from *harmos* 'joint'.

Harmsworth, Alfred Charles William, see NORTHCLIFFE.

harness ▸ **noun** a set of straps and fittings by which a horse or other draught animal is fastened to a cart, plough, etc. and is controlled by its driver. ▪ an arrangement of straps for fastening something such as a parachute to a person's body or for restraining a young child.
▸ **verb** [with obj.] **1** put a harness on (a horse or other draught animal): *how to groom a horse and harness it* | *the horse was* ***harnessed to*** *two long shafts.*
2 control and make use of (natural resources), especially to produce energy: *attempts to harness solar energy* | figurative *projects that harness the creativity of those living in the ghetto.*
– PHRASES **in harness** (of a horse or other animal) used for driving or draught work. ▪ in the routine of daily work: *a man who died in harness far beyond the normal age of retirement.* ▪ so as to achieve something together: *local and central government should work in harness.*
– DERIVATIVES **harnesser** noun.
– ORIGIN Middle English: from Old French *harneis* 'military equipment', from Old Norse, from *herr* 'army' + *nest* 'provisions'.

harness racing ▸ **noun** another term for TROTTING.

Harold the name of two kings of England: ▪ **Harold I** (d.1040), reigned 1037–40; known as **Harold Harefoot**. An illegitimate son of Canute, he acted as regent on his father's death in 1035 owing to the absence in Denmark of Hardecanute (King of Denmark and Canute's legitimate heir) and became king two years later. ▪ **Harold II** (*c.*1019–66), reigned 1066, the last Anglo-Saxon king of England. Succeeding Edward the Confessor, he was faced with two invasions within months of his accession. He resisted his half-brother Tostig and the Norse king Harald Hardrada at Stamford Bridge, but was killed and his army defeated by William of Normandy at the Battle of Hastings.

Haroun-al-Raschid /haˌruːn ˌalrəˈʃiːd/ variant spelling of HARUN AR-RASHID.

harp ▸ **noun 1** a musical instrument consisting of a frame supporting a graduated series of parallel strings, played by plucking with the fingers. The modern orchestral harp has an upright frame, with pedals which enable the strings to be retuned to different keys.
2 another term for HARMONICA: *Papa had been teaching him to play the blues harp.* [short for *mouth harp*.]
3 (also **harp shell** or **harp snail**) a marine mollusc which has a large vertically ribbed shell with a wide aperture, found chiefly in the Indo-Pacific. ● Family Harpidae, class Gastropoda.
▸ **verb** [no obj.] **1** (**harp on**) talk or write persistently and tediously on (a particular topic): *I don't want to* ***harp on about*** *the past.*
2 archaic play on a harp.
– ORIGIN Old English *hearpe*, of Germanic origin; related to Dutch *harp* and German *Harfe*.

Harper, Stephen Joseph (b.1959), Canadian Conservative statesman, Prime Minister since 2006.

harper ▸ **noun** a musician, especially a folk musician, who plays a harp.

Harpers Ferry a small town in Jefferson County, West Virginia. It is famous for a raid in October 1859 in which John Brown and a group of abolitionists captured a Federal arsenal located there.

harpist ▸ **noun** a musician who plays a harp.

Harpocrates /hɑːˈpɒkrətiːz/ Greek name for HORUS.

harpoon ▸ **noun** a barbed spear-like missile attached to a long rope and thrown by hand or fired from a gun, used for catching whales and other large sea creatures.
▸ **verb** [with obj.] spear with a harpoon.
– DERIVATIVES **harpooner** noun.
– ORIGIN early 17th cent. (denoting a barbed dart or spear): from French *harpon*, from *harpe* 'dog's claw, clamp', via Latin from Greek *harpē* 'sickle'.

harp seal ▸ **noun** a slender North Atlantic seal that typically has a dark harp-shaped mark on its grey back. ● *Pagophilus groenlandicus*, family Phocidae.

harp shell (also **harp snail**) ▸ **noun** see HARP (sense 3 of the noun).

harpsichord /ˈhɑːpsɪkɔːd/ ▸ **noun** a keyboard instrument with horizontal strings which run perpendicular to the keyboard in a long tapering case, and are plucked by points of quill, leather, or plastic operated by depressing the keys. It is used chiefly

in European classical music of the 16th to 18th centuries.
– DERIVATIVES **harpsichordist** noun.
– ORIGIN early 17th cent.: from obsolete French *harpechorde*, from late Latin *harpa* 'harp' + *chorda* 'string' (the insertion of the letter *s* being unexplained).

harpy ▶ noun (pl. **harpies**) **1** Greek & Roman Mythology a rapacious monster described as having a woman's head and body and a bird's wings and claws or depicted as a bird of prey with a woman's face.
2 a grasping, unpleasant woman: *clearly, he had us down as a couple of gold-digging harpies.*
– ORIGIN late Middle English: from Latin *harpyia*, from Greek *harpuiai* 'snatchers'.

harpy eagle ▶ noun a very large crested eagle of tropical rainforests, often preying on monkeys.
● Family Accipitridae: *Harpia harpyja* of South America, the largest eagle, and *Harpyopsis novaeguineae* of New Guinea.

harquebus /'hɑːkwɪbəs/ ▶ noun variant spelling of ARQUEBUS.

harridan /'harɪd(ə)n/ ▶ noun a strict, bossy, or belligerent old woman: *a bullying old harridan.*
– ORIGIN late 17th cent. (originally slang): perhaps from French *haridelle* 'old horse'.

H

harried ▶ adjective feeling strained as a result of having demands persistently made on one; harassed: *harried reporters are frequently forced to invent what they cannot find out.*

harrier[1] ▶ noun a person who engages in persistent attacks on others or incursions into their land.

harrier[2] ▶ noun a hound of a breed used for hunting hares. ■ (**Harriers**) used in the names of teams of cross-country runners: *Durham City Harriers.*
– ORIGIN late Middle English *hayrer*, from HARE + -ER[1]. The spelling change was due to association with HARRIER[1].

harrier[3] ▶ noun a long-winged, slender-bodied bird of prey with low quartering flight. ● Genus *Circus*, family Accipitridae: several species.
– ORIGIN mid 16th cent. (as *harrower*): from *harrow* 'harry, rob' (variant of HARRY). The spelling change in the 17th cent. was due to association with HARRIER[1].

harrier hawk ▶ noun an African bird of prey with a bare yellow face, resembling a goshawk but flying like a harrier. ● Genus *Polyboroides*, family Accipitridae: two species, in particular *P. typus*.

Harrington ▶ noun a man's short lightweight jacket with a collar and a zipped front.
– ORIGIN from the name of Rodney *Harrington*, a character in the 1960s TV serial *Peyton Place*, who was associated with the garment.

Harris[1] the southern part of the island of Lewis and Harris in the Outer Hebrides.

Harris[2], Sir Arthur Travers (1892–1984), British Marshal of the RAF; known as **Bomber Harris**. As Commander-in-Chief of Bomber Command (1942–5) in the Second World War he organized mass bombing raids against German towns which resulted in large-scale civilian casualties.

Harris[3], Frank (1856–1931), Irish writer; born *James Thomas Harris*. He gained a reputation as a fearless journalist and edited the periodical *Saturday Review* (1894–8). His autobiography *My Life and Loves* (1923–7) was notorious for its unreliability and sexual frankness.

Harrisburg /'harɪsbəːg/ the state capital of Pennsylvania, on the Susquehanna River; pop. 47,148 (est. 2008). The nearby nuclear power station at Three Mile Island suffered a serious accident in 1979.

Harris' hawk (also **Harris hawk**) ▶ noun a large chocolate-brown buzzard with chestnut shoulder patches, popular with falconers. It occurs in arid country from the southern US to South America and frequently nests in tall cacti. ● *Parabuteo unicinctus*, family Accipitridae.
– ORIGIN named after the US naturalist Edward Harris (1799–1863).

Harrison[1], Benjamin (1833–1901), American Republican statesman, 23rd President of the US 1889–93.

Harrison[2], George (1943–2001), English rock and pop guitarist, the lead guitarist of the Beatles.

Harrison[3], William Henry (1773–1841), American Whig statesman, 9th President of the US, 1841. He died of pneumonia a month after his inauguration.

Harris tweed ▶ noun [mass noun] trademark handwoven tweed made in the Outer Hebrides in Scotland, especially on the island of Lewis and Harris.

Harrod /'harəd/, Charles Henry (1800–85), English grocer and tea merchant. In 1853 he took over a shop in Knightsbridge, London, which, after expansion by his son **Charles Digby Harrod** (1841–1905), became a prestigious department store.

Harrovian /hə'rəʊvɪən/ ▶ noun a past or present member of Harrow School.
– ORIGIN early 19th cent.: from modern Latin *Harrovia* 'Harrow' + -AN.

harrow ▶ noun an implement consisting of a heavy frame set with teeth or tines which is dragged over ploughed land to break up clods, remove weeds, and cover seed.
▶ verb [with obj.] **1** draw a harrow over (land).
2 cause distress to: *Todd could take it, whereas I'm harrowed by it.*
– DERIVATIVES **harrower** noun.
– ORIGIN Middle English: from Old Norse *herfi*; obscurely related to Dutch *hark* 'rake'.

harrowing ▶ adjective acutely distressing: *a harrowing film about racism and violence.*
– DERIVATIVES **harrowingly** adverb.

Harrowing of Hell (in medieval Christian theology) the defeat of the powers of evil and the release of its victims by the descent of Christ into hell after his death.
– ORIGIN Middle English: *harrowing* from *harrow*, by-form of the verb HARRY.

Harrow School a boys' public school in NW London, founded under Queen Elizabeth I in 1571.

harrumph /hə'rʌmf/ ▶ verb [no obj.] clear the throat noisily. ■ grumpily express dissatisfaction or disapproval: *sceptics tend to harrumph at case histories like this.*
▶ noun a noisy clearing of the throat. ■ a grumpy expression of dissatisfaction or disapproval.
– ORIGIN 1930s: imitative.

harry ▶ verb (**harries, harrying, harried**) [with obj.] persistently carry out attacks on (an enemy or an enemy's territory). ■ persistently harass: *the government is being mercilessly harried by a new lobby.*
– ORIGIN Old English *herian, hergian*, of Germanic origin, probably influenced by Old French *harier*, in the same sense.

harsh ▶ adjective **1** unpleasantly rough or jarring to the senses: *drenched in a harsh white neon light | harsh guttural shouts.*
2 cruel or severe: *a time of harsh military discipline.* ■ (of a climate or conditions) difficult to survive in; hostile: *the harsh environment of the desert.* ■ (of reality or a fact) grim and unpalatable: *the harsh realities of the world news.* ■ having an undesirably strong effect: *she finds soap too harsh and drying.*
– DERIVATIVES **harshen** verb, **harshly** adverb, **harshness** noun.
– ORIGIN Middle English: from Middle Low German *harsch* 'rough', literally 'hairy', from *haer* 'hair'.

hart ▶ noun an adult male deer, especially a red deer over five years old.
– ORIGIN Old English *heorot, heort*, of Germanic origin; related to Dutch *hert* and German *Hirsch*.

hartal /'hɑːtɑːl, 'həːtɑːl/ ▶ noun (in South Asia) a closure of shops and offices as a protest or a mark of sorrow.
– ORIGIN from Hindi *haṛtāl, haṭtāl*, literally 'locking of shops', from Sanskrit *haṭṭa* 'market' + Hindi *tāla* 'lock'.

Harte /hɑːt/, (Francis) Bret (1836–1902), American short-story writer and poet. He is chiefly remembered for his stories about life in a Californian goldmining settlement.

hartebeest /'hɑːtɪbiːst/ ▶ noun a large African antelope with a long head and sloping back, related to the gnus. ● Genera *Alcelaphus, Damaliscus*, and *Sigmoceros*, family Bovidae: three or four species, in particular the **red hartebeest** (*A. buselaphus*), which typically has a reddish-brown coat.
– ORIGIN late 18th cent.: from South African Dutch, from Dutch *hert* 'hart' + *beest* 'beast'.

Hartford the state capital of Connecticut, situated on the Connecticut River; pop. 124,062 (est. 2008).

Hartlepool /'hɑːtlɪˌpuːl/ a port on the North Sea coast of NE England, in County Durham; pop. 87,800 (est. 2009).

Hartley, L. P. (1895–1972), English novelist and short-story writer; full name *Leslie Poles Hartley*. Much of his work deals with memory and the effects of childhood experience on adult life and character. Notable novels: *The Shrimp and the Anemone* (1944) and *The Go-Between* (1953).

hartshorn /'hɑːtshɔːn/ (also **spirit of hartshorn**) ▶ noun [mass noun] archaic aqueous ammonia solution used as smelling salts, formerly prepared from the horns of deer.
– ORIGIN Old English *heortes horn* (see HART, HORN).

hart's tongue (also **hart's tongue fern**) ▶ noun a common European fern whose long, narrow undivided fronds are said to resemble the tongues of deer.
● *Phyllitis* (or *Asplenium*) *scolopendrium*, family Aspleniaceae.

harum-scarum /ˌhɛːrəm'skɛːrəm/ ▶ adjective reckless; impetuous: *a wild harum-scarum youth.*
▶ noun a reckless, impetuous person.
– ORIGIN late 17th cent. (as an adverb): reduplication based on HARE and SCARE.

Harun ar-Rashid /haˌruːn ˌɑːrɑ'ʃiːd/ (also **Haroun-al-Raschid**) (763–809), fifth Abbasid caliph of Baghdad 786–809. The most powerful of the Abbasid caliphs, he was made famous by his portrayal in the *Arabian Nights*.

haruspex /hə'rʌspɛks/ ▶ noun (pl. **haruspices** /-spɪsiːz/) (in ancient Rome) a religious official who interpreted omens by inspecting the entrails of sacrificial animals.
– DERIVATIVES **haruspicy** /hə'rʌspɪsi/ noun.
– ORIGIN Latin, from an unrecorded element meaning 'entrails' (related to Sanskrit *hirā* 'artery') + *-spex* (from *specere* 'look at').

Harvard classification ▶ noun Astronomy a system of classification of stars based on their spectral types, the chief classes (O, B, A, F, G, K, M) forming a series from very hot bluish-white stars to cool dull red stars.
– ORIGIN 1960s: named after the observatory at HARVARD UNIVERSITY, where it was devised.

Harvard University /'hɑːvəd/ the oldest American university, founded in 1636 at Cambridge, Massachusetts.
– ORIGIN named after John *Harvard* (1607–38), an English settler who bequeathed his library and half his estate to the university.

harvest ▶ noun the process or period of gathering in crops: *farmers work longer hours during the harvest.* ■ the season's yield or crop: *a poor harvest.* ■ a quantity of animals caught or killed for human use: *a limited harvest of wild mink.* ■ the product or result of an action: *in terms of science, Apollo yielded a meagre harvest.*
▶ verb [with obj.] gather (a crop) as a harvest: *after harvesting, most of the crop is stored in large buildings.* ■ catch or kill (animals) for human use. ■ remove (cells, tissue, or an organ) from a person or animal for experiment or transplant.
– DERIVATIVES **harvestable** adjective, **harvester** noun.
– ORIGIN Old English *hærfest* 'autumn', of Germanic origin; related to Dutch *herfst* and German *Herbst*, from an Indo-European root shared by Latin *carpere* 'pluck' and Greek *karpos* 'fruit'.

harvester ant ▶ noun an ant that gathers and stores seeds and grain as a communal food source for the colony. ● *Messor* and other genera, family Formicidae.

harvest festival ▶ noun a celebration of the annual harvest, especially (in Britain) one held in schools and as a service in Christian churches, to which gifts of food are brought for the poor.

harvest home ▶ noun the gathering in of the final part of the year's harvest. ■ a festival marking the end of the harvest period.

harvestman ▶ noun (pl. **harvestmen**) an arachnid with a globular body and very long thin legs, typically living in leaf litter and on tree trunks. ● Order Opiliones: three suborders.

harvest mite ▶ noun a minute mite whose parasitic larvae live on or under the skin of warm-blooded animals where they cause irritation and dermatitis, and sometimes transmit scrub typhus. ● Genus *Trombicula*, family Trombiculidae: many species, including the European *T. autumnalis*, which is common at harvest time.

harvest moon ▶ noun the full moon that is seen nearest to the time of the autumn equinox.

harvest mouse ▶ noun **1** a small North Eurasian mouse with a prehensile tail, nesting among the stalks of growing cereals and other vegetation.
● *Micromys minutus*, family Muridae.
2 a nocturnal mouse found in North and Central America. ● Genus *Reithrodontomys*, family Muridae: several species.

Harvey, William (1578–1657), English physician, discoverer of the circulation of the blood. In *De Motu Cordis* (1628) Harvey described the motion of the heart and concluded that the blood left through the

– ORIGIN late 19th cent.: modern Latin, from Latin *haustor* 'thing that draws in', from the verb *haurire*.

hautboy /'(h)əʊbɔɪ/ ▶ **noun** archaic form of **OBOE**.
– ORIGIN mid 16th cent.: from French *hautbois*, from *haut* 'high' + *bois* 'wood'.

haute bourgeoisie /,əʊt bʊəʒwɑː'ziː/ ▶ **noun (the haute bourgeoisie)** [treated as sing. or pl.] the upper middle class.
– ORIGIN French, literally 'high bourgeoisie'.

haute couture /,əʊt kʊ'tjʊə/ ▶ **noun** [mass noun] the designing and making of high-quality fashionable clothes by leading fashion houses. ■ clothes of this kind.
– ORIGIN French, literally 'high dressmaking'.

haute cuisine /,əʊt kwɪ'ziːn/ ▶ **noun** [mass noun] the preparation and cooking of high-quality food following the style of traditional French cuisine. ■ food produced in such a way.
– ORIGIN French, literally 'high cookery'.

haute école /,əʊt eɪ'kɒl/ ▶ **noun** [mass noun] the art or practice of advanced classical dressage.
– ORIGIN French, literally 'high school'.

Haute-Normandie /əʊt'nɔːməndi/, French /'ɔotnɔʀmɑ̃di/ a region of northern France, on the coast of the English Channel, including the city of Rouen.

hauteur /əʊ'təː/ ▶ **noun** [mass noun] proud haughtiness of manner.
– ORIGIN French, from *haut* 'high'.

haut monde /əʊ 'mɒ̃d/ ▶ **noun (the haut monde)** fashionable society.
– ORIGIN French, literally 'high world'.

haut-relief /,əʊrɪ'liːf/ ▶ **noun** [mass noun] Sculpture another term for **HIGH RELIEF** (see **RELIEF** (sense 4)).
– ORIGIN mid 19th cent.: French, literally 'high relief'.

havala /hʌ'veɪlə/ ▶ **noun** Indian another term for **HAWALA**.
– ORIGIN from Hindi *havālā*.

havan /'havən/ ▶ **noun** Hinduism a ritual burning of offerings such as grains and ghee, which is held to mark births, marriages, and other special occasions.
– ORIGIN Hindi.

Havana[1] /hə'vanə/ the capital of Cuba, situated on the north coast; pop. 2,148,132 (2008). It was founded in 1515 by Diego Velázquez de Cuéllar. Spanish name **LA HABANA**.

Havana[2] /hə'vanə/ ▶ **noun** a cigar made in Cuba or from Cuban tobacco.

Havant /'hav(ə)nt/ a town in Hampshire, southern England; pop. 43,600 (2009).

havarti /hə'vɑːti/ ▶ **noun** [mass noun] a mild, semi-soft Danish cheese with small irregular holes.
– ORIGIN named after the farm of the Danish cheesemaker Hanne Nielsen.

Havdalah ▶ **noun** variant spelling of **HABDALAH**.

have ▶ **verb (has, having, had)** [with obj.] **1** (also **have got**) possess, own, or hold: *he had a new car and a boat | have you got a job yet? | I don't have that much money on me.* ■ possess (a quality, characteristic, or feature): *the ham had a sweet, smoky flavour | she's got blue eyes | the house has gas-fired central heating.* ■ **(have oneself)** informal, chiefly N. Amer. provide or indulge oneself with (something): *he had himself two highballs.* ■ be made up of; comprise: *in 1989 the party had 10,000 members.* ■ used to indicate a particular relationship: *he's got three children | do you have a client named Peters?* ■ be able to make use of (something available or at one's disposal): *how much time have I got for the presentation?* ■ possess as an intellectual attainment; know (a language or subject): *he knew Latin and Greek; I had only a little French.*
2 experience; undergo: *I went to a few parties and had a good time | I was having difficulty in keeping awake.* ■ (also **have got**) suffer from (an illness, ailment, or disability): *I've got a headache.* ■ (also **have got**) let (a feeling or thought) come into one's mind; hold in the mind: *he had the strong impression that someone was watching him.* ■ [with past participle] experience or suffer the specified action happening or being done to (something): *she had her bag stolen.* ■ [with obj. and complement] cause to be in a particular state or condition: *I want to have everything ready in good time | I had the TV on with the sound turned down.* ■ [with past participle] cause (something) to be done for one by someone else: *it is advisable to have your carpet laid by a professional.* ■ tell or arrange for (someone) to do something for one: [with obj. and infinitive] *he had his bodyguards throw Chris out | she's always having the builders in to do something or other.* ■ (also **have got**) informal have put (someone) at a disadvantage in an argument: *you've got me there; I've never given the matter much thought.* ■ informal cheat or deceive (someone): *I realized I'd been had.* ■ vulgar slang engage in sexual intercourse with.
3 (**have to** or **have got to do something**) be obliged or find it necessary to do the specified thing: *you don't have to accept this situation | sorry, we've got to dash.* ■ be strongly recommended to do something: *if you think that place is great, you have to try our summer house.* ■ be certain or inevitable to happen or be the case: *there has to be a catch.*
4 perform the action indicated by the noun specified (used especially in spoken English as an alternative to a more specific verb): *he had a look round | the colour green has a restful effect.* ■ organize and bring about: *are you going to have a party?* ■ eat or drink: *they had beans on toast.* ■ give birth to or be due to give birth to: *she's going to have a baby.*
5 (also **have got**) show (a personal attribute or quality) by one's actions or attitude: *he had little patience with technological gadgetry* | [with obj. and infinitive] *you never even phoned, and now you've got the cheek to come back.* ■ [often in imperative] exercise or show (mercy, pity, etc.) towards another person: *God have mercy on me!* ■ [with negative] accept or tolerate: *I can't have you insulting Tom like that.*
6 (also **have got**) [with obj. and adverbial of place] place or keep (something) in a particular position: *Mary had her back to me | I soon had the trout in a net.* ■ hold or grasp in a particular way: *he had me by the throat.*
7 be the recipient of (something sent, given, or done): *she had a letter from Mark.* ■ take or invite into one's home so as to provide care or entertainment: *we're having the children for the weekend.*
▶ **auxiliary verb** used with a past participle to form the perfect, pluperfect, and future perfect tenses, and the conditional mood: *I have finished | he had asked her | she will have left by now | I could have helped, had I known | 'Have you seen him?' 'Yes, I have.'*
▶ **noun 1** (**the haves**) informal people with plenty of money and possessions: *an increasing gap between the haves and have-nots.*
2 [in sing.] Brit. informal, dated a swindle.
– PHRASES **have a care** (or **an eye** etc.) see **CARE**, **EYE**, etc. **have got it bad** (or **badly**) informal be very powerfully affected emotionally, especially by love. **have had it** informal **1** be in a very poor condition; be beyond repair or past its best: *the car had had it.* ■ be extremely tired. ■ have lost all chance of survival: *when the lorry smashed into me, I thought I'd had it.* **2** be unable to tolerate someone or something any longer: *I've had it with him—he's humiliated me once too often!* **have it 1** [with clause] claim; express the view that: *rumour had it that although he lived in a derelict house, he was really very wealthy.* **2** win a decision, especially after a vote: *the ayes have it.* **3** have found the answer to something: *'I have it!' Rosa exclaimed.* **have it away (on one's toes)** Brit. informal leave quickly. **have it away** (or **off**) Brit. vulgar slang have sexual intercourse. **have it both ways** see **BOTH**. **have (got) it in for** informal feel a particular dislike of (someone) and behave in a hostile manner towards them. **have (got) it in one (to do something)** informal have the capacity or potential (to do something): *everyone thinks he has it in him to produce a literary classic.* **have it out** informal attempt to resolve a contentious matter by confronting someone: *give her the chance of a night's rest before you **have it out with** her.* **have a nice day** chiefly US used to express good wishes when parting. **have (got) nothing on** informal **1** be not nearly as good as. **2** (**have nothing** or **something on**) know nothing (or something) discreditable or incriminating about: *I am not worried—they've got nothing on me.* **have nothing to do with** see **DO**[1]. **have one too many** see **MANY**. **have (got) something to oneself** be able to use, occupy, or enjoy something without having to share it with anyone else. **have —— to do with** see **DO**[1].
– PHRASAL VERBS **have at** tackle or attack forcefully or aggressively. **have someone on** informal try to make someone believe something that is untrue, especially as a joke: *that's just too neat—you're having me on.* **have (got) something on 1** be wearing something: *she had a blue dress on.* **2** be committed to an arrangement: *I've got a lot on at the moment.* **have something out** undergo an operation to extract a part of one's body. **have someone up** Brit. informal bring someone before a court of justice to answer for an alleged offence: *you can **be had up for** blackmail.*
– ORIGIN Old English *habban*, of Germanic origin; related to Dutch *hebben* and German *haben*, also probably to **HEAVE**.

USAGE 1 Have and have got: there is a great deal of debate on the difference between these two forms; a traditional view is that **have got** is chiefly British, but not correct in formal writing, while **have** is chiefly American. Actual usage is more complicated: **have got** is in fact also widely used in US English. In both British and US usage **have** is more formal than **have got** and it is more appropriate in writing to use constructions such as **don't have** rather than **haven't got**.
2 A common mistake is to write the word **of** instead of **have** or **'ve**: *I **could of** told you that* instead of *I **could've** told you that*. The reason for the mistake is that the pronunciation of **have** in unstressed contexts is the same as that of **of**, and the two words are confused when it comes to writing them down. The error was recorded as early as 1837 and, though common, is unacceptable in standard English.
3 Another controversial issue is the insertion of **have** where it is superfluous, as for example *I might have missed it if you **hadn't have** pointed it out* (rather than the standard ... *if you **hadn't** pointed it out*). This construction has been around since at least the 15th and 16th centuries, but only where a hypothetical situation is presented (e.g. statements starting with **if**). More recently, there has been speculation among grammarians and linguists that this insertion of **have** may represent a kind of subjunctive and is actually making a useful distinction in the language. However, it is still regarded as an error in standard English.

H

Havel /'hɑːv(ə)l/, Václav (b.1936), Czech dramatist and statesman, President of Czechoslovakia 1989–92 and of the Czech Republic 1993–2003. His plays, such as *The Garden Party* (1963), were critical of totalitarianism and he was twice imprisoned as a dissident. He was elected president following the velvet revolution.

haveli /,hʌvə'liː/ ▶ **noun** (pl. **havelis**) Indian a mansion.
– ORIGIN via Hindi from Arabic *havelī*.

haven ▶ **noun** a place of safety or refuge: *a haven for wildlife.* ■ an inlet providing shelter for ships or boats; a harbour or small port.
– ORIGIN late Old English *hæfen*, from Old Norse *hǫfn*; related to Dutch *haven*, German *Hafen* 'harbour'.

have-nots ▶ **plural noun** (usu. **the have-nots**) informal economically disadvantaged people.

haven't ▶ **contraction** have not.

haver /'heɪvə/ ▶ **verb** [no obj.] **1** Scottish talk foolishly; babble: *Tom havered on.*
2 Brit. act in a vacillating or indecisive manner: (as noun **havering**) *she was exasperated by all this havering.*
▶ **noun** [mass noun] (also **havers**) Scottish foolish talk; nonsense.
– ORIGIN early 18th cent.: of unknown origin.

haversack /'havəsak/ ▶ **noun** a small, strong bag carried on the back or over the shoulder, used especially by soldiers and walkers.
– ORIGIN mid 18th cent.: from French *havresac*, from obsolete German *Habersack*, denoting a bag used by soldiers to carry oats as horse feed, from dialect *Haber* 'oats' + *Sack* 'sack, bag'.

Haversian canal /hə'vəːʃ(ə)n/ ▶ **noun** Anatomy any of the minute tubes which form a network in bone and contain blood vessels.
– ORIGIN mid 19th cent.: named after Clopton *Havers* (1650–1702), English anatomist.

haversine /'havəsʌɪn/ (also **haversin**) ▶ **noun** Mathematics half of a versed sine.
– ORIGIN late 19th cent.: contraction of *half versed sine*.

havildar /'havɪldɑː/ ▶ **noun** (in South Asia) a soldier or police officer corresponding to a sergeant.
– ORIGIN from Urdu *hawildār*, from Persian *ḥawāldār* 'trust-holder', from *ḥawāl* (from Arabic *ḥawāl* 'charge, assignment') + *-dār* 'holder'.

havoc ▶ **noun** [mass noun] widespread destruction: *the hurricane ripped through Florida causing havoc.* ■ great confusion or disorder: *if they weren't at school they'd be wreaking havoc in the streets.*
▶ **verb (havocs, havocking, havocked)** [with obj.] archaic lay waste to; devastate.
– PHRASES **play havoc with** completely disrupt: *shift work plays havoc with the body clock.*
– ORIGIN late Middle English: from Anglo-Norman French *havok*, alteration of Old French *havot*, of unknown origin. The word was originally used in the phrase *cry havoc* (Old French *crier havot*) 'to give

an army the order *havoc*', which was the signal for plundering.

haw¹ ▸ **noun** the red fruit of the hawthorn.
– ORIGIN Old English *haga*, of Germanic origin; probably related to **HEDGE** (compare with Dutch *haag* 'hedge').

haw² ▸ **noun** the third eyelid or nictitating membrane in certain mammals, especially dogs and cats.
– ORIGIN late Middle English (denoting a discharge from the eye): of unknown origin.

haw³ ▸ **verb** see **HUM AND HAW** at **HUM¹**.

Hawaii /həˈwʌɪi/ a state of the US comprising a group of over twenty islands in the North Pacific; capital, Honolulu (on Oahu); pop. 1,288,198 (est. 2008). First settled by Polynesians, Hawaii was visited by Captain James Cook in 1778. It was annexed by the US in 1898 and became the 50th state in 1959. Former name **SANDWICH ISLANDS**. ■ the largest island in the state of Hawaii.

Hawaiian ▸ **noun 1** a native or inhabitant of Hawaii.
2 [mass noun] the Austronesian language of Hawaii, now spoken by fewer than 2,000 people.
▸ **adjective** relating to Hawaii, its people, or their language. ■ Geology relating to or denoting a type of volcanic eruption in which very fluid basaltic lava is produced, as is typical of volcanoes in Hawaii.

H

Hawaiian goose ▸ **noun** a rare goose native to Hawaii, now breeding chiefly in captivity. Also called **NENE**. ● *Branta sandvicensis*, family Anatidae.

Hawaiian guitar ▸ **noun** a steel-stringed guitar in which a characteristic glissando effect is produced by sliding a metal bar along the strings as they are plucked.

Hawaiian honeycreeper ▸ **noun** see **HONEYCREEPER** (sense 2).

hawala /haˈwɑːlə/ ▸ **noun** [mass noun] a traditional system of transferring money used in Arab countries and South Asia, whereby the money is paid to an agent who then instructs an associate in the relevant country or area to pay the final recipient.
– ORIGIN from Arabic *ḥawāla*, literally 'assignment, bill of exchange'.

hawfinch ▸ **noun** a large Old World finch with a massive bill for cracking open cherry stones and other hard seeds. ● Genus *Coccothraustes*, family Fringillidae: three species, in particular the widespread *C. coccothraustes*.
– ORIGIN late 17th cent.: from **HAW¹** + **FINCH**.

hawk¹ ▸ **noun 1** a diurnal bird of prey with broad rounded wings and a long tail, typically taking prey by surprise with a short chase. Compare with **FALCON**. ● Family Accipitridae: several genera, especially *Accipiter*, which includes the sparrowhawk and goshawk.
■ N. Amer. a bird of prey related to the buzzards.
■ Falconry any diurnal bird of prey used in falconry.
2 a person who advocates an aggressive or warlike policy, especially in foreign affairs. Compare with **DOVE¹** (sense 2).
3 used in names of hawkmoths, e.g. **eyed hawk**.
▸ **verb** [no obj.] **1** (of a person) hunt game with a trained hawk: *he spent the afternoon hawking*.
2 (of a bird or dragonfly) hunt on the wing for food: *swifts hawked low over the water*.
– PHRASES **have eyes like a hawk** miss nothing of what is going on around one. **watch someone like a hawk** keep a vigilant eye on someone, especially to check that they do nothing wrong.
– DERIVATIVES **hawklike** adjective.
– ORIGIN Old English *hafoc*, *heafoc*, of Germanic origin; related to Dutch *havik* and German *Habicht*.

hawk² ▸ **verb** [with obj.] carry about and offer (goods) for sale, typically advertising them by shouting: *street traders were hawking costume jewellery*.
– ORIGIN late 15th cent.: probably a back-formation from **HAWKER¹**.

hawk³ ▸ **verb** [no obj.] clear the throat noisily: *he hawked and spat into the flames*. ■ [with obj.] (**hawk something up**) bring phlegm up from the throat.
– ORIGIN late 16th cent.: probably imitative.

hawk⁴ ▸ **noun** a plasterer's square board with a handle underneath for carrying plaster or mortar.
– ORIGIN late Middle English: of unknown origin.

hawkbit ▸ **noun** a Eurasian plant of the daisy family which resembles a dandelion, with a rosette of leaves and yellow flowers. ● Genus *Leontodon*, family Compositae.
– ORIGIN early 18th cent.: blend of **HAWKWEED** and **DEVIL'S BIT**.

Hawke, Bob (b.1929), Australian Labor statesman, Prime Minister 1983–91; full name *Robert James Lee Hawke*. During his premiership he pursued an economic programme based on free-market policies and tax reform.

hawk eagle ▸ **noun** a small tropical eagle with broad wings and a long tail, and typically a crest. ● Genera *Spizaetus* and *Spizastur*, family Accipitridae: several species.

Hawke Bay a bay on the east coast of the North Island, New Zealand.

hawker¹ ▸ **noun** a person who travels about selling goods, typically advertising them by shouting.
– ORIGIN early 16th cent.: probably from Low German or Dutch and related to **HUCKSTER**.

hawker² ▸ **noun 1** a falconer.
2 a slender-bodied dragonfly that remains airborne for long periods, typically patrolling a particular stretch of water. ● Aeshnidae, Gomphidae, and other families, order Odonata: several genera.
– ORIGIN Old English *hafocere*, from *hafoc* 'hawk'.

hawker centre ▸ **noun** (in South East Asia) a market at which individual vendors sell ready-to-eat food from small booths.

Hawke's Bay an administrative region on the east-ern coast of the North Island, New Zealand.

hawk-eyed ▸ **adjective** having very good eyesight. ■ watching carefully; vigilant: *a hawk-eyed police-man saved the lives of dozens of shoppers*.

Hawkeye State informal name for **IOWA**.

hawkfish ▸ **noun** (pl. **same** or **hawkfishes**) a small tropical marine fish found chiefly in the Indo-Pacific region. It typically lives in shallow water and adopts a distinctive perching or 'hovering' position just above coral. ● Family Cirrhitidae: three genera and several species.

Hawking, Stephen (William) (b.1942), English theoretical physicist. His main work has been on space–time, quantum mechanics, and black holes. He is also noted for his bestselling book *A Brief History of Time* (1988).

Hawking radiation ▸ **noun** [mass noun] Physics electromagnetic radiation which, according to theory, should be emitted by a black hole. The radiation is due to the black hole capturing one of a particle-antiparticle pair created spontaneously near to the event horizon.

Hawkins (also **Hawkyns**), Sir John (1532–95), English sailor. Involved in the slave trade and privateering, he later helped build up the fleet which defeated the Spanish Armada in 1588.

hawkish ▸ **adjective 1** resembling a hawk in nature or appearance.
2 advocating an aggressive or warlike policy, especially in foreign affairs: *the administration's hawkish stance*.
– DERIVATIVES **hawkishly** adverb, **hawkishness** noun.

hawkmoth ▸ **noun** a large swift-flying moth with a stout body and narrow forewings, typically feeding on nectar while hovering. ● Family Sphingidae: several genera and many species.

hawk-nosed ▸ **adjective** (of a person) having a nose which is curved like a hawk's beak.

hawk owl ▸ **noun** a hawklike owl with a small head and long tail. ● Family Strigidae: three genera, including *Ninox* (several species in Asia and Australasia) and *Surnia*.

Hawks, Howard (Winchester) (1896–1977), American film director, producer, and screenwriter. He directed such films as *The Big Sleep* (1946), *Gentlemen Prefer Blondes* (1953), and *Rio Bravo* (1959).

hawksbeard ▸ **noun** a plant of the daisy family which resembles a dandelion but has a branched stem with several flowers. ● Genus *Crepis*, family Compositae.

hawksbill (also **hawksbill turtle**) ▸ **noun** a small tropical sea turtle with hooked jaws and overlapping horny plates on the shell, the traditional source of tortoiseshell. ● *Eretmochelys imbricata*, family Cheloniidae.

hawkshaw ▸ **noun** informal, dated or N. Amer. a detective.
– ORIGIN early 20th cent.: from the name of a detective in the play *The Ticket-of-Leave Man* by Tom Taylor (1817–80), English dramatist; also portrayed in the comic strip *Hawkshaw the Detective* by Augustus Charles ('Gus') Mager (1878–1956), American cartoonist.

Hawksmoor, Nicholas (1661–1736), English architect. Having become a clerk to Sir Christopher Wren in 1679, in 1690 he went on to work with Vanbrugh at Castle Howard and Blenheim Palace. He later designed six London churches.

hawkweed ▸ **noun** [mass noun] a widely distributed plant of the daisy family, which typically has yellow dandelion-like flower heads and often grows as a weed. ● Genus *Hieracium*, family Compositae.
– ORIGIN late Old English, rendering Latin *hieracium*, based on Greek *hierax* 'hawk': Pliny believed that hawks fed on this plant to strengthen their eyesight.

Hawkyns variant spelling of **HAWKINS**.

hawse /hɔːz/ ▸ **noun** the part of a ship's bows through which the anchor cables pass. ■ the space between the head of an anchored vessel and the anchors.
– PHRASES **foul hawse** a situation in which an anchored ship's port and starboard cables are crossed.
– ORIGIN late Middle English *halse*, probably from Old Norse *háls* 'neck, ship's bow'.

hawsehole ▸ **noun** a hole in the deck of a ship through which an anchor cable passes.

hawsepipe ▸ **noun** an inclined pipe leading from a hawse hole to the side of a ship, containing the shank of the anchor when the anchor is raised.

hawser /ˈhɔːzə/ ▸ **noun** a thick rope or cable for mooring or towing a ship.
– ORIGIN Middle English: from Anglo-Norman French *haucer*, from Old French *haucier* 'to hoist', based on Latin *altus* 'high'.

hawser-laid ▸ **adjective** another term for **CABLE-LAID**.

hawthorn ▸ **noun** a thorny shrub or tree of the rose family, with white, pink, or red blossom and small dark red fruits (haws). Native to north temperate regions, it is commonly used for hedging in Britain. Also called **MAY¹**, **QUICKTHORN**, **WHITETHORN**. ● Genus *Crataegus*, family Rosaceae: many species, in particular the European **common hawthorn** (*C. monogyna*).
– ORIGIN Old English *hagathorn*, probably meaning literally 'hedge thorn' (see **HAW¹**, **THORN**); related to Dutch *haagdoorn*, German *Hagedorn*.

Hawthorne, Nathaniel (1804–64), American novelist and short-story writer. Much of his fiction explores guilt, sin, and morality. Notable works: *Twice-Told Tales* (short stories, 1837), *The Scarlet Letter* (1850), and *The House of the Seven Gables* (1851).

Hawthorne effect ▸ **noun** the alteration of behaviour by the subjects of a study due to their awareness of being observed.
– ORIGIN 1960s: from *Hawthorne*, the name of one of the Western Electric Company's plants in Chicago, where the phenomenon was first observed in the 1920s.

hay¹ ▸ **noun** [mass noun] grass that has been mown and dried for use as fodder.
– PHRASES **hit the hay** informal go to bed. **make hay (while the sun shines)** proverb make good use of an opportunity while it lasts.
– ORIGIN Old English *hēg*, *hieg*, *hīg*, of Germanic origin; related to Dutch *hooi* and German *Heu*, also to **HEW**.

hay² ▸ **noun** a country dance with interweaving steps similar to a reel. ■ a winding figure in such a dance.
– ORIGIN early 16th cent.: from an obsolete sense 'a kind of dance' of French *haie* 'hedge', figuratively 'row of people lining the route of a procession'.

haybox ▸ **noun** historical a box stuffed with hay in which heated food was left to continue cooking.

haycock ▸ **noun** a conical heap of hay in a field.

Hay diet ▸ **noun** a diet in which carbohydrates are eaten at separate times from fruit and proteins, in the belief that this aids digestion.
– ORIGIN 1930s: named after William Howard Hay (1866–1940), the American physician who devised it.

Haydn /ˈhʌɪd(ə)n/, Franz Joseph (1732–1809), Austrian composer. A major exponent of the classical style, he taught both Mozart and Beethoven. His work includes 108 symphonies, 67 string quartets, 12 masses, and the oratorio *The Creation* (1796–8).

Hayek /ˈhʌɪjɛk/, Friedrich August von (1899–1992), Austrian-born British economist. Strongly opposed to Keynesian economics, he was a leading advocate of the free market. Nobel Prize for Economics (1974).

Hayes, Rutherford (Birchard) (1822–93), American Republican statesman, 19th President of the US 1877–81. His administration brought the Reconstruction era in the South to an end.

hay fever ▸ **noun** [mass noun] an allergy caused by pollen or dust in which the mucous membranes of the eyes and nose are inflamed, causing running at the nose and watery eyes.

hayfield ▶ **noun** a field where grass is grown for making into hay.

haying ▶ **noun** [mass noun] the activity of mowing and drying grass to make hay.

haylage /ˈheɪlɪdʒ/ ▶ **noun** [mass noun] silage made from grass which has been partially dried.
– ORIGIN 1960s: blend of **HAY¹** and **SILAGE**.

hayloft ▶ **noun** a loft over a stable used for storing hay or straw.

haymaker ▶ **noun 1** a person who is involved in making hay, especially one who tosses and spreads it to dry after mowing. ■ an apparatus for shaking and drying hay.
2 informal a forceful blow.

haymaking ▶ **noun** [mass noun] the activity of making hay from grass grown for fodder.

haymow /ˈheɪmaʊ/ ▶ **noun** a stack of hay or part of a barn in which hay is stored.

hayrick ▶ **noun** another term for **HAYSTACK**.

hayride ▶ **noun** N. Amer. a ride taken for pleasure in a wagon carrying hay.

hayseed ▶ **noun 1** [mass noun] grass seed obtained from hay.
2 informal, chiefly N. Amer. a person from the country, especially one who is simple and unsophisticated.

haystack ▶ **noun** a packed pile of hay, typically with a pointed or ridged top.

haywire ▶ **adjective** informal erratic; out of control: *her imagination had gone haywire*.
– ORIGIN 1920s (originally US): from **HAY¹** + **WIRE**, from the use of hay-baling wire in makeshift repairs.

Hayworth, Rita (1918–87), American actress and dancer; born *Margarita Carmen Cansino*. She achieved stardom in film musicals such as *Cover Girl* (1944) before going on to play roles in film noir, notably in *Gilda* (1946) and *The Lady from Shanghai* (1948).

hazard /ˈhazəd/ ▶ **noun 1** a danger or risk: *the hazards of childbirth*. ■ a potential source of danger: *a fire hazard | a health hazard*. ■ a permanent feature of a golf course which presents an obstruction to playing a shot, such as a bunker or stream.
2 [mass noun] literary chance; probability: *we can form no calculation concerning the laws of hazard*.
3 [mass noun] a gambling game using two dice, in which the chances are complicated by arbitrary rules.
4 (in real tennis) each of the winning openings in the court.
5 Billiards a stroke with which a ball is pocketed. ■ (**losing hazard**) the pocketing of the cue ball off another ball. ■ (**winning hazard**) the pocketing of the object ball.
▶ **verb** [with obj.] **1** say (something) in a tentative way: *he hazarded a guess*.
2 put (something) at risk of being lost: *the cargo business is too risky to hazard money on*.
– ORIGIN Middle English (in sense 3 of the noun): from Old French *hasard*, from Spanish *azar*, from Arabic *az-zahr* 'chance, luck', from Persian *zār* or Turkish *zar* 'dice'.

hazard lights (also **hazard warning lights**) ▶ **plural noun** yellow flashing indicator lights on a vehicle, switched on simultaneously as a warning that the vehicle is stationary or unexpectedly slowing down or reversing.

hazardous ▶ **adjective** risky; dangerous: *we work in hazardous conditions | it is* **hazardous to** *personal safety*.
– DERIVATIVES **hazardously** adverb.
– ORIGIN mid 16th cent.: from French *hasardeux*, from *hasard* 'chance' (see **HAZARD**).

hazard pay ▶ **noun** US term for **DANGER MONEY**.

Hazchem /ˈhazkɛm/ ▶ **noun** [as modifier] denoting a system of labelling hazardous chemicals, especially during transportation.
– ORIGIN 1970s: from *hazardous chemical*.

haze¹ ▶ **noun** [mass noun] **1** a slight obscuration of the lower atmosphere, typically caused by fine suspended particles. ■ a very fine cloud of something such as vapour or smoke in the air: *the gathering haze of cigarette smoke*.
2 [in sing.] a state of mental confusion: *an alcoholic haze*.
▶ **verb** [with obj.] obscure with a haze: *a clump of islands, very green, but hazed in cloud and mist*.
– ORIGIN early 18th cent. (originally denoting fog or hoar frost): probably a back-formation from **HAZY**.

haze² ▶ **verb** N. Amer. **1** [with obj.] force (a new or potential recruit to the military or a university fraternity) to perform strenuous, humiliating, or dangerous tasks: *rookies were mercilessly hazed*.
2 [with obj. and adverbial of direction] drive (cattle) in a specified direction while on horseback.
– ORIGIN late 17th cent. (originally Scots and dialect in the sense 'frighten, scold, or beat'): perhaps related to obsolete French *haser* 'tease or insult'.

hazel ▶ **noun 1** a temperate shrub or small tree with broad leaves, bearing prominent male catkins in spring and round hard-shelled edible nuts in autumn. ● Genus *Corylus*, family Betulaceae: several species, in particular the common **Eurasian hazel** (*C. avellana*).
2 [mass noun] a reddish-brown or greenish-brown colour, especially of a person's eyes.
– ORIGIN Old English *hæsel*, of Germanic origin; related to Dutch *hazelaar* 'hazel tree', *hazelnoot* 'hazelnut', and German *Hasel*, from an Indo-European root shared by Latin *corylus*.

hazel grouse ▶ **noun** a small Eurasian woodland grouse with mainly greyish plumage. ● *Bonasa bonasia*, family Tetraonidae (or Phasianidae).

hazelnut ▶ **noun** a round brown hard-shelled nut that is the edible fruit of the hazel.

Hazlitt /ˈhazlɪt, ˈheɪz-/, William (1778–1830), English essayist and critic. His diverse essays, collected in *Table Talk* (1821), were marked by a clarity and conviction which brought new vigour to English prose writing.

hazmat /ˈhazmat/ (also **hazmats**) ▶ **noun** [mass noun] dangerous substances; hazardous material: [as modifier] *hazmat shipments*.

hazy ▶ **adjective** (**hazier**, **haziest**) covered by a haze: *it was a beautiful day but quite hazy*. ■ vague or ill-defined: *hazy memories | the picture we have of him is extremely hazy*. ■ confused; uncertain: *school-leavers were often hazy about employment*.
– DERIVATIVES **hazily** adverb, **haziness** noun.
– ORIGIN early 17th cent. (in nautical use in the sense 'foggy'): of unknown origin.

hazzan /xəˈzɑːn, ˈhɑːz(ə)n/ ▶ **noun** (pl. **hazzanim**) another term for **CANTOR** (sense 1).
– ORIGIN mid 17th cent.: from Hebrew *ḥazzān* 'cantor', possibly from Assyrian *hazannu* 'mayor, headman'.

HB ▶ **abbreviation** ■ half board. ■ (also **hb**) hardback. ■ hard black (used in describing a medium grade of pencil lead). ■ the political wing of the Basque separatist organization ETA. [abbreviation of Basque *Herri Batasuna* 'United People'.]

Hb ▶ **symbol** haemoglobin.

HBM ▶ **abbreviation** Brit. Her or His Britannic Majesty (or Majesty's).

H-bomb ▶ **noun** another term for **HYDROGEN BOMB**.
– ORIGIN 1950s: from H^2 (denoting hydrogen) + **BOMB**.

HC ▶ **abbreviation** ■ Holy Communion. ■ (in the UK) House of Commons. ■ hydrocarbon: *increasing fuel efficiency decreases the levels of HC*.

h.c. ▶ **abbreviation** honoris causa.

HCF ▶ **abbreviation** Mathematics highest common factor.

HCFC ▶ **abbreviation** hydrochlorofluorocarbon.

HCG ▶ **abbreviation** human chorionic gonadotropin.

H.D. see **DOOLITTLE**.

HDD ▶ **abbreviation** Computing hard disk drive.

HDL ▶ **abbreviation** Biochemistry high-density lipoprotein.

HDSPA ▶ **abbreviation** High-Speed Downlink Packet Access, a protocol enabling the rapid transmission of Internet data to mobile phones.

HDTV ▶ **abbreviation** high-definition television, using more lines per frame to give a sharper image.

HE ▶ **abbreviation** ■ high explosive. ■ His Eminence. ■ His or Her Excellency.

He ▶ **symbol** the chemical element helium.

he ▶ **pronoun** [third person singular] used to refer to a man, boy, or male animal previously mentioned or easily identified: *everyone liked my father—he was the perfect gentleman*. ■ used to refer to a person or animal of unspecified sex (in modern use, now chiefly replaced by 'he or she' or 'they'): see usage note below): *every child needs to know that he is loved*. ■ any person (in modern use, now chiefly replaced by 'anyone' or 'the person': see usage note below): *he who is silent consents*. ■ W. Indian him or his: *don't tell he nothing more*.
▶ **noun 1** [in sing.] a male; a man: *is that a he or a she?* ■ [in combination] male: *a he-goat*.
2 Brit. (in children's games) the player who has to catch the others; 'it'.
– ORIGIN Old English *he, hē*, of Germanic origin; related to Dutch *hij*.

> **USAGE 1** For a discussion of *I am older than* **he** versus *I am older than* **him**, see **USAGE** at **PERSONAL PRONOUN**.
> **2** Until relatively recently **he** was used to refer to a person of unspecified sex, as in *every child needs to know that he is loved*, but this is now generally regarded as old-fashioned or sexist. Since the 18th century **they** has been an alternative to **he** in this sense (*everyone needs to feel that* **they** *matter*), where it occurs after an indefinite pronoun such as **everyone** or **someone**. It is becoming more and more accepted both in speech and in writing, and is used as the norm in this dictionary. Another alternative is **he or she**, though this can become tiresomely long-winded when used frequently.

head ▶ **noun 1** the upper part of the human body, or the front or upper part of the body of an animal, typically separated from the rest of the body by a neck, and containing the brain, mouth, and sense organs. ■ the head regarded as the location of intellect, imagination, and memory: *whatever comes into my head*. ■ (**head for**) an aptitude for or tolerance of: *she had a good head for business | a head for heights*. ■ informal a headache, especially one resulting from intoxication. ■ the height or length of a head as a measure: *he was beaten by a head*. ■ (**heads**) the side of a coin bearing the image of a head (used when tossing a coin to determine a winner): *heads or tails?* ■ the antlers of a deer.
2 a thing resembling a head either in form or in relation to a whole, in particular: ■ the cutting, striking, or operational end of a tool, weapon, or mechanism. ■ the flattened or knobbed end of a nail, pin, screw, or match. ■ the ornamented top of a pillar or column. ■ a compact mass of leaves or flowers at the top of a stem, especially a capitulum: *huge heads of fluffy cream flowers*. ■ the edible leafy part at the top of the stem of such green vegetables as cabbage and lettuce.
3 the front, forward, or upper part or end of something, in particular: ■ the upper end of a table or bed: *he sat down at the head of the cot*. ■ the upper horizontal part of a window frame or door frame. ■ the flat end of a cask or drum. ■ the front of a queue or procession. ■ the top of a page. ■ short for **HEADLINE**. ■ the top of a flight of stairs or steps. ■ the foam on top of a glass of beer, or the cream on the top of milk. ■ the source of a river or stream. ■ the end of a lake or inlet at which a river enters. ■ [usu. in place names] a promontory: *Beachy Head*. ■ the top of a ship's mast. ■ the bows of a ship. ■ short for **CYLINDER HEAD**.
4 a person in charge of something; a director or leader: *the head of the Dutch Catholic Church*. ■ Brit. short for **HEADMASTER**, **HEADMISTRESS**, or **HEAD TEACHER**.
5 a person considered as a numerical unit: *they paid fifty pounds a head*. ■ [treated as pl.] a number of cattle or game as specified: *seventy head of dairy cattle*.
6 a component in an audio, video, or information system by which information is transferred from an electrical signal to the recording medium, or vice versa. ■ the part of a record player that holds the playing cartridge and stylus. ■ short for **PRINTHEAD**.
7 a body of water kept at a particular height in order to provide a supply at sufficient pressure: *an 8 m head of water in the shafts*. ■ the pressure exerted by such water or by a confined body of steam: *a good head of steam on the gauge*.
8 Nautical a toilet on a ship or boat.
9 Grammar the word that governs all the other words in a phrase in which it is used, having the same grammatical function as the whole phrase.
10 [mass noun] Geology a superficial deposit of rock fragments, formed at the edge of an ice sheet by repeated freezing and thawing and then moved downhill.
▶ **adjective** [attrib.] chief; principal: *the head waiter*.
▶ **verb** [with obj.] **1** be in the leading position on: *the St George's Day procession was headed by the mayor*. ■ be in charge of: *an organizational unit headed by a line manager | she* **headed up** *the Jubilee Year programme*.
2 give a title or caption to: *an article headed 'The Protection of Human Life'*. ■ (as adj. **headed**) having a printed heading, typically the name and address of a person or organization: *headed notepaper*.
3 [no obj., with adverbial of direction] (also **be headed**) move in a specified direction: *he was* **heading for** *the exit | we were headed in the wrong direction*. ■ (**head for**) appear to be moving inevitably towards (something, especially something undesirable): *the economy is heading for recession*. ■ [with obj. and adverbial of direction]

H

direct or steer in a specified direction: *she headed the car towards them.*
4 Soccer shoot or pass (the ball) with the head: *a corner kick that Moody headed into the net.*
5 lop off the upper part or branches of (a plant or tree).
6 [no obj.] (of a lettuce or cabbage) form a head.
– PHRASES **bang** (or **knock**) **people's heads together** reprimand people severely, especially in an attempt to stop them arguing. **be banging** (or **knocking**) **one's head against a brick wall** be doggedly attempting the impossible and suffering in the process. **be hanging over someone's head** (of something unpleasant) threaten to affect someone at any moment. **be heading for a fall** see FALL. **be on someone's** (**own**) **head** be someone's sole responsibility. **bite** (or **snap**) **someone's head off** reply sharply and brusquely to someone. **by the head** Nautical (of a boat or ship) deeper in the water forward than astern. **come to a head** reach a crisis: *the violence came to a head with the deaths of six youths.* **do someone's head in** Brit. informal make someone feel annoyed, confused, or frustrated. **enter** (or **come into**) **someone's head** [usu. with negative] occur to someone: *such an idea never entered my head.* **from head to toe** (or **foot**) all over one's body: *I was shaking from head to toe.* **get one's head down** Brit. informal **1** sleep. **2** concentrate on the task in hand. **get one's head round** (or **around**) [usu. with negative] Brit. informal understand or come to terms with: *I just can't get my head around this idea.* **get something into one's** (or **someone's**) **head** come (or cause someone) to realize or understand something: *when will you get it into your head that it's the project that counts not me?* **give someone their head** allow someone complete freedom of action. **give someone head** vulgar slang perform oral sex on someone. **go to someone's head** (of alcohol) make someone dizzy or slightly drunk. ■ (of success) make someone conceited. **hang one's head** (**in shame**) be deeply ashamed. **head first** with the head in front of the rest of the body: *she dived head first into the water | a head-first slide.* ■ without sufficient forethought. **head of hair** the hair on a person's head, regarded in terms of its appearance or quantity: *he had a fine head of hair.* **head and shoulders above** informal far superior to. **—— one's head off** talk, laugh, etc. unrestrainedly: *he was drunk as a newt and singing his head off.* **head over heels 1** turning over completely in forward motion, as in a somersault. **2** (also **head over heels in love**) madly in love: *I immediately fell head over heels for Don.* **a head start** an advantage granted or gained at the beginning of something: *our fine traditions give us a head start on the competition.* **heads I win, tails you lose** I win whatever happens. **heads will roll** people will be dismissed or forced to resign. **hold** (or **put**) **a gun to someone's head** force someone to do something by using threats. **hold up one's head** (or **hold one's head high**) be confident or unashamed: *under the circumstances I would find it impossible to hold my head up in the town.* **in one's head** by mental process without use of physical aids: *the piece he'd already written in his head.* **keep one's head** remain calm. **keep one's head above water** avoid succumbing to difficulties, typically debt. **keep one's head down** remain inconspicuous in difficult or dangerous times. **knock something on the head** dismiss an idea, project, or rumour once and for all. **lose one's head** lose self-control; panic. **make head or tail of** [usu. with negative] understand at all: *we couldn't make head nor tail of the answer.* **off** (or **out of**) **one's head** Brit. informal crazy: *my old man's going off his head, you know.* ■ extremely intoxicated by drink or drugs. **off the top of one's head** without careful thought or investigation. **over someone's head 1** beyond someone's ability to understand: *the discussion was over my head.* **2** without someone's knowledge or involvement, especially when they have a right to it: *the deal was struck over the heads of the regions concerned.* ■ with disregard for someone else's (stronger) claim: *his promotion over the heads of more senior colleagues.* **put their** (or **our** or **your**) **heads together** consult and work together: *they forced the major banks to put their heads together to sort it out.* **put something into someone's head** suggest something to someone: *who's been putting ideas into your head?* **standing on one's head** with no difficulty at all: *I could design this garden standing on my head.* **stand** (or **turn**) **something on its head** completely reverse the principles or interpretation of an idea or argument. **take it into one's head to do something** impetuously decide to do something. **turn someone's head** make someone conceited. **turn heads** attract a great deal of attention or interest: *she recently turned heads with a nude scene.*
– PHRASAL VERBS **head someone/thing off** intercept and turn aside: *he ran up the road to head off approaching cars.* ■ forestall: *they headed off a row by ordering further study of both plans.* **head up** Sailing steer towards the wind.
– DERIVATIVES **headed** adjective [in combination] *bald-headed men | woolly-headed thinking*, **headless** adjective.
– ORIGIN Old English *hēafod*, of Germanic origin; related to Dutch *hoofd* and German *Haupt*.

-head[1] ▶ suffix equivalent to -HOOD: *maidenhead.*
– ORIGIN Middle English *-hed*, *-hede*.

-head[2] ▶ combining form **1** denoting the front, forward, or upper part or end of a specified thing: *spearhead | masthead.*
2 forming informal nouns expressing disparagement of a person: *airhead | dumbhead.*
3 forming informal nouns denoting an addict or habitual user of a specified drug: *crackhead.* ■ forming informal nouns denoting an enthusiast of a particular thing: *he's a total soccer-head.*

headache ▶ noun a continuous pain in the head. ■ informal a thing or person that causes worry or difficulty; a problem: *an administrative headache.*
– DERIVATIVES **headachy** adjective.

headage ▶ noun [mass noun] [often as modifier] the number of animals held as stock on a farm.

headband ▶ noun **1** a band of fabric worn around the head as a decoration or to keep the hair or perspiration off the face.
2 an ornamental strip of coloured silk fastened to the top of the spine of a book.

headbanger ▶ noun informal **1** a fan or performer of heavy metal music.
2 a mad or eccentric person.

headbanging ▶ noun [mass noun] **1** violent rhythmic shaking of the head by fans of heavy metal music.
2 violent rocking of the body and shaking or knocking of the head, by children or mentally disordered adults.

headboard ▶ noun **1** an upright panel forming or placed behind the head of a bed.
2 a board on the front of a train bearing the name of the route or service for which it is being used.
3 Sailing a reinforcement at the top of a triangular sail such as a mainsail.

headbutt Brit. ▶ noun an aggressive and forceful thrust with the top of the head into the face or body of another person.
▶ verb [with obj.] attack (someone) with a headbutt.

headcase ▶ noun Brit. informal a mentally ill or unstable person.

headcheese ▶ noun North American term for BRAWN (sense 2).

headcount ▶ noun an instance of counting the number of people present. ■ a total number of people, especially the number of people employed in a particular organization.

headdress ▶ noun an ornamental covering or band for the head, especially one worn on ceremonial occasions.

headend ▶ noun a control centre in a cable television system where various signals are brought together and monitored before being introduced into the cable network.

header ▶ noun **1** Soccer a shot or pass made with the head.
2 informal a headlong fall or dive.
3 a brick or stone laid at right angles to the face of a wall. Compare with STRETCHER (sense 4 of the noun).
4 (also **header tank**) a raised tank of water maintaining pressure in a plumbing system.
5 a line or block of text appearing at the top of each page of a book or document. Compare with FOOTER[1] (sense 3).
6 Irish informal a mad or foolish person.

head gasket ▶ noun the gasket which fits between the cylinder head and the cylinders or cylinder block in an internal-combustion engine.

headgear ▶ noun [mass noun] hats, helmets, and other items worn on the head: *protective headgear.*

headhunt ▶ verb [with obj.] **1** (as noun **headhunting**) the practice among some peoples of collecting the heads of dead enemies as trophies.
2 identify and approach (a suitable person employed elsewhere) to fill a business position.
– DERIVATIVES **headhunter** noun.

heading ▶ noun **1** a title at the head of a page or section of a book: *chapter headings.* ■ a division of a subject; a class or category: *this topic falls under four main headings.*
2 a direction or bearing: *he crawled on a heading of 90 degrees until he came to the track.*
3 a horizontal passage made in preparation for building a tunnel. ■ Mining another term for DRIFT (sense 4 of the noun).
4 a strip of cloth at the top of a curtain above the hooks or wire by which it is suspended.

headland ▶ noun **1** a narrow piece of land that projects from a coastline into the sea.
2 a strip of land left unploughed at the end of a field.

headlight (also **headlamp**) ▶ noun a powerful light at the front of a motor vehicle or railway engine.
– PHRASES **like a deer** (or **rabbit**) **in the headlights** used to refer to a state of fear, panic, or confusion so extreme that it is impossible to act or think normally: *faced with too many choices and not enough real information, we are like deer caught in the headlights | his deer-in-the-headlights expression.*

headline ▶ noun a heading at the top of an article or page in a newspaper or magazine: *a front-page headline.* ■ (**the headlines**) the most important items of news in a newspaper or a broadcast news bulletin: *issues that are never long out of the headlines | the war at sea began to hit the headlines.*
▶ verb **1** [with obj. and complement] provide with a headline: *a feature that was headlined 'Invest in your Future'.*
2 [with obj.] appear as the star performer at (a concert): *Nirvana headlined the 1992 Reading Festival* | [no obj.] *they are headlining at the Town & Country club.*

head line ▶ noun (in palmistry) the lower of the two horizontal lines that cross the palm of the hand, linked to the nature and strength of a person's mental faculties.

headliner ▶ noun a performer or act that is promoted as the star attraction on a bill and typically perfoms last.

headlock ▶ noun a method of restraining someone by holding an arm firmly around their head, especially as a hold in wrestling.

headlong ▶ adverb & adjective **1** [as adv.] with the head foremost: *he fell headlong into the tent.*
2 in a rush; with reckless haste: [as attrib. adj.] *a headlong dash through the house* | [as adv.] *those who rush headlong to join in the latest craze.*
– ORIGIN Middle English *headling* (from HEAD + the adverbial suffix *-ling*), altered in late Middle English by association with -LONG.

head louse ▶ noun a louse which infests the hair of the human head and is especially common among schoolchildren. ● *Pediculus humanus capitis*, family Pediculidae, order Anoplura. See also BODY LOUSE.

headman ▶ noun (pl. **headmen**) the chief or leader of a community or tribe.

headmaster ▶ noun chiefly Brit. a man who is the head teacher in a school.
– DERIVATIVES **headmasterly** adjective.

headmistress ▶ noun chiefly Brit. a woman who is the head teacher in a school.
– DERIVATIVES **headmistressy** adjective.

headmost ▶ adjective archaic (chiefly of a ship) holding a position in advance of others; foremost.

headnote ▶ noun a note inserted at the head of an article or document, summarizing or commenting on the content. ■ Law a summary of a decided case prefixed to the case report, setting out the principles behind the decision and an outline of the facts.

head of state ▶ noun the chief public representative of a country, such as a president or monarch, who may also be the head of government.

head-on ▶ adjective & adverb **1** with or involving the front of a vehicle: [as attrib. adj.] *a head-on collision* | [as adv.] *they hit a bus head-on.*
2 with or involving direct confrontation: [as adv.] *she's a serious writer who frequently tackles social issues head-on.*

headphone ▶ noun (usu. **headphones**) a device consisting of a pair of earphones joined by a band placed over the head, for listening to audio signals such as music or speech.

headpiece ▶ noun **1** a device worn on the head as an ornament or to serve a function.
2 an illustration or ornamental motif printed at the head of a chapter in a book.
3 the part of a halter or bridle that fits over the top of a horse's head behind the ears.

headquarter ▶ verb [with obj. and adverbial of place] have headquarters at a specified location: *Unesco is headquartered in Paris.*

headquarters ▶ noun [treated as sing. or pl.] the premises occupied by a military commander and the commander's staff. ■ the premises serving as the managerial and administrative centre of an organization.

headrail ▶ noun a horizontal rail at the top of something.

headrest ▶ noun a padded part extending from or fixed to the back of a seat or chair, designed to support the head.

headroom ▶ noun [mass noun] the space above a driver's or passenger's head in a vehicle. ■ the space between the top of a vehicle and the underside of a bridge or other structure above it.

headsail /ˈhɛdseɪl, -s(ə)l/ ▶ noun a sail on a ship's foremast or bowsprit.

headscarf ▶ noun (pl. **headscarves**) a square of fabric worn by women as a covering for the head, often folded into a triangle and knotted under the chin.

head sea ▶ noun a mass of waves coming from directly in front of a ship: *we tried out the boat in a steep head sea.*

headset ▶ noun **1** a set of headphones, typically with a microphone attached, used especially in telephony and radio communication.
2 the bearing assembly which links the front fork of a bicycle to its frame.

headship ▶ noun the position of leader or chief. ■ chiefly Brit. the position of head teacher in a school.

headshot ▶ noun a bullet or gunshot aimed at the head.

headshrinker ▶ noun **1** historical a headhunter who preserved and shrank the heads of his dead enemies.
2 informal, chiefly N. Amer. a psychiatrist. Compare with SHRINK.

headsman ▶ noun (pl. **headsmen**) historical **1** a man who was responsible for beheading condemned prisoners.
2 a person in command of a whaling boat.

headspace ▶ noun [mass noun] **1** the air or empty space left above the contents in a sealed container.
2 informal the notional space occupied by a person's mind: *to play, you enter the headspace of a female bounty hunter.*

headspring ▶ noun **1** a spring that is the main source of a stream.
2 a somersault similar to a handspring, except that the performer lands on the head as well as the hands.

headsquare ▶ noun another term for HEADSCARF.

headstall /ˈhɛdstɔːl/ ▶ noun chiefly N. Amer. **1** a head collar or halter.
2 another term for HEADPIECE (sense 3).

headstand ▶ noun an act of balancing on one's head and hands with one's feet in the air.

headstander ▶ noun a small deep-bodied freshwater fish of the Amazon region, popular in aquaria. It swims and feeds at an oblique angle with the head down. ● Genus *Abramites*, family Anostomidae: two species.

headstay ▶ noun another term for FORESTAY.

headstock ▶ noun **1** a set of bearings in a machine, supporting a revolving part.
2 the widened piece at the end of the neck of a guitar, to which the tuning pegs are fixed.
3 the horizontal end member of the underframe of a railway vehicle.

headstone ▶ noun a slab of stone set up at the head of a grave, typically inscribed with the name of the dead person.

headstream ▶ noun a headwater stream.

headstrong ▶ adjective energetically wilful and determined: *the headstrong impulsiveness of youth.*

heads-up N. Amer. informal ▶ noun an advance warning of something: *the heads-up came just in time to stop the tanks from launching the final assault.*
▶ adjective [attrib.] showing alertness or perceptiveness: *they played a very heads-up game.*

head teacher ▶ noun chiefly Brit. the teacher in charge of a school.

headtie ▶ noun W. Indian a strip of colourful fabric worn tied around the head by women.

head-to-head ▶ adjective & adverb involving two parties confronting each other: [as adj.] *a head-to-head battle with bureaucracy.*
▶ noun a conversation, confrontation, or contest between two parties.

head-turning ▶ adjective extremely noticeable or attractive: *her skimpy, head-turning costumes.*
– DERIVATIVES **head-turner** noun.

head-up display (N. Amer. also **heads-up display**) ▶ noun a display of instrument readings in an aircraft or vehicle that can be seen without lowering the eyes, typically through being projected on to the windscreen or visor.

head voice ▶ noun [in sing.] one of the high registers of the voice in speaking or singing, above chest voice.

headward ▶ adjective in the region or direction of the head. ■ Geology denoting erosion by a stream or river occurring progressively upstream from the original source.
▶ adverb (also **headwards**) towards the head.

headwater ▶ noun (usu. **headwaters**) a tributary stream of a river close to or forming part of its source.

headway ▶ noun **1** [mass noun] (usu. in phrase **make headway**) forward movement or progress, especially when this is slow or difficult: *the ship was making very little headway against heavy seas | they appear to be* ***making headway in*** *bringing the rebels under control.*
2 the average interval between trains or buses on a regular service: *a six-minute headway.*

headwear ▶ noun [mass noun] hats and other items worn on the head.

headwind ▶ noun a wind blowing from directly in front, opposing forward motion.

headword ▶ noun a word which begins a separate entry in a reference work.

headwork ▶ noun **1** [mass noun] activities taxing the mind; mental work.
2 (**headworks**) apparatus for controlling the flow of water in a river or canal.

headwrap ▶ noun a strip of decorative material worn around the head by women.

heady ▶ adjective (**headier**, **headiest**) (of alcoholic drink) potent; intoxicating: *several bottles of heady local wine.* ■ having a strong or exhilarating effect: *a heady, exotic perfume | the heady days of my youth.*
– DERIVATIVES **headily** adverb, **headiness** noun.

heal ▶ verb [with obj.] cause (a wound, injury, or person) to become sound or healthy again: *his concern is to heal sick people.* ■ [no obj.] become sound or healthy again: *the bullet wounds had healed.* ■ alleviate (a person's distress or anguish). ■ correct or put right (an undesirable situation): *the rift between them was never really healed.*
– DERIVATIVES **healable** adjective, **healer** noun.
– ORIGIN Old English *hǣlan* (in the sense 'restore to sound health'), of Germanic origin; related to Dutch *heelen* and German *heilen*, also to WHOLE.

heal-all ▶ noun a universal remedy; a panacea. ■ informal any of a number of medicinal plants, especially roseroot and self-heal.

heald /hiːld/ ▶ noun another term for HEDDLE.
– ORIGIN Old English *hefel*, *hefeld* 'the warp and weft', of Germanic origin, from a base meaning 'raise'. The current sense dates from the mid 18th cent.

healing ▶ noun [mass noun] the process of making or becoming sound or healthy again: *the gift of healing.*
▶ adjective tending to heal; therapeutic: *a healing experience | the healing process.*

health ▶ noun [mass noun] the state of being free from illness or injury: *he was restored to health* | [as modifier] *a health risk.* ■ a person's mental or physical condition: *bad health forced him to retire* | figurative *a standard for measuring the financial health of a company.* ■ (**your health** or **your good health**) used to express friendly feelings towards one's companions before drinking.
– ORIGIN Old English *hǣlth*, of Germanic origin; related to WHOLE.

health and safety ▶ noun [mass noun] Brit. regulations and procedures intended to prevent accident or injury in workplaces or public environments.

health care ▶ noun [mass noun] [often as modifier] the organized provision of medical care to individuals or a community: *health-care professionals.*

health centre ▶ noun a building or establishment housing local medical services or the practice of a group of doctors.

health certificate ▶ noun a certificate attesting a person's good health, sometimes required when travelling between states or countries.

health club ▶ noun a private club with exercise facilities, also offering health and beauty treatments.

health farm ▶ noun chiefly Brit. a residential establishment where people seek improved health by a regimen of dieting, exercise, and treatment.

health food ▶ noun [mass noun] natural food that is thought to have health-giving qualities.

healthful ▶ adjective having or conducive to good health: *healthful methods of cooking vegetables.*
– DERIVATIVES **healthfully** adverb, **healthfulness** noun.

health maintenance organization ▶ noun (in the US) an organization which provides health care on the free market in return for a predetermined fixed insurance premium.

health physics ▶ plural noun [treated as sing.] the branch of radiology that deals with the health of people working with radioactive materials.

health service ▶ noun a public service providing medical care. ■ (**the health service**) Brit. short for NATIONAL HEALTH SERVICE.

health tourism ▶ noun [mass noun] the practice of travelling abroad in order to receive medical treatment.

health visitor ▶ noun Brit. a trained nurse who visits people in their homes to assist or advise the chronically ill or parents with very young children.

healthy ▶ adjective (**healthier**, **healthiest**) in a good physical or mental condition; in good health: *I feel fit and healthy* | figurative *the family is the basis of any healthy society.* ■ (of a part of the body) not diseased: *healthy cells.* ■ indicating or promoting good health: *a healthy appetite | a healthy balanced diet.* ■ normal, natural, and desirable: *a healthy contempt for authority | healthy competition.* ■ of a very satisfactory size or amount: *making a healthy profit.*
– DERIVATIVES **healthily** adverb, **healthiness** noun.

Heaney /ˈhiːni/, Seamus (Justin) (b.1939), Irish poet. Born in Northern Ireland, in 1972 he took Irish citizenship. Notable works: *North* (1975) and *The Haw Lantern* (1987). Nobel Prize for Literature (1995).

heap ▶ noun **1** an untidy collection of objects placed haphazardly on top of each other: ***a disordered heap of boxes*** *| her clothes lay in a heap on the floor.* ■ an amount of a particular loose substance: ***a heap of gravel.***
2 (**a heap of**/**heaps of**) informal a large amount or number of: *we have heaps of room.*
3 informal an untidy or dilapidated place or vehicle: *they climbed back in the heap and headed home.*
▶ adverb (**heaps**) Brit. informal a great deal: *'How do you like Maggie?' 'I like you heaps better!'*
▶ verb [with obj.] put (objects or a loose substance) in a heap: *she heaped logs on the fire |* ***heaped up*** *in one corner was a pile of junk.* ■ (**heap something with**) load something copiously with: *he heaped his plate with rice.* ■ (**heap something on/upon**) bestow praise, abuse, or criticism liberally on: *they once heaped praise on her.* ■ (as adj. **heaped**) chiefly Brit. (of a spoon or other container) with the contents piled above the brim or edge. ■ [no obj.] form a heap: *clouds heaped higher in the west.*
– PHRASES **at the top** (or **bottom**) **of the heap** (of a person) at the highest (or lowest) point of a society or organization. **be struck all of a heap** informal be extremely disconcerted. **heap coals of fire on someone's head** Brit. go out of one's way to cause someone remorse. [with biblical allusion to Rom. 12:20.] **in a heap** with the body completely limp: *he landed in a heap at the bottom of the stairs.*
– ORIGIN Old English *hēap* (noun), *hēapian* (verb), of Germanic origin; related to Dutch *hoop* and German *Haufen*.

hear ▶ verb (past and past participle **heard**) **1** [with obj.] perceive with the ear the sound made by (someone or something): *behind her she could hear men's voices* | [with obj. and infinitive] *she had never been heard to complain* | [no obj.] *he did not hear very well.* ■ listen or pay attention to: [with clause] *she just doesn't hear what I'm telling her.* ■ (**hear someone out**) listen to all that someone has to say: *Joseph gravely heard them out but never offered advice.* ■ Law listen to and judge (a case or plaintiff): *an all-woman jury heard the case.* ■ listen to and grant (a prayer): *our Heavenly Father has heard our prayers.*
2 be told or informed of: *have you heard the news?* | [with clause] *they heard that I had moved* | [no obj.] *I was*

H

*shocked to **hear of** her death.* ■ [no obj.] (**have heard of**) be aware of; know of the existence of: *nobody had ever heard of my college.* ■ [no obj.] (**hear from**) be contacted by (someone), especially by letter or telephone: *if you would like to join the committee, we would love to hear from you.*
3 [no obj.] (**will/would not hear of**) will or would not allow or agree to: *I won't hear of such idiocy.*
– PHRASES **be hearing things** see THING. **be unable to hear oneself think** informal used to complain about very loud noise or music: *I hate bars where you can't hear yourself think.* **hear! hear!** used to express one's wholehearted agreement with something said, especially in a speech. **hear say** (or **tell**) **of** (or **that**) be informed of or that: *I heard tell that he went out west.*
– DERIVATIVES **hearable** adjective, **hearer** noun.
– ORIGIN Old English *hīeran*, *hēran*, of Germanic origin; related to Dutch *hooren* and German *hören*.

Heard and McDonald Islands a group of uninhabited islands in the southern Indian Ocean, administered by Australia since 1947 as an external territory.

hearing ▸ noun **1** [mass noun] the faculty of perceiving sounds: *people who have very acute hearing.* ■ the range within which sounds may be heard; earshot: *she had moved out of hearing.*
2 an opportunity to state one's case: *I think I had a fair hearing.* ■ Law an act of listening to evidence in a court of law or before an official, especially a trial before a judge without a jury.

hearing aid ▸ noun a small amplifying device which fits on the ear, worn by a partially deaf person.

hearing dog ▸ noun a dog trained to alert people who are deaf or hard of hearing to such sounds as the ringing of an alarm, doorbell, or telephone.

hearing-impaired ▸ adjective partially or completely deaf.

hearken /ˈhɑːk(ə)n/ (also **harken**) ▸ verb [no obj.] **1** archaic listen: *he refused to **hearken to** Tom's words of wisdom.*
2 (**hearken back to**) another way of saying HARK BACK TO (see HARK).
– ORIGIN Old English *heorcnian*; probably related to HARK. The spelling with *ea* (dating from the 16th cent.) is due to association with HEAR.

hearsay ▸ noun [mass noun] information received from other people which cannot be substantiated; rumour: *according to hearsay, Bez had managed to break his arm.* ■ Law the report of another person's words by a witness, which is usually disallowed as evidence in a court of law: [as modifier] *hearsay evidence.*

hearse /həːs/ ▸ noun a vehicle for conveying the coffin at a funeral.
– ORIGIN Middle English: from Anglo-Norman French *herce* 'harrow, frame', from Latin *hirpex* 'a kind of large rake', from Oscan *hirpus* 'wolf' (with reference to the teeth). The earliest recorded sense in English is 'latticework canopy placed over the coffin (whilst in church) of a distinguished person', but this probably arose from the late Middle English sense 'triangular frame (shaped like the ancient harrow) for carrying candles at certain services'. The current sense dates from the mid 17th cent.

Hearst /həːst/, William Randolph (1863–1951), American newspaper publisher and tycoon. His introduction of features such as large headlines and sensational crime reporting revolutionized American journalism. He was the model for the central character of Orson Welles's film *Citizen Kane* (1941).

heart ▸ noun **1** a hollow muscular organ that pumps the blood through the circulatory system by rhythmic contraction and dilation. In vertebrates there may be up to four chambers (as in humans), with two atria and two ventricles. ■ the region of the chest above the heart: *holding hand on heart for the Pledge of Allegiance.* ■ the heart regarded as the centre of a person's thoughts and emotions, especially love or compassion: *hardening his heart, he ignored her entreaties | he poured out his heart to me |* [mass noun] *he has no heart.* ■ [mass noun] one's mood or feeling: *they had a change of heart | they found him well and in good heart.* ■ [mass noun] courage or enthusiasm: *they may **lose heart** as the work mounts up | Mary **took heart** from the encouragement handed out.*
2 the central or innermost part of something: *right in the heart of the city.* ■ the vital part or essence: *the heart of the matter.* ■ the close compact head of a cabbage or lettuce.
3 a conventional representation of a heart with two equal curves meeting at a point at the bottom and a cusp at the top. ■ (**hearts**) one of the four suits in a conventional pack of playing cards, denoted by a red heart-shaped figure. ■ a card of the suit of hearts. ■ (**hearts**) a card game similar to whist, in which players attempt to avoid taking tricks containing a card of the suit of hearts.
4 [usu. with modifier] the condition of agricultural land as regards fertility.
▸ verb [with obj.] informal like very much; love: *I totally heart this song.* [from use of the symbol ♥, first popularized by the 'I ♥ NY' advertising campaign of the late 1970s.]
– PHRASES **after one's own heart** sharing one's tastes or views. **at heart** in one's real nature, in contrast to how one may appear: *he's a good lad at heart.* **break someone's heart** overwhelm someone with sadness. **by heart** from memory. **close** (or **dear**) **to** (or **near**) **one's heart** of deep interest and concern to one. **from the** (**bottom of one's**) **heart** with sincere feeling: *their warmth and hospitality is right from the heart.* **give** (or **lose**) **one's heart to** fall in love with. **have a heart** [often in imperative] be merciful; show pity. **have a heart of gold** have a generous nature. **have the heart to do something** [usu. with negative] be insensitive or hard-hearted enough to do something: *I don't have the heart to tell her.* **have** (or **put**) **one's heart in** be (or become) keenly involved in or committed to (an enterprise): *he does not seem to have his heart in the role.* **have one's heart in one's mouth** be greatly alarmed or apprehensive. **have one's heart in the right place** be sincere or well intentioned. **heart of stone** a stern or cruel nature. **hearts and flowers** used in allusion to extreme sentimentality. **hearts and minds** used in reference to emotional and intellectual support or commitment: *a campaign to win the hearts and minds of America's college students.* **one's heart's desire** a person or thing that one greatly wishes for. **one's heart sinks** used to express a feeling of sudden sadness or dismay: *her heart sank as she thought of Craig.* **one's heartstrings** used in reference to one's deepest feelings of love or compassion: *the kitten's pitiful little squeak **tugged at her heartstrings**.* **in one's heart of hearts** in one's inmost feelings. **take something to heart** take criticism seriously and be affected or upset by it. **to one's heart's content** (or **delight**) to the full extent of one's desires: *the children could run and play to their heart's content | in an older vehicle, you can ride around to your heart's delight.* **wear one's heart on one's sleeve** make one's feelings apparent. **with all one's heart** (or **one's whole heart**) sincerely; completely. **heart to heart** candidly, intimately.
– DERIVATIVES **hearted** adjective [in combination] *a generous-hearted woman.*
– ORIGIN Old English *heorte*, of Germanic origin; related to Dutch *hart* and German *Herz*, from an Indo-European root shared by Latin *cor, cord-* and Greek *kēr, kardia*.

heartache ▸ noun [mass noun] emotional anguish or grief, typically caused by the loss or absence of someone loved.

heart attack ▸ noun a sudden occurrence of coronary thrombosis, typically resulting in the death of part of a heart muscle and sometimes fatal.

heartbeat ▸ noun the pulsation of the heart. ■ a single pulsation of the heart: *her heartbeats steadied.* ■ an animating or vital unifying force: *Ontario has long been the commercial heartbeat of Canada.*
– PHRASES **a heartbeat** (**away**) **from** very close to; on the verge of: *laughter was only a heartbeat from tears.* **in a heartbeat** instantly; immediately: *I'd do it again in a heartbeat.*

heartbreak ▸ noun [mass noun] overwhelming distress: *an unforgettable tale of joy and heartbreak.*

heartbreaker ▸ noun **1** a person who is very attractive but who is irresponsible in emotional relationships.
2 a story or event which causes overwhelming distress.

heartbreaking ▸ adjective causing overwhelming distress; very upsetting.
– DERIVATIVES **heartbreakingly** adverb [as submodifier] *the children's expectations were heartbreakingly wrong.*

heartbroken ▸ adjective suffering from overwhelming distress: *he was **heartbroken at** the thought of leaving the house.*

heartburn ▸ noun [mass noun] a form of indigestion felt as a burning sensation in the chest, caused by acid regurgitation into the oesophagus.

hearten ▸ verb [with obj.] make more cheerful or confident: [with obj. and infinitive] *she was heartened to observe that the effect was faintly comic |* (as adj. **heartening**) *this is the most heartening news of all.*
– DERIVATIVES **hearteningly** adverb.

heart failure ▸ noun [mass noun] severe failure of the heart to function properly, especially as a cause of death: *her mother had died of heart failure.*

heartfelt ▸ adjective (of a feeling or its expression) deeply and strongly felt; sincere: *our heartfelt thanks.*

hearth /hɑːθ/ ▸ noun **1** the floor of a fireplace: *a cheerful fire burning in the hearth.* ■ the area in front of a fireplace: *they were sitting around the hearth.* ■ used as a symbol of one's home: *he left **hearth and home** to train in Denmark.*
2 the base or lower part of a furnace, where molten metal collects.
– ORIGIN Old English *heorth*, of West Germanic origin; related to Dutch *haard* and German *Herd*.

hearthrug ▸ noun a rug laid in front of a fireplace to protect the carpet or floor.

hearthside ▸ noun the area round a hearth or fireplace; a fireside.

hearthstone ▸ noun a flat stone forming a hearth or part of a hearth.

heartily ▸ adverb **1** in a hearty manner: *she laughed heartily | they dined heartily.*
2 [as submodifier] to a great degree; very (especially with reference to personal feelings): *they were heartily sick of the whole subject.*

heartland ▸ noun (also **heartlands**) the central or most important part of a country, area, or field of activity. ■ the centre of support for a belief or movement: *the heartland of the rebel cause.*

heartless ▸ adjective displaying a complete lack of feeling or consideration: *heartless thieves stole the pushchair of a two-year-old boy.*
– DERIVATIVES **heartlessly** adverb, **heartlessness** noun.

heart line ▸ noun (in palmistry) the upper of the two horizontal lines that cross the palm of the hand, linked to a person's physical health and ability to form emotional relationships.

heart-lung machine ▸ noun a machine that temporarily takes over the functions of the heart and lungs, especially during heart surgery.

Heart of Dixie informal name for ALABAMA.

heart of palm ▸ noun the edible bud of a palm tree.

heart-rending ▸ adjective causing great sadness or distress: *a heart-rending story.*
– DERIVATIVES **heart-rendingly** adverb.

heart's-blood ▸ noun [mass noun] archaic the blood, as being necessary for life.

heart-searching ▸ noun [mass noun] thorough, typically painful examination of one's feelings and motives: *I began to write, but not without much heart-searching.*

heartsease /ˈhɑːtsiːz/ (also **heart's-ease**) ▸ noun a wild European pansy which typically has purple and yellow flowers. It has given rise to hybrids from which most garden pansies were developed. ● *Viola tricolor*, family Violaceae.
– ORIGIN late Middle English: origin uncertain, the term being applied by herbalists to both the pansy and the wallflower in the 16th cent.

heartsick (also **heartsore**) ▸ adjective literary very despondent, typically from grief or loss of love.
– DERIVATIVES **heartsickness** noun.

heart-stopping ▸ adjective full of suspense or excitement; thrilling: *a five-minute burst of heart-stopping action.*
– DERIVATIVES **heart-stopper** noun, **heart-stoppingly** adverb.

heart-throb ▸ noun informal a man, typically a celebrity, whose good looks excite romantic feelings in women.

heart-to-heart ▸ adjective (of a conversation) candid, intimate, and personal: *a heart-to-heart chat.*
▸ noun a candid and intimate conversation.

heart urchin ▸ noun a heart-shaped burrowing sea urchin which has a thick covering of fine spines on the shell, giving it a furry appearance. ● Class Echinoidea, order Spatangoida.

heart-warming ▶ adjective emotionally rewarding or uplifting: *heart-warming stories about life as a country vet.*

heartwood ▶ noun [mass noun] the dense inner part of a tree trunk, yielding the hardest timber.

heartworm ▶ noun a parasitic nematode worm which infests the hearts of dogs and other animals. ● *Dirofilaria immitis*, class Phasmida.

hearty ▶ adjective (**heartier**, **heartiest**) **1** loudly vigorous and cheerful: *a hearty and boisterous character | he sang in a hearty baritone.* ■ (of a feeling or an opinion) deeply or strongly felt: *he expressed his hearty agreement | hearty congratulations.* ■ (of a person) strong and healthy: *a formidably hearty spinster of fifty-five.*
2 (of food) wholesome and substantial. ■ (of a person's appetite) robust and healthy: *Jim goes for a long walk to work up a hearty appetite for dinner.*
▶ noun (pl. **hearties**) Brit. informal **1** a vigorously cheerful and sporty person.
2 (usu. **me hearties**) a form of address ascribed to sailors.
– DERIVATIVES **heartiness** noun.

heat ▶ noun [mass noun] **1** the quality of being hot; high temperature: *the fierce heat of the sun.* ■ Physics heat seen as a form of energy arising from the random motion of the molecules of bodies, which may be transferred by conduction, convection, or radiation. ■ hot weather conditions: *the oppressive heat was making both men sweat.* ■ a source or level of heat for cooking: *remove from the heat and beat in the butter.* ■ a spicy quality in food that produces a burning sensation in the mouth: *chilli peppers add taste and heat to food.* ■ technical the amount of heat that is needed to cause a specific process or is evolved in such a process: *the heat of formation.* ■ [count noun] technical a single operation of heating something, especially metal in a furnace.
2 intensity of feeling, especially of anger or excitement: *conciliation services are designed to* ***take the heat out of*** *disputes.* ■ (**the heat**) informal intensive and unwelcome pressure or criticism, especially from the authorities: *a flurry of legal proceedings* ***turned up the heat*** *in the dispute | the heat is on.*
3 [count noun] a preliminary round in a race or contest: *winners of the regional heats.*
▶ verb make or become hot or warm: [with obj.] *the room faces north and is difficult to heat* | [no obj.] *the pipes expand as they* ***heat up.*** ■ [no obj.] (**heat up**) (of a person) become excited or impassioned. ■ [no obj.] (**heat up**) become more intense and exciting: *the action really begins to heat up.* ■ [with obj.] archaic inflame; excite: *this discourse had heated them.*
– PHRASES **if you can't stand the heat, get out of the kitchen** proverb if you can't deal with the pressures and difficulties of a situation, you should leave others to deal with it rather than complaining. **in the heat of the moment** while temporarily angry, excited, or engrossed, and without stopping for thought. **on** (or N. Amer. **in**) **heat** (of a female mammal) in the receptive period of the sexual cycle; in oestrus.
– ORIGIN Old English *hǣtu* (noun), *hǣtan* (verb), of Germanic origin; related to Dutch *hitte* (noun) and German *heizen* (verb), also to **HOT**.

heat barrier ▶ noun the limitation of the speed of an aircraft or other flying object by heat resulting from air friction.

heat capacity ▶ noun another term for **THERMAL CAPACITY**.

heat death ▶ noun Physics a state of uniform distribution of energy, especially viewed as a possible fate of the universe. It is a corollary of the second law of thermodynamics.

heated ▶ adjective **1** made warm or hot: *a heated swimming pool.*
2 inflamed with passion or conviction: *she had a heated argument with an official.*
– DERIVATIVES **heatedly** adverb.

heat engine ▶ noun a device for producing motive power from heat.

heater ▶ noun **1** a device for warming the air or water: *a wall-mounted electric heater | a gas water heater.* ■ Electronics a conductor used for indirect heating of the cathode of a thermionic valve.
2 Baseball a fastball.
3 N. Amer. informal, dated a gun.

heat exchanger ▶ noun a device for transferring heat from one medium to another.

Heath, Sir Edward (Richard George) (1916–2005), British Conservative statesman, Prime Minister 1970–4. He negotiated Britain's entry into the European Economic Community and faced problems caused by a marked increase in oil prices. Attempts to restrain wage rises led to widespread strikes and he lost a general election after a second national coal strike.

heath ▶ noun **1** chiefly Brit. an area of open uncultivated land, typically on acid sandy soil, with characteristic vegetation of heather, gorse, and coarse grasses. ■ [mass noun] Ecology vegetation dominated by dwarf shrubs of the heather family: [as modifier] *heath vegetation.*
2 a dwarf shrub with small leathery leaves and small pink or purple bell-shaped flowers, characteristic of heaths and moorland. ● *Erica* and related genera, family Ericaceae: many species.
3 a small light brown and orange European butterfly which typically has eyespots on the wings, the caterpillar feeding on grasses. ● Genus *Coenonympha*, subfamily Satyrinae, family Nymphalidae: several species, including the common **small heath** (*C. pamphilus*).
4 a yellowish-brown chiefly day-flying European moth of heathland and grassland. ● Several species in the family Geometridae.
– DERIVATIVES **heathy** adjective.
– ORIGIN Old English *hǣth*, of Germanic origin; related to Dutch *heide* and German *Heide*.

heat haze ▶ noun an obscuration of the atmosphere in hot weather, especially a shimmering in the air near the ground that distorts distant views.

heathen /ˈhiːð(ə)n/ ▶ noun chiefly derogatory a person who does not belong to a widely held religion (especially one who is not a Christian, Jew, or Muslim) as regarded by those who do. ■ a follower of a polytheistic religion; a pagan. ■ informal a person regarded as lacking culture or moral principles.
▶ adjective relating to heathens: *heathen practices.*
– DERIVATIVES **heathendom** noun, **heathenish** adjective, **heathenism** noun.
– ORIGIN Old English *hǣthen*, of Germanic origin; related to Dutch *heiden* and German *Heide*; generally regarded as a specifically Christian use of a Germanic adjective meaning 'inhabiting open country', from the base of **HEATH**.

heather ▶ noun [mass noun] a purple-flowered Eurasian heath that grows abundantly on moorland and heathland. Many ornamental varieties have been developed. Also called **LING**[1]. ● *Calluna vulgaris*, family Ericaceae (the **heather family**). This family includes the rhododendrons and azaleas as well as the bilberries and many other berry-bearing dwarf shrubs.
■ informal any similar plant of the heather family; a heath.
– DERIVATIVES **heathery** adjective.
– ORIGIN Old English *hadre*, *hedre* (recorded in place names), of unknown origin. The word was chiefly Scots until the 16th cent.; the change in the first syllable in the 18th cent. was due to association with **HEATH**.

heathland ▶ noun [mass noun] (also **heathlands**) an extensive area of heath: *1,000 acres of heathland.*

Heath Robinson ▶ adjective Brit. ingeniously or ridiculously over-complicated in design or construction: *a vast Heath Robinson mechanism.*
– ORIGIN early 20th cent.: named after W. Heath Robinson (see **ROBINSON**[2]).

Heathrow an international airport situated 25 km (15 miles) west of the centre of London.

heating ▶ noun [mass noun] equipment or devices used to provide heat, especially to a building: *we had no heating in our bedrooms.*

heat lamp ▶ noun an electrical device with a bulb that emits mainly heat rather than light, used as a heat source.

heatproof ▶ adjective able to resist great heat.

heat pump ▶ noun a device that transfers heat from a colder area to a hotter area by using mechanical energy, as in a refrigerator.

heat-resistant ▶ adjective able to resist great heat; heatproof. ■ not easily becoming hot.

heat-seeking ▶ adjective (of a missile) able to detect and home in on infrared radiation emitted by a target, such as the exhaust vent of a jet aircraft.

heat shield ▶ noun a device or coating for protection from excessive heat. ■ an outer covering on a spacecraft, especially on the nose cone and leading edges, to protect it from the heat generated during re-entry into the earth's atmosphere.

heat-shock protein ▶ noun Genetics a protein induced in a living cell in response to a rise in temperature above the normal level.

heat sink ▶ noun a device or substance for absorbing excessive or unwanted heat.

heatstroke ▶ noun [mass noun] a condition marked by fever and often by unconsciousness, caused by failure of the body's temperature-regulating mechanism when exposed to excessively high temperatures.

heat treatment ▶ noun [mass noun] the use of heat for therapeutic purposes in medicine or to modify the properties of a material, especially in metallurgy.
– DERIVATIVES **heat-treat** verb.

heatwave ▶ noun a prolonged period of abnormally hot weather.

heave /hiːv/ ▶ verb (past and past participle **heaved** or chiefly Nautical **hove**) **1** [with obj. and adverbial of direction] lift or haul (something heavy) with great effort: *she heaved the sofa back into place | he* ***heaved himself*** *out of bed.* ■ informal throw (something heavy): *she heaved half a brick at him.*
2 [with obj.] produce (a sigh): *he heaved a euphoric sigh of relief.*
3 [no obj.] rise and fall rhythmically or spasmodically: *his shoulders heaved as he panted.* ■ make an effort to vomit; retch: *my stomach heaved.*
4 [with obj.] Nautical pull, raise, or move (a boat or ship) by hauling on a rope or ropes.
▶ noun **1** an act of heaving.
2 Geology a sideways displacement in a fault.
3 (**heaves**) another term for **COPD** in horses.
– PHRASES **heave in sight** (or **into view**) Nautical come into view: *they held out until a British fleet hove in sight.*
– PHRASAL VERBS **heave to** (of a boat or ship) come to a stop, especially by turning across the wind leaving the headsail backed.
– DERIVATIVES **heaver** noun.
– ORIGIN Old English *hebban*, of Germanic origin; related to Dutch *heffen* and German *heben* 'lift up'.

heave-ho ▶ exclamation a cry emitted when doing actions that take physical effort.
▶ noun (**the heave-ho**) informal dismissal or elimination from a job, institution, or contest: *conjecture over who'll get the heave-ho.*
ORIGIN late Middle English: from *heave!* (imperative) + **HO**[1], originally in nautical use when hauling a rope.

heaven ▶ noun **1** (often **Heaven**) a place regarded in various religions as the abode of God (or the gods) and the angels, and of the good after death, often traditionally depicted as being above the sky. ■ God (or the gods): *Constantine was persuaded that disunity in the Church was displeasing to heaven.* ■ Theology a state of being eternally in the presence of God after death. ■ used in various exclamations as a substitute for 'God': *heaven knows! | good heavens!*
2 (also **the heavens**) literary the sky, especially perceived as a vault in which the sun, moon, stars, and planets are situated: *Galileo used a telescope to observe the heavens.*
3 informal a place, state, or experience of supreme bliss: *lying by the pool with a good book is my idea of heaven.*
– PHRASES **the heavens open** it suddenly starts to rain very heavily. **in seventh heaven** very happy; ecstatic. **move heaven and earth to do something** make extraordinary efforts to do a specified thing: *if he had truly loved her he would have moved heaven and earth to get her back.* **stink** (or **smell**) **to high heaven** have a very strong and unpleasant odour.
– DERIVATIVES **heavenward** adjective & adverb, **heavenwards** adverb.
– ORIGIN Old English *heofon*, of Germanic origin; related to Dutch *hemel* and German *Himmel*.

heavenly ▶ adjective **1** of heaven; divine: *heavenly Father.*
2 of the heavens or sky: *heavenly constellations.*
3 informal very pleasing; wonderful: *their shampoos smell heavenly | it was a heavenly morning for a ride.*
– DERIVATIVES **heavenliness** noun.
– ORIGIN Old English *heofonlic* (see **HEAVEN**, **-LY**[1]).

heavenly body ▶ noun a planet, star, or other celestial body.

heavenly host ▶ noun see **HOST**[2].

heaven-sent ▶ adjective occurring at a very favourable time; very opportune: *she was so afraid of losing this heaven-sent opportunity.*

heavier-than-air ▶ adjective (of an aircraft) weighing more than the air it displaces.

heavily ▶ adverb **1** to a great degree; in large amounts: *it was raining heavily | he had been drinking heavily for six months.* ■ to a large extent; very

H

or very much: *the country is heavily dependent on banana exports.*
2 with a lot of force or effort; with weight: *she fell heavily to the ground* | *he sat down heavily in the chair.* ■ in a way that is mentally oppressive or hard to endure: *it is a burden that weighs heavily on his shoulders* | *tension hung heavily in the air.* ■ slowly and loudly: *she was breathing heavily.* ■ in a slow way that expresses sadness: *he sighed heavily.*

heavily built ▶ **adjective** (of a person) having a large, broad, and strong body: *he was tall and heavily built.*

heavily laden (also **heavily loaded**) ▶ **adjective** full of or loaded with heavy items: *the lorry was heavily laden with large boxes and crates.*

heaving ▶ **adjective** Brit. informal (of a place) extremely crowded: *the foyer was absolutely heaving with people.*

heaving line ▶ **noun** a lightweight line with a weight at the end, made to be thrown between a ship and the shore, or from one ship to another, and used to pull a heavier line across.

Heaviside /ˈhɛvɪsʌɪd/, Oliver (1850–1925), English physicist and electrical engineer, important in the development of telephone communication and telegraphy. In 1902 he suggested (independently of A. E. Kennelly) the existence of a layer in the atmosphere responsible for reflecting radio waves back to earth.

H

Heaviside layer (also **Heaviside–Kennelly layer**) ▶ **noun** another name for **E-LAYER**.
– ORIGIN early 20th cent.: named after O. **HEAVISIDE** and A. E. **KENNELLY**.

heavy ▶ **adjective** (**heavier**, **heaviest**) **1** of great weight; difficult to lift or move: *a heavy and bulky load* | *the pan was too heavy for me to carry.* ■ used in questions about weight: *how heavy is it?* ■ [attrib.] (of a class of thing) above the average weight; large of its kind: *heavy artillery* | *heavy woollens.* ■ [predic.] weighed down; full of something: *branches heavy with blossoms.* ■ (of a person's head or eyes) feeling weighed down by weariness: *a heavy head.*
2 of great density; thick or substantial: *heavy grey clouds* | *heavy horn-rimmed glasses.* ■ not delicate or graceful; coarse: *he had a big moustache and heavy features.* ■ (of food) hard to digest; too filling. ■ (of ground or soil) muddy or full of clay. ■ Physics of or containing atoms of an isotope of greater than the usual mass. See also **HEAVY WATER**.
3 of more than the usual size, amount, or intensity: *a heavy cold* | *the traffic was heavy and I was delayed* | *I fell into a heavy sleep.* ■ (of a smell) very strong: *a heavy scent of oil.* ■ (**heavy on**) using a lot of: *stories heavy on melodrama.* ■ doing something more, or more deeply, than usual: *a heavy smoker.*
4 striking or falling with force: *a heavy blow to the head* | *we had heavy overnight rain.* ■ (of music, especially rock) having a strong bass component and a forceful rhythm.
5 needing much physical effort: *heavy work like repairing pathways.* ■ moving slowly or with difficulty: *steering that is heavy when parking.*
6 very important or serious: *a heavy discussion.* ■ (of a literary work) overly serious or difficult. ■ mentally oppressive; hard to endure: *a heavy burden of responsibility.* ■ feeling or expressing sadness: *I left him with a heavy heart.* ■ informal serious or difficult to deal with: *things were getting pretty heavy.* ■ informal (of a person) strict or harsh: *the police were really getting heavy.* ■ informal excellent (used as a general term of approval).
▶ **noun** (pl. **heavies**) **1** informal a thing, such as a vehicle, that is large or heavy of its kind. ■ a large, strong man, especially one hired for protection: *I needed money to pay off the heavies.* ■ (**heavies**) Brit. informal serious newspapers: *reporters from the Sunday heavies.* ■ informal an important person: *music business heavies.*
2 [mass noun] chiefly Scottish strong beer, especially bitter: *a pint of heavy.*
▶ **adverb** [usu. in combination] heavily: *heavy-laden.*
– PHRASES **heavy going** difficult or boring to deal with: *she found Hilary heavy going.* **the heavy mob** Brit. informal a group of strong or violent criminals or bodyguards. **make heavy weather of** see **WEATHER**.
– DERIVATIVES **heaviness** noun, **heavyish** adjective.
– ORIGIN Old English *hefig*, of Germanic origin; related to Dutch *hevig*, also to **HEAVE**.

heavy breathing ▶ **noun** [mass noun] breathing that is audible through being deep or laboured, especially in sleep or as a result of exertion.

heavy chemicals ▶ **plural noun** bulk chemicals used in industry and agriculture.

heavy cream ▶ **noun** North American term for **DOUBLE CREAM**.

heavy-duty ▶ **adjective** (of material or an article) designed to withstand the stresses of demanding use: *heavy-duty springs.* ■ informal intense, important, or abundant: *she did some heavy-duty cleaning.*

heavy-footed ▶ **adjective** slow and laborious in movement: *the All Blacks make the Lions' pack look heavy-footed.*

heavy-handed ▶ **adjective** clumsy, insensitive, or overly forceful: *heavy-handed policing.* ■ using too much of something: *beware of being heavy-handed with the flour.*
– DERIVATIVES **heavy-handedly** adverb, **heavy-handedness** noun.

heavy-hearted ▶ **adjective** feeling depressed or melancholy: *is it better to be serious and heavy-hearted?*

heavy hitter (also **big hitter**) ▶ **noun** informal an important or powerful person.

heavy horse ▶ **noun** a large, strong, heavily built horse of a type or breed used for draught work.

heavy hydrogen ▶ **noun** another term for **DEUTERIUM**.

heavy industry ▶ **noun** [mass noun] the manufacture of large, heavy articles and materials in bulk.

heavy metal ▶ **noun 1** a metal of relatively high density, or of high relative atomic weight.
2 [mass noun] a type of highly amplified harsh-sounding rock music with a strong beat, characteristically using violent or fantastic imagery.

heavy oil ▶ **noun** any of the relatively dense hydrocarbons (denser than water) derived from petroleum, coal tar, and similar materials.

heavy petting ▶ **noun** [mass noun] erotic contact between two people involving stimulation of the genitals but stopping short of intercourse.

heavyset ▶ **adjective** (of a person) broad and strongly built.

heavy water ▶ **noun** [mass noun] water in which the hydrogen in the molecules is partly or wholly replaced by the isotope deuterium, used especially as a moderator in nuclear reactors.

heavyweight ▶ **noun 1** [mass noun] a weight in boxing and other sports, typically the heaviest category. In the amateur boxing scale it ranges from 81 to 91 kg. ■ [count noun] a heavyweight boxer or other competitor.
2 a person or thing of above-average weight. ■ a person of influence or importance in a particular sphere: *a political heavyweight with national recognition.*
▶ **adjective** of above-average weight. ■ serious, important, or influential: *heavyweight news coverage.*

Heb. ▶ **abbreviation** ■ Epistle to the Hebrews (in biblical references). ■ Hebrew.

hebdomadal /hɛbˈdɒməd(ə)l/ ▶ **adjective** formal weekly (used especially of organizations which meet weekly): *Oxford University's Hebdomadal Council.*
– ORIGIN early 17th cent. (in the sense 'lasting seven days'): from late Latin *hebdomadalis*, from Greek *hebdomas, hebdomad-* 'the number seven, seven days', from *hepta* 'seven'.

Hebe[1] /ˈhiːbi/ **1** Greek Mythology the daughter of Hera and Zeus, and cup-bearer of the gods.
2 Astronomy asteroid 6, discovered in 1847 (diameter 192 km).
– ORIGIN from Greek *hēbē* 'youthful beauty'.

Hebe[2] /hiːb/ ▶ **noun** US informal, offensive a Jewish person.
– ORIGIN early 20th cent.: abbreviation of **HEBREW**.

hebe /ˈhiːbi/ ▶ **noun** an evergreen flowering shrub with spikes of mauve, pink, or white flowers, native to New Zealand and widely grown as an ornamental.
● Genus *Hebe* (formerly *Veronica*), family Scrophulariaceae.
– ORIGIN modern Latin, named after the goddess *Hebe* (see **HEBE**[1]).

Hebei /həˈbeɪ/ (also **Hopeh**) a province of NE central China; capital, Shijiazhuang.

hebephrenia /ˌhiːbɪˈfriːnɪə/ ▶ **noun** [mass noun] a form of chronic schizophrenia involving disordered thought, inappropriate emotions, hallucinations, and bizarre behaviour.
– DERIVATIVES **hebephrenic** /-ˈfrɛnɪk/ **adjective & noun**.
– ORIGIN late 19th cent. (originally associated with behaviour in puberty): from **HEBE**[1] + Greek *phrēn* 'mind' + **-IA**[1].

hebetude /ˈhɛbɪtjuːd/ ▶ **noun** [mass noun] literary the state of being dull or lethargic.
– ORIGIN early 17th cent.: from late Latin *hebetudo*, from *hebes, hebet-* 'blunt'.

Hebraic /hɪˈbreɪɪk/ ▶ **adjective** of Hebrew or the Hebrews: *a student of Hebraic religious literature.*
– DERIVATIVES **Hebraically** adverb.
– ORIGIN via Christian Latin from late Greek *Hebraikos*, from *Hebraios* (see **HEBREW**).

Hebraism /ˈhiːbreɪɪz(ə)m/ ▶ **noun 1** a Hebrew idiom or expression.
2 [mass noun] the Jewish religion, culture, or character.
– DERIVATIVES **Hebraize** (also **Hebraise**) verb.
– ORIGIN late 16th cent.: from French *hébraïsme* or modern Latin *Hebraismus*, from late Greek *Hebraïsmos*, from *Hebraios* (see **HEBREW**).

Hebraist /ˈhiːbreɪɪst/ ▶ **noun** a scholar of the Hebrew language.

Hebrew /ˈhiːbruː/ ▶ **noun 1** a member of an ancient people living in what is now Israel and Palestine and, according to biblical tradition, descended from the patriarch Jacob, grandson of Abraham. After the Exodus (*c.*1300 BC) they established the kingdoms of Israel and Judah, and their scriptures and traditions form the basis of the Jewish religion. ■ dated or offensive a Jew.
2 [mass noun] the Semitic language spoken by the Hebrews, in its ancient or modern form.
▶ **adjective 1** of or in Hebrew.
2 of the Hebrews or the Jews.

> Hebrew is written from right to left in a characteristic alphabet of twenty-two consonants, the vowels sometimes being marked by additional signs. From about AD 500 it was almost entirely restricted to Jewish religious use, but it was revived as a spoken language in the 19th century and, with a vocabulary extended by borrowing from contemporary languages, is now the official language of the state of Israel.

– ORIGIN from Old French *Ebreu*, via Latin from late Greek *Hebraios*, from Aramaic *ʿibray*, based on Hebrew *ʿibrî* understood to mean 'one from the other side (of the river)'.

Hebrew Bible the sacred writings of Judaism, called by Christians the Old Testament, and comprising the Law (Torah), the Prophets, and the Hagiographa or Writings.

Hebrews, Epistle to the a book of the New Testament, traditionally included among the letters of St Paul but now generally held to be non-Pauline.

Hebrides /ˈhɛbrɪdiːz/ a group of about 500 islands off the NW coast of Scotland.

> The **Inner Hebrides** include the islands of Skye, Mull, Jura, Islay, Iona, Coll, Eigg, Rhum, Staffa, and Tiree. The Little Minch separates this group from the **Outer Hebrides**, which include the islands of Lewis and Harris, North and South Uist, Benbecula, Barra, and the isolated St Kilda group. The shipping forecast area **Hebrides** covers an area of the Atlantic off the NW coast of Scotland.

– DERIVATIVES **Hebridean** noun & adjective.

Hebron /ˈhɛbrɒn/ a Palestinian city on the West Bank of the Jordan; pop. 240,200 (est. 2009). As the home of Abraham it is a holy city of both Judaism and Islam.

Hebros /ˈhiːbrəs/ (also **Hebrus**) ancient Greek name for **MARITSA**.

Hecate /ˈhɛkəti/ Greek Mythology a goddess of dark places, often associated with ghosts and sorcery. She is frequently identified with Artemis and Selene.

hecatomb /ˈhɛkətuːm/ ▶ **noun** (in ancient Greece or Rome) a great public sacrifice, originally of a hundred oxen. ■ an extensive loss of life for a particular cause.
– ORIGIN late 16th cent.: via Latin from Greek *hekatombē* (from *hekaton* 'hundred' + *bous* 'ox').

heck ▶ **exclamation** expressing surprise, frustration, or dismay: *oh heck, I can't for the life of me remember.* ■ (**the heck**) used for emphasis in questions and exclamations: *what the heck's the matter?* ■ (**a heck of a ——**) used for emphasis in various statements or exclamations: *it was a heck of a lot of money.*
– ORIGIN late 19th cent. (originally northern English dialect): euphemistic alteration of **HELL**.

heckelphone /ˈhɛk(ə)lfəʊn/ ▶ **noun** a woodwind instrument resembling a large oboe, with a range about an octave lower.
– ORIGIN early 20th cent.: from German *Heckelphon*, named after Wilhelm *Heckel* (1856–1909), German instrument-maker, on the pattern of *saxophone*.

heckle ▶ **verb** [with obj.] **1** interrupt (a public speaker) with derisive or aggressive comments or abuse: *he was booed and heckled when he tried to address the*

demonstrators | [no obj.] *women round him started heckling.*
2 dress (flax or hemp) to split and straighten the fibres for spinning.
▶ **noun** a heckling comment: *heckles of 'Get stuffed!'*
– DERIVATIVES **heckler** noun.
– ORIGIN Middle English (in sense 2 of the verb): from *heckle* 'flax comb', a northern and eastern form of **HACKLE**. The sense 'interrupt (a public speaker) with aggressive comments' arose in the mid 17th cent., for the development in sense, compare with **TEASE**.

hectare /ˈhɛktɛː, -ɑː/ (abbrev.: **ha**) ▶ **noun** a metric unit of square measure, equal to 100 ares (2.471 acres or 10,000 square metres).
– DERIVATIVES **hectarage** noun.
– ORIGIN early 19th cent.: from French, formed irregularly from Greek *hekaton* 'hundred' + **ARE**².

hectic ▶ **adjective 1** full of incessant or frantic activity: *a hectic business schedule.*
2 Medicine, archaic relating to or affected by a regularly recurrent fever typically accompanying tuberculosis, with flushed cheeks and hot, dry skin.
▶ **noun** Medicine, archaic a hectic fever or flush.
– DERIVATIVES **hectically** adverb.
– ORIGIN late Middle English *etik*, via Old French from late Latin *hecticus*, from Greek *hektikos* 'habitual', from *hexis* 'habit, state of mind or body'. The original association with the symptoms of tuberculosis (*hectic fever*) gave rise to sense 1 in the early 20th century.

hecto- ▶ **combining form** (used commonly in units of measurement) a hundred: *hectometre.*
– ORIGIN from French, formed irregularly by contraction of Greek *hekaton* 'hundred'.

hectocotylus /ˌhɛktə(ʊ)ˈkɒtɪləs/ ▶ **noun** (pl. **hectocotyli** /-lʌɪ, -liː/) Zoology a modified arm used by male octopuses and some other cephalopods to transfer sperm to the female.
– ORIGIN mid 19th cent.: modern Latin, from **HECTO-** 'hundred' + Greek *kotulē* 'hollow thing', a name given by Cuvier to what he mistakenly took to be a genus of parasitic worms.

hectogram (also **hectogramme**) (abbrev.: **hg**) ▶ **noun** a metric unit of mass equal to one hundred grams.

hectolitre /ˈhɛktə(ʊ),liːtə/ (US **hectoliter**) (abbrev.: **hl**) ▶ **noun** a metric unit of capacity equal to one hundred litres, used especially for wine, beer, grain, and other agricultural produce.

hectometre /ˈhɛktə(ʊ),miːtə/ (US **hectometer**) (abbrev.: **hm**) ▶ **noun** a metric unit of length equal to one hundred metres.

Hector /ˈhɛktə/ Greek Mythology a Trojan warrior, son of Priam and Hecuba and husband of Andromache. He was killed by Achilles, who dragged his body behind his chariot three times round the walls of Troy.

hector /ˈhɛktə/ ▶ **verb** [with obj.] talk to (someone) in a bullying way: *she doesn't hector us about giving up things* | (as adj. **hectoring**) *a brusque, hectoring manner.*
– ORIGIN late Middle English: from the Trojan warrior **HECTOR**. Originally denoting a hero, the sense later became 'braggart or bully' (applied in the late 17th cent. to a member of a gang of London youths), hence 'talk to in a bullying way'.

Hecuba /ˈhɛkjʊbə/ Greek Mythology a Trojan woman, the wife of Priam and mother of children including Hector, Paris, Cassandra, and Troilus.

he'd ▶ **contraction** he had: *he'd seen all he wanted.* ■ he would: *he'd like to see you.*

heddle /ˈhɛd(ə)l/ ▶ **noun** a looped wire or cord with an eye in the centre through which a warp yarn is passed in a loom before going through the reed to control its movement and divide the threads.
– ORIGIN early 16th cent.: apparently from an alteration of Old English *hefeld* (see **HEALD**).

heder /ˈhɛdə, ˈxɛdə/ ▶ **noun** (pl. **hedarim** /hɛˈdɑːrɪm, xɛ-/ or **heders**) variant spelling of **CHEDER**.

hedge ▶ **noun 1** a fence or boundary formed by closely growing bushes or shrubs: *a privet hedge.*
2 a way of protecting oneself against financial loss or other adverse circumstances: *index-linked gilts are a useful hedge against inflation.*
3 a word or phrase used to avoid over-precise commitment, for example *etc.*, *often*, or *sometimes*.
▶ **verb** [with obj.] **1** surround with a hedge: *a garden hedged with yew.* ■ (**hedge something in**) enclose something.
2 limit or qualify (something) by conditions or exceptions: *they hedged their story about with provisos.* ■ [no obj.] avoid making a definite statement or commitment: *he hedged at every new question.*
3 protect (one's investment or an investor) against loss by making balancing or compensating contracts or transactions.
– PHRASES **hedge one's bets** avoid committing oneself when faced with a difficult choice.
– DERIVATIVES **hedger** noun.
– ORIGIN Old English *hegg*, of Germanic origin; related to Dutch *heg* and German *Hecke*.

hedge brown ▶ **noun** another term for **GATEKEEPER** (sense 2).

hedge fund ▶ **noun** an offshore investment fund, typically formed as a private limited partnership, that engages in speculation using credit or borrowed capital.

hedge garlic ▶ **noun** another term for **JACK-BY-THE-HEDGE**.

hedgehog ▶ **noun** a nocturnal insectivorous Old World mammal with a spiny coat and short legs, able to roll itself into a ball for defence. ● Family Erinaceidae: four genera and several species, including the common *Erinaceus europaeus* of western and northern Europe.
■ any other animal covered with spines, especially (N. Amer.) a porcupine. ■ used in names of plants or fruits resembling a hedgehog in having spines, e.g. **hedgehog cactus, hedgehog holly**.
– ORIGIN late Middle English: from **HEDGE** (from its habitat) + **HOG** (from its piglike snout).

hedgehog fungus ▶ **noun** an edible mushroom which has a cap with a lobed fleshy margin, the underside of which bears downward-pointing spore-bearing spines, common in both Eurasia and North America. ● *Hydnum repandum*, family Hydnaceae, class Hymenomycetes.

hedge-hop ▶ **verb** [no obj., with adverbial of direction] fly an aircraft at a very low altitude.

hedge-laying ▶ **noun** the process of making or maintaining a hedge by weaving partly cut branches through the upright stems of a row of shrubs.

hedgerow ▶ **noun** a rough or mixed hedge of wild shrubs and occasional trees, typically bordering a road or field.
– ORIGIN Old English: from **HEDGE** + obsolete *rew* 'hedgerow', assimilated to **ROW**¹.

hedge sparrow ▶ **noun** another term for **DUNNOCK**.

hedge trimmer ▶ **noun** an electric tool with a blade like a chainsaw, used for cutting back bushes, shrubs, and hedges.

hedging ▶ **noun** [mass noun] the planting or trimming of hedges: *contract work for hedging and ditching.* ■ bushes and shrubs planted to form hedges.

hedonic /hiːˈdɒnɪk, hɛ-/ ▶ **adjective** technical relating to, characterized by, or considered in terms of pleasant (or unpleasant) sensations.
– ORIGIN mid 17th cent.: from Greek *hēdonikos*, from *hēdonē* 'pleasure'.

hedonism /ˈhiːd(ə)nɪz(ə)m, ˈhɛ-/ ▶ **noun** [mass noun] the pursuit of pleasure; sensual self-indulgence. ■ Philosophy the ethical theory that pleasure (in the sense of the satisfaction of desires) is the highest good and proper aim of human life.
– ORIGIN mid 19th cent.: from Greek *hēdonē* 'pleasure' + **-ISM**.

hedonist ▶ **noun** a person who believes that the pursuit of pleasure is the most important thing in life; a pleasure-seeker: *she was living the life of a committed hedonist.*

hedonistic ▶ **adjective** engaged in the pursuit of pleasure; sensually self-indulgent: *a hedonistic existence of booze, drugs, and parties.*
– DERIVATIVES **hedonistically** adverb.

-hedron ▶ **combining form** (pl. **-hedra** or **-hedrons**) in nouns denoting geometrical solids having a specified number of plane faces: *decahedron.* ■ denoting geometrical solids having faces of a specified shape: *rhombohedron.*
– DERIVATIVES **-hedral** combining form in corresponding adjectives.
– ORIGIN from Greek *hedra* 'seat, base'.

heebie-jeebies ▶ **plural noun** (**the heebie-jeebies**) informal a state of nervous fear or anxiety: *it takes a lot more than a measly poltergeist to give me the heebie-jeebies.*
– ORIGIN 1920s (originally US): of unknown origin.

heed ▶ **verb** [with obj.] pay attention to; take notice of: *he should have heeded the warnings.*
▶ **noun** [mass noun] careful attention: *if he heard, he paid no heed* | *we must take heed of the suggestions.*
– ORIGIN Old English *hēdan*, of West Germanic origin; related to Dutch *hoeden* and German *hüten*.

heedful ▶ **adjective** aware of and attentive to: *he is heedful of his own intuitions.*
– DERIVATIVES **heedfully** adverb, **heedfulness** noun.

heedless ▶ **adjective** showing a reckless lack of care or attention: *'Elaine!' she shouted, heedless of attracting unwanted attention* | *his heedless impetuosity.*
– DERIVATIVES **heedlessly** adverb, **heedlessness** noun.

hee-haw ▶ **noun** the loud, harsh cry of a donkey or mule. ■ [as modifier] US informal relating to or denoting unsophisticated rural humour and attitudes.
▶ **verb** [no obj.] make the loud, harsh cry of a donkey or mule.
– ORIGIN early 19th cent.: imitative.

heel¹ ▶ **noun 1** the back part of the human foot below the ankle. ■ the back part of the foot in vertebrate animals. ■ the part of a shoe or boot supporting the heel: *shoes with low heels.* ■ the part of a sock covering the heel. ■ (**heels**) high-heeled shoes.
2 the part of the palm of the hand next to the wrist: *he rubbed the heel of his hand against the window.*
3 a thing resembling a heel in form or position, in particular: ■ the end of a violin bow at which it is held. ■ the part of the head of a golf club nearest the shaft. ■ a crusty end of a loaf of bread, or the rind of a cheese. ■ a piece of the main stem of a plant left attached to the base of a cutting.
4 informal, dated an inconsiderate or untrustworthy man: *what kind of a heel do you think I am?*
▶ **verb** [with obj.] **1** fit or renew a heel on (a shoe or boot).
2 (of a dog) follow closely behind its owner.
3 Rugby push or kick (the ball) out of the back of the scrum with one's heel.
4 Golf strike (the ball) with the heel of the club.
5 [no obj.] touch the ground with the heel when dancing.
▶ **exclamation** a command to a dog to walk close behind its owner.
– PHRASES **at** (or **to**) **heel** (of a dog) close to and slightly behind its owner. **at** (or **on**) **the heels of** following closely after: *he headed off with Sammy at his heels.* **bring someone to heel** bring someone under control. **cool** (or Brit. **kick**) **one's heels** be kept waiting. **in the heel of the hunt** Irish at the last minute; finally: *in the heel of the hunt, the outcome of the match was decided by a penalty.* **kick up one's heels** N. Amer. have a lively, enjoyable time. **set** (or **rock**) **someone back on their heels** astonish or disconcert someone. **take to one's heels** run away. **turn on one's heel** turn sharply round. **under the heel of** dominated or controlled by: *a population under the heel of a military dictatorship.*
– DERIVATIVES **heeled** adjective [in combination] *high-heeled shoes*, **heelless** adjective.
– ORIGIN Old English *hēla*, *hǣla*, of Germanic origin; related to Dutch *hiel*, also to **HOUGH**.

heel² ▶ **verb** [no obj.] (of a boat or ship) lean over owing to the pressure of wind or an uneven load. Compare with **LIST**². ■ [with obj.] cause (a boat or ship) to lean over.
▶ **noun** an instance of a ship heeling. ■ [mass noun] the degree of incline of a ship's leaning measured from the vertical.
– ORIGIN late 16th cent.: from obsolete *heeld*, *hield* 'incline', of Germanic origin; related to Dutch *hellen*.

heel³ ▶ **verb** [with obj.] (**heel something in**) set a plant in the ground and cover its roots.
– ORIGIN Old English *helian* 'cover, hide', of Germanic origin, from an Indo-European root shared by Latin *celare* 'hide'.

heelball ▶ **noun** [mass noun] a mixture of hard wax and lampblack used by shoemakers for polishing or in brass rubbing.

heel bar ▶ **noun** a small shop or stall where shoes are repaired, especially while the customer waits.

heel bone ▶ **noun** the calcaneus.

heelflip ▶ **noun** (in skateboarding) a manoeuvre in which the front heel is used to manipulate the board during a jump in such a way that it completes a sideways rotation before landing.

heeltap ▶ **noun 1** one of the layers of leather or other material of which a shoe heel is made.
2 dated an amount of alcohol left at the bottom of a glass after drinking.

Hefei /hɛˈfeɪ/ (also **Hofei**) an industrial city in eastern China, capital of Anhui province; pop. 1,502,800 (est. 2006).

heffalump ▶ noun a child's term for an elephant.
– ORIGIN 1920s: coined by A. A. Milne in *Winnie-the-Pooh*.

heft ▶ verb [with obj. and adverbial] lift or carry (something heavy): *he lifted crates and hefted boxes.* ■ lift or hold (something) in order to test its weight: *Anne hefted the gun in her hand.*
▶ noun [mass noun] N. Amer. the weight of someone or something. ■ ability or influence: *they lacked the political heft to get the formulation banned.*
– ORIGIN late Middle English (as a noun): probably from HEAVE, on the pattern of words such as *cleft* and *weft*.

hefty ▶ adjective (**heftier**, **heftiest**) **1** large and heavy: *a hefty young chap.* ■ (of a number or amount) impressively large: *a hefty £10 million | they could face hefty fines.*
2 done with vigour or force: *he aimed a hefty kick at the door.*
– DERIVATIVES **heftily** adverb, **heftiness** noun.

Hegel /ˈheɪɡ(ə)l/, Georg Wilhelm Friedrich (1770–1831), German philosopher. In his *Science of Logic* (1812–16) Hegel described the three-stage process of dialectical reasoning, on which Marx based his theory of dialectical materialism. He believed that history, the evolution of ideas, and human consciousness all develop through idealist dialectical processes as part of the Absolute or God coming to know itself.
– DERIVATIVES **Hegelian** /heɪˈɡiːlɪən, hɪ-, -ˈɡeɪl-/ adjective & noun, **Hegelianism** noun.

H

hegemon /ˈhɛdʒɪmɒn/ ▶ noun a supreme leader.
– ORIGIN early 20th cent.: from Greek *hēgemōn*.

hegemonic /ˌhɛdʒɪˈmɒnɪk, ˌhɛɡɪ-/ ▶ adjective ruling or dominant in a political or social context: *the bourgeoisie constituted the hegemonic class.*
– ORIGIN mid 17th cent.: from Greek *hēgemonikos* 'capable of commanding', from *hēgemōn* 'leader'.

hegemony /hɪˈdʒɛməni, -ˈɡɛ-/ ▶ noun [mass noun] leadership or dominance, especially by one state or social group over others: *Germany was united under Prussian hegemony after 1871.*
– ORIGIN mid 16th cent.: from Greek *hēgemonia*, from *hēgemōn* 'leader', from *hēgeisthai* 'to lead'.

Hegira /ˈhɛdʒɪrə/ (also **Hejira** or **Hijra**) ▶ noun Muhammad's departure from Mecca to Medina in AD 622, marking the consolidation of the first Muslim community. ■ the Muslim era reckoned from Muhammad's departure from Mecca: *the second century of the Hegira.* ■ (**hegira**) an exodus or migration.
– ORIGIN via medieval Latin from Arabic *hijra* 'departure', from *hajara* 'emigrate'.

heiau /ˈheɪəʊ/ ▶ noun (pl. **same** or **heiaus**) an ancient Hawaiian temple or sacred site.
– ORIGIN Hawaiian.

Heidegger /ˈhʌɪˌdɛɡə/, Martin (1889–1976), German philosopher. In *Being and Time* (1927) he examined the ontology of Being, in particular human existence as involvement with a world of objects (*Dasein*). His writings on *Angst* (dread) as a fundamental part of human consciousness due to radical freedom of choice and awareness of death had a strong influence on existentialist philosophers such as Sartre.

Heidelberg /ˈhʌɪd(ə)lbəːɡ/, German /ˈhaɪdlbɛrk/ a city in SW Germany, on the River Neckar in Baden-Württemberg; pop. 144,600 (est. 2006). Its university is the oldest in Germany.

heifer /ˈhɛfə/ ▶ noun (in farming) a cow that has not borne a calf, or has borne only one calf. Compare with COW[1].
– ORIGIN Old English *heahfore*, of unknown origin.

heigh ▶ exclamation archaic expressing encouragement or enquiry.
– ORIGIN natural utterance: first recorded in Middle English.

heigh-ho /ˈheɪhəʊ/ ▶ exclamation informal expressing boredom, resignation, or jollity: *heigh-ho—then it is footslogging again | how pleasant it is to have money, heigh-ho!*

height ▶ noun [mass noun] **1** the measurement of someone or something from head to foot or from base to top: *columns rising to 65 feet in height | he was of medium height.* ■ the quality of being tall or high: *her height marked her out from other women.*
2 elevation above ground or a recognized level (typically sea level): *the glider is gaining height.* ■ [count noun] a high place or position: *he's terrified of heights.*
3 [in sing.] the point or period at which something is at its best or strongest: *the height of the tourist season* | (**heights**) *they took consumerism to new heights.* ■ an extreme example of something: *it would be the height of bad manners not to attend the wedding.*
– ORIGIN Old English *hēhthu* (in the sense 'top of something'), of Germanic origin; related to Dutch *hoogte*, also to HIGH.

heighten ▶ verb **1** make or become more intense: [with obj.] *the pleasure was heightened by the sense of guilt that accompanied it* | (as adj. **heightened**) *the heightened colour of her face* | [no obj.] *concern over CFCs has heightened.*
2 [with obj.] make (something) higher.

heightism /ˈhʌɪtɪz(ə)m/ ▶ noun [mass noun] prejudice or discrimination against someone on the basis of their height.
– DERIVATIVES **heightist** adjective & noun.

height of land ▶ noun N. Amer. a watershed.

Heilbronn /ˈhʌɪlbrɒn/, German /haɪlˈbrɔn/ a city in SW Germany, on the River Neckar in Baden-Württemberg; pop. 121,400 (est. 2006).

Heilong /heɪˈlʊŋ/ Chinese name for AMUR.

Heilongjiang /ˌheɪlʊŋdʒɪˈaŋ/ (also **Heilungkiang** /ˌheɪlʊŋkɪˈaŋ/) a province of NE China, on the Russian frontier; capital, Harbin.

Heimlich manoeuvre /ˈhʌɪmlɪx/ (also **Heimlich procedure**) ▶ noun a first-aid procedure for dislodging an obstruction from a person's windpipe in which a sudden strong pressure is applied on their abdomen, between the navel and the ribcage.
– ORIGIN 1970s: named after Henry J. *Heimlich* (born 1920), the American doctor who developed the procedure.

Heine /ˈhʌɪnə/, (Christian Johann) Heinrich (1797–1856), German poet; born *Harry Heine*. Much of his early lyric poetry was set to music by Schumann and Schubert. In 1830 Heine emigrated to Paris, where his works became more political.

heinie /ˈhʌɪni/ ▶ noun US informal a person's buttocks.
– ORIGIN 1960s: alteration of HINDER[2], variant of HIND[1].

heinous /ˈheɪnəs, ˈhiːnəs/ ▶ adjective (of a person or wrongful act, especially a crime) utterly odious or wicked: *a battery of heinous crimes.*
– DERIVATIVES **heinously** adverb, **heinousness** noun.
– ORIGIN late Middle English: from Old French *haineus*, from *hair* 'to hate', of Germanic origin.

Heinz /hʌɪnz/, Henry John (1844–1919), American food manufacturer. In 1869 he established a family firm for the manufacture and sale of processed foods. Heinz devised the marketing slogan '57 Varieties' in 1896.

heir /ɛː/ ▶ noun a person legally entitled to the property or rank of another on that person's death: *his eldest son and heir | the heir to the throne.* ■ a person who inherits and continues the work of a predecessor: *they saw themselves as heirs of the Cubists.*
– DERIVATIVES **heirdom** noun, **heirless** adjective, **heirship** noun.
– ORIGIN Middle English: via Old French from Latin *heres*.

heir apparent ▶ noun (pl. **heirs apparent**) an heir whose claim cannot be set aside by the birth of another heir. Compare with HEIR PRESUMPTIVE. ■ a person who is most likely to succeed to the place of another.

heir-at-law ▶ noun (pl. **heirs-at-law**) an heir by right of blood, especially to the real property of an intestate.

heiress ▶ noun a female heir, especially to vast wealth.

heirloom ▶ noun a valuable object that has belonged to a family for several generations.
– ORIGIN late Middle English: from HEIR + LOOM[1] (which formerly had the senses 'tool, heirloom').

heir presumptive ▶ noun (pl. **heirs presumptive**) an heir whose claim may be set aside by the birth of another heir. Compare with HEIR APPARENT.

Heisenberg /ˈhʌɪz(ə)nbəːɡ/, German /ˈhaɪznbɛrk/, Werner Karl (1901–76), German mathematical physicist and philosopher. He developed a system of quantum mechanics based on matrix algebra in which he stated his famous uncertainty principle (1927). For this and his discovery of the allotropic forms of hydrogen he was awarded the 1932 Nobel Prize for Physics.

heist /hʌɪst/ informal ▶ noun a robbery: *a diamond heist.*
▶ verb [with obj.] N. Amer. steal.
– ORIGIN mid 19th cent. (originally US): representing a local pronunciation of HOIST.

hei-tiki /heɪˈtɪki/ ▶ noun a greenstone neck ornament worn by Maoris.
– ORIGIN Maori, from *hei* 'hang' + *tiki* 'image'.

Hejaz /hɪˈdʒaz/ (also **Hijaz**) a coastal region of western Saudi Arabia, extending along the Red Sea.

Hejira ▶ noun variant spelling of HEGIRA.

Hekla /ˈhɛklə/ an active volcano in SW Iceland, rising to a height of 1,491 m (4,840 ft).

HeLa cells /ˈhiːlə/ ▶ plural noun human epithelial cells of a strain maintained in tissue culture since 1951 and used in research, especially in virology.
– ORIGIN 1950s: from the name of *Henrietta Lacks*, whose cervical carcinoma provided the original cells.

held past and past participle of HOLD[1].

Heldentenor /ˈhɛld(ə)nˌtɛnɔː/ ▶ noun a powerful tenor voice suitable for heroic roles in opera. ■ a singer with a Heldentenor voice.
– ORIGIN 1920s: German, literally 'hero tenor'.

Helen Greek Mythology the daughter of Zeus and Leda, born from an egg. In the Homeric poems she was the outstandingly beautiful wife of Menelaus, and her abduction by Paris (to whom she had been promised, as a bribe, by Aphrodite) led to the Trojan War.

Helena /ˈhɛlmə/ the state capital of Montana; pop. 29,351 (est. 2008).

Helena, St /ˈhɛlmə/ (*c*. AD 255–*c*.330), Roman empress and mother of Constantine the Great. In 326 she visited the Holy Land and founded basilicas on the Mount of Olives and at Bethlehem. She is credited with the finding of the cross on which Christ was crucified. Feast day (in the Eastern Church) 21 May; (in the Western Church) 18 August.

helenium /hɛˈliːnɪəm/ ▶ noun an American plant of the daisy family, which bears many red to yellow flowers, each having a prominent central disc.
● Genus *Helenium*, family Compositae.
– ORIGIN modern Latin, from Greek *helenion*. The term originally denoted the herb *elecampane*, possibly in commemoration of Helen of Troy (said to have planted elecampane on the island of Pharos); the current designation was adopted by Linnaeus in the 18th cent.

Helgoland /ˈhɛlɡəʊlant/ German name for HELIGOLAND.

heli- ▶ combining form relating to helicopters: *heli-skiing | helipad.*

heliacal /hɪˈlʌɪək(ə)l/ ▶ adjective Astronomy relating to or near the sun.
– ORIGIN mid 16th cent.: via late Latin from Greek *hēliakos* (from *hēlios* 'sun') + -AL.

heliacal rising /hɪˈlʌɪək(ə)l/ ▶ noun the rising of a celestial object at the same time as the sun, or its first visible rising after a period of invisibility due to conjunction with the sun. The last setting before such a period is the **heliacal setting**.

helianthemum /ˌhiːlɪˈanθɪməm/ ▶ noun a low evergreen shrub with saucer-shaped flowers, which is grown as an ornamental. Also called ROCK ROSE.
● Genus *Helianthemum*, family Cistaceae.
– ORIGIN modern Latin, from Greek *hēlios* 'sun' + *anthemon* 'flower' (because the flowers open in sunlight).

helianthus /ˌhiːlɪˈanθəs/ ▶ noun a plant of the genus *Helianthus* in the daisy family, especially (in gardening) a sunflower.
– ORIGIN modern Latin, from Greek *hēlios* 'sun' + *anthos* 'flower'.

helical /ˈhɛlɪk(ə)l, ˈhiː-/ ▶ adjective having the shape or form of a helix; spiral: *helical molecules.*
– DERIVATIVES **helically** adverb.

helices plural form of HELIX.

helichrysum /ˌhɛlɪˈkrʌɪsəm/ ▶ noun an Old World plant of the daisy family. Some kinds are grown as everlastings, retaining their shape and colour when dried. ● Genus *Helichrysum*, family Compositae.
– ORIGIN Latin, from Greek *helikhrusos*, from *helix* 'spiral' + *khrusos* 'gold'. It originally denoted a yellow-flowered plant, possibly *Helichrysum stoechas*.

helicity /hiːˈlɪsɪti/ ▶ noun [mass noun] **1** chiefly Biochemistry helical character, especially of DNA.
2 Physics a combination of the spin and the linear motion of a subatomic particle.
– ORIGIN 1950s (in sense 2): from Latin *helix*, *helic-* 'spiral' + -ITY.

helicoid /ˈhiːlɪkɔɪd/ ▶ noun a helical or spiral object. ■ Geometry a surface formed by simultaneously moving a straight line along an axis and rotating it around it (like a screw thread).
▶ adjective of the form of a helix or helicoid.
– DERIVATIVES **helicoidal** adjective.

– ORIGIN late 17th cent.: from Greek *helikoeidēs* 'of spiral form', from *helix*, *helik-* (see HELIX).

helicon /ˈhɛlɪk(ə)n/ ▶ **noun** a large spiral bass tuba played encircling the player's head and resting on the shoulder.
– ORIGIN late 19th cent.: from Latin, associated with HELIX.

heliconia /ˌhɛlɪˈkəʊnɪə/ ▶ **noun** a large-leaved tropical American plant which bears spectacular flowers with brightly coloured bracts. ● Genus *Heliconia*, family Heliconiaceae (formerly Musaceae): many species, including the lobster claw.

Helicon, Mount /ˈhɛlɪk(ə)n/ a mountain in Boeotia, central Greece, to the north of the Gulf of Corinth, rising to 1,750 m (5741 ft). It was believed by the ancient Greeks to be the home of the Muses.

helicopter ▶ **noun** a type of aircraft which derives both lift and propulsion from one or two sets of horizontally revolving overhead rotors. It is capable of moving vertically and horizontally, the direction of motion being controlled by the pitch of the rotor blades.
▶ **verb** [with obj. and adverbial of direction] transport by helicopter. ■ [no obj., with adverbial of direction] fly somewhere in a helicopter.
– ORIGIN late 19th cent.: from French *hélicoptère*, from Greek *helix* 'spiral' + *pteron* 'wing'.

helicopter view ▶ **noun** informal (especially in business) a general survey of something; an overview.

helictite /hɛˈlɪktʌɪt/ ▶ **noun** Geology a distorted form of stalactite, typically resembling a twig.
– ORIGIN late 19th cent.: from Greek *heliktos* 'twisted', on the pattern of *stalactite*.

Heligoland /ˈhɛlɪɡəʊland/ a small island in the North Sea off the coast of Germany, one of the North Frisian Islands. The island was Danish from 1714 until seized by the British navy in 1807 and later ceded officially to Britain. In 1890 it was returned to Germany. German name HELGOLAND.

helio- /ˈhiːlɪəʊ/ ▶ **combining form** relating to the sun: *heliogravure* | *heliostat*.
– ORIGIN from Greek *hēlios* 'sun'.

heliocentric ▶ **adjective** having or representing the sun as the centre, as in the accepted astronomical model of the solar system. Compare with GEOCENTRIC. ■ Astronomy measured from or considered in relation to the centre of the sun: *heliocentric distance*.
– DERIVATIVES **heliocentrically** adverb.

Heliogabalus /ˌhiːlɪəˈɡabələs/ (also **Elagabalus**) (AD 204–22), Roman emperor 218–22; born *Varius Avitus Bassianus*. He took his name from the Syro-Phoenician sun god Elah-Gabal, of whom he was a hereditary priest. He became notorious for his dissipated lifestyle and neglect of state affairs; he and his mother were both murdered.

heliogram ▶ **noun** a message sent by reflecting sunlight in flashes from a movable mirror.

heliograph ▶ **noun 1** a signalling device by which sunlight is reflected in flashes from a movable mirror. ■ a message sent by heliograph; a heliogram. **2** a telescopic apparatus for photographing the sun. **3** historical a type of early photographic engraving made using a sensitized silver plate and an asphalt or bitumen varnish.
▶ **verb** [with obj.] **1** send (a message) by heliograph. **2** historical take a heliographic photograph of.
– DERIVATIVES **heliographic** adjective, **heliography** noun.

heliogravure /ˌhiːlɪəɡrəˈvjʊə, ˌhiːlɪəʊɡrəˈvjɔː/ ▶ **noun** another term for PHOTOGRAVURE.

heliometer /ˌhiːlɪˈɒmɪtə/ ▶ **noun** Astronomy a refracting telescope with a split objective lens, used for finding the angular distance between two stars.
– ORIGIN mid 18th cent.: from HELIO- 'of the sun' + -METER (because it was originally used for measuring the diameter of the sun).

heliopause ▶ **noun** Astronomy the boundary of the heliosphere.

Heliopolis /ˌhiːlɪˈɒpəlɪs/ **1** an ancient Egyptian city situated near the apex of the Nile delta at what is now Cairo. It was the original site of the obelisks known as Cleopatra's Needles. **2** ancient Greek name for BAALBEK.
– ORIGIN from Greek *hēlios* 'sun' + *polis* 'city'.

Helios /ˈhiːlɪɒs/ Greek Mythology the sun personified as a god, father of Phaethon. He is generally represented as a charioteer driving daily from east to west across the sky.
– ORIGIN Greek *hēlios* 'sun'.

heliosphere ▶ **noun** Astronomy the region of space, encompassing the solar system, in which the solar wind has a significant influence.
– DERIVATIVES **heliospheric** adjective.

heliostat /ˈhiːlɪə(ʊ)stat/ ▶ **noun** an apparatus containing a movable mirror, used to reflect sunlight in a fixed direction.

heliotherapy ▶ **noun** [mass noun] the therapeutic use of sunlight.

heliotrope /ˈhiːlɪətrəʊp, ˈhɛl-/ ▶ **noun** a plant of the borage family, cultivated for its fragrant purple or blue flowers which are used in perfume. ● Genus *Heliotropium*, family Boraginaceae. ■ [mass noun] a light purple colour, similar to that of heliotrope flowers.
– ORIGIN Old English *eliotropus* (originally applied to various plants whose flowers turn towards the sun), via Latin from Greek *hēliotropion* 'plant turning its flowers to the sun', from *hēlios* 'sun' + *trepein* 'to turn'. The spelling was influenced by French *héliotrope*.

heliotropism /ˌhiːlɪə(ʊ)ˈtrəʊpɪz(ə)m/ ▶ **noun** [mass noun] Botany the directional growth of a plant in response to sunlight. Compare with PHOTOTROPISM. ■ Zoology the tendency of an animal to move towards light.
– DERIVATIVES **heliotropic** adjective.

heliotype ▶ **noun** historical a picture obtained from a sensitized gelatin film exposed to light.

Heliozoa /ˌhiːlɪə(ʊ)ˈzəʊə/ ▶ **plural noun** Zoology a phylum of single-celled aquatic animals that are related to the radiolarians. They have a spherical shell with fine radiating needle-like projections. ● Class Heliozoa, phylum Actinopoda, kingdom Protista.
– ORIGIN modern Latin (plural), from Greek *hēlios* 'sun' + *zōion* 'animal'.

heliozoan Zoology ▶ **noun** a single-celled aquatic animal of the phylum Heliozoa.
▶ **adjective** relating to or denoting heliozoans.

helipad ▶ **noun** a landing and take-off area for helicopters.

heliport ▶ **noun** an airport or landing place for helicopters.

heli-skiing ▶ **noun** [mass noun] skiing in which the skier is taken up the mountain by helicopter.
– DERIVATIVES **heli-ski** verb.

helium /ˈhiːlɪəm/ ▶ **noun** [mass noun] the chemical element of atomic number 2, an inert gas which is the lightest member of the noble gas series. (Symbol: **He**)

> Helium occurs in traces in air, and more abundantly in natural gas deposits. It is used as a lifting gas for balloons and airships, and liquid helium (boiling point: 4.2 kelvins, −268.9°C) is used as a coolant. Helium is produced in stars as the main product of the thermonuclear fusion of hydrogen, and is the second most abundant element in the universe after hydrogen.

– ORIGIN late 19th cent.: modern Latin, from Greek *hēlios* 'sun', because its existence was inferred from an emission line in the sun's spectrum.

helix /ˈhiːlɪks/ ▶ **noun** (pl. **helices** /ˈhiːlɪsiːz, ˈhɛl-/) **1** an object having a three-dimensional shape like that of a wire wound uniformly in a single layer around a cylinder or cone, as in a corkscrew or spiral staircase. ■ Geometry a curve on a conical or cylindrical surface which would become a straight line if the surface were unrolled into a plane. ■ Biochemistry an extended spiral chain of atoms in a protein, nucleic acid, or other polymeric molecule. ■ Architecture a spiral ornament. **2** Anatomy the rim of the external ear.
– ORIGIN mid 16th cent. (in the architectural sense 'spiral ornament'): via Latin from Greek.

hell ▶ **noun** (often **Hell**) a place regarded in various religions as a spiritual realm of evil and suffering, often traditionally depicted as a place of perpetual fire beneath the earth where the wicked are punished after death. ■ a situation, experience, or place of great suffering: *I've been through hell* | *he made her life hell*.
▶ **exclamation** (also **the hell**) used for emphasis or to express anger, contempt, or surprise: *oh, hell—where will this all end?* | *who the hell are you?*
– PHRASES **all hell breaks** (or **is let**) **loose** informal suddenly there is pandemonium. **(as) —— as hell** informal used for emphasis: *he's as guilty as hell*. **be hell on** informal be very unpleasant or harmful to: *the fungus is hell on grasshoppers*. **come hell or high water** whatever difficulties may occur. **for the hell of it** informal just for fun: *she walked on window ledges for the hell of it*. **—— from hell** informal an extremely unpleasant or troublesome example of something: *neighbours from hell*. **get hell** informal be severely reprimanded. **give someone hell** informal severely reprimand or make things very unpleasant for someone. **go to hell** informal used to express angry rejection of someone or something. **go to** (or **through**) **hell and back** endure an extremely unpleasant or difficult experience. **go to hell in a handbasket** N. Amer. informal deteriorate rapidly. **hell for leather** as fast as possible. **hell's bells** informal an exclamation of annoyance or anger. **hell hath no fury like a woman scorned** proverb a woman who has been rejected by a man can be ferociously angry and vindictive. **a** (or **one**) **hell of a ——** informal used to emphasize something very bad or great: *the car cost a hell of a lot of money*. **—— the hell out of** informal used in verbal phrases to emphasize force, speed, etc.: *let's get the hell out of here*. **hell's half acre** N. Amer. a great distance. **like hell** informal **1** very fast, much, hard, etc. (used for emphasis): *my head hurts like hell*. **2** used in ironic expressions of scorn or disagreement: *like hell, he thought*. **not a hope in hell** informal no chance at all. **play hell** (or **merry hell**) Brit. informal create havoc. ■ cause damage: *the rough road played hell with the tyres*. **the road to hell is paved with good intentions** proverb promises and plans must be put into action, otherwise they are useless. **there will be hell to pay** informal serious trouble will occur as a result of a previous or proposed action. **to hell** used for emphasis: *damn it to hell*. **to hell with** informal expressing one's scorn or lack of concern for (someone or something). **until** (or **till**) **hell freezes over** forever. **what the hell** informal it doesn't matter.
– DERIVATIVES **hellward** adverb & adjective.
– ORIGIN Old English *hel*, *hell*, of Germanic origin; related to Dutch *hel* and German *Hölle*, from an Indo-European root meaning 'to cover or hide'.

he'll ▶ **contraction** he shall; he will.

hellacious /hɛˈleɪʃəs/ ▶ **adjective** N. Amer. informal very great, bad, or overwhelming: *there was this hellacious hailstorm*.
– DERIVATIVES **hellaciously** adverb.
– ORIGIN 1930s: from HELL + -ACIOUS, perhaps suggested by *bodacious*.

Helladic /hɛˈladɪk/ ▶ **adjective** Archaeology relating to or denoting the Bronze Age cultures of mainland Greece (*c.*3000–1050 BC), of which the latest period is equivalent to the Mycenaean age.
– ORIGIN early 19th cent.: from Greek *Helladikos*, from *Hellas*, *Hellad-* 'Greece'.

Hellas /ˈhɛlas/ Greek name for GREECE.

hellbender ▶ **noun** an aquatic giant salamander with greyish skin and a flattened head, native to North America. ● *Cryptobranchus alleganiensis*, family Cryptobranchidae.

hell-bent ▶ **adjective** [predic.] determined to achieve something at all costs: *she's hell-bent on leaving*.

hellcat ▶ **noun** a spiteful, violent woman.

hellebore /ˈhɛlɪbɔː/ ▶ **noun** a poisonous winter-flowering Eurasian plant of the buttercup family, typically having coarse divided leaves and large white, green, or purplish flowers. ● Genus *Helleborus*, family Ranunculaceae: several species, including the Christmas rose. ■ a false helleborine.
– ORIGIN Old English (denoting various plants supposed to cure madness), from Old French *ellebre*, *elebore* or medieval Latin *eleborus*, via Latin from Greek *helleboros*.

helleborine /ˈhɛlɪbəˌriːn, -ˌrʌɪn/ ▶ **noun** a mainly woodland orchid occurring chiefly in north temperate regions. See also FALSE HELLEBORINE. ● Two genera in the family Orchidaceae: *Epipactis* (with greenish or reddish flowers that are sometimes self-fertilized) and *Cephalanthera* (with larger white or pink flowers).
– ORIGIN late 16th cent.: French or Latin, from Greek *helleborinē*, a plant like hellebore, from *helleboros* 'hellebore'.

Hellen /ˈhɛlɪn/ Greek Mythology the son or brother of Deucalion and ancestor of all the Hellenes or Greeks.

Hellene /ˈhɛliːn/ ▶ **noun** an ancient Greek. ■ a native of modern Greece (chiefly in the title of the exiled royal family): *the King of the Hellenes*.
– ORIGIN from Greek *Hellēn* 'a Greek'. Compare with HELLEN.

Hellenic /hɛˈlɛnɪk, -ˈliːnɪk/ ▶ **adjective** Greek. ■ Archaeology relating to or denoting Iron Age and Classical Greek culture (between Helladic and Hellenistic).
▶ **noun** [mass noun] the branch of the Indo-European language family comprising classical and modern Greek. ■ the Greek language.

H

– ORIGIN from Greek *Hellēnikos*, from *Hellēn* (see **HELLENE**).

Hellenism /ˈhɛlɪnɪz(ə)m/ ▸ **noun** [mass noun] the national character or culture of Greece, especially ancient Greece. ■ the study or imitation of ancient Greek culture.
– DERIVATIVES **Hellenist** noun.
– ORIGIN early 17th cent. (denoting a Greek phrase or idiom): from Greek *Hellēnismos*, from *Hellēnizein* 'speak Greek, make Greek', from *Hellēn* 'a Greek'.

Hellenistic ▸ **adjective** relating to Greek history, language, and culture from the death of Alexander the Great to the defeat of Cleopatra and Mark Antony by Octavian in 31 BC. During this period Greek culture flourished, spreading through the Mediterranean and into the Near East and Asia and centring on Alexandria in Egypt and Pergamum in Turkey.

Hellenize /ˈhɛlɪnʌɪz/ (also **Hellenise**) ▸ **verb** [with obj.] (often as adj. **Hellenized**) make Greek or Hellenistic in form or character.
– DERIVATIVES **Hellenization** noun, **Hellenizer** noun.

Heller, Joseph (1923–99), American novelist. His experiences in the US air force during the Second World War inspired his best-known novel *Catch-22* (1961), an absurdist black comedy satirizing war and the source of the expression 'catch-22'.

heller /ˈhɛlə/ ▸ **noun** (pl. **same** or **hellers**) a former German or Austrian coin of low value. ■ another term for **HALER** or **HALIER**.
– ORIGIN from German *Heller*, earlier *haller* (see **HALER**).

Hellerwork /ˈhɛləwəːk/ ▸ **noun** [mass noun] (trademark in the US) a system involving deep tissue massage and exercise, designed to help correct posture, improve mobility, relieve pain, etc.
– ORIGIN 1980s: named after Joseph Heller (b. 1940), the US educator who developed it.

Hellespont /ˈhɛlɪspɒnt/ the ancient name for the Dardanelles, named after the legendary Helle, who fell into the strait and was drowned while escaping with her brother Phrixus from their stepmother, Ino, on a golden-fleeced ram.

hellfire ▸ **noun** [mass noun] the fire or fires regarded as existing in hell: *threats of hellfire and damnation*.

hellgrammite /ˈhɛlgrəmʌɪt/ ▸ **noun** N. Amer. the aquatic larva of a dobsonfly, often used as fishing bait.
– ORIGIN mid 19th cent.: of unknown origin.

hellhole ▸ **noun** a very unpleasant place.

hellhound ▸ **noun** a demon in the form of a dog.

hellion /ˈhɛljən/ ▸ **noun** N. Amer. informal a rowdy or mischievous person, especially a child.
– ORIGIN mid 19th cent.: perhaps from dialect *hallion* 'a worthless fellow', changed by association with **HELL**.

hellish ▸ **adjective** of or like hell: *an unearthly, hellish landscape*. ■ informal extremely difficult or unpleasant: *it had been a hellish week*.
▸ **adverb** [as submodifier] Brit. informal extremely (used for emphasis): *it was hellish expensive*.
– DERIVATIVES **hellishly** adverb, **hellishness** noun.

Hellman /ˈhɛlmən/, Lillian (Florence) (1907–84), American dramatist. Her plays, such as *The Children's Hour* (1934) and *The Little Foxes* (1939), often reflected her socialist and feminist concerns. She lived with the detective-story writer Dashiell Hammett, and both were blacklisted during the McCarthy era.

hello (also **hallo** or **hullo**) ▸ **exclamation** used as a greeting or to begin a telephone conversation: *hello there, Katie!* ■ Brit. used to express surprise: *hello, what's all this then?* ■ used as a cry to attract someone's attention: *'Hello below!' he cried*. ■ used informally to express sarcasm or anger: *Hello! Did you even get what the play was about?*
▸ **noun** (pl. **hellos**) an utterance of 'hello'; a greeting.
▸ **verb** (**helloes, helloing, helloed**) [no obj.] say or shout 'hello'.
– ORIGIN late 19th cent.: variant of earlier *hollo*; related to **HOLLA**.

hellraiser ▸ **noun** a person who causes trouble by drinking, being violent, or otherwise behaving outrageously.
– DERIVATIVES **hellraising** adjective & noun.

Hell's Angel ▸ **noun** a member of any of a number of gangs ('chapters') of male motorcycle enthusiasts, first formed in California in the 1950s and originally notorious for lawless behaviour.

Hell's Canyon a chasm in Idaho, cut by the Snake River and forming the deepest gorge in the US. Flanked by the Seven Devils Mountains, the canyon drops to a depth of 2,433 m (7,900 ft).

helluva ▸ **contraction** a hell of a (representing a non-standard pronunciation): *I'm in a helluva mess*.

helm[1] ▸ **noun** (**the helm**) a tiller or wheel for steering a ship or boat. ■ a position of leadership: *the chairman is to step down after four years* ***at the helm***. ■ Nautical a helmsman.
▸ **verb** [with obj.] steer (a boat or ship). ■ manage (an organization): *the magazine he helmed in the late eighties*. ■ chiefly N. Amer. direct (a film).
– DERIVATIVES **helmer** noun (chiefly N. Amer.).
– ORIGIN Old English *helma*; probably related to **HELVE**.

> **WORD TRENDS** Most of us still think of **helm** as primarily a nautical word, but according to the Oxford English Corpus the verb is now primarily a cinematic one. The sense 'direct a film', which dates from 1930, is dominant, with the commonest objects being *film* and *movie*. *Ship* comes in at number three, but is then followed by a long sequence of words such as *comedy*, *remake*, *adaptation*, and *thriller*.

helm[2] ▸ **noun** archaic a helmet.
– DERIVATIVES **helmed** adjective.
– ORIGIN Old English, of Germanic origin; related to Dutch *helm* and German *Helm*, also to **HELMET**, from an Indo-European root meaning 'to cover or hide'.

Helmand /ˈhɛlmənd/ the longest river in Afghanistan. Rising in the Hindu Kush, it flows 1,125 km (700 miles), generally south-west, before emptying into marshland near the Iran–Afghanistan frontier. ■ a province in SW Afghanistan.

helmet ▸ **noun** **1** a hard or padded protective hat, various types of which are worn by soldiers, police officers, motorcyclists, sports players, and others.
2 Botany the arched upper part (galea) of the corolla in some flowers, especially those of the mint and orchid families.
3 (also **helmet shell**) a predatory mollusc with a squat heavy shell, which lives in tropical and temperate seas. ● Family Cassidae, class Gastropoda.
– DERIVATIVES **helmeted** adjective.
– ORIGIN late Middle English: from Old French, diminutive of *helme*, of Germanic origin; related to **HELM**[2].

helminth /ˈhɛlmɪnθ/ ▸ **noun** a parasitic worm; a fluke, tapeworm, or nematode.
– DERIVATIVES **helminthic** adjective.
– ORIGIN mid 19th cent.: from Greek *helmins*, *helminth-* 'intestinal worm'.

helminthiasis /ˌhɛlmɪnˈθʌɪəsɪs/ ▸ **noun** [mass noun] Medicine infestation with parasitic worms.

helminthology /ˌhɛlmɪnˈθɒlədʒi/ ▸ **noun** [mass noun] the study of parasitic worms.
– DERIVATIVES **helminthologist** noun.

Helmont /ˈhɛlmɒnt/, Joannes Baptista van (1577–1644), Belgian chemist and physician. He made early studies on the conservation of matter, was the first to distinguish gases, and coined the word *gas*.

helmsman ▸ **noun** (pl. **helmsmen**) a person who steers a ship or boat.

Héloïse /ˈɛləʊiːz/ (1098–1164), French abbess. She is known for her tragic love affair with the theologian Abelard, which began after she became his pupil. When the affair came to light, Abelard persuaded her to enter a convent; she later became abbess of the community of Paraclete. See also **ABELARD**.

helot /ˈhɛlət/ ▸ **noun** a member of a class of serfs in ancient Sparta, intermediate in status between slaves and citizens. ■ a serf or slave.
– DERIVATIVES **helotage** noun, **helotism** noun, **helotry** noun.
– ORIGIN via Latin from Greek *Heilōtes* (plural), traditionally taken as referring to *Helos*, a Laconian town whose inhabitants were enslaved.

help ▸ **verb** [with obj.] **1** make it easier or possible for (someone) to do something by offering them one's services or resources: *they helped her with domestic chores* | [with obj. and infinitive] *she helped him find a buyer* | [no obj.] *the teenager* ***helped out*** *in the corner shop*. ■ improve (a situation or problem); be of benefit to: *upbeat comments about prospects helped confidence* | [no obj.] *legislation to fit all new cars with catalytic converters will help*. ■ [with obj. and adverbial of direction] assist (someone) to move: *I helped her up*. ■ (**help someone on/off with**) assist someone to put on or take off (a garment).
2 (**help someone to**) serve someone with (food or drink): *may I help you to some more meat?* | *she* ***helped herself*** *to a biscuit*. ■ (**help oneself**) take something without permission: *he* ***helped himself to*** *the wages she had brought home*.
3 (**can/could not help**) cannot or could not avoid: *he couldn't help laughing* | *I'm sorry to put you to any inconvenience, but it can't be helped*. ■ (**can/could not help oneself**) cannot or could not stop oneself from doing something: *she couldn't help herself; she burst into tears*.
▸ **noun** [mass noun] the action of helping someone to do something: *I asked for help from my neighbours*. ■ the fact of being useful: *the skimpy manual isn't much help for beginners*. ■ a person or thing that helps: *she's been given financial help with travel* | [in sing.] *he was a great help*. ■ [count noun] a domestic employee. ■ [as modifier] giving assistance to a computer user in the form of displayed instructions: *a help menu*.
▸ **exclamation** used as an appeal for urgent assistance: *Help! I'm drowning!*
– PHRASES **a helping hand** assistance: *she was always ready to lend a helping hand*. **so help me** (**God**) used to emphasize that one means what one is saying. **there is no help for it** there is no way of avoiding or remedying a situation.
– ORIGIN Old English *helpan* (verb), *help* (noun), of Germanic origin; related to Dutch *helpen* and German *helfen*.

help desk ▸ **noun** a service providing information and support to computer users, especially within a company.

helper ▸ **noun** a person who helps someone else: *there was no shortage of willing helpers*.

helper cell ▸ **noun** Physiology a T-lymphocyte that influences or controls the differentiation or activity of other cells of the immune system.

helpful ▸ **adjective** giving or ready to give help: *people are friendly and helpful* | *helpful staff*. ■ useful: *pages of helpful information*.
– DERIVATIVES **helpfully** adverb, **helpfulness** noun.

helping ▸ **noun** a portion of food served to one person at one time: *there will be enough for six helpings*. ■ a quantity of something: *it's a powerful ballad tinged with a huge helping of gospel vibes*.

helpless ▸ **adjective** unable to defend oneself or to act without help: *the cubs are born blind and helpless*. ■ uncontrollable: *they burst into helpless laughter*.
– DERIVATIVES **helplessly** adverb, **helplessness** noun.

helpline ▸ **noun** a telephone service providing help with problems.

Helpmann /ˈhɛlpmən/, Sir Robert (Murray) (1909–86), Australian ballet dancer, choreographer, director, and actor. He joined the Vic-Wells Ballet shortly after coming to England in 1933, and in 1935 began a long partnership with Margot Fonteyn.

helpmate (also **helpmeet**) ▸ **noun** a helpful companion or partner, especially one's husband or wife.
– ORIGIN late 17th cent. (as *helpmeet*): from an erroneous reading of Gen. 2:18, 20, where Adam's future wife is described as 'an help meet for him' (i.e. a suitable helper for him). The variant *helpmate* came into use in the early 18th cent.

Helsingborg /ˈhɛlsɪŋbɔːg/ a port in southern Sweden, situated on the Øresund opposite Elsinore in Denmark; pop. 126,754 (2008). Swedish name **HÄLSINGBORG**.

Helsingør /ˌhɛlsɛŋˈøːr/ Danish name for **ELSINORE**.

Helsinki /ˈhɛlsɪŋki, hɛlˈsɪŋki/ the capital of Finland, a port in the south on the Gulf of Finland; pop. 579,504 (2009). Swedish name **Helsingfors** /ˌhɛlsɪŋˈfɔrs/.

helter-skelter ▸ **adjective & adverb** in disorderly haste or confusion: [as adj.] *the helter-skelter dash to unity* | [as adv.] *hurtling helter-skelter down the pavement*.
▸ **noun** **1** Brit. a fairground amusement consisting of a tall spiral slide winding around a tower.
2 [in sing.] disorder; confusion: *the helter-skelter of a school day*.
– ORIGIN late 16th cent. (as an adverb): a rhyming jingle of unknown origin, perhaps symbolic of running feet or from Middle English *skelte* 'hasten'.

helve /hɛlv/ ▸ **noun** the handle of a weapon or tool.
– ORIGIN Old English *helfe*, of Germanic origin; related to **HALTER**.

Helvetia /hɛlˈviːʃə/ Latin name for **SWITZERLAND**.

Helvetian /hɛlˈviːʃ(ə)n/ chiefly historical ▸ **adjective** Swiss.
▸ **noun** a native of Switzerland.

Helvetic /hɛlˈvɛtɪk/ ▸ **adjective & noun** another term for **HELVETIAN**.

hem[1] ▸ **noun** the edge of a piece of cloth or clothing which has been turned under and sewn.

▸ **verb** (**hems, hemming, hemmed**) [with obj.] **1** turn under and sew the edge of (a piece of cloth).
2 (**hem someone/thing in**) surround and restrict the space or movement of someone or something: *he was hemmed in by the tables.*
– ORIGIN Old English 'border of a piece of cloth', of West Germanic origin. The verb senses date from the mid 16th cent.

hem² ▸ **exclamation** used in writing to indicate a sound made when coughing or clearing the throat to attract attention or to express hesitation.
▸ **verb** (**hems, hemming, hemmed**) [no obj.] archaic make a sound in the throat when hesitating or as a signal.
– PHRASES **hem and haw** North American term for HUM AND HAW (see HUM¹).
– ORIGIN late 15th cent.: imitative.

hemagglutination etc. ▸ **noun** US spelling of HAEMAGGLUTINATION etc.

he-man ▸ **noun** informal a well-built, muscular man.

hemato- ▸ **combining form** US spelling of HAEMATO-.

heme ▸ **noun** US spelling of HAEM.

Hemel Hempstead /ˌhɛm(ə)l ˈhɛmpstɪd/ a town in SE England, in Hertfordshire; pop. 80,500 (est. 2009). It was designated as a new town in 1947.

hemerocallis /ˌhɛm(ə)rə(ʊ)ˈkalɪs/ ▸ **noun** (pl. **same**) a plant of a genus that comprises the day lilies. ● Genus *Hemerocallis*, family Liliaceae.
– ORIGIN modern Latin, from Greek *hēmerokallis* 'a lily that flowers for a day', from *hēmera* 'day' + *kallos* 'beauty'.

hemi- ▸ **prefix** half: *hemicylindrical* | *hemiplegia.*
– ORIGIN from Greek *hēmi-*; related to Latin *semi-*.

-hemia ▸ **combining form** US spelling of -AEMIA.

hemianopia /ˌhɛmɪəˈnəʊpɪə/ (also **hemianopsia** /-ˈnɒpsɪə/) ▸ **noun** [mass noun] blindness over half the field of vision.

hemicellulose ▸ **noun** Biochemistry any of a class of substances which occur as constituents of the cell walls of plants and are polysaccharides of simpler structure than cellulose.
– ORIGIN late 19th cent.: coined in German from HEMI- + CELLULOSE.

Hemichordata /ˌhɛmɪkɔːˈdeɪtə/ ▸ **plural noun** Zoology a small phylum of marine invertebrates that comprises the acorn worms.
– ORIGIN modern Latin (see HEMI-, CHORDATA).

hemichordate Zoology ▸ **noun** a marine invertebrate of the phylum Hemichordata; an acorn worm.
▸ **adjective** relating to or denoting hemichordates.

hemicycle ▸ **noun** a semicircular shape or structure.

hemicylindrical ▸ **adjective** having the shape of half a cylinder (divided lengthways).

hemidemisemiquaver /ˌhɛmɪdɛmɪˈsɛmɪkweɪvə/ ▸ **noun** Music, chiefly Brit. a note with the time value of half a demisemiquaver, represented by a large dot with a four-hooked stem. Also called SIXTY-FOURTH NOTE.

hemihydrate /ˌhɛmɪˈhʌɪdreɪt/ ▸ **noun** Chemistry a crystalline hydrate containing one molecule of water for every two molecules of the compound in question.

hemimetabolous /ˌhɛmɪmɛˈtabələs/ ▸ **adjective** Entomology (of an insect) having no pupal stage in the transition from larva to adult.

hemimorphite /ˌhɛmɪˈmɔːfʌɪt/ ▸ **noun** [mass noun] a mineral consisting of hydrated zinc silicate, typically occurring as flat white prisms.

Hemingway, Ernest (Miller) (1899–1961), American novelist, short-story writer, and journalist. He achieved success with *The Sun Also Rises* (1926), which reflected the disillusionment of the post-war 'lost generation'. Other notable works: *A Farewell to Arms* (1929), *For Whom the Bell Tolls* (1940), and *The Old Man and the Sea* (1952, Pulitzer Prize 1953). Nobel Prize for Literature (1954).

hemiola /ˌhɛmɪˈəʊlə/ ▸ **noun** Music a musical figure in which, typically, two groups of three beats are replaced by three groups of two beats, giving the effect of a shift between triple and duple metre.
– ORIGIN late Middle English: via medieval Latin from Greek *hēmiolia* 'in the ratio of one and a half to one' (from *hēmi-* 'half' + *holos* 'whole').

hemiparasite ▸ **noun** Botany a plant which obtains or may obtain part of its food by parasitism, e.g. mistletoe, which also photosynthesizes.

hemiparesis /ˌhɛmɪpəˈriːsɪs/ ▸ **noun** another term for HEMIPLEGIA.

hemipenis /ˈhɛmɪpiːnɪs/ ▸ **noun** (pl. **hemipenes**) Zoology each of the paired male reproductive organs in snakes and lizards.

hemiplegia /ˌhɛmɪˈpliːdʒə/ ▸ **noun** [mass noun] Medicine paralysis of one side of the body.
– DERIVATIVES **hemiplegic** noun & adjective.
– ORIGIN early 17th cent.: modern Latin, from Greek *hēmiplēgia*, from *hemi-* 'half' + *plēgē* 'stroke'.

hemipode /ˈhɛmɪpəʊd/ ▸ **noun** another term for BUTTON-QUAIL.
– ORIGIN mid 19th cent.: from modern Latin *Hemipodius* (former genus name), from Greek *hēmi-* 'half' + *pous, pod-* 'foot'.

Hemiptera /hɛˈmɪpt(ə)rə/ ▸ **plural noun** Entomology a large order of insects that comprises the true bugs, which include aphids, cicadas, leafhoppers, and many others. They have piercing and sucking mouthparts and incomplete metamorphosis. See also HETEROPTERA, HOMOPTERA. ■ (**hemiptera**) insects of this order; true bugs.
– ORIGIN modern Latin (plural), from Greek *hēmi-* 'half' + *pteron* 'wing' (because of the forewing structure, partly hardened at the base and partly membranous).

hemipteran Entomology ▸ **noun** an insect of the order Hemiptera or bugs, such as an aphid, cicada, or leafhopper.
▸ **adjective** relating to or denoting hemipterans.
– DERIVATIVES **hemipterous** adjective.

hemisphere ▸ **noun** a half of a sphere. ■ a half of the earth, usually as divided into northern and southern halves by the equator, or into western and eastern halves by an imaginary line passing through the poles. ■ a half of the celestial sphere. ■ (also **cerebral hemisphere**) each of the two parts of the cerebrum (left and right) in the brain of a vertebrate.
– DERIVATIVES **hemispheric** adjective, **hemispherical** adjective, **hemispherically** adverb.
– ORIGIN late Middle English (in the sense 'half the celestial sphere, the sky'): from Old French *emisphere*, via Latin from Greek *hēmisphairion*, from *hēmi-* 'half' + *sphaira* 'sphere'.

hemistich /ˈhɛmɪstɪk/ ▸ **noun** (chiefly in Old English verse) a half of a line of verse.
– ORIGIN late 16th cent.: via late Latin from Greek *hēmistikhion*, from *hēmi-* 'half' + *stikhos* 'row, line of verse'.

Hemkund, Lake /hɛmˈkʊnd/ a lake in northern India, in the Himalayan foothills of Uttar Pradesh. It is regarded as holy by the Sikhs.

hemline ▸ **noun** the level of the lower edge of a garment such as a skirt, dress, or coat.

hemlock ▸ **noun 1** a highly poisonous European plant of the parsley family, with a purple-spotted stem, fern-like leaves, small white flowers, and an unpleasant smell. ● *Conium maculatum*, family Umbelliferae.
■ [mass noun] a sedative or poisonous potion obtained from the hemlock.
2 (also **hemlock fir** or **spruce**) a coniferous North American tree with dark green foliage which is said to smell like hemlock when crushed, grown chiefly for timber. ● Genus *Tsuga*, family Pinaceae: several species.
– ORIGIN Old English *hymlice, hemlic*, of unknown origin.

hemo- ▸ **combining form** US spelling of HAEMO-.

hemp ▸ **noun** (also **Indian hemp**) [mass noun] the cannabis plant, especially when grown for fibre. ■ the fibre of the cannabis plant, extracted from the stem and used to make rope, strong fabrics, fibreboard, and paper. ■ used in names of other plants that yield fibre, e.g. **Manila hemp**. ■ the drug cannabis.
– DERIVATIVES **hempen** adjective (archaic).
– ORIGIN Old English *henep, hænep*, of Germanic origin; related to Dutch *hennep* and German *Hanf*, also to Greek *kannabis*.

hemp agrimony ▸ **noun** an erect Eurasian plant of the daisy family, resembling a valerian, with clusters of pale purple flowers and hairy stems. ● *Eupatorium cannabinum*, family Compositae.

hemp-nettle ▸ **noun** a nettle-like Eurasian plant of the mint family. ● Genus *Galeopsis*, family Labiatae.

hempseed /ˈhɛmpsiːd/ ▸ **noun** [mass noun] the seed of hemp, particularly as used for fishing bait.

hemstitch ▸ **noun** a decorative stitch used especially alongside a hem, in which several adjacent threads are pulled out and the crossing threads are tied into bunches, making a row of small openings.
▸ **verb** [with obj.] incorporate a hemstitch in the hem of (a piece of cloth or clothing).

hen ▸ **noun 1** a female bird, especially of a domestic fowl. ■ (**hens**) domestic fowls of either sex. ■ used in names of birds, especially waterbirds of the rail family, e.g. **moorhen, native hen**. ■ Scottish used as an affectionate term of address to a girl or woman.
2 a female lobster, crab, or salmon.
– PHRASES **as rare** (or **scarce**) **as hen's teeth** extremely rare.
– ORIGIN Old English *henn*, of Germanic origin; related to Dutch *hen* and German *Henne*.

Henan /həˈnan/ (also **Honan**) a province of NE central China; capital, Zhengzhou.

hen and chickens ▸ **noun** any of a number of plants producing additional small flower heads or offshoots. ● Several species, especially the houseleek *Jovibarba sobilifera* (family Crassulaceae).

henbane /ˈhɛnbeɪn/ ▸ **noun** a poisonous Eurasian plant of the nightshade family, with sticky hairy leaves and an unpleasant smell. ● *Hyoscyamus niger*, family Solanaceae.
■ [mass noun] a narcotic drink prepared from henbane.

henbit /ˈhɛnbɪt/ ▸ **noun** a dead-nettle with purple flowers and partly prostrate stems, native to Eurasia. ● Genus *Lamium*, family Labiatae: several species, in particular *L. amplexicaule*.
– ORIGIN late 16th cent.: apparently a translation of Low German or Dutch *hoenderbeet*.

hence ▸ **adverb 1** as a consequence; for this reason: *many vehicle journeys (and hence a lot of pollution) would be saved.*
2 from now (used after a period of time): *two years hence they might say something different.*
3 (also **from hence**) archaic from here: *hence, be gone.*
– ORIGIN Middle English *hennes* (in sense 3): from earlier *henne* (from Old English *heonan*, of Germanic origin, related to HE) + -S³ (later respelled *-ce* to denote the unvoiced sound).

henceforth (also **henceforward**) ▸ **adverb** from this or that time on: *henceforth, parties which fail to get 5% of the vote will not be represented in parliament.*

henchman ▸ **noun** (pl. **henchmen**) chiefly derogatory a faithful follower or political supporter, especially one prepared to engage in crime or violence by way of service. ■ historical a squire or page of honour to a person of rank. ■ (in Scotland) the principal attendant of a Highland chief.
– ORIGIN Middle English, from Old English *hengest* 'male horse' + MAN, the original sense being probably 'groom'. In the mid 19th cent. the sense 'principal attendant of a Highland chief' was popularized by Sir Walter Scott, whence the current (originally US) usage.

hendeca- /ˈhɛndɛkə, hɛnˈdɛkə/ ▸ **combining form** eleven; having eleven: *hendecasyllable.*
– ORIGIN from Greek *hendeka* 'eleven'.

hendecagon /hɛnˈdɛkəg(ə)n/ ▸ **noun** a plane figure with eleven straight sides and angles.
– DERIVATIVES **hendecagonal** /ˌhɛndɪˈkag(ə)n(ə)l/ adjective.
– ORIGIN early 18th cent.: from HENDECA- 'eleven' + -GON, on the pattern of words such as *polygon*.

hendecasyllable /ˌhɛndɛkəˈsɪləbəl/ ▸ **noun** Prosody a line of verse containing eleven syllables.
– DERIVATIVES **hendecasyllabic** adjective.

hendiadys /hɛnˈdʌɪədɪs/ ▸ **noun** [mass noun] the expression of a single idea by two words connected with 'and', e.g. *nice and warm*, when one could be used to modify the other, as in *nicely warm*.
– ORIGIN late 16th cent.: via medieval Latin from Greek *hen dia duoin* 'one thing by two'.

Hendrix, Jimi (1942–70), American rock guitarist and singer; full name *James Marshall Hendrix*. Remembered for the flamboyance and originality of his improvisations, he greatly widened the scope of the electric guitar. Notable songs: 'Purple Haze' (1967), 'All Along the Watchtower' (1968).

henequen /ˈhɛnɪkɛn/ ▸ **noun** [mass noun] **1** a fibre resembling sisal, which is chiefly used for binder twine and paper pulp.
2 a Central American agave from which henequen is obtained. ● *Agave fourcroydes*, family Agavaceae.
– ORIGIN early 17th cent.: from Spanish *jeniquen*, from a local word.

henge /hɛn(d)ʒ/ ▸ **noun** a prehistoric monument consisting of a circle of stone or wooden uprights.
– ORIGIN mid 18th cent.: back-formation from STONEHENGE.

Hengist and Horsa /ˈhɛŋgɪst, ˈhɔːsə/ (d.488 & d.455), semi-mythological Jutish leaders. According to Bede the brothers were invited to Britain by the

H

British king Vortigern in 449 to assist in defeating the Picts and later established an independent Anglo-Saxon kingdom in Kent.

hen harrier ▶ **noun** a widespread harrier of open country, the male of which is mainly pale grey and the female brown. ● *Circus cyaneus*, family Accipitridae. North American name: **marsh hawk, northern harrier**.
– ORIGIN mid 16th cent.: so named because it was believed to prey on poultry.

henhouse ▶ **noun** a small shed for keeping poultry in.

Henle's loop ▶ **noun** another term for LOOP OF HENLE.

henley ▶ **noun** a style of casual top with a scoop neck and a short row of buttons in the centre of the neckline.
– ORIGIN late 19th cent.: originally a style associated with the Henley Royal Regatta.

Henley Royal Regatta the oldest rowing regatta in Europe, inaugurated in 1839 at Henley-on-Thames, Oxfordshire, and held annually in the first week in July.

henna ▶ **noun** [mass noun] **1** a reddish-brown dye made from the powdered leaves of a tropical shrub, used to colour the hair and decorate the body.
2 the Old World shrub which produces henna, with small pink, red, or white flowers. ● *Lawsonia inermis*, family Lythraceae.
▶ **verb** (**hennas, hennaing, hennaed**) [with obj.] dye (hair) with henna.
– ORIGIN early 17th cent.: from Arabic *ḥinnā'*.

hen night ▶ **noun** Brit. informal a celebration held for a woman who is about to get married, attended only by women.

henotheism /ˈhɛnəʊ,θiːɪz(ə)m/ ▶ **noun** [mass noun] adherence to one particular god out of several, especially by a family, tribe, or other group.
– ORIGIN mid 19th cent.: from Greek *heis, henos* 'one' + *theos* 'god' + -ISM.

hen party ▶ **noun** informal a social gathering of women, especially a hen night.

henpeck ▶ **verb** [with obj.] (usu. as adj. **henpecked**) (of a woman) continually criticize and order about (her husband or other male partner): *henpecked husbands*.

Henri /ˈhɛnri/, Robert (1865–1929), American painter. An advocate of realism, he believed that the artist must be a social force. The Ashcan School of painters was formed largely as a result of his influence.

Henrician /hɛnˈrɪʃ(ə)n/ ▶ **adjective** relating to the reign and policies of Henry VIII of England.

Henrietta Maria (1609–69), daughter of Henry IV of France, queen consort of Charles I of England 1625–49. Her Roman Catholicism heightened public anxieties about the court's religious sympathies and was a contributory cause of the English Civil War.

Henry[1] the name of eight kings of England: ■ **Henry I** (1068–1135), youngest son of William I, reigned 1100–35. His only son drowned in 1120, and although Henry extracted an oath of loyalty to his daughter Matilda from the barons in 1127, his death was followed almost immediately by the outbreak of civil war. ■ **Henry II** (1133–89), son of Matilda, reigned 1154–89. The first Plantagenet king, he restored order after the reigns of Stephen and Matilda. Opposition to his policies on reducing the power of the Church was led by Thomas à Becket, who was eventually murdered by four of Henry's knights. ■ **Henry III** (1207–72), son of John, reigned 1216–72. His ineffectual government caused widespread discontent, ending in Simon de Montfort's defeat and capture of Henry in 1264. Although he was restored a year later, real power resided with his son, who eventually succeeded him as Edward I. ■ **Henry IV** (1367–1413), son of John of Gaunt, reigned 1399–1413; known as **Henry Bolingbroke**. He overthrew Richard II, establishing the Lancastrian dynasty. His reign was marked by rebellion in Wales and the north, where the Percy family raised several uprisings. ■ **Henry V** (1387–1422), son of Henry IV, reigned 1413–22. He renewed the Hundred Years War soon after coming to the throne and defeated the French at Agincourt in 1415. ■ **Henry VI** (1421–71), son of Henry V, reigned 1422–61 and 1470–1. He was unfit to rule effectively on his own due to a recurrent mental illness. Government by the monarchy became increasingly unpopular and after intermittent civil war with the House of York (the Wars of the Roses), Henry was deposed in 1461 by Edward IV. He briefly regained his throne following a Lancastrian uprising. ■ **Henry VII** (1457–1509), the first Tudor king, son of Edmund Tudor, Earl of Richmond, reigned 1485–1509; known as **Henry Tudor**. Although the grandson of Owen Tudor, he inherited the Lancastrian claim to the throne through his mother, a great-granddaughter of John of Gaunt. He defeated Richard III at Bosworth Field and eventually established an unchallenged Tudor dynasty. ■ **Henry VIII** (1491–1547), son of Henry VII, reigned 1509–47. Henry had six wives (Catherine of Aragon, Anne Boleyn, Jane Seymour, Anne of Cleves, Catherine Howard, Katherine Parr); he executed two and divorced two. His first divorce, from Catherine of Aragon, was opposed by the Pope, leading to England's break with the Roman Catholic Church.

Henry[2] (1394–1460), Portuguese prince; known as **Henry the Navigator**. The third son of John I of Portugal, he organized many voyages of discovery, most notably south along the African coast, thus laying the foundation for Portuguese imperial expansion round Africa to East Asia.

Henry[3] the name of seven kings of the Germans, six of whom were also Holy Roman emperors: ■ **Henry I** (*c.*876–936), reigned 919–36; known as **Henry the Fowler**. He waged war successfully against the Slavs in Brandenburg, the Magyars, and the Danes. ■ **Henry II** (973–1024), reigned 1002–24, Holy Roman emperor 1014–24; also known as **Saint Henry**. ■ **Henry III** (1017–56), reigned 1039–56, Holy Roman emperor 1046–56. He brought stability and prosperity to the empire, defeating the Czechs and fixing the frontier between Austria and Hungary. ■ **Henry IV** (1050–1106), son of Henry III, reigned 1056–1105, Holy Roman emperor 1084–1105. Increasing conflict with Pope Gregory VII led Henry to call a council in 1076 to depose the Pope, who excommunicated Henry. Henry obtained absolution by doing penance before Gregory in 1077 but managed to depose him in 1084. ■ **Henry V** (1086–1125), reigned 1099–1125, Holy Roman emperor 1111–25. ■ **Henry VI** (1165–97), reigned 1169–97, Holy Roman emperor 1191–7. ■ **Henry VII** (*c.*1269/74–1313), reigned 1308–13, Holy Roman emperor 1312–3.

Henry[4], O (1862–1910), American short-story writer; pseudonym of *William Sydney Porter*. Jailed for embezzlement in 1898, he started writing short stories in prison. Collections include *Cabbages and Kings* (1904) and *The Voice of the City* (1908).

henry (abbrev.: **H**) ▶ **noun** (pl. **henries** or **henrys**) Physics the SI unit of inductance, equal to an electromotive force of one volt in a closed circuit with a uniform rate of change of current of one ampere per second.
– ORIGIN late 19th cent.: named after Joseph *Henry* (1797–1878), the American physicist who discovered the phenomenon.

Henry Bolingbroke, Henry IV of England (see HENRY[1]).

Henry IV (1553–1610), king of France 1589–1610; known as **Henry of Navarre**. Although leader of Huguenot forces in the latter stages of the French Wars of Religion, on succeeding the Catholic Henry III he became Catholic himself in order to guarantee peace. He established religious freedom with the Edict of Nantes (1598) and restored order after the prolonged civil war.

Henry's law ▶ **noun** Chemistry a law stating that the mass of a dissolved gas in a given volume of solvent at equilibrium is proportional to the partial pressure of the gas.
– ORIGIN late 19th cent.: named after William *Henry* (1774–1836), English chemist.

Henry the Fowler, Henry I, king of the Germans (see HENRY[3]).

Henry Tudor, Henry VII of England (see HENRY[1]).

hep[1] ▶ **adjective** old-fashioned term for HIP[3].

hep[2] ▶ **noun** archaic or dialect term for HIP[2].

heparin /ˈhɛpərɪn/ ▶ **noun** [mass noun] Biochemistry a compound occurring in the liver and other tissues which inhibits blood coagulation. A sulphur-containing polysaccharide, it is used as an anticoagulant in the treatment of thrombosis.
– ORIGIN early 20th cent.: via late Latin from Greek *hēpar* 'liver' + -IN[1].

heparinize (also **heparinise**) ▶ **verb** [with obj.] add heparin to (blood or a container about to be filled with blood) to prevent it from coagulating.
– DERIVATIVES **heparinization** noun.

hepatic /hɪˈpatɪk/ ▶ **adjective** relating to the liver: *right and left hepatic ducts*.
▶ **noun** Botany less common term for LIVERWORT.
– ORIGIN late Middle English: via Latin from Greek *hēpatikos*, from *hēpar, hēpat-* 'liver'.

hepatica /hɪˈpatɪkə/ ▶ **noun** a plant of the buttercup family, with anemone-like flowers, native to northern temperate regions. ● Genus *Hepatica*, family Ranunculaceae.
– ORIGIN from medieval Latin *hepatica (herba)* 'plant having liver-shaped parts, or one used to treat liver diseases', feminine of *hepaticus* (see HEPATIC).

Hepaticae /hɛˈpatɪkiː/ ▶ **plural noun** Botany a class of lower plants that comprises the liverworts.
– ORIGIN modern Latin (plural), from Greek *hēpar, hēpat-* 'liver'.

hepatic portal vein ▶ **noun** see PORTAL VEIN.

hepatitis /,hɛpəˈtʌɪtɪs/ ▶ **noun** [mass noun] a disease characterized by inflammation of the liver.
– ORIGIN early 18th cent.: modern Latin, from Greek *hēpar, hēpat-* 'liver' + -ITIS.

hepatitis A ▶ **noun** [mass noun] a form of viral hepatitis transmitted in food, causing fever and jaundice.

hepatitis B ▶ **noun** [mass noun] a severe form of viral hepatitis transmitted in infected blood, causing fever, debility, and jaundice.

hepatitis C ▶ **noun** [mass noun] a form of viral hepatitis transmitted in infected blood, causing chronic liver disease.

hepato- /ˈhɛpətəʊ, hɛˈpatə(ʊ)-/ ▶ **combining form** relating to the liver.
– ORIGIN from Greek *hēpar, hēpat-* 'liver'.

hepatocyte /ˈhɛpətəʊsʌɪt, hɛˈpatə(ʊ)-/ ▶ **noun** Physiology a liver cell.

hepatoma /,hɛpəˈtəʊmə/ ▶ **noun** (pl. **hepatomas** or **hepatomata** /-mətə/) Medicine a cancer of the cells of the liver.

hepatomegaly /,hɛpətəʊˈmɛgəli, hɛ,patəʊ-/ ▶ **noun** [mass noun] Medicine abnormal enlargement of the liver.

hepatopancreas /,hɛpətəʊˈpaŋkrɪəs, hɛ,patəʊ-/ ▶ **noun** technical term for DIGESTIVE GLAND.

hepatotoxic /,hɛpətəʊˈtɒksɪk, hɛ,patəʊ-/ ▶ **adjective** damaging or destructive to liver cells.
– DERIVATIVES **hepatotoxicity** noun, **hepatotoxin** noun.

Hepburn[1] /ˈhɛpbəːn/, Audrey (1929–93), British actress, born in Belgium. After pursuing a career as a stage and film actress in England, she moved to Hollywood, where she starred in such films as *Roman Holiday* (1953), for which she won an Oscar, and *My Fair Lady* (1964).

Hepburn[2] /ˈhɛpbəːn/, Katharine (1909–2003), American actress. She starred in a wide range of films, often opposite Spencer Tracy; films include *Woman of the Year* (1942), *The African Queen* (1951), and *On Golden Pond* (1981), for which she won her fourth Oscar.

hepcat ▶ **noun** informal, dated a stylish or fashionable person, especially in the sphere of jazz or popular music.
– ORIGIN 1930s: from HEP[1] + CAT[1].

Hephaestus /hɪˈfiːstəs/ Greek Mythology the god of fire and of craftsmen, son of Zeus and Hera. He was a divine metalworker who was lame as the result of having interfered in a quarrel between his parents. Roman equivalent VULCAN.

Hepplewhite /ˈhɛp(ə)lwʌɪt/, George (d.1786), English cabinetmaker and furniture designer. His designs, which were published posthumously in *The Cabinetmaker and Upholsterer's Guide* (1788), were characterized by light and elegant lines and encapsulate neoclassical taste.

hepta- ▶ **combining form** seven; having seven: *heptagon | heptathlon*.
– ORIGIN from Greek *hepta* 'seven'.

heptachlor /ˈhɛptəklɔː/ ▶ **noun** [mass noun] a chlorinated hydrocarbon used as an insecticide. ● Chem. formula: $C_{10}H_5Cl_7$.

heptad /ˈhɛptad/ ▶ **noun** technical a group or set of seven.
– ORIGIN mid 17th cent.: from Greek *heptas, heptad-*, from *hepta* 'seven'.

heptagon /ˈhɛptəg(ə)n/ ▶ **noun** a plane figure with seven straight sides and angles.
– DERIVATIVES **heptagonal** adjective.
– ORIGIN late 16th cent.: from Greek *heptagonon*, neuter (used as a noun) of *heptagonos* 'seven-angled'.

heptahedron /,hɛptəˈhiːdrən, -ˈhɛd-/ ▶ **noun** (pl. **heptahedra** or **heptahedrons**) a solid figure with seven plane faces.

– DERIVATIVES **heptahedral** adjective.
– ORIGIN late 17th cent.: from **HEPTA-** 'seven' + **-HEDRON**, on the pattern of words such as *polyhedron*.

heptamerous /hɛp'tamərəs/ ▸ **adjective** Botany & Zoology having parts arranged in groups of seven. ▪ consisting of seven joints or parts.

heptameter /hɛp'tamɪtə/ ▸ **noun** Prosody a line of verse consisting of seven metrical feet.
– ORIGIN late 19th cent.: via late Latin from Greek *heptametron*, from *hepta-* 'seven' + *metron* 'measure'.

heptane /'hɛpteɪn/ ▸ **noun** Chemistry a colourless liquid hydrocarbon of the alkane series, present in petroleum spirit. ● Chem. formula: C_7H_{16}; several isomers, especially the straight-chain isomer (*n*-**heptane**).
– ORIGIN late 19th cent.: from **HEPTA-** 'seven' (denoting seven carbon atoms) + **-ANE²**.

heptarchy /'hɛptɑːki/ ▸ **noun** (pl. **heptarchies**) a state or region consisting of seven autonomous regions. ▪ [mass noun] government by seven rulers.
– DERIVATIVES **heptarchic** /-'tɑːkɪk/ adjective, **heptarchical** /-'tɑːkɪk(ə)l/ adjective.
– ORIGIN late 16th cent.: from **HEPTA-** 'seven' + Greek *arkhia* 'rule', on the pattern of *tetrarchy*.

Heptateuch /'hɛptəˌtjuːk/ ▸ **noun** the first seven books of the Bible (Genesis to Judges) collectively.
– ORIGIN late 17th cent.: via late Latin from Greek *heptateukhos*, from *hepta* 'seven' + *teukhos* 'book, volume'.

heptathlon /hɛp'taθlɒn, -lən/ ▸ **noun** an athletic event, in particular one for women, in which each competitor takes part in the same prescribed seven events (100 metres hurdles, high jump, shot-put, 200 metres, long jump, javelin, and 800 metres).
– DERIVATIVES **heptathlete** noun.
– ORIGIN 1970s: from **HEPTA-** 'seven' + Greek *athlon* 'contest', on the pattern of words such as *decathlon*.

heptavalent /ˌhɛptə'veɪl(ə)nt/ ▸ **adjective** Chemistry having a valency of seven.

heptyl /'hɛptʌɪl, -tɪl/ ▸ **noun** [as modifier] Chemistry of or denoting an alkyl radical $-C_7H_{15}$, derived from heptane.

Hepworth, Dame (Jocelyn) Barbara (1903–75), English sculptor. A pioneer of abstraction in British sculpture, she worked in wood, stone, and bronze and is noted for her simple monumental works in landscape and architectural settings, including *The Family of Man* (nine-piece group, 1972).

her ▸ **pronoun** [third person singular] **1** used as the object of a verb or preposition to refer to a female person or animal previously mentioned or easily identified: *she knew I hated her* | *I told Hannah I would wait for her*. ▪ referring to a ship, country, or other inanimate thing regarded as female: *the crew tried to sail her through a narrow gap*. ▪ used after the verb 'to be' and after 'than' or 'as': *it must be her* | *he was younger than her*. See usage at **HER** below. ▪ W. Indian she: *she will get all her wants*.
2 archaic or N. Amer. dialect herself: *peevishly she flung her on her face*.
▸ **possessive determiner 1** belonging to or associated with a female person or animal previously mentioned or easily identified: *Patricia loved her job*. ▪ belonging to or associated with a ship, country, or other inanimate thing regarded as female.
2 (**Her**) used in titles: *Her Majesty*.
– PHRASES **her indoors** Brit. informal, humorous one's wife.
– ORIGIN Old English *hire*, genitive and dative of *hīo*, *hēo* 'she'.

> **USAGE** Is it incorrect to say *I am older than* **her** (rather than *I am older than* **she**) or *it's* **her** *all right* (rather than *it's* **she** *all right*) and, if so, why? For a discussion of this issue, see **USAGE** at **PERSONAL PRONOUN**.

Hera /'hɪərə/ Greek Mythology a powerful goddess, the wife and sister of Zeus and the daughter of Cronus and Rhea. She was worshipped as the queen of heaven and as a marriage goddess. Roman equivalent **JUNO**.
– ORIGIN from Greek *Hēra* 'lady', feminine of *hērōs* 'hero', perhaps used as a title.

Heracles /'hɛrəkliːz/ Greek form of **HERCULES**.

Heraclitus /ˌhɛrə'klʌɪtəs/ (*c.*500 BC), Greek philosopher. He believed that fire is the origin of all things and that permanence is an illusion, everything being in a (harmonious) process of constant change.

Heraklion /hɪ'raklɪən/ the capital of Crete, a port on the north coast of the island; pop. 138,100 (est. 2009). Greek name **IRÁKLION**.

herald ▸ **noun 1** an official employed to oversee state ceremonial, precedence, and the use of armorial bearings, and (historically) to make proclamations, carry official messages, and oversee tournaments. ▪ (in the UK) an official of the College of Arms or the Lyon Court ranking above a pursuivant.
2 a person or thing viewed as a sign that something is about to happen: *they considered the first primroses as the herald of spring*.
3 a brown moth with dull orange markings, often hibernating in houses and old buildings. ● *Scoliopteryx libatrix*, family Noctuidae.
▸ **verb** [with obj.] be a sign that (something) is about to happen: *the speech heralded a change in policy*. ▪ acclaim: *the band* ***have been heralded as*** *the great hope for the nineties*.
– ORIGIN Middle English: from Old French *herault* (noun), *herauder* (verb), of Germanic origin.

heraldic /hɛ'raldɪk/ ▸ **adjective** relating to heraldry: *heraldic devices*.
– DERIVATIVES **heraldically** adverb.

heraldist ▸ **noun** an expert in heraldry.

heraldry ▸ **noun** [mass noun] the system by which coats of arms and other armorial bearings are devised, described, and regulated. ▪ armorial bearings or other heraldic symbols.

Heralds' College informal name for **COLLEGE OF ARMS**.

Herat /hə'rat/ a city in western Afghanistan; pop. 349,000 (est. 2006).

herb ▸ **noun 1** any plant with leaves, seeds, or flowers used for flavouring, food, medicine, or perfume: *bundles of dried herbs* | [as modifier] *a herb garden*.
2 Botany any seed-bearing plant which does not have a woody stem and dies down to the ground after flowering.
– ORIGIN Middle English: via Old French from Latin *herba* 'grass, green crops, herb'. Although *herb* has always been spelled with an *h*, pronunciation without it was usual until the 19th cent. and is still standard in the US.

herbaceous /həː'beɪʃəs/ ▸ **adjective** denoting or relating to herbs (in the botanical sense).
– ORIGIN mid 17th cent.: from Latin *herbaceus* 'grassy' (from *herba* 'grass, herb') + **-OUS**.

herbaceous border ▸ **noun** a garden border containing herbaceous, typically perennial, flowering plants.

herbaceous perennial ▸ **noun** a plant whose growth dies down annually but whose roots or other underground parts survive.

herbage ▸ **noun** [mass noun] herbaceous vegetation. ▪ the succulent part of herbaceous vegetation, used as pasture. ▪ historical the right of pasture on another person's land.
– ORIGIN late Middle English: from Old French *erbage*, based on Latin *herba* 'herb, grass, crops'.

herbal ▸ **adjective** relating to or made from herbs, especially those used in cooking and medicine: *herbal remedies*.
▸ **noun** a book that describes herbs and their culinary and medicinal properties.
– DERIVATIVES **herbally** adverb.
– ORIGIN early 16th cent. (as a noun): from medieval Latin *herbalis* (adjective), from Latin *herba* 'grass, herb'.

herbalism ▸ **noun** [mass noun] the study or practice of the medicinal and therapeutic use of plants, now especially as a form of alternative medicine.

herbalist ▸ **noun** a practitioner of herbalism. ▪ a dealer in medicinal herbs. ▪ archaic a botanical writer.

herbarium /həː'bɛːrɪəm/ ▸ **noun** (pl. **herbaria** /-rɪə/) a systematically arranged collection of dried plants. ▪ a room or building housing a herbarium. ▪ a box or other receptacle in which dried plants are kept.
– ORIGIN late 18th cent.: from late Latin, from Latin *herba* 'grass, herb'.

herbary ▸ **noun** (pl. **herbaries**) archaic a herb garden.

herb bennet ▸ **noun** another term for **WOOD AVENS**.
– ORIGIN late Middle English: from Old French *herbe beneite*, from medieval Latin *herba benedicta* 'blessed herb' (apparently first applied to a plant thought to ward off the Devil).

herb Christopher ▸ **noun** the common Eurasian baneberry.
– ORIGIN late 16th cent.: translation of medieval Latin *herba Christophori* 'herb of St Christopher' (see **CHRISTOPHER, ST**).

herbed ▸ **adjective** (of food) cooked, flavoured, or seasoned with herbs: *herbed rack of lamb*.

Herbert, George (1593–1633), English metaphysical poet. He was vicar of Bemerton, near Salisbury; his poems are pervaded by simple piety and reflect the spiritual conflicts he experienced before submitting his will to God.

herbert /'həːbət/ ▸ **noun** Brit. informal an undistinguished or foolish man or youth: *a bunch of spotty herberts*.
– ORIGIN 1960s: the male given name *Herbert*.

herb Gerard /'dʒɛrɑːd/ ▸ **noun** ground elder, which was formerly used to treat gout. Compare with **GOUTWEED**.
– ORIGIN named after St *Gerard* of Toul (*c.*935–94), invoked against gout.

herbicide /'həːbɪsʌɪd/ ▸ **noun** a substance that is toxic to plants, used to destroy unwanted vegetation.

herbivore /'həːbɪvɔː/ ▸ **noun** an animal that feeds on plants.
– DERIVATIVES **herbivorous** /-'bɪv(ə)rəs/ adjective.
– ORIGIN mid 19th cent.: from Latin *herba* 'herb' + *-vore* (see **-VOROUS**).

herb Paris ▸ **noun** a European woodland plant of the lily family, which has a single unbranched stem bearing a green and purple flower above four leaves. ● *Paris quadrifolia*, family Liliaceae (or Trilliaceae).
– ORIGIN translating medieval Latin *herba paris*, probably literally 'herb of a pair', referring to the resemblance of the four leaves to a true-love knot.

herb Robert ▸ **noun** a common cranesbill with pungent-smelling red-stemmed leaves and pink flowers, native to north temperate regions. ● *Geranium robertianum*, family Geraniaceae.
– ORIGIN translating medieval Latin *herba Roberti*, variously supposed to refer to *Robert* Duke of Normandy, St *Robert*, or St Rupert.

herb tea ▸ **noun** an infusion of herbs as a refreshing or medicinal drink.

herby ▸ **adjective** (**herbier**, **herbiest**) (of food or drink) containing or tasting or smelling of herbs: *plump, herby pork sausages*.

Hercegovina variant spelling of **HERZEGOVINA**.

Herculaneum /ˌhəːkjʊ'leɪnɪəm/ an ancient Roman town, near Naples, on the lower slopes of Vesuvius. The volcano's eruption in AD 79 buried it deeply under volcanic ash, along with Pompeii, and thus largely preserved it until its accidental rediscovery by a well-digger in 1709.

Herculean /ˌhəːkjʊ'liːən, həː'kjuːlɪən/ ▸ **adjective** requiring great strength or effort: *a Herculean task*. ▪ (of a person) muscular and strong.
– ORIGIN late 16th cent. (in the sense 'relating to Hercules'): from Latin *Herculeus* 'Hercules' + **-AN**.

Hercules /'həːkjʊliːz/ **1** Greek & Roman Mythology a hero of superhuman strength and courage who performed twelve immense tasks or 'labours' imposed on him and who after death was ranked among the gods. ▪ (as noun **a Hercules**) a man of exceptional strength or size.
2 Astronomy a large northern constellation, said to represent the kneeling figure of Hercules. It contains the brightest globular cluster in the northern hemisphere, but no bright stars.
– ORIGIN Latin, from Greek *Hēraklēs*.

Hercules beetle ▸ **noun** a very large tropical American rhinoceros beetle, the male of which has two long curved horns extending from the head and one from the thorax. ● *Dynastes hercules*, family Scarabaeidae.

Hercules' club ▸ **noun** either of two tall prickly shrubs or small trees of the US: ● the southern prickly ash (*Zanthoxylum clava-herculis*, family Rutaceae). ● another term for **DEVIL'S WALKING STICK**.

Hercynian /həː'sɪnɪən/ ▸ **adjective** Geology relating to or denoting a prolonged mountain-forming period (orogeny) in western Europe, eastern North America, and the Andes in the Upper Palaeozoic era, especially the Carboniferous and Permian periods. ▪ (as noun **the Hercynian**) the Hercynian orogeny.
– ORIGIN late 16th cent.: from Latin *Hercynia silva*; the ancient name of an area of forested mountains in central Germany; later (from the late 19th cent.) applied in geology to the Harz Mountains formed in the Hercynian period.

herd ▸ **noun** a large group of animals, especially hoofed mammals, that live together or are kept together as livestock: ***a herd of elephants*** | *farms with big dairy* ***herds***. ▪ derogatory a large group of people with a shared characteristic: *I dodged* ***herds of*** *joggers* | *he is not of* ***the common herd***.
▸ **verb 1** [with adverbial of direction] (with reference to a group of people or animals) move in a group: [with obj.]

H

they were herded into a bus | [no obj.] *we all herded into a storage room.*
2 [with obj.] keep or look after (livestock).
– ORIGIN Old English *heord*, of Germanic origin; related to German *Herde*.

herd book ▶ noun Brit. a book recording the pedigrees of cattle, goats, or other livestock.

herdboy ▶ noun a boy who looks after a herd of livestock.

herder ▶ noun a person who looks after a herd of livestock or makes a living from keeping livestock, especially in open country.

herd instinct ▶ noun an inclination in people or animals to behave or think like the majority.

herdsman ▶ noun (pl. **herdsmen**) the owner or keeper of a herd of domesticated animals. ■ (**the Herdsman**) the constellation Boötes.

Herdwick /ˈhəːdwɪk/ ▶ noun a sheep of a hardy mountain breed from the north of England.
– ORIGIN early 19th cent.: from (now obsolete) *herdwick* 'pasture ground' (see HERD, WICK²), perhaps because this breed originated in the pasture grounds of Furness Abbey.

H

here ▶ adverb 1 in, at, or to this place or position: *they have lived here most of their lives* | *we leave here today* | [after prep.] *I'm getting out of here.* ■ used when gesturing to indicate the place intended: *sign here.* ■ used to draw attention to someone or something that has just arrived: *here's my brother.* ■ [with infinitive] used to indicate one's role in a particular situation: *I'm here to help you.* ■ used to refer to existence in the world in general: *what are we all doing here?*
2 (usu. **here is/are**) used when introducing something or someone: *here's a dish that is quick to make.* ■ used when giving something to someone: *here's the money I promised you.*
3 used when indicating a time, point, or situation that has arrived or is happening: *here is your opportunity* | *here we encounter the main problem.*
▶ exclamation 1 used to attract someone's attention: *here, let me hold it.*
2 indicating one's presence in a roll-call.
– PHRASES **here and now** at the present time: *we're going to settle this here and now* | [as noun] *our obsession with the here and now.* **here and there** in various places: *small bushes scattered here and there.* **here goes** said to indicate that one is about to start something difficult or exciting. **here's to someone/thing** used to wish health or success before drinking: *here's to us!* **here today, gone tomorrow** soon over or forgotten; short-lived. **here we are** said on arrival at one's destination. **here we go again** said to indicate that the same events, typically undesirable ones, are recurring. **neither here nor there** of no importance or relevance.
– ORIGIN Old English *hēr*, of Germanic origin; related to Dutch and German *hier*, also to HE.

hereabouts (also **hereabout**) ▶ adverb near this place: *there is little natural water hereabouts.*

hereafter ▶ adverb formal from now on: *he'd promised that Rachel would be the idol of his heart hereafter.* ■ at some time in the future: *this court is in no way prejudging any such defence which may hereafter be raised.* ■ after death: *the hope of **life hereafter**.*
▶ noun (**the hereafter**) life after death: *suffering is part of our preparation for the hereafter.*

hereat ▶ adverb archaic as a result of this: *greatly distressed hereat, they declared themselves to deserve a fine.*

hereby ▶ adverb formal as a result of this document or utterance: *all such warranties are hereby excluded.*

hereditable /hɪˈrɛdɪtəb(ə)l/ ▶ adjective less common term for HERITABLE.
– ORIGIN late Middle English: from Old French, or from medieval Latin *hereditabilis*, from ecclesiastical Latin *hereditare* 'inherit', from Latin *heres, hered-* 'heir'.

hereditament /ˌhɛrɪˈdɪtəm(ə)nt, hɪˈrɛdɪt-/ ▶ noun Law, dated any item of property, either a **corporeal hereditament** (land or a building) or an **incorporeal hereditament** (such as a rent), that can be inherited. ■ an item of inheritance.
– ORIGIN late Middle English: from medieval Latin *hereditamentum*, from ecclesiastical Latin *hereditare* 'inherit', from Latin *heres, hered-* 'heir'.

hereditarian /hɪˌrɛdɪˈtɛːrɪən/ ▶ adjective relating to the theory that heredity is the primary influence on human behaviour, intelligence, or other characteristics.
▶ noun an advocate of a hereditarian view.
– DERIVATIVES **hereditarianism** noun.

hereditary /hɪˈrɛdɪt(ə)ri/ ▶ adjective 1 (of a title, office, or right) conferred by or based on inheritance: *the Queen's hereditary right to the throne.* ■ [attrib.] (of a person) holding a position by inheritance: *a hereditary peer.* ■ (of a characteristic or disease) determined by genetic factors and therefore able to be passed on from parents to their offspring or descendants. ■ relating to inheritance.
2 Mathematics (of a set) defined such that every element which has a given relation to a member of the set is also a member of the set.
– DERIVATIVES **hereditarily** adverb, **hereditariness** noun.
– ORIGIN late Middle English: from Latin *hereditarius*, from *hereditas* (see HEREDITY).

heredity /hɪˈrɛdɪti/ ▶ noun [mass noun] 1 the passing on of physical or mental characteristics genetically from one generation to another. ■ a person's ancestry: *he wears a Cossack tunic to emphasize his Russian heredity.*
2 the inheritance of a title, office, or right: *a second chamber whose membership is largely based on heredity.*
– ORIGIN late 18th cent.: from French *hérédité*, from Latin *hereditas* 'heirship', from *heres, hered-* 'heir'.

Hereford¹ /ˈhɛrɪfəd/ a city in west central England, administrative centre of the county of Herefordshire, on the River Wye; pop. 55,300 (est. 2009).

Hereford² /ˈhɛrɪfəd/ ▶ noun an animal of a breed of red and white beef cattle.

Hereford and Worcester a former county of west central England, formed in 1974 from the counties of Herefordshire and Worcestershire, which were reinstated in 1998.

Herefordshire a county of west central England, between 1974 and 1998 part of the county of Hereford and Worcester.

herein ▶ adverb formal in this document or book. ■ used to introduce something that depends on or arises from what has just been mentioned: *the statues are sensual to the point of erotic and herein lies their interest.*

hereinafter ▶ adverb formal further on in this document: *grievous bodily harm (hereinafter GBH).*

hereinbefore ▶ adverb formal before this point in this document.

hereof ▶ adverb formal of this document: *in accordance with section 17 hereof.*

Herero /həˈrɛːrəʊ, -ˈrɪərəʊ/ ▶ noun (pl. **same** or **Hereros**) 1 a member of a people living in Namibia, Angola, and Botswana.
2 [mass noun] the Bantu language of the Herero, with about 75,000 speakers.
▶ adjective relating to the Herero or their language.
– ORIGIN a local name, from *Otshi-Herero*, the Herero word for the language.

heresiarch /hɛˈriːzɪɑːk/ ▶ noun the founder of a heresy or the leader of a heretical sect.
– ORIGIN mid 16th cent.: via ecclesiastical Latin from ecclesiastical Greek *hairesiarkhēs* 'leader of a sect', from *hairesis* 'heretical sect, heresy' + *arkhēs* 'ruler'.

heresy /ˈhɛrɪsi/ ▶ noun (pl. **heresies**) [mass noun] belief or opinion contrary to orthodox religious (especially Christian) doctrine: *Huss was burned for heresy* | [count noun] *the doctrine was denounced as a heresy by the pope.* ■ opinion profoundly at odds with what is generally accepted: *the heresy of being uncommitted to the right political dogma.*
– ORIGIN Middle English: from Old French *heresie*, based on Latin *haeresis*, from Greek *hairesis* 'choice' (in ecclesiastical Greek 'heretical sect'), from *haireomai* 'choose'.

heretic /ˈhɛrɪtɪk/ ▶ noun a person believing in or practising religious heresy. ■ a person holding an opinion at odds with what is generally accepted.
– ORIGIN Middle English: from Old French *heretique*, via ecclesiastical Latin from Greek *hairetikos* 'able to choose' (in ecclesiastical Greek, 'heretical'), from *haireomai* 'choose'.

heretical /hɪˈrɛtɪk(ə)l/ ▶ adjective believing in or practising religious heresy: *heretical beliefs.* ■ holding an opinion at odds with what is generally accepted: *I feel a bit heretical saying this, but I think the film has too much action.*
– DERIVATIVES **heretically** adverb.

hereto ▶ adverb formal to this matter or document: *the written consent of each of the parties hereto* | *hereto is appended an estimate of the cost.*

heretofore ▶ adverb formal before now: *diseases that heretofore were usually confined to rural areas.*

hereunder ▶ adverb formal as provided for under the terms of this document: *all expenses incurred hereunder by the bank shall be recoverable.* ■ further on in a document.

hereunto ▶ adverb archaic or formal to this document: *signed in the presence of us both who have hereunto subscribed our names as witnesses.*

hereupon ▶ adverb archaic after or as a result of this.

Hereward the Wake /ˈhɛrɪwəd/ (11th century), semi-legendary Anglo-Saxon rebel leader. A leader of Anglo-Saxon resistance to William I's new Norman regime, he is thought to have been responsible for an uprising centred on the Isle of Ely in 1070.
– ORIGIN *the Wake* apparently in the sense 'the watchful one'.

herewith ▶ adverb formal with this letter: *I enclose herewith a copy of this discussion document.*

heriot /ˈhɛrɪət/ ▶ noun historical a tribute paid to a lord out of the belongings of a tenant who died, often consisting of a live animal or, originally, military equipment that he borrowed.
– ORIGIN Old English *heregeatwa*, from *here* 'army' + *geatwa* 'trappings'.

heritable ▶ adjective 1 Biology (of a characteristic) transmissible from parent to offspring.
2 Law (of property) capable of being inherited by heirs-at-law. Compare with MOVABLE (sense 2 of the adjective).
– DERIVATIVES **heritability** noun, **heritably** adverb.
– ORIGIN late Middle English: from Old French *heriter* 'inherit', from ecclesiastical Latin *hereditare*, from Latin *heres, hered-* 'heir'.

heritage ▶ noun [in sing.] 1 property that is or may be inherited; an inheritance. ■ valued objects and qualities such as historic buildings and cultural traditions that have been passed down from previous generations: *Europe's varied cultural heritage* | [mass noun] *the estuary has a sense of history and heritage.* ■ [as modifier] denoting or relating to things of special architectural, historical, or natural value that are preserved for the nation: *a heritage centre.* ■ [as modifier] N. Amer. (of a plant variety) not hybridized with another; old-fashioned: *heritage roses.*
2 archaic a special or individual possession; an allotted portion: *God's love remains your heritage.*
3 archaic God's chosen people (the people of Israel, or the Christian Church).
– ORIGIN Middle English: from Old French *heritage*, from *heriter* 'inherit' (see HERITABLE).

heritor /ˈhɛrɪtə/ ▶ noun Scots Law a proprietor of a heritable object. ■ an heir.
– ORIGIN late Middle English: from Anglo-Norman French *heriter*, based on Latin *hereditarius* (see HEREDITARY). The spelling change in the 16th cent. was by association with words ending in -OR¹.

herky-jerky /ˈhəːkɪˌdʒəːki/ ▶ adjective N. Amer. informal characterized by or moving in sudden stops and starts: *herky-jerky black and white newsreels.*
– ORIGIN late 20th cent.: reduplication of JERKY¹.

herl /həːl/ ▶ noun a barb or filament of a feather used in dressing a fishing fly.
– ORIGIN late Middle English: apparently of Germanic origin and related to Middle Low German *harle*.

herm /həːm/ ▶ noun a squared stone pillar with a carved head on top (typically of Hermes), used in ancient Greece as a boundary marker or a signpost.
– ORIGIN from the Greek name HERMES.

hermaphrodite /həːˈmafrədʌɪt/ ▶ noun a person or animal having both male and female sex organs or other sexual characteristics, either abnormally or (in the case of some organisms) as the natural condition. ■ Botany a plant having stamens and pistils in the same flower. ■ archaic a person or thing combining opposite qualities or characteristics.
▶ adjective of or denoting a person, animal, or plant having both male and female sex organs or other sexual characteristics.
– DERIVATIVES **hermaphroditic** adjective, **hermaphroditical** adjective, **hermaphroditism** noun.
– ORIGIN late Middle English: via Latin from Greek *hermaphroditos* (see HERMAPHRODITUS).

hermaphrodite brig ▶ noun a two-masted sailing ship with a square-rigged foremast and, on the mainmast, a square topsail above a fore-and-aft gaff mainsail.

Hermaphroditus /həˌmafrəˈdʌɪtəs/ Greek Mythology a son of Hermes and Aphrodite, with whom the nymph Salmacis fell in love and prayed to be forever united. As a result Hermaphroditus and Salmacis became joined in a single body which retained characteristics of both sexes.

hermeneutic /ˌhəːmɪˈnjuːtɪk/ ▶ **adjective** concerning interpretation, especially of the Bible or literary texts.
▶ **noun** a method or theory of interpretation.
– DERIVATIVES **hermeneutical** adjective, **hermeneutically** adverb.
– ORIGIN late 17th cent.: from Greek *hermēneutikos*, from *hermēneuein* 'interpret'.

hermeneutics ▶ **plural noun** [usu. treated as sing.] the branch of knowledge that deals with interpretation, especially of the Bible or literary texts.

Hermes /ˈhəːmiːz/ Greek Mythology the son of Zeus and Maia, the messenger of the gods, and god of merchants, thieves, and oratory. He was portrayed as a herald equipped for travelling, with broad-brimmed hat, winged shoes, and a winged rod. Roman equivalent **MERCURY**.
– ORIGIN probably from Greek *herma* 'heap of stones': from early times he was represented by a carved stock or stone and was identified with **THOTH**.

Hermes Trismegistus /ˌtrɪsməˈdʒɪstəs/ a legendary figure regarded by Neoplatonists and others as the author of certain works on astrology, magic, and alchemy.
– ORIGIN Latin, 'thrice-greatest Hermes', in reference to **THOTH**, identified with **HERMES**.

hermetic /həːˈmɛtɪk/ ▶ **adjective 1** (of a seal or closure) complete and airtight. ■ insulated or protected from outside influences: *a hermetic society*.
2 (also **Hermetic**) relating to an ancient occult tradition encompassing alchemy, astrology, and theosophy. ■ difficult to understand because intended for a small number of people with specialized knowledge: *obscure and hermetic poems*.
– DERIVATIVES **hermetically** adverb, **hermeticism** noun.
– ORIGIN mid 17th cent. (in sense 2): from modern Latin *hermeticus*, from **HERMES**, identified with **THOTH**, regarded as the founder of alchemy and astrology.

hermit ▶ **noun 1** a person living in solitude as a religious discipline. ■ a reclusive or solitary person.
2 a hummingbird found in the shady lower layers of tropical forests, foraging along a regular route. ● *Phaethornis* and other genera, family Trochilidae: several species.
– DERIVATIVES **hermitic** adjective.
– ORIGIN Middle English: from Old French *hermite*, from late Latin *eremita*, from Greek *erēmitēs*, from *erēmos* 'solitary'.

hermitage ▶ **noun 1** the dwelling of a hermit, especially when small and remote.
2 (**the Hermitage**) a major art museum in St Petersburg, Russia, containing among its collections those begun by Catherine the Great. [named with reference to the 'retreat' in which the empress displayed her treasures to her friends.]
– ORIGIN Middle English: from Old French, from *hermite* (see **HERMIT**).

hermit crab ▶ **noun** a crab with a soft asymmetrical abdomen, which lives in a cast-off mollusc shell for protection. In several kinds the shell becomes covered with sponges, sea anemones, or bryozoans. ● Superfamily Paguroidea.

Hermitian /həːˈmɪtɪən/ ▶ **adjective** Mathematics denoting or relating to a matrix in which those pairs of elements which are symmetrically placed with respect to the principal diagonal are complex conjugates.
– ORIGIN early 20th cent.: from the name of Charles *Hermite* (1822–1905), French mathematician, + **-IAN**.

hermit thrush ▶ **noun** a small migratory North American thrush, noted for its melodious song. ● *Catharus guttatus*, family Turdidae.

Hermosillo /ˌɛːməˈsiːjəʊ, -ˈsiːljəʊ/ a city in NW Mexico, capital of the state of Sonora; pop. 641,791 (2005).

hernia /ˈhəːnɪə/ ▶ **noun** (pl. **hernias** or **herniae** /-nɪiː/) a condition in which part of an organ is displaced and protrudes through the wall of the cavity containing it (often involving the intestine at a weak point in the abdominal wall).
– DERIVATIVES **hernial** adjective.
– ORIGIN late Middle English: from Latin.

herniate /ˈhəːnɪeɪt/ ▶ **verb** [no obj.] (usu. as adj. **herniated**) (of an organ) suffer a hernia: *a herniated disc*.
– DERIVATIVES **herniation** noun.

Herning /ˈhəːnɪŋ/ a city in central Jutland, Denmark; pop. 45,470 (2009).

Hero[1] Greek Mythology a priestess of Aphrodite at Sestos on the European shore of the Hellespont, whose lover Leander, a youth of Abydos on the opposite shore, swam the strait nightly to visit her. One stormy night he was drowned and Hero in grief threw herself into the sea.

Hero[2] (1st century), Greek mathematician and inventor; known as **Hero of Alexandria**. His surviving works are important as a source for ancient practical mathematics and mechanics. He described a number of hydraulic, pneumatic, and other mechanical devices, including elementary applications of the power of steam.

hero ▶ **noun** (pl. **heroes**) **1** a person, typically a man, who is admired for their courage, outstanding achievements, or noble qualities: *a war hero*. ■ the chief male character in a book, play, or film, who is typically identified with good qualities, and with whom the reader is expected to sympathize. ■ (in mythology and folklore) a person of superhuman qualities and often semi-divine origin, in particular one whose exploits were the subject of ancient Greek myths.
2 (also **hero sandwich**) N. Amer. another term for **HOAGIE**.
– ORIGIN Middle English (with mythological reference): via Latin from Greek *hērōs*.

Herod /ˈhɛrəd/ the name of four rulers of ancient Palestine: ■ **Herod the Great** (*c*.74–4 BC), ruled 37–4 BC. According to the New Testament, Jesus was born during his reign, and he ordered the massacre of the innocents (Matt. 2:16). ■ **Herod Antipas** (22 BC–*c*.AD 40), son of Herod the Great, tetrarch of Galilee and Peraea 4 BC–AD 40. He married Herodias (his brother's wife) and was responsible for the beheading of John the Baptist. According to the New Testament (Luke 23:7), Pilate sent Jesus to be questioned by him before the Crucifixion. ■ ***Herod Agrippa I*** (10 BC–AD 44), grandson of Herod the Great, king of Judaea AD 41–4. He imprisoned St Peter and put St James the Great to death. ■ ***Herod Agrippa II*** (AD 27–*c*.93), son of Herod Agrippa I, king of various territories in northern Palestine 50–*c*.93. He presided over the trial of St Paul (Acts 25:13 ff.).
– DERIVATIVES **Herodian** /hɛˈrəʊdɪən/ adjective & noun.

Herodotus /hɪˈrɒdətəs/ (5th century BC), Greek historian. He was the first historian to collect his materials systematically, test their accuracy to a certain extent, and arrange them in a well-constructed and vivid narrative. His *History* tells of the Persian Wars of the early 5th century BC.

heroic ▶ **adjective 1** having the characteristics of a hero or heroine; admirably brave or determined: *heroic deeds* | *heroic bomb disposal experts*. ■ of or representing heroes or heroines: *early medieval heroic poetry*.
2 (of language or a work of art) grand or grandiose in scale or intention: *one passes under pyramids and obelisks, all on a heroic scale*. ■ Sculpture (of a statue) larger than life size but less than colossal.
▶ **noun** (**heroics**) **1** behaviour or talk that is bold or dramatic: *the England star is getting special treatment because of his World Cup heroics*.
2 short for **HEROIC VERSE**.
– DERIVATIVES **heroically** adverb.
– ORIGIN late Middle English: from Old French *heroique* or Latin *heroicus*, from Greek *hērōikos* 'relating to heroes', from *hērōs* 'hero'.

heroic age ▶ **noun** the period in Greek history and legend before the Trojan War and its aftermath, in which the legends of the heroes were set.

heroic couplet ▶ **noun** (in verse) a pair of rhyming iambic pentameters, much used by Chaucer and the poets of the 17th and 18th centuries such as Alexander Pope.

heroic verse ▶ **noun** [mass noun] a type of verse used for epic or heroic subjects, such as the hexameter, iambic pentameter, or alexandrine.

heroin ▶ **noun** [mass noun] a highly addictive analgesic drug derived from morphine, often used illicitly as a narcotic producing euphoria. ● Alternative name: **diacetylmorphine**; chem. formula: $C_{17}H_{17}NO(C_2H_3O_2)_2$.
– ORIGIN late 19th cent.: from German *Heroin*, from Latin *heros* 'hero' (because of its effects on the user's self-esteem).

heroine ▶ **noun** a woman admired for her courage, outstanding achievements, or noble qualities: *she was a true feminist heroine*. ■ the chief female character in a book, play, or film, who is typically identified with good qualities, and with whom the reader is expected to sympathize. ■ (in mythology and folklore) a woman of superhuman qualities and often semi-divine origin, in particular one whose deeds were the subject of ancient Greek myths.
– ORIGIN mid 17th cent. (in the sense 'demigoddess, venerated woman'): from French *héroïne* or Latin *heroina*, from Greek *hērōinē*, feminine of *hērōs* 'hero'.

heroism ▶ **noun** [mass noun] great bravery: *they fought with exemplary heroism*.
– ORIGIN early 18th cent.: from French *héroïsme*, from *héros*, from Latin *heros* (see **HERO**).

heroize /ˈhɪərəʊʌɪz, ˈhɛr-/ (also **heroise**) ▶ **verb** [with obj.] treat or represent as a hero: *the father is heroized for his long forbearance*.

heron ▶ **noun** a large fish-eating wading bird with long legs, a long S-shaped neck, and a long pointed bill. ● Family Ardeidae (the **heron family**): several genera and numerous species, e.g. the Old World **grey heron** (*Ardea cinerea*). The heron family also includes the bitterns and egrets.
– ORIGIN Middle English: from Old French, of Germanic origin.

heronry ▶ **noun** (pl. **heronries**) a breeding colony of herons, typically in a group of trees.

Herophilus /hɪəˈrɒfɪləs/ (4th–3rd centuries BC), Greek anatomist. He is regarded as the father of human anatomy for his fundamental discoveries concerning the anatomy of the brain, eye, and reproductive organs. Herophilus also studied the physiology of nerves, arteries, and veins.

H

hero's welcome ▶ **noun** an enthusiastic welcome for someone who has done something brave or praiseworthy.

hero worship ▶ **noun** [mass noun] excessive admiration for someone.
▶ **verb** (**hero-worship**) [with obj.] admire (someone) excessively.
– DERIVATIVES **hero-worshipper** noun.

herp ▶ **noun** short for **HERPTILE**.

herpes /ˈhəːpiːz/ ▶ **noun** [mass noun] any of a group of virus diseases caused by herpesviruses, affecting the skin (often with blisters) or the nervous system.
– DERIVATIVES **herpetic** adjective.
– ORIGIN late Middle English (originally used also of other skin conditions): via Latin from Greek *herpēs* 'shingles', literally 'creeping', from *herpein* 'to creep'.

herpes simplex ▶ **noun** [mass noun] a viral infection caused by a group of herpesviruses, which may produce cold sores, genital inflammation, or conjunctivitis.

herpesvirus /ˈhəːpiːzˌvʌɪrəs/ ▶ **noun** Medicine any of a group of DNA viruses causing herpes and other diseases.

herpes zoster /ˈzɒstə/ ▶ **noun** [mass noun] medical name for **SHINGLES**. ■ a herpesvirus that causes shingles and chickenpox.
– ORIGIN late Middle English: from **HERPES** and Latin *zoster*, from Greek *zōstēr* 'girdle, shingles'.

herpetofauna /ˈhəːpɪtə(ʊ),fɔːnə/ ▶ **noun** [mass noun] Zoology the reptiles and amphibians of a particular region, habitat, or geological period.
– DERIVATIVES **herpetofaunal** adjective.
– ORIGIN modern Latin, from Greek *herpeton* 'creeping thing, reptile' + **FAUNA**.

herpetology /ˌhəːpɪˈtɒlədʒi/ ▶ **noun** [mass noun] the branch of zoology concerned with reptiles and amphibians.
– DERIVATIVES **herpetological** adjective, **herpetologist** noun.
– ORIGIN early 19th cent.: from Greek *herpeton* 'reptile' (from *herpein* 'to creep') + **-LOGY**.

herptile /ˈhəːptʌɪl/ ▶ **noun** a reptile or amphibian.
– ORIGIN blend of **HERPETOLOGY** and **REPTILE**.

Herr /hɛː/, German /hɛr/ ▶ **noun** (pl. **Herren** /ˈhɛr(ə)n/) a title or form of address used of or to a German-speaking man, corresponding to *Mr* and also used before a rank or occupation. ■ a German man.
– ORIGIN German, from Old High German *hērro*, comparative of *hēr* 'exalted'.

Herrenvolk /ˈhɛr(ə)nfɒlk, -fəʊk/ ▶ **noun** the German nation as considered by the Nazis to be innately superior to others.
– ORIGIN German, 'master race', from *Herr* 'master' + *Volk* 'people, folk'.

Herrick /ˈhɛrɪk/, Robert (1591–1674), English poet. He is best known for his collection *Hesperides* (1648), containing both secular and religious poems.

herring ▶ **noun** a fairly small silvery fish which is most abundant in coastal waters and is of widespread commercial importance. ● *Clupea* and other genera, family

Clupeidae (the **herring family**): several species, in particular (*C. harengus*), of the North Atlantic. The herring family also includes the sprats, shads, and pilchards.
– ORIGIN Old English *hǣring, hēring*, of West Germanic origin; related to Dutch *haring* and German *Hering*.

herringbone ▶ **noun** [mass noun] [usu. as modifier] **1** a pattern consisting of columns of short parallel lines, with all the lines in one column sloping one way and all the lines in the next column sloping the other way so as to resemble the bones in a fish, for example as used in the weave of cloth: *a grey herringbone tweed jacket*. ■ (also **herringbone stitch**) a cross-stitch with a pattern resembling herringbone, used in embroidery or for securing an edge.
2 Skiing a method of ascending a slope by walking up it with the skis pointing outwards.
▶ **verb 1** [with obj.] mark with a herringbone pattern. ■ work with a herringbone stitch.
2 [no obj., with adverbial of direction] Skiing ascend a slope using the herringbone technique.

herring gull ▶ **noun** a gull with grey black-tipped wings, abundant and widespread in both Eurasia and North America. ● *Larus argentatus*, family Laridae.

Herrnhuter /ˈhɛːnhuːtə, ˈhɛːr(ə)n-/ ▶ **noun** a member of a Moravian Church.
– ORIGIN mid 18th cent.: German, from *Herrnhut* (literally 'the Lord's keeping'), the name of the first German settlement of the Moravian Church.

hers ▶ **possessive pronoun** used to refer to a thing or things belonging to or associated with a female person or animal previously mentioned: *his eyes met hers | the choice was hers | friends **of hers** warned her*.

USAGE There is no need for an apostrophe: the spelling should be **hers** not **her's**.

Herschel[1] /ˈhəːʃ(ə)l/, Sir (Frederick) William (1738–1822), German-born British astronomer. His cataloguing of the skies resulted in the discovery of the planet Uranus. He was the first to appreciate the great remoteness of stars and developed the idea that the sun belongs to the star system of the Milky Way.

Herschel[2] /ˈhəːʃ(ə)l/, Sir John (Frederick William) (1792–1871), English astronomer and physicist, son of William. He extended the sky survey to the southern hemisphere, carried out pioneering work in photography, and made contributions to meteorology and geophysics.

herself ▶ **pronoun** [third person singular] **1** [reflexive] used as the object of a verb or preposition to refer to a female person or animal previously mentioned as the subject of the clause: *she had to defend herself | Jo made herself a cup of tea*.
2 [emphatic] she or her personally: *she told me herself*.
– ORIGIN Old English (see HER, SELF).

herstory /ˈhəːst(ə)ri/ ▶ **noun** (pl. **herstories**) [mass noun] history viewed from a female or specifically feminist perspective.
– ORIGIN 1970s: from HER + STORY[1], analogous formation based on the form *history*.

Hertford /ˈhɑːtfəd/ the county town of Hertfordshire, SE England; pop. 27,900 (est. 2009).

Hertfordshire a county of SE England, one of the Home Counties; county town, Hertford.

Herts. /hɑːts/ ▶ **abbreviation** Hertfordshire.

Hertz /həːts/, German /hɛrts/, Heinrich Rudolf (1857–94), German physicist and pioneer of radio communication. He continued the work of Maxwell on electromagnetic waves and was the first to broadcast and receive radio waves. Hertz also showed that light and radiant heat were electromagnetic in nature.

hertz /həːts/ (abbrev.: **Hz**) ▶ **noun** (pl. **same**) the SI unit of frequency, equal to one cycle per second.
– ORIGIN late 19th cent.: named after H. R. HERTZ.

Hertzian wave /ˈhəːtsɪən/ ▶ **noun** former term for RADIO WAVE.

Hertzsprung–Russell diagram /ˈhəːtsˌsprʌŋ/ ▶ **noun** Astronomy a two-dimensional graph, devised independently by Ejnar Hertzsprung (1873–1967) and Henry Norris Russell (1877–1957), in which the absolute magnitudes of stars are plotted against their spectral types. Stars are found to occupy only certain regions of such a diagram.

Herut /hɛˈruːt/ a right-wing Israeli political party founded by Menachem Begin in 1948, from the remains of the Irgun group. Herut was one of the parties that combined to form the Likud coalition in 1973.
– ORIGIN Hebrew, 'freedom'.

Herzegovina /ˌhɛːtsəˈgɒvɪnə, -gəˈviːnə/ (also **Hercegovina**) a region in the Balkans forming the southern part of Bosnia and Herzegovina and separated from the Adriatic by part of Croatia. Its chief town is Mostar.
– DERIVATIVES **Herzegovinian** adjective & noun.

Herzl /ˈhəːts(ə)l/, Theodor (1860–1904), Hungarian-born journalist, dramatist, and Zionist leader. The founder of the Zionist movement (1897), he chiefly worked as a writer and journalist in Vienna, advocating the establishment of a Jewish state in Palestine.

Herzog /ˈhəːtsɒg/, German /ˈhɛrtsoːk/, Werner (b.1942), German film director; born *Werner Stipetic*. Themes of remoteness in time and space are dominant elements throughout his films, which include *Aguirre, Wrath of God* (1972) and *Fitzcarraldo* (1982).

he's ▶ **contraction** he is: *he's going to speak*. ■ he has: *he's given up his job*.

Heshvan /ˈhɛʃv(ə)n/ ▶ **noun** variant spelling of HESVAN.

Hesiod /ˈhiːsɪəd/ (*c.*700 BC), Greek poet. One of the earliest known Greek poets, he wrote the *Theogony*, a hexametric poem on the genealogies of the gods, and *Works and Days*, which gave moral and practical advice and was the chief model for later ancient didactic poetry.

hesitancy ▶ **noun** [mass noun] the quality or state of being hesitant: *Jackson took advantage of some hesitancy in the defence to rifle in a shot*.
– DERIVATIVES **hesitance** noun.

hesitant ▶ **adjective** tentative, unsure, or slow in acting or speaking: *clients are hesitant about buying | her slow, hesitant way of speaking*.
– DERIVATIVES **hesitantly** adverb.
– ORIGIN late Middle English: from Latin *haesitant-* 'being undecided', from the verb *haesitare* (see HESITATE).

hesitate ▶ **verb** [no obj.] pause in indecision before saying or doing something: *she hesitated, unsure of what to say | one **hesitates over** publicizing these things*. ■ [with infinitive] be reluctant to do something: *he hesitated to spoil the mood by being inquisitive*.
– PHRASES **he who hesitates is lost** proverb delay or vacillation may have unfortunate or disastrous consequences.
– DERIVATIVES **hesitating** adjective, **hesitatingly** adverb, **hesitative** adjective.
– ORIGIN early 17th cent.: from Latin *haesitat-* 'stuck fast, left undecided', from the verb *haesitare*, from *haerere* 'stick, stay'.

hesitation ▶ **noun** [mass noun] the action of pausing before saying or doing something: *she answered without hesitation*. ■ [usu. with negative] doubt or reluctance: *I have no hesitation in recommending him*.
– ORIGIN early 17th cent.: from Latin *haesitatio(n)-*, from *haesitare* (see HESITATE).

Hesperian /hɛˈspɪərɪən/ ▶ **adjective** Greek Mythology of or concerning the Hesperides. ■ literary western.
– ORIGIN late 15th cent.: from Latin *hesperius* (from Greek *hesperios*, from *Hesperia* 'land of the west', from *hesperos* 'western' (see HESPERUS)) + -AN.

Hesperides /hɛˈspɛrɪdiːz/ Greek Mythology a group of nymphs who were guardians, with the aid of a watchful dragon, of a tree of golden apples in a garden located beyond the Atlas Mountains at the western border of Oceanus, the river encircling the world. One of the labours of Hercules was to fetch the golden apples.

hesperidium /ˌhɛspəˈrɪdɪəm/ ▶ **noun** (pl. **hesperidia** /-dɪə/) Botany a fruit with sectioned pulp inside a separable rind, e.g. an orange or grapefruit.
– ORIGIN mid 19th cent.: based on *Hesperideae*, former name of an order of plants containing citrus fruits, named after the golden apples of the Hesperides (see HESPERIDES) + -IUM.

Hesperus /ˈhɛspərəs/ ▶ **noun** literary the planet Venus.
– ORIGIN Latin, from Greek *hesperos* 'western', (as a noun) 'the evening star'.

Hess[1] /hɛs/, Victor Francis (1883–1964), Austrian-born American physicist; born *Victor Franz Hess*. He showed that some ionizing radiation (later termed cosmic rays) was extraterrestrial in origin but did not come from the sun. Nobel Prize for Physics (1936, shared with Carl David Anderson).

Hess[2] /hɛs/, (Walther Richard) Rudolf (1894–1987), German Nazi politician, deputy leader of the Nazi Party 1934–41. In 1941, secretly and on his own initiative, he parachuted into Scotland to negotiate peace with Britain. He was imprisoned for the duration of the war and, at the Nuremberg war trials, sentenced to life imprisonment in Spandau prison, Berlin, where he died.

Hesse[1] /ˈhɛs/ a state of western Germany; capital, Wiesbaden. German name **Hessen** /ˈhɛsn/.
– DERIVATIVES **Hessian** adjective & noun.

Hesse[2] /hɛs, ˈhɛsə/, Hermann (1877–1962), German-born Swiss novelist and poet. His work reflects his interest in spiritual values as expressed in Eastern religion and his involvement in Jungian analysis. Notable works: *Siddhartha* (1922), *Der Steppenwolf* (1927), and *The Glass Bead Game* (1943). Nobel Prize for Literature (1946).

hessian ▶ **noun** [mass noun] chiefly Brit. a strong, coarse fabric made from hemp or jute, used for sacks and upholstery.
– ORIGIN late 19th cent.: from *Hesse* (see HESSE[1]) + -IAN.

Hessian boot ▶ **noun** a high tasselled leather boot, originally worn by Hessian troops.

Hessian fly ▶ **noun** a gall midge whose larvae are a pest of cereal crops, occurring in all wheat-growing areas. ● *Mayetiola destructor*, family Cecidomyiidae.
– ORIGIN late 18th cent.: so named because it was supposed (erroneously) to have been carried to America by Hessian troops during the War of Independence.

hest ▶ **noun** archaic form of BEHEST.
– ORIGIN Old English *hǣs*, of Germanic origin; related to HIGHT. The spelling change in Middle English was by association with abstract nouns ending in *-t*.

Hesvan /ˈhɛsv(ə)n/ (also **Chesvan, Heshvan**) ▶ **noun** (in the Jewish calendar) the second month of the civil and eighth of the religious year, usually coinciding with parts of October and November.
– ORIGIN from Hebrew *ḥešwān*.

Hesychast /ˈhɛsɪkast/ ▶ **noun** historical a member of a movement dedicated to interior prayer, originating among the Orthodox monks of Mount Athos in the 14th century.
– ORIGIN mid 19th cent.: from late Greek *hēsukhastēs* 'hermit', from *hēsukhazein* 'be still', from *hēsukhos* 'still'.

hetaera /hɪˈtɪərə/ (also **hetaira** /-ˈtʌɪrə/) ▶ **noun** (pl. **hetaeras** or **hetaerae** /-ˈtɪəriː/ or **hetairas** or **hetairai** /-ˈtʌɪrʌɪ/) a courtesan or mistress, especially an educated one in ancient Greece.
– ORIGIN from Greek *hetaira*, feminine of *hetairos* 'companion'.

hetero /ˈhɛt(ə)rəʊ/ ▶ **adjective & noun** (pl. **heteros**) informal short for HETEROSEXUAL.

hetero- ▶ **combining form** other; different: *heteropolar | heterosexual*. Often contrasted with HOMO-.
– ORIGIN from Greek *heteros* 'other'.

heteroaromatic /ˌhɛtərəʊarəˈmatɪk/ ▶ **adjective** Chemistry denoting an organic compound with a ring structure which is both heterocyclic and aromatic.

heterocercal /ˌhɛtərəʊˈsəːkəl/ ▶ **adjective** Zoology (of a fish's tail) having unequal upper and lower lobes, usually with the vertebral column passing into the upper. Contrasted with DIPHYCERCAL, HOMOCERCAL.
– ORIGIN mid 19th cent.: from HETERO- 'other' + Greek *kerkos* 'tail'.

heterochromatic /ˌhɛt(ə)rəʊkrəˈmatɪk/ ▶ **adjective** **1** of several different colours or (in physics) wavelengths.
2 Biochemistry relating to heterochromatin.

heterochromatin /ˌhɛtərəʊˈkrəʊmətɪn/ ▶ **noun** [mass noun] Biology chromosome material of different density from normal (usually greater), in which the activity of the genes is modified or suppressed. Compare with EUCHROMATIN.

heteroclite /ˈhɛt(ə)rə(ʊ)klʌɪt/ formal ▶ **adjective** abnormal or irregular.
▶ **noun** an abnormal thing or person. ■ an irregularly declined word, especially a Greek or Latin noun.
– DERIVATIVES **heteroclitic** adjective.
– ORIGIN late 15th cent.: via late Latin from Greek *heteroklitos*, from *heteros* 'other' + *-klitos* 'inflected' (from *klinein* 'to lean, inflect').

heterocyclic /ˌhɛt(ə)rə(ʊ)ˈsʌɪklɪk, -ˈsɪklɪk/ ▶ **adjective** Chemistry denoting a compound whose molecule contains a ring of atoms of at least two elements (one of which is generally carbon).

heterodox /ˈhɛt(ə)rə(ʊ)dɒks/ ▶ **adjective** not conforming with accepted or orthodox standards or beliefs: *heterodox views*.
– DERIVATIVES **heterodoxy** noun.

– ORIGIN early 17th cent. (originally as a noun denoting an unorthodox opinion): via late Latin from Greek *heterodoxos*, from *heteros* 'other' + *doxa* 'opinion'.

heterodyne /ˈhɛt(ə)rə(ʊ)dʌɪn/ Electronics ▶ **adjective** relating to the production of a lower frequency from the combination of two almost equal high frequencies, as used in radio transmission.
▶ **verb** [with obj.] combine (a high-frequency signal) with another to produce a lower frequency in this way.
– ORIGIN early 20th cent.: from HETERO- 'other' + *-dyne*, suffix formed irregularly from Greek *dunamis* 'power'.

heterogametic /ˌhɛt(ə)rə(ʊ)gəˈmɛtɪk/ ▶ **adjective** Biology denoting the sex which has sex chromosomes that differ in morphology, resulting in two different kinds of gamete, e.g. (in mammals) the male and (in birds) the female. The opposite of HOMOGAMETIC.

heterogamy /ˌhɛtəˈrɒgəmi/ ▶ **noun** [mass noun] **1** chiefly Zoology the alternation of generations, especially between sexual and parthenogenetic generations.
2 Botany a state in which the flowers of a plant are of two or more types. Compare with HOMOGAMY (sense 2). ■ another term for ANISOGAMY.
3 marriage between people from different sociological or educational backgrounds. Compare with HOMOGAMY (sense 1).
– DERIVATIVES **heterogamous** adjective.

heterogeneous /ˌhɛt(ə)rə(ʊ)ˈdʒiːnɪəs, -ˈdʒɛn-/ ▶ **adjective** diverse in character or content: *a large and heterogeneous collection*. ■ Chemistry of or denoting a process involving substances in different phases (solid, liquid, or gaseous): *heterogeneous catalysis*. ■ Mathematics incommensurable through being of different kinds, degrees, or dimensions.
– DERIVATIVES **heterogeneity** /-dʒɪˈniːɪti, -ˈneɪɪti/ noun, **heterogeneously** adverb, **heterogeneousness** noun.
– ORIGIN early 17th cent.: from medieval Latin *heterogeneus*, from Greek *heterogenēs*, from *heteros* 'other' + *genos* 'a kind'.

USAGE The correct spelling is **heterogeneous**, but a fairly common misspelling is **heterogenous**. The reason for the error probably relates to the pronunciation, which, in rapid speech, often misses out the extra **e**. **Heterogenous** is actually a different word, which is used in specialized medical and biological senses and means 'originating outside the organism'.

heteroglossia /ˌhɛtərəʊˈglɒsɪə/ ▶ **noun** [mass noun] the presence of two or more expressed viewpoints in a text or other artistic work.
– DERIVATIVES **heteroglossic** adjective.
– ORIGIN 1980s: from HETERO- + Greek *glōssa* 'tongue, language' + -IA[1].

heterograft ▶ **noun** another term for XENOGRAFT.

heterologous /ˌhɛtəˈrɒləgəs/ ▶ **adjective** chiefly Medicine & Biology not homologous: *heterologous antiserum*.
– DERIVATIVES **heterology** noun.

heteromerous /ˌhɛtəˈrɒm(ə)rəs/ ▶ **adjective** Biology having or composed of parts that differ in number or position.

heteromorphic /ˌhɛt(ə)rə(ʊ)ˈmɔːfɪk/ ▶ **adjective** Biology occurring in two or more different forms, especially at different stages in the life cycle.
– DERIVATIVES **heteromorph** noun, **heteromorphy** noun.

heteromorphism /ˌhɛt(ə)rə(ʊ)ˈmɔːfɪz(ə)m/ ▶ **noun** [mass noun] Biology the quality or condition of existing in various forms: *chromosomal heteromorphism*.

heteronomous /ˌhɛtəˈrɒnəməs/ ▶ **adjective** subject to a law or standard external to itself. ■ (in Kantian moral philosophy) acting in accordance with one's desires rather than reason or moral duty. Compare with AUTONOMOUS. ■ Biology subject to different laws of growth and development.
– DERIVATIVES **heteronomy** noun.

heteronormative /ˌhɛt(ə)rə(ʊ)ˈnɔːmətɪv/ ▶ **adjective** denoting or relating to a world view that promotes heterosexuality as the normal or preferred sexual orientation.
– DERIVATIVES **heteronormativity** noun.

heteronym /ˈhɛtərə(ʊ)nɪm/ ▶ **noun** Linguistics **1** each of two or more words which are spelled identically but have different sounds and meanings, such as *tear* meaning 'rip' and *tear* meaning 'liquid from the eye'.
2 each of two or more words which are used to refer to the identical thing in different geographical areas of a speech community, such as *nappy* and *diaper*.
3 each of two words having the same meaning but derived from unrelated sources, for example *preface* and *foreword*. Contrasted with PARONYM.
– DERIVATIVES **heteronymic** adjective, **heteronymous** adjective.

heteropolar /ˌhɛtərəʊˈpəʊlə/ ▶ **adjective** chiefly Physics characterized by opposite or alternating polarity. ■ (especially of an electric motor) with an armature passing north and south magnetic poles alternately.

Heteroptera /ˌhɛtəˈrɒpt(ə)rə/ ▶ **plural noun** Entomology a group of true bugs comprising those in which the forewings are non-uniform, having a thickened base and membranous tip. The predatory and water bugs belong to this group, as well as many plant bugs. Compare with HOMOPTERA. ● Suborder Heteroptera, order Hemiptera.
■ (**heteroptera**) bugs of this group.
– ORIGIN modern Latin (plural), from Greek *heteros* 'other' + *pteron* 'wing'.

heteropteran Entomology ▶ **noun** a bug of the group Heteroptera.
▶ **adjective** relating to or denoting heteropterans.
– DERIVATIVES **heteropterous** adjective.

heterosexism ▶ **noun** [mass noun] discrimination or prejudice against homosexuals on the assumption that heterosexuality is the normal sexual orientation.
– DERIVATIVES **heterosexist** adjective.

heterosexual ▶ **adjective** (of a person) sexually attracted to people of the opposite sex. ■ involving or characterized by sexual attraction between people of the opposite sex: *heterosexual relationships*.
▶ **noun** a heterosexual person.
– DERIVATIVES **heterosexuality** noun, **heterosexually** adverb.

heterosis /ˌhɛtəˈrəʊsɪs/ ▶ **noun** technical term for HYBRID VIGOUR.
– ORIGIN early 20th cent.: from Greek *heterōsis* 'alteration', from *heteros* 'other'.

heterostyly /ˈhɛtərə(ʊ)ˌstʌɪli/ ▶ **noun** [mass noun] Botany the condition (e.g. in primroses) of having styles of different lengths relative to the stamens in the flowers of different individual plants, to reduce self-fertilization.
– DERIVATIVES **heterostylous** adjective.
– ORIGIN late 19th cent.: from HETERO- 'different' + Greek *stulos* 'column' + -Y[3].

heterotic /ˌhɛtəˈrɒtɪk/ ▶ **adjective 1** Biology relating to hybrid vigour (heterosis).
2 Physics relating to a theory of cosmic strings combining elements of two earlier models.

heterotransplant ▶ **noun** another term for XENOGRAFT.

heterotroph /ˈhɛt(ə)rə(ʊ)trəʊf, -ˈtrɒf/ ▶ **noun** Biology an organism deriving its nutritional requirements from complex organic substances. Compare with AUTOTROPH.
– DERIVATIVES **heterotrophic** adjective, **heterotrophy** noun.
– ORIGIN early 20th cent.: from HETERO- 'other' + Greek *trophos* 'feeder'.

heterozygote /ˌhɛt(ə)rə(ʊ)ˈzʌɪgəʊt/ ▶ **noun** Genetics an individual having two different alleles of a particular gene or genes, and so giving rise to varying offspring. Compare with HOMOZYGOTE.
– DERIVATIVES **heterozygosity** noun, **heterozygous** adjective.

hetman /ˈhɛtmən/ ▶ **noun** (pl. **hetmen**) a Polish or Cossack military commander.
– ORIGIN Polish, probably from German *Hauptmann* 'captain'.

het up ▶ **adjective** [predic.] informal angry and agitated: *her husband is all* **het up about** *something*.
– ORIGIN mid 19th cent.: from dialect *het* 'heated, hot', surviving in Scots and northern English dialect.

heuchera /ˈhɔɪkərə, ˈhjuːk-/ ▶ **noun** a North American plant with dark green round or heart-shaped leaves and slender stems of tiny flowers. ● Genus *Heuchera*, family Saxifragaceae: many species, in particular *H. sanguinea*, with many ornamental cultivars.
– ORIGIN modern Latin, named after Johann H. von *Heucher* (1677–1747), German botanist.

heuriger /ˈhɔɪrɪgə/ (also **heurige**) ▶ **noun** (pl. **heurigen** /-g(ə)n/) [mass noun] (in Austria) wine from the latest harvest. ■ [count noun] an Austrian establishment where wine from the latest harvest is served.
– ORIGIN Austrian German, literally 'this year's (wine)'.

heuristic /ˌhjʊ(ə)ˈrɪstɪk/ ▶ **adjective** enabling a person to discover or learn something for themselves. ■ Computing proceeding to a solution by trial and error or by rules that are only loosely defined.
▶ **noun** a heuristic process or method. ■ (**heuristics**) [usu. treated as sing.] the study and use of heuristic techniques.
– DERIVATIVES **heuristically** adverb.
– ORIGIN early 19th cent.: formed irregularly from Greek *heuriskein* 'find'.

hevea /ˈhiːvɪə/ ▶ **noun** a South American tree of a genus which comprises the rubber trees. ● Genus *Hevea*, family Euphorbiaceae.
– ORIGIN modern Latin, from Quechua *hyeve*.

Hevesy /ˈhɛvəʃi/, George Charles de (1885–1966), Hungarian-born radiochemist. He studied radioisotopes and invented the technique of labelling with isotopic tracers. Hevesy was also co-discoverer of the element hafnium (1923). Nobel Prize for Chemistry (1943).

HEW ▶ **abbreviation** (the US Department of) Health, Education, and Welfare.

hew /hjuː/ ▶ **verb** (past participle **hewn** or **hewed**) **1** [with obj.] chop or cut (something, especially wood or coal) with an axe, pick, or other tool. ■ make or shape by cutting a hard material such as wood: *a seat hewn out of a fallen tree trunk*.
2 [no obj.] (**hew to**) N. Amer. conform or adhere to: *his administration would hew to high ethical standards*.
– ORIGIN Old English *hēawan*, of Germanic origin; related to Dutch *houwen* and German *hauen*.

hewer ▶ **noun** dated a person who cuts wood, stone, or other materials. ■ a miner who cuts coal from a seam.
– PHRASES **hewers of wood and drawers of water** menial drudges; labourers. [with biblical allusion to Josh. 9:21.]

hex[1] N. Amer. ▶ **verb** [with obj.] cast a spell on; bewitch: *he hexed her with his fingers*.
▶ **noun** a magic spell; a curse: *a death hex*. ■ a witch.
– ORIGIN mid 19th cent. (as a verb): from Pennsylvanian German *hexe* (verb), *Hex* (noun), from German *hexen* (verb), *Hexe* (noun).

hex[2] ▶ **adjective & noun** short for HEXADECIMAL.

hexa- (also **hex-** before a vowel) ▶ **combining form** six; having six.
– ORIGIN from Greek *hex* 'six'.

hexachord /ˈhɛksəkɔːd/ ▶ **noun** a musical scale of six notes with a semitone between the third and fourth. An overlapping series of seven such scales starting on G, C, and F formed the basis of medieval music theory.

hexad /ˈhɛksad/ ▶ **noun** technical a group or set of six.
– ORIGIN mid 17th cent. (denoting a series of six numbers): from Greek *hexas*, *hexad-*, from *hex* 'six'.

hexadecimal /ˌhɛksəˈdɛsɪm(ə)l/ ▶ **adjective** Computing relating to or using a system of numerical notation that has 16 rather than 10 as its base.
– DERIVATIVES **hexadecimally** adverb.

hexagon /ˈhɛksəg(ə)n/ ▶ **noun** a plane figure with six straight sides and angles.
– DERIVATIVES **hexagonal** adjective.
– ORIGIN late 16th cent.: via late Latin from Greek *hexagōnon*, neuter (used as a noun) of *hexagōnos* 'six-angled'.

hexagram ▶ **noun** a figure formed of six straight lines, in particular: ■ a star-shaped figure formed by two intersecting equilateral triangles. ■ any of a set of sixty-four figures made up of six parallel whole or broken lines, occurring in the ancient Chinese *I Ching*.
– ORIGIN mid 19th cent.: from HEXA- 'six' + Greek *gramma* 'line'.

hexahedron /ˌhɛksəˈhiːdrən, -ˈhɛd-/ ▶ **noun** (pl. **hexahedra** or **hexahedrons**) a solid figure with six plane faces.
– DERIVATIVES **hexahedral** adjective.
– ORIGIN late 16th cent.: from Greek *hexaedron*, neuter (used as a noun) of *hexaedros* 'six-faced'.

hexamerous /hɛkˈsam(ə)rəs/ ▶ **adjective** Botany & Zoology having parts arranged in groups of six. ■ consisting of six joints or parts.

hexameter /hɛkˈsamɪtə/ ▶ **noun** Prosody a line of verse consisting of six metrical feet.
– ORIGIN late Middle English: from Latin, from Greek *hexametros* 'of six measures' (from *hex* 'six' + *metron* 'measure').

hexane /ˈhɛkseɪn/ ▶ **noun** Chemistry a colourless liquid hydrocarbon of the alkane series, present in

petroleum spirit. ● Chem. formula: C_6H_{14}; five isomers, especially the straight-chain isomer (*n*-**hexane**).
– ORIGIN late 19th cent.: from **HEXA-** 'six' (denoting six carbon atoms) + **-ANE²**.

hexapla /ˈhɛksəplə/ ▶ **noun** a sixfold text in parallel columns, especially of the Old Testament.
– ORIGIN early 17th cent. (originally referring to Origen's edition of the Old Testament): from Greek, neuter plural of *hexaploos* 'sixfold', from *hex* 'six' + *ploos* '-fold'.

hexaploid /ˈhɛksəplɔɪd/ Genetics ▶ **adjective** (of a cell or nucleus) containing six homologous sets of chromosomes. ■ (of an organism or species) composed of hexaploid cells.
▶ **noun** a hexaploid organism, variety, or species.
– DERIVATIVES **hexaploidy** noun.

Hexapoda /ˌhɛksəˈpəʊdə/ ▶ **plural noun** Entomology a class of six-legged arthropods that comprises the insects. The name is used as another term for Insecta, especially when the primitive apterygotes are not considered to be true insects.
– DERIVATIVES **hexapod** noun.
– ORIGIN modern Latin (plural), from Greek *hexapous, hexapod-*, from *hex* 'six' + *pous* 'foot'.

hexastyle /ˈhɛksəstʌɪl/ Architecture ▶ **noun** a six-columned portico.
▶ **adjective** (of a portico) having six columns.
– ORIGIN early 18th cent.: from Greek *hexastulos*, from *hex* 'six' + *stulos* 'column'.

H

Hexateuch /ˈhɛksətjuːk/ ▶ **noun** the first six books of the Bible (Genesis to Joshua) collectively.
– ORIGIN late 19th cent.: from **HEXA-** 'six' + Greek *teukhos* 'book'.

hexavalent /ˌhɛksəˈveɪl(ə)nt/ ▶ **adjective** Chemistry having a valency of six.

hexose /ˈhɛksəʊz, -s/ ▶ **noun** Chemistry any of the class of simple sugars whose molecules contain six carbon atoms, such as glucose and fructose. They generally have the chemical formula $C_6H_{12}O_6$.
– ORIGIN late 19th cent.: from **HEXA-** 'six' + **-OSE²**.

hexyl /ˈhɛksʌɪl, -sɪl/ ▶ **noun** [as modifier] Chemistry of or denoting an alkyl radical $-C_6H_{13}$, derived from hexane.

hey ▶ **exclamation** used to attract attention, to express surprise, interest, or annoyance, or to elicit agreement: *hey, what's going on here?* ■ US used as a friendly greeting: *I just called to say hey.*
– PHRASES **hey up** N. English informal used as a greeting or as a way of drawing attention to something: *Hey up, Margaret! | Hey up! Here's the cops!* **what the hey** N. Amer. informal used as a euphemism for 'what the hell'.
– ORIGIN natural exclamation: first recorded in Middle English.

heyday ▶ **noun** (usu. **one's heyday**) the period of a person's or thing's greatest success, popularity, activity, or vigour: *the paper has lost millions of readers since its heyday in 1964.*
– ORIGIN late 16th cent. (denoting good spirits or passion): from archaic *heyday!*, an exclamation of joy, surprise, etc.

Heyerdahl /ˈheɪədɑːl/, Thor (1914–2002), Norwegian anthropologist. He is noted for his ocean voyages in primitive craft to demonstrate his theories of cultural diffusion, the best known of which was that of the balsa raft *Kon-Tiki* from Peru to the islands east of Tahiti in 1947.

hey presto ▶ **exclamation** Brit. a phrase announcing the successful completion of a trick, or to suggest that something has been done so easily that it seems to be magic: *press the start button and, hey presto, a copy comes out the other end.*

Hezbollah /ˌhɛzbəˈlɑː, ˈhɛzbʊlə/ (also **Hizbullah**) an extremist Shiite Muslim group which has close links with Iran, created after the Iranian revolution of 1979 and active especially in Lebanon.
– ORIGIN from Arabic *ḥizbullāh* 'Party of God', from *ḥezb* 'party' + *'allāh* (see **ALLAH**).

HF ▶ **abbreviation** Physics high frequency.

Hf ▶ **symbol** the chemical element hafnium.

hf ▶ **abbreviation** half.

HFC ▶ **abbreviation** hydrofluorocarbon.

HG ▶ **abbreviation** Brit. ■ Her or His Grace. ■ historical Home Guard.

Hg ▶ **symbol** the chemical element mercury.
– ORIGIN abbreviation of modern Latin *hydrargyrum*.

hg ▶ **abbreviation** hectogram(s).

HGH ▶ **abbreviation** human growth hormone.

HGV ▶ **abbreviation** Brit. heavy goods vehicle.

HH ▶ **abbreviation** ■ Brit. Her or His Highness. ■ His Holiness. ■ (used in describing grades of pencil lead) extra hard.

hh. ▶ **abbreviation** hands (as a unit of measurement of a horse's height).

hhd ▶ **abbreviation** hogshead(s).

H-hour ▶ **noun** the time of day at which an attack, landing, or other military operation is scheduled to begin.
– ORIGIN First World War: from *H* (for *hour*) + **HOUR**.

HI ▶ **abbreviation** Hawaii (in official postal use).

hi ▶ **exclamation** informal used as a friendly greeting or to attract attention: *'Hi there. How was the flight?'*
– ORIGIN natural exclamation: first recorded in late Middle English.

hiatus /hʌɪˈeɪtəs/ ▶ **noun** (pl. **hiatuses**) [usu. in sing.] a pause or break in continuity in a sequence or activity: *there was a brief hiatus in the war with France.* ■ Prosody & Grammar a break between two vowels coming together but not in the same syllable, as in *the ear* and *cooperate*.
– DERIVATIVES **hiatal** adjective.
– ORIGIN mid 16th cent. (originally denoting a physical gap): from Latin, literally 'gaping', from *hiare* 'gape'.

hiatus hernia (also **hiatal hernia**) ▶ **noun** Medicine the protrusion of an organ, typically the stomach, through the oesophageal opening in the diaphragm.

Hiawatha /ˌhʌɪəˈwɒθə/ a legendary 16th-century North American Indian teacher and chieftain, hero of a narrative poem by Henry Wadsworth Longfellow called *The Song of Hiawatha* (1855).

Hib ▶ **noun** a bacterium that causes infant meningitis. ● *Haemophilus influenzae* type B.
– ORIGIN late 20th cent.: acronym.

hiba /ˈhiːbə/ ▶ **noun** a Japanese conifer with evergreen scale-like leaves which form flattened sprays of foliage, widely planted as an ornamental and yielding durable timber. ● *Thujopsis dolabrata*, family Cupressaceae.
– ORIGIN Japanese.

hibachi /hɪˈbatʃi, ˈhɪbatʃi/ ▶ **noun** (pl. **hibachis**) a portable cooking apparatus similar to a small barbecue. ■ (in Japan) a large earthenware pan or brazier in which charcoal is burnt to provide indoor heating.
– ORIGIN mid 19th cent.: Japanese *hibachi, hi-hachi*, from *hi* 'fire' + *hachi* 'bowl, pot'.

hibakusha /ˈhɪbəˌkuːʃə/ ▶ **noun** (pl. **same**) (in Japan) a survivor of either of the atomic explosions at Hiroshima or Nagasaki in 1945.
– ORIGIN mid 20th cent.: Japanese, from *hi* 'suffer' + *baku* 'explosion' + *sha* 'person'.

hibernate ▶ **verb** [no obj.] (of an animal or plant) spend the winter in a dormant state. ■ (of a person) remain inactive or indoors for an extended period.
– DERIVATIVES **hibernation** noun, **hibernator** noun.
– ORIGIN early 19th cent. (earlier (mid 17th cent.) as *hibernation*): from Latin *hibernare*, from *hiberna* 'winter quarters', from *hibernus* 'wintry'.

Hibernian /hʌɪˈbəːnɪən/ ▶ **adjective** of or concerning Ireland (now chiefly used in names): *the Royal Hibernian Academy.*
▶ **noun** a native of Ireland (now chiefly used in names).
– ORIGIN from Latin *Hibernia* (alteration of *Iverna*, from Greek *I(w)ernē*, of Celtic origin; related to Irish *Éire, Éirinn* 'Ireland': see **EIRE, ERIN**) + **-AN**.

Hibernianism (also **Hibernicism**) ▶ **noun** an Irish idiom or expression.

Hiberno- /hʌɪˈbəːnəʊ/ ▶ **combining form** Irish; Irish and ...: *Hiberno-English.* ■ relating to Ireland.
– ORIGIN from medieval Latin *Hibernus* 'Irish'; see also **HIBERNIAN**.

hibiscus /hɪˈbɪskəs/ ▶ **noun** a plant of the mallow family, grown in warm climates for its large brightly coloured flowers or for products such as fibre or timber. ● Genus *Hibiscus*, family Malvaceae: many species, including the rose mallow.
– ORIGIN Latin, from Greek *hibiskos*, which Dioscorides identified with the marsh mallow.

hic ▶ **exclamation** used in writing to express the sound of a hiccup, especially a drunken one.
– ORIGIN late 19th cent.: imitative.

hiccup (also **hiccough** pronounced same) ▶ **noun** **1** an involuntary spasm of the diaphragm and respiratory organs, with a sudden closure of the glottis and a characteristic gulping sound: *then she got hiccups.* **2** a temporary or minor problem or setback: *just a little hiccup in our usual wonderful service.*
▶ **verb** (**hiccups, hiccuping, hiccuped**) [no obj.] have an attack of hiccups or a single hiccup.
– DERIVATIVES **hiccupy** adjective.
– ORIGIN late 16th cent.: imitative; the form *hiccough* arose by association with **COUGH**.

hic jacet /hɪk ˈdʒeɪsɛt, ˈjaket/ ▶ **noun** literary an epitaph.
– ORIGIN Latin, 'here lies', the first two words of a Latin epitaph.

hick ▶ **noun** informal, chiefly N. Amer. a person who lives in the country, regarded as being unintelligent or parochial: [as modifier] *she puts on a hick accent.*
– ORIGIN mid 16th cent.: pet form of the given name *Richard*.

hickey ▶ **noun** (pl. **hickeys**) **1** N. Amer. informal a gadget. **2** N. Amer. informal a love bite or pimple. **3** a blemish in printing, especially an area in a solid that has not been inked.
– ORIGIN early 20th cent.: of unknown origin.

Hickok, James Butler (1837–76), American frontiersman and marshal; known as **Wild Bill Hickok**. The legend of his invincibility in his encounters with frontier desperadoes became something of a challenge to gunmen, and he was eventually murdered at Deadwood, South Dakota.

hickory ▶ **noun** **1** a chiefly North American tree of the walnut family, which yields tough, heavy timber and typically bears edible nuts (pecans). ● Genus *Carya*, family Juglandaceae: several species. ■ a stick made of hickory wood. **2** (also **hickory wattle**) Austral. an acacia tree that yields tough, close-grained timber. ● Genus *Acacia*, family Leguminosae: several species, in particular *A. implexa*.
– ORIGIN late 17th cent.: abbreviation of *pohickery*, the local Virginian name, from Algonquian *pawcohiccora*.

hid past of **HIDE¹**.

Hidalgo /hɪˈdalgəʊ/ a state of southern Mexico; capital, Pachuca de Soto.

hidalgo /hɪˈdalgəʊ/ ▶ **noun** (pl. **hidalgos**) a gentleman in a Spanish-speaking country.
– ORIGIN late 16th cent.: Spanish, from *hijo de algo*, literally 'son of something' (i.e. of an important person).

Hidatsa /hɪˈdatsə/ ▶ **noun** (pl. **same** or **Hidatsas**) **1** a member of an American Indian people living on the upper Missouri River. **2** [mass noun] the Siouan language of the Hidatsa, now almost extinct.
▶ **adjective** relating to the Hidatsa or their language.
– ORIGIN from Hidatsa *hiratsa* 'willow wood lodge'.

hidden past participle of **HIDE¹**. ▶ **adjective** kept out of sight; concealed: *hidden dangers | her hidden feelings.*
– DERIVATIVES **hiddenness** noun.

hidden agenda ▶ **noun** a secret or ulterior motive for something.

hiddenite /ˈhɪd(ə)nʌɪt/ ▶ **noun** [mass noun] a rare green gem variety of spodumene (an aluminosilicate mineral).
– ORIGIN late 19th cent.: named after William E. Hidden (1832–1918), American mineralogist.

hidden reserves ▶ **plural noun** a company's funds that are not declared on its balance sheet. ■ mental or physical capabilities kept in reserve and available in exceptional circumstances: *hidden reserves of power.*

hide¹ ▶ **verb** (past **hid**; past participle **hidden**) [with obj.] put or keep out of sight: *he hid the money in the house | they swept up the pieces and hid them away.* ■ prevent (someone or something) from being seen: *clouds rolled up and hid the moon.* ■ prevent (an emotion or fact) from being apparent or known; keep secret: *Herbert could hardly hide his dislike.* ■ [no obj.] conceal oneself: *Juliet's first instinct was to hide under the blankets | he used to hide out in a cave.* ■ [no obj.] (**hide behind**) use (someone or something) to protect oneself from criticism or punishment, especially in a way considered cowardly: *companies with poor security can hide behind the law.*
▶ **noun** Brit. a camouflaged shelter used to observe wildlife at close quarters.
– PHRASES **hide one's head** cover up one's face or keep out of sight, especially from shame. **hide one's light under a bushel** keep quiet about one's talents or accomplishments. [with biblical allusion to Matt. 5:15.]
– DERIVATIVES **hider** noun.
– ORIGIN Old English *hȳdan*, of West Germanic origin.

hide² ▶ **noun** the skin of an animal, especially when tanned or dressed. ■ used to refer to a person's ability to withstand criticisms or insults: *she had never*

managed to develop a hide quite tough enough for his barbs to bounce off.
– PHRASES **hide or hair of** [with negative] the slightest trace of: *I could find neither hide nor hair of him.* **save one's hide** escape from danger or difficulty. **tan** (or **whip**) **someone's hide** beat or flog someone. ■ punish someone severely.
– DERIVATIVES **hided** adjective [in combination] *thick-hided.*
– ORIGIN Old English *hȳd*, of Germanic origin; related to Dutch *huid* and German *Haut*.

hide[3] ▶ noun a former measure of land used in England, typically equal to between 60 and 120 acres, being the amount that would support a family and its dependants.
– ORIGIN Old English *hīd, hīgid*, from the base of *hīgan, hīwan* 'household members', of Germanic origin.

hide-and-seek ▶ noun [mass noun] a children's game in which one or more players hide and the other or others have to look for them.

hideaway ▶ noun a place used for hiding in or as a retreat from other people.

hide beetle ▶ noun a dull brown scavenging beetle that feeds on stored hides and dried meat and may be a serious pest of warehouses. ● *Dermestes maculatus*, family Dermestidae.

hidebound ▶ adjective unwilling or unable to change because of tradition or convention: *they are working to change hidebound corporate cultures.*
– ORIGIN mid 16th cent. (as a noun denoting a malnourished condition of cattle): from HIDE[2] + BOUND[4]. The earliest sense of the adjective (referring to cattle) was extended to emaciated human beings, and then applied figuratively in the sense 'narrow in outlook'.

hideosity ▶ noun (pl. **hideosities**) **1** a very ugly object.
2 the quality of being hideous.

hideous ▶ adjective extremely ugly: *hideous lizard-like creatures.* ■ extremely unpleasant: *the whole hideous story.*
– DERIVATIVES **hideously** adverb [as submodifier] *a hideously expensive camera*, **hideousness** noun.
– ORIGIN Middle English: from Old French *hidos, hideus*, from *hide, hisde* 'fear', of unknown origin.

hideout ▶ noun a hiding place, especially one used by someone who has broken the law.

hidey-hole (also **hidy-hole**) ▶ noun informal a place for hiding something or oneself in, especially as a retreat from other people.

hiding[1] ▶ noun informal a physical beating: *they caught him and gave him a hiding.* ■ a severe defeat: *if they'd played badly they might have expected a hiding.*
– PHRASES **be on a hiding to nothing** Brit. be unlikely to succeed, or be unlikely to gain much advantage if one does.
– ORIGIN early 19th cent.: from HIDE[2] + -ING[1].

hiding[2] ▶ noun [mass noun] the action of concealing someone or something. ■ the state of being hidden: *the shipowner had gone into hiding.*
– ORIGIN Middle English: from HIDE[1] + -ING[1].

hiding place ▶ noun a place for concealing someone or something.

hidrosis /hɪˈdrəʊsɪs/ ▶ noun [mass noun] Medicine the action of sweating.
– DERIVATIVES **hidrotic** adjective.
– ORIGIN mid 19th cent.: from Greek *hidrōsis*, from *hidrōs* 'sweat'.

hie /hʌɪ/ ▶ verb (**hies, hieing** or **hying, hied**) [no obj., with adverbial of direction] archaic go quickly: *I hied down to New Orleans | I* ***hied me*** *to a winehouse.*
– ORIGIN Middle English: from Old English *hīgian* 'strive, pant', of unknown origin.

hielaman /ˈhiːləmən/ ▶ noun an Australian Aboriginal shield made of bark or wood.
– ORIGIN from Dharuk *yilimang*.

hierarch /ˈhʌɪərɑːk/ ▶ noun a chief priest, archbishop, or other leader.
– ORIGIN late Middle English: via medieval Latin from Greek *hierarkhēs*, from *hieros* 'sacred' + *arkhēs* 'ruler'.

hierarchical ▶ adjective of the nature of a hierarchy; arranged in order of rank: *the hierarchical bureaucracy of a local authority.*
– DERIVATIVES **hierarchically** adverb.

hierarchy /ˈhʌɪərɑːki/ ▶ noun (pl. **hierarchies**) a system in which members of an organization or society are ranked according to relative status or authority. ■ (**the hierarchy**) the clergy of the Catholic Church or of an episcopal Church. ■ (**the hierarchy**) the upper echelons of a hierarchical system: *the magazine was read quite widely even by some of the hierarchy.* ■ an arrangement or classification of things according to relative importance or inclusiveness: *a taxonomic hierarchy of phyla, classes, orders, families, genera, and species.* ■ Theology the traditional system of orders of angels and other heavenly beings.
– DERIVATIVES **hierarchic** adjective, **hierarchization** noun, **hierarchize** (also **hierarchise**) verb.
– ORIGIN late Middle English: via Old French and medieval Latin from Greek *hierarkhia*, from *hierarkhēs* 'sacred ruler' (see HIERARCH). The earliest sense was 'system of orders of angels and heavenly beings'; the other senses date from the 17th cent.

hieratic /ˌhʌɪəˈratɪk/ ▶ adjective of or concerning priests: *he raised both his arms in a hieratic gesture.* ■ of or in the ancient Egyptian writing of abridged hieroglyphics used by priests. Compare with DEMOTIC. ■ of or concerning Egyptian or Greek styles of art adhering to early methods as laid down by religious tradition.
– DERIVATIVES **hieratical** adjective, **hieratically** adverb.
– ORIGIN mid 17th cent. (earlier as *hieratical*): via Latin from Greek *hieratikos*, from *hierasthai* 'be a priest', from *hiereus* 'priest', *hieros* 'sacred'.

hiero- /ˈhʌɪ(ə)rəʊ/ ▶ combining form sacred; holy.
– ORIGIN from Greek *hieros* 'sacred'.

hierocracy /hʌɪ(ə)ˈrɒkrəsi/ ▶ noun (pl. **hierocracies**) [mass noun] rule by priests. ■ [count noun] a ruling body composed of priests.
– DERIVATIVES **hierocratic** adjective.

hieroglyph /ˈhʌɪ(ə)rəglɪf/ ▶ noun a stylized picture of an object representing a word, syllable, or sound, as found in ancient Egyptian and certain other writing systems. ■ a secret or incomprehensible symbol.
– ORIGIN late 16th cent.: back-formation from HIEROGLYPHIC.

hieroglyphic ▶ noun (**hieroglyphics**) writing consisting of hieroglyphs. ■ enigmatic or incomprehensible symbols or writing: *notebooks filled with illegible hieroglyphics.*
▶ adjective of or written in hieroglyphs. ■ of the nature of a hieroglyph; symbolic or enigmatic.
– DERIVATIVES **hieroglyphical** adjective, **hieroglyphically** adverb.
– ORIGIN late 16th cent.: from French *hiéroglyphique*, from Greek *hieroglyphikos*, from *hieros* 'sacred' + *gluphē* 'carving'.

hierogram /ˈhʌɪ(ə)rə(ʊ)gram/ ▶ noun a sacred inscription or symbol.

hierolatry /ˌhʌɪəˈrɒlətri/ ▶ noun [mass noun] the worship of saints or sacred things.

hierology /hʌɪəˈrɒlədʒi/ ▶ noun [mass noun] sacred literature or lore.

hierophant /ˈhʌɪ(ə)rə(ʊ)fant/ ▶ noun a person, especially a priest, who interprets sacred mysteries or esoteric principles.
– DERIVATIVES **hierophantic** adjective.
– ORIGIN late 17th cent.: via late Latin from Greek *hierophantēs*, from *hieros* 'sacred' + *phainein* 'show, reveal'.

hi-fi ▶ adjective of or relating to the reproduction of music or other sound with high fidelity.
▶ noun (pl. **hi-fis**) a set of equipment for playing CDs or records in high-fidelity sound.
– ORIGIN 1950s: abbreviation of HIGH FIDELITY.

higgle ▶ verb archaic spelling of HAGGLE.

higgledy-piggledy ▶ adverb & adjective in confusion or disorder: [as adv.] *bits of paper hanging higgledy-piggledy on the walls* | [as adj.] *a higgledy-piggledy mountain of newspapers.*
– ORIGIN late 16th cent.: rhyming jingle, probably with reference to the irregular herding together of pigs.

higgler ▶ noun W. Indian a person who travels around selling small items; a pedlar.

Higgs (also **Higgs boson** or **Higgs particle**) ▶ noun Physics a subatomic particle whose existence is predicted by the theory which unified the weak and electromagnetic interactions.
– ORIGIN 1970s: named after Peter W. Higgs (born 1929), English physicist.

high ▶ adjective **1** of great vertical extent: *the top of a high mountain.* ■ (after a measurement and in questions) measuring a specified distance from top to bottom: *a tree forty feet high.* ■ far above ground, sea level, or another point of reference: *a palace high up on a hill.* ■ extending above the normal level: *a round face with a high forehead.* ■ [attrib.] (of an area) inland and well above sea level: *high prairies.* ■ [attrib.] performed at, to, or from a considerable height: *high diving.* ■ (of latitude) close to 90°; near the North or South Pole.
2 great, or greater than normal, in quantity, size, or intensity: *a high temperature | sweets are very high* ***in*** *calories.* ■ of large numerical or monetary value: *they had been playing for high stakes.* ■ very favourable: *she had no very high opinion of men.* ■ extreme in religious or political views: *a man of high Tory opinions.* ■ (of a period or movement) at its peak: *high summer.*
3 great in rank, status, or importance: *both held high office under Lloyd George | financial security is* ***high on*** *your list of priorities.* ■ ranking above others of the same kind: *the last High King of Ireland.* ■ morally or culturally superior: *blurring the distinctions between high art and popular art.*
4 (of a sound or note) having a frequency at the upper end of the auditory range: *a high, squeaky voice.* ■ (of a singer or instrument) producing notes of relatively high pitch.
5 [predic.] informal feeling euphoric, especially from the effects of drugs or alcohol: *she wasn't tipsy, just a little high | some of them were* ***high on*** *Ecstasy.*
6 [predic.] (especially of food) unpleasantly strong-smelling because beginning to go bad. ■ (of game) slightly decomposed and so ready to cook.
7 Phonetics (of a vowel) produced with the tongue relatively near the palate.
▶ noun **1** a high point, level, or figure: *commodity prices were at a rare high.* ■ a high-frequency sound or musical note. ■ a high power setting: *the vent blower was on high.* ■ an area of high barometric pressure; an anticyclone.
2 a notably happy or successful moment: *the highs and lows of life.* ■ [usu. in sing.] informal a state of high spirits or euphoria: *if the stable is doing well then everybody's* ***on a high.***
3 informal, chiefly N. Amer. high school. *I go to junior high.*
4 top gear in a motor vehicle.
▶ adverb **1** at or to a considerable or specified height: *the sculpture stood about five feet high | a dish piled high with baked beans.*
2 highly: *he ranked high among the pioneers of chemical technology.* ■ at a high price: *buying shares low and selling them high.*
3 (of a sound) at or to a high pitch.
– PHRASES **ace** (or **king** or **queen** etc.) **high** (in card games) having the ace (or another specified card) as the highest-ranking. **from on high** from remote high authority or heaven: *central government programmes coming down from on high.* **high and dry** out of the water, especially stranded by the sea as it retreats. ■ without resources or help: *your family would be* ***left high and dry*** *by the death of the breadwinner.* **high and low** in many different places: *I* ***searched high and low*** *for a new teacher.* **high and mighty** informal behaving as though one is more important than others. **the high ground** a position of superiority (originally in military conflict): *he wants the EC to take the moral high ground by agreeing to an environmental tax.* **a high old ——** [attrib.] informal used for emphasis: *a high old time of it we all had.* **high, wide, and handsome** informal expansive and impressive. [from *Arizona Nights* by Stewart E. White (1873–1946), American author.] **it is high time that ——** it is past the time when something should have happened or been done: *it was high time that she faced facts.* **on high** in or to heaven or a high place: *a spotter plane circling on high.* **on one's high horse** informal behaving in an arrogant or pompous manner. **run high** (of a river) be close to overflowing, with a strong current. ■ (of feelings) be intense: *passions run high when marriages break up.*
– ORIGIN Old English *hēah*, of Germanic origin; related to Dutch *hoog* and German *hoch*.

high altar ▶ noun the chief altar of a church, typically in the chancel.

highball N. Amer. ▶ noun **1** a drink consisting of a spirit, especially whisky, and a mixer such as soda, served with ice in a tall glass.
2 informal a railway signal to proceed.
▶ verb [no obj., with adverbial of direction] informal travel fast: *they highballed north.*

high-band ▶ adjective relating to or denoting a video system using a relatively high carrier frequency, which allows more bandwidth for the signal.

high beam ▶ noun North American term for FULL BEAM.

H

highbinder /ˈhʌɪbʌɪndə/ ▸ **noun** US informal an unscrupulous person, especially a corrupt politician. ▪ an assassin, especially one belonging to a Chinese-American criminal organization.
– ORIGIN early 19th cent.: first recorded as *Highbinders*, the name of a New York gang.

high-born ▸ **adjective** having noble parents: *a high-born Portuguese family*.

highboy ▸ **noun** N. Amer. a tall chest of drawers on legs.

highbrow often derogatory ▸ **adjective** intellectual or rarefied in taste: *innovatory art had a small, mostly highbrow following*.
▸ **noun** a highbrow person.

high chair ▸ **noun** a chair with long legs for a baby or small child, fitted with a tray that is used like a table at mealtimes.

High Church ▸ **noun** [treated as sing. or pl.] a tradition within the Anglican Church emphasizing ritual, priestly authority, sacraments, and historical continuity with Catholic Christianity.
– DERIVATIVES **High Churchman noun**.

high-class ▸ **adjective** of a high standard, quality, or social class: *a high-class hotel*.

high colour (also **high colouring**) ▸ **noun** a flushed complexion: *he had a high colour to his cheeks*.

high command ▸ **noun** the commander-in-chief and associated senior staff of an army, navy, or air force.

high commission ▸ **noun** an embassy of one Commonwealth country in another.
– DERIVATIVES **high commissioner noun**.

high-concept ▸ **adjective** (especially of a film or television plot) having a striking and easily communicable idea.

high-cost ▸ **adjective** relatively expensive: *risky high-cost loans*.

high court ▸ **noun** a supreme court of justice. ▪ (in full **High Court of Justice**) (in England and Wales) the court of unlimited civil jurisdiction comprising three divisions: Queen's Bench, Chancery, and the Family Division. ▪ (in full **High Court of Justiciary**) the supreme criminal court of Scotland.

High Court of Parliament ▸ **noun** (in the UK) formal term for PARLIAMENT.

high day ▸ **noun** Brit. the day of a religious festival.
– PHRASES **high days and holidays** informal special occasions: *the drawing room is used only on high days and holidays*.

high-density lipoprotein ▸ **noun** [mass noun] a kind of lipoprotein in blood plasma that promotes the transfer of cholesterol to the liver for excretion or reuse.

high-dependency ▸ **adjective** Brit. relating to hospital patients requiring a high level of medical treatment and supervision.

high-end ▸ **adjective** denoting the most expensive of a range of products: *high-end computers*.

high enema ▸ **noun** an enema delivered into the colon.

Higher ▸ **noun** (in Scotland) the more advanced of the two main levels of the Scottish Certificate of Education. Compare with ORDINARY GRADE.

higher animals ▸ **plural noun** animals of relatively advanced or developed characteristics, such as mammals and other vertebrates.

higher court ▸ **noun** Law a court that can overrule the decision of another.

higher criticism ▸ **noun** [mass noun] the study of the literary methods and sources discernible in a text, especially as applied to biblical writings.

higher education ▸ **noun** [mass noun] education at universities or similar educational establishments, especially to degree level.

higher mathematics ▸ **plural noun** [usu. treated as sing.] advanced mathematics, such as number theory and topology, as taught at university level.

higher plants ▸ **plural noun** plants of relatively complex or advanced characteristics, especially vascular plants (including flowering plants).

higher-up ▸ **noun** informal a senior person in an organization.

highest common factor (abbrev.: **HCF**) ▸ **noun** Mathematics the highest number that can be divided exactly into each of two or more numbers.

high explosive ▸ **noun** a chemical explosive of the kind used in shells and bombs, which is more rapid and destructive in its effects than gunpowder.

highfalutin /ˌhʌɪfəˈluːtɪn/ (also **highfaluting** /-tɪŋ/) ▸ **adjective** informal (especially of speech, writing, or ideas) pompous or pretentious: *you don't want any highfalutin jargon*.
– ORIGIN mid 19th cent. (originally US): perhaps from HIGH + *fluting* (present participle of FLUTE).

high fashion ▸ **noun** another term for HAUTE COUTURE.

high fidelity ▸ **noun** [mass noun] the reproduction of sound with little distortion, giving a result very similar to the original.

high finance ▸ **noun** [mass noun] financial transactions involving large sums.

high five informal, chiefly N. Amer. ▸ **noun** a gesture of celebration or greeting in which two people slap each other's palms with their arms raised.
▸ **verb** (**high-five**) [with obj.] greet with such a gesture.

high-flown ▸ **adjective** (especially of language or ideas) extravagant and grand-sounding.

high-flyer (also **high-flier**) ▸ **noun** a person who is or has the potential to be very successful, especially academically or in business.
– DERIVATIVES **high-flying adjective**.

high forest ▸ **noun** [mass noun] forest consisting of tall trees. ▪ Forestry forest raised wholly or mainly from seed, especially as opposed to pollarded or coppiced forest.

high frequency ▸ **noun** (in radio) a frequency of 3–30 megahertz.

high gear ▸ **noun** a gear that causes a wheeled vehicle to move fast, due to a high ratio between the speed of the wheels and that of the mechanism driving them.

High German ▸ **noun** [mass noun] the standard literary and spoken form of German, originally used in the highlands in the south of Germany. The establishment of this form as a standard language owes much to the biblical translations of Martin Luther in the 16th century. See also MIDDLE HIGH GERMAN, OLD HIGH GERMAN.

high-handed ▸ **adjective** using power or authority without considering the feelings of others: *a fairly high-handed decision*.
– DERIVATIVES **high-handedly adverb**, **high-handedness noun**.

high hat ▸ **noun 1** a tall hat, especially a top hat. ▪ N. Amer. informal a snobbish or supercilious person.
2 (**high-hat**) variant form of HI-HAT.
3 a silvery marine fish with longitudinal brown stripes and a long upright dorsal fin, found in shallow rocky waters of the Caribbean. ● *Equetus acuminatus*, family Sciaenidae.
▸ **adjective** (**high-hat**) N. Amer. informal snobbish.
▸ **verb** (**high-hat**) (**high-hats**, **high-hatting**, **high-hatted**) [with obj.] N. Amer. informal act in a snobbish or supercilious manner towards (someone).

high heels ▸ **plural noun** women's shoes with tall, thin heels.
– DERIVATIVES **high-heeled adjective**.

High Holidays (also **High Holy Days**) ▸ **plural noun** the Jewish festivals of Yom Kippur and Rosh Hashana. Also called DAYS OF AWE.

high hurdles ▸ **plural noun** [treated as sing.] a race in which runners jump over hurdles 107 cm (42 inches) high.
– DERIVATIVES **high hurdler noun**.

high-impact ▸ **adjective 1** (of plastic or a similar substance) able to withstand great impact without breaking.
2 denoting exercises, typically aerobics, that place a great deal of stress on the body.

high jinks ▸ **plural noun** boisterous fun: *high jinks behind the wheel of a car*.
– ORIGIN late 17th cent.: see JINK.

high jump ▸ **noun** (**the high jump**) an athletic event in which competitors jump high over a bar which is raised until only one competitor can jump it without dislodging it.
– PHRASES **be for the high jump** Brit. informal be about to be severely reprimanded or punished.
– DERIVATIVES **high jumper noun**.

high-key (also **high-keyed**) ▸ **adjective** Art & Photography having a predominance of light or bright tones.

high kick ▸ **noun** a kick with the foot high in the air, for example in dancing or martial arts.
– DERIVATIVES **high-kicking adjective**.

highland ▸ **noun 1** [mass noun] (also **highlands**) an area of high or mountainous land: *the highlands of Madagascar* | [as modifier] *a highland region of Vietnam*.
2 (**the Highlands**) the mountainous part of Scotland, to the north of Glasgow and Stirling, often associated with Gaelic culture: [as modifier] *a Highland regiment*. ▪ (**Highland**) a council area of northern Scotland; administrative centre, Inverness.
– DERIVATIVES **highlander noun**.
– ORIGIN Old English *hēahlond* 'a high promontory' (see HIGH, LAND).

Highland cattle ▸ **plural noun** animals of a shaggy-haired breed of cattle with long, curved, widely spaced horns.

Highland clearances the forced removal of crofters from their land in the Highlands of Scotland in the late 18th and early 19th centuries. The clearances, carried out by landlords wanting to install sheep and deer on their estates, led to extreme hardship as well as to widespread emigration to North America and elsewhere.

Highland dress ▸ **noun** [mass noun] clothing in the traditional style of the Scottish Highlands, now chiefly worn on formal occasions and including the kilt.

Highland fling ▸ **noun** a vigorous Scottish dance consisting of a series of complex steps performed solo, originally to celebrate victory.

Highland Games ▸ **plural noun** a meeting for athletic events, playing of the bagpipes, and dancing, held in the Scottish Highlands or by Scots elsewhere.

highland moccasin ▸ **noun** the North American copperhead snake.

Highland pony ▸ **noun** a large sturdy pony of a breed with a long mane and tail, originally from Scotland.

high-level ▸ **adjective** at or of a level above that which is normal or average: *a high-level cistern*. ▪ relating to or involving people of high administrative rank or great authority: *high-level negotiations*. ▪ Computing denoting a programming language that is relatively accessible to the user, having instructions that resemble a natural language such as English. ▪ (of nuclear waste) highly radioactive and requiring long-term storage in isolation.

high life ▸ **noun** [mass noun] **1** (also **high living**) an extravagant social life as enjoyed by the wealthy.
2 (usu. **highlife**) a style of dance music of West African origin, influenced by rock and jazz.

highlight ▸ **noun 1** an outstanding part of an event or period of time: *he views that season as the highlight of his career*. ▪ (**highlights**) the best parts of a sporting or other event edited for broadcasting or recording: *Gary Lineker presents the highlights of today's semi-final*.
2 a bright or reflective area in a painting, picture, or design. ▪ (usu. **highlights**) a bright tint in the hair, especially one created artificially by bleaching or dyeing.
▸ **verb** [with obj.] **1** draw special attention to: *the issues highlighted by the report*. ▪ make visually prominent: *a vast backdrop with the colourful logo highlighted with lasers*. ▪ mark with a highlighter: *a photocopy with sections highlighted in green*.
2 create highlights in (hair).

highlighter ▸ **noun 1** a broad marker pen used to overlay transparent fluorescent colour on text or a part of an illustration.
2 a cosmetic used to emphasize features such as the eyes or cheekbones.

high-low ▸ **noun** historical a lace-up boot with a low heel, reaching to the ankle, worn by the military in the 18th and early 19th centuries.

highly ▸ **adverb** at or to a high degree or level: [as submodifier] *a highly dangerous substance* | *highly paid people*. ▪ favourably: *his colleagues think very highly of him*.
– ORIGIN Old English *hēalīce* (see HIGH, -LY[1]).

highly strung ▸ **adjective** Brit. very nervous and easily upset: *highly strung horses*.

high-maintenance ▸ **adjective** needing a lot of work to keep in good condition. ▪ informal (of a person) demanding a lot of attention: *if Martin could keep a high-maintenance girl like Tania happy, he must be doing something right*.

High Mass ▸ **noun** a Roman Catholic or Anglo-Catholic mass with full ceremonial, including music and incense and typically having the assistance of a deacon and subdeacon.

high-minded ▸ **adjective** having strong moral principles: *rich high-minded Victorians*.
– DERIVATIVES **high-mindedly adverb**, **high-mindedness noun**.

high muck-a-muck (also **high muckety-muck**) ▸ **noun** N. Amer. informal a person in a position of authority, especially one who is overbearing or conceited.
– ORIGIN mid 19th cent.: perhaps from Chinook *hiyu* 'plenty' + *muckamuck* 'food', from Nootka *ḥayo* 'ten' + *mar̓hor̓maq-* 'choice wheatmeal', with *high* substituted for *hiyu*.

highness ▸ **noun 1** (**His/Your** etc. **Highness**) a title given to a person of royal rank, or used in addressing them: *I am most grateful, Your Highness.*
2 [mass noun] the quality of being high: *the highness of her cheekbones.*
– ORIGIN Old English *hēanes* (see **HIGH, -NESS**).

high noon ▸ **noun 1** midday.
2 an event or confrontation which is likely to decide the final outcome of a situation: *the high noon of the peace process.* [popularized by the film *High Noon* (1952).]

high note ▸ **noun** a successful point in an event or period of time: *he wants to end his managerial career **on a high note**.*

high-octane ▸ **adjective** denoting petrol having a high octane number and thus good anti-knock properties. ■ powerful or dynamic: *a high-octane forty-year-old.*

high-pass ▸ **adjective** Electronics (of a filter) transmitting all frequencies above a certain value.

high-pitched ▸ **adjective 1** (of a sound) high: *a high-pitched wail.*
2 (of a roof) steep.

high places ▸ **plural noun** positions of power or authority: *people **in high places** were taking note.*

high point ▸ **noun** the most enjoyable or significant part of an experience or period of time: *the English lesson was **the high point of** the morning.*

high polymer ▸ **noun** a polymer having a high molecular weight, such as those used in plastics and resins.

high-powered (also **high-power**) ▸ **adjective** (of a machine or device) having greater than normal strength or capabilities: *a high-powered sports car.* ■ having a great deal of power, influence, or dynamism: *high-powered senior executives.* ■ involving a great deal of responsibility: *a very high-powered job.*

high pressure ▸ **noun** [mass noun] a condition of the atmosphere in which the pressure is above average (e.g. in an anticyclone).
▸ **adjective 1** using or containing a gas or liquid subject to great pressure: *high-pressure water jets.*
2 involving a high degree of persuasion: *high-pressure sales techniques.* ■ involving a great deal of anxiety or stress: *a high-pressure job.*

high priest ▸ **noun** the chief priest of the historic Jewish religion. ■ the head of a religious cult or similar group. ■ the chief advocate or proponent of a particular belief or practice: *the high priest of surrealism.*

high priestess ▸ **noun** a female high priest.

high profile ▸ **noun** [in sing.] a position attracting much attention or publicity: *people who have a high profile in the community.*
▸ **adjective** attracting much attention or publicity: *a high-profile military presence.*

high-quality ▸ **adjective** of very good quality: *a range of high-quality wines.*

high-ranking ▸ **adjective** having a senior or important position in a particular hierarchy: *a high-ranking government official.*

high relief ▸ **noun** see **RELIEF** (sense 4).

High Renaissance see **RENAISSANCE**.

high-res ▸ **adjective** variant spelling of **HI-RES**.

high-rise ▸ **adjective** (of a building) having many storeys: *a high-rise block of flats.* ■ taller or set higher than normal: *high-rise handlebars.*
▸ **noun** a building with many storeys: *a twelve-floor high-rise.*

high-risk ▸ **adjective** involving or exposed to a high level of danger: *high-risk activities such as skydiving and motocross racing.*

high road ▸ **noun** a main road: [in place names] *Kilburn High Road.* ■ a direct or certain route or course. ■ N. Amer. a morally superior approach towards something: *the company **took the high road**, announcing it would extend the benefits to all its workers.*

high roller ▸ **noun** informal, chiefly N. Amer. a person who gambles or spends large sums of money.
– DERIVATIVES **high-rolling** adjective.
– ORIGIN with reference to rolling dice.

high school ▸ **noun 1** N. Amer. a secondary school.
2 (in the UK except Scotland) used chiefly in names of grammar schools or independent fee-paying secondary schools, or for the lower years of a secondary school: *Wycombe High School.*
– DERIVATIVES **high schooler** noun.

high seas ▸ **plural noun** (**the high seas**) the open ocean, especially that not within any country's jurisdiction.

high season ▸ **noun** chiefly Brit. the most popular time of year at a resort, hotel, or tourist attraction, when prices are highest.

high-security ▸ **adjective** extremely secure: *a high-security jail.*

high sheriff ▸ **noun** see **SHERIFF**.

high sign ▸ **noun** N. Amer. informal a surreptitious gesture, often prearranged, giving warning or indicating that all is well: *I'm getting the high sign from my secretary—gotta go.*

Highsmith, Patricia (1921–95), American writer of detective fiction; born *Patricia Plangman.* Her novels are noted for their black humour, particularly those featuring Tom Ripley, an amoral anti-hero resident in France. *Strangers on a Train* (1949) was filmed by Alfred Hitchcock in 1951.

high society ▸ **noun** see **SOCIETY** (sense 1).

high-sounding ▸ **adjective** (of language or ideas) extravagant and grand: *high-sounding moralism.*

high-speed ▸ **adjective** moving, operating, or happening very quickly: *high-speed travel.* ■ (of photographic film) needing little light or only short exposure. ■ (of steel) suitable for drill bits and other tools that cut so fast that they become red-hot.

high spirits ▸ **plural noun** lively and cheerful behaviour or mood: *the team returned **in high spirits**.*
– DERIVATIVES **high-spirited** adjective, **high-spiritedness** noun.

high spot ▸ **noun** the most enjoyable or significant part of an experience or period of time: *the high spot of the tour was to be an audience with the Pope.*
– PHRASES **hit the high spots** informal visit the most exciting places in a town.

high-stick ▸ **verb** [with obj.] (often as noun **high-sticking**) Ice Hockey strike (an opponent) on or above the shoulders with one's stick, for which a penalty may be assessed.

high street ▸ **noun** Brit. the main street of a town, especially as the traditional site for most shops, banks, and other businesses: *the approaching festive season boosted the high street* | [in place names] *Kensington High Street.* ■ [as modifier] (of retail goods) catering to the needs of the ordinary public: *high-street fashion.*

high-strung ▸ **adjective** N. Amer. another term for **HIGHLY STRUNG**.

hight /hʌɪt/ ▸ **adjective** [predic.] archaic or literary named: *a little pest, hight Tommy Moore.*
– ORIGIN Middle English, from Old English *heht*, past tense of *hātan* 'command, call, or name', of Germanic origin; related to Dutch *heten* and German *heissen*.

high table ▸ **noun** Brit. a table in a dining hall, typically on a platform, for the most important people, such as the fellows of a college.

hightail ▸ **verb** [no obj., with adverbial of direction] informal, chiefly N. Amer. move or travel fast: *they **hightailed it** to India.*

high tea ▸ **noun** Brit. a meal eaten in the late afternoon or early evening, typically consisting of a cooked dish, bread and butter, and tea.

high-tech (also **hi-tech**) ▸ **adjective** using, requiring, or involved in high technology: *a high-tech security system.* ■ (chiefly in architecture and interior design) using styles and materials, such as steel, glass, and plastic, that are associated with industrial use.
▸ **noun** (**high tech**) short for **HIGH TECHNOLOGY**.

high technology ▸ **noun** [mass noun] advanced technological development, especially in electronics: [as modifier] *high-technology weapons.*

high-tensile ▸ **adjective** (of metal) very strong under tension: *high-tensile steel.*

high tension ▸ **noun** another term for **HIGH VOLTAGE**.

high-test ▸ **adjective** US (of petrol) high-octane. ■ meeting very high standards: *the firm's high-test offices.*

high-ticket ▸ **adjective** another term for **BIG-TICKET**.

high tide ▸ **noun** the state of the tide when at its highest level: ***at high tide** you have to go inland.* ■ the highest point of something: ***the high tide of** nationalism.*

high-toned ▸ **adjective** chiefly N. Amer. stylish or superior: *an oasis of classily high-toned culture.*

high-top ▸ **adjective** denoting a soft-soled sports shoe with a laced upper that extends some distance above the wearer's ankle.
▸ **noun** (**high-tops**) a pair of high-top shoes.

high treason ▸ **noun** see **TREASON**.

high-up ▸ **noun** informal a senior person in an organization.

highveld /ˈhʌɪvɛlt/ ▸ **noun** [mass noun] a region of veld situated at a high altitude, especially the region in the north-east of South Africa, between 1200 and 1800 metres (4000 and 6000 feet) above sea level.
– ORIGIN late 19th cent.: partial translation of Afrikaans *hoëveld*.

high voltage ▸ **noun** an electrical potential large enough to cause injury or damage.

high water ▸ **noun** another term for **HIGH TIDE**.

high-water mark ▸ **noun** the level reached by the sea at high tide, or by a lake or river in time of flood. ■ a maximum recorded level or value: *unemployment and crime both stand at a high-water mark.*

highway ▸ **noun** chiefly N. Amer. a main road, especially one connecting major towns or cities: *a six-lane highway* | figurative *the highway to success.* ■ (chiefly in official use) a public road: *the Highways Department.* ■ Computing a pathway connecting parts of one computer system or between different systems.

Highway Code (in the UK) the official set of rules and guidance for road users.

highwayman ▸ **noun** (pl. **highwaymen**) historical a man, typically on horseback, who held up travellers at gunpoint in order to rob them.

high wire ▸ **noun** a high tightrope. ■ [as modifier] denoting an activity requiring great skill or judgement: *the high-wire act performed daily by many mental health workers.*

high words ▸ **plural noun** archaic angry words: *high words passed between them.*

high yellow US offensive ▸ **adjective** denoting a light-skinned person with one black and one white parent.
▸ **noun** a person of this kind.

HIH ▸ **abbreviation** Brit. Her or His Imperial Highness.

hi-hat (also **high-hat**) ▸ **noun** a pair of foot-operated cymbals forming part of a drum kit.

hijab /hɪˈdʒɑːb/ ▸ **noun** a head covering worn in public by some Muslim women. ■ the religious code which governs the wearing of such clothing.
– ORIGIN from Persian, from Arabic *ḥajaba* 'to veil'.

hijack ▸ **verb** [with obj.] illegally seize (an aircraft, ship, or vehicle) while in transit and force it to go to a different destination or use it for one's own purposes: *a man armed with grenades hijacked the jet yesterday.* ■ steal (goods) by seizing them in transit. ■ take over (something) and use it for a different purpose: *he argues that pressure groups have hijacked the environmental debate.*
▸ **noun** an incident or act of hijacking: [as modifier] *an unsuccessful hijack attempt.*
– DERIVATIVES **hijacker** noun.
– ORIGIN 1920s (originally US): of unknown origin.

hijacking ▸ **noun** an act of illegally seizing an aircraft, vehicle, or ship while in transit; a hijack.

Hijaz variant spelling of **HEJAZ**.

Hijra /ˈhɪdʒrə/ ▸ **noun** variant spelling of **HEGIRA**.

hijra /ˈhɪdʒrə/ ▸ **noun** Indian a transvestite or eunuch.
– ORIGIN Hindi.

hike ▸ **noun 1** a long walk or walking tour: *a five-mile hike across rough terrain.* ■ informal a long distance: *it's such a hike from Adelaide to Perth.*
2 a sharp increase, especially in price or cost: *fears of a hike in interest rates.*
▸ **verb 1** [no obj., with adverbial of direction] walk for a long distance, especially across country: *they hiked across the moors* | (as noun **hiking**) *she enjoys hiking and climbing in her spare time.*
2 [with obj.] pull or lift up (something, especially clothing): *Roy **hiked up** his trousers to reveal his socks.* ■ increase (something, especially a price) sharply: *the government **hiked up** the price of milk by 40 per cent.*
– PHRASES **take a hike** [usu. in imperative] informal, chiefly N. Amer. go away (used as an expression of irritation or annoyance).

H

– DERIVATIVES **hiker** noun.
– ORIGIN early 19th cent. (originally dialect, as a verb): of unknown origin.

hikikomori /hɪˌkɪkə(ʊ)ˈmɔːri/ ▸ noun (pl. **same**) [mass noun] (in Japan) the abnormal avoidance of social contact, typically by adolescent males. ■ [count noun] a person who avoids social contact.
– ORIGIN Japanese, literally 'staying indoors, (social) withdrawal'.

hila plural form of **HILUM**.

hilar /ˈhʌɪlə/ ▸ adjective Anatomy & Botany relating to a hilus or hilum.

hilarious /hɪˈlɛːrɪəs/ ▸ adjective extremely amusing: *her hilarious novel*. ■ archaic boisterously merry: *the meal was noisy and hilarious*.
– DERIVATIVES **hilariously** adverb.
– ORIGIN early 19th cent.: from Latin *hilaris* (from Greek *hilaros* 'cheerful') + **-OUS**. The sense 'exceedingly amusing' dates from the 1920s.

hilarity /hɪˈlarɪti/ ▸ noun [mass noun] extreme amusement, especially when expressed by laughter: *his incredulous expression was the cause of much hilarity*. ■ archaic boisterous merriment: *by midnight the hilarity had increased*.
– ORIGIN late Middle English (in the sense 'cheerfulness'): from French *hilarité*, from Latin *hilaritas* 'cheerfulness, merriment', from *hilaris* (see **HILARIOUS**).

H

Hilary, St (*c*.315–*c*.367), French bishop. In *c*.350 he was appointed bishop of Poitiers, in which position he became a leading opponent of Arianism. Feast day, 13 January.

Hilary term ▸ noun Brit. (in some universities) the term beginning in January.
– ORIGIN late Middle English: named after *Hilarius* (see **HILARY, ST**).

Hilbert space ▸ noun Mathematics an infinite-dimensional analogue of Euclidean space.
– ORIGIN early 20th cent.: named after David *Hilbert* (1862–1943), German mathematician.

Hilda, St (614–80), English abbess. Related to the Anglo-Saxon kings of Northumbria, she founded a monastery for both men and women at Whitby around 658, and was one of the leaders of the Celtic Church delegation at the Synod of Whitby. Feast day, 17 November.

Hildegard of Bingen, St /ˈhɪldəɡɑːd, ˈbɪŋən/ (1098–1179), German abbess, scholar, composer, and mystic. A nun of the Benedictine order, she wrote scientific works, poetry, and music, and described her mystical experiences in *Scivias*.

Hildesheim /ˈhɪldəsˌhʌɪm/ an industrial city in Lower Saxony, NW Germany; pop. 103,200 (est. 2006).

Hiligaynon /ˌhɪlɪˈɡeɪnən/ ▸ noun (pl. **same** or **Hiligaynons**) **1** a member of a people inhabiting Panay, Negros, and other islands in the central Philippines.
2 [mass noun] the Austronesian language of the Hiligaynon, with about 5 million speakers. Also called **ILONGGO**.
▸ adjective relating to the Hiligaynon or their language.

Hill¹, Damon (b.1960), English motor-racing driver. Son of Graham Hill, he won the Formula One world championship in 1996.

Hill², (Norman) Graham (1929–75), English motor-racing driver. He became Formula One world champion in 1962 and 1975.

Hill³, Octavia (1838–1912), English housing reformer and co-founder of the National Trust (1895).

Hill⁴, Sir Rowland (1795–1879), English educationist, administrator, and inventor. He is chiefly remembered for his introduction of the penny postage-stamp system in 1840.

hill ▸ noun a naturally raised area of land, not as high or craggy as a mountain. ■ a sloping stretch of road: *they were climbing a steep hill in low gear*. ■ a heap or mound of something: ***a hill of** sliding shingle*.
▸ verb [with obj.] form (something) into a heap. ■ bank up (a plant) with soil.
– PHRASES **a hill of beans** [with negative] N. Amer. informal a thing of little value: *the problems of one old actor don't amount to a hill of beans*. **over the hill** informal old and past one's best.
– ORIGIN Old English *hyll*, of Germanic origin; from an Indo-European root shared by Latin *collis* and Greek *kolōnos* 'hill'.

Hillary, Sir Edmund (Percival) (1919–2008), New Zealand mountaineer and explorer. In 1953 Hillary and Tenzing Norgay were the first people to reach the summit of Mount Everest, as members of a British expedition.

hillbilly ▸ noun (pl. **hillbillies**) N. Amer. **1** informal, chiefly derogatory an unsophisticated country person, as associated originally with the remote regions of the Appalachians.
2 old-fashioned term for **COUNTRY MUSIC**.
– ORIGIN early 20th cent.: from **HILL** + *Billy* (pet form of the given name *William*).

hill climb ▸ noun a race for vehicles up a steep hill.
– DERIVATIVES **hill-climber** noun, **hill-climbing** noun.

hill figure ▸ noun an outline of a horse, human, or other design cut into the turf of a hill, especially in the chalk downs of southern England. The oldest of these (the White Horse at Uffington, Oxfordshire) is prehistoric.

hill fort ▸ noun a fort built on a hill, in particular an area on a hilltop enclosed by a system of defensive banks and ditches, as used by Iron Age peoples in NW Europe.

hillman ▸ noun (pl. **hillmen**) an inhabitant of hilly country.

hillock ▸ noun a small hill or mound.
– DERIVATIVES **hillocky** adjective.

hillside ▸ noun the sloping side of a hill.

hillstar ▸ noun a hummingbird that typically lives at high altitude, especially in the Andes, and is adapted to the harsher climate there. ● Family Trochilidae: two genera, in particular *Oreotrochilus*, and five species.

hill station ▸ noun a town in the low mountains of the Indian subcontinent, popular as a holiday resort during the hot season.

hilltop ▸ noun the summit of a hill.

hillwalking ▸ noun [mass noun] the pastime of walking in hilly country.
– DERIVATIVES **hillwalker** noun.

hilly ▸ adjective (**hillier**, **hilliest**) having many hills: *a remote hilly district*.
– DERIVATIVES **hilliness** noun.

hilt ▸ noun the handle of a weapon or tool, especially a sword, dagger, or knife.
– PHRASES **(up) to the hilt** completely: *the estate was mortgaged up to the hilt*.
– DERIVATIVES **hilted** adjective.
– ORIGIN Old English *hilt, hilte*, of Germanic origin.

hilum /ˈhʌɪləm/ ▸ noun (pl. **hila** /-lə/) Botany the scar on a seed marking the point of attachment to its seed vessel. ■ a point in a starch granule around which the layers of starch are deposited. ■ Anatomy another term for **HILUS**.
– ORIGIN mid 17th cent. (in the Latin sense): from Latin, literally 'little thing, trifle', once thought to mean 'that which sticks to a bean', hence the current sense (mid 18th cent.).

hilus /ˈhʌɪləs/ ▸ noun (pl. **hili** /ˈhʌɪlʌɪ/) Anatomy an indentation in the surface of a kidney, spleen, or other organ, where blood vessels, ducts, nerve fibres, etc. enter or leave it.
– ORIGIN mid 19th cent.: modern Latin, alteration of **HILUM**.

Hilversum /ˈhɪlvəsəm/ a town in the Netherlands, in North Holland province, near Amsterdam; pop. 83,815 (2008). It is the centre of the Dutch radio and television network.

HIM ▸ abbreviation Brit. Her or His Imperial Majesty.

him ▸ pronoun [third person singular] **1** used as the object of a verb or preposition to refer to a male person or animal previously mentioned or easily identified: *his wife survived him* | *he took the children with him*. Compare with **HE**. ■ referring to a person or animal of unspecified sex: *withdrawing your child from school to educate him at home may seem drastic*. ■ used after the verb 'to be' and after 'than' or 'as': *that's him all right* | *I could never be as good as him*. ■ W. Indian he: *him was a tall, bow-legged man*.
2 archaic or N. Amer. dialect himself: *in the depths of him, he too didn't want to go*.
– ORIGIN Old English, dative singular form of *he, hē* 'he' and *hit* 'it'.

> **USAGE** Why do people tell us that it is wrong to say *I could never be as good as* **him** (rather than *I could never be as good as* **he**)? If they are right, why does **he** in this context sound so odd? For a discussion of this issue, see **USAGE** at **PERSONAL PRONOUN**.

Himachal Pradesh /hɪˌmɑːtʃəl prəˈdɛʃ/ a mountainous state in northern India; capital, Shimla.

Himalayan ▸ adjective relating to the Himalayas: *the Himalayan foothills*.
▸ noun North American term for **COLOURPOINT**.

Himalayas /ˌhɪməˈleɪəz, hɪˈmɑːljəz/ a vast mountain system in southern Asia, extending 2,400 km (1,500 miles) from Kashmir eastwards to Assam.

> The Himalayas consist of a series of parallel ranges rising up from the Ganges basin to the Tibetan plateau, at over 3,000 m above sea level. The backbone is the Great Himalayan Range, the highest mountain range in the world, with several peaks rising to over 7,700 m (25,000 ft), the highest being Mount Everest.

– ORIGIN from Sanskrit *Himālaya*, from *hima* 'snow' + *ālaya* 'abode'.

himation /hɪˈmatɪɒn/ ▸ noun an outer garment worn by the ancient Greeks over the left shoulder and under the right.
– ORIGIN Greek.

Himmler /ˈhɪmlə/, Heinrich (1900–45), German Nazi leader, chief of the SS (1929–45) and of the Gestapo (1936–45). He established and oversaw the systematic genocide of over 6 million Jews and other disfavoured groups between 1941 and 1945. Captured by British forces in 1945, he committed suicide.

Hims /hɪms, hɪmz/ variant form of **HOMS**.

himself ▸ pronoun [third person singular] **1** [reflexive] used as the object of a verb or preposition to refer to a male person or animal previously mentioned as the subject of the clause: *the steward introduced himself as Pete* | *he ought to be ashamed of himself*.
2 [emphatic] he or him personally (used to emphasize a particular male person or animal mentioned): *Ben told me himself*. ■ chiefly Irish a third party of some importance, especially the master of the house: *I'll mention it to himself*.
– ORIGIN Old English (see **HIM**, **SELF**).

Himyarite /ˈhɪmjərʌɪt/ ▸ noun a member of an ancient people of the SW part of the Arabian peninsula, who ruled much of southern Arabia before the 6th century AD.
▸ adjective relating to the Himyarites.
– ORIGIN from the name *Himyar* (the name of a traditional king of Yemen) + **-ITE¹**.

hin ▸ noun a Hebrew unit of liquid capacity equal to approximately 5 litres (about one gallon).
– ORIGIN late Middle English: from biblical Hebrew *hīn*.

Hinayana /ˌhiːnəˈjɑːnə/ (also **Hinayana Buddhism**) ▸ noun [mass noun] a name given by the followers of Mahayana Buddhism to the more orthodox schools of early Buddhism. The tradition died out in India, but it survived in Ceylon (Sri Lanka) as the Theravada school and was taken from there to other regions of SE Asia. See **THERAVADA**.
– ORIGIN from Sanskrit *hīna* 'lesser' + *yāna* 'vehicle'.

hind¹ ▸ adjective [attrib.] (especially of a bodily part) situated at the back; posterior: *a hind leg*.
– PHRASES **on one's hind legs** see **LEG**.
– ORIGIN Middle English: perhaps shortened from Old English *behindan* (see **BEHIND**).

hind² ▸ noun a female deer, especially a red deer or sika in and after the third year.
– ORIGIN Old English, of Germanic origin; related to Dutch *hinde* and German *Hinde*, from an Indo-European root meaning 'hornless', shared by Greek *kemas* 'young deer'.

hind³ ▸ noun archaic, chiefly Scottish a skilled farm worker, typically married and with a tied cottage. ■ a farm steward or bailiff. ■ a peasant or rustic.
– ORIGIN late Old English *hīne* 'household servants', apparently from *hīgna*, *hīna*, genitive plural of *hīgan*, *hīwan* 'family members'.

hind- ▸ combining form (added to nouns) at the back; posterior: *hindquarters* | *hindwing*.

hindbrain ▸ noun the lower part of the brainstem, comprising the cerebellum, pons, and medulla oblongata. Also called **RHOMBENCEPHALON**.

Hindemith /ˈhɪndəmɪt/, Paul (1895–1963), German composer. A leading figure in the neoclassical trend which began in the 1920s and an exponent of *Gebrauchsmusik* ('utility music'), he believed that music should have a social purpose. Notable works: *Mathis der Maler* (opera, 1938).

Hindenburg¹ /ˈhɪndnˌbɜːk/ former German name (1915–45) for **ZABRZE**.

Hindenburg² /ˈhɪndənˌbəːɡ/, German /ˈhɪndn̩ˌbʊrk/, Paul Ludwig von Beneckendorff und von (1847–1934), German Field Marshal and statesman,

President of the Weimar Republic 1925–34. Elected President in 1925 and re-elected in 1932, he reluctantly appointed Hitler as Chancellor in 1933.

Hindenburg Line (in the First World War) a German fortified line of defence on the Western Front to which Paul von Hindenburg directed retreat and which was not breached until near the end of the war. Also called **SIEGFRIED LINE**.

hinder¹ /ˈhɪndə/ ▸ **verb** [with obj.] make it difficult for (someone) to do something or for (something) to happen: *language barriers hindered communication between scientists*.
– ORIGIN Old English *hindrian* 'injure or damage', of Germanic origin; related to German *hindern*, also to **BEHIND**.

hinder² /ˈhʌɪndə/ ▸ **adjective** [attrib.] (especially of a bodily part) rear; hind: *the hinder end of its body*.
– ORIGIN Middle English: perhaps from Old English *hinderweard* 'backward', related to **BEHIND**.

Hindi /ˈhɪndi/ ▸ **noun** [mass noun] the most widely spoken language of northern India, with over 200 million speakers; one of the official languages of India. It is an Indic language derived from Sanskrit and is written in the Devanagari script.
▸ **adjective** relating to Hindi.
– ORIGIN from Urdu *hindī*, from *Hind* 'India'.

hindlimb ▸ **noun** either of the two back limbs of an animal.

hindmost ▸ **adjective** furthest back: *the hindmost attendant*.

Hindoo ▸ **noun & adjective** archaic spelling of **HINDU**.

hindquarters ▸ **plural noun** the hind legs and adjoining parts of a quadruped.

hindrance /ˈhɪndr(ə)ns/ ▸ **noun** a thing that provides resistance, delay, or obstruction to something or someone: ***a hindrance to** the development process* | [mass noun] *the visitor can wander around without hindrance*.

hindsight ▸ **noun** [mass noun] understanding of a situation or event only after it has happened or developed: ***with hindsight**, I should never have gone*.

Hindu /ˈhɪnduː, hɪnˈduː/ ▸ **noun** (pl. **Hindus**) a follower of Hinduism.
▸ **adjective** relating to Hindus or Hinduism.
– ORIGIN Urdu, from Persian *hindū*, from *Hind* 'India'.

Hinduism ▸ **noun** [mass noun] a major religious and cultural tradition of South Asia, which developed from Vedic religion.

> Hinduism is practised primarily in India, Bangladesh, Sri Lanka, and Nepal. It is a diverse family of devotional and ascetic cults and philosophical schools, all sharing a belief in reincarnation and involving the worship of one or more of a large pantheon of gods and goddesses, including Brahma, Shiva, and Vishnu (incarnate as Rama and Krishna), Kali, Durga, Parvati, and Ganesh. Hindu society was traditionally based on a caste system.

– DERIVATIVES **Hinduize** (also **Hinduise**) **verb**.

Hindu Kush /ˌhɪnduː ˈkuːʃ, ˈkʊʃ/ a range of high mountains in northern Pakistan and Afghanistan, forming a westward continuation of the Himalayas. Several peaks exceed 6,150 m (20,000 ft), the highest being Tirich Mir.

Hindustan /ˌhɪndʊˈstɑːn, -ˈstan/ historical the Indian subcontinent in general, more specifically that part of India north of the Deccan, especially the plains of the Ganges and Jumna Rivers.

Hindustani /ˌhɪndʊˈstɑːni/ ▸ **noun** [mass noun] a group of mutually intelligible languages and dialects spoken in NW India, principally Hindi and Urdu. ■ the Delhi dialect of Hindi, widely used throughout India as a lingua franca.
▸ **adjective** relating to the culture of NW India: *Hindustani classical music*.

> **USAGE** Hindustani was the usual term in the 18th and 19th centuries for the native language of NW India. The usual modern term is **Hindi** (or **Urdu** in Muslim contexts), although **Hindustani** is still used to refer to the dialect of Hindi spoken around Delhi.

Hindutva /hɪnˈdʊtvə/ ▸ **noun** [mass noun] Indian an ideology seeking to establish the hegemony of Hindus and the Hindu way of life.
– ORIGIN Hindi.

hindwing ▸ **noun** either of the two back wings of a four-winged insect.

hinge ▸ **noun** a movable joint or mechanism on which a door, gate, or lid swings as it opens and closes or which connects linked objects. ■ Biology a natural joint that performs a similar function, for example that of a bivalve shell. ■ a central or pivotal point or principle on which everything depends: *this period can be called the hinge of history*.
▸ **verb** (**hinges**, **hingeing** or **hinging**, **hinged**) [with obj.] attach or join with or as if with a hinge: *the ironing board was set into the wall and hinged at the bottom* | (as adj. **hinged**) *a pocket watch with a hinged lid*. ■ [no obj., with adverbial of direction] (of a door or part of a structure) hang and turn on a hinge: *the skull's jaw hinged down*. ■ [no obj.] (**hinge on**) depend entirely on: *the future of the industry could hinge on the outcome of next month's election*.
– DERIVATIVES **hingeless** **adjective**.
– ORIGIN Middle English *henge*; related to **HANG**.

Hinglish /ˈhɪŋglɪʃ/ ▸ **noun** [mass noun] informal a blend of Hindi and English, in particular a variety of English used by speakers of Hindi, characterized by frequent use of Hindi vocabulary or constructions.

hinky ▸ **adjective** (**hinkier**, **hinkiest**) US informal (of a person) dishonest or suspect: *he knew the guy was hinky*. ■ (of an object) unreliable: *my brakes are a little hinky*.
– ORIGIN 1950s: of obscure origin.

hinny¹ ▸ **noun** (pl. **hinnies**) the offspring of a female donkey and a male horse.
– ORIGIN early 17th cent.: via Latin from Greek *hinnos*.

hinny² (also **hinnie**) ▸ **noun** (pl. **hinnies**) Scottish & N. English used as a term of endearment.
– ORIGIN early 19th cent.: variant of **HONEY**.

hinoki /hɪˈnəʊki/ ▸ **noun** (also **hinoki cypress**) a tall slow-growing tree native to Japan, which has bright green leaves and yields a valuable timber. ● *Chamaecyparis obtusa*, family Cupressaceae.
– ORIGIN early 18th cent.: from Japanese.

hint ▸ **noun 1** a slight or indirect indication or suggestion: *he has given no **hint of** his views*. ■ a very small trace of something: *Randall smiled with **a hint of** mockery*.
2 a small piece of practical information or advice: *handy hints on saving energy in your home*.
▸ **verb** [no obj.] suggest or indicate something indirectly or covertly: *the Minister **hinted at** a possible change of heart* | [with clause] *he hinted that the sale might be delayed*. ■ (**hint at**) be a slight or possible indication of: *the restrained fronts of the terraced houses only hinted at the wealth within*.
– PHRASES **take a** (or **the**) **hint** understand and act on what someone is implying or suggesting: *she tried to put him off but he didn't take the hint*.
– ORIGIN early 17th cent. (in the sense 'occasion, opportunity'): apparently from obsolete *hent* 'grasp, get hold of', from Old English *hentan*, of Germanic origin; related to **HUNT**. The basic notion is 'something that may be taken advantage of'.

hinterland /ˈhɪntəland/ ▸ **noun** [usu. in sing.] **1** the remote areas of a country away from the coast or the banks of major rivers: *the hinterland of southern Italy*. ■ the area around or beyond a major town or port: *a market town serving its rich agricultural hinterland*.
2 an area lying beyond what is visible or known: *the strange hinterland where life begins and ends*.
– ORIGIN late 19th cent.: from German, from *hinter* 'behind' + *Land* 'land'.

HIP ▸ **noun** (pl. **HIPs**) (in the UK) a set of information about a house or flat that a seller must provide to a potential buyer.
– ORIGIN abbreviation of *home information pack*.

hip¹ ▸ **noun 1** a projection of the pelvis and upper thigh bone on each side of the body in human beings and quadrupeds. ■ (**hips**) the circumference of the body at the buttocks: *a dark girl with big hips*. ■ a person's hip joint: *she dislocated her hip*.
2 the sharp edge of a roof from the ridge to the eaves where the two sides meet.
– PHRASES **be joined at the hip** informal (of two people) be inseparable. **on the hip** archaic at a disadvantage.
– ORIGIN Old English *hype*, of Germanic origin; related to Dutch *heup* and German *Hüfte*, also to **HOP¹**.

hip² (also **rose hip**) ▸ **noun** the fruit of a rose, especially a wild kind.
– ORIGIN Old English *hēope*, *hīope*, of West Germanic origin; related to Dutch *joop* and German *Hiefe*.

hip³ ▸ **adjective** (**hipper**, **hippest**) informal **1** very fashionable: *it's hip to be environmentally conscious*.
2 aware of or informed about: *he's trying to show how hip he is to Americana*.
– DERIVATIVES **hipness** **noun**.
– ORIGIN early 20th cent.: of unknown origin.

hip⁴ ▸ **exclamation** introducing a communal cheer: *hip hip hooray!*
– ORIGIN mid 18th cent.: of unknown origin.

hip bath ▸ **noun** a portable bath large enough to sit rather than lie down in.

hip bone ▸ **noun** a large bone forming the main part of the pelvis on each side of the body and consisting of the fused ilium, ischium, and pubis. Also called **INNOMINATE BONE**.

hip flask ▸ **noun** a small flask for spirits, of a kind intended to be carried in a hip pocket.

hip hop ▸ **noun** [mass noun] a style of popular music of US black and Hispanic origin, featuring rap with an electronic backing.
– DERIVATIVES **hip-hopper** **noun**.
ORIGIN 1980s: reduplication probably based on **HIP³**.

hip-huggers ▸ **plural noun** chiefly N. Amer. hipsters.
– DERIVATIVES **hip-hugging** **adjective**.

hip joint ▸ **noun** the ball-and-socket joint connecting a leg to the trunk of the body, in which the head of the thigh bone fits into the socket of the hip bone.

Hipparchus /hɪˈpɑːkəs/ (*c.*170–after 126 BC), Greek astronomer and geographer. He is best known for his discovery of the precession of the equinoxes and is credited with the invention of trigonometry.

hippeastrum /ˌhɪpɪˈastrəm/ ▸ **noun** see **AMARYLLIS**.
– ORIGIN modern Latin, from Greek *hippeus* 'horseman' (the leaves appearing to ride on one another) + *astron* 'star' (from the flower-shape).

hipped¹ ▸ **adjective** [in combination] having hips of a specified kind: *a thin-hipped girl*.

hipped² ▸ **adjective** (**hipped on**) informal, chiefly N. Amer. obsessed or infatuated with: *they're hipped on discipline*.
– ORIGIN 1920s: from **HIP³**, or as the past participle of *hip* 'make someone hip (i.e. aware)'.

hipped roof (also **hip roof**) ▸ **noun** a roof with a sharp edge or edges from the ridge to the eaves where the two sides meet.

hippie ▸ **noun & adjective** variant spelling of **HIPPY¹**.

hippo ▸ **noun** (pl. **same** or **hippos**) informal term for **HIPPOPOTAMUS**.

hippocampus /ˌhɪpə(ʊ)ˈkampəs/ ▸ **noun** (pl. **hippocampi** /-pɪ, -pʌɪ/) Anatomy the elongated ridges on the floor of each lateral ventricle of the brain, thought to be the centre of emotion, memory, and the autonomic nervous system.
– ORIGIN late 16th cent.: via Latin from Greek *hippokampos*, from *hippos* 'horse' + *kampos* 'sea monster'.

hip pocket ▸ **noun** a pocket in the back of a pair of trousers.
– PHRASES **in someone's hip pocket** N. Amer. completely under someone's control.

hippocras /ˈhɪpəkras/ ▸ **noun** [mass noun] historical wine flavoured with spices.
– ORIGIN late Middle English: from Old French *ipocras* 'Hippocrates' (see **HIPPOCRATES**), translating medieval Latin *vinum Hippocraticum* 'Hippocratic wine' (because it was strained through a filter called a *Hippocrates' sleeve*).

Hippocrates /hɪˈpɒkrətiːz/ (*c.*460–377 BC), Greek physician, traditionally regarded as the father of medicine. His name is associated with the medical profession's Hippocratic oath from his attachment to a body of ancient Greek medical writings, probably none of which was written by him.

Hippocratic oath /ˌhɪpəˈkratɪk/ ▸ **noun** an oath stating the obligations and proper conduct of doctors, formerly taken by those beginning medical practice. Parts of the oath are still used in some medical schools.
– ORIGIN mid 18th cent.: *Hippocratic* from medieval Latin *Hippocraticus* 'relating to Hippocrates' (see **HIPPOCRATES**).

Hippocrene /ˈhɪpəkriːn/ ▸ **noun** [mass noun] literary used to refer to poetic or literary inspiration.
– ORIGIN early 17th cent.: via Latin from Greek *Hippokrēnē*, *Hippou krēnē*, literally 'fountain of the horse' (from *hippos* 'horse' + *krēnē* 'fountain'), the name of a fountain on Mount Helicon sacred to the Muses, which according to legend was produced by a stroke of Pegasus' hoof.

hippodrome /ˈhɪpədrəʊm/ ▸ **noun 1** [as name] a theatre or concert hall: *the Birmingham Hippodrome*.

H

2 (in ancient Greece or Rome) a stadium for chariot or horse races.
– ORIGIN late 16th cent. (in sense 2): from French, via Latin from Greek *hippodromos*, from *hippos* 'horse' + *dromos* 'race, course'. The early sense led to the term's use as a grandiose name for a modern circus, later applied to other places of popular entertainment .

hippogriff /ˈhɪpə(ʊ)grɪf/ (also **hippogryph**) ▸ **noun** a mythical creature with the body of a horse and the wings and head of an eagle, born of the union of a male griffin and a filly.
– ORIGIN mid 17th cent.: from French *hippogriffe*, from Italian *ippogrifo*, from Greek *hippos* 'horse' + Italian *grifo* 'griffin'.

Hippolytus /hɪˈpɒlɪtəs/ Greek Mythology the son of Theseus, banished and cursed by his father after being accused by Phaedra of rape. He was killed when a sea monster, sent by Poseidon in response to the curse, frightened his horses as he drove his chariot along a seashore.

hippopotamus /ˌhɪpəˈpɒtəməs/ ▸ **noun** (pl. **hippopotamuses** or **hippopotami** /-mʌɪ/) a large thick-skinned semiaquatic African mammal, with massive jaws and large tusks. ● Family Hippopotamidae: the very large *Hippopotamus amphibius*, frequenting rivers and lakes, and the smaller **pygmy hippopotamus** (*Choeropsis liberiensis*), frequenting forests near fresh water in West Africa.
– ORIGIN Middle English: via Latin from Greek *hippopotamos*, earlier *hippos ho potamios* 'river horse' (from *hippos* 'horse', *potamos* 'river').

H

Hippo Regius /ˌhɪpəʊ ˈriːdʒɪəs/ see **ANNABA**.

hippus /ˈhɪpəs/ ▸ **noun** [mass noun] Medicine spasmodic or rhythmic contraction of the pupil of the eye, a symptom of some neurological conditions.
– ORIGIN late 17th cent.: modern Latin, from Greek *hippos* 'tremor of the eyes'.

hippy[1] (also **hippie**) ▸ **noun** (pl. **hippies**) (especially in the 1960s) a person of unconventional appearance, typically having long hair and wearing beads, associated with a subculture involving a rejection of conventional values and the taking of hallucinogenic drugs.
▸ **adjective** relating to hippies or the subculture associated with them: *hippy philosophy*.
– DERIVATIVES **hippiedom** noun, **hippiness** noun, **hippyish** adjective.
– ORIGIN 1950s: from **HIP**[3] + **-Y**[1].

hippy[2] ▸ **adjective** (of a woman) having large hips.

hippy-dippy ▸ **adjective** (**hippy-dippier**, **hippy-dippiest**) informal rejecting conventional practices or behaviour in a way perceived to be vague and unconsidered or foolishly idealistic.

hip roof ▸ **noun** another term form **HIPPED ROOF**.

hipshot ▸ **adjective & adverb** chiefly N. Amer. having a dislocated hip. ■ [as adv.] standing with one hip lower than the other.

hipster[1] Brit. ▸ **adjective** (of a garment) cut to fit and fasten at the hips rather than the waist.
▸ **noun** (**hipsters**) trousers cut to fit and fasten at the hips.

hipster[2] ▸ **noun** informal a person who follows the latest trends and fashions.
– DERIVATIVES **hipsterism** noun.
– ORIGIN 1940s (used originally as an equivalent term to **HEPCAT**): from **HIP**[3] + **-STER**.

hiragana /ˌhɪrəˈgɑːnə, ˌhɪərə-/ ▸ **noun** [mass noun] the more cursive form of kana (syllabic writing) used in Japanese, primarily used for function words and inflections. Compare with **KATAKANA**.
– ORIGIN Japanese, 'plain kana'.

hircine /ˈhəːsʌɪn/ ▸ **adjective** literary of or resembling a goat.
– ORIGIN mid 17th cent.: from Latin *hircinus*, from *hircus* 'he-goat'.

hire ▸ **verb** [with obj.] **1** chiefly Brit. obtain the temporary use of (something) for an agreed payment: *we flew to San Diego, hired a car, and headed for Las Vegas.* ■ (**hire something out**) grant the temporary use of something for an agreed payment: *most train stations hire out cycles.*
2 employ (someone) for wages: *management hired and fired labour in line with demand.* ■ employ for a short time to do a particular job: *Wilmot hired a private detective to follow him* | (as adj. **hired**) *a hired assassin.* ■ (**hire oneself out**) make oneself available for temporary employment.
▸ **noun 1** [mass noun] the action of hiring someone or something: *car hire is recommended* | [as modifier] *a hire charge.*
2 chiefly N. Amer. a person who is hired; an employee: *new hires go through six months of training.*
– PHRASES **for** (or **on**) **hire** available to be hired.
– DERIVATIVES **hireable** (US also **hirable**) adjective, **hirer** noun.
– ORIGIN Old English *hȳrian* 'employ someone for wages', *hȳr* 'payment under contract for the use of something', of West Germanic origin; related to Dutch *huren* (verb), *huur* (noun).

hire car ▸ **noun** Brit. a car hired, or available for hire.

hired girl ▸ **noun** N. Amer. a female domestic servant.

hired gun ▸ **noun** N. Amer. informal **1** a hired bodyguard, mercenary, or assassin.
2 an expert brought in to resolve complex legal or financial problems or to lobby for a cause.

hired hand ▸ **noun** a person hired to do short-term manual work.

hired man ▸ **noun** N. Amer. a male domestic servant.

hireling ▸ **noun** chiefly derogatory a person employed to do menial work: *he is a poorly paid hireling of a wealthy white woman.* ■ a person who works purely for material reward: *the government's paid hirelings assure us that we're on our way out of recession.*
– ORIGIN mid 16th cent.: from **HIRE** + **-LING**, on the pattern of Dutch *huurling*.

hire purchase ▸ **noun** [mass noun] Brit. a system by which one pays for a thing in regular instalments while having the use of it.

hi-res (also **high-res**) ▸ **adjective** informal (of a display or a photographic or video image) showing a large amount of detail.
– ORIGIN late 20th cent.: from *high-resolution*.

Hiri Motu ▸ **noun** see **MOTU** (sense 2 of the noun).

Hirohito /ˌhɪrəˈhiːtəʊ/ (1901–89), emperor of Japan 1926–89; full name *Michinomiya Hirohito*. Regarded as the 124th direct descendant of Jimmu, he refrained from involvement in politics, though he was instrumental in obtaining Japan's agreement to the unconditional surrender which ended the Second World War. In 1946 the new constitution imposed by America obliged him to renounce his divinity and become a constitutional monarch.

hirola /hɪˈrəʊlə/ ▸ **noun** a rare yellowish-brown antelope native to Kenya and Somalia. ● *Damaliscus hunteri*, family Bovidae. Alternative name: **Hunter's hartebeest**.
– ORIGIN late 19th cent.: from Oromo.

Hiroshima /hɪˈrɒʃɪmə, ˌhɪrəˈʃiːmə/ a city on the south coast of the island of Honshu, western Japan, capital of Chugoku region; pop. 1,144,572 (2007). It was the target of the first atom bomb, which was dropped by the United States on 6 August 1945 and resulted in the deaths of about one third of the city's population of 300,000. Together with a second attack, on Nagasaki three days later, this led to Japan's surrender and the end of the Second World War.

hirple /ˈhəːp(ə)l/ ▸ **verb** [no obj., with adverbial of direction] chiefly Scottish & N. English walk with a limp; hobble.
– ORIGIN late 15th cent.: of unknown origin.

Hirschsprung's disease /ˈhɪəʃ(s)prʊŋz/ ▸ **noun** [mass noun] a congenital condition in which the rectum and part of the colon fail to develop a normal system of nerves, leading to an accumulation of faeces in the colon following birth.
– ORIGIN early 20th cent.: named after Harald *Hirschsprung* (1830–1916), Danish paediatrician.

hirsute /ˈhəːsjuːt/ ▸ **adjective** literary or humorous hairy: *their hirsute chests.*
– DERIVATIVES **hirsuteness** noun.
– ORIGIN early 17th cent.: from Latin *hirsutus*.

hirsutism /ˈhəːsjuːtɪz(ə)m/ ▸ **noun** [mass noun] Medicine abnormal growth of hair on a woman's face and body.

hirundine /ˈhɪrʌndʌɪn, hɪˈrʌndʌɪn/ ▸ **noun** Ornithology a songbird of the swallow family (Hirundinidae).
– ORIGIN mid 19th cent.: from Latin *hirundo* 'swallow' + **-INE**[1].

his ▸ **possessive determiner 1** belonging to or associated with a male person or animal previously mentioned or easily identified: *James sold his business.* ■ belonging to or associated with a person or animal of unspecified sex (in modern use chiefly replaced by 'his or her' or 'their'): *any child with delayed speech should have his hearing checked.* See usage at **HE**.
2 (**His**) used in titles: *His Excellency* | *His Lordship.*
▸ **possessive pronoun** used to refer to a thing or things belonging to or associated with a male person or animal previously mentioned: *he took my hand in his* | *some friends of his.*
– PHRASES **his and hers** (of matching items) for husband and wife, or men and women: *his and hers towels.*
– ORIGIN Old English, genitive singular form of *he*, *hē* 'he' and *hit* 'it'.

Hispanic /hɪˈspanɪk/ ▸ **adjective** relating to Spain or to Spanish-speaking countries, especially those of Central and South America. ■ relating to Spanish-speaking people or their culture, especially in the US.
▸ **noun** a Spanish-speaking person, especially one of Latin American descent, living in the US.
– DERIVATIVES **Hispanicize** (also **Hispanicise**) verb.
– ORIGIN from Latin *Hispanicus*, from *Hispania* 'Spain'.

> **USAGE** In the US **Hispanic** is the standard accepted term when referring to Spanish-speaking people living in the US. Other, more specific terms such as **Latino** and **Chicano** are also used where occasion demands.

Hispanic American ▸ **noun** a US citizen or resident of Hispanic descent.
▸ **adjective** relating to Hispanic Americans.

Hispaniola /ˌhɪspanˈjəʊlə/ an island of the Greater Antilles in the Caribbean, divided into the states of Haiti and the Dominican Republic. After its European discovery by Columbus in 1492, Hispaniola was colonized by the Spaniards, who ceded the western part (now Haiti) to France in 1697.

Hispanist /ˈhɪspənɪst/ (also **Hispanicist** /hɪˈspanɪsɪst/) ▸ **noun** an expert in or student of the language and culture of Spain and the Spanish-speaking countries of South America.

Hispano- /hɪˈspanəʊ/ ▸ **combining form** Spanish; Spanish and ...: *Hispano-Argentine.* ■ relating to Spain.
– ORIGIN from Latin *Hispanus* 'Spanish'.

hispid /ˈhɪspɪd/ ▸ **adjective** Botany & Zoology covered with stiff hair or bristles.
– ORIGIN mid 17th cent.: from Latin *hispidus*.

hiss ▸ **verb** [no obj.] make a sharp sibilant sound as of the letter *s*: *the escaping gas was hissing.* ■ (of a person) make a sibilant sound as a sign of disapproval or derision: *the audience hissed loudly at the mention of his name.* ■ [with obj.] express disapproval of (someone) by hissing: *he was hissed off the stage.* ■ [reporting verb] whisper something in an urgent or angry way: [with direct speech] *'Get back!' he hissed.*
▸ **noun** a sharp sibilant sound: *the spit and hiss of a cornered cat.* ■ a sibilant sound used to convey disapproval or derision: *the audience greeted this comment with boos and hisses.* ■ [mass noun] electrical interference at audio frequencies: *tape hiss.*
– ORIGIN late Middle English (as a verb): imitative.

hissy fit ▸ **noun** N. Amer. informal an angry outburst; a temper tantrum: *I screamed and kicked the furniture and threw a hissy fit.*
– ORIGIN 1930s (as *hissy*): perhaps from *hysterics* (see **HYSTERIC**).

hist ▸ **exclamation** archaic used to attract attention or call for silence.
– ORIGIN natural exclamation: first recorded in English in the late 16th cent.

hist- ▸ **combining form** variant spelling of **HISTO-** shortened before a vowel (as in *histidine*).

histamine /ˈhɪstəmiːn/ ▸ **noun** [mass noun] Biochemistry a compound which is released by cells in response to injury and in allergic and inflammatory reactions, causing contraction of smooth muscle and dilation of capillaries. ● A heterocyclic amine; chem. formula: $C_5H_9N_3$.
– DERIVATIVES **histaminic** adjective.
– ORIGIN early 20th cent.: blend of **HISTIDINE** and **AMINE**.

histidine /ˈhɪstɪdiːn/ ▸ **noun** [mass noun] Biochemistry a basic amino acid which is a constituent of most proteins. It is an essential nutrient in the diet of vertebrates, and is the source from which histamine is derived in the body. ● Chem. formula: $C_6H_9N_3O_2$.
– ORIGIN late 19th cent.: from Greek *histos* 'web, tissue' + **-IDE** + **-INE**[4].

histiocyte /ˈhɪstɪə(ʊ)sʌɪt/ ▸ **noun** Physiology a stationary phagocytic cell present in connective tissue.
– ORIGIN early 20th cent.: from Greek *histion* (diminutive of *histos* 'tissue, web') + **-CYTE**.

histo- /ˈhɪstəʊ/ (also **hist-** before a vowel) ▸ **combining form** Biology relating to organic tissue: *histochemistry* | *histocompatibility*.
– ORIGIN from Greek *histos* 'web, tissue'.

histochemistry ▸ **noun** [mass noun] the branch of science concerned with the identification and distribution of the chemical constituents of tissues by means of stains, indicators, and microscopy.
– DERIVATIVES **histochemical** adjective.

histocompatibility ▸ **noun** [mass noun] Medicine compatibility between the tissues of different individuals, so that one accepts a graft from the other without giving an immune reaction.

histogenesis /ˌhɪstə(ʊ)'dʒɛnɪsɪs/ ▸ **noun** [mass noun] Biology the differentiation of cells into specialized tissues and organs during growth.
– DERIVATIVES **histogenetic** adjective.

histogeny /hɪ'stɒdʒɪni/ ▸ **noun** another term for HISTOGENESIS.
– DERIVATIVES **histogenic** adjective.

histogram ▸ **noun** Statistics a diagram consisting of rectangles whose area is proportional to the frequency of a variable and whose width is equal to the class interval.
– ORIGIN late 19th cent.: from Greek *histos* 'mast, web' + -GRAM[1].

histology /hɪ'stɒlədʒi/ ▸ **noun** [mass noun] Biology the study of the microscopic structure of tissues.
– DERIVATIVES **histologic** adjective, **histological** adjective, **histologist** noun.

histolysis /hɪ'stɒlɪsɪs/ ▸ **noun** [mass noun] Biology the breaking down of tissues (e.g. during animal metamorphosis).
– DERIVATIVES **histolytic** adjective.

histone /'hɪstəʊn/ ▸ **noun** Biochemistry any of a group of basic proteins found in chromatin.
– ORIGIN late 19th cent.: coined in German, perhaps from Greek *histanai* 'arrest' or from *histos* 'web, tissue'.

histopathology ▸ **noun** [mass noun] the study of changes in tissues caused by disease.
– DERIVATIVES **histopathological** adjective, **histopathologically** adverb, **histopathologist** noun.

histoplasmosis /ˌhɪstəʊplaz'məʊsɪs/ ▸ **noun** [mass noun] Medicine infection by a fungus found in the droppings of birds and bats in humid areas. It is not serious if confined to the lungs but can be fatal if spread throughout the body. • The fungus is *Histoplasma capsulatum*.

historian ▸ **noun** an expert in or student of history, especially that of a particular period, geographical region, or social phenomenon: *a military historian*.
– ORIGIN late Middle English: from Old French *historien*, from Latin *historia* (see HISTORY).

historiated /hɪ'stɔːrɪeɪtɪd/ ▸ **adjective** (of an initial letter in an illuminated manuscript) decorated with designs representing scenes from the text.
– ORIGIN late 19th cent.: from French *historié*, past participle of *historier* in an obsolete sense 'illustrate', from medieval Latin *historiare*, from *historia* (see HISTORY).

historic ▸ **adjective 1** famous or important in history, or potentially so: *the area's numerous historic sites* | *a historic occasion*. ▪ archaic of or concerning history; of the past: *eruptions in historic times*.
2 Grammar (of a tense) used in the narration of past events, especially Latin and Greek imperfect and pluperfect.
– ORIGIN early 17th cent. (in the sense 'relating to or in accordance with history'): via Latin from Greek *historikos*, from *historia* 'narrative, knowing by enquiry' (see HISTORY).

> **USAGE** 1 On the use of *an historic moment* or *a historic moment*, see USAGE at AN.
> **2 Historic** and **historical** are used in slightly different ways. **Historic** means 'famous or important in history', as in *a historic occasion*, whereas **historical** means 'concerning history or historical events', as in *historical evidence*: thus a *historic event* is one that was very important, whereas a *historical event* is something that happened in the past.

historical ▸ **adjective** of or concerning history or past events: *historical evidence*. ▪ belonging to the past: *famous historical figures*. ▪ (especially of a novel or film) set in the past. ▪ (of the study of a subject) based on an analysis of its development over a period: *for the Darwinians, biogeography became a historical science*.
– ORIGIN late Middle English: via Latin from Greek *historikos* (see HISTORIC).

> **USAGE** On the use of *an historical event* or *a historical event*, see USAGE at AN.

historical linguistics ▸ **plural noun** [treated as sing.] the study of the history and development of languages.

historically ▸ **adverb** with reference to past events: *a historically accurate picture of the time*. ▪ [sentence adverb] in the past: *historically, government policy has favoured urban dwellers*.

historical materialism ▸ **noun** another term for DIALECTICAL MATERIALISM.

historicism ▸ **noun** [mass noun] **1** the theory that social and cultural phenomena are determined by history. ▪ the belief that historical events are governed by natural laws.
2 the tendency to regard historical development as the most basic aspect of human existence.
3 (in artistic and architectural contexts) excessive regard for past styles.
– DERIVATIVES **historicist** noun.
– ORIGIN late 19th cent.: from HISTORIC, translating German *Historismus*.

historicity /ˌhɪstə'rɪsɪti/ ▸ **noun** [mass noun] historical authenticity: *the historicity of bible narrative*.

historicize (also **historicise**) ▸ **verb** [with obj.] treat or represent as historical.
– DERIVATIVES **historicization** noun.

historic present ▸ **noun** [mass noun] Grammar the present tense used instead of the past in vivid narrative, especially in titles, such as 'The Empire Strikes Back', and informally in speech, e.g. 'so I say to him'.

historiography /hɪˌstɔːrɪ'ɒgrəfi, -ˌstɒrɪ-/ ▸ **noun** [mass noun] the study of the writing of history and of written histories. ▪ the writing of history.
– DERIVATIVES **historiographer** noun, **historiographic** adjective, **historiographical** adjective, **historiographically** adverb.
– ORIGIN mid 16th cent.: via medieval Latin from Greek *historiographia*, from *historia* 'narrative, history' + *-graphia* 'writing'.

history ▸ **noun** (pl. **histories**) **1** [mass noun] the study of past events, particularly in human affairs: *medieval European history*. ▪ the past considered as a whole: *letters that have changed the course of history*.
2 the whole series of past events connected with a particular person or thing: *the history of the Empire* | *a patient with a complicated medical history*. ▪ an eventful past: *the group has quite a history*. ▪ a past characterized by a particular thing: *his family had a history of insanity*.
3 a continuous, typically chronological, record of important or public events or of a particular trend or institution: *a history of the labour movement*. ▪ a historical play: *Shakespeare's comedies, histories, and tragedies*.
– PHRASES **be history** be perceived as no longer relevant to the present: *the mainframe is already history*. ▪ informal used to indicate imminent departure, dismissal, or death: *an inch either way and you'd be history*. **go down in history** be remembered or recorded in history: *the 1981 Grand National has gone down in history as one of the most emotional races ever run*. **make history** do something that is remembered in or influences the course of history. **the rest is history** used to indicate that the events succeeding those already related are so well known that they need not be recounted again: *they teamed up, discovered that they could make music, and the rest is history*.
– ORIGIN late Middle English (also as a verb): via Latin from Greek *historia* 'finding out, narrative, history', from *histōr* 'learned, wise man', from an Indo-European root shared by WIT[2].

history-sheeter ▸ **noun** Indian a person with a criminal record.

histosol /'hɪstəsɒl/ ▸ **noun** Soil Science a soil of an order comprising peaty soils, with a deep surface layer of purely organic material.

histrionic /ˌhɪstrɪ'ɒnɪk/ ▸ **adjective** excessively theatrical or dramatic in character or style: *a histrionic outburst*. ▪ formal of or concerning actors or acting: *histrionic talents*. ▪ Psychiatry denoting a personality disorder marked by shallow volatile emotions and attention-seeking behaviour.
▸ **noun 1** (**histrionics**) melodramatic behaviour designed to attract attention: *by now, Anna was accustomed to her mother's histrionics*. ▪ archaic dramatic performances; the theatre.
2 archaic an actor.
– DERIVATIVES **histrionically** adverb.
– ORIGIN mid 17th cent. (in the sense 'dramatically exaggerated, hypocritical'): from late Latin *histrionicus*, from Latin *histrio(n-)* 'actor'.

hit ▸ **verb** (**hits**, **hitting**, **hit**) [with obj.] **1** bring one's hand or a tool or weapon into contact with (someone or something) quickly and forcefully: *Marius* **hit** *him* **in** *the mouth* | [no obj.] *police* **hit out** *with truncheons*. ▪ accidentally strike (part of one's body) against something, often causing injury: *she fainted and* **hit** *her head* **on** *the metal bedstead*. ▪ (of a moving object or body) come into contact with (someone or something stationary) quickly and forcefully: *a car hit the barrier*. ▪ informal touch or press (part of a machine or other device) in order to work it: *he picked up the phone and hit several buttons*.
2 cause harm or distress to: *the area has been badly hit by pit closures* | *it hit him very hard when Rosie left*. ▪ (of a disaster) occur in and cause damage to (an area) suddenly: *the country was hit by a major earthquake*. ▪ [no obj.] make a strongly worded criticism or attack: *he* **hit out at** *the club's decision to place him on the transfer list*. ▪ informal, chiefly N. Amer. attack and rob or kill: *if they're cops, maybe it's not a good idea to have them hit*.
3 (of a missile or a person aiming one) strike (a target): *the sniper fired and hit a third man*. ▪ be suddenly and vividly realized by: [with obj. and clause] *it hit her that I wanted to settle down here*.
4 informal reach (a particular level, point, or figure): *capital spending this year is likely to hit $1,800 million* | *his career hit rock bottom*. ▪ be affected by (an unfortunate and unexpected circumstance or event): *the opening of the town centre hit a snag*. ▪ arrive at or go to (a place): *it was still night when we hit the outskirts of London*. ▪ (of a product) become available and make an impact on: *the latest board game to hit the market*. ▪ [no obj.] take effect: *we sat waiting for the caffeine to hit*. ▪ give (someone) a dose of a drug or an alcoholic drink. ▪ used to convey that someone is engaging in a particular pursuit or activity with enthusiasm: *we went to Val D'Isere to hit the shops*.
5 propel (a ball) with a bat, racket, stick, etc. to score runs or points in a game. ▪ score (a run or point) in this way: *he had hit 25 home runs*.
▸ **noun 1** an instance of striking or being struck: *few structures can withstand a hit from a speeding car*. ▪ a verbal attack: *I think people will try to* **take a hit at** *my credibility*. ▪ informal, chiefly N. Amer. a murder, typically one planned and carried out by a criminal organization. ▪ Baseball short for BASE HIT.
2 an instance of striking the target aimed at: *one of the bombers had scored a direct hit*. ▪ Computing an instance of identifying an item of data which matches the requirements of a search. ▪ Computing an instance of a particular website being accessed by a user: *the site gets an average 350,000 hits a day*.
3 a successful venture, especially a film, pop record, or song: *he was the director of many big hits* | [as modifier] *a hit single*. ▪ informal a successful and popular person or thing: *he's proving to be a big hit with the fans*.
4 informal a dose of a narcotic drug.
PHRASES **hit-and-miss** done or occurring at random: *picking a remedy can be a bit hit-and-miss*. **hit-and-run** denoting a person who causes accidental or wilful damage and escapes before being discovered, or damage caused in this way: *he was struck by a hit and run driver*. **hit someone below the belt** Boxing give one's opponent an illegal low blow. ▪ behave unfairly to someone, especially so as to gain an unfair advantage. **hit the bottle** see BOTTLE. **hit someone for six** see SIX. **hit the ground running** informal start something and proceed at a fast pace with great enthusiasm. **hit the hay** see HAY[1]. **hit home** see HOME. **hit it off** informal be naturally friendly or well suited. **hit the jackpot** see JACKPOT. **hit the mark** be successful in an attempt or accurate in a guess. **hit the nail on the head** find exactly the right answer. **hit-or-miss** as likely to be unsuccessful as successful: *most drugs on the market have been found by hit-or-miss methods*. **hit the right note** see NOTE. **hit the road** (or N. Amer. **trail**) informal set out on a journey. **hit the roof** see ROOF. **hit the sack** see SACK[1]. **hit the spot** see SPOT. **hit wicket** Cricket the action of a batsman stepping on or knocking over their own wicket, resulting in their dismissal. **make a hit** be successful or popular: *you made a big hit with their daughter*.
– PHRASAL VERBS **hit on 1** (also **hit upon**) discover or think of, especially by chance: *she hit on a novel idea for fund-raising*. **2** N. Amer. make sexual advances towards. **3** (also **hit someone for**) chiefly US ask someone for: *she was waiting for the right moment to hit her mother for some cash*.
– DERIVATIVES **hitter** noun.
– ORIGIN late Old English *hittan* (in the sense 'come upon, find'), from Old Norse *hitta* 'come upon, meet with', of unknown origin.

hitch ▸ **verb 1** [with obj., and adverbial of direction] move (something) into a different position with a jerk: *she* **hitched up** *her skirt and ran*.
2 [no obj.] informal travel by hitch-hiking: *they hitched to Birmingham*. ▪ [with obj.] obtain (a lift) by hitch-hiking.

H

3 [with obj.] fasten or tether: *he returned to where he had hitched his horse.* ■ harness (a draught animal or team): *Thomas **hitched** the pony to his cart.*
▶ **noun 1** a temporary difficulty or problem: *everything went without a hitch.*
2 a knot of a particular kind, typically one used for fastening a rope to something else. ■ N. Amer. a device for attaching one thing to another, especially the tow bar of a motor vehicle.
3 informal an act of hitch-hiking.
4 N. Amer. informal a period of service: *his 12-year hitch in the navy.*
– PHRASES **get hitched** informal marry. **hitch one's wagon to a star** try to succeed by forming a relationship with someone who is already successful.
– ORIGIN Middle English (in sense 1 of the verb): of unknown origin.

Hitchcock, Sir Alfred (Joseph) (1899–1980), English film director. Acclaimed in Britain for films such as *The Thirty-Nine Steps* (1935), he moved to Hollywood in 1939. Among his later works, notable for their suspense and their technical ingenuity, are the thrillers *Strangers on a Train* (1951), *Psycho* (1960), and *The Birds* (1963).
– DERIVATIVES **Hitchcockian** adjective.

H

Hitchens /ˈhɪtʃɪnz/, Ivon (1893–1979), English painter. He is known chiefly for landscapes represented in an almost abstract style using areas of vibrant colour.

hitcher ▶ noun a hitch-hiker.

hitch-hike ▶ verb [no obj.] travel by getting free lifts in passing vehicles: *we hitch-hiked up to Scotland.*
▶ noun a journey made by hitch-hiking.
– DERIVATIVES **hitch-hiker** noun.

hi-tech ▶ adjective variant spelling of HIGH-TECH.

hither ▶ adverb archaic or literary to or towards this place: *I little knew then that such calamity would summon me hither!*
▶ adjective archaic situated on this side: *the hither side of Severn.*
– PHRASES **hither and thither** (also **hither and yon**) in various directions, especially in a disorganized way: *the entire household ran hither and thither.*
– ORIGIN Old English *hider*, of Germanic origin; related to HE and HERE.

hitherto ▶ adverb until now or until the point in time under discussion: *hitherto part of French West Africa, Benin achieved independence in 1960.*

hitherward ▶ adverb archaic to or towards this place.

Hitler, Adolf (1889–1945), Austrian-born Nazi leader, Chancellor of Germany 1933–45. ■ (as noun **a Hitler**) a person with authoritarian or tyrannical characteristics: *little Hitlers of the Trade Union movement.*

> Hitler co-founded the National Socialist German Workers' (Nazi) Party in 1919, and came to prominence through his powers of oratory. While imprisoned for an unsuccessful putsch (coup) in Munich (1923–4) he wrote *Mein Kampf* (1925), an exposition of his political ideas. Becoming Chancellor in 1933, he established the totalitarian Third Reich. His expansionist foreign policy precipitated the Second World War, while his fanatical anti-Semitism led to the Holocaust.

– DERIVATIVES **Hitlerian** adjective, **Hitlerism** noun, **Hitlerite** noun & adjective.

Hitler moustache ▶ noun a small square moustache like that worn by Adolf Hitler.

Hitler salute ▶ noun another term for NAZI SALUTE.

hit list ▶ noun a list of people to be killed for criminal or political reasons: *a terrorist hit list.*

hitmaker ▶ noun informal a successful singer or producer of popular music.

hitman ▶ noun informal a person who is paid to kill someone, especially for a criminal or political organization.

hit-out ▶ noun **1** Australian Rules an instance of hitting the ball towards a teammate after it has been bounced by the umpire or at a boundary throw-in.
2 Austral. informal a brisk run.

hit parade ▶ noun dated a weekly listing of the current bestselling pop records.

hit squad ▶ noun a team of assassins.

Hittite /ˈhɪtʌɪt/ ▶ noun **1** a member of an ancient people who established an empire in Asia Minor and Syria that flourished from *c.*1700 to *c.*1200 BC. ■ a subject of the Hittite empire or one of their descendants, including a Canaanite or Syrian people mentioned in the Bible (11th to 8th century BC).
2 [mass noun] the language of the Hittites, the oldest attested Indo-European language. Written in both hieroglyphic and cuneiform scripts, it was deciphered in the early 20th century.
▶ adjective relating to the Hittites, their empire, or their language.
– ORIGIN from Hebrew *Ḥittim*, ultimately from Hittite *Ḫatti*.

HIV ▶ abbreviation human immunodeficiency virus, a retrovirus which causes AIDS.

hive ▶ noun **1** a beehive. ■ the bees in a hive. ■ a thing that has the domed shape of a beehive.
2 a place in which people are busily occupied: *the kitchen became **a hive of activity**.*
▶ verb [with obj.] place (bees) in a hive. ■ [no obj.] (of bees) enter a hive.
– PHRASAL VERBS **hive something off** chiefly Brit. separate something from a larger group or organization: *the printing department was hived off in a management buyout.*
– ORIGIN Old English *hȳf*, of Germanic origin.

hive bee ▶ noun see BEE (sense 1).

hives ▶ plural noun [treated as sing. or pl.] another term for URTICARIA.
– ORIGIN early 16th cent. (originally Scots, denoting various conditions causing a rash, especially in children): of unknown origin.

HIV-positive ▶ adjective having had a positive result in a blood test for the AIDS virus HIV.

hiya ▶ exclamation an informal greeting.
– ORIGIN 1940s: alteration of *how are you?*

Hizbullah /ˌhɪzbʊˈlɑː, ˈhɪzbʊlə/ variant spelling of HEZBOLLAH.

HK ▶ abbreviation Hong Kong.

HKJ ▶ abbreviation Jordan (international vehicle registration).
– ORIGIN from *Hashemite Kingdom of Jordan.*

HL ▶ abbreviation (in the UK) House of Lords.

hl ▶ abbreviation hectolitre(s).

HM ▶ abbreviation ■ headmaster or headmistress. ■ Brit. heavy metal (music). ■ (in the UK) Her or His Majesty('s): *HM Forces.*

hm ▶ abbreviation hectometre(s).

h'm (also **hmm**) ▶ exclamation & noun variant spelling of HEM², HUM².

HMG ▶ abbreviation (in the UK) Her or His Majesty's Government.

HMI ▶ abbreviation historical (in the UK) Her or His Majesty's Inspector (of Schools).

HMO ▶ abbreviation health maintenance organization.

Hmong /hmɒŋ/ ▶ noun (pl. **same**) **1** a member of a people living in isolated mountain villages throughout SE Asia. Also called MIAO.
2 [mass noun] the language of the Hmong, occurring in a large number of highly distinct dialects.
▶ adjective relating to or denoting the Hmong or their language.

HMS ▶ abbreviation Her or His Majesty's Ship, used in the names of ships in the British navy: *HMS Ark Royal.*

HMSO ▶ abbreviation (in the UK) Her or His Majesty's Stationery Office, which publishes official government documents and legislation.

HNC ▶ abbreviation (in the UK) Higher National Certificate.

HND ▶ abbreviation (in the UK) Higher National Diploma.

Ho ▶ symbol the chemical element holmium.

ho¹ ▶ exclamation **1** an expression of surprise, admiration, triumph, or derision: *Ho! I'll show you.* ■ [in combination] used as the second element of various exclamations: *what ho!* | *heave ho.*
2 used to call for attention: *ho there!* ■ [in combination] chiefly Nautical used to draw attention to something seen: *land ho!*
– ORIGIN natural exclamation: first recorded in Middle English.

ho² (also **hoe**) ▶ noun (pl. **hos** or **hoes**) black slang a prostitute. ■ derogatory a woman.
– ORIGIN 1960s: representing a dialect pronunciation of WHORE.

ho. ▶ abbreviation house.

hoagie /ˈhəʊgi/ ▶ noun (pl. **hoagies**) chiefly N. Amer. a sandwich made of a long roll filled with meat, cheese, and salad.
– ORIGIN of unknown origin.

hoar /hɔː/ archaic or literary ▶ adjective greyish white; grey or grey-haired with age.
▶ noun [mass noun] hoar frost.
– ORIGIN Old English *hār*, of Germanic origin; related to German *hehr* 'majestic, noble'.

hoard ▶ noun a stock or store of money or valued objects, typically one that is secret or carefully guarded: *he came back to rescue his little **hoard of** gold.* ■ an ancient store of coins or other valuable artefacts: *a hoard of Romano-British bronzes.* ■ an amassed store of useful information, retained for future use: *a **hoard of** secret information about his work.*
▶ verb [with obj.] accumulate (money or valued objects) and hide or store away: *thousands of antiques hoarded by a compulsive collector.* ■ keep in one's mind for future use: (as adj. **hoarded**) *a year's worth of hoarded resentments and grudges.*
– ORIGIN Old English *hord* (noun), *hordian* (verb), of Germanic origin; related to German *Hort* (noun), *horten* (verb).

> **USAGE** The words **hoard** and **horde** have some similarities in meaning and are pronounced the same, so it is unsurprising that they are sometimes confused. A **hoard** is 'a secret stock or store of something', as in *a **hoard** of treasure*, while a **horde** is a disparaging word for 'a large group of people', as in *hordes of fans descended on the stage*. Instances of **hoard** being used instead of **horde** are not uncommon: around a quarter of citations for **hoard** in the Oxford English Corpus are for the incorrect use.

hoarder ▶ noun a person who hoards things: *I'm a bit of a hoarder.*

hoarding ▶ noun Brit. a large board in a public place, used to display advertisements. ■ a temporary board fence erected round a building site.
– ORIGIN early 19th cent.: from obsolete *hoard* in the same sense (probably based on Old French *hourd*; related to HURDLE) + -ING¹.

hoar frost ▶ noun [mass noun] a greyish-white crystalline deposit of frozen water vapour formed in clear still weather on vegetation, fences, etc.

hoarhound ▶ noun variant spelling of HOREHOUND.

hoarse ▶ adjective (of a person's voice) sounding rough and harsh, typically as the result of a sore throat or of shouting: *a hoarse whisper.*
– DERIVATIVES **hoarsely** adverb, **hoarseness** noun.
– ORIGIN Old English *hās*, of Germanic origin; related to Dutch *hees*. The spelling with *r* was influenced in Middle English by an Old Norse cognate.

hoarstone ▶ noun Brit. (now only in place names) an ancient boundary stone.

hoary ▶ adjective (**hoarier**, **hoariest**) **1** greyish white: *hoary cobwebs.* ■ (of a person) old and having grey or white hair: *young lasses imprisoned by hoary old husbands.* ■ [attrib.] used in names of animals and plants covered with whitish fur or short hairs, e.g. **hoary bat**, **hoary cress**.
2 overused and unoriginal; trite: *the hoary old adage often used by Fleet Street editors.*
– DERIVATIVES **hoariness** noun.

hoary marmot ▶ noun a large stocky greyish-brown marmot with a whistling call, found in the mountains of north-western North America. ● *Marmota caligata*, family Sciuridae.

hoatzin /həʊˈatsɪn/ ▶ noun a large tree-dwelling tropical American bird with weak flight. Young hoatzins have hooked claws on their wings, enabling them to climb about among the branches. ● *Opisthocomus hoazin*, the only member of the family Opisthocomidae (order Galliformes or Cuculiformes).
– ORIGIN mid 17th cent.: from American Spanish, from Nahuatl *uatzin*, probably imitative of its call.

hoax ▶ noun a humorous or malicious deception: *the evidence had been planted as part of an elaborate hoax* | [as modifier] *a hoax 999 call.*
▶ verb [with obj.] trick or deceive (someone).
– ORIGIN late 18th cent. (as a verb): probably a contraction of HOCUS.

hoaxer ▶ noun a person who tricks or deceives someone by means of a hoax: *the hoaxer claimed her mother was trapped in a burning flat.*

hob¹ ▶ noun **1** Brit. a cooking appliance, or the flat top part of a cooker, with hotplates or burners. ■ a flat metal shelf at the side of a fireplace, having its surface level with the top of the grate and used especially for heating pans.
2 a machine tool used for cutting gears or screw threads.
3 a peg or pin used as a mark in throwing games.

– ORIGIN late 16th cent. (in sense 3): alteration of **HUB**. Sense 1, 'metal shelf by a fireplace', dates from the late 17th cent.

hob² ▸ noun **1** a male ferret. Compare with **GILL⁴** (sense 1).
2 archaic or dialect a sprite or hobgoblin.
– PHRASES **play** (or **raise**) **hob** N. Amer. cause mischief.
– ORIGIN late Middle English (in the sense 'country fellow'): pet form of *Rob*, short for *Robin* or *Robert*, often referring specifically to **ROBIN GOODFELLOW**.

Hobart /ˈhəʊbɑːt/ the capital and chief port of Tasmania; pop. 209,287 (2008).
– ORIGIN named after Lord *Hobart* (1760–1816), Secretary of State for the Colonies.

Hobbema /ˈhɒbəmə/, Meindert (1638–1709), Dutch landscape painter. His painting focuses on a limited range of subject matter and reflects the influence of his teacher, Jacob van Ruisdael.

Hobbes /hɒbz/, Thomas (1588–1679), English philosopher. Hobbes was a materialist, claiming that there was no more to the mind than the physical motions discovered by science, and he believed that human action was motivated entirely by selfish concerns, notably fear of death. In *Leviathan* (1651) he argued that absolute monarchy was the most rational, hence desirable, form of government.
– DERIVATIVES **Hobbesian** adjective.

hobbit ▸ noun a member of an imaginary race similar to humans, of small size and with hairy feet, in stories by J. R. R. Tolkien.
– ORIGIN 1937: invented by Tolkien in his book *The Hobbit*, and said by him to mean 'hole-dweller'.

hobble ▸ verb **1** [no obj., with adverbial of direction] walk in an awkward way, typically because of pain from an injury: *he was hobbling around on crutches.* ■ [with obj.] cause (a person or animal) to limp: *Johnson was still hobbled slightly by an ankle injury.*
2 [with obj.] tie or strap together (the legs of a horse or other animal) to prevent it from straying. [variant of **HOPPLE**.] ■ restrict the activity or development of: *the economy was hobbled by rising oil prices.*
▸ noun **1** [in sing.] an awkward way of walking, typically due to pain from an injury: *he finished the match almost reduced to a hobble.*
2 a rope or strap used for hobbling a horse or other animal.
– DERIVATIVES **hobbler** noun.
– ORIGIN Middle English: probably of Dutch or Low German origin and related to Dutch *hobbelen* 'rock from side to side'.

hobblebush ▸ noun a North American viburnum which bears clusters of white or pink flowers and purple-black berries. ● *Viburnum alnifolium*, family Caprifoliaceae.

hobbledehoy /ˈhɒb(ə)ldɪˌhɔɪ/ informal, dated ▸ noun a clumsy or awkward youth.
▸ adjective awkward or clumsy: *his hobbledehoy hands.*
– ORIGIN mid 16th cent.: of unknown origin.

hobble skirt ▸ noun a style of skirt so narrow at the hem as to impede walking, popular in the 1910s.

Hobbs, Sir Jack (1882–1963), English cricketer; full name *John Berry Hobbs*. During his career (1905–34) he scored 61,237 runs and 197 centuries, and made 61 test appearances for England.

hobby¹ ▸ noun (pl. **hobbies**) **1** an activity done regularly in one's leisure time for pleasure: *her hobbies are reading and gardening.*
2 archaic a small horse or pony.
– ORIGIN late Middle English *hobyn*, *hoby*, from pet forms of the given name *Robin*. Originally in sense 2 (compare with **DOBBIN**), it later came to denote a toy horse or hobby horse, hence 'an activity done for pleasure'.

hobby² ▸ noun (pl. **hobbies**) a migratory Old World falcon with long, narrow wings, catching dragonflies and birds on the wing. ● Genus *Falco*, family Falconidae: four species, e.g. the (**northern**) **hobby** (*F. subbuteo*) of Eurasia.
– ORIGIN late Middle English: from Old French *hobet*, diminutive of *hobe* 'falcon'.

hobby farm ▸ noun a small farm operated primarily for pleasure rather than profit.
– DERIVATIVES **hobby farmer** noun.

hobby horse ▸ noun **1** a child's toy consisting of a stick with a model of a horse's head at one end. ■ a rocking horse. ■ a model of a horse or a horse's head, typically of wicker, used in morris dancing or pantomime.
2 a preoccupation or favourite topic: *Brennan admits that the greenhouse effect is a hobby horse of his.*

hobbyist ▸ noun a person who pursues a particular hobby: *a computer hobbyist.*

hobday ▸ verb [with obj.] Brit. operate on (a horse) to improve its breathing by pinning back the vocal fold in the larynx.
– ORIGIN 1930s: named after Sir Frederick T. G. *Hobday* (1869–1939), the British veterinary surgeon who introduced the technique.

hobgoblin ▸ noun (in mythology and fairy stories) a mischievous imp or sprite.
– ORIGIN mid 16th cent.: from **HOB²** + **GOBLIN**.

hobnail ▸ noun a short heavy-headed nail used to reinforce the soles of boots. ■ a blunt projection, especially in cut or moulded glassware. ■ [mass noun] glass decorated with blunt projections.
– DERIVATIVES **hobnailed** adjective.
– ORIGIN late 16th cent.: from **HOB¹** + **NAIL**.

hobnail liver (also **hobnailed liver**) ▸ noun a liver having many small knobbly projections due to cirrhosis.

hobnob ▸ verb (**hobnobs**, **hobnobbing**, **hobnobbed**) [no obj.] informal mix socially, especially with those of perceived higher social status: *he was hobnobbing with the great and good.*
– ORIGIN early 19th cent. (in the sense 'drink together'): from archaic *hob or nob*, *hob and nob*, probably meaning 'give and take', used by two people drinking to each other's health, from dialect *hab nab* 'have or not have'.

hobo ▸ noun (pl. **hoboes** or **hobos**) N. Amer. a homeless person; a tramp or vagrant.
– ORIGIN late 19th cent.: of unknown origin.

Hobson's choice ▸ noun a choice of taking what is available or nothing at all.
– ORIGIN mid 17th cent.: named after Thomas *Hobson* (1554–1631), a Cambridge carrier who hired out horses, giving the customer the 'choice' of the one nearest the door or none at all.

Ho Chi Minh /ˌhəʊ tʃiː ˈmɪn/, Vietnamese communist statesman (1890–1969), President of North Vietnam 1954–69; born *Nguyen That Thanh*. He led the Vietminh against the Japanese during the Second World War, fought the French until they were defeated in 1954 and Vietnam was divided into North and South Vietnam, and deployed his forces in the guerrilla struggle that became the Vietnam War.

Ho Chi Minh City official name (since 1975) for **SAIGON**.

hock¹ ▸ noun **1** the joint in a quadruped's hind leg between the knee and the fetlock, the angle of which points backwards.
2 a knuckle of meat, especially of pork or ham.
– ORIGIN late Middle English: variant of **HOUGH**.

hock² ▸ noun [mass noun] Brit. a dry white wine from the German Rhineland.
– ORIGIN abbreviation of obsolete *hockamore*, alteration of German *Hochheimer (Wein)* '(wine) from Hochheim'.

hock³ ▸ verb [with obj.] informal deposit (an object) with a pawnbroker as security for money lent.
– PHRASES **in hock** having been pawned. ■ in debt: *the women were **in hock to** extortionate moneylenders.*
– ORIGIN mid 19th cent. (in the phrase *in hock*): from Dutch *hok* 'hutch, prison, debt'.

hocket ▸ noun Music a spasmodic or interrupted effect in medieval and contemporary music, produced by dividing a melody between two parts, notes in one part coinciding with rests in the other.
– DERIVATIVES **hocketing** noun.
– ORIGIN late 18th cent.: from French *hoquet* 'hiccup'; in Old French the sense was 'hitch, sudden interruption' which also existed in Middle English.

hockey¹ /ˈhɒki/ ▸ noun [mass noun] a team game played between two teams of eleven players each, using hooked sticks with which the players try to drive a small hard ball towards goals at opposite ends of a field. In North America it is called **field hockey** to distinguish it from **ice hockey**.
– ORIGIN early 16th cent.: of unknown origin.

hockey² /ˈɒki, ˈhɒki/ ▸ noun variant spelling of **OCHE**.

hockey mom ▸ noun N. Amer. informal a mother who devotes a great deal of time and effort to supporting her children's participation in ice hockey.

Hockney, David (b.1937), English painter and draughtsman. He is best known for his association with pop art and for his Californian work of the mid 1960s, which depicts flat, almost shadowless architecture, lawns, and swimming pools.

Hocktide ▸ noun (in England) a religious festival formerly kept on the second Monday and Tuesday after Easter, during which, in pre-Reformation times, money was raised for Church and parish purposes.
– ORIGIN of unknown origin.

hocus /ˈhəʊkəs/ ▸ verb (**hocusses**, **hocussing**, **hocussed** or **hocuses**, **hocusing**, **hocused**) [with obj.] archaic **1** deceive (someone).
2 stupefy (someone) with drugs, typically for a criminal purpose.
– ORIGIN late 17th cent.: from an obsolete noun *hocus* 'trickery', from **HOCUS-POCUS**.

hocus-pocus ▸ noun [mass noun] meaningless talk or activity, typically designed to trick someone or conceal the truth of a situation: *some people still view psychology as a lot of hocus-pocus.* ■ a form of words used by a person performing conjuring tricks. ■ US deception; trickery.
– ORIGIN early 17th cent.: from *hax pax max Deus adimax*, a pseudo-Latin phrase used as a magic formula by conjurors.

hod ▸ noun a builder's V-shaped open trough on a pole, used for carrying bricks and other building materials. ■ a coal scuttle.
– ORIGIN late 16th cent.: variant of northern English dialect *hot* 'a basket for carrying earth', from Old French *hotte* 'pannier', probably of Germanic origin.

hodden /ˈhɒd(ə)n/ ▸ noun [mass noun] chiefly Scottish & N. English a coarse woollen cloth.
– ORIGIN late 16th cent.: of unknown origin.

Hodeida /həʊˈdeɪdə/ the chief port of Yemen, on the Red Sea; pop. 410,000 (est. 2004). Arabic name **AL-HUDAYDA**.

Hodge ▸ noun archaic used as a name for a typical English agricultural labourer.
– ORIGIN late Middle English: pet form of the given name *Roger*.

hodgepodge ▸ noun N. Amer. variant of **HOTCHPOTCH**.
– ORIGIN late Middle English: changed by association with **HODGE**.

Hodgkin¹, Sir Alan Lloyd (1914–98), English physiologist. With Andrew Huxley he demonstrated the role of sodium and potassium ions in the transmission of nerve impulses between cells. Nobel Prize for Physiology or Medicine (1963).

Hodgkin², Dorothy (Crowfoot) (1910–94), British chemist, born in Egypt. She developed Sir Lawrence Bragg's X-ray diffraction technique for investigating the structure of crystals and applied it to complex organic compounds. Using this method she determined the structures of penicillin, vitamin B_{12}, and insulin. Nobel Prize for Chemistry (1964).

Hodgkin's disease ▸ noun [mass noun] a malignant though often curable disease of lymphatic tissues typically causing painless enlargement of the lymph nodes, liver, and spleen.
– ORIGIN mid 19th cent.: named after Thomas *Hodgkin* (1798–1866), the English physician who first described it.

hodiernal /ˌhɒdɪˈəːn(ə)l, ˌhəʊdɪ-/ ▸ adjective rare relating to the present day.
– ORIGIN mid 17th cent.: from Latin *hodiernus* (from *hodie* 'today') + **-AL**.

hodman ▸ noun (pl. **hodmen**) Brit. a labourer who carries a hod.

hodograph /ˈhɒdəgrɑːf/ ▸ noun Mathematics a curve the radius vector of which represents in magnitude and direction the velocity of a moving object.
– ORIGIN mid 19th cent.: from Greek *hodos* 'way' + **-GRAPH**.

Hoe, Richard March (1812–86), American inventor and industrialist. In 1846 he became the first printer to develop a successful rotary press, which greatly increased the speed of printing.

hoe¹ ▸ noun a long-handled gardening tool with a thin metal blade, used mainly for weeding.
▸ verb (**hoes**, **hoeing**, **hoed**) **1** [with obj.] use a hoe to dig (earth) or thin out or dig up (plants).
2 [no obj.] (**hoe in**) Austral./NZ informal eat eagerly. ■ (**hoe into**) attack or criticize.
– DERIVATIVES **hoer** noun.
– ORIGIN Middle English: from Old French *houe*, of Germanic origin; related to German *Haue*, also to **HEW**.

hoe² ▸ noun variant spelling of **HO²**.

hoecake ▸ noun US a coarse cake of maize flour, originally baked on the blade of a hoe.

hoedown ▸ noun N. Amer. a social gathering at which lively folk dancing takes place. ■ a lively folk dance.

H

Hoek van Holland /ˌhuk vɑn ˈhɔlɑnt/ Dutch name for **Hook of Holland**.

Hofei /həʊˈfeɪ/ variant of **Hefei**.

Hoffa /ˈhɒfə/, Jimmy (1913–*c*.75), American trade union leader; full name *James Riddle Hoffa*. President of the Teamsters union from 1957, he was imprisoned in 1967–71 for attempted bribery of a federal court judge, fraud, and looting pension funds. He disappeared in 1975, and is thought to have been murdered.

Hoffman /ˈhɒfmən/, Dustin (Lee) (b.1937), American actor. A versatile method actor, he won Oscars for *Kramer vs Kramer* (1979) and *Rain Man* (1989). Other notable films: *The Graduate* (1967) and *Tootsie* (1983).

Hoffmann /ˈhɒfmən/, E. T. A. (1776–1822), German novelist, short-story writer, and music critic; full name *Ernst Theodor Amadeus Hoffmann*. His extravagantly fantastic stories provided the inspiration for Offenbach's opera *Tales of Hoffmann* (1881).

Hofmannsthal /ˈhɒfmənzˌtɑːl/, German /ˈhoːfmansˌtaːl/, Hugo von (1874–1929), Austrian poet and dramatist. He wrote the libretti for many of the operas of Richard Strauss, including *Elektra* (1909). With Strauss and Max Reinhardt he helped found the Salzburg Festival.

hog ▶ **noun 1** a domesticated pig, especially a castrated male reared for slaughter. ■ a feral pig. ■ a wild animal of the pig family, for example a warthog.
■ informal a greedy person.
2 informal a large motorcycle.
3 (also **hogg**) dialect a young sheep before the first shearing.
▶ **verb** (**hogs, hogging, hogged**) [with obj.] **1** informal take or use most or all of (something) in an unfair or selfish way: *he never hogged the limelight*.
2 cause (a ship or its keel) to curve up in the centre and sag at the ends as a result of strain.
– PHRASES **go the whole hog** informal do something completely or thoroughly. [of several origins suggested, one interprets *hog* as the American slang term for a ten cent piece; another refers to one of Cowper's poems (1779), which discusses Muslim uncertainty about which parts of the pig are acceptable as food, leading to the 'whole hog' being eaten.] **live high on** (or **off**) **the hog** N. Amer. informal have a luxurious lifestyle.
– DERIVATIVES **hogger** noun, **hoggish** adjective, **hoglike** adjective.
– ORIGIN late Old English *hogg, hocg*, perhaps of Celtic origin and related to Welsh *hwch* and Cornish *hoch* 'pig, sow'.

Hogan, Ben (1912–97), American golfer; full name *William Benjamin Hogan*. His many victories include winning the US Open, the US Masters, and the British Open in 1953, together with three other victories in the US Open, and one in the US Masters.

hogan /ˈhəʊg(ə)n/ ▶ **noun** a traditional Navajo Indian hut of logs and earth.
– ORIGIN Navajo.

Hogarth /ˈhəʊgɑːθ/, William (1697–1764), English painter and engraver. Notable works include his series of engravings on 'modern moral subjects', such as *A Rake's Progress* (1735), which satirized the vices of both high and low life in 18th-century England.
– DERIVATIVES **Hogarthian** adjective.

hogback (also **hog's back**) ▶ **noun** a long hill or mountain ridge with steep sides.

hog badger ▶ **noun** a badger with a long mobile snout and dark facial stripes, found in the forests of eastern Asia. ● *Arctonyx collaris*, family Mustelidae.

hog deer ▶ **noun** a short-legged heavily built deer having a yellow-brown coat with darker underparts, found in grasslands and paddy fields in SE Asia. ● *Cervus porcinus*, family Cervidae.

hogfish ▶ **noun** (pl. **same** or **hogfishes**) a colourful wrasse (fish) that occurs chiefly in the warm waters of the western Atlantic, often acting as a cleaner fish for other species. ● Several genera and species in the family Labridae, in particular the large edible *Lachnolaimus maximus*.

Hogg, James (1770–1835), Scottish poet. A shepherd in the Ettrick Forest whose talent was discovered by Sir Walter Scott, he is best known today for his prose work *The Confessions of a Justified Sinner* (1824).

hogg ▶ **noun** variant spelling of **hog** (sense 3 of the noun).

Hoggar Mountains /ˈhɒgə/ a mountain range in the Saharan desert of southern Algeria, rising to a height of 2,918 m (9,573 ft) at Tahat. Also called **Ahaggar Mountains**.

hogget /ˈhɒgɪt/ ▶ **noun** Brit. a yearling sheep. ■ NZ a lamb between weaning and first shearing.
– ORIGIN late Middle English (applied also to a young boar): from **hog** + **-et**[1].

hoggin ▶ **noun** [mass noun] a mixture of sand and gravel, used especially as hard core in road-building.
– ORIGIN mid 19th cent.: of unknown origin.

hog heaven ▶ **noun** [mass noun] N. Amer. informal a place or condition of foolish or idle bliss: *with all the chocolate I've gotten, I'll be in hog heaven for weeks*.

hog line ▶ **noun** (in the game of curling) a line marked across either end of a curling rink at one sixth of the rink's length from the tee. No sweeping is allowed until a stone has crossed the first line.

Hogmanay /ˈhɒgməneɪ, ˌhɒgməˈneɪ/ ▶ **noun** (in Scotland) New Year's Eve, and the celebrations that take place at this time.
– ORIGIN early 17th cent.: perhaps from *hoguinané*, Norman French form of Old French *aguillanneuf* 'last day of the year, new year's gift'.

hog-nosed bat ▶ **noun** a tiny insectivorous bat with a piglike nose and no tail, native to Thailand. It is the smallest known bat. ● *Craseonycteris thonglongyai*, the only member of the family Craseonycteridae.

hognose snake (also **hog-nosed snake**) ▶ **noun** a harmless burrowing American snake with an upturned snout. When threatened it inflates itself with air and hisses, and may feign death. Also called **puff adder** in North America. ● Genus *Heterodon*, family Colubridae: several species.

hognut ▶ **noun** another term for **earthnut** (sense 1).

hog plum ▶ **noun** a tropical tree which bears edible plum-like fruit, in particular: ● a Caribbean tree with yellow fruit (*Spondias mombin*, family Anacardiaceae). ● (**American hog plum**) an American tree with bitter fruit and timber that is used as a sandalwood substitute (*Ximenia americana*, family Olacaceae).
– ORIGIN late 17th cent.: so named because the fruit is common food for hogs in the West Indies and Brazil.

hog's back ▶ **noun** variant spelling of **hogback**.

hogshead (abbrev.: **hhd**) ▶ **noun** a large cask. ■ a measure of capacity for wine, equal to 52.5 imperial gallons or 63 US gallons (238.7 litres). ■ a measure of capacity for beer, equal to 54 imperial gallons or 64 US gallons (245.5 litres).
– ORIGIN Middle English: from **hog** + **head**; the reason for the term is unknown.

hog-tie ▶ **verb** [with obj.] N. Amer. secure (a person or animal) by fastening the hands and feet or all four feet together. ■ impede or hinder greatly: *the flood of regulations that are hog-tying our businesses*.

hogwash ▶ **noun** [mass noun] informal nonsense.
– ORIGIN mid 15th cent.: from **hog** + **wash**; the original sense was 'kitchen swill for pigs'.

hogweed ▶ **noun** [mass noun] a large white-flowered weed of the parsley family, native to north temperate regions and formerly used as forage for pigs. ● Genus *Heracleum*, family Umbelliferae: several species, in particular the common European *H. sphondylium* and the introduced **giant hogweed** (*H. mantegazzianum*).

hog-wild ▶ **adjective** N. Amer. informal out of control: *Congress will go hog-wild in its spending*.

Hohenstaufen /ˈhəʊənˌʃtaʊf(ə)n/, German /ˈhoːənˌʃtaufn/ a German dynastic family, some of whom ruled as Holy Roman emperors between 1138 and 1254, among them Frederick I (Barbarossa).

Hohenzollern /ˈhəʊənˌzɒlən/, German /ˌhoːənˈtsɔlɐn/ a German dynastic family from which came the kings of Prussia from 1701 to 1918 and German emperors from 1871 to 1918.

Hohhot /həʊˈhɒt/ (also **Huhehot**) the capital of Inner Mongolia autonomous region, NE China; pop. 825,900 (est. 2006). Former name (until 1954) **Kwesui**.

ho ho ▶ **exclamation** representing deep laughter.
■ used to express triumph, especially at a discovery: *Ho ho! A stranger in our midst!*
– ORIGIN mid 16th cent.: reduplication of **ho**[1].

ho-hum ▶ **exclamation** used to express boredom or resignation.
▶ **adjective** boring: *a ho-hum script*.
– ORIGIN 1920s: imitative of a yawn.

hoick Brit. informal ▶ **verb** [with obj. and adverbial of direction] lift or pull abruptly or with effort: *she hoicked her bag on to the desk*.
▶ **noun** an abrupt pull.
– ORIGIN late 19th cent.: perhaps a variant of **hike**.

hoicks /hɔɪks/ ▶ **exclamation** variant of **yoicks**.

hoi polloi /ˌhɔɪ pɒˈlɔɪ/ ▶ **plural noun** (usu. **the hoi polloi**) derogatory the masses; the common people: *avoid mixing with the hoi polloi*.
– ORIGIN mid 17th cent.: Greek, literally 'the many'.

> **USAGE 1** To those in the know, **hoi** is the Greek word for the definite article **the** (nominative masculine plural); the phrase **hoi polloi** thus translates as 'the many'. This knowledge has led some traditionalists to insist that **hoi polloi** should not be used in English with **the**, since that would be to state the word **the** twice. Such arguments miss the point: once established in English, expressions such as **hoi polloi** are treated as a fixed unit and are subject to the rules and conventions of English. Evidence shows that use with **the** has now become an accepted part of standard English usage.
> **2 Hoi polloi** is sometimes used incorrectly to mean 'upper class', i.e. the exact opposite of its normal meaning. It seems likely that the confusion arose by association with the similar-sounding but otherwise unrelated word **hoity-toity**.

hoisin /ˈhɔɪzɪn/ (also **hoisin sauce**) ▶ **noun** [mass noun] a sweet, spicy dark red sauce made from soya beans, vinegar, sugar, garlic, and various spices, widely used in southern Chinese cooking.

hoist ▶ **verb** [with obj.] raise (something) by means of ropes and pulleys: *a white flag was hoisted*. ■ [with obj. and adverbial] raise or haul up: *she hoisted her backpack on to her shoulder*.
▶ **noun 1** an act of raising or lifting something. ■ an apparatus for lifting or raising something. ■ an act of increasing something: *an interest rate hoist*.
2 the part of a flag nearest the staff.
3 a group of flags raised as a signal.
– PHRASES **hoist one's flag** (of an admiral) take up command. **hoist the flag** stake one's claim to discovered territory by displaying a flag. **hoist with one's own petard** see **petard**.
– DERIVATIVES **hoister** noun.
– ORIGIN late 15th cent.: alteration of dialect *hoise*, probably from Dutch *hijsen* or Low German *hiesen*, but recorded earlier.

hoity-toity ▶ **adjective** haughty or snobbish: *a hoity-toity little madam*.
– ORIGIN mid 17th cent. (as noun in the sense 'boisterous or silly behaviour', then as adjective meaning 'lively and playful'): from obsolete *hoit* 'indulge in riotous mirth', of unknown origin.

hok /hɒk, hɔːk/ (also **hokkie**) ▶ **noun** S. African an enclosure for domestic animals. ■ a small hut.
– ORIGIN Afrikaans.

Hokan /ˈhəʊkan/ ▶ **adjective** relating to or denoting a group of American Indian languages of California and western Mexico, considered as a possible language family. They include Yuman, Mojave, and several other languages now extinct or almost so.
▶ **noun** [mass noun] the hypothetical Hokan language family.
– ORIGIN from Hokan *hok* 'about two' + **-an**.

hoke /həʊk/ ▶ **verb** [with obj.] N. Amer. informal (of an actor) act (a part) in an insincere, sentimental, or melodramatic manner: *just try it straight—don't hoke it up*.
– ORIGIN early 20th cent.: back-formation from **hokum**.

hokey ▶ **adjective** (**hokier, hokiest**) N. Amer. informal mawkishly sentimental: *a hokey tear-jerker*. ■ noticeably contrived: *a hokey country-western accent*.
– DERIVATIVES **hokeyness** (also **hokiness**) noun.
– ORIGIN 1940s: from **hokum** + **-y**[1].

hokey-cokey ▶ **noun** a communal dance performed in a circle with synchronized shaking of the limbs in turn, accompanied by a simple song.
– ORIGIN 1940s: perhaps from **hocus-pocus**.

hokey-pokey ▶ **noun** informal **1** [mass noun] dated ice cream sold on the street, especially by Italian street vendors. ■ NZ a kind of brittle toffee or a type of toffee-flavoured ice cream.
2 US deception; trickery.
3 (**the hokey-pokey**) US term for **hokey-cokey**.
– ORIGIN late 19th cent.: of unknown origin.

hoki /ˈhəʊki/ ▶ **noun** an edible marine fish related to the hakes, found off the southern coasts of New Zealand. ● *Macruronus novaezeelandiae*, family Macruronidae.
– ORIGIN 19th cent.: from Maori.

Hokkaido /hɒˈkʌɪdəʊ/ the most northerly of the four main islands of Japan, constituting an administrative region; pop. 5,570,000 (est. 2007); capital, Sapporo.

Hokkien /həʊˈkiːn/ ▶ **noun 1** [mass noun] a dialect of southern Min Chinese that is also spoken in Malaysia, Singapore, Taiwan, and the Philippines.
2 (pl. **same** or **Hokkiens**) a member of a people traditionally inhabiting south-eastern China.
▶ **adjective** relating to the Hokkien or their dialect.
– ORIGIN Hokkien *hok kian*.

hokku /ˈhɒkuː/ ▶ **noun** (pl. **same**) another term for HAIKU.
– ORIGIN Japanese, literally 'opening verse' (of a linked sequence of comic verses).

hokonui /ˈhɒkənʊi/ ▶ **noun** [mass noun] NZ illicitly distilled spirits, especially whisky.
– ORIGIN from a Maori place name.

hokum /ˈhəʊkəm/ ▶ **noun** [mass noun] informal nonsense: *they dismissed such corporate homilies as boardroom hokum.* ■ trite, sentimental, or unrealistic situations and dialogue in a film or other work: *classic B-movie hokum.*
– ORIGIN early 20th cent.: of unknown origin.

Hokusai /ˈhəʊkʊsʌɪ, ˌhəʊkʊˈsʌɪ/, Katsushika (1760–1849), Japanese painter and wood engraver. A leading artist of the *ukiyo-e* school, he depicted aspects of Japanese everyday life in his woodcuts and strongly influenced European Impressionist artists.

Holarctic /hə(ʊ)ˈlɑːktɪk/ ▶ **adjective** Zoology relating to or denoting a zoogeographical region comprising the Nearctic and Palaearctic regions combined. The two continents have been linked intermittently by the Bering land bridge, and the faunas are closely related. ■ (as noun **the Holarctic**) the Holarctic region.
– ORIGIN late 19th cent.: from HOLO- 'whole' + ARCTIC.

Holbein /ˈhɒlbʌɪn/, Hans (1497–1543), German painter and engraver; known as **Holbein the Younger**. He became a well-known court portraitist in England and was commissioned by Henry VIII to supply portraits of the king's prospective brides. Notable works: *Dance of Death* (series of woodcuts, *c.*1523–6); *Anne of Cleves* (miniature, 1539).

hold[1] ▶ **verb** (past and past participle **held**) **1** [with obj.] grasp, carry, or support with one's arms or hands: *she was holding a brown leather suitcase* | [no obj.] *he held on to the back of a chair.* ■ [with obj. and adverbial] keep or sustain in a specified position: *I held the door open for him.* ■ embrace (someone): *Mark pulled her into his arms and held her close.* ■ be able to bear (the weight of a person or thing): *I reached up to the nearest branch which seemed likely to hold my weight.* ■ (of a vehicle) maintain close contact with (the road), especially when driven at speed: *the car holds the corners very well.* ■ (of a ship or an aircraft) continue to follow (a particular course): *the ship is holding a south-easterly course.* ■ [no obj., with adverbial of direction] archaic keep going in a particular direction: *he **held on his way**, close behind his friend.*
2 [with obj.] keep or detain (someone): *the police were holding him on a murder charge* | [with obj. and complement] *she was held prisoner for two days.* ■ keep possession of (something), typically in the face of a challenge or attack: *the rebels held the town for many weeks* | [no obj.] *White managed to **hold on to** his lead.* ■ keep (someone's interest or attention). ■ (of a singer or musician) sustain (a note). ■ stay or cause to stay at a certain value or level: [no obj.] *MCI shares held at 77p* | [with obj.] *they are trying to hold public spending to £244.5 billion.* ■ (in sport) manage to achieve a draw against (opponents thought likely to win): *AC Milan were **held to a 1–1 draw** by Udinese.*
3 [no obj.] remain secure, intact, or in position without breaking or giving way: *the boat's anchor would not hold.* ■ (of a favourable condition or situation) continue without changing: *let's hope her luck holds.* ■ be or remain valid or available: *I'll have that coffee now, if the offer still holds.* ■ (of an argument or theory) be logical, consistent, or convincing: *their views still seem to **hold up** extremely well.* ■ (**hold to**) refuse to abandon or change (a principle or opinion): *those who held to the view that Britain should not be part of the Common Market.* ■ [with obj.] (**hold someone to**) cause someone to adhere to (a commitment): *the role of the media ought to be to hold politicians to their promises.*
4 [with obj.] contain or be capable of containing (a specified amount): *the tank held twenty-four gallons.* ■ be able to drink (a reasonable amount of alcohol) without becoming drunk or suffering any ill effects: *I can hold my drink as well as anyone.* ■ have or be characterized by: *I don't know what the future holds.*
5 [with obj.] have in one's possession: *the managing director still holds fifty shares in the company.* ■ [no obj.] N. Amer. informal be in possession of illegal drugs: *he was holding, and the police hauled him off to jail.* ■ have or occupy (a job or position): *she held office from 1985 to 90.* ■ [with obj.] have (a belief or opinion): *I feel nothing but pity for someone who holds such chauvinistic views* | [with clause] *they hold that all literature is empty of meaning.* ■ [with obj. and complement] consider (someone) to be responsible or liable for a particular situation: *you can't hold yourself responsible for what happened.* ■ (**hold someone/thing in**) regard someone or something with (a specified feeling): *the speed limit is held in contempt by many drivers.* ■ [with clause] (of a judge or court) rule; decide: *the Court of Appeal held that there was no evidence to support the judge's assessment.*
6 [with obj.] keep or reserve for someone: *a booking can be held for twenty-four hours.* ■ maintain (a telephone connection) until the person one has telephoned is free to speak: *please **hold the line**, and I'll see if he's available* | [no obj.] *will you hold?*
7 [with obj.] prevent from going ahead or occurring: *hold your fire!* ■ N. Amer. informal refrain from adding or using (something, typically an item of food or drink): *a strawberry margarita, but hold the tequila.* ■ (**hold it**) informal wait or stop doing something: *hold it right there, mate!* ■ [no obj.] archaic restrain oneself.
8 [with obj.] arrange and take part in (a meeting or conversation): *a meeting was held at the church.*
▶ **noun 1** an act or manner of grasping something; a grip: *he **caught hold of** her arm* | *he lost his hold and fell.* ■ a particular way of grasping or restraining someone, especially an opponent in wrestling or judo. ■ a place where one can grip with one's hands or feet while climbing: *he felt carefully with his feet for a hold and swung himself up.*
2 [in sing.] power or control: *Tom had some kind of **hold over** his father.*
3 archaic a fortress.
– PHRASES **be left holding the baby** (or N. Amer. **bag**) informal be left with an unwelcome responsibility, typically without warning. **get hold of** grasp physically. ■ informal obtain: *if you can't get hold of ripe tomatoes, add some tomato purée.* ■ informal find or manage to contact (someone): *I'll try and get hold of Mark.* **hold someone/thing at bay** see BAY[5]. **hold one's breath** see BREATH. **hold someone/thing cheap** archaic have a low opinion of someone or something. **hold court** be the centre of attention amidst a crowd of one's admirers. **hold someone/thing dear** care for or value someone or something greatly: *fidelity is something most of us hold dear.* **hold fast** remain tightly secured: *the door held fast, obviously locked.* ■ continue to believe in or adhere to an idea or principle: *it is important that we **hold fast to** the policies.* **hold the field** see FIELD. **hold the fort** take responsibility for a situation while another person is temporarily absent. **hold good** (or **true**) remain true or valid: *his views still hold true today.* **hold one's ground** see GROUND[1]. **hold someone's hand** give a person comfort, guidance, or moral support in a difficult situation. **hold hands** (of two or more people) clasp each other by the hand, typically as a sign of affection. **hold hard** [as imperative] Brit. stop or wait. **hold someone/thing harmless** Law indemnify someone or something. **hold one's horses** [usu. as imperative] informal wait a moment. **hold the line** not yield to the pressure of a difficult situation. **hold one's nose** squeeze one's nostrils with one's fingers in order to avoid inhaling an unpleasant smell. **hold one's own** see OWN. **hold one's peace** see PEACE. **hold (one's) serve** (or **service**) (in tennis and other racket sports) win a game in which one is serving. **hold the stage** see STAGE. **hold sway** see SWAY. **hold thumbs** S. African fold one's fingers over one's thumb to bring good luck. **hold someone to bail** Law bind someone by bail. **hold one's tongue** [often in imperative] informal remain silent. **hold someone/thing to ransom** see RANSOM. **hold one's head up** (or **hold one's head high**) see HEAD. **hold water** [often with negative] (of a statement, theory, or line of reasoning) appear to be valid, sound, or reasonable: *this argument just does not hold water.* **no holds barred** (in wrestling) with no restrictions on the kinds of holds that are used. ■ used to convey that no rules or restrictions apply in a conflict or dispute: *no-holds-barred military action.* **on hold** waiting to be connected while making a telephone call. ■ temporarily not being dealt with or pursued: *he has had to **put** his career **on hold**.* **take hold** start to have an effect: *the reforms of the late nineteenth century had taken hold.* **there is no holding someone** used to convey that someone is particularly determined or cannot be prevented from doing something: *once Eva had found her vocation there was no holding her.*
– PHRASAL VERBS **hold something against someone** allow past actions or circumstances to have a negative influence on one's present attitude towards someone: *if he failed her, she would hold it against him forever.* **hold back** hesitate to act or speak. **hold someone/thing back** prevent or restrict the progress or development of someone or something: *my lack of experience held me back a bit.* ■ (**hold something back**) refuse or be unwilling to make something known: *you're not holding anything back from me, are you?* **hold someone down** keep someone under strict control or severely restrict their freedom: *the people are held down by a repressive military regime.* **hold something down** informal succeed in keeping a job or position for a period of time. **hold forth** talk lengthily, assertively, or tediously about a subject: *he was **holding forth on** the merits of the band's debut LP.* **hold something in** suppress an expression of emotion: *she tried to stop laughing, but it was too much to hold in.* **hold someone/thing off** resist an attacker or challenge: *he held off a late challenge by Vose to win by thirteen seconds.* **hold off** (of bad weather) fail to occur. ■ delay or postpone an action or decision. **hold on 1** [often in imperative] wait; stop: *hold on a minute, I'll be right back!* **2** endure in difficult circumstances. **hold on to** keep: *the industry is trying to hold on to experienced staff.* **hold out** resist or survive in difficult circumstances: *British troops **held out against** constant attacks.* ■ continue to be sufficient: *we can stay here for as long as our supplies hold out.* **hold out for** continue to demand (a particular thing), refusing to accept what has been offered: *he is holding out for a guaranteed 7 per cent rise.* **hold out on** informal refuse to give something, typically information, to (someone). **hold something out** offer a chance or hope: *a new drug may hold out hope for patients with lung cancer.* **hold something over 1** postpone something. **2** use a piece of information to threaten or intimidate (someone). **hold together** (or **hold something together**) remain or cause to remain united: *if your party holds together, you will probably win.* **hold up** remain strong or vigorous: *the Labour vote held up well.* **hold someone/thing up 1** support and prevent something from falling: *concrete pillars hold up the elevated section of the railway.* **2** display something by holding it above one's waist or head: *he held up the book so she could see the cover.* ■ present or expose someone or something as an example or for particular treatment: *they were **held up to** public ridicule.* **3** delay or block the movement or progress of someone or something: *our return flight was held up for seven hours.* **4** rob someone or something using threats or violence: *a masked raider held up the post office.* **5** Bridge refrain from playing a winning card for tactical reasons. **hold with** [with negative] informal approve of: *I don't hold with fighting or violence.*
– DERIVATIVES **holdable** adjective.
– ORIGIN Old English *haldan*, *healdan*, of Germanic origin; related to Dutch *houden* and German *halten*; the noun is partly from Old Norse *hald* 'hold, support, custody'.

hold[2] ▶ **noun** a large compartment or space in the lower part of a ship or aircraft in which cargo is stowed.
– ORIGIN late 16th cent.: from obsolete *holl*, from Old English *hol* (see HOLE). The addition of *-d* was due to association with HOLD[1].

holdall ▶ **noun** Brit. a large rectangular bag with handles and a shoulder strap, used for carrying clothes and other personal belongings.

holdback ▶ **noun 1** a thing serving to hold something else in place: *a curtain holdback.*
2 a sum of money withheld under certain conditions.

holder ▶ **noun 1** a device or implement for holding something: [in combination] *a cigarette-holder.*
2 a person that holds something: *a British passport holder* | *holders of two American hostages.* ■ the possessor of a trophy, championship, or record: *the FA Cup holders.*
3 a smallholder.

Hölderlin /ˈhəːldəlɪn/, German /ˈhœldɐliːn/, (Johann Christian) Friedrich (1770–1843), German poet. Most of his poems express a romantic yearning for harmony with nature and beauty. While working as a tutor he fell in love with his employer's wife, who is portrayed in his novel *Hyperion* (1797–9).

holdfast ▶ **noun** a firm grip. ■ a staple or clamp securing an object to a wall or other surface. ■ Biology a stalked organ by which an alga or other simple aquatic plant or animal is attached to a substrate.

holding ▶ **noun 1** an area of land held by lease. ■ the tenure of land held by lease.

2 (**holdings**) stocks, property, and other financial assets in someone's possession: *commercial property holdings.* ■ books, periodicals, magazines, and other material in a library.

holding company ▸ noun a company created to buy and own the shares of other companies, which it then controls.

holding ground ▸ noun Nautical an area of seabed where an anchor will hold.

holding operation ▸ noun a course of action designed to maintain the status quo under difficult circumstances.

holding pattern ▸ noun the flight path maintained by an aircraft awaiting permission to land.

holding tank ▸ noun a large container in which liquids are temporarily held.

holdout ▸ noun chiefly N. Amer. an act of resisting something or refusing to accept what is offered: *a defiant holdout against a commercial culture.* ■ a person who resists something or refuses to accept an offer.

holdover ▸ noun N. Amer. a person or thing surviving from an earlier time, especially someone surviving in office: *Young is the only holdover from the 2002 team.*

H

hold-up ▸ noun **1** a situation that causes delay: *the road closure will cause lengthy hold-ups.*
2 a robbery conducted with the use of threats or violence: *the shocked victims of an armed hold-up.*
3 (usu. **hold-ups**) a stocking held up by an elasticated top rather than by suspenders.

hole ▸ noun **1** a hollow place in a solid body or surface: *the dog had dug a hole in the ground.* ■ an aperture passing through something: *he had a hole in his sock.* ■ a cavity or receptacle on a golf course, typically one of eighteen or nine, into which the ball must be hit. ■ a cavity of this type as representing a division of a golf course or of play in golf: *Stephen lost the first three holes to Eric.* ■ an animal's burrow. ■ [in place names] a valley: *Seaton Hole.* ■ Physics a position from which an electron is absent, especially one regarded as a mobile carrier of positive charge in a semiconductor.
2 a place or position that needs to be filled because someone or something is no longer there: *she is missed terribly and her death has left a hole in all our lives.* ■ a shortcoming, weakness, or flaw in a plan, argument, etc.: *intriguing as it sounds, the theory is full of holes.*
3 informal an unpleasant place: *she had wasted a whole lifetime in this hole of a town.* ■ an awkward situation: *the team are in a bit of a hole and it's a case of seeing if they can dig themselves out.*
▸ verb [with obj.] **1** make a hole or holes in: *a fuel tank was holed by the attack and a fire started.*
2 Golf hit (the ball) into a hole: *George holed a six-iron shot from the fairway* | [no obj.] *he* ***holed out*** *for a birdie.*
– PHRASES **blow a hole in** ruin the effectiveness of: *the amendment could blow a hole in the legislation.* **in the hole** N. Amer. informal in debt: *we're still three thousand dollars in the hole.* **in holes** worn so much that holes have formed: *my clothes are in holes.* **make a hole in** use a large amount of: *holidays can make a big hole in your savings.* **need something like a hole in the head** informal used to emphasize that someone has absolutely no need or desire for something.
– PHRASAL VERBS **hole out** Cricket (of a batsman) hit the ball to a fielder and be caught. **hole up** informal hide oneself: *I holed up for two days in a tiny cottage in Snowdonia.*
– DERIVATIVES **holey** adjective.
– ORIGIN Old English *hol* (noun), *holian* (verb), of Germanic origin; related to Dutch *hol* (noun) 'cave', (adjective) 'hollow', and German *hohl* 'hollow', from an Indo-European root meaning 'cover, conceal'.

hole-and-corner ▸ adjective attempting to avoid public notice; secret: *a hole-and-corner wedding.*

hole card ▸ noun (in stud poker) a card which has been dealt face down. ■ chiefly N. Amer. a thing that is kept secret until it can be used to one's own advantage.

hole-in-one ▸ noun (pl. **holes-in-one**) Golf a shot that enters the hole from the tee with no intervening shots.

hole in the heart ▸ noun Medicine a congenital defect in the heart septum, resulting in inadequate circulation of oxygenated blood (a cause of blue baby syndrome).

hole in the wall ▸ noun informal **1** Brit. an automatic cash dispenser installed in the outside wall of a bank.
2 chiefly N. Amer. a small dingy bar, shop, or restaurant.

hole punch ▸ noun a device for punching holes in sheets of paper, so that they can be filed in a ring binder.

hole saw ▸ noun a tool for making circular holes, consisting of a metal cylinder with a toothed edge.

Holi /ˈhəʊliː/ ▸ noun a Hindu spring festival celebrated in February or March in honour of Krishna.
– ORIGIN via Hindi from Sanskrit *holī*.

Holiday /ˈhɒlɪdeɪ/, Billie (1915–59), American jazz singer; born *Eleanora Fagan*. She began her recording career with Benny Goodman's band in 1933, going on to perform with many small jazz groups.

holiday chiefly Brit. ▸ noun **1** (often **holidays**) an extended period of leisure and recreation, especially one spent away from home or in travelling: *I spent my summer holidays on a farm* | *Fred was* ***on holiday*** *in Spain.* ■ a day of festivity or recreation when no work is done: *25 December is an official public holiday.* ■ [as modifier] characteristic of a holiday; festive: *a holiday atmosphere.*
2 [with modifier] a short period during which the payment of instalments, tax, etc. may be suspended: *a pension holiday.*
▸ verb [no obj., with adverbial of place] spend a holiday in a specified place: *he is* ***holidaying in*** *Italy.*
– ORIGIN Old English *hāligdæg* 'holy day'.

holiday camp ▸ noun Brit. a site for holidaymakers with accommodation, entertainment, and leisure facilities.

holidaymaker ▸ noun Brit. a person on holiday away from home.

holiday season ▸ noun (in the US) the period of time from Thanksgiving until New Year, including such festivals as Christmas, Hanukkah, and Kwanzaa.

holiday village ▸ noun Brit. a large, modern holiday camp.

holier-than-thou ▸ adjective characterized by an attitude of moral superiority: *they had quite a critical, holier-than-thou approach.*

holiness ▸ noun [mass noun] the state of being holy: *a life of holiness and total devotion to God.* ■ (**His/Your Holiness**) a title or form of address given to the Pope, Orthodox patriarchs, and the Dalai Lama. ■ [as modifier] denoting a Christian renewal movement originating in the mid 19th century among Methodists in the US, emphasizing the Wesleyan doctrine of the sanctification of believers.
– ORIGIN Old English *hālignes* (see **HOLY**, **-NESS**).

Holinshed /ˈhɒlɪnʃɛd/, Raphael (died c.1580), English chronicler. Although the named compiler of *The Chronicles of England, Scotland, and Ireland* (1577), Holinshed wrote only the *Historie of England* and had help with the remainder. The revised (1587) edition was used by Shakespeare.

holism /ˈhəʊlɪz(ə)m, ˈhɒl-/ ▸ noun [mass noun] chiefly Philosophy the theory that parts of a whole are in intimate interconnection, such that they cannot exist independently of the whole, or cannot be understood without reference to the whole, which is thus regarded as greater than the sum of its parts. Holism is often applied to mental states, language, and ecology. The opposite of **ATOMISM**. ■ Medicine the treating of the whole person, taking into account mental and social factors, rather than just the symptoms of a disease.
– DERIVATIVES **holist** adjective & noun.
– ORIGIN 1920s: from **HOLO-** 'whole' + **-ISM**; coined by J. C. Smuts to designate the tendency in nature to produce organized 'wholes' (bodies or organisms) from the ordered grouping of units.

holistic /həʊˈlɪstɪk, hɒ-/ ▸ adjective chiefly Philosophy characterized by the belief that the parts of something are intimately interconnected and explicable only by reference to the whole. ■ Medicine characterized by the treatment of the whole person, taking into account mental and social factors, rather than just the symptoms of a disease.
– DERIVATIVES **holistically** adverb.

holla /ˈhɒlə/ ▸ exclamation archaic used to call attention to something: *'Holla! what storm is this?'*
– ORIGIN early 16th cent. (as an order to stop or cease): from French *holà*, from *ho* 'ho!' + *là* 'there'.

Holland another name for the **NETHERLANDS**. ■ a former province of the Netherlands, comprising the coastal parts of the country. It is now divided into **North Holland** and **South Holland**.

holland ▸ noun [mass noun] a kind of smooth, hard-wearing linen fabric, used chiefly for window blinds and furniture covering.
– ORIGIN Middle English: from **HOLLAND**, the name of a former province of the Netherlands where the cloth was made, from Dutch, earlier *Holtlant* (from *holt* 'wood' + *-lant* 'land').

hollandaise sauce /ˌhɒlənˈdeɪz, ˈhɒlənˌdeɪz/ ▸ noun [mass noun] a creamy sauce of melted butter, egg yolks, and vinegar, served especially with fish.
– ORIGIN French *hollandaise*, feminine of *hollandais* 'Dutch', from *Hollande* 'Holland'.

Hollander ▸ noun dated a native of the Netherlands.

Hollands ▸ noun [mass noun] archaic Dutch gin.
– ORIGIN from archaic Dutch *hollandsch genever* (earlier form of *hollands jenever*) 'Dutch gin'.

holler informal ▸ verb [no obj.] give a loud shout or cry: [with direct speech] *'I can't get down,' she hollered.*
▸ noun a loud cry or shout: *the audience responded with whoops and hollers.* ■ (also **field holler**) chiefly US a melodic cry with abrupt or swooping changes of pitch, used originally by black slaves at work in the fields and later contributing to the development of the blues.
– ORIGIN late 17th cent. (as a verb): variant of the rare verb *hollo*; related to **HALLOO**.

Hollerith /ˈhɒlərɪθ/, Herman (1860–1929), American engineer. He invented a tabulating machine using punched cards for computation, an important precursor of the electronic computer, and founded a company that later expanded to become the IBM Corporation.

hollow ▸ adjective **1** having a hole or empty space inside: *a hollow metal tube.* ■ having a concave or sunken appearance: *her cheeks were hollow and she had dark circles under her eyes.* ■ (of a sound) echoing, as though made in or on an empty container: *a hollow groan.*
2 without real significance or value: *the result was a hollow victory.* ■ insincere: *a hollow promise.*
▸ noun a hole or depression in something: *a hollow at the base of a large tree.* ■ an enclosed space within something: *he held them in the hollow of his hand.* ■ a small valley: *the village nestles in a hollow on the edge of the New Forest.*
▸ verb [with obj.] form by making a hole: *a tunnel was* ***hollowed out*** *in a mountain range.* ■ make a hollow in: *Flora's laugh hollowed her cheeks.*
– PHRASES **beat someone hollow** defeat someone thoroughly.
– DERIVATIVES **hollowly** adverb, **hollowness** noun.
– ORIGIN Old English *holh* 'cave'; obscurely related to **HOLE**.

hollow-eyed ▸ adjective (of a person) having deeply sunk eyes, typically as a result of illness or tiredness.

hollow-hearted ▸ adjective archaic insincere; false.

hollow square ▸ noun historical a body of infantry drawn up in a square with a space in the middle.

hollowware ▸ noun [mass noun] hollow articles of cookware or crockery, such as pots, kettles, and jugs.

Holly, Buddy (1936–59), American rock-and-roll singer, guitarist, and songwriter; born *Charles Hardin Holley*. He recorded such hits as 'That'll be the Day' with his band, The Crickets, before going solo in 1958. He was killed in an aircraft crash.

holly ▸ noun a widely distributed evergreen shrub, typically having prickly dark green leaves, small white flowers, and red berries. ● Genus *Ilex*, family Aquifoliaceae: many species, in particular *I. aquifolium*.
– ORIGIN Middle English *holi*, shortened form of Old English *holegn*, *holen*, of Germanic origin; related to German *Hulst*.

holly fern ▸ noun a small shield fern which has narrow glossy fronds with a double row of stiff bristle-edged lobes, found chiefly in mountainous areas of both Eurasia and North America. ● Several species in the genus *Polystichum*, family Dryopteridaceae, in particular the widespread *P. lonchitis*.

hollyhock ▸ noun a tall Eurasian plant of the mallow family, with large showy flowers. ● *Alcea rosea*, family Malvaceae.
– ORIGIN Middle English: from **HOLY** + obsolete *hock* 'mallow', of unknown origin. It originally denoted the marsh mallow which has medicinal uses (hence, perhaps, the use of 'holy'); the current sense dates from the mid 16th cent.

holly oak ▸ noun the holm oak or the kermes oak, both of which have tough evergreen leaves that are reminiscent of those of holly.

Hollywood a district of Los Angeles, the principal centre of the American film industry. ■ the American film industry and the lifestyles of the people associated with it: *he was never seduced by the glitz and money of Hollywood.*

Hollywood ending ▶ noun a conventional ending in a film, typically regarded as sentimental or simplistic and often featuring an improbably positive outcome.

holm /həʊm/ (also **holme**) ▶ noun Brit. **1** an islet, especially in a river or near a mainland.
2 a piece of flat ground by a river which is submerged in times of flood.
– ORIGIN Old English, from Old Norse *holmr*; more frequently used in Scotland and northern England, but found in place names throughout Britain.

Holmes[1] /həʊmz/, Oliver Wendell (1809–94), American physician, poet, and essayist. His best-known literary works are the humorous essays known as 'table talks', which began with *The Autocrat of the Breakfast Table* (1857–8).

Holmes[2] /həʊmz/, Sherlock, an extremely perceptive private detective in stories by Sir Arthur Conan Doyle.
– DERIVATIVES **Holmesian** adjective.

holmium /ˈhəʊlmɪəm/ ▶ noun [mass noun] the chemical element of atomic number 67, a soft silvery-white metal of the lanthanide series. (Symbol: **Ho**)
– ORIGIN late 19th cent.: modern Latin, from *Holmia*, Latinized form of STOCKHOLM (because many minerals of the yttrium group, to which holmium belongs, are found in that area); discovered by P.T. Cleve (1840–1905), Swedish chemist.

holm oak ▶ noun an evergreen southern European oak, which has dark green glossy leaves. Also called EVERGREEN OAK or ILEX. ● *Quercus ilex*, family Fagaceae.
– ORIGIN late Middle English: *holm*, alteration of dialect *hollin*, from Old English *holen* 'holly'.

holo /ˈhɒləʊ/ ▶ noun (pl. **holos**) informal a hologram.

holo- ▶ combining form whole; complete: *holocaust* | *holophytic*.
– ORIGIN from Greek *holos* 'whole'.

holocaust /ˈhɒləkɔːst/ ▶ noun **1** destruction or slaughter on a mass scale, especially caused by fire or nuclear war: *a nuclear holocaust.* ■ (**the Holocaust**) the mass murder of Jews under the German Nazi regime during the period 1941–5. More than 6 million European Jews, as well as members of other persecuted groups, were murdered at concentration camps such as Auschwitz.
2 historical a Jewish sacrificial offering which was burnt completely on an altar.
– ORIGIN Middle English: from Old French *holocauste*, via late Latin from Greek *holokauston*, from *holos* 'whole' + *kaustos* 'burnt' (from *kaiein* 'burn').

Holocaust denial ▶ noun [mass noun] the belief or assertion that the Holocaust did not happen or was greatly exaggerated.

Holocene /ˈhɒləsiːn/ ▶ adjective Geology relating to or denoting the present epoch, which is the second epoch in the Quaternary period and followed the Pleistocene. Also called RECENT. ■ (as noun **the Holocene**) the Holocene epoch or the system of deposits laid down during this time.

> The Holocene epoch has lasted from about 10,000 years ago to the present day. It covers the period since the ice retreated after the last glaciation and it is sometimes regarded as just another interglacial period.

– ORIGIN late 19th cent.: coined in French from HOLO- 'whole' + Greek *kainos* 'new'.

holoenzyme /ˌhɒləʊˈɛnzʌɪm/ ▶ noun Biochemistry a biochemically active compound formed by the combination of an enzyme with a coenzyme.

Holofernes /ˌhɒləˈfəːniːz, həˈlɒfəˌniːz/ (in the Apocrypha) the Assyrian general of Nebuchadnezzar's forces, who was killed by Judith (Judith 4:1 ff.).

hologram /ˈhɒləgram/ ▶ noun a three-dimensional image formed by the interference of light beams from a laser or other coherent light source. ■ a photograph of an interference pattern which, when suitably illuminated, produces a three-dimensional image.

holograph /ˈhɒləgrɑːf/ ▶ noun a manuscript handwritten by the person named as its author.
– ORIGIN early 17th cent.: from French *holographe*, or via late Latin from Greek *holographos*, from *holos* 'whole' + *-graphos* 'written, writing'.

holography /hɒˈlɒgrəfi/ ▶ noun [mass noun] the study or production of holograms.
– DERIVATIVES **holographic** adjective, **holographically** adverb.

holophrasis /ˌhɒlə(ʊ)ˈfreɪsɪs/ ▶ noun [mass noun] the expression of a whole phrase in a single word, for example *howdy* for *how do you do.* ■ the learning of linguistic elements as whole chunks by very young children acquiring their first language, for example *it's all gone* learned as *allgone*.
– DERIVATIVES **holophrastic** adjective.

holophytic /ˌhɒlə(ʊ)ˈfɪtɪk/ ▶ adjective Biology (of a plant or protozoan) able to synthesize complex organic compounds by photosynthesis.

holothurian /ˌhɒlə(ʊ)ˈθjʊərɪən/ ▶ noun Zoology a sea cucumber.
– ORIGIN mid 19th cent.: from the modern Latin genus name *Holothuria* (from Greek *holothourion*, denoting a kind of zoophyte) + -AN.

Holothuroidea /ˌhɒlə(ʊ)θjʊəˈrɔɪdɪə/ ▶ plural noun Zoology a class of echinoderms that comprises the sea cucumbers.
– DERIVATIVES **holothuroid** /ˈhɒlə(ʊ)θjʊərɔɪd/ noun & adjective.
– ORIGIN modern Latin (plural), based on Greek *holothourion* (see HOLOTHURIAN).

holotype /ˈhɒlətʌɪp/ ▶ noun Botany & Zoology a single type specimen upon which the description and name of a new species is based. Compare with SYNTYPE.

hols ▶ plural noun Brit. informal holidays.
– ORIGIN early 20th cent.: abbreviation.

Holst /həʊlst/, Gustav (Theodore) (1874–1934), English composer, of Swedish and Russian descent. He made his reputation with the orchestral suite *The Planets* (1914–16). Other notable works: *Choral Hymns from the Rig Veda* (1908–12).

Holstein[1] /ˈhɒlstʌɪn, -ʃtʌɪn/ a former duchy of the German kingdom of Saxony, situated in the southern part of the Jutland peninsula. A duchy of Denmark from 1474, it was taken by Prussia in 1866 and incorporated with the neighbouring duchy of Schleswig as the province of Schleswig-Holstein.

Holstein[2] /ˈhɒlstʌɪn, -iːn/ ▶ noun an animal of a black-and-white breed of large dairy cattle, originally raised in Friesland.

Holsteinian /hɒlˈstʌɪnɪən/ ▶ adjective Geology relating to or denoting an interglacial period of the Pleistocene in northern Europe, following the Elster glaciation and corresponding to the Hoxnian in Britain. ■ (as noun **the Holsteinian**) the Holsteinian interglacial or the system of deposits laid down during it.
– ORIGIN 1960s: from HOLSTEIN[1] + -IAN.

holster /ˈhəʊlstə, ˈhɒl-/ ▶ noun a holder for carrying a handgun or other firearm, typically made of leather and worn on a belt or under the arm.
▶ verb [with obj.] put (a gun) into its holster.
– ORIGIN mid 17th cent.: corresponding to and contemporary with Dutch *holster*, of unknown origin.

holt[1] /həʊlt/ ▶ noun **1** the den of an otter.
2 dialect, chiefly N. Amer. a grip or hold.
– ORIGIN late Middle English (in sense 2): variant of HOLD[1].

holt[2] /həʊlt/ ▶ noun archaic or dialect a wood or wooded hill.
– ORIGIN Old English, of Germanic origin; related to Middle Dutch *hout* and German *Holz*, from an Indo-European root shared by Greek *klados* 'twig'.

holus-bolus /ˌhəʊləsˈbəʊləs/ ▶ adverb N. Amer. or archaic all at once: *swallowing every proposal that is made holus-bolus.*
– ORIGIN mid 19th cent. (originally dialect): perhaps pseudo-Latin for 'whole bolus, whole lump'.

holy ▶ adjective (**holier**, **holiest**) **1** dedicated or consecrated to God or a religious purpose; sacred: *the Holy Bible* | *the holy month of Ramadan.* ■ (of a person) devoted to the service of God: *saints and holy men.* ■ morally and spiritually excellent: *I do not lead a holy life.*
2 dated or humorous used in exclamations of surprise or dismay: *holy smoke!*
– ORIGIN Old English *hālig*, of Germanic origin; related to Dutch and German *heilig*, also to WHOLE.

Holy Alliance a loose alliance of European powers pledged to uphold the principles of the Christian religion. It was proclaimed at the Congress of Vienna (1814–15) by the emperors of Austria and Russia and the king of Prussia and was joined by most other European monarchs.

Holy Ark ▶ noun see ARK (sense 2).

holy city ▶ noun a city held sacred by the adherents of a religion. ■ (**the Holy City**) Jerusalem. ■ (**the Holy City**) (in Christian tradition) Heaven.

Holy Communion ▶ noun see COMMUNION (sense 2).

Holy Cross Day ▶ noun the day on which the feast of the Exaltation of the Cross is held, 14 September.

holy day ▶ noun a day on which a religious observance is held.

Holy Family Christ as a child with Mary and Joseph (and often also others such as John the Baptist or St Anne), especially as a subject for a painting.

Holy Father ▶ noun the Pope.

holy fool ▶ noun a person who does not conform to social norms of behaviour because of mental disability or as a deliberate choice, regarded as having a compensating divine blessing or inspiration.
– ORIGIN translating Russian *yurodivy*, a term first used by Pushkin in the blank verse drama *Boris Godunov* (1831).

Holy Ghost ▶ noun another term for HOLY SPIRIT.

Holy Grail ▶ noun see GRAIL.

Holyhead /ˈhɒlɪhɛd/ a port on Holy Island in Wales, off Anglesey; pop. 11,800 (est. 2009). It is the chief port for ferries between the British mainland and Ireland.

H

Holy Innocents' Day ▶ noun see INNOCENTS' DAY.

Holy Island 1 another name for LINDISFARNE.
2 a small island off the western coast of Anglesey in North Wales. It contains the ferry port of Holyhead. Welsh name CAERGYBI.

Holy Joe ▶ noun informal a clergyman. ■ (also **Holy Mary**) a sanctimonious or pious person.
– ORIGIN late 19th cent.: originally nautical slang.

Holy Land a region on the eastern shore of the Mediterranean, in what is now Israel and Palestine, revered by Christians as the place in which Christ lived and taught, by Jews as the land given to the people of Israel, and by Muslims. ■ another region revered as holy, for example, Arabia in Islam.

Holy League any of various European alliances sponsored by the papacy during the 15th, 16th, and 17th centuries. They include the League of 1511–13, formed by Pope Julius II to expel Louis XII of France from Italy, and the French Holy League (also called the Catholic League) of 1576 and 1584, a Catholic extremist league formed during the French Wars of Religion.

Holy Name ▶ noun (especially in the Catholic Church) the name of Jesus as an object of formal devotion.

Holyoake /ˈhəʊlɪəʊk/, Sir Keith (Jacka) (1904–83), New Zealand statesman, Prime Minister 1957 and 1960–72, Governor General 1977–80.

Holy Office the ecclesiastical court of the Roman Catholic Church established as the final court of appeal in trials of heresy. Formed in 1542 as part of the Inquisition, it was renamed the Sacred Congregation for the Doctrine of the Faith in 1965.

holy of holies ▶ noun the inner chamber of the sanctuary in the Jewish Temple in Jerusalem, separated by a veil from the outer chamber. It was reserved for the presence of God and could be entered only by the High Priest on the Day of Atonement. ■ a place regarded as most sacred or special: *I knocked at the door and was admitted by Ms Brown to the holy of holies.*

holy orders ▶ plural noun the sacrament or rite of ordination as a member of the clergy, especially in the grades of bishop, priest, or deacon.
– PHRASES **in holy orders** having the status of an ordained member of the clergy. **take holy orders** become an ordained member of the clergy.

holy place ▶ noun a place revered as holy, typically one to which religious pilgrimage is made. ■ historical the outer chamber of the sanctuary in the Jewish Temple in Jerusalem.

holy roller ▶ noun informal, derogatory a member of an evangelical Christian group which expresses religious fervour by frenzied excitement or trances.

Holy Roman Empire the empire set up in western Europe following the coronation of Charlemagne as emperor in the year 800. It was created by the medieval papacy in an attempt to unite Christendom under one rule. At times the territory of the empire was extensive and included Germany, Austria, Switzerland, and parts of Italy and the Netherlands.

Holy Rood Day ▸ noun **1** the day on which the feast of the Invention of the Cross is held, 3 May.
2 another term for HOLY CROSS DAY.

Holy Sacrament ▸ noun see SACRAMENT.

Holy Saturday ▸ noun the Saturday preceding Easter Sunday. Also called EASTER EVE or EASTER SATURDAY.

Holy Scripture ▸ noun [mass noun] the sacred writings of Christianity contained in the Bible.

Holy See the papacy or the papal court; those associated with the Pope in the government of the Roman Catholic Church at the Vatican. Also called SEE OF ROME.

Holy Sepulchre the place in which the body of Jesus was laid after being taken down from the Cross. ■ the church in Jerusalem erected over the traditional site of this tomb.

Holy Spirit ▸ noun (in Christianity) the third person of the Trinity; God as spiritually active in the world.

Holy Spirit Association for the Unification of World Christianity another name for UNIFICATION CHURCH.

holystone /ˈhəʊlɪstəʊn/ chiefly historical ▸ noun a piece of soft sandstone used for scouring the decks of ships.
▸ verb [with obj.] scour (a deck) with a holystone.
– ORIGIN early 19th cent.: probably from HOLY + STONE. Sailors called the stones 'bibles' or 'prayer books', perhaps because they scrubbed the decks on their knees.

holy terror ▸ noun see TERROR (sense 2).

Holy Thursday ▸ noun **1** (chiefly in the Roman Catholic Church) Maundy Thursday.
2 dated (in the Anglican Church) Ascension Day.

Holy Trinity ▸ noun see TRINITY.

holy war ▸ noun a war declared or waged in support of a religious cause.

holy water ▸ noun [mass noun] water blessed by a priest and used in religious ceremonies.

Holy Week ▸ noun the week before Easter, starting on Palm Sunday.

Holy Writ ▸ noun [mass noun] the Bible. ■ writings or sayings of unchallenged authority.

Holy Year ▸ noun (in the Roman Catholic Church) a period of remission from the penal consequences of sin, granted under certain conditions for a year usually at intervals of twenty-five years.

hom /həʊm/ (also **homa** /ˈhəʊmə/) ▸ noun the soma plant. ■ [mass noun] the juice of the soma plant as a sacred drink of the Parsees.
– ORIGIN mid 19th cent.: from Persian *hūm* or Avestan *haoma*.

homage /ˈhɒmɪdʒ/ ▸ noun [mass noun] special honour or respect shown publicly: *many villagers come here to pay **homage to** the Virgin* | [count noun] *Daniel's films were a **homage to** her*. ■ historical formal public acknowledgement of feudal allegiance: *a man doing **homage to** his personal lord*.
– ORIGIN Middle English: Old French, from medieval Latin *hominaticum*, from Latin *homo*, *homin-* 'man' (the original use of the word denoted the ceremony by which a vassal declared himself to be his lord's 'man').

hombre /ˈɒmbreɪ/ ▸ noun informal, chiefly N. Amer. a man, especially one of a particular type: *the Raiders quarterback is one tough hombre*.
– ORIGIN mid 19th cent. (originally denoting a man of Spanish descent): Spanish, 'man', from Latin *homo*, *homin-*.

homburg /ˈhɒmbəːɡ/ ▸ noun a man's felt hat having a narrow curled brim and a tapered crown with a lengthwise indentation.
– ORIGIN late 19th cent.: named after *Homburg*, a town in western Germany, where such hats were first worn.

home ▸ noun **1** the place where one lives permanently, especially as a member of a family or household: *the floods forced many people to flee their homes* | *I was nineteen when I left home and went to college*. ■ the family or social unit occupying a permanent residence: *he came from a good home*. ■ a house or flat considered as a commercial property: *low-cost homes for first-time buyers* | [as modifier] *the growth in home ownership*. ■ the district or country where one was born or has settled on a long-term basis: *they have made Provence their home*. ■ a place where something flourishes, is most typically found, or from which it originates: *Montana **is home to** a surprising number of rare mammals*. ■ informal a place where an object is kept.
2 an institution for people needing professional care or supervision: *an old people's home*.
3 the finishing point in a race: *he was four fences from home*. ■ (in games) the place where a player is free from attack. ■ (in lacrosse) each of the three players stationed nearest their opponents' goal. ■ Baseball short for HOME PLATE. ■ a match played or won by a team on their own ground.
▸ adjective [attrib.] **1** relating to the place where one lives: *I don't have your home address*. ■ made, done, or intended for use in the home: *traditional home cooking* | *a home computer*. ■ relating to one's own country: *we need to stimulate demand within the UK home market*.
2 (of a sports team or player) belonging to the country or locality in which a sporting event takes place: *the home side*. ■ played on or connected with a team's own ground: *their first home match of the season*.
3 N. Amer. denoting the administrative centre of an organization: *the company has moved its home office*.
▸ adverb to or at the place where one lives: *what time did he get home last night?* ■ to the end or conclusion of a race or something difficult: *the favourite **romped home** six lengths clear*. ■ to the intended or correct position: *he slid the bolt home noisily*.
▸ verb [no obj.] **1** (of an animal) return by instinct to its territory after leaving it: *a dozen geese homing to their summer nesting grounds*. ■ (of a pigeon bred for long-distance racing) fly back to or arrive at its loft after being released at a distant point.
2 (**home in on**) move or be aimed towards (a target or destination) with great accuracy: *more than 100 missiles were launched, homing in on radar emissions*. ■ focus attention on: *a teaching style which homes in on what is of central importance for each pupil*.
3 [with obj.] provide (an animal) with a home as a pet.
– PHRASES **at home** in one's own house. ■ ready to receive and welcome visitors: *she took to her room and was not **at home to** friends*. ■ in one's own neighbourhood, town, or country: *he has been consistently successful both at home and abroad*. ■ (with reference to sports fixtures) at a team's own ground: *Spurs drew 1–1 at home to Leeds*. ■ comfortable and at ease in a place or situation: *sit down and **make yourself at home***. ■ confident or relaxed about doing or using something: *he was quite at home talking about Eisenstein or Brecht*. **bring something home to** make (someone) realize the full significance of something: *her first-hand account brought home to me the pain of the experience*. **close** (or **near**) **to home** (of a remark or topic of discussion) relevant or accurate to the point that one feels uncomfortable or embarrassed. **come home** Golf play the second nine holes in a round of eighteen holes. Compare with GO OUT (see GO[1]). **come home to someone** (of the significance of something) become fully realized by someone: *the full enormity of what was happening came home to Sara*. **drive** (or **hammer** or **press** or **ram**) **something home** make something clearly understood by the use of repeated or forcefully direct arguments: *we must drive home the message that crime doesn't pay*. **hit** (or **strike**) **home** (of a blow or a missile) reach an intended target. ■ (of words) have the intended, especially unsettling or painful, effect on their audience: *she could see that her remark had hit home*. ■ (of the significance or true nature of a situation) become fully realized by someone: *the full impact of life as a celebrity began to hit home*. **home and dry** (N. Amer. **home free**, Austral./NZ **home and hosed**) Brit. having successfully achieved or being within sight of achieving one's objective: *at 3–0 up they should have been home and dry*. **(a) home from** (N. Amer. **away from**) **home** Brit. a place where one is as happy, relaxed, or comfortable as in one's own home. **home is where the heart is** proverb your home will always be the place for which you feel the deepest affection, no matter where you are. **home sweet home** used as an expression of one's pleasure or relief at being in or returning to one's own home. **set up home** Brit. start living somewhere on a permanent basis: *the couple set up home in Chelsea eight years ago*. **when ——'s at home** Brit. used to add humorous emphasis to a question about someone's identity: *who's Peter when he's at home?*
– DERIVATIVES **homelike** adjective.
– ORIGIN Old English *hām*, of Germanic origin; related to Dutch *heem* and German *Heim*.

> **USAGE** Note that the phrasal verb meaning 'move accurately towards a target' is **home in on**, not **hone in on**. More than a third of citations for this expression in the Oxford English Corpus are for the incorrect form.

home banking ▸ noun [mass noun] a system of banking whereby transactions are performed directly by telephone or over the Internet.

home bird ▸ noun Brit. informal another term for HOMEBODY.

homebody ▸ noun (pl. **homebodies**) informal, chiefly N. Amer. a person who likes to stay at home, especially one who is perceived as unadventurous.

homeboy (or **homegirl**) ▸ noun US & S. African informal an acquaintance from one's own town or neighbourhood, or from the same social background. ■ (especially among urban black people) a member of a peer group or gang.

home brew ▸ noun [mass noun] beer or other alcoholic drink brewed at home. ■ [as modifier] informal, chiefly US made at home, rather than in a shop or factory: *a home-brew radio transmitter*.
– DERIVATIVES **home-brewed** adjective.

homebuilder ▸ noun a company whose business is the construction of private houses.
– DERIVATIVES **homebuilding** noun.

homebuyer ▸ noun a person who buys a house or flat.

home cinema ▸ noun [mass noun] chiefly Brit. television and video equipment designed to reproduce at home the experience of being in a cinema, typically including stereo speakers and a widescreen set.

homecoming ▸ noun an instance of returning home: *she spent most of the day preparing for her husband's homecoming*. ■ N. Amer. a reunion of former students of a university, college, or high school.

Home Counties the English counties surrounding London, into which London has extended. They comprise chiefly Essex, Kent, Surrey, and Hertfordshire.

home economics ▸ plural noun [often treated as sing.] cookery and other aspects of household management, especially as taught at school.

home farm ▸ noun chiefly Brit. & S. African a farm on an estate that is set aside to provide produce for the owner of the estate.

home fries (also **home-fried potatoes**) ▸ plural noun N. Amer. fried sliced potatoes.

home-grown ▸ adjective grown or produced in one's own garden or country. ■ belonging to one's own particular locality or country: *home-grown talent*.

Home Guard the British citizen army organized in 1940 to defend the UK against invasion, finally disbanded in 1957.

home help ▸ noun Brit. a person employed, especially by a local authority, to help in another's home.

home key ▸ noun **1** Music the basic key in which a work is written.
2 a key on a computer or typewriter keyboard which acts as the base position for one's fingers in touch-typing.

Homel /ˈhɒmɪl/ an industrial city in SE Belarus; pop. 488,100 (est. 2009). Russian name GOMEL.

homeland ▸ noun a person's or a people's native land: *he left his homeland to settle in London*. ■ an autonomous or semi-autonomous state occupied by a particular people: *they have been fighting for an independent homeland for nearly 30 years*. ■ historical any of ten partially self-governing areas in South Africa designated for particular indigenous African peoples under the former policy of apartheid.

homeless ▸ adjective (of a person) without a home, and therefore typically living on the streets: *the plight of young homeless people* | (as plural noun **the homeless**) *charities for the homeless*.
– DERIVATIVES **homelessness** noun.

home loan ▸ noun a loan advanced to a person to assist in buying a house or flat.

homely ▸ adjective (**homelier**, **homeliest**) **1** Brit. (of a place or surroundings) simple but cosy and comfortable, as in one's own home: *a modern hotel with a homely atmosphere*. ■ simple and unpretentious: *homely pleasures*.
2 N. Amer. (of a person) unattractive in appearance.
– DERIVATIVES **homeliness** noun.

home-made ▸ adjective made at home, rather than in a shop or factory: *home-made bread*.

homemaker ▸ noun chiefly N. Amer. a person, especially a housewife, who manages a home.
– DERIVATIVES **homemaking** noun.

home movie ▸ noun a film made at home or without professional equipment or expertise.

homeobox /ˌhɒmɪə(ʊ)ˈbɒks, ˌhəʊm-/ (also **homoeobox**) ▸ **noun** Genetics any of a class of closely similar sequences which occur in various genes and are involved in regulating embryonic development in a wide range of species.
– ORIGIN 1980s: from *homeotic* (see **HOMEOSIS**) + the noun **BOX**[1]; first discovered in homeotic genes of *Drosophila* fruit flies.

Home Office the British government department dealing with domestic affairs, including law and order, immigration, and broadcasting, in England and Wales.

Home of the Hirsel of Coldstream /ˈhəːs(ə)l/, Baron, see **DOUGLAS-HOME**.

homeomorphism /ˌhɒmɪə(ʊ)ˈmɔːfɪz(ə)m, ˌhəʊm-/ ▸ **noun** Mathematics an instance of topological equivalence.
– DERIVATIVES **homeomorphic** adjective.
– ORIGIN from Greek *homoios* 'like' + *morphē* 'form' + **-ISM**.

homeopath /ˈhəʊmɪəpaθ, ˈhɒm-/ (also **homoeopath**) ▸ **noun** a practitioner of homeopathy.
– ORIGIN mid 19th cent.: from German *Homöopath* (see **HOMEOPATHY**).

homeopathy /ˌhəʊmɪˈɒpəθi, hɒm-/ (also **homoeopathy**) ▸ **noun** a system of complementary medicine in which ailments are treated by minute doses of natural substances that in larger amounts would produce symptoms of the ailment. Often contrasted with **ALLOPATHY**.
– DERIVATIVES **homeopathic** adjective, **homeopathically** adverb, **homeopathist** noun.
– ORIGIN early 19th cent.: coined in German from Greek *homoios* 'like' + *patheia* (see **-PATHY**).

homeosis /ˌhɒmɪˈəʊsɪs/ (also **homoeosis**) ▸ **noun** (pl. **homeoses** /-siːz/) Biology the replacement of part of one segment of an insect or other segmented animal by a structure characteristic of a different segment, especially through mutation.
– DERIVATIVES **homeotic** adjective.
– ORIGIN late 19th cent.: from Greek *homoiōsis* 'becoming like', from *homoios* 'like'.

homeostasis /ˌhɒmɪə(ʊ)ˈsteɪsɪs, ˌhəʊm-/ (also **homoeostasis**) ▸ **noun** (pl. **homeostases** /-siːz/) the tendency towards a relatively stable equilibrium between interdependent elements, especially as maintained by physiological processes.
– DERIVATIVES **homeostatic** adjective.
– ORIGIN 1920s: modern Latin, from Greek *homoios* 'like' + **-STASIS**.

homeotherm /ˈhɒmɪə(ʊ)ˌθəːm/ (also **homoiotherm**) ▸ **noun** Zoology an organism that maintains its body temperature at a constant level, usually above that of the environment, by its metabolic activity. Often contrasted with **POIKILOTHERM**; compare with **WARM-BLOODED**.
– DERIVATIVES **homeothermal** adjective, **homeothermic** adjective, **homeothermy** noun.
– ORIGIN late 19th cent.: modern Latin, from Greek *homoios* 'like' + *thermē* 'heat'.

homeowner ▸ **noun** a person who owns their own home.

home page ▸ **noun** the introductory page of a website, typically serving as a table of contents for the site.

home plate ▸ **noun** Baseball the five-sided white rubber plate-like base next to which the batter stands and which must be touched in scoring a run.

home port ▸ **noun** the port from which a ship originates.

Homer[1] /ˈhəʊmə/ (8th century BC), Greek epic poet. He is traditionally held to be the author of the *Iliad* and the *Odyssey*, though modern scholarship has revealed the place of the Homeric poems in a preliterate oral tradition. In later antiquity Homer was regarded as the greatest poet, and his poems were constantly used as a model and source by others.
– PHRASES **Homer sometimes nods** proverb even the most gifted person occasionally makes mistakes.

Homer[2] /ˈhəʊmə/, Winslow (1836–1910), American painter. He is best known for his seascapes which are painted in a vigorous naturalistic style considered to express the American pioneering spirit.

homer ▸ **noun 1** Baseball a home run.
2 a homing pigeon.
3 informal a referee or official who is thought to favour the team playing at home.

home range ▸ **noun** Zoology an area over which an animal or group of animals regularly travels in search of food or mates, and which may overlap with those of neighbouring animals or groups of the same species.

Homeric /həʊˈmɛrɪk/ ▸ **adjective** of or in the style of Homer or the epic poems ascribed to him. ■ of Bronze Age Greece as described in these poems: *the mists of the Homeric age*. ■ epic and large-scale: *some of us exert a Homeric effort*.
– ORIGIN via Latin from Greek *Homērikos*, from *Homēros* (see **HOMER**[1]).

homeroom ▸ **noun** N. Amer. a classroom in which a group of students assembles daily with the same teacher before dispersing to other classes.

home rule ▸ **noun** [mass noun] the government of a colony, dependent country, or region by its own citizens, in particular as advocated for Ireland 1870–1914.

> The campaign for Irish home rule was one of the dominant forces in British politics in the late 19th and early 20th centuries, particularly in that Irish nationalists frequently held the balance of power in the House of Commons. A Home Rule Act was finally passed in 1914 but was suspended until after the First World War; after the Easter Rising of 1916 and Sinn Fein's successes in the general election of 1918, southern Ireland became the Irish Free State in 1921.

home run ▸ **noun** Baseball a hit that allows the batter to make a complete circuit of the bases and score a run.

homeschool ▸ **verb** [with obj.] educate (one's child) at home instead of sending them to a school.
– DERIVATIVES **homeschooler** noun, **homeschooling** noun.

Home Secretary ▸ **noun** (in the UK) the Secretary of State in charge of the Home Office.

Home Service one of the original programme services of the BBC (renamed *Radio 4*).

home shopping ▸ **noun** [mass noun] shopping carried out from one's own home by ordering goods advertised in a catalogue, on television, or over the Internet.
– DERIVATIVES **home shopper** noun.

homeshoring (also **homesourcing**) ▸ **noun** [mass noun] the practice of transferring employment that was previously carried out in a company's office or factory to employees' homes.
– ORIGIN early 21st cent.: on the pattern of **OFFSHORING**.

homesick ▸ **adjective** experiencing a longing for one's home during a period of absence from it: *he was homesick for America after five weeks in Europe*.
– DERIVATIVES **homesickness** noun.

home signal ▸ **noun** Brit. a railway signal controlling entry to the immediate section of the line.

homesite ▸ **noun** N. Amer. & Austral. a building plot.

homespun ▸ **adjective 1** simple and unsophisticated: *homespun philosophy*.
2 (of cloth or yarn) made or spun at home. ■ denoting a coarse handwoven fabric similar to tweed.
▸ **noun** [mass noun] homespun cloth: *clad in homespun*.

homestead ▸ **noun 1** a house, especially a farmhouse, and outbuildings. ■ Austral./NZ the owner's residence on a sheep or cattle station.
2 N. Amer. historical an area of land (usually 160 acres) granted to a settler in the West as a home.
– DERIVATIVES **homesteader** noun.
– ORIGIN Old English *hāmstede* 'a settlement' (see **HOME, STEAD**).

homesteading ▸ **noun** [mass noun] N. Amer. life as a settler on a homestead.

home straight (N. Amer. also **home stretch**) ▸ **noun** Brit. the concluding stretch of a racecourse. ■ the last part of an activity or campaign: *heading down the home stretch to Tuesday's final*.

homestyle ▸ **adjective** N. Amer. (especially of food) such as would be made or provided at home; simple and unpretentious.

home theater ▸ **noun** North American term for **HOME CINEMA**.

home town ▸ **noun** the town of one's birth or early life or present fixed residence.

home truth ▸ **noun** (usu. **home truths**) an unpleasant fact about oneself, especially as pointed out by another person: *what he needed was someone to tell him a few home truths*.

home unit ▸ **noun** Austral./NZ a flat, especially one occupied by the owner, that is one of several in a large building.

homeward ▸ **adverb** (also **homewards**) towards home: *they set off homeward*.
▸ **adjective** going or leading towards home: *their homeward journey*.
– ORIGIN Old English *hāmweard* (see **HOME, -WARD**).

homeward-bound ▸ **adjective** on the way home: *the next day we were homeward-bound*.

homework ▸ **noun** [mass noun] **1** schoolwork that a pupil is required to do at home. ■ work or study done in preparation for an event or situation: *he had evidently* ***done his homework*** *and read his predecessor's reports*.
2 paid work carried out in one's own home, especially low-paid piecework.

homeworker ▸ **noun** a person who works from home, especially doing low-paid piecework.

homey (also **homy**) ▸ **adjective** (**homier, homiest**) chiefly N. Amer. (of a place or surroundings) comfortable and cosy: *a homey atmosphere*. ■ unsophisticated: *an idealized vision of traditional peasant life as simple and homey*.
▸ **noun** (pl. **homeys**) US informal variant spelling of **HOMIE**.
– DERIVATIVES **homeyness** (also **hominess**) noun.

H

homicidal ▸ **adjective** capable of or tending towards murder; murderous: *he had homicidal tendencies*.
– DERIVATIVES **homicidally** adverb.

homicide ▸ **noun** [mass noun] chiefly N. Amer. the killing of one person by another: *he was charged with homicide* | [count noun] *knives account for a third of all homicides*. ■ (**Homicide**) the police department that deals with the crime of murder: *a man from Homicide*. ■ [count noun] dated a murderer.
– ORIGIN Middle English: from Old French, from Latin *homicidium*, from *homo, homin-* 'man'.

homie (also **homey**) ▸ **noun** (pl. **homies**) informal, chiefly US a homeboy or homegirl.

homiletic /ˌhɒmɪˈlɛtɪk/ ▸ **adjective** of the nature of or characteristic of a homily: *homiletic literature*.
▸ **noun** (**homiletics**) the art of preaching or writing sermons: *the teaching of homiletics*.
– ORIGIN mid 17th cent.: via late Latin from Greek *homilētikos*, from *homilein* 'converse with, consort', from *homilia* (see **HOMILY**).

homiliary /hɒˈmɪlɪəri/ ▸ **noun** (pl. **homiliaries**) historical a book of homilies.
– ORIGIN mid 19th cent.: from medieval Latin *homiliarius*, from ecclesiastical Latin *homilia* (see **HOMILY**).

homily /ˈhɒmɪli/ ▸ **noun** (pl. **homilies**) a religious discourse which is intended primarily for spiritual edification rather than doctrinal instruction. ■ a tedious moralizing lecture: *she delivered her homily about the need for patience*.
– DERIVATIVES **homilist** noun.
– ORIGIN late Middle English: via Old French from ecclesiastical Latin *homilia*, from Greek, 'discourse, conversation' (in ecclesiastical use, 'sermon'), from *homilos* 'crowd'.

homing ▸ **adjective** relating to an animal's ability to return to its territory after travelling away from it: *a strong homing instinct*. ■ (of a pigeon) trained to fly home from a great distance and bred for long-distance racing. ■ (of a weapon or piece of equipment) fitted with an electronic device that enables it to find and hit a target.

hominid /ˈhɒmɪnɪd/ ▸ **noun** Zoology a primate of a family (Hominidae) which includes humans and their fossil ancestors.
– ORIGIN late 19th cent.: from modern Latin *Hominidae* (plural), from Latin *homo, homin-* 'man'.

hominoid /ˈhɒmɪnɔɪd/ Zoology ▸ **noun** a primate of a group that includes humans, their fossil ancestors, and the great apes. ● Superfamily Hominoidea: families Hominidae and Pongidae.
▸ **adjective** relating to hominoid primates; hominid or pongid.
– ORIGIN early 20th cent.: from Latin *homo, homin-* 'human being' + **-OID**.

hominy /ˈhɒmɪni/ ▸ **noun** [mass noun] US coarsely ground corn (maize) used to make grits: [as modifier] *hominy grits*.
– ORIGIN shortened from Virginia Algonquian *uskatahomen*.

Homo /ˈhəʊməʊ, ˈhɒməʊ/ ▸ **noun** the genus of primates of which modern humans (*Homo sapiens*) are the present-day representatives. ■ [with Latin or pseudo-Latin modifier] denoting kinds of modern human, often humorously: *a textbook example of Homo neuroticus*.

The genus *Homo* is believed to have existed for at least two million years, and modern humans (*H. sapiens sapiens*) first appeared in the Upper Palaeolithic. Among several extinct species are *H. habilis*, *H. erectus*, and *H. neanderthalensis*.

– ORIGIN Latin, 'man'.

homo /ˈhəʊməʊ/ informal, chiefly derogatory ▶ **noun** (pl. **homos**) a homosexual man.
▶ **adjective** homosexual.
– ORIGIN 1920s: abbreviation.

homo- ▶ **combining form 1** same: *homogametic*.
2 relating to homosexual love: *homoerotic*. Often contrasted with **HETERO-**.
– ORIGIN from Greek *homos* 'same'.

homocentric[1] ▶ **adjective** having the same centre.

homocentric[2] ▶ **adjective** another term for **ANTHROPOCENTRIC**.

homocercal /ˌhɒmə(ʊ)ˈsəːk(ə)l, ˌhəʊm-/ ▶ **adjective** Zoology (of a fish's tail) appearing outwardly symmetrical but with the backbone passing into the upper lobe, as in all higher fish. Contrasted with **DIPHYCERCAL, HETEROCERCAL**.
– ORIGIN mid 19th cent.: from **HOMO-** 'same' + Greek *kerkos* 'tail' + **-AL**.

homocysteine /ˌhɒmə(ʊ)ˈsɪstiːn, ˌhəʊm-, -tɪn, -teɪn, -tiːn/ ▶ **noun** [mass noun] Biochemistry an amino acid which occurs in the body as an intermediate in the metabolism of methionine and cysteine. ● Chem. formula: $HSCH_2CH_2CH(NH_2)COOH$.

homoeobox ▶ **noun** variant spelling of **HOMEOBOX**.

homoeopath ▶ **noun** variant spelling of **HOMEOPATH**.

homoeopathy ▶ **noun** variant spelling of **HOMEOPATHY**.

homoeosis ▶ **noun** variant spelling of **HOMEOSIS**.

homoeostasis ▶ **noun** variant spelling of **HOMEOSTASIS**.

homoerotic ▶ **adjective** concerning or arousing sexual desire centred on a person of the same sex: *homoerotic images*.
– DERIVATIVES **homoeroticism** noun.

homogametic /ˌhɒmə(ʊ)gəˈmɛtɪk, -ˈmiːtɪk, ˌhəʊm-/ ▶ **adjective** Biology denoting the sex which has sex chromosomes that do not differ in morphology, resulting in only one kind of gamete, e.g. (in mammals) the female and (in birds) the male. The opposite of **HETEROGAMETIC**.

homogamy /hɒˈmɒgəmi/ ▶ **noun** [mass noun] **1** Biology inbreeding, especially as a result of isolation. ■ marriage between people from similar sociological or educational backgrounds. Compare with **HETEROGAMY** (sense 3).
2 Botany a state in which the flowers of a plant are all of one type (either hermaphrodite or of the same sex). Compare with **HETEROGAMY** (sense 2).
3 Botany the simultaneous ripening of the stamens and pistils of a flower, ensuring self-pollination. Compare with **DICHOGAMY**.
– DERIVATIVES **homogamous** adjective.
– ORIGIN late 19th cent.: from **HOMO-** 'same' + Greek *gamos* 'marriage'.

homogenate /həˈmɒdʒɪneɪt/ ▶ **noun** Biology a suspension of cell fragments and cell constituents obtained when tissue is homogenized.

homogeneity /ˌhɒmə(ʊ)dʒɪˈneɪɪti, -dʒɪˈniːɪti, ˌhəʊm-/ ▶ **noun** [mass noun] the quality or state of being homogeneous: *the cultural homogeneity of our society*.

homogeneous /ˌhɒmə(ʊ)ˈdʒiːnɪəs, -ˈdʒɛn-/ (also **homogenous** /həˈmɒdʒɪnəs/) ▶ **adjective 1** of the same kind; alike: *if all jobs and workers were homogeneous*. ■ consisting of parts all of the same kind: *a homogeneous society*. ■ Mathematics containing terms all of the same degree.
2 Chemistry denoting a process involving substances in the same phase (solid, liquid, or gaseous): *homogeneous catalysis*.
– DERIVATIVES **homogeneously** adverb, **homogeneousness** noun.
– ORIGIN early 17th cent. (as **HOMOGENEITY**): from medieval Latin *homogeneus*, from Greek *homogenēs*, from *homos* 'same' + *genos* 'race, kind'.

USAGE The usual spelling is **homogeneous**, and the spelling **homogenous** is traditionally regarded as an error. **Homogenous** is a different word, a specialized biological term meaning 'having a common descent', which has been largely replaced by **homologous**. From the evidence of the Oxford English Corpus, the spelling **homogeneous** has become significantly less common since 2000, and around a third of citations for the word now use the form **homogenous**. This can now be regarded as an established variant.

homogenize (also **homogenise**) ▶ **verb** [with obj.] **1** subject (milk) to a process in which the fat droplets are emulsified and the cream does not separate: (as adj. **homogenized**) *homogenized milk*. ■ Biology prepare a suspension of cell constituents from (tissue) by physical treatment in a liquid.
2 (often as adj. **homogenized**) make uniform or similar: *a homogenized society*.
– DERIVATIVES **homogenization** /-ˈzeɪʃ(ə)n/ noun, **homogenizer** noun.

homogenous /həˈmɒdʒɪnəs/ ▶ **adjective 1** Biology old-fashioned term for **HOMOLOGOUS**.
2 see **HOMOGENEOUS**.
– ORIGIN late 19th cent.: from **HOMO-** 'same' + Greek *genos* 'race, kind' + **-OUS**.

homogeny /həˈmɒdʒəni/ ▶ **noun** [mass noun] **1** another term for **HOMOGENEITY**.
2 Biology, dated similarity due to common descent.

homograft /ˈhɒməgrɑːft, ˈhəʊm-/ ▶ **noun** a tissue graft from a donor of the same species as the recipient. Compare with **ALLOGRAFT**.

homograph ▶ **noun** each of two or more words spelled the same but not necessarily pronounced the same and having different meanings and origins (e.g. **BOW**[1] and **BOW**[2]).
– DERIVATIVES **homographic** adjective.

homoiotherm /ˈhɒmɔɪə(ʊ),θəːm/ ▶ **noun** variant spelling of **HOMEOTHERM**.

homoiousian /ˌhɒmɔɪˈuːsɪən, -ˈaʊ-, -z-/ ▶ **noun** historical a person who held that God the Father and God the Son are of like but not identical substance. Compare with **HOMOOUSIAN**.
– ORIGIN late 17th cent. (as an adjective in the sense 'of similar but not identical substance'): via ecclesiastical Latin from Greek *homoiousios*, from *homoios* 'like' + *ousia* 'essence, substance'. The noun dates from the mid 18th cent.

homolog ▶ **noun** US variant spelling of **HOMOLOGUE**.

homologate /həˈmɒləgeɪt/ ▶ **verb** [with obj.] **1** approve (a car, engine, etc.) for sale in a particular market or use in a particular class of racing.
2 formal express agreement with or approval of.
– DERIVATIVES **homologation** noun.
– ORIGIN late 16th cent.: from medieval Latin *homologat-* 'agreed', from the verb *homologare*, from Greek *homologein* 'confess'.

homologize /hɒˈmɒlədʒʌɪz/ (also **homologise**) ▶ **verb** [with obj.] formal make or show to have the same relation, relative position, or structure.

homologous /hɒˈmɒləgəs/ ▶ **adjective** having the same relation, relative position, or structure. ■ Biology (of organs) similar in position, structure, and evolutionary origin but not necessarily in function: *a seal's flipper is **homologous with** the human arm*. Often contrasted with **ANALOGOUS**. ■ Biology (of chromosomes) pairing at meiosis and having the same structural features and pattern of genes. ■ Chemistry (of a series of chemical compounds) having the same functional group but differing in composition by a fixed group of atoms.
– DERIVATIVES **homology** noun.
– ORIGIN mid 17th cent.: via medieval Latin from Greek *homologos* 'agreeing, consistent', from *homos* 'same' + *logos* 'ratio, proportion'.

homologue /ˈhɒməlɒg/ (US **homolog**) ▶ **noun** technical a homologous thing.
– ORIGIN mid 19th cent.: from French, from Greek *homologos* (see **HOMOLOGOUS**).

homomorphic ▶ **adjective** technical of the same or similar form. ■ Mathematics relating to or of the nature of a homomorphism.
– DERIVATIVES **homomorphically** adverb.

homomorphism ▶ **noun** Mathematics a transformation of one set into another that preserves in the second set the relations between elements of the first.

homonym /ˈhɒmənɪm/ ▶ **noun** each of two or more words having the same spelling or pronunciation but different meanings and origins (e.g. **POLE**[1] and **POLE**[2]). ■ Biology a Latin name which is identical to that of a different organism, the newer of the two names being invalid.
– DERIVATIVES **homonymic** adjective, **homonymous** adjective, **homonymy** noun.
– ORIGIN late 17th cent.: via Latin from Greek *homōnumon*, neuter of *homōnumos* 'having the same name', from *homos* 'same' + *onoma* 'name'.

homoousian /ˌhɒməʊˈuːsɪən, -ˈaʊ-, -z-, ˌhəʊməʊ-/ (also **homousian**) ▶ **noun** historical a person who held that God the Father and God the Son are of the same substance. Compare with **HOMOIOUSIAN**.
– ORIGIN mid 16th cent.: from ecclesiastical Latin *homousianus*, from *homousius*, from Greek *homoousios*, from *homos* 'same' + *ousia* 'essence, substance'.

homophobia /ˌhɒməˈfəʊbɪə, ˌhəʊmə-/ ▶ **noun** [mass noun] an extreme and irrational aversion to homosexuality and homosexual people.
– DERIVATIVES **homophobe** noun, **homophobic** adjective.
– ORIGIN 1960s: from **HOMOSEXUAL** + **-PHOBIA**.

homophone /ˈhɒməfəʊn, ˈhəʊm-/ ▶ **noun** each of two or more words having the same pronunciation but different meanings, origins, or spelling (e.g. **NEW** and **KNEW**). ■ each of a set of symbols denoting the same sound or group of sounds.

homophonic ▶ **adjective 1** Music characterized by the movement of accompanying parts in the same rhythm as the melody. Often contrasted with **POLYPHONIC**.
2 another term for **HOMOPHONOUS** (sense 2).
– DERIVATIVES **homophonically** adverb.

homophonous /həˈmɒf(ə)nəs/ ▶ **adjective 1** (of music) homophonic.
2 (of a word or words) having the same pronunciation as another or others but different meaning, origin, or spelling.
– DERIVATIVES **homophony** noun.

homopolar ▶ **adjective** having equal or constant electrical polarity. ■ (of an electric generator) producing direct current without the use of commutators.

Homoptera /hɒˈmɒpt(ə)rə/ ▶ **plural noun** Entomology a group of true bugs comprising those in which the forewings are uniform in texture. Plant bugs such as aphids, whitefly, scale insects, and cicadas belong to this group. Compare with **HETEROPTERA**. ● Suborder Homoptera, order Hemiptera.
■ (**homoptera**) bugs of this group.
– ORIGIN modern Latin (plural), from **HOMO-** 'equal' + Greek *pteron* 'wing'.

homopteran Entomology ▶ **noun** a bug of the group Homoptera.
▶ **adjective** relating to or denoting homopterans.
– DERIVATIVES **homopterous** adjective.

homorganic /ˌhɒmɔːˈganɪk/ ▶ **adjective** denoting sets of speech sounds that are produced using the same vocal organs, e.g. *p*, *b*, and *m*.

Homo sapiens /ˌhəʊməʊ ˈsapɪɛnz, ˌhɒməʊ/ ▶ **noun** the primate species to which modern humans belong; humans regarded as a species. See also **HOMO**. ■ a member of this species.
– ORIGIN Latin, literally 'wise man'.

homosexual /ˌhɒmə(ʊ)ˈsɛkʃʊəl, ˌhəʊm-, -sjʊəl/ ▶ **adjective** sexually attracted to people of one's own sex. ■ involving or characterized by sexual attraction between people of the same sex: *homosexual desire*.
▶ **noun** a person who is sexually attracted to people of their own sex.
– DERIVATIVES **homosexuality** noun, **homosexually** adverb.
– ORIGIN late 19th cent.: from **HOMO-** 'same' + **SEXUAL**.

homosocial ▶ **adjective** relating to social interaction between members of the same sex, typically men.

homotransplant ▶ **noun** another term for **ALLOGRAFT**.

homousian ▶ **noun** variant spelling of **HOMOOUSIAN**.

homozygote /ˌhɒmə(ʊ)ˈzʌɪgəʊt, ˌhəʊm-/ ▶ **noun** Genetics an individual having two identical alleles of a particular gene or genes and so breeding true for the corresponding characteristic. Compare with **HETEROZYGOTE**.
– DERIVATIVES **homozygosity** noun, **homozygous** adjective.

Homs /hɒms, hɒmz/ (also **Hims**) an industrial city in western Syria, on the River Orontes; pop. 869,700 (est. 2009). It was named in 636 by the Muslims and occupies the site of ancient Emesa.

homunculus /hɒˈmʌŋkjʊləs/ (also **homuncule** /-kjuːl/) ▶ **noun** (pl. **homunculi** /-lʌɪ/ or **homuncules**) a very small human or humanoid creature. ■ historical a microscopic but fully formed human being from which a fetus was formerly believed to develop.
– ORIGIN mid 17th cent.: from Latin, diminutive of *homo, homin-* 'man'.

homy ▶ **adjective** variant spelling of **HOMEY**.

hon ▶ noun informal short for HONEY (as a form of address): *it wouldn't interest you, hon.*

Hon. ▶ abbreviation ■ Brit. (in official job titles) Honorary: *the Hon. Secretary.* ■ (in titles of the British nobility, members of parliament and some other politicians, and (in the US) judges) Honourable: *the Hon. Charles Rothschild.*

Honan /həˈnan/ 1 variant of HENAN.
2 former name for LUOYANG.

honcho /ˈhɒn(t)ʃəʊ/ N. Amer. informal ▶ noun (pl. **honchos**) a leader or manager; the person in charge: *the company's* ***head honcho*** *in the US.*
▶ verb (**honchoes, honchoing, honchoed**) [with obj.] be in charge of (a project or situation).
– ORIGIN 1940s: from Japanese *hanchō* 'group leader', a term brought back to the US by servicemen stationed in Japan during the occupation following the Second World War.

Honda /ˈhɒndə/, Soichiro (1906–92), Japanese motor manufacturer. Opening his first factory in 1934, he began motorcycle manufacture in 1948 and expanded into car production during the 1960s.

Honduras /hɒnˈdjʊərəs/ a country of Central America, bordering on the Caribbean Sea and with a short coastline on the Pacific Ocean; pop. 7,833,700 (est. 2009); official language, Spanish; capital, Tegucigalpa. See also BRITISH HONDURAS.

> Honduras was at the southern limit of the Mayan empire. It was encountered by Columbus in 1502, and became a Spanish colony. In 1821 Honduras became an independent republic, and was part of the United Provinces of Central America between 1823 and 1838.

– DERIVATIVES **Honduran** adjective & noun.

hone ▶ verb [with obj.] sharpen with a whetstone.
■ make sharper or more focused or efficient: *their appetites were honed by fresh air and exercise.*
▶ noun a whetstone, especially one used to sharpen razors.
– ORIGIN Middle English: from Old English *hān* 'stone', of Germanic origin; related to Old Norse *hein*.

> **USAGE** See USAGE at HOME.

Honecker /ˈhɒnɪkə/, German /ˈhɔːnɛkɐ/, Erich (1912–94), East German communist statesman, head of state 1976–89. His repressive regime was marked by a close allegiance to the Soviet Union. He was ousted in 1989 as communism collapsed throughout eastern Europe.

Honegger /ˈhɒnɪɡə/, French /ɔnɛɡɛʀ/, Arthur (1892–1955), French composer, of Swiss descent. He lived and worked chiefly in Paris, where he became a member of the anti-romantic group Les Six. His first major success was the orchestral work *Pacific 231* (1924).

honest ▶ adjective free of deceit; truthful and sincere: *I haven't been totally honest with you.* ■ morally correct or virtuous: *I did the only right and honest thing.* ■ [attrib.] fairly earned, especially through hard work: *he's struggling to make an honest living.* ■ (of an action) done with good intentions even if unsuccessful or misguided: *he'd made an honest mistake.* ■ [attrib.] simple, unpretentious, and unsophisticated: *good honest food with no gimmicks.*
▶ adverb informal used to persuade someone of the truth of something: *you'll like it when you get there, honest.*
– PHRASES **earn** (or **turn**) **an honest penny** earn money fairly. **make an honest woman of** dated or humorous marry a woman, especially to avoid scandal if she is pregnant. [*honest* here originally meant 'respectable', but was probably associated with the archaic sense 'chaste'.] **to be honest** speaking frankly: *to be honest, I expected to play worse.*
– ORIGIN Middle English (originally in the sense 'held in or deserving of honour'): via Old French from Latin *honestus*, from *honos* (see HONOUR).

honest broker ▶ noun an impartial mediator in international, industrial, or other disputes.
– ORIGIN late 19th cent.: translating German *ehrlicher Makler* with reference to BISMARCK[2], under whom Germany was united.

honestly ▶ adverb 1 in a truthful, fair, or honourable way: *he'd come by the money honestly.*
2 used to emphasize the sincerity of an opinion or feeling: *she honestly believed that she was making life easier for Jack.* ■ [sentence adverb] used to emphasize the truthfulness of a statement: *honestly, darling, I'm not upset.* ■ [sentence adverb] used to indicate the speaker's annoyance or impatience: *honestly, that man is the absolute limit!*

honest-to-God informal ▶ adjective [attrib.] genuine; real: *an honest-to-God celebrity.*
▶ exclamation genuinely; really: *'You mean you didn't know?' 'Honest to God!'*

honest-to-goodness ▶ adjective [attrib.] plain, genuine, and straightforward: *an honest-to-goodness family holiday in the sun.*

honesty ▶ noun [mass noun] 1 the quality of being honest: *they spoke with convincing honesty about their fears | it was not, in all honesty, an auspicious debut.* ■ denoting or relating to a way of charging for goods or services which relies on a customer to pay although there is no one to collect their payments: *an honesty bar.*
2 a European plant with purple or white flowers and round, flat, translucent seed pods which are used for indoor flower arrangements. ● Genus *Lunaria*, family Cruciferae.
– PHRASES **honesty is the best policy** proverb there are often practical as well as moral reasons for being honest.
– ORIGIN Middle English: from Old French *honeste*, from Latin *honestas*, from *honestus* (see HONEST). The original sense was 'honour, respectability', later 'decorum, virtue, chastity'. The plant is so named from its seed pods, translucency symbolizing lack of deceit.

honewort /ˈhəʊnwəːt/ ▶ noun a wild plant of the parsley family. ● Two species in the family Umbelliferae: *Cryptotaenia canadensis*, a native of North America and eastern Asia which is cultivated for food in Japan, and *Trinia glauca*, a small European plant.
– ORIGIN mid 17th cent.: from obsolete *hone* 'swelling' (for which the plant was believed to be a remedy) + WORT.

honey ▶ noun (pl. **honeys**) 1 [mass noun] a sweet, sticky yellowish-brown fluid made by bees and other insects from nectar collected from flowers. ■ a yellowish-brown or golden colour: [as modifier] *her honey skin.* ■ any sweet substance similar to bees' honey.
2 informal an excellent example of something: *it's one* ***honey of an adaptation.*** ■ an attractive girl: *she's a little honey.* ■ darling; sweetheart (usually as a form of address): *hi, honey!*
– ORIGIN Old English *hunig*, of Germanic origin; related to Dutch *honig* and German *Honig*.

honey ant ▶ noun another term for HONEYPOT ANT.

honey badger ▶ noun another term for RATEL.

honeybee ▶ noun see BEE (sense 1).

honeybird ▶ noun a small, drab African bird of the honeyguide family. ● Genus *Prodotiscus*, family Indicatoridae: three species.

honey bucket ▶ noun N. Amer. informal a toilet which does not use water and has to be emptied manually.

honeybun (also **honeybunch**) ▶ noun N. Amer. informal darling (used as a form of address).

honey buzzard ▶ noun a large Eurasian bird of prey resembling a buzzard, having a small head and long tail, feeding on bees and wasps and their nests. ● Genus *Pernis*, family Accipitridae: three species, in particular *P. apivorus*.

honeycomb ▶ noun 1 a structure of hexagonal cells of wax, made by bees to store honey and eggs.
2 a structure of adjoining cavities or cells: *a honeycomb of caves.* ■ a mass of cavities produced by corrosion or dissolution: [as modifier] *honeycomb weathering.* ■ a raised hexagonal or cellular pattern on a fabric.
3 [mass noun] tripe from the second stomach of a ruminant.
▶ verb [with obj.] fill with cavities or tunnels: *whole hillsides were honeycombed with mines.* ■ infiltrate and undermine: *their men honeycombed the army.*
– ORIGIN Old English *hunigcamb* (see HONEY, COMB).

honeycreeper ▶ noun 1 a tropical American tanager (songbird) with a long curved bill, feeding on nectar and insects. ● Genera *Cyanerpes* and *Chlorophanes*, family Emberizidae (subfamily Thraupinae): five species.
2 (also **Hawaiian honeycreeper**) a Hawaiian songbird of variable appearance and with a specialized bill, several kinds of which are now endangered.
● Family Drepanididae (or Fringillidae): several genera and species, often with Hawaiian names such as the iiwi and ou.

honeydew ▶ noun 1 [mass noun] a sweet, sticky substance excreted by aphids and often deposited on leaves and stems. ■ literary an ideally sweet substance.
2 (also **honeydew melon**) a melon of a variety with smooth pale skin and sweet green flesh.

honeyeater ▶ noun an Australasian songbird with a long brush-like tongue for feeding on nectar. ● Family Meliphagidae: numerous species and genera.

honeyed (also **honied**) ▶ adjective 1 (of food) containing or coated with honey. ■ rich and sweet in taste or smell: *as the wine matures it becomes more honeyed.* ■ having a golden or warm yellow colour.
2 (of a person's words or tone of voice) soothing, soft, and intended to please: *he wooed her with honeyed words.*

honey fungus (also **honey mushroom**) ▶ noun a widespread parasitic fungus that produces clumps of honey-coloured toadstools at the base of trees. The black string-like hyphae invade a tree, causing decay or death and spreading out to other trees. ● *Armillaria mellea*, family Tricholomataceae, class Hymenomycetes.

honeyguide ▶ noun 1 a small bird of the Old World tropics which feeds chiefly on beeswax and bee grubs. Two African kinds attract humans and other mammals, especially honey badgers, to bee nests.
● Family Indicatoridae: four genera, especially *Indicator*.
2 Botany a marking on the petal of a flower thought to guide pollinating insects to nectar.

honey locust ▶ noun a spiny tree of the pea family, grown as an ornamental for its fern-like foliage.
● Genus *Gleditsia*, family Leguminosae: several species.

honeymoon ▶ noun a holiday spent together by a newly married couple: *they flew to the West Indies* ***on honeymoon.*** ■ [often as modifier] an initial period of enthusiasm or goodwill, typically at the start of a new job: *the new President's honeymoon period.*
▶ verb [no obj., with adverbial of place] spend a honeymoon: *they are* ***honeymooning in*** *the south of France.*
– DERIVATIVES **honeymooner** noun.
– ORIGIN mid 16th cent. (originally denoting the period of time following a wedding): from HONEY + MOON. The original reference was to affection waning like the moon, but later the sense became 'the first month after marriage'.

honey parrot ▶ noun Australian term for LORIKEET.

honey possum ▶ noun a tiny shrew-like marsupial with a long pointed snout and a prehensile tail, found only in SW Australia, where it feeds exclusively upon nectar and pollen. ● *Tarsipes rostratus*, the only member of the family Tarsipedidae.

honeypot ▶ noun 1 a container for honey. ■ a place to which many people are attracted: *the tourist honeypot of St Ives.*
2 vulgar slang a woman's genitals.

honeypot ant ▶ noun an ant that stores large amounts of honeydew and nectar in its elastic abdomen, which becomes greatly distended. This is then fed to nest mates by regurgitation. ● *Myrmecocystus* and other genera, family Formicidae.

honeysucker ▶ noun any of a number of long-billed birds which feed on nectar, especially (in South Africa) a sunbird.

honeysuckle ▶ noun a widely distributed climbing shrub with tubular flowers that are typically fragrant and of two colours or shades, opening in the evening for pollination by moths. ● Genus *Lonicera*, family Caprifoliaceae (the **honeysuckle family**): many species, including the Eurasian **common honeysuckle** (*L. periclymenum*) and many cultivars. The honeysuckle family also includes such berry-bearing shrubs as guelder rose, elder, and snowberry.
– ORIGIN Middle English *honysoukil*, extension of *honysouke*, from Old English *hunigsūce* (see HONEY, SUCK). It originally denoted tubular flowers, such as the red clover, which are sucked for their nectar.

honeytrap ▶ noun a stratagem in which an attractive person entices another person into revealing information or doing something unwise.

honeywort ▶ noun a Mediterranean plant of the borage family, with greyish-green leaves and tubular yellow or purple flowers that are a favoured source of nectar for bees. ● Genus *Cerinthe*, family Boraginaceae: several species, in particular the yellow-flowered *C. major*.

hongi /ˈhɒŋi/ ▶ noun NZ a traditional Maori greeting in which people press their noses together.
– ORIGIN Maori.

Hong Kong a special administrative region on the SE coast of China, a British dependency until 1997; pop. 7,346,600 (est. 2009); official languages, English and Cantonese; capital, Victoria.

> The area comprises Hong Kong Island, ceded by China in 1841, the Kowloon peninsula, ceded in 1860, and the New Territories, additional areas of the mainland which were leased for 99 years in 1898. All were returned to China in 1997. Hong Kong has become one of the world's major financial and manufacturing centres, with the third-largest container port in the world.

Honiara /ˌhəʊnɪˈɑːrə/ a port and the capital of the Solomon Islands, situated on the NW coast of the island of Guadalcanal; pop. 66,000 (est. 2007).

honied ▸ adjective variant spelling of HONEYED.

honi soit qui mal y pense /ɒnɪ ˌswɑː kiː mal iː ˈpɒ̃s/ ▸ exclamation shame on him who thinks evil of it (the motto of the Order of the Garter).
– ORIGIN French.

Honiton lace /ˈhɒnɪt(ə)n, ˈhʌn-/ ▸ noun [mass noun] lace consisting of floral sprigs hand sewn on to fine net or joined by lacework.
– ORIGIN mid 19th cent.: from *Honiton*, the name of a town in Devon.

honk ▸ noun the cry of a wild goose. ■ the harsh sound of a car horn.
▸ verb 1 make or cause to make a honk: [no obj.] *geese circled around and honked* | [with obj.] *fans honked their horns.*
2 [no obj.] Brit. informal vomit.
– ORIGIN mid 19th cent.: imitative.

honker ▸ noun a person or thing that honks. ■ N. Amer. informal a wild goose.

honky ▸ noun (pl. **honkies**) N. Amer. informal a derogatory term used by black people for a white person or for white people collectively.
– ORIGIN 1960s: of unknown origin.

honky-tonk ▸ noun informal 1 N. Amer. a cheap or disreputable bar, club, or dance hall. ■ [as modifier] squalid and disreputable: *a honky-tonk beach resort.*
2 [mass noun] [often as modifier] ragtime piano music.
– ORIGIN late 19th cent.: of unknown origin.

honnête homme /ˌɒnɛt ˈɒm/ ▸ noun a decent, cultivated man of the world; a gentleman.
– ORIGIN French, literally 'honest man'.

Honolulu /ˌhɒnəˈluːluː/ the state capital and principal port of Hawaii, situated on the SE coast of the island of Oahu; pop. 374,676 (est. 2008).

honor ▸ noun & verb US spelling of HONOUR.

honorable ▸ adjective US spelling of HONOURABLE.

honorand /ˈɒnərand/ ▸ noun a person to be publicly honoured, especially with an honorary degree.
– ORIGIN 1950s: from Latin *honorandus* 'to be honoured', gerundive of *honorare* 'to honour', from *honor* 'honour'.

honorarium /ˌɒnəˈrɛːrɪəm/ ▸ noun (pl. **honorariums** or **honoraria** /-rɪə/) a payment given for professional services that are rendered nominally without charge.
– ORIGIN mid 17th cent.: from Latin, denoting a gift made on being admitted to public office, from *honorarius* (see HONORARY).

honorary ▸ adjective 1 conferred as an honour, without the usual requirements or functions: *an honorary doctorate.* ■ (of a person) holding an honorary title or position: *an honorary fellow of the Royal College of Surgeons.*
2 Brit. (of an office or its holder) unpaid: *Honorary Secretary of the Association.*
– ORIGIN early 17th cent.: from Latin *honorarius*, from *honor* 'honour'.

honoree /ˌɒnəˈriː/ ▸ noun N. Amer. a person who is honoured, especially by receiving an award at a public ceremony.

honorific ▸ adjective given as a mark of respect but having few or no duties: *he was elevated to the honorific status of 'Dom'.* ■ (of a form of address) showing respect: *an honorific title for addressing women.*
▸ noun a title or word implying or expressing respect.
– DERIVATIVES **honorifically** adverb.
– ORIGIN mid 17th cent.: from Latin *honorificus*, from *honor* 'honour'.

honoris causa /ɒˌnɔːrɪs ˈkaʊzə/ ▸ adverb (especially of a degree awarded without examination) as a mark of esteem.
– ORIGIN Latin, literally 'for the sake of honour'.

honour (US **honor**) ▸ noun 1 [mass noun] high respect; great esteem: *his portrait hangs in the place of honour.* ■ [in sing.] a person or thing that brings esteem: *you are an honour to our profession.* ■ (**His, Your,** etc. **Honour**) a title of respect or form of address given to a circuit judge, a US mayor, and (in Irish or rustic speech) any person of rank.
2 the quality of knowing and doing what is morally right: *I must as a matter of honour avoid any taint of dishonesty.* ■ dated a woman's chastity or her reputation for being chaste: *she died defending her honour.*
3 something regarded as a rare opportunity and bringing pride and pleasure; a privilege: *Mrs Young had the honour of being received by the Queen.* ■ a thing conferred as a distinction, especially an official award for bravery or achievement: *the highest military honours.* ■ (**honours**) a special distinction for proficiency in an examination: *she passed with honours.* ■ (**honours**) a course of degree studies more specialized than for an ordinary pass: [as modifier] *an honours degree in mathematics.* ■ Golf the right of driving off first, having won the previous hole.
4 Bridge an ace, king, queen, jack, or ten. ■ (**honours**) possession in one's hand of at least four of the ace, king, queen, jack, and ten of trumps, or of all four aces in no trumps, for which a bonus is scored. ■ (in whist) an ace, king, queen, or jack of trumps.
▸ verb [with obj.] 1 regard with great respect: *Joyce has now learned to honour her father's memory* | (as adj. **honoured**) *an honoured guest.* ■ pay public respect to: *talented writers were honoured at a special ceremony.*
2 fulfil (an obligation) or keep (an agreement): *make sure the franchisees honour the terms of the contract.* ■ accept (a bill) or pay (a cheque) when due: *the bank informed him that the cheque would not be honoured.*
– PHRASES **do the honours** informal perform a social duty for others, especially the serving of food or drink to a guest. **honour bright** Brit. dated on my honour: *I'll never do it again, honour bright, I won't.* [from Thomas Moore's *Tom Cribb's Memorial to Congress* (1819).] **honours are even** Brit. there is equality in the contest: *they are meeting in the final for the fifth time with honours even.* **in honour bound** another way of saying ON ONE'S HONOUR below. **in honour of** as a celebration of or expression of respect for. **on one's honour** under a moral obligation: *they are on their honour as gentlemen not to cheat.* ■ (**on** (or **upon**) **my honour**) used as an expression of sincerity: *I promise on my honour.* **there's honour among thieves** proverb dishonest people may have certain standards of behaviour which they will respect.
– ORIGIN Middle English: from Old French *onor* (noun), *onorer* (verb), from Latin *honos, honor.*

honourable (US **honorable**) ▸ adjective 1 bringing or deserving honour: *this is the only honourable course* | *a decent and honourable man.* ■ formal or humorous (of the intentions of a man courting a woman) directed towards marriage.
2 (**Honourable**) used as a title for certain high officials, the children of certain ranks of the nobility, and MPs: *the Honourable Alan Simpson, US Senator.*
– DERIVATIVES **honourableness** noun, **honourably** adverb.
– ORIGIN Middle English: via Old French from Latin *honorabilis*, from *honor* 'honour'.

honourable mention ▸ noun a commendation given to a candidate in an examination or competition who is not awarded a prize.

honour killing ▸ noun the killing of a relative, especially a girl or woman, who is perceived to have brought dishonour on the family.

honour point ▸ noun Heraldry the point halfway between the top of a shield and the fess point.

honours list ▸ noun a publicly issued list of people and the distinctions they are to be awarded.

honours of war ▸ plural noun privileges granted to a capitulating force, for example that of marching out with colours flying.

honour system ▸ noun a system of payment or examinations which relies solely on the honesty of those concerned.

Hon. Sec. ▸ abbreviation honorary secretary.

Honshu /ˈhɒnʃuː/ the largest of the four main islands of Japan; pop. 103,000,000 (est. 2005).

Hooch, Pieter de, see DE HOOCH.

hooch[1] (also **hootch**) ▸ noun [mass noun] informal alcoholic drink, especially inferior or illicit whisky.
– ORIGIN late 19th cent.: abbreviation of *Hoochinoo*, the name of an Alaskan Indian people who made liquor.

hooch[2] ▸ noun US informal a shelter or improvised dwelling.
– ORIGIN 1950s (originally military slang): perhaps from Japanese *uchi* 'dwelling'.

Hood, Thomas (1799–1845), English poet and humorist. He wrote much humorous verse but is chiefly remembered for serious poems such as 'The Song of the Shirt'.

hood[1] ▸ noun 1 a covering for the head and neck with an opening for the face, typically forming part of a coat or cloak. ■ a separate garment similar to this worn over a university gown or a surplice to indicate the wearer's degree. ■ Falconry a leather covering for a hawk's head.
2 a thing resembling a hood in shape or use, in particular: ■ Brit. a folding waterproof cover of a car, pram, etc. ■ N. Amer. the bonnet of a motor vehicle. ■ a canopy to protect users of machinery or to remove fumes from it. ■ a hood-like structure or marking on the head or neck of an animal. ■ the upper part of the flower of a plant such as a dead-nettle.
▸ verb [with obj.] put a hood on or over.
– DERIVATIVES **hoodless** adjective, **hood-like** adjective.
– ORIGIN Old English *hōd*, of West Germanic origin; related to Dutch *hoed*, German *Hut* 'hat', also to HAT.

hood[2] ▸ noun informal, chiefly N. Amer. a gangster or similar violent criminal.
– ORIGIN 1930s: abbreviation of HOODLUM.

hood[3] (also **'hood**) ▸ noun informal, chiefly US a neighbourhood, especially one in an urban area: *I've lived in the hood for 15 years.*
– ORIGIN 1970s: shortening of NEIGHBOURHOOD.

-hood ▸ suffix forming nouns: 1 denoting a condition or quality: *falsehood* | *womanhood.*
2 denoting a collection or group: *brotherhood.*
– ORIGIN Old English *-hād*, originally an independent noun meaning 'person, condition, quality'.

hooded ▸ adjective (of a garment) having a hood: *a hooded cloak.* ■ (of a person) wearing a hood: *a hooded figure.* ■ (of eyes) having thick, drooping upper eyelids resembling hoods: *a dark man with hooded eyes.*

hooded crow ▸ noun a bird of the North and East European race of the carrion crow, having a grey body with a black head, wings, and tail. ● *Corvus corone cornix*, family Corvidae.

hooded seal ▸ noun a seal with a grey and white blotched coat, found in the Arctic waters of the North Atlantic. The male has a nasal sac that is inflated into a hood during display. ● *Cystophora cristata*, family Phocidae.

hoodia /ˈhʊdɪə/ ▸ noun 1 a cactus-like succulent plant native to southern Africa. ● Genus *Hoodia*, family Asclepiadaceae: several species, in particular *H. gordonii.*
2 [mass noun] a compound derived from hoodia which acts as an appetite suppressant.
– ORIGIN early 20th cent.: modern Latin (genus name), from *Hood*, the surname of an English plant grower.

hoodie ▸ noun 1 Scottish term for HOODED CROW.
2 variant spelling of HOODY.

hoodlum /ˈhuːdləm/ ▸ noun a person who engages in crime and violence; a hooligan or gangster.
– ORIGIN late 19th cent.: of unknown origin.

hood mould (also **hood moulding**) ▸ noun Architecture another term for DRIPSTONE (sense 1).

hoodoo ▸ noun 1 [mass noun] voodoo or witchcraft. ■ [count noun] a run of bad luck associated with a person or activity: *when is this hoodoo going to end?* ■ [count noun] a person or thing that brings or causes bad luck.
2 chiefly N. Amer. a column or pinnacle of weathered rock: *a towering sandstone hoodoo.*
▸ verb (**hoodoos, hoodooing, hoodooed**) [with obj.] bewitch: *she's hoodooed you.* ■ bring bad luck to: *a fine player, but repeatedly hoodooed.*
– ORIGIN late 19th cent. (originally US): apparently an alteration of VOODOO. It originally denoted a person who practised voodoo, hence a hidden cause of bad luck (sense 1 of the noun). Sense 2 of the noun is apparently due to the resemblance of the rock column to a strange human form, often topped by an overhanging 'hat' of harder rock.

hoodwink ▸ verb [with obj.] deceive or trick: *staff were hoodwinked into thinking the cucumber was a sawn-off shotgun.*
– ORIGIN mid 16th cent. (originally in the sense 'to blindfold'): from the noun HOOD[1] + an obsolete sense of WINK 'close the eyes'.

hoody (also **hoodie**) ▸ noun (pl. **hoodies**) a hooded sweatshirt, jacket, or other top. ■ informal a person, especially a youth, wearing a hooded top.

hooey ▸ noun [mass noun] informal, chiefly N. Amer. nonsense: *the emphasis on family is pretentious hooey.*
– ORIGIN 1920s (originally US): of unknown origin.

hoof ▸ noun (pl. **hoofs** or **hooves**) the horny part of the foot of an ungulate animal, especially a horse: *there was a clatter of hoofs as a rider came up to them.*
▸ verb [with obj.] informal 1 kick (a ball) powerfully.
2 (**hoof it**) go on foot. ■ dance: *we hoof it reasonably fancily, and no one guffaws.*

– PHRASES **on the hoof 1** (of livestock) not yet slaughtered. **2** Brit. informal without proper thought or preparation: *policy was made on the hoof.*
– DERIVATIVES **hoofed** adjective.
– ORIGIN Old English *hōf*, of Germanic origin; related to Dutch *hoef* and German *Huf.*

hoofer ▶ noun informal a professional dancer.

hoof fungus ▶ noun another term for TINDER FUNGUS.

Hooghly /ˈhuːgli/ (also **Hugli**) the most westerly of the rivers of the Ganges delta, in West Bengal, India. It flows for 192 km (120 miles) into the Bay of Bengal and is navigable to Kolkata (Calcutta).

hoo-ha ▶ noun [in sing.] Brit. informal a commotion; a fuss: *the book was causing such a hoo-ha.*
– ORIGIN 1930s: of unknown origin.

hook ▶ noun **1** a piece of metal or other hard material curved or bent back at an angle, for catching hold of or hanging things on: *a picture hook.* ■ (also **fish hook**) a bent piece of metal, typically barbed and baited, for catching fish.
2 a thing designed to catch people's attention: *companies are looking for a sales hook.* ■ a catchy chorus or repeated instrumental passage in a piece of popular music.
3 a curved cutting instrument, especially as used for reaping or shearing.
4 a short swinging punch made with the elbow bent and rigid, especially in boxing: *a perfectly timed right hook to the chin.* ■ Cricket a stroke made to the on side with a horizontal or slightly upward swing of the bat at shoulder height. ■ Golf a stroke which makes the ball deviate in flight in the direction of the follow-through (from right to left for a right-handed player), typically inadvertently.
5 a curved stroke in handwriting. ■ Music an added stroke transverse to the stem in the symbol for a quaver or other note.
6 [usu. in place names] a curved promontory or sand spit.
▶ verb **1** [with obj. and adverbial] attach or fasten with a hook or hooks: *the truck had a red lamp hooked to its tailgate* | *she tried to* **hook up** *her bra* | [no obj.] *a ladder that hooks over the roof ridge.* ■ bend into the shape of a hook so as to fasten around or to an object: [with obj.] *he hooked his thumbs in his belt* | [no obj.] *her legs hooked around mine.* ■ [with obj.] Rugby secure (the ball) and pass it backwards with the foot in the scrum.
2 [with obj.] catch with a hook: *he hooked a 24 lb pike.* ■ informal attract and hold the attention of; captivate: *I was hooked by John's radical zeal.* ■ archaic, informal steal.
3 [with obj.] Cricket hit (the ball) round to the on side with a horizontal or slightly upward swing of the bat at shoulder height; hit a ball delivered by (the bowler) with such a stroke. ■ Golf strike (the ball) so that it deviates in the direction of the follow-through, typically inadvertently. ■ [no obj.] Boxing punch one's opponent with the elbow bent and rigid.
4 (often in imperative **hook it**) Brit. informal, dated run away.
5 [no obj.] (usu. as noun **hooking**) informal (of a woman) work as a prostitute.
– PHRASES **by hook or by crook** by any possible means: *the government intends, by hook or by crook, to hold on to the land.* **get one's hooks into** informal get hold of: *they were going to move out rather than let Mel get his hooks into them.* **get** (or **give someone**) **the hook** N. Amer. informal be dismissed (or dismiss someone) from a job. **hook, line, and sinker** used to emphasize that someone has been completely deceived or tricked: *he fell hook, line, and sinker for this year's April Fool joke.* [with allusion to the taking of bait by a fish.] **off the hook 1** informal no longer in difficulty or trouble: *I lied to get him off the hook.* **2** (of a telephone receiver) not on its rest, and so preventing incoming calls. **on the hook for** N. Amer. informal (in a financial context) responsible for: *he's on the hook for about $9.5 million.* **on one's own hook** N. Amer. informal, dated by oneself. **sling one's hook** [usu. in imperative] Brit. informal leave; go away.
– PHRASAL VERBS **hook up 1** (also **hook some-one/thing up**) link or be linked to electronic equipment: [with obj.] *Ali was hooked up to an electrocardiograph.* **2** informal (of two people) meet or form a relationship: *he hooked up with a friend in Budapest.*
– DERIVATIVES **hookless** adjective, **hooklet** noun, **hook-like** adjective.
– ORIGIN Old English *hōc*, of Germanic origin; related to Dutch *hoek* 'corner, angle, projecting piece of land', also to German *Haken* 'hook'.

hookah /ˈhʊkə/ ▶ noun an oriental tobacco pipe with a long, flexible tube which draws the smoke through water contained in a bowl.
– ORIGIN mid 18th cent.: from Urdu, from Arabic *ḥuqqa* 'casket, jar'.

hook and eye ▶ noun a small metal hook and loop used together as a fastener on a garment.

hookbait ▶ noun Brit. bait attached to a hook for fishing (as distinct from groundbait).

Hooke, Robert (1635–1703), English scientist. He formulated the law of elasticity (Hooke's law), proposed an undulating theory of light, introduced the term *cell* to biology, postulated elliptical orbits for the earth and moon, and proposed the inverse square law of gravitational attraction. He also invented or improved many scientific instruments and mechanical devices, and designed a number of buildings in London after the Great Fire.

hooked ▶ adjective **1** curved like a hook: *a golden eagle with hooked beak.* ■ having a hook or hooks: *a hooked gold earring.*
2 informal addicted: *a girl who got* **hooked on** *cocaine.* ■ devoted to or absorbed in something: *cricket fans are currently* **hooked on** *a series of college matches.*
3 (of a rug or mat) made by pulling woollen yarn through canvas with a hook.

Hooker[1], John Lee (1917–2001), American blues singer and guitarist. A major influence on British groups such as the Rolling Stones in the 1960s, he came to the attention of a new generation of fans in the 1980s.

Hooker[2], Sir Joseph Dalton (1817–1911), English botanist and pioneer in plant geography. Hooker applied Darwin's theories to plants and, with **George Bentham** (1800–84), he produced a work on classification, *Genera Plantarum* (1862–83).

hooker[1] ▶ noun **1** Rugby the player in the middle of the front row of the scrum, who tries to hook the ball.
2 informal, chiefly N. Amer. a prostitute.

hooker[2] ▶ noun a one-masted sailing boat of a kind used especially in Ireland for fishing. ■ Nautical, informal an old boat.
– ORIGIN mid 17th cent.: from Dutch *hoeker*, from *hoek* 'hook' (used earlier in *hoekboot*, denoting a two-masted Dutch fishing vessel).

hooker[3] ▶ noun N. Amer. informal a glass or drink of undiluted brandy, whisky, or other alcoholic spirit.
– ORIGIN mid 19th cent.: of unknown origin.

Hooke's law ▶ noun Physics a law stating that the strain in a solid is proportional to the applied stress within the elastic limit of that solid.

hookey (also **hooky**) ▶ noun (in phrase **play hookey**) informal, chiefly N. Amer. play truant.
– ORIGIN mid 19th cent.: of unknown origin.

hook nose ▶ noun a prominent aquiline nose.
– DERIVATIVES **hook-nosed** adjective.

Hook of Holland a cape and port of the Netherlands, near The Hague, linked by ferry to Harwich, Hull, and Dublin. Dutch name HOEK VAN HOLLAND.

hook shot ▶ noun Basketball a twisting shot started with the player's back to the basket, and completed as they pivot round towards the basket.

hooktip ▶ noun a slender moth which has hooked tips to the forewings. ● Family Drepanidae: *Drepana* and other genera.

hook-up ▶ noun a connection or link, especially to mains electricity or for communications or broadcasting equipment.

hookworm ▶ noun a parasitic nematode worm which inhabits the intestines of humans and other animals. It has hook-like mouthparts with which it attaches itself to the wall of the gut, puncturing the blood vessels and feeding on the blood. ● *Ancylostoma, Uncinaria, Necator*, and other genera, class Phasmida, including *N. americanus*, which infects millions of people in the tropics. ■ [mass noun] a disease caused by an infestation of hookworms, often resulting in severe anaemia.

hooky[1] ▶ adjective (**hookier**, **hookiest**) (of a tune) having immediate appeal and easy to remember; catchy: *a hooky bass line.*

hooky[2] ▶ noun variant spelling of HOOKEY.

hooley ▶ noun (pl. **hooleys**) informal, chiefly Irish a wild or noisy party.
– ORIGIN late 19th cent.: of unknown origin.

hooligan ▶ noun a violent young troublemaker, typically one of a gang: *a football hooligan.*
– DERIVATIVES **hooliganism** noun.
– ORIGIN late 19th cent.: perhaps from *Hooligan*, the surname of a fictional rowdy Irish family in a music-hall song of the 1890s, also of a cartoon character.

hoolock /ˈhuːlək/ (also **hoolock gibbon**) ▶ noun a gibbon with white eyebrows, the male of which has black fur and the female golden, found from NE India to Burma. ● *Hylobates hoolock*, family Hylobatidae.
– ORIGIN early 19th cent.: perhaps from Bengali and imitative of its cry.

hoon Austral./NZ informal ▶ noun a lout or hooligan, especially a young man who drives recklessly.
▶ verb [no obj.] behave in a loutish way, especially by driving recklessly.
– ORIGIN 1930s: of unknown origin.

hoop ▶ noun **1** a circular band of metal, wood, or similar material, especially one used for binding the staves of barrels or forming part of a framework. ■ a large ring formerly bowled along as a toy. ■ a large ring for circus performers to jump through. ■ historical a circle of flexible material used for expanding a woman's petticoat or skirt. ■ chiefly Brit. a metal arch through which balls are hit in croquet.
2 a horizontal band of a contrasting colour on a sports shirt or jockey's cap. ■ Austral. informal a jockey.
▶ verb [with obj.] bind or encircle with or as with hoops.
– PHRASES **jump through hoops** perform a difficult and gruelling series of tests at someone else's request or command: *the banks make you beg for a loan and they make you jump through hoops to get it.*
– DERIVATIVES **hooped** adjective.
– ORIGIN late Old English *hōp*, of West Germanic origin; related to Dutch *hoep.*

hooper ▶ noun old-fashioned term for COOPER.
– ORIGIN Middle English: from HOOP.

hoop iron ▶ noun [mass noun] flattened iron in long thin strips used for binding together the staves of casks or tubs.

hoopla /ˈhuːplɑː/ ▶ noun **1** Brit. a game in which rings are thrown from behind a line in an attempt to encircle one of several prizes.
2 [mass noun] informal, chiefly N. Amer. unnecessary fuss surrounding something.

hoopoe /ˈhuːpuː, -pəʊ/ ▶ noun a salmon-pink Eurasian bird with a long downcurved bill, a large erectile crest, and black-and-white wings and tail. ● *Upupa epops*, the only member of the family Upupidae.
– ORIGIN mid 17th cent.: alteration of obsolete *hoop*, from Old French *huppe*, from Latin *upupa*, imitative of the bird's call.

hoopster ▶ noun N. Amer. informal a basketball player.

hooptie /ˈhuːpti/ ▶ noun US informal a car, especially an old or dilapidated one.
– ORIGIN 1960s: of unknown origin.

hoor /hɔː, hʊə/ ▶ noun Irish & Scottish informal a prostitute. ■ a person (male or female) whose behaviour one disapproves of.
– ORIGIN representing a regional pronunciation of WHORE.

hooray ▶ exclamation **1** another word for HURRAH.
2 Austral./NZ goodbye.

Hooray Henry ▶ noun (pl. **Hooray Henrys** or **Hooray Henries**) Brit. informal a lively but ineffectual young upper-class man.

hooroo /hʌˈruː/ (also **hurroo**) ▶ exclamation & noun Australian word for HOORAY.

hoosegow /ˈhuːsgaʊ/ ▶ noun N. Amer. informal a prison.
– ORIGIN early 20th cent.: via Latin American Spanish from Spanish *juzgado* 'tribunal', from Latin *judicatum* 'something judged', neuter past participle of *judicare.*

Hoosier /ˈhuːʒɪə/ ▶ noun N. Amer. a native or inhabitant of the state of Indiana, US.
– ORIGIN early 19th cent.: of unknown origin.

Hoosier State informal name for INDIANA.

hoot ▶ noun a low, wavering musical sound which is the typical call of many kinds of owl. ■ a raucous sound made by a horn, siren, or steam whistle. ■ a shout expressing scorn or disapproval: *there were hoots of derision.* ■ a short outburst of laughter: *the audience broke into hoots of laughter.* ■ (**a hoot**) informal an amusing situation or person: *your mum's a real hoot.*
▶ verb [no obj.] (of an owl) utter a hoot. ■ (with reference to a car horn, siren, etc.) make or cause to make a hoot: *a car horn hooted, frightening her* | [with obj.] *Sam hooted his horn.* ■ shout loudly in scorn, disapproval, or merriment: *she began to hoot with laughter.* ■ (**hoot something down**) express loud scornful disapproval of something: *his questions were hooted down or answered obscenely.*
– PHRASES **not care** (or **give**) **a hoot** (or **two hoots**) informal not care at all.

H

– ORIGIN Middle English (in the sense 'make sounds of derision'): perhaps imitative.

hootch ▸ noun variant spelling of HOOCH[1].

hootenanny /ˈhuːt(ə),nani/ ▸ noun (pl. **hootenannies**) informal, chiefly US an informal gathering with folk music.
– ORIGIN 1920s (originally US, denoting a gadget or 'thingummy'): of unknown origin.

hooter ▸ noun **1** chiefly Brit. a siren or steam whistle, especially one used as a signal for work to begin or finish. ■ the horn of a motor vehicle.
2 informal a person's nose.
3 (**hooters**) N. Amer. vulgar slang a woman's breasts.

hoots ▸ exclamation Scottish & N. English archaic or humorous expressing dissatisfaction or impatience: *'Och, noo, hoots, Hamish! Wull yee no sing us a song?'*
– ORIGIN natural exclamation: first recorded in English in the mid 16th cent. as *hoot*; the form *hoots* dates from the early 19th cent.

Hoover[1], Herbert (Clark) (1874–1964), American Republican statesman, 31st President of the US 1929–33. As President he was faced with the long-term problems of the Depression.

Hoover[2], J. Edgar (1895–1972), American lawyer and director of the FBI 1924–72; full name *John Edgar Hoover*. He reorganized the FBI into an efficient, scientific law-enforcement agency, but came under criticism for the organization's role during the McCarthy era.

H

Hoover[3], William (Henry) (1849–1932), American industrialist. In 1908 he bought the patent of a lightweight electric cleaning machine and formed a company to manufacture it with great success. In 1910 the company was renamed Hoover.

Hoover[4] Brit. ▸ noun trademark a vacuum cleaner, properly one made by the Hoover company.
▸ verb (**hoover**) [with obj.] clean (something) with a vacuum cleaner: *he was hoovering the stairs.*
■ (**hoover something up**) suck something up with or as if with a vacuum cleaner: *hoover up all the dust.* ■ (**hoover something up**) informal consume something quickly and eagerly: *he hoovered up three slices of cake.*
– ORIGIN 1920s: named after W. H. HOOVER[3].

Hooverville ▸ noun (in the US) a shanty town built by unemployed and destitute people during the Depression of the early 1930s.
– ORIGIN named after H.C. HOOVER[1], during whose presidency such accommodation was built (see also -VILLE).

hooves plural form of HOOF.

hop[1] ▸ verb (**hops, hopping, hopped**) **1** [no obj., with adverbial of direction] (of a person) move by jumping on one foot: *he hopped along beside her.* ■ (of a bird or other animal) move by jumping with two or all feet at once: *a blackbird was hopping around in the sun.* ■ spring or leap a short distance with one jump: *he hopped down from the rock.* ■ [with obj.] N. Amer. informal jump on to (a moving vehicle): *ex-soldiers looking for work hopped freights heading west.* ■ [with obj.] jump over (something): *the cow hopped the fence.*
2 informal pass quickly from one place to another: *she hopped over the Atlantic for a bit of shopping* | [as noun, in combination] *island-hopping.* ■ (**hop it**) Brit. informal go away quickly. ■ make a quick change of position or activity: *over the years he hopped from one department to another.*
▸ noun **1** a hopping movement. ■ a short journey or distance: *a short hop by cab from Soho.*
2 an informal dance.
PHRASES **hop, skip** (or **step**), **and jump 1** old-fashioned term for TRIPLE JUMP. **2** informal a short distance: *it's just a hop, skip, and jump from my home town.* **hop the twig** (or **stick**) Brit. informal depart suddenly or die. **on the hop** Brit. informal **1** unprepared: *he was caught on the hop.* **2** bustling about; busy: *we were always kept on the hop.*
– PHRASAL VERBS **hop in** (or **out**) informal get into (or out of) a vehicle: *hop in then and we'll be off.*
– ORIGIN Old English *hoppian*, of Germanic origin; related to German dialect *hopfen* and German *hopsen*.

hop[2] ▸ noun a twining climbing plant native to north temperate regions, cultivated for the flowers borne by the female plant, which are used in brewing beer. ● *Humulus lupulus*, family Cannabaceae (or Cannabidaceae).
■ (**hops**) the dried cone-like flowers of the hop, used in brewing to give a bitter flavour and as a mild sterilant. ■ (**hops**) Austral./NZ informal beer. ■ [mass noun] US informal, dated a narcotic drug, especially opium.
▸ verb (**hops, hopping, hopped**) **1** [with obj.] flavour with hops: *a strong dark beer, heavily hopped.*
2 (**be hopped up**) informal be stimulated or intoxicated by or as if by a narcotic drug.
– DERIVATIVES **hoppy** adjective (**hoppier, hoppiest**).
– ORIGIN late Middle English *hoppe* (in the sense 'ripened hop cones for flavouring malt liquor'), from Middle Low German or Middle Dutch.

hopak ▸ noun variant spelling of GOPAK.

hop back ▸ noun a container with a perforated bottom for straining off the hops in the manufacture of beer.

hop bine (also **hop bind**) ▸ noun the climbing stem of the hop.

Hope, Bob (1903–2003), British-born American comedian; born *Leslie Townes Hope*. He often adopted the character of a cowardly incompetent, cheerfully failing to become a romantic hero, as in the series of *Road* films (1940–62).

hope ▸ noun [mass noun] **1** a feeling of expectation and desire for a particular thing to happen: *he looked through her belongings in the hope of coming across some information* | [count noun] *I had high hopes of making the Olympic team.* ■ [count noun] a person or thing that may help or save someone: *their only hope is surgery.* ■ grounds for believing that something good may happen: *he does see some hope for the future.*
2 archaic a feeling of trust.
▸ verb [no obj.] want something to happen or be the case: *he's **hoping for** an offer of compensation* | [with clause] *I hope that the kids are OK.* ■ [with infinitive] intend if possible to do something: *we're hoping to address all these issues.*
– PHRASES **hope against hope** cling to a mere possibility: *they were hoping against hope that he would find a way out.* **hope for the best** hope for a favourable outcome: *I'll just wait at home and hope for the best.* **hope springs eternal** (**in the human breast**) proverb it is human nature always to find fresh cause for optimism. **not a** (or Brit. **some**) **hope** informal no chance at all.
– DERIVATIVES **hoper** noun.
– ORIGIN late Old English *hopa* (noun), *hopian* (verb), of Germanic origin; related to Dutch *hoop* (noun), *hopen* (verb), and German *hoffen* (verb).

hope chest ▸ noun N. Amer. a chest containing household linen and clothing stored by a woman in preparation for her marriage.

hopeful ▸ adjective feeling or inspiring optimism about a future event: *a hopeful sign* | [with clause] *he remained hopeful that something could be worked out.*
▸ noun a person likely or hoping to succeed: *promotion hopefuls Huddersfield.*
– DERIVATIVES **hopefulness** noun.

hopefully ▸ adverb **1** in a hopeful manner: *he rode on hopefully.*
2 [sentence adverb] it is to be hoped that: *hopefully the road should be finished by next year.*

USAGE The traditional sense of **hopefully**, 'in a hopeful manner', has been used since the 17th century. In the second half of the 20th century a new use as a sentence adverb arose, meaning 'it is to be hoped that', as in ***hopefully**, we'll see you tomorrow.* This second use is now very much commoner than the first use, but it is still believed by some people to be incorrect. Why should this be? People do not criticize other sentence adverbs, e.g. **sadly** (as in ***sadly**, her father died last year*) or **fortunately** (as in ***fortunately**, he recovered*). Part of the reason is that **hopefully** is a rather odd sentence adverb: while many others, such as **sadly, regrettably**, and **clearly**, may be paraphrased as 'it is sad/regrettable/clear that ...', this is not possible with **hopefully**. Nevertheless, it is clear that use of **hopefully** has become a shibboleth of 'correctness' in the language—even if the arguments on which this is based are not particularly strong—and it is wise to be aware of this in formal contexts.

Hopeh /həʊˈpeɪ/ variant of HEBEI.

hopeless ▸ adjective **1** feeling or causing despair: *Jess looked at him in mute hopeless appeal.*
2 chiefly Brit. very bad or incompetent: *I'm **hopeless at** names.*
– DERIVATIVES **hopelessness** noun.

hopelessly ▸ adverb **1** in a way that shows or causes despair: *she sighed hopelessly.*
2 [as submodifier] used to emphasize that a situation is beyond hope of improvement; irredeemably: *before long, he was hopelessly lost.*

hophead ▸ noun informal **1** N. Amer. a drug addict.
2 Austral./NZ a heavy drinker.

Hopi /ˈhəʊpi/ ▸ noun (pl. **same** or **Hopis**) **1** a member of a Pueblo Indian people living chiefly in NE Arizona.
2 [mass noun] the Uto-Aztecan language of the Hopi, with around 2,000 speakers.
▸ adjective relating to the Hopi or their language.
– ORIGIN the name in Hopi.

Hopkins, Gerard Manley (1844–89), English poet. Becoming a Jesuit in 1868, he wrote little poetry until 1876, when a shipwreck inspired him to write 'The Wreck of the Deutschland'. Like his poems 'Windhover' and 'Pied Beauty' (both 1877), it makes use of Hopkins's 'sprung rhythm' technique.

hoplite /ˈhɒplʌɪt/ ▸ noun a heavily armed foot soldier of ancient Greece.
– ORIGIN from Greek *hoplitēs*, from *hoplon* 'weapon'.

Hopper, Edward (1882–1967), American realist painter. He is best known for his mature works, such as *Early Sunday Morning* (1930), often depicting isolated figures in bleak scenes from everyday urban life.

hopper[1] ▸ noun **1** a container for a loose bulk material such as grain, rock, or rubbish, typically one that tapers downward and is able to discharge its contents at the bottom. ■ chiefly historical a tapering container, working with a hopping motion, through which grain passed into a mill. ■ a railway wagon able to discharge coal or other bulk material through its floor. ■ a barge for carrying away mud or sediment from a dredging machine and discharging it. ■ (also **hopper head**) a container at the top of a vertical pipe which receives water from a gutter or waste pipe.
2 a person or thing that hops: [in combination] *island-hoppers.* ■ a hopping insect, especially a young locust.

hopper[2] ▸ noun a person who picks hops.

hopping ▸ adjective informal, chiefly N. Amer. very active or lively: *the delis do a hopping lunch business.*
– PHRASES **hopping mad** informal extremely angry.

hopping john ▸ noun [mass noun] (in the southern US and Caribbean) a stew of rice with black-eyed beans or peas, often also containing bacon and red peppers.

hopping mouse ▸ noun an Australian mouse with elongated hindlimbs and feet for jumping. ● Genus *Notomys*, family Muridae: several species.

hopple ▸ verb & noun Riding another term for HOBBLE (sense 2 of the verb, sense 2 of the noun).
– ORIGIN late 16th cent.: probably of Low German origin and related to early Flemish *hoppelen* and Middle Dutch *hobelen* 'jump, dance'; compare with HOBBLE.

hopsack ▸ noun [mass noun] a coarse clothing fabric of a loose plain weave. ■ [count noun] a coarse hemp sack used for hops.

hopscotch ▸ noun [mass noun] a children's game in which each child by turn hops into and over squares marked on the ground to retrieve a marker thrown into one of these squares.
▸ verb [no obj., with adverbial of direction] N. Amer. travel from place to place: *they hopscotched around eight Western states.*
– ORIGIN early 19th cent.: from HOP[1] + SCOTCH[1].

hop tree ▸ noun a North American shrub or small tree with bitter fruit that was formerly used in brewing as a substitute for hops. ● *Ptelea trifoliata*, family Rutaceae.

hora /ˈhɔːrə/ (also **horah**) ▸ noun a Romanian or Israeli dance in which the performers form a ring.
– ORIGIN late 19th cent.: from Romanian *horă*, Hebrew *hōrāh*.

Horace /ˈhɒrɪs/ (65–8 BC), Roman poet of the Augustan period; full name *Quintus Horatius Flaccus*. A notable satirist and literary critic, he is best known for his *Odes*, much imitated by later ages, especially by the poets of 17th-century England. His other works include *Satires* and *Ars Poetica*.

horal /ˈhɔːr(ə)l/ ▸ adjective relating to an hour or hours; hourly.
– ORIGIN early 18th cent.: from late Latin *horalis*, from Latin *hora* 'hour'.

horary /ˈhɔːrəri/ ▸ adjective archaic relating to hours as measurements of time. ■ occurring every hour: *I took horary observations of the barometer.* ■ Astrology relating to or denoting a branch of astrology in which answers are given to questions using a chart drawn up for the time a question is posed.
– ORIGIN early 17th cent.: from medieval Latin *horarius*, from Latin *hora* 'hour'.

Horatian /həˈreɪʃ(ə)n, -ʃɪən/ ▸ **adjective** relating to the Roman poet Horace or his work. ▪ (of an ode) of several stanzas each of the same metrical pattern.

horchata /ɔːˈtʃɑːtə/ ▸ **noun** [mass noun] (in Spain and Latin American countries) a milky drink made from ground almonds, tiger nuts, or rice.
– ORIGIN Spanish.

horde ▸ **noun 1** chiefly derogatory a large group of people: *a horde of beery rugby fans.* ▪ an army or tribe of nomadic warriors: *Tartar hordes.*
2 Anthropology a small loosely knit social group typically consisting of about five families.
– ORIGIN mid 16th cent. (originally denoting a tribe or troop of Tartar or other nomads): from Polish *horda*, from Turkish *ordu* '(royal) camp'.

> **USAGE** The words **hoard** and **horde** are quite distinct; see **USAGE** at **HOARD**.

horehound /ˈhɔːhaʊnd/ (also **hoarhound**) ▸ **noun** a strong-smelling hairy plant of the mint family, with a tradition of use in medicine. ● Two species in the family Labiatae: **white horehound** (*Marrubium vulgare*) and **black horehound** (*Ballota nigra*), a Eurasian plant which was formerly said to cure the bite of a mad dog.
▪ [mass noun] the bitter aromatic juice of white horehound, used especially in the treatment of coughs and colds.
– ORIGIN Old English *hāre hūne*, from *hār* (see **HOAR**) + *hūne*, the name of the white horehound, also applied to related plants.

horizon ▸ **noun 1** the line at which the earth's surface and the sky appear to meet: *the sun rose above the horizon.* ▪ (also **apparent horizon**) the circular boundary of the part of the earth's surface visible from a particular point, ignoring irregularities and obstructions. ▪ (also **true horizon**) Astronomy a great circle of the celestial sphere, the plane of which passes through the centre of the earth and is parallel to that of the apparent horizon of a place.
2 (often **horizons**) the limit of a person's knowledge, experience, or interest: *she wanted to leave home and broaden her horizons.*
3 Geology a layer of soil or rock, or a set of strata, with particular characteristics. ▪ Archaeology a level of an excavated site representing a particular period.
– PHRASES **on the horizon** imminent or just becoming apparent: *trouble could be on the horizon.*
– ORIGIN late Middle English: via Old French from late Latin *horizon*, from Greek *horizōn* (*kuklos*) 'limiting (circle)'.

horizontal ▸ **adjective 1** parallel to the plane of the horizon; at right angles to the vertical: *a horizontal line.* ▪ (of machinery) having its parts working in a horizontal direction: *a horizontal steam engine.*
2 being at or involving the same level of a hierarchy: *horizontal class loyalties.* ▪ uniform; based on uniformity: *horizontal expansion of the international community.* ▪ combining firms engaged in the same stage or type of production: *a horizontal merger.*
3 of or at the horizon: *the horizontal moon.*
▸ **noun** a horizontal line, plane, etc.
– DERIVATIVES **horizontality** noun, **horizontally** adverb.
– ORIGIN mid 16th cent. (in sense 3 of the adjective): from French, or from modern Latin *horizontalis*, from late Latin *horizon*, *horizont-* (see **HORIZON**).

horizontal gene transfer ▸ **noun** [mass noun] the acquisition by an organism of genetic information by transfer, for example via the agency of a virus, from an organism that is not its parent and is typically a member of a different species.

Horkheimer /ˈhɔːk,hʌɪmə/, German /ˈhɔrk,haɪmɐ/, Max (1895–1973), German philosopher and sociologist. A leading figure of the Frankfurt School, he wrote *Dialectic of Enlightenment* (1947), with his colleague Theodor Adorno, and *Critical Theory* (1968).

Horlicks ▸ **noun** [mass noun] trademark a drink made from malted milk powder.
– PHRASES **make a Horlicks of** Brit. informal make a mess of.
– ORIGIN late 19th cent.: named after James and William *Horlick*, British-born brothers whose company first manufactured the drink in the US.

Horlivka /ˈhɔːljuːkə/ an industrial city in SE Ukraine, in the Donets Basin; pop. 266,300 (est. 2009). Russian name **GORLOVKA**.

hormonal ▸ **adjective** relating to or containing a hormone or hormones: *a hormonal imbalance.* ▪ informal affected by one's sex hormones, especially so as to feel moody or easily aroused: *giggly, hormonal fourth formers.*
– DERIVATIVES **hormonally** adverb.

hormone ▸ **noun** a regulatory substance produced in an organism and transported in tissue fluids such as blood or sap to stimulate specific cells or tissues into action. ▪ a synthetic substance with a similar effect to that of an animal or plant hormone. ▪ (**hormones**) a person's sex hormones as held to influence behaviour or mood.
– ORIGIN early 20th cent.: from Greek *hormōn*, present participle of *horman* 'impel, set in motion'.

hormone replacement therapy (abbrev.: **HRT**) ▸ **noun** [mass noun] treatment with oestrogens with the aim of alleviating menopausal symptoms or osteoporosis.

Hormuz /ˈhɔːmʊz, hɔːˈmuːz/ (also **Ormuz**) an Iranian island at the mouth of the Persian Gulf, in the Strait of Hormuz. It is the site of an ancient city, which was an important centre of commerce in the Middle Ages.

Hormuz, Strait of a strait linking the Persian Gulf with the Gulf of Oman, which leads to the Arabian Sea, and separating Iran from the Arabian peninsula. It is of strategic and economic importance as a waterway through which sea traffic to and from the oil-rich states of the Gulf must pass.

horn ▸ **noun 1** a hard permanent outgrowth, often curved and pointed, found in pairs on the heads of cattle, sheep, goats, giraffes, etc. and consisting of a core of bone encased in keratinized skin. ▪ a woolly keratinized outgrowth, occurring singly or one behind another, on the snout of a rhinoceros. ▪ a deer's antler. ▪ a horn-like projection on the head of another animal, e.g. a snail's tentacle or the tuft of a horned owl. ▪ (**horns**) archaic a pair of horns as an emblem of a cuckold. ▪ [mass noun] W. Indian marital infidelity: *she took endless horn and pressure, but now she wants a divorce.*
2 [mass noun] the substance of which horns are composed: *powdered rhino horn.* ▪ [count noun] a receptacle made of horn, such as a drinking container or powder flask.
3 a horn-shaped projection or object. ▪ a sharp promontory or mountain peak. ▪ (**the Horn**) Cape Horn. ▪ an arm or branch of a river or bay. ▪ each of the extremities of a crescent moon. ▪ Brit. vulgar slang an erect penis.
4 a wind instrument, conical in shape or wound into a spiral, originally made from an animal horn (now typically brass) and played by lip vibration. ▪ short for **FRENCH HORN**. ▪ informal (in jazz and popular music) any wind instrument.
5 a device sounding a warning or other signal: *a car horn.*
▸ **verb** [with obj.] **1** (of an animal) butt or gore with the horns.
2 W. Indian be unfaithful to (one's husband or wife).
– PHRASES **blow** (or **toot**) **one's own horn** N. Amer. informal talk boastfully about oneself or one's achievements. **draw** (or **pull**) **in one's horns** become less assertive or ambitious. **on the horn** N. Amer. informal on the telephone: *she got on the horn to complain.* **on the horns of a dilemma** faced with a decision involving equally unfavourable alternatives.
– PHRASAL VERBS **horn in** informal intrude or interfere.
– DERIVATIVES **hornist** noun (sense 4 of the noun), **hornless** adjective, **horn-like** adjective.
– ORIGIN Old English, of Germanic origin; related to Dutch *hoorn* and German *Horn*, from an Indo-European root shared by Latin *cornu* and Greek *keras*.

Horn, Cape the southernmost point of South America, on a Chilean island south of Tierra del Fuego. The region is notorious for its storms, and until the opening of the Panama Canal in 1914 constituted the only sea route between the Atlantic and Pacific Oceans. Also called **THE HORN**.
– ORIGIN named after *Hoorn*, the birthplace of the Dutch navigator William C. Schouten who discovered it in 1616.

hornbeam ▸ **noun** a deciduous tree of north temperate regions, with oval serrated leaves, inconspicuous drooping flowers, and tough winged nuts. It yields hard pale timber. ● Genus *Carpinus*, family Betulaceae: several species.
– ORIGIN late Middle English: so named because of the tree's hard, close-grained wood.

hornbill ▸ **noun** a medium to large tropical Old World bird, having a very large curved bill that typically has a large horny or bony casque. The male often seals up the female inside the nest hole. ● Family Bucerotidae: several genera and numerous species, e.g. the **great Indian hornbill** (*Buceros bicornis*).

hornblende /ˈhɔːnblɛnd/ ▸ **noun** [mass noun] a dark brown, black, or green mineral consisting of a silicate of calcium, magnesium, and iron, occurring in many igneous and metamorphic rocks.
– ORIGIN late 18th cent.: from German, from *Horn* 'horn' + *blende* (see **BLENDE**).

hornbook ▸ **noun** historical a teaching aid consisting of a leaf of paper showing the alphabet, and often the ten digits and the Lord's Prayer, mounted on a wooden tablet and protected by a thin plate of horn. ▪ N. Amer. Law a one-volume treatise summarizing the law in a specific field.

horned ▸ **adjective 1** having a horn or horns: *horned cattle* | [in combination] *a long-horned bison.*
2 literary crescent-shaped: *the horned moon.*

horned grebe ▸ **noun** North American term for **SLAVONIAN GREBE**.

horned lark ▸ **noun** North American term for **SHORELARK**.

horned lizard ▸ **noun** another term for **HORNED TOAD** (sense 1).

horned owl (also **great horned owl**) ▸ **noun** a large owl found throughout North and South America, with horn-like ear tufts. ● *Bubo virginianus*, family Strigidae.

horned poppy ▸ **noun** a Eurasian poppy with greyish-green lobed leaves, large flowers, and a long curved seed capsule. ● Genus *Glaucium*, family Papaveraceae: several species, in particular the **yellow horned poppy** (*G. flavum*).

horned toad ▸ **noun 1** an American lizard that somewhat resembles a toad, with spiny skin and large spines on the head, typically occurring in dry open country. Also called **HORNED LIZARD**. ● Genus *Phrynosoma*, family Iguanidae: several species.
2 a large toad with horn-shaped projections of skin over the eyes, in particular: ● a SE Asian toad (*Megophrys* and other genera, family Peltobatidae). ● a South American toad (*Ceratophrys* and other genera, family Leptodactylidae).

horned viper ▸ **noun** a venomous nocturnal snake with an upright projection over each eye, native to the sandy deserts of North Africa and Arabia. It moves in the same way as the sidewinder. ● *Cerastes cerastes*, family Viperidae.

hornero /hɔːˈnɛːrəʊ/ ▸ **noun** (pl. **horneros**) a tropical American bird of the ovenbird family, often building its oven-like mud nest on the top of a fence post. Also called **OVENBIRD**. ● Genus *Furnarius*, family Furnariidae: several species.
– ORIGIN late 19th cent.: from Spanish, literally 'baker'.

Horner's syndrome ▸ **noun** [mass noun] Medicine a condition marked by a contracted pupil, drooping upper eyelid, and local inability to sweat on one side of the face, caused by damage to sympathetic nerves on that side of the neck.
– ORIGIN early 20th cent.: named after Johann F. *Horner* (1831–86), Swiss ophthalmologist.

hornet ▸ **noun** a large, fairly docile wasp which is typically red and yellow or red and black and usually nests in hollow trees. ● *Vespa* and other genera, family Vespidae: several species, including the European *V. crabro*.
– PHRASES **a hornets' nest** a situation fraught with difficulties or complications: *the move has stirred up a hornets' nest of academic fear and loathing.*
– ORIGIN Old English *hyrnet*, of Germanic origin; related to German *Hornisse*. The form of the word was probably influenced by Middle Dutch and Middle Low German *hornte*.

hornet moth ▸ **noun** a clearwing moth which resembles a hornet, with larvae that burrow under tree bark. ● Several species in the family Sesiidae.

hornfels /ˈhɔːnfɛlz/ ▸ **noun** [mass noun] a dark, fine-grained metamorphic rock consisting largely of quartz, mica, and particular feldspars.
– ORIGIN mid 19th cent.: from German, literally 'horn rock'.

Horn of Africa a peninsula of NE Africa, comprising Somalia and parts of Ethiopia. It lies between the Gulf of Aden and the Indian Ocean. Also called **SOMALI PENINSULA**.

horn of plenty ▸ **noun 1** a cornucopia.
2 an edible woodland mushroom with a funnel-shaped cap that bears spores on its greyish outer surface, found in both Eurasia and North America. ● *Craterellus cornucopioides*, family Cantharellaceae, class Hymenomycetes.

H

hornpipe ▸ noun a lively dance associated with sailors, typically performed by one person. ■ a piece of music for a hornpipe.
– ORIGIN late Middle English (denoting a wind instrument made of horn, played to accompany dancing): from HORN + PIPE.

horn-rimmed ▸ adjective (of glasses) having rims made of horn or a similar substance.

horn shell ▸ noun a mollusc with a long tapering shell, occurring in brackish and marine waters. ● Families Potamididae and Cerithidae, class Gastropoda.

hornswoggle /ˈhɔːnswɒɡ(ə)l/ ▸ verb [with obj.] informal, chiefly N. Amer. get the better of (someone) by cheating or deception.
– ORIGIN early 19th cent. (originally US): of unknown origin.

horntail ▸ noun a large wasp-like sawfly which deposits its eggs inside trees and timber. It has a long egg-laying tube but no sting. Also called WOODWASP. ● Family Siricidae, suborder Symphyta, order Hymenoptera: several species.

hornworm ▸ noun N. Amer. the caterpillar of a hawkmoth, which has a spike or 'horn' on its tail. ● Family Sphingidae: several genera and many species, in particular pests like the **tobacco hornworm** (*Manduca sexta*) and the **tomato hornworm** (*M. quinquemaculata*).

H

hornwort ▸ noun a submerged aquatic plant with narrow forked leaves that become translucent and horny as they age, occurring worldwide. ● Family Ceratophyllaceae and genus *Ceratophyllum*: two or more species, in particular *C. demersum*.

horny ▸ adjective (**hornier**, **horniest**) **1** of or resembling horn: *a horny beak*. ■ hard and rough: *horny hands* | *horny, dry skin*.
2 informal feeling or arousing sexual excitement.
– DERIVATIVES **hornily** adverb, **horniness** noun.

horologe /ˈhɒrəlɒdʒ/ ▸ noun archaic a timepiece.
– ORIGIN late Middle English: from Old French, via Latin from Greek *hōrologion*, from *hōra* 'time' + *-logos* '-telling'.

Horologium /ˌhɒrəˈləʊdʒɪəm, -ˈlɒdʒ-/ Astronomy a faint southern constellation (the Clock), between Hydrus and Eridanus.
– ORIGIN Latin.

horology /hɒˈrɒlədʒi/ ▸ noun [mass noun] **1** the study and measurement of time.
2 the art of making clocks and watches.
– DERIVATIVES **horological** adjective, **horologist** noun.
– ORIGIN early 19th cent.: from Greek *hōra* 'time' + -LOGY.

horopter /hɒˈrɒptə/ ▸ noun Optics a line or surface containing all those points in space of which images fall on corresponding points of the retinas of the two eyes.
– ORIGIN early 18th cent.: from Greek *horos* 'limit' + *optēr* 'person who looks'.

horoscope ▸ noun Astrology a forecast of a person's future, typically including a delineation of character and circumstances, based on the relative positions of the stars and planets at the time of that person's birth. ■ a short forecast for people born under a particular sign, especially as published in a newspaper or magazine. ■ a birth chart (see CHART).
– DERIVATIVES **horoscopic** /-ˈskɒpɪk/ adjective, **horoscopy** /hɒˈrɒskəpi/ noun.
– ORIGIN Old English: via Latin from Greek *hōroskopos*, from *hōra* 'time' + *skopos* 'observer'.

horrendous /hɒˈrɛndəs/ ▸ adjective extremely unpleasant, horrifying, or terrible: *she suffered horrendous injuries*.
– DERIVATIVES **horrendously** adverb.
– ORIGIN mid 17th cent.: from Latin *horrendus* (gerundive of *horrere* '(of hair) stand on end') + -OUS.

horrent /ˈhɒr(ə)nt/ ▸ adjective archaic **1** (of a person's hair) standing on end.
2 feeling or expressing horror: *a horrent cry*.
– ORIGIN mid 17th cent.: from Latin *horrent-* '(of hair) standing on end', from the verb *horrere*.

horrible ▸ adjective causing or likely to cause horror; shocking: *a horrible massacre*. ■ informal very unpleasant: *the tea tasted horrible*.
– DERIVATIVES **horribleness** noun, **horribly** adverb [as submodifier] *the plan had gone horribly wrong*.
– ORIGIN Middle English: via Old French from Latin *horribilis*, from *horrere* 'tremble, shudder' (see HORRID).

horrid ▸ adjective **1** causing horror: *a horrid nightmare*. ■ informal very unpleasant: *the teachers at school were horrid* | *a horrid brown colour*.
2 archaic rough; bristling.
– DERIVATIVES **horridly** adverb, **horridness** noun.
– ORIGIN late 16th cent. (in the sense 'rough, bristling'): from Latin *horridus*, from *horrere* 'tremble, shudder, (of hair) stand on end'.

horrific ▸ adjective causing horror: *horrific injuries*.
– DERIVATIVES **horrifically** adverb.
– ORIGIN mid 17th cent.: from Latin *horrificus*, from *horrere* 'tremble, shudder' (see HORRID).

horrify ▸ verb (**horrifies**, **horrifying**, **horrified**) [with obj.] fill with horror; shock greatly: *they were horrified by the very idea* | (as adj. **horrified**) *the horrified spectators* | (as adj. **horrifying**) *a horrifying incident*.
– DERIVATIVES **horrification** noun, **horrifiedly** adverb, **horrifyingly** adverb [as submodifier] *horrifyingly flimsy boats*.
– ORIGIN late 18th cent.: from Latin *horrificare*, from *horrificus* (see HORRIFIC).

horripilation /hɒˌrɪpɪˈleɪʃ(ə)n/ ▸ noun [mass noun] literary the erection of hairs on the skin due to cold, fear, or excitement.
– DERIVATIVES **horripilate** verb.
– ORIGIN mid 17th cent.: from late Latin *horripilatio(n-)*, from Latin *horrere* 'stand on end' (see HORRID) + *pilus* 'hair'.

horror ▸ noun **1** [mass noun] an intense feeling of fear, shock, or disgust: *children screamed in horror*. ■ a thing causing a feeling of horror: *photographs showed the horror of the tragedy* | [count noun] *the horrors of civil war*. ■ a literary or film genre concerned with arousing feelings of horror: [as modifier] *a horror film*. ■ intense dismay: *to her horror she found that a thief had stolen the machine*. ■ [as exclamation] (**horrors**) chiefly humorous used to express dismay: *horrors, two buttons were missing!* ■ [in sing.] intense dislike: *many have **a horror of** consulting a dictionary*. ■ (**the horrors**) an attack of extreme nervousness or anxiety: *the mere thought of it gives me the horrors*.
2 informal a bad or mischievous person, especially a child: *that little horror Zach was around*.
– ORIGIN Middle English: via Old French from Latin *horror*, from *horrere* 'tremble, shudder' (see HORRID).

horror-struck (also **horror-stricken**) ▸ adjective briefly paralysed with horror or shock.

horror vacui /ˌhɒrə ˈvakjuːʌɪ/ ▸ noun [in sing.] a fear or dislike of leaving empty spaces, especially in an artistic composition.
– ORIGIN modern Latin, 'horror of a vacuum'.

Horsa see HENGIST AND HORSA.

hors concours /ˌɔː kɔ̃ˈkʊə/ ▸ adjective **1** engaged in a contest but not competing for a prize.
2 literary unrivalled; unequalled.
– ORIGIN French, literally 'out of the competition'.

hors de combat /ˌɔː də ˈkɔ̃bɑː/ ▸ adjective out of action due to injury or damage: *their pilots had been rendered temporarily hors de combat*.
– ORIGIN French, literally 'out of the fight'.

hors d'oeuvre /ɔː ˈdəːv, ˈdəːvr(ə)/ ▸ noun (pl. **same** or **hors d'oeuvres** pronunc. **same** or /ˈdəːvz/) a small savoury dish, typically one served as an appetizer.
– ORIGIN French, literally 'outside the work'.

horse ▸ noun **1** a solid-hoofed plant-eating domesticated mammal with a flowing mane and tail, used for riding, racing, and to carry and pull loads. ● *Equus caballus*, family Equidae (**the horse family**), descended from the wild Przewalski's horse. The horse family also includes the asses and zebras.
■ an adult male horse; a stallion or gelding. ■ a wild mammal of the horse family. ■ [treated as sing. or pl.] cavalry: *forty horse and sixty foot*.
2 a frame or structure on which something is mounted or supported, especially a sawhorse.
■ Nautical a horizontal bar, rail, or rope in the rigging of a sailing ship. ■ short for VAULTING HORSE.
3 informal a unit of horsepower: *a 63-horse engine*.
4 [mass noun] informal heroin.
5 Mining an obstruction in a vein.
▸ verb [with obj.] provide (a person or vehicle) with a horse or horses.
– PHRASES **don't change horses in midstream** proverb choose a sensible moment to change your mind. **frighten the horses** [usu. with negative] do something likely to cause public outrage or offence: *David's views would not have frightened the horses*. **from the horse's mouth** (of information) from the person directly concerned or another authoritative source. **horses for courses** Brit. proverb different people are suited to different things. **you can lead** (or **take**) **a horse to water but you can't make him drink** proverb you can give someone an opportunity, but you can't force them to take it.
– PHRASAL VERBS **horse around** (or **about**) informal fool about: *they were talking silly and horsing around*.
– DERIVATIVES **horse-like** adjective.
– ORIGIN Old English *hors*, of Germanic origin; related to Dutch *ros* and German *Ross*.

horse-and-buggy ▸ adjective [attrib.] N. Amer. informal old-fashioned: *horse-and-buggy technology*.

horseback ▸ adjective & adverb mounted on a horse: [as adj.] *a horseback parade* | [as adv.] *they rode horseback along the trail*.
– PHRASES **on horseback** mounted on a horse.

horsebean ▸ noun a field bean of a variety with relatively large seeds, used for feeding stock.

horse-block ▸ noun archaic a mounting block.

horsebox ▸ noun Brit. a vehicle or trailer equipped with a compartment or container for transporting one or more horses.

horse brass ▸ noun see BRASS.

horse chestnut ▸ noun a deciduous tree with large leaves of five leaflets, conspicuous sticky winter buds, and upright conical clusters of white, pink, or red flowers. It bears nuts (conkers) enclosed in a fleshy case. ● Genus *Aesculus*, family Hippocastanaceae: several species, in particular *A. hippocastanum*, native east of the Balkans and widely planted.
■ another term for CONKER.
– ORIGIN late 16th cent.: translating (now obsolete) botanical Latin *Castanea equina*; its fruit is said to have been an Eastern remedy for chest diseases in horses.

horse-coper ▸ noun another term for COPER[1].

horse-drawn ▸ adjective (of a vehicle) pulled by a horse or horses: *a horse-drawn carriage*.

horseflesh ▸ noun [mass noun] horses considered collectively. ■ the flesh of a horse, especially when used as food.

horse float ▸ noun Austral./NZ a vehicle for transporting one or more horses.

horsefly ▸ noun (pl. **horseflies**) a stoutly built fly, the female of which is a bloodsucker and inflicts painful bites on horses, humans, and other large mammals. ● Family Tabanidae: numerous species, in particular the common European *Haematopota pluvialis*.

Horse Guards ▸ plural noun (in the UK) the mounted squadrons provided from the Household Cavalry for ceremonial duties.

horsehair ▸ noun [mass noun] hair from the mane or tail of a horse, typically used in furniture for padding.

horsehair worm ▸ noun a long slender worm related to the nematodes, the larvae being parasites of arthropods and the adults living in water or damp soil. ● Phylum Nematomorpha: two classes.

Horsehead Nebula Astronomy a dust nebula in the shape of a horse's head, forming a dark silhouette against a bright emission nebula in Orion.

horse latitudes ▸ plural noun a belt of calm air and sea occurring in both the northern and southern hemispheres between the trade winds and the westerlies.
– ORIGIN late 18th cent.: origin uncertain; perhaps from the fact that becalmed sailing ships on long journeys were said to have thrown horses overboard to conserve water for the crew.

horse laugh ▸ noun a loud, coarse laugh.

horseleech ▸ noun a large predatory leech of freshwater and terrestrial habitats which feeds on carrion and small invertebrates. ● Genus *Haemopis*, family Hirudidae.

horseless ▸ adjective [attrib.] (of a vehicle) not drawn by a horse or horses: *a horseless cabriolet*.

horseless carriage ▸ noun archaic or humorous a car.

horse mackerel ▸ noun a shoaling edible fish of the eastern Atlantic, which is commercially fished in southern African waters. Also called SCAD. ● *Trachurus trachurus*, family Carangidae.

horseman ▸ noun (pl. **horsemen**) a rider on horseback, especially a skilled one.
– PHRASES **the Four Horsemen of the Apocalypse** see APOCALYPSE.

horsemanship ▸ noun [mass noun] the art or practice of riding on horseback.

horsemeat ▸ noun [mass noun] the flesh of a horse as food.

horsemint ▶ noun a tall coarse kind of mint. ● Genera *Mentha* and *Monarda*, family Labiatae: several species and hybrids.
– ORIGIN Middle English: from HORSE (often used in the names of plants to denote a coarse variety) + MINT[1].

horse mushroom ▶ noun a large edible mushroom with a creamy-white cap and pinkish-grey gills, found in grassland in Eurasia and North America. ● *Agaricus arvensis*, family Agaricaceae, class Hymenomycetes.

horse mussel ▶ noun a large marine mussel which may occur in very large populations in food-rich waters. ● Genus *Modiolus*, family Mytilidae.

Horsens /ˈhɔːs(ə)nz/ a port on the east coast of Denmark, situated at the head of Horsens Fjord; pop. 52,518 (2009).

horse opera ▶ noun N. Amer. informal a western film.

horse pistol ▶ noun historical a large pistol carried at the pommel of the saddle by a rider.

horseplay ▶ noun [mass noun] rough, boisterous play: *this ridiculous horseplay has gone far enough.*

horseplayer ▶ noun N. Amer. a person who regularly bets on horse races.

horsepower (abbrev.: **h.p.**) ▶ noun (pl. **same**) an imperial unit of power equal to 550 foot-pounds per second (about 750 watts). ■ the power of an engine measured in terms of this: *a strong 140-horsepower engine.* See also BRAKE HORSEPOWER.

horse racing ▶ noun [mass noun] the sport in which horses and their riders take part in races, either on a flat course or over hurdles or fences, typically with substantial betting on the outcome.

horseradish ▶ noun a European plant of the cabbage family, with long dock-like leaves, grown for its pungent edible root. ● *Armoracia rusticana*, family Cruciferae. ■ [mass noun] horseradish root, scraped or grated as a condiment and often made into a sauce.

horse sense ▶ noun [mass noun] informal common sense.

horseshit ▶ noun [mass noun] vulgar slang, chiefly N. Amer. nonsense.

horseshoe ▶ noun a shoe for a horse formed of a narrow band of iron in the form of an extended circular arc and secured to the hoof with nails. ■ a shoe of this kind or a representation of one, regarded as bringing good luck. ■ something resembling a horseshoe in shape: [as modifier] *a horseshoe bend.* ■ (**horseshoes**) [treated as sing.] chiefly N. Amer. a game resembling quoits in which horseshoes are thrown at a peg.

horseshoe bat ▶ noun an insectivorous Old World bat with a horseshoe-shaped ridge on the nose. ● Family Rhinolophidae and genus *Rhinolophus*: numerous species.

horseshoe crab ▶ noun a large marine arthropod with a domed horseshoe-shaped shell, a long tail spine, and ten legs, little changed since the Devonian. ● Class Merostomata, subphylum Chelicerata: four species, in particular the North American *Limulus polyphemus*.

horseshoe worm ▶ noun a worm-like tube-dwelling marine animal with a horseshoe-shaped ring of ciliated tentacles (lophophore) around the mouth, extended for filter-feeding. ● Phylum Phoronida.

horse's neck ▶ noun informal a drink consisting of ginger ale, a twist of lemon peel, and spirits, typically brandy.

horsetail ▶ noun a plant with a hollow jointed stem which bears whorls of narrow leaves, producing spores in cones at the tips of the shoots. ● Genus *Equisetum*, the only surviving genus of the family Equisetaceae and class Sphenopsida, division Pteridophyta.

horse-trading ▶ noun [mass noun] the buying and selling of horses. ■ hard and shrewd bargaining, especially in politics.
– DERIVATIVES **horse-trade** verb, **horse-trader** noun.

horse walker ▶ noun a mechanically rotating arm or cage to which horses are tied in order to exercise.

horsewhip ▶ noun a long whip used for driving and controlling horses.
▶ verb (**horsewhips, horsewhipping, horsewhipped**) [with obj.] beat (a person or animal) with a horsewhip.

horsewoman ▶ noun (pl. **horsewomen**) a woman who rides on horseback, especially a skilled one.

horsey (also **horsy**) ▶ adjective (**horsier, horsiest**) **1** of or resembling a horse: *she had a long horsey face.* **2** concerned with or devoted to horses or horse racing: *the horsey fraternity.*
– DERIVATIVES **horsily** adverb, **horsiness** noun.

horst /hɔːst/ ▶ noun Geology a raised elongated block of the earth's crust lying between two faults.
– ORIGIN late 19th cent.: from German *Horst* 'heap'.

Horst Wessel Song /hɔːst ˈvɛs(ə)l/, German /ˌhɔrst ˈvɛsl/ the official song of the Nazi Party in Germany. The words were written by Horst Wessel (1907–30), a member of Hitler's Storm Troops killed by political enemies and regarded as a Nazi martyr.

Horta /ˈɔːtə/, French /ɔʀta/, Victor (1861–1947), Belgian architect. He was a leading figure in art nouveau architecture and his work was notable for its innovative use of iron and glass.

hortatory /ˈhɔːtət(ə)ri/ ▶ adjective tending or aiming to exhort: *a series of hortatory epistles.*
– DERIVATIVES **hortative** adjective.
– ORIGIN late 16th cent.: from Latin *hortatorius*, from *hortari* 'exhort'.

hortensia /hɔːˈtɛnsɪə/ ▶ noun a hydrangea of a group of varieties that have large rounded flower heads composed chiefly of sterile florets. Compare with LACECAP. ● *Hydrangea macrophylla* vars., family Hydrangeaceae.
– ORIGIN late 18th cent.: modern Latin, named after *Hortense*, wife of J.-A. Lepaute (1720–*c*.87), French clockmaker.

horticulture /ˈhɔːtɪˌkʌltʃə/ ▶ noun [mass noun] the art or practice of garden cultivation and management.
– DERIVATIVES **horticultural** adjective, **horticulturalist** noun, **horticulturist** noun.
– ORIGIN late 17th cent.: from Latin *hortus* 'garden', on the pattern of *agriculture*.

hortus siccus /ˌhɔːtəs ˈsɪkəs/ ▶ noun (pl. **horti sicci** /ˌhɔːtʌɪ ˈsɪkʌɪ, -tiː, -kiː/) an arranged collection of dried plants; a herbarium.
– ORIGIN Latin, literally 'dry garden'.

Horus /ˈhɔːrəs/ Egyptian Mythology a god regarded as the protector of the monarchy, and typically represented as a falcon-headed man. He assumed various aspects: in the myth of Isis and Osiris he was the posthumous son of the latter, whose murder he avenged.

Hos. ▶ abbreviation Hosea (in biblical references).

hosanna (also **hosannah**) ▶ exclamation (especially in biblical, Judaic, and Christian use) used to express adoration, praise, or joy.
▶ noun an expression of adoration, praise, or joy.
– ORIGIN Old English, via late Latin from Greek *hōsanna*, from Rabbinical Hebrew *hōšaʻnā*, abbreviation of biblical *hōšīʻā-nnā* 'save, we pray' (Ps. 118:25).

Hosay /həʊˈzeɪ/ ▶ noun an annual festival held by the Shiite Muslim community in the West Indies, commemorating the death of Husayn, grandson of Muhammad.
– ORIGIN representing a pronunciation of *Husayn*.

hose ▶ noun **1** a flexible tube conveying water, used chiefly for watering plants and in firefighting. **2** [treated as pl.] stockings, socks, and tights (especially in commercial use): *her hose had been laddered.* ■ historical breeches: *Elizabethan doublet and hose.*
▶ verb [with obj.] water or spray with a hose: *he was hosing down the driveway.*
– ORIGIN Old English *hosa*, of Germanic origin; related to Dutch *hoos* 'stocking, water hose' and German *Hosen* 'trousers'. Originally singular, the term denoted a covering for the leg, sometimes including the foot but sometimes reaching only to the ankle.

Hosea /həʊˈzɪə/ a Hebrew minor prophet of the 8th century BC. ■ a book of the Bible containing Hosea's prophecies.

hose-in-hose ▶ adjective (especially of a polyanthus or other primula) having petal-like sepals, and so appearing to have one corolla within another.

hosel /ˈhəʊz(ə)l/ ▶ noun the socket of a golf club head which the shaft fits into.
– ORIGIN late 16th cent.: diminutive of HOSE, in the dialect sense 'sheathing'.

hosepipe ▶ noun British term for HOSE (sense 1 of the noun).

hoser ▶ noun Canadian informal a foolish or uncultivated person.
– ORIGIN 1980s: of uncertain origin; popularized by characters on the Canadian television show *SCTV* (1980–2).

hosier /ˈhəʊzɪə/ ▶ noun a manufacturer or seller of hosiery.

hosiery ▶ noun [mass noun] stockings, socks, and tights collectively.

hospice ▶ noun a home providing care for the sick or terminally ill. ■ archaic a lodging for travellers, especially one run by a religious order.
– ORIGIN early 19th cent.: from French, from Latin *hospitium*, from *hospes, hospit-* (see HOST[1]).

hospitable /hɒˈspɪtəb(ə)l, ˈhɒspɪt-/ ▶ adjective friendly and welcoming to visitors or guests: *two friendly, hospitable brothers run the hotel.* ■ (of an environment) pleasant and favourable for living in: *one of the least hospitable places in North America.*
– DERIVATIVES **hospitably** adverb.
– ORIGIN late 16th cent.: from French, from obsolete *hospiter* 'receive a guest', from medieval Latin *hospitare* 'entertain', from *hospes, hospit-* (see HOST[1]).

hospital ▶ noun **1** an institution providing medical and surgical treatment and nursing care for sick or injured people. **2** historical a hospice, especially one run by the Knights Hospitaller. **3** [in names] Brit. a charitable institution for the education of the young: *Christ's Hospital.*
– ORIGIN Middle English (in sense 2): via Old French from medieval Latin *hospitale*, neuter of Latin *hospitalis* 'hospitable', from *hospes, hospit-* (see HOST[1]).

hospital ball ▶ noun another term for HOSPITAL PASS.

hospital corners ▶ plural noun overlapping folds used to tuck sheets neatly and securely under the mattress at the corners, in a manner typically used by nurses.

hospitaler ▶ noun US spelling of HOSPITALLER.

hospital fever ▶ noun [mass noun] historical louse-borne typhus acquired in overcrowded, insanitary conditions in an old-fashioned hospital.

hospitalism ▶ noun [mass noun] the adverse effects of a prolonged stay in hospital, such as developmental retardation in children.

hospitality ▶ noun [mass noun] the friendly and generous reception and entertainment of guests, visitors, or strangers. ■ [as modifier] relating to or denoting the business of entertaining clients, conference delegates, or other official visitors: *the BBC's hospitality suite.*
– ORIGIN late Middle English: from Old French *hospitalite*, from Latin *hospitalitas*, from *hospitalis* 'hospitable' (see HOSPITAL).

hospitalize (also **hospitalise**) ▶ verb [with obj.] admit or cause (someone) to be admitted to hospital for treatment: *Casey was hospitalized for chest pains.*
– DERIVATIVES **hospitalization** noun.

hospitaller /ˈhɒspɪt(ə)lə/ (US **hospitaler**) ▶ noun a member of a charitable religious order, originally the Knights Hospitaller.
– ORIGIN Middle English: from Old French *hospitalier*, from medieval Latin *hospitalarius*, from *hospitale* (see HOSPITAL).

hospital pass (also **hospital ball**) ▶ noun (in football) a pass to a player likely to be tackled heavily as soon as the ball is received.

hospital ship ▶ noun a ship which functions as a hospital, especially to receive or take home sick or wounded military personnel.

hospital trust ▶ noun (in the UK) a National Health Service hospital which has opted to withdraw from local authority control and be managed by a trust instead.

hospodar /ˈhɒspədɑː/ ▶ noun historical a governor of Wallachia and Moldavia under the Ottoman Porte.
– ORIGIN from Romanian, from Ukrainian *hospodar*; related to Russian *gospodar'*, from *gospod'* 'lord'.

host[1] ▶ noun **1** a person who receives or entertains other people as guests. ■ a person, place, or organization that holds an event to which others are invited: *Innsbruck once* ***played host to*** *the Winter Olympics.* ■ the presenter of a television or radio programme. **2** Biology an animal or plant on or in which a parasite or commensal organism lives. ■ (also **host cell**) a living cell in which a virus multiplies. **3** a person or animal that has received transplanted tissue or a transplanted organ. **4** (also **host computer**) a computer which mediates multiple access to databases mounted on it or provides other services to a network. **5** an area in which particular plants or animals are found: *Australia is* ***host to*** *some of the world's most dangerous animals.*
▶ verb [with obj.] **1** act as host at (an event) or for (a television or radio programme). **2** store (a website or other electronic data) on a computer connected to the Internet: *Columbia University currently hosts some 400 websites.*

H

– PHRASES **mine host** humorous the landlord or landlady of a pub.
– ORIGIN Middle English: from Old French *hoste*, from Latin *hospes, hospit-* 'host, guest'.

host² ▶ noun **1** (**a host/hosts of**) a large number of people or things: *a host of memories rushed into her mind.*
2 archaic an army.
3 (**the host** or **the heavenly host**) (in biblical use) the angels regarded collectively. See also LORD OF HOSTS at LORD. ■ the sun, moon, and stars: *the starry host of heaven.*
– ORIGIN Middle English: from Old French *ost, hoost*, from Latin *hostis* 'stranger, enemy' (in medieval Latin 'army').

host³ ▶ noun (**the Host**) the bread consecrated in the Eucharist: *the elevation of the Host.*
– ORIGIN Middle English: from Old French *hoiste*, from Latin *hostia* 'victim'.

hosta /ˈhɒstə/ ▶ noun an East Asian plant cultivated in the West for its shade-tolerant foliage and loose clusters of tubular mauve or white flowers. ● Genus *Hosta* (formerly *Funkia*), family Liliaceae.
– ORIGIN modern Latin, named after Nicolaus T. *Host* (1761–1834), Austrian physician.

H

hostage ▶ noun a person seized or held as security for the fulfilment of a condition: *they were* ***held hostage*** *by armed rebels.*
– PHRASES **hostage to fortune** an undertaking or remark seen as unwise because it invites trouble or could prove difficult to live up to.
– ORIGIN Middle English: from Old French, based on late Latin *obsidatus* 'the state of being a hostage' (the earliest sense in English), from Latin *obses, obsid-* 'hostage'.

hostel ▶ noun an establishment which provides inexpensive food and lodging for a specific group of people, such as students, workers, or travellers. ■ short for YOUTH HOSTEL. ■ archaic an inn providing accommodation.
– ORIGIN Middle English (in the general sense 'lodging, place to stay') : from Old French, from medieval Latin *hospitale* (see HOSPITAL).

hostelling (US **hosteling**) ▶ noun [mass noun] the practice of staying in youth hostels when travelling.
– DERIVATIVES **hosteller** noun.

hostelry ▶ noun (pl. **hostelries**) archaic or humorous an inn or pub.
– ORIGIN late Middle English: from Old French *hostelerie* from *hostelier* 'innkeeper', from *hostel* (see HOSTEL).

hostess ▶ noun a woman who receives or entertains guests. ■ a woman employed to welcome and entertain customers at a nightclub or bar. ■ a stewardess on an aircraft, train, etc. ■ a woman who presents a television or radio programme: *a game-show hostess.*
– ORIGIN Middle English: from Old French *(h)ostesse*, feminine of *(h)oste* (see HOST¹).

hostess trolley ▶ noun a trolley for holding food to be served at table.

hostile ▶ adjective showing or feeling opposition or dislike; unfriendly: *a hostile audience | he wrote a ferociously hostile attack.* ■ of or belonging to a military enemy: *hostile aircraft.* ■ [predic.] opposed: *people are very* ***hostile to*** *the idea.* ■ (of a takeover bid) opposed by the company to be bought.
– DERIVATIVES **hostilely** adverb.
– ORIGIN late 16th cent.: from French, or from Latin *hostilis*, from *hostis* 'stranger, enemy'.

hostile witness ▶ noun Law a witness who is antagonistic to the party calling them and, being unwilling to tell the truth, may have to be asked leading questions.

hostility ▶ noun (pl. **hostilities**) [mass noun] hostile behaviour; unfriendliness or opposition: *their hostility to all outsiders.* ■ (**hostilities**) acts of warfare: *he called for an immediate cessation of hostilities.*
– ORIGIN late Middle English: from French *hostilité* or late Latin *hostilitas*, from Latin *hostilis* (see HOSTILE).

hostler ▶ noun variant spelling of OSTLER.

hot ▶ adjective (**hotter, hottest**) **1** having a high degree of heat or a high temperature: *it was hot inside the hall | a hot day.* ■ feeling or producing an uncomfortable sensation of heat: *she felt hot and her throat was parched.* ■ (of food or drink) prepared by heating and served without cooling. ■ informal (of an electric circuit) live or at a high voltage. ■ informal radioactive.
2 (of food) containing or consisting of pungent spices or peppers which produce a burning sensation when tasted: *a very hot dish cooked with green chilli.*
3 filled with passionate excitement, anger, or other strong emotion: *the idea had been nurtured in his hot imagination | her reply came boiling out of her, hot with rage.* ■ lustful or erotic: *steamy bed scenes which may be too hot for young fans.* ■ (of popular music) strongly rhythmical and excitingly played: *hot salsa and lambada dancing.*
4 informal involving much activity, debate, or interest: *the environment has become a very hot issue.* ■ (of news) fresh and of great interest: *have I got some hot gossip for you!* ■ currently popular, fashionable, or in demand: *they know the hottest dance moves.* ■ Hunting (of the scent) fresh and strong, indicating that the quarry has passed recently. ■ [predic.] (in children's games) very close to finding or guessing something.
5 informal very knowledgeable or skilful: *Tony is very* ***hot on*** *local history.* ■ [predic.] [usu. with negative] good: *this is not so hot for business.* ■ (**hot on**) regarding (something) as very important; strict about: *local customs officers are hot on confiscations.*
6 informal difficult to deal with: *he found my story simply too hot to handle.* ■ (of goods) stolen and difficult to dispose of because easily identifiable. ■ (of a person) wanted by the police.
▶ verb (**hots, hotting, hotted**) (**hot something up** or **hot up**) Brit. informal make or become hot: [with obj.] *he hotted up the flask.* ■ become or make more lively or exciting: [no obj.] *the championship contest hotted up.*
– PHRASES **go hot and cold** experience a sudden feeling of fear or shock. **have the hots for** informal be sexually attracted to. **hot and bothered** see BOTHER. **hot and heavy** N. Amer. informal intense; with intensity. **hot on the heels of** following closely: *the gardener burst in with Mrs Cartwright hot on his heels.* **hot to trot** informal ready and eager to engage in an activity. **hot under the collar** informal angry, resentful, or embarrassed. **in hot pursuit** following closely and eagerly. **in hot water** informal in trouble or disgrace: *he* ***landed in hot water*** *for an alleged V-sign to the fans | whenever we spoke out, we* ***got into hot water.*** **make it** (or **things**) **hot for** informal stir up trouble for.
– DERIVATIVES **hotness** noun, **hottish** adjective.
– ORIGIN Old English *hāt*, of Germanic origin; related to Dutch *heet* and German *heiss*.

hot air ▶ noun [mass noun] informal empty talk that is intended to impress: *they dismissed the theory as a load of hot air.*

hot-air balloon ▶ noun see BALLOON (sense 2 of the noun).

hot-air gun ▶ noun see AIRGUN (sense 2).

hotbed ▶ noun **1** an environment promoting the growth of something, especially something unwelcome: *the country was* ***a hotbed of*** *revolt and dissension.*
2 a bed of earth heated by fermenting manure, for raising or forcing plants.

hot-blooded ▶ adjective lustful; passionate: *hot-blooded Latin lovers.*

hot button ▶ noun [often as modifier] N. Amer. informal a topic or issue that is highly charged emotionally or politically: *the hot-button issue of nuclear waste disposal.*

hot cathode ▶ noun a cathode designed to be heated in order to emit electrons.

hotchpot ▶ noun [mass noun] Law the reunion and blending together of properties for the purpose of securing equal division, especially of the property of an intestate parent.
– ORIGIN late Middle English (meaning 'hotchpotch'): from Anglo-Norman French and Old French *hochepot*, from *hocher* 'to shake' (probably of Low German origin) + *pot* 'pot'.

hotchpotch (N. Amer. **hodgepodge**) ▶ noun **1** [in sing.] a confused mixture: ***a hotchpotch of*** *uncoordinated services.*
2 a mutton stew with mixed vegetables.
– ORIGIN late Middle English: variant of HOTCHPOT.

hot cross bun ▶ noun a bun marked with a cross and containing dried fruit, traditionally eaten on Good Friday.

hot dark matter ▶ noun see DARK MATTER.

hot-desking ▶ noun [mass noun] the practice in an office of allocating desks to workers when they are required or on a rota system, rather than giving each worker their own desk.

hot dog ▶ noun **1** a hot sausage served in a long, soft roll.
2 N. Amer. informal a person, especially a skier or surfer, who performs stunts or tricks.
▶ exclamation N. Amer. informal used to express delight or enthusiastic approval.
▶ verb (**hotdog**) (**hotdogs, hotdogging, hotdogged**) [no obj.] N. Amer. informal perform stunts or tricks: *he chastised the dancers who'd been hotdogging.*
– DERIVATIVES **hotdogger** noun.

hotel ▶ noun **1** an establishment providing accommodation, meals, and other services for travellers and tourists, by the night. ■ chiefly Austral./NZ a pub.
2 a code word representing the letter H, used in radio communication.
– ORIGIN mid 18th cent.: from French *hôtel*, from Old French *hostel* (see HOSTEL).

> **USAGE** The normal pronunciation of **hotel** sounds the **h-**, which means that the preceding indefinite article is **a**. However, the older pronunciation without the **h-** is still occasionally heard, and leads to the preceding indefinite article being **an** rather than **a**. For a discussion of this, see USAGE at AN.

hotelier ▶ noun a person who owns or manages a hotel.
– ORIGIN early 20th cent.: from French *hôtelier*, from Old French *hostelier* 'innkeeper' (see HOSTELRY).

hotelling ▶ noun [mass noun] the short-term provision of office space to a temporary worker, or the short-term letting of surplus office space to employees from other companies.

hot favourite ▶ noun a competitor who is strongly fancied to win a race or other contest.

hot flush (N. Amer. also **hot flash**) ▶ noun Brit. a sudden feeling of feverish heat, typically as a symptom of the menopause.

hotfoot ▶ adverb in eager haste: *he rushed hotfoot to the planning office to object.*
▶ verb (**hotfoot it**) [with adverbial of direction] walk or run quickly and eagerly: *we hotfooted it after him.*

hot gospel ▶ noun [mass noun] informal the fervent propounding of religious beliefs; zealous evangelism.
– DERIVATIVES **hot gospeller** noun.

hothead ▶ noun a person who is impetuous or easily becomes angry and violent.

hot-headed ▶ adjective having an impetuous or quick-tempered nature: *a hot-headed youth.*
– DERIVATIVES **hot-headedly** adverb, **hot-headedness** noun.

hothouse ▶ noun a heated greenhouse in which plants that need protection from cold weather are grown. ■ an environment that encourages rapid growth or development, especially in a stifling or intense way: [as modifier] *the hothouse atmosphere of the college.*
▶ verb [with obj.] educate or teach (a child) to a high level at an earlier age than is usual.

hot key ▶ noun Computing a key or a combination of keys providing quick access to a particular function within a program.

hotline ▶ noun a direct telephone line set up for a specific purpose, especially for use in emergencies or for communication between heads of government.

hotlink Computing ▶ noun a connection between documents or applications which enables material from one source to be incorporated into another, in particular a facility which automatically updates material in a document when an alteration is made to the document from which it originated. ■ a hypertext link.
▶ verb [with obj.] connect (two documents) by means of a hotlink.

hotlist ▶ noun a personal list of favourite or most frequently accessed websites compiled by an Internet user.

hotly ▶ adverb in a passionate, intense, or angry way: *the rumours were hotly denied | hotly debated issues.*

hot metal ▶ noun a typesetting technique in which type is newly made each time from molten metal, cast by a composing machine.

hot money ▶ noun [mass noun] capital which is frequently transferred between financial institutions in an attempt to maximize interest or capital gain.

hot pants ▶ plural noun very tight, brief women's shorts, worn as a fashion garment.

hotplate ▶ **noun** a flat heated surface (or a set of these), typically metal or ceramic, used for cooking food or keeping it hot.

hotpot ▶ **noun** Brit. a casserole of meat and vegetables, typically with a topping of sliced potato.

hot potato ▶ **noun** informal a controversial issue or situation which is awkward to deal with: *dog registration has become a political hot potato.*

hot press ▶ **noun 1** a device in which paper or cloth is pressed between glazed boards and hot metal plates in order to produce a smooth or glossy surface. ■ a similar apparatus used in making plywood.
2 Irish a cupboard used for airing clothes, linen, etc.
▶ **verb** (**hot-press**) [with obj.] press (paper, cloth, etc.) with a hot press.

hot rod ▶ **noun** a motor vehicle that has been specially modified to give it extra power and speed.
▶ **verb** (**hot-rod**) (**hot-rods**, **hot-rodding**, **hot-rodded**) **1** [with obj.] modify (a vehicle or other device) to make it faster or more powerful.
2 [no obj.] drive a hot rod.
– DERIVATIVES **hot-rodder** noun.

hot seat ▶ **noun** (**the hot seat**) informal **1** the position of carrying full responsibility for something important: *it's been a bad week for the men in the hot seat.*
2 N. Amer. the electric chair.

hot shoe ▶ **noun** Photography a socket on a camera with direct electrical contacts for an attached flashgun or other accessory.

hot-short ▶ **adjective** (of a metal) brittle when hot.
– ORIGIN late 18th cent.: from HOT + *short* suggested by the earlier *red-short*, from Swedish *rödskör* (from *röd* 'red' + *skör* 'brittle').

hotshot ▶ **noun** informal an important or exceptionally able person.

hot spot ▶ **noun 1** a small area with a relatively high temperature in comparison to its surroundings. ■ Geology an area of volcanic activity. ■ a place of significant activity or danger: *a hot spot of commerce.*
2 (also **hotspot**) an area on a computer screen which can be clicked to activate a function, especially an image or piece of text acting as a hyperlink. ■ a public place where a wireless signal is made available so that the Internet can be accessed.

hot spring ▶ **noun** a spring of naturally hot water, typically heated by subterranean volcanic activity.

Hotspur /ˈhɒtspəː/ the nickname of Sir Henry Percy (see PERCY).

hotspur /ˈhɒtspəː, -spə/ ▶ **noun** archaic a rash, impetuous person.
– ORIGIN late Middle English: literally 'a person whose spur is hot from rash or constant riding'.

hot-stove ▶ **adjective** [attrib.] N. Amer. denoting a discussion about a favourite sport carried on during the off season: *hot-stove speculation.*
– ORIGIN 1950s: by association with discussions conducted around a heater in the winter.

hot stuff ▶ **noun** [mass noun] informal a person or thing of outstanding quality or skill: *he's hot stuff at arithmetic.* ■ a sexually exciting person, film, book, etc.: *Jill was reputed to be hot stuff.*

hot-swap ▶ **verb** [with obj.] informal fit or replace (a computer part) with the power still connected.
– DERIVATIVES **hot-swappable** adjective.

hotsy-totsy ▶ **adjective** US informal **1** very pleasing or good: *hotsy-totsy rhythms thrill the air.*
2 US term for HOITY-TOITY.
– ORIGIN early 20th cent.: reduplication of HOT, a fanciful formation by Billie de Beck (died 1942), American cartoonist.

hot-tempered ▶ **adjective** easily angered; quick-tempered.

Hottentot /ˈhɒt(ə)ntɒt/ ▶ **noun & adjective** offensive used to refer to Khoikhoi peoples.
– ORIGIN Dutch, perhaps a repetitive formula in a Nama dancing song, transferred by Dutch sailors to the people themselves, or from German *hotterentotteren* 'stutter' (with reference to their language, in which clicking sounds are used).

USAGE The word **Hottentot** is first recorded in the late 17th century and was a name applied by white Europeans to the Khoikhoi. It is now regarded as offensive with reference to people and should always be avoided in favour of **Khoikhoi** or the names of the particular peoples. The only standard use for **Hottentot** in modern use is in the names of animals and plants.

Hottentot fig ▶ **noun** a succulent mat-forming plant with bright yellow or lilac daisy-like flowers and edible fruit. It is native to South Africa and frequently naturalized on coastal cliffs in Europe. ● *Carpobrotus* (formerly *Mesembryanthemum*) *edulis*, family Aizoaceae.

hot ticket ▶ **noun** informal a person or thing that is much in demand: *he's the current hot ticket on the hard-core hip-hop block* | [as modifier] *a hot-ticket invitation.*

hottie (also **hotty**) ▶ **noun** (pl. **hotties**) informal **1** Brit. a hot-water bottle.
2 a sexually attractive person, especially a young woman.

hotting ▶ **noun** [mass noun] Brit. informal joyriding in stolen high-performance cars, especially for elaborate and dangerous display.
– DERIVATIVES **hotter** noun.

hot tip ▶ **noun** informal a very reliable prediction or piece of inside information.

hot tub ▶ **noun** a large tub filled with hot aerated water used for recreation or physical therapy.

hot war ▶ **noun** a war with active military hostilities.

hot-water bottle (US also **hot-water bag**) ▶ **noun** a flat, oblong container, typically made of rubber, that is filled with hot water and used for warmth, especially for warming a bed.

hot-wire ▶ **verb** [with obj.] informal start the engine of (a vehicle) by bypassing the ignition system, typically in order to steal it.

houbara /huːˈbɑːrə/ (also **houbara bustard**) ▶ **noun** a bustard of arid open country and semi-desert, found from the Canary Islands to central Asia and threatened by hunting. ● *Chlamydotis undulata*, family Otidae.
– ORIGIN early 19th cent.: modern Latin, from Arabic *ḥubārā*.

Houdini /huːˈdiːni/, Harry (1874–1926), Hungarian-born American magician and escape artist; born *Erik Weisz*. In the early 1900s he became famous for his ability to escape from all kinds of bonds and containers, from prison cells to aerially suspended straitjackets. ■ [as noun] a person skilled at escaping: *you're a regular Houdini.* ■ an ingenious escape: *he will have to* **do a Houdini** *to escape from me.*

hough /hɒk/ Brit. ▶ **noun** variant spelling of HOCK[1] (sense 1). ■ a joint of meat consisting of the part extending from the hock some way up the leg.
▶ **verb** [with obj.] archaic disable (a person or animal) by cutting the hamstrings.
– ORIGIN Old English *hōh* 'heel', of Germanic origin; related to HEEL[1].

houmous ▶ **noun** variant spelling of HUMMUS.

hound ▶ **noun 1** a dog of a breed used for hunting, especially one able to track by scent. ■ [with modifier] a person eagerly seeking something: *he has a reputation as a publicity hound.* ■ informal, dated a despicable or contemptible man.
2 used in names of dogfishes, e.g. **nurse hound**, **smooth hound**.
▶ **verb** [with obj.] harass, persecute, or pursue relentlessly: *she was hounded by the Italian press* | *his opponents used the allegations to hound him out of office.*
– ORIGIN Old English *hund* (in the general sense 'dog'), of Germanic origin; related to Dutch *hond* and German *Hund*, from an Indo-European root shared by Greek *kuōn*, *kun-* 'dog'.

houndfish ▶ **noun** (pl. **same** or **houndfishes**) a large garfish of warm inshore waters, which leaps from the water and skitters over the surface when disturbed. ● Genus *Tylosaurus*, family Belonidae: several species.

hound's tongue ▶ **noun** a tall plant of the borage family, which bears long silky hairs, small purplish flowers, and tongue-shaped leaves, and has a mousy smell. ● *Cynoglossum officinale*, family Boraginaceae.

houndstooth ▶ **noun** a large check pattern with notched corners suggestive of a canine tooth, typically used in cloth for jackets and suits.

houngan /ˈhuːŋg(ə)n/ ▶ **noun** a voodoo priest.
– ORIGIN early 20th cent.: from Fon, from *hun*, a deity represented by a fetish, + *ga* 'chief'.

hour ▶ **noun 1** a period of time equal to a twenty-fourth part of a day and night and divided into 60 minutes: *an extra hour of daylight in the winter evenings* | *rates of pay were low, starting at £3.20 an hour* | [as modifier, usu. with preceding numeral] *a two-hour operation.* ■ a more indefinite period of time: *during the early hours of the morning.* ■ the distance travelled in one hour: *Ocean City is less than an hour away.*
2 a time of day specified as an exact number of hours from midnight or midday: *the clock in the sitting room struck the hour.* ■ (**hours**) [with preceding numeral] a time so specified on the twenty-four-hour clock: *the first bomb fell at 0051 hours.* ■ the time as formerly reckoned from sunrise: *it was about the ninth hour.*
3 a fixed period of time for an activity, such as work, use of a building, etc.: *the dinner hour* | *licensing hours* | *opening hours.* ■ a particular point in time: *I wondered if my last hour had come* | *you can't turn him away at this hour.*
4 (**hours**) (in the Western (Latin) Church) a short service of psalms and prayers to be said at a particular time of day, especially in religious communities.
5 Astronomy 15° of longitude or right ascension (one twenty-fourth part of a circle).
– PHRASES **all hours** most of the time, especially outside the time considered usual: *teenagers expect to be allowed to stay out to* **all hours.** **keep late** (or **regular**) **hours** get up and go to bed late (or at the same time) every day. **on the hour** at an exact hour, or at the beginning of each hour, of the day or night: *news bulletins all day on the hour.* **within the hour** after less than an hour: *his response came within the hour.*
– ORIGIN Middle English: from Anglo-Norman French *ure*, via Latin from Greek *hōra* 'season, hour'.

hourglass ▶ **noun** a timing device with two connected glass bulbs containing sand that takes an hour to pass from the upper to the lower bulb. ■ [as modifier] shaped like an hourglass: *her hourglass figure.*

hour hand ▶ **noun** the hand on a clock or watch which indicates the hour.

houri /ˈhʊəri/ ▶ **noun** (pl. **houris**) a beautiful young woman, especially one of the virgin companions of the faithful in the Muslim Paradise.
– ORIGIN mid 18th cent.: from French, from Persian *ḥūrī*, from Arabic *ḥūr*, plural of *'aḥwar* 'having eyes with a marked contrast of black and white'.

hourly ▶ **adjective 1** done or occurring every hour: *there is an hourly bus service.* ■ (with numeral or fraction) occurring at intervals measured in hours: *he received six hourly doses of morphine* | *trains run at half-hourly intervals.*
2 reckoned by the hour: *hourly rates.*
▶ **adverb 1** every hour: *sunscreens should be applied hourly* | *a train runs hourly from 7 a.m. to 8 p.m.* ■ (with numeral or fraction) at intervals measured in hours: *temperature should be recorded four-hourly.*
2 by the hour: *hourly paid workers.*
3 very frequently or continually: *her curiosity was mounting hourly.*

house ▶ **noun** /haʊs/ **1** a building for human habitation, especially one that consists of a ground floor and one or more upper storeys. ■ the people living in a house; a household: *make yourself scarce before you wake the whole house.* ■ a noble, royal, or wealthy family or lineage; a dynasty: *the power and prestige of the House of Stewart.* ■ chiefly Scottish a dwelling that is one of several in a building. ■ [with modifier] a building in which animals live or in which things are kept: *a hen house.*
2 a building in which people meet for a particular activity: *a house of prayer.* ■ a firm or institution: *a fashion house.* ■ (**the House**) Brit. informal the Stock Exchange. ■ a restaurant or inn: *help yourself to a drink, compliments of the house!* | [as modifier] *a carafe of house wine.* ■ dated a brothel. ■ a theatre: *a hundred musicians performed in front of a full house.* ■ Brit. a performance in a theatre or cinema: *tickets for the first house.*
3 a religious community that occupies a particular building: *the Cistercian house at Clairvaux.* ■ a residential building for pupils at a boarding school. ■ Brit. each of a number of groups into which pupils at a day school are divided for games or competition. ■ Brit. formal a college of a university.
4 a legislative or deliberative assembly: *the sixty-member National Council, the country's upper house.* ■ (**the House**) (in the UK) the House of Commons or Lords; (in the US) the House of Representatives. ■ used in formal debates that mimic the procedures of a legislative assembly: *a debate on the motion 'This house would legalize cannabis'.*
5 (also **house music**) [mass noun] a style of electronic dance music typically having sparse, repetitive vocals and a fast beat.
6 Astrology a twelfth division of the celestial sphere, based on the positions of the ascendant and mid-heaven at a given time and place, and determined by any of a number of methods. ■ such a division represented as a sector on an astrological chart, used in allocating elements of character and circumstance to different spheres of human life.

H

7 [mass noun] Brit. old-fashioned term for **BINGO**. ■ [as exclamation] used by a bingo player to announce that they have won.
▶ **adjective** [attrib.] **1** (of an animal or plant) kept in, frequenting, or infesting buildings.
2 relating to a firm, institution, or society: *a house journal*. ■ (of a band or group) resident or regularly performing in a club or other venue.
▶ **verb** /haʊz/ [with obj.] **1** provide with shelter or accommodation: *they converted a disused cinema to house twelve employees*.
2 provide space for; contain or accommodate: *the museum houses a collection of Roman sculpture*. ■ fix (something) in a socket or mortise.
– PHRASES **as safe as houses** Brit. completely safe. **get on** (or **along**) **like a house on fire** informal have a very good and friendly relationship. **go** (**all**) **round the houses** Brit. take a circuitous route to one's destination. ■ take an unnecessarily long time to get to the point. **a house divided cannot stand** proverb a group or organization weakened by internal dissensions will be unable to withstand external pressures. **house of cards** a structure built out of playing cards precariously balanced together. ■ used to refer to an insubstantial or insecure situation or scheme: *the special constitutional arrangement collapsed like a house of cards*. **keep** (or **make**) **a House** Brit. secure the presence of enough members for a quorum in the House of Commons. **keep house** do the cooking, cleaning, and other tasks involved in the running of a household. **on the house** (of a drink or meal in a bar or restaurant) at the management's expense; free. **play house** (of a child) play at being a family in its home. **put** (or **set**) **one's house in order** make necessary reforms: *the Americans need to put their own economic house in order*. **set up house** make one's home in a specified place.
– DERIVATIVES **houseful** noun (pl. **housefuls**), **houseless** adjective.
– ORIGIN Old English *hūs* (noun), *hūsian* (verb), of Germanic origin; related to Dutch *huis*, German *Haus* (nouns), and Dutch *huizen*, German *hausen* (verbs).

house agent ▶ **noun** Brit. an estate agent.

house arrest ▶ **noun** [mass noun] the state of being kept as a prisoner in one's own house, rather than in a prison: *she was placed under house arrest*.

houseboat ▶ **noun** a boat which is or can be moored for use as a dwelling.

housebound ▶ **adjective** unable to leave one's house, typically due to illness or old age.

houseboy ▶ **noun** a boy or man employed to undertake domestic duties.

housebreak ▶ **verb** chiefly N. Amer. another term for **HOUSE-TRAIN**.

housebreaking ▶ **noun** [mass noun] the action of breaking into a building, especially in daytime, to commit a crime. In 1968 it was replaced as a statutory crime (in England and Wales only) by burglary.
– DERIVATIVES **housebreaker** noun.

housebuilding ▶ **noun** [mass noun] the trade or activity of building houses.
– DERIVATIVES **housebuilder** noun.

housecarl /ˈhaʊskɑːl/ (also **housecarle**) ▶ **noun** (before the Norman Conquest) a member of the bodyguard of a Danish or English king or noble.
– ORIGIN late Old English *hūscarl*, from Old Norse *húskarl* 'manservant', (plural) 'retinue, bodyguard', from *hús* 'house' + *karl* 'man'.

house church ▶ **noun** a charismatic Church independent of traditional denominations (originally meeting in a private house).

housecoat ▶ **noun** a woman's long, loose, lightweight robe for informal wear around the house.

house cricket ▶ **noun** a chiefly nocturnal cricket with a bird-like warble, native to North Africa and SW Asia. It has become established in warm buildings throughout Europe. ● *Acheta domesticus*, family Gryllidae.

housefather ▶ **noun** a man in charge of and living in a boarding school house or children's home.

house finch ▶ **noun** a red-breasted brown finch, now common from Canada to Mexico and sometimes regarded as a pest. ● *Carpodacus mexicanus*, family Fringillidae.

house flag ▶ **noun** a flag indicating the company that a ship belongs to.

housefly ▶ **noun** (pl. **houseflies**) a common small fly occurring worldwide in and around human habitation. Its eggs are laid in decaying material, and the fly can be a health hazard due to its contamination of food. ● *Musca domestica*, family Muscidae.

house gecko ▶ **noun** a large-eyed nocturnal gecko of the Old World tropics, occupying a range of habitats including houses. ● *Hemidactylus*, *Gehyra*, and other genera, family Gekkonidae: several species.

house guest ▶ **noun** a guest staying for some days in a person's private house.

household ▶ **noun** a house and its occupants regarded as a unit: *the whole household was asleep* | [as modifier] *household bills*. ■ (**the Household**) [usu. in titles] the establishment and affairs of a royal household: *Controller of the Household*.

Household Cavalry (in the British army) the two cavalry regiments with responsibility for guarding the monarch and royal palaces (and otherwise acting as part of the Royal Armoured Corps).

householder ▶ **noun** a person who owns or rents a house; the head of a household.

household gods ▶ **plural noun** gods presiding over a household, especially (in Roman history) the lares and penates.

household name (also **household word**) ▶ **noun** a person or thing that is well known by the public.

household troops ▶ **plural noun** (in the UK) troops nominally employed to guard the sovereign.

house-hunt ▶ **verb** [no obj.] seek a house to buy or rent and live in.
– DERIVATIVES **house-hunter** noun.

house husband ▶ **noun** a man who lives with a partner and carries out household duties traditionally done by a housewife rather than going out to work.

housekeeper ▶ **noun** a person, typically a woman, employed to manage a household.
– DERIVATIVES **housekeep** verb (dated).

housekeeping ▶ **noun** [mass noun] **1** the management of household affairs. ■ money set aside or given for running a household: *writing barely pays my part of the housekeeping*.
2 operations such as maintenance or record-keeping which facilitate productive work in an organization. ■ Biology the regulation of metabolic functions that are common to all cells: [as modifier] *housekeeping genes*.

houseleek /ˈhaʊsliːk/ ▶ **noun** a succulent European plant with rosettes of fleshy leaves and small pink flowers. Houseleeks grow on walls and roofs, and are popular cultivated plants. ● *Sempervivum* and related genera, family Crassulaceae: several species, in particular *S. tectorum*.

house lights ▶ **plural noun** the lights in the auditorium of a theatre.

housemaid ▶ **noun** a female domestic employee, especially one who cleans reception rooms and bedrooms.

housemaid's knee ▶ **noun** [mass noun] inflammation of the fluid-filled cavity covering the kneecap (bursitis), often due to excessive kneeling.

houseman ▶ **noun** (pl. **housemen**) **1** Brit. another term for **HOUSE OFFICER**.
2 N. Amer. another term for **HOUSEBOY**.

house martin ▶ **noun** a black-and-white Eurasian songbird of the swallow family, often building its mud nest on the walls of buildings. ● Genus *Delichon*, family Hirundinidae: three species, in particular the widespread *D. urbica*.

housemaster (also **housemistress**) ▶ **noun** chiefly Brit. a teacher in charge of a house at a boarding school.

housemate ▶ **noun** a person who shares a house with others.

housemother ▶ **noun** a woman in charge of and living in a boarding school house or children's home.

house mouse ▶ **noun** a greyish-brown mouse found abundantly as a scavenger in human dwellings. It is widely kept as a pet or experimental animal, and has been bred in many varieties. ● *Mus musculus*, family Muridae.

house music ▶ **noun** see **HOUSE** (sense 5 of the noun).

House of Commons (in the UK) the elected chamber of Parliament.

house of correction ▶ **noun** historical an institution where vagrants and minor offenders were confined and set to work.

house officer ▶ **noun** Brit. a recent medical graduate receiving supervised training in a hospital and acting as an assistant physician or surgeon. Also called **HOUSEMAN** or (N. Amer.) **INTERN**.

house of God ▶ **noun** a place of religious worship, especially a church.

house of ill fame (also **house of ill repute**) ▶ **noun** archaic or humorous a brothel.

House of Keys (in the Isle of Man) the elected chamber of Tynwald.

House of Lords (in the UK) the higher chamber of Parliament, composed of peers and bishops. ■ a committee of specially qualified members of the House of Lords, appointed as the ultimate judicial appeal court of England and Wales.

House of Representatives the lower house of the US Congress and other legislatures.

houseparent ▶ **noun** a housemother or housefather.

house party ▶ **noun** a party at which the guests stay at a house overnight or for a few days.

houseplant ▶ **noun** a plant which is grown indoors.

house-proud ▶ **adjective** attentive to, or preoccupied with, the care and appearance of one's home.

house rat ▶ **noun** another term for **BLACK RAT**, especially in South Asia.

houseroom ▶ **noun** [mass noun] space or accommodation in one's house.
– PHRASES **not give something houseroom** Brit. be unwilling to have or consider something.

house-sit ▶ **verb** [no obj.] live in and look after a house while its owner is away.
– DERIVATIVES **house-sitter** noun.

Houses of Parliament (in the UK) the Houses of Lords and Commons regarded together, or the building where they meet (the Palace of Westminster).

house sparrow ▶ **noun** a common brown and grey sparrow that nests in the eaves and roofs of houses, common from Europe to southern Asia and introduced elsewhere. ● *Passer domesticus*, family Passeridae (or Ploceidae).

house spider ▶ **noun** a large spider which frequently lives in houses, where it builds a sheet-like web: ● a common European spider which builds a large web with a tubular retreat in one corner (genus *Tegenaria*, family Ageleridae). ● a common North American spider (*Achaearanea tepidariorum*, family Theridiidae).

house style ▶ **noun** a company's preferred manner of presentation and layout of written material.

house-to-house ▶ **adjective & adverb** performed at or taken to each house in turn: [as adj.] *house-to-house inquiries*.

housetop ▶ **noun** the ridge or roof of a house.
– PHRASES **shout something from the housetops** old-fashioned way of saying **SHOUT SOMETHING FROM THE ROOFTOPS** (see **SHOUT**).

house-train ▶ **verb** [with obj.] Brit. train (a pet) to excrete outside the house or only in a special place. ■ (often as adj. **house-trained**) informal, humorous teach (someone) good manners or tidiness.

House Un-American Activities Committee (abbrev.: **HUAC**) a committee of the US House of Representatives established in 1938 to investigate subversives. It became notorious for its zealous investigations of alleged communists, particularly in the late 1940s, although it was originally intended to pursue Fascists also.

housewares ▶ **plural noun** kitchen utensils and similar household items.

house-warming ▶ **noun** [usu. as modifier] a party celebrating a move to a new home: *a house-warming party*.

housewife ▶ **noun** (pl. **housewives**) **1** a married woman whose main occupation is caring for her family, managing household affairs, and doing housework.
2 /ˈhʌzɪf/ a small case for needles, thread, and other small sewing items.
– DERIVATIVES **housewifely** adjective, **housewifery** noun.
– ORIGIN Middle English *husewif* (see **HOUSE**, **WIFE**).

housework ▶ **noun** [mass noun] regular work done in housekeeping, especially cleaning and tidying.

housey ▶ **adjective** Brit. informal in the style of house music.

housey-housey (also **housie-housie**) ▶ **noun** Brit. old-fashioned term for **BINGO**.

housing¹ ▶ **noun 1** [mass noun] houses and flats considered collectively: [as modifier] *a housing development.* ■ the provision of accommodation: [as modifier] *a housing association.*
2 a rigid casing that encloses and protects a piece of moving or delicate equipment.
3 a recess or groove cut in one piece of wood to allow another piece to be attached to it.

housing² ▶ **noun** archaic a cloth covering put on a horse for protection or ornament.
– ORIGIN late Middle English (in the general sense 'covering'): from Old French *houce*, from medieval Latin *hultia*, of Germanic origin.

housing association ▶ **noun** Brit. a non-profit organization that rents houses and flats to people on low incomes or with particular needs.

housing estate ▶ **noun** Brit. a residential area in which the houses have all been planned and built at the same time.

Housman /ˈhaʊsmən/, A. E. (1859–1936), English poet and classical scholar; full name *Alfred Edward Housman*. He is now chiefly remembered for the poems collected in *A Shropshire Lad* (1896), a series of nostalgic verses largely based on ballad forms.

Houston /ˈh(j)uːst(ə)n/ an inland port of Texas, linked to the Gulf of Mexico by the Houston Ship Canal; pop. 2,242,193 (est. 2008). Since 1961 it has been a centre for space research and manned space flight; it is the site of the NASA Space Center.
– ORIGIN named after Samuel *Houston* (1793–1863), an American politician and military leader who led the struggle to win control of Texas and make it part of the US.

houting /ˈhaʊtɪŋ/ ▶ **noun** a migratory whitefish with a pointed snout. Now rare, it is found mainly in the Baltic and adjacent rivers. ● *Coregonus oxyrhinchus*, family Salmonidae.
– ORIGIN late 19th cent.: from Dutch, from Middle Dutch *houtic*, of unknown origin.

Hove a resort on the southern coast of England, a city (with Brighton) from 2000; pop. 69,500 (est. 2009).

hove chiefly Nautical past of **HEAVE**.

hovel ▶ **noun 1** a small squalid or simply constructed dwelling. ■ archaic an open shed or outhouse, used for sheltering cattle or storing grain or tools.
2 historical a conical building enclosing a kiln.
– ORIGIN late Middle English: of unknown origin.

hover ▶ **verb** [no obj., with adverbial] remain in one place in the air: *Army helicopters hovered overhead.* ■ remain poised uncertainly in one place or between two states: *her hand hovered over the console* | *his expression hovered between cynicism and puzzlement.* ■ linger close at hand in an uncertain manner: *she hovered anxiously in the background.* ■ remain at or near a particular level: *inflation will hover around the 4 per cent mark.*
▶ **noun** [in sing.] an act of hovering.
– DERIVATIVES **hoverer** noun.
– ORIGIN late Middle English: from archaic *hove* 'hover, linger', of unknown origin.

hovercraft ▶ **noun** (pl. **same**) a vehicle or craft that travels over land or water on a cushion of air provided by a downward blast. A design was first patented by Christopher Cockerell in 1955.

hoverfly ▶ **noun** (pl. **hoverflies**) a fly which frequently hovers motionless in the air and feeds on the nectar of flowers. Most hoverflies are black and yellow, patterned to mimic various bees and wasps. ● Family Syrphidae: numerous genera and species.

hoverport ▶ **noun** a terminal for hovercraft.

hovertrain ▶ **noun** a train that travels on a cushion of air.

how¹ ▶ **adverb** [usu. interrogative adverb] **1** in what way or manner; by what means: *how does it work?* | *he did not know how he ought to behave* | [with infinitive] *he showed me how to adjust the focus.*
2 used to ask about the condition or quality of something: *how was your holiday?* | *how did they play?* ■ used to ask about someone's physical or mental state: *how are the children?* | *I asked how he was doing.*
3 [with adj. or adv.] used to ask about the extent or degree of something: *how old are you?* | *how long will it take?* | *I wasn't sure how fast to go.* ■ used to express a strong feeling such as surprise about the extent of something: *how kind it was of him* | *how I wish I had been there!*
4 [relative adverb] the way in which; that: *she told us how she had lived out of a suitcase for a week.* ■ in any way in which; however: *I'll do business how I like.*
– PHRASES **and how!** informal very much so (used to express strong agreement): *'Did you miss me?' 'And how!'* **how about 1** used to make a suggestion or offer: *how about a drink?* **2** used when asking for information or an opinion on something: *how about your company?* **the how and why** the methods and reasons for doing something: *tonight's edition demystifies the how and why of television ratings.* **how come?** see **COME**. **how do you do?** a formal greeting. **how many** what number: *how many books did you sell?* **how much** what amount or price: *how much did I win?* **how now?** archaic what is the meaning of this? **how so?** how can you show that that is so? **how's that? 1** what is your opinion of that? **2** Cricket is the batsman out or not? (said to an umpire).
– ORIGIN Old English *hū*, of West Germanic origin; related to Dutch *hoe*, also to **WHO** and **WHAT**.

how² ▶ **exclamation** a greeting attributed to North American Indians (used in humorous imitation).
– ORIGIN early 19th cent.: perhaps from Sioux *háo* or Omaha *hou*.

Howard¹, Catherine (*c.*1521–42), fifth wife of Henry VIII. She married Henry soon after his divorce from Anne of Cleves in 1540. Accused of infidelity, she confessed and was beheaded.

Howard², John (1726–90), English philanthropist and prison reformer. His tour of British prisons in 1773 culminated in two Acts of Parliament setting down sanitary standards; his work *The State of Prisons in England and Wales* (1777) gave further impetus to the movement for improvements in prisons.

Howard³, John (Winston) (b.1939), Australian Liberal statesman, Prime Minister 1996–2007 with a Liberal–National Party coalition.

howbeit ▶ **adverb** archaic nevertheless; however: *howbeit, I've no proof of the thing.*

howdah /ˈhaʊdə/ ▶ **noun** (in South Asia) a seat for riding on the back of an elephant or camel, typically with a canopy and accommodating two or more people.
– ORIGIN from Urdu *haudah*, from Arabic *hawdaj* 'litter'.

how-do-you-do (also **how-de-do** or **how-d'ye-do**) ▶ **noun** [in sing.] a greeting. ■ informal an awkward, messy, or annoying situation: *a fine how-do-you-do that would be!*

howdy ▶ **exclamation** N. Amer. an informal friendly greeting, particularly associated with the western US states: *howdy, stranger.*
– ORIGIN early 19th cent.: alteration of *how d'ye*.

Howe, Elias (1819–67), American inventor. In 1846 he patented the first sewing machine. Its principles were adapted by Isaac Merrit Singer and others in violation of Howe's patent rights, and it took a seven-year litigation battle to secure the royalties.

howe¹ ▶ **noun** N. English a tumulus or barrow. ■ [in place names] a hill.
– ORIGIN Middle English: from Old Norse *haugr* 'mound', from a Germanic base meaning 'high'.

howe² ▶ **noun** Scottish & N. English a hollow place; a depression.
– ORIGIN late Middle English: variant of Old English *hol* (see **HOLE**).

howe'er /haʊˈɛː/ literary ▶ **contraction** however.

however ▶ **adverb 1** used to introduce a statement that contrasts with or seems to contradict something that has been said previously: *People tend to put on weight in middle age. However, gaining weight is not inevitable.*
2 [relative adverb] in whatever way; regardless of how: *however you look at it, you can't criticize that.* ■ [with adj. or adv.] to whatever extent: *he was hesitant to take the risk, however small.*

> **USAGE** When **ever** is used for emphasis after **how** or **why**, it should be written as a separate word. Thus it is correct to write ***how ever** did you manage?* rather than ***however** did you manage?* (as distinct from other uses of the adverb **however**, which is always written as one word). With other words such as **what**, **where**, and **who**, the situation is not clear-cut: both two-word and one-word forms (both **what ever** and **whatever**, and so on) are well represented, and neither is regarded as particularly more correct than the other.

howff /haʊf/ ▶ **noun** Scottish a favourite meeting place or haunt, especially a pub.
– ORIGIN mid 16th cent. (as the name of the main burial ground in Dundee): of unknown origin.

howitzer /ˈhaʊɪtsə/ ▶ **noun** a short gun for firing shells on high trajectories at low velocities.
– ORIGIN late 17th cent.: from Dutch *houwitser*, from German *Haubitze*, from Czech *houfnice* 'catapult'.

howk /haʊk/ ▶ **verb** [with obj., and adverbial] chiefly Scottish dig out or up: *deep in their trenches the men stood, howking out the brown earth.* ■ [no obj., with adverbial] search about by digging or rummaging: *Frankie howked among the beer cans.*
– ORIGIN late Middle English *holk*: related to Middle Low German *holken* 'to hollow', and **HOLE**.

howl ▶ **noun** a long, doleful cry uttered by an animal such as a dog or wolf. ■ a loud cry of pain, fear, anger, or amusement: *he let out a howl of anguish* | figurative *I got howls of protest from readers.* ■ a prolonged wailing noise such as that made by a strong wind: *they listened to the howl of the gale.* ■ Electronics a wailing noise in a loudspeaker due to feedback.
▶ **verb** [no obj.] make a howling sound: *he howled in agony* | *the wind howled around the house.* ■ weep and cry out loudly: *a baby started to howl.* ■ [with obj.] (**howl someone down**) shout in disapproval in order to prevent a speaker from being heard: *they howled me down and called me a chauvinist.*
– ORIGIN Middle English *houle* (verb), probably imitative.

howler ▶ **noun 1** informal a very stupid or glaring mistake, especially an amusing one.
2 (also **howler monkey**) a fruit-eating monkey with a prehensile tail and a loud howling call, native to the forests of tropical America. ● Genus *Alouatta*, family Cebidae: several species.

howlet ▶ **noun** chiefly Scottish an owl or owlet.
– ORIGIN late 15th cent.: diminutive of **OWL**, assimilated to the verb **HOWL**.

howling ▶ **adjective** [attrib.] **1** producing a long, doleful cry or wailing sound.
2 informal extreme or great: *the meal was a howling success.*
– DERIVATIVES **howlingly** adverb.

howling dervish ▶ **noun** see **DERVISH**.

Howrah /ˈhaʊrə/ (also **Haora**) a city in eastern India; pop. 1,034,400 (est. 2009). It is situated on the Hooghly River opposite Kolkata (Calcutta).

howsoe'er /ˌhaʊsəʊˈɛː/ literary ▶ **contraction** howsoever.

howsoever formal or archaic ▶ **adverb** [with adj. or adv.] to whatever extent: *any quantity howsoever small.*
▶ **conjunction** in whatever way; regardless of how: *howsoever it came into being, it is good to look at.*

how-to informal ▶ **adjective** [attrib.] providing detailed and practical advice: *read a how-to book.*
▶ **noun** (pl. **how-tos**) a book or other guide that provides such advice.

howtowdie /haʊˈtaʊdi/ ▶ **noun** [mass noun] a Scottish dish of boiled chicken served with spinach and poached eggs.
– ORIGIN early 19th cent.: probably from Old French *estaudeau*, denoting a young chicken for the stew pot.

howzat ▶ **exclamation** Cricket shortened form of **HOW'S THAT?** (sense 2). (see **HOW¹**).

howzit ▶ **exclamation** S. African informal used as a greeting, equivalent to 'hello' or 'how are you?'.
– ORIGIN contraction of *how is it?*

Hoxha /ˈhɒdʒə/, Enver (1908–85), Albanian statesman, founder of the Albanian Communist Party 1941, Prime Minister 1944–54, and First Secretary of the Albanian Communist Party 1954–85. He rigorously isolated Albania from Western influences and implemented a Stalinist programme of nationalization and collectivization.

Hoxnian /ˈhɒksnɪən/ ▶ **adjective** Geology relating to or denoting an interglacial period of the Pleistocene in Britain, following the Anglian glaciation and identified with the Holsteinian of northern Europe. ■ (as noun **the Hoxnian**) the Hoxnian interglacial or the system of deposits laid down during it.
– ORIGIN 1950s: from *Hoxne*, the name of a village in Suffolk, + **-IAN**.

hoy¹ ▶ **exclamation** used to attract someone's attention: *'Hoy! Look!'*
▶ **noun** [mass noun] Austral. a game resembling bingo, using playing cards.
– ORIGIN natural exclamation: first recorded in late Middle English.

hoy² ▶ **noun** historical a small coastal sailing vessel, typically single-masted.
– ORIGIN Middle English: from Middle Dutch *hoei*, of unknown origin.

hoy³ ▶ **verb** [with obj.] Austral. & N. English, informal throw.
– ORIGIN mid 19th cent.: of unknown origin.

H

hoya /ˈhɔɪə/ ▶ **noun** a climbing or sprawling evergreen shrub with ornamental foliage and waxy flowers, native to SE Asia and the Pacific and grown as a greenhouse or indoor plant. ● Genus *Hoya*, family Asclepiadaceae.
– ORIGIN modern Latin, named after Thomas *Hoy* (*c.*1750–*c.*1821), English gardener.

hoyden /ˈhɔɪd(ə)n/ ▶ **noun** dated a boisterous girl.
– DERIVATIVES **hoydenish adjective**.
– ORIGIN late 16th cent. (denoting a rude or ignorant man): probably from Middle Dutch *heiden* (see **HEATHEN**).

Hoyle[1], Sir Fred (1915–2001), English astrophysicist and writer. He was one of the proponents of the steady state theory of cosmology, and, mainly with the American physicist **William A. Fowler** (1911–95), described the processes of nucleosynthesis inside stars. His later work included the controversial suggestions that life on the earth has an extraterrestrial origin, and that some viruses arrive from space.

Hoyle[2] ▶ **noun** (in phrase **according to Hoyle**) according to plan or the rules.
– ORIGIN early 20th cent.: from the name of Edmond *Hoyle* (1672–1769), English writer on card games.

H

h.p. (also **HP**) ▶ **abbreviation** ■ high pressure. ■ Brit. hire purchase. ■ horsepower.

HPV ▶ **abbreviation** human papillomavirus.

HQ ▶ **abbreviation** headquarters.

HR ▶ **abbreviation** ■ N. Amer. House of Representatives. ■ Human Resources (the personnel department of an organization).

hr ▶ **abbreviation** hour.

Hradec Králové /ˌhrɑːdɛts ˈkrɑːlɒveɪ/ a town in the northern Czech Republic, capital of East Bohemia region on the River Elbe; pop. 94,134 (2007). German name **KÖNIGGRÄTZ**.

HRH ▶ **abbreviation** Brit. Her or His Royal Highness (as a title): *HRH Prince Philip.*

Hrodna /ˈhrɒdnə/ a city in western Belarus, on the Neman River near the borders with Poland and Lithuania; pop. 338,200 (est. 2009). Russian name **GRODNO**.

hrs ▶ **abbreviation** hours.

HRT ▶ **abbreviation** hormone replacement therapy.

Hrvatska /ˈh(ə)rvaːtskaː/ Croatian name for **CROATIA**.

hryvna /ˈhrɪvnjə/ (also **hryvnia**) ▶ **noun** the basic monetary unit of Ukraine, equal to 100 kopiykas.

Hs ▶ **symbol** the chemical element hassium.

HSE ▶ **abbreviation** (in the UK) Health and Safety Executive.

HSH ▶ **abbreviation** Her or His Serene Highness (as a title): *HSH Prince Rainier.*

Hsia-men variant of **XIAMEN**.

Hsian variant of **XIAN**.

Hsiang variant of **XIANG**.

Hsining variant of **XINING**.

HST ▶ **abbreviation** ■ (in the UK) high-speed train, a design of express passenger train with integral diesel engines at either end. ■ Hubble Space Telescope.

Hsu-chou /ʃuːˈtʃaʊ/ variant of **XUZHOU**.

HT ▶ **abbreviation** (electrical) high tension.

HTH ▶ **abbreviation** informal hope this helps (used in Internet forums): *If you want to have a chat, my numbers are in my profile. HTH.*

HTML ▶ **noun** [mass noun] Computing Hypertext Markup Language, a standardized system for tagging text files to achieve font, colour, graphic, and hyperlink effects on World Wide Web pages.

HTTP ▶ **abbreviation** Computing Hypertext Transport (or Transfer) Protocol, the data transfer protocol used on the World Wide Web.

HUAC ▶ **abbreviation** House Un-American Activities Committee.

Huainan /hwʌɪˈnan/ a city in the province of Anhui, in east central China; pop. 932,200 (est. 2006).

Huallaga /hwɑːˈjɑːgə/ a river in central Peru, one of the headwaters of the Amazon. Rising in the central Andes, it flows generally north-eastwards for 1,100 km (700 miles) and emerges into the Amazon Basin at Lagunas.

Huambo /ˈhwambəʊ/ a city in the mountains in western Angola; pop. 294,100 (est. 2004). Founded in 1912, it was known by its Portuguese name of Nova Lisboa until 1978.

Huang Hai /hwaŋ ˈhʌɪ/ Chinese name for **YELLOW SEA**.

Huang Ho /hwaŋ ˈhəʊ/ (also **Huang He** /ˈhiː/) Chinese name for **YELLOW RIVER**.

huarache /waˈrɑːtʃi/ (also **guarache**) ▶ **noun** a leather-thonged sandal, originally worn by Mexican Indians.
– ORIGIN late 19th cent.: Mexican Spanish.

Huascarán /ˌhwaskəˈrɑːn/ an extinct volcano in the Peruvian Andes, west central Peru, rising to 6,768 m (22,205 ft). It is the highest peak in Peru.

hub ▶ **noun 1** the central part of a wheel, rotating on or with the axle, and from which the spokes radiate. **2** the effective centre of an activity, region, or network: *the kitchen was the hub of family life.*
– PHRASES **hub-and-spoke** denoting a system of air transportation in which local airports offer flights to a central airport where international or long-distance flights are available.
– ORIGIN early 16th cent. (denoting a shelf at the side of a fireplace used for heating pans): of unknown origin (compare with **HOB**[1]).

hubba hubba ▶ **exclamation** N. Amer. informal used to express approval, excitement, or enthusiasm, especially with regard to a person's appearance.
– ORIGIN 1940s: of unknown origin.

Hubbard squash /ˈhʌbəd/ ▶ **noun** a winter squash with a green or yellow rind and yellow flesh.

Hubble, Edwin Powell (1889–1953), American astronomer. He studied galaxies and devised a classification scheme for them. In 1929 he proposed what is now known as Hubble's law with its constant of proportionality (Hubble's constant).

hubble-bubble ▶ **noun** a hookah.
– ORIGIN mid 17th cent.: imitative repetition of **BUBBLE**.

Hubble classification Astronomy a simple method of describing the shapes of galaxies, using subdivisions of each of four basic types (elliptical, spiral, barred spiral, and irregular). Hubble's suggestion that they form an evolutionary sequence is no longer accepted.

Hubble's constant ▶ **noun** Astronomy the ratio of the speed of recession of a galaxy (due to the expansion of the universe) to its distance from the observer. The reciprocal of the constant is called **Hubble time** and represents the length of time for which the universe has been expanding, and hence the age of the universe.

Hubble's law ▶ **noun** Astronomy a law stating that the red shifts in the spectra of distant galaxies (and hence their speeds of recession) are proportional to their distance.

Hubble Space Telescope an orbiting astronomical observatory launched in 1990. The telescope's fine high-resolution images are far better than can be obtained from the earth's surface.

hubbub ▶ **noun** [in sing.] a chaotic din caused by a crowd of people: *a hubbub of laughter and shouting.* ■ a busy, noisy situation: *she fought through the hubbub.*
– ORIGIN mid 16th cent.: perhaps of Irish origin; compare with the Irish exclamations *ababú, abú*, used in battle cries.

hubby ▶ **noun** (pl. **hubbies**) informal a husband.
– ORIGIN late 17th cent.: familiar abbreviation.

hubcap ▶ **noun** a metal or plastic cover for the hub of a motor vehicle's wheel.

Hubei /huːˈbeɪ/ (also **Hupeh**) a province of eastern China; capital, Wuhan.

Hubli /ˈhuːbli/ (also **Hubli-Dharwad** /dɑːˈwɑːd/, **Hubli-Dharwar** /-ˈwɑː/) a city in SW India; pop. 892,300 (est. 2009). It was united with the adjacent city of Dharwad in 1961.

hubris /ˈhjuːbrɪs/ ▶ **noun** [mass noun] excessive pride or self-confidence. ■ (in Greek tragedy) excessive pride towards or defiance of the gods, leading to nemesis.
– DERIVATIVES **hubristic adjective**.
– ORIGIN Greek.

huchen /ˈhuːk(ə)n/ ▶ **noun** (pl. **same**) a large, slender non-migratory fish of the salmon family, which lives only in the Danube River system. ● *Hucho hucho*, family Salmonidae.
– ORIGIN early 20th cent.: from German.

huckaback ▶ **noun** [mass noun] a strong linen or cotton fabric with a rough surface, used for towelling and glass cloths.
– ORIGIN late 17th cent.: of unknown origin.

huckleberry ▶ **noun** (pl. **huckleberries**) **1** a soft edible blue-black fruit resembling a currant. **2** the low-growing North American plant of the heather family which bears the huckleberry. ● Genus *Gaylussacia*, family Ericaceae.
– ORIGIN late 16th cent.: probably originally a dialect name for the bilberry, from dialect *huckle* 'hip, haunch' (because of the plant's jointed stems).

huckster ▶ **noun 1** a person who sells small items door-to-door or from a stall. ■ a person who sells in an aggressive or ruthless way. **2** N. Amer. a publicity agent or advertising copywriter.
▶ **verb** [no obj.] N. Amer. bargain; haggle. ■ [with obj.] promote or sell (something, typically a product of questionable value).
– DERIVATIVES **hucksterism noun**.
– ORIGIN Middle English (in the sense 'retailer at a stall, hawker'): probably of Low German origin.

HUD ▶ **abbreviation** head-up display.

Huddersfield a town in West Yorkshire, northern England; pop. 136,500 (est. 2009).

huddle ▶ **verb 1** [no obj., with adverbial] crowd together; nestle closely: *they **huddled together** for warmth.* ■ curl one's body into a small space: *she **huddled up** close to him.* **2** [with obj. and adverbial] Brit. heap together in a disorderly manner: *a man with his clothes all huddled on anyhow.* **3** [no obj.] N. Amer. have a private discussion; confer: *the colonel huddled with A.J. at the dining-room table.*
▶ **noun** a close grouping of people or things: *a huddle of huts.* ■ a number of people gathered together to speak about private or secret matters. ■ a brief gathering of players during a game to receive instructions, especially in American Football. ■ [mass noun] archaic confusion; bustle.
– ORIGIN late 16th cent. (in the sense 'conceal'): perhaps of Low German origin.

Hudson, Henry (*c.*1565–1611), English explorer. He visited the North American bay, river, and strait which bear his name. In 1610 he attempted to winter in Hudson Bay, but his crew mutinied and set Hudson and a few companions adrift, never to be seen again.

Hudson Bay a large inland sea in NE Canada. It is the largest inland sea in the world and is connected to the North Atlantic Ocean via the Hudson Strait.
– ORIGIN named after the explorer Henry *Hudson* (see **HUDSON**), who visited it in 1610.

Hudsonian /hʌdˈsəʊnɪən/ ▶ **adjective** relating to Hudson Bay and the surrounding land. ■ Biology denoting a biogeographical zone represented by the territory around the bay (north of the treeline from Labrador to Alaska).

Hudson River a river of eastern North America, which rises in the Adirondack Mountains and flows southwards for 560 km (350 miles) into the Atlantic at New York.
– ORIGIN named after Henry *Hudson* (see **HUDSON**), who in 1609 sailed 240 km (150 miles) up the river as far as Albany.

Hudson's Bay blanket ▶ **noun** Canadian a durable woollen blanket, typically with a coloured border.
– ORIGIN late 19th cent.: originally sold by the *Hudson's Bay* Company and frequently used as material for coats.

Hudson's Bay Company a British colonial trading company set up in 1670 and granted all lands draining into Hudson Bay for purposes of commercial exploitation, principally trade in fur. The company handed over control to the new Canadian government in 1870 and is now a Canadian retail and wholesale operation.

hue ▶ **noun** a colour or shade: *the water is the deepest hue of aquamarine* | [mass noun] *verdigris is greenish-yellow in hue.* ■ the attribute of a colour by virtue of which it is discernible as red, green, etc., and which is dependent on its dominant wavelength and independent of intensity or lightness. ■ character or aspect: *men of all political hues submerged their feuds.*
– DERIVATIVES **hued adjective** [in combination] *rainbow-hued*, **hueless adjective**.
– ORIGIN Old English *hīw, hēow* (also 'form, appearance', obsolete except in Scots), of Germanic origin; related to Swedish *hy* 'skin, complexion'. The sense 'colour, shade' dates from the mid 19th cent.

Hué /hweɪ/ a city in central Vietnam; pop. 233,800 (est. 2009).

hue and cry ▶ **noun** a loud clamour or public outcry. ■ historical a loud cry calling for the pursuit and capture of a criminal. In former English law, the cry had to be raised by the inhabitants of a hundred in which a robbery had been committed, if they were not to become liable for the damages suffered by the victim.
– ORIGIN late Middle English: from the Anglo-Norman French legal phrase *hu e cri*, literally 'outcry and cry', from Old French *hu* 'outcry' (from *huer* 'to shout').

huevos rancheros /ˌ(h)wɛvɒs ranˈtʃɛːrɒs/ ▶ **plural noun** a dish of fried or poached eggs served on a tortilla with a spicy tomato sauce, originating in Mexico.
– ORIGIN Spanish, 'rancheros' eggs'.

huff ▶ **verb 1** [no obj.] blow out air loudly on account of exertion: *he was huffing under a heavy load* | *I was* ***huffing and puffing*** *to keep up with him.*
2 express one's feeling of petty annoyance: [with direct speech] *'Huh!' Nanny huffed.*
3 [with obj.] N. Amer. informal sniff fumes from (petrol or solvents) for a euphoric effect.
4 [with obj.] (in draughts) remove (an opponent's piece that could have made a capture) from the board as a forfeit. [from the former practice of blowing on the piece.]
▶ **noun** [usu. in sing.] a fit of petty annoyance: *she walked off* ***in a huff***.
– DERIVATIVES **huffer** noun, **huffish** adjective.
– ORIGIN late 16th cent.: imitative of the sound of blowing.

huffy ▶ **adjective** (**huffier**, **huffiest**) annoyed or irritated and quick to take offence at petty things.
– DERIVATIVES **huffily** adverb, **huffiness** noun.

hug ▶ **verb** (**hugs**, **hugging**, **hugged**) [with obj.] squeeze (someone) tightly in one's arms, typically to express affection: *he hugged her close to him* | *people kissed and* ***hugged each other*** | [no obj.] *we hugged and kissed.* ■ hold (something) tightly around or against part of one's body: *he hugged his knees to his chest.* ■ fit tightly round: *a pair of jeans that hugged the contours of his body.* ■ keep close to: *I headed north, hugging the coastline all the way.* ■ (**hug oneself**) congratulate or be pleased with oneself: *she hugged herself with secret joy.* ■ cherish or cling to (something such as a belief): *a boy hugging a secret.*
▶ **noun** an act of hugging someone. ■ a squeezing grip in wrestling.
– DERIVATIVES **huggable** adjective, **hugger** noun.
– ORIGIN mid 16th cent.: probably of Scandinavian origin and related to Norwegian *hugga* 'comfort, console'.

huge ▶ **adjective** (**huger**, **hugest**) extremely large; enormous: *a huge area* | *he made a huge difference to the team.*
DERIVATIVES **hugeness** noun.
– ORIGIN Middle English: shortening of Old French *ahuge*, of unknown origin.

hugely ▶ **adverb** [often as submodifier] very much; to a very great extent: *a hugely expensive house.*

hugger-mugger ▶ **adjective 1** confused; disorderly: *a spirit of careless frivolity where all was hugger-mugger.*
2 secret; clandestine.
▶ **noun** [mass noun] **1** disorder or confusion.
2 secrecy or secretive behaviour.
– ORIGIN early 16th cent. (in sense 2 of the noun): probably related to HUDDLE and to dialect *mucker* 'hoard money, conceal'. This is one of a number of similar formations from late Middle English to the 16th cent., including *hucker-mucker* and *hudder-mudder*, with the basic sense 'secrecy, concealment'.

Hughes[1], Ted (1930–98), English poet; full name *Edward James Hughes*. His vision of the natural world as a place of violence, terror, and beauty pervades his work. He was appointed Poet Laureate in 1984. Hughes was married to Sylvia Plath.

Hughes[2], Howard (Robard) (1905–76), American industrialist, film producer, and aviator. He made his fortune through the Hughes Tool Company, made his debut as a film director in 1926, and from 1935 to 1938 broke many world aviation records. For the last twenty-five years of his life he lived as a recluse.

Hughes[3], (James Mercer) Langston (1902–67), American writer. He began a prolific literary career with *The Weary Blues* (1926), a series of poems on black themes using blues and jazz rhythms. Other poetry collections include *The Negro Mother* (1931).

Hughie ▶ **noun** Austral./NZ informal an imaginary being held to be responsible for the weather.
– ORIGIN early 20th cent.: diminutive of the given name *Hugh*.

Hugli variant spelling of HOOGHLY.

Hugo /ˈhjuːɡəʊ/, French /ˈyɡo/, Victor (1802–85), French poet, novelist, and dramatist; full name *Victor-Marie Hugo*. A leading figure of French romanticism, he brought a new freedom to French poetry, and his belief that theatre should express both the grotesque and the sublime in human existence overturned existing conventions. His political and social concern is shown in his novels. Notable works: *Hernani* (drama, 1830) and *Les Misérables* (novel, 1862).

Huguenot /ˈhjuːɡənəʊ, -nɒt/ ▶ **noun** a French Protestant of the 16th and 17th centuries. Largely Calvinist, the Huguenots suffered severe persecution at the hands of the Catholic majority, and many thousands emigrated from France.
– ORIGIN French, alteration (by association with the name of a Geneva burgomaster, Besançon *Hugues*) of *eiguenot*, from Dutch *eedgenot*, from Swiss German *Eidgenoss* 'confederate', from *Eid* 'oath' + *Genoss* 'associate'.

huh ▶ **exclamation** used to express scorn, anger, or surprise: *'Huh,' she snorted, 'Over my dead body!'* ■ used in questions to invite agreement or further comment: *pretty devastating, huh?*
– ORIGIN natural utterance: first recorded in English in the early 17th cent.

Huhehot /ˌhuːheɪˈhɒt/ variant of HOHHOT.

hui /ˈhuːi/ ▶ **noun** (pl. **huis**) (in New Zealand) a large social or ceremonial gathering. ■ (in Hawaii) a formal club or association.
– ORIGIN Maori and Hawaiian.

huia /ˈhuːɪə/ ▶ **noun** an extinct New Zealand wattlebird with glossy black plumage, the female having a much longer and more curved bill than the male. The tail feathers were formerly prized by Maoris, and the last huia was seen in 1907. ● *Heteralocha acutirostris*, family Callaeidae.
– ORIGIN mid 19th cent.: from Maori, imitative of its cry.

hula /ˈhuːlə/ (also **hula-hula**) ▶ **noun** a dance performed by Hawaiian women, characterized by six basic steps, undulating hips, and gestures symbolizing or imitating natural phenomena or historical or mythological subjects.
– ORIGIN early 19th cent.: Hawaiian.

hula hoop (also US trademark **Hula-Hoop**) ▶ **noun** a large hoop spun round the body by gyrating the hips, for play or exercise.
▶ **verb** (**hula-hoop**) [no obj.] (usu. as noun **hula-hooping**) spin a hula hoop round the body by gyrating the hips.

hula skirt ▶ **noun** a long grass skirt as worn by a hula dancer.

hulk ▶ **noun 1** an old ship stripped of fittings and permanently moored, especially for use as storage or (formerly) as a prison. ■ a large disused structure: *hulks of abandoned machinery.*
2 a large or unwieldy boat or other object. ■ a large, clumsy-looking person: *a six-foot* ***hulk of a man***.
– ORIGIN Old English *hulc* 'fast ship', probably reinforced in Middle English by Middle Low German and Middle Dutch *hulk*; probably of Mediterranean origin and related to Greek *holkas* 'cargo ship'.

hulking ▶ **adjective** informal (of a person or object) very large, heavy, or clumsy: *a hulking young man.*

Hull a city and port in NE England, situated at the junction of the Hull and Humber Rivers; pop. 263,000 (est. 2009). Official name KINGSTON UPON HULL.

hull[1] ▶ **noun** the main body of a ship or other vessel, including the bottom, sides, and deck but not the masts, superstructure, rigging, engines, and other fittings.
▶ **verb** [with obj.] hit and pierce the hull of (a ship) with a missile.
– DERIVATIVES **hulled** adjective [in combination] *a wooden-hulled narrowboat.*
– ORIGIN Middle English: perhaps the same word as HULL[2], or related to HOLD[2].

hull[2] ▶ **noun** the outer covering of a fruit or seed, especially the pod of peas and beans, or the husk of grain. ■ the green calyx of a strawberry or raspberry.
▶ **verb** [with obj.] remove the hulls from (fruit, seeds, or grain).
– ORIGIN Old English *hulu*, of Germanic origin; related to Dutch *huls*, German *Hülse* 'husk, pod', and German *Hülle* 'covering', also to HEEL[3].

hullabaloo ▶ **noun** [in sing.] informal a commotion; a fuss: *remember all the hullabaloo over the golf ball?*
– ORIGIN mid 18th cent.: reduplication of *hallo*, *hullo*, etc.

hullo ▶ **exclamation** variant spelling of HELLO.
– ORIGIN first recorded, in this form, in T. Hughes's *Tom Brown's Schooldays* (1857).

hum[1] ▶ **verb** (**hums**, **humming**, **hummed**) [no obj.] **1** make a low, steady continuous sound like that of a bee: *the computers hummed.* ■ sing with closed lips: *he hummed softly to himself* | [with obj.] *she was humming a cheerful tune.* ■ (of a place) be filled with a low, steady continuous sound: *the room* ***hummed with*** *an expectant murmur.*
2 informal be in a state of great activity: *the house was humming with preparations for the dance.*
3 Brit. informal smell unpleasant: *when the wind drops this stuff really hums.*
▶ **noun** [in sing.] a low, steady continuous sound: *the hum of insects* | *a low hum of conversation.* ■ an unwanted low-frequency noise in an amplifier caused by variation of electric current, especially the alternating frequency of the mains.
– PHRASES **hum and haw** (or chiefly N. Amer. **hem and haw**) Brit. be indecisive.
– DERIVATIVES **hummable** adjective, **hummer** noun.
– ORIGIN late Middle English: imitative.

hum[2] ▶ **exclamation** used to express hesitation or dissent.
– ORIGIN mid 16th cent.: imitative; related to the verb HUM[1].

human ▶ **adjective** relating to or characteristic of humankind: *the human body* | *the complex nature of the human mind.* ■ of or characteristic of people as opposed to God or animals or machines, especially in being susceptible to weaknesses: *they are only human and therefore mistakes do occur* | *the risk of human error.* ■ showing the better qualities of humankind, such as kindness: *the human side of politics is getting stronger.* ■ Zoology of or belonging to the genus *Homo*.
▶ **noun** a human being.
– DERIVATIVES **humanness** noun.
– ORIGIN late Middle English *humaine*, from Old French *humain(e)*, from Latin *humanus*, from *homo* 'man, human being'. The present spelling became usual in the 18th cent.; compare with HUMANE.

human being ▶ **noun** a man, woman, or child of the species *Homo sapiens*, distinguished from other animals by superior mental development, power of articulate speech, and upright stance.

human capital ▶ **noun** [mass noun] the skills, knowledge, and experience possessed by an individual or population, viewed in terms of their value or cost to an organization or country.

human chain ▶ **noun** a line of people formed for passing things quickly from one site to another.

human chorionic gonadotrophin ▶ **noun** [mass noun] Biochemistry a hormone produced in the human placenta that maintains the corpus luteum during pregnancy.

humane /hjʊˈmeɪn/ ▶ **adjective 1** having or showing compassion or benevolence: *regulations ensuring the humane treatment of animals.* ■ inflicting the minimum of pain: *humane methods of killing.*
2 formal (of a branch of learning) intended to have a civilizing effect on people.
– DERIVATIVES **humanely** adverb, **humaneness** noun.
– ORIGIN late Middle English: the earlier form of HUMAN, restricted to the senses above in the 18th cent.

humane killer ▶ **noun** Brit. an instrument for the painless slaughter of animals.

human engineering ▶ **noun** [mass noun] the management of industrial labour, especially as regards relationships between people and machines.

Human Genome Project an international project to chart the entire genetic material of a human being, the first draft of which was completed in 2000.

human geography ▶ **noun** [mass noun] the branch of geography dealing with how human activity affects or is influenced by the earth's surface.

human interest ▶ **noun** [mass noun] the aspect of a story in the media that interests people because it describes the experiences or emotions of individuals to which others can relate.

humanism ▶ **noun** [mass noun] a rationalist outlook or system of thought attaching prime importance to human rather than divine or supernatural matters. ■ (often **Humanism**) a Renaissance cultural

movement which turned away from medieval scholasticism and revived interest in ancient Greek and Roman thought. ■ (among some contemporary writers) a system of thought criticized as being centred on the notion of the rational, autonomous self and ignoring the conditioned nature of the individual.
– DERIVATIVES **humanist** noun & adjective, **humanistic** adjective, **humanistically** adverb.

humanitarian /hjʊˌmanɪˈtɛːrɪən/ ▶ adjective concerned with or seeking to promote human welfare: *groups sending humanitarian aid.* ■ denoting an event or situation which causes or involves widespread human suffering, especially one which requires the large-scale provision of aid: *human rights groups have warned of a worsening humanitarian crisis.*
▶ noun a person who seeks to promote human welfare.
– DERIVATIVES **humanitarianism** noun.

> **USAGE** The primary sense of **humanitarian** is 'concerned with or seeking to promote human welfare'. Since the 1930s a new sense, exemplified by phrases such as *the worst* **humanitarian** *disaster this country has seen*, has been gaining currency, and is now broadly established, especially in journalism, although it is not considered good style by all. In the Oxford English Corpus the second most common collocation of **humanitarian** is **crisis**.

H

humanity ▶ noun (pl. **humanities**) [mass noun] **1** human beings collectively: *appalling crimes against humanity.* ■ the state of being human: *our differences matter but our common humanity matters more.*
2 the quality of being humane; benevolence: *he praised them for their standards of humanity and care.*
3 (**humanities**) learning concerned with human culture, especially literature, history, art, music, and philosophy.
– ORIGIN Middle English: from Old French *humanite*, from Latin *humanitas*, from *humanus* (see HUMAN).

humanize (also **humanise**) ▶ verb [with obj.] **1** make (something) more humane or civilized: *his purpose was to humanize prison conditions.*
2 give (something) a human character: *dogs are wonderful friends but why do we try to humanize them?*
– DERIVATIVES **humanization** noun.
– ORIGIN early 17th cent.: from French *humaniser*, from Latin *humanus* (see HUMAN).

humankind ▶ noun [mass noun] human beings considered collectively (used as a neutral alternative to 'mankind'): *the origin of humankind.*

humanly ▶ adverb **1** from a human point of view; in a human manner: *they can grow both humanly and spiritually.* ■ [as submodifier] within human ability: *we did all that was humanly possible.*
2 archaic with human feeling or kindness.

human nature ▶ noun [mass noun] the general psychological characteristics, feelings, and behavioural traits of humankind, regarded as shared by all humans: *he had a poor opinion of human nature.*

humanoid /ˈhjuːmənɔɪd/ ▶ adjective having an appearance or character resembling that of a human.
▶ noun (especially in science fiction) a being resembling a human in its shape.

human papillomavirus ▶ noun a virus with subtypes that cause diseases in humans ranging from common warts to cervical cancer.

human race ▶ noun (**the human race**) human beings in general; humankind: *trees are vital to the survival of the human race.*

human relations ▶ plural noun relations with or between people, particularly the treatment of people in a professional context.

human resources ▶ plural noun the personnel of a business or organization, regarded as a significant asset in terms of skills and abilities. ■ the department of a business or organization that deals with the hiring, administration, and training of staff.

human right ▶ noun (usu. **human rights**) a right which is believed to belong to every person: *a flagrant disregard for basic human rights.*

human shield ▶ noun a person or group of people held near a potential target to deter attack.

Humber /ˈhʌmbə/ an estuary in NE England. It is formed at the junction of the Rivers Ouse and Trent, near Goole, and flows 60 km (38 miles) eastwards to enter the North Sea at Spurn Head. It has the major port of Hull on its north bank and is spanned by the world's second-largest suspension bridge, opened in 1981 and having a span of 1,410 m (4,626 ft). ■ a shipping forecast area covering an area of the North Sea off eastern England, extending roughly from north Norfolk to Flamborough Head.

Humberside a former county of NE England, formed in 1974 from parts of the East and West Ridings of Yorkshire and the northern part of Lincolnshire. It was dissolved in 1996.

humble ▶ adjective (**humbler**, **humblest**) **1** having or showing a modest or low estimate of one's importance: *I felt very humble when meeting her.* ■ (of an action or thought) offered with or affected by a modest estimate of one's importance: *my humble apologies.*
2 of low social, administrative, or political rank: *she came from a humble, unprivileged background.*
3 (of a thing) of modest pretensions or dimensions: *he built the business empire from humble beginnings.*
▶ verb [with obj.] cause (someone) to feel less important or proud: *he was humbled by his many ordeals.* ■ decisively defeat (a sporting opponent previously thought to be superior).
– PHRASES **eat humble pie** make a humble apology and accept humiliation. [*humble pie* is from a pun based on UMBLES 'offal', considered inferior food.] **one's humble abode** used to refer to one's home with an ironic or humorous show of modesty. **your humble servant** archaic or humorous used at the end of a letter or as a form of ironic courtesy: *your most humble servant, George Porter.*
– DERIVATIVES **humbleness** noun, **humbly** adverb.
– ORIGIN Middle English: from Old French, from Latin *humilis* 'low, lowly', from *humus* 'ground'.

humble-bee ▶ noun another term for BUMBLEBEE.
– ORIGIN late Middle English: probably from Middle Low German *hummelbē*, from *hummel* 'to buzz' + *bē* 'bee'.

Humboldt /ˈhʌmbɒlt/, Friedrich Heinrich Alexander, Baron von (1769–1859), German explorer and scientist. He travelled in Central and South America (1799–1804) and wrote on natural history, meteorology, and physical geography.

Humboldt Current another name for PERUVIAN CURRENT.

humbug ▶ noun **1** [mass noun] deceptive or false talk or behaviour: *his comments are sheer humbug.* ■ [count noun] a hypocrite.
2 Brit. a boiled sweet, especially one flavoured with peppermint.
▶ verb (**humbugs**, **humbugging**, **humbugged**) [with obj.] deceive; trick: *poor Dave is easily humbugged.* ■ [no obj.] dated act like a fraud.
– DERIVATIVES **humbuggery** noun.
– ORIGIN mid 18th cent. (in the senses 'hoax, trick' and 'deceiver'): of unknown origin.

humdinger /hʌmˈdɪŋə/ ▶ noun informal a remarkable or outstanding person or thing of its kind: *a humdinger of a funny story.*
– ORIGIN early 20th cent. (originally US): of unknown origin.

humdrum ▶ adjective lacking excitement or variety; boringly monotonous: *humdrum routine work.*
▶ noun [mass noun] monotonous routine: *an escape from the humdrum of his life.*
– ORIGIN mid 16th cent.: probably a reduplication of HUM[1].

Hume /hjuːm/, David (1711–76), Scottish philosopher, economist, and historian. He rejected the possibility of certainty in knowledge and claimed that all the data of reason stem from experience. Notable works: *A Treatise of Human Nature* (1739–40) and *History of England* (1754–62).
– DERIVATIVES **Humean** /ˈhjuːmɪən/ adjective & noun.

humectant /hjʊˈmɛkt(ə)nt/ ▶ adjective retaining or preserving moisture.
▶ noun a substance, especially a skin lotion or a food additive, used to reduce the loss of moisture.
– ORIGIN early 19th cent. (denoting a moistening agent): from Latin *humectant-* 'moistening', from the verb *humectare*, from *humectus* 'moist, wet', from *humere* 'be moist'.

humeral /ˈhjuːm(ə)r(ə)l/ ▶ adjective [attrib.] **1** relating to the humerus: *a humeral fracture.*
2 (in Catholic use) denoting a plain vestment worn around the shoulders when administering the sacrament.
– ORIGIN late 16th cent.: from French, or from late Latin *humeralis*, from Latin *humerus* (see HUMERUS).

humerus /ˈhjuːm(ə)rəs/ ▶ noun (pl. **humeri** /-rʌɪ/) Anatomy the bone of the upper arm or forelimb, forming joints at the shoulder and the elbow. ■ Entomology the structure forming the front basal corner of an insect's wing or wing case.
– ORIGIN late Middle English: from Latin, 'shoulder'.

humic /ˈhjuːmɪk/ ▶ adjective [attrib.] relating to or consisting of humus: *humic acids.*

humid /ˈhjuːmɪd/ ▶ adjective marked by a relatively high level of water vapour in the atmosphere: *a hot and humid day.*
– DERIVATIVES **humidly** adverb.
– ORIGIN late Middle English: from French *humide* or Latin *humidus*, from *humere* 'be moist'.

humidifier ▶ noun a device for keeping the atmosphere in a room moist.

humidify ▶ verb (**humidifies**, **humidifying**, **humidified**) [with obj.] increase the level of moisture in (air).
– DERIVATIVES **humidification** noun.

humidistat /hjʊˈmɪdɪstat/ ▶ noun a machine or device which automatically regulates the humidity of the air in a room or building.

humidity ▶ noun (pl. **humidities**) [mass noun] the state or quality of being humid. ■ a quantity representing the amount of water vapour in the atmosphere or in a gas: *the temperature is seventy-seven, the humidity in the low thirties.* ■ atmospheric moisture.
– ORIGIN late Middle English: from Old French *humidite* or Latin *humiditas*, from *humidus* (see HUMID).

humidor /ˈhjuːmɪdɔː/ ▶ noun an airtight container for keeping cigars or tobacco moist.
– ORIGIN early 20th cent.: from HUMID, on the pattern of *cuspidor*.

humify /ˈhjuːmɪfʌɪ/ ▶ verb (**humifies**, **humifying**, **humified**) [with obj.] convert (plant remains) into humus.
– DERIVATIVES **humification** noun.

humiliate ▶ verb [with obj.] make (someone) feel ashamed and foolish by injuring their dignity and pride: *you'll humiliate me in front of the whole school!*
– DERIVATIVES **humiliator** noun.
– ORIGIN mid 16th cent. (earlier (late Middle English) as *humiliation*): from late Latin *humiliat-* 'made humble', from the verb *humiliare*, from *humilis* (see HUMBLE). The original meaning was 'bring low'; the current sense dates from the mid 18th cent.

humiliating ▶ adjective making someone feel ashamed and foolish by injuring their dignity and pride: *a humiliating defeat.*
– DERIVATIVES **humiliatingly** adverb.

humiliation ▶ noun [mass noun] the action of humiliating someone or the state of being humiliated: *they suffered the humiliation of losing in the opening round* | [count noun] *the conference decision was a humiliation for the union's executive.*

humility ▶ noun [mass noun] the quality of having a modest or low view of one's importance.
– ORIGIN Middle English: from Old French *humilite*, from Latin *humilitas*, from *humilis* (see HUMBLE).

humint /ˈh(j)uːmɪnt/ ▶ noun [mass noun] covert intelligence-gathering by agents or others.
– ORIGIN late 20th cent.: from *human intelligence*.

hummel /ˈhʌm(ə)l/ Scottish & N. English ▶ adjective (of a cow or stag) lacking horns or antlers.
▶ noun a stag which has failed to grow antlers, typically as a result of malnutrition when young.
– ORIGIN late 15th cent. (describing grain in the sense 'without an awn'): related to Low German *hummel*, *hommel* 'hornless animal'.

Hummer ▶ noun N. Amer. informal term for HUMVEE.

hummingbird ▶ noun a small nectar-feeding tropical American bird that is able to hover and fly backwards, and typically has colourful iridescent plumage. ● Family Trochilidae: many genera and numerous species.
– ORIGIN mid 17th cent.: so named because of the humming sound produced by the rapid vibration of the bird's wings.

hummingbird hawkmoth ▶ noun a migratory day-flying hawkmoth that makes an audible hum while hovering in front of flowers to feed on nectar. ● *Macroglossum stellatarum*, family Sphingidae.

hummock ▶ noun a hillock or knoll. ■ a hump or ridge in an ice field. ■ N. Amer. a piece of forested ground rising above a marsh.
– DERIVATIVES **hummocky** adjective.
– ORIGIN mid 16th cent. (originally in nautical use denoting a small hillock on the coast): of unknown origin.

hummus /ˈhʊməs/ (also **houmous**) ▶ noun [mass noun] a thick paste or spread made from ground chickpeas and sesame seeds, olive oil, lemon, and garlic, made originally in the Middle East.
– ORIGIN from Arabic *ḥummuṣ*.

humongous /hjuːˈmʌŋɡəs/ (also **humungous**) ▸ **adjective** informal, chiefly N. Amer. huge; enormous: *a humongous steak.*
– ORIGIN 1970s (originally US): possibly based on HUGE and MONSTROUS, influenced by the stress pattern of *stupendous.*

humor ▸ **noun** US spelling of HUMOUR.

humoral /ˈhjuːm(ə)r(ə)l/ ▸ **adjective** Medicine relating to the body fluids, especially with regard to immune responses involving antibodies in body fluids as distinct from cells (see CELL-MEDIATED). ■ historical relating to the four bodily humours. ■ historical (of diseases) caused by or attributed to a disordered state of body fluids or (formerly) the bodily humours.
– ORIGIN late Middle English (in the general sense 'relating to bodily fluids'): from Old French, or from medieval Latin *humoralis,* from Latin *humor* 'moisture' (see HUMOUR).

humoresque /ˌhjuːməˈrɛsk/ ▸ **noun** a short, lively piece of music.
– ORIGIN late 19th cent.: from German *Humoreske,* from *Humor* 'humour'.

humorist ▸ **noun** a humorous writer, performer, or artist.

humorous ▸ **adjective** causing laughter and amusement; comic: *a humorous and entertaining talk.* ■ having or showing a sense of humour: *his humorous grey eyes.*
– DERIVATIVES **humorously** adverb, **humorousness** noun.

> **USAGE** Note that although **humor** is the American spelling of **humour, humorous** is not an American form. This word is spelled the same way in both British and American English, and the spelling **humourous** is regarded as an error.

humour (US **humor**) ▸ **noun** [mass noun] **1** the quality of being amusing or comic, especially as expressed in literature or speech: *his tales are full of humour.* ■ the ability to express humour or amuse other people: *their inimitable brand of humour.*
2 a mood or state of mind: *her good humour vanished | the clash hadn't improved his humour.* ■ [count noun] archaic an inclination or whim.
3 (also **cardinal humour**) [count noun] historical each of the four chief fluids of the body (blood, phlegm, yellow bile (choler), and black bile (melancholy)) that were thought to determine a person's physical and mental qualities by the relative proportions in which they were present.
▸ **verb** [with obj.] comply with the wishes of (someone) in order to keep them content, however unreasonable such wishes might be: *she was always humouring him to prevent trouble.* ■ archaic adapt or accommodate oneself to (something).
– PHRASES **out of humour** in a bad mood. **sense of humour** a person's ability to appreciate humour: *in all the ups and downs of his life he never lost his sense of humour.*
– ORIGIN Middle English: via Old French from Latin *humor* 'moisture', from *humere* (see HUMID). The original sense was 'bodily fluid' (surviving in *aqueous humour* and *vitreous humour*); it was used specifically for any of the cardinal humours (sense 3 of the noun), whence 'mental disposition' (thought to be caused by the relative proportions of the humours). This led, in the 16th cent., to the senses 'mood' (sense 2 of the noun) and 'whim', hence *to humour someone* 'to indulge a person's whim'. Sense 1 of the noun dates from the late 16th cent.

humourless (US **humorless**) ▸ **adjective** lacking humour; not able to appreciate or express humour: *they are such a humourless bunch.*
– DERIVATIVES **humourlessly** adverb, **humourlessness** noun.

hump ▸ **noun 1** a rounded raised mass of earth or land. ■ a mound over which railway vehicles are pushed so as to run by gravity over points to the required place in a marshalling yard.
2 a rounded protuberance found on the back of a camel or other animal or as an abnormality on the back of a person.
▸ **verb 1** [with obj. and adverbial of direction] chiefly Brit. informal carry (a heavy object) with difficulty: *he continued to hump cases up and down the hotel corridor.*
2 [with obj.] make hump-shaped.
3 [with obj.] vulgar slang have sexual intercourse with.
4 (usu. in imperative **hump off**) Irish informal go away.
– PHRASES **get** (or **have** or **give someone**) **the hump** Brit. informal become, be, or make someone annoyed or moody. **over the hump** past the most difficult part of something.
– DERIVATIVES **humpless** adjective.
– ORIGIN early 18th cent.: probably related to Low German *humpe* 'hump', also to Dutch *homp,* Low German *humpe* 'lump, hunk (of bread)'.

humpback ▸ **noun 1** (also **humpback whale**) a baleen whale which has a hump (instead of a dorsal fin) and long white flippers. ● *Megaptera novaeangliae,* family Balaenopteridae.
2 (also **humpback salmon**) a small salmon with dark spots on the back, native to the North Pacific and introduced into the NW Atlantic. Also called PINK SALMON. ● *Oncorhynchus gorbuscha,* family Salmonidae.
3 another term for HUNCHBACK.
– DERIVATIVES **humpbacked** adjective.

humpback bridge ▸ **noun** Brit. a small road bridge with a steep ascent and descent.

humped ▸ **adjective** having a hump or humps; hump-shaped: *a breed of humped cattle | a humped bridge.*

Humperdinck /ˈhʌmpədɪŋk, ˈhʊm-/, Engelbert (1854–1921), German composer. Influenced by Wagner, he is remembered as the composer of the opera *Hänsel und Gretel* (1893).

humph ▸ **exclamation** used to express slightly scornful doubt or dissatisfaction: *Humph! I suppose I'd better take him.*
– ORIGIN natural utterance: first recorded in English in the mid 16th cent.

Humpty Dumpty ▸ **noun** (pl. **Humpty Dumpties**) informal **1** a short fat person.
2 a person or thing that once overthrown cannot be restored.
– ORIGIN late 18th cent.: from the egg-like nursery-rhyme character who fell off a wall, broke, and could not be put together again.

humpy[1] ▸ **adjective** (**humpier, humpiest**) humped in form; having a hump.

humpy[2] ▸ **noun** (pl. **humpies**) Austral. a makeshift hut.
– ORIGIN from Yagara (an extinct Aboriginal language), influenced by HUMP.

humungous ▸ **adjective** variant spelling of HUMONGOUS.

humus /ˈhjuːməs/ ▸ **noun** [mass noun] the organic component of soil, formed by the decomposition of leaves and other plant material by soil microorganisms.
– ORIGIN late 18th cent.: from Latin, 'soil'.

Humvee /ˈhʌmviː/ ▸ **noun** trademark, chiefly N. Amer. a modern military jeep.
– ORIGIN late 20th cent.: alteration, from the initials of *high-mobility multi-purpose vehicle.*

Hun ▸ **noun 1** a member of a warlike Asiatic nomadic people who invaded and ravaged Europe in the 4th–5th centuries.
2 informal, derogatory a German (especially during the First and Second World Wars). ■ (**the Hun**) Germans collectively.
– DERIVATIVES **Hunnish** adjective.
– ORIGIN Old English *Hūne, Hūnas* (plural), from late Latin *Hunni,* from Greek *Hounnoi,* of Middle Iranian origin.

Hunan /huːˈnan/ a province of east central China; capital, Changsha.

hunch ▸ **verb** [with obj.] raise (one's shoulders) and bend the top of one's body forward: *Eliot hunched his shoulders against a gust of snow.* ■ [no obj.] sit or stand with one's shoulders raised and the top of one's body bent forward: *he **hunched over** his glass.*
▸ **noun 1** a feeling or guess based on intuition rather than fact: *I have a hunch that someone is telling lies.*
2 a humped position or thing: *the hunch of his back.*
3 dialect a thick piece; a hunk: *a **hunch of** bread.*
– ORIGIN late 15th cent.: of unknown origin. The original meaning was 'push, shove' (noun and verb), a sense retained now in Scots as a noun, and in US dialect as a verb. Sense 1 of the noun derives probably from a US sense of the verb 'nudge someone in order to draw attention to something'.

hunchback ▸ **noun** a back deformed by a sharp forward angle, forming a hump, typically caused by collapse of a vertebra. ■ often offensive a person with a hunchback.
– DERIVATIVES **hunchbacked** adjective.

hundred ▸ **cardinal number** (pl. **hundreds** or (with numeral or quantifying word) **hundred**) (**a/one hundred**) the number equivalent to the product of ten and ten; ten more than ninety; 100: *a hundred yards away | there are just a hundred of us here.* (Roman numeral: **c** or **C**) ■ (**hundreds**) the numbers from one hundred to 999: *an unknown number, probably in the hundreds, had already been lost.* ■ (**hundreds**) several hundred things or people: *her coat cost hundreds of pounds.* ■ (usu. **hundreds**) informal an unspecified large number: *hundreds of letters poured in.* ■ (**the —— hundreds**) the years of a specified century: *the early nineteen hundreds.* ■ one hundred years old: *you must be over a hundred!* ■ one hundred miles per hour. ■ Cricket a batsman's score of a hundred runs or more. ■ (chiefly in spoken English) used to express whole hours in the twenty-four-hour system: *twelve hundred hours.*
▸ **noun** Brit. historical a subdivision of a county or shire, having its own court: *Wantage Hundred.*
– PHRASES **a** (or **one**) **hundred per cent** entirely; completely: *I'm not a hundred per cent sure.* ■ [usu. with negative] informal completely fit and healthy: *she did not feel one hundred per cent.* ■ informal maximum effort and commitment: *he always gave one hundred per cent for United.*
– DERIVATIVES **hundredfold** adjective & adverb, **hundredth** ordinal number.
– ORIGIN late Old English, from *hund* 'hundred' (from an Indo-European root shared with Latin *centum* and Greek *hekaton*) + a second element meaning 'number'; of Germanic origin and related to Dutch *honderd* and German *hundert.* The noun sense 'subdivision of a county' is of uncertain origin: it may originally have been equivalent to a hundred hides of land (see HIDE[3]).

Hundred Flowers a period of debate in China 1956–7, when, under the slogan 'Let a hundred flowers bloom and a hundred schools of thought contend', citizens were invited to voice their opinions of the communist regime. It was forcibly ended after social unrest and fierce criticism of the government, with those who had voiced their opinions being prosecuted.

hundreds and thousands ▸ **plural noun** Brit. tiny sugar beads of varying colours used for decorating cakes and desserts.

hundredweight (abbrev.: **cwt**) ▸ **noun** (pl. **same** or **hundredweights**) **1** (also **long hundredweight**) Brit. a unit of weight equal to 112 lb avoirdupois (about 50.8 kg).
2 (also **short hundredweight**) US a unit of weight equal to 100 lb (about 45.4 kg).
3 (also **metric hundredweight**) a unit of weight equal to 50 kg.

Hundred Years War a war between France and England, conventionally dated 1337–1453.

> The war consisted of a series of conflicts in which successive English kings attempted to dominate France and included an early string of English military successes, most notably at Crécy and Poitiers. In 1415 England, under Henry V, delivered a crushing victory at Agincourt and occupied much of northern France, but, with the exception of Calais, all English conquests had been lost by 1453.

hung past and past participle of HANG. ▸ **adjective 1** (of an elected body in the UK and Canada) having no political party with an overall majority: *a hung parliament.* ■ (of a jury) unable to agree on a verdict.
2 (**hung up**) informal emotionally confused or disturbed: *people are hung up in all sorts of ways.* ■ (**hung up about/on**) obsessed with or worried about: *guys are so hung up about the way they look.*
3 [predic.] informal used in similes to refer to the size of a man's genitals.

Hungarian /hʌŋˈɡɛːrɪən/ ▸ **adjective** relating to Hungary, its people, or their language.
▸ **noun 1** a native or inhabitant of Hungary, or a person of Hungarian descent.
2 [mass noun] the official language of Hungary, spoken also by some 2.5 million people in Romania. Hungarian is a Finno-Ugric language and is the only major language of the Ugric branch. Also called MAGYAR.
– ORIGIN from medieval Latin *Hungari* (a name given to the Hungarians, who called themselves the Magyar) + -AN.

Hungary a country in central Europe; pop. 9,905,600 (est. 2009); official language, Hungarian; capital, Budapest. Hungarian name MAGYARORSZÁG.

> Hungary was conquered by the Habsburgs in the 17th century, becoming an equal partner in the Austro-Hungarian Empire in 1867. Following the collapse of the empire in 1918, Hungary became an independent kingdom. After participation in the Second World War on the Axis side, Hungary was occupied by the Soviet Union, and became a communist state. A liberal reform movement was crushed by Soviet troops in 1956, but the communist system was abandoned in 1989, and the first multiparty elections

H

were held in 1990. Hungary joined NATO in 1999 and the EU in 2004.

– ORIGIN from medieval Latin *Hungaria* (see also **HUNGARIAN**).

hunger ▶ **noun** [mass noun] a feeling of discomfort or weakness caused by lack of food, coupled with the desire to eat: *she was faint with hunger.* ■ a severe lack of food: *they died from cold and hunger.* ■ a strong desire or craving: *her **hunger for** knowledge.*
▶ **verb** [no obj.] **1** (**hunger after/for**) have a strong desire or craving for: *he hungered for a sense of self-worth.*
2 archaic feel or suffer hunger.
– ORIGIN Old English *hungor* (noun), *hyngran* (verb), of Germanic origin; related to Dutch *honger* and German *Hunger.*

hunger march ▶ **noun** a march undertaken by a group of people in protest against unemployment or poverty, especially any of those by unemployed workers in Britain during the 1920s and 1930s.
– DERIVATIVES **hunger marcher** noun.

hunger strike ▶ **noun** a prolonged refusal to eat, carried out as a protest by a prisoner.
– DERIVATIVES **hunger striker** noun.

hung-over ▶ **adjective** suffering from a hangover after drinking alcohol.

hungry ▶ **adjective** (**hungrier**, **hungriest**) feeling or showing the need for food: *I was feeling ravenously hungry.* ■ [attrib.] causing hunger: *I always find art galleries hungry work.* ■ having a strong desire or craving: *a party **hungry for** power* | [in combination] *grasping, power-hungry individuals.*
– DERIVATIVES **hungrily** adverb, **hungriness** noun.
– ORIGIN Old English *hungrig*, of West Germanic origin; related to Dutch *hongerig*, German *hungrig*, also to **HUNGER**.

hunk ▶ **noun 1** a large piece of something, especially food, cut or broken off a larger piece: ***a hunk of** bread.*
2 informal a large, strong, sexually attractive man.
– ORIGIN early 19th cent.: probably of Dutch or Low German origin.

hunker ▶ **verb 1** [no obj.] squat or crouch down low: *he **hunkered down** beside her.* ■ bend the top of one's body forward; hunch.
2 (**hunker down**) apply oneself seriously to a task: *students hunkered down to prepare for the examinations.*
– ORIGIN early 18th cent.: probably related to Dutch *huiken* and German *hocken.*

hunkers ▶ **plural noun** informal haunches: *he was sitting on his hunkers.*
– ORIGIN mid 18th cent. (originally Scots): from **HUNKER**.

hunky ▶ **adjective** (**hunkier**, **hunkiest**) informal (of a man) large, strong, and sexually attractive: *the sexy stars fell out over hunky footballer Lee.*

hunky-dory ▶ **adjective** informal fine; going well: *everything is hunky-dory.*
– ORIGIN mid 19th cent. (originally US): *hunky* from Dutch *honk* 'home, base' (in games); the origin of *dory* is unknown.

Hunt, (William) Holman (1827–1910), English painter, one of the founders of the Pre-Raphaelite Brotherhood. He painted biblical scenes with extensive use of symbolism. Notable works: *The Light of the World* (1854) and *The Scapegoat* (1855).

hunt ▶ **verb 1** [with obj.] pursue and kill (a wild animal) for sport or food: *in the autumn they hunted deer.* ■ Brit. pursue (a wild animal, especially a fox or deer) on horseback using hounds. ■ Brit. use (a hound or a horse) for hunting. ■ (of an animal) chase and kill (its prey): *mice are hunted by weasels and foxes* | [no obj.] *lionesses hunt in groups.*
2 [no obj.] search determinedly for someone or something: *he desperately **hunted for** a new job.* ■ [with obj.] (of the police) search for (a criminal): *the gang is being hunted by police* | [no obj.] *police are **hunting for** her attacker.* ■ [with obj.] (**hunt someone down**) search for and capture someone.
3 [no obj.] (of a device or system) oscillate about a desired speed, position, or state. ■ (of an aircraft or rocket) oscillate about a mean flight path.
4 [no obj.] (**hunt down/up**) (in change-ringing) move the place of a bell in a simple progression.
▶ **noun 1** an act of hunting wild animals or game. ■ an association of people who meet regularly to hunt, especially with hounds. ■ an area where hunting takes place.
2 a search: *police launched a **hunt for** the killer.*
3 an oscillating motion about a desired speed, position, or state.
– ORIGIN Old English *huntian*, of Germanic origin. Sense 4 dates from the late 17th cent., and is probably based on the idea of the bells pursuing one another; it gave rise to the sense 'oscillate about a desired speed' (late 19th cent.).

hunt-and-peck ▶ **adjective** denoting or using an inexpert form of typing in which only one or two fingers are used: *hunt-and-peck computer users.*

huntaway ▶ **noun** NZ a dog trained to drive sheep forward.

hunted ▶ **adjective** being pursued or searched for. ■ appearing worn or harassed as if one is being pursued: *his eyes had a hunted look.*

Hunter, John (1728–93), Scottish anatomist, regarded as a founder of scientific surgery. He also made valuable investigations in pathology, physiology, dentistry, and biology.

hunter ▶ **noun 1** a person or animal that hunts: *a deer hunter.* ■ a person searching for something: *a bargain hunter.* ■ a horse of a breed developed for stamina in fox-hunting and ability to jump obstacles. ■ (**the Hunter**) the constellation Orion.
2 a watch with a hinged cover protecting the glass.

hunter-gatherer ▶ **noun** a member of a nomadic people who live chiefly by hunting and fishing, and harvesting wild food.

hunter-killer ▶ **adjective** (of a naval vessel, especially a submarine) equipped to locate and destroy enemy vessels, especially other submarines.

hunter's moon ▶ **noun** the first full moon after a harvest moon.

hunting ▶ **noun** [mass noun] **1** the activity of hunting wild animals or game.
2 [in combination] the activity of searching for something: *house-hunting.*
3 (also **plain hunting**) Bell-ringing a simple system of changes in which bells move through the order in a regular progression.

hunting crop (also **hunting whip**) ▶ **noun** a short rigid riding whip with a handle at right angles to the stock and a long leather thong, used chiefly in hunting.

hunting dog ▶ **noun 1** a dog of a breed developed for hunting.
2 (also **Cape hunting dog**) an African wild dog that has a dark coat with pale markings and a white-tipped tail, living and hunting in packs. ● *Lycaon pictus*, family Canidae.

Huntingdon[1] a town in Cambridgeshire, eastern England, on the River Ouse; pop. 23,100 (est. 2009).

Huntingdon[2], Selina Hastings, Countess of (1707–91), English religious leader; born *Selina Shirley*. She was instrumental in introducing Methodism to the upper classes and established many chapels and a training college for ministers.

Huntingdonshire a former county of SE England. It became part of Cambridgeshire in 1974.

hunting ground ▶ **noun** a place used or suitable for hunting. ■ a place likely to be a fruitful source of something desired or sought: *the circuit is a favourite hunting ground for talent scouts.*

hunting horn ▶ **noun** a straight horn blown to give signals during hunting.

hunting pink ▶ **noun** see **PINK**[1] (sense 1 of the noun).

Huntington a city in West Virginia, on the Ohio River; pop. 49,185 (est. 2008).

Huntington Beach a city on the Pacific coast, to the south of Long Beach, in southern California; pop. 192,620 (est. 2008). It is noted as a surfing locality.

Huntington's disease ▶ **noun** [mass noun] a hereditary disease marked by degeneration of the brain cells and causing chorea and progressive dementia.
– ORIGIN late 19th cent.: named after George *Huntington* (1851–1916), the American neurologist who first described it.

hunting whip ▶ **noun** another term for **HUNTING CROP**.

huntress ▶ **noun** a woman who hunts.

hunt saboteur ▶ **noun** a person who attempts to disrupt a hunt.

huntsman ▶ **noun** (pl. **huntsmen**) a person who hunts. ■ a hunt official in charge of hounds.

Huntsville a city in northern Alabama; pop. 176,645 (est. 2008).

hunyak /ˈhʌnjak/ ▶ **noun** N. Amer. informal, derogatory a person of Hungarian or central European origin, especially an immigrant.
– ORIGIN early 20th cent.: alteration of **HUNGARIAN**, on the pattern of *Polack*.

Huon pine /ˈhjuːɒn/ ▶ **noun** a tall Tasmanian conifer which has yew-like berries and fragrant red timber. ● *Dacrydium franklinii*, family Podocarpaceae.
– ORIGIN early 19th cent.: from *Huon*, the name of a river in the south of Tasmania.

Hupeh /huːˈpeɪ/ variant of **HUBEI**.

hurdle ▶ **noun 1** one of a series of upright frames over which athletes in a race must jump. ■ (**hurdles**) a hurdle race: *the 100 m hurdles.*
2 a problem or difficulty that must be overcome: *many would like to emigrate to the United States, but face formidable hurdles.*
3 a portable rectangular frame strengthened with withies or wooden bars, used as a temporary fence. ■ a horse race over a series of hurdles: *a handicap hurdle.*
4 Brit. historical a frame on which traitors were dragged to execution.
▶ **verb 1** [no obj.] take part in a hurdle race. ■ [with obj.] jump over (a hurdle or other obstacle) while running.
2 [with obj.] enclose or fence off with hurdles.
– PHRASES **fall at the first hurdle** meet with failure at a very early stage of an undertaking: *the campaign could fall at the first hurdle if they fail to secure planning permission.*
– DERIVATIVES **hurdler** noun.
– ORIGIN Old English *hyrdel* 'temporary fence', of Germanic origin; related to Dutch *horde* and German *Hürde*.

hurdling ▶ **noun** [mass noun] the sport of racing over hurdles.

hurdy-gurdy /ˈhəːdɪˌɡəːdi/ ▶ **noun** (pl. **hurdy-gurdies**) a musical instrument with a droning sound played by turning a handle, which is typically attached to a rosined wheel sounding a series of drone strings, with keys worked by the left hand. ■ informal a barrel organ.
– ORIGIN mid 18th cent.: probably imitative of the sound of the instrument.

hurl ▶ **verb** [with obj. and adverbial of direction] throw or impel (someone or something) with great force: *rioters hurled a brick through the windscreen* | figurative *he hurled himself into the job with enthusiasm.* ■ utter (abuse) vehemently: *the demonstrators hurled abuse at councillors.* ■ [no obj.] informal vomit: *you make me want to hurl.*
▶ **noun** Scottish informal a ride in a vehicle; a lift.
– ORIGIN Middle English: probably imitative, but corresponding in form and partly in sense with Low German *hurreln*.

hurler ▶ **noun 1** N. Amer. informal a baseball pitcher.
2 a player of hurling.

Hurler's syndrome /ˈhəːləz/ ▶ **noun** [mass noun] Medicine a defect in metabolism arising from congenital absence of an enzyme, causing accumulation of lipids and mucopolysaccharides, and resulting in mental retardation, a protruding abdomen, and bone deformities including an abnormally large head. Also called **GARGOYLISM**.
– ORIGIN 1930s: named after Gertrud *Hurler* (1889–1965), the Austrian paediatrician who first described it.

hurley ▶ **noun** a stick used in the game of hurling. ■ [mass noun] another term for **HURLING**.
– ORIGIN early 19th cent.: from **HURL**.

hurling ▶ **noun** [mass noun] an Irish game resembling hockey, played with a shorter stick with a broader oval blade. It is the national game of Ireland and may date back to the 2nd millennium BC.

hurly-burly ▶ **noun** [mass noun] busy, boisterous activity: *the hurly-burly of school life.*
– ORIGIN Middle English: reduplication based on **HURL**.

Huron /ˈhjʊərɒn/ ▶ **noun** (pl. **same** or **Hurons**) **1** a member of a confederation of native North American peoples formerly living in the region east of Lake Huron and now settled mainly in Oklahoma and Quebec.
2 [mass noun] the extinct Iroquoian language of the Huron.
▶ **adjective** relating to the Huron or their language.
– ORIGIN French, literally 'having hair standing in bristles on the head', from Old French *hure* 'head of a wild boar', of unknown ultimate origin.

Huron, Lake the second-largest of the five Great Lakes of North America, on the border between Canada and the US.

hurrah (also **hooray, hurray**) ▶ **exclamation** used to express joy or approval: *Hurrah! She's here at last!*
▶ **noun** an utterance of the word 'hurrah'.
▶ **verb** [no obj.] shout 'hurrah'.
– ORIGIN late 17th cent.: alteration of **HUZZA**; perhaps originally a sailors' cry when hauling.

Hurri /ˈhʌri/ ▶ **plural noun** the Hurrian people collectively.
– ORIGIN the name in Hittite and Akkadian.

Hurrian /ˈhʌrɪən/ ▶ **noun 1** a member of an ancient people, originally from Armenia, who settled in Syria and northern Mesopotamia during the 3rd–2nd millennia BC and were later absorbed by the Hittites and Assyrians.
2 [mass noun] the language of the Hurrians, written in cuneiform and of unknown affinity.
▶ **adjective** of or relating to the Hurrians or their language.

hurricane /ˈhʌrɪk(ə)n, -keɪn/ ▶ **noun** a storm with a violent wind, in particular a tropical cyclone in the Caribbean. ■ a wind of force 12 on the Beaufort scale (equal to or exceeding 64 knots or 118 kph).
– ORIGIN mid 16th cent.: from Spanish *huracán*, probably from Taino *hurakán* 'god of the storm'.

hurricane deck ▶ **noun** a covered deck at or near the top of a ship's superstructure.

hurricane lamp ▶ **noun** an oil lamp with a glass chimney, designed to protect the flame even in high winds.

hurricane tape ▶ **noun** [mass noun] US a strong type of adhesive tape used on windows to keep the glass in place if it is broken by strong winds.

hurried ▶ **adjective** done in a hurry; rushed: *I ate a hurried breakfast.*
– DERIVATIVES **hurriedly adverb**, **hurriedness noun**.

hurroo ▶ **exclamation & noun** variant spelling of **HOOROO**.

hurry ▶ **verb** (**hurries, hurrying, hurried**) [no obj.] move or act with great haste: *we'd better hurry | servants hurried around.* ■ (often in imperative **hurry up**) do something more quickly: *hurry up and finish your meal.* ■ [with obj.] cause to move with haste: *she hurried him across the landing.* ■ [with obj.] do or finish (something) quickly or too quickly: *formalities were hurried over.*
▶ **noun** [mass noun] great haste: *in my hurry to leave I knocked over a pile of books.* ■ [with negative and in questions] a need for haste; urgency: *there's no hurry to get back.*
– PHRASES **in a hurry** rushed; in a rushed manner. ■ eager to get a thing done quickly: *no one seemed in a hurry for the results.* ■ [usu. with negative] informal easily; readily: *an experience you won't forget in a hurry.*
– ORIGIN late 16th cent. (as a verb): imitative.

hurry-scurry archaic ▶ **noun** [mass noun] disorderly haste.
▶ **adjective & adverb** with hurry and confusion.
– ORIGIN mid 18th cent.: reduplication of **HURRY**.

hurry-up ▶ **adjective** [attrib.] US informal showing, involving, or requiring haste or urgency.

hurst ▶ **noun** (archaic except in place names) **1** a hillock. ■ a wood or wooded rise: *Cumnor Hurst.*
2 a sandbank.
– ORIGIN Old English *hyrst*, of Germanic origin; related to German *Horst*.

Hurston /ˈhəːst(ə)n/, Zora Neale (1901–60), American novelist. Her novels reflect her interest in folklore, especially that of the Deep South. Notable works: *Jonah's Gourd Vine* (1934) and *Seraph on the Suwanee* (1948).

hurt ▶ **verb** (past and past participle **hurt**) [with obj.] **1** cause pain or injury to: *Ow! You're hurting me! |* [no obj.] *does acupuncture hurt?* ■ [no obj.] (of a part of the body) suffer pain: *my back hurts.* ■ cause distress to: *she didn't want to hurt his feelings.* ■ [no obj.] (of a person) feel distress: *he was hurting badly, but he smiled through his tears.*
2 be detrimental to: *high interest rates are hurting the local economy.*
3 [no obj.] (**hurt for**) N. Amer. informal have a pressing need for: *Frank wasn't hurting for money.*
▶ **noun** [mass noun] physical injury; harm. ■ mental pain or distress: *her eyes reflected her unhappiness and hurt |* [count noun] *it's time to forgive past hurts and open your heart.*
– DERIVATIVES **hurty adjective** (informal) (**hurtier, hurtiest**).
– ORIGIN Middle English (originally in the senses 'to strike' and 'a blow'): from Old French *hurter* (verb), *hurt* (noun), perhaps ultimately of Germanic origin.

hurtful ▶ **adjective** causing distress to someone's feelings: *his hurtful remarks.*
– DERIVATIVES **hurtfully adverb**, **hurtfulness noun**.

hurtle ▶ **verb** move or cause to move at high speed, typically in an uncontrolled manner: [no obj., with adverbial of direction] *a runaway car hurtled towards them |* [with obj. and adverbial of direction] *the trucks hurtled them through the grassland to the construction sites.*
– ORIGIN Middle English (in the sense 'strike against, collide with'): frequentative of **HURT**.

Husain variant spelling of **HUSSEIN²**, **HUSSEIN³**.

Husák /ˈhuːsak/, Gustáv (1913–91), Czechoslovak statesman, leader of the Communist Party of Czechoslovakia 1969–87 and President 1975–89. He succeeded Alexander Dubček following the Prague Spring of 1968 and purged the party of its reformist elements.

husband ▶ **noun** a married man considered in relation to his wife: *she and her husband are both retired.*
▶ **verb** [with obj.] use (resources) economically: *she husbanded their financial resources through difficult times.*
– DERIVATIVES **husbander noun** (rare), **husbandhood noun**, **husbandless adjective**, **husbandly adjective**.
– ORIGIN late Old English (in the senses 'male head of a household' and 'manager, steward'), from Old Norse *húsbóndi* 'master of a house', from *hús* 'house' + *bóndi* 'occupier and tiller of the soil'. The original sense of the verb was 'till, cultivate'.

husbandman ▶ **noun** (pl. **husbandmen**) archaic a person who cultivates the land; a farmer.
– ORIGIN Middle English (originally in northern English use denoting the holder of a *husbandland*, i.e. manorial tenancy): from **HUSBAND** in the obsolete sense 'farmer' + **MAN**.

husbandry ▶ **noun** [mass noun] **1** the care, cultivation, and breeding of crops and animals: *all aspects of animal husbandry.*
2 management and conservation of resources.
– ORIGIN Middle English: from **HUSBAND** in the obsolete sense 'farmer' + **-RY**; compare with **HUSBANDMAN**.

hush ▶ **verb** [with obj.] make (someone) be quiet or stop talking: *he placed a finger before pursed lips to hush her.* ■ [no obj., often in imperative] be quiet: *Hush! Someone will hear you.* ■ (**hush something up**) suppress public mention of something: *management took steps to hush up the dangers.*
▶ **noun** [in sing.] a silence: *a hush descended over the crowd.*
– ORIGIN mid 16th cent.: back-formation from obsolete *husht* 'silent' (taken to be a past participle), from an interjection *husht* 'quiet!'.

hushaby (also **hushabye**) ▶ **exclamation** archaic used to lull a child.

hushed ▶ **adjective** (of a place) very quiet and still: *he addressed the hushed courtroom.* ■ (of a voice or conversation) quiet and serious.

hush-hush ▶ **adjective** informal (especially of an official plan or project) highly secret or confidential: *a hush-hush research unit.*

hush money ▶ **noun** [mass noun] informal money paid to someone to prevent them from disclosing embarrassing or discreditable information.

hush puppies ▶ **plural noun 1** (**Hush Puppies**) trademark lightweight casual shoes made of soft suede or leather.
2 US small cakes of maize dough which are quickly deep-fried.

husk¹ ▶ **noun** the dry outer covering of some fruits or seeds. ■ a dry or rough outer layer, especially when it is empty of its contents: *the husks of dead bugs.*
▶ **verb** [with obj.] remove the husk or husks from.
– ORIGIN late Middle English: probably from Low German *hūske* 'sheath', literally 'little house'.

husk² ▶ **noun** [mass noun] **1** bronchitis in cattle, sheep, or pigs caused by parasitic infestation, typically marked by a husky cough.
2 huskiness: *the husk in her voice.*
▶ **verb** [with direct speech] say something in a husky voice: *'What big blue eyes you have,' husked Lorenzo.*
– ORIGIN early 18th cent.: partly from **HUSKY¹**, partly from the earlier verb *husk* '(of a farm animal) cough'.

husky¹ ▶ **adjective** (**huskier, huskiest**) **1** (of a voice or utterance) sounding low-pitched and slightly hoarse.
2 (of a person) big and strong: *Paddy looked a husky, strong guy.*
3 like or consisting of a husk or husks.
– DERIVATIVES **huskily adverb**, **huskiness noun**.

husky² ▶ **noun** (pl. **huskies**) a powerful dog of a breed with a thick double coat which is typically grey, used in the Arctic for pulling sledges.
– ORIGIN mid 19th cent. (originally denoting the Eskimo language or an Eskimo): abbreviation of obsolete *Ehuskemay* or Newfoundland dialect *Huskemaw* 'Eskimo', probably from Montagnais (see **ESKIMO**). The term replaced the 18th-cent. term *Eskimo dog*.

Huss /hʌs/, John (*c.*1372–1415), Bohemian religious reformer; Czech name *Jan Hus*. A rector of Prague University, he supported the views of Wyclif, attacked ecclesiastical abuses, and was excommunicated in 1411. He was later tried and burnt at the stake. See also **HUSSITE**.

huss /hʌs/ ▶ **noun** Brit. a dogfish, especially the nurse hound (also called **BULL HUSS**). ● Genus *Scyliorhinus*, family Scyliorhinidae.
– ORIGIN Middle English *husk*, of unknown origin.

hussar /hʊˈzɑː/ ▶ **noun** historical a soldier in a light cavalry regiment which had adopted a dress uniform modelled on that of the Hungarian hussars (now only in titles): *the Queen's Royal Irish Hussars.* ■ (in the 15th century) a Hungarian light horseman.
– ORIGIN from Hungarian *huszár*, from Old Serbian *husar*, from Italian *corsaro* (see **CORSAIR**).

H

Hussein¹, Abdullah ibn, see **ABDULLAH IBN HUSSEIN**.

Hussein² /hʊˈseɪn/ (also **Husain**), ibn Talal (1935–99), king of Jordan 1953–99. Throughout his reign Hussein sought to maintain good relations both with the West and with other Arab nations. During the Gulf War he supported Iraq, but in 1994 he signed a treaty normalizing relations with Israel.

Hussein³ /hʊˈseɪn/ (also **Husain**), Saddam (1937–2006), Iraqi President, Prime Minister, and head of the armed forces 1979–2003; full name *Saddam bin Hussein at-Takriti*. During his presidency Iraq fought a war with Iran (1980–8) and invaded Kuwait (1990), from which Iraqi forces were expelled in the Gulf War of 1991. He also ordered punitive attacks on Kurdish rebels in the north of Iraq and on the Marsh Arabs in the south. He was overthrown in 2003 following the invasion and occupation of Iraq by US-led forces. He was later tried for crimes against humanity and executed.

Husserl /ˈhʊsəːl/, German /ˈhʊsɐl/, Edmund (Gustav Albrecht) (1859–1938), German philosopher. His work forms the basis of the school of phenomenology; he rejected metaphysical assumptions about what actually exists, and explanations of why it exists, in favour of pure subjective consciousness as the condition for all experience, with the world as the object of this consciousness.

Hussite /ˈhʌsʌɪt/ ▶ **noun** a member or follower of the religious movement begun by John Huss. After Huss's execution the Hussites took up arms against the Holy Roman Empire and demanded a set of reforms that anticipated the Reformation. Most of the demands were granted (1436), and a Church was established that remained independent of the Roman Catholic Church until 1620.
▶ **adjective** relating to the Hussites.
– DERIVATIVES **Hussitism noun**.

hussy ▶ **noun** (pl. **hussies**) an impudent or immoral girl or woman: *that brazen little hussy!*
– ORIGIN late Middle English: contraction of **HOUSEWIFE** (the original sense); the current sense dates from the mid 17th cent.

hustings ▶ **noun** (pl. **same**) a meeting at which candidates in an election address potential voters. ■ (**the hustings**) the campaigning associated with an election: *I was out on the hustings, talking to people.*
– ORIGIN late Old English *husting* 'deliberative assembly, council', from Old Norse *hústhing* 'household assembly held by a leader', from *hús* 'house' + *thing* 'assembly, parliament'; *hustings* was applied in Middle English to the highest court of the City of London, presided over by the Recorder of London. Subsequently it denoted the platform in Guildhall where the Lord Mayor and aldermen presided, and (early 18th cent.) a temporary platform on which parliamentary candidates were nominated; hence the sense 'electoral proceedings'.

hustle ▶ **verb 1** [with obj.] push roughly; jostle: *they were hissed and hustled as they went in.* ■ [with obj. and adverbial of direction] force (someone) to move hurriedly or unceremoniously: *I was hustled away to a cold cell.* ■ [no obj., with adverbial of direction] push one's way; bustle.
2 [with obj.] informal, chiefly N. Amer. obtain illicitly or by forceful action: *Linda hustled money from men she*

met. ■ (**hustle someone into**) pressure someone into doing something. ■ sell aggressively: *he hustled his company's oil around the country.*
3 [no obj.] N. Amer. informal engage in prostitution.
▶ **noun 1** [mass noun] a state of great activity: ***the hustle and bustle** of the big cities.*
2 N. Amer. informal a fraud or swindle.
– PHRASES **hustle one's butt** (or vulgar slang **ass**) N. Amer. informal move or act quickly.
– ORIGIN late 17th cent. (originally in the sense 'shake, toss'): from Middle Dutch *hutselen*. Sense 3 of the verb dates from the early 20th cent.

hustler ▶ **noun** informal, chiefly N. Amer. **1** a person adept at aggressive selling or illicit dealing.
2 a prostitute.

Huston /ˈhjuːst(ə)n/, John (1906–87), American-born film director, an Irish citizen from 1964. He made his debut as a film director in 1941 with *The Maltese Falcon*. Other notable films: *The African Queen* (1951) and *Prizzi's Honor* (1985).

hut ▶ **noun** a small, simple, single-storey house or shelter.
▶ **verb** (**huts, hutting, hutted**) [with obj.] provide with huts: (as adj. **hutted**) *a hutted encampment.*
– DERIVATIVES **hut-like** adjective.
– ORIGIN mid 16th cent. (in the sense 'temporary wooden shelter for troops'): from French *hutte*, from Middle High German *hütte*.

H

hutch ▶ **noun 1** a box or cage, typically with a wire mesh front, for keeping rabbits or other small domesticated animals: *a rabbit hutch.*
2 N. Amer. a storage chest. ■ a cupboard or dresser.
– ORIGIN Middle English: from Old French *huche*, from medieval Latin *hutica*, of unknown origin. The original sense was 'storage chest', surviving in North American usage (sense 2).

hutia /hʌˈtiːə/ ▶ **noun** a rodent resembling a cavy, with short legs and tail, found only in the Caribbean.
● Family Capromyidae: two genera, in particular *Capromys*, and several species, some of which are now extinct.
– ORIGIN mid 16th cent.: from Spanish, from Taino *huti, cuti*.

hutment ▶ **noun** Military an encampment of huts.

hutong /ˈhuːtɒŋ/ ▶ **noun** (pl. **same** or **hutongs**) a narrow lane or alleyway in a traditional residential area of a Chinese city, especially Beijing.
– ORIGIN Chinese *hútòng*, probably from Mongolian *gudum*.

Hutterite /ˈhʌtərʌɪt/ ▶ **noun** a member of an Anabaptist Christian sect established in Moravia in the early 16th century. ■ a member of a North American community holding beliefs similar to the Moravian Hutterites and leading a very old-fashioned communal way of life.
▶ **adjective** relating to Hutterites or their beliefs.
– ORIGIN from the name of Jacob Hutter (died 1536), a Moravian Anabaptist, + **-ITE**[1].

Hutton[1], James (1726–97), Scottish geologist. Although controversial at the time, his uniformitarian description of the processes that have shaped the surface of the earth is now accepted as showing that the earth is very much older than had previously been believed.

Hutton[2], Sir Leonard (1916–90), English cricketer. He played for Yorkshire (1934–55) and for England (1937–55), scoring a record 364 in the 1938 test against Australia.

Hutu /ˈhuːtuː/ ▶ **noun** (pl. **same** or **Hutus** or **Bahutu** /bəˈhuːtuː/) a member of a Bantu-speaking people forming the majority population in Rwanda and Burundi. They are traditionally a farming people, and were historically dominated by the Tutsi people; the antagonism between the peoples led in 1994 to large-scale ethnic violence, especially in Rwanda.
▶ **adjective** relating to the Hutu.
– ORIGIN a local name.

Huxley[1] /ˈhʌksli/, Aldous (Leonard) (1894–1963), English novelist and essayist. After writing *Antic Hay* (1923) and *Brave New World* (1932), in 1937 he moved to California, where in 1953 he experimented with psychedelic drugs, writing of his experiences in *The Doors of Perception* (1954).

Huxley[2] /ˈhʌksli/, Andrew Fielding (b.1917), English physiologist, the grandson of Thomas Henry Huxley. He worked with Sir Alan Hodgkin on the physiology of nerve transmission.

Huxley[3] /ˈhʌksli/, Thomas Henry (1825–95), English biologist. A surgeon and leading supporter of Darwinism, he coined the word *agnostic* to describe his own beliefs. Notable works: *Man's Place in Nature* (1863).

Huygens[1] /ˈhʌɪgənz/, Christiaan (1629–95), Dutch physicist, mathematician, and astronomer. His wave theory of light enabled him to explain reflection and refraction. He also patented a pendulum clock, introduced the convergent eyepiece for telescopes, discovered a satellite of Saturn, and recognized the nature of Saturn's rings, which had eluded Galileo.

Huygens[2] a European space probe which is part of the Cassini spacecraft, which detached from the orbiter and landed on Saturn's moon Titan in 2005.

Huygens eyepiece ▶ **noun** Optics a simple eyepiece consisting of two separate planoconvex lenses, used chiefly in refracting telescopes of long focal length.

huzza /hʊˈzɑː/ (also **huzzah**) archaic ▶ **exclamation** used to express approval or delight.
▶ **verb** (**huzzas, huzzaed, huzzaing**) [no obj.] cry 'huzza'.
– ORIGIN late 16th cent.: perhaps used originally as a sailor's cry when hauling.

Hwange /ˈhwaŋgi/ a town in western Zimbabwe; pop. 34,300 (est. 2009). Nearby is the Hwange National Park, established as a game reserve in 1928. Former name (until 1982) **WANKIE**.

HWM ▶ **abbreviation** high-water mark.

hwyl /ˈhuːɪl/ ▶ **noun** [mass noun] (in Welsh use) a stirring feeling of emotional motivation and energy.
– ORIGIN Welsh.

hyacinth /ˈhʌɪəsɪnθ/ ▶ **noun 1** a bulbous plant of the lily family, with strap-like leaves and a compact spike of bell-shaped fragrant flowers. Native to western Asia, hyacinths are cultivated outdoors and as houseplants. ● Genus *Hyacinthus*, family Liliaceae: several species, in particular *H. orientalis*, from which the large-flowered cultivars are derived.
■ [mass noun] a light purplish-blue colour typical of some hyacinth flowers.
2 another term for **JACINTH**.
– DERIVATIVES **hyacinthine** /-ˈsɪnθiːn, -θʌɪn/ **adjective**.
– ORIGIN mid 16th cent. (denoting a gem): from French *hyacinthe*, via Latin from Greek *huakinthos*, denoting a plant identified with the flower in the myth of **HYACINTHUS**, and a gem (perhaps the sapphire). The current sense dates from the late 16th cent.

Hyacinthus /ˌhʌɪəˈsɪnθəs/ Greek Mythology a beautiful boy whom the god Apollo loved but killed accidentally with a discus. From his blood Apollo caused the hyacinth to spring up.

Hyades /ˈhʌɪədiːz/ Astronomy an open star cluster in the constellation Taurus, appearing to surround the bright star Aldebaran.
– ORIGIN from the *Hyades* (Greek *Huades*), the five sisters of the Pleiades in Greek mythology, brothers of Hyas, who were changed into stars by Zeus.

hyaena ▶ **noun** variant spelling of **HYENA**.

hyaenodon /hʌɪˈiːnədɒn/ ▶ **noun** a large, heavily built carnivorous mammal of the Oligocene epoch.
– ORIGIN modern Latin, from Latin *hyaena* 'hyena' + Greek *odous, odont-* 'tooth'.

hyalin /ˈhʌɪəlɪn/ ▶ **noun** [mass noun] Physiology a clear substance produced especially by the degeneration of epithelial or connective tissues.
– ORIGIN mid 19th cent.: via Latin from Greek *hualinos*, from *hualos* 'glass'.

hyaline /ˈhʌɪəlɪn, -iːn, -ʌɪn/ ▶ **adjective** Anatomy & Zoology (chiefly of cartilage) glassy and translucent in appearance. ■ relating to or consisting of hyalin.
▶ **noun 1** (**the hyaline**) literary a smooth sea or a clear sky.
2 another term for **HYALIN**.
– ORIGIN mid 17th cent.: from Latin *hyalinus* (see **HYALIN**).

hyaline cartilage ▶ **noun** [mass noun] a translucent bluish-white type of cartilage present in the joints, the respiratory tract, and the immature skeleton.

hyaline membrane disease ▶ **noun** [mass noun] a condition in newborn babies in which the lungs are deficient in surfactant, which prevents their proper expansion and causes the formation of hyaline material in the lung spaces. Also called **RESPIRATORY DISTRESS SYNDROME**.

hyalite /ˈhʌɪəlʌɪt/ ▶ **noun** [mass noun] a translucent, colourless variety of opal.
– ORIGIN late 18th cent.: from Greek *hualos* 'glass' + **-ITE**[1].

hyaloid /ˈhʌɪəlɔɪd/ ▶ **adjective** Anatomy glassy; transparent.
– ORIGIN mid 19th cent.: from French *hyaloïde*, or via late Latin from Greek *hualoeidēs* 'like glass', from *hualos* 'glass'.

hyaloid membrane ▶ **noun** a thin transparent membrane enveloping the vitreous humour of the eye.

hyaluronate /ˌhʌɪəˈljʊərəneɪt/ ▶ **noun** Biochemistry a salt or ester of hyaluronic acid.

hyaluronic acid /ˌhʌɪəljʊəˈrɒnɪk/ ▶ **noun** [mass noun] Biochemistry a viscous fluid carbohydrate present in connective tissue, synovial fluid, and the aqueous and vitreous humours of the eye.
– ORIGIN 1930s: *hyaluronic* from a blend of **HYALOID** and **URONIC ACID**.

hybrid /ˈhʌɪbrɪd/ ▶ **noun 1** Biology the offspring of two plants or animals of different species or varieties, such as a mule.
2 a thing made by combining two different elements: *jungle is **a hybrid of** reggae and house music.* ■ a word formed from elements taken from different languages, for example *television* (*tele-* from Greek, *vision* from Latin). ■ (also **hybrid car**) a car with a petrol engine and an electric motor, each of which can propel it.
▶ **adjective** of mixed character; composed of different elements: *hybrid diesel-electric buses.* ■ bred as a hybrid from different species or varieties.
– DERIVATIVES **hybridism** noun, **hybridity** noun.
– ORIGIN early 17th cent. (as a noun): from Latin *hybrida* 'offspring of a tame sow and wild boar, child of a freeman and slave, etc.'.

hybridize (also **hybridise**) ▶ **verb** [with obj.] cross-breed (individuals of two different species or varieties). ■ [no obj.] (of an animal or plant) breed with an individual of another species or variety.
– DERIVATIVES **hybridizable** adjective, **hybridization** noun, **hybridizer** noun.

hybrid vigour ▶ **noun** [mass noun] Genetics the tendency of a cross-bred individual to show qualities superior to those of both parents. Also called **HETEROSIS**.

hydantoin /hʌɪˈdantəʊɪn/ ▶ **noun** Chemistry a crystalline compound present in sugar beet and used in the manufacture of some anticonvulsant drugs. ● A cyclic derivative of urea; chem. formula: $C_3H_4N_2O_2$.
– ORIGIN mid 19th cent.: from Greek *hudōr* 'water' + *allantoic* (see **ALLANTOIS**) + **-IN**[1].

hydathode /ˈhʌɪdəθəʊd/ ▶ **noun** Botany a modified pore, especially on a leaf, which exudes drops of water.
– ORIGIN late 19th cent.: from Greek *hudōr, hudat-* 'water' + *hodos* 'way'.

hydatid /ˈhʌɪdətɪd/ ▶ **noun** Medicine a cyst containing watery fluid, in particular one formed by and containing a tapeworm larva. ■ a tapeworm larva.
– ORIGIN late 17th cent.: from modern Latin *hydatis*, from Greek *hudatis, hudatid-* 'watery vesicle', from *hudōr, hudat-* 'water'.

hydatidiform mole /ˌhʌɪdəˈtɪdɪfɔːm/ ▶ **noun** Medicine a cluster of fluid-filled sacs formed in the womb by the degeneration of chorionic tissue around an aborting embryo.

Hyde[1], Edward, see **CLARENDON**.

Hyde[2], Mr, see **JEKYLL**[1].

hydel ▶ **adjective** Indian hydroelectric: *India has a massive potential to develop hydel power.*

Hyde Park the largest British royal park, in west central London. It contains the Serpentine, Marble Arch, the Albert Memorial, and Speakers' Corner.

Hyderabad /ˈhʌɪdərəbad/ **1** a city in central India, capital of the state of Andhra Pradesh; pop. 4,025,300 (est. 2009).
2 a former large princely state of south central India, divided in 1956 between Maharashtra, Mysore, and Andhra Pradesh.
3 a city in SE Pakistan, in the province of Sind, on the River Indus; pop. 1,536,400 (est. 2009).

hydr- ▶ **combining form** variant spelling of **HYDRO-** shortened before a vowel (as in *hydraulic*).

Hydra /ˈhʌɪdrə/ **1** Greek Mythology a many-headed snake whose heads grew again as they were cut off, eventually killed by Hercules. ■ (as noun **hydra**) a thing which is hard to overcome or resist because of its pervasive or enduring quality or its many aspects.
2 Astronomy the largest constellation (the Water Snake or Sea Monster), said to represent the beast slain by Hercules. Its few bright stars are close to the celestial equator. Compare with **HYDRUS**.
– ORIGIN via Latin from Greek *hudra*.

hydra ▶ **noun** a minute freshwater coelenterate with a stalk-like tubular body and a ring of tentacles around the mouth. ● Genus *Hydra*, class Hydrozoa.
– ORIGIN via Latin from Greek *hudra* 'water snake' (see **HYDRA**), named by Linnaeus because, if cut into pieces, each section can grow into a whole animal.

hydramnios /hʌɪ'dramnɪɒs/ ▶ **noun** [mass noun] Medicine a condition in which excess amniotic fluid accumulates during pregnancy.

hydrangea /hʌɪ'dreɪn(d)ʒə/ ▶ **noun** a shrub or climbing plant with rounded or flattened flowering heads of small florets, native to Asia and America. ● Genus *Hydrangea*, family Hydrangeaceae: many species, in particular the **common hydrangea** (*H. macrophylla*), with flowers that are typically blue, but often pink on alkaline soils.
– ORIGIN modern Latin, from Greek *hudro-* 'water' + *angeion* 'vessel' (from the cup shape of its seed capsule).

hydrant /'hʌɪdr(ə)nt/ ▶ **noun** a water pipe, especially one in a street, with a nozzle to which a fire hose can be attached.
– ORIGIN early 19th cent. (originally US): formed irregularly from **HYDRO-** 'relating to water' + **-ANT**.

hydrate ▶ **noun** /'hʌɪdreɪt/ Chemistry a compound, typically a crystalline one, in which water molecules are chemically bound to another compound or an element.
▶ **verb** /hʌɪ'dreɪt/ [with obj.] cause to absorb water. ■ Chemistry combine chemically with water molecules.
– DERIVATIVES **hydratable** adjective, **hydration** noun, **hydrator** noun.
– ORIGIN early 19th cent.: coined in French from Greek *hudōr* 'water'.

hydraulic /hʌɪ'drɔːlɪk, hʌɪ'drɒlɪk/ ▶ **adjective** **1** denoting or relating to a liquid moving in a confined space under pressure: *hydraulic fluid*.
2 relating to the science of hydraulics.
3 (of cement) hardening under water.
– DERIVATIVES **hydraulically** adverb, **hydraulicity** /-'lɪsɪti/ noun.
– ORIGIN early 17th cent.: via Latin from Greek *hudraulikos*, from *hudro-* 'water' + *aulos* 'pipe'.

hydraulic fracturing ▶ **noun** [mass noun] the forcing open of fissures in subterranean rocks by introducing liquid at high pressure, especially to extract oil or gas.

hydraulic ram ▶ **noun** an automatic pump in which a large volume of water flows through a valve which it periodically forces shut, the sudden pressure change being used to raise a smaller volume of water to a higher level.

hydraulics ▶ **plural noun** **1** [usu. treated as sing.] the branch of science and technology concerned with the conveyance of liquids through pipes and channels, especially as a source of mechanical force or control.
2 hydraulic systems or forces.

hydrazine /'hʌɪdrəziːn/ ▶ **noun** [mass noun] Chemistry a colourless volatile alkaline liquid with powerful reducing properties, used in chemical synthesis and in some kinds of rocket fuels. ● Chem. formula: N_2H_4.
– ORIGIN late 19th cent.: from **HYDROGEN** + **AZO-** + **-INE**[4].

hydria /'hʌɪdrɪə/ ▶ **noun** (pl. **hydriae** or **hydriai**) Archaeology an ancient Greek pitcher with three handles.
– ORIGIN via Latin from Greek *hudria*.

hydric /'hʌɪdrɪk/ ▶ **adjective** Ecology (of an environment or habitat) containing plenty of moisture; very wet. Compare with **MESIC**[1] and **XERIC**.
– ORIGIN early 20th cent.: from **HYDRO-** + **-IC**.

hydride /'hʌɪdrʌɪd/ ▶ **noun** [mass noun] Chemistry a binary compound of hydrogen with a metal.

hydriodic acid /,hʌɪdrɪ'ɒdɪk, -ʌɪ'ɒdɪk/ ▶ **noun** [mass noun] Chemistry a strongly acidic solution of the gas hydrogen iodide in water. ● Chem. formula: HI.
– ORIGIN early 19th cent.: *hydriodic* from a blend of **HYDROGEN** and **IODINE**.

hydro ▶ **noun** (pl. **hydros**) **1** Brit. a hotel or clinic originally providing hydropathic treatment.
2 a hydroelectric power plant. ■ [mass noun] hydroelectricity. ■ [mass noun] Canadian electricity.
– ORIGIN late 19th cent.: abbreviation.

hydro- (also **hydr-**) ▶ **combining form** **1** water; relating to water: *hydraulic* | *hydrocolloid*. ■ Medicine affected with an accumulation of serous fluid: *hydrocephalus*.
2 Chemistry combined with hydrogen: *hydrocarbon*.
– ORIGIN from Greek *hudōr* 'water'.

hydrobromic acid /,hʌɪdrə(ʊ)'brəʊmɪk/ ▶ **noun** [mass noun] Chemistry a strongly acidic solution of the gas hydrogen bromide in water. ● Chem. formula: HBr.

hydrocarbon ▶ **noun** Chemistry a compound of hydrogen and carbon, such as any of those which are the chief components of petroleum and natural gas.

hydrocele /'hʌɪdrə(ʊ)siːl/ ▶ **noun** [mass noun] Medicine the accumulation of serous fluid in a body sac.

hydrocephalus /,hʌɪdrə'sɛf(ə)ləs, -'kɛf-/ ▶ **noun** [mass noun] Medicine a condition in which fluid accumulates in the brain, typically in young children, enlarging the head and sometimes causing brain damage.
– DERIVATIVES **hydrocephalic** adjective, **hydrocephaly** noun.
– ORIGIN late 17th cent.: modern Latin, from Greek *hudrokephalon*, from *hudro-* 'water' + *kephalē* 'head'.

hydrochloric acid ▶ **noun** [mass noun] Chemistry a strongly acidic solution of the gas hydrogen chloride in water. ● Chem. formula: HCl.

hydrochloride ▶ **noun** Chemistry a compound of a particular organic base with hydrochloric acid: [with modifier] *cocaine hydrochloride*.

hydrochlorofluorocarbon /,hʌɪdrə,klɔːrə(ʊ)'flʊərə(ʊ)kɑːbən, -,flɔːrə(ʊ)-/ (abbrev.: **HCFC**) ▶ **noun** Chemistry any of a class of inert compounds of carbon, hydrogen, chlorine, and fluorine, used in place of CFCs as being somewhat less destructive to the ozone layer.

hydrocolloid /,hʌɪdrə(ʊ)'kɒlɔɪd/ ▶ **noun** a substance which forms a gel in the presence of water, examples of which are used in surgical dressings and in various industrial applications.

hydrocortisone ▶ **noun** [mass noun] Biochemistry a steroid hormone produced by the adrenal cortex and used medicinally to treat inflammation resulting from eczema and rheumatism.

hydroculture ▶ **noun** another term for **HYDROPONICS**.

hydrocyanic acid /,hʌɪdrə(ʊ)sʌɪ'anɪk/ ▶ **noun** [mass noun] Chemistry a highly poisonous acidic solution of hydrogen cyanide in water.

hydrodynamics ▶ **plural noun** [treated as sing.] the branch of science concerned with forces acting on or exerted by fluids (especially liquids).
– DERIVATIVES **hydrodynamic** adjective, **hydrodynamical** adjective, **hydrodynamicist** noun.
– ORIGIN late 18th cent.: from modern Latin *hydrodynamica*, from Greek *hudro-* 'water' + *dunamikos* (see **DYNAMIC**).

hydroelectric ▶ **adjective** relating to or denoting the generation of electricity using flowing water (typically from a reservoir held behind a dam or barrage) to drive a turbine which powers a generator.
– DERIVATIVES **hydroelectricity** noun.

hydrofluoric acid /,hʌɪdrə(ʊ)'flʊərɪk/ ▶ **noun** [mass noun] Chemistry an acidic, extremely corrosive solution of the liquid hydrogen fluoride in water. ● Chem. formula: HF.

hydrofluorocarbon /,hʌɪdrə(ʊ)'flʊərə(ʊ),kɑːb(ə)n, -'flɔː-/ (abbrev.: **HFC**) ▶ **noun** Chemistry any of a class of partly chlorinated and fluorinated hydrocarbons, used as an alternative to CFCs in foam production, refrigeration, and other processes.

hydrofoil ▶ **noun** a boat whose hull is fitted underneath with shaped vanes (foils) which lift the hull clear of the water at speed. ■ each of the foils of a hydrofoil.
– ORIGIN 1920s: from **HYDRO-** 'relating to water', on the pattern of *aerofoil*.

hydrofracturing ▶ **noun** another term for **HYDRAULIC FRACTURING**.

hydrogel ▶ **noun** a gel in which the liquid component is water.

hydrogen /'hʌɪdrədʒ(ə)n/ ▶ **noun** [mass noun] a colourless, odourless, highly flammable gas, the chemical element of atomic number 1. (Symbol: **H**)

> Hydrogen is the lightest of the chemical elements and has the simplest atomic structure, a single electron orbiting a nucleus consisting of a single proton. It is by far the commonest element in the universe, although not on the earth, where it occurs chiefly combined with oxygen as water.

– DERIVATIVES **hydrogenous** /-'drɒdʒɪnəs/ adjective.
– ORIGIN late 18th cent.: coined in French from Greek *hudro-* 'water' + *-genēs* (see **-GEN**).

hydrogenase /hʌɪ'drɒdʒəneɪz/ ▶ **noun** [usu. with modifier] Biochemistry an enzyme which catalyses the reduction of a particular substance by hydrogen.

hydrogenate /hʌɪ'drɒdʒəneɪt, 'hʌɪdrədʒəneɪt/ ▶ **verb** [with obj.] (often as adj. **hydrogenated**) charge with or cause to combine with hydrogen.
– DERIVATIVES **hydrogenation** noun.

hydrogen bomb ▶ **noun** an immensely powerful bomb whose destructive power comes from the rapid release of energy during the nuclear fusion of isotopes of hydrogen (deuterium and tritium), using an atom bomb as a trigger.

hydrogen bond ▶ **noun** Chemistry a weak bond between two molecules resulting from an electrostatic attraction between a proton in one molecule and an electronegative atom in the other.

hydrogen cyanide ▶ **noun** [mass noun] Chemistry a highly poisonous gas or volatile liquid with an odour of bitter almonds, made by the action of acids on cyanides. ● Chem. formula: HCN.

hydrogen peroxide ▶ **noun** [mass noun] Chemistry a colourless viscous unstable liquid with strong oxidizing properties, used in some disinfectants and bleaches. ● Chem. formula: H_2O_2.

hydrogen sulphide ▶ **noun** [mass noun] Chemistry a colourless poisonous gas with a smell of bad eggs, made by the action of acids on sulphides. ● Chem. formula: H_2S.

hydrogeology ▶ **noun** [mass noun] the branch of geology concerned with water occurring underground or on the surface of the earth.
– DERIVATIVES **hydrogeological** adjective, **hydrogeologist** noun.

H

hydrography /hʌɪ'drɒgrəfi/ ▶ **noun** [mass noun] the science of surveying and charting bodies of water, such as seas, lakes, and rivers.
– DERIVATIVES **hydrographer** noun, **hydrographic** adjective, **hydrographical** adjective.

hydroid /'hʌɪdrɔɪd/ Zoology ▶ **noun** a coelenterate of an order which includes the hydras. They are distinguished by the dominance of the polyp phase. ● Order Hydroida, class Hydrozoa.
▶ **adjective** relating to coelenterates of the hydroid group. ■ another term for **POLYPOID** (sense 1).
– ORIGIN mid 19th cent.: from **HYDRA** + **-OID**.

hydrolase /'hʌɪdrəleɪz/ ▶ **noun** [usu. with modifier] Biochemistry an enzyme that catalyses the hydrolysis of a particular substrate.

hydrology ▶ **noun** [mass noun] the branch of science concerned with the properties of the earth's water, and especially its movement in relation to land.
– DERIVATIVES **hydrologic** adjective, **hydrological** adjective, **hydrologically** adverb, **hydrologist** noun.

hydrolysate /hʌɪ'drɒlɪseɪt/ ▶ **noun** Chemistry a substance produced by hydrolysis.

hydrolyse /'hʌɪdrəlʌɪz/ (US **hydrolyze**) ▶ **verb** [with obj.] Chemistry break down (a compound) by chemical reaction with water. ■ [no obj.] undergo hydrolysis.

hydrolysis /hʌɪ'drɒlɪsɪs/ ▶ **noun** [mass noun] Chemistry the chemical breakdown of a compound due to reaction with water.
– DERIVATIVES **hydrolytic** /,hʌɪdrə'lɪtɪk/ adjective.

hydromagnetics ▶ **plural noun** another term for **MAGNETOHYDRODYNAMICS**.
– DERIVATIVES **hydromagnetic** adjective.

hydromassage ▶ **noun** [mass noun] massage using jets of water, as a health or beauty treatment.

hydromechanics ▶ **plural noun** [treated as sing.] the mechanics of liquids, hydrodynamics, especially in relation to mechanical applications.
– DERIVATIVES **hydromechanical** adjective.

hydromedusa /,hʌɪdrəʊmɪ'djuːzə/ ▶ **noun** (pl. **hydromedusae**) Zoology the medusoid phase of a hydroid coelenterate.

hydromel /'hʌɪdrəmɛl/ ▶ **noun** [mass noun] historical a drink similar to mead, made with fermented honey and water.
– ORIGIN late Middle English: from Latin, from Greek *hudromeli*, from *hudro-* 'water' + *meli* 'honey'.

hydrometeor ▶ **noun** Meteorology an atmospheric phenomenon or entity involving water or water vapour, such as rain or a cloud.

hydrometer /hʌɪ'drɒmɪtə/ ▶ **noun** an instrument for measuring the density of liquids.
– DERIVATIVES **hydrometric** adjective, **hydrometry** noun.

hydronic /hʌɪ'drɒnɪk/ ▶ **adjective** denoting a cooling or heating system in which heat is transported using circulating water.

hydronium ion /hʌɪ'drəʊnɪəm/ ▶ **noun** Chemistry another term for **HYDROXONIUM ION**.
– ORIGIN early 20th cent.: *hydronium*, from German (a contraction).

hydropathy /hʌɪˈdrɒpəθi/ ▸ **noun** [mass noun] the treatment of illness through the use of water, either internally or through external means such as steam baths (not now a part of orthodox medicine). Compare with **HYDROTHERAPY**.
– DERIVATIVES **hydropathic** adjective.
– ORIGIN mid 19th cent.: from **HYDRO-** 'of water', on the pattern of *allopathy* and *homeopathy*.

hydrophilic /ˌhʌɪdrə(ʊ)ˈfɪlɪk/ ▸ **adjective** having a tendency to mix with, dissolve in, or be wetted by water. The opposite of **HYDROPHOBIC**.
– DERIVATIVES **hydrophilicity** noun.

hydrophilous /hʌɪˈdrɒfɪl(ə)s/ ▸ **adjective** Botany (of a plant) water-pollinated.
– DERIVATIVES **hydrophily** noun.

hydrophobia /ˌhʌɪdrə(ʊ)ˈfəʊbɪə/ ▸ **noun** [mass noun] extreme or irrational fear of water, especially as a symptom of rabies in humans. ■ rabies, especially in humans.
– ORIGIN late Middle English: via late Latin from Greek *hudrophobia*, from *hudro-* 'water' + *phobos* 'fear'.

hydrophobic ▸ **adjective** **1** tending to repel or fail to mix with water. The opposite of **HYDROPHILIC**.
2 of or suffering from hydrophobia.
– DERIVATIVES **hydrophobicity** noun.

hydrophone ▸ **noun** a microphone which detects sound waves under water.

hydrophyte ▸ **noun** Botany a plant which grows only in or on water.
– DERIVATIVES **hydrophytic** adjective.

hydroplane ▸ **noun** **1** a light, fast motor boat designed to skim over the surface of water.
2 a fin-like attachment which enables a moving submarine to rise or fall in the water.
3 US a seaplane.
▸ **verb** N. Amer. another term for **AQUAPLANE**.

hydroponics /ˌhʌɪdrə(ʊ)ˈpɒnɪks/ ▸ **plural noun** [treated as sing.] the process of growing plants in sand, gravel, or liquid, with added nutrients but without soil.
– DERIVATIVES **hydroponic** adjective, **hydroponically** adverb.
– ORIGIN 1930s: from **HYDRO-** 'of water' + Greek *ponos* 'labour' + **-ICS**.

hydropower ▸ **noun** [mass noun] hydroelectric power.

hydroquinone /ˌhʌɪdrəˈkwɪnəʊn/ ▸ **noun** [mass noun] Chemistry a crystalline compound made by the reduction of benzoquinone. ● Alternative name: **benzene-1,4-diol**; chem. formula: $C_6H_4(OH)_2$.

hydrospeed (also **hydrospeeding**) ▸ **noun** [mass noun] a sport or leisure activity that involves jumping into fast-flowing white water and being carried along at high speed while buoyed up by a float.

hydrosphere ▸ **noun** (usu. **the hydrosphere**) all the waters on the earth's surface, such as lakes and seas, and sometimes including water over the earth's surface, such as clouds.

hydrostatic ▸ **adjective** relating to or denoting the equilibrium of liquids and the pressure exerted by liquid at rest.
– DERIVATIVES **hydrostatical** adjective, **hydrostatically** adverb.
– ORIGIN late 17th cent.: probably from Greek *hudrostatēs* 'hydrostatic balance', from *hudro-* 'water' + *statikos* (see **STATIC**).

hydrostatics ▸ **plural noun** [treated as sing.] the branch of mechanics concerned with the hydrostatic properties of liquids.

hydrosulphite /ˌhʌɪdrə(ʊ)ˈsʌlfʌɪt/ ▸ **noun** another term for **DITHIONITE**.

hydrotherapy ▸ **noun** **1** [mass noun] the use of exercises in a pool as part of treatment for conditions such as arthritis.
2 another term for **HYDROPATHY**.
– DERIVATIVES **hydrotherapist** noun.

hydrothermal ▸ **adjective** relating to or denoting the action of heated water in the earth's crust.
– DERIVATIVES **hydrothermally** adverb.

hydrothermal vent ▸ **noun** an opening in the sea floor out of which heated mineral-rich water flows.

hydrothorax ▸ **noun** [mass noun] the condition of having fluid in the pleural cavity.

hydrotropism /hʌɪˈdrɒtrəpɪz(ə)m/ ▸ **noun** [mass noun] Botany the growth or turning of plant roots towards or away from moisture.

hydrous ▸ **adjective** chiefly Chemistry & Geology containing water as a constituent: *a hydrous lava flow*.
– ORIGIN early 19th cent.: from Greek *hudro-* 'water' + **-OUS**.

hydroxide ▸ **noun** Chemistry a compound of a metal with the hydroxide ion OH^- (as in many alkalis) or the group $-OH$.

hydroxonium ion /ˌhʌɪdrɒkˈsəʊnɪəm/ ▸ **noun** Chemistry the ion H_3O^+, consisting of a protonated water molecule and present in all aqueous acids.
– ORIGIN 1920s: *hydroxonium* from **HYDRO-** (relating to hydrogen) + **OXY-²** + the suffix *-onium* (from **AMMONIUM**).

hydroxy- ▸ **combining form** Chemistry representing **HYDROXYL** or **HYDROXIDE**: *hydroxyapatite*.

hydroxyapatite /ˌhʌɪdrɒksɪˈapətʌɪt/ ▸ **noun** [mass noun] a mineral related to apatite which is the main inorganic constituent of tooth enamel and bone, although it is rare in rocks.

hydroxyl /hʌɪˈdrɒksɪl, -sʌɪl/ ▸ **noun** [as modifier] Chemistry of or denoting the radical $-OH$, present in alcohols and many other organic compounds: *a hydroxyl group*.
– ORIGIN mid 19th cent.: from a blend of **HYDROGEN** and **OXYGEN**, + **-YL**.

hydroxylate /hʌɪˈdrɒksɪleɪt/ ▸ **verb** [with obj.] (often as adj. **hydroxylated**) Chemistry introduce a hydroxyl group into (a molecule or compound).
– DERIVATIVES **hydroxylation** noun.

Hydrozoa /ˌhʌɪdrə(ʊ)ˈzəʊə/ ▸ **plural noun** Zoology a class of coelenterates which includes hydras and Portuguese men-of-war. Many of them are colonial and some kinds have both polypoid and medusoid phases.
– ORIGIN modern Latin (plural), from **HYDRO-** 'water' + Greek *zōion* 'animal'.

hydrozoan Zoology ▸ **noun** a coelenterate of the class Hydrozoa, such as a hydra or Portuguese man-of-war.
▸ **adjective** relating to or denoting hydrozoans.

Hydrus /ˈhʌɪdrəs/ Astronomy an inconspicuous southern constellation (the Water Snake), between the star Achernar and the south celestial pole. Compare with **HYDRA** (sense 2).
– ORIGIN Latin, from Greek *hudros*.

hyena (also **hyaena**) ▸ **noun** a doglike African mammal with forelimbs that are longer than the hindlimbs and an erect mane. Hyenas are noted as scavengers but most are also effective hunters.
● Family Hyaenidae: two genera, in particular *Hyaena*, and three species.
– ORIGIN Middle English: via Latin from Greek *huaina*, feminine of *hus* 'pig' (the transference of the term probably being because the animal's mane was thought to resemble a hog's bristles).

hygiene ▸ **noun** [mass noun] conditions or practices conducive to maintaining health and preventing disease, especially through cleanliness: *poor standards of food hygiene | personal hygiene*.
– ORIGIN late 16th cent.: via French from modern Latin *hygieina*, from Greek *hugieinē* (*tekhnē*) '(art) of health', from *hugiēs* 'healthy'.

hygienic ▸ **adjective** conducive to maintaining health and preventing disease, especially by being clean; sanitary: *hygienic conditions*.
– DERIVATIVES **hygienically** adverb.

hygienist ▸ **noun** a specialist in the promotion of clean conditions for the preservation of health.

hygro- ▸ **combining form** relating to moisture: *hygrometer*.
– ORIGIN from Greek *hugros* 'wet'.

hygrometer /hʌɪˈgrɒmɪtə/ ▸ **noun** an instrument for measuring the humidity of the air or a gas.
– DERIVATIVES **hygrometric** adjective, **hygrometry** noun.

hygrophilous /hʌɪˈgrɒfɪləs/ ▸ **adjective** Botany (of a plant) growing in damp conditions.

hygrophyte /ˈhʌɪgrəfʌɪt/ ▸ **noun** Botany a plant which grows in wet conditions.

hygroscope /ˈhʌɪgrə(ʊ)skəʊp/ ▸ **noun** an instrument which gives an indication of the humidity of the air.

hygroscopic ▸ **adjective** (of a substance) tending to absorb moisture from the air. ■ relating to humidity or its measurement.

hying present participle of **HIE**.

Hyksos /ˈhɪksɒs/ ▸ **plural noun** a people of mixed Semitic and Asian descent who invaded Egypt and settled in the Nile delta *c.*1640 BC. They formed the 15th and 16th dynasties of Egypt and ruled a large part of the country until driven out *c.*1532 BC.
– ORIGIN from Greek *Huksōs* (interpreted by Manetho as 'shepherd kings' or 'captive shepherds'), from Egyptian *heqa khoswe* 'foreign rulers'.

hyla /ˈhʌɪlə/ ▸ **noun** a tree frog of a widespread genus, typically bright green in colour. ● Genus *Hyla*, family Hylidae: many species.
– ORIGIN modern Latin, from Greek *hulē* 'timber'.

hylo- ▸ **combining form** relating to matter: *hylozoism*.
– ORIGIN from Greek *hulē* 'matter'.

hylomorphism /ˌhʌɪlə(ʊ)ˈmɔːfɪz(ə)m/ ▸ **noun** [mass noun] Philosophy the doctrine that physical objects result from the combination of matter and form.
– DERIVATIVES **hylomorphic** adjective.
– ORIGIN late 19th cent.: from **HYLO-** 'matter' + Greek *morphē* 'form'.

hylozoism /ˌhʌɪlə(ʊ)ˈzəʊɪz(ə)m/ ▸ **noun** [mass noun] Philosophy the doctrine that all matter has life.
– ORIGIN late 17th cent.: from **HYLO-** 'matter' + Greek *zōē* 'life'.

hymen /ˈhʌɪmən/ ▸ **noun** a membrane which partially closes the opening of the vagina and whose presence is traditionally taken to be a mark of virginity.
– ORIGIN mid 16th cent.: via late Latin from Greek *humēn* 'membrane'.

hymeneal /ˌhʌɪmɪˈniːəl/ ▸ **adjective** literary of or concerning marriage.
– ORIGIN early 17th cent.: from Latin *hymenaeus*, from *Hymen* (from Greek *Humēn*), the name of the god of marriage, + **-AL**.

hymenium /hʌɪˈmiːnɪəm/ ▸ **noun** (pl. **hymenia** /-nɪə/) Botany (in higher fungi) a surface consisting mainly of spore-bearing structures (asci or basidia).
– DERIVATIVES **hymenial** adjective.
– ORIGIN early 19th cent.: from Greek *humenion*, diminutive of *humēn* 'membrane'.

Hymenoptera /ˌhʌɪməˈnɒpt(ə)rə/ ▸ **plural noun** Entomology a large order of insects that includes the bees, wasps, ants, and sawflies. They have four transparent wings and the females typically have a sting.
■ (**hymenoptera**) insects of the Hymenoptera order.
– ORIGIN modern Latin (plural), from Greek *humenopteros* 'membrane-winged', from *humēn* 'membrane' + *pteron* 'wing'.

hymenopteran Entomology ▸ **noun** an insect of the order Hymenoptera, such as a bee, wasp, or ant.
▸ **adjective** relating to or denoting hymenopterans.
– DERIVATIVES **hymenopterous** adjective.

Hymie /ˈhʌɪmi/ ▸ **noun** US informal an offensive term for a Jewish person.
– ORIGIN 1980s: colloquial abbreviation of the Jewish male given name *Hyman*.

hymn ▸ **noun** a religious song or poem of praise to God or a god: *a Hellenistic **hymn to** Apollo*. ■ a formal song sung during Christian worship, typically by the whole congregation. ■ a book, film, or other composition praising someone or something: *the film is **a hymn to** blue-collar mateyness*.
▸ **verb** **1** [with obj.] praise (something): *the joys of domesticity were being hymned in magazines*.
2 [no obj.] rare sing hymns.
– DERIVATIVES **hymnic** /ˈhɪmnɪk/ adjective.
– ORIGIN Old English, via Latin from Greek *humnos* 'ode or song in praise of a god or hero', used in the Septuagint to translate various Hebrew words, and hence in the New Testament and other Christian writings.

hymnal /ˈhɪmn(ə)l/ ▸ **noun** a book of hymns.
▸ **adjective** relating to hymns: *hymnal music*.
– ORIGIN late 15th cent.: from medieval Latin *hymnale*, from Latin *hymnus* (see **HYMN**).

hymnary /ˈhɪmnəri/ ▸ **noun** (pl. **hymnaries**) another term for **HYMNAL**.

hymnody /ˈhɪmnədi/ ▸ **noun** [mass noun] the singing or composition of hymns.
– DERIVATIVES **hymnodist** noun.
– ORIGIN early 18th cent.: via medieval Latin from Greek *humnōidia*, from *humnos* 'hymn'.

hymnographer /hɪmˈnɒgrəfə/ ▸ **noun** a writer of hymns.
– DERIVATIVES **hymnography** noun.
– ORIGIN early 17th cent.: from Greek *humnographos*, from *humnos* 'hymn' + *graphos* 'writer'.

hymnology /hɪmˈnɒlədʒi/ ▸ **noun** [mass noun] the study or composition of hymns.
– DERIVATIVES **hymnological** adjective, **hymnologist** noun.
– ORIGIN mid 17th cent.: originally from Greek *humnologia* 'hymn-singing', the early sense until the mid 19th cent.

hyoid /ˈhʌɪɔɪd/ Anatomy & Zoology ▶ **noun** (also **hyoid bone**) a U-shaped bone in the neck which supports the tongue.
▶ **adjective** relating to the hyoid or structures associated with it.
– ORIGIN early 19th cent.: via French from modern Latin *hyoïdes*, from Greek *huoeidēs* 'shaped like the letter upsilon (υ)'.

hyoscine /ˈhʌɪəsiːn/ ▶ **noun** [mass noun] Chemistry a poisonous plant alkaloid used as an anti-emetic in motion sickness and as a preoperative medication for examination of the eye. ● Chem. formula: $C_{17}H_{21}NO_4$. It is obtained chiefly from plants of the genus *Scopolia*, family Solanaceae.
– ORIGIN late 19th cent.: from modern Latin *hyoscyamus* (see **HYOSCYAMINE**) + **-INE**[4].

hyoscyamine /ˌhʌɪə(ʊ)ˈsʌɪəmiːn/ ▶ **noun** [mass noun] Chemistry a poisonous compound present in henbane, with similar properties to hyoscine. ● Chem. formula: $C_{17}H_{23}NO_3$.
– ORIGIN mid 19th cent.: from modern Latin *hyoscyamus* (from Greek *huoskuamos* 'henbane', from *hus, huos* 'pig' + *kuamos* 'bean') + **-INE**[4].

hyp- ▶ **combining form** variant spelling of **HYPO-** shortened before a vowel or *h* (as in *hypaesthesia*).

hypaesthesia /ˌhʌɪpiːsˈθiːzɪə, -pɛs-/ (US **hypesthesia**) ▶ **noun** [mass noun] a diminished capacity for physical sensation, especially of the skin.
– ORIGIN late 19th cent.: from **HYPO-** 'below' + Greek *aisthēsis* 'sensation'.

hypaethral /hʌɪˈpiːθr(ə)l, hɪ-/ (also **hypethral**) ▶ **adjective** (of a classical building) having no roof: *the hypaethral temple*.
– ORIGIN late 18th cent.: via Latin from Greek *hupaithros* (from *hupo* 'under' + *aithēr* 'air') + **-AL**.

hypallage /hʌɪˈpalədʒiː, hɪ-/ ▶ **noun** Rhetoric a transposition of the natural relations of two elements in a proposition, for example in the sentence '*Melissa shook her doubtful curls*'.
– ORIGIN late 16th cent.: via late Latin from Greek *hupallagē*, from *hupo* 'under' + *allassein* 'to exchange'.

hypanthium /hɪˈpanθɪəm, hʌɪ-/ ▶ **noun** (pl. **hypanthia**) Botany a cup-like or tubular enlargement of the receptacle of a flower, loosely surrounding the gynoecium or united with it.

Hypatia /hʌɪˈpeɪʃɪə/ (*c*.370–415), Greek philosopher, astronomer, and mathematician. Head of the Neoplatonist school at Alexandria, she wrote several learned treatises as well as devising inventions such as an astrolabe.

hype[1] informal ▶ **noun** [mass noun] extravagant or intensive publicity or promotion: *his first album hit the stores amid a storm of hype*. ■ [count noun] a deception carried out for the sake of publicity.
▶ **verb** [with obj.] promote or publicize (a product or idea) intensively, often exaggerating its benefits.
– ORIGIN 1920s (originally US in the sense 'shortchange, cheat', or 'person who cheats etc.'): of unknown origin.

hype[2] informal ▶ **noun** a hypodermic needle or injection. ■ a drug addict.
▶ **verb** [with obj.] stimulate or excite (someone): *I was hyped up because I wanted to do well*.
– ORIGIN 1920s (originally US): abbreviation of **HYPODERMIC**.

hyper ▶ **adjective** informal hyperactive or unusually energetic: *eating sugar makes you hyper*.
– ORIGIN 1940s: abbreviation of **HYPERACTIVE**.

hyper- ▶ **prefix 1** over; beyond; above: *hypersonic*. ■ excessively; above normal: *hyperthyroidism*.
2 relating to hypertext: *hyperlink*.
– ORIGIN from Greek *huper* 'over, beyond'.

hyperactive ▶ **adjective** abnormally or extremely active: *a hyperactive pituitary gland*. ■ (of a child) showing constantly active and sometimes disruptive behaviour.
– DERIVATIVES **hyperactively** adverb, **hyperactivity** noun.

hyperaemia /ˌhʌɪpərˈiːmɪə/ (US **hyperemia**) ▶ **noun** [mass noun] Medicine an excess of blood in the vessels supplying an organ or other part of the body.
– DERIVATIVES **hyperaemic** adjective.
– ORIGIN mid 19th cent.: from **HYPER-** 'above normal' + **-AEMIA**.

hyperaesthesia /ˌhʌɪpəriːsˈθiːzɪə, -ɛsˈθiː-/ (US **hyperesthesia**) ▶ **noun** [mass noun] Medicine excessive physical sensitivity, especially of the skin.
– ORIGIN mid 19th cent.: from **HYPER-** 'above normal' + Greek *aisthēsis* 'sensation'.

hyperalgesia /ˌhʌɪpəralˈdʒiːzɪə/ ▶ **noun** [mass noun] Medicine abnormally heightened sensitivity to pain.
– DERIVATIVES **hyperalgesic** adjective.

hyperalimentation ▶ **noun** [mass noun] Medicine artificial supply of nutrients, typically intravenously.

hyperbaric /ˌhʌɪpəˈbarɪk/ ▶ **adjective** of or involving a gas at a pressure greater than normal.
– ORIGIN 1960s: from **HYPER-** 'above normal' + Greek *barus* 'heavy'.

hyperbaton /hʌɪˈpəːbətɒn/ ▶ **noun** Rhetoric an inversion of the normal order of words, especially for the sake of emphasis, as in the sentence '*this I must see*'.
– ORIGIN mid 16th cent.: via Latin from Greek *huperbaton* 'overstepping' (from *huper* 'over, above' + *bainein* 'go, walk').

hyperbola /hʌɪˈpəːbələ/ ▶ **noun** (pl. **hyperbolas** or **hyperbolae** /-liː/) a symmetrical open curve formed by the intersection of a circular cone with a plane at a smaller angle with its axis than the side of the cone. ■ Mathematics the pair of hyperbolas formed by the intersection of a plane with two equal cones on opposite sides of the same vertex.
– ORIGIN mid 17th cent.: modern Latin, from Greek *huperbolē* 'excess' (from *huper* 'above' + *ballein* 'to throw').

hyperbole /hʌɪˈpəːbəli/ ▶ **noun** [mass noun] exaggerated statements or claims not meant to be taken literally.
– DERIVATIVES **hyperbolical** /ˌhʌɪpəˈbɒlɪk(ə)l/ adjective, **hyperbolically** adverb, **hyperbolism** noun.
– ORIGIN late Middle English: via Latin from Greek *huperbolē* (see **HYPERBOLA**).

hyperbolic /ˌhʌɪpəˈbɒlɪk/ ▶ **adjective 1** relating to a hyperbola. ■ Mathematics denoting trigonometrical functions defined with reference to a hyperbola rather than a circle.
2 (of language) deliberately exaggerated.

hyperboloid /hʌɪˈpəːbəlɔɪd/ ▶ **noun** a solid or surface having plane sections that are hyperbolas, ellipses, or circles.
– DERIVATIVES **hyperboloidal** adjective.

hyperborean /ˌhʌɪpəbɔːˈriːən, -ˈbɔːrɪən/ literary ▶ **noun** an inhabitant of the extreme north. ■ (**Hyperborean**) Greek Mythology a member of a people worshipping Apollo and living in a land of sunshine and plenty beyond the north wind.
▶ **adjective** relating to the extreme north.
– ORIGIN late Middle English: from late Latin *hyperboreanus*, from Greek *huperboreos*, from *huper* 'beyond' + *boreas* 'north wind'.

hypercholesterolaemia /ˌhʌɪpəkəˌlɛstərɒˈliːmɪə/ (US **hypercholesterolemia**) ▶ **noun** [mass noun] Medicine an excess of cholesterol in the bloodstream.
– ORIGIN late 19th cent.: from **HYPER-** 'above normal' + **CHOLESTEROL** + **-AEMIA**.

hypercorrection ▶ **noun** [mass noun] the use of an erroneous word form or pronunciation based on a false analogy with a correct or prestigious form, such as the use of *I* instead of *me* as a grammatical object (as in *he invited my husband and I to lunch*).
– DERIVATIVES **hypercorrect** adjective.

hypercritical ▶ **adjective** excessively and unreasonably critical, especially of small faults.
– DERIVATIVES **hypercritically** adverb.

hypercube ▶ **noun** a geometrical figure in four or more dimensions which is analogous to a cube in three dimensions.

hyperdrive ▶ **noun** (in science fiction) a supposed propulsion system for travel in hyperspace. ■ [mass noun] frantic activity; overdrive: *the proliferation of house music sub-genres has gone into hyperdrive*.

hyperemia ▶ **noun** US spelling of **HYPERAEMIA**.

hyperesthesia ▶ **noun** US spelling of **HYPERAESTHESIA**.

hyperextend ▶ **verb** [with obj.] forcefully extend a limb or joint beyond its normal limits, either in exercise or therapy or so as to cause injury.
– DERIVATIVES **hyperextension** noun.

hyperfocal distance ▶ **noun** the distance between a camera lens and the closest object which is in focus when the lens is focused at infinity.

hypergamy /hʌɪˈpəːgəmi/ ▶ **noun** [mass noun] the action of marrying a person of a superior caste or class.
– ORIGIN late 19th cent.: from **HYPER-** 'above' + Greek *gamos* 'marriage'.

hyperglycaemia /ˌhʌɪpəglʌɪˈsiːmɪə/ (US **hyperglycemia**) ▶ **noun** [mass noun] Medicine an excess of glucose in the bloodstream, often associated with diabetes mellitus.
– DERIVATIVES **hyperglycaemic** adjective.
– ORIGIN late 19th cent.: from **HYPER-** 'above normal' + **GLYCO-** + **-AEMIA**.

hypergolic /ˌhʌɪpəˈgɒlɪk/ ▶ **adjective** (of a rocket propellant) igniting spontaneously on mixing with another substance.
– ORIGIN 1940s: from German *Hypergol*, probably from **HYPER-** 'beyond' + Greek *ergon* 'work' + **-OL**.

hypericin /hʌɪˈpɛrɪsɪn/ ▶ **noun** [mass noun] a substance found in St John's wort, credited with chemical and pharmacological properties similar to those of antidepressants. ● A polycyclic quinone; chem. formula: $C_{30}H_{14}O_8$.
– ORIGIN early 20th cent.: from **HYPERICUM** + **-IN**[1].

hypericum /hʌɪˈpɛrɪkəm/ ▶ **noun** a yellow-flowered plant of a genus that includes the St John's worts, tutsan, and rose of Sharon. ● Genus *Hypericum*, family Guttiferae.
– ORIGIN Latin, from Greek *hupereikon*, from *huper* 'over, above' + *ereikē* 'heath'.

hyperimmune ▶ **adjective** Medicine having a high concentration of antibodies produced in reaction to repeated injections of an antigen.

hyperinflation ▶ **noun** [mass noun] monetary inflation occurring at a very high rate.

hyperinstrument ▶ **noun** a musical instrument designed or adapted to be used with electronic sensors whose output controls the computerized generation or transformation of the sound.

Hyperion /hʌɪˈpɪərɪən/ Astronomy a satellite of Saturn, the sixteenth closest to the planet, discovered in 1848 and having an irregular shape.
– ORIGIN named after a Titan of Greek mythology.

hyperkeratosis /ˌhʌɪpəkɛrəˈtəʊsɪs/ ▶ **noun** [mass noun] Medicine abnormal thickening of the outer layer of the skin.

hyperkinesis /ˌhʌɪpəkɪˈniːsɪs, -kʌɪ-/ (also **hyperkinesia**) ▶ **noun** [mass noun] **1** Medicine muscle spasm.
2 Psychiatry a disorder of children marked by hyperactivity and inability to concentrate.
– ORIGIN mid 19th cent.: from **HYPER-** 'above normal' + Greek *kinēsis* 'motion'.

hyperkinetic /ˌhʌɪpəkɪˈnɛtɪk, -kʌɪ-/ ▶ **adjective 1** of or affected with hyperkinesis.
2 chiefly US characterized by frenetic energy or activity; hyperactive: *Hong Kong's hyperkinetic movie industry*.

hyperlink Computing ▶ **noun** a link from a hypertext document to another location, activated by clicking on a highlighted word or image.
▶ **verb** [with obj.] create a hyperlink between (documents or parts of a document).

hyperlipaemia /ˌhʌɪpəlɪˈpiːmɪə/ (US **hyperlipemia**) ▶ **noun** [mass noun] Medicine an abnormally high concentration of fats or lipids in the blood.

hyperlipidaemia /ˌhʌɪpəˌlɪpɪˈdiːmɪə/ (US **hyperlipidemia**) ▶ **noun** another term for **HYPERLIPAEMIA**.
– DERIVATIVES **hyperlipidaemic** adjective.

hypermarket ▶ **noun** Brit. a very large self-service store with a wide range of goods and a large car park, typically situated outside a town.
– ORIGIN 1970s: translation of French *hypermarché*, from **HYPER-** 'beyond, exceeding' + *marché* 'market'.

hypermedia ▶ **noun** [mass noun] Computing an extension to hypertext providing multimedia facilities, such as those handling sound and video.
– ORIGIN 1960s: from **HYPER-** 'above, beyond' + **MEDIA**[1].

hypermetropia /ˌhʌɪpəmɪˈtrəʊpɪə/ ▶ **noun** [mass noun] long-sightedness.
– DERIVATIVES **hypermetropic** adjective.
– ORIGIN mid 19th cent.: from Greek *hupermetros* 'beyond measure' (from *huper* 'over, above' + *metron* 'measure') + *ōps* 'eye'.

hypermnesia /ˌhʌɪpəmˈniːzɪə/ ▶ **noun** [mass noun] unusual power or enhancement of memory, typically under abnormal conditions such as trauma, hypnosis, or narcosis.
– ORIGIN mid 19th cent.: from **HYPER-** + Greek *mnēsia* 'memory'.

hypermutable ▶ **adjective** Genetics of or in a state in which mutation is abnormally frequent.
– DERIVATIVES **hypermutation** noun.

hypernym /ˈhʌɪpənɪm/ ▶ **noun** a word with a broad meaning constituting a category into which words with more specific meanings fall; a superordinate. For example, *colour* is a hypernym of *red*. Contrasted with **HYPONYM**.
– ORIGIN 1970s: from **HYPER-** 'beyond' + **-ONYM**.

hyperon /ˈhʌɪp(ə)rɒn/ ▶ **noun** Physics an unstable subatomic particle classified as a baryon, heavier than the neutron and proton.
– ORIGIN 1950s: from **HYPER-** 'beyond, over' + **-ON**.

hyperopia /ˌhʌɪpərˈəʊpɪə/ ▶ **noun** another term for **HYPERMETROPIA**.
– DERIVATIVES **hyperopic** adjective.
– ORIGIN late 19th cent.: from **HYPER-** 'beyond' + Greek *ōps* 'eye'.

hyperparasite ▶ **noun** Biology a parasite whose host is itself a parasite.
– DERIVATIVES **hyperparasitism** noun.

hyperparathyroidism /ˌhʌɪpəˌparəˈθʌɪrɔɪdɪz(ə)m/ ▶ **noun** [mass noun] Medicine an abnormally high concentration of parathyroid hormone in the blood, resulting in weakening of the bones through loss of calcium.
– DERIVATIVES **hyperparathyroid** adjective.

hyperpigmentation ▶ **noun** [mass noun] excessive pigmentation of the skin.

hyperplasia /ˌhʌɪpəˈpleɪzɪə/ ▶ **noun** [mass noun] Medicine & Biology the enlargement of an organ or tissue caused by an increase in the reproduction rate of its cells, often as an initial stage in the development of cancer.
– ORIGIN mid 19th cent.: from **HYPER-** 'beyond' + Greek *plasis* 'formation'.

H

hyperreal ▶ **adjective 1** exaggerated in comparison to reality: *his characters are hyperreal rather than naturalistic.*
2 (of artistic representation) extremely realistic in detail.
– DERIVATIVES **hyperrealism** noun, **hyperrealist** adjective, **hyperrealistic** adjective, **hyperreality** noun.

hypersensitive ▶ **adjective 1** having extreme physical sensitivity to particular substances or conditions.
2 easily hurt, worried, or offended: *proximity to death makes people hypersensitive and aware.*
– DERIVATIVES **hypersensitiveness** noun, **hypersensitivity** noun.

hypersonic ▶ **adjective 1** relating to speeds of more than five times the speed of sound (Mach 5).
2 relating to sound frequencies above about a thousand million hertz.
– DERIVATIVES **hypersonically** adverb.
– ORIGIN 1930s (in sense 2): from **HYPER-** 'beyond, exceeding', on the pattern of *supersonic* and *ultrasonic*.

hyperspace ▶ **noun** [mass noun] space of more than three dimensions. ■ (in science fiction) a notional space–time continuum in which it is possible to travel faster than light.
– DERIVATIVES **hyperspatial** adjective.

hypersthene /ˈhʌɪpəsθiːn/ ▶ **noun** [mass noun] a greenish rock-forming mineral of the orthopyroxene class, consisting of a magnesium iron silicate.
– ORIGIN early 19th cent.: coined in French, from **HYPER-** 'exceeding' + Greek *sthenos* 'strength' (because it is harder than hornblende).

hypertension ▶ **noun** [mass noun] Medicine abnormally high blood pressure. ■ a state of great psychological stress.

hypertensive ▶ **adjective** exhibiting hypertension.
▶ **noun** Medicine a person with high blood pressure.

hypertext ▶ **noun** [mass noun] Computing a software system allowing extensive cross-referencing between related sections of text and associated graphic material.

hyperthermia /ˌhʌɪpəˈθəːmɪə/ ▶ **noun** [mass noun] Medicine the condition of having a body temperature greatly above normal.
– DERIVATIVES **hyperthermic** adjective.
– ORIGIN late 19th cent.: from **HYPER-** 'beyond' + Greek *thermē* 'heat'.

hyperthyroidism /ˌhʌɪpəˈθʌɪrɔɪdɪz(ə)m/ ▶ **noun** [mass noun] Medicine overactivity of the thyroid gland, resulting in a rapid heartbeat and an increased rate of metabolism. Also called **THYROTOXICOSIS**.
– DERIVATIVES **hyperthyroid** adjective, **hyperthyroidic** adjective.

hypertonic /ˌhʌɪpəˈtɒnɪk/ ▶ **adjective 1** Biology having a higher osmotic pressure than a particular fluid, typically a body fluid or intracellular fluid.
2 Physiology of or in a state of abnormally high muscle tone.
– DERIVATIVES **hypertonia** noun (sense 2), **hypertonicity** noun.

hypertrophy /hʌɪˈpəːtrəfi/ ▶ **noun** [mass noun] Physiology the enlargement of an organ or tissue from the increase in size of its cells.
– DERIVATIVES **hypertrophic** adjective, **hypertrophied** adjective.
– ORIGIN mid 19th cent.: from **HYPER-** 'beyond, exceeding' + Greek *-trophia* 'nourishment'.

hyperventilate ▶ **verb 1** breathe or cause to breathe at an abnormally rapid rate, so increasing the rate of loss of carbon dioxide.
2 [no obj.] be or become overexcited: *the President was hyperventilating about a minor newspaper story.*
– DERIVATIVES **hyperventilation** noun.

hypesthesia ▶ **noun** US spelling of **HYPAESTHESIA**.

hypethral ▶ **adjective** variant spelling of **HYPAETHRAL**.

hypha /ˈhʌɪfə/ ▶ **noun** (pl. **hyphae** /-fiː/) Botany each of the branching filaments that make up the mycelium of a fungus.
– DERIVATIVES **hyphal** adjective.
– ORIGIN mid 19th cent.: modern Latin, from Greek *huphē* 'web'.

Hyphasis /ˈhʌɪfəsɪs/ ancient Greek name for **BEAS**.

hyphen /ˈhʌɪf(ə)n/ ▶ **noun** the sign (-) used to join words to indicate that they have a combined meaning or that they are linked in the grammar of a sentence (as in *a pick-me-up, rock-forming minerals*), to indicate the division of a word at the end of a line, or to indicate a missing element (as in *short- and long-term*).
– ORIGIN early 17th cent.: via late Latin from Greek *huphen* 'together', from *hupo* 'under' + *hen* 'one'.

> **USAGE** In modern English the use of hyphens is in general decreasing, especially in compound nouns: **website** is preferred to **web-site**, and **air raid** to **air-raid**. Hyphens are still often employed where a compound expression precedes a noun, as in *first-rate musicians* or *twenty-odd people* (*twenty odd people* means something quite different!), but even in this context there is a growing trend to omit them. When a phrasal verb such as *build up* is made into a noun it is usually hyphenated (*a build-up of pressure*). Note, however, that a normal phrasal verb should not be hyphenated: write *food to take away* not *food to take-away*, and *continue to build up your pension* not *continue to build-up your pension*.

hyphenate ▶ **verb** [with obj.] write or separate with a hyphen.
▶ **noun** informal a person who is active in more than one sphere or occupation: ***producer-director-businessmen hyphenates such as Spielberg.***
– DERIVATIVES **hyphenation** noun.

hyphenated American ▶ **noun** US informal an American citizen who can trace their ancestry to another part of the world, such as an African American (so called because terms such as *African American* are often written with a hyphen).

hypnagogic /ˌhɪpnəˈgɒdʒɪk/ (also **hypnogogic**) ▶ **adjective** Psychology relating to the state immediately before falling asleep.
– ORIGIN late 19th cent.: from French *hypnagogique*, from Greek *hupnos* 'sleep' + *agōgos* 'leading' (from *agein* 'to lead').

hypno- ▶ **combining form** relating to sleep: *hypnopaedia.* ■ relating to hypnosis: *hypnotherapy.*
– ORIGIN from Greek *hupnos* 'sleep'.

hypnopaedia /ˌhɪpnəʊˈpiːdɪə/ (US **hypnopedia**) ▶ **noun** [mass noun] learning by hearing while asleep or under hypnosis.

hypnopompic /ˌhɪpnə(ʊ)ˈpɒmpɪk/ ▶ **adjective** Psychology relating to the state immediately preceding waking up.
– ORIGIN early 20th cent.: from Greek *hupnos* 'sleep' + *pompē* 'sending away' + **-IC**.

Hypnos /ˈhɪpnɒs/ Greek Mythology the god of sleep, son of Nyx (Night).
– ORIGIN from Greek *hupnos* 'sleep'.

hypnosis ▶ **noun** [mass noun] the induction of a state of consciousness in which a person apparently loses the power of voluntary action and is highly responsive to suggestion or direction. Its use in therapy, typically to recover suppressed memories or to allow modification of behaviour, has been revived but is still controversial. ■ a hypnotic state.
– ORIGIN late 19th cent.: from Greek *hupnos* 'sleep' + **-OSIS**.

hypnotherapy ▶ **noun** [mass noun] the use of hypnosis as a therapeutic technique.
– DERIVATIVES **hypnotherapist** noun.

hypnotic ▶ **adjective 1** relating to or producing hypnosis: *a hypnotic state.* ■ exerting a compelling or soporific effect: *her voice had a hypnotic quality.*
2 Medicine (of a drug) sleep-inducing.
▶ **noun 1** Medicine a sleep-inducing drug.
2 a person under or open to hypnosis.
– DERIVATIVES **hypnotically** adverb.
– ORIGIN early 17th cent.: from French *hypnotique*, via late Latin from Greek *hupnōtikos* 'causing sleep', from *hupnoun* 'put to sleep', from *hupnos* 'sleep'.

hypnotism ▶ **noun** [mass noun] the study or practice of hypnosis.
– DERIVATIVES **hypnotist** noun.

hypnotize (also **hypnotise**) ▶ **verb** [with obj.] produce a state of hypnosis in (someone). ■ capture the whole attention of (someone); fascinate: *she gazed down, hypnotized by the swirling tide.*
– DERIVATIVES **hypnotizable** adjective.

hypo¹ ▶ **noun** [mass noun] Photography the chemical sodium thiosulphate (formerly called hyposulphite) used as a photographic fixer.
– ORIGIN mid 19th cent.: abbreviation of *hyposulphite*.

hypo² ▶ **noun** (pl. **hypos**) informal term for **HYPODERMIC**.
– ORIGIN early 20th cent.: abbreviation.

hypo³ ▶ **noun** (pl. **hypos**) informal an attack of hypoglycaemia.
– ORIGIN late 20th cent.: abbreviation.

hypo- (also **hyp-**) ▶ **prefix** under: *hypodermic.* ■ below normal: *hypoglycaemia.* ■ slightly: *hypomanic.* ■ Chemistry containing an element with an unusually low valency: *hypochlorous.*
– ORIGIN from Greek *hupo* 'under'.

hypoallergenic /ˌhʌɪpəʊaləˈdʒɛnɪk/ ▶ **adjective** (especially of cosmetics and textiles) relatively unlikely to cause an allergic reaction.

hypoblast /ˈhʌɪpə(ʊ)blast/ ▶ **noun** Biology former term for **ENDODERM**.

hypocalcaemia /ˌhʌɪpəʊkalˈsiːmɪə/ (US **hypocalcemia**) ▶ **noun** [mass noun] Medicine deficiency of calcium in the bloodstream.

hypocaust /ˈhʌɪpə(ʊ)kɔːst/ ▶ **noun** an ancient Roman heating system, comprising a hollow space under the floor of a building, into which hot air was directed.
– ORIGIN from Latin *hypocaustum*, from Greek *hupokauston* 'place heated from below', from *hupo* 'under' + *kau-* (base of *kaiein* 'to burn').

hypocentre ▶ **noun 1** the point within the earth where an earthquake originates.
2 the point on the earth's surface directly above or below an exploding nuclear bomb.

hypochlorous acid /ˌhʌɪpə(ʊ)ˈklɔːrəs/ ▶ **noun** [mass noun] Chemistry a weak acid with oxidizing properties formed when chlorine dissolves in cold water and used in bleaching and water treatment. ● Chem. formula: HOCl.
– DERIVATIVES **hypochlorite** noun.
– ORIGIN mid 19th cent.: *hypochlorous* from **HYPO-** (denoting an element in a low valency) + **CHLORINE** + **-OUS**.

hypochondria /ˌhʌɪpəˈkɒndrɪə/ ▶ **noun** [mass noun] abnormal chronic anxiety about one's health.
– ORIGIN late Middle English: via late Latin from Greek *hupokhondria*, denoting the soft body area below the ribs, from *hupo* 'under' + *khondros* 'sternal cartilage'. Melancholy was originally thought to arise from the liver, gall bladder, spleen, etc.

hypochondriac ▶ **noun** a person who is abnormally anxious about their health.
▶ **adjective** another term for **HYPOCHONDRIACAL**.
– ORIGIN late 16th cent.: coined in French from Greek *hupokhondriakos*, from *hupokhondria* (see **HYPOCHONDRIA**).

hypochondriacal /ˌhʌɪpə(ʊ)kɒnˈdrʌɪək(ə)l/ ▶ **adjective** of or affected by hypochondria.

hypochondriasis /ˌhʌɪpə(ʊ)kɒnˈdrʌɪəsɪs/ ▶ **noun** technical term for **HYPOCHONDRIA**.

hypocoristic /ˌhʌɪpə(ʊ)kəˈrɪstɪk/ ▶ **adjective** denoting or of the nature of a pet name or diminutive form of a name.
▶ **noun** a hypocoristic name or form.
– ORIGIN mid 19th cent.: from Greek *hupokorisma*, from *hupokorizesthai* 'play the child', from *hupo* 'under' + *korē* 'child'.

hypocotyl /ˌhʌɪpə(ʊ)ˈkɒtɪl/ ▶ **noun** Botany the part of the stem of an embryo plant beneath the stalks of the seed leaves or cotyledons and directly above the root.

hypocrisy ▶ noun (pl. **hypocrisies**) [mass noun] the practice of claiming to have higher standards or more noble beliefs than is the case.
– ORIGIN Middle English: from Old French *ypocrisie*, via ecclesiastical Latin, from Greek *hupokrisis* 'acting of a theatrical part', from *hupokrinesthai* 'play a part, pretend', from *hupo* 'under' + *krinein* 'decide, judge'.

hypocrite ▶ noun a hypocritical person.
– ORIGIN Middle English: from Old French *ypocrite*, via ecclesiastical Latin from Greek *hupokritēs* 'actor', from *hupokrinesthai* (see HYPOCRISY).

hypocritical ▶ adjective behaving in a way that suggests one has higher standards or more noble beliefs than is the case: *we don't go to church and we thought it would be hypocritical to have him christened.*
– DERIVATIVES **hypocritically** adverb.

hypocycloid /ˌhʌɪpə(ʊ)ˈsʌɪklɔɪd/ ▶ noun Mathematics the curve traced by a point on the circumference of a circle which is rolling on the interior of another circle.

hypodermic ▶ adjective [attrib.] Medicine relating to the region immediately beneath the skin. ■ (of a needle or syringe) used to inject a drug or other substance beneath the skin. ■ (of a drug or other substance) injected beneath the skin.
▶ noun a hypodermic syringe or injection.
– DERIVATIVES **hypodermically** adverb.
– ORIGIN mid 19th cent.: from HYPO- 'under' + Greek *derma* 'skin' + -IC.

hypogastrium /ˌhʌɪpə(ʊ)ˈgastrɪəm/ ▶ noun (pl. **hypogastria** /-rɪə/) Anatomy the part of the central abdomen which is situated below the region of the stomach.
– DERIVATIVES **hypogastric** adjective.
– ORIGIN late 17th cent.: modern Latin, from Greek *hupogastrion*, from *hupo* 'under' + *gastēr* 'belly'.

hypogeal /ˌhʌɪpə(ʊ)ˈdʒiːəl/ (also **hypogean**) ▶ adjective Botany underground; subterranean. Compare with EPIGEAL. ■ (of seed germination) with the seed leaves remaining below the ground.
– ORIGIN late 17th cent.: via late Latin from Greek *hupogeios* (from *hupo* 'under' + *gē* 'earth') + -AL.

hypogene /ˈhʌɪpə(ʊ)dʒiːn/ ▶ adjective Geology producing or occurring under the surface of the earth.
– ORIGIN mid 19th cent.: from HYPO- 'under' + Greek *genēs* '-born, of a certain kind'.

hypogeum /ˌhʌɪpə(ʊ)ˈdʒiːəm/ ▶ noun (pl. **hypogea**) an underground chamber.
– ORIGIN mid 17th cent.: from Latin, from Greek *hupogeion*, neuter of *hupogeios* 'underground'.

hypoglossal nerve /ˌhʌɪpə(ʊ)ˈglɒs(ə)l/ ▶ noun Anatomy each of the twelfth pair of cranial nerves, supplying the muscles of the tongue.
– ORIGIN mid 19th cent.: *hypoglossal* from HYPO- 'under' + Greek *glōssa* 'tongue' + -AL.

hypoglycaemia /ˌhʌɪpəʊglʌɪˈsiːmɪə/ (US **hypoglycemia**) ▶ noun [mass noun] Medicine deficiency of glucose in the bloodstream.
– DERIVATIVES **hypoglycaemic** adjective.
– ORIGIN late 19th cent.: from HYPO- 'below' + GLYCO- + -AEMIA.

hypogonadism /ˌhʌɪpə(ʊ)ˈgəʊnadɪz(ə)m/ ▶ noun [mass noun] Medicine reduction or absence of hormone secretion or other physiological activity of the gonads (testes or ovaries).
– DERIVATIVES **hypogonadal** adjective.

hypogynous /hʌɪˈpɒdʒɪnəs/ ▶ adjective Botany (of a plant or flower) having the stamens and other floral parts situated below the carpels (or gynoecium). Compare with EPIGYNOUS, PERIGYNOUS.
– DERIVATIVES **hypogyny** noun.
– ORIGIN early 19th cent.: from modern Latin *hypogynus*, from HYPO- 'below' + *gunē* 'woman' (used to represent 'pistil') + -OUS.

hypoid /ˈhʌɪpɔɪd/ (also **hypoid gear**) ▶ noun a bevel wheel with teeth engaging with a spiral pinion mounted at right angles to the wheel's axis, used to connect non-intersecting shafts in vehicle transmissions and other mechanisms.
– ORIGIN 1920s: perhaps a contraction of HYPERBOLOID.

hypokalaemia /ˌhʌɪpəʊkəˈliːmɪə/ (US **hypokalemia**) ▶ noun [mass noun] Medicine deficiency of potassium in the bloodstream.
– DERIVATIVES **hypokalaemic** adjective.
– ORIGIN 1940s: from HYPO- 'below' + modern Latin *kalium* 'potassium'.

hypolimnion /ˌhʌɪpə(ʊ)ˈlɪmnɪən/ ▶ noun (pl. **hypolimnia** /-nɪə/) the lower layer of water in a stratified lake, typically cooler than the water above and relatively stagnant.
– ORIGIN early 20th cent.: from HYPO- 'below' + Greek *limnion* (diminutive of *limnē* 'lake').

hypomagnesaemia /ˌhʌɪpə(ʊ)ˌmagnɪˈziːmɪə/ (US **hypomagnesemia**) ▶ noun [mass noun] Medicine & Veterinary Medicine deficiency of magnesium in the blood, important in cattle as the cause of grass tetany.
– DERIVATIVES **hypomagnesaemic** adjective.

hypomania ▶ noun [mass noun] Psychiatry a mild form of mania, marked by elation and hyperactivity.
– DERIVATIVES **hypomanic** adjective.

hyponym /ˈhʌɪpə(ʊ)nɪm/ ▶ noun a word of more specific meaning than a general or superordinate term applicable to it. For example, *spoon* is a hyponym of *cutlery*. Contrasted with HYPERNYM.
– DERIVATIVES **hyponymy** noun.

hypoparathyroidism /ˌhʌɪpəʊˌparəˈθʌɪrɔɪdɪz(ə)m/ ▶ noun [mass noun] Medicine diminished concentration of parathyroid hormone in the blood, which causes deficiencies of calcium and phosphorus compounds in the blood and results in muscular spasms.

hypophysis /hʌɪˈpɒfɪsɪs/ ▶ noun (pl. **hypophyses** /-siːz/) Anatomy technical term for PITUITARY.
– DERIVATIVES **hypophyseal** /ˌhʌɪpə(ʊ)ˈfɪzɪəl/ (also **hypophysial**) adjective.
– ORIGIN late 17th cent.: modern Latin, from Greek *hupophusis* 'offshoot', from *hupo* 'under' + *phusis* 'growth'.

hypopigmentation ▶ noun [mass noun] inadequate pigmentation of the skin.

hypopituitarism /ˌhʌɪpəʊpɪˈtjuːɪt(ə)rɪz(ə)m/ ▶ noun [mass noun] Medicine diminished hormone secretion by the pituitary gland, causing dwarfism in children and premature ageing in adults.
– DERIVATIVES **hypopituitary** adjective.

hypospadias /ˌhʌɪpəʊˈspeɪdɪəs/ ▶ noun [mass noun] Medicine a congenital condition in males in which the opening of the urethra is on the underside of the penis.
– ORIGIN early 19th cent.: from Greek *hupospadias* 'person having hypospadias', apparently from HYPO- + *span* 'to draw'.

hypospray ▶ noun (chiefly in science fiction) a device used to introduce a drug or other substance into the body through the skin without puncturing it.

hypostasis /hʌɪˈpɒstəsɪs/ ▶ noun (pl. **hypostases** /-siːz/) **1** [mass noun] Medicine the accumulation of fluid or blood in the lower parts of the body or organs under the influence of gravity, as occurs in cases of poor circulation or after death.
2 Philosophy an underlying reality or substance, as opposed to attributes or to that which lacks substance.
3 Theology (in Trinitarian doctrine) each of the three persons of the Trinity, as contrasted with the unity of the Godhead. ■ [in sing.] Theology the single person of Christ, as contrasted with his dual human and divine nature.
– ORIGIN early 16th cent. (in theological use): via ecclesiastical Latin from Greek *hupostasis* 'sediment', later 'essence, substance', from *hupo* 'under' + *stasis* 'standing'.

hypostasize (also **hypostasise**) ▶ verb [with obj.] formal treat or represent (something abstract) as a concrete reality.

hypostatic /ˌhʌɪpə(ʊ)ˈstatɪk/ ▶ adjective Theology relating to the persons of the Trinity.
– DERIVATIVES **hypostatical** adjective.

hypostatic union ▶ noun Theology the combination of divine and human natures in the single person of Christ.

hypostatize ▶ verb North American term for HYPOSTASIZE.

hypostyle /ˈhʌɪpə(ʊ)stʌɪl/ ▶ adjective Architecture (of a building) having a roof supported by pillars, typically in several rows.
▶ noun a building having a hypostyle roof.
– ORIGIN mid 19th cent.: from Greek *hupostulos*, from *hupo* 'under' + *stulos* 'column'.

hypotaxis /ˌhʌɪpə(ʊ)ˈtaksɪs/ ▶ noun [mass noun] Grammar the subordination of one clause to another. Contrasted with PARATAXIS.
– DERIVATIVES **hypotactic** adjective.
– ORIGIN late 19th cent.: from Greek *hupotaxis*, from *hupo* 'under' + *taxis* 'arrangement'.

hypotension ▶ noun [mass noun] abnormally low blood pressure.

hypotensive ▶ adjective lowering the blood pressure: *hypotensive drugs.* ■ relating to or suffering from abnormally low blood pressure.

hypotenuse /hʌɪˈpɒtənjuːz, -s/ ▶ noun the longest side of a right-angled triangle, opposite the right angle.
– ORIGIN late 16th cent.: via Latin *hypotenusa* from Greek *hupoteinousa (grammē)* 'subtending (line)', from the verb *hupoteinein* (from *hupo* 'under' + *teinein* 'stretch').

hypothalamus /ˌhʌɪpə(ʊ)ˈθaləməs/ ▶ noun (pl. **hypothalami** /-mʌɪ/) Anatomy a region of the forebrain below the thalamus which coordinates both the autonomic nervous system and the activity of the pituitary, controlling body temperature, thirst, hunger, and other homeostatic systems, and involved in sleep and emotional activity.
– DERIVATIVES **hypothalamic** adjective.

hypothec /hʌɪˈpɒθɪk, ˈhʌɪ-/ ▶ noun (in Roman and Scots law) a right established by law over a debtor's property that remains in the debtor's possession.
– ORIGIN early 16th cent.: from French *hypothèque*, via late Latin from Greek *hupothēkē* 'deposit' (from *hupo* 'under' + *tithenai* 'to place').

hypothecate /hʌɪˈpɒθɪkeɪt/ ▶ verb [with obj.] pledge (money) by law to a specific purpose.
– DERIVATIVES **hypothecation** noun.
– ORIGIN early 17th cent.: from medieval Latin *hypothecat-* 'given as a pledge', from the verb *hypothecare*, based on Greek *hupothēkē* (see HYPOTHEC).

H

hypothermia /ˌhʌɪpə(ʊ)ˈθəːmɪə/ ▶ noun [mass noun] the condition of having an abnormally (typically dangerously) low body temperature.
– DERIVATIVES **hypothermic** adjective.
– ORIGIN late 19th cent.: from HYPO- 'below' + Greek *thermē* 'heat'.

hypothesis /hʌɪˈpɒθɪsɪs/ ▶ noun (pl. **hypotheses** /-siːz/) a supposition or proposed explanation made on the basis of limited evidence as a starting point for further investigation: *his 'steady state' hypothesis of the origin of the universe.* ■ Philosophy a proposition made as a basis for reasoning, without any assumption of its truth.
– ORIGIN late 16th cent.: via late Latin from Greek *hupothesis* 'foundation', from *hupo* 'under' + *thesis* 'placing'.

hypothesize (also **hypothesise**) ▶ verb [with obj.] put (something) forward as a hypothesis.
– DERIVATIVES **hypothesizer** noun.

hypothetical /ˌhʌɪpəˈθɛtɪk(ə)l/ ▶ adjective based on or serving as a hypothesis: *let us take a hypothetical case.* ■ supposed but not necessarily real or true: *the hypothetical tenth planet.* ■ Logic denoting or containing a proposition of the logical form *if p then q*.
▶ noun (usu. **hypotheticals**) a hypothetical proposition or statement.
– DERIVATIVES **hypothetically** adverb [sentence adverb] *hypothetically, varying interpretations of the term are possible.*

hypothetical imperative ▶ noun Philosophy a moral obligation that applies only if one desires the implicated goal.

hypothetico-deductive ▶ adjective Philosophy relating to the testing of the consequences of hypotheses, to determine whether the hypotheses themselves are false or acceptable.

hypothyroidism /ˌhʌɪpəʊˈθʌɪrɔɪdɪz(ə)m/ ▶ noun [mass noun] Medicine abnormally low activity of the thyroid gland, resulting in retardation of growth and mental development in children and adults.
– DERIVATIVES **hypothyroid** noun & adjective.

hypotonic /ˌhʌɪpə(ʊ)ˈtɒnɪk/ ▶ adjective **1** Biology having a lower osmotic pressure than a particular fluid, typically a body fluid or intracellular fluid.
2 Physiology of or in a state of abnormally low muscle tone.
– DERIVATIVES **hypotonia** noun, **hypotonicity** noun.

hypoventilation ▶ noun [mass noun] Medicine breathing at an abnormally slow rate, resulting in an increased amount of carbon dioxide in the blood.

hypovolaemia /ˌhʌɪpə(ʊ)vəˈliːmɪə/ (US **hypovolemia**) ▶ noun [mass noun] Medicine a decreased volume of circulating blood in the body.
– DERIVATIVES **hypovolaemic** adjective.
– ORIGIN 1920s: from HYPO- 'under' + VOLUME + Greek *haima* 'blood'.

hypoxaemia /ˌhʌɪpɒkˈsiːmɪə/ (US **hypoxemia**) ▶ noun [mass noun] Medicine an abnormally low concentration of oxygen in the blood. ■ Ecology oxygen deficiency in a biotic environment.
– ORIGIN late 19th cent.: from HYPO- (denoting an element in a low valency) + OXYGEN + -AEMIA.

hypoxanthine /ˌhʌɪpəʊˈzanθiːn/ ▶ **noun** [mass noun] Biochemistry a compound which is an intermediate in the metabolism of purines in animals and occurs in plant tissues. ● Alternative name: **6-hydroxypurine**; chem. formula: $C_5H_4N_4O$.

hypoxia /hʌɪˈpɒksɪə/ ▶ **noun** [mass noun] Medicine deficiency in the amount of oxygen reaching the tissues. ■ oxygen deficiency in a biotic environment: *aquatic hypoxia*.
– DERIVATIVES **hypoxic** adjective.
– ORIGIN 1940s: from **HYPO-** (denoting an element in a low valency) + **OXYGEN** + **-IA**[1].

hypsilophodont /ˌhɪpsɪˈlɒfədɒnt/ (also **hypsilophodontid** /ˌhɪpsəˌlɒfəˈdɒntɪd/) ▶ **noun** a small bipedal herbivorous dinosaur of the late Jurassic and Cretaceous periods, adapted for swift running. ● Family Hypsilophodontidae, infraorder Ornithopoda, order Ornithischia.
– ORIGIN late 19th cent.: from modern Latin *Hypsilophodontidae*, from Greek *hupsilophos* 'high-crested' + *odous, odont-* 'tooth'.

hypso- ▶ **combining form** relating to height or elevation: *hypsometer*.
– ORIGIN from Greek *hupsos* 'height'.

H

hypsography /hɪpˈsɒgrəfi/ ▶ **noun** [mass noun] the branch of geography concerned with the determination and mapping of the relative elevation of areas of land.
– DERIVATIVES **hypsographic** adjective.

hypsometer /hɪpˈsɒmɪtə/ ▶ **noun** a device for calibrating thermometers at the boiling point of water at a known height above sea level or for estimating height above sea level by finding the temperature at which water boils.

hypsometric /ˌhɪpsə(ʊ)ˈmɛtrɪk/ ▶ **adjective** relating to the use of the hypsometer; hypsographic.

Hyracoidea /ˌhʌɪrəˈkɔɪdɪə/ ▶ **plural noun** Zoology a small order of mammals that comprises the hyraxes.
– ORIGIN modern Latin (plural), based on Greek *hurax, hurak-* (see **HYRAX**).

hyracotherium /ˌhʌɪrəkə(ʊ)ˈθɪərɪəm/ ▶ **noun** the earliest fossil ancestor of the horse, which was a small forest animal of the Eocene epoch, with four toes on the front feet and three on the back. ● Genus *Hyracotherium*, family Equidae.
– ORIGIN modern Latin: from *hyraco-* (combining form from **HYRAX**) + Greek *thērion* 'wild animal'.

hyrax /ˈhʌɪraks/ ▶ **noun** a small herbivorous mammal with a compact body and a very short tail, found in arid country in Africa and Arabia. The nearest relatives to hyraxes are the elephants and other subungulates. ● Family Procaviidae and order Hyracoidea: three genera and several species.
– ORIGIN mid 19th cent.: modern Latin, from Greek *hurax* 'shrew-mouse'.

hyson /ˈhʌɪs(ə)n/ ▶ **noun** [mass noun] a type of green China tea.
– ORIGIN mid 18th cent.: from Chinese *xīchūn*, literally 'bright spring'.

hyssop /ˈhɪsəp/ ▶ **noun 1** a small bushy aromatic plant of the mint family, the bitter minty leaves of which are used in cookery and herbal medicine. ● *Hyssopus officinalis*, family Labiatae.
2 (in biblical use) a wild shrub of uncertain identity whose twigs were used for sprinkling in ancient Jewish rites of purification.
– ORIGIN Old English *hysope* (reinforced in Middle English by Old French *ysope*), via Latin from Greek *hyssōpos*, of Semitic origin.

hysterectomize (also **hysterectomise**) ▶ **verb** [with obj.] perform a hysterectomy on (a woman).

hysterectomy /ˌhɪstəˈrɛktəmi/ ▶ **noun** (pl. **hysterectomies**) a surgical operation to remove all or part of the womb.
– ORIGIN late 19th cent.: from Greek *hustera* 'womb' + **-ECTOMY**.

hysteresis /ˌhɪstəˈriːsɪs/ ▶ **noun** [mass noun] Physics the phenomenon in which the value of a physical property lags behind changes in the effect causing it, as for instance when magnetic induction lags behind the magnetizing force.
– ORIGIN late 19th cent.: from Greek *husterēsis* 'shortcoming, deficiency', from *husterein* 'be behind', from *husteros* 'late'.

hysteria ▶ **noun** [mass noun] **1** exaggerated or uncontrollable emotion or excitement: *the anti-Semitic hysteria of the 1890s*.
2 an old-fashioned term for a psychological disorder characterized by conversion of psychological stress into physical symptoms (somatization) or a change in self-awareness (such as a fugue state or selective amnesia).
– ORIGIN early 19th cent.: from Latin *hystericus* (see **HYSTERIC**).

hysteric ▶ **noun 1** (**hysterics**) informal a wildly emotional and exaggerated reaction: *the widow had hysterics and the inquest was wrapped up quickly*. ■ uncontrollable laughter: *they began to giggle and fled upstairs in hysterics*.
2 a person suffering from hysteria.
▶ **adjective** another term for **HYSTERICAL** (sense 2).
– ORIGIN mid 17th cent. (as an adjective): via Latin from Greek *husterikos* 'of the womb', from *hustera* 'womb' (hysteria being thought to be specific to women and associated with the womb).

hysterical ▶ **adjective 1** affected by or deriving from wildly uncontrolled emotion: *Janet became hysterical and began screaming | the band were mobbed by hysterical fans*. ■ informal extremely funny: *her attempts to teach them to dance were hysterical*.
2 relating to or suffering from hysteria.
– DERIVATIVES **hysterically** adverb [as submodifier] *isn't it hysterically funny?*

hysteron proteron /ˌhɪstərɒn ˈprɒtərɒn/ ▶ **noun** Rhetoric a figure of speech in which what naturally would come last is put first, for example *'I die! I faint! I fail!'*
– ORIGIN mid 16th cent.: late Latin, from Greek *husteron proteron* 'the latter (put in place of) the former'.

Hystricomorpha /ˌhɪstrɪkə(ʊ)ˈmɔːfə/ ▶ **plural noun** Zoology a major division of the rodents which includes the guinea pigs, coypu, porcupines and their relatives. They occur chiefly in South America. ● Suborder Hystricomorpha, order Rodentia.
– DERIVATIVES **hystricomorph** noun & adjective.
– ORIGIN modern Latin (plural), from Latin *hystrix, hystric-* 'porcupine' (from Greek *hustrix*) + *morphē* 'form'.

Hytrel /ˈhʌɪtrɛl/ ▶ **noun** [mass noun] trademark a strong, flexible synthetic resin used in shoes, sports equipment, and other manufactured articles.

Hz ▶ abbreviation hertz.

I[1] (also **i**) ▸ **noun** (pl. **Is** or **I's**) **1** the ninth letter of the alphabet. ▪ denoting the next after H in a set of items, categories, etc.
2 the Roman numeral for one.
– PHRASES **dot the i's and cross the t's** see DOT[1].

I[2] ▸ **pronoun** [first person singular] used by a speaker to refer to himself or herself: *accept me for what I am.* ▪ W. Indian me: *Junior tell I is the army him a'work for.* ▪ (also **I and I, I man**) W. Indian (especially among Rastafarians) used in reference to oneself or to people in general: *I and I must submit to and follow Jah.*
▸ **noun** (**the I**) Philosophy (in metaphysics) the subject or object of self-consciousness; the ego.
– ORIGIN Old English, of Germanic origin; related to Dutch *ik* and German *ich*, from an Indo-European root shared by Latin *ego* and Greek *egō*.

> **USAGE** Why is it incorrect to say *between you and* **I** (rather than *between you and* **me**)? Why is it also wrong to say *John and* **me** *went to the shops* (instead of *John and* **I** *went to the shops*)? Should you say *she's much better than* **me** or *she's much better than* **I**? For a discussion of such questions, see **USAGE** at **BETWEEN** and **PERSONAL PRONOUN**.

I[3] ▸ **abbreviation** (**I.**) ▪ Island(s) or Isle(s) (chiefly on maps). ▪ Italy (international vehicle registration).
▸ **symbol** ▪ electric current: $V = I/R$. ▪ the chemical element iodine.

i ▸ **symbol** (i) Mathematics the imaginary quantity equal to the square root of minus one. Compare with J.

-i[1] ▸ **suffix** forming the plural: **1** of nouns adopted from Latin ending in *-us*: *foci* | *timpani*.
2 of nouns adopted from Italian ending in *-e* or *-o*: *dilettanti*.

> **USAGE** Many nouns derived from a foreign language retain their foreign plural, at least when they first enter English and particularly if they belong to a specialist field. Over time, though, it is quite normal for a word in general use to acquire a regular English plural. This may coexist with the foreign plural (e.g. **cactus**, plural **cacti** or **cactuses**) or it may actually oust a foreign plural. Note that not all Latin words ending in *-us* have a plural that ends in *-i*: for example, the Latin word *apparatus* is unchanged in the plural.

-i[2] ▸ **suffix** forming adjectives from names of countries or regions in the Near or Middle East: *Azerbaijani* | *Pakistani*.
– ORIGIN from Semitic and Indo-Iranian adjectival endings.

-i- ▸ **suffix** a connecting vowel chiefly forming words ending in *-ana, -ferous, -fic, -form, -fy, -gerous, -vorous*. Compare with **-o-**.

IA ▸ **abbreviation** Iowa (in official postal use).

-ia[1] ▸ **suffix 1** forming nouns adopted unchanged from Latin or Greek (such as *mania, militia*), and modern Latin terms (such as *utopia*).
2 forming names of: ▪ Medicine states and disorders: *anaemia* | *diphtheria*. ▪ Botany & Zoology genera and higher groups: *dahlia* | *Latimeria*.
3 forming names of countries: *India*.
– ORIGIN representing Latin or Greek endings.

-ia[2] ▸ **suffix** forming noun plurals: **1** from Greek neuter nouns ending in *-ion* or from those in Latin ending in *-ium* or *-e*: *paraphernalia* | *regalia*.
2 Zoology in the names of classes: *Reptilia*.

IAA ▸ **abbreviation** Biochemistry indoleacetic acid.

IAAF ▸ **abbreviation** International Association of Athletics Federations.

IAEA ▸ **abbreviation** International Atomic Energy Agency.

-ial ▸ **suffix** forming adjectives such as *celestial, primordial*.
– ORIGIN from French *-iel* or Latin *-ialis*.

iamb /ˈʌɪam(b)/ ▸ **noun** Prosody another term for IAMBUS.

iambic /ʌɪˈambɪk/ ▸ **adjective** Prosody of or using iambuses: *iambic pentameters*.
▸ **noun** iambic verse as a genre. ▪ (**iambics**) verse of this kind.
– ORIGIN mid 16th cent.: from French *iambique*, via late Latin from Greek *iambikos*, from *iambos* (see IAMBUS).

iambus /ʌɪˈambəs/ ▸ **noun** (pl. **iambuses** or **iambi** /-bʌɪ/) Prosody a metrical foot consisting of one short (or unstressed) syllable followed by one long (or stressed) syllable.
– ORIGIN late 16th cent.: Latin, from Greek *iambos* 'iambus, lampoon', from *iaptein* 'attack verbally' (because the iambic trimeter was first used by Greek satirists).

-ian ▸ **suffix** forming adjectives and nouns such as *antediluvian* and *Bostonian*. Compare with **-AN**.
– ORIGIN from French *-ien* or Latin *-ianus*.

Iapetus /ʌɪˈapɪtəs/ Astronomy a satellite of Saturn, the seventeenth closest to the planet, having one bright icy side and one very dark side, discovered by Cassini in 1671 (diameter 1,440 km).
– ORIGIN named after a Titan of Greek mythology, son of Uranus (Heaven) and Gaia (Earth).

Iaşi /ˈjaʃi/ a city in eastern Romania; pop. 316,716 (2006). From 1565 to 1859 it was the capital of the principality of Moldavia. German name **JASSY**.

-iasis ▸ **suffix** a common form of **-ASIS**.

IATA /ʌɪˈɑːtə/ ▸ **abbreviation** International Air Transport Association.

iatro- /ʌɪˈatrəʊ/ ▸ **combining form** relating to a physician or to medical treatment: *iatrogenic*.
– ORIGIN from Greek *iatros* 'physician', from *iasthai* 'heal'.

iatrochemistry ▸ **noun** [mass noun] historical a school of thought of the 16th and 17th centuries which sought to understand medicine and physiology in terms of chemistry.
– DERIVATIVES **iatrochemical** adjective, **iatrochemist** noun.

iatrogenic /ʌɪˌatrə(ʊ)ˈdʒɛnɪk/ ▸ **adjective** relating to illness caused by medical examination or treatment.
– DERIVATIVES **iatrogenesis** noun.

IB ▸ **abbreviation** International Baccalaureate.

ib. ▸ **adverb** short for IBID.

IBA ▸ **abbreviation** (in the UK) Independent Broadcasting Authority.

Ibadan /ɪˈbad(ə)n/ the second-largest city of Nigeria, situated 160 km (100 miles) north-east of Lagos; pop. 2,628,000 (est. 2007).

IBAN /ˈʌɪban/ ▸ **abbreviation** International Bank Account Number.

Iban /ˈiːban/ ▸ **noun** (pl. **same**) **1** a member of an indigenous people of Kalimantan and Sarawak. Also called **SEA DAYAK**.
2 [mass noun] the Austronesian language of the Iban, spoken by around 380,000 people.
▸ **adjective** relating to the Iban or their language.
– ORIGIN the name in Iban.

Ibárruri Gómez /ɪˌbɑːrʊri ˈɡəʊmɛz/, Spanish /iˈbarruri ˈɡəʊmeθ, -mes/, Dolores (1895–1989), Spanish communist politician and leader of the Republicans during the Spanish Civil War; known as **La Pasionaria**.

I-beam ▸ **noun** a girder which has the shape of an I when viewed in section.

Iberia /ʌɪˈbɪərɪə/ the ancient name for the Iberian peninsula.
– ORIGIN Latin, literally 'the country of the *Iberi* or *Iberes*', from Greek *Ibēres* 'Spaniards'.

Iberian ▸ **adjective** relating to or denoting Iberia, or the countries of Spain and Portugal.
▸ **noun 1** a native of Iberia, especially in ancient times.
2 [mass noun] the extinct Romance language spoken in the Iberian peninsula in late classical times. It forms an intermediate stage between Latin and modern Spanish, Catalan, and Portuguese. Also called **IBERO-ROMANCE**.
3 [mass noun] the extinct Celtic language spoken in the Iberian peninsula in ancient times, known only from a few inscriptions, place names, and references by Latin authors. Also called **CELTIBERIAN**.

Iberian peninsula the extreme SW peninsula of Europe, containing present-day Spain and Portugal. It was colonized by Carthage until the third Punic War (149–146 BC), after which it came increasingly under Roman influence. It was invaded by the Visigoths in the 4th–5th centuries AD and by the Moors in the 8th century.

iberis /ʌɪˈbɪərɪs/ ▸ **noun** (pl. **same**) a plant of a genus that comprises the candytufts. ● Genus *Iberis*, family Cruciferae.
– ORIGIN modern Latin, probably from Greek *ibēris*, denoting a kind of pepperwort.

Ibero- /ʌɪˈbɪərəʊ/ ▸ **combining form** Iberian; Iberian and ...: *Ibero-Roman*. ▪ relating to Iberia.

Ibero-Romance ▸ **noun** another term for **IBERIAN** (sense 2 of the noun).

ibex /ˈʌɪbɛks/ ▸ **noun** (pl. **ibexes**) a wild mountain goat with long, thick ridged horns and a beard, found in parts of central Asia and in Ethiopia. ● Genus *Capra*, family Bovidae: the widespread *C. ibex*, and the **Spanish ibex** (*C. pyrenaica*) of the Pyrenees.
– ORIGIN early 17th cent.: from Latin.

IBF ▸ **abbreviation** International Boxing Federation.

Ibibio /ˌɪbɪˈbiːəʊ/ ▸ **noun** (pl. **same** or **Ibibios**) **1** a member of a people of southern Nigeria.
2 [mass noun] the language of the Ibibio, belonging to the Benue-Congo group and closely related to Efik. It has around 2 million speakers.
▸ **adjective** relating to the Ibibio or their language.
– ORIGIN the name in Ibibio.

ibid. /ˈɪbɪd/ (also **ib.**) ▸ **adverb** in the same source (used to save space in textual references to a quoted work which has been mentioned in a previous reference).
– ORIGIN abbreviation of Latin *ibidem* 'in the same place'.

-ibility ▸ **suffix** forming nouns corresponding to adjectives ending in *-ible* (such as *accessibility* corresponding to *accessible*).
– ORIGIN from French *-ibilité* or Latin *-ibilitas*.

I.Biol. ▶ **abbreviation** (in the UK) Institute of Biology.

ibis /ˈʌɪbɪs/ ▶ **noun** (pl. **ibises**) a large wading bird with a long downcurved bill, long neck, and long legs.
● Family Threskiornithidae: several genera and species, including the **sacred ibis**.
– ORIGIN late Middle English: via Latin from Greek.

ibisbill ▶ **noun** an upland wading bird of central Asia, with a long downcurved bill and black, white, and blue-grey plumage on the head and breast. ● *Ibidorhyncha struthersii*, the only member of the family Ibidorhynchidae.

Ibiza /ɪˈbiːθə/, Spanish /iˈβiθa, -sa/ the westernmost of the Balearic Islands. ■ the capital city and port of Ibiza; pop. 46,835 (2008).
– DERIVATIVES **Ibizan** adjective & noun.

Ibizan hound ▶ **noun** a dog of a breed of hound from Ibiza, characterized by large, pointed, pricked ears and white, fawn, or reddish-brown colouring.

-ible ▶ **suffix** forming adjectives: **1** able to be: *audible* | *defensible*.
2 suitable for being: *reversible* | *edible*.
3 causing: *terrible* | *horrible*.
4 having the quality to: *descendible* | *passible*.
– ORIGIN from French *-ible* or Latin *-ibilis*.

-ibly ▶ **suffix** forming adverbs corresponding to adjectives ending in *-ible* (such as *audibly* corresponding to *audible*).

IBM ▶ **abbreviation** International Business Machines, a leading American computer manufacturer.

Ibn Batuta /ˌɪb(ə)n bɑːˈtuːtɑː/ (*c.*1304–68), Arab explorer. From 1325 to 1354 he journeyed through North and West Africa, India, and China, and wrote a vivid account of his travels in the *Rihlah*.

ibn Hussein, Abdullah, see **Abdullah ibn Hussein**.

Ibo /ˈiːbəʊ/ ▶ **noun & adjective** variant form of **Igbo**.

ibogaine /ɪˈbəʊgəˌiːn/ ▶ **noun** [mass noun] a hallucinogenic compound derived from the roots of a West African shrub, sometimes used as a treatment for heroin or cocaine addiction. ● The shrub is *Tabernanthe iboga*, family Apocynaceae.
– ORIGIN from a blend of *iboga* (local name for the compound) and **cocaine**.

IBRD ▶ **abbreviation** International Bank for Reconstruction and Development.

IBS ▶ **abbreviation** irritable bowel syndrome.

Ibsen /ˈɪbs(ə)n/, Henrik (1828–1906), Norwegian dramatist. He is credited with being the first major dramatist to write tragedy about ordinary people in prose. Ibsen's later works, such as *The Master Builder* (1892), deal increasingly with the forces of the unconscious and were admired by Sigmund Freud. Other notable works: *Peer Gynt* (1867), *A Doll's House* (1879), *Ghosts* (1881).

ibuprofen /ˌʌɪbjuːˈprəʊf(ə)n/ ▶ **noun** [mass noun] a synthetic compound used widely as an analgesic and anti-inflammatory drug. ● Alternative name: **2-(4-isobutylphenyl) propionic acid**; chem. formula: $C_{13}H_{18}O_2$.
– ORIGIN 1960s: from elements of the chemical name.

IC ▶ **abbreviation** ■ integrated circuit. ■ internal-combustion: *the IC engine*.

i/c ▶ **abbreviation** ■ (especially in military contexts) in charge of. ■ in command.

-ic ▶ **suffix 1** forming adjectives such as *Islamic*, *terrific*.
2 forming nouns such as *lyric*, *mechanic*.
3 denoting a particular form or instance of a noun ending in *-ics*: *aesthetic* | *dietetic* | *tactic*.
4 Chemistry denoting an element in a higher valency: *ferric* | *sulphuric*. Compare with **-ous**.
– ORIGIN from French *-ique*, Latin *-icus*, or Greek *-ikos*.

-ical ▶ **suffix** forming adjectives: **1** corresponding to nouns or adjectives usually ending in *-ic* (such as *comical* corresponding to *comic*).
2 corresponding to nouns ending in *-y* (such as *pathological* corresponding to *pathology*).

-ically ▶ **suffix** forming adverbs corresponding to adjectives ending in *-ic* or *-ical* (such as *tactically* corresponding to *tactical*).

ICAO ▶ **abbreviation** International Civil Aviation Organization.

Icarus /ˈɪkərəs/ Greek Mythology the son of Daedalus, who escaped from Crete using wings made by his father but was killed when he flew too near the sun and the wax attaching his wings melted.
– DERIVATIVES **Icarian** adjective.

ICBM ▶ **abbreviation** intercontinental ballistic missile.

ICC ▶ **abbreviation** ■ International Chamber of Commerce. ■ International Cricket Council. ■ (in the US) Interstate Commerce Commission. ■ International Criminal Court.

ICE ▶ **abbreviation** ■ (in the UK) Institution of Civil Engineers. ■ internal-combustion engine.

ice ▶ **noun 1** [mass noun] frozen water, a brittle transparent crystalline solid: *she scraped the ice off the windscreen* | *her hands were as cold as ice*. ■ a sheet or layer of ice on the surface of water: *the ice beneath him gave way*. ■ complete absence of friendliness or warmth in manner or expression: *the ice in his voice was only to hide the pain*.
2 chiefly Brit. an ice cream, ice lolly, or portion of water ice. ■ N. Amer. a frozen mixture of fruit juice or of flavoured water and sugar.
3 informal diamonds.
▶ **verb** [with obj.] **1** decorate (a cake or biscuit) with icing.
2 N. Amer. informal clinch (something such as a victory or deal).
3 N. Amer. informal kill: ***another man had been iced by the police***.
– PHRASES **break the ice** do or say something to relieve tension or get conversation going in a strained situation or when strangers meet. **ice the puck** Ice Hockey shoot the puck from one's own half of the rink to the other end without it hitting the goal or being touched by a teammate, for which a face-off is awarded in one's own end. **on ice 1** (of wine or food) kept chilled by being surrounded by ice. ■ (especially of a plan or proposal) held in reserve for future consideration: *the recommendation was put on ice*. **2** (of an entertainment) performed by skaters: *Dick Whittington on Ice*. **on thin ice** in a precarious or risky situation: *you're skating on thin ice*.
– PHRASAL VERBS **ice over/up** become covered or blocked with ice: *the wings iced over, forcing the pilot to dive*.
– ORIGIN Old English *īs*, of Germanic origin; related to Dutch *ijs* and German *Eis*.

-ice ▶ **suffix** forming nouns such as *service*, *police*, and abstract nouns such as *avarice*, *justice*.
– ORIGIN from Old French *-ice*, from Latin *-itia*, *-itius*, *-itium*, or from other sources by assimilation.

ice age ▶ **noun** a glacial episode during a past geological period. See **glacial period**. ■ (**the Ice Age**) the series of glacial episodes during the Pleistocene period.

ice axe ▶ **noun** an axe used by climbers for cutting footholds in ice, having a head with one pointed and one flattened end, and a spike at the foot.

ice bag ▶ **noun** a bag filled with ice and applied to the body to reduce swelling or lower temperature.

ice beer ▶ **noun** [mass noun] a type of strong lager brewed at sub-zero temperatures so that ice crystals form. These are then strained off to remove impurities and excess water.

iceberg ▶ **noun** a large floating mass of ice detached from a glacier or ice sheet and carried out to sea.
– PHRASES **the tip of an** (or **the**) **iceberg** the small perceptible part of a much larger situation or problem that remains hidden: *detected fraud is only the tip of the iceberg*.
– ORIGIN late 18th cent.: from Dutch *ijsberg*, from *ijs* 'ice' + *berg* 'hill'.

iceberg lettuce ▶ **noun** a lettuce of a variety having a dense round head of crisp pale leaves.

iceblink ▶ **noun** a bright appearance of the sky caused by reflection from a distant ice sheet.

iceblock ▶ **noun** Austral./NZ a block of flavoured ice on a stick.

ice blue ▶ **noun** [mass noun] a very pale blue colour.

iceboat ▶ **noun 1** a light, wind-driven vehicle with sails and runners, used for travelling on ice.
2 a boat used for breaking ice on a waterway.

ice-bound ▶ **adjective** completely surrounded or covered by ice: *the lake was ice-bound*.

icebox ▶ **noun** a chilled box or cupboard for keeping something cold, especially food. ■ Brit. a compartment in a refrigerator for making and storing ice. ■ US dated a refrigerator.

icebreaker ▶ **noun** a ship designed for breaking a channel through ice. ■ a thing that serves to relieve inhibitions or tension between people.

ice bucket ▶ **noun** a cylindrical container holding chunks of ice, the ice being used either directly in drinks or for chilling a bottle of wine.

ice cap ▶ **noun** a covering of ice over a large area, especially on the polar region of a planet.

ice chest ▶ **noun** a chilled box for keeping something cold, especially food.

ice climbing ▶ **noun** [mass noun] the sport or activity of climbing glaciers.
– DERIVATIVES **ice climber** noun.

ice-cold ▶ **adjective** very cold; as cold as ice: *ice-cold beer*.

ice cream ▶ **noun** [mass noun] a semi-soft frozen dessert made with sweetened and flavoured milk fat. ■ [count noun] a serving of ice cream.
– ORIGIN mid 18th cent.: alteration of *iced cream*.

ice cube ▶ **noun** a small block of ice made in a freezer, especially for adding to drinks.

iced ▶ **adjective** [attrib.] **1** (of a drink or other liquid) cooled in or containing pieces of ice: *jugs of iced water*. ■ (of a surface or object) covered or coated with ice: *Campari and soda in a tall, iced glass*.
2 (of a cake or biscuit) decorated with icing.

ice dancing ▶ **noun** [mass noun] a form of ice skating incorporating choreographed dance moves, typically performed by skaters in pairs.
– DERIVATIVES **ice dance** noun, **ice dancer** noun.

iced lolly ▶ **noun** variant spelling of **ice lolly**.

iced tea (N. Amer. also **ice tea**) ▶ **noun** [mass noun] a chilled drink of sweetened tea without milk, typically flavoured with lemon.

icefall ▶ **noun 1** a steep part of a glacier like a frozen waterfall.
2 an avalanche or fall of loose pieces of ice.

ice field ▶ **noun** an expanse of ice, especially in polar regions.

icefish ▶ **noun** (pl. **same** or **icefishes**) **1** another term for **capelin**.
2 a scaleless Antarctic fish of pallid appearance with spiny gill covers and a snout shaped like a duck's bill.
● *Chaenocephalus aceratus*, family Chaenichthyidae.
▶ **verb** (**ice-fish**) [no obj.] (usu. as noun **ice-fishing**) fish through holes in the ice on a lake or river.

ice floe ▶ **noun** see **floe**.

ice fog ▶ **noun** [mass noun] N. Amer. fog formed of minute ice crystals.

ice front ▶ **noun** the lower edge of a glacier.

ice hockey ▶ **noun** [mass noun] a fast contact sport played on an ice rink between two teams of six skaters, who attempt to drive a small rubber disc or puck into the opposing goal with hooked or angled sticks. It developed from field hockey in Canada in the second half of the 19th century.

icehouse ▶ **noun** a building for storing ice, typically one situated partly or wholly underground.

Iceland an island country in the North Atlantic; pop. 306,700 (est. 2009); official language, Icelandic; capital, Reykjavik. Icelandic name **Island**.

> Iceland lies just south of the Arctic Circle, and only about 20 per cent of the land area is habitable. Situated at the north end of the Mid-Atlantic Ridge, it is volcanically active. First settled by Norse colonists in the 9th century, Iceland was under Norwegian rule from 1262 to 1380, when it passed to Denmark. Granted internal self-government in 1874, it became a fully fledged independent republic in 1944.

– DERIVATIVES **Icelander** noun.

Icelandic /ʌɪsˈlandɪk/ ▶ **adjective** relating to Iceland or its language.
▶ **noun** [mass noun] the language of Iceland. A Scandinavian language, it has remained closely similar to Old Norse, due partly to the geographical isolation of Iceland and partly to a policy of avoiding loanwords.

Iceland moss (also **Iceland lichen**) ▶ **noun** a brown branching lichen with stiff spines along the margins of the fronds, growing in mountain and moorland habitats. It can be boiled to produce an edible jelly.
● *Cetraria islandica*, order Parmeliales.

Iceland poppy ▶ **noun** a tall poppy which is widely cultivated for its colourful flowers and suitability for cutting, native to arctic and north temperate regions.
● *Papaver nudicaule*, family Papaveraceae.

Iceland spar ▶ **noun** [mass noun] a transparent variety of calcite, showing strong double refraction.

ice lolly (also **iced lolly**) ▶ **noun** Brit. a piece of flavoured ice or ice cream on a stick.

iceman ▶ **noun** (pl. **icemen**) chiefly N. Amer. a man who sells or delivers ice.

ice milk ▶ **noun** [mass noun] N. Amer. a frozen dessert similar to ice cream but containing less butterfat.

Iceni /ʌɪˈsiːni, -nʌɪ/ ▶ **plural noun** a tribe of ancient Britons inhabiting an area of SE England in present-day Norfolk and Suffolk. Their queen, Boudicca, led an unsuccessful rebellion against the Romans in AD 60.

ice pack ▶ **noun 1** another term for **ICE BAG**.
2 see **PACK**[1] (sense 5 of the noun).

ice pick ▶ **noun 1** a small pick used by climbers to traverse ice-covered slopes.
2 a sharp, straight, pointed implement with a handle, used to break ice into small pieces for chilling food and drinks.

ice plant ▶ **noun 1** either of two succulent plants which are widely cultivated for their flowers: ● a South African plant which has leaves covered with glistening fluid-filled hairs that resemble ice crystals (genera *Mesembryanthemum* and *Dorotheanthus*, family Aizoaceae, in particular *M. crystallinum*). ● an Asian stonecrop which bears domed heads of tiny pink flowers (*Sedum spectabile*, family Crassulaceae).
2 a machine or installation for making ice artificially.

ice rink ▶ **noun** see **RINK**.

ice sheet ▶ **noun** a layer of ice covering an extensive tract of land for a long period of time.

ice shelf ▶ **noun** a floating sheet of ice permanently attached to a land mass.

ice show ▶ **noun** an entertainment performed by ice skaters.

ice skate ▶ **noun** a boot with a blade attached to the sole, used for skating on ice.
▶ **verb** (**ice-skate**) [no obj.] skate on ice as a sport or pastime.
– DERIVATIVES **ice skater noun**.

ice skating ▶ **noun** [mass noun] skating on ice as a sport or pastime. Ice skating became a recognized sport in 1876. Skaters are marked for technical and artistic excellence in performing a series of prescribed patterns (**figure skating**) or a choreographed series of dance moves (**ice dancing**).

ice storm ▶ **noun** chiefly N. Amer. a storm of freezing rain that leaves a coating of ice.

ice tea ▶ **noun** North American term for **ICED TEA**.

ice water ▶ **noun 1** water produced by the melting of ice.
2 [mass noun] N. Amer. drinking water with ice cubes added.

ice yacht ▶ **noun** another term for **ICEBOAT** (sense 1).

ICFTU ▶ **abbreviation** International Confederation of Free Trade Unions.

I.Chem.E. ▶ **abbreviation** (in the UK) Institution of Chemical Engineers.

I Ching /iː ˈtʃɪŋ/ ▶ **noun** an ancient Chinese manual of divination based on eight symbolic trigrams and sixty-four hexagrams, interpreted in terms of the principles of yin and yang. It was included as one of the 'five classics' of Confucianism. English name **BOOK OF CHANGES**.
– ORIGIN from Chinese *yìjīng* 'book of changes'.

ichneumon /ɪkˈnjuːmən/ ▶ **noun 1** (also **ichneumon wasp** or **ichneumon fly**) a slender parasitic wasp with long antennae, which deposits its eggs in, on, or near the larvae of other insects. ● Family Ichneumonidae, order Hymenoptera: numerous genera and species.
2 another term for **EGYPTIAN MONGOOSE**.
– ORIGIN late 15th cent. (in sense 2): via Latin from Greek *ikhneumōn* 'tracker', from *ikhneuein* 'to track', from *ikhnos* 'track, footstep'.

ichnography /ɪkˈnɒɡrəfi/ ▶ **noun** (pl. **ichnographies**) a ground plan of a building or map of a region.
– ORIGIN late 16th cent.: from French *ichnographie*, or via Latin from Greek *ikhnographia*, from *ikhnos* 'track' + *-graphia* (see **-GRAPHY**).

ichor /ˈʌɪkɔː/ ▶ **noun** [mass noun] **1** Greek Mythology the fluid which flows like blood in the veins of the gods.
2 archaic a watery discharge from a wound.
– DERIVATIVES **ichorous** /ˈʌɪk(ə)rəs/ **adjective**.
– ORIGIN mid 17th cent.: from Greek *ikhōr*.

ichthus /ˈɪkθəs/ ▶ **noun** an image of a fish used as a symbol of Christianity.
– ORIGIN from Greek *ikhthus* 'fish', an early symbol of Christianity: the initial letters of the word are sometimes taken as short for *Iesous Christos, Theou Uios, Soter* (Jesus Christ, son of God, saviour).

ichthyic /ˈɪkθɪɪk/ ▶ **adjective** archaic fishlike.
– ORIGIN mid 19th cent.: from Greek *ikhthuïkos* 'fishy', from *ikhthus* 'fish'.

ichthyo- /ˈɪkθɪəʊ/ ▶ **combining form** relating to fish; fishlike: *ichthyosaur*.
– ORIGIN from Greek *ikhthus* 'fish'.

ichthyoid /ˈɪkθɪɔɪd/ ▶ **adjective** resembling a fish; fishlike.
▶ **noun** any fishlike vertebrate.

ichthyolite /ˈɪkθɪəlʌɪt/ ▶ **noun** Palaeontology a fossil fish.
– ORIGIN early 19th cent.: from **ICHTHYO-** 'fish' + Latin *oleum* 'oil' + *lithos* 'stone'.

ichthyology /ˌɪkθɪˈɒlədʒi/ ▶ **noun** [mass noun] the branch of zoology that deals with fishes.
– DERIVATIVES **ichthyological adjective**, **ichthyologist noun**.

ichthyophagous /ˌɪkθɪˈɒfəɡəs/ ▶ **adjective** formal fish-eating: *Americans are more ichthyophagous than ever*.
– DERIVATIVES **ichthyophagy** /ˌɪkθɪˈɒfədʒi/ **noun**.

ichthyornis /ˌɪkθɪˈɔːnɪs/ ▶ **noun** a fossil gull-like fish-eating bird of the Upper Cretaceous period, with large toothed jaws. ● Genus *Ichthyornis*, order Ichthyornithiformes.
– ORIGIN modern Latin, from **ICHTHYO-** + Greek *ornis* 'bird'.

ichthyosaur /ˈɪkθɪəsɔː/ (also **ichthyosaurus** /ˌɪkθɪəˈsɔːrəs/) ▶ **noun** a fossil marine reptile of the Mesozoic era, resembling a dolphin with a long pointed head, four flippers, and a vertical tail. ● Order Ichthyosauria, subclass Diapsida: numerous genera, including *Ichthyosaurus*.
– ORIGIN mid 19th cent.: from **ICHTHYO-** 'fish' + Greek *sauros* 'lizard'.

ichthyosis /ˌɪkθɪˈəʊsɪs/ ▶ **noun** [mass noun] Medicine a congenital skin condition which causes the epidermis to become dry and horny like fish scales.
– DERIVATIVES **ichthyotic adjective**.

I-chun /iːˈtʃʊn/ variant of **YICHUN**.

ICI ▶ **abbreviation** Imperial Chemical Industries (Limited).

-ician ▶ **suffix** (forming nouns) denoting a person skilled in or concerned with a field or subject (often corresponding to a noun ending in *-ic* or *-ics*): *politician* | *statistician*.
– ORIGIN from French *-icien*.

icicle ▶ **noun** a hanging, tapering piece of ice formed by the freezing of dripping water.
– ORIGIN Middle English: from **ICE** + dialect *ickle* 'icicle' (from Old English *gicel*).

icing ▶ **noun** [mass noun] **1** a mixture of sugar with water, egg white, or butter, used as a coating for cakes or biscuits.
2 the formation of ice on an aircraft, ship, or other vehicle, or in an engine.
– PHRASES **the icing** (N. Amer. also **frosting**) **on the cake** an attractive but inessential addition or enhancement: *more goals would have been the icing on the cake*.

icing sugar ▶ **noun** [mass noun] Brit. finely powdered sugar used to make icing.

-icist ▶ **suffix** equivalent to **-ICIAN**.
– ORIGIN based on forms ending in **-IC**, + **-IST**.

-icity ▶ **suffix** forming abstract nouns especially from adjectives ending in *-ic* (such as *authenticity* from *authentic*).
– ORIGIN based on forms ending in **-IC**, + **-ITY**.

ICJ ▶ **abbreviation** International Court of Justice.

ick informal, chiefly N. Amer. ▶ **noun** [mass noun] an unpleasantly sticky or congealed substance: *she scrubbed the ick off the back of the stove*.
▶ **interjection** used to express disgust: *There are rats here? Ick!*
– ORIGIN 1940s: probably imitative.

-ick ▶ **suffix** archaic variant spelling of **-IC**.

Icknield Way /ˈɪkniːld/ an ancient pre-Roman track which crosses England in a wide curve from Wiltshire to Norfolk.

icky ▶ **adjective** (**ickier**, **ickiest**) informal unpleasantly sticky. ■ nasty or unpleasant: *the kids were eating something icky*. ■ distastefully sentimental: *a romantic subplot that is just plain icky*.
– DERIVATIVES **ickiness noun**.
– ORIGIN 1930s: perhaps related to **SICK**[1] or to the child's word *ickle* 'little'.

-icle ▶ **suffix** forming nouns which were originally diminutives: *article* | *particle*.
– ORIGIN see **-CULE**.

icon /ˈʌɪkɒn, -k(ə)n/ ▶ **noun 1** (also **ikon**) a devotional painting of Christ or another holy figure, typically executed on wood and used ceremonially in the Byzantine and other Eastern Churches.
2 a person or thing regarded as a representative symbol or as worthy of veneration: *this iron-jawed icon of American manhood*.
3 Computing a symbol or graphic representation on a screen of a program, option, or window.
4 Linguistics a sign which has a characteristic in common with the thing it signifies, for example the word *snarl* pronounced in a snarling way.
– ORIGIN mid 16th cent. (in the sense 'simile'): via Latin from Greek *eikōn* 'likeness, image'. Current senses date from the mid 19th cent. onwards.

iconic ▶ **adjective 1** relating to or of the nature of an icon: *he became an iconic figure for directors around the world*.
2 (of a classical Greek statue) depicting a victorious athlete in a conventional style.
– DERIVATIVES **iconically adverb**, **iconicity noun** (especially in linguistics).
– ORIGIN mid 17th cent.: from Latin *iconicus*, from Greek *eikonikos*, from *eikōn* 'likeness, image'.

iconify ▶ **verb** (**iconifies**, **iconifying**, **iconified**) [with obj.] Computing reduce (a window on a screen) to a small symbol or graphic representation of itself so as to make room on the screen for other windows.

iconize /ˈʌɪkənʌɪz/ (also **iconise**) ▶ **verb** [with obj.]
1 Computing another term for **ICONIFY**.
2 treat as an icon: *they have been iconized as symbols of strength, courage, and self-sacrifice*.

icono- ▶ **combining form 1** of an image or likeness: *iconology*.
2 relating to icons: *iconodule*.
– ORIGIN from Greek *eikōn* 'likeness'.

iconoclasm /ʌɪˈkɒnəklaz(ə)m/ ▶ **noun** [mass noun] **1** the action of attacking or assertively rejecting cherished beliefs and institutions or established values and practices.
2 the rejection or destruction of religious images as heretical; the doctrine of iconoclasts.
– ORIGIN late 18th cent.: from **ICONOCLAST**, on the pattern of pairs such as *enthusiast*, *enthusiasm*.

iconoclast /ʌɪˈkɒnəklast/ ▶ **noun 1** a person who attacks or criticizes cherished beliefs or institutions.
2 a destroyer of images used in religious worship, in particular: ■ historical a supporter of the 8th- and 9th-century movement in the Byzantine Church which sought to abolish the veneration of icons and other religious images. ■ historical a Puritan of the 16th or 17th century.
– ORIGIN mid 17th cent. (in sense 2): via medieval Latin from ecclesiastical Greek *eikonoklastēs*, from *eikōn* 'likeness' + *klan* 'to break'.

iconoclastic /ʌɪˌkɒnəˈklastɪk/ ▶ **adjective** criticizing or attacking cherished beliefs or institutions: *an iconoclastic filmmaker who has pushed the boundaries with every film he's made*.
– DERIVATIVES **iconoclastically adverb**.

iconodule /ˌʌɪkənə(ʊ)ˈdjuːl/ ▶ **noun** a person who favours the veneration of religious icons (especially as contrasted historically with an iconoclast).

iconography /ˌʌɪkəˈnɒɡrəfi/ ▶ **noun** (pl. **iconographies**) **1** [mass noun] the visual images and symbols used in a work of art or the study or interpretation of these. ■ the visual images, symbols, or modes of representation collectively associated with a person, cult, or movement: *the iconography of pop culture*.
2 a collection of illustrations or portraits.
– DERIVATIVES **iconographer noun**, **iconographic adjective**, **iconographical adjective**, **iconographically adverb**.
– ORIGIN early 17th cent. (denoting a drawing or plan): from Greek *eikonographia* 'sketch, description', from *eikōn* 'likeness' + *-graphia* 'writing'.

iconolatry /ˌʌɪkəˈnɒlətri/ ▶ **noun** [mass noun] chiefly derogatory the worship of icons.
– ORIGIN early 17th cent.: from ecclesiastical Greek *eikonolatreia*, from *eikōn* 'likeness' + *-latria* 'worship'.

iconology /ˌʌɪkəˈnɒlədʒi/ ▶ **noun** [mass noun] the study of visual imagery and its symbolism and interpretation, especially in social or political terms. ■ symbolism: *the iconology of a work of art*.
– DERIVATIVES **iconological adjective**.

iconostasis /ˌʌɪkəˈnɒstəsɪs/ ▶ **noun** (pl. **iconostases** /-siːz/) a screen bearing icons, separating the sanctuary of many Eastern churches from the nave.
– ORIGIN mid 19th cent.: from modern Greek *eikonostasis*, from *eikōn* 'likeness' + *stasis* 'standing, stopping'.

icosahedron /ˌʌɪkɒsəˈhiːdrən, -ˈhɛd-/ ▶ **noun** (pl. **icosahedra** or **icosahedrons**) a solid figure with twenty plane faces, especially equilateral triangular ones.
– DERIVATIVES **icosahedral** adjective.
– ORIGIN late 16th cent.: via late Latin from Greek *eikosaedron*, neuter (used as a noun) of *eikosaedros* 'twenty-faced'.

ICRC ▶ **abbreviation** International Committee of the Red Cross.

-ics ▶ **suffix** (forming nouns) denoting arts or sciences, branches of study or action: *classics* | *politics*.
– ORIGIN from French *-iques*, Latin *-ica*, or Greek *-ika*, plural forms.

> **USAGE** A noun ending in **-ics** meaning 'a subject of study or branch of knowledge' will usually take a singular rather than a plural verb, e.g. ***politics is** a blood sport*; ***classics is** hardly studied at all these days*. However, the same word may take a plural verb in cases where the sense is plural: *many of the **classics were** formerly regarded with disdain*.

ICSI ▶ **abbreviation** intracytoplasmic sperm injection, a technique for in vitro fertilization in which an individual sperm cell is introduced into an egg cell.

ICT ▶ **abbreviation** information and communications technology.

ictal /ˈɪktəl/ ▶ **adjective** Medicine relating to a seizure.
– ORIGIN 1950s: from ICTUS + -AL.

I

icterine warbler /ˈɪkt(ə)rʌɪn/ ▶ **noun** a Eurasian warbler with bright yellow underparts. ● *Hippolais icterina*, family Sylviidae.
– ORIGIN mid 19th cent.: *icterine* from ICTERUS + -INE[1].

icterus /ˈɪkt(ə)rəs/ ▶ **noun** Medicine technical term for JAUNDICE.
– DERIVATIVES **icteric** /ɪkˈtɛrɪk/ **adjective**.
– ORIGIN early 18th cent.: via Latin from Greek *ikteros*. The Latin term denoted jaundice, also a yellowish-green bird (the sight of which was thought to cure jaundice).

Ictinus /ɪkˈtʌɪnəs/ (5th century BC), Greek architect. He is said to have designed the Parthenon in Athens with the architect Callicrates and the sculptor Phidias between 448 and 437 BC.

ictus /ˈɪktəs/ ▶ **noun** (pl. **same** or **ictuses**) **1** Prosody a rhythmical or metrical stress.
2 Medicine a stroke or seizure; a fit.
– ORIGIN early 18th cent. (denoting the beat of the pulse): from Latin, literally 'blow', from *icere* 'to strike'.

ICU ▶ **abbreviation** intensive-care unit.

icy ▶ **adjective** (**icier**, **iciest**) covered with or consisting of ice: *there were icy patches on the roads*. ■ very cold: *an icy wind*. ■ very unfriendly; hostile: *her voice was icy*.
– DERIVATIVES **icily** adverb, **iciness** noun.

ID ▶ **abbreviation** ■ Idaho (in official postal use). ■ identification or identity: *they weren't carrying any ID* | [as modifier] *an ID card*.

Id ▶ **noun** variant spelling of EID.

id /ɪd/ ▶ **noun** Psychoanalysis the part of the mind in which innate instinctive impulses and primary processes are manifest. Compare with EGO and SUPEREGO.
– ORIGIN 1920s: from Latin, literally 'that', translating German *es*. The term was first used in this sense by Freud, following use in a similar sense by his contemporary, Georg Groddeck.

id. ▶ **abbreviation** idem.

I'd ▶ **contraction** I had: *I'd agreed to go*. ■ I should or I would: *I'd like a bath*.

-id[1] ▶ **suffix** forming adjectives such as *putrid*, *torrid*.
– ORIGIN from French *-ide* from Latin *-idus*.

-id[2] ▶ **suffix 1** forming nouns such as *chrysalid*, *pyramid*.
2 Biology forming names of structural constituents: *plastid*.
3 Botany forming names of plants belonging to a family with a name ending in *-idaceae*: *orchid*.
– ORIGIN from or suggested by French *-ide*, via Latin *-idis* from Greek *-is*, *-id-*.

-id[3] ▶ **suffix** forming nouns: **1** Zoology denoting an animal belonging to a family with a name ending in *-idae* or to a class with a name ending in *-ida*: *carabid* | *arachnid*.
2 denoting a member of a specified dynasty or family.
3 Astronomy denoting a meteor in a shower radiating from a specified constellation: *Geminids*. ■ denoting a star of a class like one in a specified constellation: *cepheid*.
– ORIGIN from or suggested by Latin *-ides* (plural *-idae*, *-ida*), from Greek.

IDA ▶ **abbreviation** International Development Association.

Ida /ˈʌɪdə/ **1** a mountain in central Crete, associated in classical times with the god Zeus. Rising to 2,456 m (8,058 ft), it is the highest peak on the island.
2 Astronomy asteroid 243, which is 52 km long and has a tiny moon (Dactyl), which is about 1.5 km across.

Idaho /ˈʌɪdəhəʊ/ a state of the north-western US, bordering on British Columbia to the north and containing part of the Rocky Mountains; pop. 1,523,816 (est. 2008); capital, Boise. It became the 43rd state of the US in 1890.
– DERIVATIVES **Idahoan** noun & adjective.

IDB ▶ **abbreviation** S. African illicit diamond buying (or buyer), illegal trading (or an illegal trader) in uncut diamonds.

IDE ▶ **abbreviation** Computing Integrated Drive Electronics, a standard for interfacing computers and their peripherals.

ide /ʌɪd/ ▶ **noun** another term for ORFE.
– ORIGIN mid 19th cent.: from modern Latin *idus*, from Swedish *id*.

-ide ▶ **suffix** Chemistry forming nouns: ■ denoting binary compounds of a non-metallic or more electronegative element or group: *cyanide* | *sodium chloride*. ■ denoting various other compounds: *peptide* | *saccharide*. ■ denoting elements of a series in the periodic table: *lanthanide*.
– ORIGIN originally used in *oxide*.

idea ▶ **noun 1** a thought or suggestion as to a possible course of action: *recently, the idea of linking pay to performance has caught on* | *it's a good idea to do some research before you go*. ■ [in sing.] a mental impression: *our menu list will give you some idea of how interesting a low-fat diet can be*. ■ an opinion or belief: *nineteenth-century ideas about drinking*.
2 (**the idea**) the aim or purpose: *I took a job with **the idea of** getting some money together*.
3 Philosophy (in Platonic thought) an eternally existing pattern of which individual things in any class are imperfect copies. ■ (in Kantian thought) a concept of pure reason, not empirically based in experience.
– PHRASES **get** (or **give someone**) **ideas** informal become (or make someone) ambitious, conceited, or tempted to do something: *I don't want you getting any ideas about me just because we're thrown together like this*. **have** (**got**) **no idea** informal not know at all: *she had no idea where she was going*. **not someone's idea of** informal not what someone regards as typical of: *it's not my idea of a happy ending*. **put ideas into someone's head** suggest aspirations that a person would not otherwise have had. **that's an idea** informal that suggestion or proposal is worth considering. **that's the idea** informal used to confirm that someone has understood something or they are doing something correctly: *'A sort of bodyguard?' 'That's the idea.'* **the very idea!** informal an exclamation of disapproval or disagreement.
– ORIGIN late Middle English (in sense 3): via Latin from Greek *idea* 'form, pattern', from the base of *idein* 'to see'.

ideal ▶ **adjective 1** satisfying one's conception of what is perfect; most suitable: *the swimming pool is **ideal for** a quick dip* | *this is an ideal opportunity to save money*.
2 [attrib.] existing only in the imagination; desirable or perfect but not likely to become a reality: *in an ideal world, we might have made a different decision*. ■ representing an abstract or hypothetical optimum: *mathematical modelling can determine theoretically ideal conditions*.
▶ **noun** a person or thing regarded as perfect: *you're my ideal of how a man should be*. ■ a standard or principle to be aimed at: *tolerance and freedom, the liberal ideals*.
– ORIGIN late Middle English (as a term in Platonic philosophy, in the sense 'existing as an archetype'): from late Latin *idealis*, from Latin *idea* (see IDEA).

ideal gas ▶ **noun** Chemistry a hypothetical gas whose molecules occupy negligible space and have no interactions, and which consequently obeys the gas laws exactly.

idealism ▶ **noun** [mass noun] **1** the unrealistic belief in or pursuit of perfection: *the idealism of youth*. Compare with REALISM. ■ (in art or literature) the representation of things in ideal or idealized form. Often contrasted with REALISM (sense 2).
2 Philosophy any of various systems of thought in which the objects of knowledge are held to be in some way dependent on the activity of mind. Often contrasted with REALISM (sense 3).
– ORIGIN late 18th cent. (in sense 2): from French *idéalisme* or German *Idealismus*, from late Latin *idealis* (see IDEAL).

idealist ▶ **noun 1** a person who is guided more by ideals than by practical considerations: *he came to power with the reputation of a left-wing idealist*.
2 Philosophy a person who believes in the theory of idealism.

idealistic ▶ **adjective** characterized by idealism; unrealistically aiming for perfection: *idealistic young doctors who went to work for the rebels*.
– DERIVATIVES **idealistically** adverb.

ideality /ˌʌɪdɪˈalɪti/ ▶ **noun** (pl. **idealities**) [mass noun] formal the state or quality of being ideal: *the ideality of the island of Aran*. ■ the quality of expressing or being characterized by ideals: *the loftiness and ideality of the Gettysburg Address*. ■ [count noun] an ideal or idealized thing: *they commenced their married life with idealities about love*.

idealize (also **idealise**) ▶ **verb** [with obj.] (often as adj. **idealized**) regard or represent as perfect or better than in reality: *Helen's idealized accounts of their life together*.
– DERIVATIVES **idealization** noun.

ideally ▶ **adverb 1** [as sentence adverb] preferably; in an ideal world: *ideally, you should exercise for 30 minutes every day*.
2 [as submodifier] in the best possible way; perfectly: *her experience makes her ideally suited to the job*.

ideate /ˈʌɪdɪeɪt/ ▶ **verb** [with obj.] chiefly Psychology form an idea of; imagine or conceive. ■ [no obj.] form ideas; think.
– ORIGIN late 17th cent.: from medieval Latin *ideat-* 'formed as an idea', from the verb *ideare*, from Latin *idea* (see IDEA).

ideation ▶ **noun** [mass noun] the formation of ideas or concepts.
– DERIVATIVES **ideational** adjective, **ideationally** adverb.

idée fixe /ˌiːdeɪ ˈfiːks/ ▶ **noun** (pl. **idées fixes** pronunc. **same**) an idea or desire that dominates the mind; an obsession.
– ORIGIN French, literally 'fixed idea'.

idée reçue /ˌiːdeɪ rəˈs(j)uː/ ▶ **noun** (pl. **idées reçues** pronunc. **same**) a generally accepted concept or idea.
– ORIGIN French, literally 'received idea'.

idem /ˈʌɪdɛm, ˈɪdɛm/ ▶ **adverb** used in citations to indicate an author or word that has just been mentioned.
– ORIGIN Latin, 'the same'.

idempotent /ˌʌɪdɛmˈpəʊt(ə)nt, ʌɪˈdɛmpət(ə)nt/ Mathematics ▶ **adjective** denoting an element of a set which is unchanged in value when multiplied or otherwise operated on by itself.
▶ **noun** an idempotent element.
– ORIGIN late 19th cent.: from Latin *idem* 'same' + POTENT[1].

ident /ʌɪˈdɛnt, ˈʌɪdɛnt/ ▶ **noun** short for IDENTIFICATION, especially in informal or technical use. ■ a short sequence shown on television between programmes to identify the channel.

identical ▶ **adjective 1** similar in every detail; exactly alike: *four girls in identical green outfits* | *the passage on the second floor was **identical to** the one below*. ■ (of twins) developed from a single fertilized ovum, and therefore of the same sex and usually very similar in appearance. Compare with FRATERNAL (sense 2). ■ [attrib.] (of something encountered on separate occasions) the same: *she stole a suitcase from the identical station at which she had been arrested before*.
2 Logic & Mathematics expressing an identity: *an identical proposition*.
– DERIVATIVES **identically** adverb.
– ORIGIN late 16th cent. (in sense 2): from medieval Latin *identicus*, from late Latin *identitas* (see IDENTITY).

identifiable ▶ **adjective** able to be recognized; distinguishable: *there are no easily identifiable features on the shoreline*.
– DERIVATIVES **identifiably** adverb.

identification ▶ **noun 1** [mass noun] the action or process of identifying someone or something or the fact of being identified: *each child was tagged with a number for identification* | [count noun] *it may be impossible for relatives to make positive identifications*. ■ a means of proving a person's identity, especially in the form of official papers: *do you have any identification?*

2 a person's sense of identity with someone or something: *children's **identification with** story characters.*
3 the association or linking of one thing with another: *the growing identification of anti-slavery with political liberalism.*
– ORIGIN mid 17th cent.: originally from medieval Latin *identificat-* 'identified', from the verb *identificare*; later from IDENTIFY.

identification parade ▶ noun Brit. another term for IDENTITY PARADE.

identifier ▶ noun **1** a person or thing that identifies someone or something: *the new NHS number is to be known as the 'unique patient identifier'.* ■ Computing a sequence of characters used to identify or refer to a program or an element, such as a variable or a set of data, within it.
2 a person who identifies with something or someone: *Labour identifiers and left-wingers.*

identify ▶ verb (**identifies, identifying, identified**) [with obj.] **1** establish or indicate who or what (someone or something) is: *the judge ordered that the girl should not be identified | the men **identified** themselves **as** federal police.* ■ recognize or distinguish (especially something considered worthy of attention): *a system that ensures that the pupil's real needs are identified.*
2 (**identify someone/thing with**) associate someone or something closely with; regard as having strong links with: *he was equivocal about being identified too closely with the peace movement.* ■ equate (someone or something) with: *because of my country accent, people identified me with a homely farmer's wife.* ■ [no obj.] (**identify with**) regard oneself as sharing the same characteristics or thinking as someone else: *I liked Fromm and identified with him.*
– ORIGIN mid 17th cent. (in the sense 'treat as being identical with'): from medieval Latin *identificare*, from late Latin *identitas* (see IDENTITY) + Latin *-ficare* (from *facere* 'make').

identikit /ʌɪˈdɛntɪkɪt/ ▶ noun trademark a picture of a person, especially one sought by the police, reconstructed from typical facial features according to witnesses' descriptions: [as modifier] *an identikit photograph.*
▶ adjective [attrib.] often derogatory having typical features and few unique ones; formulaic or standardized: *the pub was transformed by identikit 'Victoriana'.*
– ORIGIN 1960s: blend of IDENTITY and KIT[1].

identity ▶ noun (pl. **identities**) **1** the fact of being who or what a person or thing is: *he knows the identity of the bombers |* [mass noun] *she believes she is the victim of mistaken identity.* ■ the characteristics determining who or what a person or thing is: *he wanted to develop a more distinctive Scottish Tory identity.* ■ [as modifier] (of an object) serving to establish who the holder, owner, or wearer is by bearing their name and often other details such as a signature or photograph: *an identity card.*
2 a close similarity or affinity: *an identity between the company's own interests and those of the local community.*
3 Mathematics (also **identity operation**) a transformation that leaves an object unchanged. ■ (also **identity element**) an element of a set which, if combined with another element by a specified binary operation, leaves that element unchanged.
4 Mathematics the equality of two expressions for all values of the quantities expressed by letters, or an equation expressing this, e.g. $(x + 1)^2 = x^2 + 2x + 1$.
– ORIGIN late 16th cent. (in the sense 'quality of being identical'): from late Latin *identitas*, from Latin *idem* 'same'.

identity crisis ▶ noun Psychiatry a period of uncertainty and confusion in which a person's sense of identity becomes insecure, typically due to a change in their expected aims or role in society.

identity matrix ▶ noun Mathematics a square matrix in which all the elements of the principal diagonal are ones and all other elements are zeros. The effect of multiplying a given matrix by an identity matrix is to leave the given matrix unchanged.

identity parade ▶ noun Brit. a group of people including a suspect for a crime assembled for the purpose of having an eyewitness identify the suspect from among them.

identity politics ▶ plural noun [treated as sing.] a tendency for people of a particular religion, race, social background, etc., to form exclusive political alliances, moving away from traditional broad-based party politics.

identity theft ▶ noun [mass noun] the fraudulent practice of using another person's name and personal information in order to obtain credit, loans, etc.

ideogram /ˈɪdɪə(ʊ)gram, ˈʌɪd-/ ▶ noun a character symbolizing the idea of a thing without indicating the sounds used to say it. Examples include numerals and Chinese characters.
– ORIGIN mid 19th cent.: from Greek *idea* 'form' + -GRAM[1].

ideograph /ˈɪdɪə(ʊ)grɑːf, ˈʌɪd-/ ▶ noun another term for IDEOGRAM.
– DERIVATIVES **ideographic** adjective, **ideography** noun.
– ORIGIN mid 19th cent.: from Greek *idea* 'form' + -GRAPH.

ideologue /ˈʌɪdɪəlɒg, ˈɪd-/ ▶ noun an adherent of an ideology, especially one who is uncompromising and dogmatic: *a right-wing ideologue.*
– ORIGIN early 19th cent.: from French *idéologue*; see also IDEOLOGY.

ideology /ˌʌɪdɪˈɒlədʒi, ɪd-/ ▶ noun **1** (pl. **ideologies**) a system of ideas and ideals, especially one which forms the basis of economic or political theory and policy: *the ideology of republicanism.* ■ the set of beliefs characteristic of a social group or individual: *a critique of bourgeois ideology.*
2 [mass noun] archaic the science of ideas; the study of their origin and nature. ■ archaic visionary speculation, especially of an unrealistic or idealistic nature.
– DERIVATIVES **ideological** adjective, **ideologically** adverb, **ideologist** noun.
– ORIGIN late 18th cent. (in sense 2): from French *idéologie*, from Greek *idea* 'form, pattern' + *-logos* (denoting discourse or compilation).

ides /ʌɪdz/ ▶ plural noun (in the ancient Roman calendar) a day falling roughly in the middle of each month (the 15th day of March, May, July, and October, and the 13th of other months) from which other dates were calculated. Compare with NONES, CALENDS.
– ORIGIN late Old English: from Old French, from Latin *idus* (plural), of unknown origin.

idigbo /ɪˈdɪgbəʊ/ ▶ noun (pl. **idigbos**) a West African tree which has a distinctive pagoda-like shape and yields weather-resistant timber. ● *Terminalia ivorensis*, family Combretaceae.
– ORIGIN a local name.

idio- /ˈɪdɪəʊ/ ▶ combining form personal; own: *idiotype.*
– ORIGIN from Greek *idios* 'own, distinct'.

idiocy ▶ noun (pl. **idiocies**) [mass noun] extremely stupid behaviour: *the idiocy of decimating yew forests |* [count noun] *every aspect of public administration throws up its own idiocies.*
– ORIGIN early 16th cent. (originally denoting low intelligence): from IDIOT, probably on the pattern of pairs such as *lunatic, lunacy.*

idiographic ▶ adjective relating to the study or discovery of particular scientific facts and processes, as distinct from general laws. Often contrasted with NOMOTHETIC.

idiolect /ˈɪdɪəlɛkt/ ▶ noun the speech habits peculiar to a particular person.
– ORIGIN 1940s: from IDIO- 'own, personal' + *-lect* as in *dialect.*

idiom ▶ noun **1** a group of words established by usage as having a meaning not deducible from those of the individual words (e.g. *over the moon, see the light*). ■ [mass noun] a form of expression natural to a language, person, or group of people: *he had a feeling for phrase and idiom.* ■ the dialect of a people or part of a country.
2 a characteristic mode of expression in music or art: *they were both working in a neo-Impressionist idiom.*
– ORIGIN late 16th cent.: from French *idiome*, or via late Latin from Greek *idiōma* 'private property, peculiar phraseology', from *idiousthai* 'make one's own', from *idios* 'own, private'.

idiomatic ▶ adjective **1** using, containing, or denoting expressions that are natural to a native speaker: *he spoke fluent, idiomatic English.*
2 appropriate to the style of art or music associated with a particular period, individual, or group: *a short Bach piece containing lots of idiomatic motifs.*
– DERIVATIVES **idiomatically** adverb.
– ORIGIN early 18th cent.: from Greek *idiōmatikos* 'peculiar, characteristic', from *idiōma* (see IDIOM).

idiopathic /ˌɪdɪə(ʊ)ˈpaθɪk/ ▶ adjective Medicine relating to or denoting any disease or condition which arises spontaneously or for which the cause is unknown.

idiopathy /ˌɪdɪˈɒpəθi/ ▶ noun (pl. **idiopathies**) Medicine a disease or condition which arises spontaneously or for which the cause is unknown.
– ORIGIN late 17th cent.: from modern Latin *idiopathia*, from Greek *idiopatheia*, from *idios* 'own, private' + *-patheia* 'suffering'.

idiophone /ˈɪdɪə(ʊ)fəʊn/ ▶ noun Music an instrument the whole of which vibrates to produce a sound when struck, shaken, or scraped, such as a bell, gong, or rattle. Compare with MEMBRANOPHONE.

idiosyncrasy /ˌɪdɪə(ʊ)ˈsɪŋkrəsi/ ▶ noun (pl. **idiosyncrasies**) **1** a mode of behaviour or way of thought peculiar to an individual: *one of his little idiosyncrasies was always preferring to be in the car first.* ■ a distinctive or peculiar feature or characteristic of a place or thing: *the idiosyncrasies of the prison system.*
2 Medicine an abnormal physical reaction by an individual to a food or drug.
– ORIGIN early 17th cent. (originally in the sense 'physical constitution peculiar to an individual'): from Greek *idiosunkrasia*, from *idios* 'own, private' + *sun* 'with' + *krasis* 'mixture'.

idiosyncratic /ˌɪdɪə(ʊ)sɪŋˈkratɪk/ ▶ adjective relating to idiosyncrasy; peculiar or individual: *she emerged as one of the great, idiosyncratic talents of the nineties.*
– DERIVATIVES **idiosyncratically** adverb.
– ORIGIN late 18th cent.: from IDIOSYNCRASY, on the pattern of Greek *sunkratikos* 'mixed together'.

idiot ▶ noun informal a stupid person. ■ archaic a person of low intelligence.
– ORIGIN Middle English (denoting a person of low intelligence): via Old French from Latin *idiota* 'ignorant person', from Greek *idiōtēs* 'private person, layman, ignorant person', from *idios* 'own, private'.

idiot board (also **idiot card**) ▶ noun informal a board displaying a television script to a speaker as an aid to memory.

idiot box ▶ noun N. Amer. informal a television set.

idiotic /ɪdɪˈɒtɪk/ ▶ adjective informal very stupid: *I was able to hum its idiotic theme tune.*
– DERIVATIVES **idiotically** adverb.

idiot light ▶ noun N. Amer. informal a warning light that goes on when a fault occurs in a device.

idiot savant /ˌiːdjəʊ saˈvɒ̃, ˌɪdɪəʊ/ ▶ noun (pl. **idiot savants** or **idiots savants** pronunc. **same**) a person who has a mental disability or learning difficulties but is extremely gifted in a particular way, such as the performing of feats of memory or calculation. ■ a person who is extremely unworldly but displays natural wisdom and insight.
– ORIGIN French, literally 'knowledgeable idiot'.

idiotype /ˈɪdɪə(ʊ)tʌɪp/ ▶ noun Biology the set of genetic determinants of an individual. ■ Immunology a set of antigen-binding sites which characterizes the antibodies produced by a particular clone of antibody-producing cells.

idle ▶ adjective (**idler, idlest**) **1** (of a person) avoiding work; lazy: *idle students.* ■ (of a person) not working; unemployed. ■ (especially of a machine or factory) not active or in use: *the mill has been **standing idle** for eight years.* ■ [attrib.] (of time) characterized by inaction or absence of significant activity: *at no time in the day must there be an idle moment.*
2 without purpose or effect; pointless: *he did not want to waste valuable time in idle chatter.* ■ (especially of a threat or boast) without foundation: *I knew Ellen did not make idle threats.*
3 (of money) held in cash or in accounts paying no interest.
▶ verb **1** [no obj.] spend time doing nothing: *four men were idling outside the shop |* [with obj.] *we **idled** the afternoon **away**.* ■ [no obj., with adverbial of direction] move aimlessly or lazily: *Robert idled along the pavement.* ■ [with obj.] N. Amer. take out of use or employment: *he will close the newspaper, idling 2,200 workers.*
2 (of an engine) run slowly while disconnected from a load or out of gear: *Nadine kept the engine idling.* ■ [with obj.] cause (an engine) to idle.
– ORIGIN Old English *īdel* 'empty, useless', of West Germanic origin; related to Dutch *ijdel* 'vain, frivolous, useless' and German *eitel* 'bare, worthless'.

idleness ▶ noun [mass noun] laziness; indolence: *he was punished for his idleness at school.* ■ a state of inaction; inactivity: *we suffered a period of enforced idleness.*

idler ▶ noun **1** a person who avoids work or spends time in an aimless or lazy way.

2 a pulley that transmits no power but guides or stretches a belt or rope. ■ an idle wheel.

idle wheel ▶ **noun** an intermediate wheel between two geared wheels, especially when its purpose is to allow them to rotate in the same direction.

idli /ˈɪdliː/ ▶ **noun** (pl. **same** or **idlis**) a south Indian steamed cake of rice, usually served with sambhar.
– ORIGIN from Malayalam and Kannada *iḍḍali*.

idly ▶ **adverb** with no particular purpose, reason, or foundation: *'How was the race?' Kate asked idly.* ■ in an aimless or lazy way: *I can no longer stand idly by and let him take the blame.*

Ido /ˈiːdəʊ/ ▶ **noun** [mass noun] an artificial universal language developed from Esperanto.
– ORIGIN early 19th cent.: Ido, literally 'offspring'.

idocrase /ˈʌɪdə(ʊ)kreɪz, -s/ ▶ **noun** [mass noun] a mineral consisting of a silicate of calcium, magnesium, and aluminium, occurring typically as dark-green to brown prisms in metamorphosed limestone.
– ORIGIN early 19th cent.: from Greek *eidos* 'form' + *krasis* 'mixture'.

idol ▶ **noun** an image or representation of a god used as an object of worship. ■ a person or thing that is greatly admired, loved, or revered: *a soccer idol.*
– ORIGIN Middle English: from Old French *idole*, from Latin *idolum* 'image, form' (used in ecclesiastical Latin in the sense 'idol'), from Greek *eidōlon*, from *eidos* 'form, shape'.

idolater /ʌɪˈdɒlətə/ ▶ **noun** a person who worships an idol or idols.
– ORIGIN late Middle English: from Old French *idolatre*, based on Greek *eidōlolatrēs*, from *eidōlon* (see IDOL) + *-latrēs* 'worshipper'.

idolatrous ▶ **adjective** relating to or practising idolatry; idol-worshipping: *idolatrous religions.* ■ showing extreme admiration or reverence for something: *America's idolatrous worship of the auto.*

idolatry ▶ **noun** [mass noun] the worship of idols. ■ extreme admiration, love, or reverence for something or someone: *we must not allow our idolatry of art to obscure issues of political significance.*
– ORIGIN Middle English: from Old French *idolatrie*, based on Greek *eidōlolatreia*, from *eidōlon* (see IDOL) + *-latreia* 'worship'.

idolize (also **idolise**) ▶ **verb** [with obj.] admire, revere, or love greatly or excessively: *he idolized his mother.*
– DERIVATIVES **idolization** noun, **idolizer** noun.

Idomeneus /ʌɪˌdɒmɪˈniːəs/ Greek Mythology king of Crete, son of Deucalion and descendant of Minos. He was forced to kill his son after vowing to sacrifice the first living thing that he met on his return from the Trojan War.

IDP ▶ **abbreviation** internally displaced person, a person who has been forced to move within their own country as a result of conflict or environmental disaster.

Id ul-Adha see EID.

Id ul-Fitr see EID.

idyll /ˈɪdɪl/ ▶ **noun** an extremely happy, peaceful, or picturesque period or situation, typically an idealized or unsustainable one: *the rural idyll remains strongly evocative in most industrialized societies.* ■ a short description in verse or prose of a picturesque scene or incident, especially in rustic life.
– ORIGIN late 16th cent. (in the Latin form): from Latin *idyllium*, from Greek *eidullion*, diminutive of *eidos* 'form, picture'.

idyllic ▶ **adjective** like an idyll; extremely happy, peaceful, or picturesque: *an attractive hotel in an idyllic setting.*
– DERIVATIVES **idyllically** adverb.

i.e. ▶ **abbreviation** that is to say (used to add explanatory information or to state something in different words): *a walking boot which is synthetic, i.e. not leather.*
– ORIGIN from Latin *id est* 'that is'.

-ie ▶ **suffix 1** variant spelling of -Y[2] (as in *auntie*).
2 archaic variant spelling of -Y[1], -Y[3].
– ORIGIN earlier form of *-y*.

IEA ▶ **abbreviation** International Energy Agency.

iechyd da /ˌjɛxiːd ˈdɑː/ ▶ **exclamation** Welsh used to express good wishes before drinking.
– ORIGIN Welsh, literally 'good health'.

IED ▶ **abbreviation** improvised explosive device.

IEE ▶ **abbreviation** (in the UK) Institution of Electrical Engineers.

IEEE ▶ **abbreviation** (in the US) Institute of Electrical and Electronics Engineers.

Ieper /ˈiːpər/ Flemish name for YPRES.

-ier ▶ **suffix** forming personal nouns denoting an occupation or interest: **1** pronounced with stress on the preceding element: *grazier.* [Middle English: variant of -ER[1].]
2 pronounced with stress on the final element: *brigadier* | *cashier.* [from French *-ier*, from Latin *-arius*.]

IF ▶ **abbreviation** intermediate frequency.

if ▶ **conjunction 1** introducing a conditional clause: ■ on the condition or supposition that; in the event that: *if you have a complaint, write to the director* | *if you like I'll put in a word for you.* ■ (with past tense) introducing a hypothetical situation: *if you had stayed, this would never have happened.* ■ whenever; every time: *if I go out she gets nasty.*
2 despite the possibility that; no matter whether: *if it takes me seven years, I shall do it.*
3 (often used in indirect questions) whether: *he asked if we would like some coffee* | *I wonder if she noticed.*
4 [with modal] expressing a polite request: *if I could just use the phone, I'll get a taxi* | *if you wouldn't mind giving him a message?*
5 expressing an opinion: *that's a jolly long walk, if you don't mind my saying so* | *if you ask me, he's in love.*
6 expressing surprise or regret: *well, if it isn't Frank!*
7 with implied reservation: ■ and perhaps not: *the new leaders have little if any control.* ■ used to admit something as being possible but relatively insignificant: *if there was any weakness, it was naivety* | *'We both saw him.' 'So what if you did?'* ■ despite being (used before an adjective or adverb to introduce a contrast): *she was honest, if a little brutal.*
▶ **noun** a condition or supposition: *there are so many ifs and buts in the policy.*
– PHRASES **if and only if** used to introduce a condition which is necessary as well as sufficient: *Alice will come if and only if Charles and Edward are both going to be there.* **if and when** at a future time (should it arise): *most of these plans can be altered if and when the situation changes.* **if anything** used to suggest tentatively that something may be the case (often the opposite of something previously implied): *I haven't made much of this—if anything, I've played it down.* **if I were you** used to accompany a piece of advice: *I would go to see him if I were you.* **if not** perhaps even (used to introduce a more extreme term than one first mentioned): *hundreds if not thousands of germs.* **if only 1** even if for no other reason than: *Willy would have to tell George more, if only to stop him pestering.* **2** used to express a wish, especially regretfully: *if only I had listened to you.* **if so** if that is the case.
– ORIGIN Old English *gif*, of Germanic origin; related to Dutch *of* and German *ob*.

> **USAGE** If and whether are more or less interchangeable in sentences like *I'll see* **if** *he left an address* and *I'll see* **whether** *he left an address*, although **whether** is generally regarded as more formal and suitable for written use.

IFAD ▶ **abbreviation** International Fund for Agricultural Development.

IFC ▶ **abbreviation** International Finance Corporation.

Ife /ˈiːfeɪ/ an industrial city in SW Nigeria; pop. 258,300 (est. 2005). It was a major centre of the Yoruba kingdom from the 14th to the 17th centuries.

-iferous ▶ **combining form** common form of -FEROUS.

iff ▶ **conjunction** Logic & Mathematics if and only if.
– ORIGIN 1950s: arbitrary extension of *if*.

iffy ▶ **adjective** (**iffier**, **iffiest**) informal full of uncertainty; doubtful: *the prospect for classes resuming next Wednesday seems iffy.* ■ of doubtful quality or legality: *a good wine merchant will change the iffy bottles for sound ones.*

-ific ▶ **suffix** common form of -FIC.

-ification ▶ **suffix** common form of -FICATION.

Ifni /ˈɪfni/ a former overseas province of Spain, on the SW coast of Morocco, ceded to Morocco in 1969.

-iform ▶ **combining form** common form of -FORM.

IFP ▶ **abbreviation** Inkatha Freedom Party. See INKATHA.

IFR ▶ **abbreviation** instrument flight rules, used to regulate the flying and navigating of an aircraft using instruments alone.

iftar /ˈɪftɑː/ ▶ **noun** the meal eaten by Muslims after sunset during Ramadan.
– ORIGIN Ottoman Turkish *iftār*, from Arabic *ifṭar* 'break a fast'.

Ig ▶ **abbreviation** Biochemistry immunoglobulin.

Igbo /ˈiːbəʊ/ (also **Ibo**) ▶ **noun** (pl. **same** or **Igbos**) **1** a member of a people of SE Nigeria.
2 [mass noun] the language of the Igbo, belonging to the Kwa group and having some 12 million speakers.
▶ **adjective** relating to the Igbo or their language.
– ORIGIN a local name.

igloo ▶ **noun** a dome-shaped Eskimo house, typically built from blocks of solid snow.
– ORIGIN mid 19th cent.: from Inuit *iglu* 'house'.

Ignatius Loyola, St /ɪɡˌneɪʃəs ˈlɔɪələ, lɔɪˈəʊlə/ (1491–1556), Spanish theologian and founder of the Society of Jesus. His *Spiritual Exercises* (1548), an ordered scheme of meditations, is still used in the training of Jesuits. Feast day, 31 July.

igneous /ˈɪɡnɪəs/ ▶ **adjective** Geology (of rock) having solidified from lava or magma. ■ relating to or involving volcanic or plutonic processes: *igneous activity.* ■ rare of fire; fiery.
– ORIGIN mid 17th cent.: from Latin *igneus* (from *ignis* 'fire') + -OUS.

ignimbrite /ˈɪɡnɪmbrʌɪt/ ▶ **noun** [mass noun] Geology a volcanic rock consisting essentially of pumice fragments, formed by the consolidation of material deposited by pyroclastic flows.
– ORIGIN 1930s: from Latin *ignis* 'fire' + *imber*, *imbr-* 'shower of rain, storm cloud' + -ITE[1].

ignis fatuus /ˌɪɡnɪs ˈfatjʊəs/ ▶ **noun** (pl. **ignes fatui** /ˌɪɡniːz ˈfatjʊʌɪ, ˌɪɡneɪz, ˈfatjʊiː/) a will-o'-the-wisp.
– ORIGIN mid 16th cent.: modern Latin, literally 'foolish fire' (because of its erratic movement).

ignite /ɪɡˈnʌɪt/ ▶ **verb** catch fire or cause to catch fire: [no obj.] *furniture can give off lethal fumes when it ignites* | [with obj.] *he lit a cigarette which ignited the petrol fumes.* ■ [with obj.] arouse or inflame (an emotion or situation): *the words ignited new fury in him.*
– DERIVATIVES **ignitability** noun, **ignitable** adjective.
– ORIGIN mid 17th cent. (in the sense 'make intensely hot'): from Latin *ignire* 'set on fire', from *ignis* 'fire'.

igniter ▶ **noun 1** a device for igniting a fuel mixture in an engine.
2 a device for causing an electric arc.

ignition ▶ **noun** [mass noun] the action of setting something on fire or starting to burn: *three minutes after ignition, the flames were still growing.* ■ the process of starting the combustion of fuel in the cylinders of an internal-combustion engine. ■ [count noun] (usu. **the ignition**) the mechanism for bringing this about, typically activated by a key or switch: *she turned off the ignition.*
– ORIGIN early 17th cent. (denoting the heating of a substance to the point of combustion or chemical change): from medieval Latin *ignitio(n-)*, from the verb *ignire* 'set on fire' (see IGNITE).

ignition key ▶ **noun** a key designed to start the engine of a motor vehicle.

ignitron /ɪɡˈnʌɪtrɒn/ ▶ **noun** a kind of rectifier with a mercury cathode, able to carry large electric currents.
– ORIGIN 1930s: from IGNITE or IGNITION + -TRON.

ignoble ▶ **adjective** (**ignobler**, **ignoblest**) **1** not honourable in character or purpose: *ignoble feelings of intense jealousy.*
2 of humble origin or social status.
– DERIVATIVES **ignobility** noun, **ignobly** adverb.
– ORIGIN late Middle English (in sense 2): from French, or from Latin *ignobilis*, from *in-* 'not' + *gnobilis*, older form of *nobilis* 'noble'.

ignominious /ˌɪɡnəˈmɪnɪəs/ ▶ **adjective** deserving or causing public disgrace or shame: *no other party risked ignominious defeat.*
– DERIVATIVES **ignominiously** adverb, **ignominiousness** noun.
– ORIGIN late Middle English: from French *ignominieux*, or Latin *ignominiosus*, from *ignominia* (see IGNOMINY).

ignominy /ˈɪɡnəmɪni/ ▶ **noun** [mass noun] public shame or disgrace: *the ignominy of being imprisoned.*
– ORIGIN mid 16th cent.: from French *ignominie* or Latin *ignominia*, from *in-* 'not' + a variant of *nomen* 'name'.

ignoramus /ˌɪɡnəˈreɪməs/ ▶ **noun** (pl. **ignoramuses**) an ignorant or stupid person.
– ORIGIN late 16th cent. (as the endorsement made by a grand jury on an indictment considered backed by insufficient evidence to bring before a petty jury): Latin, literally 'we do not know' (in legal use 'we take no notice of it'), from *ignorare* (see IGNORE). The modern sense may derive from the name of a character in George Ruggle's *Ignoramus* (1615), a satirical comedy exposing lawyers' ignorance.

ignorance ▸ noun [mass noun] lack of knowledge or information: *he acted in **ignorance of** basic procedures.*
– ORIGIN Middle English: via Old French from Latin *ignorantia*, from *ignorant-* 'not knowing' (see IGNORANT).

ignorant ▸ adjective **1** lacking knowledge or awareness in general; uneducated or unsophisticated: *he was told constantly that he was ignorant and stupid.* ▪ [predic.] lacking knowledge, information, or awareness about something in particular: *I was largely **ignorant of** the effects of radiotherapy.*
2 informal discourteous or rude: *this ignorant, pin-brained receptionist.*
3 black English easily angered: *I is an ignorant man—even police don't meddle with me.*
– DERIVATIVES **ignorantly** adverb.
– ORIGIN late Middle English: via Old French from Latin *ignorant-* 'not knowing', from the verb *ignorare* (see IGNORE).

ignoratio elenchi /ˌɪgnəˈreɪʃɪəʊ ɪˈlɛŋkʌɪ/ ▸ noun (pl. **ignorationes elenchi** /-ˈəʊniːzː/) Philosophy a logical fallacy which consists in apparently refuting an opponent while actually disproving something not asserted.
– ORIGIN Latin, literally 'ignorance of the elenchus'.

ignore ▸ verb [with obj.] refuse to take notice of or acknowledge; disregard intentionally: *he ignored her outraged question.* ▪ fail to consider (something significant): *the rules ignore one important principle of cricket.*
– DERIVATIVES **ignorable** adjective, **ignorer** noun.
– ORIGIN late 15th cent. (in the sense 'be ignorant of'): from French *ignorer* or Latin *ignorare* 'not know, ignore', from *in-* 'not' + *gno-*, a base meaning 'know'. Current senses date from the early 19th cent.

ignotum per ignotius /ɪgˌnəʊtəm pər ɪgˈnəʊtɪəs/ ▸ noun [mass noun] the action of offering an explanation which is harder to understand than the thing it is meant to explain.
– ORIGIN late Latin, literally 'the unknown through something more unknown'.

Iguaçu /ˌɪgwəˈsuː/ a river of southern Brazil. It rises in the Serra do Mar in SE Brazil and flows westwards for 1,300 km (800 miles) to the Paraná River, which it joins shortly below the Iguaçu Falls, a spectacular series of waterfalls. Spanish name **Iguazú** /ˌiɣwaˈsu/.

iguana /ɪˈgwɑːnə/ ▸ noun a large arboreal tropical American lizard with a spiny crest along the back and greenish coloration. ● Genus *Iguana*, family Iguanidae: two species, in particular the common **green iguana** (*I. iguana*). ▪ any iguanid lizard.
– ORIGIN mid 16th cent.: from Spanish, from Arawak *iwana*.

iguanid /ɪˈgwɑːnɪd/ ▸ noun Zoology a lizard of the iguana family (Iguanidae). Iguanids are found mainly in the New World but also occur in Madagascar and on some Pacific islands.
– ORIGIN late 19th cent.: from modern Latin *Iguanidae* (plural), from the genus name *Iguana* (see IGUANA).

iguanodon /ɪˈgwɑːnədɒn/ ▸ noun a large partly bipedal herbivorous dinosaur of the early to mid Cretaceous period, with a broad stiff tail and the thumb developed into a spike. ● Genus *Iguanodon*, infraorder Ornithopoda, order Ornithischia.
– ORIGIN modern Latin, from IGUANA + Greek *odous*, *odont-* 'tooth' (because its teeth resemble those of the iguana).

i.h.p. ▸ abbreviation indicated horsepower.

IHS ▸ abbreviation Jesus.
– ORIGIN Middle English: from late Latin, representing Greek IHΣ as an abbreviation of *Iēsous* 'Jesus' used in manuscripts and also as a symbolic or ornamental monogram, but later often taken as an abbreviation of various Latin phrases, notably *Iesus Hominum Salvator* 'Jesus Saviour of Men', *In Hoc Signo (vinces)* 'in this sign (thou shalt conquer)', and *In Hac Salus* 'in this (cross) is salvation'.

IHT ▸ abbreviation (in the UK) inheritance tax.

iimbongi plural form of IMBONGI.

iiwi /iˈiːwi/ ▸ noun (pl. **same** or **iiwis**) a Hawaiian honeycreeper with a long downcurved bill and mainly bright red plumage. ● *Vestiaria coccinea*, family Drepanididae (or Fringillidae).
– ORIGIN late 18th cent.: from Hawaiian.

Ijo /ˈiːdʒəʊ/ (also **Ijaw**) ▸ noun (pl. **same** or **Ijos**) **1** a member of a people inhabiting the Niger delta in southern Nigeria.
2 [mass noun] the language of the Ijo, an isolated member of the Niger–Congo family with several highly distinct dialects.
▸ adjective relating to the Ijo or their language.

IJssel /ˈʌɪs(ə)l/ a river in the Netherlands. In part it is a distributary of the Rhine, which it leaves at Arnhem, joining the Oude IJssel ('Old IJssel') a few kilometres downstream, and flowing 115 km (72 miles) northwards through the eastern Netherlands to the IJsselmeer.

IJsselmeer /ˈʌɪs(ə)lmɛː, -mɪə/ a shallow lake in the NW Netherlands, created in 1932 by the building of a dam across the entrance to the old Zuider Zee. Large areas have since been reclaimed as polders.

ikat /ˈiːkat, ɪˈkat/ ▸ noun [mass noun] fabric made using an Indonesian decorative technique in which warp or weft threads, or both, are tie-dyed before weaving.
– ORIGIN 1930s: Malay, literally 'fasten, tie'.

ikebana /ˌɪkɪˈbɑːnə/ ▸ noun [mass noun] the art of Japanese flower arrangement, with formal display according to strict rules.
– ORIGIN Japanese, literally 'living flowers', from *ikeru* 'keep alive' + *hana* 'flower'.

Ikhnaton /ɪkˈnɑːt(ə)n/ variant form of AKHENATEN.

ikky ▸ adjective variant spelling of ICKY.

ikon ▸ noun variant spelling of ICON (sense 1).

IL ▸ abbreviation ▪ Illinois (in official postal use). ▪ Israel (international vehicle registration).

il- ▸ prefix variant spelling of IN-[1], IN-[2] assimilated before *l* (as in *illustrate*, *illuminate*).

-il ▸ suffix forming adjectives and nouns such as *civil* and *fossil*.
– ORIGIN from Old French, from Latin *-ilis*.

ilang-ilang ▸ noun variant spelling of YLANG-YLANG.

-ile ▸ suffix forming adjectives and nouns such as *agile* and *juvenile*. ▪ Statistics forming nouns denoting a value of a variate which divides a population into the indicated number of equal-sized groups, or one of the groups itself: *decile | percentile*.
– ORIGIN variant of -IL especially in adoptions from French.

ilea plural form of ILEUM.

Île-de-France /ˌiːldəˈfrɑːns/, French /ildəfʀɑ̃s/ a region of north central France, incorporating the city of Paris.

ileitis /ˌɪlɪˈʌɪtɪs/ ▸ noun [mass noun] Medicine inflammation of the ileum.

ileostomy /ˌɪlɪˈɒstəmi/ ▸ noun (pl. **ileostomies**) a surgical operation in which a damaged part is removed from the ileum and the cut end diverted to an artificial opening in the abdominal wall. ▪ an opening formed by an ileostomy.
– ORIGIN late 19th cent.: from ILEUM + Greek *stoma* 'mouth'.

Ilesha /ɪˈleɪʃə/ a city in SW Nigeria; pop. 192,700 (est. 2005).

ileum /ˈɪlɪəm/ ▸ noun (pl. **ilea**) Anatomy the third portion of the small intestine, between the jejunum and the caecum.
– DERIVATIVES **ileac** adjective, **ileal** adjective.
– ORIGIN late 17th cent.: from medieval Latin, variant of ILIUM.

ileus /ˈɪlɪəs/ ▸ noun [mass noun or in sing.] Medicine a painful obstruction of the ileum or other part of the intestine.
– ORIGIN late 17th cent.: from Latin, from Greek *eileos*, *ilios* 'colic', apparently from *eilein* 'to roll'.

ilex /ˈʌɪlɛks/ ▸ noun **1** the holm oak.
2 a tree or shrub of a genus that includes holly and its relatives. ● Genus *Ilex*, family Aquifoliaceae.
– ORIGIN late Middle English: from Latin, 'holm oak'.

ilia plural form of ILIUM.

iliac /ˈɪlɪak/ ▸ adjective relating to the ilium or the nearby regions of the lower body: *the iliac artery*.
– ORIGIN early 16th cent.: from late Latin *iliacus*, from *ilia* 'entrails'.

iliacus /ɪˈlʌɪəkəs/ (also **iliacus muscle**) ▸ noun Anatomy a triangular muscle which passes from the pelvis through the groin on either side and, together with the psoas, flexes the hip.
– ORIGIN early 17th cent.: from late Latin.

Iliad /ˈɪlɪəd/ a Greek hexameter epic poem in twenty-four books, traditionally ascribed to Homer, telling how Achilles killed Hector at the climax of the Trojan War.

Ilium /ˈɪlɪəm/ alternative name for TROY, especially the 7th-century BC Greek city.

ilium /ˈɪlɪəm/ ▸ noun (pl. **ilia**) the large broad bone forming the upper part of each half of the pelvis.
– ORIGIN late Middle English (originally in the Greek form *ilion*, and denoting the ileum): from Latin, singular of *ilia* 'flanks, entrails'. Current senses date from the late 16th cent.

ilk ▸ noun [in sing.] a type of person or thing similar to one already referred to: *the veiled suggestions that reporters **of his ilk** seem to be so good at | there was music by Parry and Elgar and others of that ilk.* ▪ (**of that ilk**) Scottish, chiefly archaic of the place or estate of the same name: *Sir Iain Moncreiffe of that Ilk.*
– ORIGIN Old English *ilca* 'same', of Germanic origin; related to ALIKE.

> **USAGE** Today **ilk** is used in phrases such as ***of his ilk*** and ***of that ilk*** to mean 'type' or 'sort'. This sense arose out of a misunderstanding of the earlier, Scottish use in the phrase **of that ilk**, where it means 'of the same name or place'. For this reason, some traditionalists regard the modern use as incorrect. It is, however, the only common current sense and is now part of standard English.

ill ▸ adjective **1** suffering from an illness or disease or feeling unwell: *he was **taken ill** with food poisoning* | [with submodifier] *a terminally ill patient* | (as plural noun **the ill**) *a day centre for the mentally ill.*
2 [attrib.] poor in quality: *ill judgement dogs the unsuccessful.* ▪ bad or harmful: *she had a cup of the same wine and suffered no ill effects.* ▪ not favourable or auspicious: *I have had a run of ill luck | a bird of ill omen.*
▸ adverb **1** [usu. in combination] badly, wrongly, or imperfectly: *the street is dominated by ill-lit shops | it ill becomes one so beautiful to be gloomy.* ▪ unfavourably or inauspiciously: *a look on her face which boded ill for anyone who crossed her path.*
2 only with difficulty; hardly: *she could ill afford the cost of new curtains.*
▸ noun (usu. **ills**) a problem or misfortune: *a lengthy work on the ills of society.* ▪ [mass noun] evil or harm: *how could I wish him ill?*
– PHRASES **ill at ease** uncomfortable or embarrassed. **speak** (or **think**) **ill of** say (or think) something critical about (someone).
– ORIGIN Middle English (in the senses 'wicked', 'malevolent', 'harmful', and 'difficult'): from Old Norse *illr* 'evil, difficult', of unknown origin.

Ill. ▸ abbreviation Illinois.

I'll ▸ contraction I shall; I will: *I'll arrange it.*

ill-advised ▸ adjective not sensible, wise, or prudent: *you would be ill-advised to go on your own.*
– DERIVATIVES **ill-advisedly** adverb.

ill-affected ▸ adjective archaic not inclined to be friendly or sympathetic.

ill-assorted ▸ adjective not well matched: *ill-assorted furniture.*

illation /ɪˈleɪʃ(ə)n/ ▸ noun [mass noun] archaic the action of inferring or drawing a conclusion. ▪ [count noun] an inference.
– ORIGIN mid 16th cent.: from Latin *illatio(n-)*, from *illat-* 'brought in', from the verb *inferre* (see INFER).

illative /ɪˈleɪtɪv/ ▸ adjective **1** of the nature of or stating an inference. ▪ proceeding by inference.
2 Grammar relating to or denoting a case of nouns in some languages used to express motion into something.
▸ noun the illative case, or a word in this case.
– ORIGIN late 16th cent.: from Latin *illativus*, from *illat-* 'brought in' (see ILLATION).

Illawarra /ˌɪləˈwɒrə/ ▸ noun (also **Illawarra shorthorn**) an animal of an Australian breed of red or roan dairy cattle.
– ORIGIN early 20th cent.: from the name of a coastal district south of Sydney, where the breed was developed.

ill-behaved ▸ adjective behaving badly: *an ill-behaved schoolboy.*

ill-bred ▸ adjective badly brought up or rude.
– DERIVATIVES **ill breeding** noun.

ill-conceived ▸ adjective not carefully planned or considered: *ill-conceived schemes.*

ill-considered ▸ adjective badly thought out: *an ill-considered remark.*

ill-defined ▸ adjective not having a clear description or limits; vague: *ill-defined concepts.*

ill-disposed ▸ adjective unfriendly or unsympathetic: *this fact was ignored by ill-disposed critics.*

illegal ▸ adjective contrary to or forbidden by law, especially criminal law: *illegal drugs.*

I

▸ **noun** chiefly N. Amer. an illegal immigrant.
– DERIVATIVES **illegality** noun (pl. **illegalities**), **illegally** adverb.
– ORIGIN early 17th cent.: from French *illégal* or medieval Latin *illegalis*, from Latin *in-* 'not' + *legalis* 'according to the law'.

> **USAGE** **Illegal** and **unlawful** have slightly different meanings, although they are often used interchangeably. Something that is **illegal** is against the law, whereas an **unlawful** act merely contravenes the rules that apply in a particular context. Thus handball in soccer is **unlawful**, but it is not **illegal**. A third word with a similar meaning is **illicit**: this tends to encompass things that are forbidden or disapproved of by custom or society, as in *an illicit love affair*.

illegible /ɪˈlɛdʒɪb(ə)l/ ▸ **adjective** not clear enough to be read: *his handwriting is totally illegible.*
– DERIVATIVES **illegibility** noun, **illegibly** adverb.

illegitimate /ˌɪlɪˈdʒɪtɪmət/ ▸ **adjective 1** not authorized by the law; not in accordance with accepted standards or rules: *defending workers against illegitimate managerial practices.*
2 (of a child) born of parents not lawfully married to each other.
▸ **noun** a person who is illegitimate by birth.
– DERIVATIVES **illegitimacy** noun, **illegitimately** adverb.
– ORIGIN mid 16th cent.: from late Latin *illegitimus* (from *in-* 'not' + *legitimus* 'lawful'), suggested by LEGITIMATE.

I

ill-equipped ▸ **adjective** not having the necessary resources or qualities for a particular role or task: *they feel **ill-equipped to** cope with emotional issues.*

ill fame ▸ **noun** [mass noun] dated disrepute.

ill-fated ▸ **adjective** destined to fail or have bad luck: *an ill-fated expedition.*

ill-favoured (US **ill-favored**) ▸ **adjective** unattractive: *a crotchety, ill-favoured human being.*

ill feeling ▸ **noun** [mass noun] animosity or resentment.

ill-fitting ▸ **adjective** (of a garment) of the wrong size or shape for the person wearing it: *an ill-fitting suit.*

ill-founded ▸ **adjective** (especially of an idea or belief) not based on fact or reliable evidence: *ill-founded criticism | her fear may be ill-founded.*

ill-gotten ▸ **adjective** acquired by illegal or unfair means: *the mafiosi launder their **ill-gotten gains**.*

ill health ▸ **noun** [mass noun] poor physical or mental condition: *the president was absent due to ill health.*

ill humour ▸ **noun** [mass noun] irritability or bad temper.

ill-humoured ▸ **adjective** bad-tempered; irritable: *a querulous and ill-humoured little man.*

illiberal ▸ **adjective 1** opposed to liberal principles; restricting freedom of thought or behaviour: *illiberal and anti-democratic policies.*
2 archaic uncultured or unrefined.
3 archaic not generous; mean.
– DERIVATIVES **illiberalism** noun, **illiberality** noun, **illiberally** adverb.
– ORIGIN mid 16th cent. (in the sense 'vulgar, ill-bred'): from French *illibéral*, from Latin *illiberalis* 'mean, sordid', from *in-* 'not' + *liberalis* (see LIBERAL).

Illich /ˈɪlɪtʃ/, Ivan (1926–2002), Austrian-born American educationist and writer. He advocated the deinstitutionalization of education, religion, and medicine. Notable works: *Deschooling Society* (1971) and *Limits to Medicine* (1978).

illicit ▸ **adjective** forbidden by law, rules, or custom: *illicit drugs | illicit sex.*
– DERIVATIVES **illicitly** adverb, **illicitness** noun.
– ORIGIN early 16th cent.: from French, or from Latin *illicitus*, from *in-* 'not' + *licitus* (see LICIT).

> **USAGE** On the distinctions between **illicit**, **illegal**, and **unlawful**, see **USAGE** at **ILLEGAL**.

illimitable ▸ **adjective** without limits or an end: *the illimitable human capacity for evil.*
– DERIVATIVES **illimitability** noun, **illimitably** adverb.

ill-informed ▸ **adjective** having or showing an inadequate awareness of the facts: *ill-informed opinions.*

Illinoian /ˌɪlɪˈnɔɪ(j)ən/ ▸ **adjective** Geology relating to or denoting a Pleistocene glaciation in North America, preceding the Wisconsin and approximating to the Saale of northern Europe. ▪ (as noun **the Illinoian**) the Illinoian glaciation or the system of deposits laid down during it.
– ORIGIN mid 19th cent.: from **ILLINOIS** + **-AN**.

Illinois /ˌɪlɪˈnɔɪ/ a state in the Middle West of the US; pop. 12,901,563 (est. 2008); capital, Springfield. It was colonized by the French but was ceded to Britain in 1763. It was acquired by the US in 1783 and became the 21st state in 1818.
– DERIVATIVES **Illinoisan** noun & adjective.

illiquid /ɪˈlɪkwɪd/ ▸ **adjective** (of assets) not easily converted into cash: *illiquid investments.* ▪ (of a market) with few participants and a low volume of activity.
– DERIVATIVES **illiquidity** noun.

illite /ˈɪlʌɪt/ ▸ **noun** [mass noun] a clay mineral of a group resembling micas, with a lattice structure which does not expand on absorption of water.
– ORIGIN 1930s: from **ILLINOIS** + **-ITE**[1].

illiteracy /ɪˈlɪt(ə)rəsi/ ▸ **noun** [mass noun] the inability to read or write: *the ineffective educational system meant that illiteracy was widespread.* ▪ lack of knowledge in a particular subject; ignorance: *his economic illiteracy.*

illiterate /ɪˈlɪt(ə)rət/ ▸ **adjective** unable to read or write: *his parents were illiterate.* ▪ [with submodifier] ignorant in a particular subject or activity: *the extent to which voters are politically illiterate.* ▪ (of a piece of writing) showing a lack of education; badly written.
▸ **noun** a person who is unable to read or write.
– PHRASES **functionally illiterate** lacking the literacy necessary for coping with most jobs and many everyday situations.
– DERIVATIVES **illiterately** adverb.
– ORIGIN late Middle English: from Latin *illitteratus*, from *in-* 'not' + *litteratus* (see LITERATE).

ill-judged ▸ **adjective** lacking careful consideration; unwise: *an ill-judged decision.*

ill-mannered ▸ **adjective** having bad manners; not behaving well in social situations: *ill-mannered and unruly children.*

ill-matched ▸ **adjective** (of two or more people or items) not well suited to or appropriate for each other: *an ill-matched couple.*

ill nature ▸ **noun** the quality of being bad-tempered or mean-spirited.

ill-natured ▸ **adjective** bad-tempered or mean-spirited.
– DERIVATIVES **ill-naturedly** adverb.

illness ▸ **noun** a disease or period of sickness affecting the body or mind: *he died after a long illness* | [mass noun] *I've never missed a day's work through illness.*

illocution /ˌɪləˈkjuːʃ(ə)n/ ▸ **noun** Philosophy & Linguistics an act of speaking or writing which in itself effects or constitutes the intended action, e.g. ordering, warning, or promising. Compare with PERLOCUTION.
– DERIVATIVES **illocutionary** adjective.

illogic ▸ **noun** [mass noun] reasoning or thought which is not logical.

illogical ▸ **adjective** lacking sense or clear, sound reasoning: *an illogical fear of the supernatural.*
– DERIVATIVES **illogicality** noun (pl. **illogicalities**), **illogically** adverb.

ill-omened ▸ **adjective** attended by bad omens: *ill-omened birds of prey.*

ill-prepared ▸ **adjective** not ready or prepared for something: *his light clothing left him **ill-prepared for the rain**.*

ill-starred ▸ **adjective** destined to fail or have many difficulties; unlucky: *an ill-starred expedition.*

ill-suited ▸ **adjective** unsuitable or inappropriate: *the soil is ill-suited to wheat farming.*

ill temper ▸ **noun** [mass noun] irritability; anger.

ill-tempered ▸ **adjective** irritable or grumpy.
– DERIVATIVES **ill-temperedly** adverb.

ill-timed ▸ **adjective** done or occurring at an inappropriate time: *an extremely ill-timed announcement.*

ill-treat ▸ **verb** [with obj.] act cruelly towards (a person or animal).

ill-treatment ▸ **noun** [mass noun] cruel or inhumane treatment: *he died from medical neglect and ill-treatment.*

illude /ɪˈl(j)uːd/ ▸ **verb** [with obj.] literary trick; delude: *he had allowed his imagination to illude him.*
– ORIGIN late Middle English: from Latin *illudere* 'to mock'.

illume /ɪˈl(j)uːm/ ▸ **verb** [with obj.] literary light up; illuminate: *sparks from candles illume our faces.*
– ORIGIN late Middle English: abbreviation of **ILLUMINE**.

illuminance /ɪˈl(j)uːmɪnəns/ ▸ **noun** Physics the amount of luminous flux per unit area.

illuminant ▸ **noun** technical a means of lighting or source of light: *until 1880, oil was the only illuminant in use.*
▸ **adjective** giving off light.
– ORIGIN mid 17th cent.: from Latin *illuminant-* 'illuminating', from the verb *illuminare* (see **ILLUMINATE**).

illuminate /ɪˈl(j)uːmɪneɪt/ ▸ **verb 1** [with obj.] light up: *a flash of lightning illuminated the house* | figurative *his face was illuminated by a smile.* ▪ decorate (a building or structure) with lights for a special occasion.
2 (often as adj. **illuminated**) decorate (a page or initial letter in a manuscript) with gold, silver, or coloured designs.
3 (usu. as adj. **illuminating**) help to clarify or explain: *a most illuminating discussion.*
– DERIVATIVES **illuminatingly** adverb, **illuminative** adjective, **illuminator** noun.
– ORIGIN late Middle English: from Latin *illuminat-* 'illuminated', from the verb *illuminare*, from *in-* 'upon' + *lumen, lumin-* 'light'.

illuminati /ɪˌl(j)uːmɪˈnɑːti/ ▸ **plural noun** people claiming to possess special enlightenment or knowledge of something: *some mysterious standard known only to the illuminati of the organization.* ▪ (**Illuminati**) a sect of 16th-century Spanish heretics who claimed special religious enlightenment. ▪ (**Illuminati**) a Bavarian secret society founded in 1776, organized like the Freemasons.
– DERIVATIVES **illuminism** noun, **illuminist** noun.
– ORIGIN late 16th cent.: plural of Italian *illuminato* or Latin *illuminatus* 'enlightened', past participle of *illuminare* (see **ILLUMINATE**).

illumination ▸ **noun 1** [mass noun] lighting or light: *higher levels of illumination are needed for reading.* ▪ (**illuminations**) lights used in decorating a building or other structure.
2 the art of illuminating a manuscript. ▪ [count noun] an illuminated design in a manuscript.
3 clarification: *these books form the most sustained analysis and illumination of the subject.* ▪ spiritual or intellectual enlightenment.
– ORIGIN Middle English: via Old French from late Latin *illuminatio(n-)*, from the verb *illuminare* (see **ILLUMINATE**).

illumine ▸ **verb 1** [with obj.] literary light up; brighten: *he moved her lamp so that her face was illumined.*
2 enlighten (someone) spiritually or intellectually.
– ORIGIN Middle English: from Old French *illuminer*, from Latin *illuminare* (see **ILLUMINATE**).

ill-use ▸ **verb** [with obj.] ill-treat (someone): *she felt ill-used by her former boss.*
▸ **noun** (**ill use**) [mass noun] ill-treatment.

illusion /ɪˈl(j)uːʒ(ə)n/ ▸ **noun** an instance of a wrong or misinterpreted perception of a sensory experience: *stripes embellish the surface to create the illusion of various wood-grain textures.* ▪ a deceptive appearance or impression: *the illusion of family togetherness.* ▪ a false idea or belief: *he had no illusions about the trouble she was in.*
– PHRASES **be under the illusion that** believe mistakenly that: *the world is under the illusion that the original painting still hangs in the Winter Palace.* **be under no illusion** (or **illusions**) be fully aware of the true state of affairs.
– DERIVATIVES **illusional** adjective, **illusionary** adjective.
– ORIGIN Middle English (in the sense 'deceiving, deception'): via Old French from Latin *illusio(n-)*, from *illudere* 'to mock', from *in-* 'against' + *ludere* 'play'.

illusionism ▸ **noun** [mass noun] the principle or technique by which artistic representations are made to resemble real objects or to give an appearance of space by the use of perspective.
– DERIVATIVES **illusionistic** adjective.

illusionist ▸ **noun** a person who performs tricks that deceive the eye; a magician.

illusive /ɪˈl(j)uːsɪv/ ▸ **adjective** chiefly literary deceptive; illusory: *an illusive haven.*
– ORIGIN early 17th cent.: from medieval Latin *illusivus*, from Latin *illus-* 'mocked', from the verb *illudere* (see **ILLUSION**).

illusory /ɪˈl(j)uːs(ə)ri/ ▸ **adjective** based on illusion; not real: *she knew the safety of her room was illusory.*
– DERIVATIVES **illusorily** adverb, **illusoriness** noun.

illustrate ▸ **verb 1** [with obj.] provide (a book, newspaper, etc.) with pictures: *the guide is illustrated with full-colour photographs.* ▪ explain or make (something) clear by using examples, charts, pictures, etc.: *the results are illustrated in Figure 7.*

2 serve as an example of: *the World Cup illustrated what high standards our players must achieve.*
– ORIGIN early 16th cent. (in the sense 'illuminate, shed light on'): from Latin *illustrat-* 'lit up', from the verb *illustrare*, from *in-* 'upon' + *lustrare* 'illuminate'.

illustrated ▸ **adjective** (of a book, newspaper, etc.) containing pictures or other graphical material: *an illustrated weekly magazine.*

illustration ▸ **noun 1** a picture illustrating a book, newspaper, etc.: *an illustration of a yacht.*
2 [mass noun] the action or fact of illustrating something: *by way of illustration, I refer to the following case.* ■ an illustrative example: *this accident is a graphic illustration of the disaster that's waiting to happen.*
– DERIVATIVES **illustrational** adjective.
– ORIGIN late Middle English (in the sense 'illumination; spiritual or intellectual enlightenment'): via Old French from Latin *illustratio(n-)*, from the verb *illustrare* (see ILLUSTRATE).

illustrative ▸ **adjective 1** serving as an example or explanation: *this timetable is provided for illustrative purposes only.*
2 relating to pictorial illustration: *the illustrative arts.*
– DERIVATIVES **illustratively** adverb.

illustrator ▸ **noun** a person who draws or creates pictures for magazines, books, advertising, etc.

illustrious /ɪˈlʌstrɪəs/ ▸ **adjective** well known, respected, and admired for past achievements: *his illustrious predecessor | an illustrious career.*
– DERIVATIVES **illustriously** adverb, **illustriousness** noun.
– ORIGIN mid 16th cent.: from Latin *illustris* 'clear, bright' + -OUS.

illuviation /ɪˌl(j)uːvɪˈeɪʃ(ə)n/ ▸ **noun** [mass noun] Soil Science the introduction of salts or colloids into one soil horizon from another by percolating water.
– DERIVATIVES **illuvial** adjective.
– ORIGIN early 20th cent.: from IL- 'in' + *-luvial* (on the pattern of *alluvial*) + -ATION.

ill will ▸ **noun** [mass noun] animosity or bitterness: *he didn't bear his estranged wife any ill will.*

Illyria /ɪˈlɪrɪə/ an ancient region along the east coast of the Adriatic Sea, including Dalmatia and what is now Montenegro and northern Albania.

Illyrian ▸ **adjective 1** relating to the ancient region of Illyria: *Illyrian tribes.*
2 of or denoting the branch of Indo-European languages represented by modern Albanian.
▸ **noun 1** a native or inhabitant of ancient Illyria.
2 [mass noun] the branch of the Indo-European family of languages represented by modern Albanian.

illywhacker /ˈɪlɪˌwakə/ ▸ **noun** Austral. informal, dated a small-time confidence trickster.
– ORIGIN 1940s: of unknown origin.

ilmenite /ˈɪlmənʌɪt/ ▸ **noun** [mass noun] a black mineral consisting of oxides of iron and titanium, of which it is the main ore.
– ORIGIN early 19th cent.: named after the *Ilmen* mountains in the Urals + -ITE[1].

ILO ▸ **abbreviation** International Labour Organization.

Ilocano /ˌɪləˈkɑːnəʊ/ ▸ **noun** (pl. **same** or **Ilocanos**)
1 a member of a people inhabiting NW Luzon in the Philippines.
2 [mass noun] the Austronesian language of the Ilocano, with over 5 million speakers. Also called **Iloko**.
▸ **adjective** relating to the Ilocano or their language.
– ORIGIN Philippine Spanish, from *Ilocos*, the name of two provinces in the Philippines.

Iloilo /ˌiːləʊˈiːləʊ/ a port on the south coast of the island of Panay in the Philippines; pop. 418,700 (est. 2007).

Ilonggo /ɪˈlɒŋgəʊ/ ▸ **noun** another term for HILIGAYNON.
– ORIGIN a local name.

Ilorin /ɪˈlɒrɪn/ a city in western Nigeria; pop. 771,000 (est. 2007). In the 18th century it was the capital of a Yoruba kingdom that was eventually absorbed into a Fulani state in the early 19th century.

ILP ▸ **abbreviation** Independent Labour Party.

ILR ▸ **abbreviation** Independent Local Radio.

ILS ▸ **abbreviation** instrument landing system, a system in which an aircraft's instruments interact with ground-based electronics to enable the pilot to land the aircraft safely in poor visibility.

ilvaite /ˈɪlvʌɪt/ ▸ **noun** [mass noun] a mineral consisting of a basic silicate of calcium and iron, typically occurring as black prisms.
– ORIGIN early 19th cent.: from Latin *Ilva* 'Elba' + -ITE[1].

-ily ▸ **suffix** forming adverbs corresponding to adjectives ending in *-y* (such as *happily* corresponding to *happy*).
– ORIGIN see -Y[1], -LY[2].

IM ▸ **noun** (pl. **IMs**) an instant message.
▸ **verb** [with obj.] (**IMs**, **IMing**, **IMd**) informal send (someone) an instant message: *she IMd me the other day saying she was visiting her boyfriend.*

I'm ▸ **contraction** I am: *I'm a busy woman.*

im- ▸ **prefix** variant spelling of IN-[1], IN-[2] assimilated before *b*, *m*, *p* (as in *imbibe*, *immure*, *impart*).

image ▸ **noun 1** a representation of the external form of a person or thing in art. ■ a visible impression obtained by a camera, telescope, microscope, or other device, or displayed on a computer or video screen. ■ an optical appearance or counterpart produced by light from an object reflected in a mirror or refracted through a lens. ■ Mathematics a point or set formed by mapping from another point or set. ■ Computing an exact copy of a computer's hard disk, made for backing up data or setting up new machines. ■ a mental representation or idea: *I had a sudden image of Sal bringing me breakfast in bed.* ■ [in sing.] a person or thing that closely resembles another: *he's **the image** of his father.* ■ [in sing.] semblance or likeness: *made in **the image of** God.* ■ (in biblical use) an idol.
2 the general impression that a person, organization, or product presents to the public: *she strives to project an image of youth.*
3 a simile or metaphor: *he uses the image of a hole to describe emotional emptiness.*
▸ **verb** [with obj.] make a representation of the external form of: *artworks which imaged women's bodies.* ■ make a visual representation of (something) by scanning it with a detector or electromagnetic beam: (as noun **imaging**) *medical imaging.* ■ form a mental picture or idea of: *it is possible for us to image a society in which no one committed crime.*
– DERIVATIVES **imageless** adjective.
– ORIGIN Middle English: from Old French, from Latin *imago*; related to IMITATE.

image intensifier ▸ **noun** a device used to make a brighter version of an image on a photoelectric screen.

image macro ▸ **noun** (on the Internet) a photographic image on which a humorous caption or catchphrase has been digitally superimposed.

image-maker ▸ **noun** a person employed to identify and create a favourable public image for a person, organization, or product.

image processing ▸ **noun** [mass noun] the analysis and manipulation of a digitized image, especially in order to improve its quality.

imager ▸ **noun** an electronic or other device which records images of something: *a thermal imager.*

imagery ▸ **noun 1** [mass noun] visually descriptive or figurative language, especially in a literary work: *Tennyson uses imagery to create a lyrical emotion.* ■ visual symbolism: *the film's religious imagery.*
2 visual images collectively: *the impact of computer-generated imagery on contemporary art.*
– ORIGIN Middle English (in the senses 'statuary, carved images collectively'): from Old French *imagerie*, from *imager* 'make an image', from *image* (see IMAGE).

imagesetter ▸ **noun** Computing a very high-quality type of colour printer used to print glossy magazines, newsletters, or other documents.

imaginable ▸ **adjective** possible to be thought of or believed: *the most spectacular views imaginable.*
– DERIVATIVES **imaginably** adverb.
– ORIGIN late Middle English: from late Latin *imaginabilis*, from Latin *imaginare* 'form an image of, represent', from *imago*, *imagin-* 'image'.

imaginal /ɪˈmadʒɪn(ə)l/ ▸ **adjective 1** relating to an image.
2 Entomology relating to an adult insect or imago.
– ORIGIN late 19th cent.: from Latin *imago*, *imagin-* 'image' + -AL.

imaginal disc ▸ **noun** Entomology a thickening of the epidermis of an insect larva which, on pupation, develops into a particular organ of the adult insect.

imaginary ▸ **adjective 1** existing only in the imagination: *Chris had imaginary conversations with her.*
2 Mathematics (of a number or quantity) expressed in terms of the square root of a negative number (usually the square root of -1, represented by *i* or *j*). See also COMPLEX.
– DERIVATIVES **imaginarily** adverb.
– ORIGIN late Middle English: from Latin *imaginarius*, from *imago*, *imagin-* 'image'.

imagination ▸ **noun** the faculty or action of forming new ideas, or images or concepts of external objects not present to the senses: *she'd never been blessed with a vivid imagination | her story captured the public's imagination.* ■ [mass noun] the ability of the mind to be creative or resourceful: *she was set in her ways and lacked imagination.* ■ the part of the mind that imagines things: *a girl who existed only in my imagination.*
– ORIGIN Middle English: via Old French from Latin *imaginatio(n-)*, from the verb *imaginari* 'picture to oneself', from *imago*, *imagin-* 'image'.

imaginative ▸ **adjective** having or showing creativity or inventiveness: *making imaginative use of computer software | he was imaginative beyond all other architects.*
– DERIVATIVES **imaginatively** adverb, **imaginativeness** noun.

imagine ▸ **verb** [with obj.] **1** form a mental image or concept of: *she imagined him at his desk, his head in his hands* | [with clause] *I couldn't imagine what she expected to tell them.* ■ believe (something unreal or untrue) to exist or be so: *she was overtired and imagining things* | (as adj. **imagined**) *they suffered from ill health, real or imagined, throughout their lives.*
2 [with clause] suppose or assume: *after Ned died, everyone imagined that Mabel would move away.*
– DERIVATIVES **imaginer** noun.
– ORIGIN Middle English: from Old French *imaginer*, from Latin *imaginare* 'form an image of, represent' and *imaginari* 'picture to oneself', both from *imago*, *imagin-* 'image'.

imagineer /ɪˌmadʒɪˈnɪə/ ▸ **noun** a person who devises and implements a new or highly imaginative concept or technology, in particular one who devises the attractions in Walt Disney theme parks.
▸ **verb** [with obj.] (often as noun **imagineering**) devise and implement (a new or highly imaginative concept or technology): *theme parks are benefiting from a new era of imagineering.*
– ORIGIN 1940s: from IMAGINE, on the pattern of *engineer*.

imagines plural form of IMAGO.

imaginings ▸ **plural noun** thoughts or fantasies: *this was quite beyond his worst imaginings.*

imagism /ˈɪmɪdʒɪz(ə)m/ ▸ **noun** [mass noun] a movement in early 20th-century English and American poetry which sought clarity of expression through the use of precise images. The movement derived in part from the aesthetic philosophy of T. E. Hulme and involved Ezra Pound, James Joyce, Amy Lowell, and others.
– DERIVATIVES **imagist** noun, **imagistic** adjective.

imago /ɪˈmeɪgəʊ/ ▸ **noun** (pl. **imagos** or **imagines** /ɪˈmeɪdʒɪniːz/) **1** Entomology the final and fully developed adult stage of an insect, typically winged.
2 Psychoanalysis an unconscious idealized mental image of someone, especially a parent, which influences a person's behaviour.
– ORIGIN late 18th cent. (in sense 1): modern Latin use of Latin *imago* 'image'. Sense 2 dates from the early 20th cent.

imam /ɪˈmɑːm/ ▸ **noun** the person who leads prayers in a mosque. ■ (**Imam**) a title of various Muslim leaders, especially of one succeeding Muhammad as leader of Shiite Islam: *Imam Khomeini.*
– DERIVATIVES **imamate** noun.
– ORIGIN from Arabic *'imām* 'leader', from *'amma* 'lead the way'.

Imam Bayildi /ɪˌmɑːm ˈbɑːjɪldi/ ▸ **noun** [mass noun] a Turkish dish consisting of aubergines stuffed with a garlic-flavoured onion and tomato mixture and baked.
– ORIGIN Turkish, literally 'the imam fainted' (from enjoyment or the cost of the dish).

IMAP ▸ **abbreviation** Computing Internet Mail Access Protocol.

Imari /ɪˈmɑːri/ ▸ **noun** [usu. as modifier] a type of richly decorated Japanese porcelain: *an Imari vase.*
– ORIGIN late 19th cent.: from the name of a port in NW Kyushu, Japan, from which it was shipped.

IMAX /ˈʌɪmaks/ ▸ **noun** [mass noun] trademark a technique of widescreen cinematography which produces an image approximately ten times larger than that from standard 35 mm film: [as modifier] *IMAX cinemas.*
– ORIGIN 1960s: from *i-* (probably representing a pronunciation of EYE) + *max* (short for MAXIMUM).

I

imbalance ▸ noun [mass noun] lack of proportion or relation between corresponding things: *tension is generated by the imbalance of power* | [count noun] *the condition is caused by a hormonal imbalance.*

imbecile /ˈɪmbɪsiːl/ ▸ noun informal a stupid person.
▸ adjective [attrib.] stupid; idiotic: *try not to make imbecile remarks.*
– DERIVATIVES **imbecilic** adjective, **imbecility** noun (pl. **imbecilities**).
– ORIGIN mid 16th cent. (as an adjective in the sense 'physically weak'): via French from Latin *imbecillus*, literally 'without a supporting staff', from *in-* (expressing negation) + *baculum* 'stick, staff'. The current sense dates from the early 19th cent.

imbed ▸ verb variant spelling of **EMBED**.

imbibe /ɪmˈbʌɪb/ ▸ verb [with obj.] formal, often humorous drink (alcohol): *they were imbibing far too many pitchers of beer.* ■ absorb or assimilate (ideas or knowledge): *if one does not imbibe the culture one cannot succeed.* ■ chiefly Botany (especially of seeds) absorb (water) into ultramicroscopic spaces or pores. ■ Botany place (seeds) in water in order for them to absorb it.
– DERIVATIVES **imbiber** noun, **imbibition** /ɪmbɪˈbɪʃ(ə)n/ noun (chiefly Botany).
– ORIGIN late Middle English (in the senses 'absorb or cause to absorb moisture' and 'take into solution'): from Latin *imbibere*, from *in-* 'in' + *bibere* 'to drink'.

I

imbizo /ɪmˈbiːzəʊ/ ▸ noun (pl. **imbizos**) S. African a gathering, usually called by a traditional leader.
– ORIGIN from Zulu *biza* 'summon, call'.

Imbolc /ˈɪmbɒlk/ ▸ noun an ancient Celtic festival celebrated on the second day of February.
– ORIGIN a Celtic word, literally 'in the belly or womb', the festival being dedicated to women and fertility.

imbongi /ɪmˈbɔːŋgi/ ▸ noun (pl. **izimbongi** or **iimbongi** or **imbongis**) S. African (in traditional African society) a composer and orator of poems praising a chief or other figurehead.
– ORIGIN from Xhosa (plural *iim-*) and Zulu (plural *izim-*).

imbricate chiefly Zoology & Botany ▸ verb /ˈɪmbrɪkeɪt/ [with obj.] (usu. as adj. **imbricated**) arrange (scales, sepals, plates, etc.) so that they overlap like roof tiles: *these moulds have spherical bodies composed of imbricated triangular plates.* ■ [no obj.] (usu. as adj. **imbricating**) overlap: *a coating of imbricating scales.*
▸ adjective /ˈɪmbrɪkət/ (of scales, sepals, plates, etc.) having adjacent edges overlapping. Compare with **VALVATE**.
– DERIVATIVES **imbrication** noun.
– ORIGIN early 17th cent. (in the sense 'shaped like a pantile'): from Latin *imbricat-*, 'covered with roof tiles', from the verb *imbricare*, from *imbrex*, *imbric-* 'roof tile' (from *imber* 'shower of rain').

imbroglio /ɪmˈbrəʊlɪəʊ/ ▸ noun (pl. **imbroglios**) an extremely confused, complicated, or embarrassing situation: *the abdication imbroglio of 1936.* ■ archaic a confused heap.
– ORIGIN mid 18th cent.: Italian, from *imbrogliare* 'confuse'; related to **EMBROIL**.

Imbros /ˈɪmbrɒs/ a Turkish island in the NE Aegean Sea, near the entrance to the Dardanelles. Turkish name **Imroz**.

imbrue /ɪmˈbruː/ ▸ verb (**imbrues**, **imbruing**, **imbrued**) [with obj.] archaic or literary stain (something, especially one's hands or sword): *they were unwilling to imbrue their hands in his blood.*
– ORIGIN late Middle English: from Old French *embruer* 'bedaub, bedabble', ultimately of Germanic origin and related to **BROTH**.

imbue /ɪmˈbjuː/ ▸ verb (**imbues**, **imbuing**, **imbued**) [with obj.] (often **be imbued with**) inspire or permeate with (a feeling or quality): *his works are invariably imbued with a sense of calm and serenity.*
– ORIGIN late Middle English (in the sense 'saturate'): from French *imbu* 'moistened', from Latin *imbutus*, past participle of *imbuere* 'moisten'.

I.Mech.E. ▸ abbreviation (in the UK) Institution of Mechanical Engineers.

IMEI ▸ abbreviation international mobile equipment identity.

IMF ▸ abbreviation International Monetary Fund.

IMHO ▸ abbreviation in my humble opinion.

Imhotep /ɪmˈhəʊtɛp/ (*fl.* 27th century BC), Egyptian architect and scholar, later deified. He probably designed the step pyramid built at Saqqara for the 3rd-dynasty pharaoh Djoser.

imidazole /ˌɪmɪˈdeɪzəʊl, ɪˈmɪdəzəʊl/ ▸ noun [mass noun] Chemistry a colourless crystalline compound with mildly basic properties, present as a substituent in the amino acid histidine. ● a heterocyclic compound; chem. formula: $C_3H_4N_2$.
– ORIGIN late 19th cent.: from **IMIDE** + **AZO-** + **-OLE**.

imide /ˈɪmʌɪd/ ▸ noun [mass noun] Chemistry an organic compound containing the group –CONHCO–, related to ammonia by replacement of two hydrogen atoms by acyl groups.
– ORIGIN mid 19th cent.: from French, arbitrary alteration of **AMIDE**.

imine /ˈɪmiːn/ ▸ noun [mass noun] Chemistry an organic compound containing the group –C=NH or –C=NR where R is an alkyl or other group.
– ORIGIN late 19th cent.: from **AMINE**, on the pattern of the pair *amide*, *imide*.

I.Min.E. ▸ abbreviation (in the UK) Institution of Mining Engineers.

imipramine /ɪˈmɪprəmiːn/ ▸ noun [mass noun] a synthetic compound used to treat depression. ● A tricyclic amine; chem. formula: $C_{19}H_{24}N_2$.
– ORIGIN 1950s: from *imi(ne)* + *pr(opyl)* + **AMINE**.

imitate ▸ verb [with obj.] take or follow as a model: *his style was imitated by many other writers.* ■ copy (a person's speech or mannerisms), especially for comic effect: *she imitated my Scots accent.* ■ copy or simulate: *synthetic fabrics can now imitate everything from silk to rubber.*
– DERIVATIVES **imitable** adjective.
– ORIGIN mid 16th cent.: from Latin *imitat-* 'copied', from the verb *imitari*; related to *imago* 'image'.

imitation ▸ noun 1 [mass noun] the action of using someone or something as a model: *a child learns to speak by imitation.* ■ an act of imitating a person's speech or mannerisms, especially for comic effect: *he attempted an atrocious imitation of my English accent.* ■ [mass noun] Music the repetition of a phrase or melody in another part or voice, usually at a different pitch.
2 a thing intended to simulate or copy something else: [as modifier] *an imitation sub-machine gun.*
– PHRASES **imitation is the sincerest form of flattery** proverb copying someone or something is an implicit way of paying them a compliment.
– ORIGIN late Middle English: from Latin *imitatio(n-)*, from the verb *imitari* (see **IMITATE**).

imitative /ˈɪmɪtətɪv/ ▸ adjective 1 copying or following a model or example: *the derring-do of our film heroes inspired us to imitative feats.* ■ following a model or example without any attempt at originality: *I found the film pretentious and imitative.*
2 (of a word) reproducing a natural sound (e.g. *fizz*) or pronounced in a way that is thought to correspond to the appearance or character of the object or action described (e.g. *blob*).
– DERIVATIVES **imitatively** adverb, **imitativeness** noun.

imitator ▸ noun someone who copies the behaviour or actions of another: *the show's success has sparked off many imitators.*

imli /ˈɪmli:/ ▸ noun Indian term for **TAMARIND**.
– ORIGIN via Hindi from Sanskrit *amlikā*.

immaculate ▸ adjective 1 perfectly clean, neat, or tidy: *an immaculate white suit.* ■ free from flaws or mistakes; perfect: *an immaculate safety record.* ■ Theology (in the Roman Catholic Church) free from sin.
2 Botany & Zoology uniformly coloured without spots or other marks.
– DERIVATIVES **immaculacy** noun, **immaculately** adverb, **immaculateness** noun.
– ORIGIN late Middle English (in the sense 'free from moral stain'): from Latin *immaculatus*, from *in-* 'not' + *maculatus* 'stained' (from *macula* 'spot').

Immaculate Conception ▸ noun the doctrine that God preserved the Virgin Mary from the taint of original sin from the moment she was conceived; it was defined as a dogma of the Roman Catholic Church in 1854. ■ the feast commemorating the Immaculate Conception on December 8th.

immanent /ˈɪmənənt/ ▸ adjective existing or operating within; inherent: *the protection of liberties is immanent in constitutional arrangements.* ■ (of God) permanently pervading and sustaining the universe. Often contrasted with **TRANSCENDENT**.
– DERIVATIVES **immanence** noun, **immanency** noun, **immanentism** noun, **immanentist** noun.
– ORIGIN mid 16th cent.: from late Latin *immanent-* 'remaining within', from *in-* 'in' + *manere* 'remain'.

Immanuel variant spelling of **EMMANUEL**.

immaterial ▸ adjective 1 unimportant under the circumstances; irrelevant: *the difference in our ages is immaterial.*
2 Philosophy spiritual, rather than physical: *we have immaterial souls.*
– DERIVATIVES **immateriality** noun, **immaterially** adverb.
– ORIGIN late Middle English (in sense 2): from late Latin *immaterialis*, from *in-* 'not' + *materialis* 'relating to matter'.

immaterialism ▸ noun [mass noun] the belief that matter has no objective existence.
– DERIVATIVES **immaterialist** noun.

immature ▸ adjective not fully developed: *many of the fish caught are immature.* ■ having or showing an emotional or intellectual development appropriate to someone younger: *his immature sense of humour.*
– DERIVATIVES **immaturely** adverb.
– ORIGIN mid 16th cent. (in the sense 'premature', referring to death): from Latin *immaturus* 'untimely, unripe', from *in-* 'not' + *maturus* 'ripe' (see **MATURE**).

immaturity ▸ noun [mass noun] the state of being immature or not fully grown: *the immaturity of the immune system in very young children makes them especially vulnerable.* ■ behaviour that is appropriate to someone younger: *they were shocked by such immaturity in a grown man.*

immeasurable ▸ adjective too large, extensive, or extreme to measure: *immeasurable suffering.*
– DERIVATIVES **immeasurability** noun, **immeasurably** adverb.

immediacy /ɪˈmiːdɪəsi/ ▸ noun [mass noun] the quality of bringing one into direct and instant involvement with something, giving rise to a sense of urgency or excitement: *email works because it has the immediacy of a scribbled memo.*

immediate ▸ adjective 1 occurring or done at once; instant: *the authorities took no immediate action* | *the book's success was immediate.* ■ relating to or existing at the present time: *the immediate concern was how to avoid taxes.*
2 nearest in time, relationship, or rank: *no changes are envisaged in the immediate future* | *his immediate superior in the department.* ■ nearest or next to in space: *roads in the immediate vicinity of the port.* ■ (of a relation or action) without an intervening medium or agency; direct: *coronary thrombosis was the immediate cause of death.*
3 Philosophy (of knowledge or reaction) gained or shown without reasoning; intuitive.
– DERIVATIVES **immediateness** noun.
– ORIGIN late Middle English (in the sense 'nearest in space or order'): from Old French *immediat*, or from late Latin *immediatus*, from *in-* 'not' + *mediatus* 'intervening', past participle of *mediare* (see **MEDIATE**).

immediate constituent ▸ noun Linguistics each of the constituents of a syntactic unit at the next level down in the hierarchy.

immediately ▸ adverb 1 at once; instantly: *I rang immediately for an ambulance.*
2 without any intervening time or space: *she was sitting immediately behind me.* ■ in direct or very close relation: *they would be the states most immediately affected by any such action.*
▸ conjunction chiefly Brit. as soon as: *let me know immediately she arrives.*

immedicable /ɪˈmɛdɪkəb(ə)l/ ▸ adjective archaic unable to be healed or treated; incurable.
– ORIGIN mid 16th cent.: from Latin *immedicabilis*, from *in-* 'not' + *medicabilis* (see **MEDICABLE**).

Immelmann /ˈɪm(ə)lmən/ (also **Immelmann turn**) ▸ noun an aerobatic manoeuvre consisting of a half loop followed by a half roll, resulting in reversal of direction and increased height.
– ORIGIN early 20th cent.: named after Max *Immelmann* (1890–1916), German fighter pilot.

immemorial ▸ adjective originating in the distant past; very old: *an immemorial custom.*
– DERIVATIVES **immemorially** adverb.
– ORIGIN early 17th cent.: from medieval Latin *immemorialis*, from *in-* 'not' + *memorialis* 'relating to the memory'.

immense ▸ adjective extremely large or great, especially in scale or degree: *the cost of restoration has been immense* | *a factor of immense importance.*
– DERIVATIVES **immensity** noun.
– ORIGIN late Middle English: via French from Latin *immensus* 'immeasurable', from *in-* 'not' + *mensus* 'measured' (past participle of *metiri*).

immensely ▸ adverb to a great extent; extremely: [as submodifier] *the president was immensely popular.*

immerse ▸ verb **1** [with obj.] dip or submerge in a liquid: *immerse the paper **in** water for twenty minutes.* ■ baptize (someone) by immersion in water.
2 (**immerse oneself** or **be immersed**) involve oneself deeply in a particular activity: *she immersed herself in her work | she was still immersed in her thoughts.*
– ORIGIN early 17th cent.: from Latin *immers-* 'dipped into', from the verb *immergere*, from *in-* 'in' + *mergere* 'to dip'.

immersion ▸ noun [mass noun] **1** the action of immersing someone or something in a liquid: *his back was still raw from **immersion in** the icy Atlantic sea.* ■ baptism by immersing a person bodily (but not necessarily completely) in water.
2 deep mental involvement: *her total **immersion in** work meant that she had few real friends.* ■ a method of teaching a foreign language by the exclusive use of that language.
3 Astronomy the disappearance of a celestial body in the shadow of or behind another.
– ORIGIN late 15th cent.: from late Latin *immersio(n-)*, from *immergere* 'dip into' (see IMMERSE).

immersion heater ▸ noun Brit. an electric heating element that is positioned in the liquid to be heated, typically in a domestic hot-water tank.

immersive ▸ adjective (of a computer display or system) generating a three-dimensional image which appears to surround the user.

immigrant ▸ noun a person who comes to live permanently in a foreign country.
– ORIGIN late 18th cent.: from Latin *immigrant-* 'immigrating', from the verb *immigrare*, on the pattern of *emigrant*.

immigrate ▸ verb [no obj.] chiefly N. Amer. come to live permanently in a foreign country: *an Australian who immigrated to Britain in 1982.*
– ORIGIN early 17th cent.: from Latin *immigrat-* 'immigrated', from the verb *immigrare*, from *in-* 'into' + *migrare* 'migrate'.

immigration ▸ noun [mass noun] the action of coming to live permanently in a foreign country: *a barrier to control illegal immigration from Mexico.* ■ the place at an airport or country's border where government officials check the documents of people entering that country.

imminent ▸ adjective **1** about to happen: *they were in imminent danger of being swept away.*
2 archaic overhanging.
– DERIVATIVES **imminence** noun, **imminently** adverb.
– ORIGIN late Middle English: from Latin *imminent-* 'overhanging, impending', from the verb *imminere*, from *in-* 'upon, towards' + *minere* 'to project'.

immiscible /ɪˈmɪsɪb(ə)l/ ▸ adjective (of liquids) not forming a homogeneous mixture when mixed: *benzene is immiscible with water.*
– DERIVATIVES **immiscibility** noun.
– ORIGIN late 17th cent.: from late Latin *immiscibilis*, from *in-* 'not' + *miscibilis* (see MISCIBLE).

immiseration /ɪˌmɪzəˈreɪʃ(ə)n/ ▸ noun [mass noun] economic impoverishment.
– DERIVATIVES **immiserate** verb.
– ORIGIN 1940s: translating German *Verelendung*.

immiserization /ɪˌmɪzərʌɪˈzeɪʃ(ə)n/ (also **immiserisation**) ▸ noun another term for IMMISERATION.

immitigable /ɪˈmɪtɪgəb(ə)l/ ▸ adjective archaic unable to be made less severe or serious: *the pain was immitigable.*
– ORIGIN late 16th cent.: from late Latin *immitigabilis*, from *in-* 'not' + *mitigabilis* 'able to be mitigated'.

immittance /ɪˈmɪt(ə)ns/ ▸ noun Physics admittance and impedance (as a combined concept).
– ORIGIN 1950s: blend of IMPEDANCE and ADMITTANCE.

immixture ▸ noun [mass noun] archaic the process of mixing or being involved with something.

immobile ▸ adjective not moving; motionless: *she sat immobile for a long time.* ■ incapable of moving or being moved: *an immobile workforce.*
– DERIVATIVES **immobility** noun.
– ORIGIN Middle English: from Old French, from Latin *immobilis*, from *in-* 'not' + *mobilis* (see MOBILE).

immobilism ▸ noun [mass noun] deep-seated resistance to political change.

immobilize (also **immobilise**) ▸ verb [with obj.] prevent (something or someone) from moving or operating as normal: *the car had been immobilized by a wheel clamp | fear immobilized her.* ■ restrict the movements of (a limb) to allow healing.
– DERIVATIVES **immobilization** noun.
– ORIGIN late 19th cent.: from French *immobiliser*, from *immobile* (see IMMOBILE).

immobilizer (also **immobiliser**) ▸ noun a device for immobilizing a motor vehicle in order to prevent theft.

immoderate ▸ adjective not sensible or restrained; excessive: *immoderate drinking.*
– DERIVATIVES **immoderately** adverb.
– ORIGIN late Middle English: from Latin *immoderatus*, from *in-* 'not' + *moderatus* 'reduced, controlled' (past participle of *moderare*).

immoderation ▸ noun [mass noun] the quality of being excessive and lacking in restraint; overindulgence: *he paid a high price for his immoderation.*

immodest ▸ adjective lacking humility or decorousness: *his immodest personality.*
– DERIVATIVES **immodestly** adverb, **immodesty** noun.
– ORIGIN late 16th cent.: from French *immodeste* or Latin *immodestus*, from *in-* 'not' + *modestus* (see MODEST).

immolate /ˈɪməleɪt/ ▸ verb [with obj.] kill or offer as a sacrifice, especially by burning.
– DERIVATIVES **immolation** noun, **immolator** noun.
– ORIGIN mid 16th cent. (earlier (late Middle English) as *immolation*): from Latin *immolat-* 'sprinkled with sacrificial meal', from the verb *immolare*, from *in-* 'upon' + *mola* 'meal'.

immoral ▸ adjective not conforming to accepted standards of morality: *unseemly and immoral behaviour.*
– DERIVATIVES **immorally** adverb.

> **USAGE** The words **immoral** and **amoral** are different in meaning: see USAGE at AMORAL.

immoral earnings ▸ plural noun earnings from prostitution.

immoralism ▸ noun [mass noun] a system of thought or behaviour that does not accept moral principles.
– DERIVATIVES **immoralist** noun.
– ORIGIN early 20th cent.: suggested by German *Immoralismus*.

immorality ▸ noun (pl. **immoralities**) [mass noun] the state or quality of being immoral; wickedness: *he believed his father had been punished by God for his immorality* | [count noun] *her alleged immoralities aroused a public outcry.*

immortal /ɪˈmɔːt(ə)l/ ▸ adjective living forever; never dying or decaying: *our mortal bodies are inhabited by immortal souls.* ■ deserving to be remembered forever: *the immortal children's classic, 'The Wind in the Willows'.*
▸ noun **1** an immortal being, especially a god of ancient Greece or Rome. ■ a person of enduring fame: *he will always be one of the immortals of soccer.*
2 (**Immortal**) a member of the French Academy.
3 (**Immortals**) historical the royal bodyguard of ancient Persia.
– DERIVATIVES **immortally** adverb.
– ORIGIN late Middle English: from Latin *immortalis*, from *in-* 'not' + *mortalis* (see MORTAL).

immortality /ɪmɔːˈtalɪti/ ▸ noun [mass noun] the ability to live forever; eternal life: *eating the fruit gave the gods immortality.* ■ the quality of deserving to be remembered for a long time; timelessness: *occasionally a guide book has achieved immortality.*

immortalize (also **immortalise**) ▸ verb [with obj.] (usu. **be immortalized in**) confer enduring fame upon: *he will be forever immortalized in the history books.*
– DERIVATIVES **immortalization** noun.

immortelle /ˌɪmɔːˈtɛl/ ▸ noun **1** another term for EVERLASTING (sense 2 of the noun).
2 W. Indian a Caribbean tree of the pea family, with a spiny trunk and clusters of red, orange, or pinkish flowers. ● Genus *Erythrina*, family Leguminosae: two species.
– ORIGIN French (feminine adjective), literally 'everlasting'.

immotile /ɪˈməʊtʌɪl/ ▸ adjective Biology not motile.

immovable (also **immoveable**) ▸ adjective **1** not able to be moved: *all immovable objects have graffiti sprayed on them.* ■ Law (of property) consisting of land, buildings, or other permanent items.
2 (of a person) not yielding to argument or pressure. ■ (especially of a principle) fixed or unchangeable: *an immovable article of faith.*
▸ noun (**immovables**) Law immovable property.
– DERIVATIVES **immovability** noun, **immovably** adverb.

immune ▸ adjective **1** resistant to a particular infection or toxin owing to the presence of specific antibodies or sensitized white blood cells: *they were naturally **immune to** hepatitis B.* ■ [attrib.] Biology relating to immune resistance.
2 protected or exempt, especially from an obligation or the effects of something: *they are **immune from** legal action.* ■ [predic.] not affected or influenced by something: *no one is **immune to** his immense charm.*
– ORIGIN late Middle English (in the sense 'free from (a liability)'): from Latin *immunis* 'exempt from public service or charge', from *in-* 'not' + *munis* 'ready for service'. Senses relating to physiological resistance date from the late 19th cent.

immune deficiency ▸ noun [mass noun] failure of the immune system to protect the body adequately from infection, due to the absence or insufficiency of some component process or substance.

immune response ▸ noun the reaction of the cells and fluids of the body to the presence of a substance which is not recognized as a constituent of the body itself.

immune system ▸ noun the organs and processes of the body that provide resistance to infection and toxins. Organs include the thymus, bone marrow, and lymph nodes.

immunity ▸ noun (pl. **immunities**) **1** [mass noun] the ability of an organism to resist a particular infection or toxin by the action of specific antibodies or sensitized white blood cells: ***immunity to** typhoid seems to have increased spontaneously.*
2 protection or exemption from something, especially an obligation or penalty: *the rebels were given **immunity from** prosecution.* ■ Law officially granted exemption from legal proceedings or liability. ■ lack of susceptibility, especially to something unwelcome or harmful: *products must have an adequate level of **immunity to** interference.*
– ORIGIN late Middle English: in the sense 'exemption (from a liability)': from Latin *immunitas*, from *immunis* (see IMMUNE).

immunize (also **immunise**) ▸ verb [with obj.] make (a person or animal) immune to infection, typically by inoculation: *the vaccine is used to **immunize** children **against** measles.*
– DERIVATIVES **immunization** noun, **immunizer** noun.

immuno- /ˈɪmjʊnəʊ, ɪˈmjuːnəʊ/ ▸ combining form Medicine representing IMMUNE, IMMUNITY, or IMMUNOLOGY.

immunoassay /ˌɪmjʊnəʊˈaseɪ, ɪˌmjuːnəʊ-/ ▸ noun Biochemistry a procedure for detecting or measuring specific proteins or other substances through their properties as antigens or antibodies.

immunoblotting /ˈɪmjʊnəʊblɒtɪŋ, ɪˈmjuːnəʊblɒtɪŋ/ ▸ noun [mass noun] Biochemistry a technique for analysing or identifying proteins in a mixture, involving separation by electrophoresis followed by staining with antibodies.

immunochemistry ▸ noun [mass noun] the branch of biochemistry concerned with immune responses and systems.

immunocompetent /ˌɪmjʊnəʊˈkɒmpɪt(ə)nt, ɪˌmjuːnəʊ-/ ▸ adjective Medicine having a normal immune response.
– DERIVATIVES **immunocompetence** noun.

immunocompromised ▸ adjective Medicine having an impaired immune system.

immunocytochemistry /ˌɪmjʊnəʊˌsʌɪtəʊˈkɛmɪstri, ɪˌmjuːnəʊ-/ ▸ noun [mass noun] the range of microscopical techniques used in the study of the immune system.
– DERIVATIVES **immunocytochemical** adjective.

immunodeficiency ▸ noun another term for IMMUNE DEFICIENCY.

immunodiffusion ▸ noun [mass noun] Biochemistry a technique for detecting or measuring antibodies and antigens by their precipitation when diffused together through a gel or other medium.

immunoelectrophoresis /ˌɪmjʊnəʊɪˌlɛktrə(ʊ)fəˈriːsɪs, ɪˌmjuːnəʊ-/ ▸ noun [mass noun] Biochemistry a technique for the identification of proteins in serum or other fluid by electrophoresis and subsequent immunodiffusion.

immunofluorescence /ˌɪmjʊnəʊˌflʊəˈrɛs(ə)ns, ɪˌmjuːnəʊ-, -flɔː-/ ▸ noun [mass noun] Biochemistry a technique for determining the location of an antigen (or antibody) in tissues by reaction with an antibody (or antigen) labelled with a fluorescent dye.
– DERIVATIVES **immunofluorescent** adjective.

I

I

immunogenic /ˌɪmjʊnəʊˈdʒɛnɪk, ɪˌmjuːnəʊ-/ ▸ adjective relating to or denoting substances able to produce an immune response.
– DERIVATIVES **immunogenicity** noun.

immunoglobulin /ˌɪmjʊnəʊˈɡlɒbjʊlɪn, ɪˌmjuːnəʊ-/ ▸ noun [mass noun] Biochemistry any of a class of proteins present in the serum and cells of the immune system, which function as antibodies.

immunology ▸ noun [mass noun] the branch of medicine and biology concerned with immunity.
– DERIVATIVES **immunologic** adjective, **immunological** adjective, **immunologically** adverb, **immunologist** noun.

immunosorbent ▸ adjective Biochemistry relating to or denoting techniques making use of the absorption of antibodies by insoluble preparations of antigens.

immunosuppression ▸ noun [mass noun] Medicine the partial or complete suppression of the immune response of an individual. It is induced to help the survival of an organ after a transplant operation.
– DERIVATIVES **immunosuppressant** noun, **immunosuppressed** adjective.

immunosuppressive ▸ adjective Medicine (chiefly of drugs) partially or completely suppressing the immune response of an individual.
▸ noun an immunosuppressive drug.

immunotherapy ▸ noun [mass noun] Medicine the prevention or treatment of disease with substances that stimulate the immune response.

immure /ɪˈmjʊə, ɪˈmjɔː/ ▸ verb [with obj.] enclose or confine (someone) against their will: *her brother was immured in a lunatic asylum.*
– DERIVATIVES **immurement** noun.
– ORIGIN late 16th cent.: from French *emmurer* or medieval Latin *immurare*, from *in-* 'in' + *murus* 'wall'.

immutable /ɪˈmjuːtəb(ə)l/ ▸ adjective unchanging over time or unable to be changed: *an immutable fact.*
– DERIVATIVES **immutability** noun, **immutably** adverb.
– ORIGIN late Middle English: from Latin *immutabilis*, from *in-* 'not' + *mutabilis* (see MUTABLE).

IMO ▸ abbreviation **1** International Maritime Organization.
2 informal in my opinion: *this was the best episode of the entire series, IMO.*

i-mode ▸ noun [mass noun] trademark a technology that allows data to be transferred to and from Internet sites via mobile phones.
– ORIGIN early 21st cent.: from **I²** (referring to the user's ability to interact directly with the Internet) + MODE.

IMP ▸ abbreviation Bridge International Match Point.

imp ▸ noun a small, mischievous devil or sprite. ■ a mischievous child: *a cheeky young imp.*
▸ verb [with obj.] repair a damaged feather in (the wing or tail of a trained hawk) by attaching part of a new feather.
– ORIGIN Old English *impa*, *impe* 'young shoot, scion', *impian* 'to graft', based on Greek *emphuein* 'to implant'. In late Middle English, the noun denoted a descendant, especially of a noble family, and later a child of the devil or a person regarded as such; hence a 'little devil' or mischievous child (early 17th cent.).

impact ▸ noun /ˈɪmpakt/ **1** the action of one object coming forcibly into contact with another: *there was the sound of a third impact* | [mass noun] *bullets which expand and cause devastating injury on impact.*
2 a marked effect or influence: *our regional measures have had a significant* ***impact on*** *unemployment.*
▸ verb /ɪmˈpakt/ [no obj.] **1** come into forcible contact with another object: *the shell impacted twenty yards away.* ■ [with obj.] chiefly N. Amer. come into forcible contact with: *an asteroid impacted the earth some 60 million years ago.* ■ [with obj.] press (something) firmly: *the animals' feet do not impact and damage the soil as cows' hooves do.*
2 (**impact on**) have a strong effect on someone or something: *high interest rates have impacted on retail spending* | [with obj.] *the move is not expected to impact the company's employees.*
– ORIGIN early 17th cent. (as a verb in the sense 'press closely, fix firmly'): from Latin *impact-* 'driven in', from the verb *impingere* (see IMPINGE).

impact crater ▸ noun a crater on a planet or satellite caused by the impact of a meteorite or other object.

impacted ▸ adjective **1** chiefly Medicine pressed firmly together, in particular: ■ (of a tooth) wedged between another tooth and the jaw. ■ (of a fractured bone) having the parts crushed together. ■ (of faeces) lodged in the intestine.
2 strongly affected by something: *the planners' lamentable failure to consult with the impacted population.*

impactful /ɪmˈpaktf(ʊ)l/ ▸ adjective having a major impact or effect: *an eye-catching and impactful design.*

impaction ▸ noun [mass noun] Medicine the condition of being or process of becoming impacted, especially of faeces in the intestine.

impactive ▸ adjective having a strong effect or influence; making an impression: *impactive colour radiates from the sculptures.*

impactor ▸ noun chiefly Astronomy an object (such as a meteorite) which collides with another body.

impair ▸ verb [with obj.] weaken or damage (something, especially a faculty or function): *a noisy job could permanently impair their hearing.*
– ORIGIN Middle English *enpeire*, from Old French *empeirier*, based on late Latin *pejorare* (from Latin *pejor* 'worse'). The current spelling is due to association with words derived from Latin beginning with *im-*.

impaired ▸ adjective having a disability of a specified kind: [in combination] *speech-impaired children.*

impairment ▸ noun [mass noun] the state or fact of being impaired, especially in a specified faculty: *a degree of physical or mental impairment* | [count noun] *a speech impairment.*

impala /ɪmˈpɑːlə, -ˈpalə/ ▸ noun (pl. **same**) a graceful antelope often seen in large herds in open woodland in southern and East Africa. ● *Aepyceros melampus*, family Bovidae.
– ORIGIN late 19th cent.: from Zulu *impala*.

impale ▸ verb [with obj.] **1** transfix or pierce with a sharp instrument: *his head was* ***impaled on*** *a pike and exhibited for all to see.*
2 Heraldry display (a coat of arms) side by side with another on the same shield, separated by a vertical line. ■ (of a coat of arms) adjoin (another coat of arms) on the same shield.
– DERIVATIVES **impalement** noun, **impaler** noun.
– ORIGIN mid 16th cent. (in the sense 'enclose with stakes or pales'): from French *empaler* or medieval Latin *impalare*, from Latin *in-* 'in' + *palus* 'a stake'.

impalpable ▸ adjective unable to be felt by touch: *an impalpable ghost.* ■ not easily comprehended.
– DERIVATIVES **impalpability** noun, **impalpably** adverb.
– ORIGIN early 16th cent.: from French, or from late Latin *impalpabilis*, from *in-* 'not' + *palpabilis* (see PALPABLE).

impanation /ˌɪmpəˈneɪʃ(ə)n/ ▸ noun [mass noun] Theology the medieval and Reformation doctrine that the body of Christ is present within the Eucharistic bread and does not replace it. Compare with CONSUBSTANTIATION.
– ORIGIN mid 16th cent.: from medieval Latin *impanatio(n-)*, from *impanare* 'embody in bread', from *in-* 'in' + *panis* 'bread'.

impanel (also **empanel**) ▸ verb (**impanels**, **impanelling**, **impanelled**; US **impaneling**, **impaneled**) [with obj.] enlist or enrol (a jury). ■ enrol (someone) on to a jury.
– ORIGIN late Middle English (originally as *empanel*): from Anglo-Norman French *empaneller*, from *em-* 'in' + Old French *panel* 'panel'.

impark ▸ verb [with obj.] historical enclose (animals) in a park. ■ enclose (land) to make it into a park.
– ORIGIN late Middle English: from Old French *emparquer*, from *em-* 'within' + *parc* 'park'.

impart ▸ verb [with obj.] make (information) known: *the teachers* ***imparted*** *a great deal of knowledge* ***to*** *their pupils.* ■ bestow (a quality): *shiitake mushrooms* ***impart*** *a wonderfully woody flavour* ***to*** *the salad.*
– DERIVATIVES **impartation** noun.
– ORIGIN late Middle English (in the sense 'give a share of'): from Old French *impartir*, from Latin *impartire*, from *in-* 'in' + *pars*, *part-* 'part'.

impartial ▸ adjective treating all rivals or disputants equally: *the minister cannot be impartial in the way that a judge would be.*
– DERIVATIVES **impartiality** noun, **impartially** adverb.

impassable ▸ adjective impossible to travel along or over: *the narrow channels are* ***impassable to*** *ocean-going ships.*
– DERIVATIVES **impassability** noun, **impassably** adverb.

impasse /amˈpɑːs, ˈampɑːs/ ▸ noun a situation in which no progress is possible, especially because of disagreement; a deadlock: *the current political impasse.*
– ORIGIN mid 19th cent.: from French, from *im-* (expressing negation) + the stem of *passer* 'to pass'.

impassible /ɪmˈpasɪb(ə)l/ ▸ adjective chiefly Theology incapable of suffering or feeling pain: *belief in an impassible God.* ■ archaic incapable of feeling or emotion.
– DERIVATIVES **impassibility** noun, **impassibly** adverb.
– ORIGIN Middle English: via Old French from ecclesiastical Latin *impassibilis*, from Latin *in-* 'not' + *passibilis* (see PASSIBLE).

impassion ▸ verb [with obj.] make passionate: *her body had once pleased and impassioned him.*
– ORIGIN late 16th cent.: from Italian *impassionnare*, from *im-* (expressing intensive force) + *passione* 'passion', from Christian Latin *passio* (see PASSION).

impassioned ▸ adjective filled with or showing great emotion: *she made an impassioned plea for help.*

impassive ▸ adjective not feeling or showing emotion: *his cold, impassive face.*
– DERIVATIVES **impassively** adverb, **impassiveness** noun, **impassivity** noun.

impasto /ɪmˈpastəʊ/ ▸ noun [mass noun] Art the process or technique of laying on paint or pigment thickly so that it stands out from a surface. ■ paint applied thickly.
– ORIGIN late 18th cent.: from Italian, from *impastare*, from *im-* 'upon' + *pasta* 'a paste', from late Latin.

impatience ▸ noun [mass noun] the tendency to be impatient; irritability or restlessness: *she crumpled up the pages in a burst of impatience.*

impatiens /ɪmˈpatɪɛnz/ ▸ noun a plant of a genus that includes busy Lizzie and its many hybrids. ● Genus *Impatiens*, family Balsaminaceae.
– ORIGIN modern Latin, from Latin, literally 'impatient' (because the capsules of the plant readily burst open when touched).

impatient ▸ adjective **1** having or showing a tendency to be quickly irritated or provoked: *an impatient motorist blaring his horn* | *she can be* ***impatient with*** *people who don't see things her way.* ■ (**impatient of**) intolerant of: *a man impatient of bureaucracy.*
2 restlessly eager: *they are* ***impatient for*** *change* | [with infinitive] *he was impatient to be on his way.*
– DERIVATIVES **impatiently** adverb.
– ORIGIN late Middle English (in the senses 'lacking patience' and 'unbearable'): via Old French from Latin *impatient-* 'not bearing, impatient', from *in-* 'not' + *pati* 'suffer, bear'.

impeach ▸ verb [with obj.] call into question the integrity or validity of (a practice): *there is no desire to impeach the privileges of the House of Commons.* ■ Brit. charge (someone) with treason or another crime against the state. ■ chiefly US charge (the holder of a public office) with misconduct.
– DERIVATIVES **impeachable** adjective, **impeachment** noun.
– ORIGIN late Middle English (also in the sense 'hinder, prevent'; earlier as *empeche*): from Old French *empecher* 'impede', from late Latin *impedicare* 'catch, entangle' (based on *pedica* 'a fetter', from *pes*, *ped-* 'foot'). Compare with IMPEDE.

impeccable /ɪmˈpɛkəb(ə)l/ ▸ adjective in accordance with the highest standards; faultless: *he had impeccable manners.* ■ Theology, rare not liable to sin.
– DERIVATIVES **impeccability** noun, **impeccably** adverb.
– ORIGIN mid 16th cent. (in the theological sense): from Latin *impeccabilis*, from *in-* 'not' + *peccare* 'to sin'.

impecunious /ˌɪmpɪˈkjuːnɪəs/ ▸ adjective having little or no money: *a titled but impecunious family.*
– DERIVATIVES **impecuniosity** noun, **impecuniousness** noun.
– ORIGIN late 16th cent.: from IN-¹ 'not' + obsolete *pecunious* 'having money, wealthy' (from Latin *pecuniosus*, from *pecunia* 'money').

impedance /ɪmˈpiːd(ə)ns/ ▸ noun the effective resistance of an electric circuit or component to alternating current, arising from the combined effects of ohmic resistance and reactance. See also ACOUSTIC IMPEDANCE. ● Impedance is usually expressed as a complex quantity $Z = R + jX$, where R is resistance, X is reactance, and j is the imaginary square root of −1.

impede /ɪmˈpiːd/ ▸ verb [with obj.] delay or prevent (someone or something) by obstructing them;

hinder: *the sap causes swelling which can impede breathing.*
– ORIGIN late 16th cent.: from Latin *impedire* 'shackle the feet of', based on *pes, ped-* 'foot'. Compare with **IMPEACH**.

impediment /ɪmˈpɛdɪm(ə)nt/ ▸ **noun 1** a hindrance or obstruction in doing something: *a serious **impediment to** scientific progress.*
2 (also **speech impediment**) a defect in a person's speech, such as a lisp or stammer.
– ORIGIN late Middle English: from Latin *impedimentum*, from *impedire* (see **IMPEDE**).

impedimenta /ɪmˌpɛdɪˈmɛntə/ ▸ **plural noun** equipment for an activity or expedition, especially when considered as bulky or an encumbrance.
– ORIGIN early 17th cent.: from Latin, plural of *impedimentum* 'impediment', from *impedire* (see **IMPEDE**).

impel /ɪmˈpɛl/ ▸ **verb** (**impels, impelling, impelled**) [with obj.] drive, force, or urge (someone) to do something: *financial difficulties **impelled him to** desperate measures* | [with obj. and infinitive] *a lack of equality impelled the oppressed to fight.* ■ drive forward; propel: *vital energies impel him in unforeseen directions.*
– ORIGIN late Middle English (in the sense 'propel'): from Latin *impellere*, from *in-* 'towards' + *pellere* 'to drive'.

impeller (also **impellor**) ▸ **noun** the rotating part of a centrifugal pump, compressor, or other machine designed to move a fluid by rotation. ■ a device turned by the flow of water past a ship's hull, used to measure speed or distance travelled.

impend /ɪmˈpɛnd/ ▸ **verb** [no obj.] (usu. as adj. **impending**) be about to happen: *my impending departure.* ■ archaic (of something bad) be looming: *the melancholy fate which **impended over** his nephew.*
– ORIGIN late 16th cent.: from Latin *impendere*, from *in-* 'towards, upon' + *pendere* 'hang'.

impenetrable /ɪmˈpɛnɪtrəb(ə)l/ ▸ **adjective** impossible to pass through or enter: *a dark, impenetrable forest.* ■ impossible to understand: *her expression was impenetrable* | *impenetrable jargon.* ■ Physics (of matter) incapable of occupying the same space as other matter at the same time.
– DERIVATIVES **impenetrability** noun, **impenetrably** adverb.
– ORIGIN late Middle English: via French from Latin *impenetrabilis*, from *in-* 'not' + *penetrabilis* 'able to be pierced', from the verb *penetrare* (see **PENETRATE**).

impenitent ▸ **adjective** not feeling shame or regret about one's actions or attitudes.
– DERIVATIVES **impenitence** noun, **impenitency** noun, **impenitently** adverb.
– ORIGIN late Middle English: from ecclesiastical Latin *impaenitent-* 'not repenting', from Latin *in-* 'not' + *paenitere* 'repent'.

imperative ▸ **adjective 1** of vital importance; crucial: *immediate action was imperative* | [with clause] *it is imperative that standards are maintained.*
2 giving an authoritative command; peremptory: *the bell pealed again, a final imperative call.* ■ Grammar denoting the mood of a verb that expresses a command or exhortation, as in *come here!*
▸ **noun 1** an essential or urgent thing: *free movement of labour was an economic imperative.* ■ a factor or influence making something necessary: *the biological imperatives which guide male and female behaviour.*
2 Grammar a verb or phrase in the imperative mood. ■ (**the imperative**) the imperative mood.
– DERIVATIVES **imperatival** /ɪmˌpɛrəˈtʌɪv(ə)l/ adjective, **imperatively** adverb, **imperativeness** noun.
– ORIGIN late Middle English (as a grammatical term): from late Latin *imperativus* (literally 'specially ordered', translating Greek *prostatikē enklisis* 'imperative mood'), from *imperare* 'to command', from *in-* 'towards' + *parare* 'make ready'.

imperator /ˌɪmpəˈrɑːtɔː/ ▸ **noun** Roman History commander (a title conferred under the Republic on a victorious general and under the Empire on the emperor).
– DERIVATIVES **imperatorial** /ˌɪmpɛrəˈtɔːrɪəl, ɪmˌpɛrə-/ adjective.
– ORIGIN Latin, from *imperare* 'to order, command'.

imperceptible ▸ **adjective** so slight, gradual, or subtle as not to be perceived: *his head moved in an almost imperceptible nod.*
– DERIVATIVES **imperceptibility** /-ˈbɪlɪti/ noun, **imperceptibly** adverb.
– ORIGIN late Middle English: from French, or from medieval Latin *imperceptibilis*, from *in-* 'not' + *perceptibilis*, from the verb *percipere* (see **PERCEIVE**).

imperceptive ▸ **adjective** lacking in perception or insight.

impercipient ▸ **adjective** failing to perceive something.
– DERIVATIVES **impercipience** noun.

imperfect ▸ **adjective 1** not perfect; faulty or incomplete: *an imperfect grasp of English.*
2 Grammar (of a tense) denoting a past action in progress but not completed at the time in question.
3 Music (of a cadence) ending on the dominant chord.
4 Law (of a gift, title, etc.) transferred without all the necessary conditions or requirements being met.
▸ **noun** (**the imperfect**) Grammar the imperfect tense.
– DERIVATIVES **imperfectly** adverb.
– ORIGIN Middle English *imparfit, imperfet*, from Old French *imparfait*, from Latin *imperfectus*, from *in-* 'not' + *perfectus* (see **PERFECT**). The spelling change in the 16th cent. was due to association with the Latin form.

imperfect competition ▸ **noun** [mass noun] the situation prevailing in a market in which elements of monopoly allow individual producers or consumers to exercise some control over market prices.

imperfection ▸ **noun** a fault, blemish, or undesirable feature: *the imperfections and injustices in our political system.* ■ [mass noun] the state of being faulty or incomplete: *he accepted me without question, in all my imperfection.*
– ORIGIN late Middle English: via Old French from late Latin *imperfectio(n-)*, from *imperfectus* (see **IMPERFECT**).

imperfective Grammar ▸ **adjective** relating to or denoting an aspect of verbs in Slavic languages that expresses action without reference to its completion. The opposite of **PERFECTIVE**.
▸ **noun** (**the imperfective**) the imperfective aspect.

imperfect rhyme ▸ **noun** a rhyme that only partly satisfies the usual criteria (e.g. *love* and *move*).

imperforate /ɪmˈpəːf(ə)rət/ ▸ **adjective** not perforated, in particular: ■ Anatomy & Zoology lacking the normal opening: *unicellular spores of these parasites have an imperforate wall.* ■ (of a postage stamp or a block or sheet of stamps) lacking perforations, especially as an error.

imperial ▸ **adjective 1** relating to an empire: *Britain's imperial past.* ■ relating to an emperor: *the imperial family.* ■ majestic or magnificent: *the bedroom is huge and very imperial.* ■ imperious or domineering: *the party and its autocratic—many would say imperial—ways.*
2 relating to or denoting the system of non-metric weights and measures (the ounce, pound, stone, inch, foot, yard, mile, acre, pint, gallon, etc.) formerly used for all measures in the UK, and still used for some.
3 chiefly historical (of a size of paper, in the UK) measuring 762 × 559 mm (30 × 22 inches).
▸ **noun** a small pointed beard growing below the lower lip (associated with Napoleon III of France).
– DERIVATIVES **imperially** adverb.
– ORIGIN late Middle English: via Old French from Latin *imperialis*, from *imperium* 'command, authority, empire'; related to *imperare* 'to command'. Compare with **EMPEROR**, **EMPIRE**, also with **IMPERIOUS**.

imperial gallon ▸ **noun** see **GALLON** (sense 1).

imperialism ▸ **noun** [mass noun] a policy of extending a country's power and influence through colonization, use of military force, or other means: *the struggle against imperialism* | figurative *French ministers protested at US cultural imperialism.* ■ chiefly historical rule by an emperor.
– DERIVATIVES **imperialistic** adjective, **imperialistically** adverb.

imperialist ▸ **adjective** relating to, supporting, or practising imperialism: *an imperialist regime.*
▸ **noun** a person who supports or practises imperialism.

imperialize (also **imperialise**) ▸ **verb** [with obj.] (usu. as adj. **imperialized**) subject to imperial rule or influence: *people of an imperialized culture.*

imperial pigeon ▸ **noun** a tropical fruit-eating pigeon that typically has a pale greyish head and breast and a dark back, occurring in Australasia, Indonesia, and southern Asia. ● Genus *Ducula*, family Columbidae.

imperial preference ▸ **noun** [mass noun] historical a system of tariff concessions granted by members of the British Empire or Commonwealth to one another.

imperil ▸ **verb** (**imperils, imperilling, imperilled**; US **imperiling, imperiled**) [with obj.] put at risk of being harmed, injured, or destroyed.
– ORIGIN late Middle English: from **PERIL**, probably on the pattern of *endanger*.

imperious /ɪmˈpɪərɪəs/ ▸ **adjective** arrogant and domineering: *his imperious demands.*
– DERIVATIVES **imperiously** adverb, **imperiousness** noun.
– ORIGIN mid 16th cent.: from Latin *imperiosus*, from *imperium* 'command, authority, empire'; related to *imperare* 'to command'. Compare with **IMPERIAL**.

imperishable ▸ **adjective** enduring forever: *imperishable truths.*
– DERIVATIVES **imperishability** /-ˈbɪlɪti/ noun, **imperishably** adverb.

imperium /ɪmˈpɪərɪəm/ ▸ **noun** [mass noun] absolute power.
– ORIGIN mid 17th cent.: from Latin, 'command, authority, empire'; related to *imperare* 'to command'.

impermanent ▸ **adjective** not permanent.
– DERIVATIVES **impermanence** noun, **impermanency** noun, **impermanently** adverb.

impermeable /ɪmˈpəːmɪəb(ə)l/ ▸ **adjective** not allowing fluid to pass through: *an impermeable membrane.*
– DERIVATIVES **impermeability** noun.
– ORIGIN late 17th cent.: from French *imperméable*, or from late Latin *impermeabilis*, from *in-* 'not' + *permeabilis* (see **PERMEABLE**).

impermissible ▸ **adjective** not permitted or allowed: *forcing a woman to continue a pregnancy that will almost certainly kill her is impermissible.*
– DERIVATIVES **impermissibility** noun.

I

impersonal ▸ **adjective 1** not influenced by, showing, or involving personal feelings: *the impersonal power of a government.* ■ (of a place or organization) featureless and anonymous: *an impersonal tower block.*
2 not existing as a person: *he gradually came to believe in an impersonal God.*
3 Grammar (of a verb) used only with a formal subject (in English usually *it*) and expressing an action not attributable to a definite subject (as in *it is snowing*).
– DERIVATIVES **impersonality** noun, **impersonally** adverb.
– ORIGIN late Middle English (in sense 3): from late Latin *impersonalis*, from Latin *in* 'not' + *personalis* (see **PERSONAL**).

impersonal pronoun ▸ **noun** the pronoun *it* when used without definite reference or antecedent, as in *it was snowing* and *it seems hard to believe.*

impersonate ▸ **verb** [with obj.] pretend to be (another person) for entertainment or fraud: *it's a very serious offence to impersonate a police officer.*
– DERIVATIVES **impersonator** noun.
– ORIGIN early 17th cent. (in the sense 'personify'): from **IN-²** 'into' + Latin *persona* 'person', on the pattern of *incorporate*.

impersonation ▸ **noun** an act of pretending to be another person for the purpose of entertainment or fraud: *he did an impersonation of Fred Astaire* | [mass noun] *he was tried on charges of impersonation and forgery.*

impertinence ▸ **noun** [mass noun] lack of respect; rudeness: *they gasped at the impertinence of the suggestion.*

impertinent ▸ **adjective 1** not showing proper respect; rude: *an impertinent question.*
2 formal not pertinent to a particular matter; irrelevant: *talk of 'rhetoric' and 'strategy' is **impertinent to** this process.*
– DERIVATIVES **impertinently** adverb.
– ORIGIN late Middle English (in sense 2): from Old French, or from late Latin *impertinent-* 'not having reference to', from Latin *in-* 'not' + *pertinere* 'pertain'.

imperturbable /ˌɪmpəˈtəːbəb(ə)l/ ▸ **adjective** unable to be upset or excited; calm: *an imperturbable tranquillity.*
– DERIVATIVES **imperturbability** noun **imperturbably** adverb.
– ORIGIN late Middle English: from late Latin *imperturbabilis*, from *in-* 'not' + *perturbare* (see **PERTURB**).

impervious /ɪmˈpəːvɪəs/ ▸ **adjective 1** not allowing fluid to pass through: *an impervious layer of basaltic clay.*
2 (**impervious to**) unable to be affected by: *he worked, apparently impervious to the heat.*
– DERIVATIVES **imperviously** adverb, **imperviousness** noun.
– ORIGIN mid 17th cent.: from Latin *impervius* (from *in-* 'not' + *pervius* 'pervious') + **-OUS**.

impetigo /ˌɪmpɪˈtʌɪgəʊ/ ▸ **noun** [mass noun] a contagious bacterial skin infection forming pustules and yellow

crusty sores. ● This disease is caused by the bacteria *Streptococcus pyogenes* or *S. aureus*.
– ORIGIN late Middle English: from Latin, from *impetere* 'to assail, attack'.

impetrate /ˈɪmpətreɪt/ ▶ **verb** [with obj.] archaic beseech or beg for: *a slight testimonial which I thought fit to impetrate from that worthy nobleman.*
– ORIGIN late 15th cent.: from Latin *impetrat-* 'brought to pass', from the verb *impetrare* (based on *patrare* 'bring to pass').

impetuous ▶ **adjective** acting or done quickly and without thought or care: *she might live to rue this impetuous decision.* ■ moving forcefully or rapidly: *an impetuous but controlled flow of water.*
– DERIVATIVES **impetuosity** noun, **impetuously** adverb, **impetuousness** noun.
– ORIGIN late Middle English: from Old French *impetueux*, from late Latin *impetuosus*, from *impetere* 'to attack'.

impetus ▶ **noun** [mass noun] the force or energy with which a body moves: *hit the booster coil before the flywheel loses all its impetus.* ■ something that makes a process or activity happen or happen more quickly: *the ending of the Cold War gave new* ***impetus to*** *idealism.*
– ORIGIN mid 17th cent.: from Latin, 'assault, force', from *impetere* 'assail', from *in-* 'towards' + *petere* 'seek'.

I

Imphal /ˈɪmfəl, ɪmˈfɑːl/ the capital of the state of Manipur in the far north-east of India, lying close to the border with Burma (Myanmar); pop. 236,400 (est. 2009). It was the scene of an important victory in 1944 by Anglo-Indian forces over the Japanese.

impi /ˈɪmpi/ ▶ **noun** (pl. **impis**) a body of Zulu warriors. ■ an armed band of Zulus involved in urban or rural conflict.
– ORIGIN Zulu, 'regiment, armed band'.

impiety /ɪmˈpʌɪɪti/ ▶ **noun** (pl. **impieties**) [mass noun] lack of piety or reverence: *he blamed the fall of the city on the impiety of the people.*
– ORIGIN Middle English: from Old French *impiete* or Latin *impietas*, from *impius* 'impious'.

impinge ▶ **verb** (**impinges, impinging, impinged**) [no obj.] have an effect, especially a negative one: *several factors* ***impinge on*** *market efficiency.* ■ advance over an area belonging to someone or something else; encroach: *the proposed fencing would* ***impinge on*** *a public bridleway.* ■ (**impinge on/upon**) Physics strike: *the gases impinge on the surface of the liquid.*
– DERIVATIVES **impingement** noun, **impinger** noun.
– ORIGIN mid 16th cent.: from Latin *impingere* 'drive something in or at', from *in-* 'into' + *pangere* 'fix, drive'. The word originally meant 'thrust at forcibly', then 'come into forcible contact'; hence 'encroach' (mid 18th cent.).

impious /ˈɪmpɪəs, ɪmˈpʌɪəs/ ▶ **adjective** showing a lack of respect for God or religion: *the emperor's impious attacks on the Church.* ■ (of a person or act) wicked: *impious villains.*
– DERIVATIVES **impiously** adverb, **impiousness** noun.
– ORIGIN mid 16th cent.: from Latin *impius* (from *in-* 'not' + *pius*: see PIOUS) + -OUS.

impish ▶ **adjective** inclined to do slightly naughty things for fun; mischievous: *he had an impish look about him.*
– DERIVATIVES **impishly** adverb, **impishness** noun.

implacable ▶ **adjective** unable to be appeased or placated: *he was an implacable enemy of Ted's.* ■ unable to be stopped; relentless: *the implacable advance of the enemy.*
– DERIVATIVES **implacability** noun, **implacably** adverb.
– ORIGIN late Middle English: from Latin *implacabilis*, from *in-* 'not' + *placabilis* (see PLACABLE).

implant ▶ **verb** /ɪmˈplɑːnt/ [usu. with obj.] insert or fix (tissue or an artificial object) in a person's body, especially by surgery: *electrodes had been* ***implanted in*** *his brain.* ■ (**implant someone/thing with**) provide someone or something with (something) by implantation. ■ [no obj.] (of a fertilized egg) become attached to the wall of the uterus. ■ establish (an idea) in a person's mind.
▶ **noun** /ˈɪmplɑːnt/ a thing implanted in something else, especially a piece of tissue, prosthetic device, or other object implanted in the body: *a silicone breast implant.*
– ORIGIN late Middle English: from late Latin *implantare* 'engraft', from Latin *in-* 'into' + *plantare* 'to plant'.

implantation ▶ **noun** [mass noun] the action of implanting or state of being implanted. ■ Zoology & Medicine (in a mammal) the attachment of the fertilized egg or blastocyst to the wall of the womb at the start of pregnancy. Also called NIDATION.
– ORIGIN late 16th cent.: from French, from *implanter* 'to implant'.

implausible ▶ **adjective** (of an argument or statement) not seeming reasonable or probable; failing to convince: *this is a blatantly implausible claim.*
– DERIVATIVES **implausibility** noun, **implausibly** adverb.

implead ▶ **verb** [with obj.] Law prosecute or take proceedings against.
– ORIGIN late Middle English *emplede*, from Old French *empleidier*, based on *plaid* (see PLEA).

implement ▶ **noun** /ˈɪmplɪm(ə)nt/ **1** a tool, utensil, or other piece of equipment that is used for a particular purpose: *garden implements.*
2 [mass noun] Scots Law performance of an obligation.
▶ **verb** /ˈɪmplɪmɛnt/ [with obj.] put (a decision, plan, agreement, etc.) into effect: *the scheme to implement student loans.*
– DERIVATIVES **implementer** noun.
– ORIGIN late Middle English (in the sense 'article of furniture, equipment, or dress'): partly from medieval Latin *implementa* (plural), partly from late Latin *implementum* 'filling up, fulfilment', both from Latin *implere* 'fill up' (later 'employ'), from *in-* 'in' + Latin *plere* 'fill'. The verb dates from the early 18th cent.

implementation /ɪmplɪmɛnˈteɪʃ(ə)n/ ▶ **noun** [mass noun] the process of putting a decision or plan into effect; execution: *she was responsible for the implementation of the plan.*

implicate ▶ **verb** /ˈɪmplɪkeɪt/ [with obj.] **1** show (someone) to be involved in a crime: *he* ***implicated*** *his government* ***in*** *the murders of three judges.* ■ (**be implicated in**) bear some of the responsibility for (an action or process, especially a criminal or harmful one): *viruses are known to be implicated in the development of certain cancers.*
2 [with clause] convey (a meaning) indirectly through what one says, rather than stating it explicitly: *by saying that coffee would keep her awake, Mary implicated that she didn't want any.*
▶ **noun** /ˈɪmplɪkət/ Logic a thing implied.
– DERIVATIVES **implicative** /ɪmˈplɪkətɪv/ adjective.
– ORIGIN late Middle English: from Latin *implicatus* 'folded in', past participle of *implicare* (see IMPLY). The original sense was 'entwine'; compare with EMPLOY and IMPLY. The earliest modern (sense 2 of the verb), dates from the early 17th cent.

implication ▶ **noun 1** the conclusion that can be drawn from something although it is not explicitly stated: *the implication is that no one person at the bank is responsible.* ■ a likely consequence of something.
2 [mass noun] the action or state of being involved in something: *our implication in the problems.*
– PHRASES **by implication** by what is implied rather than by explicit expression: *he criticized her and, by implication, her country.*
– DERIVATIVES **implicational** adjective.
– ORIGIN late Middle English (in the sense 'entwining, being entwined'): from Latin *implicatio(n-)*, from the verb *implicare* (see IMPLICATE).

implicature /ˈɪmplɪˌkətʃə, -ˌkeɪtʃə/ ▶ **noun** [mass noun] the action of implying a meaning beyond the literal sense of what is explicitly stated, for example saying *the frame is nice* and implying *I don't like the picture in it.* ■ [count noun] an implied meaning.

implicit /ɪmˈplɪsɪt/ ▶ **adjective 1** suggested though not directly expressed: *comments seen as implicit criticism of the policies.*
2 (**implicit in**) always to be found in; essentially connected with: *the values implicit in the school ethos.*
3 with no qualification or question; absolute: *an implicit faith in God.*
4 Mathematics (of a function) not expressed directly in terms of independent variables.
– DERIVATIVES **implicitness** noun.
– ORIGIN late 16th cent.: from French *implicite* or Latin *implicitus*, later form of *implicatus* 'entwined', past participle of *implicare* (see IMPLY).

implicitly /ɪmˈplɪsɪtli/ ▶ **adverb 1** in a way that is not directly expressed; tacitly: *she implicitly suggested that he was responsible for the error.*
2 without qualification: absolutely: *he trusted Sarah implicitly.*

implied ▶ **adjective** suggested but not directly expressed; implicit: *she was aware of his implied criticism.*
– DERIVATIVES **impliedly** adverb.

implode /ɪmˈpləʊd/ ▶ **verb** collapse or cause to collapse violently inwards: [no obj.] *both the windows had imploded* | [with obj.] *the plasma implodes the fuel.*
– DERIVATIVES **implosion** noun.
– ORIGIN late 19th cent.: from IN-² 'within' + Latin *plodere*, *plaudere* 'to clap', on the pattern of *explode*.

implore ▶ **verb** [reporting verb] beg someone earnestly or desperately to do something: [with obj. and infinitive] *he implored her to change her mind* | [with direct speech] *'Hold me,' Ellen implored* | (as adj. **imploring**) *an imploring look.* ■ [with obj.] archaic beg earnestly for: *I implore mercy.*
– DERIVATIVES **imploringly** adverb.
– ORIGIN early 16th cent.: from French *implorer* or Latin *implorare* 'invoke with tears'.

implosive ▶ **adjective 1** formed by implosion; tending to implode.
2 Phonetics denoting a type of consonant produced in the glottis with an ingressive air flow.

impluvium /ɪmˈpluːvɪəm/ ▶ **noun** (pl. **impluvia** /-vɪə/) the square basin in the centre of the atrium of an ancient Roman house, which received rainwater from an opening in the roof.
– ORIGIN Latin, from *impluere* 'rain into'.

imply ▶ **verb** (**implies, implying, implied**) [with obj.] indicate the truth or existence of (something) by suggestion rather than explicit reference: *salesmen who use jargon to imply superior knowledge* | [with clause] *the report implies that two million jobs might be lost.* ■ (of a fact or occurrence) suggest (something) as a logical consequence: *the forecasted traffic increase implied more roads and more air pollution.*
– ORIGIN late Middle English: from Old French *emplier*, from Latin *implicare*, from *in-* 'in' + *plicare* 'to fold'. The original sense was 'entwine'; in the 16th and 17th cents the word also meant 'employ'. Compare with EMPLOY and IMPLICATE.

> **USAGE** Imply and infer do not mean the same thing and should not be used interchangeably: see USAGE at INFER.

impolite ▶ **adjective** not having or showing good manners; rude: *it would have been impolite to refuse.*
– DERIVATIVES **impolitely** adverb, **impoliteness** noun.
– ORIGIN early 17th cent. (in the sense 'unpolished'): from Latin *impolitus*, from *in-* 'not' + *politus* (see POLITE).

impolitic /ɪmˈpɒlɪtɪk/ ▶ **adjective** failing to possess or display prudence; unwise: *it was impolitic to pay the slightest tribute to the enemy.*

imponderable ▶ **noun** a factor that is difficult or impossible to estimate or assess: *there are too many imponderables for an overall prediction.*
▶ **adjective 1** difficult or impossible to estimate or assess: *imponderable longer-term prospects.*
2 archaic very light.
– DERIVATIVES **imponderability** /-ˈbɪlɪti/ noun, **imponderably** adverb.

import ▶ **verb** /ɪmˈpɔːt, ˈɪm-/ [with obj.] **1** bring (goods or services) into a country from abroad for sale: *supermarkets may no longer import cheap jeans from Bulgaria* | (as adj. **imported**) *imported cigarettes.*
2 introduce (an idea) from a different place or context: *new beliefs were often imported by sailors.* ■ Computing transfer (data) into a file or document.
3 archaic indicate or signify: *having thus seen, what is imported in a Man's trusting his Heart.* ■ express or make known.
▶ **noun** /ˈɪmpɔːt/ **1** (usu. **imports**) a commodity, article, or service brought in from abroad for sale: *cheap imports from eastern Europe.* ■ (**imports**) sales of imported goods or services, or the revenue from such sales: *this surplus pushes up the yen, which ought to boost imports.* ■ [mass noun] the action or process of importing goods or services: *the import of live cattle from Canada.*
2 [in sing.] the implicit meaning or significance of something: *the import of her message is clear.* ■ [mass noun] great significance; importance: *pronouncements of world-shaking import.*
– DERIVATIVES **importable** adjective, **importation** noun, **importer** noun.
– ORIGIN late Middle English (in the sense 'signify'): from Latin *importare* 'bring in' (in medieval Latin 'imply, mean, be of consequence'), from *in-* 'in' + *portare* 'carry'.

importance ▶ **noun** [mass noun] the state or fact of being of great significance or value: *the importance of a good education* | *an issue of great importance.*

– PHRASES **full of one's own importance** having a very high opinion of oneself; self-important.
– ORIGIN early 16th cent.: from French, from medieval Latin *importantia*, from *important-* 'being of consequence', from the verb *importare* (see IMPORT).

important ▶ adjective of great significance or value: *important habitats for wildlife* | *it is important to avoid monosyllabic answers* | [sentence adverb] *the speech had passion and, more important, compassion.* ■ (of a person) having high rank or status. ■ (of an artist or artistic work) significantly original and influential.
– ORIGIN late Middle English: from medieval Latin *important-* 'being of consequence', from the verb *importare* (see IMPORT).

importantly ▶ adverb **1** [sentence adverb] used to emphasize a significant point: *a non-drinking, non-smoking, and, importantly, non-political sportsman.* **2** in a manner designed to draw attention to one's importance: *Kruger strutted forward importantly.*

importunate /ɪmˈpɔːtjʊnət/ ▶ adjective persistent, especially to the point of annoyance: *importunate creditors.*
– DERIVATIVES **importunately** adverb, **importunity** /ˌɪmpɔːˈtjuːnɪti/ noun (pl. **importunities**).
– ORIGIN early 16th cent.: from Latin *importunus* 'inconvenient, unseasonable', based on *Portunus*, the name of the god who protected harbours (from *portus* 'harbour'); compare with OPPORTUNE.

importune /ˌɪmpɔːˈtjuːn/ ▶ verb [with obj.] harass (someone) persistently for or to do something: *she importuned a waiter for profiteroles.* ■ (usu. as noun **importuning**) approach (someone) to offer one's services as a prostitute.
– ORIGIN mid 16th cent.: from French *importuner* or medieval Latin *importunari*, from Latin *importunus* 'inconvenient, unseasonable' (see IMPORTUNATE).

impose ▶ verb **1** [with obj.] force (an unwelcome decision or ruling) on someone: *the decision was theirs and was not* ***imposed on*** *them by others.* ■ put (a restriction) in place: *sanctions imposed on South Africa.* ■ require (a duty, charge, or penalty) to be undertaken or paid. ■ (**impose oneself on**) exert firm control over: *the director was unable to impose himself on the production.*
2 [no obj.] take advantage of someone by demanding their attention or commitment: *she realized that she had* ***imposed on*** *Mark's kindness.*
3 [with obj.] Printing arrange (pages of type) so as to be in the correct order after printing and folding.
– ORIGIN late 15th cent. (in the sense 'impute'): from French *imposer*, from Latin *imponere* 'inflict, deceive' (from *in-* 'in, upon' + *ponere* 'put'), but influenced by *impositus* 'inflicted' and Old French *poser* 'to place'.

imposing ▶ adjective grand and impressive in appearance: *an imposing 17th-century manor house.*
– DERIVATIVES **imposingly** adverb.

imposition ▶ noun **1** [mass noun] the action or process of imposing something or of being imposed: *the imposition of martial law.*
2 a thing that is imposed, in particular an unfair or unwelcome demand or burden: *I'd like to see you, if that wouldn't be too much of an imposition.* ■ a tax or duty.
3 [mass noun] Printing the imposing of pages of type. ■ [count noun] a particular arrangement of imposed pages: *samples of 16-page impositions.*
ORIGIN late Middle English: from Latin *impositio(n-)*, from the verb *imponere* (see IMPOSE).

impossibilism ▶ noun [mass noun] belief in ideas or policy, especially on social reform, that are held to be unrealizable or impractical.
– DERIVATIVES **impossibilist** noun.

impossibility ▶ noun (pl. **impossibilities**) [mass noun] the state or fact of being impossible: *the impossibility of finding reliable staff.* ■ [count noun] an impossible thing: *they believe that a world at peace is an impossibility.*
– ORIGIN late Middle English: from French *impossibilite* or Latin *impossibilitas*, from *impossibilis*, from *in-* 'not' + *possibilis* (see POSSIBLE).

impossible ▶ adjective not able to occur, exist, or be done: *a seemingly impossible task* | [with infinitive] *it was almost impossible to keep up with him.* ■ very difficult to deal with: *she was in an impossible situation.* ■ informal (of a person) very unreasonable: *'Impossible woman!' the doctor complained.*
– ORIGIN Middle English: from Old French, or from Latin *impossibilis*, from *in-* 'not' + *possibilis* (see POSSIBLE).

impossibly ▶ adverb **1** [as submodifier] so as to be impossible: *every task seemed impossibly difficult.* ■ [sentence adverb] used to describe an event or action that is so difficult or unlikely one would not expect it to be possible: *he held her and, impossibly, she fell asleep.*
2 [as submodifier] possessing the specified quality to an unbelievably high degree: *her impossibly blonde hair.*

impost[1] /ˈɪmpəʊst/ ▶ noun **1** a tax or similar compulsory payment.
2 Horse Racing the weight carried by a horse as a handicap.
– ORIGIN mid 16th cent.: from French (earlier form of *impôt*), from medieval Latin *impostus*, from Latin *impositus*, past participle of *imponere* (see IMPOSE).

impost[2] /ˈɪmpəʊst/ ▶ noun Architecture the top course of a pillar that supports an arch.
– ORIGIN late 15th cent.: from Italian *imposta*, feminine past participle of *imporre*, from Latin *imponere* (see IMPOSE).

impostor (also **imposter**) ▶ noun a person who pretends to be someone else in order to deceive others, especially for fraudulent gain.
– ORIGIN late 16th cent. (in early use spelled *imposture*, and sometimes confused with IMPOSTURE in meaning): from French *imposteur*, from late Latin *impostor*, contraction of *impositor*, from Latin *imponere* (see IMPOSE).

imposture ▶ noun an instance of pretending to be someone else in order to deceive others.
– ORIGIN mid 16th cent.: via French from late Latin *impostura*, from Latin *imposit-* 'imposed upon', from the verb *imponere* (see IMPOSE).

impotent /ˈɪmpət(ə)nt/ ▶ adjective **1** unable to take effective action; helpless or powerless: *he was seized with an impotent anger.*
2 (of a man) abnormally unable to achieve an erection or orgasm. ■ (of a male animal) unable to copulate.
– DERIVATIVES **impotence** noun, **impotency** noun, **impotently** adverb.
– ORIGIN late Middle English: via Old French from Latin *impotent-* 'powerless', from *in-* 'not' + *potent-* (see POTENT[1]).

impound ▶ verb [with obj.] **1** seize and take legal custody of (something, especially a vehicle, goods, or documents) because of an infringement of a law: *vehicles parked where they cause an obstruction will be impounded.*
2 shut up (domestic animals) in a pound or enclosure. ■ lock up (someone).
3 (of a dam) hold back (water).
– DERIVATIVES **impoundable** adjective, **impounder** noun, **impoundment** noun.

impoverish ▶ verb [with obj.] make (a person or area) poor: *the wars had impoverished him* | (as adj. **impoverished**) *impoverished villages.* ■ exhaust the strength or vitality of: *the soil was impoverished by annual burning* | (as adj. **impoverished**) *an impoverished and debased language.*
– DERIVATIVES **impoverishment** noun.
– ORIGIN late Middle English (formerly also as *empoverish*): from Old French *empoveriss-*, lengthened stem of *empoverir*, based on *povre* 'poor'.

impracticable ▶ adjective (of a course of action) impossible in practice to do or carry out: *it was impracticable to widen the road here.*
– DERIVATIVES **impracticability** noun, **impracticably** adverb.

> **USAGE** Although there is considerable overlap, **impracticable** and **impractical** are not used in exactly the same way. **Impracticable** means 'impossible to carry out' and is normally used of a specific procedure or course of action, as in *poor visibility made the task difficult, even impracticable*. **Impractical**, on the other hand, tends to be used in more general senses, often to mean simply 'unrealistic' or 'not sensible', as in *in windy weather an umbrella is impractical*.

impractical ▶ adjective **1** not adapted for use or action; not sensible or realistic: *impractical high heels* | *his impractical romanticism.* ■ (of a person) not skilled or interested in doing practical work.
2 chiefly N. Amer. impossible to do; impracticable.
– DERIVATIVES **impracticality** noun, **impractically** adverb.

imprecate /ˈɪmprɪkeɪt/ ▶ verb [with obj.] archaic utter (a curse) or invoke (evil) against someone or something.
– ORIGIN early 17th cent.: from Latin *imprecat-* 'invoked', from the verb *imprecari*.

imprecation ▶ noun formal a spoken curse: *I pushed my way through, screaming imprecations.*
– DERIVATIVES **imprecatory** adjective.
– ORIGIN late Middle English: from Latin *imprecatio(n-)*, from *imprecari* 'invoke (evil)', from *in-* 'towards' + *precari* 'pray'.

imprecise ▶ adjective lacking exactness and accuracy of expression or detail: *the witness could give only vague and imprecise descriptions.*
– DERIVATIVES **imprecisely** adverb, **impreciseness** noun, **imprecision** noun.

impregnable ▶ adjective (of a fortified position) unable to be captured or broken into: *a massive and impregnable fortress* | figurative *the seat I was offered appeared to be an impregnable Tory stronghold.* ■ unable to be defeated or overcome: *Liverpool used their good fortune to forge an impregnable lead.*
– DERIVATIVES **impregnability** noun, **impregnably** adverb.
– ORIGIN late Middle English: from Old French *imprenable*, from *in-* 'not' + *prendre* 'take' (from Latin *prehendere*). The current spelling arose in the 16th cent., perhaps influenced by Old French variants.

impregnate /ˈɪmprɛgneɪt/ ▶ verb [with obj.] **1** soak or saturate (something) with a substance: *wood which had been impregnated with preservative.* ■ fill with a feeling or quality: *an atmosphere impregnated with tension.*
2 make (a woman or female animal) pregnant. ■ Biology fertilize (an ovum).
– DERIVATIVES **impregnation** noun.
– ORIGIN early 17th cent. (in the sense 'fill'; earlier (Middle English) as *impregnation*): from late Latin *impregnat-* 'made pregnant', from the verb *impregnare*.

impresario /ˌɪmprɪˈsɑːrɪəʊ/ ▶ noun (pl. **impresarios**) a person who organizes and often finances concerts, plays, or operas. ■ chiefly historical the manager of a musical, theatrical, or operatic company.
– ORIGIN mid 18th cent.: from Italian, from *impresa* 'undertaking'.

imprescriptible /ˌɪmprɪˈskrɪptɪb(ə)l/ ▶ adjective Law (of rights) not subject to being taken away by prescription or by lapse of time.
– ORIGIN late 16th cent.: from medieval Latin *imprescriptibilis*, from *in-* 'not' + Latin *praescript-* (from *praescribere* 'prescribe').

impress[1] ▶ verb /ɪmˈprɛs/ [with obj.] **1** make (someone) feel admiration and respect: *their performance impressed the judges* | [no obj.] *he has to put on an act to impress.*
2 make a mark or design on (an object) using a stamp or seal: *the company should impress the cards with a stamp.* ■ apply (a mark) to something with pressure: *Andean cultures used seals to* ***impress*** *designs* ***on*** *pottery.*
3 (**impress something on**) fix an idea in the mind of (someone): *nobody impressed on me the need to save.*
4 apply (an electric current or potential) from an external source.
▶ noun /ˈɪmprɛs/ [in sing.] an act of making an impression or mark: *bluish marks made by the impress of his fingers.* ■ a mark made by a seal or stamp. ■ a person's characteristic quality: *his desire to put his own impress on the films he made.*
– DERIVATIVES **impressible** adjective.
– ORIGIN late Middle English (in the sense 'apply with pressure'): from Old French *empresser*, from *em-* 'in' + *presser* 'to press', influenced by Latin *imprimere* (see IMPRINT). Sense 1 of the verb dates from the mid 18th cent.

impress[2] ▶ verb [with obj.] historical force (someone) to serve in an army or navy: *a number of Poles, impressed into the German army.* ■ commandeer (goods or equipment) for public service.
– DERIVATIVES **impressment** noun.
– ORIGIN late 16th cent.: from IN-[2] 'into' + PRESS[2].

impression ▶ noun **1** an idea, feeling, or opinion about something or someone, especially one formed without conscious thought or on the basis of little evidence: *his first impressions of Manchester were very positive* | *I got the impression that he was sorely disappointed.* ■ an effect produced on someone: *her courtesy had made a good impression.* ■ [mass noun] a difference made by the action or presence of someone or something: *the floor was too dirty for the mop to make much impression.*
2 an imitation of a person or thing, done to entertain: *he did an impression of Shirley Bassey.*
3 a mark impressed on a surface: *the impression of his body on the leaves.* ■ Dentistry a negative copy of the teeth or mouth made by pressing them into a soft substance.

I

4 a graphic or pictorial representation of someone or something: *police issued an artist's impression of the attacker.*
5 the printing of a number of copies of a book, periodical, or picture for issue at one time. ■ [usu. with modifier] chiefly Brit. a particular printed version of a book, especially one reprinted from existing type, plates, or film with no or only minor alteration. ■ a print taken from an engraving.
6 an instance of a pop-up or other Web advertisement being seen on an Internet user's monitor.
– PHRASES **under the impression that** believing, mistakenly or on the basis of little evidence, that something is the case: *he was under the impression that they had become friends.*
– DERIVATIVES **impressional** adjective.
– ORIGIN late Middle English: via Old French from Latin *impressio(n-)*, from *impress-* 'pressed in', from the verb *imprimere* (see IMPRINT).

impressionable ▶ adjective easily influenced: *a girl of eighteen is highly impressionable.*
– DERIVATIVES **impressionability** noun **impressionably** adverb.
– ORIGIN mid 19th cent.: from French, from *impressionner*, from Latin *impressio(n-)*, from the verb *imprimere* 'press into' (see IMPRINT).

Impressionism ▶ noun [mass noun] a style or movement in painting originating in France in the 1860s, characterized by a concern with depicting the visual impression of the moment, especially in terms of the shifting effect of light and colour. ■ a literary or artistic style that seeks to capture a feeling or experience rather than to achieve accurate depiction. ■ Music a style of composition (associated especially with Debussy) in which clarity of structure and theme is subordinate to harmonic effects, characteristically using the whole-tone scale.

> The Impressionist painters repudiated both the precise academic style and the emotional concerns of romanticism, and their interest in objective representation, especially of landscape, was influenced by early photography. Impressionism met at first with scorn, but soon became highly influential. Its chief exponents included Monet, Renoir, Pissarro, Cézanne, and Degas.

– ORIGIN from French *impressionnisme*, from *impressionniste*, originally applied unfavourably with reference to Monet's painting *Impression: soleil levant* (1872).

Impressionist ▶ noun a painter, writer, or composer who is an exponent of Impressionism.
▶ adjective relating to Impressionism or its exponents.

impressionist ▶ noun an entertainer who impersonates famous people.

impressionistic ▶ adjective **1** based on subjective reactions presented unsystematically: *a personal and impressionistic view of the war.*
2 (**Impressionistic**) in the style of Impressionism.
– DERIVATIVES **impressionistically** adverb.

impressive ▶ adjective evoking admiration through size, quality, or skill; grand, imposing, or awesome: *an impressive view of the mountains | impressive achievements in science.*
– DERIVATIVES **impressively** adverb, **impressiveness** noun.

imprest ▶ noun a fund used by a business for small items of expenditure and restored to a fixed amount periodically. ■ a sum of money advanced to a person for a particular purpose.
– ORIGIN mid 16th cent.: from the earlier phrase *in prest* 'as a loan', influenced by Italian or medieval Latin *imprestare* 'lend'.

imprimatur /ˌɪmprɪˈmeɪtə, -ˈmɑːtə, -ˈmɑːtʊə/ ▶ noun an official licence issued by the Roman Catholic Church to print an ecclesiastical or religious book. ■ a person's authoritative approval: *the original LP enjoyed the imprimatur of the composer.*
– ORIGIN mid 17th cent.: from Latin, 'let it be printed', from the verb *imprimere* (see IMPRINT).

imprint ▶ verb **1** [with obj.] impress or stamp (a mark or outline) on a surface: *tyre marks were **imprinted** in the snow.* ■ make an impression or mark on: *clothes **imprinted with** the logos of sports teams.* ■ fix (an idea) firmly in someone's mind: *he'd always have this ghastly image **imprinted on** his mind.*
2 [no obj.] (**imprint on**) Zoology (of a young animal) come to recognize (another animal, person, or thing) as a parent or other object of habitual trust.
▶ noun **1** a mark or outline made by pressing something on to a softer substance: *he made imprints of the keys in bars of soap.* ■ a lasting effect: *years in the colonies had left their imprint.*
2 a printer's or publisher's name, address, and other details in a book or other publication. ■ a brand name under which books are published, typically the name of a former publishing house that is now part of a larger group.
– ORIGIN late Middle English (originally as *emprint*): from Old French *empreinter*, based on Latin *imprimere*, from *in-* 'into' + *premere* 'to press'.

imprison ▶ verb [with obj.] put or keep in prison or a place like a prison: *he was imprisoned three times for his activities.*
– ORIGIN Middle English *emprison*, from Old French *emprisoner*, from *em-* 'in' + *prison*.

imprisoned ▶ adjective kept in prison: captive: *an imprisoned dissident.*

imprisonment ▶ noun [mass noun] the state of being imprisoned; captivity: *he was sentenced to two months' imprisonment.*

impro ▶ noun (pl. **impros**) [mass noun] informal improvisation, especially as a theatrical technique.
– ORIGIN 1970s: abbreviation.

improbability ▶ noun (pl. **improbabilities**) [mass noun] the quality of being improbable; unlikelihood: *his belief in the improbability of war in Europe.* ■ an improbable event: [count noun] *the film is full of improbabilities.*

improbable ▶ adjective not likely to be true or to happen: *this account of events was seen by the jury as most improbable.* ■ unexpected and apparently inauthentic: *the characters have improbable names.*
– DERIVATIVES **improbably** adverb.
– ORIGIN late 16th cent.: from French, or from Latin *improbabilis* 'hard to prove', from *in-* 'not' + *probabilis* (see PROBABLE).

improbity /ɪmˈprəʊbɪti, -ˈprɒb-/ ▶ noun [mass noun] formal lack of honesty and moral integrity.
– ORIGIN late 16th cent.: from Latin *improbitas*, from *improbus* 'wicked', from *in-* 'not' + *probus* 'good'. Compare with PROBITY.

impromptu /ɪmˈprɒm(p)tjuː/ ▶ adjective & adverb done without being planned or rehearsed: [as adj.] *an impromptu press conference* | [as adv.] *he spoke impromptu.*
▶ noun (pl. **impromptus**) a short piece of instrumental music, especially a solo, that is reminiscent of an improvisation.
– ORIGIN mid 17th cent. (as an adverb): from French, from Latin *in promptu* 'in readiness', from *promptus* (see PROMPT).

improper ▶ adjective not in accordance with accepted standards, especially of morality or honesty: *the improper use of public funds | it was considered improper to leave one's house on Christmas Day.* ■ lacking in modesty or decency: *an improper suggestion.*
– DERIVATIVES **improperly** adverb.
– ORIGIN late Middle English: from French *impropre* or Latin *improprius*, from *in-* 'not' + *proprius* 'one's own, proper'.

improper fraction ▶ noun a fraction in which the numerator is greater than the denominator, such as $^5/_4$.

impropriate /ɪmˈprəʊprɪeɪt/ ▶ verb [with obj.] (usu. as adj. **impropriated**) grant (an ecclesiastical benefice) to a corporation or person as their property. ■ place (tithes or ecclesiastical property) in lay hands.
– DERIVATIVES **impropriation** noun.
– ORIGIN early 16th cent.: from Anglo-Latin *impropriat-* 'appropriated', from the verb *impropriare*, based on Latin *proprius* 'one's own, proper'.

impropriator ▶ noun a person to whom a benefice is granted as their property.

impropriety /ˌɪmprəˈprʌɪəti/ ▶ noun (pl. **improprieties**) [mass noun] failure to observe standards of honesty or modesty; improper behaviour or character: *she was scandalized at the impropriety of the question* | [count noun] *there are no demonstrable legal improprieties.*
– ORIGIN early 17th cent. (also in the sense 'inaccuracy'): from French *impropriété* or Latin *improprietas*, from *improprius* (see IMPROPER).

improv ▶ noun another term for IMPRO.

improve ▶ verb make or become better: [with obj.] *efforts to improve relations between the countries* | (as adj. **improved**) *an improved design* | [no obj.] *communications improved during the 18th century.* ■ [with obj.] develop or increase in mental capacity by education or experience: *I subscribed to two magazines to improve my mind.* ■ [no obj.] (**improve on/upon**) achieve or produce something better than: *they are trying to improve on the tired old style.*
– DERIVATIVES **improvability** noun, **improvable** adjective, **improver** noun.
– ORIGIN early 16th cent. (as *emprowe* or *improwe*): from Anglo-Norman French *emprower* (based on Old French *prou* 'profit', ultimately from Latin *prodest* 'is of advantage'); *-owe* was changed to *-ove* under the influence of PROVE. The original sense was 'make a profit, increase the value of'; subsequently 'make greater in amount or degree'.

improvement ▶ noun an example of improving or being improved: *an improvement in East–West relations.* ■ [mass noun] the action of improving or being improved: *there's still **room for improvement**.* ■ a thing that makes something better or is better than something else: *home improvements | it's an improvement on the last cake I made.*
– ORIGIN late Middle English *emprowement* (in the sense 'profitable management or use; profit'), from Anglo-Norman French, from *emprower* (see IMPROVE).

improvident ▶ adjective not having or showing foresight; spendthrift or thoughtless: *improvident and undisciplined behaviour.*
– DERIVATIVES **improvidence** noun, **improvidently** adverb.

improving ▶ adjective giving moral or intellectual benefit: *a large, improving picture hung opposite.*

improvisation ▶ noun [mass noun] the action of improvising. ■ [count noun] something that is improvised, in particular a piece of music, drama, etc. created spontaneously or without preparation: *free-form jazz improvisations.*
– DERIVATIVES **improvisational** adjective.

improvise ▶ verb [with obj.] create and perform (music, drama, or verse) spontaneously or without preparation: *he invited actors to improvise dialogue* | [no obj.] *he was improvising to a backing of guitar chords.* ■ produce or make (something) from whatever is available: *I improvised a costume for myself out of an old blue dress.*
– DERIVATIVES **improvisatory** adjective, **improviser** noun.
– ORIGIN early 19th cent. (earlier (late 18th cent.) as *improvisation*): from French *improviser* or its source, Italian *improvvisare*, from *improvviso* 'extempore', from Latin *improvisus* 'unforeseen', based on *provisus*, past participle of *providere* 'make preparation for'.

improvised ▶ adjective created and performed spontaneously or without preparation; impromptu: *an improvised short speech.* ■ done or made using whatever is available; makeshift: *we slept on improvised beds.*

imprudent ▶ adjective not showing care for the consequences of an action; rash: *it would be imprudent to leave her winter coat behind.*
– DERIVATIVES **imprudence** noun, **imprudently** adverb.
– ORIGIN late Middle English: from Latin *imprudent-* 'not foreseeing', from *in-* 'not' + *prudent-* (see PRUDENT).

impudence /ˈɪmpjʊd(ə)ns/ ▶ noun [mass noun] the quality of being impudent; impertinence: *his arrogance and impudence had offended many.*

impudent /ˈɪmpjʊd(ə)nt/ ▶ adjective not showing due respect for another person; impertinent: *he could have strangled this impudent upstart.*
– DERIVATIVES **impudently** adverb.
– ORIGIN late Middle English (in the sense 'immodest, indelicate'): from Latin *impudent-*, from *in-* 'not' + *pudent-* 'ashamed, modest' (from *pudere* 'be ashamed').

impudicity /ˌɪmpjʊˈdɪsɪti/ ▶ noun [mass noun] formal lack of modesty.
– ORIGIN early 16th cent.: from French *impudicité*, from Latin *impudicitia*, from *impudicus* 'shameless', from *in-* 'not' + *pudere* 'be ashamed'.

impugn /ɪmˈpjuːn/ ▶ verb [with obj.] dispute the truth, validity, or honesty of (a statement or motive); call into question: *the father does not impugn her capacity as a good mother.*
– DERIVATIVES **impugnable** adjective.
– ORIGIN late Middle English (also in the sense 'assault, attack physically'): from Latin *impugnare* 'assail', from *in-* 'towards' + *pugnare* 'fight'.

impuissant /ɪmˈpjuːɪs(ə)nt, -ˈpwiː-, -ˈpwɪs-/ ▶ adjective literary unable to take effective action; powerless.
– DERIVATIVES **impuissance** noun.
– ORIGIN early 17th cent.: French, from *im-* 'not' + *puissant* 'powerful'.

impulse ▸ noun **1** a sudden strong and unreflective urge or desire to act: *I had an almost irresistible impulse to giggle.* ■ [mass noun] the tendency to act impulsively: *he was a man of impulse, not premeditation.*
2 something that causes something to happen or happen more quickly; an impetus: *an added impulse to this process of renewal.*
3 a pulse of electrical energy; a brief current: *nerve impulses | electrical impulses.*
4 Physics a force acting briefly on a body and producing a finite change of momentum. ■ a change of momentum produced by an impulse, equivalent to the average value of the force multiplied by the time during which it acts.
– PHRASES **on impulse** (or **on an impulse**) suddenly and without forethought; impulsively.
– ORIGIN early 17th cent. (as a verb in the sense 'give an impulse to'): the verb from Latin *impuls-* 'driven on', the noun from *impulsus* 'impulsion', both from the verb *impellere* (see **IMPEL**).

impulse buying ▸ noun [mass noun] the buying of goods without planning to do so in advance, as a result of a sudden whim or impulse.
– DERIVATIVES **impulse buy** noun.

impulsion ▸ noun a strong urge to do something: *the impulsion of the singers to govern the pace.* ■ [mass noun] the motive or influence behind an action or process: *attitudes changed under the impulsion of humanitarian considerations.*
– ORIGIN late Middle English (in the sense 'the action or an instance of impelling'): via Old French from Latin *impulsio(n-)*, from the verb *impellere* (see **IMPEL**).

impulsive ▸ adjective **1** acting or done without forethought: *they'd married as impulsive teenagers | he regretted his impulsive offer.*
2 Physics acting as an impulse.
– DERIVATIVES **impulsively** adverb, **impulsiveness** noun, **impulsivity** noun.
– ORIGIN late Middle English (in the sense 'tending to impel'): from French *impulsif, -ive* or late Latin *impulsivus*, from Latin *impuls-* 'driven onwards' (see **IMPULSE**). Sense 1 dates from the mid 18th cent.

impunity /ɪmˈpjuːnɪti/ ▸ noun [mass noun] exemption from punishment or freedom from the injurious consequences of an action: *the impunity enjoyed by military officers implicated in civilian killings | protestors burned flags on the streets* ***with impunity.***
– ORIGIN mid 16th cent.: from Latin *impunitas*, from *impunis* 'unpunished', from *in-* 'not' + *poena* 'penalty' or *punire* 'punish'.

impure ▸ adjective **1** mixed with foreign matter; adulterated: *an impure form of heroin.* ■ dirty. ■ (of a colour) mixed with another colour.
2 morally wrong, especially in sexual matters: *citizens suspected of harbouring impure thoughts.* ■ defiled or contaminated according to ritual prescriptions: *the perception of woman as impure.*
– DERIVATIVES **impurely** adverb.
– ORIGIN late Middle English (in the sense 'dirty, containing offensive matter'): from Latin *impurus*, from *in-* 'not' + *purus* 'pure'.

impurity ▸ noun (pl. **impurities**) [mass noun] the state or quality of being impure. ■ [count noun] a constituent which impairs the purity of something: *aluminium and lead are impurities frequently found in tap water.* ■ [count noun] Electronics a trace element deliberately added to a semiconductor; a dopant.
– ORIGIN late Middle English: from French *impurite* or Latin *impuritas*, from *impurus* (see **IMPURE**).

impute /ɪmˈpjuːt/ ▸ verb [with obj.] **1** represent (something, especially something undesirable) as being done or possessed by someone; attribute: *the crimes* ***imputed to*** *Richard.* ■ Theology ascribe (righteousness, guilt, etc.) to someone by virtue of a similar quality in another: *Christ's righteousness has been imputed to us.*
2 Finance assign (a value) to something by inference from the value of the products or processes to which it contributes: (as adj. **imputed**) *recovering the initial outlay plus imputed interest.*
– DERIVATIVES **imputable** adjective, **imputation** noun.
– ORIGIN late Middle English: from Old French *imputer*, from Latin *imputare* 'enter in the account', from *in-* 'in, towards' + *putare* 'reckon'.

Imroz /ɪmˈrɒz/ Turkish name for **IMBROS**.

imshi /ˈɪmʃiː/ ▸ exclamation military slang, chiefly Austral. go away; be off.
– ORIGIN from colloquial Arabic *'mšī* 'go!', imperative of *mišī*.

I.Mun.E. ▸ abbreviation (in the UK) Institution of Municipal Engineers.

IN ▸ abbreviation Indiana (in official postal use).

In ▸ symbol the chemical element indium.

in ▸ preposition **1** expressing the situation of something that is or appears to be enclosed or surrounded by something else: *I'm living in London | dressed in their Sunday best | she saw the bus in the rear-view mirror.* ■ expressing motion with the result that something ends up within or surrounded by something else: *don't put coal in the bath | he got in his car and drove off.*
2 expressing a period of time during which an event happens or a situation remains the case: *they met in 1885 | at one o'clock in the morning | I hadn't seen him in years.*
3 expressing the length of time before a future event is expected to happen: *I'll see you in fifteen minutes.*
4 (often followed by a noun without a determiner) expressing a state or condition: *to be in love | I've got to put my affairs in order | a woman in her thirties.* ■ indicating the quality or aspect with respect to which a judgement is made: *no discernible difference in quality.*
5 expressing inclusion or involvement: *I read it in a book | acting in a film.*
6 indicating someone's occupation or profession: *she works in publishing.*
7 indicating the language or medium used: *say it in French | put it in writing.* ■ indicating the key in which a piece of music is written: *Mozart's Piano Concerto in E flat.*
8 [with verbal noun] as an integral part of (an activity): *in planning public expenditure it is better to be prudent.*
9 expressing a value as a proportion of (a whole): *a local income tax running at six pence in the pound.*
▸ adverb **1** expressing movement with the result that someone or something becomes enclosed or surrounded by something else: *come in | presently the admiral breezed in.*
2 expressing the situation of being enclosed or surrounded by something: *we were locked in.*
3 expressing arrival: *the train got in very late.*
4 (of the tide) rising or at its highest level.
▸ adjective **1** [predic.] present at one's home or office: *we knocked at the door but there was no one in.*
2 informal fashionable: *pastels and light colours are in this year | the in thing to do.*
3 [predic.] (of the ball in tennis and similar games) landing within the designated playing area.
4 [predic.] Cricket batting: *which side is in?*
– PHRASES **be in for** have good reason to expect (something, typically something unpleasant): *she's in for a shock.* ■ (**be in for it**) have good reason to expect trouble or retribution. **have it in for someone** informal have hostile feelings towards someone. **in all** see **ALL**. **in and out of** being a frequent visitor to (a house) or frequent inmate of (an institution). **in on** privy to (a secret). **in so far as** see **FAR**. **in that** for the reason that: *I was fortunate in that I had friends.* **in with** informal on friendly terms with: *the Krays were in with a couple of MPs.* **the ins and outs** informal all the details.
– ORIGIN Old English *in* (preposition), *inn, inne* (adverb), of Germanic origin; related to Dutch and German *in* (preposition), German *ein* (adverb), from an Indo-European root shared by Latin *in* and Greek *en*.

in. ▸ abbreviation inch(es).

in-[1] ▸ prefix **1** (added to adjectives) not: *infertile | inapt.*
2 (added to nouns) without; a lack of: *inappreciation.*
– ORIGIN from Latin.

in-[2] ▸ prefix in; into; towards; within: *induce | influx | inborn.*
– ORIGIN representing **IN** or the Latin preposition *in*.

-in[1] ▸ suffix Chemistry forming names of organic compounds, pharmaceutical products, proteins, etc.: *insulin | penicillin | dioxin.*
– ORIGIN alteration of **-INE**[4].

-in[2] ▸ combining form denoting a gathering of people having a common purpose, typically as a form of protest: *sit-in | sleep-in | love-in.*

-ina ▸ suffix **1** denoting feminine names and titles: *tsarina.*
2 denoting names of musical instruments: *concertina.*
3 denoting names of plant and animal groups: *globigerina.*
– ORIGIN from Italian, Spanish, or Latin.

inability ▸ noun [with infinitive] the state of being unable to do something: *his inability to accept new ideas.*

in absentia /ˌɪn abˈsɛntɪə/ ▸ adverb while not present at the event being referred to: *two foreign suspects will be tried in absentia.*
– ORIGIN Latin, 'in absence'.

inaccessible ▸ adjective **1** unable to be reached: *a remote and inaccessible cave | the city centre is* ***inaccessible to*** *traffic in most places.* ■ unable to be used: *such costs would make litigation inaccessible to private individuals.*
2 (of language or an artistic work) difficult to understand or appreciate.
3 (of a person) not open to advances or influence; unapproachable.
– DERIVATIVES **inaccessibility** noun, **inaccessibly** adverb.
– ORIGIN late Middle English: from French, or from late Latin *inaccessibilis*, from *in-* 'not' + *accessibilis* (see **ACCESSIBLE**).

inaccuracy ▸ noun (pl. **inaccuracies**) [mass noun] the quality or state of not being accurate: *a weapon of notorious inaccuracy.* ■ [count noun] an aspect of something that is not accurate: *reference works full of inaccuracies.*

inaccurate ▸ adjective not accurate: *false or inaccurate descriptions of goods | a forecast that proved wildly inaccurate.*
– DERIVATIVES **inaccurately** adverb.

inaction ▸ noun [mass noun] lack of action where some is expected or appropriate.

inactivate ▸ verb [with obj.] make inactive or inoperative: *household bleach does not inactivate the virus |* (as adj. **inactivated**) *inactivated polio vaccine.*
– DERIVATIVES **inactivation** noun, **inactivator** noun.

inactive ▸ adjective not engaging in or involving any or much physical activity: *an inactive lifestyle.* ■ not working; inoperative: *the device remains inactive while the computer is started up.* ■ not engaging in political or other activity: *an inactive Russian spy.* ■ having no chemical or biological effect: *the inactive X chromosome.* ■ (of a disease) not exhibiting symptoms.
– DERIVATIVES **inactively** adverb.

inactivity ▸ noun [mass noun] the state of being inactive; idleness: *don't suddenly take up violent exercise after years of inactivity.* ■ reluctance to take action; apathy: *people are frustrated with government inactivity.*

inadequacy ▸ noun (pl. **inadequacies**) [mass noun] the state or quality of being inadequate; lack of the quantity or quality required: *the inadequacy of available resources |* [count noun] *the inadequacies of the present system.* ■ inability to deal with a situation or with life: *her feelings of personal inadequacy.*

inadequate ▸ adjective lacking the quality or quantity required; insufficient for a purpose: *these labels prove to be wholly inadequate | inadequate funding.* ■ (of a person) unable to deal with a situation or with life: *a sad, solitary, inadequate man | I felt like a fraud,* ***inadequate to*** *the task.*
– DERIVATIVES **inadequately** adverb.

inadmissible ▸ adjective **1** (especially of evidence in court) not accepted as valid.
2 not to be allowed or tolerated: *an inadmissible interference in the affairs of the Church.*
– DERIVATIVES **inadmissibility** noun, **inadmissibly** adverb.

inadvertent ▸ adjective not resulting from or achieved through deliberate planning: *he was pardoned for inadvertent manslaughter.*
– DERIVATIVES **inadvertence** noun, **inadvertency** noun.
– ORIGIN mid 17th cent. (earlier (late Middle English) as *inadvertence*): from **IN-**[1] 'not' + Latin *advertent-* 'turning the mind to' (from the verb *advertere*).

inadvertently ▸ adverb without intention; accidentally: *his name had been inadvertently omitted from the list.*

inadvisable ▸ adjective likely to have unfortunate consequences; unwise: [with infinitive] *it would be inadvisable to involve more than one architect.*
– DERIVATIVES **inadvisability** noun.

inalienable ▸ adjective not subject to being taken away from or given away by the possessor: *the shareholders have the inalienable right to dismiss directors.*
– DERIVATIVES **inalienability** noun, **inalienably** adverb.

inalterable ▸ adjective unable to be changed.
– DERIVATIVES **inalterability** noun, **inalterably** adverb.

inamorata /ɪˌnaməˈrɑːtə/ ▶ **noun** a person's female lover.
– ORIGIN mid 17th cent.: Italian, literally 'enamoured', feminine of *inamorato* (see INAMORATO).

inamorato /ɪˌnaməˈrɑːtəʊ/ ▶ **noun** (pl. **inamoratos**) a person's male lover.
– ORIGIN late 16th cent.: Italian, literally 'enamoured', past participle of the verb *inamorare* (now *innamorare*), based on Latin *amor* 'love'.

in-and-out ▶ **adjective** informal **1** involving rapid inward and outward movement: *smuggling drugs was a quick in-and-out operation.*
2 inconsistent and unreliable: *this horse is a notoriously in-and-out performer.*

inane ▶ **adjective** lacking sense or meaning; silly: *don't badger people with inane questions.*
– DERIVATIVES **inanely** adverb, **inaneness** noun, **inanity** noun (pl. **inanities**).
– ORIGIN mid 16th cent.: from Latin *inanis* 'empty, vain'.

inanga /ˈiːnaŋə/ ▶ **noun** NZ a small edible Australasian fish which spends its first year in the sea, thereafter living mainly in fresh water. The young are caught as whitebait. Also called JOLLYTAIL. ● *Galaxias maculatus*, family Galaxiidae.
– ORIGIN Maori.

inanimate ▶ **adjective** not alive: *inanimate objects like stones.* ■ showing no sign of life; lifeless.
– DERIVATIVES **inanimately** adverb.
– ORIGIN late Middle English: from late Latin *inanimatus* 'lifeless', from *in-* 'not' + *animatus* (see ANIMATE).

inanition /ˌɪnəˈnɪʃ(ə)n/ ▶ **noun** [mass noun] formal exhaustion caused by lack of nourishment. ■ lack of mental or spiritual vigour and enthusiasm: *she was thinking that old age bred inanition.*
– ORIGIN late Middle English: from late Latin *inanitio(n-)*, from Latin *inanire* 'make empty', from *inanis* 'empty, vain'.

inapparent ▶ **adjective** Medicine causing no noticeable signs or symptoms: *many worm infections are clinically inapparent.*

inappetence ▶ **noun** [mass noun] chiefly Veterinary Medicine lack of appetite.

inapplicable ▶ **adjective** not relevant or appropriate: *the details are likely to be **inapplicable to** other designs.*
– DERIVATIVES **inapplicability** noun, **inapplicably** adverb.

inapposite /ɪnˈapəzɪt/ ▶ **adjective** out of place; inappropriate: *the Shakespearean allusions are inapposite.*
– DERIVATIVES **inappositely** adverb, **inappositeness** noun.

inappreciable ▶ **adjective 1** too small or insignificant to be valued or perceived: *they are few in number and those numbers are inappreciable.*
2 archaic too valuable to be properly estimated.
– DERIVATIVES **inappreciably** adverb.

inappreciative ▶ **adjective** another term for UNAPPRECIATIVE.
– DERIVATIVES **inappreciation** noun.

inappropriate ▶ **adjective** not suitable or proper in the circumstances: *there are penalties for inappropriate behaviour | it would be inappropriate for me to comment.*
– DERIVATIVES **inappropriately** adverb, **inappropriateness** noun.

inapt ▶ **adjective** not suitable or appropriate in the circumstances: *a more inapt name I cannot imagine.*
– DERIVATIVES **inaptitude** noun, **inaptly** adverb.

inarch ▶ **verb** [with obj.] Horticulture graft (a plant) by connecting a growing branch without separating it from its parent stock.
– ORIGIN early 17th cent. (formerly also as *enarch*): from EN-[1], IN-[2] 'into' + the verb ARCH[1].

inarguable ▶ **adjective** another term for UNARGUABLE.
– DERIVATIVES **inarguably** adverb.

inarticulate /ˌɪnɑːˈtɪkjʊlət/ ▶ **adjective 1** unable to express one's ideas or feelings clearly or easily: *an inarticulate man of action.* ■ not clearly expressed or pronounced: *Fay gave a faint, inarticulate cry.* ■ not expressed in words: *mention of her mother filled her with inarticulate irritation.*
2 without joints or articulations. ■ Zoology denoting a brachiopod in which the valves of the shell have no hinge and are held together by muscles.
– DERIVATIVES **inarticulacy** noun, **inarticulately** adverb, **inarticulateness** noun.
– ORIGIN early 17th cent.: from IN-[1] 'not' + the adjective ARTICULATE; the sense 'not clearly pronounced' corresponds to that of late Latin *inarticulatus*.

inartistic ▶ **adjective** having or showing a lack of skill or talent in art.
– DERIVATIVES **inartistically** adverb.

inasmuch ▶ **adverb** (in phrase **inasmuch as**) to the extent that; in so far as: *these provisions apply only inasmuch as trade between Member States is affected.* ■ considering that; since: *a most unusual astronomer inasmuch as he was deaf mute.*
– ORIGIN Middle English: originally as *in as much*, translating Old French *en tant (que)* 'in so much (as)'.

inattention ▶ **noun** [mass noun] lack of attention; distraction: *a moment of inattention which could have cost lives.* ■ failure to attend to one's responsibilities; negligence: *his **inattention to** duty.*

inattentive ▶ **adjective** not paying attention to something: *a particularly dull and inattentive pupil.* ■ failing to attend to the comfort or wishes of others: *I was disappointed by the food and the inattentive service.*
– DERIVATIVES **inattentively** adverb, **inattentiveness** noun.

inaudible ▶ **adjective** unable to be heard: *inaudible pulses of high-frequency sound.*
– DERIVATIVES **inaudibility** noun, **inaudibly** adverb.
– ORIGIN late Middle English: from late Latin *inaudibilis*, from *in-* 'not' + *audibilis* (see AUDIBLE).

inaugural /ɪˈnɔːgjʊr(ə)l/ ▶ **adjective** [attrib.] marking the beginning of an institution, activity, or period of office: *his inaugural concert as Music Director.*
▶ **noun** an inaugural speech, especially one made by an incoming US president.
– ORIGIN late 17th cent.: from French (from *inaugurer* 'inaugurate', from Latin *inaugurare*) + -AL.

inaugurate /ɪˈnɔːgjʊreɪt/ ▶ **verb** [with obj.] begin or introduce (a system, policy, or period): *he inaugurated a new policy of trade and exploration.* ■ admit (someone) formally to office. ■ mark the beginning or first public use of (an organization or project) with a special event or ceremony: *the museum was inaugurated on September 12.*
– DERIVATIVES **inaugurator** noun, **inauguratory** adjective.
– ORIGIN late 16th cent.: from Latin *inaugurat-* 'interpreted as omens (from the flight of birds)', based on *augurare* 'to augur'.

inauguration /ɪˌnɔːgjʊˈreɪʃ(ə)n/ ▶ **noun** [mass noun] the beginning or introduction of a system, policy, or period: *the inauguration of an independent prosecution service.* ■ the formal admission of someone to office: *the President's inauguration.* ■ [count noun] a ceremony to mark the beginning or introduction of something: *the inauguration of the Modern Art Museum.*

inauspicious ▶ **adjective** not conducive to success; unpromising: *following this inauspicious start the British, outnumbered, withdrew.* ■ unlucky.
– DERIVATIVES **inauspiciously** adverb, **inauspiciousness** noun.

inauthentic ▶ **adjective** not in fact what it is said to be: *the Holy Shroud of Turin is thought to have been proved inauthentic by radiocarbon dating.* ■ not genuinely belonging to a style or period: *baroque harpsichord pieces played on the decidedly inauthentic modern Steinway.* ■ lacking sincerity: *people close to death could not waste time being inauthentic.*
– DERIVATIVES **inauthentically** adverb, **inauthenticity** noun.

in-between informal ▶ **adjective** situated somewhere between two extremes or categories; intermediate: *I am not unconscious, but in some in-between state.*
▶ **noun** an intermediate thing.
– DERIVATIVES **in-betweener** noun.

inboard ▶ **adverb & adjective** within a ship, aircraft, or vehicle: [as adv.] *the spray was coming inboard now* | [as adj.] *the uncovered inboard engine.* ■ towards the centre of a ship, aircraft, or vehicle: [as adv.] *move the clew inboard along the boom.*
▶ **noun** a boat's engine housed inside its hull. ■ a boat with an inboard engine.

inborn ▶ **adjective** existing from birth: *an inborn defect in the formation of collagen.* ■ natural to a person or animal: *people think doctors have inborn compassion.*

inbound ▶ **adjective & adverb** travelling towards a particular place, especially when returning to the original point of departure: [as adj.] *inbound traffic* | [as adv.] *we have three enemy planes inbound on bearing two ninety.*
▶ **verb** [with obj.] Basketball throw (the ball) from out of bounds, putting it into play.

inbounds ▶ **adjective** Basketball denoting or relating to a throw which puts the ball into play from out of bounds: *an inbounds pass.*

inbox ▶ **noun** N. Amer. an in tray. ■ a folder in which emails received by an individual are held.

inbreathe ▶ **verb** [with obj.] literary breathe in or absorb: *he felt himself inbreathing power from on high.*

inbred ▶ **adjective 1** produced by inbreeding: *inbred dogs will be more likely to have some genetic maladies.*
2 existing from birth.

inbreed ▶ **verb** (past and past participle **inbred**) [no obj.] (often as noun **inbreeding**) breed from closely related people or animals, especially over many generations.

inbuilt ▶ **adjective** existing as an original or essential part of something or someone: *the body's inbuilt ability to heal itself.*

in-bye (also **in-by**) ▶ **adjective** Scottish & N. English (of farmland or farming) situated or carried out near to the farm buildings.

Inc. ▶ **abbreviation** N. Amer. Incorporated: *Northeast Airlines Inc.*

Inca ▶ **noun 1** a member of a South American Indian people living in the central Andes before the Spanish conquest.

> The Incas arrived in the Cuzco valley in Peru c. AD 1200. When the Spanish invaded in the early 1530s, the Inca empire covered most of modern Ecuador and Peru, much of Bolivia, and parts of Argentina and Chile. Inca technology and architecture were highly developed despite a lack of wheeled vehicles and of writing. Their descendants, speaking Quechua, still make up about half of Peru's population.

2 the supreme ruler of the Incas.
– DERIVATIVES **Incaic** /ɪŋˈkeɪɪk/ adjective, **Incan** adjective.
– ORIGIN the name in Quechua, literally 'lord, royal person'.

inca ▶ **noun** a South American hummingbird having mainly blackish or bronze-coloured plumage with one or two white breast patches. ● Genus *Coeligena*, family Trochilidae: four species.

incalculable ▶ **adjective 1** too great to be calculated or estimated: *an archive of incalculable value.*
2 not able to be calculated or estimated: *the odds against such an event are incalculable.* ■ (of a person or their character) unpredictable.
– DERIVATIVES **incalculability** noun, **incalculably** adverb.

in camera ▶ **adverb** see CAMERA[2].

incandesce /ˌɪnkanˈdɛs/ ▶ **verb** [no obj.] glow with heat: *the lights of the town lay incandescing across the prairie.*
– ORIGIN late 19th cent.: back-formation from INCANDESCENT.

incandescent ▶ **adjective 1** emitting light as a result of being heated: *plumes of incandescent liquid rock.* ■ (of an electric light) containing a filament which glows white-hot when heated by a current passed through it.
2 full of strong emotion; passionate: *she felt an incandescent love for life.* ■ extremely angry: *I am incandescent at the way I've been treated.*
– DERIVATIVES **incandescence** noun, **incandescently** adverb.
– ORIGIN late 18th cent.: from French, from Latin *incandescent-* 'glowing', from the verb *incandescere*, from *in-* (expressing intensive force) + *candescere* 'become white' (from *candidus* 'white').

incant /ɪnˈkant/ ▶ **verb** [with obj.] chant or intone: *priests were incanting psalms round her body.*
– ORIGIN mid 16th cent. (in the sense 'use enchantment on'): from Latin *incantare* 'to chant, charm', from *in-* (expressing intensive force) + *cantare* 'sing'. The current sense dates from the mid 20th cent.

incantation ▶ **noun** a series of words said as a magic spell or charm: *an incantation to raise the dead.* ■ [mass noun] the use of words as a magic spell: *there was no magic in such incantation.*
– DERIVATIVES **incantatory** adjective.
– ORIGIN late Middle English: via Old French from late Latin *incantatio(n-)*, from *incantare* 'chant, bewitch' (see INCANT).

incapable ▶ **adjective 1** (**incapable of**) unable to do or achieve (something): *Wilson blushed and was*

incapable of speech. ■ not allowing the possibility of (a particular action): *with the battery removed the car was incapable of being driven.* ■ (of a person) too caring or moral to do (something): *a man incapable of any kind of prejudice.*
2 unable to behave rationally or manage one's affairs: *the pilot may become incapable from the lack of oxygen.*
– DERIVATIVES **incapability** noun, **incapably** adverb.
– ORIGIN late 16th cent.: from French, or from late Latin *incapabilis*, from *in-* 'not' + *capabilis* (see CAPABLE).

incapacitant ▶ noun a substance capable of temporarily incapacitating a person without wounding or killing them.
– ORIGIN 1960s: from INCAPACITATE + -ANT.

incapacitate /ˌɪnkəˈpasɪteɪt/ ▶ verb [with obj.] prevent from functioning in a normal way: *he was incapacitated by a heart attack.* ■ Law deprive (someone) of their legal capacity.
– DERIVATIVES **incapacitation** noun.
– ORIGIN mid 17th cent.: from INCAPACITY + -ATE[3].

incapacitated /ˌɪnkəˈpasɪteɪtɪd/ ▶ adjective deprived of strength or power; debilitated: *Richard was temporarily incapacitated.*

incapacity ▶ noun (pl. **incapacities**) [mass noun]
1 physical or mental inability to do something or to manage one's affairs: *they can be sacked only for incapacity or misbehaviour.*
2 legal disqualification.
– ORIGIN early 17th cent.: from French *incapacité* or late Latin *incapacitas*, from *in-* (expressing negation) + *capacitas* (see CAPACITY).

incapacity benefit ▶ noun [mass noun] (in the UK) a state benefit paid to people who are unable to work due to illness or disability for a period of more than twenty-eight consecutive weeks.

in-car ▶ adjective [attrib.] occurring, situated, or carried in a car: *an in-car navigation system.*

incarcerate /ɪnˈkɑːsəreɪt/ ▶ verb [with obj.] imprison or confine: *many are incarcerated for property offences.*
– DERIVATIVES **incarcerator** noun.
– ORIGIN mid 16th cent. (earlier (late Middle English) as *incarceration*): from medieval Latin *incarcerat-* 'imprisoned', from the verb *incarcerare*, from *in-* 'into' + Latin *carcer* 'prison'.

incarceration /ɪnˌkɑːsəˈreɪʃ(ə)n/ ▶ noun [mass noun] the state of being confined in prison; imprisonment: *the public would not be served by her incarceration.*

incarnadine /ɪnˈkɑːnədʌɪn/ literary ▶ noun [mass noun] a bright crimson or pinkish-red colour.
▶ verb [with obj.] colour (something) a bright crimson or pinkish-red.
– ORIGIN late 16th cent.: from French *incarnadin(e)*, from Italian *incarnadino*, variant of *incarnatino* 'flesh colour', based on Latin *incarnare* (see INCARNATE).

incarnate ▶ adjective /ɪnˈkɑːnət/ [often postpositive] (especially of a deity or spirit) embodied in human form: *God incarnate.* ■ [postpositive] represented in the most fundamental or extreme form: *here is capitalism incarnate.*
▶ verb /ˈɪnkɑːneɪt, -ˈkɑːneɪt/ [with obj.] embody or represent (a deity or spirit) in human form: *the idea that God incarnates himself in man.* ■ put (a concept or quality) into concrete form: *a desire to make things which will incarnate their personality.* ■ (of a person) be the living embodiment of (a quality): *the man who incarnates the pain of the entire community.*
– ORIGIN late Middle English: from ecclesiastical Latin *incarnat-* 'made flesh', from the verb *incarnare*, from *in-* 'into' + *caro, carn-* 'flesh'.

incarnation ▶ noun 1 a person who embodies in the flesh a deity, spirit, or quality: *Rama was Vishnu's incarnation on earth | Beethoven was an incarnation of artistic genius.* ■ **(the Incarnation)** (in Christian theology) the embodiment of God the Son in human flesh as Jesus Christ.
2 (with reference to reincarnation) each of a series of earthly lifetimes: *in my next incarnation, I'd like to be the Minister of Fun.* ■ the form taken by a person or thing during an incarnation.
– ORIGIN Middle English (as a term in Christian theology): via Old French from ecclesiastical Latin *incarnatio(n-)*, from the verb *incarnare* (see INCARNATE).

incase ▶ verb variant spelling of ENCASE.

incautious ▶ adjective (of a person or an action) heedless of potential problems or risks: *he blames incautious borrowing during the boom.*
– DERIVATIVES **incaution** noun, **incautiously** adverb, **incautiousness** noun.
– ORIGIN mid 17th cent.: on the pattern of Latin *incautus*.

incendiary /ɪnˈsɛndɪəri/ ▶ adjective 1 (of a device or attack) designed to cause fires: *incendiary bombs.*
2 tending to stir up conflict: *incendiary rhetoric.* ■ very exciting: *an incendiary live performer.*
▶ noun (pl. **incendiaries**) 1 an incendiary bomb or device.
2 a person who starts fires. ■ a person who stirs up conflict.
– DERIVATIVES **incendiarism** noun.
– ORIGIN late Middle English: from Latin *incendiarius*, from *incendium* 'conflagration', from *incendere* 'set fire to'.

incense[1] /ˈɪnsɛns/ ▶ noun [mass noun] a gum, spice, or other substance that is burned for the sweet smell it produces. ■ the smoke or perfume of incense.
▶ verb [with obj.] perfume with incense or a similar fragrance: *the aroma of cannabis incensed the air.*
– DERIVATIVES **incensation** noun.
– ORIGIN Middle English (originally as *encense*): from Old French *encens* (noun), *encenser* (verb), from ecclesiastical Latin *incensum* 'something burnt, incense', neuter past participle of *incendere* 'set fire to', from *in-* 'in' + the base of *candere* 'to glow'.

incense[2] /ɪnˈsɛns/ ▶ verb [with obj.] make very angry: *locals are incensed at the suggestion.*
– ORIGIN late Middle English (in the general sense 'inflame or excite someone with a strong feeling'): from Old French *incenser*, from Latin *incendere* 'set fire to'.

incense cedar ▶ noun a columnar North American cedar with scale-like leaves that smell of turpentine when crushed, grown as an ornamental in Europe.
● *Calocedrus decurrens*, family Cupressaceae.

incensed /ɪnˈsɛnst/ ▶ adjective very angry; enraged: *Leonora glared back at him, incensed.*

incensory /ˈɪnsɛns(ə)ri/ ▶ noun (pl. **incensories**) another term for CENSER.
– ORIGIN early 17th cent. (denoting a burnt offering, or an altar for it): from medieval Latin *incensorium*, from *incensum* (see INCENSE[1]).

incentive ▶ noun a thing that motivates or encourages someone to do something: *give farmers an incentive to improve their land.* ■ a payment or concession to stimulate greater output or investment: *tax incentives for investing in depressed areas.*
– ORIGIN late Middle English: from Latin *incentivum* 'something that sets the tune or incites', from *incantare* 'to chant or charm'.

incentivize (also **incentivise**) ▶ verb [with obj.] provide (someone) with an incentive for doing something: *this is likely to incentivize management to find savings.*

incentre (US **incenter**) ▶ noun Geometry the centre of the incircle of a triangle or other figure.

incept /ɪnˈsɛpt/ ▶ verb [no obj.] Brit. historical graduate from a university with an academic degree.
– ORIGIN mid 16th cent. (in the sense 'undertake, begin'): from Latin *incept-* 'begun', from the verb *incipere*. The current sense dates from the mid 19th cent.

inception ▶ noun [in sing.] the establishment or starting point of an institution or activity: *she has been on the board since its inception two years ago.*
– ORIGIN late Middle English: from Latin *inceptio(n-)*, from *incipere* 'begin'.

inceptisol /ɪnˈsɛptɪsɒl/ ▶ noun Soil Science a soil of an order comprising freely draining soils in which the formation of distinct horizons is not far advanced, such as brown earth.
– ORIGIN 1960s: from Latin *inceptum* 'beginning' (from the verb *incipere*) + -SOL.

inceptive ▶ adjective relating to or marking the beginning of something; initial: *the inceptive period of the program.* ■ Grammar (of a verb) expressing the beginning of an action.
▶ noun Grammar an inceptive verb.
– ORIGIN early 17th cent. (as a noun): from late Latin *inceptivus*, from *incept-* 'begun', from the verb *incipere*.

incertitude ▶ noun [mass noun] a state of uncertainty or hesitation: *some schools broke down under the stresses of policy incertitude.*
– ORIGIN late Middle English: from Old French, or from late Latin *incertitudo*, from *in-* (expressing negation) + *certitudo* (see CERTITUDE).

incessant ▶ adjective (of something regarded as unpleasant) continuing without pause or interruption: *the incessant beat of the music.*
– DERIVATIVES **incessancy** noun, **incessantness** noun.
– ORIGIN late Middle English: via Old French from late Latin *incessant-*, from *in-* 'not' + Latin *cessant-* 'ceasing' (from the verb *cessare*).

incessantly ▶ adverb without interruption; constantly: *she talked about him incessantly.*

incest ▶ noun [mass noun] sexual relations between people classed as being too closely related to marry each other. ■ the crime of having sexual intercourse with a parent, child, sibling, or grandchild.
– ORIGIN Middle English: from Latin *incestus*, *incestum* 'unchastity, incest', from *in-* 'not' + *castus* 'chaste'.

incestuous /ɪnˈsɛstjʊəs/ ▶ adjective 1 involving or guilty of incest: *the child of an incestuous relationship.*
2 (of human relations) excessively close and resistant to outside influence: *the incestuous nature of literary journalism.*
– DERIVATIVES **incestuously** adverb, **incestuousness** noun.
– ORIGIN early 16th cent.: from late Latin *incestuosus*, from Latin *incestus* (see INCEST).

inch[1] ▶ noun 1 a unit of linear measure equal to one twelfth of a foot (2.54 cm): *the toy train is four inches long | eighteen inches of thread.* ■ **(inches)** informal a person's height or waist measurement: *my only reservation is the goalkeeper's lack of inches.* ■ [often with negative] a very small amount or distance: *I had no intention of budging an inch.*
2 a unit used to express other quantities, in particular: ■ (as a unit of rainfall) a quantity that would cover a horizontal surface to a depth of one inch, equivalent to 253.7 cubic metres per hectare. ■ (also **inch of mercury**) (as a unit of atmospheric pressure) an amount that would support a column of mercury one-inch high in a barometer (equal to 33.86 millibars, 29.5 inches being equal to one bar). ■ (as a unit of map scale) so many inches representing one mile on the ground: [in combination] *one-inch maps of the east Midland counties.*
▶ verb [no obj., with adverbial of direction] move along slowly and carefully: *he inched away as I approached |* figurative *Spain's conservatives are inching ahead.* ■ [with obj. and adverbial of direction] cause (something) to move slowly and carefully: *he inched the car forward.*
– PHRASES **by inches** only just: *the shot missed her by inches.* **every inch 1** the whole surface, distance, or area: *between them they know every inch of the country.* **2** entirely; very much so: *he's every inch the gentleman.* **give someone an inch and he (or she) will take a mile** proverb once concessions have been made to someone they will demand a great deal. **inch by inch** gradually. **within an inch of** very close to: *her mouth was within an inch of his chin.* **(to) within an inch of one's life** almost to the point of death: *he was beaten within an inch of his life.*
– ORIGIN late Old English *ynce*, from Latin *uncia* 'twelfth part', from *unus* 'one' (probably denoting a unit). Compare with OUNCE[1].

inch[2] ▶ noun [in place names] chiefly Scottish a small island or a small area of high land: *Inchkeith.*
– ORIGIN Middle English: from Scottish Gaelic *innis*.

-in-chief ▶ combining form supreme: *commander-in-chief.*

inchmeal ▶ adverb by inches; little by little.
– ORIGIN mid 16th cent.: from INCH[1] + *-meal* from Old English *mǣlum*, in the sense 'measure, quantity taken at one time'.

inchoate /ɪnˈkəʊeɪt, ˈɪnk-, -ət/ ▶ adjective 1 just begun and so not fully formed or developed; rudimentary: *a still inchoate democracy.* ■ confused or incoherent: *inchoate proletarian protest.*
2 Law (of an offence, such as incitement or conspiracy) anticipating or preparatory to a further criminal act.
– DERIVATIVES **inchoately** adverb, **inchoateness** noun.
– ORIGIN mid 16th cent.: from Latin *inchoatus*, past participle of *inchoare*, variant of *incohare* 'begin'.

inchoative /ɪnˈkəʊətɪv/ ▶ adjective Grammar denoting an aspect of a verb expressing the beginning of an action, typically one occurring of its own accord. Compare with ERGATIVE.
▶ noun an inchoative verb.

Inchon /ɪnˈtʃɒn/ a port on the west coast of South Korea, on the Yellow Sea near Seoul; pop. 2,741,200 (est. 2008).

inchworm ▶ noun North American term for LOOPER.

incidence ▶ noun 1 the occurrence, rate, or frequency of a disease, crime, or other undesirable thing: *an increased incidence of cancer.* ■ the way in which the

I

burden of a tax falls upon the population: *the entire incidence falls on the workers.*
2 [mass noun] Physics the intersection of a line, or something moving in a straight line, such as a beam of light, with a surface.
– ORIGIN late Middle English (denoting a casual or subordinate event): from Old French, or from medieval Latin *incidentia*, from Latin *incidere* 'fall upon, happen to' (see INCIDENT). Sense 1 dates from the early 19th cent.

incident ▶ **noun 1** an instance of something happening; an event or occurrence: *several amusing incidents | there was not one incident of teasing from the 90 pupils.* ■ a violent event, such as a fracas or assault: *one person was stabbed in the incident.* ■ a hostile clash between forces of rival countries. ■ [mass noun] the occurrence of dangerous or exciting things: *my period in Egypt wasn't without incident.*
2 Law a privilege, burden, or right attaching to an office, estate, or other holding.
▶ **adjective 1** (**incident to**) liable to happen because of; resulting from: *the changes incident to economic development.* ■ Law attaching to.
2 (especially of light or other radiation) falling on or striking something: *when an ion beam is **incident on** a surface.* ■ Physics relating to incidence: *the incident angle.*
– ORIGIN late Middle English: via Old French from Latin *incident-* 'falling upon, happening to', from the verb *incidere*, from *in-* 'upon' + *cadere* 'to fall'.

I

incidental ▶ **adjective 1** happening as a minor accompaniment to something else: *for the fieldworker who deals with real problems, paperwork is incidental | incidental expenses.* ■ occurring by chance in connection with something else: *the incidental catch of dolphins in the pursuit of tuna.*
2 (**incidental to**) happening as a result of (an activity): *the ordinary risks incidental to a fireman's job.*
▶ **noun** (usu. **incidentals**) an incidental expense, event, etc.: *an allowance to cover meals, taxis, and other incidentals.*
– ORIGIN early 17th cent.: originally from medieval Latin *incidentalis*, from Latin *incident-* 'falling upon, happening to' (from the verb *incidere*).

incidentally ▶ **adverb 1** [sentence adverb] used to add a further comment or a remark unconnected to the current subject; by the way: *incidentally, it was many months before the whole truth was discovered.*
2 in an incidental manner; as a chance occurrence: *the infection was discovered only incidentally at post-mortem examination.*

incidental music ▶ **noun** [mass noun] music used in a film or play as a background to create or enhance a particular atmosphere.

incident room ▶ **noun** a centre set up by the police to coordinate operations connected with a particular crime, accident, or other incident.

incinerate /ɪnˈsɪnəreɪt/ ▶ **verb** [with obj.] destroy (something, especially waste material) by burning: *waste packaging is to be incinerated rather than buried in landfills.*
– DERIVATIVES **incineration** noun.
– ORIGIN late 15th cent.: from medieval Latin *incinerat-* 'burnt to ashes', from the verb *incinerare*, from *in-* 'into, towards' + *cinis, ciner-* 'ashes'.

incinerator ▶ **noun** an apparatus for burning waste material, especially industrial waste, at high temperatures until it is reduced to ash.

incipient /ɪnˈsɪpɪənt/ ▶ **adjective** beginning to happen or develop: *he could feel incipient anger building up | an incipient black eye.* ■ (of a person) developing into a specified type or role: *we seemed more like friends than incipient lovers.*
– DERIVATIVES **incipience** noun, **incipiency** noun, **incipiently** adverb.
– ORIGIN late 16th cent. (as a noun denoting a beginner): from Latin *incipient-* 'undertaking, beginning', from the verb *incipere*, from *in-* 'into, towards' + *capere* 'take'.

incipit /ˈɪnsɪpɪt/ ▶ **noun** the opening of a manuscript, early printed book, or chanted liturgical text. Compare with EXPLICIT.
– ORIGIN Latin, literally '(here) begins'.

incircle ▶ **noun** Geometry a circle inscribed in a triangle or other figure so as to touch (but not cross) each side.

incise ▶ **verb** [with obj.] mark or decorate (an object or surface) with a cut or cuts: *a button incised with a skull.* ■ cut (a mark or decoration) into a surface: *figures incised on upright stones.* ■ cut (skin or flesh) with a surgical instrument.
– ORIGIN mid 16th cent.: from French *inciser*, from Latin *incis-* 'cut into, engraved', from the verb *incidere*, from *in-* 'into' + *caedere* 'to cut'.

incised meander ▶ **noun** Geology a river meander which has been cut abnormally deeply into the landscape because uplift of the land has led to renewed downward erosion by the river.

incision ▶ **noun** a surgical cut made in skin or flesh: *an abdominal incision.* ■ a mark or decoration cut into a surface: *a block of marble delicately decorated with incisions.* ■ [mass noun] the action or process of cutting into something: *the method is associated with less blood loss during incision.*
– DERIVATIVES **incisional** adjective.
– ORIGIN late Middle English: from late Latin *incisio(n-)*, from Latin *incidere* 'cut into' (see INCISE).

incisive ▶ **adjective 1** (of a person or mental process) intelligently analytical and clear-thinking: *she was an incisive critic.* ■ (of an account) accurate and sharply focused: *the songs offer incisive pictures of American ways.*
2 (of an action) quick and direct: *the most incisive move of a tight match.*
– DERIVATIVES **incisively** adverb, **incisiveness** noun.
– ORIGIN late Middle English (in the sense 'cutting, penetrating'): from medieval Latin *incisivus*, from Latin *incidere* 'cut into' (see INCISE).

incisor (also **incisor tooth**) ▶ **noun** a narrow-edged tooth at the front of the mouth, adapted for cutting. In humans there are four incisors in each jaw.
– ORIGIN late 17th cent.: from medieval Latin, literally 'cutter', from Latin *incis-* (see INCISE).

incisure /ɪnˈsɪʒə/ (also **incisura** /ˌɪnsɪˈʒʊərə/) ▶ **noun** (pl. **incisures** or **incisurae** /-riː/) Anatomy a deep indentation or notch in an edge or surface.

incite ▶ **verb** [with obj.] encourage or stir up (violent or unlawful behaviour): *they conspired to incite riots.* ■ urge or persuade (someone) to act in a violent or unlawful way: *he **incited** loyal subjects **to** rebellion.*
– DERIVATIVES **inciter** noun.
– ORIGIN late 15th cent. (earlier (late Middle English) as *incitation*): from French *inciter*, from Latin *incitare*, from *in-* 'towards' + *citare* 'rouse'.

inciteful ▶ **adjective** (of words, actions, etc.) offering incitement.

incitement ▶ **noun** [mass noun] [often with infinitive] the action of provoking unlawful behaviour or urging someone to behave unlawfully: *this amounted to an incitement to commit murder.*

incivility ▶ **noun** (pl. **incivilities**) [mass noun] rude or unsociable speech or behaviour: *absenteeism and incivility were not tolerated.* ■ [count noun] (often **incivilities**) an impolite or offensive comment.
– ORIGIN mid 16th cent.: from French *incivilité* or late Latin *incivilitas*, from Latin *incivilis*, from *in-* 'not' + *civilis* 'of a citizen' (see CIVIL).

incl. (also **inc.**) ▶ **abbreviation** including.

inclement /ɪnˈklɛm(ə)nt/ ▶ **adjective** (of the weather) unpleasantly cold or wet.
– DERIVATIVES **inclemency** noun (pl. **inclemencies**).
– ORIGIN early 17th cent.: from French *inclément* or Latin *inclement-*, from *in-* 'not' + *clement-* 'clement'.

inclination ▶ **noun** [mass noun] **1** a person's natural tendency or urge to act or feel in a particular way; a disposition: *John was a scientist by training and inclination | Fanny showed little inclination to talk about anything serious |* [count noun] *he was free to follow his inclinations.* ■ (**inclination for/to/towards**) an interest in or liking for (something): *my inborn inclination for things with moving parts.*
2 the fact or degree of sloping: *changes in inclination of the line on the graph.* ■ the angle at which a straight line or plane is inclined to another. ■ the dip of a magnetic needle. ■ Astronomy the angle between the orbital plane of a planet, comet, etc. and the ecliptic, or between the orbital plane of a satellite and the equatorial plane of its primary.
3 an act of inclining the body or head: *the questioner's inclination of his head.*
– ORIGIN late Middle English: from Latin *inclinatio(n-)*, from *inclinare* 'bend towards' (see INCLINE).

incline ▶ **verb 1** (usu. **be inclined to/towards/to do something**) be favourably disposed towards or willing to do something: *he was inclined to accept the offer | Lucy was inclined to a belief in original sin.* ■ [with infinitive] (especially as a polite formula) tend to have a specified opinion: *I'm inclined to agree with you.* ■ [with obj.] make (someone) disposed to do something: *his prejudice inclines him to overlook obvious facts.* ■ [no obj.] feel favourably disposed towards someone or something: *I **incline to** the view that this conclusion is untenable.*
2 (usu. **be inclined to/to do something**) have a tendency to do something: *she's inclined to gossip with complete strangers.* ■ [with adverbial] have a specified disposition or talent: *some people are very mathematically inclined.*
3 [no obj., usu. with adverbial of direction] lean or turn away from a given plane or direction, especially the vertical or horizontal: *the bunker doors incline outwards |* (as adj. **inclined**) *an inclined ramp.* ■ [with obj.] bend (one's head) forwards and downwards.
▶ **noun** an inclined surface or plane; a slope, especially on a road or railway: *the road climbs a long incline through a forest.*
– DERIVATIVES **inclinable** adjective, **incliner** noun.
– ORIGIN Middle English (originally in the sense 'bend (the head or body) towards something'; formerly also as *encline*): from Old French *encliner*, from Latin *inclinare*, from *in-* 'towards' + *clinare* 'to bend'.

inclined plane ▶ **noun** a plane inclined at an angle to the horizontal. ■ a sloping ramp up which heavy loads can be raised by ropes or chains.

inclinometer /ˌɪnklɪˈnɒmɪtə/ ▶ **noun** a device for measuring the angle of inclination of something, especially from the horizontal.
– ORIGIN mid 19th cent.: from Latin *inclinare* 'to incline' + -METER.

inclose ▶ **verb** variant spelling of ENCLOSE.

inclosure ▶ **noun** variant spelling of ENCLOSURE.

include ▶ **verb** [with obj.] **1** comprise or contain as part of a whole: *the price includes dinner, bed, and breakfast | other changes included the abolition of the death penalty.*
2 make part of a whole or set: *we have included some hints for beginners in this section.* ■ allow (someone) to share in an activity or privilege: *there were doubts as to whether she was included in the invitation.* ■ (**include someone out**) informal specifically exclude someone from a group or activity.
– ORIGIN late Middle English (also in the sense 'shut in'): from Latin *includere*, from *in-* 'into' + *claudere* 'to shut'.

> **USAGE** **Include** has a broader meaning than **comprise**. In the sentence *the accommodation **comprises** 2 bedrooms, bathroom, kitchen, and living room*, the word **comprise** implies that there is no accommodation other than that listed. **Include** can be used in this way too, but it is also used in a non-restrictive way, implying that there may be other things not specifically mentioned that are part of the same category, as in *the price **includes** a special welcome pack.*

included ▶ **adjective** [postpositive] contained as part of a whole being considered: *all of Europe (Britain included) | service tax included.*

including ▶ **preposition** containing as part of the whole being considered: *languages including Welsh and Gaelic | weapons were recovered from the house, including a shotgun.*

inclusion ▶ **noun 1** [mass noun] the action or state of including or of being included within a group or structure: *they have been selected for inclusion in the scheme.* ■ [count noun] a person or thing that is included within a whole: *the exhibition features such inclusions as the study of the little girl.*
2 chiefly Geology a body or particle of distinct composition embedded in a rock or other material.
– DERIVATIVES **inclusionary** adjective.
– ORIGIN early 17th cent.: from Latin *inclusio(n-)*, from *includere* 'shut in'.

inclusive ▶ **adjective** including all the services or items normally expected or required: *menus stating fully inclusive prices.* ■ (**inclusive of**) containing (a specified element) as part of a whole: *all prices are inclusive of VAT.* ■ [postpositive] including the limits specified: *between the ages of 55 and 59 inclusive.* ■ not excluding any section of society or any party involved in something: *only an inclusive peace process will end the conflict.* ■ (of language) deliberately avoiding usages that could be seen as excluding a particular social group, for example avoiding the use of masculine pronouns to cover both men and women.
– DERIVATIVES **inclusively** adverb, **inclusiveness** noun, **inclusivity** noun.
– ORIGIN late 16th cent.: from medieval Latin *inclusivus*, from Latin *includere* (see INCLUDE).

inclusive fitness ▶ **noun** [mass noun] Genetics the ability of an individual organism to pass on its genes to the next generation, taking into account the shared genes passed on by the organism's close relatives.

inclusivism ▶ **noun** [mass noun] the practice of trying to incorporate diverse or unreconciled elements into a single system.
– DERIVATIVES **inclusivist** noun & adjective.

incog ▶ adjective, adverb, & noun informal, dated short for INCOGNITO.

incognito /ˌɪnkɒɡˈniːtəʊ, ɪnˈkɒɡnɪtəʊ/ ▶ **adjective & adverb** (of a person) having one's true identity concealed: [as adj.] *in order to observe you have to be incognito* | [as adv.] *he is now operating incognito.*
▶ **noun** (pl. **incognitos**) an assumed or false identity.
– ORIGIN mid 17th cent.: from Italian, literally 'unknown', from Latin *incognitus*, from *in-* 'not' + *cognitus* (past participle of *cognoscere* 'know').

incognizant (also **incognisant**) ▶ **adjective** formal lacking knowledge or awareness: *the government appears **incognizant of** the growing threat to our agricultural industry.*
– DERIVATIVES **incognizance** noun.

incoherent ▶ **adjective 1** (of spoken or written language) expressed in an incomprehensible or confusing way; unclear: *he screamed some incoherent threat.* ■ (of a person) unable to speak intelligibly: *he was incoherent with sentiment.*
2 not logical or internally consistent: *the film is ideologically incoherent.*
3 Physics (of waves) having no definite or stable phase relationship.
– DERIVATIVES **incoherence** noun, **incoherency** noun (pl. **incoherencies**), **incoherently** adverb.

incohesion ▶ **noun** [mass noun] lack of social cohesion: *anxiety about national decline and incohesion.*

incombustible ▶ **adjective** (especially of a building material or component) consisting or made of material that does not burn if exposed to fire.
– DERIVATIVES **incombustibility** noun.
– ORIGIN late 15th cent.: from medieval Latin *incombustibilis*, from *in-* 'not' + *combustibilis* (see COMBUSTIBLE).

income ▶ **noun** money received, especially on a regular basis, for work or through investments: *he has a nice home and an adequate income* | [mass noun] *figures showed an overall increase in income this year.*
– ORIGIN Middle English (in the sense 'entrance, arrival', now only Scots): in early use from Old Norse *innkoma*, later from IN + COME. The current sense dates from the late 16th cent.

income group ▶ **noun** a section of the population classified according to their level of income.

incomer ▶ **noun** Brit. a person who has come to live in an area in which they have not grown up, especially in a close-knit rural community.

-incomer /ˈɪnkʌmə/ ▶ **combining form** Brit. denoting a person with a specified level of income: *middle-incomer.*

income support ▶ **noun** [mass noun] (in the UK and Canada) payment made by the state in particular circumstances to people who are on a low income.

income tax ▶ **noun** [mass noun] tax levied directly on personal income.

incoming ▶ **adjective** in the process of coming in: *incoming passengers.* ■ (of a communication) being received rather than sent: *an incoming call.* ■ (of an official or administration) having just been elected or appointed to succeed another: *the incoming Labour government.* ■ Brit. coming to settle in a country; immigrant.
▶ **noun** (**incomings**) revenue; income: *keep an account of your incomings and outgoings.*

incommensurable /ˌɪnkəˈmɛnʃ(ə)rəb(ə)l, -sjə-/ ▶ **adjective 1** not able to be judged by the same standards; having no common standard of measurement: *the two types of science are incommensurable and thus cannot be integrated.*
2 Mathematics (of numbers) in a ratio that cannot be expressed as a ratio of integers. ■ irrational.
▶ **noun** (usu. **incommensurables**) an incommensurable quantity.
– DERIVATIVES **incommensurability** noun, **incommensurably** adverb.
– ORIGIN mid 16th cent. (in the mathematical sense): from late Latin *incommensurabilis*, from *in-* 'not' + *commensurabilis* (see COMMENSURABLE).

incommensurate /ˌɪnkəˈmɛnʃ(ə)rət, -sjə-/ ▶ **adjective 1** (**incommensurate with**) out of keeping or proportion with: *man's influence on the earth's surface seems incommensurate with his scale.*
2 another term for INCOMMENSURABLE (sense 1 of the adjective).
– DERIVATIVES **incommensurately** adverb, **incommensurateness** noun.

incommode ▶ **verb** [with obj.] formal inconvenience (someone): *they are incommoded by the traffic.*
– ORIGIN late 16th cent.: from French *incommoder* or Latin *incommodare*, from *in-* 'not' + *commodus* 'convenient'.

incommodious ▶ **adjective** formal or dated causing inconvenience or discomfort.
– DERIVATIVES **incommodiously** adverb.

incommunicable ▶ **adjective** not able to be communicated to others: *the pain of separation took the form of an incommunicable depression.*
– DERIVATIVES **incommunicability** noun, **incommunicably** adverb.
– ORIGIN mid 16th cent. (in the sense 'incommunicative'): from late Latin *incommunicabilis* 'not to be imparted', from *in-* 'not' + *communicabilis* (see COMMUNICABLE).

incommunicado /ˌɪnkəmjuːnɪˈkɑːdəʊ/ ▶ **adjective** not able, wanting, or allowed to communicate with other people: *they were separated and detained incommunicado.*
– ORIGIN mid 19th cent.: from Spanish *incomunicado*, past participle of *incomunicar* 'deprive of communication'.

incommunicative ▶ **adjective** another term for UNCOMMUNICATIVE.
– DERIVATIVES **incommunicatively** adverb, **incommunicativeness** noun.

incommutable ▶ **adjective** not capable of being changed or exchanged.
– DERIVATIVES **incommutably** adverb.
– ORIGIN late Middle English: from Latin *incommutabilis*, from *in-* 'not' + *commutabilis* (see COMMUTABLE).

in-company ▶ **adjective** occurring or existing within a company: *in-company training programmes.*

incomparable /ɪnˈkɒmp(ə)rəb(ə)l/ ▶ **adjective**
1 without an equal in quality or extent; matchless: *the incomparable beauty of Venice.*
2 unable to be compared; totally different: *censorship still exists, but now it's **incomparable with** what it was.*
– DERIVATIVES **incomparability** noun.
– ORIGIN late Middle English: via Old French from Latin *incomparabilis*, from *in-* 'not' + *comparabilis* (see COMPARABLE).

incomparably /ˌɪnkəmˈparəbli, ɪnˈkɒmp(ə)rəbli/ ▶ **adverb** [as submodifier] immeasurably; by far: *this beach is incomparably superior to the others on the island.*

incompatible ▶ **adjective** (of two things) so different in nature as to be incapable of coexisting: *cleverness and femininity were seen as incompatible.* ■ (of two people) unable to live together harmoniously. ■ (**incompatible with**) (of one thing or person) not consistent or able to coexist with (another): *long hours are simply incompatible with family life.* ■ (of equipment, computer programs, etc.) not capable of being used in combination.
– DERIVATIVES **incompatibility** noun, **incompatibly** adverb.
– ORIGIN late Middle English: from medieval Latin *incompatibilis*, from *in-* 'not' + *compatibilis* (see COMPATIBLE).

incompetence ▶ **noun** [mass noun] inability to do something successfully; ineptitude: *allegations of professional incompetence.*
– DERIVATIVES **incompetency** noun.

incompetent ▶ **adjective** [mass noun] not having or showing the necessary skills to do something successfully: *a forgetful and utterly incompetent assistant.* ■ Law not qualified to act in a particular capacity: *the patient is deemed legally incompetent.* ■ Medicine (especially of a valve or sphincter) not able to perform its function.
▶ **noun** an incompetent person.
– DERIVATIVES **incompetently** adverb.
– ORIGIN late 16th cent. (in the sense 'not legally competent'): from French, or from late Latin *incompetent-*, from *in-* 'not' + Latin *competent-* 'being fit or proper' (see COMPETENT).

incompletable ▶ **adjective** rare unable to be completed.
– DERIVATIVES **incompletability** noun.

incomplete ▶ **adjective** not having all the necessary or appropriate parts: *incomplete carvings of cattle.* ■ not full or finished: *the analysis remains incomplete.*
– DERIVATIVES **incompletely** adverb, **incompleteness** noun.
– ORIGIN late Middle English: from late Latin *incompletus*, from Latin *in-* 'not' + *completus* 'filled, finished' (see COMPLETE).

incompleteness theorem (also **Gödel's incompleteness theorem**) ▶ **noun** Logic the theorem that in any sufficiently powerful, logically consistent formulation of logic or mathematics there must be true formulas which are neither provable nor disprovable. The theorem entails the corollary that the consistency of a logical system cannot be proved within that system.

incompletion ▶ **noun 1** [mass noun] the state of lacking something or of having failed to complete something.
2 American Football a forward pass which is not caught.

incomprehensible ▶ **adjective** not able to be understood; not intelligible: *a language which is **incomprehensible to** anyone outside the office.*
– DERIVATIVES **incomprehensibility** noun, **incomprehensibleness** noun, **incomprehensibly** adverb.
– ORIGIN late Middle English (earlier than *comprehensible*): from Latin *incomprehensibilis*, from *in-* 'not' + *comprehensibilis* (see COMPREHENSIBLE).

incomprehension ▶ **noun** [mass noun] failure to understand something: *they gave him a look of complete incomprehension.*

incompressible ▶ **adjective** not able to be compressed.
– DERIVATIVES **incompressibility** noun.

incomputable ▶ **adjective** rare unable to be calculated or estimated: *incomputable riches.*
– ORIGIN early 17th cent.: from IN-[1] 'not' + Latin *computabilis* 'able to be counted' (see COMPUTE).

inconceivable ▶ **adjective** not capable of being imagined or grasped mentally; unbelievable: [with clause] *it seemed inconceivable that the president had been unaware of what was going on* | *they behaved with inconceivable cruelty.*
– DERIVATIVES **inconceivability** noun, **inconceivableness** noun, **inconceivably** adverb [as submodifier] *a crisis of inconceivably devastating proportions.*

inconclusive ▶ **adjective** not leading to a firm conclusion or result; not ending doubt or dispute: *three years of inconclusive negotiations* | *the medical evidence is inconclusive.*
– DERIVATIVES **inconclusively** adverb, **inconclusiveness** noun.

Inconel /ˈɪnkənɛl/ ▶ **noun** [mass noun] trademark an alloy of nickel containing chromium and iron, resistant to corrosion at high temperatures.
– ORIGIN 1930s: apparently from *I(nternational) N(ickel) Co(mpany)*, on the pattern of *nickel*.

incongruent /ɪnˈkɒŋɡrʊənt/ ▶ **adjective** incongruous; incompatible. ■ Chemistry (of melting, dissolution, or other process) affecting the components of an alloy or other substance differently.
– DERIVATIVES **incongruence** noun, **incongruently** adverb.
– ORIGIN late Middle English: from Latin *incongruent-*, from *in-* 'not' + *congruent-* 'meeting together' (see CONGRUENT).

incongruity /ˌɪnkɒŋˈɡruːɪti/ ▶ **noun** (pl. **incongruities**) [mass noun] the state of being incongruous; incompatibility: *the incongruity of his fleshy face and skinny body disturbed her.*

incongruous /ɪnˈkɒŋɡrʊəs/ ▶ **adjective** not in harmony or keeping with the surroundings or other aspects of something: *the duffel coat looked incongruous with the black dress she wore underneath.*
– DERIVATIVES **incongruously** adverb.
– ORIGIN early 17th cent.: from Latin *incongruus* (from *in-* 'not' + *congruus* 'agreeing, suitable', from the verb *congruere*) + **-ous**.

inconnu /ˈãkɒnuː, ˌãkɒˈn(j)uː/ ▶ **noun 1** an unknown person or thing.
2 (pl. **same**) an edible predatory freshwater whitefish related to the salmon, native to Eurasian and North American lakes close to the Arctic Circle.
• *Stenodus leucichthys*, family Salmonidae.
– ORIGIN early 19th cent.: French, literally 'unknown'.

inconsequent ▶ **adjective** not connected or following logically; irrelevant: *people say the most stupid, inconsequent things when surprised.* ■ another term for INCONSEQUENTIAL.
– DERIVATIVES **inconsequence** noun, **inconsequently** adverb.

I

– ORIGIN late 16th cent.: from Latin *inconsequent-*, from *in-* 'not' + *consequent-* 'overtaking, following closely' (see CONSEQUENT).

inconsequential ▸ adjective not important or significant: *they talked about inconsequential things.*
– DERIVATIVES **inconsequentiality** noun (pl. **inconsequentialities**), **inconsequentially** adverb, **inconsequentialness** noun.

inconsiderable ▸ adjective [with negative] of small size, amount, or extent: *a not inconsiderable amount of money.* ■ unimportant or insignificant: *a not inconsiderable artist.*
– ORIGIN late 16th cent. (in the sense 'impossible to imagine'): from French, or from late Latin *inconsiderabilis*, from *in-* 'not' + *considerabilis* 'worthy of consideration' (see CONSIDERABLE).

inconsiderate ▸ adjective thoughtlessly causing hurt or inconvenience to others: *it's **inconsiderate of** her to go away without telling us.*
– DERIVATIVES **inconsiderately** adverb, **inconsiderateness** noun, **inconsideration** noun.
– ORIGIN late Middle English (originally in the sense 'not properly considered'): from Latin *inconsideratus*, from *in-* 'not' + *consideratus* 'examined, considered' (see CONSIDERATE).

inconsistency ▸ noun (pl. **inconsistencies**) [mass noun] the fact or state of being inconsistent: *the inconsistency between his expressed attitudes and his actual behaviour.* ■ [count noun] an inconsistent aspect or element: *a book riddled with inconsistencies and contradictions.*
– ORIGIN mid 17th cent.: from INCONSISTENT, on the pattern of *consistency*.

inconsistent ▸ adjective **1** not staying the same throughout: *police interpretation of the law was often inconsistent.* ■ acting at variance with one's own principles or former behaviour: *parents can become inconsistent and lacking in control over their children.*
2 (**inconsistent with**) not compatible or in keeping with: *he had done nothing inconsistent with his morality.*
– DERIVATIVES **inconsistently** adverb.

inconsolable ▸ adjective (of a person or their grief) not able to be comforted or alleviated: *his widow, Jane, was inconsolable.*
– DERIVATIVES **inconsolability** noun, **inconsolably** adverb.
– ORIGIN late 16th cent.: from French, or from Latin *inconsolabilis*, from *in-* 'not' + *consolabilis* 'able to be consoled', from the verb *consolari* (see CONSOLE[1]).

inconsonant ▸ adjective rare not in agreement or harmony; not compatible.
– DERIVATIVES **inconsonance** noun.

inconspicuous ▸ adjective not clearly visible or attracting attention: *an inconspicuous red-brick building.*
– DERIVATIVES **inconspicuously** adverb, **inconspicuousness** noun.
– ORIGIN early 17th cent. (in the sense 'invisible, indiscernible'): from Latin *inconspicuus* (from *in-* 'not' + *conspicuus* 'clearly visible') + -OUS.

inconstant ▸ adjective frequently changing; variable or irregular: *the exact dimensions aren't easily measured since they are inconstant.* ■ (of a person or their behaviour) not faithful and dependable.
– DERIVATIVES **inconstancy** noun (pl. **inconstancies**), **inconstantly** adverb.
– ORIGIN late Middle English: via Old French from Latin *inconstant-*, from *in-* 'not' + *constant-* 'standing firm' (see CONSTANT).

incontestable ▸ adjective not able to be disputed.
– DERIVATIVES **incontestability** noun, **incontestably** adverb.
– ORIGIN late 17th cent.: from French, or from medieval Latin *incontestabilis*, from *in-* 'not' + *contestabilis* 'able to be called upon in witness', from the verb *contestari* (see CONTEST).

incontinent ▸ adjective **1** having no or insufficient voluntary control over urination or defecation.
2 lacking self-restraint; uncontrolled: *the incontinent hysteria of the massed pop fans.*
– DERIVATIVES **incontinence** noun, **incontinently** adverb.
– ORIGIN late Middle English (in sense 2): from Old French, or from Latin *incontinent-*, from *in-* 'not' + *continent-* 'holding together' (see CONTINENT[2]). Sense 1 dates from the early 19th cent.

incontrovertible ▸ adjective not able to be denied or disputed: *incontrovertible proof.*
– DERIVATIVES **incontrovertibility** noun, **incontrovertibly** adverb.

inconvenience ▸ noun [mass noun] the state or fact of being troublesome or difficult with regard to one's personal requirements or comfort: *the inconvenience of having to change trains.* ■ [count noun] a cause of trouble or difficulty: *the inconveniences of life in a remote city.*
▸ verb [with obj.] cause trouble or difficulty to: *noise and fumes from traffic would inconvenience residents.*
– ORIGIN late Middle English (originally in the sense 'incongruity', also 'unsuitability'): via Old French from late Latin *inconvenientia* 'incongruity, inconsistency', from *in-* 'not' + Latin *convenient-* 'agreeing, fitting' (see CONVENIENT).

inconvenient ▸ adjective causing trouble, difficulties, or discomfort: *she telephoned frequently, usually at inconvenient times.*
– DERIVATIVES **inconveniently** adverb.
– ORIGIN late Middle English (originally in the sense 'incongruous' or 'unsuitable'): via Old French from Latin *inconvenient-*, from *in-* 'not' + *convenient-* 'agreeing, fitting' (see CONVENIENT). Current senses date from the mid 17th cent.

inconvertible ▸ adjective not able to be changed in form, function, or character. ■ (of currency) not able to be converted into another form on demand.
– DERIVATIVES **inconvertibly** adverb.
– ORIGIN mid 17th cent.: from French, or from late Latin *inconvertibilis*, from *in-* 'not' + *convertibilis* (see CONVERTIBLE).

incoordination ▸ noun [mass noun] technical lack of coordination, especially the inability to use different parts of the body together smoothly and efficiently.

incorporate ▸ verb [with obj.] **1** take in or contain (something) as part of a whole; include: *he has **incorporated in** his proposals a number of measures | some schemes incorporated all these variations.* ■ combine (ingredients) into one substance: *add the cheeses and butter and process briefly to incorporate them.*
2 constitute (a company, city, or other organization) as a legal corporation.
▸ adjective **1** another term for INCORPORATED.
2 literary having a bodily form; embodied.
– DERIVATIVES **incorporation** noun, **incorporator** noun.
– ORIGIN late Middle English: from late Latin *incorporat-* 'embodied', from the verb *incorporare*, from *in-* 'into' + Latin *corporare* 'form into a body' (from *corpus, corpor-* 'body').

incorporated ▸ adjective (of a company or other organization) formed into a legal corporation: *the Incorporated Society of Musicians |* [postpositive] *Adobe Systems Incorporated.*

incorporative ▸ adjective tending to incorporate or include things.

incorporeal /ˌɪnkɔːˈpɔːrɪəl/ ▸ adjective not composed of matter; having no material existence: *a supreme but incorporeal being called God.* ■ Law having no physical existence.
– DERIVATIVES **incorporeality** noun, **incorporeally** adverb.
– ORIGIN late Middle English: from Latin *incorporeus*, from *in-* 'not' + *corporeus* (from *corpus, corpor-* 'body') + -AL.

incorrect ▸ adjective **1** not in accordance with fact; wrong: *the doctor gave you incorrect advice.*
2 not in accordance with particular standards or rules: *strictly speaking, the form of address was incorrect.*
– DERIVATIVES **incorrectly** adverb, **incorrectness** noun.
– ORIGIN late Middle English: from Latin *incorrectus*, from *in-* 'not' + *correctus* 'made straight, amended' (see CORRECT). Originally in the general sense 'uncorrected', the word was later applied specifically to a book containing many errors because it had not been corrected for the press; hence sense 2 (late 17th cent.).

incorrigible ▸ adjective (of a person or their behaviour) not able to be changed or reformed: *she's an incorrigible flirt.*
▸ noun an incorrigible person.
– DERIVATIVES **incorrigibility** noun **incorrigibly** adverb.
– ORIGIN Middle English: from Old French, or from Latin *incorrigibilis*, from *in-* 'not' + *corrigibilis* (see CORRIGIBLE).

incorrupt ▸ adjective rare (especially of a human body) not having undergone decomposition.
– ORIGIN late Middle English: from Latin *incorruptus*, from *in-* 'not' + *corruptus* 'destroyed, marred' (see CORRUPT).

incorruptible ▸ adjective **1** not susceptible to corruption, especially by bribery.
2 not subject to death or decay; everlasting.
– DERIVATIVES **incorruptibility** /ˈbɪlɪti/ noun, **incorruptibly** adverb.
– ORIGIN Middle English: from Old French, or from ecclesiastical Latin *incorruptibilis*, from *in-* 'not' + *corruptibilis* 'corruptible'.

in-country ▸ adjective & adverb in a country rather than operating from outside it: [as adv.] *selection for the posts takes place in London, or occasionally in-country.*

incrassate /ɪnˈkraseɪt/ ▸ adjective rare thickened in form or consistency.
– ORIGIN late 15th cent.: from late Latin *incrassatus* 'made thick', past participle of *incrassare*.

increase ▸ verb /ɪnˈkriːs/ become or make greater in size, amount, or degree: [no obj.] *car use is increasing at an alarming rate |* [with obj.] *we are aiming to increase awareness of social issues |* (as adj. **increasing**) *the increasing numbers of students.*
▸ noun /ˈɪŋkriːs/ a rise in the size, amount, or degree of something: *an increase of 28.3 per cent |* [mass noun] *some increase in inflation is expected.*
– PHRASES **on the increase** becoming greater, more common, or more frequent.
– DERIVATIVES **increasable** adjective.
– ORIGIN Middle English (formerly also as *encrease*): from Old French *encreistre*, from Latin *increscere*, from *in-* 'into' + *crescere* 'grow'.

increasingly /ɪnˈkriːsɪŋli/ ▸ adverb to an increasing extent; more and more: [sentence adverb] *increasingly, attention is paid to health |* [as submodifier] *an increasingly difficult situation.*

increate /ˌɪnkriːˈeɪt/ ▸ adjective literary not yet created.
– ORIGIN late Middle English: from ecclesiastical Latin *increatus*, from Latin *in-* 'not' + *creatus* (past participle of *creare* 'create').

incredible ▸ adjective **1** impossible to believe: *an almost incredible tale of triumph and tragedy.*
2 difficult to believe; extraordinary: *the noise from the crowd was incredible.* ■ informal very good; wonderful: *I was mesmerized: she looked so incredible.*
– DERIVATIVES **incredibility** noun.
– ORIGIN late Middle English: from Latin *incredibilis*, from *in-* 'not' + *credibilis* (see CREDIBLE).

incredibly ▸ adverb **1** [as submodifier] to a great degree; extremely: *Michele was incredibly brave.*
2 [sentence adverb] used to introduce a statement that is hard to believe; strangely: *incredibly, he was still alive.*

incredulity ▸ noun [mass noun] the state of being unwilling or unable to believe something: *he stared down the street in incredulity.*

incredulous ▸ adjective (of a person or their manner) unwilling or unable to believe something: *an incredulous gasp.*
– DERIVATIVES **incredulously** adverb, **incredulousness** noun.
– ORIGIN 16th cent.: from Latin *incredulus* (from *in-* 'not' + *credulus* 'believing, trusting', from *credere* 'believe') + -OUS.

increment /ˈɪŋkrɪm(ə)nt/ ▸ noun an increase or addition, especially one of a series on a fixed scale: *all sizes from 4–30 mm in 1 mm increments.* ■ a regular increase in salary on an incremental scale: *your first increment will be payable six months from your date of commencement.* ■ Mathematics a small positive or negative change in a variable quantity or function.
▸ verb [with obj.] chiefly Computing cause a discrete increase in (a numerical quantity).
– DERIVATIVES **incremental** adjective, **incrementally** adverb.
– ORIGIN late Middle English: from Latin *incrementum*, from the stem of *increscere* 'grow' (see INCREASE).

incremental backup ▸ noun Computing a security copy which contains only those files which have been altered since the last full backup.

incrementalism ▸ noun [mass noun] belief in or advocacy of change by degrees; gradualism.
– DERIVATIVES **incrementalist** noun & adjective.

incriminate /ɪnˈkrɪmɪneɪt/ ▸ verb [with obj.] make (someone) appear guilty of a crime or wrongdoing: *he refused to answer questions in order not to incriminate himself |* (as adj. **incriminating**) *incriminating evidence.*
– DERIVATIVES **incrimination** noun, **incriminatory** adjective.

– ORIGIN mid 18th cent. (earlier (mid 17th cent.) as *incrimination*): from late Latin *incriminat-* 'accused', from the verb *incriminare*, from *in-* 'into, towards' + Latin *crimen* 'crime'.

in-crowd ▶ noun (**the in-crowd**) informal a small group of people perceived by others to be particularly fashionable, informed, or popular.

incrust ▶ verb variant spelling of ENCRUST.

incrustation ▶ noun variant spelling of ENCRUSTATION.

incubate /ˈɪŋkjʊbeɪt/ ▶ verb **1** [with obj.] (of a bird) sit on (eggs) in order to keep them warm and bring them to hatching. ■ (in a laboratory or other controlled situation) keep (eggs, bacteria, embryos, etc.) at a suitable temperature so that they develop. ■ N. Amer. give support and aid the development of (a new small business).
2 (**be incubating something**) be developing an infectious disease before symptoms appear: *the possibility that she was incubating early syphilis.* ■ [no obj.] develop slowly without outward or perceptible signs: *the BSE bug incubates for around three years.*
– ORIGIN mid 17th cent.: from Latin *incubat-* 'lain on', from the verb *incubare*, from *in-* 'upon' + *cubare* 'to lie'.

incubation ▶ noun [mass noun] the process of incubating eggs, cells, bacteria, a disease, etc.: *the chick hatches after a month's incubation.*
– DERIVATIVES **incubatory** /ˈɪŋkjʊbeɪt(ə)ri/ adjective.
– ORIGIN early 17th cent.: from Latin *incubatio(n-)* 'brooding', from the verb *incubare* (see INCUBATE).

incubation period ▶ noun the period over which eggs, cells, etc. are incubated. ■ the period between exposure to an infection and the appearance of the first symptoms.

incubator ▶ noun **1** an enclosed apparatus in which premature or unusually small babies are placed and which provides a controlled and protective environment for their care. ■ an apparatus used to hatch eggs or grow microorganisms under controlled conditions.
2 N. Amer. a place, especially with support staff and equipment, made available at low rent to new small businesses.

incubous /ˈɪŋkjʊbəs/ ▶ adjective Botany (of a liverwort) having leaves which point forward so that their upper edges overlap the lower edges of the leaves above. Often contrasted with SUCCUBOUS.
– ORIGIN mid 19th cent.: from Latin *incubare* 'lie on' + -OUS.

incubus /ˈɪŋkjʊbəs/ ▶ noun (pl. **incubi** /-bʌɪ/) a male demon believed to have sexual intercourse with sleeping women. ■ a cause of difficulty or anxiety: *debt is a big incubus in developing countries.* ■ archaic a nightmare.
– ORIGIN Middle English: late Latin form of Latin *incubo* 'nightmare', from *incubare* 'lie on' (see INCUBATE).

incudes plural form of INCUS.

inculcate /ˈɪnkʌlkeɪt/ ▶ verb [with obj.] instil (an idea, attitude, or habit) by persistent instruction: *I tried to inculcate in my pupils an attitude of enquiry.* ■ teach (someone) an attitude, idea, or habit by persistent instruction: *they will try to **inculcate** you **with** a respect for culture.*
– DERIVATIVES **inculcation** noun, **inculcator** noun.
– ORIGIN mid 16th cent.: from Latin *inculcat-* 'pressed in', from the verb *inculcare*, from *in-* 'into' + *calcare* 'to tread' (from *calx, calc-* 'heel').

inculpate /ˈɪnkʌlpeɪt/ ▶ verb [with obj.] accuse or blame. ■ incriminate: *someone placed the pistol in your room in order to inculpate you.*
– DERIVATIVES **inculpation** noun, **inculpatory** adjective.
– ORIGIN late 18th cent.: from late Latin *inculpat-* 'made culpable', from the verb *inculpare*, from *in-* 'upon, towards' + *culpare* 'to blame' (from *culpa* 'fault').

inculturation /ɪnˌkʌltʃəˈreɪʃ(ə)n/ (also **enculturation**) ▶ noun [mass noun] the gradual acquisition of the characteristics and norms of a culture or group by a person, another culture, etc. ■ the adaptation of Christian liturgy to a non-Christian cultural background.

incumbency ▶ noun (pl. **incumbencies**) the holding of an office or the period during which one is held.

incumbent /ɪnˈkʌmb(ə)nt/ ▶ adjective **1** (**incumbent on/upon**) necessary for (someone) as a duty or responsibility: *the government realized that it was incumbent on them to act.*
2 [attrib.] (of an official or regime) currently holding office: *the incumbent President was defeated.*
3 [attrib.] (of a company) having a sizeable share of a market: *powerful incumbent airlines.*
▶ noun the holder of an office or post. ■ Christian Church the holder of an ecclesiastical benefice.
– ORIGIN late Middle English (as a noun): from Anglo-Latin *incumbens, incumbent-*, from Latin *incumbere* 'lie or lean on', from *in-* 'upon' + a verb related to *cubare* 'lie'.

incunabulum /ˌɪnkjʊˈnabjʊləm/ (also **incunable** /ɪnˈkjuːnəb(ə)l/) ▶ noun (pl. **incunabula**) an early printed book, especially one printed before 1501.
– ORIGIN early 19th cent.: from Latin *incunabula* (neuter plural) 'swaddling clothes, cradle', from *in-* 'into' + *cunae* 'cradle'.

incur ▶ verb (**incurs, incurring, incurred**) [with obj.] become subject to (something unwelcome or unpleasant) as a result of one's own behaviour or actions: *I will pay any expenses incurred.*
– DERIVATIVES **incurrence** noun.
– ORIGIN late Middle English: from Latin *incurrere*, from *in-* 'towards' + *currere* 'run'.

incurable ▶ adjective (of a sick person or a disease) not able to be cured. ■ (of a person or behaviour) unable to be changed: *an incurable optimist.*
▶ noun a person who cannot be cured.
– DERIVATIVES **incurability** noun **incurably** adverb [as submodifier] *incurably ill patients.*
– ORIGIN Middle English: from Old French, or from late Latin *incurabilis*, from *in-* 'not' + *curabilis* (see CURABLE).

incurious ▶ adjective not eager to know something; lacking curiosity.
– DERIVATIVES **incuriosity** noun, **incuriously** adverb, **incuriousness** noun.
– ORIGIN late 16th cent. (in the sense 'careless'): partly from Latin *incuriosus* 'careless, indifferent', from *in-* 'not' + Latin *curiosus* 'careful' (see CURIOUS); partly from IN-[1] 'not' + CURIOUS.

incurrent ▶ adjective chiefly Zoology (of a vessel or opening) conveying fluid inwards. The opposite of EXCURRENT.
– ORIGIN late 16th cent. (in the sense 'falling within (a period)'): from Latin *incurrent-* 'running in', from the verb *incurrere* (see INCUR).

incursion /ɪnˈkəːʃ(ə)n/ ▶ noun an invasion or attack, especially a sudden or brief one.
– DERIVATIVES **incursive** adjective.
– ORIGIN late Middle English (formerly also as *encursion*): from Latin *incursio(n-)*, from the verb *incurrere* (see INCUR).

incurvate ▶ verb /ˈɪnkəːveɪt/ [no obj.] curve inwards.
▶ adjective /ɪnˈkəːvət/ curved inwards.
– DERIVATIVES **incurvation** noun.
– ORIGIN late Middle English (as an adjective): from Latin *incurvat-* 'bent into a curve', from the verb *incurvare*.

incurve ▶ verb [no obj.] (usu. as adj. **incurved**) curve inwards: *incurved horns.*
– ORIGIN late Middle English: from Latin *incurvare*, from *in-* 'in, towards' + *curvare* 'to curve'.

incus /ˈɪŋkəs/ ▶ noun (pl. **incudes** /ˈɪŋkjʊdiːz, ɪnˈkjuːdiːz/) Anatomy a small anvil-shaped bone in the middle ear, transmitting vibrations between the malleus and stapes.
– ORIGIN mid 17th cent.: from Latin, literally 'anvil'.

incuse /ɪnˈkjuːz/ ▶ noun an impression hammered or stamped on a coin.
▶ verb [with obj.] mark (a coin) with a figure by impressing it with a stamp.
– ORIGIN early 19th cent.: from Latin *incusus* 'forged with a hammer', past participle of *incudere*, from *in-* 'into' + *cudere* 'to forge'.

IND ▶ abbreviation India (international vehicle registration).

Ind. ▶ abbreviation ■ Independent. ■ India. ■ Indian. ■ Indiana.

indaba /ɪnˈdɑːbə/ ▶ noun S. African **1** a discussion or conference.
2 informal one's own problem or concern: *this country is our indaba and no one else's.*
– ORIGIN Xhosa and Zulu, 'discussion'.

indebted ▶ adjective owing money: *heavily indebted countries.* ■ owing gratitude for a service or favour: *I am **indebted to** her for her help in indexing my book.*
– DERIVATIVES **indebtedness** noun.
– ORIGIN Middle English *endetted*, from Old French *endette* 'involved in debt', past participle of *endetter*. The spelling change in the 16th cent. was due to association with medieval Latin *indebitare* (based on Latin *debitum* 'debt').

indecency ▶ noun (pl. **indecencies**) [mass noun] indecent behaviour. ■ [count noun] an indecent act or expression.

indecent ▶ adjective **1** not conforming with generally accepted standards of behaviour, especially in relation to sexual matters: *indecent acts.*
2 not appropriate or fitting: *they leaped on the suggestion with indecent haste.*
– DERIVATIVES **indecently** adverb.
– ORIGIN late 16th cent.: from French *indécent* or Latin *indecent-*, from *in-* 'not' + *decent-* 'being fitting' (see DECENT).

indecent assault ▶ noun [mass noun] sexual assault that does not involve rape.

indecent exposure ▶ noun [mass noun] the crime of intentionally showing one's sexual organs in public. ■ the act of outraging public decency by being naked in a public place.

indecipherable /ˌɪndɪˈsʌɪf(ə)rəb(ə)l/ ▶ adjective not able to be read or understood.
– DERIVATIVES **indecipherability** noun, **indecipherably** adverb.

indecision ▶ noun [mass noun] the inability to make a decision quickly.
– ORIGIN mid 18th cent.: from French *indécision*, from *in-* (expressing negation) + *décision*, from Latin *decisio(n-)*, from the verb *decidere* (see DECIDE).

indecisive ▶ adjective **1** not providing a clear and definite result: *an indecisive battle.*
2 (of a person) not able to make decisions quickly and effectively.
– DERIVATIVES **indecisively** adverb, **indecisiveness** noun.

indeclinable /ˌɪndɪˈklʌɪnəb(ə)l/ ▶ adjective Grammar (of a noun, pronoun, or adjective in a highly inflected language) having no inflections.
– ORIGIN late Middle English: via French from Latin *indeclinabilis*, from *in-* 'not' + *declinabilis* 'able to be inflected' (see DECLINE).

indecomposable /ˌɪndiːkəmˈpəʊzəb(ə)l/ ▶ adjective Mathematics unable to be expressed as a product of factors or otherwise decomposed into simpler elements.

indecorous ▶ adjective not in keeping with good taste and propriety; improper.
– DERIVATIVES **indecorously** adverb, **indecorousness** noun.
– ORIGIN late 17th cent.: from Latin *indecorus* (from *in-* 'not' + *decorus* 'seemly') + -OUS.

indecorum /ˌɪndɪˈkɔːrəm/ ▶ noun [mass noun] failure to conform to good taste, propriety, or etiquette.
– ORIGIN late 16th cent. (denoting an indecorous act): from Latin, neuter of *indecorus* (see INDECOROUS).

indeed ▶ adverb **1** used to emphasize a statement or response confirming something already suggested: *it was not expected to last long, and indeed it took less than three weeks* | *'She should have no trouble hearing him.' 'No indeed.'* ■ used to emphasize a description: *it was a very good buy indeed.*
2 used to introduce a further and stronger or more surprising point: *the idea is attractive to many men and indeed to many women.*
3 used in a response to express interest, surprise, or contempt: *'A ghost indeed! I've never heard anything so silly.'* ■ expressing interest of an ironical kind with repetition of a question just asked: *'Who'd believe it?' 'Who indeed?'*
– ORIGIN Middle English: originally as *in deed*.

indeedy ▶ adverb N. Amer. informal term for INDEED (sense 1): *Yes, indeedy! That was a good question.*

indefatigable /ˌɪndɪˈfatɪɡəb(ə)l/ ▶ adjective (of a person or their efforts) persisting tirelessly: *an indefatigable defender of human rights.*
– DERIVATIVES **indefatigability** noun, **indefatigably** adverb.
– ORIGIN early 17th cent.: from French, or from Latin *indefatigabilis*, from *in-* 'not' + *de-* 'away, completely' + *fatigare* 'wear out'.

indefeasible /ˌɪndɪˈfiːzɪb(ə)l/ ▶ adjective chiefly Law & Philosophy not subject to being lost, annulled, or overturned: *an indefeasible right.*
– DERIVATIVES **indefeasibility** noun, **indefeasibly** adverb.

indefectible /ˌɪndɪˈfɛktɪb(ə)l/ ▶ adjective formal **1** not liable to fail, end, or decay.
2 having no defects; perfect.

indefensible ▶ adjective **1** not justifiable by argument: *this behaviour is morally indefensible.*

I

2 not able to be protected against attack: *the towns were tactically indefensible.*
– DERIVATIVES **indefensibility** noun, **indefensibly** adverb.

indefinable ▸ **adjective** not able to be defined or described exactly: *she reminds me, in some indefinable way, of my grandmother.*
– DERIVATIVES **indefinably** adverb.

indefinite ▸ **adjective 1** lasting for an unknown or unstated length of time: *they may face indefinite detention.*
2 not clearly expressed or defined; vague: *an indefinite number of generations.* ■ Grammar (of a word, inflection, or phrase) not determining the person, thing, time, etc. referred to.
– DERIVATIVES **indefiniteness** noun.
– ORIGIN mid 16th cent.: from Latin *indefinitus*, from *in-* 'not' + *definitus* 'defined, set within limits' (see DEFINITE).

indefinite article ▸ **noun** Grammar a determiner (*a* and *an* in English) that introduces a noun phrase and implies that the thing referred to is non-specific (as in *she bought me a book*; *government is an art*; *he went to a public school*). Typically, the indefinite article is used to introduce new concepts into a discourse. Compare with DEFINITE ARTICLE.

indefinite integral ▸ **noun** Mathematics an integral expressed without limits, and so containing an arbitrary constant.

indefinitely ▸ **adverb** for an unlimited or unspecified period of time: *talks cannot go on indefinitely.* ■ [as submodifier] to an unlimited or unspecified degree or extent: *an indefinitely large number of channels.*

indefinite pronoun ▸ **noun** Grammar a pronoun that does not refer to any person, amount, or thing in particular, e.g. *anything, something, anyone, everyone.*

indehiscent /ˌɪndɪˈhɪs(ə)nt/ ▸ **adjective** Botany (of a pod or fruit) not splitting open to release the seeds when ripe.
– DERIVATIVES **indehiscence** noun.

indelible /ɪnˈdɛlɪb(ə)l/ ▸ **adjective** (of ink or a pen) making marks that cannot be removed. ■ not able to be forgotten: *the story made an indelible impression on me.*
– DERIVATIVES **indelibility** noun, **indelibly** adverb.
– ORIGIN late 15th cent. (as *indeleble*): from French, or from Latin *indelebilis*, from *in-* 'not' + *delebilis* (from *delere* 'efface, delete'). The ending was altered under the influence of -IBLE.

indelicacy ▸ **noun** (pl. **indelicacies**) [mass noun] **1** a lack of sensitive understanding or tact: *the magazine printed the photographs with manifest indelicacy for commercial ends.*
2 the quality of being slightly indecent: *the play's cynicism and sexual indelicacy* | [count noun] *such crude indelicacies.*

indelicate ▸ **adjective 1** having or showing a lack of sensitive understanding or tact: *forgive me asking an indelicate question, but how are you off for money?*
2 slightly indecent: *an earthy, often indelicate sense of humour.*
– DERIVATIVES **indelicately** adverb.

indemnify /ɪnˈdɛmnɪfʌɪ/ ▸ **verb** (**indemnifies, indemnifying, indemnified**) [with obj.] compensate (someone) for harm or loss: *each of the parties shall indemnify me for all reasonable costs of defending such actions and proceedings.* ■ secure (someone) against legal responsibility for their actions: *the company has taken out insurance to **indemnify** its directors **against** liability when acting for the group.*
– DERIVATIVES **indemnification** noun, **indemnifier** noun.
– ORIGIN early 17th cent.: from Latin *indemnis* 'unhurt, free from loss or damage', from *in-* (expressing negation) + *damnum* 'loss, damage'.

indemnity /ɪnˈdɛmnɪti/ ▸ **noun** (pl. **indemnities**) [mass noun] security or protection against a loss or other financial burden: *no indemnity will be given for loss of cash.* ■ security against or exemption from legal responsibility for one's actions: *a deed of indemnity* | [count noun] *even warranties and indemnities do not provide complete protection.* ■ [count noun] a sum of money paid as compensation, especially one paid by a country defeated in war as a condition of peace.
– ORIGIN late Middle English: from French *indemnite*, from late Latin *indemnitas*, from *indemnis* 'unhurt, free from loss'.

indemonstrable /ˌɪndɪˈmɒnstrəb(ə)l, ɪnˈdɛmən-/ ▸ **adjective** not able to be proved or demonstrated. ■ Philosophy (of a truth) axiomatic and hence unprovable.

indene /ˈɪndiːn/ ▸ **noun** [mass noun] Chemistry a colourless liquid hydrocarbon, obtained from coal tar and used in making synthetic resins. ● A bicyclic aromatic compound; chem. formula: C_9H_8.
– ORIGIN late 19th cent.: from INDOLE + -ENE.

indent[1] ▸ **verb** /ɪnˈdɛnt/ [with obj.] **1** start (a line of text) or position (a block of text) further from the margin than the main part of the text.
2 form deep recesses or notches in (a line or surface): *a coastline indented by many fjords.*
3 [no obj.] Brit. make a requisition or written order for something.
4 historical divide (a document drawn up in duplicate) into its two copies with a zigzag line, thus ensuring identification and preventing forgery. ■ draw up (a legal document) in exact duplicate.
▸ **noun** /ˈɪndɛnt/ **1** Brit. an official order or requisition for goods.
2 a space left by indenting text.
3 an indentation: *every indent in the coastline.*
4 an indenture.
– DERIVATIVES **indentor** noun.
– ORIGIN late Middle English (as a verb in the sense 'give a zigzag outline to, divide by a zigzag line'): from Anglo-Norman French *endenter* or medieval Latin *indentare*, from *en-*, *in-* 'into' + Latin *dens, dent-* 'tooth'.

indent[2] /ɪnˈdɛnt/ ▸ **verb** [with obj.] make a dent or impression in (something).

indentation ▸ **noun 1** [mass noun] the action of indenting or the state of being indented: *paragraphs are marked off by indentation* | [count noun] *an indentation for each change of speaker.*
2 a deep recess or notch on the edge or surface of something: *coastal indentations.*

indented ▸ **adjective** Heraldry divided or edged with a zigzag line.

indenter ▸ **noun** a small hard object used for producing an indentation in a solid in an indentation test.

indention ▸ **noun** archaic term for INDENTATION.

indenture /ɪnˈdɛntʃə/ ▸ **noun** a legal agreement, contract, or document, in particular: ■ historical a deed or contract of which copies were made for the contracting parties with the edges indented for identification and to prevent forgery. ■ a formal list, certificate, or inventory. ■ an agreement binding an apprentice to a master. ■ [mass noun] the state of being bound to service by an indenture: *the bracelet on his wrist represented his **indenture to** his master.* ■ historical a contract by which a person agreed to work for a set period for a landowner in a British colony in exchange for passage to the colony.
▸ **verb** [with obj.] (usu. **be indentured to**) chiefly historical bind (someone) by an indenture as an apprentice or labourer.
– DERIVATIVES **indentureship** noun.
– ORIGIN late Middle English *endenture*, via Anglo-Norman French from medieval Latin *indentura*, from *indentatus*, past participle of *indentare* (see INDENT[1]).

independence ▸ **noun** [mass noun] the fact or state of being independent: *Argentina gained independence from Spain in 1816* | *I've always valued my independence.*
– ORIGIN mid 17th cent.: from INDEPENDENT, partly on the pattern of French *indépendance*.

Independence Day ▸ **noun** a day celebrating the anniversary of national independence. ■ another term for FOURTH OF JULY.

Independence Hall a building in Philadelphia where the US Declaration of Independence was proclaimed and outside which the Liberty Bell is kept.

independency ▸ **noun** (pl. **independencies**) **1** rare an independent state.
2 archaic term for INDEPENDENCE.

independent ▸ **adjective 1** free from outside control; not subject to another's authority: *an independent nuclear deterrent* | *the study is totally **independent of** central government.* ■ (of a country) self-governing: *India became independent in 1947.* ■ not belonging to or supported by a political party: *the independent candidate.* ■ (of broadcasting, a school, etc.) not supported by public funds. ■ (**Independent**) historical Congregational.
2 not depending on another for livelihood or subsistence: *I wanted to remain independent in old age.* ■ (of income or resources) making it unnecessary to earn one's living: *a woman of independent means.*
3 capable of thinking or acting for oneself: *advice for independent travellers.* ■ not influenced by others; impartial: *a thorough and independent investigation of the case.*
4 not connected with another or with each other; separate: *treating each factory as an independent unit of production* | *the legislature and the judicature are **independent of** one another.* ■ not depending on something else for strength or effectiveness; free-standing: *an independent electric shower.* ■ Mathematics (of one of a set of axioms, equations, or quantities) incapable of being expressed in terms of, or derived or deduced from, the others.
▸ **noun** an independent person or body. ■ an independent political candidate. ■ (**Independent**) historical a Congregationalist.
– ORIGIN early 17th cent. (as an adjective): partly on the pattern of French *indépendant*.

Independent Broadcasting Authority (abbrev.: **IBA**) (in the UK) the body responsible for regulating commercial television and radio, until its replacement in 1991 by the Independent Television Commission and the Radio Authority.

Independent Labour Party (abbrev.: **ILP**) a British socialist political party formed in 1893 under the leadership of Keir Hardie. It was instrumental in the formation of the Labour Party in 1906, but tension between the two parties grew in the 1930s over the questions of pacifism and support for communism, and by the early 1950s the Independent Labour Party had lost all its parliamentary representation.

independently ▸ **adverb 1** in a way that is free from outside control or influence: *the government must prove its ability to govern independently.*
2 without outside help; unaided: *disabled people living independently in their own homes.*
3 in a way that is not connected with another; individually: *decisions are made **independently of** consumers.*

independent suspension ▸ **noun** [mass noun] a form of vehicle suspension in which each wheel is supported independently of the others.

Independent Television Commission (abbrev.: **ITC**) (in the UK) an organization responsible for licensing and regulating commercial television. It merged with Ofcom in 2003.

independent variable ▸ **noun** Mathematics a variable (often denoted by *x*) whose variation does not depend on that of another.

in-depth ▸ **adjective** comprehensive and thorough: *in-depth analysis of the figures.*

indescribable ▸ **adjective** too unusual, extreme, or indefinite to be adequately described: *most prisoners suffered indescribable hardship.*
– DERIVATIVES **indescribability** noun, **indescribably** adverb.

indestructible ▸ **adjective** not able to be destroyed: *indestructible plastic containers.*
– DERIVATIVES **indestructibility** noun, **indestructibly** adverb.

indeterminable ▸ **adjective** not able to be definitely ascertained, calculated, or identified: *a woman of indeterminable age.* ■ (of a dispute or difficulty) not able to be resolved.
– DERIVATIVES **indeterminably** adverb.
– ORIGIN late 15th cent. (in the sense 'unable to be limited'): from late Latin *indeterminabilis*, from *in-* 'not' + *determinabilis* (see DETERMINABLE).

indeterminacy principle ▸ **noun** another term for UNCERTAINTY PRINCIPLE.

indeterminate /ˌɪndɪˈtəːmɪnət/ ▸ **adjective 1** not exactly known, established, or defined: *the carpet is an indeterminate dull shade* | *the date of manufacture is indeterminate.* ■ (of a judicial sentence) not of a fixed length but dependent on the convicted person's conduct. ■ Mathematics (of a quantity) having no definite or definable value. ■ Medicine (of a condition) from which a diagnosis of the underlying cause cannot be made: *indeterminate colitis.*
2 Botany (of a shoot) not having all the axes terminating in a flower bud and so potentially of indefinite length.
– DERIVATIVES **indeterminacy** noun, **indeterminately** adverb, **indeterminateness** noun.
– ORIGIN early 17th cent.: from late Latin *indeterminatus*, from *in-* 'not' + Latin *determinatus* 'limited, determined' (see DETERMINATE).

indeterminate vowel ▸ **noun** Phonetics the vowel /ə/ heard in '*a* moment *ago*'; a schwa.

indetermination ▸ **noun** [mass noun] the state of being uncertain or undecided.

indeterminism ▶ noun [mass noun] **1** Philosophy the doctrine that not all events are wholly determined by antecedent causes.
2 the state of being uncertain or undecided.
– DERIVATIVES **indeterminist** noun, **indeterministic** adjective.

index /ˈɪndɛks/ ▶ noun (pl. **indexes** or especially in technical use **indices** /ˈɪndɪsiːz/) **1** (in a book or set of books) an alphabetical list of names, subjects, etc. with reference to the pages on which they are mentioned. ■ an alphabetical list by title, author, or other category of a collection of books or documents, for example in a library. ■ Computing a set of items each of which specifies one of the records of a file and contains information about its address.
2 a sign or measure of something: *exam results may serve as an index of the teacher's effectiveness.* ■ a figure in a system or scale representing the average value of specified prices, shares, or other items as compared with some reference figure: *the hundred-shares index closed down 9.3.* ■ [with modifier] a number giving the magnitude of a physical property or other measured phenomenon in terms of a standard: *the oral hygiene index was calculated as the sum of the debris and calculus indices.*
3 Mathematics an exponent or other superscript or subscript number appended to a quantity.
4 a pointer on an instrument, showing a quantity, a position on a scale, etc. ■ Printing a symbol shaped like a pointing hand, used to draw attention to a note.
▶ verb [with obj.] **1** record (names, subjects, etc.) in an index: *the list indexes theses under regional headings.* ■ provide an index to.
2 link the value of (prices, wages, or other payments) automatically to the value of a price index.
3 [no obj.] (often as noun **indexing**) (of a machine or part of one) move from one predetermined position to another in order to carry out a sequence of operations.
– DERIVATIVES **indexation** noun, **indexer** noun.
– ORIGIN late Middle English: from Latin *index*, *indic-* 'forefinger, informer, sign', from *in-* 'towards' + a second element related to *dicere* 'say' or *dicare* 'make known'; compare with **INDICATE**. The original sense 'index finger' (with which one points), came to mean 'pointer' (late 16th cent.), and figuratively something that serves to point to a fact or conclusion; hence a list of topics in a book ('pointing' to their location).

index case ▶ noun Medicine the first identified case in a group of related cases of a particular communicable or heritable disease.

index finger ▶ noun the finger next to the thumb; the forefinger.

index fossil ▶ noun Geology a fossil that is useful for dating and correlating the strata in which it is found.

index futures ▶ plural noun contracts to buy a range of shares at an agreed price but delivered and paid for later.

indexical /ɪnˈdɛksɪk(ə)l/ ▶ adjective & noun Linguistics another term for **DEICTIC**.
– ORIGIN early 20th cent.: coined in this sense by the American philosopher C. S. Peirce.

Index Librorum Prohibitorum /ˌɪndɛks lɪˌbrɔːrʊm prəʊˌhɪbɪˈtɔːrʊm/ an official list of books which Roman Catholics were forbidden to read or which were to be read only in expurgated editions, as contrary to Catholic faith or morals. The first Index was issued in 1557; it was revised at intervals until abolished in 1966.
– ORIGIN Latin, 'index of forbidden books'.

index-linked ▶ adjective Brit. adjusted according to the value of a retail price index: *an index-linked pension.*
– DERIVATIVES **index-linking** noun.

India a country in southern Asia occupying the greater part of the Indian subcontinent; pop. 1,156,897,800 (est. 2009); official languages, Hindi and English (fourteen other languages are recognized as official in certain regions; of these, Bengali, Gujarati, Marathi, Tamil, Telugu, and Urdu have most first-language speakers); capital, New Delhi. Hindi name **BHARAT**.

> Much of India was united under a Muslim sultanate based around Delhi from the 12th century until incorporated in the Mogul empire in the 16th century. Colonial intervention began in the late 17th century, particularly by the British; in 1765 the East India Company acquired the right to administer Bengal. In 1858, after the Indian Mutiny, the Crown took over the Company's authority, and in 1876 Queen Victoria was proclaimed Empress of India. Independence was won in 1947, at which time India was partitioned, Pakistan being created from mainly Muslim territories in the north-east (now Bangladesh) and the north-west. A member of the Commonwealth, India is the second most populous country in the world.

■ a code word representing the letter I, used in radio communication.
– ORIGIN via Latin from Greek *India*, from *Indos*, the name of the River Indus, from Persian *Hind*, from Sanskrit *sindhu* 'river', specifically 'the Indus', also 'the region around the Indus' (compare with **SINDHI**). Both the Greeks and the Persians extended the name to include all the country east of the Indus. Compare with **HINDI** and **HINDU**.

India ink ▶ noun North American term for **INDIAN INK**.

Indiaman ▶ noun (pl. **Indiamen**) historical a ship engaged in trade with India or the East or West Indies, especially an East Indiaman.
– ORIGIN early 18th cent.: from **INDIA** + *-man* from **MAN-OF-WAR**.

Indian ▶ adjective **1** relating to India or to the subcontinent comprising India, Pakistan, and Bangladesh.
2 relating to the indigenous peoples of America.
▶ noun **1** a native or inhabitant of India, or a person of Indian descent.
2 an American Indian.
3 Brit. informal an Indian meal or restaurant.
– DERIVATIVES **Indianization** (also **Indianisation**) noun, **Indianize** (also **Indianise**) verb, **Indianness** noun.

> **USAGE** The native peoples of America came to be described as Indian as a result of Christopher Columbus and other voyagers in the 15th–16th centuries believing that, when they reached the east coast of America, they had reached part of India by a new route. The terms **Indian** and **Red Indian** are today regarded as old-fashioned and inappropriate, recalling, as they do, the stereotypical portraits of the Wild West. **American Indian**, however, is well established, although the preference where possible is to make reference to specific peoples, such as **Apache**, **Delaware**, and so on. See also **USAGE** at **AMERICAN INDIAN** and **NATIVE AMERICAN**.

Indiana /ˌɪndɪˈanə/ a state in the Middle West of the US; pop. 6,376,792 (est. 2008); capital, Indianapolis. It was colonized by the French in the 18th century and ceded to Britain in 1763. It passed to the US in 1783 and became the 19th state in 1816.
– DERIVATIVES **Indianan** noun & adjective.

Indianapolis /ˌɪndɪəˈnapəlɪs/ the state capital of Indiana; pop. 798,382 (est. 2008). The city hosts an annual 500-mile (804.5-km) motor race, known as the Indy 500.

Indian bean tree ▶ noun a North American catalpa which is widely planted in urban parks in Europe. ● *Catalpa bignonioides*, family Bignoniaceae.

Indian bison ▶ noun another term for **GAUR**.

Indian club ▶ noun each of a pair of bottle-shaped clubs swung to exercise the arms in gymnastics.

Indian cobra ▶ noun another term for **SPECTACLED COBRA**.

Indian corn ▶ noun chiefly N. Amer. a type of maize with large brown and yellow grains, not usually eaten but used to make decorations at festivals such as Thanksgiving.

Indian defence ▶ noun [usu. with modifier] Chess a defence in which Black responds to White's advance of the queen's pawn by moving the king's knight to square *f6*, usually following with a fianchetto.

Indian elephant ▶ noun the elephant of southern Asia, which is smaller than the African elephant, with smaller ears and only one lip to the trunk. It is often tamed as a beast of burden in India. Also called **ASIAN ELEPHANT**. ● *Elephas maximus*, family Elephantidae.

Indian file ▶ noun another term for **SINGLE FILE**.

Indian hemp ▶ noun see **HEMP**.

Indian ink (N. Amer. also **India ink**) ▶ noun [mass noun] deep black ink containing dispersed carbon particles, used especially in drawing and technical graphics.
– ORIGIN mid 17th cent.: originally applied to Chinese and Japanese pigments prepared in solid blocks and imported to Europe via India.

Indianism ▶ noun **1** [mass noun] devotion to or adoption of the customs and culture of North American Indians.
2 a word or idiom characteristic of Indian English or North American Indians.

Indian meal ▶ noun [mass noun] N. Amer. meal ground from maize.

Indian Mutiny a revolt of Indians against British rule, 1857–8. Also called **SEPOY MUTINY**.

> Discontent with British administration resulted in widespread mutinies in British garrison towns, with accompanying massacres of white soldiers and inhabitants. After a series of sieges (most notably that of Lucknow) and battles, the revolt was put down; it was followed by the institution of direct rule by the British Crown in place of the East India Company administration.

Indian National Congress a broad-based political party in India. Founded in 1885, it dominated the independence movement in the 1930s under Mahatma Gandhi, and has been the principal party in government since 1947. Following splits in the party the Indian National Congress (I), formed by Indira Gandhi as a breakaway group (the *I* standing for *Indira*), was confirmed in 1981 as the official Congress party.

Indian Ocean the ocean to the south of India, extending from the east coast of Africa to the East Indies and Australia.

Indian paintbrush ▶ noun see **PAINTBRUSH** (sense 2).

Indian pipe ▶ noun a plant with a yellowish stem and a single drooping flower, native to North America and NE Asia. It lacks chlorophyll and obtains nourishment via symbiotic fungi in its roots. ● *Monotropa uniflora*, family Monotropaceae.

Indian poke ▶ noun see **POKE**[3] (sense 2).

Indian red ▶ noun [mass noun] a red ferric oxide pigment made typically by roasting ferrous salts.

Indian rhinoceros ▶ noun a large one-horned rhinoceros with prominent skin folds and a prehensile upper lip, found in NE India and Nepal. ● *Rhinoceros unicornis*, family Rhinocerotidae.

Indian rope trick ▶ noun the feat supposed to have been performed in India in the 19th century of climbing a length of unattached rope hanging vertically in the air.

Indian runner ▶ noun a duck of a slender upright breed, typically with white or fawn plumage, kept for egg laying.

Indian shot ▶ noun see **CANNA**.

Indian sign ▶ noun dated a magic spell or curse.

Indian subcontinent the part of Asia south of the Himalayas which forms a peninsula extending into the Indian Ocean, between the Arabian Sea and the Bay of Bengal. Historically forming the whole territory of greater India, the region is now divided between India, Pakistan, and Bangladesh.

Indian summer ▶ noun a period of unusually dry, warm weather occurring in late autumn. ■ a period of happiness or success occurring late in life.

Indian yellow ▶ noun [mass noun] an orange-yellow pigment originally obtained from the urine of cows fed on mango leaves.

India paper ▶ noun [mass noun] soft, absorbent paper, originally imported from China and used for proofs of engravings. ■ very thin, tough, opaque printing paper, used especially for Bibles.

India rubber ▶ noun [mass noun] natural rubber.

India rubber tree ▶ noun another term for **RUBBER PLANT** (sense 2).

Indic /ˈɪndɪk/ ▶ adjective relating to or denoting the group of Indo-European languages comprising Sanskrit and the modern Indian languages which are its descendants.
▶ noun [mass noun] the Indic language group.
– ORIGIN via Latin from Greek *Indikos*, from *India* (see **INDIA**).

indican /ˈɪndɪkan/ ▶ noun [mass noun] Biochemistry a potassium salt present in urine, in which it occurs as a product of the metabolism of indole. ● Alternative name: **potassium indoxylsulphate**; chem. formula $C_8H_6NOSO_2OH$.
– ORIGIN mid 19th cent.: from Latin *indicum* 'indigo' (because of its early use denoting an indoxyl glucoside occurring in the leaves of indigo plants) + **-AN**.

indicant ▶ noun a thing which indicates something.
– ORIGIN early 17th cent.: from Latin *indicant-* 'pointing out', from the verb *indicare* (see **INDICATE**).

indicate ▶ verb [with obj.] **1** point out; show: *dotted lines indicate the text's margins.* ■ be a sign of; strongly suggest: *sales indicate a growing market for such art* | [with clause] *his tone indicated that he didn't hold out much hope.* ■ mention indirectly or briefly: *the president indicated his willingness to use force against the rebels.* ■ direct attention to (someone or something)

I

by means of a gesture: *he indicated Cindy with a brief nod of the head.* ■ (of a gauge or meter) register a reading of (a quantity, dimension, etc.).
2 suggest as a desirable or necessary course of action: *treatment for shock may be indicated.*
3 [no obj.] Brit. (of a driver or motor vehicle) signal an intention to change lanes or turn using an indicator.
– ORIGIN early 17th cent.: from Latin *indicat-* 'pointed out', from the verb *indicare*, from *in-* 'towards' + *dicare* 'make known'.

indicated horsepower ▸ **noun** [mass noun] the power produced in a reciprocating engine by the working of the cylinders.

indication ▸ **noun 1** a sign or piece of information that indicates something: *the visit was an **indication of** the improvement in relations between the countries.* ■ a reading given by a gauge or meter.
2 a symptom that suggests certain medical treatment is necessary: *heavy bleeding is a common **indication for** hysterectomy.*

indicative /ɪnˈdɪkətɪv/ ▸ **adjective 1** serving as a sign or indication of something: *having recurrent dreams is not necessarily **indicative of** any psychological problem.*
2 Grammar denoting a mood of verbs expressing simple statement of a fact. Compare with SUBJUNCTIVE.
▸ **noun** Grammar a verb in the indicative mood. ■ (**the indicative**) the indicative mood.
– DERIVATIVES **indicatively** adverb.
– ORIGIN late Middle English: from French *indicatif*, *-ive*, from late Latin *indicativus*, from the verb *indicare* (see INDICATE).

indicator ▸ **noun 1** a thing that indicates the state or level of something: *car ownership is frequently used as an **indicator of** affluence.*
2 a device providing specific information on the state or condition of something, in particular: ■ [usu. with modifier] a gauge or meter of a specified kind: *a speed indicator.* ■ Brit. a board or screen in a railway station, airport, etc. giving current information.
3 Brit. a flashing light or (formerly) other device on a vehicle to show that it is about to change lanes or turn.
4 Chemistry a compound which changes colour at a specific pH value or in the presence of a particular substance, and can be used to monitor acidity, alkalinity, or the progress of a reaction.
5 (also **indicator species**) an animal or plant species which can be used to infer conditions in a particular habitat.

indicator diagram ▸ **noun** a diagram of the variation of pressure and volume within a cylinder of a reciprocating engine.

indicatory /ɪnˈdɪkət(ə)ri, ˌɪndɪˈkeɪt(ə)ri/ ▸ **adjective** rare term for INDICATIVE.

indicatrix /ˌɪndɪˈkeɪtrɪks, ɪnˈdɪkətrɪks/ (also **optical indicatrix**) ▸ **noun** (pl. **indicatrices** /-trɪsiːz/) Crystallography an imaginary ellipsoidal surface whose axes represent the refractive indices of a crystal for light following different directions with respect to the crystal axes.
– ORIGIN late 19th cent.: modern Latin, feminine of Latin *indicator* 'something that points out'.

indices plural form of INDEX.

indicia /ɪnˈdɪʃɪə, -sɪə/ ▸ **plural noun** formal signs, indications, or distinguishing marks: *the indicia of predictive child abuse.*
– ORIGIN early 17th cent.: plural of Latin *indicium*, from *index*, *indic-* 'informer, sign'.

indicolite /ɪnˈdɪkəlʌɪt/ ▸ **noun** [mass noun] an indigo-blue gem variety of tourmaline.
– ORIGIN early 19th cent.: from Latin *indicum* 'indigo' + -LITE.

indict /ɪnˈdʌɪt/ ▸ **verb** [with obj.] chiefly N. Amer. formally accuse of or charge with a crime: *his former manager was **indicted for** fraud.*
– DERIVATIVES **indictee** noun.
– ORIGIN Middle English *endite*, *indite*, from Anglo-Norman French *enditer*, based on Latin *indicere* 'proclaim, appoint', from *in-* 'towards' + *dicere* 'pronounce, utter'.

indictable ▸ **adjective** (of an offence) rendering the person who commits it liable to be charged with a serious crime that warrants a trial by jury.

indiction /ɪnˈdɪkʃ(ə)n/ ▸ **noun** historical a fiscal period of fifteen years used as a means of dating events and transactions in the Roman Empire and in the papal and some royal courts. The system was instituted by the Emperor Constantine in AD 313 and was used in some places until the 16th century. ■ [with numeral] a particular year in an indiction period.
– ORIGIN from Latin *indictio(n-)*, from the verb *indicere* (see INDICT).

indictment /ɪnˈdʌɪtm(ə)nt/ ▸ **noun 1** chiefly N. Amer. a formal charge or accusation of a serious crime: *an **indictment for** conspiracy.* ■ [mass noun] the action of indicting or being indicted: *the indictment of twelve people who had imported cocaine.*
2 a thing that serves to illustrate that a system or situation is bad and deserves to be condemned: *these rapidly escalating crime figures are an indictment of our society.*
– ORIGIN Middle English *enditement*, *inditement*, from Anglo-Norman French *enditement*, from *enditer* (see INDICT).

indie ▸ **adjective** (of a pop group, record label, or film company) not belonging or affiliated to a major record or film company. ■ characteristic of the deliberately unpolished or uncommercialized style of small independent pop groups.
▸ **noun** a small independent pop group, record label, or film company. ■ [mass noun] indie music regarded as a genre.
– ORIGIN 1920s (first used with reference to film production): abbreviation of INDEPENDENT.

Indies archaic another term for EAST INDIES (sense 2).
– ORIGIN plural of *Indy*, an obsolete variant of INDIA.

indifference ▸ **noun** [mass noun] **1** lack of interest, concern, or sympathy: *she shrugged, feigning indifference.* ■ unimportance: *it cannot be regarded as a matter of indifference.*
2 mediocrity: *the indifference of Chelsea's midfield.*
– ORIGIN late Middle English (in the sense 'being neither good nor bad'): from Latin *indifferentia*, from *in-* 'not' + *different-* 'differing, deferring' (from the verb *differre*).

indifference curve ▸ **noun** Economics a curve on a graph (the axes of which represent quantities of two commodities) linking those combinations of quantities which the consumer regards as of equal value.

indifferent ▸ **adjective 1** having no particular interest or sympathy; unconcerned: *he gave an indifferent shrug | most workers were **indifferent to** foreign affairs.*
2 neither good nor bad; mediocre: *a pair of indifferent watercolours.* ■ not good; fairly bad: *in spite of very indifferent weather.*
– DERIVATIVES **indifferently** adverb.
– ORIGIN late Middle English (in the sense 'having no partiality for or against'): via Old French from Latin *indifferent-* 'not making any difference', from *in-* 'not' + *different-* 'differing' (see DIFFERENT).

indifferentism ▸ **noun** [mass noun] the belief that differences of religious belief are of no importance.
– DERIVATIVES **indifferentist** noun.

indigence /ˈɪndɪdʒ(ə)ns/ ▸ **noun** [mass noun] a state of extreme poverty; destitution: *he did valuable work towards the relief of indigence.*

indigene /ˈɪndɪdʒiːn/ ▸ **noun** an indigenous person.
– ORIGIN late 16th cent.: from French *indigène*, from Latin *indigena*, from *indi-* (strengthened form of *in-* 'into') + an element related to *gignere* 'beget'.

indigenize /ɪnˈdɪdʒɪnʌɪz/ (also **indigenise**) ▸ **verb** [with obj.] bring (something) under the control, dominance, or influence of indigenous or local people: *English has been indigenized in different parts of the world.*
– DERIVATIVES **indigenization** noun.

indigenous /ɪnˈdɪdʒɪnəs/ ▸ **adjective** originating or occurring naturally in a particular place; native: *the indigenous peoples of Siberia | coriander is **indigenous to** southern Europe.*
– DERIVATIVES **indigeneity** /ɪnˌdɪdʒɪˈneɪɪti/ noun, **indigenously** adverb, **indigenousness** noun.
– ORIGIN mid 17th cent.: from Latin *indigena* 'a native' (see INDIGENE) + -OUS.

indigent /ˈɪndɪdʒ(ə)nt/ ▸ **adjective** poor; needy.
▸ **noun** a needy person.
– ORIGIN late Middle English: via Old French from late Latin *indigent-* 'lacking', from the verb *indigere*, from *indi-* (strengthened form of *in-* 'into') + *egere* 'to need'.

indigested ▸ **adjective** archaic term for UNDIGESTED.

indigestible ▸ **adjective 1** (of food) difficult or impossible to digest.
2 too complex or awkward to read or understand easily: *a turgid and indigestible book.*
– DERIVATIVES **indigestibility** noun, **indigestibly** adverb.
– ORIGIN late 15th cent.: via French from late Latin *indigestibilis*, from *in-* 'not' + *digestibilis* (see DIGESTIBLE).

indigestion ▸ **noun** [mass noun] pain or discomfort in the stomach associated with difficulty in digesting food.
– DERIVATIVES **indigestive** adjective.
– ORIGIN late Middle English: from late Latin *indigestio(n-)*, from *in-* (expressing negation) + *digestio* (see DIGESTION).

Indigirka /ˌɪndɪˈgɪəkə/ a river of far eastern Siberia, which flows northwards for 1,779 km (1,112 miles) to the Arctic Ocean, where it forms a wide delta.

indignant ▸ **adjective** feeling or showing anger or annoyance at what is perceived as unfair treatment: *he was indignant at being the object of suspicion.*
– DERIVATIVES **indignantly** adverb.
– ORIGIN late 16th cent.: from Latin *indignant-* 'regarding as unworthy', from the verb *indignari*, from *in-* 'not' + *dignus* 'worthy'.

indignation ▸ **noun** [mass noun] anger or annoyance provoked by what is perceived as unfair treatment: *the letter filled Lucy with indignation.*
– ORIGIN late Middle English (also in the sense 'disdain, contempt'): from Latin *indignatio(n-)*, from *indignari* 'regard as unworthy'.

indignity ▸ **noun** (pl. **indignities**) [mass noun] treatment or circumstances that cause one to feel shame or to lose one's dignity: *the indignity of needing financial help* | [count noun] *he was subjected to all manner of indignities.*
– ORIGIN late 16th cent.: from French *indignité* or Latin *indignitas*, from *indignari* 'regard as unworthy'.

indigo /ˈɪndɪgəʊ/ ▸ **noun** (pl. **indigos** or **indigoes**) **1** a tropical plant of the pea family, which was formerly widely cultivated as a source of dark blue dye.
● Genus *Indigofera*, family Leguminosae: several species, in particular *I. tinctoria*.
2 [mass noun] the dark blue dye obtained from the indigo plant. ■ a colour between blue and violet in the spectrum: *the deepest indigo of the horizon.*
– ORIGIN mid 16th cent.: from Portuguese *índigo*, via Latin from Greek *indikon*, from *indikos* 'Indian (dye)' (see INDIC).

indigobird (also **indigo finch**) ▸ **noun** an African weaver related to the whydahs, the male having black plumage with blue or purple iridescence.
● Genus *Vidua*, family Ploceidae: four species.

indigoid /ˈɪndɪgɔɪd/ ▸ **adjective** (of a dye) related to indigotin in molecular structure.

indigo snake ▸ **noun** a large harmless American snake that typically has bluish-black skin which may be patterned. Also called CRIBO. ● *Drymarchon corais*, family Colubridae. Alternative name: **blue gopher snake**.

indigotin /ɪnˈdɪgətɪn, ˌɪndɪˈgəʊtɪn/ ▸ **noun** [mass noun] Chemistry a dark blue crystalline compound which is the main constituent of the dye indigo. ● Chem. formula: $(C_8H_5NO)_2$.
– ORIGIN mid 19th cent.: from INDIGO + *-t-* (for ease of pronunciation) + -IN[1].

Indio /ˈɪndɪəʊ/ ▸ **noun** (pl. **Indios**) a member of any of the indigenous peoples of America or eastern Asia in areas formerly subject to Spain or Portugal.
– ORIGIN mid 19th cent.: from Spanish and Portuguese, literally 'Indian'.

Indira Gandhi Canal /ɪnˌdɪərə, ˌɪndərə/ a massive canal in NW India, bringing water to the Thar Desert of Rajasthan from the Harike Barrage on the Sutlej River. The canal, which is 650 km (406 miles) long, was completed in 1986. Former name RAJASTHAN CANAL.

indirect ▸ **adjective 1** not directly caused by or resulting from something: *full employment would have an indirect effect on wage levels.* ■ not done directly; conducted through intermediaries: *local government under the indirect control of the British.* ■ (of costs) deriving from overhead charges or subsidiary work. ■ (of taxation) levied on goods and services rather than income or profits.
2 (of a route) not straight; not following the shortest way. ■ (of lighting) from a concealed source and diffusely reflected.
3 avoiding direct mention or exposition of a subject: *an indirect attack on the Archbishop.*
4 Soccer denoting a free kick from which a goal may not be scored directly.
– DERIVATIVES **indirectness** noun.
– ORIGIN late Middle English (in the sense 'not in full grammatical concord'): from medieval Latin *indirectus*, from *in-* 'not' + *directus* (see DIRECT).

indirection ▸ **noun** [mass noun] indirectness or lack of straightforwardness in action, speech, or progression: *his love of intrigue and sly indirection.*

– ORIGIN late 16th cent.: from INDIRECT, on the pattern of *direction*.

indirectly ▶ adverb **1** in a way that is not directly caused by something; incidentally: *the losses indirectly affect us all.*
2 without having had direct experience; at second hand: *I heard of the damage indirectly.*
3 through implication; obliquely: *both writers refer, if only indirectly, to a wealth of other art.*

indirect object ▶ noun Grammar a noun phrase referring to someone or something that is affected by the action of a transitive verb (typically as a recipient), but is not the primary object (e.g. *him* in *give him the book*). Compare with DIRECT OBJECT.

indirect question ▶ noun Grammar a question in reported speech (e.g. *they asked who I was*).

indirect rule ▶ noun [mass noun] a system of government of one nation by another in which the governed people retain certain administrative, legal, and other powers.

indirect speech ▶ noun another term for REPORTED SPEECH.

indirect tax ▶ noun a tax levied on goods and services rather than on income or profits.

indiscernible /ˌɪndɪˈsəːnɪb(ə)l/ ▶ adjective impossible to see or clearly distinguish.
– DERIVATIVES **indiscernibility** noun, **indiscernibly** adverb.

indiscipline ▶ noun [mass noun] lack of discipline.

indiscreet ▶ adjective having, showing, or proceeding from too great a readiness to reveal things that should remain private or secret.
– DERIVATIVES **indiscreetly** adverb.
– ORIGIN late Middle English (originally as *indiscrete* in the sense 'lacking discernment or judgement'): from late Latin *indiscretus* 'not separate or distinguishable' (in medieval Latin 'careless, indiscreet'), from *in-* 'not' + *discretus* 'separate' (see DISCREET). Compare with INDISCRETE.

indiscrete ▶ adjective rare not divided into distinct parts.
– ORIGIN early 17th cent. (in the sense 'not separate or distinguishable'; originally as *indiscreet*): from Latin *indiscretus*, from *in-* 'not' + *discretus* 'separate' (see DISCREET). Compare with INDISCREET.

indiscretion ▶ noun [mass noun] behaviour or speech that is indiscreet or displays a lack of good judgement: *he knew himself all too prone to indiscretion* | [count noun] *sexual indiscretions.*
– ORIGIN Middle English: from late Latin *indiscretio(n-)*, from *in-* (expressing negation) + *discretio* 'separation' (in late Latin 'discernment'), from *discernere* 'separate out, discern'.

indiscriminate /ˌɪndɪˈskrɪmɪnət/ ▶ adjective done at random or without careful judgement: *the indiscriminate use of antibiotics can cause problems.* ■ (of a person) not using or exercising discrimination: *she was indiscriminate with her affections.*
– DERIVATIVES **indiscriminateness** noun, **indiscrimination** noun.
– ORIGIN late 16th cent. (in the sense 'haphazard, not selective'): from IN-[1] 'not' + Latin *discriminatus*, past participle of *discriminare* (see DISCRIMINATE).

indiscriminately /ˌɪndɪˈskrɪmɪnətli/ ▶ adverb in a random manner; unsystematically: *his armies slaughtered men, women, and children indiscriminately.* ■ in a way that does not show care or judgement: *people who are sedentary and who eat indiscriminately.*

indiscriminating ▶ adjective making no distinctions; indiscriminate.

indispensable ▶ adjective absolutely necessary: *he made himself indispensable to the parish priest.*
– DERIVATIVES **indispensability** noun, **indispensably** adverb.
– ORIGIN mid 16th cent. (in the sense 'not to be allowed or provided for by ecclesiastical dispensation'): from medieval Latin *indispensabilis*, from *in-* 'not' + *dispensabilis* (see DISPENSABLE).

indispose ▶ verb [with obj.] archaic **1** make (someone) unfit for or unable to do something.
2 make (someone) averse to something.

indisposed ▶ adjective **1** slightly unwell: *my mother is indisposed.*
2 averse; unwilling: [with infinitive] *the potential audience seemed indisposed to attend.*
– ORIGIN late Middle English: from IN-[1] 'not' + DISPOSED, or past participle of *indispose* 'make unwell or unwilling'.

indisposition ▶ noun [mass noun] **1** mild illness: *she was chiefly confined by indisposition to her bedroom.*
2 lack of enthusiasm or inclination; reluctance: *indisposition to motion, exertion, or change* | [count noun] *an utter indisposition to do anything whatever.*

indisputable ▶ adjective unable to be challenged or denied: *a far from indisputable fact.*
– DERIVATIVES **indisputability** noun, **indisputably** adverb.
– ORIGIN mid 16th cent.: from late Latin *indisputabilis*, from *in-* 'not' + *disputabilis* (see DISPUTABLE).

indissociable ▶ adjective unable to be dissociated.

indissoluble /ˌɪndɪˈsɒljʊb(ə)l/ ▶ adjective unable to be destroyed; lasting: *an indissoluble friendship.*
– DERIVATIVES **indissolubility** noun, **indissolubly** adverb.
– ORIGIN late 15th cent.: from Latin *indissolubilis*, from *in-* 'not' + *dissolubilis* (see DISSOLUBLE).

indistinct ▶ adjective not clear or sharply defined: *his speech was slurred and indistinct.*
– DERIVATIVES **indistinctly** adverb, **indistinctness** noun.
– ORIGIN mid 16th cent.: from Latin *indistinctus*, from *in-* 'not' + *distinctus* 'separated, distinguished' (see DISTINCT).

indistinctive ▶ adjective not having a distinctive character or features.
– DERIVATIVES **indistinctiveness** noun.

indistinguishable ▶ adjective not able to be identified as different or distinct: *the counterfeit bills were virtually* ***indistinguishable from*** *the real thing.*
– DERIVATIVES **indistinguishably** adverb.

indite /ɪnˈdʌɪt/ ▶ verb [with obj.] archaic write; compose: *he indites the wondrous tale of Our Lord.*
– ORIGIN Middle English *endite*, from Old French *enditier*, based on Latin *indicere* (see INDICT).

indium /ˈɪndɪəm/ ▶ noun [mass noun] the chemical element of atomic number 49, a soft silvery-white metal occurring naturally in association with zinc and some other metals. (Symbol: **In**)
– ORIGIN mid 19th cent.: from INDIGO (because there are two characteristic indigo lines in its spectrum) + -IUM.

individual ▶ adjective **1** [attrib.] single; separate: *individual tiny flowers.*
2 of or for a particular person: *the individual needs of the children.* ■ designed for use by one person: *a casserole served in individual portions.* ■ characteristic of a particular person or thing: *she was surprised at how individual the others' bodies were.* ■ having a striking or unusual character; original: *she creates her own, highly individual landscapes.*
▶ noun a single human being as distinct from a group: *boat trips for parties and individuals.* ■ a single member of a class: *they live in a group or as individuals, depending on the species.* ■ [with adj.] informal a person of a specified kind: *the most selfish, egotistical individual I have ever met.* ■ a distinctive or original person.
– ORIGIN late Middle English (in the sense 'indivisible'): from medieval Latin *individualis*, from Latin *individuus*, from *in-* 'not' + *dividuus* 'divisible' (from *dividere* 'to divide').

individualism ▶ noun [mass noun] **1** the habit or principle of being independent and self-reliant. ■ self-centred feeling or conduct; egoism.
2 a social theory favouring freedom of action for individuals over collective or state control.
– DERIVATIVES **individualist** noun & adjective.

individualistic ▶ adjective **1** more interested in individual people than in society as a whole: *individualistic cultures where individuals strive for self-realization.*
2 marked by or expressing individuality; unconventional: *her work is quirky and genuinely individualistic.*
– DERIVATIVES **individualistically** adverb.

individuality ▶ noun [mass noun] **1** the quality or character of a particular person or thing that distinguishes them from others of the same kind, especially when strongly marked: *clothes with real style and individuality.* ■ (**individualities**) individual characteristics.
2 separate existence.
– ORIGIN early 17th cent.: in early use from medieval Latin *individualitas*.

individualize (also **individualise**) ▶ verb [with obj.] give an individual character to: *have your shirt individualized with your own club name.* ■ (usu. as adj. **individualized**) tailor (something) to suit the individual: *an individualized learning programme.*
– DERIVATIVES **individualization** noun.

individually ▶ adverb **1** one by one; singly; separately: *individually wrapped cheeses.* ■ in a distinctive manner: *Dublin people dress more individually than people in London.*
2 personally; in an individual capacity: *partnerships and individually owned firms.*

individuate ▶ verb [with obj.] distinguish from others of the same kind; single out: *it is easy to individuate and enumerate the significant elements.*
– DERIVATIVES **individuation** noun.
– ORIGIN early 17th cent.: from medieval Latin *individuat-* 'singled out', from the verb *individuare*, from Latin *individuus*, from *in-* 'into' + *dividuus* 'divisible' (from *dividere* 'to divide').

indivisible ▶ adjective unable to be divided or separated: *privilege was indivisible from responsibility.* ■ (of a number) unable to be divided by another number exactly without leaving a remainder.
– DERIVATIVES **indivisibility** noun, **indivisibly** adverb.
– ORIGIN late Middle English: from late Latin *indivisibilis*, from *in-* 'not' + *divisibilis* (see DIVISIBLE).

Indo- /ˈɪndəʊ/ ▶ combining form (used commonly in linguistic and ethnological terms) Indian; Indian and ...: *Indo-Iranian.* ■ relating to India.
– ORIGIN from Latin *Indus*, from Greek *Indos* 'Indian'.

Indo-Aryan ▶ adjective **1** relating to or denoting an Indo-European people who invaded NW India in the 2nd millennium BC. See ARYAN.
2 another term for INDIC.

Indo-China (also **Indochina**) the peninsula of SE Asia containing Burma (Myanmar), Thailand, Malaya, Laos, Cambodia, and Vietnam; especially, the part of this area consisting of Laos, Cambodia, and Vietnam, which was a French dependency (**French Indo-China**) from 1862 to 1954.
– DERIVATIVES **Indo-Chinese** adjective & noun.

indochinite /ˌɪndəʊˈtʃʌɪnʌɪt/ ▶ noun Geology a tektite from the strewn field in Indo-China.
– ORIGIN 1940s: from INDO-CHINA + -ITE[1].

indocile ▶ adjective difficult to teach or discipline; not submissive.
– DERIVATIVES **indocility** noun.
– ORIGIN early 17th cent.: from French, or from Latin *indocilis*, from *in-* 'not' + *docilis* (see DOCILE).

indoctrinate /ɪnˈdɒktrɪneɪt/ ▶ verb [with obj.] teach (a person or group) to accept a set of beliefs uncritically: *broadcasting was a vehicle for indoctrinating the masses.* ■ archaic teach or instruct (someone): *he indoctrinated them in systematic theology.*
– DERIVATIVES **indoctrination** noun, **indoctrinator** noun.
– ORIGIN early 17th cent.: formerly also as *endoctrinate*: from EN-[1], IN-[2] 'into' + DOCTRINE + -ATE[3], or from obsolete *indoctrine* (verb), from French *endoctriner*, based on *doctrine* 'doctrine'.

Indo-European ▶ adjective relating to the family of languages spoken over the greater part of Europe and Asia as far as northern India. ■ another term for PROTO-INDO-EUROPEAN.

> The Indo-European languages have a history of over 3,000 years. Their unattested, reconstructed ancestor, Proto-Indo-European, is believed to have been spoken well before 4000 BC in a region somewhere to the north or south of the Black Sea. The family comprises twelve branches: Indic (including Sanskrit and its descendants), Iranian, Anatolian (including Hittite and other extinct languages), Armenian, Hellenic (Greek), Albanian (or Illyrian), Italic (including Latin and the Romance languages), Celtic, Tocharian (an extinct group from central Asia), Germanic (including English, German, Dutch, and the Scandinavian languages), Baltic, and Slavic (including Russian, Polish, Czech, Bulgarian, Serbian, and Croatian).

▶ noun **1** [mass noun] the ancestral Proto-Indo-European language. ■ the Indo-European family of languages.
2 a speaker of an Indo-European language, especially Proto-Indo-European.

Indo-Germanic ▶ adjective & noun former term for INDO-EUROPEAN.

Indo-Iranian ▶ adjective relating to a subfamily of Indo-European languages spoken in northern India and Iran.
▶ noun [mass noun] the Indo-Iranian subfamily of languages, divided into the Indic group and the Iranian group. Also called ARYAN.

indole /ˈɪndəʊl/ ▶ noun [mass noun] Chemistry a crystalline organic compound with an unpleasant odour, present

I

in coal tar and in faeces. ● A heteroaromatic compound with fused benzene and pyrrole rings; chem. formula: C_8H_7N.
– ORIGIN mid 19th cent.: blend of **INDIGO** (because obtained artificially from indigo blue) and Latin *oleum* 'oil'.

indoleacetic acid /ˌɪndəʊləˈsiːtɪk, -ˈsɛtɪk/ ▸ **noun** [mass noun] Biochemistry a compound which is an acetic acid derivative of indole, especially one found as a natural growth hormone (auxin) in plants. ● Chem. formula: $C_8H_6(CH_3COOH)N$; seven isomers; auxin is **indole-3-acetic acid**.

indolence /ˈɪnd(ə)l(ə)ns/ ▸ **noun** [mass noun] avoidance of activity or exertion; laziness: *my failure is probably due to my own indolence*.

indolent /ˈɪnd(ə)l(ə)nt/ ▸ **adjective 1** wanting to avoid activity or exertion; lazy.
2 Medicine (of a disease or condition) causing little or no pain. ■ (especially of an ulcer) slow to develop, progress, or heal; persistent.
– DERIVATIVES **indolently** adverb.
– ORIGIN mid 17th cent.: from late Latin *indolent-*, from *in-* 'not' + *dolere* 'suffer or give pain'. The sense 'idle' arose in the early 18th cent.

Indology /ɪnˈdɒlədʒi/ ▸ **noun** [mass noun] the study of Indian history, literature, philosophy, and culture.
– DERIVATIVES **Indologist** noun.

Indo-Malaysian (also **Indo-Malayan**) ▸ **adjective** relating to both India and Malaya, in particular: ■ denoting an ethnological region comprising Sri Lanka, the Malay peninsula, and the Malaysian islands. ■ (also **Indo-Malesian**) Biology denoting a major biogeographical region comprising Malesia and East, South, and SE Asia.

I

indomethacin /ˌɪndəʊˈmɛθəsɪn/ ▸ **noun** [mass noun] Medicine a compound with anti-inflammatory, antipyretic, and analgesic properties, used chiefly to treat rheumatoid arthritis and gout. ● Chem. formula: $C_{19}H_{16}NO_4Cl$.
– ORIGIN 1960s: from *indo(le)* + *meth(yl)* + *ac(etic)* + **-IN**[1].

indomitable /ɪnˈdɒmɪtəb(ə)l/ ▸ **adjective** impossible to subdue or defeat: *a woman of indomitable spirit*.
– DERIVATIVES **indomitability** noun, **indomitableness** noun, **indomitably** adverb.
– ORIGIN mid 17th cent. (in the sense 'untameable'): from late Latin *indomitabilis*, from *in-* 'not' + Latin *domitare* 'to tame'.

Indonesia /ˌɪndəˈniːʒə, -ˈniːzɪə/ a SE Asian country consisting of many islands in the Malay Archipelago; pop. 240,271,500 (est. 2009); languages, Indonesian (official), Malay, Balinese, Chinese, Javanese, and others; capital, Jakarta (on Java). Former name (until 1949) **DUTCH EAST INDIES**.

> Indonesia consists of the territories of the former Dutch East Indies, of which the largest are Java, Sumatra, southern Borneo, western New Guinea, the Moluccas, and Sulawesi. The Dutch established control over the area in the 17th century. Independence was won in 1949, although Irian Jaya (now the province of Papua) was not handed over until 1963. An attempted communist coup was crushed by the army in 1965 and East Timor was annexed in 1976. The end of the 20th century saw the introduction of democratic elections and the gaining of full independence by East Timor. In 2004 more than 200,000 people were killed when an earthquake off the coast of Sumatra led to a tsunami that caused devastation in many countries around the Indian Ocean.

– ORIGIN from **INDO-** + Greek *nēsos* 'island'.

Indonesian ▸ **adjective** relating to Indonesia, Indonesians, or their languages.
▸ **noun 1** a native or inhabitant of Indonesia.
2 [mass noun] the group of Austronesian languages, closely related to Malay, which are spoken in Indonesia and neighbouring islands. ■ another term for **BAHASA INDONESIA**.

indoor ▸ **adjective** [attrib.] situated, conducted, or used within a building or under cover: *indoor sports*. ■ relating to sports played indoors: *the national indoor champion*.
– ORIGIN early 18th cent. (superseding earlier *within-door*): from **IN** (as a preposition) + **DOOR**.

indoors ▸ **adverb** into or within a building: *they went indoors and explored the house*.
▸ **noun** the area or space inside a building.
– ORIGIN late 18th cent. (superseding earlier *within doors*): from **INDOOR**.

Indo-Pacific ▸ **adjective** relating to the Indian Ocean and the adjacent parts of the Pacific. ■ another term for **AUSTRONESIAN**.
▸ **noun** [mass noun] the Indo-Pacific seas or ocean.

Indore /ɪnˈdɔː/ a manufacturing city of Madhya Pradesh in central India; pop. 1,811,500 (est. 2009).

indorse ▸ **verb** US spelling of **ENDORSE**.

indorsement ▸ **noun** chiefly US variant spelling of **ENDORSEMENT**.

indoxyl /ɪnˈdɒksʌɪl, -sɪl/ ▸ **noun** [as modifier] Chemistry of or denoting the radical $-ONC_8H_6$, derived from a hydroxy derivative of indole and present in indigotin.

Indra /ˈɪndrə/ Hinduism the warrior king of the heavens, god of war and storm, to whom many of the prayers in the Rig Veda are addressed.

indraught /ˈɪndrɑːft/ (US **indraft**) ▸ **noun** [mass noun] the drawing in of something. ■ [count noun] an inward flow, especially of air.

indrawn ▸ **adjective 1** [attrib.] (of breath) taken in.
2 (of a person) shy and introspective.

indri /ˈɪndri/ ▸ **noun** (pl. **indris**) a large, short-tailed Madagascan lemur which jumps from tree to tree in an upright position and rarely comes to the ground. ● *Indri indri*, family Indriidae.
– ORIGIN mid 19th cent.: from Malagasy *indry!* 'behold!' or *indry izy!* 'there he is!', mistaken for its name. The Malagasy name is *babakoto*.

indricothere /ˈɪndrɪkə(ʊ),θɪə/ ▸ **noun** a large ungulate fossil mammal of the Oligocene epoch, related to the rhinoceros. ● Family Hyracodontidae, order Paracatheriinae.
– ORIGIN 1960s: from modern Latin *Indricotherium* (genus name), from Russian *indrik* 'giant mythical animal' + Greek *thērion* 'wild beast'.

indubitable /ɪnˈdjuːbɪtəb(ə)l/ ▸ **adjective** impossible to doubt; unquestionable: *an indubitable truth*.
– DERIVATIVES **indubitably** adverb [sentence adverb] *indubitably, liberalism parades under many guises*.
– ORIGIN late Middle English: from Latin *indubitabilis*, from *in-* 'not' + *dubitabilis* (see **DUBITABLE**).

induce /ɪnˈdjuːs/ ▸ **verb** [with obj.] **1** [with obj. and infinitive] succeed in persuading or leading (someone) to do something: *the pickets induced many workers to stay away*.
2 bring about or give rise to: *none of these measures induced a change of policy*. ■ produce (an electric charge or current or a magnetic state) by induction. ■ (usu. as adj. **induced**) Physics cause (radioactivity) by bombardment with radiation.
3 Medicine bring on (the birth of a baby) artificially, typically by the use of drugs. ■ bring on childbirth in (a pregnant woman) artificially, typically by the use of drugs.
4 Logic derive by inductive reasoning.
– DERIVATIVES **inducer** noun, **inducible** adjective.
– ORIGIN late Middle English (formerly also as *enduce*): from Latin *inducere* 'lead in', from *in-* 'into' + *ducere* 'to lead', or from French *enduire*. Compare with **ENDUE**.

induced drag ▸ **noun** [mass noun] Aeronautics that part of the drag on an aerofoil which arises from the development of lift.

inducement ▸ **noun** a thing that persuades or leads someone to do something: *companies were prepared to build only in return for massive inducements* | [mass noun] [with infinitive] *there is no inducement to wait for payment*. ■ a bribe.

induct /ɪnˈdʌkt/ ▸ **verb** [with obj.] **1** admit (someone) formally to a post or organization: *arrangements for inducting new members to an organization*. ■ formally introduce (a member of the clergy) into possession of a benefice. ■ US enlist (someone) for military service. ■ (**induct someone in/into**) introduce someone to (a difficult or obscure subject): *my master inducted me into the skills of magic*.
2 archaic install in a seat or room.
– DERIVATIVES **inductee** noun.
– ORIGIN late Middle English: from Latin *induct-* 'led into', from the verb *inducere* (see **INDUCE**).

inductance ▸ **noun** [mass noun] Physics the property of an electric conductor or circuit that causes an electromotive force to be generated by a change in the current flowing. ■ [count noun] a component with the property of inductance.
– ORIGIN late 19th cent.: from **INDUCTION** + **-ANCE**.

induction ▸ **noun** [mass noun] **1** the action or process of inducting someone to a post or organization: *induction into membership of a Masonic brotherhood*. ■ [usu. as modifier] a formal introduction to a new job or position: *an induction course*. ■ US enlistment into military service.
2 the process or action of bringing about or giving rise to something: *the induction of malformations by radiation*. ■ Medicine the process of bringing on the birth of a baby by artificial means, typically by the use of drugs.
3 Logic the inference of a general law from particular instances. Often contrasted with **DEDUCTION**. ■ the production of facts to prove a general statement. ■ (also **mathematical induction**) Mathematics a means of proving a theorem by showing that if it is true of any particular case it is true of the next case in a series, and then showing that it is indeed true in one particular case.
4 the production of an electric or magnetic state by the proximity (without contact) of an electrified or magnetized body. See also **MAGNETIC INDUCTION**. ■ the production of an electric current in a conductor by varying the magnetic field applied to the conductor.
5 the stage of the working cycle of an internal-combustion engine in which the fuel mixture is drawn into the cylinders.
– ORIGIN late Middle English: from Latin *inductio(n-)*, from the verb *inducere* 'lead into' (see **INDUCE**).

induction coil ▸ **noun** a coil for generating intermittent high voltage from a direct current.

induction hardening ▸ **noun** [mass noun] Metallurgy a process for hardening steel surfaces by induction heating followed by quenching.

induction heating ▸ **noun** [mass noun] heating of a material by inducing an electric current within it.

induction loop ▸ **noun** a sound system in which a loop of wire around an area in a building, such as a cinema or theatre, produces an electromagnetic signal received directly by hearing aids used by the partially deaf.

inductive ▸ **adjective 1** characterized by the inference of general laws from particular instances: *instinct rather than inductive reasoning marked her approach to life*.
2 relating to or caused by electric or magnetic induction. ■ possessing inductance.
– DERIVATIVES **inductively** adverb, **inductiveness** noun.
– ORIGIN late Middle English (in the sense 'leading to'): from Old French *inductif, -ive* or late Latin *inductivus* 'hypothetical' (later 'inducing, leading to'), from Latin *inducere* (see **INDUCE**). Sense 1 dates from the mid 18th cent.

inductivism ▸ **noun** [mass noun] the use of or preference for inductive methods of reasoning, especially in science.
– DERIVATIVES **inductivist** noun & adjective.

inductor ▸ **noun 1** a component in an electric or electronic circuit which possesses inductance.
2 a substance that promotes an equilibrium reaction by reacting with one of the substances produced.
– ORIGIN mid 17th cent. (in the sense 'a person who inducts or initiates'): from late Latin, from Latin *inducere* (see **INDUCE**), or from **INDUCT** + **-OR**[1]. Current senses date from the early 20th cent.

indue ▸ **verb** variant spelling of **ENDUE**.

indulge ▸ **verb 1** [no obj.] (**indulge in**) allow oneself to enjoy the pleasure of: *we indulged in a cream tea*. ■ (**indulge in**) become involved in (an activity, typically one that is undesirable or disapproved of): *I don't indulge in idle gossip*. ■ informal allow oneself to enjoy a particular pleasure, especially that of alcohol: *I only indulge on special occasions*. ■ [with obj.] satisfy or yield freely to (a desire or interest): *she was able to indulge a growing passion for literature*.
2 [with obj.] allow (someone) to enjoy something desired: *a luxury service used to indulge the chief executive*.
– DERIVATIVES **indulger** noun.
– ORIGIN early 17th cent. (in the sense 'treat with excessive kindness'): from Latin *indulgere* 'give free rein to'.

indulgence ▸ **noun 1** [mass noun] the action or fact of indulging: *indulgence in self-pity*. ■ the state or attitude of being indulgent or tolerant: *she regarded his affairs with a casual, slightly amused indulgence*. ■ [count noun] a thing that is indulged in; a luxury: *Claire collects shoes—it is her indulgence*.
2 chiefly historical (in the Roman Catholic Church) a grant by the Pope of remission of the temporal punishment in purgatory still due for sins after absolution. The unrestricted sale of indulgences by pardoners was a widespread abuse during the later Middle Ages.
3 an extension of the time in which a bill or debt has to be paid.

– ORIGIN late Middle English: via Old French from Latin *indulgentia*, from the verb *indulgere* (see INDULGE).

indulgent ▶ adjective having or indicating a readiness or over-readiness to be generous to or lenient with someone: *indulgent parents.* ■ self-indulgent: *sheer indulgent nostalgia.*
– DERIVATIVES **indulgently** adverb.
– ORIGIN early 16th cent.: from French, or from Latin *indulgent-* 'giving free rein to', from the verb *indulgere.*

indult /ɪnˈdʌlt/ ▶ noun (in the Roman Catholic Church) a licence granted by the Pope authorizing an act that the common law of the Church does not sanction.
– ORIGIN late 15th cent.: from French, from late Latin *indultum* 'grant, concession', neuter past participle of Latin *indulgere* 'indulge'.

indumentum /ˌɪndjʊˈmɛntəm/ ▶ noun (pl. **indumenta**) Botany & Zoology a covering of hairs (or feathers) on an animal or plant.
– ORIGIN mid 19th cent.: from Latin, literally 'garment', from *induere* 'put on, don'.

induna /ɪnˈduːnə/ ▶ noun S. African a tribal councillor or headman. ■ an African foreman. ■ a person in authority.
– ORIGIN Xhosa and Zulu, from the nominal prefix *in-* + *duna* 'captain, councillor'.

indurate /ˈɪndjʊreɪt/ ▶ verb [with obj.] (usu. as adj. **indurated**) harden: *a bed of indurated clay.*
– DERIVATIVES **induration** noun.
– ORIGIN mid 16th cent. (earlier Middle English) as *induration*: from Latin *indurat-* 'made hard', from the verb *indurare* (based on *durus* 'hard').

Indus[1] /ˈɪndəs/ a river of southern Asia, about 2,900 km (1,800 miles) in length, flowing from Tibet through Kashmir and Pakistan to the Arabian Sea. Along its valley an early civilization flourished from *c.*2600 to 1760 BC.

Indus[2] /ˈɪndəs/ Astronomy an inconspicuous southern constellation (the Indian), between Capricornus and Pavo.
– ORIGIN Latin.

indusium /ɪnˈdjuːzɪəm/ ▶ noun (pl. **indusia**) chiefly Botany a thin membranous covering, especially a shield covering a sorus on a fern frond.
– ORIGIN early 18th cent.: from Latin, literally 'tunic', from *induere* 'put on, don'.

industrial ▶ adjective **1** relating to or characterized by industry: *industrial waste | a small industrial town.* ■ having highly developed industries: *the major industrial nations.* ■ designed or suitable for use in industry: *industrial heating oil.* ■ (of a disease or injury) contracted or sustained in the course of employment, especially in a factory.
2 relating to or denoting a type of harsh, uncompromising rock music incorporating sounds resembling those produced by industrial machinery.
▶ noun (**industrials**) shares in industrial companies.
– DERIVATIVES **industrially** adverb.
– ORIGIN late 15th cent.: from INDUSTRY + -AL; in later use influenced by French *industriel.*

industrial action ▶ noun [mass noun] Brit. action taken by employees of a company as a protest, especially striking or working to rule.

industrial archaeology ▶ noun [mass noun] the study of equipment and buildings formerly used in industry.

industrial democracy ▶ noun [mass noun] the involvement of employees in the running of an industry, factory, company, etc.

industrial diamond ▶ noun a small diamond, not of gem quality, used in abrasives and in cutting and drilling tools.

industrial dispute ▶ noun a dispute between employers and employees.

industrial espionage ▶ noun [mass noun] spying directed towards discovering the secrets of a rival manufacturer or other industrial company.

industrial estate ▶ noun Brit. an area of land developed as a site for factories and other industrial businesses.

industrialism ▶ noun [mass noun] a social or economic system in which manufacturing industries are prevalent.

industrialist ▶ noun a person involved in the ownership and management of industry.

industrialize (also **industrialise**) ▶ verb [with obj.] (often as adj. **industrialized**) develop industries in (a country or region) on a wide scale: *the industrialized nations.* ■ [no obj.] (of a country or region) build up a system of industries.
– DERIVATIVES **industrialization** noun.

industrial language ▶ noun [mass noun] Brit. informal bad language; swearing.

industrial melanism ▶ noun [mass noun] Zoology the prevalence of dark-coloured varieties of animals (especially moths) in industrial areas where they are better camouflaged than paler forms.

industrial park ▶ noun North American term for INDUSTRIAL ESTATE.

industrial relations ▶ plural noun the relations between management and workers in industry.

Industrial Revolution the rapid development of industry that occurred in Britain in the late 18th and 19th centuries, brought about by the introduction of machinery. It was characterized by the use of steam power, the growth of factories, and the mass production of manufactured goods.

industrial-strength ▶ adjective very strong or powerful: *an industrial-strength cleaner.*

Industrial Workers of the World (abbrev.: **IWW**) a radical US labour movement, founded in 1905 and, as part of the syndicalist movement, dedicated to the overthrow of capitalism. Also called the WOBBLIES.

industrious ▶ adjective diligent and hard-working.
– DERIVATIVES **industriously** adverb, **industriousness** noun.
– ORIGIN late 15th cent. (in the sense 'skilful, clever, ingenious'): from French *industrieux* or late Latin *industriosus*, from Latin *industria* 'diligence'.

industry ▶ noun (pl. **industries**) **1** [mass noun] economic activity concerned with the processing of raw materials and manufacture of goods in factories: *new investment incentives for British industry.* ■ [count noun] [with adj. or noun modifier] a particular form or branch of economic or commercial activity: *the car industry.* ■ [count noun] [with adj. or noun modifier] informal an activity or domain in which a great deal of effort is expended: *the Shakespeare industry.*
2 [mass noun] hard work: *the kitchen became **a hive of industry**.*
– ORIGIN late Middle English (in sense 2): from French *industrie* or Latin *industria* 'diligence'.

indwell ▶ verb (past and past participle **indwelt**) **1** [with obj.] be permanently present in (someone's soul or mind); possess spiritually.
2 (as adj. **indwelling**) Medicine (of a catheter, needle, etc.) fixed in a person's body for a sustained period of time.
– DERIVATIVES **indweller** noun.
– ORIGIN late Middle English: originally translating Latin *inhabitare.*

Indy ▶ noun [mass noun] a form of motor racing in which cars are driven round a banked, regular oval circuit which allows for racing at exceptionally high speeds. It takes place chiefly in the US.
– ORIGIN 1950s: named after INDIANAPOLIS, where the principal Indy race is held.

IndyCar ▶ noun a type of car used in Indy racing: [as modifier] *the IndyCar championship.*

-ine[1] /ʌɪn, ɪn, iːn/ ▶ suffix **1** (forming adjectives) belonging to; resembling in nature: *Alpine | asinine | canine.*
2 forming adjectives from the names of genera (such as *bovine* from the genus *Bos*) or from the names of subfamilies (such as *colubrine* from the subfamily *Colubrinae*).
– ORIGIN from French *-in, -ine*, or from Latin *-inus.*

-ine[2] /ʌɪn/ ▶ suffix forming adjectives from the names of minerals, plants, etc.: *crystalline | hyacinthine.*
– ORIGIN from Latin *-inus*, from Greek *-inos.*

-ine[3] /ɪn, iːn/ ▶ suffix forming feminine nouns such as *heroine, margravine.*
– ORIGIN from French, via Latin *-ina* from Greek *-inē*, or from German *-in.*

-ine[4] /iːn, ɪn/ ▶ suffix **1** forming chiefly abstract nouns and diminutives such as *doctrine, medicine, figurine.*
2 Chemistry forming names of alkaloids, halogens, amines, amino acids, and other substances: *cocaine | chlorine | thymine.*
– ORIGIN from French, from the Latin feminine form *-ina.*

inebriate formal or humorous ▶ verb /ɪˈniːbrɪeɪt/ [with obj.] (often as adj. **inebriated**) make (someone) drunk; intoxicate: *I got mildly inebriated.*
▶ noun /ɪˈniːbrɪət/ a drunkard.
▶ adjective /ɪˈniːbrɪət/ drunk; intoxicated.
– DERIVATIVES **inebriety** noun.
– ORIGIN late Middle English (as an adjective): from Latin *inebriatus*, past participle of *inebriare* 'intoxicate' (based on *ebrius* 'drunk').

inebriation /ɪˌniːbrɪˈeɪʃ(ə)n/ ▶ noun [mass noun] formal or humorous drunkenness; intoxication: *they were in an advanced state of inebriation.*

inedible ▶ adjective not fit or suitable for eating: *an inedible variety of mushroom.*
– DERIVATIVES **inedibility** noun.

ineducable /ɪnˈɛdjʊkəb(ə)l/ ▶ adjective considered incapable of being educated, especially (formerly) as a result of mental disability.
– DERIVATIVES **ineducability** noun.

ineffable /ɪnˈɛfəb(ə)l/ ▶ adjective too great or extreme to be expressed or described in words: *the ineffable mysteries of the soul.* ■ not to be uttered: *the ineffable Hebrew name that gentiles write as Jehovah.*
– DERIVATIVES **ineffability** noun, **ineffably** adverb.
– ORIGIN late Middle English: from Old French, or from Latin *ineffabilis*, from *in-* 'not' + *effabilis* (see EFFABLE).

ineffaceable /ɪnɪˈfeɪsəb(ə)l/ ▶ adjective unable to be erased or forgotten.

ineffective ▶ adjective not producing any significant or desired effect: *the legal sanctions against oil spills are virtually ineffective | a weak and ineffective president.*
– DERIVATIVES **ineffectively** adverb, **ineffectiveness** noun.

ineffectual ▶ adjective not producing any significant or desired effect: *an ineffectual campaign.* ■ (of a person) lacking the ability or qualities to fulfil a role or handle a situation: *she was neglectful and ineffectual as a parent.*
– DERIVATIVES **ineffectuality** noun, **ineffectually** adverb, **ineffectualness** noun.
– ORIGIN late Middle English: from medieval Latin *ineffectualis*, from *in-* 'not' + *effectualis*, from Latin *effectus* (see EFFECT); in later use from IN-[1] 'not' + EFFECTUAL.

inefficacious /ˌɪnɛfɪˈkeɪʃəs/ ▶ adjective not producing the desired effect.
– DERIVATIVES **inefficacy** noun.

inefficient ▶ adjective not achieving maximum productivity; wasting or failing to make the best use of time or resources: *inefficient transport systems | the government was both inefficient and corrupt.*
– DERIVATIVES **inefficiency** noun, **inefficiently** adverb.

inegalitarian /ˌɪnɪgalɪˈtɛːrɪən/ ▶ adjective characterized by or promoting inequality between people.

inelastic ▶ adjective **1** (of a substance or material) not elastic.
2 Economics (of demand or supply) insensitive to changes in price or income.
3 Physics (of a collision) involving an overall loss of translational kinetic energy.
– DERIVATIVES **inelastically** adverb, **inelasticity** noun.

inelegant ▶ adjective having or showing a lack of physical grace, elegance, or refinement: *he came skidding to an inelegant halt | an inelegant bellow of laughter.* ■ (of language) unpolished: *an inelegant title.*
– DERIVATIVES **inelegance** noun, **inelegantly** adverb.
– ORIGIN early 16th cent.: from French *inélégant*, from Latin *inelegant-*, from *in-* 'not' + Latin *elegant-* 'fastidious, refined' (see ELEGANT).

ineligible ▶ adjective legally or officially unable to be considered for a position or benefit: *they were **ineligible for** jury service.* ■ dated not suitable or desirable, especially as a marriage partner: *as a son-in-law he was quite ineligible.*
– DERIVATIVES **ineligibility** noun.

ineliminable /ɪnɪˈlɪmɪnəb(ə)l/ ▶ adjective incapable of being removed or excluded from consideration: *an ineliminable feature of the human condition.*

ineluctable /ˌɪnɪˈlʌktəb(ə)l/ ▶ adjective unable to be resisted or avoided; inescapable: *the ineluctable facts of history.*
– DERIVATIVES **ineluctability** /-ˈbɪlɪti/ noun, **ineluctably** adverb.
– ORIGIN early 17th cent.: from Latin *ineluctabilis*, from *in-* 'not' + *eluctari* 'struggle out'.

ineludible /ˌɪnɪˈl(j)uːdɪb(ə)l/ ▶ adjective rare unavoidable; inescapable.

inept ▶ adjective having or showing no skill; clumsy: *the referee's inept handling of the match.*

I

– DERIVATIVES **ineptitude** noun, **ineptly** adverb, **ineptness** noun.
– ORIGIN mid 16th cent. (in the sense 'not apt, unsuitable'): from Latin *ineptus*, from *in-* 'not' + *aptus* (see APT).

inequable ▶ adjective not equal or evenly distributed: *the inequable temperature of rivers and lakes.*
– ORIGIN early 18th cent.: from Latin *inaequabilis* 'uneven', from *in-* 'not' + *aequabilis* (see EQUABLE).

inequality ▶ noun (pl. **inequalities**) [mass noun] difference in size, degree, circumstances, etc.; lack of equality: *social inequality* | [count noun] *the widening inequalities in income.* ■ Mathematics the relation between two expressions that are not equal, employing a sign such as ≠ 'not equal to', > 'greater than', or < 'less than'. ■ [count noun] Mathematics a symbolic expression of the fact that two quantities are not equal.
– ORIGIN late Middle English: from Old French *inequalite*, or from Latin *inaequalitas*, from *in-* 'not' + *aequalis* (see EQUAL).

inequitable ▶ adjective unfair; unjust: *the present taxes are inequitable.*
– DERIVATIVES **inequitably** adverb.

inequity ▶ noun (pl. **inequities**) [mass noun] lack of fairness or justice: *policies aimed at redressing racial inequity* | [count noun] *inequities in school financing.*

inequivalve /ɪnˈiːkwɪvalv/ ▶ adjective Zoology (of a bivalve shell) having valves of different sizes.

ineradicable /ˌɪnɪˈradɪkəb(ə)l/ ▶ adjective unable to be destroyed or removed: *ineradicable hostility.*
– DERIVATIVES **ineradicably** adverb.

inerrant ▶ adjective incapable of being wrong.
– DERIVATIVES **inerrancy** noun, **inerrantist** noun.
– ORIGIN mid 19th cent.: from Latin *inerrant-* 'fixed', from *in-* 'not' + *errant-* 'erring' (see ERRANT).

inert ▶ adjective **1** lacking the ability or strength to move: *she lay inert in her bed.* ■ lacking vigour: *an inert political system.*
2 chemically inactive.
– DERIVATIVES **inertly** adverb, **inertness** noun.
– ORIGIN mid 17th cent.: from Latin *iners, inert-* 'unskilled, inactive', from *in-* (expressing negation) + *ars, art-* 'skill, art'.

inert gas ▶ noun another term for NOBLE GAS.

inertia /ɪˈnəːʃə/ ▶ noun [mass noun] **1** a tendency to do nothing or to remain unchanged: *the bureaucratic inertia of the various tiers of government.*
2 Physics a property of matter by which it continues in its existing state of rest or uniform motion in a straight line, unless that state is changed by an external force. See also MOMENT OF INERTIA. ■ [with modifier] resistance to change in some other physical property: *the* ***thermal inertia*** *of the oceans will delay the full rise in temperature for a few decades.*
– DERIVATIVES **inertialess** adjective.
– ORIGIN early 18th cent. (in sense 2): from Latin, from *iners, inert-* (see INERT).

inertial ▶ adjective chiefly Physics relating to or arising from inertia. ■ (of navigation or guidance) depending on internal instruments which measure a craft's acceleration and compare the calculated position with stored data. ■ (of a frame of reference) in which bodies continue at rest or in uniform straight motion unless acted on by a force.

inertia reel ▶ noun a reel device which allows a vehicle seat belt to unwind freely but which locks under force of impact or rapid deceleration.

inertia selling ▶ noun [mass noun] Brit. the sending of unsolicited goods to potential customers in the hope of making a sale.

inescapable ▶ adjective unable to be avoided or denied.
– DERIVATIVES **inescapability** noun, **inescapably** adverb.

inescutcheon /ˌɪnɪˈskʌtʃ(ə)n, ˌɪnɛ-/ ▶ noun Heraldry a small shield placed within a larger one.

-iness ▶ suffix forming nouns corresponding to adjectives ending in *-y* (such as *clumsiness* corresponding to *clumsy*).
– ORIGIN see -Y¹, -NESS.

in esse /ɪn ˈɛsi, ˈɛseɪ/ ▶ adverb in actual existence.
– ORIGIN Latin.

inessential ▶ adjective not absolutely necessary.
▶ noun (usu. **inessentials**) a thing that is not absolutely necessary.

inestimable ▶ adjective too great to calculate: *a treasure of inestimable value.*
– DERIVATIVES **inestimably** adverb.
– ORIGIN late Middle English: via Old French from Latin *inaestimabilis*, from *in-* 'not' + *aestimabilis* (see ESTIMABLE).

inevitable ▶ adjective certain to happen; unavoidable: *war was inevitable.* ■ informal so frequently experienced or seen that it is completely predictable: *the inevitable letter from the bank.*
▶ noun (**the inevitable**) a situation that is unavoidable.
– DERIVATIVES **inevitability** noun.
– ORIGIN late Middle English: from Latin *inevitabilis*, from *in-* 'not' + *evitabilis* 'avoidable' (from *evitare* 'avoid').

inevitably ▶ adverb [often as sentence adverb] as is certain to happen; unavoidably: *inevitably some details are already out of date* | *war inevitably has casualties.* ■ informal as one would expect; predictably: *inevitably, the phone started to ring just as we sat down.*

inexact ▶ adjective not quite accurate or correct: *an inexact description.*
– DERIVATIVES **inexactitude** noun, **inexactly** adverb, **inexactness** noun.

inexcusable ▶ adjective too bad to be justified or tolerated: *Matt's behaviour was inexcusable.*
– DERIVATIVES **inexcusably** adverb.
– ORIGIN late Middle English: from Latin *inexcusabilis*, from *in-* 'not' + *excusabilis* 'able to be excused' (see EXCUSE).

inexhaustible ▶ adjective (of an amount or supply of something) unable to be used up because existing in abundance: *his inexhaustible energy.*
– DERIVATIVES **inexhaustibility** noun, **inexhaustibly** adverb.

inexistent ▶ adjective rare non-existent.

inexorable /ɪnˈɛks(ə)rəb(ə)l/ ▶ adjective impossible to stop or prevent: *the seemingly inexorable march of new technology.* ■ (of a person) impossible to persuade; unrelenting: *the doctors were inexorable, and there was nothing to be done.*
– DERIVATIVES **inexorability** noun, **inexorably** adverb.
– ORIGIN mid 16th cent.: from French, or from Latin *inexorabilis*, from *in-* 'not' + *exorabilis* (from *exorare* 'entreat').

inexpedient ▶ adjective not practical, suitable, or advisable.
– DERIVATIVES **inexpediency** noun.

inexpensive ▶ adjective not costing a great deal; cheap: *a simple and inexpensive solution.*
– DERIVATIVES **inexpensively** adverb, **inexpensiveness** noun.

inexperience ▶ noun [mass noun] lack of experience.
– ORIGIN late 16th cent.: from French *inexpérience*, from late Latin *inexperientia*, from *in-* (expressing negation) + *experientia* 'experience'.

inexperienced ▶ adjective having little knowledge or experience of a particular thing: *an inexperienced driver.*

inexpert ▶ adjective having or showing a lack of skill or knowledge: *an inexpert transcription from the real music.*
– DERIVATIVES **inexpertly** adverb.
– ORIGIN late Middle English (in the sense 'inexperienced'): via Old French from Latin *inexpertus*, from *in-* 'not' + *expertus* (see EXPERT).

inexpiable /ɪnˈɛkspɪəb(ə)l/ ▶ adjective (of an offence or feeling) so bad as to be impossible to expiate.
– DERIVATIVES **inexpiably** adverb.
– ORIGIN late Middle English: from Latin *inexpiabilis*, from *in-* 'not' + *expiabilis* 'able to be appeased' (from *expiare* 'expiate').

inexplicable /ˌɪnɪkˈsplɪkəb(ə)l, ˌɪnɛk-, ɪnˈɛksplɪ-/ ▶ adjective unable to be explained or accounted for: *for some inexplicable reason her mind went completely blank.*
– DERIVATIVES **inexplicability** noun, **inexplicably** adverb [sentence adverb] *inexplicably, the pumps started to malfunction.*
– ORIGIN late Middle English: from French, or from Latin *inexplicabilis* 'that cannot be unfolded', from *in-* 'not' + *explicabilis* (see EXPLICABLE).

inexplicit ▶ adjective not definitely or clearly expressed or explained.

inexpressible ▶ adjective (of a feeling) too strong to be described or conveyed in words: *a mood of inexpressible longing.*
– DERIVATIVES **inexpressibly** adverb.

inexpressive ▶ adjective showing no expression: *an inexpressive face.*
– DERIVATIVES **inexpressively** adverb, **inexpressiveness** noun.

inexpugnable /ˌɪnɪkˈspʌgnəb(ə)l, ˌɪnɛk-/ ▶ adjective archaic impregnable.
– ORIGIN late Middle English: via Old French from Latin *inexpugnabilis*, from *in-* 'not' + *expugnabilis* 'able to be taken by assault'.

inextensible /ˌɪnɪkˈstɛnsɪb(ə)l, ˌɪnɛk-/ ▶ adjective unable to be stretched or drawn out in length.

in extenso /ˌɪn ɛkˈstɛnsəʊ/ ▶ adverb in full; at length: *the paper covered their speeches in extenso.*
– ORIGIN Latin, from *in* 'in' + *extensus*, past participle of *extendere* 'stretch out'.

inextinguishable ▶ adjective unable to be extinguished or quenched: *a small inextinguishable candle.*

in extremis /ˌɪn ɛkˈstriːmɪs/ ▶ adverb in an extremely difficult situation. ■ at the point of death.
– ORIGIN Latin, from *in* 'in' + *extremis*, ablative plural of *extremus* 'outermost'.

inextricable /ɪnˈɛkstrɪkəb(ə)l, ˌɪnɪkˈstrɪk-, ˌɪnɛk-/ ▶ adjective impossible to disentangle or separate: *the past and the present are inextricable.* ■ impossible to escape from: *an inextricable situation.*
– DERIVATIVES **inextricability** noun, **inextricably** adverb.
– ORIGIN mid 16th cent.: from Latin *inextricabilis*, from *in-* 'not' + *extricare* 'unravel' (see EXTRICATE).

INF ▶ abbreviation intermediate-range nuclear force(s).

infall ▶ noun [mass noun] Astronomy the falling of small objects or other matter on to or into a larger body.

infallibility ▶ noun [mass noun] the quality of being infallible; the inability to be wrong: *his judgement became impaired by faith in his own infallibility.* ■ (also **papal infallibility**) (in the Roman Catholic Church) the doctrine that in specified circumstances the Pope is incapable of error in pronouncing dogma.
– ORIGIN early 17th cent.: from obsolete French *infallibilité* or medieval Latin *infallibilitas* (based on Latin *fallere* 'deceive').

infallible /ɪnˈfalɪb(ə)l/ ▶ adjective incapable of making mistakes or being wrong: *doctors are not infallible.* ■ never failing; always effective: *infallible cures.* ■ (in the Roman Catholic Church) credited with papal infallibility.
– DERIVATIVES **infallibly** adverb.
– ORIGIN late 15th cent.: from French *infaillible* or late Latin *infallibilis*, from *in-* 'not' + Latin *fallere* 'deceive'.

infamous /ˈɪnfəməs/ ▶ adjective well known for some bad quality or deed: *an infamous war criminal.* ■ wicked; abominable: *the medical council disqualified him for infamous misconduct.* ■ Law, historical (of a person) deprived of all or some citizens' rights as a consequence of conviction for a serious crime.
– DERIVATIVES **infamously** adverb.
– ORIGIN late Middle English: from medieval Latin *infamosus*, from Latin *infamis* (based on *fama* 'fame').

infamy /ˈɪnfəmi/ ▶ noun (pl. **infamies**) [mass noun] the state of being well known for some bad quality or deed: *a day that will live in infamy.* ■ [count noun] an evil or wicked act: *one of history's greatest infamies.*

infancy ▶ noun [mass noun] the state or period of babyhood or early childhood: *a son who died in infancy.* ■ the early stage in the development or growth of something: *opinion polls were* ***in their infancy.*** ■ Law the condition of being a minor.
– ORIGIN late Middle English: from Latin *infantia* 'childhood, inability to speak', from *infans, infant-* (see INFANT).

infant ▶ noun a very young child or baby. ■ Brit. a schoolchild between the ages of about four and eight: [as modifier] *their first year at infant school.* ■ [as modifier] denoting something in an early stage of its development: *the infant Labour Party.* ■ Law a person who has not attained legal majority.
– ORIGIN late Middle English: from Old French *enfant*, from Latin *infant-* 'unable to speak', from *in-* 'not' + *fant-* 'speaking' (from the verb *fari*).

infanta /ɪnˈfantə/ ▶ noun historical a daughter of the ruling monarch of Spain or Portugal, especially the eldest daughter who was not heir to the throne.
– ORIGIN late 16th cent.: Spanish and Portuguese, feminine of INFANTE.

infante /ɪnˈfanteɪ/ ▶ noun historical a son of the ruling monarch of Spain or Portugal other than the heir to the throne, specifically the second son.
– ORIGIN mid 16th cent.: Spanish and Portuguese, from Latin *infans, infant-* (see INFANT).

infanticide /ɪnˈfantɪsʌɪd/ ▸ **noun 1** [mass noun] the crime of a mother killing her child within a year of birth. ▪ the practice in some societies of killing unwanted children soon after birth.
2 a person who kills an infant, especially their own child.
– DERIVATIVES **infanticidal adjective**.
– ORIGIN mid 17th cent.: via French from late Latin *infanticidium*, from Latin *infant-* (see **INFANT**) + *-cidium* (see **-CIDE**).

infantile /ˈɪnf(ə)ntʌɪl/ ▸ **adjective** of or occurring among babies or very young children: *infantile colic*. ▪ derogatory childish: *infantile jokes*.
– DERIVATIVES **infantility noun** (pl. **infantilities**).
– ORIGIN late Middle English: from French, or from Latin *infantilis*, from *infans*, *infant-* (see **INFANT**).

infantile paralysis ▸ **noun** [mass noun] dated poliomyelitis.

infantilism /ɪnˈfantɪlɪz(ə)m/ ▸ **noun** [mass noun] childish behaviour. ▪ Psychology the persistence of infantile characteristics or behaviour in adult life.

infantilize /ɪnˈfantɪlʌɪz/ (also **infantilise**) ▸ **verb** [with obj.] treat (someone) as a child or in a way which denies their maturity in age or experience.
– DERIVATIVES **infantilization noun**.

infantine /ˈɪnf(ə)ntʌɪn/ ▸ **adjective** archaic term for **INFANTILE**.
– ORIGIN early 17th cent.: from obsolete French *infantin*, variant of Old French *enfantin*, from Latin *infans*, *infant-* (see **INFANT**).

infant mortality ▸ **noun** [mass noun] the death of children under the age of one year.

infantry ▸ **noun** [mass noun] soldiers marching or fighting on foot; foot soldiers collectively.
– ORIGIN late 16th cent.: from French *infanterie*, from Italian *infanteria*, from *infante* 'youth, infantryman', from Latin *infant-* (see **INFANT**).

infantryman ▸ **noun** (pl. **infantrymen**) a soldier belonging to an infantry regiment.

infarct /ˈɪnfɑːkt, ɪnˈfɑːkt/ ▸ **noun** Medicine a small localized area of dead tissue resulting from failure of blood supply.
– ORIGIN late 19th cent.: from modern Latin *infarctus*, from *infarcire* 'stuff into or with', from *in-* 'into' + Latin *farcire* 'to stuff'.

infarction /ɪnˈfɑːkʃ(ə)n/ ▸ **noun** [mass noun] obstruction of the blood supply to an organ or region of tissue, typically by a thrombus or embolus, causing local death of the tissue.

infatuate /ɪnˈfatʃʊeɪt, -tjʊ-/ ▸ **verb** (**be infatuated with**) be inspired with an intense but short-lived passion or admiration for: *she is infatuated with a handsome police chief* | (as adj. **infatuated**) *an infatuated teenager*.
– ORIGIN mid 16th cent.: from Latin *infatuat-* 'made foolish', from the verb *infatuare*, from *in-* 'into' + *fatuus* 'foolish'.

infatuation /ɪn,fatʃʊˈeɪʃ(ə)n, -tjʊ-/ ▸ **noun** an intense but short-lived passion or admiration for someone or something: *he had developed an infatuation with the girl*.

infauna /ˈɪnfɔːnə/ ▸ **noun** [mass noun] Ecology the animals living in the sediments of the ocean floor or river or lake beds. Compare with **EPIFAUNA**.
– DERIVATIVES **infaunal adjective**.

infeasible ▸ **adjective** not possible to do easily or conveniently; impracticable.
– DERIVATIVES **infeasibility noun**.

infect ▸ **verb** [with obj.] affect (a person, organism, etc.) with a disease-causing organism: *the chance that a child may have been infected with HIV*. ▪ contaminate (air, water, etc.) with harmful organisms: (as adj. **infected**) *the bacteria can get into a crop from an infected water supply*. ▪ Computing affect with a virus. ▪ (of a negative feeling or idea) take hold of or be communicated to (someone): *the panic in his voice infected her*.
– DERIVATIVES **infector noun**.
– ORIGIN late Middle English: from Latin *infect-* 'tainted', from the verb *inficere*, from *in-* 'into' + *facere* 'put, do'.

infection ▸ **noun** [mass noun] the process of infecting or the state of being infected: *strict hygiene will limit the risk of infection* | *a reddening of the skin at the site of infection*. ▪ [count noun] an infectious disease: *a chest infection*. ▪ Computing the presence of a virus in, or its introduction into, a computer system.
– ORIGIN late Middle English: from late Latin *infectio(n-)*, from Latin *inficere* 'dip in, taint' (see **INFECT**).

infectious ▸ **adjective 1** (of a disease or disease-causing organism) liable to be transmitted to people, organisms, etc. through the environment. ▪ liable to spread infection: *the dogs may still be infectious*.
2 likely to spread or influence others in a rapid manner: *a loud infectious laugh* | *her enthusiasm is infectious*.
– DERIVATIVES **infectiously adverb**, **infectiousness noun**.

> **USAGE** On the differences in meaning between **infectious** and **contagious**, see **USAGE** at **CONTAGIOUS**.

infective ▸ **adjective** capable of causing infection. ▪ dated infectious: *infective hepatitis*.
– DERIVATIVES **infectivity noun**.
– ORIGIN late Middle English: from Latin *infectivus*, from *inficere* 'to taint' (see **INFECT**).

infecund ▸ **adjective** Medicine & Zoology (of a woman or female animal) having low or zero fecundity; unable to bear children or young.
– DERIVATIVES **infecundity noun**.
– ORIGIN late Middle English: from Latin *infecundus*, from *in-* 'not' + *fecundus* 'fecund'.

infeed ▸ **noun** [mass noun] the action or process of supplying material to a machine. ▪ [count noun] a mechanism which supplies material to a machine.

infelicitous ▸ **adjective** unfortunate; inappropriate: *his illustration is singularly infelicitous*.
– DERIVATIVES **infelicitously adverb**.

infelicity ▸ **noun** (pl. **infelicities**) **1** a thing that is inappropriate, especially a remark or expression: *she winced at their infelicities and at the clumsy way they talked*.
2 [mass noun] archaic unhappiness; misfortune.
– ORIGIN late Middle English (in the sense 'unhappiness'): from Latin *infelicitas*, from *infelix*, *infelic-* 'unhappy', from *in-* 'not' + *felix* 'happy'.

infer ▸ **verb** (**infers**, **inferring**, **inferred**) [with obj.] deduce or conclude (something) from evidence and reasoning rather than from explicit statements: [with clause] *from these facts we can infer that crime has been increasing*.
– DERIVATIVES **inferable** (also **inferrable**) **adjective**.
– ORIGIN late 15th cent. (in the sense 'bring about, inflict'): from Latin *inferre* 'bring in, bring about' (in medieval Latin 'deduce'), from *in-* 'into' + *ferre* 'bring'.

> **USAGE** There is a distinction in meaning between **infer** and **imply**. In the sentence *the speaker **implied** that the General had been a traitor*, **implied** means that the speaker subtly **suggested** that this man was a traitor (though nothing so explicit was actually stated). However, in *we **inferred** from his words that the General had been a traitor*, **inferred** means that something in the speaker's words enabled the listeners to **deduce** that the man was a traitor. The two words **infer** and **imply** can describe the same event, but from different angles. Use of **infer** to mean **imply**, as in *are you **inferring** that I'm a liar?* (instead of *are you **implying** that I'm a liar?*), is an extremely common error.

inference /ˈɪnf(ə)r(ə)ns/ ▸ **noun** a conclusion reached on the basis of evidence and reasoning. ▪ [mass noun] the process of inferring something: *his emphasis on order and health, and **by inference** cleanliness*.
– DERIVATIVES **inferential adjective**, **inferentially adverb**.
– ORIGIN late 16th cent.: from medieval Latin *inferentia*, from *inferent-* 'bringing in', from the verb *inferre* (see **INFER**).

inferior ▸ **adjective 1** lower in rank, status, or quality: *schooling in inner-city areas was **inferior to** that in the rest of the country*. ▪ of low standard or quality: *inferior goods*. ▪ Law (of a court or tribunal) susceptible to having its decisions overturned by a higher court. ▪ Economics denoting goods or services which are in greater demand during a recession than in a boom, for example second-hand clothes.
2 chiefly Anatomy low or lower in position. ▪ Botany (of the ovary of a flower) situated below the sepals and enclosed in the receptacle.
3 (of a letter, figure, or symbol) written or printed below the line.
▸ **noun 1** a person lower than another in rank, status, or ability: *her social and intellectual inferiors*.
2 Printing an inferior letter, figure, or symbol.
– DERIVATIVES **inferiorly adverb** (sense 2 of the adjective).
– ORIGIN late Middle English (in sense 2 of the adjective): from Latin, comparative of *inferus* 'low'.

inferior conjunction ▸ **noun** Astronomy a conjunction of Mercury or Venus with the sun, in which the planet and the earth are on the same side of the sun.

inferiority ▸ **noun** [mass noun] the condition of being lower in status or quality than another or others.
– ORIGIN late 16th cent.: probably from medieval Latin *inferioritas*, from Latin *inferior* 'lower'.

inferiority complex ▸ **noun** an unrealistic feeling of general inadequacy caused by actual or supposed inferiority in one sphere, sometimes marked by aggressive behaviour in compensation.

inferior planet ▸ **noun** Astronomy either of the two planets Mercury and Venus, whose orbits are closer to the sun than the earth's.

infernal ▸ **adjective 1** relating to or characteristic of hell or the underworld: *the infernal regions* | *the infernal heat of the forge*.
2 [attrib.] informal irritating and tiresome (used for emphasis): *you're an infernal nuisance*.
– DERIVATIVES **infernally adverb**.
– ORIGIN late Middle English: from Old French, from Christian Latin *infernalis*, from Latin *infernus* 'below, underground', used by Christians to mean 'hell', on the pattern of *inferni* (masculine plural) 'the shades' and *inferna* (neuter plural) 'the lower regions'.

inferno ▸ **noun** (pl. **infernos**) **1** a large fire that is dangerously out of control.
2 (usu. **Inferno**) hell (with reference to Dante's *Divine Comedy*). ▪ a place or situation that is too hot, chaotic, or noisy: *the inferno of the Friday evening rush hour*.
– ORIGIN mid 19th cent.: from Italian, from Christian Latin *infernus* (see **INFERNAL**).

infertile ▸ **adjective** (of a person, animal, or plant) unable to reproduce itself; unable to have young. ▪ (of land) unable to sustain crops or vegetation.
– DERIVATIVES **infertility noun**.
– ORIGIN late 16th cent.: from French, or from late Latin *infertilis*, from *in-* 'not' + *fertilis* (see **FERTILE**).

infest ▸ **verb** [with obj.] (of insects or animals) be present (in a place or site) in large numbers, typically so as to cause damage or disease: *the house is **infested with** cockroaches* | (as adj., in combination **-infested**) *shark-infested waters*.
– DERIVATIVES **infestation noun**.
– ORIGIN late Middle English (in the sense 'torment, harass'): from French *infester* or Latin *infestare* 'assail', from *infestus* 'hostile'. The current sense dates from the mid 16th cent.

infibulate /ɪnˈfɪbjʊleɪt/ ▸ **verb** [with obj.] (usu. as adj. **infibulated**) perform infibulation on (a girl or woman).
– ORIGIN early 17th cent.: from Latin *infibulat-* 'fastened with a clasp', from the verb *infibulare*, from *in-* 'into' + *fibula* 'brooch'.

infibulation ▸ **noun** [mass noun] the practice of excising the clitoris and labia of a girl or woman and stitching together the edges of the vulva to prevent sexual intercourse. It is traditional in some NE African cultures but is highly controversial.

infidel /ˈɪnfɪd(ə)l/ chiefly archaic ▸ **noun** a person who has no religion or whose religion is not that of the majority: *a crusade against infidels and heretics*.
▸ **adjective** adhering to a religion other than that of the majority: *the infidel foe*.
– ORIGIN late 15th cent.: from French *infidèle* or Latin *infidelis*, from *in-* 'not' + *fidelis* 'faithful' (from *fides* 'faith', related to *fidere* 'to trust'). The word originally denoted a person of a religion other than one's own, specifically a Muslim (to a Christian), a Christian (to a Muslim), or a Gentile (to a Jew).

infidelity ▸ **noun** (pl. **infidelities**) [mass noun] **1** the action or state of being unfaithful to a spouse or other sexual partner: *her infidelity continued after her marriage* | [count noun] *I ought not to have tolerated his infidelities*.
2 disbelief in a particular religion, especially Christianity.
– ORIGIN late Middle English (in the senses 'lack of faith' and 'disloyalty'): from Old French *infidelite* or Latin *infidelitas*, from *infidelis* 'not faithful' (see **INFIDEL**).

infield ▸ **noun 1** the inner part of the field of play in various sports, in particular: ▪ Cricket the part of the field closer to the wicket. ▪ Baseball the area within and near the four bases. ▪ the players stationed in the infield, collectively.
2 the land around or near a farmstead, especially arable land.

▸ **adverb** into or towards the inner part of the field of play.
– DERIVATIVES **infielder noun** (sense 1 of the noun).

infighting ▸ **noun** [mass noun] hidden conflict or competitiveness within an organization. ■ boxing closer to an opponent than at arm's length.
– DERIVATIVES **infighter noun**.

infill ▸ **noun** (also **infilling**) [mass noun] material that fills or is used to fill a space or hole. ■ buildings constructed to occupy the space between existing structures.
▸ **verb** [with obj.] fill or block up (a space or hole). ■ construct new buildings between (existing structures).

infiltrate /ˈɪnfɪltreɪt/ ▸ **verb** [with obj.] **1** enter or gain access to (an organization, place, etc.) surreptitiously and gradually, especially in order to acquire secret information: *the organization has been infiltrated by informers*. ■ introduce (someone) into an organization, place, etc. surreptitiously, in order for them to acquire secret information. ■ Medicine (of a tumour, cells, etc.) spread into or invade (a tissue or organ).
2 (of a liquid) permeate (something) by filtration: *virtually no water infiltrates deserts such as the Sahara*. ■ cause (a liquid) to permeate something by filtration: *lignocaine was* ***infiltrated into*** *the wound*.
3 gradually permeate or become a part of: *computing has infiltrated most professions now*.
▸ **noun** Medicine an infiltrating substance or a number of infiltrating cells.
– DERIVATIVES **infiltration noun**, **infiltrator noun**.
– ORIGIN Middle English (as *infiltration*): from IN-[2] + FILTRATE.

infimum /ɪnˈfʌɪməm/ ▸ **noun** Mathematics the largest quantity that is less than or equal to each of a given set or subset of quantities. The opposite of SUPREMUM.
– ORIGIN 1940s: from Latin, literally 'lowest part', neuter (used as a noun) of *infimus* 'lowest'.

in fine /ɪn ˈfʌɪni, ˈfiːneɪ/ ▸ **adverb** finally; in short; to sum up.
– ORIGIN Latin.

infinite /ˈɪnfɪnɪt/ ▸ **adjective 1** limitless or endless in space, extent, or size; impossible to measure or calculate: *the infinite mercy of God* | *the infinite number of stars in the universe*. ■ very great in amount or degree: *he bathed the wound with infinite care*. ■ Mathematics greater than any assignable quantity or countable number. ■ Mathematics (of a series) able to be continued indefinitely.
2 Grammar another term for NON-FINITE.
▸ **noun** (**the infinite**) a space or quantity that is infinite. ■ (**the Infinite**) God.
– DERIVATIVES **infinitely adverb** [as submodifier] *the pay is infinitely better*, **infiniteness noun**.
– ORIGIN late Middle English: from Latin *infinitus*, from *in-* 'not' + *finitus* 'finished, finite' (see FINITE).

infinite regress ▸ **noun** chiefly Logic a sequence of reasoning or justification which can never come to an end.

infinitesimal /ˌɪnfɪnɪˈtɛsɪm(ə)l/ ▸ **adjective** extremely small: *an infinitesimal pause*.
▸ **noun** Mathematics an indefinitely small quantity; a value approaching zero.
– DERIVATIVES **infinitesimally adverb**.
– ORIGIN mid 17th cent.: from modern Latin *infinitesimus*, from Latin *infinitus* (see INFINITE), on the pattern of *centesimal*.

infinitesimal calculus ▸ **noun** see CALCULUS.

infinitive /ɪnˈfɪnɪtɪv/ ▸ **noun** the basic form of a verb, without an inflection binding it to a particular subject or tense (e.g. *see* in *we came to see*, *let him see*).
▸ **adjective** having or involving the basic form of a verb.
– DERIVATIVES **infinitival** /-ˈtʌɪv(ə)l/ **adjective**.
– ORIGIN late Middle English (as an adjective): from Latin *infinitivus*, from *infinitus* (see INFINITE). The noun dates from the mid 16th cent.

infinitude /ɪnˈfɪnɪtjuːd/ ▸ **noun** [mass noun] the state or quality of being infinite or having no limit: *the infinitude of the universe*.
– ORIGIN mid 17th cent.: from Latin *infinitus* (see INFINITE), on the pattern of *magnitude*.

infinity ▸ **noun** (pl. **infinities**) **1** [mass noun] the state or quality of being infinite: *the infinity of space*. ■ [count noun] an infinite or very great number or amount: *an infinity of combinations*. ■ a point in space or time that is or seems infinitely distant: *the lawns stretched into infinity*.
2 Mathematics a number greater than any assignable quantity or countable number (symbol ∞).
– ORIGIN late Middle English: from Old French *infinite* or Latin *infinitas*, from *infinitus* (see INFINITE).

infinity pool ▸ **noun** a swimming pool whose positioning gives the impression that it merges into the surrounding landscape, especially the sea.

infirm ▸ **adjective** not physically or mentally strong, especially through age or illness. ■ archaic (of a person or their judgement) weak; irresolute: *he was infirm of purpose*.
– DERIVATIVES **infirmly adverb**.
– ORIGIN late Middle English (in the general sense 'weak, frail'): from Latin *infirmus*, from *in-* 'not' + *firmus* 'firm'.

infirmarer /ɪnˈfəːm(ə)rə/ ▸ **noun** historical a person in charge of the infirmary in a medieval monastery.
– ORIGIN late Middle English: from Old French *enfermerier*, from *enfermerie* 'infirmary', based on Latin *infirmus* (see INFIRM).

infirmary ▸ **noun** (pl. **infirmaries**) a hospital. ■ a place in a large institution for the care of those who are ill: *the prison infirmary*.
– ORIGIN late Middle English: from medieval Latin *infirmaria*, from Latin *infirmus* (see INFIRM).

infirmity ▸ **noun** (pl. **infirmities**) [mass noun] physical or mental weakness: *old age and infirmity come to men and women alike* | [count noun] *the infirmities of old age*.

infix ▸ **verb** /ɪnˈfɪks/ [with obj.] **1** implant or insert firmly in something.
2 Grammar insert (a formative element) into the body of a word.
▸ **noun** /ˈɪnfɪks/ Grammar a formative element inserted in a word.
– DERIVATIVES **infixation noun** (Grammar).
– ORIGIN early 16th cent.: from Latin *infix-* 'fixed in', from the verb *infigere*, from *in-* 'into' + *figere* 'fasten', reinforced by IN-[2] 'into' + FIX. The noun is on the pattern of *prefix* and *suffix*.

in flagrante delicto /ɪn fləˌgranteɪ dɪˈlɪktəʊ, fləˌgranti/ (also informal **in flagrante**) ▸ **adverb** in the very act of wrongdoing, especially in an act of sexual misconduct: *he had been* ***caught in flagrante*** *with the wife of the Association's Treasurer*.
– ORIGIN Latin, 'in the heat of the crime' (literally 'in blazing crime').

inflame ▸ **verb** [with obj.] **1** provoke or intensify (strong feelings, especially anger) in someone: *high fines further inflamed public feelings*. ■ provoke (someone) to strong feelings: *her sister was inflamed with jealousy*. ■ make (a situation) worse: *comments that inflame what is already a sensitive situation*.
2 cause inflammation in (a part of the body): *the finger joints were inflamed with rheumatoid arthritis* | (as adj. **inflamed**) *inflamed eyes and lips*.
3 literary light up with or as if with flames.
– ORIGIN Middle English *enflaume*, *inflaume*, from Old French *enflammer*, from Latin *inflammare*, from *in-* 'into' + *flamma* 'flame'.

inflammable ▸ **adjective** easily set on fire: *inflammable materials*.
▸ **noun** (usu. **inflammables**) a substance which is easily set on fire.
– DERIVATIVES **inflammability noun**.
– ORIGIN early 17th cent.: from French, or from Latin *inflammare* (see INFLAME).

> **USAGE** The words **inflammable** and **flammable** both have the same meaning, 'easily set on fire'. This might seem surprising, given that the prefix **in-** normally has a negative meaning (as in **indirect** and **insufficient**), and so it might be expected that **inflammable** would mean the opposite of **flammable**, i.e. 'not easily set on fire'. In fact, **inflammable** is formed using a different Latin prefix **in-**, which has the meaning 'into' and here has the effect of intensifying the meaning of the word in English. **Flammable** is a far commoner word than **inflammable** and carries less risk of confusion.

inflammation ▸ **noun** [mass noun] a localized physical condition in which part of the body becomes reddened, swollen, hot, and often painful, especially as a reaction to injury or infection.
– ORIGIN late Middle English: from Latin *inflammatio(n-)*, from the verb *inflammare* (see INFLAME).

inflammatory ▸ **adjective 1** relating to or causing inflammation of a part of the body.
2 (especially of speech or writing) arousing or intended to arouse angry or violent feelings: *inflammatory remarks*.

inflatable ▸ **adjective** capable of being filled with air: *an inflatable mattress*.
▸ **noun** a plastic or rubber object that must be filled with air before use.

inflate ▸ **verb** [usu. with obj.] **1** fill (a balloon, tyre, or other expandable structure) with air or gas so that it becomes distended. ■ [no obj.] become distended with air or gas.
2 increase (something) by a large or excessive amount: *objectives should be clearly set out so as not to duplicate work and inflate costs*. ■ exaggerate: *numbers have been grossly inflated by the local press*.
3 bring about inflation of (a currency) or in (an economy).
– DERIVATIVES **inflater** (also **inflator**) **noun**.
– ORIGIN late Middle English: from Latin *inflat-* 'blown into', from the verb *inflare*, from *in-* 'into' + *flare* 'to blow'.

inflated ▸ **adjective 1** distended through being filled with air or gas: *a partially inflated balloon*.
2 excessively or unreasonably high: *inflated salaries*. ■ exaggerated: *you have a very inflated opinion of your worth*.

inflation ▸ **noun** [mass noun] **1** the action of inflating something or the condition of being inflated: *the inflation of a balloon* | *the gross inflation of salaries*. ■ Astronomy (in some theories of cosmology) a very brief exponential expansion of the universe postulated to have interrupted the standard linear expansion shortly after the Big Bang.
2 Economics a general increase in prices and fall in the purchasing value of money.
– DERIVATIVES **inflationism noun**, **inflationist noun & adjective**.
– ORIGIN Middle English (in the sense 'the condition of being inflated with a gas'): from Latin *inflatio(n-)*, from *inflare* 'blow in to' (see INFLATE). Sense 2 dates from the mid 19th cent.

inflationary ▸ **adjective 1** characterized by or tending to cause monetary inflation.
2 Astronomy relating to or involving inflation.

inflect ▸ **verb** [with obj.] **1** Grammar change the form of (a word) to express a particular grammatical function or attribute, typically tense, mood, person, number, and gender. ■ [no obj.] (of a word or language) undergo inflection.
2 vary the intonation or pitch of (the voice), especially to express mood or feeling. ■ vary the pitch of (a musical note). ■ influence or colour (music or writing) in tone or style.
3 technical bend or deflect (something), especially inwards.
– DERIVATIVES **inflective adjective**.
– ORIGIN late Middle English (in sense 3): from Latin *inflectere*, from *in-* 'into' + *flectere* 'to bend'.

inflection (chiefly Brit. also **inflexion**) ▸ **noun 1** Grammar a change in the form of a word (typically the ending) to express a grammatical function or attribute such as tense, mood, person, number, case, and gender. ■ [mass noun] the process or practice of inflecting words.
2 [mass noun] the modulation of intonation or pitch in the voice: *she spoke slowly and without inflection* | [count noun] *the variety of his vocal inflections*. ■ the variation of the pitch of a musical note.
3 chiefly Mathematics a change of curvature from convex to concave at a particular point on a curve.
– DERIVATIVES **inflectional adjective**, **inflectionless adjective**.
– ORIGIN late Middle English (in the sense 'the action of bending inwards'): from Latin *inflexio(n-)*, from the verb *inflectere* 'bend in, curve' (see INFLECT).

inflection point ▸ **noun 1** (also **point of inflection**) Mathematics a point of a curve at which a change in the direction of curvature occurs.
2 chiefly US (in business) a time of significant change in a situation; a turning point.

inflexed ▸ **adjective** technical bent or curved inwards.

inflexible ▸ **adjective 1** unwilling to change or compromise: *once she had made up her mind, she was inflexible*. ■ not able to be changed or adapted to particular circumstances: *inflexible rules*.
2 not able to be bent; stiff: *heavy inflexible armour*.
– DERIVATIVES **inflexibility noun**, **inflexibly adverb**.
– ORIGIN late Middle English: from Latin *inflexibilis*, from *in-* 'not' + *flexibilis* 'flexible'.

inflict ▸ **verb** [with obj.] cause (something unpleasant or painful) to be suffered by someone or something: *they* ***inflicted*** *serious injuries* ***on*** *three other men*. ■ (**inflict something on**) impose something unwelcome on: *she is wrong to inflict her beliefs on everyone else*.
– DERIVATIVES **inflicter** (also **inflictor**) **noun**.
– ORIGIN mid 16th cent. (in the sense 'afflict, trouble'): from Latin *inflict-* 'struck against', from the verb *infligere*, from *in-* 'into' + *fligere* 'to strike'.

infliction ▶ **noun** [mass noun] the action of inflicting something unpleasant or painful on someone or something: *the repeated infliction of pain.* ■ [count noun] informal, dated a nuisance: *what an infliction he must be!*

in-flight ▶ **adjective** occurring or provided during an aircraft flight: *in-flight catering.*

inflorescence /ˌɪnflɔːˈrɛs(ə)ns, -flə-/ ▶ **noun** Botany the complete flower head of a plant including stems, stalks, bracts, and flowers. ■ the arrangement of the flowers on a plant. ■ [mass noun] the process of flowering.
– ORIGIN mid 18th cent. (denoting the arrangement of a plant's flowers): from modern Latin *inflorescentia*, from late Latin *inflorescere* 'come into flower', from Latin *in-* 'into' + *florescere* 'begin to flower'.

inflow ▶ **noun** the movement of liquid or air into a place: *an inflow of less salty water.* ■ the movement of a large number of people or things or a large amount of money into a place: *enormous inflows of foreign investment* | [mass noun] *the inflow of migrant workers.*
– DERIVATIVES **inflowing** noun & adjective.

influence ▶ **noun 1** [mass noun] the capacity to have an effect on the character, development, or behaviour of someone or something, or the effect itself: *the influence of television violence* | *I was still* **under the influence of** *my parents* | [count noun] *their friends are having a bad* **influence on** *them.* ■ the power to shape policy or ensure favourable treatment from someone, especially through status, contacts, or wealth: *the institute has considerable influence with teachers.* ■ [count noun] a person or thing with the capacity to have an influence on someone or something: *Fiona was a good* **influence on** *her.*
2 Physics, archaic electrical or magnetic induction.
▶ **verb** [with obj.] have an influence on: *feminist ideas have influenced the law-makers.*
– PHRASES **under the influence** informal affected by alcoholic drink or drugs: *he was charged with driving under the influence.*
– DERIVATIVES **influenceable** adjective, **influencer** noun.
– ORIGIN late Middle English: from Old French, or from medieval Latin *influentia* 'inflow', from Latin *influere*, from *in-* 'into' + *fluere* 'to flow'. The word originally had the general sense 'an influx, flowing matter', also specifically (in astrology) 'the flowing in of ethereal fluid (affecting human destiny)'. The sense 'imperceptible or indirect action exerted to cause changes' was established in Scholastic Latin by the 13th cent., but not recorded in English until the late 16th cent.

influence peddling ▶ **noun** [mass noun] N. Amer. the use of position or political influence on someone's behalf in exchange for money or favours.
– DERIVATIVES **influence peddler** noun.

influent /ˈɪnflʊənt/ ▶ **adjective** flowing in.
▶ **noun** a stream, especially a tributary, which flows into another stream or lake.
– ORIGIN late Middle English (as an adjective): from Latin *influent-* 'flowing in', from *influere* (see **INFLUENCE**). The noun is recorded from the mid 19th cent.

influential ▶ **adjective** having great influence on someone or something: *her work is influential in feminist psychology.*
▶ **noun** (usu. **influentials**) an influential person.
– DERIVATIVES **influentially** adverb.
– ORIGIN late 16th cent. (referring to astral influence): from medieval Latin *influentia* (see **INFLUENCE**).

influenza ▶ **noun** [mass noun] a highly contagious viral infection of the respiratory passages causing fever, severe aching, and catarrh, and often occurring in epidemics.
– DERIVATIVES **influenzal** adjective.
– ORIGIN mid 18th cent.: from Italian, literally 'influence', from medieval Latin *influentia* (see **INFLUENCE**). The Italian word also has the sense 'an outbreak of an epidemic', hence 'epidemic'. It was applied specifically to an influenza epidemic which began in Italy in 1743, later adopted in English as the name of the disease.

influx /ˈɪnflʌks/ ▶ **noun 1** an arrival or entry of large numbers of people or things: *a massive influx of tourists.*
2 an inflow of water into a river, lake, or the sea.
– ORIGIN late 16th cent. (denoting an inflow of liquid, gas, or light): from late Latin *influxus*, from *influere* 'flow in' (see **INFLUENCE**).

influx control ▶ **noun** [mass noun] (in South Africa during the apartheid era) the rigid limitation and control imposed upon the movement of black people into urban areas.

info ▶ **noun** [mass noun] informal information.
– ORIGIN early 20th cent.: abbreviation.

infolded ▶ **adjective** technical turned or folded inwards.

infolding ▶ **noun** technical a turning or folding inwards; an inward fold.

infomediary /ˌɪnfə(ʊ)ˈmiːdɪəri/ ▶ **noun** an Internet company that gathers and links information on particular subjects on behalf of commercial organizations and their potential customers.
– ORIGIN 1980s: after **INTERMEDIARY**.

infomercial /ˌɪnfə(ʊ)ˈməːʃ(ə)l/ ▶ **noun** chiefly N. Amer. an advertising film which promotes a product in an informative and supposedly objective style.
– ORIGIN 1980s: blend of **INFORMATION** and **COMMERCIAL**.

inform ▶ **verb 1** [reporting verb] give (someone) facts or information; tell: [with obj.] *he wrote to her, informing her of the situation* | [with obj. and direct speech] *'That's nothing new,' she informed him* | [with obj. and clause] *they were informed that no risk was involved.* ■ [no obj.] give incriminating information about someone to the police or other authority: *he had been recruited by the KGB to* **inform on** *his fellow students.*
2 [with obj.] give an essential or formative principle or quality to: *religion informs every aspect of their lives.*
– ORIGIN Middle English *enforme, informe* 'give form or shape to', also 'form the mind of, teach', from Old French *enfourmer*, from Latin *informare* 'shape, fashion, describe', from *in-* 'into' + *forma* 'a form'.

informal ▶ **adjective 1** having a relaxed, friendly, or unofficial style, manner, or nature: *an informal atmosphere* | *an informal agreement between the two companies.* ■ (of dress) casual; suitable for everyday wear.
2 denoting the grammatical structures, vocabulary, and idiom suitable to everyday language and conversation rather than to official or formal contexts.
3 (of economic activity) carried on by self-employed or independent people on a small scale, especially unofficially or illegally: *Peru's huge and dense informal sector of street vendors and cottage industries.*
– DERIVATIVES **informally** adverb.

informality ▶ **noun** [mass noun] relaxed, friendly, or unofficial style or nature; absence of formality: *he enjoyed the informality of the occasion.*

informal settlement ▶ **noun** another term for **SHACKLAND**.

informal vote ▶ **noun** Austral./NZ an invalid vote or voting paper.

informant ▶ **noun** a person who gives information to another. ■ another term for **INFORMER**. ■ a person from whom a linguist or anthropologist obtains information about language, dialect, or culture.

informatics /ˌɪnfəˈmatɪks/ ▶ **plural noun** [treated as sing.] Computing the science of processing data for storage and retrieval; information science.
– ORIGIN 1960s: from **INFORMATION** + **-ICS**, translating Russian *informatika*.

information ▶ **noun** [mass noun] **1** facts provided or learned about something or someone: *a vital piece of information.* ■ [count noun] Law a charge lodged with a magistrates' court: *the tenant may* **lay an information against** *his landlord.*
2 what is conveyed or represented by a particular arrangement or sequence of things: *genetically transmitted information.* ■ Computing data as processed, stored, or transmitted by a computer. ■ (in information theory) a mathematical quantity expressing the probability of occurrence of a particular sequence of symbols, impulses, etc., as against that of alternative sequences.
– DERIVATIVES **informational** adjective, **informationally** adverb.
– ORIGIN late Middle English (also in the sense 'formation of the mind, teaching'), via Old French from Latin *informatio(n-)*, from the verb *informare* (see **INFORM**).

information retrieval ▶ **noun** [mass noun] Computing the tracing and recovery of specific information from stored data.

information revolution ▶ **noun** the proliferation of the availability of information and the accompanying changes in its storage and dissemination owing to the use of computers.

information science ▶ **noun** [mass noun] Computing the study of processes for storing and retrieving information.

information superhighway ▶ **noun** see **SUPERHIGHWAY**.

information technology ▶ **noun** [mass noun] the study or use of systems (especially computers and telecommunications) for storing, retrieving, and sending information.

information theory ▶ **noun** [mass noun] the mathematical study of the coding of information in the form of sequences of symbols, impulses, etc. and of how rapidly such information can be transmitted, for example through computer circuits or telecommunications channels.

informative ▶ **adjective** providing useful or interesting information: *a thought-provoking, informative article.*
– DERIVATIVES **informatively** adverb, **informativeness** noun.
– ORIGIN late Middle English (in the sense 'formative, giving life or shape'): from medieval Latin *informativus*, from Latin *informare* 'give form to, instruct' (see **INFORM**).

informatory /ɪnˈfɔːmət(ə)ri/ ▶ **adjective** giving information; informative. ■ Bridge (of a double) intended to convey information to one's partner rather than to score a penalty.
– ORIGIN late Middle English (but rare before the late 19th cent.): from Latin *informat-* 'shaped, described' (from the verb *informare*) + **-ORY**[2].

informed ▶ **adjective** having or showing knowledge of a subject or situation: *an informed readership.* ■ (of a decision or judgement) based on an understanding of the facts of the situation.
– DERIVATIVES **informedly** /ɪnˈfɔːmɪdli/ adverb, **informedness** /ɪnˈfɔːmɪdnɪs/ noun.

informer ▶ **noun** a person who informs on another person to the police or other authority.

infotainment ▶ **noun** [mass noun] broadcast material which is intended both to entertain and to inform.
– ORIGIN 1980s (originally US): blend of **INFORMATION** and **ENTERTAINMENT**.

infotech ▶ **noun** short for **INFORMATION TECHNOLOGY**.

infowar ▶ **noun 1** another term for **CYBERWAR**.
2 a propaganda war waged via electronic media.

infra ▶ **adverb** (in a written document) below; further on: *see note, infra.*
– ORIGIN Latin, 'below'.

infra- /ˈɪnfrə/ ▶ **prefix** below: *infraorder* | *infrasonic.* ■ Anatomy below or under a part of the body: *infrarenal.*
– ORIGIN from Latin *infra* 'below'.

infraclass ▶ **noun** Biology a taxonomic category that ranks below a subclass.

infraction ▶ **noun** chiefly Law a violation or infringement of a law or agreement.
– ORIGIN late Middle English: from Latin *infractio(n-)*, from the verb *infringere* (see **INFRINGE**).

infradian /ɪnˈfreɪdɪən/ ▶ **adjective** Physiology (of a rhythm or cycle) having a period of recurrence longer than a day; occurring less than once a day. Compare with **ULTRADIAN**.
– ORIGIN mid 20th cent.: from **INFRA-** 'below' (i.e. expressing a lower frequency), on the pattern of *circadian*.

infra dig /ˌɪnfrə ˈdɪg/ ▶ **adjective** [predic.] informal, chiefly Brit. beneath one; demeaning: *she regarded playing for the Pony Club as deeply infra dig.*
– ORIGIN early 19th cent.: abbreviation of Latin *infra dignitatem* 'beneath (one's) dignity'.

infralapsarian /ˌɪnfrəlapˈsɛːrɪən/ Theology ▶ **noun** a Calvinist holding the view that God's election of only some to everlasting life was not originally part of the divine plan, but a consequence of the Fall of Man.
▶ **adjective** relating to the infralapsarians or their doctrine.
– ORIGIN mid 18th cent.: from **INFRA-** 'below' + Latin *lapsus* 'fall' + **-ARIAN**.

infrangible /ɪnˈfran(d)ʒɪb(ə)l/ ▶ **adjective** formal unbreakable; inviolable.
– ORIGIN late 16th cent.: from French, or from medieval Latin *infrangibilis*, from *in-* 'not' + *frangibilis* (see **FRANGIBLE**).

infraorder ▶ **noun** Biology a taxonomic category that ranks below a suborder.

infrared ▶ **adjective** (of electromagnetic radiation) having a wavelength just greater than that of the red end of the visible light spectrum but less than that of microwaves. Infrared radiation has a wavelength from about 800 nm to 1 mm, and is emitted particularly by heated objects. ■ (of equipment or

I

techniques) using or concerned with infrared radiation: *infrared cameras.*
▶ **noun** [mass noun] the infrared region of the spectrum; infrared radiation.

infrarenal ▶ **adjective** Anatomy below the kidney.

infrasonic ▶ **adjective** relating to or denoting sound waves with a frequency below the lower limit of human audibility.

infrasound ▶ **noun** [mass noun] sound waves with frequencies below the lower limit of human audibility.

infraspecific ▶ **adjective** Biology at a taxonomic level below that of species, e.g. subspecies, variety, cultivar, or form. In botany, Latin names at this level usually require the addition of a term denoting the rank. ■ occurring within a species: *infraspecific variation.*

infrastructure ▶ **noun** the basic physical and organizational structures and facilities (e.g. buildings, roads, power supplies) needed for the operation of a society or enterprise.
– DERIVATIVES **infrastructural** adjective.
– ORIGIN early 20th cent.: from French (see **INFRA-**, **STRUCTURE**).

infrequent ▶ **adjective** not occurring often; rare: *her visits were so infrequent.*
– DERIVATIVES **infrequency** noun, **infrequently** adverb.
– ORIGIN mid 16th cent. (in the sense 'little used, seldom done, uncommon'): from Latin *infrequent-* from *in-* 'not' + *frequent-* 'frequent'.

infringe /ɪnˈfrɪn(d)ʒ/ ▶ **verb** (**infringes**, **infringing**, **infringed**) [with obj.] **1** actively break the terms of (a law, agreement, etc.): ***making an unauthorized copy would infringe copyright.***
2 act so as to limit or undermine (something); encroach on: *such widespread surveillance could infringe personal liberties* | [no obj.] *I wouldn't* ***infringe on*** *his privacy.*
– DERIVATIVES **infringer** noun.
– ORIGIN mid 16th cent.: from Latin *infringere*, from *in-* 'into' + *frangere* 'to break'.

infringement /ɪnˈfrɪn(d)ʒm(ə)nt/ ▶ **noun** [mass noun] **1** the action of breaking the terms of a law, agreement, etc.; violation: *copyright infringement* | [count noun] *an infringement of the rules.*
2 the action of limiting or undermining something: [count noun] *this bill is an infringement of our civil liberties.*

infructescence /ˌɪnfrʌkˈtɛs(ə)ns/ ▶ **noun** Botany an aggregate fruit.
– ORIGIN late 19th cent.: from **IN-**[2] 'in' + Latin *fructus* 'fruit', on the pattern of *inflorescence.*

infula /ˈɪnfjʊlə/ ▶ **noun** (pl. **infulae** /-liː/) (in the Christian Church) either of the two ribbons on a bishop's mitre.
– ORIGIN early 17th cent.: from Latin, denoting a woollen fillet worn by a priest or placed on the head of a sacrificial victim.

infundibulum /ˌɪnfʌnˈdɪbjʊləm/ ▶ **noun** (pl. **infundibula** /-ˈdɪbjʊlə/) Anatomy & Zoology a funnel-shaped cavity or structure. ■ the hollow stalk which connects the hypothalamus and the posterior pituitary gland.
– DERIVATIVES **infundibular** adjective.
– ORIGIN mid 16th cent.: from Latin, 'funnel', from *infundere* 'pour in'.

infuriate ▶ **verb** /ɪnˈfjʊərɪeɪt/ [with obj.] make (someone) extremely angry and impatient: *I was infuriated by your article.*
– ORIGIN mid 17th cent.: from medieval Latin *infuriat-* 'made angry', from the verb *infuriare*, from *in-* 'into' + Latin *furia* 'fury'.

infuriating ▶ **adjective** making one extremely angry and impatient: *that infuriating half-smile on his face.*
– DERIVATIVES **infuriatingly** adverb [as submodifier] *the truth is infuriatingly hard to pin down.*

infuse ▶ **verb** [with obj.] **1** fill; pervade: *her work is infused with an anger born of pain and oppression.* ■ instil (a quality) in someone or something: *he did his best to infuse good humour into his voice.*
2 soak (tea, herbs, etc.) in liquid to extract the flavour or healing properties. ■ [no obj.] (of tea, herbs, etc.) release flavour or healing properties while being soaked.
3 Medicine allow (a liquid) to flow into a vein or tissue: *saline was* ***infused into*** *the aorta.*
– DERIVATIVES **infuser** noun.
– ORIGIN late Middle English: from Latin *infus-* 'poured in', from the verb *infundere*, from *in-* 'into' + *fundere* 'pour'.

infusible ▶ **adjective** (of a substance) not able to be melted or fused.

infusion ▶ **noun 1** a drink, remedy, or extract prepared by soaking tea leaves or herbs in liquid. ■ [mass noun] the process of preparing an infusion.
2 [mass noun] the introduction of a new element or quality into something: *the infusion of $6.3 million for improvements* | [count noun] *an infusion of youthful talent.*
3 Medicine the slow injection of a substance into a vein or tissue.
– ORIGIN late Middle English (denoting the pouring in of a liquid): from Latin *infusio(n-)*, from the verb *infundere* (see **INFUSE**).

infusoria /ˌɪnfjʊˈzɔːrɪə, -ˈsɔːrɪə/ ▶ **plural noun** Zoology, dated single-celled organisms of the former group Infusoria, which consisted mainly of ciliate protozoans.
– ORIGIN modern Latin, from Latin *infundere* (see **INFUSE**); so named because they were originally found in infusions of decaying organic matter.

-ing[1] ▶ **suffix 1** denoting a verbal action, an instance of this, or its result: *fighting* | *outing* | *building.* ■ denoting a verbal action relating to an occupation, skill, etc.: *banking* | *ice skating* | *welding.*
2 denoting material used for or associated with a process etc.: *cladding* | *piping.* ■ denoting something involved in an action or process but with no corresponding verb: *sacking.*
3 forming the gerund of verbs (such as *painting* as in *I love painting*).
– ORIGIN Old English *-ung, -ing*, of Germanic origin.

-ing[2] ▶ **suffix 1** forming the present participle of verbs: *doing* | *calling.* ■ forming present participles used as adjectives: *charming.*
2 forming adjectives from nouns: *hulking.*
– ORIGIN Middle English: alteration of earlier *-ende*, later *-inde.*

-ing[3] ▶ **suffix** (used especially in names of coins and fractional parts) a thing belonging to or having the quality of: *farthing* | *riding.*
– ORIGIN Old English, of Germanic origin.

ingather ▶ **verb** [with obj.] formal gather (something) in or together: *it may not be possible to ingather that information within the time.*

ingeminate /ɪnˈdʒɛmɪneɪt/ ▶ **verb** [with obj.] archaic repeat or reiterate (a word or statement), typically for emphasis.
– PHRASES **ingeminate peace** call repeatedly for peace.
– ORIGIN late 16th cent. (originally as *engeminate*): from Latin *ingeminat-* 'redoubled', from the verb *ingeminare*, from *in-* (expressing intensive force) + *geminare* (see **GEMINATE**).

Ingenhousz /ˈɪŋənˌhuːs/, Jan (1730–99), Dutch scientist. He is best known for his work on photosynthesis, in which he discovered that sunlit green plants take in carbon dioxide, fix the carbon, and 'restore' the air (oxygen).

ingenious /ɪnˈdʒiːnɪəs/ ▶ **adjective** (of a person) clever, original, and inventive: *he was ingenious enough to overcome the limited budget.* ■ (of a machine or idea) cleverly and originally devised and well suited to its purpose.
– DERIVATIVES **ingeniously** adverb, **ingeniousness** noun.
– ORIGIN late Middle English: from French *ingénieux* or Latin *ingeniosus*, from *ingenium* 'mind, intellect'; compare with **ENGINE**.

ingénue /ˈãʒən(j)uː/ ▶ **noun** an innocent or unsophisticated young woman.
– ORIGIN French, feminine of *ingénu* 'ingenuous', from Latin *ingenuus* (see **INGENUOUS**).

ingenuity /ˌɪndʒɪˈnjuːɪti/ ▶ **noun** [mass noun] the quality of being clever, original, and inventive.
– ORIGIN late 16th cent. (also in the senses 'nobility' and 'ingenuousness'): from Latin *ingenuitas* 'ingenuousness', from *ingenuus* 'inborn'. The current meaning arose by confusion of **INGENUOUS** with **INGENIOUS**.

ingenuous /ɪnˈdʒɛnjʊəs/ ▶ **adjective** (of a person or action) innocent and unsuspecting.
– DERIVATIVES **ingenuously** adverb, **ingenuousness** noun.
– ORIGIN late 16th cent.: from Latin *ingenuus* literally 'native, inborn', from *in-* 'into' + an element related to *gignere* 'beget'. The original sense was 'noble, generous', giving rise to 'honourably straightforward, frank', hence 'innocently frank' (late 17th cent.).

ingest ▶ **verb** [with obj.] take (food, drink, or another substance) into the body by swallowing or absorbing it. ■ absorb (information).
– DERIVATIVES **ingestion** noun, **ingestive** adjective.
– ORIGIN early 17th cent.: from Latin *ingest-* 'brought in', from the verb *ingerere*, from *in-* 'into' + *gerere* 'carry'.

ingesta /ɪnˈdʒɛstə/ ▶ **plural noun** Medicine & Zoology substances taken into the body as nourishment; food and drink.
– ORIGIN early 18th cent.: from Latin, 'things brought in', neuter plural of *ingestus*, past participle of *ingerere.*

ingle ▶ **noun** chiefly dialect a domestic fire or fireplace. ■ an inglenook.
– ORIGIN early 16th cent. (originally Scots): perhaps from Scottish Gaelic *aingeal* 'light, fire', Irish *aingeal* 'live ember'.

inglenook ▶ **noun** a space on either side of a large fireplace.
– ORIGIN late 18th cent.: from Scots **INGLE** + **NOOK**.

inglorious ▶ **adjective 1** (of an action or situation) causing shame or a loss of honour: *an inglorious episode in British imperial history.*
2 not famous or renowned.
– DERIVATIVES **ingloriously** adverb, **ingloriousness** noun.
– ORIGIN mid 16th cent.: from Latin *inglorius* (from *in-* (expressing negation) + *gloria* 'glory') + **-OUS**.

-ingly ▶ **suffix** forming adverbs denoting manner, nature, or condition: *startlingly* | *unwittingly.*

in-goal area ▶ **noun** Rugby the area between the goal line and the dead-ball line.

ingoing ▶ **adjective** [attrib.] going into or towards a particular place: *the paths of ingoing and outgoing rays.*

ingot /ˈɪŋgət/ ▶ **noun** a block of steel, gold, silver, or other metal, typically oblong in shape.
– ORIGIN late Middle English (denoting a mould in which metal is cast): perhaps from **IN** + Old English *goten*, past participle of *geotan* 'pour, cast'.

ingraft ▶ **verb** variant spelling of **ENGRAFT**.

ingrain ▶ **verb** (also **engrain**) [with obj.] firmly fix or establish (a habit, belief, or attitude) in a person.
▶ **adjective** (of a textile) composed of fibres which have been dyed different colours before being woven.
– ORIGIN late Middle English (originally as *engrain* in the sense 'dye with cochineal or in fast colours'): from **EN-**[1], **IN-**[2] (as an intensifier) + the verb **GRAIN**. The adjective is from *in grain* 'fast-dyed', from the old use of *grain* meaning 'kermes, cochineal'.

ingrain carpet ▶ **noun** a reversible carpet in which the pattern appears on both sides.

ingrained ▶ **adjective** (also **engrained**) **1** (of a habit, belief, or attitude) firmly fixed or established; difficult to change: *his deeply ingrained Catholic convictions.*
2 (of dirt or a stain) deeply embedded and thus difficult to remove: *the ingrained dirt on the flaking paintwork.*

ingrate /ˈɪngreɪt, ɪnˈgreɪt/ formal or literary ▶ **noun** an ungrateful person.
▶ **adjective** ungrateful.
– ORIGIN late Middle English (as an adjective): from Latin *ingratus*, from *in-* 'not' + *gratus* 'grateful'.

ingratiate /ɪnˈgreɪʃɪeɪt/ ▶ **verb** (**ingratiate oneself**) bring oneself into favour with someone by flattering or trying to please them: *a sycophantic attempt to* ***ingratiate herself with*** *the local aristocracy.*
– DERIVATIVES **ingratiation** noun.
– ORIGIN early 17th cent.: from Latin *in gratiam* 'into favour', on the pattern of obsolete Italian *ingratiare*, earlier form of *ingraziare.*

ingratiating ▶ **adjective** intended to gain approval or favour; sycophantic: *an ingratiating manner.*
– DERIVATIVES **ingratiatingly** adverb.

ingratitude ▶ **noun** [mass noun] a discreditable lack of gratitude: *he returned his daughter's care with ingratitude and unkindness.*
– ORIGIN Middle English: from Old French, or from late Latin *ingratitudo*, from Latin *ingratus* 'ungrateful' (see **INGRATE**).

ingredient ▶ **noun** any of the foods or substances that are combined to make a particular dish. ■ a component part or element of something: *the affair contains all the ingredients of an insoluble mystery.*
– ORIGIN late Middle English: from Latin *ingredient-* 'entering', from the verb *ingredi*, from *in-* 'into' + *gradi* 'walk'.

Ingres /ˈaŋgrə/, French /ɛ̃gʀ/, Jean Auguste Dominique (1780–1867), French painter. A pupil of Jacques-Louis David, he vigorously upheld neoclassicism in opposition to Delacroix's romanticism. Notable works: *Ambassadors of Agamemnon* (1801) and *The Bather* (1808).

ingress /ˈɪŋɡrɛs/ ▶ **noun 1** [mass noun] the action or fact of going in or entering; the capacity or right of entrance. ■ a place or means of access; an entrance. ■ [mass noun] the unwanted introduction of water, foreign bodies, contaminants, etc.
2 Astronomy & Astrology the arrival of the sun, moon, or a planet in a specified constellation or part of the sky. ■ the beginning of a transit.
– DERIVATIVES **ingression** noun.
– ORIGIN late Middle English (in the sense 'an entrance or beginning'): from Latin *ingressus*, from the verb *ingredi* 'enter'.

ingressive ▶ **adjective 1** relating to ingress; having the quality or character of entering.
2 Phonetics (of a speech sound) made with an intake of air rather than an exhalation. ■ (of an airflow) inward.
▶ **noun** an ingressive sound, e.g. a click.

in-group ▶ **noun** an exclusive, typically small, group of people with a shared interest or identity.

ingrowing ▶ **adjective** growing inwards or within something, especially (of a toenail) growing abnormally so as to press into the flesh.

ingrown ▶ **adjective 1** growing or having grown within; innate: *as ingrown habit would have dictated.* ■ (of a toenail) having grown into the flesh. ■ inward looking: *a clubby, ingrown world in which everybody knows everybody.*
2 Geology (of an incised meander) asymmetric in cross section due to lateral erosion.

ingrowth ▶ **noun** a thing which has grown inwards or within something. ■ [mass noun] the action of growing inwards.

inguinal /ˈɪŋɡwɪn(ə)l/ ▶ **adjective** [attrib.] Anatomy of the groin: *inguinal lymph nodes.*
– ORIGIN late Middle English: from Latin *inguinalis*, from *inguen*, *inguin-* 'groin'.

ingulf ▶ **verb** archaic spelling of **ENGULF**.

ingurgitate /ɪnˈɡəːdʒɪteɪt/ ▶ **verb** [with obj.] literary swallow (something) greedily.
– DERIVATIVES **ingurgitation** noun.
– ORIGIN late 16th cent.: from Latin *ingurgitat-* 'poured in, drenched', from the verb *ingurgitare*, from *in-* 'into' + *gurges*, *gurgit-* 'whirlpool, gulf'.

Ingush /ˈɪŋɡʊʃ/ ▶ **noun** (pl. **same** or **Ingushes**) **1** a member of a people living mainly in Ingushetia in the central Caucasus.
2 [mass noun] the North Caucasian language of the Ingush.
▶ **adjective** relating to the Ingush or their language.
– ORIGIN Russian.

Ingushetia /ɪŋɡʊˈʃɛtɪə/ an autonomous republic of Russia in the central Caucasus between Chechnya and North Ossetia; pop. 506,600 (est. 2009). Also called **Ingush Republic**.

inhabit ▶ **verb** (**inhabits, inhabiting, inhabited**) [with obj.] (of a person, animal, or group) live in or occupy (a place or environment): *a bird that inhabits North America* | *the region was inhabited by Indians.*
– DERIVATIVES **inhabitation** noun.
– ORIGIN late Middle English *inhabite*, *enhabite*, from Old French *enhabiter* or Latin *inhabitare*, from *in-* 'in' + *habitare* 'dwell' (from *habere* 'have').

inhabitable ▶ **adjective** suitable to live in; habitable: *soon we will run out of inhabitable space on the planet.*
– DERIVATIVES **inhabitability** noun.

inhabitancy (also **inhabitance**) ▶ **noun** [mass noun] archaic living in a certain place as an inhabitant, especially during a specified period so as to acquire certain rights.

inhabitant ▶ **noun** a person or animal that lives in or occupies a place. ■ US a person who fulfils the residential or legal requirements for being a member of a state or parish.
– ORIGIN late Middle English: from Old French, from Latin *inhabitare* 'inhabit'.

inhalant ▶ **noun** a medicinal preparation for inhaling. ■ a solvent or other material producing vapour that is inhaled by drug abusers.
▶ **adjective** [attrib.] chiefly Zoology serving for inhalation: *an inhalant siphon.*

inhalation ▶ **noun** the action of inhaling or breathing in: [mass noun] *the inhalation of airborne particles* | [count noun] *with every inhalation air passes over the vocal cords.* ■ Medicine the inhaling of medicines or anaesthetics in the form of a gas or vapour. ■ [count noun] Medicine a preparation to be inhaled in the form of a vapour or spray.
– ORIGIN early 17th cent.: from medieval Latin *inhalatio(n-)*, from *inhalare* 'inhale'.

inhalator /ˈɪnhəˌleɪtə/ ▶ **noun** a device for inhaling something; a respirator or inhaler.

inhale /ɪnˈheɪl/ ▶ **verb** breathe in (air, gas, smoke, etc.): [with obj.] *they were taken to hospital after inhaling fumes* | [no obj.] *she took the cigarette and inhaled deeply.* ■ [with obj.] N. Amer. informal eat (food) greedily or rapidly.
– ORIGIN early 18th cent.: from Latin *inhalare* 'breathe in', from *in-* 'in' + *halare* 'breathe'.

inhaler ▶ **noun** a portable device for administering a drug which is to be breathed in, used for relieving asthma and other bronchial or nasal congestion.

inharmonic ▶ **adjective** chiefly Music not harmonic.
– DERIVATIVES **inharmonicity** noun.

inharmonious ▶ **adjective** not forming or contributing to a pleasing whole; discordant: *an inharmonious, negative state of mind.*
– DERIVATIVES **inharmoniously** adverb.

inhaul ▶ **noun** Sailing a rope used to haul in the clew of a sail.

inhere /ɪnˈhɪə/ ▶ **verb** [no obj.] (**inhere in/within**) formal exist essentially or permanently in: *the potential for change that inheres within the adult education world.* ■ Law (of rights, powers, etc.) be vested in a person or group or attached to the ownership of a property.
– ORIGIN mid 16th cent. (in the sense 'stick, cling to'): from Latin *inhaerere* 'stick to'.

inherent /ɪnˈhɪər(ə)nt, -ˈhɛr(ə)nt/ ▶ **adjective** existing in something as a permanent, essential, or characteristic attribute: *any form of mountaineering has its inherent dangers.* ■ Law vested in (someone) as a right or privilege. ■ Linguistics (of an adjective) having the same meaning in both attributive and predicative uses.
– DERIVATIVES **inherence** noun, **inherently** adverb.
– ORIGIN late 16th cent.: from Latin *inhaerent-* 'sticking to', from the verb *inhaerere*, from *in-* 'in, towards' + *haerere* 'to stick'.

inherit ▶ **verb** (**inherits, inheriting, inherited**) **1** [with obj.] receive (money, property, or a title) as an heir at the death of the previous holder: *she inherited a fortune from her father.*
2 derive (a quality, characteristic, or predisposition) genetically from one's parents or ancestors: (as adj. **inherited**) *inherited diseases.*
3 receive or be left with (a situation, object, etc.) from a predecessor or former owner: *spending commitments inherited from previous governments.* ■ N. Amer. come into possession of (belongings) from someone else: *she inherits all her clothes from her older sisters.* ■ archaic come into possession of (something) as a right (especially in biblical translations and allusions).
– ORIGIN Middle English *enherite* 'receive as a right', from Old French *enheriter*, from late Latin *inhereditare* 'appoint as heir', from Latin *in-* 'in' + *heres*, *hered-* 'heir'.

inheritable ▶ **adjective** capable of being inherited: *these characteristics are inheritable* | *inheritable property.*
– DERIVATIVES **inheritability** noun.
– ORIGIN late Middle English (formerly also as *enheritable*): from Anglo-Norman French *enheritable* 'able to be made heir', from Old French *enheriter* (see **INHERIT**).

inheritance ▶ **noun** a thing that is inherited. ■ [mass noun] the action of inheriting: *the inheritance of traits.*
– ORIGIN late Middle English (formerly also as *enheritance*): from Anglo-Norman French *enheritaunce* 'being admitted as heir', from Old French *enheriter* (see **INHERIT**).

inheritance tax ▶ **noun** [mass noun] (in the UK) tax levied on property and money acquired by gift or inheritance (introduced in 1986 to replace capital transfer tax).

inheritor ▶ **noun** a person who inherits something; an heir: *we are the inheritors of these cultural traditions.*

inhesion /ɪnˈhiːʒ(ə)n/ ▶ **noun** formal the action or state of inhering in something.
– ORIGIN mid 17th cent.: from late Latin *inhaesio(n-)*, from Latin *inhaerere* 'stick to'.

inhibin /ɪnˈhɪbɪn/ ▶ **noun** [mass noun] Biochemistry a gonadal hormone which inhibits the secretion of follicle-stimulating hormone, under consideration as a potential male contraceptive.
– ORIGIN 1930s: from Latin *inhibere* 'hinder' + **-IN**[1].

inhibit ▶ **verb** (**inhibits, inhibiting, inhibited**)
1 [with obj.] hinder, restrain, or prevent (an action or process): *cold inhibits plant growth.* ■ chiefly Physiology & Biochemistry (of a substance) slow down or prevent (a process, reaction, or function) or reduce the activity of (an enzyme or other agent).
2 make (someone) self-conscious and unable to act in a relaxed and natural way: *they felt inhibited by the presence of healthcare professionals.*
3 (in ecclesiastical law) forbid (a member of the clergy) to exercise clerical functions.
– DERIVATIVES **inhibitive** adjective, **inhibitory** adjective.
– ORIGIN late Middle English (in the sense 'forbid (a person) to do something'): from Latin *inhibere* 'hinder', from *in-* 'in' + *habere* 'hold'.

inhibited ▶ **adjective** unable to act in a relaxed and natural way because of self-consciousness or mental restraint: *I could never appear nude, I'm far too inhibited.*

inhibition ▶ **noun 1** a feeling that makes one self-conscious and unable to act in a relaxed and natural way: *the children, at first shy, soon lost their inhibitions* | [mass noun] *she showed an enthusiasm for sex and a lack of inhibition which was entirely alien to him.* ■ Psychology a restraint on the direct expression of an instinct. ■ [mass noun] the slowing or prevention of a process, reaction, or function by a particular substance.
2 [mass noun] the action of inhibiting a process.
3 Law, Brit. an order or writ of prohibition, especially against dealing with a specified piece of land or property.
– ORIGIN late Middle English (in the sense 'forbidding, a prohibition'): from Latin *inhibitio(n-)*, from the verb *inhibere* (see **INHIBIT**).

inhibitor ▶ **noun** a thing which inhibits someone or something. ■ a substance which slows down or prevents a particular chemical reaction or other process or which reduces the activity of a particular reactant, catalyst, or enzyme. ■ Scots Law a person who takes out an inhibition.

in-home ▶ **adjective** [attrib.] (of a service or activity) provided or taking place within a person's home: *in-home haircuts for children.*

inhomogeneous /ˌɪnhɒmə(ʊ)ˈdʒiːnɪəs, -ˈdʒɛn-, ˌɪnhəʊm-/ ▶ **adjective** not uniform in character or content; diverse. ■ Mathematics consisting of terms that are not all of the same degree or dimensions.
– DERIVATIVES **inhomogeneity** noun.

inhospitable /ˌɪnhɒˈspɪtəb(ə)l, ɪnˈhɒspɪt-/ ▶ **adjective**
1 (of an environment) harsh and difficult to live in: *the inhospitable landscape.*
2 (of a person) unfriendly and unwelcoming towards people.
– DERIVATIVES **inhospitableness** noun, **inhospitably** adverb, **inhospitality** noun.
– ORIGIN late 16th cent.: French, from *in-* 'not' + *hospitable* (see **HOSPITABLE**).

in-house ▶ **adjective** /ˈɪnhaʊs/ [attrib.] done or existing within an organization: *in-house publications.*
▶ **adverb** /ɪnˈhaʊs/ without assistance from outside an organization; internally: *services previously provided in-house are being contracted out.*

inhuman ▶ **adjective 1** lacking human qualities of compassion and mercy; cruel and barbaric: *the inhuman treatment meted out to political prisoners.*
2 not human in nature or character: *the inhuman scale of the dinosaurs.*
– DERIVATIVES **inhumanly** adverb.
– ORIGIN late Middle English (originally as *inhumane*): from Latin *inhumanus*, from *in-* 'not' + *humanus* (see **HUMAN**).

inhumane ▶ **adjective** without compassion for misery or suffering; cruel: *confining wild horses is inhumane.*
– DERIVATIVES **inhumanely** adverb.
– ORIGIN late Middle English (in the sense 'inhuman, brutal'): originally a variant of **INHUMAN** (rare after 1700); in modern use from **IN-**[1] 'not' + **HUMANE** (the current sense dating from the early 19th cent.).

inhumanity ▶ **noun** (pl. **inhumanities**) [mass noun] extremely cruel and brutal behaviour: *man's inhumanity to man* | [count noun] *an elaborate review of man's inhumanities.*
– ORIGIN late 15th cent.: from Old French *inhumanite* or Latin *inhumanitas*, from *inhumanus* 'inhuman'.

inhumation /ˌɪnhjʊˈmeɪʃ(ə)n/ ▶ **noun** [mass noun] chiefly Archaeology the action or practice of burying the dead; the fact of being buried. ■ [count noun] a burial or

I

buried corpse: *more than thirty human inhumations from various sites.*

inhume /ɪnˈhjuːm/ ▶ **verb** [with obj.] literary bury: *no hand his bones shall gather or inhume.*
– ORIGIN early 17th cent.: from Latin *inhumare*, from *in-* 'into' + *humus* 'ground'.

inimical /ɪˈnɪmɪk(ə)l/ ▶ **adjective** tending to obstruct or harm: *the policy was* **inimical to** *Britain's real interests.* ■ unfriendly; hostile: *an inimical alien power.*
– DERIVATIVES **inimically** adverb.
– ORIGIN early 16th cent.: from late Latin *inimicalis*, from Latin *inimicus* (see ENEMY).

inimitable /ɪˈnɪmɪtəb(ə)l/ ▶ **adjective** so good or unusual as to be impossible to copy; unique: *they took the charts by storm with their inimitable style.*
– DERIVATIVES **inimitability** noun, **inimitably** adverb.
– ORIGIN late 15th cent.: from French, or from Latin *inimitabilis*, from *in-* 'not' + *imitabilis* (from *imitari* 'imitate').

inion /ˈɪnɪɒn/ ▶ **noun** Anatomy the projecting part of the occipital bone at the base of the skull.
– ORIGIN early 19th cent.: from Greek, literally 'nape of the neck'.

iniquitous ▶ **adjective** grossly unfair and morally wrong: *an iniquitous tax.*
– DERIVATIVES **iniquitousness** noun.

iniquity /ɪˈnɪkwɪti/ ▶ **noun** (pl. **iniquities**) [mass noun] immoral or grossly unfair behaviour: *a den of iniquity* | [count noun] *the iniquities of British taxation.*
– ORIGIN Middle English: from Old French *iniquite*, from Latin *iniquitas*, from *iniquus*, from *in-* 'not' + *aequus* 'equal, just'.

I

initial ▶ **adjective** [attrib.] existing or occurring at the beginning: *our initial impression was favourable.* ■ (of a letter) at the beginning of a word.
▶ **noun** (usu. **initials**) the first letter of a name or word, typically a person's given name or a word forming part of a phrase: *they carved their initials into the desktops.*
▶ **verb** (**initials, initialling, initialled**; US **initialing, initialed**) [with obj.] mark or sign (a document) with one's initials in order to authorize or validate it. ■ agree to or ratify (a treaty or contract) by signing it.
– ORIGIN early 16th cent.: from Latin *initialis*, from *initium* 'beginning', from *inire* 'go in', from *in-* 'into' + *ire* 'go'.

initialism ▶ **noun** an abbreviation consisting of initial letters pronounced separately (e.g. *BBC*).

initialize (also **initialise**) ▶ **verb** [with obj.] Computing **1** (often **be initialized to**) set to the value or put in the condition appropriate to the start of an operation: *the counter is initialized to one.*
2 format (a computer disk).
– DERIVATIVES **initialization** noun.

initially ▶ **adverb** [usu. sentence adverb] at first: *initially, he thought the new concept was nonsense.*

initial public offering ▶ **noun** chiefly US the act of offering the stock of a company on a public stock exchange for the first time.

initial teaching alphabet ▶ **noun** a 44-letter phonetic alphabet used to help those beginning to read and write English. It was used in many British primary schools in the 1960s but is now rarely seen.

initiate ▶ **verb** /ɪˈnɪʃieɪt/ [with obj.] **1** cause (a process or action) to begin: *he proposes to initiate discussions on planning procedures.*
2 admit (someone) into a secret or obscure society or group, typically with a ritual: *she had been formally* **initiated into** *the movement.* ■ (as plural noun **the initiated**) a small group of people who share obscure knowledge: *it's a secret sign to the initiated.* ■ (**initiate someone in/into**) introduce someone to (a particular activity or skill, especially a difficult or obscure one): *they were initiated into the mysteries of mathematics.*
▶ **noun** /ɪˈnɪʃɪət/ a person who has been initiated into an organization or activity: *an initiate of the cult.*
– DERIVATIVES **initiatory** adjective.
– ORIGIN mid 16th cent. (in sense 2 of the verb): from Latin *initiat-* 'begun', from the verb *initiare*, from *initium* 'beginning'.

initiation ▶ **noun** [mass noun] **1** the action of admitting someone into a secret or obscure society or group, typically with a ritual: *rituals of initiation* | [as modifier] *an initiation ceremony.* ■ the introduction of someone to a particular activity or skill: *his initiation into the world of martial arts.*
2 the action of beginning something: *the initiation of criminal proceedings.*

initiative ▶ **noun 1** [mass noun] the ability to assess and initiate things independently: *use your initiative, imagination, and common sense.*
2 [in sing.] the power or opportunity to act or take charge before others do: *anti-hunting groups have seized the initiative in the dispute.*
3 an act or strategy intended to resolve a difficulty or improve a situation; a fresh approach to something: *a new initiative against car crime.* ■ a proposal made by one nation to another in an attempt to improve relations: *a Middle East peace initiative.*
4 (**the initiative**) (especially in Switzerland and some US states) the right of citizens outside the legislature to originate legislation.
– PHRASES **on one's own initiative** without being prompted by others.
– ORIGIN late 18th cent.: from French, from Latin *initiare*, from *initium* 'beginning'.

initiator ▶ **noun** a person or thing that initiates someone or something. ■ Chemistry a substance which starts a chain reaction. ■ an explosive or device used to detonate a larger one.

inject ▶ **verb** [with obj.] **1** introduce (a liquid, especially a drug or vaccine) into the body with a syringe: *the doctor injected a painkilling drug.* ■ administer a drug or medicine by syringe to (a person or animal): *he was forcibly* **injected with** *a sedative.* ■ [no obj.] inject oneself with a narcotic drug, especially habitually: *people who want to stop injecting.*
2 introduce (something) under pressure into a passage, cavity, or solid material: *inject the foam and allow it to expand.* ■ Physics introduce or feed (a current, beam of particles, etc.) into a substance or device.
3 introduce (a new or different element) into something: *she tried to* **inject** *scorn* **into** *her tone.*
4 place (a spacecraft or other object) into an orbit or trajectory.
– DERIVATIVES **injectable** adjective & noun.
– ORIGIN late 16th cent. (in the sense 'throw or cast on something'): from Latin *inject-* 'thrown in', from the verb *inicere*, from *in-* 'into' + *jacere* 'throw'.

injection ▶ **noun 1** an instance of injecting or being injected: *painkilling injections* | *an injection of capital was needed.* ■ a thing that is injected: *a morphine injection.* ■ [mass noun] the action of injecting: *the walls have been damp-proofed by injection.* ■ short for FUEL INJECTION.
2 [mass noun] the entry or placing of a spacecraft or other object into an orbit or trajectory.
3 Mathematics a one-to-one mapping.
– ORIGIN late Middle English: from Latin *injectio(n-)*, from the verb *inicere* (see INJECT).

injection moulding ▶ **noun** [mass noun] the shaping of rubber or plastic articles by injecting heated material into a mould.
– DERIVATIVES **injection-moulded** adjective.

injective ▶ **adjective** Mathematics of the nature of or relating to an injection or one-to-one mapping.

injector ▶ **noun** a person or thing that injects something. ■ (also **fuel injector**) (in an internal-combustion engine) the nozzle and valve through which fuel is sprayed into a combustion chamber. ■ (in a steam engine) a system of nozzles that uses steam to inject water into a pressurized boiler.

injera /ˈɪndʒiːrə/ ▶ **noun** [mass noun] a white leavened Ethiopian bread made from teff flour, similar to a crêpe.
– ORIGIN Amharic.

in-joke ▶ **noun** a joke that is shared exclusively by a small group of people.

injudicious ▶ **adjective** showing very poor judgement; unwise: *I took a few injudicious swigs of potent cider.*
– DERIVATIVES **injudiciously** adverb, **injudiciousness** noun.

Injun /ˈɪndʒ(ə)n/ ▶ **noun** US informal, offensive an American Indian.
– PHRASES **honest Injun** dated honestly; really: *I won't run away, honest Injun.*
– ORIGIN late 17th cent.: alteration of INDIAN.

injunct /ɪnˈdʒʌŋ(k)t/ ▶ **verb** [with obj.] issue a legal injunction against.
– ORIGIN late 19th cent.: from Latin *injunct-* 'imposed', from the verb *injungere* (see ENJOIN).

injunction ▶ **noun** an authoritative warning or order. ■ Law a judicial order restraining a person from beginning or continuing an action threatening or invading the legal right of another, or compelling a person to carry out a certain act, e.g. to make restitution to an injured party.
– DERIVATIVES **injunctive** adjective.
– ORIGIN late Middle English: from late Latin *injunctio(n-)*, from Latin *injungere* 'enjoin, impose'.

injure ▶ **verb 1** [with obj.] do physical harm or damage to (someone): *the explosion injured several people.* ■ suffer physical harm or damage to (a part of one's body).
2 harm or impair (something): *a libel calculated to injure the company's reputation.* ■ archaic do injustice or wrong to (someone).
– DERIVATIVES **injurer** noun.
– ORIGIN late Middle English: back-formation from INJURY.

injured ▶ **adjective 1** harmed, damaged, or impaired: *a road accident left him severely injured.*
2 offended: *his injured pride.*

injurious /ɪnˈdʒʊərɪəs/ ▶ **adjective** causing or likely to cause damage or harm: *food which is injurious to health.* ■ (of language) maliciously insulting; libellous.
– DERIVATIVES **injuriously** adverb, **injuriousness** noun.
– ORIGIN late Middle English: from French *injurieux* or Latin *injuriosus*, from *injuria* 'a wrong' (see INJURY).

injury ▶ **noun** (pl. **injuries**) **1** an instance of being injured: *she suffered an injury to her back.* ■ [mass noun] the fact of being injured; harm or damage: *all escaped without serious injury.*
2 damage to a person's feelings.
– PHRASES **do oneself an injury** informal suffer physical harm or damage.
– ORIGIN late Middle English: from Anglo-Norman French *injurie*, from Latin *injuria* 'a wrong', from *in-* (expressing negation) + *jus, jur-* 'right'.

injury time ▶ **noun** [mass noun] Brit. (in soccer and other sports) extra playing time allowed by a referee to compensate for time lost in dealing with injuries.

injustice ▶ **noun** [mass noun] lack of fairness or justice: *she was taken aback by the injustice of Nora's remark.* ■ [count noun] an unjust act or occurrence: *brooding over life's injustices.*
– PHRASES **do someone an injustice** judge a person unfairly.
– ORIGIN late Middle English: from Old French, from Latin *injustitia*, from *in-* 'not' + *justus* 'just, right'.

ink ▶ **noun** [mass noun] a coloured fluid or paste used for writing, drawing, printing, or duplicating: *the names are written in ink* | [count noun] *a picture executed in coloured inks.* ■ informal publicity in the written media: *the story got lots of ink and plenty of air time.* ■ Zoology a black liquid ejected by a cuttlefish, octopus, or squid to confuse a predator.
▶ **verb 1** [with obj.] mark (words or a design) with ink: *the cork has the name of the château inked on to the side.* ■ cover (type or a stamp) with ink before printing: *a raised image is inked to produce an impression.*
2 N. Amer. informal sign (a contract): *she's just inked a deal to host her own talk show.* ■ secure the services of (someone) with a contract.
– DERIVATIVES **inker** noun.
– ORIGIN Middle English *enke, inke*, from Old French *enque*, via late Latin from Greek *enkauston*, denoting the purple ink used by Roman emperors for signatures, from *enkaiein* 'burn in'.

Inkatha /ɪnˈkɑːtə/ (in full **Inkatha Freedom Party**) a mainly Zulu political party and organization in South Africa, founded in 1928 and revived in 1975 by Dr Mangosuthu Buthelezi. It was active in the struggle for racial equality and universal franchise during the apartheid years, although in this it clashed with members of the rival ANC.
– ORIGIN from Zulu *inkatha* 'crown of woven grass', a tribal emblem symbolizing the force unifying the Zulu nation.

inkberry ▶ **noun** (pl. **inkberries**) a low-growing North American holly with black berries and nearly spineless leaves. ● *Ilex glabra*, family Aquifoliaceae.

ink-blot test ▶ **noun** another term for RORSCHACH TEST.

ink cap ▶ **noun** a widely distributed mushroom with a tall, narrow cap and slender white stem, turning into a black liquid after the spores are shed. ● Genus *Coprinus*, family Coprinaceae, class Hymenomycetes: several species, including the **common ink cap** (*C. atramentarius*). See also SHAGGY INK CAP.

inkhorn ▶ **noun** historical a small portable container for ink. ■ [as modifier] denoting words or expressions used only in academic writing: *I will avoid many of the inkhorn terms coined by the narratologists.*

inkjet printer ▶ **noun** a printer in which the characters are formed by minute jets of ink.

inkle /ˈɪŋk(ə)l/ ▸ noun [mass noun] a kind of linen tape formerly used to make laces, or the linen yarn from which this is manufactured.
– ORIGIN mid 16th cent.: of unknown origin.

inkling ▸ noun a slight knowledge or suspicion; a hint: *the records give us an inkling of how people saw the world.*
– ORIGIN late Middle English (in the sense 'a mention in an undertone, a hint'): from the rare verb *inkle* 'utter in an undertone', of unknown origin.

ink pad ▸ noun an ink-soaked pad in a shallow box, used for inking a rubber stamp or taking fingerprints.

inkstand ▸ noun a stand for one or more ink bottles, typically incorporating a pen tray.

inkwell ▸ noun a pot for ink housed in a hole in a desk.

inky ▸ adjective (**inkier**, **inkiest**) **1** as dark as ink: *the cold inky blackness of a Mexican cave.*
2 stained with ink: *bureaucrats with inky fingers.*
– DERIVATIVES **inkiness** noun.

INLA ▸ abbreviation Irish National Liberation Army.

inlaid past and past participle of **INLAY**.

inland /ˈɪnlənd, -land/ ▸ adjective situated in the interior of a country rather than on the coast: *the inland port of Gloucester.* ■ [attrib.] chiefly Brit. carried on within the limits of a country; domestic: *a network of waterways that allowed inland trade.*
▸ adverb also /ɪnˈland/ in or towards the interior of a country: *the path turned inland and met the road.*
▸ noun (**the inland**) the parts of a country remote from the sea or frontiers; the interior.
– DERIVATIVES **inlander** noun.

inland navigation ▸ noun [mass noun] transportation by canals and rivers.

inland revenue ▸ noun [mass noun] Brit. public revenue consisting of income tax and some other direct taxes. ■ (**Inland Revenue**) (in the UK) the government department responsible for assessing and collecting inland revenue.

Inland Sea an almost landlocked arm of the Pacific Ocean, surrounded by the Japanese islands of Honshu, Shikoku, and Kyushu. Its chief port is Hiroshima.

inland sea ▸ noun an entirely landlocked large body of salt or fresh water.

in-law ▸ noun a relative by marriage.

inlay ▸ verb /ɪnˈleɪ/ (past and past participle **inlaid**) [with obj.] ornament (an object) by embedding pieces of a different material in it, flush with its surface: *mahogany panelling **inlaid with** rosewood.* ■ embed (material or a design) flush with the surface of an object: *a small silver crown was inlaid in the wood.*
▸ noun /ˈɪnleɪ/ **1** a design, pattern, or piece of material inlaid in something: *ivory inlays that decorated wooden furnishings.* ■ a material or substance that is used as an inlay. ■ [mass noun] inlaid work: *the cathedral was decorated with mosaic and inlay.* ■ [mass noun] the technique of inlaying material.
2 a filling shaped to fit a tooth cavity.
3 a printed card or paper insert supplied with a CD, video, etc.
– ORIGIN mid 16th cent. (in the sense 'lay something in a place in order to hide or preserve it'): from **IN-²** 'into' + **LAY¹**.

inlet ▸ noun **1** a small arm of the sea, a lake, or a river.
2 a place or means of entry: *an air inlet.*
3 (chiefly in tailoring and dressmaking) a piece of material inserted into a garment.
– ORIGIN Middle English (denoting admission): from **IN** + the verb **LET¹**.

inlier /ˈɪnlʌɪə/ ▸ noun Geology an older rock formation isolated among newer rocks.
– ORIGIN mid 19th cent.: from **IN**, on the pattern of *outlier*.

in-line ▸ adjective **1** having parts arranged in a line.
2 constituting an integral part of a continuous sequence of operations or machines. ■ constituting an integral part of a computer program: *the parameters can be set up as in-line code.*

inline engine ▸ noun a type of internal-combustion engine used chiefly in aircraft, having its cylinders arranged in a row.

in-liner ▸ noun an in-line skater. ■ an in-line skate.

in-line skates ▸ plural noun a pair of roller skates in which the wheels on each boot are fixed in a single line along its sole.
– DERIVATIVES **in-line skater** noun, **in-line skating** noun.

in loco parentis /ɪn ˌləʊkəʊ pəˈrɛntɪs/ ▸ adverb (of a teacher or other adult responsible for children) in the place of a parent: *he was used to acting in loco parentis.*
– ORIGIN Latin.

inly /ˈɪnli/ ▸ adverb literary inwardly: *inly stung with anger and disdain.*
– ORIGIN Old English *innlīce* (see **IN**, **-LY²**).

inlying /ˈɪnlʌɪɪŋ/ ▸ adjective [attrib.] situated within or near a centre.

Inmarsat /ˈɪnmɑːsat/ an international organization founded in 1978 that provides telecommunication services, as well as distress and safety communication services, to the world's shipping, aviation, and offshore industries.
– ORIGIN from initials of *International Maritime Satellite Organization.*

inmate ▸ noun a person living in an institution such as a prison or hospital. ■ archaic one of several occupants of a house.
– ORIGIN late 16th cent. (denoting a person who shared a house, specifically a lodger or subtenant): probably originally from **INN** + **MATE¹**, later associated with **IN**.

in medias res /ɪn ˌmiːdɪas ˈreɪz/ ▸ adverb into the middle of a narrative; without preamble: *having begun his story in medias res.* ■ into the midst of things.
– ORIGIN Latin.

in memoriam /ˌɪn mɪˈmɔːrɪam/ ▸ noun [often as modifier] an article written in memory of a dead person; an obituary: *in memoriam notices in the paper.*
▸ preposition in memory of (a dead person): *an openly revolutionary work in memoriam Che Guevara.*
– ORIGIN Latin.

inmost ▸ adjective literary innermost.
– ORIGIN Old English *innemest* (see **IN**, **-MOST**).

inn ▸ noun [usu. in names] a pub, typically one in the country, in some cases providing accommodation: *the Swan Inn.* ■ historical a house providing accommodation, food, and drink, especially for travellers.
– ORIGIN Old English (in the sense 'dwelling place, lodging'): of Germanic origin; related to **IN**. In Middle English the word was used to translate Latin *hospitium* (see **HOSPICE**), denoting a house of residence for students: this sense is preserved in the names of some buildings formerly used for this purpose, notably *Gray's Inn* and *Lincoln's Inn*, two of the **INNS OF COURT**. The current sense dates from late Middle English.

innards ▸ plural noun informal entrails. ■ the internal workings of a device or machine.
– ORIGIN early 19th cent.: representing a dialect pronunciation of **INWARDS**, used as a noun.

innate /ɪˈneɪt, ˈɪneɪt/ ▸ adjective inborn; natural: *her innate capacity for organization.* ■ Philosophy originating in the mind.
– DERIVATIVES **innately** adverb, **innateness** noun.
– ORIGIN late Middle English: from Latin *innatus*, past participle of *innasci*, from *in-* 'into' + *nasci* 'be born'.

inner ▸ adjective [attrib.] **1** situated inside or further in; internal: *an inner courtyard | the inner thigh.* ■ close to the centre: *inner London.* ■ close to the centre of power: *the inner cabinet.*
2 mental or spiritual: *a test of inner strength.* ■ (of thoughts or feelings) private and not expressed or discernible. ■ denoting a concealed or unacknowledged part of a person's personality: *it's time to get in touch with your inner geek | join a choir and give voice to that inner diva who has been hidden away too long.*
▸ noun the inner part of something: *using his rock shoes as inners for his double boots.* ■ (in archery and shooting) a division of the target next to the bullseye. ■ a shot that strikes the inner.
– DERIVATIVES **innerly** adverb (literary), **innerness** noun (literary).
– ORIGIN Old English *innerra, innra*, comparative of **IN**.

inner bar ▸ noun (in the UK) all Queen's or King's Counsel collectively.

inner child ▸ noun a person's supposed original or true self, especially when regarded as concealed in adulthood.

inner circle ▸ noun an exclusive group close to the centre of power of an organization or movement, regarded as elitist and secretive.

inner city ▸ noun [usu. as modifier] the area near the centre of a city, especially when associated with social and economic problems: *inner-city areas.*

inner ear ▸ noun the semicircular canals and cochlea, which form the organs of balance and hearing and are embedded in the temporal bone.

Inner Hebrides see **HEBRIDES**.

Inner House (in full **the Inner House of the Court of Session**) (in Scotland) either of two law courts that correspond to the Court of Appeal in England and Wales, each presided over by three judges.

inner light ▸ noun [in sing.] personal spiritual revelation; a source of enlightenment within oneself.
– ORIGIN mid 19th cent.: originally in Quaker doctrine.

Inner Mongolia an autonomous region of northern China, on the border with Mongolia; capital, Hohhot.

innermost ▸ adjective [attrib.] **1** (of thoughts or feelings) most private and deeply felt: *innermost beliefs and convictions.*
2 furthest in; closest to the centre: *the innermost layer.*

inner planet ▸ noun a planet whose orbit lies within the asteroid belt, i.e. Mercury, Venus, Earth, or Mars.

inner sanctum ▸ noun the most sacred place in a temple or church. ■ a private or secret place to which few other people are admitted: *he walked into the inner sanctum of the editor's office.*

inner space ▸ noun **1** the region between the earth and outer space, or below the surface of the sea.
2 the part of the mind not normally accessible to consciousness.

Inner Temple one of the two Inns of Court on the site of the Temple in London. Compare with **MIDDLE TEMPLE**.

inner tube ▸ noun a separate inflatable tube inside a pneumatic tyre.

innervate /ˈɪnəveɪt, ɪˈnəːveɪt/ ▸ verb [with obj.] Anatomy & Zoology supply (an organ or other body part) with nerves.
– DERIVATIVES **innervation** noun.
– ORIGIN late 19th cent.: from **IN-²** 'into' + **NERVE** + **-ATE³**.

inning ▸ noun Baseball each division of a game during which both sides have a turn at batting.
– ORIGIN Old English *innung* 'a putting or getting in', related to **IN**. The current sense dates from the mid 19th cent.

innings ▸ noun (pl. **same** or informal **inningses**) **1** Cricket each of two or four divisions of a game during which one side has a turn at batting: *the highlight of the Surrey innings.* ■ a player's turn at batting: *he had played his greatest innings.* ■ the score achieved during a player's turn at batting: *a solid innings of 78 by Marsh.*
2 a period during which a person or group is active or effective.
– PHRASES **have had a good innings** Brit. informal have had a long and fulfilling life or career.

innit ▸ contraction Brit. informal isn't it (often used in conversation when seeking confirmation or as a general filler): *it's the easiest way, innit? | we all want to get highly paid jobs, innit?*

> **WORD TRENDS** Few words induce such rage and consternation in traditionalists as the contraction **innit**. The word first emerged in the mid 20th century as an informal way of saying 'isn't it', particularly in questions seeking agreement or confirmation: *it's a publicity stunt, innit?* More recently it has developed into an all-purpose 'filler', with a range of meanings including 'don't I?' and 'hasn't he/she?', often used simply for emphasis: *I get on with everyone, innit | she's got this boyfriend Joe, innit?* Though usually found in informal spoken English, these extended meanings are also well represented in the Oxford English Corpus, appearing in blogs, news, and fiction, with the 'filler' use now more common than the direct contraction of 'isn't it'.

innkeeper ▸ noun chiefly archaic a person who runs an inn.

innocence ▸ noun [mass noun] the state, quality, or fact of being innocent of a crime or offence: *they must prove their innocence.* ■ lack of guile or corruption; purity: *the healthy bloom in her cheeks gave her an aura of innocence.* ■ euphemistic a person's virginity: *all the boys lost their innocence with her.*
– PHRASES **in all innocence** without knowledge of something's significance or possible consequences: *she knew the gift had been chosen in all innocence.*
– DERIVATIVES **innocency** noun (archaic).
– ORIGIN Middle English: from Old French, from Latin *innocentia*, from *innocent-* 'not harming' (based on *nocere* 'injure').

I

innocent ▸ adjective **1** not guilty of a crime or offence: *the prisoners were later found innocent | he is innocent of Sir Thomas's death.* ■ (**innocent of**) without experience or knowledge of: *a man innocent of war's cruelties.* ■ (**innocent of**) without; lacking: *a street quite innocent of bookshops.*
2 [attrib.] not responsible for or directly involved in an event yet suffering its consequences: *an innocent bystander.*
3 free from moral wrong; not corrupted: *an innocent child.* ■ simple; naive: *she is a poor, innocent young creature.*
4 not involving or intended to cause harm or offence; harmless: *an innocent mistake.*
▸ noun **1** a pure, guileless, or naive person: *a young innocent abroad.*
2 a person involved by chance in a situation, especially a victim of crime or war: *they are prepared to kill or maim innocents in pursuit of a cause.* ■ (**the Innocents**) the young children killed by Herod after the birth of Jesus (Matt. 2:16).
– DERIVATIVES **innocently** adverb.
– ORIGIN Middle English: from Old French, or from Latin *innocent-* 'not harming', from *in-* 'not' + *nocere* 'to hurt'.

Innocents' Day (also **Holy Innocents' Day**) ▸ noun a Christian festival commemorating the massacre of the Innocents, 28 December.

I

innocuous /ɪˈnɒkjʊəs/ ▸ adjective not harmful or offensive: *it was an innocuous question.*
– DERIVATIVES **innocuously** adverb, **innocuousness** noun.
– ORIGIN late 16th cent.: from Latin *innocuus*, from *in-* 'not' + *nocuus* 'injurious' (see NOCUOUS).

Inn of Court ▸ noun (in the UK) each of the four legal societies having the exclusive right of admitting people to the English bar. ■ any of the sets of buildings in London occupied by the Inns of Court.

innominate /ɪˈnɒmɪnət/ ▸ adjective not named or classified.
– ORIGIN mid 17th cent.: from late Latin *innominatus*, from *in-* 'not' + *nominatus* 'named' (past participle of *nominare*).

innominate artery ▸ noun Anatomy a large artery which branches from the aortic arch and divides into the right common carotid and right subclavian arteries.

innominate bone ▸ noun Anatomy the bone formed from the fusion of the ilium, ischium, and pubis; the hip bone.

innominate vein ▸ noun Anatomy either of two large veins of the neck formed by the junction of the external jugular and subclavian veins.

innovate /ˈɪnəveɪt/ ▸ verb [no obj.] make changes in something established, especially by introducing new methods, ideas, or products: *the company's failure to diversify and innovate competitively.* ■ [with obj.] introduce (something new, especially a product).
– DERIVATIVES **innovatory** adjective.
– ORIGIN mid 16th cent.: from Latin *innovat-* 'renewed, altered', from the verb *innovare*, from *in-* 'into' + *novare* 'make new' (from *novus* 'new').

innovation ▸ noun [mass noun] the action or process of innovating. ■ [count noun] a new method, idea, product, etc.: *technological innovations designed to save energy.*
– DERIVATIVES **innovational** adjective.
– ORIGIN late Middle English: from Latin *innovatio(n-)*, from the verb *innovare* (see INNOVATE).

innovative /ˈɪnəvətɪv/ ▸ adjective (of a product, idea, etc.) featuring new methods; advanced and original: *innovative designs | innovative ways to help unemployed people.* ■ (of a person) introducing new ideas; original and creative in thinking: *writers who are now viewed as innovative.*
– DERIVATIVES **innovatively** adverb, **innovativeness** noun.

innovator ▸ noun a person who introduces new methods, ideas, or products: *he was one of the great innovators in jazz.*

Innsbruck /ˈɪnzbrʊk, ˈɪns-/ a city in western Austria, capital of Tyrol; pop. 116,239 (2006).

Inns of Chancery ▸ plural noun historical (in the UK) the buildings in London formerly used as hostels for law students.

Inns of Court ▸ plural noun see INN OF COURT.

innuendo /ˌɪnjʊˈɛndəʊ/ ▸ noun (pl. **innuendoes** or **innuendos**) an allusive or oblique remark or hint, typically a suggestive or disparaging one: *she's always making sly innuendoes* | [mass noun] *a constant torrent of innuendo, gossip, lies, and half-truths.*
– ORIGIN mid 16th cent. (as an adverb in the sense 'that is to say, to wit', used in legal documents to introduce an explanation): Latin, 'by nodding at, by pointing to', ablative gerund of *innuere*, from *in-* 'towards' + *nuere* 'to nod'. The noun dates from the late 17th cent.

innumerable ▸ adjective too many to be counted (often used hyperbolically): *innumerable flags of all colours.*
– DERIVATIVES **innumerably** adverb.
– ORIGIN Middle English: from Latin *innumerabilis*, from *in-* 'not' + *numerabilis* (see NUMERABLE).

innumerate ▸ adjective without a basic knowledge of mathematics and arithmetic.
▸ noun an innumerate person.
– DERIVATIVES **innumeracy** noun.

innutrition ▸ noun [mass noun] rare lack of nourishment.

innutritious ▸ adjective (of food) lacking in nutrients; not nourishing.

inobservance ▸ noun [mass noun] archaic failure to observe or notice; inattention. ■ failure to observe a law, custom, etc.
– ORIGIN early 17th cent.: from French, or from Latin *inobservantia*, from *in-* (expressing negation) + *observantia* 'observance' (from *observare* 'observe').

inoculant ▸ noun a substance suitable for inoculating.

inoculate /ɪˈnɒkjʊleɪt/ ▸ verb [with obj.] treat with a vaccine to produce immunity against a disease; vaccinate: *he **inoculated** his tenants **against** smallpox.* ■ introduce (an infective agent) into an organism. ■ introduce (cells or organisms) into a culture medium.
– DERIVATIVES **inoculative** /-lətɪv/ adjective, **inoculator** noun.
– ORIGIN late Middle English (in the sense 'graft a bud or shoot into a different plant'): from Latin *inoculat-* 'engrafted', from the verb *inoculare*, from *in-* 'into' + *oculus* 'eye, bud'. The sense 'vaccinate' dates from the early 18th cent.

inoculation ▸ noun [mass noun] the action of inoculating or of being inoculated; vaccination: *inoculation against flu was readily available* | [count noun] *a course of inoculations.*

inoculum /ɪˈnɒkjʊləm/ ▸ noun (pl. **inocula**) Medicine a substance used for inoculation.
– ORIGIN early 20th cent.: modern Latin, from Latin *inoculare* (see INOCULATE), on the pattern of the pair *coagulate, coagulum.*

inodorous ▸ adjective having no smell; odourless.
– ORIGIN mid 17th cent.: from Latin *inodorus*, from *in-* 'not' + *odorus* 'odorous', or from IN-^{1} 'not' + ODOROUS.

in-off ▸ noun Billiards & Snooker the pocketing of the cue ball (a scoring stroke in billiards, a foul in snooker) by bouncing it off another ball: *he attempted a very difficult in-off* | [as adv.] *going in-off on the penultimate red.*

inoffensive ▸ adjective not objectionable or harmful: *a shy, inoffensive, and sensitive girl.*
– DERIVATIVES **inoffensively** adverb, **inoffensiveness** noun.

inoperable ▸ adjective **1** Medicine not able to be suitably operated on: *inoperable cancer.*
2 not able to be used: *the airfield was bombed and made inoperable.*
3 not able to be implemented; impractical: *the procedures were inoperable.*
– DERIVATIVES **inoperability** noun, **inoperably** adverb.

inoperative ▸ adjective not working or taking effect: *the Act may be rendered inoperative.*

inopportune ▸ adjective occurring at an inconvenient or inappropriate time: *a storm blew up at an inopportune moment.*
– DERIVATIVES **inopportunely** adverb.
– ORIGIN early 16th cent.: from Latin *inopportunus*, from *in-* 'not' + *opportunus* (see OPPORTUNE).

inordinate /ɪˈnɔːdɪnət/ ▸ adjective **1** unusually or disproportionately large; excessive: *the case had taken up an inordinate amount of time.*
2 archaic (of a person) unrestrained in feelings or behaviour.
– DERIVATIVES **inordinately** adverb [as submodifier] *an inordinately expensive business.*
– ORIGIN late Middle English: from Latin *inordinatus*, from *in-* 'not' + *ordinatus* 'arranged, set in order' (past participle of *ordinare*).

inorganic ▸ adjective **1** not consisting of or deriving from living matter. ■ without organized physical structure.
2 Chemistry relating to or denoting compounds which are not organic (broadly, compounds not containing carbon).
– DERIVATIVES **inorganically** adverb.

inorganic chemistry ▸ noun [mass noun] the branch of chemistry that deals with inorganic compounds.

inosculate /ɪˈnɒskjʊleɪt/ ▸ verb [no obj.] formal join by intertwining or fitting closely together.
– DERIVATIVES **inosculation** noun.
– ORIGIN late 17th cent.: from IN-^{2} 'into' + Latin *osculare* 'provide with a mouth or outlet' (from *osculum*, diminutive of *os* 'mouth'), on the pattern of Greek *anastomoun*, in the same sense.

inosine /ˈɪnə(ʊ)siːn/ ▸ noun [mass noun] Biochemistry a compound which is an intermediate in the metabolism of purine and is used in kidney transplantation to provide a temporary source of sugar. It is a nucleoside consisting of hypoxanthine linked to ribose.
– ORIGIN early 20th cent.: from Greek *is, in-* 'fibre, muscle' + -OSE^{2} + -INE^{4}.

inositol /ʌɪˈnəʊsɪtɒl/ ▸ noun [mass noun] Biochemistry a simple carbohydrate which occurs in animal and plant tissue and is a vitamin of the B group. ● Alternative name: **hexahydroxycyclohexane**; chem. formula: $C_6H_{12}O_6$.
– ORIGIN late 19th cent.: from the earlier name *inosite* + -OL.

inotropic /ˌɪnə(ʊ)ˈtrəʊpɪk, -ˈtrɒpɪk/ ▸ adjective Physiology modifying the force or speed of contraction of muscles.

inpatient ▸ noun a patient who lives in hospital while under treatment.

in personam /ˌɪn pəːˈsəʊnam/ ▸ adjective & adverb Law made or availing against or affecting a specific person only; imposing a personal liability: [as postpositive adj.] *rights and duties in personam* | [as adv.] *the view that trusts operate in personam.* Compare with IN REM.
– ORIGIN Latin, 'against a person'.

in potentia /ˌɪn pəˈtɛnʃɪə/ ▸ adverb as a possibility; potentially.
– ORIGIN Latin, 'in potentiality'.

inpouring ▸ noun [mass noun] the action of pouring something in: *vast inpouring of public money.*

in propria persona /ɪn ˌprəʊprɪə pəːˈsəʊnə/ ▸ adverb in his or her own person.
– ORIGIN Latin.

input ▸ noun **1** [mass noun] what is put in, taken in, or operated on by any process or system: *there is little input from other members of the team | data input.* ■ a contribution of work or information: *her input on issues was appreciated.* ■ energy supplied to a device or system; an electrical signal. ■ the action of putting something in: *the input of data to the system.* ■ the information put into a computer.
2 Electronics a place where, or a device through which, energy or information enters a system: *the signal being fed through the main input.*
▸ verb (**inputs, inputting**; past and past participle **input** or **inputted**) [with obj.] put (data) into a computer.
– DERIVATIVES **inputter** noun.

input-output ▸ adjective Electronics relating to or for both input and output.

inquest ▸ noun **1** Law a judicial inquiry to ascertain the facts relating to an incident. ■ Brit. an inquiry by a coroner's court into the cause of a death. ■ Brit. a coroner's jury.
2 informal a discussion or investigation into something that has happened, especially something undesirable.
– ORIGIN Middle English from Old French *enqueste*, based on Latin *inquirere* (see ENQUIRE).

inquietude /ɪnˈkwʌɪətjuːd/ ▸ noun [mass noun] physical or mental restlessness or disturbance.
– ORIGIN late Middle English (in the sense 'disturbance of one's quietness or rest'): from Old French, or from late Latin *inquietudo*, from Latin *inquietus*, from *in-* 'not' + *quietus* 'quiet'.

inquilab /ˈɪŋkɪlɑːb/ ▸ noun Indian a revolution or uprising (often used as a political slogan).
– ORIGIN Urdu *inqalāb, inqilāb* 'change, turn, revolution'.

inquiline /ˈɪnkwɪlʌɪn/ ▸ noun Zoology an animal exploiting the living space of another, e.g. an insect that lays its eggs in a gall produced by another.
– ORIGIN mid 17th cent.: from Latin *inquilinus* 'temporary resident', from *in-* 'into' + *colere* 'dwell'.

inquire ▸ verb another term for ENQUIRE.

– DERIVATIVES **inquirer** noun.
– ORIGIN Middle English *enquere* (later *inquere*), from Old French *enquerre*, from a variant of Latin *inquirere*, based on *quaerere* 'seek'. The spelling with *in-*, influenced by Latin, dates from the 15th cent.

USAGE On the difference between **inquire** and **enquire**, see **USAGE** at **ENQUIRE**.

inquiring ▸ adjective another term for **ENQUIRING**.

inquiry ▸ noun (pl. **inquiries**) another term for **ENQUIRY**.

inquisition ▸ noun **1** a period of prolonged and intensive questioning: *she relented in her determined inquisition and offered help*. ■ historical a judicial or official inquiry.
2 (**the Inquisition**) an ecclesiastical tribunal established by Pope Gregory IX *c.*1232 for the suppression of heresy. It was active chiefly in northern Italy and southern France, becoming notorious for the use of torture. In 1542 the papal Inquisition was revived to combat Protestantism, eventually becoming an organ of papal government. See also **SPANISH INQUISITION**.
– DERIVATIVES **inquisitional** adjective.
– ORIGIN late Middle English (denoting a searching examination): via Old French from Latin *inquisitio(n-)* 'examination', from the verb *inquirere* (see **ENQUIRE**).

inquisitive ▸ adjective having or showing an interest in learning things; curious: *his poems reveal an intensely inquisitive mind*. ■ unduly curious about the affairs of others; prying.
– DERIVATIVES **inquisitively** adverb, **inquisitiveness** noun.
– ORIGIN late Middle English: from Old French *inquisitif, -ive*, from late Latin *inquisitivus*, from the verb *inquirere* (see **ENQUIRE**).

inquisitor /ɪnˈkwɪzɪtə/ ▸ noun a person making an inquiry, especially one seen to be excessively harsh or searching: *the professional inquisitors of the press*. ■ historical an officer of the Inquisition.
– ORIGIN late Middle English: from French *inquisiteur*, from Latin *inquisitor*, from the verb *inquirere* (see **ENQUIRE**).

Inquisitor General ▸ noun the head of the Spanish Inquisition.

inquisitorial ▸ adjective of or like an inquisitor, especially in questioning someone in a harsh or intensive manner. ■ Law (of a trial or legal procedure) characterized by the judge performing an examining role. Compare with **ACCUSATORIAL, ADVERSARIAL**.
– DERIVATIVES **inquisitorially** adverb.
– ORIGIN mid 18th cent.: from medieval Latin *inquisitorius* (from Latin *inquisitor*, from *inquirere* 'inquire') + **-AL**.

inquorate /ɪnˈkwɔːrət, -eɪt/ ▸ adjective Brit. (of an assembly) unable to proceed effectively because not enough members are present to make up a quorum: *they had boycotted the debate, leaving the house inquorate*.

in re /ɪn ˈriː, ˈreɪ/ ▸ preposition in the legal case of; with regard to: *the decision of the Court of Appeal in re Midland Railway Co's Agreement*.
– ORIGIN Latin, 'in the matter of'.

in rem /ɪn ˈrɛm/ ▸ adjective [often postpositive] Law made or availing against or affecting a thing, and therefore other people generally; imposing a general liability: *it confers a right in rem*. Compare with **IN PERSONAM**.
– ORIGIN Latin, 'against a thing'.

INRI ▸ abbreviation Jesus of Nazareth, King of the Jews (a traditional representation in art of the inscription over Christ's head at the Crucifixion).
– ORIGIN from the initials of Latin *Iesus Nazarenus Rex Iudaeorum*.

inro /ˈɪnrəʊ/ ▸ noun (pl. **same** or **inros**) an ornamental box with compartments for items such as seals and medicines, worn suspended from a girdle as part of traditional Japanese dress.
– ORIGIN early 17th cent.: from Japanese *inrō*, from *in* 'seal' + *rō* 'basket'.

inroad ▸ noun **1** (usu. **make inroads in/into/on**) an instance of something being encroached on or reduced by something else: *the firm is beginning to make inroads into the UK market* | *serious inroads had now been made into my pitiful cash reserves*.
2 a hostile attack; a raid.
– ORIGIN mid 16th cent. (in sense 2): from **IN** + **ROAD** (from an early use in the sense 'riding').

inrush ▸ noun [in sing.] the sudden arrival or entry of something: *a great inrush of water occurred*.
– DERIVATIVES **inrushing** adjective & noun.

INS ▸ abbreviation Immigration and Naturalization Service, a US government agency.

insalata /ˌɪnsəˈlɑːtə/ ▸ noun an Italian-style salad: *insalata verde*.
– ORIGIN Italian, 'salad'.

insalubrious /ˌɪnsəˈluːbrɪəs/ ▸ adjective (of a place) seedy and run-down; unwholesome: *a poor area full of insalubrious hotels*.
– DERIVATIVES **insalubrity** noun.
– ORIGIN mid 17th cent.: from Latin *insalubris* (from *in-* 'not' + *salubris* 'salubrious') + **-OUS**.

insane ▸ adjective in a state of mind which prevents normal perception, behaviour, or social interaction; seriously mentally ill: *he had gone insane*. ■ (of an action or quality) characterized or caused by madness: *his eyes were glowing with insane fury*. ■ extremely annoyed: *a fly whose buzzing had been driving me insane*. ■ extremely foolish; irrational: *she had an insane desire to giggle*.
– DERIVATIVES **insanely** adverb.
– ORIGIN mid 16th cent.: from Latin *insanus*, from *in-* 'not' + *sanus* 'healthy'.

insanitary ▸ adjective so dirty or germ-ridden as to be a danger to health: *insanitary conditions*.

insanity ▸ noun [mass noun] the state of being seriously mentally ill; madness: *he suffered from bouts of insanity*. ■ extreme foolishness or irrationality: *it might be pure insanity to take this loan* | [count noun] *the insanities of our time*.
– ORIGIN late 16th cent.: from Latin *insanitas*, from *insanus* (see **INSANE**).

insatiable /ɪnˈseɪʃəb(ə)l/ ▸ adjective (of an appetite or desire) impossible to satisfy: *an insatiable hunger for success*. ■ (of a person) having an insatiable appetite or desire for something, especially sex.
– DERIVATIVES **insatiability** noun, **insatiably** adverb.
– ORIGIN late Middle English: from Old French *insaciable* or Latin *insatiabilis*, from *in-* 'not' + *satiare* 'fill, satisfy' (see **SATIATE**).

insatiate /ɪnˈseɪʃɪət/ ▸ adjective literary never satisfied: *your strong desire is insatiate*.
– ORIGIN late Middle English: from Latin *insatiatus*, from *in-* 'not' + *satiatus* 'filled, satisfied', past participle of *satiare* (see **SATIATE**).

inscape ▸ noun literary the unique inner nature of a person or object as shown in a work of art, especially a poem.
– ORIGIN mid 19th cent. (originally in the poetic theory of Gerard Manley Hopkins): perhaps from **IN-**[2] 'within' + **-SCAPE**.

inscribe ▸ verb [with obj.] **1** write or carve (words or symbols) on something, especially as a formal or permanent record: *his name was inscribed on the new silver trophy*. ■ mark (a surface or object) with characters: *the memorial is **inscribed with** ten names* | (as adj. **inscribed**) *an inscribed watch*. ■ write a dedication to someone in (a book). ■ archaic enter the name of (someone) on a list or in a book.
2 Geometry draw (a figure) within another so that their boundaries touch but do not intersect: *a regular polygon inscribed in a circle*. Compare with **CIRCUMSCRIBE**.
3 (usu. as adj. **inscribed**) Brit. issue (loan stock) in the form of shares whose holders are listed in a register rather than issued with certificates.
– DERIVATIVES **inscribable** adjective, **inscriber** noun.
– ORIGIN late Middle English: from Latin *inscribere*, from *in-* 'into' + *scribere* 'write'.

inscription ▸ noun a thing inscribed, as on a monument or in a book: *the inscription on her headstone*. ■ [mass noun] the action of inscribing something: *the inscription of memorable utterances on durable materials*.
– DERIVATIVES **inscriptional** adjective, **inscriptive** adjective.
– ORIGIN late Middle English (denoting a short descriptive or dedicatory passage at the beginning of a book): from Latin *inscriptio(n-)*, from the verb *inscribere* (see **INSCRIBE**).

inscrutable /ɪnˈskruːtəb(ə)l/ ▸ adjective impossible to understand or interpret: *Guy looked blankly inscrutable*.
– DERIVATIVES **inscrutability** noun, **inscrutably** adverb.
– ORIGIN late Middle English: from ecclesiastical Latin *inscrutabilis*, from *in-* 'not' + *scrutari* 'to search' (see **SCRUTINY**).

inseam ▸ noun N. Amer. another term for **INSIDE LEG**.

insect ▸ noun a small arthropod animal that has six legs and generally one or two pairs of wings. ■ informal any small invertebrate animal such as a spider or tick.

Insects are usually placed in the class Insecta (see also **HEXAPODA**). The body of a typical adult insect is divided into head, thorax (bearing the legs and wings), and abdomen. The class includes many familiar forms, such as flies, bees, wasps, moths, beetles, grasshoppers, and cockroaches. Insects are the most numerous animals in both numbers of individuals and of different kinds, with more than a million species in all habitats except the sea, and they are of enormous economic importance as pests and carriers of disease, and also as pollinators.

– ORIGIN early 17th cent. (originally denoting any small cold-blooded creature with a segmented body): from Latin (*animal*) *insectum* 'segmented (animal)' (translating Greek *zōion entomon*), from *insecare* 'cut up or into', from *in-* 'into' + *secare* 'to cut'.

insectan ▸ adjective Zoology relating to insects: *the insectan orders*.

insectarium /ˌɪnsɛkˈtɛːrɪəm/ (also **insectary** /ɪnˈsɛktəri/) ▸ noun (pl. **insectariums** or **insectaries**) a place where insects are kept, exhibited, and studied.

insecticide ▸ noun a substance used for killing insects.
– DERIVATIVES **insecticidal** adjective.

insectile ▸ adjective resembling or reminiscent of an insect or insects: *his insectile hands*.

Insectivora /ˌɪnsɛkˈtɪvərə/ ▸ plural noun Zoology an order of small mammals that comprises the shrews, moles, hedgehogs, tenrecs, moonrats, and solenodons. They are distinguished by mainly terrestrial habits and an insectivorous diet.

insectivore /ɪnˈsɛktɪvɔː/ ▸ noun an animal that feeds on insects, worms, and other invertebrates. ■ Zoology a mammal of the order Insectivora.
– ORIGIN mid 19th cent.: from modern Latin *insectivorus*, from *insectum* (see **INSECT**) + *-vorus* 'devouring', on the pattern of Latin *carnivorus* 'carnivorous'.

insectivorous /ˌɪnsɛkˈtɪv(ə)rəs/ ▸ adjective (of an animal) feeding on insects, worms, and other invertebrates. ■ (of a plant such as the sundew) able to capture and digest insects.

insecure ▸ adjective **1** uncertain or anxious about oneself; not confident: *a rather gauche, insecure young man* | *a top model who is notoriously insecure about her looks*.
2 (of a thing) not firm or fixed; liable to give way or break: *an insecure footbridge*. ■ not sufficiently protected; easily broken into: *an insecure computer system*.
3 (of a job or situation) liable to change for the worse; not permanent or settled.
– DERIVATIVES **insecurely** adverb.
– ORIGIN mid 17th cent.: from medieval Latin *insecurus* 'unsafe', from *in-* 'not' + Latin *securus* 'free from care', or from **IN-**[1] 'not' + **SECURE**.

insecurity ▸ noun (pl. **insecurities**) [mass noun] **1** uncertainty or anxiety about oneself; lack of confidence: *she had a deep sense of insecurity* | [count noun] *he's plagued with insecurities*.
2 the state of being open to danger or threat; lack of protection: *growing job insecurity* | *the insecurity of wireless networks*.

inselberg /ˈɪns(ə)lbəːg, -z-/ ▸ noun Geology an isolated hill or mountain rising abruptly from a plain.
– ORIGIN early 20th cent.: from German, from *Insel* 'island' + *Berg* 'mountain'.

inseminate /ɪnˈsɛmɪneɪt/ ▸ verb [with obj.] introduce semen into (a woman or a female animal) by natural or artificial means.
– DERIVATIVES **insemination** noun, **inseminator** noun.
– ORIGIN early 17th cent.: from Latin *inseminat-* 'sown', from the verb *inseminare*, from *in-* 'into' + *seminare* 'plant, sow' (from *semen, semin-* 'seed, semen').

insensate ▸ adjective **1** lacking physical sensation: *a patient who was permanently unconscious and insensate*. ■ lacking sympathy or compassion; unfeeling: *a positively insensate hatred*.
2 completely lacking sense or reason: *insensate jabbering*.
– ORIGIN late 15th cent.: from ecclesiastical Latin *insensatus*, from *in-* 'not' + *sensatus* 'having senses' (see **SENSATE**).

insensibility ▸ noun **1** [mass noun] unconsciousness: *I flogged him into insensibility*. ■ inability to be moved emotionally.

I

2 lack of awareness or concern; indifference: *your* ***insensibility to*** *the extreme importance of the mission we are on.*
– ORIGIN late Middle English: partly from Old French *insensibilite* or late Latin *insensibilitas* (from *in-* 'not' + Latin *sensibilis* 'sensible', from *sensus* 'sense'), partly from IN-[1] 'without' + SENSIBILITY.

insensible ▶ adjective **1** [usu. as complement] without one's mental faculties, typically as a result of injury or intoxication; unconscious: *they knocked each other insensible with their fists.* ■ (of a person or bodily extremity) without feeling; numb: *the horny and insensible tip of the beak.*
2 (**insensible of/to**) unaware of or indifferent to: *they slept on, insensible to the headlight beams.*
3 too small or gradual to be perceived; inappreciable: *varying by insensible degrees.*
– DERIVATIVES **insensibly** adverb.
– ORIGIN late Middle English (also in the senses 'unable to be perceived' and 'incapable of physical sensation'): partly from Old French *insensible* (from Latin *insensibilis*, from *in-* 'not' + *sensibilis*, from *sensus* 'sense'), partly from IN-[1] 'not' + SENSIBLE.

insensitive ▶ adjective **1** showing or feeling no concern for others' feelings: *an insensitive remark.*
2 not sensitive to a physical sensation: *she was remarkably* ***insensitive to*** *pain.* ■ not aware of or able to respond to something: *both were in many ways* ***insensitive to*** *painting.*
– DERIVATIVES **insensitively** adverb, **insensitiveness** noun, **insensitivity** noun.

insentient ▶ adjective incapable of feeling or understanding things; inanimate: *it's arrogant to presume animals to be insentient.*
– DERIVATIVES **insentience** noun.

inseparable ▶ adjective **1** unable to be separated or treated separately: *research and higher education seem inseparable.* ■ (of people) unwilling to be separated; very close: *they met 18 months ago and have been inseparable ever since.*
2 Grammar (of a prefix) not used as a separate word or (in German) not separated from the base verb when inflected. ■ (of a German verb) consisting of a prefix and a base verb which are not separated when inflected, for example *wiederholen*.
▶ noun a person or thing inseparable from another.
– DERIVATIVES **inseparability** noun, **inseparably** adverb.
– ORIGIN late Middle English: from Latin *inseparabilis*, from *in-* 'not' + *separabilis* (see SEPARABLE).

insert ▶ verb /ɪnˈsəːt/ [with obj.] **1** place, fit, or push (something) into something else: *Claudia* ***inserted*** *her key* ***in*** *the lock.* ■ include (text) in a piece of writing: *he immediately inserted a clause into later contracts.* ■ Biology incorporate (a piece of genetic material) into a chromosome.
2 (**be inserted**) Anatomy & Zoology (of a muscle or other organ) be attached to a part, especially that which is moved: *the muscle that raises the wing is* ***inserted on*** *the dorsal surface of the humerus.*
▶ noun /ˈɪnsəːt/ a thing that has been inserted, in particular: ■ a loose page or section in a magazine or other publication, typically one carrying an advertisement. ■ an ornamental section of cloth or needlework inserted into a garment. ■ a shot inserted in a film or video.
– DERIVATIVES **insertable** adjective, **inserter** noun.
– ORIGIN late 15th cent. (in the sense 'include (text) in a piece of writing'): from Latin *insert-* 'put in', from the verb *inserere*, from *in-* 'into' + *serere* 'to join'.

insertion ▶ noun **1** [mass noun] the action of inserting something: *he didn't notice the insertion of the envelope into his pocket.*
2 a thing that is inserted, in particular: ■ an amendment or addition inserted in a text. ■ each appearance of an advertisement in a newspaper or periodical. ■ an ornamental section of cloth or needlework inserted into a garment.
3 Anatomy & Zoology the place or manner of attachment of an organ. ■ the place or manner of attachment of a muscle to the part which it moves: *the names of the muscles and their* ***insertions on*** *the eyeball.*
– ORIGIN mid 16th cent. (in sense 2): from late Latin *insertio(n-)*, from Latin *inserere* (see INSERT).

in-service ▶ adjective (of training) intended for those actively engaged in the profession or activity concerned: *in-service training of library staff.*

INSET /ˈɪnsɛt/ ▶ noun [mass noun] training during term time for teachers in British and South African state schools.
– ORIGIN 1970s: acronym from *in-service education and training*.

inset ▶ noun /ˈɪnsɛt/ a thing that is put in or inserted: *a pair of doors with their original stained-glass insets.* ■ a small picture or map inserted within the border of a larger one. ■ a section of cloth or needlework inserted into a garment: *elastic insets in the waistband.* ■ an insert in a magazine or other publication.
▶ verb /ɪnˈsɛt/ (**insets, insetting**; past and past participle **inset** or **insetted**) put in (something) as an inset: *washbasins are usually inset into a toilet table to form a vanity unit.* ■ decorate with an inset: *tables inset with ceramic tiles.*

inshallah /ɪnˈʃalə/ ▶ exclamation if Allah wills it.
– ORIGIN from Arabic *in šā' Allāh*.

inshore ▶ adjective at sea but close to the shore: *inshore waters around Shetland.* ■ used at sea but close to the shore: *an inshore lifeboat.*
▶ adverb towards or closer to the shore: *birds heading inshore to their breeding sites.*
– PHRASES **inshore of** nearer to shore than.

inside ▶ noun /ɪnˈsʌɪd/ **1** [usu. in sing.] the inner side or surface of something: *wipe the inside of the windscreen.* ■ the part of a road furthest from the centre: *overtaking* ***on the inside.*** ■ the part of a path nearer to a wall or further from a road. ■ the side of a bend where the edge or surface is shorter: *the inside of the bend.*
2 the inner part; the interior: *the inside of the car was like an oven.* ■ (**insides**) informal a person's stomach and bowels: *my insides are out of order.*
▶ adjective /ˈɪnsʌɪd/ [attrib.] **1** situated on or in the inside: *an inside pocket.* ■ (in hockey, soccer, and other sports) denoting positions nearer to the centre of the field: *an inside forward.*
2 known or done by someone within a group or organization: *they were accused of selling shares while in possession of inside information.*
▶ preposition & adverb /ɪnˈsʌɪd/ **1** situated within the confines of (something): [as prep.] *a radio was playing inside the flat* | [as adv.] *Mr Jackson is waiting for you inside.* ■ moving so as to end up within (something): [as prep.] *Anatoly reached inside his shirt and brought out a map* | [as adv.] *we walked inside.* ■ within (a person's body or mind), typically with reference to sensations of self-awareness: [as prep.] *she felt a stirring of life inside her* | *I just roll the phrases round inside my head* | [as adv.] *I was screaming inside.* ■ informal in prison: *she was sentenced to three years inside.* ■ (in soccer, rugby, and other sports) closer to the centre of the field than (another player): [as prep.] *he went inside Graves and scored near the post.*
2 [prep.] in less than (the period of time specified): *the oven will have paid for itself inside 18 months.*
– PHRASES **inside of** informal within: *something inside of me wanted to believe him.* ■ in less than (the period of time specified): *preparing a ship for a voyage inside of a week.* **on the inside** informal in a position affording private information: *will you be my spy on the inside?*
– ORIGIN late Middle English (denoting the interior of the body): from IN + SIDE.

inside job ▶ noun informal a crime committed by or with the assistance of a person living or working on the premises where it occurred.

inside leg ▶ noun the length of a person's leg from crotch to ankle, or of the equivalent part of a pair of trousers.

inside money ▶ noun [mass noun] Economics money held in a form such as bank deposits which is an asset to the holder but also represents a liability for someone else.

inside out ▶ adverb with the inner surface turned outwards: *she put her dress on inside out.*
▶ adjective having the inner surface turned outwards: *inside-out clothes.*
– PHRASES **know something inside out** know something very thoroughly. **turn something inside out** turn the inner surface of something outwards. ■ change something utterly: *it is not so easy to turn your whole life inside out.*

insider ▶ noun a person within a group or organization, especially someone privy to information unavailable to others: *political insiders.*

insider dealing (also **insider trading**) ▶ noun [mass noun] the illegal practice of trading on the stock exchange to one's own advantage through having access to confidential information.

inside track ▶ noun the inner, shorter side of a racecourse. ■ a position of advantage: *he always had the inside track for the starring role.*

insidious /ɪnˈsɪdɪəs/ ▶ adjective proceeding in a gradual, subtle way, but with very harmful effects: *sexual harassment is a serious and insidious problem.*
– DERIVATIVES **insidiously** adverb, **insidiousness** noun.
– ORIGIN mid 16th cent.: from Latin *insidiosus* 'cunning', from *insidiae* 'an ambush or trick', from *insidere* 'lie in wait for', from *in-* 'on' + *sedere* 'sit'.

insight ▶ noun [mass noun] the capacity to gain an accurate and deep understanding of someone or something: *his mind soared to previously unattainable heights of insight.* ■ [count noun] an accurate and deep understanding: *his work provides important insights into language use* | [mass noun] *the town offers some insight into Finnish rural life.* ■ [mass noun] Psychiatry awareness by a mentally ill person that their mental experiences are not based in external reality.
– ORIGIN Middle English (in the sense 'inner sight, wisdom'): probably of Scandinavian and Low German origin and related to Swedish *insikt*, Danish *indsigt*, Dutch *inzicht*, and German *Einsicht*.

insightful ▶ adjective having or showing an accurate and deep understanding; perceptive: *thank you for all the insightful comments.*
– DERIVATIVES **insightfully** adverb.

insignia /ɪnˈsɪɡnɪə/ ▶ noun (pl. **same** or **insignias**) a distinguishing badge or emblem of military rank, office, or membership of an organization: *a khaki uniform with colonel's insignia on the collar* | *the royal insignia of Scotland.* ■ a sign or token of something: *the ruins are devoid of moss and ivy, the romantic insignia of age and decay.*
– ORIGIN mid 17th cent.: from Latin, plural of *insigne* 'sign, badge of office', neuter of *insignis* 'distinguished (as if by a mark)', from *in-* 'towards' + *signum* 'sign'.

insignificant ▶ adjective **1** too small or unimportant to be worth consideration: *the sum required was insignificant compared with military spending.* ■ (of a person) without power or influence.
2 meaningless: *insignificant yet enchanting phrases.*
– DERIVATIVES **insignificance** noun, **insignificantly** adverb.

insincere ▶ adjective not expressing genuine feelings: *she flashed him an insincere smile.*
– DERIVATIVES **insincerely** adverb, **insincerity** noun (pl. **insincerities**).
– ORIGIN mid 17th cent.: from Latin *insincerus*, from *in-* 'not' + *sincerus* 'sincere'.

insinuate /ɪnˈsɪnjʊeɪt/ ▶ verb [with obj.] **1** suggest or hint (something bad) in an indirect and unpleasant way: [with clause] *he was insinuating that she slept her way to the top* | (as adj. **insinuating**) *dirty, insinuating laughter.*
2 (**insinuate oneself into**) manoeuvre oneself into (a favourable position) by subtle manipulation: *he insinuated himself into the king's confidence.*
3 [with obj. and adverbial of direction] slide (oneself or a thing) slowly and smoothly into a particular place: *I insinuated my shoulder in the gap.*
– DERIVATIVES **insinuatingly** adverb, **insinuator** noun.
– ORIGIN early 16th cent. (in the sense 'enter (a document) on the official register'): from Latin *insinuat-* 'introduced tortuously', from the verb *insinuare*, from *in-* 'in' + *sinuare* 'to curve'.

insinuation ▶ noun an unpleasant hint or suggestion of something bad: *I've done nothing to deserve all your vicious insinuations* | [mass noun] *a piece of filthy insinuation.*
– ORIGIN mid 16th cent.: from Latin *insinuatio(n-)*, from *insinuare* (see INSINUATE).

insinuendo /ɪnˌsɪnjʊˈɛndəʊ/ ▶ noun (pl. **insinuendos**) chiefly humorous informal term for INSINUATION.
– ORIGIN late 19th cent.: blend of INSINUATION and INNUENDO.

insipid /ɪnˈsɪpɪd/ ▶ adjective lacking flavour; weak or tasteless: *mugs of insipid coffee.* ■ lacking vigour or interest: *many artists continued to churn out insipid, shallow works.*
– DERIVATIVES **insipidity** noun, **insipidly** adverb, **insipidness** noun.
– ORIGIN early 17th cent.: from French *insipide* or late Latin *insipidus*, from *in-* 'not' + *sapidus* (see SAPID).

insist ▶ verb [no obj.] demand something forcefully, not accepting refusal: *she* ***insisted on*** *carrying her own bag* | [with clause] *he insisted that she came.* ■ (**insist on**) demand forcefully to have (something): *he insisted on answers to his allegations.* ■ (**insist on**) persist in (doing something): *the heavy studded boots she insisted on wearing.* ■ [reporting verb] state positively and assertively: [with clause] *the chairman insisted that*

all was not doom and gloom | [with direct speech] *'I really am all right now,' Isabel insisted.*
– ORIGIN late 16th cent. (in the sense 'persist, persevere'): from Latin *insistere* 'persist', from *in-* 'upon' + *sistere* 'stand'.

insistence ▶ **noun** [mass noun] the fact or quality of insisting that something is the case or should be done: *Alison's insistence on doing the washing-up straight after the meal.*
– DERIVATIVES **insistency** noun.

insistent ▶ **adjective 1** insisting on or demanding something; not allowing refusal: *Tony's soft, insistent questioning* | [with clause] *she was very insistent that I call her.*
2 continuing in a prolonged and demanding way: *a telephone started ringing, loud and insistent.*
– DERIVATIVES **insistently** adverb.

in situ /ɪn ˈsɪtjuː/ ▶ **adverb & adjective** in the original place: [as adv.] *frescoes have been left in situ* | [as adj.] *a collection of in situ pumping engines.* ■ in the appropriate position: [as adv.] *her guests were all in situ.*
– ORIGIN Latin.

insobriety ▶ **noun** [mass noun] drunkenness.

insofar ▶ **adverb** variant spelling of **so far as** (see **far**).

insolation /ˌɪnsəˈleɪʃ(ə)n/ ▶ **noun** [mass noun] technical exposure to the sun's rays. ■ the amount of solar radiation reaching a given area.
– ORIGIN early 17th cent.: from Latin *insolatio(n-)*, from the verb *insolare*, from *in-* 'towards' + *sol* 'sun'.

insole ▶ **noun** a removable sole worn in a shoe for warmth, as a deodorizer, or to improve the fit. ■ the fixed inner sole of a boot or shoe.

insolence ▶ **noun** [mass noun] rude and disrespectful behaviour: *she was sacked for insolence.*

insolent ▶ **adjective** showing a rude and arrogant lack of respect: *she hated the insolent tone of his voice.*
– DERIVATIVES **insolently** adverb.
– ORIGIN late Middle English (also in the sense 'extravagant, going beyond acceptable limits'): from Latin *insolent-* 'immoderate, unaccustomed, arrogant', from *in-* 'not' + *solent-* 'being accustomed' (from the verb *solere*).

insoluble ▶ **adjective 1** impossible to solve: *the problem is not insoluble.*
2 (of a substance) incapable of being dissolved: *once dry, the paints become* ***insoluble in*** *water.*
– DERIVATIVES **insolubility** noun, **insolubly** adverb.
– ORIGIN late Middle English: from Old French, or from Latin *insolubilis*, from *in-* 'not' + *solubilis* (see **soluble**).

insolvable ▶ **adjective** rare term for **insoluble** (sense 1).

insolvency ▶ **noun** (pl. **insolvencies**) [mass noun] the state of being insolvent: *the club was facing insolvency* | [count noun] *insolvencies in the media sector rose by 8%.*

insolvent ▶ **adjective** unable to pay debts owed: *the company became insolvent.* ■ relating to insolvency: *insolvent liquidation.*
▶ **noun** an insolvent person.

insomnia ▶ **noun** [mass noun] habitual sleeplessness; inability to sleep.
– ORIGIN early 17th cent.: from Latin, from *insomnis* 'sleepless', from *in-* (expressing negation) + *somnus* 'sleep'.

insomniac ▶ **noun** a person who is regularly unable to sleep: *I'm a terrible insomniac, I often write from four in the morning to seven.*
▶ **adjective** regularly unable to sleep.

insomuch ▶ **adverb 1** (**insomuch that**) to the extent that.
2 (**insomuch as**) inasmuch as; since.
– ORIGIN late Middle English: originally as *in so much*, translating French *en tant (que)* 'in so much (as)'.

insouciance /ɪnˈsuːsɪəns/ ▶ **noun** [mass noun] casual lack of concern; indifference: *an impression of boyish insouciance.*
– ORIGIN late 18th cent.: French, from *insouciant*, from *in-* 'not' + *souciant* 'worrying' (present participle of *soucier*).

insouciant /ɪnˈsuːsɪənt, ɪnˈsuːsɪɒ̃/ ▶ **adjective** showing a casual lack of concern: *an insouciant shrug.*
– DERIVATIVES **insouciantly** adverb.

insourcing ▶ **noun** [mass noun] the reallocation of work previously done by an outside supplier to in-house staff.
– DERIVATIVES **insource** verb.

Insp. ▶ **abbreviation** Inspector (as part of a police officer's title).

inspan /ɪnˈspan/ ▶ **verb** (**inspans, inspanning, inspanned**) [with obj.] S. African yoke (draught animals, typically oxen) in a team to a vehicle. ■ harness an animal or animals to (a vehicle).
– ORIGIN early 19th cent.: from Dutch *inspannen* 'to stretch', from *in-* 'in' + *spannen* 'to span'.

inspect ▶ **verb** [with obj.] look at (someone or something) closely, typically to assess their condition or to discover any shortcomings: *they inspected the paintwork for cracks and flaws.* ■ examine (someone or something) to ensure that they reach an official standard: *customs officers came aboard to inspect our documents.*
– ORIGIN early 17th cent. (earlier (late Middle English) as *inspection*): from Latin *inspect-* 'looked into, examined', from the verb *inspicere* (from *in-* 'in' + *specere* 'look at'), or from its frequentative, *inspectare*.

inspection ▶ **noun** [mass noun] careful examination or scrutiny: *on closer inspection it looked like a fossil* | [count noun] *we carry out regular safety inspections.*

inspection chamber ▶ **noun** a manhole sited at a junction or bend in a drain to allow clearance of blockages.

inspector ▶ **noun 1** an official employed to ensure that official regulations are obeyed, especially in public services: *a prison inspector.* ■ Brit. an official who examines bus or train tickets to check that they are valid.
2 a police officer ranking below a chief inspector: [as title] *Inspector Simmons.*
– DERIVATIVES **inspectorial** adjective, **inspectorship** noun.

inspectorate ▶ **noun** chiefly Brit. a body that ensures that the official regulations applying to a particular type of institution or activity are obeyed: *the factory inspectorate.*

inspector general ▶ **noun** the head of an inspectorate. ■ Military a staff officer responsible for conducting inspections and investigations.

inspector of taxes (also **tax inspector**) ▶ **noun** (in the UK) an official of the Inland Revenue responsible for assessing and collecting income tax and some other taxes.

inspiration ▶ **noun 1** [mass noun] the process of being mentally stimulated to do or feel something, especially to do something creative: *Helen had one of her flashes of inspiration* | *the Malvern Hills have provided inspiration for many artists.* ■ the quality of being inspired: *a rare moment of inspiration in an otherwise dull display.* ■ [count noun] a person or thing that inspires: *he is an inspiration to everyone.* ■ divine influence, especially that supposed to have led to the writing of the Bible.
2 a sudden brilliant or timely idea: *then I had an inspiration.*
3 [mass noun] the drawing in of breath; inhalation.
– ORIGIN Middle English (in the sense 'divine guidance'): via Old French from late Latin *inspiratio(n-)*, from the verb *inspirare* (see **inspire**).

inspirational ▶ **adjective** providing or showing creative or spiritual inspiration: *the team's inspirational captain.*
– DERIVATIVES **inspirationally** adverb.

inspiratory /ɪnˈspʌɪrət(ə)ri/ ▶ **adjective** Physiology relating to the act of breathing in.

inspire ▶ **verb** [with obj.] **1** fill (someone) with the urge or ability to do or feel something, especially to do something creative: *his philosophy inspired a later generation of environmentalists* | [with obj. and infinitive] *his passion for literature inspired him to begin writing.* ■ create (a feeling, especially a positive one) in a person: *their past record does not inspire confidence.* ■ (**inspire someone with**) animate someone with (a feeling): *he inspired his students with a vision of freedom.* ■ give rise to: *the film was successful enough to inspire a sequel.*
2 breathe in (air); inhale.
– DERIVATIVES **inspirer** noun.
– ORIGIN Middle English *enspire*, from Old French *inspirer*, from Latin *inspirare* 'breathe or blow into' from *in-* 'into' + *spirare* 'breathe'. The word was originally used of a divine or supernatural being, in the sense 'impart a truth or idea to someone'.

inspired ▶ **adjective 1** of extraordinary quality, as if arising from some external creative impulse: *they had to thank the goalkeeper for some inspired saves.* ■ (of a person) displaying a creative impulse in the activity specified: *she was an inspired gardener.*
2 (of air or another substance) that is breathed in.
– DERIVATIVES **inspiredly** adverb.

inspiring ▶ **adjective** having the effect of inspiring someone: *he was an inspiring teacher* | *the scenery is not very inspiring.*
– DERIVATIVES **inspiringly** adverb.

inspirit ▶ **verb** (**inspirits, inspiriting, inspirited**) [with obj.] (usu. as adj. **inspiriting**) encourage and enliven (someone): *the inspiriting beauty of Gothic architecture.*

inspissate /ɪnˈspɪseɪt/ ▶ **verb** [with obj.] (usu. as adj. **inspissated**) thicken or congeal: *inspissated secretions.*
– DERIVATIVES **inspissation** noun.
– ORIGIN early 17th cent.: from late Latin *inspissat-* 'made thick', from the verb *inspissare* (based on Latin *spissus* 'thick, dense').

inspissator /ˈɪnspɪˌseɪtə/ ▶ **noun** a heating device for thickening or congealing a liquid.

inst. ▶ **abbreviation** ■ dated (in business letters) instant: *we are pleased to acknowledge receipt of your letter of 14 inst.* ■ institute; institution.

instability ▶ **noun** (pl. **instabilities**) [mass noun] the state of being unstable; lack of stability: *political and economic instability.* ■ tendency to unpredictable behaviour or erratic changes of mood.
– ORIGIN late Middle English: from French *instabilité*, from Latin *instabilitas*, from *instabilis*, from *in-* 'not' + *stabilis* (see **stable**[1]).

install (also **instal**) ▶ **verb** (**installs** or **instals, installing, installed**) [with obj.] **1** place or fix (equipment or machinery) in position ready for use: *we're planning to install a new shower.*
2 place (someone) in a new position of authority, especially with ceremony: *he was installed as Prime Minister in 1966.* ■ establish (someone) in a new place or condition: *Ashley installed herself behind her table.*
– DERIVATIVES **installer** noun.
– ORIGIN late Middle English (in sense 2): from medieval Latin *installare*, from *in-* 'into' + *stallum* 'place, stall'. Sense 1 dates from the mid 19th cent.

I

installation ▶ **noun 1** [mass noun] the action of installing someone or something, or the state of being installed: *the installation of a central heating system* | [count noun] *the use of the system could be followed by installations on other vehicles.*
2 a large piece of equipment installed for use: *computer installations.* ■ a military or industrial establishment: *nuclear installations.* ■ an art exhibit constructed within a gallery: *a video installation.*

instalment (US also **installment**) ▶ **noun 1** a sum of money due as one of several equal payments for something, spread over an agreed period of time: *the first instalment of a grant for housing* | *the purchase price is paid* ***in instalments.***
2 any of several parts of something which are published, broadcast, or made public in sequence at intervals: *filming the final instalment in his Vietnam trilogy.*
3 [mass noun] the process of installing something; installation: *instalment will begin early next year.*
– ORIGIN mid 18th cent. (denoting the arrangement of payment by instalments): alteration of obsolete *estalment* (probably by association with **installation**), from Anglo-Norman French *estalement*, from Old French *estaler* 'to fix'.

instalment credit ▶ **noun** [mass noun] credit for a fixed sum to be repaid in instalments, e.g. for hire purchase.

instance ▶ **noun** an example or single occurrence of something: *a serious instance of corruption* | *the search finds every instance where the word appears.* ■ a particular case: *in this instance it mattered little.*
▶ **verb** [with obj.] cite (a fact, case, etc.) as an example: *I instanced Bob as someone whose commitment had certainly got things done.*
– PHRASES **at first instance** Law at the first court hearing concerning a case. See also **court of first instance**. **at the instance of** formal at the request or instigation of: *prosecution at the instance of the police.* **for instance** as an example: *take Canada, for instance.* **in the first** (or **second** etc.) **instance** in the first (or second etc.) place or stage of a proceeding: *the appointment will be for three years in the first instance.*
– ORIGIN Middle English: via Old French from Latin *instantia* 'presence, urgency', from *instare* 'be present, press upon', from *in-* 'upon' + *stare* 'to stand'. The original sense was 'urgency, urgent entreaty', surviving in *at the instance of*. In the late 16th cent. the word denoted a particular case cited to disprove a general assertion, derived from medieval Latin

instantia 'example to the contrary' (translating Greek *enstasis* 'objection'); hence the meaning 'single occurrence'.

instance court ▶ noun old-fashioned term for COURT OF FIRST INSTANCE. ■ (**Instance Court**) (in the UK) a branch of the former Admiralty Court dealing with private maritime matters.

instancy ▶ noun [mass noun] archaic urgency: *he told his servants to press the message with greater instancy.*
– ORIGIN early 16th cent.: from Latin *instantia* (see INSTANCE).

instant ▶ adjective **1** happening or coming immediately: *the offence justified instant dismissal.* ■ prepared quickly and with little effort: *we can't promise instant solutions.* ■ (of food) processed to allow very quick preparation: *instant coffee.* ■ (of a person) becoming a specified thing immediately: *become an instant millionaire.*
2 dated urgent; pressing.
3 [postpositive] dated (in business letters) of the current month: *your letter of the 6th instant.*
4 archaic of the present moment.
▶ noun **1** a precise moment of time: *come here this instant!* | *at that instant the sun came out.*
2 a very short time; a moment: *for an instant the moon disappeared.*
3 [mass noun] informal instant coffee.
– PHRASES **on the instant** archaic instantly; immediately: *he was thrown into the water, and on the instant the sea grew calm.*
– ORIGIN late Middle English (in sense 2 of the adjective, sense 3 of the adjective, sense 4 of the adjective): via Old French from Latin *instant-* 'being at hand', from the verb *instare*, from *in-* 'in, at' + *stare* 'to stand'.

I

instantaneity /ɪnˌstantəˈneɪɪti/ ▶ noun [mass noun] the quality of being instant or immediate.

instantaneous /ˌɪnst(ə)nˈteɪnɪəs/ ▶ adjective
1 occurring or done instantly: *modern methods of instantaneous communication* | *her reaction was almost instantaneous.*
2 Physics existing or measured at a particular instant: *measurement of the instantaneous velocity.*
– DERIVATIVES **instantaneously** adverb, **instantaneousness** noun.
– ORIGIN mid 17th cent.: from medieval Latin *instantaneus*, from Latin *instant-* 'being at hand' (from the verb *instare*), on the pattern of ecclesiastical Latin *momentaneus*.

instanter /ɪnˈstantə/ ▶ adverb archaic or humorous at once; immediately: *we sealed the bargain instanter.*
– ORIGIN Latin.

instantiate /ɪnˈstanʃɪeɪt/ ▶ verb [with obj.] represent as or by an instance: *a study of two groups who seemed to instantiate productive aspects of this.* ■ (**be instantiated**) Philosophy (of a universal or abstract concept) be represented by an actual example.
– DERIVATIVES **instantiation** noun.
– ORIGIN 1940s: from Latin *instantia* (see INSTANCE) + -ATE[3].

instantly ▶ adverb **1** at once; immediately: *she fell asleep almost instantly.*
2 archaic urgently or persistently.

instant message ▶ noun a message sent via the Internet that appears on the recipient's screen as soon as it is transmitted.
▶ verb (**instant-message**) [with obj.] send (someone) an instant message.

instant replay ▶ noun N. Amer. an immediate playback of part of a television broadcast, typically one in slow motion showing an incident in a sporting event.

instar /ˈɪnstɑː/ ▶ noun Zoology a phase between two periods of moulting in the development of an insect larva or other invertebrate animal.
– ORIGIN late 19th cent.: from Latin, literally 'form, likeness'.

instate ▶ verb [with obj.] set up in position; install or establish.
– ORIGIN early 17th cent. (formerly also as *enstate*): from EN-[1], IN-[2] 'into' + the noun STATE. Compare with earlier REINSTATE.

in statu pupillari /ɪn ˌstatjuː ˌpjuːpɪˈlɑːriː/ ▶ adjective [often postpositive] **1** under guardianship, especially as a pupil.
2 in a junior position at university; not having a master's degree.
– ORIGIN Latin.

instauration /ˌɪnstɔːˈreɪʃ(ə)n/ ▶ noun [mass noun] formal the action of restoring or renewing something.
– DERIVATIVES **instaurator** /ˈɪnstɔːreɪtə/ noun.
– ORIGIN early 17th cent.: from Latin *instauratio(n-)*, from *instaurare* 'renew', from *in-* 'in, towards' + *staur-* (a stem also found in *restaurare* 'restore').

instead ▶ adverb as an alternative or substitute: *do not use lotions, but put on a clean dressing instead* | *she never married, preferring instead to remain single.* ■ (**instead of**) as a substitute or alternative to; in place of: *walk to work instead of going by car.*
– ORIGIN Middle English (originally as two words): from IN + STEAD.

instep ▶ noun the part of a person's foot between the ball and the ankle. ■ the part of a shoe which fits over or under the instep. ■ a thing shaped like the inner arch of a foot.
– ORIGIN late Middle English: of unknown origin; compare with West Frisian *ynstap* 'opening in a shoe for insertion of the foot'.

instigate /ˈɪnstɪgeɪt/ ▶ verb [with obj.] bring about or initiate (an action or event): *they instigated a reign of terror* | *I will be instigating legal proceedings.*
■ (**instigate someone to/to do something**) incite someone to do something, especially something bad: *instigating men to refuse allegiance to the civil powers.*
– ORIGIN mid 16th cent. (in the sense 'urge on'): from Latin *instigat-* 'urged, incited', from the verb *instigare*, from *in-* 'towards' + *stigare* 'prick, incite'.

instigation ▶ noun [mass noun] the action or process of instigating an action or event: *the Domesday Survey was compiled **at the instigation of** William I.*
– ORIGIN late Middle English (in the sense 'incitement'): from Old French, or from Latin *instigatio(n-)*, from the verb *instigare* (see INSTIGATE).

instigator ▶ noun a person who brings about or initiates something: *he was not the instigator of the incident.*

instil /ɪnˈstɪl/ (also **instill**) ▶ verb (**instils, instilling, instilled**) [with obj.] **1** gradually but firmly establish (an idea or attitude) in a person's mind: *the standards her parents had **instilled into** her.*
2 put (a substance) into something in the form of liquid drops.
– DERIVATIVES **instillation** noun, **instilment** noun.
– ORIGIN late Middle English (in sense 2): from Latin *instillare*, from *in-* 'into' + *stillare* 'to drop' (from *stilla* 'a drop').

instinct ▶ noun /ˈɪnstɪŋ(k)t/ an innate, typically fixed pattern of behaviour in animals in response to certain stimuli: *the homing instinct.* ■ a natural or intuitive way of acting or thinking: *they retain their old authoritarian instincts.* ■ a natural propensity or skill of a specified kind: *his **instinct for** making the most of his chances.* ■ [mass noun] the fact or quality of possessing innate behaviour patterns: *instinct told her not to ask the question.*
▶ adjective /ɪnˈstɪŋ(k)t/ (**instinct with**) formal imbued or filled with (a quality, especially a desirable one): *these canvases are instinct with passion.*
– DERIVATIVES **instinctual** adjective, **instinctually** adverb.
– ORIGIN late Middle English (also in the sense 'instigation, impulse'): from Latin *instinctus* 'impulse', from the verb *instinguere*, from *in-* 'towards' + *stinguere* 'to prick'.

instinctive ▶ adjective relating to or prompted by instinct; done without conscious thought: *an instinctive distaste for conflict.* ■ (of a person) doing or being a specified thing apparently naturally or automatically: *he was an instinctive cook.*
– DERIVATIVES **instinctively** adverb.

institute ▶ noun [often in names] **1** an organization having a particular purpose, especially one that is involved with science, education, or a specific profession: *the Institute of Architects* | *a research institute.*
2 (usu. **institutes**) archaic a commentary, treatise, or summary of principles, especially concerning law.
▶ verb [with obj.] **1** introduce or establish (a scheme, undertaking, or policy): *the state instituted a national lottery* | *the award was instituted in 1900.* ■ begin (legal proceedings) in a court.
2 appoint (someone) to a position, especially as a cleric: *his sons were **instituted to** the priesthood* | [with complement] *a testator who has instituted his daughter heir.*
– ORIGIN Middle English (in sense 2 of the verb): from Latin *institut-* 'established', from the verb *instituere*, from *in-* 'in, towards' + *statuere* 'set up'. The noun is from Latin *institutum* 'something designed, precept', neuter past participle of *instituere*; sense 1 dates from the early 19th cent.

institution ▶ noun **1** an organization founded for a religious, educational, professional, or social purpose. ■ an organization providing residential care for people with special needs: *about 5 per cent of elderly people live in institutions.* ■ an established official organization having an important role in a society, such as the Church or parliament: *the institutions of democratic government.* ■ a large company or other organization involved in financial trading: *City institutions.*
2 an established law or practice: *the institution of marriage.* ■ informal a well-established and familiar person or custom: *he soon became something of a national institution.*
3 [mass noun] the action of instituting something: *a delay in the institution of proceedings.*
– ORIGIN late Middle English (in sense 2, sense 3): via Old French from Latin *institutio(n-)*, from the verb *instituere* (see INSTITUTE). Sense 1 dates from the early 18th cent.

institutional ▶ adjective **1** of, in, or like an institution or institutions: *institutional care* | *an institutional investor.* ■ (especially of surroundings) impersonal and unappealing: *the rooms are rather drab and institutional.* ■ expressed through or organized in the form of institutions: *institutional religion.*
2 (of advertising) intended to create prestige rather than immediate sales.
– DERIVATIVES **institutionalism** noun, **institutionally** adverb.

institutionalize (also **institutionalise**) ▶ verb [with obj.] **1** establish (something, typically a practice or activity) as a convention or norm in an organization or culture: *he institutionalized the practice of collaborative research on a grand scale* | (as adj. **institutionalized**) *institutionalized religion.*
2 place or keep (someone) in a residential institution. ■ (as adj. **institutionalized**) (of a person) apathetic and dependent after a long period in an institution.
– DERIVATIVES **institutionalization** noun.

in-store ▶ adjective & adverb within a store (shop): [as adj.] *an in-store bakery* | [as adv.] *the goods are promoted in-store.*

Inst.P. ▶ abbreviation (in the UK) Institute of Physics.

INSTRAW International Research and Training Institute for the Advancement of Women, a United Nations agency.

instruct ▶ verb **1** [reporting verb] tell or order someone to do something, especially in a formal or official way: [with obj. and infinitive] *she instructed him to wait* | [with direct speech] *'Look at me,' he instructed* | [with clause] *I instructed that she should be given hot, sweet tea.*
2 [with obj.] teach (someone) a subject or skill: *he **instructed** them **in** the use of firearms* | [with obj. and clause] *instructing electors how to record their votes.*
3 [with obj.] Law (of a client) employ or authorize (a solicitor or barrister) to act on one's behalf. ■ (of a solicitor) give directions or information to (a barrister) regarding a court case.
4 [with obj.] give information to (someone): [with clause] *the bank was instructed that the money from the deposit account was now held by the company.*
– ORIGIN late Middle English (in sense 2): from Latin *instruct-* 'constructed, equipped, taught', from the verb *instruere*, from *in-* 'upon, towards' + *struere* 'pile up'.

instruction ▶ noun **1** (often **instructions**) a direction or order: *he issued instructions to the sheriff* | *he was acting on my instructions.* ■ (**instructions**) Law directions to a solicitor or counsel, or to a jury. ■ Computing a code in a program which defines and carries out an operation.
2 (**instructions**) detailed information about how something should be done or operated: *always study the instructions supplied.*
3 [mass noun] teaching; education: *instruction in the Roman Catholic faith.*
– DERIVATIVES **instructional** adjective.
– ORIGIN late Middle English: via Old French from late Latin *instructio(n-)*, from the verb *instruere* (see INSTRUCT).

instruction set ▶ noun Computing the complete set of all the instructions in machine code that can be recognized and executed by a central processing unit.

instructive ▶ adjective useful and informative: *it is instructive to compare the two projects.*
– DERIVATIVES **instructively** adverb, **instructiveness** noun.

instructor ▶ noun a person who teaches something: *a driving instructor.* ■ N. Amer. a university teacher ranking below assistant professor.
– DERIVATIVES **instructorship** noun.

instructress ▶ noun a woman who teaches something: *a riding instructress.*

instrument ▶ noun **1** a tool or implement, especially one for precision work: *a surgical instrument | instruments of torture | writing instruments.*
2 a measuring device used to gauge the level, position, speed, etc. of something, especially a motor vehicle or aircraft.
3 (also **musical instrument**) an object or device for producing musical sounds: *a percussion instrument.*
4 a means of pursuing an aim: *the failure of education as an instrument of social reform.* ■ a person who is exploited or made use of: *he was a mere instrument acting under coercion.*
5 a formal or legal document: *execution involves signature and unconditional delivery of the instrument.*
▶ verb [with obj.] equip (something) with measuring instruments.
– ORIGIN Middle English: from Old French, or from Latin *instrumentum* 'equipment, implement', from the verb *instruere* 'construct, equip'.

instrumental ▶ adjective **1** serving as a means of pursuing an aim: *the Society was* ***instrumental in*** *bringing about legislation.* ■ relating to something's function as a means to an end: *a very instrumental view of education and how it relates to their needs.*
2 (of music) performed on instruments, with no vocals: *a largely instrumental piece.* ■ relating to musical instruments: *brilliance of instrumental colour.*
3 relating to an implement or measuring device: *instrumental error | instrumental delivery of a baby.*
4 Grammar denoting or relating to a case of nouns and pronouns (and words in grammatical agreement with them) indicating a means or instrument.
▶ noun **1** a piece of (usually non-classical) music performed by instruments, with no vocals.
2 (**the instrumental**) Grammar the instrumental case. ■ a noun in the instrumental case.
– DERIVATIVES **instrumentally** adverb.

instrumental conditioning ▶ noun [mass noun] Psychology a learning process in which behaviour is modified by the reinforcing or inhibiting effect of its consequence.

instrumentalism ▶ noun [mass noun] **1** a pragmatic philosophical approach which regards an activity (such as science, law, or education) chiefly as an instrument or tool for some practical purpose, rather than in more absolute or ideal terms: ■ Philosophy the pragmatic philosophy of John Dewey which supposes that thought is an instrument for solving practical problems, and that truth is not fixed but changes as the problems change. ■ (especially in Marxist theory) the view that the state and social organizations are tools which are exploited by the ruling class or by individuals in their own interests.
2 Music, rare instrumental technique.

instrumentalist ▶ noun **1** a player of a musical instrument.
2 an adherent of instrumentalism.
▶ adjective of or in terms of instrumentalism.

instrumentality ▶ noun (pl. **instrumentalities**) [mass noun] the fact or quality of serving as an instrument or means to an end; agency: *a corporate body can act only through the instrumentality of human beings.* ■ [count noun] a thing which serves as a means to an end.

instrumentation ▶ noun [mass noun] **1** the particular instruments used in a piece of music: *Telemann's specified instrumentation of flute, violin, and continuo.* ■ the arrangement or composition of a piece of music for particular instruments: *an experiment in instrumentation.*
2 measuring instruments regarded collectively: *the controls and instrumentation of an aircraft.* ■ the design, provision, or use of measuring instruments.

instrument panel (also **instrument board**) ▶ noun a surface in front of a driver's or pilot's seat, on which the vehicle's or aircraft's instruments are situated.

insubordinate ▶ adjective defiant of authority; disobedient to orders: *an insubordinate attitude.*
– DERIVATIVES **insubordinately** adverb.

insubordination ▶ noun [mass noun] defiance of authority; refusal to obey orders: *he was dismissed for insubordination.*

insubstantial ▶ adjective lacking strength and solidity: *the huts are relatively few and insubstantial | insubstantial evidence.* ■ not having physical existence: *the flickering light made her face seem insubstantial.*
– DERIVATIVES **insubstantiality** noun, **insubstantially** adverb.
– ORIGIN early 17th cent.: from late Latin *insubstantialis*, from *in-* 'not' + *substantialis* (see SUBSTANTIAL).

insufferable ▶ adjective too extreme to bear; intolerable: *the heat would be insufferable by July.* ■ having or showing unbearable arrogance or conceit: *an insufferable bully.*
– DERIVATIVES **insufferableness** noun, **insufferably** adverb.
– ORIGIN late Middle English: perhaps via French (now dialect) *insouffrable*, based on Latin *sufferre* 'endure' (see SUFFER).

insufficiency ▶ noun (pl. **insufficiencies**) [mass noun] the condition of being insufficient: *insufficiency of adequate housing* | [count noun] *there have been demands to redress such insufficiencies.* ■ Medicine the inability of an organ to perform its normal function: *renal insufficiency.*
– ORIGIN early 16th cent. (in the sense 'incompetence, inability'): from late Latin *insufficientia*, from *in-* 'not' + Latin *sufficere* 'be sufficient'.

insufficient ▶ adjective not enough; inadequate: *there was insufficient evidence to convict him.*
– DERIVATIVES **insufficiently** adverb.
– ORIGIN late Middle English (in the sense 'incapable, incompetent'): via Old French from late Latin *insufficient-* 'not sufficing', from *in-* 'not' + Latin *sufficere* (see SUFFICE).

insufflate /ˈɪnsəfleɪt/ ▶ verb [with obj.] **1** Medicine blow or breathe (air, vapour, or a powdered medicine) into or through a body cavity. ■ blow or breathe something into or through (a part of the body).
2 Theology breathe on (someone) to symbolize spiritual influence.
– DERIVATIVES **insufflation** noun.
– ORIGIN late 17th cent.: from late Latin *insufflat-* 'blown into', from the verb *insufflare*, from *in-* 'into' + *sufflare* 'blow' (from *sub-* 'from below' + *flare* 'to blow'). Sense 2 dates from the early 20th cent.

insufflator ▶ noun **1** a device for blowing powder on to a surface in order to make fingerprints visible.
2 an instrument for medical insufflation.

insula /ˈɪnsjʊlə/ ▶ noun (pl. **insulae** /-liː/) **1** (in ancient Rome) a tenement in a city.
2 Anatomy a region of the brain deep in the cerebral cortex.
– ORIGIN Latin, literally 'island'.

insulant ▶ noun an insulating material.

insular ▶ adjective **1** ignorant of or uninterested in cultures, ideas, or peoples outside one's own experience: *a stubbornly insular farming people.* ■ lacking contact with other people: *people living restricted and sometimes insular existences.*
2 relating to or from an island: *goods of insular origin.* ■ relating to a form of Latin handwriting used in Britain and Ireland in the early Middle Ages: *insular illumination of the 6th century.* ■ (of climate) equable because of the influence of the sea.
3 Anatomy relating to the insula of the brain.
– DERIVATIVES **insularly** adverb.
– ORIGIN mid 16th cent. (as a noun denoting an islander): from late Latin *insularis*, from *insula* 'island'.

insularity ▶ noun [mass noun] **1** ignorance of or lack of interest in cultures, ideas, or peoples outside one's own experience: *an example of British insularity.* ■ lack of contact with other people: *the stifling insularity of the children's existence.*
2 the state or condition of being an island.

insulate ▶ verb [with obj.] **1** protect (something) by interposing material that prevents the loss of heat or the intrusion of sound: *insulate and draught-proof your home* | (as adj. **insulated**) *an insulated loft.* ■ prevent the passage of electricity to or from (something) by covering it in non-conducting material: *the case is carefully insulated to prevent short circuits.* ■ protect (someone or something) from unpleasant influences or experiences: *the service is* ***insulated from*** *outside pressures.*
2 archaic make (land) into an island: *the village was insulated by every flood of the river.*
– ORIGIN mid 16th cent. (in sense 2): from Latin *insula* 'island' + -ATE[3].

insulating tape ▶ noun [mass noun] adhesive tape used chiefly to cover exposed electric wires.

insulation ▶ noun [mass noun] the action of insulating something: *keep your home warmer through insulation.* ■ the state of being insulated: *his comparative insulation from the world.* ■ material used to insulate something: *fit insulation to all exposed pipes.*

insulator ▶ noun a substance which does not readily allow the passage of heat or sound: *cotton is a poor insulator.* ■ a substance or device which does not readily conduct electricity. ■ a block of glass, ceramic, or other insulating material enclosing a wire carrying an electric current where it crosses a support.

insulin ▶ noun [mass noun] Biochemistry a hormone produced in the pancreas by the islets of Langerhans, which regulates the amount of glucose in the blood. The lack of insulin causes a form of diabetes. ■ an animal-derived or synthetic form of this substance used to treat diabetes.
– ORIGIN early 20th cent.: from Latin *insula* 'island' + -IN[1].

insulin shock ▶ noun [mass noun] Medicine an acute physiological condition resulting from excess insulin in the blood, involving low blood sugar, weakness, convulsions, and potentially coma.

insulitis /ˌɪnsjʊˈlʌɪtɪs/ ▶ noun [mass noun] Medicine disease of the pancreas caused by the infiltration of lymphocytes.

insult ▶ verb /ɪnˈsʌlt/ [with obj.] speak to or treat with disrespect or scornful abuse: *you're insulting the woman I love.*
▶ noun /ˈɪnsʌlt/ **1** a disrespectful or scornfully abusive remark or act: *he hurled insults at us | he saw the book as a deliberate* ***insult to*** *the Church.* ■ a thing so worthless or contemptible as to be offensive: *the present offer is an absolute insult.*
2 Medicine an event which causes damage to a tissue or organ: *the movement of the bone causes a severe tissue insult.*
– PHRASES **add insult to injury** act in a way that makes a bad situation worse.
– DERIVATIVES **insulter** noun.
– ORIGIN mid 16th cent. (as a verb in the sense 'exult, act arrogantly'): from Latin *insultare* 'jump or trample on', from *in-* 'on' + *saltare*, frie *salire* 'to leap'. The noun (in the early 17th cent. denoting an attack) is from French *insulte* or ecclesiastical Latin *insultus*. The main current senses date from the 17th cent., the medical use dating from the early 20th cent.

insulting ▶ adjective disrespectful or scornfully abusive: *insulting remarks | their language is* ***insulting to*** *women.*
– DERIVATIVES **insultingly** adverb [as submodifier] *an insultingly low salary.*

insuperable /ɪnˈsuːp(ə)rəb(ə)l/ ▶ adjective (of a difficulty or obstacle) impossible to overcome: *insuperable financial problems.*
– DERIVATIVES **insuperability** noun, **insuperably** adverb.
– ORIGIN Middle English (in the general sense 'invincible'): from Old French, or from Latin *insuperabilis*, from *in-* 'not' + *superabilis* (from *superare* 'overcome')

insupportable ▶ adjective **1** unable to be supported or justified: *he had arrived at a wholly insupportable conclusion.*
2 unable to be endured; intolerable: *the heat was insupportable.*
– DERIVATIVES **insupportably** adverb.
– ORIGIN mid 16th cent.: from French, from *in-* 'not' + *supportable* (from *supporter* 'to support').

insurance ▶ noun [mass noun] **1** an arrangement by which a company or the state undertakes to provide a guarantee of compensation for specified loss, damage, illness, or death in return for payment of a specified premium: *many new borrowers take out* ***insurance against*** *unemployment or sickness.* ■ the business of providing insurance: *Howard is in insurance.* ■ money paid for insurance. ■ money paid out as compensation under an insurance policy: *when will I be able to collect the insurance?*
2 a thing providing protection against a possible eventuality: *jackets were hung on the back of their chairs,* ***insurance against*** *an encounter with air-conditioning* | [count noun] *a marquee was hired as an* ***insurance against*** *the weather.*
– ORIGIN late Middle English (originally as *ensurance* in the sense 'ensuring, assurance, a guarantee'): from Old French *enseurance*, from *enseurer* (see ENSURE). Sense 1 dates from the mid 17th cent.

> **USAGE** There is a technical distinction between **insurance** and **assurance** in the context of life insurance: see **USAGE** at **ASSURANCE**.

insurance broker ▶ **noun** a person or company registered as an adviser on matters of insurance and as an arranger of insurance cover with an insurer on behalf of a client.

insurance carrier ▶ **noun** N. Amer. an insurer; an insurance company.

insurance policy ▶ **noun** a document detailing the terms and conditions of a contract of insurance.

insurance stamp ▶ **noun** Brit. a stamp which certifies that a weekly payment has been made towards National Insurance.

insure /ɪnˈʃɔː, ɪnˈʃʊə/ ▶ **verb** [with obj.] **1** arrange for compensation in the event of damage to or loss of (property), or injury to or the death of (someone), in exchange for regular payments to a company or to the state: *the table should be **insured for** £2,500 | the company had **insured** itself **against** a fall of the dollar* | [no obj.] *businesses can **insure against** exchange rate fluctuations.* ■ secure the payment of (an amount in compensation) in this way: *your new sum insured is shown on your renewal notice.* ■ provide insurance cover in respect of: *subsidiaries set up to insure the risks of a group of companies.*
2 (**insure someone against**) secure or protect someone against (a possible contingency): *by appeasing Celia they might insure themselves against further misfortune* | [no obj.] *such changes could insure against further unrest.*
3 another term for **ENSURE**.
– DERIVATIVES **insurability** noun, **insurable** adjective.
– ORIGIN late Middle English (in the sense 'assure someone of something'): alteration of **ENSURE**.

> **USAGE** There is considerable overlap between the meaning and use of **insure** and **ensure**. In both British and US English the primary meaning of **insure** is the commercial sense of providing financial compensation in the event of damage to property; **ensure** is not used at all in this sense. For the more general senses, **ensure** is the more usual word, but **insure** is also sometimes used, particularly in US English, e.g. *bail is posted to **insure** that the defendant appears for trial; the system is run to **ensure** that a good quality of service is maintained.*

insured ▶ **adjective** covered by insurance: *the insured car.*
▶ **noun** (**the insured**) (pl. **same**) a person or organization covered by insurance.

insurer ▶ **noun** a person or company that underwrites an insurance risk; the party in an insurance contract undertaking to pay compensation.

insurgent /ɪnˈsəːdʒ(ə)nt/ ▶ **noun** a person fighting against a government or invading force; a rebel or revolutionary: *an attack by armed insurgents.*
▶ **adjective** [attrib.] rising in active revolt: *alleged links with insurgent groups.* ■ relating to rebels: *a series of insurgent attacks.*
– DERIVATIVES **insurgence** noun, **insurgency** noun (pl. **insurgencies**).
– ORIGIN mid 18th cent.: via French from Latin *insurgent-* 'arising', from the verb *insurgere*, from *in-* 'into, towards' + *surgere* 'to rise'.

> **WORD TRENDS** See **FIGHTER**.

insurmountable /ˌɪnsəˈmaʊntəb(ə)l/ ▶ **adjective** too great to be overcome: *an insurmountable problem.*
– DERIVATIVES **insurmountably** adverb.

insurrection /ˌɪnsəˈrɛkʃ(ə)n/ ▶ **noun** a violent uprising against an authority or government: *the insurrection was savagely put down* | [mass noun] *opposition to the new regime led to armed insurrection.*
– DERIVATIVES **insurrectionary** adjective, **insurrectionist** noun & adjective.
– ORIGIN late Middle English: via Old French from late Latin *insurrectio(n-)*, from *insurgere* 'rise up'.

insusceptible ▶ **adjective** not likely to be affected: *the larvae are **insusceptible to** most treatments.*
– DERIVATIVES **insusceptibility** noun.

inswinger ▶ **noun** Cricket a ball bowled with a swing from the off to the leg side.
– DERIVATIVES **inswing** noun, **inswinging** adjective.

int. ▶ **abbreviation** ■ interior. ■ internal. ■ international.

intact ▶ **adjective** [often as complement] not damaged or impaired in any way; complete: *the church was in ruins but its tower remained intact.*
– DERIVATIVES **intactness** noun.
– ORIGIN late Middle English: from Latin *intactus*, from *in-* 'not' + *tactus* (past participle of *tangere* 'touch').

intagliated /ɪnˈtalɪeɪtɪd/ ▶ **adjective** archaic carved or engraved on the surface.
– ORIGIN late 18th cent.: from Italian *intagliato* 'engraved', past participle of *intagliare*, from *in-* 'into' + *tagliare* 'to cut'.

intaglio /ɪnˈtalɪəʊ, -ˈtɑːl-/ ▶ **noun** (pl. **intaglios**) a design incised or engraved into a material. ■ a gem with an incised design. ■ [mass noun] a printing process in which the type or design is etched or engraved, such as photogravure.
▶ **verb** (**intaglioes, intaglioing, intaglioed**) [with obj.] (usu. as adj. **intaglioed**) engrave or represent by an engraving: *a carved box with little intaglioed pineapples on it.*
– ORIGIN mid 17th cent.: Italian, from *intagliare* 'engrave'.

intake ▶ **noun 1** an amount of food, air, or another substance taken into the body: *your daily intake of calories | his alcohol intake.* ■ an act of taking something into the body: *she heard his **sharp intake of breath*** | [mass noun] *a protective factor is the intake of cereal fibre.*
2 [treated as sing. or pl.] the people taken into an organization at a particular time: *the new intake of MPs.* ■ an act of taking people into an organization: *the first intake of women was in 1915.*
3 a place or structure through which something is taken in, e.g. water into a channel or pipe from a river, fuel or air into an engine, etc.: *cut rectangular holes for the air intake.* ■ [mass noun] the action of taking something in: *facilities for the intake of grain by road.*
4 [mass noun] N. English land reclaimed from a moor or common.
– ORIGIN Middle English (originally Scots and northern English): from **IN** + **TAKE**.

intangible ▶ **adjective** unable to be touched; not having physical presence: *the moonlight made things seem intangible.* ■ difficult or impossible to define or understand; vague and abstract: *the rose symbolized something intangible about their relationship.* ■ (of an asset or benefit) not constituting or represented by a physical object and of a value not precisely measurable: *intangible business property like patents.*
▶ **noun** (usu. **intangibles**) an intangible thing: *intangibles like self-confidence and responsibility.*
– DERIVATIVES **intangibility** noun, **intangibly** adverb.
– ORIGIN early 17th cent. (as an adjective): from French, or from medieval Latin *intangibilis*, from *in-* 'not' + late Latin *tangibilis* (see **TANGIBLE**).

intarsia /ɪnˈtɑːsɪə/ ▶ **noun** [mass noun] [often as modifier]
1 a method of knitting with a number of colours, in which a separate length or ball of yarn is used for each area of colour (as opposed to different yarns being carried at the back of the work): *an intarsia design.*
2 an elaborate form of marquetry using inlays in wood, especially as practised in 15th-century Italy. ■ similar inlaid work in stone, metal, or glass.
– ORIGIN from Italian *intarsio*; in sense 2 superseding earlier *tarsia* (from Italian, 'marquetry'); the knitting term dates from the mid 19th cent.

integer /ˈɪntɪdʒə/ ▶ **noun 1** a number which is not a fraction; a whole number.
2 a thing complete in itself.
– ORIGIN early 16th cent. (as an adjective meaning 'entire, whole'): from Latin, 'intact, whole', from *in-* (expressing negation) + the root of *tangere* 'to touch'. Compare with **ENTIRE**, also with **INTEGRAL, INTEGRATE**, and **INTEGRITY**.

integral ▶ **adjective** /ˈɪntɪgr(ə)l, ɪnˈtɛgr(ə)l/ **1** necessary to make a whole complete; essential or fundamental: *games are an integral part of the school's curriculum | systematic training should be **integral to** library management.* ■ included as part of a whole rather than supplied separately: *the unit comes complete with integral pump and heater.* ■ having all the parts that are necessary to be complete: *the first integral recording of the ten Mahler symphonies.*
2 Mathematics of or denoted by an integer. ■ involving only integers, especially as coefficients of a function.
▶ **noun** /ˈɪntɪgr(ə)l/ Mathematics a function of which a given function is the derivative, i.e. which yields that function when differentiated, and which may express the area under the curve of a graph of the function. See also **DEFINITE INTEGRAL, INDEFINITE INTEGRAL**. ■ a function satisfying a given differential equation.
– DERIVATIVES **integrality** noun, **integrally** adverb.
– ORIGIN mid 16th cent.: from late Latin *integralis*, from *integer* 'whole' (see **INTEGER**). Compare with **INTEGRATE** and **INTEGRITY**.

> **USAGE** There are two possible pronunciations for **integral** as an adjective: one with the stress on the **in-** and the other with the stress on the **-teg-**. In British English, the second pronunciation is sometimes frowned on, but both are acceptable as standard.

integral calculus ▶ **noun** [mass noun] a branch of mathematics concerned with the determination, properties, and application of integrals. Compare with **DIFFERENTIAL CALCULUS**.

integrand /ˈɪntɪgrand/ ▶ **noun** Mathematics a function that is to be integrated.
– ORIGIN late 19th cent.: from Latin *integrandus*, gerundive of *integrare* (see **INTEGRATE**).

integrant /ˈɪntɪgr(ə)nt/ ▶ **adjective** (of parts) making up or contributing to a whole; constituent.
▶ **noun** a component.
– ORIGIN mid 17th cent. (as an adjective): from French *intégrant*, from the verb *intégrer*, from Latin *integrare* (see **INTEGRATE**).

integrate /ˈɪntɪgreɪt/ ▶ **verb** [with obj.] **1** combine (one thing) with another to form a whole: *transport planning should be **integrated with** energy policy | a fully equipped laboratory is being **integrated into** the development.* ■ combine (two things) so that they form a whole: *the problem of integrating the two approaches.* ■ [no obj.] (of a thing) combine with another to form a whole: *the stone will blend with the environment and integrate into the landscape.*
2 bring (people or groups with particular characteristics or needs) into equal participation in or membership of a social group or institution: ***integrating** children with special needs **into** ordinary schools.* ■ [no obj.] come into equal participation in or membership of a social group or institution: *she was anxious to **integrate** well **into** her husband's family.* ■ desegregate (a school, area, etc.), especially racially: *the protest forced the bus companies to desegregate the buses* | [no obj.] *cities' efforts to integrate.*
3 Mathematics find the integral of.
– DERIVATIVES **integrability** /ˌɪntɪgrəˈbɪlɪti/ noun, **integrable** /ˈɪntɪgrəb(ə)l/ adjective, **integrative** /ˈɪntɪgrətɪv/ adjective.
– ORIGIN mid 17th cent.: from Latin *integrat-* 'made whole', from the verb *integrare*, from *integer* 'whole' (see **INTEGER**). Compare with **INTEGRAL** and **INTEGRITY**.

integrated ▶ **adjective 1** (of an institution, body, etc.) desegregated, especially racially: *integrated education.*
2 with various parts or aspects linked or coordinated: *an integrated public transport system.*
3 chiefly Physics indicating the mean value or total sum of a variable quantity of property: *integrated electron density along the line of sight.*

integrated circuit ▶ **noun** an electronic circuit formed on a small piece of semiconducting material, which performs the same function as a larger circuit made from discrete components.

integrated services digital network (abbrev.: **ISDN**) ▶ **noun** a telecommunications network through which sound, images, and data can be transmitted as digitized signals.

integrating ▶ **adjective** (of an instrument) indicating the mean value or total sum of a measured quantity.

integration ▶ **noun** [mass noun] **1** the action or process of integrating: *economic and political integration | **integration of** individual countries **into** trading blocs.* ■ the intermixing of people who were previously segregated: *integration is the best hope for both black and white Americans.*
2 Mathematics the finding of an integral or integrals.
3 Psychology the coordination of processes in the nervous system, including diverse sensory information and motor impulses: *visuomotor integration.* ■ Psychoanalysis the process by which a well-balanced psyche becomes whole as the developing ego organizes the id, and the state which results or which treatment seeks to create by countering the fragmenting effect of defence mechanisms.
– DERIVATIVES **integrationist** noun.

integrator ▶ **noun** a person or thing that integrates, in particular: ■ (also **system integrator** or **systems integrator**) Computing a company which markets commercial integrated software and hardware systems. ■ Electronics a computer chip or circuit which performs mathematical integration. ■ an instrument for indicating or registering the total amount or mean value of a physical quality such as area or temperature.

integrin /ˈɪntəgrɪn, ɪnˈtɛgrɪn/ ▸ **noun** Biochemistry any of a class of animal transmembrane proteins involved in the adhesion of cells to each other and to their substrate.
– ORIGIN 1980s: from *integr-* in **INTEGRAL** + **-IN**[1].

integrity /ɪnˈtɛgrɪti/ ▸ **noun** [mass noun] **1** the quality of being honest and having strong moral principles: *a gentleman of complete integrity.*
2 the state of being whole and undivided: *upholding territorial integrity and national sovereignty.* ▪ the condition of being unified or sound in construction: *the structural integrity of the novel.* ▪ internal consistency or lack of corruption in electronic data: [as modifier] *integrity checking.*
– ORIGIN late Middle English (in sense 2): from French *intégrité* or Latin *integritas*, from *integer* 'intact' (see **INTEGER**). Compare with **ENTIRETY**, **INTEGRAL**, and **INTEGRATE**.

integument /ɪnˈtɛgjʊm(ə)nt/ ▸ **noun** a tough outer protective layer, especially that of an animal or plant.
– DERIVATIVES **integumental** adjective, **integumentary** adjective.
– ORIGIN early 17th cent. (denoting a covering or coating): from Latin *integumentum*, from the verb *integere*, from *in-* 'in' + *tegere* 'to cover'.

intein /ˈɪntiːn/ ▸ **noun** Biochemistry an internal segment of amino acids that is excised from a protein precursor to generate a new protein.
– ORIGIN 1990s: from **INTERNAL** + **PROTEIN**.

intel /ˈɪntɛl/ ▸ **noun** [mass noun] [often as modifier] Military, informal military intelligence; information.
– ORIGIN 1980s: abbreviation.

intellect ▸ **noun** [mass noun] the faculty of reasoning and understanding objectively, especially with regard to abstract matters: *he was a man of action rather than of intellect.* ▪ [count noun] a person's mental powers: *her keen intellect.* ▪ [count noun] a clever person: *sapping our country of some of its brightest intellects.*
– ORIGIN late Middle English: from Latin *intellectus* 'understanding', from *intellegere* 'understand' (see **INTELLIGENT**).

intellection ▸ **noun** [mass noun] the action or process of understanding, as opposed to imagination.
– DERIVATIVES **intellective** adjective.

intellectual /ˌɪntəˈlɛktʃʊəl, -tjʊəl/ ▸ **adjective** relating to the intellect: *children need intellectual stimulation.* ▪ appealing to or requiring use of the intellect: *the film wasn't very intellectual, but it caught the mood of the times.* ▪ possessing a highly developed intellect: *you are an intellectual girl, like your mother.*
▸ **noun** a person possessing a highly developed intellect.
– DERIVATIVES **intellectuality** noun, **intellectually** adverb.
– ORIGIN late Middle English: from Latin *intellectualis*, from *intellectus* 'understanding', from *intellegere* 'understand' (see **INTELLIGENT**).

intellectualism ▸ **noun** [mass noun] the exercise of the intellect at the expense of the emotions. ▪ Philosophy the theory that knowledge is wholly or mainly derived from pure reason; rationalism.
– DERIVATIVES **intellectualist** noun.

intellectualize (also **intellectualise**) ▸ **verb 1** [with obj.] give an intellectual character to: *belief was a gut feeling—it couldn't be intellectualized.*
2 [no obj.] talk, write, or think intellectually: *people who intellectualize about fashion.*

intellectual property ▸ **noun** [mass noun] Law intangible property that is the result of creativity, such as patents, copyrights, etc.

intelligence ▸ **noun** [mass noun] **1** the ability to acquire and apply knowledge and skills: *an eminent man of great intelligence.* ▪ [count noun] a person or being with the ability to acquire and apply knowledge and skills: *extraterrestrial intelligences.*
2 the collection of information of military or political value: *the chief of military intelligence.* ▪ people employed in the collection of military or political information: *British intelligence has secured numerous local informers.* ▪ military or political information: *the gathering of intelligence.* ▪ archaic information in general; news.
– DERIVATIVES **intelligential** adjective (archaic).
– ORIGIN late Middle English: via Old French from Latin *intelligentia*, from *intelligere* 'understand' (see **INTELLIGENT**).

intelligence quotient (abbrev.: **IQ**) ▸ **noun** a number representing a person's reasoning ability (measured using problem-solving tests) as compared to the statistical norm or average for their age, taken as 100.

intelligencer ▸ **noun** archaic a person who gathers intelligence, especially an informer, spy, or secret agent.

intelligent ▸ **adjective** having or showing intelligence, especially of a high level: *Anna is intelligent and hard-working | an intelligent guess.* ▪ (of a device or building) able to vary its state or action in response to varying situations and past experience. ▪ (of a computer terminal) incorporating a microprocessor and having its own processing capability. Often contrasted with **DUMB**.
– DERIVATIVES **intelligently** adverb.
– ORIGIN early 16th cent.: from Latin *intelligent-* 'understanding', from the verb *intelligere*, variant of *intellegere* 'understand', from *inter* 'between' + *legere* 'choose'.

intelligent design ▸ **noun** [mass noun] the theory that life, or the universe, cannot have arisen by chance and was designed and created by some intelligent entity.

intelligentsia /ɪnˌtɛlɪˈdʒɛntsɪə/ ▸ **noun** [treated as sing. or pl.] (usu. **the intelligentsia**) intellectuals or highly educated people as a group, especially when regarded as possessing culture and political influence.
– ORIGIN early 20th cent.: from Russian *intelligentsiya*, from Polish *inteligencja*, from Latin *intelligentia* (see **INTELLIGENCE**).

intelligibility ▸ **noun** [mass noun] the state or quality of being intelligible: *being able to see a speaker can improve intelligibility.*

intelligible /ɪnˈtɛlɪdʒɪb(ə)l/ ▸ **adjective** able to be understood; comprehensible: *use vocabulary that is intelligible to your audience | a barely intelligible reply.* ▪ Philosophy able to be understood only by the intellect, not by the senses.
– DERIVATIVES **intelligibly** adverb.
– ORIGIN late Middle English (also in the sense 'capable of understanding'): from Latin *intelligibilis*, from *intelligere* 'understand' (see **INTELLIGENT**).

Intelsat /ˈɪntɛlsat/ an international organization of more than 100 countries, formed in 1964, which owns and operates the worldwide commercial communications satellite system.
– ORIGIN from *In(ternational) Tel(ecommunications) Sat(ellite Consortium).*

intemperance ▸ **noun** [mass noun] lack of moderation or restraint: *his occasional intemperance of tone.* ▪ excessive indulgence, especially in alcohol.

intemperate ▸ **adjective** having or showing a lack of self-control; immoderate: *intemperate outbursts concerning global conspiracies.* ▪ given to or characterized by excessive indulgence, especially in alcohol: *an intemperate social occasion.*
– DERIVATIVES **intemperately** adverb, **intemperateness** noun.
– ORIGIN late Middle English (in the sense 'inclement'): from Latin *intemperatus*, from *in-* 'not' + *temperatus* (see **TEMPERATE**).

intend ▸ **verb** [with obj.] **1** have (a course of action) as one's purpose or intention; plan: [with infinitive] *the company intends to cut 400 jobs* | [with clause] *it was not intended that colleges should have to revise their current schemes.* ▪ (**intend something as/to do something**) plan that something should be or do something: *a series of questions intended as a checklist.* ▪ plan that speech should have (a particular meaning): *no offence was intended, I assure you.*
2 (usu. **be intended for/to do something**) design or destine something for a particular purpose: *pigs intended for human consumption | a one-roomed cottage intended to accommodate a family.* ▪ (**be intended for**) be meant or designed for the use of (a particular person or group): *this benefit is intended for people incapable of work.*
– DERIVATIVES **intender** noun.
– ORIGIN Middle English *entend* (in the sense 'direct the attention to'), from Old French *entendre*, from Latin *intendere* 'intend, extend, direct', from *in-* 'towards' + *tendere* 'stretch, tend'.

intendant ▸ **noun 1** the administrator of an opera house or theatre.
2 chiefly historical a title given to a high-ranking official or administrator, especially in France, Spain, Portugal, or one of their colonies.
– DERIVATIVES **intendancy** noun.
– ORIGIN mid 17th cent.: from French, from Latin *intendere* 'to direct' (see **INTEND**).

intended ▸ **adjective** [attrib.] planned or meant: *the intended victim escaped.*
▸ **noun** (**one's intended**) informal the person one intends to marry; one's fiancé or fiancée.
– DERIVATIVES **intendedly** adverb.

intendment ▸ **noun** [mass noun] Law the sense in which the law understands or interprets something, such as the true intention of an Act.
– ORIGIN late Middle English (denoting an intended meaning): from Old French *entendement*, from *entendre* 'intend'.

intense ▸ **adjective** (**intenser**, **intensest**) **1** of extreme force, degree, or strength: *the job demands intense concentration | the heat was intense | an intense blue.* ▪ (of an action) highly concentrated: *a phase of intense activity.*
2 having or showing strong feelings or opinions; extremely earnest or serious: *an intense young woman, passionate about her art | a burning and intense look.*
– DERIVATIVES **intensely** adverb, **intenseness** noun.
– ORIGIN late Middle English: from Old French, or from Latin *intensus* 'stretched tightly, strained', past participle of *intendere* (see **INTEND**).

> **USAGE** **Intense** and **intensive** are clearly similar in meaning, but they differ in emphasis. **Intense** tends to relate to subjective responses—emotions and how we feel—while **intensive** tends to relate to objective descriptions. Thus, *an **intensive** course* simply describes the type of course: one that is designed to cover a lot of ground in a short time, e.g. by being full-time rather than part-time. On the other hand, in *the course was **intense***, **intense** describes how someone felt about the course.

intensification ▸ **noun** [mass noun] the action of making or becoming more intense: *the intensification of the conflict.*

intensifier ▸ **noun** a person or thing that intensifies. ▪ Photography a chemical used to intensify a negative. ▪ Grammar an adverb used to give force or emphasis, for example *really* in *my feet are really cold.*

intensify ▸ **verb** (**intensifies**, **intensifying**, **intensified**) **1** become or make more intense: [no obj.] *the dispute began to intensify* | [with obj.] *they had intensified their military campaign.*
2 [with obj.] Photography increase the opacity of (a negative) using a chemical.
– ORIGIN early 19th cent.: coined by Coleridge.

intension ▸ **noun 1** Logic the internal content of a concept. Often contrasted with **EXTENSION**.
2 [mass noun] archaic resolution or determination.
– DERIVATIVES **intensional** adjective, **intensionally** adverb.
– ORIGIN early 17th cent. (also in the sense 'straining, stretching'): from Latin *intensio(n-)*, from *intendere* (see **INTEND**). Sense 1 dates from the mid 19th cent.

intensity ▸ **noun** (pl. **intensities**) [mass noun] **1** the quality of being intense: *the pain grew in intensity* | [in sing.] *there's an intensity in his eyes that's downright scary.*
2 the measurable amount of a property, such as force, brightness, or a magnetic field: *hydrothermal processes of low intensity* | [count noun] *different light intensities.*

intensive ▸ **adjective 1** concentrated on a single subject or into a short time; very thorough or vigorous: *she undertook an intensive Arabic course | eight days of intensive arms talks.* ▪ (of agriculture) aiming to achieve maximum production within a limited area, especially by using chemical and technological aids: *intensive farming.* Often contrasted with **EXTENSIVE** (sense 2). ▪ [usu. in combination] (typically in business and economics) concentrating on or making much use of a specified thing: *computer-intensive methods.*
2 Grammar (of an adjective, adverb, or particle) giving force or emphasis.
3 chiefly Physics denoting a property which is measured in terms of intensity (e.g. concentration) rather than of extent (e.g. volume), and so is not simply increased by addition of one thing to another.
▸ **noun** Grammar an intensive adjective, adverb, or particle; an intensifier.
– DERIVATIVES **intensively** adverb, **intensiveness** noun.
– ORIGIN late Middle English (in the sense 'vehement, intense'): from French *intensif, -ive* or medieval Latin *intensivus*, from *intendere* (see **INTEND**).

> **USAGE** On the difference between **intensive** and **intense**, see **USAGE** at **INTENSE**.

intensive care ▸ **noun** [mass noun] special medical treatment of a dangerously ill patient, with constant monitoring.

intent ▶ noun [mass noun] intention or purpose: *with alarm she realized his intent* | [count noun] *a real intent to cut back on social programmes.*
▶ adjective **1** (**intent on/upon**) determined to do (something): *the government was intent on achieving greater efficiency.* ■ attentively occupied with: *Gill was intent on her gardening magazine.*
2 (of a look or expression) showing earnest and eager attention: *a curiously intent look on her face.*
– PHRASES **to all intents and purposes** in all important respects: *a man who was to all intents and purposes illiterate.* **with intent** Law with the intention of committing a crime: *he denied arson with intent to endanger life.*
– DERIVATIVES **intentness** noun.
– ORIGIN Middle English: from Old French *entent*, *entente*, based on Latin *intendere* (see INTEND). The adjective is from Latin *intentus*, past participle of *intendere*.

intention ▶ noun **1** a thing intended; an aim or plan: *she was full of good intentions* | [with infinitive] *he announced his intention to stand for re-election.* ■ [mass noun] the action or fact of intending: *intention is just one of the factors that will be considered.* ■ (**someone's intentions**) a person's plans, especially a man's, in respect to marriage: *if his intentions aren't honourable, I never want to see him again.*
2 Medicine the healing process of a wound. See FIRST INTENTION, SECOND INTENTION.
3 (**intentions**) Logic conceptions formed by directing the mind towards an object.
– DERIVATIVES **intentioned** adjective [in combination] *a well-intentioned remark.*
– ORIGIN late Middle English: from Old French *entencion*, from Latin *intentio(n-)* 'stretching, purpose', from *intendere* (see INTEND).

intentional ▶ adjective done on purpose; deliberate: *intentional wrongdoing and harm.*
– ORIGIN mid 16th cent. (in the sense 'existing only in intention'): from French *intentionnel* or medieval Latin *intentionalis*, from Latin *intentio(n-)*, from *intendere* (see INTEND).

intentional fallacy ▶ noun (**the intentional fallacy**) (in literary theory) the fallacy of basing an assessment of a work on the author's intention rather than on one's response to the actual work.

intentionalism ▶ noun [mass noun] the theory that a literary work should be judged in terms of the author's intentions.

intentionality ▶ noun [mass noun] the fact of being deliberate or purposive. ■ Philosophy the quality of mental states (e.g. thoughts, beliefs, desires, hopes) which consists in their being directed towards some object or state of affairs.

intentionally ▶ adverb deliberately; on purpose: *I didn't do it intentionally.*

intention tremor ▶ noun a trembling of a part of the body when attempting a precise movement, associated especially with disease of the cerebellum.

intently ▶ adverb with earnest and eager attention: *he gazed at her intently.*

inter /ɪn'tə:/ ▶ verb (**inters, interring, interred**) [with obj.] place (a corpse) in a grave or tomb, typically with funeral rites.
– ORIGIN Middle English: from Old French *enterrer*, based on Latin *in-* 'into' + *terra* 'earth'.

inter. ▶ abbreviation intermediate.

inter- ▶ prefix **1** between; among: *inter-agency* | *interblend.*
2 mutually; reciprocally: *interactive.*
– ORIGIN from Old French *entre-* or Latin *inter* 'between, among'.

interact ▶ verb [no obj.] act in such a way as to have an effect on each other: *all the stages in the process interact.* ■ communicate or be involved directly: *the user **interacts** directly **with** the library* | *people who interact daily.*
– DERIVATIVES **interactant** adjective & noun.

interaction ▶ noun [mass noun] reciprocal action or influence: *ongoing **interaction between** the two languages.* ■ Physics a particular way in which matter, fields, and atomic and subatomic particles affect one another, e.g. through gravitation or electromagnetism.
– DERIVATIVES **interactional** adjective.

interactionism ▶ noun [mass noun] Philosophy the theory that there are two entities, mind and body, each of which can have an effect on the other.
– DERIVATIVES **interactionist** noun & adjective.

interactive ▶ adjective (of two people or things) influencing each other: *fully sighted children in interactive play with others with defective vision.* ■ (of a computer or other electronic device) allowing a two-way flow of information between it and a user; responding to the user's input: *interactive video.*
– DERIVATIVES **interactively** adverb, **interactivity** noun.
– ORIGIN mid 19th cent.: from INTERACT, on the pattern of *active*.

interactive whiteboard ▶ noun see WHITEBOARD.

inter-agency ▶ adjective occurring between different agencies: *inter-agency cooperation.* ■ constituted from more than one agency: *inter-agency groups.*

inter alia /ˌɪntər 'eɪlɪə, 'ɑːlɪə/ ▶ adverb among other things: *the study includes, inter alia, computers, aircraft, and pharmaceuticals.*
– ORIGIN Latin.

inter alios /ˌɪntər 'eɪlɪəʊs, 'ɑːlɪəʊs/ ▶ adverb among other people: *tuition to be given to them by, inter alios, a volunteer retired teacher.*
– ORIGIN Latin.

inter-allied ▶ adjective relating to two or more states formally cooperating for military purposes.

interarticular /ˌɪntərɑː'tɪkjʊlə/ ▶ adjective Anatomy existing or acting between the adjacent surfaces of a joint.

interatomic ▶ adjective Physics existing or acting between atoms.

interbank ▶ adjective arranged or operating between banks: *an interbank transfer.*

interbed ▶ verb (**be interbedded**) Geology (of a stratum) be embedded among or between others.

interbreed ▶ verb (past and past participle **interbred**) (with reference to an animal) breed or cause to breed with another of a different race or species: [no obj.] *wolves and dogs can interbreed.* ■ (of an animal) inbreed.

intercalary /ɪn'təːkəl(ə)ri, ˌɪntə'kal(ə)ri/ ▶ adjective **1** (of a day or a month) inserted in the calendar to harmonize it with the solar year, e.g. 29 February in leap years.
2 (of an academic year or period) additional to the standard course and taken at a different institution.
3 of the nature of an insertion.
4 Botany (of the meristem of a plant) located between its daughter cells, especially (in a grass) at or near the base of a leaf.
– ORIGIN early 17th cent.: from Latin *intercalarius*, from *intercalare* (see INTERCALATE).

intercalate /ɪn'təːkəleɪt, ˌɪntəkə'leɪt/ ▶ verb [with obj.] **1** insert (an intercalary period) in a calendar.
2 insert (something) between layers in a crystal lattice, geological formation, or other structure.
– DERIVATIVES **intercalation** noun.
– ORIGIN early 17th cent.: from Latin *intercalat-* 'proclaimed as inserted in the calendar', from the verb *intercalare*, from *inter-* 'between' + *calare* 'proclaim solemnly'.

intercede /ˌɪntə'siːd/ ▶ verb [no obj.] intervene on behalf of another: *I prayed that she would intercede for us.*
– DERIVATIVES **interceder** noun.
– ORIGIN late 16th cent.: from French *intercéder* or Latin *intercedere* 'intervene', from *inter-* 'between' + *cedere* 'go'.

intercellular ▶ adjective Biology located or occurring between cells: *intercellular spaces.*

intercensal /ˌɪntə'sɛns(ə)l/ ▶ adjective relating to the interval between two censuses.

intercept ▶ verb /ˌɪntə'sɛpt/ [with obj.] obstruct (someone or something) so as to prevent them from continuing to a destination: *intelligence agencies intercepted a series of telephone calls* | *I intercepted Edward on his way to work.* ■ chiefly Physics cut off or deflect (light or other electromagnetic radiation). ■ Mathematics (of a line or surface) mark or cut off (part of a space, line, or surface).
▶ noun /'ɪntəsɛpt/ an act or instance of intercepting something: *he read the file of radio intercepts.* ■ Mathematics the point at which a given line cuts a coordinate axis; the value of the coordinate at that point.
– DERIVATIVES **interception** noun, **interceptive** adjective.
– ORIGIN late Middle English (in the senses 'contain between limits' and 'halt (an effect)'): from Latin *intercept-* 'caught between', from the verb *intercipere*, from *inter-* 'between' + *capere* 'take'.

interceptor ▶ noun a person or thing that intercepts. ■ a fast aircraft for stopping or repelling hostile aircraft.

intercession /ˌɪntə'sɛʃ(ə)n/ ▶ noun [mass noun] the action of intervening on behalf of another: *he only escaped ruin by the intercession of his peers with the king.* ■ the action of saying a prayer on behalf of another.
– DERIVATIVES **intercessional** adjective, **intercessory** adjective.
– ORIGIN late Middle English: from Latin *intercessio(n-)*, from the verb *intercedere* (see INTERCEDE).

intercessor ▶ noun a person who intervenes on behalf of another, especially by prayer.

interchange ▶ verb /ɪntə'tʃeɪn(d)ʒ/ [with obj.] (of two or more people) exchange (things) with each other: *superior and subordinates freely interchange information.* ■ put each of (two things) in the other's place: *the terms are often interchanged.* ■ [no obj.] (of a thing) be able to be exchanged with another: *diesel units will **interchange with** the petrol ones.*
▶ noun /'ɪntətʃeɪn(d)ʒ/ **1** [mass noun] the action of interchanging people or things: *the interchange of ideas* | [count noun] *we have a significant interchange of staff with the nearby college.* ■ [count noun] an exchange of words: *I listened in shock to this venomous interchange.*
2 [mass noun] alternation: *the interchange of woods and meadows.*
3 a road junction designed on several levels so that traffic streams do not intersect.
4 a station where passengers may change from one railway line, bus service, etc. to another.
– ORIGIN late Middle English: from Old French *entrechangier*, from *entre-* 'between' + *changier* 'to change'.

interchangeable /ɪntə'tʃeɪn(d)ʒəbl/ ▶ adjective (of two things) able to be interchanged: *eyepieces are interchangeable and one can use any eyepiece with any telescope* | *the V8 engines are all **interchangeable with** each other.* ■ apparently identical; very similar: *anonymous DJs and interchangeable disco divas.*
– DERIVATIVES **interchangeability** noun, **interchangeably** adverb.

intercity ▶ adjective existing or travelling between cities. ■ (also trademark **InterCity**) denoting express passenger rail services in the UK.

inter-class ▶ adjective existing or conducted between different social classes.

intercollegiate ▶ adjective N. Amer. existing or conducted between colleges or universities: *intercollegiate sports.*

intercolonial ▶ adjective existing or conducted between colonies: *an intercolonial railway.*

intercolumniation /ˌɪntəkəlʌmnɪ'eɪʃ(ə)n/ ▶ noun [mass noun] Architecture the distance between adjacent columns of a building.
– DERIVATIVES **intercolumnar** adjective.

intercom ▶ noun an electrical device allowing one-way or two-way communication.
– ORIGIN Second World War: abbreviation of INTERCOMMUNICATION.

intercommunicate ▶ verb [no obj.] **1** engage in two-way communication: *Dr Haber gazed at this while **intercommunicating with** his receptionist.*
2 (often as adj. **intercommunicating**) (of two rooms) have a common connecting door.
– DERIVATIVES **intercommunication** noun, **intercommunicative** /-kətɪv/ adjective.
– ORIGIN late 16th cent.: from Anglo-Latin *intercommunicat-* 'mutually communicated', from the verb *intercommunicare*.

intercommunion ▶ noun [mass noun] participation in Holy Communion or other services by members of different religious denominations.

intercommunity ▶ adjective existing or conducted between communities: *intercommunity relations.*

interconnect ▶ verb [no obj.] connect with each other: *the way human activities **interconnect with** the environment* | [with obj.] *the lakes are interconnected by trails filled with joggers.*
▶ noun a device used to connect two things together.
– DERIVATIVES **interconnected** adjective, **interconnectedness** noun, **interconnection** noun.

intercontinental ▶ adjective relating to or travelling between continents: *an intercontinental flight* | *intercontinental ballistic missiles.*
– DERIVATIVES **intercontinentally** adverb.

interconvert ▶ verb [with obj.] cause (two things) to be converted into each other: *oestrogens and androgens are easily interconverted in the laboratory.*

– DERIVATIVES **interconversion** noun, **interconvertible** adjective.

intercooler ▶ noun an apparatus for cooling gas between successive compressions, especially in a supercharged vehicle engine.
– DERIVATIVES **intercool** verb.

intercorrelation /ˌɪntəkɒrəˈleɪʃ(ə)n/ ▶ noun a mutual relationship or connection between two or more things: *analyses showing intercorrelations between sets of variables.*
– DERIVATIVES **intercorrelate** verb.

intercostal /ˌɪntəˈkɒst(ə)l/ Anatomy ▶ adjective situated between the ribs: *the fifth left intercostal space.*
▶ noun a muscle situated between the ribs.

intercourse ▶ noun **1** [mass noun] communication or dealings between individuals or groups: *everyday social intercourse.*
2 short for **SEXUAL INTERCOURSE**.
– ORIGIN late Middle English: from Old French *entrecours* 'exchange, commerce', from Latin *intercursus*, from *intercurrere* 'intervene', from *inter-* 'between' + *currere* 'run'. The specifically sexual use arose in the late 18th cent.

intercrop ▶ verb (**intercrops, intercropping, intercropped**) [with obj.] (often as noun **intercropping**) grow (a crop) among plants of a different kind: *lettuce is particularly good for intercropping among Brussels sprouts.*
▶ noun a crop grown among plants of a different kind.

intercross ▶ verb (with reference to animals or plants of different breeds or varieties) interbreed or cause to interbreed.
▶ noun an instance of intercrossing. ■ an animal or plant resulting from intercrossing.

intercrural /ˌɪntəˈkrʊər(ə)l/ ▶ adjective between the legs.

intercultural ▶ adjective taking place between cultures, or derived from different cultures: *intercultural communication.*
– DERIVATIVES **interculturalism** noun.

intercurrent ▶ adjective **1** Medicine (of a disease) occurring during the progress of another disease: *intercurrent infection with other microbes.*
2 rare (of a time or event) intervening.
– ORIGIN early 17th cent.: from Latin *intercurrent-* 'intervening', from the verb *intercurrere*.

intercut ▶ verb (**intercuts, intercutting**; past and past participle **intercut**) [with obj.] alternate (scenes or shots) with contrasting scenes or shots to make one composite scene in a film: *pieces of archive film are intercut with brief interviews* | [no obj.] *the action intercuts between the time periods.*

interdenominational /ˌɪntədɪnɒmɪˈneɪʃ(ə)n(ə)l/ ▶ adjective relating to more than one religious denomination: *an interdenominational service.*
– DERIVATIVES **interdenominationally** adverb.

interdental ▶ adjective situated or placed between the teeth. ■ Phonetics (of a consonant) pronounced by placing the tip of the tongue between the teeth, such as the 'th' sounds in the English words 'thaw' and 'though'.
▶ noun Phonetics an interdental consonant.

interdepartmental ▶ adjective relating to more than one department.
– DERIVATIVES **interdepartmentally** adverb.

interdependent ▶ adjective (of two or more people or things) dependent on each other: *we in Europe are all increasingly interdependent.*
– DERIVATIVES **interdepend** verb, **interdependence** noun, **interdependency** noun.

interdict ▶ noun /ˈɪntədɪkt/ an authoritative prohibition, in particular: ■ Law, chiefly Scottish a court order forbidding an act; a negative injunction. ■ (in the Roman Catholic Church) a sentence debarring a person or place from ecclesiastical functions and privileges: *a papal interdict.*
▶ verb /ˌɪntəˈdɪkt/ [with obj.] chiefly N. Amer. **1** prohibit or forbid (something): *society will never interdict sex.* ■ (**interdict someone from**) prohibit someone from (doing something): *I have not been interdicted from consuming alcoholic beverages.*
2 intercept and prevent the movement of (a prohibited commodity or person): *army efforts to interdict enemy supply shipments.* ■ Military impede (an enemy force), especially by bombing lines of communication or supply.
– DERIVATIVES **interdiction** noun.
– ORIGIN Middle English *entredite* (in the ecclesiastical sense), from Old French *entredit*, from Latin *interdictum*, past participle of *interdicere* 'interpose, forbid by decree', from *inter-* 'between' + *dicere* 'say'. The spelling change in the 16th cent. was due to association with the Latin form.

interdictor /ˌɪntəˈdɪktə/ ▶ noun Military an aircraft designed to interrupt enemy supply operations by aerial bombing.
– DERIVATIVES **interdictory** /-ˈdɪkt(ə)ri/ adjective.

interdigital ▶ adjective between the fingers or toes.

interdigitate /ˌɪntəˈdɪdʒɪteɪt/ ▶ verb [no obj.] (of two or more things) interlock like the fingers of two clasped hands: (as adj. **interdigitating**) *interdigitating metal bars.*
– ORIGIN mid 19th cent.: from **INTER-** 'between' + **DIGIT** + **-ATE**[3].

interdisciplinary ▶ adjective relating to more than one branch of knowledge: *an interdisciplinary research programme.*

interest ▶ noun **1** [mass noun] the feeling of wanting to know or learn about something or someone: *she looked about her with interest* | [in sing.] *he developed an interest in art.* ■ the quality of exciting curiosity or holding the attention: *a tale full of interest.* ■ [count noun] an activity or subject which one enjoys doing or studying: *their sole interests are soccer, drink, and cars.*
2 [mass noun] money paid regularly at a particular rate for the use of money lent, or for delaying the repayment of a debt: *the monthly rate of interest* | [as modifier] *interest payments.*
3 the advantage or benefit of a person or group: *the merger is not contrary to the public interest* | *it is* ***in your interest*** *to keep your insurance details to hand* | *we are acting in the best interests of our customers.* ■ archaic the selfish pursuit of one's own welfare; self-interest.
4 a stake or involvement in an undertaking, especially a financial one: *holders of voting rights must disclose their interests* | *he must have no personal* ***interest in*** *the outcome of the case.* ■ a legal concern, title, or right in property.
5 (usu. **interests**) a group or organization having a common concern, especially in politics or business: *food interests in Scotland must continue to invest.*
▶ verb [with obj.] excite the curiosity or attention of (someone): *I thought the book might interest Eliot.* ■ (**interest someone in**) persuade someone to undertake or acquire (something): *efforts were made to interest her in a purchase.*
– PHRASES **at interest** (of money borrowed) on the condition that interest is payable. **declare an** (or **one's**) **interest** make known one's financial interests in an undertaking before it is discussed. **in the interests** (or **interest**) **of something** for the benefit of: *in the interests of security we are keeping the information confidential.* **of interest** interesting: *his book should be of interest to historians.* **with interest** with interest charged or paid. ■ (of an action) reciprocated with more force or vigour than the original one: *she returned his look with interest.*
– ORIGIN late Middle English (originally as *interess*): from Anglo-Norman French *interesse*, from Latin *interesse* 'differ, be important', from *inter-* 'between' + *esse* 'be'. The *-t* was added partly by association with Old French *interest* 'damage, loss', apparently from Latin *interest* 'it is important'. The original sense was 'the possession of a share in or a right to something'; hence sense 4 of the noun. Sense 1 of the noun and the verb arose in the 18th cent. Sense 2 of the noun was influenced by medieval Latin *interesse* 'compensation for a debtor's defaulting'.

interested ▶ adjective **1** showing curiosity or concern about something or someone; having a feeling of interest: *I had always been* ***interested in*** *history.*
2 [attrib.] having an interest or involvement; not impartial: *seeking views from all interested parties.*
– DERIVATIVES **interestedly** adverb, **interestedness** noun.

interest-free ▶ adjective & adverb with no interest charged on money that has been borrowed: [as adj.] *interest-free credit* | [as adv.] *he lent the money interest-free.*

interesting ▶ adjective arousing curiosity or interest; holding or catching the attention: *an interesting debate* | *it will be very interesting to see what they come up with.*
– PHRASES **in an interesting condition** archaic, euphemistic (of a woman) pregnant.
– DERIVATIVES **interestingly** adverb *he talked interestingly and learnedly* | [sentence adverb] *interestingly, the researchers did notice a link*, **interestingness** noun.

interface ▶ noun **1** a point where two systems, subjects, organizations, etc. meet and interact: *the* ***interface between*** *accountancy and the law.* ■ chiefly Physics a surface forming a common boundary between two portions of matter or space, for example between two immiscible liquids: *the surface tension of a liquid at its air/liquid interface.*
2 Computing a device or program enabling a user to communicate with a computer. ■ a device or program for connecting two items of hardware or software so that they can be operated jointly or communicate with each other.
▶ verb [no obj.] (**interface with**) **1** interact with (another system, person, etc.): *you will interface with counterparts from sister companies.*
2 Computing connect with (another computer or piece of equipment) by an interface.

interfacial ▶ adjective **1** included between two faces of a crystal or other solid.
2 relating to or forming a common boundary between two portions of matter or space.

interfacing ▶ noun [mass noun] an extra layer of material or an adhesive stiffener that is applied to the facing of a garment to add support.

interfaith ▶ adjective relating to or involving different religions or members of different religions: *action to encourage interfaith dialogue.*

interfere ▶ verb [no obj.] **1** (**interfere with**) prevent (a process or activity) from continuing or being carried out properly: *a holiday job would interfere with his studies.* ■ (of a thing) strike against or impede (something) when working: *the rotors are widely separated and do not interfere with one another.* ■ handle or adjust (something) without permission, especially so as to cause damage: *he admitted interfering with a van.*
2 intervene in a situation without invitation or necessity: *she tried not to* ***interfere in*** *her children's lives.*
3 (**interfere with**) Brit., euphemistic sexually molest (someone, especially a child).
4 (**interfere with**) Law attempt to bribe or intimidate (a witness).
5 Physics (of light or other electromagnetic waveforms) interact to produce interference. ■ cause interference to a broadcast radio signal.
6 (of a horse) knock one foot against the fetlock of another leg.
– DERIVATIVES **interferer** noun.
– ORIGIN late Middle English: from Old French *s'entreferir* 'strike each other', from *entre-* 'between' + *ferir* (from Latin *ferire* 'to strike').

interference ▶ noun [mass noun] **1** the action of interfering or the process of being interfered with: *concerns about government* ***interference in*** *church life* | [count noun] *an unwarranted* ***interference with*** *personal liberty.* ■ American Football the legal blocking of an opponent to clear a way for the ball carrier. ■ (in ice hockey and other sports) the illegal hindering of an opponent not in possession of the puck or ball.
2 Physics the combination of two or more electromagnetic waveforms to form a resultant wave in which the displacement is either reinforced or cancelled. ■ the fading or disturbance of received radio signals caused by unwanted signals from other sources, such as unshielded electrical equipment, or broadcasts from other channels.
– PHRASES **run interference** American Football move in such a way as to cause interference. ■ N. Amer. informal intervene on someone's behalf, typically so as to protect them from distraction or annoyance: *Elizabeth was quick to run interference and said that the Professor would be very busy.*
– DERIVATIVES **interferential** adjective.
– ORIGIN mid 18th cent.: from **INTERFERE**, on the pattern of words such as *difference*.

interference fit ▶ noun a fit between two parts in which the external dimension of one part slightly exceeds the internal dimension of the part into which it has to fit.

interfering ▶ adjective (of a person) tending to interfere in other people's affairs: *interfering busybodies.*
– DERIVATIVES **interferingly** adverb.

interferogram /ˌɪntəˈfɪərə(ʊ)gram/ (also **interferogramme**) ▶ noun Physics a pattern formed by wave interference, especially one represented in a photograph or diagram.

interferometer /ˌɪntəfəˈrɒmɪtə/ ▶ noun Physics an instrument in which wave interference is employed to make precise measurements of length of displacement in terms of the wavelength.

– DERIVATIVES **interferometric** adjective, **interferometrically** adverb, **interferometry** noun.

interferon /ˌɪntəˈfɪərɒn/ ▸ noun [mass noun] Biochemistry a protein released by animal cells, usually in response to the entry of a virus, which has the property of inhibiting virus replication.
– ORIGIN 1950s: from INTERFERE + -ON.

interfile ▸ verb [with obj.] file (two or more sequences) together. ▪ file (one or more items) into an existing sequence: *this index is interfiled with the main card catalogue.*

interflow ▸ verb [no obj.] literary mix or mingle: *the thousand varying shades interflowing like a lighted water.*

interfluve /ˈɪntəfluːv/ ▸ noun Geology a region between the valleys of adjacent watercourses, especially in a dissected upland.
– ORIGIN early 20th cent.: back-formation from *interfluvial*.

interfuse ▸ verb [with obj.] literary join or mix (two or more things) together: (as adj. **interfused**) *nowhere do art and life seem so interfused.*
– DERIVATIVES **interfusion** noun.
– ORIGIN late 16th cent.: from Latin *interfus-* 'poured among', from the verb *interfundere*, from *inter-* 'between' + *fundere* 'pour'.

intergalactic ▸ adjective relating to, moving, or situated between two or more galaxies: *intergalactic gas.*
– DERIVATIVES **intergalactically** adverb.

intergenerational ▸ adjective relating to, involving, or affecting several generations: *the intergenerational conflict and political turmoil of the 1960s.*

intergeneric /ˌɪntədʒɪˈnɛrɪk/ ▸ adjective Biology existing between or obtained from different genera: *intergeneric differences | an intergeneric hybrid.*

interglacial Geology ▸ adjective relating to a period of milder climate between two glacial periods. Compare with INTERSTADIAL.
▸ noun an interglacial period.

intergovernmental /ˌɪntəɡʌv(ə)nˈmɛnt(ə)l, -ɡʌv(ə)ˈmɛnt(ə)l/ ▸ adjective relating to or conducted between two or more governments: *an intergovernmental conference.*
– DERIVATIVES **intergovernmentally** adverb.

intergrade ▸ verb [no obj.] Biology pass into another form by a series of intervening forms.
▸ noun a form resulting from intergrading.
– DERIVATIVES **intergradation** noun.

intergrow ▸ verb (past **intergrew**; past participle **intergrown**) [no obj.] (usu. as adj. **intergrown**) (chiefly of crystals) grow into each other: *finely intergrown siderite.*

intergrowth ▸ noun a thing produced by intergrowing, especially of mineral crystals in rock.

interim /ˈɪnt(ə)rɪm/ ▸ noun 1 the intervening time: *in the interim I'll just keep my fingers crossed.*
2 (usu. **interims**) chiefly Brit. an interim dividend, profit, etc.
▸ adjective 1 in or for the intervening period; provisional: *an interim arrangement.*
2 relating to less than a full year's business activity: *an interim dividend.*
▸ adverb archaic meanwhile.
– ORIGIN mid 16th cent. (denoting a provisional arrangement, originally for the adjustment of religious differences between the German Protestants and the Roman Catholic Church): from Latin, 'meanwhile'.

interior ▸ adjective 1 situated on or relating to the inside of something; inner: *the interior lighting is not adequate.* ▪ (**interior to**) chiefly technical situated further in or within: *the layer immediately interior to the epidermis.* ▪ (in filming) indoor: *interior scenes.*
2 [attrib.] remote from the coast or frontier; inland: *the interior jungle regions.*
3 relating to a country's internal affairs: *the interior minister.*
4 existing or taking place in the mind or soul; mental: *an interior monologue.*
▸ noun 1 the inner part of something; the inside: *the interior has been much restored.* ▪ an artistic representation of the inside of a building or room: *a few still lifes, interiors, and landscapes.*
2 (**the interior**) the inland part of a country or region: *the plains of the interior.*
3 (**the interior**) the internal affairs of a country: *the Minister of the Interior.*
– DERIVATIVES **interiorize** (also **interiorise**) verb, **interiorly** adverb.
– ORIGIN late 15th cent.: from Latin, 'inner', comparative adjective from *inter* 'within'.

interior angle ▸ noun the angle between adjacent sides of a rectilinear figure.

interior decoration ▸ noun [mass noun] the decoration of the interior of a building or room, especially with regard for colour combination and artistic effect.
– DERIVATIVES **interior decorator** noun.

interior design ▸ noun [mass noun] the art or process of designing the interior decoration of a room or building.
– DERIVATIVES **interior designer** noun.

interiority ▸ noun [mass noun] the quality of being interior or inward. ▪ inner character; subjectivity: *the profound interiority of faith.*
– ORIGIN early 18th cent.: from medieval Latin *interioritas*, from Latin *interior* 'inner'.

interior monologue ▸ noun a piece of writing expressing a character's inner thoughts.

interject /ˌɪntəˈdʒɛkt/ ▸ verb [with obj.] say (something) abruptly, especially as an aside or interruption: *she interjected the odd question here and there* | [no obj.] *Christina felt bound to interject before there was open warfare.*
– DERIVATIVES **interjectory** adjective.
– ORIGIN late 16th cent.: from Latin *interject-* 'interposed', from the verb *interjicere*, from *inter-* 'between' + *jacere* 'to throw'.

interjection ▸ noun an abrupt remark, especially as an aside or interruption. ▪ an exclamation, especially as a part of speech (e.g. *ah!*, *dear me!*).
– DERIVATIVES **interjectional** adjective.
– ORIGIN late Middle English: via Old French from Latin *interjectio(n-)*, from the verb *interjicere* (see INTERJECT).

interknit ▸ verb (**interknits**, **interknitting**; past and past participle **interknitted** or **interknit**) [with obj.] knit (things) together; intertwine.

interlace ▸ verb cross or be crossed intricately together; interweave: [with obj.] *Jane interlaced her fingers to form a cup* | (as adj. **interlacing**) *closely interlacing branches.* ▪ [with obj.] (**interlace something with**) mingle or intersperse something with: *discussion interlaced with esoteric mathematics.* ▪ [with obj.] Electronics scan (a video image) in such a way that alternate lines form one sequence which is followed by the other lines in a second sequence: (as adj. **interlaced**) *interlaced displays.*
– ORIGIN late Middle English: from Old French *entrelacier*, from *entre-* 'between' + *lacier* 'to lace'.

Interlaken /ˈɪntəˌlɑːk(ə)n/, German /ˈɪntɐˌlakn/ the chief town of the Bernese Alps in central Switzerland, situated on the River Aare between Lake Brienz and Lake Thun; pop. 5,286 (2007).

interlanguage ▸ noun a language or form of language having features of two others, typically a pidgin or a version produced by a foreign learner.

interlap ▸ verb (**interlaps**, **interlapping**, **interlapped**) [no obj.] overlap.

interlard ▸ verb [with obj.] (**interlard something with**) intersperse or embellish speech or writing with different material: *a compendium of advertisements and reviews, interlarded with gossip.*
– ORIGIN late Middle English (in the sense 'mix with alternate layers of fat'): from French *entrelarder*, from *entre-* 'between' + *larder* 'to lard'.

interlay ▸ verb (past and past participle **interlaid**) [with obj.] lay between or among; interpose: *strips of granite are interlaid with creamy Sardinian stone.*
▸ noun [mass noun] an inserted layer: *use interlay under foam-backed carpets.* ▪ [count noun] Printing a sheet of paper placed between a letterpress printing plate and its base to give increased pressure on certain areas.

interlayer ▸ noun a layer situated between two others.

interleaf ▸ noun (pl. **interleaves**) an extra page, typically a blank one, between the leaves of a book.

interleave ▸ verb [with obj.] 1 insert pages, typically blank ones, between the pages of (a book): *books of maps interleaved with tracing paper.* ▪ place something between the layers of (something): *pasta interleaved with strips of courgette.*
2 Telecommunications & Computing mix (digital signals) by alternating between them. ▪ Computing divide (memory or processing power) between a number of tasks by allocating segments of it to each task in turn.

interleukin /ˌɪntəˈluːkɪn/ ▸ noun Biochemistry any of a class of glycoproteins produced by leucocytes for regulating immune responses.
– ORIGIN 1970s: from INTER- 'occurring between' + *leukocyte* (variant of LEUCOCYTE) + -IN[1].

interlibrary ▸ adjective between libraries.

interline[1] ▸ verb [with obj.] insert words between the lines of (a document or other text).
– ORIGIN late Middle English: from medieval Latin *interlineare*, from *inter-* 'between' + Latin *linea* 'line'.

interline[2] ▸ verb [with obj.] put an extra lining between the ordinary lining and the fabric of (a garment, curtain, etc.), typically to provide extra strength.

interlinear ▸ adjective written or printed between the lines of a text: *interlinear glosses.* ▪ (of a book) having the same text in different languages printed on alternate lines.
– ORIGIN late Middle English: from medieval Latin *interlinearis*, from *inter-* 'between' + Latin *linearis* (from *linea* 'line').

interlineate /ˌɪntəˈlɪnɪeɪt/ ▸ verb another term for INTERLINE[1].
– DERIVATIVES **interlineation** noun.
– ORIGIN late 17th cent.: from medieval Latin *interlineat-* 'interlined', from the verb *interlineare*.

interlingua /ˌɪntəˈlɪŋɡwə/ ▸ noun an artificial language, devised for machine translation, that makes explicit the distinctions necessary for successful translation into a target language, even where they are not present in the source language. ▪ (**Interlingua**) [mass noun] an artificial international language formed of elements common to the Romance languages, designed primarily for scientific and technical use.
– ORIGIN early 20th cent.: from INTER- 'between' + Latin *lingua* 'tongue'.

interlingual ▸ adjective between or relating to two languages: *interlingual dictionaries.* ▪ relating to an interlingua or artificial interlanguage.

interlining ▸ noun [mass noun] material used as an extra lining between the ordinary lining and the fabric of a garment, curtain, etc.

interlink ▸ verb [with obj.] join or connect (two or more things) together: *the department's postgraduate work is closely interlinked with the MSc programme.*
– DERIVATIVES **interlinkage** noun.

interlobular /ˌɪntəˈlɒbjʊlə/ ▸ adjective Anatomy situated between lobes (e.g. of the kidney or liver).

interlock ▸ verb [no obj.] (of two or more things) engage with each other by overlapping or by the fitting together of projections and recesses: *their fingers interlocked* | (as adj. **interlocking**) *a design of interlocking leaves.* ▪ [with obj.] lock or join (things) together: *the two planes were almost interlocked as they climbed together.*
▸ noun 1 a device or mechanism for connecting or coordinating the function of different components.
2 (also **interlock fabric**) [mass noun] a fabric knitted with closely interlocking stitches allowing it to stretch.
– DERIVATIVES **interlocker** noun.

interlocutor /ˌɪntəˈlɒkjʊtə/ ▸ noun formal a person who takes part in a dialogue or conversation.
– DERIVATIVES **interlocution** noun.
– ORIGIN early 16th cent.: modern Latin, from Latin *interlocut-* 'interrupted (by speech)', from the verb *interloqui*, from *inter-* 'between' + *loqui* 'speak'.

interlocutory /ˌɪntəˈlɒkjʊt(ə)ri/ ▸ adjective 1 Law (of a decree or judgement) given provisionally during the course of a legal action.
2 rare relating to dialogue.
– ORIGIN late 15th cent.: from medieval Latin *interlocutorius*, from Latin *interloqui* 'interrupt' (see INTERLOCUTOR).

interloper /ˈɪntələʊpə/ ▸ noun a person who becomes involved in a place or situation where they are not wanted or are considered not to belong.
– DERIVATIVES **interlope** verb.
– ORIGIN late 16th cent. (denoting an unauthorized trader trespassing on the rights of a trade monopoly): from INTER- 'amid' + *-loper* as in archaic *landloper* 'vagabond' (from Middle Dutch *landlooper*).

interlude ▸ noun 1 an intervening period of time; an interval: *enjoying a lunchtime interlude.* ▪ a pause between the acts of a play.
2 a thing occurring or done during an interval. ▪ something performed during a theatre interval: *an orchestral interlude.* ▪ a piece of music played between other pieces or between the verses of a hymn. ▪ a temporary amusement or diversion that contrasts with what goes before or after: *the romantic interlude palled rapidly once he was back in town.*

– ORIGIN Middle English (originally denoting a light dramatic entertainment): from medieval Latin *interludium*, from *inter-* 'between' + *ludus* 'play'.

intermarriage ▶ noun [mass noun] marriage between people of different races, castes, or religions: *intermarriage between Scots and English borderers was officially forbidden.* ■ marriage between close relations.

intermarry ▶ verb (**intermarries, intermarrying, intermarried**) [no obj.] (of people belonging to different races, castes, or religions) become connected by marriage: *over the centuries the Greeks* ***intermarried with*** *the natives.* ■ (of close relations) marry each other.

intermediary /ˌɪntəˈmiːdɪəri/ ▶ noun (pl. **intermediaries**) a person who acts as a link between people in order to try and bring about an agreement; a mediator: *negotiations took place through an intermediary.*
▶ adjective intermediate: *an intermediary stage.*
– ORIGIN late 18th cent.: from French *intermédiaire*, from Italian *intermediario*, from Latin *intermedius* (see INTERMEDIATE).

intermediate /ˌɪntəˈmiːdɪət/ ▶ adjective coming between two things in time, place, character, etc.: *an intermediate stage of development | a cooled liquid* ***intermediate between*** *liquid and solid.* ■ having or suitable for a level of knowledge or skill between basic and advanced: *intermediate skiers | an intermediate course.*
▶ noun an intermediate thing. ■ a person at an intermediate level of knowledge or skill. ■ a chemical compound formed by one reaction and then taking part in another, especially during synthesis.
▶ verb /ˌɪntəˈmiːdɪeɪt/ [no obj.] act as intermediary; mediate: *groups which* ***intermediated between*** *the individual and the state.*
– DERIVATIVES **intermediacy** noun, **intermediately** adverb, **intermediateness** noun, **intermediation** noun, **intermediator** noun.
– ORIGIN late Middle English: from medieval Latin *intermediatus*, from Latin *intermedius*, from *inter-* 'between' + *medius* 'middle'.

intermediate frequency ▶ noun the frequency to which a radio signal is converted during heterodyne reception.

intermediate host ▶ noun Biology an organism that supports the immature or non-reproductive forms of a parasite. Compare with DEFINITIVE HOST.

intermediate technology ▶ noun [mass noun] technology suitable for use in developing countries, typically making use of locally available resources.

intermedium /ˌɪntəˈmiːdɪəm/ ▶ noun (pl. **intermedia** /-ˈmiːdɪə/) Zoology (in tetrapods) a carpal in the centre of the wrist joint, or a tarsal in the centre of the ankle joint.
– ORIGIN late 16th cent. (denoting an intervening action or performance): from late Latin, neuter (used as a noun) of Latin *intermedius* 'intermediate'.

interment /ɪnˈtəːm(ə)nt/ ▶ noun [mass noun] the burial of a corpse in a grave or tomb, typically with funeral rites: *the day of interment* | [count noun] *interments took place in the churchyard.*

intermesh ▶ verb [no obj.] (of two or more things) mesh with one another.

intermezzo /ˌɪntəˈmɛtsəʊ/ ▶ noun (pl. **intermezzi** /-ˈmɛtsi/ or **intermezzos**) a short connecting instrumental movement in an opera or other musical work. ■ a short piece for a solo instrument. ■ a light dramatic, musical, or other performance inserted between the acts of a play.
– ORIGIN late 18th cent.: from Italian, from Latin *intermedium* 'interval', neuter of *intermedius* (see INTERMEDIATE).

interminable ▶ adjective endless or apparently endless (often used hyperbolically): *we got bogged down in interminable discussions.*
– DERIVATIVES **interminably** adverb.
– ORIGIN late Middle English: from Old French, or from late Latin *interminabilis*, from *in-* 'not' + *terminare* (see TERMINATE).

intermingle ▶ verb mix or mingle together: [no obj.] *daisies* ***intermingled with*** *huge expanses of gorse and foxgloves* | [with obj.] *Riesling grapes were always* ***intermingled with*** *other varieties.*

intermission ▶ noun a pause or break: *he was granted an intermission in his studies* | [mass noun] *the daily work goes on without intermission.* ■ an interval between parts of a play, film, or concert.
– ORIGIN late Middle English: from Latin *intermissio(n-)*, from the verb *intermittere* (see INTERMIT).

intermit /ˌɪntəˈmɪt/ ▶ verb (**intermits, intermitting, intermitted**) [with obj.] suspend or discontinue (an action or practice) for a time: *he was urged to intermit his application.* ■ [no obj.] (especially of a fever or pulse) stop for a time.
– ORIGIN mid 16th cent.: from Latin *intermittere*, from *inter-* 'between' + *mittere* 'let go'.

intermittent ▶ adjective occurring at irregular intervals; not continuous or steady: *intermittent rain.*
– DERIVATIVES **intermittence** noun, **intermittency** noun, **intermittently** adverb.
– ORIGIN mid 16th cent.: from Latin *intermittent-* 'ceasing', from the verb *intermittere* (see INTERMIT).

intermittent claudication ▶ noun see CLAUDICATION.

intermix ▶ verb mix together: [with obj.] *the ore had to be handled so that it was not inadvertently* ***intermixed with*** *other material* | [no obj.] *along its southern edge low trees* ***intermix with*** *the shrubs.*
– DERIVATIVES **intermixture** noun.
– ORIGIN mid 16th cent. (originally as the past participle *intermixt*): from Latin *intermixtus*, past participle of *intermiscere* 'mix together', from *inter-* 'between' + *miscere* 'to mix'.

intermodal ▶ adjective involving two or more different modes of transport in conveying goods.

intermolecular ▶ adjective existing or taking place between molecules.

intern ▶ noun /ˈɪntəːn/ a student or trainee who works, sometimes without pay, in order to gain work experience or satisfy requirements for a qualification. ■ N. Amer. a recent medical graduate receiving supervised training in a hospital and acting as an assistant physician or surgeon. Compare with HOUSE OFFICER.
▶ verb **1** /ɪnˈtəːn/ [with obj.] confine (someone) as a prisoner, especially for political or military reasons.
2 /ˈɪntəːn/ [no obj.] N. Amer. serve as an intern.
– DERIVATIVES **internment** noun (sense 1 of the verb), **internship** noun.
– ORIGIN early 16th cent. (as an adjective in the sense 'internal'): from French *interne* (adjective), *interner* (verb), from Latin *internus* 'inward, internal'. Current senses date from the 19th cent.

internal ▶ adjective **1** of or situated on the inside: *the tube had an internal diameter of 1.1 mm.* ■ inside the body: *internal bleeding.* ■ existing or occurring within an organization: *an internal telephone system.* ■ relating to affairs and activities within a country rather than with other countries; domestic: *internal flights.* ■ experienced in one's mind; inner rather than expressed: *internal feelings.* ■ of the inner nature of a thing; intrinsic: *the party suffered from grave internal weaknesses.*
2 Brit. (of a student) attending a university as well as taking its examinations.
▶ noun (**internals**) inner parts or features: *all the weapon's internals are well finished and highly polished.*
– DERIVATIVES **internality** noun, **internally** adverb.
– ORIGIN early 16th cent. (in the sense 'intrinsic'): from modern Latin *internalis*, from Latin *internus* 'inward, internal'.

internal clock ▶ noun a person's innate sense of time. ■ another term for BIOLOGICAL CLOCK.

internal-combustion engine ▶ noun an engine which generates motive power by the burning of petrol, oil, or other fuel with air inside the engine, the hot gases produced being used to drive a piston or do other work as they expand.

internal energy ▶ noun [mass noun] Physics the energy in a system arising from the relative positions and interactions of its parts.

internal evidence ▶ noun [mass noun] evidence derived from the contents of the thing discussed.

internal exile ▶ noun [mass noun] penal banishment from a part of one's own country.

internalize (also **internalise**) ▶ verb [with obj.] **1** Psychology make (attitudes or behaviour) part of one's nature by learning or unconscious assimilation. ■ acquire knowledge of (the rules of a language).
2 Economics incorporate (costs) as part of a pricing structure, especially social costs resulting from a product's manufacture and use.
– DERIVATIVES **internalization** noun.

internal market ▶ noun **1** another term for SINGLE MARKET.
2 (in the UK) a system of decentralized funding in the National Health Service whereby hospital departments purchase each other's services contractually.

internal rhyme ▶ noun a rhyme involving a word in the middle of a line and another at the end of the line or in the middle of the next.

international ▶ adjective existing, occurring, or carried on between nations: *international trade.* ■ agreed on by all or many nations: *a violation of international law.* ■ used by people of many nations: *large international hotels.*
▶ noun **1** Brit. a game or contest between teams representing different countries in a sport. ■ a player who has taken part in an international game or contest.
2 (**International**) any of four associations founded (1864–1936) to promote socialist or communist action.

> The First International was formed by Karl Marx in London in 1864 as an international working men's association. The Second International was formed in Paris in 1889 to celebrate the 100th anniversary of the French Revolution and still survives as a loose association of social democrats. The Third International, also known as the Comintern, was formed by the Bolsheviks in 1919 to further the cause of world revolution. It was abolished in 1943. The Fourth International, a body of Trotskyist organizations, was formed in 1938 in opposition to the policies of the Stalin-dominated Third International.

– DERIVATIVES **internationality** noun, **internationally** adverb.

International Atomic Energy Agency (abbrev.: **IAEA**) an international organization set up in 1957 to promote research into and the development of atomic energy for peaceful purposes.

International Baccalaureate (abbrev.: **IB**) ▶ noun trademark a set of examinations intended to qualify successful candidates for higher education in any of several countries.

International Bank for Reconstruction and Development (abbrev.: **IBRD**) an agency of the United Nations which constitutes the main part of the World Bank. It was established in 1945 and its headquarters are in Washington DC.

International Brigade a group of volunteers which was raised internationally by foreign communist parties and which fought on the Republican side in the Spanish Civil War.

international candle ▶ noun see CANDLE.

International Civil Aviation Organization an agency of the United Nations, founded in 1947 to study problems of international civil aviation and establish standards and regulations.

International Confederation of Free Trade Unions (abbrev.: **ICFTU**) an association formed in 1949 to promote free trade unionism worldwide. Its headquarters are in Brussels.

International Court of Justice a judicial court of the United Nations which replaced the Cour Permanente de Justice in 1945 and meets at The Hague.

International Date Line ▶ noun see DATE LINE.

International Development Association (abbrev.: **IDA**) an affiliate of the International Bank for Reconstruction and Development (World Bank) established in 1960 to provide assistance primarily in the poorer developing countries.

Internationale /ˌɪntənaʃəˈnɑːl/ **1** (**the Internationale**) a revolutionary song composed in France in the late 19th century. It was adopted by French socialists and subsequently by others, and was the official anthem of the USSR until 1944.
2 variant spelling of INTERNATIONAL (sense 2 of the noun).
– ORIGIN French, feminine of *international* 'international'.

International Energy Agency (abbrev.: **IEA**) an agency founded in 1974, within the framework of the OECD, to coordinate energy supply and demand worldwide. Its headquarters are in Paris.

International Finance Corporation (abbrev.: **IFC**) an affiliate of the International Bank for Reconstruction and Development (World Bank) established in 1956 to assist developing member countries by promoting the growth of the private sector of their economies.

International Fund for Agricultural Development (abbrev.: **IFAD**) an agency of the United Nations whose purpose is to mobilize additional funds for agricultural and rural development in developing countries through programmes that directly benefit the poorest rural populations. It began operations in 1977.

internationalism ▸ noun [mass noun] **1** the state or process of being international: *the internationalism of popular music.* ■ the advocacy of cooperation and understanding between nations.
2 (**Internationalism**) the principles of any of the four Internationals.
– DERIVATIVES **internationalist** noun.

internationalize (also **internationalise**) ▸ verb [with obj.] **1** make (something) international.
2 bring (a place) under the protection or control of two or more nations: (as adj. **internationalized**) *an internationalized city.*
– DERIVATIVES **internationalization** noun.

International Labour Organization (abbrev.: **ILO**) an organization established in 1919 whose aim is to promote lasting peace through social justice, awarded the Nobel Peace Prize in 1969.

international law ▸ noun [mass noun] a body of rules established by custom or treaty and recognized by nations as binding in their relations with one another.

International Maritime Association an agency of the United Nations established in 1958 for co-operation and exchange of information among governments on matters relating to international shipping. Its headquarters are in London.

International Monetary Fund (abbrev.: **IMF**) an international organization established in 1945 which aims to promote international trade and monetary cooperation and the stabilization of exchange rates.

> Member countries contribute in gold and in their own currencies to provide a reserve on which they may draw to meet foreign obligations during periods of deficit in their international balance of payments. Payments are usually made on the basis of the country's acceptance of stipulated measures for economic correction, which often entail cuts in public expenditure and an increased cost of living, and have frequently caused controversy. It is affiliated to the United Nations, with headquarters in Washington DC.

International Organization for Standardization an organization founded in 1946 to standardize measurements for international industrial, commercial, and scientific purposes.

International Phonetic Alphabet (abbrev.: **IPA**) an internationally recognized set of phonetic symbols developed in the late 19th century, based on the principle of strict one-to-one correspondence between sounds and symbols.

International Society for Krishna Consciousness see **Hare Krishna**.

International Style ▸ noun [mass noun] a functional style of 20th-century architecture, so called because it crossed national and cultural barriers. It is characterized by the use of steel and reinforced concrete, wide windows, uninterrupted interior spaces, simple lines, and strict geometric forms.

International System of Units ▸ noun a system of physical units (**SI units**) based on the metre, kilogram, second, ampere, kelvin, candela, and mole, together with a set of prefixes to indicate multiplication or division by a power of ten.
– ORIGIN translating French *Système International d'Unités.*

International Telecommunication Union (abbrev.: **ITU**) an organization whose purpose is to promote international cooperation in the use and improvement of telecommunications of all kinds. Founded in Paris in 1865 as the International Telegraph Union, it became an agency of the United Nations in 1947.

international unit ▸ noun a unit of activity or potency for vitamins, hormones, or other substances, defined individually for each substance in terms of the activity of a standard quantity or preparation.

interne ▸ noun variant spelling of **intern**.

internecine /ˌɪntəˈniːsʌɪn/ ▸ adjective destructive to both sides in a conflict: *the region's history of savage internecine warfare.* ■ relating to conflict within a group.
– ORIGIN mid 17th cent. (in the sense 'deadly, characterized by great slaughter'): from Latin *internecinus*, based on *inter-* 'among' + *necare* 'to kill'.

internee /ˌɪntəːˈniː/ ▸ noun a person who is confined as a prisoner, especially for political or military reasons.

internegative ▸ noun Photography a second negative of an image made from the original negative.

Internet ▸ noun (**the Internet**) a global computer network providing a variety of information and communication facilities, consisting of interconnected networks using standardized communication protocols.
– ORIGIN 1970s (denoting a computer network connecting two or more smaller networks): from **inter-** 'reciprocal, mutual' + **network**.

Internet appliance ▸ noun a small computer designed especially to provide easy access to the Internet.

Internet cafe ▸ noun a simple cafe in which customers pay to use computer terminals to access the Internet.

Internet Protocol ▸ noun a set of rules governing the format of data sent over the Internet or other network.

interneuron /ˌɪntəˈnjʊərɒn/ (also **interneurone** /-rəʊn/) ▸ noun Physiology a neuron which transmits impulses between other neurons, especially as part of a reflex arc.
– DERIVATIVES **interneuronal** adjective.
– ORIGIN 1930s: from **internuncial** + **neuron**.

internist ▸ noun N. Amer. a medical specialist in internal diseases.
– ORIGIN early 20th cent.: from **internal** + **-ist**.

internode /ˈɪntənəʊd/ ▸ noun a slender part between two nodes or joints, in particular: ■ Botany a part of a plant stem between two of the nodes from which leaves emerge. ■ Anatomy a stretch of a nerve cell axon sheathed in myelin, between two nodes of Ranvier.
– ORIGIN mid 17th cent.: from Latin *internodium*, from *inter-* 'between' + *nodus* 'knot'.

internuclear ▸ adjective between nuclei (especially of atoms).

internuncial /ˌɪntəˈnʌnʃ(ə)l/ ▸ adjective Physiology (of neurons) forming connections between other neurons in the central nervous system.
– ORIGIN mid 19th cent.: from Latin *internuntius* (from *inter-* 'between' + *nuntius* 'messenger') + **-al**.

interoceanic ▸ adjective between or connecting two oceans.

interoceptive /ˌɪntərəʊˈsɛptɪv/ ▸ adjective Physiology relating to stimuli produced within an organism, especially in the gut and other internal organs. Compare with **exteroceptive**.
– ORIGIN early 20th cent.: from **interior** + **receptive**.

interoceptor /ˌɪntərəʊˈsɛptə/ ▸ noun Physiology a sensory receptor which receives stimuli from within the body, especially from the gut and other internal organs. Compare with **exteroceptor**.

interoperable ▸ adjective (of computer systems or software) able to exchange and make use of information.
– DERIVATIVES **interoperability** noun, **interoperate** verb.

interosseous /ˌɪntərˈɒsɪəs/ ▸ adjective situated between bones, in particular: ■ Anatomy of or denoting certain muscles of the hand and foot. ■ of or denoting certain arteries of the forearm.

interpellate /ɪnˈtəːpɪleɪt/ ▸ verb [with obj.] **1** (in a parliament) interrupt the order of the day by demanding an explanation from (the minister concerned).
2 Philosophy (of an ideology or discourse) bring into being or give identity to (an individual or category).
– DERIVATIVES **interpellation** noun.
– ORIGIN late 16th cent. (in the sense 'interrupt'): from Latin *interpellat-* 'interrupted (by speech)', from the verb *interpellare*, from *inter-* 'between' + *pellere* 'to drive'. Sense 1 dates from the late 19th cent.; sense 2 is from the works of Althusser.

interpenetrate ▸ verb mix or merge together: [no obj.] *the two concepts interpenetrate in interesting ways* | [with obj.] *fibres of meaning interpenetrate every strand of sound.*
– DERIVATIVES **interpenetration** noun, **interpenetrative** adjective.

interpersonal ▸ adjective relating to relationships or communication between people: *you will need good interpersonal skills.*
– DERIVATIVES **interpersonally** adverb.

interphase ▸ noun [mass noun] Biology the resting phase between successive mitotic divisions of a cell, or between the first and second divisions of meiosis.

interplanetary ▸ adjective situated or travelling between planets: *interplanetary missions.*

interplant ▸ verb [with obj.] plant (a crop or plant) together with another crop or plant. ■ plant (land) with a mixture of crops or plants.

interplay ▸ noun [mass noun] the way in which two or more things have an effect on each other: *the interplay between inheritance and learning.*

interpleader ▸ noun Law a suit pleaded between two parties to determine a matter of claim or right to property held by a third party.
– ORIGIN mid 16th cent.: from Anglo-Norman French *enterpleder*, from *enter-* 'between' + *pleder* 'to plead'.

Interpol /ˈɪntəpɒl/ an organization based in France that coordinates investigations made by the police forces of member countries into crimes with an international dimension.
– ORIGIN originally as the telegraphic address of the International Criminal Police Commission, founded in 1923; from *Inter(national) pol(ice).*

interpolate /ɪnˈtəːpəleɪt/ ▸ verb [with obj.] **1** insert (something of a different nature) into something else: *illustrations were interpolated in the text.* ■ insert (words) in a book or other text, especially in order to give a false impression as to its date. ■ alter or enlarge (a text) by insertion of new material. ■ Mathematics insert (an intermediate value or term) into a series by estimating or calculating it from surrounding known values.
2 interject (a remark) in a conversation: [with direct speech] *'I dare say,' interpolated her employer.*
– DERIVATIVES **interpolation** noun, **interpolative** adjective.
– ORIGIN early 17th cent.: from Latin *interpolat-* 'refurbished, altered', from the verb *interpolare*, from *inter-* 'between' + *-polare* (related to *polire* 'to polish').

interpolator ▸ noun **1** a person who interpolates something.
2 a device which guides a tool through a smooth curve when provided with a set of points defining the curve.

interpole ▸ noun an auxiliary pole of a commutator placed between the main poles to increase its efficiency.

interpose ▸ verb **1** [with obj.] place or insert between one thing and another: *she interposed herself between the newcomers.* ■ say (words) as an interruption: *if I might interpose a personal remark here.*
2 [no obj.] intervene between parties: [with infinitive] *the legislature interposed to suppress these amusements.* ■ [with obj.] exercise or advance (a veto or objection): *the memo interposes no objection to issuing a discharge.*
– ORIGIN late 16th cent.: from French *interposer*, from Latin *interponere* 'put in' (from *inter-* 'between' + *ponere* 'put'), but influenced by *interpositus* 'inserted' and Old French *poser* 'to place'.

interposition ▸ noun [mass noun] the action of interposing someone or something: *the interposition of members between tiers of management.* ■ interference or intervention.
– ORIGIN late Middle English: from Latin *interpositio(n-)*, from the verb *interponere* (see **interpose**).

interpret ▸ verb (**interprets**, **interpreting**, **interpreted**) [with obj.] **1** explain the meaning of (information or actions): *the evidence is difficult to interpret.* ■ understand (an action, mood, or way of behaving) as having a particular meaning: *he would no longer interpret her silence as indifference.* ■ perform (a dramatic role or piece of music) in a way that conveys one's understanding of the creator's ideas.
2 [no obj.] translate orally or into sign language the words of a person speaking a different language: *I agreed to interpret for Jean-Claude.*
– DERIVATIVES **interpretability** noun, **interpretable** adjective.
– ORIGIN late Middle English: from Old French *interpreter* or Latin *interpretari* 'explain, translate', from *interpres, interpret-* 'agent, translator, interpreter'.

interpretation ▸ noun [mass noun] the action of explaining the meaning of something: *the interpretation of data.* ■ [count noun] an explanation or way of explaining: *this action is open to a number of interpretations.* ■ [count noun] a stylistic representation of a creative work or dramatic role: *his unique interpretation of the Liszt études.*
– DERIVATIVES **interpretational** adjective.
– ORIGIN late Middle English: from Old French *interpretation* or Latin *interpretatio(n-)*, from the verb *interpretari* (see **interpret**).

interpretative (also **interpretive**) ▸ adjective relating to or providing an interpretation: *activities designed to reinforce students' interpretative skills.*
– DERIVATIVES **interpretatively** adverb.

interpreter ▶ **noun** **1** a person who interprets, especially one who translates speech orally or into sign language.
2 Computing a program that can analyse and execute a program line by line.
– ORIGIN late Middle English: from Old French *interpreteur*, from late Latin *interpretator*, from Latin *interpretari* (see INTERPRET).

interprovincial ▶ **adjective** existing or carried on between provinces of the same country.
▶ **noun** (usu. **interprovincials**) a sports tournament between the provinces of a country. ■ a competitor in an interprovincial tournament.

interquartile /ˌɪntəˈkwɔːtʌɪl/ ▶ **adjective** Statistics situated between the first and third quartiles of a distribution.

interracial ▶ **adjective** existing between or involving different races: *interracial conflict*.
– DERIVATIVES **interracially** adverb.

interregnum /ˌɪntəˈrɛɡnəm/ ▶ **noun** (pl. **interregnums** or **interregna** /-nə/) a period when normal government is suspended, especially between successive reigns or regimes. ■ (**the Interregnum**) the period in English history from the execution of Charles I in 1649 to the Restoration of Charles II in 1660. ■ an interval between the periods of office of two incumbents in a parish.
– ORIGIN late 16th cent. (denoting temporary rule between reigns or during suspension of normal government): from Latin, from *inter-* 'between' + *regnum* 'reign'.

interrelate ▶ **verb** relate or connect to one other: *each component* ***interrelates with*** *all the others* | [with obj.] *shared values and mechanisms that interrelate peoples in all corners of the world*.
– DERIVATIVES **interrelatedness** noun.

interrelationship ▶ **noun** the way in which each of two or more things is related to the other or others: *the* ***interrelationship between*** *the comprehension and production of early vocabulary*.
– DERIVATIVES **interrelation** noun.

interrogate ▶ **verb** [with obj.] **1** ask questions of (someone) closely, aggressively, or formally: *he was interrogated by MI6*.
2 obtain data from (a computer file, database, storage device, or terminal). ■ (of an electronic device) transmit a signal to (another device, especially one on a vehicle) to obtain information about identity, condition, etc.
– DERIVATIVES **interrogator** noun.
– ORIGIN late 15th cent.: from Latin *interrogat-* 'questioned', from the verb *interrogare*, from *inter-* 'between' + *rogare* 'ask'.

interrogation ▶ **noun** [mass noun] the action of interrogating or the process of being interrogated: *would he keep his mouth shut* ***under interrogation****?* | [count noun] *he had conducted hundreds of criminal interrogations*.
– DERIVATIVES **interrogational** adjective.

interrogation point (also **interrogation mark**) ▶ **noun** another term for QUESTION MARK.

interrogative /ˌɪntəˈrɒɡətɪv/ ▶ **adjective** having the force of a question: *a hard, interrogative stare*. ■ Grammar used in questions: *an interrogative adverb*. Contrasted with AFFIRMATIVE and NEGATIVE.
▶ **noun** a word used in questions, such as *how* or *what*. ■ a construction that has the force of a question.
– DERIVATIVES **interrogatively** adverb.
– ORIGIN early 16th cent.: from late Latin *interrogativus*, from Latin *interrogare* (see INTERROGATE).

interrogatory /ˌɪntəˈrɒɡət(ə)ri/ ▶ **adjective** conveying a question; questioning: *she abandoned her interrogatory monologue*.
▶ **noun** (pl. **interrogatories**) Law a written question which is formally put to one party in a case by another party and which must be answered.
– ORIGIN mid 16th cent.: the noun from medieval Latin *interrogatoria*, plural of *interrogatorium*; the adjective from late Latin *interrogatorius*, based on Latin *interrogare* (see INTERROGATE).

interrupt ▶ **verb** [with obj.] **1** stop the continuous progress of (an activity or process): *the buzzer interrupted his thoughts*. ■ stop (someone speaking) by saying or doing something: *'Of course ...' Shepherd began, but his son interrupted him*.
2 break the continuity of (a line or surface): *the coastal plain is interrupted by chains of large lagoons*. ■ obstruct (something, especially a view).
– DERIVATIVES **interruptible** adjective, **interruptive** adjective.
– ORIGIN late Middle English: from Latin *interrupt-* 'broken, interrupted', from the verb *interrumpere*, from *inter-* 'between' + *rumpere* 'to break'.

interrupted ▶ **adjective** **1** Botany (of a compound leaf or other plant organ) made discontinuous by smaller interposed leaflets or intervals of bare stem.
2 Music (of a cadence) having a penultimate dominant chord that is followed not by the expected chord of the tonic but by another, usually that of the submediant.

interrupter (also **interruptor**) ▶ **noun** a person or thing that interrupts. ■ a device that automatically breaks an electric circuit if a fault develops.

interruption ▶ **noun** [mass noun] the action of interrupting or being interrupted: *a chance to study without interruption*. ■ [count noun] an act, utterance, or period that interrupts someone or something: *she ignored the interruption and carried on* | *students returning to education after an interruption in their career*.

inter se /ˌɪntə ˈseɪ/ ▶ **adverb** between or among themselves: *covenants entered into by all the shareholders inter se*.
– ORIGIN Latin.

intersect ▶ **verb** [with obj.] divide (something) by passing or lying across it: *the area is intersected only by minor roads*. ■ [no obj.] (of two or more things) pass or lie across each other: *lines of latitude and longitude intersect at right angles*.
– ORIGIN early 17th cent.: from Latin *intersect-* 'cut, intersected', from the verb *intersecare*, from *inter-* 'between' + *secare* 'to cut'.

intersection ▶ **noun** a point or line common to lines or surfaces that intersect: *the intersection of a plane and a cone*. ■ a point at which two or more things intersect, especially a road junction: *a red light at the intersection with Brompton Road*. ■ an act of intersecting.
– DERIVATIVES **intersectional** adjective.
– ORIGIN mid 16th cent.: from Latin *intersectio(n-)*, from *intersecare* (see INTERSECT).

intersegmental /ˌɪntəsɛɡˈmɛnt(ə)l/ ▶ **adjective** chiefly Zoology situated or occurring between segments.

interseptal /ɪntəˈsɛpt(ə)l/ ▶ **adjective** Anatomy & Zoology situated between septa or partitions.

intersession ▶ **noun** **1** US a short period between university terms, sometimes used by students to engage in projects outside the normal academic programme.
2 Canadian a short university term in which thirteen weeks of course material is covered in five or six weeks of intensive study.

intersex ▶ **noun** [mass noun] the abnormal condition of being intermediate between male and female; hermaphroditism. ■ [count noun] an individual in this condition; a hermaphrodite.

intersexual ▶ **adjective** **1** existing or occurring between the sexes.
2 relating to or having the condition of being intermediate between male and female.
– DERIVATIVES **intersexuality** noun.

interspace ▶ **noun** a space between things.
▶ **verb** [with obj.] put or occupy a space between (two or more things): *the four-storey houses were interspaced with the ramshackle cottages of the workmen*.

interspecific /ˌɪntəspəˈsɪfɪk/ ▶ **adjective** Biology existing or occurring between different species: *interspecific differences*.
– DERIVATIVES **interspecifically** adverb.

intersperse ▶ **verb** [with obj.] scatter among or between other things; place here and there: *deep pools interspersed by shallow shingle banks*. ■ diversify (a thing or things) with other things at intervals: *the debate was interspersed with angry exchanges*.
– DERIVATIVES **interspersion** noun.
– ORIGIN mid 16th cent. (in the sense 'diversify (something) by introducing other things at intervals'): from Latin *interspers-* 'scattered between', from *interspergere*, from *inter-* 'between' + *spargere* 'scatter'.

interspinal ▶ **adjective** Anatomy situated between the spines or spinose protuberances of the vertebrae.
– DERIVATIVES **interspinous** adjective.

interstadial /ˌɪntəˈsteɪdɪəl/ Geology ▶ **adjective** relating to a minor period of less cold climate during a glacial period. Compare with INTERGLACIAL.
▶ **noun** an interstadial period.
– ORIGIN early 20th cent.: from INTER- 'between' + *stadial* from Latin *stadialis*, from *stadium* 'stage'.

interstate ▶ **adjective** existing or carried on between states, especially of the US: *interstate travel*. ■ US in a different state from one referred to or understood: *their interstate rivals*.
▶ **noun** (also **interstate highway**) one of a system of motorways running between US states.
▶ **adverb** Austral. from one state to another.

interstellar /ˌɪntəˈstɛlə/ ▶ **adjective** occurring or situated between stars: *interstellar travel*.

interstice /ɪnˈtəːstɪs/ ▶ **noun** (usu. **interstices**) an intervening space, especially a very small one: *sunshine filtered through the interstices of the arching trees*.
– ORIGIN late Middle English: from Latin *interstitium*, from *intersistere* 'stand between', from *inter-* 'between' + *sistere* 'to stand'.

interstitial /ˌɪntəˈstɪʃ(ə)l/ ▶ **adjective** of, forming, or occupying interstices: *the interstitial space*. ■ Ecology (of minute animals) living in the spaces between individual sand grains in the soil or aquatic sediments: *interstitial fauna*.
▶ **noun** Computing an advertisement that appears while a chosen website or page is downloading.
– DERIVATIVES **interstitially** adverb.

intersubjective ▶ **adjective** Philosophy existing between conscious minds; shared by more than one conscious mind.
– DERIVATIVES **intersubjectively** adverb, **intersubjectivity** noun.

intertextuality /ˌɪntətɛkstjʊˈalɪti/ ▶ **noun** [mass noun] the relationship between texts, especially literary ones.
– DERIVATIVES **intertextual** adjective, **intertextually** adverb.

intertidal ▶ **adjective** Ecology of or denoting the area of a seashore which is covered at high tide and uncovered at low tide.

intertrack ▶ **adjective** (of betting, especially on horse races) involving bets placed at racecourses other than the one at which the race betted on is being run.

intertribal ▶ **adjective** existing or occurring between different tribes: *intertribal conflict*. ■ involving members of more than one tribe: *an intertribal group*.

intertrigo /ˌɪntəˈtrʌɪɡəʊ/ ▶ **noun** [mass noun] Medicine inflammation caused by the rubbing of one area of skin on another.
– ORIGIN early 18th cent.: from Latin, 'a sore place caused by rubbing', from *interterere* 'rub against each other'.

intertropical convergence zone ▶ **noun** a narrow zone near the equator where northern and southern air masses converge, typically producing low atmospheric pressure.

intertwine ▶ **verb** twist or twine together: [with obj.] *a net made of cotton* ***intertwined with*** *other natural fibres* | [no obj.] *the coils* ***intertwine with*** *one another like strands of spaghetti*. ■ [with obj.] connect or link (two or more things) closely: *as with most traditions, fact and fiction have become inextricably intertwined*.
– DERIVATIVES **intertwinement** noun.

intertwist ▶ **verb** [with obj.] (usu. as adj. **intertwisted**) twisted together: *intertwisted trees*.

interval ▶ **noun** **1** an intervening time: *after his departure, there was an interval of many years without any meetings* | *the day should be dry with sunny intervals*.
2 a pause or break in activity: *an interval of mourning*. ■ Brit. a period of time separating parts of a theatrical or musical performance. ■ a break between the parts of a sports match.
3 a space between two things; a gap.
4 the difference in pitch between two sounds.
– PHRASES **at intervals 1** with time between; not continuously: *the light flashed at intervals*. **2** with spaces between: *the path is marked with rocks at intervals*.
– DERIVATIVES **intervallic** adjective.
– ORIGIN Middle English: from Old French *entrevalle*, based on Latin *intervallum* 'space between ramparts, interval', from *inter-* 'between' + *vallum* 'rampart'.

interval estimate ▶ **noun** Statistics an interval within which the value of a parameter of a population has a stated probability of occurring. Compare with POINT ESTIMATE.

intervalometer /ˌɪntəvəˈlɒmɪtə/ ▶ **noun** Photography an attachment or facility on a camera that operates the shutter regularly at set intervals over a period. On a cine camera the device is used for time-lapse photography.

I

interval training ▶ **noun** [mass noun] physical training consisting of alternating periods of high- and low-intensity activity.

intervene ▶ **verb** [no obj.] **1** take part in something so as to prevent or alter a result or course of events: *he acted outside his authority when he* **intervened in** *the dispute* | [with infinitive] *their forces intervened to halt the attack.* ■ (of an event or circumstance) occur as a delay or obstacle to something being done: *Christmas intervened and the investigation was suspended.* ■ interrupt verbally: [with direct speech] *'It's true!' he intervened.* ■ Law become involved in a lawsuit as a third party.
2 (usu. as adj. **intervening**) occur in the time between events: *to occupy the intervening months she took a job in a hospital.* ■ be situated between things: *they heard the sound of distant gunfire, muffled by the intervening trees.*
– DERIVATIVES **intervener** noun, **intervenient** adjective, **intervenor** noun.
– ORIGIN late 16th cent. (in the sense 'come in as an extraneous factor or thing'): from Latin *intervenire*, from *inter-* 'between' + *venire* 'come'.

intervention ▶ **noun** [mass noun] the action or process of intervening: *a high degree of state intervention in the economy* | [count noun] *repeated interventions by central banks.* ■ interference by a state in another's affairs: *the government was reported to be considering military intervention.* ■ action taken to improve a medical disorder: *two patients were referred for surgical intervention.*
– DERIVATIVES **interventional** adjective.
– ORIGIN late Middle English: from Latin *interventio(n-)*, from the verb *intervenire* (see INTERVENE).

interventionist ▶ **adjective** favouring intervention, especially by a government in its domestic economy or by one state in the affairs of another.
▶ **noun** a person who favours intervention of this kind.
– DERIVATIVES **interventionism** noun.

intervertebral /ˌɪntəˈvəːtɪbr(ə)l/ ▶ **adjective** situated between vertebrae: *intervertebral joints.*

intervertebral disc ▶ **noun** see DISC (sense 2).

interview ▶ **noun** a meeting of people face to face, especially for consultation. ■ a conversation between a journalist or radio or television presenter and a person of public interest, used as the basis of a broadcast or publication: *a half-hour interview* **with** *the prime minister.* ■ an oral examination of an applicant for a job, college place, etc.: *I am pleased to advise you that you have been selected for interview.* ■ a session of formal questioning of a person by the police.
▶ **verb** [with obj.] hold an interview with (someone): *she was interviewed by a reporter from the Daily News* | *police are keen to interview two men seen nearby.* ■ [no obj., with adverbial] perform (well or badly) at an interview.
– DERIVATIVES **interviewee** noun, **interviewer** noun.
– ORIGIN early 16th cent. (formerly also as *enterview*): from French *entrevue*, from *s'entrevoir* 'see each other', from *voir* 'to see', on the pattern of *vue* 'a view'.

inter vivos /ˌɪntə ˈviːvəʊs/ ▶ **adverb & adjective** (especially of a gift as opposed to a legacy) between living people.
– ORIGIN Latin.

intervocalic /ˌɪntəvə(ʊ)ˈkalɪk/ ▶ **adjective** Phonetics occurring between vowels.
– DERIVATIVES **intervocalically** adverb.

interwar ▶ **adjective** existing in the period between two wars, especially the two world wars (i.e. between 1918 and 1939).

interweave ▶ **verb** (past **interwove**; past participle **interwoven**) weave or become woven together: [with obj.] *the rugs are made by tightly interweaving the strands* | [no obj.] *the branches met and interwove above his head.* ■ [with obj.] blend closely: *Wordsworth's political ideas are often* **interwoven with** *his philosophical and religious beliefs.*

Interweb ▶ **noun** humorous the Internet.

interwind /ˌɪntəˈwʌɪnd/ ▶ **verb** (past and past participle **interwound**) [with obj.] (usu. as adj. **interwound**) wind together: *a transformer consists of two interwound coils.*

interwork ▶ **verb** [no obj.] Computing (of items of hardware or software) be able to connect, communicate, or exchange data.

intestate /ɪnˈtɛsteɪt/ ▶ **adjective** not having made a will before one dies: *he died intestate.*
▶ **noun** a person who has died without having made a will.
– DERIVATIVES **intestacy** /-təsi/ noun.
– ORIGIN late Middle English: from Latin *intestatus*, from *in-* 'not' + *testatus* 'testified, witness' (see TESTATE).

intestinal /ɪntɛˈstʌɪn(ə)l, ɪnˈtɛstɪn(ə)l/ ▶ **adjective** relating to or affecting the intestine: *the intestinal tract.*
– DERIVATIVES **intestinally** adverb.

intestinal flora ▶ **plural noun** [usu. treated as sing.] the symbiotic bacteria occurring naturally in the gut.

intestine (also **intestines**) ▶ **noun** (in vertebrates) the lower part of the alimentary canal from the end of the stomach to the anus. See also LARGE INTESTINE, SMALL INTESTINE. ■ (especially in invertebrates) the whole alimentary canal from the mouth downward.
– ORIGIN late Middle English: from Latin *intestinum*, neuter of *intestinus*, from *intus* 'within'.

intichiuma /ˌɪntɪtʃɪˈuːmə/ ▶ **plural noun** sacred ceremonies performed by some Central Australian Aborigines with the purpose of increasing the number of totemic plants or animals and thus ensuring a good food supply.
– ORIGIN Arrernte.

intifada /ˌɪntɪˈfɑːdə/ ▶ **noun** the Palestinian uprising against Israeli occupation of the West Bank and Gaza Strip. The first intifada lasted from 1987 to 1993, and the second began in 2000.
– ORIGIN Arabic *intifāḍa* 'an uprising' (literally 'a jumping up as a reaction to something'), from *intifaḍa* 'be shaken, shake oneself'.

intima /ˈɪntɪmə/ ▶ **noun** (pl. **intimae** /-miː/) Anatomy & Zoology the innermost coating or membrane of a part or organ, especially of a vein or artery.
– DERIVATIVES **intimal** adjective.
– ORIGIN late 19th cent.: shortening of modern Latin *tunica intima* 'innermost sheath'.

intimacy ▶ **noun** (pl. **intimacies**) [mass noun] close familiarity or friendship: *the intimacy between a husband and wife.* ■ a cosy and private or relaxed atmosphere: *the room had a peaceful sense of intimacy about it.* ■ euphemistic sexual intercourse. ■ [count noun] an intimate remark: *here she was sitting swapping intimacies with a stranger.* ■ [in sing.] closeness of observation or knowledge of a subject: *he acquired an intimacy with Swahili literature.*

intimate[1] /ˈɪntɪmət/ ▶ **adjective** **1** closely acquainted; familiar: *intimate friends* | *they are on intimate terms.* ■ (of a place or setting) having a cosy and private or relaxed atmosphere: *an intimate little Italian restaurant.* ■ involving very close connection: *their intimate involvement with their community.* ■ (of knowledge) detailed or thorough: *an intimate knowledge of the software.*
2 private and personal: *going into intimate details of his sexual encounters.* ■ [predic.] euphemistic having a sexual relationship: *he was sickened by the thought of others having been* **intimate with** *her.*
▶ **noun** a very close friend: *his circle of intimates.*
– DERIVATIVES **intimately** adverb.
– ORIGIN early 17th cent. (as a noun): from late Latin *intimatus*, past participle of Latin *intimare* 'impress, make familiar', from *intimus* 'inmost'.

intimate[2] /ˈɪntɪmeɪt/ ▶ **verb** [with obj.] state or make known: *Mr Hutchison has intimated his decision to retire.* ■ [with clause] imply or hint: *he had already intimated that he might not be able to continue.*
– ORIGIN early 16th cent.: (earlier (late Middle English) as *intimation*) from late Latin *intimat-* 'made known', from the verb *intimare* (see INTIMATE[1]).

intimation ▶ **noun** an indication or hint: *the first intimations of trouble* | *no one gave any intimation that there had been any problems.* ■ [mass noun] the action of making something known, especially in an indirect way.

intimidate ▶ **verb** frighten or overawe (someone), especially in order to make them do what one wants: *the forts are designed to intimidate the nationalist population* | (as adj. **intimidating**) *the intimidating defence barrister.*
– DERIVATIVES **intimidatingly** adverb, **intimidator** noun, **intimidatory** adjective.
– ORIGIN mid 17th cent.: from medieval Latin *intimidat-* 'made timid', from the verb *intimidare* (based on *timidus* 'timid').

intimidation ▶ **noun** [mass noun] the action of intimidating someone, or the state of being intimidated: *the intimidation of witnesses and jurors.*

intimism /ˈɪntɪmɪz(ə)m/ ▶ **noun** [mass noun] a style of painting showing intimate views of domestic interiors using Impressionist techniques, used by artists such as Bonnard in the early 20th century.
– DERIVATIVES **intimist** adjective & noun.
– ORIGIN early 20th cent.: from French *intimisme*, from Latin *intimus* 'innermost'.

intinction /ɪnˈtɪŋ(k)ʃ(ə)n/ ▶ **noun** [mass noun] the action of dipping the bread in the wine at a Eucharist so that a communicant receives both together.
– ORIGIN mid 16th cent.: from late Latin *intinctio(n-)*, from Latin *intingere*, from *in-* 'into' + *tingere* 'dip'. The word originally denoted the general action of dipping, especially into something coloured; compare with TINGE. The current sense dates from the late 19th cent.

intitule /ɪnˈtɪtjuːl/ ▶ **verb** [with obj.] Brit. give a specified title to (an Act of Parliament).
– ORIGIN late 15th cent. (formerly also as *entitule*): from Old French *entituler*, *intituler* (see ENTITLE).

into ▶ **preposition** **1** expressing movement or action with the result that someone or something becomes enclosed or surrounded by something else: *cover the bowl and put it into the fridge* | *Sara got into her car and shut the door.*
2 expressing movement or action with the result that someone or something makes physical contact with something else: *he crashed into a parked car.*
3 indicating a route by which someone or something may arrive at a particular destination: *the narrow road which led down into the village.*
4 indicating the direction towards which someone or something is turned when confronting something else: *with the wind blowing into your face* | *sobbing into her skirt.*
5 indicating an object of attention or interest: *a clearer insight into what is involved* | *an inquiry into the squad's practices.*
6 expressing a change of state: *a peaceful protest which turned into a violent confrontation* | *the fruit can be made into jam.*
7 expressing the result of an action: *they forced the club into a humiliating special general meeting.*
8 expressing division: *three into twelve goes four.*
9 informal (of a person) taking a lively and active interest in (something): *he's into surfing and jet-skiing.*
– ORIGIN Old English *intō* (see IN, TO).

intolerable ▶ **adjective** unable to be endured: *the intolerable pressures of his work.*
– DERIVATIVES **intolerably** adverb.
– ORIGIN late Middle English: from Old French, or from Latin *intolerabilis*, from *in-* 'not' + *tolerabilis* (see TOLERABLE).

intolerance ▶ **noun** [mass noun] unwillingness to accept views, beliefs, or behaviour that differ from one's own: *a struggle against religious intolerance.* ■ an inability to eat a food or take a drug without adverse effects: *young children with lactose intolerance.*

intolerant ▶ **adjective** not tolerant of views, beliefs, or behaviour that differ from one's own: *as a society we are more* **intolerant of** *certain types of violence than we were in the past.* ■ unable to be given (a medicine or other treatment) or to eat (a food) without adverse effects. ■ (of a plant or animal) unable to survive exposure to (a particular physical influence).
– DERIVATIVES **intolerantly** adverb.
– ORIGIN mid 18th cent.: from Latin *intolerant-*, from *in-* 'not' + *tolerant-* 'enduring' (see TOLERANT).

intonation ▶ **noun** [mass noun] **1** the rise and fall of the voice in speaking: *she spoke English with a German intonation.* ■ the action of intoning or reciting in a singing voice.
2 accuracy of pitch in playing or singing, or on a stringed instrument such as a guitar: *poor woodwind intonation at the opening.*
3 the opening phrase of a plainsong melody.
– DERIVATIVES **intonate** verb, **intonational** adjective.
– ORIGIN early 17th cent. (in sense 3): from medieval Latin *intonatio(n-)*, from *intonare* (see INTONE).

intone /ɪnˈtəʊn/ ▶ **verb** [with obj.] say or recite with little rise and fall of the pitch of the voice: *he intoned a short Latin prayer* | [with direct speech] *'All rise,' intoned the usher.*
– ORIGIN late 15th cent. (originally as *entone*): from Old French *entoner* or medieval Latin *intonare*, from *in-* 'into' + Latin *tonus* 'tone'.

in toto /ɪn ˈtəʊtəʊ/ ▶ **adverb** as a whole: *such proposals should be subjected to specific criticism rather than rejected in toto.* ■ in all; overall: *there was, in toto, an increase in legal regulation and public surveillance.*
– ORIGIN Latin.

intoxicant ▶ **noun** an intoxicating substance.

intoxicate ▶ **verb 1** [with obj.] (usu. as adj. **intoxicated**) (of alcoholic drink or a drug) cause (someone) to lose control of their faculties or behaviour. ■ excite or exhilarate (someone): *he became intoxicated with his own power.*
2 archaic poison (someone).
– ORIGIN late Middle English (in the sense 'poison'): from medieval Latin *intoxicare*, from *in-* 'into' + *toxicare* 'to poison', from Latin *toxicum* (see **TOXIC**).

intoxicating ▶ **adjective** (of alcoholic drink or a drug) liable to cause intoxication. ■ exhilarating or exciting: *an intoxicating sense of freedom.*
– DERIVATIVES **intoxicatingly** adverb.

intoxication ▶ **noun** [mass noun] the state of being intoxicated, especially by alcohol: *signs of intoxication.*

intoximeter /ɪnˈtɒksɪmiːtə/ ▶ **noun** a non-portable instrument for measuring the alcohol content of a person's breath, especially in cases of suspected drunken driving, usually sited at a police station.
– ORIGIN 1950s: from *intoxication* (see **INTOXICATE**) + **-METER**.

intra- /ˈɪntrə/ ▶ **prefix** (added to adjectives) on the inside; within: *intramural | intrauterine.*
– ORIGIN from Latin *intra* 'inside'.

intracellular ▶ **adjective** Biology located or occurring within a cell or cells: *intracellular calcium.*
– DERIVATIVES **intracellularly** adverb.

intracranial ▶ **adjective** within the skull: *intracranial haemorrhage.*
– DERIVATIVES **intracranially** adverb.

intractable /ɪnˈtraktəb(ə)l/ ▶ **adjective** hard to control or deal with: *intractable economic problems.* ■ (of a person) difficult or stubborn.
– DERIVATIVES **intractability** noun, **intractableness** noun, **intractably** adverb.
– ORIGIN late 15th cent.: from Latin *intractabilis*, from *in-* 'not' + *tractabilis* (see **TRACTABLE**).

intraday ▶ **adjective** Stock Exchange, N. Amer. occurring within one day: *the dollar slipped from an intraday high of 104.*

intradermal /ˌɪntrəˈdəːm(ə)l/ ▶ **adjective** situated or applied within the layers of the skin.
– DERIVATIVES **intradermally** adverb.

intrados /ɪnˈtreɪdɒs/ ▶ **noun** Architecture the lower or inner curve of an arch. Often contrasted with **EXTRADOS**.
– ORIGIN late 18th cent.: from French, from *intra-* 'on the inside' + *dos* 'the back' (from Latin *dorsum*).

intramolecular ▶ **adjective** existing or taking place within a molecule.
– DERIVATIVES **intramolecularly** adverb.

intramural /ˌɪntrəˈmjʊər(ə)l/ ▶ **adjective 1** situated or done within the walls of a building: *both intramural and churchyard graves.*
2 chiefly N. Amer. taking place within a single educational institution: *recreational intramural games.* ■ forming part of normal university or college studies. ■ situated or done within a community: *an intramural social symbol within the tribe.*
3 Medicine & Biology situated within the wall of a hollow organ or a cell: *an intramural haematoma.*
– DERIVATIVES **intramurally** adverb.
– ORIGIN mid 19th cent.: from **INTRA-** 'within' + Latin *murus* 'wall' + **-AL**.

intramuscular ▶ **adjective** situated or taking place within, or administered into, a muscle: *an intramuscular injection.*
– DERIVATIVES **intramuscularly** adverb.

intranet /ˈɪntrənɛt/ ▶ **noun** Computing a local or restricted communications network, especially a private network created using World Wide Web software.

intransigent /ɪnˈtransɪdʒ(ə)nt, -ˈtrɑː-, -nz-/ ▶ **adjective** unwilling or refusing to change one's views or to agree about something.
▶ **noun** an intransigent person.
– DERIVATIVES **intransigence** noun, **intransigency** noun, **intransigently** adverb.
– ORIGIN late 19th cent.: from French *intransigeant*, from Spanish *los intransigentes* (a name adopted by the extreme republicans in the Cortes, 1873–4); based on Latin *in-* 'not' + *transigere* 'come to an understanding'.

intransitive /ɪnˈtransɪtɪv, -ˈtrɑː-, -nz-/ ▶ **adjective** (of a verb or a sense or use of a verb) not taking a direct object, e.g. *look* in *look at the sky*. The opposite of **TRANSITIVE**.
– DERIVATIVES **intransitively** adverb, **intransitivity** noun.
– ORIGIN early 17th cent.: from late Latin *intransitivus* 'not passing over', from *in-* 'not' + *transitivus* (see **TRANSITIVE**).

intrapersonal ▶ **adjective** taking place or existing within the mind.

intrapreneur /ˌɪntrəprəˈnəː/ ▶ **noun** a manager within a company who promotes innovative product development and marketing.
– ORIGIN 1970s (originally US): from **INTRA-** 'within' + a shortened form of **ENTREPRENEUR**.

intraspecific ▶ **adjective** Biology produced, occurring, or existing within a species or between individuals of a single species: *intraspecific competition.*

intrathecal /ˌɪntrəˈθiːk(ə)l/ ▶ **adjective** Medicine occurring within or administered into the spinal theca: *intrathecal injection.*
– DERIVATIVES **intrathecally** adverb.

intrauterine /ˌɪntrəˈjuːtərʌɪn, -rɪn/ ▶ **adjective** within the uterus.

intrauterine device (abbrev.: **IUD**) ▶ **noun** a contraceptive device fitted inside the uterus and physically preventing the implantation of fertilized ova.

intravascular /ˌɪntrəˈvaskjʊlə/ ▶ **adjective** Medicine & Biology situated or occurring within a vessel or vessels of an animal or plant, especially within a blood vessel or blood vascular system.
– DERIVATIVES **intravascularly** adverb.

intravenous /ˌɪntrəˈviːnəs/ (abbrev.: **IV**) ▶ **adjective** existing or taking place within, or administered into, a vein or veins: *an intravenous drip.*
– DERIVATIVES **intravenously** adverb.

in tray ▶ **noun** chiefly Brit. a tray on a person's desk for letters and documents that have to be dealt with.

intrazonal ▶ **adjective** Soil Science (of a soil) having a well-developed structure different from that expected for its climatic and vegetational zone owing to the overriding influence of relief, parent material, or some other local factor.

intrepid ▶ **adjective** fearless; adventurous (often used for rhetorical or humorous effect): *our intrepid reporter.*
– DERIVATIVES **intrepidity** noun, **intrepidly** adverb.
– ORIGIN late 17th cent.: from French *intrépide* or Latin *intrepidus*, from *in-* 'not' + *trepidus* 'alarmed'.

intricacy /ˈɪntrɪkəsi/ ▶ **noun** (pl. **intricacies**) [mass noun] the quality of being intricate: *the intricacy of the procedure.* ■ (**intricacies**) details, especially of an involved or perplexing subject: *the intricacies of economic policymaking.*

intricate ▶ **adjective** very complicated or detailed: *an intricate network of canals.*
– DERIVATIVES **intricately** adverb.
– ORIGIN late Middle English: from Latin *intricat-* 'entangled', from the verb *intricare*, from *in-* 'into' + *tricae* 'tricks, perplexities'.

intrigant /ˈɪntrɪg(ə)nt/ ▶ **noun** a person who makes secret plans to do something illicit or detrimental to someone else.
– ORIGIN late 18th cent.: variant of French *intriguant*, from *intriguer* 'to intrigue'.

intrigue ▶ **verb** /ɪnˈtriːg/ (**intrigues**, **intriguing**, **intrigued**) **1** [with obj.] arouse the curiosity or interest of; fascinate: *I was intrigued by your question.*
2 [no obj.] make secret plans to do something illicit or detrimental to someone: *Henry and Louis intrigued with the local nobles.*
▶ **noun** /ˈɪntriːg, ˈɪn-/ [mass noun] **1** the secret planning of something illicit or detrimental: *the cabinet was a nest of intrigue.* ■ [count noun] a secret love affair.
2 a mysterious or fascinating quality: *within the region's borders is a wealth of interest and intrigue.*
– DERIVATIVES **intriguer** noun.
– ORIGIN early 17th cent. (in the sense 'deceive, cheat'): from French *intrigue* 'plot', *intriguer* 'to tangle, to plot', via Italian from Latin *intricare* (see **INTRICATE**). Sense 1 of the verb, which was influenced by a later French sense 'to puzzle, make curious', arose in the late 19th cent.

intriguing ▶ **adjective** arousing one's curiosity or interest; fascinating: *an intriguing story.*
– DERIVATIVES **intriguingly** adverb [sentence adverb] *intriguingly, he agreed on one condition.*

intrinsic /ɪnˈtrɪnsɪk/ ▶ **adjective** belonging naturally; essential: *access to the arts is **intrinsic to** a high quality of life.*
– DERIVATIVES **intrinsically** adverb.
– ORIGIN late 15th cent. (in the general sense 'interior, inner'): from French *intrinsèque*, from late Latin *intrinsecus*, from the earlier adverb *intrinsecus* 'inwardly, inwards'.

intrinsic factor ▶ **noun** [mass noun] Biochemistry a substance secreted by the stomach which enables the body to absorb vitamin B_{12}. It is a glycoprotein.

intro ▶ **noun** (pl. **intros**) informal an introduction.
– ORIGIN early 19th cent.: abbreviation.

intro- ▶ **prefix** into; inwards: *introgression | introvert.*
– ORIGIN from Latin *intro* 'to the inside'.

introduce ▶ **verb** [with obj.] **1** bring (something, especially a product, measure, or concept) into use or operation for the first time: *various new taxes were introduced | measures were introduced to help families with children.* ■ bring (a plant, animal, or disease) to a place for the first time: *horses and sheep **introduced to** the island did not survive.* ■ (**introduce something to**) bring a subject to the attention of (someone) for the first time: *the programme is a bid to introduce opera to the masses.* ■ present (a new piece of legislation) for debate in a legislative assembly: *bills can be introduced in either House of Parliament.*
2 make (someone) known by name to another in person, especially formally: *I must **introduce** you **to** my wife | he introduced himself as Detective Sergeant Fraser.*
3 insert or bring into something: *a device which introduces chlorine into the pool automatically.*
4 occur at the start of; open: *a longer, more lyrical opening which introduces a courting song.* ■ (of a person) provide an opening explanation or announcement for (a television or radio programme, book, etc.).
– DERIVATIVES **introducer** noun.
– ORIGIN late Middle English (in the sense 'bring (a person) into a place or group'): from Latin *introducere*, from *intro-* 'to the inside' + *ducere* 'to lead'.

introduction ▶ **noun 1** [mass noun] the action of introducing something: *issues arising from the introduction of new technology | the introduction of muskrats into central Europe.* ■ [count noun] a thing newly brought into use or introduced to a place for the first time: *despite the new introductions, many of the older species remain firm favourites.*
2 a formal presentation of one person to another, in which each is told the other's name: *he returned to his desk, leaving Michael to make the introductions |* [mass noun] *a letter of introduction.*
3 a thing preliminary to something else, especially an explanatory section at the beginning of a book, report, or speech. ■ a preliminary section in a piece of music, often thematically different from the main section. ■ a book or course of study intended to introduce a subject to a person: *a good general introduction to the subject is A Social History of England.* ■ [in sing.] a person's first experience of a subject or thing: ***my introduction to** drama was through an amateur dramatic society.*
– ORIGIN late Middle English: from Latin *introductio(n-)*, from the verb *introducere* (see **INTRODUCE**).

introductory ▶ **adjective** serving as an introduction to a subject or topic; basic or preliminary: *a two-day introductory course.* ■ intended to persuade someone to purchase something for the first time: *we are making a special introductory offer of a reduced subscription.*
– ORIGIN late Middle English (as a noun denoting an introductory text): from late Latin *introductorius*, from Latin *introducere* (see **INTRODUCE**).

introgression /ˌɪntrə(ʊ)ˈgrɛʃ(ə)n/ ▶ **noun** [mass noun] Biology the transfer of genetic information from one species to another as a result of hybridization between them and repeated backcrossing.
– DERIVATIVES **introgressive** adjective.
– ORIGIN mid 17th cent.: from Latin *introgredi* 'step in', from *intro-* 'to the inside' + *gradi* 'proceed, walk', on the pattern of *egression, ingression.*

introit /ˈɪntrɔɪt, ɪnˈtrəʊɪt/ ▶ **noun** a psalm or antiphon sung or said while the priest approaches the altar for the Eucharist.
– ORIGIN late Middle English (denoting an entrance or the action of going in): via Old French from Latin *introitus*, from *introire* 'enter', from *intro-* 'to the inside' + *ire* 'go'.

introjection /ˌɪntrə(ʊ)ˈdʒɛkʃ(ə)n/ ▶ **noun** [mass noun] Psychoanalysis the unconscious adoption of the ideas or attitudes of others.
– DERIVATIVES **introject** verb.
– ORIGIN mid 19th cent.: from **INTRO-** 'into', on the pattern of *projection.*

I

intromission ▶ noun the action or process of inserting the penis into the vagina in sexual intercourse.

intromittent organ /ˌɪntrə(ʊ)ˈmɪt(ə)nt/ ▶ noun Zoology the male copulatory organ of an animal.
– ORIGIN mid 19th cent.: *intromittent* from Latin *intromittent-* 'introducing', from the verb *intromittere*, from *intro-* 'to the inside' + *mittere* 'send'.

intron /ˈɪntrɒn/ ▶ noun Biochemistry a segment of a DNA or RNA molecule which does not code for proteins and interrupts the sequence of genes. Compare with EXON[1].
– DERIVATIVES **intronic** adjective.
– ORIGIN 1970s: from INTRA- 'within' + -ON.

introrse /ɪnˈtrɔːs/ ▶ adjective Botany & Zoology turned inwards. The opposite of EXTRORSE. ■ (of anthers) releasing their pollen towards the centre of the flower.
– ORIGIN mid 19th cent.: from Latin *introrsus*, from *introversus* 'turned inwards'.

introspect /ˌɪntrə(ʊ)ˈspɛkt/ ▶ verb [no obj.] examine one's own thoughts or feelings: *what they don't do is introspect much about the reasons for their plight*.
– ORIGIN late 17th cent.: from Latin *introspect-* 'looked into', from the verb *introspicere*, or from *introspectare* 'keep looking into'.

introspection ▶ noun [mass noun] the examination or observation of one's own mental and emotional processes: *quiet introspection can be extremely valuable*.

introspective ▶ adjective characterized by or given to introspection: *he grew withdrawn and introspective*.
– DERIVATIVES **introspectively** adverb, **introspectiveness** noun.

introvert ▶ noun a shy, reticent person. ■ Psychology a person predominantly concerned with their own thoughts and feelings rather than with external things. Compare with EXTROVERT.
▶ adjective another term for INTROVERTED.
– DERIVATIVES **introversion** noun, **introversive** /-ˈvəːsɪv/ adjective.
– ORIGIN mid 17th cent. (as a verb in the general sense 'turn one's thoughts inwards (in spiritual contemplation)'): from modern Latin *introvertere*, from *intro-* 'to the inside' + *vertere* 'to turn'. Its use as a term in psychology dates from the early 20th cent.

introverted ▶ adjective **1** of, denoting, or typical of an introvert. ■ (of a community, company, or other group) concerned principally with its own affairs; inward-looking or parochial.
2 Anatomy & Zoology (of an organ or other body part) turned or pushed inward on itself.

intrude ▶ verb **1** [no obj.] put oneself deliberately into a place or situation where one is unwelcome or uninvited: *he had no right to* ***intrude into*** *their lives | she felt awkward at* ***intruding on*** *private grief*. ■ enter with disruptive or adverse effect: *the noise began to* ***intrude into*** *her thoughts*. ■ [with obj.] introduce (something) into a situation with disruptive or adverse effect: *to* ***intrude*** *political criteria* ***into*** *military decisions risks reducing efficiency*.
2 [with obj.] Geology (of igneous rock) be forced or thrust into (an existing formation): *the granite may have intruded these rock layers*. ■ force or thrust (igneous rock) into an existing formation.
– ORIGIN mid 16th cent. (in the sense 'usurp an office or right'; originally as *entrude*): from Latin *intrudere*, from *in-* 'into' + *trudere* 'to thrust'.

intruder ▶ noun a person who intrudes, especially into a building with criminal intent.

intrusion ▶ noun [mass noun] **1** the action of intruding: *he was furious about this* ***intrusion into*** *his private life | [count noun] unacceptable intrusions of privacy*. ■ [count noun] a thing that intrudes: *villagers say the noise is an intrusion on their lives*.
2 Geology the action or process of forcing a body of igneous rock between or through existing formations, without reaching the surface. ■ [count noun] a body of igneous rock which has intruded the surrounding strata.
– ORIGIN late Middle English (in the sense 'invasion, usurpation'): from medieval Latin *intrusio(n-)*, from Latin *intrudere* 'thrust in' (see INTRUDE).

intrusive ▶ adjective **1** causing disruption or annoyance through being unwelcome or uninvited: *that was an intrusive question | tourist attractions that are environmentally intrusive*.
2 Phonetics (of a sound) pronounced between words or syllables to facilitate pronunciation, such as an *r* in *saw a film*.
3 Geology relating to or formed by intrusion.
– DERIVATIVES **intrusively** adverb, **intrusiveness** noun.

intrust ▶ verb archaic spelling of ENTRUST.

intubate /ˈɪntjʊbeɪt/ ▶ verb [with obj.] Medicine insert a tube into (a person or a body part, especially the trachea for ventilation).
– DERIVATIVES **intubation** noun.
– ORIGIN late 19th cent.: from IN-[2] 'into' + Latin *tuba* 'tube' + -ATE[3].

intuit /ɪnˈtjuːɪt/ ▶ verb [with obj.] understand or work out by instinct: *I intuited his real identity*.
– DERIVATIVES **intuitable** adjective.
– ORIGIN late 18th cent. (in the sense 'instruct, teach'): from Latin *intuit-* 'contemplated', from the verb *intueri*, from *in-* 'upon' + *tueri* 'to look'.

intuition ▶ noun [mass noun] the ability to understand something instinctively, without the need for conscious reasoning: *we shall allow our intuition to guide us*. ■ [count noun] a thing that one knows or considers likely from instinctive feeling rather than conscious reasoning: *your insights and intuitions as a native speaker are positively sought*.
– DERIVATIVES **intuitional** adjective.
– ORIGIN late Middle English (denoting spiritual insight or immediate spiritual communication): from late Latin *intuitio(n-)*, from Latin *intueri* 'consider' (see INTUIT).

intuitionism (also **intuitionalism**) ▶ noun [mass noun] Philosophy the theory that primary truths and principles (especially those of ethics and metaphysics) are known directly by intuition. ■ the theory that mathematical knowledge is based on intuition and mental construction, rejecting certain modes of reasoning and the notion of independent mathematical objects.
– DERIVATIVES **intuitionist** noun & adjective.

intuitive ▶ adjective using or based on what one feels to be true even without conscious reasoning; instinctive: *his intuitive understanding of the readers' real needs*. ■ (chiefly of computer software) easy to use and understand.
– DERIVATIVES **intuitively** adverb, **intuitiveness** noun.
– ORIGIN late 15th cent. (originally used of sight, in the sense 'accurate, unerring'): from medieval Latin *intuitivus*, from Latin *intueri* (see INTUIT).

intumesce /ˌɪntjʊˈmɛs/ ▶ verb [no obj.] rare swell up.
– DERIVATIVES **intumescence** noun.
– ORIGIN late 18th cent.: from Latin *intumescere*, from *in-* 'into' + *tumescere* 'begin to swell' (from *tumere* 'swell').

intumescent ▶ adjective (of a coating or sealant) swelling up when heated, thus protecting the material underneath or sealing a gap in the event of a fire.

intussusception /ˌɪntəsəˈsɛpʃ(ə)n/ ▶ noun **1** Medicine an instance of the inversion of one portion of the intestine within another.
2 [mass noun] Botany the growth of a cell wall by the deposition of cellulose.
– ORIGIN early 18th cent. (in the sense 'absorption'): from modern Latin *intussusceptio(n-)*, from Latin *intus* 'within' + *susceptio(n-)* (from *suscipere* 'take up').

intwine ▶ verb archaic spelling of ENTWINE.

Inuit /ˈɪnjʊɪt, ˈɪnʊɪt/ ▶ noun **1** [as plural noun] the members of an indigenous people of northern Canada and parts of Greenland and Alaska.
2 [mass noun] the language of the Inuit, one of the three branches of the Eskimo-Aleut language family, with about 60,000 speakers. It is also known as **Inupiaq** or (especially to its speakers) as **Inuktitut**.
▶ adjective relating to the Inuit or their language.
– ORIGIN Inuit, plural of *inuk* 'person'.

> **USAGE** The peoples inhabiting the regions from the central Canadian Arctic to western Greenland prefer to be called **Inuit** rather than **Eskimo**, and this term now has official status in Canada. By analogy, the term **Inuit** is also used as a synonym for **Eskimo** in general. However, this latter use, in including people from Siberia who are not Inupiaq-speakers, is, strictly speaking, not accurate. See also USAGE at ESKIMO.

Inuk /ˈɪnʊk/ ▶ noun (pl. **Inuit**) a member of the Inuit people.
– ORIGIN Inuit, literally 'person'.

Inuktitut /ɪˈnʊktɪtʊt/ (also **Inuktituk** /-tʊk/) ▶ noun [mass noun] the Inuit language.
– ORIGIN Inuit, literally 'the Inuk way', used as the title of a periodical.

inulin /ˈɪnjʊlɪn/ ▶ noun [mass noun] Biochemistry a complex of sugar present in the roots of various plants and used medically to test kidney function. It is a polysaccharide based on fructose.
– ORIGIN early 19th cent.: from Latin *inula* (identified by medieval herbalists with elecampane) + -IN[1].

inunction /ɪˈnʌŋ(k)ʃ(ə)n/ ▶ noun [mass noun] chiefly Medicine the rubbing of ointment or oil into the skin.
– ORIGIN late 15th cent.: from Latin *inunctio(n-)*, from *inunguere* 'smear on'.

inundate /ˈɪnʌndeɪt/ ▶ verb [with obj.] **1** overwhelm (someone) with things or people to be dealt with: *we've been* ***inundated with*** *complaints from listeners*.
2 flood: *the islands may be the first to be inundated as sea levels rise*.
– ORIGIN late 16th cent.: (earlier (late Middle English) as *inundation*) from Latin *inundat-* 'flooded', from the verb *inundare*, from *in-* 'into, upon' + *undare* 'to flow' (from *unda* 'a wave').

inundation ▶ noun **1** an overwhelming abundance of people or things: *an inundation of rugby fans*.
2 flooding: *the annual inundation of the Nile | [mass noun] areas were at risk of inundation*.

Inupiaq /ɪˈnuːpɪak/ (also **Inupiat** /-pɪat/, **Inupik** /-pɪk/) ▶ noun (pl. **same**) **1** a member of a group of Inuit people inhabiting northern Alaska.
2 [mass noun] the Inuit language.
▶ adjective relating to the Inupiaq or their language.
– ORIGIN Inuit, from *inuk* 'person' + *piaq* 'genuine'.

inure /ɪˈnjʊə, ɪˈnjɔː/ ▶ verb [with obj.] **1** (usu. **be inured to**) accustom (someone) to something, especially something unpleasant: *these children have been inured to violence*.
2 Law variant spelling of ENURE (sense 1).
– DERIVATIVES **inurement** noun.
– ORIGIN late Middle English *inure, enure*, from an Anglo-Norman French phrase meaning 'in use or practice', from *en* 'in' + Old French *euvre* 'work' (from Latin *opera*).

inurn ▶ verb [with obj.] place or bury (something, especially ashes after cremation) in an urn.

in utero /ɪn ˈjuːtərəʊ/ ▶ adverb & adjective in a woman's uterus; before birth: [as adv.] *this damage may occur in utero* | [as adj.] *the in utero development of the gastrointestinal tract*.
– ORIGIN Latin.

inutile /ɪnˈjuːtɪl/ ▶ adjective formal useless; pointless.
– DERIVATIVES **inutility** noun.
– ORIGIN late Middle English: from Old French, from Latin *inutilis*, from *in-* 'not' + *utilis* 'useful'.

in vacuo /ɪn ˈvakjʊəʊ/ ▶ adverb in a vacuum. ■ away from or without the normal context or environment: *instead of dealing with individual aspects of lifestyle in vacuo, social factors are taken into account*.
– ORIGIN Latin.

invade ▶ verb [with obj.] (of an armed force) enter (a country or region) so as to subjugate or occupy it: *during the Second World War the island was invaded by the Axis powers*. ■ enter (a place, situation, or sphere of activity) in large numbers, especially with intrusive effect: *demonstrators invaded the Presidential Palace*. ■ (of a parasite or disease) spread into (an organism or bodily part). ■ encroach or intrude on: *he felt his privacy was being invaded*.
– ORIGIN late Middle English (in the sense 'attack or assault (a person)'): from Latin *invadere*, from *in-* 'into' + *vadere* 'go'.

invader ▶ noun a person or group that invades a country, region, or other place: *it is a country that has repelled all invaders*.

invaginate /ɪnˈvadʒɪneɪt/ ▶ verb (**be invaginated**) chiefly Anatomy & Biology be turned inside out or folded back on itself to form a cavity or pouch.
– ORIGIN mid 17th cent.: back-formation from INVAGINATION.

invagination ▶ noun [mass noun] chiefly Anatomy & Biology the action or process of being turned inside out or folded back on itself to form a cavity or pouch. ■ [count noun] a cavity or pouch so formed.
– ORIGIN mid 17th cent.: from modern Latin *invaginatio(n-)*, based on IN-[2] 'into' + Latin *vagina* 'sheath'.

invalid[1] /ˈɪnvəlɪd/ ▶ noun a person made weak or disabled by illness or injury.
▶ verb (**invalids, invaliding, invalided**) [with obj.] remove (someone) from active service in the armed forces because of injury or illness: *he was badly wounded and* ***invalided out of*** *the infantry*. ■ disable (someone) by injury or illness: *an officer invalided by a chest wound*.
– DERIVATIVES **invalidism** noun.

– ORIGIN mid 17th cent. (as an adjective in the sense 'infirm or disabled'): a special sense of **INVALID²**, with a change of pronunciation.

invalid² /ɪnˈvalɪd/ ▶ **adjective** not valid, in particular: ■ (especially of an official document or procedure) not legally recognized because it contravenes a regulation or law: *the vote was declared invalid due to a technicality.* ■ (especially of an argument, statement, or theory) not true because based on erroneous information or unsound reasoning: *a comparison is invalid if we are not comparing like with like.* ■ (of computer instructions, data, etc.) not conforming to the correct format or specifications.
– DERIVATIVES **invalidly** adverb.
– ORIGIN mid 16th cent. (earlier than *valid*): from Latin *invalidus*, from *in-* 'not' + *validus* 'strong' (see **VALID**).

invalidate ▶ **verb** [with obj.] **1** make or prove (an argument, statement, or theory) unsound or erroneous. **2** deprive (an official document or procedure) of legal validity because it contravenes a regulation or law: *a technical flaw in her papers invalidated her nomination.*
– DERIVATIVES **invalidation** noun.
– ORIGIN mid 17th cent.: from medieval Latin *invalidat-* 'annulled', from the verb *invalidare* (based on Latin *validus* 'strong').

invalidity ▶ **noun** [mass noun] **1** Brit. the condition of being an invalid.
2 the fact of not being valid.

invaluable ▶ **adjective** extremely useful; indispensable: *an invaluable source of information.*
– DERIVATIVES **invaluably** adverb.

Invar /ˈɪnvɑː/ ▶ **noun** [mass noun] trademark an alloy of iron and nickel with a negligible coefficient of expansion, used in the making of clocks and scientific instruments.
– ORIGIN early 20th cent.: abbreviation of **INVARIABLE**.

invariable ▶ **adjective** never changing: *his routine was invariable.* ■ Grammar (of a noun in an inflected language) having the same form in both the singular and the plural, as does *relais* in French. ■ Mathematics (of a quantity) constant.
– DERIVATIVES **invariability** noun, **invariableness** noun.
– ORIGIN late Middle English: from French, or from late Latin *invariabilis*, from *in-* 'not' + *variabilis* (see **VARIABLE**).

invariably ▶ **adverb** in every case or on every occasion; always: *ranch meals are invariably big and hearty.*

invariant ▶ **adjective** never changing: *the pattern of cell divisions was found to be invariant.*
▶ **noun** Mathematics a function, quantity, or property which remains unchanged when a specified transformation is applied.
– DERIVATIVES **invariance** noun.

invasion ▶ **noun** an instance of invading a country or region with an armed force: *Napoleon's disastrous invasion of Russia in 1812* | [mass noun] *in 1546 England had to be defended from invasion.* ■ an incursion by a large number of people or things into a place or sphere of activity: *there was a brief pitch invasion when Sunderland scored.* ■ an unwelcome intrusion into another's domain: *random drug testing of employees is an unwarranted invasion of privacy.*
– ORIGIN late Middle English: from late Latin *invasio(n-)*, from the verb *invadere* (see **INVADE**).

invasive ▶ **adjective** tending to spread very quickly and undesirably or harmfully: *patients suffering from invasive cancer.* ■ tending to intrude on a person's thoughts or privacy: *the sound of the piano was invasive.* ■ (of medical procedures) involving the introduction of instruments or other objects into the body or body cavities: *minimally invasive surgery.*
– DERIVATIVES **invasively** adverb, **invasiveness** noun.
– ORIGIN late Middle English: from obsolete French *invasif*, *-ive* or medieval Latin *invasivus*, from Latin *invadere* (see **INVADE**).

invected ▶ **adjective** [usu. postpositive] Heraldry having convex semicircular projections along the edge. Compare with **ENGRAILED**.

invective ▶ **noun** [mass noun] insulting, abusive, or highly critical language: *he let out a stream of invective.*
– ORIGIN late Middle English (originally as an adjective meaning 'reviling, abusive'): from Old French *invectif*, *-ive*, from late Latin *invectivus* 'attacking', from *invehere* (see **INVEIGH**). The noun is from late Latin *invectiva (oratio)* 'abusive or censorious (language)'.

inveigh /ɪnˈveɪ/ ▶ **verb** [no obj.] (**inveigh against**) speak or write about (something) with great hostility: *he liked to inveigh against all forms of academic training.*
– ORIGIN late 15th cent. (in the sense 'carry in, introduce'; formerly also as *enveigh*): from Latin *invehere* 'carry in', *invehi* 'be carried into, assail', from *in-* 'into' + *vehere* 'carry'.

inveigle /ɪnˈviːɡ(ə)l, ɪnˈveɪɡ(ə)l/ ▶ **verb** [with obj. and adverbial] persuade (someone) to do something by means of deception or flattery: *he inveigled her back to his room.* ■ (**inveigle oneself** or **one's way into**) gain entrance to (a place) by using such methods: *Jones had inveigled himself into her house.*
– ORIGIN late 15th cent. (in the sense 'beguile, deceive'; formerly also as *enveigle*): from Anglo-Norman French *envegler*, alteration of Old French *aveugler* 'to blind', from *aveugle* 'blind'.

invent ▶ **verb** [with obj.] create or design (something that has not existed before); be the originator of: *he invented an improved form of the steam engine.* ■ make up (an idea, name, story, etc.), especially so as to deceive someone: *I did not have to invent any tales about my past.*
– ORIGIN late 15th cent. (in the sense 'find out, discover'): from Latin *invent-* 'contrived, discovered', from the verb *invenire*, from *in-* 'into' + *venire* 'come'.

invention ▶ **noun** [mass noun] the action of inventing something, typically a process or device: *the invention of printing in the 15th century.* ■ [count noun] something, typically a process or device, that has been invented: *medieval inventions included spectacles for reading and the spinning wheel.* ■ creative ability: *his powers of invention were rather limited.* ■ [count noun] something fabricated or made up: *you know my story is an invention.* ■ used as a title for a short piece of music: *Bach's two-part Inventions.*
– ORIGIN Middle English (in the sense 'finding out, discovery'): from Latin *inventio(n-)*, from *invenire* 'discover' (see **INVENT**).

Invention of the Cross ▶ **noun** a festival, held on 3 May (Holy Rood Day), commemorating the reputed finding of the Cross of Christ by Helena, mother of the emperor Constantine, in AD 326.

inventive ▶ **adjective** having the ability to create or design new things or to think originally: *the most inventive composer of his time.* ■ showing creativity or original thought: *a courageous and inventive piece of film-making.*
– DERIVATIVES **inventively** adverb.
– ORIGIN late Middle English: from French *inventif*, *-ive* or medieval Latin *inventivus*, from Latin *invenire* 'discover' (see **INVENT**).

inventiveness ▶ **noun** [mass noun] the quality of being inventive; creativity: *the inventiveness of the staging.*

inventor ▶ **noun** a person who invented a particular process or device or who invents things as an occupation.

inventory /ˈɪnv(ə)nt(ə)ri/ ▶ **noun** (pl. **inventories**) a complete list of items such as property, goods in stock, or the contents of a building. ■ chiefly N. Amer. a quantity of merchandise or goods held in stock. ■ (in accounting) the entire stock of a business, including materials, components, work in progress, and finished product.
▶ **verb** (**inventories**, **inventorying**, **inventoried**) [with obj.] make a complete list of. ■ enter in a list: *every book was inventoried.*
– ORIGIN late Middle English: from medieval Latin *inventorium*, alteration of late Latin *inventarium*, literally 'a list of what is found', from Latin *invenire* 'come upon'.

inventress ▶ **noun** rare a female inventor.

inveracity /ˌɪnvəˈrasɪti/ ▶ **noun** (pl. **inveracities**) formal a lie. ■ [mass noun] untruthfulness.

Invercargill /ˌɪnvəˈkɑːɡɪl/ a city in New Zealand, in the South Island; pop. 50,328 (2006).

Inverness /ˌɪnvəˈnɛs/ a city in Scotland, administrative centre of Highland council area, situated at the mouth of the River Ness; pop. 41,200 (est. 2009).

inverse /ˈɪnvəːs, ɪnˈvəːs/ ▶ **adjective** [attrib.] opposite or contrary in position, direction, order, or effect: *numerous studies have shown an inverse relationship between exercise and the risk of heart disease.* ■ chiefly Mathematics produced from or related to something else by a process of inversion: *inverse logarithms.*
▶ **noun 1** [usu. in sing.] something that is the opposite or reverse of something else: *power is the inverse of dependence.*
2 Mathematics a reciprocal quantity, mathematical expression, geometric figure, etc. which is the result of inversion. ■ an element which, when combined with a given element in an operation, produces the identity element for that operation.
– DERIVATIVES **inversely** adverb.
– ORIGIN late Middle English: from Latin *inversus*, past participle of *invertere* (see **INVERT¹**).

inverse proportion (also **inverse ratio**) ▶ **noun** a relation between two quantities such that one increases in proportion as the other decreases.

inverse square law ▶ **noun** Physics a law stating that the intensity of an effect such as illumination or gravitational force changes in inverse proportion to the square of the distance from the source.

inversion ▶ **noun 1** [mass noun] the action of inverting something or the state of being inverted: *the inversion of the normal domestic arrangement* | [count noun] *an inversion of traditional customer–supplier relationships.* ■ reversal of the normal order of words, typically for rhetorical effect but also found in the regular formation of questions in English. ■ Music the process of inverting an interval, chord, or phrase. ■ [count noun] Music an inverted interval, chord, or phrase. ■ Physics (also **population inversion**) a transposition in the relative numbers of atoms, molecules, etc. occupying particular energy levels. ■ Chemistry a reaction causing a change from one optically active configuration to the opposite configuration, especially the hydrolysis of dextrose to give a laevorotatory solution of fructose and glucose.
2 (also **temperature** or **thermal inversion**) a reversal of the normal decrease of air temperature with altitude, or of water temperature with depth. ■ (also **inversion layer**) a layer of the atmosphere in which temperature increases with height.
3 [mass noun] Mathematics the process of finding a quantity, function, etc. from a given one such that the product of the two under a particular operation is the identity. ■ the interchanging of numerator and denominator of a fraction, or antecedent and consequent of a ratio. ■ the process of finding the expression which gives a given expression under a given transformation. ■ [count noun] Geometry a transformation in which each point of a given figure is replaced by another point on the same straight line from a fixed point, especially in such a way that the product of the distances of the two points from the centre of inversion is constant.
4 (also **sexual inversion**) Psychology, dated homosexuality.
– DERIVATIVES **inversive** adjective.
– ORIGIN mid 16th cent. (as a term in rhetoric, denoting the turning of an argument against the person who put it forward): from Latin *inversio(n-)*, from the verb *invertere* (see **INVERT¹**).

I

inversion temperature ▶ **noun** Physics the temperature at which the Joule–Thomson effect for a given gas changes sign, so that the gas is neither heated nor cooled when allowed to expand without expending energy.

invert¹ ▶ **verb** /ɪnˈvəːt/ [with obj.] put upside down or in the opposite position, order, or arrangement: *invert the mousse on to a serving plate.* ■ Music modify (a phrase) by reversing the direction of pitch changes. ■ Music alter (an interval or triad) by changing the relative position of the notes in it. ■ chiefly Mathematics subject to inversion; transform into its inverse.
▶ **noun** /ˈɪnvəːt/ **1** an arch constructed in an upside-down position to provide lateral support, e.g. in a tunnel. ■ the concave lower surface of a sewer or drain.
2 Psychology, dated a homosexual.
3 Philately a postage stamp printed with an error such that all or part of its design is upside down.
– DERIVATIVES **invertibility** noun, **invertible** adjective.
– ORIGIN mid 16th cent. (in the sense 'turn back to front'): from Latin *invertere*, literally 'turn inside out', from *in-* 'into' + *vertere* 'to turn'.

invert² /ˈɪnvəːt/ ▶ **noun** informal short for **INVERTEBRATE**.

invertase /ˈɪnvəːteɪz, ɪnˈvəːt-/ ▶ **noun** [mass noun] Biochemistry an enzyme produced by yeast which catalyses the hydrolysis of sucrose, forming invert sugar.

invertebrate /ɪnˈvəːtɪbrət/ ▶ **noun** an animal lacking a backbone, such as an arthropod, mollusc, annelid, coelenterate, etc. The invertebrates constitute an artificial division of the animal kingdom, comprising 95 per cent of animal species and about thirty different phyla. Compare with **VERTEBRATE**.
▶ **adjective** relating to or belonging to this division of animals.

– ORIGIN early 19th cent. (as a noun): from modern Latin *invertebrata* (plural) 'the invertebrates' (former taxonomic group), from French *invertébrés*, from *in-* 'without' + Latin *vertebra* (see VERTEBRA).

inverted comma ▶ noun chiefly Brit. another term for QUOTATION MARK.

inverted snobbery ▶ noun [mass noun] derogatory the attitude of seeming to despise anything associated with wealth or social status, while at the same time elevating those things associated with lack of wealth and social position.
– DERIVATIVES **inverted snob** noun.

inverter ▶ noun **1** an apparatus which converts direct current into alternating current.
2 Electronics a device that converts either of the two binary digits or signals into the other.

invert sugar ▶ noun [mass noun] a mixture of glucose and fructose obtained by the hydrolysis of sucrose.
– ORIGIN late 19th cent.: *invert* from *inverted*, because of the reversal of optical activity involved in its formation (see the chemical sense of INVERSION).

invest ▶ verb [with obj.] **1** put (money) into financial schemes, shares, property, or a commercial venture with the expectation of achieving a profit: *the company is to **invest** £12 m **in** its manufacturing site at Linlithglow* | [no obj.] *getting workers to **invest in** private pension funds.* ■ devote (one's time, effort, or energy) to a particular undertaking with the expectation of a worthwhile result: *we have **invested** a considerable amount of time **in** demonstrating the value of the system.* ■ [no obj.] (**invest in**) informal buy (a relatively expensive product) whose usefulness will repay the cost: *I invested in an expensive moisturizer and tried to drink more water.*
2 (**invest someone/thing with**) provide or endow someone or something with (a particular quality or attribute): *the passage of time has invested the words with an unintended humour.* ■ formally confer a rank or office on (someone): *he was invested as Head of State on 1 October 1936.* ■ (**invest something in**) confer a right or power on (someone or something): *all executive powers were invested in the Secretary of State.*
3 archaic clothe or cover with a garment: *he stands before you **invested in** the full canonicals of his calling.*
4 archaic surround (a place) in order to besiege or blockade it: *Fort Pulaski was invested and captured.*
– DERIVATIVES **investable** adjective, **investible** adjective, **investor** noun.
– ORIGIN mid 16th cent. (in the senses 'clothe', 'clothe with the insignia of a rank', and 'endow with authority'): from French *investir* or Latin *investire*, from *in-* 'into, upon' + *vestire* 'clothe' (from *vestis* 'clothing'). Sense 1 (early 17th cent.) is influenced by Italian *investire*.

investigable ▶ adjective open to investigation, inquiry, or research.
– ORIGIN late 16th cent.: from late Latin *investigabilis*, from *investigare* (see INVESTIGATE).

investigate ▶ verb [with obj.] carry out a systematic or formal inquiry to discover and examine the facts of (an incident, allegation, etc.) so as to establish the truth: *police are investigating a claim that the man was beaten unconscious by a gang.* ■ carry out research or study into (a subject or problem, typically one in a scientific or academic field): [with clause] *future studies will investigate whether long-term use of the drugs could prevent cancer.* ■ make inquiries as to the character, activities, or background of (someone): *everyone with a possible interest in your brother's death must be thoroughly investigated.* ■ [no obj.] make a check to find out something: *when you didn't turn up I thought I'd better come back to investigate.*
– DERIVATIVES **investigatory** adjective.
– ORIGIN early 16th cent.: from Latin *investigat-* 'traced out', from the verb *investigare*, from *in-* 'into' + *vestigare* 'track, trace out'.

investigation ▶ noun [mass noun] the action of investigating something or someone; formal or systematic examination or research: *he is **under investigation** for receiving illicit funds.* ■ [count noun] a formal inquiry or systematic study: *an **investigation into** fresh allegations of malpractice* | *a murder investigation.*
– DERIVATIVES **investigational** adjective.
– ORIGIN late Middle English: from Latin *investigatio(n-)*, from the verb *investigare* (see INVESTIGATE).

investigative /ɪnˈvɛstɪɡətɪv, -ɡeɪtɪv/ ▶ adjective of or concerned with investigating something: *a special investigative committee to look into the strikers' demands.* ■ (of journalism or a journalist) inquiring intensively into and seeking to expose malpractice, the miscarriage of justice, or other controversial issues.

investigator ▶ noun a person who carries out a formal inquiry or investigation: *accident investigators are at the crash site.*

investiture /ɪnˈvɛstɪtjə, -tʃə/ ▶ noun [mass noun] the action of formally investing a person with honours or rank: *the investiture of bishops.* ■ [count noun] a ceremony at which honours or rank are formally conferred on a particular person.
– ORIGIN late Middle English: from medieval Latin *investitura*, from *investire* (see INVEST).

investment ▶ noun **1** [mass noun] the action or process of investing money for profit: *a debate over private **investment in** road-building* | *the need to attract foreign investment* | [count noun] *a total investment of £50,000.* ■ [count noun] a thing that is worth buying because it may be profitable or useful in the future: *freezers really are a good investment for the elderly.* ■ [count noun] an act of devoting time, effort, or energy to a particular undertaking with the expectation of a worthwhile result: *the time spent in attending the seminar is an investment in our professional futures.*
2 [mass noun] archaic the surrounding of a place by a hostile force in order to besiege or blockade it.

investment bank ▶ noun a bank that purchases large holdings of newly issued shares and resells them to investors.
– DERIVATIVES **investment banker** noun, **investment banking** noun.

investment bond ▶ noun (in the UK) a single-premium life insurance policy linked to a unit trust for long-term investment.

investment casting ▶ noun [mass noun] technical a technique for making small, accurate castings in refractory alloys using a mould formed around a pattern of wax or similar material which is then removed by melting.

investment grade ▶ noun [mass noun] a level of credit rating for stocks regarded as carrying a minimal risk to investors.

investment trust ▶ noun a limited company whose business is the investment of shareholders' funds, the shares being traded like those of any other public company.

inveterate /ɪnˈvɛt(ə)rət/ ▶ adjective [attrib.] having a particular habit, activity, or interest that is long-established and unlikely to change: *an inveterate gambler.* ■ (of a feeling or habit) long-established and unlikely to change.
– DERIVATIVES **inveteracy** noun, **inveterately** adverb.
– ORIGIN late Middle English (referring to disease, in the sense 'of long standing, chronic'): from Latin *inveteratus* 'made old', past participle of *inveterare* (based on *vetus, veter-* 'old').

inviable ▶ adjective not viable.
– DERIVATIVES **inviability** noun.

invidious /ɪnˈvɪdɪəs/ ▶ adjective (of an action or situation) likely to arouse or incur resentment or anger in others: *she'd put herself in an invidious position.* ■ (of a comparison or distinction) unfairly discriminating; unjust: *it seems invidious to make special mention of one aspect of his work.*
– DERIVATIVES **invidiously** adverb, **invidiousness** noun.
– ORIGIN early 17th cent.: from Latin *invidiosus*, from *invidia* (see ENVY).

invigilate /ɪnˈvɪdʒɪleɪt/ ▶ verb [no obj.] Brit. supervise candidates during an examination.
– DERIVATIVES **invigilation** noun, **invigilator** noun.
– ORIGIN mid 16th cent. (in the general sense 'watch over, keep watch'): from Latin *invigilat-* 'watched over', from the verb *invigilare*, from *in-* 'upon, towards' + *vigilare* 'watch' (from *vigil* 'watchful').

invigorate /ɪnˈvɪɡəreɪt/ ▶ verb [with obj.] give strength or energy to: *the shower had invigorated her.*
– DERIVATIVES **invigoration** noun, **invigorator** noun.
– ORIGIN mid 17th cent.: from medieval Latin *invigorat-* 'made strong', from the verb *invigorare*, from *in-* 'towards' + Latin *vigorare* 'make strong' (from *vigor* 'vigour').

invigorating ▶ adjective making one feel strong, healthy, and full of energy: *a brisk, invigorating walk.*
– DERIVATIVES **invigoratingly** adverb.

invincible /ɪnˈvɪnsɪb(ə)l/ ▶ adjective too powerful to be defeated or overcome: *an invincible warrior.*
– DERIVATIVES **invincibility** noun, **invincibly** adverb.
– ORIGIN late Middle English (earlier than *vincible*): via Old French from Latin *invincibilis*, from *in-* 'not' + *vincibilis* (see VINCIBLE).

in vino veritas /ɪn ˌviːnəʊ ˈvɛrɪtɑːs/ ▶ exclamation under the influence of alcohol, a person tells the truth.
– ORIGIN Latin, literally 'truth in wine'.

inviolable /ɪnˈvʌɪələb(ə)l/ ▶ adjective never to be broken, infringed, or dishonoured: *an inviolable rule of chastity* | *the Polish–German border was inviolable.*
– DERIVATIVES **inviolability** noun, **inviolably** adverb.
– ORIGIN late Middle English: from French, or from Latin *inviolabilis*, from *in-* 'not' + *violabilis* 'able to be violated' (from the verb *violare*).

inviolate /ɪnˈvʌɪələt/ ▶ adjective free or safe from injury or violation: *an international memorial which must remain inviolate.*
– DERIVATIVES **inviolacy** noun, **inviolately** adverb.
– ORIGIN late Middle English: from Latin *inviolatus*, from *in-* 'not' + *violare* 'violate'.

inviscid /ɪnˈvɪsɪd/ ▶ adjective Physics having no or negligible viscosity.

invisible ▶ adjective **1** unable to be seen: *this invisible gas is present to some extent in every home.* ■ concealed from sight; hidden: *he lounged in a doorway, invisible in the dark.* ■ treated as if unable to be seen; ignored or not taken into consideration: *before 1971 women artists were pretty well invisible.*
2 Economics relating to or denoting earnings which a country makes from the sale of services or other items not constituting tangible commodities: *invisible exports.*
▶ noun (**invisibles**) invisible exports and imports.
– DERIVATIVES **invisibility** noun, **invisibly** adverb.
– ORIGIN Middle English: from Old French, or from Latin *invisibilis*, from *in-* 'not' + *visibilis* (see VISIBLE).

invisible ink ▶ noun [mass noun] a type of ink used to produce writing that cannot be seen until the paper is heated or otherwise treated.

invitation ▶ noun a written or verbal request inviting someone to go somewhere or to do something: *a wedding invitation.* ■ [mass noun] the action of inviting someone to go somewhere or to do something: *a club with membership by invitation only* | *a herb garden where guests can only go **at the invitation of** the chef.* ■ [in sing.] a situation or action that tempts someone to do something or makes a particular outcome likely: *tactics like those of the colonel would have been an **invitation to** disaster.*
– ORIGIN late Middle English: from French, or from Latin *invitatio(n-)*, from *invitare* (see INVITE).

invitational N. Amer. ▶ adjective (especially of a competition) open only to those invited.
▶ noun an invitational competition.

invitatory /ɪnˈvʌɪtət(ə)ri/ ▶ adjective containing or conveying an invitation. ■ (in the Christian Church) denoting a psalm or versicle acting as an invitation to worshippers, especially Psalm 95 (the Venite).
– ORIGIN Middle English: from late Latin *invitatorius*, from Latin *invitare* (see INVITE).

invite ▶ verb [with obj.] make a polite, formal, or friendly request to (someone) to go somewhere or to do something: *we were **invited to** a dinner at the Embassy* | [with obj. and infinitive] *she invited Patrick to sit down.* ■ make a formal or polite request for (something) from someone: *applications are invited for the post of Director.* ■ (of an action or situation) tend to elicit (a particular reaction or response) or to tempt (someone) to do something: *his use of the word did little but invite criticism.*
▶ noun informal an invitation.
– DERIVATIVES **invitee** noun, **inviter** noun.
– ORIGIN mid 16th cent.: from Old French *inviter*, or from Latin *invitare*.

inviting ▶ adjective offering the promise of an attractive or enjoyable experience: *the sea down there looks so inviting.*
– DERIVATIVES **invitingly** adverb.

in vitro /ɪn ˈviːtrəʊ/ ▶ adjective & adverb Biology (of processes or reactions) taking place in a test tube, culture dish, or elsewhere outside a living organism: [as adj.] *in vitro fertilization.* The opposite of IN VIVO.
– ORIGIN Latin, literally 'in glass'.

in vivo /ɪn ˈviːvəʊ/ ▶ adverb & adjective Biology (of processes) taking place in a living organism. The opposite of IN VITRO.
– ORIGIN Latin, 'in a living thing'.

invocation ▶ noun [mass noun] the action of invoking someone or something: *his invocation of the ancient powers of Callanish.* ■ [count noun] an incantation used

to invoke a deity or the supernatural. ■ [count noun] (in the Christian Church) a form of words such as 'In the name of the Father' introducing a prayer, sermon, etc.
– DERIVATIVES **invocatory** /ɪnˈvɒkət(ə)ri/ **adjective**.
– ORIGIN late Middle English: via Old French from Latin *invocatio(n-)*, from the verb *invocare* (see INVOKE).

invoice ▸ **noun** a list of goods sent or services provided, with a statement of the sum due for these; a bill.
▸ **verb** [with obj.] send an invoice to (someone). ■ send an invoice for (goods or services provided).
– ORIGIN mid 16th cent.: originally the plural of obsolete *invoy*, from obsolete French *envoy* from *envoyer* 'send' (see ENVOY).

invoke /ɪnˈvəʊk/ ▸ **verb** [with obj.] **1** call on (a deity or spirit) in prayer, as a witness, or for inspiration. ■ summon (a spirit) by charms or incantation.
2 cite or appeal to (someone or something) as an authority for an action or in support of an argument: *the antiquated defence of insanity is rarely invoked in England.* ■ call earnestly for: *she invoked his help against this attack.* ■ give rise to; evoke: *how could she explain how the accident happened without invoking his wrath?*
3 Computing cause (a procedure) to be carried out.
– DERIVATIVES **invoker** **noun**.
– ORIGIN late 15th cent.: from French *invoquer*, from Latin *invocare*, from *in-* 'upon' + *vocare* 'to call'.

involatile ▸ **adjective** not volatile; unable to be vaporized.

involucre /ˈɪnvəl(j)uːkə/ ▸ **noun 1** Anatomy a membranous envelope.
2 Botany a whorl or rosette of bracts surrounding an inflorescence (especially a capitulum) or at the base of an umbel.
– ORIGIN late 16th cent.: from French, or from Latin *involucrum*, from *involvere* 'roll in, envelop' (see INVOLVE).

involuntary ▸ **adjective 1** done without will or conscious control: *she gave an involuntary shudder.* ■ (especially of muscles or nerves) concerned in bodily processes that are not under the control of the will.
2 done against someone's will; compulsory: *a policy of involuntary repatriation.*
– DERIVATIVES **involuntarily** **adverb**, **involuntariness** **noun**.

involute /ˈɪnvəl(j)uːt/ ▸ **adjective 1** formal involved or intricate: *the art novel has grown increasingly involute.*
2 technical curled spirally. ■ Zoology (of a shell) having the whorls wound closely round the axis. ■ Botany (of a leaf or the cap of a fungus) rolled inwards at the edges.
▸ **noun** Geometry the locus of a point considered as the end of a taut string being unwound from a given curve in the plane of that curve. Compare with EVOLUTE.
– ORIGIN mid 17th cent.: from Latin *involutus*, past participle of *involvere* (see INVOLVE).

involuted ▸ **adjective** complicated or abstruse: *his involuted prose.*

involution ▸ **noun 1** [mass noun] Physiology the shrinkage of an organ in old age or when inactive, e.g. of the womb after childbirth.
2 Mathematics a function, transformation, or operator that is equal to its inverse, i.e. which gives the identity when applied to itself.
3 [mass noun] formal the process of complicating something, or the state of being complicated: *periods of artistic involution.*
– DERIVATIVES **involutional** **adjective**.
– ORIGIN late Middle English (in the sense ('part) curling inwards'): from Latin *involutio(n-)*, from *involvere* (see INVOLVE).

involve ▸ **verb** [with obj.] have or include (something) as a necessary or integral part or result: *my job involves a lot of travelling* | *a bill proposing harsher penalties for crimes involving firearms and drugs.* ■ cause to participate in an activity or situation: *an opportunity to involve as many people as possible in all aspects of music-making.* ■ (**be/get involved**) be or become occupied or engrossed in something: *her husband had been very **involved in** his work.* ■ (**be involved**) be engaged in an emotional or personal relationship: *Angela told me she was **involved with** someone else.*
– ORIGIN late Middle English (in the senses 'enfold' and 'entangle'; formerly also as *envolve*): from Latin *involvere*, from *in-* 'into' + *volvere* 'to roll'.

involved ▸ **adjective** difficult to understand; complicated: *a long, involved conversation.*

involvement ▸ **noun** [mass noun] the fact or condition of being involved with or participating in something: *US officials produced evidence of his involvement in drug trafficking.* ■ emotional or personal association with someone: *she knew that involvement with Adam would only complicate her life.*

invulnerable ▸ **adjective** impossible to harm or damage: *no state in the region is now invulnerable to attack by another.*
– DERIVATIVES **invulnerability** **noun**, **invulnerably** **adverb**.
– ORIGIN late 16th cent. (earlier than *vulnerable*): from Latin *invulnerabilis*, from *in-* 'not' + *vulnerabilis* (see VULNERABLE).

-in-waiting ▸ **combining form 1** denoting a position as attendant to a royal personage: *lady-in-waiting.*
2 awaiting a turn, confirmation of a process, etc.: *a political administration-in-waiting.* ■ about to happen: *an explosion-in-waiting.*

inwale /ˈɪnweɪl/ ▸ **noun** a longitudinal structural piece on the inside of a boat; an internal gunwale.

inward ▸ **adjective** [attrib.] directed or proceeding towards the inside; coming in from outside: *inward mail* | *a graceful inward movement of her wrist.* ■ existing within the mind, soul, or spirit, and often not expressed: *she felt an inward sense of release.*
▸ **adverb** variant of INWARDS.
– ORIGIN Old English *inweard, inneweard, innanweard* (see IN, -WARD).

inward investment ▸ **noun** [mass noun] investment made within a country from outside.

inward-looking ▸ **adjective** not interested in or taking account of other people or groups.

inwardly ▸ **adverb** within the mind: *inwardly seething, he did as he was told.*
– ORIGIN Old English *inweardlīce* (see INWARD, -LY[2]).

inwardness ▸ **noun** [mass noun] preoccupation with one's inner self; concern with spiritual or philosophical matters rather than externalities.

inwards (also **inward**) ▸ **adverb** towards the inside: *the door began to swing inwards.* ■ into or towards the mind, spirit, or soul: *people must look inwards to gain insight into their own stress.*

inwrap ▸ **verb** archaic spelling of ENWRAP.

inwrought /ɪnˈrɔːt, ˈɪnrɔːt/ ▸ **adjective** literary (of a fabric or garment) intricately embroidered with a pattern or decoration: *robes inwrought with gold.*

inyanga /ɪnˈjaŋgə, ɪnˈjɑːŋgə/ ▸ **noun** (pl. **inyangas** or **izinyanga**) S. African a traditional healer or diviner, especially one specializing in herbalism.
– ORIGIN Zulu, 'doctor, herbalist'.

Io /ˈʌɪəʊ/ **1** Greek Mythology a priestess of Hera who was loved by Zeus. Trying to protect her from the jealousy of Hera, Zeus turned Io into a heifer. Hera sent a gadfly to torture the heifer, which then fled across the world and finally reached Egypt, where Zeus turned her back into human form.
2 Astronomy one of the Galilean moons of Jupiter, the fifth-closest satellite to the planet, being actively volcanic and coloured red and yellow with sulphur compounds (diameter 3,630 km).

I/O ▸ **abbreviation** Electronics input-output.

IOC ▸ **abbreviation** International Olympic Committee.

iod- ▸ **combining form** variant spelling of IODO- shortened before a vowel (as in *iodic*).

iodate ▸ **noun** Chemistry a salt or ester of iodic acid.

iodic acid /ʌɪˈɒdɪk/ ▸ **noun** [mass noun] Chemistry a crystalline acid with strong oxidizing properties, made by oxidation of iodine. ● Chem. formula: HIO_3.

iodide /ˈʌɪədʌɪd/ ▸ **noun** [mass noun] Chemistry a compound of iodine with another element or group, especially a salt of the anion I^-.

iodinate /ˈʌɪədɪneɪt, ʌɪˈɒdɪneɪt/ ▸ **verb** [with obj.] (usu. as adj. **iodinated**) Chemistry introduce iodine into (a compound).
– DERIVATIVES **iodination** **noun**.

iodine /ˈʌɪədiːn, -ʌɪn, -ɪn/ ▸ **noun** [mass noun] the chemical element of atomic number 53, a non-metallic element forming black crystals and a violet vapour. (Symbol: **I**) ■ a solution of this in alcohol, used as a mild antiseptic.

> A member of the halogen group, iodine occurs chiefly as salts in seawater and brines. As a constituent of thyroid hormones it is required in small amounts in the body, and deficiency can lead to goitre.

– ORIGIN early 19th cent.: from French *iode* (from Greek *iōdēs* 'violet-coloured', from *ion* 'violet' + *-eidēs* 'like') + -INE[4].

iodism /ˈʌɪədɪz(ə)m/ ▸ **noun** [mass noun] Medicine iodine poisoning, causing thirst, diarrhoea, weakness, and convulsions.

iodize (also **iodise**) ▸ **verb** [with obj.] (usu. as adj. **iodized**) treat or impregnate with iodine.
– DERIVATIVES **iodization** **noun**.

iodo- (usu. **iod-** before a vowel) ▸ **combining form** Chemistry representing IODINE.

iodoform /ʌɪˈəʊdə(ʊ)fɔːm, ˈʌɪədə(ʊ)-, ʌɪˈɒdə(ʊ)-/ ▸ **noun** [mass noun] a volatile pale yellow sweet-smelling crystalline organic compound of iodine, with antiseptic properties. ● Alternative name: **triiodomethane**; chem. formula: CHI_3.
– ORIGIN mid 19th cent.: from IODINE, on the pattern of *chloroform*.

iodometry /ʌɪəˈdɒmɪtri/ ▸ **noun** [mass noun] Chemistry the quantitative analysis of a solution of an oxidizing agent by adding an iodide which reacts to form iodine, which is then titrated.
– DERIVATIVES **iodometric** **adjective**.

iodophor /ʌɪˈəʊdə(ʊ)fɔː, ˈʌɪəd-/ ▸ **noun** any of a group of disinfectants containing iodine in combination with a surfactant.

IOM ▸ **abbreviation** Isle of Man.

io moth /ˈʌɪəʊ/ ▸ **noun** a large, mainly yellow North American moth of the silk moth family, with prominent eyespots on the hindwings. ● *Automeris io*, family Saturniidae.
– ORIGIN late 19th cent.: named after the Greek priestess Io.

ion /ˈʌɪən/ ▸ **noun** an atom or molecule with a net electric charge due to the loss or gain of one or more electrons. See also CATION, ANION.
– ORIGIN mid 19th cent.: from Greek, neuter present participle of *ienai* 'go'.

-ion ▸ **suffix** forming nouns denoting verbal action: *communion.* ■ denoting an instance of this: *a rebellion.* ■ denoting a resulting state or product: *oblivion* | *opinion.*
– ORIGIN via French from Latin *-ion-*.

> **USAGE** The suffix **-ion** is usually found preceded by **s** (**-sion**), **t** (**-tion**), or **x** (**-xion**).

Iona /ʌɪˈəʊnə/ a small island in the Inner Hebrides, off the west coast of Mull. It is the site of a monastery founded by St Columba in about 563.

Ionesco /ˌiːəˈnɛskəʊ/, Eugène (1912–94), Romanian-born French dramatist, a leading exponent of the Theatre of the Absurd. Notable plays: *The Bald Prima Donna* (1950), *Rhinoceros* (1960).

ion exchange ▸ **noun** [mass noun] the exchange of ions of the same charge between an insoluble solid and a solution in contact with it, used in water-softening and other purification and separation processes.

ion exchanger ▸ **noun** a solid used in ion exchange, typically a special cross-linked synthetic resin or a zeolite.

Ionia /ʌɪˈəʊnɪə/ in classical times, the central part of the west coast of Asia Minor, which had long been inhabited by Hellenic people (the Ionians) and was again colonized by Greeks from the mainland from about the 8th century BC.

Ionian ▸ **noun 1** a member of an ancient Hellenic people inhabiting Attica, parts of western Asia Minor, and the Aegean islands in pre-classical times. Apparently displaced from some areas by the Dorians in the 11th or 12th century BC, they retained their settlements in Attica, especially Athens, where they were responsible for some of the greatest achievements of classical Greece.
2 a native or inhabitant of the Ionian Islands.
▸ **adjective** relating to the Ionians, Ionia, or the Ionian Islands.

Ionian Islands a chain of about forty Greek islands off the western coast of mainland Greece, in the Ionian Sea, including Corfu, Cephalonia, Ithaca, and Zakinthos.

Ionian mode ▸ **noun** Music the mode represented by the natural diatonic scale C–C (the major scale).

Ionian Sea the part of the Mediterranean Sea between western Greece and southern Italy, at the mouth of the Adriatic.
– ORIGIN named, according to legend, after the priestess Io.

Ionic /ʌɪˈɒnɪk/ ▸ **adjective 1** relating to or denoting a classical order of architecture characterized by a

column with scroll shapes (volutes) on either side of the capital.
2 another term for **Ionian**.
▸ **noun** [mass noun] **1** the Ionic order of architecture.
2 the ancient Greek dialect used in Ionia.
– ORIGIN late 16th cent.: via Latin from Greek *Iōnikos*, from *Iōnia* (see **Ionia**).

ionic /ʌɪˈɒnɪk/ ▸ **adjective** relating to or using ions. ■ (of a chemical bond) formed by the electrostatic attraction of oppositely charged ions. Often contrasted with **covalent**.
– DERIVATIVES **ionically** adverb.

ionic strength ▸ **noun** Chemistry a quantity representing the strength of the electric field in a solution, equal to the sum of the molalities of each type of ion present multiplied by the square of their charges.

ionization chamber ▸ **noun** an instrument for detecting ionizing radiation.

ionize /ˈʌɪənʌɪz/ (also **ionise**) ▸ **verb** [with obj.] convert (an atom, molecule, or substance) into an ion or ions, typically by removing one or more electrons. ■ [no obj.] become converted into an ion or ions in this way.
– DERIVATIVES **ionizable** adjective, **ionization** noun.

ionizer (also **ioniser**) ▸ **noun** a device which produces ionization, especially one used to improve the quality of the air in a room.

ionizing radiation ▸ **noun** [mass noun] radiation consisting of particles, X-rays, or gamma rays with sufficient energy to cause ionization in the medium through which it passes.

ionomer /ʌɪˈɒnəmə/ ▸ **noun** any of a class of polymer materials consisting of thermoplastic resins stabilized by ionic cross-linkages, used to make dental cement and sealants.

ionopause /ʌɪˈɒnə(ʊ)pɔːz/ ▸ **noun** Astronomy the upper boundary of the ionosphere of a planet, comet, or other celestial object.

ionophore /ʌɪˈɒnə(ʊ)fɔː/ ▸ **noun** Biochemistry a substance which is able to transport particular ions across a lipid membrane in a cell.

ionosphere /ʌɪˈɒnəsfɪə/ ▸ **noun** the layer of the earth's atmosphere which contains a high concentration of ions and free electrons and is able to reflect radio waves. It lies above the mesosphere and extends from about 80 to 1,000 km above the earth's surface.
– DERIVATIVES **ionospheric** adjective.

iontophoresis /ʌɪˌɒntə(ʊ)fəˈriːsɪs/ ▸ **noun** [mass noun] Medicine a technique of introducing ionic medicinal compounds into the body through the skin by applying a local electric current.
– ORIGIN early 20th cent.: from **ion**, on the pattern of *electrophoresis*.

-ior ▸ **suffix** forming adjectives of comparison: *anterior* | *senior*.
– ORIGIN from Latin.

iora /ʌɪˈɔːrə/ ▸ **noun** a small insectivorous Asian songbird with greenish back and yellow underparts.
● Genus *Aegithina*, family Irenidae (or Chloropseidae): four species.
– ORIGIN of obscure origin.

iota /ʌɪˈəʊtə/ ▸ **noun 1** the ninth letter of the Greek alphabet (Ι, ι), transliterated as 'i'. ■ (**Iota**) [followed by Latin genitive] Astronomy the ninth star in a constellation: *Iota Piscium*.
2 [in sing.] [usu. with negative] an extremely small amount: *nothing she said seemed to make an iota of difference*.
– ORIGIN from Greek *iōta*. Sense 2 arose because *iota* is the smallest letter of the Greek alphabet: compare with **jot**.

iota subscript ▸ **noun** (in Greek) a small iota written beneath a long vowel, forming the second element of a diphthong but not pronounced and not always represented in transliteration.

IOU ▸ **noun** a signed document acknowledging a debt.
– ORIGIN late 18th cent.: representing the pronunciation of *I owe you*.

-ious ▸ **suffix** (forming adjectives) characterized by; full of: *cautious* | *vivacious*.
– ORIGIN from French *-ieux*, from Latin *-iosus*.

IOW ▸ **abbreviation 1** Isle of Wight.
2 informal in other words: *no one wants to commit to anything longer than short-term, IOW about a month*.

Iowa /ˈʌɪəwə/ a state in the Middle West of the US, acquired as part of the Louisiana Purchase in 1803; pop. 3,002,555 (est. 2008); capital, Des Moines. It became the 29th state of the US in 1846.
– DERIVATIVES **Iowan** adjective & noun.

Iowa City a city in eastern Iowa; pop. 67,831 (est. 2008). Founded in 1838, it was the state capital until replaced by Des Moines in 1858.

IPA ▸ **abbreviation** ■ India pale ale, a type of light-coloured beer similar to bitter. [said to have been brewed originally for the British colonies.] ■ International Phonetic Alphabet.

IP address ▸ **noun** Computing a unique string of numbers separated by full stops that identifies each computer using the Internet Protocol to communicate over a network.
– ORIGIN *IP*, abbreviation of **Internet Protocol**.

ipecac /ˈɪpɪkak/ ▸ **noun** short for **ipecacuanha**.

ipecacuanha /ˌɪpɪkakjʊˈanə/ ▸ **noun** [mass noun]
1 the dried rhizome of a South American shrub, or a drug prepared from this, used as an emetic and expectorant.
2 the shrub that produces this rhizome, native to Brazil and cultivated elsewhere. ● *Cephaelis ipecacuanha*, family Rubiaceae.
■ used in names of other plants with similar uses, e.g. **American ipecacuanha**.
– ORIGIN early 17th cent.: from Portuguese, from Tupi-Guarani *ipekaaguéne* 'emetic creeper', from *ipe* 'small' + *kaa* 'leaves' + *guéne* 'vomit'.

Iphigenia /ˌɪfɪdʒɪˈnʌɪə/ Greek Mythology the daughter of Agamemnon, who was obliged to offer her as a sacrifice to Artemis when the Greek fleet was becalmed on its way to the Trojan War. However, Artemis saved her life and took her to Tauris in the Crimea, where she became a priestess until rescued by her brother Orestes.

Ipiros /ˈɪpɪrɔs/ Greek name for **Epirus**.

IPMS ▸ **abbreviation** (in the UK) Institution of Professionals, Managers, and Specialists.

IPO ▸ **abbreviation** chiefly US initial public offering.

iPod ▸ **noun** trademark a small electronic device for playing and storing digital audio and video files.

Ipoh /ˈiːpəʊ/ the capital of the state of Perak in western Malaysia; pop. 702,500 (est. 2009). It replaced Taiping as state capital in 1937.

ipomoea /ˌɪpəˈmiːə/ ▸ **noun** a plant of the genus *Ipomoea* in the convolvulus family, especially (in gardening) a morning glory.
– ORIGIN modern Latin, from Greek *ips* 'worm' + *homoios* 'like'.

ippon /ˈɪpɒn/ ▸ **noun** a full point scored in judo, karate, and other martial sports.
– ORIGIN Japanese.

IPR ▸ **abbreviation** intellectual property rights.

iproniazid /ˌʌɪprə(ʊ)ˈnʌɪəzɪd/ ▸ **noun** [mass noun] Medicine a synthetic compound used as a drug to treat depression. ● A derivative of isoniazid; chem. formula: $(CH_3)_2CHNHNHCOC_5H_4N$.
– ORIGIN 1950s: from *i(so)pro(pyl)* + *(iso)niazid*.

ipse dixit /ˌɪpseɪ ˈdɪksɪt, ˌɪpsiː/ ▸ **noun** a dogmatic and unproven statement.
– ORIGIN Latin, literally 'he himself said it', translating Greek *autos epha*, a phrase used of Pythagoras by his followers.

ipsilateral /ˌɪpsɪˈlat(ə)r(ə)l/ ▸ **adjective** belonging to or occurring on the same side of the body.
– ORIGIN early 20th cent.: formed irregularly from Latin *ipse* 'self' + **lateral**.

ipsissima verba /ɪpˌsɪsɪmə ˈvəːbə/ ▸ **plural noun** the precise words.
– ORIGIN Latin.

ipso facto /ˌɪpsəʊ ˈfaktəʊ/ ▸ **adverb** by that very fact or act: *the enemy of one's enemy may be ipso facto a friend*.
– ORIGIN Latin.

Ipswich /ˈɪpswɪtʃ/ the county town of Suffolk, a port and industrial town on the estuary of the River Orwell; pop. 145,700 (est. 2009).

Ipswichian /ɪpˈswɪtʃɪən/ ▸ **adjective** relating to or denoting the most recent interglacial period of the Pleistocene in Britain, preceding the Devensian glaciation and identified with the Eemian of northern Europe. ■ (as noun **the Ipswichian**) the Ipswichian interglacial or the system of deposits laid down during it.

IQ ▸ **abbreviation** intelligence quotient.

Iqbal /ˈɪkbal/, Sir Muhammad (1875–1938), Indian poet and philosopher, generally regarded as the father of Pakistan. As president of the Muslim League in 1930, he advocated the creation of a separate Muslim state in NW India; the demands of the League led ultimately to the establishment of Pakistan in 1947.

-ique ▸ **suffix** archaic spelling of **-ic**.

Iquitos /ɪˈkiːtɒs/ a city in NE Peru, a river port on the west bank of the Amazon; pop. 371,000 (est. 2007).

IR ▸ **abbreviation** ■ infrared. ■ Iran (international vehicle registration).

Ir ▸ **symbol** the chemical element iridium.

ir- ▸ **prefix** variant spelling of **in-**[1], **in-**[2] assimilated before *r* (as in *irradiate*, *irrelative*).

IRA ▸ **abbreviation** ■ (in the US) Individual Retirement Account. ■ Irish Republican Army.

irade /ɪˈrɑːdi/ ▸ **noun** historical a written decree of the sultan of Turkey.
– ORIGIN Turkish, from Arabic *'irāda* 'will, decree', from *'arāda* 'intend'.

Iráklion /iˈrakliɒn/ Greek name for **Heraklion**.

Iran /ɪˈrɑːn, ɪˈran/ a country in the Middle East, between the Caspian Sea and the Persian Gulf; pop. 66,429,300 (est. 2009); languages, Farsi (Persian) (official), Azerbaijani, Kurdish, Arabic, and others; capital, Tehran.

> Previously known as Persia, the country adopted the name Iran in 1935. Iran was a monarchy until 1979, when the shah was overthrown in a popular uprising, headed by Ayatollah Khomeini, which led soon after to the establishment of an Islamic republic. From 1980 to 1988 Iran was at war with its neighbour Iraq. See also **Persia**, **Iran–Iraq War**.

Irangate /ɪˈrɑːngeɪt, ɪˈran-/ a US political scandal of 1987 involving the covert sale by the US of arms to Iran. The proceeds of the arms sales were used by officials to give arms to the anti-communist Contras in Nicaragua, despite Congressional prohibition. Also called **Iran-Contra affair** or **scandal**.

Iranian ▸ **adjective** relating to Iran or its people. ■ relating to or denoting the group of Indo-European languages that includes Persian (Farsi), Pashto, Avestan, and Kurdish.
▸ **noun** a native or inhabitant of Iran, or a person of Iranian descent.

Iran–Iraq War the war of 1980–8 between Iran and Iraq in the general area of the Persian Gulf. It ended inconclusively after great hardship and loss of life on both sides. Also called **Gulf War**.

Iraq /ɪˈrɑːk, ɪˈrak/ a country in the Middle East, on the Persian Gulf; pop. 28,945,600 (est. 2009); official language, Arabic; capital, Baghdad.

> Iraq is traversed by the Rivers Tigris and Euphrates, whose valley was the site of the ancient civilizations of Mesopotamia. It was conquered by Arabia in the 7th century and from 1534 formed part of the Ottoman Empire. After the First World War a kingdom was established, although the country was under British administration until 1932. Saddam Hussein came to power as President in 1979. From 1980 to 1988 the country was at war with its eastern neighbour Iran. In 1990 Iraq invaded Kuwait; it was expelled by an international coalition of forces in the Gulf War of 1991. In 2003 the country was invaded and occupied by US-led forces in response to its failure to comply fully with a UN resolution that it should disarm.

Iraqi ▸ **adjective** relating to Iraq, its people, or their language.
▸ **noun** (pl. **Iraqis**) **1** a native or inhabitant of Iraq, or a person of Iraqi descent.
2 [mass noun] the form of Arabic spoken in Iraq.

IRAS a satellite launched in 1983 to map the distribution of infrared radiation in the sky.
– ORIGIN abbreviation of *Infrared Astronomical Satellite*.

irascible /ɪˈrasɪb(ə)l/ ▸ **adjective** having or showing a tendency to be easily angered: *an irascible and difficult man*.
– DERIVATIVES **irascibility** noun, **irascibly** adverb.
– ORIGIN late Middle English: via French from late Latin *irascibilis*, from Latin *irasci* 'grow angry', from *ira* 'anger'.

irate /ʌɪˈreɪt/ ▸ **adjective** feeling or characterized by great anger: *a barrage of irate letters*.
– DERIVATIVES **irately** adverb, **irateness** noun.
– ORIGIN mid 19th cent.: from Latin *iratus*, from *ira* 'anger'.

IRBM ▸ **abbreviation** intermediate-range ballistic missile.

IRC ▸ **abbreviation** Internet Relay Chat.

ire /ˈʌɪə/ ▸ **noun** [mass noun] anger: *the plans provoked the ire of conservationists*.

– DERIVATIVES **ireful** adjective.
– ORIGIN Middle English: via Old French from Latin *ira*.

Ireland an island of the British Isles, lying west of Great Britain. Approximately four fifths of the area of Ireland forms the Republic of Ireland, with the remaining one fifth forming Northern Ireland.

> Ireland was inhabited by Celts from about the 6th century BC. English invasions began in the 12th century under Henry II, although the whole of the island was not conquered until the time of the Tudors. Revolts against English rule led to English and Scottish families being settled on confiscated land; in parts of Ulster the descendants of Protestant settlers form a majority. After an unsuccessful rebellion in 1798, union of Britain and Ireland followed in 1801. Increased prosperity was experienced in Protestant Ulster, but not in the rest of the island, and after the failure of the potato crop in the 1840s thousands died in a famine, and thousands more emigrated. In 1922 Ireland was partitioned by the Anglo-Irish Treaty.

Ireland, Republic of a country comprising approximately four fifths of Ireland; pop. 4,203,200 (est. 2009); languages, Irish (official), English; capital, Dublin. Also called IRISH REPUBLIC.

> The Anglo-Irish Treaty by which Ireland was partitioned in 1922 gave the southern part of Ireland dominion status as the Irish Free State. The treaty was followed by civil war between the Free State government and republicans, led by Eamon de Valera, who rejected partition. The war ended in victory for the government in 1923. A new constitution as a sovereign state (Eire) was adopted in 1937. Eire remained neutral during the Second World War; in 1949 it left the Commonwealth and became fully independent as the Republic of Ireland. The Republic of Ireland joined the EC in 1973.

Irenaeus, St /ˌʌɪrəˈniːəs/ (*c.*130–*c.*200 AD), Greek theologian, the author of *Against Heresies* (*c.*180), a detailed attack on Gnosticism. Feast day (in the Eastern Church) 23 August; (in the Western Church) 28 June.

irenic /ʌɪˈrɛnɪk, -ˈriː-/ (also **eirenic**) ▶ **adjective** formal aiming or aimed at peace.
▶ **noun** (**irenics**) a part of Christian theology concerned with reconciling different denominations and sects.
– DERIVATIVES **irenical** adjective.
– ORIGIN mid 19th cent.: from Greek *eirēnikos*, from *eirēnē* 'peace'. Compare with EIRENICON.

irenicon /ʌɪˈriːnɪkɒn/ (also **eirenicon**) ▶ **noun** formal a proposal made as a means of achieving peace.
– ORIGIN early 17th cent. (as *irenicon*): from Greek *eirēnikon*, neuter of *eirēnikos* 'promoting peace', from *eirēnē* 'peace'. Compare with IRENIC.

Irgun /ɪəˈgʊn/ a right-wing Zionist organization founded in 1931. During the period when it was active (1937–48) it carried out violent attacks on Arabs and Britons in its campaign to establish a Jewish state; it was disbanded after the creation of Israel in 1948.
– ORIGIN from modern Hebrew *'irgūn (šĕḇā'ī lĕ'ummī)* '(national military) organization'.

Irian Jaya /ˌɪrɪən ˈdʒʌɪə/ former name for the province of PAPUA (sense 1). Also called WEST IRIAN.

iridaceous /ˌʌɪrɪˈdeɪʃəs, ˌɪrɪ-/ ▶ **adjective** Botany relating to or denoting plants of the iris family (Iridaceae), which grow from bulbs, corms, or rhizomes.
– ORIGIN mid 19th cent.: from modern Latin *Iridaceae* (plural), based on Greek *iris*, *irid-* 'rainbow', + -OUS.

iridectomy /ˌʌɪrɪˈdɛktəmi, ˌɪrɪ-/ ▶ **noun** (pl. **iridectomies**) a surgical procedure to remove part of the iris.

iridescent /ˌɪrɪˈdɛs(ə)nt/ ▶ **adjective** showing luminous colours that seem to change when seen from different angles.
– DERIVATIVES **iridescence** noun, **iridescently** adverb.
– ORIGIN late 18th cent.: from Latin *iris*, *irid-* 'rainbow' + -ESCENT.

iridium /ɪˈrɪdɪəm, ʌɪ-/ ▶ **noun** [mass noun] the chemical element of atomic number 77, a hard, dense silvery-white metal. (Symbol: **Ir**)
– ORIGIN early 19th cent.: modern Latin, from Latin *iris*, *irid-* 'rainbow' (so named because it forms compounds of various colours).

iridology /ˌʌɪrɪˈdɒlədʒi, ˌɪrɪ-/ ▶ **noun** [mass noun] (in alternative medicine) diagnosis by examination of the iris of the eye.
– DERIVATIVES **iridologist** noun.
– ORIGIN early 20th cent.: from Greek *iris*, *irid-* 'iris' + -LOGY.

irie /ˈʌɪriː/ black English ▶ **adjective** nice, good, or pleasing (used as a general term of approval): *the place is jumping with irie vibes | I feeling irie*.
▶ **exclamation** used by Rastafarians as a friendly greeting.
– ORIGIN perhaps representing a pronunciation of *all right*.

Iris Greek Mythology the goddess of the rainbow, who acted as a messenger of the gods.

iris ▶ **noun 1** a flat, coloured, ring-shaped membrane behind the cornea of the eye, with an adjustable circular opening (pupil) in the centre. ■ (also **iris diaphragm**) an adjustable diaphragm of thin overlapping plates for regulating the size of a central hole, especially for the admission of light to a lens.
2 a plant with showy flowers, typically of purple or yellow, and sword-shaped leaves. Irises are native to both Eurasia and North America and widely cultivated as ornamentals. ● Genus *Iris*, family Iridaceae (the **iris family**): many species and numerous hybrids. The iris family also includes the gladioli, crocuses, and freesias.
▶ **verb** [no obj., with adverbial of direction] (of an aperture, typically that of a lens) open or close in the manner of an iris or iris diaphragm.
– ORIGIN modern Latin, via Latin from Greek *iris* 'rainbow, iris'.

irised ▶ **adjective** literary coloured like a rainbow; iridescent.

Irish ▶ **adjective** relating to Ireland, its people, or the Celtic language traditionally and historically spoken there. ■ offensive (of a statement or action) paradoxical; illogical or apparently so.
▶ **noun** [mass noun] **1** (also **Irish Gaelic**) the Celtic language of Ireland.
2 (as plural noun **the Irish**) the people of Ireland; Irish people collectively.

> Irish is now spoken regularly only in a few isolated areas in the west of Ireland, having elsewhere been displaced by English. It is, however, the first official language of the Republic of Ireland and is taught in all state schools. Scottish Gaelic was descended from it.

– DERIVATIVES **Irishness** noun.
– ORIGIN Middle English: from Old English *Īr-* (stem of *Īras* 'the Irish' and *Īrland* 'Ireland', obscurely related to HIBERNIAN) + -ISH[1].

Irish coffee ▶ **noun** [mass noun] coffee mixed with a dash of Irish whiskey and served with cream on top.

Irish elk ▶ **noun** an extinct giant European and North African deer of the Pleistocene epoch, with massive antlers up to 3 m (10 ft) across. Also called GIANT DEER. ● *Megaloceros giganteus*, family Cervidae.

Irish Free State the name for the independent part of southern Ireland from 1922 until 1937 (see IRELAND, REPUBLIC OF).

Irishman ▶ **noun** (pl. **Irishmen**) a male native or inhabitant of Ireland, or a man of Irish descent.

Irish moss ▶ **noun** another term for CARRAGEEN.

Irish National Liberation Army (abbrev.: **INLA**) a small paramilitary organization seeking union between Northern Ireland and the Republic of Ireland. It was formed in the early 1970s, probably as an offshoot of the Provisional IRA.

Irish Republic see IRELAND, REPUBLIC OF.

Irish Republican Army (abbrev.: **IRA**) the military arm of Sinn Fein, aiming for union between the Republic of Ireland and Northern Ireland.

> The IRA was formed during the struggle for independence from Britain in 1916–21; in 1969 it split into Official and Provisional wings. The Official IRA became virtually inactive, while the Provisional IRA stepped up the level of violence against military and civilian targets in Northern Ireland, Britain, and Europe. The IRA declared a ceasefire in 1994 and another in 1997, and in 2005 announced that it had ended its armed campaign.

Irish Republican Brotherhood see FENIAN.

Irish Sea the sea separating Ireland from England and Wales.

Irish setter ▶ **noun** a dog of a breed of setter with a long, silky dark red coat and a long feathered tail.

Irish stew ▶ **noun** [mass noun] a stew made with mutton, potatoes, and onions.

Irish Sweepstake (also **Irish Sweep**) a sweepstake on the results of certain major horse races, authorized since 1930 by the government of the Republic of Ireland in order to benefit Irish hospitals. It is the largest international lottery.

Irish terrier ▶ **noun** a terrier of a rough-haired light reddish-brown breed.

Irish wolfhound ▶ **noun** a large, typically greyish hound of a rough-coated breed.

Irishwoman ▶ **noun** (pl. **Irishwomen**) a female native or inhabitant of Ireland, or a woman of Irish descent.

iritis /ʌɪˈrʌɪtɪs/ ▶ **noun** [mass noun] Medicine inflammation of the iris of the eye.

irk /əːk/ ▶ **verb** [with obj.] irritate; annoy: *it irks her to think of the runaround she received*.
– ORIGIN Middle English (in the sense 'be annoyed or disgusted'): perhaps from Old Norse *yrkja* 'to work'.

irksome ▶ **adjective** irritating; annoying: *an irksome journey | petty regulations were becoming very irksome*.
– DERIVATIVES **irksomely** adverb, **irksomeness** noun.

Irkutsk /ɪəˈkʊtsk/ the chief city of Siberia, situated on the western shore of Lake Baikal in eastern Russia; pop. 575,800 (est. 2008).

IRL ▶ **abbreviation** the Republic of Ireland (international vehicle registration).

IRO ▶ **abbreviation** ■ (in the UK) Inland Revenue Office. ■ International Refugee Organization.

iroko /ɪˈrəʊkəʊ, iː-/ ▶ **noun** (pl. **irokos**) a tropical African tree which yields pale timber that is sometimes used as an oak or teak substitute. ● Genus *Chlorophora*, family Moraceae: several species.
– ORIGIN late 19th cent.: from Yoruba.

iron ▶ **noun 1** [mass noun] a strong, hard magnetic silvery-grey metal, the chemical element of atomic number 26, much used as a material for construction and manufacturing, especially in the form of steel. (Symbol: **Fe**) ■ used figuratively as a symbol or type of firmness, strength, or resistance: *her father had a will of iron* | [as modifier] *the iron grip of religion on minority cultures*.

> Iron is widely distributed as ores such as haematite, magnetite, and siderite, and the earth's core is believed to consist largely of metallic iron and nickel. Besides steel, other important forms of the metal are cast iron and wrought iron. Chemically a transition element, iron is a constituent of some biological molecules, notably haemoglobin.

2 a tool or implement now or originally made of iron: *a caulking iron*. ■ (**irons**) fetters or handcuffs. ■ (**irons**) metal supports for a malformed leg. ■ (**irons**) informal stirrups.
3 a handheld implement, typically an electrical one, with a heated flat steel base, used to smooth clothes, sheets, etc.
4 a golf club with a metal head (typically with a numeral indicating the degree to which the head is angled in order to loft the ball): [in combination] *a four-iron*. ■ a shot made with such a club.
5 Astronomy a meteorite containing a high proportion of iron.
▶ **verb** [with obj.] smooth (clothes, sheets, etc.) with an iron.
– PHRASES **have many** (or **other**) **irons in the fire** have a range of options or courses of action available, or be involved in many activities or commitments at the same time. **in irons 1** having the feet or hands fettered. **2** (of a sailing vessel) stalled head to wind and unable to come about or tack either way. **iron hand** (or **fist**) used to refer to firmness or ruthlessness of attitude or behaviour: *he ruled with an iron hand*. **an iron hand** (or **fist**) **in a velvet glove** firmness or ruthlessness cloaked in outward gentleness.
– PHRASAL VERBS **iron something out** solve or settle difficulties or problems: *they had ironed out their differences*.
– DERIVATIVES **ironer** noun, **iron-like** adjective.
– ORIGIN Old English *īren*, *īsen*, *īsern*, of Germanic origin; related to Dutch *ijzer* and German *Eisen*, and probably ultimately from Celtic.

Iron Age a prehistoric period that followed the Bronze Age, when weapons and tools came to be made of iron.

> The Iron Age is conventionally taken as beginning in the early 1st millennium BC, but iron-working began with the Hittites in Anatolia in *c.*1400 BC. Its arrival in Britain was associated with the first Celtic immigrants in about the 6th century BC. In much of Europe it ended at the Roman period, but outside the Roman Empire it continued to the 4th–6th centuries AD.

ironbark ▶ **noun** an Australian eucalyptus tree with thick, solid bark and hard, dense, durable timber. ● Genus *Eucalyptus*, family Myrtaceae: several species, including the **grey ironbark** (*E. paniculata*).

iron-bound ▶ **adjective** bound with iron: *an old iron-bound chest*. ■ rigorous or inflexible: *iron-bound* *rules.* ■ archaic (of a coast) faced or enclosed with rocks.

Iron Chancellor see BISMARCK².

ironclad ▶ **adjective** covered or protected with iron. ■ impossible to contradict, weaken, or change: *an ironclad guarantee.*
▶ **noun** historical a 19th-century warship with armour plating.

Iron Cross ▶ **noun** the highest German military decoration for bravery, instituted in 1813.

Iron Curtain ▶ **noun** (**the Iron Curtain**) a notional barrier separating the former Soviet bloc and the West prior to the decline of communism that followed the political events in eastern Europe in 1989.

Iron Duke see WELLINGTON².

Iron Gate a gorge through which a section of the River Danube flows, forming part of the boundary between Romania and Serbia. Navigation was improved by means of a ship canal constructed through it in 1896. Romanian name **PORŢILE DE FIER**, Serbian name **GVOZDENA VRATA**.

iron grey ▶ **noun** [mass noun] a dark grey colour.

Iron Guard a fascist Romanian political party that was founded in 1927 and ceased to exist after the Second World War.

iron horse ▶ **noun** literary a steam railway locomotive.

I

ironic /ʌɪˈrɒnɪk/ ▶ **adjective** using or characterized by irony: *his mouth curved into an ironic smile.* ■ happening in a way contrary to what is expected, and typically causing wry amusement because of this: [with clause] *it was ironic that now everybody had plenty of money for food they couldn't obtain it because everything was rationed.*
– DERIVATIVES **ironical** adjective.
– ORIGIN mid 17th cent.: from French *ironique* or late Latin *ironicus*, from Greek *eirōnikos* 'dissembling, feigning ignorance', from *eirōneia* (see IRONY¹).

ironically ▶ **adverb** in an ironic manner: *'How very noble,' Oliver said ironically.* ■ used in reference to a paradoxical, unexpected, or coincidental situation: [sentence adverb] *ironically, the rescue craft which saved her was the boat she was helping to pay for.*

ironing ▶ **noun** [mass noun] the activity or task of ironing clothes, sheets, etc. ■ clothes, sheets, etc. that need to be or have just been ironed.

ironing board ▶ **noun** a long, narrow board covered with soft material and having folding legs, on which clothes, sheets, etc. are ironed.

ironist /ˈʌɪr(ə)nɪst/ ▶ **noun** a person who uses irony.

ironize /ˈʌɪr(ə)nʌɪz/ (also **ironise**) ▶ **verb** [with obj.] use ironically: *this novel follows and yet ironizes many of the conventions of the picaresque narrative.*

Iron Lady the nickname of Margaret Thatcher while she was British Prime Minister.

iron lung ▶ **noun** a rigid case fitted over a patient's body, used for administering prolonged artificial respiration by means of mechanical pumps.

iron maiden ▶ **noun** (in historical contexts) an instrument of torture consisting of a coffin-shaped box lined with iron spikes.

iron man ▶ **noun** (especially in sporting contexts) an exceptionally strong or robust man. ■ [often as modifier] trademark (**Ironman**) a multi-event sporting contest demanding stamina, in particular a consecutive triathlon of swimming, cycling, and running.

ironmaster ▶ **noun** a manufacturer of iron, especially (in former times) the proprietor of an ironworks.

ironmonger ▶ **noun** Brit. a person or shop selling hardware such as tools and household implements.
– DERIVATIVES **ironmongery** noun (pl. **ironmongeries**).

iron mould (US **iron mold**) ▶ **noun** a spot caused by rust or an ink stain, especially on fabric.

iron-on ▶ **adjective** able to be fixed to the surface of a fabric by ironing.

iron ore ▶ **noun** [mass noun] a rock or mineral from which iron can be profitably extracted.

iron pan ▶ **noun** Geology a hardpan in which iron oxides are the chief cementing agents.

iron pyrites ▶ **noun** see PYRITES.

iron rations ▶ **plural noun** a small emergency supply of food.

Ironsides a nickname for Oliver Cromwell. ■ [as plural noun] (in the English Civil War) Cromwell's cavalry troopers, so called by their Royalist opponents in allusion to their hardiness in battle.

ironstone ▶ **noun** [mass noun] **1** sedimentary rock containing a substantial proportion of iron compounds.
2 [usu. as modifier] a kind of dense, opaque stoneware.

ironware ▶ **noun** [mass noun] articles made of iron, typically domestic implements.

ironwood ▶ **noun** any of a number of trees that produce very hard timber, in particular: ● a southern African tree of the olive family (*Olea laurifolia*, family Oleaceae). ● a North American tree related to the hornbeam (*Ostrya virginiana*, family Betulaceae).

ironwork ▶ **noun** [mass noun] things or parts made of iron.

ironworks ▶ **noun** [treated as sing. or pl.] a place where iron is smelted or iron goods are made.

irony¹ /ˈʌɪrəni/ ▶ **noun** (pl. **ironies**) [mass noun] the expression of one's meaning by using language that normally signifies the opposite, typically for humorous or emphatic effect: *'Don't go overboard with the gratitude,' he rejoined with heavy irony.* ■ a state of affairs or an event that seems deliberately contrary to what one expects and is often wryly amusing as a result: *the irony is that I thought he could help me* | [count noun] *one of life's little ironies.* ■ (also **dramatic** or **tragic irony**) a literary technique, originally used in Greek tragedy, by which the full significance of a character's words or actions is clear to the audience or reader although unknown to the character.
– ORIGIN early 16th cent. (also denoting Socratic irony): via Latin from Greek *eirōneia* 'simulated ignorance', from *eirōn* 'dissembler'.

irony² /ˈʌɪəni/ ▶ **adjective** of or like iron: *an irony grey colour.*

Iroquoian ▶ **noun** [mass noun] a language family of eastern North America, including Cherokee and Mohawk. With the exception of Cherokee, all its members are extinct or nearly so.
▶ **adjective** relating to the Iroquois people or the Iroquoian language family.

Iroquois /ˈɪrəkwɔɪ, -kɔɪ/ ▶ **noun** (pl. **same**) **1** a member of a former confederacy of six American Indian peoples (Mohawk, Oneida, Seneca, Onondaga, Cayuga, and Tuscarora) who lived mainly in southern Ontario and Quebec and northern New York State.
2 [mass noun] any of the Iroquoian languages of these peoples.
▶ **adjective** relating to the Iroquois or their languages.
– ORIGIN French, from an Algonquian language.

IRQ ▶ **abbreviation** Iraq (international vehicle registration).

irradiance ▶ **noun** [mass noun] **1** Physics the flux of radiant energy per unit area (normal to the direction of flow of radiant energy through a medium).
2 literary the fact of shining brightly.

irradiant ▶ **adjective** literary shining brightly.
– ORIGIN early 16th cent.: from Latin *irradiant-* 'shining upon', from the verb *irradiare* (based on *radius* 'ray').

irradiate ▶ **verb** [with obj.] **1** expose (someone or something) to radiation. ■ expose (food) to gamma rays to kill microorganisms.
2 illuminate (something) by or as if by shining light on it: *happiness filled her, irradiating her whole face.*
– ORIGIN late 16th cent. (in the sense 'emit rays, shine upon'): from Latin *irradiat-* 'shone upon', from the verb *irradiare*, from *in-* 'upon' + *radiare* 'to shine' (from *radius* 'ray').

irradiation ▶ **noun** [mass noun] **1** the process or fact of irradiating or being irradiated.
2 Optics the apparent extension of the edges of an illuminated object seen against a dark background.

irrational ▶ **adjective** **1** not logical or reasonable: *irrational feelings of hostility.* ■ not endowed with the power of reason.
2 Mathematics (of a number, quantity, or expression) not expressible as a ratio of two integers, and having an infinite and non-recurring expansion when expressed as a decimal. Examples of irrational numbers are the number π and the square root of 2.
▶ **noun** Mathematics an irrational number or quantity; a surd.
– DERIVATIVES **irrationality** noun, **irrationalize** (also **irrationalise**) verb, **irrationally** adverb.
– ORIGIN late Middle English: from Latin *irrationalis*, from *in-* 'not' + *rationalis* (see RATIONAL).

irrationalism ▶ **noun** [mass noun] a system of belief or action that disregards or contradicts rational principles.
– DERIVATIVES **irrationalist** noun & adjective.

Irrawaddy /ˌɪrəˈwɒdi/ the principal river of Burma (Myanmar), 2,090 km (1,300 miles) long. It flows in a large delta into the eastern part of the Bay of Bengal.

irrebuttable /ˌɪrɪˈbʌtəb(ə)l/ ▶ **adjective** unable to be rebutted.

irreclaimable ▶ **adjective** not able to be reclaimed or reformed.
– DERIVATIVES **irreclaimably** adverb.

irreconcilable ▶ **adjective** (of ideas or statements) so different from each other that they cannot be made compatible: *these two views of the economy are irreconcilable.* ■ incapable of being resolved: *irreconcilable differences.* ■ (of people) implacably hostile to each other: *irreconcilable enemies.*
▶ **noun** (usu. **irreconcilables**) any of two or more ideas or statements that cannot be made compatible.
– DERIVATIVES **irreconcilability** noun, **irreconcilably** adverb.

irrecoverable ▶ **adjective** not able to be recovered, regained, or remedied: *his liquid assets had to be written off as irrecoverable.*
– DERIVATIVES **irrecoverably** adverb.

irrecusable /ˌɪrɪˈkjuːzəb(ə)l/ ▶ **adjective** rare (of evidence or a statement) not able to be challenged or rejected.
– ORIGIN late 18th cent.: via French from late Latin *irrecusabilis*, from *in-* 'not' + *recusabilis* 'that should be refused' (from the verb *recusare*).

irredeemable ▶ **adjective** **1** not able to be saved, improved, or corrected: *so many irredeemable mistakes have been made.*
2 (of paper currency) for which the issuing authority does not undertake to pay coin. ■ (of securities) on which no date is given for repayment of the capital sum.
– DERIVATIVES **irredeemability** /-ˈbɪlɪti/ noun, **irredeemably** adverb.

irredentist /ˌɪrɪˈdɛntɪst/ ▶ **noun** [usu. as modifier] a person advocating the restoration to their country of any territory formerly belonging to it. ■ historical (in 19th-century Italian politics) an advocate of the return to Italy of all Italian-speaking districts subject to other countries.
– DERIVATIVES **irredentism** noun.
– ORIGIN from Italian *irredentista*, from (*Italia*) *irredenta* 'unredeemed (Italy)'.

irreducible ▶ **adjective** not able to be reduced or simplified: *literature is often* ***irreducible to*** *normative ideas.*
– DERIVATIVES **irreducibility** noun, **irreducibly** adverb.

irreflexive /ɪrɪˈflɛksɪv/ ▶ **adjective** Logic denoting a relation which never holds between a term and itself.

irreformable ▶ **adjective** (chiefly of religious dogma) unable to be revised or altered.

irrefragable /ɪˈrɛfrəgəb(ə)l/ ▶ **adjective** not able to be refuted or disproved; indisputable.
– DERIVATIVES **irrefragably** adverb.
– ORIGIN mid 16th cent.: from late Latin *irrefragabilis*, from *in-* 'not' + *refragari* 'oppose'.

irrefrangible /ˌɪrɪˈfran(d)ʒɪb(ə)l/ ▶ **adjective** rare (of a rule) inviolable: *an irrefrangible law of country etiquette.*

irrefutable /ɪˈrɛfjʊtəb(ə)l, ˌɪrɪˈfjuː-/ ▶ **adjective** impossible to deny or disprove: *irrefutable evidence.*
– DERIVATIVES **irrefutability** noun, **irrefutably** adverb.
– ORIGIN early 17th cent.: from late Latin *irrefutabilis*, from *in-* 'not' + *refutabilis* (from *refutare* 'repel, rebut').

irregardless ▶ **adjective & adverb** informal regardless: *the photographer always says,* ***irregardless of*** *how his subjects are feeling, 'Smile!'.*
– ORIGIN mid 19th cent.: probably a blend of IRRESPECTIVE and REGARDLESS.

> **USAGE** **Irregardless** means the same as **regardless**, but the negative prefix *ir-* merely duplicates the suffix *-less*, and is unnecessary. The word dates back to the 19th century, but is regarded as incorrect in standard English.

irregular ▶ **adjective** **1** not even or balanced in shape or arrangement: *his strong, irregular features.* ■ occurring at uneven or varying rates or intervals: *an irregular heartbeat.* ■ Botany (of a flower) having the petals differing in size and shape; zygomorphic.
2 contrary to the rules or to that which is normal or established: *their involvement in irregular financial dealings.* ■ (of troops) not belonging to regular or established army units.

3 Grammar (of a verb or other word) having inflections that do not conform to the usual rules.
▶ noun (usu. **irregulars**) **1** a member of an irregular military force.
2 chiefly N. Amer. an imperfect piece of merchandise sold at a reduced price.
– DERIVATIVES **irregularly** adverb.
– ORIGIN late Middle English (in the sense 'not conforming to rule (especially that of the Church')): via Old French from medieval Latin *irregularis*, from *in-* 'not' + *regularis* (see **REGULAR**).

irregularity ▶ noun (pl. **irregularities**) [mass noun] the state or quality of being irregular: *there is evidence that fraud and irregularity continue on a large scale* | *the irregularity of his breathing.* ■ [count noun] (usu. **irregularities**) a thing that is irregular in form or nature: *irregularities of the heartbeat* | *financial irregularities.*
– ORIGIN Middle English: from Old French *irregularite*, from late Latin *irregularitas*, from *irregularis* (see **IRREGULAR**).

irrelative ▶ adjective rare unconnected or unrelated. ■ irrelevant.
– DERIVATIVES **irrelatively** adverb.

irrelevance ▶ noun [mass noun] the quality or state of being irrelevant: *the document was withheld on grounds of irrelevance.* ■ [count noun] a person or thing that is irrelevant: *he regarded religion as an irrelevance.*
– DERIVATIVES **irrelevancy** noun (pl. **irrelevancies**).

irrelevant ▶ adjective not connected with or relevant to something: *an irrelevant comment* | *theory can sometimes be hastily dismissed as* ***irrelevant to the*** *classroom.*
– DERIVATIVES **irrelevantly** adverb.

irreligious ▶ adjective indifferent or hostile to religion: *an irreligious man.*
– DERIVATIVES **irreligion** noun, **irreligiously** adverb, **irreligiousness** noun.
– ORIGIN late Middle English: from Latin *irreligiosus*, from *in-* 'not' + *religiosus* (see **RELIGIOUS**).

irremediable /ˌɪrɪˈmiːdɪəb(ə)l/ ▶ adjective impossible to cure or put right: *irremediable marital breakdowns.*
– DERIVATIVES **irremediably** adverb.
– ORIGIN late Middle English: from Latin *irremediabilis*, from *in-* 'not' + *remediabilis* 'curable' (from *remedium* 'remedy').

irremissible ▶ adjective **1** (of a crime) unpardonable.
2 (of an obligation or duty) binding.
– ORIGIN late Middle English: from Old French, or from ecclesiastical Latin *irremissibilis*, from *in-* 'not' + *remissibilis* (from *remittere* 'remit').

irremovable ▶ adjective incapable of being removed: *the irremovable taint of corruption.* ■ (of an official) unable to be displaced from office.
– DERIVATIVES **irremovability** noun, **irremovably** adverb.

irreparable /ɪˈrɛp(ə)rəb(ə)l/ ▶ adjective (of an injury or loss) impossible to rectify or repair: *they were doing irreparable damage to my heart and lungs.*
– DERIVATIVES **irreparability** /-ˈbɪlɪti/ noun, **irreparably** adverb.
– ORIGIN late Middle English: via Old French from Latin *irreparabilis*, from *in-* 'not' + *reparabilis* (see **REPARABLE**).

irreplaceable ▶ adjective impossible to replace if lost or damaged: *do not send valuable or irreplaceable photographs* | *some favourite old books are irreplaceable.*
– DERIVATIVES **irreplaceably** adverb.

irrepressible ▶ adjective not able to be controlled or restrained: *an irrepressible rogue* | *a great shout of irrepressible laughter.*
– DERIVATIVES **irrepressibility** noun, **irrepressibly** adverb.

irreproachable ▶ adjective beyond criticism; faultless: *his private life was irreproachable.*
– DERIVATIVES **irreproachability** noun, **irreproachably** adverb.
– ORIGIN mid 17th cent.: from French *irréprochable*, from *in-* 'not' + *reprochable* (from *reprocher* 'to reproach').

irreproducible ▶ adjective not reproducible.

irresistible ▶ adjective too attractive and tempting to be resisted: *he found the delicious-looking cakes irresistible.* ■ too powerful or convincing to be resisted: *she felt an irresistible urge to object.*
– DERIVATIVES **irresistibility** noun, **irresistibly** adverb.
– ORIGIN late 16th cent.: from medieval Latin *irresistibilis*, from *in-* 'not' + *resistibilis* (from *resistere* 'resist').

irresoluble /ˌɪrɪˈzɒljʊb(ə)l/ ▶ adjective unable to be resolved.
– ORIGIN mid 17th cent.: from Latin *irresolubilis* 'indissoluble'.

irresolute ▶ adjective showing or feeling hesitancy; uncertain: *she stood irresolute outside his door.*
– DERIVATIVES **irresolutely** adverb, **irresoluteness** noun.
– ORIGIN late 16th cent.: from Latin *irresolutus* 'not loosened', or from **IN-**[1] 'not' + **RESOLUTE**.

irresolution ▶ noun [mass noun] hesitancy; uncertainty: *a moment of irresolution.*

irresolvable ▶ adjective (of a problem or dilemma) impossible to solve or settle.

irrespective ▶ adjective (**irrespective of**) not taking (something) into account; regardless of: *child benefit is paid irrespective of income levels.*
– DERIVATIVES **irrespectively** adverb.

irresponsible ▶ adjective (of a person, attitude, or action) not showing a proper sense of responsibility: [with infinitive] *it would have been irresponsible just to drive on.*
– DERIVATIVES **irresponsibility** noun, **irresponsibly** adverb.

irresponsive ▶ adjective not responsive to someone or something.
– DERIVATIVES **irresponsiveness** noun.

irretrievable ▶ adjective not able to be retrieved or put right: *the irretrievable breakdown of their marriage.*
– DERIVATIVES **irretrievability** noun, **irretrievably** adverb.

irreverence ▶ noun [mass noun] a lack of respect for people or things that are generally taken seriously: *an attitude of irreverence towards politicians.*

irreverent /ɪˈrɛv(ə)r(ə)nt/ ▶ adjective showing a lack of respect for people or things that are generally taken seriously: *she is irreverent about the whole business of politics.*
– DERIVATIVES **irreverential** adjective, **irreverently** adverb.
– ORIGIN late Middle English: from Latin *irreverent-* 'not revering', from *in-* 'not' + *reverent-* 'revering' (see **REVERENT**).

irreversible ▶ adjective not able to be undone or altered: *she suffered irreversible damage to her health.*
– DERIVATIVES **irreversibility** noun, **irreversibly** adverb.

irreversible binomial ▶ noun Grammar a noun phrase consisting of two nouns joined by a conjunction, in which the conventional order is fixed. Examples include *bread and butter* and *kith and kin*.

irrevocable /ɪˈrɛvəkəb(ə)l/ ▶ adjective not able to be changed, reversed, or recovered; final: *an irrevocable step.*
– DERIVATIVES **irrevocability** noun, **irrevocably** adverb.
– ORIGIN late Middle English: from Old French, or from Latin *irrevocabilis*, from *in-* 'not' + *revocabilis* 'able to be revoked' (from the verb *revocare*).

irrigate /ˈɪrɪgeɪt/ ▶ verb [with obj.] **1** supply water to (land or crops) to help growth, typically by means of channels. ■ (of a river or stream) supply (land) with water.
2 Medicine wash out (an organ or wound) with a continuous flow of water or medication.
– DERIVATIVES **irrigable** adjective, **irrigation** noun, **irrigator** noun.
– ORIGIN early 17th cent.: from Latin *irrigat-* 'moistened', from the verb *irrigare*, from *in-* 'into' + *rigare* 'moisten, wet'.

irritability ▶ noun [mass noun] the quality or state of being irritable: *symptoms include insomnia and irritability.*

irritable ▶ adjective **1** having or showing a tendency to be easily annoyed: *she was tired and irritable.*
2 Medicine (of a body part) abnormally sensitive. ■ (of a condition) caused by such sensitivity. ■ Biology (of a living organism) having the property of responding actively to physical stimuli.
– DERIVATIVES **irritably** adverb.
– ORIGIN mid 17th cent.: from Latin *irritabilis*, from the verb *irritare* (see **IRRITATE**).

irritable bowel syndrome ▶ noun [mass noun] a widespread condition involving recurrent abdominal pain and diarrhoea or constipation, often associated with stress, depression, anxiety, or previous intestinal infection.

irritant ▶ noun **1** a substance that causes slight inflammation or other discomfort to the body.
2 a thing that is continually annoying or distracting: *in 1966 Vietnam was becoming an irritant to the government.*
▶ adjective causing slight inflammation or other discomfort to the body.
– DERIVATIVES **irritancy** noun.

irritate ▶ verb [with obj.] **1** make (someone) annoyed or a little angry: *his tone irritated her.*
2 cause inflammation or other discomfort in (a part of the body). ■ Biology stimulate (an organism, cell, or organ) to produce an active response.
– DERIVATIVES **irritative** adjective.
– ORIGIN mid 16th cent. (in the sense 'excite, provoke'): from Latin *irritat-* 'irritated', from the verb *irritare*.

irritated ▶ adjective showing or feeling slight anger; annoyed: *the irritated look on Alec's face.*
– DERIVATIVES **irritatedly** adverb.

irritating ▶ adjective **1** causing annoyance, impatience, or mild anger: *an irritating child.*
2 causing irritation to a body part: *the substance may be irritating to eyes and skin.*
– DERIVATIVES **irritatingly** adverb.

irritation ▶ noun [mass noun] **1** the state of feeling annoyed, impatient, or slightly angry: *much to my irritation, Chris fell asleep.* ■ [count noun] a cause of this: *the minor irritations of life.*
2 inflammation or other discomfort in a body part caused by reaction to an irritant substance. ■ Biology the stimulation of an organism, cell, or organ to produce an active response.
– ORIGIN late Middle English: from Latin *irritatio(n-)*, from the verb *irritare* (see **IRRITATE**).

irrotational /ˌɪrəʊˈteɪʃ(ə)n(ə)l/ ▶ adjective Physics (especially of fluid motion) not rotational; having no rotation.

irrupt /ɪˈrʌpt/ ▶ verb [no obj.] enter somewhere forcibly or suddenly. ■ (of a bird or other animal) migrate into an area in abnormally large numbers.
– DERIVATIVES **irruption** noun, **irruptive** adjective.
– ORIGIN mid 19th cent.: (earlier (mid 16th cent.) as *irruption*) from Latin *irrupt-* 'broken into', from the verb *irrumpere*, from *in-* 'into' + *rumpere* 'break'.

IRS ▶ abbreviation (in the US) Internal Revenue Service.

Irtysh /ɪəˈtɪʃ/ a river of central Asia, which rises in the Altai Mountains in northern China and flows westwards into NE Kazakhstan, where it turns north-west into Russia, joining the River Ob near its mouth. Its length is 4,248 km (2,655 miles).

Irving[1] /ˈəːvɪŋ/, Sir Henry (1838–1905), English actor-manager; born *John Henry Brodribb*. He managed the Lyceum Theatre from 1878 to 1902, during which period he entered into a celebrated acting partnership with Ellen Terry.

Irving[2] /ˈəːvɪŋ/, Washington (1783–1859), American writer. He is best known for *The Sketch Book of Geoffrey Crayon, Gent* (1819–20), which contains such tales as 'Rip Van Winkle' and 'The Legend of Sleepy Hollow'.

Irvingite ▶ noun a member of the Catholic Apostolic Church, which followed the teachings of Edward Irving (1792–1834), who was originally a minister of the Church of Scotland.

IS ▶ abbreviation Iceland (international vehicle registration).
– ORIGIN from Icelandic *Ísland*.

is third person singular present of **BE**.

Is. ▶ abbreviation ■ (also **Isa.**) Isaiah (in biblical references). ■ Island(s). ■ Isle(s).

ISA ▶ noun (in the UK) an individual savings account, a scheme allowing individuals to hold cash, shares, and unit trusts free of tax on dividends, interest, and capital gains; in 1999 it replaced both personal equity plans (PEPs) and tax-exempt special savings accounts (TESSAs).
▶ abbreviation Computing industry standard architecture, a standard for connecting computers and their peripherals.

Isaac /ˈʌɪzək/ (in the Bible) a Hebrew patriarch, son of Abraham and Sarah and father of Jacob and Esau.

Isabella I (1451–1504), queen of Castile 1474–1504 and of Aragon 1479–1504. Her marriage in 1469 to Ferdinand of Aragon helped to join together the

Christian kingdoms of Castile and Aragon, marking the beginning of the unification of Spain. They instituted the Spanish Inquisition (1478) and supported Columbus's famous expedition of 1492.

Isabella of France (1292–1358), daughter of Philip IV of France and wife of Edward II of England (1308–27). After returning to France in 1325, she organized an invasion of England in 1326 with her lover Roger de Mortimer, murdering Edward and replacing him with her son, Edward III. Edward took control in 1330, executing Mortimer and sending Isabella into retirement.

isabgul ▸ **noun** variant spelling of **ISPAGHULA**.

isagogics /ˌʌɪsəˈɡɒdʒɪks/ ▸ **plural noun** [treated as sing.] introductory study, especially of the literary and external history of the Bible prior to exegesis.
– ORIGIN mid 19th cent.: plural of *isagogic*, via Latin from Greek *eisagōgikos*, from *eisagōgē* 'introduction', from *eis* 'into' + *agein* 'to lead'.

Isaiah /ʌɪˈzʌɪə/ a major Hebrew prophet of Judah in the 8th century BC, who taught the supremacy of the God of Israel and emphasized the moral demands on worshippers. ■ a book of the Bible containing his prophecies (and, it is generally thought, those of at least one later prophet: see **DEUTERO-ISAIAH**).

isallobar /ʌɪˈsalə(ʊ)bɑː/ ▸ **noun** Meteorology a line on a map connecting points at which the barometric pressure has changed by an equal amount during a specified time.
– ORIGIN early 20th cent.: from **ISO-** 'equal' + **ALLO-** 'other' + **BAR²**.

isangoma /ˌɪsaŋˈɡɔːma/ ▸ **noun** (pl. **same** or **isangomas**) variant spelling of **SANGOMA**.

isatin /ˈʌɪsətɪn/ ▸ **noun** [mass noun] Chemistry a red crystalline compound used in the manufacture of dyes. ● An indole derivative; chem. formula: $C_8H_5NO_2$.
– ORIGIN mid 19th cent.: from Latin *isatis* 'woad' (from Greek) + **-IN¹**.

ISBN ▸ **abbreviation** international standard book number, a ten-digit number assigned to every book before publication, recording such details as language, provenance, and publisher.

ischaemia /ɪˈskiːmɪə/ (US **ischemia**) ▸ **noun** [mass noun] Medicine an inadequate blood supply to an organ or part of the body, especially the heart muscles.
– DERIVATIVES **ischaemic** adjective.
– ORIGIN late 19th cent. (denoting the staunching of bleeding): modern Latin, from Greek *iskhaimos* 'stopping blood', from *iskhein* 'keep back' + *haima* 'blood'.

Ischia /ˈɪskɪə/ an island in the Tyrrhenian Sea off the west coast of Italy, about 26 km (16 miles) west of Naples.

ischiorrhogic /ˌɪskɪə(ʊ)ˈrɒdʒɪk/ ▸ **adjective** Prosody (of an iambic line) having a spondee as its second, fourth, or sixth foot.
– ORIGIN mid 19th cent.: from Greek *iskhiorrhōgikos*, literally 'having broken hips, limping', from *iskhion* 'hip joint' + *rhōx, rhōg-* 'broken'.

ischium /ˈɪskɪəm/ ▸ **noun** (pl. **ischia** /-kɪə/) the curved bone forming the base of each half of the pelvis.
– DERIVATIVES **ischial** adjective.
– ORIGIN early 17th cent.: from Latin, from Greek *iskhion* 'hip joint', later 'ischium'.

ISDN ▸ **abbreviation** integrated services digital network.

Ise /ˈiːseɪ/ a city in central Honshu island, Japan, on Ise Bay; pop. 134,573 (2007). Former name (until 1956) **UJIYAMADA**.

-ise¹ ▸ **suffix** variant spelling of **-IZE**.

> **USAGE** There are some verbs which must be spelled **-ise** and are not variants of the **-ize** ending. Most reflect a French influence; they include **advertise**, **televise**, **compromise**, and **improvise**. For more details, see **USAGE** at **-IZE**.

-ise² ▸ **suffix** forming nouns of quality, state, or function: *expertise* | *franchise* | *merchandise*.
– ORIGIN from Old French *-ise*, from Latin *-itia, -itium*.

isentropic /ˌʌɪsɛnˈtrɒpɪk/ ▸ **adjective** Physics having equal entropy.

Iseult /ɪˈzuːlt, ɪˈsuːlt/ a princess in medieval legend. According to one account, she was the sister or daughter of the king of Ireland, the wife of King Mark of Cornwall, and loved by Tristram. In another account, she was the daughter of the king of Brittany and wife of Tristram. Also called **ISOLDE**.

Isfahan /ˌɪsfəˈhɑːn/ (also **Esfahan**, **Ispahan**) an industrial city in central Iran, the country's third-largest city; pop. 1,602,110 (2006). It was the capital of Persia from 1598 until 1722.

ish ▸ **adverb** informal to some extent: *'Are you busy?' 'Ish.'*

-ish¹ ▸ **suffix** forming adjectives: **1** (from nouns) having the qualities or characteristics of: *apish* | *girlish*. ■ of the nationality of: *Swedish*.
2 (from adjectives) somewhat: *yellowish*. ■ informal denoting an approximate age or time of day: *sixish*.
– ORIGIN Old English *-isc*, of Germanic origin; related to Old Norse *-iskr*, German and Dutch *-isch*, also to Greek *-iskos* (suffix forming diminutive nouns).

-ish² ▸ **suffix** forming verbs such as *abolish*, *establish*.
– ORIGIN from French *-iss-* (from stems of verbs ending in *-ir*), from Latin *-isc-* (suffix forming inceptive verbs); compare with **-ISH¹**.

Isherwood /ˈɪʃəwʊd/, Christopher (William Bradshaw) (1904–86), British-born American novelist. Notable novels: *Mr Norris Changes Trains* (1935), *Goodbye to Berlin* (1939; filmed as *Cabaret*, 1972).

Ishihara test /ɪʃɪˈhɑːrə/ ▸ **noun** a test for colour blindness in which the subject is asked to distinguish numbers or pathways printed in coloured spots on a background of spots of a different colour or colours.
– ORIGIN early 20th cent.: named after Shinobu *Ishihara* (1879–1963), Japanese ophthalmologist.

Ishmael /ˈɪʃmeɪəl/ (in the Bible) a son of Abraham and Hagar, his wife Sarah's maid, driven away with his mother after the birth of Isaac (Gen. 16:12). Ishmael (or Ismail) is also important in Islamic belief as the traditional ancestor of Muhammad and of the Arab peoples.
– DERIVATIVES **Ishmaelite** /ˈɪʃməˌlʌɪt/ noun.

Ishtar /ˈɪʃtɑː/ a Babylonian and Assyrian goddess of love and war whose name and functions correspond to those of the Phoenician goddess Astarte.

Isidore of Seville, St /ˈɪzɪdɔː/ (*c.*560–636), Spanish archbishop and Doctor of the Church; also called *Isidorus Hispalensis*. He is noted for his *Etymologies*, an encyclopedic work used by many medieval authors. Feast day, 4 April.

isinglass /ˈʌɪzɪŋˌɡlɑːs/ ▸ **noun** [mass noun] **1** a kind of gelatin obtained from fish, especially sturgeon, and used in making jellies, glue, etc. and for fining real ale.
2 chiefly US mica or a similar material in thin transparent sheets.
– ORIGIN mid 16th cent.: alteration (by association with **GLASS**) of obsolete Dutch *huysenblas* 'sturgeon's bladder', from *huysen* 'sturgeon' + *blas* 'bladder'.

Isis /ˈʌɪsɪs/ Egyptian Mythology a goddess of fertility, wife of Osiris and mother of Horus. Her worship spread to western Asia, Greece, and Rome, where she was identified with various local goddesses.

Iskenderun /ɪsˈkɛndəruːn/ a port and naval base in southern Turkey, on the Mediterranean coast; pop. 177,300 (est. 2007). Formerly named Alexandretta, it lies on or near the site of Alexandria ad Issum, founded by Alexander the Great in 333 BC.

Islam /ˈɪzlɑːm, ɪzˈlɑːm, ˈɪslɑːm, ɪsˈlɑːm, -lam/ ▸ **noun** [mass noun] the religion of the Muslims, a monotheistic faith regarded as revealed through Muhammad as the Prophet of Allah. ■ the Muslim world: *the most enormous complex of fortifications in all Islam*.

> Founded in the Arabian peninsula in the 7th century AD, Islam is now the professed faith of more than a billion people worldwide, particularly in North Africa, the Middle East, and parts of Asia. The ritual observances and moral code of Islam were said to have been given to Muhammad as a series of revelations, which were codified in the Koran. Islam is regarded by its adherents as the last of the revealed religions, and Muhammad is seen as the last of the prophets, building on and perfecting the examples and teachings of Abraham, Moses, and Jesus. There are two major branches in Islam, Sunni and Shia.

– DERIVATIVES **Islamization** noun, **Islamize** verb (also **Islamise**).
– ORIGIN from Arabic *'islām* 'submission', from *'aslama* 'submit (to God)'.

Islamabad /ɪzˈlɑːməbad/ the capital of Pakistan, a modern planned city in the north of the country, which replaced Rawalpindi as capital in 1967; pop. 673,800 (est. 2009).

Islamic /ɪzˈlamɪk, ɪzˈlɑːmɪk, ɪs-/ ▸ **adjective** relating to Islam: *the Islamic world* | *Islamic law*.
– DERIVATIVES **Islamicization** noun, **Islamicize** (also **Islamicise**) verb.

Islamic Jihad (also **Jehad**) a Muslim fundamentalist group within the Shiite Hezbollah association.

Islamism /ˈɪzləmɪz(ə)m, ˈɪs-/ (also **Islamicism**) ▸ **noun** [mass noun] Islamic militancy or fundamentalism.
– DERIVATIVES **Islamist** noun & adjective.

Islamophobia /ɪzˌlaməˈfəʊbɪə/ ▸ **noun** [mass noun] a hatred or fear of Islam or Muslims, especially as a political force.
– DERIVATIVES **Islamophobe** noun, **Islamophobic** adjective.

Ísland /ˈiːsland/ Icelandic name for **ICELAND**.

island ▸ **noun 1** a piece of land surrounded by water: *the island of Crete* | [as modifier] *this island nation*.
2 a thing regarded as resembling an island, especially in being isolated, detached, or surrounded in some way: *the university is the last island of democracy in this country*. ■ a traffic island. ■ a free-standing kitchen unit with a worktop, allowing access from all sides.
3 Anatomy a detached portion of tissue or group of cells. Compare with **ISLET**.
– ORIGIN Old English *īegland*, from *īeg* 'island' (from a base meaning 'watery, watered') + **LAND**. The change in the spelling of the first syllable in the 16th cent. was due to association with the unrelated word **ISLE**.

island arc ▸ **noun** Geology a curved chain of volcanic islands located at a tectonic plate margin, typically with a deep ocean trench on the convex side.

island area ▸ **noun** each of three administrative areas in Scotland (Orkney, Shetland, Western Isles), consisting of groups of islands.

Island Carib ▸ **noun** see **CARIB** (sense 3 of the noun).

islander ▸ **noun** a native or inhabitant of an island.

island-hop ▸ **verb** [no obj.] (usu. as noun **island-hopping**) travel from one island to another, especially as a tourist in an area of small islands.

Islands of the Blessed (in classical mythology) a land, traditionally located near the place where the sun sets, to which the souls of the good were taken to enjoy a life of eternal bliss.

Islay /ˈʌɪlə/ a large island which is the southernmost of the Inner Hebrides, south of Jura.

isle ▸ **noun** chiefly literary an island or peninsula, especially a small one: *Crusoe's fabled isle* | [in place names] *the British Isles*.
– ORIGIN Middle English *ile*, from Old French, from Latin *insula*. The spelling with *s* (also in 15th-cent. French) is influenced by Latin.

Isle of Man an island in the Irish Sea which is a British Crown dependency having home rule, with its own legislature (the Tynwald) and judicial system; pop. 82,000 (est. 2009); capital, Douglas. The island was part of the Norse kingdom of the Hebrides in the Middle Ages, passing into Scottish hands in 1266 for a time, until the English gained control in the early 15th century. Its ancient language, Manx, is still occasionally used for ceremonial purposes.

Isle of Wight /wʌɪt/ an island off the south coast of England, a county since 1974; pop. 131,700 (est. 2009); administrative centre, Newport. It lies at the entrance to Southampton Water and is separated from the mainland by the Solent and Spithead.

Isle of Wight disease ▸ **noun** [mass noun] a disease of bees that is caused by a parasitic mite. ● The mite is *Acarapis woodi*, order (or subclass) Acari.
– ORIGIN so named because it was first observed in the Isle of Wight in 1904.

islesman ▸ **noun** (pl. **islesmen**) a male native or inhabitant of a group of islands, especially the Hebrides, the Orkneys, or Shetland.

Isles of Scilly another name for the **SCILLY ISLES**.

islet /ˈʌɪlɪt/ ▸ **noun 1** a small island.
2 Anatomy a portion of tissue structurally distinct from surrounding tissues. ■ (**islets**) short for **ISLETS OF LANGERHANS**.
– ORIGIN mid 16th cent.: from Old French, diminutive of *isle* (see **ISLE**).

islets of Langerhans /ˈlaŋəhanz/ ▸ **plural noun** groups of pancreatic cells secreting insulin and glucagon.
– ORIGIN late 19th cent.: named after Paul *Langerhans* (1847–88), the German anatomist who first described them.

ism /ˈɪz(ə)m/ ▸ **noun** informal, chiefly derogatory a distinctive practice, system, or philosophy, typically a political ideology or an artistic movement: *he loathed isms and any form of dogma*.
– DERIVATIVES **ist** noun.
– ORIGIN late 17th cent.: independent usage of **-ISM**.

-ism ▶ suffix forming nouns: **1** denoting an action or its result: ***baptism*** | ***exorcism***. ■ denoting a state or quality: ***barbarism***.
2 denoting a system, principle, or ideological movement: ***Anglicanism*** | ***feminism*** | ***hedonism***. ■ denoting a basis for prejudice or discrimination: ***racism***.
3 denoting a peculiarity in language: ***colloquialism*** | ***Americanism***.
4 denoting a pathological condition: ***alcoholism***.
– ORIGIN from French *-isme*, via Latin from Greek *-ismos*, *-isma*.

Ismail Arabic spelling of **ISHMAEL**.

Ismaili /ˌɪsmʌɪˈiːli, ˌɪsmɑː-/ ▶ noun (pl. **Ismailis**) a member of a branch of Shiite Muslims that seceded from the main group in the 8th century because of their belief that Ismail, the son of the sixth Shiite imam, should have become the seventh imam.

Ismail Samani Peak /ˈɪsmʌɪl ˌsəˈmɑːni/ one of the principal peaks in the Pamir Mountains of Tajikistan, rising to 7,495 m (24,590 ft). It was the highest mountain in the Soviet Union. Former names **GARMO, MOUNT**, **STALIN PEAK**, **COMMUNISM PEAK**.
– ORIGIN named after the 9th-century founder of the Tajik nation.

Isnik ▶ adjective variant spelling of **IZNIK**.

isn't ▶ contraction is not.

ISO[1] International Organization for Standardization.
– ORIGIN from Greek *isos* 'equal'; the term is often erroneously thought to be an abbreviation.

ISO[2] ▶ abbreviation historical (in the UK) Imperial Service Order, awarded to British and commonwealth civil servants (discontinued in 1993).

iso- ▶ combining form equal: *isochron* | *isosceles*. ■ Chemistry (chiefly of hydrocarbons) isomeric: *isooctane*.
– ORIGIN from Greek *isos* 'equal'.

isoagglutination /ˌʌɪsəʊəˌgluːtɪˈneɪʃ(ə)n/ ▶ noun [mass noun] Physiology agglutination of sperms, erythrocytes, or other cells of an individual caused by a substance from another individual of the same species.

isobar /ˈʌɪsə(ʊ)bɑː/ ▶ noun **1** Meteorology a line on a map connecting points having the same atmospheric pressure at a given time or on average over a given period. ■ Physics a curve or formula representing a physical system at constant pressure.
2 Chemistry each of two or more isotopes of different elements, with the same atomic weight.
– DERIVATIVES **isobaric** adjective.
– ORIGIN mid 19th cent.: from Greek *isobaros* 'of equal weight', from *isos* 'equal' + *baros* 'weight'.

isobutane /ˌʌɪsəʊˈbjuːteɪn/ ▶ noun [mass noun] Chemistry a gaseous hydrocarbon isomeric with butane. ● Chem. formula: $CH_3CH(CH_3)_2$.

isobutyl /ˌʌɪsəʊˈbjuːtʌɪl, -tɪl/ ▶ noun [as modifier] Chemistry of or denoting the alkyl radical $-CH_2CH(CH_3)_2$, derived from isobutane.

isobutylene /ˌʌɪsəʊˈbjuːtʌɪliːn, ˌʌɪsəʊˈbjuːtɪliːn/ ▶ noun [mass noun] Chemistry an easily liquefied hydrocarbon gas used in the making of butyl rubber. ● Chem. formula: $(CH_3)_2C{=}CH_2$.

isocheim /ˈʌɪsə(ʊ)kʌɪm/ ▶ noun Meteorology a line on a map connecting points having the same average temperature in winter.
– ORIGIN mid 19th cent.: from **ISO-** 'equal' + Greek *kheima* 'winter weather'.

isochromatic /ˌʌɪsə(ʊ)krəˈmatɪk/ ▶ adjective of a single colour.

isochron /ˈʌɪsə(ʊ)krɒn/ ▶ noun chiefly Geology a line on a diagram or map connecting points relating to the same time or equal times.
– ORIGIN late 17th cent. (as an adjective in the sense 'isochronous'): from Greek *isokhronos*, from *isos* 'equal' + *khronos* 'time'.

isochronous /ʌɪˈsɒkrənəs/ ▶ adjective occurring at the same time. ■ occupying equal time.
– DERIVATIVES **isochronously** adverb.
– ORIGIN early 18th cent. (in the sense 'equal in duration or in frequency'): from modern Latin *isochronus* (from Greek *isokhronos*, from *isos* 'equal' + *khronos* 'time') + **-OUS**.

isoclinal /ˌʌɪsə(ʊ)ˈklʌɪn(ə)l/ ▶ adjective Geology denoting a fold in which the two limbs are parallel.
– ORIGIN mid 19th cent. (denoting 'equal magnetic inclination'): from **ISO-** 'equal' + Greek *klinein* 'to lean, slope' + **-AL**.

isocline /ˈʌɪsə(ʊ)klʌɪn/ ▶ noun a line on a diagram or map connecting points of equal gradient or inclination.
– DERIVATIVES **isoclinic** adjective.
– ORIGIN late 19th cent. (denoting an isoclinal line or fold): from Greek *isoklinēs* 'equally balanced', from *klinein* 'to lean, slope'.

isoclinic line ▶ noun a line on a map connecting points where the dip of the earth's magnetic field is the same.

Isocrates /ʌɪˈsɒkrətiːz/ (436–338 BC), Athenian orator whose written speeches are among the earliest political pamphlets.

isocratic /ˌʌɪsə(ʊ)ˈkratɪk/ ▶ adjective Chemistry (of a chromatographic method) involving a mobile phase whose composition is kept constant and uniform.
– ORIGIN early 19th cent.: from Greek *isokratia* 'equality of power' (from *isos* 'equal' + *kratos* 'strength') + **-IC**.

isocyanate /ˌʌɪsə(ʊ)ˈsʌɪəneɪt/ ▶ noun Chemistry a salt or ester of isocyanic acid.

isocyanic acid /ˌʌɪsə(ʊ)sʌɪˈanɪk/ ▶ noun [mass noun] Chemistry a volatile pungent liquid, isomeric with cyanic acid. ● Chem. formula: HNCO. See also **FULMINIC ACID**.

isocyanide ▶ noun Chemistry an organic compound containing the group –NC bonded to an alkyl group. Such compounds are typically toxic, malodorous liquids.

isodiametric /ˌʌɪsə(ʊ)dʌɪəˈmɛtrɪk/ ▶ adjective chiefly Botany (of a cell, spore, etc.) roughly spherical or polyhedral.

isodynamic ▶ adjective Geography indicating or connecting points on the earth's surface at which the intensity of the magnetic force is the same.

isoelectric ▶ adjective having or involving no net electric charge or difference in electrical potential.

isoelectric focusing ▶ noun [mass noun] Biochemistry a technique of electrophoresis in which the resolution is improved by maintaining a pH gradient between the electrodes.

isoelectronic ▶ adjective Chemistry having the same numbers of electrons or the same electronic structure.

isoenzyme ▶ noun Biochemistry each of two or more enzymes with identical function but different structure.

isoflavone /ˌʌɪsə(ʊ)ˈfleɪvəʊn/ ▶ noun Chemistry a crystalline compound whose derivatives occur in many plants (especially pulses), often as glycosides. ● A tricyclic ketone; chem. formula: $C_{15}H_{10}O_2$.

isogamy /ʌɪˈsɒgəmi/ ▶ noun [mass noun] Biology sexual reproduction by the fusion of similar gametes. Compare with **ANISOGAMY**.
– DERIVATIVES **isogamete** noun, **isogamous** adjective.
– ORIGIN late 19th cent.: from **ISO-** 'equal' + Greek *-gamia* (from *gamos* 'marriage').

isogenic /ˌʌɪsə(ʊ)ˈdʒɛnɪk/ ▶ adjective Biology (of organisms) having the same or closely similar genotypes.

isogeotherm /ˌʌɪsə(ʊ)ˈdʒiːə(ʊ)θəːm/ ▶ noun Geography a line or surface on a diagram connecting points representing those in the interior of the earth having the same temperature.
– DERIVATIVES **isogeothermal** adjective.
– ORIGIN mid 19th cent.: from **ISO-** 'equal' + **GEO-** 'earth' + Greek *thermē* 'heat'.

isogloss /ˈʌɪsə(ʊ)glɒs/ ▶ noun Linguistics a line on a map marking an area having a distinct linguistic feature.
– ORIGIN early 20th cent.: from **ISO-** 'equal' + Greek *glōssa* 'tongue, word'.

isogonic /ˌʌɪsə(ʊ)ˈgɒnɪk/ ▶ adjective Geography indicating or connecting points of the earth's surface at which the magnetic declination is the same.
– ORIGIN mid 19th cent.: from Greek *isogōnios* 'equiangular' + **-IC**.

isohel /ˈʌɪsə(ʊ)hɛl/ ▶ noun Meteorology a line on a map connecting points having the same duration of sunshine.
– ORIGIN early 20th cent.: from **ISO-** 'equal' + Greek *hēlios* 'sun'.

isohyet /ˌʌɪsə(ʊ)ˈhʌɪɪt/ ▶ noun Meteorology a line on a map connecting points having the same amount of rainfall in a given period.
– ORIGIN late 19th cent.: from **ISO-** 'equal' + Greek *huetos* 'rain'.

isokinetic /ˌʌɪsə(ʊ)kɪˈnɛtɪk/ ▶ adjective characterized by or producing a constant speed. ■ Physiology relating to muscular action with a constant rate of movement.

isolate ▶ verb [with obj.] **1** cause (a person or place) to be or remain alone or apart from others: ***a country which is isolated from the rest of the world***. ■ place (a person or animal) in quarantine as a precaution against infectious or contagious disease.
2 identify (something) and examine or deal with it separately: ***his difficulty will be to isolate the factors which are most significant***. ■ cut off the electrical or other connection to (something, especially a part of a supply network). ■ Chemistry & Biology obtain or extract (a compound, microorganism, etc.) in a pure form.
▶ noun **1** a person or thing which has been or become isolated: ***social isolates often become careless of their own welfare***.
2 Biology a culture of microorganisms isolated for study.
– DERIVATIVES **isolable** adjective, **isolatable** adjective, **isolator** noun.
– ORIGIN early 19th cent. (as a verb): back-formation from **ISOLATED**.

isolated ▶ adjective far away from other places, buildings, or people; remote: ***isolated farms and villages***. ■ having minimal contact or little in common with others: ***he lived a very isolated existence***. ■ single; exceptional: ***isolated incidents of student unrest***.
– ORIGIN mid 18th cent.: from French *isolé*, from Italian *isolato*, from late Latin *insulatus* 'made into an island', from Latin *insula* 'island'.

isolating ▶ adjective (of a language) tending to have each element as an independent word without inflections.

isolation ▶ noun [mass noun] the process or fact of isolating or being isolated: ***isolation from family and friends may also contribute to anxiety***. ■ [as modifier] denoting a hospital or ward for patients with contagious or infectious diseases. ■ [count noun] an instance of isolating something, especially a compound or microorganism.
– PHRASES **in isolation** without relation to other people or things; separately: ***environmental problems must not be seen in isolation from social ones***.
– ORIGIN mid 19th cent.: from **ISOLATE**, partly on the pattern of French *isolation*.

isolationism ▶ noun [mass noun] a policy of remaining apart from the affairs or interests of other groups, especially the political affairs of other countries.
– DERIVATIVES **isolationist** noun.

Isolde /ɪˈzɒld, ɪˈzəʊldə/ another name for **ISEULT**.

isoleucine /ˌʌɪsə(ʊ)ˈluːsiːn/ ▶ noun [mass noun] Biochemistry a hydrophobic amino acid that is a constituent of most proteins. It is an essential nutrient in the diet of vertebrates. ● Chem. formula: $CH_3CH_2CH(CH_3)CH(NH_2)COOH$.

isoline /ˈʌɪsə(ʊ)lʌɪn/ ▶ noun another term for **ISOPLETH**.

isomer /ˈʌɪsəmə/ ▶ noun **1** Chemistry each of two or more compounds with the same formula but a different arrangement of atoms in the molecule and different properties.
2 Physics each of two or more atomic nuclei that have the same atomic number and the same mass number but different energy states.
– DERIVATIVES **isomeric** adjective, **isomerism** noun, **isomerize** (also **isomerise**) verb.
– ORIGIN mid 19th cent.: from Greek *isomerēs* 'sharing equally', from *isos* 'equal' + *meros* 'a share'.

isomerase /ʌɪˈsɒməreɪz/ ▶ noun Biochemistry an enzyme which catalyses the conversion of a specified compound to an isomer.

isomerous /ʌɪˈsɒm(ə)rəs/ ▶ adjective Biology having or composed of parts that are similar in number or position.
– ORIGIN mid 19th cent.: from Greek *isomerēs* (see **ISOMER**) + **-OUS**.

isometric ▶ adjective **1** of or having equal dimensions.
2 Physiology relating to or denoting muscular action in which tension is developed without contraction of the muscle.
3 (in technical or architectural drawing) incorporating a method of showing projection or perspective in which the three principal dimensions are represented by three axes 120° apart.
4 Mathematics (of a transformation) without change of shape or size.
– DERIVATIVES **isometrically** adverb, **isometry** noun (sense 4).
– ORIGIN mid 19th cent.: from Greek *isometria* 'equality of measure' (from *isos* 'equal' + *-metria* 'measuring') + **-IC**.

isometrics ▶ plural noun a system of physical exercises in which muscles are caused to act against each other or against a fixed object.

isomorph /ˈʌɪsə(ʊ)mɔːf/ ▶ noun Biology & Crystallography a substance or organism that exactly corresponds in form with another.

isomorphic /ˌʌɪsə(ʊ)ˈmɔːfɪk/ ▶ **adjective** corresponding or similar in form and relations. ■ having the same crystalline form.
– DERIVATIVES **isomorphism** noun, **isomorphous** adjective.

-ison ▶ suffix (forming nouns) equivalent to **-ATION** (as in *comparison, jettison*).
– ORIGIN from Old French *-aison, -eison*, etc., from Latin *-atio(n)-*.

isoniazid /ˌʌɪsə(ʊ)ˈnʌɪəzɪd/ ▶ **noun** [mass noun] Medicine a synthetic compound used as a bacteriostatic drug, chiefly to treat tuberculosis. ● A derivative of nicotinic acid and hydrazine; chem. formula: $C_5H_5NCONHNH_2$.
– ORIGIN 1950s: from **ISO-** 'equal' + *ni(cotinic)* + *(hydr)azine* + **-IDE**.

isonitrile /ˌʌɪsə(ʊ)ˈnʌɪtrʌɪl/ ▶ **noun** Chemistry another term for **ISOCYANIDE**.

isooctane /ˌʌɪsəʊˈɒkteɪn/ ▶ **noun** [mass noun] Chemistry a liquid hydrocarbon present in petroleum. It serves as a standard in the system of octane numbers. ● Chem. formula: $(CH_3)_3CCH_2CH(CH_3)CH_3$.

isopach /ˈʌɪsə(ʊ)pak/ ▶ **noun** Geology a line on a map or diagram connecting points beneath which a particular stratum or group of strata has the same thickness.
– ORIGIN early 20th cent.: from **ISO-** 'equal' + Greek *pakhus* 'thick'.

isophote /ˈʌɪsə(ʊ)fəʊt/ ▶ **noun** a line in a diagram connecting points where the intensity of light is the same.
– ORIGIN early 20th cent.: from **ISO-** 'equal' + Greek *phōs, phōt-* 'light'.

isopleth /ˈʌɪsə(ʊ)plɛθ/ ▶ **noun** Meteorology a line on a map connecting points having equal incidence of a specified meteorological feature.
– ORIGIN early 20th cent.: from Greek *isoplēthēs* 'equal in quantity', from Greek *isos* 'equal' + *plēthos* 'multitude, quantity'.

isopod ▶ **noun** Zoology a crustacean of the order Isopoda, such as a woodlouse.

Isopoda /ˌʌɪsəˈpəʊdə/ ▶ **plural noun** Zoology an order of mainly aquatic crustaceans that includes the woodlice and sea slaters. They have a flattened segmented body with seven similar pairs of legs, and many kinds are marine.
– ORIGIN modern Latin (plural), from Greek *isos* 'equal' + *pous, pod-* 'foot'.

isoprenaline /ˌʌɪsə(ʊ)ˈprɛnəliːn/ ▶ **noun** [mass noun] Medicine a synthetic derivative of adrenalin, used for the relief of bronchial asthma and pulmonary emphysema.
– ORIGIN 1950s: from elements of the systematic name *N-isopropylnoradrenaline*.

isoprene /ˈʌɪsə(ʊ)priːn/ ▶ **noun** [mass noun] Chemistry a volatile liquid hydrocarbon obtained from petroleum, whose molecule forms the basic structural unit of natural and synthetic rubbers. ● Chem. formula: $CH_2{=}C(CH_3)CH{=}CH_2$.
– ORIGIN mid 19th cent.: apparently from **ISO-** 'equal' + *pr(opyl)ene*.

isopropanol /ˌʌɪsə(ʊ)ˈprəʊpənɒl/ ▶ **noun** [mass noun] Chemistry a liquid alcohol, used as a solvent and in the industrial production of acetone. ● Chem. formula: $CH_3CHOHCH_3$.

isopropyl /ˌʌɪsəʊˈprəʊpʌɪl, -pɪl/ ▶ **noun** [as modifier] Chemistry of or denoting the alkyl radical $-CH(CH_3)_2$, derived from propane by removal of a hydrogen atom from the middle carbon atom.

isopropyl alcohol ▶ **noun** [mass noun] Chemistry another term for **ISOPROPANOL**.

isoproterenol /ˌʌɪsə(ʊ)prəʊtəˈriːnɒl/ ▶ **noun** another term for **ISOPRENALINE**.
– ORIGIN 1950s: from elements of the semi-systematic name *N-isopropylarterenol*.

Isoptera /ʌɪˈsɒptərə/ ▶ **plural noun** Entomology an order of insects that comprises the termites.
– DERIVATIVES **isopteran** noun & adjective.
– ORIGIN modern Latin (plural), from Greek *isos* 'equal' + *pteron* 'wing'.

isopycnal /ˌʌɪsə(ʊ)ˈpɪkn(ə)l/ ▶ **adjective** Oceanography (especially of an imaginary line or surface on a map or chart) connecting points in the ocean where the water has the same density.
– ORIGIN early 20th cent.: from **ISO-** 'equal' + Greek *puknos* 'dense' + **-AL**.

isopycnic /ˌʌɪsə(ʊ)ˈpɪknɪk/ ▶ **adjective** Biochemistry of or denoting ultracentrifugal separation techniques making use of differences in density between the components of a mixture.
– ORIGIN late 19th cent.: from **ISO-** 'equal' + Greek *puknos* 'dense' + **-IC**.

isorhythmic ▶ **adjective** Music (of a composition or part) in which the rhythm is often repeated but the pitch of the notes is varied each time.

isosbestic point /ˌʌɪsə(ʊ)sˈbɛstɪk/ ▶ **noun** Chemistry a wavelength at which the absorption of light by a mixed solution remains constant as the equilibrium between the components in the solution changes.
– ORIGIN early 20th cent.: *isosbestic* from **ISO-** 'equal' + Greek *sbestos* 'extinguished' (from *sbennunai* 'quench') + **-IC**.

isosceles /ʌɪˈsɒsɪliːz/ ▶ **adjective** (of a triangle) having two sides of equal length.
– ORIGIN mid 16th cent.: via late Latin from Greek *isoskelēs*, from *isos* 'equal' + *skelos* 'leg'.

isoseismal /ˌʌɪsə(ʊ)ˈsʌɪzm(ə)l/ ▶ **adjective** Geology relating to or denoting lines on a map connecting places where an earthquake was experienced with equal strength.
– DERIVATIVES **isoseismic** adjective.

isosmotic /ˌʌɪsɒzˈmɒtɪk/ ▶ **adjective** Biology having the same osmotic pressure.

isospin /ˈʌɪsə(ʊ)spɪn/ ▶ **noun** [mass noun] Physics a vector quantity or quantum number assigned to subatomic particles and atomic nuclei and having values such that similar particles differing only in charge-related properties (independent of the strong interaction between particles) can be treated as different states of a single particle.
– ORIGIN 1960s: contraction of *isotopic spin, isobaric spin*.

isostasy /ʌɪˈsɒstəsi/ ▶ **noun** [mass noun] Geology the equilibrium that exists between parts of the earth's crust, which behaves as if it consists of blocks floating on the underlying mantle, rising if material (such as an ice cap) is removed and sinking if material is deposited.
– DERIVATIVES **isostatic** adjective.
– ORIGIN late 19th cent.: from **ISO-** 'equal' + Greek *stasis* 'station'.

isotactic /ˌʌɪsə(ʊ)ˈtaktɪk/ ▶ **adjective** Chemistry denoting a polymer in which all the repeating units have the same stereochemical configuration.
– ORIGIN 1950s: from **ISO-** 'equal' + Greek *taktos* 'arranged' + **-IC**.

isothere /ˈʌɪsə(ʊ)θɪə/ ▶ **noun** Meteorology a line on a map connecting points having the same average temperature in summer.
– ORIGIN mid 19th cent.: from French *isothère*, from Greek *isos* 'equal' + *theros* 'summer'.

isotherm /ˈʌɪsə(ʊ)θəːm/ ▶ **noun** a line on a map connecting points having the same temperature at a given time or on average over a given period. ■ Physics a curve on a diagram joining points representing states of equal temperature.
– DERIVATIVES **isothermal** adjective & noun, **isothermally** adverb.
– ORIGIN mid 19th cent.: from French *isotherme*, from Greek *isos* 'equal' + *thermē* 'heat'.

isothiocyanate /ˌʌɪsə(ʊ)ˌθʌɪə(ʊ)ˈsʌɪəneɪt/ ▶ **noun** Chemistry a compound containing the group $-N{=}C{=}S$ as a substituent or ligand.

isotonic /ˌʌɪsə(ʊ)ˈtɒnɪk/ ▶ **adjective** **1** Physiology (of muscle action) taking place with normal contraction. **2** Physiology denoting or relating to a solution having the same osmotic pressure as some other solution, especially one in a cell or a body fluid. **3** (of a drink) containing essential salts and minerals in the same concentration as in the body and intended to replace those lost as a result of sweating during vigorous exercise.
– DERIVATIVES **isotonically** adverb, **isotonicity** noun.
– ORIGIN early 19th cent. (as a musical term designating a system of tuning, characterized by equal intervals): from Greek *isotonos*, from *isos* 'equal' + *tonos* 'tone'.

isotope /ˈʌɪsətəʊp/ ▶ **noun** Chemistry each of two or more forms of the same element that contain equal numbers of protons but different numbers of neutrons in their nuclei, and hence differ in relative atomic mass but not in chemical properties; in particular, a radioactive form of an element.
– DERIVATIVES **isotopic** adjective, **isotopically** adverb, **isotopy** noun.
– ORIGIN 1913: coined by F. Soddy, from **ISO-** 'equal' + Greek *topos* 'place' (because the isotopes occupy the same place in the periodic table of elements).

isotropic /ˌʌɪsə(ʊ)ˈtrɒpɪk/ ▶ **adjective** Physics (of an object or substance) having a physical property which has the same value when measured in different directions. Often contrasted with **ANISOTROPIC**. ■ (of a property or phenomenon) not varying in magnitude according to the direction of measurement.
– DERIVATIVES **isotropically** adverb, **isotropy** /ʌɪˈsɒtrəpi/ noun.
– ORIGIN mid 19th cent.: from **ISO-** 'equal' + Greek *tropos* 'a turn' + **-IC**.

isozyme /ˈʌɪsə(ʊ)zʌɪm/ ▶ **noun** Biochemistry another term for **ISOENZYME**.

ISP ▶ **abbreviation** Internet service provider.

ispaghula /ˌɪspəˈguːlə/ (also **ispaghul** /ˈɪspəguːl/, **isabgul** /ˈɪsəbguːl/) ▶ **noun** [mass noun] the dried seeds of a southern Asian plantain, chiefly used medicinally in the treatment of dysentery. ● The plantain is *Plantago ovata*, family Plantaginaceae.
– ORIGIN early 19th cent.: from Persian and Urdu *ispağol*, from *asp* 'horse' + *ğol* 'ear' (because of the shape of the leaves).

Ispahan /ˌɪspəˈhɑːn/ variant spelling of **ISFAHAN**.

I spy ▶ **noun** [mass noun] a children's game in which one player specifies the first letter of an object they can see, the other players then having to guess the identity of this object.

Israel¹ /ˈɪzreɪəl/ **1** (also **children of Israel**) the Hebrew nation or people. According to tradition they are descended from the twelve sons of the patriarch Jacob (also named Israel).
2 the northern kingdom of the Hebrews (*c.*930–721 BC), formed after the reign of Solomon, whose inhabitants were carried away to captivity in Assyria. See also **JUDAH** (sense 2).
– ORIGIN from Hebrew *Yiśrā'ēl* 'he that strives with God' (see Gen. 32:28).

Israel² /ˈɪzreɪəl/ a country in the Middle East, on the Mediterranean Sea; pop. 7,233,700 (est. 2009); languages, Hebrew (official), English, Arabic; capital (not recognized as such by the United Nations), Jerusalem.

> The modern state of Israel was established as a Jewish homeland in 1948, on land that was at that time part of the British mandated territory of Palestine. Israel was immediately attacked by the surrounding Arab states, which it defeated. The continuing conflict with the neighbouring Arabs, mainly over the rights of the Palestinians displaced from their homes or living under Israeli rule, has caused continual tension and intermittent terrorist and military activity. Further wars occurred in 1956, 1967, and 1973, which resulted in Israeli occupation of eastern Jerusalem, the West Bank, the Gaza Strip, and the Golan Heights. In 1993 Israel and the Palestine Liberation Organization signed an agreement for limited Palestinian autonomy in the West Bank and the Gaza Strip, but this proved unsuccessful in bringing about an end to conflict. See also **PALESTINE**.

Israeli /ɪzˈreɪli/ ▶ **adjective** relating to the modern country of Israel.
▶ **noun** (pl. **Israelis**) a native or inhabitant of Israel, or a person of Israeli descent.

Israelite /ˈɪzrəlʌɪt/ ▶ **noun** a member of the ancient Hebrew nation, especially in the period from the Exodus to the Babylonian Captivity (*c.*12th to 6th centuries BC). ■ an old-fashioned and sometimes offensive term for a Jew.
▶ **adjective** relating to the Israelites.
– ORIGIN via late Latin from Greek *Israēlitēs*.

Israfel /ˈɪzrəfɛl/ (in Muslim tradition) the angel who will sound the trumpet on the Day of Judgement.

Issa /ˈiːsɑː/ ▶ **noun** (pl. **same** or **Issas**) a member of a Somali people living in the Republic of Djibouti.
▶ **adjective** relating to the Issa.
– ORIGIN the name in Somali.

Issachar /ˈɪsəkə/ (in the Bible) a Hebrew patriarch, son of Jacob and Leah (Gen. 30:18). ■ the tribe of Israel traditionally descended from him.

issei /ˈiːseɪ/ ▶ **noun** (pl. **same**) N. Amer. a Japanese immigrant to North America. Compare with **NISEI** and **SANSEI**.
– ORIGIN Japanese, literally 'generation'.

Issigonis /ˌɪsɪˈgəʊnɪs/, Sir Alec (Arnold Constantine) (1906–88), Turkish-born British car designer. His most famous designs were the Morris Minor (1948) and the Mini (1959).

ISSN ▶ **abbreviation** international standard serial number, an eight-digit number assigned to many serial publications such as newspapers, magazines, annuals, and series of books.

issuant /ˈɪʃ(j)ʊənt, ˈɪsjʊ-/ ▶ **adjective** [predic.] Heraldry (of the upper part of an animal) shown rising up or out

from another bearing, especially from the bottom of a chief or from behind a fess.
– ORIGIN early 17th cent.: from ISSUE + -ANT (on the pattern of French present participles ending in *-ant*).

issue /ˈɪʃ(j)uː, ˈɪsjuː/ ▸ **noun 1** an important topic or problem for debate or discussion: *the issue of racism | raising awareness of environmental issues.* ▪ **(issues)** informal personal problems or difficulties: *emotions and intimacy issues that were largely dealt with through alcohol.* ▪ **(issues)** problems or difficulties, especially with a service or facility: *a small number of users are experiencing connectivity issues.*
2 [mass noun] the action of supplying or distributing an item for use, sale, or official purposes: *the issue of notes by the Bank of England.* ▪ [count noun] a number or set of items distributed at one time: *a share issue has been launched.* ▪ [count noun] each of a regular series of publications: *the December issue of the magazine.*
3 a result or outcome of something: *the chance of carrying such a scheme to a successful issue was small.*
4 the action of flowing or coming out: *a point of issue.*
5 [mass noun] formal or Law children of one's own: *the earl died without male issue.*
▸ **verb (issues, issuing, issued) 1** [with obj.] supply or distribute (something) for use or sale: *licences were **issued** indiscriminately **to** any company | Christmas stamps to be issued in November.* ▪ **(issue someone with)** supply someone with (something): *everyone was issued with a gas mask.* ▪ formally send out or make known: *the minister issued a statement.*
2 [no obj.] **(issue from)** come, go, or flow out from: *exotic smells issued from a nearby building.* ▪ result or be derived from: *the struggles of history issue from the divided heart of humanity.*
– PHRASES **at issue** under discussion; in dispute. **make an issue of** treat too seriously or as a problem. **take issue with** disagree with; challenge: *she takes issue with the notion of crime as unique to contemporary society.*
– DERIVATIVES **issuable** adjective, **issuance** noun, **issueless** adjective, **issuer** noun.
– ORIGIN Middle English (in the sense 'outflowing'): from Old French, based on Latin *exitus*, past participle of *exire* 'go out'.

> **WORD TRENDS** To say that someone has **issues** is to imply that they suffer from emotional or psychological difficulties: *she's got issues from her childhood | he has serious issues with monogamy.* Use of the term is a euphemistic way of avoiding the word **problem**, seen as negative and stigmatizing. The exact nature of the issues is generally left vague and mysterious, even when narrowed down by a modifier (*intimacy issues, emotional issues, mental issues*). More generally **issues** are problems or difficulties, particularly with the provision of a service (*devices on the company's network are experiencing performance issues*): again, the word has a euphemistic feel, perhaps implying that what is occurring is not so serious or specific as to amount to an actual problem. See also SOLUTION.

issue of fact ▸ **noun** Law a dispute in court in which the significance of a fact or facts is denied.

issue of law ▸ **noun** Law a dispute in court in which the application of the law is contested.

-ist ▸ **suffix** forming personal nouns and some related adjectives: **1** denoting an adherent of a system of beliefs, principles, etc. expressed by nouns ending in *-ism*: *hedonist | Calvinist.* See -ISM (sense 2). ▪ denoting a person who subscribes to a prejudice or practises discrimination: *sexist.*
2 denoting a member of a profession or business activity: *dentist | dramatist | florist.* ▪ denoting a person who uses a thing: *flautist | motorist.* ▪ denoting a person who does something expressed by a verb ending in *-ize*: *plagiarist.*
– ORIGIN from Old French *-iste*, Latin *-ista*, from Greek *-istēs*.

-ista ▸ **suffix** informal forming nouns denoting a person associated with a particular activity, often with a derogatory force: *fashionista.*
– ORIGIN from the Spanish ending *-ista*, as in SANDINISTA.

Istanbul /ˌɪstanˈbʊl/ a port in Turkey on the Bosporus, lying partly in Europe, partly in Asia; pop. 10,757,300 (est. 2007). Formerly the Roman city of Constantinople (330–1453), it was built on the site of the ancient Greek city of Byzantium. It was captured by the Ottoman Turks in 1453 and was the capital of Turkey from that time until 1923.
– ORIGIN Turkish, from Greek *eis tēn polin* 'into the city'.

isthmian /ˈɪsθmɪən, ˈɪstm-, ˈɪsm-/ ▸ **adjective** relating to an isthmus. ▪ **(Isthmian)** relating to the Isthmus of Corinth in southern Greece.

Isthmian games games held by the ancient Greeks every other year near the Isthmus of Corinth.

isthmus /ˈɪsθməs, ˈɪstməs, ˈɪsməs/ ▸ **noun** (pl. **isthmuses**) **1** a narrow strip of land with sea on either side, forming a link between two larger areas of land.
2 (pl. **isthmi**) Anatomy a narrow organ, passage, or piece of tissue connecting two larger parts.
– ORIGIN mid 16th cent.: via Latin from Greek *isthmos*.

istle /ˈɪstli/ ▸ **noun** variant spelling of IXTLE.

ISV ▸ **abbreviation** independent software vendor.

IT ▸ **abbreviation** information technology.

it[1] ▸ **pronoun** [third person singular] **1** used to refer to a thing previously mentioned or easily identified: *a room with two beds in it | this approach is refreshing because it breaks down barriers.* ▪ referring to an animal or child of unspecified sex: *she was holding the baby, cradling it and smiling into its face.* ▪ referring to a fact or situation previously mentioned, known, or happening: *stop it, you're hurting me.*
2 used to identify a person: *it's me | it's a boy!*
3 used in the normal subject position in statements about time, distance, or weather: *it's half past five | it was two miles to the island | it's raining.*
4 used in the normal subject or object position when a more specific subject or object is given later in the sentence: *it is impossible to assess the problem | she found it interesting to learn about their strategy.*
5 [with clause] used to emphasize a following part of a sentence: *it is the child who is the victim.*
6 the situation or circumstances; things in general: *no one can stay here—it's too dangerous now | he would like to see you straight away if it's convenient.*
7 exactly what is needed or desired: *they thought they were it | you've either got it or you haven't.*
8 (usu. **'it'**) informal sexual intercourse or sex appeal.
9 (usu. **'it'**) (in children's games) the player who has to catch the others.
– PHRASES **at it** see AT[1]. **that's it 1** that is the main point or difficulty: *'Is she going?' 'That's just it—she can't make up her mind.'* **2** that is enough or the end: *okay, that's it, you've cried long enough.* **this is it 1** the expected event is about to happen: *this is it—the big sale.* **2** this is enough or the end: *this is it, I'm going.* **3** this is the main point or difficulty.
– ORIGIN Old English *hit*, neuter of HE, of Germanic origin; related to Dutch *het*.

it[2] ▸ **noun** [mass noun] Brit. informal, dated Italian vermouth: *he poured a **gin and it**.*
– ORIGIN 1930s: abbreviation.

ITA ▸ **abbreviation** initial teaching alphabet.

Itaipu /iːˈtʌɪpuː/ a dam on the Paraná River in SW Brazil, one of the world's largest hydroelectric installations, formally opened in 1982.

ital /ˈɪtal/ ▸ **noun** [mass noun] (in Rastafarian culture) organically grown vegetarian food, cooked without salt.
– ORIGIN from *I* (used by Rastafarians to signify value) + VITAL or VITTLE.

ital. ▸ **abbreviation** italic (used as an instruction for a typesetter).

Italia /iˈtalja/ Italian name for ITALY.

Italian ▸ **adjective** relating to Italy, its people, or their language.
▸ **noun 1** a native or inhabitant of Italy, or a person of Italian descent.
2 [mass noun] the Romance language of Italy, descended from Latin and with roughly 60 million speakers worldwide. It is also one of the official languages of Switzerland.
– DERIVATIVES **Italianist** noun, **Italianize** (also **Italianise**) verb.
– ORIGIN late Middle English: from Italian *italiano*, from *Italia* 'Italy'.

Italianate ▸ **adjective** Italian in character or appearance: *an Italianate staircase with triple loggia.*
– ORIGIN late 16th cent.: from Italian *italianato*, from *Italia* 'Italy'.

Italian garden ▸ **noun** a type of garden characterized by clipped trees, box-edged beds of flowers, paved paths, statues, fountains, etc., and often arranged in terraces.

Italianism ▸ **noun 1** an Italian characteristic, expression, or custom.
2 [mass noun] attachment to Italy or Italian ideas or practices.

Italian parsley ▸ **noun** another term for FLAT-LEAVED PARSLEY.

Italian vermouth ▸ **noun** [mass noun] a type of bittersweet vermouth made in Italy.

Italic /ɪˈtalɪk/ ▸ **adjective** relating to or denoting the branch of Indo-European languages that includes Latin, Oscan, Umbrian, and the Romance languages.
▸ **noun** [mass noun] the Italic group of languages.
– ORIGIN late 19th cent.: via Latin from Greek *Italikos*, from *Italia* 'Italy'.

italic /ɪˈtalɪk/ ▸ **adjective** of the sloping kind of typeface used especially for emphasis or distinction and in foreign words. ▪ (of handwriting) modelled on 16th-century Italian handwriting, typically cursive and sloping and with elliptical or pointed letters.
▸ **noun** (also **italics**) [mass noun] an italic typeface or letter: *the key words are **in italics**.*
– ORIGIN late Middle English (in the general sense 'Italian'): via Latin from Greek *Italikos*, from *Italia* 'Italy'. Senses relating to writing date from the early 17th cent.

italicize /ɪˈtalɪsʌɪz/ (also **italicise**) ▸ **verb** [with obj.] print (text) in italics.
– DERIVATIVES **italicization** noun.

Italiot /ɪˈtalɪət/ ▸ **noun** an inhabitant of any of the Greek colonies in ancient Italy.
▸ **adjective** relating to these people.
– ORIGIN from Greek *Italiōtēs*, from *Italia* 'Italy'.

Italo- /ˈɪtələʊ, ɪˈtaləʊ/ ▸ **combining form** Italian; Italian and ...: *Italophile | Italo-Grecian.* ▪ relating to Italy.

Italy a country in southern Europe; pop. 58,126,200 (est. 2009); official language, Italian; capital, Rome. Italian name ITALIA.

> Italy was united under Rome from the 1st century BC to the collapse of the empire in AD 476. In the Middle Ages it was dominated by several city-states and the papacy and was the centre of the Renaissance. Modern Italy was created in the mid 19th century by a movement led by Garibaldi; the Sardinian monarch, Victor Emmanuel II, became king of Italy in 1861. Italy entered the First World War on the Allied side in 1915. In 1922 the country was taken over by the Fascist dictator Mussolini; participation in support of Germany during the Second World War resulted in defeat and Mussolini's downfall. Italy was a founder member of the EEC.

Itanagar /ˌiːtəˈnʌgə/ a city in the far north-east of India, north of the Brahmaputra River, capital of the state of Arunachal Pradesh; pop. 55,500 (est. 2009).

ITAR-Tass /ˈʌɪtɑː/ the official news agency of Russia, founded in 1925 in Leningrad as Tass, and renamed in 1992.
– ORIGIN from the initials of Russian *Informatsionnoe telegrafnoe agentstvo Rossii* 'Information Telegraph Agency of Russia', + TASS.

itch ▸ **noun** [usu. in sing.] an uncomfortable sensation on the skin that causes a desire to scratch. ▪ [mass noun] [usu. with modifier] a skin disease or condition of which itching is a symptom. ▪ informal a restless or strong desire to do something: *an itch to write fiction.*
▸ **verb** [no obj.] be the site of or cause an itch: *the bite itched like crazy.* ▪ (of a person) experience an itch: *I itched all over.* ▪ informal feel a restless or strong desire to do something: [with infinitive] *Paul was itching to get outside.*
– PHRASES **an itching palm** an avaricious nature.
– ORIGIN Old English *gycce* (noun), *gyccan* (verb), of West Germanic origin; related to Dutch *jeuk* (noun) and Dutch *jeuken*, German *jucken* (verb).

itching powder ▸ **noun** [mass noun] a powder used to make someone's skin itch, typically as a practical joke.

itch mite ▸ **noun** a parasitic mite which burrows under the skin, causing scabies in humans and sarcoptic mange in animals. • *Sarcoptes scabiei*, family Sarcoptidae.

itchy ▸ **adjective (itchier, itchiest)** having or causing an itch: *dry, itchy skin | an itchy rash.*
– PHRASES **have** (or **get**) **itchy feet** informal have or develop a strong urge to travel or move from place to place.
– DERIVATIVES **itchiness** noun.

it'd ▸ **contraction** it had: *it'd been there for years.* ▪ it would: *it'd be great to see you.*

-ite[1] ▸ **suffix 1** forming names denoting natives of a country: *Israelite.* ▪ often derogatory denoting followers of a movement, doctrine, etc.: *Luddite | Thatcherite.*
2 used in scientific and technical terms: ▪ forming names of fossil organisms: *ammonite.* ▪ forming names of minerals: *graphite.* ▪ forming names of

constituent parts of a body or organ: *somite*. ▪ forming names of explosives and other commercial products: *dynamite* | *vulcanite*. ▪ Chemistry forming names of salts or esters of acids ending in *-ous*: *sulphite*.
– ORIGIN from French *-ite*, via Latin *-ita* from Greek *ites*.

-ite² ▸ suffix **1** forming adjectives such as *composite*, *erudite*.
2 forming nouns such as *appetite*.
3 forming verbs such as *unite*.
– ORIGIN from Latin *-itus*, past participle of verbs ending in *-ere* and *-ire*.

item ▸ noun an individual article or unit, especially one that is part of a list, collection, or set: *the items on the agenda* | *an item of clothing*. ▪ a piece of news or information. ▪ an entry in an account.
▸ adverb archaic used to introduce each item in a list: *item two statute books ... item two drums*.
– PHRASES **be an item** informal (of a couple) be involved in an established romantic or sexual relationship.
– ORIGIN late Middle English (as an adverb): from Latin, 'in like manner, also'. The noun sense arose (late 16th cent.) from the use of the adverb to introduce each statement in a list.

itemize (also **itemise**) ▸ verb [with obj.] present as a list of individual items: *I have itemized the morning's tasks*. ▪ break down (a whole) into its constituent parts. ▪ specify (an individual item or items).
– DERIVATIVES **itemization** /-ˈzeɪʃ(ə)n/ noun, **itemizer** noun.

I

iterate /ˈɪtəreɪt/ ▸ verb [with obj.] perform or utter repeatedly. ▪ [no obj.] make repeated use of a mathematical or computational procedure, applying it each time to the result of the previous application; perform iteration.
▸ noun Mathematics a quantity arrived at by iteration.
– ORIGIN mid 16th cent.: from Latin *iterat-* 'repeated', from the verb *iterare*, from *iterum* 'again'.

iteration ▸ noun [mass noun] the repetition of a process or utterance. ▪ repetition of a mathematical or computational procedure applied to the result of a previous application, typically as a means of obtaining successively closer approximations to the solution of a problem. ▪ [count noun] a new version of a piece of computer hardware or software.
– ORIGIN late Middle English: from Latin *iteratio(n-)*, from the verb *iterare* (see ITERATE).

iterative ▸ adjective relating to or involving iteration, especially of a mathematical or computational process. ▪ Linguistics denoting a grammatical rule that can be applied repeatedly. ▪ Grammar another term for FREQUENTATIVE.
– DERIVATIVES **iteratively** adverb.
– ORIGIN late 15th cent.: from French *itératif, -ive*, from Latin *iterare* 'to repeat'; the grammar term is from late Latin *iterativus*.

It girl ▸ noun informal a young woman who has achieved celebrity because of her socialite lifestyle.
– ORIGIN coined by the American screenwriter Elinor Glyn (1864–1943) with reference to the American actress and sex symbol Clara Bow, who made her name in such films as *It* (1927). The current use dates from the 1960s.

Ithaca /ˈɪθəkə/ an island off the western coast of Greece in the Ionian Sea, the legendary home of Odysseus.

ithyphallic /ˌɪθɪˈfalɪk/ ▸ adjective (especially of a statue or other representation of a deity) having an erect penis.
– ORIGIN early 17th cent. (as a noun denoting a sexually explicit poem): via late Latin from Greek *ithuphallikos*, from *ithus* 'straight' + *phallos* 'phallus'.

Iti ▸ noun (pl. **Ities**) & adjective variant spelling of EYETIE.

-itic ▸ suffix forming adjectives and nouns corresponding to nouns ending in *-ite* (such as *Semitic* corresponding to *Semite*). ▪ corresponding to nouns ending in *-itis* (such as *arthritic* corresponding to *arthritis*). ▪ from other bases: *syphilitic*.
– ORIGIN from French *-itique*, via Latin *-iticus* from Greek *-itikos*.

itinerant /ɪˈtɪn(ə)r(ə)nt, ʌɪ-/ ▸ adjective travelling from place to place: *itinerant traders*.
▸ noun a person who travels from place to place.
– DERIVATIVES **itineracy** noun, **itinerancy** noun.
– ORIGIN late 16th cent. (used to describe a judge travelling on a circuit): from late Latin *itinerant-* 'travelling', from the verb *itinerari*, from Latin *iter*, *itiner-* 'journey, road'.

itinerary /ʌɪˈtɪn(ə)(rə)ri, ɪ-/ ▸ noun (pl. **itineraries**) a planned route or journey. ▪ a travel document recording a route or journey.
– ORIGIN late Middle English: from late Latin *itinerarium*, neuter of *itinerarius* 'of a journey or roads', from Latin *iter*, *itiner-* 'journey, road'.

itinerate /ɪˈtɪnəreɪt, ʌɪ-/ ▸ verb [no obj.] (especially of a Church minister or a magistrate) travel from place to place to perform one's professional duty.
– DERIVATIVES **itineration** noun.
– ORIGIN early 17th cent.: from late Latin *itinerat-* 'travelled', from the verb *itinerari* (see ITINERANT).

-ition ▸ suffix (forming nouns) equivalent to -ATION (as in *audition*, *rendition*).
– ORIGIN from French, or from Latin *-itio(n)-*.

-itious¹ ▸ suffix forming adjectives corresponding to nouns ending in *-ition* (such as *ambitious* corresponding to *ambition*).
– ORIGIN from Latin *-itiosus*.

-itious² ▸ suffix (forming adjectives) related to; having the nature of: *fictitious* | *suppositious*.
– ORIGIN from late Latin *-itius*, alteration of Latin *-icius*.

-itis ▸ suffix forming names of inflammatory diseases: *cystitis* | *hepatitis*. ▪ informal used with reference to a tendency or state of mind that is compared to a disease: *creditcarditis*.
– ORIGIN from Greek feminine form of adjectives ending in *-itēs* (combined with *nosos* 'disease' implied).

-itive ▸ suffix (forming adjectives) equivalent to -ATIVE (as in *genitive*, *positive*).
– ORIGIN from French *-itif*, *-itive* or Latin *-itivus* (from past participial stems ending in *-it*).

it'll ▸ contraction it shall; it will.

ITN ▸ abbreviation (in the UK) Independent Television News.

Ito /ˈiːtəʊ/, Prince Hirobumi (1841–1909), Japanese statesman, Premier four times between 1884 and 1901. He was prominent in drafting the Japanese constitution (1889) and helped to establish a bicameral national diet (1890). He was assassinated by a member of the Korean independence movement.

-itous ▸ suffix forming adjectives corresponding to nouns ending in *-ity* (such as *calamitous* corresponding to *calamity*).
– ORIGIN from French *-iteux*, from Latin *-itosus*.

its ▸ possessive determiner belonging to or associated with a thing previously mentioned or easily identified: *turn the camera on its side* | *he chose the area for its atmosphere*. ▪ belonging to or associated with a child or animal of unspecified sex: *a baby in its mother's womb*.

> **USAGE** A common error in writing is to confuse the possessive **its** (as in *turn the camera on **its** side*) with the contraction **it's** (short for either **it is** or **it has**, as in ***it's** my fault; **it's** been a hot day*). The confusion is at least partly understandable since other possessive forms (singular nouns) do take an apostrophe + **-s**, as in *the **girl's** bike*; *the **President's** smile*.

it's ▸ contraction it is: *it's my fault*. ▪ it has: *it's been a hot day*.

itself ▸ pronoun [third person singular] **1** [reflexive] used as the object of a verb or preposition to refer to a thing or animal previously mentioned as the subject of the clause: *his horse hurt itself* | *the company has established itself as a leader in the field*.
2 [emphatic] used to emphasize a particular thing or animal mentioned: *the roots are several inches long, though the plant itself is only a foot tall*. ▪ used after a quality to emphasize what a perfect example of that quality someone or something is: *Mrs Vincent was kindness itself*.
– PHRASES **by itself** see BY ONESELF at BY. **in itself** viewed in its essential qualities; considered separately from other things: *some would say bringing up a family was a full-time job in itself*.
– ORIGIN Old English (see IT¹, SELF).

itsy-bitsy (also **itty-bitty**) ▸ adjective informal very small; tiny.
– ORIGIN 1930s: from a child's form of LITTLE + *bitsy* (from BIT¹ + -SY).

ITU ▸ abbreviation ▪ Brit. intensive therapy unit. ▪ International Telecommunication Union.

ITV ▸ abbreviation ▪ (in the UK) Independent Television. ▪ (also **iTV**) interactive television.

-ity ▸ suffix forming nouns denoting quality or condition: *humility* | *probity*. ▪ denoting an instance or degree of this: *a profanity*.
– ORIGIN from French *-ité*, from Latin *-itas*, *-itatis*.

IU ▸ abbreviation international unit.

IUCN ▸ abbreviation International Union for the Conservation of Nature.

IUD ▸ abbreviation ▪ intrauterine death (of the fetus before birth). ▪ intrauterine device.

-ium ▸ suffix **1** forming nouns adopted unchanged from Latin (such as *alluvium*) or based on Latin or Greek words (such as *euphonium*).
2 (also **-um**) forming names of metallic elements: *cadmium* | *magnesium*.
3 denoting a region of the body: *pericardium*.
4 denoting a biological structure: *mycelium*.
– ORIGIN modern Latin in sense 2, sense 3, sense 4, via Latin from Greek *-ion*.

IUPAC ▸ abbreviation International Union of Pure and Applied Chemistry.

IV ▸ abbreviation intravenous or intravenously.

Ivan¹ /ˈʌɪv(ə)n/ the name of six rulers of Russia:
▪ **Ivan I** (*c.*1304–41), grand duke of Muscovy 1328–40. He strengthened and enlarged the duchy, making Moscow the ecclesiastical capital in 1326.
▪ **Ivan II** (1326–59), grand duke of Muscovy 1353–9; known as **Ivan the Red**. ▪ **Ivan III** (1440–1505), grand duke of Muscovy 1462–1505; known as **Ivan the Great**. He consolidated and enlarged his territory, defending it against a Tartar invasion in 1480 and adopting the title 'Ruler of all Russia' in 1472. ▪ **Ivan IV** (1530–84), grand duke of Muscovy 1533–47 and first tsar of Russia 1547–84; known as **Ivan the Terrible**. He captured Kazan, Astrakhan, and Siberia, but the Tartar siege of Moscow and the Polish victory in the Livonian War (1558–82) left Russia weak and divided. In 1581 he killed his eldest son Ivan in a fit of rage, the succession passing to his mentally disturbed second son Fyodor.
▪ **Ivan V** (1666–96), nominal tsar of Russia 1682–96.
▪ **Ivan VI** (1740–64), infant tsar of Russia 1740–1.

Ivan² /ˈʌɪv(ə)n/ ▸ noun informal a Russian man, especially a Russian soldier.

I've ▸ contraction I have.

-ive ▸ suffix (forming adjectives, also nouns derived from them) tending to; having the nature of: *active* | *corrosive* | *palliative*.
– DERIVATIVES **-ively** suffix forming corresponding adverbs, **-iveness** suffix forming corresponding nouns.
– ORIGIN from French *-if*, *-ive*, from Latin *-ivus*.

ivermectin /ˌʌɪvəˈmɛktɪn/ ▸ noun [mass noun] a compound of the avermectin group, used as an anthelmintic in veterinary medicine and as a treatment for river blindness.

Ives /ʌɪvz/, Charles (Edward) (1874–1954), American composer, noted for his use of polyrhythms, polytonality, quarter-tones, and aleatoric techniques. Notable works: *The Unanswered Question* (chamber work, 1906) and *Three Places in New England* (for orchestra, 1903–14).

IVF ▸ abbreviation in vitro fertilization.

ivied ▸ adjective covered in ivy: *the ivied rectory*.
▪ US relating to the academic institutions of the Ivy League.

IVM ▸ abbreviation in vitro maturation, a fertility treatment in which immature eggs are extracted from a woman's body and matured in a laboratory before being fertilized.

Ivorian ▸ adjective relating to Côte d'Ivoire (Ivory Coast) or its people.
▸ noun a native or inhabitant of Côte d'Ivoire.

ivorine /ˈʌɪvəriːn, -ʌɪn/ ▸ noun [mass noun] trademark an artificial product resembling ivory in colour or texture.

Ivory, James (b.1928), American film director. He has made a number of films in partnership with the producer Ismail Merchant, including *Heat and Dust* (1983) and *Howard's End* (1992).

ivory ▸ noun (pl. **ivories**) [mass noun] **1** a hard creamy-white substance composing the main part of the tusks of an elephant, walrus, or narwhal, often (especially formerly) used to make ornaments and other articles. ▪ [count noun] an object made of ivory. ▪ (**the ivories**) informal the keys of a piano: ***Derek tinkled the ivories for us***. ▪ (**ivories**) informal a person's teeth.
2 the creamy-white colour of ivory: [as modifier] *an ivory silk blouse*.
– DERIVATIVES **ivoried** adjective.
– ORIGIN Middle English: from Anglo-Norman French *ivurie*, based on Latin *ebur*.

ivory black ▶ **noun** [mass noun] a black carbon pigment made from charred ivory or (now usually) bone, used in drawing and painting.

Ivory Coast another name for **Côte d'Ivoire**.

ivory nut ▶ **noun** the seed of a tropical American palm, which, when hardened, is a source of vegetable ivory. Also called **tagua nut**. ● The palm is *Phytelephas macrocarpa*, family Palmae.

ivory tower ▶ **noun** a state of privileged seclusion or separation from the facts and practicalities of the real world: *the ivory tower of academia*.
– ORIGIN early 20th cent.: translating French *tour d'ivoire*, used by the writer Sainte-Beuve.

ivy ▶ **noun** [mass noun] a woody evergreen Eurasian climbing plant, typically having shiny, dark green five-pointed leaves. ● Genus *Hedera*, family Araliaceae: several species, in particular the common *H. helix*, which is often seen climbing on tree trunks and walls.
■ used in names of similar climbing plants, e.g. **poison ivy**, **Boston ivy**.
– ORIGIN Old English *ifig*, of Germanic origin; related to the first elements of Dutch *eiloof* and German *Efeu*.

Ivy League ▶ **noun** a group of long-established universities in the eastern US having high academic and social prestige. It includes Harvard, Yale, Princeton, and Columbia.
– ORIGIN with reference to the ivy traditionally growing over the walls of these establishments.

IWC ▶ **abbreviation** International Whaling Commission.

iwi /ˈiːwi/ ▶ **noun** (pl. **same**) NZ a Maori community or people.
– ORIGIN Maori.

Iwo Jima /ˌiːwəʊ ˈdʒiːmə/ a small volcanic island, the largest of the Volcano Islands in the western Pacific, 1,222 km (760 miles) south of Tokyo. During the Second World War it was the heavily fortified site of a Japanese airbase, and its attack and capture in 1944–5 was one of the severest US campaigns. It was returned to Japan in 1968.

IWW ▶ **abbreviation** Industrial Workers of the World.

ixia /ˈɪksɪə/ ▶ **noun** a South African plant of the iris family, which bears showy six-petalled starlike flowers on tall wiry stems and has sword-shaped leaves. ● Genus *Ixia*, family Iridaceae: many cultivars.
– ORIGIN modern Latin, from Latin, denoting a kind of thistle, from Greek.

Ixion /ɪkˈsʌɪən/ Greek Mythology a king punished by Zeus for attempting to seduce Hera by being pinned to a fiery wheel that revolved unceasingly through the underworld.

ixnay /ˈɪksneɪ/ US informal ▶ **exclamation** (**ixnay on/to**) used in rejecting something specified: *ixnay to corporate control!*
▶ **verb** [with obj.] cancel or stop: *the group has ixnayed the rest of its North American tour*.
– ORIGIN 1920s: pig Latin for **nix**[1].

ixtle /ˈɪkstli/ (also **istle**) ▶ **noun** [mass noun] (in Mexico and Central America) a plant fibre used for cordage, nets, and carpets. ● This fibre is obtained chiefly from *Agave* species (family Agavaceae), in particular *A. funkiana* and *A. lecheguilla*.
– ORIGIN late 19th cent.: via American Spanish from Nahuatl *ixtli*.

Iyengar /ɪˈjɛŋgɑː/ ▶ **noun** [mass noun] a type of hatha yoga focusing on the correct alignment of the body, making use of straps, wooden blocks, and other objects as aids to achieving the correct postures.
– ORIGIN named after B. K. S. *Iyengar* (born 1918), the Indian yoga teacher who devised this method.

Iyyar /ˈiːjɑː/ ▶ **noun** (in the Jewish calendar) the eighth month of the civil and second of the religious year, usually coinciding with parts of April and May.
– ORIGIN from Hebrew *ʾiyyār*.

izard /ˈɪzəd/ ▶ **noun** (in the Pyrenees) a chamois.
– ORIGIN late 18th cent.: from French *isard* or Gascon *isart*, of unknown origin.

-ize (also **-ise**) ▶ **suffix** forming verbs meaning: **1** make or become: *fossilize* | *privatize*. ■ cause to resemble: *Americanize*.
2 treat in a specified way: *pasteurize*. ■ treat or cause to combine with a specified substance: *carbonize* | *oxidize*.
3 follow a specified practice: *agonize* | *theorize*. ■ subject to a practice: *hospitalize*.
– DERIVATIVES **-ization suffix** forming corresponding nouns, **-izer suffix** forming agent nouns.
– ORIGIN from French *-iser*, via late Latin *-izare* from Greek verbs ending in *-izein*.

USAGE 1 The form **-ize** has been in use in English since the 16th century; although it is widely used in American English, it is not an Americanism. The alternative spelling **-ise** (reflecting a French influence) is in common use, especially in British English. It is obligatory in certain cases: first, where it forms part of a larger word element, such as **-mise** (= sending) in **compromise**, and **-prise** (= taking) in **surprise**; and second, in verbs corresponding to nouns with **-s-** in the stem, such as **advertise** and **televise**.
2 Adding **-ize** to a noun or adjective has been a standard way of forming new verbs for centuries, and verbs such as **characterize**, **terrorize**, and **sterilize** were all formed in this way hundreds of years ago. For some reason, people object to recent formations of this type: during the 20th century, objections were raised against **prioritize**, **finalize**, and **hospitalize**, among others. There doesn't seem to be any coherent reason for this, except that verbs formed from nouns tend, inexplicably, to be criticized as vulgar formations. Despite objections, it is clear that **-ize** forms are an accepted part of the standard language.

Izhevsk /ɪˈʒɛfsk/ an industrial city in central Russia, capital of the republic of Udmurtia; pop. 612,400 (est. 2009). Former name (1984–87) **Ustinov**.

izimbongi plural form of **imbongi**.

izinyanga plural form of **inyanga**.

Izmir /ˈɪzmɪə/ a seaport and naval base in western Turkey, on an inlet of the Aegean Sea; pop. 2,606,300 (est. 2007). It is the third-largest city in Turkey. Former name **Smyrna**.

Izmit /ˈɪzmɪt/ a city in NW Turkey, situated on the Gulf of Izmit, an inlet of the Sea of Marmara; pop. 248,400 (est. 2007).

Iznik /ˈɪznɪk/ (also **Isnik**) ▶ **adjective** denoting colourful pottery and ceramic tiles produced during the 16th and 17th centuries in Iznik (ancient Nicaea), a town in NW Turkey.

Izod test /ˈʌɪzɒd/ ▶ **noun** a material strength test in which a notched specimen is broken by a blow from a pendulum, the energy absorbed being determined from the decrease in the swing of the pendulum.
– ORIGIN early 20th cent.: named after Edwin G. *Izod*, the British engineer who devised the test.

Izvestia /ɪzˈvɛstɪə/ (also **Izvestiya**) a Russian daily newspaper founded in 1917 as the official organ of the Soviet government. It has continued to be published independently since the collapse of communist rule and the break-up of the Soviet Union.
– ORIGIN from Russian *izvestiya* 'news'.

izzat /ˈɪzʌt/ ▶ **noun** [mass noun] Indian honour, reputation, or prestige.
– ORIGIN Persian and Urdu, from Arabic *ʿizza* 'glory'.

I

Jj

J¹ (also **j**) ▶ **noun** (pl. **Js** or **J's**) **1** the tenth letter of the alphabet. ■ denoting the next after I (or H if I is omitted) in a set of items, categories, etc.
2 (**J**) a shape like that of a capital J (without a crosspiece).
3 archaic used instead of I as the Roman numeral for one in final position: *between ij and iij of the clock*.

J² ▶ **abbreviation** ■ jack (used in describing play in card games). ■ Japan (international vehicle registration). ■ Physics joule(s). ■ (in titles) Journal (of): *J. Biol. Chem.*

j ▶ **symbol** (*j*) (in electrical engineering and electronics) the imaginary quantity equal to the square root of minus one. Compare with **I**.

JA ▶ **abbreviation** Jamaica (international vehicle registration).

ja /jɑː/ ▶ **exclamation** informal South African term for **YES**: *'Let's go swimming.' 'Ja!'* | *ja, this is the life!*
– PHRASES **ja well** used as an expression of embarrassment, apology, or world-weariness. **ja well no fine** used to express a non-committal, resigned, or ironical attitude.
– ORIGIN Dutch.

jab ▶ **verb** (**jabs, jabbing, jabbed**) [with obj. and adverbial] poke roughly or quickly, especially with something sharp or pointed: *she jabbed him in his ribs* | [no obj.] *he jabbed at the air with his finger*. ■ roughly or quickly thrust (a sharp or pointed object) someone or something: *she jabbed the fork into the earth*.
▶ **noun** a quick, sharp blow, especially with the fist: *a jab in the stomach*. ■ Brit. informal a hypodermic injection, especially a vaccination: *an anti-tetanus jab*. ■ a sharp, painful sensation or feeling: *a jab of envy*.
– ORIGIN early 19th cent. (originally Scots): variant of **JOB²**.

Jabalpur /ˌdʒʌb(ə)lˈpʊə/ an industrial city and military post in Madhya Pradesh, central India; pop. 1,067,000 (est. 2009).

jabber ▶ **verb** [no obj.] talk in a rapid, excited, and often incomprehensible way: *he jabbered on about football*.
▶ **noun** [mass noun] rapid, excited, and often incomprehensible speech.
– ORIGIN late 15th cent.: imitative.

jabberwocky /ˈdʒabəˌwɒki/ ▶ **noun** (pl. **jabberwockies**) [mass noun] invented or meaningless language; nonsense.
– ORIGIN early 20th cent.: from the title of a nonsense poem in Lewis Carroll's *Through the Looking Glass* (1871).

jabiru /ˈdʒabɪruː/ ▶ **noun** a large Central and South American stork with a black neck, mainly white plumage, and a large black upturned bill. ● *Jabiru mycteria*, family Ciconiidae.
■ either of two related storks found in Asia, Australasia, and Africa.
– ORIGIN late 18th cent.: from Tupi-Guarani *jabirú*, from *j* 'that which has' + *abirú* 'swollen' (suggested by the bird's large neck).

jab jab ▶ **noun** W. Indian a devil, in particular as represented in a carnival masquerade.
– ORIGIN French Creole, from French *diable diable* 'devil devil'.

jaborandi /ˌdʒabəˈrandi/ ▶ **noun 1** [mass noun] a drug made from the dried leaves of certain South American plants, which contain the alkaloid pilocarpine and promote salivation when chewed.
2 any of the plants that yield this drug. ● Several genera and species, in particular *Pilocarpus jaborandi* (family Rutaceae).
– ORIGIN early 17th cent.: from Tupi-Guarani *jaburandi*, literally 'a person who spits'.

jabot /ˈʒabəʊ/ ▶ **noun** an ornamental frill or ruffle on the front of a shirt or blouse, typically made of lace.
– ORIGIN early 19th cent. (denoting a frill on a man's shirt): French, originally 'crop of a bird'.

jacal /həˈkɑːl/ ▶ **noun** (pl. **jacales** /həˈkɑːleɪz/) (in Mexico and the south-western US) a thatched wattle-and-daub hut.
– ORIGIN Mexican Spanish, from Nahuatl *xacalli*, contraction of *xamitl calli* 'adobe house'.

jacamar /ˈdʒakəmɑː/ ▶ **noun** an insectivorous bird of tropical American forests, with a long pointed bill, a long tail, and plumage that is typically iridescent green above. ● Family Galbulidae: several genera and species.
– ORIGIN early 19th cent.: from French, apparently from Tupi.

jacana /ˈdʒakənə/ (also **jaçana** /ˌdʒasəˈnɑː/) ▶ **noun** a small tropical wading bird with greatly elongated toes and claws that enable it to walk on floating vegetation. Also called **LILY-TROTTER**. ● Family Jacanidae: several genera and species.
– ORIGIN mid 18th cent.: from Portuguese *jaçanã*, from Tupi-Guarani *jasanã*.

jacaranda /ˌdʒakəˈrandə/ ▶ **noun** a tropical American tree which has blue trumpet-shaped flowers, fern-like leaves, and fragrant timber. ● Genus *Jacaranda*, family Bignoniaceae.
– ORIGIN mid 18th cent.: from Portuguese, from Tupi-Guarani *jakara'nda*.

jacinth /ˈdʒasɪnθ, ˈdʒeɪ-/ ▶ **noun** [mass noun] a reddish-orange gem variety of zircon.
– ORIGIN Middle English: from Old French *iacinte* or medieval Latin *iacintus*, alteration of Latin *hyacinthus* (see **HYACINTH**).

jack¹ ▶ **noun 1** a device for lifting heavy objects, especially one for raising the axle of a motor vehicle off the ground so that a wheel can be changed or the underside inspected.
2 a playing card bearing a representation of a soldier, page, or knave, normally ranking next below a queen.
3 (also **jack socket**) a socket with two or more pairs of terminals designed to receive a jack plug.
4 a small white ball in bowls, at which the players aim.
5 (also **jackstone**) a small round pebble or star-shaped piece of metal or plastic used in games involving tossing and catching. ■ (**jacks**) a game played by tossing and catching such pebbles or pieces of metal.
6 (**Jack**) informal used to typify an ordinary man: *he had that world-weary look of the working Jack who'd seen everything*. ■ chiefly US used as a form of address to a man whose name is not known. ■ N. Amer. a lumberjack. ■ a detective or police officer. ■ archaic a steeplejack. ■ the figure of a man striking the bell on a clock.
7 a small version of a national flag flown at the bow of a vessel in harbour to indicate its nationality.
8 [mass noun] N. Amer. informal money.
9 a device for turning a spit.
10 a part of the mechanism in a spinet or harpsichord that connects a key to its corresponding string and causes the string to be plucked when the key is pressed down.
11 a marine fish that is typically laterally compressed with a row of large spiky scales along each side, important in many places as food or game fish. Also called **POMPANO, SCAD**. [originally a West Indian term.] ● Family Carangidae (the **jack family**): many genera and numerous species. The jack family also includes the horse mackerel, pilotfish, kingfishes, and trevallies.
12 the male of various animals, especially a merlin or (*US*) an ass.
13 used in names of animals that are smaller than similar kinds, e.g. **jack snipe**.
14 US informal short for **JACK SHIT**.
– PHRASES **before one can say Jack Robinson** informal very quickly or suddenly. **every man jack** informal each and every person (used for emphasis): *they're spies, every man jack of them*. **I'm all right, Jack** informal used to express selfish complacency. **jack of all trades (and master of none)** a person who can do many different types of work but who is not necessarily very competent at any of them. **on one's jack** (or **Jack Jones**) Brit. rhyming slang on one's own.
– PHRASAL VERBS **jack someone around** N. Amer. informal cause someone inconvenience or problems, especially by acting unfairly or indecisively. **jack in** (or **into**) informal log into or connect up (a computer or electronic device). **jack something in** Brit. informal give up or stop doing something, especially a job. **jack off** vulgar slang masturbate. **jack up** informal **1** inject oneself with a narcotic drug. **2** Austral. give up or refuse to participate in something. **jack something up 1** raise something, especially a vehicle, with a jack. ■ informal increase something by a considerable amount: *France jacked up its key bank interest rate*. **2** NZ informal arrange or organize something.
– ORIGIN late Middle English: from *Jack*, pet form of the given name *John*. The term was used originally to denote an ordinary man (sense 6), also a youth (mid 16th cent.), hence the 'knave' in cards and 'male animal'. The word also denoted various devices saving human labour, as though one had a helper (sense 1, sense 3, sense 9, sense 10, and in compounds such as **JACKHAMMER** and **JACKKNIFE**); the general sense 'labourer' arose in the early 18th cent. and survives in **CHEAPJACK, LUMBERJACK, STEEPLEJACK**, etc. Since the mid 16th cent. a notion of 'smallness' has arisen, hence sense 4, sense 5, sense 7, sense 13.

jack² ▶ **noun** historical **1** another term for **BLACKJACK** (sense 5).
2 a sleeveless padded tunic worn by foot soldiers. [late Middle English: from Old French *jaque*; origin uncertain, perhaps based on Arabic.]

jack³ ▶ **adjective** [predic.] Austral. informal tired of or bored with someone or something: *people are getting jack of strikes*.
– ORIGIN late 19th cent.: from *jack up* 'give up'.

jack⁴ ▶ **verb** [with obj.] N. Amer. informal take (something) illicitly; steal: *what's wrong is to jack somebody's lyrics and not acknowledge the fact*. ■ rob (someone).
– ORIGIN 1990s: from **HIJACK**.

jackal /ˈdʒakəl, -kɔːl/ ▶ **noun** a slender long-legged wild dog that feeds on carrion, game, and fruit and often hunts cooperatively, found in Africa and southern Asia. ● Genus *Canis*, family Canidae: four species.
– ORIGIN early 17th cent.: from Turkish *çakal*, from Persian *šagāl*. The change in the first syllable was due to association with **JACK¹**.

jackanapes /ˈdʒakəneɪps/ ▶ **noun 1** dated a cheeky or impertinent person.
2 archaic a tame monkey.
– ORIGIN early 16th cent. (originally as *Jack Napes*): perhaps from a playful name for a tame ape, the initial *n-* by elision of *an ape* (compare with **NEWT**), and the final *-s* as in surnames such as *Hobbes*: applied to a person whose behaviour resembled that of an ape.

jack arch ▶ **noun** a small arch only one brick in thickness, especially as used in numbers to support a floor.

jackaroo /ˌdʒakəˈruː/ (also **jackeroo**) Austral./NZ informal ▶ **noun** a young man working on a sheep or cattle station to gain experience.
▶ **verb** (usu. **jackeroo**) [no obj.] work as a jackaroo.
– ORIGIN late 19th cent.: perhaps a blend of **JACK**[1] and **KANGAROO**.

jackass ▶ **noun 1** a stupid person.
2 a male ass or donkey.
3 Austral. short for **LAUGHING JACKASS**.

jack bean ▶ **noun** a tropical American climbing plant of the pea family, which yields an edible bean and pod and is widely grown for fodder in tropical countries. ● Genus *Canavalia*, family Leguminosae: in particular *C. ensiformis*.

jackboot ▶ **noun** a large leather military boot reaching to the knee. ■ used as a symbol of cruel or authoritarian behaviour or rule: *a country under the jackboot of colonialism*.
– DERIVATIVES **jackbooted** adjective.

Jack-by-the-hedge ▶ **noun** a white-flowered European plant of the cabbage family, which grows typically in hedgerows and has leaves that smell of garlic when crushed. Also called **HEDGE GARLIC**. ● *Alliaria petiolata*, family Cruciferae.

Jack cheese ▶ **noun** North American term for **MONTEREY JACK**.

jackdaw ▶ **noun** a small grey-headed crow that typically nests in tall buildings and chimneys, noted for its inquisitiveness. ● Genus *Corvus*, family Corvidae: two species, in particular the Eurasian *C. monedula*.

jackeen /dʒaˈkiːn/ ▶ **noun** Irish, chiefly derogatory a city-dweller, especially a Dubliner.
– ORIGIN mid 19th cent.: diminutive of the pet name *Jack* (see **JACK**[1], **-EEN**).

jackeroo ▶ **noun & verb** variant spelling of **JACKAROO**.

jacket ▶ **noun 1** an outer garment extending either to the waist or the hips, typically having sleeves and a fastening down the front.
2 an outer covering, especially one placed round a tank or pipe to insulate it. ■ the dust jacket of a book. ■ a record sleeve.
3 Brit. the skin of a potato: *potatoes cooked in their jackets*. ■ informal a jacket potato.
4 US a folder or envelope containing an official document or file.
5 a steel frame fixed to the seabed, forming the support structure of an oil production platform.
▶ **verb** (**jackets, jacketing, jacketed**) [with obj.] cover with a jacket.
– ORIGIN late Middle English: from Old French *jaquet*, diminutive of *jaque* (see **JACK**[2]).

jacket potato ▶ **noun** Brit. a baked potato served with the skin on.

jackfish ▶ **noun** (pl. **same** or **jackfishes**) chiefly N. Amer. a pike or sauger, especially the northern pike.

Jack Frost ▶ **noun** a personification of frost: *the seedlings battled with Jack Frost*.

jackfruit ▶ **noun** a fast-growing tropical Asian tree related to the breadfruit. ● *Artocarpus heterophyllus*, family Moraceae.
■ the very large edible fruit of this tree, resembling a breadfruit and important as food in the tropics.
– ORIGIN late 16th cent.: from Portuguese *jaca* (from Malayalam *chakka*) + **FRUIT**.

jackhammer chiefly N. Amer. ▶ **noun** a portable pneumatic hammer or drill.
▶ **verb** [with obj.] beat or hammer heavily or loudly and repeatedly.

jackie hangman ▶ **noun** South African term for **FISCAL** (sense 2 of the noun).
– ORIGIN early 20th cent.: apparently so named because of the bird's habit of impaling its prey on long sharp thorns.

jack-in-office ▶ **noun** Brit. a self-important minor official.

jack-in-the-box ▶ **noun** a toy consisting of a box containing a figure on a spring which pops up when the lid is opened.

Jack-in-the-pulpit ▶ **noun** either of two small plants of the arum family: ● another term for **CUCKOO PINT**. ● a North American arum with a green or purple-brown spathe (*Arisaema triphyllum*, family Araceae).
– ORIGIN mid 19th cent.: so named because the erect spadix overarched by the spathe resembles a person in a pulpit.

jackknife ▶ **noun** (pl. **jackknives**) **1** a large knife with a folding blade.
2 a dive in which the body is first bent at the waist and then straightened.
3 Statistics a method of assessing the variability of data by repeating a calculation on the sets of data obtained by removing one value from the complete set.
▶ **verb** (**jackknifes, jackknifing, jackknifed**) [no obj.] move one's body into a bent or doubled-up position: *she jackknifed into a sitting position*. ■ (of an articulated vehicle) bend into a V-shape in an uncontrolled skidding movement. ■ (of a diver) perform a jackknife.

jackknife clam ▶ **noun** North American term for **RAZOR SHELL**.

jackknife fish ▶ **noun** a strikingly marked fish with a long upright dorsal fin, which lives among rocks and corals in the warm waters of the western Atlantic. ● *Equetus lanceolatus*, family Sciaenidae.

jackleg ▶ **noun** US informal an incompetent, unskilful, or dishonest person.

jack light ▶ **noun** N. Amer. a portable light, especially one used for fishing at night.

Jacklin, Tony (b.1944), English golfer; full name *Antony Jacklin*. He won the British Open in 1969 and in 1970 became the first British player to win the US Open for fifty years.

jack mackerel ▶ **noun** a game fish of the jack family, occurring in the eastern Pacific. ● *Trachurus symmetricus*, family Carangidae.

jack-o'-lantern ▶ **noun 1** a lantern made from a hollowed-out pumpkin or turnip in which holes are cut to represent facial features, typically made at Halloween.
2 archaic a will-o'-the-wisp.

jack pine ▶ **noun** a small, hardy North American pine with short needles. ● *Pinus banksiana*, family Pinaceae.

jack plane ▶ **noun** a medium-sized plane for use in rough joinery.

jack plug ▶ **noun** a plug consisting of a single shaft used to make a connection which transmits a signal, typically used in sound equipment.

jackpot ▶ **noun** a large cash prize in a game or lottery, especially one that accumulates until it is won.
– PHRASES **hit the jackpot** informal **1** win a jackpot. **2** have great or unexpected success, especially in making a lot of money quickly: *the theatre hit the jackpot with its first musical*.
– ORIGIN late 19th cent.: from **JACK**[1] + **POT**[1]. The term was originally used in a form of poker, where the pool or pot accumulated until a player could open the bidding with two jacks or better.

jackrabbit ▶ **noun** a hare found on the prairies and steppes of North America. ● Genus *Lepus*, family Leporidae: several species.
– ORIGIN mid 19th cent.: abbreviation of *jackass-rabbit*, because of its long ears.

Jack Russell (also **Jack Russell terrier**) ▶ **noun** a terrier of a small working breed with short legs.
– ORIGIN early 20th cent.: named after the Revd John (*Jack*) *Russell* (1795–1883), an English clergyman famed in fox-hunting circles as a breeder of such terriers.

jacks ▶ **noun** Irish a toilet.
– ORIGIN variant form of **JAKES**.

jack screw ▶ **noun 1** a screw which can be turned to adjust the position of an object into which it fits.
2 another term for **SCREW JACK**.

jack shaft ▶ **noun** a small auxiliary or intermediate shaft in machinery.

jack shit ▶ **noun** [mass noun] [usu. with negative] US vulgar slang anything at all.

jacksie (also **jacksy**) ▶ **noun** Brit. informal a person's bottom.
– ORIGIN late 19th cent.: diminutive of **JACK**[1].

jack snipe ▶ **noun** a small dark Eurasian snipe. ● *Lymnocryptes minima*, family Scolopacidae.
■ N. Amer. any similar wader, e.g. the pectoral sandpiper or the common snipe.

jack socket ▶ **noun** see **JACK**[1] (sense 3).

Jackson[1] the state capital of Mississippi; pop. 173,861 (est. 2008).
– ORIGIN originally known as *Le Fleur's Bluff*, it was later named after President Andrew *Jackson*.

Jackson[2], Andrew (1767–1845), American general and Democratic statesman, 7th President of the US 1829–37; known as **Old Hickory**. As President he replaced an estimated 20 per cent of those in public office with Democrat supporters, a practice that became known as the spoils system.

Jackson[3], Michael (Joe) (1958–2009), American pop singer and songwriter. Having started singing with his four brothers, as the Jackson Five, he became the most commercially successful American star of the 1980s with the albums *Thriller* (1982) and *Bad* (1987).

Jackson[4], Thomas Jonathan (1824–63), American Confederate general; known as **Stonewall Jackson**. During the American Civil War he made his mark as a commander at the first battle of Bull Run in 1861 and later became the deputy of Robert E. Lee.

Jacksonian /dʒakˈsəʊnɪən/ ▶ **adjective** Medicine relating to or denoting a form of epilepsy in which seizures begin at one site (typically a digit or the angle of the mouth).
– ORIGIN late 19th cent.: from the name of John H. *Jackson* (1835–1911), English physician and neurologist, + **-IAN**.

Jacksonville an industrial city and port in NE Florida; pop. 807,815 (est. 2008).
– ORIGIN named in honour of President Andrew Jackson.

J

jackstaff ▶ **noun** a short staff at a ship's bow, on which a jack is hoisted.

jackstay ▶ **noun** Nautical a rope, bar, or batten placed along a ship's yard to bend the head of a square sail to. ■ a line secured at both ends to serve as a support, e.g. for an awning.

jackstone ▶ **noun** see **JACK**[1] (sense 5).

jackstraw ▶ **noun** another term for **SPILLIKIN**.

jacksy ▶ **noun** (pl. **jacksies**) variant spelling of **JACKSIE**.

Jack tar ▶ **noun** Brit. informal, dated a sailor.

Jack the Lad ▶ **noun** Brit. informal a brash, cocky young man.
– ORIGIN nickname of *Jack Sheppard*, an 18th-cent. thief.

Jack the Ripper an unidentified 19th-century English murderer. In 1888 at least six prostitutes were brutally killed in the East End of London, the bodies being mutilated in a way that indicated a knowledge of anatomy. The authorities received taunting notes from a person calling himself Jack the Ripper and claiming to be the murderer, but the cases remain unsolved.

jack-up ▶ **noun 1** (also **jack-up rig**) an offshore drilling rig the legs of which are lowered to the seabed from the operating platform.
2 NZ informal a dishonest or underhand way of achieving something.

Jacky (also **Jacky Jacky**) ▶ **noun** (pl. **Jackies**) Austral. offensive an Aborigine.
– ORIGIN mid 19th cent.: diminutive of the pet name *Jack* (see **JACK**[1]).

Jacky lizard ▶ **noun** a brownish SE Australian lizard which becomes paler as the temperature rises. When threatened it puffs itself up and opens its orange mouth. ● *Amphibolus muricatus*, family Agamidae.

Jacky Winter ▶ **noun** an Australasian flycatcher which has a grey-brown back and whitish underside and constantly wags its white-edged tail. ● *Microeca leucophaea*, family Eopsaltridae (or Muscicapidae). Alternative name: **Australian brown flycatcher**.
– ORIGIN late 19th cent.: diminutive form of the pet name *Jack* (see **JACK**[1]) + *Winter* (imitative of the bird's cry).

Jacob /ˈdʒeɪkəb/ (in the Bible) a Hebrew patriarch, the younger of the twin sons of Isaac and Rebecca, who persuaded his brother Esau to sell him his birthright and tricked him out of his father's blessing (Gen. 25, 27). The twelve tribes of ancient Israel were descended from his twelve sons.
– ORIGIN from Hebrew *ya'ăqōḇ* 'following after, supplanter'.

Jacobean /ˌdʒakəˈbiːən/ ▶ **adjective** relating to the reign of James I of England: *a Jacobean mansion*.
■ denoting the architectural style prevalent during the reign of James I, consisting of a blend of Gothic and classical features. ■ (of furniture) in the style

prevalent during the reign of James I, characterized by the use of dark oak.
▸ **noun** a person who lived in the Jacobean period.
– ORIGIN mid 19th cent. (in use earlier with reference to St James): from modern Latin *Jacobaeus* (from ecclesiastical Latin *Jacobus* 'James', from Greek *Iakōbos* 'Jacob') + **-AN**.

Jacobethan /ˌdʒakəˈbiːθ(ə)n/ ▸ **adjective** (especially of architecture) displaying a combination of Elizabethan and Jacobean styles.
– ORIGIN 1930s: blend of **JACOBEAN** and **ELIZABETHAN**.

Jacobi /dʒaˈkəʊbi/, Karl Gustav Jacob (1804–51), German mathematician. He worked on the theory of elliptic functions, in competition with Niels Abel.

Jacobian /dʒəˈkəʊbɪən/ Mathematics ▸ **adjective** relating to the work of the mathematician K. G. J. Jacobi.
▸ **noun** a determinant whose constituents are the derivatives of a number of functions (*u, v, w*, ...) with respect to each of the same number of variables (*x, y, z*, ...).

Jacobin /ˈdʒakəbɪn/ ▸ **noun 1** historical a member of a democratic club established in Paris in 1789. The Jacobins were the most radical and ruthless of the political groups formed in the wake of the French Revolution, and in association with Robespierre they instituted the Terror of 1793–4. ■ an extreme political radical.
2 chiefly historical a Dominican friar.
3 (**jacobin**) a pigeon of a breed with reversed feathers on the back of its neck like a cowl.
4 (**jacobin**) a mainly green Central and South American hummingbird, with blue feathers on the head. ● *Florisuga mellivora* and *Melanotrichilus fuscus*, family Trochilidae.
– DERIVATIVES **Jacobinic** adjective, **Jacobinical** adjective, **Jacobinism** noun.
– ORIGIN Middle English (in sense 2): from Old French, from medieval Latin *Jacobinus*, from ecclesiastical Latin *Jacobus* 'James'. The term was applied to the Dominicans in Old French on account of their church in Paris, St Jacques, near which they built their first convent; the latter eventually became the headquarters of the French revolutionary group.

Jacobite¹ /ˈdʒakəbʌɪt/ ▸ **noun** a supporter of the deposed James II and his descendants in their claim to the British throne after the Revolution of 1688. Drawing most of their support from Catholic clans of the Scottish Highlands, Jacobites made attempts to regain the throne in 1689–90, 1715, 1719, and 1745–6, finally being defeated at the Battle of Culloden.
– DERIVATIVES **Jacobitical** adjective, **Jacobitism** noun.
– ORIGIN from Latin *Jacobus* 'James' (see **JACOBEAN**) + **-ITE¹**.

Jacobite² /ˈdʒakəbʌɪt/ ▸ **noun** a member of the Syrian Orthodox Church (Monophysite).
– ORIGIN early 15th cent.: from medieval Latin *Jacobita*, from the name of *Jacobus* Baradaeus, a 6th-cent. Syrian monk.

Jacobsen /ˈjakəbsən/, Arne (1902–1971), Danish architect and furniture designer. His buildings include the SAS tower in Copenhagen and St Catherine's College in Oxford, both of which are expressive of his interest in modernism.

Jacob sheep ▸ **noun** a four-horned sheep of a piebald breed, kept as an ornamental animal or for its wool.

Jacob's ladder ▸ **noun 1** a herbaceous Eurasian plant with blue or white flowers and slender pointed leaves, rows of which are said to resemble a ladder. ● *Polemonium caeruleum*, family Polemoniaceae.
2 a rope ladder with wooden rungs.
– ORIGIN mid 18th cent.: with biblical allusion to Jacob's dream of a ladder reaching to heaven (Gen. 28:12).

Jacobson's organ ▸ **noun** Zoology a scent organ consisting of a pair of sacs or tubes typically in the roof of the mouth. Such organs are present in many vertebrates, notably snakes and lizards.
– ORIGIN mid 19th cent.: named after Ludwig L. *Jacobson* (1783–1843), Dutch anatomist.

Jacob's staff ▸ **noun** a rod with a sliding cursor formerly used for measuring distances and heights.
– ORIGIN mid 16th cent. (denoting a pilgrim's staff): alluding to St James (*Jacobus* in ecclesiastical Latin), whose symbols are a pilgrim's staff and a scallop shell.

jaconet /ˈdʒakənɪt/ ▸ **noun** [mass noun] a lightweight cotton cloth with a smooth and slightly stiff finish.
– ORIGIN mid 18th cent.: from Hindi *Jagannāth(purī)* (now *Puri*) in India, its place of origin; see also **JUGGERNAUT**.

Jacopo della Quercia see **DELLA QUERCIA**.

jacquard /ˈdʒakɑːd, -kəd/ ▸ **noun** an apparatus with perforated cards, fitted to a loom to facilitate the weaving of figured and brocaded fabrics. ■ [mass noun] a fabric made on a loom with such a device, with an intricate variegated pattern. ■ (also **jacquard loom**) a loom fitted with such a device.
– ORIGIN early 19th cent.: named after Joseph M. *Jacquard* (1787–1834), French weaver and inventor.

jacquerie /ˈdʒeɪk(ə)ri/ ▸ **noun** a communal uprising or revolt.
– ORIGIN early 16th cent. (referring to the 1357 peasants' revolt against the nobles in northern France): from Old French, literally 'villeins', from *Jacques*, a given name used in the sense 'peasant'.

jactitation¹ /ˌdʒaktɪˈteɪʃ(ə)n/ ▸ **noun** [mass noun] Medicine the restless tossing of the body in illness. ■ the twitching of a limb or muscle.
– ORIGIN mid 17th cent.: expressive extension of earlier *jactation* 'restless tossing', from Latin *jactare* 'to throw'.

jactitation² ▸ **noun** (in phrase **jactitation of marriage**) archaic false declaration that one is married to a specified person.
– ORIGIN late 17th cent.: from medieval Latin *jactitatio(n-)* 'false declaration', from Latin *jactitare* 'to boast'.

Jacuzzi /dʒəˈkuːzi/ ▸ **noun** (pl. **Jacuzzis**) trademark a large bath with a system of underwater jets of water to massage the body.
– ORIGIN 1960s: named after Candido *Jacuzzi* (*c.*1903–86), Italian-born American inventor.

jade¹ ▸ **noun** [mass noun] a hard, typically green stone used for ornaments and implements and consisting of the minerals jadeite or nephrite. ■ [count noun] an ornament made of jade. ■ (also **jade green**) a light bluish-green.
– ORIGIN late 16th cent.: from French *le jade* (earlier *l'ejade*), from Spanish *piedra de ijada* 'stone of the flank' (i.e. stone for colic, which it was believed to cure).

jade² ▸ **noun** archaic **1** a bad-tempered or disreputable woman.
2 an old or worn-out horse.
– ORIGIN late Middle English: of unknown origin.

jaded ▸ **adjective** bored or lacking enthusiasm, typically after having had too much of something: *meals to tempt the most jaded appetites*. ■ Irish informal physically tired; exhausted.
– DERIVATIVES **jadedly** adverb, **jadedness** noun.
– ORIGIN late 16th cent. (in the sense 'disreputable'): from **JADE²**.

jadeite /ˈdʒeɪdʌɪt/ ▸ **noun** [mass noun] a green, blue, or white mineral which is one of the forms of jade. It is a silicate of sodium, aluminium, and iron and belongs to the pyroxene group.

j'adoube /ʒɑːˈduːb/ ▸ **exclamation** Chess a declaration by a player intending to adjust the placing of a chessman without making a move with it.
– ORIGIN French, literally 'I adjust'.

jaeger /ˈdʒeɪgə/ ▸ **noun** N. Amer. any of the smaller kinds of Arctic-breeding skuas. ● Genus *Stercorarius*, family Stercorariidae: three species, e.g. the **parasitic jaeger** or Arctic skua (*S. parasiticus*).
– ORIGIN mid 19th cent. (applied to any predatory seabird): from German *Jäger* 'hunter', from *jagen* 'to hunt'.

Jaffa¹ /ˈdʒafə/ a city and port on the Mediterranean coast of Israel, forming a southern suburb of the Tel Aviv conurbation and since 1949 united with Tel Aviv; pop. (with Tel Aviv) 392,500 (est. 2008). Inhabited since prehistoric times, Jaffa was a Byzantine bishopric until captured by the Arabs in 636; later, it was a stronghold of the Crusaders. Hebrew name **YAFO**; biblical name **JOPPA**.

Jaffa² /ˈdʒafə/ (also **Jaffa orange**) ▸ **noun** Brit. trademark a large oval orange of a thick-skinned variety.

Jaffa cake ▸ **noun** Brit. a sponge biscuit with an orange-flavoured jelly and chocolate topping.

jaffle ▸ **noun** Austral. a toasted sandwich.
– ORIGIN 1950s: from the proprietary name for a toaster.

Jaffna /ˈdʒafnə/ a city and port on the Jaffna peninsula at the northern tip of Sri Lanka; pop. 151,600 (est. 2007).

JAG ▸ **abbreviation** Judge Advocate General.

Jag ▸ **noun** informal a Jaguar car: *an E-type Jag*.
– ORIGIN 1950s: abbreviation.

jag¹ ▸ **noun** a sharp projection. ■ chiefly Scottish an injection.
▸ **verb** (**jags, jagging, jagged**) [with obj.] stab, pierce, or prick: *she jagged herself in the mouth*.
– DERIVATIVES **jagger** noun.
– ORIGIN late Middle English (in the sense 'stab, pierce'): perhaps symbolic of sudden movement or unevenness (compare with **JAM¹** and **RAG¹**).

jag² ▸ **noun** informal, chiefly N. Amer. **1** a bout of unrestrained or excessive indulgence in alcohol or drugs, or in a particular emotion or activity: *a thirty-five minute crying jag*.
2 dialect a bundle: *a jag of hay*.
– ORIGIN late 16th cent. (in sense 2): of unknown origin. In the late 18th cent. the sense was 'portion, quantity', later 'as much alcohol as one can hold', hence 'a binge'. Sense 1 dates from the early 20th cent.

Jagannatha /ˌdʒagəˈnɑːθə/ another name for **JUGGERNAUT**.

jagged /ˈdʒagɪd/ ▸ **adjective** with rough, sharp points protruding: *the jagged edges gashed their fingers* | figurative *her jagged nerves*.
– DERIVATIVES **jaggedly** adverb, **jaggedness** noun.
– ORIGIN late Middle English: from **JAG¹**.

Jagger, Sir Mick (b.1943), English rock singer and songwriter; full name *Michael Philip Jagger*. He formed the Rolling Stones *c.*1962 with guitarist Keith Richards (b.1943), a childhood friend.

jaggery /ˈdʒag(ə)ri/ ▸ **noun** [mass noun] a coarse dark brown sugar made in India by evaporation of the sap of palm trees.
– ORIGIN late 16th cent.: from Portuguese *xagara, jag(a)ra*, from Malayalam *cakkarā*, from Sanskrit *śarkarā* 'sugar'.

jaggy ▸ **adjective** (**jaggier, jaggiest**) jagged. ■ (also **jaggie**) Scottish prickly.
▸ **plural noun** (**jaggies**) Computing, informal another term for **ALIASING** (sense 3).

jaguar /ˈdʒagjʊə/ ▸ **noun** a large heavily built cat that has a yellowish-brown coat with black spots, found mainly in the dense forests of Central and South America. ● *Panthera onca*, family Felidae.
– ORIGIN early 17th cent.: from Portuguese, from Tupi-Guarani *yaguára*.

jaguarundi /ˌdʒagwəˈrʌndi/ ▸ **noun** (pl. **jaguarundis**) a small American wild cat with a uniform red or grey coat, slender body, and short legs, found from Arizona to Argentina. ● *Felis yagouaroundi*, family Felidae.
– ORIGIN mid 19th cent.: from Portuguese, from Tupi-Guarani, from *yaguára* 'jaguar' + *undi* 'dark'.

Jah /dʒɑː, jɑː/ ▸ **noun** the Rastafarian name of God.
– ORIGIN representing Hebrew *Yāh*, abbreviation of **YAHWEH**. The current use was popularized in the mid 20th cent.

Jai /dʒʌɪ/ ▸ **exclamation** Indian victory! (used as an expression of praise or support, especially in political slogans).
– ORIGIN Hindi, literally 'long live!'.

jai alai /ˌhʌɪ əˈlʌɪ/ ▸ **noun** [mass noun] a game like pelota played with large curved wicker baskets.
– ORIGIN Spanish, from Basque *jai* 'festival' + *alai* 'merry'.

jail (Brit. also **gaol**) ▸ **noun** a place for the confinement of people accused or convicted of a crime: *he spent 15 years in jail* | [as modifier] *a jail sentence*.
▸ **verb** [with obj.] put (someone) in jail: *the driver was jailed for two years*.
– ORIGIN Middle English: based on Latin *cavea* (see **CAGE**). The word came into English in two forms, *jaiole* from Old French and *gayole* from Anglo-Norman French *gaole* (surviving in the spelling *gaol*), originally pronounced with a hard *g*, as in *goat*.

jailbait ▸ **noun** [mass noun treated as sing. or pl.] informal a young woman, or young women collectively, considered in sexual terms but under the age of consent.

jailbird ▸ **noun** informal a person who is or has been in prison, especially a criminal who has been jailed repeatedly.

jailbreak ▸ **noun** an escape from jail.

jailer (Brit. also **gaoler**) ▸ **noun** a person in charge of a jail or of the prisoners in it.

jailhouse ▸ **noun** N. Amer. a prison.

Jain /dʒeɪn/ ▸ **noun** an adherent of Jainism.
▸ **adjective** relating to Jainism.
– ORIGIN via Hindi from Sanskrit *jaina* 'of or concerning a *Jina*' (a great Jain teacher or holy man, literally 'victor'), from *ji-* 'conquer' or *jyā-* 'overcome'.

Jainism ▶ **noun** [mass noun] a non-theistic religion founded in India in the 6th century BC by the Jina Vardhamana Mahavira as a reaction against the teachings of orthodox Brahmanism, and still practised there. The Jain religion teaches salvation by perfection through successive lives, and non-injury to living creatures, and is noted for its ascetics. See also **SVETAMBARA** and **DIGAMBARA**.
– DERIVATIVES **Jainist** noun.

Jaipur /dʒʌɪˈpʊə/ a city in western India, the capital of Rajasthan; pop. 3,102,800 (est. 2009).

Jakarta /dʒəˈkɑːtə/ (also **Djakarta**) the capital of Indonesia, situated in NW Java; pop. 9,125,000 (est. 2009). Former name (until 1949) **BATAVIA**.

jake /dʒeɪk/ ▶ **adjective** [predic.] N. Amer. & Austral./NZ informal all right; satisfactory: *everything was jake again*.
– ORIGIN early 20th cent.: of unknown origin.

jakes /dʒeɪks/ ▶ **noun** archaic a toilet, especially an outdoor one.
– ORIGIN mid 16th cent.: perhaps from the given name *Jacques*, or as the genitive of the pet name *Jack* (see **JACK**[1]).

Jakobson /ˈjakəbs(ə)n/, Roman (Osipovich) (1896–1982), Russian-born American linguist. His most influential work described universals in phonology.

Jalalabad /dʒəˈlaləbad/ a city in eastern Afghanistan, situated east of Kabul, near the border with Pakistan; pop. 168,600 (est. 2006).

Jalal ad-Din ar Rumi /dʒəˌlal adˌdɪn ɑːˈruːmi/ (1207–73), Persian poet and Sufi mystic, founder of the order of whirling dervishes; also called *Mawlana*.

Jalandhar /ˈdʒʌləndə/ (also **Jullundur**) a city in Punjab, NW India; pop. 880,500 (est. 2009).

jalap /ˈdʒaləp, ˈdʒɒləp/ ▶ **noun** [mass noun] a purgative drug obtained chiefly from the tuberous roots of a Mexican climbing plant. ● This drug is obtained from *Ipomoea purga*, family Convolvulaceae.
– ORIGIN mid 17th cent.: from French, from Spanish (*purga de*) *Jalapa* (see **JALAPA**).

Jalapa /həˈlɑːpə/, Spanish /xaˈlapa/ a city in east central Mexico, capital of the state of Veracruz; pop. 387,879 (2005). Full name **Jalapa Enríquez** /ɛnˈriːkɛz/, Spanish /enˈrrikes, -keθ/.

jalapeño /ˌhaləˈpeɪnjəʊ, -ˈpiːnəʊ/ (also **jalapeño pepper**) ▶ **noun** (pl. **jalapeños**) a very hot green chilli pepper, used especially in Mexican-style cooking.
– ORIGIN from Mexican Spanish (*chile*) *jalapeño*.

jalebi /dʒəˈleɪbi/ ▶ **noun** (pl. **jalebis**) an Indian sweet made of a coil of batter fried and steeped in syrup.
– ORIGIN from Hindi *jalebī*.

jaleo /haˈleɪəʊ/, Spanish /xaˈleo/ ▶ **noun** (pl. **jaleos**) a lively dance of Andalusian origin, or the music or handclapping which accompanies it. ■ a fast instrumental chorus in merengue music.
– ORIGIN mid 19th cent.: Spanish, literally 'halloo'.

jalfrezi /dʒalˈfreɪzi/ ▶ **noun** (pl. **jalfrezis**) a medium-hot Indian dish consisting of chicken or lamb with fresh chillies, tomatoes, and onions.
– ORIGIN Bengali, from *jhal* 'hot'.

jali /ˈdʒɑːli/ ▶ **noun** [mass noun] Indian intricate ornamental openwork in wood, metal, stone, etc.: [as modifier] *a bamboo jali bedside cabinet*.
– ORIGIN Urdu, from *jaal* 'a net'.

Jalisco /həˈliːskəʊ/ a state of west central Mexico, on the Pacific coast; capital, Guadalajara.

jalopy /dʒəˈlɒpi/ ▶ **noun** (pl. **jalopies**) informal an old car in a dilapidated condition.
– ORIGIN 1920s (originally US): of unknown origin.

jalousie /ˈʒalʊziː/ ▶ **noun** a blind or shutter made of a row of angled slats.
– ORIGIN mid 18th cent.: French, literally 'jealousy', from Italian *geloso* 'jealous', also (by extension) 'screen', associated with the screening of women from view in the Middle East.

jam[1] ▶ **verb** (**jams, jamming, jammed**) **1** [with obj. and adverbial] squeeze or pack tightly into a specified space: *four of us were jammed in one compartment* | *people jammed their belongings into cars* | [no obj., with adverbial] *mum, dad, and I jammed into the pickup truck*. ■ push (something) roughly and forcibly into position or a space: *he jammed his hat on*. ■ [with obj.] crowd on to (a road or area) so as to block it: *the streets were jammed with tourist coaches*. ■ [with obj.] cause (telephone lines) to be continuously engaged with a large number of calls: *listeners jammed a radio station's switchboard with calls*.
2 become or make unable to move or work due to a part seizing up or becoming stuck: [no obj.] *the photocopier jammed* | [with obj.] *the doors were jammed open*. ■ [with obj.] make (a radio transmission) unintelligible by causing interference.
3 [no obj.] informal improvise with other musicians, especially in jazz or blues.
▶ **noun 1** an instance of a thing seizing or becoming stuck: *paper jams*. ■ short for **TRAFFIC JAM**. ■ Climbing a hold obtained by jamming a part of the body such as a hand or foot into a crack in the rock.
2 informal an awkward situation or predicament: *I'm in a jam*.
3 (also **jam session**) an improvised performance by a group of musicians, especially in jazz or blues.
– PHRASES **jam on the brakes** operate the brakes of a vehicle suddenly and forcibly, typically in response to an emergency.
– DERIVATIVES **jammer** noun.
– ORIGIN early 18th cent.: probably symbolic; compare with **JAG**[1] and **CRAM**.

jam[2] ▶ **noun** [mass noun] a sweet spread or conserve made from fruit and sugar boiled to a thick consistency. ■ Brit. used in reference to something easy or pleasant: *they want it all, both ways and with jam on the top*.
▶ **verb** (**jam, jamming, jammed**) [with obj.] make (fruit) into jam.
– PHRASES **jam tomorrow** Brit. a pleasant thing which is often promised but rarely materializes. [phrase from Lewis Carroll's *Through the Looking Glass* (1871).]
– ORIGIN mid 18th cent.: perhaps from **JAM**[1].

Jam. ▶ **abbreviation** ■ Jamaica. ■ James (in biblical references).

jamadar /ˈdʒʌməˌdɑː/ (also **jemadar**) ▶ **noun** Indian **1** a minor official or junior officer. ■ historical an Indian officer in a sepoy regiment.
2 a person who sweeps homes or offices as a job.
– ORIGIN from Urdu *jam(a)'dār*, from Persian, from Arabic *jamā'*, *jamā'a(t)* 'muster' + *-dār* 'holder'.

Jamaica /dʒəˈmeɪkə/ an island country in the Caribbean Sea, south-east of Cuba; pop. 2,825,900 (est. 2009); official language, English; capital, Kingston.

> Visited by Columbus in 1494, Jamaica was colonized by the Spanish, who enslaved or killed the native people. Both the Spanish and the British, who took the island by force in 1655, imported slaves, mainly to work on sugar plantations. Self-government was achieved in 1944, and in 1962 Jamaica became an independent Commonwealth state.

– DERIVATIVES **Jamaican** adjective & noun.

Jamaica pepper ▶ **noun** another term for **ALLSPICE** (sense 1 and sense 2).

jamb /dʒam/ ▶ **noun** a side post or surface of a doorway, window, or fireplace.
– ORIGIN Middle English: from Old French *jambe* 'leg, vertical support', based on Greek *kampē* 'joint'.

jambalaya /ˌdʒambəˈlʌɪə/ ▶ **noun** [mass noun] a Cajun dish of rice with shrimps, chicken, and vegetables.
– ORIGIN Louisiana French, from Provençal *jambalaia*.

jambeau /ˈʒambəʊ/ ▶ **noun** (pl. **jambeaux** pronunc. **same** or **jambeaus**) historical a piece of armour for the leg.
– ORIGIN late Middle English: apparently an Anglo-Norman French derivative of French *jambe* 'leg'.

jamboree /ˌdʒambəˈriː/ ▶ **noun 1** a large celebration or party, typically a lavish and boisterous one: *the film industry's annual jamboree in Cannes*.
2 a large rally of Scouts or Guides.
– ORIGIN mid 19th cent. (originally US slang): of unknown origin.

James[1] the name of seven Stuart kings of Scotland: ■ **James I** (1394–1437), son of Robert III, reigned 1406–37. A captive of the English until 1424, he returned to a country divided by baronial feuds, but managed to restore some measure of royal authority. ■ **James II** (1430–60), son of James I, reigned 1437–60. He considerably strengthened the position of the Crown by crushing the powerful Douglas family (1452–5). ■ **James III** (1451–88), son of James II, reigned 1460–88. His nobles raised an army against him in 1488, using his son, the future James IV, as a figurehead. The king was defeated and killed in battle. ■ **James IV** (1473–1513), son of James III, reigned 1488–1513. He forged a dynastic link with England through his marriage to Margaret Tudor, the daughter of Henry VII, and revitalized the traditional pact with France. When England and France went to war in 1513 he invaded England, but died in defeat at Flodden. ■ **James V** (1512–42), son of James IV, reigned 1513–42. During his reign Scotland was dominated by French interests. Relations with England deteriorated in the later years, culminating in an invasion by Henry VIII's army. ■ **James VI** (1566–1625), James I of England (see **JAMES**[2]). ■ **James VII** (1633–1701), James II of England (see **JAMES**[2]).

James[2] the name of two kings of England, Ireland, and Scotland: ■ **James I** (1566–1625), son of Mary, Queen of Scots, king of Scotland (as James VI) 1567–1625, and of England and Ireland 1603–25. He inherited the throne of England from Elizabeth I, as great-grandson of Margaret Tudor, daughter of Henry VII. His declaration of the divine right of kings and his intended alliance with Spain made him unpopular with Parliament. ■ **James II** (1633–1701), son of Charles I, king of England, Ireland, and (as James VII) Scotland 1685–8. His Catholic beliefs led to the rebellion of the Duke of Monmouth in 1685 and to James' later deposition in favour of William of Orange and Mary II. Attempts to regain the throne resulted in James's defeat at the Battle of the Boyne in 1690.

James[3], C. L. R. (1901–89), Trinidadian historian, journalist, political theorist, and novelist; full name *Cyril Lionel Robert James*. After working as a cricket columnist he established a reputation as a historian with his study of the Haitian revolution, *Black Jacobins* (1938).

James[4], Henry (1843–1916), American-born British novelist and critic. His early novels, notably *The Portrait of a Lady* (1881), deal with the relationship between European civilization and American life, while later works such as *What Maisie Knew* (1897) depict English life. He was the brother of William James.
– DERIVATIVES **Jamesian** adjective.

James[5], Jesse (Woodson) (1847–82), American outlaw. He joined with his brother **Frank** (1843–1915) and others to form a notorious band of outlaws which specialized in bank and train robberies and inspired many westerns.

James[6], M. R. (1862–1936), English scholar and writer of ghost stories; full name *Montague Rhodes James*. He is noted for eerie tales collected in such volumes as *Ghost Stories of an Antiquary* (1904).

James[7], William (1842–1910), American philosopher and psychologist. A leading exponent of pragmatism, he sought a functional definition of truth, and in psychology he is credited with introducing the concept of the stream of consciousness. He was the brother of Henry James.

James, St[1], an Apostle, son of Zebedee and brother of John; known as **St James the Great**. He was put to death by Herod Agrippa I; afterwards, according to a Spanish tradition, his body was taken to Santiago de Compostela. Feast day, 25 July.

James, St[2], an Apostle; known as **St James the Less**. Feast day (in the Eastern Church) 9 October; (in the Western Church) 1 May.

James, St[3] leader of the early Christian Church at Jerusalem; known as **St James the Just** or **the Lord's brother**. He was put to death by the Sanhedrin. Feast day, 1 May. ■ the epistle of the New Testament traditionally ascribed to St James.

James Bay a shallow southern arm of Hudson Bay, Canada.
– ORIGIN named after Captain Thomas *James* (*c.*1593–*c.*1635), who explored the region in 1631.

Jameson Raid /ˈdʒeɪms(ə)n/ an abortive raid into Boer territory made in 1895–6 by pro-British extremists led by Dr L. S. Jameson (1853–1917) in an attempt to incite an uprising among recent, non-Boer immigrants. The raid contributed to the eventual outbreak of the Second Boer War.

Jamestown 1 a British settlement established in Virginia in 1607, abandoned when the state capital of Virginia was moved to Williamsburg at the end of the 17th century.
2 the capital and chief port of the island of St Helena; pop. 700 (est. 2008).

jam jar ▶ **noun** Brit. rhyming slang a car.

Jammu /ˈdʒʌmuː/ a town in NW India; pop. 542,200 (est. 2009). It is the winter capital of the state of Jammu and Kashmir.

Jammu and Kashmir a mountainous state of NW India at the western end of the Himalayas, formerly part of Kashmir; capitals, Srinagar (in summer) and Jammu (in winter).

jammy ▶ **adjective** (**jammier, jammiest**) **1** covered with, filled with, or resembling jam: *a jammy doughnut*.

J

2 Brit. informal lucky: *you always were a jammy beggar when it came to women.*

Jamnagar /dʒʌmˈnʌɡə/ a port and walled city in the state of Gujarat, western India; pop. 529,600 (est. 2009).

jam-packed ▶ **adjective** informal extremely crowded or full to capacity: *trains were* ***jam-packed with*** *holidaymakers.*

jamrool /dʒamˈruːl/ ▶ **noun** Indian term for ROSEAPPLE.

jam session ▶ **noun** see JAM¹ (sense 3 of the noun).

Jamshedpur /ˌdʒʌmʃɛdˈpʊə/ an industrial city in the state of Jharkhand, NE India; pop. 666,700 (est. 2009).

Jamshid /dʒamˈʃiːd/ a legendary early king of Persia, reputed inventor of the arts of medicine, navigation, and iron-working.

jamun /ˈdʒamʌn/ (also **jamun tree**) ▶ **noun** a large evergreen Asian tree of the myrtle family, which yields edible fruit, tanbark, and fuelwood. ● *Syzygium cumini*, family Myrtaceae.
■ the purplish edible berry of this tree.
– ORIGIN early 19th cent.: from Hindi *jāmun*.

Jan. ▶ **abbreviation** January.

Janáček /ˈjanəˌtʃɛk/, Leoš (1854–1928), Czech composer. His works, much influenced by Moravian folk songs, include the opera *The Cunning Little Vixen* (1924) and the *Glagolitic Mass* (1927).

jandal ▶ **noun** NZ trademark a light sandal with a thong between the big and second toe; a flip-flop.
– ORIGIN 1950s: probably from *J(apanese) (s)andal.*

jane ▶ **noun** informal, chiefly US a woman.
– PHRASES **plain Jane** an unattractive girl or woman.
– ORIGIN early 20th cent.: from the given name *Jane.*

Jane Doe ▶ **noun** US Law an anonymous female party, typically the plaintiff, in a legal action. ■ informal a hypothetical average woman.
– ORIGIN mid 19th cent.: the female equivalent of JOHN DOE.

jangle ▶ **verb** make or cause to make a ringing metallic sound, typically a discordant one: [no obj.] *a bell jangled loudly* | [with obj.] *Ryan stood on the terrace jangling his keys.* ■ (with reference to a person's nerves) set or be set on edge: [no obj.] *now it's over my nerves are jangling.*
▶ **noun** [in sing.] a ringing metallic sound: *the shrill jangle of the door bell.*
– DERIVATIVES **jangly adjective** (**janglier, jangliest**).
– ORIGIN Middle English (in the sense 'talk excessively or noisily, squabble'): from Old French *jangler*, of unknown origin.

janissary /ˈdʒanɪs(ə)ri/ (also **janizary** /-z(ə)ri/) ▶ **noun** (pl. **janissaries**) historical a member of the Turkish infantry forming the Sultan's guard between the 14th and 19th centuries. ■ a devoted follower or supporter.
– ORIGIN early 16th cent.: from French *janissaire*, based on Turkish *yeniçeri*, from *yeni* 'new' + *çeri* 'troops'.

janitor /ˈdʒanɪtə/ ▶ **noun** chiefly N. Amer. a caretaker or doorkeeper of a building.
– DERIVATIVES **janitorial adjective.**
– ORIGIN mid 16th cent.: from Latin, from *janua* 'door'.

Janjaweed a grouping of Arabic-speaking fighters in conflict with rebel groups in the Darfur region of western Sudan.

jankers /ˈdʒaŋkəz/ ▶ **noun** [mass noun] Brit. military slang punishment for those who have committed a military offence: *the sergeant put me on jankers.*
– ORIGIN early 20th cent.: of unknown origin.

Jan Mayen /jan ˈmʌɪən/ a barren and virtually uninhabited island in the Arctic Ocean between Greenland and Norway, annexed by Norway in 1929.
– ORIGIN named after Jan *May*, the Dutch sea captain who claimed the island for his company and his country in 1614.

Jansen /ˈdʒans(ə)n/, Cornelius Otto (1585–1638), Flemish Roman Catholic theologian and founder of Jansenism. A strong opponent of the Jesuits, he proposed a reform of Christianity through a return to St Augustine.

Jansenism ▶ **noun** a Christian movement of the 17th and 18th centuries, based on Jansen's writings and characterized by moral rigour and asceticism.
– DERIVATIVES **Jansenist noun.**

Jansens /ˈdʒans(ə)nz/ (also **Janssen van Ceulen** /ˌdʒans(ə)n van ˈkəːlən/) variant spelling of JOHNSON³.

January /ˈdʒanjʊ(ə)ri/ ▶ **noun** (pl. **Januaries**) the first month of the year, in the northern hemisphere usually considered the second month of winter: *Sophie was two in January* | *last January my grandmother died.*
– ORIGIN Old English, from Latin *Januarius (mensis)* '(month) of *Janus*' (see JANUS), the Roman god who presided over doors and beginnings.

Janus /ˈdʒeɪnəs/ Roman Mythology an ancient Italian deity, guardian of doorways and gates and protector of the state in time of war. He is usually represented with two faces, so that he looks both forwards and backwards.

Janus-faced ▶ **adjective** having two sharply contrasting aspects or characteristics: *the Janus-faced nature of American society.* ■ insincere or deceitful: *a Janus-faced politician.*

Jap ▶ **noun & adjective** informal, offensive short for JAPANESE.

Japan a country in East Asia, occupying a festoon of islands in the Pacific roughly parallel with the east coast of the Asiatic mainland; pop. 127,078,700 (est. 2009); official language, Japanese; capital, Tokyo. Japanese name NIPPON.

> From the late 19th century Japan began a modernizing process which eventually made it into a major world power. It fought wars against China (1894–5) and Russia (1904–5), and after the First World War occupied Manchuria (1931) and invaded China (1937). Japan entered the Second World War on the Axis side with a surprise attack on Pearl Harbor in 1941. The country surrendered in 1945 after the dropping of atom bombs by the US on Hiroshima and Nagasaki. Japan is now the most highly industrialized country and the leading economic power in the region.

japan ▶ **noun** [mass noun] a hard, dark, enamel-like varnish containing asphalt, used to give a black gloss to metal objects. ■ a kind of varnish in which pigments are ground, typically used to imitate lacquer on wood. ■ articles made in a Japanese style, especially when decorated with lacquer or enamel-like varnish.
▶ **verb** (**japans, japanning, japanned**) [with obj.] cover (something) with a hard black varnish: (as adj. **japanned**) *a japanned tin tray.*
– ORIGIN late 17th cent.: from JAPAN.

Japan, Sea of the sea between Japan and the mainland of Asia. Referred to in Korea as the EAST SEA.

Japan Current another name for KUROSHIO.

Japanese ▶ **adjective** relating to Japan or its language, culture, or people.
▶ **noun** (pl. **same**) **1** a native or inhabitant of Japan, or a person of Japanese descent.
2 [mass noun] the language of Japan, spoken by almost all of its population.

> Probably related to Korean, Japanese has many Chinese loanwords, and is usually written in vertical columns using Chinese characters (kanji) supplemented by two sets of syllabic characters (kana).

Japanese anemone ▶ **noun** an autumn-flowering anemone with large pink or white flowers. It is native to China and naturalized in Japan, and several cultivars have been developed. ● *Anemone hupehensis* var. *japonica*, family Ranunculaceae.

Japanese cedar ▶ **noun** see CRYPTOMERIA.

Japanese Current another name for KUROSHIO.

Japanese knotweed ▶ **noun** [mass noun] a tall fast-growing Japanese plant of the dock family, with bamboo-like stems and small white flowers. It has been grown as an ornamental but tends to become an aggressive weed. ● *Reynoutria japonica*, family Polygonaceae.

Japanese lantern ▶ **noun** another term for CHINESE LANTERN (sense 1).

Japanese paper ▶ **noun** [mass noun] paper of a kind traditionally handmade in Japan, typically from vegetable fibres such as mulberry bark and without being sized, used for art and craft work.

Japanese quince ▶ **noun** another term for JAPONICA.

Japanese wax tree ▶ **noun** see WAX TREE.

Japanimation /dʒəˌpanɪˈmeɪʃ(ə)n/ ▶ **noun** another term for ANIME.
– ORIGIN 1980s: blend of JAPAN and ANIMATION.

jape ▶ **noun** a practical joke.
▶ **verb** [no obj.] say or do something in jest or mockery.
– DERIVATIVES **japery noun.**
– ORIGIN Middle English: apparently combining the form of Old French *japer* 'to yelp, yap' with the sense of Old French *gaber* 'to mock'.

Japheth /ˈdʒeɪfɛθ/ (in the Bible) a son of Noah (Gen. 10:1), traditional ancestor of the peoples living round the Mediterranean.

Japlish /ˈdʒaplɪʃ/ ▶ **noun** [mass noun] informal a blend of Japanese and English, either Japanese speech that makes liberal use of English expressions or unidiomatic English spoken by a Japanese person.

japonica /dʒəˈpɒnɪkə/ ▶ **noun** an Asian shrub of the rose family, with bright red flowers followed by round white, green, or yellow edible fruits. Also called JAPANESE QUINCE. ● Genus *Chaenomeles*, family Rosaceae: several species, in particular *C. speciosa*, which is grown as an ornamental.
– ORIGIN early 19th cent.: modern Latin, feminine of *japonicus* 'Japanese'.

Jaques-Dalcroze /ˌʒakdalˈkrəʊz/, Émile (1865–1950), Austrian-born Swiss music teacher and composer. He evolved the eurhythmics method of teaching music and dance, establishing a school for eurhythmics instruction in 1910.

jar¹ ▶ **noun** a wide-mouthed cylindrical container made of glass or pottery, especially one used for storing food. ■ the contents of such a container: *a jar of coffee.* ■ Brit. informal a glass of beer: *let's have a jar.*
– DERIVATIVES **jarful noun** (pl. **jarfuls**).
– ORIGIN late 16th cent.: from French *jarre*, from Arabic *jarra*.

jar² ▶ **verb** (**jars, jarring, jarred**) **1** [with obj.] send a painful or damaging shock through (something, especially a part of the body): *he jarred the knee in training.* ■ [no obj.] strike against something with an unpleasant vibration or jolt: *the stick jarred on the bottom of the pond.*
2 [no obj.] have an unpleasant or disturbing effect: *a laugh which* ***jarred on*** *the ears* | *the difference in their background began to jar.* ■ be incongruous in a striking or shocking way: *the play's symbolism* ***jarred with*** *the realism of its setting.*
▶ **noun** a physical shock or jolt. ■ [mass noun] archaic discord or disagreement.
– ORIGIN late 15th cent. (as a noun in the sense 'disagreement, dispute'): probably imitative.

jar³ ▶ **noun** (in phrase **on the jar**) informal or dialect ajar.
– ORIGIN late 17th cent.: later form of obsolete *char* 'turn' (see also AJAR¹ and CHARWOMAN).

jardinière /ˌʒɑːdɪnˈjɛː/ ▶ **noun 1** an ornamental pot or stand for the display of growing plants.
2 a garnish of mixed vegetables.
– ORIGIN mid 19th cent.: French, literally 'female gardener'.

jargon¹ /ˈdʒɑːɡ(ə)n/ ▶ **noun** [mass noun] special words or expressions used by a profession or group that are difficult for others to understand: *legal jargon.* ■ archaic a form of language regarded as barbarous, debased, or hybrid.
– DERIVATIVES **jargonistic adjective.**
– ORIGIN late Middle English (originally in the sense 'twittering, chattering', later 'gibberish'): from Old French *jargoun*, of unknown origin. The main sense dates from the mid 17th cent.

jargon² /ˈdʒɑːɡ(ə)n/ (also **jargoon** /dʒɑːˈɡuːn/) ▶ **noun** [mass noun] a translucent, colourless, or smoky gem variety of zircon.
– ORIGIN mid 18th cent.: from French, from Italian *giargone*; probably ultimately related to ZIRCON.

Jargonelle /ˌdʒɑːɡəˈnɛl/ ▶ **noun** Brit. a pear of an early-ripening variety.
– ORIGIN late 17th cent.: from French, diminutive of JARGON² (with reference to the colour).

jargonize (also **jargonise**) ▶ **verb** [with obj.] use jargon to talk about: (as adj. **jargonized**) *the jargonized world of information superhighways.*

jarhead ▶ **noun** US informal a marine.
– ORIGIN early 20th cent. (originally US dialect, in the sense 'mule'): from JAR¹ + HEAD. The word originally referred to members of the US army, on account of the mule mascot of the Army football teams.

jarl /jɑːl/ ▶ **noun** historical a Norse or Danish chief.
– ORIGIN Old Norse, literally 'man of noble birth'; related to EARL.

Jarlsberg /ˈjɑːlzbəːɡ/ ▶ **noun** [mass noun] trademark a kind of hard yellow Norwegian cheese with many small holes and a mild, nutty flavour.
– ORIGIN named after the town of *Jarlsberg*, Norway.

jarrah /ˈdʒarə/ ▶ **noun** a eucalyptus tree native to western Australia, yielding durable timber. ● *Eucalyptus marginata*, family Myrtaceae.
– ORIGIN mid 19th cent.: from Nyungar *djarryl, jerrhyl.*

jarring ▶ adjective **1** incongruous in a striking or shocking way; clashing: *the telephone* ***struck a jarring note*** *in those Renaissance surroundings.*
2 causing a physical shock, jolt, or vibration: *the van came to a jarring halt.*
– DERIVATIVES **jarringly** adverb.

Jarrow a town in NE England, on the Tyne estuary; pop. 27,000 (est. 2009). From the 7th century until the Viking invasions its monastery was a centre of Northumbrian Christian culture. Its name is associated with a series of hunger marches to London by the unemployed during the Depression of the 1930s.

Jarry /ˈdʒari/, French /ʒaʀi/, Alfred (1873–1907), French dramatist. His satirical farce *Ubu Roi* (1896) anticipated surrealism and the Theatre of the Absurd.

jarul /dʒəˈruːl/ (also **jarool**) ▶ noun a tropical Asian tree which bears large clusters of purple or white flowers. ● *Lagerstroemia speciosa*, family Lythraceae.
– ORIGIN mid 19th cent.: from Hindi.

Jaruzelski /ˌjarʊˈzɛlski/, Wojciech (b.1923), Polish general and statesman, Prime Minister 1981–5, head of state 1985–9, and President 1989–90. He responded to the rise of Solidarity by imposing martial law and banning trade union operation, but following the victory of Solidarity in the 1989 elections he supervised Poland's transition to a democracy.

Jas. ▶ abbreviation James (in biblical references and generally).

jasmine /ˈdʒazmɪn, ˈdʒas-/ ▶ noun an Old World shrub or climbing plant which is popular as an ornamental and bears fragrant white, pink, or yellow flowers.
● Genus *Jasminum*, family Oleaceae: many species, including the **winter jasmine**.
■ used in names of other shrubs or climbers with fragrant flowers, e.g. **Cape jasmine**, **yellow jasmine**.
– ORIGIN mid 16th cent.: from French *jasmin* and obsolete French *jessemin*, from Arabic *yāsamīn*, from Persian *yāsamīn*.

jasmine tea ▶ noun [mass noun] a tea perfumed with dried jasmine blossom.

Jason Greek Mythology the son of the king of Iolcos in Thessaly, and leader of the Argonauts in the quest for the Golden Fleece.

jaspé /ˈdʒaspeɪ/ ▶ adjective randomly mottled or variegated, like jasper.
– ORIGIN mid 19th cent.: French, past participle of *jasper* 'to marble', from *jaspe* (see **JASPER**).

jasper ▶ noun [mass noun] **1** an opaque reddish-brown semi-precious stone consisting of a variety of chalcedony.
2 (also **jasperware**) a kind of fine hard porcelain developed by Josiah Wedgwood and used for Wedgwood cameos and other delicate work.
– ORIGIN Middle English (originally denoting any bright-coloured chalcedony other than carnelian): from Old French *jasp(r)e*, from Latin *iaspis*, from Greek, of oriental origin.

Jassy /ˈjasi/ German name for **IAŞI**.

Jat /dʒɑːt/ ▶ noun a member of a people widely scattered throughout the north-west of India and Pakistan.
– ORIGIN Hindi *Jāṭ*.

Jataka /ˈdʒʌtəkə/ ▶ noun any of the various stories of the former lives of the Buddha found in Buddhist literature.
– ORIGIN from Sanskrit *jātaka* 'born under'.

jatha /ˈdʒɑːtə/ ▶ noun Indian an armed parade, especially of Sikhs. ■ a long march, usually aimed at spreading a message.
– ORIGIN from Punjabi, from Hindi *jāthā*.

jati /ˈdʒɑːti/ ▶ noun (pl. **same** or **jatis**) Indian a caste or subcaste.
– ORIGIN via Hindi from Sanskrit *jāti* 'birth'.

jato /ˈdʒeɪtəʊ/ ▶ noun (pl. **jatos**) [mass noun] Aeronautics jet-assisted take-off. ■ [count noun] an auxiliary power unit providing extra thrust at take-off.
– ORIGIN Second World War (originally US): acronym.

jatropha /ˈjatrəfə/ ▶ noun any of various plants or shrubs of the genus *Jatropha* (family Euphorbiaceae), one species of which (*Jatropha curcas*) produces seeds that can be used in the production of biodiesel.
– ORIGIN mid 18th cent.: modern Latin (genus name), from Greek *iatros* 'physician' + *trophē* 'nourishment'.

jaundice /ˈdʒɔːndɪs/ ▶ noun [mass noun] **1** a medical condition with yellowing of the skin or whites of the eyes, arising from excess of the pigment bilirubin and typically caused by obstruction of the bile duct, by liver disease, or by excessive breakdown of red blood cells.
2 bitterness, resentment, or cynicism.
– ORIGIN Middle English *jaunes*, from Old French *jaunice* 'yellowness', from *jaune* 'yellow'.

jaundiced ▶ adjective **1** affected by jaundice, in particular unnaturally yellow in complexion.
2 affected by bitterness, resentment, or cynicism: *they looked on politicians with* ***a jaundiced eye***.

jaunt ▶ noun a short excursion or journey made for pleasure: *her regular jaunts to Europe.*
▶ verb [no obj.] make such an excursion or journey.
– ORIGIN late 16th cent.: of unknown origin. Originally depreciatory, early senses included 'tire a horse out by riding it up and down', 'traipse about', and (as a noun) 'troublesome journey'. The current positive sense dates from the mid 17th cent.

jaunting car ▶ noun historical a light two-wheeled horse-drawn vehicle formerly used in Ireland.

jaunty ▶ adjective (**jauntier**, **jauntiest**) having or expressing a lively, cheerful, and self-confident manner: *there was no mistaking that jaunty walk.*
– DERIVATIVES **jauntily** adverb, **jauntiness** noun.
– ORIGIN mid 17th cent. (in the sense 'well-bred, genteel'): from French *gentil* (see **GENTLE**[1], **GENTEEL**).

Java[1] /ˈdʒɑːvə/ a large island in the Malay Archipelago, forming part of Indonesia; pop. 120,000,000 (est. 2008) (with Madura).
– DERIVATIVES **Javan** noun & adjective.

Java[2] /ˈdʒɑːvə/ ▶ noun [mass noun] trademark a general-purpose computer programming language designed to produce programs that will run on any computer system.
– ORIGIN 1990s: with allusion to **JAVA**.

java /ˈdʒɑːvə/ ▶ noun [mass noun] N. Amer. informal coffee.

Java man ▶ noun a fossil hominid of the Middle Pleistocene period, whose remains were found in Java in 1891. ● An early form of *Homo erectus* (formerly *Pithecanthropus*), family Hominidae.

Javanese ▶ noun (pl. **same**) **1** a native or inhabitant of Java, or a person of Javanese descent.
2 [mass noun] the Indonesian language of central Java, spoken by about 70 million people.
▶ adjective relating to Java, its people, or their language.

Javan rhinoceros ▶ noun a rare one-horned rhinoceros that is now confined to the lowland rainforests of Java. ● *Rhinoceros sondaicus*, family Rhinocerotidae.

JavaScript ▶ noun [mass noun] trademark an object-oriented computer programming language commonly used to create interactive effects within web browsers.
– ORIGIN 1990s: from **JAVA**[2] + **SCRIPT**[1].

Java Sea a sea in the Malay Archipelago of SE Asia, surrounded by the islands of Borneo, Java, and Sumatra.

Java sparrow ▶ noun a waxbill with a large red bill and black-and-white head, native to Java and Bali but introduced elsewhere and popular as a cage bird.
● *Padda oryzivora*, family Estrildidae.

javelin /ˈdʒav(ə)lɪn/ ▶ noun a light spear thrown in a competitive sport or as a weapon. ■ (**the javelin**) the athletic event or sport of throwing the javelin: *his nearest rival in the javelin.*
– ORIGIN late Middle English: from Old French *javeline*, of Celtic origin.

javelina /ˌhavəˈliːnə/ ▶ noun North American term for **PECCARY**.
– ORIGIN early 19th cent.: from Spanish *jabalina*, from the feminine form of *jabalí* 'wild boar', from Arabic *jabalī* 'mountaineer'.

jaw ▶ noun **1** each of the upper and lower bony structures in vertebrates forming the framework of the mouth and containing the teeth. ■ the lower movable bone of the jaw, or the part of the face containing it: *she suffered a broken jaw.* ■ (**jaws**) the mouth with its bones and teeth. ■ (**jaws**) the grasping, biting, or crushing mouthparts of an invertebrate. ■ (usu. **jaws**) the gripping parts of a tool or machine, such as a wrench or vice. ■ (**jaws**) the grasping or destructive power of something: *victory was snatched* ***from the jaws of*** *defeat.* ■ (**jaws**) an opening likened to a mouth: *a passenger stepping from the jaws of a car ferry.*
2 [mass noun] informal talk or gossip, especially when lengthy or tedious: *committee work is just endless jaw.*
▶ verb [no obj.] informal talk at length; chatter: *I was too busy to spend time jawing with the rest of the crew.*
– PHRASES **one's jaw drops** one feels or appears amazed or shocked: *Laurel's jaw dropped despite her attempts to hide her surprise.*
– DERIVATIVES **jawed** adjective [in combination] *square-jawed young men*, **jawless** adjective.
– ORIGIN late Middle English: from Old French *joe* 'cheek, jaw', of unknown origin.

jawan /dʒəˈwɑːn/ ▶ noun Indian a male police constable or soldier.
– ORIGIN from Urdu *jawān* 'young man', from Persian; ultimately related to **YOUNG**.

jawbone ▶ noun a bone of the jaw, especially that of the lower jaw (the mandible), or either half of this.
▶ verb [with obj.] N. Amer. informal use one's position or authority to pressure (someone) to do something: *the Treasury could jawbone the banks into lending more to small businesses.*

jawbreaker ▶ noun **1** informal a word that is very long or hard to pronounce.
2 chiefly N. Amer. a large gobstopper.

jaw-dropping ▶ adjective informal amazing: *a jaw-dropping display of slick trickery.*
– DERIVATIVES **jaw-droppingly** adverb.

jawfish ▶ noun (pl. **same** or **jawfishes**) a small fish with very large jaws which lives in shallow tropical seas. It often inhabits a burrow in the sand, the walls of which are lined with pieces of shell and stone.
● Family Opistognathidae: several genera and species.

jaw-jaw informal ▶ noun [mass noun] talking, especially lengthy and pointless discussion.
▶ verb talk, especially at length.
– ORIGIN mid 19th cent.: reduplication of **JAW**.

jawline ▶ noun the contour of the lower edge of a person's jaw: *he had a dark, unshaven jawline.*

Jaws of Life ▶ noun N. Amer. trademark a hydraulic apparatus used to pry apart the wreckage of crashed vehicles in order to free people trapped inside.

jay ▶ noun **1** a bird of the crow family with boldly patterned plumage, typically having blue feathers in the wings or tail. ● Family Corvidae: several genera and numerous species, in particular the Eurasian *Garrulus glandarius*, with a crest, mainly pinkish-brown plumage, and a harsh screech.
2 informal, dated a person who talks at length in a foolish or impertinent way.
– ORIGIN late 15th cent.: via Old French from late Latin *gaius*, *gaia*, perhaps from the Latin given name *Gaius*.

Jaycee /dʒeɪˈsiː/ ▶ noun N. Amer. informal a member of a Junior Chamber of Commerce, a civic organization for business and community leaders.
– ORIGIN 1940s: representing the initials of *Junior Chamber*.

jaywalk ▶ verb [no obj., with adverbial of direction] chiefly N. Amer. cross or walk in the street or road unlawfully or without regard for approaching traffic.
– DERIVATIVES **jaywalker** noun.
– ORIGIN early 20th cent.: from **JAY** in the colloquial sense 'silly person' + **WALK**.

jazz ▶ noun [mass noun] a type of music of black American origin which emerged at the beginning of the 20th century, characterized by improvisation, syncopation, and usually a regular or forceful rhythm. Brass and woodwind instruments and piano are particularly associated with jazz, although guitar and occasionally violin are also used; styles include Dixieland, swing, bebop, and free jazz. ■ (also **jazz ballet** or **jazz dance**) a style of theatrical dance performed to jazz or popular music.
▶ verb [no obj.] dated play or dance to jazz music.
– PHRASES **and all that jazz** informal and such similar things: *oh, love, life, and all that jazz.*
– PHRASAL VERBS **jazz something up** make something more lively or cheerful: *jazz up an all-white kitchen with red tiles.*
– DERIVATIVES **jazzer** noun.
– ORIGIN early 20th cent.: of unknown origin.

Jazz Age ▶ noun the 1920s in the US characterized as a period of carefree hedonism, wealth, freedom, and youthful exuberance, reflected in the novels of writers such as F. Scott Fitzgerald.

jazzbo ▶ noun (pl. **jazzbos**) informal **1** a jazz musician or jazz enthusiast.
2 US archaic a person, especially a black man.
– ORIGIN early 20th cent.: of unknown origin.

Jazzercise ▶ noun trademark a type of fitness training combining aerobic exercise and jazz dancing.
– ORIGIN 1970s: blend of **JAZZ** and **EXERCISE**.

jazz funk ▶ noun [mass noun] a style of popular dance music incorporating elements of jazz and funk.

jazzman ▶ noun (pl. **jazzmen**) a male jazz musician.

jazzy ▶ adjective (**jazzier**, **jazziest**) **1** of, resembling, or in the style of jazz: *a jazzy piano solo.*

2 bright, colourful, and showy: *jazzy ties.*
– DERIVATIVES **jazzily** adverb, **jazziness** noun.

JCB ▸ noun Brit. trademark a type of mechanical excavator with a shovel at the front and a digging arm at the rear.
– ORIGIN 1960s: the initials of *J. C. Bamford*, the makers.

JCL ▸ abbreviation Computing job control language.

J-cloth ▸ noun (trademark in the UK) a type of cloth used for household cleaning.
– ORIGIN 1970s: *J* from *Johnson and Johnson*, the original makers.

JCR ▸ abbreviation Brit. Junior Common (or Combination) Room.

JCS ▸ abbreviation Joint Chiefs of Staff, the chief military advisory body to the President of the United States.

jealous ▸ adjective feeling or showing an envious resentment of someone or their achievements, possessions, or perceived advantages: *she was always jealous of me.* ■ feeling or showing a resentful suspicion that one's partner is attracted to or involved with someone else: *a jealous husband.* ■ fiercely protective of one's rights or possessions: *the men were proud of their achievements and jealous of their independence.* ■ (of God) demanding faithfulness and exclusive worship.
– DERIVATIVES **jealously** adverb.
– ORIGIN Middle English: from Old French *gelos*, from medieval Latin *zelosus* (see ZEALOUS).

jealousy ▸ noun (pl. **jealousies**) [mass noun] the state or feeling of being jealous: *a sharp pang of jealousy* | [count noun] *resentments and jealousies festered.*
– ORIGIN Middle English: from Old French *gelosie*, from *gelos* (see JEALOUS).

jean ▸ noun [mass noun] heavy twilled cotton cloth, especially denim: [as modifier] *a jean jacket.* ■ [count noun] (in commercial use) a pair of jeans: *a button-fly jean.*
– ORIGIN late 15th cent. (as an adjective): from Old French *Janne* (now *Gênes*), from medieval Latin *Janua* 'Genoa', the place of original production. The noun sense comes from *jean fustian*, literally 'fustian from Genoa', used in the 16th cent. to denote a heavy twilled cotton cloth.

Jean Paul /ʒɒn ˈpɔːl/ (1763–1825), German novelist; pseudonym of *Johann Paul Friedrich Richter*. He is noted for his romantic novels, including *Hesperus* (1795), and for comic works such as *Titan* (1800–3).

jeans ▸ plural noun hard-wearing casual trousers made of denim or other cotton fabric: *he wore a pair of faded jeans and a white T-shirt.*
– ORIGIN mid 19th cent.: plural of JEAN.

jebel /ˈdʒɛbɛl/ (also **djebel**) ▸ noun (in the Middle East and North Africa) a mountain or hill, or a range of hills.
– ORIGIN colloquial Arabic form of *jabal* 'mountain'.

Jeddah /ˈdʒɛdə/ variant spelling of JIDDAH.

Jedi /ˈdʒɛdʌɪ/ (also **Jedi knight**) ▸ noun (pl. **same** or **Jedis**) a member of the mystical knightly order in the *Star Wars* films, trained to guard peace and justice in the Universe.

jeep ▸ noun trademark a small, sturdy motor vehicle with four-wheel drive, especially one used by the military.
– ORIGIN Second World War (originally US): from the initials *GP*, standing for *general purpose*, influenced by 'Eugene the Jeep', a creature of great resourcefulness and power represented in the *Popeye* comic strip.

jeepers (also **jeepers creepers**) ▸ exclamation informal, chiefly N. Amer. used to express surprise or alarm: *Jeepers! Do you think she saw?*
– ORIGIN 1920s: alteration of JESUS.

jeer ▸ verb [no obj.] make rude and mocking remarks, typically in a loud voice: *some of the younger men jeered at him* | (as adj. **jeering**) *the jeering crowds.* ■ [with obj.] shout such remarks at (someone): *councillors were jeered and heckled.*
▸ noun a rude and mocking remark.
– DERIVATIVES **jeeringly** adverb.
– ORIGIN mid 16th cent.: of unknown origin.

jeera /ˈdʒiːrə/ (also **zeera**) ▸ noun Indian term for CUMIN.
– ORIGIN from Hindi *jīrā*.

jeet kune do /ˈdʒiːt kuːn duː/ ▸ noun [mass noun] a modern martial art incorporating elements of kung fu, fencing, and boxing, devised by the American actor Bruce Lee.
– ORIGIN from Cantonese, literally 'the way of the intercepting fist'.

Jeeves the resourceful and influential valet of Bertie Wooster in the novels of P. G. Wodehouse.

jeez (also **jeeze** or **geez**) ▸ exclamation informal a mild expression used to show surprise or annoyance.
– ORIGIN 1920s: abbreviation of JESUS.

jefe /ˈhɛfeɪ/ ▸ noun US informal a boss or leader; a person in charge of something.
– ORIGIN late 19th cent.: Spanish from French *chef* CHIEF.

Jefferies, (John) Richard (1848–87), English writer and naturalist renowned for his observation of English rural life. Notable works: *Bevis* (novel, 1882) and *The Story of my Heart* (autobiography, 1883).

Jefferson, Thomas (1743–1826), American Democratic Republican statesman, 3rd President of the US 1801–9. He played a key role in the American leadership during the War of Independence and was the principal drafter of the Declaration of Independence (1776).
– DERIVATIVES **Jeffersonian** adjective & noun.

Jefferson City the state capital of Missouri; pop. 40,771 (est. 2008).

Jeffreys, George, 1st Baron (*c.*1645–89), Welsh judge. Chief Justice of the King's Bench from 1683, he took part in the Popish Plot prosecutions and later became infamous for his brutal sentencing at the Bloody Assizes.

jehad ▸ noun variant spelling of JIHAD.

Jehoshaphat /dʒɪˈhɒʃəfat/ (also **Jehosaphat**) a king of Judah in the mid 9th century BC. ■ [as exclamation] (also **jumping Jehoshaphat**) a mild expletive: *Jehoshaphat! That would be ghastly.* [probably a euphemism for JESUS.]

Jehovah /dʒɪˈhəʊvə/ ▸ noun a form of the Hebrew name of God used in some translations of the Bible.
– ORIGIN from medieval Latin *Iehouah, Iehoua*, from Hebrew *YHWH* or *JHVH*, the consonants of the name of God, with the inclusion of vowels taken from *'ădōnāy* 'my lord'; see also YAHWEH.

Jehovah's Witness ▸ noun a member of a Christian movement (the Watch Tower Bible and Tract Society) founded in the US by Charles Taze Russell (1852–1916). Jehovah's Witnesses deny many traditional Christian doctrines (including the divinity of Christ) and refuse military service and blood transfusion on religious grounds.

Jehovist /dʒɪˈhəʊvɪst/ ▸ noun another name for YAHWIST.

Jehu /ˈdʒiːhjuː/ (842–815 BC), king of Israel. He was famous for driving his chariot furiously (2 Kings 9).

jejune /dʒɪˈdʒuːn/ ▸ adjective **1** naive, simplistic, and superficial: *their entirely predictable and usually jejune opinions.*
2 (of ideas or writings) dry and uninteresting.
– DERIVATIVES **jejunely** adverb, **jejuneness** noun.
– ORIGIN early 17th cent.: from Latin *jejunus* 'fasting, barren'. The original sense was 'without food', hence 'not intellectually nourishing'.

jejunoileal /dʒɪˌdʒuːnəʊˈɪlɪəl/ ▸ adjective Medicine of or involving the jejunum and the ileum, usually with reference to a bypass operation in which they are connected.

jejunum /dʒɪˈdʒuːnəm/ ▸ noun Anatomy the part of the small intestine between the duodenum and ileum.
– DERIVATIVES **jejunal** adjective.
– ORIGIN mid 16th cent.: from medieval Latin, neuter of *jejunus* 'fasting' (because it is usually found to be empty after death).

Jekyll[1] /ˈdʒɛk(ə)l/, Dr, the central character of Robert Louis Stevenson's story *The Strange Case of Dr Jekyll and Mr Hyde* (1886). He discovers a drug which creates a separate personality (appearing in the character of Mr Hyde) into which Jekyll's evil impulses are channelled.
– PHRASES **a Jekyll and Hyde** a person alternately displaying opposing good and evil personalities.

Jekyll[2] /ˈdʒiːk(ə)l/, Gertrude (1843–1932), English horticulturalist and garden designer. She created over 300 gardens for buildings designed by Edwin Lutyens, promoting colour design in garden planning and 'wild' gardens.

jell ▸ verb variant spelling of GEL[2].
– ORIGIN mid 18th cent.: back-formation from JELLY.

jellaba ▸ noun variant spelling of DJELLABA.

Jellicoe /ˈdʒɛlɪkəʊ/, John Rushworth, 1st Earl (1859–1935), British admiral, commander of the Grand Fleet at the Battle of Jutland.

jello (also trademark **Jell-O**) ▸ noun [mass noun] N. Amer. a fruit-flavoured gelatin dessert made up from a commercially prepared powder.

jelly ▸ noun (pl. **jellies**) **1** [mass noun] chiefly Brit. a fruit-flavoured dessert made by warming and then cooling a liquid containing gelatin or a similar setting agent in a mould or dish so that it sets into a semi-solid, somewhat elastic mass. ■ a substance with a similar consistency made with fruit or other ingredients as a condiment: *roast pheasant with redcurrant jelly.* ■ a similar savoury preparation made by boiling meat and bones. ■ any substance of a similar consistency: *petroleum jelly.*
2 a small sweet made with gelatin. ■ Brit. informal a tablet of the drug Temazepam.
3 US term for JAM[2].
4 Brit. informal gelignite.
5 (**jellies**) jelly shoes.
▸ verb (**jellies, jellying, jellied**) [with obj.] (usu. as adj. **jellied**) set (food) as or in a jelly: *jellied cranberry sauce* | *jellied eels.*
– DERIVATIVES **jellify** verb (**jellifies, jellifying, jellified**), **jelly-like** adjective.
– ORIGIN late Middle English: from Old French *gelee* 'frost, jelly', from Latin *gelata* 'frozen', from *gelare* 'freeze', from *gelu* 'frost'.

jelly baby ▸ noun Brit. a jelly-like sweet in the stylized shape of a baby.

jelly bag ▸ noun a fine mesh bag used for straining the juice from cooked fruit, especially so that this liquid can be made into jelly.

jelly bean ▸ noun a bean-shaped sweet with a jelly-like centre and a firm sugar coating.

jellyfish ▸ noun (pl. **same** or **jellyfishes**) **1** a free-swimming marine coelenterate with a jelly-like bell- or saucer-shaped body that is typically transparent and has stinging tentacles around the edge. ● Classes Scyphozoa and Cubozoa.
2 informal a feeble person.

jelly roll ▸ noun N. Amer. a Swiss roll.

jelly shoe (also **jelly sandal**) ▸ noun a sandal made from brightly coloured or translucent moulded plastic.

jelutong /dʒɛˈluːtɒŋ/ ▸ noun a Malaysian tree with pale lightweight timber. ● Genus *Dyera*, family Apocynaceae: several species, in particular *D. costulata*, from which a latex is obtained.
– ORIGIN mid 19th cent.: from Malay.

jemadar /ˈdʒɛməˌdɑː/ ▸ noun variant spelling of JAMADAR.

jemmy (also **jimmy**) ▸ noun (pl. **jemmies**) a short crowbar used by a burglar to force open a window or door.
▸ verb (**jemmies, jemmying, jemmied**) [with obj.] informal force open (a window or door) with a jemmy.
– ORIGIN early 19th cent.: pet form of the given name *James* (compare with JACK[1]).

Jena /ˈjeɪnə/, German /ˈjeːna/ a university town in central Germany, in Thuringia; pop. 102,500 (est. 2006). It is noted as a manufacturing centre for optical and precision instruments.

je ne sais quoi /ˌʒə nə seɪ ˈkwɑː/, French /ʒən sɛ kwa/ ▸ noun a quality that cannot be described or named easily: *that je ne sais quoi which makes a professional.*
– ORIGIN French, literally 'I do not know what'.

Jenkins's Ear, War of a war between England and Spain (1739). It was precipitated by a British sea captain, Robert Jenkins, who appeared before Parliament to produce what he claimed was his ear, cut off by the Spanish while they were carrying out a search of his ship in the Caribbean.

Jenner /ˈdʒɛnə/, Edward (1749–1823), English physician, the pioneer of vaccination. Jenner deliberately infected people with small amounts of cowpox as he believed it would protect them from catching smallpox. The practice was eventually accepted throughout the world, leading to the widespread use of vaccination for other diseases and eventually to the eradication of smallpox in the late 20th century.

jennet /ˈdʒɛnɪt/ ▸ noun a kind of small Spanish horse.
– ORIGIN late Middle English: via French from Spanish *jinete* 'light horseman', from Spanish Arabic *Zenāta*, the name of a Berber people famous for horsemanship.

jenny ▸ noun (pl. **jennies**) **1** a female donkey or ass.
2 short for SPINNING JENNY.
– ORIGIN early 17th cent. (used to denote a female mammal or bird): pet form of the given name *Janet* (compare with JACK[1]).

jenny wren ▸ **noun** Brit. informal a wren.

jeon /dʒʌn/ ▸ **noun** (pl. **same**) a monetary unit of South Korea, equal to one hundredth of a won.
– ORIGIN Korean.

jeopardize /ˈdʒɛpədʌɪz/ (also **jeopardise**) ▸ **verb** [with obj.] put (someone or something) into a situation in which there is a danger of loss, harm, or failure: *a devaluation of the dollar would jeopardize New York's position as a financial centre.*

jeopardy /ˈdʒɛpədi/ ▸ **noun** [mass noun] danger of loss, harm, or failure: *the whole peace process is in jeopardy.* ■ Law danger arising from being on trial for a criminal offence.
– ORIGIN Middle English *iuparti*, from Old French *ieu parti* '(evenly) divided game'. The term was originally used in chess and other games to denote a problem, or a position in which the chances of winning or losing were evenly balanced, hence 'a dangerous situation'.

Jephthah /ˈdʒɛfθə/ (in the Bible) a judge of Israel who sacrificed his daughter in consequence of a vow that if victorious in battle he would sacrifice the first living thing that met him on his return (Judges 11, 12).

Jer. ▸ **abbreviation** Jeremiah (in biblical references).

Jerba variant spelling of **DJERBA**.

jerboa /dʒəːˈbəʊə, ˈdʒəːbəʊə/ ▸ **noun** a desert-dwelling rodent with very long hind legs that enable it to walk upright and perform long jumps, found from North Africa to central Asia. ● Family Dipodidae: several genera and species.
– ORIGIN mid 17th cent.: modern Latin, from Arabic *yarbū'*.

jeremiad /ˌdʒɛrɪˈmʌɪad/ ▸ **noun** a long, mournful complaint or lamentation; a list of woes.
– ORIGIN late 18th cent.: from French *jérémiade*, from *Jérémie* 'Jeremiah', from ecclesiastical Latin *Jeremias*, with reference to the Lamentations of Jeremiah in the Old Testament.

Jeremiah /ˌdʒɛrɪˈmʌɪə/ (*c.*650–*c.*585 BC) a Hebrew major prophet who foresaw the fall of Assyria, the conquest of his country by Egypt and Babylon, and the destruction of Jerusalem. The biblical Lamentations are traditionally ascribed to him. ■ a book of the Bible containing his prophecies. ■ (as noun **a Jeremiah**) a person who complains continually or foretells disaster.

jerepigo /ˌdʒɛrɪˈpiːɡəʊ/ ▸ **noun** [mass noun] S. African a heavy, sweet fortified dessert wine.
– ORIGIN alteration of *geropiga* (from Portuguese, *jeropiga*), a grape juice mixture added during the port-making process.

Jerez /hɛˈrɛθ/, Spanish /xeˈreθ, -ˈres/ a town in Andalusia, Spain; pop. 205,364 (2008). It is the centre of the sherry-making industry. Full name **Jerez de la Frontera** /deɪ la frɒnˈtɛːrə/, Spanish /de la fronˈtera/.

Jericho /ˈdʒɛrɪkəʊ/ a town in Palestine, in the West Bank north of the Dead Sea.

> According to the Bible, Jericho was a Canaanite city destroyed by the Israelites after they crossed the Jordan into the Promised Land; its walls were flattened by the shout of the army and the blast of the trumpets. Occupied by the Israelis since the Six Day War of 1967, in 1994 Jericho was the first area given partial autonomy under the PLO–Israeli peace accord.

jerk[1] ▸ **noun 1** a quick, sharp, sudden movement: *he gave a sudden jerk of his head.* ■ a spasmodic muscular twitch. ■ Weightlifting the raising of a barbell above the head from shoulder level by an abrupt straightening of the arms and legs, typically as the second part of a clean and jerk.
2 informal a contemptibly foolish person.
▸ **verb** [with adverbial of direction] move or cause to move with a jerk: [no obj.] *the van jerked forward* | [with obj.] *she jerked her chin up* | figurative *the thud jerked her back to reality.* ■ [with obj.] Weightlifting raise (a weight) from shoulder level to above the head.
– PHRASAL VERBS **jerk someone around** N. Amer. informal deal with someone dishonestly or unfairly. **jerk off** vulgar slang, chiefly N. Amer. masturbate.
– DERIVATIVES **jerker** noun.
– ORIGIN mid 16th cent. (denoting a stroke with a whip): probably imitative.

jerk[2] ▸ **verb** [with obj.] **1** cure (meat) by cutting it into strips and drying it (originally in the sun).
2 (usu. as adj. **jerked**) prepare (pork or chicken) by marinating it in spices and barbecuing it over a wood fire.
▸ **noun** [mass noun] [often as modifier] jerked meat: *jerk chicken.*
– ORIGIN early 18th cent.: from Latin American Spanish *charquear*, from *charqui*, from Quechua *echarqui* 'dried flesh'.

jerkin ▸ **noun** a sleeveless jacket. ■ historical a man's close-fitting jacket, typically made of leather.
– ORIGIN early 16th cent.: of unknown origin.

jerkin head ▸ **noun** Architecture the end of a roof that is hipped for only part of its height, leaving a truncated gable.
– ORIGIN mid 19th cent.: perhaps from an alteration of *jerking* (from the **JERK[1]** (verb)) + **HEAD**; compare also with earlier *kirkin-head* (apparently arbitrarily formed from **KIRK**) in the same sense.

jerkwater ▸ **adjective** [attrib.] N. Amer. informal of or associated with small, remote, and insignificant rural settlements: *some jerkwater town.*
– ORIGIN mid 19th cent.: from **JERK[1]** + **WATER**, from the need for early railway engines to be supplied with water in remote areas, by dipping a bucket into a stream and 'jerking' it out by rope.

jerky[1] ▸ **adjective** (**jerkier**, **jerkiest**) characterized by abrupt stops and starts: *the coach drew to a jerky halt.*
– DERIVATIVES **jerkily** adverb, **jerkiness** noun.

jerky[2] ▸ **noun** [mass noun] meat that has been cured by being cut into long, thin strips and dried: *beef jerky.*
– ORIGIN mid 19th cent.: from American Spanish *charqui*, from Quechua.

jeroboam /ˌdʒɛrəˈbəʊəm/ ▸ **noun** a wine bottle with a capacity four times larger than that of an ordinary bottle.
– ORIGIN early 19th cent.: named after *Jeroboam*, a king of Israel, 'who made Israel to sin' (1 Kings 11:28, 14:16).

Jerome /dʒəˈrəʊm/, Jerome K. (1859–1927), English novelist and dramatist; full name *Jerome Klapka Jerome*. He is chiefly remembered for his humorous novel *Three Men in a Boat* (1889).

Jerome, St (*c.*342–420), Doctor of the Church. He is chiefly known for his compilation of the Vulgate. Feast day, 30 September.

Jerry ▸ **noun** (pl. **Jerries**) Brit. informal, derogatory a German (especially in military contexts). ■ [in sing.] the Germans collectively.
– ORIGIN First World War: probably an alteration of **GERMAN**.

jerry ▸ **noun** (pl. **jerries**) Brit. informal, dated a chamber pot.
– ORIGIN mid 19th cent.: probably a diminutive of **JEROBOAM**.

jerry-built ▸ **adjective** badly or hastily built with materials of poor quality.
– DERIVATIVES **jerry-builder** noun, **jerry-building** noun.
– ORIGIN mid 19th cent.: origin unknown; sometimes said to be from the name of a firm of builders in Liverpool, or to allude to the walls of Jericho, which fell down at the sound of Joshua's trumpets (Josh. 6:20).

jerrycan (also **jerrican**) ▸ **noun** a large flat-sided metal container for storing or transporting liquids, typically petrol or water.
– ORIGIN Second World War: from **JERRY** + **CAN[2]**, because such containers were first used in Germany.

jerrymander ▸ **verb** Brit. variant spelling of **GERRYMANDER**.

Jersey the largest of the Channel Islands; pop. 87,200 (2001); capital, St Helier.

jersey ▸ **noun** (pl. **jerseys**) **1** a knitted garment with long sleeves, worn over the upper body. ■ a distinctive shirt worn by a player or competitor in certain sports. ■ [mass noun] a soft, fine knitted fabric.
2 (**Jersey**) an animal of a breed of light brown dairy cattle from Jersey.
– ORIGIN late 16th cent. (denoting woollen worsted fabric made in Jersey): from **JERSEY**.

Jersey City an industrial city in NE New Jersey, on the Hudson River opposite New York City; pop. 241,114 (est. 2008).

Jerusalem /dʒəˈruːsələm/ the holy city of the Jews, sacred also to Christians and Muslims, lying in the Judaean hills about 30 km (20 miles) from the River Jordan; pop. 763,600 (est. 2008).

> The city was captured from the Canaanites by King David of the Israelites (*c.*1000 BC), who made it his capital. As the site of the Temple, built by Solomon (957 BC), it became also the centre of the Jewish religion. Since then it has shared the troubled history of the area—destroyed by the Babylonians in 586 BC and by the Romans in AD 70, and fought over by Saracens and Crusaders in the Middle Ages. From 1947 the city was divided between the states of Israel and Jordan until the Israelis occupied the whole city in June 1967 and proclaimed it the capital of Israel. It is revered by Christians as the place of Christ's death and resurrection, and by Muslims as the site of the Dome of the Rock.

Jerusalem artichoke ▸ **noun 1** a knobbly edible tuber with white flesh, eaten as a vegetable.
2 the tall North American plant, closely related to the sunflower, which produces this tuber. ● *Helianthus tuberosus*, family Compositae.
– ORIGIN early 17th cent.: *Jerusalem*, alteration of Italian *girasole* 'sunflower'.

Jerusalem Bible ▸ **noun** a modern English translation of the Bible by mainly Roman Catholic scholars, published in 1966 and revised (as the **New Jerusalem Bible**) in 1985.

Jerusalem cross ▸ **noun** a cross with arms of equal length each ending in a bar; a cross potent.

Jerusalem thorn ▸ **noun** a thorny tropical American tree of the pea family, grown as an ornamental. ● *Parkinsonia aculeata*, family Leguminosae.

Jervis /ˈdʒɑːvɪs/, John, Earl St Vincent (1735–1823), British admiral. In 1797, as commander of the British fleet, he defeated a Spanish fleet off Cape St Vincent, for which he was created Earl St Vincent.

Jervis Bay Territory a territory on Jervis Bay on the SE coast of Australia. Incorporated in 1915 as a sea outlet for the Australian Capital Territory, it separated from the Capital Territory in 1988.

Jespersen /ˈjɛspəs(ə)n/, (Jens) Otto (Harry) (1860–1943), Danish philologist, grammarian, and educationist. He promoted the use of the 'direct method' in language teaching with the publication of his theoretical work *How to Teach a Foreign Language* (1904). Other notable works: *Modern English Grammar* (1909–49).

jess Falconry ▸ **noun** (usu. **jesses**) a short leather strap fastened round each leg of a hawk, usually also having a ring or swivel to which a leash may be attached.
▸ **verb** [with obj.] put jesses on (a hawk).
– ORIGIN Middle English: from Old French *ges*, based on Latin *jactus* 'a throw', from *jacere* 'to throw'.

jessamine /ˈdʒɛsəmɪn/ ▸ **noun** another term for **JASMINE**.

Jesse /ˈdʒɛsi/ (in the Bible) the father of David (1 Sam. 16), represented as the first in the genealogy of Jesus Christ.

Jesse tree ▸ **noun** a representation in carving or stained glass of the genealogy of Jesus as a tree with Jesse at the base and intermediate descendants on branching scrolls of foliage.

Jesse window ▸ **noun** a church window showing Jesus's descent from Jesse, typically in the form of a Jesse tree.

jessie (also **jessy**) ▸ **noun** (pl. **jessies**) Brit. informal, derogatory an effeminate, weak, or oversensitive man.
– ORIGIN 1920s: from the female given name *Jessie*.

jest ▸ **noun** a thing said or done for amusement; a joke: *he laughed uproariously at his own jest* | [mass noun] *it was said in jest.* ■ archaic an object of derision: *lowly virtue is the jest of fools.*
▸ **verb** [no obj.] speak in a joking way: *you jest, surely?*
– DERIVATIVES **jesting** adjective & noun, **jestingly** adverb.
– ORIGIN late Middle English: from earlier *gest*, from Old French *geste*, from Latin *gesta* 'actions, exploits', from *gerere* 'do'. The original sense was 'heroic deed', hence 'a narrative of such deeds'; later the term denoted an idle tale, hence a joke.

jester ▸ **noun** historical a professional joker or 'fool' at a medieval court, typically wearing a cap with bells on it and carrying a mock sceptre. ■ a person who habitually plays the fool.

Jesu /ˈdʒiːzjuː/ archaic form of **JESUS**.
– ORIGIN Middle English: from Old French. *Jesus* became the usual spelling in the 16th cent., but *Jesu* was often retained in translations of the Bible, reflecting Latin vocative use.

Jesuit /ˈdʒɛz(j)ʊɪt/ ▸ **noun** a member of the Society of Jesus, a Roman Catholic order of priests founded by St Ignatius Loyola, St Francis Xavier, and others in 1534, to do missionary work. The order was zealous in opposing the Reformation. Despite periodic persecution it has retained an important influence in Catholic thought and education.

– ORIGIN from French *jésuite* or modern Latin *Jesuita*, from Christian Latin *Iesus* (see **JESUS**).

Jesuitical ▶ adjective of or concerning the Jesuits. ■ dissembling or equivocating, in the manner once associated with Jesuits.
– DERIVATIVES **Jesuitically** adverb.

Jesuits' bark ▶ noun [mass noun] archaic cinchona bark.

Jesus (also **Jesus Christ** or **Jesus of Nazareth**), the central figure of the Christian religion.

> Jesus conducted a mission of preaching and healing (with reported miracles) in Palestine in about AD 28–30, which is described in the Gospels, as are his arrest, death by crucifixion, and Resurrection from the dead. His followers considered him to be the Christ or Messiah and the Son of God, and belief in his Resurrection became a central tenet of Christianity.

■ [as exclamation] an oath used to express irritation, dismay, or surprise.
– ORIGIN from Christian Latin *Iesus*, from Greek *Iēsous*, from a late Hebrew or Aramaic analogous formation based on *Yĕhōšûaʿ* 'Joshua'.

Jesus freak ▶ noun informal, chiefly derogatory a fervent evangelical Christian, especially one who adopts a lifestyle like that of a hippy.

JET ▶ abbreviation Joint European Torus, a machine for conducting experiments in nuclear fusion, at Culham in Oxfordshire.

jet[1] ▶ noun **1** a rapid stream of liquid or gas forced out of a small opening: *a jet of boiling water spurted over his hand*. ■ a nozzle or narrow opening for sending out such a stream.
2 a jet engine. ■ an aircraft powered by one or more jet engines: *a private jet*.
▶ verb (**jets, jetting, jetted**) [no obj., with adverbial of direction] **1** spurt out in jets: *blood jetted from his nostrils*.
2 travel by jet aircraft: *the newly weds jetted off for a honeymoon in New York*.
– ORIGIN late 16th cent. (as a verb meaning 'jut out'): from French *jeter* 'to throw', based on Latin *jactare*, frequentative of *jacere* 'to throw'.

jet[2] ▶ noun [mass noun] a hard black semi-precious variety of lignite, capable of being carved and highly polished. ■ (also **jet black**) a glossy black colour: [as modifier] *her jet-black hair*.
– ORIGIN Middle English: from Old French *jaiet*, from Latin *Gagates*, from Greek *gagatēs* 'from *Gagai*', a town in Asia Minor.

jetboat ▶ noun a motor boat of shallow draught propelled by a jet of water pumped forcefully out from below the stern waterline.

jeté /ˈʒɛteɪ, ʒəˈteɪ/ ▶ noun Ballet a jump in which a dancer springs from one foot to land on the other with one leg extended outwards from the body while in the air. See also **GRAND JETÉ, PETIT JETÉ**.
– ORIGIN French, past participle of *jeter* 'to throw'.

jet engine ▶ noun an engine using jet propulsion for forward thrust, mainly used for aircraft.

jetfoil ▶ noun a type of passenger-carrying hydrofoil.
– ORIGIN 1970s: blend of **JET**[1] and **HYDROFOIL**.

jet lag ▶ noun [mass noun] extreme tiredness and other physical effects felt by a person after a long flight across different time zones.
– DERIVATIVES **jet-lagged** adjective.

jetliner ▶ noun a large jet aircraft carrying passengers.
– ORIGIN 1940s: blend of **JET**[1] and **AIRLINER**.

jet-propelled ▶ adjective moved by jet propulsion.

jet propulsion ▶ noun [mass noun] propulsion by the backward ejection of a high-speed jet of gas or liquid.

jetsam /ˈdʒɛts(ə)m/ ▶ noun [mass noun] unwanted material or goods that have been thrown overboard from a ship and washed ashore, especially material that has been discarded to lighten the vessel. Compare with **FLOTSAM**.
– ORIGIN late 16th cent. (as *jetson*): from **JETTISON**.

jet set ▶ noun (**the jet set**) informal wealthy and fashionable people who travel widely and frequently for pleasure: [as modifier] *the jet-set lifestyle*.
– DERIVATIVES **jet-setter** noun, **jet-setting** adjective.

jet ski ▶ noun trademark a small jet-propelled vehicle which skims across the surface of water and is ridden in a similar way to a motorcycle.
▶ verb (**jet-ski**) [no obj.] ride on a jet-ski.
– DERIVATIVES **jet-skier** noun, **jet-skiing** noun.

jet stream ▶ noun **1** a narrow variable band of very strong predominantly westerly air currents encircling the globe several miles above the earth. There are typically two or three jet streams in each of the northern and southern hemispheres.
2 a flow of exhaust gases from a jet engine.

jettison /ˈdʒɛtɪs(ə)n, -z(ə)n/ ▶ verb [with obj.] throw or drop (something) from an aircraft or ship: *six aircraft jettisoned their loads in the sea*. ■ abandon or discard (someone or something that is no longer wanted): *the scheme was jettisoned*.
▶ noun [mass noun] the action of jettisoning something.
– ORIGIN late Middle English (as a noun denoting the throwing of goods overboard to lighten a ship in distress): from Old French *getaison*, from Latin *jactatio(n-)*, from *jactare* 'to throw' (see **JET**[1]). The verb dates from the mid 19th cent.

jetton /ˈdʒɛt(ə)n/ ▶ noun a counter or token used as a gambling chip or to operate slot machines.
– ORIGIN mid 18th cent.: from French *jeton*, from *jeter* 'throw, add up accounts' (see **JET**[1]); so named because the term was formerly used in accounting.

jetty ▶ noun (pl. **jetties**) a landing stage or small pier at which boats can dock or be moored. ■ a bridge or staircase used by passengers boarding an aircraft. ■ a breakwater constructed to protect or defend a harbour, stretch of coast, or riverbank.
– ORIGIN late Middle English: from Old French *jetee*, feminine past participle of *jeter* 'to throw' (see **JET**[1]).

jetway ▶ noun (trademark in the UK) another term for **AIR BRIDGE**.

jeu d'esprit /ʒəː dɛˈspriː/, French /ʒø dɛspʀi/ ▶ noun (pl. **jeux d'esprit** pronunc. **same**) a light-hearted display of wit and cleverness, especially in a work of literature.
– ORIGIN French, literally 'game of the mind'.

jeunesse dorée /ʒəːˌnɛs ˈdɔːreɪ/, French /ʒœnɛs dɔʀe/ ▶ noun French term for **GILDED YOUTH**.

Jew ▶ noun a member of the people and cultural community whose traditional religion is Judaism and who trace their origins to the ancient Hebrew people of Israel.
– ORIGIN Middle English: from Old French *juiu*, via Latin from Greek *Ioudaios*, via Aramaic from Hebrew *yĕhūḏī*, from *yĕhūḏāh* 'Judah' (see **JUDAH**).

jewel ▶ noun a precious stone, typically a single crystal or piece of a hard lustrous or translucent mineral cut into shape with flat facets or smoothed and polished for use as an ornament. ■ (usu. **jewels**) an ornament or piece of jewellery containing a precious stone or stones. ■ a hard precious stone used as a bearing in a watch, compass, or other device. ■ a very pleasing or valued person or thing; a very fine example: *she was a jewel of a nurse*.
– PHRASES **the jewel in the** (or **one's**) **crown** the most valuable or successful part of something: *Galway is the jewel in the crown of the Irish racing industry*.
– ORIGIN Middle English: from Old French *joel*, from *jeu* 'game, play', from Latin *jocus* 'jest'.

jewel beetle ▶ noun a chiefly tropical beetle that has bold metallic colours and patterns. The larvae are mainly wood-borers and may be serious pests of timber. ● Family Buprestidae: numerous genera.

jewel box ▶ noun **1** a bivalve mollusc which has a robust shell with a rough or spiny surface. It lives in warm seas, attached to rock or coral. ● Family Chamidae: *Chama* and other genera.
2 (also **jewel case**) a storage box for a CD.

jewelfish ▶ noun (pl. **same** or **jewelfishes**) a scarlet and green tropical freshwater cichlid fish. ● *Hemichromis bimaculatus*, family Cichlidae.

jewelled (US **jeweled**) ▶ adjective adorned, set with, or made from jewels: *a jewelled dagger*.

jeweller (US **jeweler**) ▶ noun a person or company that makes or sells jewels or jewellery.
– ORIGIN Middle English: from Old French *juelier*, from *joel* (see **JEWEL**).

jeweller's rouge ▶ noun [mass noun] finely ground ferric oxide, used as a polish for metal and optical glass.

jewellery (US also **jewelry**) ▶ noun [mass noun] personal ornaments, such as necklaces, rings, or bracelets, that are typically made from or contain jewels and precious metal.
– ORIGIN late Middle English: from Old French *juelerie*, from *juelier* 'jeweller', from *joel* (see **JEWEL**).

Jewess ▶ noun often offensive a Jewish woman or girl.

jewfish ▶ noun (pl. **same** or **jewfishes**) a large sporting or food fish of warm coastal waters: ● a fish of the Atlantic and Pacific coasts of North America (*Epinephelus itajara*, family Serranidae). ● a fish of the Indo-Pacific (family Sciaenidae: several species), in particular the mulloway.

Jewish ▶ adjective relating to, associated with, or denoting Jews or Judaism: *the Jewish people*.
– DERIVATIVES **Jewishly** adverb, **Jewishness** noun.

Jewish calendar ▶ noun a complex ancient calendar in use among Jewish people.

> It is a lunar calendar adapted to the solar year, normally consisting of twelve months but having thirteen months in leap years, which occur seven times in every cycle of nineteen years. The years are reckoned from the Creation (which is placed at 3761 BC); the months are Nisan, Iyyar, Sivan, Thammuz, Ab, Elul, Tishri, Hesvan, Kislev, Tebet, Sebat, and Adar, with an intercalary month (First Adar) being added in leap years. The religious year begins with Nisan and ends with Adar, while the civil year begins with Tishri and ends with Elul.

Jewish New Year ▶ noun another term for **ROSH HASHANA**.

Jewison /ˈdʒuːɪs(ə)n/, Norman (b.1926), Canadian film director and producer. He is known particularly for the drama *In the Heat of the Night* (1967), which won five Oscars, the musical *Fiddler on the Roof* (1971), and the romantic comedy *Moonstruck* (1987).

Jewry /ˈdʒʊəri/ ▶ noun (pl. **Jewries**) **1** [mass noun] Jews collectively.
2 historical a Jewish quarter in a town or city.
– ORIGIN Middle English: from Old French *juierie*, from *juiu* (see **JEW**).

Jew's ear ▶ noun a common fungus with a brown rubbery cup-shaped fruiting body, growing on dead or dying trees in both Eurasia and North America. ● *Auricularia auricula-judae*, family Auriculariaceae, class Hymenomycetes.
– ORIGIN mid 16th cent.: a mistranslation of medieval Latin *auricula Judae* 'Judas's ear', from its shape, and because it grows on the elder, which was said to be the tree from which Judas Iscariot hanged himself.

Jew's harp ▶ noun a small lyre-shaped musical instrument held between the teeth and struck with a finger. It can produce only one note, but harmonics are sounded by the player altering the shape of the mouth cavity.

Jezebel /ˈdʒɛzəbɛl/ (*fl.* 9th century BC), a Phoenician princess, traditionally the great-aunt of Dido and in the Bible the wife of Ahab king of Israel. She was denounced by Elijah for introducing the worship of Baal into Israel (1 Kings 16:31, 21:5–15, 2 Kings 9:30–7). Her use of make-up was especially condemned by Puritan England. ■ (as noun **a Jezebel**) a shameless or immoral woman.

Jhansi /ˈdʒɑːnsi/ a city in the state of Uttar Pradesh, northern India; pop. 442,400 (est. 2009).

Jharkhand /dʒɑːˈkand/ a state in NE India, formed in 2000 from the southern part of Bihar; capital, Ranchi.

Jhelum /ˈdʒiːləm/ a river which rises in the Himalayas and flows through the Vale of Kashmir into Punjab, where it meets the Chenab River. It is one of the five rivers that gave Punjab its name. In ancient times it was called the Hydaspes.

Jheri curl ▶ noun a black male hairstyle in which the hair is styled into tight ringlets with a glossy finish.
– ORIGIN from the nickname of Robert William Redding (1907–98), the American developer of the haircare product used to create the style.

jhil /dʒiːl/ (also **jheel**) ▶ noun Indian a pool or lake.
– ORIGIN Hindi *jhīl*.

jhuggi /ˈdʒʌgi/ ▶ noun (pl. **jhuggis**) Indian a slum dwelling typically made of mud and corrugated iron.
– ORIGIN Hindi.

-ji /dʒi/ ▶ combining form Indian used with names and titles to show respect: *Lalitaji | guruji*.
– ORIGIN via Hindi from Sanskrit *jaya* 'conquering'.

Jiang Jie Shi /ˌdʒjaŋ dʒiː ˈʃiː/ variant form of **CHIANG KAI-SHEK**.

Jiangsu /ˌdʒjaŋˈsuː/ (also **Kiangsu**) a province of eastern China; capital, Nanjing. It includes much of the Yangtze delta.

Jiangxi /ˌdʒjaŋˈʃiː/ (also **Kiangsi**) a province of SE China; capital, Nanchang.

jiao /dʒaʊ/ ▶ noun (pl. **same**) a monetary unit of China, equal to one tenth of a yuan.
– ORIGIN from Chinese *jiǎo*.

jib[1] ▶ noun **1** Sailing a triangular staysail set forward of the mast.
2 the projecting arm of a crane.
– ORIGIN mid 17th cent.: of unknown origin.

jib[2] ▸ **verb** (**jibs, jibbing, jibbed**) [no obj.] (of an animal, especially a horse) stop and refuse to go on: *he jibbed at the final fence.* ■ (of a person) be unwilling to do or accept something: *he jibs at paying large bills.*
– DERIVATIVES **jibber** noun.
– ORIGIN early 19th cent.: perhaps related to French *regimber* (earlier *regiber*) 'to buck, rear'; compare with JIBE[1].

jibba /ˈdʒɪbə/ (also **jibbah, djibba,** or **djibbah**) ▸ **noun** a long coat worn by Muslim men.
– ORIGIN mid 19th cent.: Egyptian variant of Arabic *jubba*.

jib boom ▸ **noun** Sailing a spar run out forward as an extension of the bowsprit.

jibe[1] (also **gibe**) ▸ **noun** an insulting or mocking remark; a taunt: *a jibe at his old rivals.*
▸ **verb** [no obj.] make insulting or mocking remarks; jeer: *some cynics in the media might jibe.*
– ORIGIN mid 16th cent. (as a verb): perhaps from Old French *giber* 'handle roughly' (in modern dialect 'kick'); compare with JIB[2].

jibe[2] ▸ **verb & noun** US variant of GYBE.

jibe[3] ▸ **verb** [no obj.] N. Amer. informal be in accord; agree: *the verdict does not jibe with the medical evidence.*
– ORIGIN early 19th cent.: of unknown origin.

jib sheet ▸ **noun** Sailing a rope by which a jib is trimmed.

Jibuti variant spelling of DJIBOUTI.

jicama /ˈhiːkəmə/ ▸ **noun** [mass noun] the crisp white-fleshed edible tuber of the yam bean, used especially in Mexican cookery.
– ORIGIN early 17th cent.: from Mexican Spanish *jícama*, from Nahuatl *xicama*.

Jiddah /ˈdʒɪdə/ (also **Jeddah**) a seaport on the Red Sea coast of Saudi Arabia, near Mecca; pop. 3,012,000 (est. 2007).

jiffy (also **jiff**) ▸ **noun** [in sing.] informal a moment: *we'll be back in a jiffy.*
– ORIGIN late 18th cent.: of unknown origin.

Jiffy bag ▸ **noun** Brit. trademark a padded envelope for protecting fragile items in the post.

jig ▸ **noun 1** a lively dance with leaping movements. ■ a piece of music for a jig, typically in compound time.
2 a device that holds a piece of work and guides the tool operating on it.
3 Fishing a type of artificial bait that is jerked up and down through the water.
▸ **verb** (**jigs, jigging, jigged**) **1** [no obj.] dance a jig. ■ [with adverbial] move up and down with a quick jerky motion: *we were jigging about in our seats.*
2 [with obj.] equip (a factory or workshop) with a jig or jigs.
3 [no obj.] fish with a jig: *a man jigged for squid.*
– PHRASES **in jig time** N. Amer. informal extremely quickly; in a very short time. **the jig is up** N. Amer. informal the scheme or deception is revealed or foiled.
– ORIGIN mid 16th cent.: of unknown origin.

jigaboo /ˈdʒɪɡəbuː/ ▸ **noun** N. Amer. offensive a black person.
– ORIGIN early 20th cent.: related to slang *jig* (in the same sense); compare with the pair *bug, bugaboo*.

jigger[1] ▸ **noun 1** a machine or vehicle with a part that rocks or moves to and fro, e.g. a jigsaw.
2 a person who dances a jig.
3 a small sail set at the stern of a ship. ■ a small tackle consisting of a double and single block with a rope.
4 a measure or small glass of spirits or wine.
5 informal a rest for a billiard cue.
6 Golf, dated a metal golf club with a narrow face.
7 Canadian & NZ a small hand- or power-operated railway vehicle used by railway workers.
▸ **verb** [with obj.] informal rearrange or tamper with.
– ORIGIN mid 16th cent. (originally a slang word for a door): from the verb JIG.

jigger[2] ▸ **noun** variant spelling of CHIGGER.

jiggered ▸ **adjective** Brit. informal damaged; broken: *the lens is totally jiggered.* ■ (of a person) exhausted.
– PHRASES **well, I'll be** (or **I'm**) **jiggered** used to express one's astonishment.
– ORIGIN mid 19th cent.: from JIGGER[1]; its use to mean 'exhausted' is probably euphemistic for *buggered*.

jiggery-pokery ▸ **noun** [mass noun] informal, chiefly Brit. deceitful or dishonest behaviour.
– ORIGIN late 19th cent.: probably a variant of Scots *joukery-pawkery*, from JOUK.

jiggle ▸ **verb** [no obj.] move about quickly from side to side or up and down: *the car jiggled on its springs.* ■ [with obj.] shake (something) lightly up and down or from side to side: *he was jiggling his car keys in his hand.*
▸ **noun** [in sing.] a quick light shake: *give that rack a jiggle.*
– DERIVATIVES **jiggly** adjective.
– ORIGIN mid 19th cent.: partly an alteration of JOGGLE[1], reinforced by JIG.

jiggy /ˈdʒɪɡi/ ▸ **adjective** US informal **1** uninhibited, especially in a sexual manner: *the script required her to get jiggy with Leonardo.*
2 trembling or nervous, especially as the result of drug withdrawal.
– ORIGIN 1930s: from JIG + -Y[1].

jigsaw ▸ **noun 1** (also **jigsaw puzzle**) a puzzle consisting of a picture printed on cardboard or wood and cut into various pieces of different shapes that have to be fitted together. ■ a mystery that can only be resolved by assembling various pieces of information: *help the police put all the pieces of the jigsaw together.*
2 a machine saw with a fine blade enabling it to cut curved lines in a sheet of wood, metal, or plastic.
– ORIGIN late 19th cent.: from the verb JIG + the noun SAW[1].

jihad /dʒɪˈhɑːd/ (also **jehad**) ▸ **noun** (among Muslims) a war or struggle against unbelievers. ■ (also **greater jihad**) Islam the spiritual struggle within oneself against sin.
– ORIGIN from Arabic *jihād*, literally 'effort', expressing, in Muslim thought, struggle on behalf of God and Islam.

jihadi /dʒɪˈhɑːdi/ (also **jehadi**) ▸ **noun** (pl. **jihadis**) a person involved in a jihad; an Islamic militant.
– DERIVATIVES **jihadism** noun, **jihadist** noun.
– ORIGIN from Arabic *jihādī*, from *jihād* (see JIHAD).

jilbab /dʒɪlˈbɑːb/ ▸ **noun** a full-length outer garment, traditionally covering the head and hands, worn in public by some Muslim women.
– ORIGIN Persian *jilbāb*, from Arabic, 'garment, dress, veil'.

Jilin /dʒiːˈlɪn/ (also **Kirin**) a province of NE China; capital, Changchun. ■ a city in Jilin province; pop. 1,263,900 (est. 2006).

jill ▸ **noun** variant spelling of GILL[4].

jillaroo /ˌdʒɪləˈruː/ ▸ **noun** Austral. informal a female novice on a cattle station or sheep station.
– ORIGIN 1940s: from the given name *Jill*, on the pattern of *jackaroo*.

jillion /ˈdʒɪljən/ ▸ **cardinal number** informal, chiefly N. Amer. an extremely large number: *they ran jillions of ads.*
– ORIGIN 1940s: fanciful formation on the pattern of *billion* and *million*.

jilt ▸ **verb** [with obj.] suddenly reject or abandon (a lover): *he was jilted at the altar by his bride-to-be.*
▸ **noun** archaic a person, especially a woman, who capriciously rejects a lover.
– ORIGIN mid 17th cent.: (in the sense 'deceive, trick'): of unknown origin.

Jim Crow ▸ **noun** US **1** [mass noun] the former practice of segregating black people in the US. ■ [count noun] offensive a black person.
2 an implement for straightening iron bars or bending rails by screw pressure.
– DERIVATIVES **Jim Crowism** noun.
– ORIGIN mid 19th cent.: the name of a black character in a 19th-cent. plantation song.

jim-dandy N. Amer. informal ▸ **adjective** fine, outstanding, or excellent.
▸ **noun** an excellent or notable person or thing.
– ORIGIN late 19th cent.: from the given name *Jim* (pet form of *James*) + DANDY.

Jiménez de Cisneros /hɪˌmenez deɪ sɪsˈneːrɒs/, Spanish /xiˌmeneθ de θisˈneɾos, xiˈmenes, sisˈneɾos/ (also **Ximenes de Cisneros**), Francisco (1436–1517), Spanish cardinal and statesman, regent of Spain 1516–17. He was Grand Inquisitor for Castile and Léon from 1507 to 1517, during which time he undertook a massive campaign against heresy, having some 2,500 alleged heretics put to death.

Jiminy /ˈdʒɪmɪni/ ▸ **exclamation** used in phrases as an expression of surprise: *by Jiminy, she was right* | *Jiminy Cricket!*
– ORIGIN early 19th cent.: alteration of GEMINI used as a mild oath in the mid 17th cent., a euphemistic form of *Jesus* (*Christ*).

jim-jams[1] ▸ **plural noun** informal a fit of depression or nervousness: *pre-race jim-jams.*
– ORIGIN mid 16th cent. (originally denoting a small article or knick-knack): fanciful reduplication. The current sense dates from the late 19th cent.

jim-jams[2] ▸ **plural noun** Brit. informal pyjamas.
– ORIGIN early 20th cent.: abbreviation of *pie-jim-jams*, alteration of PYJAMAS.

Jimmu /ˈdʒɪmuː/ the legendary first emperor of Japan (660 BC), descendant of the sun goddess Amaterasu and founder of the imperial dynasty.

Jimmy ▸ **noun** Brit. informal **1** an act of urination. [1930s: from *Jimmy Riddle*, rhyming slang for 'piddle'.]
2 chiefly Scottish used as a term of address to a male stranger.

jimmy ▸ **noun & verb** US spelling of JEMMY.

Jimmy Woodser /ˈwʊdzə/ ▸ **noun** Austral./NZ informal a person who drinks alone or a drink taken on one's own.
– ORIGIN late 19th cent.: from a line in the poem *Jimmy Wood* (1892) by Barcroft Boake: 'Who drinks alone, drinks toast to Jimmy Wood, sir'.

jimson weed /ˈdʒɪms(ə)n/ (also **jimpson weed**) ▸ **noun** [mass noun] North American term for THORN APPLE.
– ORIGIN late 17th cent. (originally as *Jamestown weed*): named after JAMESTOWN in Virginia.

Jin /dʒɪn/ (also **Chin**) **1** a dynasty that ruled China AD 265–420, commonly divided into **Western Jin** (265–317) and **Eastern Jin** (317–420).
2 a dynasty that ruled Manchuria and northern China AD 1115–1234.

Jina /ˈdʒɪnə/ ▸ **noun** (in Jainism) a great teacher who has attained liberation from karma.
– ORIGIN from Sanskrit (see also JAIN).

Jinan /dʒiːˈnan/ (also **Tsinan**) a city in eastern China, the capital of Shandong province; pop. 2,726,400 (est. 2006).

jing /dʒɪŋ/ ▸ **exclamation** variant of JINGS.

jingbang ▸ **noun** (in phrase **the whole jingbang**) informal the whole lot.
– ORIGIN mid 19th cent.: of unknown origin.

jingle ▸ **noun 1** a light ringing sound such as that made by metal objects being shaken together.
2 a short slogan, verse, or tune designed to be easily remembered, especially as used in advertising.
3 (also **jingle shell**) a bivalve mollusc with a fragile, slightly translucent shell. ● Family Anomiidae: *Anomia* and other genera.
▸ **verb** make or cause to make a light metallic ringing sound: [no obj.] *her bracelets were jingling* | [with obj.] *he jingled the coins in his purse.* ■ [no obj.] (of writing) be full of alliteration or rhymes.
– DERIVATIVES **jingly** adjective.
– ORIGIN late Middle English: imitative.

jingo /ˈdʒɪŋɡəʊ/ ▸ **noun** (pl. **jingoes**) dated, chiefly derogatory a vociferous supporter of policy favouring war, especially in the name of patriotism.
– PHRASES **by jingo!** an exclamation of surprise.
– ORIGIN late 17th cent. (originally a conjuror's word): *by jingo* (and the noun sense) come from a popular song adopted by those supporting the sending of a British fleet into Turkish waters to resist Russia in 1878. The chorus ran: 'We don't want to fight, yet by Jingo! if we do, We've got the ships, we've got the men, and got the money too'.

jingoism ▸ **noun** [mass noun] chiefly derogatory extreme patriotism, especially in the form of aggressive or warlike foreign policy.
– DERIVATIVES **jingoist** noun, **jingoistic** adjective.

jings /dʒɪŋz/ (also **jing**) ▸ **exclamation** (often **by jings**) chiefly Scottish used to express surprise.
– ORIGIN late 18th cent.: alteration of JINGO.

jink /dʒɪŋk/ ▸ **verb** [no obj.] change direction suddenly and nimbly, as when dodging a pursuer: *she was too quick for him and jinked away every time.*
▸ **noun** a sudden quick change of direction.
– ORIGIN late 17th cent. (originally Scots as *high jinks*, denoting antics at drinking parties): probably symbolic of nimble motion. Current senses date from the 18th cent.

jinker /ˈdʒɪŋkə/ Austral./NZ ▸ **noun** a wheeled conveyance for moving heavy logs. ■ a light two-wheeled cart.
▸ **verb** [with obj. and adverbial of direction] convey in a jinker.
– ORIGIN late 19th cent.: variant of early 19th-cent. Scots *janker*, a long pole on wheels for carrying logs.

jinn /dʒɪn/ (also **djinn**) ▸ **noun** (pl. **same** or **jinns**) (in Arabian and Muslim mythology) an intelligent spirit of lower rank than the angels, able to appear in human and animal forms and to possess humans. Compare with GENIE.
– ORIGIN from Arabic *jinnī*, plural *jinn*.

J

Jinnah /ˈdʒɪnə, ˈdʒɪnɑː/, Muhammad Ali (1876–1948), Indian statesman and founder of Pakistan. He headed the Muslim League in its struggle with the Hindu-oriented Indian National Congress over Indian independence, and in 1947 he became the first Governor General and President of Pakistan.

jinricksha /dʒɪnˈrɪkʃə/ (also **jinrikisha** /dʒɪnˈrɪkɪʃə/) ▸ **noun** another term for RICKSHAW.
– ORIGIN Japanese, from *jin* 'man' + *riki* 'strength' + *sha* 'vehicle'.

jinx ▸ **noun** a person or thing that brings bad luck.
▸ **verb** [with obj.] bring bad luck to; cast an evil spell on: *the play is jinxed*.
– ORIGIN early 20th cent. (originally US): probably a variant of *jynx* 'wryneck' (because the bird was used in witchcraft).

jird /dʒəːd/ ▸ **noun** a long-tailed burrowing rodent related to the gerbils, found in deserts and steppes from North Africa to China. ● Genus *Meriones*, family Muridae: several species.
– ORIGIN from Berber *(a)gherda*.

jism /ˈdʒɪz(ə)m/ (also **jissom** /ˈdʒɪsəm/ or **jizz**) ▸ **noun** [mass noun] vulgar slang semen.
– ORIGIN mid 19th cent.: of unknown origin.

JIT ▸ **abbreviation** (of manufacturing systems) just-in-time.

jit /dʒɪt/ (also **jit jive**) ▸ **noun** [mass noun] a style of dance music popular in Zimbabwe.
– ORIGIN Shona, from *jit* 'to dance'.

jitney /ˈdʒɪtni/ ▸ **noun** (pl. **jitneys**) N. Amer. informal a bus or other vehicle carrying passengers for a low fare.
– ORIGIN early 20th cent. (originally denoting a five-cent piece): of unknown origin.

J

jitter informal ▸ **noun 1** (**jitters**) feelings of extreme nervousness: *a bout of the jitters*.
2 [mass noun] slight irregular movement, variation, or unsteadiness, especially in an electrical signal or electronic device.
▸ **verb 1** [no obj.] act nervously: *an anxious student who jittered at any provocation*.
2 (of a signal or device) suffer from jitter.
– ORIGIN 1920s: of unknown origin.

jitterbug ▸ **noun 1** a fast dance popular in the 1940s, performed chiefly to swing music. ■ dated a person fond of dancing the jitterbug.
2 informal, dated a nervous person.
▸ **verb** (**jitterbugs, jitterbugging, jitterbugged**) [no obj.] dance the jitterbug.
– ORIGIN 1930s (originally US): from the verb JITTER + BUG.

jittery ▸ **adjective** nervous or unable to relax: *caffeine makes me jittery*.
– DERIVATIVES **jitteriness** noun.

jiu-jitsu ▸ **noun** variant spelling of JU-JITSU.

Jivaro /ˈhiːvərəʊ/ ▸ **noun** (pl. **same** or **Jivaros**) **1** a member of an indigenous people living widely scattered throughout the Amazon jungle.
2 [mass noun] any of the group of languages spoken by the Jivaro.
▸ **adjective** relating to the Jivaro or their language.
– DERIVATIVES **Jivaroan** adjective & noun.
– ORIGIN from Spanish *jíbaro*, probably from the local name *Shuara, Shiwora*.

jive ▸ **noun 1** a lively style of dance popular especially in the 1940s and 1950s, performed to swing music or rock and roll. ■ [mass noun] swing music. ■ [mass noun] a style of dance music popular in South Africa: *township jive*.
2 (also **jive talk**) [mass noun] a form of slang associated with black American jazz musicians. ■ N. Amer. informal deceptive or worthless talk: *a single image says more than any amount of blather and jive*.
▸ **verb 1** [no obj.] perform the jive or a similar dance to popular music: *people were jiving in the aisles*.
2 [with obj.] N. Amer. informal taunt or sneer at: *Willy kept jiving him until Jimmy left*. ■ [no obj.] talk nonsense: *he wasn't jiving about that bartender*.
▸ **adjective** N. Amer. informal deceitful or worthless.
– DERIVATIVES **jiver** noun, **jivey** adjective.
– ORIGIN 1920s (originally US denoting meaningless or misleading speech): of unknown origin; the later musical sense 'jazz' gave rise to 'dance performed to jazz' (1940s).

jizz[1] ▸ **noun** informal (among birdwatchers and naturalists) the characteristic impression given by a particular species of animal or plant.
– ORIGIN 1920s: of unknown origin.

jizz[2] ▸ **noun** vulgar slang variant of JISM.

Jn ▸ **abbreviation** ■ (with preceding numeral) an Epistle of John (in biblical references). ■ the Gospel of John.

Jnr ▸ **abbreviation** Junior (in names).

jo ▸ **noun** (pl. **joes**) Scottish archaic a sweetheart.
– ORIGIN early 16th cent.: variant of JOY.

Joachim, St /ˈdʒəʊəkɪm/ (in Christian tradition) the husband of St Anne and father of the Virgin Mary. He is first mentioned in an apocryphal work of the 2nd century, and then rarely referred to until much later times.

joanna ▸ **noun** Brit. rhyming slang a piano.

Joan of Arc, St (*c*.1412–31), French national heroine; known as **the Maid of Orleans**. She led the French armies against the English in the Hundred Years War, relieving besieged Orleans (1429) and ensuring that Charles VII could be crowned in previously occupied Reims. Captured by the Burgundians in 1430, she was handed over to the English, convicted of heresy, and burnt at the stake. She was canonized in 1920. Feast day, 30 May.

João Pessoa /ˌʒwaʊ peˈsəʊə/ a city in NE Brazil, on the Atlantic coast, capital of the state of Paraíba; pop. 674,762 (2007).

Job /dʒəʊb/ (in the Bible) a prosperous man whose patience and piety were tried by undeserved misfortunes, and who, in spite of his bitter lamentations, remained confident in the goodness and justice of God. ■ a book of the Bible telling of Job.

job[1] ▸ **noun 1** a paid position of regular employment: *the scheme could create 200 jobs | a part-time job*.
2 a task or piece of work, especially one that is paid: *she wants to be left alone to get on with the job*. ■ a responsibility or duty: *it's our job to find things out*. ■ [in sing.] informal a difficult task: *we thought you'd have a job getting there*. ■ [with modifier] informal a procedure to improve the appearance of something: *someone had done a skilful paint job*. ■ informal a crime, especially a robbery: *a series of daring bank jobs*. ■ Computing an operation or group of operations treated as a single and distinct unit.
3 [with modifier] informal a thing of a specified nature: *the car was a blue malevolent-looking job*.
▸ **verb** (**jobs, jobbing, jobbed**) **1** [no obj.] (usu. as adj. **jobbing**) do casual or occasional work: *a jobbing builder*.
2 [with obj.] buy and sell (stocks) as a broker-dealer, especially on a small scale.
3 [with obj.] N. Amer. informal cheat; betray.
4 [no obj.] archaic turn a public office or a position of trust to private advantage.
– PHRASES **between jobs** a euphemistic way of referring to a person being temporarily unemployed: *public money should be used to lend a hand to people who find themselves between jobs*. **big jobs** Brit. informal a euphemistic way of referring to faeces or defecation. **do the job** informal achieve the required result: *a piece of board will do the job*. **give something up as a bad job** informal decide that it is futile to devote further time or energy to something. **a good job** informal, chiefly Brit. a fortunate fact or circumstance: *it was a good job she hadn't brought the car*. **jobs for the boys** Brit. derogatory used in reference to the practice of giving paid employment to one's friends, supporters, or relations. **just the job** Brit. informal exactly what is needed. **make the best of a bad job** see BEST. **on the job** while working; at work. ■ Brit. informal engaged in sexual intercourse. **out of a job** unemployed; redundant.
– PHRASAL VERBS **job something out** N. Amer. assign separate elements of a piece of work to different companies or workers: *all the work done by the middleman can be jobbed out at a much lower cost*.
– ORIGIN mid 16th cent. (in sense 2 of the noun): of unknown origin.

job[2] archaic ▸ **verb** (**jobs, jobbing, jobbed**) [with obj.] prod or stab: *he prepared to job the huge brute*.
■ thrust (something pointed) at or into something.
▸ **noun** an act of prodding, thrusting, or wrenching.
– ORIGIN late Middle English: apparently symbolic of a brief forceful action (compare with JAB).

job analyst ▸ **noun** a person employed to assess the essential factors of particular jobs and the qualifications needed to carry them out.

jobber ▸ **noun 1** historical (in the UK) a principal or wholesaler who dealt only on the Stock Exchange with brokers, not directly with the public.
2 N. Amer. a wholesaler.
3 a person who does casual or occasional work.
– ORIGIN late 17th cent. (in the sense 'broker, middleman', originally not derogatory): from JOB[1].

> **USAGE** On the UK Stock Exchange the term **jobber** was officially replaced by **broker-dealer** in 1986, broker-dealers being entitled to act as both agents and principals in share dealings.

jobbery ▸ **noun** [mass noun] the practice of using a public office or position of trust for one's own gain or advantage.

jobbie ▸ **noun** informal **1** [with adj. or noun modifier] an object or product of a specified kind: *I just got the hang of these computer jobbies*.
2 Brit. a lump of excrement.

jobcentre ▸ **noun** (in the UK) a government office in a town displaying information and giving advice about available jobs and being involved in the administration of benefits to unemployed people.

job club ▸ **noun** (in the UK) an organization providing support and practical help for the long-term unemployed in seeking work.

job control language ▸ **noun** Computing a language enabling the user to define the tasks to be undertaken by the operating system.

job creation ▸ **noun** [mass noun] the provision of new opportunities for paid employment, especially for those who are unemployed.

job description ▸ **noun** a formal account of an employee's responsibilities.

job-hunt ▸ **verb** [no obj.] (usu. as noun **job-hunting**) informal seek employment.
– DERIVATIVES **job-hunter** noun (also **job-seeker**).

jobless ▸ **adjective** unemployed.
– DERIVATIVES **joblessness** noun.

job lot ▸ **noun** a miscellaneous group of articles, especially when sold or bought together: *a job lot of stuff I bought from a demolition firm*.

job reservation ▸ **noun** [mass noun] (in South Africa during the apartheid era) the setting aside by law of certain skilled grades of employment for certain ethnic groups, particularly whites.

job rotation ▸ **noun** [mass noun] the practice of moving employees between different tasks to promote experience and variety.

Jobs /dʒɒbz/, Steven (Paul) (b.1955), American computer entrepreneur. Jobs set up the Apple computer company in 1976 with Steve Wozniak (b.1950), remaining chairman of the company until 1985 and returning in 1997 as CEO.

Job's comforter /dʒəʊbz/ ▸ **noun** a person who aggravates distress under the guise of giving comfort.
– ORIGIN mid 18th cent.: alluding to the biblical story (Job 16:2) of the patriarch JOB.

jobseeker ▸ **noun** a person who is unemployed and looking for work.

jobseeker's allowance ▸ **noun** Brit. a benefit paid by the state to a person who is unemployed and looking for work.

job-share ▸ **verb** [no obj.] (of two part-time employees) share the work and pay of a single full-time job.
▸ **noun** an arrangement in which two people share the work and pay of a single full-time job.
– DERIVATIVES **job-sharer** noun.

Job's tears /dʒəʊbz/ ▸ **plural noun** a SE Asian grass which bears its seeds inside hollow pear-shaped receptacles, which are grey and shiny and sometimes used as beads. ● *Coix lacryma-jobi*, family Gramineae.
– ORIGIN late 16th cent.: named after the patriarch JOB.

jobsworth ▸ **noun** Brit. informal an official who upholds petty rules even at the expense of humanity or common sense.
– ORIGIN 1970s: from 'it's more than my *job's worth* (not) to'.

Joburg /ˈdʒəʊbəːg/ informal name for JOHANNESBURG.

jobwork ▸ **noun** old-fashioned term for PIECEWORK.

Jocasta /dʒəˈkastə/ Greek Mythology a Theban woman, the wife of Laius and mother and later wife of Oedipus.

Jock ▸ **noun** informal, often offensive a Scotsman (often as a form of address).
– ORIGIN early 16th cent.: Scots form of the given name *Jack*, originally as a name for an ordinary man (compare with JACK[1]). The current sense dates from the late 18th cent.

jock[1] ▸ **noun** informal **1** a disc jockey.
2 N. Amer. an enthusiast or participant in a specified activity: *a computer jock*. ■ US a pilot or astronaut.

– ORIGIN late 18th cent. (denoting a rider in horse races): abbreviation.

jock² ▸ noun N. Amer. informal **1** another term for JOCKSTRAP.
2 an enthusiastic male athlete or sports fan, especially one with few other interests.
– DERIVATIVES **jockish** adjective.

jockey ▸ noun (pl. **jockeys**) a person who rides in horse races, especially as a profession.
▸ verb (**jockeys, jockeying, jockeyed**) [no obj.] struggle by every available means to gain or achieve something: *both men will be jockeying for the two top jobs.* ■ [with obj. and adverbial] handle or manipulate (someone or something) in a skilful manner: *he jockeyed his machine into a dive.*
– DERIVATIVES **jockeyship** noun.
– ORIGIN late 16th cent.: diminutive of JOCK. Originally the name for an ordinary man, lad, or underling, the word came to mean 'mounted courier', hence the current sense (late 17th cent.). Another early use 'horse-dealer' (long a byword for dishonesty) probably gave rise to the verb sense 'manipulate', whereas the main verb sense probably relates to the behaviour of jockeys manoeuvring for an advantageous position during a race.

jockey cap ▸ noun a strengthened cap with a long peak of a kind worn by jockeys.

Jockey Club an organization whose stewards are the central authority for the administration of horse racing in Britain. It was founded in 1750.

jockey shorts ▸ plural noun trademark men's close-fitting underpants with a short leg.

jock itch ▸ noun [mass noun] N. Amer. informal a fungal infection of the groin area.
– ORIGIN 1970s: *jock* from JOCKSTRAP.

jocks ▸ plural noun informal jockey shorts.

jockstrap ▸ noun a support or protection for the male genitals, worn especially by sportsmen.
– ORIGIN late 19th cent.: from slang *jock* 'genitals' (of unknown origin) + STRAP.

jocose /dʒəˈkəʊs/ ▸ adjective formal playful or humorous: *a jocose allusion.*
– DERIVATIVES **jocosely** adverb, **jocosity** /-ˈkɒsɪti/ noun (pl. **jocosities**).
– ORIGIN late 17th cent.: from Latin *jocosus*, from *jocus* (see JOKE).

jocular /ˈdʒɒkjʊlə/ ▸ adjective fond of or characterized by joking; humorous or playful: *she sounded in a jocular mood | his voice was jocular.*
– DERIVATIVES **jocularity** noun, **jocularly** adverb.
– ORIGIN early 17th cent.: from Latin *jocularis*, from *joculus*, diminutive of *jocus* (see JOKE).

jocund /ˈdʒɒk(ə)nd, ˈdʒəʊk-/ ▸ adjective formal cheerful and light-hearted: *a jocund wedding party.*
– DERIVATIVES **jocundity** noun (pl. **jocundities**), **jocundly** adverb.
– ORIGIN late Middle English: via Old French from Latin *jocundus*, variant (influenced by *jocus* 'joke') of *jucundus* 'pleasant, agreeable', from *juvare* 'to delight'.

Jodhpur /ˈdʒɒdpʊə/ **1** a city in western India, in Rajasthan; pop. 1,006,700 (est. 2009).
2 a former princely state of India, now part of Rajasthan.

jodhpurs /ˈdʒɒdpəz/ ▸ plural noun full-length trousers worn for horse riding, which are close-fitting below the knee and have reinforced patches on the inside of the leg.
– ORIGIN late 19th cent.: named after JODHPUR, where similar garments are worn by Indian men as part of everyday dress.

Jodrell Bank /ˈdʒɒdrəl/ the site in Cheshire of one of the world's largest radio telescopes, with a fully steerable dish 76 m (250 ft) in diameter.

joe ▸ noun N. Amer. informal **1** an ordinary man: *the average joe.*
2 [mass noun] coffee.
– ORIGIN mid 19th cent.: pet form of the given name *Joseph*; compare with JOE BLOGGS. Sense 2 arose in the 1940s.

Joe Blake ▸ noun rhyming slang **1** Austral. a snake.
2 (**Joe Blakes**) Austral./NZ the shakes; delirium tremens.

Joe Bloggs ▸ noun Brit. informal a name for a hypothetical average man.

Joe Blow ▸ noun North American term for JOE BLOGGS.

joe job ▸ noun Canadian informal a menial or monotonous task.

Joel /ˈdʒəʊəl/ a Hebrew minor prophet of the 5th or possibly 9th century BC. ■ a book of the Bible containing his prophecies.

Joe Public ▸ noun Brit. informal a name for a hypothetical representative member of the general public, or the general public personified.

joe-pye weed ▸ noun [mass noun] N. Amer. a tall perennial plant of the daisy family, which bears clusters of small purple flowers. ● *Eupatorium purpureum* and *E. maculatum*, family Compositae.
– ORIGIN early 19th cent.: of unknown origin.

Joe Sixpack ▸ noun informal, chiefly US a name for a hypothetical ordinary working man.

joey¹ ▸ noun (pl. **joeys**) Austral. a young kangaroo, wallaby, or possum. ■ informal a baby or young child.
– ORIGIN of unknown origin.

joey² ▸ noun historical a silver threepenny bit.
– ORIGIN 1930s: diminutive of the pet name *Joe*: the derivation remains unknown. The term (originally London slang) denoted a fourpenny piece in the 19th cent.

Joffre /ˈʒɒfrə/, French /ʒɔfʀ/, Joseph Jacques Césaire (1852–1931), French Marshal, Commander-in-Chief of the French army on the Western Front during the First World War.

jog ▸ verb (**jogs, jogging, jogged**) **1** [no obj.] run at a steady gentle pace, especially on a regular basis as a form of physical exercise: *he began to jog along the road* | (as noun **jogging**) *try cycling or gentle jogging.* ■ (of a horse) move at a slow trot. ■ move in an unsteady way: *the bus jogged and jolted.* ■ (**jog along/on**) continue in a steady, uneventful way: *our marriage worked and we jogged along.*
2 [with obj.] nudge or knock slightly: *a hand jogged his elbow.*
▸ noun **1** a spell of jogging: *his morning jog.* ■ [in sing.] a gentle running pace: *he set off along the bank at a jog.*
2 a slight push or nudge.
– PHRASES **jog someone's memory** cause someone to remember something suddenly.
– ORIGIN late Middle English (in the sense 'stab, pierce'): variant of JAG¹.

jogger ▸ noun a person who jogs as a form of physical exercise. ■ (**joggers**) loose trousers made of a stretchy fabric and typically elasticated at the waist and ankles, worn especially for jogging.

joggle¹ ▸ verb move or cause to move with repeated small bobs or jerks: [no obj.] *helium balloons were joggling above the crowds.*
▸ noun a bobbing or jerking movement.
– ORIGIN early 16th cent.: frequentative of JOG.

joggle² ▸ noun a joint between two pieces of stone, concrete, or timber consisting of a projection in one of the pieces fitting into a notch in the other or a small piece let in between the two.
▸ verb [with obj.] join (pieces of stone, concrete, or timber) by means of a joggle.
– ORIGIN early 18th cent.: perhaps related to JAG¹.

Jogjakarta /ˌdʒɒgdʒəˈkɑːtə/ variant spelling of YOGYAKARTA.

jogtrot ▸ noun a slow trot.

Johannesburg /dʒəʊˈhanɪsbəːg/ a city in South Africa, the capital of the province of Gauteng; pop. 2,023,500 (est. 2009).

Johannine /dʒəʊˈhanʌɪn/ ▸ adjective relating to the Apostle St John the Evangelist, or to the Gospel or Epistles of John in the New Testament.
– ORIGIN mid 19th cent.: from the medieval Latin given name *Johannes* 'John' + -INE¹.

Johannisberg /dʒəˈhanɪsbəːg/ (also **Johannisberg Riesling**) ▸ noun the chief variety of the Riesling wine grape, originating in Germany and widely grown in California and elsewhere. ■ [mass noun] a white wine made from this grape.
– ORIGIN from the name of a castle and village on the Rhine, Germany, where it was originally produced.

Johannisberger /dʒəˈhanɪsˌbəːgə/ ▸ noun variant of JOHANNISBERG.

John¹ (1165–1216), son of Henry II, king of England 1199–1216; known as **John Lackland**. He lost most of his French possessions, including Normandy, to Philip II of France. In 1209 he was excommunicated for refusing to accept Stephen Langton as Archbishop of Canterbury. Forced to sign Magna Carta by his barons (1215), he ignored its provisions and civil war broke out.

John² the name of six kings of Portugal: ■ **John I** (1357–1433), reigned 1385–1433; known as **John the Great**. Reinforced by an English army, he defeated the Castilians at Aljubarrota (1385), winning independence for Portugal. ■ **John II** (1455–95), reigned 1481–95. ■ **John III** (1502–57), reigned 1521–57. ■ **John IV** (1604–56), reigned 1640–56; known as **John the Fortunate**. The founder of the Braganza dynasty, he expelled a Spanish usurper and proclaimed himself king. ■ **John V** (1689–1750), reigned 1706–50. ■ **John VI** (1767–1826), reigned 1816–26.

John³, Augustus (Edwin) (1878–1961), Welsh painter. Frequent subjects of his work are the Gypsies of Wales; he was also noted for his portraits of the wealthy and famous, particularly prominent writers. He was the brother of Gwen John.

John⁴, Barry (b.1945), Welsh rugby union player. During his international career (1966–72) he played at half back and scored a record ninety points for his country.

John⁵, Sir Elton (Hercules) (b.1947), English pop and rock singer, pianist, and songwriter; born *Reginald Kenneth Dwight*. His many hit songs include 'Your Song' (1970) and 'Nikita' (1985). His tribute to Diana, Princess of Wales, 'Candle in the Wind' (1997), became the highest-selling single in history.

John⁶, Gwen (1876–1939), Welsh painter. The sister of Augustus John, she settled in France. In 1913 she converted to Catholicism; her paintings, noted for their grey tonality, often depict nuns or girls in interior settings.

john ▸ noun informal **1** chiefly N. Amer. a toilet.
2 a prostitute's client.
– ORIGIN early 20th cent. (in sense 2): from the given name *John*, used from late Middle English as a form of address to a man, or to denote various occupations, including that of priest (late Middle English) and policeman (mid 17th cent.).

J

John III (1624–96), king of Poland 1674–96; known as **John Sobieski**. In 1683 he relieved Vienna when it was besieged by the Turks, thereby becoming the hero of the Christian world.

John, St an Apostle, son of Zebedee and brother of James; known as **St John the Evangelist** or **St John the Divine**. He has traditionally been credited with the authorship of the fourth Gospel, Revelation, and three epistles of the New Testament. Feast day, 27 December. ■ the fourth Gospel (see GOSPEL (sense 2)). ■ any of the three epistles of the New Testament attributed to St John.

John Barleycorn ▸ noun a personification of barley, or of malt liquor.

johnboat ▸ noun N. Amer. a small flat-bottomed boat with square ends, used chiefly on inland waterways.

John Bull ▸ noun a personification of England or the typical Englishman, represented as a stout red-faced farmer in a top hat and high boots.
– ORIGIN late 18th cent.: from the name of a character representing the English nation in John Arbuthnot's satire *Law is a Bottomless Pit; or, the History of John Bull* (1712).

John Chrysostom, St see CHRYSOSTOM, ST JOHN.

John Citizen ▸ noun a hypothetical ordinary man.

John Crow ▸ noun West Indian term for TURKEY VULTURE.

John Doe ▸ noun N. Amer. Law an anonymous party, typically the plaintiff, in a legal action. ■ informal a hypothetical average man.
– ORIGIN mid 18th cent.: originally in legal use as a name of a fictitious plaintiff, corresponding to *Richard Roe*, used to represent the defendant.

John Dory ▸ noun (pl. **John Dories**) an edible dory (fish) of the eastern Atlantic and Mediterranean, with a black oval mark on each side. ● *Zeus faber*, family Zeidae.

Johne's disease /ˈjəʊnəz/ ▸ noun [mass noun] a form of chronic enteritis in cattle and sheep, caused by a mycobacterium.
– ORIGIN early 20th cent.: named after Heinrich A. *Johne* (1839–1910), German veterinary surgeon.

johnny ▸ noun (pl. **johnnies**) informal **1** Brit. used as a name for an unknown man, often suggesting that he is unimportant or insignificant: *the security johnny insists that you sign the visitors' book.*
2 (also **rubber johnny**) a condom.
3 US a gown fastened at the back, worn by hospital patients.
– ORIGIN late 17th cent. (in sense 1): pet form of the given name *John*; sense 2 dates from the 1960s.

johnnycake ▸ noun **1** [mass noun] N. Amer. maize flour bread typically baked or fried on a griddle.

J

2 (**johnny cake**) Austral./NZ a small, thin unleavened wheat loaf baked in wood ashes.
– ORIGIN early 18th cent.: also referred to as *journey cake*, which may be the original form.

johnny-come-lately ▸ **noun** informal a newcomer to or late starter at a particular place or sphere of activity.

Johnny-on-the-spot ▸ **noun** N. Amer. informal, dated a person who is at hand whenever needed.

Johnny Reb ▸ **noun** another term for **REB[2]**.

John of Damascus, St (*c*.675–*c*.749), Syrian theologian and Doctor of the Church. A champion of image worship against the iconoclasts, he wrote the influential encyclopedic work on Christian theology *The Fount of Wisdom*. Feast day, 4 December.

John of Gaunt (1340–99), son of Edward III. John of Gaunt was effective ruler of England during the final years of his father's reign and the minority of Richard II. His son Henry Bolingbroke later became King Henry IV.

John of the Cross, St (1542–91), Spanish mystic and poet; born *Juan de Yepis y Alvarez*. A Carmelite monk and priest, he joined with St Teresa of Ávila in founding the 'discalced' Carmelite order in 1568. Feast day, 14 December.

John o'Groats /əˈɡrəʊts/ a village at the extreme NE point of the Scottish mainland.
– ORIGIN said to be named after *John de Groat* and his two brothers, who came from Holland with a royal letter of protection and built a house on the site in the 16th cent.

John Paul II (1920–2005), Polish cleric, pope 1978–2005; born *Karol Jozef Wojtyla*. The first non-Italian pope since 1522, he upheld the Roman Catholic Church's traditional opposition to artificial means of contraception and abortion, homosexuality, the ordination of women, and the relaxation of the rule of celibacy for priests.

John Q. Public ▸ **noun** North American term for **JOE PUBLIC**.

Johns, Jasper (b.1930), American painter, sculptor, and printmaker. A key figure in the development of pop art, he depicted commonplace and universally recognized images.

Johnson[1], Amy (1903–41), English aviator. In 1930 she became the first woman to fly solo to Australia. She later set records with her solo flights to Tokyo (1931) and to Cape Town (1932).

Johnson[2], Andrew (1808–75), American Democratic statesman, 17th President of the US 1865–9. His lenient policy towards the Southern states after the American Civil War led him to be impeached by the Republican majority in Congress; he was acquitted by a single vote.

Johnson[3] (also **Jansens** or **Janssen van Ceulen**), Cornelius (1593–*c*.1661), English-born Dutch portrait painter. He painted for the court of Charles I; after the outbreak of the English Civil War he emigrated to Holland (1643).

Johnson[4], Earvin (b.1959), American basketball player; known as **Magic Johnson**. He played for the Los Angeles Lakers from 1979 to 1991. After being diagnosed HIV-positive he won an Olympic gold medal in 1992 and then returned to the Lakers.

Johnson[5], Jack (1878–1946), American boxer. He was the first black world heavyweight champion (1908–15).

Johnson[6], Lyndon Baines (1908–73), American Democratic statesman, 36th President of the US 1963–9; known as **LBJ**. He continued the programme of reforming initiated by John F. Kennedy, but the increasing involvement of the US in the Vietnam War undermined his popularity.

Johnson[7], Michael (b.1967), American sprinter, winner of five Olympic gold medals between 1992 and 2000.

Johnson[8], Robert (1911–38), American blues singer and guitarist. Despite his mysterious early death, he was very influential on the 1960s blues movement. Notable songs: 'I Was Standing at the Crossroads'.

Johnson[9], Samuel (1709–84), English lexicographer, writer, critic, and conversationalist; known as **Dr Johnson**. A leading figure in the literary London of his day, he is noted particularly for his *Dictionary of the English Language* (1755), edition of Shakespeare (1765), and *The Lives of the English Poets* (1777). James Boswell's biography of Johnson records details of his life and conversation.
– DERIVATIVES **Johnsonian** adjective.

johnson ▸ **noun** US vulgar slang a man's penis.
– ORIGIN mid 19th cent.: of unknown origin.

John the Baptist, St, Jewish preacher and prophet, a contemporary of Jesus. In *c*.27 AD he preached and baptized on the banks of the River Jordan. Among those whom he baptized was Christ. He was beheaded by Herod Antipas after denouncing the latter's marriage to Herodias, the wife of Herod's brother Philip (Matt. 14:1–12). Feast day, 24 June.

John the Evangelist, St (also **John the Divine**) see **JOHN, ST**.

John the Fortunate, John IV of Portugal (see **JOHN[2]**).

John the Great, John I of Portugal (see **JOHN[2]**).

Johor /dʒəʊˈhɔː/ (also **Johore**) a state of Malaysia, at the southernmost point of mainland Asia, joined to Singapore by a causeway; capital, Johor Baharu.

Johor Baharu /bəˈhɑːruː/ the capital of the state of Johor in Malaysia; pop. 895,500 (est. 2009).

joie de vivre /ˌʒwɑː də ˈviːvr(ə)/, French /ʒwad vivʀ/ ▸ **noun** [mass noun] exuberant enjoyment of life.
– ORIGIN French, literally 'joy of living'.

join ▸ **verb** [with obj.] link; connect: *the tap was* ***joined to*** *a pipe* | ***join*** *the paragraphs* ***together***. ■ become linked or connected to: *where the River Drave joins the Danube*. ■ [no obj., with adverbial] unite to form one entity or group: *they* ***joined up with*** *local environmentalists* | *countries* ***join together*** *to abolish restrictions on trade*. ■ become a member or employee of: *she joined the department last year*. ■ take part in: *I joined the demonstration* | [no obj.] *I* ***joined in*** *and sang along*. ■ [no obj.] (**join up**) become a member of the armed forces: *her brothers joined up in 1914*. ■ come into the company of: *after the show we were joined by Jessica's sister*. ■ support (someone) in an activity: *I am sure you will* ***join me in*** *wishing him every success*.
▸ **noun** a place or line where two or more things are connected or fastened together.
– PHRASES **join battle** formal begin fighting. **join the club** see **CLUB[1]**. **join forces** combine efforts. **join hands** hold each other's hands. ■ work together: *education has been shy to join hands with business*.
– DERIVATIVES **joinable** adjective.
– ORIGIN Middle English: from Old French *joindre*, from Latin *jungere* 'to join'.

joinder /ˈdʒɔɪndə/ ▸ **noun** [mass noun] Law the action of bringing parties together; union.
– ORIGIN late Middle English: from Anglo-Norman French, from Old French *joindre* 'to join'.

joined-up ▸ **adjective** (of handwriting) written with the characters joined; cursive. ■ (especially of a policy) characterized by coordination and coherence of thought; integrated: *a joined-up approach to rural poverty, public services and employment*.

joiner ▸ **noun 1** chiefly Brit. a person who constructs the wooden components of a building, such as stairs, doors, and door and window frames.
2 informal a person who readily joins groups or campaigns: *a compulsive joiner of revolutionary movements*.
– ORIGIN Middle English: from Old French *joigneor*, from *joindre* 'to join'.

joinery ▸ **noun** [mass noun] the wooden components of a building, such as stairs, doors, and door and window frames, viewed collectively. ■ the activity or skill of a joiner.

joint ▸ **noun 1** a point at which parts of an artificial structure are joined. ■ a particular arrangement of parts of a structure at the point where they are joined. ■ Geology a break or fracture in a mass of rock, with no relative displacement of the parts. ■ a piece of flexible material forming the hinge of a book cover.
2 a structure in the human or animal body at which two parts of the skeleton are fitted together. ■ each of the distinct sections of a body or limb between the places at which they are connected: *the top two joints of his index finger*. ■ Brit. a large piece of meat cooked whole or ready for cooking: *a* ***joint of*** *ham*. ■ the part of a stem of a plant from which a leaf or branch grows. ■ a section of a plant stem between such parts; an internode.
3 informal an establishment of a specified kind, especially one where people meet for eating, drinking, or entertainment: *a burger joint*. ■ (**the joint**) N. Amer. prison.
4 informal a cannabis cigarette: *he rolled a joint*.
5 chiefly black slang a piece of creative work, especially a film or piece of music: *listen to one of his joints nowadays and you don't even need to see the production credit*.
▸ **adjective** [attrib.] shared, held, or made by two or more people together: *a joint statement*. ■ sharing in a position, achievement, or activity: *a joint winner*. ■ Law applied or regarded together. Often contrasted with **SEVERAL**.
▸ **verb** [with obj.] **1** provide or fasten (something) with joints: (as adj. **jointed**) *jointed lever arms*. ■ fill up the joints of (masonry or brickwork) with mortar; point. ■ prepare (a board) for being joined to another by planing its edge.
2 cut (the body of an animal) into joints for cooking.
– PHRASES **out of joint** (of a joint of the body) out of position; dislocated: *he put his hip out of joint*. ■ in a state of disorder or disorientation: *time was thrown completely out of joint*.
– DERIVATIVES **jointless** adjective.
– ORIGIN Middle English: from Old French, past participle of *joindre* 'to join' (see **JOIN**).

joint account ▸ **noun** a bank account held by more than one person, each individual having the right to deposit and withdraw funds.

joint and several ▸ **adjective** (of a legal obligation) undertaken by two or more people, each individual having liability for the whole.

jointer ▸ **noun 1** a plane used for preparing a wooden edge for fixing or joining to another. ■ a tool used for pointing masonry and brickwork.
2 a worker employed in jointing pipes or wires.

jointing ▸ **noun** [mass noun] **1** the action of providing with, connecting by, or preparing for a joint.
2 an arrangement of joints.

jointly ▸ **adverb** with another person or people; together: *a report prepared jointly by Harvard and Yale universities*.

jointress ▸ **noun** Law, dated a widow who holds a jointure.
– ORIGIN early 17th cent.: feminine of obsolete *jointer* 'joint owner'.

joint-stock company ▸ **noun** Finance a company whose stock is owned jointly by the shareholders.

joint tenancy ▸ **noun** the holding of an estate or property jointly by two or more parties, the share of each passing to the other or others on death.
– DERIVATIVES **joint tenant** noun.

jointure /ˈdʒɔɪntʃə/ ▸ **noun** Law an estate settled on a wife for the period during which she survives her husband, in lien of a dower.
– ORIGIN Middle English (in the sense 'junction, joint'): from Old French, from Latin *junctura* (see **JUNCTURE**). In late Middle English the term denoted the joint holding of property by a husband and wife for life, whence the current sense.

joint venture ▸ **noun** a commercial enterprise undertaken jointly by two or more parties which otherwise retain their distinct identities.

joist /dʒɔɪst/ ▸ **noun** a length of timber or steel supporting part of the structure of a building, typically arranged in parallel series to support a floor or ceiling.
– DERIVATIVES **joisted** adjective.
– ORIGIN late Middle English *giste*, from Old French, 'beam supporting a bridge', based on Latin *jacere* 'lie down'.

jojoba /həˈhəʊbə, həʊ-/ ▸ **noun 1** (also **jojoba oil**) [mass noun] an oil extracted from the seeds of an American shrub, widely used in cosmetics.
2 the leathery-leaved evergreen shrub or small tree that produces the seeds from which jojoba is obtained, native to south-western North America.
● *Simmondsia chinensis*, the only member of the family Simmondsiaceae.
– ORIGIN early 20th cent.: from Mexican Spanish.

joke ▸ **noun** a thing that someone says to cause amusement or laughter, especially a story with a funny punchline: *she was in a mood to tell jokes*. ■ a trick played on someone for fun. ■ [in sing.] informal a person or thing that is ridiculously inadequate: *public transport is a joke*.
▸ **verb** [no obj.] make jokes; talk humorously or flippantly: *she could laugh and* ***joke with*** *her colleagues* | (as adj. **joking**) *a joking manner*. ■ [with obj.] archaic poke fun at: *he was pretending to joke his daughter*.
– PHRASES **be no joke** informal be a serious matter or difficult undertaking: *trying to shop with three children in tow is no joke*. **can** (or **can't**) **take a joke** be able (or unable) to receive humorous remarks or tricks in the spirit in which they are intended. **get** (or **be** or **go**) **beyond a joke** informal become (or be) something that is serious or worrying: *this rain's*

getting beyond a joke. **joking apart** said to indicate that one is being serious, especially after making a joke: *joking apart, I really appreciate this sort of help.* **make a joke of** laugh or be humorous about (something that is not funny in itself).
– DERIVATIVES **jokingly** adverb.
– ORIGIN late 17th cent. (originally slang): perhaps from Latin *jocus* 'jest, wordplay'.

joker ▶ noun **1** a person who is fond of joking. ■ informal a foolish or inept person: *a bunch of jokers.*
2 a playing card, typically bearing the figure of a jester, used in some games as a wild card.
3 US a clause unobtrusively inserted in a bill or document and affecting its operation in a way not immediately apparent.
– PHRASES **the joker in the pack** a person or factor likely to have an unpredictable effect on events.

jokey (also **joky**) ▶ adjective (**jokier**, **jokiest**) not serious; teasing or humorous: *a brief exchange of jokey comments.*
– DERIVATIVES **jokily** adverb, **jokiness** noun.

jol /dʒɔːl/ S. African informal ▶ noun an occasion of celebration and enjoyment; a good time.
▶ verb (**jols**, **jolling**, **jolled**) [no obj.] **1** [with adverbial of direction] set off; go: *you could jol to the lake on a Sunday.*
2 have a good time; celebrate in a lively way: *everyone goes to clubs and jols till late.* ■ engage in a flirtation or a casual love affair.
– DERIVATIVES **joller** noun.
– ORIGIN Afrikaans, literally 'party'.

jolie laide /ˌʒɒli ˈlɛd/ ▶ noun (pl. **jolies laides** pronunc. **same**) a woman whose face is attractive despite having ugly features.
– ORIGIN French, from *jolie* 'pretty' and *laide* 'ugly', feminine adjectives.

Joliot /ˈʒɒlɪəʊ/, French /ʒɔljo/, Jean-Frédéric (1900–58), French nuclear physicist. As Marie Curie's assistant at the Radium Institute he worked with her daughter **Irène** (1897–1956), whom he married (taking the name Joliot-Curie); together they discovered artificial radioactivity. Nobel Prize for Chemistry (1935, shared with his wife).

joliotium /ˌdʒɒlɪˈəʊtɪəm/ ▶ noun [mass noun] the name proposed by IUPAC for the chemical element of atomic number 105, now called **dubnium**.
– ORIGIN 1990s: modern Latin, from the name of J.F. **JOLIOT**.

jollification ▶ noun [mass noun] lively celebration with others; merrymaking.

jollity ▶ noun (pl. **jollities**) [mass noun] lively and cheerful activity or celebration: *a night of riotous jollity.* ■ the quality of being cheerful: *he was full of false jollity.*
– ORIGIN Middle English: from Old French *jolite*, from *joli* (see **JOLLY**[1]).

jollof rice /ˈdʒɒləf rʌɪs/ ▶ noun a West African stew made with rice, chilli peppers, and meat or fish.
– ORIGIN *jollof*, variant of **WOLOF**.

jolly[1] ▶ adjective (**jollier**, **jolliest**) happy and cheerful: *he was a jolly man full of jokes.* ■ informal lively and entertaining: *we had a very jolly time.*
▶ verb (**jollies**, **jollying**, **jollied**) [with obj. and adverbial] informal encourage (someone) in a friendly way: *he jollied people along | they were trying to jolly her out of her torpor.* ■ (**jolly someone/thing up**) make someone or something more lively or cheerful: *ideas to jolly up a winter's party.*
▶ adverb [as submodifier] Brit. informal very; extremely: *that's a jolly good idea.*
▶ noun (pl. **jollies**) Brit. informal a party or celebration.
– PHRASES **get one's jollies** informal have fun or find pleasure. **jolly well** Brit. informal used for emphasis, especially when one is angry or irritated: *I'm going to keep on eating as much sugar as I jolly well like.*
– DERIVATIVES **jollily** adverb, **jolliness** noun.
– ORIGIN Middle English: from Old French *jolif*, an earlier form of *joli* 'pretty', perhaps from Old Norse *jól* (see **YULE**).

jolly[2] (also **jolly boat**) ▶ noun (pl. **jollies**) a clinker-built ship's boat that is smaller than a cutter, typically hoisted at the stern of the ship.
– ORIGIN early 18th cent.: perhaps related to **YAWL**.

Jolly Roger ▶ noun a pirate's flag with a white skull and crossbones on a black background.
– ORIGIN late 18th cent.: of unknown origin.

jollytail ▶ noun another term for **INANGA**.

Jolson /ˈdʒəʊls(ə)n/, Al (1886–1950), Russian-born American singer, film actor, and comedian; born *Asa Yoelson.* He made the Gershwin song 'Swanee' his trademark, and appeared in the first full-length talking film, *The Jazz Singer* (1927).

jolt /dʒəʊlt, dʒɒlt/ ▶ verb [with obj.] push or shake (someone or something) abruptly and roughly: *a surge in the crowd behind him jolted him forwards.* ■ give a surprise or shock to (someone) in order to make them act or change: *she tried to jolt him out of his depression.* ■ [no obj., with adverbial] move with sudden lurches: *the train jolted into motion.*
▶ noun an abrupt rough or violent movement. ■ an unpleasant surprise or shock: *that information gave her a severe jolt.*
– DERIVATIVES **jolty** adjective (**joltier**, **joltiest**).
– ORIGIN late 16th cent.: of unknown origin.

Jomon /ˈdʒəʊmən/ ▶ noun [usu. as modifier] Archaeology an early Mesolithic-type culture in Japan (*c.*10,000–300 BC), preceding the Yayoi period. It is characterized by pottery decorated with a distinctive cord pattern.
– ORIGIN from Japanese *jōmon* 'cord pattern'.

Jon. ▶ abbreviation ■ Jonah (in biblical references). ■ Jonathan.

Jonagold /ˈdʒɒnəˌgəʊld/ ▶ noun a dessert apple of a variety with greenish-gold skin and crisp flesh.
– ORIGIN 1960s: blend of **JONATHAN**[2] and **GOLDEN DELICIOUS**.

Jonah /ˈdʒəʊnə/ (in the Bible) a Hebrew minor prophet. He was called by God to preach in Nineveh, but disobeyed and attempted to escape by sea; in a storm he was thrown overboard as a bringer of bad luck and swallowed by a great fish, only to be saved and finally succeed in his mission. ■ a book of the Bible telling of Jonah.

Jonathan[1] (in the Bible) a son of Saul, noted for his friendship with David (1 Sam. 18–20, 2 Sam. 1) and killed at the battle of Mount Gilboa (1 Sam. 31).

Jonathan[2] ▶ noun a cooking apple of a red-skinned variety first grown in the US.
– ORIGIN mid 19th cent.: named after *Jonathan* Hasbrouk (died 1846), American lawyer.

Jones[1], Bobby (1902–71), American golfer; full name *Robert Tyre Jones.* In a short competitive career (1923–30), and as an amateur, he won thirteen major competitions, including four American and three British open championships.

Jones[2], Daniel (1881–1967), British phonetician. He developed the International Phonetic Alphabet from 1907 and went on to invent the system of cardinal vowels and produce the *English Pronouncing Dictionary* (1917).

Jones[3], Inigo (1573–1652), English architect and stage designer. He introduced the Palladian style to England; notable buildings include the Queen's House at Greenwich (1616) and the Banqueting Hall at Whitehall (1619).

Jones[4], John Paul (1747–92), Scottish-born American admiral; born *John Paul.* He became famous for his raids off the northern coasts of Britain during the War of American Independence.

jones US, chiefly black slang ▶ noun a fixation on or compulsive desire for someone or something, typically a drug; an addiction: *a two-year amphetamine jones.*
▶ verb [no obj.] (**jones on/for**) have a fixation on; be addicted to: *Palmer was jonesing for some coke again.*
– ORIGIN 1960s: said to come from *Jones* Alley, in Manhattan, associated with drug addicts.

Joneses ▶ plural noun (usu. **the Joneses**) a person's neighbours or social equals.
– PHRASES **keep up with the Joneses** try to emulate or not be outdone by one's neighbours.
– ORIGIN late 19th cent.: from *Jones*, a commonly found British surname.

jong /jɒŋ/ S. African ▶ noun **1** chiefly historical a young black male servant. ■ offensive a black man.
2 informal used as a form of address to both men and women, expressing affection or exasperation: *there are sharks out there, jong.* ■ a boyfriend or lover.
▶ exclamation used to express surprise, pleasure, or anger, or to add emphasis to a statement.
– ORIGIN Afrikaans, from earlier South African Dutch *jongen* 'lad'.

jongleur /ʒɒ̃ˈgləː/ ▶ noun historical an itinerant minstrel.
– ORIGIN French, variant of *jougleur* 'juggler', earlier *jogleor* 'pleasant, smiling', from Latin *joculator* 'joker'.

Jönköping /ˈjəːnˌtʃəːpɪŋ/ an industrial city in southern Sweden, at the south end of Lake Vättern; pop. 125,154 (2008).

jonquil /ˈdʒɒŋkwɪl/ ▶ noun a narcissus with clusters of small fragrant yellow flowers and cylindrical leaves, native to southern Europe and NE Africa.
● *Narcissus jonquilla*, family Liliaceae (or Amaryllidaceae).
– ORIGIN early 17th cent.: from modern Latin *jonquilla* or French *jonquille*, from Spanish *junquillo*, diminutive of *junco*, from Latin *juncus* 'rush, reed'.

Jonson, Ben (1572–1637), English dramatist and poet; full name *Benjamin Jonson.* With his play *Every Man in his Humour* (1598) he established his 'comedy of humours', whereby each character is dominated by a particular obsession. He became the first Poet Laureate in the modern sense. Other notable works: *Volpone* (1606) and *Bartholomew Fair* (1614).
– DERIVATIVES **Jonsonian** adjective.

jook ▶ verb [with obj.] W. Indian pierce, poke, or stab.
– ORIGIN of uncertain origin: perhaps from a West African language, or related to **JOUK**.

Joplin[1] /ˈdʒɒplɪn/, Janis (1943–70), American rock singer. She died from a heroin overdose just before her most successful album, *Pearl*, and her number-one single 'Me and Bobby McGee' were released.

Joplin[2] /ˈdʒɒplɪn/, Scott (1868–1917), American pianist and composer. He was the first of the creators of ragtime to write down his compositions. Notable compositions: 'Maple Leaf Rag' (1899), 'The Entertainer' (1902), and 'Gladiolus Rag' (1907).

Joppa /ˈdʒɒpə/ biblical name for **JAFFA**[1].

Jordaens /jɔːˈdɑːns/, Jacob (1593–1678), Flemish painter. Influenced by Rubens, he is noted for his boisterous peasant scenes painted in warm colours. Notable works: *The King Drinks* (1638).

J

Jordan[1] **1** a country in the Middle East east of the River Jordan; pop. 6,269,300 (est. 2009); official language, Arabic; capital, Amman. Official name **HASHEMITE KINGDOM OF JORDAN**.

> Romans, Arabs, Crusaders, and Turks dominated the area successively until it was made a British protectorate in 1916 and achieved independence in 1946. During the war of 1948–9 that followed the establishment of the state of Israel, Jordan took over the area of the West Bank; this was recovered by Israel in the Six Day War of 1967, after which many Palestinian refugees entered the country. A peace treaty with Israel was signed in 1994, ending an official state of war between the two countries.

2 a river flowing southward for 320 km (200 miles) from the Anti-Lebanon Mountains through the Sea of Galilee into the Dead Sea. John the Baptist baptized Christ in the River Jordan. It is regarded as sacred not only by Christians but also by Jews and Muslims.
– DERIVATIVES **Jordanian** /dʒɔːˈdeɪnɪən/ adjective & noun.

Jordan[2], Michael (Jeffrey) (b.1963), American basketball player. Playing for the Chicago Bulls from 1984, he was the National Basketball Association's Most Valuable Player five times.

jorum /ˈdʒɔːrəm/ ▶ noun historical a large bowl or jug used for serving drinks such as tea or punch.
– ORIGIN early 18th cent.: perhaps from *Joram* (2 Sam. 8:10), who 'brought with him vessels of silver, and vessels of gold' to King David.

Jorvik /ˈjɔːvɪk/ (also **Yorvik**) Viking name for **YORK**.

Jos. ▶ abbreviation ■ Joseph. ■ Joshua (in biblical references).

Joseph (in the Bible) a Hebrew patriarch, son of Jacob. He was given a coat of many colours by his father, but was then sold by his jealous brothers into captivity in Egypt, where he attained high office (Gen. 30–50).

Joseph, St, husband of the Virgin Mary. A carpenter of Nazareth, he was betrothed to Mary at the time of the Annunciation. Feast day, 19 March.

Josephine (1763–1814), Empress of France 1804–9; full name *Marie Joséphine Rose Tascher de la Pagerie.* She married Napoleon in 1796. Their marriage proved childless and she was divorced by Napoleon in 1809.

Joseph of Arimathea, St /ˌarɪməˈθiːə/ a member of the council at Jerusalem who, after the Crucifixion, asked Pilate for Christ's body, which he buried. He is also known from the medieval story that he came to England with the Holy Grail and built the first church at Glastonbury. Feast day, 17 March.

Josephson junction ▶ noun Physics an electrical device in which two superconducting metals are separated by a thin layer of insulator, across which an electric current may flow in the absence of a

potential difference. The current may be made to oscillate in proportion to an applied potential difference.
– ORIGIN 1960s: named after Brian D. *Josephson* (born 1940), British physicist.

Josephus /dʒəʊˈsiːfəs/, Flavius (*c.*37–*c.*100), Jewish historian, general, and Pharisee; born *Joseph ben Matthias*. His *Jewish War* gives an eyewitness account of the events leading up to the Jewish revolt against the Romans in 66, in which he was a leader.

josh informal ▶ **verb** [with obj.] tease (someone) in a playful way: *he loved to josh people.* ■ [no obj.] engage in joking or playful talk with others.
▶ **noun** [mass noun] N. Amer. good-natured banter.
– DERIVATIVES **josher** noun.
– ORIGIN mid 19th cent. (as a verb): of unknown origin.

Josh. ▶ **abbreviation** Joshua (in biblical references).

Joshua /ˈdʒɒʃʊə/ (*fl. c.*13th century BC), the Israelite leader who succeeded Moses and led his people into the Promised Land. ■ the sixth book of the Bible, telling of the conquest of Canaan and its division among the twelve tribes of Israel.

Joshua tree ▶ **noun** a yucca which grows as a tree and has clusters of spiky leaves, native to arid regions of south-western North America. ● *Yucca brevifolia*, family Agavaceae.
– ORIGIN mid 19th cent.: apparently from **JOSHUA** (Josh. 8:18), the plant being likened to a man brandishing a spear.

Josquin des Prez see **DES PREZ**.

J

joss[1] ▶ **noun** a Chinese religious statue or idol.
– ORIGIN early 18th cent.: from Javanese *dejos*, from obsolete Portuguese *deos*, from Latin *deus* 'god'.

joss[2] ▶ **noun** informal, chiefly Austral. a person of influence or importance.
– ORIGIN mid 19th cent.: from dialect *joss* 'foreman', of unknown origin.

josser ▶ **noun** Brit. informal a man, typically an old man or one regarded with some contempt: *an old josser.*
– ORIGIN late 19th cent. (in Australian sense 'a clergyman'): from **JOSS**[1] + **-ER**[1].

joss house ▶ **noun** a Chinese temple.

joss stick ▶ **noun** a thin stick consisting of a substance that burns slowly and with a fragrant smell, used as incense.

jostle ▶ **verb** [with obj.] push, elbow, or bump against (someone) roughly, typically in a crowd: *he was jostled by passengers rushing for the gates* | [no obj.] *people **jostled against** us.* ■ [no obj.] **(jostle for)** struggle or compete forcefully for: *a jumble of images jostled for attention.*
▶ **noun** [mass noun] the action of jostling.
– ORIGIN late Middle English *justle*, from *just*, an earlier form of **JOUST**. The original sense was 'have sexual intercourse with'; current senses date from the mid 16th cent.

jot ▶ **verb** (**jots, jotting, jotted**) [with obj.] write (something) quickly: *when you've found the answers, **jot** them **down**.*
▶ **noun** [usu. with negative] a very small amount: *you didn't care a jot* | *I have yet to see **one jot of** evidence.*
– ORIGIN late 15th cent. (as a noun): via Latin from Greek *iōta*, the smallest letter of the Greek alphabet: see **IOTA**.

jota /ˈxəʊtə/ ▶ **noun** a folk dance from northern Spain, danced by couples in fast triple time.
– ORIGIN Spanish.

jotter ▶ **noun** Brit. a small pad or notebook used for notes or jottings.

jotting ▶ **noun** (usu. **jottings**) a brief note.

Jotun /ˈjəʊtʊn/ ▶ **noun** Scandinavian Mythology a member of the race of giants, enemies of the gods.
– ORIGIN from Old Norse *jǫtunn*, related to Old English *eoten*, of Germanic origin.

Jotunheim /ˈjəʊtʊnˌhʌɪm/ **1** Scandinavian Mythology a region of the universe, inhabited by giants.
2 a mountain range in south central Norway.

joual /ʒwal, ʒuːˈɑːl/ ▶ **noun** [mass noun] a non-standard form of popular Canadian French, influenced by English vocabulary and grammar.
– ORIGIN Canadian French dialect, from French *cheval* 'horse', apparently from the way *cheval* is pronounced in rural areas of Quebec.

jougs /dʒuːgz/ ▶ **plural noun** historical a hinged iron collar chained to a wall or post, used in medieval Scotland as an instrument of punishment.
– ORIGIN late 16th cent.: from French *joug* or Latin *jugum* 'yoke'.

jouissance /ˈʒwiːsɒ̃s/, French /ʒwisɑ̃s/ ▶ **noun** [mass noun] formal physical or intellectual pleasure, delight, or ecstasy.
– ORIGIN French, from *jouir* 'enjoy'.

jouk /dʒuːk/ ▶ **verb** [no obj., with adverbial of direction] Scottish & N. English turn or bend quickly, typically to avoid someone or something: *I jouked around the corner.*
– ORIGIN early 16th cent.: perhaps related to the verb **DUCK**[2].

Joule /dʒuːl/, James Prescott (1818–89), English physicist. Joule established that all forms of energy were interchangeable—the first law of thermodynamics. The Joule–Thomson effect, discovered with William Thomson, later Lord Kelvin, in 1852, led to the development of the refrigerator and to the science of cryogenics. Joule also measured and described the heating effects of an electric current passing through a resistance.

joule /dʒuːl/ (abbrev.: **J**) ▶ **noun** the SI unit of work or energy, equal to the work done by a force of one newton when its point of application moves one metre in the direction of action of the force, equivalent to one 3600th of a watt-hour.
– ORIGIN late 19th cent.: named after J. P. **JOULE**.

Joule effect ▶ **noun** Physics the heating that occurs when an electric current flows through a resistance.

Joule's law ▶ **noun** Physics a law stating that the heat produced by an electric current *i* flowing through a resistance *R* for a time *t* is proportional to i^2Rt.

Joule–Thomson effect ▶ **noun** Physics the change of temperature of a gas when it is allowed to expand without doing any external work. The gas becomes cooler if it was initially below a certain temperature (the **inversion temperature**), or hotter if initially above it.

jounce /dʒaʊns/ ▶ **verb** jolt or bounce: [no obj.] *the car jounced wildly* | [with obj.] *the pilot jounced the ship through turbulence.*
– ORIGIN late Middle English: probably symbolic; compare with **BOUNCE**.

journal /ˈdʒəːn(ə)l/ ▶ **noun 1** a newspaper or magazine that deals with a particular subject or professional activity: *medical journals* | [in names] *the Wall Street Journal.*
2 a daily record of news and events of a personal nature; a diary. ■ Nautical a logbook. ■ (**the Journals**) a record of the daily proceedings in the Houses of Parliament. ■ (in bookkeeping) a daily record of business transactions with a statement of the accounts to which each is to be debited and credited.
3 the part of a shaft or axle that rests on bearings.
▶ **verb** (**journals, journaling, journaled**) [no obj.] write in a journal or diary.
– ORIGIN late Middle English (originally denoting a book containing the appointed times of daily prayers): from Old French *jurnal*, from late Latin *diurnalis* (see **DIURNAL**).

journalese ▶ **noun** [mass noun] informal a hackneyed style of writing supposedly characteristic of that in newspapers and magazines.

journalism ▶ **noun** [mass noun] the activity or profession of writing for newspapers or magazines or of broadcasting news on radio or television. ■ the product of the activity of journalism: *a collection of journalism.*

journalist ▶ **noun** a person who writes for newspapers or magazines or prepares news to be broadcast on radio or television.
– DERIVATIVES **journalistic** adjective, **journalistically** adverb.

journalize (also **journalise**) ▶ **verb** [with obj.] dated enter (notes or information) in a journal or account book: *I would gladly journalize some of my proceedings.*

journey ▶ **noun** (pl. **journeys**) an act of travelling from one place to another: *an eight-hour train journey.* ■ a long and often difficult process of personal change and development: *her spiritual journey towards Roman Catholicism* | *I was excited with my character's journey in the film.*
▶ **verb** (**journeys, journeying, journeyed**) [no obj., with adverbial of direction] travel somewhere: *they journeyed south.*
– DERIVATIVES **journeyer** noun.
– ORIGIN Middle English: from Old French *jornee* 'day, a day's travel, a day's work' (the earliest senses in English), based on Latin *diurnum* 'daily portion', from *diurnus* (see **DIURNAL**).

journeyman ▶ **noun** (pl. **journeymen**) **1** a worker or sports player who is reliable but not outstanding: [as modifier] *a solid journeyman professional.*
2 a trained worker who is employed by someone else.
– ORIGIN late Middle English: from **JOURNEY** (in the obsolete sense 'day's work') + **MAN**; so named because the journeyman was no longer bound by indentures but was paid by the day.

journo ▶ **noun** (pl. **journos**) informal a journalist.

joust /dʒaʊst/ ▶ **verb** [no obj.] **1** (often as noun **jousting**) historical (of a medieval knight) engage in a sporting contest in which two opponents on horseback fight with lances.
2 compete closely for superiority: *the guerrillas **jousted for** supremacy.*
▶ **noun** a medieval sporting contest in which two opponents on horseback fought with lances.
– DERIVATIVES **jouster** noun.
– ORIGIN Middle English (originally in the sense 'join battle, engage'): from Old French *jouster* 'bring together', based on Latin *juxta* 'near'.

J'Ouvert /dʒuːˈveɪ/ ▶ **noun** (in the Caribbean) the official start of carnival, at dawn on the Monday preceding Lent.
– ORIGIN French Creole, from French *jour ouvert* 'day opened'.

Jove /ˈdʒəʊv/ another name for **JUPITER**.
– PHRASES **by Jove** dated an exclamation indicating surprise or used for emphasis: *by Jove, yes, it's been warm all right.*
– ORIGIN from Latin *Jov-*, stem of Old Latin *Jovis*, replaced later by *Jupiter*. The exclamation *by Jove* dates from the late 16th cent.

jovial /ˈdʒəʊvɪəl, -vj(ə)l/ ▶ **adjective** cheerful and friendly: *she was in a jovial mood.*
– DERIVATIVES **joviality** noun, **jovially** adverb.
– ORIGIN late 16th cent.: from French, from late Latin *jovialis* 'of Jupiter' (see **JOVE**), with reference to the supposed influence of the planet Jupiter on those born under it.

Jovian /ˈdʒəʊvɪən/ ▶ **adjective 1** Roman Mythology of or like the god Jove (or Jupiter).
2 relating to the planet Jupiter or the class of giant planets to which Jupiter belongs.
▶ **noun** a hypothetical or fictional inhabitant of the planet Jupiter.

jowar /dʒaʊˈɑː/ ▶ **noun** another term for **DURRA**.
– ORIGIN from Hindi *jauār*.

jowl ▶ **noun** (often **jowls**) the lower part of a person's or animal's cheek, especially when it is fleshy or drooping: *she had a large nose and heavy jowls.*
■ N. Amer. the cheek of a pig used as meat. ■ the loose fleshy part of the neck of certain animals, such as the dewlap of cattle or the wattle of birds.
– DERIVATIVES **jowled** adjective [in combination] *ruddy-jowled*, **jowly** adjective (**jowlier, jowliest**).
– ORIGIN Old English *ceole* (related to German *Kehle* 'throat, gullet'), partly merged with Old English *ceafl* 'jaw' (related to Dutch *kevels* 'cheekbones').

joy ▶ **noun** [mass noun] a feeling of great pleasure and happiness: *tears of joy* | *the joy of being alive.* ■ [count noun] a thing that causes joy: *the joys of country living.* ■ [usu. with negative] Brit. informal success or satisfaction: *you'll get no joy out of her.*
▶ **verb** [no obj.] literary rejoice: *I felt shame that I had ever joyed in his discomfiture or pain.*
– PHRASES **be full of the joys of spring** be lively and cheerful. **wish someone joy** Brit., chiefly ironic congratulate someone.
– ORIGIN Middle English: from Old French *joie*, based on Latin *gaudium*, from *gaudere* 'rejoice'.

Joyce, James (Augustine Aloysius) (1882–1941), Irish writer. One of the most important writers of the modernist movement, he made his name with *Dubliners* (short stories, 1914). His novel *Ulysses* (1922) revolutionized the structure of the modern novel and developed the stream-of-consciousness technique. Other notable novels: *A Portrait of the Artist as a Young Man* (1914–15) and *Finnegans Wake* (1939).
– DERIVATIVES **Joycean** adjective & noun.

joyful ▶ **adjective** feeling, expressing, or causing great pleasure and happiness: *joyful music.*
– DERIVATIVES **joyfully** adverb, **joyfulness** noun.

joyless ▶ **adjective** not giving or feeling any pleasure or satisfaction; grim or dismal: *she had to face the thought of a joyless future.*
– DERIVATIVES **joylessly** adverb.

joyous ▶ **adjective** chiefly literary full of happiness and joy: *scenes of joyous celebration.*

– DERIVATIVES **joyously** adverb, **joyousness** noun.

joypad ▸ noun an input device for a computer games console which uses buttons to control the motion of an image on the screen.
– ORIGIN late 20th cent.: blend of JOYSTICK and KEYPAD.

joyride ▸ noun a ride for enjoyment in a vehicle or aircraft. ■ informal a fast and dangerous ride in a stolen vehicle: *they went for a joyride.*

joyriding ▸ noun [mass noun] the action or practice of driving fast and dangerously in a stolen car for enjoyment.
– DERIVATIVES **joyrider** noun.

joystick ▸ noun informal the control column of an aircraft. ■ a lever that can be moved in several directions to control the movement of an image on a computer or similar display screen.

JP ▸ abbreviation (in the UK) Justice of the Peace.

JPEG /ˈdʒeɪpɛg/ ▸ noun [mass noun] Computing a format for compressing image files: [as modifier] *a JPEG image.* ■ [count noun] a file in this format.
– ORIGIN 1990s: abbreviation of *Joint Photographic Experts Group.*

J-pop ▸ noun [mass noun] Japanese pop music.

Jr ▸ abbreviation chiefly N. Amer. junior (in names): *John Smith Jr.*

jua kali /dʒʊə ˈkali/ ▸ noun [mass noun] [usu. as modifier] (in Kenya) small-scale craft or artisanal work, such as making tools or textiles.
– ORIGIN Kiswahili, literally 'hot sun' (referring to the outdoor nature of the work).

Juan Carlos /ˌhwɑːn ˈkɑːlɒs/ (b.1938), grandson of Alfonso XIII, king of Spain since 1975; full name *Juan Carlos Victor María de Borbón y Borbón.* Franco's chosen successor, he became king after Franco's death. His reign has seen Spain's increasing liberalization and its entry into NATO and the European Community.

Juan Fernandez Islands /ˌhwɑːn fəˈnandɛz/ a group of three almost uninhabited islands in the Pacific Ocean 640 km (400 miles) west of Chile.

Juárez /ˈhwɑːrɛz/, Benito Pablo (1806–72), Mexican statesman, President 1861–4 and 1867–72. Between 1864 and 1867 he was replaced as emperor by Maximilian, who was supported by the French.

Juba /ˈdʒuːbə/ the capital of the southern region of Sudan, on the White Nile; pop. 250,000 (est. 2005).

juba /ˈdʒuːbə/ ▸ noun [mass noun] a dance originating among plantation slaves in the southern US, featuring rhythmic handclapping and slapping of the thighs.
– ORIGIN late 19th cent.: of unknown origin.

Jubba /ˈdʒʊbə, ˈdʒuːbə/ a river in East Africa, rising in the highlands of central Ethiopia and flowing southwards for about 1,600 km (1,000 miles) through Somalia to the Indian Ocean.

jube ▸ noun Austral./NZ a jujube lozenge.
– ORIGIN 1930s: shortened form.

jubilant ▸ adjective feeling or expressing great happiness and triumph: *a large number of jubilant fans ran on to the pitch.*
– DERIVATIVES **jubilance** noun, **jubilantly** adverb.
– ORIGIN mid 17th cent. (originally in the sense 'making a joyful noise'): from Latin *jubilant-* 'calling, hallooing', from the verb *jubilare* (see JUBILATE).

Jubilate /ˌdʒuːbɪˈlɑːteɪ/ ▸ noun Psalm 100, beginning *Jubilate deo* 'rejoice in God', especially as used as a canticle in the Anglican service of matins. ■ a musical setting of the Jubilate.
– ORIGIN Latin, 'shout for joy!', imperative of *jubilare* (see JUBILATE).

jubilate /ˈdʒuːbɪleɪt/ ▸ verb [no obj.] archaic show great happiness; rejoice: *sing and jubilate aloud before God.*
– ORIGIN mid 17th cent.: from Latin *jubilat-* 'called out', from the verb *jubilare*, used by Christian writers to mean 'shout for joy'.

jubilation ▸ noun [mass noun] a feeling of great happiness and triumph: *unbelievable scenes of jubilation.*

jubilee ▸ noun **1** a special anniversary of an event, especially one celebrating twenty-five or fifty years of a reign or activity.
2 Judaism a year of emancipation and restoration, kept every fifty years.
3 a period of remission from the penal consequences of sin, granted by the Roman Catholic Church under certain conditions for a year, usually at intervals of twenty-five years.
– ORIGIN late Middle English: from Old French *jubile*, from late Latin *jubilaeus (annus)* '(year) of jubilee', based on Hebrew *yōḇēl*, originally 'ram's-horn trumpet', with which the jubilee year was proclaimed.

Jubilee clip ▸ noun trademark a type of adjustable steel band secured with a screw.

Jubran /ʒuˈbrɑːn/ variant form of GIBRAN.

Jud. ▸ abbreviation ■ Judges (in biblical references). ■ Judith (Apocrypha) (in biblical references).

Judaea /dʒuːˈdiːə/ the southern part of ancient Palestine, corresponding to the former kingdom of Judah.
– DERIVATIVES **Judaean** adjective.

Judaeo- /dʒuːˈdiːəʊ/ (US **Judeo-**) ▸ combining form Jewish; Jewish and ...: *Judaeo-Christian.* ■ relating to Judaea.
– ORIGIN from Latin *Judaeus* 'Jewish'.

Judah /ˈdʒuːdə/ **1** (in the Bible) a Hebrew patriarch, the fourth son of Jacob. ■ the tribe of Israel traditionally descended from him, the most powerful of the twelve tribes of Israel.
2 the southern part of ancient Palestine, occupied by the tribe of Judah. After the reign of Solomon (*c.*930 BC) it formed a separate kingdom from Israel. Later known as JUDAEA.

Judaic /dʒuːˈdeɪɪk/ ▸ adjective relating to Judaism or the ancient Jews: *tenets of Judaic law.*
– ORIGIN early 17th cent.: from Latin *Judaicus*, from Greek *Ioudaïkos*, from *Ioudaios* (see JEW).

Judaism /ˈdʒuːdeɪɪz(ə)m/ ▸ noun [mass noun] the monotheistic religion of the Jews. ■ the Jews collectively.

> For its origins Judaism looks to the biblical covenant made by God with Abraham, and to the laws revealed to Moses and recorded in the Torah (supplemented by the rabbinical Talmud), which established the Jewish people's special relationship with God. Since the destruction of the Temple in Jerusalem in AD 70, the rituals of Judaism have centred on the home and the synagogue, the chief day of worship being the Sabbath (sunset on Friday to sunset on Saturday), and the annual observances including Yom Kippur and Passover.

– DERIVATIVES **Judaist** noun.
– ORIGIN from late Latin *Judaismus*, from Greek *Ioudaïsmos*, from *Ioudaios* (see JEW).

Judaize /ˈdʒuːdeɪʌɪz/ (also **Judaise**) ▸ verb [with obj.] make Jewish; convert to Judaism. ■ [no obj.] follow Jewish customs or religious rites.
– DERIVATIVES **Judaization** noun.
– ORIGIN late 16th cent.: from Christian Latin *judaizare*, from Greek *ioudaizein*, from *Ioudaios* (see JEW).

Judas[1] /ˈdʒuːdəs/ an Apostle; full name **Judas Iscariot**. He betrayed Christ to the Jewish authorities in return for thirty pieces of silver; the Gospels leave his motives uncertain. Overcome with remorse, he later committed suicide. ■ (as noun usu. **a Judas**) a person who betrays a friend or comrade.

Judas[2] see JUDE, ST.

judas (also **judas hole**) ▸ noun a peephole in a door.
– ORIGIN mid 19th cent.: from *Judas* Iscariot (see JUDAS[1]), because of his association with betrayal.

Judas kiss ▸ noun an act of betrayal, especially one disguised as a gesture of friendship.
– ORIGIN early 15th cent.: with biblical allusion (Matt. 26:48) to the betrayal of Christ by Judas Iscariot.

Judas Maccabaeus /ˌmakəˈbiːəs/ (died *c.*161 BC), Jewish leader. Leading a Jewish revolt in Judaea against Antiochus IV Epiphanes from around 167 BC, he recovered Jerusalem and dedicated the Temple anew. He is the hero of the two books of the Maccabees in the Apocrypha.

Judas tree ▸ noun a Mediterranean tree of the pea family, with purple flowers that typically appear before the rounded leaves. ● *Cercis siliquastrum*, family Leguminosae.

judder ▸ verb [no obj.] (especially of something mechanical) shake and vibrate rapidly and with force: *the steering wheel juddered in his hand.*
▸ noun an instance of rapid and forceful shaking and vibration: *the car gave a judder.*
– DERIVATIVES **juddery** adjective.
– ORIGIN 1930s: imitative; compare with SHUDDER.

judder bar ▸ noun NZ a speed bump.

Jude, St /dʒuːd/ an Apostle, supposed brother of James; also known as **Judas**. Thaddaeus is traditionally identified with him. According to tradition, he was martyred in Persia with St Simon. Feast day (with St Simon), 28 October. ■ the last epistle of the New Testament, ascribed to St Jude.

Judenrat /ˈjuːd(ə)nrɑːt/, German /ˈjuːdnraːt/ ▸ noun (pl. **Judenrate**) a council representing a Jewish community, especially in German-occupied territory during the Second World War.
– ORIGIN German, 'Jewish council'.

judenrein /ˈjuːd(ə)nrʌɪn/ ▸ adjective from which Jews are excluded (originally with reference to organizations in Nazi Germany).
– ORIGIN German, 'free of Jews'.

Judeo- ▸ combining form US spelling of JUDAEO-.

Judezmo /dʒuːˈdɛzməʊ/ ▸ noun another term for LADINO.
– ORIGIN Old Spanish, 'the Jewish manner'.

Judg. ▸ abbreviation Judges (in biblical references).

judge ▸ noun **1** a public officer appointed to decide cases in a law court. ■ a person who decides the results of a competition. ■ a person able or qualified to give an opinion on something: *she was a good judge of character.*
2 a leader having temporary authority in ancient Israel in the period between Joshua and the kings. See also JUDGES.
▸ verb [with obj.] form an opinion or conclusion about: *a production can be judged according to the canons of aesthetic criticism* | [with clause] *it is hard to judge whether such opposition is justified* | [no obj.] *judging from his letters home, Monty was in good spirits.* ■ decide (a case) in a law court: *other cases were judged by tribunal.* ■ [with obj. and complement] give a verdict on (someone) in a law court: *she was judged innocent of murder.* ■ decide the results of (a competition).
– DERIVATIVES **judgeship** noun.
– ORIGIN Middle English: from Old French *juge* (noun), *juger* (verb), from Latin *judex, judic-*, from *jus* 'law' + *dicere* 'to say'.

J

judge advocate ▸ noun Law a barrister who advises a court martial on points of law and sums up the case.

judge advocate general ▸ noun an officer in supreme control of the courts martial in the armed forces, excluding (in the UK) the navy.

judge-made ▸ adjective Law constituted by judicial decisions rather than explicit legislation.

judgement (also **judgment**) ▸ noun **1** [mass noun] the ability to make considered decisions or come to sensible conclusions: *an error of judgement* | *that is not, in my judgement, the end of the matter.* ■ [count noun] an opinion or conclusion: *they make subjective judgements about children's skills.* ■ [count noun] a decision of a law court or judge: *county court judgements against individuals in debt.*
2 a misfortune or calamity viewed as a divine punishment: *the events of last week are a judgement on us for our sinful ways.*
– PHRASES **against one's better judgement** contrary to what one feels to be wise or sensible. **pass judgement** (of a law court or judge) give a decision concerning a defendant or legal matter: *he passed judgement on the accused.* ■ criticize or condemn someone from a position of assumed moral superiority: *we're here to help, not to pass judgement.* **reserve judgement** delay the process of judging or giving one's opinion. **sit in judgement** assume the right to judge someone, especially in a critical manner.
– ORIGIN Middle English: from Old French *jugement*, from *juger* 'to judge'.

> **USAGE** In British English the normal spelling in general contexts is **judgement**. However, the spelling **judgment** is conventional in legal contexts, and in North American English.

judgemental (also **judgmental**) ▸ adjective of or concerning the use of judgement: *judgemental decisions about the likelihood of company survival.* ■ having or displaying an overly critical point of view: *I don't like to sound judgemental, but it was a big mistake.*
– DERIVATIVES **judgementally** adverb.

Judgement Day ▸ noun the time of the Last Judgement; the end of the world.

judgement in default ▸ noun [mass noun] Law judgement awarded to the plaintiff on the defendant's failure to plead.

Judgement of Solomon (in the Bible) the arbitration of King Solomon over a baby claimed by two women (1 Kings 3:16–28). He proposed cutting the baby in half, and then gave it to the woman who showed concern for its life.

judgement seat ▸ noun chiefly literary a judge's seat; a tribunal. ■ the place where the souls of the dead are judged by God: *a sin for which he would have to give an account at the Judgement Seat.*

Judges the seventh book of the Bible, describing the conquest of Canaan under the leaders called 'judges' in an account that is parallel to that of the Book of Joshua and is probably more accurate historically. The book includes the stories of Deborah, Jael, Gideon, Jephthah, and Samson.

Judges' Rules ▶ **plural noun** English Law rules regarding the admissibility of an accused's statements as evidence.

judgment ▶ **noun** variant spelling of **JUDGEMENT**.

judgmental ▶ **adjective** variant spelling of **JUDGEMENTAL**.

judicature /'dʒuːdɪkə,tʃə, dʒʊ'dɪk-/ ▶ **noun** [mass noun] the administration of justice. ■ (**the judicature**) judges collectively; the judiciary.
– DERIVATIVES **judicatory** **adjective**.
– ORIGIN mid 16th cent.: from medieval Latin *judicatura*, from Latin *judicare* 'to judge'.

judicial /dʒuː'dɪʃ(ə)l/ ▶ **adjective** of, by, or appropriate to a law court or judge; relating to the administration of justice: *a judicial inquiry into the allegations* | *a judicial system*.
– DERIVATIVES **judicially** **adverb**.
– ORIGIN late Middle English: from Latin *judicialis*, from *judicium* 'judgement', from *judex* (see **JUDGE**).

> **USAGE** See **USAGE** at **JUDICIOUS**.

Judicial Committee of the Privy Council (in the UK) a court made up of members of the House of Lords and others, which considers appeals made to the Sovereign in Council concerning decisions of some Commonwealth courts outside the UK.

judicial factor ▶ **noun** Scots Law an agent legally appointed to administer a person's estate.

judicial review ▶ **noun** [mass noun] (in the UK) a procedure by which a court can review an administrative action by a public body and (in England) secure a declaration, order, or award. ■ (in the US) review by the Supreme Court of the constitutional validity of a legislative act.

judicial separation ▶ **noun** another term for **LEGAL SEPARATION**.

judiciary /dʒʊ'dɪʃ(ə)ri/ ▶ **noun** (pl. **judiciaries**) (usu. **the judiciary**) the judicial authorities of a country; judges collectively.
– ORIGIN early 19th cent.: from Latin *judiciarius*, from *judicium* 'judgement'.

judicious /dʒʊ'dɪʃəs/ ▶ **adjective** having, showing, or done with good judgement or sense: *the judicious use of public investment*.
– DERIVATIVES **judiciously** **adverb**, **judiciousness** **noun**.
– ORIGIN late 16th cent.: from French *judicieux*, from Latin *judicium* 'judgement' (see **JUDICIAL**).

> **USAGE** **Judicious** means 'using good judgement, careful and sensible', as in *the judicious use of public investment* or *the judicious use of pesticides*; it should not be confused with **judicial**, which means 'relating to the administration of justice', as in *the judicial system*.

Judith (in the Apocrypha) a rich Israelite widow who saved the town of Bethulia from Nebuchadnezzar's army by seducing the besieging general Holofernes and cutting off his head while he slept. ■ a book of the Apocrypha recounting the story of Judith.

judo ▶ **noun** [mass noun] a sport of unarmed combat derived from ju-jitsu and intended to train the body and mind. It involves using holds and leverage to unbalance the opponent.
– DERIVATIVES **judoist** **noun**.
– ORIGIN late 19th cent.: Japanese, from *jū* 'gentle' + *dō* 'way'.

judoka /'dʒuːdəʊka/ ▶ **noun** a person who practises or is an expert in judo.
– ORIGIN Japanese, from **JUDO** + *-ka* 'person, profession'.

Judy ▶ **noun** (pl. **Judies**) the wife of Punch in the Punch and Judy show. ■ Brit. informal, dated a woman.
– ORIGIN early 19th cent.: pet form of the given name *Judith*.

jug ▶ **noun** **1** Brit. a cylindrical container with a handle and a lip, used for holding and pouring liquids. ■ N. Amer. a large container for liquids, with a narrow mouth and typically a stopper or cap. ■ the contents of a jug: *she gave us a big jug of water*.
2 (**the jug**) informal prison: *three months in the jug*.
3 (**jugs**) vulgar slang a woman's breasts.
4 (also **jug handle**) Climbing a secure hold that is cut into rock for climbing.
▶ **verb** (**jugs**, **jugging**, **jugged**) [with obj.] **1** (usu. as adj. **jugged**) stew or boil (a hare or rabbit) in a covered container: *jugged hare*.
2 N. Amer. informal prosecute and imprison (someone).
– DERIVATIVES **jugful** **noun** (pl. **jugfuls**).
– ORIGIN mid 16th cent.: perhaps from *Jug*, pet form of the given names *Joan*, *Joanna*, and *Jenny*.

jugal /'dʒuːg(ə)l/ ▶ **adjective** **1** Anatomy relating to the zygoma (the bony arch of the cheek).
2 Entomology relating to the jugum of an insect's forewing.
– ORIGIN late 16th cent.: from Latin *jugalis*, from *jugum* 'yoke'.

jug band ▶ **noun** a group of jazz, blues, or folk musicians using simple or improvised instruments such as jugs and washboards.

Jugendstil /'juːgənd,ʃtiːl/, German /'juːgnt,ʃtil/ ▶ **noun** German term for **ART NOUVEAU**.
– ORIGIN German, from *Jugend* 'youth' + *Stil* 'style'.

Juggernaut /'dʒʌgənɔːt/ Hinduism the form of Krishna worshipped in Puri, Orissa, where in the annual festival his image is dragged through the streets on a heavy chariot; devotees are said formerly to have thrown themselves under its wheels. Also called **JAGANNATHA**.
– ORIGIN via Hindi from Sanskrit *Jagannātha* 'Lord of the world'.

juggernaut /'dʒʌgənɔːt/ ▶ **noun** Brit. a large, heavy vehicle, especially an articulated lorry. ■ a huge, powerful, and overwhelming force: *the juggernaut of public expenditure*.
– ORIGIN mid 19th cent.: extension of **JUGGERNAUT**.

juggins ▶ **noun** Brit. informal, dated a simple-minded or gullible person: *you silly juggins*.
– ORIGIN late 19th cent.: perhaps from the surname *Juggins*, from *Jug* (see **JUG**); compare with **MUGGINS**.

juggle ▶ **verb** [with obj.] continuously toss into the air and catch (a number of objects) so as to keep at least one in the air while handling the others: *Charles juggled five tangerines, his hands a frantic blur* | [no obj.] *he can't juggle*. ■ cope with by adroitly balancing (several activities): *she works full time, juggling her career with raising children*. ■ organize (information or figures) in order to give a particular impression: *the average first-time buyer spends many hours juggling figures as they try to budget for their first home*.
▶ **noun** [in sing.] an act of juggling.
– DERIVATIVES **juggler** **noun**, **jugglery** **noun**.
– ORIGIN late Middle English (in the sense 'entertain with jesting, tricks, etc.'): back-formation from *juggler*, or from Old French *jogler*, from Latin *joculari* 'to jest', from *joculus*, diminutive of *jocus* 'jest'. Current senses date from the late 19th cent.

jug kettle ▶ **noun** Brit. a tall, narrow electric kettle like a jug with a lid.

Jugoslav ▶ **noun & adjective** old-fashioned variant spelling of **YUGOSLAV**.

Jugoslavia old-fashioned variant spelling of **YUGOSLAVIA**.

jugular /'dʒʌgjʊlə/ ▶ **adjective** **1** of the neck or throat.
2 Zoology (of fish's pelvic fins) located in front of the pectoral fins.
▶ **noun** short for **JUGULAR VEIN**.
– PHRASES **go for the jugular** be aggressive or unrestrained in making an attack.
– ORIGIN late 16th cent.: from late Latin *jugularis*, from Latin *jugulum* 'collarbone, throat', diminutive of *jugum* 'yoke'.

jugular vein ▶ **noun** any of several large veins in the neck, carrying blood from the head and face.

jugulate /'dʒʌgjʊleɪt/ ▶ **verb** [with obj.] archaic kill (someone) by cutting the throat.
– ORIGIN early 17th cent.: from Latin *jugulat-* 'slain by a cut to the throat', from the verb *jugulare*, from *jugulum* 'throat' (see **JUGULAR**).

jugum /'dʒuːgəm/ ▶ **noun** (pl. **juga**) chiefly Zoology a connecting ridge or projection, especially on a bone. ■ Entomology a lobe on the forewing of some moths which interlocks with the hindwing in flight.
– ORIGIN mid 19th cent.: from Latin, literally 'yoke'.

Jugurtha /dʒə'gəːθə/ (d.104 BC), joint king of Numidia *c.*118–104. His attacks on his royal partners prompted intervention by Rome and led to the outbreak of the Jugurthine War (112–105). He was eventually captured by the Roman general Marius and executed in Rome.
– DERIVATIVES **Jugurthine** /-θʌɪn/ **adjective**.

juice ▶ **noun** [mass noun] the liquid obtained from or present in fruit or vegetables: *add the juice of a lemon*. ■ a drink made from fruit or vegetable juice: *a carton of orange juice*. ■ (**juices**) the liquid that comes from meat or other food when cooked. ■ (**juices**) fluid secreted by the body, especially in the stomach to help digest food. ■ (**juices**) a person's vitality or creative faculties: *it saps the creative juices*. ■ informal electrical energy: *the batteries have run out of juice*. ■ petrol: *he ran out of juice on the last lap*. ■ N. Amer. informal alcoholic drink.
▶ **verb** [with obj.] **1** extract the juice from (fruit or vegetables): *juice one orange at a time*.
2 (**juice something up**) N. Amer. informal liven something up: *they juiced it up with some love interest*.
3 (as adj. **juiced**) N. Amer. informal drunk.
– PHRASES **get one's creative juices flowing** start thinking in a creative and lively way: *the workshops allow staff to get away from their desks and get their creative juices flowing*.
– DERIVATIVES **juiceless** **adjective**.
– ORIGIN Middle English: via Old French from Latin *jus* 'broth, vegetable juice'.

juicer ▶ **noun** **1** an appliance for extracting juice from fruit and vegetables.
2 N. Amer. informal a person who drinks alcohol excessively.

juicy ▶ **adjective** (**juicier**, **juiciest**) (of food) full of juice; succulent: *a juicy apple* | *a juicy steak*. ■ informal interestingly scandalous: *juicy gossip*. ■ informal temptingly appealing: *the promise of juicy returns*.
– DERIVATIVES **juicily** **adverb**, **juiciness** **noun**.

ju-jitsu /dʒuː'dʒɪtsuː/ (also **jiu-jitsu** or **ju-jutsu** /-'jʌtsuː/) ▶ **noun** [mass noun] a Japanese system of unarmed combat and physical training. Compare with **JUDO**.
– ORIGIN Japanese *jūjutsu*, from *jū* 'gentle' + *jutsu* 'skill'.

juju[1] /'dʒuːdʒuː/ ▶ **noun** a charm or fetish, especially of a type used by some West African peoples. ■ [mass noun] supernatural power attributed to a charm or fetish: *juju and witchcraft*.
– ORIGIN early 17th cent.: of West African origin, perhaps from French *joujou* 'toy'.

juju[2] /'dʒuːdʒuː/ ▶ **noun** [mass noun] a style of music popular among the Yoruba in Nigeria and characterized by the use of guitars and variable-pitch drums.
– ORIGIN perhaps from Yoruba *jo jo* 'dance'.

jujube /'dʒuːdʒuːb/ ▶ **noun** **1** the edible berry-like fruit of a Eurasian plant, formerly taken as a cough cure. ■ N. Amer. a jujube-flavoured lozenge or sweet.
2 (also **jujube bush**) the shrub or small tree that produces the jujube fruit, native to the warmer regions of Eurasia. ● *Ziziphus jujuba*, family Rhamnaceae.
– ORIGIN late Middle English: from French, or from medieval Latin *jujuba*, based on Greek *zizuphos*.

juke N. Amer. informal ▶ **noun** (also **juke joint**) a roadhouse, nightclub, or bar, especially one providing food, drinks, and music for dancing.
▶ **verb** [no obj.] **1** dance, especially to the music of a jukebox: *a middle-aged couple shook and juked to the music*.
2 (in sport) make a sham move to mislead an opponent. ■ move in a zigzag fashion: *I juked down an alley*.
– ORIGIN 1930s: from Gullah *juke* 'disorderly'.

jukebox ▶ **noun** a machine that automatically plays a selected musical recording when a coin is inserted. ■ Computing a device which stores several computer disks in such a way that data can be read from any of them.
– ORIGIN 1930s: from Gullah *juke* 'disorderly' + **BOX**[1].

jukskei /'jəkskeɪ/ ▶ **noun** [mass noun] S. African a game in which a peg is thrown at a stake.
– ORIGIN South African Dutch, from Dutch *juk* 'yoke' + *skei* 'pin'; the game was originally played with sticks from an animal's yoke.

juku /'dʒʊkuː/ ▶ **noun** (pl. **same**) (in Japan) a private school or college attended in addition to an ordinary educational institution.
– ORIGIN Japanese.

Jul. ▶ **abbreviation** July.

julep /'dʒuːlɛp/ ▶ **noun** a sweet flavoured drink made from a sugar syrup, sometimes containing alcohol or medication. ■ short for **MINT JULEP**.
– ORIGIN late Middle English: from Old French, from medieval Latin *julapium*, via Arabic from Persian *gulāb*, from *gul* 'rose' + *āb* 'water'.

julia /'dʒuːlɪə/ ▶ **noun** an orange and black American butterfly with long, narrow forewings, found chiefly in tropical regions. ● *Dryas julia*, subfamily Heliconiinae, family Nymphalidae.

Julian[1] /ˈdʒuːlɪən/ ▸ adjective of or associated with Julius Caesar.
– ORIGIN from Latin *Julianus*, from the given name *Julius*.

Julian[2] /ˈdʒuːlɪən/ (*c.*331–63 AD), Roman emperor 360–3, nephew of Constantine; full name *Flavius Claudius Julianus*; known as **the Apostate**. He restored paganism as the state cult in place of Christianity, but this move was reversed after his death on campaign against the Persians.

Julian Alps an Alpine range in western Slovenia and NE Italy, rising to a height of 2,863 m (9,395 ft) at Triglav.

Julian calendar ▸ noun a calendar introduced by the authority of Julius Caesar in 46 BC, in which the year consisted of 365 days, every fourth year having 366 days. It was superseded by the Gregorian calendar, though it is still used by some Orthodox Churches. Dates in the Julian calendar are sometimes designated 'Old Style'.

Julian of Norwich (*c.*1342–*c.*1413), English mystic. She is said to have lived as a recluse outside St Julian's Church, Norwich. She is chiefly associated with the *Revelations of Divine Love* (*c.*1393), a description of a series of visions she had in which she depicts the Holy Trinity as Father, Mother, and Lord.

Julia set /ˈdʒuːlɪə/ ▸ noun Mathematics a set of complex numbers which do not converge to any limit when a given mapping is repeatedly applied to them. In some cases the result is a connected fractal set.
– ORIGIN 1970s: named after Gaston M. *Julia* (1893–1978), Algerian-born French mathematician.

julienne /ˌdʒuːlɪˈɛn/ ▸ noun a portion of food cut into short, thin strips: *a julienne of vegetables*.
▸ verb [with obj.] cut (food) into short, thin strips.
– ORIGIN early 18th cent. (originally as an adjective designating soup made of chopped vegetables, especially carrots): French, from the male given names *Jules* or *Julien*, of obscure development.

Juliet /ˈdʒuːlɪɛt/ ▸ noun a code word representing the letter J, used in radio communication.

Juliet balcony ▸ noun a very shallow balcony with a safety railing on an upper storey of a building.

Juliet cap ▸ noun a type of women's small ornamental cap, typically made of lace or net and often worn by brides.
– ORIGIN early 20th cent.: so named because it forms part of the usual costume of the heroine of Shakespeare's *Romeo and Juliet*.

Julius Caesar /ˌdʒuːlɪəs/, Gaius (100–44 BC), Roman general and statesman.

> He established the First Triumvirate with Pompey and Crassus (60), and became consul in 59. Between 58 and 51 he fought the Gallic Wars, invaded Britain (55–54), and acquired immense power. After civil war with Pompey, which ended in Pompey's defeat at Pharsalus (48), Caesar became dictator of the Roman Empire; he was murdered on the Ides (15th) of March in a conspiracy led by Brutus and Cassius.

Jullundur /ˈdʒʌləndə/ variant spelling of **JALANDHAR**.

July ▸ noun (pl. **Julys**) the seventh month of the year, in the northern hemisphere usually considered the second month of summer: *I had a letter from him in July | a festival held every July*.
– ORIGIN Middle English: from Latin *Julius* (*mensis*) '(month) of July', named after Julius Caesar.

jumar /ˈdʒuːmə/ Climbing ▸ noun a clamp that is attached to a fixed rope and automatically tightens when weight is applied and relaxes when it is removed.
▸ verb (**jumars**, **jumaring**, **jumared**) [no obj.] climb with the aid of a jumar.
– ORIGIN 1960s: originally in Swiss use, of unknown origin.

jumbie /ˈdʒʌmbi/ ▸ noun W. Indian a spirit of a dead person, typically an evil one.
– ORIGIN from Kikongo *zumbi* 'fetish'.

jumbie bird ▸ noun W. Indian a bird of ill omen, especially a pygmy owl. ● *Glaucidium brasilianum*, family Strigidae. Alternative name: **ferruginous pygmy owl**.

jumble ▸ noun an untidy collection or pile of things: *the books were in a chaotic jumble*. ■ [mass noun] Brit. articles collected for a jumble sale.
▸ verb [with obj.] mix up in a confused or untidy way: *a drawer full of letters jumbled together*.
– ORIGIN early 16th cent.: probably symbolic.

jumble sale ▸ noun Brit. a sale of miscellaneous second-hand articles, typically held in order to raise money for a charity or a special event.

jumbo informal ▸ noun (pl. **jumbos**) a very large person or thing. ■ (also **jumbo jet**) a very large airliner (originally and specifically a Boeing 747).
▸ adjective [attrib.] very large: *a jumbo pad*.
– ORIGIN early 19th cent. (originally of a person): probably the second element of **MUMBO JUMBO**. Originally denoting a large and clumsy person, the term was popularized as the name of an elephant at London Zoo, sold in 1882 to the Barnum and Bailey circus.

jumbuck /ˈdʒʌmbʌk/ ▸ noun Austral. informal a sheep.
– ORIGIN early 19th cent.: of unknown origin, possibly Australian pidgin for *jump up*.

Jumna /ˈdʒʌmnə/ a river of northern India, which rises in the Himalayas and flows in a large arc southwards and south-eastwards, through Delhi, joining the Ganges below Allahabad. Its source (Yamunotri) and its confluence with the Ganges are both Hindu holy places. Hindi name **YAMUNA**.

jump ▸ verb **1** [no obj., usu. with adverbial of direction] push oneself off a surface and into the air by using the muscles in one's legs and feet: *the cat jumped off his lap | he jumped twenty-five feet to the ground*. ■ [with obj.] pass over (an obstacle or barrier) by jumping: *one of the deer tried to jump the ditch*. ■ [with adverbial] (of an athlete or horse) perform in a competition involving jumping over obstacles: *his horse jumped well and won by five lengths*. ■ (especially of prices or figures) rise suddenly and by a large amount: *pre-tax profits jumped from £51,000 to £1.03 million*. ■ informal (of a place) be full of lively activity: *the bar is jumping on Fridays and Saturdays*. ■ [with obj.] informal (of driver or a vehicle) fail to stop at (a red traffic light). ■ [with obj.] get on or off (a train or other vehicle) quickly, typically illegally or dangerously. ■ [with obj.] N. Amer. take summary possession of (a mining concession or other piece of land) after alleged abandonment or forfeiture by the former occupant.
2 [no obj., usu. with adverbial] (of a person) move suddenly and quickly in a specified way: *Juliet jumped to her feet | they jumped back into the car and drove off*. ■ (of a person) make a sudden involuntary movement in reaction to something that causes surprise or shock: *an owl hooted nearby, making her jump*. ■ pass quickly or abruptly from one idea, subject, or state to another: *the book jumps constantly from Brooklyn to Harlem*. ■ [with obj.] omit or skip over (part of something) and pass on to a further point or stage. ■ (of a machine or device) move or jerk suddenly and abruptly: *the vibration can cause the needle to jump*. ■ (of a person) make a sudden, impulsive rush to do something: *Gordon jumped to my defence*. ■ Bridge make a bid that is higher than necessary, in order to signal a strong hand: *East jumped to four spades*. ■ [with obj.] informal attack (someone) suddenly and unexpectedly.
3 vulgar slang, N. Amer. have sexual intercourse with (someone).
4 [with obj.] N. Amer. informal start (a vehicle) using jump leads: *I jumped his saloon from my car's battery*.
▸ noun **1** an act of jumping from a surface by pushing upwards with one's legs and feet: *in making the short jump across the gully he lost his balance*. ■ an obstacle to be jumped, especially by a horse and rider in an equestrian competition. ■ an act of descending from an aircraft by parachute. ■ a sudden dramatic rise in amount, price, or value: *a 51 per cent jump in annual profits*. ■ a large or sudden transition or change: *the jump from county to Test cricket*. ■ Bridge a bid that is higher than necessary, signalling strength.
2 N. Amer. vulgar slang an act of sexual intercourse.
3 a sudden involuntary movement caused by shock or surprise: *I woke up with a jump*. ■ (**the jumps**) informal extreme nervousness or anxiety.
– PHRASES **be jumping up and down** informal be very angry, upset, or excited. **get** (or **have**) **the jump on someone** N. Amer. informal get (or have) an advantage over someone as a result of one's prompt action. **jump bail** see **BAIL**[1]. **jump someone's bones** N. Amer. vulgar slang have sexual intercourse with someone. **jump down someone's throat** informal respond to what someone has said in a sudden and angrily critical way. **jump for joy** be ecstatically happy. **jump the gun** see **GUN**. **jump in with both feet** get started enthusiastically. **jump into bed with** informal engage readily in sexual intercourse with. **jump on the bandwagon** see **BANDWAGON**. **jump out of one's skin** informal be extremely startled. **jump the queue** (or US **jump in line**) push into a queue of people in order to be served or dealt with before one's turn. ■ take unfair precedence over others: *the old boy networks were one way of jumping the promotion queue*. **jump the rails** (or **track**) (of a train) become dislodged from the track. **jump the shark** informal (of a television series or film) reach a point when far-fetched events are included merely for the sake of novelty, indicative of a decline in quality. [said to be with allusion to the long-running US television series *Happy Days*, in which the central character (the Fonz) jumped over a shark when waterskiing.] **jump ship** (of a sailor) leave the ship on which one is serving without having obtained permission to do so: *he jumped ship in Cape Town*. **jump through hoops** go through an elaborate or complicated procedure in order to achieve an objective. **jump** (or **leap**) **to conclusions** (or **the conclusion**) form an opinion hastily, before one has learned or considered all the facts. **jump to it!** informal used to exhort someone to prompt or immediate action. **one jump ahead** one step or stage ahead of someone else and so having the advantage over them: *the Americans were **one jump ahead** of the British in this*.
– PHRASAL VERBS **jump at** accept (an opportunity or offer) with great eagerness: *I'd jump at the chance of a career in football*. **jump off** (of a military campaign) begin. **jump on** informal attack or take hold of (someone) suddenly. ■ criticize (someone) suddenly and severely. ■ seize on (something) eagerly; give sudden (typically critical) attention to: *the paper jumped on the inconsistencies of his stories*. **jump out** have a strong visual or mental impact; be very striking: *advertising posters that really jump out at you*.
– DERIVATIVES **jumpable** adjective.
– ORIGIN early 16th cent. (in the sense 'be moved or thrown with a sudden jerk'): probably imitative of the sound of feet coming into contact with the ground.

jump ball ▸ noun Basketball a ball put in play by the referee, who throws it up between two opposing players.

jump blues ▸ noun [mass noun] a style of popular music combining elements of swing and blues.

jump cut ▸ noun (in film or television) an abrupt transition from one scene to another.
▸ verb (**jump-cut**) [no obj.] make a jump cut.

jumped-up ▸ adjective informal denoting someone who considers themselves to be more important than they really are, or who has suddenly and undeservedly risen in status: *she's not really a journalist, more a jumped-up PR woman*.

jumper[1] ▸ noun **1** Brit. a knitted garment typically with long sleeves, worn over the upper body.
2 historical a loose outer jacket worn by sailors.
3 N. Amer. a pinafore dress.
– ORIGIN mid 19th cent. (in sense 2): probably from dialect *jump* 'short coat', perhaps from Scots *jupe* 'a man's (later also a woman's) loose jacket or tunic', via Old French from Arabic *jubba*. Compare with **JIBBA**.

jumper[2] ▸ noun **1** a person or animal that jumps.
2 (also **jumper wire**) a short wire used to shorten an electric circuit or close it temporarily.
3 Nautical a rope made fast to keep a yard or mast from jumping.
4 a heavy chisel-ended iron bar for drilling blast holes.
5 a mushroom-shaped brass part in a tap which supports the washer.

jumper cable ▸ noun North American term for **JUMP LEAD**.

jumping bean ▸ noun a plant seed that jumps as a result of the movement of a moth larva which is developing inside it. ● Affected seeds are found in several plants of the family Euphorbiaceae, in particular the Mexican plant *Sebastiana pavoniana*, the seeds of which can contain larvae of the moth *Cydia saltitans*.

jumping gene ▸ noun informal term for **TRANSPOSON**.

jumping jack ▸ noun **1** a jump done from a standing position with the arms and legs pointing outwards.
2 Brit. dated a small firework producing repeated explosions.
3 a toy figure of a man, with movable limbs.

jumping Jehoshaphat ▸ exclamation see **JEHOSHAPHAT**.

jumping mouse ▸ noun a mouse-like rodent that has long back feet and typically moves in short hops, found in North America and China. ● Family Zapodidae: three genera, in particular *Zapus*, and several species.

jumping-off point (also **jumping-off place**) ▸ noun the point from which a new undertaking or activity is begun.

J

jumping plant louse ▸ noun a minute hopping bug with wings, resembling a miniature cicada. Many kinds are pests of cultivated plants. ● Family Psyllidae, suborder Homoptera.

jumping spider ▸ noun a large-eyed spider which hunts prey by stalking and pouncing on it. ● Family Salticidae, order Araneae.

jump instruction ▸ noun Computing an instruction in a computer program that causes processing to move to a different place in the program sequence.

jump jet ▸ noun a jet aircraft that can take off and land vertically, without need of a runway.

jump jockey ▸ noun a jockey who rides in steeplechases.

jump lead ▸ noun Brit. each of a pair of thick electric cables fitted with clips at either end, used for recharging a battery in a motor vehicle by connecting it to the battery in another.

jump-off ▸ noun a deciding round in a showjumping competition.

jump ring ▸ noun a wire ring made by bringing the two ends together without soldering or welding.

jump rope N. Amer. ▸ noun a skipping rope.
▸ verb [no obj.] play or exercise using a skipping rope.

jump seat ▸ noun chiefly N. Amer. an extra seat in a car or taxi that folds back when not in use.

jump shift ▸ noun Bridge a bid that is both in a different suit from that bid by oneself or one's partner and at a higher level than necessary, indicating a strong hand.

J

jump shot ▸ noun **1** Basketball a shot made while jumping.
2 Billiards & Snooker a shot in which the cue ball is made to jump over another ball.

jump-start ▸ verb [with obj.] start (a car with a flat battery) with jump leads or by a sudden release of the clutch while the car is being pushed. ■ give an added impetus to (something that is proceeding slowly or is at a standstill): *she suggests ways to jump-start the sluggish educational system.*
▸ noun an act of jump-starting a car. ■ an added impetus.

jumpstation ▸ noun a site on the World Wide Web containing a collection of hypertext links, usually to pages on a particular topic.

jumpsuit ▸ noun a garment incorporating trousers and a sleeved top in one piece, worn as a fashion item, protective garment, or uniform.
– ORIGIN 1940s (originally US): so named because it was first used to denote a parachutist's garment.

jump-up ▸ noun **1** a jump in an upward direction. ■ an informal Caribbean dance or celebration.
2 Austral. informal an escarpment.

jumpy ▸ adjective (**jumpier**, **jumpiest**) informal (of a person) anxious and uneasy: *he was tired and jumpy.* ■ characterized by abrupt stops and starts or an irregular course: *a jumpy pulse.*
– DERIVATIVES **jumpily** adverb, **jumpiness** noun.

jun /dʒʌn/ ▸ noun (pl. **same**) a monetary unit of North Korea, equal to one hundredth of a won.
– ORIGIN Korean.

Jun. ▸ abbreviation ■ June. ■ junior (in names): *John Smith Jun.*

junco /ˈdʒʌŋkəʊ/ ▸ noun (pl. **juncos** or **juncoes**) a North American songbird related to the buntings, with mainly grey and brown plumage. ● Genus *Junco*, family Emberizidae (subfamily Emberizinae): three or four species.
– ORIGIN early 18th cent. (originally 'reed bunting'): from Spanish, from Latin *juncus* 'rush, reed'.

junction ▸ noun **1** a point where two or more things are joined: *the junction of the two rivers.* ■ a place where two or more roads or railway lines meet.
2 Electronics a region of transition in a semiconductor between a part where conduction is mainly by electrons and a part where it is mainly by holes.
3 [mass noun] the action or fact of joining or being joined.
– ORIGIN early 18th cent. (in sense 3): from Latin *junctio(n-)*, from *jungere* 'to join'.

junction box ▸ noun a box containing a junction of electric wires or cables.

juncture /ˈdʒʌŋ(k)tʃə/ ▸ noun **1** a particular point in events or time: *it is difficult to say at this juncture whether this upturn can be sustained.*
2 a place where things join: *the plane crashed at the juncture of two mountains.*
3 Phonetics the set of features in speech that enable a hearer to detect a word or phrase boundary (e.g. distinguishing *I scream* from *ice cream*).
– ORIGIN late Middle English (in the sense 'act of joining'): from Latin *junctura*, 'joint', from *jungere* 'to join'.

June ▸ noun the sixth month of the year, in the northern hemisphere usually considered the first month of summer: *the roses flower in June* | *each June the group meet for an informal reunion.*
– ORIGIN Middle English: from Old French *juin*, from Latin *Junius* (*mensis*) '(month) of June', variant of *Junonius* 'sacred to Juno'.

Juneau /ˈdʒuːnəʊ/ the state capital of Alaska, a seaport on an inlet of the Pacific Ocean in the south of the state; pop. 30,988 (est. 2008).
– ORIGIN named after Joseph *Juneau*, who discovered gold there in 1880.

juneberry ▸ noun (pl. **juneberries**) a North American shrub of the rose family, some kinds of which are grown for their showy white flowers and bright autumn colours. ● Genus *Amelanchier*, family Rosaceae: many species, including *A. laevis*, which has naturalized in England.
■ the edible berry of this plant.

June bug ▸ noun another term for GARDEN CHAFER.

juneteenth /dʒuːnˈtiːnθ/ ▸ noun (in the US) a festival held annually on the nineteenth of June by African Americans (especially in the southern states), to commemorate emancipation from slavery in Texas on that day in 1865.
– ORIGIN 1930s: blend of JUNE and NINETEENTH (see NINETEEN).

June War Arab name for SIX DAY WAR.

Jung /jʊŋ/, Carl (Gustav) (1875–1961), Swiss psychologist.

> Jung originated the concept of introvert and extrovert personality, and of the four psychological functions of sensation, intuition, thinking, and feeling. He collaborated with Sigmund Freud in developing the psychoanalytic theory of personality, but later disassociated himself from Freud's preoccupation with sexuality as the determinant of personality, preferring to emphasize a mystical or religious factor in the unconscious.

– DERIVATIVES **Jungian** adjective & noun.

Jungfrau /ˈjʊŋfraʊ/ a mountain in the Swiss Alps, 4,158 m (13,642 ft) high.

jungle ▸ noun **1** an area of land overgrown with dense forest and tangled vegetation, typically in the tropics: *we set off into the jungle* | [mass noun] *the lakes are hidden in dense jungle.* ■ a wild tangled mass of vegetation or other things: *the garden was a jungle of bluebells.* ■ a situation or place of bewildering complexity or brutal competitiveness: *it's a jungle out there.*
2 (also **jungle music**) [mass noun] a style of dance music incorporating elements of ragga, hip hop, and hard core and consisting of very fast electronic drum tracks and slower synthesized bass lines, originating in Britain in the early 1990s.
– PHRASES **the law of the jungle** the principle that those who are strong and apply ruthless self-interest will be most successful.
– DERIVATIVES **jungled** adjective, **junglist** noun & adjective (sense 2), **jungly** adjective (**junglier**, **jungliest**).
– ORIGIN late 18th cent.: via Hindi from Sanskrit *jāṅgala* 'rough and arid (terrain)'.

jungle cat ▸ noun a small wild cat that has a yellowish or greyish coat with dark markings on the legs and tail, living in dry forests from Egypt to SE Asia. ● *Felis chaus*, family Felidae.

jungle fever ▸ noun [mass noun] a severe form of malaria.

junglefowl ▸ noun (pl. **same**) a southern Asian game bird related to the domestic fowl, typically frequenting forested country. ● Genus *Gallus*, family Phasianidae: four species, in particular the **red junglefowl** (*G. gallus*), which is the ancestor of the domestic fowl.

jungle gym ▸ noun N. Amer. a climbing frame for children.
– ORIGIN 1920s: formerly a US trademark.

jungle juice ▸ noun [mass noun] informal powerful or roughly prepared alcoholic drink.

jungle telegraph ▸ noun another term for BUSH TELEGRAPH.

jungli /ˈdʒʌŋgli/ ▸ adjective Indian uncultured; wild.
– ORIGIN from JUNGLE + the suffix *-i* (as in *Hindi*); compare with Hindi *janglī*.

junior ▸ adjective **1** for or denoting young or younger people: *junior tennis.* ■ Brit. for or denoting schoolchildren between the ages of about 7 and 11. ■ N. Amer. of or for students in the third year of a course lasting four years at college or high school: *his junior year in college.* ■ (often **Junior**) [postpositive] [in names] denoting the younger of two who have the same name in a family, especially a son as distinct from his father: *John F. Kennedy Junior.*
2 low or lower in rank or status: *a junior minister* | *part of my function is to supervise those **junior to** me.*
▸ noun **1** a person who is a specified number of years younger than someone else: *he's five years her junior.* ■ Brit. a child attending a junior school. ■ N. Amer. a student in the third year at college or high school. ■ (in sport) a young competitor, typically under sixteen or eighteen. ■ N. Amer. informal used as a nickname or form of address for one's son.
2 a person with low rank or status compared with others: *an office junior.*
– DERIVATIVES **juniority** /-ˈɒrɪti/ noun.
– ORIGIN Middle English (as an adjective following a family name): from Latin, comparative of *juvenis* 'young'.

junior barrister ▸ noun (in the UK) a barrister who has not taken silk, i.e. is not a Queen's (or King's) Counsel.

junior college ▸ noun (in the US) a college offering courses for two years beyond high school, either as a complete training or in preparation for completion at a senior college.

junior combination room ▸ noun term used in Cambridge University for JUNIOR COMMON ROOM.

junior common room ▸ noun Brit. a room used for social purposes by the undergraduates of a college. ■ [treated as sing. or pl.] the undergraduates of a college regarded collectively.

junior high school ▸ noun (in the US and Canada) a school intermediate between an elementary school and a high school, generally for children in the seventh, eighth, and ninth grades.

junior lightweight ▸ noun [mass noun] a weight in professional boxing of 57.1–59 kilograms. ■ [count noun] a professional boxer of this weight.

junior middleweight ▸ noun [mass noun] a weight in professional boxing of 66.7–69.8 kilograms. ■ [count noun] a professional boxer of this weight.

junior school ▸ noun a school for young or younger children, in particular (in England and Wales) a school for children aged between 7 and 11.

junior technician ▸ noun a rank in the RAF, above senior aircraftman or senior aircraftwoman and below corporal.

junior welterweight ▸ noun [mass noun] a weight in professional boxing of 61.2–63.5 kilograms. ■ [count noun] a professional boxer of this weight.

juniper /ˈdʒuːnɪpə/ ▸ noun an evergreen shrub or small tree which bears berry-like cones, widely distributed throughout Eurasia and North America. Many kinds have aromatic cones or foliage. ● Genus *Juniperus*, family Cupressaceae: many species, including the **common juniper** (*J. communis*), the berries of which are used for flavouring gin.
– ORIGIN late Middle English: from Latin *juniperus*.

junk[1] ▸ noun [mass noun] **1** informal old or discarded articles that are considered useless or of little value. ■ worthless writing, talk, or ideas: *I can't write this kind of junk.*
2 informal heroin.
3 the lump of oily fibrous tissue in a sperm whale's head, containing spermaceti.
▸ verb [with obj.] informal discard or abandon unceremoniously: *sort out what could be sold off and junk the rest.*
– ORIGIN late Middle English (denoting an old or inferior rope): of unknown origin. Sense 1 of the noun dates from the mid 19th cent.

junk[2] ▸ noun a flat-bottomed sailing vessel of a kind typical of China and the East Indies, with a prominent stem and lugsails.
– ORIGIN mid 16th cent.: from obsolete French *juncque* or Portuguese *junco*, from Malay *jong*, reinforced by Dutch *jonk*.

Junkanoo /ˈdʒʌŋka,nuː, ˈdʒɒŋka,nuː/ ▸ noun (chiefly in Jamaica, Belize, and the Bahamas) a masquerade held at Christmas, consisting of a street procession of characters in traditional costumes and dancing to drums, bells, and whistles.
– ORIGIN probably from Ewe.

junk bond ▶ noun a high-yielding high-risk security, typically issued by a company seeking to raise capital quickly in order to finance a takeover.

junk DNA ▶ noun [mass noun] Genetics DNA that does not code for a protein, usually occurs in repetitive sequences of nucleotides, and does not seem to serve any useful purpose.

Junker /ˈjʊŋkə/ ▶ noun historical a German nobleman or aristocrat, especially a member of the Prussian aristocracy.
– DERIVATIVES **junkerism** noun.
– ORIGIN German, earlier *Junkher*, from Middle High German *junc* 'young' + *herre* 'lord'.

junket /ˈdʒʌŋkɪt/ ▶ noun **1** [mass noun] a dish of sweetened and flavoured curds of milk.
2 informal an extravagant trip or celebration, in particular one enjoyed by government officials at public expense.
▶ verb (**junkets, junketing, junketed**) [no obj.] (often as noun **junketing**) informal attend or go on a trip or celebration at public expense.
– ORIGIN late Middle English: from Old French *jonquette* 'rush basket', from *jonc* 'rush', from Latin *juncus*. Originally denoting a rush basket, especially one for fish (remaining in dialect use), the term also denoted a cream cheese, formerly made in a rush basket or served on a rush mat. A later extended sense, 'feast, merrymaking', gave rise to sense 2 of the noun.

junk food ▶ noun [mass noun] pre-prepared or packaged food that has low nutritional value.

junkie (also **junky**) ▶ noun informal a drug addict. ■ [with modifier] a person with a compulsive habit or obsessive dependency on something: *power junkies*.
– ORIGIN 1920s (originally US): from JUNK[1].

junk mail ▶ noun [mass noun] informal unsolicited advertising or promotional material received through the post.

junk science ▶ noun [mass noun] untested or unproven theories when presented as scientific fact.

junk shop ▶ noun informal a shop selling second-hand goods or inexpensive antiques.

junky informal ▶ adjective N. Amer. regarded as useless or of little value.
▶ noun (pl. **junkies**) variant spelling of JUNKIE.

junkyard ▶ noun N. Amer. a scrapyard.

Juno /ˈdʒuːnəʊ/ **1** Roman Mythology the most important goddess of the Roman state, wife of Jupiter. Greek equivalent **Hera**.
2 Astronomy asteroid 3, discovered in 1804 (diameter 244 km).

Junoesque /ˌdʒuːnəʊˈɛsk/ ▶ adjective (of a woman) imposingly tall and shapely.
– ORIGIN mid 19th cent.: from JUNO + -ESQUE.

Junr ▶ abbreviation Junior (in names).

junta /ˈdʒʌntə, ˈhʊ-/ ▶ noun **1** a military or political group that rules a country after taking power by force: *the country's ruling military junta*.
2 historical a deliberative or administrative council in Spain or Portugal.
– ORIGIN early 17th cent. (in sense 2): from Spanish and Portuguese, from Latin *juncta*, feminine past participle of *jungere* 'to join'.

junto /ˈdʒʌntəʊ/ ▶ noun (pl. **juntos**) historical a political grouping or faction, especially in 17th- and 18th-century Britain.
– ORIGIN alteration of JUNTA, on the pattern of Spanish nouns ending in *-o*.

Jupiter /ˈdʒuːpɪtə/ **1** Roman Mythology the chief god of the Roman state religion, originally a sky god associated with thunder and lightning. His wife was Juno. Also called **Jove**. Greek equivalent **Zeus**.
2 Astronomy the largest planet in the solar system, a gas giant which is the fifth in order from the sun and one of the brightest objects in the night sky.

> Jupiter orbits between Mars and Saturn at an average distance of 778 million km from the sun. Although it has an equatorial diameter of 142,800 km the planet rotates in less than ten hours. Its upper atmosphere consists mainly of hydrogen with swirling clouds of ammonia and methane, with a circulation system that results in a number of distinct latitudinal bands. There are at least sixteen satellites, four of which (the Galilean moons) are visible through binoculars, and a faint ring system.

– ORIGIN Latin, from *Jovis pater*, literally 'Father Jove'.

Jura[1] /ˈʒʊərə/, French /ʒyʀa/ a system of mountain ranges on the border of France and Switzerland.

Jura[2] /ˈdʒʊərə/ an island of the Inner Hebrides, north of Islay and south of Mull, separated from the west coast of Scotland by the Sound of Jura.

jural /ˈdʒʊər(ə)l/ ▶ adjective formal relating to the law. ■ Philosophy relating to rights and obligations.
– ORIGIN mid 17th cent.: from Latin *jus, jur-* 'law, right' + -AL.

Jurassic /dʒʊˈrasɪk/ ▶ adjective Geology relating to or denoting the second period of the Mesozoic era, between the Triassic and Cretaceous periods. ■ (as noun **the Jurassic**) the Jurassic period or the system of rocks deposited during it.

> The Jurassic lasted from about 208 to 146 million years ago. Large reptiles, including the largest known dinosaurs, were dominant on both land and sea. Ammonites were abundant, and the first birds (including Archaeopteryx) appeared.

– ORIGIN mid 19th cent.: from French *jurassique*; named after the *Jura* Mountains (see JURA[1]).

jurat /ˈdʒʊərat/ ▶ noun Law **1** chiefly historical a person who has taken an oath or who performs a duty on oath, e.g. a juror. ■ (in the Channel Islands) a magistrate or other public official.
2 a statement on an affidavit of when, where, and before whom it was sworn.
– ORIGIN late Middle English: based on Latin *juratus* 'sworn', past participle of Latin *jurare*.

juridical /dʒʊˈrɪdɪk(ə)l/ ▶ adjective Law relating to judicial proceedings and the administration of the law.
– DERIVATIVES **juridically** adverb.
– ORIGIN early 16th cent.: from Latin *juridicus* (from *jus, jur-* 'law' + *dicere* 'say') + -AL.

jurisconsult /ˌdʒʊərɪskənˈsʌlt/ ▶ noun Law, chiefly historical an expert on law.
– ORIGIN early 17th cent.: from Latin *jurisconsultus*, from *jus, jur-* 'law' + *consultus* 'skilled' (from *consulere* 'take counsel').

jurisdiction /ˌdʒʊərɪsˈdɪkʃ(ə)n/ ▶ noun [mass noun] the official power to make legal decisions and judgements: *the English court had no **jurisdiction over** the defendants*. ■ [count noun] a system of law courts; a judicature. ■ [count noun] the territory or sphere of activity over which the legal authority of a court or other institution extends.
– DERIVATIVES **jurisdictional** adjective.
– ORIGIN Middle English: from Old French *jurediction*, from Latin *jurisdictio(n-)*, from *jus, jur-* 'law' + *dictio* 'saying' (from *dicere* 'say').

jurisprudence /ˌdʒʊərɪsˈpruːd(ə)ns/ ▶ noun [mass noun] the theory or philosophy of law. ■ a legal system: *American jurisprudence*.
– DERIVATIVES **jurisprudent** adjective & noun, **jurisprudential** adjective.
– ORIGIN early 17th cent.: from late Latin *jurisprudentia*, from Latin *jus, jur-* 'law' + *prudentia* 'knowledge'.

jurist /ˈdʒʊərɪst/ ▶ noun an expert in or writer on law. ■ N. Amer. a lawyer or a judge.
– DERIVATIVES **juristic** adjective.
– ORIGIN late 15th cent. (in the sense 'lawyer'): from French *juriste*, medieval Latin *jurista*, from *jus, jur-* 'law'.

juror ▶ noun **1** a member of a jury.
2 historical a person taking an oath, especially one of allegiance. Compare with NONJUROR.
– ORIGIN late Middle English: from Old French *jureor*, from Latin *jurator*, from *jurare* 'swear', from *jus, jur-* 'law'.

jury[1] ▶ noun (pl. **juries**) a body of people (typically twelve in number) sworn to give a verdict in a legal case on the basis of evidence submitted to them in court: *the jury returned unanimous guilty verdicts*. ■ a body of people selected to judge a competition.
▶ verb (**juries, jurying, juried**) [with obj.] N. Amer. judge (an art or craft exhibition or exhibit).
– PHRASES **the jury is out** a decision has not yet been reached on a controversial subject: *the jury is still out on whether self-regulation by doctors is adequate*.
– ORIGIN late Middle English: from Old French *juree* 'oath, inquiry', from Latin *jurata*, feminine past participle of *jurare* 'swear' (see JUROR).

jury[2] ▶ adjective Nautical (of a mast or other fitting) improvised or temporary: *we need to get that jury rudder fixed*.
– ORIGIN early 19th cent.: independent usage of the first element of early 17th-cent. *jury-mast* 'temporary mast', of uncertain origin (compare with JURY-RIGGED).

jury box ▶ noun a segregated area in which the jury sits in a court of law.

juryman (or **jurywoman**) ▶ noun (pl. **jurymen** or **jurywomen**) a person serving on a jury.

jury-rigged ▶ adjective (of a ship) having temporary makeshift rigging. ■ chiefly N. Amer. makeshift; improvised: *jury-rigged classrooms in gymnasiums*.
– ORIGIN late 18th cent.: *jury* perhaps based on Old French *ajurie* 'aid'.

jus /ʒuː/, French /ʒy/ ▶ noun (especially in French cuisine) a thin gravy or sauce made from meat juices: *chicken with a rich game jus*.
– ORIGIN French.

jus cogens /ˌdʒʌs ˈkəʊdʒɛnz/ ▶ noun [mass noun] Law the principles which form the norms of international law that cannot be set aside.
– ORIGIN Latin, literally 'compelling law'.

jus gentium /ˌdʒʌs ˈdʒɛntɪəm, -ʃɪəm, ˈgɛntɪəm/ ▶ noun [mass noun] Law international law.
– ORIGIN Latin, literally 'law of nations'.

Jussieu /ʒuːˈsjəː/, French /ʒusjœ/, Antoine Laurent de (1748–1836), French botanist. Jussieu grouped plants into families on the basis of common essential properties and, in *Genera Plantarum* (1789), developed the system on which modern plant classification is based.

jussive /ˈdʒʌsɪv/ ▶ adjective Grammar (of a form of a verb) expressing a command.
– ORIGIN mid 19th cent.: from Latin *juss-* 'commanded' (from the verb *jubere*) + -IVE.

just ▶ adjective based on or behaving according to what is morally right and fair: *a just and democratic society | fighting for a just cause*. ■ (of treatment) deserved or appropriate in the circumstances: *we all get our just deserts*. ■ (of an opinion or appraisal) well founded; justifiable: *these simplistic approaches have been the subject of just criticism*.
▶ adverb **1** exactly: *that's just what I need | you're a human being, just like everyone else*. ■ exactly or almost exactly at this or that moment: *she's just coming | we were just finishing breakfast*.
2 very recently; in the immediate past: *I've just seen the local paper*.
3 barely; by a little: *inflation fell to just over 4 per cent | I **only just** caught the train*.
4 simply; only; no more than: *just a bad day in the office | they were just interested in making money*. ■ really; absolutely (used for emphasis): *they're just great*. ■ used as a polite formula for giving permission or making a request: *just help yourselves*. ■ [with modal] possibly (used to indicate a slight chance of something happening or being true): *it might just help*.
5 expressing agreement: *'Simon really messed things up.' 'Didn't he just?'*
– PHRASES **just about** informal almost exactly; nearly: *he can do just about anything*. **just as well** a good or fortunate thing: *it was just as well I didn't know at the time*. **just in case** as a precaution. **just a minute** (or **moment**, or **second**, etc.) used to ask someone to wait or pause for a short time. ■ used to interrupt someone, especially in protest or disagreement. **just now** **1** at this moment: *it's pretty hectic just now*. **2** a little time ago: *she was talking to me just now*. **3** S. African in a little while; very soon: *I'll come just now but I want breakfast first*. **just on** (with reference to time and numbers) exactly: *it was just on midnight*. **just so** **1** arranged or done very neatly and carefully: *polishing the furniture and making everything just so*. **2** formal used to express agreement.
– DERIVATIVES **justness** noun.
– ORIGIN late Middle English: via Old French from Latin *justus*, from *jus* 'law, right'.

juste milieu /ˌʒuːst mɪˈljəː/, French /ʒystə miljø/ ▶ noun the happy medium; judicious moderation.
– ORIGIN French, literally 'correct mean'.

justice ▶ noun **1** [mass noun] just behaviour or treatment: *a concern for justice, peace, and genuine respect for people*. ■ the quality of being fair and reasonable: *the justice of his case*. ■ the administration of the law or authority in maintaining this: *a tragic miscarriage of justice*.
2 a judge or magistrate, in particular a judge of the Supreme Court of a country or state.
– PHRASES **bring someone to justice** arrest someone for a crime and ensure that they are tried in court. **do oneself justice** perform as well as one is able to. **do someone/thing justice** do, treat, or represent someone or something with due fairness or appreciation: *the brief menu does not do justice to the food*. **in justice to** out of fairness to: *I say this in justice to both of you*. **Mr** (or **Mrs**) **Justice** Brit. a form of address or reference to a judge of the supreme court (e.g. a High Court judge). **rough justice** see ROUGH.

– DERIVATIVES **justiceship** noun (sense 2).
– ORIGIN late Old English *iustise* 'administration of the law', via Old French from Latin *justitia*, from *justus* (see JUST).

Justice of the Peace ▸ noun (in the UK) a lay magistrate appointed to hear minor cases, grant licences, etc., in a town, county, or other local district.

justiciable /dʒʌˈstɪʃəb(ə)l/ ▸ adjective Law (of a state or action) subject to trial in a court of law.
– DERIVATIVES **justiciability** noun.
– ORIGIN late Middle English: from Old French, from *justicier* 'bring to trial', from medieval Latin *justitiare*, from Latin *justitia* 'equity', from *justus* (see JUST).

justiciar /dʒʌˈstɪʃə/ ▸ noun historical an administrator of justice, in particular: ■ a regent and deputy presiding over the court of a Norman or early Plantagenet king of England. ■ either of two supreme judges in medieval Scotland.
– ORIGIN late 15th cent.: from medieval Latin *justitiarius* (see JUSTICIARY).

justiciary /dʒʌˈstɪʃ(ə)ri/ ▸ noun (pl. **justiciaries**) chiefly Scottish an administrator of justice. ■ [mass noun] the administration of justice: [as modifier] *justiciary cases*.
– ORIGIN mid 16th cent.: from medieval Latin *justitiarius*, from Latin *justitia*, from *justus* (see JUST).

justifiable ▸ adjective able to be shown to be right or reasonable; defensible: *it is not financially justifiable | their justifiable fears*.
– DERIVATIVES **justifiability** noun, **justifiableness** noun, **justifiably** adverb *he was justifiably angry*.
– ORIGIN early 16th cent. (in the sense 'justiciable'): from French, from *justifier* 'to justify'.

J

justifiable homicide ▸ noun [mass noun] the killing of a person in circumstances which allow the act to be regarded in law as without criminal guilt.

justification /dʒʌstɪfɪˈkeɪʃ(ə)n/ ▸ noun [mass noun]
1 the action of showing something to be right or reasonable: *the justification of revolutionary action | he made a speech **in justification of** his career*. ■ good reason for something that exists or has been done: *there is no **justification for** an increase in charges* | [count noun] *all these incidents were used again as a justification for my sacking*.
2 Theology the action of declaring or making righteous in the sight of God.
3 Printing the action or manner of justifying a line of type or piece of text.

justified ▸ adjective **1** having, done for, or marked by a good or legitimate reason: *the doctors were **justified** in treating her*.
2 Theology declared or made righteous in the sight of God.
3 Printing having been adjusted so that the print fills a space evenly or forms a straight line at the margin.

justify /ˈdʒʌstɪfʌɪ/ ▸ verb (**justifies, justifying, justified**) [with obj.] **1** show or prove to be right or reasonable: *the person appointed has fully justified our confidence*. ■ be a good reason for: *the situation was grave enough to justify further investigation*.
2 Theology declare or make righteous in the sight of God.
3 Printing adjust (a line of type or piece of text) so that the print fills a space evenly or forms a straight edge at the margin.
– DERIVATIVES **justificatory** adjective, **justifier** noun.
– ORIGIN Middle English (in the senses 'administer justice to' and 'inflict a judicial penalty on'): from Old French *justifier*, from Christian Latin *justificare* 'do justice to', from Latin *justus* (see JUST).

Justin, St (*c.*100–165), Christian philosopher; known as **St Justin the Martyr**. According to tradition he was martyred in Rome together with some of his followers. He is remembered for his *Apologia* (*c.*150). Feast day, 1 June.

Justinian /dʒʌˈstɪnɪən/ (483–565), Byzantine emperor 527–65; Latin name *Flavius Petrus Sabbatius Justinianus*. Through his general Belisarius he regained North Africa and Spain. He codified Roman law (529) and carried out a building programme throughout the Empire, of which St Sophia at Constantinople (532) was a part.

just-in-time ▸ adjective denoting a manufacturing system in which materials or components are delivered immediately before they are required in order to minimize storage costs.

justly ▸ adverb according to what is morally right or fair; fairly: *we deal justly with complaints*. ■ in a way that is well founded; justifiably: *we can justly be proud of our achievements*.

just war ▸ noun a war that is deemed to be morally or theologically justifiable.

jut ▸ verb (**juts, jutting, jutted**) [no obj., with adverbial] extend out, over, or beyond the main body or line of something: *a rock jutted out from the side of the bank*. ■ [with obj.] cause (something) to protrude: *she put up her head and **jutted out** her chin with determination*.
▸ noun a point that sticks out.
– ORIGIN mid 16th cent.: variant of JET¹.

Jute /dʒuːt/ ▸ noun a member of a Germanic people that (according to Bede) joined the Angles and Saxons in invading Britain in the 5th century, settling in a region including Kent and the Isle of Wight. They may have come from Jutland.
– DERIVATIVES **Jutish** adjective.
– ORIGIN Old English *Eotas, Iotas*, influenced later in spelling by medieval Latin *Jutae, Juti*.

jute /dʒuːt/ ▸ noun [mass noun] **1** rough fibre made from the stems of a tropical Old World plant, used for making twine and rope or woven into sacking or matting.
2 the herbaceous plant which is cultivated for this fibre, with edible young shoots. ● Genus *Corchorus*, family Tiliaceae: several species.
■ used in names of other plants that yield fibre, e.g. **Chinese jute**.
– ORIGIN mid 18th cent.: from Bengali *jhuṭo* 'matted hair', from Prakrit *juṣṭi*.

Jutland /ˈdʒʌtlənd/ a peninsula of NW Europe, forming the mainland of Denmark together with the north German state of Schleswig-Holstein. Danish name JYLLAND.

Jutland, Battle of a major naval battle in the First World War, fought between the British Grand Fleet under Admiral Jellicoe and the German High Seas Fleet in the North Sea west of Jutland on 31 May 1916. Although the battle was indecisive the German fleet never again sought a full-scale engagement, and the Allies retained control of the North Sea.

Juvenal /ˈdʒuːvɪn(ə)l/ (*c.*60–*c.*140), Roman satirist; Latin name *Decimus Junius Juvenalis*. His sixteen verse satires present a savage attack on the vice and folly of Roman society, chiefly in the reign of the emperor Domitian.

juvenescence /ˌdʒuːvəˈnɛs(ə)ns/ ▸ noun [mass noun] formal the state or period of being young.
– DERIVATIVES **juvenescent** adjective.
– ORIGIN early 19th cent.: from Latin *juvenescent-* 'reaching the age of youth', from the verb *juvenescere*, from *juvenis* 'young'.

juvenile /ˈdʒuːvənʌɪl/ ▸ adjective **1** for or relating to young people: *juvenile crime*. ■ denoting a theatrical or film role representing a young person: *the romantic juvenile lead*. ■ relating to young birds and animals.
2 childish; immature: *she's bored with my juvenile conversation*.
▸ noun a young person. ■ Law a person below the age at which ordinary criminal prosecution is possible (18 in most countries). ■ an actor playing a juvenile role. ■ a young bird or animal.
– DERIVATIVES **juvenility** /-ˈnɪlɪti/ noun.
– ORIGIN early 17th cent.: from Latin *juvenilis*, from *juvenis* 'young, a young person'.

juvenile court ▸ noun a court of law responsible for the trial or legal supervision of children under a specified age (18 in most countries). Compare with YOUTH COURT.

juvenile delinquency ▸ noun [mass noun] the habitual committing of criminal acts or offences by a young person, especially one below the age at which ordinary criminal prosecution is possible.
– DERIVATIVES **juvenile deliquent** noun.

juvenile hormone ▸ noun Entomology any of a number of hormones regulating larval development in insects and inhibiting metamorphosis.

juvenile offender ▸ noun a person below a specific age (18 in most countries) who has committed a crime.

juvenilia /ˌdʒuːvəˈnɪlɪə/ ▸ plural noun works produced by an author or artist while still young.
– ORIGIN early 17th cent.: from Latin, neuter plural of *juvenilis* (see JUVENILE).

juvenilize /ˈdʒuːvənɪlʌɪz/ (also **juvenilise**) ▸ verb [with obj.] make or keep young or youthful; arrest the development of. ■ (as adj. **juvenilized**) Entomology (of an insect or part of one) having a juvenile appearance or physiology; showing arrested or reversed development.

juvie /ˈdʒuːvi/ ▸ noun (pl. **juvies**) informal a youth, especially a juvenile delinquent.
– ORIGIN 1940s: abbreviation of JUVENILE.

juxtaglomerular /ˌdʒʌkstəglɒˈmɛrʊlə/ ▸ adjective Anatomy denoting a group of structures secreting regulatory hormones into the arteriole which leads into a glomerulus in the kidney.
– ORIGIN 1930s: from Latin *juxta* 'near to' + *glomerular* (see GLOMERULUS).

juxtapose /ˌdʒʌkstəˈpəʊz/ ▸ verb [with obj.] place or deal with close together for contrasting effect: *black-and-white photos of slums were starkly **juxtaposed** with colour images*.
– ORIGIN mid 19th cent. (earlier (Middle English) as *juxtaposition*): from French *juxtaposer*, from Latin *juxta* 'next' + French *poser* 'to place'.

juxtaposition /ˌdʒʌkstəpəˈzɪʃ(ə)n/ ▸ noun the fact of two things being seen or placed close together with contrasting effect: *the juxtaposition of these two images*.
– DERIVATIVES **juxtapositional** adjective.

Jylland /ˈjylan/ Danish name for JUTLAND.

Jyväskylä /ˈjuːvasˌkʊlə/ a city in central Finland; pop. 128,211 (2009).

Kk

K¹ (also **k**) ▶ **noun** (pl. **Ks** or **K's**) the eleventh letter of the alphabet. ■ denoting the next after J in a set of items, categories, etc.

K² ▶ **abbreviation** ■ Cambodia (international vehicle registration). [from *Kampuchea*.] ■ kelvin(s) ■ Computing kilobyte(s). ■ kilometre(s). ■ N. Amer. kindergarten. ■ king (used especially in describing play in card games and recording moves in chess): *declarer overruffed with ♦K and led another spade* | *18.Ke2.* ■ knit (as an instruction in knitting patterns): *K 42 rows.* ■ Köchel (catalogue of Mozart's works): *the Sinfonia Concertante, K364.* ■ (also **k**) informal thousand (used chiefly in expressing salaries or other sums of money): *he earns about £50K a year.* [from **KILO-** 'thousand'.]
▶ **symbol** the chemical element potassium. [from modern Latin *kalium*.]

k ▶ **abbreviation** [in combination] ■ (in units of measurement) kilo-: *a distance of 700 kpc.* ■ see **K²** (abbreviation).
▶ **symbol** ■ a constant in a formula or equation. ■ Chemistry Boltzmann's constant.

K2 the highest mountain in the Karakoram range, on the border between Pakistan and China. It is the second-highest peak in the world, rising to 8,611 m (28,250 ft). It was discovered in 1856 and named K2 because it was the second peak to be surveyed in the Karakoram range. It was also formerly known as Mount Godwin-Austen after Col. H. H. Godwin-Austen, who first surveyed it. Also called **DAPSANG**.

ka /kɑː/ ▶ **noun** (in ancient Egypt) the supposed spiritual part of an individual human being or god, which survived (with the soul) after death and could reside in a statue of the person. See also **BA**.

Kaaba /ˈkɑːəbə/ (also **Caaba**) a square stone building in the centre of the Great Mosque at Mecca, the site most holy to Muslims and towards which they must face when praying. It stands on the site of a pre-Islamic shrine said to have been built by Abraham, and a sacred Black Stone is set in its south-eastern corner.
– ORIGIN from Arabic *(al-)kaʻba*, literally '(the) cubic house'.

Kaapenaar /ˈkɑːpəˌnɑː/ ▶ **noun** S. African an inhabitant of Cape Town or of the Western Cape Province.
– ORIGIN Afrikaans, from *kaap* 'Cape' + the personal suffix *-enaar*.

kabaddi /kəˈbadi, kəˈbʌdi/ ▶ **noun** [mass noun] a sport of Indian origin played by teams of seven on a circular sand court. The players attempt to tag or capture opponents and must hold their breath while running, repeating the word 'kabaddi' to show that they are doing so.
– ORIGIN of uncertain origin; compare with Kannada *kabalisu* 'to gulp' and Hindi *kabaḍḍī* 'shout "kabaddi"'.

kabaka /kəˈbɑːkə/ ▶ **noun** the traditional ruler of the Baganda people of Uganda.
– ORIGIN a local title.

Kabalega Falls /ˌkabəˈleɪgə/ a waterfall on the lower Victoria Nile near Lake Albert, in NW Uganda. Former name **MURCHISON FALLS**.

Kabardian /kəˈbɑːdɪən/ ▶ **adjective** relating to an indigenous people of the NW Caucasus.
▶ **noun 1** a member of the Kabardian people.
2 [mass noun] the North Caucasian language of the Kabardian people, with about 350,000 speakers.
– ORIGIN from Russian *Kabarda*, a district in SW Russia.

Kabardino-Balkaria /ˌkabəˈdiːnəʊ balˈkɑːrɪə/ an autonomous republic of SW Russia, on the border with Georgia; pop. 893,100 (est. 2009); capital, Nalchik. Also called **Kabarda-Balkar Republic** /ˌkabədə balˈkɑː/.

Kabbalah /kəˈbɑːlə, ˈkabələ/ (also **Kabbala**, **Cabbala**, **Cabala**, or **Qabalah**) ▶ **noun** the ancient Jewish tradition of mystical interpretation of the Bible, first transmitted orally and using esoteric methods (including ciphers). It reached the height of its influence in the later Middle Ages and remains significant in Hasidism.
– DERIVATIVES **Kabbalism noun**, **Kabbalist noun**, **Kabbalistic adjective**.
– ORIGIN from medieval Latin *cabala*, *cabbala*, from Rabbinical Hebrew *qabbālāh* 'tradition', from *qibbēl* 'receive, accept'.

kabeljou /ˌkab(ə)lˈjəʊ/ ▶ **noun** (pl. **same**) S. African a large predatory marine fish of the drum family, found in the Mediterranean, East Atlantic, and SW Indian Ocean. It is an important food fish in southern Africa. ● *Argyrosomus hololepidotus*, family Sciaenidae.
– ORIGIN early 18th cent.: from Afrikaans, from Dutch, 'cod'.

Kabila /kəˈbiːlə/, Laurent-Désiré (1939–2001), African statesman, President of the Democratic Republic of the Congo (formerly Zaire) 1997–2001. After his forces overthrew President Mobutu in 1997, Kabila took power and changed the name of the country to the Democratic Republic of the Congo. He was assassinated by one of his army officers and was succeeded as President by his son **Joseph Kabila** (b.1971).

Kabinett /ˌkabɪˈnɛt/, German /ˌkabɪˈnɛt/ ▶ **noun** a wine of German origin or style of superior or reserve quality, especially one made from a specified quality of grape must, without added sugar.
– ORIGIN from German *Kabinettwein*, literally 'chamber wine'.

kabloona /kəˈbluːnə/ ▶ **noun** (pl. **kabloonas**, **kabloonat** /-nat/) Canadian (among Inuit people) a person who is not a member of the Inuit; a white person.
– ORIGIN from Inuit *kabluna* 'big eyebrow'.

kabob /kəˈbɑːb/ ▶ **noun** US spelling of **KEBAB**.

kaboodle /kəˈbuːd(ə)l/ ▶ **noun** variant spelling of **CABOODLE**.

kaboom /kəˈbuːm/ ▶ **exclamation** used to represent the sound of a loud explosion.

kabuki /kəˈbuːki/ ▶ **noun** [mass noun] a form of traditional Japanese drama with highly stylized song, mime, and dance, now performed only by male actors, using exaggerated gestures and body movements to express emotions, and including historical plays, domestic dramas, and dance pieces.
– ORIGIN Japanese, originally as a verb meaning 'act dissolutely', later interpreted as if from *ka* 'song' + *bu* 'dance' + *ki* 'art'.

Kabul /ˈkɑːbʊl/ the capital of Afghanistan; pop. 2,536,000 (est. 2006). It is situated in the north-east of the country, with a strategic position commanding the mountain passes through the Hindu Kush, especially the Khyber Pass. It was capital of the Mogul empire 1504–1738 and in 1773 replaced Kandahar as capital of an independent Afghanistan. It suffered severe damage following the Soviet invasion of Afghanistan in 1979 and during the rise and fall of the Taliban regime.

Kabwe /ˈkabweɪ/ a town in central Zambia, situated to the north of Lusaka; pop. 211,500 (est. 2009). It is the site of a cave which has yielded human fossils associated with the Upper Pleistocene period. Former name (1904–65) **BROKEN HILL**.

Kabyle /kəˈbʌɪl/ ▶ **noun 1** (pl. **same**) a member of a Berber people inhabiting northern Algeria.
2 [mass noun] the Berber dialect of the Kabyle people.
▶ **adjective** relating to the Kabyle or their language.
– ORIGIN probably from Arabic *qabā'il*, plural of *qabīla* 'tribe'.

kachha ▶ **noun** variant spelling of **KUCCHA**.

Kachin /ˈkatʃɪn/ ▶ **noun 1** (pl. **same**) a member of an indigenous people living in northern Burma (Myanmar) and adjacent parts of China and India.
2 [mass noun] the Tibeto-Burman language of the Kachin people, with about 500,000 speakers.
▶ **adjective** relating to the Kachin or their language.

kachina /kəˈtʃiːnə/ (also **katsina**) ▶ **noun** (pl. **kachinas**) a deified ancestral spirit in the mythology of Pueblo Indians. ■ (also **kachina dancer**) a person who represents a kachina in ceremonial dances. ■ (also **kachina doll**) a small carved figure representing a kachina.
– ORIGIN from Hopi *kacina* 'supernatural', of Keres origin.

ka-ching /kəˈtʃɪŋ/ (also **ker-ching**) ▶ **noun** used to represent the sound of a cash register, especially with reference to making money: *the highlight will be a month-long gig at a casino in the US Virgin Islands ka-ching!*
– ORIGIN imitative; compare with **CHING**.

kachori /ˈkatʃəri/ ▶ **noun** (pl. **kachoris**) (in Indian cookery) a puri stuffed with spiced lentils, potato, or beans.
– ORIGIN Hindi *kacaurī*.

kadai /kʌˈdʌɪ/ ▶ **noun** variant spelling of **KARAHI**.

kadaitcha /kəˈdʌɪtʃə/ (also **kurdaitcha**) ▶ **noun** Austral.
1 (among Aborigines) a malignant spirit.
2 [mass noun] an Aboriginal mission of vengeance or punishment. ■ the ritual accompanying this mission. ■ (also **kadaitcha man**) [count noun] a man empowered to carry out vengeance or punishment.
– ORIGIN probably from Arrernte.

Kádár /ˈkɑːdɑː/, János (1912–89), Hungarian statesman, First Secretary of the Hungarian Socialist Workers' Party 1956–88 and Prime Minister 1956–8 and 1961–5. After crushing the Hungarian uprising of 1956, Kádár consistently supported the Soviet Union. His policy of 'consumer socialism' made Hungary the most affluent state in eastern Europe.

Kaddish /ˈkadɪʃ/ ▶ **noun** an ancient Jewish prayer sequence regularly recited in the synagogue service, including thanksgiving and praise and concluding with a prayer for universal peace. ■ a form of the Kaddish recited for the dead.
– ORIGIN from Aramaic *qaddīš* 'holy'.

kadi ▶ **noun** (pl. **kadis**) variant spelling of **CADI**.

Kadiköy /kaˈdikœj/ Turkish name for **CHALCEDON**.

kaffeeklatsch /ˈkafeɪˌklatʃ/ ▶ **noun** another term for **KLATCH**.
– ORIGIN German, from *Kaffee* 'coffee' + *Klatsch* 'gossip'.

Kaffir /ˈkafə/ ▶ **noun** offensive, chiefly S. African an insulting and contemptuous term for a black African.
– ORIGIN from Arabic *kāfir* 'infidel', from *kafara* 'not believe'.

> **USAGE** The word **Kaffir** is first recorded in the 16th century (as **Caffre**) and was originally simply a descriptive term for a particular ethnic group. Now it is always a racially abusive and offensive term when used of people, and in South Africa its use is actionable.

Kaffir lily ▶ **noun** either of two South African plants with strap-like leaves and stems bearing a number of red, pink, or orange flowers: ● a plant with star-shaped flowers (*Schizostylis coccinea*, family Iridaceae). ● another term for CLIVIA.

Kaffir lime ▶ **noun** a SE Asian citrus tree whose fragrant leaves are used in Thai and Indonesian cooking. ● *Citrus hystrix*, family Rutaceae.

kaffiyeh ▶ **noun** variant spelling of KEFFIYEH.

Kafir /ˈkafə/ ▶ **noun** a member of a people of the Hindu Kush mountains of NE Afghanistan.
– ORIGIN from Arabic *kāfir* (see KAFFIR).

kafir /ˈkafɪə/ ▶ **noun** a person who is not a Muslim (used chiefly by Muslims).
– ORIGIN from Arabic *kāfir* 'infidel, unbeliever'. Compare with KAFFIR.

Kafka /ˈkafkə/, Franz (1883–1924), Czech novelist, who wrote in German. His work is characterized by its portrayal of an enigmatic and nightmarish reality where the individual is perceived as lonely, perplexed, and threatened. Notable works: *The Metamorphosis* (1917) and *The Trial* (1925).
– DERIVATIVES **Kafkaesque** /ˌkafkəˈɛsk/ **adjective**.

kaftan /ˈkaftan/ (also **caftan**) ▶ **noun** a man's long belted tunic, worn in countries of the Near East. ■ a woman's long loose dress. ■ a loose shirt or top.
– ORIGIN late 16th cent.: from Turkish, from Persian *ḳaftān*, partly influenced by French *cafetan*.

Kagoshima /ˌkagəˈʃiːmə/ a city and port in Japan; pop. 601,122 (2007). Situated on the southern coast of Kyushu island, on the Satsuma Peninsula, it is noted for its porcelain (Satsuma ware).

kagoul (also **kagoule**) ▶ **noun** variant spelling of CAGOULE.

kagu /ˈkɑːguː/ ▶ **noun** a crested, almost flightless bluish-grey bird related to the rails, which is found only on the Pacific island of New Caledonia, and is now endangered. ● *Rhynochetos jubatus*, the only member of the family Rhynochetidae.
– ORIGIN mid 19th cent.: from Melanesian.

kahawai /ˈkɑːwʌɪ/ ▶ **noun** (pl. **same**) New Zealand term for AUSTRALIAN SALMON (see SALMON (sense 2)).
– ORIGIN Maori.

kahikatea /ˌkʌɪkəˈtiːə/ ▶ **noun** a tall coniferous New Zealand tree which is used for its timber and resin. ● *Podocarpus* (or *Dacrycarpus*) *dacrydioides*, family Podocarpaceae.
– ORIGIN early 19th cent.: from Maori.

Kahlo /ˈkɑːləʊ/, Frida (1907–54), Mexican painter. She is noted for her brightly coloured self-portraits, which were influenced by Mexican primitive art. She was married to Diego Rivera.

Kahlúa /kɑːˈluːə/ ▶ **noun** [mass noun] trademark a coffee-flavoured liqueur.

kahuna /kəˈhuːnə/ ▶ **noun** (in Hawaii) a wise man or shaman. ■ N. Amer. informal an important person; the person in charge: *one big kahuna runs the whole show*. ■ N. Amer. informal (in surfing) a very large wave.
– ORIGIN Hawaiian.

kai /kʌɪ/ (also **kaikai** /ˈkʌɪkʌɪ/) ▶ **noun** [mass noun] NZ informal food.
– ORIGIN Maori.

Kaifeng /kʌɪˈfɛŋ/ a city in Henan province, eastern China, on the Yellow River; pop. 591,300 (est. 2006). Established in the 4th century BC, it is one of the oldest cities in China.

kail ▶ **noun** variant spelling of KALE.

kainga /kɑːˈɪŋə/ ▶ **noun** NZ a Maori village or settlement.
– ORIGIN Maori.

kainic acid /ˈkʌɪnɪk/ ▶ **noun** [mass noun] Medicine an organic acid extracted from a red alga, used to kill intestinal worms. ● Chem. formula: $C_{10}H_{15}NO_4$.
– ORIGIN 1950s: *kainic* from Japanese *kainin* (from *kainin-sō*, name of the alga *Digenea simplex* from which it is extracted) + -IC.

kainite /ˈkʌɪnʌɪt, ˈkeɪnʌɪt/ ▶ **noun** [mass noun] a white mineral consisting of a double salt of hydrated magnesium sulphate and potassium chloride.
– ORIGIN mid 19th cent.: from German *Kainit*, from Greek *kainos* 'new, recent', because of the mineral's recent formation.

kairomone /ˈkʌɪrəməʊn/ ▶ **noun** Biology a chemical substance emitted by an organism and detected by another of a different species which gains advantage from this, e.g. a parasite seeking a host.
– ORIGIN late 20th cent.: from Greek *kairos* 'advantage, opportunity', on the pattern of *pheromone*.

kairos /ˈkʌɪrɒs/ ▶ **noun** a propitious moment for decision or action.
– ORIGIN 1930s: Greek, literally 'opportunity'.

Kairouan /ˌkʌɪərʊˈɑːn/ a city in NE Tunisia; pop. 117,900 (est. 2004). It is the site of some of the earliest mosques, and became a centre of Islamic law.

kaiseki /kʌɪˈsɛkiː/ ▶ **noun** [mass noun] a style of traditional Japanese cuisine in which a series of very small, intricate dishes are prepared.
– ORIGIN Japanese, from *kai* (from *kaichu* 'kimono pocket') + *seki* 'stone'.

kaiser /ˈkʌɪzə/ ▶ **noun 1** historical the German Emperor, the Emperor of Austria, or the head of the Holy Roman Empire: [as title] *Kaiser Wilhelm*.
2 (also **kaiser roll**) N. Amer. a crisp bread roll in the shape of a pinwheel, made by folding the corners of a square of dough into the centre before baking.
– ORIGIN Middle English *cayser*, from Old Norse *keisari*, based on Latin *Caesar* (see CAESAR), and later reinforced by Middle Dutch *keiser*. The modern English form (early 19th cent.) derives from German *Kaiser*.

Kaiserslautern /ˌkʌɪzəsˈlaʊt(ə)n/, German /ˌkaɪzɐsˈlaʊtɐn/ a city in western Germany, in Rhineland-Palatinate; pop. 98,000 (est. 2006).

Kaiser Wilhelm, Wilhelm II of Germany (see WILHELM II).

kaizen /kʌɪˈzɛn/ ▶ **noun** [mass noun] a Japanese business philosophy of continuous improvement of working practices, personal efficiency, etc.
– ORIGIN Japanese, literally 'improvement'.

kajal /ˈkʌdʒəl/ ▶ **noun** [mass noun] a black powder used in South Asia as a cosmetic, either around the eyes or as a mark on the forehead.
– ORIGIN from Hindi *kājal*.

kaka /ˈkɑːkɑː/ ▶ **noun** a large New Zealand parrot with olive-brown and dull green upper parts and reddish underparts. ● *Nestor meridionalis*, family Psittacidae.
– ORIGIN late 18th cent.: from Maori.

kakapo /ˈkɑːkəpəʊ/ ▶ **noun** (pl. **kakapos**) a large flightless New Zealand parrot with greenish plumage, which is nocturnal, ground-dwelling, and now endangered. Also called OWL PARROT. ● *Strigops habroptilus*, family Psittacidae.
– ORIGIN mid 19th cent.: from Maori, literally 'night kaka'.

kakemono /ˌkɑːkɪˈməʊnəʊ, ˌkakɪ-/ ▶ **noun** (pl. **kakemonos**) a Japanese unframed painting made on paper or silk and displayed as a wall hanging.
– ORIGIN late 19th cent.: Japanese, from *kake-* 'hang, suspend' + *mono* 'thing'.

kaki /ˈkɑːki/ ▶ **noun** the Japanese persimmon.
– ORIGIN early 18th cent.: from Japanese.

Kakiemon /kəˈkiːəmɒn/ ▶ **adjective** [attrib.] relating to a style of Japanese porcelain with sparse asymmetrical designs on a white ground, developed in the early 17th century.
– ORIGIN named after Sakaida *Kakiemon* (1596–1666), the first Japanese potter to work in this style.

kakuro /ˈkakərəʊ, kəˈkjʊərəʊ, -ˈʊərəʊ/ ▶ **noun** [mass noun] a type of number puzzle in which players have to insert numbers into a crossword-like grid, with numbered clues and some blank squares.
– ORIGIN early 21st cent.: blend of Japanese *kasan* 'addition' and *kurosu*, representing a Japanese pronunciation of *cross*.

kala /kəˈlɑː/ ▶ **noun** Indian **1** a skilled craft.
2 a performing art such as singing, dance, or drama.
– ORIGIN from Hindi.

Kalaallit Nunaat /kəˌlɑːlɪt nəˈnɑːt/ Inuit name for GREENLAND.

kala-azar /ˌkɑːləˌəˈzɑː/ ▶ **noun** [mass noun] a form of the disease leishmaniasis marked by emaciation, anaemia, fever, and enlargement of the liver and spleen. ● This is caused by *Leishmania donovani*, phylum Kinetoplastida, kingdom Protista.
– ORIGIN late 19th cent.: from Assamese, from *kālā* 'black' + *āzār* 'disease' (because of the bronzing of the skin often associated with it).

Kalahari Desert /ˌkaləˈhɑːri/ a high, vast, arid plateau in southern Africa north of the Orange River. It comprises most of Botswana with parts in Namibia and South Africa.

kalamkari /ˈkʌləmˌkɑːri/ ▶ **noun** [mass noun] a type of cotton cloth printed by hand, originally made in southern India.
– ORIGIN from Hindi *kalamkārī*, literally 'painting'.

kalanchoe /ˌkalənˈkəʊi/ ▶ **noun** a tropical succulent plant with clusters of tubular flowers, sometimes producing miniature plants along the edges of the leaves and grown as an indoor or greenhouse plant. ● Genus *Kalanchoe*, family Crassulaceae.
– ORIGIN mid 19th cent.: modern Latin, from French, based on Chinese *gāláncài*.

Kalashnikov /kəˈlaʃnɪkɒf, -ˈlɑːʃ-/ ▶ **noun** a type of rifle or sub-machine gun made in Russia.
– ORIGIN 1970s: named after Mikhail T. *Kalashnikov* (born 1919), the Russian designer of the weapons.

kale /keɪl/ (also **kail**) ▶ **noun** [mass noun] **1** a hardy cabbage of a variety which produces erect stems with large leaves and no compact head. See also CURLY KALE.
2 N. Amer. informal, dated money.
– ORIGIN Middle English: northern English form of COLE.

kaleidoscope /kəˈlʌɪdəskəʊp/ ▶ **noun** a toy consisting of a tube containing mirrors and pieces of coloured glass or paper, whose reflections produce changing patterns when the tube is rotated. ■ a constantly changing pattern or sequence of elements: *the dancers moved in* ***a kaleidoscope of*** *colour*.
– ORIGIN early 19th cent.: from Greek *kalos* 'beautiful' + *eidos* 'form' + -SCOPE.

kaleidoscopic /kəlʌɪdəˈskɒpɪk/ ▶ **adjective** having complex patterns of colours; multicoloured: *kaleidoscopic diamond patterns*. ■ made up of a complex mix of elements; multifaceted: *a kaleidoscopic range of topics*.
– DERIVATIVES **kaleidoscopically** **adverb**.

kalends ▶ **plural noun** variant spelling of CALENDS.

Kalevala /ˈkɑːlɛˌvɑːlə/ a collection of Finnish legends transmitted orally until published in the 19th century, and now regarded as the Finnish national epic.
– ORIGIN of Karelian origin.

Kaleyard School (also **Kailyard School**) a group of late 19th-century fiction writers, including J. M. Barrie, who described local town life in Scotland in a romantic vein and with much use of the vernacular.
– ORIGIN from Scots *kaleyard* or *kailyard*, literally 'kitchen garden'.

Kalgan /kɑːlˈgɑːn/ Mongolian name for ZHANGJIAKOU.

Kalgoorlie /kalˈgʊəli/ a gold-mining town in Western Australia; pop. 28,200 (est. 2006). Gold was discovered there in 1887, leading to a gold rush in the 1890s.

Kali /ˈkɑːli/ Hinduism the most terrifying goddess, wife of Shiva, often identified with Durga, and in her benevolent aspect with Parvati. She is typically depicted as black, naked, old, and hideous.
– ORIGIN from Sanskrit *Kālī* 'black'.

kali /ˈkeɪlʌɪ, ˈkali/ ▶ **noun** old-fashioned term for SALTWORT.
– ORIGIN late 16th cent.: from colloquial Arabic *qalī* 'calcined ashes of Salsola (and similar plants)'; compare with ALKALI.

Kalidasa /ˌkalɪˈdɑːsə/ (probably *fl.* 5th century AD), Indian poet and dramatist. He is best known for his drama *Sakuntala*, the love story of King Dushyanta and the maiden Sakuntala.

Kalimantan /ˌkalɪˈmantan/ a region of Indonesia, comprising the southern part of the island of Borneo.

kalimba /kəˈlɪmbə/ ▶ **noun** a type of African thumb piano.
– ORIGIN 1950s: a local word; related to MARIMBA.

Kalinin[1] /kəˈliːnɪn/ former name (1931–91) for TVER.

Kalinin[2] /kəˈliːnɪn/, Mikhail (Ivanovich) (1875–1946), Soviet statesman, head of state of the USSR 1919–46. He founded the newspaper *Pravda* (1912).

Kaliningrad /kəˈliːnɪngrad/ **1** a port on the Baltic coast of eastern Europe, capital of the Russian region of Kaliningrad; pop. 421,700 (est. 2008). It was known by its German name of Königsberg until 1946, when it was ceded to the Soviet Union under the Potsdam Agreement and renamed in honour of Kalinin. Its port is ice-free all the year round and is a significant naval base for the Russian fleet.
2 a region of Russia, an enclave situated on the Baltic coast of eastern Europe; capital, Kaliningrad. It

shares its borders with Lithuania and Poland and is separated from Russia by the intervening countries of Lithuania, Latvia, and Belarus.

Kalisz /ˈkɑːlɪʃ/ a city in central Poland; pop. 108,311 (2007).

Kalmar /ˈkalmɑː/ a port in SE Sweden, on the Kalmar Sound opposite Öland; pop. 61,693 (2008).

Kalmar Sound a narrow strait between the mainland of SE Sweden and the island of Öland, in the Baltic Sea.

Kalmar, Union of the treaty which joined together the Crowns of Denmark, Sweden, and Norway in 1397, dissolved in 1523.

kalmia /ˈkalmɪə/ ▸ **noun** an evergreen leathery-leaved shrub of the heather family, bearing large clusters of pink or red flowers. It is native to North America and Cuba and widely grown as an ornamental. ● Genus *Kalmia*, family Ericaceae.
– ORIGIN modern Latin, named after Pehr *Kalm* (1716–1779), Swedish botanist.

Kalmyk /ˈkalmʌk/ (also **Kalmuck**) ▸ **noun** (pl. **same**, **Kalmyks**, or **Kalmucks**) **1** a member of a Buddhist people of Mongolian origin living chiefly in Kalmykia.
2 [mass noun] the Altaic language of the Kalmyk.
▸ **adjective** relating to the Kalmyk or their language.
– ORIGIN from Russian *kalmyk*.

Kalmykia /kalˈmɪkɪə/ an autonomous republic in SW Russia, on the Caspian Sea; pop. 285,800 (est. 2009); capital, Elista .

kalong /ˈkɑːlɒŋ/ ▸ **noun** a flying fox found in SE Asia and Indonesia. ● Genus *Pteropus*, family Pteropodidae, in particular the large flying fox (*P. vampyrus*).
– ORIGIN early 19th cent.: from Javanese.

kalpa /ˈkalpə/ ▸ **noun** (in Hindu and Buddhist tradition) an immense period of time, reckoned as 4,320 million human years, and considered to be the length of a single cycle of the cosmos (or 'day of Brahma') from creation to dissolution.
– ORIGIN Sanskrit.

kalsomine /ˈkalsəmʌɪn/ (also **calcimine**) ▸ **noun** [mass noun] a kind of white or pale blue wash for walls and ceilings.
▸ **verb** [with obj.] whitewash (a wall or ceiling) with kalsomine.
– ORIGIN mid 19th cent.: of unknown origin.

Kaluga /kəˈluːɡə/ an industrial city and river port in European Russia, on the River Oka south-west of Moscow; pop. 326,900 (est. 2008).

Kalyan /kʌlˈjɑːn/ a city on the west coast of India, in the state of Maharashtra, north-east of Mumbai (Bombay); pop. 1,328,000 (est. 2009).

Kama /ˈkɑːmə/ Hinduism the god of love, typically represented as a youth with a bowl of sugar cane, a bowstring of bees, and arrows of flowers.

kamacite /ˈkaməsʌɪt/ ▸ **noun** [mass noun] an alloy of iron and nickel occurring in some meteorites.
– ORIGIN late 19th cent.: from Greek *kamax*, *kamak-* 'vine pole' (because of the occurrence of the alloy in bar-shaped masses) + **-ITE**[1].

kamahi /ˈkɑːməhi/ ▸ **noun** a tall New Zealand forest tree with small cream-coloured flowers and dark timber. ● *Weinmannia racemosa*, family Cunoniaceae.
– ORIGIN mid 19th cent.: from Maori.

Kama Sutra /ˌkɑːmə ˈsuːtrə/ an ancient Sanskrit treatise on the art of love and sexual technique.
– ORIGIN Sanskrit, from *kāma* 'love' + *sūtra* 'thread'.

Kamba /ˈkambə/ ▸ **noun** (pl. **same**, **Kambas**, or **Wakamba**) **1** a member of a people of central Kenya, ethnically related to the Kikuyu.
2 [mass noun] the Bantu language of the Kamba, with around 2.5 million speakers.
▸ **adjective** relating to the Kamba or their language.
– ORIGIN a local name.

Kamchatka /kamˈtʃatkə/ a vast mountainous peninsula of the NE coast of Siberian Russia, separating the Sea of Okhotsk from the Bering Sea; chief port, Petropavlovsk.

kame /keɪm/ ▸ **noun** Geology a steep-sided mound of sand and gravel deposited by a melting ice sheet.
– ORIGIN late 18th cent.: Scots form of **COMB**.

kameez /kəˈmiːz/ ▸ **noun** (pl. **same** or **kameezes**) a long tunic worn by many people from South Asia, typically with a salwar or churidars.
– ORIGIN from Arabic *qamīṣ*, perhaps from late Latin *camisia* (see **CHEMISE**).

Kamenskoye /kaˈmjɛnˌskɒjə/ former name (until 1936) for **DNIPRODZERZHINSK**.

Kamensk-Uralsky /ˌkɑːmɪnskʊˈralski/ an industrial city in central Russia, in the eastern foothills of the Urals; pop. 180,900 (est. 2008).

kami /ˈkɑːmi/ ▸ **noun** (pl. **same**) a divine being in the Shinto religion.
– ORIGIN Japanese.

kamikaze /ˌkamɪˈkɑːzi/ ▸ **noun** (in the Second World War) a Japanese aircraft loaded with explosives and making a deliberate suicidal crash on an enemy target. ■ the pilot of a kamikaze aircraft.
▸ **adjective** [attrib.] relating to or denoting a kamikaze attack or pilot. ■ reckless or potentially self-destructive: *he made a kamikaze run across three lanes of traffic*.
– ORIGIN Japanese, from *kami* 'divinity' + *kaze* 'wind', originally referring to the gale that, in Japanese tradition, destroyed the fleet of invading Mongols in 1281.

Kamilaroi /kəˈmɪlərɔɪ/ ▸ **noun** (pl. **same**) **1** a member of a group of Australian Aboriginal peoples of north-eastern New South Wales.
2 [mass noun] the extinct language of the Kamilaroi.
▸ **adjective** relating to the Kamilaroi or their language.
– ORIGIN the name in Kamilaroi.

Kampala /kamˈpɑːlə/ the capital of Uganda; pop. 1,533,600 (est. 2009). It is situated on the northern shores of Lake Victoria and replaced Entebbe as capital when the country became independent in 1963.

kampong /kamˈpɒŋ, ˈkampɒŋ/ (also **kampung** /kamˈpʌŋ, ˈkampʌŋ/) ▸ **noun** a Malaysian enclosure or village.
– ORIGIN Malay; compare with **COMPOUND**[2].

Kampuchea /ˌkampʊˈtʃiːə/ former name (1976–89) for **CAMBODIA**.
– DERIVATIVES **Kampuchean noun & adjective.**

Kan. ▸ **abbreviation** Kansas.

kana /ˈkɑːnə/ ▸ **noun** [mass noun] the system of syllabic writing used for Japanese, having two forms, hiragana and katakana. Compare with **KANJI**.
– ORIGIN Japanese.

kanaka /kəˈnakə, -ˈnɑːkə/ ▸ **noun 1** a native or inhabitant of Hawaii.
2 historical a Pacific islander employed as an indentured labourer in Australia, especially in the sugar and cotton plantations of Queensland.
– ORIGIN Hawaiian, literally 'man'.

kanamycin /ˌkanəˈmʌɪsɪn/ ▸ **noun** [mass noun] Medicine a broad-spectrum antibiotic obtained from a strain of bacteria.
– ORIGIN 1950s: from modern Latin *Streptomyces kanamyceticus*, the name of the source bacterium (see also **-MYCIN**).

Kanarese /ˌkanəˈriːz/ (also **Canarese**) ▸ **noun** (pl. **same**) **1** a member of a people living mainly in Kanara, a district in SW India.
2 another term for **KANNADA**.
▸ **adjective** relating to Kanara, its people, or their language.

kanban /ˈkanban/ ▸ **noun** (also **kanban system**) [mass noun] a Japanese manufacturing system in which the supply of components is regulated through the use of an instruction card sent along the production line. ■ [count noun] an instruction card used in a kanban system.
– ORIGIN late 20th cent.: Japanese, literally 'billboard, sign'.

Kanchenjunga /ˌkantʃɛnˈdʒʌŋɡə/ (also **Kangchenjunga** or **Kinchinjunga**) a mountain in the Himalayas, on the border between Nepal and Sikkim. Rising to a height of 8,598 m (28,209 ft), it is the world's third-highest mountain.
– ORIGIN Tibetan, literally 'the five treasures of the snows', referring to the five separate peaks of the summit.

Kandahar /ˌkandəˈhɑː/ a city in southern Afghanistan; pop. 324,800 (est. 2006). From 1748 it was Afghanistan's first capital after independence, until being replaced by Kabul in 1773.

Kandinsky /kanˈdɪnski/, Wassily (1866–1944), Russian painter and theorist. A pioneer of abstract art, he urged the expression of inner and essential feelings in art, rather than the representation of surface appearances. In 1911 he co-founded the Munich-based *Blaue Reiter* group of artists.

Kandy /ˈkandi/ a city in Sri Lanka; pop. 121,300 (est. 2007). It was the capital (1480–1815) of the former independent kingdom of Kandy and contains one of the most sacred Buddhist shrines, the Dalada Maligava (Temple of the Tooth).
– DERIVATIVES **Kandyan adjective.**

kanga[1] ▸ **noun** Austral. informal **1** a kangaroo.
2 a prison warder.
– ORIGIN 1920s: abbreviation; sense 2 from rhyming slang *kangaroo* 'screw'.

kanga[2] ▸ **noun** variant spelling of **KHANGA**.

Kangar /ˈkaŋɡɑː/ the capital of the state of Perlis in northern Malaysia, near the west coast of the Malay Peninsula; pop. 65,500 (est. 2009).

kangaroo ▸ **noun** a large plant-eating marsupial with a long powerful tail and strongly developed hindlimbs that enable it to travel by leaping, found only in Australia and New Guinea. ● Genus *Macropus*, family Macropodidae: several species.
– PHRASES **have kangaroos in the** (or **one's**) **top paddock** Austral. informal be mad or eccentric.
– ORIGIN late 18th cent.: the name of a specific kind of kangaroo in an extinct Aboriginal language of North Queensland.

kangaroo care ▸ **noun** [mass noun] a method of caring for a premature baby in which the infant is held in skin-to-skin contact with a parent, typically the mother, for as long as possible each day.

kangaroo court ▸ **noun** an unofficial court held by a group of people in order to try someone regarded, especially without good evidence, as guilty of a crime or misdemeanour.

kangaroo grass ▸ **noun** [mass noun] a fodder grass which grows in very tall tussocks. ● Genus *Themeda*, family Gramineae: several species, in particular *T. australis*.

kangaroo mouse ▸ **noun** a small seed-eating hopping rodent with large cheek pouches and long hind legs, found in North America. ● Genus *Microdipodops*, family Heteromyidae: two species.

kangaroo paw ▸ **noun** an Australian plant which has long strap-like leaves and tubular flowers with woolly outer surfaces. ● Genera *Anigozanthos* and *Macropidia*, family Haemodoraceae: several species.

kangaroo rat ▸ **noun** a seed-eating hopping rodent with large cheek pouches and long hind legs, found from Canada to Mexico. ● Genus *Dipodomys*, family Heteromyidae: several species.

kangaroo vine ▸ **noun** an Australian evergreen climbing plant of the vine family, grown as a houseplant. ● *Cissus antarctica*, family Vitaceae.

Kangchenjunga /ˌkaŋtʃɛnˈdʒʌŋɡə/ variant spelling of **KANCHENJUNGA**.

kangha /ˈkʌŋhə/ ▸ **noun** a comb worn in the hair as one of the five distinguishing signs of the Sikh Khalsa.
– ORIGIN from Punjabi *kanghā*.

Kango /ˈkaŋɡəʊ/ ▸ **noun** (pl. **Kangoes**) trademark a heavy electrically powered hammer.
– ORIGIN 1920s: of unknown origin.

kangri /ˈkaŋɡri/ ▸ **noun** Indian a small pot filled with lighted charcoal, used to transport fire or (in Kashmir) carried close to the body as a means of keeping warm.
– ORIGIN from Hindi *kāṁgṛī*.

KaNgwane /ˌkɑːəŋˈɡwɑːneɪ/ a former homeland established in South Africa for the Swazi people, now part of the province of Mpumalanga.

kanji /ˈkandʒi, ˈkɑːn-/ ▸ **noun** [mass noun] a system of Japanese writing using Chinese characters, used primarily for content words. Compare with **KANA**.
– ORIGIN Japanese, from *kan* 'Chinese' + *ji* 'character'.

Kannada /ˈkanədə/ ▸ **noun** [mass noun] a Dravidian language related to Telugu and using a similar script, spoken by about 43 million people, mainly in Karnataka in SW India. Also called **KANARESE**.
▸ **adjective** relating to Kannada and its speakers.
– ORIGIN the name in Kannada.

Kano /ˈkɑːnəʊ/ a city in northern Nigeria; pop. 2,359,200 (est. 2009).

Kanpur /kɑːnˈpʊə/ a city in Uttar Pradesh, northern India, on the River Ganges; pop. 3,144,300 (est. 2009). It was the site of a massacre of British soldiers and European families in July 1857, during the Indian Mutiny. Former name **CAWNPORE**.

Kans. ▸ **abbreviation** Kansas.

Kansas /ˈkanzəs/ a state in the central US; pop. 2,802,134 (est. 2008); capital, Topeka. Acquired as part of the Louisiana Purchase in 1803, it became the 34th state of the US in 1861.
– DERIVATIVES **Kansan adjective & noun.**

Kansas City each of two adjacent cities in the US, situated at the junction of the Missouri and Kansas Rivers, one in NE Kansas; pop. 142,562 (est. 2008),

K

and the other in NW Missouri; pop. 451,572 (est. 2008).

Kansu /kan'su:/ variant of **GANSU**.

Kant /kant/, Immanuel (1724–1804), German philosopher. In the *Critique of Pure Reason* (1781) he countered Hume's sceptical empiricism by arguing that any affirmation or denial regarding the ultimate nature of reality ('noumenon') makes no sense. All we can know are the objects of experience ('phenomena'), interpreted by space and time and ordered according to twelve key concepts. Kant's *Critique of Practical Reason* (1788) affirms the existence of an absolute moral law—the categorical imperative.
– DERIVATIVES **Kantian** adjective & noun, **Kantianism** noun.

Kanto /kan'təʊ/ a region of Japan, on the island of Honshu.

KANU /'kɑ:nu:/ ▶ abbreviation Kenya African National Union.

kanuka /'kɑ:nʊkə/ ▶ noun a small evergreen New Zealand tree with white flowers, yielding useful timber and products used in herbal medicine. ● *Leptospermum ericoides*, family Myrtaceae.
– ORIGIN early 20th cent.: from Maori.

kanzu /'kanzu:/ ▶ noun a long white cotton or linen robe worn by East African men.
– ORIGIN early 20th cent.: from Kiswahili.

Kaohsiung /kaʊ'ʃjʊŋ/ the chief port of Taiwan, on the SW coast; pop. 1,520,600 (est. 2007).

kaoliang /'keɪəʊ,ljaŋ/ ▶ noun [mass noun] sorghum of a variety grown in China and used to make dough and alcoholic drinks. ● *Sorghum bicolor* var. *nervosum*, family Gramineae.
– ORIGIN early 20th cent.: from Chinese *gāoliang*, from *gāo* 'high' + *liáng* 'fine grain'.

K

kaolin /'keɪəlɪn/ ▶ noun [mass noun] a fine soft white clay, resulting from the natural decomposition of other clays or feldspar. It is used for making porcelain and china, as a filler in paper and textiles, and in medicinal absorbents. Also called **CHINA CLAY**.
– ORIGIN early 18th cent.: from French, from Chinese *gāolǐng*, literally 'high hill', the name of a mountain in Jiangxi province where the clay is found.

kaolinite /'keɪəlɪnʌɪt/ ▶ noun [mass noun] a white or grey clay mineral which is the chief constituent of kaolin.

kaon /'keɪɒn/ ▶ noun Physics a meson having a mass several times that of a pion.
– ORIGIN 1950s: from *ka* representing the letter *K* (as a symbol for the particle) + **-ON**.

Kaonde /ka'ɒndeɪ/ ▶ noun (pl. **same**) **1** a member of a people living mainly in north-western Zambia.
2 [mass noun] the Bantu language of the Kaonde, with around 200,000 speakers.
▶ adjective relating to the Kaonde or their language.

Kapachira Falls /,kapə'tʃɪərə/ a waterfall on the Shire River in southern Malawi. Former name **MURCHISON RAPIDS**.

kapai /'kɑ:pʌɪ/ NZ ▶ adjective very pleasant; good, fine.
▶ adverb in a pleasant way; very well.
– ORIGIN mid 19th cent.: from Maori *ka pai*.

kapellmeister /kə'pɛl,mʌɪstə/ ▶ noun (in German-speaking countries) the leader or conductor of an orchestra or choir. ■ historical a leader of a chamber ensemble or orchestra attached to a German court.
– ORIGIN mid 19th cent.: German, from *Kapelle* 'court orchestra' (from medieval Latin *capella* 'chapel') + *Meister* 'master'.

Kap Farvel /,kab far'vɛl/ Danish name for Cape Farewell (see **FAREWELL, CAPE** (sense 1)).

Kapil Dev /,kapɪl 'dɛv/ (b.1959), Indian cricketer; full name *Kapil Dev Nikhanj*. Originally a medium-pace bowler, he soon developed into an all-rounder. As captain (1983–4) he led India to victory in the 1983 World Cup. In 1994 he set a new record of 432 Test match wickets.

kapok /'keɪpɒk/ ▶ noun [mass noun] a fine, fibrous cotton-like substance which grows around the seeds of the ceiba tree, used as stuffing for cushions, soft toys, etc. ■ (also **kapok tree**) another term for **CEIBA**.
– ORIGIN mid 18th cent.: from Malay *kapuk*.

Kaposi's sarcoma /kə'pəʊsɪz/ ▶ noun [mass noun] Medicine a form of cancer involving multiple tumours of the lymph nodes or skin, occurring chiefly in people with depressed immune systems, e.g. as a result of AIDS.
– ORIGIN late 19th cent.: named after Moritz K. *Kaposi* (1837–1902), Hungarian dermatologist.

kappa /'kapə/ ▶ noun the tenth letter of the Greek alphabet (Κ, κ), transliterated as 'k'. ■ (**Kappa**) [followed by Latin genitive] Astronomy the tenth star in a constellation: *Kappa Orionis*. ■ [as modifier] Biochemistry denoting one of the two types of light polypeptide chain present in all immunoglobulin molecules (the other being lambda).
– ORIGIN Greek.

kapu /'kapu:/ ▶ noun [mass noun] (in Hawaiian traditional culture and religion) a set of rules and prohibitions for everyday life.
– ORIGIN Hawaiian.

kapur /'kapə/ ▶ noun a large tropical Old World tree which yields light brown timber, edible fruit, and camphor. ● Genus *Dryobalanops*, family Dipterocarpaceae.
– ORIGIN Malay.

kaput /kə'pʊt/ ▶ adjective [predic.] informal broken and useless; no longer working or effective.
– ORIGIN late 19th cent.: from German *kaputt*, from French (*être*) *capot* '(be) without tricks in a card game'; compare with **CAPOT**.

kara /'kɑ:rə/ ▶ noun a steel bangle worn on the right wrist as one of the five distinguishing signs of the Sikh Khalsa.
– ORIGIN from Punjabi *karā*.

karabiner /,karə'bi:nə/ (also **carabiner**) ▶ noun a coupling link with a safety closure, used by rock climbers.
– ORIGIN 1930s: shortened from German *Karabinerhaken* 'spring hook'.

Karachai /,karə'tʃʌɪ/ (also **Karachay**) ▶ noun **1** a member of an indigenous people living in Karachai-Cherkessia.
2 (also **Karachay-Balkar**) [mass noun] the Turkic language of the Karachai, with under 200,000 speakers.
▶ adjective relating to the Karachai or their language.
– ORIGIN from Turkic, from *kara*, *qara* 'back' and *chai* 'brook'.

Karachai-Cherkessia /,karətʃʌɪ,tʃɛ:'kɛsɪə/ an autonomous republic in the northern Caucasus, SW Russia; pop. 427,100 (est. 2009); capital, Cherkessk. Official name **Karachai-Cherkess Republic**.

Karachi /kə'rɑ:tʃi/ a major city and port in Pakistan, capital of Sind province; pop. 12,827,900 (est. 2009). Situated on the Arabian Sea, it was the capital of Pakistan 1947–59 before being replaced by Rawalpindi.

Karafuto /,karə'fu:təʊ/ the Japanese name for the southern part of the island of Sakhalin.

Karaganda /karəgan'da/ Russian name for **QARAGHANDY**.

karahi /kʌ'rʌɪ/ (also **kadai** or **karai**) ▶ noun (pl. **karahis**) a bowl-shaped frying pan with two handles used in Indian cookery, chiefly for balti dishes.
– ORIGIN from Hindi *karāhī*.

Karaite /'kɛ:rəʌɪt/ ▶ noun a member of a Jewish sect founded in the 8th century and located chiefly in the Crimea and nearby areas, and in Israel, which rejects rabbinical interpretation in favour of a literal interpretation of the scriptures.
– ORIGIN early 18th cent.: from Hebrew *Qārā'īm* (from *qārā'* 'read') + **-ITE**[1].

Karaj /ka'rɑ:dʒ/ a city in northern Iran, to the west of Tehran; pop. 1,386,030 (2006).

Karajan /'karəjan/, Herbert von (1908–89), Austrian conductor, chiefly remembered as the principal conductor of the Berlin Philharmonic Orchestra (1955–89).

karaka /kə'rakə/ ▶ noun a New Zealand tree with orange berries containing seeds which are poisonous unless roasted. ● *Corynocarpus laevigata*, family Corynocarpaceae.
– ORIGIN mid 19th cent.: from Maori.

Karakalpak /,karə'kalpak/ ▶ noun (pl. **same** or **Karakalpaks**) **1** a member of an indigenous people living in the Karakalpak autonomous republic of Russia, south of the Aral Sea.
2 [mass noun] the Turkic language of the Karakalpaks, with about 300,000 speakers.
▶ adjective relating to the Karakalpaks or their language.

Karakoram /,karə'kɔ:rəm/ a great mountain system of central Asia, extending over 480 km (300 miles) south-eastwards from NE Afghanistan to Kashmir and forming part of the borders of India and Pakistan with China. One of the highest mountain systems in the world, it consists of a group of parallel ranges, forming a westwards continuation of the Himalayas, with many peaks over 7,900 m (26,000 ft), the highest being K2.

Karakorum /,karə'kɔ:rəm/ an ancient city in central Mongolia, now ruined, which was the capital of the Mongol empire, established by Genghis Khan in 1220. The capital was moved to Khanbaliq (modern Beijing) in 1267, and Karakorum was destroyed by Chinese forces in 1388.

karakul /'karəkʊl/ (also **caracul**) ▶ noun a sheep of an Asian breed with a dark curled fleece when young. ■ [mass noun] cloth or fur made from or resembling the fleece of the karakul. Also called **PERSIAN LAMB**.
– ORIGIN mid 19th cent.: from Russian, from the name of an oasis in Uzbekistan and of two lakes in Tadjikistan, based on Turkic.

Kara Kum /,karə 'ku:m/ a desert in central Asia, to the east of the Caspian Sea, covering much of Turkmenistan. Russian name **Karakumy** /kəra'kumij/.

karanga /'karaŋə/ ▶ noun NZ a Maori ritual chant of welcome.
– ORIGIN Maori.

karaoke /,karɪ'əʊki/ ▶ noun [mass noun] a form of entertainment, offered typically by bars and clubs, in which people take turns to sing popular songs into a microphone over pre-recorded backing tracks.
– ORIGIN 1970s: from Japanese, literally 'empty orchestra'.

Kara Sea /'kɑ:rə/ an arm of the Arctic Ocean off the northern coast of Russia, bounded to the east by the islands of Severnaya Zemlya and to the west by Novaya Zemlya.

karat ▶ noun US spelling of **CARAT** (sense 2).

karate /kə'rɑ:ti/ ▶ noun [mass noun] an oriental system of unarmed combat using the hands and feet to deliver and block blows, widely practised as a sport.

> It was formalized in Okinawa in the 17th century, and popularized via Japan after about 1920. Karate is performed barefoot in loose padded clothing, with a coloured belt indicating the level of skill, and involves mental as well as physical training.

– ORIGIN Japanese, from *kara* 'empty' + *te* 'hand'.

karate-chop ▶ verb [with obj.] strike sharply with the side of the hand.

karateka /kə'rɑ:tɪkɑ:/ ▶ noun (pl. **same** or **karatekas**) a practitioner of karate.

Karbala /'kɑ:bələ/ a city in southern Iraq; pop. 475,000 (est. 2003). A holy city for Shiite Muslims, it is the site of the tomb of Husayn, grandson of Muhammad, who was killed there in AD 680.

karee ▶ noun variant spelling of **KARREE**.

Karelia /kə'reɪlɪə, -'ri:lɪə/ a region of NE Europe on the border between Russia and Finland. Following Finland's declaration of independence in 1917, part of Karelia became a region of Finland and part an autonomous republic of the Soviet Union. After the Russo-Finnish war of 1939–40 the greater part of Finnish Karelia was ceded to the Soviet Union. The remaining part of Karelia constitutes a province of eastern Finland.
– DERIVATIVES **Karelian** adjective & noun.

Karen /kə'rɛn/ ▶ noun (pl. **same** or **Karens**) **1** a member of an indigenous people of eastern Burma (Myanmar) and western Thailand.
2 [mass noun] the language of the Karen, which probably belongs to the Sino-Tibetan family. Its highly distinct dialects have over 5 million speakers altogether.
▶ adjective relating to the Karen or their language.
– ORIGIN from Burmese *ka-reng* 'wild unclean man'.

Karen State a state in SE Burma (Myanmar), on the border with Thailand; capital, Pa-an. Inaugurated in 1954 as an autonomous state of Burma, the state was given the traditional Karen name of Kawthoolay in 1964, but reverted to Karen after the 1974 constitution limited its autonomy. The people are engaged in armed conflict with the Burmese government in an attempt to gain independence. Also called **KAWTHOOLAY, KAWTHULEI**.

karez /'kɑ:rɛz/ ▶ noun (pl. **same**) (in parts of central southern Asia) a qanat.
– ORIGIN Pashto, from Persian.

karezza /kə'rɛtsə/ ▶ noun [mass noun] sexual intercourse in which ejaculation is avoided.
– ORIGIN late 19th cent.: from Italian *carezza* 'a caress'.

Kariba, Lake /kə'ri:bə/ a large, man-made lake on the Zambia–Zimbabwe border in central Africa. It was created by the damming of the Zambezi River by the Kariba Dam, and it is the chief source of hydroelectric power for Zimbabwe and Zambia.

Kariba Dam a concrete arch dam on the Zambezi River, 385 km (240 miles) downstream from the Victoria Falls. It was built in 1955–9, creating Lake Kariba and providing a bridge over the Zambezi between Zambia and Zimbabwe.

Karitane /ˌkarɪˈtɑːni/ ▶ **adjective** [attrib.] NZ trained or administered according to the principles of child care and nutrition advocated by the Royal New Zealand Society for the Health of Women and Children (the Plunket Society): *a Karitane hospital.*
– ORIGIN early 20th cent.: from the name of a township in the South Island, New Zealand.

kark ▶ **verb** variant form of **CARK**.

Karl XII /kɑːl/ variant spelling of **CHARLES XII**.

Karl-Marx-Stadt /kɑːlˈmɑːksˌʃtat/, German /karlˈmarksˌʃtat/ former name (1953–90) for **CHEMNITZ**.

Karloff /ˈkɑːlɒf/, Boris (1887–1969), British-born American actor; born *William Henry Pratt.* His name is chiefly linked with horror films, such as *Frankenstein* (1931) and *The Body Snatcher* (1945).

Karlovy Vary /ˌkɑːləvɪ ˈvɑːri/ a spa town in the western Czech Republic; pop. 50,940 (2007). It is famous for its alkaline thermal springs. German name **Karlsbad** /ˈkarlsbaːt/.

Karlsruhe /ˈkɑːlzˌruːə/, German /ˈkarlsˌruːə/ an industrial town and port on the Rhine in western Germany; pop. 286,300 (est. 2006).

karma /ˈkɑːmə, ˈkəːmə/ ▶ **noun** [mass noun] (in Hinduism and Buddhism) the sum of a person's actions in this and previous states of existence, viewed as deciding their fate in future existences. ■ informal good or bad luck, viewed as resulting from one's actions.
– DERIVATIVES **karmic** adjective, **karmically** adverb.
– ORIGIN from Sanskrit *karman* 'action, effect, fate'.

karma yoga ▶ **noun** [mass noun] Hinduism the discipline of selfless action as a way to perfection.

Karnak /ˈkɑːnak/ a village in Egypt on the Nile, now largely amalgamated with Luxor. It is the site of the northern complex of monuments of ancient Thebes, including the great temple of Amun.

Karnataka /kəˈnɑːtəkə/ a state in SW India; capital, Bangalore. Former name (until 1973) **MYSORE**.

Karnaugh map /ˈkɑːnɔː/ (also **Karnaugh diagram**) ▶ **noun** Mathematics & Electronics a diagram consisting of a rectangular array of squares each representing a different combination of the variables of a Boolean function.
– DERIVATIVES **Karnaugh mapping** noun.
– ORIGIN 1950s: named after Maurice *Karnaugh* (born 1924), American physicist.

Kärnten /ˈkɛrntn/ German name for **CARINTHIA**.

karo /ˈkarəʊ/ ▶ **noun** (pl. **karos**) an ornamental evergreen shrub or small tree with leathery leaves and clusters of small dark red flowers, native to New Zealand and naturalized in parts of Europe. ● *Pittosporum crassifolium*, family Pittosporaceae.
– ORIGIN mid 19th cent.: from Maori.

Karoo /kəˈruː/ (also **Karroo**) an elevated semi-desert plateau in South Africa. ■ [as mass noun] (**karoo**) S. African semi-desert land like that of the Karoo.
– ORIGIN from Khoikhoi, literally 'hard, dry'.

karoshi /kaˈrəʊʃi/ ▶ **noun** [mass noun] (in Japan) death caused by overwork or job-related exhaustion.
– ORIGIN Japanese, from *ka* 'excess' + *rō* 'labour' + *shi* 'death'.

kaross /kəˈrɒs/ ▶ **noun** S. African a rug or blanket of sewn animal skins, formerly worn as a garment by African people, now used as a bed or floor covering.
– ORIGIN South African Dutch, from Khoikhoi *karos.*

Karpov /ˈkɑːpɒf/, Anatoli (Yevgenevich) (b.1951), Russian chess player. He was world champion from 1975 until defeated by Garry Kasparov in 1985.

karree /kəˈriː/ (also **karee**) ▶ **noun** S. African an evergreen African tree related to sumac, with willow-like foliage and useful timber. ● Genus *Rhus*, family Anacardiaceae, in particular *R. lancea.*
– ORIGIN early 19th cent.: from Afrikaans, from Nama *karib.*

karren /ˈkarən/ ▶ **plural noun** Geology grooves and fissures, typically separated by sharp ridges, produced in a hard limestone surface by water erosion.
– ORIGIN late 19th cent.: from German *Karren.*

karri /ˈkari/ ▶ **noun** (pl. **karris**) a tall Australian eucalyptus with hard red wood. ● *Eucalyptus diversicolor*, family Myrtaceae.
– ORIGIN late 19th cent.: from Nyungar.

karroid /ˈkarɔɪd/ ▶ **adjective** S. African, chiefly technical of or characteristic of the Karoo.

Karroo variant spelling of **KAROO**.

Kars /kɑːs/ a city and province in NE Turkey; pop. 77,000 (est. 2007).

karst /kɑːst/ ▶ **noun** [mass noun] Geology landscape underlain by limestone which has been eroded by dissolution, producing ridges, towers, fissures, sinkholes and other characteristic landforms.
– DERIVATIVES **karstic** adjective, **karstification** noun, **karstify** verb (**karstifies**, **karstifying**, **karstified**).
– ORIGIN late 19th cent.: from German *der Karst*, the name of a limestone region in Slovenia.

kart ▶ **noun** a small unsprung motor-racing vehicle typically having four wheels and consisting of a tubular frame with a rear-mounted engine.
– DERIVATIVES **karting** noun.
– ORIGIN 1950s: shortening of **GO-KART**.

Kartvelian /kɑːtˈviːlɪən/ ▶ **adjective & noun** another term for **SOUTH CAUCASIAN** (see **CAUCASIAN**).
– ORIGIN from Georgian *k'art'velebi* 'Georgians' + **-IAN**.

karyo- ▶ **combining form** Biology denoting the nucleus of a cell: *karyotype.*
– ORIGIN from Greek *karuon* 'kernel'.

karyokinesis /ˌkarɪəʊkɪˈniːsɪs, -kʌɪ-/ ▶ **noun** [mass noun] Biology division of a cell nucleus during mitosis.
– ORIGIN late 19th cent.: from **KARYO-** 'cell nucleus' + Greek *kinēsis* 'movement' (from *kinein* 'to move').

karyolysis /ˌkarɪˈɒlɪsɪs/ ▶ **noun** [mass noun] Biology dissolution of a cell nucleus, especially during mitosis.

karyotype /ˈkarɪə(ʊ)tʌɪp/ ▶ **noun** Biology & Medicine the number and visual appearance of the chromosomes in the cell nuclei of an organism or species.
– DERIVATIVES **karyotypic** adjective.

karyotyping ▶ **noun** [mass noun] Biology & Medicine the determination of a karyotype, e.g. to detect chromosomal abnormalities.

karzy ▶ **noun** variant spelling of **KHAZI**.

kasbah /ˈkazbɑː/ (also **casbah**) ▶ **noun** the citadel of a North African city. ■ (**the kasbah**) the area surrounding a North African citadel.
– ORIGIN mid 18th cent.: from French *casbah*, from Arabic *qaṣaba* 'citadel'.

Kasha /ˈkaʃə/ ▶ **noun** [mass noun] trademark a soft napped fabric of wool and hair. ■ a kind of cotton flannel used as a lining material.
– ORIGIN early 20th cent.: of unknown origin.

kasha /ˈkaʃə/ ▶ **noun** [mass noun] (in Russia and Poland) porridge made from cooked buckwheat or similar grain. ■ uncooked buckwheat groats.
– ORIGIN Russian.

Kashmir /kaʃˈmɪə/ a region on the northern border of India and NE Pakistan. Formerly a state of India, it has been disputed between India and Pakistan since partition in 1947, with sporadic outbreaks of fighting. The north-western part is controlled by Pakistan, most of it forming the state of Azad Kashmir, while the remainder is incorporated into the Indian state of Jammu and Kashmir.

Kashmir goat ▶ **noun** a goat of a Himalayan breed yielding fine, soft wool, which is used to make cashmere.

Kashmiri /kaʃˈmɪəri/ ▶ **adjective** relating to Kashmir, its people, or their language.
▶ **noun 1** a native or inhabitant of Kashmir.
2 [mass noun] the Indic language of Kashmir, spoken by over 3 million people and written in both Devanagari and Arabic script.

kashrut /kaʃˈruːt/ (also **kashruth**) ▶ **noun** [mass noun] the body of Jewish religious laws concerning the suitability of food, the use of ritual objects, etc. ■ the observance of the Kashrut laws.
– ORIGIN Hebrew, literally 'legitimacy (in religion)'; see also **KOSHER**.

Kashubian /kəˈʃuːbɪən/ ▶ **noun 1** a native or inhabitant of Kashubia, a region of Poland west and north-west of Gdansk.
2 [mass noun] the Western Slavic vernacular language spoken by about 200,000 people in Kashubia. It is closely related to Polish.
▶ **adjective** relating to Kashubia, its people, or their language.

Kasparov /ˈkaspərɒf/, Garry (b.1963), Azerbaijani chess player of Armenian-Jewish descent; born *Garry Weinstein.* At the age of 22 he became the youngest-ever world champion, defeating Anatoli Karpov in 1985; he held the title until 2000. He won a match against the IBM computer Deep Blue in 1996 but in 1997 was beaten by Deeper Blue.

Kassel /ˈkas(ə)l/ a city in central Germany, in Hesse; pop. 193,500 (est. 2006). It was the capital of the kingdom of Westphalia (1807–13) and of the Prussian province of Hesse-Nassau (1866–1944).

Kasur /kəˈsʊə/ a city in Punjab province, NE Pakistan; pop. 322,000 (est. 2009).

kata /ˈkɑːtɑː/ ▶ **noun** [mass noun] a system of individual training exercises in karate and other martial arts. ■ [count noun] (pl. **same** or **katas**) an individual training exercise in karate and other martial arts.
– ORIGIN Japanese.

katabatic /ˌkatəˈbatɪk/ ▶ **adjective** Meteorology (of a wind) caused by local downward motion of cool air.
– ORIGIN late 19th cent.: from Greek *katabatikos*, from *katabainein* 'go down'.

katakana /ˌkatəˈkɑːnə/ ▶ **noun** [mass noun] the more angular form of kana (syllabic writing) used in Japanese, primarily used for words of foreign origin. Compare with **HIRAGANA**.
– ORIGIN early 18th cent.: Japanese, literally 'side kana'.

katana /kəˈtɑːnə/ ▶ **noun** a long, single-edged sword used by Japanese samurai.
– ORIGIN early 17th cent.: Japanese.

Katanga /kəˈtaŋgə/ a copper-mining region of the Democratic Republic of the Congo (Zaire); capital, Lubumbashi. It was known as Shaba 1972–97.

Katangese /ˌkataŋˈgiːz/ ▶ **noun** (pl. **same**) a native or inhabitant of Katanga.
▶ **adjective** relating to the Katangese.

Kathak /ˈkʌtək/ ▶ **noun 1** [mass noun] a type of northern Indian classical dance, with alternating passages of mime and dancing.
2 (pl. **same** or **Kathaks**) a member of a northern Indian caste of storytellers and musicians.
– ORIGIN from Sanskrit *kathaka* 'professional storyteller', from *kathā* 'story'.

Kathakali /ˌkɑːtəˈkɑːli, ˌkʌtəˈkʌli/ ▶ **noun** [mass noun] a form of dramatic dance of southern India, based on Hindu literature and characterized by masks, stylized costume and make-up, and frequent use of mime.
– ORIGIN from Malayalam, from Sanskrit *kathā* 'story' + Malayalam *kaḷi* 'play'.

katharevousa /ˌkaθəˈrɛvuːsə/ ▶ **noun** [mass noun] a heavily archaized form of modern Greek used in traditional literary writing, as opposed to the form which is spoken and used in everyday writing (called demotic).
– ORIGIN early 20th cent.: modern Greek, literally 'purified', feminine of *kathareuōn*, present participle of Greek *kathareuein* 'be pure', from *katharos* 'pure'.

katharometer /ˌkaθəˈrɒmɪtə/ ▶ **noun** an instrument for detecting a gas or measuring its concentration in a mixture, by measuring changes in thermal conductivity.
– ORIGIN early 20th cent.: from Greek *katharos* 'pure' + **-METER**.

Kathiawar /ˌkatɪəˈwɑː/ a peninsula on the western coast of India, in the state of Gujarat, separating the Gulf of Kutch from the Gulf of Cambay.

Kathmandu /ˌkatmanˈduː/ (also **Katmandu**) the capital of Nepal; pop. 895,000 (est. 2007). It is situated in the Himalayas at an altitude of 1,370 m (4,450 ft).

kathode ▶ **noun** archaic spelling of **CATHODE**.

katipo /ˈkatɪpəʊ/ ▶ **noun** (pl. **katipos**) a highly venomous New Zealand spider which is black with a red spot on the back, closely related to the American black widow. ● *Latrodectus mactans katipo*, family Theridiidae.
– ORIGIN mid 19th cent.: from Maori.

Katmandu variant spelling of **KATHMANDU**.

Katowice /ˌkatəˈviːtsə/ a city in SW Poland; pop. 313,461 (2007). It is the industrial centre of the Silesian coal-mining region.

katsina ▶ **noun** (pl. **katsinam**) variant of **KACHINA**.

katsuobushi /ˌkatswəʊˈbʊʃi/ ▶ **noun** [mass noun] dried fish prepared in hard blocks from skipjack tuna and used in Japanese cookery.
– ORIGIN Japanese.

katsura /katˈsʊərə/ ▶ **noun 1** an ornamental East Asian tree which has leaves that resemble those of the Judas tree and light, fine-grained timber. ● *Cercidiphyllum japonicum*, the only member of the family Cercidiphyllaceae.

K

2 a type of Japanese wig worn mainly by women.
– ORIGIN early 20th cent.: from Japanese.

Kattegat /ˈkatɪɡat/ a strait, 225 km (140 miles) in length, between Sweden and Denmark. It is linked to the North Sea by the Skagerrak and to the Baltic Sea by the Øresund.

katydid /ˈkeɪtɪdɪd/ ▶ **noun** a large, typically green, bush cricket that is native to North America. The male makes a characteristic sound which resembles the name. ● *Microcentrum* and other genera, family Tettigoniidae.

katzenjammer /ˈkatzənˌdʒamə/ ▶ **noun** US informal, dated **1** [mass noun] confusion; uproar.
2 a hangover; a severe headache resulting from a hangover.
– ORIGIN mid 19th cent.: from German *Katzen* (combining form of *Katze* 'cat') + *Jammer* 'distress'; popularized by the cartoon *Katzenjammer Kids*, drawn by Rudolf Dirks in 1897 for the *New York Journal*, featuring two incorrigible children.

Kauai /kaʊˈwɑːi/ an island in the state of Hawaii, separated from Oahu by the Kauai Channel; chief town, Lihue.

Kauffmann /ˈkaʊfman/ (also **Kauffman**), (Maria Anna Catherina) Angelica (1740–1807), Swiss painter. In London from 1766, she became well known for her neoclassical and allegorical paintings. She was a founder member of the Royal Academy of Arts (1768).

kaumatua /kaʊˈmɑːtʊə/ ▶ **noun** NZ a Maori elder.
– ORIGIN Maori.

Kaunas /ˈkaʊnəs/ an industrial city and river port in southern Lithuania, at the confluence of the Viliya and Neman Rivers; pop. 352,279 (2009).

Kaunda /kɑːˈʊndə/, Kenneth (David) (b.1924), Zambian statesman, President 1964–91. He led the United National Independence Party to electoral victory in 1964, becoming Prime Minister and the first President of independent Zambia.

kaupapa /ˈkaʊpapa/ ▶ **noun** NZ a principle or policy.
– ORIGIN Maori.

kauri /ˈkaʊri/ ▶ **noun** (pl. **kauris**) (also **kauri pine**) a tall coniferous forest tree with broad leathery leaves, which produces valuable timber and dammar resin. It grows in warm countries from Malaysia to New Zealand. ● Genus *Agathis*, family Araucariaceae: several species, in particular *A. australis* of New Zealand.
– ORIGIN early 19th cent.: from Maori.

kauri gum (also **kauri resin**) ▶ **noun** [mass noun] the resin of the kauri tree, used as a varnish, and often also found in fossilized form where the tree formerly grew.

kava /ˈkɑːvə/ ▶ **noun 1** [mass noun] a narcotic sedative drink made in Polynesia from the crushed roots of a plant of the pepper family.
2 the Polynesian shrub from which kava is obtained. ● *Piper methysticum*, family Piperaceae.
– ORIGIN late 18th cent.: from Tongan.

Kaválla /kəˈvalə/ a port on the Aegean coast of NE Greece; pop. 54,900 (est. 2009). Originally a Byzantine city and fortress, it was Turkish until 1912, when it was ceded to Greece.

Kaveri variant spelling of **Cauvery**.

kawaii /kəˈwʌɪ/ ▶ **adjective** (in the context of Japanese popular culture) cute: *she paints elephants that are extremely kawaii.*
▶ **noun** [mass noun] the quality of being cute, or items that are cute.
– ORIGIN Japanese.

kawa-kawa /ˈkɑːwəˌkɑːwə/ ▶ **noun** a New Zealand shrub of the pepper family with aromatic leaves, cultivated as an ornamental. Also called **pepper tree**. ● *Macropiper excelsum*, family Piperaceae.
– ORIGIN mid 19th cent.: from Maori.

Kawasaki /ˌkɑːwəˈsɑːki/ an industrial city on the SE coast of the island of Honshu, Japan; pop. 1,316,006 (2007).

Kawasaki disease ▶ **noun** [mass noun] a disease in young children with an unknown cause, giving rise to a rash, glandular swelling, and sometimes damage to the heart.
– ORIGIN 1960s: named after Tomisaku *Kawasaki*, Japanese physician.

Kawthoolay /ˌkɔːθuːˈleɪ/ (also **Kawthulei**) former name (1964–74) for **Karen State**.

kayak /ˈkʌɪak/ ▶ **noun** a canoe of a type used originally by the Inuit, made of a light frame with a watertight covering having a small opening in the top to sit in.
▶ **verb** (**kayaks**, **kayaking**, **kayaked**) [no obj.] (usu. as noun **kayaking**) travel in or use a kayak.
– DERIVATIVES **kayaker** noun.
– ORIGIN mid 18th cent.: from Inuit *qayaq*.

kayakeet /ˈkʌɪəkiːt, ˈkaja-/ ▶ **noun** W. Indian the common lantana, a scrambling shrub with prickly stems and flowers that turn from yellow to orange and finally to pinkish-red. ● *Lantana camara*, family Verbenaceae.
– ORIGIN French Creole, from Latin American Spanish *cariaquito*.

kayo /keɪˈəʊ/ Boxing, informal ▶ **noun** (pl. **kayos**) a knockout.
▶ **verb** (**kayoes**, **kayoing**, **kayoed**) [with obj.] knock (someone) out.
– ORIGIN 1920s: representing the pronunciation of *KO*.

Kayseri /ˈkʌɪsəri/ a city in central Turkey, capital of a province of the same name; pop. 696,800 (est. 2007). Known as Kayseri since the 11th century, it was formerly called Caesarea Mazaca and was the capital of Cappadocia.

kazachok /ˌkazəˈtʃɒk/ ▶ **noun** a Slavic dance with a fast and typically quickening tempo, featuring a step in which a squatting dancer kicks out each leg alternately to the front.
– ORIGIN early 20th cent.: Russian, diminutive of *kazak* 'Cossack'.

Kazakh /kəˈzak, ˈkazak/ ▶ **noun 1** a member of a people living chiefly in Kazakhstan. Traditionally nomadic, Kazakhs are predominantly Sunni Muslims.
2 [mass noun] the Turkic language of the Kazakhs, with over 7 million speakers.
▶ **adjective** relating to the Kazakhs or their language.
– ORIGIN Russian, from Turkic; see **Cossack**.

Kazakhstan /ˌkazəkˈstɑːn, -ˈstan/ a republic in central Asia, on the southern border of Russia, extending from the Caspian Sea eastwards to the Altai Mountains and China; pop. 15,399,400 (est. 2009); languages, Kazakh (official), Russian; capital Astana.

> The Turkic tribes of Kazakhstan were overrun by the Mongols in the 13th century, and the region was eventually absorbed into the Russian empire. Kazakhstan formed a constituent republic of the Soviet Union, becoming an independent republic within the Commonwealth of Independent States in 1991.

Kazan[1] /kəˈzan, -ˈzɑːn/ a port situated on the River Volga to the east of Nizhni Novgorod in Russia, capital of the autonomous republic of Tatarstan; pop. 1,120,200 (est. 2008).

Kazan[2] /kəˈzan/, Elia (1909–2003), Turkish-born American film and theatre director; born *Elia Kazanjoglous*. In 1947 he co-founded the Actors' Studio in New York City, one of the leading centres of method acting. Kazan directed *A Streetcar Named Desire* on stage (1947) and then on film (1953). Other notable films: *On the Waterfront* (1954) and *East of Eden* (1955).

kazillion /kəˈzɪljən/ ▶ **cardinal number** another term for **gazillion**.

kazoo /kəˈzuː/ ▶ **noun** a small, simple musical instrument consisting of a hollow pipe with a hole in it, over which is a thin covering that vibrates and adds a buzzing sound when the player sings or hums into the pipe.
– ORIGIN late 19th cent.: apparently imitative of the sound produced.

KB ▶ **abbreviation** ■ (also **Kb**) kilobit(s) or kilobyte(s). ■ (in the UK) King's Bench.

kb ▶ **abbreviation** Biochemistry kilobase(s).

KBE ▶ **abbreviation** (in the UK) Knight Commander of the Order of the British Empire.

Kbps ▶ **abbreviation** kilobits per second.

kbyte ▶ **abbreviation** kilobyte(s).

KC ▶ **abbreviation** King's Counsel.

kc ▶ **abbreviation** kilocycle(s).

kcal ▶ **abbreviation** kilocalorie(s).

KCB ▶ **abbreviation** (in the UK) Knight Commander of the Order of the Bath.

KCMG ▶ **abbreviation** (in the UK) Knight Commander of the Order of St Michael and St George.

kc/s ▶ **abbreviation** kilocycles per second.

KCVO ▶ **abbreviation** (in the UK) Knight Commander of the Royal Victorian Order.

KE ▶ **abbreviation** kinetic energy.

kea /ˈkiːə/ ▶ **noun** a New Zealand mountain parrot with a long, narrow bill and mainly olive-green plumage, sometimes feeding on carrion. ● *Nestor notabilis*, family Psittacidae.
– ORIGIN mid 19th cent.: from Maori, imitative of its call.

keaki /keɪˈɑːki, keɪˈaki/ ▶ **noun** a Japanese tree of the elm family, which is cultivated as an ornamental, for its timber, and as a bonsai tree. ● *Zelkova serrata*, family Ulmaceae.
– ORIGIN Japanese.

Kean, Edmund (1787–1833), English actor, renowned for his interpretations of Shakespearean tragic roles, notably those of Macbeth and Iago.

Keating, Paul (John) (b.1944), Australian Labor statesman, Prime Minister 1991–6. He resigned from parliament in 1996, having been defeated in the general election by the Liberal-National coalition.

Keaton, Buster (1895–1966), American actor and director; born *Joseph Francis Keaton*. His deadpan face and acrobatic skills made him one of the biggest comedy stars of the silent-film era. He starred in and directed films including *The Navigator* (1924) and *The General* (1926).

Keats, John (1795–1821), English poet. A principal figure of the romantic movement, he wrote all of his most famous poems, including 'La Belle Dame sans Merci', 'Ode to a Nightingale', and 'Ode on a Grecian Urn', in 1818 (published in 1820).
– DERIVATIVES **Keatsian** adjective.

kebab /kɪˈbab, kəˈbɑːb/ (N. Amer. also **kabob**) ▶ **noun** a dish of pieces of meat, fish, or vegetables roasted or grilled on a skewer or spit.
– ORIGIN late 17th cent.: from Arabic *kabāb*, partly via Urdu, Persian, and Turkish.

kebaya /kəˈbɑːjə/ ▶ **noun** a light, loose tunic worn by women in Malaysia, Indonesia, and other SE Asian countries.
– ORIGIN Malay, ultimately of Persian or Arabic origin.

Keble /ˈkiːb(ə)l/, John (1792–1866), English churchman. His sermon on national apostasy (1833) is generally held to mark the beginning of the Oxford Movement, which he founded with John Henry Newman and Edward Pusey.

Kebnekaise /ˌkɛbnəˈkʌɪsə/ the highest peak in Sweden, in the north of the country, rising to a height of 2,117 m (6,962 ft).

keck[1] ▶ **verb** [no obj.] informal feel as if one is about to vomit; retch.
– ORIGIN early 17th cent.: imitative.

keck[2] ▶ **noun** dialect cow parsley or a similar plant.
– ORIGIN early 17th cent.: from earlier dialect *kex* (perhaps of Celtic origin), interpreted as plural.

kecks ▶ **plural noun** Brit. informal trousers, knickers, or underpants.
– ORIGIN 1960s: phonetic respelling of obsolete *kicks* 'trousers'.

ked ▶ **noun** a wingless louse fly, especially one that is a parasite of sheep. ● Several species in the family Hippoboscidae, in particular the **sheep ked** (*Melophagus ovinus*).
– ORIGIN late 16th cent.: of unknown origin.

Kedah /ˈkɛdə/ a state of NW Malaysia, on the west coast of the Malay Peninsula; capital, Alor Setar.

keddah ▶ **noun** variant spelling of **kheda**.

kedge /kɛdʒ/ ▶ **verb** [with obj.] move (a boat) by hauling in a hawser attached at a distance to a small anchor. ■ [no obj.] (of a boat) be moved in such a way.
▶ **noun** (also **kedge anchor**) a small anchor used for kedging.
– ORIGIN late 15th cent.: perhaps a specific use of dialect *cadge* 'bind, tie'.

kedgeree /ˈkɛdʒəriː/ ▶ **noun** [mass noun] **1** a European dish consisting chiefly of fish, rice, and hard-boiled eggs.
2 another term for **khichri**.
– ORIGIN from Hindi *khicṛī*; see **khichri**.

keech /kiːx/ ▶ **noun** [mass noun] Scottish informal excrement. ■ rubbish: *maybe this keech about 'microclimate' was true.*
– ORIGIN early 19th cent.: from *cach*, Scots variant of **cack**.

keek Scottish ▶ **verb** [no obj.] peep surreptitiously: *he keeked through the window.*
▶ **noun** a surreptitious glance.
– ORIGIN late Middle English: perhaps related to Dutch *kijken* 'have a look'.

keel[1] ▶ **noun 1** the lengthwise timber or steel structure along the base of a ship, supporting the

framework of the whole, in some vessels extended downwards as a ridge to increase stability. ▪ literary a ship.
2 Zoology a ridge along the breastbone of many birds to which the flight muscles are attached; the carina.
3 Botany a prow-shaped pair of petals present in flowers of the pea family.
▸ **verb** [no obj.] (**keel over**) (of a boat or ship) turn over on its side; capsize. ▪ informal (of a person or thing) fall over; collapse.
– DERIVATIVES **keeled adjective** [in combination] *a deep-keeled yacht*, **keelless adjective**.
– ORIGIN Middle English: from Old Norse *kjǫlr*, of Germanic origin.

keel² ▸ **noun** Brit. a flat-bottomed boat of a kind formerly used on the Rivers Tyne and Wear for loading ships carrying coal.
– ORIGIN Middle English: from Middle Low German *kēl*, Middle Dutch *kiel* 'ship, boat'.

keelback ▸ **noun** a harmless Australian snake which lives close to water, where it feeds exclusively on frogs and the cane toad, whose venom it is immune to. ● *Amphiesma mairii*, family Colubridae.
– ORIGIN so named because each scale on the back has a keel.

keelboat ▸ **noun 1** a yacht built with a permanent keel rather than a centreboard.
2 a large, flat freight boat used on American rivers.

Keeler, Christine (b.1942), English model and show girl. She achieved notoriety through her affair with the Conservative cabinet minister John Profumo in 1963 when she was also mistress of a Soviet attaché. Profumo resigned and Keeler was imprisoned on related charges.

keeler ▸ **noun** [often in combination] a boat having a keel, especially one of a specified type: *a long-keeler*.

keelhaul ▸ **verb** [with obj.] historical punish (someone) by dragging them through the water under the keel of a ship, either across the width or from bow to stern. ▪ humorous punish or reprimand severely.
– ORIGIN mid 17th cent.: from Dutch *kielhalen*.

keelie¹ /'ki:li/ ▸ **noun** (pl. **keelies**) Scottish & N. English a disreputable inhabitant of a town or city, especially one from Glasgow.
– ORIGIN early 19th cent.: perhaps related to GILLIE.

keelie² /'ki:li/ ▸ **noun** (pl. **keelies**) Scottish & N. English a small hawk or falcon, such as the sparrowhawk or kestrel.
– ORIGIN early 19th cent.: perhaps imitative of its call.

Keeling Islands /'ki:lɪŋ/ another name for **COCOS ISLANDS**.

keelson /'ki:ls(ə)n/ (also **kelson**) ▸ **noun** a structure running the length of a ship and fastening the timbers or plates of the floor to its keel.
– ORIGIN Middle English *kelswayn*, related to Low German *kielswīn*, from *kiel* 'keel of a ship' + *swīn* 'swine' (used as the name of a timber).

keema /'ki:mə/ ▸ **noun** [mass noun] Indian minced meat.
– ORIGIN from Hindi *kīmā*.

Keemun /'ki:mu:n/ ▸ **noun** [mass noun] a black tea grown in Keemun, China.

keen¹ ▸ **adjective 1** chiefly Brit. having or showing eagerness or enthusiasm: *a keen gardener* | *John was keen to help*. ▪ (**keen on**) interested in or attracted by (someone or something): *Bob makes it obvious he's keen on her*.
2 sharp or penetrating, in particular: ▪ (of a sense) highly developed: *I have keen eyesight*. ▪ (of mental faculties) quick to understand: *her keen intellect*. ▪ (of the edge or point of a blade) sharp. ▪ (of the air or wind) extremely cold; biting. ▪ literary (of a smell, light, or sound) penetrating; clear.
3 Brit. (of activity or feeling) intense: *there could be keen competition to provide the service*. (of prices) very low; competitive.
4 [predic.] N. Amer. informal, dated excellent.
– PHRASES **(as) keen as mustard** Brit. informal extremely eager or enthusiastic.
– DERIVATIVES **keenly adverb**.
– ORIGIN Old English *cēne* 'wise, clever', also 'brave, daring', of Germanic origin; related to Dutch *koen* and German *kühn* 'bold, brave'. Current senses date from Middle English.

keen² ▸ **verb** [no obj.] wail in grief for a dead person. ▪ (usu. as noun **keening**) make an eerie wailing sound: *the keening of the cold night wind*.
▸ **noun** an Irish funeral song accompanied by wailing in lamentation for the dead.
– DERIVATIVES **keener noun**.
– ORIGIN mid 19th cent.: from Irish *caoinim* 'I wail'.

Keene, Charles Samuel (1823–91), English illustrator and caricaturist. He is remembered for his work in the weekly journal *Punch* from 1851.

keenness ▸ **noun** [mass noun] the quality of being eager or enthusiastic; eagerness: *he has expressed his keenness to retain his job*.

keep ▸ **verb** (past and past participle **kept** /kɛpt/) [with obj.] **1** have or retain possession of: *my father would keep the best for himself* | *she had trouble keeping her balance*. ▪ retain or reserve for future use: *return one copy to me, keeping the other for your files*. ▪ put or store in a regular place: *the stand where her umbrella was kept*.
2 continue or cause to continue in a specified condition, position, course, etc.: [no obj., with complement] *I kept quiet while Emily talked on* | *keep left along the wall* | [with obj. and complement] *she might be kept alive artificially by machinery*. ▪ [no obj., with present participle] continue doing or do repeatedly: *he keeps going on about the murder*. ▪ [no obj.] (of a perishable commodity) remain in good condition. ▪ [with obj.] retain one's place in or on (a seat or saddle, the ground, etc.) in spite of difficulty. ▪ [no obj., with adverbial] chiefly Brit. be in a specified state of health: *he had not been keeping well*. ▪ [with obj.] cause to be late; delay: *I won't keep you, I know you've got a busy evening*. ▪ [with obj. and present participle] make (someone) do something for a period of time: *I have kept her waiting too long*. ▪ archaic continue to follow (a path or course).
3 provide for the sustenance of (someone): *he had to keep his large family in the manner he had chosen*. ▪ provide (someone) with a regular supply of a commodity: *the money should* **keep** *him* **in** *cigarettes for a week*. ▪ own and look after (an animal) for pleasure or profit. ▪ own and manage (a shop or business). ▪ guard; protect: *his only thought is to* **keep** *the boy* **from** *harm*. ▪ support (someone, especially a woman) financially in return for sexual favours.
4 honour or fulfil (a commitment or undertaking): *I'll keep my promise, naturally*. ▪ observe (a religious occasion) in the prescribed manner: *today's consumers do not keep the Sabbath*. ▪ pay due regard to (a law or custom).
5 make written entries in (a diary) on a regular basis. ▪ write down as (a record): *keep a note of each item*.
▸ **noun 1** [mass noun] food, clothes, and other essentials for living: *the Society are paying for your keep*. ▪ the cost of the essentials for living.
2 [mass noun] archaic charge; control: *if from shepherd's keep a lamb strayed far*.
3 the strongest or central tower of a castle, acting as a final refuge.
– PHRASES **you can't keep a good man** (or **woman**) **down** informal a competent person will always recover well from setbacks. **for keeps** informal permanently; indefinitely. **keep one's feet** manage not to fall. **keep goal** chiefly Soccer act as a goalkeeper. **keep going** make an effort to live normally in spite of difficulty. **keep to oneself** avoid contact with others. **keep something to oneself** refuse to disclose or share something. **keep up with the Joneses** see JONESES. **keep wicket** Cricket act as a wicketkeeper.
– PHRASAL VERBS **keep at** (or **keep someone at**) persist (or force someone to persist) with: *it was the best part of a day's work but I kept at it*. **keep away** (or **keep someone away**) stay away (or make someone stay away): *keep away* **from** *the edge of the cliff*. **keep back** (or **keep someone/thing back**) remain (or cause someone or something to remain) at a distance: *he had kept back from the river when he could*. **keep someone back** N. Amer. make a pupil repeat a year at school because of poor marks. **keep something back** retain or withhold something: *he kept back £5 for himself*. ▪ decline to disclose something. **keep down** stay hidden by crouching or lying down. **keep someone down 1** make a pupil repeat a year at school because of poor marks. **2** cause someone to remain in a state of oppression or subjection. **keep something down 1** cause something to remain at a low level: *the population of aphids is normally kept down by other animals*. **2** retain food or drink in one's stomach without vomiting. **keep from** (or **keep someone from**) avoid (or cause someone to avoid) doing something: *Dinah bit her lips to keep from screaming*. **keep something from 1** cause something to remain a secret from (someone). **2** cause something to stay out of: *she could not keep the dismay from her voice*. **keep in with** remain on good terms with (someone). **keep someone in** confine someone indoors or in a particular place: *he should be kept in overnight for observation*. **keep something in** restrain oneself from expressing a feeling: *he wanted to make me mad, but I kept it all in*. **keep off 1** avoid encroaching on or touching. ▪ avoid consuming or smoking: *the first thing was to keep off alcohol*. ▪ avoid (a subject). **2** (of bad weather) fail to occur. **keep someone/thing off** prevent someone or something from encroaching on or touching: *keep your hands off me*. **keep someone off** prevent someone from attending (school). **keep on** continue to do something: *he kept on moving*. **keep on about** speak about (something) repeatedly. **keep on at** Brit. annoy (someone) by making frequent requests: *he'd kept on at her, wanting her to go out with him*. **keep someone/thing on** continue to use or employ someone or something. **keep out** (or **keep someone/thing out**) remain (or cause someone or something to remain) outside. **keep to** avoid leaving (a path, road, or place). ▪ adhere to (a schedule). ▪ observe (a promise). ▪ confine or restrict oneself to: *nothing is more irritating than people who do not keep to the point*. **keep someone under** cause someone to remain in a state of oppression or subjection: *the local people are kept under by the army*. **keep up** (also **keep up with**) **1** move or progress at the same rate as someone or something else: *often they had to pause to allow him to keep up*. **2** meet a commitment to pay or do something regularly: *if you do not* **keep up with** *the payments, the loan company can make you sell your home*. **keep up with** learn about or be aware of (current events or developments). ▪ continue to be in contact with (someone). **keep someone up** prevent someone from going to bed or to sleep. **keep something up** continue a course of action: *keep up the good work*. ▪ keep something in an efficient or proper state: *the rector could not afford to keep up the grounds*. ▪ make something remain at a high level: *he was whistling to keep up his spirits*.
– DERIVATIVES **keepable adjective**.
– ORIGIN late Old English *cēpan* 'seize, take in', also 'care for, attend to', of unknown origin.

keeper ▸ **noun 1** a person who manages or looks after something or someone. ▪ a custodian of a museum or gallery collection. ▪ an animal attendant employed in a zoo. ▪ short for GAMEKEEPER.
2 short for GOALKEEPER or WICKETKEEPER.
3 a plain ring worn to preserve a hole in a pierced ear lobe; a sleeper. ▪ a ring worn to keep a more valuable one on the finger. ▪ a bar of soft iron placed across the poles of a horseshoe magnet to maintain its strength.
4 [with adj.] a food or drink that remains in a specified condition if stored: *hazelnuts are good keepers*.
5 a fish large enough to be kept when caught. ▪ informal a person or thing that is valuable and to be cherished: *this disc is a keeper and one that belongs on every serious DVD collector's shelf* | *if he's a good communicator and a great listener, he's a keeper*.
6 American Football a play in which the quarterback receives the ball from the centre and runs with it.
– DERIVATIVES **keepership noun**.

keep-fit ▸ **noun** [mass noun] chiefly Brit. regular exercises to improve personal fitness and health.

keeping ▸ **noun** [mass noun] the action or fact of owning, maintaining, or protecting something: *the keeping of dogs* | [in combination] *careful record-keeping is needed*.
– PHRASES **in someone's keeping** in someone's care or custody. **in** (or **out of**) **keeping with** in (or out of) harmony or conformity with: *the cuisine is in keeping with the hotel's Edwardian character*.

keepnet ▸ **noun** Fishing a net for keeping fish alive until they are returned to the water.

keepsake ▸ **noun** a small item kept in memory of the person who gave it or originally owned it.

keeshond /'keɪshɒnd/ ▸ **noun** a dog of a Dutch breed with long thick grey hair, resembling a large Pomeranian.
– ORIGIN 1920s: Dutch, from *Kees* (pet form of the given name *Cornelius*) + *hond* 'dog'.

keester /'ki:stə/ ▸ **noun** variant spelling of KEISTER.

kef /kɛf/ ▸ **noun & adjective** variant spelling of KIF.

Kefallinía /ˌkɛfali'nia/ Greek name for **CEPHALONIA**.

keffiyeh /kə'fi:(j)ə/ (also **kaffiyeh**) ▸ **noun** a headdress worn by Arab men, consisting of a square of fabric fastened by a band round the crown of the head.
– ORIGIN early 19th cent.: from Arabic *keffiyya*, *kūfiyya*.

Keflavik /'kɛfləvɪk/ a fishing port in SW Iceland; pop. 14,183 (2009). Iceland's international airport is located nearby.

K

keftedes /kɛfˈtɛðiːz/ ▶ **plural noun** (in Greek cookery) small meatballs made with herbs and onions.
– ORIGIN from Greek *kephtedes*, plural of *kephtes*, via Turkish from Persian *koftah* (see **KOFTA**).

keg ▶ **noun** a small barrel, especially one of less than 10 gallons or (in the US) 30 gallons. ■ Brit. short for **KEG BEER**.
– ORIGIN early 17th cent.: variant of Scots and US dialect *cag*, from Old Norse *kaggi*.

keg beer ▶ **noun** [mass noun] Brit. beer supplied in a keg, to which carbon dioxide has been added.

Kegel exercises /ˈkeɪɡ(ə)l/ ▶ **plural noun** exercises performed to strengthen a woman's pelvic floor muscles.
– ORIGIN 1950s: named after the US physician Dr Arnold *Kegel* (1894–1976), who developed the exercises.

kegger ▶ **noun** US informal a party at which beer is served, typically from kegs. ■ a keg of beer.

keiretsu /keɪˈrɛtsuː/ ▶ **noun** (pl. **same**) (in Japan) a conglomeration of businesses linked together by cross-shareholdings to form a robust corporate structure.
– ORIGIN Japanese, from *kei* 'systems' + *retsu* 'tier'.

keirin /keɪˈrɪn/ ▶ **noun** [mass noun] Cycling a racing event in which cyclists ride several laps around an indoor track behind a motorized pacemaker before sprinting to the finish.
– ORIGIN 1950s: Japanese, literally 'bicycle race'.

keister /ˈkiːstə/ (also **keester**) ▶ **noun** N. Amer. informal
1 a person's buttocks.
2 dated a suitcase, bag, or box for carrying possessions or merchandise.
– ORIGIN late 19th cent. (in sense 2): of unknown origin.

K

keitai /ˈkeɪtʌɪ/ ▶ **noun** (pl. **same** or **keitais**) (in Japan) a mobile phone.
– ORIGIN Japanese, literally 'portable', short for *keitai denwa* 'mobile phone'.

Kejia /keɪˈdʒjɑː/ ▶ **noun** another term for **HAKKA**.

Kekulé /ˈkɛkjʊleɪ/, German /ˈkeːkule/, Friedrich August (1829–96), German chemist; full name *Friedrich August Kekulé von Stradonitz*. One of the founders of structural organic chemistry, he is best known for discovering the ring structure of benzene.

Kelantan /kəˈlantən/ a state of northern Malaysia, on the east coast of the Malay Peninsula; capital, Kota Baharu.

kelim ▶ **noun** variant spelling of **KILIM**.

Keller /ˈkɛlə/, Helen (Adams) (1880–1968), American writer, social reformer, and academic. Blind and deaf from the age of nineteen months, she learned how to read, type, and speak with the help of a tutor. She went on to champion the cause of blind and deaf people throughout the world.

Kellogg /ˈkɛlɒɡ/, Will Keith (1860–1951), American food manufacturer. He collaborated with his brother, a doctor, to develop a breakfast cereal for sanatorium patients, of crisp flakes of rolled and toasted wheat and corn. Its success led to the establishment of the W. K. Kellogg company in 1906.

Kellogg Pact (also **Kellogg–Briand Pact**) a treaty renouncing war as an instrument of national policy, signed in Paris in 1928 by representatives of fifteen nations. It grew out of a proposal made by the French Premier Aristide Briand (1862–1932) to Frank B. Kellogg (1856–1937), US Secretary of State.

Kells, Book of /kɛlz/ an illuminated manuscript of the Gospels, perhaps made by Irish monks in Iona in the 8th or early 9th century, now kept at Trinity College, Dublin.
– ORIGIN *Kells*, the name of a town in County Meath, Ireland, where the manuscript was formerly kept.

Kelly[1], Ned (1855–80), Australian outlaw; full name *Edward Kelly*. Leader of a band of horse and cattle thieves and bank raiders operating in Victoria, he was eventually hanged in Melbourne.

Kelly[2], Gene (1912–96), American dancer and choreographer; full name *Eugene Curran Kelly*. He performed in and choreographed many film musicals, including *An American in Paris* (1951) and *Singin' in the Rain* (1952).

Kelly[3], Grace (Patricia) (1928–82), American film actress; also called (from 1956) **Princess Grace of Monaco**. She starred in *High Noon* (1952) and also made three Hitchcock films, including *Rear Window* (1954), before retiring from films in 1956 on her marriage to Prince Rainier III of Monaco. She died in a road accident.

keloid /ˈkiːlɔɪd/ ▶ **noun** Medicine an area of irregular fibrous tissue formed at the site of a scar or injury.
– ORIGIN mid 19th cent.: via French from Greek *khēlē* 'crab's claw' + **-OID**.

kelp ▶ **noun** [mass noun] a large brown seaweed that typically has a long, tough stalk with a broad frond divided into strips. ● Family Laminariaceae, class Phaeophyceae, including the genera *Laminaria* (used in some areas as manure) and *Macrocystis* (harvested in the US as a source of algin).
■ the calcined ashes of seaweed, used as a source of various salts.
– ORIGIN late Middle English: of unknown origin.

kelpfish ▶ **noun** (pl. **same** or **kelpfishes**) any of a number of fish that live among kelp or other marine algae, in particular: ● a small fish with the dorsal fin running the length of the body, of the Pacific coast of North America (*Gibbonsia* and other genera, family Clinidae). ● an Australian fish which lives among seagrass and algae (family Chironemidae: several genera).

kelpie /ˈkɛlpi/ ▶ **noun** **1** a water spirit of Scottish folklore, typically taking the form of a horse and reputed to delight in the drowning of travellers.
2 a sheepdog of an Australian breed with a smooth coat, originally bred from a Scottish collie.
– ORIGIN late 17th cent.: perhaps from Scottish Gaelic *cailpeach, colpach* 'bullock, colt'. Sense 2 apparently comes from the name of a particular bitch, *King's Kelpie* (c.1879).

kelson /ˈkɛls(ə)n/ ▶ **noun** variant spelling of **KEELSON**.

kelt ▶ **noun** a salmon or sea trout after spawning and before returning to the sea.
– ORIGIN Middle English: of unknown origin.

Kelvin, William Thomson, 1st Baron (1824–1907), British physicist and natural philosopher. He is best known for introducing the absolute scale of temperature. He also restated the second law of thermodynamics and was involved in the laying of the first Atlantic cable, for which he invented several instruments.

kelvin (abbrev.: **K**) ▶ **noun** (pl. **same** or **kelvins**) the SI base unit of thermodynamic temperature, equal in magnitude to the degree Celsius.
– ORIGIN late 19th cent.: named after Lord **KELVIN**.

Kelvin scale ▶ **noun** a scale of temperature with absolute zero as zero, and the triple point of water as exactly 273.16 degrees.

Kemal Pasha /kɛˈmɑːl ˌpɑːʃə/ see **ATATÜRK**.

Kemble[1] /ˈkɛmb(ə)l/, Fanny (1809–93), English actress; full name *Frances Anne Kemble*. The daughter of Charles Kemble and the niece of Sarah Siddons, she was a success in both Shakespearean comedy and tragedy.

Kemble[2] /ˈkɛmb(ə)l/, John Philip (1757–1823), English actor-manager, brother of Sarah Siddons. Noted for his performances in Shakespearean tragedy, he was manager of Drury Lane (1788–1803) and Covent Garden (1803–17) theatres. His younger brother **Charles Kemble** (1775–1854) was also a successful actor-manager.

Kemerovo /ˈkɛmɪrəvə/ an industrial city in south central Russia, to the east of Novosibirsk; pop. 515,100 (est. 2009).

kemp ▶ **noun** a coarse hair or fibre in wool.
– ORIGIN late Middle English (originally denoting a coarse human hair): from Old Norse *kampr* 'beard, whisker'.

Kempe, Margery (c.1373–c.1440), English mystic. From about 1432 to 1436 she dictated one of the first autobiographies in English, *The Book of Margery Kempe*. It gives an account of her series of pilgrimages, as well as details of her mystic self-transcendent visions.

Kempis, Thomas à, see **THOMAS À KEMPIS**.

kempt ▶ **adjective** (of a person or a place) maintained in a neat and clean condition; well cared for: *she was looking as thoroughly kempt as ever*.
– ORIGIN Old English *cemd-*, past participle of *cemban* 'to comb', of Germanic origin; related to **COMB**. The Middle English form *kemb* survives in dialect.

ken ▶ **noun** [in sing.] one's range of knowledge or understanding: *politics are **beyond my ken***.
▶ **verb** (**kens, kenning**; past and past participle **kenned** or **kent**) [with obj.] Scottish & N. English know: *d'ye ken anyone who can boast of that?* ■ recognize; identify: *that's him—d'ye ken him?*
– ORIGIN Old English *cennan* 'tell, make known', of Germanic origin; related to Dutch and German *kennen* 'know, be acquainted with', from an Indo-European root shared by **CAN**[1] and **KNOW**. Current senses of the verb date from Middle English; the noun from the mid 16th cent.

kenaf /kəˈnaf/ ▶ **noun** [mass noun] a brown plant fibre similar to jute, used to make ropes and coarse cloth.
– ORIGIN late 19th cent.: from Persian, variant of *kanab* 'hemp'.

Kendal /ˈkɛnd(ə)l/ a town in Cumbria, NW England; pop. 31,100 (est. 2009).

Kendal Green ▶ **noun** [mass noun] a kind of rough green woollen cloth. ■ the green colour of Kendal Green cloth.

Kendall /ˈkɛnd(ə)l/, Edward Calvin (1886–1972), American biochemist. He isolated crystalline thyroxine from the thyroid gland, and from the adrenal cortex he obtained a number of steroid hormones, one of which was later named cortisone. Nobel Prize for Physiology or Medicine (1950).

Kendal mint cake ▶ **noun** [mass noun] a hard peppermint-flavoured sweet which is sold in flat rectangular blocks and is popular with ramblers and hill climbers.

kendo /ˈkɛndəʊ/ ▶ **noun** [mass noun] a Japanese form of fencing with two-handed bamboo swords, originally developed as a safe form of sword training for samurai.
– DERIVATIVES **kendoist** noun.
– ORIGIN Japanese, from *ken* 'sword' + *dō* 'way'.

Keneally /kəˈnali, -ˈniːli/, Thomas (Michael) (b.1935), Australian novelist. He first gained recognition for *The Chant of Jimmie Blacksmith* (1972), but is probably best known for his Booker Prize-winning novel *Schindler's Ark* (1982), filmed by Steven Spielberg in 1993 as *Schindler's List*.

Kennedy the name of a family of US Democratic politicians: ■ **John F.** (1917–63), 35th President of the US 1961–3; in full *John Fitzgerald Kennedy*; known as **JFK**. The youngest man ever to be elected US President (at 43), he was a popular advocate of civil rights. In foreign affairs he recovered from the Bay of Pigs fiasco to demand successfully the withdrawal of Soviet missiles from Cuba (the Cuban Missile Crisis). Kennedy was assassinated while riding in a motorcade through Dallas, Texas. ■ **Robert** (1925–68), US Attorney General 1961–4; full name *Robert Francis Kennedy*. He closely assisted his brother John in domestic policy, and was also a champion of the civil rights movement. He was assassinated during his campaign as a prospective presidential candidate. ■ **Ted** (1932–2009), brother of John and Robert, US Senator since 1962; full name *Edward Moore Kennedy*. His political career was overshadowed by his involvement in a car accident at Chappaquiddick Island (1969), in which his assistant Mary Jo Kopechne drowned.

Kennedy, Cape former name (1963–73) for **CANAVERAL, CAPE**.

kennel ▶ **noun** a small shelter for a dog. ■ (usu. **kennels**) [treated as sing. or pl.] a boarding or breeding establishment for dogs.
▶ **verb** (**kennels, kennelling, kennelled**; US **kennels, kenneling, kenneled**) [with obj.] put (a dog) in a kennel or kennels.
– ORIGIN Middle English: from an Old Northern French variant of Old French *chenil*, from Latin *canis* 'dog'.

Kennelly /ˈkɛnəli/, Arthur Edwin (1861–1939), American electrical engineer. His principal work was on the theory of alternating currents. Independently of Oliver Heaviside, he also discovered the layer in the atmosphere responsible for reflecting radio waves back to the earth.

Kennelly layer (also **Kennelly–Heaviside layer**) ▶ **noun** another name for **E-LAYER**.

kennelmaid ▶ **noun** a woman who works in a kennels.

kennelman ▶ **noun** (pl. **kennelmen**) a man who works in a kennels, especially for a hunt.

Kenneth I (d.858), king of Scotland c.844–58; known as **Kenneth MacAlpin**. He is traditionally viewed as the founder of the kingdom of Scotland, which was established following his defeat of the Picts in about 844.

kenning ▶ **noun** a compound expression in Old English and Old Norse poetry with metaphorical meaning, e.g. *oar-steed* = ship.
– ORIGIN late 19th cent.: from Old Norse, from *kenna* 'know, perceive'; related to **KEN**.

keno /ˈkiːnəʊ/ ▶ **noun** [mass noun] a game of chance similar to bingo, based on the drawing of numbers and covering of corresponding numbers on cards.
– ORIGIN early 19th cent.: from French *quine*, denoting a set of five winning lottery numbers.

kenosis /kɪˈnəʊsɪs/ ▶ **noun** [mass noun] (in Christian theology) the renunciation of the divine nature, at least in part, by Christ in the Incarnation.
– DERIVATIVES **kenotic** adjective.
– ORIGIN late 19th cent.: from Greek *kenōsis* 'an emptying', from *kenoein* 'to empty', from *kenos* 'empty', with biblical allusion (Phil. 2:7) to Greek *heauton ekenōse*, literally 'emptied himself'.

Kensington /ˈkɛnzɪŋtən/ a fashionable residential district in central London. Part of the borough of Kensington and Chelsea, it contains Kensington Palace, Kensington Gardens, and the Victoria and Albert Museum, Natural History Museum, and Science Museum.

kenspeckle /ˈkɛnˌspɛk(ə)l/ ▶ **adjective** Scottish easily recognizable; conspicuous.
– ORIGIN mid 16th cent.: of Scandinavian origin, probably based on Old Norse *kenna* 'know, perceive' and *spak-*, *spek-* 'wise or wisdom'.

Kent[1] a county on the SE coast of England; county town, Maidstone.
– DERIVATIVES **Kentish** adjective.
– ORIGIN from Latin *Cantium*, of Celtic origin.

Kent[2], William (*c*.1685–1748), English architect and landscape gardener. Chiefly remembered for his landscape gardens at Stowe House in Buckinghamshire (*c*.1730), he also promoted the Palladian style of architecture in England.

kent past and past participle of KEN.

kente /ˈkɛntə/ ▶ **noun** [mass noun] a brightly coloured cloth consisting of separate strips sewn together, made in Ghana. ■ [count noun] a long garment made from kente, worn loosely around the shoulders and waist.
– ORIGIN from Akan, literally 'cloth'.

kentia palm /ˈkɛntɪə/ (also **kentia**) ▶ **noun** an Australasian palm tree which is popular as a houseplant while it is young. ● *Howeia* (or *Howea*, formerly *Kentia*) *forsteriana*, family Palmae.
– ORIGIN late 19th cent.: modern Latin, named after William *Kent* (died 1828), botanical collector.

Kentish glory ▶ **noun** a large European moth with orange-brown and white markings, occurring chiefly on moorland and in open woodland. ● *Endromis versicolora*, the only member of the family Endromidae.

Kentish plover ▶ **noun** a small white-breasted plover related to the ringed plover, found on most continents. ● *Charadrius alexandrinus*, family Charadriidae; American races are sometimes treated as a different species. North American name: **snowy plover**.
– ORIGIN early 19th cent.: so named because of its first discovery in Kent, but now extinct in Britain.

Kentish ragstone (also **Kentish rag**) ▶ **noun** [mass noun] a hard, compact limestone found in Kent, used for paving and building.

Kentucky /kɛnˈtʌki/ a state in the south-eastern US; pop. 4,269,245 (est. 2008); capital, Frankfort. Ceded by the French to the British in 1763, Kentucky entered the Union as the 15th state in 1792.
– DERIVATIVES **Kentuckian** adjective.

Kentucky Derby ▶ **noun** an annual horse race for three-year-olds at Louisville, Kentucky. First held in 1875, it is the oldest horse race in the US.

Kenya /ˈkɛnjə/ an equatorial country in East Africa, on the Indian Ocean; pop. 39,002,800 (est. 2009); languages, Swahili (official), English (official), Kikuyu; capital, Nairobi.

> Populated largely by Bantu-speaking peoples, Kenya became a British Crown Colony in 1920. The demands made on land by European settlers led to the Mau Mau rebellion of the 1950s. Kenya became an independent state within the Commonwealth in 1963, and a republic was established the following year.

– DERIVATIVES **Kenyan** adjective & noun.

Kenya, Mount a mountain in central Kenya, just south of the equator, rising to a height of 5,200 m (17,058 ft). The second-highest mountain in Africa, it gave its name to the country Kenya.

Kenya African National Union (abbrev.: **KANU**) a Kenyan political party formed in 1960 and led first by Jomo Kenyatta. KANU won the first Kenyan elections and took the country into independence in 1963; it has since dominated Kenyan politics, ruling as the sole legal party 1982–91.

Kenyatta /kɛnˈjatə/, Jomo (*c*.1891–1978), Kenyan statesman, Prime Minister of Kenya 1963 and President 1964–78. Imprisoned for alleged complicity in the Mau Mau uprising (1952–61), on his release he was elected president of the Kenya African National Union and led Kenya to independence in 1963, subsequently serving as its first President.

kep /kɛp/ ▶ **verb** (**keps**, **kepping**, **kepped**) [with obj.] Scottish & N. English catch.
– ORIGIN late Middle English (originally in the sense 'meet, receive the force of a blow'): differentiated form of the verb KEEP.

kepi /ˈkɛpi, ˈkeɪpi/ ▶ **noun** (pl. **kepis**) a French military cap with a horizontal peak.
– ORIGIN mid 19th cent.: from French *képi*, from Swiss German *Käppi*, diminutive of *Kappe* 'cap'.

Kepler /ˈkɛplə/, German /ˈkɛplɐ/, Johannes (1571–1630), German astronomer. His analysis of Tycho Brahe's planetary observations led him to discover the three laws governing orbital motion.
– DERIVATIVES **Keplerian** adjective.

Kepler's laws ▶ **plural noun** Astronomy three theorems describing orbital motion. The first law states that planets move in elliptical orbits with the sun at one focus. The second states that the radius vector of a planet sweeps out equal areas in equal times. The third law relates the distances of the planets from the sun to their orbital periods.

kept past and past participle of KEEP.

Kerala /ˈkɛrələ/ a state on the coast of SW India; capital, Thiruvananthapuram. It was created in 1956 from the former state of Travancore-Cochin and part of Madras.
– DERIVATIVES **Keralite** adjective & noun.

kerat- ▶ **combining form** variant spelling of KERATO- shortened before a vowel (as in *keratectomy*).

keratectomy /ˌkɛrəˈtɛktəmi/ ▶ **noun** [mass noun] surgical removal of a section or layer of the cornea, usually performed using a laser to correct myopia.

keratin /ˈkɛrətɪn/ ▶ **noun** [mass noun] a fibrous protein forming the main structural constituent of hair, feathers, hoofs, claws, horns, etc.
– ORIGIN mid 19th cent.: from Greek *keras*, *kerat-* 'horn' + -IN[1].

keratinize /ˈkɛrətɪnʌɪz, kəˈrat-/ (also **keratinise**) ▶ **verb** Biology change or become changed into a form containing keratin: [with obj.] *the products of the epidermal line are ultimately keratinized* | [no obj.] *the cells keratinize under oestrogenic action.*
– DERIVATIVES **keratinization** noun.
– ORIGIN late 19th cent.: from Greek *keratinos* 'horny' + -IZE.

keratinocyte /ˌkɛrəˈtɪnə(ʊ)sʌɪt/ ▶ **noun** Biology an epidermal cell which produces keratin.

keratinous /kəˈratɪnəs/ ▶ **adjective** Biology containing or made from keratin.

keratitis /ˌkɛrəˈtʌɪtɪs/ ▶ **noun** [mass noun] Medicine inflammation of the cornea of the eye.

kerato- (also **kerat-**) ▶ **combining form 1** relating to keratin or horny tissue.
2 relating to the cornea.
– ORIGIN from Greek *keras*, *kerat-* 'horn'.

keratomileusis /ˌkɛrətəʊmʌɪˈluːsɪs/ ▶ **noun** [mass noun] the surgical reshaping of the cornea, carried out in order to correct a refractive error.
– ORIGIN 1990s: from KERATO- + Greek *smileusis* 'carving'.

keratoplasty /ˈkɛrətə(ʊ)ˌplasti/ ▶ **noun** [mass noun] Medicine surgery carried out on the cornea, especially corneal transplantation.

keratosis /ˌkɛrəˈtəʊsɪs/ ▶ **noun** (pl. **keratoses**) Medicine a horny growth, especially on the skin.

keratotomy /ˌkɛrəˈtɒtəmi/ ▶ **noun** [mass noun] a surgical operation involving cutting into the cornea of the eye. The most common form is **radial keratotomy**, performed to correct myopia.

kerb (US **curb**) ▶ **noun** a stone edging to a pavement or raised path.
– ORIGIN mid 17th cent. (denoting a raised border or frame): variant of CURB.

kerb-crawling ▶ **noun** [mass noun] Brit. the action or practice of driving slowly along the edge of the road in search of a prostitute.
– DERIVATIVES **kerb-crawler** noun.

kerb drill ▶ **noun** Brit. a set of precautions, especially looking to right and left, taken before crossing the road and typically taught to children.

kerbing ▶ **noun** [mass noun] **1** the stones collectively forming a kerb.
2 the action of hitting a kerb with a car tyre, leading to possible damage to the tyre.

kerb market ▶ **noun** a market for selling shares not dealt with on the normal stock exchange, or for dealing after hours.

kerbside (US **curbside**) ▶ **noun** the side of a road or pavement that is nearer to the kerb.

kerbstone (US **curbstone**) ▶ **noun** a long, narrow stone or concrete block, laid end to end with others to form a kerb.

kerb weight ▶ **noun** the weight of a car without occupants or baggage.

Kerch /kəːtʃ/ a city in southern Ukraine, the chief port and industrial centre of the Crimea, at the eastern end of the Kerch peninsula; pop. 148,100 (est. 2009).

kerchief /ˈkəːtʃɪf/ ▶ **noun** a piece of fabric used to cover the head. ■ literary a handkerchief.
– DERIVATIVES **kerchiefed** adjective.
– ORIGIN Middle English *kerchef*, from Old French *cuevrechief*, from *couvrir* 'to cover' + *chief* 'head'.

kereru /ˈkɛrəruː/ ▶ **noun** NZ a New Zealand pigeon which has mainly greenish metallic plumage with white underparts and a purplish-crimson bill and feet. ● *Hemiphaga novaeseelandiae*, family Columbidae. Alternative name: **New Zealand pigeon**.
– ORIGIN late 19th cent.: from Maori.

Keres /ˈkɛrɛs/ ▶ **noun** (pl. **same**) **1** a member of a Pueblo Indian people inhabiting parts of New Mexico.
2 [mass noun] the language of the Keres, of unknown affinity, with fewer than 8,000 speakers.
▶ **adjective** relating to the Keres or their language.
– DERIVATIVES **Keresan** noun & adjective.
– ORIGIN from American Spanish *Queres*, from American Indian.

K

kerf /kəːf/ ▶ **noun 1** a slit made by cutting with a saw.
2 the cut end of a felled tree.
– DERIVATIVES **kerfed** adjective.
– ORIGIN Old English *cyrf* 'cutting, a cut', of West Germanic origin; related to CARVE.

kerfuffle /kəˈfʌf(ə)l/ ▶ **noun** [in sing.] Brit. informal a commotion or fuss, especially one caused by conflicting views: *there was a kerfuffle over the chairmanship.*
– ORIGIN early 19th cent.: perhaps from Scots *curfuffle* (probably from Scottish Gaelic *car* 'twist, bend' + imitative Scots *fuffle* 'to disorder'), or related to Irish *cior thual* 'confusion, disorder'.

Kerguelen Islands /ˈkəːgɪlɪn, kəːˈgeɪlən/ a group of islands in the southern Indian Ocean, comprising the island of Kerguelen and some 300 small islets, forming part of French Southern and Antarctic Territories.
– ORIGIN named after the Breton navigator Yves-Joseph de *Kerguélen*-Trémarec, who discovered the islands in 1772.

Kérkira /ˈkɛrkɪrə/ modern Greek name for CORFU.

Kerkrade /ˈkəːkrɑːdə/ a mining town in the southern Netherlands, on the German border; pop. 48,334 (2008). An international music competition is held there every four years.

Kermadec Islands /kəːˈmadək/ a group of uninhabited islands in the western South Pacific, north of New Zealand, administered by New Zealand since 1887.

kermes /ˈkəːmɪz/ ▶ **noun 1** [mass noun] a red dye obtained from the crushed dried bodies of a female scale insect, used for colouring fabrics and manuscripts.
2 (**oak kermes**) the scale insect from which kermes is obtained, forming berry-like galls on the kermes oak. ● *Kermes illicis*, family Eriococcidae, suborder Homoptera.
– ORIGIN late 16th cent. (denoting the kermes oak): from French *kermès*, from Arabic *qirmiz*; related to CRIMSON.

kermes oak ▶ **noun** a very small evergreen Mediterranean oak which sometimes remains as a shrub. It has prickly holly-like leaves and was formerly prized as a host plant for kermes insects. ● *Quercus coccifera*, family Fagaceae.

kermis /ˈkəːmɪs/ ▶ **noun** a summer fair held in towns and villages in the Netherlands. ■ US a fair or carnival, especially one held to raise money for a charity.
– ORIGIN late 16th cent.: Dutch, originally denoting a mass on the anniversary of the dedication of a church, when a fair was held, from *kerk* 'church' + *mis* 'Mass'.

Kern, Jerome (David) (1885–1945), American composer. A major influence in the development of the musical, he wrote several musical comedies, including *Showboat* (1927).

kern[1] Printing ▶ **verb** [with obj.] **1** (usu. as noun **kerning**) adjust the spacing between (characters) in a piece of text to be printed.
2 provide (metal type or a printed character) with a kern.
▶ **noun** the part of a metal type projecting beyond the body or shank, or a part of a printed character that overlaps its neighbours.
– ORIGIN late 17th cent.: perhaps from French *carne* 'corner', from Latin *cardo*, *cardin-* 'hinge'.

kern[2] (also **kerne**) ▶ **noun 1** historical a light-armed Irish foot soldier.
2 archaic a peasant; a rustic.
– ORIGIN late Middle English: from Irish *ceithearn*, from Old Irish *ceithern* 'band of foot soldiers'.

kernel /ˈkəːn(ə)l/ ▶ **noun 1** a softer, usually edible part of a nut, seed, or fruit stone contained within its shell. ■ the seed and hard husk of a cereal, especially wheat.
2 the central or most important part of something: *this is the kernel of the argument*. ■ Computing the most basic level or core of an operating system, responsible for resource allocation, file management, and security. ■ [as modifier] Linguistics denoting a basic unmarked linguistic string.
– ORIGIN Old English *cyrnel*, diminutive of CORN[1].

kernite /ˈkəːnʌɪt/ ▶ **noun** [mass noun] a transparent crystalline mineral which consists of hydrated sodium borate and is a major source of borax.
– ORIGIN early 20th cent.: from *Kern* (the name of the Californian county where it was discovered) + -ITE[1].

Kernow /ˈkəːnəʊ/ ▶ **noun** Cornish name for CORNWALL.

kerogen /ˈkɛrədʒ(ə)n/ ▶ **noun** [mass noun] a complex fossilized organic material, found in oil shale and other sedimentary rock, which is insoluble in common organic solvents and yields petroleum products on distillation.
– ORIGIN early 20th cent.: from Greek *kēros* 'wax' + -GEN.

kerosene /ˈkɛrəsiːn/ (also **kerosine**) ▶ **noun** [mass noun] chiefly N. Amer. a light fuel oil obtained by distilling petroleum, used especially in jet engines and domestic heating boilers; paraffin oil.
– ORIGIN mid 19th cent.: from Greek *kēros* 'wax' (because the solid form of paraffin is wax-like) + -ENE.

Kerouac /ˈkɛrʊak/, Jack (1922–69), American novelist and poet, of French-Canadian descent; born *Jean-Louis Lebris de Kérouac*. A leading figure of the beat generation, he is best known for his semi-autobiographical novel *On the Road* (1957).

Kerr effect /kəː/ ▶ **noun** Physics **1** the rotation of the plane of polarization of light when reflected from a magnetized surface.
2 the production of double refraction in a substance by an electric field.
– ORIGIN early 20th cent.: named after John *Kerr* (1824–1907), the Scottish physicist who studied these effects.

kerria /ˈkɛrɪə/ ▶ **noun** an East Asian shrub of the rose family, which is cultivated for its yellow flowers, especially as the double-flowered variety. ● *Kerria japonica*, family Rosaceae.
– ORIGIN early 19th cent.: modern Latin, named after William *Ker(r)* (died 1814), English botanical collector.

Kerry[1] a county of the Republic of Ireland, on the SW coast in the province of Munster; county town, Tralee.

Kerry[2] ▶ **noun** (pl. **Kerries**) an animal of a breed of small black dairy cattle.

Kerry blue ▶ **noun** a terrier of a breed with a silky blue-grey coat.

Kerry Hill ▶ **noun** a sheep of a breed having a thick fleece and black markings near the muzzle and feet.
– ORIGIN early 20th cent.: from *Kerry*, the name of a town and neighbouring hill range in Powys, Wales.

kersey /ˈkəːzi/ ▶ **noun** [mass noun] a kind of coarse, ribbed cloth with a short nap, woven from short-stapled wool.
– ORIGIN late Middle English: probably from *Kersey*, a town in Suffolk where woollen cloth was made.

kerseymere /ˈkəːzɪmɪə/ ▶ **noun** [mass noun] a fine twilled woollen cloth.
– ORIGIN late 18th cent.: alteration of *cassimere*, variant of CASHMERE, changed by association with KERSEY.

keruing /ˈkɛrʊɪŋ/ ▶ **noun** a timber tree related to the gurjun, growing in Malaysia, Sabah, and Indonesia. ● Genus *Dipterocarpus*, family Dipterocarpaceae: several species.
– ORIGIN early 20th cent.: from Malay.

kesh /keɪʃ/ (also **kes**) ▶ **noun** [mass noun] the uncut hair and beard worn as one of the five distinguishing signs of the Sikh Khalsa.
– ORIGIN from Punjabi *keś*.

kestrel ▶ **noun** a small falcon that hovers with rapidly beating wings while searching for prey on the ground. ● Genus *Falco*, family Falconidae: several species, in particular the **common kestrel** (*F. tinnunculus*) of Eurasia and Africa, and the **American kestrel** (*F. sparverius*).
– ORIGIN late Middle English *castrel*, perhaps from *casserelle*, dialect variant of Old French *crecerelle*, perhaps imitative of its call.

Keswick /ˈkɛzɪk/ a market town and tourist centre on the northern shores of Derwent Water in Cumbria, NW England; pop. 5,000 (est. 2009).

ketamine /ˈkiːtəmiːn/ ▶ **noun** [mass noun] a synthetic compound used as an anaesthetic and analgesic drug and also (illicitly) as a hallucinogen. ● Chem. formula: $C_{13}H_{16}NOCl$.
– ORIGIN 1960s: blend of KETONE and AMINE.

ketch ▶ **noun** a two-masted, fore-and-aft rigged sailing boat with a mizzenmast stepped forward of the rudder and smaller than its foremast.
– ORIGIN mid 17th cent.: later form of obsolete *catch*, probably from CATCH.

ketchup /ˈkɛtʃəp, -ʌp/ (US also **catsup**) ▶ **noun** [mass noun] a spicy sauce made chiefly from tomatoes and vinegar, used as a relish.
– ORIGIN late 17th cent.: perhaps from Chinese (Cantonese dialect) *k'ē chap* 'tomato juice'.

ketene /ˈkiːtiːn/ ▶ **noun** [mass noun] Chemistry a pungent colourless reactive gas, used as an intermediate in chemical synthesis. ● Chem. formula: $CH_2{=}C{=}O$.
– ORIGIN early 20th cent.: from KETONE + -ENE.

keto acid /ˈkiːtəʊ/ ▶ **noun** Chemistry a compound whose molecule contains both a carboxyl group (–COOH) and a ketone group (–CO–).

ketonaemia /ˌkiːtə(ʊ)ˈniːmɪə/ (US **ketonemia**) ▶ **noun** [mass noun] Medicine the presence of an abnormally high concentration of ketone bodies in the blood.

ketone /ˈkiːtəʊn/ ▶ **noun** Chemistry an organic compound containing a carbonyl group =C=O bonded to two hydrocarbon groups, made by oxidizing secondary alcohols. The simplest such compound is acetone.
– DERIVATIVES **ketonic** /kɪˈtɒnɪk/ **adjective**.
– ORIGIN mid 19th cent.: from German *Keton*, alteration of *Aketon* 'acetone'.

ketone bodies ▶ **plural noun** Biochemistry three related compounds (one of which is acetone) produced during the metabolism of fats.

ketonuria /ˌkiːtə(ʊ)ˈnjʊərɪə/ ▶ **noun** [mass noun] Medicine the excretion of abnormally large amounts of ketone bodies in the urine, characteristic of diabetes mellitus, starvation, or other medical conditions.

ketosis /kɪˈtəʊsɪs/ ▶ **noun** [mass noun] Medicine a condition characterized by raised levels of ketone bodies in the body, associated with abnormal fat metabolism and diabetes mellitus.
– DERIVATIVES **ketotic adjective**.

kettle ▶ **noun 1** a metal or plastic container with a lid, spout, and handle, used for boiling water.
2 a bowl- or saucer-shaped container in which operations are carried out on metals or other substances with a low melting point.
– PHRASES **a different kettle of fish** informal a completely different type of person or thing from the one previously mentioned: *he's certainly a different kettle of fish from old Rowell*. **the pot calling the kettle black** see POT[1]. **a pretty** (or **fine**) **kettle of fish** informal an awkward state of affairs.
– DERIVATIVES **kettleful noun** (pl. **kettlefuls**).
– ORIGIN Old English *cetel*, *cietel*, of Germanic origin, based on Latin *catillus*, diminutive of *catinus* 'deep container for cooking or serving food'. In Middle English the word's form was influenced by Old Norse *ketill*.

kettlebell ▶ **noun** Weightlifting a large cast-iron ball-shaped weight with a single handle.

kettledrum ▶ **noun** a large drum shaped like a bowl, with a membrane adjustable for tension (and so pitch) stretched across. Also collectively called TIMPANI.

kettle hole ▶ **noun** Geology a hollow, typically filled by a lake, resulting from the melting of a mass of ice trapped in glacial deposits.

kettling ▶ **noun** [mass noun] a method used by police to maintain order during a large demonstration by confining demonstrators to a small area.

Keuper /ˈkɔɪpə/ ▶ **noun** [mass noun] Geology a European series of sedimentary rocks of Upper Triassic age, represented in England chiefly by marls and sandstones.
– ORIGIN mid 19th cent. (originally a miners' term): German.

keurboom /ˈkɪəbʊəm/ ▶ **noun** S. African a small southern African tree which typically bears drooping clusters of scented mauve flowers. ● Genus *Virgilia*, family Leguminosae.
– ORIGIN early 18th cent.: from Afrikaans, from *keur* 'choice' + *boom* 'tree'.

keV ▶ **abbreviation** kilo-electronvolt(s).

kevel /ˈkɛv(ə)l/ ▶ **noun** a large cleat fitted to the gunwale of a ship and used for securing ropes.
– ORIGIN Middle English: of unknown origin.

Kevlar /ˈkɛvlɑː/ ▶ **noun** [mass noun] trademark a synthetic fibre of high tensile strength used especially as a reinforcing agent in the manufacture of tyres and other rubber products.

Kew Gardens the Royal Botanic Gardens at Kew, in Richmond, London. Developed by the mother of George III with the aid of Sir Joseph Banks, the gardens are now an important botanical institution.

kewpie /ˈkjuːpi/ (also **kewpie doll**) ▶ **noun** (trademark in the US) a type of doll characterized by a large head, big eyes, chubby cheeks, and a curl or topknot on top of its head.
– ORIGIN early 20th cent. (originally US): from CUPID + -IE.

Key, John (Phillip) (b.1961), New Zealand National Party statesman, Prime Minister of New Zealand since 2008.

key[1] ▶ **noun** (pl. **keys**) **1** a small piece of shaped metal with incisions cut to fit the wards of a particular lock, which is inserted into a lock and turned to open or close it. ■ a shaped metal implement for operating a switch in the form of a lock, especially one operating the ignition of a motor vehicle. ■ an instrument for grasping and turning a screw, peg, or nut, especially one for winding a clock or turning a valve. ■ a pin, bolt, or wedge inserted into a hole or between parts so as to lock the parts together.
2 each of several buttons on a panel for operating a computer, typewriter, or telephone. ■ a lever depressed by the finger in playing an instrument such as the organ, piano, flute, or concertina. ■ a lever operating a mechanical device for making or breaking an electric circuit, for example in telegraphy.
3 a thing that provides a means of achieving or understanding something: *discipline seems to be the **key** to her success*. ■ an explanatory list of symbols used in a map, table, etc. ■ a set of answers to exercises or problems. ■ a word or system for solving a cipher or code. ■ the first move in the solution of a chess problem. ■ Computing a field in a record which is used to identify that record uniquely.
4 Music a group of notes based on a particular note and comprising a scale, regarded as forming the tonal basis of a piece of music: *the key of E minor*. ■ the tone or pitch of someone's voice: *his voice had changed to a lower key*. ■ the prevailing tone of a piece of writing, situation, etc.: *it was like the sixties all over again, in a new, more austerely intellectual key*. ■ the prevailing range of tones in a painting: *these mauves, lime greens, and saffron yellows recall the high key of El Greco's palette*.
5 the dry winged fruit of an ash, maple, or sycamore, typically growing in bunches; a samara.
6 the part of a first coat of wall plaster that passes between the laths and so secures the rest. ■ the roughness of a surface, helping the adhesion of plaster or other material.
7 Basketball the keyhole-shaped area marked on the court near each basket.
▶ **adjective** of crucial importance: *she became a key figure in the suffragette movement*.
▶ **verb** (**keys, keying, keyed**) [with obj.] **1** enter or operate on (data) by means of a computer keyboard or telephone keypad: *she **keyed in** a series of commands* | [no obj.] *a hacker caused disruption after **keying into** a vital database*.
2 [with obj. and adverbial] fasten (something) in position with a pin, wedge, or bolt: *the coils may be keyed into the slots by fibre wedges*.
3 roughen (a surface) to help the adhesion of plaster or other material.

4 word (an advertisement in a periodical), typically by varying the form of the address given, so as to identify the publication generating particular responses.
5 informal vandalize (a car) by scraping its paint with a key.
6 N. Amer. informal be the crucial factor in achieving: *Ewing keyed a 73–35 advantage on the boards with twenty rebounds*.
– PHRASES **in** (or **out of**) **key** in (or out of) harmony: *this uplifting conclusion is out of key with the body of his book*.
– PHRASAL VERBS **key someone/thing into** (or **in with**) cause someone or something to be in harmony with: *to those who are keyed into his lunatic sense of humour, the arrival of any Bergman movie is a major comic event*. **key something to** chiefly N. Amer. link something to: *courses keyed to the needs of health professionals*. **be keyed up** be nervous, tense, or excited, especially before an important event: *he was keyed up at the thought of seeing Rosemary*.
– DERIVATIVES **keyed** adjective, **keyer** noun, **keyless** adjective.
– ORIGIN Old English *cǣg*, *cǣge*, of unknown origin.

key² ▸ noun a low-lying island or reef, especially in the Caribbean. Compare with CAY.
– ORIGIN late 17th cent.: from Spanish *cayo* 'shoal, reef', influenced by QUAY.

keyboard ▸ noun 1 a panel of keys that operate a computer or typewriter.
2 a set of keys on a piano or similar musical instrument. ■ an electronic musical instrument with keys arranged as on a piano: *she plays keyboards and guitar*.
▸ verb [with obj.] enter (data) by means of a keyboard.
– DERIVATIVES **keyboarder** noun (sense 1 of the noun), **keyboardist** noun (sense 2 of the noun).

key card (also **card key**) ▸ noun a small plastic card, sometimes used instead of a door key in hotels, bearing magnetically encoded data that can be read and processed by an electronic device.

key grip ▸ noun the person in a film crew who is in charge of the camera equipment.

keyholder ▸ noun a person who is entrusted with keeping a key to commercial or industrial premises.

keyhole ▸ noun a hole in a lock into which the key is inserted. ■ a circle cut out of a garment as a decorative effect, typically at the front or back neckline.

keyhole limpet ▸ noun a limpet which has an aperture at the apex of the shell, sometimes extending to the margin. ● Family Fissurellidae, class Gastropoda.

keyhole saw ▸ noun a saw with a long, narrow blade for cutting small holes such as keyholes.

keyhole surgery ▸ noun [mass noun] minimally invasive surgery carried out through a very small incision, with special instruments and techniques including fibre optics.

key industry ▸ noun an industry that is essential to the functioning of others, such as the manufacture of machine tools.

Key Largo a resort island off the south coast of Florida, the northernmost and the longest of the Florida Keys.

key light ▸ noun the main source of light in a photograph or film.

Key lime ▸ noun a small yellowish lime with a sharp flavour.
– ORIGIN named after the Florida *Keys*.

keylogger ▸ noun a computer program that records every keystroke made by a computer user, especially in order to gain fraudulent access to passwords and other confidential information.
– DERIVATIVES **keylogging** noun.

key map ▸ noun a map drawn in bare outline, to simplify the use of a full map.

key money ▸ noun [mass noun] informal money paid to a landlord as an inducement by a person wishing to rent a property. ■ Brit. a payment required from a new tenant of rented accommodation in exchange for the provision of a key to the premises.

Keynes /keɪnz/, John Maynard, 1st Baron (1883–1946), English economist. He laid the foundations of modern macroeconomics with *The General Theory of Employment, Interest and Money* (1936), in which he argued that full employment is determined by effective demand and requires government spending on public works to stimulate this.
– DERIVATIVES **Keynesian** adjective & noun, **Keynesianism** noun.

keynote ▸ noun 1 a prevailing tone or central theme: *individuality is the keynote of the Nineties*. ■ [as modifier] (of a speech) setting out the central theme of a conference.
2 Music the note on which a key is based.
– DERIVATIVES **keynoter** noun.

keypad ▸ noun a miniature keyboard or set of buttons for operating a portable electronic device, telephone, or other equipment.

keypal ▸ noun informal a person with whom one becomes friendly by exchanging emails; an email penfriend.
– ORIGIN 1990s: from KEY¹ + PAL, by analogy with PEN PAL.

keypunch ▸ noun a device for transferring data by means of punched holes or notches on a series of cards or paper tape.
▸ verb [with obj.] put (data) into the form of punched cards or paper tape with a keypunch.
– DERIVATIVES **keypuncher** noun.

key ring ▸ noun a metal ring on to which keys may be threaded in order to keep them together.

key signature ▸ noun Music any of several combinations of sharps or flats after the clef at the beginning of each stave, indicating the key of a composition.

Key Stage ▸ noun (in the UK) any of the four fixed stages into which the national curriculum is divided, each having its own prescribed course of study. At the end of each stage, pupils are required to complete standard assessment tasks.

Keystone a US film company formed in 1912, remembered for its silent slapstick comedy films, many featuring the bumbling Keystone Kops police characters.

keystone ▸ noun a central stone at the summit of an arch, locking the whole together. ■ the central principle or part of a policy, system, etc., on which all else depends: *cooperation remains the keystone of the government's security policy*.

Keystone State informal name for PENNSYLVANIA.

keystroke ▸ noun a single depression of a key on a keyboard, especially as a measure of work.

keyway ▸ noun a slot cut in a part of a machine or an electrical connector, to ensure correct orientation with another part which is fitted with a key.

Key West a city in southern Florida, at the southern tip of the Florida Keys; pop. 22,364 (est. 2008). It is the southernmost city in the continental US.

keyword ▸ noun 1 a word which acts as the key to a cipher or code.
2 a word or concept of great significance: *homes and jobs are the keywords in the campaign*. ■ a word used in an information retrieval system to indicate the content of a document. ■ a significant word mentioned in an index.

key worker ▸ noun an employee who provides a vital service, especially in the police, health, or education sectors.

KG ▸ abbreviation (in the UK) Knight of the Order of the Garter.

kg ▸ abbreviation kilogram(s).

KGB the state security police (1954–91) of the former Soviet Union with responsibility for external espionage, internal counter-intelligence, and internal 'crimes against the state'.
– ORIGIN Russian, abbreviation of *Komitet gosudarstvennoĭ bezopasnosti* 'Committee of State Security'.

Kgs ▸ abbreviation Kings (in biblical references).

khabar /ˈkʌbə/ ▸ noun [mass noun] Indian the latest information; news.
– ORIGIN mid 19th cent.: from Urdu and Persian *ḵabar*, from Arabic.

Khabarovsk /kəˈbɑːrɒfsk/ a krai (administrative territory) on the east coast of Siberian Russia. ■ the capital of Khabarovsk, a city on the Amur River, on the Chinese border; pop. 577,300 (est. 2008).

Khachaturian /ˌkatʃəˈtʃʊərɪən/, Aram (Ilich) (1903–78), Soviet composer, born in Georgia. His music is richly romantic and reflects his lifelong interest in the folk music of Armenia, Georgia, and Russia. Notable works include *Gayane* (ballet, 1942), his Second Symphony (1943), and *Spartacus* (ballet, 1954).

khadi /ˈkadə/ (also **khaddar**) ▸ noun [mass noun] an Indian homespun cotton cloth.
– ORIGIN from Punjabi, from Hindi *khādī*.

Khakassia /kɑːˈkasɪə/ an autonomous republic in south central Russia; pop. 533,000 (est. 2009); capital, Abakan.

khaki /ˈkɑːki/ ▸ noun (pl. **khakis**) [mass noun] 1 a strong cotton or wool fabric of a dull brownish-yellow colour, used especially in military clothing. ■ (**khakis**) trousers or other clothing made of khaki.
2 a dull greenish or brownish-yellow colour: [as modifier] *a pair of khaki Bermuda shorts*.
– ORIGIN mid 19th cent.: from Urdu *khākī* 'dust-coloured', from *khāk* 'dust', from Persian.

Khaki Campbell ▸ noun a duck of a light brown breed, kept for egg laying.

khalasi /kəˈlasi/ ▸ noun (pl. **khalasis**) (in South Asia) a manual worker, especially a docker, porter, or sailor.
– ORIGIN from Urdu *ḵalāṣī*, *ḵalāšī*.

Khalistan /ˈkalɪstɑːn, -stan/ the name given by Sikh nationalists to a proposed independent Sikh state.
– ORIGIN compare with Arabic *ḵālṣa* 'pure, real, proper'.

Khalkha /ˈkalkə/ ▸ noun (pl. **same** or **Khalkhas**) 1 a member of a section of the Mongolian people, constituting the bulk of the population of Mongolia.
2 [mass noun] the language of the Khalkha, a demotic form of Mongolian adopted as the official language of Mongolia.
▸ adjective relating to the Khalkha or their language.
– ORIGIN of unknown origin.

Khalkís /xalˈkis/ Greek name for CHALCIS.

Khalsa /ˈkʌlsə/ ▸ noun the body or company of fully initiated Sikhs, to which devout orthodox Sikhs are ritually admitted at puberty. The Khalsa was founded in 1699 by the last Guru (Gobind Singh). Members show their allegiance by five signs (called the five Ks): kangha (comb), kara (steel bangle), kesh (uncut hair, covered by a turban, and beard), kirpan (short sword) and kuccha (short trousers, originally for riding).
– ORIGIN via Urdu from Persian, from the feminine form of Arabic *ḵāliṣ* 'pure, belonging to'.

K

Khama /ˈkɑːmə/, Sir Seretse (1921–80), Botswanan statesman, Prime Minister of Bechuanaland 1965 and first President of Botswana 1966–80.

Khambat, Gulf of /kɑːmˈbɑːt/ another name for CAMBAY, GULF OF.

khamsin /ˈkamsɪn/ ▸ noun an oppressive, hot southerly or south-easterly wind blowing in Egypt in spring.
– ORIGIN late 17th cent.: from Arabic *ḵamsīn*, from *ḵamsūn* 'fifty' (being the approximate duration in days).

Khan¹, Ayub, see AYUB KHAN.

Khan² /kɑːn/, Imran (b.1952), Pakistani cricketer; full name *Imran Ahmad Khan Niazi*. An all-rounder, he served as Pakistan's captain in four periods between 1982 and 1992. After retiring from cricket in 1992, he entered politics in Pakistan.

khan¹ /kɑːn, kan/ ▸ noun a title given to rulers and officials in central Asia, Afghanistan, and certain other Muslim countries. ■ any of the successors of Genghis Khan, supreme rulers of the Turkish, Tartar, and Mongol peoples and emperors of China in the Middle Ages.
– DERIVATIVES **khanate** noun.
– ORIGIN late Middle English: from Old French *chan*, medieval Latin *canus*, *caanus*, from Turkic *ḵān* 'lord, prince'.

khan² /kɑːn, kan/ ▸ noun (in the Middle East) an inn for travellers, built around a central courtyard.
– ORIGIN from Persian *ḵān*.

khana /ˈkɑːnə/ ▸ noun [mass noun] Indian food. ■ [count noun] a meal.
– ORIGIN via Hindi from the Sanskrit root *khād-* 'eat'.

khanda /ˈkandə, ˈkɑːndə/ ▸ noun an emblem of Sikhism, representing a vertical two-edged sword with its blade surrounded by a circle and its hilt intersected by the crossing hilts of two single-edged swords.
– ORIGIN from Persian *khanjar* 'dagger'.

khanga /ˈkaŋɡə/ (also **kanga**) ▸ noun [mass noun] a light East African cotton fabric printed with coloured designs, used mainly for women's clothing.
– ORIGIN Kiswahili.

Khaniá /xaˈnja/ Greek name for CHANIA.

khansama /ˈkɑːnsəˌmɑː/ ▸ noun Indian a male cook, who often also assumes the role of house steward.
– ORIGIN from Urdu and Persian *ḵānsāmān*, from *ḵān* 'master' + *sāmān* 'household goods'.

khapra beetle /ˈkaprə/ ▸ **noun** a small dark brown beetle, the larva of which is a serious pest of stored grain and cereal products. ● *Trogoderma granarium*, family Dermestidae.
– ORIGIN late 19th cent.: from Hindi *khaprā*, from Sanskrit *kharpara* 'thief'.

Kharg Island /kɑːɡ/ a small island at the head of the Persian Gulf, site of Iran's principal deep-water oil terminal.

kharif /kaˈriːf/ ▸ **noun** [mass noun] (in South Asia) the autumn crop sown at the beginning of the summer rains.
– ORIGIN Persian and Urdu, from Arabic *karīf* 'autumn, autumnal rain'.

Kharkiv /ˈhɑːkɪv/ an industrial city in NE Ukraine, in the Donets basin; pop. 1,456,000 (est. 2009). Russian name **Kharkov** /ˈxarʲkəf/.

Khartoum /kɑːˈtuːm/ the capital of Sudan, situated at the junction of the Blue Nile and the White Nile; pop. 2,737,500 (est. 2007).

> In 1885 a British and Egyptian force under the command of General Gordon was besieged in Khartoum for ten months by the Mahdists, who eventually stormed the garrison, killing most of the defenders. It remained under the control of the Mahdists until they were defeated by the British in 1898 and the city was recaptured by General Kitchener.

khat /kɑːt/ (also **qat**) ▸ **noun 1** [mass noun] the leaves of an Arabian shrub, which are chewed (or drunk as an infusion) as a stimulant.
2 the shrub that produces khat, growing in mountainous regions and often cultivated. ● *Catha edulis*, family Celastraceae.
– ORIGIN mid 19th cent.: from Arabic *qāt*.

khayal /kəˈjɑːl/ (also **khyal**) ▸ **noun** a traditional type of song from the northern part of the Indian subcontinent, with instrumental accompaniment and typically having two main stanzas.
– ORIGIN from Hindi *khayāl*.

K

Khayelitsha /ˌkʌɪjəˈlɪtʃə/ a township 40 km (25 miles) south-east of Cape Town, South Africa; pop. 2,100,000 (est. 2009). Designed to accommodate 250,000 people, it was built in 1983 for black Africans from the squatter camps of Crossroads, Langa, and KTC.

Khazar /kəˈzɑː/ ▸ **noun** a member of a Turkic people who occupied a large part of southern Russia from the 6th to the 11th centuries and who converted to Judaism in the 8th century.
▸ **adjective** relating to the Khazars.
– ORIGIN of unknown origin.

khazi /ˈkɑːzi/ (also **karzy**) ▸ **noun** (pl. **khazies**) Brit. informal a toilet.
– ORIGIN 1960s: from Italian *casa* 'house'.

kheda /ˈkeɪdə/ (also **keddah** or **kheddah**) ▸ **noun** (in South Asia) an enclosure used for the capture of wild elephants.
– ORIGIN from Assamese and Bengali *khedā*.

Khedive /kɪˈdiːv/ ▸ **noun** the title of the viceroy of Egypt under Turkish rule 1867–1914.
– DERIVATIVES **Khedival** adjective, **Khedivial** adjective.
– ORIGIN via French from Ottoman Turkish *ḳediv*, from Persian *ḳadiw* 'prince' (variant of *ḳudaiw* 'minor god', from *ḳudā* 'god').

Kherson /kɪəˈsɒn/ a port on the south coast of Ukraine, on the Dnieper estuary; pop. 306,600 (est. 2009).

khichri /ˈkɪtʃriː/ ▸ **noun** an Indian dish consisting chiefly of rice and split pulses.
– ORIGIN from Hindi *khichṛī*, from Sanskrit *khiccā*, a dish of rice and sesame.

khimar /kɪˈmɑː/ ▸ **noun** a head covering or veil worn in public by some Muslim women, typically covering the head, neck, and shoulders.
– ORIGIN Arabic *khimār*.

Khios /ˈxiɒs/ Greek name for **CHIOS**.

khir /ˈkɪə/ ▸ **noun** [mass noun] an Indian dish of sweet rice pudding.
– ORIGIN from Hindi *khīr*.

Khitai /kɪˈtʌɪ/ variant of **CATHAY**.

Khmer /kmɛː/ ▸ **noun** (pl. **same** or **Khmers**) **1** an ancient kingdom in SE Asia which reached the peak of its power in the 11th century, when it ruled over the entire Mekong valley from the capital at Angkor. It was destroyed by Siamese conquests in the 12th and 14th centuries.
2 a native or inhabitant of the ancient Khmer kingdom.
3 a native or inhabitant of Cambodia.
4 [mass noun] the language of the Khmer, belonging to the Mon-Khmer family. It is the official language of Cambodia, spoken by about 7 million people. Also called **CAMBODIAN**.
▸ **adjective** relating to the Khmer or their language.
– ORIGIN the name in Khmer.

Khmer Republic former official name (1970–5) for **CAMBODIA**.

Khmer Rouge /ruːʒ/ a communist guerrilla organization which opposed the Cambodian government in the 1960s and waged a civil war from 1970, taking power in 1975.

> Under Pol Pot the Khmer Rouge undertook a forced reconstruction of Cambodian society, involving mass deportations from the towns to the countryside and mass executions. More than two million died before the regime was overthrown by the Vietnamese in 1979. Khmer Rouge forces have continued a programme of guerrilla warfare from bases in Thailand.

– ORIGIN from **KHMER** + French *rouge* 'red'.

Khoikhoi /ˈkɔɪkɔɪ/ (also **Khoi-khoin** /-kɔɪn/, **Khoi**) ▸ **noun** (pl. **same**) a member of a group of indigenous peoples of South Africa and Namibia, traditionally nomadic herders and hunter-gatherers, including the Nama people and the ancestors of the Griquas.
▸ **adjective** relating to the Khoikhoi or their languages.
– ORIGIN Nama, literally 'men of men'.

> **USAGE** Khoikhoi should be used in preference to **Hottentot**, since the latter is likely to cause offence: see **USAGE** at **HOTTENTOT**.

Khoisan /ˈkɔɪsɑːn/ ▸ **noun 1** [usu. treated as pl.] a collective term for the Khoikhoi and San peoples of southern Africa.
2 [mass noun] a language family of southern Africa, including the languages of the Khoikhoi and San, now having fewer than a million speakers altogether, and notable for the use of clicks (made by suction with the tongue) as additional consonants.
▸ **adjective** relating to the Khoisan or their languages.
– ORIGIN blend of **KHOIKHOI** and **SAN**.

Khoja /ˈkəʊdʒə/ ▸ **noun** a member of an Ismaili sect found mainly in western India.
– ORIGIN early 17th cent. (in the sense 'Muslim scribe or teacher'): from Turkish *hoca*, from Persian.

kho-kho /ˈkəʊkəʊ/ ▸ **noun** [mass noun] an Indian game of tag played with two teams of twelve people.
– ORIGIN from Marathi *khō-khō*.

Khomeini /xɒˈmeɪni/, Ruhollah (1900–89), Iranian Shiite Muslim leader; known as **Ayatollah Khomeini**. After sixteen years in exile he returned to Iran in 1979 to lead an Islamic revolution which overthrew the shah. He established Iran as a fundamentalist Islamic republic and relentlessly pursued the Iran–Iraq War 1980–8.

Khonsu /ˈkɒnsuː/ Egyptian Mythology a moon god worshipped especially at Thebes, a member of a triad as the divine son of Amun and Mut.

Khorramshahr /ˌxɔːrəmˈʃɑː/ an oil port on the Shatt al-Arab waterway in western Iran. It was almost totally destroyed during the Iran–Iraq War of 1980–8. Former name (until 1924) **MOHAMMERAH**.

khoum /kuːm/ ▸ **noun** a monetary unit of Mauritania, equal to one fifth of an ouguiya.
– ORIGIN from Arabic *ḵums* 'one fifth'.

Khrushchev /ˈkrʊʃtʃɒf, ˌkrʊsˈtʃɒf/, Nikita (Sergeevich) (1894–1971), Soviet statesman, Premier of the USSR 1958–64. He was First Secretary of the Communist Party of the USSR 1953–64 after the death of Stalin, whom he denounced in 1956. He came close to war with the US over the Cuban Missile Crisis in 1962 and also clashed with China, which led to his being ousted by Brezhnev and Kosygin.
– DERIVATIVES **Khrushchevian** adjective.

Khufu /ˈkuːfuː/ see **CHEOPS**.

khula /kuːˈlɑː/ ▸ **noun** [mass noun] (in Islamic law) a form of divorce initiated by the wife, which is effected by the return of her husband's wedding gift. Compare with **TALAQ**.
– ORIGIN from Arabic *ḵul* 'retreat, renunciation'.

Khulna /ˈkʊlnɑː/ an industrial city in southern Bangladesh, on the Ganges delta; pop. 855,650 (est. 2008).

Khunjerab Pass /ˈkʌnjərɑːb/ a high-altitude pass through the Himalayas, on the Karakoram highway at a height of 4,900 m (16,088 ft), linking China and Pakistan.

khus-khus /ˈkʌskʌs/ ▸ **noun** another term for **VETIVER**.
– ORIGIN early 19th cent.: from Urdu and Persian *ḵasḵas*.

khyal /kɪˈɑːl/ ▸ **noun** variant spelling of **KHAYAL**.

Khyber Pass /ˈkʌɪbə/ a mountain pass in the Hindu Kush, on the border between Pakistan and Afghanistan at a height of 1,067 m (3,520 ft). In the past the pass was of great commercial and strategic importance and formed the route by which successive invaders entered India; it was garrisoned by the British intermittently between 1839 and 1947.

kHz ▸ **abbreviation** kilohertz.

ki ▸ **noun** variant spelling of **CHI2**.

kiaat /kɪˈɑːt/ ▸ **noun** a tree with fragrant yellow flowers and useful timber that resembles teak, native to tropical and southern Africa. ● *Pterocarpus angolensis*, family Leguminosae.
– ORIGIN mid 19th cent.: via Dutch from Malay *kayu jati* 'teak wood'.

kiang /kɪˈaŋ/ ▸ **noun** an animal of a large race of the Asian wild ass with a thick furry coat, native to the Tibetan plateau. ● *Equus hemionus kiang*, family Equidae; sometimes treated as a separate species. Compare with **ONAGER**, **KULAN**.
– ORIGIN mid 19th cent.: from Tibetan *kyang*.

Kiangsi /kjaŋˈsiː/ variant of **JIANGXI**.

Kiangsu /kjaŋˈsuː/ variant of **JIANGSU**.

kia ora /ˌkɪə ˈɔːrə/ ▸ **exclamation** (in New Zealand) a greeting wishing good health.
– ORIGIN Maori.

kiasu /ˈkiːəsuː/ SE Asian ▸ **noun** a grasping, selfish attitude.
▸ **adjective** (of a person) very anxious not to miss an opportunity; grasping.
– ORIGIN from Chinese, 'scared to lose'.

kibbeh /ˈkɪbeɪ/ ▸ **noun** [mass noun] (in Middle Eastern cookery) a mixture of minced meat, bulgar or rice, and seasonings, typically served in the form of croquettes stuffed with a filling.
– ORIGIN from Egyptian Arabic *kubba* 'ball, lump'.

kibble1 /ˈkɪb(ə)l/ ▸ **verb** [with obj.] (usu. as adj. **kibbled**) grind or chop (beans, grain, etc.) coarsely.
▸ **noun** [mass noun] N. Amer. ground meal shaped into pellets, especially for pet food.
– ORIGIN late 18th cent.: of unknown origin.

kibble2 /ˈkɪb(ə)l/ ▸ **noun** Brit. an iron hoisting bucket used in mines.
– ORIGIN late Middle English: from Middle High German *kübel*, from medieval Latin *cupellus* 'corn measure', diminutive of *cuppa* 'cup'.

kibbutz /kɪˈbʊts/ ▸ **noun** (pl. **kibbutzim** /-ˈtsiːm/) a communal settlement in Israel, typically a farm.
– ORIGIN 1930s: from modern Hebrew *qibbūṣ* 'gathering'.

kibbutznik /kɪˈbʊtsnɪk/ ▸ **noun** a member of a kibbutz.

kibe /kʌɪb/ ▸ **noun** an ulcerated chilblain, especially one on the heel.
– ORIGIN late Middle English: of unknown origin.

kibitka /kɪˈbɪtkə/ ▸ **noun 1** a type of covered Russian sledge.
2 a circular tent, covered with felt, formerly used by Tartars.
– ORIGIN late 18th cent.: Russian, from Tartar and Kyrgyz *kibit* (from Arabic *qubbat* 'dome') + the Russian suffix *-ka*.

kibitz /ˈkɪbɪts/ ▸ **verb** [no obj.] informal, chiefly N. Amer. **1** look on and offer unwelcome advice, especially at a card game.
2 speak informally; chat: *she **kibitzed** with friends.*
– DERIVATIVES **kibitzer** noun.
– ORIGIN 1920s: Yiddish, from colloquial German, from German *Kiebitz* 'interfering onlooker' (literally 'lapwing').

kiblah ▸ **noun** variant spelling of **QIBLAH**.

kibosh /ˈkʌɪbɒʃ/ (also **kybosh**) ▸ **noun** (in phrase **put the kibosh on**) informal put an end to; dispose of decisively: *he put the kibosh on the deal.*
– ORIGIN mid 19th cent.: of unknown origin.

kick1 ▸ **verb 1** [with obj. and adverbial] strike or propel forcibly with the foot: *police **kicked** down the door* | [with obj. and complement] *he **kicked** the door open.* ■ [no obj.] strike out with the foot or feet: *she **kicked** out at him* | [with obj.] *he **kicked** his feet free of a vine.*
■ (chiefly in rugby) score (a goal) by a kick.
2 [with obj.] informal succeed in giving up (a habit or addiction).
3 [no obj.] (of a gun) recoil when fired.

▸ **noun 1** a blow or forceful thrust with the foot: *a kick in the head.* ■ (in sport) an instance of striking the ball with the foot: *Scott's kick went wide of the goal.* ■ Brit. (chiefly in rugby) a player of specified kicking ability.
2 [in sing.] a sudden forceful jolt: *the shuttle accelerated with a kick.* ■ the recoil of a gun when discharged. ■ Billiards & Snooker an irregular movement of the ball caused by dust.
3 informal the sharp stimulant effect of alcohol or a drug. ■ a thrill of pleasurable, often reckless excitement: *rich kids turning to crime just **for kicks** | I get such **a kick out of** driving a racing car.* ■ [with modifier] a temporary interest in a particular thing: *the jogging kick.*
– PHRASES **kick against the pricks** see PRICK. **kick (some) ass** (or **butt**) N. Amer. vulgar slang act in a forceful or aggressive manner. **kick someone's ass** (or **butt**) N. Amer. vulgar slang punish, dominate, or defeat someone. **a kick at the can** (or **cat**) Canadian informal an opportunity to achieve something. **kick the bucket** informal die. **kick one's heels** see HEEL[1]. **a kick in the pants** (or **up the backside**) informal an unwelcome surprise that prompts fresh effort: *the competition will be healthy—we need a kick in the pants.* **a kick in the teeth** informal a grave setback or disappointment. **kick something into touch** Brit. informal reject something firmly. [with reference to rugby, the ball in touch being out of play.] **kick oneself** be annoyed with oneself for doing something foolish or missing an opportunity. **kick over the traces** see TRACE[2]. **kick the shit out of** vulgar slang see SHIT. **kick someone/thing to the curb** N. Amer. informal reject or cast aside: *things get complicated for Alfie when he's kicked to the curb by his girlfriend.* **kick up a fuss** (or **a stink**) informal object loudly or publicly to something. **kick up one's heels** see HEEL[1]. **kick someone upstairs** informal remove someone from an influential position by giving them an ostensible promotion. **kick someone when they are down** cause further misfortune to someone who is already in a difficult situation.
– PHRASAL VERBS **kick against** protest against or resist (something). **kick around** (or **about**) (of a thing) lie unwanted or unexploited: *the idea has been kicking around for over a year.* ■ (of a person) drift idly from place to place. **kick someone around** treat someone roughly or without respect. **kick something around** (or **about**) discuss a proposal informally. **kick back** N. Amer. informal be at leisure; relax. **kick down** Brit. change quickly into a lower gear in a car with an automatic transmission by a sudden full depression of the accelerator. **kick in** come into effect or operation: *the hospital's emergency generators kicked in.* **kick something in** N. Amer. informal contribute something, especially money. **kick off 1** (of a football match) be started or resumed by a player kicking the ball from the centre spot. ■ (of a team or player) begin or resume a match by kicking the ball from the centre spot. ■ (also **kick something off**) informal begin or cause something to begin. **2** Brit. informal become angry. **kick someone out** informal expel or dismiss someone. **kick up** (of the wind) become stronger.
– DERIVATIVES **kickable** adjective.
– ORIGIN late Middle English: of unknown origin.

kick[2] ▸ **noun** archaic an indentation in the bottom of a glass bottle, diminishing the internal capacity.
– ORIGIN mid 19th cent.: of unknown origin.

kick-and-rush ▸ **adjective** denoting soccer played vigorously but with little skill.

Kickapoo /ˈkɪkəpuː/ ▸ **noun** (pl. **same** or **Kickapoos**) **1** a member of an American Indian people formerly living in Wisconsin, and now in Kansas, Oklahoma, and northern central Mexico.
2 [mass noun] the Algonquian language of the Kickapoo, now nearly extinct.
▸ **adjective** relating to the Kickapoo or their language.
– ORIGIN from Kickapoo *kiikaapoa.*

kick-ass ▸ **adjective** informal, chiefly N. Amer. forceful, vigorous, and aggressive.

kickback ▸ **noun 1** a sudden forceful recoil.
2 informal an illicit payment made to someone in return for facilitating a transaction or appointment.

kickball ▸ **noun** [mass noun] N. Amer. an informal game combining elements of baseball and soccer, in which a soccer ball is thrown to a person who kicks it and proceeds to run the bases.

kick-boxing ▸ **noun** [mass noun] a form of martial art which combines boxing with elements of karate, in particular kicking with bare feet.
– DERIVATIVES **kick-boxer** noun.

kick-down ▸ **noun** Brit. a device for changing gear in a motor vehicle with automatic transmission by full depression of the accelerator.

kick drum ▸ **noun** informal a bass drum played using a pedal.

kicker ▸ **noun 1** a person or animal that kicks. ■ the player in a team who scores or gains positional advantage by kicking.
2 N. Amer. informal an unexpected and unwelcome discovery or turn of events: *the kicker was you couldn't get a permit.* ■ an extra clause in a contract.
3 informal a small outboard motor.
4 (in poker) a high third card retained in the hand with a pair at the draw.

kickflip ▸ **noun** (in skateboarding) a manoeuvre in which the board is manipulated by the feet during a jump so that it spins sideways through 360 degrees before landing.

kicking ▸ **noun** an assault in which the victim is kicked repeatedly: *they gave him a good kicking.*
▸ **adjective** informal lively and exciting: *their seriously kicking debut, 'Paradise'.*

kicking strap ▸ **noun 1** a strap used to prevent a horse from kicking.
2 Sailing a rope lanyard fixed to a boom to prevent it from rising.

kick-off ▸ **noun** the start or resumption of a football match, in which a player kicks the ball from the centre spot. ■ informal the start of an event or activity.

kick plate ▸ **noun** a metal plate at the base of a door or panel to protect it from damage or wear.

kick-pleat ▸ **noun** an inverted pleat in a narrow skirt to allow freedom of movement.

kickshaw ▸ **noun** archaic a fancy but insubstantial cooked dish, especially one of foreign origin. ■ chiefly N. Amer. an elegant but insubstantial trinket.
– ORIGIN late 16th cent.: from French *quelque chose* 'something'. The French spelling was common in the 17th cent.; the present form results from interpretation of *quelque chose* as plural.

kicksorter ▸ **noun** informal a device for analysing electrical pulses according to amplitude.

kickstand ▸ **noun** a metal rod attached to a bicycle or motorcycle, lying horizontally when not in use, that may be kicked into a vertical position to support the vehicle when it is stationary.

kick-start ▸ **verb** [with obj.] start (a motorcycle engine) with a downward thrust of a pedal. ■ provide an impetus to start or resume (a process): *they need to kick-start the economy.*
▸ **noun** a device to start an engine by the downward thrust of a pedal, as in older motorcycles. ■ an act of kick-starting an engine. ■ an impetus given to start or resume a process: *new investment will provide the kick-start needed to escape from recession.*

kick-turn ▸ **noun** Skiing a turn carried out while stationary by lifting first one and then the other ski through 180°. ■ (in skateboarding) a turn performed with the front wheels lifted off the ground.

kicky ▸ **adjective** (**kickier**, **kickiest**) N. Amer. informal exciting; fashionable.

kid[1] ▸ **noun 1** informal a child or young person. ■ used as an informal form of address: *we'll be seeing ya, kid!*
2 a young goat. ■ [mass noun] leather made from a young goat's skin: [as modifier] *white kid gloves.*
▸ **verb** (**kids**, **kidding**, **kidded**) [no obj.] (of a goat) give birth.
– PHRASES **kids' stuff** (N. Amer. **kid stuff**) informal a thing regarded as very easy or simple to do: *all this was kids' stuff compared to the directing.* **our kid** Brit. informal one's younger brother or sister (often used as a form of address): *come here, our kid.*
– ORIGIN Middle English (in sense 2 of the noun): from Old Norse *kith*, of Germanic origin; related to German *Kitze.*

kid[2] ▸ **verb** (**kids**, **kidding**, **kidded**) [with obj.] informal deceive (someone) in a playful way; tease: *you're kidding me!* ■ [with obj. and clause] fool (someone) into believing something: *he likes to kid everyone he's the big macho tough guy.* ■ [no obj.] (**kid around**) behave in a silly way.
– PHRASES **no kidding** used to emphasize the truth of a statement: *no kidding, she's gone.*
– DERIVATIVES **kidder** noun, **kiddingly** adverb.
– ORIGIN early 19th cent.: perhaps from KID[1], expressing the notion 'make a child or goat of'.

kid[3] ▸ **noun** archaic a small wooden tub, especially a sailor's mess tub for grog or rations.
– ORIGIN mid 18th cent.: perhaps a variant of KIT[1].

kid brother ▸ **noun** informal one's younger brother.

Kidd, William (1645–1701), Scottish pirate; known as **Captain Kidd**. Sent to the Indian Ocean in 1695 in command of an anti-pirate expedition, Kidd became a pirate himself. In 1699 he went to Boston in the hope of obtaining a pardon, but was arrested and later hanged in London.

Kidderminster /ˈkɪdəˌmɪnstə/ a town in west central England, in Worcestershire, on the River Stour; pop. 58,000 (est. 2009).

Kidderminster carpet ▸ **noun** a reversible carpet made of two cloths of different colours woven together.
– ORIGIN late 17th cent.: named after KIDDERMINSTER, a centre of carpet-making.

kiddie (also **kiddy**) ▸ **noun** (pl. **kiddies**) informal a young child.

kiddiewink ▸ **noun** Brit. humorous a small child.
– ORIGIN 1950s: a familiar extension of KIDDIE.

kiddle /ˈkɪd(ə)l/ ▸ **noun** a dam or other barrier in a river, with an opening fitted with nets to catch fish. ■ an arrangement of fishing nets hung on stakes along the seashore to catch fish.
– ORIGIN Middle English: from Old French *quidel.*

kiddo ▸ **noun** (pl. **kiddos** or **kiddoes**) informal a friendly or slightly condescending form of address.

kiddush /ˈkɪdʊʃ/ ▸ **noun** a ceremony of prayer and blessing over wine, performed by the head of a Jewish household at the meal ushering in the Sabbath (on a Friday night) or a holy day, or at the lunch preceding it.
– ORIGIN mid 18th cent.: from Hebrew *qiddûš* 'sanctification'.

kiddy ▸ **noun** variant spelling of KIDDIE.

kid gloves ▸ **plural noun** gloves made of fine kid leather. ■ (also **kid-glove**) [as modifier] used in reference to careful and delicate treatment of a person or situation: *the star is getting kid-glove treatment.*
– PHRASES **handle** (or **treat**) **someone/thing with kid gloves** deal with someone or something very carefully or tactfully.

kidnap ▸ **verb** (**kidnaps**, **kidnapping**, **kidnapped**; US also **kidnaps**, **kidnaping**, **kidnaped**) [with obj.] abduct (someone) and hold them captive, typically to obtain a ransom.
▸ **noun** [mass noun] the action of kidnapping someone: *they were arrested for robbery and kidnap.*
– DERIVATIVES **kidnapper** noun.
– ORIGIN late 17th cent.: back-formation from *kidnapper*, from KID[1] + slang *nap* 'nab, seize'.

kidnapping ▸ **noun** an act of abducting someone and holding them captive: *the recent kidnapping of a Dutch industrialist.*

kidney ▸ **noun** (pl. **kidneys**) **1** each of a pair of organs in the abdominal cavity of mammals, birds, and reptiles, that excrete urine. ■ [mass noun] the kidney of a sheep, ox, or pig as food.

> The kidneys' main function is to purify the blood by removing nitrogenous waste products and excreting them in the urine. They also control the fluid and ion levels in the body, by excreting any excesses. In the past the kidneys were thought to control disposition and temperament.

2 [mass noun] nature or temperament: *I hoped that he would not prove of similar kidney.*
– ORIGIN Middle English: of obscure origin.

kidney bean ▸ **noun** a kidney-shaped bean, especially a dark red one from a dwarf French bean plant.

kidney dialysis ▸ **noun** see DIALYSIS.

kidney dish ▸ **noun** a kidney-shaped dish used as a receptacle in an operating theatre or doctor's surgery.

kidney machine ▸ **noun** an apparatus that performs the functions of the human kidney (outside the body), when one or both organs are damaged; an artificial kidney or dialysis machine.

kidney ore ▸ **noun** [mass noun] haematite occurring in rounded, kidney-shaped masses.

kidney-shaped ▸ **adjective** shaped like a kidney, with one side concave and the other convex and with rounded ends.

kidney stone ▸ **noun** a hard mass formed in the kidneys, typically consisting of insoluble calcium compounds; a renal calculus.

kidney tubule ▸ **noun** Anatomy each of the long, fine, convoluted tubules conveying urine from the glomeruli to the renal pelvis in the vertebrate kidney. Water and salts are reabsorbed into the blood along their length. Also called RENAL TUBULE, URINIFEROUS TUBULE.

kidney vetch ▶ **noun** a yellow- or orange-flowered grassland plant of the pea family. Native to Europe and the Mediterranean, it is sometimes grown as a fodder crop. Also called LADY'S FINGER. ● *Anthyllis vulneraria*, family Leguminosae.

kidney worm ▶ **noun** a parasitic nematode worm which infests the kidneys of mammals. ● Several species in the class Phasmida, in particular *Stephanurus dentatus* (in pigs) and the large *Dioctophyma renale* (in humans and other mammals).

kidology /kɪˈdɒlədʒi/ ▶ **noun** [mass noun] informal, chiefly Brit. the art or practice of deliberately deceiving or teasing people.
– ORIGIN 1960s: formed irregularly from the verb KID[2] + -LOGY.

kid sister ▶ **noun** informal one's younger sister.

kidskin ▶ **noun** another term for KID[1] (sense 2 of the noun).

kidstakes /ˈkɪdsteɪks/ ▶ **plural noun** Austral./NZ informal nonsense; pretence.
– ORIGIN early 20th cent.: probably a humorous formation based on slang *kid* 'humbug'.

kidult ▶ **noun** informal an adult with childish tastes.
■ [mass noun] [often as modifier] a genre of television programmes, films, or games intended to appeal to both children and adults: *high-tech kidult entertainment*.
– ORIGIN 1960s: blend of KID[1] and ADULT.

kiekie /ˈkiːkiː/ ▶ **noun** a New Zealand climbing plant with edible bracts, and leaves which are used for basket-making and weaving. ● *Freycinetia banksii*, family Pandanaceae.
– ORIGIN mid 19th cent.: from Maori.

K

Kiel /kiːl/ a naval port in northern Germany, capital of Schleswig-Holstein, on the Baltic Sea coast at the eastern end of the Kiel Canal; pop. 235,400 (est. 2006).

kielbasa /kiːlˈbasə/ ▶ **noun** [mass noun] a type of highly seasoned Polish sausage, typically containing garlic.
– ORIGIN Polish, literally 'sausage'.

Kiel Canal a man-made waterway, 98 km (61 miles) in length, in NW Germany, running westwards from Kiel to Brunsbüttel at the mouth of the Elbe. It connects the North Sea with the Baltic and was constructed in 1895 to provide the German navy with a shorter route between these two seas.

Kielce /ˈkjɛltsə/ an industrial city in southern Poland; pop. 206,796 (2007).

kier /kɪə/ ▶ **noun** a vat.
– ORIGIN late 16th cent.: from Old Norse *ker* 'container, tub'.

kierie /ˈkɪri/ ▶ **noun** (pl. **kieries**) S. African a short, thick stick with a knobbed head, traditionally used as a club or missile by the indigenous peoples of South Africa.
– ORIGIN from Khoikhoi *kirri* 'walking stick'.

Kierkegaard /ˈkɪəkəˌgɑːd/, Søren (Aabye) (1813–55), Danish philosopher. A founder of existentialism, he affirmed the importance of individual experience and choice and believed one could know God only through a 'leap of faith', and not through doctrine. Notable works: *Either-Or* (1843) and *The Sickness unto Death* (1849).
– DERIVATIVES **Kierkegaardian** adjective.

kieselguhr /ˈkiːz(ə)lˌgʊə/ ▶ **noun** [mass noun] a form of diatomaceous earth used in various manufacturing and laboratory processes, chiefly as a filter, filler, or insulator.
– ORIGIN late 19th cent.: from German, from *Kiesel* 'gravel' + dialect *Guhr* (literally 'yeast') used to denote a loose earthy deposit, found in the cavities of rocks.

kieserite /ˈkiːzərʌɪt/ ▶ **noun** [mass noun] a fine-grained white mineral consisting of hydrated magnesium sulphate, occurring often in salt mines.
– ORIGIN mid 19th cent.: from the name of Dietrich G. *Kieser* (1779–1862), German physician, + -ITE[1].

Kieslowski /kɪˈslɒfski/, Krzysztof (1941–96), Polish film director. Noted for their mannered style and their artistic, philosophical nature, his films include the series *Dekalog* (1988), each film being a visual interpretation of one of the Ten Commandments, and the trilogy *Three Colours* (1993–4).

Kiev /ˈkiːɛf/ the capital of Ukraine, an industrial city and port on the River Dnieper; pop. 2,765,500 (est. 2009). Founded in the 8th century, it became capital of the Ukrainian Soviet Socialist Republic in 1934. In 1991 it became capital of independent Ukraine. Ukrainian name KYIV.

kif /kɪf/ (also **kef**) ▶ **noun** [mass noun] a substance, especially cannabis, smoked to produce a drowsy state.
▶ **adjective** S. African informal very good (used as a general term of approval): *that T-shirt's kif*.
– ORIGIN early 19th cent.: from Arabic *kayf* 'enjoyment, well-being'.

Kigali /kɪˈgɑːli/ the capital of Rwanda; pop. 860,000 (est. 2007).

kike /kʌɪk/ ▶ **noun** N. Amer. informal an offensive term for a Jewish person.
– ORIGIN early 20th cent.: of unknown origin.

Kikládhes /kiˈklaðɛs/ Greek name for CYCLADES.

kikoi /kɪˈkɔɪ/ ▶ **noun** (pl. **kikois**) [mass noun] a distinctive East African striped cloth with an end fringe.
■ [count noun] a garment made of kikoi, worn around the waist.
– ORIGIN Kiswahili.

Kikongo /kɪˈkɒŋgəʊ/ ▶ **noun** [mass noun] either of two similar Bantu languages spoken in Congo, the Democratic Republic of the Congo (Zaire), and adjacent areas, with around 4.7 million speakers altogether.
▶ **adjective** relating to Kikongo.
– ORIGIN the name in Kikongo.

Kikuyu /kɪˈkuːjuː/ ▶ **noun** (pl. **same** or **Kikuyus**) **1** a member of a people forming the largest ethnic group in Kenya.
2 [mass noun] the Bantu language of the Kikuyu, with over 5 million speakers.
3 (**kikuyu** or **kikuyu grass**) a creeping perennial grass which is native to Kenya and cultivated elsewhere as a lawn and fodder grass. ● *Pennisetum clandestinum*, family Gramineae.
▶ **adjective** relating to the Kikuyu or their language.
– ORIGIN a local name.

Kilauea /ˌkiːlaʊˈeɪə/ a volcano with a crater roughly 8 km (5 miles) long by 5 km (3 miles) broad on the island of Hawaii, situated on the eastern flanks of Mauna Loa at an altitude of 1,247 m (4,090 ft).

Kildare /kɪlˈdɛː/ a county of the Republic of Ireland, in the east, in the province of Leinster; county town, Naas.

kilderkin /ˈkɪldəkɪn/ ▶ **noun** a cask for liquids or other substances, holding 16 or 18 gallons. ■ this amount as a unit of measurement.
– ORIGIN late Middle English: from Middle Dutch *kinderkin*, variant of *kinerkijn*, diminutive of *kintal* (see QUINTAL).

kilim /kɪˈliːm, ˈkiːlɪm/ (also **kelim**) ▶ **noun** a flat-woven carpet or rug made in Turkey, Kurdistan, and neighbouring areas.
– ORIGIN late 19th cent.: via Turkish from Persian *gelīm*.

Kilimanjaro, Mount /ˌkɪlɪmənˈdʒɑːrəʊ/ an extinct volcano in northern Tanzania. It has twin peaks, the higher of which, Kibo (5,895 m, 19,340 ft), is the highest mountain in Africa.

Kilkenny /kɪlˈkɛni/ a county of the Republic of Ireland, in the south-east, in the province of Leinster.
■ the county town of Kilkenny; pop. 8,661 (2006).

Kilkenny cats two cats which, according to legend, fought until only their tails remained.

kill ▶ **verb** [with obj.] **1** cause the death of (a person, animal, or other living thing): *her father was killed in a car crash* | [no obj.] *a robber armed with a shotgun who kills in cold blood*. ■ (**kill someone**/**thing off**) get rid of or destroy completely, especially in large numbers: *there is every possibility all river life would be killed off for generations*. ■ (**kill someone off**) (of a writer) bring about the 'death' of a fictional character. ■ [no obj.] (**kill out**) (of an animal) yield (a specified amount of meat) when slaughtered.
2 put an end to or cause the failure or defeat of (something): *two fast goals from Dublin killed any hopes of a famous Sligo victory*. ■ stop (a computer programme or process). ■ informal switch off (a light or engine). ■ informal delete (a line, paragraph, or file) from a document or computer. ■ (in soccer or other ball games) make (the ball) stop: *after killing the ball with his chest, he brushed past Reeves*. ■ Tennis hit (the ball) so that it cannot be returned. ■ neutralize or subdue (an effect or quality): *the sauce would kill the taste of the herbs*. ■ informal consume the entire contents of (a bottle containing an alcoholic drink).
3 informal overwhelm (someone) with an emotion: *the suspense is killing me*. ■ (**kill oneself**) overexert oneself: *I killed myself carrying those things home*. ■ used hyperbolically to indicate that someone will be extremely angry with (another person): *my boss will kill me for saying this*. ■ cause pain or anguish to: *my feet are killing me*.
4 pass (time, or a specified amount of it), typically while waiting for a particular event: *when he reached the station he found he actually had an hour to kill*.
▶ **noun** [usu. in sing.] an act of killing, especially of one animal by another: *a lion has **made a kill***. ■ an animal or animals killed: *the vulture is able to survey the land and locate a fresh kill*. ■ informal an act of destroying or disabling an enemy aircraft, submarine, etc.
– PHRASES **be in at the kill** be present at or benefit from the successful conclusion of an enterprise. **go** (or **move in** or **close in**) **for the kill** take ruthless or decisive action to turn a situation to one's advantage. **if it kills one** informal whatever the problems or difficulties involved: *we are going to smile and be pleasant if it kills us*. **kill oneself laughing** informal, chiefly Brit. be overcome with laughter. **kill or cure** Brit. (of a remedy for a problem) likely to either work well or fail catastrophically, with no possibility of partial success: *the spring Budget will be kill or cure*. **kill two birds with one stone** proverb achieve two aims at once. **kill someone with** (or **by**) **kindness** spoil someone by overindulging them.
– ORIGIN Middle English (in the sense 'strike, beat', also 'put to death'): probably of Germanic origin and related to QUELL. The noun originally denoted a stroke or blow.

Killarney /kɪˈlɑːni/ a town in the south-west of the Republic of Ireland, in County Kerry, famous for the beauty of the nearby lakes and mountains; pop. 13,497 (2006).

Killarney fern ▶ **noun** a rare bristle fern which grows on rocks by streams in a few parts of western Europe. ● *Trichomanes speciosum*, family Hymenophyllaceae.

killdeer /ˈkɪldɪə/ (also **killdeer plover**) ▶ **noun** a widespread American plover with a plaintive call that resembles its name. ● *Charadrius vociferus*, family Charadriidae.
– ORIGIN mid 18th cent.: imitative of its call.

killer ▶ **noun 1** a person, animal, or thing that kills: [as modifier] *a killer virus*.
2 informal a formidable, impressive or difficult thing: *his new novel is a killer*. ■ a hilarious joke.
3 Austral./NZ informal an animal that has been selected for slaughter.

killer app ▶ **noun** informal a feature, function, or application of a new technology or product which is presented as virtually indispensable or much superior to rival products.

killer bee ▶ **noun** informal, chiefly US an Africanized honeybee. See AFRICANIZE (sense 2).

killer cell ▶ **noun** Physiology a white blood cell (a type of lymphocyte) which destroys infected or cancerous cells.

killer instinct ▶ **noun** a ruthless determination to succeed or win.

killer whale ▶ **noun** a large toothed whale with distinctive black-and-white markings and a prominent dorsal fin. It lives in groups that hunt fish, seals, and penguins cooperatively. Also called ORCA. ● *Orcinus orca*, family Delphinidae.

kill file Computing ▶ **noun** (in a Usenet program) a file into which one may put particular email addresses or keywords, posts from or containing which are then automatically deleted without being displayed.
▶ **verb** (**killfile**) [with obj.] place (something) in a kill file.

killick /ˈkɪlɪk/ ▶ **noun** a heavy stone used by small craft as an anchor. ■ a small anchor. ■ Brit. Nautical slang a leading seaman. [so named because the leading seaman's badge bore the symbol of an anchor.]
– ORIGIN mid 17th cent.: of unknown origin.

killifish /ˈkɪlɪfɪʃ/ ▶ **noun** (pl. **same** or **killifishes**) a small toothcarp of fresh or brackish water, typically brightly coloured. They are mainly native to America and include many popular aquarium fishes. ● Families Cyprinodontidae (or Fundulidae), which includes numerous genera of egg-laying killifishes, and Poeciliidae, which includes a few live-bearing species.
– ORIGIN early 19th cent.: apparently from KILL and FISH[1].

killing ▶ **noun** an act of causing death, especially deliberately.
▶ **adjective 1** causing death: *a killing disease*.
2 informal exhausting or unbearable: *a killing schedule*. ■ dated extremely funny.
– PHRASES **make a killing** informal have a great financial success.
– DERIVATIVES **killingly** adverb.

killing field ▸ **noun** (usu. **killing fields**) a place where a heavy loss of life has occurred, typically as the result of massacre or genocide.

killing zone (also **kill zone**) ▸ **noun 1** the area of a military engagement with a high concentration of fatalities.
2 an area of the human body where entry of a projectile would cause death, especially as indicated on a target for shooting practice.

killjoy ▸ **noun** a person who deliberately spoils the enjoyment of others.

kill ratio ▸ **noun** the proportion of casualties on each side in a military action.

Kilmarnock /kɪl'mɑːnək/ a town in west central Scotland, administrative centre of East Ayrshire; pop. 45,200 (est. 2009).

kiln ▸ **noun** a furnace or oven for burning, baking, or drying, especially one for calcining lime or firing pottery.
– ORIGIN Old English *cylene*, from Latin *culina* 'kitchen, cooking stove'.

kiln-dry ▸ **verb** [with obj.] (usu. as adj. **kiln-dried**) dry (a material such as wood or sand) in a kiln.

Kilner jar /'kɪlnə/ ▸ **noun** trademark a glass preserving jar with a metal lid which forms an airtight seal, used to bottle fruit and vegetables.
– ORIGIN 1930s: from the name of the manufacturing company.

kilo ▸ **noun** (pl. **kilos**) **1** a kilogram.
2 rare a kilometre.
3 a code word representing the letter K, used in radio communication.
– ORIGIN late 19th cent.: from French, abbreviation of *kilogramme*, *kilomètre*.

kilo- /'kɪləʊ, 'kiːləʊ/ ▸ **combining form** (used commonly in units of measurement) denoting a factor of 1,000: *kilojoule* | *kilolitre*.
– ORIGIN via French from Greek *khilioi* 'thousand'.

kilobase (abbrev.: **kb**) ▸ **noun** Biochemistry (in expressing the lengths of nucleic acid molecules) one thousand bases.

kilobit (abbrev.: **Kb** or **KB**) ▸ **noun** a unit of computer memory or data equal to 1,024 bits.

kilobyte (abbrev.: **Kb** or **KB**) ▸ **noun** Computing a unit of memory or data equal to 1,024 bytes.

kilocalorie (abbrev.: **kcal**) ▸ **noun** a unit of energy of one thousand calories (equal to one large calorie).

kilocycle (abbrev.: **kc**) ▸ **noun** a former measure of frequency, equivalent to 1 kilohertz.

kilogram (also **kilogramme**) (abbrev.: **kg**) ▸ **noun** the SI unit of mass, equivalent to the international standard kept at Sèvres near Paris (approximately 2.205 lb).
– ORIGIN late 18th cent.: from French *kilogramme* (see KILO-, GRAM[1]).

kilohertz (abbrev.: **kHz**) ▸ **noun** a measure of frequency equivalent to 1,000 cycles per second.

kilojoule (abbrev.: **kJ**) ▸ **noun** 1,000 joules, especially as a measure of the energy value of foods.

kilolitre (US **kiloliter**) (abbrev.: **kl**) ▸ **noun** 1,000 litres (equivalent to 220 imperial gallons).

kilometre /'kɪləˌmiːtə, kɪ'lɒmɪtə/ (US **kilometer**) (abbrev.: **km**) ▸ **noun** a metric unit of measurement equal to 1,000 metres (approximately 0.62 miles).
– DERIVATIVES **kilometric** adjective.
– ORIGIN late 18th cent.: from French *kilomètre* (see KILO-, METRE[1]).

> **USAGE** There are two possible pronunciations for **kilometre**: one with the stress on the **ki-** and the other with the stress on the **-lo-**. The first is traditionally considered correct, with a stress pattern similar to other units of measurement such as **centimetre**. The second pronunciation, which originated in US English and is now also very common in British English, is still regarded as incorrect by some people, especially in British English.

kiloton (also **kilotonne**) ▸ **noun** a unit of explosive power equivalent to 1,000 tons of TNT.

kilovolt (abbrev.: **kV**) ▸ **noun** 1,000 volts.

kilowatt (abbrev.: **kW**) ▸ **noun** a measure of one thousand watts of electrical power.

kilowatt-hour (abbrev.: **kWh**) ▸ **noun** a measure of electrical energy equivalent to a power consumption of one thousand watts for one hour.

Kilroy a mythical person, popularized by American servicemen in the Second World War, who left such inscriptions as 'Kilroy was here' on walls all over the world.
– ORIGIN of the many unverifiable accounts of the source of the term, one claims that James J. *Kilroy* of Halifax, Massachusetts, a shipyard employee, wrote 'Kilroy was here' on sections of warships after inspection; the phrase is said to have been reproduced by shipyard workers who entered the armed services.

kilt ▸ **noun** a knee-length skirt of pleated tartan cloth, traditionally worn by men as part of Scottish Highland dress and now also worn by women and girls.
▸ **verb** [with obj.] **1** gather (a garment or material) in vertical pleats: (as adj. **kilted**) *kilted skirts*.
2 (usu. **kilt something up**) tuck up one's skirts around one's body.
– DERIVATIVES **kilted** adjective.
– ORIGIN Middle English (as a verb in the sense 'tuck up around the body'): of Scandinavian origin; compare with Danish *kilte (op)* 'tuck (up)' and Old Norse *kilting* 'a skirt'. The noun dates from the mid 18th cent.

kilter ▸ **noun** (in phrase **out of kilter**) out of harmony or balance: *daylight saving throws everybody's body clock out of kilter*.
– ORIGIN early 17th cent.: of unknown origin.

kiltie /'kɪlti/ (also **kilty**) ▸ **noun** informal a person who wears a kilt (often used as a humorous or slightly derogatory term for a Scot).

Kimberley /'kɪmbəli/ **1** a city in South Africa, the capital of Northern Cape; pop. 183,000 (est. 2009). It has been a diamond-mining centre since the early 1870s. [named after the 1st Earl of *Kimberley*, a British Colonial Secretary.]
2 (also **the Kimberleys**) a plateau region in the far north of Western Australia. It was the scene of a gold rush in 1885.

kimberlite /'kɪmbəlʌɪt/ ▸ **noun** [mass noun] Geology a rare, blue-tinged, coarse-grained intrusive igneous rock sometimes containing diamonds, found in South Africa and Siberia. Also called BLUE GROUND.
– ORIGIN late 19th cent.: from KIMBERLEY + -ITE[1].

Kimbundu see MBUNDU.

kimchi /'kɪmtʃi/ ▸ **noun** [mass noun] a Korean dish of spicy pickled cabbage.
– ORIGIN Korean.

Kim Il-sung /ˌkɪm ɪl'sʊŋ/ (1912–94), Korean communist statesman, first Premier of North Korea 1948–72 and President 1972–94; born *Kim Song-ju*. He precipitated the Korean War (1950–3), and remained committed to the reunification of the country. He maintained a one-party state and created a personality cult around himself and his family; on his death he was quickly replaced in power by his son Kim Jong-il (b.1942).

kimono /kɪ'məʊnəʊ/ ▸ **noun** (pl. **kimonos**) a long, loose traditional Japanese robe with wide sleeves, tied with a sash. ■ a similar garment worn elsewhere as a dressing gown.
– DERIVATIVES **kimonoed** adjective.
– ORIGIN mid 17th cent.: Japanese, from *ki* 'wearing' + *mono* 'thing'.

Ki-moon, Ban, see BAN KI-MOON.

kin ▸ **noun** [treated as pl.] one's family and relations: *many elderly people have no kin to turn to for assistance*. ■ animals or plants that are related to a particular species or kind: *dolphins, whales, and their kin*.
▸ **adjective** [predic.] (of a person) related: *he was* **kin** *to the brothers*.
– DERIVATIVES **kinless** adjective.
– ORIGIN Old English *cynn*, of Germanic origin; related to Dutch *kunne*, from an Indo-European root meaning 'give birth to', shared by Greek *genos* and Latin *genus* 'race'.

-kin ▸ **suffix** forming diminutive nouns such as *bumpkin, catkin*.
– ORIGIN from Middle Dutch *-kijn*, *-ken*, Middle Low German *-kin*.

kina[1] /'kiːnə/ ▸ **noun** (pl. **same**) the basic monetary unit of Papua New Guinea, equal to 100 toea.
– ORIGIN Papuan.

kina[2] /'kiːnə/ ▸ **noun** (pl. **same**) an edible sea urchin occurring on New Zealand coasts. ● *Evechinus chloroticus*, class Echinoidea.
– ORIGIN Maori.

Kinabalu, Mount /ˌkɪnəbə'luː/ a mountain in the state of Sabah in eastern Malaysia, on the north coast of Borneo. Rising to 4,094 m (13,431 ft), it is the highest peak of Borneo and of SE Asia.

kinaesthesia /ˌkɪnɪs'θiːzɪə, ˌkʌɪn-/ (US **kinesthesia**) ▸ **noun** [mass noun] awareness of the position and movement of the parts of the body by means of sensory organs (proprioceptors) in the muscles and joints.
– DERIVATIVES **kinaesthetic** adjective.
– ORIGIN late 19th cent.: from Greek *kinein* 'to move' + *aisthēsis* 'sensation'.

kinase /'kʌɪneɪz/ ▸ **noun** [usu. with modifier] Biochemistry an enzyme that catalyses the transfer of a phosphate group from ATP to a specified molecule.
– ORIGIN early 20th cent.: from Greek *kinein* 'to move' + -ASE.

Kincardineshire /kɪn'kɑːdɪnʃɪə, -ʃə/ a former county of eastern Scotland. In 1975 it became part of Grampian region and in 1996 part of Aberdeenshire.

Kinchinjunga /ˌkɪntʃɪn'dʒʌŋgə/ variant of KANCHENJUNGA.

kind[1] ▸ **noun 1** a group of people or things having similar characteristics: *all kinds of music* | *more data of this kind would be valuable*. ■ [mass noun] character or nature: *the trials were different* **in kind** *from any that preceded them*.
2 each of the elements (bread and wine) of the Eucharist: *communion* **in both kinds**.
– PHRASES **in kind 1** in the same way; with something similar: *if he responded positively, they would respond in kind*. **2** (of payment) in goods or services as opposed to money. **one's (own) kind** people with whom one has a great deal in common. **someone's kind** used to express disapproval of a certain type of person: *I don't apologize to her kind ever*. **kind of** informal rather; to some extent: *it got kind of cosy*. **a kind of** something resembling: *teaching based on a kind of inspired guesswork*. **nothing of the kind** not at all like the thing in question: *my son had done nothing of the kind before*. ■ used to express an emphatic denial: *'He made you do that?' 'He did nothing of the kind.'* **of its kind** within the limitations of its class: *this new building was no doubt excellent of its kind*. **of a kind** used to indicate that something is not as good as it might be expected to be: *there is tribute, of a kind, in such popularity*. **one of a kind** unique. **something of the kind** something like the thing in question: *they had always suspected something of the kind*. **two** (or **three, four**, etc.) **of a kind** the same or very similar: *she and her sister were two of a kind*. ■ (of cards) having the same face value but of a different suit.
– ORIGIN Old English *cynd(e)*, *gecynd(e)*, of Germanic origin; related to KIN. The original sense was 'nature, the natural order', also 'innate character, form, or condition' (compare with KIND[2]); hence 'a class or race distinguished by innate characteristics'.

> **USAGE** The plural of **kind** often causes difficulty. With *this* or *that*, speaking of one kind, use a singular construction: ***this kind of*** *question* ***is*** *not relevant*; ***that kind of*** *fabric* ***doesn't*** *need ironing*. With *these* or *those*, speaking of more than one kind, use a plural construction: *we refuse to buy* ***these kinds of*** *books*; *I've given up* ***those kinds of*** *ideas*. The ungrammatical use *these kind* rather than *these kinds* (as in ***these kind of*** *questions* ***are*** *not relevant*) has been recorded since the 14th century, and although often encountered today, it should be avoided.

kind[2] ▸ **adjective** having or showing a friendly, generous, and considerate nature: *she was a good, kind woman* | *he was very* **kind to** *me*. ■ [predic.] used in a polite request: *would you be kind enough to repeat what you said?* ■ (**kind to**) (of a consumer product) gentle on (a part of the body): *look for rollers that are kind to hair*. ■ archaic affectionate or loving.
– ORIGIN Old English *gecynde* 'natural, native'; in Middle English the earliest sense is 'well born or well bred', whence 'well disposed by nature, courteous, gentle, benevolent'.

kinda informal ▸ **contraction** kind of: *I think it's kinda funny*.
– ORIGIN early 20th cent. (originally US): alteration.

kinder /'kɪndə/ ▸ **noun** Austral. informal short for KINDERGARTEN.

kindergarten /'kɪndəˌgɑːt(ə)n/ ▸ **noun** (in Britain and Australia) an establishment where children below the age of compulsory education play and learn; a nursery school. ■ (in North America) a class or school that prepares children, usually five- or six-year-olds, for the first year of formal education.
– DERIVATIVES **kindergartener** (US also **kindergartner**) noun.
– ORIGIN mid 19th cent.: from German, literally 'children's garden'.

kind-hearted ▶ adjective having a kind and sympathetic nature.
– DERIVATIVES **kind-heartedly** adverb, **kind-heartedness** noun.

kindie ▶ noun (pl. **kindies**) variant spelling of KINDY.

kindle[1] /ˈkɪnd(ə)l/ ▶ verb [with obj.] set (something) on fire. ■ arouse or inspire (an emotion or feeling): *a love of art was kindled in me.* ■ [no obj.] (of an emotion) be aroused: *she hesitated, suspicion kindling within her.*
– DERIVATIVES **kindler** noun.
– ORIGIN Middle English: based on Old Norse *kynda*, influenced by Old Norse *kindill* 'candle, torch'.

kindle[2] /ˈkɪnd(ə)l/ ▶ verb [no obj.] (of a hare or rabbit) give birth.
– ORIGIN Middle English: apparently a frequentative of KIND[1].

kindliness ▶ noun [mass noun] the quality of being kind, warm-hearted, or gentle; kindness.

kindling ▶ noun [mass noun] **1** small sticks or twigs used for lighting fires.
2 (in neurology) a process by which a seizure or other brain event is both initiated and its recurrence made more likely.

kindly ▶ adverb in a kind manner: *'Never mind,' she said kindly.* ■ please (used in a polite request or demand, often ironically): *would you kindly explain what you're talking about?*
▶ adjective (**kindlier**, **kindliest**) kind, warm-hearted, or gentle: *he was a quiet, kindly man.*
– PHRASES **look kindly on** regard (someone or something) sympathetically. **not take kindly to** not welcome or be pleased by: *she does not take kindly to criticism.* **take something kindly** like or be pleased by something. **thank someone kindly** thank someone very much.
– ORIGIN Old English: adverb from *gecyndelīce* 'naturally, characteristically' (see KIND[2], -LY[2]); adjective from *gecyndelīc* 'natural' (see KIND[1], -LY[1]).

kindness ▶ noun [mass noun] the quality of being friendly, generous, and considerate: *he thanked them for their kindness and support.* ■ [count noun] a kind act: *it would be a kindness on your part to invite her.*

kindred /ˈkɪndrɪd/ ▶ noun [treated as pl.] one's family and relations. ■ [mass noun] relationship by blood: *ties of kindred.*
▶ adjective [attrib.] similar in kind; related: *books on kindred subjects.*
– ORIGIN Middle English: from KIN + *-red* (from Old English *rǣden* 'condition'), with insertion of *-d-* in the modern spelling through phonetic development (as in *thunder*).

kindred spirit ▶ noun a person whose interests or attitudes are similar to one's own.

kindy /ˈkɪndi/ ▶ noun (pl. **kindies**) Austral./NZ informal short for KINDERGARTEN.

kine /kʌɪn/ ▶ plural noun archaic cows collectively.

kinematics /ˌkɪnɪˈmatɪks, ˌkʌɪn-/ ▶ plural noun [usu. treated as sing.] the branch of mechanics concerned with the motion of objects without reference to the forces which cause the motion. Compare with DYNAMICS. ■ [usu. treated as pl.] the features or properties of motion in an object, regarded in such a way.
– DERIVATIVES **kinematic** adjective, **kinematically** adverb.
– ORIGIN mid 19th cent.: from Greek *kinēma*, *kinēmat-* 'motion' (from *kinein* 'to move') + -ICS.

kinematic viscosity ▶ noun Mechanics a quantity representing the dynamic viscosity of a fluid per unit density.

kinematograph /ˌkɪnɪˈmatəgrɑːf/ ▶ noun variant spelling of CINEMATOGRAPH.

kinescope /ˈkɪnɪskəʊp/ ▶ noun US dated a television tube. ■ a film recording of a television broadcast.
– ORIGIN 1930s: originally a proprietary name, from Greek *kinēsis* 'movement' + -SCOPE.

kinesics /kɪˈniːsɪks, kʌɪ-/ ▶ plural noun [usu. treated as sing.] the study of the way in which certain body movements and gestures serve as a form of non-verbal communication. ■ [usu. treated as pl.] body movements and gestures regarded as a form of non-verbal communication.
– ORIGIN 1950s: from Greek *kinēsis* 'motion' (from *kinein* 'to move') + -ICS.

kinesiology /kɪˌniːsɪˈɒlədʒi, kʌɪ-/ ▶ noun [mass noun] the study of the mechanics of body movements.
– DERIVATIVES **kinesiological** adjective, **kinesiologist** noun.
– ORIGIN late 19th cent.: from Greek *kinēsis* 'movement' (from *kinein* 'to move') + -LOGY.

kinesis /kɪˈniːsɪs, kʌɪ-/ ▶ noun (pl. **kineses**) [mass noun] movement; motion. ■ [count noun] Biology an undirected movement of a cell, organism, or part in response to an external stimulus. Compare with TAXIS. ■ Zoology mobility of the bones of the skull, as in some birds and reptiles.
– ORIGIN early 17th cent.: from Greek *kinēsis* 'movement', from *kinein* 'to move'.

kinesthesia ▶ noun US spelling of KINAESTHESIA.

kinetic /kɪˈnɛtɪk, kʌɪ-/ ▶ adjective relating to or resulting from motion. ■ (of a work of art) depending on movement for its effect.
– DERIVATIVES **kinetically** adverb.
– ORIGIN mid 19th cent.: from Greek *kinētikos*, from *kinein* 'to move'.

kinetic art ▶ noun [mass noun] a form of art that depends on movement for its effect. The term was coined by Naum Gabo and Antoine Pevsner in 1920 and is associated with the work of Alexander Calder.

kinetic energy ▶ noun [mass noun] Physics energy which a body possesses by virtue of being in motion. Compare with POTENTIAL ENERGY.

kinetics /kɪˈnɛtɪks, kʌɪ-/ ▶ plural noun [usu. treated as sing.] the branch of chemistry or biochemistry concerned with measuring and studying the rates of reactions. ■ [usu. treated as pl.] the rates of chemical or biochemical reaction. ■ Physics another term for DYNAMICS (sense 1).

kinetic theory ▶ noun [mass noun] the body of theory which explains the physical properties of matter in terms of the motions of its constituent particles.

kinetin /ˈkʌɪnɪtɪn/ ▶ noun [mass noun] a synthetic compound similar to kinin, used to stimulate cell division in plants.
– ORIGIN 1950s: from Greek *kinetos* 'movable' (from *kinein* 'to move') + -IN[1].

kineto- ▶ combining form relating to movement.
– ORIGIN from Greek *kinētos* 'movable'.

kinetochore /kɪˈniːtəʊkɔː, kʌɪ-/ ▶ noun another term for CENTROMERE.
– ORIGIN 1930s: from KINETO- 'of movement' + Greek *khōros* 'place'.

kinetoplast /kɪˈniːtəʊplast, -plɑːst, kʌɪ-/ ▶ noun Biology a mass of mitochondrial DNA lying close to the nucleus in some flagellate protozoa.

kinetoscope /kɪˈniːtəʊskəʊp, kʌɪ-/ ▶ noun an early motion-picture device in which the images were viewed through a peephole.

kinfolk ▶ plural noun another term for KINSFOLK.

King[1], B. B. (b.1925), American blues singer and guitarist; born *Riley B. King*. An established blues performer, he came to the notice of a wider audience in the late 1960s, when his style of guitar playing was imitated by rock musicians.

King[2], Billie Jean (b.1943), American tennis player. She won a record twenty Wimbledon titles, including six singles titles (1966–8; 1972–3; 1975), ten doubles titles, and four mixed doubles titles.

King[3], Martin Luther (1929–68), American Baptist minister and civil rights leader. He opposed discrimination against blacks by organizing non-violent resistance and peaceful mass demonstrations and was a notable orator. He was assassinated in Memphis. Nobel Peace Prize (1964).

King[4], William Lyon Mackenzie (1874–1950), Canadian Liberal statesman, Prime Minister 1921–6, 1926–30, and 1935–48. The grandson of William Lyon Mackenzie, he played an important role in establishing the status of the self-governing nations of the Commonwealth.

king ▶ noun **1** the male ruler of an independent state, especially one who inherits the position by right of birth: [as title] *King Henry VIII.* ■ a person or thing regarded as the finest or most important in their sphere or group: *a country where football is king | the king of rock.* ■ (**the King**) dated (in the UK) the national anthem when there is a male sovereign. ■ [attrib.] used in names of animals and plants that are particularly large, e.g. **king cobra**.
2 the most important chess piece, of which each player has one, which the opponent has to checkmate in order to win. The king can move in any direction, including diagonally, to any adjacent square that is not attacked by an opponent's piece or pawn. ■ a piece in draughts with extra capacity for moving, made by crowning an ordinary piece that has reached the opponent's baseline. ■ a playing card bearing a representation of a king, normally ranking next below an ace.
▶ verb **1** [with obj.] archaic make (someone) king.
2 [no obj.] (**king it**) dated act in an unpleasantly superior and domineering way: *he kings it over the natives on his atoll.*
– PHRASES **a king's ransom** see RANSOM. **live like a king** (or **queen**) live in great comfort and luxury.
– DERIVATIVES **kinghood** noun, **kingless** adjective, **kinglike** adjective, **kingship** noun.
– ORIGIN Old English *cyning*, *cyng*, of Germanic origin; related to Dutch *koning* and German *König*, also to KIN.

King Alfred's cakes ▶ plural noun another term for CRAMP BALLS.

kingbird ▶ noun a large American tyrant flycatcher, typically with a grey head and back and yellowish or white underparts. ● Genus *Tyrannus*, family Tyrannidae: several species.

kingbolt ▶ noun a kingpin in a mechanical structure.

King Charles spaniel ▶ noun a spaniel of a small breed, typically with a white, black, and tan coat.

king cobra ▶ noun a brownish cobra with an orange-cream throat patch, native to southern Asia. It is the largest of all venomous snakes. Also called HAMADRYAD. ● *Ophiophagus hannah*, family Elapidae.

king crab ▶ noun **1** another term for HORSESHOE CRAB.
2 N. Amer. an edible crab of the North Pacific, resembling a spider crab. ● Genus *Paralithodes*, family Lithodidae.

kingcraft ▶ noun [mass noun] archaic the art of ruling as a king, especially with reference to the use of clever or crafty diplomacy in dealing with subjects.

kingcup ▶ noun British term for MARSH MARIGOLD.

kingdom ▶ noun **1** a country, state, or territory ruled by a king or queen. ■ a realm associated with or regarded as being under the control of a particular person or thing: *the kingdom of dreams.*
2 the spiritual reign or authority of God. ■ the rule of God or Christ in a future age. ■ heaven as the abode of God and of the faithful after death.
3 each of the three traditional divisions (animal, vegetable, and mineral) in which natural objects have conventionally been classified. ■ Biology the highest category in taxonomic classification.
– PHRASES **come into** (or **to**) **one's kingdom** achieve recognition or supremacy. **till** (or **until**) **kingdom come** informal forever. **to kingdom come** informal into the next world: *the truck was blown to kingdom come.*
– ORIGIN Old English *cyningdōm* 'kingship' (see KING, -DOM).

King Edward ▶ noun an oval potato of a variety with a white skin mottled with red.
– ORIGIN 1920s: named after *King Edward* VII.

king eider ▶ noun an Arctic eider duck, the male of which has a red bill and colourful plumage on the head. ● *Somateria spectabilis*, family Anatidae.

kingfish ▶ noun (pl. **same** or **kingfishes**) any of a number of large sporting fish, many of which are edible: ● a fish of the jack family (Carangidae), including the **yellowtail kingfish** (*Seriola grandis*) of the South Pacific. ● (**northern kingfish**) a fish of the drum family (*Menticirrhus saxatilis*, family Sciaenidae), of the east coast of North America. ● a western Atlantic fish of the mackerel family (*Scomberomorus cavalla*, family Scombridae).

kingfisher ▶ noun an often brightly coloured bird with a large head and long sharp beak, typically diving for fish from a perch. Many of the tropical kinds live in forests and feed on terrestrial prey such as insects and lizards. ● Family Alcedinidae: many genera and numerous species, e.g. the small **river kingfisher** (*Alcedo atthis*), with bright blue and orange plumage, found from Europe to Australasia.

kingfisher blue ▶ noun [mass noun] a brilliant blue colour.

king-hit Austral./NZ informal ▶ noun a sudden knockout blow.
▶ verb [with obj.] punch (someone) suddenly and hard.

King in Council ▶ noun (in the UK) in the reign of a king, the term for QUEEN IN COUNCIL.

King James Bible (also **King James Version**) ▶ noun another name for AUTHORIZED VERSION.

kingklip /ˈkɪŋklɪp/ ▶ noun a cusk-eel of South African waters, which is an important commercial food fish. ● *Genypterus capensis*, family Ophidiidae.
– ORIGIN early 19th cent.: abbreviation of *kingklipfish*, partly translating Afrikaans *koningklipvis* 'king rock fish'.

King Kong ▸ noun informal someone or something of outstanding size or strength: *a King Kong of a man* | [as modifier] *a King Kong spider legged it across the floor*.
– ORIGIN from the name of a huge apelike monster featuring in the film *King Kong* (1933).

kinglet ▸ noun 1 chiefly derogatory a minor king.
2 chiefly N. Amer. a very small warbler of a group that includes the goldcrest, having an orange or yellow crown. ● Genus *Regulus*, family Sylviidae: several species, e.g. the American **golden-crowned kinglet** (*R. satrapa*).

King Log ▸ noun a ruler or leader noted for extreme laxity.
– ORIGIN from a classical fable in which the frogs wanted a king, and Jupiter gave them a log of wood; when they complained, he sent them a stork, which promptly gobbled them up. See also **King Stork**.

kingly ▸ adjective (**kinglier**, **kingliest**) associated with or typical of a king; regal: *his kingly duties*.
– DERIVATIVES **kingliness** noun.

kingmaker ▸ noun a person who brings leaders to power through the exercise of political influence.
– ORIGIN used originally with reference to the Earl of Warwick (see **Warwick**[2]).

King of Arms ▸ noun Heraldry (in the UK) a chief herald. Those now at the College of Arms are the Garter, Clarenceux, and Norroy and Ulster Kings of Arms; the Lyon King of Arms has jurisdiction in Scotland.

king of beasts ▸ noun chiefly literary the lion.

king of birds ▸ noun chiefly literary the eagle.

King of Kings ▸ noun 1 (in the Christian Church) a name or form of address for God.
2 a title assumed by certain kings who rule over lesser kings.

King of the Castle ▸ noun [mass noun] Brit. a children's game in which the object is to beat one's rivals to an elevated position at the top of a mound or other high place.

king of the herrings ▸ noun another term for **allis shad** and **oarfish**.

king penguin ▸ noun a large penguin native to the Falklands and other Antarctic islands. ● *Aptenodytes patagonica*, family Spheniscidae.

kingpin ▸ noun 1 a main or large bolt in a central position. ■ a vertical bolt used as a pivot.
2 a person or thing that is essential to the success of an organization or operation: *the kingpins of the television industry*.

king post ▸ noun an upright post in the centre of a roof truss, extending from the tie beam to the apex of the truss.

king prawn ▸ noun a large edible prawn which is of great commercial value. ● Genus *Penaeus*, class Malacostraca.

Kings the name of two books of the Bible, recording the history of Israel from the accession of Solomon to the destruction of the Temple in 586 BC.

King's Bench ▸ noun (in the UK) in the reign of a king, the term for **Queen's Bench**.

king's bishop ▸ noun Chess each player's bishop on the kingside of the board at the start of a game.

King's bounty ▸ noun historical (in the UK) a sum of money given from royal funds to a mother who had had a multiple birth of three or more.

Kings Canyon National Park a national park in the Sierra Nevada, California, to the north of Sequoia National Park. Established in 1940, it preserves groves of ancient sequoia trees, including some of the largest in the world.

King's Champion ▸ noun another term for **Champion of England**.

King's Counsel (abbrev.: **KC**) ▸ noun (in the UK) in the reign of a king, the term for **Queen's Counsel**.

King's English ▸ noun in the reign of a king, the term for **Queen's English**.

King's evidence ▸ noun in the reign of a king, the term for **Queen's evidence**.

king's evil ▸ noun [mass noun] archaic scrofula, formerly held to be curable by the royal touch.

King's highway ▸ noun in the reign of a king, the term for **Queen's highway**.

kingside ▸ noun Chess the half of the board on which both kings stand at the start of a game (the right-hand side for White, left for Black).

king-sized (also **king-size**) ▸ adjective (especially of a commercial product) of a larger size than the standard; very large: *a king-sized bed*.

king's knight ▸ noun Chess each player's knight on the kingside of the board at the start of a game.

Kingsley /ˈkɪŋzli/, Charles (1819–75), English novelist and clergyman. He is remembered for his historical novel *Westward Ho!* (1855) and for his classic children's story *The Water-Babies* (1863).

kingsnake ▸ noun a large, smooth-scaled North American constrictor which typically has shiny dark brown or black skin with lighter markings. ● Genus *Lampropeltis*, family Colubridae: several species, in particular *L. getulus*. Compare with **milk snake**.

king's pawn ▸ noun Chess the pawn occupying the square immediately in front of each player's king at the start of a game.

king's rook ▸ noun Chess each player's rook on the kingside of the board at the start of a game.

king's shilling ▸ noun a shilling formerly given to a recruit when enlisting in the army during the reign of a king.
– PHRASES **take the King's shilling** see **shilling**.

King's Speech ▸ noun (in the UK) in the reign of a king, the term for **Queen's Speech**.

Kingston 1 the capital and chief port of Jamaica; pop. 580,000 (est. 2007). Founded in 1693, it became capital in 1870.
2 a port in SE Canada, on Lake Ontario, at the head of the St Lawrence River; pop. 117,207 (2006).
3 (also **Kingston upon Thames**) a town and London borough on the south bank of the Thames, county town of Surrey.

Kingston upon Hull official name for **Hull**.

King Stork ▸ noun a tyrannical ruler or leader noted for extremes of oppression. See also **King Log**.

Kingstown the capital and chief port of St Vincent in the Caribbean; pop. 26,000 (est. 2007).

kinin /ˈkʌɪnɪn/ ▸ noun 1 Biochemistry any of a group of substances formed in body tissue in response to injury. They are polypeptides and cause vasodilation and smooth muscle contraction.
2 Botany a compound that promotes cell division and inhibits ageing in plants. Also called **cytokinin**.
– ORIGIN 1950s: from Greek *kinein* 'to move' + **-in**[1].

kink ▸ noun 1 a sharp twist or curve in something that is otherwise straight: *a kink in the road*. ■ a flaw or obstacle in a plan, operation, etc.: *though the system is making some headway, there are still some kinks to iron out*. ■ a quirk of character or behaviour. ■ informal a person's unusual sexual preference.
2 N. Amer. a crick in the neck.
▸ verb form or cause to form a sharp twist or curve: [no obj.] *the river kinks violently in a right angle* | [with obj.] *take care to avoid kinking the wire*.
– ORIGIN late 17th cent.: from Middle Low German *kinke*, probably from Dutch *kinken* 'to kink'.

kinkajou /ˈkɪŋkəˌdʒuː/ ▸ noun an arboreal nocturnal fruit-eating mammal with a prehensile tail and a long tongue, found in the tropical forests of Central and South America. ● *Potos flavus*, family Procyonidae.
– ORIGIN late 18th cent.: from French *quincajou*, alteration of **carcajou**.

Kinki /ˈkiːŋkiː/ a region of Japan, on the island of Honshu; capital, Osaka.

kinky ▸ adjective (**kinkier**, **kinkiest**) 1 informal involving or given to unusual sexual behaviour. ■ (of clothing) sexually provocative in an unusual way: *kinky underwear*.
2 having kinks or twists: *long and kinky hair*.
– DERIVATIVES **kinkily** adverb, **kinkiness** noun.
– ORIGIN mid 19th cent. (in sense 2): from **kink** + **-y**[1].

Kinneret, Lake /ˈkɪnərɛt/ another name for the Sea of Galilee (see **Galilee, Sea of**).

kinnikinnick /ˌkɪnɪkɪˈnɪk/ (also **kinnikinnic** or **kinnikinnik**) ▸ noun [mass noun] a substance used by North American Indians as a substitute for tobacco or for mixing with it, typically consisting of dried sumac leaves and the inner bark of willow or dogwood. ■ [count noun] N. Amer. the bearberry, which was also sometimes used in kinnikinnick.
– ORIGIN late 18th cent.: from a Delaware (Unami) word meaning 'admixture'.

kino /ˈkiːnəʊ/ ▸ noun [mass noun] a gum obtained from certain tropical trees by tapping, used locally as an astringent in medicine and in tanning. ● The trees belong to genera in various families, in particular *Pterocarpus* and *Butea* (family Leguminosae).
– ORIGIN late 18th cent.: apparently from a West African language.

Kinorhyncha /ˌkʌɪnə(ʊ)ˈrɪŋkə/ ▸ plural noun Zoology a small phylum of minute marine invertebrates that have a spiny body and burrow in sand or mud.
– DERIVATIVES **kinorhynch** /ˈkʌɪnə(ʊ)rɪŋk/ noun.
– ORIGIN modern Latin (plural), from Greek *kinein* 'set in motion' + *rhunkos* 'snout'.

Kinross-shire /kɪnˈrɒsʃɪə, -ʃə/ a former county of east central Scotland.

-kins ▸ suffix equivalent to **-kin**, often expressing endearment.

kin selection ▸ noun [mass noun] Zoology natural selection in which an apparently disadvantageous characteristic (especially altruistic behaviour) increases in the population due to increased survival of individuals genetically related to those possessing the characteristic.

Kinsey /ˈkɪnzi/, Alfred Charles (1894–1956), American zoologist and sex researcher. He carried out pioneering studies into sexual behaviour by interviewing large numbers of people. His best-known work, *Sexual Behaviour in the Human Male* (1948, also known as the *Kinsey Report*), was controversial but highly influential.

kinsfolk (also **kinfolk**) ▸ plural noun (in anthropological or formal use) a person's blood relations, regarded collectively. ■ a group of people related by blood.

Kinshasa /kɪnˈʃɑːsə, -ˈʃɑːzə/ the capital of the Democratic Republic of the Congo (Zaire), a port on the River Congo, in the south-west; pop. 7,273,900 (est. 2004). Founded in 1881 by the explorer Sir Henry Morton Stanley, it became the country's capital in 1960. Former name (until 1966) **Léopoldville**.

kinship ▸ noun [mass noun] blood relationship. ■ [count noun] a sharing of characteristics or origins: *they felt a kinship with architects*.

kinship group ▸ noun Anthropology a family, clan, or other group based on kinship.

kinsman (or **kinswoman**) ▸ noun (pl. **kinsmen** or **kinswomen**) (in anthropological or formal use) one of a person's blood relations.

Kintyre /kɪnˈtʌɪə/ a peninsula on the west coast of Scotland, to the west of Arran, extending southwards for 64 km (40 miles) into the North Channel and separating the Firth of Clyde from the Atlantic Ocean. Its southern tip is the Mull of Kintyre.

kiosk /ˈkiːɒsk/ ▸ noun 1 a small open-fronted hut or cubicle from which newspapers, refreshments, tickets, etc. are sold. ■ a small structure in a public area used for providing information or displaying advertisements, often incorporating an interactive display screen or screens.
2 (usu. **telephone kiosk**) Brit. a public telephone booth.
3 archaic (in Turkey and Iran) a light open pavilion or summer house.
– ORIGIN early 17th cent. (in the sense 'pavilion'): from French *kiosque*, from Turkish *köşk* 'pavilion', from Persian *kuš*.

kip[1] informal ▸ noun 1 Brit. a sleep or nap: *I might have a little kip* | [mass noun] *he was trying to get some kip*. ■ chiefly Scottish a bed.
2 Irish an unpleasant, dirty, or sordid place: *he couldn't get a start in this kip of a city*.
▸ verb (**kips**, **kipping**, **kipped**) [no obj.] Brit. sleep: *he can kip on her sofa*.
– ORIGIN mid 18th cent. (in the sense 'brothel'): perhaps related to Danish *kippe* 'hovel, tavern'.

kip[2] ▸ noun (in leather-making) the hide of a young or small animal. ■ a set or bundle of such hides.
– ORIGIN late Middle English: perhaps related to Middle Dutch *kip*, *kijp* 'bundle (of hides)'.

kip[3] ▸ noun (pl. **same** or **kips**) the basic monetary unit of Laos, equal to 100 ats.
– ORIGIN Thai.

kip[4] ▸ noun (in Australia) a small piece of wood from which coins are spun in the game of two-up.
– ORIGIN late 19th cent.: perhaps related to Irish *cipin* 'small stick, dibble'.

Kipling, (Joseph) Rudyard (1865–1936), British novelist, short-story writer, and poet. Born in India, he is known for his poems, such as 'If' and 'Gunga Din' and his children's tales, notably *The Jungle Book* (1894) and the *Just So Stories* (1902). Nobel Prize for Literature (1907).
– DERIVATIVES **Kiplingesque** adjective.

kippa /kɪˈpɑː/ (also **kipa**, **kipah**, or **kippah**) ▸ noun a skullcap worn by Orthodox male Jews.
– ORIGIN from modern Hebrew *kippāh*.

K

kipper[1] ▶ **noun 1** a kippered fish, especially a herring. **2** a male salmon in the spawning season.
▶ **verb** [with obj.] (usu. as adj. **kippered**) cure (a herring or other fish) by splitting it open and salting and drying it in the open air or in smoke.
– ORIGIN Old English *cypera* (in sense 2 of the noun), of Germanic origin; related to Old Saxon *kupiro*, perhaps also to COPPER[1].

kipper[2] ▶ **noun** Austral. historical an Aboriginal youth who has been initiated into manhood.
– ORIGIN from Dharuk *gibara*, from *giba* 'a stone' (because of its use in the ceremonial extraction of teeth).

kipper tie ▶ **noun** a brightly coloured and very wide tie.

Kir /kɪə/ ▶ **noun** [mass noun] trademark a drink made from dry white wine and cassis.
– ORIGIN 1960s: named after Canon Félix *Kir* (1876–1968), a mayor of Dijon who is said to have invented the recipe.

kirby grip /ˈkəːbi/ (also trademark **Kirbigrip**) ▶ **noun** Brit. a type of hairgrip consisting of a thin folded and sprung metal strip or wire.
– ORIGIN 1920s: named after *Kirby*, Beard & Co. Ltd, of Birmingham, England, the original manufacturers.

Kirchhoff /ˈkɪəxhɒf/, German /ˈkɪrçhɔf/, Gustav Robert (1824–87), German physicist, a pioneer in spectroscopy. He developed the concept of black-body radiation and discovered the elements caesium and rubidium.

Kirchner /ˈkɪəxnə/, German /ˈkɪrçnɐ/, Ernst Ludwig (1880–1938), German expressionist painter. In 1905 he was a founder of the first group of German expressionists. His paintings are characterized by the use of bright, contrasting colours and angular outlines, and often depict claustrophobic street scenes.

K

Kirghiz ▶ **noun & adjective** variant spelling of KYRGYZ.

Kirghizia /kɪəˈɡɪzɪə/ (also **Kyrgyzia**) former name for KYRGYZSTAN.

Kiribati /ˌkɪrɪˈbɑːti, ˌkɪrɪˈbas/ a country in the SW Pacific including the Gilbert Islands, the Line islands, the Phoenix Islands, and Banaba (Ocean Island); pop. 112,900 (est. 2009); official languages, English and I-Kiribati (local Austronesian language); capital, Bairiki (on Tarawa).

> Inhabited by Micronesian people, the islands were sighted by the Spaniards in the mid 16th century. Britain declared a protectorate over the Gilbert and Ellice Islands in 1892, and they became a colony in 1915. British links with the Ellice Islands (now Tuvalu) ended in 1975, and in 1979 Kiribati became an independent republic within the Commonwealth.

Kirin /kiːˈrɪn/ variant of JILIN.

Kiritimati /kɪˈrɪsɪməs, ˌkɪrɪtɪˈmɑːti/ an island in the Pacific Ocean, one of the Line Islands of Kiribati; pop. 5,115 (2005). The largest atoll in the world, it was discovered by Captain James Cook on Christmas Eve 1777 and was British until it became part of an independent Kiribati in 1979. Former name (until 1981) CHRISTMAS ISLAND.

kirk /kəːk/ ▶ **noun** Scottish & N. English **1** a church. **2** (**the Kirk** or **the Kirk of Scotland**) the Church of Scotland as distinct from the Church of England or from the Episcopal Church in Scotland.
– ORIGIN Middle English: from Old Norse *kirkja*, from Old English *cirice* (see CHURCH).

Kirkcaldy /kəːˈkɒdi/ an industrial town and port in Fife, SE Scotland, on the north shore of the Firth of Forth; pop. 47,600 (est. 2009).

Kirkcudbright /kəːˈkuːbrɪ/ a town in Dumfries and Galloway, SW Scotland, on the River Dee; pop. 3,400 (est. 2009).

Kirkcudbrightshire /kəːˈkuːbrɪʃɪə, -ʃə/ a former county of SW Scotland. It became part of Dumfries and Galloway in 1975.

kirkman /ˈkəːkmən/ ▶ **noun** (pl. **kirkmen**) Scottish a clergyman or member of the Church of Scotland.

Kirk session ▶ **noun** the lowest court in the Church of Scotland, composed of the minister and elders of the parish. ■ historical a court of this type in other Presbyterian Churches.

Kirkuk /kəːˈkʊk/ an industrial city in northern Iraq, centre of the oil industry in that region; pop. 600,000 (est. 2003).

Kirkwall /ˈkəːkwɔːl/ a port in the Orkney Islands; pop. 6,600 (est. 2009). Situated on Mainland, it is the chief town of the islands.

kirkyard ▶ **noun** Scottish a churchyard.

Kirlian photography /ˈkəːlɪən/ ▶ **noun** [mass noun] a technique for recording photographic images of corona discharges and hence, supposedly, the auras of living creatures.
– ORIGIN late 20th cent.: from the name of Semyon D. and Valentina K. *Kirlian*, Russian electricians.

Kirman /kɪəˈmɑːn/ ▶ **noun** a carpet of a kind typically having soft, delicate colouring and naturalistic designs.
– ORIGIN late 19th cent.: from *Kirman*, the name of a province and town in SE Iran.

Kirov /ˈkɪərɒf/ former name (1934–92) for VYATKA.

Kirovabad /ˌkɪrəvəˈbad/ former name (1935–89) for GÄNCÄ.

kirpan /kəːˈpɑːn/ ▶ **noun** a short sword or knife with a curved blade, worn (sometimes in miniature form) as one of the five distinguishing signs of the Sikh Khalsa.
– ORIGIN from Punjabi and Hindi *kirpān*, from Sanskrit *kṛpāṇa* 'sword'.

Kir royal /kɪə rɔɪˈɑːl/ (also **Kir royale**) ▶ **noun** a cocktail made from champagne or sparkling white wine and cassis.
– ORIGIN French, literally 'royal Kir'.

kirsch /kɪəʃ/ (also **kirschwasser** /ˈkɪəʃvasə/) ▶ **noun** [mass noun] brandy distilled from the fermented juice of cherries.
– ORIGIN German, abbreviation of *Kirschenwasser*, from *Kirsche* 'cherry' + *Wasser* 'water'.

kirtan /ˈkɪətʌn/ ▶ **noun** Hinduism a devotional song, typically about the life of Krishna, in which a group repeats lines sung by a leader.
– ORIGIN from Sanskrit *kīrtana*.

kirtle /ˈkəːt(ə)l/ ▶ **noun** archaic a woman's gown or outer petticoat. ■ a man's tunic or coat.
– ORIGIN Old English *cyrtel*, of Germanic origin, probably based on Latin *curtus* 'short'.

Kiruna /ˈkɪərʊnə/ the northernmost town of Sweden, situated in the Lapland iron-mining region; pop. 23,099 (2008).

Kirundi /kɪˈrʊndi/ ▶ **noun** [mass noun] an official language of Burundi, belonging to the Bantu language family and spoken by around 5 million people.

kisan /kɪˈsɑːn/ ▶ **noun** Indian an agricultural worker; a peasant.
– ORIGIN 1930s: Hindi *kisān*, from Sanskrit *kṛṣāṇa* 'person who ploughs'.

Kisangani /ˌkɪsaŋˈɡɑːni/ a city in the north of the Democratic Republic of the Congo (Zaire), on the River Congo; pop. 682,600 (est. 2004). Former name (until 1966) STANLEYVILLE.

kish /kɪʃ/ ▶ **noun** [mass noun] a scum of impure graphite, formed on molten iron during smelting.
– ORIGIN early 19th cent.: of uncertain origin; compare with French dialect *quiasse* 'scum on metal' (French *chiasse* 'insect excrement').

Kishinyov /kʲiʃiˈnʲɔf/ Russian name for CHIȘINĂU.

kishke /ˈkɪʃkə/ ▶ **noun** a beef intestine stuffed with a savoury filling. ■ (usu. **kishkes**) US informal a person's guts.
– ORIGIN Yiddish, from Polish *kiszka* or Ukrainian *kishka*.

kiskadee /ˌkɪskəˈdiː/ ▶ **noun** a large tyrant flycatcher with a black-and-white-striped head and bright yellow breast, found mainly in tropical America.
● The **greater kiskadee** (*Pitangus sulphuratus*) and the **lesser kiskadee** (*Philohydor lictor*), family Tyrannidae.
– ORIGIN late 19th cent.: imitative of its call.

Kislev /ˈkɪslɛf/ (also **Kislew**) ▶ **noun** (in the Jewish calendar) the third month of the civil and ninth of the religious year, usually coinciding with parts of November and December.
– ORIGIN from Hebrew *kislēw*.

kismet /ˈkɪzmɛt, -mɪt, -s-/ ▶ **noun** [mass noun] destiny; fate: *what chance did I stand against kismet?*
– ORIGIN early 19th cent.: from Turkish, from Arabic *qisma* 'division, portion, lot', from *qasama* 'to divide'.

kiss ▶ **verb** [with obj.] touch or caress with the lips as a sign of love, sexual desire, or greeting: *he kissed her on the lips* | [with obj. and complement] *she kissed the children goodnight* | [no obj.] *we started kissing.* ■ Billiards & Snooker (of a ball) lightly touch (another ball) in passing.
▶ **noun 1** a touch or caress with the lips: *a quick kiss on the cheek.* ■ used to express affection at the end of a letter (conventionally represented by the letter X): *she sent lots of love and a whole line of kisses.*
2 Billiards & Snooker a slight touch of a ball against another ball.
3 N. Amer. a small cake, biscuit, or sweet.
– PHRASES **kiss and make up** become reconciled. **kiss and tell** recount one's sexual exploits, especially to the media concerning a famous person. **kiss someone's arse** (or N. Amer. **ass**) vulgar slang behave obsequiously towards someone. **kiss ass** N. Amer. vulgar slang behave in an obsequious or sycophantic way. **kiss something better** informal comfort a sick or injured person, especially a child, by kissing the sore or injured part of their body as a gesture of removing pain. **kiss something goodbye** (or **kiss goodbye to something**) informal accept the certain loss of something: *I could kiss my career goodbye.* **kiss of death** an action or event that causes certain failure for an enterprise: *it would be the kiss of death for the company if it could be proved that the food was unsafe.* **kiss of life** mouth-to-mouth resuscitation. ■ an action or event that revives a failing enterprise: *good ratings gave the programme the kiss of life.* **kiss of peace** a ceremonial kiss given or exchanged as a sign of unity, especially the act of kissing the consecrated elements during the Christian Eucharist. **kiss the rod** accept punishment submissively.
– PHRASAL VERBS **kiss someone/thing off** N. Amer. informal dismiss or reject someone or something abruptly. **kiss up to** N. Amer. informal behave sycophantically or obsequiously towards (someone) in order to obtain something.
– DERIVATIVES **kissable** adjective.
– ORIGIN Old English *cyssan* (verb), of Germanic origin; related to Dutch *kussen* and German *küssen*.

kiss-ass ▶ **adjective** N. Amer. vulgar slang having or showing an obsequious or sycophantic eagerness to please.

kiss-curl ▶ **noun** a small curl of hair trained to lie flat on the forehead, at the nape of the neck, or in front of the ear.

kissel /ˈkɪs(ə)l/ ▶ **noun** [mass noun] a Russian dessert made from fruit juice or purée boiled with sugar and water and thickened with potato or cornflour.
– ORIGIN from Russian *kisel'*, from a base shared by *kislyĭ* 'sour'.

kisser ▶ **noun 1** a person who kisses someone, especially in a particular way: *he's a good kisser.* [mid 16th cent.: from the verb KISS + -ER[1].]
2 informal a person's mouth: *I belted him one, right on the kisser.* [originally boxing slang.]

kissing bug ▶ **noun** a bloodsucking North American assassin bug which can inflict a painful bite on humans and often attacks the face. ● *Melanolestes picipes*, family Reduviidae, suborder Heteroptera.

kissing cousin ▶ **noun** a relative known well enough to be given a kiss in greeting.

kissing disease ▶ **noun** informal a disease transmitted by contact with infected saliva, especially mononucleosis.

Kissinger /ˈkɪsɪndʒə/, Henry (Alfred) (b.1923), German-born American statesman and diplomat, Secretary of State 1973–7. In 1973 he helped negotiate the withdrawal of US troops from South Vietnam, for which he shared the Nobel Peace Prize. He later restored US diplomatic relations with Egypt in the wake of the Yom Kippur War and headed the commission investigating the attacks of September 11.

kissing gate ▶ **noun** Brit. a small gate hung in a U- or V-shaped enclosure, letting one person through at a time.

kissing gourami ▶ **noun** an edible SE Asian freshwater fish which is widely kept in aquaria. Individuals sometimes press their fleshy lips together, probably as a threat display. ● *Helostoma temminckii*, family Helostomatidae.

kiss-off ▶ **noun** informal, chiefly N. Amer. a rude or abrupt dismissal or rejection.

kissogram ▶ **noun** a novelty greeting or message delivered by a man or woman who accompanies it with a kiss, prearranged as a humorous surprise for the recipient.

kissy ▶ **adjective** informal characterized by or given to kissing; amorous: *Dean and I were just getting kissy.*

kissy-face ▶ **noun** N. Amer. informal a puckering of the lips as if to kiss someone.
– PHRASES **play kissy-face** engage in kissing or petting, especially in public.

kist ▶ **noun 1** chiefly Scottish & S. African a chest used for storing clothes and linen.
2 variant spelling of CIST.
– ORIGIN Middle English: northern English form of CHEST.

Kiswahili /ˌkiːswəˈhiːli, ˌkɪswɑː-/ ▶ **noun** another term for SWAHILI (sense 1 of the noun).

– ORIGIN from the Bantu prefix *ki-* (used in names of languages) + **Swahili**.

kit[1] ▶ **noun 1** a set of articles or equipment needed for a specific purpose: *a first-aid kit.* ■ a set of articles forming part of a soldier's equipment. ■ a set of all the parts needed to assemble something: *an aircraft kit.*
2 Brit. the clothing used for an activity such as a sport: *a football kit.*
3 Brit. a large basket, box, or other container, especially for fish.
▶ **verb** [with obj.] (**kit someone/thing out/up**) chiefly Brit. provide someone or something with the appropriate clothing or equipment: *we were all kitted out in life jackets.*
– PHRASES **get one's kit off** Brit. informal take off all one's clothes.
– ORIGIN Middle English: from Middle Dutch *kitte* 'wooden vessel', of unknown origin. The original sense 'wooden tub' was later applied to other containers; the use denoting a soldier's equipment (late 18th cent.) probably arose from the idea of a set of articles packed in a container.

kit[2] ▶ **noun** the young of certain animals, such as the beaver, ferret, and mink. ■ informal a kitten.

kit[3] ▶ **noun** historical a small violin, especially one used by a dancing master.
– ORIGIN early 16th cent.: perhaps from Latin *cithara* (see **cittern**).

kitab /kɪ'tɑːb/ ▶ **noun** the Koran. ■ (among Muslims) a sacred book of certain other religions, such as the Bible. ■ Indian any book or text.
– ORIGIN Arabic *kitāb* 'piece of writing, book'.

Kitakyushu /ˌkiːtə'kjuːʃuː/ a port in southern Japan, on the north coast of Kyushu island; pop. 986,755 (2007).

kitbag ▶ **noun** a long, cylindrical canvas bag, used especially for carrying a soldier's clothes and personal possessions.

kit car ▶ **noun** a car sold as a set of separate components, designed to be assembled by the purchaser.

kit-cat ▶ **noun** a canvas of a standard size (typically 36 × 28 in., 91.5 × 71 cm), especially as used for a life-size portrait (**kit-cat portrait**) showing the sitter's head, shoulders, and one or both hands.
– ORIGIN mid 18th cent.: named after a series of portraits of the members of the **Kit-Cat Club**.

Kit-Cat Club an association of prominent Whigs and literary figures founded in the early part of the 18th century. According to Alexander Pope its members included Richard Steele, Joseph Addison, William Congreve, and John Vanbrugh.
– ORIGIN named after *Kit* (= Christopher) *Cat* or *Catling*, who kept the pie house in Shire Lane, by Temple Bar, the original meeting place of the club.

kitchen ▶ **noun 1** a room or area where food is prepared and cooked. ■ a set of fitments and units that are sold together and fixed in place in a kitchen: *a fully fitted kitchen at a bargain price.* ■ [in sing.] the cuisine of a particular country or region: *the dried shrimp pastes of the Thai kitchen.*
2 informal the percussion section of an orchestra.
3 [as modifier] (of a language) in an uneducated or domestic form: *kitchen Swahili.*
– ORIGIN Old English *cycene*, of West Germanic origin; related to Dutch *keuken* and German *Küche*, based on Latin *coquere* 'to cook'.

kitchenalia ▶ **plural noun** cooking utensils and other items associated with the kitchen.

kitchen cabinet ▶ **noun** a group of unofficial advisers to the holder of an elected office who are considered to be unduly influential.

kitchen-diner ▶ **noun** a room used as both a kitchen and a dining room.

Kitchener[1] /'kɪtʃɪnə/ a city in Ontario, southern Canada; pop. 204,668 (2006). Settled by German Mennonites in 1806, as Dutch Sand Hills, it was renamed Berlin in 1830 and Kitchener in 1916, in honour of Field Marshal Kitchener.

Kitchener[2] /'kɪtʃɪnə/, (Horatio) Herbert, 1st Earl Kitchener of Khartoum (1850–1916), British soldier and statesman. At the outbreak of the First World War he was made Secretary of State for War. He had previously defeated the Mahdist forces at Omdurman in 1898, served as Chief of Staff in the Second Boer War, and been Commander-in-Chief (1902–9) in India.

kitchener ▶ **noun** historical a range fitted with various appliances such as ovens, plate-warmers, water heaters, etc.

kitchenette ▶ **noun** a small kitchen or part of a room equipped as a kitchen.

kitchen garden ▶ **noun** a garden or area where vegetables, fruit, or herbs are grown for domestic use.

kitchen midden ▶ **noun** a prehistoric refuse heap which marks an ancient settlement, chiefly containing bones, shells, and stone implements.

kitchen paper ▶ **noun** [mass noun] Brit. absorbent paper used for drying and cleaning.

kitchen police ▶ **noun** [usu. treated as pl.] US military slang enlisted men detailed to help the cook by washing dishes, peeling vegetables, and other kitchen duties.

kitchen porter ▶ **noun** a person employed to wash dishes and carry out other menial duties in the kitchen of a restaurant or hotel.

kitchen roll ▶ **noun** [mass noun] Brit. kitchen paper.

kitchen sink ▶ **noun** a sink in a kitchen, used for washing dishes and preparing food: *the traditional view of women as dedicated housewives tied to the kitchen sink is all but extinct.* ■ [as modifier] (of art forms) characterized by great realism in the depiction of drab or sordid subjects. The term is most used of post-war British drama, such as John Osborne's *Look Back in Anger* (1956) and Arnold Wesker's *Roots* (1959), which used working-class domestic settings rather than the drawing rooms of conventional middle-class drama.
– PHRASES **everything but the kitchen sink** humorous everything imaginable.

kitchen tea ▶ **noun** Austral./NZ & S. African a party held before a wedding to which female guests bring items of kitchen equipment as presents for the bride-to-be.

kitchenware ▶ **noun** [mass noun] the utensils used in a kitchen.

kite ▶ **noun 1** a toy consisting of a light frame with thin material stretched over it, flown in the wind at the end of a long string. ■ Brit. informal, dated an aircraft. ■ Sailing, informal a spinnaker or other high, light sail.
2 a medium to large long-winged bird of prey which typically has a forked tail and frequently soars on updraughts of air. ● *Milvus* and other genera, family Accipitridae: many species, in particular the **red kite** and **black kite**.
3 informal a fraudulent cheque, bill, or receipt. ■ an illicit or surreptitious letter or note. ■ archaic a person who exploits or preys on others.
4 Geometry a quadrilateral figure having two pairs of equal adjacent sides, symmetrical only about one diagonal.
▶ **verb 1** [no obj.] (usu. as noun **kiting**) fly a kite. ■ [with adverbial of direction] fly; move quickly: *he kited into England on Concorde.*
2 [with obj.] N. Amer. informal write or use (a cheque, bill, or receipt) fraudulently.
– PHRASES **(as) high as a kite** informal intoxicated with drugs or alcohol.
– ORIGIN Old English *cȳta* (in sense 2 of the noun); probably of imitative origin and related to German *Kauz* 'screech owl'. The toy was so named because it hovers in the air like the bird.

kite-flying ▶ **noun** [mass noun] **1** the action of flying a kite on a string. ■ the action of trying something out to test public opinion.
2 informal the fraudulent writing or using of a cheque, bill, or receipt.

Kitemark ▶ **noun** trademark (in the UK) an official kite-shaped mark on goods approved by the British Standards Institution.

kitenge /kɪ'tɛŋgi/ ▶ **noun** [mass noun] an East African cotton fabric printed in various colours and designs with distinctive borders, used especially for women's clothing.
– ORIGIN from Kiswahili *kitengele*.

kitesurfing (also **kiteboarding**) ▶ **noun** [mass noun] the sport or pastime of riding on a modified surfboard while holding on to a specially designed kite, using the wind for propulsion.
– DERIVATIVES **kitesurfer** (also **kiteboarder**) noun.

kit fox ▶ **noun** a small nocturnal fox with a yellowish-grey back and large, close-set ears, found in the deserts and steppes of the south-western US. ● *Vulpes macrotis*, family Canidae.
– ORIGIN early 19th cent.: *kit* probably from **kit**[2] (because of its small size).

kith /kɪθ/ ▶ **noun** (in phrase **kith and kin** or **kith or kin**) one's relations: *a widow without kith or kin.*
– ORIGIN Old English *cȳthth*, of Germanic origin; related to **couth**. The original senses were 'knowledge', 'one's native land', and 'friends and neighbours'. The phrase *kith and kin* originally denoted one's country and relatives; later one's friends and relatives.

kitke /'kɪtkə/ ▶ **noun** South African term for **challah**.
– ORIGIN perhaps from Hebrew *kikkār* 'loaf'.

kitsch /kɪtʃ/ ▶ **noun** [mass noun] art, objects, or design considered to be in poor taste because of excessive garishness or sentimentality, but sometimes appreciated in an ironic or knowing way: *the lava lamp is a bizarre example of sixties kitsch* | [as modifier] *kitsch knickknacks.*
– DERIVATIVES **kitschiness** noun, **kitschy** adjective (**kitschier**, **kitschiest**).
– ORIGIN 1920s: German.

kitten ▶ **noun 1** a young cat. ■ the young of several other animals, such as the rabbit and beaver.
2 a stout furry grey and white moth, the caterpillar of which resembles that of the puss moth. ● Genus *Furcula*, family Notodontidae.
▶ **verb** [no obj.] (of a cat or certain other animals) give birth.
– PHRASES **have kittens** Brit. informal be extremely nervous or upset.
– ORIGIN late Middle English *kitoun*, *ketoun*, from an Anglo-Norman French variant of Old French *chitoun*, diminutive of *chat* 'cat'.

kitten heel ▶ **noun** a type of low stiletto heel.

kittenish ▶ **adjective** playful, lively, or flirtatious: *her voice had that kittenish quality.*
– DERIVATIVES **kittenishly** adverb, **kittenishness** noun.

kittiwake /'kɪtɪweɪk/ ▶ **noun** a small gull that nests in colonies on sea cliffs, having a loud call that resembles its name. ● Genus *Rissa*, family Laridae: two species, in particular the black-legged *Rissa tridactyla* of the North Atlantic and North Pacific.
– ORIGIN early 17th cent. (originally Scots): imitative of its call.

K

kittle /'kɪt(ə)l/ (also **kittle-cattle** /'kɪt(ə)lkat(ə)l/) ▶ **adjective** archaic difficult to deal with; prone to erratic behaviour.
– ORIGIN mid 16th cent.: from *kittle* 'to tickle' (now Scots and dialect), probably from Old Norse *kitla*.

kitty[1] ▶ **noun** (pl. **kitties**) **1** a fund of money for communal use, made up of contributions from a group of people. ■ a pool of money in some gambling card games.
2 (in bowls) the jack.
– ORIGIN early 19th cent. (denoting a jail): of unknown origin.

kitty[2] ▶ **noun** (pl. **kitties**) a pet name or a child's name for a kitten or cat.

kitty-corner ▶ **adjective & adverb** N. Amer. another term for **cater-cornered**.

Kitty Hawk a town on a narrow sand peninsula on the Atlantic coast of North Carolina from where, in 1903, the Wright brothers made the first powered aeroplane flight.

kitty party ▶ **noun** chiefly Indian a regular social gathering of women in which each member contributes money to a central pool and lots are drawn to decide which member will get the entire sum.

Kitwe /'kɪtweɪ/ a city in the Copperbelt mining region of northern Zambia; pop. 508,700 (est. 2009).

Kitzbühel /'kɪtsˌbjʊəl/, German /'kɪtsˌbyːəl/ a town in the Tyrol, western Austria; pop. 8,398 (2006). It is a popular winter sports resort.

kiva /'kiːvə/ ▶ **noun** a chamber, built wholly or partly underground, used by male Pueblo Indians for religious rites.
– ORIGIN late 19th cent.: from Hopi *kíva*.

Kivu, Lake /'kiːvuː/ a lake in central Africa, on the Democratic Republic of the Congo (Zaire)–Rwanda frontier.

Kiwanis /kɪ'wɑːnɪs/ (in full **Kiwanis Club**) ▶ **noun** a North American society of business and professional people formed to maintain commercial ethics and as a social and charitable organization.
– DERIVATIVES **Kiwanian** noun & adjective.
– ORIGIN early 20th cent.: of unknown origin.

kiwi ▶ **noun** (pl. **kiwis**) **1** a flightless New Zealand bird with hair-like feathers, having a long downcurved bill with sensitive nostrils at the tip. ● Family Apterygidae and genus *Apteryx*: three species.
2 (**Kiwi**) informal a New Zealander.
– ORIGIN mid 19th cent.: from Maori.

kiwi fruit ▶ **noun** (pl. **same**) a fruit with a thin hairy skin, green flesh, and black seeds. Formerly called **Chinese gooseberry**. ● This fruit is obtained from the East Asian climbing plant *Actinidia chinensis* (family Actinidiaceae).

kJ ▸ abbreviation kilojoule(s).

KKK ▸ abbreviation Ku Klux Klan.

KL ▸ abbreviation informal Kuala Lumpur.

kl ▸ abbreviation kilolitre(s).

Klagenfurt /ˈklɑːɡənfʊət/, German /ˈklaːɡnˌfʊrt/ a city in southern Austria, capital of Carinthia; pop. 92,427 (2006).

Klaipeda /ˈklʌɪpədə/ a city and port in Lithuania, on the Baltic Sea; pop. 183,433 (2009). Former name (1918–23 and 1941–4, when under German control) **MEMEL**.

Klamath /ˈklaməθ/ ▸ noun (pl. **same** or **Klamaths**)
1 a member of an American Indian people of the Oregon–California border.
2 [mass noun] the Penutian language of the Klamath, now extinct or very nearly so.
▸ **adjective** relating to the Klamath or their language.
– ORIGIN from Chinook.

Klan ▸ noun the Ku Klux Klan or a large organization within it.

Klansman (or **Klanswoman**) ▸ noun (pl. **Klansmen** or **Klanswomen**) a member of the Ku Klux Klan.

Klaproth /ˈklaprəʊt/, Martin Heinrich (1743–1817), German chemist, one of the founders of analytical chemistry. He discovered three new elements (zirconium, uranium, and titanium) in certain minerals, and contributed to the identification of others. A follower of Lavoisier, he helped to introduce the latter's new system of chemistry into Germany.

klatch /klatʃ/ (also **klatsch**) ▸ noun N. Amer. an informal social gathering at which coffee is served.
– ORIGIN 1950s: from German *Klatsch* 'gossip'.

Klausenburg /ˈklaʊz(ə)n,bəːɡ/, German /ˈklaʊzn,bʊrk/ German name for **CLUJ-NAPOCA**.

K

klaxon /ˈklaks(ə)n/ ▸ noun trademark an electric horn or warning hooter.
– ORIGIN early 20th cent.: from the name of the manufacturing company.

klebsiella /ˌklɛbzɪˈɛlə/ ▸ noun [mass noun] a bacterium which causes respiratory, urinary, and wound infections. ● Genus *Klebsiella*; non-motile Gram-negative rods.
– ORIGIN modern Latin, from the name *Klebs* (see **KLEBS–LÖFFLER BACILLUS**).

Klebs–Löffler bacillus /klɛbzˈləːflə/ ▸ noun (pl. **Klebs–Löffler bacilli**) a bacterium that causes diphtheria in humans and similar diseases in other animals. ● *Corynebacterium diphtheriae*; non-motile Gram-positive rods.
– ORIGIN late 19th cent.: named after Theodore A. E. *Klebs* (1834–1913) and Friedrich A. J. *Löffler* (1852–1915), German bacteriologists.

Klee /kleɪ/, Paul (1879–1940), Swiss painter, resident in Germany 1906–33. He joined Kandinsky's *Blaue Reiter* group in 1912 and later taught at the Bauhaus (1920–33). His work is characterized by his sense of colour and moves freely between abstraction and figuration.

Kleenex ▸ noun (pl. **same** or **Kleenexes**) trademark an absorbent disposable paper tissue.

Klein¹ /klʌɪn/, Calvin (Richard) (b.1942), American fashion designer, known for his understated fashions for both men and women.

Klein² /klʌɪn/, Melanie (1882–1960), Austrian-born psychoanalyst. Klein was the first psychologist to specialize in the psychoanalysis of small children. Her discoveries led to an understanding of the more severe mental disorders found in children.

Klein bottle ▸ noun Mathematics a closed surface with only one side, formed by passing one end of a tube through the side of the tube and joining it to the other end.
– ORIGIN 1940s: named after Felix *Klein* (1849–1925), the German mathematician who first described it.

Klemperer /ˈklɛmpərə/, German /ˈklɛmpərɐ/, Otto (1885–1973), German-born conductor and composer. He became an American citizen in 1937 and subsequently became known for his interpretations of Beethoven, Brahms, and Mahler.

klepht /klɛft/ ▸ noun **1** a Greek independence fighter, especially one who fought the Turks in the 15th century or during the war of independence (1821–8).
2 historical a Greek brigand or bandit.
– ORIGIN from modern Greek *klephtēs*, from Greek *kleptēs* 'thief'. The original klephts led an outlaw existence in the mountains; those who maintained this after the war of independence became bandits.

kleptocrat /ˈklɛptə(ʊ)krat/ ▸ noun a ruler who uses their power to steal their country's resources.
– DERIVATIVES **kleptocracy** noun, **kleptocratic** adjective.
– ORIGIN 1960s: from Greek *kleptēs* 'thief' + **-CRAT**.

kleptomania /ˌklɛptə(ʊ)ˈmeɪnɪə/ ▸ noun [mass noun] a recurrent urge to steal, typically without regard for need or profit.
– DERIVATIVES **kleptomaniac** noun & adjective.
– ORIGIN mid 19th cent.: from Greek *kleptēs* 'thief' + **-MANIA**.

kleptoparasite ▸ noun Zoology a bird, insect, or other animal which habitually robs animals of other species of food.
– DERIVATIVES **kleptoparasitic** adjective, **kleptoparasitism** noun.
– ORIGIN late 20th cent.: from Greek *kleptēs* 'thief' + **PARASITE**.

Klerk, F. W. de, see **DE KLERK**.

Klerksdorp /ˈkləːksdɔːp/ a city in South Africa, in North West, south-west of Johannesburg; pop. 174,900 (est. 2009).

kletterschuh /ˈklɛtəʃuː/ ▸ noun (pl. **kletterschuhe**) a light boot with a cloth or felt sole, worn especially for rock climbing.
– ORIGIN early 20th cent.: from German *Kletterschuh* 'climbing shoe'.

klezmer /ˈklɛzmə/ ▸ noun (pl. **klezmorim** /-rɪm/) [mass noun] traditional eastern European Jewish music.
■ [count noun] a musician who plays klezmer music.
– ORIGIN 1920s: Yiddish, contraction of Hebrew *kĕlē zemer* 'musical instruments'.

klick (also **klik**) ▸ noun informal a kilometre.
– ORIGIN 1960s: of unknown origin; the term was originally used in the Vietnam War.

klieg /kliːɡ/ (also **klieg light**) ▸ noun a powerful electric lamp used in filming.
– ORIGIN 1920s: named after the American brothers, Anton T. *Kliegl* (1872–1927) and John H. *Kliegl* (1869–1959), who invented it.

Klimt /klɪmt/, Gustav (1862–1918), Austrian painter and designer. Co-founder of the Vienna Secession (1897), he is known for his decorative and allegorical paintings and his portraits of women. Notable works: *The Kiss* (1908).

Klinefelter's syndrome /ˈklʌɪnˌfɛltəz/ ▸ noun [mass noun] Medicine a syndrome affecting males in which the cells have an extra X chromosome (in addition to the normal XY), characterized by a tall thin physique, small infertile testes, and enlarged breasts.
– ORIGIN 1940s: named after Harry F. *Klinefelter* (born 1912), American physician.

Klingon /ˈklɪŋɒn/ ▸ noun **1** a member of a warlike humanoid alien species in the US television series *Star Trek* and its derivatives and sequels.
2 [mass noun] the language of the Klingons.
– ORIGIN 1960s: invented name.

klipfish /ˈklɪpfɪʃ, ˈkləp-/ ▸ noun a small bottom-dwelling fish, typically found in shallow water or rock pools. ● *Clinus* and other genera, family Clinidae: several species, in particular the brightly coloured *C. superciliosus*.
– ORIGIN late 18th cent.: partial translation of Dutch *klipvis* or Danish *klipfisk* 'rock fish'.

klipspringer /ˈklɪpˌsprɪŋə/ ▸ noun a small rock-dwelling antelope with a yellowish-grey coat, an arched back, and a stiff bouncing gait, native to southern Africa. ● *Oreotragus oreotragus*, family Bovidae.
– ORIGIN late 18th cent.: from Afrikaans, from Dutch *klip* 'rock' + *springer* 'jumper'.

Klondike /ˈklɒndʌɪk/ **1** a tributary of the Yukon River, in Yukon Territory, NW Canada, which rises in the Ogilvie mountains and flows 160 km (100 miles) westwards to join the Yukon at Dawson. It gave its name to the surrounding region, which became famous when gold was found in nearby Bonanza Creek in 1896. In the ensuing gold rush of 1897–8 thousands settled in the area to mine gold. ■ [as noun] a source of valuable material: *the surrounding area was still an archaeological Klondike*.
2 [as noun] chiefly N. Amer. a form of the card game patience or solitaire.

klong /klɒŋ/ ▸ noun (in Thailand) a canal.
– ORIGIN Thai.

kloof /kluːf/ S. African ▸ noun a steep-sided, wooded ravine or valley.
▸ **verb** [no obj.] (usu. as noun **kloofing**) explore kloofs as a sport.
– ORIGIN Afrikaans, from Middle Dutch *clove* 'cleft'.

Klosters /ˈkləʊstəz/, German /ˈkloːstɐs/ an Alpine winter-sports resort in eastern Switzerland, near the Austrian border.

kludge /klʌdʒ, kluːdʒ/ informal ▸ noun an ill-assorted collection of parts assembled to fulfil a particular purpose. ■ Computing a machine, system, or program that has been badly put together, especially a clumsy but temporarily effective solution to a particular fault or problem.
▸ **verb** [with obj.] improvise or put together from an ill-assorted collection of parts.
– ORIGIN 1960s: invented word, perhaps influenced by **BODGE** and **FUDGE**.

klutz /klʌts/ ▸ noun informal, chiefly N. Amer. a clumsy, awkward, or foolish person.
– DERIVATIVES **klutziness** noun, **klutzy** adjective (**klutzier**, **klutziest**).
– ORIGIN 1960s: from Yiddish *klots* 'wooden block'.

Kluxer /ˈklʌksə/ ▸ noun a member of the Ku Klux Klan.

klystron /ˈklʌɪstrɒn/ ▸ noun Physics an electron tube that generates or amplifies microwaves by velocity modulation.
– ORIGIN 1930s: from Greek *kluzein*, *klus-* 'wash over' + **-TRON**.

km ▸ abbreviation kilometre(s).

K-meson ▸ noun another term for **KAON**.
– ORIGIN 1950s: from *K* (for **KAON**) + **MESON**.

km/h (also **kmph**) ▸ abbreviation kilometres per hour.

kn. ▸ abbreviation knot(s).

knack ▸ noun [usu. in sing.] an acquired or natural skill at doing something: *he had a **knack** for communicating*. ■ a tendency to do something: *John had the enviable **knack** of falling asleep anywhere*.
– ORIGIN late Middle English (originally denoting a clever or deceitful trick): probably related to obsolete *knack* 'sharp blow or sound', of imitative origin (compare with Dutch *knak* 'crack, snap').

knacker Brit. ▸ noun **1** a person whose business is the disposal of dead or unwanted animals, especially those whose flesh is not fit for human consumption.
2 (**knackers**) vulgar slang testicles.
3 Irish informal an uncouth or loutish person.
▸ **verb** [with obj.] informal tire (someone) out: *this weekend has really knackered me*. ■ damage (something) severely: *I knackered my ankle playing on Sunday*.
– ORIGIN late 16th cent. (originally denoting a harness-maker, then a slaughterer of horses): possibly from obsolete *knack* 'trinket'. The word also had the sense 'old worn-out horse' (late 18th cent.). Sense 2 of the noun may be from dialect *knacker* 'castanet', from obsolete *knack* 'make a sharp abrupt noise', of imitative origin. It is unclear whether the verb represents a figurative use of 'slaughter', from sense 1 of the noun, or of 'castrate', from sense 2 of the noun.

knackered ▸ adjective Brit. informal extremely tired: *you look absolutely knackered*. ■ worn out or damaged by overuse: *a knackered CD player*.

knacker's yard ▸ noun Brit. a place where old or injured animals are taken to be slaughtered.

knackwurst /ˈnakwəːst/ (also **knockwurst**) ▸ noun [mass noun] a type of short, fat, highly seasoned German sausage.
– ORIGIN German, from *knacken* 'make a cracking noise' + *Wurst* 'sausage'.

knag /naɡ/ ▸ noun a short projection from the trunk or branch of a tree, such as a dead branch. ■ a knot in wood.
– ORIGIN late Middle English: from Low German *knagge*.

knaidel /ˈkneɪd(ə)l/ (also **kneidel**) ▸ noun (pl. **knaidlach** /ˈkneɪdlax/ or **knaidels**) a type of dumpling eaten in Jewish households during Passover.
– ORIGIN from Yiddish *kneydel*.

knap¹ /nap/ ▸ noun archaic the crest of a hill.
– ORIGIN Old English *cnæpp*, *cnæp*.

knap² /nap/ ▸ verb (**knaps**, **knapping**, **knapped**) [with obj.] Architecture & Archaeology shape (a piece of stone, typically flint) by striking it, so as to make a tool or weapon or a flat-faced stone for building walls.
■ archaic strike with a hard short sound; knock.
– DERIVATIVES **knapper** noun.
– ORIGIN late Middle English (in the sense 'to knock, rap'): imitative; compare with Dutch and German *knappen* 'crack, crackle'.

knapsack ▸ noun a soldier's or hiker's bag with shoulder straps, carried on the back, and typically made of canvas or other weatherproof material.
– ORIGIN early 17th cent.: from Middle Low German, from Dutch *knapzack*, probably from German *knappen* 'to bite' + *zak* 'sack'.

knapsack sprayer ▸ noun a sprayer consisting of a handheld nozzle supplied from a pressurized reservoir that is carried on the back like a knapsack.

knapweed ▸ noun [mass noun] a tough-stemmed Eurasian plant that typically has purple thistle-like flower heads, occurring chiefly in grassland and on roadsides. ● Genus *Centaurea*, family Compositae: several species, including the widespread **common** (or **lesser**) **knapweed** (*C. nigra*) (also called **HARDHEADS**).
– ORIGIN late Middle English (originally as *knop-weed*): from **KNOP** (because of its hard rounded involucre or 'head') + **WEED**.

knar /nɑː/ (also **knur**) ▸ noun archaic a knot or protuberance on a tree trunk or root.
– ORIGIN Middle English *knarre* (denoting a rugged rock or stone); related to Middle Low German *knarre* 'knobbly protuberance'; compare with **KNUR**.

knave /neɪv/ ▸ noun **1** archaic a dishonest or unscrupulous man.
2 (in cards) a jack.
– DERIVATIVES **knavery** noun (pl. **knaveries**).
– ORIGIN Old English *cnafa* 'boy, servant', of West Germanic origin; related to German *Knabe* 'boy'.

knavish /'neɪvɪʃ/ ▸ adjective archaic dishonest or unscrupulous: *his knavish tricks will be frustrated*.
– DERIVATIVES **knavishly** adverb, **knavishness** noun.

knawel /'nɔːɪl/ ▸ noun a low-growing inconspicuous plant of the pink family, which grows in temperate regions of the northern hemisphere. ● Genus *Scleranthus*, family Caryophyllaceae.
– ORIGIN late 16th cent.: from German *Knauel*, *Knäuel* 'knotgrass'.

knead ▸ verb [with obj.] work (moistened flour or clay) into dough or paste with the hands. ■ make (bread or pottery) by such a process. ■ massage or squeeze with the hands: *she kneaded his back*.
– DERIVATIVES **kneadable** adjective, **kneader** noun.
– ORIGIN Old English *cnedan*, of Germanic origin; related to Dutch *kneden* and German *kneten*.

knee ▸ noun **1** the joint between the thigh and the lower leg in humans. ■ the corresponding or analogous joint in other animals. ■ the upper surface of someone's thigh when they are sitting; a person's lap: *they were eating their suppers on their knees*. ■ the part of a garment covering the knee.
2 an angled piece of wood or metal frame used to connect and support the beams and timbers of a wooden ship.
3 an abrupt obtuse or approximately right-angled bend in a graph between parts where the slope varies smoothly.
▸ verb (**knees**, **kneeing**, **kneed**) [with obj.] hit (someone) with one's knee: *she kneed him in the groin*.
– PHRASES **at one's mother's** (or **father's**) **knee** at an early age. **bend** (or **bow**) **the** (or **one's**) **knee** (**to**) kneel in submission; submit. **bring some-one/thing to their/its knees** reduce someone or something to a state of weakness or submission. **fall** (or **drop**, or **sink**, etc.) **to one's knees** assume a kneeling position. **on bended knee(s)** kneeling, especially in entreaty or worship: *did your guy propose on bended knee?* **on one's knees** in a kneeling position. ■ on the verge of collapse: *when they took over, the newspaper was on its knees*. **weak at the knees** overcome by a strong feeling, typically desire.
– ORIGIN Old English *cnēow*, *cnēo*, of Germanic origin; related to Dutch *knie* and German *Knie*, from an Indo-European root shared by Latin *genu* and Greek *gonu*.

kneeboard ▸ noun a short board for surfing or water-skiing in a kneeling position.
– DERIVATIVES **kneeboarder** noun, **kneeboarding** noun.

knee breeches ▸ plural noun archaic short trousers worn by men and fastened at or just below the knee.

kneecap ▸ noun the convex bone in front of the knee joint; the patella.
▸ verb (**kneecaps**, **kneecapping**, **kneecapped**) [with obj.] shoot (someone) in the knee or leg as a form of punishment.

knee-deep ▸ adjective & adverb of or at a depth or height to reach the knees: [as adj.] *the snow was almost knee-deep* | [as adv.] *his leg plunged knee-deep into the water*. ■ [as adj.] having more than one needs or wants of something: *we shall soon be knee-deep in conflicting legal views*.

knee-high ▸ adjective & adverb so high as to reach the knees: [as adj.] *knee-high boots* | [as adv.] *they were wading knee-high in the water*.
▸ noun (usu. **knee-highs**) a nylon stocking with an elasticated top that reaches to a person's knee.
– PHRASES **knee-high to a grasshopper** informal very small or very young.

kneehole ▸ noun a space for the knees, especially one under a desk: [as modifier] *a kneehole desk*.

knee-jerk ▸ adjective [attrib.] (of a response) automatic and unthinking: *a knee-jerk reaction*. ■ (of a person) responding to situations in an automatic and unthinking way: *knee-jerk radicals*.
▸ noun a sudden involuntary reflex kick caused by a blow on the tendon just below the knee.

kneel ▸ verb (past and past participle **knelt** or chiefly N. Amer. also **kneeled**) [no obj.] be in or assume a position in which the body is supported by a knee or the knees, as when praying or showing submission: *they knelt down and prayed*.
– ORIGIN Old English *cnēowlian*, from *cnēow* (see **KNEE**).

knee-length ▸ adjective (of footwear or an item of clothing) reaching the knees: *knee-length boots*.

kneeler ▸ noun a person who kneels, especially in prayer. ■ a cushion or bench for kneeling on.

knee-pan ▸ noun old-fashioned term for **KNEECAP**.

knee-slapper ▸ noun N. Amer. informal an uproariously funny joke.
– DERIVATIVES **knee-slapping** adjective.

knees-up ▸ noun [in sing.] Brit. informal a lively party or gathering.

knee-trembler ▸ noun informal an act of sexual intercourse between people in a standing position.

kneidel ▸ noun (pl. **kneidlach**) variant spelling of **KNAIDEL**.

knell /nɛl/ literary ▸ noun [in sing.] the sound of a bell, especially when rung solemnly for a death or funeral. ■ used in reference to an announcement, event, or sound that warns of the end of something: *emails and text messages are **sounding the knell for** the written word*.
▸ verb [no obj.] (of a bell) ring solemnly, especially for a death or funeral. ■ [with obj.] proclaim (something) by or as if by a knell.
– ORIGIN Old English *cnyll* (noun), *cnyllan* (verb), of West Germanic origin; related to Dutch *knal* (noun), *knallen* (verb) 'bang, pop, crack'. The current spelling (dating from the 16th cent.) is perhaps influenced by **BELL**[1].

knelt past and past participle of **KNEEL**.

Knesset /'knɛsɛt/ the parliament of modern Israel, established in 1949. It consists of 120 members elected every four years.
– ORIGIN Hebrew, literally 'gathering'.

knew past of **KNOW**.

knickerbocker ▸ noun **1** (**knickerbockers**) loose-fitting breeches gathered at the knee or calf.
2 (**Knickerbocker**) informal a New Yorker. ■ a descendant of the original Dutch settlers in New York.
– DERIVATIVES **knickerbockered** adjective.
– ORIGIN mid 19th cent. (originally in sense 2): named after Diedrich *Knickerbocker*, pretended author of W. Irving's *History of New York* (1809). Sense 1 is said to have arisen from the resemblance of knickerbockers to the knee breeches worn by Dutch men in George Cruikshank's illustrations in Irving's book.

Knickerbocker Glory ▸ noun Brit. a dessert consisting of ice cream served with fruit, cream, and other sweet ingredients in a tall glass.

knickers ▸ plural noun **1** Brit. a woman's or girl's undergarment, covering the body from the waist or hips to the top of the thighs and having two holes for the legs. ■ [as exclamation] informal expressing contempt or annoyance: *oh, knickers to the lot of them!*
2 N. Amer. knickerbockers.
– PHRASES **get one's knickers in a twist** Brit. informal become upset or angry.
– DERIVATIVES **knickerless** adjective.
– ORIGIN late 19th cent. (in the sense 'short trousers'): abbreviation of *knickerbockers* (see **KNICKERBOCKER**).

knick-knack (also **nick-nack**) ▸ noun (usu. **knick-knacks**) small worthless objects, especially household ornaments.
– DERIVATIVES **knick-knackery** noun.
– ORIGIN late 16th cent. (in the sense 'a petty trick'): reduplication of **KNACK**.

knicks ▸ plural noun Brit. informal short for **KNICKERS**.

knife ▸ noun (pl. **knives**) a cutting instrument composed of a blade and a handle into which it is fixed, either rigidly or with a joint. ■ an instrument such as this used as a weapon. ■ a cutting blade forming part of a machine.
▸ verb [with obj.] stab (someone) with a knife: *he was knifed to death during the argument*. ■ [no obj., with adverbial] cut or move cleanly through something with a knife-like action: *a shard of steel knifed through the mainsail*.
– PHRASES **before you can say knife** informal very quickly; almost instantaneously. **that one could cut with a knife 1** (of an atmosphere) very tense or oppressive. **2** (of an accent) very obvious or strong. **get** (or **stick**) **the knife into** (or **in**) **someone** informal be malicious or vindictive towards someone. **go** (or **be**) **under the knife** informal have surgery. **the knives are out** (**for someone**) informal there is open hostility (towards someone). **like a** (**hot**) **knife through butter** very easily; without any resistance or difficulty. **twist** (or **turn**) **the knife** (**in the wound**) deliberately make someone's sufferings worse.
– DERIVATIVES **knife-like** adjective, **knifer** noun.
– ORIGIN late Old English *cnīf*, from Old Norse *knífr*, of Germanic origin.

knife block ▸ noun a block of wood or other solid material, containing long hollow grooves in which kitchen knives can be inserted up to the handle.

knife-edge ▸ noun **1** the edge of a knife. ■ [as modifier] (of creases or pleats in a garment) very narrow or sharp.
2 [in sing.] a very tense or dangerous situation: *worried investors could be living on a knife-edge for the next twelve months*.
3 a sharp mountain ridge; an arête.
4 a steel wedge on which a pendulum or other device oscillates or is balanced.

knifefish ▸ noun (pl. **same** or **knifefishes**) a semi-nocturnal freshwater fish with a reduced or absent dorsal fin and a long anal fin which reaches from the belly to the tail: ● a New World fish with a narrow eel-like body (families Rhamphichthyidae and Gymnotidae: several genera). ● another term for **FEATHERBACK**.

knifeman ▸ noun (pl. **knifemen**) a man who uses a knife to commit a crime.

knife pleat ▸ noun a sharp, narrow pleat on a skirt, typically one of many folded in the same direction and overlapping each other.

knifepoint ▸ noun (in phrase **at knifepoint**) while threatening someone or being threatened with a knife: *she was raped at knifepoint*.

knife rest ▸ noun a metal or glass support for a carving knife or carving fork at table.

knife-throwing ▸ noun [mass noun] a circus act or other entertainment in which knives are thrown at a target.
– DERIVATIVES **knife-thrower** noun.

knight ▸ noun **1** (in the Middle Ages) a man who served his sovereign or lord as a mounted soldier in armour. ■ (in the Middle Ages) a man raised by a sovereign to honourable military rank after service as a page and squire. ■ (also **knight of the shire**) historical a gentleman representing a shire or county in Parliament. ■ literary a man devoted to the service of a woman or a cause: *in all your quarrels I will be your knight*.
2 (in the UK) a man awarded a non-hereditary title by the sovereign in recognition of merit or service and entitled to use the honorific 'Sir' in front of his name.
3 a chess piece, typically with its top shaped like a horse's head, that moves by jumping to the opposite corner of a rectangle two squares by three. Each player starts the game with two knights.
4 (in ancient Rome) a member of the class of equites. ■ (in ancient Greece) a citizen of the second class in Athens, called *hippeus* in Greek.
▸ verb [with obj.] invest (someone) with the title of knight: *he was knighted for his services to industry*.
– PHRASES **knight in shining armour** (or **knight on a white charger**) an idealized or chivalrous man who comes to the rescue of a woman in a difficult situation. **knight of the road** informal a man who frequents the roads, for example a travelling sales representative, tramp, or (formerly) a highwayman.
– ORIGIN Old English *cniht* 'boy, youth, servant', of West Germanic origin; related to Dutch *knecht* and German *Knecht*. Sense 2 of the noun dates from the mid 16th cent.; the uses relating to Greek and Roman history derive from comparison with medieval knights.

knightage ▸ noun rare a list of knights.

knight bachelor ▸ noun (pl. **knights bachelor**) a knight not belonging to any particular order.

K

knight commander ▸ noun a very high class in some orders of knighthood.

knight errant ▸ noun (pl. **knights errant**) a medieval knight wandering in search of chivalrous adventures.
– DERIVATIVES **knight-errantry** noun.

knighthood ▸ noun the title, rank, or status of a knight: *he received a knighthood in the Birthday Honours* | [mass noun] *the basis of feudal knighthood.*

knightly ▸ adjective (**knightlier**, **knightliest**) associated with or typical of a knight; chivalrous: *a knightly quest.*
– DERIVATIVES **knightliness** noun.

knight marshal ▸ noun historical an officer of the royal household with judicial functions.

knight of the shire ▸ noun see **KNIGHT** (sense 1 of the noun).

Knightsbridge a district in the West End of London, to the south of Hyde Park, noted for its fashionable and expensive shops.

knight service ▸ noun [mass noun] (in the Middle Ages) the tenure of land by a knight on condition of performing military service.

Knights Hospitaller a military and religious order founded as the Knights of the Order of the Hospital of St John of Jerusalem in the 11th century.

> Originally protectors of pilgrims, they also undertook the care of the sick. During the Middle Ages they became a powerful and wealthy military force, with foundations in various European countries. In England, the order was revived in 1831 and was responsible for the foundation of the St John Ambulance Brigade in 1888.

Knights Templar a religious and military order for the protection of pilgrims to the Holy Land, founded as the Poor Knights of Christ and of the Temple of Solomon in 1118.

> The order became powerful and wealthy, but its members' arrogance towards rulers, together with their wealth and their rivalry with the Knights Hospitaller, led to their downfall; the order was suppressed in 1312, many of its possessions being given to the Knights Hospitaller.

K

kniphofia /nɪˈfəʊfɪə, nʌɪ-, nɪpˈhəʊfɪə/ ▸ noun a plant of a genus that comprises the red-hot pokers. ● Genus *Kniphofia*, family Liliaceae (or Aloaceae).
– ORIGIN modern Latin; named after Johann H. *Kniphof* (1704–1763), German botanist.

knish /knɪʃ/ ▸ noun a dumpling of flaky dough with a savoury filling that is baked or fried.
– ORIGIN Yiddish, from Russian *knish*, *knysh*, denoting a kind of bun or dumpling.

knit ▸ verb (**knits**, **knitting**; past and past participle **knitted** or (especially in sense 2) **knit**) **1** [with obj.] make (a garment or other item) by interlocking loops of wool or other yarn with knitting needles or on a machine: *she was knitting a sweater.* ■ make (a stitch or row of stitches) in such a way. ■ make (a plain stitch) in knitting: *knit one, purl one.*
2 unite or cause to unite: [no obj.] *disparate regions had begun to **knit together** under the king* | [with obj.] *the experience **knitted the men together*** | (as adj., with submodifier **knit**) *a closely knit family.* ■ [with obj.] (of parts of a broken bone) become joined.
3 [with obj.] tighten (one's eyebrows) in a frown of concentration, disapproval, or anxiety.
▸ noun (**knits**) knitted garments.
– DERIVATIVES **knitter** noun.
– ORIGIN Old English *cnyttan*, of West Germanic origin; related to German dialect *knütten*, also to **KNOT**[1]. The original sense was 'tie in or with a knot', hence 'join, unite' (sense 2 of the verb); an obsolete Middle English sense 'knot string to make a net' gave rise to sense 1 of the verb.

knitbone ▸ noun another term for **COMFREY**.

knitting ▸ noun [mass noun] the craft or action of knitting. ■ material which is in the process of being knitted: *I put down my knitting.*
– PHRASES **stick to the** (or **one's**) **knitting** informal (of an organization) concentrate on a familiar area of activity rather than diversify.

knitting machine ▸ noun a machine with a bank of needles on which garments can be knitted.

knitting needle ▸ noun a long, thin, pointed rod used as part of a pair for knitting by hand.

knitwear ▸ noun [mass noun] knitted garments.

knives plural form of **KNIFE**.

knob ▸ noun **1** a rounded lump or ball, especially at the end or on the surface of something. ■ a ball-shaped handle on a door or drawer. ■ a round button for adjusting or controlling a machine. ■ a small lump of a substance: *add a knob of butter.*
2 chiefly N. Amer. a prominent round hill.
3 vulgar slang a man's penis.
▸ verb (**knobs**, **knobbing**, **knobbed**) [with obj.] Brit. vulgar slang (of a man) have sexual intercourse with (someone).
– PHRASES **with** (**brass**) **knobs on** Brit. informal and something more: *it is the rock 'n' roll statement with knobs on.* ■ used as a way of returning and intensifying an insult: *'Lazy tyke!' 'Lazy yourself with brass knobs on!'* [with allusion to the addition of decorative knobs to an object as an embellishment.]
– DERIVATIVES **knobbed** adjective, **knobby** adjective (**knobbier**, **knobbiest**), **knob-like** adjective.
– ORIGIN late Middle English: from Middle Low German *knobbe* 'knot, knob, bud'.

knobble ▸ noun Brit. a small knob or lump on something.
– ORIGIN late Middle English: diminutive of **KNOB**.

knobbly ▸ adjective (**knobblier**, **knobbliest**) having lumps which give a misshapen appearance: *knobbly knees* | *knobbly potatoes.*

knobhead ▸ noun Brit. vulgar slang a stupid person.

knobkerrie /ˈnɒbˌkɛri/ (also **knobkierie**) ▸ noun a short stick with a knob at the top, traditionally used as a weapon by the indigenous peoples of South Africa.
– ORIGIN mid 19th cent.: from **KNOB** + *-kerrie* (from Nama *kieri* 'knobkerrie'), suggested by Afrikaans *knopkierie*.

knobstick ▸ noun **1** another term for **KNOBKERRIE**.
2 archaic term for **BLACKLEG** (sense 1 of the noun).

knock ▸ verb **1** [no obj.] strike a surface noisily to attract attention, especially when waiting to be let in through a door: *he strolled over and **knocked on** a door marked Enquiries.* ■ strike or thump together or against something: *her heart knocked painfully behind her ribs.* ■ (of a motor or other engine) make a regular thumping or rattling noise, e.g. through pinking.
2 [with obj.] collide with (someone or something), giving them a hard blow: *he deliberately ran against her, knocking her shoulder* | [no obj.] *he **knocked into** an elderly man with a walking stick.* ■ [with obj. and adverbial of direction] force to move or fall with a deliberate or accidental blow or collision: *he'd **knocked over** a glass of water.* ■ injure or damage by striking: *she knocked her knee painfully on the table* | figurative *you have had a setback that has knocked your self-esteem.* ■ make (a hole or a dent) in something by striking it forcefully: *you'll need to knock a hole in the wall.* ■ demolish the barriers between (rooms or buildings): *two of the downstairs rooms had been **knocked into one**.*
3 [with obj.] informal talk disparagingly about; criticize.
4 [with obj.] informal approach (a specified age): *he's younger than his brother—knocking seventy.*
▸ noun **1** a sudden short sound caused by a blow, especially on a door to attract attention or gain entry. ■ [mass noun] a continual thumping or rattling sound made by an engine.
2 a blow or collision: *the casing is tough enough to withstand knocks.* ■ a discouraging experience; a setback: *the region's industries have taken a severe knock.* ■ informal a critical comment.
3 Cricket, informal an innings, especially of an individual batsman: *a splendid knock of 117 against Somerset.*
– PHRASES **knock someone's block off** informal hit someone very hard. **knock the bottom out of** see **BOTTOM**. **knock someone dead** informal greatly impress someone. **knock someone for six** see **SIX**. **knock people's heads together** see **BANG PEOPLE'S HEADS TOGETHER** at **BANG**[1]. **knock something into a cocked hat** see **COCKED HAT**. **knock someone into the middle of next week** informal hit someone very hard. **knock someone/thing into shape** see **SHAPE**. **knock it off** informal stop doing something. **knock someone on the head** stun or kill someone by a blow to the head. **knock something on the head** Brit. informal prevent an idea, plan, or proposal from being developed or carried out. **knock on wood** see **TOUCH WOOD** at **WOOD**. **knock someone's socks off** see **SOCK**. **knock spots off** Brit. informal easily outdo. **the school of hard knocks** painful or difficult experiences that are seen to be useful in teaching someone about life. **you could have knocked me** (or **her**, **him**, etc.) **down with a feather** informal used to express great surprise.
– PHRASAL VERBS **knock about** (or **around**) informal travel without a specific purpose: *for a couple of years she and I knocked around the Mediterranean.* ■ happen to be present: *it gets confusing when there are too many people knocking about.* ■ chiefly Brit. spend time with someone: *she **knocked around with** artists.* **knock someone/thing about** (or **around**) injure or damage by rough treatment. **knock someone back** Brit. informal **1** reject or discourage a person or their request or suggestion. **2** cost someone a specified, typically large, amount of money: *buying that house must have knocked them back a bit.* **knock something back 1** informal consume a drink quickly. **2** work risen dough by vigorous kneading to expel air before baking. **knock someone down** (or **over**) chiefly Brit. (especially of a vehicle) strike or collide with someone so as to cause them to fall to the ground: *I was nearly knocked down by a bus.* **knock something down 1** demolish a building or other structure: *the closely packed terraced houses were knocked down in the interests of 'progress'.* **2** (at an auction) confirm the sale of an article to a bidder by a knock with a hammer. ■ informal reduce the price of an article. **3** US informal earn a specified sum as a wage. **4** Austral./NZ informal spend a pay cheque freely. **knock off** informal stop work. **knock someone off 1** informal kill someone. **2** Brit. vulgar slang have sexual intercourse with a woman. **knock something off 1** informal produce a piece of work quickly and without much effort. **2** informal deduct an amount from a total: *when the bill came they knocked off £600 because of a little scratch.* **3** Brit. informal steal something. ■ N. Amer. informal rob a shop or similar establishment. ■ informal make an illegal copy of a product. **knock on 1** informal grow old: *she's knocking on a bit.* **2** (also **knock the ball on**) Rugby illegally drive the ball with the hand or arm towards the opponents' goal line. **knock someone out 1** make a person unconscious, typically with a blow to the head. ■ knock down (a boxer) for a count of ten, thereby winning the contest. ■ (**knock oneself out**) informal work so hard that one is exhausted. ■ informal astonish or greatly impress someone. **2** defeat a competitor in a knockout competition: *England had been **knocked out of** the World Cup.* **knock something out 1** destroy, damage, or disable a machine or piece of equipment. **2** informal produce work at a steady fast rate: *if you knock out a thousand words a day you'll soon have finished.* **3** empty a tobacco pipe by tapping it against a surface. **4** Austral./NZ informal earn a specified sum of money. **knock someone over** another way of saying **KNOCK SOMEONE DOWN**. **knock something over** N. Amer. informal rob a shop or similar establishment. **knock someone sideways** informal astonish someone. **knock something together** assemble something in a hasty and makeshift way. **knock up** Brit. informal (in a racket game) practise before formal play begins. **knock someone up 1** Brit. wake or attract the attention of someone by knocking at their door. **2** informal make a woman pregnant. **knock something up 1** Brit. make something in a hurry. **2** Cricket score runs rapidly.
– ORIGIN Old English *cnocian*, of imitative origin.

knockabout ▸ adjective **1** denoting rough, slapstick comedy.
2 (of clothes) suitable for rough use.
▸ noun **1** a rough, slapstick comic performance.
2 US a tramp.
3 Austral./NZ a farm or station handyman.
4 N. Amer. a small yacht or dinghy.

knock-back ▸ noun informal a refusal, rejection, or setback: *don't despair if you have a few knock-backs.*

knock-down ▸ adjective [attrib.] **1** informal (of a price) very low. [used earlier to refer to reserve prices set at an auction.]
2 capable of knocking down or overwhelming someone or something: *repeated knock-down blows.* ■ (of furniture) easily dismantled and reassembled.
▸ noun **1** Boxing an act of knocking an opponent down. ■ Soccer an instance of a striker heading a high ball down to a nearby teammate. ■ Sailing an instance of a boat toppling over as a result of the force of the wind.
2 Austral./NZ informal an introduction to someone.

knock-down-drag-out ▸ noun informal a free-for-all fight.

knocker ▸ noun **1** a metal or wooden object hinged to a door and rapped by visitors to attract attention and gain entry. ■ informal a person who buys or sells from door to door, especially with intent to deceive.
2 informal a person who continually finds fault.
3 (**knockers**) informal a woman's breasts.
– PHRASES **on the knocker** informal **1** Brit. going from door to door canvassing, buying, or selling. **2** Austral./NZ (of payment) immediately; on demand: *he has to pay cash on the knocker.*

knocker-up ▸ **noun** (pl. **knockers-up**) Brit. historical a person employed to rouse workers by knocking at their doors or windows.

knock-for-knock agreement ▸ **noun** Brit. an agreement between insurance companies by which each pays its own policyholders regardless of liability.

knocking copy ▸ **noun** [mass noun] advertising or publicity that discredits a competitor's product.

knocking shop ▸ **noun** Brit. informal a brothel.

knock knees ▸ **plural noun** a condition in which the legs curve inwards so that the feet are apart when the knees are touching.
– DERIVATIVES **knock-kneed adjective**.

knock-off ▸ **noun** informal a copy or imitation, especially of an expensive product.

knock-on ▸ **noun 1** [usu. as modifier] chiefly Brit. a secondary, indirect, or cumulative effect: *movements in oil prices have knock-on effects on other fuels*.
2 Rugby an act of knocking on, for which a penalty or scrum is awarded to the opposition.

knockout ▸ **noun 1** an act of knocking someone out, especially in boxing: [as modifier] *a knockout blow*. ■ informal an extremely attractive or impressive person or thing: *he must have been a knockout when he was young*.
2 Brit. a tournament in which the loser in each round is eliminated.

knockout drops ▸ **plural noun** a drug in liquid form added to a drink to cause unconsciousness.

knockout mouse ▸ **noun** Genetics a mouse whose DNA has been genetically engineered so that it does not express particular proteins.

knock-up ▸ **noun** Brit. (in tennis or other racket sports) a period of practice play, especially before formal play begins.

knockwurst /ˈnɒkwəːst/ ▸ **noun** variant spelling of **KNACKWURST**.

Knole sofa /nəʊl/ ▸ **noun** a sofa with adjustable sides which allow it to be converted into a bed.
– ORIGIN 1940s: named after *Knole* Park, Kent, where the prototype of the sofa originated (*c*.1605–20).

knoll[1] /nəʊl/ ▸ **noun** a small hill or mound.
– ORIGIN Old English *cnoll* 'hilltop', of Germanic origin; related to German *Knolle* 'clod, lump, tuber' and Dutch *knol* 'tuber, turnip'.

knoll[2] /nəʊl/ ▸ **verb & noun** archaic form of **KNELL**.
– ORIGIN Middle English: probably an imitative alteration of **KNELL**.

knop /nɒp/ ▸ **noun** a knob, especially an ornamental one, for example in the stem of a wine glass. ■ an ornamental loop or tuft in yarn.
– ORIGIN Middle English: from Middle Low German and Middle Dutch *knoppe*.

knopper gall /ˈnɒpə/ ▸ **noun** a hard, irregular umbrella-like gall which forms on an oak acorn in response to the developing larva of a gall wasp. ● The wasp is *Andricus quercuscalicis*, family Cynipidae.
– ORIGIN late 19th cent.: *knopper* from German *Knopper* 'gall'.

Knossos /ˈknɒsəs, ˈnɒs-/ the principal city of Minoan Crete, the remains of which are situated on the north coast of Crete. The city site was occupied from Neolithic times until *c*.1200 BC. Excavations by Sir Arthur Evans from 1899 onwards revealed the remains of a luxurious palace, which he called the Palace of Minos.

knot[1] ▸ **noun 1** a fastening made by looping a piece of string, rope, or something similar on itself and tightening it: *tie a knot at the end of the cord* | figurative *a complicated knot of racial politics and pride*. ■ a particular method of making a knot: *you need to master two knots, the clove hitch and the sheet bend*. ■ an ornamental ribbon.
2 a tangled mass in something such as hair or wool.
3 a knob, protuberance, or node in a stem, branch, or root. ■ a hard mass formed in a tree trunk at the intersection with a branch, resulting in a round cross-grained piece in timber when cut through. ■ a hard lump of tissue in the body.
4 an unpleasant feeling of tightness or tension in a part of the body: *her stomach was* **in knots** *as she unlocked the door*.
5 a small tightly packed group of people: *a knot of spectators was gathering*.
6 a unit of speed equivalent to one nautical mile per hour, used especially of ships, aircraft, or winds. ■ chiefly historical a length marked by knots on a log line, as a measure of speed.
▸ **verb** (**knots, knotting, knotted**) [with obj.] **1** fasten with a knot: *the scarves were knotted loosely around their throats* | (as adj. **knotted**) *a knotted rope*. ■ make (a carpet or other decorative item) with knots.
2 make (something, especially hair) tangled: (as adj. **knotted**) *he brushed through his knotted hair*.
3 cause (a muscle) to become tense and hard. ■ [no obj.] (of the stomach) tighten as a result of nervousness or tension.
– PHRASES **at a rate of knots** Brit. informal very fast. **get knotted** Brit. informal used to express contemptuous rejection of someone. **tie someone** (**up**) **in knots** informal make someone completely confused. **tie the knot** informal get married.
– DERIVATIVES **knotless adjective**, **knotter noun**.
– ORIGIN Old English *cnotta*, of West Germanic origin; related to Dutch *knot*.

knot[2] ▸ **noun** (pl. **same** or **knots**) a small, relatively short-billed sandpiper, with a reddish-brown or blackish breast in the breeding season. ● Genus *Calidris*, family Scolopacidae: two species, in particular the **red knot** (*C. canutus*), which breeds in the Arctic and winters in the southern hemisphere.
– ORIGIN late Middle English: of unknown origin.

knot garden ▸ **noun** a formal garden laid out in an intricate design.

knotgrass ▸ **noun** [mass noun] a common Eurasian plant of the dock family, with jointed creeping stems and small pink flowers. It is a serious weed in some areas. ● Genus *Polygonum*, family Polygonaceae: several species, in particular *P. aviculare*. ■ any of a number of other plants, especially grasses, with jointed stems.

knothole ▸ **noun** a hole in a piece of timber where a knot has fallen out, or in a tree trunk where a branch has decayed.

knotted wrack ▸ **noun** [mass noun] a dark olive-green seaweed with flat branching fronds which bear air bladders, occurring on rocky seashores. ● *Ascophyllum nodosum*, class Phaeophyceae.

knotting ▸ **noun** [mass noun] **1** the action or craft of tying knots in yarn to make carpets or other decorative items. ■ the knots tied in a carpet or other item.
2 a preparation applied to knots in wooden boards prior to painting to prevent resin from oozing through, typically consisting of shellac dissolved in methylated spirits.

knotty ▸ **adjective** (**knottier, knottiest**) **1** full of knots: *panelling in knotty pine*.
2 extremely difficult or complex: *a knotty legal problem*.
– DERIVATIVES **knottily adverb**, **knottiness noun**.

knotweed ▸ **noun** [mass noun] a plant of the dock family, which typically has sheaths where the leaves join the stems and is often an invasive weed. ● *Polygonum* and other genera, family Polygonaceae: several species, in particular **Japanese knotweed**. ■ knotgrass.

knotwork ▸ **noun** [mass noun] ornamental work consisting of or representing intertwined and knotted cords.

knout /naʊt/ ▸ **noun** (in imperial Russia) a whip used to inflict punishment, often causing death.
▸ **verb** [with obj.] flog (someone) with such a knout.
ORIGIN mid 17th cent.: via French from Russian *knut*, from Old Norse *knútr*; related to **KNOT**[1].

know ▸ **verb** (past **knew**; past participle **known**) **1** [with clause] be aware of through observation, inquiry, or information: *most people know that CFCs can damage the ozone layer* | *I know what I'm doing*. ■ [with obj.] have knowledge or information concerning: *I would write to him if I knew his address* | [no obj.] *I* **know of** *one local who shot himself*. ■ be absolutely certain or sure about something: *I just knew it was something I wanted to do* | [with obj.] *I knew it!*
2 [with obj.] have developed a relationship with (someone) through meeting and spending time with them; be familiar or friendly with: *he knew and respected Laura*. ■ have a good command of (a subject or language). ■ recognize (someone or something): *Isabel couldn't hear the words clearly but she knew the voice*. ■ be familiar or acquainted with (something): *a little restaurant she knew near Leicester Square*. ■ have personal experience of (an emotion or situation): *a man who had known better times*. ■ (usu. **be known as**) regard or perceive as having a specified characteristic: *the loch is known as a dangerous area for swimming*. ■ (usu. **be known as**) give (someone or something) a particular name or title: *the doctor was universally known as 'Hubert'*. ■ (**know someone/thing from**) be able to distinguish one person or thing from (another): *you are convinced you know your own baby from any other in the world*.
3 [with obj.] archaic have sexual intercourse with (someone). [a Hebraism which has passed into modern languages; compare with German *erkennen*, French *connaître*.]
– PHRASES **and one knows it** said to emphasize that someone is well aware of a fact although they might pretend otherwise: *that's nonsense and you know it*. **—— as we know it** as is familiar or customary in the present: *apocalyptic expectations, envisaging the end of the world as we know it*. **before one knows where one is** (or **before one knows it**) informal with baffling speed. **be in the know** be aware of something known only to a few people: *he had a tip from a friend in the know: the horse was a cert*. **be not to know** have no way of being aware of: *you weren't to know he was about to die*. **don't I know it!** informal used as an expression of rueful assent or agreement. **don't you know** informal, dated used to emphasize what one has just said or is about to say: *I was, don't you know, a great motoring enthusiast in those days*. **for all someone knows** used to express the limited scope or extent of one's information: *she could be dead for all I know*. **God** (or **goodness** or **heaven**) **knows 1** used to emphasize that one does not know something: *God knows what else they might find*. **2** used to emphasize the truth of a statement: *goodness knows, I haven't been perfect*. **have been known to do something** have occasionally in the past done something. **I know 1** I agree: *'It's not the same without Rosie.' 'I know.'* **2** (also **I know what**) I have a new idea or suggestion: *I know what, let's do it now*. **know something backwards** see **BACKWARDS**. **know best** have better knowledge or more appropriate skills. **know better than** be wise or polite enough to avoid doing a particular thing: *you ought to know better than to ask that*. **know someone by sight** recognize someone by their appearance without knowing their name or being so well acquainted as to talk to them. **know different** (or **otherwise**) be aware of information or evidence to the contrary. **know something for a fact** be aware of something that is irrefutable or beyond doubt: *I know for a fact that he can't speak a word of Japanese*. **know someone in the biblical sense** informal, humorous have sexual intercourse with someone. **know no bounds** have no limits: *their courage knows no bounds*. **know one's own mind** be decisive and certain. **know one's way around** be familiar with (an area, procedure, or subject). **know the ropes** have experience of the appropriate procedures. [with reference to ropes used in sailing.] **know what's what** informal be experienced and competent in a particular area. **know who's who** be aware of the identity and status of each person. **let it be** (or **make something**) **known** ensure that people are informed about something, especially via a third party: [with clause] *the Minister let it be known that he was not seeking reappointment*. **not know from nothing** N. Amer. informal be totally ignorant: *she shakes her head while you talk, as if to say you don't know from nothing*. **not know the first thing about** have not the slightest idea about (something). **not know that** informal used to express one's doubts about one's ability to do something: *I don't know that I can sum up my meaning on paper*. **not know what hit one** be very shocked or surprised by a sudden attack or event. **not know what to do with oneself** be at a loss as to know what to do, typically through boredom, embarrassment, or anxiety. **not know where** (or **which way**) **to look** feel great embarrassment and not know how to react. **not want to know** informal refuse to react or take notice: *they just didn't want to know when I gave my side of the story*. **what does —— know?** informal used to indicate that someone knows nothing about the subject in question: *what does he know about football, anyway?* **what do you know** (**about that**)? N. Amer. informal used as an expression of surprise. **wouldn't you like to know?** informal used to express one's intention to keep something secret despite another's curiosity: *'You're loaded, aren't you, Bella?' 'Wouldn't you like to know?'* **you know** informal used to indicate that what is being referred to is known to or understood by the listener: *when in Rome, you know*. ■ used as a filler in conversation: *oh well, you know, I was wondering if you had any jobs for me*. **you know something** (or **what**)? informal used to indicate that one is going to say something interesting or surprising: *You know what? I believed her*. **you never know** informal you can never be certain.
– DERIVATIVES **knowable adjective**, **knower noun**.

– ORIGIN Old English *cnāwan* (earlier *gecnāwan*) 'recognize, identify', of Germanic origin; from an Indo-European root shared by Latin *(g)noscere*, Greek *gignōskein*, also by CAN[1] and KEN.

know-all ▶ noun Brit. informal a person who behaves as if they know everything.

knowbot /ˈnəʊbɒt/ ▶ noun Computing (trademark in the US) a program designed to search through large numbers of databases in response to requests for information by users of a network.
– ORIGIN 1980s: from *knowledgeable robot*.

know-how ▶ noun [mass noun] practical knowledge or skill; expertise: *technical know-how*.

knowing ▶ adjective **1** showing or suggesting that one has knowledge or awareness that is secret or known to only a few people: *a knowing smile*. ■ chiefly derogatory experienced or shrewd, especially excessively or prematurely so: *today's society is too knowing, too corrupt*.
2 done in full awareness or consciousness: *a knowing breach of the order by the appellants*.
▶ noun [mass noun] the state of being aware or informed.
– PHRASES **there is no knowing** no one can tell: *if we go there's no knowing what will happen*.
– DERIVATIVES **knowingness** noun.

knowingly ▶ adverb **1** in a way that suggests one has secret knowledge or awareness: *Amy looked at me knowingly*.
2 in full awareness or consciousness; deliberately: *when a journalist knowingly misleads their readers*.

know-it-all ▶ noun another term for KNOW-ALL.

knowledge ▶ noun [mass noun] **1** facts, information, and skills acquired through experience or education; the theoretical or practical understanding of a subject: *a thirst for knowledge | her considerable knowledge of antiques*. ■ the sum of what is known: *the transmission of knowledge*. ■ information held on a computer system. ■ Philosophy true, justified belief; certain understanding, as opposed to opinion.
2 awareness or familiarity gained by experience of a fact or situation: *the programme had been developed without his knowledge | he denied all knowledge of the incidents*.
3 archaic sexual intercourse.
– PHRASES **come to one's knowledge** become known to one. **to (the best of) one's knowledge** as far as one knows; judging from the information one has.
– ORIGIN Middle English (originally as a verb in the sense 'acknowledge, recognize', later as a noun): from an Old English compound based on *cnāwan* (see KNOW).

knowledgeable (also **knowledgable**) ▶ adjective intelligent and well informed: *she is very knowledgeable about livestock and pedigrees*.
– DERIVATIVES **knowledgeability** noun, **knowledgeably** adverb.

knowledge base ▶ noun [mass noun] **1** a store of information or data that is available to draw on.
2 the underlying set of facts, assumptions, and rules which a computer system has available to solve a problem.

knowledge economy ▶ noun an economy in which growth is dependent on the quantity, quality, and accessibility of the information available, rather than the means of production.

knowledge management ▶ noun [mass noun] efficient handling of information and resources within a commercial organization.

knowledge worker ▶ noun a person whose job involves handling or using information.

known past participle of KNOW. ▶ adjective recognized, familiar, or within the scope of knowledge: *plants little known to western science | the known world*. ■ [attrib.] publicly acknowledged to be: *a known criminal*. ■ Mathematics (of a quantity or variable) having a value that can be stated.

know-nothing ▶ noun **1** an ignorant person.
2 (**Know-Nothing**) N. Amer. historical a member of a political party in the US, prominent from 1853 to 1856, which was antagonistic towards Roman Catholics and recent immigrants, and whose members preserved its secrecy by denying its existence.
– DERIVATIVES **know-nothingism** noun.

Knox /nɒks/, John (*c.*1505–72), Scottish Protestant reformer. Knox played a central part in the establishment of the Church of Scotland within a Scottish Protestant state, and led opposition to the Catholic Mary, Queen of Scots when she returned to rule in her own right in 1561.

Knoxville /ˈnɒksvɪl/ a port on the Tennessee River, in eastern Tennessee; pop. 184,802 (est. 2008).

Knt ▶ abbreviation Knight.

knuckle ▶ noun a part of a finger at a joint where the bone is near the surface, especially where the finger joins the hand. ■ a projection of the carpal or tarsal joint of a quadruped. ■ a joint of meat consisting of the knuckle of an animal together with the adjoining parts: *a knuckle of pork*.
▶ verb [with obj.] rub or press (something, especially the eyes) with the knuckles.
– PHRASES **near the knuckle** Brit. informal verging on the indecent or offensive.
– PHRASAL VERBS **knuckle down** apply oneself seriously to a task. **knuckle under** submit to someone else's authority.
– DERIVATIVES **knuckly** adjective.
– ORIGIN Middle English *knokel* (originally denoting the rounded shape when a joint such as the elbow or knee is bent), from Middle Low German, Middle Dutch *knökel*, diminutive of *knoke* 'bone'. In the mid 18th cent. the verb *knuckle (down)* expressed setting the knuckles down to shoot the taw in a game of marbles, hence the notion of applying oneself with concentration.

knuckleball ▶ noun Baseball a slow pitch which moves erratically, made by releasing the ball from the knuckles of the first joints of the index and middle finger.
– DERIVATIVES **knuckleballer** noun.

knucklebone ▶ noun **1** a bone forming or corresponding to a knuckle. ■ a knuckle of meat.
2 (**knucklebones**) animal knucklebones used in the game of jacks. ■ the game of jacks.

knuckle-dragger ▶ noun informal a stupid or loutish man.
– DERIVATIVES **knuckle-dragging** adjective.

knuckleduster ▶ noun a metal guard worn over the knuckles in fighting to increase the effect of blows.

knucklehead ▶ noun informal a stupid person.
– DERIVATIVES **knuckleheaded** adjective.

knuckle joint ▶ noun a joint connecting two parts of a mechanism, in which a projection in one fits into a recess in the other.

knuckle sandwich ▶ noun informal a punch in the mouth.

knur /nəː/ ▶ noun **1** a small wooden or porcelain ball used in a game (**knur and spell**) resembling trapball, played in northern England.
2 variant form of KNAR.
– ORIGIN late Middle English *knorre*, variant of *knarre* (see KNAR).

knurl /nəːl/ ▶ noun a small projecting knob or ridge, especially in a series around the edge of something.
– DERIVATIVES **knurled** adjective.
– ORIGIN early 17th cent.: apparently a derivative of KNUR.

Knut variant spelling of CANUTE.

KO[1] ▶ abbreviation kick-off.

KO[2] Boxing ▶ noun a knockout in a boxing match. See also KAYO.
▶ verb (**KO's, KO'ing, KO'd**) [with obj.] knock (an opponent) out in a boxing match.
– ORIGIN 1920s: abbreviation.

koa /ˈkəʊə/ ▶ noun a large Hawaiian forest tree which yields dark red timber. ● *Acacia koa*, family Leguminosae.
– ORIGIN early 19th cent.: from Hawaiian.

koala /kəʊˈɑːlə/ ▶ noun a bear-like arboreal Australian marsupial that has thick grey fur and feeds on eucalyptus leaves. Also called NATIVE BEAR in Australia. ● *Phascolarctos cinereus*, the only member of the family Phascolarctidae.
– ORIGIN early 19th cent.: from Dharuk.

> **USAGE** In non-technical contexts **koala bear** (as opposed to **koala**) is widely used. Zoologists, however, regard this form as incorrect on the grounds that, despite appearances, koalas are completely unrelated to bears.

koan /ˈkəʊɑːn, ˈkəʊan/ ▶ noun a paradoxical anecdote or riddle without a solution, used in Zen Buddhism to demonstrate the inadequacy of logical reasoning and provoke enlightenment.
– ORIGIN Japanese, literally 'matter for public thought', from Chinese *gōngàn* 'official business'.

kob[1] ▶ noun (pl. **same**) an antelope with a reddish coat and lyre-shaped horns, found on the savannah of southern Africa. ● *Kobus kob*, family Bovidae.
– ORIGIN late 18th cent.: from Wolof *kooba*.

kob[2] (also **cob**) ▶ noun (pl. **same**) S. African a fish of the drum family, especially the kabeljou.
– ORIGIN early 20th cent.: abbreviation of KABELJOU, with anglicization of the vowel.

Kobe /ˈkəʊbi/ a port in central Japan, on the island of Honshu; pop. 1,502,772 (2007). The city was severely damaged by an earthquake in 1995.

København /ˌkøbənˈhaʊn/ Danish name for COPENHAGEN.

kobo /ˈkəʊbəʊ/ ▶ noun (pl. **same**) a monetary unit of Nigeria, equal to one hundredth of a naira.
– ORIGIN corruption of COPPER[1].

kobold /ˈkəʊbəld/ ▶ noun (in Germanic mythology) a spirit who haunts houses or lives underground in caves or mines.
– ORIGIN from German *Kobold*.

Köchel number /ˈkəːx(ə)l/ ▶ noun Music a number given to each of Mozart's compositions in the complete catalogue of his works compiled by the Austrian scientist L. von Köchel (1800–77) and his successors.

Kochi /kəʊˈtʃi, kɒˈtʃi/ a seaport and naval base on the Malabar Coast of SW India, in the state of Kerala; pop. 254,500 (est. 2009). Former name COCHIN[1].

kochia /ˈkəʊkɪə, ˈkɒtʃɪə/ ▶ noun a shrubby Eurasian plant of the goosefoot family, grown for its decorative foliage which turns deep fiery red in the autumn. Also called BURNING BUSH, SUMMER CYPRESS. ● *Bassia* (formerly *Kochia*) *scoparia*, family Chenopodiaceae.
– ORIGIN late 19th cent.: named after Wilhelm D. J. *Koch* (1771–1849), German botanist.

Kodály /ˈkəʊdʌɪ/, Zoltán (1882–1967), Hungarian composer. His main source of inspiration was his native land; he was also involved in the collection and publication of Hungarian folk songs. Notable works: *Psalmus Hungaricus* (choral, 1923) and *Háry János* (opera, 1925–7).

Kodiak bear /ˈkəʊdɪak/ ▶ noun an animal of a large race of the North American brown bear or grizzly, found on islands to the south of Alaska. ● *Ursus arctos middendorffi*, family Ursidae.
– ORIGIN late 19th cent.: named after *Kodiak* Island, Alaska.

koeksister /ˈkʊksɪstə/ (also **koesister** /ˈkuːsɪstə/) ▶ noun S. African a plaited doughnut dipped in syrup.
– ORIGIN from Afrikaans *koe(k)sister*, perhaps from *koek* 'cake' + *sissen* 'to sizzle'.

koel /ˈkəʊəl/ ▶ noun an Asian and Australasian cuckoo with a call that resembles its name, the male typically having all-black plumage. ● Genus *Eudynamys*, family Cuculidae: one or two species, in particular *E. scolopacea*.
– ORIGIN early 19th cent.: from Hindi *koēl*, from Sanskrit *kokila* in the same sense.

Koestler /ˈkəːstlə/, Arthur (1905–83), Hungarian-born British novelist and essayist. His best-known novel *Darkness at Noon* (1940) exposed the Stalinist purges of the 1930s. He left money in his will to found a university chair in parapsychology.

kofta /ˈkɒftə, ˈkəʊftə/ ▶ noun (pl. **same** or **koftas**) (in Middle Eastern and Indian cookery) a savoury ball made with minced meat, paneer, or vegetables.
– ORIGIN from Urdu and Persian *koftah* 'pounded meat'.

koftgari /ˈkəʊftgəˌriː/ ▶ noun [mass noun] a kind of damascene work made in South Asia, in which a pattern traced on steel is inlaid with gold.
– ORIGIN late 19th cent.: from Urdu and Persian *kuftgarī* 'beaten work'.

kohanga reo /kəˌhaŋə ˈreɪəʊ/ ▶ noun (pl. **kohanga reos**) NZ a kindergarten where lessons are conducted in Maori.
– ORIGIN Maori, literally 'language nest'.

kohen /ˈkɒhɛn, kɔɪn/ (also **cohen**) ▶ noun (pl. **kohanim** /-nɪm/ or **cohens**) Judaism a member of the priestly caste, having certain rights and duties in the synagogue.
– ORIGIN from Hebrew, literally 'priest'.

Kohima /kəʊˈhiːmə/ a city in the far north-east of India, capital of the state of Nagaland; pop. 103,200 (est. 2009).

Koh-i-noor /ˈkəʊɪˌnʊə, ˈkəʊɪˌnɔː/ a famous Indian diamond which has a history going back to the 14th century. It passed into British possession on the annexation of Punjab in 1849, and was set in the queen's state crown for the coronation of George VI (1937).
– ORIGIN from Persian *kōh-i nūr* 'mountain of light'.

Kohl /kəʊl/, Helmut (b.1930), German statesman, Chancellor of the Federal Republic of Germany

1982–90, and of Germany 1990–8. As Chancellor he showed a strong commitment to NATO and to closer European union within the EU.

kohl /kəʊl/ ▶ noun [mass noun] a black powder, usually antimony sulphide or lead sulphide, used as eye make-up especially in Eastern countries.
– ORIGIN late 18th cent.: from Arabic *kuḥl*.

kohlrabi /kəʊlˈrɑːbi/ ▶ noun (pl. **kohlrabies**) a cabbage of a variety with an edible turnip-like swollen stem.
– ORIGIN early 19th cent.: via German from Italian *cavoli rape*, plural of *cavola rapa*, from medieval Latin *caulorapa*, from Latin *caulis* (see COLE) + *rapum*, *rapa* 'turnip'; compare with French *chou-rave*.

koi /kɔɪ/ (also **koi carp**) ▶ noun (pl. **same**) a common carp of a large ornamental variety, originally bred in Japan.
– ORIGIN early 18th cent.: from Japanese, 'carp'.

Koil /kɔɪl/ see ALIGARH.

koine /ˈkɔɪniː/ ▶ noun [mass noun] the common language of the Greeks from the close of the classical period to the Byzantine era. ■ [count noun] a common language shared by various peoples; a lingua franca.
– ORIGIN late 19th cent.: from Greek *koinē (dialektos)* 'common (language)'.

koinonia /kɔɪˈnəʊnɪə/ ▶ noun [mass noun] Theology Christian fellowship or communion, with God or, more commonly, with fellow Christians.
– ORIGIN early 20th cent.: from Greek *koinōnia* 'fellowship'.

kokako /ˈkɔːkakəʊ/ ▶ noun (pl. **kokakos**) a large New Zealand wattlebird with dark blue-grey plumage, a black downcurved bill, and two blue or orange wattles. ● *Callaeas cinerea*, family Callaeidae.
– ORIGIN late 19th cent.: from Maori.

kokanee /ˈkəʊkani/ ▶ noun (pl. **same** or **kokanees**) a sockeye salmon of a dwarf variety which lives in landlocked lakes in western North America.
– ORIGIN late 19th cent.: from Shuswap (a Salish language).

kokowai /ˈkɔːkɔːˌwʌɪ/ ▶ noun [mass noun] NZ red ochre (burnt red clay) used to decorate wood or other materials.
– ORIGIN Maori.

kola ▶ noun variant spelling of COLA (sense 2).

Kola Peninsula /ˈkəʊlə/ a peninsula on the NW coast of Russia, separating the White Sea from the Barents Sea. The port of Murmansk lies on its northern coast.

Kolhapur /ˌkəʊlhɑːˈpʊə/ an industrial city in the state of Maharashtra, western India; pop. 562,000 (est. 2009).

kolinsky /kəˈlɪnski/ ▶ noun (pl. **kolinskies**) a dark brown weasel with a bushy tail, found from Siberia to Japan. ● *Mustela sibirica*, family Mustelidae. Alternative name: **Siberian weasel**.
■ [mass noun] the fur of the kolinsky.
– ORIGIN mid 19th cent.: from the place name *Kola*, a port in NW Russia, + the pseudo-Russian ending *-insky*.

Kolkata /kɒlˈkɑːtə/ a port and industrial centre in eastern India, capital of the state of West Bengal and the second-largest city in India; pop. 5,080,500 (est. 2009). It is situated on the Hooghly River near the Bay of Bengal. Former name (until 2000) CALCUTTA.
– DERIVATIVES **Kolkatan** noun & adjective.

Kolkhis /ˈkɒlxis/ Greek name for COLCHIS.

kolkhoz /ˈkɒlkɒz, kʌlkˈhɔːz/ ▶ noun (pl. **same** or **kolkhozes** or **kolkhozy**) a collective farm in the former Soviet Union.
– ORIGIN 1920s: Russian, from *kol(lektivnoe) khoz(yaĭstvo)* 'collective farm'.

Köln /kœln/ German name for COLOGNE.

Kol Nidre /kɒl ˈniːdreɪ/ ▶ noun an Aramaic prayer annulling vows made before God, sung by Jews at the opening of the Day of Atonement service on the eve of Yom Kippur.
– ORIGIN from Aramaic *kol nidrē* 'all the vows' (the opening words of the prayer).

kolo /ˈkəʊləʊ/ ▶ noun (pl. **kolos**) a Slavic dance performed in a circle.
– ORIGIN late 18th cent.: Croatian, literally 'wheel'.

Kolozsvár /ˈkɒlɒʒvɑːr/ Hungarian name for CLUJ-NAPOCA.

Kolyma /ˌkɒlɪˈmɑː/ a river of far eastern Siberia, which flows approximately 2,415 km (1,500 miles) northwards to the Arctic Ocean.

komatiite /kəˈmatɪʌɪt/ ▶ noun [mass noun] Geology a magnesium-rich extrusive rock, typically with a characteristic texture of criss-crossing olivine crystals.
– DERIVATIVES **komatiitic** adjective.
– ORIGIN 1960s: from *Komati* (the name of a river in southern Africa) + -ITE[1].

komatik /ˈkɒmətɪk/ ▶ noun a sledge drawn by dogs, used by the people of Labrador.
– ORIGIN early 19th cent.: from Inuit *qamutik*.

kombi /ˈkɒmbi, ˈkʊmbi/ (also **combi**) ▶ noun (pl. **kombis**) S. African a minibus, especially one used to transport passengers commercially.
– ORIGIN from Volkswagen's proprietary name, abbreviation of German *Kombiwagen* 'combination car'.

kombu /ˈkɒmbuː/ ▶ noun [mass noun] a brown seaweed used in Japanese cooking, especially as a base for stock. ● Genus *Laminaria*, class Phaeophyceae.
– ORIGIN late 19th cent.: Japanese.

Komi[1] /ˈkəʊmi/ an autonomous republic of NW Russia; pop. 959,500 (est. 2009); capital, Syktyvkar.

Komi[2] /ˈkəʊmi/ ▶ noun (pl. **same**) **1** a member of an indigenous people of northern Russia, from an area west of the Urals.
2 [mass noun] the Finno-Ugric language of the Komi, with about 350,000 speakers. Formerly called ZYRIAN.
▶ adjective relating to the Komi or their language.
– ORIGIN the name in Komi.

Komodo /kəˈməʊdəʊ/ a small island in Indonesia, in the Lesser Sunda Islands, situated between the islands of Sumbawa and Flores.

Komodo dragon ▶ noun a heavily built monitor lizard which captures large prey such as pigs by ambush. Occurring only on Komodo and neighbouring Indonesian islands, it is the largest extant lizard. ● *Varanus komodoensis*, family Varanidae.

Komondor /ˈkɒmənˌdɔː/ ▶ noun a powerful sheepdog of a white breed with a dense coat.
– ORIGIN Hungarian.

Komsomol /ˈkɒmsəmɒl/ historical an organization for communist youth in the former Soviet Union.
– ORIGIN Russian, from *Kom(munisticheskiĭ) So(yuz) Mol(odëzhi)* 'Communist League of Youth'.

Komsomolsk /ˌkɒmsəˈmɒlsk/ an industrial city in the far east of Russia, on the Amur River; pop. 272,400 (est. 2008). It was built in 1932 by members of the Komsomol on the site of the village of Permskoe. Also called **Komsomolsk-on-Amur** /-ˌɒnəˈmʊə/.

Kondratiev /kɒnˈdrɑːtjɛf/ ▶ noun [usu. as modifier] Economics each of a series of cycles or waves of economic contraction and expansion lasting about fifty years, postulated by Kondratiev in the 1920s.
– ORIGIN 1930s: named after Nikolai D. *Kondratiev* (1892–c.1935), Russian economist.

koneke /ˈkɒnɛki/ ▶ noun NZ a farm or logging wagon, usually with runners at the front and wheels at the back.
– ORIGIN Maori.

konfyt /kɒnˈfeɪt/ ▶ noun [mass noun] S. African a preserve containing whole fruit or pieces of fruit.
– ORIGIN mid 19th cent.: Afrikaans, from Dutch *konfijt*, probably from French *confiture*.

Kongo /ˈkɒŋgəʊ/ ▶ noun (pl. **same** or **Kongos**) **1** a member of an indigenous people inhabiting the region of the River Congo in west central Africa.
2 [mass noun] Kikongo, the Bantu language of the Kongo.
▶ adjective relating to the Kongo or their language.
– ORIGIN the name in Kikongo.

kongoni /kɒŋˈgəʊni/ ▶ noun (pl. **same**) a hartebeest, in particular one of a pale yellowish-brown race found in Kenya and Tanzania. ● *Alcelaphus buselaphus cokii*, family Bovidae.
– ORIGIN early 20th cent.: from Kiswahili.

Königgrätz /ˈkøːnɪçˌgrɛts/ German name for HRADEC KRÁLOVÉ.

Königsberg /ˈkøːnɪçsbɛrk/ German name for KALININGRAD.

konimeter /kəˈnɪmɪtə/ ▶ noun an instrument for collecting dust samples which directs a measured volume of air on to a greased slide to which any dust present will stick.
– ORIGIN early 20th cent.: from Greek *konis* 'dust' + -METER.

Konkani /ˈkəʊŋkəni/ ▶ noun [mass noun] an Indic language that is the main language of Goa and adjacent parts of Maharashtra, with about 5 million speakers. Also called GOANESE (see GOA).
▶ adjective relating to Konkani.
– ORIGIN from Marathi and Hindi *koṅkaṇī*, from Sanskrit *koṅkaṇa* 'Konkan' (a coastal region of western India).

Kon-Tiki /kɒnˈtɪki/ the raft made of balsa logs in which Thor Heyerdahl sailed from the western coast of Peru to the islands of Polynesia in 1947.
– ORIGIN named after an Inca god.

Konya /ˈkɒnjə/ a city in SW central Turkey; pop. 967,100 (est. 2007). An ancient Phrygian settlement, it became the capital of the Seljuk sultans towards the end of the 11th century.

kook ▶ noun N. Amer. informal a mad or eccentric person.
– ORIGIN 1960s: probably from CUCKOO.

kookaburra /ˈkʊkəˌbʌrə/ ▶ noun a very large Australasian kingfisher that feeds on terrestrial prey such as reptiles and birds. ● Genus *Dacelo*, family Alcedinidae: two species, in particular the **laughing kookaburra** or laughing jackass (*D. novaeguineae*), which has a loud cackling call.
– ORIGIN late 19th cent.: from Wiradhuri *gugubarra*.

kooky ▶ adjective (**kookier**, **kookiest**) informal strange or eccentric: *I like kooky foreign films*.
– DERIVATIVES **kookily** adverb, **kookiness** noun.

Kooning, Willem de, see DE KOONING.

Koori /ˈkʊəri/ ▶ noun (pl. **Kooris**) Austral. an Aborigine (used by some Aborigines to refer to themselves).
– ORIGIN from Awabakal (an Aboriginal language), literally 'man'.

kop ▶ noun **1** (usu. **the Kop**) Brit. a high bank of terracing at certain soccer grounds where spectators formerly stood, notably at Liverpool Football Club.
2 S. African (especially in place names) a hill or peak.
– ORIGIN Sense 2 from Afrikaans, from Dutch, literally 'head' (compare with COP[2]). Sense 1 comes from the name of *Spioen Kop*, site of a Boer War battle in which troops from Lancashire led the assault (Liverpool then being part of Lancashire).

kopek /ˈkəʊpɛk, ˈkɒpɛk/ (also **copeck** or **kopeck**) ▶ noun a monetary unit of Russia and some other countries of the former Soviet Union, equal to one hundredth of a rouble.
– ORIGIN from Russian *kopeĭka*, diminutive of *kop'ë* 'lance' (from the figure on the coin (1535) of Tsar Ivan IV, bearing a lance instead of a sword).

kopiyka /kɒˈpiːkə/ ▶ noun a monetary unit of Ukraine, equal to one hundredth of a hryvna.
– ORIGIN 1990s: Ukrainian, from Russian *kopeĭka* KOPEK.

koppie /ˈkɒpi/ (also **kopje**) ▶ noun S. African a small hill in a generally flat area.
– ORIGIN Afrikaans, from Dutch *kopje*, diminutive of *kop* 'head'.

kora /ˈkɔːrə/ ▶ noun a West African musical instrument shaped like a lute, with 21 strings passing over a high bridge, and played like a harp.
– ORIGIN late 18th cent.: a local word.

koradji /ˈkɒrədʒi, kəˈradʒi/ ▶ noun Austral. (pl. **koradjis**) an Aborigine who has recognized skills in traditional medicine and an important role in ceremonial life.
– ORIGIN from Dharuk *garraaji* 'doctor'.

Koran /kɔːˈrɑːn, kə-/ (also **Quran** or **Qur'an** /kʊ-/) ▶ noun the Islamic sacred book, believed to be the word of God as dictated to Muhammad by the archangel Gabriel and written down in Arabic. The Koran consists of 114 units of varying lengths, known as *suras*; the first sura is said as part of the ritual prayer. These touch upon all aspects of human existence, including matters of doctrine, social organization, and legislation.
– DERIVATIVES **Koranic** /-ˈranɪk, -ˈrɑːnɪk/ adjective.
– ORIGIN from Arabic *qur'ān* 'recitation', from *qara'a* 'read, recite'.

Korbut /ˈkɔːbət/, Olga (b.1955), Soviet gymnast, born in Belarus. She won two individual gold medals at the 1972 Olympic Games.

Korchnoi /ˈkɔːtʃnɔɪ/, Viktor (Lvovich) (b.1931), Russian chess player. He ranked third (c.1967–75) and then second (c.1975–80) in the world.

Korda /ˈkɔːdə/, Sir Alexander (1893–1956), Hungarian-born British film producer and director; born *Sándor Kellner*. He produced *The Third Man* (1949) and produced and directed *The Private Life of Henry VIII* (1933).

Kordofan /ˌkɔːdəˈfɑːn/ a region of central Sudan.

kore /ˈkɔːreɪ/ ▶ noun (pl. **korai**) an ancient Greek statue of a young woman, standing and clothed in long loose robes.
– ORIGIN from Greek *korē* 'maiden'.

Korea /kəˈrɪə/ a region of East Asia forming a peninsula between the Sea of Japan (East Sea) and the

Yellow Sea, now divided into the countries of North Korea and South Korea.

Ruled from the 14th century by the Korean Yi dynasty but more recently dominated by the Chinese and Japanese in turn, Korea was annexed by Japan in 1910. Following the Japanese surrender at the end of the Second World War, Korea was partitioned along the 38th parallel in 1948.

Korea, Democratic People's Republic of official name for **North Korea**.

Korea, Republic of official name for **South Korea**.

Korean ▶ adjective relating to North or South Korea or its people or language.
▶ noun **1** a native or inhabitant of North or South Korea, or a person of Korean descent.
2 [mass noun] the language of Korea, which has roughly 68 million speakers worldwide. It has its own writing system, and is now generally regarded as distantly related to Japanese.

Korean War the war of 1950–3 between North and South Korea.

UN troops, dominated by US forces, countered the invasion of South Korea by North Korean forces by invading North Korea, while China intervened on the side of the North. Peace negotiations were begun in 1951, and the war ended two years later with the restoration of previous boundaries.

korero /'kɔːrərəʊ/ ▶ noun (pl. **koreros**) NZ a conversation, discussion, or meeting.
– ORIGIN Maori.

korfball /'kɔːfbɔːl/ ▶ noun [mass noun] a game similar to basketball, played by teams each consisting of six men and six women.
– ORIGIN early 20th cent.: from Dutch *korfbal*, from *korf* 'basket' + *bal* 'ball'.

K

korhaan /kɔː'hɑːn, kə'rɑːn/ ▶ noun S. African a small crested bustard, which is typically boldly marked and has penetrating repetitive calls. ● Genus *Eupodotis*, family Otididae: several species.
– ORIGIN mid 18th cent.: Afrikaans, from the imitative base *kor-*, *knor-* (compare with Dutch *korren* 'coo') + *haan* 'cock'.

kori /'kɔːri/ (also **kori bustard**) ▶ noun a very large bustard with a crested head, native to sub-Saharan Africa. ● *Ardeotis kori*, family Otididae.
– ORIGIN early 19th cent.: from Setswana *kgori*.

Kórinthos /'korinθɔs/ Greek name for **Corinth**.

korma /'kɔːmə/ ▶ noun a mildly spiced Indian curry dish of meat or fish marinaded in yogurt or curds.
– ORIGIN from Urdu *ḳormā*, from Turkish *kavurma*.

Korsakoff's syndrome /'kɔːsakɒfs/ (also **Korsakoff's psychosis**) ▶ noun [mass noun] Psychiatry a serious mental illness, typically the result of chronic alcoholism, characterized by disorientation and a tendency to invent explanations to cover a loss of memory of recent events.
– ORIGIN early 20th cent.: named after Sergei S. *Korsakoff* (1854–1900), Russian psychiatrist.

Kortrijk /'kɔːtrʌɪk/ a city in western Belgium, in West Flanders; pop. 73,941 (2008). French name **Courtrai**.

koru /'kɒrʊ/ ▶ noun a stylized fern-leaf motif in Maori carving and tattooing.
– ORIGIN Maori.

koruna /'kɒrʊnə, kə'ruːnə/ ▶ noun the basic monetary unit of the Czech Republic, equal to 100 halers.
– ORIGIN Czech, literally 'crown'.

Korup National Park /'kɒrəp/ a national park in western Cameroon, on the border with Nigeria. It was established in 1961 to protect a large area of tropical rainforest.

Koryak /'kɒrjak/ ▶ noun (pl. **same** or **Koryaks**) **1** a member of an indigenous people of the northern Kamchatka peninsula.
2 [mass noun] the language of the Koryak, which has about 5,000 speakers and is related to Chukchi.
▶ adjective relating to the Koryaks or their language.
– ORIGIN from Russian *koryaki* (plural).

Kos /kɒs/ (also **Cos**) a Greek island in the SE Aegean, one of the Dodecanese group.

Kosciusko /ˌkɒʃ'tʃʊskəʊ/, Thaddeus (1746–1817), Polish soldier and patriot; full Polish name *Tadeusz Andrzej Bonawentura Kościuszko*. After fighting for the Americans during the War of American Independence, he led a nationalist uprising against Russia in Poland in 1794.

Kosciusko, Mount /ˌkɒzɪ'ʌskəʊ/ a mountain in SE Australia, in the Great Dividing Range in SE New South Wales. Rising to a height of 2,228 m (7,234 ft), it is the highest mountain in Australia.
– ORIGIN named by the explorer Sir Paul Edmund de Strzelecki (1797–1873), in honour of T. **Kosciusko**.

kosher /'kəʊʃə/ ▶ adjective **1** (of food, or premises in which food is sold, cooked, or eaten) satisfying the requirements of Jewish law: *a kosher kitchen.* ■ (of a person) observing Jewish food laws.
2 informal genuine and legitimate: *she consulted lawyers to make sure everything was kosher.*

Restrictions on the foods suitable for Jews are derived from rules in the books of Leviticus and Deuteronomy. Animals must be slaughtered and prepared in the prescribed way, in which the blood is drained from the body, while certain creatures, notably pigs and shellfish, are forbidden altogether. Meat and milk must not be cooked or consumed together, and separate utensils must be kept for each. Strict observance of these rules is today confined mainly to Orthodox Jews.

▶ verb [with obj.] prepare (food) according to the requirements of Jewish law.
– PHRASES **keep** (or **eat**) **kosher** observe the Jewish food regulations (kashrut).
– ORIGIN mid 19th cent.: from Hebrew *kāšēr* 'proper'.

Košice /'kɒʃɪtsə/ an industrial city in southern Slovakia; pop. 234,237 (2007).

Kosovo /'kɒsəvə, 'kɒsəvəʊ/ an autonomous area in the Balkans, formerly a part of Yugoslavia; pop. 1,804,800 (est. 2009); capital, Priština. It borders on Albania and the majority of the people are of Albanian descent. In 1998 Kosovo was attacked by Serbian forces intent on expelling the Albanian population; the aggression was halted by NATO bombing in 1999, and Kosovo was put under UN administration. In 2008 it declared itself independent.
– DERIVATIVES **Kosovan** noun & adjective, **Kosovar** noun.

Kossuth /'kɒsuːθ, 'kɒʃuːt/, Lajos (1802–94), Hungarian statesman and patriot. He led the 1848 insurrection against the Hapsburgs, but after brief success the uprising was crushed and he began a lifelong period of exile.

Kostroma /ˌkɒstrə'mɑː/ an industrial city in European Russia, situated on the River Volga to the north-west of Nizhni Novgorod; pop. 271,700 (est. 2008).

Kosygin /kɒ'siːgɪn/, Aleksei (Nikolaevich) (1904–80), Soviet statesman, Premier of the USSR 1964–80. He devoted most of his attention to internal economic affairs, being gradually eased out of the leadership by Brezhnev.

Kota /'kəʊtə/ an industrial city in Rajasthan state, in NW India, on the Chambal River; pop. 827,400 (est. 2009).

Kota Baharu /ˌkəʊtə bə'hɑːruː/ a city in Malaysia, on the east coast of the Malay Peninsula, the capital of the state of Kelantan; pop. 277,300 (est. 2009).

Kota Kinabalu /ˌkɪnəbə'luː/ a port in Malaysia, on the north coast of Borneo, capital of the state of Sabah; pop. 579,300 (est. 2009).

Kotka /'kɒtkə/ a port on the south coast of Finland; pop. 54,781 (2009).

koto /'kəʊtəʊ/ ▶ noun (pl. **kotos**) a Japanese zither about six feet long, with thirteen strings passed over small movable bridges.
– ORIGIN late 18th cent.: Japanese.

kotwal /'kɒtwʌl/ ▶ noun Indian a police officer.
– ORIGIN via Hindi from Sanskrit *koṭṭapāla*.

kotwali /kɒt'wɑːli/ ▶ noun Indian a police station.
– ORIGIN from Hindi *koṭvālī*, from *koṭvāl* (see **kotwal**).

Kotzebue /'kɒtsɪb(j)uː/, August von (1761–1819), German dramatist. His many plays were popular in both Germany and England. He was a political informant to Tsar Alexander I and was assassinated by the Germans.

koulibiac ▶ noun variant spelling of **coulibiac**.

koumiss /'kuːmɪs/ (also **kumiss** or **kumis**) ▶ noun [mass noun] a fermented liquor prepared from mare's milk, used as a drink and medicine by Asian nomads.
– ORIGIN late 16th cent.: based on Tartar *kumiz*.

kouprey /'kuːpreɪ/ ▶ noun a very rare grey ox found in the forests of SE Asia. ● *Bos sauveli*, family Bovidae.
– ORIGIN 1940s: from Khmer.

kourbash /'kʊəbaʃ/ ▶ noun variant spelling of **kurbash**.

kouros /'kuːrɒs/ ▶ noun (pl. **kouroi** /-rɔɪ/) an ancient Greek statue of a young man, standing and often naked.
– ORIGIN Greek, Ionic form of *koros* 'boy'.

Kourou /kʊ'ruː/ a town on the north coast of French Guiana; pop. 23,800 (est. 2006). Nearby is a satellite-launching station of the European Space Agency, established in 1967.

kowari /kə'wɑːri/ ▶ noun (pl. **kowaris**) a small carnivorous marsupial with a pointed snout, large eyes, and a black bushy tip to the tail, found in central Australia. ● *Dasycercus byrnei*, family Dasyuridae.
– ORIGIN from Diyari and Ngamini (Aboriginal languages) *kariri*.

kowhai /'kəʊwʌɪ, 'kɔːfʌɪ/ ▶ noun a tree of the pea family, which bears hanging clusters of yellow flowers. It is native to New Zealand and Chile and yields useful timber. ● *Sophora tetraptera*, family Leguminosae.
– ORIGIN mid 19th cent.: from Maori.

Kowloon /kaʊ'luːn/ a densely populated peninsula on the SE coast of China, forming part of Hong Kong. It is separated from Hong Kong Island by Victoria Harbour.

kowtow /kaʊ'taʊ/ ▶ verb [no obj.] **1** act in an excessively subservient manner: *she didn't have to kowtow to a boss.*
2 historical kneel and touch the ground with the forehead in worship or submission as part of Chinese custom.
▶ noun historical an act of kowtowing as part of Chinese custom.
– ORIGIN early 19th cent.: from Chinese *kētóu*, from *kē* 'knock' + *tóu* 'head'.

Kozhikode /'kəʊʒəˌkəʊd/ a seaport in the state of Kerala in SW India, on the Malabar Coast; pop. 440,900 (est. 2009). Formerly called **Calicut**.

KP ▶ abbreviation kitchen police.

kph ▶ abbreviation kilometres per hour.

Kr ▶ symbol the chemical element krypton.

Kra, Isthmus of /krɑː/ the narrowest part of the Malay Peninsula, forming part of southern Thailand.

kraal /krɑːl/ S. African ▶ noun **1** a traditional African village of huts, typically enclosed by a fence.
2 an enclosure for cattle or sheep.
▶ verb [with obj.] drive (cattle or sheep) into an enclosure.
– ORIGIN Dutch, from Portuguese *curral* (see **corral**).

Krafft-Ebing /kraft'ɛbɪŋ/, Richard von (1840–1902), German physician and psychologist. He established the relationship between syphilis and general paralysis and pioneered the systematic study of aberrant sexual behaviour.

kraft /krɑːft/ (also **kraft paper**) ▶ noun [mass noun] a kind of strong, smooth brown wrapping paper.
– ORIGIN early 20th cent.: from Swedish, literally 'strength', used to form the term *kraftpapper* 'kraft paper'.

Kragujevac /'kraguːjəˌvats/ a city in central Serbia; pop. 145,400 (est. 2008). It was the capital of Serbia 1818–39.

krai /krʌɪ/ (also **kray**) ▶ noun (pl. **krais**) an administrative territory of Russia. In pre-revolutionary times krais were each made up of a number of provinces, becoming in 1924 large administrative units in the Soviet territorial system.
– ORIGIN from Russian *kraĭ* 'edge, border'.

krait /krʌɪt/ ▶ noun a highly venomous Asian snake of the cobra family. ● Genus *Bungarus*, family Elapidae: several species, including the black and yellow **banded krait** (*B. fasciatus*). See also **sea krait**.
– ORIGIN late 19th cent.: from Hindi *karait*.

Krakatoa /ˌkrakə'təʊə/ a small volcanic island in Indonesia, lying between Java and Sumatra, scene of a great eruption in 1883 which destroyed most of the island. Indonesian name **Krakatau**.

kraken /'krɑːk(ə)n/ ▶ noun an enormous mythical sea monster said to appear off the coast of Norway.
– ORIGIN Norwegian.

Kraków /'krakuf/ Polish name for **Cracow**.

krantz /krɑːns/ (also **krans**) ▶ noun S. African a precipitous or overhanging wall of rocks.
– ORIGIN South African Dutch, from Dutch *krans*, literally 'coronet'.

Krasnodar /ˌkrasnə'dɑː/ a krai (administrative territory) in the northern Caucasus, on the Black Sea in southern Russia. ■ the capital of Krasnodar, a port on the lower Kuban River; pop. 705,500 (est. 2009). It was known until 1922 as Yekaterinodar (Ekaterinodar).

Krasnoyarsk /ˌkrasnəˈjɑːsk/ a krai (administrative territory) in central Siberian Russia. ■ the capital of Krasnoyarsk, a port on the Yenisei River; pop. 936,400 (est. 2008).

Kraut /kraʊt/ ▸ **noun** informal, offensive a German.
– ORIGIN First World War: shortening of SAUERKRAUT.

Krautrock /ˈkraʊtrɒk/ ▸ **noun** [mass noun] an experimental style of rock music associated with German groups of the 1970s, characterized by improvisation and strong, hypnotic rhythms.
– DERIVATIVES **Krautrocker** noun.

Krav Maga /ˌkrɑːv ˈmɑːgə/ ▸ **noun** [mass noun] a form of self-defence and physical training, first developed by the Israeli army in the 1940s, based on the use of reflexive responses to threatening situations.
– ORIGIN from Hebrew, 'contact combat'.

kray ▸ **noun** variant spelling of KRAI.

Krebs cycle /krɛbz/ ▸ **noun** Biochemistry the sequence of reactions by which most living cells generate energy during the process of aerobic respiration. It takes place in the mitochondria, using up oxygen and producing carbon dioxide and water as waste products, and ADP is converted to energy-rich ATP.
– ORIGIN 1940s: named after Sir Hans A. *Krebs* (1900–81), German-born British biochemist.

kreef /kriːf/ ▸ **noun** S. African informal a spiny lobster of southern Africa. ● *Jasus lalandii*, family Palinuridae.
– ORIGIN mid 19th cent.: from Afrikaans, from Dutch *kreeft* 'lobster'.

Krefeld /ˈkreɪfɛlt/ an industrial town and port on the Rhine in western Germany, in North Rhine-Westphalia; pop. 237,100 (est. 2006).

Kremenchuk /ˌkrɛmənˈtʃuːk, ˌkrɪmɪn-/ an industrial city in east central Ukraine, on the River Dnieper; pop. 228,500 (est. 2009). Russian name **Kremenchug**.

kremlin /ˈkrɛmlɪn/ ▸ **noun** a citadel within a Russian town. ■ (**the Kremlin**) the citadel in Moscow. ■ the Russian or (formerly) USSR government.
– ORIGIN mid 17th cent.: via French from Russian *kreml'* 'citadel'.

Kremlinology /ˌkrɛmlɪˈnɒlədʒi/ ▸ **noun** [mass noun] the study and analysis of Soviet or Russian policies.
– DERIVATIVES **Kremlinologist** noun.

kreplach /ˈkrɛplɑːx/ ▸ **plural noun** (in Jewish cookery) triangular noodles filled with chopped meat or cheese and served with soup.
– ORIGIN from Yiddish *kreplekh*, plural of *krepel*, from German dialect *Kräppel* 'fritter'.

kriegspiel /ˈkriːgspiːl/ ▸ **noun** [mass noun] **1** a war game in which blocks representing armies or other military units are moved about on maps.
2 a form of chess in which each player has a separate board and can only infer the position of the opponent's forces from limited information given by an umpire.
– ORIGIN late 19th cent.: from German, from *Krieg* 'war' + *Spiel* 'game'.

Kriemhild /ˈkriːmhɪlt/ (in the Nibelungenlied) a Burgundian princess, wife of Siegfried and later of Etzel (Attila the Hun), whom she marries in order to be revenged on her brothers for Siegfried's murder.

krill ▸ **noun** (pl. **same**) a small shrimp-like planktonic crustacean of the open seas. It is eaten by a number of larger animals, notably the baleen whales. ● Many species in the class Malacostraca, especially *Meganyctiphanes norvegica*.
– ORIGIN early 20th cent.: from Norwegian *kril* 'small fish fry'.

krimmer /ˈkrɪmə/ ▸ **noun** [mass noun] tightly curled grey or black fur made from the wool of young Crimean lambs.
– ORIGIN mid 19th cent.: from German, from *Krim* 'Crimea'.

Krio /ˈkriːəʊ/ ▸ **noun** [mass noun] an English-based Creole language of Sierra Leone. It is the first language of about 350,000 people and is used as a lingua franca by over 3 million.
▸ **adjective** relating to Krio.
– ORIGIN probably an alteration of CREOLE.

kris /kriːs/ (also archaic **creese**) ▸ **noun** a Malay or Indonesian dagger with a wavy-edged blade.
– ORIGIN late 16th cent.: based on Malay *keris*.

Krishna /ˈkrɪʃnə/ Hinduism one of the most popular gods, the eighth and most important avatar or incarnation of Vishnu.

> He is worshipped in several forms: as the child god whose miracles and pranks are extolled in the Puranas; as the divine cowherd whose erotic exploits, especially with his favourite, Radha, have produced both romantic and religious literature; and as the divine charioteer who preaches to Arjuna on the battlefield in the Bhagavadgita.

– ORIGIN from Sanskrit *Kṛṣṇa*, literally 'black'.

Krishnaism /ˈkrɪʃnəɪz(ə)m/ ▸ **noun** [mass noun] Hinduism the worship of the god Krishna as an incarnation of Vishnu.

Krishnamurti /ˌkrɪʃnəˈmʊəti/, Jiddu (1895–1986), Indian spiritual leader. His spiritual philosophy is based on a rejection of organized religion and the attainment of self-realization by introspection.

Krishna River a river which rises in the Western Ghats of southern India and flows generally eastwards for 1,288 km (805 miles) to the Bay of Bengal.

Kristallnacht /ˈkrɪst(ə)lˌnɑːxt/, German /krɪsˈtalnaxt/ the occasion of concerted violence by Nazis throughout Germany and Austria against Jews and their property on the night of 9–10 November 1938.
– ORIGIN German, literally 'night of crystal', referring to the broken glass produced by the smashing of shop windows.

Kristiania variant spelling of CHRISTIANIA.

Kristiansand /ˈkrɪstʃənˌsand/ a ferry port on the south coast of Norway, in the Skagerrak; pop. 65,636 (2007).

Kríti /ˈkriːti/ Greek name for CRETE.

Krivoi Rog /krʲiˌvɔj ˈrɔk/ (also **Krivoy Rog**) Russian name for KRYVYI RIH.

kromesky /krə(ʊ)ˈmɛski, ˈkrɒmɛski/ ▸ **noun** (pl. **kromeskies**) a croquette of minced meat or fish, rolled in bacon and fried.
– ORIGIN from Polish *kromeczka* 'small slice'.

krona /ˈkrəʊnə/ ▸ **noun 1** (pl. **kronor** pronunc. **same**) the basic monetary unit of Sweden, equal to 100 öre. [Swedish, 'crown'.]
2 (pl. **kronur** pronunc. **same**) the basic monetary unit of Iceland, equal to 100 aurar. [from Icelandic *króna*, 'crown'.]

krone /ˈkrəʊnə/ ▸ **noun** (pl. **kroner** pronunc. **same**) the basic monetary unit of Denmark and Norway, equal to 100 øre.
– ORIGIN Danish and Norwegian, literally 'crown'.

Kronos variant spelling of CRONUS.

Kronstadt /ˈkrəʊnʃtat/ German name for BRAŞOV.

kroon /kruːn/ ▸ **noun** (pl. **kroons** or **krooni**) the basic monetary unit of Estonia, equal to 100 sents.
– ORIGIN Estonian, literally 'crown'; compare with KRONA, KRONE.

Kropotkin /krəˈpɒtkɪn/, Prince Peter (1842–1921), Russian anarchist. Imprisoned in 1874, he escaped abroad in 1876 and did not return to Russia until after the Revolution. His works include *Modern Science and Anarchism* (1903).

Kru /kruː/ ▸ **noun** (pl. **same**) **1** a member of a seafaring people of the coast of Liberia and Côte d'Ivoire (Ivory Coast).
2 [mass noun] the Niger–Congo language of the Kru, consisting of a large number of highly differentiated dialects.
▸ **adjective** relating to the Kru or their language.
– ORIGIN from a West African language.

Kru Coast a section of the coast of Liberia to the north-west of Cape Palmas, inhabited by the Kru people.

Kruger /ˈkruːgə/, Stephanus Johannes Paulus (1825–1904), South African soldier and statesman, President of Transvaal (1883–99). He led the Afrikaners to victory in the First Boer War in 1881. His refusal to allow equal rights to non-Boer immigrants was one of the causes of the Second Boer War.

Kruger National Park a national park in eastern South Africa, on the Mozambique border. It was originally a game reserve established in 1898 by President Kruger.

Krugerrand /ˈkruːgərand/ (also **Kruger**) ▸ **noun** a South African gold coin with a portrait of President Kruger on the obverse.
– ORIGIN 1967: from the name of S. J. P. KRUGER + RAND[1].

krummholz /ˈkrʌmhɒlts/ ▸ **noun** [mass noun] stunted wind-blown trees growing near the treeline on mountains.
– ORIGIN early 20th cent.: from German, literally 'crooked wood'.

krummhorn /ˈkrʌmhɔːn, ˈkrʊm-/ (also **crumhorn**) ▸ **noun** a medieval wind instrument with an enclosed double reed and an upward-curving end, producing an even, nasal sound.
– ORIGIN from German, from *krumm* 'crooked' + *Horn* 'horn'.

Krung Thep /ˌgrʊŋ ˈteɪp/ Thai name for BANGKOK. Situated to the east across the Chao Phraya river from the old capital of Bangkok, this was the site of the new capital founded by King Rama I in 1782. The modern city encompasses both sites.

Krupp /krʊp/, Alfred (1812–87), German arms manufacturer. His company played a pre-eminent part in German arms production from the 1840s through to the end of the Second World War.

krypton /ˈkrɪptɒn/ ▸ **noun** [mass noun] the chemical element of atomic number 36, a member of the noble gas series. It is obtained by distillation of liquid air, and is used in some kinds of electric light. (Symbol: **Kr**)
– ORIGIN late 19th cent.: from Greek *krupton*, neuter of *kruptos* 'hidden'.

kryptonite /ˈkrɪptənʌɪt/ ▸ **noun** [mass noun] (in science fiction) an alien mineral with the property of depriving Superman of his powers.

krytron /ˈkrʌɪtrɒn/ ▸ **noun** Physics a high-speed solid-state switching device which is triggered by a pulse of coherent light and is used in the triggers of nuclear devices.
– ORIGIN late 20th cent.: first element of obscure derivation + -TRON.

Kryvyi Rih /krɪˌviː ˈrɪx/ an industrial city in southern Ukraine, at the centre of an iron-ore mining region; pop. 675,600 (est. 2009). Russian name KRIVOI ROG.

KS ▸ **abbreviation** ■ Kansas (in official postal use). ■ Kaposi's sarcoma. ■ (in the UK) King's Scholar.

Kshatriya /ˈkʃatrɪə/ ▸ **noun** a member of the second of the four great Hindu castes, the military caste. The traditional function of the Kshatriyas is to protect society by fighting in wartime and governing in peacetime.
– ORIGIN late 18th cent.: from Sanskrit *kṣatriya*, from *kṣhatra* 'rule, authority'.

KStJ ▸ **abbreviation** Knight of the Order of St John, an international organization of Christian people which undertakes charitable work.

KT ▸ **abbreviation** ■ (in the UK) Knight of the Order of the Thistle. ■ Knight Templar.

Kt ▸ **abbreviation** Knight.

kt ▸ **abbreviation** knot(s): *a cruising speed of 240 kt.*

K/T boundary short for CRETACEOUS–TERTIARY BOUNDARY.
– ORIGIN late 20th cent.: *K/T*, from the symbols for *Cretaceous* and *Tertiary*.

Kuala Lumpur /ˌkwɑːlə ˈlʊmpʊə/ the capital of Malaysia, in the south-west of the Malay Peninsula; pop. 1,469,000 (est. 2009).

Kuala Trengganu /trɛŋˈgɑːnuː/ (also **Kuala Terengganu**) the capital of the state of Trengganu in Malaysia, on the east coast of the Malay Peninsula at the mouth of the Trengganu River; pop. 286,400 (est. 2009).

Kuantan /kwɑːnˈtɑːn/ the capital of the state of Pahang in Malaysia, on the east coast of the Malay Peninsula; pop. 407,800 (est. 2009).

Kuan Yin /kwɑːn ˈjɪn/ (in Chinese Buddhism) the goddess of compassion.

Ku-band /ˈkeɪjuːband/ ▸ **noun** [mass noun] a microwave frequency band used for satellite communication and broadcasting, using frequencies of about 12 gigahertz for terrestrial reception and 14 gigahertz for transmission.
– ORIGIN 1990s: from *Ku* (arbitrary serial designation) + BAND[1].

Kublai Khan /ˌkuːblʌɪ ˈkɑːn/ (1215–94), Mongol emperor of China, grandson of Genghis Khan. With his brother Mangu (then Mongol Khan) he conquered southern China (1252–9). After Mangu's death in 1259 he completed the conquest of China, founded the Yuan dynasty, and established his capital on the site of modern Beijing.

Kubrick /ˈkjuːbrɪk/, Stanley (1928–99), American film director, producer, and writer. Notable films: *2001: A Space Odyssey* (1968) and *A Clockwork Orange* (1971).

kuccha /ˈkʌtʃtʃʌ/ (also **kachha**) ▸ **plural noun** short trousers ending above the knee, worn as one of the five distinguishing signs of the Sikh Khalsa.
– ORIGIN Punjabi.

K

kuchen /ˈkuːx(ə)n/ ▶ **noun** (pl. **same**) a cake, especially one eaten with coffee.
– ORIGIN from German *Kuchen*.

Kuching /ˈkuːtʃɪŋ/ a port in Malaysia, on the Sarawak River near the NW coast of Borneo, capital of the state of Sarawak; pop. 658,600 (est. 2009).

kudos /ˈkjuːdɒs/ ▶ **noun** [mass noun] praise and honour received for an achievement: *she was looking for kudos rather than profit*. ■ informal, chiefly N. Amer. compliments or congratulations: *kudos to everyone who put the event together*.
– ORIGIN late 18th cent.: Greek.

> **USAGE** Kudos comes from Greek and means 'praise'. Despite appearances, it is not a plural form. This means that there is no singular form **kudo** and that the use of **kudos** as a plural, as in the following sentence, is incorrect: *he received* ***many kudos*** *for his work* (correct use is *he received* ***much kudos*** *for his work*).

kudu /ˈkuːduː, ˈkʊduː/ ▶ **noun** (pl. **same** or **kudus**) an African antelope that has a greyish or brownish coat with white vertical stripes, and a short bushy tail. The male has long spirally curved horns. ● Genus *Tragelaphus*, family Bovidae: two species.
– ORIGIN late 18th cent.: from Afrikaans *koedoe*, from Xhosa *i-qudu*.

kudzu /ˈkʊdzuː/ (also **kudzu vine**) ▶ **noun** a quick-growing East Asian climbing plant with reddish-purple flowers, used as a fodder crop and for erosion control. ● *Pueraria lobata*, family Leguminosae.
– ORIGIN late 19th cent.: from Japanese *kuzu*.

Kufic /ˈkjuːfɪk/ (also **Cufic**) ▶ **noun** [mass noun] an early angular form of the Arabic alphabet found chiefly in decorative inscriptions.
▶ **adjective** of or in Kufic.
– ORIGIN early 18th cent.: from the name *Kufa*, a city south of Baghdad, Iraq (because it was attributed to the city's scholars), + **-IC**.

kugel /ˈkuːg(ə)l/ ▶ **noun 1** [mass noun] (in Jewish cookery) a kind of savoury pudding of potatoes or other vegetables.
2 S. African derogatory a spoilt and materialistic young woman, typically Jewish, with a distinctive nasal accent.
– ORIGIN Yiddish, literally 'ball'.

Kuibyshev /ˈkuːɪbɪˌʃɛf/ former name (1935–91) for **SAMARA**.

Kuiper belt /ˈkʌɪpə bɛlt/ ▶ **noun** a region of the solar system beyond the orbit of Neptune, believed to contain many comets, asteroids, and other small bodies made largely of ice.
– ORIGIN 1990s: named after Gerard P. *Kuiper* (1905–73), Dutch-born US astronomer.

Ku Klux Klan /ˌkuː klʌks ˈklan/ (abbrev.: **KKK**) an extremist right-wing secret society in the US.

> The Ku Klux Klan was originally founded in the Southern states after the Civil War to oppose social change and black emancipation by violence and terrorism. Although disbanded twice, it re-emerged in the 1950s and 1960s and continues at a local level. Members disguise themselves in white robes and hoods, and often use a burning cross as a symbol of their organization.

– DERIVATIVES **Ku Kluxer** noun, **Ku Klux Klansman** noun (pl. **Klansmen**).
– ORIGIN perhaps from Greek *kuklos* 'circle' and **CLAN**.

kukri /ˈkʊkri/ ▶ **noun** (pl. **kukris**) a curved knife broadening towards the point, used by Gurkhas.
– ORIGIN early 19th cent.: from Nepalese *khukuri*.

kuku /ˈkuːkuː/ ▶ **noun** NZ another term for **KERERU**.

kula /ˈkuːlə/ ▶ **noun** [mass noun] (in some Pacific communities) an inter-island system of ceremonial gift exchange as a prelude to or at the same time as regular trading.
– ORIGIN Melanesian.

kulak /ˈkuːlak/ ▶ **noun** historical a peasant in Russia wealthy enough to own a farm and hire labour. Emerging after the emancipation of serfs in the 19th century the kulaks resisted Stalin's forced collectivization, but millions were arrested, exiled, or killed.
– ORIGIN Russian, literally 'fist, tight-fisted person', from Turkic *ḳol* 'hand'.

kulan /ˈkuːlən/ ▶ **noun** an animal of a race of the Asian wild ass, native to the central Asian steppes. ● *Equus hemionus kulan*, family Equidae. Compare with **ONAGER, KIANG**.
– ORIGIN late 18th cent.: from Turkic.

kulcha /ˈkʊltʃə/ ▶ **noun** a small, round Indian bread made from flour, milk, and butter, typically stuffed with meat or vegetables.
– ORIGIN from Persian *kulīca*.

kulfi /ˈkʊlfi/ ▶ **noun** [mass noun] a type of Indian ice cream, typically served in the shape of a cone.
– ORIGIN from Hindi *kulfī*.

kultarr /ˈkʊltɑː/ ▶ **noun** a nocturnal carnivorous marsupial mouse with long hindlimbs and a plumed tail, found in arid regions of Australia. ● *Antechinomys laniger*, family Dasyuridae.
– ORIGIN probably from Yitha-yitha (an Aboriginal language).

Kultur /kʊlˈtʊə/, German /kʊlˈtuːɐ/ ▶ **noun** [mass noun] German civilization and culture (sometimes used in a derogatory sense to suggest elements of racism, authoritarianism, or militarism).
– ORIGIN German, from Latin *cultura* or French *culture* (see **CULTURE**).

Kulturkampf /kʊlˈtʊəkampf/, German /kʊlˈtuːɐkampf/ a conflict from 1872 to 1887 between the German government (headed by Bismarck) and the papacy for the control of schools and Church appointments, in which Bismarck was forced to concede to the Catholic Church.
– ORIGIN German, from **KULTUR** + *Kampf* 'struggle'.

Kum variant spelling of **QOM**.

Kumamoto /ˌkuːməˈməʊtəʊ/ a city in southern Japan, on the west coast of Kyushu island; pop. 662,565 (2007).

kumara /ˈkuːmərə/ ▶ **noun** (pl. **same**) NZ a sweet potato.
– ORIGIN late 18th cent.: from Maori.

Kumasi /kuˈmasi/ a city in southern Ghana; pop. 1,517,000 (est. 2005). It is the capital of the Ashanti region.

Kumayri /kuˈmajri/ Russian name for **GYUMRI**.

Kumbh Mela /kʊm ˈmeɪlɑː/ ▶ **noun** a Hindu festival and assembly, held once every twelve years at four locations in India, at which pilgrims bathe in the waters of the Ganges and Jumna Rivers.
– ORIGIN from Sanskrit, literally 'pitcher festival', from *kumbh* 'pitcher' + *melā* 'assembly'.

Kumina /ˈkʌmiːnə/ ▶ **noun** a Jamaican religious ceremony involving music, dancing, and supposed possession by spirits.
– ORIGIN perhaps from a Kimbundu word meaning 'possession, to see'.

kumis (also **kumiss**) ▶ **noun** variant spelling of **KOUMISS**.

kumite /ˈkuːmɪteɪ/ ▶ **noun** [mass noun] (in martial arts) freestyle fighting.
– ORIGIN Japanese, literally 'sparring'.

kumkum /ˈkʊmkʊm/ ▶ **noun** [mass noun] a red pigment used by Hindu women to make a round mark on the forehead.
– ORIGIN from Sanskrit *kuṅkuma* 'saffron'.

kümmel /ˈkʊm(ə)l/ ▶ **noun** [mass noun] a sweet liqueur flavoured with caraway and cumin seeds.
– ORIGIN from German, from Old High German *kumil*, variant of *kumīn* (see **CUMIN**).

kumquat /ˈkʌmkwɒt/ (also **cumquat**) ▶ **noun 1** an orange-like fruit related to the citruses, with an edible sweet rind and acid pulp.
2 the East Asian shrub or small tree which yields the kumquat. ● Genus *Fortunella*, family Rutaceae.
– ORIGIN late 17th cent.: from Chinese (Cantonese dialect) *kam kwat* 'little orange'.

Kuna /ˈkuːnə/ (also **Cuna**) ▶ **noun** (pl. **same** or **Kunas**)
1 a member of an American Indian people of the isthmus of Panama.
2 [mass noun] the Chibchan language of the Kuna, with about 35,000 speakers.
▶ **adjective** relating to the Kuna or their language.
– ORIGIN the name in Kuna.

kuna /ˈkuːnə/ ▶ **noun** (pl. **kune**) the basic monetary unit of Croatia, equal to 100 lipa.
– ORIGIN Croatian, literally 'marten' (the fur of the marten was formerly a medium of exchange).

kund /kʊnd/ ▶ **noun** Indian a tank or small reservoir in which rainwater is collected for drinking.
– ORIGIN from Hindi.

kundalini /ˈkʊndəˌliːni/ ▶ **noun** [mass noun] (in yoga) latent female energy believed to lie coiled at the base of the spine. ■ (also **kundalini yoga**) a system of meditation directed towards the release of kundalini energy.
– ORIGIN Sanskrit, literally 'snake'.

Kundera /ˈkʊndərə/, Milan (b.1929), Czech novelist. He emigrated to France in 1975 after his books were banned in Czechoslovakia following the Soviet military invasion of 1968. Notable works: *The Book of Laughter and Forgetting* (1979) and *The Unbearable Lightness of Being* (1984).

Kung /kʊŋ/ ▶ **noun** (pl. **same**) **1** a member of a San (Bushman) people of the Kalahari Desert in southern Africa.
2 [mass noun] the Khoisan language of the Kung, with about 10,000 speakers.
▶ **adjective** relating to the Kung or their language.
– ORIGIN Khoikhoi *!Kung*, literally 'people'.

kung fu /kʊŋ ˈfuː, kʌŋ/ ▶ **noun** [mass noun] a primarily unarmed Chinese martial art resembling karate.
– ORIGIN from Chinese *gongfu*, from *gong* 'merit' + *fu* 'master'.

K'ung Fu-tzu /ˌkʊŋ fuːˈtsuː/ see **CONFUCIUS**.

Kunlun Shan /ˌkʊnlʊn ˈʃɑːn/ a range of mountains in western China, on the northern edge of the Tibetan plateau, extending eastwards for over 1,600 km (1,000 miles) from the Pamir Mountains. Its highest peak is Muztag, which rises to 7,723 m (25,338 ft).

Kunming /kʊnˈmɪŋ/ a city in SW China, capital of Yunnan province; pop. 1,700,200 (est. 2006).

kunzite /ˈkʌntsʌɪt, ˈkʌnzʌɪt/ ▶ **noun** [mass noun] a lilac-coloured gem variety of spodumene which fluoresces or changes colour when irradiated.
– ORIGIN early 20th cent.: from the name of George F. *Kunz* (1856–1932), American gemmologist, + **-ITE**[1].

Kuomintang /ˌkwəʊmɪnˈtaŋ/ (also **Guomindang**) a nationalist party founded in China under Sun Yat-sen in 1912, and led by Chiang Kai-shek from 1925. It held power from 1928 until the Communist Party took power in October 1949 and subsequently formed the central administration of Taiwan.
– ORIGIN from Chinese, 'national people's party'.

Kuopio /kʊˈəʊpɪəʊ/ a city in southern Finland, capital of a province of the same name; pop. 91,930 (2009).

Kupffer cell /ˈkʊpfə/ ▶ **noun** Anatomy a phagocytic cell which forms the lining of the sinusoids of the liver and is involved in the breakdown of red blood cells.
– ORIGIN early 20th cent.: named after Karl Wilhelm von *Kupffer* (1829–1902), Bavarian anatomist.

kurbash /ˈkʊəbaʃ/ (also **kourbash**) ▶ **noun** a whip, typically of hippopotamus hide, formerly used as an instrument of punishment in Turkey and Egypt.
– ORIGIN early 19th cent.: from Arabic *kurbāj*, from Turkish *kırbaç* 'whip'.

kurchatovium /ˌkəːtʃəˈtəʊvɪəm/ ▶ **noun** [mass noun] historical a name proposed in the Soviet Union for the artificial radioactive element of atomic number 104, now called **rutherfordium**.
– ORIGIN 1960s: named after Igor V. *Kurchatov* (1903–60), Russian nuclear physicist.

Kurd /kəːd/ ▶ **noun** a member of a mainly Islamic people living in Kurdistan.
– ORIGIN the name in Kurdish.

kurdaitcha /kəˈdʌɪtʃə/ ▶ **noun** variant spelling of **KADAITCHA**.

Kurdish /ˈkəːdɪʃ/ ▶ **adjective** relating to the Kurds or their language.
▶ **noun** [mass noun] the Iranian language of the Kurds.

Kurdistan /ˌkəːdɪˈstɑːn, -ˈstan/ an extensive region in the Middle East south of the Caucasus, the traditional home of the Kurdish people.

> The area includes large parts of eastern Turkey, northern Iraq, western Iran, eastern Syria, Armenia, and Azerbaijan. The creation of a separate state of Kurdistan, proposed by the Allies after the First World War, is opposed by Iraq, Iran, Syria, and Turkey. Following persecution of the Kurds by Iraq in the aftermath of the Gulf War of 1991, certain areas designated safe havens were established for the Kurds in northern Iraq, although these havens are not officially recognized as a state.

Kure /kuːˈreɪ/ a city in southern Japan, on the south coast of the island of Honshu, near Hiroshima; pop. 250,345 (2007).

Kurgan /kʊəˈgɑːn/ a city in central Russia, commercial centre for an agricultural region; pop. 324,100 (est. 2008).

kurgan /kʊəˈgɑːn/ ▶ **noun** Archaeology a prehistoric burial mound of a type found in southern Russia and Ukraine. ■ (**Kurgan**) a member of the ancient people who built such burial mounds.
▶ **adjective** relating to the ancient Kurgans.
– ORIGIN Russian, of Turkic origin; compare with Turkish *kurgan* 'castle'.

kuri /ˈkʊri/ ▶ **noun** (pl. **kuris**) NZ a dog, especially a mongrel. ■ informal an unpleasant or disliked person.
– ORIGIN Maori, 'dog'.

Kuril Islands /kʊə'riːl/ (also **Kurile Islands** or **the Kurils**) a chain of 56 islands between the Sea of Okhotsk and the North Pacific, stretching from the southern tip of the Kamchatka peninsula to the north-eastern corner of the Japanese island of Hokkaido. They are the subject of dispute between Russia and Japan.

Kurosawa /ˌkʊrə'sɑːwə/, Akira (1910–98), Japanese film director. Notable films: *Rashomon* (1950) and *Ran* (1985), a Japanese version of Shakespeare's *King Lear*.

Kuroshio /ˌkʊrə'ʃiːəʊ/ a warm current flowing in the Pacific Ocean north-eastwards past Japan and towards Alaska. Also called **JAPANESE CURRENT, JAPAN CURRENT**.
– ORIGIN late 19th cent.: Japanese, from *kuro* 'black' + *shio* 'tide'.

kurrajong /'kʌrədʒɒŋ/ (also **currajong**) ▶ **noun** an Australian plant which produces useful tough fibre.
● Several species, in particular a small tree with shiny pointed leaves and boat-shaped leathery seed cases (*Brachychiton populneus*, family Sterculiaceae).
– ORIGIN early 19th cent.: from Dharuk *garrajung* 'fibre fishing line'.

kursaal /'kʊəsɑːl, -z-/ ▶ **noun** (in Germany) a public building at a spa, in which entertainment is provided.
– ORIGIN mid 19th cent.: from German, from *Kur* 'cure' + *Saal* 'room'.

Kursk /kʊəsk/ an industrial city in SW Russia; pop. 408,100 (est. 2008). It was the scene of an important Soviet victory in the Second World War.

kurta /'kəːtə/ (also **kurtha**) ▶ **noun** a loose collarless shirt worn by people from South Asia, usually with a salwar, churidars, or pyjama.
– ORIGIN from Urdu and Persian *kurtah*.

kurtosis /kəː'təʊsɪs/ ▶ **noun** [mass noun] Statistics the sharpness of the peak of a frequency-distribution curve.
– ORIGIN early 20th cent.: from Greek *kurtōsis* 'a bulging', from *kurtos* 'bulging, convex'.

kuru /'kʊruː/ ▶ **noun** [mass noun] Medicine a fatal disease of the brain occurring in some peoples in New Guinea and thought to be caused by a virus-like agent such as a prion.
– ORIGIN 1950s: a local word.

kurus /kə'ruːʃ/ ▶ **noun** (pl. **same**) a monetary unit of Turkey, equal to one hundredth of a Turkish lira.
– ORIGIN from Turkish *kuruş*.

Kuşadasi /'kʊʃəˌdɑsi/ a resort town on the Aegean coast of western Turkey; pop. 54,700 (est. 2007).

Kushan /'kʊʃɑːn/ ▶ **noun** (pl. **same** or **Kushans**) a member of an Iranian dynasty which invaded the Indian subcontinent and established a powerful empire in the north-west between the 1st and 3rd centuries AD.
▶ **adjective** relating to the Kushan or their dynasty.
– ORIGIN from Prakrit *kuṣāṇa* (adjective), from Iranian.

kusti /'kʊstiː/ ▶ **noun** (pl. **kustis**) a cord worn round the waist by Parsees, consisting of seventy-two threads to represent the chapters of one of the portions of the Zend-Avesta.
– ORIGIN mid 19th cent.: Persian and Gujarati.

Kutaisi /ˌkʊtə'iːsi/ an industrial city in central Georgia; pop. 190,100 (est. 2006). One of the oldest cities in Transcaucasia, it has been the capital of various kingdoms, including Colchis and Abkhazia.

Kutani /kʊ'tɑːni/ ▶ **noun** [mass noun] (also **Kutani ware**) a kind of richly decorated Japanese porcelain, especially that of the 17th century, or of a 19th-century red and gold style.
– ORIGIN late 19th cent.: from *Kutani-mura*, the name of a Japanese village in the former province of Kaga.

Kutch, Gulf of /kʌtʃ, kʊtʃ/ an inlet of the Arabian Sea on the west coast of India.

Kutch, Rann of /kʌtʃ, kʊtʃ, ran/ a vast salt marsh on the shores of the Arabian Sea, extending over the boundary between SE Pakistan and the state of Gujarat in NW India.

Kuwait /kʊ'weɪt/ a country on the NW coast of the Persian Gulf; pop. 2,692,500 (est. 2009); official language, Arabic; capital, Kuwait City.

> Kuwait has been an autonomous Arab sheikhdom, under the rule of an amir, from the 18th century, although the British established a protectorate from 1897 until 1961. One of the world's leading oil-producing countries, Kuwait was invaded by Iraq in August 1990, the occupying forces being expelled in the Gulf War of 1991.

– DERIVATIVES **Kuwaiti** adjective & noun.

Kuwait City a port on the Persian Gulf, the capital of Kuwait; pop. 32,400 (est. 2005).

Kuzbass /kʊz'bas/ another name for **KUZNETS BASIN**.

Kuznets Basin /kʊz'njɛts/ (also **Kuznetsk** /-'njɛtsk/) an industrial region of southern Russia, situated in the valley of the Tom River, between Tomsk and Novokuznetsk. The region is rich in iron and coal deposits. Also called **KUZBASS**.

kV ▶ **abbreviation** kilovolt(s).

kvass /kvɑːs/ ▶ **noun** [mass noun] (especially in Russia) a fermented drink, low in alcohol, made from rye flour or bread with malt.
– ORIGIN from Russian *kvas*.

kvell /kvɛl/ ▶ **verb** [no obj.] N. Amer. informal feel happy and proud.
– ORIGIN 1960s: from Yiddish *kveln*, from Middle High German, literally 'well up'.

kvetch /kvɛtʃ/ N. Amer. informal ▶ **noun** a person who complains a great deal. ■ a complaint.
▶ **verb** [no obj.] complain persistently.
– ORIGIN 1960s: from Yiddish *kvetsh* (noun), *kvetshn* (verb), from Middle High German *quetschen*, literally 'crush'.

kW ▶ **abbreviation** kilowatt(s).

Kwa /kwɑː/ ▶ **noun** [mass noun] a major branch of the Niger–Congo family of languages, spoken from Côte d'Ivoire (Ivory Coast) to Nigeria and including Igbo and Yoruba.
▶ **adjective** relating to this group of languages.
– ORIGIN the name in Kwa.

kwacha /'kwɑːtʃə/ ▶ **noun** the basic monetary unit of Zambia and Malawi, equal to 100 ngwee in Zambia and 100 tambala in Malawi.
– ORIGIN previously used as a Zambian nationalist slogan calling for a new 'dawn' of freedom, later applied to the currency of the newly independent state.

kwaito /'kwʌɪtəʊ/ ▶ **noun** [mass noun] S. African a style of popular music similar to hip hop, featuring vocals recited over an instrumental backing with strong bass lines.
– ORIGIN 1990s: named after the *Amakwaito*, a group of 1950s gangsters in Sophiatown (a former quarter of Johannesburg), or from Afrikaans *kwaai* 'angry, vicious', slang 'excellent, great'.

Kwakiutl /'kwɑːˌkjʊt(ə)l/ ▶ **noun** (pl. **same** or **Kwakiutls**) **1** a member of an American Indian people of the NW Pacific coast, living mainly on Vancouver Island.
2 [mass noun] the Wakashan language of the Kwakiutl, now with few speakers.
▶ **adjective** relating to the Kwakiutl or their language.
– ORIGIN the name in Kwakiutl.

KwaNdebele /ˌkwɑː(ə)ndə'biːli/ a former homeland established in South Africa for the Ndebele people, now part of the province of Mpumalanga.

Kwangchow /kwaŋ'tʃaʊ/ variant of **GUANGZHOU**.

Kwangju /kwaŋ'dʒuː/ a city in SW South Korea; pop. 1,434,600 (est. 2008).

Kwangsi Chuang /ˌkwaŋsiː 'tʃwaŋ/ variant of **GUANGXI ZHUANG**.

Kwangtung /kwaŋ'tʊŋ/ variant of **GUANGDONG**.

kwanza /'kwanzə/ ▶ **noun** (pl. **same** or **kwanzas**) the basic monetary unit of Angola, equal to 100 lwei.
– ORIGIN perhaps from a Kiswahili word meaning 'first'.

Kwanzaa /'kwanzɑː/ ▶ **noun** N. Amer. a secular festival observed by many African Americans from 26 December to 1 January as a celebration of their cultural heritage and traditional values.
– ORIGIN from Kiswahili *matunda ya kwanza*, literally 'first fruits (of the harvest)', from *kwanza* 'first'.

kwashiorkor /ˌkwɒʃɪ'ɔːkɔː, ˌkwa-/ ▶ **noun** [mass noun] a form of malnutrition caused by protein deficiency in the diet, typically affecting young children in the tropics.
– ORIGIN 1930s: a local word in Ghana.

KwaZulu /kwɑː'zuːluː/ a former homeland established in South Africa for the Zulu people, now part of the province of KwaZulu-Natal. The general area was formerly known as Zululand.

KwaZulu-Natal a province of eastern South Africa, on the Indian Ocean; capital, Pietermaritzburg. Formerly called Natal, it became one of the new provinces of South Africa following the democratic elections of 1994. See also **NATAL**.

Kweichow /kweɪ'tʃaʊ/ variant of **GUIZHOU**.

Kweilin /kweɪ'lɪn/ variant of **GUILIN**.

Kweiyang /kweɪ'jaŋ/ variant of **GUIYANG**.

kwela /'kweɪlə/ ▶ **noun** [mass noun] a style of rhythmical, repetitive popular music of central and southern Africa, resembling jazz, in which the lead part is usually played on the penny whistle. ■ [count noun] a type of dance performed to kwela.
– ORIGIN 1950s: Afrikaans, perhaps from Zulu *khwela* 'mount, climb'.

Kwesui /kweɪ'sweɪ/ former name (until 1954) for **HOHHOT**.

kWh ▶ **abbreviation** kilowatt-hour(s).

KWIC ▶ **noun** [mass noun] [as modifier] Computing denoting a database search in which the keyword is shown highlighted in the middle of the display, with the text forming its context on either side.
– ORIGIN 1950s: acronym from *key word in centre*.

KWT ▶ **abbreviation** Kuwait (international vehicle registration).

KY ▶ **abbreviation** Kentucky (in official postal use).

Ky ▶ **abbreviation** Kentucky.

kyanite /'kʌɪənʌɪt/ ▶ **noun** [mass noun] a blue or green crystalline mineral consisting of aluminium silicate, used in heat-resistant ceramics.
– ORIGIN late 18th cent.: from Greek *kuanos*, *kuaneos* 'dark blue' + **-ITE**[1].

kyat /kɪ'ɑːt/ ▶ **noun** (pl. **same** or **kyats**) the basic monetary unit of Burma (Myanmar), equal to 100 pyas.
– ORIGIN Burmese.

kybosh ▶ **noun** variant spelling of **KIBOSH**.

Kyd, Thomas (1558–94), English dramatist. His play *The Spanish Tragedy* (published anonymously in 1592) was an early example of revenge tragedy and was very popular on the Elizabethan stage.

Kyiv /'kɪjɪf/ Ukrainian name for **KIEV**.

kyle /kʌɪl/ ▶ **noun** Scottish a narrow sea channel.
– ORIGIN mid 16th cent.: from Scottish Gaelic *caol* 'strait', (as an adjective) 'narrow'.

kylie /'kʌɪli/ ▶ **noun** Austral. (in Western Australia) a boomerang.
– ORIGIN from Nyungar (and other Aboriginal languages) *garli*.

kylin /'kiːlɪn/ ▶ **noun** a mythical composite animal, often figured on Chinese and Japanese ceramics.
– ORIGIN mid 19th cent.: from Chinese *qilin*, from *qi* 'male' + *lin* 'female'.

kylix /'kʌɪlɪks, 'kɪl-/ ▶ **noun** (pl. **kylikes** or **kylixes**) an ancient Greek cup with a shallow bowl and a tall stem.
– ORIGIN from Greek *kulix*.

kyloe /'kʌɪləʊ/ ▶ **noun** Scottish name for **HIGHLAND CATTLE**.
– ORIGIN early 19th cent.: from Scottish Gaelic *gaidhealach* 'Gaelic, Highland'.

kymograph /'kʌɪmə(ʊ)grɑːf/ ▶ **noun** an instrument for recording variations in pressure, e.g. in sound waves or in blood within blood vessels, by the trace of a stylus on a rotating cylinder.
– ORIGIN mid 19th cent.: from Greek *kuma* 'wave' + **-GRAPH**.

Kyoto /kɪ'əʊtəʊ/ an industrial city in central Japan, on the island of Honshu; pop. 1,389,595 (2007). Founded in the 8th century, it was the imperial capital from 794 until 1868.

kype /kʌɪp/ ▶ **noun** a hook formed on the lower jaw of adult male salmon and trout during the breeding season.
– ORIGIN mid 20th cent.: variant of Scots *kip*, perhaps influenced by **PIKE**[1].

kyphosis /kʌɪ'fəʊsɪs/ ▶ **noun** [mass noun] Medicine excessive outward curvature of the spine, causing hunching of the back. Compare with **LORDOSIS**.
– DERIVATIVES **kyphotic** adjective.
– ORIGIN mid 19th cent.: from Greek *kuphōsis*, from *kuphos* 'bent, hunchbacked'.

Kyrgyz /kɪə'giːz, 'kəːgɪz/ (also **Kirghiz**) ▶ **noun** (pl. **same**) **1** a member of an indigenous people of central Asia, living chiefly in Kyrgyzstan.
2 [mass noun] the Turkic language of the Kyrgyz, with approximately 2 million speakers.
▶ **adjective** relating to the Kyrgyz or their language.
– ORIGIN the name in Kyrgyz.

Kyrgyz Republic another name for **KYRGYZSTAN**.

Kyrgyzstan /ˌkɪəgɪ'stɑːn, ˌkəːgɪ-, -'stan/ a mountainous country in central Asia, on the north-western border of China; pop. 5,431,700 (est. 2009); official

K

language, Kyrgyz; capital, Bishkek. Also called **Kyrgyz Republic** or (formerly) **Kirghizia**.

The region was annexed by Russia in 1864, and became a constituent republic of the Soviet Union. On the break-up of the Soviet Union in 1991 Kyrgyzstan became an independent republic within the Commonwealth of Independent States.

Kyrie /ˈkɪrɪeɪ/ (also **Kyrie eleison** /ɪˈleɪɪzɒn, -sɒn, ɛˈleɪ-/) ▶ **noun** a short repeated invocation (in Greek or in translation) used in many Christian liturgies, especially at the beginning of the Eucharist or as a response in a litany.
– ORIGIN from Greek *Kuriē eleēson* 'Lord, have mercy'.

kyte /kʌɪt/ ▶ **noun** Scottish a person's belly or stomach.
– ORIGIN mid 16th cent.: of unknown origin.

kyu /kjuː/ ▶ **noun** a numbered grade of the less advanced level of proficiency in judo, karate, and other martial arts. ■ a person who has achieved a kyu.
– ORIGIN from Japanese *kyū* 'class'.

kyudo /ˈkjuːdəʊ/ ▶ **noun** [mass noun] the Japanese martial art of longbow archery, incorporating set rhythmic movements and practised in a meditative state.
– ORIGIN Japanese, literally 'way of the bow', from *kyū* 'bow' + *dō* 'way, method'.

Kyushu /kɪˈuːʃuː/ the most southerly of the four main islands of Japan, constituting an administrative region; pop. 13,232,000 (est. 2006); capital, Fukuoka.

Kyzyl /kəˈzɪl/ a city in south central Russia, on the Yenisei River, capital of the republic of Tuva; pop. 108,100 (est. 2008).

Kyzyl Kum /kəˌzɪl ˈkuːm/ an arid desert region in central Asia, extending eastwards from the Aral Sea to the Pamir Mountains and covering part of Uzbekistan and southern Kazakhstan.

K

L

L[1] (also **l**) ▶ **noun** (pl. **Ls** or **L's**) **1** the twelfth letter of the alphabet. ■ denoting the next after K in a set of items, categories, etc.
2 (**L**) a shape like that of a capital L: [in combination] *an L-shaped building.* ■ (usu. **ell**) N. Amer. an extension of a building or room that is at right angles to the main part. ■ (usu. **ell**) N. Amer. a bend or joint for connecting two pipes at right angles.
3 the Roman numeral for 50. [originally a symbol identified with the letter *L*, because of coincidence of form. In ancient Roman notation, *L* with a stroke above denoted 50,000.]

L[2] ▶ **abbreviation** ■ (in tables of sports results) games lost. ■ Chemistry laevorotatory: *L-tryptophan.* ■ (**L.**) Lake, Loch, or Lough (chiefly on maps): *L. Ontario.* ■ large (as a clothes size). ■ Brit. (on a motor vehicle) learner driver. ■ (**L.**) Linnaeus (as the source of names of animal and plant species): *Swallowtail Butterfly Papilio machaon (L., 1758).* ■ lire. ■ Luxembourg (international vehicle registration).
▶ **symbol** ■ Chemistry Avogadro's constant. ■ Physics inductance.

l ▶ **abbreviation** ■ (giving position or direction) left: *l to r: Gordon, Anthony, and Mark.* ■ (chiefly in horse racing) length(s). ■ (**l.**) (in textual references) line: *l. 648.* ■ Chemistry liquid. ■ litre(s). ■ (**l.**) archaic pound(s).
▶ **symbol** (in mathematical formulae) length.

LA ▶ **abbreviation** ■ Library Association. ■ Los Angeles. ■ Louisiana (in official postal use).

La ▶ **abbreviation** (**La.**) Louisiana.
▶ **symbol** the chemical element lanthanum.

la ▶ **noun** Music variant spelling of **LAH**.

laager /ˈlɑːɡə/ ▶ **noun 1** S. African historical an encampment formed by a circle of wagons.
2 an entrenched position or viewpoint that is defended against opponents: *an educational laager, isolated from the outside world.*
▶ **verb** [with obj.] S. African historical form (vehicles) into a laager. ■ [no obj.] make camp.
– ORIGIN South African Dutch, from Dutch *leger*, *lager* 'camp'. Compare with **LAGER**, **LAIR**[1], and **LEAGUER**[2].

laaitie ▶ **noun** variant spelling of **LIGHTY**.

Laayoune /lɑːˈjuːn/ (also **La'youn**) the capital of Western Sahara; pop. 200,000 (est. 2007). Arabic name **EL-AAIÚN**.

Lab ▶ **noun** a Labrador dog.

lab ▶ **noun** informal a laboratory: *a science lab.*
– ORIGIN late 19th cent.: abbreviation.

Lab. ▶ **abbreviation** Brit. (following a politician's name) Labour.

Laban /ˈlɑːb(ə)n/, Rudolf von (1879–1958), Hungarian choreographer and dancer. A pioneer of the central European school of modern dance, in 1920 he published the first of several volumes outlining his system of dance notation.

la Barca, Pedro Calderón de see **CALDERÓN DE LA BARCA**.

labarum /ˈlabərəm/ ▶ **noun** historical the imperial standard of Constantine the Great, which bore Christian symbolic imagery fused with the military symbols of the Roman Empire.
– ORIGIN early 17th cent.: from late Latin, of unknown origin.

labdanum /ˈlabdənəm/ ▶ **noun** variant spelling of **LADANUM**.

labefaction /ˌlabɪˈfakʃ(ə)n/ ▶ **noun** [mass noun] archaic deterioration or downfall.
– ORIGIN early 17th cent.: from Latin *labefactio(n-)*, from *labefacere* 'weaken', from *labi* 'to fall' + *facere* 'make'.

label ▶ **noun 1** a small piece of paper, fabric, plastic, or similar material attached to an object and giving information about it. ■ a piece of fabric sewn inside a garment and bearing the brand name, size, or instructions for care. ■ the piece of paper in the centre of a record giving the artist and title. ■ a company that produces recorded music: *independent labels.* ■ the name or trademark of a fashion company: *she plans to launch her own designer clothes label.*
2 a classifying phrase or name applied to a person or thing, especially one that is inaccurate or restrictive: *the label 'salsa' seems especially meaningless when applied to musicians like Tito Puente.* ■ (in a dictionary entry) a word or words used to specify the subject area, register, or geographical origin of the word being defined. ■ Computing a string of characters used to refer to a particular instruction in a program. ■ Biology & Chemistry a radioactive isotope, fluorescent dye, or enzyme used to make something identifiable for study.
3 Heraldry a narrow horizontal strip, typically with three downward projections, that is superimposed on a coat of arms by an eldest son during the life of his father.
4 Architecture another term for **DRIPSTONE**.
▶ **verb** (**labels**, **labelling**, **labelled**; US **labels**, **labeling**, **labeled**) [with obj.] **1** attach a label to (something). ■ assign to a category, especially inaccurately or restrictively: *many pupils felt that they were labelled as failures* | [with obj. and complement] *the critics labelled him a loser.*
2 Biology & Chemistry make (a substance, molecule, or cell) identifiable by replacing an atom with one of a distinctive radioactive isotope, or by attaching a fluorescent dye, enzyme, or other molecule.
– DERIVATIVES **labeller** noun.
– ORIGIN Middle English (denoting a narrow strip): from Old French, 'ribbon', probably of Germanic origin and related to **LAP**[1].

La Belle Province /la ˌbɛl prɒˈvɑ̃s/, French /la bɛl prɔvɛ̃s/ informal name for **QUEBEC**.
– ORIGIN French, literally 'the Beautiful Province'.

labellum /ləˈbɛləm/ ▶ **noun** (pl. **labella**) **1** Entomology each of a pair of lobes at the tip of the proboscis in some insects.
2 Botany a central petal at the base of an orchid flower, typically larger than the other petals and of a different shape.
– ORIGIN early 19th cent.: from Latin, diminutive of *labrum* 'lip'.

labelmate ▶ **noun** a musician, group, or singer that is signed to the same record label as another.

labia /ˈleɪbɪə/ ▶ **plural noun 1** Anatomy the inner and outer folds of the vulva, at either side of the vagina.
2 plural form of **LABIUM**.

labial /ˈleɪbɪəl/ ▶ **adjective 1** chiefly Anatomy relating to the lips. ■ Dentistry (of the surface of a tooth) adjacent to the lips. ■ Zoology resembling or serving as a lip, lip-like part, or labium.
2 Phonetics (of a consonant) requiring partial or complete closure of the lips (e.g. *p*, *b*, *f*, *v*, *m*, *w*), or (of a vowel) requiring rounded lips (e.g. *oo* in moon).
▶ **noun** Phonetics a labial sound.
– DERIVATIVES **labialize** (also **labialise**) verb (sense 2 of the adjective), **labially** adverb.
– ORIGIN late 16th cent.: from medieval Latin *labialis*, from Latin *labium* 'lip'.

labia majora /məˈdʒɔːrə/ ▶ **plural noun** Anatomy the larger outer folds of the vulva.

labia minora /mɪˈnɔːrə/ ▶ **plural noun** Anatomy the smaller inner folds of the vulva.

labiate /ˈleɪbɪət/ ▶ **noun** Botany a plant of the mint family (Labiatae), with a distinctive two-lobed flower.
▶ **adjective 1** Botany relating to or denoting plants of the mint family.
2 Botany & Zoology resembling or possessing a lip or labium.
– ORIGIN early 18th cent. (as an adjective in the sense 'two-lipped', describing a corolla or calyx): from modern Latin *labiatus*, from *labium* 'lip'.

labile /ˈleɪbɪl, -ʌɪl/ ▶ **adjective** technical liable to change; easily altered. ■ of or characterized by emotions which are easily aroused, freely expressed, and tend to alter quickly and spontaneously. ■ Chemistry easily broken down or displaced.
– DERIVATIVES **lability** /ləˈbɪlɪti/ noun.
– ORIGIN late Middle English (in the sense 'liable to err or sin'): from late Latin *labilis*, from *labi* 'to fall'.

labio- /ˈleɪbɪəʊ/ ▶ **combining form** relating to the lips: *labiodental.*
– ORIGIN from Latin *labium* 'lip'.

labiodental ▶ **adjective** Phonetics (of a sound) made with the lips and teeth, for example *f* and *v*.

labiovelar ▶ **adjective** Phonetics (of a sound) made with the lips and soft palate, for example *w*.

labium /ˈleɪbɪəm/ ▶ **noun** (pl. **labia** /-bɪə/) **1** Entomology a fused mouthpart which forms the floor of the mouth of an insect.
2 Botany the lower lip of the flower of a plant of the mint family.
– ORIGIN late 16th cent. (in the general sense 'lip, lip-like structure'): from Latin, 'lip'; related to **LABRUM**.

lablab /ˈlablab/ ▶ **noun** [mass noun] an Asian plant of the pea family, which is widely grown in the tropics for its edible seeds and pods and as a fodder crop.
● *Lablab purpureus*, family Leguminosae.
– ORIGIN early 19th cent.: from Arabic *lablāb*.

labor etc. ▶ **noun** US spelling of **LABOUR** etc.

laboratory /ləˈbɒrəˌt(ə)ri, ˈlab(ə)rəˌt(ə)ri/ ▶ **noun** (pl. **laboratories**) a room or building equipped for scientific experiments, research, or teaching, or for the manufacture of drugs or chemicals: [as modifier] *laboratory tests.* ■ [as modifier] (of an animal) bred for or used in experiments in laboratories: *laboratory rats.*
– ORIGIN early 17th cent.: from medieval Latin *laboratorium*, from Latin *laborare* 'to labour'.

labored ▶ **adjective** US spelling of **LABOURED**.

laborer ▶ **noun** US spelling of **LABOURER**.

laborious /ləˈbɔːrɪəs/ ▶ **adjective** requiring considerable time and effort: *years of laborious training* | *the work is very slow and laborious.* ■ (of speech or writing style) showing obvious signs of effort and lacking in fluency: *she wrote in laborious, dictionary-assisted English.*
– DERIVATIVES **laboriously** adverb, **laboriousness** noun.
– ORIGIN late Middle English (also in the sense 'industrious, assiduous'): from Old French *laborieux*, from Latin *laboriosus*, from *labor* 'labour'.

laborism ▸ noun US spelling of LABOURISM.

Laborite ▸ noun US spelling of LABOURITE.

Labor Party, Australian see AUSTRALIAN LABOR PARTY.

labour (US **labor**) ▸ noun [mass noun] **1** work, especially physical work: *the price of repairs includes labour, parts, and VAT | manual labour*. ■ workers, especially manual workers, considered collectively: *non-union casual labour*. ■ workers considered as a social class or political force: [as modifier] *the labour movement*. ■ [as modifier] (**Labour**) a government department concerned with a nation's workforce: *the Labour Secretary*.
2 (**Labour**) [treated as sing. or pl.] the Labour Party: [as modifier] *the Labour leader*.
3 the process of childbirth from the start of uterine contractions to delivery: *a woman **in labour***.
▸ verb [no obj.] **1** work hard; make great effort: *they laboured from dawn to dusk | she was patiently **labouring over** her sketchbooks*. ■ work at an unskilled manual occupation: *he was eking out an existence by labouring* | (as adj. **labouring**) *the labouring classes*. ■ [with obj.] archaic till (the ground): *the land belonged to him who laboured it*.
2 have difficulty in doing something despite working hard: *United laboured against confident opponents*. ■ [with adverbial of direction] move or proceed with difficulty: *they **laboured up** a steep, tortuous track*. ■ (of an engine) work noisily and with difficulty. ■ (of a ship) roll or pitch heavily.
– PHRASES **a labour of Hercules** see HERCULES. **a labour of love** a task done for pleasure, not reward. **labour the point** explain or discuss something at excessive length.
– PHRASAL VERBS **labour under 1** carry (a very heavy load) with difficulty. **2** be misled by (a mistaken belief): *you've been labouring under a misapprehension*.
– ORIGIN Middle English: from Old French *labour* (noun), *labourer* (verb), both from Latin *labor* 'toil, trouble'.

L

labour camp ▸ noun a prison camp in which a regime of hard labour is enforced.

Labour Day ▸ noun a public holiday or day of festivities held in honour of working people, in many countries on 1 May, in the US and Canada on the first Monday in September.

laboured (US **labored**) ▸ adjective done with great effort and difficulty: *his breathing was laboured*. ■ (especially of humour or a performance) not spontaneous or fluent: *one of Alan's laboured jokes*.

labourer (US **laborer**) ▸ noun a person doing unskilled manual work for wages: *a farm labourer*.

labour exchange ▸ noun former term for JOBCENTRE.

labour force ▸ noun all the members of a particular organization or country who are able to work, viewed collectively.

labour-intensive ▸ adjective (of a form of work) needing a large workforce or a large amount of work in relation to output.

labourism (US **laborism**) ▸ noun [mass noun] the principles of a Labour Party or the labour movement.
– DERIVATIVES **labourist** noun & adjective.

Labourite (US **Laborite**) ▸ noun a member or supporter of a Labour Party.

Labour Party ▸ noun a left-of-centre political party formed to represent the interests of ordinary working people, in particular a major British party that since the Second World War has been in power 1945–51, 1964–70, 1974–9, and since 1997. Arising from the trade union movement at the end of the 19th century, it replaced the Liberals as the country's second party after the First World War.

labour-saving ▸ adjective (of an appliance) designed to reduce the amount of work needed to do something.

labour theory of value ▸ noun [mass noun] the Marxist theory that the value of a commodity should be determined by the amount of human labour used in its production.

labour union ▸ noun N. Amer. a trade union.

labra plural form of LABRUM.

labradoodle ▸ noun a dog of a breed developed as a cross between a Labrador retriever and a poodle.
– ORIGIN 1980s: blend of LABRADOR^{2} and POODLE.

Labrador^{1} /ˈlabrədɔː/ a coastal region of eastern Canada, which forms the mainland part of the province of Newfoundland and Labrador.

Labrador^{2} /ˈlabrədɔː/ (also **Labrador dog** or **retriever**) ▸ noun a retriever of a breed that most typically has a black or yellow coat, widely used as a gun dog or as a guide for a blind person.
– ORIGIN early 20th cent.: named after the LABRADOR PENINSULA, where the breed was developed. The name *Labrador dog* had been applied in the 19th cent. to a much larger breed, similar to the Newfoundland.

Labrador Current a cold ocean current which flows southwards from the Arctic Ocean along the NE coast of North America. It meets the warm Gulf Stream in an area off the coast of Newfoundland which is noted for its dense fogs.

labradorescence /ˌlabrədɔːˈrɛs(ə)ns/ ▸ noun [mass noun] Mineralogy the brilliant iridescence exhibited by some specimens of labradorite and other feldspars.

labradorite /ˌlabrəˈdɔːrʌɪt/ ▸ noun [mass noun] a mineral of the plagioclase feldspar group, found in many igneous rocks.
– ORIGIN early 19th cent.: from LABRADOR PENINSULA, where it was found, + -ITE^{1}.

Labrador Peninsula a broad peninsula of eastern Canada, between Hudson Bay, the Atlantic, and the Gulf of St Lawrence. Consisting of the Ungava Peninsula and Labrador, it contains most of Quebec and the mainland part of the province of Newfoundland and Labrador. Also called **Labrador-Ungava** /ʊŋˈɡɑːvə/.

Labrador tea ▸ noun a low-growing northern shrub of the heather family, with fragrant leathery evergreen leaves which are sometimes used locally in Canada as a tea substitute. ● Genus *Ledum*, family Ericaceae.

labret /ˈleɪbrɪt/ ▸ noun an object such as a small piece of shell, bone, or stone inserted into the lip as an ornament in some cultures.
– ORIGIN mid 19th cent.: diminutive of LABRUM.

labrish /ˈlabrɪʃ/ ▸ noun [mass noun] W. Indian gossip.
– ORIGIN probably a corruption of the verb BLABBER.

labrum /ˈleɪbrəm/ ▸ noun (pl. **labra** /-brə/) Zoology a structure corresponding to a lip, especially the upper border of the mouthparts of a crustacean or insect.
– DERIVATIVES **labral** adjective.
– ORIGIN early 18th cent.: from Latin, literally 'lip'; related to LABIUM.

Labrusca /ləˈbrʊskə/ ▸ noun [mass noun] a variety of grape obtained from a wild vine native to the eastern US. ● *Vitis labrusca*, family Vitaceae. ■ a wine made from the Labrusca grape.
– ORIGIN from Latin *labrusca*, denoting a wild vine.

La Bruyère /ˌla bruːˈjɛː/, French /la bʀyjɛʀ/, Jean de (1645–96), French writer and moralist. He is known for his *Caractères* (1688), based on a translation of the *Characters* of Theophrastus and exposing the vanity and corruption of human behaviour by satirizing Parisian society.

Labuan /ləˈbuːən/ a small Malaysian island off the north coast of Borneo; pop. 85,000 (est. 2009); capital, Victoria.

laburnum /ləˈbəːnəm/ ▸ noun a small European tree which has hanging clusters of yellow flowers followed by slender pods containing poisonous seeds. The hard timber is sometimes used as an ebony substitute. ● Genus *Laburnum*, family Leguminosae.
– ORIGIN modern Latin, from Latin.

labyrinth /ˈlab(ə)rɪnθ/ ▸ noun **1** a complicated irregular network of passages or paths in which it is difficult to find one's way; a maze: *you lose yourself **in a labyrinth of** little streets*. ■ an intricate and confusing arrangement: ***a labyrinth of** conflicting laws and regulations*.
2 Anatomy a complex structure in the inner ear which contains the organs of hearing and balance. It consists of bony cavities (the **bony labyrinth**) filled with fluid and lined with sensitive membranes (the **membranous labyrinth**). ■ Zoology an accessory respiratory organ of certain fish.
– DERIVATIVES **labyrinthian** adjective.
– ORIGIN late Middle English (referring to the maze constructed by Daedalus to house the Minotaur): from French *labyrinthe* or Latin *labyrinthus*, from Greek *laburinthos*.

labyrinth fish ▸ noun a freshwater fish with poorly developed gills and a labyrinthine accessory breathing organ, native to Africa and Asia. ● Suborder Anabantoidei: Belontiidae and related families, with many species, including such popular aquarium fishes as the gouramis and the fighting fish.

labyrinthine /ˌlabəˈrɪnθʌɪn/ ▸ adjective (of a network) like a labyrinth; irregular and twisting: *labyrinthine streets and alleys*. ■ (of a system) intricate and confusing: *labyrinthine plots and counterplots*.

labyrinthitis /ˌlab(ə)rɪnˈθʌɪtɪs/ ▸ noun [mass noun] Medicine inflammation of the labyrinth or inner ear.

labyrinthodont /ˌlabəˈrɪnθədɒnt/ ▸ adjective Zoology (of teeth) having the enamel deeply folded to form a labyrinthine structure. ■ Palaeontology relating to a group of large fossil amphibians of the late Devonian to early Triassic periods having labyrinthodont teeth.
▸ noun a labyrinthodont amphibian. ● Former subclass Labyrinthodontia: several families, but no longer considered to be a single group.
– ORIGIN mid 19th cent.: from modern Latin *Labyrinthodontia*, from Greek *laburinthos* 'labyrinth' + *odous, odont-* 'tooth'.

LAC ▸ abbreviation Leading Aircraftman.

lac^{1} ▸ noun [mass noun] a resinous substance secreted as a protective covering by the lac insect, used to make varnish, shellac, sealing wax, dyes, etc.
– ORIGIN late Middle English: from medieval Latin *lac, lac(c)a*, from Portuguese *laca*, based on Hindi *lākh* or Persian *lāk*.

lac^{2} ▸ adjective Biology denoting the ability of normal strains of the bacterium *E. coli* to metabolize lactose, or the genetic factors involved in this ability (which is lost in some mutant strains): *the lac operon*.
– ORIGIN 1940s: abbreviation of LACTOSE.

lac^{3} ▸ noun variant spelling of LAKH.

Lacan /laˈkɒ̃/, French /lakɑ̃/, Jacques (1901–81), French psychoanalyst and writer. A notable post-structuralist, he reinterpreted Freudian psychoanalysis, especially the theory of the unconscious, in the light of structural linguistics and anthropology.
– DERIVATIVES **Lacanian** /laˈkeɪnɪən/ adjective & noun, **Lacanianism** noun.

Laccadive Islands /ˈlakədɪv/ one of the groups of islands forming the Indian territory of Lakshadweep in the Indian Ocean.

laccase /ˈlakeɪz/ ▸ noun [mass noun] Biochemistry a copper-containing enzyme which oxidizes hydroquinones to quinones, involved in the setting of lac.
– ORIGIN late 19th cent.: from medieval Latin *lacca* (see LAC^{1}) + -ASE.

laccolith /ˈlakəlɪθ/ ▸ noun Geology a mass of igneous rock, typically lens-shaped, that has been intruded between rock strata causing uplift in the shape of a dome.
– ORIGIN late 19th cent.: from Greek *lakkos* 'reservoir' + -LITH.

lace ▸ noun **1** [mass noun] a fine open fabric of cotton or silk, made by looping, twisting, or knitting thread in patterns and used especially for trimming garments. ■ braid used for trimming, especially on military dress uniforms.
2 (usu. **laces**) a cord or leather strip passed through eyelets or hooks on opposite sides of a shoe or garment and then pulled tight and fastened.
▸ verb [with obj.] **1** fasten or tighten (a shoe or garment) by tying the laces: *he put the shoes on and **laced** them **up***. ■ tighten a laced corset around the waist of: *Rosina **laced** her **up** tight to show off her neat waist*. ■ (**lace someone into**) fasten someone into (a garment) by tightening the laces: *she couldn't breathe, laced into this frock*. ■ [no obj.] (of a garment or shoe) be fastened by means of laces: *the shoes laced at the front*.
2 [with obj. and adverbial] entwine (things, especially fingers) together: *she laced her fingers **together***. ■ (**lace something through**) pass a lace or cord through (a hole).
3 (usu. **be laced with**) add an ingredient, especially alcohol, to (a drink or dish) to enhance its flavour or strength: *coffee laced with brandy*. ■ give (something) a large amount or degree of a feature or quality: *the script is laced with expletives | his voice was laced with derision*.
– PHRASAL VERBS **lace into** informal attack verbally or physically: *Brady laced into his teammates for playing with a lack of passion*.
– ORIGIN Middle English: from Old French *laz, las* (noun), *lacier* (verb), based on Latin *laqueus* 'noose' (also an early sense in English). Compare with LASSO.

lacebark ▸ noun any of a number of trees or shrubs which possess a lacy bark or inner bark, in particular: ● an evergreen Caribbean shrub with a lacy inner bark that is used ornamentally (*Lagetta lagetto*, family Thymelaeaceae). ● a small ornamental New Zealand tree (genus *Hoheria*, family Malvaceae).

lace bug ▶ noun a small plant-eating bug that has a raised net-like pattern on the wings and upper surface. ● Family Tingidae, suborder Heteroptera: several genera.

lacecap ▶ noun a hydrangea of a group of varieties that have flat flower heads with fertile florets in the centre surrounded by sterile florets. Compare with HORTENSIA. ● *Hydrangea macrophylla* vars., family Hydrangeaceae.

laced ▶ adjective trimmed or fitted with lace or laces: *heavy laced boots*.

Lacedaemonian /ˌlasɪdɪˈməʊnɪən/ ▶ noun a native or inhabitant of Lacedaemon, an area of ancient Greece comprising the city of Sparta and its surroundings.
▶ adjective of Lacedaemon or its inhabitants; Spartan.

lace glass ▶ noun [mass noun] a type of Venetian glass, having designs resembling lace.

La Ceiba /la ˈseɪbə/ a seaport on the Caribbean coast of Honduras; pop. 167,300 (est. 2008).

lacemaking ▶ noun [mass noun] the activity or occupation of making lace.
– DERIVATIVES **lacemaker** noun.

lace pillow ▶ noun a cushion placed on the lap to provide support in lacemaking.

lacerate /ˈlasəreɪt/ ▶ verb [with obj.] tear or deeply cut (something, especially flesh or skin): *the point had lacerated his neck* | (as adj. **lacerated**) *his badly lacerated hands and knees*.
– ORIGIN late Middle English: from Latin *lacerat-* 'mangled', from the verb *lacerare*, from *lacer* 'mangled, torn'.

laceration /lasəˈreɪʃ(ə)n/ ▶ noun a deep cut or tear, especially in skin; a gash: *he suffered lacerations to his head and face*. ■ [mass noun] the action of making such a cut.

Lacerta /ləˈsəːtə/ Astronomy a small and inconspicuous northern constellation (the Lizard), on the edge of the Milky Way between Cygnus and Andromeda.
– ORIGIN Latin.

lacertid /ləˈsəːtɪd/ ▶ noun Zoology a typical lizard of a large family (Lacertidae) to which most European lizards belong.
– ORIGIN late 19th cent.: from modern Latin *Lacertidae* (plural), from Latin *lacerta* 'lizard'.

Lacertilia /ˌlasəˈtɪlɪə/ ▶ plural noun Zoology a group of reptiles that comprises the lizards. Also called SAURIA. ● Suborder Lacertilia (or Sauria), order Squamata.
– ORIGIN modern Latin (plural), from Latin *lacerta* 'lizard'.

lacertilian /ˌlasəˈtɪlɪən/ Zoology ▶ noun a reptile of the suborder Lacertilia, a lizard.
▶ adjective relating to or denoting lacertilians.

lace-up ▶ adjective (of a shoe or garment) fastened with laces: *flat lace-up shoes*.
▶ noun chiefly Brit. a shoe or boot that is fastened with laces: ***brown leather lace-ups***.

lacewing ▶ noun a slender delicate insect with large clear membranous wings. Both the adults and larvae are typically predators of aphids. ● Several families in the order Neuroptera, in particular Chrysopidae (the **green lacewings**).

lacewood ▶ noun [mass noun] the timber of the plane tree.

lacework ▶ noun [mass noun] fabric or decorative items made of lace. ■ the process of making lace.

laches /ˈlatʃɪz, ˈleɪ-/ ▶ noun [mass noun] Law unreasonable delay in asserting a claim, which may result in its dismissal.
– ORIGIN late Middle English (in the sense 'slackness, negligence'): from Old French *laschesse*, from *lasche* 'loose, lax', based on Latin *laxus*. The current sense dates from the late 16th cent.

Lachesis /ˈlakɪsɪs/ Greek Mythology one of the three Fates.
– ORIGIN Greek, literally 'getting by lot'.

Lachlan /ˈlaklən/ a river of New South Wales, Australia, which rises in the Great Dividing Range and flows some 1,472 km (920 miles) north-west then south-west to join the Murrumbidgee River near the border with Victoria.
– ORIGIN named after *Lachlan* Macquarie, the governor of New South Wales from 1810 to 1821.

lachrymal /ˈlakrɪm(ə)l/ (also **lacrimal** or **lacrymal**) ▶ adjective **1** formal or literary connected with weeping or tears.
2 (**lacrimal**) Physiology & Anatomy concerned with the secretion of tears: *lacrimal cells*.
▶ noun **1** (**lacrimal** or **lacrimal bone**) Anatomy a small bone forming part of the eye socket.
2 short for LACHRYMAL VASE.
– ORIGIN late Middle English (in sense 2 of the adjective): from medieval Latin *lachrymalis*, from Latin *lacrima* 'tear'.

lachrymal vase ▶ noun historical a phial holding the tears of mourners at a funeral.

lachrymation /ˌlakrɪˈmeɪʃ(ə)n/ (also **lacrimation** or **lacrymation**) ▶ noun [mass noun] literary or Medicine the flow of tears.
– ORIGIN late 16th cent.: from Latin *lacrimatio(n-)*, from *lacrimare* 'weep', from *lacrima* 'tear'.

lachrymator /ˈlakrɪˌmeɪtə/ (also **lacrimator**) ▶ noun chiefly Medicine a substance that irritates the eyes and causes tears to flow.

lachrymatory /ˈlakrɪmə,t(ə)ri/ (also **lacrimatory**) ▶ adjective technical or literary relating to, causing, or containing tears: *a lachrymatory secretion*.
▶ noun (pl. **lachrymatories**) a phial of a kind found in ancient Roman tombs and thought to be a lachrymal vase.
– ORIGIN mid 17th cent. (as a noun): from Latin *lacrima*.

lachrymose /ˈlakrɪməʊs, -z/ ▶ adjective tearful or given to weeping: *she was pink-eyed and lachrymose*. ■ inducing tears; sad: *a lachrymose children's classic*.
– DERIVATIVES **lachrymosely** adverb, **lachrymosity** noun.
– ORIGIN mid 17th cent. (in the sense 'like tears; liable to exude in drops'): from Latin *lacrimosus*, from *lacrima* 'tear'.

lacing ▶ noun **1** [mass noun] the laced fastening of a shoe or garment.
2 lace trimming, especially on a uniform.
3 a dash of spirits added to a drink: *black coffee with a generous lacing of rum*.

lacing course ▶ noun a strengthening course of bricks built into an arch or wall.

laciniate /ləˈsɪnɪət/ (also **laciniated** /-eɪtɪd/) ▶ adjective Botany & Zoology divided into deep narrow irregular segments.
– ORIGIN mid 18th cent.: from Latin *lacinia* 'fringe, hem, flap of a garment' + -ATE[2].

lac insect ▶ noun an Asian scale insect which lives on croton trees and produces secretions that are used in the production of shellac. ● *Laccifer lacca*, family Lacciferidae, suborder Homoptera.

lack ▶ noun [mass noun] (usu. **lack of**) the state of being without or not having enough of something: *there is **no lack of** entertainment aboard ship* | *the case was dismissed for lack of evidence* | [in sing.] *there is a lack of parking space in the town*.
▶ verb [with obj.] be without or deficient in: *the novel lacks imagination* | [no obj.] *she **lacks in** patience* | *Sam did not **lack for** friends*.
– ORIGIN Middle English: corresponding to, and perhaps partly from, Middle Dutch and Middle Low German *lak* 'deficiency', Middle Dutch *laken* 'lack, blame'.

lackadaisical /ˌlakəˈdeɪzɪk(ə)l/ ▶ adjective lacking enthusiasm and determination; carelessly lazy: *a lackadaisical defence left Spurs adrift in the second half*.
– DERIVATIVES **lackadaisically** adverb.
– ORIGIN mid 18th cent. (also in the sense 'feebly sentimental'): from LACKADAY or its obsolete extended form *lackadaisy*.

lackaday ▶ exclamation archaic an expression of surprise, regret, or grief.
– ORIGIN late 17th cent.: shortening of *alack-a-day*.

lackey ▶ noun (pl. **lackeys**) **1** a servant, especially a liveried footman or manservant. ■ derogatory a person who is obsequiously willing to obey or serve another person.
2 (also **lackey moth**) a brownish European moth of woods and hedgerows, the caterpillars of which live communally in a silken tent on the food tree. [mid 19th cent.: from the resemblance of the coloured stripes of its caterpillars to a footman's livery.] ● *Malacosoma neustria*, family Lasiocampidae.
▶ verb (**lackeys, lackeying, lackeyed**) [with obj.] archaic behave servilely towards; wait on as a lackey.
– ORIGIN early 16th cent.: from French *laquais*, perhaps from Catalan *alacay*, from Arabic *al-qā'id* 'the chief'.

lacking ▶ adjective [predic.] not available or in short supply: *adequate resources are sadly lacking*. ■ (of a quality) absent: *there was something lacking in our marriage*. ■ deficient or inadequate: *the students are not **lacking in** intellectual ability* | *workers were asked in what way they found their managers **lacking***.

lacklustre (US **lackluster**) ▶ adjective **1** lacking in vitality, force, or conviction; uninspired or uninspiring: *no excuses were made for the team's lacklustre performance*.
2 (of the hair or the eyes) not shining; dull.

Lac Léman /lak lemɑ̃/ French name for Lake Geneva (see GENEVA, LAKE).

Laclos /laˈkləʊ/, French /laklo/, Pierre Choderlos de (1741–1803), French novelist; full name *Pierre-Ambroise-François Choderlos de Laclos*. He is chiefly remembered for his epistolary novel *Les Liaisons dangereuses* (1782).

Laconia /ləˈkəʊnɪə/ (also **Lakonia**) a modern department and ancient region of Greece, in the SE Peloponnese. Throughout the classical period the region was dominated by its capital, Sparta.
– DERIVATIVES **Laconian** adjective & noun.

laconic /ləˈkɒnɪk/ ▶ adjective (of a person, speech, or style of writing) using very few words: *his laconic reply suggested a lack of interest in the topic*.
– DERIVATIVES **laconically** adverb, **laconicism** noun, **laconism** noun.
– ORIGIN mid 16th cent. (in the sense 'Laconian'): via Latin from Greek *Lakōnikos*, from *Lakōn* 'Laconia, Sparta', the Spartans being known for their terse speech.

laconicum /ləˈkɒnɪkəm/ ▶ noun (pl. **laconica**) a room in an ancient Roman baths used for hot-air or steam baths.
– ORIGIN Latin, neuter of *Laconicus* 'Laconic', this type of room being first used by the Spartans.

La Coruña /la kəʊˈruːnjə/ Spanish name for CORUNNA.

lacquer /ˈlakə/ ▶ noun [mass noun] **1** a liquid made of shellac dissolved in alcohol, or of synthetic substances, that dries to form a hard protective coating for wood, metal, etc.
2 the sap of the lacquer tree used as a varnish. ■ decorative wooden articles coated with lacquer: [as modifier] *a lacquer box*.
3 (also **hair lacquer**) a chemical substance sprayed on hair to keep it in place.
▶ verb [with obj.] (often as adj. **lacquered**) **1** coat with lacquer: *a small lacquered table*.
2 spray (the hair) with lacquer.
– DERIVATIVES **lacquerer** noun.
– ORIGIN late 16th cent. (denoting lac): from obsolete French *lacre* 'sealing wax', from Portuguese *laca* (see LAC[1]).

lacquer tree ▶ noun an East Asian tree with white sap that turns dark on exposure to air, producing a hard-wearing varnish traditionally used in lacquerwork. ● *Rhus verniciflua*, family Anacardiaceae.

lacquerware (also **lacquerwork**) ▶ noun [mass noun] decorative articles, typically made of wood, that have been coated with lacquer.

lacquey ▶ noun & verb archaic spelling of LACKEY.

lacrimal ▶ adjective & noun variant spelling of LACHRYMAL.

lacrimation ▶ noun variant spelling of LACHRYMATION.

lacrimator ▶ noun variant spelling of LACHRYMATOR.

lacrimatory ▶ adjective variant spelling of LACHRYMATORY.

lacrosse /ləˈkrɒs/ ▶ noun [mass noun] a team game, originally played by North American Indians, in which the ball is thrown, carried, and caught with a long-handled stick having a curved L-shaped or triangular frame at one end with a piece of shallow netting in the angle.
– ORIGIN mid 19th cent.: from French (*le jeu de*) *la crosse* '(the game of) the hooked stick'. Compare with CROSSE.

lacrymal ▶ adjective & noun variant spelling of LACHRYMAL.

lacrymation ▶ noun variant spelling of LACHRYMATION.

lactalbumin /lakˈtalbjʊmɪn/ ▶ noun [mass noun] Biochemistry a protein or mixture of similar proteins occurring in milk, obtained after the removal of casein and soluble in a salt solution.
– ORIGIN late 19th cent.: from LACTO- 'of milk' + ALBUMIN.

lactam /ˈlaktam/ ▶ noun Chemistry an organic compound containing an amide group –NHCO– as part of a ring.
– ORIGIN late 19th cent.: blend of LACTONE and AMIDE.

lactase /ˈlakteɪz/ ▶ noun [mass noun] Biochemistry an enzyme which catalyses the hydrolysis of lactose to glucose and galactose.
– ORIGIN late 19th cent.: from LACTOSE + -ASE.

L

lactate¹ /lak'teɪt/ ▸ **verb** [no obj.] (of a female mammal) secrete milk.
– ORIGIN late 19th cent.: back-formation from **LACTATION**.

lactate² /'lakteɪt/ ▸ **noun** [mass noun] Chemistry a salt or ester of lactic acid.
– ORIGIN late 18th cent.: from **LACTIC** + **-ATE¹**.

lactation ▸ **noun** [mass noun] the secretion of milk by the mammary glands. ■ the action of suckling an infant.
– DERIVATIVES **lactational** adjective.
– ORIGIN mid 17th cent.: from Latin *lactatio(n-)*, from *lactare* 'suckle', from *lac, lact-* 'milk'.

lacteal /'laktɪəl/ ▸ **adjective** of milk. ■ Anatomy (of a vessel) conveying chyle or other milky fluid.
▸ **plural noun (lacteals)** Anatomy the lymphatic vessels of the small intestine which absorb digested fats.
– ORIGIN mid 17th cent.: from Latin *lacteus* (from *lac, lact-* 'milk') + **-AL**.

lactescent /lak'tɛs(ə)nt/ ▸ **adjective** milky in appearance. ■ Botany yielding a milky latex.
– ORIGIN mid 17th cent.: from Latin *lactescent-* 'being milky', from the verb *lactere*, from *lac, lact-* 'milk'.

lactic /'laktɪk/ ▸ **adjective** relating to or obtained from milk.
– ORIGIN late 18th cent.: from Latin *lac, lact-* 'milk' + **-IC**.

lactic acid ▸ **noun** [mass noun] Biochemistry a colourless syrupy organic acid formed in sour milk, and produced in the muscle tissues during strenuous exercise. ● Chem. formula: $CH_3CH(OH)COOH$.

lactiferous /lak'tɪf(ə)rəs/ ▸ **adjective** chiefly Anatomy forming or conveying milk or milky fluid: *lactiferous ducts*.
– ORIGIN late 17th cent.: from Latin *lac, lact-* 'milk' + **-FEROUS**.

lacto- ▸ **combining form 1** relating to milk: *lactoscope*.
2 from or relating to lactic acid or lactose: *lactobacillus*.
– ORIGIN from Latin *lac, lact-* 'milk'.

L

lactobacillus /ˌlaktəʊbə'sɪləs/ ▸ **noun** (pl. **lactobacilli** /-lʌɪ/) Biology a rod-shaped bacterium which produces lactic acid from the fermentation of carbohydrates.
● Genus *Lactobacillus*; non-motile Gram-positive bacteria.

lactoferrin /ˌlaktəʊ'fɛrɪn/ ▸ **noun** [mass noun] Biochemistry a protein present in milk and other secretions, with bactericidal and iron-binding properties.

lactoflavin /ˌlaktəʊ'fleɪvɪn/ ▸ **noun** another term for **RIBOFLAVIN**.

lactogenic /ˌlaktə(ʊ)'dʒɛnɪk/ ▸ **adjective** Physiology (of a hormone or other substance) inducing the secretion of milk.

lactoglobulin /ˌlaktə(ʊ)'glɒbjʊlɪn/ ▸ **noun** [mass noun] Biochemistry a protein or mixture of similar proteins occurring in milk, obtained after the removal of casein and precipitated in a salt solution.

lactometer /lak'tɒmɪtə/ ▸ **noun** an instrument for measuring the density of milk.

lactone /'laktəʊn/ ▸ **noun** Chemistry an organic compound containing an ester group –OCO– as part of a ring.

lacto-ovo-vegetarian ▸ **noun** a person who eats vegetables, eggs, and dairy products but who does not eat meat.

lactoprotein ▸ **noun** [mass noun] the protein component of milk.

lactose /'laktəʊz, -s/ ▸ **noun** [mass noun] Chemistry a sugar present in milk. It is a disaccharide containing glucose and galactose units.

lactosuria /ˌlaktə(ʊ)'sjʊərɪə/ ▸ **noun** [mass noun] the presence of lactose in the urine.

lacto-vegetarian ▸ **noun** a person who abstains from eating meat and eggs.

lactulose /'laktjʊləʊz/ ▸ **noun** [mass noun] Chemistry a synthetic sugar with laxative properties. It is a disaccharide consisting of glucose and fructose units.
– ORIGIN 1930s: from **LACTO-** 'of milk', perhaps on the pattern of *cellulose*.

lacuna /lə'kjuːnə/ ▸ **noun** (pl. **lacunae** /-niː/ or **lacunas**) **1** an unfilled space; a gap: *the journal has filled a lacuna in Middle Eastern studies*. ■ a missing portion in a book or manuscript.
2 Anatomy a cavity or depression, especially in bone.
– DERIVATIVES **lacunal** adjective, **lacunary** adjective, **lacunose** adjective.
– ORIGIN mid 17th cent.: from Latin, 'pool', from *lacus* 'lake'.

lacunar¹ /lə'kjuːnə/ ▸ **adjective** relating to a lacuna.

lacunar² /lə'kjuːnə/ ▸ **noun** a vault or ceiling consisting of recessed panels. ■ a panel in a lacunar.

lacustrine /lə'kʌstrʌɪn, -trɪn/ ▸ **adjective** technical or literary relating to or associated with lakes.
– ORIGIN early 19th cent.: from Latin *lacus* 'lake' (the stem *lacustr-* influenced by Latin *palustris* 'marshy') + **-INE¹**.

LACW ▸ **abbreviation** Leading Aircraftwoman.

lacy ▸ **adjective** (**lacier, laciest**) made of, resembling, or trimmed with lace: *a lacy petticoat*.
– DERIVATIVES **lacily** adverb, **laciness** noun.

lad ▸ **noun 1** informal a boy or young man (often as a form of address): *come in, lad, and shut the door*. ■ (**lads**) Brit. a group of men sharing recreational, working, or other interests: *she wouldn't let him go out with* ***the lads*** *any more | a furious row ensued between the referee and our lads*. ■ Brit. a boisterously macho or high-spirited young man: *Tony was* ***a bit of a lad****—always had an eye for the women*.
2 Brit. a stable worker (regardless of age or sex).
– ORIGIN Middle English: of unknown origin.

Ladakh /lə'dɑːk/ a high-altitude region of NW India, Pakistan, and China, containing the Ladakh and Karakoram mountain ranges and the upper Indus valley; chief town, Leh (in India).

Ladakhi /lə'dɑːki/ ▸ **noun** (pl. **Ladakhis**) **1** a native or inhabitant of Ladakh.
2 [mass noun] the language of Ladakh, a dialect of Tibetan.
▸ **adjective** relating to Ladakh, the Ladakhis, or their language.
– ORIGIN the name in Ladakhi.

ladanum /'lad(ə)nəm/ (also **labdanum**) ▸ **noun** [mass noun] a gum resin obtained from the twigs of a southern European rock rose, used in perfumery and for fumigation. ● The rock rose is usually *Cistus ladanifer*, family Cistaceae.
– ORIGIN mid 16th cent.: via Latin from Greek *ladanon, lēdanon*, from *lēdon* 'mastic'.

ladder ▸ **noun 1** a piece of equipment consisting of a series of bars or steps between two upright lengths of wood, metal, or rope, used for climbing up or down something. ■ a series of ascending stages by which someone or something may progress: *employees on their way up the career ladder*.
2 Brit. a vertical strip of unravelled fabric in tights or stockings.
▸ **verb** Brit. (with reference to tights or stockings) develop or cause to develop a ladder: (as adj. **laddered**) *her tights were always laddered* | [no obj.] *they laddered the minute I put them on*.
– ORIGIN Old English *hlǣd(d)er*, of West Germanic origin; related to Dutch *leer* and German *Leiter*.

ladder-back (also **ladder-back chair**) ▸ **noun** an upright chair with a back resembling a ladder.

ladder stitch ▸ **noun** [mass noun] a stitch in embroidery consisting of transverse bars.

laddertron /'ladətrɒn/ ▸ **noun** a device used to carry charge to the terminals of some electrostatic accelerators, consisting of a series of metal bars joined at each end by non-conducting links to form a closed loop.
– ORIGIN 1970s: from **LADDER** + **-TRON**.

laddie ▸ **noun** informal, chiefly Scottish a boy or young man (often as a form of address): *he's just a wee laddie*.

laddish ▸ **adjective** denoting or characteristic of a young man who behaves in a boisterously macho manner.
– DERIVATIVES **laddishness** noun.

laddu /'lʌduː/ (also **laddoo** or **ladoo**) ▸ **noun** (pl. **laddus**) an Indian sweet made from a mixture of flour, sugar, and shortening, which is shaped into a ball.
– ORIGIN from Hindi *laḍḍū*.

lade /leɪd/ ▸ **verb** (past participle **laden**) [with obj.] archaic put cargo on board (a ship). ■ ship (goods) as cargo: *the surplus products must be laden on board the vessels*. ■ [no obj.] (of a ship) take on cargo.
– ORIGIN Old English *hladan*, of West Germanic origin; related to Dutch and German *laden* 'to load', also to **LADLE** and perhaps to **LATHE**.

laden ▸ **adjective** heavily loaded or weighed down: *a tree laden with apples* | [in combination] *the moisture-laden air*.
– ORIGIN late 16th cent.: past participle of **LADE**.

ladette ▸ **noun** Brit. informal a young woman who behaves in a boisterously assertive or crude manner and engages in heavy drinking sessions.
– ORIGIN 1990s: from **LAD** + **-ETTE**.

la-di-da (also **lah-di-dah**) ▸ **adjective** informal pretentious or snobbish in manner or speech: *do I really sound like a la-di-da society lawyer?*
– ORIGIN late 19th cent.: imitative of an affected manner of speech.

ladies plural form of **LADY**.

ladies' chain ▸ **noun** a figure in a quadrille or other dance.

ladies' fingers ▸ **plural noun** Brit. another term for **OKRA**.

ladies' man (also **lady's man**) ▸ **noun** informal a man who enjoys spending time and flirting with women.

ladies' night ▸ **noun** a function at a men's institution or club to which women are invited. ■ an evening on which women are given free or reduced admission to a nightclub.

ladies' room ▸ **noun** chiefly N. Amer. a toilet for women in a public or institutional building.

ladies' tresses ▸ **noun** US spelling of **LADY'S TRESSES**.

ladified ▸ **adjective** variant spelling of **LADYFIED**.

Ladin /lə'diːn/ ▸ **noun** [mass noun] the Rhaeto-Romance dialect spoken in northern Italy and the Engadine region of SE Switzerland.
– ORIGIN mid 19th cent.: from Latin *Latinus* (see **LATIN**).

lading /'leɪdɪŋ/ ▸ **noun** [mass noun] archaic the action of loading a ship with cargo. ■ [count noun] a cargo.

Ladino /lə'diːnəʊ/ ▸ **noun** (pl. **Ladinos**) **1** [mass noun] the language of some Sephardic Jews, especially formerly in Mediterranean countries. It is based on medieval Spanish, with some Hebrew, Greek, and Turkish words, and is written in modified Hebrew characters. Also called **JUDEZMO**.
2 a mestizo or Spanish-speaking white person in Central America.
– ORIGIN Spanish, from Latin *Latinus* (see **LATIN**).

ladino /lə'diːnəʊ/ ▸ **noun** (pl. **ladinos**) a white (or Dutch) clover of a large variety native to Italy and cultivated for fodder in North America.
– ORIGIN 1920s: from Italian.

Ladislaus I /'ladɪsˌlɔːs/ (*c.*1040–95), king of Hungary 1077–95; canonized as **St Ladislaus**. He extended Hungarian power and advanced the spread of Christianity. Feast day, 27 June.

Ladislaus II /'ladɪsˌlaʊs/ (*c.*1351–1434), king of Poland 1386–1434; Polish name **Władysław**. As grand duke of Lithuania, he acceded to the Polish throne on his marriage to the Polish monarch, Queen Jadwiga, thus uniting Lithuania and Poland.

ladle ▸ **noun** a large long-handled spoon with a cup-shaped bowl, used for serving soup or sauce. ■ a container for transporting molten metal in a foundry.
▸ **verb** [with obj. and adverbial] serve (soup, stew, or sauce) with a ladle: *she ladled out onion soup*. ■ provide (information, advice, etc.) lavishly or overgenerously: *he was* ***ladling out*** *his personal philosophy of life*.
– DERIVATIVES **ladleful** noun (pl. **ladlefuls**).
– ORIGIN Old English *hlædel*, from *hladan* (see **LADE**).

Ladoga, Lake /'lɑːdəgə/ a large lake in NW Russia, north-east of St Petersburg, near the border with Finland. It is the largest lake in Europe, with an area of 17,700 sq. km (6,837 sq. miles).

ladoo ▸ **noun** variant spelling of **LADDU**.

lad's love ▸ **noun** another term for **SOUTHERNWOOD**.

lady ▸ **noun** (pl. **ladies**) **1** a polite or formal way of referring to a woman: *I spoke to the lady at the travel agency* | [as modifier] *a lady doctor*. ■ used as a courteous designation for a female fellow member of the House of Commons: *the Right Honourable Lady promised me her support*. ■ chiefly N. Amer. used as an informal, often brusque, form of address to a woman: *I'm sorry, lady, but you have the wrong number*.
2 a woman of good social position. ■ a courteous, decorous, or genteel woman: *his wife was a real lady, with such nice manners*. ■ (**Lady**) (in the UK) a title used by peeresses, female relatives of peers, the wives and widows of knights, etc.: *Lady Caroline Lamb*. ■ a woman at the head of a household.
3 (**one's lady**) dated a man's wife: *welcoming the vice-president and his lady*. ■ (also **lady friend**) a female lover or sweetheart. ■ historical a woman to whom a man, especially a knight, is chivalrously devoted.
4 (**the Ladies**) Brit. a women's public toilet.
– PHRASES **find the lady** another term for **THREE-CARD TRICK**. **it isn't over till the fat lady sings** used to convey that there is still time for a situation to change. [by association with the final aria in tragic opera.] **ladies who lunch** informal, often derogatory

women with both the means and free time to meet socially for lunch in expensive restaurants. **Lady Bountiful** a woman who engages in ostentatious acts of charity to impress others. [early 19th cent.: from the name of a character in Farquhar's *The Beaux' Stratagem* (1707).] **Lady Luck** chance personified as a controlling power in human affairs: *it seemed Lady Luck was still smiling on them.* **Lady Muck** Brit. informal a haughty or socially pretentious woman. **My Lady** a polite form of address to female judges and certain noblewomen.
– DERIVATIVES **ladyhood** noun.
– ORIGIN Old English *hlǣfdīge* (denoting a woman to whom homage or obedience is due, such as the wife of a lord, also specifically the Virgin Mary), from *hlāf* 'loaf' + a Germanic base meaning 'knead', related to DOUGH; compare with LORD. In LADY DAY and other compounds where it signifies possession, it represents the Old English genitive *hlǣfdīgan* '(Our) Lady's'.

Lady altar ▸ noun the altar in a Lady chapel.

ladybird ▸ noun Brit. a small beetle with a domed back which is typically red or yellow with black spots. Both the adults and larvae are important predators of aphids. Called LADYBUG in North America. ● Family Coccinellidae: several genera and species, including the common European **seven-spot ladybird** (*Coccinella septempunctata*).

ladyboy ▸ noun (in Thailand) a transvestite or transsexual.

ladybug ▸ noun North American term for LADYBIRD.

Lady chapel ▸ noun a chapel dedicated to the Virgin Mary in a church or cathedral, typically to the east of the high altar in a cathedral and to the south of it in a church.

Lady Day ▸ noun 25 March (the feast of the Annunciation), a quarter day in England, Wales, and Ireland.
– ORIGIN with reference to *Our Lady*, the Virgin Mary.

lady fern ▸ noun a tall, graceful fern of worldwide distribution which favours moist shady habitats. ● *Athyrium* and other genera, family Woodsiaceae: several species, in particular *A. filix-femina*.

ladyfied (also **ladified**) ▸ adjective having the manner of a socially superior woman; pretentiously refined.

ladyfinger ▸ noun North American term for LADY'S FINGER (sense 2).

ladyfish ▸ noun (pl. **same** or **ladyfishes**) any of a number of marine fishes of warm coastal waters, several of which are popular with anglers, notably: ■ a tenpounder. ■ a bonefish.

lady-in-waiting ▸ noun (pl. **ladies-in-waiting**) a woman who attends a queen or princess.

ladykiller ▸ noun informal an attractive, charming man who habitually seduces women.

ladylike ▸ adjective appropriate for or typical of a well-bred, decorous woman or girl: *her antics were considered very undignified by her ladylike peers | it wasn't ladylike to be too interested in men.*
– DERIVATIVES **ladylikeness** noun.

lady-love ▸ noun dated a female lover or sweetheart.

Lady Mayoress ▸ noun the title of the wife of a Lord Mayor.

lady of the bedchamber ▸ noun (in the UK) a female attendant to the queen or queen mother, ranking in the royal household above woman of the bedchamber.

lady of the night ▸ noun euphemistic a prostitute.

lady's bedstraw ▸ noun a yellow-flowered Eurasian bedstraw which smells of hay when dried and was formerly used to make a mattress for sleeping on. ● *Galium verum*, family Rubiaceae.

lady's companion ▸ noun Brit. a small case or bag containing needlework items.

lady's finger ▸ noun Brit. **1** another term for KIDNEY VETCH.
2 a finger-shaped sponge cake with a sugar topping.

ladyship ▸ noun (**Her/Your Ladyship**) a respectful form of reference or address to a woman who has a title: *the car is outside, Your Ladyship.* ■ Brit. ironic a form of reference or address to a woman thought to be acting in a grand or self-important way: *bow everyone, Her Ladyship's actually gracing us with her presence!*

lady's maid ▸ noun chiefly historical a maid who attended to the personal needs of her mistress.

lady's man ▸ noun variant spelling of LADIES' MAN.

lady's mantle ▸ noun a herbaceous European plant of the rose family, with lobed rounded leaves and inconspicuous greenish flowers, and formerly valued in herbal medicine. ● *Alchemilla vulgaris*, family Rosaceae.

Ladysmith /ˈleɪdɪˌsmɪθ/ a town in eastern South Africa, in KwaZulu-Natal. It was subjected to a four-month siege by Boer forces during the Second Boer War.
– ORIGIN named after the wife of the governor of Natal, Sir Harry *Smith* (1787–1860).

lady's slipper ▸ noun an orchid of north temperate regions, the flower of which has a conspicuous pouch- or slipper-shaped lip. Also called SLIPPER ORCHID. ● Genus *Cypripedium*, family Orchidaceae.

lady's smock ▸ noun another term for CUCKOOFLOWER.

lady's tresses (US also **ladies' tresses**) ▸ plural noun [usu. treated as sing.] a short orchid with small white flowers, growing chiefly in north temperate regions. ● Genus *Spiranthes* (and *Goodyera*), family Orchidaceae.

Lady Superior ▸ noun the head of a convent or nunnery in certain orders.

Lae /ˈlɑːeɪ/ an industrial seaport on the east coast of Papua New Guinea, the country's second-largest city; pop. 73,000 (est. 2009).

Laennec's cirrhosis /laˈɛnɛks/ ▸ noun [mass noun] Medicine a type of cirrhosis of the liver characterized by a nodular appearance of the liver surface, associated with alcoholism.
– ORIGIN early 19th cent.: named after René T. H. *Laënnec* (1781–1826), the French physician who described the condition.

Laetrile /ˈleɪtrʌɪl/ ▸ noun [mass noun] trademark a compound extracted from peach stones, formerly used controversially to treat cancer.
– ORIGIN 1950s: from a blend of LAEVOROTATORY and NITRILE.

laevo- /ˈliːvəʊ/ (also **levo-**) ▸ combining form on or to the left: *laevorotatory*.
– ORIGIN from Latin *laevus* 'left'.

laevorotatory /ˌliːvəʊˈrəʊtət(ə)ri/ (US **levorotatory**) ▸ adjective Chemistry (of a compound) having the property of rotating the plane of a polarized light ray to the left, i.e. anticlockwise facing the oncoming radiation. The opposite of DEXTROROTATORY.
– DERIVATIVES **laevorotation** noun.

laevulose /ˈliːvjʊləʊz, -s/ (US **levulose**) ▸ noun Chemistry another term for FRUCTOSE.

Lafayette /ˌlafʌɪˈ(j)ɛt/ (also **La Fayette**), Marie Joseph Paul Yves Roch Gilbert du Motier, Marquis de (1757–1834), French soldier and statesman. He fought alongside the American colonists in the War of Independence and commanded the National Guard (1789–91) in the French Revolution.

Laffer curve /ˈlafə/ ▸ noun Economics a supposed relationship between economic activity and the rate of taxation which suggests that there is an optimum tax rate which maximizes tax revenue.
– ORIGIN 1970s: named after Arthur *Laffer* (born 1942), American economist.

La Fontaine /ˌla fɒnˈtɛn, -teɪn/, French /la fɔ̃tɛn/, Jean de (1621–95), French poet. He is chiefly remembered for his *Fables* (1668–94), drawn from oriental, classical, and contemporary sources.

lag[1] ▸ verb (**lags, lagging, lagged**) [no obj.] **1** fail to keep up with another or others in movement or development: *they waited for Tim who was lagging behind.*
2 N. Amer. another term for STRING (sense 6 of the verb).
▸ noun **1** (also **time lag**) a period of time between one event and another: *a time lag between infection and symptoms.*
2 Physics a retardation in an electric current or movement.
– DERIVATIVES **lagger** noun.
– ORIGIN early 16th cent. (as a noun in the sense 'hindmost person in a game, race, etc.', also 'dregs'): related to the dialect adjective *lag* (perhaps from a fanciful distortion of LAST[1], or of Scandinavian origin: compare with Norwegian dialect *lagga* 'go slowly').

lag[2] ▸ verb (**lags, lagging, lagged**) [with obj.] enclose or cover (a boiler, pipes, etc.) with material that provides heat insulation.
– DERIVATIVES **lagger** noun.
– ORIGIN late 19th cent.: from earlier *lag* 'piece of insulating cover'.

lag[3] Brit. informal ▸ noun a person who has been frequently convicted and sent to prison: *both old lags were sentenced to ten years' imprisonment.*
▸ verb (**lags, lagging, lagged**) [with obj.] archaic arrest or send to prison.
– ORIGIN late 16th cent. (as a verb in the sense 'carry off, steal'): of unknown origin. Current senses date from the 19th cent.

lagan /ˈlag(ə)n/ ▸ noun [mass noun] archaic (in legal contexts) goods or wreckage lying on the bed of the sea.
– ORIGIN mid 16th cent.: from Old French, perhaps of Scandinavian origin and related to LAY[1].

lagar /laˈgɑː/ ▸ noun (pl. **lagares**) (in Spain and Portugal) a large, typically stone trough in which grapes are trodden.
– ORIGIN Spanish, from Latin *lacus*, denoting a vat for freshly pressed wine.

Lag b'Omer /lɑːg ˈbəʊmə/ ▸ noun a Jewish festival held on the 33rd day of the Omer (the period between Passover and Pentecost), traditionally regarded as celebrating the end of a plague in the 2nd century.
– ORIGIN from Hebrew *lāg* (pronunciation of the letters L (*lamed*) and G (*gimel*) symbolizing 33) + *bā* 'in the' + *'ōmer* (see OMER).

lagena /laˈdʒiːnə/ ▸ noun (pl. **lagenae** /-niː/) Zoology an extension of the saccule of the ear in some vertebrates, corresponding to the cochlear duct in mammals.
– ORIGIN late 19th cent.: from Latin, literally 'flagon', from Greek *lagunos*.

lager ▸ noun [mass noun] a kind of effervescent beer which is light in colour and body.
– ORIGIN mid 19th cent.: from German *Lagerbier* 'beer brewed for keeping', from *Lager* 'storehouse'. Compare with LAAGER, LAIR[1], and LEAGUER[2].

lager lout ▸ noun Brit. informal a young man who behaves in an unpleasant or violent way as a result of excessive drinking.

laggard /ˈlagəd/ ▸ noun a person who makes slow progress and falls behind others.
▸ adjective slower than desired or expected: *a bell to summon laggard children to school.*
– DERIVATIVES **laggardly** adjective & adverb, **laggardness** noun.
– ORIGIN early 18th cent. (as an adjective): from LAG[1].

lagged ▸ adjective Economics showing a delayed effect: *a lagged measure of unemployment.*

lagging ▸ noun [mass noun] material providing heat insulation for a water tank, pipes, etc.
– ORIGIN mid 19th cent.: from LAG[2].

La Gioconda /ˌla dʒɪəˈkɒndə/ another name for MONA LISA.

lagniappe /laˈnjap/ ▸ noun N. Amer. something given as a bonus or gratuity.
– ORIGIN Louisiana French, from Spanish *la ñapa*.

lagomorph /ˈlagəmɔːf/ Zoology ▸ noun a mammal of the order Lagomorpha, which comprises the hares, rabbits, and pikas.
▸ adjective relating to or denoting lagomorphs.

Lagomorpha /ˌlagəˈmɔːfə/ ▸ plural noun Zoology an order of mammals that comprises the hares, rabbits, and pikas. They are distinguished by the possession of double incisor teeth, and were formerly placed with the rodents.
– ORIGIN modern Latin (plural), from Greek *lagōs* 'hare' + *morphē* 'form'.

lagoon ▸ noun a stretch of salt water separated from the sea by a low sandbank or coral reef. ■ N. Amer. & Austral./NZ a small freshwater lake near a larger lake or river. ■ an artificial pool for the treatment of effluent or to accommodate an overspill from surface drains during heavy rain.
– DERIVATIVES **lagoonal** adjective.
– ORIGIN early 17th cent.: from Italian and Spanish *laguna*, from Latin *lacuna* (see LACUNA).

Lagos /ˈleɪgɒs/ the chief city of Nigeria, a port on the Gulf of Guinea; pop. 7,439,300 (est. 2007). Originally a centre of the slave trade, it became capital of the newly independent Nigeria in 1960. It was replaced as capital by Abuja in 1991.

Lagrange /laˈgrɒ̃ʒ/, French /lagrɑ̃ʒ/, Joseph Louis, Comte de (1736–1813), Italian-born French mathematician. He is remembered for his proof that every positive integer can be expressed as a sum of at most four squares, and for his work on mechanics and its application to the description of planetary and lunar motion.

Lagrangian point /ləˈgrɒ̃ʒɪən/ ▸ noun one of five points in the plane of orbit of one body around another (e.g. the moon around the earth) at which a small third body can remain stationary with respect to both.

lah (also **la**) ▶ **noun** Music (in tonic sol-fa) the sixth note of a major scale. ■ the note A in the fixed-doh system.
– ORIGIN Middle English: representing (as an arbitrary name for the note) the first syllable of Latin *labii*, taken from a Latin hymn (see SOLMIZATION).

La Habana /la aˈβana/ Spanish name for HAVANA[1].

lahar /ˈlɑːhɑː/ ▶ **noun** Geology a destructive mudflow on the slopes of a volcano.
– ORIGIN 1920s: from Javanese.

lah-di-dah ▶ **adjective** variant spelling of LA-DI-DA.

Lahnda /ˈlɑːndə/ ▶ **noun** [mass noun] an Indic language of the western Punjab and adjacent areas of Pakistan, with some 58 million speakers. It is sometimes classified as a dialect of Punjabi.
▶ **adjective** relating to Lahnda.
– ORIGIN early 20th cent.: from Punjabi *lahandā*, literally 'western'.

Lahore /ləˈhɔː/ the capital of Punjab province and second-largest city of Pakistan, situated near the border with India; pop. 6,926,600 (est. 2009).
– DERIVATIVES **Lahori** adjective.

Lahu /lɑːˈhuː/ ▶ **noun** (pl. **same** or **Lahus**) **1** a member of an indigenous people of SW China and Laos.
2 [mass noun] the Tibeto-Burman language of the Lahu.
▶ **adjective** relating to the Lahu or their language.
– ORIGIN the name in Lahu.

Laibach /ˈlaɪbax/ German name for LJUBLJANA.

laic /ˈleɪɪk/ formal ▶ **adjective** of the laity; secular.
▶ **noun** a person who is not a member of the clergy; a layperson.
– DERIVATIVES **laical** adjective.
– ORIGIN mid 16th cent.: from late Latin *laicus* (see LAY[2]).

laicity /leɪˈɪsɪti/ ▶ **noun** [mass noun] formal the status or influence of the laity.

laicize /ˈleɪɪsʌɪz/ (also **laicise**) ▶ **verb** [with obj.] formal withdraw clerical character, control, or status from: *when his priestly vocation no longer satisfied him he had asked to be laicized.*
– DERIVATIVES **laicism** noun, **laicization** noun.

laid past and past participle of LAY[1].

laid-back ▶ **adjective** informal relaxed and easy-going: *he was being very laid-back about it all.*

laid paper ▶ **noun** [mass noun] paper that has a finely ribbed appearance. Compare with WOVE PAPER.

lain past participle of LIE[1].

Laing /laŋ/, R. D. (1927–89), Scottish psychiatrist; full name *Ronald David Laing*. He became famous for his controversial views on madness and in particular on schizophrenia, linking what society calls insanity with politics and family structure.

lair[1] ▶ **noun** a place where a wild animal lives. ■ a secret or private place in which a person seeks concealment or seclusion.
– ORIGIN Old English *leger* 'resting place, bed', of Germanic origin; related to Dutch *leger* 'bed, camp' and German *Lager* 'storehouse', also to LIE[1]. Compare with LAAGER, LAGER, and LEAGUER[2].

lair[2] Austral./NZ informal ▶ **noun** a flashily dressed man who enjoys showing off.
▶ **verb** [no obj.] dress or behave in a flashy manner: *some of us **laired up** in Assam silk suits.*
– ORIGIN 1930s: back-formation from LAIRY.

lairage /ˈlɛːrɪdʒ/ ▶ **noun** a place where cattle or sheep may be rested on the way to market or slaughter.

laird /lɛːd/ ▶ **noun** (in Scotland) a person who owns a large estate.
– DERIVATIVES **lairdship** noun.
– ORIGIN late Middle English: Scots form of LORD.

lairy ▶ **adjective** (**lairier**, **lairiest**) Brit. informal **1** cunning or conceited.
2 ostentatiously attractive; flashy.
3 aggressive or rowdy: *a couple of lairy people pushed me around.*
– ORIGIN mid 19th cent. (originally Cockney slang): alteration of LEERY. Sense 2 was originally Australian slang and dates from the early 20th cent.

laissez-aller /ˌlɛseɪˈaleɪ/, French /leseale/ ▶ **noun** [mass noun] absence of restraint; unconstrained freedom.
– ORIGIN French, literally 'allow to go'.

laissez-faire /ˌlɛseɪˈfɛː/, French /lɛsefɛʀ/ ▶ **noun** [mass noun] [usu. as modifier] the policy of leaving things to take their own course, without interfering: *a laissez-faire attitude to life.* ■ Economics abstention by governments from interfering in the workings of the free market: *laissez-faire capitalism.*
– DERIVATIVES **laissez-faireism** noun.
– ORIGIN French, literally 'allow to do'.

laissez-passer /ˌlɛseɪˈpɑːseɪ/, French /lɛsepase/ ▶ **noun** a document allowing the holder to pass; a permit.
– ORIGIN French, literally 'allow to pass'.

laissez vibrer /ˌlɛse ˈviːbreɪ/, French /lɛse vibʀe/ ▶ **verb** [in imperative] a musical instruction used to indicate that a note made by striking or plucking should be allowed to fade away without damping.
– ORIGIN French, literally 'allow to vibrate'.

laity /ˈleɪɪti/ ▶ **noun** [usu. treated as pl.] (**the laity**) **1** lay people, as distinct from the clergy.
2 ordinary people, as distinct from professionals or experts.
– ORIGIN late Middle English: from LAY[2] + -ITY.

Laius /ˈlʌɪəs/ Greek Mythology a king of Thebes, the father of Oedipus and husband of Jocasta.

lake[1] ▶ **noun** a large area of water surrounded by land: *boys were swimming in the lake* | [in names] *Lake Victoria.* ■ (**the Lakes**) the Lake District. ■ a pool of liquid: *the fish was served in a lake of spicy sauce.* ■ [with modifier] a large surplus of a liquid commodity: *the EU wine lake.*
– DERIVATIVES **lakelet** noun.
– ORIGIN late Old English (denoting a pond or pool), from Old French *lac*, from Latin *lacus* 'basin, pool, lake'.

lake[2] ▶ **noun** [often with modifier] an insoluble pigment made by combining a soluble organic dye and an insoluble mordant. ■ [mass noun] a purplish-red pigment of this kind, originally one made with lac.
– ORIGIN early 17th cent.: variant of LAC[1].

Lake Albert, Lake Baikal, etc. see ALBERT, LAKE; BAIKAL, LAKE, etc.

Lake District a region of lakes and mountains in Cumbria.

lake dwelling ▶ **noun** a prehistoric hut built on piles driven into the bed or shore of a lake.
– DERIVATIVES **lake-dweller** noun.

lakefront ▶ **noun** the land along the edge of a lake.

Lakeland another term for LAKE DISTRICT.

Lakeland terrier ▶ **noun** a terrier of a small stocky breed originating in the Lake District.

Lake of the Woods a lake on the border between Canada and the US, to the west of the Great Lakes.

Lake Poets (also **Lake School**) the poets Samuel Taylor Coleridge, Robert Southey, and William Wordsworth, who lived in and were inspired by the Lake District.

laker ▶ **noun** N. Amer. informal **1** a lake trout.
2 a ship constructed for sailing on the Great Lakes.

lakeside ▶ **noun** the land adjacent to a lake.

lake trout ▶ **noun** any of a number of fishes of the salmon family, which live in large lakes and are highly prized as a game fish and as food: ● a European brown trout of a large race. ● a North American charr (*Salvelinus namaycush*, family Salmonidae).

lakh /lak, lɑːk/ (also **lac**) ▶ **noun** (pl. **lakhs**, **same**) Indian a hundred thousand: *they fixed the price at five lakhs of rupees.*
– ORIGIN via Hindi from Sanskrit *lakṣa*.

Lakonia variant spelling of LACONIA.

Lakota /ləˈkəʊtə/ ▶ **noun** (pl. **same** or **Lakotas**) **1** a member of an American Indian people of western South Dakota (also called **Teton Sioux**).
2 [mass noun] the Siouan language of the Lakota, with about 6,000 speakers.
▶ **adjective** relating to the Lakota or their language.
– ORIGIN the name in Lakota, related to the word DAKOTA[1].

laksa /ˈlɑːksa/ ▶ **noun** [mass noun] a Malaysian dish of Chinese origin, consisting of rice noodles served in a curry sauce or hot soup.
– ORIGIN Malay.

Lakshadweep /lakˈʃadwiːp, ˌlʌkʃədˈwiːp/ a group of islands off the Malabar Coast of SW India, constituting a Union Territory in India; pop. 67,400 (est. 2009); capital, Kavaratti. The group consists of the Laccadive, Minicoy, and Amindivi Islands.

Lakshmi /ˈlʌkʃmi/ Hinduism the goddess of prosperity, consort of Vishnu. She assumes different forms (e.g. Radha, Sita) in order to accompany her husband in his various incarnations.

la-la land ▶ **noun** [mass noun] N. Amer. informal Los Angeles or Hollywood, especially with regard to the film and television industry. ■ a fanciful state or dreamworld.
– ORIGIN *la-la*, reduplication of LA (i.e. Los Angeles).

lalapalooza ▶ **noun** variant spelling of LOLLAPALOOZA.

laldy /ˈlaldi/ ▶ **noun** [mass noun] Scottish a beating: *'Give him laldy!' yelled a voice.*
– PHRASES **give it laldy** do something with vigour or enthusiasm.
– ORIGIN late 19th cent.: perhaps imitative, or from Old English *læl* 'whip, weal'.

Lalique /laˈliːk/, René (1860–1945), French jeweller, famous for his art nouveau brooches and combs and his decorative glassware.

Lallans /ˈlalənz/ ▶ **noun** [mass noun] a distinctive Scottish literary form of English, based on standard older Scots.
▶ **adjective** relating to or in Lallans.
– ORIGIN early 18th cent. (also, as an adjective, *Lallan*): Scots variant of *Lowlands*, with reference to a central Lowlands dialect.

lallation /laˈleɪʃ(ə)n/ ▶ **noun** [mass noun] imperfect speech, especially the repetition of meaningless sounds by babies. ■ the pronunciation of *r* as *l*.
– ORIGIN mid 17th cent.: from Latin *lallatio(n-)*, from *lallare* 'sing a lullaby'.

lallygag /ˈlalɪgag/ ▶ **verb** variant spelling of LOLLYGAG.

La Louvière /ˌla luːˈvjɛː/, French /la luvjɛʀ/ an industrial city in SW Belgium, in the province of Hainaut west of Charleroi; pop. 77,616 (2008).

lam[1] ▶ **verb** (**lams**, **lamming**, **lammed**) [with obj.] informal hit hard; strike: *I'll lam you in the mouth in a minute* | [no obj.] *they surged along, **lamming into** anyone in their path.*
– ORIGIN late 16th cent.: perhaps of Scandinavian origin and related to Norwegian and Danish *lamme* 'paralyse'.

lam[2] N. Amer. informal ▶ **noun** (in phrase **on the lam**) in flight, especially from the police: *he **went on the lam** and is living under a false name.*
▶ **verb** (**lams**, **lamming**, **lammed**) [no obj.] escape; flee.
– ORIGIN late 19th cent.: from LAM[1].

Lam. ▶ **abbreviation** Lamentations (in biblical references).

lama /ˈlɑːmə/ ▶ **noun** **1** an honorific title applied to a spiritual leader in Tibetan Buddhism, whether a reincarnate lama or one who has earned the title in life.
2 a Tibetan or Mongolian Buddhist monk.
– ORIGIN mid 17th cent.: from Tibetan *bla-ma* (the initial *b* being silent), literally 'superior one'.

Lamaism /ˈlɑːməˌɪz(ə)m/ ▶ **noun** [mass noun] the system of doctrine and observances inculcated and maintained by lamas; Tibetan Buddhism.
– DERIVATIVES **Lamaist** noun & adjective.

Lamarck /laˈmɑːk/, French /lamaʀk/, Jean Baptiste de (1744–1829), French naturalist. He was an early proponent of organic evolution, although his theory is not widely accepted today. He suggested that species could have evolved from each other by small changes in their structure, and that the mechanism of such change (not now generally considered possible) was that characteristics acquired in order to survive could be passed on to offspring.
– DERIVATIVES **Lamarckian** noun & adjective, **Lamarckism** noun.

Lamartine /ˌlamɑːˈtiːn/, French /lamaʀtin/, Alphonse Marie Louis de (1790–1869), French poet, statesman, and historian. He was Minister of Foreign Affairs in the provisional government following the Revolution of 1848. Notable works: *Méditations poétiques* (1820).

lamasery /ˈlɑːməs(ə)ri, ləˈmɑːs(ə)ri/ ▶ **noun** (pl. **lamaseries**) a monastery of lamas.

Lamaze /ləˈmɑːz, laˈmaz/ ▶ **adjective** relating to a method of childbirth involving exercises and breathing control to give pain relief without drugs.
– ORIGIN 1950s: from the name of Fernand *Lamaze* (1891–1957), French physician.

Lamb, Charles (1775–1834), English essayist and critic. Together with his sister Mary he wrote *Tales from Shakespeare* (1807). Other notable works: *Essays of Elia* (1823).

lamb ▶ **noun** a young sheep. ■ [mass noun] the flesh of a lamb as food. ■ used figuratively as a symbol of meekness or innocence: *he accepted her decision like a lamb.* ■ used to describe or address someone regarded with affection or pity, especially a young child: *the poor lamb is very upset.*
▶ **verb** **1** [no obj.] (of a ewe) give birth to lambs. ■ [with obj.] tend (ewes) at lambing time.

2 [with obj.] (**lamb someone down**) Austral./NZ informal, dated encourage someone to squander their money, especially on alcohol: *Pitt had been lambed down at the Pig and Whistle*.
– PHRASES **in lamb** (of a ewe) pregnant. **the Lamb of God** (also **the Lamb**) a title of Jesus Christ (see John 1:29). **like a lamb to the slaughter** as a helpless victim.
– DERIVATIVES **lamber** noun, **lamblike** adjective.
– ORIGIN Old English, of Germanic origin; related to Dutch *lam* and German *Lamm*.

lambada /lam'bɑːdə/ ▶ noun a fast erotic Brazilian dance which couples perform in close physical contact.
– ORIGIN 1980s: Portuguese, literally 'a beating', from *lambar* 'to beat'.

lambaste /lam'beɪst/ (also **lambast** /-'bast/) ▶ verb [with obj.] criticize (someone or something) harshly: *they lambasted the report as a gross distortion of the truth*.
– DERIVATIVES **lambasting** noun.
– ORIGIN mid 17th cent. (in the sense 'beat, thrash'): from LAM[1] + BASTE[3]. The current sense dates from the late 19th cent.

lambda /'lamdə/ ▶ noun the eleventh letter of the Greek alphabet (Λ, λ), transliterated as 'l'.
■ (**Lambda**) [followed by Latin genitive] Astronomy the eleventh star in a constellation: *Lambda Tauri*. ■ Biology a type of bacteriophage virus used in genetic research: [as modifier] *lambda phage*. ■ Anatomy the point at the back of the skull where the parietal bones and the occipital bone meet. ■ [as modifier] Biochemistry denoting one of the two types of light polypeptide chain present in all immunoglobulin molecules (the other being kappa).
▶ symbol ■ (λ) wavelength. ■ (λ) Astronomy celestial longitude.
– ORIGIN Greek.

lambdoid /'lamdɔɪd/ ▶ adjective resembling the Greek letter lambda in form. ■ Anatomy relating to or denoting the suture near the back of the skull, which connects the parietal bones with the occipital.
– DERIVATIVES **lambdoidal** adjective.

lambent /'lamb(ə)nt/ ▶ adjective literary (of light or fire) glowing, gleaming, or flickering with a soft radiance.
– DERIVATIVES **lambency** noun, **lambently** adverb.
– ORIGIN mid 17th cent.: from Latin *lambent*- 'licking', from the verb *lambere*.

Lambert /'lambət/, (Leonard) Constant (1905–51), English composer, conductor, and critic. He wrote the music for the ballet *Romeo and Juliet* (1926) and the jazz work *The Rio Grande* (1929), later becoming musical director of Sadler's Wells (1930–47).

lambert /'lambət/ ▶ noun a former unit of luminance, equal to the emission or reflection of one lumen per square centimetre.
– ORIGIN early 20th cent.: named after Johann H. *Lambert* (1728–77), German physicist.

Lambeth Conference ▶ noun an assembly of bishops from the Anglican Communion, usually held every ten years (since 1867) at Lambeth Palace and presided over by the Archbishop of Canterbury.

Lambeth Palace a palace in the London borough of Lambeth, the residence of the Archbishop of Canterbury since 1197.

Lambeth Walk ▶ noun a social dance with a walking step, popular in the late 1930s.
– ORIGIN created for the revue *Me and My Girl* and named after a street in the London borough of Lambeth.

Lambic /'lɑ̃bɪk, 'lambɪk/ ▶ noun [mass noun] a strong, sweet Belgian beer.
– ORIGIN French.

lambing ▶ noun [mass noun] the birth of lambs on a farm: *lambing begins in mid January*.

lambkin ▶ noun a small or young lamb. ■ used as a term of endearment for a young child.

lambrequin /'lambrɪkɪn/ ▶ noun **1** N. Amer. a short piece of decorative drapery hung over the top of a door or window or draped from a shelf or mantelpiece.
2 a cloth covering the back of a medieval knight's helmet, represented in heraldry as the mantling.
– ORIGIN early 18th cent. (in sense 2): from French, from the Dutch diminutive of *lamper* 'veil'.

Lambrusco /lam'brʊskəʊ/ ▶ noun [mass noun] a variety of wine grape grown in the Emilia-Romagna region of North Italy. ■ a sparkling red wine made from the Lambrusco grape. ■ a red or white wine resembling Lambrusco, produced outside North Italy.
– ORIGIN Italian, literally 'grape of the wild vine'.

lamb's ears ▶ plural noun [usu. treated as sing.] a SW Asian plant of the mint family, which has grey-green woolly leaves and is cultivated as an ornamental, particularly for ground cover. ● *Stachys byzantina*, family Labiatae.

lamb's fry ▶ noun [mass noun] lamb's offal as food, in particular: ■ Brit. lamb's testicles. ■ Austral./NZ lamb's liver.

lambskin ▶ noun [mass noun] prepared skin from a lamb with the wool on or as leather: [as modifier] *lambskin gloves*.

lamb's lettuce ▶ noun [mass noun] a small blue-flowered herbaceous plant of dry soils, native to Europe and the Mediterranean and sometimes eaten in salads. Also called CORN SALAD. ● *Valerianella locusta*, family Valerianaceae.

lamb's quarter (also **lamb's quarters**) ▶ noun North American term for FAT HEN.

lamb's-tails ▶ plural noun Brit. catkins from the hazel tree.

lamb's tongue ▶ noun another term for LAMB'S EARS.

lambswool ▶ noun [mass noun] fine, soft wool from lambs, used to make knitted garments, blankets, etc.

lame ▶ adjective **1** (of a person or animal) unable to walk without difficulty as the result of an injury or illness affecting the leg or foot: *his horse went lame*.
■ (of a leg or foot) affected by injury or illness.
2 (of an explanation or excuse) unconvincingly feeble: *the TV licensing teams hear a lot of lame excuses*. ■ (of something intended to be entertaining) uninspiring and dull. ■ N. Amer. informal (of a person) naive or socially inept.
▶ verb [with obj.] make (a person or animal) lame.
– DERIVATIVES **lamely** adverb, **lameness** noun.
– ORIGIN Old English *lama*, of Germanic origin, related to Dutch *lam* and German *lahm*.

lamé /'lɑːmeɪ/ ▶ noun [mass noun] fabric with interwoven gold or silver threads.
– ORIGIN 1920s: French, from Latin *lamina* (see LAMINA).

lamebrain ▶ noun informal a stupid person.
– DERIVATIVES **lamebrained** adjective.

lame duck ▶ noun an ineffectual or unsuccessful person or thing: *most of her boyfriends have been lame ducks*. ■ chiefly N. Amer. a politician or administration in the final period of office, after the election of a successor: [as modifier] *a lame-duck president*.

lamella /lə'mɛlə/ ▶ noun (pl. **lamellae** /-liː/) a thin layer, membrane, or plate of tissue, especially in bone. ■ Botany a membranous fold in a chloroplast.
– DERIVATIVES **lamellar** adjective, **lamellate** adjective, **lamelliform** adjective, **lamellose** adjective.
– ORIGIN late 17th cent.: from Latin, diminutive of *lamina* 'thin plate'.

lamellibranch /lə'mɛlɪbraŋk/ ▶ noun another term for BIVALVE.
– ORIGIN mid 19th cent.: from modern Latin *Lamellibranchia* (former class name), from Latin *lamella* (diminutive of *lamina* 'thin plate') + Greek *brankhia* 'gills'.

lamellicorn /lə'mɛlɪkɔːn/ ▶ noun former term for SCARABAEOID.
– ORIGIN mid 19th cent.: from modern Latin *Lamellicornia* (former taxonomic name), from Latin *lamella* 'thin plate' + *cornu* 'horn'.

lamellipodium /lə,mɛlɪ'pəʊdɪəm/ ▶ noun (pl. **lamellipodia**) Zoology a flattened extension of a cell, by which it moves over or adheres to a surface.
– DERIVATIVES **lamellipodial** adjective.
– ORIGIN 1970s: from LAMELLA, on the pattern of *pseudopodium*.

lament ▶ noun **1** a passionate expression of grief or sorrow: *his mother's night-long laments for his father* | [mass noun] *a song full of lament and sorrow*. ■ a song, piece of music, or poem expressing grief or sorrow: *the piper played a lament*.
2 a complaint: *there were constant laments about the conditions of employment*.
▶ verb **1** [with obj.] express passionate grief about: *he was lamenting the death of his infant daughter* | [no obj.] *the women wept and lamented over him*.
2 [reporting verb] express regret or disappointment about something: [with obj.] *she lamented the lack of shops in the town* | [with direct speech] *'We could have won,' lamented the England captain*.
– DERIVATIVES **lamenter** noun.
– ORIGIN late Middle English (as a verb): from French *lamenter* or Latin *lamentari*, from *lamenta* (plural) 'weeping, wailing'.

lamentable /'laməntəb(ə)l/ ▶ adjective **1** (of circumstances or conditions) very bad; deplorable: *the industry is in a lamentable state*. ■ (of an event, action, or attitude) unfortunate; regrettable: *her open prejudice showed lamentable immaturity*.
2 archaic full of or expressing sorrow or grief.
– DERIVATIVES **lamentably** adverb.
– ORIGIN late Middle English (in the sense 'mournful', also 'pitiable, regrettable'): from Old French, or from Latin *lamentabilis*, from the verb *lamentari* (see LAMENT).

lamentation /laman'teɪʃ(ə)n/ ▶ noun [mass noun] the passionate expression of grief or sorrow; weeping: *scenes of lamentation*. ■ (**Lamentations** or **Lamentations of Jeremiah**) a book of the Bible telling of the desolation of Judah after the fall of Jerusalem in 586 BC.

lamented ▶ adjective (often **the late lamented**) a conventional way of describing someone who has died or something that has ceased to exist: *the late and much lamented Leonard Bernstein*.

lamer ▶ noun informal, chiefly US a stupid, inept, or dull person.

lamia /'leɪmɪə/ ▶ noun (pl. **lamias** or **lamiae** /-ɪiː/) a mythical monster supposed to have the body of a woman, and to prey on human beings and suck the blood of children.
– ORIGIN via Latin from Greek, denoting a carnivorous fish or mythical monster.

lamina /'lamɪnə/ ▶ noun (pl. **laminae** /-niː/) technical a thin layer, plate, or scale of sedimentary rock, organic tissue, or other material.
– ORIGIN mid 17th cent.: from Latin.

laminal /'lamɪn(ə)l/ ▶ adjective Phonetics (of a consonant) formed with the blade of the tongue touching the alveolar ridge.
– ORIGIN 1950s: from LAMINA + -AL.

laminar /'lamɪnə/ ▶ adjective **1** consisting of laminae.
2 Physics (of a flow) taking place along constant streamlines, without turbulence.

laminate ▶ verb /'lamɪneɪt/ [with obj.] (often as adj. **laminated**) overlay (a flat surface) with a layer of plastic or some other protective material. ■ manufacture (something) by bonding layers of material together: *windows fitted with laminated glass*. ■ split into layers or leaves. ■ beat or roll (metal) into thin plates.
▶ noun /'lamɪnət/ a laminated structure or material. ■ a small badge made of laminated plastic bearing the wearer's name.
▶ adjective /'lamɪnət/ in the form of a lamina or laminae.
– DERIVATIVES **lamination** noun, **laminator** noun.
– ORIGIN mid 17th cent.: from LAMINA + -ATE[4].

laminectomy /,lamɪ'nɛktəmi/ ▶ noun (pl. **laminectomies**) a surgical operation to remove the back of one or more vertebrae, usually to give access to the spinal cord or to relieve pressure on nerves.

lamington /'lamɪŋtən/ ▶ noun Austral./NZ a square of sponge cake dipped in melted chocolate and grated coconut.
– ORIGIN apparently from the name of Lord *Lamington*, Governor of Queensland (1895–1901).

laminin /'lamɪnɪn/ ▶ noun [mass noun] Biochemistry a fibrous protein present in the basal lamina of the epithelia.

laminitis /,lamɪ'nʌɪtɪs/ ▶ noun [mass noun] inflammation of sensitive layers of tissue (laminae) inside the hoof in horses and other animals. It is particularly prevalent in ponies feeding on rich spring grass and can cause extreme lameness.

lamium /'leɪmɪəm/ ▶ noun (pl. **lamiums**) a plant of a genus which comprises the dead-nettles. ● Genus *Lamium*, family Labiatae.
– ORIGIN modern Latin, from Latin, from Greek *lamia* 'gaping mouth' (because of the shape of the flowers).

Lammas /'laməs/ (also **Lammas Day**) ▶ noun the first day of August, formerly observed as harvest festival.
– ORIGIN Old English *hlāfmæsse* (see LOAF[1], MASS), later interpreted as if it were from LAMB + MASS.

lammergeier /'lamə,gʌɪə/ (also **lammergeyer**) ▶ noun a large Old World vulture of mountainous country, with a wingspan of 3 m (10 ft) and dark beard-like feathers, noted for its habit of dropping bones from a height to break them. Also called BEARDED VULTURE. ● *Gypaetus barbatus*, family Accipitridae.

L

– ORIGIN early 19th cent.: from German *Lämmergeier*, from *Lämmer* (plural of *Lamm* 'lamb') + *Geier* 'vulture'.

lamp[1] ▶ noun a device for giving light, either one consisting of an electric bulb together with its holder and shade or cover, or one burning gas or oil and consisting of a wick or mantle and a glass shade: *a table lamp*. ■ an electrical device producing ultraviolet, infrared, or other radiation, used for therapeutic purposes. ■ literary a source of spiritual or intellectual inspiration.
▶ verb 1 [with obj.] supply with lamps; illuminate: *inspectors can lamp the lines between the manholes for routine maintenance observations*. ■ [no obj.] literary shine: *an evil fire out of their eyes came lamping*.
2 [no obj.] (often as noun **lamping**) hunt at night using lamps, especially for rabbits.
– DERIVATIVES **lamper** noun, **lampless** adjective.
– ORIGIN Middle English: via Old French from late Latin *lampada*, from Latin *lampas*, *lampad-* 'torch', from Greek.

lamp[2] ▶ verb [with obj.] chiefly N. English hit or beat (someone).
– ORIGIN early 19th cent.: of uncertain origin; perhaps related to LAM[1].

lampas[1] /ˈlampəs/ ▶ noun [mass noun] a condition of horses, in which there is swelling of the fleshy lining of the roof of the mouth behind the front teeth.
– ORIGIN early 16th cent.: from French, probably via French dialect from the Germanic base of the verb LAP[3].

lampas[2] /ˈlampəs/ ▶ noun [mass noun] a patterned drapery and upholstery fabric similar to brocade, made of silk, cotton, or rayon.
– ORIGIN mid 19th cent.: from French *lampas*, *lampasse*, of unknown origin.

lampblack ▶ noun [mass noun] a black pigment made from soot.

lamp chimney ▶ noun a glass cylinder positioned over the wick of an oil lamp to encircle and provide a draught for the flame.

L

Lampedusa /ˌlampɪˈduːzə/, Giuseppe Tomasi di (1896–1957), Italian novelist. His only novel *Il Gattopardo* (*The Leopard*) was originally rejected by publishers but won worldwide acclaim on its posthumous publication in 1958.

lampern /ˈlampən/ ▶ noun a lamprey of rivers and coastal waters in NW Europe. ● *Lampetra fluviatilis*, family Petromyzonidae.
– ORIGIN Middle English: from Old French *lampreion*, diminutive of *lampreie* 'lamprey'.

lamplight ▶ noun [mass noun] the light cast from a lamp: *he was working in the stables by lamplight*.
– DERIVATIVES **lamplit** adjective.

lamplighter ▶ noun historical a person employed to light street gaslights by hand.

lampoon /lamˈpuːn/ ▶ verb [with obj.] publicly criticize (someone or something) by using ridicule, irony, or sarcasm: *the actor was lampooned by the press*.
▶ noun a speech or text lampooning someone or something.
– DERIVATIVES **lampooner** noun, **lampoonery** noun, **lampoonist** noun.
– ORIGIN mid 17th cent.: from French *lampon*, said to be from *lampons* 'let us drink' (used as a refrain), from *lamper* 'gulp down', nasalized form of *laper* 'to lap (liquid)'.

lamp post ▶ noun a tall pole with a light at the top; a street light.

lamprey /ˈlampri/ ▶ noun (pl. **lampreys**) an eel-like aquatic jawless vertebrate that has a sucker mouth with horny teeth and a rasping tongue. The adult is often parasitic, attaching itself to other fish and sucking their blood. ● Family Petromyzonidae: several genera and species.
– ORIGIN Middle English: from Old French *lampreie*, from medieval Latin *lampreda*, probably from Latin *lambere* 'to lick' + *petra* 'stone' (because the lamprey attaches itself to stones by its mouth).

lamprophyre /ˈlamprəˌfʌɪə/ ▶ noun [mass noun] Geology a porphyritic igneous rock consisting of a fine-grained feldspathic groundmass with phenocrysts chiefly of biotite.
– ORIGIN late 19th cent.: from Greek *lampros* 'bright, shining' + *porphureos* 'purple'.

lampshade ▶ noun a cover for a lamp, used to soften or direct its light.

lamp shell ▶ noun a marine invertebrate which superficially resembles a bivalve mollusc but has two or more arms of ciliated tentacles (lophophores) that are extended for filter-feeding. Lamp shells are common as fossils. Also called BRACHIOPOD. ● Phylum Brachiopoda: numerous groups in the Palaeozoic era but few surviving to the present day.
– ORIGIN mid 19th cent.: from its resemblance to an ancient oil lamp.

lamp standard ▶ noun another term for LAMP POST.

LAN ▶ abbreviation local area network.

lanai /ləˈnʌɪ/ ▶ noun (pl. **lanais**) a porch or veranda.
– ORIGIN Hawaiian.

Lanarkshire /ˈlanəkʃɪə, -ʃə/ a former county of SW central Scotland, now divided into the council areas of **North Lanarkshire** and **South Lanarkshire**.

Lancashire[1] /ˈlaŋkəʃɪə, -ʃə/ a county of NW England, on the Irish Sea; administrative centre, Preston.

Lancashire[2] /ˈlaŋkəʃə/ ▶ noun [mass noun] a mild white cheese with a crumbly texture.

Lancashire hotpot ▶ noun a stew of meat, onions, and potatoes, typically covered with a layer of sliced potato.

Lancaster[1] /ˈlaŋkastə/ the county town of Lancashire, a city on the estuary of the River Lune; pop. 44,500 (est. 2009).

Lancaster[2] /ˈlaŋkastə/, Burt (1913–94), American film actor; full name *Burton Stephen Lancaster*. He starred in films such as *From Here to Eternity* (1953), *Elmer Gantry* (1960), for which he won an Oscar, and *Field of Dreams* (1989).

Lancaster, House of the English royal house descended from John of Gaunt, Duke of Lancaster, that ruled England from 1399 (Henry IV) until 1461 (the deposition of Henry VI) and again on Henry's brief restoration in 1470–1. With the red rose as its emblem it fought the Wars of the Roses with the House of York; Lancaster's descendants, the Tudors, eventually prevailed through Henry VII's accession to the throne in 1485.

Lancaster, Duchy of an estate vested in the Crown, consisting of properties in Lancashire and elsewhere in England.

Lancaster House Agreement an agreement which brought about the establishment of the independent state of Zimbabwe, reached in September 1979 at Lancaster House in London.

Lancastrian /laŋˈkastrɪən/ ▶ noun 1 a native of Lancashire or Lancaster.
2 historical a follower of the House of Lancaster in the Wars of the Roses.
▶ adjective relating to Lancashire or Lancaster, or the House of Lancaster.

lance ▶ noun 1 a long weapon with a wooden shaft and a pointed steel head, formerly used by a horseman in charging. ■ a weapon resembling a lance used in hunting fish or whales. ■ another term for LANCER (sense 1).
2 [usu. with modifier] a metal pipe supplying a jet of oxygen to a furnace or to make a very hot flame for cutting.
3 a rigid tube at the end of a hose for pumping or spraying liquid.
▶ verb [with obj.] Medicine prick or cut open (an abscess or boil) with a lancet or other sharp instrument. ■ pierce with or as if with a lance: *the teenager had been lanced by a wooden splinter* | [no obj.] *pain lanced through her*. ■ [no obj., with adverbial of direction] move suddenly and quickly: *he lanced through Harlequins' midfield to score Swansea's lone try*. ■ [with obj.] archaic throw; hurl: *he affirms to have lanced darts at the sun*.
– ORIGIN Middle English: from Old French *lance* (noun), *lancier* (verb), from Latin *lancea* (noun).

lance bombardier ▶ noun a rank of non-commissioned officer in an artillery regiment of the British army, corresponding to that of a lance corporal in the infantry.

lance corporal ▶ noun a rank of non-commissioned officer in the British army, above private and below corporal.
– ORIGIN late 18th cent.: on the analogy of obsolete *lancepesade*, the lowest grade of non-commissioned officer, based on Italian *lancia spezzata* 'broken lance'.

lancejack ▶ noun Brit. military slang a lance corporal or lance bombardier.

lancelet /ˈlɑːnslɪt/ ▶ noun a small elongated marine invertebrate that resembles a fish but lacks jaws and obvious sense organs. Lancelets possess a notochord and are among the most primitive chordates. ● Subphylum Cephalochordata, phylum Chordata: several species, including amphioxus.
– ORIGIN mid 19th cent.: from the noun LANCE (because of its long narrow form) + -LET.

Lancelot /ˈlɑːnsələt, -lɒt/ (also **Launcelot** /ˈlɔːn-/) (in Arthurian legend) the most famous of Arthur's knights, lover of Queen Guinevere and father of Galahad.

lanceolate /ˈlɑːnsɪələt/ ▶ adjective technical shaped like a lance head; of a narrow oval shape tapering to a point at each end: *lanceolate leaves*.
– ORIGIN mid 18th cent.: from late Latin *lanceolatus*, from Latin *lanceola*, diminutive of *lancea* 'a lance'.

lancer ▶ noun 1 historical a soldier of a cavalry regiment armed with lances. ■ (**Lancer**) a soldier of a regiment originally armed with lances: *the Queen's Royal Lancers*.
2 (**lancers**) [treated as sing.] a quadrille for eight or sixteen pairs.
– ORIGIN late 16th cent.: from French *lancier*, from *lance* 'a lance'.

lance sergeant ▶ noun a rank in the Foot Guards equivalent to corporal.

lancet /ˈlɑːnsɪt/ ▶ noun 1 a small, broad two-edged surgical knife or blade with a sharp point.
2 a lancet arch or window. ■ [as modifier] shaped like a lancet arch: *a lancet clock*.
– ORIGIN late Middle English (also denoting a small lance): from Old French *lancette*, diminutive of *lance* 'a lance'.

lancet arch ▶ noun a narrow arch with a pointed crown.

lancetfish ▶ noun (pl. **same** or **lancetfishes**) a long slender predatory fish with a large sail-like dorsal fin, living in the deeper waters of open oceans. ● Family Alepisauridae and genus *Alepisaurus*: two or three species.

lancet window ▶ noun a slender pointed arched window.

lancewood ▶ noun any of a number of hardwood trees with tough elastic timber, in particular: ● a Caribbean tree (*Oxandra lanceolata*, family Annonaceae). ● a New Zealand tree (*Pseudopanax crassifolius*, family Araliaceae).

Lanchow /lanˈtʃaʊ/ variant of LANZHOU.

Lancs. ▶ abbreviation Lancashire.

Land /land/, German /lant/ ▶ noun (pl. **Länder** /ˈlɛndə/, German /ˈlɛndɐ/) a state of Germany or Austria.
– ORIGIN German, literally 'land'.

land ▶ noun 1 [mass noun] the part of the earth's surface that is not covered by water: *the reptiles lay their eggs on land* | *after four weeks at sea we sighted land*. ■ [as modifier] living or travelling on land rather than in water or the air: *a land force*. ■ an area of ground, especially in terms of its ownership or use: *he bought 360 acres of land* | *waste land* | (**lands**) *measures to reduce logging on federal lands*. ■ (**the land**) ground or soil used as a basis for agriculture: *my family had worked the land for many years*. ■ (**the land**) rural areas and the rural way of life. ■ [count noun] S. African an area fenced off for cultivation; a field. [from Dutch *land* 'piece of ground'.]
2 a country or state: *the valley is one of the most beautiful in the land* | *the lands of the Middle East*. ■ [in combination] a particular sphere of activity or group of people: *the blunt, charmless climate of techno-land*. ■ a conceptual area: *you're living in a fantasy land*.
3 the space between the rifling grooves in a gun.
▶ verb 1 [with obj.] put (someone or something) on land from a boat: *he landed his troops at Hastings*. ■ [no obj.] go ashore; disembark: *the marines landed at a small jetty*. ■ bring (a fish) to land with a net or rod. ■ informal succeed in obtaining or achieving (something desirable), especially in the face of competition: *she landed the starring role in a new film*.
2 [no obj.] come down through the air and rest on the ground or another surface: *we will shortly be landing at Gatwick* | *a fly **landed on** Tom's nose*. ■ [with obj.] bring (an aircraft or spacecraft) to the ground or the surface of water in a controlled way. ■ reach the ground after falling or jumping: *he leapt over the fence and landed nimbly on his feet*. ■ [with adverbial of place] (of an object) come to rest after falling or being thrown: *the plate landed in her lap*.
3 [no obj.] informal (of something undesirable or unexpected) arrive suddenly: *there were more problems than ever landing on her desk*.
4 [with obj.] (**land someone in**) informal cause someone to be in (a difficult situation): *his exploits always landed him in trouble*. ■ (**land someone with**) inflict (an unwelcome task or difficult situation) on someone: *the mistake landed the company with a massive bill*.

5 [with obj.] informal inflict (a blow) on someone: *I won the fight without landing a single punch.*
– PHRASES **how the land lies** Brit. what the situation is: *let's keep it to ourselves until we see how the land lies.* **in the land of the living** humorous alive or awake. **the land of the free** the United States of America. **the land of Nod** humorous a state of sleep. [punningly, with biblical allusion to the place name *Nod* (Gen. 4:16).] **land** (or **fall**) **on one's feet** have good luck or success. **live off the land** live on whatever food one can obtain by hunting, gathering, or subsistence farming.
– PHRASAL VERBS **land up** reach a place or situation: *the ship landed up on the south coast of Devon* | *I landed up in prison.* **land up with** end up with (an unwelcome situation): *I landed up with three broken ribs.*
– ORIGIN Old English, of Germanic origin; related to Dutch *land* and German *Land*.

Land Acts a series of British parliamentary acts concerning land tenure in Ireland, passed in 1870, 1881, 1903, and 1909, intended to give tenants greater security and further rights.

land agent ▸ noun Brit. **1** a person employed to manage an estate on behalf of its owners.
2 a person who deals with the sale of land.
– DERIVATIVES **land agency** noun.

landau /ˈlandɔː, -aʊ/ ▸ noun a horse-drawn four-wheeled enclosed carriage with a removable front cover and a back cover that can be raised and lowered.
– ORIGIN mid 18th cent.: named after *Landau*, near Karlsruhe in Germany, where it was first made.

landaulet /ˌlandɔːˈlɛt, -də-/ ▸ noun a small landau.
■ chiefly historical a car with a folding hood over the rear seats.

land bank ▸ noun **1** a large area of land held by a public or private organization for future development or disposal.
2 a bank that provides loans for the purchase of land, especially by farmers.

landbanking ▸ noun [mass noun] the practice of buying land as an investment, holding it for future use and making no specific plans for its development.

land breeze ▸ noun a breeze blowing towards the sea from the land. Compare with SEA BREEZE.

land bridge ▸ noun a connection between two land masses, especially a prehistoric one that allowed humans and animals to colonize new territory before being cut off by the sea, as across the Bering Strait and the English Channel.

land crab ▸ noun a crab that lives in burrows inland and migrates in large numbers to the sea to breed.
● Family Gecarcinidae: *Cardisoma* and other genera.

land drain ▸ noun a drain made of porous or perforated piping and placed in a gravel-filled trench, used for subsoil drainage.

landed ▸ adjective [attrib.] owning much land, especially through inheritance: *the landed aristocracy.*
■ consisting of or relating to land owned through inheritance: *the decline of landed estates.*

lander ▸ noun a spacecraft designed to land on the surface of a planet or moon: *a lunar lander.* Compare with ORBITER.

Länder plural form of LAND.

landfall ▸ noun **1** an arrival at land on a sea or air journey.
2 a collapse of a mass of land; a landslide.

landfill ▸ noun [mass noun] the disposal of waste material by burying it, especially as a method of filling in and reclaiming excavated pits: [as modifier] *landfill sites.*
■ waste material used in landfill sites. ■ [count noun] an area filled in by landfill.
▸ verb [with obj.] bury in a landfill: *many tons of edible food are landfilled* | [as adj.] *landfilled waste.*

landform ▸ noun a natural feature of the earth's surface.

land girl ▸ noun historical (in the UK) a woman doing farm work, especially during the Second World War.

land-grabber ▸ noun historical a person who took the land of an evicted Irish tenant.
– DERIVATIVES **land-grab** noun, **land-grabbing** noun.

land grant ▸ noun N. Amer. a grant of public land, especially to an institution or to American Indians.

landgrave /ˈlan(d)greɪv/ ▸ noun historical a count having jurisdiction over a territory. ■ the title of certain German princes.
– ORIGIN late Middle English: from Middle Low German, from *land* 'land' + *grave* 'count' (used as a title).

landholder ▸ noun a person who owns land, especially one who either makes their living from it or rents it out to others.

landholding ▸ noun a piece of land owned or rented.
■ [mass noun] possession or rental of land.

landing ▸ noun **1** an instance of coming or bringing something to land, either from the air or from water: *we made a perfect landing at the airstrip* | [mass noun] *the landing of men on the moon.* ■ an act of unloading troops in enemy territory as part of a military operation: *the D-Day landings.* ■ (also **landing place**) a place where people and goods can be landed from a boat: *the ferry landing.*
2 a level area at the top of a staircase or between one flight of stairs and another.

landing craft ▸ noun a boat specially designed for putting troops and military equipment ashore on a beach.

landing gear ▸ noun the undercarriage of an aircraft.

landing light ▸ noun (usu. **landing lights**) a bright light on an aircraft that is switched on prior to landing. ■ a light of a kind that is arranged in rows along each side of an aircraft runway.

landing net ▸ noun a net for landing a large fish which has been hooked.

landing pad ▸ noun a small area designed for helicopters to land on and take off from.

landing stage ▸ noun chiefly Brit. a platform, typically a floating one, on to which passengers from a boat disembark or cargo is unloaded.

landing strip ▸ noun an airstrip.

landlady ▸ noun (pl. **landladies**) a woman who rents out land, a building, or accommodation. ■ a woman who keeps lodgings, a boarding house, or (Brit.) a pub.

land law ▸ noun [mass noun] (also **land laws**) the law governing real property.

Land League an Irish organization formed in 1879 to campaign for tenants' rights. Its techniques included the use of a boycott against anyone taking on a farm from which the tenant had been evicted. The Land Act of 1881 met many of the League's demands.

ländler /ˈlɛndlə/ ▸ noun an Austrian folk dance in triple time, a precursor of the waltz.
– ORIGIN late 19th cent.: German, from *Landl* 'Upper Austria'.

landless ▸ adjective (especially of an agricultural worker) owning no land.
– DERIVATIVES **landlessness** noun.

landline ▸ noun a conventional telecommunications connection by cable laid across land.

landlocked ▸ adjective (of a country or region) almost or entirely surrounded by land: *I was raised in landlocked Winnipeg.* ■ (of a lake or harbour) enclosed by land and having no navigable route to the sea. ■ (of a fish, especially a North American salmon) cut off from the sea in the past and now confined to fresh water.

landlord ▸ noun a man (in legal use also a woman) who rents out land, a building, or accommodation.
■ a man who keeps lodgings, a boarding house, or (Brit.) a pub.

landlordism ▸ noun [mass noun] the system whereby land (or property) is owned by landlords to whom tenants pay a fixed rent.

landlubber ▸ noun informal a person unfamiliar with the sea or sailing.

landmark ▸ noun **1** an object or feature of a landscape or town that is easily seen and recognized from a distance, especially one that enables someone to establish their location: *the spire was once a landmark for ships sailing up the river.* ■ N. Amer. a building or monument of historical importance. ■ historical the boundary of an area of land, or an object marking this.
2 an event or discovery marking an important stage or turning point in something: *the vaccine is a landmark in the history of preventive medicine.*

land mass ▸ noun a continent or other large body of land.

landmine ▸ noun an explosive mine laid on or just under the surface of the ground.

land mullet ▸ noun a large burrowing lizard of the skink family, with shiny fishlike scales, native to the coastal regions of eastern Australia. ● *Egernia major*, family Scincidae.

Land of Enchantment informal name for NEW MEXICO.

land office ▸ noun N. Amer. a government office recording dealings in public land.
– PHRASES **do a land-office business** informal do a lot of successful trading.

Land of Opportunity informal name for ARKANSAS.

Landor /ˈlandɔː/, Walter Savage (1775–1864), English poet and essayist. His works include the oriental epic poem *Gebir* (1798), and *Imaginary Conversations of Literary Men and Statesmen* (prose, 1824–8).

landowner ▸ noun a person who owns land, especially a large amount of land.
– DERIVATIVES **landownership** noun, **landowning** adjective & noun.

landplane ▸ noun an aircraft which can only operate from or alight on land.

landrace ▸ noun **1** a pig of a white lop-eared breed, originally developed in Denmark.
2 a local cultivar or animal breed that has been improved by traditional agricultural methods.
– ORIGIN 1930s: from Danish.

landrail ▸ noun another term for CORNCRAKE.

land reform ▸ noun [mass noun] the statutory division of agricultural land and its reallocation to landless people.

Land Registry Brit. a government department with which titles to or charges upon land must be registered.

Landsat a series of artificial satellites that monitor the earth's resources by photographing the surface at different wavelengths. The resulting images provide information about agriculture, geology, ecological changes, etc.

landscape ▸ noun **1** all the visible features of an area of land, often considered in terms of their aesthetic appeal: *the soft colours of the Northumbrian landscape* | *a bleak urban landscape.* ■ a picture representing an area of countryside. ■ [mass noun] the genre of landscape painting. ■ the distinctive features of a sphere of activity: *the event transformed the political landscape.*
2 [as modifier] denoting a format of printed matter which is wider than it is high. Compare with PORTRAIT (sense 2).
▸ verb [with obj.] improve the aesthetic appearance of (an area) by changing its contours, adding ornamental features, or planting trees and shrubs: *the site has been tastefully landscaped.*
– DERIVATIVES **landscaper** noun, **landscapist** noun.
– ORIGIN late 16th cent. (denoting a picture of scenery): from Middle Dutch *lantscap*, from *land* 'land' + *scap* (equivalent of -SHIP).

landscape architecture ▸ noun [mass noun] the art and practice of designing the outdoor environment, especially designing parks or gardens to harmonize with buildings and roads.
– DERIVATIVES **landscape architect** noun.

landscape gardening ▸ noun [mass noun] the art and practice of laying out grounds in a way which is ornamental or which imitates natural scenery.
– DERIVATIVES **landscape gardener** noun.

landscape history ▸ noun [mass noun] the history of the rural landscape, as determined from visible features, ecological and archaeological evidence, and documentary records.

land scrip ▸ noun see SCRIP[1] (sense 2).

Landseer /ˈlandsɪə/, Sir Edwin Henry (1802–73), English painter and sculptor. He is best known for his animal subjects such as *The Monarch of the Glen* (1851). As a sculptor he is chiefly remembered for the bronze lions in Trafalgar Square (1867).

Land's End a rocky promontory in SW Cornwall, which forms the westernmost point of England. The approximate distance by road from Land's End to John o'Groats is 1,400 km (876 miles).

landside ▸ noun the side of an airport terminal to which the general public has unrestricted access. Contrasted with AIRSIDE.

landsknecht /ˈlan(t)sknɛkt/ ▸ noun historical a member of a class of mercenary soldiers in the German and other continental armies in the 16th and 17th centuries.
– ORIGIN from German *Landsknecht*, literally 'soldier of the land'.

landslide ▸ noun **1** a collapse of a mass of earth or rock from a mountain or cliff.
2 an overwhelming majority of votes for one party or candidate in an election: *they won by a landslide.*

L

landslip ▶ noun chiefly Brit. another term for **LANDSLIDE** (sense 1).

Landsmål /ˈlantsmɔːl/ ▶ noun another term for **NYNORSK**.
– ORIGIN Norwegian, literally 'language of the land'.

landsman ▶ noun (pl. **landsmen**) a person unfamiliar with the sea or sailing.

land tax ▶ noun [mass noun] tax levied on landed property.

landtie ▶ noun a beam or piece of masonry supporting a wall or other vertical structure by connecting it with the ground.

landward ▶ adverb (also **landwards**) towards land: *the ship turned landward*.
▶ adjective facing towards land as opposed to sea: *the landward side of the road*.

land yacht ▶ noun a wind-powered wheeled vehicle with sails, used for recreation and sport. ■ N. Amer. informal a very large car.

lane ▶ noun **1** a narrow road, especially in a rural area: *she drove along the winding lane*. ■ [in place names] an urban street: *Park Lane*.
2 a division of a road marked off with painted lines and intended to separate single lines of traffic according to speed or direction: *the car moved into the outside lane* | *a bus lane*. ■ each of a number of parallel strips of track or water for runners, rowers, or swimmers in a race. ■ a route prescribed for or regularly followed by ships or aircraft: *the shipping lanes of the South Atlantic*. ■ (in tenpin bowling) a long, narrow strip of floor down which the ball is bowled. ■ Biochemistry each of a number of notional parallel strips in the gel of an electrophoresis plate, occupied by a single sample. ■ Astronomy a dark streak or band which shows up against a bright background, especially in a spiral galaxy.
– PHRASES **it's a long lane that has no turning** proverb nothing goes on forever; change is inevitable.
– DERIVATIVES **laned** adjective [in combination] *multi-laned motorways*.
– ORIGIN Old English, related to Dutch *laan*; of unknown ultimate origin.

L

Lang, Fritz (1890–1976), Austrian-born film director, resident in the US from 1933. He directed the silent dystopian film *Metropolis* (1927), making the transition to sound in 1931 with the thriller *M*. His later work included *The Big Heat* (1953).

langar /ˈlʌŋgər/ ▶ noun Indian (among Sikhs) a communal free kitchen. ■ a communal meal.
– ORIGIN from Hindi.

langer /ˈlaŋə/ ▶ noun Irish vulgar slang **1** a man's penis.
2 a stupid or contemptible person.
– ORIGIN 1980s: of uncertain origin.

Langland /ˈlaŋlənd/, William (*c*.1330–*c*.1400), English poet. He is best known for *Piers Plowman* (*c*.1367–70), a long allegorical poem which takes the form of a spiritual pilgrimage.

langlauf /ˈlaŋlaʊf/ ▶ noun [mass noun] cross-country skiing.
– ORIGIN 1920s: from German, literally 'long run'.

Langley, Samuel Pierpoint (1834–1906), American astronomer and aviation pioneer. He invented the bolometer (1879–81) and contributed to the design of early aircraft.

langosta /laŋˈgɒstə/ ▶ noun chiefly US another term for **LANGOUSTE**.
– ORIGIN Spanish.

langouste /ˈlɒŋguːst/ ▶ noun a spiny lobster, especially when prepared and cooked.
– ORIGIN French, from Old Provençal *lagosta*, based on Latin *locusta* 'locust, crustacean'.

langoustine /ˈlɒŋgʊstiːn/ ▶ noun another term for **NORWAY LOBSTER**, especially when prepared and cooked.
– ORIGIN French, from *langouste* (see **LANGOUSTE**).

langra /ˈlɑːŋgrə, ˈlaŋgrə/ ▶ noun **1** a mango of a variety which has pale green skin when ripe.
2 Indian a person who is lame or unable to walk.
– ORIGIN from Hindi *lāngra* 'lame'.

lang syne /laŋ ˈsʌɪn/ Scottish archaic ▶ adverb in the distant past: *we talked of races run lang syne*.
▶ noun [mass noun] times gone by.
– ORIGIN early 16th cent.: from *lang*, Scots variant of **LONG**[1] + **SYNE**.

Langton, Stephen (*c*.1150–1228), English churchman, Archbishop of Canterbury 1207–15 and 1218–28. A champion of the English Church, he was involved in the negotiations leading to the signing of Magna Carta.

Langtry /ˈlaŋtri/, Lillie (1853–1929), British actress; born *Emilie Charlotte le Breton*. She made her stage debut in 1881 and later became the mistress of the Prince of Wales, later Edward VII.

language ▶ noun **1** [mass noun] the method of human communication, either spoken or written, consisting of the use of words in a structured and conventional way: *a study of the way children learn language* | [as modifier] *language development*. ■ a non-verbal method of expression or communication: *body language*.
2 a system of communication used by a particular country or community: *the book was translated into twenty-five languages*. ■ Computing a system of symbols and rules for writing programs or algorithms.
3 [mass noun] the style of a piece of writing or speech: *he explained the procedure in simple, everyday language*. ■ the phraseology and vocabulary of a particular profession, domain, or group: *legal language*. ■ (usu. as **bad/foul/strong language**) coarse or offensive language.
– PHRASES **speak the same language** understand one another as a result of shared opinions or values.
– ORIGIN Middle English: from Old French *langage*, based on Latin *lingua* 'tongue'.

language area ▶ noun **1** Physiology the area of the cerebral cortex thought to be particularly involved in the processing of language.
2 a region where a particular language is spoken.

language engineering ▶ noun [mass noun] any of a variety of computing procedures that use tools such as machine-readable dictionaries and sentence parsers in order to process natural languages for industrial applications such as speech recognition and speech synthesis.

language laboratory ▶ noun a room equipped with audio and visual equipment, such as tape and video recorders, for learning a foreign language.

language of flowers ▶ noun [mass noun] a set of symbolic meanings attached to different flowers when they are given or arranged.

langue /lɒ̃g/ ▶ noun (pl. pronunc. **same**) Linguistics a language viewed as an abstract system used by a speech community, in contrast to the actual linguistic behaviour of individuals. Contrasted with **PAROLE**.
– ORIGIN 1920s: French, from Latin *lingua* 'language, tongue'.

langued /ˈlaŋgd/ ▶ adjective Heraldry having the tongue of a specified tincture.
– ORIGIN late Middle English: from French *langué* 'tongued' + **-ED**[2].

langue de chat /ˌlɒ̃(g) də ˈʃɑː/ ▶ noun a very thin finger-shaped crisp biscuit or piece of chocolate.
– ORIGIN French, literally 'cat's tongue'.

Languedoc /ˌlɒ̃g(ə)ˈdɒk/, French /lɑ̃gdɔk/ a former province of southern France, which extended from the Rhône valley to the northern foothills of the eastern Pyrenees.

langue d'oc /lɒ̃(g) ˈdɒk/, French /lɑ̃g dɔk/ ▶ noun [mass noun] the form of medieval French spoken south of the Loire, generally characterized by the use of *oc* to mean 'yes', and forming the basis of modern Provençal. Compare with **OCCITAN**.
– ORIGIN from Old French *langue* 'language' (from Latin *lingua* 'tongue'), *d'* (from *de* 'of'), and *oc* (from Latin *hoc*) 'yes'. Compare with **LANGUE D'OÏL**.

Languedoc-Roussillon /ˌruːsiːˈjɒ̃/, French /rusijɔ̃/ a region of southern France, on the Mediterranean coast, extending from the Rhône delta to the border with Spain.

langue d'oïl /lɒ̃(g) ˈdɔɪl/, French /lɑ̃g dɔjl/ ▶ noun [mass noun] the form of medieval French spoken north of the Loire, generally characterized by the use of *oïl* to mean 'yes', and forming the basis of modern French.
– ORIGIN from Old French *langue* 'language' (from Latin *lingua* 'tongue'), *d'* (from *de* 'of'), and *oïl* (from Latin *hoc ille*) 'yes'. Compare with **LANGUE D'OC**.

languid ▶ adjective **1** (of a person, manner, or gesture) having or showing a disinclination for physical exertion or effort: *his languid demeanour irritated her*. ■ (of a period of time) relaxed and peaceful: *the terrace was perfect for languid days in the Italian sun*.
2 weak or faint from illness or fatigue.
– DERIVATIVES **languidly** adverb, **languidness** noun.
– ORIGIN late 16th cent. (in sense 2): from French *languide* or Latin *languidus*, from *languere* (see **LANGUISH**).

languish ▶ verb [no obj.] **1** (of a person, animal, or plant) lose or lack vitality; grow weak: *plants may appear to be languishing simply because they are dormant*. ■ fail to make progress or be successful: *Kelso languish near the bottom of the Scottish First Division* | (as adj. **languishing**) *the country's languishing stock market*. ■ archaic pine with love or grief: *she still **languished after** Richard*. ■ archaic assume a sentimentally tender or melancholy expression or tone.
2 be forced to remain in an unpleasant place or situation: *he has been **languishing in jail** since 1974*.
– DERIVATIVES **languishingly** adverb, **languishment** noun (archaic).
– ORIGIN Middle English (in the sense 'become faint, feeble, or ill'): from Old French *languiss-*, lengthened stem of *languir* 'languish', from a variant of Latin *languere*, related to *laxus* 'loose, lax'.

languor /ˈlaŋgə/ ▶ noun [mass noun] **1** tiredness or inactivity, especially when pleasurable: *her whole being was pervaded by a dreamy languor*.
2 an oppressive stillness of the air: *the afternoon was hot, quiet, and heavy with languor*.
– DERIVATIVES **languorous** adjective, **languorously** adverb.
– ORIGIN Middle English: via Old French from Latin, from *languere* (see **LANGUISH**). The original sense was 'illness, distress', later 'faintness, lassitude'; current senses date from the 18th cent., when such lassitude became associated with a romantic yearning.

langur /ˈlaŋgə, laŋˈgʊə/ ▶ noun a long-tailed arboreal Asian monkey with a characteristic loud call. ● *Presbytis* and other genera, family Cercopithecidae: several species. Compare with **LEAF MONKEY**.
– ORIGIN early 19th cent.: via Hindi from Sanskrit *lāṅgūla*.

laniard ▶ noun variant spelling of **LANYARD**.

La Niña /lɑː ˈniːnjə/ ▶ noun a cooling of the water in the equatorial Pacific, which occurs at irregular intervals, and is associated with widespread changes in weather patterns complementary to those of El Niño, but less extensive and damaging in their effects.
– ORIGIN Spanish, literally 'the girl child', after **EL NIÑO**.

lank[1] ▶ adjective **1** (of hair) long, limp, and straight.
2 (of a person) lanky.
– DERIVATIVES **lankly** adverb, **lankness** noun.
– ORIGIN Old English *hlanc* 'thin', of Germanic origin; related to High German *lenken* 'to bend, turn', also to **FLINCH** and **LINK**[1].

lank[2] ▶ adjective S. African informal **1** very numerous or plentiful: *come and share our braai—we've got lank meat*.
2 very good; fantastic: *dad's got a lank new car*.
– ORIGIN sense 1 is perhaps from Afrikaans *geld lank* 'money galore'; sense 2 may be related to Afrikaans *lank nie sleg nie* 'not at all bad'.

lanky ▶ adjective (**lankier**, **lankiest**) (of a person) ungracefully thin and tall.
– DERIVATIVES **lankily** adverb, **lankiness** noun.

lanner /ˈlanə/ (also **lanner falcon**) ▶ noun a falcon with a dark brown back and buff cap, found in SE Europe, the Middle East, and Africa. ● *Falco biarmicus*, family Falconidae.
■ Falconry a female lanner.
– ORIGIN late Middle English: from Old French *lanier*, perhaps a noun use of *lanier* 'cowardly', from a derogatory use of *lanier* 'wool merchant', from Latin *lanarius*, from *lana* 'wool'.

lanneret /ˈlanərɪt/ ▶ noun Falconry a male lanner, which is smaller than the female.
– ORIGIN late Middle English: from Old French *laneret*, diminutive of *lanier* (see **LANNER**).

lanolin ▶ noun [mass noun] a fatty substance found naturally on sheep's wool. It is extracted as a yellowish viscous mixture of esters and used as a base for ointments.
– ORIGIN late 19th cent.: coined in German from Latin *lana* 'wool' + *oleum* 'oil' + **-IN**[1].

Lansing /ˈlansɪŋ/ the state capital of Michigan; pop. 113,968 (est. 2008).

lansquenet /ˈlɑːnskəˌnɛt, ˈlans-/ ▶ noun **1** [mass noun] historical a gambling game of German origin involving betting on cards turned up by the dealer.
2 archaic variant of **LANDSKNECHT**.
– ORIGIN early 17th cent. (in sense 2): via French from German *Landsknecht* (see **LANDSKNECHT**).

lantana /lanˈtɑːnə, -ˈteɪnə/ ▶ noun a tropical evergreen shrub of the verbena family, several kinds of which are cultivated as ornamentals. ● Genus *Lantana*, family Verbenaceae: many species, in particular the South American scrambler *L. camara*, grown as an ornamental and sometimes becoming a serious weed.

– ORIGIN modern Latin, from the specific name of the wayfaring tree *Viburnum lantana*, which it resembles superficially.

Lantau /lan'taʊ/ an island of Hong Kong, situated to the west of Hong Kong Island and forming part of the New Territories. Chinese name **TAI YUE SHAN**.

lantern ▸ noun **1** a lamp with a transparent case protecting the flame or electric bulb, and typically having a handle by which it may be carried or hung: *a paper lantern*.
2 a square, curved, or polygonal structure on the top of a dome or a room, with the sides glazed or open so as to admit light. ■ the light chamber at the top of a lighthouse.
– ORIGIN Middle English: from Old French *lanterne*, from Latin *lanterna*, from Greek *lamptēr* 'torch, lamp', from *lampein* 'to shine'.

Lantern Festival ▸ noun another name for **BON**.

lanternfish ▸ noun (pl. **same** or **lanternfishes**) a deep-sea fish that has light organs on its body, seen chiefly when it rises to the surface at night. ● Family Myctophidae: several genera and species.

lantern fly ▸ noun a chiefly tropical bug which is typically brightly coloured and may have a large bizarrely shaped head. It was formerly thought to be luminescent. ● Family Fulgoridae, suborder Homoptera.

lantern jaw ▸ noun a long, thin jaw and prominent chin.
– DERIVATIVES **lantern-jawed** adjective.

lantern slide ▸ noun historical a mounted photographic transparency for projection by a magic lantern.

lantern wheel ▸ noun a cylindrical gearwheel.

lanthanide /'lanθənʌɪd/ ▸ noun Chemistry any of the series of fifteen metallic elements from lanthanum to lutetium in the periodic table (atomic numbers 57–71). See also **RARE EARTH**.
– ORIGIN 1920s: from **LANTHANUM** + **-IDE**.

lanthanum /'lanθənəm/ ▸ noun [mass noun] the chemical element of atomic number 57, a silvery-white rare earth metal. (Symbol: **La**)
– ORIGIN mid 19th cent.: from Greek *lanthanein* 'escape notice' (because it was long undetected in cerium oxide) + **-UM**.

lanthorn ▸ noun archaic spelling of **LANTERN**.

lanugo /lə'nju:gəʊ/ ▸ noun [mass noun] fine, soft hair, especially that which covers the body and limbs of a human fetus.
– ORIGIN late 17th cent.: from Latin, 'down', from *lana* 'wool'.

lanyard /'lanjəd/ ▸ noun a rope used to secure or raise and lower something such as the shrouds and sails of a sailing ship or a flag on a flagpole. ■ a cord passed round the neck, shoulder, or wrist for holding a knife, whistle, or similar object.
– ORIGIN late Middle English *lanyer*, in the general sense 'a short length of rope for securing something', from Old French *laniere*. The change in the ending in the 17th cent. was due to association with **YARD**[1].

Lanzarote /ˌlanzə'rɒti/, Spanish /lanθa'roəte, lansa-/ one of the Canary Islands, the most easterly island of the group; chief town, Arrecife. A series of volcanic eruptions in about 1730 dramatically altered the island's landscape, creating an area of volcanic cones in the south-west known as the 'Mountains of Fire'.

Lanzhou /lan'dʒəʊ/ (also **Lanchow**) a city in northern China, on the upper Yellow River, capital of Gansu province; pop. 1,708,200 (est. 2006).

LAO ▸ abbreviation Laos (international vehicle registration).

Lao /laʊ/ ▸ noun (pl. **same** or **Laos**) **1** a member of an indigenous people of Laos and NE Thailand.
2 [mass noun] the language of the Lao, closely related to Thai, with about 3 million speakers. Also called **LAOTIAN**.
▸ adjective relating to the Lao or their language.
– ORIGIN the name in Lao.

Laocoon /leɪ'ɒkəʊɒn/ Greek Mythology a Trojan priest who, with his two sons, was crushed to death by two great sea serpents as a penalty for warning the Trojans against drawing the wooden horse of the Greeks into Troy.

Laodicean /ˌleɪə(ʊ)dɪ'si:ən/ archaic ▸ adjective half-hearted or indifferent, especially with respect to religion or politics.
▸ noun a person with a Laodicean attitude.
– ORIGIN early 17th cent.: from Latin *Laodicea* in Asia Minor, with reference to the early Christians there (Rev. 3:16), + **-AN**.

laogai /laʊ'gʌɪ/ ▸ noun (**the laogai**) (in China) a system of labour camps, many of whose inmates are political dissidents.
– ORIGIN Chinese, 'reform through labour'.

Laois /li:ʃ/ (also **Laoighis**, **Leix**) a county of the Republic of Ireland, in the province of Leinster; county town, Portlaoise. Former name **QUEEN'S COUNTY**.

Laos /laʊs, 'lɑ:ɒs/ a landlocked country in SE Asia; pop. 6,834,300 (est. 2009); official language, Laotian; capital, Vientiane.

> Part of French Indo-China, Laos became independent in 1949, but for most of the next twenty-five years was torn by civil strife between the communist Pathet Lao movement and government supporters. In 1975 the Pathet Lao achieved total control and a communist republic was established.

– DERIVATIVES **Laotian** /leɪ'əʊʃ(ə)n/ adjective & noun.

Lao-tzu /laʊ'tsu:/ (also **Laoze** /-'tseɪ/) (*fl.* 6th century BC), Chinese philosopher traditionally regarded as the founder of Taoism and author of the Tao-te-Ching, its most sacred scripture.
– ORIGIN Chinese, literally 'Lao the Master'.

lap[1] ▸ noun **1** (usu. **one's lap**) the flat area between the waist and knees of a seated person: *come and sit on my lap*. ■ the part of an item of clothing, especially a skirt or dress, covering the lap.
2 archaic a hanging flap on a garment or a saddle.
– PHRASES **fall** (or **drop**) **into someone's lap** (of something desirable) be acquired by or happen to someone without any effort being made on their part: *women fall at his feet, power falls into his lap*. **in someone's lap** as someone's responsibility: *she dumped the problem in my lap*. **in the lap of the gods** (of the success of a plan or event) depending on factors that one cannot control; open to chance. **in the lap of luxury** in conditions of great comfort and wealth.
– DERIVATIVES **lapful** noun (pl. **lapfuls**).
– ORIGIN Old English *læppa*, of Germanic origin; related to Dutch *lap*, German *Lappen* 'piece of cloth'. The word originally denoted a fold or flap of a garment (compare with **LAPEL**), later specifically one that could be used as a pocket or pouch, or the front of a skirt when held up to carry something (Middle English), hence the area between the waist and knees as a place where a child could be nursed or an object held.

lap[2] ▸ noun **1** one circuit of a track during a race. ■ a stage in a swim consisting of two lengths of a pool. ■ a part of a journey or other undertaking: *we caught a cab for the last lap of our journey*.
2 an overlapping or projecting part. ■ [mass noun] the amount by which one thing overlaps a part of another. ■ Metallurgy a defect formed in rolling when a projecting part is accidentally folded over and pressed against the surface of the metal.
3 a single turn of rope, thread, or cable round a drum or reel. ■ a layer or sheet of cotton or wool, wound on a roller during manufacture.
4 (in a lapping machine) a rotating disc with a coating of fine abrasive for polishing. ■ a polishing tool of a special shape, coated or impregnated with an abrasive.
▸ verb (**laps**, **lapping**, **lapped**) [with obj.] **1** overtake (a competitor in a race) to become one or more laps ahead: *she lapped all of her rivals in the 3,000 metres*. ■ [no obj.] (of a competitor in a race) complete a lap, especially in a specified time: *Mansell lapped two tenths of a second faster than anyone else*.
2 (**lap someone/thing in**) literary wrap or enfold someone or something in (something soft): *he was lapped in blankets*.
3 [no obj.] project beyond or overlap something: *the water lapped over the edges*.
4 polish (metal, glass, or a gem) with a lapping machine.
– ORIGIN Middle English (as a verb in the sense 'coil, fold, or wrap'): from **LAP**[1]. Sense 1 of the noun and verb date from the mid 19th cent.

lap[3] ▸ verb (**laps**, **lapping**, **lapped**) [with obj.] **1** (of an animal) take up (liquid) with quick movements of the tongue: *the cat was* **lapping up** *a saucer of milk*. ■ (**lap something up**) accept something eagerly and with obvious pleasure: *she's lapping up the attention*.
2 (of water) wash against (something) with a gentle rippling sound: *the waves lapped the shore* | [no obj.] *the sound of the river lapping against the banks*.
▸ noun [in sing.] the action or sound of water washing gently against something: *listening to the comfortable lap of the waves against the shore*.
– ORIGIN Old English *lapian*, of Germanic origin; related to Middle Low German and Middle Dutch *lapen*.

lapa /'lɑ:pə/ ▸ noun S. African a courtyard or similar enclosure, especially the first of two courtyards in a traditional Sotho homestead.
– ORIGIN from Sotho *lelapa*.

La Palma /lɑ: 'pɑ:lmə, 'pɑ:mə/ one of the Canary Islands, the most north-westerly in the group; chief town, Santa Cruz de la Palma. It is the site of an astronomical observatory.

laparoscopy /ˌlapə'rɒskəpi/ ▸ noun (pl. **laparoscopies**) a surgical procedure in which a fibre-optic instrument is inserted through the abdominal wall to view the organs in the abdomen or permit small-scale surgery.
– DERIVATIVES **laparoscope** noun, **laparoscopic** adjective, **laparoscopically** adverb.
– ORIGIN mid 19th cent.: from Greek *lapara* 'flank' + **-SCOPY**.

laparotomy /ˌlapə'rɒtəmi/ ▸ noun (pl. **laparotomies**) a surgical incision into the abdominal cavity, for diagnosis or in preparation for major surgery.
– ORIGIN mid 19th cent.: from Greek *lapara* 'flank' + **-TOMY**.

La Paz /la 'paz, lɑ: 'pɑ:z/ **1** the capital of Bolivia, in the north-west of the country near the border with Peru; pop. 835,301 (2009). (The judicial capital is Sucre.) Situated in the Andes at an altitude of 3,660 m (12,000 ft), La Paz is the highest capital city in the world.
2 a city in Mexico, near the southern tip of the Baja California peninsula, capital of the state of Baja California Sur; pop. 189,176 (2005).

lap belt ▸ noun a safety belt worn across the lap.

lap dance ▸ noun an erotic dance or striptease performed close to, or sitting on the lap of, a paying customer.
– DERIVATIVES **lap dancer** noun, **lap dancing** noun.

lap dissolve ▸ noun a fade-out of a scene in a film that overlaps with a fade-in of a new scene, so that one appears to dissolve into the other.

lapdog ▸ noun a small pampered pet dog. ■ a person or organization which is influenced or controlled by another: *the government and its media lapdogs*.

lapel ▸ noun the part on each side of a coat or jacket immediately below the collar which is folded back on either side of the front opening.
– DERIVATIVES **lapelled** adjective [in combination] *a narrow-lapelled suit*.
– ORIGIN mid 17th cent.: diminutive of **LAP**[1].

lapidary /'lapɪd(ə)ri/ ▸ adjective relating to the engraving, cutting, or polishing of stones and gems. ■ (of language) elegant and concise, and therefore suitable for engraving on stone: *a lapidary statement*.
▸ noun (pl. **lapidaries**) a person who cuts, polishes, or engraves gems.
– ORIGIN Middle English (as a noun): from Latin *lapidarius* (in late Latin 'stonecutter'), from *lapis, lapid-* 'stone'. The adjective dates from the early 18th cent.

lapilli /lə'pɪlʌɪ/ ▸ plural noun Geology rock fragments ejected from a volcano.
– ORIGIN mid 18th cent. (in the general sense 'stones, pebbles'): via Italian from Latin, plural of *lapillus*, diminutive of *lapis* 'stone'.

lapis lazuli /ˌlapɪs 'lazjʊlʌɪ, -li/ (also **lapis**) ▸ noun [mass noun] a bright blue metamorphic rock consisting largely of lazurite, used for decoration and in jewellery. ■ a bright blue pigment formerly made by crushing lapis lazuli. ■ a bright blue colour.
– ORIGIN late Middle English: from Latin *lapis* 'stone' and medieval Latin *lazuli*, genitive of *lazulum*, from Persian *lāžward* 'lapis lazuli'. Compare with **AZURE**.

Lapita /la'pi:tə/ ▸ noun [usu. as modifier] Archaeology a prehistoric Oceanic culture centred on Melanesia, dated to about *c.*1500–500 BC. It is characterized by pottery distinctively stamped with a toothed instrument.
– ORIGIN 1960s: from the name of a site in New Caledonia.

Lapith /'lapɪθ/ ▸ noun Greek Mythology a member of a Thessalian people who fought and defeated the centaurs.
– ORIGIN via Latin from Greek *Lapithai* (plural).

lap joint ▸ noun a joint made by halving the thickness of each member at the joint and fitting them together.

Laplace /la'plɑ:s/, French /laplas/, Pierre Simon, Marquis de (1749–1827), French applied mathematician and theoretical physicist. His treatise *Mécanique*

L

céleste (1799–1825) is an extensive mathematical analysis of geophysical matters and of planetary and lunar motion.

Lapland /ˈlapland/ a region of northern Europe which extends from the Norwegian Sea to the White Sea and lies mainly within the Arctic Circle. It consists of the northern parts of Norway, Sweden, and Finland, and the Kola Peninsula of Russia.
– DERIVATIVES **Laplander** noun.
– ORIGIN late 16th cent.: from Swedish *Lappland*, from *Lapp* (see **LAPP**) + *land* 'land'.

La Plata /lɑː ˈplɑːtə/ a port in Argentina, on the River Plate (Río de la Plata) south-east of Buenos Aires; pop. 654,800 (est. 2008).

lap of honour ▶ **noun** a celebratory circuit of a sports field or track by the person or team that has won a contest.

Lapp ▶ **noun 1** a member of an indigenous people of the extreme north of Scandinavia, traditionally associated with the herding of reindeer.
2 [mass noun] the Finno-Ugric language of the Lapps, with nine distinct dialects spoken by around 25,000 people altogether.
▶ **adjective** relating to the Lapps or their language.
– ORIGIN Swedish, perhaps originally a term of contempt and related to Middle High German *lappe* 'simpleton'.

> **USAGE** Although the term **Lapp** is still widely used and is the most familiar term to many people, the people themselves prefer to be called **Sami**.

lappet /ˈlapɪt/ ▶ **noun 1** a fold or hanging piece of flesh in some animals. ■ a loose or overlapping part of a garment.
2 (also **lappet moth**) a brownish moth, the hairy caterpillars of which have fleshy lappets along each side of the body. ● *Gastropacha quercifolia* and other species in the family Lasiocampidae.
– ORIGIN late Middle English (denoting a lobe of the ear, liver, etc.): diminutive of **LAP**[1].

lapping machine ▶ **noun** a machine with a rotating abrasive disc for polishing gems, metal, and optical glass.

Lappish ▶ **adjective** relating to the Lapps (Sami) or their language.
▶ **noun** [mass noun] the Lapp language.

lap robe ▶ **noun** N. Amer. a travelling rug.

lapsang souchong /ˈlapsaŋ/ ▶ **noun** [mass noun] a variety of souchong tea with a smoky flavour.
– ORIGIN late 19th cent.: from an invented first element + **SOUCHONG**.

lapse ▶ **noun 1** a brief or temporary failure of concentration, memory, or judgement: *a lapse of concentration in the second set cost her the match.* ■ a decline from previously high standards: *tracing his **lapse into** petty crime.* ■ Law the termination of a right or privilege through disuse or failure to follow appropriate procedures.
2 an interval or passage of time: *there was a considerable lapse of time between the two events.*
▶ **verb** [no obj.] **1** (of a right, privilege, or agreement) become invalid because it is not used, claimed, or renewed; expire: *he let his membership of CND lapse.* ■ (of a state or activity) fail to be maintained; come to an end: *if your diet has lapsed it's time you revived it.* ■ cease to follow the rules and practices of a religion or doctrine.
2 (**lapse into**) pass gradually into (an inferior state or condition): *the country has lapsed into chaos.* ■ revert to (a previous or more familiar style of speaking or behaviour): *the girls lapsed into French.*
– ORIGIN late Middle English: from Latin *lapsus*, from *labi* 'to glide, slip, or fall'; the verb reinforced by Latin *lapsare* 'to slip or stumble'.

lapsed ▶ **adjective** no longer valid; expired: *a lapsed insurance policy.* ■ no longer following the rules and practices of a religion or doctrine; non-practising: *a lapsed Catholic.*

lapse rate ▶ **noun** the rate at which air temperature falls with increasing altitude.

lap steel (also **lap steel guitar**) ▶ **noun** another term for **PEDAL STEEL**.

lapstone ▶ **noun** a shoemaker's stone held in the lap and used to beat leather on.

lapstrake chiefly N. Amer. ▶ **noun** a clinker-built boat.
▶ **adjective** (also **lapstraked**) clinker-built.

lapsus calami /ˌlapsəs ˈkaləmʌɪ/ ▶ **noun** (pl. **same**) formal a slip of the pen.
– ORIGIN Latin.

lapsus linguae /ˌlapsəs ˈlɪŋgwʌɪ/ ▶ **noun** (pl. **same**) formal a slip of the tongue.
– ORIGIN Latin.

Laptev Sea /ˈlaptɛf/ a part of the Arctic Ocean, which lies to the north of Russia between the Taimyr Peninsula and the New Siberian Islands.

laptop (also **laptop computer**) ▶ **noun** a computer that is portable and suitable for use while travelling.

lap-weld ▶ **verb** [with obj.] weld (something) with the edges overlapping.
▶ **noun** (**lap weld**) a weld with overlapping edges.

lapwing ▶ **noun** a large plover, typically having a black-and-white head and underparts and a loud call. ● Genus *Vanellus*, family Charadriidae: several species, in particular the (**northern**) **lapwing** (*V. vanellus*) of Eurasia (also called the **GREEN PLOVER** or **PEEWIT**), which has a dark green back and a crest.
– ORIGIN Old English *hlēapewince*, from *hlēapan* 'to leap' and a base meaning 'move from side to side' (whence also **WINK**); so named because of the way it flies. The spelling was changed in Middle English by association with **LAP**[2] and **WING**.

L'Aquila /ˈlakwila/ Italian name for **AQUILA**[2].

LAR ▶ **abbreviation** Libya (international vehicle registration).
– ORIGIN from *Libyan Arab Republic*.

lar (also **lar gibbon**) ▶ **noun** the common gibbon, which has white hands and feet and is found in Thailand and Malaysia. ● *Hylobates lar*, family Hylobatidae.
– ORIGIN early 19th cent.: from Latin, literally 'household god'.

Lara /ˈlɑːrə/, Brian (Charles) (b.1969), West Indian cricketer. He scored 375 against England in Antigua (1994), breaking the record Test score, and 501 not out, a world record in first-class cricket, for Warwickshire against Durham (1994).

Laramie /ˈlarəmi/ a city in SE Wyoming; pop. 27,664 (est. 2008). It was first settled in 1868, during the construction of the Union Pacific Railroad.

larboard /ˈlɑːbɔːd, -bəd/ ▶ **noun** Nautical archaic term for **PORT**[3].
– ORIGIN Middle English *ladebord* (see **LADE**, **BOARD**), referring to the side on which cargo was put aboard. The change to *lar-* in the 16th cent. was due to association with **STARBOARD**.

larceny /ˈlɑːs(ə)ni/ ▶ **noun** (pl. **larcenies**) [mass noun] theft of personal property. In English law larceny was replaced as a statutory crime by theft in 1968. See also **GRAND LARCENY**, **PETTY LARCENY**.
– DERIVATIVES **larcenist** noun, **larcenous** adjective.
– ORIGIN late 15th cent.: from Old French *larcin*, from Latin *latrocinium*, from *latro(n-)* 'robber', earlier 'mercenary soldier', from Greek *latreus*.

larch ▶ **noun** a coniferous tree with bunches of deciduous bright green needles, found in cool regions of the northern hemisphere. It is grown for its tough timber and its resin (which yields turpentine).
● Genus *Larix*, family Pinaceae: several species, including the **common** (or **European**) **larch** (*L. decidua*).
– ORIGIN mid 16th cent.: from Middle High German *larche*, based on Latin *larix*.

lard ▶ **noun** [mass noun] fat from the abdomen of a pig that is rendered and clarified for use in cooking.
■ informal excess fat in a person.
▶ **verb** [with obj.] **1** insert strips of fat or bacon in (meat) before cooking. ■ smear or cover (a foodstuff) with lard or fat to prevent it drying out during storage.
2 (usu. **be larded with**) embellish (talk or writing) with an excessive number of esoteric or technical expressions: *his conversation is larded with quotations from Coleridge.* ■ cover or fill thickly or excessively: *the pages were larded with corrections and crossings-out.*
– DERIVATIVES **lardy** adjective (**lardier**, **lardiest**).
– ORIGIN Middle English (also denoting fat bacon or pork): from Old French 'bacon', from Latin *lardum*, *laridum*, related to Greek *larinos* 'fat'.

lardass /ˈlɑːdɑːs, ˈlɑːdas/ ▶ **noun** N. Amer. informal, derogatory a fat person, especially one with large buttocks.

larder ▶ **noun** a room or large cupboard for storing food.
– ORIGIN Middle English (denoting a store of meat): from Old French *lardier*, from medieval Latin *lardarium*, from *laridum* (see **LARD**).

larder beetle ▶ **noun** a brownish scavenging beetle which is a pest of stored products, especially meat and hides. ● *Dermestes lardarius*, family Dermestidae.

lardon /ˈlɑːdən/ (also **lardoon** /-ˈduːn/) ▶ **noun** a chunk or cube of bacon used to lard meat.
– ORIGIN late Middle English: from French, from *lard* 'bacon' (see **LARD**).

lardy cake ▶ **noun** Brit. a cake made with bread dough, lard, and currants.

lares /ˈlɑːriːz/ ▶ **plural noun** gods of the household worshipped in ancient Rome. See also **PENATES**.
– PHRASES **lares and penates** a person's home and household possessions.
– ORIGIN Latin.

Largactil /lɑːˈgaktɪl/ ▶ **noun** trademark for **CHLORPROMAZINE**.
– ORIGIN 1950s: of unknown origin.

large ▶ **adjective 1** of considerable or relatively great size, extent, or capacity: *add a large clove of garlic* | *the concert attracted large crowds* | *the jumper comes in small, medium, and large sizes.* ■ pursuing a commercial activity on a significant scale: *many large investors are likely to take a different view.*
2 of wide range or scope: *we can afford to take a larger view of the situation.*
▶ **verb** [no obj.] (**large it**) Brit. informal enjoy oneself in a lively way with drink or drugs and music.
– PHRASES **at large 1** (especially of a criminal or dangerous animal) at liberty; escaped or not yet captured: *the fugitive was still at large.* **2** as a whole; in general: *there has been a loss of community values in society at large.* **3** US in a general way; without particularizing: *he served as an ambassador at large in the Reagan Administration.* **4** dated at length; in great detail: *writing at large on the policies he wished to pursue.* **have** (or **give**) **it large** Brit. informal go out and enjoy oneself, typically with drink or drugs; go clubbing. **in large measure** (or **part**) to a great extent: *the success of the conference was due in large part to its organizers.* (**as**) **large as life** see **LIFE**. **larger than life** see **LIFE**.
– DERIVATIVES **largeness** noun, **largish** adjective.
– ORIGIN Middle English (in the sense 'liberal in giving, lavish, ample in quantity'): via Old French from Latin *larga*, feminine of *largus* 'copious'.

large calorie ▶ **noun** see **CALORIE**.

large-hearted ▶ **adjective** sympathetic and generous.

large intestine ▶ **noun** Anatomy the caecum, colon, and rectum collectively.

largely ▶ **adverb** [sentence adverb] to a great extent; on the whole; mostly: *he was soon arrested, largely through the efforts of Tom Poole.*

large-minded ▶ **adjective** open to and tolerant of other people's ideas; liberal.

largemouth ▶ **noun** N. Amer. the largemouth bass (see **BLACK BASS**).

large-scale ▶ **adjective 1** involving large numbers or a large area; extensive: *large-scale commercial farming.*
2 (of a map or model) made to a scale large enough to show certain features in detail.

largesse /lɑːˈ(d)ʒɛs/ (also **largess**) ▶ **noun** [mass noun] generosity in bestowing money or gifts upon others: *presumably public money is not dispensed with such largesse to anyone else.* ■ money or gifts given generously: *the distribution of largesse to the local population.*
– ORIGIN Middle English: from Old French, from Latin *largus* 'copious'.

larghetto /lɑːˈgɛtəʊ/ Music ▶ **adverb & adjective** (especially as a direction) in a fairly slow tempo.
▶ **noun** (pl. **larghettos**) a passage or movement marked to be performed in this way.
– ORIGIN Italian, diminutive of *largo* 'broad'.

largo /ˈlɑːgəʊ/ Music ▶ **adverb & adjective** (especially as a direction) in a slow tempo and dignified in style.
▶ **noun** (pl. **largos**) a passage, movement, or composition marked to be performed in this way.
– ORIGIN Italian, from Latin *largus* 'copious, abundant'.

lari /ˈlɑːriː/ ▶ **noun** (pl. **same** or **laris**) **1** the basic monetary unit of Georgia, equal to 100 tetri.
2 a monetary unit of the Maldives, equal to one hundredth of a rufiyaa.
– ORIGIN from Persian.

Lariam /ˈlarɪəm/ ▶ **noun** trademark for **MEFLOQUINE**.
– ORIGIN 1980s: probably from partial rearrangement of **MALARIA**.

lariat /ˈlarɪət/ ▶ **noun** a rope used as a lasso or for tethering.
– ORIGIN mid 19th cent.: from Spanish *la reata* from *la* 'the' and *reatar* 'tie again' (based on Latin *aptare* 'adjust', from *aptus* 'apt, fitting').

La Rioja /ˌlɑː rɪˈɒhə/ an autonomous region of northern Spain, in the wine-producing valley of the River Ebro; capital, Logroño.

Larissa /ləˈrɪsə/ a city in Greece, the chief town of Thessaly; pop. 134,100 (est. 2009). Greek name **Lárisa** /ˈlarisa/.

lark[1] ▶ **noun** a small ground-dwelling songbird with elongated hind claws and a song that is delivered on the wing, typically crested and with brown streaky plumage. ● Family Alaudidae: many genera and numerous species, e.g. the **skylark** and **shorelark**.
■ used in names of similar birds of other families, e.g. **meadowlark**. ■ informal a person who habitually gets up early and feels energetic early in the day. Often contrasted with **OWL**.
– PHRASES **be up with the lark** Brit. get out of bed very early in the morning.
– ORIGIN Old English *laferce, læwerce*; related to Dutch *leeuwerik* and German *Lerche*; of unknown ultimate origin.

lark[2] informal ▶ **noun** something done for fun, especially something mischievous or daring; an amusing adventure or escapade: *I only went along* ***for a lark***. ■ [usu. with modifier] Brit. informal an activity regarded as foolish or a waste of time: ***he's serious about this music lark***.
▶ **verb** [no obj.] (**lark about/around**) Brit. enjoy oneself by behaving in a playful and mischievous way: *he's always joking and larking about in the office.*
– DERIVATIVES **larky** adjective.
– ORIGIN early 19th cent.: perhaps from dialect *lake* 'play', from Old Norse *leika*, but compare with **SKYLARK** in the same sense, which is recorded earlier.

Larkin, Philip (Arthur) (1922–85), English poet. His poetry is characterized by an air of melancholy and bitterness, and by stoic wit. Notable works: *The Whitsun Weddings* (1964) and *High Windows* (1974).

larkspur ▶ **noun** an annual Mediterranean plant of the buttercup family, which bears spikes of spurred flowers. It is closely related to the delphiniums, with which it has been bred to produce a number of cultivated hybrids. ● Genus *Consolida* (formerly *Delphinium*), family Ranunculaceae.

larn ▶ **verb** dialect form of **LEARN**.

larney /ˈlɑːni/ (also **larnie**) S. African informal ▶ **adjective** suggesting wealth and high status; smart and elegant.
▶ **noun** (pl. **larneys** or **larnies**) derogatory a white man.
■ an employer or a member of the upper classes.
– ORIGIN from Isicamtho (a South African urban argot) *lani(e)* 'white man', of unknown ultimate origin; perhaps related to Malay *rani* 'rich'.

La Rochefoucauld /la ˈrɒʃfuːkəʊ/, French /la ʀɔʃfukəʊ/, François de Marsillac, Duc de (1613–80), French writer and moralist. Notable works: *Réflexions, ou sentences et maximes morales* (1665).

La Rochelle /ˌla rɒˈʃɛl/, French /la ʀɔʃɛl/ a port on the Atlantic coast of western France; pop. 80,014 (2006).

Larousse /laˈruːs/, French /laʀus/, Pierre (1817–75), French lexicographer and encyclopedist. He edited the fifteen-volume *Grand dictionnaire universel du XIXe siècle* (1866–76), which aimed to treat every area of human knowledge. In 1852 he co-founded the publishing house of Larousse.

larrikin /ˈlarɪkɪn/ ▶ **noun** Austral./NZ a boisterous, often badly behaved young man. ■ Austral. a person with apparent disregard for convention; a maverick: [as modifier] *the larrikin trade union leader.*
– ORIGIN mid 19th cent.: from English dialect, perhaps from the given name *Larry* (pet form of *Lawrence*) + **-KIN**, or from a pronunciation of *larking*.

larrup /ˈlarəp/ ▶ **verb** (**larrups, larruping, larruped**) [with obj.] informal thrash or whip (a person or animal).
– ORIGIN early 19th cent. (originally dialect): perhaps related to **LATHER** or **LEATHER**.

larva /ˈlɑːvə/ ▶ **noun** (pl. **larvae** /-viː/) the active immature form of an insect, especially one that differs greatly from the adult and forms the stage between egg and pupa, e.g. a caterpillar or grub. Compare with **NYMPH** (sense 2). ■ an immature form of other animals that undergo some metamorphosis, e.g. a tadpole.
– DERIVATIVES **larval** adjective, **larvicide** noun.
– ORIGIN mid 17th cent. (denoting a disembodied spirit or ghost): from Latin, literally 'ghost, mask'.

Larvacea /lɑːˈveɪʃə/ ▶ **plural noun** Zoology a class of minute transparent planktonic animals related to the sea squirts. They have a tadpole-like body which is typically enclosed in a gelatinous 'house' that is regularly shed and replaced.
– DERIVATIVES **larvacean** adjective & noun.
– ORIGIN modern Latin (plural), from **LARVA**.

Larwood, Harold (1904–95), English cricketer. A fast bowler for Nottinghamshire, in the 1932–3 MCC tour of Australia he bowled fast short-pitched 'bodyline' deliveries, and was involved in controversy when several of the home batsmen were badly injured.

laryngeal /ləˈrɪn(d)ʒɪəl/ ▶ **adjective** relating to the larynx: *the laryngeal artery.* ■ Phonetics (of a speech sound) made in the larynx with only the front part of the vocal cords vibrating, giving a very low frequency and producing what is known as 'creaky voice': *laryngeal consonants.*
– ORIGIN late 18th cent.: from modern Latin *laryngeus* 'relating to the larynx' + **-AL**.

laryngitis /ˌlarɪnˈdʒʌɪtɪs/ ▶ **noun** [mass noun] inflammation of the larynx, typically resulting in huskiness or loss of the voice, harsh breathing, and a painful cough.
– DERIVATIVES **laryngitic** /-ˈdʒɪtɪk/ adjective.

laryngology /ˌlarɪŋˈɡɒlədʒi/ ▶ **noun** [mass noun] the branch of medicine that deals with the larynx and its diseases.
– DERIVATIVES **laryngologist** noun.

laryngoscope /ləˈrɪŋɡəskəʊp/ ▶ **noun** an instrument for examining the larynx, or for inserting a tube through it.
– DERIVATIVES **laryngoscopy** noun.

laryngotomy /ˌlarɪŋˈɡɒtəmi/ ▶ **noun** [mass noun] surgical incision into the larynx, typically to provide an air passage when breathing is obstructed.

larynx /ˈlarɪŋks/ ▶ **noun** (pl. **larynges** /ləˈrɪn(d)ʒiːz/) Anatomy the hollow muscular organ forming an air passage to the lungs and holding the vocal cords in humans and other mammals; the voice box.
– ORIGIN late 16th cent.: modern Latin, from Greek *larunx*.

lasagne /ləˈzanjə, -ˈsan-, -ˈsɑːn-, -ˈzɑːn-/ (also **lasagna**) ▶ **noun** [mass noun] pasta in the form of sheets or wide strips. ■ an Italian dish consisting of lasagne baked with meat or vegetables and a cheese sauce.
– ORIGIN Italian, plural of *lasagna*, based on Latin *lasanum* 'chamber pot', perhaps also 'cooking pot'.

La Salle /la ˈsal/, René-Robert Cavelier, Sieur de (1643–87), French explorer. He sailed down the Ohio and Mississippi Rivers to the sea from Canada in 1682, naming the Mississippi basin Louisiana in honour of Louis XIV.

La Scala /la ˈskɑːlə/ an opera house in Milan built 1776–8 on the site of the church of Santa Maria della Scala.

lascar /ˈlaskə/ ▶ **noun** dated a sailor from India or SE Asia.
– ORIGIN early 17th cent.: from Portuguese *lascari*, from Urdu and Persian *laškarī* 'soldier', from *laškar* 'army'.

Lascaux /laˈskəʊ/, French /laskəʊ/ the site of a cave in the Dordogne, France, which is richly decorated with Palaeolithic wall paintings of animals dated to the Magdalenian period.

lascivious /ləˈsɪvɪəs/ ▶ **adjective** feeling or revealing an overt sexual interest or desire: *he gave her a lascivious wink.*
– DERIVATIVES **lasciviously** adverb, **lasciviousness** noun.
– ORIGIN late Middle English: from late Latin *lasciviosus*, from Latin *lascivia* 'lustfulness', from *lascivus* 'lustful, wanton'.

lase /leɪz/ ▶ **verb** [no obj.] (of a substance, especially a gas or crystal) undergo the physical processes employed in a laser; function as or in a laser.
– ORIGIN 1960s: back-formation from **LASER**, interpreted as an agent noun.

laser ▶ **noun** a device that generates an intense beam of coherent monochromatic light (or other electromagnetic radiation) by stimulated emission of photons from excited atoms or molecules. Lasers are used in drilling and cutting, alignment and guidance, and in surgery; the optical properties are exploited in holography, reading barcodes, and in recording and playing compact discs.
– ORIGIN 1960s: acronym from *light amplification by stimulated emission of radiation*, on the pattern of *maser*.

laserdisc ▶ **noun** a disc resembling a larger CD but able to store video, now generally replaced by the DVD.

laser gun ▶ **noun 1** a handheld device incorporating a laser beam, used for reading a barcode or for determining the distance or speed of an object.
2 (in science fiction) a weapon that uses a powerful laser beam.

laser printer ▶ **noun** a printer linked to a computer producing good-quality printed material by using a laser to form a pattern of electrostatically charged dots on a light-sensitive drum, which attract toner (or dry ink powder). The toner is transferred to a piece of paper and fixed by a heating process.

lash ▶ **verb 1** [with obj.] strike or beat with a whip or stick: *they lashed him repeatedly about the head.*
■ beat forcefully against: *waves lashed the coast.*
■ (**lash someone into**) drive someone into (a particular state or condition): *fear lashed him into a frenzy.*
2 [with obj.] (of an animal) move (a part of the body, especially the tail) quickly and violently: *the cat was lashing its tail back and forth.* ■ [no obj.] (of a part of the body) move in this way.
3 [with obj. and adverbial] fasten (something) securely with a cord or rope: *the hatch was securely* ***lashed down*** | *he lashed the flag to the mast.*
▶ **noun 1** a sharp blow or stroke with a whip or rope: *he was sentenced to fifty lashes for his crime* | figurative *she felt the lash of my tongue.* ■ the flexible leather part of a whip, used for administering blows. ■ (**the lash**) punishment in the form of a beating with a whip or rope: *they were living under the threat of the lash.*
2 (usu. **lashes**) an eyelash: *she fluttered her long dark lashes.*
– PHRASES **be** (or **go**) **on the lash** Brit. informal be engaged in (or go on) a heavy drinking session.
– PHRASAL VERBS **lash down** (of rain) fall very heavily: *torrential rain was lashing down.* **lash out 1** hit or kick out at someone or something: *the woman had lashed out in fear.* ■ address someone angrily: *in his speech, he lashed out at his enemies.* **2** Brit. spend money extravagantly: *I decided to lash out and treat myself* | *let's* ***lash out on*** *a taxi.*
– DERIVATIVES **lasher** noun, **lashless** adjective.
– ORIGIN Middle English (in the sense 'make a sudden movement'): probably imitative.

lashed[1] ▶ **adjective** [in combination] having eyelashes of a specified kind: *long-lashed eyes.*

lashed[2] ▶ **adjective** Brit. informal very drunk.

lashing ▶ **noun 1** a beating with a stick or whip: *I threatened to give him a good lashing!* | figurative *he was on the receiving end of a verbal lashing yesterday.*
2 (usu. **lashings**) a cord used to fasten something securely.

lashings ▶ **plural noun** Brit. informal a copious amount of something, especially food or drink: *chocolate cake with* ***lashings of*** *cream.*

lash-up ▶ **noun** informal, chiefly Brit. a makeshift, improvised structure or arrangement.

LASIK /ˈleɪzɪk/ ▶ **noun** [mass noun] corrective eye surgery in which a flap of the corneal surface is raised and a thin layer of underlying tissue is removed using a laser.
– ORIGIN 1990s: acronym from *laser-assisted in situ keratomileusis*.

Las Palmas /lɑːs ˈpɑːməs, ˈpɑːlməs/ a port and resort on the north coast of the island of Gran Canaria, capital of the Canary Islands; pop. 381,123 (2008). Full name **Las Palmas de Gran Canaria** /də ˌɡran kəˈnɛːrɪə/.

La Spezia /la ˈspɛtsɪə/ an industrial port in NW Italy; pop. 95,372 (2008). Since 1861 it has been Italy's chief naval station.

lasque /lɑːsk/ (also **lasque diamond**) ▶ **noun** a flat, ill-formed, or veiny diamond.
– ORIGIN late 17th cent.: perhaps from Persian *lašk* 'piece'.

lass ▶ **noun** chiefly Scottish & N. English a girl or young woman: *he married a lass from Yorkshire* | *village lasses.*
– ORIGIN Middle English: based on Old Norse *laskura* (feminine adjective) 'unmarried'.

Lassa fever /ˈlasə/ ▶ **noun** [mass noun] an acute and often fatal viral disease, with fever, occurring chiefly in West Africa. It is usually acquired from infected rats.
– ORIGIN 1970s: named after the village of *Lassa*, in NW Nigeria, where it was first reported.

lassi /ˈlasi/ ▶ **noun** [mass noun] a sweet or savoury Indian drink made from a yogurt or buttermilk base with water.
– ORIGIN from Hindi *lassī*.

lassie ▸ **noun** chiefly Scottish & N. English another term for LASS.

lassitude /ˈlasɪtjuːd/ ▸ **noun** [mass noun] a state of physical or mental weariness; lack of energy: *she was overcome by lassitude and retired to bed.*
– ORIGIN late Middle English: from French, from Latin *lassitudo*, from *lassus* 'tired'.

lasso /ləˈsuː, ˈlasəʊ/ ▸ **noun** (pl. **lassos** or **lassoes**) a rope with a noose at one end, used especially in North America for catching cattle.
▸ **verb** (**lassoes, lassoing, lassoed**) [with obj.] catch (an animal) with a lasso.
– ORIGIN mid 18th cent.: representing an American Spanish pronunciation of Spanish *lazo*, based on Latin *laqueus* 'noose'. Compare with LACE.

Lassus /ˈlasəs/, Orlande de (*c.*1532–94), Flemish composer; Italian name *Orlando di Lasso*. A notable composer of polyphonic music, he wrote over 2,000 secular and sacred works.

last[1] ▸ **adjective** [attrib.] **1** coming after all others in time or order; final: *they caught the last bus.* ■ met with or encountered after any others: *the last house in the village.* ■ the lowest in importance or rank: *finishing in last place* | [as complement] *he **came last** in the race.* ■ (**the last**) the least likely or suitable: *he's the last person I'd turn to for help* | ***the last thing** she needed was a husband.*
2 most recent in time; latest: *last year* | [postpositive] *your letter of Sunday last.* ■ immediately preceding in order; previous in a sequence or enumeration: *their last album* | *this last point is critical.*
3 only remaining: *it's our last hope.*
▸ **adverb 1** on the last occasion before the present; previously: *a woman last heard of in Cornwall.*
2 [in combination] after all others in order or sequence: *the last-named film.*
3 (especially in enumerating points) lastly: *and last, I'd like to thank you all for coming.*
▸ **noun** (pl. **same**) the last person or thing; the one occurring, mentioned, or acting after all others: *the last of their guests had gone* | *he was eating as if every mouthful were his last.* ■ (**the last of**) the only part of something that remains: *they drank the last of the wine.* ■ [in sing.] the last position or finisher in a race or competition: *Lion Cavern came from last in a slowly run race.* ■ (**the last**) the end or last moment, especially death: *he was dead, having refused morphia **to the last**.* ■ (**the last**) the last mention or sight of someone or something: *that was **the last we saw of** her.*
– PHRASES **at last** (or **at long last**) in the end; after much delay: *you've come back to me at last!* **in the** (or **as a**) **last resort** see RESORT. —— **one's last** do something for the last time: *the dying embers sparked their last.* **last but not least** last in order of mention or occurrence but not of importance. **one's** (or **the**) **last gasp** see GASP. **the last minute** the latest possible time before an event: *the visit was cancelled at the last minute.* **last orders** (N. Amer. also **last call**) (in a bar or pub) an expression used to inform customers that closing time is approaching and that any further drinks should be purchased immediately: *last orders, gentlemen, please.* **the last straw** see STRAW. **last thing** late in the evening, especially as a final act before going to bed: *I think having that cup of tea **last thing at night** really helps.* **the last word 1** the final or definitive pronouncement on or decision about a subject: *he's always determined to **have the last word**.* **2** the finest or most modern, fashionable, or advanced example of something: *the new flat is **the last word in** luxury.* **on one's last legs** see LEG.
– ORIGIN Old English *latost* (adverb) 'after all others in a series', of Germanic origin; related to Dutch *laatst*, *lest* and German *letzt*, also to LATE.

last[2] ▸ **verb** [no obj.] **1** [with adverbial] (of a process, activity, or state) continue for a specified period of time: *the guitar solo lasted for twenty minutes* | *childhood seems to last forever.*
2 continue to operate or remain usable for a considerable or specified length of time: *the car is built to last* | *a lip pencil lasts longer than lipstick.* ■ manage to continue in a state or position; survive or endure: *she managed to **last out** until the end of the programme* | *his condition is so serious that he won't last the night* | *how long does he reckon he'll last as manager?* ■ (of provisions or resources) be adequate or sufficient for a specified length of time: *green peppers which had been served with their rice while supplies lasted* | [with obj.] *he filled the freezer with enough food to last him for three months.*
– ORIGIN Old English *lǣstan*, of Germanic origin, related to German *leisten* 'afford, yield', also to LAST[3].

last[3] ▸ **noun** a shoemaker's model for shaping or repairing a shoe or boot.
– ORIGIN Old English *lǣste*, of Germanic origin, from a base meaning 'follow'; related to Dutch *leest* and German *Leisten*.

last-ditch ▸ **adjective** denoting a final, often desperate attempt to achieve something: *a last-ditch effort to break the deadlock.*

last-gasp ▸ **adjective** done at the last possible moment, typically in desperation: *Wilson levelled with a last-gasp try.*

last hurrah ▸ **noun** informal a final act, performance, or effort: *the election campaign was his last hurrah.*

lasting ▸ **adjective** enduring or able to endure over a long period of time: *they left a lasting impression* | *a lasting, happy marriage.*
– DERIVATIVES **lastingly** adverb, **lastingness** noun.

Last Judgement ▸ **noun** the judgement of humankind expected in some religious traditions to take place at the end of the world.

lastly ▸ **adverb** in the last place (used to introduce the last of a series of points or actions): *lastly, I would like to thank my parents.*

last-minute ▸ **adjective** done or occurring at the latest possible time before an event: *a last-minute change of plan.*

last name ▸ **noun** one's surname.

last number redial ▸ **noun** see REDIAL.

last offices ▸ **plural noun** the preparation of a dead person for burial.

last post ▸ **noun** (in the British armed forces) the second of two bugle calls giving notice of the hour of retiring at night, played also at military funerals and acts of remembrance.

last rites ▸ **plural noun** (in the Christian Church) rites administered to a person who is about to die.

Last Supper the supper eaten by Jesus and his disciples on the night before the Crucifixion, as recorded in the New Testament and commemorated by Christians in the Eucharist.

last trump ▸ **noun** the trumpet blast that in some religious beliefs is thought will wake the dead on Judgement Day.

Las Vegas /las ˈveɪɡəs/ a city in southern Nevada; pop. 558,383 (est. 2008). It is noted for its casinos and nightclubs.

lat[1] /lat/ ▸ **noun** (pl. **lati** /ˈlati/ or **lats**) the basic monetary unit of Latvia, equal to 100 santims.
– ORIGIN from the first syllable of *Latvija* 'Latvia'.

lat[2] /lat/ ▸ **noun** (usu. **lats**) informal (in bodybuilding) a latissimus muscle.
– ORIGIN 1930s: abbreviation.

lat. ▸ **abbreviation** latitude: *between approximately 40° and 50° S. lat.*

Latakia /ˌlatəˈkiːə/ a seaport on the coast of western Syria, opposite the north-eastern tip of Cyprus; pop. 366,600 (est. 2009).

latch ▸ **noun 1** a metal bar with a catch and lever used for fastening a door or gate. ■ a spring lock for an outer door, which catches when the door is closed and can only be opened from the outside with a key.
2 Electronics a circuit which retains whatever output state results from a momentary input signal until reset by another signal.
▸ **verb** [with obj.] **1** fasten (a door or gate) with a latch: *she latched the door carefully.*
2 [no obj.] Electronics (of a device) become fixed in a particular state.
– PHRASES **on the latch** Brit. (of a door or gate) closed but not locked: *let yourself in, the door's on the latch.*
– PHRASAL VERBS **latch on** (of a breastfeeding baby) get its mouth into the correct position around the nipple. **latch on to** informal **1** attach oneself to (someone) as a constant and usually unwelcome companion: *he spent the whole evening trying to latch on to my friends.* ■ take up (an idea or trend) enthusiastically: *the newspapers latched on to the idea of healthy eating.* ■ Brit. (of a football or rugby player) take advantage of (another player's move) when attacking: *Nevin latched on to a miscued header to smash home the winning goal.* ■ (of one substance) cohere with (another). **2** understand the meaning of (something): [with clause] *she'll soon latch on to what is happening.*
– ORIGIN Old English *læccan* 'take hold of, grasp (physically or mentally)', of Germanic origin.

latchet /ˈlatʃɪt/ ▸ **noun** archaic a narrow thong or lace for fastening a shoe or sandal.
– ORIGIN late Middle English: from Old French *lachet*, variant of *lacet*, from *laz* 'lace'.

latchkey ▸ **noun** (pl. **latchkeys**) a key of an outer door of a house.

latchkey child ▸ **noun** a child who is at home without adult supervision for some part of the day, especially after school until a parent returns from work.

late ▸ **adjective 1** doing something or taking place after the expected, proper, or usual time: *his late arrival* | *she was half an hour **late for** her lunch appointment.*
2 belonging or taking place far on in a particular period: *they won the game with a late goal* | *an elegantly dressed woman in her late fifties.* ■ denoting or belonging to the advanced stage of a historical period or cultural movement: *the late 1960s* | *late Gothic style.* ■ far on in the day or night: *I'm sorry the call is so late* | *it's **too late for** sherry.* ■ flowering or ripening towards the end of the season: *the last late chrysanthemums.*
3 (**the/one's late**) (of a specified person) no longer alive: *the late Francis Bacon* | *her late husband's grave.* ■ no longer having the specified status; former: *a late colleague of mine.*
4 (**latest**) of most recent date: *the latest news.*
▸ **adverb 1** after the expected, proper, or usual time: *she arrived late.*
2 far on in time; towards the end of a period: *it happened late in 1994.* ■ at or until a time far on in the day or night: *now I'm old enough to stay up late.* ■ (**later**) at a time in the near future; soon or afterwards: *I'll see you later* | ***later on** it will be easier.*
3 (**late of**) formerly but not now living or working in a specified place or institution: *Mrs Halford, late of the County Records Office.*
▸ **noun** (**the latest**) the most recent news or fashion: *have you heard the latest?*
– PHRASES **at the latest** no later than the time specified: *all new cars will be required to meet this standard by 1997 at the latest.* **late in the day** (or N. Amer. **game**) at a late stage in proceedings, especially too late to be useful: *it's a bit late in the day to go into all this.* **of late** recently: *she'd been drinking too much of late.*
– ORIGIN Old English *læt* (adjective; also in the sense 'slow, tardy'), *late* (adverb), of Germanic origin; related to German *lass*, from an Indo-European root shared by Latin *lassus* 'weary', LET[1], and LET[2].

latecomer ▸ **noun** a person who arrives late: *latecomers were not admitted before the interval.*

late cut Cricket ▸ **noun** a cut made with a delayed action so as to send the ball to the off side behind the wicket.
▸ **verb** (**late-cut**) [with obj.] hit (the ball) with such a stroke; hit a ball delivered by (the bowler) with such a stroke.

lateen /ləˈtiːn/ (also **lateen sail**) ▸ **noun** a triangular sail on a long yard at an angle of 45° to the mast.
– ORIGIN mid 16th cent.: from French (*voile*) *Latine* 'Latin (sail)', so named because it was common in the Mediterranean.

late-glacial ▸ **adjective** Geology relating to the later stages of the final (Weichsel or Devensian) glaciation, from the beginning of the rise in temperature about 15,000 years ago to the beginning of the Flandrian about 10,000 years ago. Compare with POSTGLACIAL.

lateish ▸ **adjective & adverb** variant spelling of LATISH.

late Latin ▸ **noun** [mass noun] Latin of about AD 200–600.

lately ▸ **adverb** recently; not long ago: *she hasn't been looking too well lately.*
– ORIGIN Old English *lætlīce* 'slowly, tardily' (see LATE, -LY[2]).

late-model ▸ **adjective** chiefly N. Amer. (especially of a car) recently made or of a recent design.

La Tène /la ˈtɛn/ ▸ **noun** [usu. as modifier] Archaeology the second cultural phase of the European Iron Age, following the Hallstatt period (*c.*480 BC) and lasting until the coming of the Romans. This culture represents the height of Celtic power, being characterized by hill forts, rich and elaborate burials, and distinctively crafted artefacts.
– ORIGIN late 19th cent.: named after a district in Switzerland, where remains of the culture were first identified.

lateness ▸ **noun** [mass noun] **1** the fact or quality of happening or arriving after the expected or usual time; unpunctuality: *she wouldn't tolerate lateness in her class.*

2 the fact of being far on in the day or night: *she noticed the lateness of the hour.*

latent ▶ **adjective** (of a quality or state) existing but not yet developed or manifest; hidden or concealed: *they have a huge reserve of latent talent.* ■ Biology lying dormant or hidden until circumstances are suitable for development or manifestation. ■ (of a disease) not yet manifesting the usual symptoms. ■ Physiology (of a microorganism, especially a virus) present in the body without causing disease, but capable of doing so at a later stage, or when transmitted to another body.
– DERIVATIVES **latency** noun, **latently** adverb.
– ORIGIN late Middle English: from Latin *latent-* 'being hidden', from the verb *latere.*

latent heat ▶ **noun** [mass noun] Physics the heat required to convert a solid into a liquid or vapour, or a liquid into a vapour, without change of temperature.

latent image ▶ **noun** Photography an image on an exposed film or print that has not yet been made visible by developing.

latent period ▶ **noun 1** Medicine the period between infection with a virus or other microorganism and the onset of symptoms, or between exposure to radiation and the appearance of a cancer.
2 Physiology the delay between the receipt of a stimulus by a sensory nerve and the response to it.

later (Brit. also **laters**) ▶ **exclamation** informal goodbye for the present; see you later.

-later ▶ **combining form** denoting a person who worships a specified thing: *idolater.*
– ORIGIN from Greek *-latrēs* 'worshipper'.

lateral ▶ **adjective 1** of, at, towards, or from the side or sides: *the plant takes up water through its lateral roots.* ■ Anatomy & Zoology situated on one side or other of the body or of an organ, especially in the region furthest from the median plane. The opposite of MEDIAL. ■ Medicine (of a disease or condition) affecting the side or sides of the body, or confined to one side of the body. ■ Physics acting or placed at right angles to the line of motion or of strain.
2 chiefly Brit. involving lateral thinking: *he's very creative in a lateral way.*
3 Phonetics (of a consonant, especially the English clear *l*) pronounced with partial closure of the air passage by the tongue, which is so placed as to allow the breath to flow on one or both sides of the point of contact.
▶ **noun 1** a side part of something, especially a shoot or branch growing out from the side of a stem.
2 Phonetics a lateral consonant.
3 American Football a pass thrown either sideways or back.
– DERIVATIVES **laterally** adverb.
– ORIGIN late Middle English: from Latin *lateralis,* from *latus, later-* 'side'.

laterality ▶ **noun** [mass noun] dominance of one side of the brain in controlling particular activities or functions, or of one of a pair of organs such as the eyes or hands.

lateralize (also **lateralise**) ▶ **verb** (**be lateralized**) (of the brain) show laterality. ■ [with adverbial] (of an organ, function, or activity) be largely under the control of one or other side of the brain: *this is a function which is usually lateralized on the right.* ■ [with adverbial] Medicine (of a lesion or pathological process) be diagnosed as localized to one or other side of the brain.
– DERIVATIVES **lateralization** noun.

lateral line ▶ **noun** Zoology a visible line along the side of a fish consisting of a series of sense organs which detect pressure and vibration.

lateral thinking ▶ **noun** [mass noun] chiefly Brit. the solving of problems by an indirect and creative approach, typically through viewing the problem in a new and unusual light. Contrasted with VERTICAL THINKING.
– DERIVATIVES **lateral thinker** noun.

lateral ventricle ▶ **noun** Anatomy each of the first and second ventricles in the centre of each cerebral hemisphere of the brain.

Lateran /ˈlatərən/ the site in Rome containing the cathedral church of Rome (a basilica dedicated to St John the Baptist and St John the Evangelist) and the Lateran Palace, where the popes resided until the 14th century.

Lateran Council any of five general councils of the Western Church held in the Lateran Palace in 1123, 1139, 1179, 1215, and 1512–17. The council of 1215 condemned the Albigenses as heretical and clarified the Church doctrine on transubstantiation, the Trinity, and the Incarnation.

Lateran Treaty a concordat signed in 1929 in the Lateran Palace between the kingdom of Italy (represented by Mussolini) and the Holy See (represented by Pope Pius XI), which recognized the papal state under the name Vatican City as fully sovereign and independent.

laterite /ˈlatərʌɪt/ ▶ **noun** [mass noun] a reddish clayey material, hard when dry, forming a topsoil in some tropical or subtropical regions and sometimes used for building. ■ Geology a clayey soil horizon rich in iron and aluminium oxides, formed by weathering of igneous rocks in moist warm climates.
– DERIVATIVES **lateritic** adjective.
– ORIGIN early 19th cent.: from Latin *later* 'brick' + -ITE[1].

latex /ˈleɪtɛks/ ▶ **noun** (pl. **latexes** or **latices** /-tɪsiːz/) [mass noun] a milky fluid found in many plants, such as poppies and spurges, which exudes when the plant is cut and coagulates on exposure to the air. The latex of the rubber tree is the chief source of natural rubber. ■ a synthetic product resembling latex used to make paints, coatings, etc.
– ORIGIN mid 17th cent. (denoting various bodily fluids, especially the watery part of blood): from Latin, literally 'liquid, fluid'.

lath /lɑːθ, laθ/ ▶ **noun** (pl. **laths** /lɑːθs, lɑːðz, laθs/) a thin flat strip of wood, especially one of a series forming a foundation for the plaster of a wall. ■ [mass noun] laths collectively as a building material.
▶ **verb** [with obj.] cover with laths.
– ORIGIN Old English *lætt,* of Germanic origin; related to Dutch *lat* and German *Latte,* also to LATTICE.

lathe /leɪð/ ▶ **noun** a machine for shaping wood, metal, or other material by means of a rotating drive which turns the piece being worked on against changeable cutting tools.
▶ **verb** [with obj.] shape with a lathe.
– ORIGIN Middle English: probably from Old Danish *lad* 'structure, frame', perhaps from Old Norse *hlath* 'pile, heap', related to *hlatha* (see LADE).

lather /ˈlɑːðə, ˈlaðə/ ▶ **noun 1** [mass noun] a frothy white mass of bubbles produced by soap, washing powder, etc. when mixed with water. ■ heavy sweat visible on a horse's coat as a white foam.
2 (**a lather**) informal a state of agitation or nervous excitement: *Dad had got into a right lather by the time I got home.*
▶ **verb 1** form or cause to form a lather: [no obj.] *soap will not lather in hard water.* ■ [with obj.] rub soap on to (the body) until a lather is produced: *she was lathering herself languidly beneath the shower.* ■ (**be/become lathered**) (of a horse) be or become covered with sweat: *his horse was* ***lathered up*** *by the end of the day.*
2 [with obj.] spread (a substance) thickly or liberally: *we lathered the cream on our scones.* ■ cover (something) with liberal amounts of a substance: *she lathered a slice of toast with butter.*
3 [with obj.] informal thrash (someone).
– DERIVATIVES **lathery** adjective.
– ORIGIN Old English *læthor* (denoting washing soda or its froth), *lēthran* (verb), of Germanic origin; related to Old Norse *lauthr* (noun), from an Indo-European root shared by Greek *loutron* 'bath'.

lathi /ˈlɑːtiː/ ▶ **noun** (pl. **lathis**) (in South Asia) a long, heavy iron-bound bamboo stick used as a weapon, especially by police.
– ORIGIN from Hindi *lāṭhī.*

lathyrism /ˈlaθɪrɪz(ə)m/ ▶ **noun** [mass noun] a tropical disease marked by tremors, muscular weakness, and paraplegia, especially prevalent in South Asia. It is commonly attributed to continued consumption of the seeds of the grass pea.
– ORIGIN late 19th cent.: from modern Latin *Lathyrus* (genus name of various leguminous plants) + -ISM.

latices plural form of LATEX.

laticifer /laˈtɪsɪfə/ ▶ **noun** Botany a cell, tissue, or vessel that contains or conducts latex.
– DERIVATIVES **laticiferous** /latɪˈsɪf(ə)rəs/ adjective.
– ORIGIN mid 19th cent.: from Latin *latex, latic-* 'fluid' + *-fer* 'bearing'.

latifundium /ˌlɑːtɪˈfʌndɪəm, ˌlatɪ-/ ▶ **noun** (pl. **latifundia**) a large landed estate or ranch in ancient Rome or more recently in Spain or Latin America, typically worked by peasants or slaves.
– ORIGIN mid 17th cent.: from Latin, from *latus* 'broad' + *fundus* 'landed estate', partly via Spanish.

Latimer /ˈlatɪmə/, Hugh (*c.*1485–1555), English Protestant prelate and martyr. One of Henry VIII's chief advisers when the king broke with the papacy, under Mary I he was condemned for heresy and burnt at the stake at Oxford with Nicholas Ridley.

Latin ▶ **noun 1** [mass noun] the language of ancient Rome and its empire, widely used historically as a language of scholarship and administration.

> Latin is a member of the Italic branch of the Indo-European family of languages. After the decline of the Roman Empire it continued to be a medium of communication among educated people throughout the Middle Ages in Europe and elsewhere, and remained the liturgical language of the Roman Catholic Church until the reforms of the second Vatican Council (1962–5); it is still used for scientific names in biology and astronomy. The Romance languages are derived from it.

2 a native or inhabitant of a country whose language developed from Latin, especially a Latin American. ■ historical an inhabitant of ancient Latium.
3 [mass noun] music of a kind originating in Latin America, characterized by dance rhythms and extensive use of indigenous percussion instruments.
▶ **adjective 1** relating to Latin: *Latin poetry.* ■ relating to the countries using languages, such as French and Spanish, that developed from Latin. ■ relating to the Western or Roman Catholic Church (as historically using Latin for its rites): *the Latin patriarch of Antioch.* ■ historical relating to ancient Latium.
2 relating to or characteristic of Latin American music: *snapping his fingers to a Latin beat.*
– DERIVATIVES **Latinism** noun, **Latinist** noun.
– ORIGIN from Latin *Latinus* 'of Latium' (see LATIUM).

Latina /ləˈtiːnə/ ▶ **noun & adjective** feminine form of LATINO.

Latin America the parts of the American continent where Spanish or Portuguese is the main national language (i.e. Mexico and, in effect, the whole of Central and South America including many of the Caribbean islands).
– DERIVATIVES **Latin American** noun & adjective.

Latinate /ˈlatɪneɪt/ ▶ **adjective** (of language) having the character of Latin: *Latinate oaths.*

Latin Church the Christian Church which originated in the Western Roman Empire, giving allegiance to the Pope of Rome, and historically using Latin for the liturgy; the Roman Catholic Church as distinguished from Orthodox and Uniate Churches.

Latin cross ▶ **noun** a plain cross in which the vertical part below the horizontal is longer than the other three parts.

Latinity ▶ **noun** [mass noun] the use of Latin style or words of Latin origin.

Latinize (also **Latinise**) ▶ **verb** [with obj.] **1** give a Latin or Latinate form to (a word): *his name was Latinized into Confucius.* ■ archaic translate into Latin. ■ [no obj.] archaic use Latin forms or idiom.
2 make (a people) conform to the ideas and customs of the ancient Romans, the Latin peoples, or the Latin Church.
– DERIVATIVES **Latinization** noun.
– ORIGIN late 16th cent.: from late Latin *Latinizare,* from Latin *Latinus* (see LATIN).

Latin lover ▶ **noun** a Mediterranean man popularly characterized as having a romantic, passionate temperament and great sexual prowess.

Latino /ləˈtiːnəʊ/ chiefly N. Amer. ▶ **noun** (fem. **Latina**; pl. **Latinos** or **Latinas**) a Latin American inhabitant of the United States.
▶ **adjective** relating to Latinos or Latinas.
– ORIGIN Latin American Spanish, probably a special use of Spanish *latino* (see LATIN).

Latin square ▶ **noun** an arrangement of letters or symbols that each occur *n* times, in a square array of n^2 compartments so that no letter appears twice in the same row or column.

latish (also **lateish**) ▶ **adjective & adverb** fairly late: [as adv.] *Margaret came in latish.*

latissimus /lɑːˈtɪsɪməs/ (also **latissimus dorsi** /ˈdɔːsʌɪ, -siː/) ▶ **noun** (pl. **latissimi** /lɑːˈtɪsɪmʌɪ, -miː/) Anatomy either of a pair of large, roughly triangular muscles covering the lower part of the back, extending from the sacral, lumbar, and lower thoracic vertebrae to the armpits.
– ORIGIN early 17th cent.: modern Latin, from *musculus latissimus dorsi,* literally 'broadest muscle of the back'.

latitude /ˈlatɪtjuːd/ ▶ **noun 1** the angular distance of a place north or south of the earth's equator, or of the equator of a celestial object, usually expressed in degrees and minutes: *at a latitude of 51° N* | [mass noun]

L

lines of latitude. ■ (**latitudes**) regions, especially with reference to their temperature and distance from the equator: *temperate latitudes* | *northern latitudes*.

2 [mass noun] scope for freedom of action or thought: *journalists have considerable latitude in criticizing public figures*.

3 Photography the range of exposures for which an emulsion or printing paper will give acceptable contrast.

– DERIVATIVES **latitudinal** adjective, **latitudinally** adverb.

– ORIGIN late Middle English: from Latin *latitudo* 'breadth', from *latus* 'broad'.

latitudinarian /ˌlatɪtjuːdɪˈnɛːrɪən/ ▶ **adjective** allowing latitude in religion; showing no preference among varying creeds and forms of worship.

▶ **noun** a person with a latitudinarian attitude.

– DERIVATIVES **latitudinarianism** noun.

– ORIGIN mid 17th cent.: from Latin *latitudo* 'breadth' (see LATITUDE) + -ARIAN. The term was first applied in a derogatory sense to more liberal and tolerant Anglican clerics.

Latium /ˈleɪʃɪəm/ an ancient region of west central Italy, west of the Apennines and south of the River Tiber. Settled during the early part of the 1st millennium BC by a branch of the Indo-European people known as the Latini, it had become dominated by Rome by the end of the 4th century BC; it is now part of the modern region of Lazio.

latke /ˈlʌtkə/ ▶ **noun** (in Jewish cookery) a pancake, especially one made with grated potato.

– ORIGIN Yiddish.

Latona /ləˈtəʊnə/ Roman Mythology Roman name for LETO.

La Tour /la ˈtʊə/, French /la tuʀ/, Georges de (1593–1652), French painter. He is best known for his nocturnal religious scenes and his subtle portrayal of candlelight. Notable works: *St Joseph the Carpenter* (1645) and *The Denial of St Peter* (1650).

latria /ləˈtrʌɪə, ˈlatrɪə/ ▶ **noun** [mass noun] (in the Roman Catholic Church) supreme worship allowed to God alone. Compare with DULIA.

– ORIGIN early 16th cent.: from late Latin, from Greek *latreia* 'worship', from *latreuein* 'serve'.

latrine /ləˈtriːn/ ▶ **noun** a toilet, especially a communal one in a camp or barracks.

– ORIGIN Middle English (rare before the mid 19th cent.): via French from Latin *latrina*, contraction of *lavatrina*, from *lavare* 'to wash'.

-latry ▶ **combining form** denoting worship of a specified thing: *idolatry*.

– ORIGIN from Greek *-latria* 'worship'.

latte /ˈlɑːteɪ, ˈlateɪ/ ▶ **noun** a drink made by adding a shot of espresso coffee to a glass or cup of frothy steamed milk.

– ORIGIN from Italian (*caffè*) *latte*, literally 'milk (coffee)'.

latten /ˈlat(ə)n/ ▶ **noun** [mass noun] historical an alloy of copper and zinc resembling brass, hammered into thin sheets and used to make monumental brasses and church ornaments.

– ORIGIN Middle English: from Old French *laton*, of unknown origin.

latter ▶ **adjective** [attrib.] **1** occurring or situated nearer to the end of something than to the beginning: *the latter half of 1989* | *heart disease dogged his latter years*. ■ recent: *the project has had low cash flows in latter years*.

2 (**the latter**) denoting the second or second mentioned of two people or things: *the Russians could advance into either Germany or Austria—they chose the latter option* | [as noun] *the President appoints the Prime Minister and, on the latter's advice, the rest of the government*.

– ORIGIN Old English *lætra* 'slower', comparative of *læt* (see LATE).

> **USAGE** It is not considered good writing style to use **latter** to refer to more than two things. For an explanation, see **USAGE** at **FORMER¹**.

latter-day ▶ **adjective** [attrib.] modern or contemporary, especially when mirroring some person or thing of the past: *the book is built round the story of the Flood and a latter-day Noah*.

Latter-Day Saints (abbrev.: **LDS**) ▶ **plural noun** the Mormons' name for themselves.

latterly ▶ **adverb** recently: *latterly, his painting has shown a new freedom of expression*. ■ in the later stages of something, especially of a person's life: *he worked on the paper for fifty years, latterly as its political editor*.

lattice ▶ **noun** a structure consisting of strips of wood or metal crossed and fastened together with square or diamond-shaped spaces left between, used as a screen or fence or as a support for climbing plants. ■ an interlaced structure or pattern resembling a lattice: *the lattice of branches above her*. ■ Physics a regular repeated three-dimensional arrangement of atoms, ions, or molecules in a metal or other crystalline solid.

– ORIGIN Middle English: from Old French *lattis*, from *latte* 'lath', of Germanic origin.

latticed ▶ **adjective** decorated with or in the form of a lattice: *a latticed screen*.

lattice energy ▶ **noun** Chemistry a measure of the energy contained in the crystal lattice of a compound, equal to the energy that would be released if the component ions were brought together from infinity.

lattice frame (also **lattice girder**) ▶ **noun** an iron or steel structure consisting of two horizontal beams connected by diagonal struts.

lattice window ▶ **noun** a window with small panes set in diagonally crossing strips of lead.

latticework ▶ **noun** [mass noun] interlacing strips of wood, metal, or other material forming a lattice.

latticinio /ˌlatɪˈtʃiːnjəʊ/ (also **latticino** /-nəʊ/) ▶ **noun** [mass noun] an opaque white glass used in threads to decorate clear Venetian glass.

– ORIGIN Italian, literally 'dairy produce', from medieval Latin *lacticinium*.

Latvia /ˈlatvɪə/ a country on the eastern shore of the Baltic Sea, between Estonia and Lithuania; pop. 2,231,500 (est. 2009); official language, Latvian; capital, Riga.

> Latvia was annexed by Russia in the 18th century after periods of Polish and Swedish rule. It was proclaimed an independent republic in 1918, but in 1940 was annexed by the Soviet Union as a constituent republic. In 1991, on the break-up of the Soviet Union, Latvia became an independent republic once again.

Latvian ▶ **noun 1** a native or inhabitant of Latvia.

2 [mass noun] the official language of Latvia, which belongs to the Baltic branch of the Indo-European family and has about 1.5 million speakers.

▶ **adjective** relating to Latvia or its language.

Laud /lɔːd/, William (1573–1645), English prelate, Archbishop of Canterbury 1633–45. His attempts to restore some pre-Reformation practices in England and Scotland aroused great hostility and were a contributory cause of the English Civil War. He was executed for treason.

laud /lɔːd/ ▶ **verb** [with obj.] formal praise (a person or their achievements) highly: *the obituary lauded him as a great statesman and soldier* | (as adj., with submodifier **lauded**) *her much-lauded rendering of Lady Macbeth*.

▶ **noun** [mass noun] archaic praise: *all glory, laud, and honour to Thee Redeemer King*.

– ORIGIN late Middle English: the noun from Old French *laude*, the verb from Latin *laudare*, both from Latin *laus*, *laud-* 'praise' (see also LAUDS).

laudable ▶ **adjective** (of an action, idea, or aim) deserving praise and commendation: *laudable though the aim might be, the results have been criticized*.

– DERIVATIVES **laudability** noun, **laudably** adverb.

– ORIGIN late Middle English: from Latin *laudabilis*, from *laus*, *laud-* 'praise'.

laudanum /ˈlɔːd(ə)nəm, ˈlɒ-/ ▶ **noun** [mass noun] an alcoholic solution containing morphine, prepared from opium and formerly used as a narcotic painkiller.

– ORIGIN mid 16th cent. (applied to various preparations containing opium): modern Latin, the name given by Paracelsus to a costly medicament of which opium was believed to be the active ingredient; perhaps a variant of Latin *ladanum* (see LADANUM).

laudation /lɔːˈdeɪʃ(ə)n/ ▶ **noun** [mass noun] formal praise; commendation.

– ORIGIN late Middle English: from Latin *laudatio(n-)*, from the verb *laudare* (see LAUD).

laudatory /ˈlɔːdət(ə)ri/ ▶ **adjective** (of speech or writing) expressing praise and commendation.

– ORIGIN mid 16th cent.: from late Latin *laudatorius*, from *laudat-* 'praised', from the verb *laudare* (see LAUD).

Lauder /ˈlɔːdə/, Sir Harry (1870–1950), Scottish music-hall comedian; born *Hugh MacLennan Lauder*. He became highly popular singing songs such as 'Roamin' in the Gloamin'', and entertained troops at home and abroad in both world wars.

lauds /lɔːdz/ ▶ **noun** a service of morning prayer in the Divine Office of the Western Christian Church, traditionally said or chanted at daybreak, though historically it was often held with matins on the previous night.

– ORIGIN Middle English: from the frequent use, in Psalms 148–150, of the Latin imperative *laudate!* 'praise ye!' (see also LAUD).

laugh ▶ **verb** [no obj.] make the spontaneous sounds and movements of the face and body that are the instinctive expressions of lively amusement and sometimes also of derision: *he rarely smiled or laughed* | *she couldn't help* **laughing at** *his jokes* | *we* **fell about laughing**. ■ (**laugh at**) treat with ridicule or scorn. ■ (**laugh something off**) dismiss something by treating it in a light-hearted way: *he laughed off suggestions that the company was in trouble*. ■ (**be laughing**) informal be in a fortunate or successful position: *if next year's model is as successful, Ford will be laughing*.

▶ **noun 1** an act of laughing: *she gave a loud, silly laugh*.

2 (**a laugh**) informal something that causes laughter; a source of fun, amusement, or derision: *come along, it'll be a laugh* | *she decided to play along with him* **for a laugh** | *that's a laugh, the idea of you cooking a meal!* ■ a person who is good fun or amusing company: *I like Peter—he's* **a good laugh**.

– PHRASES **be laughing all the way to the bank** informal be making a great deal of money very easily. **have the last laugh** be finally vindicated, thus confounding earlier scepticism. **he who laughs last laughs longest** proverb don't rejoice too soon, in case your delight at your own good fortune is premature. **laugh one's head off** laugh heartily or uncontrollably. **laugh in someone's face** show open contempt for someone by laughing rudely at them in their presence: *I remonstrated with him but he just laughed in my face* | figurative *vandals and muggers who laugh in the face of the law*. **the laugh is on me** (or **you**, **him**, etc.) the tables are turned and now the other person is the one who appears ridiculous: *all the critics had laughed at him—well, the laugh was on them now*. **laugh like a drain** Brit. informal laugh raucously. **a laugh a minute** very funny: *it's a laugh a minute when Lois gets together with her dad*. **laugh on the other side of one's face** (or N. Amer. **out of the other side of one's mouth**) be discomfited after feeling satisfaction or confidence about something. **laugh someone/thing out of court** Brit. dismiss with contempt as being obviously ridiculous. **laugh oneself silly** (or **sick**) laugh uncontrollably or for a long time. **laugh something to scorn** dated ridicule something. **laugh up one's sleeve** be secretly or inwardly amused. **no laughing matter** something serious that should not be joked about: *heavy snoring is no laughing matter*. **play something for laughs** (of a performer) try to arouse laughter in an audience, especially in inappropriate circumstances.

– ORIGIN Old English *hlæhhan*, *hliehhan*, of Germanic origin; related to Dutch and German *lachen*, also to LAUGHTER.

laughable ▶ **adjective** so ludicrous as to be amusing: *if it didn't make me so angry it would be laughable*.

– DERIVATIVES **laughably** adverb [as submodifier] *his antics were laughably pretentious*.

laugher ▶ **noun 1** a person who laughs.

2 N. Amer. informal a sporting match or competition which is so easily won by one team or competitor that it seems absurd.

laughing gas ▶ **noun** non-technical term for NITROUS OXIDE.

laughing hyena ▶ **noun** another term for SPOTTED HYENA.

laughing jackass ▶ **noun** Austral. dated the laughing kookaburra. See KOOKABURRA.

laughingly ▶ **adverb** in an amused way; with laughter. ■ with amused ridicule or ludicrous inappropriateness: *we finally reached what we laughingly called civilization*.

laughing stock ▶ **noun** a person subjected to general mockery or ridicule.

laughing-thrush ▶ **noun** a gregarious thrush-like babbler of South and SE Asia, typically with dark grey or brown plumage and a boldly marked head, and a cackling call. ● Genus *Garrulax*, family Timaliidae: many species.

laughter ▶ **noun** [mass noun] the action or sound of laughing: *he roared with laughter*.

L

– ORIGIN Old English *hleahtor*, of Germanic origin; related to German *Gelächter*, also to LAUGH.

Laughton /ˈlɔːt(ə)n/, Charles (1899–1962), British-born American actor. He is remembered for character roles such as Henry VIII (*The Private Life of Henry VIII*, 1933); he also played Quasimodo in *The Hunchback of Notre Dame* (1939).

launce /lɑːns, lans/ ▶ **noun** another term for SAND EEL.
– ORIGIN early 17th cent.: early variant of LANCE (because of its shape).

Launcelot variant spelling of LANCELOT.

Launceston /ˈlɔːns(ə)stən/ a city in northern Tasmania, on the Tamar estuary, the second-largest city of the island; pop. 99,647 (2008).

launch[1] ▶ **verb** [with obj.] **1** set (a boat) in motion by pushing it or allowing it to roll into the water: *the town's lifeboat was launched to rescue the fishermen.* ■ set (a newly built ship or boat) afloat for the first time with an official ceremony: *the ship was launched in 1843 by Prince Albert.* ■ send (a missile, satellite, or spacecraft) on its course: *they launched two Scud missiles.* ■ [with obj. and adverbial of direction] hurl (something) forcefully: *a chair was launched at him.* ■ [with adverbial of direction] (**launch oneself**) make a sudden energetic movement: *I launched myself out of bed.* ■ utter (criticism or a threat) vehemently: *he launched a biting attack on BBC chiefs.*
2 start or set in motion (an activity or enterprise): *the government is to launch a £1.25 million publicity campaign.* ■ introduce (a new product or publication) to the public for the first time: *two new Ford models are to be launched in the US next year.*
▶ **noun** an act or instance of launching something: *the launch of a new campaign against drinking and driving.* ■ an occasion at which a new product or publication is introduced to the public: *a book launch.*
– PHRASAL VERBS **launch into** begin (something) energetically and enthusiastically: *he launched into a two-hour sales pitch.* **launch out** make a start on a new and challenging enterprise: *she wasn't brave enough to launch out by herself.*
– ORIGIN Middle English (in the sense 'hurl a missile, discharge with force'): from Anglo-Norman French *launcher*, variant of Old French *lancier* (see LANCE).

launch[2] ▶ **noun** a large motor boat used for short trips. ■ historical the largest boat carried on an armed sailing ship.
– ORIGIN late 17th cent.: from Spanish *lancha* 'pinnace', perhaps from Malay *lancharan*, from *lanchar* 'swift, nimble'.

launcher ▶ **noun** a structure that holds a rocket or missile, typically one used as a weapon, during launching: *a rocket launcher* | *a grenade launcher.* ■ a rocket that is used to convey a satellite or spacecraft into orbit.

launch pad (also **launching pad**) ▶ **noun** the area on which a rocket stands for launching, typically consisting of a platform with a supporting structure.

launch vehicle ▶ **noun** a rocket-powered vehicle used to send artificial satellites or spacecraft into space.

launder ▶ **verb** [with obj.] **1** wash and iron (clothes or linen): *he wasn't used to laundering his own bed linen* | (as adj., with submodifier **laundered**) *freshly laundered sheets.*
2 informal conceal the origins of (money obtained illegally) by transfers involving foreign banks or legitimate businesses. ■ alter (information) to make it appear more acceptable: *we began to notice attempts to launder the data retrospectively.*
▶ **noun** a trough for holding or conveying water, especially (in mining) one used for washing ore. ■ a channel for conveying molten metal from a furnace or container to a ladle or mould.
– DERIVATIVES **launderer** noun.
– ORIGIN Middle English (as a noun denoting a person who washes linen): contraction of *lavender*, from Old French *lavandier*, based on Latin *lavanda* 'things to be washed', from *lavare* 'to wash'.

launderette (also **laundrette**) ▶ **noun** Brit. an establishment with coin-operated washing machines and dryers for public use.

laundress ▶ **noun** a woman who is employed to launder clothes and linen.

laundromat ▶ **noun** N. Amer. (trademark in the US) a launderette.
– ORIGIN 1940s (originally US, as the proprietary name of a washing machine): blend of LAUNDER and AUTOMATIC.

laundry ▶ **noun** (pl. **laundries**) **1** [mass noun] clothes and linen that need to be washed or that have been newly washed: *piles of dirty laundry.* ■ the action or process of washing clothes: *cooking and laundry were undertaken by domestic staff.*
2 a room in a house, hotel, or institution where clothes and linen can be washed and ironed. ■ a company washing and ironing clothes and linen commercially.
– ORIGIN early 16th cent.: contraction of Middle English *lavendry*, from Old French *lavanderie*, from *lavandier* 'person who washes linen' (see LAUNDER).

laundry list ▶ **noun** a long or exhaustive list of people or things.

laundryman ▶ **noun** (pl. **laundrymen**) a man who is employed to launder clothes and linen.

Laurasia /lɔːˈreɪʒə, -ʃə/ a vast continental area believed to have existed in the northern hemisphere and to have resulted from the break-up of Pangaea in Mesozoic times. It comprised the present North America, Greenland, Europe, and most of Asia north of the Himalayas.
– DERIVATIVES **Laurasian** adjective.

laureate /ˈlɒrɪət, ˈlɔː-/ ▶ **noun** a person who is honoured with an award for outstanding creative or intellectual achievement: *a Nobel laureate.* ■ short for POET LAUREATE.
▶ **adjective** literary wreathed with laurel as a mark of honour. ■ (of a crown or wreath) consisting of laurel.
– DERIVATIVES **laureateship** noun.
– ORIGIN late Middle English (as an adjective): from Latin *laureatus*, from *laurea* 'laurel wreath', from *laurus* 'laurel'.

laurel ▶ **noun 1** any of a number of shrubs and other plants with dark green glossy leaves, in particular: ● short for CHERRY LAUREL ● the bay tree. See BAY[2].
2 an aromatic evergreen shrub related to the bay tree, several kinds of which form forests in tropical and warm countries. ● Family Lauraceae: many genera and species.
3 (usu. **laurels**) the foliage of the bay tree woven into a wreath or crown and worn on the head as an emblem of victory or mark of honour in classical times. ■ honour or praise for an achievement: *she has rightly won laurels for this brilliantly perceptive first novel.*
▶ **verb** (**laurels, laurelling, laurelled**; US **laurels, laureling, laureled**) [with obj.] honour by adorning with a laurel or presenting with an award.
– PHRASES **look to one's laurels** be careful not to lose one's superior position to a rival. **rest on one's laurels** be so satisfied with what one has already done or achieved that one makes no further effort.
– ORIGIN Middle English *lorer*, from Old French *lorier*, from Provençal *laurier*, from earlier *laur*, from Latin *laurus*.

Laurel and Hardy an American comedy duo consisting of **Stan Laurel** (born *Arthur Stanley Jefferson*) (1890–1965) and **Oliver Hardy** (1892–1957). British-born Stan Laurel played the scatterbrained and often tearful innocent, Oliver Hardy his pompous, overbearing, and frequently exasperated friend. They brought their distinctive slapstick comedy to many films from 1927 onwards.

Laurence, (Jean) Margaret (1926–87), Canadian novelist. Her life in Somalia and Ghana (1950–7) influenced her early work, including *This Side Jordan* (1960). Other notable works: *The Stone Angel* (1964).

Laurentian Plateau /lɒˈrɛnʃ(ə)n/ another name for CANADIAN SHIELD.
– ORIGIN *Laurentian* from Latin *Laurentius* 'Lawrence' (from St *Lawrence* River) + -AN.

Laurier /ˈlɔːrɪeɪ/, Sir Wilfrid (1841–1919), Canadian Liberal statesman, Prime Minister 1896–1911. He was Canada's first French-Canadian and Roman Catholic Prime Minister.

laurustinus /ˌlɒrəˈstʌɪnəs, ˌlɔː-/ ▶ **noun** an evergreen winter-flowering viburnum with dense glossy green leaves and white or pink flowers, native to the Mediterranean area. ● *Viburnum tinus*, family Caprifoliaceae.
– ORIGIN early 17th cent.: modern Latin, from Latin *laurus* 'laurel' + *tinus* 'wild laurel'.

Lausanne /ləʊˈzan/ a town in SW Switzerland, on the north shore of Lake Geneva; pop. 119,180 (2007).

Lausitzer Neisse /ˌlaʊzɪtsə ˈnʌɪsə/ German name for NEISSE (sense 1).

lav ▶ **noun** informal a lavatory.
– ORIGIN early 20th cent.: abbreviation.

lava ▶ **noun** [mass noun] hot molten or semi-fluid rock erupted from a volcano or fissure, or solid rock resulting from cooling of this.
– ORIGIN mid 18th cent.: from Italian (Neapolitan dialect), denoting the lava stream from Vesuvius, but originally denoting a stream caused by sudden rain, from *lavare* 'to wash', from Latin.

lavabo /ləˈveɪbəʊ, ləˈvɑː-/ ▶ **noun** (pl. **lavabos**) **1** (in the Roman Catholic Church) a towel or basin used for the ritual washing of the celebrant's hands at the offertory of the Mass. ■ [mass noun] ritual washing of this type.
2 /ˈlavəbəʊ/ a trough for washing in a monastery. ■ dated a washbasin or toilet.
– ORIGIN mid 18th cent.: from Latin, literally 'I will wash', in *Lavabo inter innocentes manus meas* 'I will wash my hands in innocence' (Ps. 26:6), which was recited at the washing of hands in the Roman rite.

lava dome ▶ **noun** a mound of viscous lava which has been extruded from a volcanic vent.

lava flow ▶ **noun** a mass of flowing or solidified lava.

lavage /ˈlavɪdʒ, ləˈvɑːʒ/ ▶ **noun** Medicine washing out of a body cavity, such as the colon or stomach, with water or a medicated solution.
– ORIGIN late 18th cent. (in the general sense 'washing, a wash'): from French, from *laver* 'to wash'.

lava lamp ▶ **noun** a transparent electric lamp containing a viscous liquid in which a brightly coloured waxy substance is suspended, rising and falling in irregular and constantly changing shapes.

lavatera /ˌlavəˈtɛːrə/ ▶ **noun** a plant of a genus that includes the tree mallow. ● Genus *Lavatera*, family Malvaceae.
– ORIGIN modern Latin, named after the brothers *Lavater*, 17th- and 18th-cent. Swiss naturalists.

lavatorial ▶ **adjective** relating to or resembling lavatories: *the lavatorial utility that was a feature of subway design.* ■ chiefly Brit. (of conversation or humour) characterized by undue reference to toilets and their use: *the comic's lavatorial schoolboy humour appealed to many people.*

L

lavatory ▶ **noun** (pl. **lavatories**) a toilet.
– ORIGIN late Middle English: from late Latin *lavatorium* 'place for washing', from Latin *lavare* 'to wash'. The word originally denoted something in which to wash, such as a bath or piscina, later (mid 17th cent.) a room with washing facilities; the current sense dates from the 19th cent.

lavatory paper ▶ **noun** Brit. toilet paper.

lava tube (also **lava tunnel**) ▶ **noun** a natural tunnel within a solidified lava flow, formerly occupied by flowing molten lava.

lave /leɪv/ ▶ **verb** [with obj.] literary wash: *she ran cold water in the basin, laving her face and hands.* ■ (of water) wash against or over (something): *the sea below laved the shore with small, agitated waves.*
– DERIVATIVES **lavation** noun.
– ORIGIN Old English *lafian*, from Latin *lavare* 'to wash'; reinforced in Middle English by Old French *laver*.

lavender ▶ **noun** [mass noun] **1** a small aromatic evergreen shrub of the mint family, with narrow leaves and bluish-purple flowers, used in perfumery and medicine. ● Genus *Lavandula*, family Labiatae. ■ (also **lavender oil**) a scented oil distilled from lavender flowers. ■ used in names of similar plants, e.g. **cotton lavender**, **sea lavender**. ■ informal used in reference to effeminacy or homosexuality: *Rick is so hard-boiled that any touch of lavender is wiped away.* ■ dated used in reference to refinement or gentility: [as modifier] *she had a certain lavender charm.*
2 a pale blue colour with a trace of mauve.
▶ **verb** [with obj.] perfume with lavender.
– ORIGIN Middle English: from Anglo-Norman French *lavendre*, based on medieval Latin *lavandula*.

lavender cotton ▶ **noun** another term for COTTON LAVENDER.

lavender water ▶ **noun** [mass noun] a perfume made from distilled lavender, alcohol, and ambergris.

Laver /ˈleɪvə/, Rod (b.1938), Australian tennis player; full name *Rodney George Laver*. In 1962 he became the second man (after Don Budge in 1938) to win the four major singles championships (British, American, French, and Australian) in one year; in 1969 he was the first to repeat this.

laver[1] /ˈlɑːvə, ˈleɪvə/ (also **purple laver**) ▶ **noun** [mass noun] an edible seaweed with thin sheet-like fronds of a reddish-purple and green colour which becomes black when dry. Laver typically grows on exposed

shores, but in Japan it is cultivated in estuaries.
● *Porphyra umbilicaulis*, division Rhodophyta.
– ORIGIN late Old English (as the name of a water plant mentioned by Pliny), from Latin. The current sense dates from the early 17th cent.

laver² /ˈleɪvə/ ▶ noun archaic or literary a basin or similar container used for washing oneself. ■ (in biblical use) a large brass bowl used by Jewish priests for ritual washing.
– ORIGIN Middle English: from Old French *laveoir*, from late Latin *lavatorium* 'place for washing' (see LAVATORY).

laver bread ▶ noun [mass noun] a Welsh dish of laver which is boiled, dipped in oatmeal, and fried.
– ORIGIN early 18th cent.: *laver* from LAVER¹.

lavish ▶ adjective sumptuously rich, elaborate, or luxurious: *a lavish banquet.* ■ (of a person) very generous or extravagant: *he was lavish with his hospitality.* ■ spent or given in profusion: *lavish praise.*
▶ verb [with obj.] (**lavish something on**) bestow something in generous or extravagant quantities on: *the media couldn't lavish enough praise on the film.* ■ (**lavish someone with**) give someone generous amounts of: *he was lavished with gifts.*
– DERIVATIVES **lavishly** adverb, **lavishness** noun.
– ORIGIN late Middle English (as a noun denoting profusion): from Old French *lavasse* 'deluge of rain', from *laver* 'to wash', from Latin *lavare*.

Lavoisier /laˈvwʌzɪeɪ/, French /lavwazje/, Antoine Laurent (1743–94), French scientist, regarded as the father of modern chemistry. He caused a revolution in chemistry by his description of combustion as the combination of substances with air, or more specifically the gas oxygen.

Law, (Andrew) Bonar (1858–1923), Canadian-born British Conservative statesman, Prime Minister 1922–3. He was leader of the Conservative Party 1911–21. He retired in 1921, but returned in 1922, following Lloyd George's resignation, to become Prime Minister for six months.

L

law ▶ noun **1** [mass noun] (often **the law**) the system of rules which a particular country or community recognizes as regulating the actions of its members and which it may enforce by the imposition of penalties: ***shooting the birds is against the law*** | *they were taken to court for* ***breaking the law*** | [as modifier] *law enforcement.* ■ [count noun] an individual rule as part of such a system: *a new law was passed to make divorce easier and simpler.* ■ such systems as a subject of study or as the basis of the legal profession: *he was still practising law* | [as modifier] *a law firm.* ■ statute law and the common law. Compare with EQUITY. ■ something regarded as having binding force or effect: *he had supreme control—what he said was law.* ■ (**the law**) informal the police: *he'd never been in trouble with the law in his life.*
2 a rule defining correct procedure or behaviour in a sport: *the laws of the game.*
3 a statement of fact, deduced from observation, to the effect that a particular natural or scientific phenomenon always occurs if certain conditions are present: *the second law of thermodynamics.* ■ a generalization based on a fact or event perceived to be recurrent: *the first law of American corporate life is that dead wood floats.*
4 [mass noun] the body of divine commandments as expressed in the Bible or other religious texts. ■ (**the Law**) the Pentateuch as distinct from the other parts of the Hebrew Bible (the Prophets and the Writings). ■ (also **the Law of Moses**) the precepts of the Pentateuch.
– PHRASES **at** (or **in**) **law** according to or concerned with the laws of a country: *an agreement enforceable at law* | *a barrister-at-law.* **be a law unto oneself** behave in a manner that is not conventional or predictable. **go to law** Brit. resort to legal action in order to settle a matter. **law and order** a situation characterized by respect for and obedience to the rules of a society. **the law of the jungle** see JUNGLE. **lay down the law** issue instructions to other people in an authoritative or dogmatic way. **take the law into one's own hands** punish someone for an offence according to one's own ideas of justice, especially in an illegal or violent way. **take someone to law** initiate legal proceedings against someone. **there's no law against it** informal said to assert that one is doing nothing wrong, especially in response to an actual or implied criticism.
– ORIGIN Old English *lagu*, from Old Norse *lag* 'something laid down or fixed', of Germanic origin and related to LAY¹.

law-abiding ▶ adjective obedient to the laws of society: *a law-abiding citizen.*
– DERIVATIVES **law-abidingness** noun.

law agent ▶ noun (in Scotland) a solicitor.

lawbreaker ▶ noun a person who breaks the law.
– DERIVATIVES **lawbreaking** noun & adjective.

law centre ▶ noun (in the UK) an independent publicly funded advisory service on legal matters.

Law Commission (in the UK) a body of legal advisers responsible for systematically reviewing the law of England and Wales, or of Scotland, which recommends changes and the removal of obsolete legislation.

law court ▶ noun a court of law.

Lawd (also **Lawdy**) ▶ exclamation non-standard spelling of LORD, used in representing black speech: *Good Lawd, Zora!*

lawful ▶ adjective conforming to, permitted by, or recognized by law or rules: *it is an offence to carry a weapon in public without lawful authority.* ■ dated (of a child) born within a lawful marriage.
– DERIVATIVES **lawfully** adverb, **lawfulness** noun.

lawgiver ▶ noun a person who draws up and enacts laws.

lawks ▶ exclamation dated (especially among cockneys) expressing surprise, awe, or consternation: *Lawks, girl, where've you sprung from?*
– ORIGIN mid 18th cent.: alteration of LORD.

lawless ▶ adjective not governed by or obedient to laws; characterized by a lack of civic order: *it was a lawless, anarchic city.*
– DERIVATIVES **lawlessly** adverb, **lawlessness** noun.

law lord ▶ noun (in the UK) a member of the House of Lords qualified to perform its legal work.

lawmaker ▶ noun a legislator.
– DERIVATIVES **lawmaking** adjective & noun.

lawman ▶ noun (pl. **lawmen**) (in the US) a law-enforcement officer, especially a sheriff.

lawn¹ ▶ noun an area of short, regularly mown grass in the garden of a house or park.
– DERIVATIVES **lawned** adjective, **lawny** adjective.
– ORIGIN mid 16th cent.: alteration of dialect *laund* 'glade, pasture', from Old French *launde* 'wooded district, heath', of Celtic origin. The current sense dates from the mid 18th cent.

lawn² ▶ noun [mass noun] a fine linen or cotton fabric used for making clothes.
– DERIVATIVES **lawny** adjective.
– ORIGIN Middle English: probably from *Laon*, the name of a city in France important for linen manufacture.

lawn bowling ▶ noun North American term for BOWLS.

lawn chair ▶ noun N. Amer. a folding chair for use out of doors.

lawnmower ▶ noun a machine for cutting the grass on a lawn.

lawn party ▶ noun N. Amer. a garden party.

lawn tennis ▶ noun [mass noun] dated or formal the usual form of tennis, played with a soft ball on an open court.

law of averages ▶ noun the supposed principle that future events are likely to turn out so that they balance any past deviation from a presumed average.

law office ▶ noun N. Amer. a lawyer's office.

Law Officer (in full **Law Officer of the Crown**) ▶ noun (in England and Wales) the Attorney General or the Solicitor General, or (in Scotland) the Lord Advocate or the Solicitor General for Scotland.

law of mass action Chemistry ▶ noun the principle that the rate of a chemical reaction is proportional to the concentrations of the reacting substances.

law of nations ▶ noun [mass noun] Law international law.

law of nature ▶ noun **1** another term for NATURAL LAW (sense 1, sense 2).
2 informal a regularly occurring or apparently inevitable phenomenon observable in human society.

law of parsimony ▶ noun see PARSIMONY.

law of succession ▶ noun the law regulating the inheritance of property. ■ (**Law of Succession**) the law regulating the appointment of a new monarch or head of state.

Lawrence¹, D. H. (1885–1930), English novelist, poet, and essayist; full name *David Herbert Lawrence.* His work is characterized by its condemnation of industrial society and by its frank exploration of sexual relationships, as in *Lady Chatterley's Lover*, originally published in Italy in 1928, but not available in England in unexpurgated form until 1960. Other notable works: *Sons and Lovers* (1913) and *Women in Love* (1921).
– DERIVATIVES **Lawrentian** adjective.

Lawrence², Sir Thomas (1769–1830), English painter. He achieved success with his full-length portrait (1789) of Queen Charlotte, the wife of King George III, and by 1810 he was recognized as the leading portrait painter of his time.

Lawrence³, T. E. (1888–1935), British soldier and writer; full name *Thomas Edward Lawrence*; known as **Lawrence of Arabia**. From 1916 onwards he helped to organize the Arab revolt against the Turks in the Middle East, contributing to General Allenby's eventual victory in Palestine in 1918. Lawrence described this period in *The Seven Pillars of Wisdom* (1926).

Lawrence, St (d.258), Roman martyr and deacon of Rome; Latin name *Laurentius.* According to tradition, Lawrence was ordered by the prefect of Rome to deliver up the treasure of the Church; when in response to this order he presented the poor people of Rome to the prefect, he was roasted to death on a gridiron. Feast day, 10 August.

lawrencium /lɒˈrɛnsɪəm/ ▶ noun [mass noun] the chemical element of atomic number 103, a radioactive metal of the actinide series. Lawrencium does not occur naturally and was first made by bombarding californium with boron nuclei. (Symbol: **Lr**)
– ORIGIN 1960s: modern Latin, named after the American physicist E. O. *Lawrence*, who founded the laboratory in which it was produced.

Law Society the professional body responsible for regulating solicitors in England and Wales, established in 1825.

Lawson's cypress ▶ noun a slender North American conifer with dense foliage and lower branches arising at ground level. It is widely grown for timber and as an ornamental with many cultivars. ● *Chamaecyparis lawsoniana*, family Cupressaceae.
– ORIGIN mid 19th cent.: named after Peter *Lawson* (died 1820) and his son Charles (1794–1873), the Scottish nurserymen who first cultivated it.

lawsuit ▶ noun a claim or dispute brought to a law court for adjudication.

law term ▶ noun Brit. a period appointed for the sitting of law courts.

lawyer ▶ noun a person who practises or studies law, especially (in the UK) a solicitor or a barrister or (in the US) an attorney.
▶ verb [no obj.] N. Amer. practise law; work as a lawyer. ■ [with obj.] (of a lawyer) work on the legal aspects of (a contract, lawsuit, etc.).
– DERIVATIVES **lawyerly** adjective.

lawyer's wig ▶ noun another term for SHAGGY INK CAP.

lawyer vine (also **lawyer cane**) ▶ noun an Australian climbing palm which is thickly covered in sharp spines and recurved hooks. It grows in rainforest, where groups may form dense tangled thickets.
● Genus *Calamus*, family Palmae.
– ORIGIN early 20th cent.: probably so named by humorous analogy with 'tortuous' legal arguments.

lax ▶ adjective **1** not sufficiently strict, severe, or careful: *lax security arrangements at the airport* | *he'd been a bit lax about discipline in school lately.*
2 (of the limbs or muscles) relaxed. ■ (of the bowels) loose. ■ Phonetics (of a speech sound, especially a vowel) pronounced with the vocal muscles relaxed. The opposite of TENSE¹.
– DERIVATIVES **laxity** noun, **laxly** adverb, **laxness** noun.
– ORIGIN late Middle English (in the sense 'loose', said of the bowels): from Latin *laxus*.

laxative ▶ adjective (chiefly of a drug or medicine) tending to stimulate or facilitate evacuation of the bowels.
▶ noun a medicine which has a laxative effect.
– ORIGIN late Middle English: via Old French *laxatif, -ive* or late Latin *laxativus*, from Latin *laxare* 'loosen' (from *laxus* 'loose').

lay¹ ▶ verb (past and past participle **laid**) **1** [with obj. and adverbial of place] put (something) down gently or carefully: *she laid the baby in his cot.* ■ [with obj.] prevent (something) from rising off the ground: *there may have been the odd light shower just to lay the dust.*

2 [with obj.] put down and set in position for use: *it is advisable to have your carpet laid by a professional.* ■ Brit. set cutlery, crockery, etc. on (a table) in preparation for a meal: *she laid the table for dinner.* ■ (often **be laid with**) cover (a surface) with objects or a substance: *the floor was laid with mattresses.* ■ put the material for (a fire) in place and arrange it. ■ prepare (a trap) for someone: *she wouldn't put it past him to lay a trap for her.* ■ work out (an idea or suggestion) in detail ready for use or presentation: *I'd like more time to lay my plans.* ■ (**lay something before**) present information or suggestions to be considered and acted upon by (someone): *he laid before Parliament proposals for the establishment of the committee.* ■ locate (an episode in a play, novel, etc.) in a particular place: *no one who knew the area could be in doubt where the scene was laid.* ■ [with obj.] stake (an amount of money) in a bet: *she suspected he was pulling her leg, but she wouldn't have laid money on it.*

3 [with obj.] used with an abstract noun so that the phrase formed has the same meaning as the verb related to the noun used, e.g. 'lay the blame on' means 'to blame': *she laid great stress on little courtesies.*

4 [with obj.] (of a female bird, insect, reptile, or amphibian) produce (an egg) from inside the body: *flamingos lay only one egg* | [no obj.] *the hens were laying at the same rate as usual.*

5 [with obj.] vulgar slang have sexual intercourse with.

6 [with obj.] Nautical follow (a specified course).

7 [with obj.] trim (a hedge) back, cutting the branches half through, bending them down, and interweaving them.

▶ **noun 1** [in sing.] the general appearance of an area of land: *the lay of the surrounding countryside.* ■ the position or direction in which something lies: *roll the carpet against the lay of the nap.* ■ the direction or amount of twist in rope strands.

2 vulgar slang an act of sexual intercourse. ■ [with adj.] a person with a particular ability or availability as a sexual partner.

3 [mass noun] the laying of eggs or the period during which they are laid.

– PHRASES **in lay** (of a hen) laying eggs regularly. **lay something at someone's door** see DOOR. **lay something bare** bring something out of concealment; expose something: *the sad tale of failure was laid bare.* **lay a charge** make an accusation: *we could lay a charge of gross negligence.* **lay claim to** assert that one has a right to (something): *four men laid claim to the leadership.* ■ assert that one possesses (a skill or quality): *she has never laid claim to medical knowledge.* **lay down one's arms** (or **weapons**) cease fighting. **lay down the law** see LAW. **lay down one's life** sacrifice one's life for a cause: *the willingness of British troops to lay down their lives for their country is a humbling thought.* **lay eyes on** see EYE. **lay a** (or **the**) **ghost** exorcise a ghost. ■ finally cease to be troubled by the memory of an unpleasant situation or event: *by claiming victory, they **laid to rest the ghosts of** five previous defeats.* **lay hands on** (also **lay** or **put one's hands on**) 1 find and take possession of: *they huddled trying to keep warm under anything they could lay hands on.* 2 place one's hands on or over, especially in confirmation, ordination, or spiritual healing. **lay hold of** (or **on**) catch or gain possession of: *he was afraid she might vanish if he did not lay hold of her.* **lay it on the line** see LINE[1]. **lay someone low** (of an illness) reduce someone to inactivity: *he was laid low by a stomach bug.* ■ bring to an end the high position or good fortune formerly enjoyed by someone: *she reflected on how quickly fate can lay a person low.* **lay something on the table** see TABLE. **lay something on thick** (or **with a trowel**) informal grossly exaggerate or overemphasize something. **lay someone open to** expose someone to the risk of (something): *his position could lay him open to accusations of favouritism.* **lay oneself out to do something** chiefly Brit. make a special effort to do something: *she's laying herself out to be pleasant.* **lay siege to** see SIEGE. **lay store by** see STORE. **lay someone/thing to rest** bury a body in a grave. ■ soothe and dispel fear, anxiety, etc.: *suspicion will be laid to rest by fact rather than hearsay.* **lay something (to) waste** see WASTE.

– PHRASAL VERBS **lay about** Brit. beat or attack (someone) violently. ■ (**lay about one**) strike out wildly on all sides: *the mare laid about her with her front legs and teeth.* **lay something aside** put something to one side: *he laid aside his book* | figurative *the situation gave them a good reason to lay aside their differences.* ■ reserve money for the future or for a particular cause. **lay something down 1** put something down. 2 formulate and enforce or insist on a rule or principle: *stringent criteria have been laid down.* 3 pay or bet money. 4 begin to construct a ship or railway. ■ build up a deposit of a substance: *these cells lay down new bone tissue.* 5 store wine in a cellar. 6 informal record a piece of music: *he was invited to the studio to lay down some backing vocals.* **lay something in/up** build up a stock of something in case of need. **lay into** informal attack violently with words or blows: *three youths laid into him.* **lay off** informal give up or stop doing something: *I laid off smoking for seven years.* **lay someone off** discharge a worker temporarily or permanently because of a shortage of work. **lay something off 1** chiefly Soccer pass the ball to a teammate. 2 paint the final layer on a wall or other surface. 3 (of a bookmaker) insure against a loss resulting from a large bet by placing a similar bet with another bookmaker. **lay something on 1** Brit. provide a service or amenity: *the council provides a grant to lay on a bus.* 2 informal require (someone) to endure or deal with a responsibility or difficulty: *this is an absurdly heavy guilt trip to lay on anyone.* **lay someone out 1** prepare someone for burial after death. 2 informal knock someone unconscious: *he was lucky that the punch didn't lay him out.* **lay something out 1** spread something out to its full extent. 2 construct or arrange buildings or gardens according to a plan. ■ arrange and present material for printing and publication: *the brochure is beautifully laid out.* ■ explain something clearly and carefully: *we need a paper laying out our priorities.* 3 informal spend a sum of money: *look at the money I had to lay out for your uniform.* **lay over** US break one's journey. **lay up** Golf hit the ball deliberately to a lesser distance than possible, typically in order to avoid a hazard. **lay someone up** put someone out of action through illness or injury: *he was laid up with the flu.* **lay something up 1** see LAY SOMETHING IN/UP. 2 take a ship or other vehicle out of service: *our boats were laid up during the winter months.* 3 assemble plies or layers in the arrangement required for the manufacture of plywood or other laminated material.

– ORIGIN Old English *lecgan*, of Germanic origin; related to Dutch *leggen* and German *legen*, also to LIE[1].

USAGE The verb **lay** means, broadly, 'put something down', as in *they are going to **lay** the carpet*. The past tense and the past participle of this verb is **laid**, as in *they **laid** the groundwork* or *she had **laid** careful plans*. The verb **lie**, on the other hand, means 'be in a horizontal position to rest', as in *why don't you **lie** on the floor?* The past tense of this verb is **lay** (*he **lay** on the floor*) and the past participle is **lain** (*she had **lain** on the bed for hours*). Thus, in correct use, **lay** can be either the past tense of **lie** or the base form of **lay**. In practice many people make the mistake of using **lay**, **laying**, and **laid** as if they meant **lie**, **lying**, and **lain**. Examples of incorrect use: *why don't you **lay** on the bed?* (correct form is **lie**); *she was **laying** on the bed* (correct form is **lying**); *he had **laid** on the floor for hours* (correct form is **lain**).

lay[2] ▶ **adjective** [attrib.] **1** not ordained into or belonging to the clergy: *a lay preacher.*

2 not having professional qualifications or expert knowledge, especially in law or medicine: *a lay member of the Health Authority.*

– ORIGIN Middle English: from Old French *lai*, via late Latin from Greek *laïkos*, from *laos* 'people'. Compare with LAIC.

lay[3] ▶ **noun** a short lyric or narrative poem meant to be sung. ■ literary a song: *on his lips there died the cheery lay.*

– ORIGIN Middle English: from Old French *lai*, corresponding to Provençal *lais*, of unknown origin.

lay[4] past of LIE[1].

layabout ▶ **noun** Brit. derogatory a person who habitually does little or no work.

Layamon /ˈlʌɪəmən/ (late 12th century), English poet and priest. He wrote the verse chronicle known as the *Brut*, a history of England which introduces for the first time in English the story of King Arthur.

layaway ▶ **noun 1** [mass noun] N. Amer. a system of paying a deposit to secure an article for later purchase: *she picked up a coat she had **on layaway**.*

2 Climbing a handhold that is used to best effect by leaning out to the side of it.

layback ▶ **noun** [mass noun] Climbing a method of climbing a crack in rock by leaning back and pulling with the hands on one face, with the feet against the other face.

lay brother (or **lay sister**) ▶ **noun** a person who has taken the vows of a religious order but is not ordained or obliged to take part in the full cycle of liturgy and is employed in ancillary or manual work.

lay-by ▶ **noun** (pl. **lay-bys**) **1** Brit. an area at the side of a road where vehicles may pull off the road and stop.

2 [mass noun] Austral./NZ & S. African a system of paying a deposit to secure an article for later purchase.

layer ▶ **noun 1** a sheet, quantity, or thickness of material, typically one of several, covering a surface or body: *arrange a layer of aubergines in a dish.* ■ a level of seniority in the hierarchy of an organization: *a managerial layer.*

2 [in combination] a person or thing that lays something: *the majority of fish are egg-layers.*

3 a shoot fastened down to take root while attached to the parent plant.

▶ **verb** [with obj.] (often as adj. **layered**) **1** arrange in a layer or layers: *the current trend for layered clothes.* ■ cut (hair) in overlapping layers: *her layered, shoulder-length hair.*

2 propagate (a plant) as a layer: *a layered shoot.*

– ORIGIN Middle English (denoting a mason): from LAY[1] + -ER[1]. The sense 'stratum of material covering a surface' (early 17th cent.) may represent a respelling of an obsolete agricultural use of LAIR[1] denoting quality of soil.

layer cake ▶ **noun** chiefly N. Amer. a cake of two or more layers with jam, cream, or icing between.

layering ▶ **noun** [mass noun] **1** the action of arranging something in layers. ■ Geology the presence or formation of layers in sedimentary or igneous rock.

2 a method of propagating a plant in which a shoot is fastened down to form roots while still attached to the parent plant.

layer-out ▶ **noun** (pl. **layers-out**) dated a person who prepares a dead body for burial.

layette ▶ **noun** a set of clothing, bedclothes, and sometimes toiletries for a newborn child.

– ORIGIN mid 19th cent.: from French, diminutive of Old French *laie* 'drawer', from Middle Dutch *laege*.

L

lay figure ▶ **noun** a dummy or jointed manikin of a human body used by artists, especially for arranging drapery on.

– ORIGIN late 18th cent.: from obsolete *layman*, from Dutch *leeman*, from obsolete *led*, earlier form of *lid* 'joint'.

layman (also **laywoman** or **layperson**) ▶ **noun** (pl. **laymen, laywomen, laypersons**, or **laypeople**) **1** a non-ordained member of a Church.

2 a person without professional or specialized knowledge in a particular subject: *the book seems well suited to the interested layman.*

lay-off ▶ **noun 1** a temporary or permanent discharge of a worker or workers.

2 a period during which someone is unable to take part in a sport or other activity due to injury or illness.

La'youn variant spelling of LAAYOUNE.

layout ▶ **noun** the way in which the parts of something are arranged or laid out: *the road layout.* ■ the way in which text or pictures are set out on a page: *the layout is uncluttered and the illustrations are helpful.* ■ [mass noun] the process of setting out material on a page: *doing layout for newspapers and magazines.* ■ a thing arranged or set out in a particular way: *a model railway layout.*

layover ▶ **noun** N. Amer. a period of rest or waiting before a further stage in a journey.

layperson ▶ **noun** see LAYMAN.

lay reader ▶ **noun** (in the Anglican Church) a layperson licensed to preach and to conduct some religious services, but not licensed to celebrate the Eucharist.

layshaft ▶ **noun** Brit. a second or intermediate transmission shaft in a machine.

lay sister ▶ **noun** see LAY BROTHER.

lay-up ▶ **noun 1** [mass noun] the state whereby a ship is laid up.

2 Basketball a one-handed shot made from near the basket, especially one that rebounds off the backboard.

lazar /ˈleɪzə, ˈlazə/ ▶ **noun** archaic a poor and diseased person, especially one afflicted by an unpleasant disease such as leprosy.

– ORIGIN Middle English: from medieval Latin *lazarus*, with biblical allusion to *Lazarus*, the name of a beggar covered in sores (Luke 16:20).

lazarette /ˌlazəˈrɛt/ (also **lazaret**) ▶ **noun 1** the rear part of a ship's hold, used for stores.

2 a lazaretto.

– ORIGIN early 17th cent. (denoting an isolation hospital): from French *lazaret*, from Italian *lazaretto* (see LAZARETTO).

lazaretto /ˌlazəˈrɛtəʊ/ ▸ **noun** (pl. **lazarettos**) historical an isolation hospital for people with infectious diseases, especially leprosy or plague. ■ a military or prison hospital.
– ORIGIN mid 16th cent.: from Italian, diminutive of *lazzaro* 'beggar', from medieval Latin *lazarus* (see LAZAR).

Lazarist /ˈlazərɪst/ ▸ **noun** a member of the Congregation of the Mission, a Catholic organization founded at the priory of St Lazare in Paris by St Vincent de Paul to preach to the rural poor and train candidates for the priesthood. Also called **VINCENTIAN**.
– ORIGIN from French *Lazariste*, from the biblical name *Lazarus* (see LAZAR).

laze ▸ **verb** [no obj.] spend time in a relaxed, lazy manner: *she spent the day at home, reading the papers and generally* ***lazing around***. ■ [with obj.] (**laze something away**) pass time in a relaxed, lazy way: *laze away a long summer day*.
▸ **noun** [in sing.] a spell of lazing around.
– ORIGIN late 16th cent.: back-formation from LAZY.

laziness ▸ **noun** [mass noun] the quality of being unwilling to work or use energy; idleness: *it was sheer laziness on my part*.

Lazio /ˈlatsɪəʊ/ an administrative region of west central Italy, on the Tyrrhenian Sea, including the ancient region of Latium; capital, Rome.

lazuli /ˈlazjʊlʌɪ, -li/ ▸ **noun** short for LAPIS LAZULI.

lazurite /ˈlazjʊrʌɪt/ ▸ **noun** [mass noun] a bright blue mineral which is the chief constituent of lapis lazuli and consists chiefly of a silicate and sulphate of sodium and aluminium.

lazy ▸ **adjective** (**lazier**, **laziest**) **1** unwilling to work or use energy: *he was too lazy to cook*. ■ characterized by lack of effort or activity: *they were enjoying a really lazy holiday*. ■ showing a lack of care: *lazy writing*. ■ (of a river) slow-moving.
2 N. Amer. (of a brand on livestock) placed on its side rather than upright.
– DERIVATIVES **lazily** adverb.
– ORIGIN mid 16th cent.: perhaps related to Low German *lasich* 'languid, idle'.

lazybones ▸ **noun** (pl. **same**) informal a lazy person (often as a form of address).

lazy daisy stitch ▸ **noun** [mass noun] an embroidery stitch in the form of a flower petal.

lazy eye ▸ **noun** an eye with poor vision that is mainly caused by underuse, especially the unused eye in a squint.

lazy jack ▸ **noun** Sailing a small rope extending vertically from the topping lift to the boom for holding a fore-and-aft sail when it is being taken down.

lazy locking ▸ **noun** a car safety feature involving the automatic closing of its electric windows when the car is locked.

lazy Susan ▸ **noun** a revolving stand or tray on a table, used especially for holding condiments.

lazy tongs ▸ **noun** a set of extending tongs for grasping objects at a distance, with several connected pairs of levers pivoted like scissors.

LB ▸ **abbreviation** Liberia (international vehicle registration).

lb ▸ **abbreviation** ■ pound(s) (in weight). [from Latin *libra*.] ■ Cricket leg bye(s).

LBD ▸ **noun** (pl. **LBDs**) informal a little black dress: *you can't go wrong with an LBD for premières or parties*.

LBDR ▸ **abbreviation** Lance Bombardier.

LBO ▸ **abbreviation** leveraged buyout.

lbw ▸ **abbreviation** Cricket leg before wicket.

l.c. ▸ **abbreviation** ■ in the passage cited. [from Latin *loco citato*.] ■ letter of credit. ■ lower case.

LCC ▸ **abbreviation** historical London County Council.

LCD ▸ **abbreviation** ■ Electronics & Computing liquid crystal display. ■ Mathematics lowest (or least) common denominator.

LCM ▸ **abbreviation** Mathematics lowest (or least) common multiple.

LCpl ▸ **abbreviation** Lance Corporal.

LD ▸ **abbreviation** ■ N. Amer. learning disability (or disabled). ■ lethal dose (of a toxic compound, drug, or pathogen). It is usually written with a following numeral indicating the percentage of a group of animals or cultured cells or microorganisms killed by such a dose, typically standardized at 50 per cent (**LD**$_{50}$).

Ld ▸ **abbreviation** Lord: *Ld Lothian*.

LDC ▸ **abbreviation** less-developed country.

Ldg ▸ **abbreviation** Leading (in navy ranks).

LDL ▸ **abbreviation** Biochemistry low-density lipoprotein.

l-dopa ▸ **noun** [mass noun] Biochemistry the laevorotatory form of dopa, used to treat Parkinson's disease. Also called LEVODOPA.

L-driver ▸ **noun** Brit. a learner driver.

LDS ▸ **abbreviation** ■ Latter-Day Saints. ■ Licentiate in Dental Surgery.

LE ▸ **abbreviation** language engineering.

-le[1] ▸ **suffix 1** forming names of appliances or instruments: *bridle* | *thimble*.
2 forming names of animals and plants: *beetle*.
– ORIGIN Old English, of Germanic origin.

-le[2] (also **-el**) ▸ **suffix** forming nouns having or originally having a diminutive sense: *mantle* | *battle* | *castle*.
– ORIGIN Middle English *-el*, *-elle*, partly from Old English and partly from Old French (based on Latin forms).

-le[3] ▸ **suffix** (forming adjectives from an original verb) apt to; liable to: *brittle* | *nimble*.
– ORIGIN Middle English: from earlier *-el*, of Germanic origin.

-le[4] ▸ **suffix** forming verbs, chiefly those expressing repeated action or movement (as in *babble*, *dazzle*), or having diminutive sense (as in *nestle*).
– ORIGIN Old English *-lian*, of Germanic origin.

LEA ▸ **abbreviation** (in the UK) Local Education Authority.

lea ▸ **noun** literary an open area of grassy or arable land: *the lowing herd winds slowly o'er the lea*.
– ORIGIN Old English *lēa(h)*, of Germanic origin; related to Old High German *loh* 'grove', from an Indo-European root shared by Sanskrit *lokás* 'open space', Latin *lucus* 'grove', and perhaps also LIGHT[1].

leach ▸ **verb** [with adverbial of direction] (with reference to a soluble chemical or mineral) drain away from soil, ash, or similar material by the action of percolating liquid, especially rainwater: [with obj.] *the nutrient is quickly leached away* | [no obj.] *pesticides and fertilizers that leach into rivers*. ■ [with obj.] subject (soil, ash, etc.) to this process.
– ORIGIN Old English *leccan* 'to water', of West Germanic origin. The current sense dates from the mid 19th cent.

leachate ▸ **noun** [mass noun] technical water that has percolated through a solid and leached out some of the constituents.

Leacock, Stephen (Butler) (1869–1949), Canadian humorist and economist. He is chiefly remembered for his many humorous short stories, parodies, and essays. Notable works: *Sunshine Sketches of a Little Town* (1912).

lead[1] /liːd/ ▸ **verb** (past and past participle **led** /lɛd/) [with obj.] **1** cause (a person or animal) to go with one by holding them by the hand, a halter, a rope, etc. while moving forward: *she emerged leading a bay horse*. ■ [with obj. and adverbial of direction] show (someone or something) the way to a destination by going in front of or beside them: *she stood up and led her friend to the door*.
2 [no obj., with adverbial of direction] (usu. **lead to**) be a route or means of access to a particular place or in a particular direction: *the door led to a better-lit corridor* | *a farm track* ***led off to*** *the left*. ■ [with obj.] be a reason or motive for (someone): *nothing that I have read about the case leads me to the conclusion that anything untoward happened* | [with obj. and infinitive] *a fascination for art led him to start a collection of paintings*. ■ [no obj.] culminate or result in (a particular event or consequence): *closing the plant will lead to 300 job losses* | *fashioning a policy appropriate to the situation entails understanding the forces that* ***led up to*** *it*.
3 be in charge or command of: *a military delegation was led by the Chief of Staff*. ■ organize and direct: *the conference included sessions led by people with personal knowledge of the area*. ■ be the principal player of (a group of musicians): *since the forties he has led his own big bands*. ■ set (a process) in motion: *they are waiting for an expansion of world trade to lead a recovery*. ■ [no obj.] (**lead (off) with**) begin a report or text with a particular item: *the radio news led with the murder*. ■ [no obj.] (**lead with**) Boxing make an attack with (a particular punch or fist): *Adam led with a left*. ■ (in card games) play (the first card) in a trick or round of play.
4 [no obj.] have the advantage over competitors in a race or game: [with complement] *he followed up with a break of 105 to lead 3-0* | [with obj.] *the Wantage jockey was leading the field*. ■ [with obj.] be superior to (competitors or colleagues): *there will be specific areas or skills in which other nations* ***lead the world***.
5 have or experience (a particular way of life): *she's led a completely sheltered life*.
▸ **noun 1** the initiative in an action; an example for others to follow: *Britain is now* ***taking the lead*** *in environmental policies*. ■ a clue to be followed in the resolution of a problem: *detectives investigating the murder are chasing new leads*. ■ (in card games) an act or right of playing first in a trick or round of play: *it's your lead*. ■ the card played first in a trick or round.
2 (**the lead**) a position of advantage in a contest; first place: *the team burst into life and* ***took the lead*** | *they were beaten 5-3 after twice being* ***in the lead***. ■ an amount by which a competitor is ahead of the others: *the team held a slender one-goal lead*.
3 the chief part in a play or film: *she had the lead in a new film* | [as modifier] *the lead role*. ■ the person playing the chief part: *he still looked like a romantic lead*. ■ [usu. as modifier] the chief performer or instrument of a specified type: *a lead guitarist*. ■ [often as modifier] the item of news given the greatest prominence in a newspaper or magazine: *the lead story*.
4 Brit. a strap or cord for restraining and guiding a dog or other domestic animal.
5 Brit. a wire that conveys electric current from a source to an appliance, or that connects two points of a circuit together.
6 the distance advanced by a screw in one turn.
7 an artificial watercourse leading to a mill. ■ a channel of water in an ice field.
– PHRASES **lead someone astray** cause someone to act or think foolishly or wrongly. **lead someone by the nose** informal control someone totally, especially by deceiving them. **lead from the front** take an active role in what one is urging and directing others to do. **lead someone up** (or **down**) **the garden path** informal give someone misleading clues or signals. **lead with one's chin** informal (of a boxer) leave one's chin unprotected. ■ behave or speak incautiously.
– PHRASAL VERBS **lead off** Baseball bat first in a game or inning. ■ (of a base runner) be in a position to run from a base while standing off the base. **lead someone on** mislead or deceive someone, especially into believing that one is in love with or attracted to them: *she flirted with him and led him on*. **lead up to** immediately precede: *the weeks leading up to the elections*.
– ORIGIN Old English *lǣdan*, of Germanic origin; related to Dutch *leiden* and German *leiten*, also to LOAD and LODE.

lead[2] /lɛd/ ▸ **noun 1** [mass noun] a soft, heavy, ductile bluish-grey metal, the chemical element of atomic number 82. It has been used in roofing, plumbing, ammunition, storage batteries, radiation shields, etc., and its compounds have been used in crystal glass, as an anti-knock agent in petrol, and (formerly) in paints. (Symbol: **Pb**) ■ used figuratively as a symbol of something heavy: *Joe's feet felt like lumps of lead*.
2 an item or implement made of lead, in particular: ■ (**leads**) Brit. sheets or strips of lead covering a roof. ■ Brit. a piece of lead-covered roof. ■ (**leads**) lead frames holding the glass of a lattice or stained-glass window. ■ Nautical a lump of lead suspended on a line to determine the depth of water.
3 [mass noun] graphite used as the part of a pencil that makes a mark.
4 Printing a blank space between lines of print. [originally with reference to the metal strip used to create this space.]
– PHRASES **get the lead out** N. Amer. informal move or work more quickly. **go down** (or N. Amer. **over**) **like a lead balloon** informal (of a speech, proposal, or joke) be poorly received. **lead in one's pencil** informal vigour or energy, especially sexual energy in a man.
– ORIGIN Old English *lēad*, of West Germanic origin; related to Dutch *lood* 'lead' and German *Lot* 'plummet, solder'.

lead-acid ▸ **adjective** denoting a secondary cell or battery in which the electrodes are plates or grids of lead (or lead alloy) immersed in dilute sulphuric acid. The anode is coated with lead dioxide and the cathode with spongy lead.

Leadbeater's possum /ˈlɛdbɛtəz/ ▶ **noun** a small grey and white Australian possum, living only in high-altitude eucalyptus forests in eastern Victoria, where it feeds on gum. ● *Gymnobelidus leadbeateri*, family Petauridae.
– ORIGIN named after John *Leadbeater* (*c.*1832–88), Australian taxidermist.

lead crystal ▶ **noun** another term for LEAD GLASS.

leaded ▶ **adjective 1** (of windowpanes or a roof) framed, covered, or weighted with lead: *Georgian-style leaded windows*.
2 (of petrol) containing tetraethyl lead.
3 Printing (of print) having the lines separated by spaces.

leaded light ▶ **noun** a window consisting of a lattice of small panes held within strips of lead.

leaden ▶ **adjective 1** dull, heavy, or slow: *his eyelids were leaden with sleep*.
2 of the colour of lead; dull grey: *a leaden sky*.
■ archaic made of lead: *a leaden coffin*.
– ORIGIN Old English *lēaden* (see LEAD[2], -EN[2]).

leaden seal ▶ **noun** chiefly historical a seal made of lead, used especially for papal documents.

leader ▶ **noun 1** the person who leads or commands a group, organization, or country: *the leader of a protest group* | *a natural leader*. ■ (also **Leader of the House**) Brit. a member of the government officially responsible for initiating business in Parliament. ■ the person or team that is winning a sporting competition at a particular time: *Nora was up among the leaders*. ■ an organization or company that is the most advanced or successful in a particular area: *a leader in the use of video conferencing*.
2 the principal player in a music group. ■ Brit. the principal first violinist in an orchestra. ■ N. Amer. a conductor of a small musical group.
3 Brit. a leading article in a newspaper.
4 a short strip of non-functioning material at each end of a reel of film or recording tape for connection to the spool. ■ a length of filament attached to the end of a fishing line to carry the hook or fly.
5 a shoot of a plant at the apex of a stem or main branch.
6 (**leaders**) Printing a series of dots or dashes across the page to guide the eye, especially in tabulated material.
– DERIVATIVES **leaderless** adjective.

leader board ▶ **noun** a scoreboard showing the names and current scores of the leading competitors, especially in a golf match.

leaderene /ˌliːdəˈriːn/ ▶ **noun** Brit. humorous a female leader, especially an autocratic one.
– ORIGIN 1980s (originally a humorous or ironic name for Margaret Thatcher): from LEADER + *-ene*, on the pattern of female given names such as *Marlene*.

leadership ▶ **noun** [mass noun] the action of leading a group of people or an organization, or the ability to do this: *different styles of leadership*. ■ the state or position of being a leader: *the party prospered under his leadership*. ■ [treated as sing. or pl.] the leaders of an organization, country, etc.: *the leadership was divided into two camps*.

lead-footed ▶ **adjective** N. Amer. informal **1** slow; clumsy: *the most lead-footed guy can try aerobic moves*.
2 tending to drive too quickly.

lead-free ▶ **adjective** (of petrol) without added tetraethyl lead.

lead glass ▶ **noun** [mass noun] glass containing a substantial proportion of lead oxide, making it more refractive. Also called LEAD CRYSTAL.

lead-in ▶ **noun 1** an introduction or preamble which allows one to move smoothly on to the next part of something: [as modifier] *the lead-in note*.
2 a wire leading in from outside, especially from an aerial to a receiver or transmitter.

leading[1] /ˈliːdɪŋ/ ▶ **adjective** [attrib.] most important: *a number of leading politicians*.
▶ **noun** [mass noun] guidance or leadership, especially in a spiritual context.

leading[2] /ˈlɛdɪŋ/ ▶ **noun** [mass noun] the amount of blank space between lines of print. ■ the distance from the bottom of one line of type to the bottom of the next.

leading aircraftman (or **leading aircraftwoman**) ▶ **noun** a rank in the RAF, above aircraftman and below senior aircraftman.

leading article ▶ **noun** Brit. a newspaper article giving the editorial opinion.

leading counsel ▶ **noun** the senior barrister of the team which represents either party in a legal case.

leading dog ▶ **noun** Austral./NZ a sheepdog trained to run ahead of a flock of sheep to control its speed.

leading edge ▶ **noun 1** Aeronautics the foremost edge of an aerofoil, especially a wing or propeller blade. Compare with TRAILING EDGE.
2 the forefront or vanguard, especially of technological development: [as modifier] *leading-edge research*.
3 Electronics the part of a pulse in which the amplitude increases.

leading lady ▶ **noun** the actress playing the principal female part in a film or play.

leading light ▶ **noun** a person who is prominent or influential in a particular field or organization: *Lesley is a leading light in a local netball team*.

leading man ▶ **noun** the actor playing the principal male part in a film or play.

leading note ▶ **noun** Music another term for SUBTONIC.

leading question ▶ **noun** a question that prompts or encourages the answer wanted.

leading rein ▶ **noun** a rein used to lead a horse along, especially when ridden by an inexperienced rider.

leading seaman ▶ **noun** a rank in the Royal Navy, above able seaman and below petty officer.

leading tone ▶ **noun** Music North American term for SUBTONIC.

lead-off ▶ **adjective** beginning a series or a process: *the album's lead-off track*. ■ Baseball denoting the first batter in a line-up or of an inning.

lead poisoning ▶ **noun** [mass noun] acute or chronic poisoning due to the absorption of lead into the body. Also called PLUMBISM.

lead shot ▶ **noun** another term for SHOT[1] (sense 3).

lead tetraethyl ▶ **noun** Chemistry another term for TETRAETHYL LEAD.

lead time ▶ **noun** the time between the initiation and completion of a production process.

lead-up ▶ **noun** [in sing.] an event, point, or sequence that leads up to something else: ***the lead-up to the*** *elections*.

leadwort /ˈlɛdwəːt/ ▶ **noun** another term for PLUMBAGO (sense 2).

leaf ▶ **noun** (pl. **leaves**) **1** a flattened structure of a higher plant, typically green and blade-like, that is attached to a stem directly or via a stalk. Leaves are the main organs of photosynthesis and transpiration. ■ any of a number of similar plant structures, e.g. bracts, sepals, and petals. ■ [mass noun] foliage regarded collectively. ■ [mass noun] the state of having leaves: *the trees are still in leaf*. ■ [mass noun] the leaves of tobacco or tea: [as modifier] *leaf tea*.
2 a thing that resembles a leaf in being flat and thin. ■ a single thickness of paper, especially in a book with each side forming a page. ■ [mass noun] [with modifier] gold, silver, or other specified metal in the form of very thin foil: *gold leaf*. ■ the hinged part or flap of a door, shutter, or table. ■ an extra section inserted to extend a table. ■ the inner or outer part of a cavity wall or double-glazed window.
▶ **verb** [no obj.] **1** (of a plant, especially a deciduous one in spring) put out new leaves.
2 (**leaf through**) turn over (the pages of a book or the papers in a pile), reading them quickly or casually: *he leafed through the stack of notes*.
– PHRASES **shake** (or **tremble**) **like a leaf** (of a person) tremble greatly, especially from fear.
– DERIVATIVES **leafage** noun, **leafed** adjective [in combination] *purple-leafed dahlias*, **leafless** adjective, **leaf-like** adjective.
– ORIGIN Old English *lēaf*, of Germanic origin; related to Dutch *loof* and German *Laub*.

leaf beetle ▶ **noun** a small beetle that feeds chiefly on leaves and typically has bright metallic colouring. Some kinds are serious crop pests. ● Family Chrysomelidae: numerous species.

leafbird ▶ **noun** a tree-dwelling songbird of South and SE Asia with mainly green plumage and a black bill, the male typically having a black throat. ● Genus *Chloropsis*, family Irenidae (or Chloropseidae): several species.

leaf curl ▶ **noun** [mass noun] a plant condition distinguished by the presence of curling leaves, caused by environmental stress or disease.

leafcutter ant ▶ **noun** a tropical ant which cuts pieces from leaves and carries them back to the nest for use as a culture medium for growing food fungi. ● Genus *Atta*, family Formicidae.

leafcutter bee ▶ **noun** a solitary bee which cuts pieces from leaves, typically of roses, and uses them to construct cells in its nest. ● Genus *Megachile*, family Megachilidae.

leaf-fall ▶ **noun** [mass noun] the shedding of leaves by a plant.

leaf fat ▶ **noun** [mass noun] dense fat occurring in layers around the kidneys of some animals, especially pigs.

leaf fish ▶ **noun** a small deep-bodied predatory freshwater fish, with mottled brownish-green coloration which gives it a leaf-like appearance. ● Two species in the family Nandidae: *Monocirrhus polyacanthus* of South America, and *Polycentropsis abbreviata* of Africa.

leaf green ▶ **noun** [mass noun] a bright, deep green colour.

leafhopper ▶ **noun** a small plant bug which is typically brightly coloured and leaps when disturbed. It can be a serious crop pest in warm regions. ● Family Cicadellidae, suborder Homoptera: numerous genera.

leaf insect ▶ **noun** a large slow-moving tropical insect related to the stick insects, with a flattened body that is leaf-like in shape and colour. ● Family Phylliidae, order Phasmida: *Phyllium* and other genera.

leaflet ▶ **noun 1** a printed sheet of paper containing information or advertising and usually distributed free.
2 Botany each of the leaflike structures that together make up a compound leaf, such as in the ash and horse chestnut. ■ (in general use) a young leaf.
▶ **verb** (**leaflets, leafleting, leafleted**) [with obj.] distribute leaflets to (people or an area): *tourists visiting the area are being leafleted* | [no obj.] *they were leafleting in Victoria Square*.

leaf litter ▶ **noun** see LITTER (sense 4 of the noun).

leaflove ▶ **noun** an African bulbul (songbird) that frequents dense thickets, with mainly drab brown plumage and a loud bubbling call. ● The **leaflove** (*Phyllastrephus scandens*) and the **yellow-throated leaflove** (*Chlorocichla flavicollis*), family Pycnonotidae.

L

leaf miner ▶ **noun** a small fly, moth, or sawfly whose larvae burrow between the two surfaces of a leaf.

leaf monkey ▶ **noun** a leaf-eating arboreal Asian monkey that is related to the langurs. ● Genus *Presbytis*, family Cercopithecidae: several species.

leaf mould ▶ **noun** [mass noun] **1** soil consisting chiefly of decayed leaves.
2 a fungal disease of tomatoes in which mould develops on the leaves. ● The fungus is *Fulvia fulva* (formerly *Cladosporium fulvum*), subdivision Deuteromycotina.

leaf-nosed bat ▶ **noun** a bat with a leaf-like appendage on the snout. ● Families Hipposideridae (Old World) and Phyllostomatidae (New World): numerous species.

leaf peeper ▶ **noun** US informal a person who visits particular areas, especially in New England, to view the autumn foliage.
– DERIVATIVES **leaf peeping** noun.

leaf roll ▶ **noun** [mass noun] a virus disease of potatoes marked by upward curling of the leaves.

leaf roller ▶ **noun** an insect, especially a small moth, whose larvae roll up the leaves of plants which they feed upon.

leaf spot ▶ **noun** [mass noun] [usu. with modifier] any of a large number of fungal, bacterial, or viral plant diseases which cause leaves to develop discoloured spots.

leaf spring ▶ **noun** a spring made of a number of strips of metal curved slightly upwards and clamped together one above the other.

leaf-tailed gecko ▶ **noun** a gecko with a wide, flat leaf-shaped tail and skin that serves to camouflage it. ● Genus *Phyllurus* (four Australian species), family Pygopodidae, and *Uroplatus* (several Madagascan species), family Gekkonidae.

leaf trace ▶ **noun** Botany a strand of conducting vessels extending from the stem to the base of a leaf.

leaf warbler ▶ **noun** a small, slender Old World songbird with a brown or greenish back and whitish or yellowish underparts. ● Genus *Phylloscopus*, family Sylviidae: many species, including the chiffchaff and willow warbler.

leafy ▶ **adjective** (**leafier, leafiest**) having many leaves or much foliage: *a leafy glade* | *leafy bushes* | *the leafy suburbs*. ■ (of a plant) producing or grown for its broad-bladed leaves: *green leafy vegetables*. ■ resembling a leaf or leaves: *a three-pointed leafy bract*.
– DERIVATIVES **leafiness** noun.

league[1] ▸ **noun** **1** a collection of people, countries, or groups that combine for mutual protection or cooperation: *the League of Nations.* ▪ archaic an agreement or alliance.
2 a group of sports clubs which play each other over a period for a championship: *the leading goalscorer in the league* | [as modifier] *the league championship.* ▪ the contest for the championship of a league: *the year we won the league.* ▪ short for RUGBY LEAGUE.
3 a class or category of quality or excellence: *the two men were **not in the same league** | Austin's in a league of his own.*
▸ **verb** (**leagues, leaguing, leagued**) [no obj.] join in a league or alliance: *Oscar had **leagued with** other construction firms.*
– PHRASES **in league** conspiring with another or others: *he is in league with the devil.*
– ORIGIN late Middle English (denoting a compact for mutual protection or advantage): via French from Italian *lega*, from *legare* 'to bind', from Latin *ligare*.

league[2] ▸ **noun** a former measure of distance by land, usually about three miles.
– ORIGIN late Middle English: from late Latin *leuga, leuca*, late Greek *leugē*, or from Provençal *lega* (modern French *lieue*).

League of Arab States an organization of Arab states, founded in 1945 in Cairo, whose purpose is to ensure cooperation among its member states and protect their independence and sovereignty. Also called ARAB LEAGUE.

League of Nations an association of countries established in 1919 by the Treaty of Versailles to promote international cooperation and achieve international peace and security. It was powerless to stop Italian, German, and Japanese expansionism leading to the Second World War, and was replaced by the United Nations in 1945.

leaguer[1] ▸ **noun** [with adj. or noun modifier] chiefly N. Amer. a member of a particular league, especially a sports player: *an assembly of minor leaguers in spring training.*

L

leaguer[2] ▸ **noun & verb** variant of LAAGER.
– ORIGIN late 16th cent.: from Dutch *leger* 'camp'. Compare with LAAGER, LAGER, and LAIR[1].

league table ▸ **noun** Brit. a list of the competitors in a league, showing their ranking according to performance in a particular season. ▪ a comparison of achievement or merit in a competitive area: *a national league table of school results.*

leak ▸ **verb** [no obj.] **1** (of a container or covering) accidentally lose or admit contents, especially liquid or gas, through a hole or crack: *the roof leaked* | (as adj. **leaking**) *a leaking gutter* | [with obj.] *the drums were leaking an unidentified liquid.* ▪ [with adverbial of direction] (of liquid, gas, etc.) pass in or out through a hole or crack in such a way: *water kept leaking in.*
2 (of secret information) become known: *worrying stories leaked out.* ▪ [with obj.] intentionally disclose (secret information): *a report was leaked to the press* | (as adj. **leaked**) *a leaked government document.*
▸ **noun** **1** a hole in a container or covering through which contents may accidentally pass: *I checked all of the pipework for leaks.* ▪ an instance of leaking in such a way: *a gas leak* | [mass noun] *the leak of fluid may occur.*
2 an intentional disclosure of secret information: *one of the employees was responsible for the leak.*
– PHRASES **have** (or **take**) **a leak** informal urinate.
– DERIVATIVES **leaker** noun.
– ORIGIN late Middle English: probably of Low German or Dutch origin and related to LACK.

leakage ▸ **noun** [mass noun] **1** the accidental admission or escape of liquid or gas through a hole or crack: *we're saving water by reducing leakage* | [count noun] *there have been no leakages of radioactive material.* ▪ Physics the gradual escape of an electric charge or current, or magnetic flux.
2 deliberate disclosure of confidential information.

Leakey a family of eminent Kenyan archaeologists and anthropologists. **Louis (Seymour Bazett)** (1903–72) pioneered the investigation of human origins in East Africa. He began excavations at Olduvai Gorge and together with Mary discovered the remains of early hominids and their implements, including *Australopithecus* (or *Zinjanthropus*) *boisei* in 1959. His British-born wife **Mary (Douglas)** (1913–96) discovered *Homo habilis* and *Homo erectus* at Olduvai in 1960. Their son **Richard (Erskine)** (b.1944) was director of the Kenya Wildlife Service 1989–94.

leakproof ▸ **adjective** closely sealed or fitted so as to prevent leaks.

leaky ▸ **adjective** (**leakier, leakiest**) **1** having a leak or leaks: *a leaky roof.*
2 given to disclosing secrets: *leaky sources at the company.*
– DERIVATIVES **leakiness** noun.

leal /liːl/ ▸ **adjective** Scottish archaic loyal and honest: *his leal duty to the King.*
– ORIGIN Middle English: from Old French *leel*, earlier form of *loial* (see LOYAL).

Leamington Spa /ˈlɛmɪŋtən/ a town in central England, in Warwickshire, south-east of Birmingham; pop. 59,100 (est. 2009). Noted for its saline springs, it was granted the status of royal spa after a visit by Queen Victoria in 1838. Official name ROYAL LEAMINGTON SPA.

Lean, Sir David (1908–91), English film director. He made many notable films, including *Lawrence of Arabia* (1962), *Doctor Zhivago* (1965), and *A Passage to India* (1984).

lean[1] ▸ **verb** (past and past participle **leaned** or chiefly Brit. **leant**) [no obj., with adverbial] be in or move into a sloping position: *he leaned back in his chair.* ▪ (**lean against/on**) incline from the perpendicular and rest for support against (something): *a man was leaning against the wall.* ▪ [with obj.] (**lean something against/on**) cause something to rest against: *he leaned his elbows on the table.*
▸ **noun** a deviation from the perpendicular; an inclination: *the vehicle has a definite lean to the left.*
– PHRASES **lean over backwards** see BACKWARDS.
– PHRASAL VERBS **lean on 1** rely on or derive support from: *they have learned to lean on each other for support.* **2** informal put pressure on (someone) to act in a certain way: *a determination not to allow the majority to lean on the minority.* **lean to/towards** incline or be partial to (a view or position): *I now lean towards sabotage as the cause of the crash.*
– ORIGIN Old English *hleonian, hlinian*, of Germanic origin; related to Dutch *leunen* and German *lehnen*, from an Indo-European root shared by Latin *inclinare* and Greek *klinein*.

lean[2] ▸ **adjective** **1** (of a person or animal) thin, especially healthily so; having no superfluous fat: *his lean, muscular body.* ▪ (of meat) containing little fat: *lean bacon.* ▪ (of an industry or company) efficient and with no wastage: *staff were pruned, ostensibly to produce a leaner and fitter organization.*
2 offering little reward, substance, or nourishment; meagre: *the lean winter months* | *keep a small reserve to tide you over the lean years.*
3 (of a vaporized fuel mixture) having a high proportion of air: *lean air-to-fuel ratios.*
▸ **noun** [mass noun] the lean part of meat.
– DERIVATIVES **leanly** adverb, **leanness** noun.
– ORIGIN Old English *hlǣne*, of Germanic origin.

lean-burn ▸ **adjective** relating to an internal-combustion engine designed to run on a lean mixture to reduce pollution: *lean-burn technology.*

Leander /lɪˈandə/ **1** Greek Mythology a young man, the lover of the priestess Hero. He was drowned swimming across the Hellespont to visit her.
2 (also **Leander Club**) the oldest amateur rowing club in the world, founded early in the 19th century, now based in Henley-on-Thames. Membership is a mark of distinction in the rowing world.

leaning ▸ **noun** (often **leanings**) a tendency or partiality of a particular kind: *his early leanings towards socialism.*

lean-to ▸ **noun** (pl. **lean-tos**) a building sharing one wall with a larger building, and having a roof that leans against that wall: [as modifier] *a lean-to garage.* ▪ a temporary shelter, either supported or free-standing.

leap ▸ **verb** (past or past participle **leaped** or **leapt**) [no obj., with adverbial] **1** jump or spring a long way, to a great height, or with great force: *he leapt on to the parapet* | figurative *Fabia's heart leapt excitedly.* ▪ [with obj.] jump across: *Peter leapt the last few stairs.*
2 move quickly and suddenly: *Polly leapt to her feet.* ▪ make a sudden rush to do something; act eagerly and suddenly: *everybody leapt into action.* ▪ (**leap at**) accept (an opportunity) eagerly: *they leapt at the opportunity to combine fun with fund-raising.* ▪ (of a price, amount, etc.) increase dramatically: *sales leapt by a third last year.* ▪ (**leap out**) (especially of writing) be conspicuous; stand out: *amid the notes, a couple of items leap out.*
▸ **noun** a forceful jump or quick movement: *she came downstairs in a series of flying leaps.* ▪ a dramatic increase in price, amount, etc.: *a leap of 75 per cent in two years.* ▪ a sudden abrupt change or transition: *a leap of faith.* ▪ [in place names] a thing to be leaped over or from: *Lover's Leap.*
– PHRASES **a leap in the dark** a daring step or enterprise whose consequences are unpredictable. **by** (or **in**) **leaps and bounds** with startlingly rapid progress: *productivity improved in leaps and bounds.* **leap to the eye** (especially of writing) be immediately apparent.
– DERIVATIVES **leaper** noun.
– ORIGIN Old English *hlēapan* (verb), *hlȳp* (noun), of Germanic origin; related to Dutch *lopen*, German *laufen* (verb), and Dutch *loop*, German *Lauf* (noun), all meaning 'run', also to LOPE.

leap day ▸ **noun** the intercalary day in a leap year; 29 February.

leapfrog ▸ **noun** [mass noun] a game in which players in turn vault with parted legs over others who are bending down.
▸ **verb** (**leapfrogs, leapfrogging, leapfrogged**) [no obj.] perform such a vault: *they leapfrogged around the courtyard.* ▪ [no obj., with adverbial] surpass or overtake another to move into a leading or dominant position: *she leapfrogged into a sales position.* ▪ [with obj.] pass over (a stage or obstacle): *attempts to leapfrog the barriers of class.*

leap second ▸ **noun** a second which is occasionally inserted into the atomic scale of reckoning time in order to bring it into line with solar time. It is indicated by an additional bleep in the time signal at the end of some years.

leap year ▸ **noun** a year, occurring once every four years, which has 366 days including 29 February as an intercalary day.
– ORIGIN late Middle English: probably from the fact that feast days after February in such a year fell two days later than in the previous year, rather than one day later as in other years, and could be said to have 'leaped' a day.

Lear[1] /lɪə/ a legendary early king of Britain, the central figure in Shakespeare's tragedy *King Lear*. He is mentioned by the chronicler Geoffrey of Monmouth.

Lear[2] /lɪə/, Edward (1812–88), English humorist and illustrator. He wrote *A Book of Nonsense* (1845) and *Laughable Lyrics* (1877). He also published illustrations of birds and of his travels around the Mediterranean.

learn ▸ **verb** (past and past participle **learned** or chiefly Brit. **learnt**) [with obj.] **1** gain or acquire knowledge of or skill in (something) by study, experience, or being taught: *they'd started learning French* | [with infinitive] *she is learning to play the piano* | [no obj.] *we learn from experience.* ▪ commit to memory: *I'd learned too many grim poems in school.* ▪ become aware of (something) by information or from observation: [with clause] *I learned that they had eaten already* | [no obj.] *the trading standards office **learned of** the illegal network.*
2 archaic or informal teach (someone): *'That'll learn you,' he chuckled* | [with obj. and infinitive] *we'll have to learn you to milk cows.*
– DERIVATIVES **learnability** noun, **learnable** adjective.
– ORIGIN Old English *leornian* 'learn' (in Middle English also 'teach'), of West Germanic origin; related to German *lernen*, also to LORE[1].

> **USAGE** In modern standard English it is wrong to use **learn** to mean **teach**, as in *that'll **learn** you* (correct use is *that'll **teach** you*). This meaning has been recorded since the 13th century and has been used by writers such as Spenser, Bunyan, and Samuel Johnson, but it fell into disfavour in the early 19th century and is now found only in non-standard and dialect use.

learned /ˈləːnɪd/ ▸ **adjective** (of a person) having acquired much knowledge through study. ▪ showing, requiring, or characterized by learning; scholarly: *an article in a learned journal.* ▪ Brit. used as a courteous description of a lawyer in certain formal contexts: *my learned friend.*
– DERIVATIVES **learnedly** adverb, **learnedness** noun.
– ORIGIN Middle English: from LEARN, in the sense 'teach'.

learned helplessness ▸ **noun** [mass noun] Psychiatry a condition in which a person suffers from a sense of powerlessness, arising from a traumatic event or persistent failure to succeed. It is thought to be one of the underlying causes of depression.

learner ▸ **noun** a person who is learning a subject or skill: *a fast learner.* ▪ (also **learner driver**) a person who is learning to drive a motor vehicle and has not yet passed a driving test.

learner's dictionary ▸ **noun** a dictionary designed for the use of foreign students.

learnfare ▸ **noun** [mass noun] N. Amer. a welfare system in which attendance at school, college, or a training programme is necessary in order to receive benefits.
– ORIGIN 1980s: from LEARN, on the pattern of WORKFARE.

learning ▸ **noun** [mass noun] the acquisition of knowledge or skills through study, experience, or being taught: *these children experienced difficulties in learning* | [as modifier] *an important learning process.* ■ knowledge acquired in this way: *I liked to parade my learning in front of my sisters.*
– ORIGIN Old English *leornung* (see LEARN, -ING[1]).

learning curve ▸ **noun** the rate of a person's progress in gaining experience or new skills: *the latest software packages have a steep learning curve.*

learning difficulties ▸ **plural noun** Brit. difficulties in acquiring knowledge and skills to the normal level expected of those of the same age, especially because of mental disability or cognitive disorder.

> **USAGE** The phrase **learning difficulties** became prominent in the 1980s. It is broad in scope, covering general conditions such as Down's syndrome as well as more specific cognitive or neurological conditions such as dyslexia and attention deficit disorder. In emphasizing the difficulty experienced rather than any perceived 'deficiency', it is considered less discriminatory and more positive than other terms such as **mentally handicapped**, and is now the standard accepted term in Britain in official contexts. **Learning disability** is the standard accepted term in North America.

learning disability ▸ **noun** a condition giving rise to learning difficulties, especially when not associated with physical disability.
– DERIVATIVES **learning-disabled** adjective.

Leary, Timothy (Francis) (1920–96), American psychologist and drug pioneer. After experimenting with consciousness-altering drugs including LSD, he was dismissed from his teaching post at Harvard University in 1963 and became a figurehead for the hippy drug culture.

lease ▸ **noun** a contract by which one party conveys land, property, services, etc. to another for a specified time, usually in return for a periodic payment.
▸ **verb** [with obj.] grant (property) on lease; let: *she* ***leased*** *the site* ***to*** *a local company.* ■ take (property) on lease; rent: *land was* ***leased from*** *the Duchy of Cornwall.*
– PHRASES **a new lease of** (or N. Amer. **on**) **life** a substantially improved prospect of life or use after rejuvenation or repair.
– DERIVATIVES **leasable** adjective, **leaser** noun.
– ORIGIN late Middle English: from Old French *lais, leis*, from *lesser, laissier* 'let, leave', from Latin *laxare* 'make loose', from *laxus* 'loose, lax'.

leaseback ▸ **noun** [often as modifier] the leasing of a property, especially one recently purchased, back to the seller: *leaseback agreements.*

leasehold ▸ **noun** [mass noun] chiefly Brit. the holding of property by lease: *a form of leasehold* | [as modifier] *leasehold premises.* Often contrasted with FREEHOLD. ■ [count noun] a property held by lease.
– DERIVATIVES **leaseholder** noun.
– ORIGIN early 18th cent.: from LEASE, on the pattern of *freehold.*

Lease-Lend historical another term for LEND-LEASE.

leash ▸ **noun** a dog's lead. ■ Falconry a thong or string attached to the jesses of a hawk, used for tying it to a perch or a creance. ■ a restraint: *her bristling temper was kept* ***on a leash*** | *the state needs to let business* ***off the leash.***
▸ **verb** [with obj.] put a leash on (a dog). ■ restrain: *his violence was barely leashed.*
– PHRASES **strain at the leash** be eager to begin or do something.
– ORIGIN Middle English: from Old French *lesse, laisse*, from *laissier* in the specific sense 'let run on a slack lead' (see LEASE).

least ▸ **determiner & pronoun** (usu. **the least**) smallest in amount, extent, or significance: [as determiner] *who has the least money?* | *he never had the least idea what to do about it* | [as pronoun] *how others see me is* ***the least of my worries*** | *it's the least I can do.*
▸ **adverb** to the smallest extent or degree: *my best routine was the one I had practised* ***the least*** | *turning up when he was least expected* | *only the least expensive lot sold* | *I never hid the truth,* ***least of all*** *from you.*
▸ **adjective** used in names of very small animals and plants, e.g. **least shrew**.
– PHRASES **at least 1** not less than; at the minimum: *clean the windows at least once a week.* **2** if nothing else (used to add a positive comment about a generally negative situation): *the options aren't complete, but at least they're a start.* **3** anyway (used to modify something just stated): *they seldom complained—officially at least.* **at the least** (or **very least**) **1** (used after amounts) not less than; at the minimum: *stay ten days at the least.* **2** taking the most pessimistic or unfavourable view: *a programme which is, at the very least, excellent PR for the hospital.* **least said, soonest mended** proverb a difficult situation will be resolved more quickly if there is no more discussion of it. **not in the least** not in the smallest degree; not at all: *he was not in the least taken aback.* **not least** in particular; notably: *there is a great deal at stake, not least in relation to the environment.* **to say the least (of it)** used as an understatement (implying the reality is more extreme, usually worse): *his performance was disappointing to say the least.*
– ORIGIN Old English *lǣst, lǣsest*, of Germanic origin; related to LESS.

least common denominator ▸ **noun** another term for LOWEST COMMON DENOMINATOR.

least common multiple ▸ **noun** another term for LOWEST COMMON MULTIPLE.

least significant bit (abbrev.: **LSB**) ▸ **noun** Computing the bit in a binary number which is of the lowest numerical value.

least squares ▸ **noun** [mass noun] a method of estimating a quantity or fitting a graph to data so as to minimize the sum of the squares of the differences between the observed values and the estimated values.

leastways (also **leastwise**) ▸ **adverb** dialect or informal at least: *I don't hold with foreigners, leastways not here in King's Magnum Parva.*

leat /liːt/ ▸ **noun** Brit. an open watercourse conducting water to a mill.
– ORIGIN late 16th cent.: from Old English *-gelǣt* (recorded in *wætergelǣt* 'water channel'), related to *lǣtan* 'to let'.

leather ▸ **noun 1** [mass noun] a material made from the skin of an animal by tanning or a similar process: [as modifier] *a leather jacket.* ■ (**leathers**) leather clothes, especially those worn by a motorcyclist.
2 a piece of leather as a polishing cloth.
3 short for STIRRUP LEATHER.
▸ **verb** [with obj.] **1** (usu. as adj. **leathered**) cover with leather: *his leathered foot.*
2 informal beat or thrash (someone): *he caught me and leathered me black and blue* | (as noun **leathering**) *go, before you get a leathering.*
– ORIGIN Old English *lether*, of Germanic origin; related to Dutch *leer* and German *Leder*, from an Indo-European root shared by Irish *leathar* and Welsh *lledr*.

leatherback (also **leatherback turtle**) ▸ **noun** a very large black turtle with a thick leathery shell, living chiefly in tropical seas. ● *Dermochelys coriacea*, the only member of the family Dermochelyidae.

leather-bound ▸ **adjective** (especially of a book) strengthened by a leather binding.

leather carp ▸ **noun** a carp of a variety which lacks scales.

leathercloth ▸ **noun** [mass noun] strong, coated fabric embossed to resemble leather.

leatherette ▸ **noun** [mass noun] imitation leather.

leather-hard ▸ **adjective** (of unfired pottery) dried and hardened enough to be decorated or trimmed with slip but not enough to be fired.

leatherjacket ▸ **noun 1** Brit. the tough-skinned larva of a large crane fly. It lives in the soil, where it feeds on plant matter and can seriously damage the roots of grasses and crops. ● Genus *Tipula*, family Tipulidae.
2 any of a number of tough-skinned marine fishes, in particular: ● a fish of the jack family (Carangidae), in particular a slender fish of American coastal waters, with a greenish back and a bright yellow tail (*Oligoplites saurus*). ● a filefish or triggerfish (family Balistidae).

leathern ▸ **adjective** archaic made of leather.

leatherneck ▸ **noun** US informal a marine.
– ORIGIN late 19th cent.: with allusion to the leather lining inside the collar of a marine's uniform.

leatherwear ▸ **noun** [mass noun] articles of clothing made of leather.

leatherwood ▸ **noun 1** an evergreen American shrub or small tree with tough, flexible bark. ● *Cyrilla racemiflora*, family Cyrillaceae.
2 a Tasmanian eucryphia tree which bears fragrant white flowers and yields tough pinkish timber. ● *Eucryphia lucida*, family Eucryphiaceae.

leathery ▸ **adjective** having a tough, hard texture like leather: *brown, leathery skin.*
– DERIVATIVES **leatheriness** noun.

leathery turtle ▸ **noun** another term for LEATHERBACK.

leave[1] ▸ **verb** (past and past participle **left**) **1** [with obj.] go away from: *she left London on June 6* | [no obj.] *we were almost the last to leave* | *the England team* ***left for*** *Pakistan on Monday.* ■ depart from permanently: *at the age of sixteen he left home.* ■ cease attending (a school or college) or working for (an organization): *she is leaving the BBC after 20 years.*
2 [with obj.] allow or cause to remain: *the parts he disliked he would alter and the parts he didn't dislike he'd leave.* ■ (**be left**) remain to be used or dealt with: *we've even got one of the Christmas puddings* ***left over*** *from last year* | [with infinitive] *a retired person with no mortgage left to pay.* ■ [with obj. and adverbial of place] go away from a place without taking (someone or something): *we had not* ***left*** *any of our belongings* ***behind*** | figurative *women had been* ***left behind*** *in the struggle for pay equality.* ■ abandon (a spouse or partner): *her boyfriend* ***left*** *her* ***for*** *another woman.* ■ have as (a surviving relative) after one's death: *he leaves a wife and three children.* ■ bequeath: *he left £500 to the National Asthma Campaign* | [with two objs] *Cornelius had left her fifty pounds a year for life.*
3 [with obj. and adverbial or complement] cause (someone or something) to be in a particular state or position: *he'll leave you in no doubt about what he thinks* | *I'll leave the door open* | *the children were* ***left with*** *feelings of loss.* ■ [with obj. and infinitive] let (someone) do or deal with something without offering help or assistance: *infected people are often rejected by family and friends, leaving them to face this chronic condition alone.* ■ [with obj.] cause to remain as a trace or record: *dark fruit that would leave purple stains on the table napkins* | figurative *they leave the impression that they can be bullied.* ■ [with obj.] deposit or entrust to be kept, collected, or attended to: *she left a note for me.* ■ [with obj.] (**leave something to**) entrust a decision, choice, or action to (someone else, especially someone considered better qualified): *the choice of which link to take is generally* ***left up to*** *the reader.*
▸ **noun** (in snooker, croquet, and other games) the position in which a player leaves the balls for the next player.
– PHRASES **be left at the post** be beaten from the start of a race or competition. **be left for dead** be abandoned as being almost dead or certain to die. **be left to oneself** be alone or solitary: *left to himself he removed his shirt and tie.* ■ be allowed to do what one wants: *women, left to themselves, would make the world a beautiful place to live in.* **leave someone/thing alone** see ALONE. **leave someone be** informal refrain from disturbing or interfering with someone. **leave someone cold** fail to interest someone: *the Romantic poets left him cold.* **leave go** Brit. informal remove one's hold or grip: *leave go of me!* **leave hold of** cease holding. **leave it at that** abstain from further comment or action: *if you are not sure of the answers, say so, and leave it at that.* **leave much** (or **a lot**) **to be desired** be highly unsatisfactory.
– PHRASAL VERBS **leave off** discontinue (an activity): *the dog left off chasing the sheep* | *he resumed the other story at the point where the previous author had left off.* **leave someone/thing out** fail to include: *it seemed unkind to leave Daisy out, so she was invited too* | (as adj. **left out**) *Olivia was feeling rather left out.* ■ (usu. in imperative **leave it out**) Brit. informal stop it: *'Leave it out,' I said sternly, pushing him off.*
– DERIVATIVES **leaver** noun.
– ORIGIN Old English *lǣfan* 'bequeath', also 'allow to remain, leave in place' of Germanic origin; related to German *bleiben* 'remain'.

leave[2] ▸ **noun** [mass noun] **1** (also **leave of absence**) time when one has permission to be absent from work or from duty in the armed forces: *Joe was home* ***on leave*** | *maternity leave.*
2 [often with infinitive] permission: *leave from the court to commence an action.*
– PHRASES **by** (or **with**) **your leave 1** with your permission: *with your leave, I will send him your address.* **2** informal an apology for rude or unwelcome behaviour: *she came in without so much as a by your leave.* **take one's leave** formal say goodbye: *he went to* ***take his leave of*** *his hostess.* **take leave of one's senses** see SENSE. **take leave to do something** formal

L

venture or presume to do something: *whether this amounts to much, one may take leave to doubt.*
– ORIGIN Old English *lēaf* 'permission', of West Germanic origin; related to LIEF and LOVE.

leaved ▶ adjective [in combination] having a leaf or leaves of a particular kind: *ivy-leaved toadflax.*

leaven /ˈlɛv(ə)n/ ▶ noun [mass noun] **1** a substance, typically yeast, that is added to dough to make it ferment and rise. ■ dough that is reserved from an earlier batch in order to start a later one fermenting.
2 a pervasive influence that modifies something or transforms it for the better: *they acted as an intellectual leaven to the warriors who dominated the city.*
▶ verb [with obj.] **1** (usu. as adj. **leavened**) cause (dough or bread) to ferment and rise by adding leaven: *leavened breads are forbidden during Passover.*
2 permeate and modify or transform (something) for the better: *the proceedings should be leavened by humour* | (as noun **leavening**) *companies of Territorial Army volunteers with a leavening of regular soldiers.*
– ORIGIN Middle English: from Old French *levain*, based on Latin *levamen* 'relief' (literally 'means of raising'), from *levare* 'to lift'.

leaves plural form of LEAF.

leave-taking ▶ noun an act of saying goodbye: *the leave-taking was formal, with none of her earlier displays of emotion.*

leavings ▶ plural noun things that have been left as worthless: *she dropped her lunch leavings into a bin.*

Leavis /ˈliːvɪs/, F. R. (1895–1978), English literary critic; full name *Frank Raymond Leavis*. Founder and editor of the quarterly *Scrutiny* (1932–53), he emphasized the value of critical study of English literature to preserving cultural continuity. Notable works: *The Great Tradition* (1948).
– DERIVATIVES **Leavisite** noun & adjective.

Lebanon /ˈlɛbənən/ a country in the Middle East with a coastline on the Mediterranean Sea; pop. 4,017,100 (est. 2009); official language, Arabic; capital, Beirut.

L

> Part of the Ottoman Empire from the early 16th century, Lebanon became a French mandate after the First World War and achieved independence in 1943. Until the mid 1970s the country prospered, but conflict between the Christian and Muslim communities, the influx of Palestinian refugees, and repeated Middle Eastern wars chronically destabilized the country. The first general elections for twenty years were held in 1992.

– DERIVATIVES **Lebanese** adjective & noun.

Lebanon Mountains a range of mountains in Lebanon. Running parallel to the Mediterranean coast, it rises to a height of 3,087 m (10,022 ft) at Qornet es Saouda. It is separated from the Anti-Lebanon Mountains, on the border with Syria, by the Bekaa valley.

Lebensraum /ˈleɪb(ə)nzˌraʊm/, German /ˈleːbnsˌraʊm/ ▶ noun [mass noun] the territory which a state or nation believes is needed for its natural development.
– ORIGIN German, literally 'living space' (originally with reference to Germany).

lebkuchen /ˈleːbkuːk(ə)n/ ▶ noun (pl. **same**) a type of biscuit with a cake-like texture, typically glazed and containing spices and honey.
– ORIGIN German *Lebkuchen*, from Kuchen 'cake'; the origin of the first element is uncertain.

Leblanc /ləˈblɒ̃(k)/, French /ləblɑ̃/, Nicolas (1742–1806), French surgeon and chemist. He developed a process for making soda ash (sodium carbonate) from common salt, enabling the large-scale manufacture of glass, soap, paper, and other chemicals.

Lebowa /ləˈbəʊə/ a former homeland established in South Africa for the North Sotho people, now part of the province of Limpopo.

Lebrun /ləˈbrəːn/, French /ləbrœ̃/, Charles (1619–90), French painter, designer, and decorator. He was prominent in the development and institutionalization of French art and was a leading exponent of French classicism. In 1648 he helped to found the Royal Academy of Painting and Sculpture in Paris.

Le Carré /lə ˈkareɪ/, John (b.1931), English novelist; pseudonym of *David John Moore Cornwell*. He is known for his thoughtful spy novels, which often feature the British agent George Smiley and include *The Spy Who Came in from the Cold* (1963) and *Tinker, Tailor, Soldier, Spy* (1974).

leccy /ˈlɛki/ ▶ noun [mass noun] Brit. informal electricity.

lech /lɛtʃ/ (also **letch**) informal, derogatory ▶ noun a lecher. ■ a lecherous urge or desire: *I think he has a kind of lech for you.*
▶ verb [no obj.] act in a lecherous or lustful manner: *businessmen leching after bimbos.*
– ORIGIN late 18th cent. (denoting a strong desire, particularly sexually): back-formation from LECHER.

Le Chatelier's principle /ˌlə ʃaˈtɛljeɪz/ Chemistry a principle stating that if a constraint (such as a change in pressure, temperature, or concentration of a reactant) is applied to a system in equilibrium, the equilibrium will shift so as to tend to counteract the effect of the constraint.
– ORIGIN early 20th cent.: named after Henri *le Chatelier* (1850–1936), French chemist.

lecher /ˈlɛtʃə/ ▶ noun a lecherous man.
– ORIGIN Middle English: from Old French *lichiere*, *lecheor*, from *lechier* 'live in debauchery or gluttony', ultimately of West Germanic origin and related to LICK.

lecherous ▶ adjective having or showing excessive or offensive sexual desire: *she ignored his lecherous gaze.*
– DERIVATIVES **lecherously** adverb, **lecherousness** noun.
– ORIGIN Middle English: from Old French *lecheros*, from *lecheor* (see LECHER).

lechery ▶ noun [mass noun] excessive or offensive sexual desire; lustfulness.
– ORIGIN Middle English: from Old French *lecherie*, from *lecheor* (see LECHER).

lechwe /ˈliːtʃwi/ ▶ noun (pl. **same**) a rough-coated grazing antelope with pointed hoofs and long horns, found in swampy grassland in southern Africa and Sudan. ● Genus *Kobus*, family Bovidae: two species, in particular *K. leche*.
– ORIGIN mid 19th cent.: from Setswana.

lecithin /ˈlɛsɪθɪn/ ▶ noun Biochemistry another term for PHOSPHATIDYLCHOLINE.
– ORIGIN mid 19th cent.: from Greek *lekithos* 'egg yolk' + -IN[1].

lecithinase /ˈlɛsɪθɪˌneɪz/ ▶ noun Biochemistry another term for PHOSPHOLIPASE.

lecker ▶ adjective variant spelling of LEKKER.

Leclanché cell /ləˈklɒ̃ʃeɪ/ ▶ noun a primary electrochemical cell having a zinc cathode in contact with zinc chloride, ammonium chloride (as a solution or a paste) as the electrolyte, and a carbon anode in contact with a mixture of manganese dioxide and carbon powder.
– ORIGIN late 19th cent.: named after Georges *Leclanché* (1839–82), French chemist.

Leconte de Lisle /ləˌkɒnt də ˈliːl/, French /ləkɔ̃t də lil/, Charles Marie René (1818–94), French poet and leader of the Parnassians. His poetry often draws inspiration from mythology, biblical history, and exotic Eastern landscape.

Le Corbusier /ˌlə kɔːˈbjuːzɪeɪ/, French /lə kɔʀbyzje/ (1887–1965), French architect and town planner, born in Switzerland; born *Charles Édouard Jeanneret*. A pioneer of the International Style, he developed theories on functionalism, the use of new materials and industrial techniques, and the Modulor, a modular system of standard-sized units.

lectern /ˈlɛkt(ə)n, -təːn/ ▶ noun a tall stand with a sloping top to hold a book or notes, from which someone, typically a preacher or lecturer, can read while standing up.
– ORIGIN Middle English: from Old French *letrun*, from medieval Latin *lectrum*, from *legere* 'to read'.

lectin ▶ noun Biochemistry any of a class of proteins, chiefly of plant origin, which bind specifically to certain sugars and so cause agglutination of particular cell types.
– ORIGIN 1950s: from Latin *lect-* 'chosen' (from the verb *legere*) + -IN[1].

lection /ˈlɛkʃ(ə)n/ ▶ noun archaic a reading of a text found in a particular copy or edition.
– ORIGIN Middle English (in the sense 'election'): from Latin *lectio(n-)* 'choosing, reading', from the verb *legere*. The current sense dates from the mid 17th cent.

lectionary /ˈlɛkʃ(ə)n(ə)ri/ ▶ noun (pl. **lectionaries**) a list or book of portions of the Bible appointed to be read at divine service.
– ORIGIN late 18th cent.: from medieval Latin *lectionarium*, from Latin *lect-* 'chosen, read', from the verb *legere*.

lector /ˈlɛktɔː/ ▶ noun **1** a reader, especially someone who reads lessons in a church service.
2 a lecturer, especially one employed in a foreign university to teach in their native language.
– ORIGIN late Middle English: from Latin, from *lect-* 'read, chosen', from the verb *legere*.

lectrice /lɛkˈtriːs/ ▶ noun a female lector in a university.
– ORIGIN late 19th cent.: from French, literally 'female reader'.

lecture ▶ noun **1** an educational talk to an audience, especially one of students in a university.
2 a long serious speech, especially one given as a scolding or reprimand: *the usual lecture on table manners.*
▶ verb **1** [no obj.] deliver an educational lecture or lectures: *he was lecturing at the University of Birmingham.* ■ [with obj.] give a lecture to (a class or other audience): *he was lecturing future generations of health-service professionals.*
2 [with obj.] talk seriously or reprovingly to (someone): *I do not wish to be lectured about smoking.*
– ORIGIN late Middle English (in the sense 'reading, a text to read'): from Old French, or from medieval Latin *lectura*, from Latin *lect-* 'read, chosen', from the verb *legere*.

lecturer ▶ noun a person who gives lectures, especially (Brit.) as an occupation at a university or college of higher education.

lectureship ▶ noun a post as a lecturer: *a three-year lectureship in English Literature.*

lecture theatre ▶ noun see THEATRE.

lecythus /ˈlɛsɪθəs/ ▶ noun (pl. **lecythi** /-θʌɪ/) a thin narrow-necked vase or flask from ancient Greece.
– ORIGIN via late Latin from Greek *lēkuthos*.

LED ▶ abbreviation light-emitting diode, a semiconductor diode which glows when a voltage is applied.

led past and past participle of LEAD[1].

Leda /ˈliːdə/ Greek Mythology the wife of Tyndareus king of Sparta. She was loved by Zeus, who visited her in the form of a swan; among her children were the Dioscuri, Helen, and Clytemnestra.

lederhosen /ˈleɪdəˌhəʊz(ə)n/ ▶ plural noun leather shorts with H-shaped braces, traditionally worn by men in Alpine regions such as Bavaria.
– ORIGIN from German, from *Leder* 'leather' + *Hosen* 'trousers'.

ledge ▶ noun **1** a narrow horizontal surface projecting from a wall, cliff, or other surface: *he heaved himself up over a ledge.* ■ a window ledge.
2 an underwater ridge, especially of rocks beneath the sea near the shore: *a reef ledge.*
3 Mining a stratum of metal- or ore-bearing rock; a vein of quartz or other mineral.
– DERIVATIVES **ledged** adjective, **ledgy** adjective.
– ORIGIN Middle English (denoting a strip of wood or other material fixed across a door, gate, etc.): perhaps from an early form of LAY[1]. Sense 1 dates from the mid 16th cent.

ledger ▶ noun **1** a book or other collection of financial accounts: *the total balance of the purchases ledger.*
2 a flat stone slab covering a grave.
3 a horizontal scaffolding pole, parallel to the face of the building.
4 a weight used on a fishing line without a float, to anchor the bait in a particular place: [as modifier] *ledger tackle.*
▶ verb [no obj.] fish using a ledger.
– ORIGIN late Middle English *legger*, *ligger* (denoting a large bible or breviary), probably from variants of LAY[1] and LIE[1], influenced by Dutch *legger* and *ligger*. Current senses date from the 16th cent., except the fishing senses, known from the 17th cent.

ledger line ▶ noun Music variant spelling of LEGER LINE.

Lee[1], Bruce (1941–73), American actor; born *Lee Yuen Kam*. An expert in kung fu, he starred in a number of martial arts films, such as *Enter the Dragon* (1973).

Lee[2], Gypsy Rose (1914–70), American striptease artist; born *Rose Louise Hovick*. In the 1930s she became famous on Broadway for her sophisticated striptease act.

Lee[3], (Nelle) Harper (b.1926), American novelist. She won a Pulitzer Prize with her only novel, *To Kill a Mockingbird* (1960), about the sensational trial of a black man falsely charged with raping a white woman.

Lee[4], Laurie (1914–97), English writer. He is best known for his autobiographical novels *Cider With Rosie* (1959) and *As I Walked Out One Midsummer Morning* (1969), evocative accounts of his childhood in rural Gloucestershire and his travelling experiences in pre-war Europe.

Lee[5], Robert E. (1807–70), American general; full name *Robert Edward Lee*. He was the commander of the Confederate army of Northern Virginia for most of the American Civil War. His invasion of the North was repulsed at the Battle of Gettysburg (1863) and he surrendered in 1865.

lee ▸ noun [mass noun] (also **lee side**) the sheltered side of something; the side away from the wind: *ducks were taking shelter on the lee of the island*. Contrasted with WEATHER. ■ shelter from wind or weather given by an object: *he went round the front of the cab to be out of the wind and lit a cigarette in its lee*.
– ORIGIN Old English *hlēo*, *hlēow* 'shelter', of Germanic origin; probably related to *luke-* in LUKEWARM.

leeboard ▸ noun a plank frame fixed to the side of a flat-bottomed boat and let down into the water to reduce drifting to the leeward side.

leech[1] ▸ noun **1** an aquatic or terrestrial annelid worm with suckers at both ends. Many species are bloodsucking parasites, especially of vertebrates, and others are predators. ● Class Hirudinea: many species. See also MEDICINAL LEECH.
2 a person who extorts profit from or sponges on others: *they are leeches feeding off the hard-working majority*.
▸ verb [no obj.] (**leech on/off**) habitually exploit or rely on: *he's leeching off the abilities of others*.
– PHRASES **like a leech** very closely and persistently: *you've been clinging to me like a leech all these months*.
– ORIGIN Old English *lǣce*, *lȳce*; related to Middle Dutch *lake*, *lieke*.

leech[2] ▸ noun archaic a doctor or healer.
– ORIGIN Old English *lǣce*, of Germanic origin.

leech[3] ▸ noun Sailing the after or leeward edge of a fore-and-aft sail, the leeward edge of a spinnaker, or a vertical edge of a square sail.
– ORIGIN late 15th cent.: probably of Scandinavian origin and related to Swedish *lik*, Danish *lig*, denoting a rope sewn round the edge of a sail to stop the canvas tearing.

leechcraft ▸ noun [mass noun] archaic the art of healing.
– ORIGIN Old English *lǣcecræft* (see LEECH[2], CRAFT).

Leeds an industrial city in West Yorkshire, northern England; pop. 441,100 (est. 2009). It developed as a wool town in the Middle Ages, becoming a centre of the clothing trade in the Industrial Revolution.

Lee–Enfield (also **Lee–Enfield rifle**) ▸ noun a bolt-action rifle of a type formerly used by the British army.
– ORIGIN from J. P. *Lee* (1831–1904), US designer of the bolt action + *Enfield* in north London, where it was made.

lee gage ▸ noun see GAUGE (sense 3 of the noun).

lee helm ▸ noun [mass noun] Sailing the tendency of a ship to turn its bow to the leeward side.

lee ho ▸ exclamation Sailing a command or warning given by a helmsman to indicate the moment of going about.

leek ▸ noun a plant related to the onion, with flat overlapping leaves forming an elongated cylindrical bulb which together with the leaf bases is eaten as a vegetable. It is used as a Welsh national emblem. ● *Allium porrum*, family Liliaceae (or Alliaceae).
– ORIGIN Old English *lēac*, of Germanic origin; related to Dutch *look* and German *Lauch*.

leer[1] ▸ verb [no obj.] look or gaze in a lascivious or unpleasant way: *bystanders were leering at the nude painting* | (as adj. **leering**) *every leering eye in the room was on her*.
▸ noun a lascivious or unpleasant look.
– DERIVATIVES **leeringly** adverb.
– ORIGIN mid 16th cent. (in the general sense 'look sideways or askance'): perhaps from obsolete *leer* 'cheek', from Old English *hlēor*, as though the sense were 'to glance over one's cheek'.

leer[2] ▸ noun variant spelling of LEHR.

leervis /ˈlɪərfəs/ ▸ noun (pl. **same**) S. African a large greyish marine fish with small scales which give the skin a leathery appearance. It lives in the Mediterranean and around the western and southern coasts of Africa, where it is a popular game fish. ● *Lichia amia*, family Carangidae.
– ORIGIN mid 19th cent.: from Afrikaans, from Dutch *leer* 'leather' + *vis* 'fish'.

leery ▸ adjective (**leerier**, **leeriest**) informal cautious or wary due to realistic suspicions: *a city leery of gang violence*.
– DERIVATIVES **leeriness** noun.
– ORIGIN late 17th cent.: from obsolete *leer* 'looking askance', from LEER[1] + -Y[1].

lees ▸ plural noun the sediment of wine in the barrel; dregs. ■ the most worthless part or parts of something: *the lees of the Venetian underworld*.
– ORIGIN late Middle English: plural of obsolete *lee* in the same sense, from Old French *lie*, from medieval Latin *liae* (plural), of Gaulish origin.

lee shore ▸ noun a shore lying on the leeward side of a ship (and on to which a ship could be blown in foul weather).

lee side ▸ noun see LEE.

leet[1] (also **court leet**) ▸ noun historical a yearly or half-yearly court of record that the lords of certain manors held.
– ORIGIN Middle English: from Anglo-Norman French *lete* or Anglo-Latin *leta*, of unknown origin.

leet[2] ▸ noun Scottish a list of candidates selected for a post.
– ORIGIN late Middle English: probably from Old French *lit(t)e*, variant of *liste* 'list'.

leet[3] (also **leetspeak**) ▸ noun [mass noun] an informal language or code used on the Internet, in which standard letters are often replaced by numerals or special characters.
– ORIGIN early 21st cent.: from *leet*, representing a pronunciation of ELITE + -SPEAK.

Leeuwenhoek /ˈleɪv(ə)nhuːk/, Antoni van (1632–1723), Dutch naturalist. He developed a lens for scientific purposes and was the first to observe bacteria, protozoa, and yeast. He accurately described red blood cells, capillaries, striated muscle fibres, spermatozoa, and the crystalline lens of the eye.

leeward /ˈliːwəd, ˈluːəd/ ▸ adjective & adverb on or towards the side sheltered from the wind; downwind: [as adj.] *the leeward side of the house* | [as adv.] *we pitched our tents* ***leeward of*** *a hill*. Contrasted with WINDWARD.
▸ noun [mass noun] the side sheltered or away from the wind: *the ship was drifting* ***to leeward***.

Leeward Islands /ˈliːwəd/ a group of islands in the Caribbean, constituting the northern part of the Lesser Antilles. The group includes Guadeloupe, Antigua, St Kitts, and Montserrat.
– ORIGIN *Leeward* with reference to the islands' situation further downwind (in terms of the prevailing south-easterly winds) than the Windward Islands.

leewardly /ˈliːwədli, ˈluːədli/ ▸ adjective (of a ship) liable to drift to leeward when sailing close to the wind.

lee wave ▸ noun a standing wave generated on the sheltered side of a mountain by an air current passing over or around it, and often made visible by the formation of clouds.

leeway ▸ noun [mass noun] **1** the amount of freedom to move or act that is available: *the government had greater leeway to introduce reforms*. ■ margin of safety: *there is little leeway if anything goes wrong*.
2 the sideways drift of a ship to leeward of the desired course: *the leeway is only about 2°*.
– PHRASES **make up (the) leeway** Brit. struggle out of a bad position, especially by recovering lost time.

Le Fanu /ˈlɛfənjuː, lə ˈfɑːnuː/, Joseph Sheridan (1814–73), Irish novelist. He is best known for his stories of mystery, suspense, and the supernatural, such as *The House by the Churchyard* (1861) and *Uncle Silas* (1864).

left[1] ▸ adjective **1** on, towards, or relating to the side of a human body or of a thing which is to the west when the person or thing is facing north: *her left eye* | *the left side of the road*.
2 relating to a person or group favouring radical, reforming, or socialist views. [see LEFT WING.]
▸ adverb on or to the left side: *turn left here* | *keep left*.
▸ noun **1** (**the left**) the left-hand part, side, or direction: *turn to the left* | (**one's left**) *the general sat to his left*. ■ (in football or a similar sport) the left-hand half of the field when facing the opponents' goal: *a free kick from the left*. ■ the left wing of an army: *a token attack on the Russian left*. ■ a left turn: *take a left here*. ■ a road, entrance, etc. on the left: *my road's the first left*. ■ a person's left fist, especially a boxer's: *a dazzler with the left*. ■ a blow given with the left fist: *a left to the body*.
2 (often **the Left**) [treated as sing. or pl.] a group or party favouring radical, reforming, or socialist views: *the Left is preparing to fight presidential elections* | *he is on the left of the party*.
– PHRASES **have two left feet** be clumsy or awkward. **left, right, and centre** (also **left and right** or **right and left**) on all sides: *deals were being done left, right, and centre*.
– DERIVATIVES **leftish** adjective, **leftward** adjective & adverb, **leftwards** adverb.
– ORIGIN Old English *lyft*, *left* 'weak' (the left-hand side being regarded as the weaker side of the body), of West Germanic origin.

left[2] past and past participle of LEAVE[1].

left back ▸ noun a defender in soccer or field hockey who plays primarily in a position on the left of the field.

Left Bank a district of the city of Paris, situated on the left bank of the River Seine, to the south of the river. It is an area noted for its intellectual and artistic life.

left bank ▸ noun the bank of a river on the left as one faces downstream.

left brain ▸ noun the left-hand side of the human brain, which is believed to be associated with linear and analytical thought.

left-brained ▸ adjective having the left part of the brain as the dominant or more efficient part.

left-click ▸ verb [no obj.] Computing click on a link or other screen object by depressing the left-hand button of the mouse: *left-click on any of the thumbnails to see a photo*.

left field ▸ noun **1** Baseball the part of the outfield to the left of the batter when facing the pitcher: *a high fly to left field*.
2 N. Amer. informal a surprising or unconventional position or style: *seldom do so many witty touches come out of left field*. ■ a position of ignorance, error, or confusion: *he's way over in left field on these issues*.
▸ adjective (of artistic work) radical or experimental: *left-field guitar-based music*.

left-footed ▸ adjective (of a person) using the left foot more naturally than the right. ■ (of a kick) done with the left foot: *he drove a left-footed shot into the net*.

left hand ▸ noun the hand of a person's left side. ■ the region or direction on the left side of a person or thing: *there was a vast forest on the left hand*.
▸ adjective [attrib.] on or towards the left side of a person or thing: *his left-hand pocket*. ■ done with or using the left hand: *an excellent left-hand catch by Smith*.
– PHRASES **marry with the left hand** Brit. marry morganatically. [from a German custom by which the bridegroom gave the bride his left hand in such marriages.]

left-hand drive ▸ noun [mass noun] a motor-vehicle steering system with the steering wheel and other controls fitted on the left side, designed for use in countries where vehicles drive on the right-hand side of the road. ■ [count noun] a vehicle with left-hand drive steering.

left-handed ▸ adjective **1** (of a person) using the left hand more naturally than the right: *a left-handed batsman*. ■ (of a tool or item of equipment) made to be used with the left hand: *left-handed golf clubs*. ■ made or done with the left hand: *my left-handed scrawl*.
2 (of a screw) advanced by turning anticlockwise. ■ Biology (of a spiral shell or helix) sinistral. ■ (of a racecourse) turning anticlockwise.
3 perverse: *we take a left-handed pleasure in our errors*. ■ (especially of a compliment) ambiguous.
▸ adverb with the left hand: *a significant number play the game left-handed*.
– DERIVATIVES **left-handedly** adverb, **left-handedness** noun.

left-hander ▸ noun **1** a left-handed person. ■ a blow struck with a person's left hand.
2 a corner on a road or racing circuit that bends to the left.

leftie ▸ noun variant spelling of LEFTY.

leftism ▸ noun [mass noun] the political views or policies of the left.
– DERIVATIVES **leftist** noun & adjective.

left-leaning ▸ adjective sympathetic to or tending towards the left in politics: *a left-leaning professor*.

left luggage ▸ noun [mass noun] Brit. travellers' luggage left in temporary storage at a railway station, bus station, or airport. ■ a room where left luggage may be stored temporarily for a small charge: *I picked up my parcel from left luggage*.

leftmost ▸ adjective [attrib.] furthest to the left: *the leftmost edge of the screen*.

leftover ▸ noun (usu. **leftovers**) something, especially food, remaining after the rest has been used.
▸ adjective [attrib.] remaining; surplus: *yesterday's leftover bread*.

L

left turn ▶ noun a turn that brings a person's front to face the way their left side did before: *take a left turn into Cumberland Road.*

left wing ▶ noun (**the left wing**) **1** the radical, reforming, or socialist section of a political party or system. [with reference to the National Assembly in France (1789–91), where the nobles sat to the president's right and the commons to the left.]
2 the left side of a team on the field in soccer, rugby, and field hockey: *his usual position on the left wing.* ■ the left side of an army: *the Allied left wing.*
▶ adjective radical, reforming, or socialist: *left-wing activists.*
– DERIVATIVES **left-winger** noun.

lefty (also **leftie**) ▶ noun (pl. **lefties**) informal **1** chiefly Brit. a person with left-wing political views.
2 chiefly N. Amer. a left-handed person.

leg ▶ noun **1** each of the limbs on which a person or animal walks and stands: *Adams broke his leg* | *he was off as fast as his legs would carry him* | [as modifier] *a leg injury.* ■ a leg of an animal or bird as food: *a roast leg of lamb.* ■ a part of a garment covering a leg or part of a leg: *his trouser leg.* ■ (**legs**) informal (with reference to a ball, especially in golf) sufficient momentum to reach the desired point. ■ (**legs**) informal (with reference to a product or idea) sustained popularity or success: *some books have legs, others don't.*
2 each of the supports of a chair, table, or other structure: *table legs* | *the house was set on legs.*
3 a section or stage of a journey or process: *the return leg of his journey.* ■ Sailing a run made on a single tack. ■ (in soccer and other sports) each of two games constituting a round of a competition. ■ a section of a relay or other race done in stages: *one leg of its race round the globe.* ■ a single game in a darts match.
4 a branch of a forked object.
5 (also **leg side**) Cricket the half of the field (as divided lengthways through the pitch) away from which the batsman's feet are pointed when standing to receive the ball. The opposite of OFF.
6 archaic a deferential gesture made by drawing back one leg and bending it while keeping the front leg straight.
▶ verb (**legs, legging, legged**) [with obj.] **1** (**leg it**) Brit. informal travel by foot; walk. ■ run away: *he legged it after someone shouted at him.*
2 chiefly historical propel (a boat) through a tunnel on a canal by pushing with one's legs against the tunnel roof or sides.
– PHRASES **feel** (or **find**) **one's legs** become able to stand or walk. **get one's leg over** Brit. vulgar slang (of a man) have sexual intercourse. **have the legs of** Brit. be able to go faster or further than (a rival). **not have a leg to stand on** have no facts or sound reasons to support one's argument or justify one's actions. **on one's hind legs** Brit. informal, dated standing up to make a speech: *he wasn't afraid to get up on his hind legs at a social gathering and talk.* **on one's last legs** near the end of life, usefulness, or existence: *the foundry business was on its last legs.*
– DERIVATIVES **legged** adjective [in combination] *a four-legged animal*, **legger** noun [in combination] *a three-legger.*
– ORIGIN Middle English (superseding SHANK): from Old Norse *leggr* (compare with Danish *læg* 'calf (of the leg)'), of Germanic origin.

legacy ▶ noun (pl. **legacies**) an amount of money or property left to someone in a will. ■ something left or handed down by a predecessor: *the legacy of centuries of neglect.*
▶ adjective Computing denoting or relating to software or hardware that has been superseded but is difficult to replace because of its wide use.
– ORIGIN late Middle English (also denoting the function or office of a deputy, especially a papal legate): from Old French *legacie*, from medieval Latin *legatia* 'legateship', from *legatus* 'person delegated' (see LEGATE).

legal ▶ adjective **1** [attrib.] relating to the law: *the European legal system.* ■ appointed or required by the law: *a legal requirement.* ■ Law recognized by common or statute law, as distinct from equity. ■ relating to theological legalism.
2 permitted by law: *he claimed that it had all been legal.*
3 N. Amer. denoting a size of paper that measures 22 × 35.5 cm (8.5 × 14 inches).
– DERIVATIVES **legally** adverb.
– ORIGIN late Middle English (in the sense 'to do with Mosaic law'): from French, or from Latin *legalis*, from *lex, leg-* 'law'. Compare with LOYAL.

legal aid ▶ noun [mass noun] payment from public funds allowed, in cases of need, to help pay for legal advice or proceedings.

legal capacity ▶ noun [mass noun] a person's authority under law to engage in a particular undertaking or maintain a particular status.

legal clinic ▶ noun N. Amer. a place where one can obtain legal advice and assistance, paid for by legal aid.

legal eagle (also **legal beagle**) ▶ noun informal a lawyer, especially one who is keen and astute.

legalese /ˌliːɡəˈliːz/ ▶ noun [mass noun] informal the formal and technical language of legal documents.

legal fiction ▶ noun an assertion that is accepted as true for legal purposes, even though it may be untrue or unproven.

legal holiday ▶ noun N. Amer. a public holiday established by law.

legalism ▶ noun [mass noun] excessive adherence to law or formula. ■ Theology adherence to moral law rather than to personal religious faith.
– DERIVATIVES **legalist** noun & adjective, **legalistic** adjective, **legalistically** adverb.

legality ▶ noun (pl. **legalities**) [mass noun] the quality or state of being in accordance with the law: *documentation testifying to the legality of the arms sale.* ■ (**legalities**) obligations imposed by law.
– ORIGIN late Middle English: from French *légalité* or medieval Latin *legalitas* 'relating to the law', from Latin *legalis* (see LEGAL).

legalize (also **legalise**) ▶ verb [with obj.] make (something that was previously illegal) permissible by law: *homosexuality and abortion have been legalized.*
– DERIVATIVES **legalization** noun.

legal pad ▶ noun N. Amer. a pad of lined paper, typically yellow, that measures 22 × 35.5 cm (8.5 × 14 inches).

legal person ▶ noun Law an individual, company, or other entity which has legal rights and is subject to obligations.

legal separation ▶ noun an arrangement by which a husband and wife remain married but live apart, following a court order. Also called JUDICIAL SEPARATION.

legal tender ▶ noun [mass noun] coins or banknotes that must be accepted if offered in payment of a debt.

legate /ˈlɛɡət/ ▶ noun **1** a member of the clergy, especially a cardinal, representing the Pope. ■ archaic an ambassador or messenger.
2 a general or governor of an ancient Roman province, or their deputy: *the Roman legate of Syria.*
– DERIVATIVES **legateship** noun, **legatine** /-tɪn/ adjective.
– ORIGIN late Old English, from Old French *legat*, from Latin *legatus*, past participle of *legare* 'depute, delegate, bequeath'.

legate a latere /ˌlɛɡət ɑː ˈlatəreɪ, -ri/ ▶ noun a papal legate of the highest class, with full powers.
– ORIGIN early 16th cent.: from LEGATE + Latin *a latere* 'by a third party'.

legatee /ˌlɛɡəˈtiː/ ▶ noun a person who receives a legacy.
– ORIGIN late 17th cent.: from 15th-cent. *legate* 'bequeath' (from Latin *legare* 'delegate, bequeath') + -EE.

legation ▶ noun **1** a diplomatic minister, especially one below the rank of ambassador, and their staff. ■ the official residence of a diplomatic minister.
2 archaic the position or office of legate; a legateship.
– ORIGIN late Middle English (denoting the sending of a papal legate; also the mission itself): from Latin *legatio(n-)*, from *legare* 'depute, delegate, bequeath'.

legato /lɪˈɡɑːtəʊ/ Music ▶ adverb & adjective in a smooth flowing manner, without breaks between notes. Compare with STACCATO.
▶ noun (pl. **legatos**) a piece or passage marked to be performed legato.
– ORIGIN Italian, literally 'bound'.

legator /lɪˈɡeɪtə/ ▶ noun rare a testator, especially one who leaves a legacy.
– ORIGIN mid 17th cent.: from Latin, from *legat-* 'deputed, delegated, bequeathed', from the verb *legare.*

leg before wicket (also **leg before**) (abbrev.: **lbw**) ▶ adverb & adjective Cricket (of a batsman) adjudged by the umpire to be out through obstructing the ball with the leg (or other part of the body) rather than the bat, when the ball would otherwise have hit the wicket.

leg break ▶ noun Cricket a ball which deviates from the leg side towards the off side after pitching.

leg bye ▶ noun Cricket a run scored from a ball that has touched part of the batsman's body (apart from the hand) without touching the bat, the batsman having made an attempt to hit it.

leg-cutter ▶ noun Cricket a fast leg break.

legend ▶ noun **1** a traditional story sometimes popularly regarded as historical but not authenticated: *the legend of King Arthur* | [mass noun] *according to legend he banished all the snakes from Ireland.* ■ historical the story of a saint's life.
2 an extremely famous or notorious person, especially in a particular field: *the man was a living legend* | *a screen legend.*
3 an inscription, especially on a coin or medal. ■ a caption: *a picture of a tiger with the legend 'Go ahead make my day'.* ■ the wording on a map or diagram explaining the symbols used: *see legend to Fig. 1.*
▶ adjective [predic.] very well known: *his speed and ferocity in attack were legend.*
– ORIGIN Middle English (in the sense 'story of a saint's life'): from Old French *legende*, from medieval Latin *legenda* 'things to be read', from Latin *legere* 'read'. Sense 1 of the noun dates from the early 17th cent.

legendary ▶ adjective **1** described in or based on legends: *a legendary British king of the 4th century.*
2 remarkable enough to be famous; very well known: *her wisdom in matters of childbirth was legendary.*
– DERIVATIVES **legendarily** adverb.
– ORIGIN early 16th cent. (as a noun denoting a collection of legends, especially of saints' lives): from medieval Latin *legendarius*, from *legenda* 'things to be read' (see LEGEND).

Léger /ˈleɪʒeɪ/, French /leʒe/, Fernand (1881–1955), French painter. From about 1909 he was associated with the cubist movement, but then developed a style inspired by machinery and modern technology; works include the *Contrast of Forms* series (1913).

legerdemain /ˌlɛdʒədɪˈmeɪn/ ▶ noun [mass noun] skilful use of one's hands when performing conjuring tricks. ■ deception; trickery.
– ORIGIN late Middle English: from French *léger de main* 'dexterous', literally 'light of hand'.

leger line /ˈlɛdʒə/ (also **ledger line**) ▶ noun Music a short line added for notes above or below the range of a stave.
– ORIGIN late 19th cent.: *leger*, variant of LEDGER.

leggings ▶ plural noun **1** tight-fitting stretch trousers worn by women and children.
2 strong protective overgarments for the legs.

leggy ▶ adjective (**leggier, leggiest**) **1** having long legs: *a leggy type of collie.* ■ (of a woman) having attractively long legs: *a leggy redhead.*
2 (of a plant) having an excessively long and straggly stem.
– DERIVATIVES **legginess** noun.

leghold trap ▶ noun a type of trap with a mechanism that catches and holds an animal by one of its legs.

Leghorn /ˈlɛɡhɔːn/ old-fashioned name for LIVORNO.

leghorn /lɛˈɡɔːn, ˈlɛɡhɔːn/ ▶ noun **1** [mass noun] fine plaited straw. ■ (also **leghorn hat**) [count noun] a hat made of leghorn.
2 (**Leghorn**) a chicken of a small hardy breed.
– ORIGIN mid 18th cent.: from LEGHORN (Livorno), from where the straw and fowls were imported.

legibility ▶ noun [mass noun] the quality of being clear enough to read: *we've increased the type size for greater legibility.*

legible ▶ adjective (of handwriting or print) clear enough to read: *the original typescript is scarcely legible.*
– DERIVATIVES **legibly** adverb.
– ORIGIN late Middle English: from late Latin *legibilis*, from *legere* 'to read'.

legion ▶ noun **1** a division of 3,000–6,000 men, including a complement of cavalry, in the ancient Roman army. ■ (**the Legion**) the Foreign Legion. ■ (**the Legion**) a national association of former servicemen and servicewomen instituted after the First World War, such as the Royal British Legion or the American Legion.
2 (**a legion/legions of**) a vast number of people or things: *legions of photographers and TV cameras.*
▶ adjective [predic.] great in number: *her fans are legion.*
– ORIGIN Middle English: via Old French from Latin *legio(n-)*, from *legere* 'choose, levy'. The adjective dates from the late 17th cent., in early use often in

L

the phrase *my, their, etc. name is legion*, i.e. 'we, they, etc. are many' (Mark 5:9).

legionary ▶ **noun** (pl. **legionaries**) a soldier in a Roman legion.
▶ **adjective** of an ancient Roman legion.
– ORIGIN late Middle English: from Latin *legionarius*, from *legio(n-)* (see LEGION).

legioned ▶ **adjective** literary arrayed in legions.

legionella /ˌliːdʒəˈnɛlə/ ▶ **noun** (pl. **legionellae** /-liː/) [mass noun] the bacterium which causes legionnaires' disease, flourishing in air conditioning and central heating systems. ● *Legionella pneumophila*, a motile aerobic rod-shaped (or filamentous) Gram-negative bacterium. ■ informal legionnaires' disease.
– ORIGIN 1970s: modern Latin, from LEGION + the diminutive suffix *-ella*.

legionnaire /ˌliːdʒəˈnɛː/ ▶ **noun** a member of a legion, in particular an ancient Roman legion or the French Foreign Legion.
– ORIGIN early 19th cent.: from French *légionnaire*, from *légion* 'legion', from Latin *legio* (see LEGION).

legionnaires' disease ▶ **noun** [mass noun] a form of bacterial pneumonia first identified after an outbreak at an American Legion meeting in 1976. It is spread chiefly by water droplets through air conditioning and similar systems. See also LEGIONELLA.

Legion of Honour a French order of distinction founded in 1802.
– ORIGIN translation of French *Légion d'honneur*.

leg iron ▶ **noun** (usu. **leg irons**) a metal band or chain placed around a prisoner's ankle as a restraint.

legislate /ˈlɛdʒɪsleɪt/ ▶ **verb 1** [no obj.] make or enact laws: *they legislated against discrimination in the workplace.* ■ [with obj.] bring about by making or enacting laws: *constitutional changes will be legislated.*
2 (**legislate for/against**) provide or prepare for (an occurrence): *you cannot legislate for bad luck like that.*
– ORIGIN early 18th cent.: back-formation from LEGISLATION.

legislation ▶ **noun** [mass noun] laws, considered collectively: *housing legislation.* ■ the process of making or enacting laws.
– ORIGIN mid 17th cent. (denoting the enactment of laws): from late Latin *legis latio(n-)*, literally 'proposing of a law', from *lex* 'law' and *latus* 'raised' (past participle of *tollere*).

legislative /ˈlɛdʒɪslətɪv/ ▶ **adjective** having the power to make laws: *the country's supreme legislative body.* Often contrasted with EXECUTIVE. ■ relating to legislation: *legislative proposals.* ■ relating to a legislature: *legislative elections.*
– DERIVATIVES **legislatively** adverb.

legislator ▶ **noun** a person who makes laws; a member of a legislative body.
– ORIGIN late 15th cent.: from Latin *legis lator*, literally 'proposer of a law', from *lex* 'law' and *lator* 'proposer, mover' (see also LEGISLATION).

legislature /ˈlɛdʒɪslətʃə/ ▶ **noun** the legislative body of a country or state.
– ORIGIN late 17th cent.: from LEGISLATION, on the pattern of *judicature*.

legit /lɪˈdʒɪt/ ▶ **adjective** informal conforming to the rules; legal: *is this car legit?* ■ (of a person) not engaging in illegal activity or attempting to deceive; honest: *he used to be a bad boy, but now he's totally legit.*
– ORIGIN early 20th cent.: abbreviation of LEGITIMATE.

legitimacy /lɪˈdʒɪtɪməsi/ ▶ **noun** [mass noun] **1** conformity to the law or to rules: *refusal to recognize the legitimacy of both governments.* ■ (with reference to a child) the quality of being legitimate: *disputes over the legitimacy of heirs.*
2 ability to be defended with logic or justification; validity: *it is difficult to judge the legitimacy of the rumour.*

legitimate ▶ **adjective** /lɪˈdʒɪtɪmət/ **1** conforming to the law or to rules: *his claims to legitimate authority.* ■ (of a child) born of parents lawfully married to each other. ■ (of a sovereign) having a title based on strict hereditary right.
2 able to be defended with logic or justification; valid: *a legitimate excuse for being late.*
3 constituting or relating to serious drama as distinct from musical comedy, revue, etc.: *the legitimate theatre.*
▶ **verb** /lɪˈdʒɪtɪmeɪt/ [with obj.] make lawful or justify: *the regime was not legitimated by popular support.*
– DERIVATIVES **legitimately** adverb, **legitimation** noun, **legitimatization** noun, **legitimatize** (also **legitimatise**) verb.
– ORIGIN late Middle English (in the sense 'born of parents lawfully married to each other'): from medieval Latin *legitimatus* 'made legal', from the verb *legitimare*, from Latin *legitimus* 'lawful', from *lex, leg-* 'law'.

legitimism ▶ **noun** [mass noun] support for a sovereign or pretender whose claim to a throne is based on direct descent.
– DERIVATIVES **legitimist** noun & adjective.
– ORIGIN late 19th cent.: from French *légitimisme*, from *légitime*, from Latin *legitimus* (see LEGITIMATE).

legitimize (also **legitimise**) ▶ **verb** [with obj.] make legitimate: *voters legitimize the government through the election of public officials.*
– DERIVATIVES **legitimization** noun.

legless ▶ **adjective 1** having no legs.
2 Brit. informal extremely drunk.

legless lizard ▶ **noun** a lizard which lacks legs and has a snake-like or worm-like appearance, in particular: ● an Australian lizard of a group that includes the scalyfoots (several genera in the family Pygopodidae). ● a North American lizard of California and Baja California (genus *Anniella* and family Anniellidae).

legman ▶ **noun** (pl. **legmen**) a person employed to do simple tasks such as running errands. ■ N. Amer. a reporter whose job it is to gather information about news stories at the scene of the event or from an original source.

Lego ▶ **noun** [mass noun] trademark a construction toy consisting of interlocking plastic building blocks.
– ORIGIN 1950s: from Danish *leg godt* 'play well', from *lege* 'to play'.

leg-of-mutton sleeve ▶ **noun** a sleeve which is full and loose on the upper arm but close-fitting on the forearm and wrist.

leg-over ▶ **noun** Brit. vulgar slang an instance of sexual intercourse.

leg-pull ▶ **noun** informal a trick or practical joke.
– DERIVATIVES **leg-pulling** noun.

legroom ▶ **noun** [mass noun] space in which a seated person can put their legs.

leg show ▶ **noun** informal, dated a theatrical production in which dancing girls display their legs.

leg side ▶ **noun** see LEG (sense 5 of the noun).

leg slip ▶ **noun** Cricket a fielding position just behind the batsman on the leg side. ■ a fielder at this position.

leg spin ▶ **noun** [mass noun] Cricket a type of spin bowling which causes the ball to deviate from the leg side towards the off side after pitching; leg breaks.
– DERIVATIVES **leg-spinner** noun.

leg stump ▶ **noun** Cricket the stump on the leg side of a wicket.

leg trap ▶ **noun** Cricket a group of fielders close to the wicket on the leg side.

leguan /ˈlɛgjʊən/ (also **leguaan** or **likkewaan**) ▶ **noun** S. African a large African monitor lizard. ● Genus *Varanus*, family Varanidae: the **water leguan** or Nile monitor, and *V. exanthematicus*, which lives in burrows in savannah and semi-desert habitats.
– ORIGIN late 18th cent.: from Dutch, probably from French *l'iguane* 'the iguana'.

legume /ˈlɛgjuːm/ ▶ **noun** a leguminous plant, especially one grown as a crop. ■ a seed, pod, or other edible part of a leguminous plant, used as food. ■ Botany the long seed pod of a leguminous plant.
– ORIGIN mid 17th cent. (denoting the edible portion of the plant): from French *légume*, from Latin *legumen*, from *legere* 'to pick' (because the fruit may be picked by hand).

leguminous /lɪˈgjuːmɪnəs/ ▶ **adjective** Botany relating to or denoting plants of the pea family (Leguminosae). These have seeds in pods, distinctive flowers, and typically root nodules containing symbiotic bacteria able to fix nitrogen. Compare with PAPILIONACEOUS.
– ORIGIN late Middle English (in the sense 'relating to pulses'): from medieval Latin *leguminosus*, from *legumen* (see LEGUME).

leg-up ▶ **noun** [in sing.] Brit. an act of helping someone to mount a horse or high object: *give me a leg-up over the wall.* ■ an act of helping someone or something to improve their situation: *he gave hip hop a much-needed leg-up.*
– PHRASES **have** (or **get**) **a leg-up on** US informal have (or get) an advantage over: *he'd certainly have a leg-up on the competition.*

leg warmer ▶ **noun** each of a pair of tubular knitted garments designed to cover the leg from ankle to knee or thigh, typically worn by dancers during rehearsal.

legwork ▶ **noun** [mass noun] work that involves much travelling about to collect information, especially when such work is difficult but boring.

Leh /leɪ/ a town in Jammu and Kashmir, northern India, to the east of Srinagar near the Indus River; pop. 46,500 (est. 2009). It is the chief town of the Himalayan region of Ladakh, and the administrative centre of Ladakh district.

Lehár /ˈleɪhɑː/, Franz (Ferenc) (1870–1948), Hungarian composer. He is chiefly known for his operettas, of which the most famous is *The Merry Widow* (1905).

Le Havre /lə ˈhɑːvr(ə)/, French /lə ˈɑvʀ/ a port in northern France, on the English Channel at the mouth of the Seine; pop. 185,311 (2006).

lehnga /ˈlɛŋgə/ (also **lehenga**) ▶ **noun** a full ankle-length skirt worn by Indian women, usually on formal or ceremonial occasions.
– ORIGIN Punjabi *lehnga*.

lehr /lɪə/ (also **leer**) ▶ **noun** a furnace used for the annealing of glass.
– ORIGIN mid 17th cent.: of unknown origin.

lei[1] /leɪ, ˈleɪi/ ▶ **noun** a Polynesian garland of flowers.
– ORIGIN Hawaiian.

lei[2] plural form of LEU.

Leibniz /ˈlʌɪbnɪts/, Gottfried Wilhelm (1646–1716), German rationalist philosopher, mathematician, and logician. He argued that the world is composed of single units (monads), each of which is self-contained but acts in harmony with every other, as ordained by God, and so this world is the best of all possible worlds. Leibniz also made the important distinction between necessary and contingent truths and devised a method of calculus independently of Newton.
– DERIVATIVES **Leibnizian** adjective & noun.

Leibovitz /ˈliːbəvɪts/, Annie (b.1950), American photographer. She was chief photographer of *Rolling Stone* magazine (1973–83) before moving to *Vanity Fair*, and has produced portraits of many celebrities.

Leicester[1] /ˈlɛstə/ a city in central England, on the River Soar, the county town of Leicestershire; pop. 294,900 (est. 2009). It was founded as a Roman settlement where the Fosse Way crosses the Soar (AD 50–100).

Leicester[2] /ˈlɛstə/, Earl of, see DUDLEY[2].

Leicester[3] /ˈlɛstə/ ▶ **noun 1** (also **Red Leicester**) [mass noun] a kind of mild, firm orange cheese originally made in Leicestershire.
2 (also **Border Leicester**) a sheep of a breed often crossed with other breeds to produce lambs for the meat industry.
3 (also **Blue-faced Leicester**) a sheep of a breed similar to the Border Leicester, but with finer wool and a darker face.

Leicestershire /ˈlɛstəʃɪə, -ʃə/ a county of central England; county town, Leicester.

Leichhardt /ˈlʌɪkhɑːt/, (Friedrich Wilhelm) Ludwig (1813–48), Australian explorer, born in Prussia. After emigrating to Australia in 1841, he began a series of geological surveys; he disappeared during an attempt at a transcontinental crossing.

Leics. ▶ **abbreviation** Leicestershire.

Leiden /ˈlʌɪd(ə)n/ (also **Leyden**) a city in the west Netherlands, 15 km (9 miles) north-east of The Hague; pop. 116,878 (2008). It is the site of the country's oldest university, founded in 1575.

Leif Ericsson see ERICSSON[2].

Leigh /liː/, Vivien (1913–67), British actress, born in India; born *Vivian Mary Hartley*. She won Oscars for her performances in *Gone with the Wind* (1939) and *A Streetcar Named Desire* (1951). She was married to Laurence Olivier from 1940 to 1961.

Leighton /ˈleɪt(ə)n/, Frederic, 1st Baron Leighton of Stretton (1830–96), English painter and sculptor. He was a leading exponent of Victorian neoclassicism and chiefly painted large-scale mythological and genre scenes. Notable works: *Flaming June* (painting, c.1895).

L

Leinster /ˈlɛnstə/ a province of the Republic of Ireland, in the south-east of the country, centred on Dublin.

leiothrix /ˈlʌɪə(ʊ)θrɪks/ (also **red-billed leiothrix**) ▶ **noun** an Asian bird of the babbler family, with orange-yellow underparts and a melodious song, popular as a cage bird. Also called PEKIN ROBIN. ● *Leiothrix lutea*, family Timaliidae.
– ORIGIN modern Latin, from Greek *leios* 'smooth' + *thrix* 'hair'.

Leipzig /ˈlʌɪpsɪɡ/, German /ˈlaiptsɪç/ an industrial city in east central Germany; pop. 506,600 (est. 2006).

leishmania /liːʃˈmeɪnɪə/ ▶ **noun** (pl. **same** or **leishmanias** or **leishmaniae** /-ˈmeɪnɪʌɪ/) a single-celled parasitic protozoan which spends part of its life cycle in the gut of a sandfly and part in the blood and other tissues of a vertebrate. ● Genus *Leishmania*, phylum Kinetoplastida, kingdom Protista.
– ORIGIN modern Latin, from the name of William B. *Leishman* (1856–1926), British pathologist.

leishmaniasis /ˌliːʃməˈnʌɪəsɪs/ ▶ **noun** [mass noun] a tropical and subtropical disease caused by leishmania and transmitted by the bite of sandflies. It affects either the skin or the internal organs.

Leisler's bat /ˈlʌɪzləz/ ▶ **noun** a small blackish bat related to the noctule, found from Europe and North Africa to central Asia. ● *Nyctalus leisleri*, family Vespertilionidae.
– ORIGIN early 20th cent.: named after T. P. *Leisler*, 19th-cent. German zoologist.

leister /ˈliːstə/ ▶ **noun** a pronged spear used for catching salmon.
▶ **verb** [with obj.] spear (a fish) with a leister.
– ORIGIN mid 16th cent.: from Old Norse *ljóstr*, from *ljósta* 'to strike'.

leisure /ˈlɛʒə/ ▶ **noun** [mass noun] time when one is not working or occupied; free time. ■ use of free time for enjoyment: *increased opportunities for leisure* | [as modifier] *leisure activities*. ■ (**leisure for/to do something**) opportunity afforded by free time to do something: *writers with enough leisure to practise their art*.
– PHRASES **at leisure 1** not occupied; free: *the rest of the day can be spent at leisure*. **2** in an unhurried manner: *the poems were left for others to read at leisure*. **at one's leisure** at one's convenience. **lady** (or **man** or **gentleman**) **of leisure** a person who does not need to earn a living.
– ORIGIN Middle English: from Old French *leisir*, based on Latin *licere* 'be allowed'.

leisure centre ▶ **noun** Brit. a large public building with many different sports and exercise facilities.

leisure complex ▶ **noun** a large establishment (or group of establishments) that provides facilities for a wide range of entertainment, exercise, and sport.

leisured ▶ **adjective** having ample leisure, especially through being rich: *the leisured classes*. ■ leisurely: *the leisured life of his college*.

leisurely ▶ **adjective** acting or done at leisure; unhurried or relaxed: *a leisurely breakfast at our hotel*.
▶ **adverb** without hurry.
– DERIVATIVES **leisureliness** noun.

leisurewear ▶ **noun** [mass noun] casual clothes designed to be worn for leisure activities.

leitmotif /ˈlʌɪtməʊˌtiːf/ (also **leitmotiv**) ▶ **noun** a recurrent theme throughout a musical or literary composition, associated with a particular person, idea, or situation.
– ORIGIN late 19th cent.: from German *Leitmotiv*, from *leit-* 'leading' (from *leiten* 'to lead') + *Motiv* 'motive'.

Leitrim /ˈliːtrɪm/ a county of the Republic of Ireland, in the province of Connacht; county town, Carrick-on-Shannon.

Leix variant spelling of LAOIS.

lek¹ /lɛk/ ▶ **noun** the basic monetary unit of Albania, equal to 100 qintars.
– ORIGIN Albanian.

lek² /lɛk/ ▶ **noun** a patch of ground used for communal display in the breeding season by the males of certain birds and mammals, especially black grouse.
▶ **verb** [no obj.] (usu. as noun **lekking**) take part in a communal display on a lek.
– ORIGIN late 19th cent.: perhaps from Swedish *leka* 'to play'.

lekker /ˈlɛkə, ˈlʌkə/ S. African informal ▶ **adjective 1** good; pleasant: *the lekker local flavour of South Africa*.
2 slightly intoxicated.
▶ **adverb 1** well: *we got on lekker*.
2 [as submodifier] extremely: *he was lekker drunk*.
– ORIGIN Afrikaans, from Dutch, literally 'delicious'.

Lely /ˈliːli/, Sir Peter (1618–80), Dutch portrait painter, resident in England from 1641; Dutch name *Pieter van der Faes*. He became principal court painter to Charles II. Notable works include *Windsor Beauties*, a series painted during the 1660s.

LEM ▶ **abbreviation** lunar excursion module.

leman /ˈlɛmən, ˈliː-/ ▶ **noun** (pl. **lemans**) archaic a lover or sweetheart. ■ an illicit lover, especially a mistress.
– ORIGIN Middle English *lēofman*, from *lēof* (see LIEF) + MAN.

Le Mans /lə ˈmɒ̃/ an industrial city in NW France; pop. 148,169 (2006). It is the site of a motor-racing circuit, on which a 24-hour endurance race (established in 1923) is held each summer.

Lemberg /ˈlɛmbɛrk/ German name for LVIV.

lemma¹ /ˈlɛmə/ ▶ **noun** (pl. **lemmas** or **lemmata** /-mətə/) **1** a subsidiary or intermediate theorem in an argument or proof.
2 a heading indicating the subject or argument of a literary composition or annotation.
3 a word or phrase defined in a dictionary or entered in a word list.
– ORIGIN late 16th cent.: via Latin from Greek *lēmma* 'something assumed'; related to *lambanein* 'take'.

lemma² /ˈlɛmə/ ▶ **noun** (pl. **lemmas** or **lemmata** /-mətə/) Botany the lower bract of the floret of a grass. Compare with PALEA.
– ORIGIN mid 18th cent. (denoting the husk or shell of a fruit): from Greek, from *lepein* 'to peel'.

lemmatize (also **lemmatise**) ▶ **verb** [with obj.] sort so as to group together inflected or variant forms of the same word.
– DERIVATIVES **lemmatization** noun.

lemme informal ▶ **contraction** let me: *lemme ask you something*.

lemming ▶ **noun** a small, short-tailed, thickset rodent related to the voles, found in the Arctic tundra. ● *Lemmus*, *Dicrostonyx*, and other genera, family Muridae: several species, in particular the **Norway lemming** (*L. lemmus*), noted for its fluctuating populations and periodic mass migrations, which in popular belief sometimes culminate in the animals jumping off cliffs into the sea.
■ a person who unthinkingly joins a mass movement, especially a headlong rush to destruction.
– ORIGIN early 18th cent.: from Norwegian and Danish; related to Old Norse *lómundr*.

Lemnos /ˈlɛmnɒs/ a Greek island in the northern Aegean Sea; chief town, Kástron. Greek name LÍMNOS.

lemon ▶ **noun 1** a pale yellow oval citrus fruit with thick skin and fragrant, acidic juice. ■ [mass noun] a drink made from or flavoured with lemon juice: *a port and lemon*.
2 (also **lemon tree**) the evergreen citrus tree which produces lemons, widely cultivated in warm climates. ● *Citrus limon*, family Rutaceae.
3 [mass noun] a pale yellow colour: [as modifier] *a lemon T-shirt*.
4 informal an unsatisfactory or feeble person or thing: *car-makers cannot afford to create lemons*.
– DERIVATIVES **lemony** adjective.
– ORIGIN Middle English: via Old French *limon* (in modern French denoting a lime) from Arabic *līmūn* (a collective term for fruits of this kind); compare with LIME².

lemonade ▶ **noun** [mass noun] a drink made from lemon juice and water sweetened with sugar. ■ Brit. a sweet colourless carbonated drink containing lemon flavouring.
– ORIGIN mid 17th cent.: from French *limonade*, from *limon* 'lemon'.

lemon balm ▶ **noun** see BALM (sense 3).

lemon curd (Brit. also **lemon cheese**) ▶ **noun** [mass noun] a thick conserve made from lemons, butter, eggs, and sugar.

lemon grass ▶ **noun** [mass noun] a fragrant tropical grass which yields an oil that smells of lemon. It is widely used in Asian cooking and in perfumery and medicine. ● *Cymbopogon citratus*, family Gramineae.

lemon sole ▶ **noun** a common European flatfish of the plaice family. It is an important food fish. ● *Microstomus kitt*, family Pleuronectidae.
– ORIGIN mid 19th cent.: *lemon* from French *limande*, of unknown origin.

lemon-squeezer ▶ **noun** Brit. a small kitchen device for extracting the juice from lemons.

lemon thyme ▶ **noun** thyme of a hybrid variety having lemon-scented leaves. ● *Thymus* × *citriodorus*, family Labiatae.

lemon verbena ▶ **noun** a South American shrub of the verbena family, with lemon-scented leaves that are used as flavouring and to make a sedative tea. ● *Aloysia triphylla*, family Verbenaceae.

lemonwood ▶ **noun** a small evergreen New Zealand tree whose leaves produce a lemon-like smell when crushed. Also called TARATA in New Zealand. ● *Pittosporum eugenoides*, family Pittosporaceae.

lempira /lɛmˈpɪərə/ ▶ **noun** the basic monetary unit of Honduras, equal to 100 centavos.
– ORIGIN named after *Lempira*, a 16th-cent. Indian chieftain who opposed the Spanish conquest of Honduras.

lemur /ˈliːmə/ ▶ **noun** an arboreal primate with a pointed snout and typically a long tail, found only in Madagascar. Compare with FLYING LEMUR. ● Lemuridae and other families, suborder Prosimii; includes also the sifaka, indri, and aye-aye.
– ORIGIN late 18th cent.: modern Latin, from Latin *lemures* (plural) 'spirits of the dead' (from its spectre-like face).

Lena /ˈleɪnə/ a river in Siberia, which rises in the mountains on the western shore of Lake Baikal and flows for 4,400 km (2,750 miles) into the Laptev Sea. It is famous for the goldfields in its basin.

Lenclos /lɒ̃ˈkləʊ/, French /lɑ̃klo/, Ninon de (1620–1705), French courtesan; born *Anne de Lenclos*. She was a famous wit and beauty who advocated a form of Epicureanism in her book *La Coquette vengée* (1659), and later presided over one of the most distinguished literary salons of the age.

lend ▶ **verb** (past and past participle **lent**) [with two objs]
1 grant to (someone) the use of (something) on the understanding that it will be returned: *Stewart asked me to lend him my car* | *the pictures were lent to each museum in turn*. ■ allow (a person or organization) the use of (a sum of money) under an agreement to pay it back later, typically with interest: *no one would lend him the money* | [no obj.] *banks lend only to their current account customers* | (as noun **lending**) *balance sheets weakened by unwise lending*.
2 contribute or add (a quality) to: *the smile lent his face a boyish charm*.
3 (**lend oneself to**) accommodate or adapt oneself to: *John stiffly lent himself to her aromatic embraces*. ■ (**lend itself to**) (of a thing) be suitable for: *bay windows lend themselves to blinds*.
– PHRASES **lend an ear** (or **one's ears**) listen sympathetically or attentively. **lend a hand** (or **a helping hand**) see GIVE A HAND at HAND. **lend one's name to** allow oneself to be publicly associated with: *he lent his name and prestige to the project*.
– DERIVATIVES **lendable** adjective.
– ORIGIN Old English *lǣnan*, of Germanic origin; related to Dutch *lenen*, also to LOAN¹. The addition of the final *-d* in late Middle English was due to association with verbs such as *bend* and *send*.

lender ▶ **noun** an organization or person that lends money: *a mortgage lender*.

lending library ▶ **noun** a public library from which books may be borrowed and taken away for a short time.

Lend-Lease historical an arrangement made in 1941 whereby the US supplied military equipment and armaments to the UK and its allies, originally as a loan in return for the use of British-owned military bases. Also called LEASE-LEND.

lengha ▶ **noun** variant spelling of LEHNGA.

length /lɛŋθ, lɛŋkθ/ ▶ **noun 1** [mass noun] the measurement or extent of something from end to end; the greater of two or the greatest of three dimensions of an object: *the delta is twenty kilometres* ***in length*** | [count noun] *the fish reaches a length of 10 inches*. ■ the quality of being long: *the length of the waiting list*. ■ [count noun] the length of a swimming pool as a measure of the distance swum: *fifty lengths of the pool*. ■ [count noun] the length of a horse, boat, etc., as a measure of the lead in a race: *the mare won the race by seven lengths*. ■ the extent of a garment in a vertical direction when worn. ■ the full distance that a thing extends for: *the muscles running the length of my spine*. ■ (**one's length**) the full extent of one's body: *he awkwardly lowered his length into the small car*. ■ Prosody & Phonetics the metrical quantity or duration of a vowel or syllable.
2 the amount of time occupied by something: *delivery must be within a reasonable length of time*.

L

3 a piece or stretch of something: ***a length of** brown satin* | *the surviving **length of** track.*
4 an extreme to which a course of action is taken: *they **go to great lengths** to avoid the press.*
5 Cricket the distance from the batsman at which a well-bowled ball pitches: *Lewis tended to bowl short of a length.*
6 (in bridge or whist) the number of cards of a suit held in one's hand, especially when five or more.
– PHRASES **at length 1** in detail; fully: *these aspects have been discussed at length.* **2** after a long time: *at length she laid down the pencil.* **the length and breadth of** the whole extent of: *women from the length and breadth of Russia.*
– ORIGIN Old English *lengthu*, of Germanic origin; related to Dutch *lengte*, also to LONG[1].

-length ▶ **combining form** reaching up to or down to the place specified: *knee-length.* ■ of the size, duration, or extent specified: *full-length* | *feature-length.*

lengthen ▶ **verb** make or become longer: [with obj.] *the mascara will lengthen your lashes* | [no obj.] *in the spring when the days are lengthening* | (as adj. **lengthening**) *the lengthening shadows.*
– DERIVATIVES **lengthener** noun.

lengthman ▶ **noun** (pl. **lengthmen**) archaic a person employed to maintain a section of road or railway.

lengthways ▶ **adverb** in a direction parallel with a thing's length: *cut the courgettes in half lengthways.*

lengthwise ▶ **adverb** lengthways: *halve the potatoes lengthwise.*
▶ **adjective** [attrib.] lying or moving lengthways.

lengthy ▶ **adjective** (**lengthier**, **lengthiest**) (especially in reference to time) of considerable or unusual length, especially so as to be tedious: *lengthy delays.*
– DERIVATIVES **lengthily** adverb, **lengthiness** noun.

leniency /ˈliːnɪənsi/ ▶ **noun** [mass noun] the fact or quality of being more merciful or tolerant than expected; clemency: *the court could show leniency.*
– DERIVATIVES **lenience** noun.

lenient /ˈliːnɪənt/ ▶ **adjective 1** (of a punishment or person in authority) more merciful or tolerant than expected: *in the view of the Court the sentence was too lenient* | *lenient magistrates.*
2 archaic mild or soothing; emollient.
– DERIVATIVES **leniently** adverb.
– ORIGIN mid 17th cent. (in sense 2): from Latin *lenient-* 'soothing', from the verb *lenire*, from *lenis* 'mild, gentle'.

Lenin /ˈlɛnɪn/, Vladimir Ilich (1870–1924), the principal figure in the Russian Revolution and first Premier of the Soviet Union 1918–24; born *Vladimir Ilich Ulyanov.*

> Lenin was the first political leader to attempt to put Marxist principles into practice. In 1917 he established Bolshevik control after the overthrow of the tsar, and in 1918 became head of state (Chairman of the Council of People's Commissars). With Trotsky he defeated counter-revolutionary forces in the Russian Civil War, but was forced to moderate his policies to allow the country to recover from the effects of war and revolution.

Leninakan /ˌlɛnɪnəˈkɑːn/ former name (1924–91) for GYUMRI.

Leningrad /ˈlɛnɪngrad/ former name (1924–91) for ST PETERSBURG.

Leninism ▶ **noun** [mass noun] Marxism as interpreted and applied by Lenin.
– DERIVATIVES **Leninist** noun & adjective.
– ORIGIN early 20th cent.: named after LENIN.

lenis /ˈlɛnɪs, ˈleɪnɪs, ˈliːnɪs/ ▶ **adjective** Phonetics (of a consonant, especially a voiced consonant) weakly articulated, especially denoting the less or least strongly articulated of two or more similar consonants. The opposite of FORTIS.
– ORIGIN early 20th cent.: from Latin, literally 'mild, gentle'.

lenite /ˈliːnʌɪt, lɪˈnʌɪt/ ▶ **verb** (**be lenited**) (of a consonant in a Celtic language) be pronounced with palatalization.
– ORIGIN early 20th cent.: back-formation from LENITION.

lenition /lɪˈnɪʃ(ə)n/ ▶ **noun** [mass noun] (in Celtic languages) the process or result of palatalizing a consonant.
– ORIGIN early 20th cent.: from Latin *lenis* 'soft' + -ITION, suggested by German *Lenierung.*

lenitive /ˈlɛnɪtɪv/ Medicine, archaic ▶ **adjective** (of a medicine) laxative.
▶ **noun** a laxative.
– ORIGIN late Middle English: from medieval Latin *lenitivus*, from *lenit-* 'softened', from the verb *lenire*.

lenity /ˈlɛnɪti/ ▶ **noun** [mass noun] literary the quality of being kind or gentle.
– ORIGIN late Middle English: from Old French *lenite*, or from Latin *lenitas*, from *lenis* 'gentle'.

Lennon, John (1940–80), English pop and rock singer, guitarist, and songwriter. A founder member of the Beatles, he wrote most of their songs in collaboration with Paul McCartney. He was assassinated outside his home in New York.

leno /ˈliːnəʊ/ ▶ **noun** (pl. **lenos**) [mass noun] an openwork fabric with the warp threads twisted in pairs before weaving.
– ORIGIN late 18th cent.: from French *linon*, from *lin* 'flax', from Latin *linum*. Compare with LINEN.

Le Nôtre /lə ˈnəʊtr(ə)/, French /lə nɔtʀ/, André (1613–1700), French landscape gardener. He designed many formal gardens, including the parks of Vaux-le-Vicomte and Versailles. These incorporated his ideas on geometric formality and equilibrium.

lens ▶ **noun** a piece of glass or other transparent material with curved sides for concentrating or dispersing light rays, used singly (as in a magnifying glass) or with other lenses (as in a telescope). ■ the light-gathering device of a camera, typically containing a group of compound lenses. ■ Anatomy short for CRYSTALLINE LENS. ■ short for CONTACT LENS. ■ Physics an object or device which focuses or otherwise modifies the direction of movement of light, sound, electrons, etc.
– DERIVATIVES **lensed** adjective, **lensless** adjective.
– ORIGIN late 17th cent.: from Latin, 'lentil' (because of the similarity in shape).

lens hood ▶ **noun** a tube or ring attached to the front of a camera lens to prevent unwanted light from reaching the film.

lensman ▶ **noun** (pl. **lensmen**) a professional photographer or cameraman.

Lent ▶ **noun** (in the Christian Church) the period preceding Easter, which is devoted to fasting, abstinence, and penitence in commemoration of Christ's fasting in the wilderness. In the Western Church it runs from Ash Wednesday to Holy Saturday, and so includes forty weekdays. ■ (**Lents**) the boat races held at Cambridge University in the Lent term.
– ORIGIN Middle English: abbreviation of LENTEN.

lent past and past participle of LEND.

-lent ▶ **suffix** forming adjectives such as *pestilent, violent.* Compare with -ULENT.

Lenten ▶ **adjective** of, in, or appropriate to Lent: *Lenten food.*
– ORIGIN Old English *lencten* 'spring, Lent', of Germanic origin, related to LONG[1] (perhaps with reference to the lengthening of the day in spring); now interpreted as being from LENT + -EN[2].

Lenten fare ▶ **noun** [mass noun] chiefly archaic food appropriate to Lent, especially that without meat.

Lenten rose ▶ **noun** a hellebore that is cultivated for its flowers which appear in late winter or early spring. ● *Helleborus orientalis*, family Ranunculaceae.

lentic /ˈlɛntɪk/ ▶ **adjective** Ecology (of organisms or habitats) inhabiting or situated in still fresh water. Compare with LOTIC.
– ORIGIN 1930s: from Latin *lentus* 'calm, slow' + -IC.

lenticel /ˈlɛntɪsɛl/ ▶ **noun** Botany one of many raised pores in the stem of a woody plant that allows gas exchange between the atmosphere and the internal tissues.
– ORIGIN mid 19th cent.: from modern Latin *lenticella*, diminutive of Latin *lens, lent-* 'lentil'.

lenticular /lɛnˈtɪkjʊlə/ ▶ **adjective 1** shaped like a lentil, especially by being biconvex: *lenticular lenses.*
2 relating to the lens of the eye.
– ORIGIN late Middle English: from Latin *lenticularis*, from *lenticula*, diminutive of *lens, lent-* 'lentil'.

lentiform nucleus ▶ **noun** Anatomy the lower of the two grey nuclei of the corpus striatum.
– ORIGIN early 18th cent.: *lentiform* from Latin *lens, lent-* 'lentil' + -IFORM.

lentigo /lɛnˈtʌɪɡəʊ/ ▶ **noun** (pl. **lentigines** /-ˈtɪdʒɪniːz/) [mass noun] a condition marked by small brown patches on the skin, typically in elderly people.
– ORIGIN late Middle English (denoting a freckle or pimple): from Latin, from *lens, lent-* 'lentil'.

lentil ▶ **noun 1** a high-protein pulse which is dried and then soaked and cooked prior to eating.
2 the plant which yields lentils, native to the Mediterranean and Africa and grown also for fodder. ● *Lens culinaris*, family Leguminosae.
– ORIGIN Middle English: from Old French *lentille*, from Latin *lenticula*, diminutive of *lens, lent-* 'lentil'.

lentisk /lɛnˈtɪsk/ ▶ **noun** the mastic tree.
– ORIGIN late Middle English: from Latin *lentiscus*.

lentivirus /ˈlɛntɪˌvʌɪrəs/ ▶ **noun** Medicine any of a group of retroviruses producing illnesses characterized by a delay in the onset of symptoms after infection.
– ORIGIN 1970s: from Latin *lentus* 'slow' + VIRUS.

lent lily ▶ **noun** Brit. the European wild daffodil, which typically has pale creamy-white outer petals. ● *Narcissus pseudonarcissus*, family Liliaceae (or Amaryllidaceae).

lento /ˈlɛntəʊ/ ▶ **adverb & adjective** Music (especially as a direction) slow or slowly.
▶ **noun** (pl. **lentos**) a passage or movement marked to be performed slowly.
– ORIGIN Italian.

lentoid /ˈlɛntɔɪd/ ▶ **adjective** another term for LENTICULAR (sense 1).
– ORIGIN late 19th cent.: from Latin *lens, lent-* 'lentil' + -OID.

Lent term ▶ **noun** Brit. the university term in which Lent falls.

Lenz's law /ˈlɛntsɪz, ˈlɛnzɪz/ ▶ **noun** Physics a law stating that the direction of an induced current is always such as to oppose the change in the circuit or the magnetic field that produces it.
– ORIGIN mid 19th cent.: named after Heinrich F. E. *Lenz* (1804–65), German physicist.

Leo[1] the name of thirteen popes, notably: ■ **Leo I** (d.461), pope from 440 and Doctor of the Church; known as **Leo the Great**; canonized as **St Leo I**. He defined the doctrine of the Incarnation at the Council of Chalcedon (451) and extended the power of the Roman see to Africa, Spain, and Gaul. Feast day (in the Eastern Church) 18 February; (in the Western Church) 11 April. ■ **Leo X** (1475–1521), pope from 1513; born *Giovanni de' Medici*. He excommunicated Martin Luther and bestowed on Henry VIII of England the title of Defender of the Faith. He was a noted patron of learning and the arts.

L

Leo[2] 1 Astronomy a large constellation (the Lion), said to represent the lion slain by Hercules. It contains the bright stars Regulus and Denebola and numerous galaxies.
2 Astrology the fifth sign of the zodiac, which the sun enters about 23 July. ■ (**a Leo**) (pl. **Leos**) a person born when the sun is in the sign of Leo.
– DERIVATIVES **Leonian** noun & adjective (sense 2).
– ORIGIN Latin.

Leo III (c.680–741), Byzantine emperor 717–41. He repulsed several Muslim invasions and carried out an extensive series of reforms. In 726 he banned icons and other religious images; the resulting iconoclastic controversy led to over a century of political and religious turmoil.

Leo Minor /ˌliːəʊ ˈmʌɪnə/ Astronomy a small and inconspicuous northern constellation (the Little Lion), immediately north of Leo.
– ORIGIN Latin.

León /leɪˈɒn/ **1** a city in northern Spain; pop. 135,119 (2008). It is the capital of the province and former kingdom of León, now part of Castilla-León region.
2 an industrial city in central Mexico; pop. 1,137,465 (2005).
3 a city in western Nicaragua, the second-largest city in the country; pop. 174,051 (2006).

Leonard, Elmore (John) (b.1925), American thriller writer. After working as an advertising copywriter, in 1967 he turned to writing screenplays and novels. Notable works: *Freaky Deaky* (1988) and *Get Shorty* (1990).

Leonardo da Vinci /lɪəˌnɑːdəʊ də ˈvɪntʃi/ (1452–1519), Italian painter, scientist, and engineer.

> His paintings are notable for their blended colour and shading in the technique known as *sfumato*; they include *The Virgin of the Rocks* (1483–5), *The Last Supper* (1498), and the enigmatic *Mona Lisa* (1504–5). He devoted himself to a wide range of other subjects, from anatomy and biology to mechanics and hydraulics: his nineteen notebooks include studies of the human circulatory system and plans for a type of aircraft and a submarine.

Leonberg /ˈliːənbəːɡ/ ▶ **noun** a large dog of a breed typically having a golden coat, produced by crossing a St Bernard and a Newfoundland.

– ORIGIN early 20th cent.: named after a town in SW Germany.

Leoncavallo /ˌleɪɒnkəˈvaləʊ/, Ruggiero (1857–1919), Italian composer. His opera *Pagliacci* (1892) introduced verismo or realism to Italian opera and brought him immediate acclaim.

leone /liːˈəʊn/ ▶ **noun** the basic monetary unit of Sierra Leone, equal to 100 cents.

Leonids /ˈliːənɪdz/ Astronomy an annual meteor shower with a radiant in the constellation Leo, reaching a peak about 17 November.
– ORIGIN late 19th cent.: from Latin *leo, leon-* (see **LEO²**) + **-ID³**.

Leonine /ˈliːənʌɪn/ ▶ **adjective 1** relating to any of the popes named Leo, in particular denoting the part of Rome fortified by Leo IV (d.855).
2 Prosody (of medieval Latin verse) in hexameter or elegiac metre with internal rhyme. ■ (of English verse) with internal rhyme.
▶ **noun (Leonines)** Prosody Leonine verse.
– ORIGIN late Middle English: from the name *Leo*, from Latin *leo* 'lion'. Sense 2 of the adjective may be from the name of a medieval poet, but his identity is not known.

leonine /ˈliːənʌɪn/ ▶ **adjective** of or resembling a lion or lions: *a handsome, leonine profile*.
– ORIGIN late Middle English: from Old French, or from Latin *leoninus*, from *leo, leon-* 'lion'.

Leonine City the part of Rome in which the Vatican stands, walled and fortified by Pope Leo IV.

leopard ▶ **noun** a large solitary cat that has a fawn or brown coat with black spots, native to the forests of Africa and southern Asia. Also called **PANTHER**.
● *Panthera pardus*, family Felidae. See also **BLACK PANTHER**.
■ Heraldry the leopard as a heraldic device. ■ Heraldry a lion passant guardant as in the arms of England. ■ [as modifier] spotted like a leopard: *a leopard-print outfit*.
– PHRASES **a leopard can't change his spots** proverb people can't change their basic nature.
L
– ORIGIN Middle English: via Old French from late Latin *leopardus*, from late Greek *leopardos*, from *leōn* 'lion' + *pardos* (see **PARD**).

leopard cat ▶ **noun** a small East Asian wild cat that has a yellowish-brown coat with black spots and often lives near water. ● *Felis bengalensis*, family Felidae.

leopardess ▶ **noun** a female leopard.

leopard frog ▶ **noun** a common greenish-brown North American frog which has dark leopard-like spots with a pale border. ● *Rana pipiens*, family Ranidae.

leopard lily ▶ **noun** a spotted lily resembling a tiger lily, native to the south-western US. ● *Lilium pardalinum*, family Liliaceae.

leopard moth ▶ **noun** a large white European moth with black spots, the larvae of which tunnel into trees and can cause damage. ● *Zeuzera pyrina*, family Cossidae.

leopard's bane ▶ **noun** a herbaceous Eurasian plant of the daisy family, with large yellow flowers which typically bloom early in the spring. ● Genus *Doronicum*, family Compositae.

leopard seal ▶ **noun** a large grey Antarctic seal which has leopard-like spots and preys on penguins and other seals. ● *Hydrurga leptonyx*, family Phocidae.

leopard-skin ▶ **adjective** (of a garment) made of a fabric resembling the spotted skin of a leopard: *leopard-skin pedal pushers*.

Leopold I /ˈliːəpəʊld/ (1790–1865), first king of Belgium 1831–65. The fourth son of the Duke of Saxe-Coburg-Saalfeld, Leopold was an uncle of Queen Victoria. In 1830 he refused the throne of Greece, but a year later accepted that of the newly independent Belgium.

Léopoldville /ˈliːəpəʊldˌvɪl/ former name (until 1966) for **KINSHASA**.

leotard /ˈliːətɑːd/ ▶ **noun** a close-fitting one-piece garment, made of a stretchy fabric, which covers a person's body from the shoulders to the top of the thighs, worn by dancers or people exercising indoors.
– ORIGIN early 20th cent.: named after Jules *Léotard* (1839–70), French trapeze artist.

Leo the Great Pope Leo I (see **LEO¹**).

lepak /ˈlɛpak/ ▶ **verb (lepaks, lepaking, lepaked)** [no obj.] SE Asian (especially of a young person) spend one's time aimlessly loitering or loafing around.
– ORIGIN from Malay *lepa* 'lazy'.

Lepanto, Battle of /lɪˈpantəʊ/ a naval battle fought in 1571 close to the port of Lepanto at the entrance to the Gulf of Corinth. The Christian forces of Rome, Venice, and Spain defeated a large Turkish fleet, ending for the time being Turkish naval domination in the eastern Mediterranean.

Lepanto, Gulf of another name for the Gulf of Corinth (see **CORINTH, GULF OF**).

Lepcha /ˈlɛptʃə/ ▶ **noun** (pl. **same** or **Lepchas**) **1** a member of a people living mainly in mountain valleys in Sikkim, western Bhutan, and parts of Nepal and West Bengal.
2 [mass noun] the Tibeto-Burman language of the Lepcha, with over 50,000 speakers.
▶ **adjective** relating to the Lepcha or their language.
– ORIGIN from Nepali *lāpche*.

leper ▶ **noun** a person suffering from leprosy. ■ a person who is shunned or rejected by others for moral or social reasons: *the story made her out to be a social leper*.
– ORIGIN late Middle English: probably from an attributive use of *leper* 'leprosy', from Old French *lepre*, via Latin from Greek *lepra*, feminine of *lepros* 'scaly', from *lepos, lepis* 'scale'.

lepidocrocite /ˌlɛpɪdə(ʊ)ˈkrəʊsʌɪt/ ▶ **noun** [mass noun] a red to reddish-brown mineral consisting of ferric hydroxide, typically occurring as scaly or fibrous crystals.
– ORIGIN early 19th cent.: from Greek *lepis, lepid-* 'scale' + *krokis* 'fibre'.

lepidolite /ˈlɛpɪdəlʌɪt, lɪˈpɪdəlʌɪt/ ▶ **noun** [mass noun] a mineral of the mica group containing lithium, typically grey or lilac in colour.
– ORIGIN late 18th cent.: from Greek *lepis, lepid-* 'scale' + **-LITE**.

Lepidoptera /ˌlɛpɪˈdɒpt(ə)rə/ ▶ **plural noun** Entomology an order of insects that comprises the butterflies and moths. They have four large scale-covered wings that bear distinctive markings, and larvae that are caterpillars. ■ **(lepidoptera)** insects of the Lepidoptera order.
– DERIVATIVES **lepidopteran** adjective & noun, **lepidopterous** adjective.
– ORIGIN modern Latin (plural), from Greek *lepis, lepid-* 'scale' + *pteron* 'wing'.

lepidopterist /ˌlɛpɪˈdɒptərɪst/ ▶ **noun** a person who studies or collects butterflies and moths.

Lepidus /ˈlɛpɪdəs/, Marcus Aemilius (died *c.*13 BC), Roman statesman and triumvir. A supporter of Julius Caesar in the civil war against Pompey, he was elected consul in 46, and appointed one of the Second Triumvirate with Octavian and Antony in 43.

leporine /ˈlɛpərʌɪn/ ▶ **adjective** of or resembling a hare or hares.
– ORIGIN mid 17th cent.: from Latin *leporinus*, from *lepus, lepor-* 'hare'.

lepospondyl /ˌlɛpə(ʊ)ˈspɒndɪl/ ▶ **noun** an early fossil amphibian of the Carboniferous and Permian periods, distinguished by vertebrae shaped liked hourglasses. ● Microsauria and related orders, formerly placed in the subclass Lepospondyli.
– ORIGIN 1930s: from modern Latin *Lepospondyli* (plural), from Greek *lepos* 'husk' + *spondulos* 'vertebra'.

leprechaun /ˈlɛprəkɔːn/ ▶ **noun** (in Irish folklore) a small, mischievous sprite.
– ORIGIN early 17th cent.: from Irish *leipreachán*, based on Old Irish *luchorpán*, from *lu* 'small' + *corp* 'body'.

lepromatous /lɛˈprəʊmətəs/ ▶ **adjective** Medicine relating to or denoting the more severe of the two principal forms of leprosy, marked by thickening of the skin and nerves, the formation of lumps on the skin, and often severe loss of feeling and paralysis leading to disfigurement. Compare with **TUBERCULOID**.

leprosarium /ˌlɛprəˈsɛːrɪəm/ ▶ **noun** a hospital for people with leprosy.
– ORIGIN mid 19th cent.: from late Latin *leprosus* 'leprous' + **-ARIUM**.

leprosy ▶ **noun** [mass noun] **1** a contagious disease that affects the skin, mucous membranes, and nerves, causing discoloration and lumps on the skin and, in severe cases, disfigurement and deformities. Leprosy is now mainly confined to tropical Africa and Asia. Also called **HANSEN'S DISEASE**. ● Leprosy is caused by the bacterium *Mycobacterium leprae*, which is Gram-positive, non-motile, and acid-fast.
2 a state of corruption or decay.
– ORIGIN mid 16th cent. (superseding Middle English *lepry*): from **LEPROUS** + **-Y³**.

leprous ▶ **adjective** suffering from leprosy. ■ relating to or resembling leprosy: *leprous growths*.
– ORIGIN Middle English: via Old French from late Latin *leprosus*, from Latin *lepra* 'scaly' (see **LEPER**).

lepta plural form of **LEPTON¹**.

leptin ▶ **noun** [mass noun] Biochemistry a protein produced by fatty tissue which is believed to regulate fat storage in the body.
– ORIGIN 1990s: from Greek *leptos* 'fine, thin' + **-IN¹**.

Leptis Magna /ˌlɛptɪs ˈmagnə/ an ancient seaport and trading centre on the Mediterranean coast of North Africa, near present-day al-Khums in Libya. Founded by the Phoenicians, it became one of the three chief cities of Tripolitania and was later a Roman colony under Trajan.

lepto- ▶ **combining form** small; narrow: *leptocephalic*.
– ORIGIN from Greek *leptos* 'fine, thin, delicate'.

leptocephalic /ˌlɛptə(ʊ)sɪˈfalɪk, -kɛˈfalɪk-/ (also **leptocephalous** /-ˈsɛf(ə)ləs, -ˈkɛf-/) ▶ **adjective** narrow-skulled.

leptomeninges /ˌlɛptəʊmɪˈnɪndʒiːz/ ▶ **plural noun** Anatomy the inner two meninges, the arachnoid and the pia mater, between which circulates the cerebrospinal fluid.
– DERIVATIVES **leptomeningeal** adjective.

lepton¹ /ˈlɛptɒn/ ▶ **noun** (pl. **lepta**) a former monetary unit of Greece used only in calculations, worth one hundredth of a drachma.
– ORIGIN from Greek *lepton*, neuter of *leptos* 'small'.

lepton² /ˈlɛptɒn/ ▶ **noun** Physics a subatomic particle, such as an electron, muon, or neutrino, which does not take part in the strong interaction.
– ORIGIN 1940s: from Greek *leptos* 'small' + **-ON**.

lepton number ▶ **noun** Physics a quantum number assigned to subatomic particles that is ±1 for leptons and 0 for other particles and is conserved in all known interactions.

leptospirosis /ˌlɛptə(ʊ)spʌɪˈrəʊsɪs/ ▶ **noun** [mass noun] an infectious bacterial disease occurring in rodents, dogs, and other mammals, which can be transmitted to humans. See also **WEIL'S DISEASE**. ● The bacterium is a spirochaete of the genus *Leptospira*.
– ORIGIN 1920s: from **LEPTO-** 'narrow' + Greek *speira* 'coil' + **-OSIS**.

leptotene /ˈlɛptə(ʊ)tiːn/ ▶ **noun** [mass noun] Biology the first stage of the prophase of meiosis, during which each chromosome becomes visible as two fine threads (chromatids).
– ORIGIN early 20th cent.: from **LEPTO-** 'narrow, fine' + Greek *tainia* 'band, ribbon'.

Lepus /ˈliːpəs/ Astronomy a small constellation (the Hare) at the foot of Orion, said to represent the hare pursued by Orion.
– ORIGIN Latin.

Lerner /ˈləːnə/, Alan J. (1918–86), American lyricist and dramatist; full name *Alan Jay Lerner*. He wrote a series of musicals with composer Frederick Loewe (1904–88) which were also filmed, including *My Fair Lady* (1956; filmed 1964). He won Oscars for the films *An American in Paris* (1951) and *Gigi* (1958).

Lerwick /ˈləːwɪk/ the capital of the Shetland Islands, on the island of Mainland; pop. 6,200 (est. 2009). The most northerly town in the British Isles, it is a fishing centre and a service port for the oil industry.

les (also **lez**) ▶ **noun** informal a lesbian.

Lesage /ləˈsɑːʒ/, French /ləsaʒ/, Alain-René (1668–1747), French novelist and dramatist. He is best known for the picaresque novel *Gil Blas* (1715–35).

Lesbian ▶ **adjective** from or relating to the island of Lesbos.

lesbian ▶ **noun** a homosexual woman.
▶ **adjective** relating to homosexual women or to homosexuality in women: *a lesbian relationship*.
– DERIVATIVES **lesbianism** noun.
– ORIGIN late 19th cent.: via Latin from Greek *Lesbios*, from **LESBOS**, home of Sappho, who expressed affection for women in her poetry, + **-IAN**.

lesbigay informal ▶ **adjective** relating to or denoting lesbians, bisexuals, and male homosexuals.
▶ **noun** a lesbian, bisexual, or male homosexual.
– ORIGIN 1990s: from *les(bian), bi(sexual)*, and *gay*.

lesbo ▶ **noun** (pl. **lesbos**) informal a lesbian.

Lesbos /ˈlɛzbɒs/ a Greek island in the eastern Aegean, off the coast of NW Turkey; chief town, Mytilene. Its artistic golden age of the late 7th and early 6th centuries BC produced the poets Alcaeus and Sappho. Greek name **Lésvos**.

Lesch–Nyhan syndrome /lɛʃˈnʌɪhən/ ▶ **noun** [mass noun] a rare hereditary disease which affects young boys, usually causing early death. It is marked by compulsive self-mutilation of the head and hands,

together with learning difficulties and involuntary muscular movements.
– ORIGIN 1960s: named after Michael *Lesch* (born 1939) and William L. *Nyhan* (born 1926), American physicians.

lese-majesty /liːz'madʒɪsti/ ▶ **noun** [mass noun] the insulting of a monarch or other ruler; treason. ■ presumptuous or disrespectful behaviour.
– ORIGIN late Middle English: from French *lèse-majesté*, from Latin *laesa majestas* 'injured sovereignty'.

lesion /'liːʒ(ə)n/ ▶ **noun** chiefly Medicine a region in an organ or tissue which has suffered damage through injury or disease, such as a wound, ulcer, abscess, or tumour.
– ORIGIN late Middle English: via Old French from Latin *laesio(n-)*, from *laedere* 'injure'.

Lesotho /lə'suːtuː/ a landlocked mountainous country forming an enclave in South Africa; pop. 2,130,800 (est. 2009); official languages, Sesotho and English; capital, Maseru.

> The region was settled by the Sotho people in the 16th century, coming under British rule (as Basutoland) in 1868. The country became an independent kingdom within the Commonwealth in 1966, changing its name to Lesotho.

less ▶ **determiner & pronoun** a smaller amount of; not as much: [as determiner] *the less time spent there, the better* | [as pronoun] *storage is **less of** a problem than it used to be* | *they returned in **less than** an hour.* ■ fewer in number: [as pronoun] *a population of **less than** 200,000.* See usage at **LESS** below.
▶ **adjective** archaic of lower rank or importance: *James the Less.*
▶ **adverb** to a smaller extent; not so much: *cut out less important material* | *that this is a positive stereotype makes it **no less** a stereotype.* ■ (**less than**) far from; certainly not: *Mitch looked less than happy.*
▶ **preposition** before subtracting (something); minus: *£900,000 less tax.*
– PHRASES **less and less** at a continually decreasing rate. **less is more** used to express the view that a minimalist approach to artistic or aesthetic matters is more effective. **much** (or **still**) **less** used to introduce something as being even less likely than something already mentioned: *what woman would consider a date with him, much less a marriage?* **no less** used to suggest, often ironically, that something is surprising or impressive: *Peter cooked dinner—fillet steak and champagne, no less.* ■ (**no less than**) used to emphasize a surprisingly large amount.
– ORIGIN Old English *lǣssa*, of Germanic origin; related to Old Frisian *lēssa*, from an Indo-European root shared by Greek *loisthos* 'last'.

> **USAGE** In standard English **less** should only be used with uncountable things (*less money, less time*). With countable things it is incorrect to use **less** (*less people* and *less words*); strictly speaking, correct use is *fewer people* and *fewer words*. See also **USAGE** at **FEW**.

-less ▶ **suffix** forming adjectives and adverbs: **1** (from nouns) not having; free from: *flavourless* | *skinless.* **2** (from verbs) not affected by or not carrying out the action of the verb: *fathomless* | *tireless.*
– DERIVATIVES **-lessly suffix** forming corresponding adverbs., **-lessness suffix** forming corresponding nouns.
– ORIGIN Old English *-lēas*, from *lēas* 'devoid of'.

less-developed country ▶ **noun** a Third World or non-industrialized country.

lessee /lɛ'siː/ ▶ **noun** a person who holds the lease of a property; a tenant.
– ORIGIN late 15th cent.: from Old French *lesse*, past participle of *lesser* 'to let, leave', + **-EE**.

lessen ▶ **verb** make or become less; diminish: [with obj.] *the years have lessened the gap in age between us* | [no obj.] *the warmth of the afternoon lessened.*

Lesseps /'lɛsəps/, French /lesɛp/, Ferdinand Marie, Vicomte de (1805–94), French diplomat. From 1854 onwards, while in the consular service in Egypt, he devoted himself to the project of the Suez Canal. In 1881 he embarked on the building of the Panama Canal, but the project was abandoned in 1889.

lesser ▶ **adjective** [attrib.] not so great or important as the other or the rest: *he was convicted of a lesser assault charge* | *they nest mostly in Alaska and **to a lesser extent** in Siberia.* ■ lower in rank or quality: *you're looking down your nose at us lesser mortals.* ■ used in names of animals and plants which are smaller than similar kinds, e.g. **lesser spotted woodpecker, lesser celandine.**
– PHRASES **the lesser evil** (or **the lesser of two evils**) the less unpleasant of two undesirable possibilities: *authoritarianism may seem a lesser evil than abject poverty.*
– ORIGIN Middle English: a double comparative, from **LESS** + **-ER²**.

Lesser Antilles see **ANTILLES**.

Lesser Bairam ▶ **noun** another term for **EID UL-FITR** (see **EID**).

lesser celandine ▶ **noun** see **CELANDINE**.

lesser-known ▶ **adjective** not as well or widely known as others of the same kind.

lesser noctule ▶ **noun** another term for **LEISLER'S BAT**.

lesser panda ▶ **noun** another term for **RED PANDA**.

Lesser Sunda Islands see **SUNDA ISLANDS**.

Lessing, Gotthold Ephraim (1729–81), German dramatist and critic. In his critical works, such as *Laokoon* (1766), he suggested that German writers look to English literature rather than the French classical school. He also wrote both tragedy and comedy.

Les Six /leɪ 'siːs/, French /le sis/ (also **the Six**) a group of six Parisian composers (Louis Durey, Arthur Honegger, Darius Milhaud, Germaine Tailleferre, Georges Auric, and Francis Poulenc) formed after the First World War, whose music represents a reaction against romanticism and Impressionism.
– ORIGIN French, literally 'the Six'.

lesson ▶ **noun 1** a period of learning or teaching: *an advanced lesson in maths* | *a driving lesson.* ■ a thing learned or to be learned by a pupil. ■ a thing learned by experience: *lessons should have been learned from two similar collisions.* ■ an experience or event that serves as a warning or encouragement: *let that be a lesson to you!*
2 a passage from the Bible read aloud during a church service, especially either of two readings at morning and evening prayer in the Anglican Church.
▶ **verb** [with obj.] archaic instruct or teach (someone). ■ rebuke (someone).
– PHRASES **teach someone a lesson** punish or hurt someone as a deterrent or warning: *they were teaching me a lesson for daring to complain.*
– ORIGIN Middle English: from Old French *leçon*, from Latin *lectio* (see **LECTION**).

lessor /lɛ'sɔː, 'lɛsɔː/ ▶ **noun** a person who leases or lets a property to another; a landlord.
– ORIGIN late Middle English: from Anglo-Norman French, from Old French *lesser* 'let, leave'.

lest ▶ **conjunction** formal with the intention of preventing (something undesirable); to avoid the risk of: *he spent whole days in his room, wearing headphones lest he disturb anyone.* ■ (after a clause indicating fear) because of the possibility of something undesirable happening; in case: *she sat up late worrying lest he be murdered on the way home.*
– ORIGIN Old English *thy lǣs the* 'whereby less that', later *the lǣste.*

> **USAGE** There are very few contexts in English where the subjunctive mood is, strictly speaking, required: **lest** remains one of them. Thus the standard use is *she was worrying **lest** he **be** attacked* (not ***lest** he **was** ...*) or *she is using headphones **lest** she **disturb** anyone* (not *... **lest** she **disturbs** anyone*). See also **SUBJUNCTIVE**.

Lésvos /'lɛzvɒs/ Greek name for **LESBOS**.

let¹ ▶ **verb** (**lets, letting**; past and past participle **let**) **1** [with obj. and infinitive] not prevent or forbid; allow: *my boss let me leave early* | *you mustn't let yourself get so involved.* ■ [with obj. and adverbial of direction] allow to pass in a particular direction: *could you let the dog out?* | *a tiny window that let in hardly any light.*
2 [with obj. and infinitive] used in the imperative to formulate various expressions: ■ (**let us** or **let's**) used as a polite way of making or responding to a suggestion, giving an instruction, or introducing a remark: *let's have a drink* | *'Shall we go?' 'Yes, let's.'* ■ (**let me** or **let us**) used to make an offer of help: *'Here, let me,' offered Bruce.* ■ used to express one's strong desire for something to happen or be the case: *'Dear God,' Jessica prayed, 'let him be all right.'* ■ used as a way of expressing defiance or challenge: *if he wants to walk out, well let him!* ■ used to express an assumption upon which a theory or calculation is to be based: *let A and B stand for X and Y respectively.*
3 [with obj.] chiefly Brit. allow someone to have the use of (a room or property) in return for regular payments: *she let the flat to a tenant* | *they've **let out** their house.* ■ award (a contract for a project) to an applicant.
▶ **noun** Brit. a period during which a room or property is rented: *I've taken a month's let on the flat.* ■ a property available for rent: *an unfurnished let.*
– PHRASES **let alone** used to indicate that something is far less likely or suitable than something else already mentioned: *he was incapable of leading a bowling team, let alone a country.* **let someone/thing alone** see **ALONE**. **let someone/thing be** stop interfering with someone or something. **let someone down gently** seek to give someone bad news in a way that avoids causing them too much distress. **let something drop** (or **fall**) casually reveal a piece of information: *from the things he let drop I think there was a woman in his life.* **let fall** Geometry draw (a perpendicular) from an outside point to a line. **let fly** attack physically or verbally: *Mary opened her mouth to let fly at Jim.* **let oneself go 1** act in a relaxed or uninhibited way: *you need to unwind and let yourself go.* **2** become careless or untidy in one's habits or appearance: *he's really let himself go since my mother died.* **let someone/thing go 1** allow someone or something to escape or go free: *they let the hostages go.* ■ euphemistic dismiss an employee. **2** (also **let go** or **let go of**) relinquish one's grip on someone or something: *Adam let go of the reins* | figurative *you must let the past go.* **let someone have it** informal attack someone physically or verbally. **let in** (or **out**) **the clutch** engage (or release) the clutch of a vehicle by releasing pressure on (or applying it to) the clutch pedal. **let something drop** (or **rest**) say or do no more about a matter. **let something go** (or **pass**) choose not to react to an action or remark: *the decision worried us, but we let it go.* **let someone know** inform someone. **let someone/thing loose** release someone or something. ■ allow someone freedom of action in a particular place or situation: *Ellen was laughing like a child let loose in a sweet shop.* ■ suddenly utter a sound or remark: *he let loose a stream of abuse.* **let me see** (or **think**) used when one is trying to remember something or considering one's next words: *now let me see, where did I put it?* **let me tell you** used to emphasize a statement: *let me tell you, I was very scared!* **let off steam** see **STEAM**. **let rip** see **RIP¹**. **let's face it** (or **let's be honest**) informal used to convey that one must be realistic about an unwelcome fact or situation. **let slip** see **SLIP¹**. **let's pretend** a game or situation in which one behaves as though a fictional or unreal situation is a real one. **let's say** (or **let us say**) used as a way of introducing a hypothetical situation: *let's say we agreed to go our separate ways.* **to let** (of a room or property) available for rent.
– PHRASAL VERBS **let down** (of an aircraft or a pilot) descend prior to making a landing. **let someone down** fail to support or help someone as they had hoped. ■ (**let someone/thing down**) have a detrimental effect on the overall quality or success of someone or something: *the whole machine is let down by the tacky keyboard.* **let something down 1** lower something slowly: *they let down a basket on a chain.* **2** make a garment longer by lowering the hem. **3** Brit. deflate a tyre. **let someone in** admit someone to a room, building, or area: *I had to wake up my flatmate Veronica to let me in.* **let oneself in for** informal involve oneself in (something likely to be difficult or unpleasant): *I didn't know what I was letting myself in for.* **let someone in on/into** allow someone to know or share (something secret). **let something into** set something back into (the surface to which it is fixed), so that it does not project: *the basin is partly let into the wall.* **let someone off 1** punish someone lightly or not at all for a misdemeanour or offence: *he was let off with a caution.* **2** excuse someone from a task or obligation: *he let me off work for the day.* **let something off** cause a gun, firework, or bomb to fire or explode. **let on** informal **1** reveal information: *she knows a lot more than she lets on.* **2** pretend: [with clause] *they all let on they didn't hear me.* **let out** N. Amer. (of lessons at school, a meeting, or an entertainment) finish, so that those attending are able to leave: *his classes let out at noon.* **let someone out** release someone from obligation or suspicion: *they've started looking for motives—that lets me out.* **let something out 1** utter a sound or cry. **2** make a garment looser or larger, typically by adjusting a seam. **3** reveal information: [with clause] *she let out that he'd given her a lift home.* **let up** informal (of something undesirable) become less intense: *the rain's letting up—it'll be clear soon.* ■ relax one's efforts: *she was so far ahead she could afford to let up a bit.* ■ (**let up on**) informal treat in a more lenient manner: *she didn't let up on Cunningham.*

– ORIGIN Old English *lǣtan* 'leave behind, leave out', of Germanic origin; related to Dutch *laten* and German *lassen*, also to LATE.

let² ▸ noun (in racket sports) a circumstance under which a service is nullified and has to be taken again, especially (in tennis) when the ball clips the top of the net and falls within bounds.
▸ verb (**lets, letting**; past and past participle **letted** or **let**) [with obj.] archaic hinder: *pray you let us not; we fain would greet our mother*.
– PHRASES **play a let** (in tennis, squash, etc.) play a point again because the ball or one of the players has been obstructed. **without let or hindrance** formal without obstruction or impediment: *rats scurried about the house without let or hindrance*.
– ORIGIN Old English *lettan* 'hinder', of Germanic origin; related to Dutch *letten*, also to LATE.

-let ▸ suffix **1** (forming nouns) denoting a smaller or lesser kind: *booklet* | *starlet*.
2 denoting articles of ornament or dress: *anklet* | *necklet*.
– ORIGIN originally corresponding to French *-ette* added to nouns ending in *-el*.

letch ▸ noun & verb variant spelling of LECH.

let-down ▸ noun **1** a disappointment: *the election was a bit of a let-down*.
2 [mass noun] the release of milk in a nursing mother or lactating animal as a reflex response to suckling or massage.
3 Aeronautics the descent of an aircraft or spacecraft prior to landing.

lethal ▸ adjective sufficient to cause death: *a lethal cocktail of drink and pills*. ■ very harmful or destructive: *the Krakatoa eruption was the most lethal on record*. ■ (in a sporting context) very accurate or skilful: *a lethal drop-shot*.
– DERIVATIVES **lethality** noun, **lethally** adverb.
– ORIGIN late 16th cent. (in the sense 'causing spiritual death'): from Latin *lethalis*, from *lethum*, a variant (influenced by Greek *lēthē* 'forgetfulness'), of *letum* 'death'.

L

lethal chamber ▸ noun an enclosed space in which animals may be killed painlessly with gas.

lethal injection ▸ noun an injection administered for the purposes of euthanasia or as a means of capital punishment.

lethargic /lɪˈθɑːdʒɪk/ ▸ adjective affected by lethargy; sluggish and apathetic: *I felt tired and a little lethargic*.
– DERIVATIVES **lethargically** adverb.
– ORIGIN late Middle English: via Latin from Greek *lēthargikos*, from *lēthargos* 'forgetful'.

lethargy /ˈlɛθədʒi/ ▸ noun [mass noun] a lack of energy and enthusiasm: *there was an air of lethargy about him*. ■ Medicine a pathological state of sleepiness or deep unresponsiveness and inactivity.
– ORIGIN late Middle English: via Old French from late Latin *lethargia*, from Greek *lēthargia*, from *lēthargos* 'forgetful', from the base of *lanthanesthai* 'forget'.

Lethe /ˈliːθi/ Greek Mythology a river in Hades whose water when drunk made the souls of the dead forget their life on earth.
– DERIVATIVES **Lethean** /liːˈθiːən/ adjective.
– ORIGIN via Latin from Greek *lēthē* 'forgetfulness', from the base of *lanthanesthai* 'forget'.

Leticia /ləˈtiːsɪə/, Spanish /leˈtisja, -ˈtiθja/ a town and river port at the southern tip of Colombia, on the upper reaches of the Amazon on the border with Brazil and Peru; pop. 32,450 (2005).

Leto /ˈliːtəʊ/ Greek Mythology the daughter of a Titan, mother (by Zeus) of Artemis and Apollo. Roman name LATONA.

let-off ▸ noun informal a chance to escape or avoid something, especially defeat: *the team had two let-offs as shots rebounded to strike the defenders' legs*.

let-out ▸ noun Brit. informal an opportunity to escape from or avoid a difficult situation.

let-out clause ▸ noun informal a clause specifying a circumstance in which the terms of an agreement or contract shall not apply.

let's ▸ contraction let us: *let's meet for a drink sometime*.

Lett ▸ noun old-fashioned term for LATVIAN.
– DERIVATIVES **Lettish** adjective.
– ORIGIN from German *Lette*, from Latvian *Latvi*.

letter ▸ noun **1** a character representing one or more of the sounds used in speech; any of the symbols of an alphabet: *a capital letter*. ■ (**letters**) Brit. informal the initials of a degree or other qualification: *your personality matters far more than letters after your name*. ■ US a school or college initial as a mark of proficiency, especially in sport: [as modifier] *a letter jacket*.
2 a written, typed, or printed communication, sent in an envelope by post or messenger: *he sent a letter to Mrs Falconer*. ■ (**letters**) a legal or formal document.
3 (**the letter**) the precise terms of a statement or requirement; the strict verbal interpretation: *we must keep the spirit of the law as well as the letter*.
4 (**letters**) literature: *the world of letters*. ■ archaic scholarly knowledge; erudition.
5 [mass noun] Printing a style of typeface.
▸ verb **1** [with obj.] inscribe letters or writing on: *her name was lettered in gold*. ■ classify with letters: *he numbered and lettered the paragraphs*.
2 [no obj.] US informal be given a school or college initial as a mark of proficiency in sport.
– PHRASES **to the letter** with adherence to every detail: *the method was followed to the letter*.
– ORIGIN Middle English: from Old French *lettre*, from Latin *litera*, *littera* 'letter of the alphabet', (plural) 'epistle, literature, culture'.

letter bomb ▸ noun an explosive device hidden in a small package and sent to someone with the intention of harming or killing them.

letter box ▸ noun **1** Brit. a box attached to an outside wall, or a slot in the door of a building, into which mail is delivered.
2 (**letterbox**) [mass noun] [usu. as modifier] a format for presenting widescreen films on a standard television screen, in which the image is displayed in approximately its original proportions across the middle of the screen, leaving horizontal black bands above and below.
▸ verb (**letterbox**) [with obj.] record (a widescreen film) on to video in letterbox format.

letter carrier ▸ noun N. Amer. a postman or postwoman.

lettered ▸ adjective dated formally educated: *though not lettered, he read widely*.

letterform ▸ noun the graphic form of a letter of the alphabet, either as written or in a particular type font.

letterhead (also **letter heading**) ▸ noun a printed heading on stationery, stating a person or organization's name and address. ■ [mass noun] stationery with a printed heading.

lettering ▸ noun [mass noun] the letters inscribed on something, especially decorative ones.

letter missive (also **letters missive**) ▸ noun a letter from the monarch to a dean and chapter nominating a person to be elected bishop.

letter of comfort ▸ noun an assurance about a debt, short of a legal guarantee, given to a bank by a third party.

letter of credence ▸ noun a letter of introduction or recommendation, especially of an ambassador.

letter of credit ▸ noun a letter issued by a bank to another bank (especially one in a different country) to serve as a guarantee for payments made to a specified person under specified conditions.

letter of intent ▸ noun a document containing a declaration of the intentions of the writer.

letter of marque ▸ noun (usu. **letters of marque**) historical a licence to fit out an armed vessel and use it in the capture of enemy merchant shipping and to commit acts which would otherwise have constituted piracy. ■ a ship carrying a letter of marque.
– ORIGIN late Middle English: Law French *marque*, from Old French *marque* 'right of reprisal'.

letter-perfect ▸ adjective North American term for WORD-PERFECT.

letterpress ▸ noun [mass noun] **1** printing from a hard raised image under pressure, using viscous ink.
2 Brit. printed text as opposed to illustrations.

letterset ▸ noun [mass noun] a method of printing in which ink is transferred from a raised surface to a blanket wrapped round a cylinder and from that to the paper.
– ORIGIN 1960s: blend of LETTERPRESS and OFFSET.

letters missive ▸ noun variant of LETTER MISSIVE.

letters of administration ▸ plural noun Law authority to administer the estate of someone who has died without making a will.

letters patent ▸ plural noun an open document issued by a monarch or government conferring a patent or other right.
– ORIGIN late Middle English: from medieval Latin *litterae patentes*, literally 'letters lying open'.

letters rogatory /ˈrəʊɡət(ə)ri/ ▸ plural noun Law documents making a request through a foreign court to obtain information or evidence from a specified person within the jurisdiction of that court.
– ORIGIN mid 19th cent.: *rogatory* from medieval Latin *rogatorius* 'interrogatory'.

letting ▸ noun [mass noun] Brit. the action of renting out a property. ■ [count noun] a property that is let or available to be let.

lettuce ▸ noun a cultivated plant of the daisy family, with edible leaves that are eaten in salads. ● *Lactuca sativa*, family Compositae.
■ used in names of other plants with edible green leaves, e.g. **lamb's lettuce**, **sea lettuce**.
– ORIGIN Middle English: from Old French *letues*, *laitues*, plural of *laitue*, from Latin *lactuca*, from *lac*, *lact-* 'milk' (because of its milky juice).

let-up ▸ noun [in sing.] informal a pause or reduction in the intensity of something dangerous, difficult, or tiring: *there had been no **let-up** in the eruption*.

Letzeburgesch /ˌlɛts(ə)bəːˈɡɛʃ, ˈlɛts(ə),bəːɡɪʃ/ (also **Letzebuergesch**) ▸ noun & adjective another term for LUXEMBURGISH.
– ORIGIN from a local name for LUXEMBOURG + *-esch* (equivalent of -ISH¹).

leu /ˈleɪuː/ ▸ noun (pl. **lei** /leɪ/) the basic monetary unit of Romania, equal to 100 bani.
– ORIGIN Romanian, literally 'lion'.

leucine /ˈluːsiːn/ ▸ noun [mass noun] Biochemistry a hydrophobic amino acid which is a constituent of most proteins. It is an essential nutrient in the diet of vertebrates. ● Chem. formula: $(CH_3)_2CHCH_2CH(NH_2)COOH$.
– ORIGIN early 19th cent.: coined in French from Greek *leukos* 'white' + -INE⁴.

leucistic /luːˈsɪstɪk/ ▸ adjective Zoology (of an animal) having whitish fur, plumage, or skin due to a lack of pigment.
– ORIGIN from LEUCO- 'white' + the adjectival suffix *-istic*.

leucite /ˈluːsʌɪt/ ▸ noun [mass noun] a potassium aluminosilicate mineral, crystallizing in the tetrahedral system and typically found as grey or white glassy trapezohedra in volcanic rocks.
– ORIGIN late 18th cent.: from Greek *leukos* 'white' + -ITE¹.

leuco- (also **leuko-**) ▸ combining form **1** white: *leucoma*.
2 representing LEUCOCYTE.
– ORIGIN from Greek *leukos* 'white'.

leucocyte /ˈluːkə(ʊ)sʌɪt/ (also **leukocyte**) ▸ noun Physiology a colourless cell which circulates in the blood and body fluids and is involved in counteracting foreign substances and disease; a white (blood) cell. There are several types, all amoeboid cells with a nucleus, including lymphocytes, granulocytes, and monocytes.
– DERIVATIVES **leucocytic** adjective.

leucocytosis /ˌluːkə(ʊ)sʌɪˈtəʊsɪs/ (also **leukocytosis**) ▸ noun [mass noun] Medicine an increase in the number of white cells in the blood, especially during an infection.

leucoderma /ˌluːkə(ʊ)ˈdəːmə/ ▸ noun another term for VITILIGO.

leucoma /luːˈkəʊmə/ ▸ noun Medicine a white opacity in the cornea of the eye.
– ORIGIN early 18th cent.: modern Latin, from Greek *leukōma*.

leucopenia /ˌluːkə(ʊ)ˈpiːnɪə/ (also **leukopenia**) ▸ noun [mass noun] Medicine a reduction in the number of white cells in the blood, typical of various diseases.
– DERIVATIVES **leucopenic** adjective.
– ORIGIN late 19th cent.: from Greek *leukos* 'white' + *penia* 'poverty'.

leucoplast /ˈluːkə(ʊ)plast, -plɑːst/ ▸ noun Botany a colourless organelle found in plant cells, used for the storage of starch or oil.

leucorrhoea /ˌluːkəˈriːə/ (US **leucorrhea**, **leukorrhea**) ▸ noun [mass noun] a whitish or yellowish discharge of mucus from the vagina.

leucosis /luːˈkəʊsɪs/ (also **leukosis**) ▸ noun [mass noun] a leukaemic disease of animals, especially one of a group of malignant viral diseases of poultry or cattle.

leucotomy /luːˈkɒtəmi/ ▸ noun (pl. **leucotomies**) [mass noun] the surgical cutting of white nerve fibres within the brain, especially prefrontal lobotomy, formerly used to treat mental illness.

leukaemia /luːˈkiːmɪə/ (US **leukemia**) ▸ noun [mass noun] a malignant progressive disease in which the bone marrow and other blood-forming organs produce

increased numbers of immature or abnormal leucocytes. These suppress the production of normal blood cells, leading to anaemia and other symptoms.
– DERIVATIVES **leukaemic** adjective.
– ORIGIN mid 19th cent.: coined in German from Greek *leukos* 'white' + *haima* 'blood'.

leukaemogenic /luːˌkiːmə(ʊ)ˈdʒɛnɪk/ (US **leukemogenic**) ▸ adjective Medicine relating to or promoting the development of leukaemia.
– DERIVATIVES **leukaemogenesis** noun.

leuko- ▸ combining form variant spelling of LEUCO-.

leukotriene /ˌluːkə(ʊ)ˈtrʌɪiːn/ ▸ noun Biochemistry any of a group of biologically active compounds, originally isolated from leucocytes. They are metabolites of arachidonic acid, containing three conjugated double bonds.

Leuven /ˈləːv(ə)n/ a town in Belgium, east of Brussels; pop. 92,704 (2008). French name LOUVAIN.

lev /lɛv, lɛf/ ▸ noun the basic monetary unit of Bulgaria, equal to 100 stotinki.
– ORIGIN Bulgarian, variant of *lăv* 'lion'.

Lev. ▸ abbreviation Leviticus (in biblical references).

levade /ləˈvɑːd/ ▸ noun a movement performed in classical riding, in which the horse lifts its forelegs from the ground and balances on its deeply bent hind legs.
– ORIGIN 1940s: from French, from *lever* 'raise'.

Levallois /ləˈvalwɑː/ ▸ noun [usu. as modifier] Archaeology a flint-working technique associated with the Mousterian culture of the Neanderthals, in which a flint is trimmed so that a flake of predetermined size and shape can be struck from it.
– ORIGIN early 20th cent.: named after a suburb of northern Paris.

levamisole /lɪˈvamɪsəʊl/ ▸ noun [mass noun] Medicine a synthetic compound used as an anthelmintic drug (especially in animals) and in cancer chemotherapy.
● A polycyclic imidazole derivative; chem. formula: $C_{11}H_{12}N_2S$.
– ORIGIN 1960s: from LEVO- (it being a laevorotatory isomer) + *(tetra)misole*, the name of an anthelmintic drug.

Levant /lɪˈvant/ archaic the eastern part of the Mediterranean with its islands and neighbouring countries.
– ORIGIN late 15th cent.: from French, literally 'rising', present participle of *lever* 'to lift' used as a noun in the sense 'point of sunrise, east'.

levant /lɪˈvant/ ▸ verb [no obj.] archaic run away, typically leaving unpaid debts.
– ORIGIN early 17th cent.: perhaps from LEVANT: compare with French *faire voile en Levant* 'be stolen or spirited away', literally 'set sail for the Levant'.

levanter¹ /lɪˈvantə/ ▸ noun a strong easterly wind in the Mediterranean region.

levanter² /lɪˈvantə/ ▸ noun archaic a person who runs away leaving unpaid debts.

Levantine /lɪˈvantʌɪn, ˈlɛv(ə)n-, -tɪn/ chiefly archaic
▸ adjective relating to the Levant or eastern Mediterranean: *the Levantine coast.*
▸ noun a person who lives in or comes from the Levant.

Levant morocco ▸ noun [mass noun] high-grade large-grained morocco leather.

Levant storax ▸ noun see STORAX (sense 1).

levator /lɪˈveɪtə/ (also **levator muscle**) ▸ noun Anatomy a muscle whose contraction causes the raising of a part of the body.
– ORIGIN early 17th cent.: from Latin, literally 'a person who lifts', from *levare* 'raise, lift'.

levee¹ /ˈlɛvi, ˈlɛveɪ/ ▸ noun archaic or N. Amer. a formal reception of visitors or guests. ■ historical an afternoon assembly for men held by the British monarch or their representative. ■ archaic a reception of visitors just after rising from bed.
– ORIGIN late 17th cent. (denoting a reception of visitors after rising from bed) : from French *levé*, variant of *lever* 'rising', from the verb *lever*.

levee² /ˈlɛvi, lɪˈviː/ ▸ noun an embankment built to prevent the overflow of a river. ■ a ridge of sediment deposited naturally alongside a river by overflowing water. ■ N. Amer. a landing place; a quay.
– ORIGIN early 18th cent. (originally US): from French *levée*, feminine past participle of *lever* 'to lift'.

level ▸ noun **1** a horizontal plane or line with respect to the distance above or below a given point: *the front garden is* **on a level with** *this floor.* ■ a height or distance from the ground or another stated or understood base: *storms caused river levels to rise.* ■ a floor within a multistorey building.
2 a position on a scale of amount, quantity, extent, or quality: *a high level of unemployment* | *debt rose to unprecedented levels.* ■ an intellectual, social, or moral standard: *at six he could play chess at an advanced level* | [mass noun] *women do better at degree level.* ■ a position in a hierarchy: *a junior level of management.*
3 an instrument marked with a line parallel to the plane of the horizon for testing whether things are horizontal. ■ Surveying an instrument for giving a horizontal line of sight.
4 a flat tract of land: [in place names] *the Somerset Levels.*
▸ adjective **1** having a flat, horizontal surface: *we had reached level ground.* ■ (of a quantity of a dry substance) with the contents not rising above the brim of the measure: *a level teaspoon of salt.*
2 at the same height as someone or something else: *his eyes were* **level with** *hers.*
3 having the same relative position; not in front of or behind: *the car backed rapidly until it was* **level with** *me.* ■ chiefly Brit. having the same position or score in a contest: *the two teams finished level on points.* ■ not having risen or fallen; unchanged: *earnings were level at 17.5p a share.*
4 calm and steady: *the cold, level gaze he had given her.*
▸ verb (**levels, levelling, levelled**; US **levels, leveling, leveled**) **1** [with obj.] give a flat and even surface to: *contractors started levelling the ground for the new power station.* ■ demolish (a building or town): *bulldozers are now waiting to level their home.*
2 [no obj.] (**level off/out**) begin to fly horizontally after climbing or diving. ■ (of a path, road, or incline) cease to slope: *the track levelled out and there below us was the bay.* ■ remain at a steady level after falling or rising: *inflation has levelled out at an acceptable rate.*
3 [with obj.] chiefly Brit. make (something, especially a score in sport) equal or similar: *Woods sliced the ball into the net to level the score* | [no obj.] *Ardsley deservedly levelled with two minutes remaining.* ■ (**level something up/down**) increase or reduce something in order to remove a disparity.
4 [with obj.] aim (a weapon): *he* **levelled** *a pistol* **at** *us.* ■ direct (a criticism or accusation): *accusations of corruption had been* **levelled against** *him.*
5 [no obj.] (**level with**) informal be frank or honest with (someone).
6 [with obj.] Surveying ascertain differences in the height of (land).
– PHRASES **do one's level best** make all possible efforts. **find its (own) level** (of a liquid) reach the same height in containers which are interconnected. ■ reach a stable level, value, or position without interference. **find one's (own) level** (of a person) reach a position that seems appropriate in relation to one's associates. **level of attainment** Brit. a rating of the ability of a school pupil, on a scale of 1 to 10. **be level pegging** Brit. be equal in score or achievement during a contest: *the two were level pegging after three heats.* **a level playing field** a situation in which everyone has a fair and equal chance of succeeding. **on the level** informal honest; truthful: *Eddie said my story was on the level.* **on a level with** equal with: *they were treated as menials, on a level with cooks.*
– DERIVATIVES **levelly** adverb, **levelness** noun.
– ORIGIN Middle English (denoting an instrument to determine whether a surface is horizontal): from Old French *livel*, based on Latin *libella*, diminutive of *libra* 'scales, balance'.

level crossing ▸ noun Brit. a place where a railway and a road, or two railway lines, cross at the same level.

level-headed ▸ adjective calm and sensible.
– DERIVATIVES **level-headedly** adverb, **level-headedness** noun.

leveller (US **leveler**) ▸ noun **1** a person or thing that levels something. ■ a situation or activity in which distinctions of class, age, or ability are immaterial: *he valued the sport because it was a great leveller.*
2 (**Leveller**) a member of a group of radical dissenters in the English Civil War (1642–9) who called for the abolition of the monarchy, social and agrarian reforms, and religious freedom.

levelling screw ▸ noun a screw, typically one of three, for adjusting part of a machine or instrument to a precise level.

lever /ˈliːvə/ ▸ noun a rigid bar resting on a pivot, used to move a heavy or firmly fixed load with one end when pressure is applied to the other. ■ a projecting arm or handle that is moved to operate a mechanism: *a control lever.* ■ a means of pressurizing someone into doing something: *rich countries use foreign aid as a lever to promote political pluralism.*
▸ verb [with obj. and adverbial] lift or move with a lever: *she levered the lid off the pot with a screwdriver.* ■ move (someone or something) with a concerted physical effort: *she levered herself up against the pillows.* ■ [no obj.] use a lever: *the men levered at the coffin with crowbars.* ■ pressurize (someone) to do something: *another sticking point is the money that will be required to lever the unions into accepting a deal.*
– ORIGIN Middle English: from Old French *levier, leveor*, from *lever* 'to lift'.

leverage /ˈliːv(ə)rɪdʒ/ ▸ noun [mass noun] **1** the exertion of force by means of a lever: *my spade hit something solid that wouldn't respond to leverage.* ■ mechanical advantage gained by leverage: *use a metal bar to increase the leverage.* ■ the power to influence a person or situation: *the right wing had lost much of its political leverage in the Assembly.*
2 Finance the ratio of a company's loan capital (debt) to the value of its ordinary shares (equity); gearing. ■ the use of credit or borrowed capital to increase the earning potential of shares.
▸ verb [with obj.] **1** (usu. as adj. **leveraged**) use borrowed capital for (an investment), expecting the profits made to be greater than the interest payable: *a leveraged takeover bid.*
2 use (something) to maximum advantage: *the organization needs to leverage its key resources.*

leveraged buyout ▸ noun the purchase of a controlling share in a company by its management using outside capital.

lever escapement ▸ noun a mechanism in a watch connecting the escape wheel and the balance wheel using two levers.

leveret /ˈlɛv(ə)rɪt/ ▸ noun a young hare in its first year.
– ORIGIN late Middle English: from Anglo-Norman French, diminutive of *levre*, from Latin *lepus, lepor-* 'hare'.

L

Leverhulme /ˈliːvəhjuːm/, 1st Viscount (1851–1925), English industrialist and philanthropist; born *William Hesketh Lever*. He and his brother manufactured soap under the trade name Sunlight; their company, Lever Bros., came to form the basis of the international corporation Unilever. Leverhulme founded the model village Port Sunlight for his company's workers.

Leverkusen /ˈleɪvəˌkuːz(ə)n/, German /ˈleːvɐˌkuːzn/ an industrial city in western Germany, in North Rhine-Westphalia, on the River Rhine north of Cologne; pop. 161,300 (est. 2006).

Le Verrier /lə ˈvɛrɪeɪ/, French /lə vɛrje/, Urbain (1811–77), French mathematician. His analysis of the motions of the planets suggested that an unknown body was disrupting the orbit of Uranus. Le Verrier prompted the German astronomer **Johann Galle** (1812–1910) to investigate, and the planet Neptune was discovered in 1846.

lever watch ▸ noun a watch with a lever escapement.

Levi¹ /ˈliːvʌɪ/ (in the Bible) a Hebrew patriarch, son of Jacob and Leah (Gen. 29:34). ■ the tribe of Israel traditionally descended from Levi.

Levi² /ˈleɪvi/, Primo (1919–87), Italian novelist and poet, of Jewish descent. His experiences as a survivor of Auschwitz are recounted in his first book *If This is a Man* (1947).

leviathan /lɪˈvʌɪəθ(ə)n/ ▸ noun (in biblical use) a sea monster, identified in different passages with the whale and the crocodile (e.g. Job 41, Ps. 74:14), and with the Devil (after Isa. 27:1). ■ a very large aquatic creature, especially a whale: *the great leviathans of the deep.* ■ a thing that is very large or powerful, especially an organization or vehicle. ■ an autocratic monarch or state. [with allusion to Hobbes's *Leviathan* (1651).]
– ORIGIN via late Latin from Hebrew *liwyāṯān*.

levigate /ˈlɛvɪgeɪt/ ▸ verb [with obj.] archaic reduce (a substance) to a fine powder or smooth paste.
– ORIGIN mid 16th cent.: from Latin *levigat-* 'made smooth, polished', from the verb *levigare*, from *levis* 'smooth'.

levin /ˈlɛvɪn/ ▸ noun [mass noun] archaic lightning; thunderbolts.
– ORIGIN Middle English: probably of Scandinavian origin.

levirate /ˈliːvɪrət, ˈlɛv-/ ▸ noun (usu. **the levirate**) a custom of the ancient Hebrews and some other peoples by which a man may be obliged to marry his brother's widow: [as modifier] *levirate marriages.*

– ORIGIN early 18th cent.: from Latin *levir* 'brother-in-law' + **-ATE**[1].

Levi's /ˈliːvʌɪz/ ▶ **plural noun** trademark a brand of denim jeans.
– ORIGIN 1920s: named after *Levi* Strauss, original US manufacturer in the 1860s.

Lévi-Strauss /ˌlɛvɪˈstraʊs/, French /levistʀaʊs/, Claude (1908–2009), French social anthropologist. A pioneer in the use of a structuralist analysis to study cultural systems, he regarded language as an essential common denominator underlying cultural phenomena.

levitate /ˈlɛvɪteɪt/ ▶ **verb** rise or cause to rise and hover in the air, typically by means of supposed magical powers: [no obj.] *I swear to God he levitated over the bar* | [with obj.] *I focused on levitating the rucksack*.
– DERIVATIVES **levitation** noun, **levitator** noun.
– ORIGIN late 17th cent.: from Latin *levis* 'light', on the pattern of *gravitate*.

Levite /ˈliːvʌɪt/ ▶ **noun** a member of the Hebrew tribe of Levi, especially of that part of it which provided assistants to the priests in the worship in the Jewish temple.
– ORIGIN Middle English: from late Latin *levita*, from Greek *leuitēs*, from Hebrew *Lēwī* 'Levi'.

Levitical /lɪˈvɪtɪk(ə)l/ ▶ **adjective 1** relating to the Levites or the tribe of Levi: *a Levitical priest*.
2 Judaism (of a rule of conduct, temple ritual, etc.) derived from the biblical Book of Leviticus: *a Levitical edict*.
– ORIGIN mid 16th cent.: via late Latin from Greek *levitikos*, from *Levi* (see **LEVITE**), + **-AL**.

Leviticus /lɪˈvɪtɪkəs/ the third book of the Bible, containing details of law and ritual.

levity /ˈlɛvɪti/ ▶ **noun** (pl. **levities**) [mass noun] the treatment of a serious matter with humour or lack of due respect: *as an attempt to introduce a note of levity, the words were a disastrous flop*.
– ORIGIN mid 16th cent.: from Latin *levitas*, from *levis* 'light'.

L

levo- ▶ **combining form** US spelling of **LAEVO-**.

levodopa /ˌliːvə(ʊ)ˈdəʊpə/ ▶ **noun** another term for **L-DOPA**.

levonorgestrel /ˌliːvəʊnɔːˈdʒɛstr(ə)l/ ▶ **noun** [mass noun] Biochemistry a synthetic steroid hormone which has a similar effect to progesterone and is used in some contraceptive pills.
– ORIGIN 1970s: from **LEVO-** (it being a laevorotatory isomer) + *norgestrel*, a synthetic steroid hormone.

levulose ▶ **noun** US spelling of **LAEVULOSE**.

levy /ˈlɛvi/ ▶ **verb** (**levies**, **levying**, **levied**) [with obj.] **1** impose (a tax, fee, or fine): *a tax of two per cent was levied on all cargoes*. ■ impose a tax, fee, or fine on: *there will be powers to levy the owner*. ■ [no obj.] (**levy on/upon**) seize (property) to satisfy a legal judgement.
2 archaic enlist (someone) for military service. ■ begin to wage (war).
▶ **noun** (pl. **levies**) **1** an act of levying a tax, fee, or fine: *police forces receive 49 per cent of their funding via a levy on the rates*. ■ a tax raised by levying. ■ a sum collected as a supplement to an existing subscription: *the trade-union political levy*. ■ an item or items of property seized to satisfy a legal judgement.
2 historical an act of enlisting troops. ■ (usu. **levies**) a body of troops that have been enlisted: *lightly armed local levies*.
– DERIVATIVES **leviable** adjective.
– ORIGIN Middle English (as a noun): from Old French *levee*, feminine past participle of *lever* 'raise', from Latin *levare*, from *levis* 'light'.

lewd ▶ **adjective** crude and offensive in a sexual way: *she began to gyrate to the music and sing a lewd song*.
– DERIVATIVES **lewdly** adverb, **lewdness** noun.
– ORIGIN Old English *lǣwede*, of unknown origin. The original sense was 'belonging to the laity'; in Middle English, 'belonging to the common people, vulgar', and later 'worthless, vile, evil', leading to the current sense.

Lewes /ˈluːɪs/ a town in southern England on the River Ouse eight miles north-east of Brighton, the county town of East Sussex; pop. 17,000 (est. 2009). It was the site in 1264 of a battle in which the younger Simon de Montfort defeated Henry III.

Lewis[1] the northern part of the island of Lewis and Harris in the Outer Hebrides.

Lewis[2], Cecil Day, see **DAY LEWIS**.

Lewis[3], C. S. (1898–1963), British novelist, religious writer, and literary scholar; full name *Clive Staples Lewis*. He broadcast and wrote on religious and moral issues, and created the imaginary land of Narnia for a series of children's books, which began with *The Lion, the Witch, and the Wardrobe* (1950).

Lewis[4], Carl (b.1961), American athlete; full name *Frederick Carleton Lewis*. He won Olympic gold medals in 1984, 1988, 1992, and 1996 (his ninth) for sprinting and the long jump, and broke the world record for the 100 metres on several occasions.

Lewis[5], Jerry Lee (b.1935), American rock-and-roll singer and pianist. In 1957 he had hits with 'Whole Lotta Shakin' Going On' and 'Great Balls of Fire'. His career was interrupted when his marriage to his fourteen-year-old cousin caused a public outcry.

Lewis[6], Lennox (b.1965), English boxer, world heavyweight champion three times from 1999.

Lewis[7], (Harry) Sinclair (1885–1951), American novelist, known for satirical works such as *Main Street* (1920), *Babbitt* (1922), and *Elmer Gantry* (1927). He was the first American writer to receive the Nobel Prize for Literature (1930).

Lewis[8], Meriwether (1774–1809), American explorer. Together with William Clark he led an expedition to explore the newly acquired Louisiana Purchase (1804–6). They travelled from St Louis to the Pacific Coast and back.

Lewis[9], (Percy) Wyndham (1882–1957), British novelist, critic, and painter, born in Canada. He was a leader of the Vorticist movement, and with Ezra Pound edited the magazine *Blast* (1914–15). Notable novels: *The Apes of God* (1930).

lewis ▶ **noun** a steel device for gripping heavy blocks of stone or concrete for lifting, consisting of three pieces arranged to form a dovetail, the outside pieces being fixed in a dovetail mortise by the insertion of the middle piece.
– ORIGIN late Middle English: probably from Old French *lous*, plural of *lou(p)* 'wolf', the name of a kind of siege engine.

Lewis acid ▶ **noun** Chemistry a compound or ionic species which can accept an electron pair from a donor compound.
– ORIGIN 1940s: named after Gilbert N. *Lewis* (1875–1946), American chemist.

Lewis and Harris (also **Lewis with Harris**) the largest and northernmost island of the Outer Hebrides in Scotland; chief town, Stornoway. The island, which is separated from the mainland by the Minch, consists of a northern part, Lewis, and a smaller and more mountainous southern part, Harris.

Lewis base ▶ **noun** Chemistry a compound or ionic species which can donate an electron pair to an acceptor compound.
– ORIGIN 1960s: named after G. N. *Lewis* (see **LEWIS ACID**).

Lewis gun ▶ **noun** a light air-cooled machine gun with a magazine operated by gas from its own firing, used mainly in the First World War.
– ORIGIN early 20th cent.: named after its inventor, Isaac N. *Lewis* (1858–1931), a colonel in the US army.

Lewisian /luːˈɪsɪən/ ▶ **adjective** Geology relating to or denoting the earlier stage of the Proterozoic aeon in NW Scotland, from about 2,500 to 1,100 million years ago, when the oldest rocks in Britain were deposited. ■ (as noun **the Lewisian**) the Lewisian stage or the system of rocks deposited during it.
– ORIGIN mid 19th cent.: from the name of the island of *Lewis and Harris* in the Outer Hebrides (where the chief outcrops of these rocks are found) + **-IAN**.

lewisite /ˈluːɪsʌɪt/ ▶ **noun** [mass noun] a dark oily liquid producing an irritant gas that causes blisters, developed for use in chemical warfare. ● An organic compound of arsenic; chem. formula: $ClCH{=}CHAsCl_2$.
– ORIGIN 1920s: named after Winford L. *Lewis* (1878–1943), American chemist.

Lewis with Harris another name for **LEWIS AND HARRIS**.

Lexan /ˈlɛksan/ ▶ **noun** [mass noun] trademark a transparent plastic (polycarbonate) of high impact strength, used for cockpit canopies, bulletproof screens, etc.
– ORIGIN 1950s: an invented name.

lexeme /ˈlɛksiːm/ ▶ **noun** Linguistics a basic lexical unit of a language consisting of one word or several words, the elements of which do not separately convey the meaning of the whole.
– ORIGIN 1940s: from **LEXICON** + **-EME**.

lex fori /lɛks ˈfɔːrʌɪ/ ▶ **noun** [mass noun] Law the law of the country in which an action is brought.
– ORIGIN Latin, 'law of the court'.

lexical /ˈlɛksɪk(ə)l/ ▶ **adjective** relating to the words or vocabulary of a language: *lexical analysis*. ■ relating to or of the nature of a lexicon or dictionary: *a lexical entry*.
– DERIVATIVES **lexicalize** (also **lexicalise**) verb, **lexically** adverb.
– ORIGIN mid 19th cent.: from Greek *lexikos* 'of words' (from *lexis* 'word') + **-AL**.

lexical meaning ▶ **noun** the meaning of a word considered in isolation from the sentence containing it, and regardless of its grammatical context, e.g. of *love* in or as represented by *loves, loved, loving*, etc.

lexicographer ▶ **noun** a person who compiles dictionaries.

lexicography /ˌlɛksɪˈkɒgrəfi/ ▶ **noun** [mass noun] the activity or occupation of compiling dictionaries.
– DERIVATIVES **lexicographic** adjective, **lexicographical** /-kəˈgrafɪk(ə)l/ adjective, **lexicographically** adverb.

lexicology ▶ **noun** [mass noun] the study of the form, meaning, and behaviour of words.
– DERIVATIVES **lexicological** adjective, **lexicologically** adverb.

lexicon /ˈlɛksɪk(ə)n/ ▶ **noun** the vocabulary of a person, language, or branch of knowledge: *the size of the English lexicon*. ■ a dictionary, especially of Greek, Hebrew, Syriac, or Arabic: *a Greek–Latin lexicon*.
– ORIGIN early 17th cent.: modern Latin, from Greek *lexikon (biblion)* '(book) of words', from *lexis* 'word', from *legein* 'speak'.

lexigram /ˈlɛksɪgram/ ▶ **noun** a symbol representing a word, especially one used in learning a language.

Lexington 1 a city in central Kentucky; pop. (with Fayette) 282,114 (est. 2008). It is a noted horse-breeding centre.
2 a residential town north-west of Boston, Massachusetts; pop. 30,272 (est. 2008). It was the scene in 1775 of the first battle fought in the War of American Independence.

lexis /ˈlɛksɪs/ ▶ **noun** [mass noun] the total stock of words in a language. ■ the level of language consisting of vocabulary, as opposed to grammar or syntax.
– ORIGIN 1950s (denoting the wording in a piece of writing): from Greek, literally 'word' (see **LEXICON**).

lex loci /lɛks ˈləʊsʌɪ/ ▶ **noun** [mass noun] Law the law of the country in which a transaction is performed, a tort is committed, or a property is situated.
– ORIGIN Latin, 'law of the place'.

lex talionis /lɛks ˌtalɪˈəʊnɪs/ ▶ **noun** [mass noun] the law of retaliation, whereby a punishment resembles the offence committed in kind and degree.
– ORIGIN Latin, from *lex* 'law' and *talio(n-)* 'retaliation' (from *talis* 'such').

ley[1] /leɪ/ (also **temporary ley**) ▶ **noun** a piece of land put down to grass, clover, etc., for a single season or a limited number of years, in contrast to permanent pasture.
– ORIGIN Old English *lǣge* 'fallow' (recorded in *lǣghrycg* 'ridge left at the edge of a ploughed field'); related to **LAY**[1] and **LIE**[1].

ley[2] /leɪ, liː/ (also **ley line**) ▶ **noun** a supposed straight line connecting three or more prehistoric or ancient sites, sometimes regarded as the line of a former track and associated by some with lines of energy and other paranormal phenomena.
– ORIGIN 1920s: variant of **LEA**.

Leyden variant spelling of **LEIDEN**.

Leyden jar /ˈlʌɪd(ə)n/ ▶ **noun** an early form of capacitor consisting of a glass jar with layers of metal foil on the outside and inside.
– ORIGIN mid 18th cent.: named after *Leyden* (see **LEIDEN**), where it was invented (1745).

ley farming ▶ **noun** [mass noun] chiefly Brit. the alternate growing of crops and grass.

Leyland cypress /ˈleɪlənd/ ▶ **noun** a fast-growing hybrid conifer which is narrowly conical with a dense growth of shoots bearing scale-like leaves, widely grown as a screening plant or for shelter. Also called **LEYLANDII**. ● × *Cupressocyparis leylandii*, family Cupressaceae; a hybrid between the Nootka cypress and the Monterey cypress (macrocarpa).
– ORIGIN 1930s: named after Christopher J. *Leyland* (1849–1926), British horticulturist.

leylandii /leɪˈlandɪʌɪ/ ▶ **noun** (pl. **same**) a Leyland cypress.
– ORIGIN from the modern Latin taxonomic name.

ley line ▶ **noun** see **LEY**[2].

Leyte /ˈleɪti/ an island in the central Philippines; pop. 1,790,400 (est. 2009); chief town, Tacloban.

lez ▶ noun variant spelling of LES.

lezzy ▶ noun (pl. **lezzies**) informal a lesbian.

LF ▶ abbreviation low frequency.

LGBT ▶ abbreviation lesbian, gay, bisexual, or transgendered.

LGV ▶ abbreviation Brit. large goods vehicle.

LH ▶ abbreviation Biochemistry luteinizing hormone.

l.h. ▶ abbreviation left hand.

Lhasa /ˈlɑːsə/ the capital of Tibet; pop. 156,100 (est. 2006). It is situated in the northern Himalayas at an altitude of 3,600 m (*c.*11,800 ft), on a tributary of the Brahmaputra.

> Its inaccessibility and the unwillingness of the Tibetan Buddhist priests to receive foreign visitors—to whom Lhasa was closed until the 20th century—earned it the title of the Forbidden City. The spiritual centre of Tibetan Buddhism, Lhasa was the seat of the Dalai Lama until 1959, when direct Chinese administration was imposed on the city.

Lhasa apso /ˈapsəʊ/ ▶ noun (pl. **Lhasa apsos**) a dog of a small long-coated breed, typically gold or grey and white, originating at Lhasa.
– ORIGIN 1930s: from LHASA + Tibetan *a-sob*.

LHD ▶ abbreviation left-hand drive.

LI ▶ abbreviation ■ Light Infantry. ■ (in the US) Long Island.

Li ▶ symbol the chemical element lithium.

li /liː/ ▶ noun (pl. **same**) a Chinese unit of distance, equal to about 0.6 km (0.4 mile).
– ORIGIN from Chinese *lǐ*.

liability ▶ noun (pl. **liabilities**) **1** [mass noun] the state of being legally responsible for something: *once you contact the card protection scheme your **liability for** any loss ends.* ■ [count noun] (usu. **liabilities**) a thing for which someone is responsible, especially an amount of money owed: *valuing the company's liabilities and assets.*
2 [usu. in sing.] a person or thing whose presence or behaviour is likely to put one at a disadvantage: *she said the party had become a liability to green politics.*

liable ▶ adjective [predic.] **1** responsible by law; legally answerable: *the credit-card company is **liable for** any breach of contract.* ■ (**liable to**) subject by law to: *non-resident trustees are liable to the basic rate of tax.*
2 [with infinitive] likely to do or to be something: *patients were liable to faint if they stood up too suddenly.* ■ (**liable to**) likely to experience (something undesirable): *areas liable to flooding.*
– ORIGIN late Middle English: perhaps from Anglo-Norman French, from French *lier* 'to bind', from Latin *ligare*.

liaise /lɪˈeɪz/ ▶ verb [no obj.] cooperate on a matter of mutual concern: *she will **liaise with** teachers across the country.* ■ (**liaise between**) act as a link to assist communication between (people or groups): *civil servants who liaise between the prime minister and departmental ministers.*
– ORIGIN 1920s (originally military slang): back-formation from LIAISON.

liaison ▶ noun [mass noun] **1** communication or cooperation which facilitates a close working relationship between people or organizations: *the head porter works in close **liaison with** the reception office.* ■ [count noun] a person who acts as a link to assist communication or cooperation between people: *he's our liaison with a number of interested parties.* ■ [count noun] a sexual relationship, especially one that is secret or illicit.
2 the binding or thickening agent of a sauce, often based on egg yolks.
3 Phonetics (in French and other languages) the sounding of a consonant that is normally silent at the end of a word, because the next word begins with a vowel. ■ introduction of a consonant between a word that ends in a vowel and another that begins with a vowel, as in English *law and order*.
– ORIGIN mid 17th cent. (as a cookery term): from French, from *lier* 'to bind'.

liaison officer ▶ noun a person who is employed to form a working relationship between two organizations to their mutual benefit.

liana /lɪˈɑːnə/ (also **liane** /-ˈɑːn/) ▶ noun a woody climbing plant that hangs from trees, especially in tropical rainforests. ■ the free-hanging stem of a liana.
– ORIGIN late 18th cent.: from French *liane* 'clematis, liana', of unknown origin.

Liao[1] /ljaʊ/ a river of NE China, which rises in Inner Mongolia and flows about 1,450 km (900 miles) east and south to the Gulf of Liaodong at the head of the gulf of Bo Hai.

Liao[2] /ljaʊ/ a dynasty which ruled much of Manchuria and part of NE China AD 947–1125.

Liaodong Peninsula /ˌljaʊˈdʊŋ/ a peninsula in NE China, which extends southwards into the Yellow Sea between Bo Hai and Korea Bay.

Liaoning /ˌljaʊˈnɪŋ/ a province of NE China, bordered on the east by North Korea; capital, Shenyang.

liar ▶ noun a person who tells lies.
– ORIGIN Old English *lēogere* (see LIE[2], -AR[4]).

liard /ljɑː, ljɑːd/ ▶ noun historical a small coin formerly used in France, worth three deniers or a quarter of a sou.
– ORIGIN French, of unknown origin.

liar dice ▶ noun [mass noun] a gambling game resembling poker dice, in which the thrower conceals the dice thrown and sometimes declares a false score.

lias /ˈlʌɪəs/ ▶ noun (**the Lias**) Geology the earliest epoch of the Jurassic period, lasting from about 208 to 178 million years ago. ■ the system of rocks deposited during the Lias, consisting of shales and limestones rich in fossils. ■ (also **blue lias**) [mass noun] a blue-grey clayey limestone derived from marl deposited in the Lower Jurassic, found chiefly in SW England.
– DERIVATIVES **liassic** adjective.
– ORIGIN late Middle English (denoting blue lias): from Old French *liais* 'hard limestone', probably from *lie* (see LEES).

liatris /lʌɪˈatrɪs/ ▶ noun (pl. **same**) a plant of a genus which includes the blazing stars of the daisy family.
● Genus *Liatris*, family Compositae.
– ORIGIN modern Latin, of unknown origin.

lib ▶ noun [mass noun] informal (in the names of political movements) liberation: *I'm all for **women's lib**.*
– ORIGIN 1970s: abbreviation.

Lib. ▶ abbreviation Liberal.

libation /lʌɪˈbeɪʃ(ə)n/ ▶ noun a drink poured out as an offering to a deity. ■ [mass noun] the pouring out of a libation: *gin was poured in libation.* ■ humorous a drink: *tequila is a favourite libation throughout the West.*
– ORIGIN late Middle English: from Latin *libatio(n-)*, from *libare* 'pour as an offering'.

libber ▶ noun [usu. with modifier] informal a member or advocate of a movement calling for the liberation of people or animals: *a women's libber.*

Lib Dem ▶ noun informal (in the UK) Liberal Democrat: *I'm voting Lib Dem.*

libeccio /lɪˈbɛtʃɪəʊ/, Italian /liˈbettʃo/ ▶ noun a strong south-westerly wind blowing on the sea to the west of Italy.
– ORIGIN Italian.

libel ▶ noun **1** Law a published false statement that is damaging to a person's reputation; a written defamation. Compare with SLANDER. ■ [mass noun] the action or crime of publishing a libel: *she sued two newspapers for libel* | [as modifier] *a libel action.* ■ a false and typically malicious statement about a person. ■ a thing that brings undeserved discredit on a person by misrepresentation.
2 (in admiralty and ecclesiastical law) a plaintiff's written declaration.
▶ verb (**libels**, **libelling**, **libelled**; US **libels**, **libeling**, **libeled**) [with obj.] **1** Law defame (someone) by publishing a libel: *the jury found that he was libelled by a newspaper.* ■ make a false and typically malicious statement about.
2 (in admiralty and ecclesiastical law) bring a suit against.
– DERIVATIVES **libeller** noun.
– ORIGIN Middle English (in the general sense 'a document, a written statement'): via Old French from Latin *libellus*, diminutive of *liber* 'book'.

libellous /ˈlʌɪb(ə)ləs/ (US also **libelous**) ▶ adjective containing or constituting a libel: *a libellous newspaper story.*
– DERIVATIVES **libellously** adverb.

liberal ▶ adjective **1** willing to respect or accept behaviour or opinions different from one's own; open to new ideas: *liberal views towards divorce.* ■ favourable to or respectful of individual rights and freedoms: *liberal citizenship laws.* ■ (in a political context) favouring individual liberty, free trade, and moderate political and social reform: *a liberal democratic state.* ■ (**Liberal**) relating to Liberals or a Liberal Party, especially (in the UK) relating to the Liberal Democrat party. ■ Theology regarding many traditional beliefs as dispensable, invalidated by modern thought, or liable to change.
2 [attrib.] (of education) concerned with broadening a person's general knowledge and experience, rather than with technical or professional training.
3 (especially of an interpretation of a law) broadly construed or understood; not strictly literal: *they could have given the 1968 Act a more liberal interpretation.*
4 given, used, or occurring in generous amounts: *liberal amounts of wine had been consumed.* ■ (of a person) giving generously: *Sam was too **liberal with** the wine.*
▶ noun a person of liberal views. ■ (**Liberal**) a supporter or member of a Liberal Party, especially (in the UK) a Liberal Democrat.
– DERIVATIVES **liberalism** noun, **liberalist** noun, **liberalistic** adjective, **liberally** adverb, **liberalness** noun.
– ORIGIN Middle English: via Old French from Latin *liberalis*, from *liber* 'free (man)'. The original sense was 'suitable for a free man', hence 'suitable for a gentleman' (one not tied to a trade), surviving in *liberal arts*. Another early sense 'generous' (compare with sense 4 of the adjective) gave rise to an obsolete meaning 'free from restraint', leading to sense 1 of the adjective (late 18th cent.).

liberal arts ▶ plural noun **1** chiefly N. Amer. arts subjects such as literature and history, as distinct from science and technology.
2 historical the medieval trivium and quadrivium.
– ORIGIN *liberal*, as distinct from *servile* or *mechanical* (i.e. involving manual labour) and originally referring to arts and sciences considered 'worthy of a free man'; later the word related to general intellectual development rather than vocational training.

Liberal Democrat ▶ noun (in the UK) a member of a party (formerly the Social and Liberal Democrats) formed from the Liberal Party and members of the Social Democratic Party.

liberality ▶ noun [mass noun] **1** the quality of giving or spending freely.
2 the quality of being open to new ideas and free from prejudice: *liberality towards bisexuality.*
– ORIGIN Middle English: from Old French *liberalite*, or from Latin *liberalitas*, from *liberalis* (see LIBERAL).

liberalize (also **liberalise**) ▶ verb [with obj.] remove or loosen restrictions on (something, typically an economic or political system): *several agreements to liberalize trade were signed.*
– DERIVATIVES **liberalization** noun, **liberalizer** noun.

Liberal Party ▶ noun a political party advocating liberal policies, in particular a British party that emerged in the 1860s from the old Whig Party and until the First World War was one of the two major parties in Britain. In 1988 the party regrouped with elements of the Social Democratic Party to form the Social and Liberal Democrats, now known as the Liberal Democrats; a small Liberal Party still exists.

Liberal Party of Australia an Australian political party established in its modern form by Robert Menzies in 1944, in opposition to the Australian Labor Party. It first gained power in 1949.

Liberal Party of Canada a Canadian political party generally taking a moderate, left-of-centre position. The party emerged in the mid 19th century, and held power for most of the period 1963–84.

liberal studies ▶ plural noun [usu. treated as sing.] Brit. an additional course in arts subjects taken by students studying for a qualification in science, technology, or the humanities.

Liberal Unionist ▶ noun a member of a group of British Liberal MPs who left the party in 1886 because of Gladstone's support for Irish Home Rule. Led by Joseph Chamberlain from 1891, they formed an alliance with the Conservative Party in Parliament, and merged officially with them in 1909 as the Conservative and Unionist Party.

liberate ▶ verb [with obj.] **1** set (someone) free from imprisonment, slavery, or oppression. ■ free (a place or people) from enemy occupation: *twelve months earlier Paris had been liberated.* ■ release (someone) from a situation which limits freedom of thought or behaviour: *she is **liberated from** the constraints of an unhappy marriage* | (as adj. **liberating**) *the arts can have a liberating effect on people.* ■ free (someone) from social conventions, especially those concerned with accepted sexual roles: *ways of working politically that liberate women.*
2 Chemistry & Physics release (gas, energy, etc.) as a result of chemical reaction or physical decomposition.

L

3 informal steal (something): *the drummer's wearing a beret he's liberated from Lord knows where.*
– ORIGIN late 16th cent.: from Latin *liberat-* 'freed', from the verb *liberare*, from *liber* 'free'.

liberated ▶ adjective 1 (of a person) free from social conventions or traditional ideas, especially with regard to sexual roles: *the modern image of the independent, liberated woman.*
2 (of a place or people) freed from enemy occupation: *liberated areas of the country.*

liberation ▶ noun [mass noun] the act of setting someone free from imprisonment, slavery, or oppression; release: *the liberation of all political prisoners.* ■ freedom from limits on thought or behaviour: *the struggle for women's liberation.*
– DERIVATIVES **liberationist** noun.

liberation theology ▶ noun [mass noun] a movement in Christian theology, developed mainly by Latin American Roman Catholics, which attempts to address the problems of poverty and social injustice as well as spiritual matters.

Liberation Tigers of Tamil Eelam another name for **TAMIL TIGERS**.

liberator ▶ noun a person who liberates a person or place from imprisonment or oppression: *they were seen as liberators.*

Liberia /lʌɪˈbɪərɪə/ a country on the Atlantic coast of West Africa; pop. 3,441,800 (est. 2009); languages, English (official), English-based pidgin; capital, Monrovia.

> Liberia was founded in 1822 as a settlement for freed slaves from the US, and was proclaimed independent in 1847. Indigenous peoples, however, form the majority of the population. In 1980 a coup overthrew the predominant Liberian–American elite, and a civil war began in 1990, ending with a ceasefire in 1996.

– DERIVATIVES **Liberian** adjective & noun.
– ORIGIN from Latin *liber* 'free'.

L

libero /ˈliːbərəʊ/ ▶ noun (pl. **liberos**) Soccer another term for **SWEEPER** (sense 2).
– ORIGIN 1960s: from Italian, abbreviation of *battitore libero* 'free defender', literally 'free beater'.

libertarian /ˌlɪbəˈtɛːrɪən/ ▶ noun 1 an adherent of libertarianism: [as modifier] *libertarian philosophy.* ■ a person who advocates civil liberty.
2 a person who believes in free will.
– ORIGIN late 18th cent. (in sense 2): from **LIBERTY**, on the pattern of words such as *unitarian.*

libertarianism ▶ noun [mass noun] an extreme laissez-faire political philosophy advocating only minimal state intervention in the lives of citizens.

> Its adherents believe that private morality is not the state's affair, and that therefore activities such as drug use and prostitution that arguably harm no one but the participants should not be illegal. Libertarianism shares elements with anarchism, although it is generally associated more with the political right (chiefly in the US); it lacks the concern of traditional liberalism with social justice.

libertine /ˈlɪbətiːn, -tɪn, -tʌɪn/ ▶ noun 1 a person, especially a man, who freely indulges in sensual pleasures without regard to moral principles.
2 a freethinker in matters of religion.
▶ adjective 1 characterized by free indulgence in sensual pleasures: *his more libertine impulses.*
2 freethinking.
– DERIVATIVES **libertinage** noun, **libertinism** noun.
– ORIGIN late Middle English (denoting a freed slave or the son of one): from Latin *libertinus* 'freedman', from *liber* 'free'. In the mid 16th cent., imitating French *libertin*, the term denoted a member of any of various antinomian sects in France; hence sense 2 of the noun.

liberty ▶ noun (pl. **liberties**) [mass noun] 1 the state of being free within society from oppressive restrictions imposed by authority on one's behaviour or political views: *compulsory retirement would interfere with individual liberty.* ■ the state of not being imprisoned or enslaved: *people who attacked phone boxes would lose their liberty.* ■ the power or scope to act as one pleases: *individuals should enjoy the liberty to pursue their own preferences.* ■ Philosophy a person's freedom from control by fate or necessity.
2 [count noun] (usu. **liberties**) a right or privilege, especially a statutory one: *the Bill of Rights was intended to secure basic civil liberties.*
3 [count noun] informal a presumptuous remark or action: *how did he know what she was thinking?—it was a liberty!*
4 Nautical shore leave granted to a sailor.
– PHRASES **at liberty 1** not imprisoned. **2** allowed or entitled to do something: *he's not at liberty to discuss his real work.* **take liberties 1** behave in an unduly familiar or easy manner towards someone or something: *you've taken too many liberties with me.* **2** treat something freely, without strict faithfulness to the facts or to an original: *the scriptwriter has taken few liberties with the original narrative.* **take the liberty** venture to do something without first asking permission: *I took the liberty of checking out a few convalescent homes for him.*
– ORIGIN late Middle English: from Old French *liberte*, from Latin *libertas*, from *liber* 'free'.

Liberty, Statue of a statue at the entrance to New York harbour, a symbol of welcome to immigrants, representing a draped female figure carrying a book of laws in her left hand and holding aloft a torch in her right. Dedicated in 1886, it was designed by Frédéric-Auguste Bartholdi and was the gift of the French, commemorating the alliance of France and the US during the War of American Independence.

Liberty Bell a bell in Philadelphia first rung on 8 July 1776 to celebrate the first public reading of the Declaration of Independence. It bears the legend 'Proclaim liberty throughout all the land unto all the inhabitants thereof' (Leviticus 25:10).

liberty boat ▶ noun Brit. a boat carrying sailors who have leave to go on shore.

liberty bodice ▶ noun Brit. trademark a girl's or woman's close-fitting sleeveless bodice made from thick cotton, formerly worn as a warm undergarment.

liberty cap ▶ noun 1 a common small European toadstool which has a greyish-brown cap with a distinct boss and a long, thin stem, containing the hallucinogen psilocybin. See also **MAGIC MUSHROOM**. ● *Psilocybe semilanceata*, family Strophariaceae, class Hymenomycetes.
2 another term for **CAP OF LIBERTY** (see **CAP**[1]).

Liberty Hall ▶ noun a place where one may do as one likes.

liberty horse ▶ noun a horse that performs in a circus without a rider.

liberty man ▶ noun Brit. a sailor with leave to go ashore.

liberty of the subject ▶ noun chiefly Brit. the rights of a subject under constitutional rule.

Liberty ship ▶ noun a prefabricated US-built freighter of the Second World War.

libidinous /lɪˈbɪdɪnəs/ ▶ adjective showing excessive sexual drive; lustful: *libidinous teenagers.*
– DERIVATIVES **libidinously** adverb, **libidinousness** noun.
– ORIGIN late Middle English: from Latin *libidinosus*, from *libido* 'desire, lust'.

libido /lɪˈbiːdəʊ, lɪˈbʌɪdəʊ/ ▶ noun (pl. **libidos**) [mass noun] sexual desire: *loss of libido* | [count noun] *a deficient libido.* ■ Psychoanalysis the energy of the sexual drive as a component of the life instinct.
– DERIVATIVES **libidinal** adjective, **libidinally** adverb.
– ORIGIN early 20th cent.: from Latin, literally 'desire, lust'.

Li Bo /liː ˈbəʊ/ variant of **LI PO**.

LIBOR /ˈlʌɪbɔː/ ▶ abbreviation London interbank offered rate, the basic rate of interest used in lending between banks on the London interbank market.

Libra /ˈliːbrə, ˈlɪb-, ˈlʌɪb-/ 1 Astronomy a small constellation (the Scales or Balance), said to represent the pair of scales which is the symbol of justice. It contains no bright stars.
2 Astrology the seventh sign of the zodiac, which the sun enters at the northern autumnal equinox (about 23 September). ■ (**a Libra**) a person born when the sun is in the sign of Libra.
– DERIVATIVES **Libran** noun & adjective (sense 2).
– ORIGIN Latin.

libra /ˈlʌɪbrə/ ▶ noun (pl. **librae** /ˈlʌɪbriː/) (in ancient Rome) a unit of weight, equivalent to 12 ounces (0.34 kg). It was the forerunner of the pound.
– ORIGIN Latin, 'pound, balance'.

librarian ▶ noun a person in charge of or assisting in a library.
– DERIVATIVES **librarianship** noun.
– ORIGIN late 17th cent. (denoting a scribe or copyist): from Latin *librarius* 'relating to books', (used as a noun) 'bookseller, scribe', + **-AN**.

library ▶ noun (pl. **libraries**) a building or room containing collections of books, periodicals, and sometimes films and recorded music for use or borrowing by the public or the members of an institution: *a university library* | [as modifier] *a library book.* ■ a collection of books and periodicals held in a library. ■ a room in a private house where books are kept. ■ a series of books or recordings issued by a company as a set. ■ a collection of films, recorded music, etc., organized systematically and kept for research or borrowing: *a record library.* ■ (also **software library**) Computing a collection of programs and software packages made generally available, often loaded and stored on disk for immediate use.
– ORIGIN late Middle English: via Old French from Latin *libraria* 'bookshop', feminine (used as a noun) of *librarius* 'relating to books', from *liber, libr-* 'book'.

library edition ▶ noun an edition of a book which is of large size and has good-quality print and binding, especially the standard edition of a writer's works.

Library of Congress the US national library, in Washington DC.

library science ▶ noun [mass noun] the study of librarianship.

libration /lʌɪˈbreɪʃ(ə)n/ ▶ noun Astronomy an apparent or real oscillation of the moon, by which parts near the edge of the disc that are often not visible from the earth sometimes come into view.
– DERIVATIVES **librate** verb.
– ORIGIN early 17th cent. (denoting an oscillating motion, or equilibrium): from Latin *libratio(n-)*, from the verb *librare*, from *libra* 'a balance'.

libretto /lɪˈbrɛtəʊ/ ▶ noun (pl. **libretti** /-ti/ or **librettos**) the text of an opera or other long vocal work.
– DERIVATIVES **librettist** noun.
– ORIGIN mid 18th cent.: from Italian, diminutive of *libro* 'book', from Latin *liber*.

Libreville /ˈliːbrəvɪl/ the capital of Gabon, a port on the Atlantic coast at the mouth of the Gabon River; pop. 576,000 (est. 2007).

Librium /ˈlɪbrɪəm/ ▶ noun trademark for **CHLORDIAZEPOXIDE**.
– ORIGIN 1960s: of unknown origin.

Libya /ˈlɪbɪə/ a country in North Africa; pop. 6,324,400 (est. 2009); official language, Arabic; capital, Tripoli. ■ ancient North Africa west of Egypt.

> Much of Libya forms part of the Sahara Desert, with a narrow coastal plain bordering the Mediterranean; the country has major oil deposits. The area came under Turkish domination in the 16th century, was annexed by Italy in 1912, and became an independent kingdom in 1951.

– DERIVATIVES **Libyan** adjective & noun.

lice plural form of **LOUSE**.

licence (US **license**) ▶ noun 1 a permit from an authority to own or use something, do a particular thing, or carry on a trade (especially in alcoholic drink): *a gun licence* | [as modifier] *a television licence fee.* ■ [mass noun] formal or official permission to do something: *a subsidiary company manufactured cranes under licence from a Norwegian firm.*
2 [mass noun] freedom to behave as one wishes, especially in a way which results in excessive or unacceptable behaviour: *the government was criticized for giving the army too much licence.* ■ a writer's or artist's freedom to deviate from fact, or from conventions such as grammar, for effect: *artistic licence.* ■ licentiousness. ■ (**a licence to do something**) a reason or excuse to do something unacceptable: *police say that the lenient sentence is a licence to assault.*
– PHRASES **licence to print money** a very lucrative commercial activity, regarded as requiring little effort.
– ORIGIN late Middle English: via Old French from Latin *licentia* 'freedom, licentiousness' (in medieval Latin 'authority, permission'), from *licere* 'be lawful or permitted'.

license (also **licence**) ▶ verb [with obj.] grant a licence to: *a pub has to be licensed by the local justices* | [with obj. and infinitive] *he ought not to have been licensed to fly a plane* | (as adj. **licensing**) *a licensing authority.* ■ authorize the use, performance, or release of (something): *the company expect that the drug will soon be licensed for use in the USA.* ■ dated permit (someone) to do something: [with obj. and infinitive] *he was licensed to do no more than send a message.*
– DERIVATIVES **licensable** adjective, **licenser** noun, **licensor** noun.
– ORIGIN late Middle English: from **LICENCE**. The spelling *-se* arose by analogy with pairs such as *practice, practise.*

licensed (also **licenced**) ▶ adjective having an official licence: *a licensed taxi operator.* ■ Brit. (of premises) having a licence for the sale of alcohol: *a licensed restaurant*.

licensed victualler ▸ noun see VICTUALLER (sense 1).

licensee ▸ noun the holder of a licence, especially to sell alcoholic drinks.

license number ▸ noun North American term for REGISTRATION (sense 2).

license plate ▸ noun North American term for NUMBER PLATE.

licensure ▸ noun [mass noun] chiefly N. Amer. the granting of a licence, especially to carry out a trade or profession.

licentiate /lʌɪˈsɛnʃɪət/ ▸ noun **1** the holder of a certificate of competence to practise a particular profession. ■ (in certain universities, especially abroad) a degree between that of bachelor and master or doctor. ■ the holder of a licentiate degree.
2 a licensed preacher not yet having an appointment, especially in a Presbyterian Church.
– ORIGIN late 15th cent.: from medieval Latin, noun use of *licentiatus* 'having freedom', based on *licentia* 'freedom'.

licentious /lʌɪˈsɛnʃəs/ ▸ adjective **1** promiscuous and unprincipled in sexual matters.
2 archaic disregarding accepted conventions, especially in grammar or literary style.
– DERIVATIVES **licentiously** adverb, **licentiousness** noun.
– ORIGIN late Middle English: from Latin *licentiosus*, from *licentia* 'freedom'.

lichee ▸ noun variant spelling of LYCHEE.

lichen /ˈlʌɪk(ə)n, ˈlɪtʃ(ə)n/ ▸ noun **1** a simple slow-growing plant which typically forms a low crust-like, leaf-like, or branching growth on rocks, walls, and trees.

> Lichens are composite plants consisting of a fungus that contains photosynthetic algal cells. Their classification is based upon that of the fungal partner, which in most cases belongs to the subdivision Ascomycotina, and the algal partners are either green algae or cyanobacteria.

2 [mass noun] [usu. with modifier] a skin disease in which small, hard round lesions occur close together.
– DERIVATIVES **lichened** adjective (sense 1), **lichenology** noun (sense 1), **lichenous** adjective (sense 2).
– ORIGIN early 17th cent.: via Latin from Greek *leikhēn*.

Lichfield /ˈlɪtʃfiːld/ a town in central England, in Staffordshire north of Birmingham; pop. 29,500 (est. 2009). It was the birthplace of Samuel Johnson.

licht /lɪxt/ ▸ noun, adjective, & verb Scottish variant of LIGHT[1], LIGHT[2].

Lichtenstein /ˈlɪktənˌstʌɪn/, Roy (1923–97), American painter and sculptor. A leading exponent of pop art, he became known for paintings inspired by comic strips. Notable works: *Whaam!* (1963).

-licious ▸ combining form forming adjectives denoting someone or something delightful or extremely attractive: *babelicious* | *bootylicious*.
– ORIGIN 1950s: from DELICIOUS.

licit /ˈlɪsɪt/ ▸ adjective not forbidden; lawful: *usage patterns differ between licit and illicit drugs*.
– DERIVATIVES **licitly** adverb.
– ORIGIN late 15th cent.: from Latin *licitus* 'allowed', from the verb *licere*.

lick ▸ verb [with obj.] **1** pass the tongue over (something) in order to taste, moisten, or clean it: *he licked the stamp and stuck it on the envelope*. ■ [no obj., with adverbial of direction] (of a flame, wave, or breeze) move lightly and quickly like a tongue: *the flames licked around the wood*.
2 informal overcome (a person or problem) decisively: *all right Mary, I know when I'm licked* | *the Chancellor said that the government **had** inflation **licked***. ■ beat or thrash (someone). ■ (**lick someone/thing down**) W. Indian cut or knock someone or something down.
▸ noun **1** an act of licking something with the tongue: *Sammy gave his fingers a lick*. ■ a quick movement of flame, water, etc.
2 informal a light coating or quick application of something, especially paint: *she needed to give the kitchen **a lick of paint***. ■ [in sing.] [usu. with negative] US an extremely small amount of something abstract: *there's not a lick of suspense in the entire plot*.
3 (often **licks**) informal a short phrase or solo in jazz or popular music: *cool guitar licks*.
4 informal a smart blow: *his mother gave him several licks for daring to blaspheme*.
– PHRASES **at a lick** informal at a fast pace. **a lick and a promise** informal an act of cleaning or washing something in a hasty manner. **lick someone's boots** (or vulgar slang **arse**) be excessively obsequious towards someone. **lick someone/thing into shape** see SHAPE. **lick one's lips** (or **chops**) look forward to something with eager anticipation. **lick one's wounds** retire to recover one's strength or confidence after a humiliating experience: *the party was licking its wounds after electoral defeat*. **not be able to do something a lick** US informal be totally incompetent at the specified activity: *I couldn't sing a lick*.
– DERIVATIVES **licker** noun [usu. in combination].
– ORIGIN Old English *liccian*, of West Germanic origin; related to Dutch *likken* and German *lecken*, from an Indo-European root shared by Greek *leikhein* and Latin *lingere*.

lickerish /ˈlɪkərɪʃ/ ▸ adjective **1** lecherous: *lickerish grins and dirty jokes*.
2 W. Indian or archaic fond of eating; greedy.
– ORIGIN late 15th cent.: alteration of obsolete *lickerous*, in the same sense, from an Anglo-Norman French variant of Old French *lecheros* (see LECHEROUS).

lickety-split ▸ adverb N. Amer. informal as fast as possible: *I took off lickety-split across the lawn*.
– ORIGIN early 19th cent. (in the phrase *as fast as lickety* 'at full speed'): from a fanciful extension of LICK + SPLIT (verb).

lick hole ▸ noun Austral. a salt lick, or a place where a block of salt is placed for stock to lick.

licking ▸ noun informal a heavy defeat or beating.

lickspittle ▸ noun a person who behaves obsequiously to those in power.

licorice ▸ noun US spelling of LIQUORICE.

lictor /ˈlɪktə/ ▸ noun (in ancient Rome) an officer attending the consul or other magistrate, bearing the fasces, and executing sentence on offenders.
– ORIGIN Latin, perhaps related to *ligare* 'to bind'.

lid ▸ noun a removable or hinged cover for the top of a container: *a dustbin lid*. ■ (usu. **lids**) an eyelid: *eyes hooded beneath heavy lids*. ■ the top crust of a pie. ■ Botany the operculum of a moss capsule. ■ informal a hat or crash helmet.
– PHRASES **keep a** (or **the**) **lid on** informal keep (an emotion or process) from going out of control: *she couldn't keep the lid on her simmering anger*. ■ keep secret: *she keeps a very tight lid on her private life*. **put a** (or **the**) **lid on** informal put a stop to: *it's time to put the lid on all the talk*. **put the lid** (or **the tin lid**) **on it** Brit. informal be the culmination of a series of acts or events that makes a situation unbearable. **take** (or **lift**) **the lid off** (or **lift the lid on**) informal reveal unwelcome secrets about.
– DERIVATIVES **lidded** adjective, **lidless** adjective.
– ORIGIN Old English *hlid*, of Germanic origin, from a base meaning 'cover'; related to Dutch *lid*.

lidar /ˈlʌɪdɑː/ ▸ noun [mass noun] a detection system which works on the principle of radar, but uses light from a laser.
– ORIGIN 1960s: blend of LIGHT[1] and RADAR.

Liddell /ˈlɪd(ə)l/, Eric (Henry) (1902–45), British athlete and missionary, born in China. In the 1924 Olympic Games he won the 400 metres in a world record time. His exploits were celebrated in the film *Chariots of Fire* (1981).

Liddell Hart /ˌlɪd(ə)l ˈhɑːt/, Sir Basil Henry (1895–1970), British military historian and theorist. He developed principles of mobile warfare, which were adopted by both sides in the Second World War.

Lidingö /ˈliːdɪŋəː/ an island suburb of Stockholm in Sweden, in the north-east of the city; pop. 43,111 (2008).

Lido /ˈliːdəʊ/ **1** an island reef off the coast of NE Italy, in the northern Adriatic. It separates the Lagoon of Venice from the Gulf of Venice. Full name **Lido di Malamocco** /dɪ ˌmaləˈmɒkəʊ/.
2 (also **the Lido**) a town and beach resort in NE Italy, on the Lido reef opposite Venice; pop. 20,000 (est. 2008).

lido /ˈliːdəʊ, ˈlʌɪ-/ ▸ noun (pl. **lidos**) Brit. a public open-air swimming pool or bathing beach.
– ORIGIN late 17th cent.: from Italian LIDO, from *lido* 'shore', from Latin *litus*.

lidocaine /ˈlɪdə(ʊ)keɪn/ ▸ noun chiefly N. Amer. another term for LIGNOCAINE.
– ORIGIN 1940s: from *(acetani)lid(e)* + *-caine* (from COCAINE).

Lie /liː/, Trygve Halvdan (1896–1968), Norwegian Labour politician, first Secretary General of the United Nations 1946–53.

lie[1] ▸ verb (**lies, lying**; past **lay**; past participle **lain**) [no obj., with adverbial] **1** (of a person or animal) be in or assume a horizontal or resting position on a supporting surface: *the body lay face downwards on the grass* | *I had to lie down because I was groggy* | *Lily lay back on the pillows and watched him*. ■ (of a thing) rest flat on a surface: *a book lay open on the table*. ■ (of a dead person) be buried in a particular place.
2 be, remain, or be kept in a specified state: *the abbey lies in ruins today* | *putting homeless families into private houses that would otherwise lie empty*. ■ (of something abstract) reside or be found: *the solution lies in a return to traditional values*.
3 (of a place) be situated in a specified position or direction: *Kexby lies about five miles due east of York*. ■ (of a scene) extend from the observer's viewpoint in a specified direction: *stand here, and all of Amsterdam lies before you*. ■ Brit. (of a competitor or team) be in a specified position during a competition or within a group: *United are currently lying in fifth place*.
4 Law (of an action, charge, or claim) be admissible or sustainable.
▸ noun (usu. **the lie**) the way, direction, or position in which something lies: *he was familiarizing himself with **the lie of** the streets*. ■ Golf the position in which a golf ball comes to rest, especially as regards the ease of the next shot. ■ the lair or place of cover of an animal or a bird.
– PHRASES **let something lie** take no action regarding a problematic matter. **lie heavy on one** cause one to feel troubled or uncomfortable. **lie in state** (of the corpse of a person of national importance) be laid in a public place of honour before burial. **lie low** (especially of a criminal) keep out of sight; avoid detection or attention. **the lie** (N. Amer. **lay**) **of the land** the features or characteristics of an area. ■ the current situation: *she was beginning to see the lie of the land with her in-laws*. **take something lying down** [usu. with negative] accept an insult, setback, or rebuke without protest.
– PHRASAL VERBS **lie ahead** be going to happen: *I'm excited by what lies ahead*. **lie around/about** (of an object) be left carelessly out of place. ■ (of a person) pass the time lazily or aimlessly: *you all just lay around all day on your backsides, didn't you?* **lie behind** be the real, often hidden, reason for (something): *a subtle strategy lies behind such silly claims*. **lie in** Brit. remain in bed after the normal time for getting up. ■ archaic (of a pregnant woman) go to bed to give birth. **lie off** Nautical (of a ship) stand some distance from shore or from another ship. **lie over** US break one's journey: *we'll lie over in New York, then fly to London*. **lie to** Nautical (of a ship) come almost to a stop with its head towards the wind. **lie up** (of a ship) go into dock or be out of commission. ■ (**lie something up**) put a boat in dock or out of commission. **lie with 1** (of a responsibility) be attributable to (someone): *ultimate responsibility for the violence lies with the President*. **2** archaic have sexual intercourse with.
– ORIGIN Old English *licgan*, of Germanic origin; related to Dutch *liggen* and German *liegen*, from an Indo-European root shared by Greek *lektron*, *lekhos* and Latin *lectus* 'bed'.

> **USAGE** The verb **lie** is often confused with the verb **lay**, giving rise to incorrect uses such as *he is **laying** on the bed* (correct use is *he is **lying** on the bed*) or *why don't you **lie** it on the bed?* (correct use is *why don't you **lay** it on the bed?*). See USAGE at LAY[1].

lie[2] ▸ noun an intentionally false statement: *they hint rather than **tell outright lies*** | *the whole thing is a **pack of lies***. ■ used with reference to a situation involving deception or founded on a mistaken impression: *all their married life she had been **living a lie***.
▸ verb (**lies, lying, lied**) [no obj.] tell a lie or lies: *why had Ashenden lied about his visit to London?* | [with direct speech] *'I am sixty-five,' she lied*. ■ (of a thing) present a false impression: *the camera cannot lie*.
– PHRASES **give the lie to** serve to show that (something previously assumed to be the case) is not true: *these figures give the lie to the notion that Britain is excessively strike-ridden*. **I tell a lie** (or **that's a lie**) Brit. informal used to correct oneself immediately when one realizes that one has made an incorrect remark: *I never used to dream—I tell a lie, I did dream when I was little*. **lie through one's teeth** informal tell an outright lie without remorse.
– ORIGIN Old English *lyge* (noun), *lēogan* (verb), of Germanic origin; related to Dutch *liegen* and German *lügen*.

L

Liebchen /ˈliːbtʃ(ə)n/, German /ˈliːpçən/ ▸ **noun** a person who is very dear to another (often used as a term of endearment).
– ORIGIN German, diminutive of *lieb* 'dear'.

Liebfraumilch /ˈliːbfraʊmɪlʃ/, German /ˈliːpfraʊˌmɪlç/ ▸ **noun** [mass noun] a light white wine from the Rhine region.
– ORIGIN German, from *lieb* 'dear' + *Frau* 'lady' (referring to the Virgin Mary, patroness of the convent where it was first made) + *Milch* 'milk'.

Liebig /ˈliːbɪx/, German /ˈliːbɪç/, Justus, Baron von (1803–73), German chemist and teacher. With Friedrich Wöhler he discovered the benzoyl radical, and demonstrated that such radicals were groups of atoms that remained unchanged in many chemical reactions.

Liechtenstein /ˈlɪktənˌstʌɪn/, German /ˈlɪçtn̩ʃtaɪn/ a small independent principality in the Alps, between Switzerland and Austria; pop. 34,800 (est. 2009); official language, German; capital, Vaduz.

> The principality was created in 1719 within the Holy Roman Empire, becoming independent of the German confederation in 1866. Liechtenstein is economically integrated with Switzerland.

– DERIVATIVES **Liechtensteiner** noun.

lied /liːd, -t/ ▸ **noun** (pl. **lieder** /ˈliːdə/) a type of German song, especially of the Romantic period, typically for solo voice with piano accompaniment.
– ORIGIN from German *Lied*.

lie detector ▸ **noun** an instrument for determining whether a person is telling the truth by testing for physiological changes considered to be associated with lying. The results of lie-detector tests are generally not accepted for judicial purposes. Compare with POLYGRAPH.

lie-down ▸ **noun** Brit. a short rest in which one lies down on a bed, sofa, etc.: *he felt badly in need of a lie-down.*

lief /liːf/ ▸ **adverb** (**as lief**) archaic as happily; as gladly: *he would just as lief eat a pincushion.*
– ORIGIN Old English *lēof* 'dear, pleasant', of Germanic origin: related to LEAVE[2] and LOVE.

liege /liːdʒ/ historical ▸ **adjective** concerned with or relating to the relationship between a feudal superior and a vassal: *an oath of fealty and liege homage.*
▸ **noun** (also **liege lord**) a feudal superior or sovereign. ■ a vassal or subject: *the king's lieges.*
– ORIGIN Middle English: via Old French *lige*, *liege* from medieval Latin *laeticus*, probably of Germanic origin.

Liège /lɪˈɛʒ/, French /ljɛʒ/ a province of eastern Belgium. Formerly ruled by independent prince-bishops, it became a part of the Netherlands in 1815 and of Belgium in 1830. Flemish name LUIK. ■ the capital of Liège; pop. 190,102 (2008).

liegeman ▸ **noun** (pl. **liegemen**) historical a vassal who owed feudal service or allegiance to a nobleman.

lie-in ▸ **noun** Brit. a prolonged stay in bed in the morning.

lien /liːn, ˈliːən/ ▸ **noun** Law a right to keep possession of property belonging to another person until a debt owed by that person is discharged.
– ORIGIN mid 16th cent.: from French, via Old French *loien* from Latin *ligamen* 'bond', from *ligare* 'to bind'.

lierne /lɪˈəːn/ ▸ **noun** [usu. as modifier] Architecture (in vaulting) a short rib connecting the bosses and intersections of the principal ribs: *a fine lierne vault.*
– ORIGIN late Middle English: from French, perhaps a transferred use of dialect *lierne* (standard French *liane*) 'clematis'.

lieu /ljuː, luː/ ▸ **noun** (**in lieu**) instead: *the company issued additional shares to shareholders **in lieu of** a cash dividend.*
– ORIGIN Middle English: via French from Latin *locus* 'place'.

Lieut. ▸ **abbreviation** Lieutenant.

lieutenant /lɛfˈtɛnənt/ ▸ **noun** a deputy or substitute acting for a superior: *one of the Prime Minister's most trusted lieutenants.* ■ a rank of officer in the British army, above second lieutenant and below captain. ■ a rank of officer in the navy, above sub lieutenant and below lieutenant commander. ■ (in the US) a police officer next in rank below captain.
– DERIVATIVES **lieutenancy** noun (pl. **lieutenancies**).
– ORIGIN late Middle English: from Old French (see LIEU, TENANT).

> **USAGE** In the normal British pronunciation of **lieutenant** the first syllable sounds like **lef-**. In the standard US pronunciation the first syllable, in contrast, rhymes with **do**. It is difficult to explain where the **f** in the British pronunciation comes from. Probably, at some point before the 19th century, the **u** at the end of Old French **lieu** was read and pronounced as a **v**, and the **v** later became an **f**.

lieutenant colonel ▸ **noun** a rank of officer in the army and the US air force, above major and below colonel.

lieutenant commander ▸ **noun** a rank of officer in the navy, above lieutenant and below commander.

lieutenant general ▸ **noun** a high rank of officer in the army, above major general and below general.

lieutenant governor ▸ **noun** the acting or deputy governor of a state or province, under a governor or Governor General.
– DERIVATIVES **lieutenant governorship** noun.

Lieutenant of the Tower ▸ **noun** (in the UK) the acting commandant of the Tower of London.

life ▸ **noun** (pl. **lives**) **1** [mass noun] the condition that distinguishes animals and plants from inorganic matter, including the capacity for growth, reproduction, functional activity, and continual change preceding death: *the origins of life | cats require visual experience during the first few weeks of life.* ■ living things and their activity: *lower forms of life | the ice-cream vendors were the only signs of life | the valley is teeming with bird life.*
2 the existence of an individual human being or animal: *a disaster that claimed the lives of 266 people |* [mass noun] *she didn't want to die; she loved life.* ■ [with adj. or noun modifier] a particular type or aspect of human existence: *his father decided to start a new life in California |* [mass noun] *a teacher will help you settle into school life | revelations about his private life.* ■ a biography: *a life of Shelley.* ■ (in Christianity and some other religious traditions) either of the two states of a person's existence separated by death: *he departed this life on 28 March 1912.* ■ (in Hinduism and some other religious traditions) any of a number of successive existences in which a soul is held to be reincarnated. ■ a chance to live after narrowly escaping death (with reference to the nine lives traditionally attributed to cats). ■ (in various games) one of a specified number of chances each player has before being put out.
3 (usu. **one's life**) the period between the birth and death of a living thing, especially a human being: *she has lived all her life in the country | they became friends **for life**.* ■ the period during which something inanimate or abstract continues to exist, function, or be valid: *underlay helps to prolong the life of a carpet.* ■ [mass noun] informal a sentence of imprisonment for life.
4 vitality, vigour, or energy: *she was beautiful and full of life.*
5 [mass noun] (in art) the depiction of a subject from a real model, rather than from an artist's imagination: *the pose and clothing were sketched **from life**.* See also STILL LIFE.
– PHRASES **bring** (or **come**) **to life** regain or cause to regain consciousness. ■ (with reference to a fictional character or inanimate object) cause or seem to be alive or real: *he brings the character of MacDonald to life with power and precision.* ■ make or become active, lively, or interesting: *soon, with the return of the fishermen, the village comes to life again | bring any room to life with these coordinating cushions.* **do anything for a quiet life** make any concession to avoid being disturbed. **for dear** (or **one's**) **life** as if or in order to escape death: *I clung on to the tree for dear life | Sue ran for her life.* **for the life of me** [with modal and negative] informal however hard I try; even if my life depended on it: *I can't for the life of me understand what you see in her.* **frighten the life out of** terrify. **get a life** [often in imperative] informal start living a fuller existence: *if he's a waster then get yourself out of there and get a life.* **give one's life for** die for. (**as**) **large as life** informal used to emphasize that a person is conspicuously present: *he was standing nearby, large as life.* **larger than life** (of a person) attracting special attention because of unusual and flamboyant appearance or behaviour. **life and limb** see LIMB[1]. **the life and soul of the party** (US **the life of the party**) a vivacious and sociable person. **life in the fast lane** informal an exciting and eventful lifestyle, especially one bringing wealth and success. **one's life's work** the work (especially that of an academic or artistic nature) accomplished in or pursued throughout someone's lifetime. **lose one's life** be killed: *he lost his life in a car accident.* **a matter of life and death** a matter of vital importance. **not on your life** informal said to emphasize one's refusal to comply with a request: *'I want to see Clare alone.' 'Not on your life,' said Buzz.* **save someone's** (or **one's own**) **life** prevent someone's (or one's own) death. ■ informal provide much-needed relief from boredom or a difficult situation. **see life** gain a wide experience of the world. **take one's life in one's hands** risk being killed. **take someone's** (or **one's own**) **life** kill someone (or oneself). **that's life** an expression of one's acceptance of a situation, however difficult: *we'll miss each other, but still, that's life.* **this is the life** an expression of contentment with one's present circumstances: *Ice cubes clinked in crystal glasses. 'This is the life,' she said.* **to the life** exactly like the original: *there he was, Nathan to the life, sitting at a table.* **to save one's life** [with modal and negative] even if one's life were to depend on it: *she couldn't stop crying now to save her life.*
– ORIGIN Old English *līf*, of Germanic origin; related to Dutch *lijf*, German *Leib* 'body', also to LIVE[1].

life-affirming ▸ **adjective** having an emotionally or spiritually uplifting effect: *meeting these people was a life-affirming experience.*

life-and-death ▸ **adjective** deciding whether someone lives or dies; vitally important.

life assurance ▸ **noun** Brit. another term for LIFE INSURANCE.

> **USAGE** There is a technical distinction between **life assurance** and **life insurance**: see **USAGE** at **ASSURANCE**.

lifebelt ▸ **noun** a ring of buoyant or inflatable material used to help a person who has fallen into water to stay afloat.

lifeblood ▸ **noun** [mass noun] literary the blood, as being necessary to life. ■ the indispensable factor or influence that gives something its strength and vitality: *the movement of coal was the lifeblood of British railways.*

lifeboat ▸ **noun** a specially constructed boat launched from land to rescue people in distress at sea. ■ a small boat kept on a ship for use in emergency, typically one of a number on deck or suspended from davits.
– DERIVATIVES **lifeboatman** noun (pl. **lifeboatmen**).

lifebuoy ▸ **noun** a buoyant support such as a lifebelt for keeping a person afloat in water.

life coach ▸ **noun** a person employed to help people attain their goals in life.
– DERIVATIVES **life-coaching** noun.

life cycle ▸ **noun** the series of changes in the life of an organism including reproduction.

life expectancy ▸ **noun** the average period that a person may expect to live.

life-expired ▸ **adjective** Brit. (especially of locomotives or other railway equipment) worn out or outdated: *life-expired signalling.*

life force ▸ **noun** [mass noun] the force that gives something its vitality or strength: *the passionate life force of the symphony.* ■ the spirit which animates living creatures; the soul.

life form ▸ **noun** any living thing.

life-giving ▸ **adjective** sustaining or revitalizing life: *the life-giving water of baptism.*

lifeguard ▸ **noun** an expert swimmer employed to rescue bathers who get into difficulty at a beach or swimming pool.
– DERIVATIVES **lifeguarding** noun.

Life Guards ▸ **plural noun** (in the UK) a regiment of the Household Cavalry.

life history ▸ **noun** the series of changes undergone by an organism during its lifetime.

life imprisonment ▸ **noun** [mass noun] a long term of imprisonment, which (in the UK) is now the only sentence for murder and the maximum for any crime. It is indeterminate in length, and in practice is rarely for the whole of a criminal's remaining life.

life instinct ▸ **noun** Psychoanalysis an innate desire for self-preservation, manifest in hunger, self-defensive aggression, and the sexual instincts. Compare with DEATH INSTINCT.

life insurance ▸ **noun** [mass noun] insurance that pays out a sum of money either on the death of the insured person or after a set period.

> **USAGE** There is a technical distinction between **life insurance** and **life assurance**: see **USAGE** at **ASSURANCE**.

life interest ▸ **noun** [mass noun] Law a right to property that a person holds for life but cannot dispose of further.

life jacket ▸ noun a sleeveless buoyant or inflatable jacket for keeping a person afloat in water.

lifeless ▸ adjective **1** dead or apparently dead: *his lifeless body was taken from the river.* ▪ lacking vigour, vitality, or excitement: *dull and lifeless hair.*
2 devoid of living things.
– DERIVATIVES **lifelessly** adverb, **lifelessness** noun.
– ORIGIN Old English *lifléas* (see LIFE, -LESS).

lifelike ▸ adjective very similar to the person or thing represented: *the artist had etched a lifelike horse.*
– DERIVATIVES **lifelikeness** noun.

lifeline ▸ noun **1** a rope or line used for life-saving, typically one thrown to rescue someone in difficulties in water or one used by sailors to secure themselves to a boat. ▪ a line used by a diver for sending signals to the surface.
2 a thing on which someone or something depends or which provides a means of escape from a difficult situation: *the telephone has always been a lifeline for Gabby and me.*
3 (in palmistry) a line on the palm of a person's hand, regarded as indicating how long they will live.
– PHRASES **throw a lifeline to** provide (someone) with a means of escaping from a difficult situation.

life list ▸ noun Ornithology a list of all the kinds of birds observed by a person during his or her life.

lifelong ▸ adjective lasting or remaining in a particular state throughout a person's life: *the two men were to remain lifelong friends* | *a lifelong Conservative.*

life member ▸ noun a person who has lifelong membership of a society.
– DERIVATIVES **life membership** noun.

life office ▸ noun an office or company dealing in life insurance.

life peer ▸ noun (in the UK) a peer whose title cannot be inherited.
– DERIVATIVES **life peerage** noun.

life peeress ▸ noun a woman holding a life peerage.

life preserver ▸ noun **1** Brit. a short truncheon with a heavily loaded end.
2 N. Amer. a buoyant device such as a lifebelt or life jacket.

lifer ▸ noun **1** informal a person serving a life sentence.
2 N. Amer. a person who spends their life in a particular career, especially in one of the armed forces.

life raft ▸ noun a raft, typically inflatable, for use in an emergency at sea.

life ring ▸ noun another term for LIFEBELT.

lifesaver ▸ noun **1** informal a thing that saves one from serious difficulty: *a microwave could be a lifesaver this Christmas.*
2 (also **surf lifesaver**) Austral./NZ a lifeguard working on a beach.

life sciences ▸ plural noun the sciences concerned with the study of living organisms, including biology, botany, zoology, microbiology, physiology, biochemistry, and related subjects. Often contrasted with PHYSICAL SCIENCES.
– DERIVATIVES **life scientist** noun.

life sentence ▸ noun a punishment of life imprisonment or of imprisonment for a specified long period.

life-size (also **life-sized**) ▸ adjective of the same size as the person or thing represented: *a life-size model of a discus-thrower.*

life skill ▸ noun (usu. **life skills**) a skill that is necessary or desirable for full participation in everyday life: *sharing with a sibling can help children learn important life skills.*

lifespan ▸ noun the length of time for which a person or animal lives or a thing functions: *the human lifespan.*

lifestyle ▸ noun the way in which a person lives: *the benefits of a healthy lifestyle.* ▪ [as modifier] denoting advertising or products designed to appeal to a consumer by association with a desirable lifestyle.

lifestyle drug ▸ noun a pharmaceutical product characterized as improving the quality of life rather than alleviating or curing disease.

life support ▸ noun [mass noun] Medicine maintenance of a patient's vital functions following disablement or in an adverse environment: [as modifier] *a life-support machine.* ▪ informal equipment in a hospital used for life support: *a patient on life support.*

life table ▸ noun a table of statistics relating to life expectancy and mortality for a given category of people. ▪ Zoology a similar table for a population of animals divided into cohorts of given age.

life-threatening ▸ adjective (especially of an illness or injury) potentially fatal.

lifetime ▸ noun the duration of a person's life: *a reward for a lifetime's work.* ▪ the duration of a thing's existence or usefulness: *fifteen shops closed during the lifetime of the scheme.* ▪ informal a very long period of time: *five weeks was a lifetime, anything could have happened.*
– PHRASES **of a lifetime** (of a chance or experience) such as does not occur more than once in a person's life: *because of Frankie she had rejected the opportunity of a lifetime.*

life vest ▸ noun North American term for LIFE JACKET.

lifeworld ▸ noun Philosophy all the immediate experiences, activities, and contacts that make up the world of an individual or corporate life.
– ORIGIN 1940s: translating German *Lebenswelt.*

Liffey /ˈlɪfi/ a river of eastern Ireland, which flows for 80 km (50 miles) from the Wicklow Mountains to Dublin Bay. The city of Dublin is situated at its mouth.

Lifford /ˈlɪfəd/ the county town of Donegal, in the Republic of Ireland; pop. 1,448 (2006).

LIFO /ˈlʌɪfəʊ/ ▸ abbreviation last in, first out (chiefly with reference to methods of stock valuation and data storage). Compare with **FIFO**.

lift ▸ verb **1** [with obj.] raise to a higher position or level: *he lifted his trophy over his head.* ▪ move (one's eyes or face) to face upwards and look at someone or something: *he lifted his eyes for an instant.* ▪ [no obj.] move upwards; be raised: *Thomas's eyelids drowsily lifted.* ▪ [no obj.] (of a cloud, fog, etc.) move upwards or away: *the factory smoke hung low, never lifted.* ▪ increase the volume of (one's voice). ▪ increase (a price or amount): *the building society lifted its interest rates by 0.75 of a point.* ▪ perform cosmetic surgery on (part of the body) to reduce sagging. ▪ dig up (plants or root vegetables).
2 [with obj. and adverbial of direction] pick up and move to a different position: *he lifted her down from the pony's back.* ▪ transport by air: *a helicopter lifted 11 crew to safety from the ship.* ▪ enable (someone or something) to escape from an unpleasant situation: *the best way to **lift** nations **out of** poverty is through trade.* ▪ improve the rank or position of (a person or team): *this victory lifted United into third place.*
3 [with obj.] raise (a person's spirits or confidence): *we heard inspiring talks which lifted our spirits.* ▪ [no obj.] (of a person's mood) become happier: *suddenly his heart lifted and he could have wept with relief.*
4 [with obj.] formally remove or end (a legal restriction, decision, or ban): *the European Community lifted its oil embargo against South Africa.*
5 [with obj.] carry off or win (a prize or event): *she staged a magnificent comeback to lift the British Open title.* ▪ use (a person's work or ideas) without permission or acknowledgement: *this is a hackneyed adventure lifted straight from a vintage Lassie episode.* ▪ informal steal (something): *the shirt she had lifted from a supermarket.* ▪ informal arrest (someone).
▸ noun **1** Brit. a platform or compartment housed in a shaft for raising and lowering people or things to different levels. ▪ a device incorporating a moving cable for carrying people up or down a mountain. ▪ a built-up heel or device worn in a boot or shoe to make the wearer appear taller or to correct shortening of a leg.
2 an act of lifting: *weightlifters attempting a particularly heavy lift.* ▪ [mass noun] upward force exerted by the air on an aerofoil or other structure, counteracting gravity: *separate engines provide lift and generate forward speed.* ▪ the maximum weight that an aircraft can raise. ▪ [mass noun] Cricket the tendency of a ball bowled to rise sharply on bouncing. ▪ a rise in price, level, or amount: *the company has already produced a 10 per cent lift in profits.* ▪ informal an instance of stealing or plagiarizing something.
3 a free ride in another person's vehicle: *Miss Green is giving me a lift to school.*
4 [in sing.] a feeling of confidence or cheerfulness: *winning this match has **given** everyone **a lift**.*
– PHRASES **lift a finger** (or **hand**) [usu. with negative] make the slightest effort to do something, especially to help someone: *he never lifted a finger to get Jimmy released from prison.* **lift his** (or **its**) **leg** informal (of a male dog) urinate.
– PHRASAL VERBS **lift off** (of an aircraft, spacecraft, or rocket) take off, especially vertically: *the helicopters lifted off at 1030 hours.*
– DERIVATIVES **liftable** adjective, **lifter** noun.
– ORIGIN Middle English: from Old Norse *lypta*, of Germanic origin; related to LOFT.

lift-off ▸ noun the vertical take-off of a spacecraft, rocket, or helicopter.

lift pump ▸ noun a simple pump consisting of a piston moving in a cylinder, both parts incorporating a valve.

lig Brit. informal ▸ verb (**ligs**, **ligging**, **ligged**) [no obj.] take advantage of free parties, travel, or other benefits offered by companies for publicity purposes.
▸ noun a free party or show provided for publicity.
– DERIVATIVES **ligger** noun.
– ORIGIN 1960s: from a dialect variant of LIE[1], literally 'lie about, loaf', whence 'freeload'.

ligament /ˈlɪgəm(ə)nt/ ▸ noun Anatomy a short band of tough, flexible fibrous connective tissue which connects two bones or cartilages or holds together a joint. ▪ a membranous fold that supports an organ and keeps it in position.
– DERIVATIVES **ligamental** adjective, **ligamentary** adjective, **ligamentous** adjective.
– ORIGIN late Middle English: from Latin *ligamentum* 'bond', from *ligare* 'to bind'.

ligand /ˈlɪg(ə)nd/ ▸ noun Chemistry an ion or molecule attached to a metal atom by coordinate bonding. ▪ Biochemistry a molecule that binds to another (usually larger) molecule.
– ORIGIN 1950s: from Latin *ligandus* 'that can be tied', gerundive of *ligare* 'to bind'.

ligase /ˈlɪgeɪz/ ▸ noun Biochemistry an enzyme which brings about ligation of DNA or another substance.
– ORIGIN 1960s: from Latin *ligare* 'to bind' + -ASE.

ligate /lɪˈgeɪt/ ▸ verb [with obj.] Surgery tie up (an artery or vessel).
– ORIGIN late 16th cent.: from Latin *ligat-* 'tied', from the verb *ligare*.

ligation ▸ noun [mass noun] **1** the surgical procedure of tying a ligature tightly around a blood vessel or other duct or tube in the body.
2 Biochemistry the joining of two DNA strands or other molecules by a phosphate ester linkage.
– ORIGIN late Middle English: from late Latin *ligatio(n-)*, from the verb *ligare* (see LIGATE).

ligature /ˈlɪgətʃə/ ▸ noun **1** a thing used for tying or binding something tightly. ▪ a cord or thread used in surgery, especially to tie up a bleeding artery.
2 Music a slur or tie.
3 Printing a character consisting of two or more joined letters, e.g. *æ, fl*. ▪ a stroke that joins adjacent letters in writing or printing.
▸ verb [with obj.] bind or connect with a ligature.
– ORIGIN Middle English: via late Latin *ligatura* from Latin *ligat-* 'bound', from the verb *ligare*.

liger /ˈlʌɪgə/ ▸ noun the hybrid offspring of a male lion and a tigress. Compare with TIGON.
– ORIGIN 1930s: blend of LION and TIGER.

Ligeti /ˈlɪgəti/, György Sándor (1923–2006), Hungarian composer. His orchestral works *Apparitions* (1958–9) and *Atmosphères* (1961) dispense with the formal elements of melody, harmony, and rhythm.

light[1] ▸ noun **1** [mass noun] the natural agent that stimulates sight and makes things visible: *the light of the sun* | [in sing.] *the lamps in the street shed a faint light into the room.* ▪ [count noun] a source of illumination, especially an electric lamp: *a light came on in his room.* ▪ (**lights**) decorative illuminations: *Christmas lights.* ▪ [count noun] (usu. **lights**) a traffic light: *turn right at the lights.* ▪ the amount or quality of light in a place: *the plant requires good light* | [count noun] *in some lights she could look beautiful.* ▪ Law the light falling on the windows of a house. See ANCIENT LIGHTS.

> Visible light is electromagnetic radiation whose wavelength falls within the range to which the human retina responds, i.e. between about 390 nm (violet light) and 740 nm (red). White light consists of a roughly equal mixture of all visible wavelengths, which can be separated to yield the colours of the spectrum, as was first demonstrated conclusively by Newton. In the 20th century it became apparent that light consists of energy quanta called photons which behave partly like waves and partly like particles. The velocity of light in a vacuum is 299,792 km per second.

2 [in sing.] an expression in someone's eyes indicating a particular emotion or mood: *a shrewd light entered his eyes.* ▪ (**lights**) a person's opinions, standards, and abilities: *leaving the police to do the job **according to their lights**.*
3 [mass noun] understanding of a problem or mystery; enlightenment: *she saw light dawn on the woman's face.* ▪ spiritual illumination by divine truth.

L

4 an area of something that is brighter or paler than its surroundings: *sunshine will brighten the natural lights in your hair.*
5 a device used to produce a flame or spark: *he asked me for a light.*
6 a window or opening to let light in. ■ a perpendicular division of a mullioned window. ■ a pane of glass forming the roof or side of a greenhouse or the top of a cold frame.
7 a person eminent in a particular sphere of activity: *such lights of Liberalism as the historian Goldwin Smith.*
8 Brit. (in a crossword puzzle) a blank space to be filled by a letter.
▸ verb (past **lit**; past participle **lit** or **lighted**) [with obj.] **1** provide with light or lighting; illuminate: *the room was lit by a number of small lamps* | *lightning suddenly lit up the house.* ■ switch on (an electric light). ■ [with obj. and adverbial] provide a light for (someone) so that they can see where they are going: *I'll light you down to the gate.* ■ [no obj.] (**light up**) become illuminated.
2 make (something) start burning; ignite: *Alan gathered sticks and lit a fire* | (as adj. **lighted** or **lit**) *a lit cigarette.* ■ [no obj.] begin to burn; be ignited: *the gas wouldn't light properly.* ■ (**light something up**) ignite a cigarette, cigar, or pipe and begin to smoke it: *she lit up a cigarette and puffed on it serenely* | [no obj.] *workers who light up in prohibited areas face dismissal.*
▸ adjective **1** having a considerable or sufficient amount of natural light; not dark: *the bedrooms are light and airy.*
2 (of a colour) pale: *her eyes were light blue.*
– PHRASES **bring** (or **come**) **to light** make or become widely known or evident: *no new facts came to light.* **go out like a light** informal fall asleep or lose consciousness suddenly. **in a —— light** so as to give a specified impression: *the audit portrayed the company in a favourable light.* **in the light of** (or **in light of**) taking (something) into consideration: *the exorbitant prices are explainable in the light of the facts.* **light a fire under someone** see FIRE. **light at the end of the tunnel** an indication that a long period of difficulty is nearing an end. **light the fuse** see FUSE². **the light of day** daylight. ■ general public attention: *bringing old family secrets into the light of day.* **the light of one's life** a much loved person. **lights out** bedtime in a school dormitory, military barracks, or other institution, when lights should be switched off. **lit up** informal, dated drunk. **see the light** understand or realize something after prolonged thought or doubt. ■ undergo religious conversion. **see the light of day** be born. ■ begin to exist or to become publicly known or available: *this software first saw the light of day back in 1993.* **throw** (or **cast** or **shed**) **light on** help to explain (something) by providing further information about it.
– PHRASAL VERBS **light up** (of a person's face or eyes) suddenly become animated with liveliness or joy: *his eyes lit up and he smiled* | *a smile of delight lit up her face.*
– DERIVATIVES **lightish** adjective, **lightless** adjective, **lightness** noun.
– ORIGIN Old English *lēoht, līht* (noun and adjective), *līhtan* (verb), of Germanic origin; related to Dutch *licht* and German *Licht*, from an Indo-European root shared by Greek *leukos* 'white' and Latin *lux* 'light'.

light² ▸ adjective **1** of little weight; not heavy: *light alloy wheels* | *you're **as light as a feather**.* ■ deficient in weight, especially by a specified amount: *the sack of potatoes is 5 kilos light.* ■ carrying or suitable for small loads: *light commercial vehicles.* ■ carrying only light armaments: *light infantry.* ■ (of a vehicle, ship, or aircraft) travelling unladen or with less than a full load. ■ (of soil) friable, porous, and workable. ■ (of an isotope) having not more than the usual mass; (of a compound) containing such an isotope.
2 not strongly or heavily built or made: *light, impractical clothes* | *light armour.*
3 relatively low in density, amount, or intensity: *passenger traffic was light* | *light autumn rains.* ■ (of food or a meal) small in quantity and easy to digest: *a light supper.* ■ (of a foodstuff) low in fat, cholesterol, sugar, or other rich ingredients: *stick to a light diet.* ■ (of drink) not strongly alcoholic or heavy on the stomach: *a light Hungarian wine.* ■ (of pastry or cake) fluffy or well aerated during cooking.
4 gentle or delicate: *she planted a light kiss on his cheek* | *my breathing was steady and light.* ■ (of type) having thin strokes; not bold.
5 (of entertainment) requiring little mental effort; not profound or serious: *pop is thought of as light entertainment* | *some light reading.* ■ not solemn or unhappy; cheerful: *I left the island with a light heart.* ■ easily borne or done: *he received a light sentence* | *some light housework.*
6 (of sleep or a sleeper) easily disturbed.
7 archaic (of a woman) promiscuous.
– PHRASES **be light on** be rather short of: *we're light on fuel.* **be light on one's feet** (of a person) be quick or nimble. **a light touch** the ability to deal with something tactfully or in an understated way: *a novel which handles its tricky subject with a light touch.* **make light of** treat as unimportant: *I didn't mean to make light of your problems.* **make light work of** accomplish (a task) quickly and easily. **travel light** travel with a minimum load or minimum luggage.
– DERIVATIVES **lightish** adjective, **lightness** noun.
– ORIGIN Old English *lēocht, līht* (noun), *lēohte* (adverb), of Germanic origin; related to Dutch *licht* and German *leicht*, from an Indo-European root shared by LUNG.

light³ ▸ verb (past and past participle **lit** or **lighted**) [no obj.] **1** (**light on/upon**) come upon or discover by chance: *he lit on a possible solution.*
2 archaic descend: *from the horse he lit down.* ■ (**light on**) fall and settle or land on (a surface).
– PHRASAL VERBS **light into** N. Amer. informal criticize severely; attack: *he lit into him for his indiscretion.* **light out** N. Amer. informal depart hurriedly.
– ORIGIN Old English *līhtan* (in sense 2; also 'lessen the weight of'), from LIGHT²; compare with ALIGHT¹.

light air ▸ noun a wind of force 1 on the Beaufort scale (1–3 knots or 1–6 kph).

light box ▸ noun a flat box having a side of translucent glass or plastic and containing an electric light, so as to provide an evenly lighted flat surface or even illumination, such as in a studio.

light breeze ▸ noun a wind of force 2 on the Beaufort scale (4–6 knots or 7–12 kph).

Light Brigade, Charge of the see CHARGE OF THE LIGHT BRIGADE.

light bulb ▸ noun a glass bulb inserted into a lamp or a socket in a ceiling, which provides light by passing an electric current through a pocket of inert gas.

light cone ▸ noun Physics a surface in space–time, represented as a cone in three dimensions, comprising all the points from which a light signal would reach a given point (at the apex) simultaneously, and which therefore appear simultaneous to an observer at the apex.

light curve ▸ noun Astronomy a graph showing the variation in the light received over a period of time from a variable star or other varying celestial object.

light-emitting diode ▸ noun see **LED**.

lighten¹ ▸ verb make or become lighter in weight, pressure, or severity: [with obj.] *efforts to lighten the burden of regulation* | [no obj.] *the strain had lightened.* ■ make or become more cheerful or less serious: [with obj.] *she attempted a joke to lighten the atmosphere* | [no obj.] *try to **lighten up** and think positive.*

lighten² ▸ verb **1** make or become lighter or brighter: [no obj.] *the sky began to lighten in the east* | [with obj.] *she had lightened her hair.* ■ [with obj.] archaic enlighten spiritually.
2 [no obj.] (**it lightens, it is lightening**, etc.) rare flash with lightning: *it thundered and lightened.*

light engine ▸ noun a railway locomotive running with no vehicles attached.

lightening ▸ noun a drop in the level of the womb during the last weeks of pregnancy as the head of the fetus engages in the pelvis.

lighter¹ ▸ noun a device that produces a small flame, used to light cigarettes.

lighter² ▸ noun a flat-bottomed barge or other unpowered boat used to transfer goods to and from ships in harbour.
– DERIVATIVES **lighterman** noun (pl. **lightermen**).
– ORIGIN late Middle English: from LIGHT² (in the sense 'unload'), or from Middle Low German *luchter*.

lighterage ▸ noun [mass noun] the transference of cargo by means of a lighter.

lighter-than-air ▸ adjective relating to or denoting a balloon or other aircraft weighing less than the air it displaces, and so flying as a result of its own buoyancy.

lightfast ▸ adjective (of a dye or pigment) not prone to discolour when exposed to light.
– DERIVATIVES **lightfastness** noun.

light-fingered ▸ adjective **1** informal prone to steal: *light-fingered shoplifters.*
2 having or showing delicate skill with the hands.

light flyweight ▸ noun [mass noun] the lowest weight in amateur boxing, ranging up to 48 kg. ■ [count noun] an amateur boxer of this weight.

light-footed ▸ adjective fast, nimble, or stealthy on one's feet: *a light-footed leap.*
– DERIVATIVES **light-footedly** adverb.

light gun ▸ noun a handheld gunlike photosensitive device used chiefly in computer games, held to the display screen for passing information to the computer.

light-headed ▸ adjective dizzy and slightly faint: *she felt light-headed with relief.*
– DERIVATIVES **light-headedly** adverb, **light-headedness** noun.

light-hearted ▸ adjective amusing and entertaining: *a light-hearted speech.* ■ (of a person) cheerful or carefree.
– DERIVATIVES **light-heartedly** adverb, **light-heartedness** noun.

light heavyweight ▸ noun [mass noun] a weight in boxing and other sports intermediate between middleweight and heavyweight. In the amateur boxing scale it ranges from 75 to 81 kg. Also called CRUISERWEIGHT. ■ [count noun] a boxer or other competitor of this weight.

lighthouse ▸ noun a tower or other structure containing a beacon light to warn or guide ships at sea.

light industry ▸ noun [mass noun] the manufacture of small or light articles.

lighting ▸ noun [mass noun] equipment in a room, building, or street for producing light: *fluorescent bulbs for street lighting.* ■ the arrangement or effect of lights: *the lighting was very flat.*

lighting cameraman ▸ noun (in films) a person in charge of the lighting of sets being filmed.

lighting-up time ▸ noun Brit. the time at which motorists are required by law to switch their vehicles' lights on.

lightly ▸ adverb **1** gently, delicately or softly: *she placed her hand lightly on my shoulder.*
2 in relatively small amounts or in low density; sparingly: *it was snowing lightly.*
3 in a way that is not serious or solemn; carelessly: *it is not something that should be taken lightly.*
4 without severe punishment; leniently: *some people are let off lightly.*

light meter ▸ noun an instrument for measuring the intensity of light, used chiefly to show the correct exposure when taking a photograph.

light middleweight ▸ noun [mass noun] a weight in amateur boxing ranging from 67 to 71 kg. ■ an amateur boxer of this weight.

lightning ▸ noun [mass noun] the occurrence of a natural electrical discharge of very short duration and high voltage between a cloud and the ground or within a cloud, accompanied by a bright flash and typically also thunder: *a tremendous flash of lightning.* ■ [count noun] literary a flash or discharge of lightning: *the sky was a mass of black cloud out of which lightnings flashed.*
▸ adjective [attrib.] very quick: *a lightning cure for his hangover* | *galloping across the country at lightning speed.*
– PHRASES **lightning never strikes twice in the same place** proverb an unusual situation or event is unlikely to happen again in exactly the same circumstances or to the same person. **like** (**greased**) **lightning** very quickly.
– ORIGIN Middle English: special use of *lightening* (verbal noun from LIGHTEN²).

> **USAGE** The form **lightning** is historically a contracted form of **lightening** (it was at one time spelled **light'ning**) but the two forms are now two distinct words. In the sense *thunder and **lightning*** and ***lightning** speed*, the spelling is always **lightning**, while in the sense 'make or become lighter' the spelling is always **lightening**.

lightning bug ▸ noun North American term for FIREFLY.

lightning chess ▸ noun [mass noun] a form of chess in which moves must be made at very short intervals.

lightning conductor (also chiefly N. Amer. **lightning rod**) ▸ noun Brit. a metal rod or wire fixed to an exposed part of a building or other tall structure to divert lightning harmlessly into the ground. ■ a person or thing that attracts criticism, especially in order to divert attention from more serious issues or allow a more important public figure to appear blameless.

lightning strike ▸ noun Brit. a strike by workers after little or no warning, especially without official union backing.

light opera ▸ noun another term for OPERETTA.

light pen ▸ noun **1** a handheld pen-like photosensitive device held to the display screen of a computer terminal for passing information to the computer.
2 a handheld light-emitting device used for reading barcodes.

light pollution ▸ noun [mass noun] brightening of the night sky that inhibits the observation of stars and planets, caused by street lights and other man-made sources.

lightproof ▸ adjective able to block out light completely.

light railway ▸ noun a railway constructed for light traffic.

light reaction ▸ noun **1** [mass noun] the reaction of something, especially the iris of the eye, to different intensities of light.
2 (**the light reaction**) Biochemistry the reaction which occurs as the first phase of photosynthesis, in which energy in the form of light is absorbed and converted to chemical energy in the form of ATP.

lights ▸ plural noun the lungs of sheep, pigs, or bullocks, used as food, especially for pets.
– PHRASES **punch someone's lights out** beat someone up.
– ORIGIN Middle English: use of LIGHT² as a noun (so named because of their lightness). Compare with LUNG.

light-sensitive ▸ adjective (of a surface or substance) changing physically or chemically when exposed to light. ■ Biology (of a cell, organ, or tissue) able to detect the presence or intensity of light.

lightship ▸ noun a moored or anchored boat with a beacon light to warn or guide ships at sea.

light show ▸ noun a spectacle of coloured lights that move and change, especially at a pop concert.

lightsome ▸ adjective literary **1** happy and carefree.
2 gracefully nimble.
– DERIVATIVES **lightsomely** adverb.

light stick ▸ noun another term for GLOW STICK.

light trap ▸ noun **1** an illuminated trap for attracting and catching nocturnal flying insects.
2 Photography a device for excluding light from a darkroom without preventing entry into it.

light vessel ▸ noun another term for LIGHTSHIP.

light water ▸ noun [mass noun] **1** water containing the normal proportion (or less) of deuterium oxide, i.e. about 0.02 per cent, especially to distinguish it from heavy water.
2 foam formed by water and a fluorocarbon surfactant, which floats on flammable liquids lighter than water and is used in firefighting.

lightweight ▸ noun **1** [mass noun] a weight in boxing and other sports intermediate between featherweight and welterweight. In the amateur boxing scale it ranges from 57 to 60 kg. ■ [count noun] a boxer or other competitor of this weight.
2 a person or thing that is lightly built or constructed. ■ informal a person of little importance or influence, especially in a particular sphere: *he was regarded as a political lightweight.*
▸ adjective **1** of thin material or build and weighing less than average: *a lightweight grey suit.*
2 lacking seriousness, depth, or influence: *the film was entertaining, if rather lightweight.*

light well ▸ noun an open area or vertical shaft in the centre of a building, typically roofed with glass, bringing natural light to the lower floors or basement.

light welterweight ▸ noun [mass noun] a weight in amateur boxing ranging from 60 to 63.5 kg. ■ [count noun] an amateur boxer of this weight.

lightwood ▸ noun **1** chiefly Austral. a tree yielding timber that is pale in colour or light in weight. ● Several species, in particular the hickory wattle.
2 [mass noun] US firewood that burns easily and with a bright flame; kindling.

lighty /ˈlʌɪti/ (also **laaitie, litie**) ▸ noun (pl. **lighties**) S. African informal a boy or young male adult.
– ORIGIN apparently from the adjective LIGHT² from *light of heart* + -Y²; the variant *laaitie* shows Afrikaans influence.

light year ▸ noun Astronomy a unit of astronomical distance equivalent to the distance that light travels in one year, which is 9.4607 × 10^{12} km (nearly 6 million million miles). ■ (**light years**) informal a long distance or great amount: *the new range puts them **light years ahead of** the competition.*

ligneous /ˈlɪgnɪəs/ ▸ adjective made, consisting of, or resembling wood; woody.
– ORIGIN early 17th cent.: from Latin *ligneus* 'relating to wood' + -OUS.

ligni- ▸ combining form relating to wood: *lignify.*
– ORIGIN from Latin *lignum* 'wood'.

lignify /ˈlɪgnɪfʌɪ/ ▸ verb (**lignifies, lignifying, lignified**) [with obj.] (usu. as adj. **lignified**) Botany make rigid and woody by the deposition of lignin in cell walls.
– DERIVATIVES **lignification** noun.

lignin /ˈlɪgnɪn/ ▸ noun [mass noun] Botany a complex organic polymer deposited in the cell walls of many plants, making them rigid and woody.
– ORIGIN early 19th cent.: from LIGNI- 'of wood' + -IN¹.

lignite /ˈlɪgnʌɪt/ ▸ noun [mass noun] a soft brownish coal showing traces of plant structure, intermediate between bituminous coal and peat.
– DERIVATIVES **lignitic** adjective.
– ORIGIN early 19th cent.: coined in French from Latin *lignum* 'wood' + -ITE¹.

ligno- ▸ combining form relating to wood: *lignotuber.* ■ representing LIGNIN: *lignocellulose.*
– ORIGIN from Latin *lignum* 'wood'.

lignocaine /ˈlɪgnə(ʊ)keɪn/ ▸ noun [mass noun] Medicine a synthetic compound used as a local anaesthetic, e.g. for dental surgery, and in treating abnormal heart rhythms. ● An aromatic amide; chem. formula: $C_{14}H_{22}N_2O$.
– ORIGIN 1950s: from LIGNO- (Latin equivalent of XYLO-, used in the earlier name *xylocaine* and reflecting chemical similarity to XYLENE) + *-caine* (from COCAINE).

lignocellulose /ˌlɪgnə(ʊ)ˈsɛljʊləʊz, -s/ ▸ noun [mass noun] Botany a complex of lignin and cellulose present in the cell walls of woody plants.

lignotuber /ˈlɪgnəʊˌtjuːbə/ ▸ noun Botany a rounded woody growth at or below ground level on some shrubs and trees that grow in areas subject to fire or drought, containing a mass of buds and food reserves.

lignum vitae /ˌlɪgnəm ˈvʌɪtiː, ˈviːtʌɪ/ ▸ noun another term for GUAIACUM.
– ORIGIN Latin, 'wood of life'.

ligroin /ˈlɪgrəʊɪn/ ▸ noun [mass noun] Chemistry a volatile hydrocarbon mixture obtained from petroleum, used as a solvent.
– ORIGIN late 19th cent.: of unknown origin.

ligula /ˈlɪgjʊlə/ ▸ noun (pl. **ligulae** /-liː/) Entomology the strap-shaped terminal part of an insect's labium, typically lobed.
– ORIGIN mid 18th cent.: from Latin, 'strap'.

ligulate /ˈlɪgjʊlət/ ▸ adjective chiefly Botany strap-shaped, as in the ray florets of plants of the daisy family. ■ (of a plant) having ray florets or ligules.

ligule /ˈlɪgjuːl/ ▸ noun Botany a narrow strap-shaped part of a plant, especially a membranous scale on the inner side of the leaf sheath at its junction with the blade in most grasses and sedges.
– ORIGIN early 19th cent.: from Latin *ligula* 'strap'.

Liguria /lɪˈg(j)ʊərɪə/ a coastal region of NW Italy, which extends along the Mediterranean coast from Tuscany to the border with France; capital, Genoa. In ancient times Liguria extended as far as the Atlantic seaboard.
– DERIVATIVES **Ligurian** adjective & noun.

Ligurian Sea a part of the northern Mediterranean, between Corsica and the NW coast of Italy.

ligustrum /lɪˈgʌstrəm/ ▸ noun a plant of a genus that comprises the privets. ● Genus *Ligustrum*, family Oleaceae.
– ORIGIN mid 17th cent.: from Latin.

likable ▸ adjective chiefly US variant spelling of LIKEABLE.

like¹ ▸ preposition **1** having the same characteristics or qualities as; similar to: *he used to have a car like mine | they were like brothers | she looked nothing like Audrey Hepburn.* ■ in the manner of; in the same way or to the same degree as: *he was screaming like a banshee.* ■ in a way appropriate to: *students were angry at being treated like children.* ■ such as one might expect from; characteristic of: *just like you to put a damper on people's enjoyment.* ■ used in questions to ask about the characteristics or nature of someone or something: *what is it like to be a tuna fisherman? | what's she like?*
2 used to draw attention to the nature of an action or event: *I apologize for coming over unannounced like this | why are you talking about me like that?*
3 such as; for example: *the cautionary vision of works like Animal Farm and 1984.*
▸ conjunction informal **1** in the same way that; as: *people who change countries like they change clothes.*
2 as though; as if: *I felt like I'd been kicked by a camel.*
▸ noun used with reference to a person or thing of the same kind as another: *the quotations could be arranged to put **like with like** | I know him—him and his like.* ■ (**the like**) a thing or things of the same kind (often used to express surprise or for emphasis): *did you ever hear the like? | a church interior **the like of which** he had never seen before.*
▸ adjective [attrib.] (of a person or thing) having similar qualities or characteristics to another person or thing: *I responded in like manner | the grouping of children of like ability together.* ■ [predic.] (of a portrait or other image) having a faithful resemblance to the original: *'Who painted the dog's picture? It's very like.'*
▸ adverb **1** informal used in speech as a meaningless filler or to signify the speaker's uncertainty about an expression just used: *there was this funny smell—sort of dusty like.*
2 informal used to convey a person's reported attitude or feelings in the form of direct speech (whether or not representing an actual quotation): *so she comes into the room and she's like 'Where is everybody?'*
3 (**like as/to**) archaic in the manner of: *like as a ship with dreadful storm long tossed.*
– PHRASES **and the like** and similar things; et cetera: *the preservation of endangered species in zoos, botanical gardens, and the like.* **like anything** Brit. informal to a great degree: *they would probably worry like anything.* **(as) like as not** probably: *she would be in bed by now, like as not.* **like enough** (or **most like**) archaic probably: *he'll have lost a deal of blood, I dare say, and like enough he's still losing it.* **like ——, like —— as —— is, so is ——:** *like father, like son.* **like so** informal in this manner: *the votive candles are arranged like so.* **the likes of** informal someone or something regarded as a type: *she didn't want to associate with the likes of me.* **more like** informal nearer to (a specified number or description) than one previously given: *he believes the figure should be more like £10 million.* ■ (**more like it**) nearer to what is required or expected; more satisfactory. **of (a) like mind** (of a person) sharing the same opinions or tastes. **what is he** (or **she** etc.) **like?** Brit. informal used as an expression of light-hearted incredulity at behaviour regarded as foolish or eccentric: *What are you like? I don't believe you are doing this.*
– ORIGIN Middle English: from Old Norse *líkr*; related to ALIKE.

> **USAGE** In the sentence *he's behaving **like** he owns the place*, **like** is a conjunction meaning 'as if', a usage regarded as incorrect in standard English. Although **like** has been used as a conjunction in this way since the 15th century by many respected writers, it is still frowned upon and considered unacceptable in formal English, where **as if** should be used instead.

like² ▸ verb [with obj.] **1** find agreeable, enjoyable, or satisfactory: *all his classmates liked him* | [with present participle] *people who don't like reading books* | [with infinitive] *I like to be the centre of attention.*
2 wish for; want: *would you like a cup of coffee?* | [with infinitive] *I'd like to hire a car* | [with obj. and infinitive] *I'd like you to stay.* ■ (**would like to do something**) used as a polite formula: *we would like to apologize for the late running of this service.* ■ (**not like doing/to do something**) feel reluctant to do something: *I don't like leaving her on her own too long.* ■ choose to have (something); prefer: *how do you like your coffee?* ■ [in questions] feel about or regard (something): *how would you like it if it happened to you?*
▸ noun (**likes**) the things one likes or prefers: *a wide variety of likes, dislikes, tastes, and income levels.*
– PHRASES **if you like 1** if it suits or pleases you: *we could go riding if you like.* **2** used when expressing something in a new or tentative way: *it's a whole new branch of chemistry, a new science if you like.* **I like that!** used as an exclamation expressing affront. **like it or not** informal used to indicate that someone has no choice in a matter: *you're celebrating with us, like it or not.* **not like the look** (or **sound**) **of** find worrying or alarming: *I don't like the look of that head injury.* **what's not to like?** informal used as a rhetorical expression of approval or satisfaction: *cleaner air, cooler temperatures and mountain views—what's not to like?*
– ORIGIN Old English *lician* 'be pleasing', of Germanic origin; related to Dutch *lijken*.

-like ▸ combining form (added to nouns) similar to; characteristic of: *pealike | crust-like.*

L

likeable (also chiefly US **likable**) ▸ adjective (especially of a person) pleasant, friendly, and easy to like.
– DERIVATIVES **likeability** noun, **likeableness** noun, **likeably** adverb.

likelihood ▸ noun [mass noun] the state or fact of something's being likely; probability: *young people who can see no* ***likelihood of*** *finding employment* | [in sing.] *situations where there is* ***a likelihood of*** *violence.*
– PHRASES **in all likelihood** very probably.

likely ▸ adjective (**likelier**, **likeliest**) **1** such as well might happen or be true; probable: *speculation on the likely effect of opting out* | [with clause] ***it was likely that*** *he would make a televised statement* | [with infinitive] *sales are likely to drop further.*
2 apparently suitable; promising: *a likely-looking spot.*
▸ adverb probably: *we will most likely go to a bar.*
– PHRASES **a likely story** used to express disbelief of an account or excuse: *'She's your lodger? A likely story!'.* **as likely as not** probably: *I won't take their pills, because as likely as not they'd poison me.* **not likely!** informal certainly not; I refuse: *'Are you going home?' 'Not likely!'.*
– DERIVATIVES **likeliness** noun.
– ORIGIN Middle English: from Old Norse *líkligr*, from *líkr* (see LIKE[1]).

> **USAGE** In standard British English, when **likely** is used as an adverb it must be preceded by a submodifier such as **very**, **most**, or **more**, as in *we will* ***most likely*** *see him later*. In informal US English, use without a submodifier is very common and not regarded as incorrect, as in *we will* ***likely*** *see him later*.

like-minded ▸ adjective having similar tastes or opinions: *a radio ham with like-minded friends all over the world.*
– DERIVATIVES **like-mindedness** noun.

liken ▸ verb [with obj.] (**liken someone/thing to**) point out the resemblance of someone or something to: *racism is likened to a contagious disease.*
– ORIGIN Middle English: from LIKE[1] + -EN[1].

L

likeness ▸ noun [mass noun] the fact or quality of being alike; resemblance: *her* ***likeness to*** *him was astonishing* | [count noun] *a family likeness can be seen in all the boys.* ▪ the semblance, guise, or outward appearance of: *humans are described as being made in God's likeness.* ▪ [count noun] a portrait or representation: *the only known likeness of Dorothy as a young woman.*
– ORIGIN Old English *gelīknes* (see ALIKE, -NESS).

Likert scale /ˈlʌɪkət/ ▸ noun Psychology a scale used to represent people's attitudes to a topic.
– ORIGIN 1940s: named after Rensis *Likert* (1903–81), American psychologist.

likewise ▸ adverb **1** in the same way; also: *the programmes of study will apply from five years of age, likewise the attainment targets.* ▪ used to introduce a point similar or related to one just made: *The banks advise against sending cash. Likewise, sending British cheques may cause problems.*
2 in a like manner; similarly: *I stuck out my tongue and Frankie* ***did likewise***.
– ORIGIN late Middle English: from the phrase *in like wise*.

liking ▸ noun [usu. in sing.] a feeling of regard or fondness: *she'd* ***taken an instant liking to*** *Arnie's new girlfriend.* ▪ (**a liking for**) a taste for: *Mrs Parsons had a liking for gin and tonic.*
– PHRASES **for one's liking** to suit one's taste or wishes: *he is a little too showy for my liking.* **to one's liking** to one's taste; pleasing: *his coffee was just to his liking.*
– ORIGIN Old English *līcung* (see LIKE[2], -ING[1]).

likkewaan /ˈlɪkəvɑːn/ ▸ noun variant spelling of LEGUAN.

Likud /lɪˈkuːd/ a coalition of right-wing Israeli political parties, formed in 1973.
– ORIGIN Hebrew, literally 'consolidation, unity'.

lilac ▸ noun a Eurasian shrub or small tree of the olive family, which has fragrant violet, pink, or white blossom and is a popular garden ornamental. ● Genus *Syringa*, family Oleaceae; several species, in particular the **common lilac** (*S. vulgaris*), with many cultivars.
▪ [mass noun] a pale pinkish-violet colour.
– ORIGIN early 17th cent.: from obsolete French, via Spanish and Arabic from Persian *līlak*, variant of *nīlak* 'bluish', from *nīl* 'blue'.

lilangeni /ˌliːlaŋˈgeɪni/ ▸ noun (pl. **emalangeni** /ɪˌmalaŋˈgeɪni/) the basic monetary unit of Swaziland, equal to 100 cents.
– ORIGIN from the Bantu prefix *li-* (used to denote a singular) + *-langeni* 'member of a royal family'.

liliaceous /ˌlɪlɪˈeɪʃəs/ ▸ adjective Botany relating to or denoting plants of the lily family (Liliaceae). These have elongated leaves which grow from a corm, bulb, or rhizome.
– ORIGIN mid 18th cent.: from modern Latin *Liliaceae* (plural), based on Latin *lilium* 'lily', + -OUS.

Lilienthal /ˈliːlɪəntɑːl/, Otto (1848–96), German pioneer in the design and flying of gliders. Working with his brother, he made over 2,000 flights in various gliders before being killed in a crash.

Lilith /ˈlɪlɪθ/ a female demon of Jewish folklore, who tries to kill newborn children. In the Talmud she is the first wife of Adam, dispossessed by Eve.

Lille /liːl/ an industrial city in northern France, near the border with Belgium; pop. 232,432 (2006).

Lillee /ˈlɪli/, Dennis (Keith) (b.1949), Australian cricketer. A fast bowler, he took 355 wickets in seventy matches during his career in Test cricket (1971–84).

Lilliburlero /ˌlɪlɪbəˈlɛːrəʊ/ a song ridiculing the Irish, popular at the end of the 17th century. With different words the song has remained associated with the Orange Party, as 'Protestant Boys'.

Lilliputian /ˌlɪlɪˈpjuːʃ(ə)n/ ▸ adjective trivial or very small: *America's banks look Lilliputian in comparison with Japan's.*
▸ noun a trivial or very small person or thing.
– ORIGIN early 18th cent.: from the imaginary country of *Lilliput* in Swift's *Gulliver's Travels*, inhabited by people 6 inches (15 cm) high, + -IAN.

lilly-pilly ▸ noun (pl. **lilly-pillies**) an Australian evergreen tree of the myrtle family, with edible pink, purple, or white berries. ● *Acmena smithii*, family Myrtaceae.
– ORIGIN mid 19th cent.: of unknown origin.

lilo /ˈlʌɪləʊ/ (also trademark **Li-lo**) ▸ noun (pl. **lilos**) Brit. a type of inflatable mattress which is used as a bed or for floating on water.
– ORIGIN 1930s: alteration of *lie low*.

Lilongwe /lɪˈlɒŋweɪ/ the capital of Malawi; pop. 669,021 (2008).

lilt ▸ noun a characteristic rising and falling of the voice when speaking; a pleasant gentle accent: *he spoke with a faint but recognizable Irish lilt.* ▪ a pleasant, gently swinging rhythm in a song or tune: *the lilt of the Hawaiian music.* ▪ archaic, chiefly Scottish a cheerful tune.
▸ verb [no obj.] (often as adj. **lilting**) speak, sing, or sound with a lilt: *a lilting Irish accent.*
– ORIGIN late Middle English *lulte* (in the senses 'sound an alarm' or 'lift up the voice'), of unknown origin.

lily ▸ noun (pl. **lilies**) **1** a bulbous plant with large trumpet-shaped, typically fragrant, flowers on a tall, slender stem. ● Genus *Lilium*, family Liliaceae (the **lily family**). This family includes many flowering bulbs, such as bluebells, hyacinths, and tulips. Several plants are often placed in different families, especially the Alliaceae (onions and their relatives), Aloaceae (aloes), and Amaryllidaceae (amaryllis, daffodils, jonquil), and as many as 38 families are sometimes recognized.
▪ short for WATER LILY. ▪ used in names of other plants with similar flowers or leaves, e.g. **arum lily**.
2 a heraldic fleur-de-lis.
– DERIVATIVES **lilied** adjective.
– ORIGIN Old English *lilie*, from Latin *lilium*, from Greek *leirion*.

lily-livered ▸ adjective weak and cowardly.

lily of the valley ▸ noun a European plant of the lily family, with broad leaves and arching stems of fragrant white bell-shaped flowers. ● Genus *Convallaria*, family Liliaceae.

lily pad ▸ noun a round floating leaf of a water lily.

lily-trotter ▸ noun (especially in Africa) a jacana.

lily-white ▸ adjective pure or ideally white. ▪ without fault or corruption; totally innocent or immaculate.

Lima /ˈliːmə/ the capital of Peru; pop. 7,605,700 (est. 2007). Founded in 1535 by Francisco Pizarro, it was the capital of the Spanish colonies in South America until the 19th century. ▪ a code word representing the letter L, used in radio communication.

lima bean /ˈliːmə/ ▸ noun **1** an edible flat whitish bean. See also BUTTER BEAN.
2 the tropical American plant which yields lima beans. ● *Phaseolus lunatus* (or *limensis*), family Leguminosae.
– ORIGIN mid 18th cent.: *lima* from the name of the Peruvian capital LIMA.

Limassol /ˈlɪməsɒl/ a port on the south coast of Cyprus, on Akrotiri Bay; pop. 179,900 (est. 2005).

limb[1] ▸ noun **1** an arm or leg of a person or four-legged animal, or a bird's wing.
2 a large branch of a tree. ▪ a branch of a cross. ▪ each half of an archery bow.
3 a projecting landform such as a spur of a mountain range, or each of two or more such projections as in a forked peninsula or archipelago. ▪ a projecting section of a building.
– PHRASES **life and limb** life and all bodily faculties: *a burglar risking life and limb to scramble into an open third-floor window.* **out on a limb 1** isolated: *Aberdeen is rather out on a limb.* **2** in or into a position where one is not joined or supported by anyone else: *I wouldn't* ***go out on a limb*** *like this if I didn't have the data to justify it.* **tear someone limb from limb** violently dismember someone.
– DERIVATIVES **limbed** adjective [in combination] *long-limbed*, **limbless** adjective.
– ORIGIN Old English *lim* (also in the sense 'organ or part of the body'), of Germanic origin.

limb[2] ▸ noun **1** Astronomy the edge of the disc of a celestial object, especially the sun or moon.
2 Botany the blade or broad part of a leaf or petal. ▪ the spreading upper part of a tube-shaped flower.
3 the graduated arc of a quadrant or other scientific instrument, used for measuring angles.
– ORIGIN late Middle English: from French *limbe* or Latin *limbus* 'hem, border'.

Limba /ˈlɪmbə/ ▸ noun (pl. **same** or **Limbas**) **1** a member of a West African people of Sierra Leone and Guinea.
2 [mass noun] the Niger–Congo language of the Limba, with about 300,000 speakers.
▸ adjective relating to the Limba or their language.
– ORIGIN the name in Limba.

limba ▸ noun another term for AFARA.
– ORIGIN 1930s: from *limbo*, the name used in Gabon.

limber[1] /ˈlɪmbə/ ▸ adjective (of a person or body part) lithe or supple: *I have to practise to keep myself limber.* ▪ (of a thing) flexible: *limber graphite fishing rods.*
▸ verb [no obj.] warm up in preparation for exercise or activity, especially sport or athletics: *the acrobats were* ***limbering up*** *for the big show.*
– DERIVATIVES **limberness** noun.
– ORIGIN mid 16th cent. (as an adjective): perhaps from LIMBER[2] in the dialect sense 'cart shaft', with allusion to the to-and-fro motion.

limber[2] /ˈlɪmbə/ ▸ noun the detachable front part of a gun carriage, consisting of two wheels and an axle, a pole, and a frame holding one or more ammunition boxes.
▸ verb [with obj.] attach a limber to (a gun).
– ORIGIN Middle English *lymour*, apparently related to medieval Latin *limonarius* from *limo, limon-* 'shaft'.

limberneck ▸ noun [mass noun] a kind of botulism affecting poultry.

limber pine ▸ noun a small pine tree with tough pliant branches, which is native to the Rocky Mountains of North America. ● *Pinus flexilis*, family Pinaceae.

limbic system /ˈlɪmbɪk/ ▸ noun a complex system of nerves and networks in the brain, involving several areas near the edge of the cortex concerned with instinct and mood. It controls the basic emotions (fear, pleasure, anger) and drives (hunger, sex, dominance, care of offspring).
– ORIGIN late 19th cent.: *limbic* from French *limbique*, from Latin *limbus* 'edge'.

limbo[1] ▸ noun [mass noun] **1** (in some Christian beliefs) the supposed abode of the souls of unbaptized infants, and of the just who died before Christ's coming.
2 an uncertain period of awaiting a decision or resolution; an intermediate state or condition: *the legal battle could leave the club in limbo until next year.* ▪ a state of neglect or oblivion: *these prisoners are in limbo: no one is responsible for their welfare.*
– ORIGIN late Middle English: from the medieval Latin phrase *in limbo*, from *limbus* 'hem, border, limbo'.

limbo[2] ▸ noun (pl. **limbos**) a West Indian dance in which the dancer bends backwards to pass under a horizontal bar which is progressively lowered to a position just above the ground.
▸ verb [no obj.] perform the limbo.
– ORIGIN 1950s: from LIMBER[1].

Limburg /ˈlɪmbəːg/ a former duchy of Lorraine, divided in 1839 between Belgium and the Netherlands. It now forms a province of NE Belgium (capital,

Hasselt) and a province of the SE Netherlands (capital, Maastricht). French name **Limbourg** /lɛ̃buʀ/.

Limburger ▶ **noun** [mass noun] a soft white cheese with a characteristic strong smell, originally made in Limburg.

limbus /ˈlɪmbəs/ ▶ **noun** (pl. **limbi** /-bʌɪ/) Anatomy the border or margin of a structure, especially the junction of the cornea and sclera in the eye.
– ORIGIN late Middle English (denoting limbo): from Latin, 'edge, border'. The current sense dates from the late 17th cent.

lime¹ ▶ **noun 1** (also **quicklime**) [mass noun] a white caustic alkaline substance consisting of calcium oxide, which is obtained by heating limestone and which combines with water with the production of much heat. ■ (also **slaked lime**) a white alkaline substance consisting of calcium hydroxide, made by adding water to quicklime and used in traditional building methods to make plaster, mortar, and limewash. ■ (in general use) any of a number of calcium compounds, especially calcium hydroxide, used as an additive to soil or water.
2 archaic birdlime.
▶ **verb** [with obj.] **1** treat (soil or water) with lime to reduce acidity and improve fertility or oxygen levels. ■ (often as adj. **limed**) give (wood) a bleached appearance by treating it with lime: *limed oak dining furniture.*
2 archaic catch (a bird) with birdlime.
– DERIVATIVES **limy** adjective (**limier**, **limiest**).
– ORIGIN Old English *līm*, of Germanic origin; related to Dutch *lijm*, German *Leim*, also to LOAM.

lime² ▶ **noun 1** a rounded citrus fruit similar to a lemon but greener, smaller, and with a distinctive acid flavour. ■ [mass noun] a drink made from or flavoured with lime juice: *lager and lime.*
2 (also **lime tree**) the evergreen citrus tree which produces limes, widely cultivated in warm climates. ● *Citrus aurantifolia*, family Rutaceae.
3 (also **lime green**) [mass noun] a bright light green colour like that of a lime: [as modifier] *a lime-green bikini.*
– ORIGIN mid 17th cent.: from French, from modern Provençal *limo*, Spanish *lima*, from Arabic *līma*; compare with LEMON.

lime³ (also **lime tree**) ▶ **noun** a deciduous tree with heart-shaped leaves and fragrant yellowish blossom, native to north temperate regions. The pale timber is used for carving and inexpensive furniture.
Also called LINDEN. ● Genus *Tilia*, family Tiliaceae: many species, including the widely grown hybrid **common lime** (*T.* × *europaea*), and the **small-leaved lime** (*T. cordata*), which dominated the pre-Neolithic forests of much of lowland England.
– ORIGIN early 17th cent.: alteration of obsolete *line*, from Old English *lind* (see LINDEN).

lime⁴ W. Indian ▶ **verb** [no obj., with adverbial] sit or stand around talking with others: *boys and girls were liming along the roadside as if they didn't have anything to do.*
▶ **noun** an informal social gathering characterized by semi-ritualized talking.
– ORIGIN origin uncertain; said to be from LIMEY (because of the number of British sailors present during the Second World War), or from *suck a lime*, expressing bitterness at not being invited to a gathering.

limeade ▶ **noun** [mass noun] a drink made from lime juice sweetened with sugar.

limeburner ▶ **noun** historical a person whose job was burning limestone in order to obtain lime.

limekiln ▶ **noun** a kiln in which limestone is burnt or calcined to produce quicklime.

limelight ▶ **noun 1** (**the limelight**) the focus of public attention: *the shock win has thrust him into the limelight.*
2 intense white light obtained by heating lime, formerly used in theatres.

limen /ˈlʌɪmɛn, ˈliː-/ ▶ **noun** (pl. **limens** or **limina** /ˈlʌɪmɪnə, ˈliː-/) Psychology a threshold below which a stimulus is not perceived or is not distinguished from another.
– ORIGIN mid 17th cent.: from Latin, 'threshold'.

limepit ▶ **noun** historical a pit containing lime in which hides were placed to remove hair and fur.

Limerick /ˈlɪmərɪk/ a county of the Republic of Ireland, in the west of the province of Munster. ■ the county town of Limerick, on the River Shannon; pop. 52,539 (2006).

limerick /ˈlɪm(ə)rɪk/ ▶ **noun** a humorous five-line poem with a rhyme scheme *aabba.*
– ORIGIN late 19th cent.: said to be from the chorus 'will you come up to Limerick?', sung between improvised verses at a gathering.

limescale ▶ **noun** [mass noun] Brit. a hard white substance consisting chiefly of calcium carbonate, deposited by water on the inside of pipes, kettles, etc.

limestone ▶ **noun** [mass noun] a hard sedimentary rock, composed mainly of calcium carbonate or dolomite, used as building material and in the making of cement.

limestone pavement ▶ **noun** a horizontal or gently sloping expanse of bare limestone, consisting of large blocks (clints) separated by deep eroded fissures (grikes).

lime sulphur ▶ **noun** [mass noun] an insecticide and fungicide containing calcium polysulphides, made by boiling lime and sulphur in water.

limewash ▶ **noun** [mass noun] a mixture of lime and water used for coating walls.
▶ **verb** [with obj.] apply limewash to (a surface or structure): (as adj. **limewashed**) *limewashed cottages.*

lime water ▶ **noun** [mass noun] Chemistry a solution of calcium hydroxide in water, which is alkaline and turns milky in the presence of carbon dioxide.

Limey ▶ **noun** (pl. **Limeys**) N. Amer. & Austral. informal a British person.
– ORIGIN late 19th cent.: from LIME² + -Y¹, because of the former enforced consumption of lime juice in the British navy.

liminal /ˈlɪmɪn(ə)l/ ▶ **adjective** technical **1** relating to a transitional or initial stage of a process.
2 occupying a position at, or on both sides of, a boundary or threshold.
– DERIVATIVES **liminality** noun.
– ORIGIN late 19th cent.: from Latin *limen, limin-* 'threshold' + -AL.

limit ▶ **noun 1** a point or level beyond which something does not or may not extend or pass: *the failure showed the* **limits of** *British power | the 10-minute* **limit on** *speeches | there was no* **limit to** *his imagination.* ■ (often **limits**) the terminal point or boundary of an area or movement: *the city limits | the upper limit of the tidal reaches.* ■ the furthest extent of one's physical or mental endurance: *Mary Ann tried everyone's patience* **to the limit**.
2 a restriction on the size or amount of something permissible or possible: *an age limit | a weight limit.* ■ a speed limit: *a 30 mph limit.* ■ (also **legal limit**) the maximum concentration of alcohol in the blood that the law allows in the driver of a motor vehicle: *the risk of drinkers inadvertently going* **over the limit**.
3 Mathematics a point or value which a sequence, function, or sum of a series can be made to approach progressively, until they are as close to it as desired.
▶ **verb** (**limits**, **limiting**, **limited**) [with obj.] set or serve as a limit to: *try to limit the amount you drink | class sizes are* **limited to** *a maximum of 10* | (as adj. **limiting**) *a limiting factor.*
– PHRASES **be the limit** informal be intolerably troublesome or irritating. **off limits** out of bounds: *the site was off limits to the public.* ■ not to be mentioned or discussed: *it was apparent that the whole topic was off limits.* **within limits** moderately; up to a point. **without limit** with no restriction.
– DERIVATIVES **limitary** adjective, **limitative** adjective.
– ORIGIN late Middle English: from Latin *limes, limit-* 'boundary, frontier'. The verb is from Latin *limitare*, from *limes*.

limitation ▶ **noun 1** (often **limitations**) a limiting rule or circumstance; a restriction: *severe* **limitations on** *water use.* ■ a condition of limited ability; a defect or failing: *she knew her limitations better than she knew her worth.* ■ [mass noun] the action of limiting something: *the limitation of local authorities' powers.*
2 (also **limitation period**) Law a legally specified period beyond which an action may be defeated or a property right does not continue. See also STATUTE OF LIMITATIONS.
– ORIGIN late Middle English: from Latin *limitatio(n-)*, from the verb *limitare* (see LIMIT).

limit bid ▶ **noun** Bridge a bid showing that the value of the bidder's hand is only just sufficient for a bid.

limited ▶ **adjective 1** restricted in size, amount, or extent; few, small, or short: *a limited number of places are available | the legislation has had a limited effect.* ■ (of a monarchy or government) exercised under limitations of power prescribed by a constitution. ■ (of a person) having restricted ability or talents: *I think he is a very limited man.*
2 (**Limited**) Brit. denoting a limited company (used after a company name): *Times Newspapers Limited.*
– DERIVATIVES **limitedness** noun.

limited company (also **limited liability company**) ▶ **noun** Brit. a private company whose owners are legally responsible for its debts only to the extent of the amount of capital they invested. See also PUBLIC LIMITED COMPANY.

limited edition ▶ **noun** an edition of a book, or reproduction of a print or object, limited to a specific number of copies.

limited liability ▶ **noun** [mass noun] Brit. the condition by which shareholders are legally responsible for the debts of a company only to the extent of the nominal value of their shares.

limited partner ▶ **noun** a partner in a company or venture whose liability towards its debts is legally limited to the extent of their investment.
– DERIVATIVES **limited partnership** noun.

limited war ▶ **noun** a war in which the weapons used, the nations or territory involved, or the objectives pursued are restricted in some way, in particular one in which the use of nuclear weapons is avoided.

limiter ▶ **noun** a person or thing that limits something. ■ Electronics a circuit whose output is restricted to a certain range of values irrespective of the size of the input. Also called CLIPPER. ■ (also **speed limiter**) a device that prevents a vehicle from being driven above a specified speed.

limitless ▶ **adjective** without end, limit, or boundary: *our resources are not limitless.*
– DERIVATIVES **limitlessly** adverb, **limitlessness** noun.

limit point ▶ **noun** Mathematics a point for which every neighbourhood contains at least one point belonging to a given set.

limit switch ▶ **noun** a switch preventing the travel of an object in a mechanism past some predetermined point, mechanically operated by the motion of the object itself.

L

limn /lɪm/ ▶ **verb** [with obj.] literary depict or describe in painting or words. ■ suffuse or highlight (something) with a bright colour or light: *a crescent moon limned each shred with white gold.*
– ORIGIN late Middle English (in the sense 'illuminate a manuscript'): alteration of obsolete *lumine* 'illuminate', via Old French *luminer* from Latin *luminare* 'make light'.

limner /ˈlɪmnə/ ▶ **noun** archaic a painter, especially of portraits or miniatures.

limnology /lɪmˈnɒlədʒi/ ▶ **noun** [mass noun] the study of the biological, chemical, and physical features of lakes and other bodies of fresh water.
– DERIVATIVES **limnological** adjective, **limnologist** noun.
– ORIGIN late 19th cent.: from Greek *limnē* 'lake' + -LOGY.

Límnos /ˈlimnɔs/ Greek name for LEMNOS.

limo ▶ **noun** (pl. **limos**) short for LIMOUSINE.

Limoges /lɪˈməʊʒ/, French /limɔʒ/ a city in west central France, the principal city of Limousin; pop. 139,026 (2006). Famous in the late Middle Ages for enamel work, it has been noted since the 18th century for the production of porcelain.

Limón /lɪˈmɒn/ a port on the Caribbean coast of Costa Rica; pop. 69,786 (2007). Also called PUERTO LIMÓN.

limoncello /ˌlɪm(ə)nˈtʃɛləʊ/ ▶ **noun** (pl. **limoncellos**) [mass noun] a lemon-flavoured Italian liqueur.
– ORIGIN Italian, from *limone* 'lemon' + the diminutive suffix *-cello*.

limonene /ˈlɪməniːn/ ▶ **noun** [mass noun] Chemistry a colourless liquid hydrocarbon with a lemon-like scent, present in lemon oil, orange oil, and similar essential oils. ● A terpene; chem. formula: $C_{10}H_{16}$.
– ORIGIN early 20th cent.: from German *Limonen*, from *Limone* 'lemon', + -ENE.

limonite /ˈlʌɪmənʌɪt/ ▶ **noun** [mass noun] an amorphous brownish secondary mineral consisting of a mixture of hydrous ferric oxides, important as an iron ore.
– DERIVATIVES **limonitic** adjective.
– ORIGIN early 19th cent.: from German *Limonit*, probably from Greek *leimōn* 'meadow' (suggested by the earlier German name *Wiesenerz*, literally 'meadow ore').

Limousin¹ /ˈlɪmuːzã/, French /limuzɛ̃/ a region and former province of central France, centred on Limoges.

Limousin² /ˈlɪmʊzã/, French /limuzɛ̃/ ▶ **noun 1** a native or inhabitant of Limousin.
2 [mass noun] the French dialect of Limousin.
3 an animal of a French breed of beef cattle.
▶ **adjective** relating to the Limousins or their dialect.

limousine /ˈlɪməziːn, ˌlɪməˈziːn/ ▶ **noun** a large, luxurious car, especially one driven by a chauffeur who is separated from the passengers by a partition. ■ chiefly N. Amer. a passenger vehicle carrying people to and from an airport.
– ORIGIN early 20th cent.: from French, feminine adjective meaning 'of Limousin', originally denoting a caped cloak worn in *Limousin* (see **LIMOUSIN¹**): originally the driver's seat of the car was outside in a separate compartment, covered with a canopy.

limousine liberal ▶ **noun** US derogatory a wealthy liberal.

limp¹ ▶ **verb** [no obj., usu. with adverbial of direction] walk with difficulty, typically because of a damaged or stiff leg or foot: *he limped heavily as he moved* | [with adverbial of direction] *he limped off during Saturday's game.* ■ [with adverbial of direction] (of a damaged ship, aircraft, or vehicle) proceed with difficulty: *the badly damaged aircraft limped back to Sicily.*
▶ **noun** a tendency to limp; a gait impeded by injury or stiffness: *the accident left him with a pronounced limp.*
– ORIGIN late Middle English (in the sense 'fall short of'): related to obsolete *limphalt* 'lame', and probably of Germanic origin.

limp² ▶ **adjective** lacking internal strength or structure; not stiff or firm: *she let her whole body go limp* | *the flags hung limp and still.* ■ having or denoting a book cover that is not stiffened with board. ■ without energy or vigour: *a limp handshake.*
– DERIVATIVES **limply** adverb, **limpness** noun.
– ORIGIN early 18th cent.: of unknown origin; perhaps related to **LIMP¹**, having the basic sense 'hanging loose'.

L

limpet ▶ **noun** a marine mollusc which has a shallow conical shell and a broad muscular foot, proverbial for the way it clings tightly to rocks. ● Patellidae, Fissurellidae (the keyhole limpets), and other families, class Gastropoda: numerous species, including the **common limpet** (*Patella vulgata*).
– ORIGIN Old English *lempedu*, from medieval Latin *lampreda* 'limpet, lamprey'.

limpet mine ▶ **noun** a mine designed to be attached magnetically to a ship's hull and set to explode after a certain time.

limpid ▶ **adjective** (of a liquid) completely clear and transparent: *the limpid waters of the Caribbean.* ■ (of a person's eyes) unclouded; clear. ■ (especially of writing or music) clear and accessible or melodious: *the limpid notes of a recorder.*
– DERIVATIVES **limpidity** noun, **limpidly** adverb.
– ORIGIN late Middle English: from Latin *limpidus*; perhaps related to **LYMPH**.

limpkin ▶ **noun** a wading marshbird related to the rails, with long legs and a long bill, found in the south-eastern US and tropical America. ● *Aramus guarauna*, the only member of the family Aramidae.
– ORIGIN late 19th cent.: from **LIMP¹** (with reference to the bird's limping gait) + **-KIN**.

Limpopo /lɪmˈpəʊpəʊ/ **1** a river of SE Africa. Rising as the Crocodile River near Johannesburg, it flows 1,770 km (1,100 miles) in a sweeping curve to the north and east to meet the Indian Ocean in Mozambique, north of Maputo. For much of its course it forms South Africa's boundary with Botswana and Zimbabwe.
2 a province of northern South Africa, formerly part of Transvaal; capital Polokwane. It was known as the Northern Province until 2002.

limp-wristed ▶ **adjective** informal, derogatory (of a man, especially a homosexual) effeminate.

limulus /ˈlɪmjʊləs/ ▶ **noun** (pl. **limuli**) an arthropod of a genus that comprises the North American horseshoe crab and its extinct relatives. ● Genus *Limulus*, class Merostomata.
– ORIGIN modern Latin, from Latin *limulus* 'somewhat oblique', from *limus* 'oblique'.

linac /ˈlɪnak/ ▶ **noun** short for **LINEAR ACCELERATOR**.

Linacre /ˈlɪnəkə/, Thomas (*c.*1460–1524), English physician and classical scholar. In 1518 he founded the College of Physicians in London, and became its first president. He translated Galen's Greek works on medicine and philosophy into Latin, reviving studies in anatomy, botany, and clinical medicine in Britain.

linage /ˈlʌɪnɪdʒ/ ▶ **noun** [mass noun] the number of lines in printed or written matter, especially when used to calculate payment.

Lin Biao /lɪn ˈbjaʊ/ (also **Lin Piao**) (1908–71), Chinese communist statesman and general. He was nominated to become Mao's successor in 1969. Having staged an unsuccessful coup in 1971, he was reported to have been killed in a plane crash while fleeing to the Soviet Union.

linchpin (also **lynchpin**) ▶ **noun 1** a pin passed through the end of an axle to keep a wheel in position.
2 a person or thing vital to an enterprise or organization: *nurses are the linchpin of the National Health Service.*
– ORIGIN late Middle English: from Old English *lynis* (in the sense 'linchpin') + **PIN**.

Lincoln¹ /ˈlɪŋk(ə)n/ **1** a city in eastern England, the county town of Lincolnshire; pop. 86,800 (est. 2009). It was founded by the Romans as Lindum Colonia.
2 the state capital of Nebraska; pop. 251,624 (est. 2008). Founded as Lancaster in 1856, it was made state capital in 1867 and renamed in honour of Abraham Lincoln.

Lincoln² /ˈlɪŋk(ə)n/, Abraham (1809–65), American Republican statesman, 16th President of the US 1861–5. His election as President on an anti-slavery platform helped precipitate the American Civil War; he was assassinated shortly after the war ended. Lincoln was noted for his succinct, eloquent speeches, including the Gettysburg Address of 1863.

Lincoln green ▶ **noun** [mass noun] historical bright green woollen cloth originally made at Lincoln.

Lincoln Memorial a monument in Washington DC to Abraham Lincoln, designed by Henry Bacon (1866–1924).

Lincoln red ▶ **noun** an animal of a breed of red shorthorn cattle, producing both meat and milk.

Lincolnshire /ˈlɪŋkənʃɪə, -ʃə/ a county on the east coast of England; county town, Lincoln. The former northern part of the county, included in Humberside 1974–96, is now divided into the unitary authorities of **North Lincolnshire** and **North East Lincolnshire**.

Lincoln's Inn one of the Inns of Court in London.

Lincrusta /lɪŋˈkrʌstə/ ▶ **noun** [mass noun] trademark a type of thick embossed wallpaper.
– ORIGIN late 19th cent.: from Latin *linum* 'flax' + *crusta* 'bark', the paper originally incorporating a mixture of oil and cork.

Lincs. ▶ **abbreviation** Lincolnshire.

linctus /ˈlɪŋktəs/ ▶ **noun** [mass noun] Brit. thick liquid medicine, especially cough mixture.
– ORIGIN late 17th cent.: from Latin, from *lingere* 'to lick'.

Lind¹, James (1716–94), Scottish physician. He laid the foundations for the discovery of vitamins by performing experiments on scurvy in sailors. After his death the Royal Navy officially adopted the practice of giving lime juice to sailors.

Lind², Jenny (1820–87), Swedish soprano; born *Johanna Maria Lind Goldschmidt*. She was known as 'the Swedish nightingale' for the purity and agility of her voice.

lindane /ˈlɪndeɪn/ ▶ **noun** [mass noun] a synthetic organochlorine insecticide, now generally restricted in use owing to its toxicity and persistence in the environment. Also called **GAMMA-HCH**. ● An isomer of benzene hexachloride; chem. formula: $C_6H_{12}Cl_6$.
– ORIGIN 1940s: named after Teunis van der *Linden*, 20th-cent. Dutch chemist.

Lindbergh /ˈlɪndbəːg/, Charles (Augustus) (1902–74), American aviator. In 1927 he made the first solo transatlantic flight in a single-engined monoplane, *Spirit of St Louis*. He moved to Europe with his wife to escape the publicity surrounding the kidnap and murder of his two-year-old son in 1932.

Lindemann /ˈlɪndəmən/, Frederick Alexander, see **CHERWELL**.

linden ▶ **noun** another term for the lime tree (**LIME³**), especially in North America.
– ORIGIN Old English (as an adjective in the sense 'made of wood from the lime tree'): from *lind* 'lime tree' (compare with **LIME³**) + **-EN³**, reinforced by obsolete Dutch *lindenboom* and German *Lindenbaum*.

Lindisfarne /ˈlɪndɪsˌfɑːn/ a small island off the coast of Northumberland, north of the Farne Islands. Linked to the mainland by a causeway exposed only at low tide, it is the site of a church and monastery founded by St Aidan in 635. Also called **HOLY ISLAND**.

Lindsay /ˈlɪndzi/ a family of Australian artists. **Sir Lionel Lindsay** (1874–1961) was an art critic, watercolour painter, and graphic artist. His brother, **Norman Lindsay** (1874–1969), was a graphic artist, painter, critic, and novelist.

Lindum Colonia /ˌlɪndəm kəˈləʊnɪə/ Roman name for **LINCOLN¹**.

line¹ ▶ **noun 1** a long, narrow mark or band: *a row of closely spaced dots will look like a continuous line* | *I can't draw a straight line.* ■ Mathematics a straight or curved continuous extent of length without breadth. ■ a direct course: *the ball rose in a straight line.* ■ a furrow or wrinkle in the skin, especially on the face. ■ a contour or outline considered as a feature of design or composition: *crisp architectural lines* | [mass noun] *the artist's use of clean line and colour.* ■ (on a map or graph) a curve connecting all points having a specified common property. ■ a line marking the starting or finishing point in a race. ■ (in football, hockey, etc.) the goal line: *video evidence suggests the ball did not cross the line.* ■ (**the Line**) the equator. ■ a notional limit or boundary: *the issue of peace cut across class lines* | *television blurs the line between news and entertainment.* ■ each of the very narrow horizontal sections forming a television picture. ■ Physics a narrow range of the spectrum that is noticeably brighter or darker than the adjacent parts. ■ (**the line**) the level of the base of most letters, such as *h* and *x*, in printing and writing. ■ [as modifier] Printing & Computing denoting an image consisting of lines and solid areas, with no gradation of tone: *a line block* | *line art.* ■ each of (usually five) horizontal lines forming a stave in musical notation. ■ a sequence of notes or tones forming an instrumental or vocal melody: *a powerful melodic line.* ■ informal a dose of a powdered narcotic drug, especially cocaine, laid out in a line ready to be taken.
2 a length of cord, rope, wire, or other material serving a particular purpose: *Lily pegged the washing on the line.* ■ a telephone connection or service: *I've got Inspector Jackson* ***on the line*** *for you* | *a freephone advice line.* ■ a railway track: *passengers were hit by delays caused by leaves on the line.* ■ a branch or route of a railway system: *the Glasgow to London line.* ■ a company that provides ships, aircraft, or buses on particular routes on a regular basis: *a major shipping line.*
3 a horizontal row of written or printed words. ■ a part of a poem or song forming one such row: *each stanza has eight lines.* ■ (**lines**) the words of an actor's part in a play or film. ■ (**lines**) Brit. an amount of text or number of repetitions of a sentence written out as a school punishment.
4 a row of people or things: *a line of altar boys proceeded down the aisle.* ■ N. Amer. a queue. ■ a connected series of people following one another in time (used especially of several generations of a family): *we follow the history of a family through the male line.* ■ a series of related things: *the bill is the latest in a long line of measures to protect society from criminals.* ■ a range of commercial goods: *the company intends to hire more people and expand its product line.*
5 an area or branch of activity: *the stresses unique to their* ***line of work.*** ■ a direction, course, or channel: *he opened another line of attack.* ■ (**lines**) a manner of doing or thinking about something: *you can't run a business* ***on these lines*** | *the superintendent was thinking* ***along the same lines.*** ■ an agreed approach; a policy: *the official line is that there were no chemical attacks on allied troops.* ■ informal a false or exaggerated remark or story: *he fed me a line about some nightclubbing Japanese photographer* | *none of my chat-up lines ever worked.*
6 a connected series of military fieldworks or defences facing an enemy force: *raids behind enemy lines.* ■ an arrangement of soldiers or ships in a column or line formation; a line of battle. ■ (**the line**) regular army regiments (as opposed to auxiliary forces or household troops).
▶ **verb** [with obj.] **1** stand or be positioned at intervals along: *a processional route lined by people waving flags.*
2 (usu. as adj. **lined**) mark or cover with lines: *a thin woman with a lined face* | *lined paper.*
– PHRASES **above the line 1** Finance denoting or relating to money spent on items of current expenditure. **2** Bridge denoting bonus points and penalty points, which do not count towards the game. **all (the way) down** (or **along**) **the line** at every point or stage: *the mistakes were due to lack of care all down the line.* **along** (or **down**) **the line** at a further, later, or unspecified point: *I knew that somewhere*

down the line there would be an inquest. **below the line 1** Finance denoting or relating to money spent on items of capital expenditure. **2** Bridge denoting points for tricks bid and won, which count towards the game. **bring someone/thing into line** cause someone or something to conform: *the change in the law will bring Britain into line with Europe.* **come down to the line** (of a race) be closely fought right until the end. **come into line** conform: *Britain has come into line with other Western democracies in giving the vote to its citizens living abroad.* **do a line with** Irish & NZ informal have a regular romantic or sexual romantic relationship with (someone). **the end of the line** the point at which further effort is unproductive or one can go no further. **get a line on** informal learn something about. **in line 1** under control: *that threat kept a lot of people in line.* **2** chiefly N. Amer. in a queue: *we stood in line at the counter.* **in line for** likely to receive: *the club are in line for a windfall of three hundred thousand pounds.* **in the line of duty** while one is working (used mainly of police officers or soldiers). **in** (or **out of**) **line with** in (or not in) alignment or accordance with: *remuneration is in line with comparable international organizations.* **lay** (or **put**) **it on the line** speak frankly. (**draw**) **a line in the sand** (state that one has reached) a point beyond which one will not go. **line abreast** Nautical a formation in which a number of ships travel side by side. **line ahead** Nautical a formation in which a number of ships follow one another in a line. **line astern** a formation in which a number of aircraft or ships follow one another in a line. **line of battle** a disposition of troops for action in battle. ▪ historical a battle formation of warships following one another in a line. **line of communications** a means of connection between an army in the field and its bases. **line of credit** an amount of credit extended to a borrower. **line of fire** the expected path of gunfire or a missile: *residents within line of fire were evacuated from their homes.* **line of flight** a route taken through the air. **line of force** an imaginary line which represents the strength and direction of a magnetic, gravitational, or electric field at any point. **the line of least resistance** see RESISTANCE. **line of march** the route taken in marching. **line of scrimmage** American Football the imaginary line separating the teams at the beginning of a play. **line of sight** a straight line along which an observer has unobstructed vision: *a building which obstructs our line of sight.* **line of vision** the straight line along which an observer looks: *Jimmy moved forward into Len's line of vision.* **on the line 1** at serious risk: *their careers were on the line.* **2** (of a picture in an exhibition) hung with its centre about level with the spectator's eye. **out of line** informal behaving in a way that breaks the rules or is considered inappropriate: *he had never stepped out of line with her before.*

– PHRASAL VERBS **line out** Baseball be caught out after hitting a line drive. **line something out** transplant seedlings from beds into nursery lines, where they are grown before being moved to their permanent position. **line someone/thing up 1** arrange a number of people or things in a straight row: *they lined them up and shot them.* ▪ (**line up**) (of a number of people or things) stand or be arranged in a straight row: *we would line up across the parade ground, shoulder to shoulder.* **2** have someone or something ready or prepared: *have you got any work lined up?*

– ORIGIN Old English *līne* 'rope, series', probably of Germanic origin, from Latin *linea* (*fibra*) 'flax (fibre)', from Latin *linum* 'flax', reinforced in Middle English by Old French *ligne*, based on Latin *linea*.

line² ▸ **verb** [with obj.] cover the inside surface of (a container or garment) with a layer of different material: *a basket lined with polythene.* ▪ form a layer on the inside surface of (an area); cover as if with a lining: *hundreds of telegrams lined the walls.*

– PHRASES **line one's pocket** informal make money, especially by dishonest means. **line one's stomach** informal fill one's stomach.

– ORIGIN late Middle English: from obsolete *line* 'flax', with reference to the common use of linen for linings.

lineage /ˈlɪnɪɪdʒ/ ▸ **noun 1** [mass noun] direct descent from an ancestor; ancestry or pedigree. ▪ [count noun] Anthropology a social group tracing its descent from a single ancestor.

2 Biology a sequence of species each of which is considered to have evolved from its predecessor: *the chimpanzee and gorilla lineages.* ▪ a sequence of cells in the body which developed from a common ancestral cell: *the myeloid lineage.*

– ORIGIN Middle English: from Old French *lignage*, from Latin *linea* 'a line' (see LINE¹).

lineal /ˈlɪnɪəl/ ▸ **adjective 1** in a direct line of descent or ancestry: *a lineal descendant.*

2 relating to or consisting of lines; linear.

– DERIVATIVES **lineally** adverb.

– ORIGIN late Middle English: via Old French from late Latin *linealis*, from *linea* 'a line' (see LINE¹).

lineament /ˈlɪnɪəm(ə)nt/ ▸ **noun 1** (usu. **lineaments**) literary a distinctive feature or characteristic, especially of the face.

2 Geology a linear feature on the earth's surface, such as a fault.

– ORIGIN late Middle English: from Latin *lineamentum*, from *lineare* 'make straight', from *linea* 'a line' (see LINE¹).

linear /ˈlɪnɪə/ ▸ **adjective 1** arranged in or extending along a straight or nearly straight line: *linear movement.* ▪ consisting of or predominantly formed using lines or outlines: *simple linear designs.* ▪ involving one dimension only: *linear elasticity.* ▪ Mathematics able to be represented by a straight line on a graph: *linear functions.* ▪ Mathematics involving or exhibiting directly proportional change in two related quantities: *linear relationship.*

2 progressing from one stage to another in a single series of steps; sequential: *a linear narrative.*

– DERIVATIVES **linearity** noun, **linearly** adverb.

– ORIGIN mid 17th cent.: from Latin *linearis*, from *linea* 'a line' (see LINE¹).

Linear A the earlier of two related forms of writing discovered at Knossos in Crete between 1894 and 1901, found on tablets and vases dating from *c.*1700 to 1450 BC and still largely unintelligible.

linear accelerator ▸ **noun** Physics an accelerator in which particles travel in straight lines, not in closed orbits.

Linear B a form of Bronze Age writing discovered on tablets in Crete, dating from *c.*1400 to 1200 BC. In 1952 it was shown to be a syllabic script composed of linear signs, derived from Linear A and older Minoan scripts, representing a form of Mycenaean Greek.

linear equation ▸ **noun** an equation between two variables that gives a straight line when plotted on a graph.

linearize (also **linearise**) ▸ **verb** [with obj.] technical make linear; represent in or transform into a linear form.

– DERIVATIVES **linearization** noun, **linearizer** noun.

linear motor ▸ **noun** an electric induction motor which produces straight-line motion (as opposed to rotary motion) by means of a linear stator and rotor placed in parallel.

linear perspective ▸ **noun** [mass noun] a type of perspective used by artists, in which the relative size, shape, and position of objects is determined by drawn or imagined lines converging at a point on the horizon.

linear programming ▸ **noun** [mass noun] a mathematical technique for maximizing or minimizing a linear function of several variables, such as output or cost.

lineation /ˌlɪnɪˈeɪʃ(ə)n/ ▸ **noun** [mass noun] the action or process of drawing lines or marking with lines. ▪ [count noun] a line or linear marking; an arrangement or group of lines: *magnetic lineations.* ▪ [count noun] a contour or outline. ▪ the division of text into lines: *the punctuation and lineation are reproduced accurately.*

– ORIGIN late Middle English: from Latin *lineatio(n-)*, from *lineare* 'make straight'.

linebacker ▸ **noun** American Football a defensive player positioned just behind the line of scrimmage.

line breeding ▸ **noun** [mass noun] the selective breeding of animals for a desired feature by mating them within a closely related line.

line dancing ▸ **noun** [mass noun] a type of country and western dancing in which dancers line up in a row without partners and follow a choreographed pattern of steps to music.

– DERIVATIVES **line dance** noun, **line-dance** verb, **line dancer** noun.

line drawing ▸ **noun** a drawing done using only narrow lines, without blocks of shading.

line drive ▸ **noun** Baseball a powerfully struck shot that travels close to the ground.

line engraving ▸ **noun** [mass noun] the art or technique of engraving by lines incised on the plate, as distinguished from etching and mezzotint. ▪ [count noun] an engraving executed in this manner.

– DERIVATIVES **line-engraved** adjective, **line engraver** noun.

linefeed ▸ **noun** [mass noun] **1** the action of advancing paper in a printing machine or text on a screen by the space of one line.

2 the distance from the bottom of one line of type to the bottom of the next.

linefish ▸ **noun** [mass noun] S. African fish of smaller species, caught from the shore or with lines from boats rather than by trawlers.

line-in ▸ **noun** an input socket in an electrical device.

line integral ▸ **noun** Mathematics the integral, taken along a line, of any function that has a continuously varying value along that line.

Line Islands a group of eleven islands in the central Pacific, straddling the equator south of Hawaii. Eight of the islands, including Kiritimati (Christmas Island), form part of Kiribati; the remaining three are uninhabited dependencies of the US.

lineman ▸ **noun** (pl. **linemen**) **1** a person employed in laying and maintaining railway track. ▪ North American term for LINESMAN (sense 2).

2 American Football a player positioned on the line of scrimmage.

line manager ▸ **noun** chiefly Brit. a person with direct managerial responsibility for a particular employee. ▪ a manager involved in running the main business activities of a company.

– DERIVATIVES **line management** noun.

linen ▸ **noun** [mass noun] cloth woven from flax. ▪ articles such as sheets or clothes made, or originally made, of linen.

– ORIGIN Old English *līnen* (as an adjective in the sense 'made of flax'), of West Germanic origin; related to Dutch *linnen*, German *Leinen*, also to obsolete *line* 'flax'.

linen basket ▸ **noun** chiefly Brit. a receptacle with a lid, for holding soiled clothing.

linenfold ▸ **noun** [mass noun] carved or moulded ornaments, especially on a panel, representing folds or scrolls of linen.

line-out ▸ **noun 1** Rugby a formation of parallel lines of opposing forwards at right angles to the touchline when the ball is thrown in. ▪ an occasion when the ball is thrown in to such a formation.

2 an output socket in an electrical device.

line printer ▸ **noun** a machine that prints output from a computer a line at a time rather than character by character.

liner¹ ▸ **noun 1** (also **ocean liner**) a large luxurious passenger ship of a type formerly used on a regular line.

2 a fine paintbrush used for painting thin lines and for outlining. ▪ a cosmetic used for outlining or accentuating a facial feature, or a brush or pencil for applying this.

3 a boat engaged in sea fishing with lines as opposed to nets.

4 a ferret held on a leash or line while rabbiting, used to help recover another ferret lost underground.

liner² ▸ **noun** a lining in a device, container, or other object, especially a removable one. ▪ the lining of a garment. ▪ (also **cylinder liner**) a replaceable metal sleeve placed within the cylinder of an engine, forming a durable surface to withstand wear from the piston.

-liner ▸ **combining form** informal denoting a text of a specified number of lines such as an advertisement or a spoken passage in a play, dialogue, etc.: *a two-liner.*

liner note ▸ **noun** (usu. **liner notes**) the text printed on a paper insert issued as part of the packaging of a CD or on the sleeve of a record.

lineside ▸ **noun** Brit. the area adjacent to a railway track.

linesman ▸ **noun** (pl. **linesmen**) **1** (in games played on a field or court) an official who assists the referee or umpire from the touchline, especially in deciding whether the ball is out of play.

2 Brit. a person employed for the repair and maintenance of telephone or electricity power lines.

line spectrum ▸ **noun** Physics an emission spectrum consisting of separate isolated lines. ▪ an emission (of light, sound, or other radiation) composed of a number of discrete frequencies or energies.

line squall ▸ **noun** Meteorology a violent local storm occurring as one of a number along a cold front.

line-up ▸ **noun 1** a group of people or things brought together for a particular purpose, especially the members of a sports team or a group of musicians or

L

other entertainers: *the instrumental line-up is piano, drums, and lead and bass guitar.*
2 chiefly N. Amer. a line or queue of people or things. ■ another term for IDENTITY PARADE.

ling¹ ▶ **noun** any of a number of long-bodied edible marine fishes: ● a large East Atlantic fish related to the cod (genus *Molva*, family Gadidae), in particular *M. molva*, which is of commercial importance. ● a related Australian fish (*Lotella callarias*, family Gadidae). ● a similar but unrelated Australian fish (*Genypterus blacodes*, family Ophidiidae).
– ORIGIN Middle English *lenge*, probably from Middle Dutch; related to LONG¹.

ling² ▶ **noun** the common heather of Eurasia.
– ORIGIN Middle English: from Old Norse *lyng*, of unknown origin.

-ling ▶ **suffix 1** forming nouns from nouns (such as *hireling, sapling*).
2 forming nouns from adjectives and adverbs (such as *darling, sibling, underling*).
3 forming diminutive words: *gosling*. ■ often with depreciatory reference: *princeling*.
– ORIGIN Old English; sense 3 from Old Norse.

Lingala /lɪŋˈɡɑːlə/ ▶ **noun** [mass noun] a Bantu language used by over 8 million people as a lingua franca in northern parts of Congo and the Democratic Republic of the Congo (Zaire).
– ORIGIN a local name.

lingam /ˈlɪŋɡam/ (also **linga** /ˈlɪŋɡə/) ▶ **noun** Hinduism a symbol of divine generative energy, especially a phallus or phallic object as a symbol of Shiva. Compare with YONI.
– ORIGIN from Sanskrit *liṅga*, literally 'mark, (sexual) characteristic'.

lingcod /ˈlɪŋkɒd/ ▶ **noun** (pl. **same**) a large slender greenling (fish), which has large teeth and is greenish-brown with golden spots. It lives along the Pacific coast of North America, where it is a valuable commercial and sporting fish. ● *Ophiodon elongatus*, family Hexagrammidae.

linger ▶ **verb** [no obj.] stay in a place longer than necessary because of a reluctance to leave: *she lingered in the yard, enjoying the warm sunshine* | figurative *she let her eyes linger on him suggestively*. ■ (**linger over**) spend a long time over (something): *she lingered over her meal*. ■ be slow to disappear or die: *the tradition seems to linger on* | *we are thankful that she didn't linger on and suffer*.
– DERIVATIVES **lingerer** noun.
– ORIGIN Middle English (in the sense 'dwell, abide'): frequentative of obsolete *leng* 'prolong', of Germanic origin; related to German *längen* 'make long(er)', also to LONG¹.

lingerie /ˈlãʒ(ə)ri/ ▶ **noun** [mass noun] women's underwear and nightclothes.
– ORIGIN mid 19th cent.: from French, from *linge* 'linen'.

lingering ▶ **adjective** lasting for a long time or slow to end: *there are still some lingering doubts in my mind* | *a painful and lingering death*.
– DERIVATIVES **lingeringly** adverb.

lingo ▶ **noun** (pl. **lingos** or **lingoes**) informal, often humorous a foreign language or local dialect: *it doesn't matter if you can't speak the lingo*. ■ the vocabulary or jargon of a particular subject or group of people: *computer lingo*.
– ORIGIN mid 17th cent.: probably via Portuguese *lingoa* from Latin *lingua* 'tongue'.

lingonberry /ˈlɪŋ(ə)nˌb(ə)ri, -ˌbɛri/ ▶ **noun** (pl. **lingonberries**) another term for the cowberry, especially in Scandinavia where the berries are much used in cookery.
– ORIGIN 1950s: from Swedish *lingon* 'cowberry' + BERRY.

lingua franca /ˌlɪŋɡwə ˈfraŋkə/ ▶ **noun** (pl. **lingua francas**) a language that is adopted as a common language between speakers whose native languages are different. ■ [mass noun] historical a mixture of Italian with French, Greek, Arabic, and Spanish, formerly used in the eastern Mediterranean.
– ORIGIN late 17th cent.: from Italian, literally 'Frankish tongue'.

lingual /ˈlɪŋɡw(ə)l/ ▶ **adjective** technical **1** chiefly Anatomy relating to, near, or on the side towards the tongue. ■ (of a sound) formed by the tongue.
2 relating to speech or language: *his demonstrations of lingual dexterity*.
– DERIVATIVES **lingually** adverb.
– ORIGIN mid 17th cent.: from medieval Latin *lingualis*, from Latin *lingua* 'tongue, language'.

linguine /lɪŋˈɡwiːneɪ, -ni/ ▶ **plural noun** small pieces of pasta in the form of narrow ribbons.
– ORIGIN Italian, plural of *linguina*, diminutive of *lingua* 'tongue'.

linguist ▶ **noun 1** a person skilled in foreign languages.
2 a person who studies linguistics.
– ORIGIN late 16th cent.: from Latin *lingua* 'language' + -IST.

linguistic ▶ **adjective** relating to language or linguistics.
– DERIVATIVES **linguistically** adverb.

linguistic competence ▶ **noun** see COMPETENCE.

linguistic performance ▶ **noun** see PERFORMANCE (sense 2).

linguistics /lɪŋˈɡwɪstɪks/ ▶ **plural noun** [treated as sing.] the scientific study of language and its structure, including the study of grammar, syntax, and phonetics. Specific branches of linguistics include sociolinguistics, dialectology, psycholinguistics, computational linguistics, comparative linguistics, and structural linguistics.
– DERIVATIVES **linguistician** /-ˈstɪʃ(ə)n/ **noun**.

lingulate /ˈlɪŋɡjʊleɪt/ ▶ **adjective 1** Botany & Zoology tongue-shaped.
2 Zoology denoting a type of burrowing brachiopod with an inarticulate shell and a long pedicle.
– ORIGIN mid 19th cent.: from Latin *lingulatus*, based on *lingua* 'tongue', from *lingere* 'to lick'.

linhay /ˈlɪni/ ▶ **noun** dialect a shed or other farm building open in front, typically with a lean-to roof.
– ORIGIN late 17th cent.: of unknown origin.

liniment /ˈlɪnɪm(ə)nt/ ▶ **noun** [mass noun] an embrocation for rubbing on the body to relieve pain, especially one made with oil.
– ORIGIN late Middle English: from late Latin *linimentum*, from Latin *linire* 'to smear'.

lining ▶ **noun** a layer of different material covering the inside surface of something: *self-clean oven linings*. ■ an additional layer of different material attached to the inside of a garment or curtain to make it warmer or hang better: *leather gloves with fur linings*.

linish /ˈlɪnɪʃ/ ▶ **verb** [with obj.] technical polish or remove excess material from (something) by contact with an abrasive moving belt.
– ORIGIN 1970s (as a verb): blend of LINEN and FINISH.

link¹ ▶ **noun 1** a relationship between two things or situations, especially where one affects the other: *a commission to investigate a link between pollution and forest decline*. ■ a relationship or connection between people, countries, or organizations: *he retained strong links with the media*. ■ something that enables communication between people: *sign language interpreters represent a vital link between the deaf and hearing communities*. ■ a means of contact, travel, or transport between two places: *they set up a satellite link with Tokyo* | *a high-speed rail link to the Channel Tunnel*. ■ Computing a code or instruction which connects one part of a program or an element in a list to another. ■ short for HYPERLINK.
2 a ring or loop in a chain. ■ a unit of measurement of length equal to one hundredth of a surveying chain (7.92 inches).
▶ **verb** [with obj.] make, form, or suggest a connection with or between: *rumours that **linked** his name **with** Judith* | *foreign and domestic policy are linked* | [no obj.] *she **linked up with** an artistic group*. ■ connect or join physically: *a network of routes linking towns and villages* | *the cows are **linked up to** milking machines*. ■ clasp; intertwine: *once outside he linked arms with her*.
– ORIGIN late Middle English (denoting a loop; also as a verb in the sense 'connect physically'): from Old Norse *hlekkr*, of Germanic origin; related to German *Gelenk* 'joint'.

link² ▶ **noun** historical a torch of pitch and tow for lighting the way in dark streets.
– ORIGIN early 16th cent.: perhaps from medieval Latin *li(n)chinus* 'wick', from Greek *lukhnos* 'light'.

linkage ▶ **noun** [mass noun] the action of linking or the state of being linked. ■ [count noun] a system of links: *a complex linkage of nerves*. ■ the linking of different issues in political negotiations. ■ Genetics the tendency of groups of genes on the same chromosome to be inherited together.

linkage disequilibrium ▶ **noun** [mass noun] Genetics the occurrence in members of a population of combinations of linked genes in non-random proportions.

linked list ▶ **noun** Computing an ordered set of data elements, each containing a link to its successor (and sometimes its predecessor).

linker ▶ **noun** a thing which links other things. ■ Computing a program used with a compiler or assembler to provide links to the libraries needed for an executable program.

linking ▶ **adjective** connecting or joining something to something else. ■ Phonetics denoting a consonant that is sounded at a boundary between two words or morphemes where two vowels would otherwise be adjacent, as in *law(r) and order*. See also LIAISON.

linkman ▶ **noun** (pl. **linkmen**) Brit. a person serving as a connection between groups of people. ■ a person providing continuity between items in a radio or television programme or between such programmes.

Linköping /ˈlɪnˌtʃəːpɪŋ/ an industrial town in SE Sweden; pop. 141,863 (2008). It was a noted cultural and ecclesiastical centre in the Middle Ages.

links ▶ **plural noun** (also **golf links**) [treated as sing. or pl.] a golf course, especially one on grass-covered sandy ground near the sea. ■ another term for LINKSLAND.
– ORIGIN Old English *hlinc* 'rising ground', perhaps related to LEAN¹.

linksland ▶ **noun** [mass noun] Scottish level or undulating sandy ground covered by coarse grass and near the sea.

linkspan ▶ **noun** a hinged bridge on the quay at a port or ferry terminal which can be connected with a ramp on a vessel to allow loading or unloading.

link-up ▶ **noun** an instance of two or more people or things connecting or joining. ■ a connection enabling two or more people or machines to communicate with each other: *a live satellite link-up*.

linkwork ▶ **noun** [mass noun] a kind of gearing which transmits motion by a series of links rather than by wheels or bands.

linn ▶ **noun** Scottish archaic a waterfall. ■ the pool below a waterfall. ■ a steep precipice.
– ORIGIN early 16th cent., from Scottish Gaelic *linne*, Irish *linn*, related to Welsh *llyn* 'lake'.

Linnaeus /lɪˈniːəs, -ˈneɪəs/, Carolus (1707–78), Swedish botanist, founder of modern systematic botany and zoology; Latinized name of *Carl von Linné*. He devised an authoritative classification system for flowering plants involving binomial Latin names (later superseded by that of Antoine Jussieu), and also a classification method for animals.
– DERIVATIVES **Linnaean** (also **Linnean**) **adjective & noun**.

linnet ▶ **noun** a mainly brown and grey finch with a reddish breast and forehead. ● Genus *Acanthis*, family Fringillidae: three species, in particular the Eurasian *A. cannabina*.
– ORIGIN early 16th cent.: from Old French *linette*, from *lin* 'flax' (because the bird feeds on flaxseeds).

lino ▶ **noun** (pl. **linos**) chiefly Brit. informal term for LINOLEUM.

linocut ▶ **noun** a design or form carved in relief on a block of linoleum. ■ a print made from a linocut block.

linocutting ▶ **noun** [mass noun] the action or technique of making a print from a linocut block.

linoleate /ˈlɪnəlɪeɪt/ ▶ **noun** Chemistry a salt or ester of linoleic acid.

linoleic acid /ˌlɪnə(ʊ)ˈliːɪk, -ˈleɪɪk/ ▶ **noun** [mass noun] Chemistry a polyunsaturated fatty acid present as a glyceride in linseed oil and other oils and essential in the human diet. ● Chem. formula: $C_{17}H_{31}COOH$.
– ORIGIN mid 19th cent.: from Latin *linum* 'flax' + OLEIC ACID.

linolenate /ˌlɪnəˈlɛneɪt/ ▶ **noun** Chemistry a salt or ester of linolenic acid.

linolenic acid /ˌlɪnə(ʊ)ˈlɛnɪk, -ˈliːnɪk/ ▶ **noun** [mass noun] Chemistry a polyunsaturated fatty acid (with one more double bond than linoleic acid) present as a glyceride in linseed and other oils and essential in the human diet. ● Chem. formula: $C_{17}H_{29}COOH$; several isomers, notably **gamma-linolenic acid**, present in evening primrose oil.
– ORIGIN late 19th cent.: from German *Linolensaüre*, from *Linolsaüre* 'linoleic acid', with the insertion of *-en-* (from -ENE).

linoleum /lɪˈnəʊlɪəm/ ▶ **noun** [mass noun] a material consisting of a canvas backing thickly coated with a preparation of linseed oil and powdered cork, used especially as a floor covering.
– DERIVATIVES **linoleumed** adjective.

– ORIGIN late 19th cent.: from Latin *linum* 'flax' + *oleum* 'oil'.

Linotype /ˈlʌɪnə(ʊ)tʌɪp/ ▸ **noun** Printing, trademark a composing machine producing lines of words as single strips of metal, used chiefly for newspapers. It is now rarely used.
– ORIGIN late 19th cent.: alteration of the phrase *line o' type*.

Lin Piao /lɪn ˈpjaʊ/ variant of LIN BIAO.

linsang /ˈlɪnsaŋ/ ▸ **noun** a small, secretive relation of the civet, with a spotted or banded coat and a long tail, found in the forests of SE Asia and West Africa. ● Family Viverridae: genera *Prionodon* (two Asian species) and *Poiana* (one African species).
– ORIGIN early 19th cent.: via Javanese from Malay.

linseed ▸ **noun** [mass noun] the seeds of the flax plant, which are the source of linseed oil and linseed cake. ■ the flax plant, especially when grown for linseed oil.
– ORIGIN Old English *līnsǣd*, from *līn* 'flax' + *sǣd* 'seed'.

linseed cake ▸ **noun** [mass noun] pressed linseed used as cattle food.

linseed oil ▸ **noun** [mass noun] a pale yellow oil extracted from linseed, used especially in paint and varnish.

linsey-woolsey /ˌlɪnzɪˈwʊlzi/ (also **linsey-wolsey**) ▸ **noun** [mass noun] a strong, coarse fabric with a linen or cotton warp and a woollen weft.
– ORIGIN late 15th cent.: from *linsey*, originally denoting a coarse linen fabric (probably from *Lindsey*, a village in Suffolk where the material was first made) + WOOL + *-sey* as a rhyming suffix.

linstock ▸ **noun** historical a long pole used to hold a match for firing a cannon.
– ORIGIN late 16th cent.: from earlier *lintstock*, from Dutch *lontstok*, from *lont* 'match' + *stok* 'stick'. The change in the first syllable was due to association with LINT.

lint ▸ **noun** [mass noun] **1** short, fine fibres which separate from the surface of cloth or yarn during processing. ■ Scottish flax fibres prepared for spinning. ■ the fibrous material of a cotton boll.
2 a fabric, originally of linen, with a raised nap on one side, used for dressing wounds.
– DERIVATIVES **linty** adjective.
– ORIGIN late Middle English *lynnet* 'flax prepared for spinning', perhaps from Old French *linette* 'linseed', from *lin* 'flax'.

lintel ▸ **noun** a horizontal support of timber, stone, concrete, or steel across the top of a door or window.
– DERIVATIVES **lintelled** (US **linteled**) adjective.
– ORIGIN Middle English: from Old French, based on late Latin *liminare*, from Latin *limen* 'threshold'.

linter ▸ **noun** a machine for removing the short fibres from cotton seeds after ginning. ■ (**linters**) fibres of this kind.

lintie /ˈlɪnti/ ▸ **noun** (pl. **linties**) Scottish term for LINNET.

Linux /ˈlɪnʌks, ˈlʌɪnʌks/ ▸ **noun** [mass noun] Computing (trademark in the US) an open-source operating system modelled on UNIX.
– ORIGIN 1990s: from the name of *Linus* Benedict Torvalds (born 1969), a Finnish software engineer who wrote the first version of the system, + *-x*, as in *Unix*.

liny ▸ **adjective** (**linier**, **liniest**) informal marked with lines; wrinkled.

Linz /lɪnts/ an industrial city in northern Austria, on the River Danube, capital of the state of Upper Austria; pop. 188,430 (2006).

lion ▸ **noun 1** a large tawny-coloured cat that lives in prides, found in Africa and NW India. The male has a flowing shaggy mane and takes little part in hunting, which is done cooperatively by the females. ● *Panthera leo*, family Felidae.
■ the lion as an emblem (e.g. of English or Scottish royalty) or as a charge in heraldry. ■ (**the Lion**) the zodiacal sign or constellation Leo. ■ a brave, strong, or fierce person. ■ (usu. **literary lion**) a notable or famous author.
2 (**Lion** or **British Lion**) a member of a touring international rugby union team representing the British Isles.
3 (**Lion**) a member of a Lions Club.
– PHRASES **the lion's den** a demanding, intimidating, or unpleasant place or situation. **the lion's share** Brit. the largest part of something. **throw someone to the lions** cause someone to be in an extremely dangerous or unpleasant situation. [with reference to the throwing of Christians to the lions in Roman times.]
– DERIVATIVES **lion-like** adjective.
– ORIGIN Middle English: from Anglo-Norman French *liun*, from Latin *leo*, *leon-*, from Greek *leōn*, *leont-*.

lion dance ▸ **noun** a traditional Chinese dance in which the dancers are masked and costumed to resemble lions.

lioness ▸ **noun** a female lion.

lionhead ▸ **noun** a goldfish of a large-headed variety.

lionhearted ▸ **adjective** brave and determined.
– DERIVATIVES **lionheart** noun.

lionize /ˈlʌɪənʌɪz/ (also **lionise**) ▸ **verb** [with obj.] give a lot of public attention and approval to (someone); treat as a celebrity: *modern sportsmen are lionized and feted*.
– DERIVATIVES **lionization** noun, **lionizer** noun.

Lions Club ▸ **noun** a worldwide charitable society devoted to social and international service, taking its membership primarily from business and professional groups.

lion tamarin ▸ **noun** a rare tamarin with a golden or black and golden coat and an erect mane, found only in Brazil. ● Genus *Leontopithecus*, family Callitrichidae (or Callithricidae): the **golden lion tamarin** (*L. rosalia*), and three other species that have been recently recognized or discovered.

lip ▸ **noun 1** either of the two fleshy parts which form the upper and lower edges of the opening of the mouth: *he kissed her on the lips*. ■ (**lips**) used to refer to a person's speech or to current topics of conversation: *downsizing is on everyone's lips at the moment*. ■ another term for LABIUM (sense 1, sense 2).
2 the edge of a hollow container or an opening: *the lip of the cup*. ■ a rounded, raised, or extended piece along an edge: *the cockpit is protected by a lip extending from the roof*.
3 [mass noun] informal insolent or impertinent talk: *don't give me any of your lip!*
▸ **verb** (**lips**, **lipping**, **lipped**) [with obj.] **1** (of water) lap against: *beaches lipped by the surf rimming the Pacific*.
2 Golf (of the ball) hit the rim of (a hole) but fail to go in.
– PHRASES **bite one's lip** repress an emotion; stifle laughter or a retort: *she bit her lip to stop the rush of bitter words*. **curl one's lip** raise a corner of one's upper lip to show contempt; sneer. **lick one's lips** look forward to something with relish. **my** (or **his** etc.) **lips are sealed** see SEAL[1]. **pass one's lips** be eaten, drunk, or spoken. **pay lip service to** express approval of or support for (something) insincerely or without taking any significant action.
– DERIVATIVES **lipless** adjective, **lip-like** adjective, **lipped** adjective [in combination] *her pale-lipped mouth*.
– ORIGIN Old English *lippa*, of Germanic origin; related to Dutch *lip* and German *Lippe*, from an Indo-European root shared by Latin *labia*, *labra* 'lips'.

lipa /ˈliːpə/ ▸ **noun** (pl. **same** or **lipas**) a monetary unit of Croatia, equal to one hundredth of a kuna.
– ORIGIN Croatian, literally 'lime tree'.

lipaemia /lɪˈpiːmɪə/ (US **lipemia**) ▸ **noun** [mass noun] Medicine the presence in the blood of an abnormally high concentration of emulsified fat.
– ORIGIN late 19th cent.: from Greek *lipos* 'fat' + -AEMIA.

Lipari Islands /ˈlɪpəri/ a group of seven volcanic islands in the Tyrrhenian Sea, off the NE coast of Sicily, and in Italian possession. Believed by the ancient Greeks to be the home of Aeolus, the islands were formerly known as the Aeolian Islands.

lipase /ˈlɪpeɪz, ˈlʌɪp-/ ▸ **noun** [mass noun] Biochemistry a pancreatic enzyme that catalyses the breakdown of fats to fatty acids and glycerol or other alcohols.
– ORIGIN late 19th cent.: from Greek *lipos* 'fat' + -ASE.

lip brush ▸ **noun** a small brush designed for applying lipstick.

Lipchitz /ˈlɪpʃɪts/, Jacques (1891–1973), Lithuanian-born French sculptor; born *Chaim Jacob Lipchitz*. After producing cubist works such as *Sailor with a Guitar* (1914), he explored the interpenetration of solids and voids in his series of 'transparent' sculptures of the 1920s.

lipectomy /lʌɪˈpɛktəmi, lɪ-/ ▸ **noun** (pl. **lipectomies**) any surgical procedure carried out to remove unwanted body fat, usually by suction.
– ORIGIN 1990s: from LIPO- + -ECTOMY.

Lipetsk /ˈlɪpɪtsk/ an industrial city in SW Russia, on the Voronezh River; pop. 502,500 (est. 2008).

lip gloss ▸ **noun** [mass noun] a cosmetic applied to the lips to provide a glossy finish and sometimes colour.

lipid ▸ **noun** Chemistry any of a class of organic compounds that are fatty acids or their derivatives and are insoluble in water but soluble in organic solvents. They include many natural oils, waxes, and steroids.
– ORIGIN early 20th cent.: from French *lipide*, based on Greek *lipos* 'fat'.

lipidosis /ˌlɪpɪˈdəʊsɪs/ (also **lipoidosis**) ▸ **noun** [mass noun] (pl. **lipidoses** /-siːz/) Medicine a disorder of lipid metabolism in the body tissues.

Lipizzaner /ˌlɪpɪˈtsɑːnə, ˌlɪpɪˈzeɪnə/ (also **Lippizaner**) ▸ **noun** a horse of a fine white breed used especially in displays of dressage.
– ORIGIN early 20th cent.: from German, from *Lippiza*, site of the former Austrian Imperial stud near Trieste.

lipline ▸ **noun** the outline of a person's lips, especially with reference to the application of cosmetics.

lip liner ▸ **noun** [mass noun] a cosmetic applied to the outline of the lips, mainly to prevent the unwanted spreading of lipstick or lip gloss.

lip microphone ▸ **noun** a small microphone designed to be held or worn close to a person's mouth.

lipo- /ˈlɪpəʊ, ˈlʌɪpəʊ/ ▸ **combining form** relating to fat or other lipids: *liposuction* | *lipoprotein*.
– ORIGIN from Greek *lipos* 'fat'.

Li Po /liː ˈpəʊ/ (also **Li Bo** or **Li T'ai Po**) (AD 701–62), Chinese poet. Typical themes in his poetry are wine, women, and the beauties of nature.

lipogenesis /ˌlɪpə(ʊ)ˈdʒɛnɪsɪs, ˌlʌɪ-/ ▸ **noun** [mass noun] Physiology the metabolic formation of fat.
– DERIVATIVES **lipogenic** adjective.

lipogram ▸ **noun** a composition from which the writer systematically omits a certain letter or certain letters of the alphabet.
– DERIVATIVES **lipogrammatic** adjective.
– ORIGIN early 18th cent.: back-formation from Greek *lipogrammatos* 'lacking a letter', from *lip-* (stem of *leipein* 'to leave (out)') + *gramma* 'letter'.

lipoid /ˈlɪpɔɪd/ ▸ **adjective** Biochemistry relating to or resembling fat.
– ORIGIN late 19th cent.: from Greek *lipos* 'fat' + -OID.

lipoidosis /ˌlɪpɔɪˈdəʊsɪs/ ▸ **noun** variant spelling of LIPIDOSIS.

lipolysis /lɪˈpɒlɪsɪs/ ▸ **noun** [mass noun] Physiology the breakdown of fats and other lipids by hydrolysis to release fatty acids.
– DERIVATIVES **lipolytic** adjective.

lipoma /lɪˈpəʊmə/ ▸ **noun** (pl. **lipomas** or **lipomata** /-mətə/) Medicine a benign tumour of fatty tissue.

lipophilic /ˌlɪpə(ʊ)ˈfɪlɪk, ˌlʌɪ-/ ▸ **adjective** Biochemistry tending to combine with or dissolve in lipids or fats.

lipopolysaccharide /ˌlɪpəʊpɒlɪˈsakərʌɪd, ˌlʌɪ-/ ▸ **noun** Biochemistry a complex molecule containing both lipid and polysaccharide parts.

lipoprotein ▸ **noun** Biochemistry any of a group of soluble proteins that combine with and transport fat or other lipids in the blood plasma.

liposculpture /ˈlɪpə(ʊ)ˌskʌlptʃə, ˈlʌɪ-/ ▸ **noun** [mass noun] the use of liposuction to accentuate specific bodily features.

liposome /ˈlɪpəsəʊm, ˈlʌɪ-/ ▸ **noun** Biochemistry a minute spherical sac of phospholipid molecules enclosing a water droplet, especially as formed artificially to carry drugs or other substances into the tissues.

liposuction /ˈlɪpə(ʊ)ˌsʌkʃ(ə)n, ˈlʌɪ-/ ▸ **noun** [mass noun] a technique in cosmetic surgery for removing excess fat from under the skin by suction.

lipotropin /ˌlɪpəʊˈtrəʊpɪn, ˌlʌɪ-/ (also **lipotrophin** /-ˈtrəʊfɪn/) ▸ **noun** Biochemistry a hormone secreted by the anterior pituitary gland which promotes the release of fat reserves from the liver into the bloodstream.

Lippes loop /ˈlɪpɪz/ ▸ **noun** a type of intrauterine contraceptive device made of inert plastic in a double S-shape, which can be inserted for long periods.
– ORIGIN 1960s: named after Jack *Lippes* (born 1924), American obstetrician.

Lippi[1] /ˈlɪpi/, Filippino (*c.*1457–1504), Italian painter, son of Fra Filippo Lippi. Having trained with his father and Botticelli he completed a fresco cycle begun by Masaccio in the Brancacci Chapel, Florence; other works include the series of frescoes in the Carafa Chapel in Rome and the painting *The Vision of St Bernard* (*c.*1486).

L

Lippi² /ˈlɪpi/, Fra Filippo (*c.*1406–69), Italian painter. He was a pupil of Masaccio, whose influence can be seen in the fresco *The Relaxation of the Carmelite Rule* (*c.*1432); his later style is more decorative and less monumental than his early work.

Lippizaner ▶ noun variant spelling of LIPIZZANER.

lippy informal ▶ adjective (**lippier**, **lippiest**) insolent or impertinent.
▶ noun (also **lippie**) [mass noun] lipstick.

lip-read ▶ verb [no obj.] (of a deaf person) understand speech from observing a speaker's lip movements.
– DERIVATIVES **lip-reader** noun.

lipsalve ▶ noun [mass noun] Brit. a preparation, typically in stick form, to prevent or relieve sore lips.

lipslide ▶ noun (in skateboarding and snowboarding) a manoeuvre in which the board slides along a rail, ledge, edge of a ramp, etc. on the underside of the lip of the board at either the front or the back.

lipstick ▶ noun [mass noun] coloured cosmetic applied to the lips from a small solid stick.

lipstick lesbian ▶ noun informal a lesbian who favours a glamorous, traditionally feminine style.

lip-sync (also **lip-synch**) ▶ verb [no obj.] (of an actor or singer) move the lips silently in synchronization with a pre-recorded soundtrack.
– DERIVATIVES **lip-syncer** noun.

liquate /lɪˈkweɪt/ ▶ verb [with obj.] Metallurgy separate or purify (a metal) by melting it.
– DERIVATIVES **liquation** noun.
– ORIGIN mid 19th cent.: from Latin *liquat-* 'made liquid', from the verb *liquare*; related to LIQUOR.

liquefied petroleum gas (abbrev.: **LPG**) ▶ noun [mass noun] a mixture of light gaseous hydrocarbons (ethane, propane, butane, etc.) made liquid by pressure and used as fuel.

liquefy /ˈlɪkwɪfʌɪ/ (also **liquify**) ▶ verb (**liquefies**, **liquefying**, **liquefied**) make or become liquid: [with obj.] *the minimum pressure required to liquefy a gas* | [no obj.] *as the fungus ripens, the cap turns black and liquefies.*
– DERIVATIVES **liquefaction** noun, **liquefactive** adjective, **liquefiable** adjective, **liquefier** noun.
– ORIGIN late Middle English: from French *liquéfier* from Latin *liquefacere* 'make liquid', from *liquere* 'be liquid'.

liquescent /lɪˈkwɛs(ə)nt/ ▶ adjective literary becoming or apt to become liquid.
– ORIGIN early 18th cent.: from Latin *liquescent-* 'becoming liquid', from the verb *liquescere* (see LIQUEFY).

liqueur /lɪˈkjʊə/ ▶ noun a strong, sweet flavoured alcoholic spirit, usually drunk after a meal. ■ a chocolate with a liqueur filling: *a box of liqueurs.*
– ORIGIN mid 18th cent.: from French, 'liquor'.

liquid ▶ noun **1** a substance that flows freely but is of constant volume, having a consistency like that of water or oil: *drink plenty of liquids* | [mass noun] *washing-up liquid.*
2 Phonetics a consonant produced by allowing the airstream to flow over the sides of the tongue, typically *l* and *r* (in British English pronunciation).
▶ adjective **1** having the consistency of a liquid: *liquid fertilizer* | *liquid refreshments.* ■ having the translucence of water; clear: *looking into those liquid dark eyes.* ■ denoting a substance normally a gas that has been liquefied by cold or pressure: *liquid oxygen.* ■ not fixed or stable; fluid.
2 (of a sound) clear, pure, and flowing; harmonious: *the liquid song of the birds.*
3 (of assets) held in cash or easily converted into cash. ■ having ready cash or liquid assets. ■ (of a market) having a high volume of activity.
– DERIVATIVES **liquidly** adverb, **liquidness** noun.
– ORIGIN late Middle English: from Latin *liquidus*, from *liquere* 'be liquid'.

liquidambar /ˌlɪkwɪdˈambə/ ▶ noun a deciduous North American and Asian tree with maple-like leaves and bright autumn colours, yielding aromatic resinous balsam. ● Genus *Liquidambar*, family Hamamelidaceae: several species, including *L. orientalis* of Asia, which yields Levant storax, and the sweet gum of North America.
■ [mass noun] liquid balsam obtained chiefly from the Asian liquidambar tree, used medicinally and in perfume. Also called STORAX.
– ORIGIN late 16th cent.: modern Latin, apparently formed irregularly from Latin *liquidus* 'liquid' + medieval Latin *ambar* 'amber'.

liquidate ▶ verb [with obj.] **1** wind up the affairs of (a business) by ascertaining liabilities and apportioning assets. ■ [no obj.] (of a business) undergo such a process. ■ convert (assets) into cash: *a plan to liquidate £1 billion worth of property over seven years.* ■ pay off (a debt).
2 informal kill (someone), typically by violent means: *nationalist rivals and critics were liquidated in bloody purges.*
– ORIGIN mid 16th cent. (in the sense 'set out (accounts) clearly'): from medieval Latin *liquidat-* 'made clear', from the verb *liquidare*, from Latin *liquidus* (see LIQUID). Sense 1 was influenced by Italian *liquidare* and French *liquider*, sense 2 by Russian *likvidirovat'*.

liquidation ▶ noun [mass noun] **1** the process of liquidating a business: *the company **went into liquidation**.* ■ the conversion of assets into cash (i.e. by selling them). ■ the clearing of a debt.
2 informal the killing of someone, typically by violent means.
– ORIGIN mid 16th cent.: from French, from *liquider* 'liquidate', based on Latin *liquidus* (see LIQUID).

liquidator ▶ noun a person appointed to wind up the affairs of a company or firm.

liquid crystal ▶ noun a substance which flows like a liquid but has some degree of ordering in the arrangement of its molecules.

liquid crystal display (abbrev.: **LCD**) ▶ noun a form of visual display used in electronic devices, in which a layer of a liquid crystal is sandwiched between two transparent electrodes.

liquidity /lɪˈkwɪdɪti/ ▶ noun [mass noun] Finance the availability of liquid assets to a market or company. ■ liquid assets; cash. ■ a high volume of activity in a market.
– ORIGIN early 17th cent.: from French *liquidité* or medieval Latin *liquiditas*, from Latin *liquidus* (see LIQUID).

liquidity preference ▶ noun [mass noun] Economics (in Keynesian theory) the preference of investors for holding liquid assets rather than securities or long-term interest-bearing investments.

liquidity ratio ▶ noun Finance the ratio between the liquid assets and the liabilities of a bank or other institution.

liquidize (also **liquidise**) ▶ verb [with obj.] Brit. convert (solid food) into a liquid or purée, typically by using a liquidizer: *liquidize the soup until quite smooth.*

liquidizer (also **liquidiser**) ▶ noun Brit. a machine for liquidizing food or other material.

liquid lunch ▶ noun informal, humorous a drinking session at lunchtime taking the place of a meal.

liquid measure ▶ noun a unit for measuring the volume of liquids.

liquid paraffin ▶ noun [mass noun] chiefly Brit. a colourless, odourless oily liquid consisting of a mixture of hydrocarbons obtained from petroleum, used as a laxative.

liquid storax ▶ noun see STORAX (sense 1).

liquify ▶ verb variant spelling of LIQUEFY.

liquor /ˈlɪkə/ ▶ noun [mass noun] **1** alcoholic drink, especially distilled spirits.
2 a liquid produced or used in a process, in particular: ■ liquid in which something has been steeped or cooked. ■ liquid which drains from food during cooking. ■ the liquid from which a substance has been crystallized or extracted. ■ water used in brewing.
▶ verb [with obj.] **1** dress (leather) with grease or oil.
2 steep (something, especially malt) in water.
– PHRASAL VERBS **be/get liquored up** N. Amer. informal be or get drunk.
– ORIGIN Middle English (denoting liquid or something to drink): from Old French *lic(o)ur*, from Latin *liquor*; related to *liquare* 'liquefy', *liquere* 'be fluid'.

liquorice /ˈlɪk(ə)rɪʃ, -rɪs/ (US **licorice**) ▶ noun **1** [mass noun] a sweet, chewy, aromatic black substance made by evaporation from the juice of a root and used as a sweet and in medicine. ■ a sweet flavoured with liquorice.
2 the widely distributed plant of the pea family from which liquorice is obtained. ● Genus *Glycyrrhiza*, family Leguminosae; many species are used locally to obtain liquorice, the chief commercial source being the cultivated *G. glabra*.
– ORIGIN Middle English: from Old French *licoresse*, from late Latin *liquiritia*, from Greek *glukurrhiza*, from *glukus* 'sweet' + *rhiza* 'root'.

liquorish /ˈlɪkərɪʃ/ ▶ adjective **1** archaic form of LICKERISH.
2 fond of or indicating a fondness for alcoholic drink.

lira /ˈlɪərə/ ▶ noun (pl. **lire** /ˈlɪərə, ˈlɪəreɪ, ˈlɪəri/) **1** (until the introduction of the euro in 2002) the basic monetary unit of Italy, notionally equal to 100 centesimos.
2 the basic monetary unit of Turkey, equal to 100 kurus.
– ORIGIN Italian, from Provençal *liura*, from Latin *libra* 'pound'.

liriodendron /ˌlɪrɪə(ʊ)ˈdɛndrɒn/ ▶ noun a tree of a small genus which includes the tulip tree. ● Genus *Liriodendron*, family Magnoliaceae.
– ORIGIN modern Latin, from Greek *leirion* 'lily' + *dendron* 'tree'.

liripipe /ˈlɪrɪpʌɪp/ ▶ noun a long tail hanging from the back of a hood, especially in medieval or academic dress.
– ORIGIN early 17th cent.: from medieval Latin *liripipium* 'tippet of a hood, cord', of unknown origin.

lis¹ /lɪs/ ▶ noun (pl. **same** or **lisses**) short for FLEUR-DE-LIS.

lis² /lɪs/ ▶ noun Law a lawsuit. See also LIS PENDENS.
– ORIGIN mid 18th cent.: from Latin *lis* 'dispute'.

lis alibi pendens /lɪs ˌalɪbʌɪ ˈpɛndɛnz/ ▶ noun Law a lawsuit pending elsewhere.
– ORIGIN Latin.

Lisbon /ˈlɪzbən/ the capital and chief port of Portugal, on the Atlantic coast at the mouth of the River Tagus; pop. 499,700 (2007). Portuguese name **Lisboa** /lɪʒˈbəʊə/.

Lisburn /ˈlɪzbəːn/ a city in Northern Ireland, to the south-west of Belfast, on the border between Antrim and Down; pop. 83,200 (est. 2009).

Lisdoonvarna /ˌlɪsduːnˈvɑːnə/ a spa town in the Republic of Ireland, in County Clare; pop. 767 (2006).

lisente plural form of SENTE.

-lish ▶ suffix forming nouns denoting a blend of a particular language with English, as used by native speakers of the first language: *Japlish.*

lisle /lʌɪl/ (also **lisle thread**) ▶ noun [mass noun] a fine, smooth cotton thread used especially for stockings.
– ORIGIN mid 16th cent.: from *Lisle*, former spelling of LILLE, the original place of manufacture.

Lisp ▶ noun [mass noun] a high-level computer programming language devised for list processing.
– ORIGIN 1950s: from *lis(t) p(rocessor)*.

lisp ▶ noun a speech defect in which *s* is pronounced like *th* in *thick* and *z* is pronounced like *th* in *this*.
▶ verb [no obj.] speak with a lisp.
– DERIVATIVES **lisper** noun, **lisping** adjective, **lispingly** adverb.
– ORIGIN Old English *wlispian* (recorded in *āwlyspian*), from *wlisp* (adjective) 'lisping', of imitative origin; compare with Dutch *lispen* and German *lispeln*.

lis pendens /lɪs ˈpɛndɛnz/ ▶ noun Law a pending legal action, or a formal notice of one.
– ORIGIN Latin.

Lissajous figure /ˈlɪsaʒuː/ ▶ noun Mathematics any of a number of characteristic looped or curved figures traced out by a point undergoing two independent simple harmonic motions at right angles with frequencies in a simple ratio.
– ORIGIN late 19th cent.: named after Jules A. Lissajous (1822–80), French physicist.

lissom (also **lissome**) ▶ adjective (of a person or their body) thin, supple, and graceful: *the kind of outfit that should be left to lissom teenagers.*
– DERIVATIVES **lissomness** noun.
– ORIGIN late 18th cent.: contraction, from LITHE + -SOME¹.

list¹ ▶ noun **1** a number of connected items or names written or printed consecutively, typically one below the other: *consult the list of drugs on page 326* | figurative *if you're buying a new car, put security high on your list of priorities.* ■ Computing a formal structure analogous to a list, by which items of data can be stored or processed in a definite order.
2 (**lists**) historical palisades enclosing an area for a tournament. ■ the scene of a contest or combat.
3 a selvedge of a piece of fabric.
▶ verb **1** [with obj.] make a list of: *I have listed four reasons below.* ■ include or enter in a list: *local offices are listed in the phone book.* ■ [no obj.] (**list at/for**) be on a list of products at (a specified price): *the bottom-of-the-line Mercedes lists for $52,050.* ■ give (a building, company, etc.) listed status.
2 [no obj.] archaic enlist for military service.
– PHRASES **enter the lists** issue or accept a challenge.
– DERIVATIVES **listable** adjective.

L

– ORIGIN Middle English (in sense 3 of the noun): from Old English *liste* 'border', of Germanic origin; related to Dutch *lijst* and German *Leiste*. Sense 2 of the noun is late Middle English, from Old French *lisse*; sense 1 of the noun is late 16th cent., from French *liste*, of Germanic origin.

list[2] ▶ **verb** [no obj.] (of a ship) lean over to one side, typically because of a leak or unbalanced cargo. Compare with HEEL[2].
▶ **noun** an instance of a ship listing to one side.
– ORIGIN early 17th cent.: of unknown origin.

list[3] archaic ▶ **verb** [no obj.] want; like: [with clause] *let them think what they list.*
▶ **noun** [mass noun] desire or inclination: *I have little list to write.*
– ORIGIN Old English *lystan* (verb), of Germanic origin, from a base meaning 'pleasure'.

list box ▶ **noun** Computing a box on the screen that contains a list of options, only one of which can be selected.

list broking ▶ **noun** [mass noun] trading in mailing lists for marketing or publicity by direct mail.
– DERIVATIVES **list broker** noun.

listed ▶ **adjective 1** (of a building in the UK) officially designated as being of architectural or historical importance and having protection from demolition or major alterations.
2 relating to or denoting companies whose shares are quoted on the main market of the London Stock Exchange. *listed securities.*

listel /ˈlɪstəl/ ▶ **noun** Architecture a narrow flat strip between mouldings; a fillet.
– ORIGIN late 16th cent.: from Italian *listello*, diminutive of *lista* 'strip, band'.

listen ▶ **verb** [no obj.] give one's attention to a sound: *evidently he was not listening* | *sit and listen to the radio.* ■ take notice of and act on what someone says; respond to advice or a request: *I told her over and over again, but she wouldn't listen.* ■ **(listen for** or **listen out for)** make an effort to hear something; be alert and ready to hear something: *they listened for sounds from the baby's room.* ■ (also N. Amer. **listen up**) [in imperative] used to urge someone to pay attention to what one is going to say: *listen, I've had an idea.*
▶ **noun** [in sing.] an act of listening to something.
– PHRASAL VERBS **listen in** listen to a private conversation, especially secretly. ■ use a radio receiving set to listen to a broadcast or conversation.
– ORIGIN Old English *hlysnan* 'pay attention to', of Germanic origin.

listenable ▶ **adjective** easy or pleasant to listen to: *all the tracks prove eminently listenable.*
– DERIVATIVES **listenability** noun.

listener ▶ **noun** a person who listens, especially someone who does so in an attentive manner. ■ a person listening to a radio station or programme.
– DERIVATIVES **listenership** noun.

listening post ▶ **noun** a station for intercepting electronic communications. ■ a point near an enemy's lines for detecting movements by sound.

Lister, Joseph, 1st Baron (1827–1912), English surgeon, inventor of antiseptic techniques in surgery. He realized the significance of Louis Pasteur's germ theory in connection with sepsis and in 1865 he used carbolic acid dressings on patients who had undergone surgery.

lister ▶ **noun** US a plough with a double mouldboard.
– ORIGIN late 19th cent.: from LIST[1] in the late 18th-cent. sense 'prepare land for a crop' + -ER[1].

listeria /lɪˈstɪərɪə/ ▶ **noun** [mass noun] a type of bacterium which infects humans and other warm-blooded animals through contaminated food. ● *Listeria monocytogenes*; motile aerobic Gram-positive rods.
■ informal food poisoning or other disease caused by infection with listeria; listeriosis.
– ORIGIN 1940s: modern Latin, named after Joseph LISTER.

listeriosis /lɪˌstɪərɪˈəʊsɪs/ ▶ **noun** [mass noun] disease caused by infection with listeria, which can resemble influenza or meningitis and may cause miscarriage.

listing ▶ **noun 1** a list or catalogue. ■ [mass noun] the drawing up of a list. ■ an entry in a list or register. ■ an entry for a company in the Official List of Securities of the London Stock Exchange, for which certain requirements must be satisfied.
2 a selvedge of a piece of fabric.

listless ▶ **adjective** (of a person or their manner) lacking energy or enthusiasm: *bouts of listless depression.*
– DERIVATIVES **listlessly** adverb, **listlessness** noun.
– ORIGIN Middle English: from LIST[3] + -LESS.

Liston /ˈlɪst(ə)n/, Sonny (1932–70), American boxer; born *Charles Liston*. In 1962 he became world heavyweight champion but in 1964 lost his title to Muhammad Ali (then Cassius Clay).

list price ▶ **noun** the price of an article as shown in a list issued by the manufacturer.

list processing ▶ **noun** [mass noun] Computing the manipulation of data organized as lists.

LISTSERV ▶ **noun** [mass noun] trademark an electronic mailing list of people who wish to receive information about or discuss a specific topic. ■ [count noun] (**listserv**) any similar application.

list system ▶ **noun** a system of voting (used in several European countries) in which votes are cast for a list of candidates rather than an individual, to allow a degree of proportional representation.

Liszt /lɪst/, Franz (1811–86), Hungarian composer and pianist. He was a key figure in the romantic movement; many of his piano compositions combine lyricism with great technical complexity, while his twelve symphonic poems (1848–58) created a new musical form.
– DERIVATIVES **Lisztian** adjective & noun.

lit[1] past and past participle of LIGHT[1], LIGHT[3].

lit[2] ▶ **noun** short for LITERATURE: *chick lit.*

Li T'ai Po /ˌliː tʌɪ ˈpəʊ/ variant of LI PO.

litany /ˈlɪt(ə)ni/ ▶ **noun** (pl. **litanies**) **1** a series of petitions for use in church services or processions, usually recited by the clergy and responded to in a recurring formula by the people. ■ **(the Litany)** such petitions and responses contained in the Book of Common Prayer.
2 a tedious recital or repetitive series: *a litany of complaints.*
– ORIGIN Middle English: from Old French *letanie*, via ecclesiastical Latin from Greek *litaneia* 'prayer', from *litē* 'supplication'.

litas /ˈliːtas/ ▶ **noun** (pl. **same**) the basic monetary unit of Lithuania, equal to 100 centas.
– ORIGIN Lithuanian.

litchi ▶ **noun** variant spelling of LYCHEE.

lit. crit. ▶ **abbreviation** literary criticism.

lite ▶ **adjective** denoting a low-fat or low-sugar version of a manufactured food or drink product: *lite beer.* ■ informal denoting a simpler or less challenging version of a particular thing or person: *I am the happy feminist who likes men, the feminist lite.*
▶ **noun** [mass noun] light beer with relatively few calories.
– ORIGIN 1950s: a commercial respelling of LIGHT[1], LIGHT[2].

-lite ▶ **suffix** forming names of rocks, minerals, and fossils: *rhyolite* | *zeolite.*
– ORIGIN from French, from Greek *lithos* 'stone'.

liter ▶ **noun** US spelling of LITRE.

literacy ▶ **noun** [mass noun] the ability to read and write. ■ competence or knowledge in a specified area: *computer literacy is essential.*
– ORIGIN late 19th cent.: from LITERATE, on the pattern of *illiteracy*.

literacy hour ▶ **noun** a period in school set aside for developing reading skills, introduced as a daily requirement in English primary schools in 1998.

Literae Humaniores /ˌlɪtərʌɪ hjuːˌmanɪˈɔːriːz/ ▶ **plural noun** [treated as sing.] the honours course in classics, philosophy, and ancient history at Oxford University.
– ORIGIN Latin, literally 'the more humane studies'.

literal ▶ **adjective 1** taking words in their usual or most basic sense without metaphor or exaggeration: *dreadful in its literal sense, full of dread.* ■ free from exaggeration or distortion: *you shouldn't take this as a literal record of events.* ■ informal absolute (used to emphasize that a strong expression is deliberately chosen to convey one's feelings): *fifteen years of literal hell.*
2 (of a translation) representing the exact words of the original text. ■ (of a visual representation) exactly copied; realistic as opposed to abstract or impressionistic.
3 (also **literal-minded**) (of a person or performance) lacking imagination; prosaic.
4 of, in, or expressed by a letter or the letters of the alphabet: *literal mnemonics.*
▶ **noun** Printing, Brit. a misprint of a letter.
– DERIVATIVES **literality** noun, **literalize** (also **literalise**) verb, **literalness** noun.
– ORIGIN late Middle English: from Old French, or from late Latin *litteralis*, from Latin *littera* (see LETTER).

literalism ▶ **noun** [mass noun] the interpretation of words in their literal sense: *biblical literalism.* ■ literal representation in literature or art.
– DERIVATIVES **literalist** noun, **literalistic** adjective.

literally ▶ **adverb** in a literal manner or sense; exactly: *the driver **took it literally** when asked to go straight over the roundabout* | *tiramisu, literally translated 'pull-me-up'.* ■ informal used for emphasis while not being literally true: *I have received literally thousands of letters.*

> **USAGE** In its standard use **literally** means 'in a literal sense, as opposed to a non-literal or exaggerated sense', as for example in *I told him I never wanted to see him again, but I didn't expect him to take it **literally**.* In recent years an extended use of **literally** (and also **literal**) has become very common, where **literally** (or **literal**) is used deliberately in non-literal contexts, for added effect, as in *they bought the car and **literally** ran it into the ground.* This use can lead to unintentional humorous effects (*we were **literally** killing ourselves laughing*) and is not acceptable in formal contexts, though it is widespread.

literary ▶ **adjective 1** [attrib.] concerning the writing, study, or content of literature, especially of the kind valued for quality of form: *the great literary works of the nineteenth century.* ■ concerned with literature as a profession: *the newspaper's literary editor.*
2 (of language) associated with literary works or other formal writing; having a marked style intended to create a particular emotional effect.
– DERIVATIVES **literarily** adverb, **literariness** noun.
– ORIGIN mid 17th cent. (in the sense 'relating to the letters of the alphabet'): from Latin *litterarius*, from *littera* (see LETTER).

literary agent ▶ **noun** a professional agent who acts on behalf of an author in dealing with publishers and others involved in promoting the author's work.

literary criticism ▶ **noun** [mass noun] the art or practice of judging and commenting on the qualities and character of literary works.
– DERIVATIVES **literary critic** noun.

literary executor ▶ **noun** a person entrusted with a dead writer's papers and copyrighted and unpublished works.

literary history ▶ **noun** [mass noun] the history of the treatment of, and references to, a particular subject in literature: *lesbian literary history.*
– DERIVATIVES **literary historian** noun.

literate ▶ **adjective** able to read and write. ■ having education or knowledge, typically in a specified area: *we need people who are economically and politically literate.*
▶ **noun** a literate person.
– DERIVATIVES **literately** adverb.
– ORIGIN late Middle English: from Latin *litteratus*, from *littera* (see LETTER).

literati /ˌlɪtəˈrɑːtiː/ ▶ **plural noun** well-educated people who are interested in literature.
– ORIGIN early 17th cent.: from Latin, plural of *literatus* 'acquainted with letters', from *littera* (see LETTER).

literatim /ˌlɪtəˈrɑːtɪm, -ˈreɪtɪm/ ▶ **adverb** formal (of the copying of a text) letter by letter.
– ORIGIN from medieval Latin.

literature ▶ **noun** [mass noun] written works, especially those considered of superior or lasting artistic merit: *a great work of literature.* ■ books and writings published on a particular subject: *the **literature** on environmental epidemiology.* ■ leaflets and other printed matter used to advertise products or give advice.
– ORIGIN late Middle English (in the sense 'knowledge of books'): via French from Latin *litteratura*, from *littera* (see LETTER).

lith ▶ **noun** [mass noun] photographic film with a very thin coat of emulsion, producing images of high contrast and density.
– ORIGIN 1950s: abbreviation of LITHOGRAPHY, LITHOGRAPHIC.

-lith ▶ **suffix** denoting types of stone: *laccolith* | *monolith.*
– ORIGIN from Greek *lithos* 'stone'.

litharge /ˈlɪθɑːdʒ/ ▶ **noun** [mass noun] lead monoxide, especially a red form used as a pigment and in glass and ceramics. ● Chem. formula: PbO.
– ORIGIN Middle English: from Old French *litarge*, via Latin from Greek *litharguros*, from *lithos* 'stone' + *arguros* 'silver'.

lithe ▶ **adjective** (especially of a person's body) thin, supple, and graceful: *she lay gazing up at his tall, lithe figure.*
– DERIVATIVES **lithely** adverb, **litheness** noun.

L

– ORIGIN Old English *lithe* 'gentle, meek' also 'mellow', of Germanic origin; related to German *lind* 'soft, gentle'.

lithesome ▸ adjective another term for LITHE.

lithia /ˈlɪθɪə/ ▸ noun [mass noun] Chemistry lithium oxide, a white alkaline solid. • Chem. formula: Li_2O.
– ORIGIN early 19th cent.: modern Latin, alteration of earlier *lithion*, from Greek, neuter of *litheios*, from *lithos* 'stone', on the pattern of words such as *soda*.

lithiasis /lɪˈθʌɪəsɪs/ ▸ noun [mass noun] Medicine the formation of stony concretions (calculi) in the body, most often in the gall bladder or urinary system.
– ORIGIN mid 17th cent.: from medieval Latin, based on Greek *lithos* 'stone'.

lithic /ˈlɪθɪk/ ▸ adjective **1** chiefly Archaeology & Geology of the nature of or relating to stone.
2 Medicine, dated relating to calculi.
– ORIGIN late 18th cent.: from Greek *lithikos*, from *lithos* 'stone'.

lithify /ˈlɪθɪfʌɪ/ ▸ verb (**lithifies**, **lithifying**, **lithified**) [with obj.] chiefly Geology transform (a sediment or other material) into stone.
– DERIVATIVES **lithification** noun.
– ORIGIN late 19th cent.: from Greek *lithos* 'stone' + -FY.

lithium /ˈlɪθɪəm/ ▸ noun [mass noun] the chemical element of atomic number 3, a soft silver-white metal. It is the lightest of the alkali metals. (Symbol: **Li**)
■ lithium carbonate or another lithium salt, used as a mood-stabilizing drug.
– ORIGIN early 19th cent.: from LITHIA + -IUM.

litho /ˈlʌɪθəʊ, ˈlɪθ-/ informal ▸ noun (pl. **lithos**) short for LITHOGRAPHY or LITHOGRAPH.
▸ adjective short for LITHOGRAPHIC.
▸ verb (**lithoes**, **lithoing**, **lithoed**) short for LITHOGRAPH.

litho- ▸ combining form **1** relating to stone: *lithosol*.
2 relating to a calculus: *lithotomy*.
– ORIGIN from Greek *lithos* 'stone'.

lithograph /ˈlɪθəgrɑːf, ˈlʌɪ-/ ▸ noun a lithographic print.
▸ verb [with obj.] print by lithography: (as adj. **lithographed**) *a set of lithographed drawings*.
– ORIGIN early 19th cent.: back-formation from LITHOGRAPHY.

lithographic ▸ adjective relating to or produced by lithography: *lithographic prints*.
– DERIVATIVES **lithographically** adverb.

lithographic limestone ▸ noun [mass noun] a compact fine-grained yellowish limestone used in lithography. It sometimes contains finely preserved Upper Jurassic fossils.

lithography /lɪˈθɒgrəfi/ ▸ noun [mass noun] the process of printing from a flat surface treated so as to repel the ink except where it is required for printing.
■ Electronics a method analogous to lithography, used in making printed circuits.

> The earliest forms of lithography used greasy ink to form an image on a piece of limestone which was then etched with acid and treated with gum arabic. In a modern press, rollers transfer ink to a thin aluminium plate wrapped round a cylinder. In **offset lithography** the image is transferred to an intermediate rubber-covered cylinder before being printed.

– DERIVATIVES **lithographer** noun.
– ORIGIN early 19th cent.: from German *Lithographie* (see LITHO-, -GRAPHY).

lithology /lɪˈθɒlədʒi/ ▸ noun [mass noun] the study of the general physical characteristics of rocks. Compare with PETROLOGY. ■ the general physical characteristics of a rock or the rocks in a particular area: *the lithology of South Wales*.
– DERIVATIVES **lithologic** adjective, **lithological** adjective, **lithologically** adverb.

lithophane /ˈlɪθəfeɪn, ˈlʌɪ-/ ▸ noun [mass noun] a kind of ornamentation of porcelain visible when held to the light, produced by pressing designs into it when soft. ■ [count noun] an object with such a decoration.
– ORIGIN 1940s: from Greek *lithos* 'stone' + *-phanēs* 'appearing'.

lithophyte /ˈlɪθə(ʊ)fʌɪt, ˈlʌɪ-/ ▸ noun Botany a plant that grows on bare rock or stone.

lithopone /ˈlɪθəpəʊn/ ▸ noun [mass noun] a white pigment made from zinc sulphide and barium sulphate.
– ORIGIN late 19th cent.: from LITHO- 'stone, crystals' + Greek *ponos* '(thing) produced by work'.

lithosol /ˈlɪθəsɒl/ ▸ noun Soil Science a thin soil consisting mainly of partially weathered rock fragments.

lithosphere /ˈlɪθəsfɪə/ ▸ noun Geology the rigid outer part of the earth, consisting of the crust and upper mantle.
– DERIVATIVES **lithospheric** adjective.

lithotomy /lɪˈθɒtəmi/ ▸ noun [mass noun] surgical removal of a calculus (stone) from the bladder, kidney, or urinary tract.
– DERIVATIVES **lithotomist** noun.
– ORIGIN mid 17th cent.: via late Latin from Greek *lithotomia* (see LITHO-, -TOMY).

lithotomy position ▸ noun a supine position of the body with the legs separated, flexed, and supported in raised stirrups, originally used for lithotomy and later also for childbirth.

lithotomy stirrups ▸ plural noun see STIRRUP (sense 2).

lithotripsy /ˈlɪθəˌtrɪpsi/ ▸ noun [mass noun] Surgery a treatment, typically using ultrasound shock waves, by which a kidney stone or other calculus is broken into small particles that can be passed out by the body.
– DERIVATIVES **lithotripter** (also **lithotriptor**) noun, **lithotriptic** adjective.
– ORIGIN mid 19th cent.: from LITHO- 'of stone' + Greek *tripsis* 'rubbing', from *tribein* 'to rub'.

lithotrity /lɪˈθɒtrɪti/ ▸ noun [mass noun] Surgery a surgical procedure involving the mechanical breaking down of gallstones or other calculi.
– ORIGIN early 19th cent.: from LITHO- 'of stone' + Latin *tritor* 'thing that rubs' + -Y[3].

Lithuania /ˌlɪθ(j)uːˈeɪnɪə/ a country on the SE shore of the Baltic sea; pop. 3,555,200 (est. 2009); languages, Lithuanian (official), Russian; capital, Vilnius.

> Lithuania was absorbed into the Russian empire in 1795, having been united with Poland since 1386. It was declared an independent republic in 1918, but in 1940 was annexed by the Soviet Union as a constituent republic. In 1991, on the break-up of the USSR, Lithuania became an independent republic once again.

Lithuanian ▸ adjective relating to Lithuania or its people or language.
▸ noun **1** a native or citizen of Lithuania, or a person of Lithuanian descent.
2 [mass noun] the language of Lithuania, which belongs to the Baltic branch of the Indo-European family and has about 3.5 million speakers.

litie ▸ noun variant spelling of LIGHTY.

litigant ▸ noun a person involved in a lawsuit.
▸ adjective [postpositive] archaic involved in a lawsuit: *the parties litigant*.
– ORIGIN mid 17th cent.: from French, from Latin *litigant-* 'carrying on a lawsuit', from the verb *litigare* (see LITIGATE).

litigate /ˈlɪtɪgeɪt/ ▸ verb [no obj.] resort to legal action to settle a matter; be involved in a lawsuit. ■ [with obj.] take (a claim or a dispute) to a law court.
– DERIVATIVES **litigator** noun.
– ORIGIN early 17th cent.: from Latin *litigat-* 'disputed in a lawsuit', from the verb *litigare*, from *lis*, *lit-* 'lawsuit'.

litigation /lɪtɪˈgeɪʃ(ə)n/ ▸ noun [mass noun] the process of taking legal action: *the company wishes to avoid litigation*.

litigious /lɪˈtɪdʒəs/ ▸ adjective tending or too ready to take legal action to settle disputes: *our increasingly litigious society*. ■ concerned with lawsuits or litigation. ■ suitable to become the subject of a lawsuit.
– DERIVATIVES **litigiously** adverb, **litigiousness** noun.
– ORIGIN late Middle English: from Old French *litigieux* or Latin *litigiosus* from *litigium* 'litigation', from *lis*, *lit-* 'lawsuit'.

litmus /ˈlɪtməs/ ▸ noun [mass noun] a dye obtained from certain lichens that is red under acid conditions and blue under alkaline conditions.
– ORIGIN Middle English: from Old Norse *lit-mosi*, from *litr* 'dye' + *mosi* 'moss'.

litmus paper ▸ noun paper stained with litmus which is used to indicate the acidity or alkalinity of a substance.

litmus test ▸ noun **1** Chemistry a test for acidity or alkalinity using litmus.
2 a decisively indicative test: *effectiveness in these areas is often a good litmus test of overall quality*.

litoptern /lɪˈtɒptəːn/ ▸ noun an extinct South American hoofed mammal resembling a horse or camel, found from the Palaeocene to the Pleistocene epochs. • Order Litopterna: several families.
– ORIGIN early 20th cent.: from modern Latin *Litopterna*, from Greek *litos* 'smooth' + *pternē* 'heel bone'.

litotes /lʌɪˈtəʊtiːz/ ▸ noun [mass noun] ironical understatement in which an affirmative is expressed by the negative of its contrary (e.g. *I shan't be sorry* for *I shall be glad*).
– ORIGIN late 16th cent.: via late Latin from Greek *litotēs*, from *litos* 'plain, meagre'.

litre (US **liter**) (abbrev.: **l**) ▸ noun a metric unit of capacity, formerly defined as the volume of one kilogram of water under standard conditions, now equal to 1,000 cubic centimetres (about 1.75 pints).
– DERIVATIVES **litreage** /ˈliːt(ə)rɪdʒ/ noun.
– ORIGIN late 18th cent.: from French, alteration of *litron* (an obsolete measure of capacity), via medieval Latin from Greek *litra*, a Sicilian monetary unit.

LittD ▸ abbreviation Doctor of Letters.
– ORIGIN from Latin *Litterarum Doctor*.

litter ▸ noun **1** [mass noun] rubbish such as paper, tins, and bottles left lying in an open or public place: *always clear up after a picnic and never drop litter* | [as modifier] *a litter bin*. ■ [in sing.] an untidy collection of things lying about: *a litter of sleeping bags on the floor*.
2 a number of young animals born to an animal at one time: *a litter of five kittens*.
3 (also **cat litter**) [mass noun] granular absorbent material lining a tray in which a cat can urinate and defecate when indoors.
4 [mass noun] straw or other plant matter used as bedding for animals. ■ (also **leaf litter**) decomposing but recognizable leaves and other debris forming a layer on top of the soil, especially in forests.
5 historical a structure used to transport people, containing a bed or seat enclosed by curtains and carried on men's shoulders or by animals. ■ a framework with a couch for transporting the sick and wounded.
▸ verb [with obj.] **1** make (a place or area) untidy with rubbish or a large number of objects left lying about: *clothes and newspapers littered the floor* | *the sitting room was **littered with** books*. ■ [with obj. and adverbial] leave (rubbish or a number of objects) lying untidily in a place: *there was broken glass littered about*.
■ (usu. **be littered with**) fill with examples of a particular thing, typically something bad or unpleasant: *news pages have been littered with doom and gloom about company collapses*.
2 archaic provide (a horse or other animal) with litter as bedding.
– ORIGIN Middle English (in sense 5 of the noun): from Old French *litiere*, from medieval Latin *lectaria*, from Latin *lectus* 'bed'. Sense 1 dates from the mid 18th cent.

littérateur /ˌlɪtərɑːˈtəː/ ▸ noun a person who is interested in and knowledgeable about literature.
– ORIGIN early 19th cent.: French.

litterbug (Brit. also **litter lout**) ▸ noun informal a person who carelessly drops litter in a public place.

little ▸ adjective small in size, amount, or degree (often used to convey an appealing diminutiveness or express an affectionate or condescending attitude): *the plants will grow into little bushes* | *a little puppy dog* | *a boring little man*. ■ (of a person) young or younger: *my little brother* | *when she was little she was always getting into scrapes*. ■ [attrib.] denoting something, especially a place, that is the smaller or smallest of those so named or is named after a similar larger one: *the village of Little Chesterton*.
■ [attrib.] used in names of animals and plants that are smaller than related kinds, e.g. **little grebe**. ■ [attrib.] of short distance or duration: *stay for a little while* | *we climbed up a little way*. ■ [attrib.] relatively unimportant or trivial (often used ironically): *we have a little problem* | *I can't remember every little detail*.
▸ determiner & pronoun **1** (**a little**) a small amount of: [as determiner] *we got a little help from a training scheme* | [as pronoun] *you only see **a little of** what he can do*.
■ [pronoun] a short time or distance: *after a little, the rain stopped*.
2 used to emphasize how small an amount is: [as determiner] *I have little doubt of their identity* | *there was very little time to be lost* | [as pronoun] *he ate and drank very little* | *the rouble is worth so little these days*.
▸ adverb (**less**, **least**) **1** (**a little**) to a small extent: *he reminded me a little of my parents* | *I was always a little afraid of her*.
2 only to a small extent; not much or often (used for emphasis): *he was little known in this country* | *he had slept little these past weeks*. ■ hardly or not at all: ***little did he know** what wheels he was putting into motion*.

– PHRASES **in little** archaic on a small scale; in miniature. **little by little** by degrees; gradually: *little by little the money dried up.* **little or nothing** hardly anything. **make little of** treat as unimportant: *they made little of their royal connection.* **no little** considerable: *a factor of no little importance.* **not a little** a great deal (of); much: *not a little consternation was caused.* ■ very: *it was not a little puzzling.* **quite a little** a fairly large amount of: *some spoke quite a little English.* ■ a considerable: *it turned out to be quite a little bonanza.* **quite the little ——** used as a condescending or ironic recognition that someone has a particular quality or accomplishment: *you've become quite the little horsewoman.*
– DERIVATIVES **littleness** noun.
– ORIGIN Old English *lȳtel*, of Germanic origin; related to Dutch *luttel*, German dialect *lützel*.

Little Ararat see ARARAT, MOUNT.

little auk ▶ noun a small, stubby short-billed auk (seabird) with black plumage and white underparts, breeding in the Arctic. ● *Alle alle*, family Alcidae.

Little Bear the constellation Ursa Minor.

Little Bighorn, Battle of a battle in which General George Custer and his forces were defeated by Sioux warriors on 25 June 1876, popularly known as Custer's Last Stand. It took place in the valley of the Little Bighorn River in Montana.

little black dress ▶ noun informal a woman's short or medium-length black dress suitable for almost any social engagement.

Little Corporal a nickname for Napoleon.

little end ▶ noun (in a piston engine) the smaller end of the connecting rod, attached to the piston.

Little Englander ▶ noun a person who opposes an international role or policy for England (or, in practice, for Britain).

little finger ▶ noun the smallest finger, at the outer side of the hand, furthest from the thumb.
– PHRASES **twist** (or **wind** or **wrap**) **someone around one's little finger** have the ability to make someone do whatever one wants.

Little Gem ▶ noun a small compact lettuce of a variety of the cos type.

little grebe ▶ noun a small, dumpy Old World grebe with a short neck and bill and a trilling call. ● Genus *Tachybaptus*, family Podicipedidae: three species, in particular the widespread *T. ruficollis* (also called DABCHICK).

little green man ▶ noun informal an imaginary or hypothetical being from outer space.

little hours ▶ plural noun (in the Western Church) the offices of prime, terce, sext, and none.

little ice age ▶ noun a comparatively cold period occurring between major glacial periods, in particular one such period which reached its peak during the 17th century.

Little League ▶ noun [mass noun] N. Amer. organized baseball played by children aged between 8 and 12.

Little Lord Fauntleroy see FAUNTLEROY.

Little Masters a group of 16th-century Nuremberg engravers, followers of Dürer, who worked small-dimension plates with biblical, mythological, and genre scenes.
– ORIGIN mistranslation of German *Kleinmeister* 'masters in small (prints)'.

Little Minch see MINCH.

little ones ▶ plural noun young children.

Little Ouse another name for OUSE (sense 4).

little owl ▶ noun a small owl with speckled plumage, native to Eurasia and Africa and introduced to Britain. ● *Athene noctua*, family Strigidae.

little people ▶ plural noun **1** the ordinary people in a country, organization, etc. who do not have much power.
2 (**the little people**) small supernatural creatures such as fairies and leprechauns.

Little Rhody informal name for RHODE ISLAND.

Little Rock the state capital of Arkansas; pop. 189,515 (est. 2008).

Little Russian ▶ noun & adjective former term for UKRAINIAN.

Little St Bernard Pass see ST BERNARD PASS.

little slam ▶ noun Bridge another term for SMALL SLAM.

little theatre ▶ noun a small independent theatre used for experimental or avant-garde drama, or for community, non-commercial productions.

Little Tibet another name for BALTISTAN.

little toe ▶ noun the smallest toe, on the outer side of the foot.

littoral /ˈlɪt(ə)r(ə)l/ ▶ adjective relating to or situated on the shore of the sea or a lake: *the littoral states of the Indian Ocean.* ■ Ecology relating to or denoting the zone of the seashore between high- and low-water marks, or the zone near a lake shore with rooted vegetation: *limpets and other littoral molluscs.*
▶ noun a region lying along a shore: *irrigated regions of the Mediterranean littoral.* ■ Ecology the littoral zone.
– ORIGIN mid 17th cent.: from Latin *littoralis*, from *litus, litor-* 'shore'.

Littré /ˈlɪtreɪ/, French /litʀe/, Émile (1801–81), French lexicographer and philosopher. He was the author of the major *Dictionnaire de la langue française* (1863–77). A follower of Auguste Comte, he became the leading exponent of positivism after Comte's death.

liturgical /lɪˈtəːdʒɪk(ə)l/ ▶ adjective relating to liturgy or public worship.
– DERIVATIVES **liturgically** adverb, **liturgist** /ˈlɪtədʒɪst/ noun.
– ORIGIN mid 17th cent.: via medieval Latin from Greek *leitourgikos* (see LITURGY) + -AL.

liturgics /lɪˈtəːdʒɪks/ ▶ plural noun [treated as sing.] the study of liturgies.

liturgiology /lɪˌtəːdʒɪˈɒlədʒi/ ▶ noun [mass noun] another term for LITURGICS.
– DERIVATIVES **liturgiological** adjective, **liturgiologist** noun.

liturgy /ˈlɪtədʒi/ ▶ noun (pl. **liturgies**) **1** a form or formulary according to which public religious worship, especially Christian worship, is conducted. ■ a religious service conducted according to such a form or formulary. ■ (**the Liturgy**) the service of the Eucharist in the Orthodox Church. ■ (**the Liturgy**) archaic the Book of Common Prayer.
2 (in ancient Greece) a public office or duty performed voluntarily by a rich Athenian.
– ORIGIN mid 16th cent.: via French or late Latin from Greek *leitourgia* 'public service, worship of the gods', from *leitourgos* 'minister', from *lēitos* 'public' + *-ergos* 'working'.

Litvak /ˈlɪtvak/ ▶ noun a Jew from Lithuania or the surrounding region.
– ORIGIN Yiddish, from Polish *Litwak* 'Lithuanian'.

Liuzhou /ljuːˈdʒəʊ/ (also **Liuchow** /-ˈtʃaʊ/) an industrial city in southern China, in Guangxi Zhuang province north-east of Nanning; pop. 871,600 (est. 2006).

livable ▶ adjective variant spelling of LIVEABLE.

live[1] /lɪv/ ▶ verb **1** [no obj.] remain alive: *the doctors said she had only six months to live | both cats lived to a ripe age.* ■ [with adverbial] be alive at a specified time: *he lived four centuries ago.* ■ [with adverbial] spend one's life in a particular way or under particular circumstances: *people are living in fear in the wake of the shootings* | [with obj. and adverbial] *he was living a life of luxury in Australia.* ■ (**live in** (or **out**)) (of an employee or student) reside at (or away from) the place where one works or studies. ■ supply oneself with the means of subsistence: *they **live by** hunting and fishing.* ■ (**live through**) survive (an unpleasant experience or period): *both men lived through the Depression.* ■ survive in someone's mind; be remembered: *only the name **lived on**.* ■ have an exciting or fulfilling life: *he couldn't wait to get out of school and really start living.* ■ (**live for**) regard as the purpose or most important aspect of one's life: *Tony lived for his painting.* ■ archaic (of a ship) escape destruction; remain afloat.
2 [no obj., with adverbial] make one's home in a particular place or with a particular person: *I've lived in the East End all my life | they lived with his grandparents.* ■ informal (of an object) be kept in a particular place: *I told her where the coffee lived and went back to sleep.*
– PHRASES **as I live and breathe** used to express surprise at encountering someone or something: *good God, Jack Stone, as I live and breathe!* **be living on borrowed time** see BORROW. **live and breathe something** devote a great deal of one's time to a particular subject or activity: *they live and breathe Italy and all things Italian.* **live and let live** proverb you should tolerate the opinions and behaviour of others so that they will similarly tolerate your own. **live by one's wits** see WIT[1]. **live dangerously** do something risky, especially on a habitual basis. **live for the moment** see MOMENT. **live in hope** be or remain optimistic about something. **live in the past** have old-fashioned or outdated ideas and attitudes. ■ dwell on or reminisce at length about past events. **live in sin** see SIN[1]. **live it up** informal spend one's time in an extremely enjoyable way, typically by being extravagant or engaging in an exciting social life. **live off** (or **on**) **the fat of the land** see FAT. **live off the land** see LAND. **live out of a suitcase** live or stay somewhere on a temporary basis and with only a limited selection of one's belongings. **live one's own life** follow one's own plans and principles independently of others. **live rough** live and sleep outdoors as a consequence of having no proper home. **live to fight another day** survive a particular experience or ordeal. **live to regret something** come to wish that one had not done something: *those who put work before their family life often live to regret it.* **live to tell the tale** survive a dangerous experience and be able to tell others about it. **live with oneself** be able to retain one's self-respect as a consequence of one's actions: *taking money from children—how can you live with yourself?* **long live ——!** said to express loyalty or support for a specified person or thing: *long live the Queen!* **where one lives** N. Amer. informal at, to, or in the right, vital, or most vulnerable spot: *it gets me where I live.* **you** (or **we**) **live and learn** used to acknowledge that a fact is new to one.
– PHRASAL VERBS **live something down** [usu. with negative] succeed in making others forget something embarrassing that has happened: *I'd never live it down if Lily got wind of this.* **live off** (or **on**) depend on as a source of income or support: *if you think you're going to live off me for the rest of your life, you're mistaken.* ■ have (a particular amount of money) with which to buy food and other necessities. ■ subsist on (a particular type of food). ■ (of a person) eat, or seem to eat, only (a particular type of food): *she used to live on bacon and tomato sandwiches.* **live something out 1** do in reality that which one has imagined: *your wedding day is the one time that you can live out your most romantic fantasies.* **2** spend the rest of one's life in a particular place or particular circumstances: *he lived out his days as a happy family man.* **live together** (especially of a couple not married to each other) share a home and have a sexual relationship. **live up to** fulfil (expectations). ■ fulfil (an undertaking): *the president lived up to his promise to set America swiftly on a new path.* **live with 1** share a home and have a sexual relationship with (someone to whom one is not married). **2** accept or tolerate (something unpleasant): *our marriage was a failure—you have to learn to live with that fact.*
– ORIGIN Old English *libban, lifian*, of Germanic origin; related to Dutch *leven* and German *leben*, also to LIFE and LEAVE[1].

L

live[2] /lʌɪv/ ▶ adjective **1** [attrib.] not dead or inanimate; living: *live animals.* ■ (of a vaccine) containing viruses or bacteria that are living but of a mild or attenuated strain. ■ (of yogurt) containing the living microorganisms by which it is formed.
2 relating to a musical performance given in concert, not on a recording: *there is traditional live music played most nights | a live album.* ■ (of a broadcast) transmitted at the time of occurrence, not from a recording: *live coverage of the match.*
3 (of a wire or device) connected to a source of electric current. ■ of, containing, or using undetonated explosive: *live ammunition.* ■ (of coals) burning or glowing. ■ (of a match) unused. ■ (of a wheel or axle in machinery) moving or imparting motion. ■ (of a ball in a game) in play, esp. in contrast to being foul or out of bounds.
4 (of a question or subject) of current or continuing interest and importance: *the future organization of Europe has become a live issue.*
▶ adverb as or at an actual event or performance: *the match will be televised live.*
– PHRASES **go live** (of a computer system) become operational.
– ORIGIN mid 16th cent.: shortening of ALIVE.

liveable (US also **livable**) ▶ adjective worth living: *fatherhood makes life more liveable.* ■ (also **liveable in**) (of an environment or climate) fit to live in: *one of the most liveable cities in the world.* ■ (**liveable with**) informal easy or bearable to live with.
– DERIVATIVES **liveability** noun.

live action ▶ noun [mass noun] action in films involving filming real people or animals, as contrasted with animation or computer-generated effects.

live bait ▶ noun [mass noun] small living fish or worms used to entice prey.

livebearer ▶ noun a small, chiefly freshwater American toothcarp that has internal fertilization and gives birth to live young. Many livebearers, including the guppy, swordtail, mollies, platies, and gambusias, are popular in aquaria. ● Family Poeciliinae: many genera and species.

live-bearing ▸ adjective (of an animal) bearing live young rather than laying eggs; viviparous or ovoviviparous.

live birth ▸ noun a birth at which a child is born alive.

live-born ▸ adjective born alive, not stillborn.

lived-in ▸ adjective (of a room or building) showing comforting signs of wear and habitation. ■ informal (of a person's face) marked by experience.

live-in ▸ adjective [attrib.] (of a domestic employee) resident in an employer's house: *a live-in housekeeper*. ■ (of a person) living with another in a sexual relationship: *a live-in lover*. ■ residential: *a live-in treatment program*.
▸ noun informal a person who shares another's living accommodation as a sexual partner or as an employee.

livelihood ▸ noun a means of securing the necessities of life: *people whose livelihoods depend on the rainforest*.
– ORIGIN Old English *līflād* 'way of life', from *līf* 'life' + *lād* 'course' (see LODE). The change in the word's form in the 16th cent. was due to association with LIVELY and -HOOD.

live load ▸ noun the weight of people or goods in a building or vehicle. Often contrasted with DEAD LOAD.

livelong[1] /ˈlɪvlɒŋ/ ▸ adjective [attrib.] literary (of a period of time) entire: *all this **livelong day** I lay in the sun*.
– ORIGIN late Middle English *leve longe* 'dear long' (see LIEF, LONG[1]). The change in spelling of the first word was due to association with LIVE[1].

livelong[2] /ˈlɪvlɒŋ/ ▸ noun a stonecrop, especially orpine.

lively ▸ adjective (**livelier**, **liveliest**) full of life and energy; active and outgoing: *a lively and uninhibited girl*. ■ (of a place or atmosphere) full of activity and excitement: *Barcelona's many lively bars*. ■ intellectually stimulating or perceptive: *a lively discussion* | *her lively mind*. ■ ironic, chiefly Brit. difficult or challenging: *a lively homeward passage dodging aircraft and E-boats*. ■ (of a boat) rising lightly to the waves.
– PHRASES **look lively** [usu. in imperative] informal move more quickly and energetically: *'Look lively, lads, keep in step,' Charlie shouted*.
– DERIVATIVES **liveliness** noun.
– ORIGIN Old English *līflic* 'living, animate' (see LIFE, -LY[1]).

L

liven ▸ verb make or become more lively or interesting: [with obj.] ***liven up** bland foods with a touch of mustard* | [no obj.] *the match didn't **liven up** until the second half*.

live oak ▸ noun a large, spreading, evergreen North American oak, which typically supports a large quantity of Spanish moss and other epiphytes. ● *Quercus virginiana*, family Fagaceae.

liver[1] ▸ noun a large lobed glandular organ in the abdomen of vertebrates, involved in many metabolic processes. ■ a similar organ in other animals. ■ [mass noun] the flesh of an animal's liver as food: [as modifier] *liver pâté*. ■ [mass noun] a dark reddish brown.

> The liver's main role is in the processing of the products of digestion into substances useful to the body. It also neutralizes harmful substances in the blood, secretes bile for the digestion of fats, synthesizes plasma proteins, and stores glycogen and some minerals and vitamins. It was formerly supposed to be the seat of love and violent emotion.

– ORIGIN Old English *lifer*, of Germanic origin; related to German *Leber*, Dutch *lever*.

liver[2] ▸ noun [with adj. or noun modifier] a person who lives in a specified way: *a clean liver* | *high livers*.

liver chestnut ▸ noun a horse of a dark chestnut colour.

liver fluke ▸ noun a fluke which has a complex life cycle and is of medical and veterinary importance. The adult lives within the liver tissues of a vertebrate, and the larva within one or more secondary hosts such as a snail or fish. ● Many species in the subclass Digenea, class Trematoda, including the **Chinese liver fluke** (*Opisthorchis sinensis*), which infests humans, and *Fasciola hepatica*, which infests sheep and cattle.

liverish ▸ adjective **1** slightly ill, as though having a disordered liver. ■ unhappy and bad-tempered.
2 resembling liver in colour: *a liverish red*.
– DERIVATIVES **liverishly** adverb, **liverishness** noun.

liver of sulphur ▸ noun [mass noun] archaic a liver-coloured mixture containing potassium sulphide, used in medicinal ointment.

Liverpool[1] /ˈlɪvəpuːl/ a city and seaport in NW England, situated at the east side of the mouth of the River Mersey; pop. 454,700 (est. 2009). Liverpool developed as a port in the 17th century with the import of cotton from America and the export of textiles produced in Lancashire and Yorkshire, and in the 18th century became an important centre of shipbuilding and engineering.

Liverpool[2] /ˈlɪvəpuːl/, Robert Banks Jenkinson, 2nd Earl of (1770–1828), British Tory statesman, Prime Minister 1812–27.

Liverpudlian /ˌlɪvəˈpʌdlɪən/ ▸ noun a native of Liverpool. ■ [mass noun] the dialect or accent of people from Liverpool.
▸ adjective relating to Liverpool.
– ORIGIN mid 19th cent.: humorous formation from LIVERPOOL[1] + PUDDLE.

liver rot ▸ noun [mass noun] disease of the liver, especially that caused in sheep by the liver fluke.

liver salts ▸ plural noun Brit. salts taken in water to relieve indigestion or nausea.

liver sausage ▸ noun [mass noun] Brit. a savoury meat paste in the form of a sausage containing cooked liver, or a mixture of liver and pork.

liver spot ▸ noun a small brown spot on the skin, especially as caused by a skin condition such as lentigo.
– DERIVATIVES **liver-spotted** adjective.

liverwort /ˈlɪvəwəːt/ ▸ noun a small flowerless green plant with leaf-like stems or lobed leaves, occurring in moist habitats. They lack true roots and reproduce by means of spores released from capsules. ● Class Hepaticae, division Bryophyta.
– ORIGIN late Old English, from LIVER[1] + WORT, translating medieval Latin *hepatica*.

livery[1] ▸ noun (pl. **liveries**) **1** a special uniform worn by a servant, an official, or a member of a City Company: *yeomen of the guard wearing a royal red and gold livery* | [mass noun] *pageboys in scarlet and green livery*. ■ a special design and colour scheme used on the vehicles, aircraft, or products of a particular company.
2 N. Amer. short for LIVERY STABLE.
3 (in the UK) the members of a City livery company collectively.
4 historical a provision of food or clothing for servants.
5 (in full **livery of seisin**) Brit. historical the ceremonial procedure at common law of conveying freehold land to a grantee.
– PHRASES **at livery** (of a horse) kept for the owner and fed and cared for at a fixed charge.
– DERIVATIVES **liveried** adjective (sense 1).
– ORIGIN Middle English: from Old French *livree* 'delivered', feminine past participle of *livrer*, from Latin *liberare* 'liberate' (in medieval Latin 'hand over'). The original sense was 'the dispensing of food, provisions, or clothing to servants'; hence sense 4, also 'allowance of provender for horses', surviving in the phrase *at livery* and in LIVERY STABLE. Sense 1 arose because medieval nobles provided matching clothes to distinguish their servants from others'.

livery[2] ▸ adjective **1** resembling liver in colour or consistency: *he was short with livery lips*. ■ informal liverish: *port always makes you livery*.
2 dialect (of soil) heavy.

livery company ▸ noun (in the UK) any of a number of Companies of the City of London descended from the medieval trade guilds. They are now largely social and charitable organizations.
– ORIGIN mid 18th cent.: so named because of the distinctive costume formerly used for special occasions.

liveryman ▸ noun (pl. **liverymen**) **1** (in the UK) a member of a livery company.
2 an owner of or attendant in a livery stable.

livery stable (also **livery yard**) ▸ noun a stable where horses are kept at livery or let out for hire.

lives plural form of LIFE.

livestock ▸ noun [mass noun] farm animals regarded as an asset: *markets for the trading of livestock*.

liveware ▸ noun [mass noun] informal working personnel, especially computer personnel, as distinct from the inanimate or abstract things they work with.

live weight ▸ noun [mass noun] the weight of an animal before it has been slaughtered and prepared as a carcass.

live wire ▸ noun informal an energetic and unpredictable person.

live-work ▸ adjective denoting or relating to property which combines residential living space with commercial or manufacturing space: *housing on the site might include live-work units for small businesses*.

livid ▸ adjective **1** furiously angry: *he was livid that Garry had escaped*.
2 dark bluish grey in colour: *livid bruises*.
– DERIVATIVES **lividity** noun, **lividly** adverb, **lividness** noun.
– ORIGIN late Middle English (in the sense 'of a bluish leaden colour'): from French *livide* or Latin *lividus*, from *livere* 'be bluish'. The sense 'furiously angry' dates from the early 20th cent.

living ▸ noun **1** [usu. in sing.] an income sufficient to live on or the means of earning it: *she was struggling to **make a living** as a dancer* | *what does he **do for a living**?* ■ Brit. (in church use) a position as a vicar or rector with an income or property.
2 [mass noun] [with adj. or noun modifier] the pursuit of a lifestyle of the specified type: *the benefits of country living*.
▸ adjective alive: *living creatures* | (as plural noun **the living**) *flowers were for the living*. ■ [attrib.] (of a place) used for living rather than working in: *the living quarters of the pub*. ■ (of a language) still spoken and used. ■ [attrib.] literary (of water) perennially flowing: *streams of living water*.
– PHRASES **be (the) living proof that** (or **of**) show by one's existence and qualities that something is the case: *she is living proof that hard work need not be ageing*. **in** (or **within**) **living memory** within or during a time that is remembered by people still alive: *the worst recession in living memory*. **the living image of** an exact copy or likeness of.

living death ▸ noun a state of existence that is as bad as being dead; a life of hopeless and unbroken misery.

living rock ▸ noun [mass noun] rock that is not detached but still forms part of the earth.

living room ▸ noun a room in a house for general and informal everyday use.

Livingstone[1] former name for MARAMBA.

Livingstone[2], David (1813–73), Scottish missionary and explorer. He went to Bechuanaland as a missionary in 1841. On extensive travels, he discovered Lake Ngami (1849), the Zambezi River (1851), and the Victoria Falls (1855). In 1866 he went in search of the source of the Nile, and was found in poor health by Sir Henry Morton Stanley in 1871.

living stone ▸ noun a small succulent southern African plant which resembles a pebble in appearance. It consists of two fleshy cushion-like leaves divided by a slit through which a daisy-like flower emerges. ● Genus *Lithops*, family Aizoaceae.

Livingstone daisy ▸ noun a low spreading succulent plant which bears glistening daisy-like flowers in many colours, native to southern Africa. ● *Dorotheanthus* (formerly *Mesembryanthemum*) *bellidiformis*, family Aizoaceae.
– ORIGIN 1930s: of unknown origin.

living wage ▸ noun a wage which is high enough to maintain a normal standard of living.

living will ▸ noun a written statement detailing a person's desires regarding future medical treatment in circumstances in which they are no longer able to express informed consent, especially an advance directive.

Livonia /lɪˈvəʊnɪə/ a region on the east coast of the Baltic Sea, north of Lithuania, comprising most of present-day Latvia and Estonia. German name **Livland** /ˈliːflant/.
– DERIVATIVES **Livonian** adjective & noun.

Livorno /lɪˈvɔːnəʊ/, Italian /liˈvɔrno/ a port in west central Italy, in Tuscany, on the Ligurian Sea; pop. 161,095 (2008). It is the site of the Italian Naval Academy.

Livy /ˈlɪvi/ (59 BC–AD 17), Roman historian; Latin name *Titus Livius*. His history of Rome from its foundation to his own time contained 142 books, of which thirty-five survive (including the earliest history of the war with Hannibal).

lixiviate /lɪkˈsɪvɪeɪt/ ▸ verb [with obj.] Chemistry, archaic separate (a substance) into soluble and insoluble constituents by the percolation of liquid.
– DERIVATIVES **lixiviation** noun.
– ORIGIN mid 17th cent.: from modern Latin *lixiviat-* 'impregnated with lye', from the verb *lixiviare*, from *lixivius* 'made into lye', from *lix* 'lye'.

Lizard a promontory in SW England, in Cornwall. Its southern tip, Lizard Point, is the southernmost point of the British mainland.

lizard ▶ **noun** a reptile that typically has a long body and tail, four legs, movable eyelids, and a rough, scaly, or spiny skin. ● Suborder Lacertilia (or Sauria), order Squamata: many families.
– ORIGIN late Middle English: from Old French *lesard(e)*, from Latin *lacertus* 'lizard, sea fish', also 'muscle'.

lizardfish ▶ **noun** (pl. **same** or **lizardfishes**) a fish with a broad bony head, pointed snout, and heavy, shiny scales. It lives in warm shallow seas, where it often rests on the bottom propped up on its pelvic fins. ● Family Synodontidae: several genera and species, including the widespread *Trachinocephalus myops* (also called **SNAKEFISH**).

lizard orchid ▶ **noun** a tall orchid with greenish flowers that have a very long twisted lip and a goat-like smell. It has spread from the Mediterranean area to more northern parts of Europe. ● *Himantoglossum hircinum*, family Orchidaceae.

lizard's tail ▶ **noun** a North American bog plant with long tapering spikes of fragrant white flowers. ● *Saururus cernuus*, family Saururaceae.

LJ ▶ **abbreviation** (pl. **L JJ**) (in the UK) Lord Justice.

Ljubljana /ljuːˈbljɑːnə/ the capital of Slovenia; pop. 267,760 (2007). The city was founded (as Emona) by the Romans in 34 BC. German name **LAIBACH**.

Lk. ▶ **abbreviation** the Gospel of Luke (in biblical references).

ll. ▶ **abbreviation** (in textual references) lines.

'll ▶ **contraction** shall; will: *I'll get the food in.*

llama /ˈlɑːmə/ ▶ **noun** a domesticated pack animal of the camel family found in the Andes, valued for its soft woolly fleece. ● *Lama glama*, family Camelidae, probably descended from the wild guanaco.
■ [mass noun] the wool of the llama. ■ [mass noun] cloth made from the wool of the llama.
– ORIGIN early 17th cent.: from Spanish, probably from Quechua.

Llandudno /lanˈdɪdnəʊ, hlan-/ a resort town in Conwy, northern Wales, on the Irish Sea; pop. 15,200 (est. 2009).

llanero /laˈnɛːrəʊ, lj-/ ▶ **noun** (pl. **llaneros**) (in South America) an inhabitant of a llano, in particular one who works as a cowboy.
– ORIGIN Spanish.

llano /ˈlɑːnəʊ, ˈljɑː-/ ▶ **noun** (pl. **llanos**) (in South America) a treeless grassy plain.
– ORIGIN Spanish, from Latin *planum* 'plain'.

LLB ▶ **abbreviation** Bachelor of Laws.
– ORIGIN from Latin *legum baccalaureus*.

LLD ▶ **abbreviation** Doctor of Laws.
– ORIGIN from Latin *legum doctor*.

Llewelyn /luːˈɛlɪn, hluː-/ (d.1282), prince of Gwynedd in North Wales; also known as **Llywelyn ap Gruffydd**. Proclaiming himself prince of all Wales in 1258, he was recognized by Henry III in 1265. His refusal to pay homage to Edward I led the latter to invade and subjugate Wales (1277–84); Llewelyn died in an unsuccessful rebellion.

LLM ▶ **abbreviation** Master of Laws.
– ORIGIN from Latin *legum magister*.

Llosa, Mario Vargas, see **VARGAS LLOSA**.

Lloyd[1] /lɔɪd/, Harold (Clayton) (1893–1971), American film comedian. Performing his own hair-raising stunts, he used physical danger as a source of comedy in silent movies such as *High and Dizzy* (1920), *Safety Last* (1923), and *The Freshman* (1925).

Lloyd[2] /lɔɪd/, Marie (1870–1922), English music-hall entertainer; born *Matilda Alice Victoria Wood*. She achieved fame for her risqué songs and extravagant costumes and took her act to the US, South Africa, and Australia.

Lloyd George, David, 1st Earl Lloyd-George of Dwyfor (1863–1945), British Liberal statesman, Prime Minister 1916–22. As Chancellor of the Exchequer (1908–15), he introduced old-age pensions (1908) and national insurance (1911). His coalition government was threatened by economic problems and trouble in Ireland, and he resigned when the Conservatives withdrew their support in 1922.

Lloyd's an incorporated society of insurance underwriters in London, made up of private syndicates. Founded in 1871, Lloyd's originally dealt only in marine insurance. ■ short for **LLOYD'S REGISTER**.
– ORIGIN named after the coffee house of Edward Lloyd (*fl.* 1688–1726), in which underwriters and merchants congregated and where *Lloyd's List* was started in 1734.

Lloyd's List ▶ **noun** a daily newsletter relating to shipping, published in London.

Lloyd's Register (in full **Lloyd's Register of Shipping**) a classified list of merchant ships over a certain tonnage, published annually in London. ■ the corporation that produces this list and lays down the specifications for ships on which it is based.

Lloyd Webber, Sir Andrew, Baron Lloyd-Webber of Sydmonton (b.1948), English composer. His many successful musicals, several of them written in collaboration with the lyricist Sir Tim Rice, include *Jesus Christ Superstar* (1970), *Cats* (1981), and *The Phantom of the Opera* (1986).

Llywelyn ap Gruffydd /luːˈɛlɪn ap ˈɡrɪfɪð, hluː-/ see **LLEWELYN**.

LM /lɛm/ ▶ **abbreviation** ■ long metre. ■ lunar module.

lm ▶ **abbreviation** lumen(s).

LMAO ▶ **abbreviation** vulgar slang laughing my arse (or N. Amer. ass) off.

LMS ▶ **abbreviation** ■ (in the UK) local management of schools. ■ historical (in the UK) London Midland and Scottish (Railway).

LMT ▶ **abbreviation** Local Mean Time, the standard time in the relevant time zone.

ln ▶ **abbreviation** Mathematics natural logarithm.
– ORIGIN from modern Latin *logarithmus naturalis*.

LNB ▶ **abbreviation** low noise blocker, a circuit on a satellite dish which selects the required signal from the transmission.

LNER ▶ **abbreviation** historical (in the UK) London and North Eastern Railway.

LNG ▶ **abbreviation** liquefied natural gas.

lo ▶ **exclamation** archaic used to draw attention to an interesting or amazing event: *and lo, the star, which they saw in the east, went before them.*
– PHRASES **lo and behold** used to present a new scene, situation, or turn of events, often with the suggestion that, though surprising, it could in fact have been predicted: *you took me out and, lo and behold, I got home to find my house had been ransacked.*
– ORIGIN natural exclamation: first recorded as *lā* in Old English; reinforced in Middle English by a shortened form of *loke* 'look!', imperative of **LOOK**.

loa /ˈləʊə/ ▶ **noun** (pl. **same** or **loas**) a god in the voodoo cult of Haiti.
– ORIGIN Haitian Creole.

loach /ləʊtʃ/ ▶ **noun** a small elongated bottom-dwelling freshwater fish with several barbels near the mouth, found in Eurasia and NW Africa. ● Family Cobitidae and Homalopteridae (or Balitoridae): several genera and numerous species.
– ORIGIN Middle English: from Old French *loche*, of unknown origin.

load ▶ **noun 1** a heavy or bulky thing that is being carried or is about to be carried: *in addition to their own food, they must carry a load of up to eighty pounds.* ■ [in combination] the total number or amount that can be carried in something, typically a vehicle or container: *a lorry-load of soldiers.* ■ a quantity of items washed or to be washed in a washing machine or dishwasher at one time: *I do at least six **loads of** washing a week.* ■ the material carried along by a stream, glacier, ocean current, etc.
2 a weight or source of pressure borne by someone or something: *the increased **load on** the heart caused by a raised arterial pressure | the arch has hollow spandrels to lighten the **load on** the foundations.* ■ the amount of work to be done by a person or machine: *Arthur has a light teaching load.* ■ a burden of responsibility, worry, or grief.
3 (**a load of**) informal a lot of: *she was talking **a load of** rubbish.* ■ (**a load/loads**) plenty: *she spends **loads of** money on clothes | there's loads to see here, even when it rains.*
4 the amount of power supplied by a source; the resistance of moving parts to be overcome by a motor. ■ the amount of electricity supplied by a generating system at any given time. ■ Electronics an impedance or circuit that receives or develops the output of a transistor or other device.
▶ **verb** [with obj.] **1** fill (a vehicle, ship, container, etc.) with a large amount of something: *they go to Calais to **load up** their vans with cheap beer.* ■ [with obj. and adverbial] place (a load or large quantity of something) on or in a vehicle, ship, container, etc.: *stolen property from a burglary was loaded into a taxi.* ■ [no obj.] (of a ship or vehicle) take on a load: *when we came to the quay the ship was still loading.* ■ [no obj.] (**load up on**) informal take, buy, or consume a large amount of: *I just went down to the store and loaded up on beer.*
2 make (someone or something) carry or hold a large or excessive quantity of heavy things: *Elaine was **loaded down with** bags full of shopping.* ■ (**load someone/thing with**) supply someone or something with (something) in overwhelming abundance or to excess: *the King and Queen loaded Columbus with wealth and honours.* ■ bias towards a particular outcome: *the odds were loaded against them before the match.*
3 charge (a firearm) with ammunition. ■ insert something into (a device) so that it can be operated: *load your camera before you start | following breakfast we clear the table and load the dishwasher.* ■ insert (something) into a device so that it will operate: *load the cassette into the camcorder.* ■ Computing transfer (a program or data) into memory, or into the central processor from storage.
4 add an extra charge to (an insurance premium) to take account of a factor that increases the risk.
– PHRASES **get a load of** informal used to draw attention to someone or something: *get a load of that blonde girl!* **get** (or **have**) **a load on** US informal become drunk. **load the bases** Baseball have base runners on all three bases. **load the dice against/in favour of someone** put someone at a disadvantage or advantage. **take a** (or **the**) **load off one's feet** sit or lie down. **take a load off someone's mind** bring someone relief from anxiety. **under load** subject to a mechanical or electrical load.
– ORIGIN Old English *lād* 'way, journey, conveyance', of Germanic origin: related to German *Leite*, also to **LEAD**[1]; compare with **LODE**. The verb dates from the late 15th cent.

load-bearing ▶ **adjective** (especially of a wall) supporting much of the weight of the overlying parts of a building or other structure. ■ relating to the carrying of a load: *the road's load-bearing capacity.*

loaded ▶ **adjective 1** carrying or bearing a load, especially a large one: *a heavily loaded freight train.* ■ (of a firearm) charged with ammunition: *a loaded gun.* ■ [predic.] informal having a lot of money; wealthy: *she doesn't really have to work—they're loaded.* ■ [predic.] informal, chiefly N. Amer. drunk: *it's Friday night, and we want to **get loaded**.* ■ N. Amer. informal (of a car) equipped with many optional extras; deluxe: *1989 Ford 250 LXT: low miles, loaded.*
2 weighted or biased towards a particular outcome: *a trick like the one with the loaded dice.* ■ (of a word, statement, or question) charged with an underlying meaning or implication: *avoid politically loaded terms like 'nation' | 'Anything else?' It was a loaded question and Kelly knew it.*
– PHRASES **loaded for bear** see **BEAR**[2].

loader ▶ **noun 1** a machine or person that loads something. ■ an attendant who loads guns at a shoot.
2 [in combination] a gun, machine, or lorry which is loaded in a specified way: *a front-loader.*

load factor ▶ **noun** the ratio of the average or actual amount of some quantity and the maximum possible or permissible. ■ the ratio between the lift and the weight of an aircraft.

loading ▶ **noun** [mass noun] **1** the application of a mechanical load or force to something. ■ the amount of electric current or power delivered to a device. ■ the maximum electric current or power taken by an appliance. ■ the provision of extra electrical inductance to improve the properties of a transmission wire or aerial.
2 an increase in an insurance premium due to a factor increasing the risk involved. ■ Austral. an increment added to a basic wage for special skills or qualifications.
▶ **adjective** [in combination] (of a gun, machine, or lorry) loaded in a specified way: *a front-loading dishwasher.*

loading bay ▶ **noun** a bay or recess in a building where vehicles are loaded and unloaded.

loading coil ▶ **noun** a coil used to provide additional inductance in an electric circuit, in order to reduce distortion and attenuation of transmitted signals or to reduce the resonant frequency of an aerial.

loading dock ▶ **noun** see **DOCK**[1].

loading gauge ▶ **noun** the maximum permitted height and width for rolling stock on a railway. ■ a frame suspended above a railway track to indicate these limits.

L

loading shovel ▸ noun a vehicle with a power-operated shovel for scooping up material and carrying it short distances.

load line ▸ noun another term for PLIMSOLL LINE.

loadmaster ▸ noun the member of an aircraft's crew responsible for the cargo.

loadsa ▸ contraction loads of (in the sense 'lots' representing non-standard use): *Bond gets to shoot loadsa bad guys.*

load-shedding ▸ noun [mass noun] action to reduce the load on something, especially the interruption of an electricity supply to avoid excessive load on the generating plant.

loadspace ▸ noun the space in a motor vehicle for carrying a load.

loadstone ▸ noun variant spelling of LODESTONE.

loaf[1] ▸ noun (pl. **loaves**) a quantity of bread that is shaped and baked in one piece and usually sliced before being eaten: ***a loaf of bread*** | *a granary loaf.* ■ an item of food formed into an oblong shape and sliced into portions.
– PHRASES **half a loaf is better than no bread** proverb it is better to accept less than one wants or expects than to have nothing at all. **use one's loaf** Brit. informal use one's common sense. [probably from *loaf of bread*, rhyming slang for 'head'.]
– ORIGIN Old English *hlāf*, of Germanic origin; related to German *Laib*.

loaf[2] ▸ verb [no obj.] spend one's time in an aimless, idle way: *don't let him see you* ***loafing about*** *with your hands in your pockets.*
– ORIGIN mid 19th cent.: probably a back-formation from LOAFER.

loafer ▸ noun **1** a person who avoids work and spends their time idly.
2 trademark a leather shoe shaped like a moccasin, with a flat heel.
– ORIGIN mid 19th cent.: perhaps from German *Landläufer* 'tramp', from *Land* 'land' + *laufen* (dialect *lofen*) 'to run'.

L

loaf sugar ▸ noun [mass noun] sugar from or comprising a sugarloaf.

loam ▸ noun [mass noun] a fertile soil of clay and sand containing humus. ■ Geology a soil with roughly equal proportions of sand, silt, and clay. ■ a paste of clay and water with sand, chopped straw, etc., used in making bricks and plastering walls.
– DERIVATIVES **loaminess** noun, **loamy** adjective (**loamier**, **loamiest**).
– ORIGIN Old English *lām* 'clay', of West Germanic origin: related to Dutch *leem* and German *Lehm*, also to LIME[1].

loan[1] ▸ noun a thing that is borrowed, especially a sum of money that is expected to be paid back with interest: *borrowers can* ***take out a loan*** *for £84,000.* ■ an act of lending something to someone: *she offered to buy him dinner in return for the loan of the flat.* ■ short for LOANWORD.
▸ verb [with obj.] lend (a sum of money or item of property): *the computer was loaned to us by the theatre* | [with two objs] *he knew Rab would not loan him money.*
– PHRASES **on loan** (of a thing) being borrowed: *the painting is at present* ***on loan to*** *the Tate Gallery.* ■ (of a worker or sports player) on secondment to another organization or team, typically for an agreed fixed period.
– DERIVATIVES **loanable** adjective, **loanee** noun, **loaner** noun.
– ORIGIN Middle English (also denoting a gift from a superior): from Old Norse *lán*, of Germanic origin; related to Dutch *leen*, German *Lehn*, also to LEND.

loan[2] (also **loaning**) ▸ noun [usu. in place names] Scottish a lane or narrow path, especially one leading to open ground: *Whitehouse Loan.* ■ an open, uncultivated piece of land where cows are milked.
– ORIGIN late Middle English variant of LANE.

loan capital ▸ noun [mass noun] money required to run a business which is raised from loans rather than shares.

loan collection ▸ noun a collection of works of art or other objects lent by various owners for an exhibition.

loanholder ▸ noun a person or organization holding the securities for a loan; a mortgagee.

loaning (also **lonning**) ▸ noun another term for LOAN[2].

loan shark ▸ noun informal, derogatory a moneylender who charges extremely high rates of interest, typically under illegal conditions.

loan translation ▸ noun an expression adopted by one language from another in a more or less literally translated form. Also called CALQUE.

loanword ▸ noun a word adopted from a foreign language with little or no modification.

loath /ləʊθ/ (also **loth**) ▸ adjective [predic., with infinitive] reluctant; unwilling: *I was loath to leave.*
– ORIGIN Old English *lāth* 'hostile, spiteful', of Germanic origin; related to Dutch *leed*, German *Leid* 'sorrow'.

> **USAGE** Although different in meaning, **loath** and **loathe** are often confused. **Loath** is an adjective (also spelled **loth**) meaning 'reluctant or unwilling', as in *I was loath to leave*, whereas **loathe** is a verb meaning 'feel intense dislike or disgust for', as in *she loathed him on sight*.

loathe /ləʊð/ ▸ verb [with obj.] feel intense dislike or disgust for: *she loathed him on sight.*
– DERIVATIVES **loather** noun.
– ORIGIN Old English *lāthian*, of Germanic origin; related to LOATH.

loathing /ˈləʊðɪŋ/ ▸ noun [mass noun] a feeling of intense dislike or disgust; hatred: *the thought filled him with loathing.*

loathsome ▸ adjective causing hatred or disgust; repulsive: *this loathsome little swine.*
– DERIVATIVES **loathsomely** adverb, **loathsomeness** noun.
– ORIGIN Middle English: from archaic *loath* 'disgust, loathing' + -SOME[1].

loaves plural form of LOAF[1].

lob ▸ verb (**lobs**, **lobbing**, **lobbed**) [with obj. and adverbial of direction] throw or hit (a ball or missile) in a high arc: *he lobbed the ball over their heads.* ■ [with obj.] (in soccer or tennis) kick or hit the ball over (an opponent) in a high arc: *he managed to lob the keeper.*
▸ noun (in sport) a ball lobbed over an opponent or a stroke producing this result. ■ Cricket a ball bowled with a slow underarm action.
– ORIGIN late 16th cent. (in the senses 'cause or allow to hang heavily' and 'behave like a lout'): from the archaic noun *lob* 'lout', 'pendulous object', probably from Low German or Dutch (compare with modern Dutch *lubbe* 'hanging lip'). The current sense dates from the mid 19th cent.

Lobachevsky /ˌlɒbəˈtʃɛfski/, Nikolai Ivanovich (1792–1856), Russian mathematician. At about the same time as Gauss and **János Bolyai** (1802–60), he independently discovered non-Euclidean geometry. His work was not widely recognized until the non-Euclidean nature of space–time was revealed by the general theory of relativity.

lobar /ˈləʊbə/ ▸ adjective chiefly Anatomy & Medicine relating to or affecting a lobe, especially a whole lobe of a lung.

lobate /ˈləʊbeɪt/ ▸ adjective Biology having a lobe or lobes: *lobate oak leaves.*
– DERIVATIVES **lobation** noun.

lobby ▸ noun (pl. **lobbies**) **1** a room providing a space out of which one or more other rooms or corridors lead, typically one near the entrance of a public building.
2 (in the UK) any of several large halls in the Houses of Parliament in which MPs may meet members of the public. ■ (also **division lobby**) (in the UK) each of two corridors in the Houses of Parliament to which MPs retire to vote. ■ (**the lobby**) informal (in the UK) lobby correspondents collectively.
3 a group of people seeking to influence legislators on a particular issue: *members of the anti-abortion lobby.* ■ [in sing.] an organized attempt by members of the public to influence legislators: *a recent* ***lobby of*** *Parliament by pensioners.*
▸ verb (**lobbies**, **lobbying**, **lobbied**) [with obj.] seek to influence (a legislator) on an issue: *they insist on their right to lobby Congress* | [no obj.] *the organization was formed to* ***lobby for*** *student concerns.*
– DERIVATIVES **lobbyist** noun.
– ORIGIN mid 16th cent. (in the sense 'monastic cloister'): from medieval Latin *lobia*, *lobium* 'covered walk, portico'. The verb sense (originally US) derives from the practice of frequenting the lobby of a house of legislature to influence its members into supporting a cause.

lobby correspondent ▸ noun (in the UK) a senior political journalist of a group receiving direct but unattributable briefings from the government.

lobe ▸ noun a roundish and flattish projecting or hanging part of something, typically one of two or more such parts divided by a fissure. See also EARLOBE. ■ each of the parts of the cerebrum of the brain.
– DERIVATIVES **lobed** adjective.
– ORIGIN late Middle English: via late Latin from Greek *lobos* 'lobe, pod'.

lobectomy ▸ noun (pl. **lobectomies**) [mass noun] surgical removal of a lobe of an organ such as the thyroid gland, lung, liver, or brain.

lobe-finned fish (also **lobefin**) ▸ noun a fish of a largely extinct group having fleshy lobed fins, including the probable ancestors of the amphibians. Compare with RAY-FINNED FISH. ● Subclass Crossopterygia (or Actinistia or Coelacanthimorpha): the only living representative is the coelacanth.

lobelia /ləˈbiːlɪə/ ▸ noun a chiefly tropical or subtropical plant of the bellflower family, in particular an annual widely grown as a bedding plant. Some kinds are aquatic, and some grow as thick-trunked shrubs or trees on African mountains. ● Genus *Lobelia*, family Campanulaceae: many species, including the popular blue-flowered *L. erinus*.
– ORIGIN modern Latin, named after Matthias de *Lobel* (1538–1616), Flemish botanist to James I.

Lobito /lʊˈbiːtəʊ/ a seaport and natural harbour on the Atlantic coast of Angola; pop. 128,600 (est. 2004).

loblolly /ˈlɒblɒli/ ▸ noun (pl. **loblollies**) **1** (also **loblolly pine**) a pine tree of the southern US that has very long slender needles and is an important source of timber. ● *Pinus taeda*, family Pinaceae.
2 (also **loblolly bay**) a small evergreen tree of the tea family, with bay-like leaves and white flowers resembling those of the camellia, native to the south-eastern US. ● *Gordonia lasianthus*, family Theaceae.
– ORIGIN late 16th cent. (denoting thick gruel): the reason for the application of the word to the two plants, and the word's origin, are unknown.

lobo /ˈləʊbəʊ/ ▸ noun (pl. **lobos**) N. Amer. (in the south-western US and Mexico) a timber wolf.
– ORIGIN mid 19th cent.: from Spanish, from Latin *lupus* 'wolf'.

lobola /ləˈbəʊlə/ (also **lobolo** /ləˈbəʊləʊ/) ▸ noun (among southern African peoples) a bride price, traditionally one paid with cattle. ■ [mass noun] the practice of paying a bride price.
– ORIGIN Zulu and Xhosa.

lobopod /ˈləʊbə(ʊ)pɒd/ ▸ noun Zoology the lobopodium of an onychophoran. ■ an onychophoran: [as modifier] *a lobopod animal.*

lobopodium /ˌləʊbə(ʊ)ˈpəʊdɪəm/ ▸ noun (pl. **lobopodia** /-ɪə/) Zoology a blunt limb or organ resembling a limb, in particular: ■ the primitive leg of an onychophoran. ■ a lobe-like pseudopodium in an amoeba.
– ORIGIN early 20th cent.: from modern Latin *lobosus* 'having many lobes, large lobed' + PODIUM.

lobotomize (also **lobotomise**) ▸ verb [with obj.] Surgery perform a lobotomy on. ■ informal make (someone) less able to function mentally or emotionally: *couples we knew who had been lobotomized by the birth of their children.*
– DERIVATIVES **lobotomization** noun.

lobotomy /ləˈbɒtəmi/ ▸ noun (pl. **lobotomies**) a surgical operation involving incision into the prefrontal lobe of the brain, formerly used to treat mental illness. Compare with LEUCOTOMY.

lobscouse /ˈlɒbskaʊs/ ▸ noun [mass noun] a stew formerly eaten by sailors, consisting of meat, vegetables, and ship's biscuit.
– ORIGIN early 18th cent.: of unknown origin; compare with Dutch *lapskous*, Danish and Norwegian *lapskaus*, and German *Lapskaus*.

lobster ▸ noun a large marine crustacean with a cylindrical body, stalked eyes, and the first of its five pairs of limbs modified as pincers. ● *Homarus* and other genera, class Malacostraca.
■ [mass noun] the flesh of the lobster as food. ■ Austral./NZ a marine crayfish, especially one whose claws are eaten as food. ■ [mass noun] a deep red colour typical of a cooked lobster.
▸ verb [no obj.] catch lobsters.
– ORIGIN Old English *lopustre*, alteration of Latin *locusta* 'crustacean, locust'.

lobster claw ▸ noun a tropical American plant with brightly coloured flowers which resemble a lobster's claw, each being composed of boat-shaped bracts. ● *Heliconia bihai*, family Heliconiaceae.

lobster moth ▸ noun a brown woodland European moth with a caterpillar that has long legs and an upturned tail reminiscent of a lobster. ● *Stauropus fagi*, family Notodontidae.

lobster Newburg /ˈnjuːbəːg/ ▶ **noun** [mass noun] a dish of lobster cooked in a thick cream sauce containing sherry or brandy.
– ORIGIN probably named after *Newburgh*, New York.

lobster pot ▶ **noun** a basket-like trap in which lobsters are caught.

lobster thermidor /ˈθəːmɪdɔː/ ▶ **noun** [mass noun] a dish of lobster cooked in a cream sauce, returned to its shell, sprinkled with cheese, and browned under the grill.
– ORIGIN *thermidor* from THERMIDOR.

lobule /ˈlɒbjuːl/ ▶ **noun** chiefly Anatomy a small lobe.
– DERIVATIVES **lobular** adjective, **lobulate** /-lət/ adjective, **lobulated** adjective.
– ORIGIN late 17th cent.: from LOBE, on the pattern of words such as *globule*.

lobworm ▶ **noun** a large earthworm used as fishing bait.
– ORIGIN mid 17th cent.: from LOB in the obsolete sense 'pendulous object'.

local ▶ **adjective 1** relating or restricted to a particular area or one's neighbourhood: *researching local history | the local post office.* ■ denoting a telephone call made to a nearby place and charged at a relatively low rate. ■ denoting a train or bus serving a particular district, with frequent stops.
2 (in technical use) relating to a particular region or part, or to each of any number of these: *a local infection | migration can regulate the local density of animals.* ■ Computing denoting a variable or other entity that is only available for use in one part of a program. ■ Computing denoting a device that can be accessed without the use of a network. Compare with REMOTE.
▶ **noun** a local person or thing, in particular: ■ an inhabitant of a particular area or neighbourhood: *the street was full of locals and tourists.* ■ Brit. informal a pub convenient to a person's home: *a pint in the local.* ■ a local train or bus service. ■ N. Amer. a local branch of an organization, especially a trade union. ■ Stock Exchange slang a floor trader who trades on their own account, rather than on behalf of other investors.
– DERIVATIVES **locally** adverb, **localness** noun.
– ORIGIN late Middle English: from late Latin *localis*, from Latin *locus* 'place'.

local anaesthetic ▶ **noun** [mass noun] an anaesthetic that affects a restricted area of the body. Compare with GENERAL ANAESTHETIC.

local area network (abbrev.: **LAN**) ▶ **noun** a computer network that links devices within a building or group of adjacent buildings, especially one with a radius of less than 1 km.

local authority ▶ **noun** Brit. an administrative body in local government.

local bus ▶ **noun** Computing a high-speed data connection directly linking peripheral devices to the processor and memory, allowing activities that require high data transmission rates such as video display.

local colour ▶ **noun** [mass noun] **1** the customs, manner of speech, dress, or other typical features of a place or period that contribute to its particular character: *reporters in search of local colour and gossip.*
2 Art the actual colour of a thing in ordinary daylight, uninfluenced by the proximity of other colours.

local derby ▶ **noun** see DERBY².

locale /ləʊˈkɑːl/ ▶ **noun** a place where something happens or is set, or that has particular events associated with it: *her summers were spent in a variety of exotic locales.*
– ORIGIN late 18th cent.: from French *local* (noun), respelled to indicate stress on the final syllable; compare with MORALE.

local government ▶ **noun** [mass noun] the administration of a particular county or district, with representatives elected by those who live there.

Local Group Astronomy the cluster of galaxies of which our Galaxy is a member.

localism ▶ **noun** [mass noun] preference for one's own area or region, especially when this results in a limitation of outlook. ■ [count noun] a characteristic of a particular locality, such as a local idiom or custom.
– DERIVATIVES **localist** noun & adjective.

locality ▶ **noun** (pl. **localities**) the position or site of something: *the rock's size and locality.* ■ an area or neighbourhood: *she had few friends in the locality | a working-class locality.*
– ORIGIN early 17th cent.: from French *localité* or late Latin *localitas*, from *localis* 'relating to a place' (see LOCAL).

localize (also **localise**) ▶ **verb** [with obj.] (often as adj. **localized**) restrict (something) to a particular place: *symptoms include localized pain and numbness.* ■ make (something) local in character: *there'd now be a more localized news service.* ■ assign (something) to a particular place: *most vertebrates localize sounds by orienting movements.*
– DERIVATIVES **localizable** adjective, **localization** noun, **localizer** noun.

local option ▶ **noun** a choice available to a local administration to accept or reject national legislation (e.g. concerning the sale of alcoholic drink).

local preacher ▶ **noun** a Methodist layperson authorized to conduct services in a particular circuit.

local time ▶ **noun** time as reckoned in a particular region or time zone. ■ time at a particular place as measured from the sun's transit over the meridian at that place, defined as noon.

Locarno /ləˈkɑːnəʊ/, Italian /lɔˈkarnɔ/ a resort in southern Switzerland, at the northern end of Lake Maggiore; pop. 14,909 (2007).

Locarno Pact a series of agreements made in Locarno in 1925 between the UK, Germany, France, Belgium, Poland, and Czechoslovakia in an attempt to ensure the future peace of Europe. The Pact guaranteed the common borders of France, Germany, and Belgium and the demilitarization of the Rhineland, as specified by the Treaty of Versailles.

locate /lə(ʊ)ˈkeɪt/ ▶ **verb** [with obj.] discover the exact place or position of: *engineers were working to locate the fault.* ■ [with obj. and adverbial of place] situate in a particular place: *these popular apartments are centrally located.* ■ [with obj. and adverbial] place within a particular context: *they locate their policies in terms of wealth creation.* ■ [no obj., with adverbial of place] N. Amer. establish oneself or one's business in a specified place: *his marketing strategy has been to locate in small towns.*
– DERIVATIVES **locatable** adjective.
– ORIGIN early 16th cent.: from Latin *locat-* 'placed', from the verb *locare*, from *locus* 'place'. The original sense was as a legal term meaning 'let out on hire', later (late 16th cent.) 'assign to a particular place', then (particularly in North American usage) 'establish in a place'. The sense 'discover the exact position of' dates from the late 19th cent.

location ▶ **noun 1** a particular place or position: *the property is set in a convenient location.* ■ an actual place or natural setting in which a film or broadcast is made, as distinct from a simulation in a studio: *the movie was filmed entirely* ***on location.*** ■ [mass noun] the action of locating someone or something: *the location of new housing beyond the existing built-up areas.* ■ a position or address in computer memory.
2 S. African dated an area where black South Africans were obliged by apartheid laws to live, usually on the outskirts of a town or city. The term was later replaced by *township*.
– DERIVATIVES **locational** adjective.
– ORIGIN late 16th cent.: from Latin *locatio(n-)*, from the verb *locare* (see LOCATE).

locative /ˈlɒkətɪv/ Grammar ▶ **adjective** relating to or denoting a case in some languages of nouns, pronouns, and adjectives, expressing location.
▶ **noun** (**the locative**) the locative case. ■ a word in the locative case.
– ORIGIN early 19th cent.: from LOCATE, on the pattern of *vocative*.

locator ▶ **noun** a device or system for locating something, typically by means of radio signals.

locavore /ˈləʊkəvɔː/ ▶ **noun** N. Amer. a person whose diet consists only or principally of locally grown or produced food.
– ORIGIN early 21st cent.: on the pattern of *carnivore*, *herbivore*, etc.

loc. cit. ▶ **abbreviation** in the passage already cited.
– ORIGIN from Latin *loco citato*.

loch /lɒk, lɒx/ ▶ **noun** Scottish a lake. ■ (also **sea loch**) an arm of the sea, especially when narrow or partially landlocked.
– ORIGIN late Middle English: from Scottish Gaelic.

lochan /ˈlɒk(ə)n, ˈlɒx(ə)n/ ▶ **noun** Scottish a small loch.
– ORIGIN late 17th cent.: from Scottish Gaelic, diminutive of *loch*.

lochia /ˈlɒkɪə, ˈləʊ-/ ▶ **noun** [mass noun] Medicine the normal discharge from the uterus after childbirth.
– DERIVATIVES **lochial** adjective.
– ORIGIN late 17th cent.: modern Latin, from Greek *lokhia*, neuter plural (used as a noun) of *lokhios* 'of childbirth'.

Loch Ness a deep lake in NW Scotland, in the Great Glen. Forming part of the Caledonian Canal, it is 38 km (24 miles) long, with a maximum depth of 230 m (755 ft).

Loch Ness monster a large creature alleged to live in the deep waters of Loch Ness. Reports of its existence date from the time of St Columba (6th century); despite recent scientific expeditions, there is still no proof of its existence.

loci plural form of LOCUS.

loci classici plural form of LOCUS CLASSICUS.

locie /ˈləʊki/ (also **lokey**) ▶ **noun** (pl. **locies** or **lokeys**) N. Amer. & NZ informal a locomotive.

lock¹ ▶ **noun 1** a mechanism for keeping a door, window, lid, or container fastened, typically operated by a key. ■ a similar device used to prevent the operation or movement of a vehicle or other machine: *a steering lock | a bicycle lock.* ■ (in wrestling and martial arts) a hold that prevents an opponent from moving a limb. ■ [in sing.] archaic a number of interlocked or jammed items: *I have seen all Albermarle Street closed by a lock of carriages.*
2 a short section of a canal or river with gates and sluices at each end which can be opened or closed to change the water level, used for raising and lowering boats.
3 [mass noun] Brit. the turning of the front wheels of a vehicle to change its direction of motion. ■ (also **full lock**) the maximum extent that the front wheels of a vehicle can be turned.
4 (also **lock forward**) Rugby a player in the second row of a scrum.
5 (**a lock**) N. Amer. informal a person or thing that is certain to succeed; a certainty.
6 historical a mechanism for exploding the charge of a gun.
▶ **verb 1** [with obj.] fasten or secure (something) with a lock: *she closed and locked her desk* | (as adj. **locked**) *behind locked doors.* ■ [no obj.] (of a door, window, etc.) become or be able to be secured with a lock: *the door will automatically lock behind you.* ■ [with obj. and adverbial] enclose or shut in by locking or fastening a door, lid, etc.: *the prisoners are* ***locked in*** *overnight | Phil* ***locked away*** *the takings.*
2 make or become rigidly fixed or immovable: [with obj.] *he locked his hands behind her neck* | [no obj.] *their gaze locked for several long moments.*
3 [no obj.] [with adverbial of direction] go through a lock on a canal: *we locked through at Moore Haven.*
– PHRASES **have a lock on** N. Amer. informal have total control over. **lock horns** engage in conflict. **lock, stock, and barrel** including everything; completely: *the place is owned lock, stock, and barrel by an oil company.* [referring to the complete mechanism of a firearm.] **under lock and key** securely locked up.
– PHRASAL VERBS **lock someone down** N. Amer. confine a prisoner to their cell. **lock someone/thing in** (or **into**) involve someone or something in (a difficult or competitive situation): *they were locked in a legal battle.* ■ oblige a person or company to abide by the terms of a contract for a specific period: *you're locked in to the society's standard variable rate throughout that time.* **lock on to** locate and then track (a target) by radar or similar means. **lock someone out 1** keep someone out of a room or building by locking the door. **2** (of an employer) subject employees to a lockout. **lock someone out of** exclude someone from: *those now locked out of the job market.* **lock someone up** (or **away**) imprison someone. **lock something up** (also **lock up**) shut and secure a building by fastening its doors with locks: *they locked up the building and walked off | you could lock up for me when you leave.* ■ (**lock something away**) invest money in something so that it is not easily accessible: *vast sums of money locked up in pension funds.*
– DERIVATIVES **lockable** adjective, **lockless** adjective.
– ORIGIN Old English *loc*, of Germanic origin; related to German *Loch* 'hole'.

lock² ▶ **noun** a piece of a person's hair that coils or hangs together: *she pushed back* ***a lock of hair.*** ■ (**locks**) literary a person's hair: *flowing locks and a long white beard.* ■ a tuft of wool or cotton.
– DERIVATIVES **locked** adjective [in combination] *his curly-locked comrades.*
– ORIGIN Old English *locc*, of Germanic origin; related to Dutch *lok*, German *Locke*, possibly also to LOCK¹.

lockage ▶ **noun** [mass noun] the construction or use of locks on waterways. ■ the amount of rise and fall of water levels resulting from the use of locks. ■ money paid as a toll for the use of a lock.

L

lockbox ▶ **noun** N. Amer. a lockable container; a safe. ■ a delivery letter box provided with a lock. ■ [mass noun] a service provided by a bank, whereby the bank receives, processes, and deposits all of a company's mail receipts.

lockdown ▶ **noun** N. Amer. the confining of prisoners to their cells, typically in order to regain control during a riot. ■ a state of isolation or restricted access instituted as a security measure: *the university is on lockdown and nobody has been able to leave.*

Locke[1], John (1632–1704), English philosopher, a founder of empiricism and political liberalism. His *Two Treatises of Government* (1690) argues that the authority of rulers has a human origin and is limited. In *An Essay concerning Human Understanding* (1690) he argued that all knowledge is based on experience derived from the senses.
– DERIVATIVES **Lockean** adjective.

Locke[2], Joseph (1805–60), English civil engineer. A pioneer in railways, he enjoyed a lifelong association with Thomas Brassey, building important lines in England, Scotland, and France.

locker ▶ **noun 1** a small lockable cupboard or compartment, typically as one of a number placed together for public use, e.g. in schools or railway stations. ■ a chest or compartment on a ship or boat for clothes, stores, equipment, or ammunition.
2 a device that locks something.
– ORIGIN late Middle English: probably related to Flemish *loker*.

Lockerbie /ˈlɒkəbi/ a town in SW Scotland, in Dumfries and Galloway; pop. 4,500 (est. 2009). In 1988 the wreckage of an American airliner, destroyed by a terrorist bomb, crashed on the town, killing all those on board and eleven people on the ground.

locker room ▶ **noun** chiefly N. Amer. a room containing lockers, especially a sports changing room. ■ [as modifier] characteristic of or suited to a men's locker room, especially in being coarse or ribald: *locker-room humour.*

L

locket ▶ **noun 1** a small ornamental case, typically made of gold or silver, worn round a person's neck on a chain and used to hold things of sentimental value, such as a photograph.
2 a metal plate or band on a scabbard.
– ORIGIN late Middle English (in sense 2): from Old French *locquet*, diminutive of *loc* 'latch, lock', of Germanic origin; related to LOCK[1]. Sense 1 dates from the late 17th cent.

lockfast ▶ **adjective** Scottish secured with a lock: *lockfast areas in which to store equipment.*

lock forward ▶ **noun** another term for LOCK[1] (sense 4 of the noun).

lock-in ▶ **noun 1** an arrangement according to which a person or company is obliged to deal only with a specific company. ■ a period during which a person or company is bound by the terms of a contract: [as modifier] *a lock-in period.*
2 Brit. a period during which customers are locked into a bar or pub after closing time to continue drinking privately.
3 a protest demonstration in which a group locks itself within an office or factory.

lockjaw ▶ **noun** non-technical term for TRISMUS.

lock-keeper ▶ **noun** a person who is employed to attend and maintain a lock on a river or canal.

lock-knit ▶ **adjective** (of a fabric) knitted with an interlocking stitch.

locknut ▶ **noun** a nut screwed down on another to keep it tight. ■ a nut designed so that, once tightened, it cannot be accidentally loosened.

lockout ▶ **noun** the exclusion of employees by their employer from their place of work until certain terms are agreed to.

locksmith ▶ **noun** a person who makes and repairs locks.

lockstep ▶ **noun** [mass noun] chiefly N. Amer. a way of marching with each person as close as possible to the one in front: *the trio marched in lockstep.* ■ close adherence to and emulation of another's actions: *they raised prices in lockstep with those of foreign competitors.*

lock stitch ▶ **noun** [mass noun] a stitch made by a sewing machine by firmly linking together two threads or stitches.

lock-up ▶ **noun 1** a jail, especially a temporary one.
2 Brit. non-residential premises that can be locked up, typically a small shop or garage.
3 [mass noun] the locking up of premises for the night. ■ the time when premises are locked up: *hurrying back to their houses before lock-up.*
4 [mass noun] the action of becoming fixed or immovable: *anti-lock braking helps prevent wheel lock-up.*
5 an investment in assets which cannot readily be realized or sold on in the short term.

loco[1] ▶ **noun** (pl. **locos**) informal a locomotive.
– ORIGIN mid 19th cent.: abbreviation.

loco[2] ▶ **adjective** informal crazy.
– ORIGIN late 19th cent.: from Spanish, 'insane'.

locomotion ▶ **noun** [mass noun] movement or the ability to move from one place to another: *the muscles that are concerned with locomotion* | *he preferred walking to other forms of locomotion.*
– ORIGIN mid 17th cent.: from Latin *loco*, ablative of *locus* 'place' + *motio* (see MOTION).

locomotive ▶ **noun** a powered railway vehicle used for pulling trains: *a diesel locomotive.*
▶ **adjective** [attrib.] relating to or effecting locomotion: *locomotive power.* ■ archaic (of a machine, vehicle, or animal) having the power of progressive motion: *locomotive bivalves have the strongest hinges.*
– ORIGIN early 17th cent. (as an adjective): from modern Latin *locomotivus*, from Latin *loco* (ablative of *locus* 'place') + late Latin *motivus* 'motive', suggested by medieval Latin *in loco moveri* 'move by change of position'.

locomotor ▶ **adjective** chiefly Biology relating to locomotion: *locomotor organs.*
– ORIGIN early 19th cent.: from LOCOMOTION + MOTOR.

locomotor ataxia ▶ **noun** [mass noun] Medicine loss of coordination of movement, especially as a result of syphilitic infection of the spinal cord. Also called TABES DORSALIS.

locomotory ▶ **adjective** chiefly Zoology relating to or having the power of locomotion: *locomotory cilia.*

locoweed ▶ **noun** [mass noun] **1** a plant of the pea family which can cause a brain disorder if eaten by livestock, found in the western and south-western US. ● Genus *Astragalus* (and *Oxytropis*), family Leguminosae.
2 US informal cannabis.

Locrian mode /ˈlɒkrɪən/ ▶ **noun** Music the mode represented by the natural diatonic scale B–B (containing a minor 2nd, 3rd, 6th, and 7th, and a diminished 5th).
– ORIGIN late 19th cent.: *Locrian* from Greek *Locris*, a division of ancient Greece, + -IAN; named after an ancient Greek mode but not identifiable with it.

locule /ˈlɒkjuːl/ ▶ **noun** another term for LOCULUS.

loculus /ˈlɒkjʊləs/ ▶ **noun** (pl. **loculi** /-lʌɪ, -liː/) chiefly Botany each of a number of small separate cavities, especially in an ovary.
– DERIVATIVES **locular** adjective.
– ORIGIN mid 19th cent.: from Latin, 'compartment', diminutive of *locus* 'place'.

locum /ˈləʊkəm/ ▶ **noun** Brit. a person who stands in temporarily for someone else of the same profession, especially a cleric or doctor.
– ORIGIN early 20th cent.: short for LOCUM TENENS.

locum tenens /ˌləʊkəm ˈtiːnɛnz, ˈtɛn-/ ▶ **noun** (pl. **locum tenentes** /tɪˈnɛntiːz, tɛ-/) full form of LOCUM.
– DERIVATIVES **locum tenency** noun.
– ORIGIN mid 17th cent.: from medieval Latin, literally 'one holding a place' (see LOCUS, TENANT).

locus /ˈləʊkəs/ ▶ **noun** (pl. **loci** /-sʌɪ, -kʌɪ, -kiː/)
1 technical a particular position or place where something occurs or is situated: *it is impossible to specify the exact locus in the brain of these neural events.* ■ the effective or perceived location of something abstract: *the real locus of power is the informal council.* ■ Genetics the position of a gene or mutation on a chromosome.
2 Mathematics a curve or other figure formed by all the points satisfying a particular equation of the relation between coordinates, or by a point, line, or surface moving according to mathematically defined conditions.
3 Law short for LOCUS STANDI.
– ORIGIN early 18th cent.: from Latin, 'place'.

locus classicus /ˌləʊkəs ˈklasɪkəs, ˌlɒkəs/ ▶ **noun** (pl. **loci classici** /ˌləʊsʌɪ ˈklasɪsʌɪ, ˌlɒkiː ˈklasɪkiː/) a passage considered to be the best known or most authoritative on a particular subject.
– ORIGIN Latin, literally 'classical place'.

locus standi /ˌləʊkəs ˈstandʌɪ, ˌlɒkəs/ ▶ **noun** (pl. **loci standi** /ˌləʊsʌɪ ˈstandʌɪ, ˌlɒkiː ˈstandiː/) Law the right or capacity to bring an action or to appear in a court.
– ORIGIN Latin, literally 'place of standing'.

locust ▶ **noun 1** a large, mainly tropical grasshopper with strong powers of flight. It is usually solitary, but from time to time there is a population explosion and it migrates in vast swarms which cause extensive damage to vegetation. ● Several species in the family Acrididae, including the **migratory locust** (*Locusta migratoria*). ■ (also **seventeen-year locust**) US the periodical cicada.
2 (also **locust bean**) the large edible pod of some plants of the pea family, in particular the carob bean, which is said to resemble a locust.
3 (also **locust tree**) a carob tree, false acacia, or similar pod-bearing tree of the pea family.
– ORIGIN Middle English: via Old French *locuste* from Latin *locusta* 'locust, crustacean'.

locust years ▶ **plural noun** years of hardship or poverty.

locution /ləˈkjuːʃ(ə)n/ ▶ **noun 1** a word or phrase, especially with regard to style or idiom. ■ [mass noun] a person's style of speech: *his impeccable locution.*
2 an utterance regarded in terms of its intrinsic meaning or reference, as distinct from its function or purpose in context. Compare with ILLOCUTION, PERLOCUTION.
– DERIVATIVES **locutionary** adjective.
– ORIGIN late Middle English: from Old French, or from Latin *locutio(n-)*, from *loqui* 'speak'.

lode /ləʊd/ ▶ **noun** a vein of metal ore in the earth. ■ a rich source of something: *a rich lode of scandal and alleged crime.*
– ORIGIN Old English *lād* 'way, course', variant of LOAD. The term denoted a watercourse in late Middle English and a lodestone in the early 16th cent. The current sense dates from the early 17th cent.

loden /ˈləʊd(ə)n/ ▶ **noun** [mass noun] a thick waterproof woollen cloth. ■ the dark green colour typical of loden cloth.
– ORIGIN early 20th cent.: from German *Loden*.

lodestar ▶ **noun** a star that is used to guide the course of a ship, especially the pole star.
– ORIGIN Middle English: from LODE in the obsolete sense 'way, course' + STAR.

lodestone (also **loadstone**) ▶ **noun** a piece of magnetite or other naturally magnetized mineral, able to be used as a magnet. ■ [mass noun] a naturally magnetized mineral; magnetite. ■ a person or thing that is the focus of attention or attraction.

lodge ▶ **noun 1** a small house at the gates of a park or in the grounds of a large house, occupied by a gatekeeper, gardener, or other employee. ■ a small country house occupied in season for sports such as hunting, shooting, or skiing. ■ [in names] a large house or hotel: *Cumberland Lodge.* ■ a porter's quarters at the main entrance of a college or other large building. ■ the residence of a head of a college, especially at Cambridge. ■ an American Indian tent or wigwam. ■ a beaver's den.
2 a branch or meeting place of an organization such as the Freemasons.
▶ **verb 1** [with obj.] present (a complaint, appeal, claim, etc.) formally to the proper authorities: *he has 28 days in which to lodge an appeal.* ■ (**lodge something in/with**) leave money or a valuable item in (a place) or with (someone) for safekeeping.
2 [with adverbial of place] make or become firmly fixed or embedded in a place: [with obj.] *they had to remove a bullet lodged near his spine* | [no obj.] figurative *the image had lodged in her mind.*
3 [no obj., with adverbial] rent accommodation in another person's house: *the man who lodged in the room next door.* ■ [with obj. and adverbial] provide (someone) with accommodation in return for payment.
4 [with obj.] (of wind or rain) flatten (a standing crop): (as adj. **lodged**) *rain that soaks standing or lodged crops.*
– ORIGIN Middle English *loge*, via Old French *loge* 'arbour, hut' from medieval Latin *laubia, lobia* (see LOBBY), of Germanic origin; related to German *Laube* 'arbour'.

lodgement (US **lodgment**) ▶ **noun 1** chiefly literary a place in which a person or thing is located or lodged: *they found a lodgement for the hook in the parapet.*
2 [mass noun] the action of depositing or lodging something.
– ORIGIN late 16th cent.: from French *logement* 'dwelling', from Old French *loge* 'arbour' (see LODGE).

lodgepole pine ▶ **noun** a straight-trunked pine tree which grows in the mountains of western North America, widely grown for timber and traditionally used by some American Indians in the construction of lodges. ● *Pinus contorta* var. *latifolia*, family Pinaceae.

lodger ▶ **noun** chiefly Brit. a person who rents accommodation in another person's house.

lodging ▶ **noun** [mass noun] temporary accommodation: *a fee for **board and lodging**.* ■ [count noun] (usu. **lodgings**) a room or rooms rented out to someone, usually in the same residence as the owner: *he was looking for lodgings and a job.*

lodging house ▶ **noun** a private house in which furnished rooms are rented for living or staying in temporarily.

lodicule /ˈlɒdɪkjuːl/ ▶ **noun** Botany a small green or white scale below the ovary of a grass flower.
– ORIGIN mid 19th cent.: from Latin *lodicula*, diminutive of *lodix* 'coverlet'.

Łódź /wʊtʃ/ an industrial city in central Poland, south-west of Warsaw, the second-largest city in the country; pop. 756,666 (2007).

loerie ▶ **noun** (pl. **loeries**) variant spelling of LOURIE.

loess /ˈləʊɪs, ləːs/ ▶ **noun** [mass noun] Geology a loosely compacted yellowish-grey deposit of wind-blown sediment of which extensive deposits occur e.g. in eastern China and the American Midwest.
– DERIVATIVES **loessial** adjective, **loessic** adjective.
– ORIGIN mid 19th cent.: from German *Löss*, from Swiss German *lösch* 'loose'.

lo-fi (also **low-fi**) ▶ **adjective** of or employing sound reproduction of a lower quality than hi-fi: *lo-fi recording techniques.* ■ (of popular music) recorded and produced with basic equipment and thus having a raw and unsophisticated sound.
▶ **noun** [mass noun] lo-fi sound reproduction or music.
– ORIGIN 1950s: from an alteration of LOW[1] + *-fi* on the pattern of *hi-fi*.

Lofoten Islands /ləˈfəʊt(ə)n/ an island group off the NW coast of Norway. They are situated within the Arctic Circle, south-west of the Vesterålen group.

loft ▶ **noun 1** a room or space directly under the roof of a house or other building, used for accommodation or storage. ■ a gallery in a church or hall: *a choir loft.* ■ a large, open area in a warehouse, factory, or other large building that has been converted into living space. ■ a pigeon house. ■ US part of a room on a higher level than the rest of the room.
2 [mass noun] Golf upward inclination given to the ball in a stroke. ■ backward slope of the head of a club, designed to give upward inclination to the ball.
3 [mass noun] the thickness of insulating matter in an object such as a sleeping bag.
▶ **verb 1** [with obj. and adverbial of direction] kick, hit, or throw (a ball or missile) high up: *he lofted the ball over the goalkeeper.*
2 [with obj.] (usu. as adj. **lofted**) give backward slope to the head of (a golf club): *a lofted metal club.*
– ORIGIN late Old English, from Old Norse *lopt* 'air, sky, upper room', of Germanic origin; related to Dutch *lucht* and German *Luft*.

lofter ▶ **noun 1** a decoy placed in a tree to attract pigeons.
2 Golf, dated a nine-iron or similar lofted club.

lofting ▶ **noun** [mass noun] the work carried out by a loftsman.

loftsman ▶ **noun** (pl. **loftsmen**) a person who draws up full-size outlines from the drawing or plans for parts of a ship or aircraft.

lofty ▶ **adjective** (**loftier**, **loftiest**) **1** of imposing height: *the elegant square was shaded by lofty palms.* ■ of a noble or elevated nature: *an extraordinary mixture of harsh reality and lofty ideals.* ■ haughty and aloof: *lofty intellectual disdain.*
2 (of wool and other textiles) thick and resilient.
– DERIVATIVES **loftily** adverb, **loftiness** noun.
– ORIGIN Middle English: from LOFT, influenced by ALOFT.

log[1] ▶ **noun 1** a part of the trunk or a large branch of a tree that has fallen or been cut off.
2 (also **logbook**) an official record of events during the voyage of a ship or aircraft: *a ship's log.* ■ a regular or systematic record of incidents or observations: *keep a detailed log of your activities.*
3 an apparatus for determining the speed of a ship, originally one consisting of a float attached to a knotted line that is wound on a reel, the distance run out in a certain time being used as an estimate of the vessel's speed.
▶ **verb** (**logs, logging, logged**) [with obj.] **1** enter (an incident or fact) in the log of a ship or aircraft or in another systematic record: *the incident has to be logged.* ■ (of a ship, aircraft, or pilot) achieve (a certain distance, speed, or time): *she had logged more than 12,000 miles since her launch.* ■ make a systematic recording of events, observations, or measurements: *the virus can log keystrokes that you make when you log on to all sorts of services.*
2 cut down (an area of forest) in order to exploit the timber commercially.
– PHRASES (**as**) **easy as falling off a log** informal very easy.
– PHRASAL VERBS **log in** (or **on**) go through the procedures to begin use of a computer, database, or system. **log off** (or **out**) go through the procedures to conclude use of a computer, database, or system.
– ORIGIN Middle English (in the sense 'bulky mass of wood'): of unknown origin; perhaps symbolic of the notion of heaviness. Sense 3 of the noun originally denoted a thin quadrant of wood loaded to float upright in the water, whence 'ship's journal' in which information derived from this device was recorded.

> **WORD TRENDS** The verb **log** has become part of the vocabulary of modern paranoia. As the Oxford English Corpus shows, the word is now primarily associated with technology, in particular that used for surveillance: *the spyware secretly records your keystrokes, logging sensitive information such as online banking passwords.* Hackers are not the only ones responsible for the logging of information. Increasingly, those in authority are accused of systematically recording people's details without reason or permission: *the government is logging details of every man, woman and child in 'Big Brother' computers.*

log[2] ▶ **noun** short for LOGARITHM: [as modifier] *log tables* | [prefixed to a number or algebraic symbol] *log x*.

log$_e$ ▶ **symbol** natural logarithm.

-log ▶ **combining form** US spelling of -LOGUE.

logan /ˈlɒɡ(ə)n, ˈləʊɡ(ə)n/ (also **logan stone**) ▶ **noun** another term for ROCKING STONE.
– ORIGIN mid 18th cent.: from *logging* (from dialect *log* 'to rock').

Logan, Mount /ˈləʊɡ(ə)n/ a mountain in SW Yukon Territory, Canada, near the border with Alaska. Rising to 6,054 m (19,850 ft), it is the highest peak in Canada and the second-highest peak in North America.

loganberry /ˈləʊɡ(ə)nˌb(ə)ri, -ˌbɛri/ ▶ **noun** (pl. **loganberries**) **1** an edible dull-red soft fruit, considered to be a hybrid of a raspberry and an American dewberry.
2 the scrambling blackberry-like plant which bears the loganberry. ● *Rubus loganobaccus*, family Rosaceae.
– ORIGIN late 19th cent.: from the name of John H. *Logan* (1841–1928), American horticulturalist, + BERRY.

logarithm /ˈlɒɡərɪð(ə)m, -rɪθ-/ (abbrev.: **log**) ▶ **noun** a quantity representing the power to which a fixed number (the base) must be raised to produce a given number.

> Logarithms can be used to simplify calculations, as the addition and subtraction of logarithms is equivalent to multiplication and division, though the use of printed tables of logarithms for this has declined with the spread of electronic calculators. They also allow a geometric relationship to be represented conveniently by a straight line. The base of a **common logarithm** is 10, and that of a **natural logarithm** is the number *e* (2.71828 ...).

– ORIGIN early 17th cent.: from modern Latin *logarithmus*, from Greek *logos* 'reckoning, ratio' + *arithmos* 'number'.

logarithmic ▶ **adjective** relating to or expressed in terms of logarithms. ■ (of a scale) constructed so that successive points along an axis, or graduations which are an equal distance apart, represent values which are in an equal ratio. ■ (of a curve) forming a straight line when plotted on a logarithmic scale; exponential.
– DERIVATIVES **logarithmically** adverb.

logarithmic spiral ▶ **noun** another term for EQUIANGULAR SPIRAL.

logbook ▶ **noun** another term for LOG[1] (sense 2 of the noun). ■ Brit. another term for REGISTRATION DOCUMENT.

log cabin ▶ **noun** a hut built of whole or split logs. ■ [usu. as modifier] a pattern of squares used for patchwork quilts resembling the patterning of wood in a log cabin.

loge /ləʊʒ/ ▶ **noun** a private box or enclosure in a theatre.
– ORIGIN mid 18th cent.: from French.

-loger ▶ **combining form** equivalent to -LOGIST.
– ORIGIN on the pattern of words such as *(astro)loger*.

log flume ▶ **noun** a water chute ride at an amusement park.

logger ▶ **noun 1** a person who fells trees for timber; a lumberjack.
2 a device or computer program for making a systematic recording of events, observations, or measurements.

loggerhead ▶ **noun 1** (also **loggerhead turtle**) a reddish-brown turtle with a very large head, occurring chiefly in warm seas. ● *Caretta caretta*, family Cheloniidae.
2 (also **loggerhead shrike**) a widespread North American shrike, having mainly grey plumage with a black eyestripe, wings, and tail. ● *Lanius ludovicianus*, family Laniidae.
3 archaic a foolish person.
– PHRASES **at loggerheads** in violent dispute or disagreement: *councillors were **at loggerheads with** the government over the grant allocation.* [perhaps a use of *loggerhead* in the late 17th-cent. sense 'long-handled iron instrument for heating liquids and tar' (when wielded as a weapon).]
– ORIGIN late 16th cent. (in sense 3): from dialect *logger* 'block of wood for hobbling a horse' + HEAD.

loggia /ˈləʊdʒə, ˈlɒ-, -dʒɪə/ ▶ **noun** a gallery or room with one or more open sides, especially one that forms part of a house and has one side open to the garden.
– ORIGIN mid 18th cent.: from Italian, 'lodge'.

logging ▶ **noun** [mass noun] the activity or business of felling trees and cutting and preparing the timber.

logia plural form of LOGION.

logic ▶ **noun** [mass noun] **1** reasoning conducted or assessed according to strict principles of validity: *experience is a better guide to this than deductive logic* | *the logic of the argument is faulty.* ■ a particular system or codification of the principles of proof and inference: *Aristotelian logic.* ■ the systematic use of symbolic and mathematical techniques to determine the forms of valid deductive argument. ■ the quality of being justifiable by reason: *there seemed to be a lack of logic in his remarks.* ■ (**the logic of**) the course of action suggested by or following as a necessary consequence of: *the logic of private competition was to replace small firms by larger firms.*
2 a system or set of principles underlying the arrangements of elements in a computer or electronic device so as to perform a specified task. ■ logical operations collectively.
– DERIVATIVES **logician** noun.
– ORIGIN late Middle English: via Old French *logique* and late Latin *logica* from Greek *logikē* (*tekhnē*) '(art) of reason', from *logos* 'word, reason'.

-logic ▶ **combining form** equivalent to -LOGICAL (as in *pharmacologic*).
– ORIGIN from Greek *-logikos*.

logical ▶ **adjective** of or according to the rules of logic or formal argument: *a logical impossibility.* ■ characterized by or capable of clear, sound reasoning: *her logical mind* | *the information is displayed in a simple and logical fashion.* ■ (of an action, decision, etc.) expected or sensible under the circumstances: *the polar expedition is a logical extension of his Arctic travels.*
– DERIVATIVES **logicality** /-ˈkalɪtɪ/ noun, **logically** adverb [sentence adverb] *such a situation is logically impossible.*
– ORIGIN late Middle English: from medieval Latin *logicalis* from late Latin *logica* (see LOGIC).

-logical ▶ **combining form** in adjectives corresponding chiefly to nouns ending in *-logy* (such as *pharmacological* corresponding to *pharmacology*).

logical atomism ▶ **noun** [mass noun] Philosophy the theory that all propositions can be analysed into simple independent elements of meaning corresponding to elements making up facts about the world. It formed part of the early thought of Wittgenstein and Bertrand Russell.

logical empiricism ▶ **noun** see LOGICAL POSITIVISM.

logical form ▶ **noun** Logic the abstract form in which an argument or proposition may be expressed in logical terms, as distinct from its particular content.

logical necessity ▶ **noun** [mass noun] that state of things which obliges something to be as it is because no alternative is logically possible. ■ [count noun] a thing which logically must be so.

logical operation ▶ **noun** an operation of the kind used in logic, e.g. conjunction or negation. ■ Computing an operation that acts on binary numbers to produce

L

a result according to the laws of Boolean logic (e.g. the AND, OR, and NOT functions).

logical positivism ▶ **noun** [mass noun] a form of positivism, developed by members of the Vienna Circle, which considers that the only meaningful philosophical problems are those which can be solved by logical analysis. Also called **LOGICAL EMPIRICISM**.

logic bomb ▶ **noun** Computing a set of instructions secretly incorporated into a program so that if a particular condition is satisfied they will be carried out, usually with harmful effects.

logic chopping ▶ **noun** [mass noun] the practice of engaging in excessively pedantic argument.

logic circuit ▶ **noun** Electronics a circuit for performing logical operations on input signals.

logicism /ˈlɒdʒɪsɪz(ə)m/ ▶ **noun** [mass noun] Philosophy the theory that all mathematics can ultimately be deduced from purely formal logical axioms, introduced by Frege and developed by Bertrand Russell.
– DERIVATIVES **logicist** **noun**.

login (also **logon**) ▶ **noun** an act of logging in to a computer, database, or system. ■ a password or code used when logging in: *you need to remember your user login*.

logion /ˈlɒgɪɒn, ˈləʊ-/ ▶ **noun** (pl. **logia** /-gɪə/) a saying attributed to Christ, especially one not recorded in the canonical Gospels.
– ORIGIN late 19th cent.: from Greek, 'oracle', from *logos* 'word'.

-logist ▶ **combining form** indicating a person skilled or involved in a branch of study denoted by a noun ending in *-logy* (such as *biologist* corresponding to *biology*).

logistic ▶ **adjective** relating to logistics: *logistic problems*.
– DERIVATIVES **logistical** **adjective**, **logistically** **adverb**.

L

logistic curve ▶ **noun** Statistics a sigmoid curve used in population studies which increases exponentially for small values of the variable, and approaches a constant value asymptotically for large values.

logistics /ləˈdʒɪstɪks/ ▶ **plural noun** [treated as sing. or pl.] the detailed organization and implementation of a complex operation: *the logistics of a large-scale rock show demand certain necessities*. ■ the activity of organizing the movement, equipment, and accommodation of troops. ■ the commercial activity of transporting goods to customers.
– ORIGIN late 19th cent.: from French *logistique*, from *loger* 'to lodge'.

logjam ▶ **noun 1** a crowded mass of logs blocking a river.
2 a situation that seems irresolvable: *the president can use his power to* ***break the logjam*** *over this issue*. ■ a backlog: *keeping a diary may ease the logjam of work*.

log line ▶ **noun** a line to which a ship's log is attached.

log-log ▶ **adjective** Mathematics denoting a graph or graph paper having or using a logarithmic scale along both axes.

log-normal ▶ **adjective** Statistics of or denoting a set of data in which the logarithm of the variate is distributed according to a normal distribution.
– DERIVATIVES **log-normality** **noun**, **log-normally** **adverb**.

logo /ˈlɒgəʊ, ˈləʊgəʊ/ ▶ **noun** (pl. **logos**) a symbol or other small design adopted by an organization to identify its products, uniform, vehicles, etc.: *the Olympic logo was emblazoned across the tracksuits*.
– DERIVATIVES **logoed** **adjective**.
– ORIGIN 1930s: abbreviation of **LOGOGRAM** or **LOGOTYPE**.

logocentric ▶ **adjective** regarding words and language as a fundamental expression of an external reality (especially applied as a negative term to traditional Western thought by postmodernist critics).
– DERIVATIVES **logocentrism** **noun**.
– ORIGIN 1930s: from Greek *logos* 'word, reason' + **-CENTRIC**.

logoff ▶ **noun** another term for **LOGOUT**.

logogram ▶ **noun** a sign or character representing a word or phrase, such as those used in shorthand and some ancient writing systems.
– ORIGIN mid 19th cent.: from Greek *logos* 'word' + **-GRAM**[1].

logograph ▶ **noun** another term for **LOGOGRAM**.
– DERIVATIVES **logographic** **adjective**.

logomachy /ləˈgɒməki/ ▶ **noun** (pl. **logomachies**) rare an argument about words.
– ORIGIN mid 16th cent.: from Greek *logomakhia*, from *logos* 'word' + *-makhia* 'fighting'.

logon ▶ **noun** another term for **LOGIN**.

logophile /ˈlɒgə(ʊ)fʌɪl/ ▶ **noun** a lover of words.

logorrhoea /ˌlɒgəˈrɪə/ (US **logorrhea**) ▶ **noun** [mass noun] a tendency to extreme loquacity.
– ORIGIN early 20th cent.: from Greek *logos* 'word' + *rhoia* 'flow'.

Logos /ˈlɒgɒs/ ▶ **noun** [mass noun] **1** Theology the Word of God, or principle of divine reason and creative order, identified in the Gospel of John with the second person of the Trinity incarnate in Jesus Christ.
2 (in Jungian psychology) the principle of reason and judgement, associated with the animus. Often contrasted with **EROS**.
– ORIGIN Greek, 'word, reason'.

logotype ▶ **noun** Printing a single piece of type that prints a word, a group of separate letters, or a logo. ■ a logo.
– ORIGIN early 19th cent.: from Greek *logos* 'word' + **TYPE**.

logout (also **logoff**) ▶ **noun** an act of logging out of a computer system.

logrolling ▶ **noun** [mass noun] N. Amer. **1** informal the practice of exchanging favours, especially in politics by reciprocal voting for each other's proposed legislation. [from the phrase *you roll my log and I'll roll yours*.]
2 a sport in which two contestants stand on a floating log and try to knock each other off by spinning it with their feet.
– DERIVATIVES **logroller** **noun**.

Logroño /lɒˈgrɒnjəʊ/ a market town in northern Spain, on the River Ebro, capital of La Rioja region; pop. 150,071 (2008).

logrunner ▶ **noun** a ground-dwelling Australasian songbird, having a blackish or mottled brown back and a spine-tipped tail. Also called **SPINETAIL**. ● Genus *Orthonyx*, family Orthonychidae (the **logrunner family**): two species; the logrunner family also includes whipbirds, quail-thrushes, and rail-babblers.

-logue (US also **-log**) ▶ **combining form 1** denoting discourse of a specified type: *dialogue*.
2 denoting compilation: *catalogue*.
3 equivalent to **-LOGIST**.
– ORIGIN from French *-logue*, from Greek *-logos*, *-logon*.

logwood ▶ **noun** a spiny Caribbean tree of the pea family, the dark heartwood of which yields haematoxylin and other dyes. ● *Haematoxylon campechianum*, family Leguminosae.

logy /ˈləʊgi/ ▶ **adjective** (**logier**, **logiest**) N. Amer. dull and heavy in motion or thought; sluggish.
– ORIGIN mid 19th cent.: of uncertain origin; compare with Dutch *log* 'heavy, dull'.

-logy ▶ **combining form 1** (usu. as **-ology**) denoting a subject of study or interest: *psychology*.
2 denoting a characteristic of speech or language: *eulogy*. ■ denoting a type of discourse: *trilogy*.
– ORIGIN from French *-logie* or medieval Latin *-logia*, from Greek.

Lohengrin /ˈləʊənˌgrɪn/, German /ˈloːənˌgriːn/ (in medieval French and German romances) the son of Perceval (Parsifal). He was summoned from the temple of the Holy Grail and taken in a boat to Antwerp, where he consented to marry Elsa of Brabant on condition that she did not ask who he was. Elsa broke this condition and he was carried away again in the boat.

loiasis /ləʊˈʌɪəsɪs/ ▶ **noun** [mass noun] a tropical African disease caused by infestation with eye worms, which cause transient subcutaneous swellings, often accompanied by pain or fever.
– ORIGIN early 20th cent.: modern Latin, from *loa* (a local Angolan word for the parasite) + **-IASIS**.

loin ▶ **noun** (usu. **loins**) the part of the body on both sides of the spine between the lowest (false) ribs and the hip bones. ■ (**loins**) chiefly literary the region of the sexual organs regarded as the source of erotic or procreative power: *he felt a stirring in his loins at the thought*. ■ a joint of meat that includes the vertebrae of the loins: ***loin of pork***.
– ORIGIN Middle English: from Old French *loigne*, based on Latin *lumbus*.

loincloth ▶ **noun** a single piece of cloth wrapped round the hips, typically worn by men in some hot countries as their only garment.

Loire /lwɑː/, French /lwaʀ/ a river of west central France. France's longest river, it rises in the Massif Central and flows 1,015 km (630 miles) north and west to the Atlantic at St-Nazaire.

loiter ▶ **verb** [no obj., with adverbial of place] stand or wait around without apparent purpose: *she saw Mary loitering near the cloakrooms*. ■ [with adverbial of direction] walk slowly and with no apparent purpose; dawdle: *the weather had tempted them to loiter along the banks of the Cherwell*.
– PHRASES **loiter with intent** English Law, dated stand or wait around with the intention of committing an offence.
– DERIVATIVES **loiterer** **noun**.
– ORIGIN late Middle English: perhaps from Middle Dutch *loteren* 'wag about'.

lokey ▶ **noun** variant spelling of **LOCIE**.

Loki /ˈləʊki/ Scandinavian Mythology a mischievous and sometimes evil god who contrived the death of Balder and was punished by being bound to a rock.

Lok Sabha /ˌləʊk səˈbɑː/ the lower house of the Indian Parliament. Compare with **RAJYA SABHA**.
– ORIGIN from Hindi *lok* 'the public' and *sabhā* 'assembly'.

LOL ▶ **abbreviation** informal laughing (or laugh) out loud.

Lolita /lə(ʊ)ˈliːtə/ ▶ **noun** a sexually precocious young girl.
– ORIGIN from the name of a character in the novel *Lolita* (1958) by Vladimir Nabokov.

loll ▶ **verb** [no obj., with adverbial] sit, lie, or stand in a lazy, relaxed way: *the two girls lolled in their chairs*. ■ (of a part of the body) hang loosely; droop: *he slumped against a tree trunk, his head lolling back*. ■ [with obj.] stick out (one's tongue) so that it hangs loosely out of the mouth.
– ORIGIN late Middle English: probably symbolic of dangling.

Lolland /ˈlɒlɑːn/ a Danish island in the Baltic Sea, to the south of Zealand and west of Falster.
– ORIGIN Danish, literally 'low land'.

lollapalooza /ˌlɒləpəˈluːzə/ (also **lalapalooza**) ▶ **noun** N. Amer. informal a person or thing that is particularly impressive or attractive: *it's a lollapalooza, just like your other books*.
– ORIGIN late 19th cent.: of fanciful formation.

Lollard /ˈlɒləd/ ▶ **noun** a follower of John Wyclif. The Lollards believed that the Church should help people to live a life of evangelical poverty and imitate Christ. Their ideas influenced the thought of John Huss, who in turn influenced Martin Luther.
– DERIVATIVES **Lollardism** **noun**, **Lollardy** **noun**.
– ORIGIN originally a derogatory term, derived from a Dutch word meaning 'mumbler', based on *lollen* 'to mumble'.

lollipop ▶ **noun** a large, flat, rounded boiled sweet on the end of a stick. ■ British term for **ICE LOLLY**. ■ informal a short, entertaining, but undemanding piece of classical music.
– ORIGIN late 18th cent.: perhaps from dialect *lolly* 'tongue' + **POP**[1].

lollipop lady (also **lollipop woman** or **man**) ▶ **noun** Brit. informal a woman (or man) who is employed to help children cross the road safely near a school by holding up a circular sign on a pole to stop the traffic.

lollop ▶ **verb** (**lollops**, **lolloping**, **lolloped**) [no obj., with adverbial of direction] move in an ungainly way in a series of clumsy paces or bounds: *the bear lolloped along the path*.
– ORIGIN mid 18th cent.: probably from **LOLL**, associated with **TROLLOP**.

lollo rosso /ˌlɒləʊ ˈrɒsəʊ/ ▶ **noun** [mass noun] lettuce of a variety with deeply divided red-edged leaves.
– ORIGIN Italian, from *lolla* 'husk, chaff' + *rosso* 'red'.

lolly ▶ **noun** (pl. **lollies**) informal **1** Brit. a lollipop. ■ Austral./NZ a small piece of confectionery; a sweet.
2 [mass noun] Brit. money: *you've done brilliantly raising all that lovely lolly*.
– ORIGIN mid 19th cent.: abbreviation. Sense 2 dates from the 1940s.

lollygag (also **lallygag**) ▶ **verb** (**lollygags**, **lollygagging**, **lollygagged**) [no obj.] N. Amer. informal spend time aimlessly; idle: *she goes to Arizona every January to lollygag in the sun*. ■ [with adverbial of direction] dawdle: *we're lollygagging along*.
– ORIGIN mid 19th cent.: of unknown origin.

Lollywood ▶ **noun** a name for the Pakistani popular film industry, based in Lahore.
– ORIGIN 1990s: blend of **LAHORE** and **BOLLYWOOD**.

Lombard /ˈlɒmbəd, -bɑːd/ ▸ **noun 1** a member of a Germanic people who invaded Italy in the 6th century.
2 a native of Lombardy in northern Italy.
3 [mass noun] the Italian dialect of Lombardy.
▸ **adjective** relating to Lombardy, or to the Lombards or their language.
– DERIVATIVES **Lombardic** adjective (sense 1 of the noun).
– ORIGIN from Italian *lombardo*, representing late Latin *Langobardus*, of Germanic origin, from the base of **LONG**[1] + the ethnic name *Bardi*.

Lombard Street a street in the City of London containing many of the principal London banks.
– ORIGIN so named because formerly occupied by bankers from *Lombardy*.

Lombardy /ˈlɒmbədi/ a region of central northern Italy, between the Alps and the River Po; capital, Milan. Italian name **Lombardia** /ˌlɔmbarˈdia/.

Lombardy poplar ▸ **noun** a black poplar of a variety which has a distinctive tall, slender columnar form. It arose as a mutation in Italy and is widely cultivated. • *Populus nigra* var. *italica*, family Salicaceae.

Lombok /ˈlɒmbɒk/ a volcanic island of the Lesser Sunda group in Indonesia, between Bali and Sumbawa; pop. 2,950,100 (est. 2005); chief town, Mataram.

Lomé /ˈləʊmeɪ/ the capital and chief port of Togo, on the Gulf of Guinea; pop. 1,452,000 (est. 2007)

Lomé Convention an agreement on trade and development aid, reached in Lomé in 1975, between the EC and forty-six African, Caribbean, and Pacific Ocean states, aiming for technical cooperation and the provision of development aid. Further agreements have been signed by a larger group.

loment /ˈləʊmənt/ (also **lomentum** /lə(ʊ)ˈmɛntəm/) ▸ **noun** Botany the pod of some leguminous plants, breaking up when mature into one-seeded sections.
– ORIGIN mid 19th cent.: from Latin, literally 'bean-meal', from *lavare* 'to wash'.

Lomond, Loch /ˈləʊmənd/ a lake in west central Scotland, to the north-west of Glasgow. It is the largest freshwater lake in Scotland.

Lomu /ˈləʊmuː/, Jonah Tali (b.1975), New Zealand rugby player. He became the youngest Test player for the All Blacks when he joined the team in 1994.

London[1] **1** the capital of the United Kingdom, situated in SE England on the River Thames; pop. (Greater London) 7,619,800 (est. 2008).

> London was settled as a river port and trading centre, called Londinium, shortly after the Roman invasion of AD 43, and, since the Middle Ages, has been a flourishing centre. It is divided administratively into the City of London, which is the country's financial centre, and thirty-two boroughs.

2 an industrial city in SW Ontario, Canada, situated to the north of Lake Erie; pop. 353,395 (2006).
– DERIVATIVES **Londoner** noun.

London[2], Jack (1876–1916), American novelist; pseudonym of *John Griffith Chaney*. The Klondike gold rush of 1897 provided the material for his famous works depicting struggle for survival. Notable works: *The Call of the Wild* (1903) and *White Fang* (1906).

London broil ▸ **noun** N. Amer. a grilled steak served cut diagonally in thin slices.

London clay ▸ **noun** [mass noun] clay forming an extensive layer in SE England, dating from the lower Eocene period.

Londonderry /ˈlʌnd(ə)nˌdɛri/ one of the Six Counties of Northern Ireland, formerly an administrative area. ■ the chief town of Londonderry, a city and port on the River Foyle near its outlet on the north coast; pop. 89,900 (est. 2009). It was formerly called Derry, a name still used by many. In 1613 it was granted to the City of London for colonization and became known as Londonderry.

London plane ▸ **noun** a plane tree which is considered to be a hybrid between the American and the oriental planes. Its flaking bark renders it resistant to pollution and it is widely planted in towns. • *Platanus* × *hispanica*, family Platanaceae.

London pride ▸ **noun** a European saxifrage with rosettes of fleshy leaves and stems of pink starlike flowers. • *Saxifraga* × *urbium*, family Saxifragaceae.

lone ▸ **adjective** [attrib.] **1** having no companions; solitary or single: *I approached a lone drinker across the bar* | *we sheltered under a lone tree.* ■ lacking the support of others; isolated: *I am by no means a lone voice.* ■ Brit. (of a parent) not having a partner to share the care of one's child or children.
2 literary (of a place) unfrequented and remote: *houses in lone rural settings.*
– ORIGIN late Middle English: shortening of **ALONE**.

lone hand ▸ **noun** (in euchre or quadrille) a hand played against the rest, or a player playing such a hand.
– PHRASES **play a lone hand** act on one's own.

loneliness ▸ **noun** [mass noun] **1** sadness because one has no friends or company: *feelings of depression and loneliness.* ■ the fact of being without companions; solitariness: *the loneliness of a sailor's life.*
2 (of a place) the quality of being unfrequented and remote; isolation: *the loneliness of the farm.*

lonely ▸ **adjective** (**lonelier**, **loneliest**) **1** sad because one has no friends or company: *lonely old people whose families do not care for them.* ■ without companions; solitary: *passing long lonely hours looking on to the street.*
2 (of a place) unfrequented and remote: *a lonely country lane.*
– ORIGIN late 16th cent.: from **LONE** + **-LY**[1].

lonely heart ▸ **noun** [usu. as modifier] a person looking for a lover or friend by advertising in a newspaper: *a lonely hearts column.*

lone pair ▸ **noun** Chemistry a pair of electrons occupying an orbital in an atom or molecule and not directly involved in bonding.

loner ▸ **noun** a person that prefers not to associate with others.

lonesome ▸ **adjective** chiefly N. Amer. **1** solitary or lonely: *she felt lonesome and out of things.*
2 remote and unfrequented: *a lonesome, unfriendly place.*
– PHRASES **by** (or Brit. **on**) **one's lonesome** informal all alone.
– DERIVATIVES **lonesomely** adverb, **lonesomeness** noun.

Lone Star State informal name for **TEXAS**.

lone wolf ▸ **noun** a person who prefers to act alone.

long[1] ▸ **adjective** (**longer**, **longest**) **1** measuring a great distance from end to end: *a long corridor* | *long black hair* | *the queue for tickets was long.* ■ (after a measurement and in questions) measuring a specified distance from end to end: *a boat 150 feet long.* ■ (of a journey) covering a great distance: *I went for a long walk.* ■ (of a ball in sport) travelling a great distance, or further than expected or intended: *he tried to head a long ball back to the keeper.* ■ (of a garment or sleeves on a garment) covering the whole of a person's legs or arms. ■ of elongated shape: *shaped like a torpedo, long and thin.*
2 lasting or taking a great amount of time: *a long and distinguished career* | *she took a long time to dress.* ■ (after a noun of duration and in questions) lasting or taking a specified amount of time: *a week-long course* | *the debates will be 90 minutes long.* ■ [attrib.] seeming to last more time than is the case; lengthy: *serving long hours on the committee.* ■ (of a person's memory) retaining things for a great amount of time.
3 relatively great in extent: *write a long report* | *a long list of candidates.* ■ (after a noun of extent and in questions) having a specified extent: *the statement was three pages long.*
4 Phonetics (of a vowel) categorized as long with regard to quality and length (e.g. in standard British English the vowel /uː/ in *food* is long as distinct from the short vowel /ʊ/ in *good*). ■ Prosody (of a vowel or syllable) having the greater of the two recognized durations.
5 (of odds or a chance) reflecting or representing a low level of probability: *winning against long odds.*
6 Finance (of shares, bonds, or other assets) bought in advance, with the expectation of a rise in price. ■ (of a broker or their position in the market) buying or based on long stocks. ■ (of a security) maturing at a distant date.
7 (of a drink) large and refreshing, and in which alcohol, if present, is not concentrated.
8 (**long on**) informal well supplied with: *an industry that's long on ideas but short on cash.*
▸ **noun 1** [mass noun] a long period: *see you **before long*** | *it will not be **for long**.*
2 a long sound such as a long signal in Morse code or a long vowel or syllable: *two longs and a short.*
3 (**longs**) Finance long-dated securities, especially gilts. ■ assets held in a long position.
▸ **adverb** (**longer**, **longest**) **1** for a long time: *we hadn't known them long* | *an experience they will long remember* | *his long-awaited Grand Prix debut.* ■ in questions about a period of time: ***how long have you been working?*** ■ at a time distant from a specified event or time: *her son died long ago* | *the work was compiled long after his death.* ■ [comparative] [with negative] after an implied point of time: *he couldn't wait any longer.* ■ (after a noun of duration) throughout a specified period: *it rained all day long.*
2 (with reference to the ball in sport) at, to, or over a great distance: *the Cambridge side played the ball long.* ■ beyond the point aimed at; too far: *he threw the ball long.*
– PHRASES **as** (or **so**) **long as 1** during the whole time that: *they have been there as long as anyone can remember.* **2** provided that: *as long as you fed him, he would be cooperative.* **be long** take a long time to happen or arrive: *sit down, tea won't be long.* **in the long run** over or after a long period of time; eventually: *it saves money in the long run.* **the long and the short of it** all that can or need be said: *the long and short of it is, I must make something or be miserable.* **long in the tooth** rather old. [originally said of horses, from the receding of the gums with age.] **long time no see** informal it's a long time since we last met (used as a greeting). [in humorous imitation of broken English spoken by an American Indian.] **so long** see **so**. **take the long view** think beyond the current situation.
– DERIVATIVES **longish** adjective.
– ORIGIN Old English *lang, long* (adjective), *lange, longe* (adverb), of Germanic origin; related to Dutch and German *lang*.

long[2] ▸ **verb** [no obj.] have a strong wish or desire: *she **longed for** a little more excitement* | [with infinitive] *we are longing to see the new baby.*
– ORIGIN Old English *langian* 'grow long, prolong', also 'dwell in thought, yearn', of Germanic origin; related to Dutch *langen* 'present, offer' and German *langen* 'reach, extend'.

long. ▸ **abbreviation** longitude.

-long ▸ **combining form** (added to nouns) for the duration of: *lifelong.*

long-acting ▸ **adjective** (chiefly of a drug) having effects that last for a long time.

longan /ˈlɒŋg(ə)n/ ▸ **noun** an edible juicy fruit from a plant related to the lychee, cultivated in SE Asia. • The plant is *Dimocarpus longan*, family Sapindaceae.
– ORIGIN mid 18th cent.: from Chinese *lóngyǎn*, literally 'dragon's eye'.

long-and-short work ▸ **noun** [mass noun] Architecture alternating tall and horizontal stone quoins forming a corner of a building, characteristic of Anglo-Saxon architecture.

long-awaited ▸ **adjective** having been hoped for or expected for a long time: *their long-awaited debut album.*

Long Beach a port and resort in California, situated on the south side of the Los Angeles conurbation; pop. 463,789 (est. 2008).

longboard ▸ **noun** a type of long surfboard.

longboat ▸ **noun 1** a large boat which may be launched from a sailing ship.
2 another term for **LONGSHIP**.

longbow ▸ **noun** a large bow drawn by hand and shooting a long feathered arrow. It was the chief weapon of English armies from the 14th century until the introduction of firearms.

longcase clock ▸ **noun** another term for **GRANDFATHER CLOCK**.

long corner ▸ **noun** (in field hockey) a penalty hit taken from the back line within 5 yards of the corner.

long-dated ▸ **adjective** (of securities) not due for early payment or redemption.

long-day ▸ **adjective** (of a plant) needing a long period of light each day to initiate flowering, which therefore happens naturally as the days lengthen in the spring.

long distance ▸ **adjective 1** travelling or operating between distant places: *a long-distance lorry driver* | *long-distance phone calls.*
2 Athletics denoting or relating to a race distance of 6 miles or 10,000 metres (6 miles 376 yds), or longer: *a long-distance runner.*
▸ **adverb** between distant places: *travelling long distance.*

long division ▸ **noun** [mass noun] arithmetical division in which the divisor has two or more figures, and a series of workings is made as successive groups of

L

digits of the dividend are divided by the divisor, to avoid excessive mental calculation.

longdog ▸ **noun** informal a greyhound or other hound of similar body shape.

long dozen ▸ **noun** (**a long dozen**) thirteen.

long-drawn (also **long-drawn-out**) ▸ **adjective** continuing for a long time, especially for longer than is necessary: *long-drawn-out negotiations*.

long drop ▸ **noun** informal a pit toilet.

longe ▸ **noun** variant of LUNGE².

long-eared bat ▸ **noun** an insectivorous bat with ears that are very long in proportion to the body.
● *Plecotus* and other genera, family Vespertilionidae: several species, in particular the **common** (or **brown**) **long-eared bat** (*P. auritus*) of Eurasia.

longeron /ˈlɒn(d)ʒərɒn/ ▸ **noun** a longitudinal structural component of an aircraft's fuselage.
– ORIGIN early 20th cent.: from French, literally 'girder'.

longevity /lɒnˈdʒɛvɪti/ ▸ **noun** [mass noun] long life: *the greater longevity of women compared with men.* ■ long existence or service: *her longevity in office now appeared as a handicap to the party.*
– ORIGIN early 17th cent.: from late Latin *longaevitas*, from Latin *longus* 'long' + *aevum* 'age'.

long face ▸ **noun** an unhappy or disappointed expression.
– DERIVATIVES **long-faced** adjective.

Longfellow /ˈlɒŋfɛləʊ/, Henry Wadsworth (1807–82), American poet. He is known for 'The Wreck of the Hesperus' and 'The Village Blacksmith' (both 1841) and *The Song of Hiawatha* (1855).

Longford /ˈlɒŋfəd/ a county of the Republic of Ireland, in the province of Leinster. ■ the county town of Longford; pop. 7,622 (2006).

longhair ▸ **noun 1** informal, often derogatory a person with long hair or characteristics associated with it, such as a hippy.
2 a cat of a long-haired breed.

L

longhand ▸ **noun** [mass noun] ordinary handwriting (as opposed to shorthand, typing, or printing): *he wrote out the reply in longhand* | [as modifier] *a longhand draft.*

long haul ▸ **noun** a long distance (in reference to the transport of goods or passengers): [as modifier] *a long-haul flight.* ■ a prolonged and difficult effort or task: *implementing the White Paper is likely to be a long haul.*
– PHRASES **over the long haul** chiefly N. Amer. over an extended period of time.

long-headed ▸ **adjective** dated having or showing foresight and good judgement.

long hop ▸ **noun** Cricket a short-pitched, easily hit ball.

longhorn ▸ **noun** an animal of a breed of cattle with long horns.

longhorn beetle ▸ **noun** an elongated beetle with long antennae, the larva of which typically bores in wood. ● Family Cerambycidae, formerly in the superfamily Longicornia; many species.

long-horned grasshopper ▸ **noun** former term for BUSH CRICKET.

longhouse ▸ **noun 1** historical the traditional dwelling of the Iroquois and other North American Indians.
2 a large communal village house in parts of Malaysia and Indonesia.

long hundredweight ▸ **noun** see HUNDREDWEIGHT.

longicorn /ˈlɒn(d)ʒɪkɔːn/ ▸ **noun** former term for LONGHORN BEETLE.
– ORIGIN mid 19th cent.: from modern Latin *longicornis*, from Latin *longus* 'long' + *cornu* 'horn'.

longing ▸ **noun** a yearning desire: *Miranda felt a wistful* ***longing for*** *the old days* | [mass noun] *a tale of love and longing.*
▸ **adjective** [attrib.] having or showing a yearning desire: *her longing eyes.*
– DERIVATIVES **longingly** adverb.

Longinus /lɒnˈdʒʌɪnəs/ (*fl.* 1st century AD), Greek scholar. He is the supposed author of a Greek literary treatise *On the Sublime*, concerned with the moral function of literature, which influenced Augustan writers such as Dryden and Pope.

Long Island an island on the coast of New York State. Its western tip, comprising the New York districts of Brooklyn and Queens, is separated from Manhattan and the Bronx by the East River and is linked to Manhattan by the Brooklyn Bridge.

Long Island iced tea ▸ **noun** a cocktail consisting of rum, vodka, gin, and other spirits mixed with cola and lemon juice.

longitude /ˈlɒn(d)ʒɪtjuːd, ˈlɒŋgɪ-/ ▸ **noun** the angular distance of a place east or west of the Greenwich meridian, or west of the standard meridian of a celestial object, usually expressed in degrees and minutes: *at a longitude of 2° W* | [mass noun] *lines of longitude.*
– ORIGIN late Middle English (also denoting length and tallness): from Latin *longitudo*, from *longus* 'long'.

longitudinal /ˌlɒn(d)ʒɪˈtjuːdɪn(ə)l, ˌlɒŋgɪ-/ ▸ **adjective**
1 running lengthwise rather than across: *longitudinal muscles* | *longitudinal stripes.*
2 relating to longitude; measured from east to west: *longitudinal positions.*
3 (of research or data) involving information about an individual or group gathered over a long period of time.
– DERIVATIVES **longitudinally** adverb.

longitudinal wave ▸ **noun** Physics a wave vibrating in the direction of propagation.

long johns ▸ **plural noun** informal underpants with closely fitted legs that extend to the wearer's ankles.

long jump ▸ **noun** (**the long jump**) an athletic event in which competitors jump as far as possible along the ground in one leap.
– DERIVATIVES **long jumper** noun.

long-lasting ▸ **adjective** enduring or having endured for a long period of time: *long-lasting effects* | *a long-lasting friendship.*

longleaf pine ▸ **noun** a large North American pine tree with long needles and cones, which is an important source of turpentine. Also called PITCH PINE.
● *Pinus palustris*, family Pinaceae.

long leg ▸ **noun** Cricket a fielding position far behind the batsman on the leg side. ■ a fielder at long leg.

long lens ▸ **noun** a lens with a long focal length, especially as a camera attachment for taking photographs from a great distance.

long-life ▸ **adjective** (of food) treated so as to stay fresh for longer than usual: *long-life milk.* ■ (of a product) able to continue working for longer than others of the same kind: *long-life batteries.*

longline ▸ **noun** a deep-sea fishing line from which are suspended many short lines with baited hooks.

longliner ▸ **noun** chiefly N. Amer. a person or fishing vessel that uses longlines.

longlist ▸ **noun** a list of selected names or things from which a shortlist is to be compiled.
▸ **verb** [with obj.] place on a longlist.

long-lived ▸ **adjective** living or lasting a long time.

long-lost ▸ **adjective** [attrib.] lost or absent for a long time: *a long-lost friend* | *his long-lost youth.*

Long March the epic withdrawal of the Chinese communists from SE to NW China in 1934–5, over a distance of 9,600 km (6,000 miles). 100,000 people, led by Mao Zedong, left the communist rural base after it was almost destroyed by the Kuomintang; 20,000 people survived the journey.

long mark ▸ **noun** informal term for MACRON.

long measure ▸ **noun** archaic a measure of length; a linear measure.

long metre ▸ **noun 1** a metrical pattern for hymns in which the stanzas have four lines with eight syllables each.
2 Prosody a quatrain of iambic tetrameters with alternate lines rhyming.

longneck ▸ **noun** N. Amer. informal a beer bottle with a long, narrow neck and a capacity of 330 ml.

long off ▸ **noun** Cricket a fielding position far behind the bowler and towards the off side. ■ a fielder at long off.

long on ▸ **noun** Cricket a fielding position far behind the bowler and towards the on side. ■ a fielder at long on.

Long Parliament the English Parliament which sat from November 1640 to March 1653, was restored for a short time in 1659, and finally voted its own dissolution in 1660. It was summoned by Charles I and sat through the English Civil War and on into the interregnum which followed.

long pig ▸ **noun** a translation of a term formerly used in some Pacific islands for human flesh as food.

long-playing ▸ **adjective** (of a record) about 30 cm in diameter and designed to rotate at 33⅓ revolutions per minute.
– DERIVATIVES **long-player** noun.

long-range ▸ **adjective 1** (especially of vehicles or missiles) able to be used or be effective over long distances: *long-range bombers.*
2 relating to a period of time that extends far into the future: *long-range forecasts.*

long reins ▸ **plural noun** a pair of long reins used to school a horse from the ground.

long-running ▸ **adjective** continuing for a long time: *a long-running dispute over EU subsidies.*

long s ▸ **noun** an obsolete form of lower-case s, written or printed as ſ. It was used in initial and medial but not final position in a word, and was generally abandoned in English-language printing shortly before 1800.

Longshan /lɒŋˈʃan/ ▸ **noun** [usu. as modifier] Archaeology a Neolithic civilization of the Yellow River valley in China (*c.*2500–1700 BC), between the Yangshao and Shang periods. It is characterized by pottery kiln-fired to a uniform black colour and by the establishment of towns.

longship ▸ **noun** a long, narrow warship, powered by both oar and sail with many rowers, used by the Vikings and other ancient northern European peoples.

longshore ▸ **adjective** existing on, frequenting, or moving along the seashore: *longshore currents.*
– ORIGIN early 19th cent.: from *along shore*.

longshore drift ▸ **noun** [mass noun] the movement of material along a coast by waves which approach at an angle to the shore but recede directly away from it.

longshoreman ▸ **noun** (pl. **longshoremen**) N. Amer. a docker.

long shot ▸ **noun** [in sing.] an attempt or guess that has only the slightest chance of succeeding or being accurate: *it's a long shot, but well worth trying.*
– PHRASES **(not) by a long shot** informal (not) by far or at all.

long sight ▸ **noun** [mass noun] the inability to see things clearly, especially if they are relatively close to the eyes, owing to the focusing of rays of light by the eye at a point behind the retina. Also called HYPERMETROPIA.

long-sighted ▸ **adjective** Brit. having long sight. ■ having imagination or foresight.
– DERIVATIVES **long-sightedly** adverb, **long-sightedness** noun.

long-sleeved ▸ **adjective** having sleeves that reach to the wrist: *a long-sleeved shirt.*

long-sleever ▸ **noun** Austral./NZ informal a large glass of beer.

longspur ▸ **noun** a mainly Canadian songbird related to the buntings, with brownish plumage and a boldly marked head in the male. ● Genus *Calcarius*, family Emberizidae (subfamily Emberizinae): three or four species.

long-standing ▸ **adjective** having existed or continued for a long time: *a long-standing tradition.*

long-stay ▸ **adjective** denoting or relating to people staying somewhere for a long time: *long-stay patients.*

longstop ▸ **noun** Cricket a fielding position (not normally used in the modern game) directly behind the wicketkeeper. ■ a fielder at longstop.

long-suffering ▸ **adjective** having or showing patience in spite of troubles, especially those caused by other people: *his long-suffering wife.*
– DERIVATIVES **long-sufferingly** adverb.

long suit ▸ **noun 1** (in bridge or whist) a holding of several cards of one suit in a hand, typically 5 or more out of the 13.
2 [usu. with negative] (**one's long suit**) one's outstanding personal quality or achievement: *tact was not his long suit.*

long-tailed duck ▸ **noun** a marine diving duck that breeds in Arctic Eurasia and North America, the male having very long tail feathers and mainly white plumage in winter. ● *Clangula hyemalis*, family Anatidae. North American name: **oldsquaw**.

long-tailed tit ▸ **noun** a small Eurasian songbird that resembles a tit, having black, white, and pink plumage and a long slender tail, and building a domed nest. ● Genus *Aegithalos*, family Aegithalidae: several species, in particular *A. caudatus*.

long-term ▸ adjective occurring over or relating to a long period of time: *the long-term unemployed* | *the long-term effects of smoking*.

long-termism ▸ noun [mass noun] the practice of making decisions with a view to long-term objectives or consequences.

long-time ▸ adjective (especially of a person) having had a specified role or identity for a long time: *his long-time friend and colleague*.

long tom ▸ noun informal, historical **1** a large cannon with a long range.
2 a trough for washing gold-bearing deposits.

long ton ▸ noun see **TON**[1].

longueur /lɒ̃(ŋ)ˈgəː/ ▸ noun a tedious passage in a book, piece of music, etc.: *its brilliant comedy passages do not cancel out the occasional longueurs*. ■ a tedious period of time: *frustrated by the longueurs, many rail-users take to the roads instead*.
– ORIGIN French, literally 'length'.

long vacation ▸ noun Brit. the summer break of three months taken by universities and (formerly) law courts.

long waist ▸ noun a low waist on a dress or a person's body.
– DERIVATIVES **long-waisted** adjective.

longwall ▸ adjective Mining of or involving a single long face worked (usually mechanically) along its whole length.

long wave ▸ noun a radio wave of a wavelength above one kilometre (and a frequency below 300 kHz): [as modifier] *long-wave radio*. ■ [mass noun] broadcasting using radio waves of 1 to 10 km wavelength: *listening to BBC Radio 4 **on long wave***.

longways (also **longwise**) ▸ adverb lengthways: *it has been sliced longways to show the internal structure*.

long-winded ▸ adjective **1** (of speech or writing) continuing at tedious length: *a long-winded question*.
2 archaic capable of doing something for a long time without becoming breathless.
– DERIVATIVES **long-windedly** adverb, **long-windedness** noun.

longwool ▸ noun a sheep of a breed with long wool.

lonicera /lɒˈnɪs(ə)rə/ ▸ noun a plant of a genus which comprises the honeysuckles. ● Genus *Lonicera*, family Caprifoliaceae.
– ORIGIN modern Latin, named after Adam *Lonitzer* (1528–86), German botanist.

lonning ▸ noun another term for **LOAN**[2].

Lonsdale belt ▸ noun Boxing an ornate belt awarded to a professional boxer winning a British title fight. A fighter winning three title fights in one weight division is given a belt to keep.
– ORIGIN early 20th cent.: named after the fifth Earl of Lonsdale, Hugh Cecil Lowther (1857–1944), who presented the first one.

loo[1] ▸ noun Brit. informal a toilet.
– ORIGIN 1940s: many theories have been put forward about the word's origin: one suggests the source is *Waterloo*, a trade name for iron cisterns in the early part of the century; the evidence remains inconclusive.

loo[2] ▸ noun [mass noun] a gambling card game, popular from the 17th to the 19th centuries, in which a player who fails to win a trick must pay a sum to a pool.
– ORIGIN late 17th cent.: abbreviation of obsolete *lanterloo* from French *lanturlu*, a meaningless song refrain.

looey (also **looie**) ▸ noun (pl. **looeys** or **looies**) US military slang short for **LIEUTENANT**.

loofah /ˈluːfə/ ▸ noun **1** the fibrous matter of the fluid-transport system of a marrow-like fruit, which is dried and used as a bath sponge.
2 the tropical Old World climbing plant of the gourd family which produces loofahs, which are also edible. ● *Luffa cylindrica*, family Cucurbitaceae.
– ORIGIN late 19th cent.: from Egyptian Arabic *lūfa*, denoting the plant.

look ▸ verb **1** [no obj., usu. with adverbial of direction] direct one's gaze in a specified direction: *people were **looking at** him* | *they looked up as he came into the room*. ■ (**look through**) ignore (someone) by pretending not to see them: *he glanced up once but **looked right through** me*. ■ [with obj.] dated express (something) by one's gaze: *Poirot looked a question*. ■ [with obj.] (**look something over**) inspect something with a view to establishing its merits: *they looked over a property in Great Marlborough Street*. ■ (**look through**) peruse (a book or other written material). ■ (**look round/around**) walk round (a place or building) in order to view any interesting features: *he spent the day looking round Edinburgh*. ■ [with clause] ascertain with a quick glance: *people finishing work don't **look where** they're going*.
2 (**look at/on**) regard in a specified way: *I look at tennis differently from some coaches*. ■ (**look at**) examine (a matter) and consider what action to take: *a committee is looking at the financing of the BBC*. ■ (**look into**) investigate: *the police looked into his business dealings*. ■ (usu. **look for**) attempt to find: *Howard has been looking for you*.
3 [with complement or adverbial] have the appearance or give the impression of being: *mum looked unhappy* | *the home **looked like** a prison* | (as adj., in combination **-looking**) *a funny-looking bloke*. ■ (**look like**) informal show a likelihood of: [with present participle] *Leeds didn't look like scoring from any of their corners* | [with clause] *it doesn't look like you'll be moving to Liverpool*. ■ (**look oneself**) appear one's normal, healthy self: *he just didn't look himself at all*.
4 (**look to**) rely on (someone) to do or provide something: *she will look to you for help*. ■ [with infinitive] hope or expect to do something: *universities are looking to expand their intakes*. ■ [with clause] archaic take care; make sure: *Look ye obey the masters of the craft*.
5 (of a building or room) have an outlook in a specified direction: *the room **looks out over** Mylor Harbour*.
▸ noun **1** an act of directing one's gaze in order to see someone or something: *let me get a closer look*. ■ an expression of a feeling or thought by looking: *the orderly gave me a funny look*. ■ a scrutiny or examination: *the government should **take a look at** the amount of grant the council receives*.
2 the appearance of someone or something, especially as expressing a particular quality: *the bedraggled look of the village*. ■ (**looks**) a person's facial appearance considered aesthetically: *he had charm, **good looks**, and an amusing insouciance*. ■ a style or fashion: *Italian designers unveiled their latest look*.
▸ exclamation (also **look here!**) used to call attention to what one is going to say: *'Look, this is ridiculous.'*
– PHRASES **look one's age** appear to be as old as one really is. **look alive** see **LOOK LIVELY**. **look before you leap** proverb you shouldn't act without first considering the possible consequences or dangers. **look daggers at** see **DAGGER**. **look down one's nose at** another way of saying **LOOK DOWN ON**. **look for trouble** see **TROUBLE**. **look someone in the eye** (or **face**) look directly at someone without showing embarrassment, fear, or shame. **look lively** (or dated **alive**) informal used to tell someone to be quick in doing something. **look the other way** deliberately ignore wrongdoing by others: *they do look the other way at corrupt practices here*. **look sharp** be quick. **look small** see **SMALL**. **look to the future** consider and plan for what is in the future, rather than worrying about the past or present. **look someone up and down** scrutinize someone carefully.
– PHRASAL VERBS **look after** take care of: *women who stay at home to look after children*. **look back** [with negative] suffer a setback or interrupted progress: *she launched her own company in 1981 and has never looked back*. **look back at/on** think of (past events). **look down on** regard (someone) with a feeling of superiority. **look forward to** await eagerly: *we look forward to seeing you*. **look in** make a short visit or call: *I will **look in on** you tomorrow*. **look on** watch without getting involved. **look out** [usu. in imperative] be vigilant and take notice: *'Look out!' warned Billie, seeing a movement from the room beyond*. **look something out** Brit. search for and produce something: *I've got a catalogue somewhere and I'll look it out if you're interested*. **look up** (of a situation) improve: *things seemed to be looking up at last*. **look someone up** informal make social contact with someone. **look something up** search for and find a piece of information in a book or database. **look up to** have a great deal of respect for (someone).
– ORIGIN Old English *lōcian* (verb), of West Germanic origin; related to German dialect *lugen*.

lookalike ▸ noun a person or thing that closely resembles another, especially someone who looks very similar to a famous person: *an Elvis Presley lookalike*.

look-and-say ▸ noun [mass noun] [as modifier] denoting a method of teaching reading based on the visual recognition of words rather than the association of sounds and letters. Compare with **PHONIC**.

lookbook ▸ noun a set of photographs displaying a fashion designer's new collection, assembled for marketing purposes.

looker ▸ noun **1** a person who looks: *it depends on whether you are a listener, a looker or a doer*.
2 [with adj.] a person with a specified appearance: *a tough looker is not necessarily a tough fighter*. ■ informal a very attractive person: *she was a real looker, good for the eyes*.

looker-on ▸ noun (pl. **lookers-on**) a person who is a spectator rather than a participant in a situation.

look-in ▸ noun [in sing.] [often with negative] Brit. informal a chance to take part or succeed in something: *they didn't let the other side **get a look-in** in the final*.

looking glass ▸ noun a mirror. ■ [as modifier] opposite to what is normal or expected: *looking-glass logic*.

lookism ▸ noun [mass noun] prejudice or discrimination on the grounds of a person's appearance.
– DERIVATIVES **lookist** noun & adjective.

lookit N. Amer. informal ▸ verb [with obj., in imperative] look at: *Hey, lookit that!*
▸ exclamation used to draw attention to what one is about to say: *lookit, Pete, this is serious*.

lookout ▸ noun **1** a place from which to keep watch or view the landscape. ■ a person stationed to keep watch for danger or trouble: *they acted as lookouts at the post office*. ■ archaic a view over a landscape.
2 [in sing.] [with adj.] informal, chiefly Brit. used to indicate whether a likely outcome is good or bad: *'What if he gets fits?' 'It's a bad lookout in that case.'*
– PHRASES **be one's (own) lookout** Brit. informal be a person's own responsibility or problem: *if you can't take an interest in local affairs, that's your lookout*. **be on the lookout** (or **keep a lookout**) **for** be alert to (danger or trouble). ■ keep searching for (something that is wanted): *we kept a sharp lookout for animals and saw several waterbuck*.

look-see ▸ noun informal a brief look or inspection: *we are just about to take a little look-see around the hotel*.
– ORIGIN late 19th cent.: from, or in imitation of, pidgin English.

L

lookup ▸ noun [mass noun] [usu. as modifier] the action of systematic electronic information retrieval. ■ a facility for lookup: *dictionary with fast phonetic lookup*.

looky ▸ exclamation informal used to draw attention to what one is about to say: *Looky there! You've gone and broken it*.

loom[1] ▸ noun an apparatus for making fabric by weaving yarn or thread.
ORIGIN Old English *gelōma* 'tool', shortened to *lome* in Middle English.

loom[2] ▸ verb [no obj., with adverbial] appear as a vague form, especially one that is large or threatening: *vehicles loomed out of the darkness*. ■ [no obj.] (of an event regarded as threatening) seem about to happen: *there is a crisis looming* | *dearer mortgages **loomed large** last night*.
▸ noun [in sing.] a vague and often exaggerated first appearance of an object seen in darkness or fog, especially at sea: *the loom of the land*. ■ the dim reflection by cloud or haze of a light which is not directly visible, e.g. from a lighthouse over the horizon.
– ORIGIN mid 16th cent.: probably from Low German or Dutch; compare with East Frisian *lōmen* 'move slowly', Middle High German *lüemen* 'be weary'.

loon[1] ▸ noun informal a silly or foolish person.
– ORIGIN late 19th cent.: from **LOON**[2] (referring to the bird's actions when escaping from danger), perhaps influenced by **LOONY**.

loon[2] ▸ noun North American term for **DIVER** (sense 2).
– ORIGIN mid 17th cent.: probably by alteration of Shetland dialect *loom*, denoting especially a guillemot or a diver, from Old Norse.

loon[3] ▸ verb [no obj., with adverbial] Brit. informal act in a foolish or desultory way: *he decided to loon around London*.
– ORIGIN 1960s: of unknown origin.

loonie ▸ noun (pl. **loonies**) Canadian informal a Canadian one-dollar coin, introduced in 1987.
– ORIGIN from **LOON**[2] (because of the image on the coin) + **-IE**.

loons (also **loon pants**) ▸ plural noun Brit. dated close-fitting casual trousers widely flared from the knees downwards.
– ORIGIN 1970s: from **LOON**[3].

loony informal ▸ noun (pl. **loonies**) a mad or silly person.

▸ adjective (**loonier, looniest**) mad or silly: *loony drivers.*
– DERIVATIVES **looniness** noun.
– ORIGIN mid 19th cent.: abbreviation of **LUNATIC**.

loony bin ▸ noun informal, offensive a home or hospital for people with mental illnesses.

loony tunes N. Amer. informal ▸ adjective crazy; deranged: *it sounds a little loony tunes.*
▸ plural noun crazy or deranged people.
– ORIGIN 1980s: from *Looney Tunes*, the name of a US animated cartoon series that began in the 1930s, featuring Bugs Bunny and other characters.

loop ▸ noun **1** a shape produced by a curve that bends round and crosses itself. ■ a length of thread, rope, or similar material, doubled or crossing itself, used as a fastening or handle. ■ a curved stroke forming part of a letter (e.g. *b, p*). ■ (also **loop line**) Brit. a length of railway track which is connected at either end to the main line and on to which trains can be diverted to allow others to pass. ■ (also **loop road**) Brit. a stretch of road that diverges from a main road and joins it again. ■ (also **loop-the-loop**) a manoeuvre in which an aircraft describes a vertical circle in the air. ■ Skating a manoeuvre describing a curve that crosses itself, made on a single edge.
2 a structure, series, or process, the end of which is connected to the beginning: *a feedback loop.* ■ an endless strip of tape or film allowing continuous repetition. ■ a complete circuit for an electric current. ■ Computing a programmed sequence of instructions that is repeated until or while a particular condition is satisfied.
▸ verb [with obj. and adverbial] form (something) into a loop or loops; encircle: *she looped her arms around his neck.* ■ [no obj., with adverbial] follow a course that forms a loop or loops: *the canal loops for two miles through the city.* ■ put into or execute a loop of tape, film, or computing instructions.
– PHRASES **in** (or **out of**) **the loop** informal aware (or unaware) of information known to only a privileged few. **loop the loop** (of an aircraft) describe a vertical circle in the air. **throw** (or **knock**) **someone for a loop** N. Amer. informal surprise or astonish someone.
– ORIGIN late Middle English: of unknown origin; compare with Scottish Gaelic *lùb* 'loop, bend'.

loop diuretic ▸ noun Medicine a powerful diuretic which inhibits resorption of water and sodium from the loop of Henle.

looper ▸ noun **1** a caterpillar of a geometrid moth, which moves forward by arching itself into loops. Also called **MEASURING WORM** or (N. Amer.) **INCHWORM**.
2 a device for making loops.

loophole ▸ noun **1** an ambiguity or inadequacy in the law or a set of rules: *they exploited tax loopholes.*
2 historical an arrow slit in a wall.
▸ verb [with obj.] make arrow slits in (a wall).
– ORIGIN late 16th cent. (denoting an arrow slit): from obsolete *loop* 'embrasure' + **HOLE**.

loop of Henle /ˈhɛnli/ ▸ noun Anatomy the part of a kidney tubule which forms a long loop in the medulla of the kidney, from which water and salts are resorbed into the blood.
– ORIGIN mid 19th cent.: named after Friedrich G. J. *Henle* (1809–85), German anatomist.

loop stitch ▸ noun [mass noun] a method of sewing or knitting in which each stitch incorporates a free loop of thread, for ornament or to give a thick pile.
– DERIVATIVES **loop stitching** noun.

loopy ▸ adjective (**loopier, loopiest**) **1** informal mad or silly: *a loopy grin.*
2 having many loops: *a big, loopy signature.*
– DERIVATIVES **loopily** adverb, **loopiness** noun.

loose /luːs/ ▸ adjective **1** not firmly or tightly fixed in place; detached or able to be detached: *a loose tooth | the lorry's trailer came loose.* ■ not held or tied together or contained within something: *wear your hair loose | pockets bulging with loose change.* ■ (of a person or animal) not tied up or shut in: *the bull was loose with cattle in the field | the tethered horses* **broke loose**. ■ (of the ball in a game) in play but not in any player's possession.
2 (of a garment) not fitting tightly or closely: *she slipped into a loose T-shirt.*
3 not close, compact, or solid in structure or formation: *the fabric's loose weave | loose soil.* ■ not rigidly organized: *a loose federation of political groups.* ■ (of play, especially in rugby) with the players not close together.
4 relaxed; physically slack: *she swung into her easy, loose stride.* ■ not strict or exact: *a loose interpretation.* ■ careless and indiscreet in what is said: *there is too much loose talk about the situation.* ■ (of play in cricket) inaccurate or careless: *Lucas punished some loose bowling severely.*
5 dated promiscuous: *a loose woman.*
6 (of faeces) containing excessive liquid.
▸ noun (**the loose**) Rugby loose play: *he was in powerful form in the loose.*
▸ verb [with obj.] **1** set free; release: *the hounds have been loosed.* ■ make (something) loose; untie or undo: *the ropes were loosed.* ■ relax (one's grip): *he loosed his grip suddenly.*
2 (usu. **loose off**) fire (a bullet, arrow, etc.): *he loosed off a shot at the vehicle.*
– PHRASES **hang** (or **stay**) **loose** [often as imperative] informal, chiefly N. Amer. be relaxed; refrain from taking anything too seriously: *hang loose, baby!* **on the loose** having escaped from confinement: *a serial killer is on the loose.*
– DERIVATIVES **loosely** adverb, **looseness** noun.
– ORIGIN Middle English *loos* 'free from bonds', from Old Norse *lauss*, of Germanic origin; related to Dutch and German *los*.

> **USAGE** The words **loose** and **lose** are different and should not be confused: see **USAGE** at **LOSE**.

loose box ▸ noun Brit. a stable, or an enclosed area in a stable building, in which a horse is kept and within which it does not need to be tied.

loose cannon ▸ noun an unpredictable or uncontrolled person who is liable to cause unintentional damage.

loose cover ▸ noun Brit. a removable fitted cloth cover for a chair or sofa.

loose end ▸ noun a detail that is not yet settled or explained: *Mark arrived back at his office to tie up any loose ends.*
– PHRASES **be at a loose end** (or N. Amer. **at loose ends**) have nothing specific to do.

loose-footed ▸ adjective (of a boat's sail) having no boom or not secured to a boom at the foot.

loose forward ▸ noun Rugby a forward who plays at the back of the scrum.

loose head ▸ noun Rugby the forward in the front row of a scrummage who is nearest to the scrum half as the ball is put in.

loose housing ▸ noun [mass noun] partly covered barns or sheds for livestock with access to a feeding area (as distinct from individual pens or crates).

loose-knit ▸ adjective connected in a tenuous or vague way: *a loose-knit grouping of independent states.*

loose-leaf ▸ adjective (of a notebook or folder) having each sheet of paper separate and removable.

loose-limbed ▸ adjective supple and physically relaxed: *his loose-limbed, athletic body exudes fitness and energy.*

loosen ▸ verb [with obj.] **1** make (something tied, fastened, or fixed in place) less tight or firm: *loosen your collar and tie.* ■ relax (one's grip or muscles): *he loosened his hold so she could pull her arms free.* ■ [no obj.] become relaxed or less tight: *the stiffness in his shoulders had loosened.* ■ (with reference to the bowels) make or become relaxed prior to excretion.
2 make less strict: *his main mistake was to loosen monetary policy.* ■ make (a connection) less strong: *he wanted to strengthen rather than loosen union links.*
– PHRASES **loosen someone's tongue** make someone talk freely.
– PHRASAL VERBS **loosen up** relax one's muscles before taking exercise: *arrive early to loosen up and hit some practice shots.* ■ become mentally relaxed: *they taught me to have fun and loosen up.*

loosener ▸ noun a person or thing that loosens something. ■ informal a relatively undemanding challenge early in a game or competition, before the participants are fully settled or warmed up.

loose rein ▸ noun [in sing.] a manner of riding in which the reins are held slackly, allowing the horse to relax. ■ a lack of strict control: *he ran foreign affairs* **on a loose rein**.

loose scrum (also **loose scrummage**) ▸ noun Rugby a scrum formed by the players round the ball during play, not ordered by the referee.

loosestrife /ˈluːsˌstrʌɪf/ ▸ noun any of a number of tall plants which bear upright spikes of flowers and grow by water and in wet ground: ● several plants of the genus *Lythrum* (family Lythraceae), in particular the **purple loosestrife** (*L. salicaria*) of the Old World. ● several plants of the genus *Lysimachia* (family Primulaceae), in particular the **yellow loosestrife** (*L. vulgaris*) of Eurasia.
– ORIGIN mid 16th cent.: from **LOOSE** + **STRIFE**, taking the Greek name *lusimakheion* (actually from *Lusimakhos*, the name of its discoverer) to be directly from *luein* 'undo' + *makhē* 'battle'.

loose tongue ▸ noun a tendency to speak indiscreetly.

loosey-goosey /luːsɪˈguːsi/ ▸ adjective N. Amer. informal relaxed and comfortable.
– ORIGIN 1980s: fanciful formation from **LOOSE** + **GOOSEY**.

loot ▸ noun [mass noun] private property taken from an enemy in war. ■ stolen money or valuables: *the gang escaped with their loot.* ■ informal money: *ten thousand quid is a lot of loot.*
▸ verb [with obj.] steal goods from (a place), typically during a war or riot: *police confronted the protestors who were looting shops.* ■ steal (goods) in a war, riot, etc.: *tonnes of food aid awaiting distribution had been looted.* ■ Indian steal (something) from someone: *a gang looted Rs. 1.5 lakh from a passenger.*
– DERIVATIVES **looter** noun.
– ORIGIN early 19th cent. (as a verb): from Hindi *lūṭ*, from Sanskrit *luṇṭh-* 'rob'.

loo table ▸ noun a circular table for playing the card game loo on, or a table made in a similar style.

lop¹ ▸ verb (**lops, lopping, lopped**) [with obj.] cut off (a branch, limb, or twig) from the main body of a tree: *they* **lopped off** *more branches to save the tree.* ■ remove branches from (a tree). ■ informal remove (something regarded as unnecessary or burdensome): *the new rail link* **lops** *an hour* **off** *journey times.*
▸ noun [mass noun] (also **lop and top**) branches and twigs lopped off trees.
– ORIGIN late Middle English (as a noun): of unknown origin.

lop² ▸ verb (**lops, lopping, lopped**) [no obj.] N. Amer. or archaic hang loosely or limply; droop: *a stomach that lopped over his belt.* ■ [with adverbial of direction] move in a loping or slouching way: *he lopped towards the plane.*
– ORIGIN late 16th cent.: probably symbolic of limpness; compare with **LOB**.

lope ▸ verb [no obj., with adverbial of direction] walk or run with a long bounding stride: *the dog was loping along by his side* | (as adj. **loping**) *a loping stride.*
▸ noun [in sing.] a long bounding stride: *they set off at a fast lope.*
– ORIGIN Middle English: variant of Scots *loup*, from Old Norse *hlaupa* 'leap'.

lop-eared ▸ adjective (of an animal) having drooping ears.
– DERIVATIVES **lop ears** plural noun.

loperamide /ləʊˈpɛrəmʌɪd/ ▸ noun [mass noun] Medicine a synthetic drug of the opiate class which inhibits peristalsis and is used to treat diarrhoea.
– ORIGIN 1970s: probably from *(ch)lo(ro-)* + *(pi)per(idine)* + **AMIDE**.

lopho- ▸ combining form Zoology crested: *lophodont.*
– ORIGIN from Greek *lophos* 'crest'.

lophodont /ˈləʊfə(ʊ)dɒnt, ˈlɒf-/ ▸ adjective Zoology (of molar teeth) having transverse ridges on the grinding surfaces, characteristic of some ungulates. ■ (of an ungulate) having lophodont teeth.
▸ noun an animal with lophodont teeth.
– ORIGIN late 19th cent.: from **LOPHO-** 'crest' + Greek *odous, odont-* 'tooth'.

lophophorate /ləˈfɒfəreɪt, ˌləʊfəˈfɔːreɪt/ Zoology ▸ adjective denoting small aquatic invertebrates belonging to a group of phyla characterized by the possession of lophophores. They include bryozoans, brachiopods, and horseshoe worms.
▸ noun a lophophorate animal.

lophophore /ˈləʊfəˌfɔː, ˈlɒf-/ ▸ noun Zoology a structure in certain small marine invertebrates, having the shape of a horseshoe and bearing ciliated tentacles around the mouth.

Lop Nor /lɒp ˈnɔː/ (also **Lop Nur** /ˈnʊə/) a dried-up salt lake in the arid basin of the Tarim River in NW China, used since 1964 for nuclear testing.

lopolith /ˈlɒpə(ʊ)lɪθ/ ▸ noun Geology a large saucer-shaped intrusion of igneous rock.
– ORIGIN early 20th cent.: from Greek *lopas* 'basin' + **-LITH**.

loppers ▸ plural noun a cutting tool, especially for pruning trees: *a good pair of loppers.*

lopsided ▸ adjective with one side lower or smaller than the other: *a lopsided grin.*

– DERIVATIVES **lopsidedly** adverb, **lopsidedness** noun.
– ORIGIN early 18th cent.: from LOP² + SIDE + -ED¹.

loquacious /ləˈkweɪʃəs/ ▶ adjective tending to talk a great deal; talkative.
– DERIVATIVES **loquaciously** adverb, **loquaciousness** noun.
– ORIGIN mid 17th cent.: from Latin *loquax, loquac-* (from *loqui* 'talk') + -IOUS.

loquacity /ləˈkwasɪti/ ▶ noun [mass noun] the quality of talking a great deal; talkativeness: *he was renowned for loquacity.*

loquat /ˈləʊkwɒt/ ▶ noun 1 a small yellow egg-shaped acidic fruit.
2 the evergreen East Asian tree of the rose family which bears the loquat, cultivated both for its fruit and as an ornamental. ● *Eriobotrya japonica*, family Rosaceae.
– ORIGIN early 19th cent.: from Chinese dialect *luh kwat* 'rush orange'.

loquitur /ˈlɒkwɪtə/ (abbrev.: **loq.**) ▶ verb (he or she) speaks (with the speaker's name following, as a stage direction or to inform the reader).
– ORIGIN Latin, from *loqui* 'talk, speak'.

lor ▶ exclamation Brit. informal used to indicate surprise or dismay: *Lor, look at that! Isn't it horrible?*
– ORIGIN mid 19th cent.: abbreviation of LORD.

Loran /ˈlɔːran, ˈlɒ-/ ▶ noun [mass noun] a system of long-distance navigation in which position is determined from the intervals between signal pulses received from widely spaced radio transmitters.
– ORIGIN 1940s: from *lo(ng-)ra(nge) n(avigation)*.

loranthus /lɔːˈranθəs/ ▶ noun a semi-parasitic Asian plant of the mistletoe family, which has orange or red flowers and oval berries. ● Family Loranthaceae; most species formerly in the genus *Loranthus* are now placed in other genera.
– ORIGIN modern Latin (genus name), from Latin *lorum* 'strap' + Greek *anthos* 'flower'.

lorazepam /lɔːˈreɪzɪpam, -ˈrazə-/ ▶ noun [mass noun] Medicine a drug of the benzodiazepine group, used especially to treat anxiety.
– ORIGIN 1960s: from *(ch)lor(o-)* ('chlorine') + *-azepam*, on the pattern of words such as *diazepam*.

Lorca /ˈlɔːkə/, Federico García (1898–1936), Spanish poet and dramatist. His works include *Gypsy Ballads* (verse, 1928) and intense, poetic tragedies evoking the passionate emotions of Spanish life, notably *Blood Wedding* (1933). He was killed by nationalists in the Spanish Civil War.

lord ▶ noun a man of noble rank or high office; a nobleman. ■ (**Lord**) (in the UK) a title given formally to a baron, and less formally to a marquess, earl, or viscount (prefixed to a family or territorial name): *Lord Derby.* ■ (**the Lords**) (in the UK) the House of Lords, or its members collectively. ■ (**Lord**) (in the UK) a courtesy title given to a younger son of a duke or marquess (prefixed to a Christian name): *Lord John Russell.* ■ used in compound titles of other people of authority: *Lord High Executioner.* ■ historical a feudal superior, especially the owner of a manor house. ■ a master or ruler: *our lord the king.* ■ (**Lord**) a name for God or Christ: *give thanks to the Lord.*
▶ exclamation (**Lord**) used in exclamations expressing surprise or worry, or for emphasis: *Lord, I'm cold!*
▶ verb 1 (**lord it over**) act in a superior and domineering manner towards (someone).
2 [with obj.] archaic confer the title of Lord upon.
– PHRASES **live like a lord** live sumptuously. **Lord (God) of hosts** God as Lord over earthly or heavenly armies. **lord of the manor** the owner of a manor house (formerly the master of a feudal manor). **Lord of Misrule** historical a person presiding over Christmas games and revelry in a wealthy household. **Lord Muck** Brit. informal a haughty or socially pretentious man. **the Lord's Day** Sunday. **the Lord's Prayer** the prayer taught by Christ to his disciples, beginning 'Our Father'. **the Lord's Supper** the Eucharist; Holy Communion (especially in Protestant use). **My Lord** (in the UK) a polite form of address to judges, bishops, and certain noblemen. **Our Lord** used as a title for God or Jesus Christ.
– DERIVATIVES **lordless** adjective, **lord-like** adjective.
– ORIGIN Old English *hlāford*, from *hlāfweard* 'bread-keeper', from a Germanic base (see LOAF¹, WARD). Compare with LADY.

Lord Advocate ▶ noun the principal Law Officer of the Crown in Scotland.

Lord Bishop ▶ noun the formal title of a bishop, in particular of a diocesan bishop (as distinct from a suffragan).

Lord Chamberlain (also **Lord Chamberlain of the Household**) ▶ noun (in the UK) the official in charge of the royal household, formerly the licenser of plays.

Lord Chancellor ▶ noun (in the UK) the highest officer of the Crown, responsible for the efficient functioning and independence of the courts, and formerly presiding over the House of Lords, the Chancery Division, or the Court of Appeal. ■ historical an officer of state acting as head of the judiciary and administrator of the royal household.

Lord Chief Justice ▶ noun (in the UK) the officer presiding over the Queen's Bench Division and the Court of Appeal (Criminal Division).

Lord Commissioner ▶ noun 1 the representative of the Crown at the General Assembly of the Church of Scotland.
2 (**Lords Commissioners**) (in the UK) the members of a board performing the duties of a high state office put in commission.

Lord Fauntleroy see FAUNTLEROY.

Lord Great Chamberlain of England ▶ noun the hereditary holder of a ceremonial office whose responsibilities include attendance on the monarch at a coronation.

Lord High Admiral ▶ noun a title of the British monarch, originally the title of an officer who governed the Royal Navy and had jurisdiction over maritime causes.

Lord High Chancellor ▶ noun another term for LORD CHANCELLOR.

Lord High Commissioner ▶ noun another term for LORD COMMISSIONER.

Lord High Treasurer ▶ noun see TREASURER.

Lord Howe Island a volcanic island in the SW Pacific off the east coast of Australia, administered as part of New South Wales; pop. 347 (2006).
– ORIGIN named after Admiral *Lord Howe* (1726–99), who was First Lord of the Admiralty when it was first visited.

Lord Justice (also **Lord Justice of Appeal**) ▶ noun (pl. **Lords Justices**) (in the UK) a judge in the Court of Appeal.

Lord Lieutenant ▶ noun (in the UK) the chief executive authority and head of magistrates in each county. ■ historical the viceroy of Ireland.

lordling ▶ noun archaic, chiefly derogatory a minor lord.

lordly ▶ adjective (**lordlier**, **lordliest**) of, characteristic of, or suitable for a lord: *lordly titles | they were putting on lordly airs.*
– DERIVATIVES **lordliness** noun.
– ORIGIN Old English *hlāfordlic* (see LORD, -LY¹).

Lord Lyon ▶ noun see LYON.

Lord Mayor ▶ noun the title of the mayor in London and some other large British cities.

Lord of Appeal (in full **Lord of Appeal in Ordinary**) ▶ noun formal term for LAW LORD.

Lord Ordinary ▶ noun (in Scotland) any of the judges of the Outer House of the Court of Session.

lordosis /lɔːˈdəʊsɪs/ ▶ noun [mass noun] Medicine excessive inward curvature of the spine. Compare with KYPHOSIS. ■ a posture assumed by some female mammals during mating, in which the back is arched downward.
– DERIVATIVES **lordotic** adjective.
– ORIGIN early 18th cent.: modern Latin, from Greek *lordōsis*, from *lordos* 'bent backwards'.

Lord President of the Council ▶ noun (in the UK) the cabinet minister presiding at the Privy Council.

Lord Privy Seal ▶ noun (in the UK) a senior cabinet minister without specified official duties.

Lord Protector of the Commonwealth ▶ noun see PROTECTOR (sense 2).

Lord Provost ▶ noun the head of a municipal corporation or borough in certain Scottish cities.

Lord's a cricket ground in St John's Wood, north London, headquarters since 1814 of the MCC.
– ORIGIN named after the cricketer Thomas *Lord* (1755–1832).

lords and ladies ▶ noun another term for CUCKOO PINT.

lordship ▶ noun 1 [mass noun] supreme power or rule: *his lordship over the other gods.* ■ archaic the authority or state of being a lord. ■ [count noun] historical a piece of land belonging to or under the jurisdiction of a lord: *lands including the lordship of Denbigh.*
2 (**His/Your** etc. **Lordship**) (in the UK) a respectful form of reference or address to a judge, a bishop, or a man with a title: *if Your Lordship pleases.* ■ Brit. ironic a form of address or reference to a man thought to be acting in a pretentious way.
– ORIGIN Old English *hlāfordscipe* (see LORD, -SHIP).

Lords of Session ▶ plural noun (in Scotland) the judges of the Court of Session.

Lords spiritual ▶ plural noun the bishops in the House of Lords.

Lords temporal ▶ plural noun the members of the House of Lords other than the bishops.

Lord Treasurer ▶ noun see TREASURER.

Lordy ▶ exclamation informal used to express surprise or dismay: *Lordy! Whatever happened?*

lore¹ ▶ noun [mass noun] a body of traditions and knowledge on a subject or held by a particular group, typically passed from person to person by word of mouth: *the jinns of Arabian lore | baseball lore.*
– ORIGIN Old English *lār* 'instruction', of Germanic origin: related to Dutch *leer*, German *Lehre*, also to LEARN.

lore² ▶ noun Zoology the surface on each side of a bird's head between the eye and the upper base of the beak, or between the eye and nostril in snakes.
– ORIGIN early 19th cent.: from Latin *lorum* 'strap'.

Lorelei /ˈlɒrəlʌɪ/ a rock on the bank of the Rhine, held by legend to be the home of a siren whose song lures boatmen to destruction. ■ the siren said to live on the Lorelei rock.

Loren /ləˈrɛn/, Sophia (b.1934), Italian actress; born *Sofia Scicolone*. She has starred in both Italian and American films, including the slapstick comedy *The Millionairess* (1960) and the wartime drama *La Ciociara* (1961), for which she won an Oscar.

Lorentz /ˈlɒrənts/, Hendrik Antoon (1853–1928), Dutch theoretical physicist. He worked on the forces affecting electrons and realized that electrons and cathode rays were the same thing. For their work on electromagnetic theory he and his pupil **Pieter Zeeman** (1865–1943) shared the 1902 Nobel Prize for Physics.

Lorentz contraction ▶ noun another term for FITZGERALD CONTRACTION.

Lorentz force ▶ noun Physics the force which is exerted by a magnetic field on a moving electric charge.

Lorentz transformation ▶ noun Physics the set of equations which in Einstein's special theory of relativity relate the space and time coordinates of one frame of reference to those of another.

Lorenz /ˈlɒrənts/, Konrad (Zacharias) (1903–89), Austrian zoologist. He pioneered the science of ethology, emphasizing innate rather than learned behaviour or conditioned reflexes. Lorenz extrapolated his studies in ornithology to human behaviour patterns, and compared the ill effects of the domestication of animals to human civilizing processes. He shared a Nobel Prize in 1973 with Karl von Frisch and Nikolaas Tinbergen.

Lorenz attractor ▶ noun Mathematics a strange attractor in the form of a two-lobed figure formed by a trajectory which spirals around the two lobes, passing randomly between them.
– ORIGIN 1970s: named after Edward N. *Lorenz* (born 1917), American meteorologist.

Lorenz curve ▶ noun Economics a graph on which the cumulative percentage of total national income (or some other variable) is plotted against the cumulative percentage of the corresponding population (ranked in increasing size of share). The extent to which the curve sags below a straight diagonal line indicates the degree of inequality of distribution.
– ORIGIN early 20th cent.: named after Max O. *Lorenz*, the American statistician who devised the curve.

Lorenzo de' Medici /ləˈrɛnzəʊ/ (1449–92), Italian statesman and scholar. A patron of the arts and humanist learning, he supported Botticelli, Leonardo da Vinci, and Michelangelo among others. He was also a noted poet and scholar in his own right.

lo-res (also **low-res**) ▶ adjective informal (of a display or an image) showing a small amount of detail.
– ORIGIN late 20th cent.: from *low-resolution*.

Loreto /ləˈrɛtəʊ/ a town in eastern Italy, near the Adriatic coast to the south of Ancona; pop. 12,285 (2008). It is the site of the 'Holy House', said to be the home of the Virgin Mary and to have been brought from Nazareth by angels in 1295.

L

lorgnette /lɔːˈnjɛt/ (also **lorgnettes**) ▶ **noun** a pair of glasses or opera glasses held in front of a person's eyes by a long handle at one side.
– ORIGIN early 19th cent.: from French, from *lorgner* 'to squint'.

lorica /ləˈrʌɪkə/ ▶ **noun** (pl. **loricae** /-kiː/ or **loricas**) **1** historical a Roman corselet or cuirass of leather. **2** Zoology the rigid case or shell of some rotifers and protozoans.
– ORIGIN Latin, literally 'breastplate'.

loricate /ˈlɒrɪkeɪt, -kət/ ▶ **adjective** Zoology (of an animal) having a lorica or other protective covering of plates or scales.
– ORIGIN early 19th cent.: from Latin *loricatus*, from *lorica* 'breastplate', from *lorum* 'strap'.

Lorient /ˈlɒrɪɒ̃/ a port in NW France, on the south coast of Brittany; pop. 60,286 (2006).

lorikeet /ˈlɒrɪkiːt/ ▶ **noun** a small bird of the lory family, found chiefly in New Guinea. ● *Charmosyna* and other genera, family Loridae (or Psittacidae): several species. ■ Australian term for **LORY**.
– ORIGIN late 18th cent.: diminutive of **LORY**, on the pattern of *parakeet*.

loriner /ˈlɒrmə/ (also **lorimer**) ▶ **noun** archaic a maker of small iron objects, especially bits, spurs, stirrups, and mountings for horse's bridles.
– ORIGIN Middle English: from Old French *lorenier*, from *lorain* 'harness strap', from Latin *lorum* 'strap'.

loris /ˈlɔːrɪs/ ▶ **noun** (pl. **lorises**) a small, slow-moving nocturnal Asian primate with a short or absent tail, living in dense vegetation. ● Genera *Loris* and *Nycticebus*, family Lorisidae, suborder Prosimii: the **slender loris** (*L. tardigradus*) of South India and Sri Lanka, and the **slow loris** (genus *Nycticebus*, two species) of SE Asia.
– ORIGIN late 18th cent.: from French, perhaps from obsolete Dutch *loeris* 'clown'.

lorn ▶ **adjective** literary lonely and abandoned; forlorn.
– ORIGIN Middle English: past participle of obsolete *lese* from Old English *lēosan* 'lose'.

L

Lorrain, Claud see **CLAUDE LORRAIN**.

Lorraine /ləˈreɪn/, French /lɔʀɛn/ a region of NE France, between Champagne and the Vosges mountains. The modern region corresponds to the southern part of the medieval kingdom of Lorraine, which extended from the North Sea to Italy.
– ORIGIN from Latin *Lotharingia*, from *Lothair*, the name of a king (825–69).

Lorraine cross ▶ **noun** a cross with one vertical and two horizontal bars. It was the symbol of Joan of Arc, and in the Second World War was adopted by the Free French forces of General de Gaulle.

lorry /ˈlɒri/ ▶ **noun** (pl. **lorries**) Brit. a large, heavy motor vehicle for transporting goods or troops; a truck.
– PHRASES **fall off the back of a lorry** informal (of goods) be acquired in dubious circumstances.
– ORIGIN mid 19th cent.: perhaps from the given name *Laurie*.

lory /ˈlɔːri/ ▶ **noun** (pl. **lories**) a small Australasian and SE Asian parrot with a brush-tipped tongue for feeding on nectar and pollen, having mainly green plumage with patches of bright colour. Called **LORIKEET** in Australia. ● Family Loridae (or Psittacidae): several genera and species, e.g. the brightly coloured **rainbow lory** or **rainbow lorikeet** (*Trichoglossus haematodus*).
– ORIGIN late 17th cent.: from Malay *lūri*.

Los Alamos /lɒs ˈaləmɒs/ a town in northern New Mexico; pop. 11,600 (est. 2009). It has been a centre for nuclear research since the 1940s, when it was the site of the development of the first atomic and hydrogen bombs.

Los Angeleno ▶ **noun** variant of **ANGELENO**.

Los Angeles /lɒs ˈandʒɪliːz, -lɪs/ a city on the Pacific coast of southern California, the second-largest city in the US; pop. 3,833,995 (est. 2008). It became a major centre of industry, film-making, and television in the 20th century, its metropolitan area having expanded to include towns such as Beverly Hills, Hollywood, Santa Monica, and Pasadena.

lose /luːz/ ▶ **verb** (past and past participle **lost**) [with obj.] **1** be deprived of or cease to have or retain (something): *I've lost my appetite* | *Linda was very upset about losing her job* | *the company may find itself losing customers to cheaper rivals.* ■ [with two objs] cause (someone) to fail to gain or retain (something): *you lost me my appointment at London University.* ■ be deprived of (a relative or friend) through their death: *she lost her husband in the fire.* ■ (of a pregnant woman) miscarry (a baby) or suffer the death of (a baby) during childbirth. ■ (**be lost**) be destroyed or killed, especially as a result of an accident or military action: *a fishing disaster in which 129 men were lost.* ■ decrease in (body weight); undergo a reduction of (a specified amount of weight). ■ (of a watch or clock) become slow by (a specified amount of time): *this clock will neither gain nor lose a second.* ■ (**lose it**) informal become unable to control one's temper or emotions: *I completely lost it—I was screaming at them.*
2 become unable to find (something or someone): *I've lost the car keys.* ■ cease or become unable to follow (the right route). ■ evade or shake off (a pursuer): *he came after me waving his revolver, but I easily lost him.* ■ N. Amer. informal get rid of (an undesirable person or thing): *lose that creep!* ■ informal cause (someone) to be unable to follow an argument or explanation: *sorry, Tim, you've lost me there.* ■ (**lose oneself in**/**be lost in**) be or become deeply absorbed in (something): *he had been lost in thought.*
3 fail to win (a game or contest): *England lost the first Test match* | [no obj.] *they lost by one vote* | (as adj. **losing**) *the losing side.* ■ [with two objs] cause (someone) to fail to win (a game or contest): *that shot lost him the championship.*
4 earn less (money) than one is spending or has spent: *the paper is losing £1.5 million a month* | [no obj.] *he lost heavily on box office flops.*
5 waste or fail to take advantage of (time or an opportunity): *he has lost his chance of becoming world No. 1* | *the government* ***lost no time in*** *holding fresh elections.*
– PHRASES **have nothing to lose** be in a situation that is so bad that even if an action is unsuccessful it cannot make it any worse. **lose face** come to be less highly respected: *the US must act or lose face.* **lose heart** become discouraged. **lose one's heart to** see **HEART**. **lose height** (of an aircraft) descend to a lower level in flight. **lose one's mind** (or **one's marbles**) informal go insane. **lose sleep** [usu. with negative] worry about something: *no one is losing any sleep over what he thinks of us.* **lose one's** (or **the**) **way** become unable to find one's way. ■ no longer have a clear idea of one's purpose or motivation in an activity: *the company has lost its way and should pull out of general insurance.*
– PHRASAL VERBS **lose out 1** be beaten in competition: *they* ***lost out to*** *France in the finals.* **2** be deprived of an opportunity; be disadvantaged: *youngsters who were* ***losing out on*** *regular schooling.*
– ORIGIN Old English *losian* 'perish, destroy', also 'become unable to find', from *los* 'loss'.

> **USAGE** The verb **lose** is sometimes mistakenly written as **loose**, as in *this would cause them to* ***loose*** *20 to 50 per cent* (correct form is ... *to* ***lose*** *20 to 50 per cent*). There is a word **loose**, but it is very different—normally an adjective, meaning 'untethered; not held in place; detached', as in *loose cobbles; the handle was* ***loose***; *set* ***loose***.

losel /ˈləʊz(ə)l/ ▶ **noun** archaic or dialect a worthless person.
– ORIGIN late Middle English: apparently from *los-*, stem of obsolete *lese* 'lose', + **-EL**.

lose-lose ▶ **adjective** of or denoting a situation which is disadvantageous or damaging to all those involved: *he even gets his way in what would clearly be a lose-lose situation.*

loser ▶ **noun** a person or thing that loses or has lost something, especially a game or contest. ■ [with adj.] a person who accepts defeat with good or bad grace: *they should concede that we won and be good losers.* ■ a person who is disadvantaged by a particular situation or course of action: *children are the losers when politicians keep fiddling around with education.* ■ informal a person who fails frequently or is generally unsuccessful in life: *a ragtag community of rejects and losers.* ■ Bridge a card that is expected to be part of a losing trick.
– PHRASES **be on** (or **on to**) **a loser** informal be involved in a course of action that is bound to fail.

losing battle ▶ **noun** a struggle that seems certain to end in failure: *the police force is fighting a losing battle against a rising tide of crime.*

losingest /ˈluːzɪŋɪst/ ▶ **adjective** N. Amer. informal losing more often than others of its kind; least successful: *the losingest club in baseball history.*

loss ▶ **noun** [mass noun] the fact or process of losing something or someone: *avoiding loss of time* | [count noun] *funding cuts will lead to job losses.* ■ an amount of money lost by a business or organization: *insurance can protect you against financial loss* | [count noun] *we have incurred huge losses* | [in combination] *loss-making industries.* ■ the feeling of grief after losing someone or something of value: *I feel a terrible sense of loss.* ■ [in sing.] a person who or thing that is badly missed when lost: *he will be a great loss to many people.*
– PHRASES **at a loss 1** puzzled or uncertain what to think, say, or do: [with infinitive] *she became popular, and was at a loss to know why* | *he was* ***at a loss for*** *words.* **2** making less money than is spent buying, operating, or producing something: *a railway running at a loss.*
– ORIGIN Old English *los* 'destruction', of Germanic origin; related to Old Norse *los* 'breaking up of the ranks of an army' and **LOOSE**; later probably a back-formation from *lost*, past participle of **LOSE**.

loss adjuster ▶ **noun** Brit. an insurance agent who assesses the amount of compensation that should be paid after a person has claimed on their insurance policy.

loss-leader ▶ **noun** a product sold at a loss to attract customers.

lossless ▶ **adjective** having or involving no dissipation of electrical or electromagnetic energy. ■ Computing (of data compression) without loss of information.

loss-making ▶ **adjective** (especially of a business) losing money, rather than making a profit: *subsidies to loss-making industries.*
– DERIVATIVES **loss-maker** noun.

lossy ▶ **adjective** having or involving the dissipation of electrical or electromagnetic energy. ■ Computing (of data compression) in which unnecessary information is discarded.

lost past and past participle of **LOSE**. ▶ **adjective** **1** unable to find one's way; not knowing one's whereabouts: *Help! We're lost!* ■ unable to be found: *he turned up with my lost golf clubs.* ■ [predic.] unable to understand or to cope with a situation: *she stood there clutching a drink, feeling completely lost* | *I'd* ***be lost without*** *her.*
2 that has been taken away or cannot be recovered: *if only one could recapture one's lost youth.* ■ (of time or an opportunity) not used advantageously; wasted. ■ having died or been destroyed: *a memorial to the lost crewmen.*
– PHRASES **all is not lost** used to suggest that there is still some chance of success or recovery. **be lost for words** be so surprised, confused, or upset that one cannot think what to say. **be lost on** fail to be noticed or appreciated by (someone): *the significance of his remarks was not lost on Scott.* **get lost** [often in imperative] informal go away (used as an expression of anger or impatience). **give someone up for lost** stop expecting that a missing person will be found alive. **make up for lost time** do something faster or more often in order to compensate for not having done it quickly or often enough before.

lost and found ▶ **noun** North American term for **LOST PROPERTY**.

lost cause ▶ **noun** a person or thing that can no longer hope to succeed or be changed for the better.

lost generation ▶ **noun** the generation reaching maturity during and just after the First World War, a high proportion of whose men were killed during those years. ■ an unfulfilled generation coming to maturity during a period of instability.
– ORIGIN phrase applied by Gertrude Stein to disillusioned young American writers, such as Ernest Hemingway, Scott Fitzgerald, and Ezra Pound, who went to live in Paris in the 1920s.

lost property ▶ **noun** Brit. a place where lost articles are stored to await retrieval by their owners.

Lost Tribes (also **Ten Lost Tribes of Israel**) the ten tribes of Israel taken away *c.*720 BC by Sargon II to captivity in Assyria (2 Kings 17:6), from which they are believed never to have returned, while the tribes of Benjamin and Judah remained. See also **TRIBES OF ISRAEL**.

lost wax ▶ **noun** another term for **CIRE PERDUE**.

Lot[1] /lɒt, ləʊ/ a river of southern France, which rises in the Auvergne and flows 480 km (300 miles) west to meet the Garonne south-east of Bordeaux.

Lot[2] /lɒt/ (in the Bible) the nephew of Abraham, who was allowed to escape from the destruction of Sodom (Gen. 19). His wife, who disobeyed orders and looked back, was turned into a pillar of salt.

lot ▶ **pronoun** (**a lot** or **lots**) informal a large number or amount; a great deal: *there are* ***a lot of*** *actors in the cast* | *they took* ***a lot of*** *abuse* | *a lot can happen in eight months* | *we had* ***lots of*** *fun.* ■ (**the lot** or **the whole lot**) the whole number or quantity that is involved or implied: *you might as well take the whole lot.*

▶ **adverb** (**a lot** or **lots**) informal a great deal; much: *he played tennis a lot last year | thanks a lot.*

▶ **noun 1** [treated as sing. or pl.] informal a particular group or set of people or things: *it's just one lot of rich people stealing from another | he will need a second lot of tills to handle the second currency.* ■ [with adj.] chiefly Brit. a group of a specified kind (used in a derogatory or dismissive way): *an inefficient lot, our Council.*
2 an item or set of items for sale at an auction: *nineteen lots failed to sell.*
3 [mass noun] the making of a decision by random selection, especially by a method involving the choice of one from a number of pieces of folded paper, one of which has a concealed mark: *officers were elected rather than selected* **by lot**. ■ [in sing.] the choice resulting from deciding something by lot: *eventually the lot fell on the King's daughter.*
4 [in sing.] a person's luck, situation, or destiny in life: *schemes to improve the lot of the disadvantaged.*
5 chiefly N. Amer. a plot of land assigned for sale or for a particular use: *a vacant lot.* ■ (also **parking lot**) a car park. ■ an area of land near a film studio where outside filming may be done. ■ the area at a car dealership where cars for sale are kept.

▶ **verb** (**lots, lotting, lotted**) [with obj.] divide (items) into lots for sale at an auction: *the contents have already been lotted up, and the auction takes place on Monday.*

– PHRASES **all over the lot** US informal in a disorganized or confused state. **a bad lot** Brit. informal a dishonest person. **draw** (or **cast**) **lots** decide by lot: *we drew lots to decide the order.* **fall to someone's lot** become someone's task or responsibility. **throw in one's lot with** decide to ally oneself closely with and share the fate of (a person or group).

– ORIGIN Old English *hlot* (noun), of Germanic origin; related to Dutch *lot*, German *Los*. The original meanings were sense 3 of the noun and (by extension) the sense 'a portion assigned to someone'; the latter gave rise to the other noun senses. The pronoun and adverb uses date from the early 19th cent.

> **USAGE** 1 The expressions **a lot of** and **lots of** are used before nouns to mean 'a large number or amount of'. In common with other words denoting quantities, **lot** itself does not normally function as a head noun, meaning that it does not itself determine whether the following verb is singular or plural. Thus, although **lot** is singular in *a lot of people*, the verb which follows is not singular. In this case the word **people** acts as the head noun and, being plural, ensures that the following verb is also plural: *a lot of people* ***were*** *assembled* (not *a lot of people was assembled*). See also **USAGE** at **NUMBER**
> 2 **A lot of** and **lots of** are very common in speech and writing but they still have a distinctly informal feel and are generally not considered acceptable for formal English, where alternatives such as **many** or **a large number** are used instead.
> 3 Written as one word **alot** is incorrect, although not uncommon.

lota /ˈləʊtə/ ▶ **noun** Indian a round water pot, typically of polished brass.
– ORIGIN from Hindi *loṭā*.

lo-tech ▶ **adjective & noun** variant spelling of **LOW-TECH**.

loth ▶ **adjective** variant spelling of **LOATH**.

Lothario /ləˈθɑːrɪəʊ, -ˈθɛː-/ ▶ **noun** (pl. **Lotharios**) a man who behaves selfishly and irresponsibly in his sexual relationships with women.
– ORIGIN from a character in Rowe's *Fair Penitent* (1703).

Lothian /ˈləʊðɪən/ a former local government region in central Scotland, now divided into **East Lothian**, **Midlothian**, and **West Lothian**.

loti /ˈləʊti, ˈluːti/ ▶ **noun** (pl. **maloti** /məˈləʊti, -ˈluːti/) the basic monetary unit of Lesotho, equal to 100 lisente.
– ORIGIN Sesotho.

lotic /ˈləʊtɪk/ ▶ **adjective** Ecology (of organisms or habitats) inhabiting or situated in rapidly moving fresh water. Compare with **LENTIC**.
– ORIGIN early 20th cent.: from Latin *lotus* 'washing' + **-IC**.

lotion ▶ **noun** [mass noun] a thick, smooth liquid preparation designed to be applied to the skin for medicinal or cosmetic purposes.
– ORIGIN late Middle English: from Old French, or from Latin *lotio(n-)*, from *lot-* 'washed', from the verb *lavare*.

Lotka–Volterra /ˌlɒtkəvɒlˈtɛrə/ ▶ **adjective** Ecology relating to a mathematical model which uses coupled differential equations to describe and predict the variation of two interacting populations, especially a predator and a prey species.
– ORIGIN 1950s: from the names of Alfred J. *Lotka* (1880–1949), Austrian-born American statistician, and Vito *Volterra* (1860–1940), Italian mathematician.

lotta (also **lotsa**) informal ▶ **contraction** lots of (representing non-standard use): *I saw a lotta courage out there, and a lotta hard work.*

lottery ▶ **noun** (pl. **lotteries**) a means of raising money by selling numbered tickets and giving prizes to the holders of numbers drawn at random. ■ [in sing.] a situation whose success or outcome is governed by chance: *you can appeal, but the procedure is something of a lottery.*
– ORIGIN mid 16th cent.: probably from Dutch *loterij*, from *lot* 'lot'.

Lotto /ˈlɒtəʊ/, Lorenzo (*c.*1480–1556), Italian painter. He chiefly painted religious subjects, though he also produced a number of notable portraits, such as *A Lady as Lucretia* (*c.*1533).

lotto ▶ **noun 1** [mass noun] a children's game similar to bingo, in which numbered or illustrated counters or cards are drawn by the players.
2 a lottery.
– ORIGIN late 18th cent.: from Italian.

lotus ▶ **noun 1** either of two large water lilies: ● (also **sacred lotus**) a red-flowered Asian lily (*Nelumbo nucifera*, family Nelumbonaceae). ● (also **Egyptian lotus**) a lily regarded as sacred in ancient Egypt (the white-flowered *Nymphaea lotus* and the blue-flowered *N. caerulea*, family Nymphaeaceae).
2 Greek Mythology a plant whose fruit induced a dreamy forgetfulness and an unwillingness to leave.
3 the flower of the sacred lotus as a symbol in Asian art and religion.
– ORIGIN late 15th cent. (denoting a type of clover or trefoil, described by Homer as food for horses): via Latin from Greek *lōtos*, of Semitic origin. The term was used by classical writers to denote various trees and plants; the legendary plant (sense 2), mentioned by Homer, was thought by later Greek writers to be *Ziziphus lotus*, a relative of the jujube.

lotusbird ▶ **noun** Austral. a jacana with a pink comb on the forehead, found in Australasia and Indonesia.
● *Irediparra gallinacea*, family Jacanidae. Alternative name: **comb-crested jacana**.

lotus-eater ▶ **noun** a person who spends their time indulging in pleasure and luxury rather than dealing with practical concerns.
– DERIVATIVES **lotus-eating** adjective.

lotus position (also **lotus posture**) ▶ **noun** a cross-legged position for meditation, with the feet resting on the thighs.

Lotus Sutra ▶ **noun** Buddhism one of the most important texts in Mahayana Buddhism, significant particularly in China and Japan and given special veneration by the Nichiren sect.

Louangphrabang variant spelling of **LUANG PRABANG**.

louche /luːʃ/ ▶ **adjective** disreputable or sordid in a rakish or appealing way: *the louche world of the theatre.*
– DERIVATIVES **loucheness** noun.
– ORIGIN early 19th cent.: from French, literally 'squinting'.

loud ▶ **adjective** producing or capable of producing much noise: *they were kept awake by loud music | his voice is loud and challenging.* ■ strong or emphatic in expression: *there were loud protests from the lumber barons.* ■ vulgarly obtrusive; flashy: *a man in a loud checked suit.*

▶ **adverb** with a great deal of volume: *they shouted as loud as they could.*
– PHRASES **out loud** aloud; audibly: *she laughed out loud.*
– DERIVATIVES **louden** verb, **loudly** adverb, **loudness** noun.
– ORIGIN Old English *hlūd*, of West Germanic origin; related to Dutch *luid*, German *laut*, from an Indo-European root meaning 'hear', shared by Greek *kluein* 'hear', *klutos* 'famous' and Latin *cluere* 'be famous'.

loudhailer ▶ **noun** Brit. an electronic device used to amplify the sound of a person's voice so that it can be heard at a distance; a megaphone.

loudmouth ▶ **noun** informal a person who tends to talk too much in an offensive or tactless way.
– DERIVATIVES **loud-mouthed** adjective.

loudspeaker ▶ **noun** an apparatus that converts electrical impulses into sound, typically as part of a public address system.

Lou Gehrig's disease ▶ **noun** [mass noun] a form of motor neurone disease; amyotrophic lateral sclerosis.
– ORIGIN 1940s: named after H. L. **GEHRIG**.

lough /lɒk, lɒx/ ▶ **noun** Irish spelling of **LOCH**.
– ORIGIN Middle English: from Irish *loch*. The spelling *lough* survived in Ireland but the pronunciation was replaced by that of the Irish word.

Loughborough /ˈlʌfb(ə)rə/ a town in Leicestershire, on the River Soar north of Leicester; pop. 59,300 (est. 2009).

Louis[1] /ˈluːi/ the name of eighteen kings of France: ■ **Louis I** (778–840), son of Charlemagne, king of the West Franks and Holy Roman Emperor 814–40. ■ **Louis II** (846–79), reigned 877–9. ■ **Louis III** (863–82), son of Louis II, reigned 879–82. ■ **Louis IV** (921–54), reigned 936–54. ■ **Louis V** (967–87), reigned 979–87. ■ **Louis VI** (1081–1137), reigned 1108–37. ■ **Louis VII** (1120–80), reigned 1137–80. ■ **Louis VIII** (1187–1226), reigned 1223–6. ■ **Louis IX** (1214–70), son of Louis VIII, reigned 1226–70; canonized as **St Louis**. He conducted two unsuccessful crusades, dying of plague in Tunis during the second. Feast day, 25 August. ■ **Louis X** (1289–1316), reigned 1314–16. ■ **Louis XI** (1423–83), son of Charles VII, reigned 1461–83. He continued his father's work in laying the foundations of a united France ruled by an absolute monarchy. ■ **Louis XII** (1462–1515), reigned 1498–1515. ■ **Louis XIII** (1601–43), son of Henry IV of France, reigned 1610–43. During his minority the country was ruled by his mother Marie de Médicis. From 1624 he was heavily influenced in policy-making by his chief minister Cardinal Richelieu. ■ **Louis XIV** (1638–1715), son of Louis XIII, reigned 1643–1715; known as **the Sun King**. His reign represented the high point of the Bourbon dynasty and of French power in Europe, and in this period French art and literature flourished. His almost constant wars of expansion united Europe against him, however, and gravely weakened France's financial position. ■ **Louis XV** (1710–74), great-grandson and successor of Louis XIV, reigned 1715–74. He led France into the Seven Years War (1756–63). ■ **Louis XVI** (1754–93), grandson and successor of Louis XV, reigned 1774–92. His minor concessions and reforms in the face of the emerging French Revolution proved disastrous. As the Revolution became more extreme, he was executed with his wife, Marie Antoinette, and the monarchy was abolished. ■ **Louis XVII** (1785–95), son of Louis XVI, titular king who died in prison during the Revolution. ■ **Louis XVIII** (1755–1824), brother of Louis XVI, reigned 1814–24. After his nephew Louis XVII's death he became titular king in exile until the fall of Napoleon in 1814, when he returned to Paris on the summons of Talleyrand and was officially restored to the throne.

L

Louis[2] /ˈluːɪs/, Joe (1914–81), American boxer; born *Joseph Louis Barrow*; known as the **Brown Bomber**. He was heavyweight champion of the world 1937–49, defending his title twenty-five times during that period.

louis /ˈluːi/ (also **louis d'or** /-ˈdɔː/) ▶ **noun** (pl. **same** /ˈluːɪz/) a gold coin issued in France between 1640 and 1793. ■ another term for **NAPOLEON** (sense 1).
– ORIGIN from **LOUIS**[1].

Louis I (1326–82), king of Hungary 1342–82 and of Poland 1370–82; known as **Louis the Great**. Under his rule Hungary became a powerful state; he fought two successful wars against Venice (1357–8; 1378–81), and the rulers of Serbia, Wallachia, Moldavia, and Bulgaria became his vassals.

Louis, St, Louis IX of France (see **LOUIS**[1]).

Louisiana /luːˌiːzɪˈanə/ a state in the southern US, on the Gulf of Mexico; pop. 4,410,796 (est. 2008); capital, Baton Rouge. Louisiana originally denoted the large region of the Mississippi basin claimed for France by the explorer La Salle in 1682. It was sold by the French to the US in the Louisiana Purchase of 1803. The smaller area now known as Louisiana became the 18th state in 1812.
– DERIVATIVES **Louisianan** (also **Louisianian**) adjective & noun.
– ORIGIN named in honour of *Louis* XIV.

Louisiana Purchase the territory sold by France to the US in 1803, comprising the western part of the Mississippi valley and including the modern state of Louisiana.

Louis Philippe /ˌluːi fɪˈliːp/ (1773–1850), king of France 1830–48. After the restoration of the Bourbons he became the focus for liberal discontent and was made king, replacing Charles X. His regime was gradually undermined by radical discontent and eventually overthrown.

Louis the Great, Louis I of Hungary (see **Louis I**).

Louisville /ˈluːɪvɪl/ an industrial city and river port in northern Kentucky, on the Ohio River just south of the border with Indiana; pop. 557,200 (est. 2008). It is the site of the annual Kentucky Derby.

lounge ▶ **verb** [no obj., with adverbial of place] lie, sit, or stand in a relaxed or lazy way: *several students were lounging about reading papers.*
▶ **noun 1** a public room in a hotel, theatre, or club in which to sit and relax. ■ a seating area in an airport for waiting passengers: *the departure lounge.* ■ Brit. a sitting room in a house.
2 [in sing.] Brit. an act or spell of lounging.
– ORIGIN early 16th cent. (in the sense 'move indolently'): perhaps symbolic of slow movement. Sense 1 of the noun dates from the late 19th cent.

lounge bar ▶ **noun** Brit. the smarter and more comfortably furnished bar in a pub. Compare with **PUBLIC BAR**.

lounge lizard ▶ **noun** informal an idle man who spends his time in places frequented by rich and fashionable people.

lounger ▶ **noun** a comfortable chair for relaxing on, especially an outdoor chair that adjusts or extends, allowing a person to recline. ■ a person spending their time lazily or in a relaxed way.

lounge suit ▶ **noun** Brit. a man's suit consisting of a matching jacket and trousers, worn during the day, especially in the workplace.

loungewear ▶ **noun** [mass noun] casual, comfortable clothing suitable for wearing at home.

loungey ▶ **adjective** informal (of a place) conducive to lounging; comfortable: *a loungey bar with low seating.* ■ denoting or relating to easy-listening music.

L

loup /laʊp/ ▶ **verb & noun** Scottish and northern English variant of **LEAP**.
– ORIGIN Middle English: from Old Norse *hlaupa* (verb), *hlaup* (noun).

loupe /luːp/ ▶ **noun** a small magnifying glass used by jewellers and watchmakers.
– ORIGIN late 19th cent.: from French.

louping-ill /ˈlaʊpɪŋɪl/ ▶ **noun** [mass noun] a viral disease attacking animals, especially sheep, which is transmitted by ticks and causes staggering and jumping.
– ORIGIN late Middle English: from **LOUP** (because of the symptom of spasmodic jumping) + the noun **ILL**.

lour /ˈlaʊə/ (also **lower**) ▶ **verb** [no obj.] look angry or sullen; scowl: *the lofty statue lours at patients in the infirmary.* ■ (of the sky or landscape) look dark and threatening.
▶ **noun** a scowl. ■ a dark and gloomy appearance of the sky or landscape.
– ORIGIN Middle English: of unknown origin.

Lourdes /lʊəd/, French /luʀd/ a town in SW France, at the foot of the Pyrenees; pop. 15,698 (2006). It has been a major place of Roman Catholic pilgrimage since in 1858 a young peasant girl, Marie Bernarde Soubirous (St Bernadette), claimed to have had a series of visions of the Virgin Mary.

Lourenço Marques /ləˌrɛnsəʊ ˈmɑːks/ former name (until 1976) for **MAPUTO**.

lourie /ˈlaʊəri/ (also **loerie**) ▶ **noun** (pl. **louries**) S. African another term for **TURACO** and **GO-AWAY BIRD**.
– ORIGIN Afrikaans, from Dutch *lori*. Compare with **LORY**.

louring /ˈlaʊərɪŋ/ (also **lowering**) ▶ **adjective** (of the sky) dark and threatening: *a day of louring cloud.*
– DERIVATIVES **louringly** adverb.

louse ▶ **noun 1** (pl. **lice**) either of two small wingless parasitic insects that live on the skin of mammals and birds: ● **(sucking louse)** an insect with piercing mouthparts, found only on mammals (order Anoplura or Siphunculata). See also **BODY LOUSE, HEAD LOUSE** ● **(biting louse)** an insect with a large head and jaws, found chiefly on birds (order Mallophaga).
■ used in names of small invertebrates that parasitize aquatic animals or infest plants, e.g. **fish louse**.
2 (pl. **louses**) informal a contemptible or unpleasant person.
▶ **verb** [with obj.] **1 (louse something up)** informal spoil or ruin something: *he loused up my promotion chances.*
2 archaic remove lice from.
– ORIGIN Old English *lūs*, (plural) *lȳs*, of Germanic origin; related to Dutch *luis*, German *Laus*.

louse fly ▶ **noun** a flattened bloodsucking fly which may have reduced or absent wings and typically spends much of its life on one individual of the host species. ● Family Hippoboscidae: several genera.

louser ▶ **noun** informal, chiefly Irish a mean, unpleasant, or contemptible person.

lousewort ▶ **noun** a partially parasitic herbaceous plant of the figwort family, typically favouring damp habitats. It is native to both Eurasia and North America and was formerly reputed to harbour lice.
● Genus *Pedicularis*, family Scrophulariaceae: several species, including the red rattle.

lousy ▶ **adjective** (**lousier**, **lousiest**) **1** informal very poor or bad: *the service is usually lousy | lousy weather.*
■ used to express anger, contempt, or annoyance: *you lousy creeps.* ■ [predic.] unwell: *she felt lousy.*
2 infested with lice. ■ **(lousy with)** informal teeming with (something regarded as undesirable): *the town is lousy with tourists.*
– DERIVATIVES **lousily** adverb, **lousiness** noun.

lout ▶ **noun** an uncouth and aggressive man or boy.
– ORIGIN mid 16th cent.: perhaps from archaic *lout* 'to bow down', of Germanic origin.

Louth /laʊθ/ a county of the Republic of Ireland, on the east coast in the province of Leinster; county town, Dundalk.

loutish ▶ **adjective** (of a man or boy) uncouth and aggressive; thuggish: *youths responsible for awful, loutish behaviour.*
– DERIVATIVES **loutishly** adverb, **loutishness** noun.

Louvain /luvɛ̃/ French name for **LEUVEN**.

louvar /ˈluːvɑː/ ▶ **noun** a large brightly coloured fish with a distinctive high forehead. It lives in warm open seas, feeding on jellyfishes and comb jellies.
● *Luvarus imperialis*, the only member of the family Luvaridae.
– ORIGIN alteration of Latin name.

Louvre /ˈluːvr(ə)/, French /luvʀ/ the principal museum and art gallery of France, in Paris, housed in the former royal palace built by Francis I. The Louvre holds the Mona Lisa and the Venus de Milo.

louvre /ˈluːvə/ (US also **louver**) ▶ **noun 1** each of a set of angled slats fixed or hung at regular intervals in a door, shutter, or screen to allow air or light to pass through.
2 (in a medieval house) a structure in a roof incorporating openings for the passage of smoke.
– DERIVATIVES **louvred** adjective.
– ORIGIN Middle English (in sense 2): from Old French *lover, lovier* 'skylight', probably of Germanic origin and related to **LODGE**.

lovable (also **loveable**) ▶ **adjective** inspiring or deserving love or affection: *a naughty but lovable child | he has a lovable, sweet personality.*
– DERIVATIVES **lovability** noun, **lovableness** noun, **lovably** adverb.

lovage /ˈlʌvɪdʒ/ ▶ **noun** a large edible white-flowered plant of the parsley family. ● Several species in the family Umbelliferae, in particular a Mediterranean herb (*Levisticum officinale*), which is chiefly used for flavouring liqueurs.
– ORIGIN Middle English *loveache*, alteration (as if from **LOVE** + obsolete *ache* 'parsley') of Old French *luvesche, levesche*, via late Latin *levisticum* from Latin *ligusticum*, neuter of *ligusticus* 'Ligurian'.

lovat /ˈlʌvət/ (also **lovat green**) ▶ **noun** [mass noun] a muted green colour used especially in tweed and woollen garments.
– ORIGIN early 20th cent.: from *Lovat*, a place name in Highland Scotland.

love ▶ **noun** [mass noun] **1** a strong feeling of affection: *babies fill parents with intense feelings of love | their **love for** their country.* ■ a strong feeling of affection and sexual attraction for someone: *they were both **in love with** her | we were slowly **falling in love**.*
■ affectionate greetings conveyed to someone on one's behalf: *give her my love.* ■ a formula for ending an affectionate letter: *take care, lots of love, Judy.*
2 a great interest and pleasure in something: *his love for football | we share a **love of** music.*
3 [count noun] a person or thing that one loves: *she was **the love of his life** | their two great loves are tobacco and whisky.* ■ Brit. informal a friendly form of address: *it's all right, love.* ■ **(a love)** informal used in affectionate requests: *don't fret, there's a love.*
4 (in tennis, squash, and some other sports) a score of zero; nil: *love fifteen.* [apparently from the phrase *play for love* (i.e. the love of the game, not for money); folk etymology has connected the word with French *l'oeuf* 'egg', from the resemblance in shape between an egg and a zero.]
▶ **verb** [with obj.] feel deep affection or sexual love for (someone): *do you love me?* ■ like or enjoy very much: *I'd love a cup of tea | I just love dancing.*
– PHRASES **for love** for pleasure rather than profit: *he played **for the love of** the game.* **for the love of God** used to accompany an urgent request or to express annoyance or surprise: *for the love of God, get me out of here!* **for the love of Mike** Brit. informal used to accompany an exasperated request or to express dismay. **love me, love my dog** proverb if you love someone, you must accept everything about them, even their faults. **make love 1** have sexual intercourse. **2 (make love to)** dated pay amorous attention to (someone). **not for love or money** informal not in any circumstances: *they'll not return for love or money.* **there's no** (or **little** or **not much**) **love lost between** there is mutual dislike between (the people mentioned).
– ORIGIN Old English *lufu*, of Germanic origin; from an Indo-European root shared by Sanskrit *lubhyati* 'desires', Latin *libet* 'it is pleasing', *libido* 'desire', also by **LEAVE²** and **LIEF**.

loveable ▶ **adjective** variant spelling of **LOVABLE**.

love affair ▶ **noun** a romantic or sexual relationship between two people who are not married to each other. ■ an intense enthusiasm or liking for something: *he had a lifelong love affair with the cinema.*

love apple ▶ **noun** archaic a tomato.

lovebird ▶ **noun 1** a very small African and Madagascan parrot with mainly green plumage and typically a red or black face, noted for the affectionate behaviour of mated birds. ● Genus *Agapornis*, family Psittacidae: several species.
2 (lovebirds) informal an openly affectionate couple.

love bite ▶ **noun** Brit. a temporary red mark on a person's skin caused by a lover biting or sucking it as a sexual act.

love child ▶ **noun** a child born to parents who are not married to each other.

loved-up ▶ **adjective** Brit. informal under the influence of the drug Ecstasy, typically with the result of feeling euphoric and affectionate. ■ in love, or behaving very amorously.

love feast ▶ **noun** historical a feast in token of fellowship among early Christians; an agape. ■ a religious service or gathering imitating a love feast, especially among early Methodists.

love game ▶ **noun** (in tennis and similar sports) a game in which the loser does not score.

love handles ▶ **plural noun** informal deposits of excess fat at a person's waistline.

love-hate ▶ **adjective** (of a relationship) characterized by ambivalent feelings of love and hate felt by one or each of two or more parties.

love-in ▶ **noun** informal, dated a gathering or party at which people are encouraged to express feelings of friendship and physical attraction, associated with the hippies of the 1960s.

love-in-a-mist ▶ **noun** a Mediterranean plant of the buttercup family, which bears blue flowers surrounded by delicate thread-like green bracts, giving a hazy appearance to the flowers. ● *Nigella damascena*, family Ranunculaceae.

love-in-idleness ▶ **noun** another term for **HEARTSEASE**.

love interest ▶ **noun** an actor whose main role in a story or film is that of a lover of the central character. ■ [mass noun] a theme or subsidiary plot in a story or film in which the main element is the affection of lovers.

Lovelace¹, Augusta Ada King, Countess of (1815–52), English mathematician. The daughter of Lord Byron, she became assistant to Charles Babbage and worked with him on his mechanical computer.

Lovelace², Richard (1618–57), English poet. A Royalist, he was imprisoned in 1642, when he probably wrote his famous poem 'To Althea, from Prison'.

loveless ▶ **adjective** having no feelings of love: *a young wife trapped in a loveless marriage.*
– DERIVATIVES **lovelessly** adverb, **lovelessness** noun.

love-lies-bleeding ▶ **noun** a South American plant with long drooping tassels of crimson flowers. Cultivated today as an ornamental, its seeds and leaves were formerly eaten in the Andes. ● *Amaranthus caudatus*, family Amaranthaceae.

love life ▶ **noun** the area of a person's life concerning their relationships with lovers.

Lovell /ˈlʌv(ə)l/, Sir (Alfred Charles) Bernard (b.1913), English astronomer and physicist, and pioneer of radio astronomy. He founded Manchester University's radio observatory at Jodrell Bank, where he directed the construction of the large radio telescope that is now named after him.

Lovelock, James (Ephraim) (b.1919), English scientist. He is best known for the **Gaia hypothesis**, first presented by him in 1972 and discussed in several popular books, including *Gaia* (1979).

lovelock ▶ **noun** archaic a curl of hair worn on the temple or forehead.

lovelorn ▶ **adjective** unhappy because of unrequited love.

lovely ▶ **adjective** (**lovelier**, **loveliest**) very beautiful or attractive: *lovely views* | *she looked lovely.* ■ informal very pleasant or enjoyable; delightful: *we've had a lovely day* | *how lovely to see you!*
▶ **noun** (pl. **lovelies**) informal an attractive woman or girl: *a bevy of lovelies.* ■ used as an affectionate form of address: *don't worry, my lovely.*
– PHRASES **lovely jubbly** Brit. informal used to express delight or approbation; excellent: *fish and chips and a few beers on the way back from a match—lovely jubbly!* [from *lubbly Jubbly*, a 1950s advertising slogan for *Jubbly*, an orange-flavoured soft drink; adopted by comedy writer John Sullivan in his BBC television series *Only Fools & Horses*.]
– DERIVATIVES **lovelily** adverb, **loveliness** noun.
– ORIGIN Old English *luflic* (see LOVE, -LY[1]).

lovemaking ▶ **noun** [mass noun] **1** sexual activity, especially sexual intercourse.
2 archaic courtship.

love match ▶ **noun** a marriage based on the mutual love of the couple rather than social or financial considerations.

love nest ▶ **noun** informal a place where two lovers spend time together, especially in secret.

lover ▶ **noun** a partner in a sexual or romantic relationship outside marriage. ■ a person who likes or enjoys a specified thing: *he was a great lover of cats* | *music lovers.*
– DERIVATIVES **loverless** adjective.

lovers' rock ▶ **noun** [mass noun] a gentle, melodic style of reggae incorporating elements of soul and usually featuring lyrics with a romantic theme.

love seat ▶ **noun** a small sofa for two people, especially one designed in an S-shape so that the couple can face each other.

lovesick ▶ **adjective** in love, or missing the person one loves, so much that one is unable to act normally: *you're mooning around like some lovesick teenager.*
– DERIVATIVES **lovesickness** noun.

lovesome ▶ **adjective** literary lovely or lovable.

love vine ▶ **noun** [mass noun] N. Amer. & W. Indian the dodder, which is sometimes used medicinally and as a love charm.

lovey ▶ **noun** (pl. **loveys**) Brit. informal used as an affectionate form of address: *Ruth, lovey, are you there?*

lovey-dovey ▶ **adjective** informal very affectionate or romantic, especially excessively so: *a lovey-dovey couple.*

loving ▶ **adjective** feeling or showing love or great care: *a loving father* | *the cargo was described in loving detail.* ■ (in combination **-loving**) enjoying the specified activity or thing: *a fun-loving girl.*
– DERIVATIVES **lovingly** adverb, **lovingness** noun.

loving cup ▶ **noun** a large two-handled cup, passed round at banquets for each guest to drink from in turn.

loving-kindness ▶ **noun** [mass noun] tenderness and consideration towards others.
– ORIGIN from usage in Coverdale's translation of the Psalms.

Low, Sir David (Alexander Cecil) (1891–1963), New-Zealand-born British cartoonist famous for his political cartoons and for inventing the character Colonel Blimp.

low[1] ▶ **adjective 1** of less than average height from top to bottom or to the top from the ground: *the school is a long, low building* | *a low table.* ■ situated not far above the ground, the horizon, or sea level: *the sun was low in the sky.* ■ located at or near the bottom of something: *low back pain* | *he smashed a pane low down in the window.* ■ (of women's clothing) cut so as to reveal the neck and the upper part of the breasts: *the low neckline of her blouse* | [in combination] *a low-cut black dress.* ■ (of latitude) near the equator. ■ Phonetics (of a vowel) pronounced with the tongue held low in the mouth; open.
2 below average in amount, extent, or intensity: *bringing up children on a low income* | *borrowing fell to a low level* | *cook over low heat.* ■ (of a river or lake) below the usual water level. ■ (of a substance or food) containing smaller quantities than usual of a specified ingredient: *vegetables are **low in** calories* | [in combination] *low-fat spreads.* ■ (of a supply) small or reduced in quantity: *food and ammunition were **running low**.* ■ having a small or reduced quantity of a supply: *they were **low on** fuel.*
3 ranking below other people or things in importance or class: *jobs with low status* | *training will be given low priority.* ■ (of art or culture) considered to be inferior in quality and refinement: *the dual traditions of high and low art.* ■ less good than is expected or desired; inferior: *the standard of living is low.* ■ unscrupulous or dishonest: *practise a little low cunning.* ■ (of an opinion) unfavourable.
4 (of a sound or voice) not loud or high: *keep the volume very low* | *his low, husky voice.*
5 depressed or lacking in energy: *I was feeling low.*
▶ **noun 1** a low point, level, or figure: *his popularity ratings are at an all-time low.* ■ an area of low barometric pressure; a depression.
2 a difficult time in a person's life: *the highs and lows of an actor's life.* ■ informal a state of depression.
▶ **adverb 1** in or into a low position or state: *she pressed on, bent low to protect her face.*
2 in a low voice or at a low pitch: *we were talking low so we wouldn't wake Dean.*
– PHRASES **the lowest of the low** the people regarded as the most immoral or socially inferior of all.
– DERIVATIVES **lowish** adjective, **lowness** noun.
– ORIGIN Middle English: from Old Norse *lágr*, of Germanic origin; related to Dutch *laag*, also to LIE[1].

low[2] ▶ **verb** [no obj.] (of a cow) make a characteristic deep sound.
▶ **noun** a sound made by cattle; a moo.
– ORIGIN Old English *hlōwan*, of Germanic origin; related to Dutch *loeien*, from an Indo-European root shared by Latin *clamare* 'to shout'.

lowan ▶ **noun** Austral. another term for MALLEEFOWL.

lowball ▶ **noun** Baseball a ball pitched so as to pass over the plate below the level of the batter's knees. ■ [as modifier] N. Amer. informal (of an estimate, bid, etc.) deceptively or unrealistically low.
▶ **verb** [with obj.] N. Amer. informal offer a deceptively or unrealistically low bid or estimate.

low-born ▶ **adjective** born to a family that has a low social status.

lowboy ▶ **noun** N. Amer. **1** a low chest or table with drawers and short legs.
2 (also **lowboy trailer**) a trailer with a low frame for transporting very tall or heavy loads.

lowbrow often derogatory ▶ **adjective** not highly intellectual or cultured: *lowbrow tabloids.*
▶ **noun** a lowbrow person.

low-carb ▶ **adjective** informal denoting or relating to food or drink that is low in carbohydrates: *a low-carb diet.*

Low Church ▶ **noun** [treated as sing. or pl.] a tradition within the Anglican Church (and some other denominations) which is Protestant in outlook and gives relatively little emphasis to ritual, sacraments, and the authority of the clergy.
– DERIVATIVES **Low Churchman** noun (pl. **Low Churchmen**).

low-class ▶ **adjective** of a low or inferior standard, quality, or social class: *low-class places of amusement.*

low comedy ▶ **noun** [mass noun] comedy in which the subject and its treatment border on farce.

low-cost ▶ **adjective** relatively inexpensive; cheap: *a low-cost airline.*

Low Countries the region of NW Europe comprising the Netherlands, Belgium, and Luxembourg.

low-density lipoprotein ▶ **noun** [mass noun] the form of lipoprotein in which cholesterol is transported in the blood.

low-down informal ▶ **adjective** mean and unfair: *dirty low-down tricks.*
▶ **noun** (**the low-down**) the true facts or relevant information about something: *you get **the low-down on** where to go and where to stay away from.*

Lowell[1] /ˈləʊəl/, Amy (Lawrence) (1874–1925), American poet. A leading imagist poet, she is known for her polyphonic prose and sensuous imagery.

Lowell[2] /ˈləʊəl/, James Russell (1819–91), American poet and critic. His works include the satirical *Biglow Papers* (1848 and 1867; prose and verse) and volumes of essays including *Among my Books* (1870).

Lowell[3] /ˈləʊəl/, Percival (1855–1916), American astronomer. Lowell inferred the existence of a ninth planet beyond Neptune, and when it was eventually discovered in 1930 it was given the name Pluto, with a symbol that also included his initials. He was the brother of Amy Lowell.

Lowell[4] /ˈləʊəl/, Robert (Traill Spence) (1917–77), American poet. His poetry, often describing his manic depression, is notable for its intense confessional nature and for its complex imagery.

low-end ▶ **adjective** denoting the cheaper products of a range, especially of audio or computer equipment.

lower[1] comparative of LOW[1]. ▶ **adjective** less high in position: *the lower levels of the building.* ■ less high in status or amount: *managers lower down the hierarchy* | *lower costs will encourage people to buy.* ■ (of an animal or plant) showing relatively primitive or simple characteristics. ■ (often **Lower**) Geology & Archaeology denoting an older (and hence usually deeper) part of a stratigraphic division or archaeological deposit or the period in which it was formed or deposited: *Lower Cretaceous* | *Lower Palaeolithic.* ■ [in place names] situated to the south: *the union of Upper and Lower Egypt.*
▶ **adverb** in or into a lower position: *the sun sank lower.*
– DERIVATIVES **lowermost** adjective.

lower[2] ▶ **verb** [with obj.] move (someone or something) in a downward direction: *he watched the coffin being lowered into the ground.* ■ make or become less in amount, intensity, or degree: [with obj.] *traffic speeds must be lowered* | *she lowered her voice to a whisper* | [no obj.] *temperatures lowered.* ■ (**lower oneself**) behave in a way that is perceived as unworthy or debased.
– PHRASES **lower the boom on** N. Amer. informal treat (someone) severely. ■ put a stop to (an activity): *let's lower the boom on high-level corruption.* **lower the tone** diminish the general spirit or moral character of a conversation, place, etc.: *trust you to lower the tone of the conversation.*

lower[3] ▶ **verb & noun** variant spelling of LOUR.

lower animals ▶ **plural noun** animals of relatively simple or primitive characteristics as contrasted with humans or with more advanced animals such as mammals or vertebrates.

Lower Austria a state of NE Austria; capital, St Pölten. German name NIEDERÖSTERREICH.

Lower California another name for BAJA CALIFORNIA.

Lower Canada the mainly French-speaking region of Canada around the lower St Lawrence River, in what is now southern Quebec.

lower case ▶ **noun** [mass noun] small letters as opposed to capital letters (upper case): *the name may be typed in lower case* | [as modifier] *lower-case letters.*
– ORIGIN referring originally to the lower of two cases of type positioned on an angled stand for use by a compositor (see UPPER CASE).

lower chamber ▶ **noun** another term for LOWER HOUSE.

lower class ▶ **noun** [treated as sing. or pl.] the social group that has the lowest status; the working class.
▶ **adjective** relating to or characteristic of such a group: *a lower-class area.*

lower court ▶ **noun** Law a court whose decisions may be overruled by another court on appeal.

lower criticism ▶ **noun** [mass noun] dated term for TEXTUAL CRITICISM, in contrast to HIGHER CRITICISM.

lower deck ▶ **noun** the deck of a ship situated immediately above the hold. ■ the petty officers and crew of a ship, collectively.

lower house ▶ **noun** the larger of two sections of a bicameral parliament or similar legislature, typically with elected members and having the primary responsibility for legislation. ■ (**the Lower House**) (in the UK) the House of Commons.

Lower Hutt /hʌt/ a city in New Zealand, near Wellington; pop. 97,701 (2006).

lower orders ▶ **plural noun** dated the lower classes of society.

lower plants ▶ **plural noun** plants of relatively simple or primitive characteristics, especially those which are not vascular plants, i.e. algae, mosses, liverworts, and sometimes fungi.

lower regions ▶ **plural noun** archaic hell or the underworld.

Lower Saxony a state of NW Germany; capital, Hanover. It corresponds to the north-western part of the former kingdom of Saxony. German name **NIEDERSACHSEN**.

lower school ▶ noun the section of a larger school which comprises or caters for the younger pupils, especially those below the fifth form.

lowest common denominator ▶ noun 1 Mathematics the lowest common multiple of the denominators of several vulgar fractions.
2 derogatory the level of the least discriminating audience or consumer group.

lowest common multiple (abbrev.: **LCM**) ▶ noun Mathematics the lowest quantity that is a multiple of two or more given quantities (e.g. 12 is the lowest common multiple of 2, 3, and 4).

Lowestoft /ˈləʊɪstɒft/ a fishing port and resort town on the North Sea coast of eastern England, in Suffolk; pop. 75,200 (est. 2009). It is the most easterly English town.

low-fi ▶ adjective variant spelling of **LO-FI**.

low frequency ▶ noun (in radio) 30–300 kilohertz.

low gear ▶ noun a gear that causes a wheeled vehicle to move slowly, due to a low ratio between the speed of the wheels and that of the mechanism driving them.

Low German ▶ noun [mass noun] a vernacular language spoken in much of northern Germany, more closely related to Dutch than to standard German. Also called **PLATTDEUTSCH**.

low-grade ▶ adjective of low quality or standard: *low-grade steel.* ■ at a low level in a salary or employment structure: *low-grade clerical jobs.* ■ (of a medical condition) of a less serious kind; minor: *a low-grade malignancy.*

low-hanging fruit ▶ noun (pl. **same**) informal the most easily achieved of a set of tasks, measures, goals, etc.: *it's more difficult to produce new drugs—all the low-hanging fruit has been picked.*

L

low-impact ▶ adjective 1 (of exercises, typically aerobics) designed to put little harmful stress on the body.
2 (of an activity, industry, or product) affecting or altering the environment as little as possible.

low-key (also **low-keyed**) ▶ adjective not elaborate, showy, or intensive; modest or restrained: *their marriage was a very quiet, low-key affair.* ■ Art & Photography having a predominance of dark or muted tones.

lowland /ˈləʊlənd/ ▶ noun [mass noun] (also **lowlands**) low-lying country: *economic power gravitated towards the lowlands* | [as modifier] *lowland farming.* ■ (**the Lowlands**) the region of Scotland lying south and east of the Highlands.
– DERIVATIVES **lowlander** noun.

Low Latin ▶ noun [mass noun] medieval and later forms of Latin.

low-level ▶ adjective at or of a level below that which is normal or average: *low-level flying was banned.* ■ relating to or involving people of low administrative rank or authority: *opportunities to progress beyond low-level jobs.* ■ Computing denoting programming languages or operations which are relatively close to machine code in form. ■ (of nuclear waste) having a small degree of radioactivity.

low life ▶ noun [mass noun] people or activities characterized as being disreputable and often criminal: *crackheads, loafers, and general Nineties low life.* ■ (**lowlife**) [count noun] informal a person of such a kind.
– DERIVATIVES **low-lifer** noun.

lowlight ▶ noun 1 (**lowlights**) darker streaks in a person's hair produced by dyeing.
2 informal a particularly disappointing or dull event or feature.
– ORIGIN 1920s: from **LOW**[1], suggested by **HIGHLIGHT**.

low-loader ▶ noun Brit. a lorry with a low floor and no sides, for transporting heavy loads.

lowly ▶ adjective (**lowlier**, **lowliest**) low in status or importance; humble: *she'd been too good for her lowly position.* ■ (of an organism) primitive or simple.
▶ adverb to a low degree; in a low manner: *lowly paid workers.*
– DERIVATIVES **lowlily** adverb, **lowliness** noun.

low-lying ▶ adjective at low altitude above sea level: *flooding problems in low-lying areas.*

low-maintenance ▶ adjective requiring little work to keep in good condition: *low-maintenance lawns.* ■ informal (of a person) independent and not demanding a lot of attention.

Low Mass ▶ noun (in the Catholic Church) Mass with no music and a minimum of ceremony.

low-minded ▶ adjective vulgar or sordid in mind or character.

low-pass ▶ adjective Electronics (of a filter) transmitting all frequencies below a certain value.

low-pitched ▶ adjective 1 (of a sound) deep or relatively quiet.
2 (of a roof) having only a slight slope.

low post ▶ noun Basketball an offensive position on the court close to the basket.

low pressure ▶ noun [mass noun] a condition of the atmosphere in which the pressure is below average (e.g. in a depression).

low profile ▶ noun [in sing.] a position of avoiding or not attracting much attention or publicity: *he's not the sort of politician to **keep a low profile**.*
▶ adjective 1 avoiding attention or publicity: *a low-profile campaign.*
2 (of an object) lower or slimmer than is usual for objects of its type. ■ (of a motor-vehicle tyre) of smaller diameter and greater width than usual, for high-performance use.

low-ranking ▶ adjective having a low rank or position in a particular hierarchy: *low-ranking police officers.*

low relief ▶ noun see **RELIEF** (sense 4).

low-rent ▶ adjective (of a property) costing relatively little to rent: *a low-rent apartment.* ■ informal having little prestige; inferior or shoddy: *low-rent reality shows.*

low-res ▶ adjective variant spelling of **LO-RES**.

low-residue ▶ adjective (of a meal or diet) designed to produce relatively little faeces and urine.

low-rider ▶ noun US a customized vehicle with hydraulic jacks that allow the chassis to be lowered nearly to the road.
– DERIVATIVES **low-riding** noun.

low-rise ▶ adjective 1 (of a building) having few storeys: *low-rise apartment blocks.*
2 (of trousers) cut so as to fit low on the hips rather than on the waist: *low-rise jeans.*
▶ noun a building having few storeys.

Lowry[1] /ˈlaʊəri/, (Clarence) Malcolm (1909–57), English novelist. His experiences living in Mexico in the 1930s provided the background for his symbolic semi-autobiographical novel *Under the Volcano* (1947).

Lowry[2] /ˈlaʊəri/, L. S. (1887–1976), English painter; full name *Laurence Stephen Lowry*. He painted small matchstick figures set against the iron and brick expanse of urban and industrial landscapes, settings provided by his life in Salford, near Manchester.

low season ▶ noun Brit. the least popular time of year at a resort, hotel, or tourist attraction, when prices are lowest.

low-slung ▶ adjective 1 lower in height or closer to the ground than usual: *a low-slung Mercedes with blacked-out windows.*
2 (of clothes, especially trousers) cut to fit low on the hips rather than the waist: *a pair of low-slung jeans.*

low-spirited ▶ adjective sad and despondent; depressed: *he was a bit low-spirited.*

low spirits ▶ plural noun a feeling of sadness and despondency: *he was **in low spirits**.*

Low Sunday ▶ noun the Sunday after Easter.
– ORIGIN perhaps so named in contrast to the high days of Holy Week and Easter.

low-tech (also **lo-tech**) ▶ adjective using or requiring only low technology: *low-tech water-purifying and solar-heating systems.*
▶ noun (**low tech**) short for **LOW TECHNOLOGY**.

low technology ▶ noun [mass noun] less advanced or relatively unsophisticated technological development or equipment.

low tension (also **low voltage**) ▶ noun an electrical potential not large enough to cause injury or damage if diverted.

low tide ▶ noun the state of the tide when at its lowest level: *islets visible **at low tide**.*

lowveld /ˈləʊvɛlt, -fɛlt/ ▶ noun [mass noun] a region of veld situated at a low altitude, especially the low-lying region of north-eastern South Africa and Swaziland.
– ORIGIN partly translating Afrikaans *laeveld*, from *lae* 'low' + *veld* (see **VELD**).

low water ▶ noun another term for **LOW TIDE**.

low-water mark ▶ noun the level reached by the sea at low tide, or by a lake or river during a drought or dry season. ■ a minimum recorded level or value: *the market was approaching its low-water mark.*

Low Week ▶ noun the week that begins with Low Sunday.

lox[1] /lɒks/ ▶ noun [mass noun] liquid oxygen.
– ORIGIN early 20th cent.: acronym from *liquid oxygen explosive*, later interpreted as being from *liquid oxygen*.

lox[2] /lɒks/ ▶ noun [mass noun] N. Amer. smoked salmon.
– ORIGIN 1940s: from Yiddish *laks*.

loxodrome /ˈlɒksədrəʊm/ ▶ noun another term for **RHUMB** (sense 1).

loyal ▶ adjective giving or showing firm and constant support or allegiance to a person or institution: *he remained **loyal to** the government* | *loyal service.*
– DERIVATIVES **loyally** adverb.
– ORIGIN mid 16th cent.: from French, via Old French *loial* from Latin *legalis* (see **LEGAL**).

loyalist ▶ noun a person who remains loyal to the established ruler or government, especially in the face of a revolt. ■ (**Loyalist**) a supporter of union between Great Britain and Northern Ireland. ■ (**Loyalist**) a colonist of the American revolutionary period who supported the British cause.
– DERIVATIVES **loyalism** noun.

loyal toast ▶ noun a toast proposed and drunk to the sovereign of one's country.

loyalty ▶ noun (pl. **loyalties**) [mass noun] the quality of being loyal: *his extreme **loyalty to** the Crown.* ■ [count noun] (often **loyalties**) a strong feeling of support or allegiance: *rows with in-laws are distressing because they cause divided loyalties.*

loyalty card ▶ noun Brit. an identity card issued by a retailer to its customers as part of a consumer incentive scheme, whereby credits are accumulated for future discounts every time a transaction is recorded.

Loyalty Islands a group of islands in the SW Pacific, forming part of the French overseas territory of New Caledonia; pop. 22,080 (2004).

lozenge /ˈlɒzɪn(d)ʒ/ ▶ noun a rhombus or diamond shape. ■ a small medicinal tablet, originally in the shape of a lozenge, taken for sore throats and dissolved in the mouth: *throat lozenges.* ■ Heraldry a charge in the shape of a solid diamond, in particular one on which the arms of an unmarried or widowed woman are displayed.
– ORIGIN Middle English: from Old French *losenge*, probably derived from the base of Spanish *losa*, Portuguese *lousa* 'slab', late Latin *lausiae (lapides)* 'stone slabs'.

Lozi /ˈləʊzi/ ▶ noun (pl. **same** or **Lozis**) 1 a member of an African people living mainly in western Zambia.
2 [mass noun] the Bantu language of the Lozi, with about 450,000 speakers.
▶ adjective relating to the Lozi or their language.
– ORIGIN a local name.

LP ▶ abbreviation ■ long-playing (record): *two LP records* | *a collection of LPs.* ■ low pressure.

l.p. ▶ abbreviation low pressure.

LPG ▶ abbreviation liquefied petroleum gas.

L-plate ▶ noun Brit. a sign bearing the letter L, attached to the front and rear of a motor vehicle to indicate that it is being driven by a learner.

LPN ▶ abbreviation (in North America) Licensed Practical Nurse. See **PRACTICAL NURSE**.

LPO ▶ abbreviation London Philharmonic Orchestra.

Lr ▶ symbol the chemical element lawrencium.

LS ▶ abbreviation Lesotho (international vehicle registration).

LSB ▶ abbreviation Computing least significant bit.

LSD ▶ noun [mass noun] a synthetic crystalline compound, lysergic acid diethylamide, which is a powerful hallucinogenic drug. ● Chem. formula: $C_{20}H_{25}N_3O$.
– ORIGIN 1950s: abbreviation.

l.s.d. ▶ noun [mass noun] Brit. pounds, shillings, and pence (in former British currency). ■ dated money.
– ORIGIN mid 19th cent.: from Latin *librae* ('pounds'), *solidi*, *denarii* (both denoting Roman coins).

LSE ▶ abbreviation ■ London School of Economics. ■ London Stock Exchange.

LSO ▶ abbreviation London Symphony Orchestra.

Lt ▶ abbreviation ■ Lieutenant. ■ (also **lt**) Military light.

LTA ▸ **abbreviation** Lawn Tennis Association.

Ltd ▸ **abbreviation** Brit. (after a company name) Limited.

LTP ▸ **abbreviation** Physiology long-term potentiation.

LTR ▸ **abbreviation** long-term relationship (used in personal advertisements).

Lu ▸ **symbol** the chemical element lutetium.

Lualaba /ˌluːəˈlɑːbə/ a river of central Africa, which rises near the southern border of the Democratic Republic of the Congo (Zaire) and flows northwards for about 640 km (400 miles), joining the Lomami to form the River Congo.

Luanda /luːˈandə/ the capital of Angola, a port on the Atlantic coast; pop. 1,729,500 (est. 2006).

Luang Prabang /luːˌaŋ prəˈbaŋ/ (also **Louangphrabang**) a city in NW Laos, on the Mekong River; pop. 60,800 (est. 2009). It was the royal residence and Buddhist religious centre of Laos until the end of the monarchy in 1975.

luau /ˈluːaʊ/ ▸ **noun** (pl. **same** or **luaus**) a Hawaiian party or feast, especially one accompanied by some form of entertainment.
– ORIGIN from Hawaiian *lu'au*.

Luba /ˈluːbə/ ▸ **noun** (pl. **same** or **Lubas**) **1** a member of a people living mainly in SE Democratic Republic of the Congo (Zaire).
2 [mass noun] the Bantu language of the Luba, with about 8 million speakers. Also called **CHILUBA**.
▸ **adjective** relating to the Luba or their language.
– ORIGIN a local name.

lubber ▸ **noun 1** archaic or dialect a big, clumsy person.
2 short for **LANDLUBBER**.
– DERIVATIVES **lubberlike adjective**, **lubberly adjective & adverb**.
– ORIGIN late Middle English: perhaps via Old French *lobeor* 'swindler, parasite' from *lober* 'deceive'.

lubber line (also **lubber's line**) ▸ **noun** a line marked on the compass in a ship or aircraft, showing the direction straight ahead.

Lubbock /ˈlʌbək/ a city in NW Texas; pop. 220,483 (est. 2008).

lube /luːb/ informal ▸ **noun** a lubricant. ■ [mass noun] lubrication. ■ US & Austral. an oil change for a vehicle.
▸ **verb** [with obj.] lubricate (something).
– ORIGIN 1930s: abbreviation.

Lübeck /ˈluːbɛk/, German /ˈlyːbɛk/ a port in northern Germany, on the Baltic coast in Schleswig-Holstein, north-east of Hamburg; pop. 211,200 (est. 2006). Between the 14th and 19th centuries it was an important city within the Hanseatic League.

Lubianka variant spelling of **LUBYANKA**.

Lublin /ˈlʊblɪn/ a manufacturing city in eastern Poland; pop. 352,786 (2007).

lubra /ˈluːbrə/ ▸ **noun** Austral. offensive an Aboriginal woman.
– ORIGIN mid 19th cent.: from Tasmanian *lubura*.

lubricant ▸ **noun** a substance used for lubricating an engine or component, such as oil or grease.
▸ **adjective** lubricating: *a thin lubricant film*.
– ORIGIN early 19th cent.: from Latin *lubricant-* 'making slippery', from the verb *lubricare* (see **LUBRICATE**).

lubricate /ˈluːbrɪkeɪt/ ▸ **verb** [with obj.] apply a substance such as oil or grease to (an engine or component) so as to minimize friction and allow smooth movement: *remove the nut and lubricate the thread* | (as adj. **lubricating**) *lubricating oils*. ■ make (a process) run smoothly: *the availability of credit lubricated the channels of trade*. ■ informal make (someone) convivial with alcohol: *men lubricated with alcohol speak their true feelings*.
– DERIVATIVES **lubrication noun**, **lubricator noun**.
– ORIGIN early 17th cent.: from Latin *lubricat-* 'made slippery', from the verb *lubricare*, from *lubricus* 'slippery'.

lubricious /luːˈbrɪʃəs/ ▸ **adjective 1** offensively displaying or intended to arouse sexual desire.
2 smooth and slippery with oil or a similar substance.
– DERIVATIVES **lubriciously adverb**, **lubricity noun**.
– ORIGIN late 16th cent.: from Latin *lubricus* 'slippery' + **-IOUS**.

Lubumbashi /ˌluːbʊmˈbaʃi/ a city in SE Democratic Republic of the Congo (Zaire), near the border with Zambia, capital of the region of Shaba; pop. 1,283,400 (est. 2004). Former name (until 1966) **ELISABETHVILLE**.

Lubyanka /luːˈbjaŋkə/ (also **Lubianka**) a building in Moscow used as a prison and as the headquarters of the KGB and other Russian secret police organizations since the Russian Revolution.

Lucan[1] /ˈluːk(ə)n/ (AD 39–65), Roman poet, born in Spain; Latin name *Marcus Annaeus Lucanus*. His major work is *Pharsalia*, a hexametric epic in ten books dealing with the civil war between Julius Caesar and Pompey.

Lucan[2] /ˈluːk(ə)n/ ▸ **adjective** relating to St Luke.
– ORIGIN via ecclesiastical Latin from Greek *Loukas* 'Luke' + **-AN**.

Lucas, George (Walton) (b.1944), American film director, producer, and screenwriter. He wrote and directed the science-fiction film *Star Wars* (1977), and wrote and produced Steven Spielberg's *Raiders of the Lost Ark* (1981) and the sequels of each film.

Lucas van Leyden /ˌluːkəs van ˈlʌɪd(ə)n/ (*c.*1494–1533), Dutch painter and engraver. He produced his most significant work as an engraver, including *Ecce Homo* (1510). His paintings include portraits, genre scenes, and religious subjects.

Lucca /ˈluːkə/ a city in west central Italy, in Tuscany to the west of Florence; pop. 84,186 (2008).

luce /luːs/ ▸ **noun** (pl. **same**) a pike (fish), especially when full-grown.
– ORIGIN late Middle English: via Old French *lus*, *luis* from late Latin *lucius*.

lucent /ˈluːs(ə)nt/ ▸ **adjective** literary glowing with or giving off light: *the moon was lucent in the background*.
– DERIVATIVES **lucency noun**.
– ORIGIN late Middle English: from Latin *lucent-* 'shining', from the verb *lucere* (see **LUCID**).

Lucerne /luːˈsəːn/, French /lysɛʀn/ a resort on the western shore of Lake Lucerne, in central Switzerland; pop. 58,381 (2007). German name **LUZERN**.

lucerne /luːˈsəːn/ ▸ **noun** another term for **ALFALFA**.
– ORIGIN mid 17th cent.: from French *luzerne*, from modern Provençal *luzerno* 'glow-worm' (with reference to its shiny seeds).

Lucerne, Lake a lake in central Switzerland, surrounded by the four cantons of Lucerne, Nidwalden, Uri, and Schwyz. Also called **FOUR CANTONS, LAKE OF THE**; German name **VIERWALDSTÄTTERSEE**.

lucid /ˈluːsɪd/ ▸ **adjective 1** expressed clearly; easy to understand: *a lucid account* | *write in a clear and lucid style*. ■ showing or having the ability to think clearly, especially in intervals between periods of confusion or insanity: *he has a few lucid moments every now and then*. ■ Psychology (of a dream) experienced with the dreamer feeling awake, aware of dreaming, and able to control events consciously.
2 literary bright or luminous: *birds dipped their wings in the lucid flow of air*.
– DERIVATIVES **lucidity noun**, **lucidly adverb**.
– ORIGIN late 16th cent. (in sense 2): from Latin *lucidus* (perhaps via French *lucide* or Italian *lucido*) from *lucere* 'shine', from *lux*, *luc-* 'light'.

Lucifer /ˈluːsɪfə/ ▸ **noun 1** another name for **SATAN**.
2 literary the planet Venus when it rises in the morning.
3 (**lucifer**) archaic a match struck by rubbing it on a rough surface.
– ORIGIN Old English, from Latin, 'light-bringing, morning star', from *lux*, *luc-* 'light' + *-fer* 'bearing'. Sense 1 is by association with the 'son of the morning' (Isa. 14:12), believed by Christian interpreters to be a reference to Satan.

lucifugous /luːˈsɪfjʊɡəs/ ▸ **adjective** chiefly Zoology shunning the light.
– ORIGIN mid 17th cent.: from Latin *lucifugus* (from *lux*, *luc-* 'light' + *fugere* 'to fly') + **-OUS**.

lucine /ˈluːsiːn/ ▸ **noun** a bivalve mollusc which typically has a rounded white shell with radial and concentric ridges, found in tropical and temperate seas. ● Family Lucinidae: *Lucina* and other genera.

lucite /ˈluːsʌɪt/ ▸ **noun** [mass noun] trademark, chiefly N. Amer. a solid transparent plastic made of polymethyl methacrylate (the same material as perspex or plexiglas).
– ORIGIN 1930s: from Latin *lux*, *luc-* 'light' + **-ITE**[1].

luck ▸ **noun** [mass noun] success or failure apparently brought by chance rather than through one's own actions: *it was just luck that the first kick went in* | *they're supposed to bring good luck*. ■ chance considered as a force that causes good or bad things to happen. ■ something regarded as bringing about or portending good or bad things: *I don't like Friday—it's bad luck*.
▸ **verb** [no obj.] (**luck into/upon**) informal chance to find or acquire: *he lucked into a disc-jockey job*. ■ (**luck out**) N. Amer. achieve success or advantage by good luck: *I lucked out and found a wonderful woman*.
– PHRASES **as luck would have it** used to indicate the fortuitousness of a situation: *as luck would have it, his route took him very near where they lived*. **bad** (or **tough** or **rotten**) **luck** informal used to express sympathy or commiserations. **be in** (or **out of**) **luck** be fortunate (or unfortunate). **for luck** to bring good fortune: *I wear this crystal under my costume for luck*. **good** (or **the best of**) **luck** used to express wishes for success: ***good luck with your studies!*** **good luck to ——** used to indicate one's support for someone's actions despite the difficulties or risks they pose. **one's luck is in** one is fortunate. **the luck of the draw** the outcome of chance rather than something one can control: *quality of care depends largely on the luck of the draw*. **no such luck** informal used to express disappointment that something has not happened or is unlikely to happen. **ride one's luck** let favourable events take their course without taking undue risks. **try one's luck** do something that involves risk or luck, hoping to succeed: *he thought he'd **try his luck** at farming in Canada*. **with** (**any** or **a bit of**) **luck** expressing the hope that something will happen in the way described: *with luck we should be there in time for breakfast*. **worse luck** informal used to express regret about something: *I have to go to secretarial school, worse luck*.
– ORIGIN late Middle English (as a verb): perhaps from Middle Low German or Middle Dutch *lucken*. The noun use (late 15th cent.) is from Middle Low German *lucke*, related to Dutch *geluk*, German *Glück*, of West Germanic origin and possibly related to **LOCK**[1].

luckily ▸ **adverb** [sentence adverb] it is fortunate that: *luckily they didn't recognize me* | ***luckily for me** it's worked out*.

luckless ▸ **adjective** having bad luck; unfortunate: *an osprey seized the luckless fish with its talons*.
– DERIVATIVES **lucklessly adverb**, **lucklessness noun**.

Lucknow /ˈlʌknaʊ/ a city in northern India, capital of the state of Uttar Pradesh; pop. 2,685,500 (est. 2009). In 1857, during the Indian Mutiny, its British residency was twice besieged by Indian insurgents.

lucky ▸ **adjective** (**luckier**, **luckiest**) having, bringing, or resulting from good luck: *you had a very lucky escape* | *three's my lucky number*.
– PHRASES **you** (or **he** etc.) **will be lucky** (or **should be so lucky**) used to imply in an ironic or resigned way that someone's wishes or expectations are unlikely to be fulfilled: *'A shirt would be nice.' 'You'll be lucky.'* **lucky devil** (or **lucky you**, **her**, etc.) used to express envy at someone else's good fortune.
– DERIVATIVES **luckiness noun**.

lucky bag ▸ **noun** Brit. another term for **GRAB BAG**.

lucky bean ▸ **noun** a plant of the pea family which produces poisonous shiny scarlet beans with a black eye, sometimes used as amulets. ● *Abrus* and other genera, family Leguminosae: several species.
■ the beans of any of these plants.

lucky dip ▸ **noun** Brit. a game in which small prizes are concealed in a container and chosen at random by participants. ■ a process of choosing or deciding something purely at random.

lucrative /ˈluːkrətɪv/ ▸ **adjective** producing a great deal of profit: *a lucrative career as a stand-up comedian*.
– DERIVATIVES **lucratively adverb**, **lucrativeness noun**.
– ORIGIN late Middle English: from Latin *lucrativus*, from *lucrat-* 'gained', from the verb *lucrari*, from *lucrum* (see **LUCRE**).

lucre /ˈluːkə/ ▸ **noun** [mass noun] money, especially when regarded as sordid or distasteful or gained in a dishonourable way: *officials getting their hands grubby with filthy lucre*.
– ORIGIN late Middle English: from French *lucre* or Latin *lucrum*; the phrase *filthy lucre* is with biblical allusion to Tit. 1:11.

Lucretia /luːˈkriːʃə/ (in Roman legend) a woman who was raped by a son of Tarquinius Superbus and took her own life; this led to the expulsion of the Tarquins from Rome by a rebellion under Brutus.

Lucretius /luːˈkriːʃəs/ (*c.*94–*c.*55 BC), Roman poet and philosopher; full name *Titus Lucretius Carus*. His didactic hexametric poem *On the Nature of Things* is an exposition of the materialist atomist physics of Epicurus, which aims to give peace of mind by showing that fear of the gods and of death is without foundation.

L

lucubrate /ˈluːkjʊbreɪt/ ▶ **verb** [no obj.] archaic write or study, especially by night. ■ produce learned written material.
– ORIGIN early 17th cent.: from Latin *lucubrat-* ‘(having) worked by lamplight’, from the verb *lucubrare*.

lucubration ▶ **noun** [mass noun] archaic writing or study: *after sixteen years' lucubration he produced this account.* ■ [count noun] (usu. **lucubrations**) a learned or pedantic piece of writing.
– ORIGIN late 16th cent.: from Latin *lucubratio(n-)*, from the verb *lucubrare* (see LUCUBRATE).

luculent /ˈluːkjʊl(ə)nt/ ▶ **adjective** rare **1** (of writing or speech) clearly expressed.
2 brightly shining.
– ORIGIN late Middle English (in sense 2): from Latin *luculentus*, from *lux, luc-* ‘light’.

Lucullan /luːˈkʌlən, lʊ-/ ▶ **adjective** (especially of food) extremely luxurious: *a Lucullan repast for one.*
– ORIGIN mid 19th cent.: from the name of Licinius *Lucullus*, Roman general of the 1st cent. BC, famous for giving lavish banquets, + **-AN**.

Lucy the nickname of a partial female skeleton of a fossil hominid found in Ethiopia in 1974, about 3.2 million years old and 1.2 m (4 ft) in height.
● *Australopithecus afarensis*, family Hominidae. This species is regarded by many as the ancestor of all subsequent *Australopithecus* and *Homo* species.

lud ▶ **noun** (**m'lud** or **my lud**) Brit. used to address a judge in a court of law: *so it is alleged, m'lud.*
– ORIGIN early 18th cent.: alteration of LORD.

Luda /luːˈdɑː/ an industrial conurbation and port in NE China, in the province of Liaoning at the south-eastern tip of the Liaodong Peninsula; pop. 2,407,345 (2006). It comprises the cities of Lushun and Dalian.

Luddite /ˈlʌdʌɪt/ ▶ **noun** a member of any of the bands of English workers who destroyed machinery, especially in cotton and woollen mills, which they believed was threatening their jobs (1811–16).
■ derogatory a person opposed to increased industrialization or new technology: *a small-minded Luddite resisting progress.*
– DERIVATIVES **Luddism** noun, **Ludditism** noun.
– ORIGIN perhaps named after Ned *Lud*, a participant in the destruction of machinery, + **-ITE**[1].

Ludendorff /ˈluːd(ə)nˌdɔːf/, German /ˈluːdnˌdɔrf/, Erich (1865–1937), German general, Chief of Staff to General von Hindenburg during the First World War and later a Nazi Party MP (1924–8).

luderick /ˈluːd(ə)rɪk, ˈlʌdrɪk/ ▶ **noun** (pl. **same**) an edible herbivorous fish of Australasian coastal waters and estuaries. Also called BLACKFISH. ● *Girella tricuspidata*, family Kyphosidae.
– ORIGIN late 19th cent.: from Ganay (an Aboriginal language) *ludarag*.

Ludhiana /ˌlʊdɪˈɑːnə/ a city in NW India, in Punjab south-east of Amritsar; pop. 1,701,200 (est. 2009).

ludic /ˈluːdɪk/ ▶ **adjective** formal showing spontaneous and undirected playfulness.
– ORIGIN 1940s: from French *ludique*, from Latin *ludere* ‘to play’, from *ludus* ‘sport’.

ludicrous ▶ **adjective** so foolish, unreasonable, or out of place as to be amusing: *it's ludicrous that I have been fined | every night he wore a ludicrous outfit.*
– DERIVATIVES **ludicrously** adverb [as submodifier] *a ludicrously inadequate army*, **ludicrousness** noun.
– ORIGIN early 17th cent. (in the sense ‘sportive, intended as a jest’): from Latin *ludicrus* (probably from *ludicrum* ‘stage play’) + **-OUS**.

ludo ▶ **noun** [mass noun] Brit. a simple game in which players move counters round a board according to throws of a dice.
– ORIGIN late 19th cent.: from Latin, ‘I play’.

Ludwig /ˈlʊdvɪg/, German /ˈluːtvɪç/ the name of three kings of Bavaria: ■ **Ludwig I** (1786–1868), reigned 1825–48. He became unpopular due to his reactionary policies, lavish expenditure, and his domination by the dancer Lola Montez, and he was forced to abdicate in favour of his son. ■ **Ludwig II** (1845–86), reigned 1864–86. A patron of the arts, he became a recluse and built a series of elaborate castles. He was declared insane and deposed in 1886. ■ **Ludwig III** (1845–1921), reigned 1913–8.

Ludwigshafen /ˈlʊdvɪgzˌhɑːf(ə)n/, German /ˈluːtvɪçsˌhaːfn/ an industrial river port in west central Germany, south-west of Mannheim, on the River Rhine in the state of Rhineland-Palatinate; pop. 163,600 (est. 2006).

lues /ˈl(j)uːiːz/ (also **lues venerea** /vɪˈnɪərɪə/) ▶ **noun** [mass noun] dated a serious infectious disease, particularly syphilis.
– DERIVATIVES **luetic** /l(j)uːˈɛtɪk/ adjective.
– ORIGIN mid 17th cent.: from Latin, literally ‘plague’.

luff Sailing ▶ **noun** the edge of a fore-and-aft sail next to the mast or stay.
▶ **verb** [with obj.] steer (a yacht) nearer the wind: *I came aft and luffed her for the open sea.* ■ obstruct (an opponent in yacht racing) by sailing closer to the wind.
– ORIGIN Middle English: from Old French *lof*, probably from Low German.

Luftwaffe /ˈlʊftwafə/, German /ˈlʊftvafə/ the German air force.
– ORIGIN German, from *Luft* ‘air’ + *Waffe* ‘weapon’.

lug[1] ▶ **verb** (**lugs, lugging, lugged**) [with obj. and adverbial of direction] carry or drag (a heavy or bulky object) with great effort: *she began to lug her suitcase down the stairs.* ■ be encumbered with: *he had lugged his poor wife round for so long.*
▶ **noun** a box or crate used for transporting fruit.
– DERIVATIVES **luggable** adjective.
– ORIGIN late Middle English: probably of Scandinavian origin: compare with Swedish *lugga* ‘pull a person's hair’ (from *lugg* ‘forelock’).

lug[2] ▶ **noun 1** (usu. **lugs**) Scottish & N. English or informal a person's ear.
2 a projection on an object by which it may be carried or fixed in place.
3 informal, chiefly N. Amer. a loutish man.
– ORIGIN late 15th cent. (denoting the ear flap of a hat): probably of Scandinavian origin: compare with Swedish *lugg* ‘forelock, nap of cloth’. Sense 3 is perhaps from the 19th-cent. term denoting the lowest grade of tobacco.

lug[3] ▶ **noun** short for LUGWORM.

Luganda /luːˈgandə/ ▶ **noun** [mass noun] the Bantu language of the Baganda people, widely used in Uganda and having over 2 million speakers.

Lugano /luːˈgɑːnəʊ/ a town in southern Switzerland, on the northern shore of Lake Lugano; pop. 50,603 (2007).

Lugansk /luˈgansk/ Russian name for LUHANSK.

Lugdunum /lʊgˈduːnəm/ Roman name for LYONS.

luge /luːʒ/ ▶ **noun** a light toboggan for one or two people, ridden in a sitting or supine position. ■ [mass noun] a sport in which competitors make a timed descent of a course riding luges.
▶ **verb** [no obj.] ride on a luge.
– ORIGIN late 19th cent. (as a verb): from Swiss French.

Luger /ˈluːgə/ ▶ **noun** (trademark in the US) a type of German automatic pistol.
– ORIGIN early 20th cent.: named after George *Luger* (1849–1923), German firearms expert.

luggage ▶ **noun** [mass noun] suitcases or other bags in which to pack personal belongings for travelling.
■ past experiences or long-held ideas and opinions perceived as burdensome encumbrances: *carrying emotional luggage from the past.*
– ORIGIN late 16th cent. (originally denoting inconveniently heavy baggage): from LUG[1] + **-AGE**.

lugger ▶ **noun** a small sailing ship with two or three masts and a lugsail on each.
– ORIGIN mid 18th cent.: from LUGSAIL + **-ER**[1].

lughole ▶ **noun** Brit. informal a person's ear.

Lugosi /ləˈgəʊsi/, Bela (1884–1956), Hungarian-born American actor; born *Béla Ferenc Blasko*. He is famous for his roles in horror films such as *Dracula* (1931) and *The Wolf Man* (1940).

lugsail /ˈlʌgseɪl, -s(ə)l/ ▶ **noun** an asymmetrical four-sided sail which is bent on and hoisted from a steeply inclined yard.
– ORIGIN late 17th cent.: probably from LUG[2] + the noun SAIL.

lugubrious /lʊˈguːbrɪəs/ ▶ **adjective** looking or sounding sad and dismal: *his face looked even more lugubrious than usual.*
– DERIVATIVES **lugubriously** adverb, **lugubriousness** noun.
– ORIGIN early 17th cent.: from Latin *lugubris* (from *lugere* ‘mourn’) + **-OUS**.

lugworm ▶ **noun** a bristle worm that lives in muddy sand, leaving characteristic worm casts on lower shores. It is widely used as bait by fishermen.
● *Arenicola marina*, class Polychaeta.
– ORIGIN early 19th cent.: from earlier *lug* ‘lugworm’ (of unknown origin) + WORM.

Luhansk /luːˈhansk/ an industrial city in eastern Ukraine, in the Donets Basin; pop. 438,000 (est. 2009). Former name VOROSHILOVGRAD. Russian name LUGANSK.

Luik /lœyk/ Flemish name for LIÈGE.

Lukács /ˈluːkatʃ/, György (1885–1971), Hungarian philosopher, literary critic, and politician. His best-known work is *History and Class Consciousness* (1923), in which he stresses the central role of alienation in Marxist thought.

Luke, St an evangelist, closely associated with St Paul and traditionally the author of the third Gospel and the Acts of the Apostles. Feast day, 18 October. ■ the third Gospel (see GOSPEL (sense 2)).

lukewarm ▶ **adjective** (of liquid or food that should be hot) only moderately warm; tepid: *they drank bitter lukewarm coffee.* ■ (of a person, attitude, or action) unenthusiastic: *Britain is lukewarm about the proposal.*
– DERIVATIVES **lukewarmly** adverb, **lukewarmness** noun.
– ORIGIN late Middle English: from dialect *luke* (probably from dialect *lew* ‘lukewarm’ and related to LEE) + WARM.

lull ▶ **verb** [with obj.] calm or send to sleep, typically with soothing sounds or movements: *the rhythm of the boat lulled her to sleep.* ■ make (someone) feel deceptively secure or confident: *the rarity of earthquakes there has lulled people into a false sense of security.*
■ [no obj.] (of noise or a storm) abate or fall quiet: *conversation lulled for an hour.*
▶ **noun** a temporary interval of quiet or lack of activity: *for two days there had been* ***a lull in the fighting.***
– PHRASES **the lull before the storm** see STORM.
– ORIGIN Middle English: imitative of sounds used to quieten a child; compare with Latin *lallare* ‘sing to sleep’, Swedish *lulla* ‘hum a lullaby’, and Dutch *lullen* ‘talk nonsense’. The noun (first recorded in the sense ‘soothing drink’) dates from the mid 17th cent.

lullaby ▶ **noun** (pl. **lullabies**) a quiet, gentle song sung to send a child to sleep.
▶ **verb** (**lullabies, lullabying, lullabied**) [with obj.] rare sing to (someone) to get them to go to sleep: *she lullabied us, she fed us.*
– ORIGIN mid 16th cent.: from LULL + *bye-bye*, a sound used as a refrain in lullabies; compare with BYE-BYES.

Lully /ˈlʊli/, French /lyli/, Jean-Baptiste (1632–87), French composer, born in Italy; Italian name *Giovanni Battista Lulli*. His operas, which include *Alceste* (1674) and *Armide* (1686), mark the beginning of the French operatic tradition.

lulu ▶ **noun** informal an outstanding example of a particular type of person or thing: *as far as nightmares went, this one was a lulu.*
– ORIGIN late 19th cent.: perhaps from *Lulu*, pet form of the given name *Louise*.

lum /lʌm/ ▶ **noun** Scottish & N. English a chimney.
– ORIGIN early 16th cent.: perhaps from Old French *lum* ‘light’, from Latin *lumen*.

luma /ˈluːma/ ▶ **noun** (pl. **same** or **lumas**) a monetary unit of Armenia, equal to one hundredth of a dram.
– ORIGIN Armenian.

lumbago /lʌmˈbeɪgəʊ/ ▶ **noun** [mass noun] pain in the muscles and joints of the lower back.
– ORIGIN late 17th cent.: from Latin, from *lumbus* ‘loin’.

lumbar /ˈlʌmbə/ ▶ **adjective** relating to the lower part of the back: *backache in the lumbar region.*
– ORIGIN mid 17th cent.: from medieval Latin *lumbaris*, from Latin *lumbus* ‘loin’.

lumbar puncture ▶ **noun** Medicine, Brit. the procedure of taking fluid from the spine in the lower back through a hollow needle, usually done for diagnostic purposes.

lumber[1] ▶ **verb** [no obj., with adverbial of direction] move in a slow, heavy, awkward way: *a truck lumbered past.*
– ORIGIN late Middle English *lomere*, perhaps symbolic of clumsy movement.

lumber[2] ▶ **noun** [mass noun] **1** Brit. articles of furniture or other household items that are no longer useful and inconveniently take up storage space.
2 chiefly N. Amer. timber sawn into rough planks or otherwise partly prepared.
▶ **verb 1** [with obj.] (usu. **be lumbered with**) Brit. informal burden (someone) with something unwanted: *the banks do not want to be lumbered with a building that they cannot sell.*
2 [no obj.] (usu. as noun **lumbering**) chiefly N. Amer. cut and prepare forest timber for transport and sale.
– ORIGIN mid 16th cent.: perhaps from LUMBER[1]; later associated with obsolete *lumber* ‘pawnbroker's shop’.

lumber³ Scottish informal ▸ **verb** [with obj.] casually strike up a relationship with (a prospective sexual partner).
▸ **noun** a person regarded as a prospective sexual partner.
– ORIGIN 1960s: of unknown origin.

lumberer ▸ **noun** chiefly N. Amer. a person engaged in the lumber trade, especially a lumberjack.

lumbering ▸ **adjective** moving in a slow, heavy, awkward way: *Bob was the big, lumbering, gentle sort* | figurative *a lumbering bureaucracy*.

lumberjack (also **lumberman**) ▸ **noun** (especially in North America) a person who fells trees, cuts them into logs, or transports them to a sawmill.

lumberjacket ▸ **noun** a warm, thick jacket, typically in a bright colour with a check pattern, of the kind worn by lumberjacks.

lumberjack shirt ▸ **noun** a shirt of brushed cotton or flannel, typically with a check pattern.

lumber room ▸ **noun** Brit. a room where disused or bulky things are kept.

lumbersome ▸ **adjective** bulky and awkward to handle or use.

lumen¹ /ˈluːmɛn/ (abbrev.: **lm**) ▸ **noun** Physics the SI unit of luminous flux, equal to the amount of light emitted per second in a unit solid angle of one steradian from a uniform source of one candela.
– ORIGIN late 19th cent.: from Latin, literally 'light'.

lumen² /ˈluːmən/ ▸ **noun** (pl. **lumina** /-mɪnə/) Anatomy the central cavity of a tubular or other hollow structure in an organism or cell.
– DERIVATIVES **luminal** /ˈluːmɪn(ə)l/ **adjective**.
– ORIGIN late 19th cent.: from Latin, literally 'opening'.

lum hat ▸ **noun** Scottish informal a top hat.

Lumière /ˈluːmɪɛː/, French /lymjɛʀ/, Auguste Marie Louis Nicholas (1862–1954) and Louis Jean (1864–1948), French inventors and pioneers of cinema. In 1895 the brothers patented their 'Cinématographe', a cine camera and projector in one. They also invented the improved 'autochrome' process of colour photography.

luminaire /ˈluːmɪnɛː, ˌluːmɪˈnɛː/ ▸ **noun** a complete electric light unit (used especially in technical contexts).
– ORIGIN early 20th cent.: from French.

Luminal /ˈluːmɪn(ə)l/ ▸ **noun** trademark for PHENOBARBITONE.
– ORIGIN early 20th cent.: probably from Latin *lumen* 'light' (rendering *phen-*, from Greek *phaino-* 'shining'), + -AL.

luminance /ˈluːmɪn(ə)ns/ ▸ **noun** [mass noun] Physics the intensity of light emitted from a surface per unit area in a given direction. ■ the component of a television signal which carries information on the brightness of the image.
– ORIGIN late 19th cent. (as a general term meaning 'light, brightness'): from Latin *luminant-* 'illuminating' (from the verb *luminare*) + -ANCE.

luminary /ˈluːmɪn(ə)ri/ ▸ **noun** (pl. **luminaries**) **1** a person who inspires or influences others, especially one prominent in a particular sphere: *one of the luminaries of child psychiatry*.
2 archaic a natural light-giving body, especially the sun or moon. ■ an artificial light.
– ORIGIN late Middle English: from Old French *luminarie* or late Latin *luminarium*, from Latin *lumen, lumin-* 'light'.

luminesce /ˌluːmɪˈnɛs/ ▸ **verb** [no obj.] emit light by luminescence.
– ORIGIN late 19th cent.: back-formation from LUMINESCENCE.

luminescence /ˌluːmɪˈnɛs(ə)ns/ ▸ **noun** [mass noun] the emission of light by a substance that has not been heated, as in fluorescence and phosphorescence.
– DERIVATIVES **luminescent** **adjective**.
– ORIGIN late 19th cent.: from Latin *lumen, lumin-* 'light' + *-escence* (denoting a state).

luminiferous /ˌluːmɪˈnɪf(ə)rəs/ ▸ **adjective** chiefly archaic producing or transmitting light.

luminosity ▸ **noun** (pl. **luminosities**) [mass noun] luminous quality: *acrylic colours retain freshness and luminosity*. ■ Astronomy the intrinsic brightness of a celestial object (as distinct from its apparent brightness diminished by distance). ■ Physics the rate of emission of radiation, visible or otherwise.

luminous /ˈluːmɪnəs/ ▸ **adjective** giving off light; bright or shining: *the luminous dial on his watch* | *a luminous glow* | figurative *her eyes were **luminous with** joy*. ■ very bright in colour; lurid: *he wore luminous green socks*. ■ Physics relating to light as it is perceived by the eye, rather than in terms of its actual energy.
– DERIVATIVES **luminously** **adverb**, **luminousness** **noun**.
– ORIGIN late Middle English: from Old French *lumineux* or Latin *luminosus*, from *lumen, lumin-* 'light'.

lumme /ˈlʌmi/ ▸ **exclamation** Brit. informal, dated an expression of surprise or interest: *'Lumme!' said Quigley. 'She isn't half a size!'*.
– ORIGIN late 19th cent.: from *(Lord) love me*.

lummox /ˈlʌməks/ ▸ **noun** informal, chiefly N. Amer. a clumsy, stupid person: *watch it, you great lummox!*
– ORIGIN early 19th cent.: of unknown origin.

lump¹ ▸ **noun** **1** a compact mass of a substance, especially one without a definite or regular shape: *there was a **lump of** ice floating in the milk*. ■ a swelling under the skin, especially one caused by injury or disease: *he was unhurt apart from a huge lump on his head*. ■ a small cube of sugar. ■ informal a heavy, ungainly, or slow-witted person: *I won't stand a chance against a big lump like you*.
2 (**the lump**) Brit. informal the state of being self-employed and paid without deduction of tax, especially in the building industry: *'Working?' 'Only on the lump, here and there'* | [as modifier] *lump labour*.
▸ **verb** **1** [with obj. and adverbial] put in an indiscriminate mass or group; treat as alike without regard for particulars: *Hong Kong and Bangkok tend to **be lumped together** in holiday brochures* | *Nigel didn't like being **lumped in with** prisoners*. ■ [no obj.] (in taxonomy) classify plants or animals in relatively inclusive groups, disregarding minor variations.
2 [with obj. and adverbial of direction] Brit. carry (a heavy load) somewhere with difficulty: *the coalman had to lump one-hundredweight sacks right through the house*.
– PHRASES **a lump in the throat** a feeling of tightness or dryness in the throat caused by strong emotion, especially sadness: *there was a lump in her throat as she gazed down at her uncle's gaunt features*. **take** (or **get**) **one's lumps** informal, chiefly N. Amer. suffer punishment; be attacked or defeated.
– ORIGIN Middle English: perhaps from a Germanic base meaning 'shapeless piece'; compare with Danish *lump* 'lump', Norwegian and Swedish dialect *lump* 'block, log', and Dutch *lomp* 'rag'.

lump² ▸ **verb** (**lump it**) informal accept or tolerate a disagreeable situation whether one likes it or not: *you can **like it or lump it** but I've got to work*.
– ORIGIN late 16th cent. (in the sense 'look sulky'): symbolic of displeasure; compare with words such as *dump* and *grump*. The current sense dates from the early 19th cent.

lumpectomy ▸ **noun** (pl. **lumpectomies**) a surgical operation in which a lump is removed from the breast, typically when cancer is present but has not spread.

lumpen ▸ **adjective** **1** (in Marxist contexts) uninterested in revolutionary advancement. ■ boorish and stupid.
2 Brit. lumpy and misshapen; ugly and ponderous: *her own body was lumpen and awkward*.
▸ **plural noun** (**the lumpen**) the lumpenproletariat.
– ORIGIN 1940s: back-formation from LUMPENPROLETARIAT; the sense 'misshapen, ponderous' is by association with LUMPISH.

lumpenproletariat /ˌlʌmpənprəʊlɪˈtɛːrɪət/ ▸ **noun** [treated as sing. or pl.] (especially in Marxist terminology) the unorganized and unpolitical lower orders of society who are not interested in revolutionary advancement.
– ORIGIN 1920s: from German (a term originally used by Karl Marx), from *Lumpen* 'rag, rogue' + PROLETARIAT.

lumper ▸ **noun** **1** a docker, especially one who unloads cargoes from fishing boats.
2 a person (especially a taxonomist) who attaches more importance to similarities than to differences in classification. Contrasted with SPLITTER.

lumpfish ▸ **noun** (pl. **same** or **lumpfishes**) a North Atlantic lumpsucker, the roe of which is sometimes used as a substitute for caviar. ● *Cyclopterus lumpus*, family Cyclopteridae.
– ORIGIN early 17th cent.: from Middle Low German *lumpen*, Middle Dutch *lompe* + FISH¹.

lumpish ▸ **adjective** roughly or clumsily formed or shaped: *those large and lumpish hands could produce exquisitely fine work*. ■ (of a person) stupid and lethargic.
– DERIVATIVES **lumpishly** **adverb**, **lumpishness** **noun**.

lumpsucker ▸ **noun** a globular fish of cooler northern waters, typically having a ventral sucker and spiny fins; a lumpfish. ● Family Cyclopteridae: several genera and species.

lump sugar ▸ **noun** [mass noun] sugar in the form of small cubes.

lump sum ▸ **noun** a single payment made at a particular time, as opposed to a number of smaller payments or instalments.

lumpy ▸ **adjective** (**lumpier**, **lumpiest**) full of or covered with lumps: *he lay on the lumpy mattress*. ■ Nautical (of water) formed by the wind into small waves: *there's a lumpy sea running*.
– DERIVATIVES **lumpily** **adverb**, **lumpiness** **noun**.

lumpy jaw ▸ **noun** [mass noun] infection of the jaw with actinomycete bacteria, common in cattle.

Luna /ˈluːnə/ a series of Soviet moon probes launched in 1959–76. They made the first hard and soft landings on the moon (1959 and 1966).

lunacy ▸ **noun** (pl. **lunacies**) [mass noun] the state of being a lunatic; insanity (not in technical use): *it has been suggested that originality demands a degree of lunacy*. ■ extreme folly or eccentricity: *such an economic policy would be sheer lunacy*.
– ORIGIN mid 16th cent. (originally referring to insanity of an intermittent kind attributed to changes of the moon): from LUNATIC + -ACY.

luna moth ▸ **noun** a large North American moon moth which has pale green wings with long tails and transparent eyespots bearing crescent-shaped markings. ● *Actias luna*, family Saturniidae.
– ORIGIN late 19th cent.: *luna* from Latin *luna* 'moon' (from its markings).

lunar /ˈluːnə/ ▸ **adjective** of, determined by, or resembling the moon: *a lunar eclipse* | *a lunar landscape*.
– ORIGIN late Middle English: from Latin *lunaris*, from *luna* 'moon'.

lunar caustic ▸ **noun** [mass noun] Chemistry, archaic silver nitrate, especially fused in the form of a stick.
– ORIGIN early 19th cent.: *lunar* in the sense 'containing silver'.

L

lunar cycle ▸ **noun** another term for METONIC CYCLE.

lunar day ▸ **noun** the interval of time between two successive crossings of the meridian by the moon (roughly 24 hours and 50 minutes).

lunar distance ▸ **noun** the angular distance of the moon from the sun, a planet, or a star, used in finding longitude at sea.

lunar eclipse ▸ **noun** an eclipse in which the moon appears darkened as it passes into the earth's shadow.

Lunarian /luːˈnɛːrɪən/ ▸ **noun** (in science fiction) an imagined inhabitant of the moon.

lunar module ▸ **noun** a small craft used for travelling between the moon's surface and an orbiting spacecraft (formerly known as **lunar excursion module** or **LEM**).

lunar month ▸ **noun** a month measured between successive new moons (roughly $29^1/_2$ days). ■ (in general use) a period of four weeks.

lunar node ▸ **noun** Astronomy each of the two points at which the moon's orbit cuts the ecliptic.

lunar observation ▸ **noun** a measurement of the position of the moon in order to calculate longitude from lunar distance.

lunar roving vehicle (also **lunar rover**) ▸ **noun** a vehicle designed for use by astronauts on the moon's surface, used on the last three missions of the *Apollo* project. Also called MOON BUGGY.

lunar year ▸ **noun** a period of twelve lunar months (approximately 354 days).

lunate /ˈluːneɪt/ ▸ **adjective** crescent-shaped.
▸ **noun** **1** Archaeology a crescent-shaped prehistoric stone implement.
2 (also **lunate bone**) Anatomy a crescent-shaped carpal bone situated in the centre of the wrist and articulating with the radius.
– ORIGIN late 18th cent.: from Latin *lunatus*, from *luna* 'moon'.

lunatic ▸ **noun** a person who is mentally ill (not in technical use). ■ an extremely foolish or eccentric person: *this lunatic just accelerated out from the side of the road*.
▸ **adjective** mentally ill (not in technical use). ■ extremely foolish or eccentric: *he would be asked to acquiesce in some lunatic scheme*.
– ORIGIN Middle English: from Old French *lunatique*, from late Latin *lunaticus*, from Latin *luna* 'moon'

(from the belief that changes of the moon caused intermittent insanity).

lunatic asylum ▸ noun dated a psychiatric hospital.

lunatic fringe ▸ noun an extreme or eccentric minority within society or a group.

lunation /luːˈneɪʃ(ə)n/ ▸ noun Astronomy another term for LUNAR MONTH.
– ORIGIN late Middle English: from medieval Latin *lunatio(n-)*, from Latin *luna* 'moon'.

lunch ▸ noun a meal eaten in the middle of the day, typically one that is lighter or less formal than an evening meal: *a light lunch* | [mass noun] *do join us for lunch.*
▸ verb [no obj., with adverbial] eat lunch: *he told his wife he was lunching with a client.* ■ [with obj.] take (someone) out for lunch: *public relations people lunch their clients there.*
– PHRASES **do lunch** informal, chiefly N. Amer. meet for lunch. **out to lunch** informal temporarily not in command of one's mental faculties. **there's no such thing as a free lunch** proverb it isn't possible to get something for nothing.
– DERIVATIVES **luncher** noun.
– ORIGIN early 19th cent.: abbreviation of LUNCHEON.

lunch box ▸ noun a container in which to carry a packed meal. ■ a portable computer slightly larger than a laptop. ■ Brit. humorous a man's genitals.

luncheon ▸ noun a formal lunch, or a formal word for lunch.
– ORIGIN late 16th cent. (in the sense 'thick piece, hunk'): possibly an extension of obsolete *lunch* 'thick piece, hunk', from Spanish *lonja* 'slice'.

luncheonette ▸ noun N. Amer. a small, informal restaurant serving light lunches.

luncheon meat ▸ noun [mass noun] finely minced cooked pork mixed with cereal, sold in a tin and typically eaten cold in slices.

luncheon voucher ▸ noun Brit. a document issued to employees by their employer as part of their pay and exchangeable for food at restaurants and shops.

L

lunch hour ▸ noun a period in the middle of the day, when people stop work to have lunch.

lunch pail N. Amer. ▸ noun a lunch box.
▸ adjective (**lunch-pail**) informal working-class; blue-collar: *lunch-pail labourers.*

lunchroom ▸ noun N. Amer. a room or establishment in which lunch is served or in which it may be eaten; a school or office canteen.

lunchtime ▸ noun the time in the middle of the day when lunch is eaten.

Lund /lʊnd/ a city in SW Sweden, just north-east of Malmö; pop. 107,351 (2008). Its university was founded in 1666.

Lunda /ˈlʊndə, ˈluːndə/ ▸ noun (pl. **same** or **Balunda** /baˈlʊndə, -luːndə/ or **Lundas**) **1** a member of any of several peoples living mainly in northern Zambia and adjoining parts of the Democratic Republic of the Congo (Zaire) and Angola.
2 [mass noun] any of several Bantu languages of the Lunda, especially one spoken by about 200,000 people mainly in NW Zambia.
▸ adjective relating to or denoting the Lunda or their language.
– ORIGIN a local name.

Lundy /ˈlʌndi/ **1** a granite island in the Bristol Channel, off the coast of north Devon.
2 a shipping forecast area covering the Bristol Channel and the eastern Celtic Sea.

lune /luːn/ ▸ noun a crescent-shaped figure formed on a sphere or plane by two arcs intersecting at two points.
– ORIGIN early 18th cent.: from French, from Latin *luna* 'moon'.

lunette /luːˈnɛt/ ▸ noun **1** an arched aperture or window, especially one in a domed ceiling. ■ a crescent-shaped or semicircular alcove containing something such as a painting or statue.
2 a fortification with two faces forming a projecting angle, and two flanks.
3 Christian Church a holder for the consecrated host in a monstrance.
4 a broad, shallow, typically crescent-shaped mound of wind-blown material along the leeward side of a lake or dry lake basin.
5 a ring fixed to a vehicle, by which it can be towed.
– ORIGIN late 16th cent. (denoting a semicircular horseshoe): from French, diminutive of *lune* 'moon', from Latin *luna*.

lung ▸ noun each of the pair of organs situated within the ribcage, consisting of elastic sacs with branching passages into which air is drawn, so that oxygen can pass into the blood and carbon dioxide be removed. Lungs are characteristic of vertebrates other than fish, though similar structures are present in some other animal groups.
– DERIVATIVES **lunged** adjective [in combination] *strong-lunged*, **lungful** noun (pl. **lungfuls**), **lungless** adjective.
– ORIGIN Old English *lungen*, of Germanic origin; related to Dutch *long* and German *Lunge*, from an Indo-European root shared by LIGHT²; compare with LIGHTS.

lunge¹ ▸ noun a sudden forward thrust of the body, typically with an arm outstretched to attack someone or seize something: *Lucy made a lunge for Gabriel's wrist* | *a crude lunge at United's goalscorer.* ■ the basic attacking move in fencing, in which the leading foot is thrust forward close to the floor with the knee bent while the back leg remains straightened. ■ an exercise or gymnastic movement resembling the lunge of a fencer.
▸ verb (**lunges, lungeing** or **lunging, lunged**) [no obj., with adverbial of direction] make a lunge: *McCulloch raised his cudgel and lunged at him* | *John lunged forward and grabbed him by the throat.* ■ [with obj. and adverbial of direction] make a sudden forward thrust with (a part of the body or a weapon): *Billy lunged his spear at the fish.*
– ORIGIN mid 18th cent.: from earlier *allonge*, from French *allonger* 'lengthen'.

lunge² (also **longe**) ▸ noun a long rein on which a horse is held and made to move in a circle round its trainer.
▸ verb (**lunges, lungeing, lunged**) [with obj.] exercise (a horse) on a lunge.
– ORIGIN early 18th cent.: from French *longe*, from *allonge* 'lengthening out'.

lunge³ ▸ noun N. Amer. short for MUSKELLUNGE.

lungfish ▸ noun (pl. **same** or **lungfishes**) an elongated freshwater fish with one or two sacs which function as lungs, enabling it to breathe air. It lives in poorly oxygenated water and can aestivate in mud for long periods to survive drought. ● Subclass Dipnoi: families Ceratodontidae (one Australian species), Lepidosirenidae (one South American species), and Protopteridae (four African species).

lungi /ˈlʊŋgiː/ ▸ noun (pl. **lungis**) a sarong-like garment wrapped around the waist and extending to the ankles, worn by both sexes in India and in Burma (Myanmar), where it is the national dress.
– ORIGIN Urdu.

lungless salamander ▸ noun a slender-bodied chiefly aquatic salamander native to America and southern Europe. Having neither lungs nor gills, it breathes through the skin and lining of the mouth. ● Family Plethodontidae: numerous genera, including *Plethodon* (the American woodland salamanders) and *Hydromantes* (two European species).

lungworm ▸ noun a parasitic nematode worm found in the lungs of mammals, especially farm and domestic animals. ● *Dictyocaulus* and other genera, class Phasmida.

lungwort ▸ noun **1** a bristly herbaceous European plant of the borage family, typically having white-spotted leaves and pink flowers which turn blue as they age. [so named because the leaves were said to have the appearance of a diseased lung.] ● Genus *Pulmonaria*, family Boraginaceae: several species, in particular *P. officinalis*.
2 (also **tree lungwort**) a large lichen which grows on trees, forming lobed fronds which are green or brown above and orange-brown below. [so named because of its former use to treat lung disease, because of its apparent resemblance to lung tissue.] ● *Lobaria pulmonaria*, order Peltigerales.

lunisolar /ˌluːnɪˈsəʊlə/ ▸ adjective of or concerning the combined motions or effects of the sun and moon. ■ of or employing a calendar year divided according to the phases of the moon, but adjusted in average length to fit the length of the solar cycle. ■ of or denoting a 532-year period over which both the lunar months and the days of the week return to the same point in relation to the solar year.
– ORIGIN late 17th cent.: from Latin *luna* 'moon' + SOLAR¹.

lunitidal /ˌluːnɪˈtʌɪd(ə)l/ ▸ adjective denoting the interval between the time at which the moon crosses a meridian and the time of high tide at that meridian.

lunk ▸ noun short for LUNKHEAD.

lunker ▸ noun N. Amer. informal an exceptionally large specimen of something, in particular (among anglers) a fish.
– ORIGIN early 20th cent.: of unknown origin.

lunkhead ▸ noun informal a slow-witted person.
– ORIGIN mid 19th cent.: probably from an alteration of LUMP¹ + HEAD.

lunula /ˈluːnjʊlə/ ▸ noun (pl. **lunulae** /-liː/) **1** the white area at the base of a fingernail.
2 a crescent-shaped Bronze Age ornament worn as a necklace.
– DERIVATIVES **lunulate** adjective.
– ORIGIN late 16th cent. (denoting a crescent-shaped geometrical figure): from Latin, diminutive of *luna* 'moon'.

lunule /ˈluːnjuːl/ ▸ noun another term for LUNULA.

Luo /ˈluːəʊ/ ▸ noun (pl. **same** or **Luos**) **1** a member of an East African people of Kenya and the upper Nile valley.
2 [mass noun] the Nilotic language of the Luo, with more than 3 million speakers.
▸ adjective relating to the Luo or their language.
– ORIGIN the name in Luo.

Luoyang /laʊˈjaŋ/ an industrial city in east central China, in Henan province on the Luo River; pop. 1,065,100 (est. 2006). Between the 4th and 6th centuries AD the construction of cave temples to the south of the city made it an important Buddhist centre. Former name HONAN.

lupara /lʊˈpɑːrə/ ▸ noun a sawn-off shotgun, especially as used by the Mafia.
– ORIGIN Italian, slang term from *lupa* 'she-wolf'.

Lupercalia /ˌluːpəˈkeɪlɪə/ (also in sing. **Lupercal** /ˈluːpəkal/) ▸ plural noun [usu. treated as sing.] an ancient Roman festival of purification and fertility, held annually on 15 February.
– DERIVATIVES **Lupercalian** adjective.
– ORIGIN Latin, neuter plural of *lupercalis* 'relating to *Lupercus*', Roman equivalent of the Greek god Pan.

lupin /ˈluːpɪn/ (N. Amer. also **lupine** /-pɪn/) ▸ noun a plant of the pea family with deeply divided leaves and tall colourful tapering spikes of flowers. ● Genus *Lupinus*, family Leguminosae: several species.
– ORIGIN late Middle English: from Latin *lupinus*.

lupine /ˈluːpʌɪn/ ▸ adjective of, like, or relating to a wolf or wolves.
– ORIGIN mid 17th cent.: from Latin *lupinus*, from *lupus* 'wolf'.

lupulin /ˈluːpjʊlɪn/ ▸ noun [mass noun] a bitter yellowish powder found on glandular hairs beneath the scales of the flowers of the female hop plant.
– ORIGIN early 19th cent.: from the modern Latin use as an epithet of Latin *lupulus* (as in *Humulus lupulus*), a plant mentioned by Pliny and perhaps denoting 'wild hops', + -IN¹.

Lupus /ˈluːpəs/ Astronomy a southern constellation (the Wolf), lying partly in the Milky Way between Scorpius and Centaurus.
– ORIGIN Latin.

lupus /ˈluːpəs/ ▸ noun [mass noun] any of various diseases or conditions marked by inflammation of the skin, especially lupus vulgaris or lupus erythematosus.
– DERIVATIVES **lupoid** adjective.
– ORIGIN late 16th cent.: from Latin, literally 'wolf'.

lupus erythematosus /ˌɛrɪθiːməˈtəʊsəs/ ▸ noun [mass noun] an autoimmune inflammatory disease causing scaly red patches on the skin, especially on the face, and sometimes affecting connective tissue in the internal organs.
– ORIGIN mid 19th cent.: from LUPUS + modern Latin *erythematosus*, from Greek *eruthēma* 'reddening'.

lupus vulgaris /vʌlˈgɑːrɪs, -ˈgɛːrɪs/ ▸ noun [mass noun] chronic direct infection of the skin with tuberculosis, causing dark red patches.
– ORIGIN mid 19th cent.: from LUPUS + Latin *vulgaris* 'common'.

lur /lʊə/ (also **lure**) ▸ noun a Scandinavian S-shaped bronze trumpet dating from the Bronze Age.
– ORIGIN Danish and Norwegian, originally denoting a wooden shepherd's horn.

lurch¹ ▸ verb [no obj., with adverbial] make an abrupt, unsteady, uncontrolled movement or series of movements; stagger: *the car lurched forward* | *Stuart lurched to his feet* | figurative *he was lurching from one crisis to the next.*
▸ noun [usu. in sing.] an abrupt uncontrolled movement, especially an unsteady tilt or roll: *the boat gave a violent lurch and he missed his footing.*

– ORIGIN late 17th cent. (as a noun denoting the sudden leaning of a ship to one side): of unknown origin.

lurch[2] ▸ **noun** (in phrase **leave someone in the lurch**) leave an associate or friend abruptly and without assistance or support when they are in a difficult situation.
– ORIGIN mid 16th cent. (denoting a state of discomfiture): from French *lourche*, the name of a game resembling backgammon, used in the phrase *demeurer lourche* 'be discomfited'.

lurcher ▸ **noun 1** Brit. a cross-bred dog, typically a retriever, collie, or sheepdog crossed with a greyhound, of a kind originally used for hunting and by poachers for catching rabbits.
2 archaic a prowler, swindler, or petty thief.
– ORIGIN early 16th cent. (in sense 2): from obsolete *lurch* 'remain in a place furtively', variant of LURK.

lurdan /'lə:dən/ (also **lurdane**) archaic ▸ **noun** an idle or incompetent person.
▸ **adjective** lazy; good-for-nothing.
– ORIGIN Middle English: from Old French *lourdin*, from *lourd* 'heavy', *lort* 'foolish', from Latin *luridus* 'lurid'.

lure[1] /l(j)ʊə/ ▸ **verb** [with obj. and adverbial] tempt (a person or animal) to do something or to go somewhere, especially by offering some form of reward: *the child was lured into a car but managed to escape.*
▸ **noun 1** something that tempts or is used to tempt a person or animal to do something: *the film industry always has been a glamorous lure for young girls.* ■ the strongly attractive quality of a person or thing: *the lure of the exotic East.*
2 a type of bait used in fishing or hunting. ■ Falconry a bunch of feathers with a piece of meat attached to a long string, swung around the head of the falconer to recall a hawk.
– ORIGIN Middle English: from Old French *luere*, of Germanic origin; probably related to German *Luder* 'bait'.

lure[2] /lʊə/ ▸ **noun** variant spelling of LUR.

lurex /'l(j)ʊərɛks/ ▸ **noun** [mass noun] trademark a type of yarn or fabric which incorporates a glittering metallic thread.
– ORIGIN 1940s: of unknown origin.

lurgy /'lə:gi/ ▸ **noun** (pl. **lurgies**) Brit. humorous an unspecified or indeterminate illness: *I had caught the **dreaded lurgy**.*
– ORIGIN 1950s (originally spelled *lurgi*): used in the British radio series *The Goon Show* and probably invented by its writers, though possibly from an English dialect term.

lurid /'l(j)ʊərɪd/ ▸ **adjective** unpleasantly bright in colour, especially so as to create a harsh or unnatural effect: *lurid food colourings | a pair of lurid shorts.* ■ presented in vividly shocking or sensational terms: *the more lurid details of the massacre were too frightening for the children.*
– DERIVATIVES **luridly** adverb, **luridness** noun.
– ORIGIN mid 17th cent. (in the sense 'pale and dismal in colour'): from Latin *luridus*; related to *luror* 'wan or yellow colour'.

lurk ▸ **verb** [no obj., with adverbial of place] be or remain hidden so as to wait in ambush for someone or something: *a ruthless killer still lurked in the darkness.* ■ (of an unpleasant quality) be present in a latent or barely discernible state, although still presenting a threat: *danger lurks beneath the surface* | (as adj. **lurking**) *he lives with a lurking fear of exposure as a fraud.* ■ [no obj.] informal read the postings on an Internet message board or in a chat room without making any contribution oneself.
▸ **noun** Austral./NZ informal a profitable stratagem; a dodge or scheme: *you'll soon learn the lurks and perks.*
– DERIVATIVES **lurker** noun.
– ORIGIN Middle English: perhaps from LOUR + the frequentative suffix *-k* (as in *talk*). The noun is from British slang *lurk* 'method of fraud'.

lurve ▸ **noun & verb** non-standard spelling of LOVE (used in humorous reference to romantic infatuation).
– ORIGIN 1930s: as a parody of the pronunciation of *love* in popular romantic songs.

Lusaka /lu:'sɑ:kə/ the capital of Zambia; pop. 1,420,000 (est. 2009).

Lusatian /lu:'seɪʃ(ə)n/ ▸ **adjective & noun** another term for SORBIAN.

luscious ▸ **adjective** (of food or drink) having a pleasingly rich, sweet taste: *a luscious and fragrant dessert wine.* ■ appealing strongly to the senses; pleasingly rich: *the luscious brush strokes and warm colours of these late masterpieces.* ■ (of a woman) very sexually attractive.
– DERIVATIVES **lusciously** adverb, **lusciousness** noun.
– ORIGIN late Middle English: perhaps an alteration of obsolete *licious*, shortened form of DELICIOUS.

lush[1] ▸ **adjective 1** (of vegetation, especially grass) growing luxuriantly: *lush greenery and cultivated fields.* ■ very rich and providing great sensory pleasure: *lush orchestrations.*
2 Brit. informal sexually attractive. ■ very good: *I had some really lush pressies.*
– DERIVATIVES **lushly** adverb, **lushness** noun.
– ORIGIN late Middle English: perhaps an alteration of obsolete *lash* 'soft, lax', from Old French *lasche* 'lax', by association with LUSCIOUS.

lush[2] informal, chiefly N. Amer. ▸ **noun** a heavy drinker, especially a habitual one.
▸ **verb** [with obj.] dated make (someone) drunk: *Mr Hobart **got so lushed up** he was spilling drinks down his shirt.*
– ORIGIN late 18th cent.: perhaps a humorous use of LUSH[1].

Lushai /lu:'ʃʌɪ/ ▸ **noun** another name for MIZO (sense 2 of the noun).

Lushun /lu:'ʃʊn/ a port on the Liaodong Peninsula in NE China, now part of the urban complex of Luda. It was leased by Russia for use as a Pacific naval port from 1898 until 1905, when it was known as Port Arthur.

Lusitania[1] /,lu:sɪ'teɪnɪə/ an ancient Roman province in the Iberian peninsula, corresponding to modern Portugal.
– DERIVATIVES **Lusitanian** adjective & noun.

Lusitania[2] /,lu:sɪ'teɪnɪə/ a Cunard liner which was sunk by a German submarine in the Atlantic in May 1915 with the loss of over 1,000 lives.

lusophone /'lu:səfəʊn/ ▸ **adjective** Portuguese-speaking.
– ORIGIN 1970s: from *luso-* (representing LUSITANIA[1]) + -PHONE.

lust ▸ **noun** [mass noun] strong sexual desire: *he knew that his **lust for** her had returned.* ■ [in sing.] a passionate desire for something: *a **lust for** power.* ■ (usu. **lusts**) chiefly Theology a sensuous appetite regarded as sinful: *lusts of the flesh.*
▸ **verb** [no obj.] have strong sexual desire for someone: *he really **lusted after** me in those days.* ■ have a strong desire for something: *pregnant women **lusting for** pickles and ice cream.*
– ORIGIN Old English (also in the sense 'pleasure, delight'), of Germanic origin; related to Dutch *lust* and German *Lust*.

luster ▸ **noun** US spelling of LUSTRE[1], LUSTRE[2].

lusterware ▸ **noun** US spelling of LUSTREWARE.

lustful ▸ **adjective** having or showing strong feelings of sexual desire: *lustful glances.*
– DERIVATIVES **lustfully** adverb, **lustfulness** noun.

lustily ▸ **adverb** in a strong, healthy, vigorous way; heartily: *fans cheered lustily.*

lustra plural form of LUSTRUM.

lustral /'lʌstr(ə)l/ ▸ **adjective** relating to or used in ceremonial purification.
– ORIGIN mid 16th cent.: from Latin *lustralis*, from *lustrum* (see LUSTRUM).

lustrate /'lʌstreɪt/ ▸ **verb** [with obj.] rare purify by expiatory sacrifice, ceremonial washing, or some other ritual action: *a soul lustrated in the baptismal waters.*
– DERIVATIVES **lustration** noun.
– ORIGIN early 17th cent.: from Latin *lustrat-* 'purified by lustral rites', from the verb *lustrare*, from *lustrum* (see LUSTRUM).

lustre[1] (US **luster**) ▸ **noun** [mass noun] **1** a gentle sheen or soft glow: *the lustre of the Milky Way | she couldn't eat and her hair lost its lustre.* ■ the manner in which the surface of a mineral reflects light. ■ glory or distinction: *a celebrity player to **add lustre to** the line-up.*
2 a thin coating containing unoxidized metal which gives an iridescent glaze to ceramics. ■ ceramics with such a glaze; lustreware: [as modifier] *lustre jugs.*
3 a fabric or yarn with a sheen or gloss. ■ Brit. a thin dress material with a cotton warp, woollen weft, and a glossy surface.
4 [count noun] a prismatic glass pendant on a chandelier or other ornament. ■ a cut-glass chandelier or candelabrum.
– ORIGIN early 16th cent.: from French, from Italian *lustro*, from the verb *lustrare*, from Latin *lustrare* 'illuminate'.

lustre[2] (US **luster**) ▸ **noun** another term for LUSTRUM.

lustred ▸ **adjective** (especially of ceramics) having an iridescent surface; shining.

lustreless (US **lusterless**) ▸ **adjective** not bright or shiny; dull: *her uncombed, lustreless black hair.*

lustreware (US **lusterware**) ▸ **noun** [mass noun] ceramic articles with an iridescent metallic glaze.

lustring (also **lustrine** /'lʌstri:n/ or **lutestring**) ▸ **noun** [mass noun] historical a glossy silk fabric, or a satin-weave fabric resembling it.
– ORIGIN late 17th cent.: from French *lustrine* or from Italian *lustrino*, from *lustro* 'lustre'.

lustrous ▸ **adjective** having lustre; shining: *large, lustrous eyes.*
– DERIVATIVES **lustrously** adverb, **lustrousness** noun.

lustrum /'lʌstrəm/ ▸ **noun** (pl. **lustra** /-trə/ or **lustrums**) chiefly literary or historical a period of five years.
– ORIGIN late 16th cent.: from Latin, originally denoting a purificatory sacrifice after a quinquennial census.

lusty ▸ **adjective** (**lustier**, **lustiest**) healthy and strong; full of vigour: *the other farmsteads had lusty young sons to work the land | lusty singing.*
– DERIVATIVES **lustiness** noun.
– ORIGIN Middle English: from LUST (in the early sense 'vigour') + -Y[1].

lusus naturae /,lu:səs nə'tjʊəri:, -rʌɪ/ ▸ **noun** (pl. same /-su:s/ or **lususes**) rare a freak of nature.
– ORIGIN Latin, literally 'a sport of nature'.

lutanist ▸ **noun** variant spelling of LUTENIST.

lutchet /'lʌtʃɪt/ ▸ **noun** a fitting on the deck of a barge or wherry to which the foot of the mast is fixed, allowing the mast to be lowered by pivoting when passing under bridges.
– ORIGIN early 19th cent.: perhaps from the northern English dialect verb *lutch* 'lift', or an alteration of LATCHET.

lute[1] ▸ **noun** a plucked stringed instrument with a long neck bearing frets and a rounded body with a flat front, rather like a halved egg in shape.
– ORIGIN Middle English: from Old French *lut*, *leut*, probably via Provençal from Arabic *al-'ūd*.

lute[2] ▸ **noun** (also **luting**) [mass noun] liquid clay or cement used to seal a joint, coat a crucible, or protect a graft. ■ [count noun] a rubber seal for a jar.
▸ **verb** [with obj.] seal, join, or coat with lute.
– ORIGIN late Middle English: from Old French *lut* or medieval Latin *lutum*, a special use of Latin *lutum* 'potter's clay'.

luteal /lu:'tɪəl/ ▸ **adjective** Anatomy relating to the corpus luteum.

lutecium ▸ **noun** variant spelling of LUTETIUM.

lutein /'lu:tɪɪn/ ▸ **noun** [mass noun] Biochemistry a deep yellow pigment of the xanthophyll class, found in the leaves of plants, in egg yolk, and in the corpus luteum.
– ORIGIN mid 19th cent.: from Latin *luteum* 'yolk of egg' (neuter of *luteus* 'yellow') + -IN[1].

luteinizing hormone /'lu:tənʌɪzɪŋ/ (also **luteinising hormone**) ▸ **noun** [mass noun] Biochemistry a hormone secreted by the anterior pituitary gland that stimulates ovulation in females and the synthesis of androgen in males.

lutenist /'lu:t(ə)nɪst/ (also **lutanist**) ▸ **noun** a lute player.
– ORIGIN early 17th cent.: from medieval Latin *lutanista*, from *lutana* 'lute'.

luteo- /'lu:tɪəʊ/ ▸ **combining form 1** yellow-coloured: *luteofulvous.*
2 relating to the corpus luteum: *luteotrophic.*
– ORIGIN from Latin *luteus* (or neuter *luteum*) 'yellow'.

luteofulvous /,lu:tɪəʊ'fʌlvəs/ ▸ **adjective** of an orange-tawny colour.

luteotrophic hormone /,lu:tɪə(ʊ)'trəʊfɪk, -'trɒfɪk/ (also **luteotropic hormone** /-'trəʊpɪk, -'trɒpɪk/) ▸ **noun** another term for PROLACTIN.

luteous /'lu:tɪəs, 'lju:-/ ▸ **adjective** Biology of an orange-yellow or greenish yellow colour.
– ORIGIN mid 17th cent.: from Latin *luteus* 'yellow' + -OUS.

lutestring /'lu:tstrɪŋ/ ▸ **noun** variant spelling of LUSTRING.

Lutetia /lu:'ti:ʃə/ Roman name for PARIS[1].

lutetium /lu:'ti:ʃɪəm, -sɪəm/ (also **lutecium**) ▸ **noun** [mass noun] the chemical element of atomic number 71, a rare silvery-white metal of the lanthanide series. (Symbol: **Lu**)

– ORIGIN early 20th cent.: from French *lutécium*, from Latin *Lutetia*, the ancient name of Paris, the home of its discoverer.

Luther /ˈluːθə/, German /ˈlʊtɐ/, Martin (1483–1546), German Protestant theologian, the principal figure of the German Reformation. He preached the doctrine of justification by faith rather than by works and attacked the sale of indulgences (1517) and papal authority. In 1521 he was excommunicated at the Diet of Worms. His translation of the Bible into High German (1522–34) contributed significantly to the development of German literature in the vernacular.

Lutheran ▸ **noun** a follower of Martin Luther. ■ a member of the Lutheran Church.
▸ **adjective** of or characterized by the theology of Martin Luther. ■ relating to the Lutheran Church.
– DERIVATIVES **Lutheranism** noun.

Lutheran Church the Protestant Church accepting the Augsburg Confession of 1530, with justification by faith alone as a cardinal doctrine. The Lutheran Church is the largest Protestant body, with substantial membership in Germany, Scandinavia, and the US.

luthern /ˈluːθən/ ▸ **noun** old-fashioned term for DORMER.
– ORIGIN mid 17th cent.: perhaps an alteration of earlier *lucarne* 'skylight', from Old French.

luthier /ˈluːtɪə/ ▸ **noun** a maker of stringed instruments such as violins or guitars.
– ORIGIN late 19th cent.: from French, from *luth* 'lute'.

Luthuli /luːˈtuːli/ (also **Lutuli**), Albert John (*c.*1898–1967), South African political leader. His presidency of the African National Congress (1952–60) was marked by a programme of civil disobedience for which he was awarded the Nobel Peace Prize (1960).

Lutine Bell /ˈluːtiːn/ a bell kept at Lloyd's in London and rung whenever there is an important announcement to be made to the underwriters. It was salvaged from HMS *Lutine*, which sank in 1799 with a large cargo of gold and bullion.

L

luting ▸ **noun** see LUTE[2].

lutino /luːˈtiːnəʊ/ ▸ **noun** (pl. **lutinos**) [often as modifier] a bird (especially a cage bird of the parrot family) with more yellow in the plumage than usual for the species.
– ORIGIN early 20th cent.: from Latin *luteus* 'yellow' + *-ino*, on the pattern of *albino*.

lutist ▸ **noun 1** a lute player.
2 a maker of lutes; a luthier.

Lutomer Riesling /ˈluːtəmə/ ▸ **noun** [mass noun] a Riesling wine produced in the Ljutomer region of northern Slovenia.

Luton an industrial town in Bedfordshire, England, to the north-west of London; pop. 187,800 (est. 2009).

Lutuli variant spelling of LUTHULI.

Lutyens[1] /ˈlʌtjənz/, (Agnes) Elisabeth (1906–83), English composer. She was one of the first English composers to use the twelve-note system, as in her *Chamber Concerto No. 1* (1939). She was the daughter of Sir Edwin Lutyens.

Lutyens[2] /ˈlʌtjənz/, Sir Edwin (Landseer) (1869–1944), English architect. He established his reputation designing country houses, but is particularly known for his plans for New Delhi (1912), where he introduced an open garden-city layout, and for the Cenotaph in London (1919–21).

lutz /lʊts/ ▸ **noun** a jump in skating from the backward outside edge of one skate to the backward outside edge of the other, with one or more full turns in the air.
– ORIGIN 1930s: named after the Austrian skater Alois *Lutz* (1899–1918).

luv ▸ **noun & verb** Brit. non-standard spelling of LOVE (representing informal or dialect use).

Luvale /lʊˈvɑːleɪ/ ▸ **noun** (pl. **same**) **1** a member of a people living mainly in eastern Angola and western Democratic Republic of the Congo (Zaire).
2 [mass noun] the Bantu language of the Luvale, with around 600,000 speakers. Also called LWENA.
▸ **adjective** relating to the Luvale or their language.

luvvy (also **luvvie**) ▸ **noun** (pl. **luvvies**) Brit. informal
1 often derogatory an actor or actress, especially one who is particularly effusive or affected.
2 (as a form of address) variant spelling of LOVEY.
– DERIVATIVES **luvviedom** noun.

Luwian /ˈluːwɪən/ (also **Luvian** /ˈluːvɪən/) ▸ **noun** [mass noun] an ancient Anatolian language of the 2nd millennium BC, related to Hittite. It is recorded in both cuneiform and hieroglyphic scripts, and may have been the language spoken in Troy at the time of the Homeric war.
– ORIGIN from *Luwia*, part of Asia Minor, + -AN.

lux /lʌks/ (abbrev.: **lx**) ▸ **noun** (pl. **same**) the SI unit of illuminance, equal to one lumen per square metre.
– ORIGIN late 19th cent.: from Latin, literally 'light'.

luxate /ˈlʌkseɪt/ ▸ **verb** [with obj.] Medicine dislocate.
– DERIVATIVES **luxation** noun.
– ORIGIN early 17th cent.: from Latin *luxat-* 'dislocated', from the verb *luxare*, from *luxus* 'out of joint'.

luxe /lʌks, lʊks/ ▸ **adjective** expensive and of high quality; luxurious: *the luxe 65-room Four Seasons hotel*.
▸ **noun** [mass noun] luxury.
– ORIGIN mid 16th cent.: from French, from Latin *luxus* 'abundance'. Compare with DELUXE.

Luxembourg /ˈlʌksəmbəːg/ a country in western Europe, situated between Belgium, Germany, and France; pop. 491,800 (est. 2009); official languages, Luxemburgish, French, and German; capital, Luxembourg. ■ the capital of Luxembourg; pop. 88,600 (est. 2009). It is the seat of the European Court of Justice. ■ a province of SE Belgium, until 1839 a province of Luxembourg; capital, Arlon.

> Annexed by France in 1795, Luxembourg became an independent grand duchy as a result of the Treaty of Vienna in 1815. It formed a customs union with Belgium in 1922, extended in 1948 into the Benelux Customs Union with the Netherlands. It was a founder member of the EEC in 1957.

– DERIVATIVES **Luxembourger** noun.

Luxemburg /ˈlʌksəmbəːg/, Rosa (1871–1919), Polish-born German revolutionary leader. Together with the German socialist **Karl Liebknecht** (1871–1919) she founded the revolutionary group known as the Spartacus League in 1916 and the German Communist Party in 1918.

Luxemburgish /ˈlʌksəmˌbəːgɪʃ/ ▸ **noun** [mass noun] the local language of Luxembourg, a form of German with a strong admixture of French. Also called LETZEBURGESCH.

Luxor /ˈlʌksɔː/ a city in eastern Egypt, on the east bank of the Nile; pop. 202,200 (est. 2006). It is the site of the southern part of ancient Thebes and contains the ruins of the temple built by Amenhotep III and of monuments erected by Ramses II. Arabic name EL-UQSUR.

luxuriant /lʌgˈʒʊərɪənt, lʌgˈzjʊə-, lʌkˈsjʊə-/ ▸ **adjective** (of vegetation) rich and profuse in growth; lush. ■ (of hair) thick and healthy.
– DERIVATIVES **luxuriance** noun, **luxuriantly** adverb.
– ORIGIN mid 16th cent.: from Latin *luxuriant-* 'growing rankly', from the verb *luxuriare*, from *luxuria* 'luxury, rankness'.

luxuriate /lʌgˈʒʊərɪeɪt, lʌgˈzjʊə-, lʌkˈsjʊə-/ ▸ **verb** [no obj.] (**luxuriate in/over**) enjoy (something) as a luxury; take self-indulgent delight in: *she was luxuriating in a long bath*.
– ORIGIN early 17th cent.: from Latin *luxuriat-* 'grown in abundance', from the verb *luxuriare*.

luxurious ▸ **adjective** extremely comfortable or elegant, especially when involving great expense: *the island's most luxurious hotel*. ■ giving self-indulgent or sensual pleasure: *a luxurious wallow in a scented bath*.
– DERIVATIVES **luxuriously** adverb, **luxuriousness** noun.
– ORIGIN Middle English (in the sense 'lascivious'): from Old French *luxurios*, from Latin *luxuriosus*, from *luxuria* 'luxury'

> **USAGE** **Luxurious** and **luxuriant** are sometimes confused. **Luxurious** chiefly means 'very comfortable, elegant, and involving great expense', as in *a luxurious hotel*, whereas **luxuriant** means 'rich and profuse in growth', as in *acres of luxuriant gardens*.

luxury ▸ **noun** (pl. **luxuries**) [mass noun] a state of great comfort or elegance, especially when involving great expense: *he lived a life of luxury*. ■ [count noun] an inessential, desirable item which is expensive or difficult to obtain: *luxuries like chocolate, scent, and fizzy wine*. ■ [in sing.] a pleasure obtained only rarely: *they actually had* **the luxury of** *a whole day together*.
▸ **adjective** [attrib.] luxurious or of the nature of a luxury: *a luxury yacht | luxury goods*.
– ORIGIN Middle English (denoting lechery): from Old French *luxurie*, *luxure*, from Latin *luxuria*, from *luxus* 'excess'. The earliest current sense dates from the mid 17th cent.

Luzern /luˈtsɛrn/ German name for LUCERNE.

Luzon /luːˈzɒn/ the most northerly and the largest island in the Philippines; pop. 47,245,500 (est. 2007). Its chief towns are Quezon City and Manila, the country's capital.

LV ▸ **abbreviation** (in the UK) luncheon voucher.

Lviv /lvɪv/ an industrial city in western Ukraine, near the border with Poland; pop. 734,500 (est. 2009). Russian name **Lvov** /ljvɒf/.

LVO ▸ **abbreviation** Lieutenant of the Royal Victorian Order.

LW ▸ **abbreviation** long wave.

LWB ▸ **abbreviation** long wheelbase.

lwei /ləˈweɪ/ ▸ **noun** (pl. **same**) a monetary unit of Angola, equal to one hundredth of a kwanza.
– ORIGIN a local word.

Lwena ▸ **noun** another term for LUVALE (the language).

LWM ▸ **abbreviation** low-water mark.

L-word ▸ **noun** US informal, humorous used in place of the word 'liberal' in a political context where this word is regarded as having negative connotations.

Lwów /lvuf/ Polish name for LVIV.

lx ▸ **abbreviation** Physics lux.

LXX ▸ **symbol** Septuagint.
– ORIGIN special use of the Roman numeral for 70.

-ly[1] ▸ **suffix** forming adjectives meaning: **1** having the qualities of: *brotherly | rascally*.
2 recurring at intervals of: *hourly | quarterly*.
– ORIGIN Old English *-lic*, of Germanic origin; related to LIKE[1].

-ly[2] ▸ **suffix** forming adverbs from adjectives, chiefly denoting manner or degree: *greatly | happily | pointedly*.
– ORIGIN Old English *-līce*, of Germanic origin.

Lyallpur /ˌlʌɪəlˈpʊə/ former name (until 1979) for FAISALABAD.

lyase /ˈlʌɪeɪz/ ▸ **noun** Biochemistry an enzyme which catalyses the joining of specified molecules or groups by a double bond.
– ORIGIN 1960s: from LYSIS + -ASE.

lycaenid /lʌɪˈsiːnɪd/ ▸ **noun** Entomology a small butterfly of a family (Lycaenidae) that includes the blues, coppers, hairstreaks, and arguses.
– ORIGIN late 19th cent.: from modern Latin *Lycaenidae* (plural), from the genus name *Lycaena*, apparently from Greek *lukaina* 'she-wolf'.

lycanthrope /ˈlʌɪk(ə)nˌθrəʊp/ ▸ **noun** a werewolf.
– ORIGIN early 17th cent.: from modern Latin *lycanthropus*, from Greek *lukanthrōpos* 'wolf man' (see LYCANTHROPY).

lycanthropy /lʌɪˈkanθrəpi/ ▸ **noun** [mass noun] the mythical transformation of a person into a wolf. ■ archaic a form of madness involving the delusion of being an animal, usually a wolf, with correspondingly altered behaviour.
– DERIVATIVES **lycanthropic** adjective.
– ORIGIN late 16th cent. (as a supposed form of madness): from modern Latin *lycanthropia*, from Greek *lukanthrōpia*, from *lukos* 'wolf' + *anthrōpos* 'man'.

lycée /ˈliːseɪ/, French /lise/ ▸ **noun** (pl. **lycées** pronunc. **same**) a secondary school in France that is funded by the state.
– ORIGIN French, from Latin *lyceum* (see LYCEUM).

Lyceum /lʌɪˈsiːəm/ the garden at Athens in which Aristotle taught philosophy. ■ (as noun **the Lyceum**) Aristotelian philosophy and its followers. ■ (as noun **a lyceum**) US archaic a literary institution, lecture hall, or teaching place.
– ORIGIN via Latin from Greek *Lukeion*, neuter of *Lukeios*, epithet of Apollo (from whose neighbouring temple the Lyceum was named).

lychee /ˈlʌɪtʃiː, ˈlɪ-/ (also **litchi** or **lichee**) ▸ **noun 1** a small rounded fruit with sweet white scented flesh, a large central stone, and a thin rough skin.
2 the Chinese tree which bears lychees. ● *Nephelium litchi* (or *Litchi chinensis*), family Sapindaceae.
– ORIGIN late 16th cent.: from Chinese *lìzhī*.

lychgate /ˈlɪtʃgeɪt/ (also **lichgate**) ▸ **noun** a roofed gateway to a churchyard, formerly used at burials for sheltering a coffin until the clergyman's arrival.
– ORIGIN late 15th cent.: from Old English *līc* 'body' + GATE[1].

lychnis /ˈlɪknɪs/ ▸ **noun** a plant of a genus which includes the campions, ragged robin, and a number of cultivated ornamental flowers. ● Genus *Lychnis*, family Caryophyllaceae.

– ORIGIN modern Latin, via Latin from Greek *lukhnis*, denoting a red flower, from *lukhnos* 'lamp'.

Lycia /ˈlɪsɪə/ an ancient region on the coast of SW Asia Minor, between Caria and Pamphylia.
– DERIVATIVES **Lycian** adjective & noun.

lycopene /ˈlʌɪkə(ʊ)piːn/ ▶ noun [mass noun] Biochemistry a red carotenoid pigment present in tomatoes and many berries and fruits.
– ORIGIN 1930s: from the variant *lycopin* (from modern Latin *Lycopersicon*, a genus name including the tomato) + -ENE.

lycopod /ˈlʌɪkə(ʊ)pɒd/ ▶ noun Botany a clubmoss, especially a lycopodium. Giant lycopods the size of trees were common in the Carboniferous period. ● Class Lycopsida: several families.
– ORIGIN mid 19th cent.: anglicized form of LYCOPODIUM.

lycopodium /ˌlʌɪkə(ʊ)ˈpəʊdɪəm/ ▶ noun a plant of a genus that includes the common clubmosses. ● Genus *Lycopodium*, family Lycopodiaceae.
■ (usu. **lycopodium powder** or **lycopodium seed**) [mass noun] a fine flammable powder consisting of clubmoss spores, formerly used as an absorbent in surgery, in experiments in the physical sciences, and in making fireworks.
– ORIGIN modern Latin, from Greek *lukos* 'wolf' + *pous, pod-* 'foot' (because of the claw-like shape of the root).

Lycopsida /lʌɪˈkɒpsɪdə/ ▶ plural noun Botany a class of pteridophyte plants that comprises the clubmosses and their extinct relatives.
– DERIVATIVES **lycopsid** noun & adjective.
– ORIGIN modern Latin (plural), from Greek *lukos* 'wolf' + *opsis* 'appearance'.

Lycra /ˈlʌɪkrə/ ▶ noun [mass noun] trademark an elastic polyurethane fibre or fabric used especially for close-fitting sports clothing.
– ORIGIN 1950s: of unknown origin.

Lycurgus /lʌɪˈkəːgəs/ (9th century BC), Spartan lawgiver. He is traditionally held to have been the founder of the constitution and military regime of ancient Sparta.

lyddite /ˈlɪdʌɪt/ ▶ noun [mass noun] a high explosive containing picric acid, used chiefly by the British during the First World War.
– ORIGIN late 19th cent.: named after *Lydd*, a town in Kent where the explosive was first tested, + -ITE[1].

Lydgate /ˈlɪdgeɪt/, John (*c.*1370–*c.*1450), English poet and monk. His copious output of verse, often in Chaucerian style, includes the poetical translations the *Troy Book* (1412–20) and *The Fall of Princes* (1431–8).

Lydia /ˈlɪdɪə/ an ancient region of western Asia Minor, south of Mysia and north of Caria. It became a powerful kingdom in the 7th century BC but in 546 its final king, Croesus, was defeated by Cyrus and it was absorbed into the Persian empire. Lydia was probably the first realm to use coined money.
– DERIVATIVES **Lydian** noun & adjective.

Lydian mode ▶ noun Music the mode represented by the natural diatonic scale F–F (containing an augmented 4th).

lye ▶ noun [mass noun] a strongly alkaline solution, especially of potassium hydroxide, used for washing or cleansing.
– ORIGIN Old English *lēag*, of Germanic origin: related to Dutch *loog*, German *Lauge*, also to LATHER.

Lyell /ˈlʌɪəl/, Sir Charles (1797–1875), Scottish geologist. His textbook *Principles of Geology* (1830–3) influenced a generation of geologists and held that the earth's features were shaped over a long period of time by natural processes, thus clearing the way for Darwin's theory of evolution.

lying[1] present participle of LIE[1].

lying[2] present participle of LIE[2]. ▶ adjective not telling the truth: *he's a lying, cheating, snake in the grass.*
– DERIVATIVES **lyingly** adverb.

lying-in ▶ noun archaic seclusion before and after childbirth; confinement.

lying-in-state ▶ noun the display of the corpse of a public figure for public tribute before it is buried or cremated.

lyke wake /lʌɪk/ ▶ noun Brit. a night spent watching over a dead body, typically acting as a celebration to mark the passing of the person's soul.
– ORIGIN late Middle English: from *lyke* (from Old English *līc* 'body': compare with LYCHGATE) and the noun WAKE[1].

Lyly /ˈlɪli/, John (*c.*1554–1606), English prose writer and dramatist. His prose romance in two parts, *Euphues, The Anatomy of Wit* (1578) and *Euphues and his England* (1580), was written in an elaborate style that became known as *euphuism*.

Lyman series /ˈlʌɪmən/ Physics a series of lines in the ultraviolet spectrum of atomic hydrogen, between 122 and 91 nanometres.
– ORIGIN early 20th cent.: named after Theodore *Lyman* (1874–1954), American physicist.

Lyme disease /lʌɪm/ ▶ noun [mass noun] a form of arthritis caused by bacteria that are transmitted by ticks. ● Lyme disease is caused by the spirochaete *Borrelia burgdorferi*.
– ORIGIN 1970s: named after *Lyme*, a town in Connecticut, US, where an outbreak occurred.

lymph /lɪmf/ ▶ noun [mass noun] **1** Physiology a colourless fluid containing white blood cells, which bathes the tissues and drains through the lymphatic system into the bloodstream. ■ fluid exuding from a sore or inflamed tissue.
2 literary pure water.
– ORIGIN late 16th cent. (in sense 2): from French *lymphe* or Latin *lympha, limpa* 'water'.

lymph- ▶ combining form variant spelling of LYMPHO- shortened before a vowel, as in *lymphangiography*.

lymphadenitis /ˌlɪmfadɪˈnʌɪtɪs/ ▶ noun [mass noun] Medicine inflammation of the lymph nodes.
– ORIGIN late 19th cent.: from LYMPH- + Greek *adēn* 'gland' + -ITIS.

lymphadenopathy /ˌlɪmfadɪˈnɒpəθi/ ▶ noun [mass noun] Medicine a disease affecting the lymph nodes.

lymphangiography /ˌlɪmfandʒɪˈɒgrəfi/ ▶ noun [mass noun] Medicine X-ray examination of the vessels of the lymphatic system after injection of a substance opaque to X-rays.
– DERIVATIVES **lymphangiogram** noun.

lymphangitis /ˌlɪmfanˈdʒʌɪtɪs/ ▶ noun [mass noun] Medicine inflammation of the walls of the lymphatic vessels.

lymphatic ▶ adjective **1** Physiology relating to lymph or its secretion: *lymphatic vessels | lymphatic drainage.*
2 archaic (of a person) pale, flabby, or sluggish.
▶ noun a vein-like vessel conveying lymph in the body.
– ORIGIN mid 17th cent. (in the sense 'frenzied, mad'): from Latin *lymphaticus* 'mad', from Greek *numpholēptos* 'seized by nymphs'; now associated with LYMPH, on the pattern of words such as *spermatic*.

lymphatic system ▶ noun the network of vessels through which lymph drains from the tissues into the blood.

lymph gland ▶ noun less technical term for LYMPH NODE.

lymph node ▶ noun Physiology each of a number of small swellings in the lymphatic system where lymph is filtered and lymphocytes are formed.

lympho- (also **lymph-** before a vowel) ▶ combining form representing LYMPH: *lymphocyte*.

lymphoblast /ˈlɪmfə(ʊ)blast/ ▶ noun Medicine an abnormal cell resembling a large lymphocyte, produced in large numbers in a form of leukaemia.
– DERIVATIVES **lymphoblastic** adjective.

lymphocyte /ˈlɪmfə(ʊ)sʌɪt/ ▶ noun Physiology a form of small leucocyte (white blood cell) with a single round nucleus, occurring especially in the lymphatic system.
– DERIVATIVES **lymphocytic** adjective.

lymphoid /ˈlɪmfɔɪd/ ▶ adjective Anatomy & Medicine relating to or denoting the tissue responsible for producing lymphocytes and antibodies. This tissue occurs in the lymph nodes, thymus, tonsils, and spleen, and dispersed elsewhere in the body.

lymphokine /ˈlɪmfə(ʊ)kʌɪn/ ▶ noun Physiology a substance of a type produced by lymphocytes and having an effect on other cells of the immune system.
– ORIGIN 1960s: from LYMPHO- + Greek *kinein* 'to move'.

lymphoma /lɪmˈfəʊmə/ ▶ noun (pl. **lymphomas** or **lymphomata** /-mətə/) [mass noun] Medicine cancer of the lymph nodes.

lymphoreticular /ˌlɪmfə(ʊ)rɪˈtɪkjʊlə/ ▶ adjective another term for RETICULOENDOTHELIAL.

lynch ▶ verb [with obj.] (of a group of people) kill (someone) for an alleged offence without a legal trial, especially by hanging.
– DERIVATIVES **lyncher** noun.
– ORIGIN mid 19th cent.: from *Lynch's law*, named after Capt. William *Lynch*, head of a self-constituted judicial tribunal in Virginia *c.*1780.

lynchet /ˈlɪn(t)ʃɪt/ ▶ noun a ridge or ledge formed along the downhill side of a plot by ploughing in ancient times.
– ORIGIN late 17th cent.: probably from dialect *linch* 'rising ground'; compare with LINKS.

lynch mob ▶ noun a band of people intent on lynching someone.

lynchpin ▶ noun variant spelling of LINCHPIN.

Lynn, Dame Vera (b.1917), English singer; born *Vera Margaret Welch*. She is known chiefly for her rendering of such songs as 'We'll Meet Again' and 'White Cliffs of Dover', which she sang to the troops in the Second World War.

Lynx /lɪŋks/ Astronomy an inconspicuous northern constellation (the Lynx), between Ursa Major and Gemini.
– ORIGIN via Latin from Greek *lunx*.

lynx ▶ noun a wild cat with yellowish-brown fur (sometimes spotted), a short tail, and tufted ears, found chiefly in the northern latitudes of North America and Eurasia. ● Genus *Felis*, family Felidae: the **Eurasian lynx** (*F. lynx*) and the **Canadian lynx** (*F. canadensis* or *F. lynx*).
■ [mass noun] the fur of the lynx. ■ **(African lynx)** another term for CARACAL.
– ORIGIN Middle English: via Latin from Greek *lunx*.

lynx-eyed ▶ adjective keen-sighted.

lyocell /ˈlʌɪə(ʊ)sɛl/ ▶ noun [mass noun] (trademark in the US) a synthetic fibre and fabric made from wood pulp.
– ORIGIN 1990s: probably from Greek *luein* 'loosen' + *cell* as in CELLULOSE.

Lyon (in full **Lord Lyon** or **Lyon King of Arms**) ▶ noun the chief herald of Scotland.
– ORIGIN late Middle English: archaic variant of LION, named from the lion on the royal shield.

Lyon Court ▶ noun the court over which the Lyon King of Arms presides.

lyonnaise /ˌliːəˈneɪz/ ▶ adjective (of food, especially sliced potatoes) cooked with onions or with a white wine and onion sauce.
– ORIGIN French, 'characteristic of the city of Lyons'.

L

Lyons /ˈliːɒ̃/, French /ljɔ̃/ an industrial city and river port in SE France, situated at the confluence of the Rhône and Saône Rivers; pop. 480,778 (2006). Founded by the Romans in AD 43 as Lugdunum, it was an important city of Roman Gaul. French name **Lyon** /ljɔ̃/.

lyophilic /ˌlʌɪə(ʊ)ˈfɪlɪk/ ▶ adjective Chemistry (of a colloid) readily dispersed by a solvent and not easily precipitated.
– ORIGIN early 20th cent.: from Greek *luein* 'loosen, dissolve' + *philos* 'loving'.

lyophilize /lʌɪˈɒfɪlʌɪz/ (also **lyophilise**) ▶ verb [with obj.] technical freeze-dry (a substance).
– DERIVATIVES **lyophilization** noun.

lyophobic /ˌlʌɪəˈfəʊbɪk/ ▶ adjective Chemistry (of a colloid) not lyophilic.

Lyotard /ˈljɒtɑː/, French /ljɔtaʀ/, Jean-François (1924–98), French philosopher and literary critic. He outlined his 'philosophy of desire', based on the politics of Nietzsche, in *L'Économie libidinale* (1974). In later books he adopted a postmodern quasi-Wittgensteinian linguistic philosophy.

Lyra /ˈlʌɪrə/ Astronomy a small northern constellation (the Lyre), said to represent the lyre invented by Hermes. It contains the bright star Vega.
– ORIGIN Latin.

lyrate /ˈlʌɪreɪt/ ▶ adjective Biology lyre-shaped.
– ORIGIN mid 18th cent.: from Latin *lyra* 'lyre' + -ATE[2].

lyre ▶ noun a stringed instrument like a small U-shaped harp with strings fixed to a crossbar, used especially in ancient Greece. Modern instruments of this type are found mainly in East Africa.
– ORIGIN Middle English: via Old French *lire* and Latin *lyra* from Greek *lura*.

lyrebird ▶ noun a large Australian songbird, the male of which has a long lyre-shaped tail and is noted for its remarkable song and display. ● Family Menuridae and genus *Menura*: two species, in particular the **superb lyrebird** (*M. novaehollandiae*).

lyretail ▶ noun a small African killifish which is popular in aquaria. The colour pattern and shape of the tail, especially in the brightly coloured male, are suggestive of a lyre. ● Several genera and species, family Cyprinodontidae.

lyric ▶ adjective **1** (of poetry) expressing the writer's emotions, usually briefly and in stanzas or recognized forms. ■ writing in this manner: *a lyric poet.*

2 (of a singing voice) using a light register: *a lyric soprano with a light, clear timbre.*
▶ **noun** (usu. **lyrics**) **1** a lyric poem or verse. ■ [mass noun] lyric poetry as a literary genre.
2 the words of a popular song: *she has published both music and lyrics for a number of songs.*
– ORIGIN late 16th cent.: from French *lyrique* or Latin *lyricus*, from Greek *lurikos*, from *lura* 'lyre'.

lyrical ▶ **adjective 1** (of literature, art, or music) expressing the writer's emotions in an imaginative and beautiful way: *he gained a devoted following for his lyrical cricket writing.* ■ (of poetry or a poet) lyric: *Wordsworth's Lyrical Ballads.*
2 relating to the words of a popular song: *the lyrical content of his songs.*
– PHRASES **wax lyrical** talk in a highly enthusiastic and effusive way: *he waxed lyrical about his splendid son-in-law.*
– DERIVATIVES **lyrically** adverb.

lyricism ▶ **noun** [mass noun] an artist's expression of emotion in an imaginative and beautiful way; the quality of being lyrical.

lyricist ▶ **noun** a person who writes the words to a popular song or musical.

lyrist ▶ **noun 1** /ˈlʌɪərɪst/ a person who plays the lyre. **2** /ˈlɪrɪst/ a lyric poet.
– ORIGIN mid 17th cent.: from Latin *lyrista*, from Greek *luristēs*, from *lura* 'lyre'.

Lysander /lʌɪˈsandə/ (d.395 BC) Spartan general. He defeated the Athenian navy in 405 and captured Athens in 404, so bringing the Peloponnesian War to an end.

lysate /ˈlʌɪzeɪt/ ▶ **noun** Biology a preparation containing the products of lysis of cells.

lyse /lʌɪz/ ▶ **verb** Biology undergo or cause to undergo lysis.
– ORIGIN early 20th cent.: back-formation from LYSIS.

Lysenko /lɪˈsɛŋkəʊ/, Trofim Denisovich (1898–1976), Soviet biologist and geneticist. He was an adherent of Lamarck's theory of evolution by the inheritance of acquired characteristics. Since his ideas harmonized with Marxist ideology he was favoured by Stalin and dominated Soviet genetics for many years.
– DERIVATIVES **Lysenkoism** noun.

lysergic acid /lʌɪˈsəːdʒɪk/ (abbrev.: **LSD**) ▶ **noun** [mass noun] a crystalline compound prepared from natural ergot alkaloids or synthetically, from which the drug LSD (**lysergic acid diethylamide**) can be made.
● A tetracyclic acid; chem. formula: $C_{16}H_{16}N_2O_2$.
– ORIGIN 1930s: *lysergic* from *(hydro)lys(is)* + *erg(ot)* + -IC.

lysimeter /lʌɪˈsɪmɪtə/ ▶ **noun** an apparatus for measuring changes due to moisture loss, percolation, etc. undergone by a body of soil under controlled conditions.
– ORIGIN late 19th cent.: from Greek *lusis* 'loosening' + -METER.

lysin /ˈlʌɪsɪn/ ▶ **noun** Biology an antibody or other substance able to cause lysis of cells (especially bacteria).
– ORIGIN early 20th cent.: from German *Lysine*.

lysine /ˈlʌɪsiːn/ ▶ **noun** [mass noun] Biochemistry a basic amino acid which is a constituent of most proteins. It is an essential nutrient in the diet of vertebrates.
● Chem. formula: $NH_2(CH_2)_4CH(NH_2)COOH$.
– ORIGIN late 19th cent.: from German *Lysin*, based on LYSIS.

Lysippus /lʌɪˈsɪpəs/ (4th century BC), Greek sculptor. He is said to have introduced a naturalistic scheme of proportions for the human body into Greek sculpture.

lysis /ˈlʌɪsɪs/ ▶ **noun** [mass noun] Biology the disintegration of a cell by rupture of the cell wall or membrane.
– ORIGIN early 19th cent.: from Latin, from Greek *lusis* 'loosening', from *luein* 'loosen'.

-lysis ▶ **combining form** denoting disintegration or decomposition: ■ in nouns specifying an agent: *hydrolysis.* ■ in nouns specifying a reactant: *haemolysis.* ■ in nouns specifying the nature of the process: *autolysis.*
– ORIGIN via Latin from Greek *lusis* 'loosening'.

Lysol /ˈlʌɪsɒl/ ▶ **noun** [mass noun] trademark a disinfectant consisting of a mixture of cresols and soft soap.
– ORIGIN late 19th cent.: from -LYSIS + -OL.

lysosome /ˈlʌɪsəsəʊm/ ▶ **noun** Biology an organelle in the cytoplasm of eukaryotic cells containing degradative enzymes enclosed in a membrane.
– DERIVATIVES **lysosomal** adjective.

lysozyme /ˈlʌɪsəzʌɪm/ ▶ **noun** [mass noun] Biochemistry an enzyme which catalyses the destruction of the cell walls of certain bacteria, and occurs notably in tears and egg white.
– ORIGIN early 20th cent.: from LYSIS + a shortened form of ENZYME.

lytic /ˈlɪtɪk/ ▶ **adjective** Biology relating to or causing lysis: *the lytic activity of bile acids.*
– DERIVATIVES **lytically** adverb.

-lytic ▶ **combining form** in adjectives corresponding to nouns ending in *-lysis* (such as *hydrolytic* corresponding to *hydrolysis*).
– ORIGIN from Greek *-lutikos* 'able to loosen'.

Lytton /ˈlɪt(ə)n/, 1st Baron (1803–73), British novelist, dramatist, and statesman; born *Edward George Earle Bulwer-Lytton*. He achieved literary success with *Pelham* (1828), a novel of fashionable society, and also wrote historical romances (such as *The Last Days of Pompeii*, 1834) and plays. He became an MP in 1831.

L

Contents

Countries of the World

Population figures are based on 2009 estimates.

Independent countries

Country	Capital	Area (sq. km)	Population	Currency unit
Afghanistan	Kabul	648,000	28,395,700	afghani = 100 puls
Albania	Tirana	28,700	3,639,500	lek = 100 qintars
Algeria	Algiers	2,319,000	34,178,200	dinar = 100 centimes
Andorra	Andorra la Vella	468	83,900	euro = 100 cents
Angola	Luanda	1,246,000	12,799,300	kwanza = 100 lwei
Antigua and Barbuda	St John's	442	85,600	dollar = 100 cents
Argentina	Buenos Aires	2,780,000	40,913,600	peso = 100 centavos
Armenia	Yerevan	29,800	2,967,000	dram = 100 luma
Australia	Canberra	7,692,000	21,262,600	dollar = 100 cents
Austria	Vienna	83,900	8,210,300	euro = 100 cents
Azerbaijan	Baku	86,600	8,238,700	manat = 100 gopik
Bahamas	Nassau	13,900	307,600	dollar = 100 cents
Bahrain	Manama	620	728,700	dinar = 1,000 fils
Bangladesh	Dhaka	144,000	156,050,900	taka = 100 poisha
Barbados	Bridgetown	431	284,600	dollar = 100 cents
Belarus	Minsk	208,000	9,648,500	Belarusian rouble
Belgium	Brussels	30,500	10,414,300	euro = cents
Belize	Belmopan	23,000	307,900	dollar = 100 cents
Benin	Porto Novo	113,000	8,791,800	franc = 100 centimes
Bhutan	Thimphu	46,600	691,100	ngultrum = 100 chetrum, Indian rupee
Bolivia	La Paz	1,099,000	9,775,200	boliviano = 100 centavos
Bosnia and Herzegovina	Sarajevo	51,100	4,613,400	mark = 100 fening
Botswana	Gaborone	600,000	1,990,900	pula = 100 thebe
Brazil	Brasilia	8,512,000	198,739,300	real = 100 centavos
Brunei	Bandar Seri Begawan	5,770	388,200	dollar = 100 sen
Bulgaria	Sofia	111,000	7,204,700	lev = 100 stotinki
Burkina Faso	Ouagadougou	274,000	15,746,200	franc = 100 centimes
Burma (Myanmar)	Naypyidaw	677,000	48,137,700	kyat = 100 pyas
Burundi	Bujumbura	27,800	9,511,300	franc = 100 centimes
Cambodia	Phnom Penh	181,000	14,494,300	riel = 100 sen
Cameroon	Yaoundé	475,000	18,879,300	franc = 100 centimes
Canada	Ottawa	9,976,000	33,487,200	dollar = 100 cents
Cape Verde Islands	Praia	4,030	429,500	escudo = 100 centavos
Central African Republic	Bangui	625,000	4,511,500	franc = 100 centimes
Chad	N'Djamena	1,284,000	10,329,200	franc = 100 centimes
Chile	Santiago	757,000	16,601,700	peso = 100 centavos
China	Beijing	9,561,000	1,338,613,000	yuan = 10 jiao or 100 fen
Colombia	Bogotá	1,140,000	43,677,400	peso = 100 centavos
Comoros	Moroni	1,790	752,400	franc = 100 centimes
Congo	Brazzaville	342,000	4,012,800	franc = 100 centimes
Congo, Democratic Republic of the (Zaire)	Kinshasa	2,344,000	68,692,500	franc = 100 centimes
Costa Rica	San José	51,000	4,253,900	colón = 100 centimos
Côte d'Ivoire	Yamoussoukro	322,000	20,617,100	franc = 100 centimes
Croatia	Zagreb	56,500	4,489,400	kuna = 100 lipa
Cuba	Havana	111,000	11,451,700	peso = 100 centavos
Cyprus	Nicosia	9,250	1,084,700	euro = 100 cents
Czech Republic	Prague	78,900	10,211,900	koruna = 100 halers
Denmark	Copenhagen	43,100	5,500,500	krone = 100 øre
Djibouti	Djibouti	23,300	724,600	franc = 100 centimes
Dominica	Roseau	751	72,700	dollar = 100 cents
Dominican Republic	Santo Domingo	48,400	9,650,100	peso = 100 centavos
East Timor	Dili	14,874	1,131,600	dollar = 100 centavos
Ecuador	Quito	271,000	14,573,100	dollar = 100 centavos
Egypt	Cairo	1,002,000	78,866,600	pound = 100 piastres or 1,000 milliemes

Countries of the World

Country	Capital	Area (sq. km)	Population	Currency unit
El Salvador	San Salvador	21,400	7,185,200	dollar = 100 centavos
Equatorial Guinea	Malabo	28,100	633,400	franc = 100 centimes
Eritrea	Asmara	118,000	5,647,200	nakfa = 100 cents
Estonia	Tallinn	45,100	1,299,400	kroon = 100 sents
Ethiopia	Addis Ababa	1,224,000	85,237,300	birr = 100 cents
Fiji	Suva	18,300	944,700	dollar = 100 cents
Finland	Helsinki	338,000	5,250,300	euro = 100 cents
France	Paris	547,000	64,420,100	euro = 100 cents
Gabon	Libreville	268,000	1,515,000	franc = 100 centimes
Gambia	Banjul	11,300	1,778,100	dalasi = 100 butut
Georgia	Tbilisi	69,700	4,615,800	lari = 100 tetri
Germany	Berlin	357,000	82,329,800	euro = 100 cents
Ghana	Accra	239,000	23,887,800	cedi = 100 pesewas
Greece	Athens	131,000	10,737,400	euro = 100 cents
Grenada	St George's	345	90,700	dollar = 100 cents
Guatemala	Guatemala City	109,000	13,276,500	quetzal = 100 centavos
Guinea	Conakry	246,000	10,058,000	franc = 100 centimes
Guinea-Bissau	Bissau	36,000	1,534,000	franc = 100 centimes
Guyana	Georgetown	215,000	752,900	dollar = 100 cents
Haiti	Port-au-Prince	27,800	9,035,500	gourde = 100 centimes
Honduras	Tegucigalpa	112,000	7,833,700	lempira = 100 centavos
Hungary	Budapest	93,000	9,905,600	forint = 100 filler
Iceland	Reykjavik	103,000	306,700	krona = 100 aurar
India	New Delhi	3,185,000	1,156,897,800	rupee = 100 paisa
Indonesia	Jakarta	1,905,000	240,271,500	rupiah = 100 sen
Iran	Tehran	1,648,000	66,429,300	rial = 100 dinars
Iraq	Baghdad	438,000	28,945,600	dinar = 1,000 fils
Ireland, Republic of	Dublin	70,300	4,203,200	euro = 100 cents
Israel	Jerusalem	20,800	7,233,700	shekel = 100 agora
Italy	Rome	301,000	58,126,200	euro = 100 cents
Ivory Coast (see Côte d'Ivoire)				
Jamaica	Kingston	11,000	2,825,900	dollar = 100 cents
Japan	Tokyo	378,000	127,078,700	yen
Jordan	Amman	97,700	6,269,300	dinar = 1,000 fils
Kazakhstan	Astana	2,717,000	15,399,400	tenge = 100 teins
Kenya	Nairobi	583,000	39,002,800	shilling = 100 cents
Kiribati	Bairiki	717	112,900	Australian dollar
Kuwait	Kuwait City	17,800	2,692,500	dinar = 1,000 fils
Kyrgyzstan	Bishkek	199,000	5,431,700	som = 100 tiyin
Laos	Vientiane	237,000	6,834,300	kip = 100 ats
Latvia	Riga	64,600	2,231,500	lat = 100 santims
Lebanon	Beirut	10,500	4,017,100	pound = 100 piastres
Lesotho	Maseru	30,300	2,130,800	loti = 100 lisente
Liberia	Monrovia	111,000	3,441,800	dollar = 100 cents
Libya	Tripoli	1,776,000	6,324,400	dinar = 1,000 dirhams
Liechtenstein	Vaduz	160	34,800	franc = 100 centimes
Lithuania	Vilnius	65,200	3,555,200	litas = 100 centas
Luxembourg	Luxembourg	2,590	491,800	euro = 100 cents
Macedonia	Skopje	25,700	2,066,700	denar = 100 deni
Madagascar	Antananarivo	587,000	20,653,600	ariary = 5 iraimbilanja
Malawi	Lilongwe	118,000	15,028,800	kwacha = 100 tambala
Malaysia	Kuala Lumpur	330,000	25,715,800	ringgit = 100 sen
Maldives	Male	298	396,300	rufiyaa = 100 laris
Mali	Bamako	1,240,000	13,443,200	franc = 100 centimes
Malta	Valletta	316	405,200	euro = 100 cents
Marshall Islands	Majuro	181	64,500	US dollar
Mauritania	Nouakchott	1,031,000	3,129,500	ouguiya = 5 khoums
Mauritius	Port Louis	2,040	1,284,300	rupee = 100 cents
Mexico	Mexico City	1,958,000	111,211,800	peso = 100 centavos
Micronesia	Palikir	701	107,400	US dollar
Moldova	Chişinău	33,700	4,320,700	leu = 100 bani
Monaco	–	1.5	33,000	euro = 100 cents
Mongolia	Ulan Bator	1,565,000	3,041,100	tugrik = 100 mongos
Montenegro	Podgorica	13,812	672,200	euro = 100 cents

Country	Capital	Area (sq. km)	Population	Currency unit
Morocco	Rabat	459,000	31,285,200	dirham = 100 centimes
Mozambique	Maputo	799,000	21,669,300	metical = 100 centavos
Myanmar (see Burma)				
Namibia	Windhoek	824,000	2,108,700	dollar = 100 cents
Nauru	–	21	14,000	Australian dollar
Nepal	Kathmandu	147,000	28,563,400	rupee = 100 paisa
Netherlands	Amsterdam	37,000	16,716,000	euro = 100 cents
New Zealand	Wellington	268,000	4,213,400	dollar = 100 cents
Nicaragua	Managua	120,000	5,891,200	cordoba = 100 centavos
Niger	Niamey	1,267,000	15,306,300	franc = 100 centimes
Nigeria	Abuja	924,000	149,229,100	naira = 100 kobo
North Korea	Pyongyang	121,000	22,665,300	won = 100 jun
Norway	Oslo	324,000	4,660,500	krone = 100 øre
Oman	Muscat	212,000	3,418,100	rial = 1,000 baiza
Pakistan	Islamabad	804,000	174,578,600	rupee = 100 paisa
Palau	Melekeok	459	20,800	dollar = 100 cents
Panama	Panama City	77,100	3,360,500	balboa = 100 centésimos
Papua New Guinea	Port Moresby	463,000	5,940,800	kina = 100 toea
Paraguay	Asunción	407,000	6,995,700	guarani = 100 centimos
Peru	Lima	1,285,000	29,547,000	sol = 100 cents
Philippines	Manila	300,000	97,976,600	peso = 100 centavos
Poland	Warsaw	304,000	38,482,900	zloty = 100 groszy
Portugal	Lisbon	92,000	10,707,900	euro = 100 cents
Qatar	Doha	11,400	833,300	riyal = 100 dirhams
Romania	Bucharest	229,000	22,215,400	leu = 100 bani
Russia	Moscow	17,075,000	140,041,200	rouble = 100 copecks
Rwanda	Kigali	26,300	10,746,300	franc = 100 centimes
St Kitts and Nevis	Basseterre	261	40,100	dollar = 100 cents
St Lucia	Castries	616	160,300	dollar = 100 cents
St Vincent and the Grenadines	Kingstown	389	104,600	dollar = 100 cents
Samoa	Apia	2,840	220,000	tala = 100 sene
San Marino	San Marino	61	30,200	euro = 100 cents
São Tomé and Principe	São Tomé	964	212,700	dobra = 100 centavos
Saudi Arabia	Riyadh	2,150,000	28,686,600	riyal = 20 qursh or 100 halalas
Senegal	Dakar	197,000	13,711,600	franc = 100 centimes
Serbia	Belgrade	88,361	7,379,300	dinar = 100 paras
Seychelles	Victoria	453	87,500	rupee = 100 cents
Sierra Leone	Freetown	71,700	5,132,100	leone = 100 cents
Singapore	Singapore City	618	4,657,500	dollar = 100 cents
Slovakia	Bratislava	49,000	5,463,000	euro = 100 cents
Slovenia	Ljubljana	20,300	2,005,700	euro = 100 cents
Solomon Islands	Honiara	276,000	595,600	dollar = 100 cents
Somalia	Mogadishu	638,000	9,832,000	shilling = 100 cents
South Africa	Pretoria	1,221,000	49,052,500	rand= 100 cents
South Korea	Seoul	99,300	48,509,000	won = 100 jeon
Spain	Madrid	505,000	40,525,000	euro = 100 cents
Sri Lanka	Colombo	64,000	21,324,800	rupee = 100 cents
Sudan	Khartoum	2,506,000	41,087,800	pound = 100 piastres
Suriname	Paramaribo	163,000	481,300	dollar = 100 cents
Swaziland	Mbabane	17,000	1,337,200	lilangeni = 100 cents
Sweden	Stockholm	450,000	9,059,700	krona = 100 öre
Switzerland	Berne	41,000	7,604,500	franc = 100 centimes
Syria	Damascus	184,000	21,763,000	pound = 100 piastres
Taiwan	Taipei	36,000	22,974,300	New Taiwan dollar = 100 cents
Tajikistan	Dushanbe	143,000	7,349,100	somoni = 100 dirams
Tanzania	Dodoma	940,000	41,048,500	shilling = 100 cents
Thailand	Bangkok	513,000	65,998,400	baht = 100 satangs
Togo	Lomé	57,000	6,031,800	franc = 100 centimes
Tonga	Nuku'alofa	668	120,900	pa'anga = 100 seniti
Trinidad and Tobago	Port-of-Spain	5,130	1,230,000	dollar = 100 cents
Tunisia	Tunis	164,000	10,486,300	dinar = 1,000 milliemes
Turkey	Ankara	779,000	76,805,500	lira = 100 kurus
Turkmenistan	Ashgabat	488,000	4,884,900	manat = 100 tenesi
Tuvalu	Funafuti	26	12,400	dollar = 100 cents

Country	Capital	Area (sq. km)	Population	Currency unit
Uganda	Kampala	241,000	32,369,600	shilling = 100 cents
Ukraine	Kiev	604,000	45,700,400	hryvna = 100 kopiykas
United Arab Emirates	Abu Dhabi	77,770	4,798,500	dirham = 100 fils
United Kingdom	London	244,000	61,113,200	pound = 100 pence
United States	Washington DC	9,373,000	304,059,724	dollar = 100 cents
Uruguay	Montevideo	176,000	3,494,400	peso = 100 centésimos
Uzbekistan	Tashkent	447,000	27,606,000	som = 100 tiyin
Vanuatu	Vila	14,800	218,500	vatu = 100 centimes
Vatican City	–	0.44	800	euro = 100 cents
Venezuela	Caracas	912,000	26,814,800	bolivar = 100 centimos
Vietnam	Hanoi	330,000	88,576,800	dong = 100 xu
Yemen	Sana'a	540,000	22,858,200	riyal = 100 fils
Zambia	Lusaka	753,000	11,862,700	kwacha = 100 ngwee
Zimbabwe	Harare	391,000	11,392,600	dollar = 100 cents

Principal dependencies

Country	Capital	Area	Population	Currency unit
American Samoa (US)	Fagatogo	197	65,600	US dollar
Anguilla (UK)	The Valley	155	14,400	East Caribbean dollar
Aruba (Netherlands)	Oranjestad	193	103,100	florin
Bermuda (UK)	Hamilton	53	67,800	Bermudian dollar
Cayman Islands (UK)	George Town	259	49,000	Cayman Islands dollar
Christmas Island (Australia)	–	135	1,400	Australian dollar
Cocos Islands (Australia)	–	14	600	Australian dollar
Cook Islands (NZ)	Avarua	238	11,900	NZ dollar
Falkland Islands (UK)	Stanley	12,200	3,100	pound
Faroe Islands (Denmark)	Tórshavn	1,400	48,900	Danish krone
French Guiana (France)	Cayenne	91,000	202,000	euro
French Polynesia (France)	Papeete	3,940	287,000	franc
Gibraltar (UK)	Gibraltar	5.9	28,800	pound
Greenland (Denmark)	Nuuk	2,186,100	57,600	Danish krone
Guadeloupe (France)	Basse-Terre	1,780	445,000	euro
Guam (US)	Agaña	541	178,400	US dollar
Martinique (France)	Fort-de-France	1,080	399,000	euro
Mayotte (France)	Mamoutzu	362	223,800	euro
Montserrat (UK)	Plymouth	102	5,100	East Caribbean dollar
Netherlands Antilles (Netherlands)	Willemstad	800	227,000	guilder
New Caledonia (France)	Nouméa	18,600	227,400	franc
Niue (NZ)	Alofi	263	1,400	NZ dollar
Norfolk Island (Australia)	–	35	2,100	Australian dollar
Northern Marianas (US)	Saipan	477	51,500	US dollar
Pitcairn Islands (UK)	–	4.6	50	NZ dollar
Puerto Rico (US)	San Juan	8,960	3,966,200	US dollar
Réunion (France)	Saint-Denis	2,510	807,000	euro
St Helena and dependencies (UK)	Jamestown	420	7,600	pound
St Pierre and Miquelon (France)	St-Pierre	242	7,100	euro
Svalbard (Norway)	Longyearbyen	62,000	2,100	Norwegian krone
Turks and Caicos Islands (UK)	Cockburn Town	430	22,900	US dollar
Virgin Islands (US)	Charlotte Amalie	342	109,800	US dollar
Virgin Islands, British (UK)	Road Town	153	24,500	US dollar
Wallis and Futuna Islands (France)	Mata-Utu	274	15,300	franc
Western Sahara (Morocco)	Laayoune	252,000	405,200	Moroccan dirham

The Commonwealth

THE COMMONWEALTH

The Commonwealth of Nations is a free association of the fifty-four sovereign independent states listed below, together with their associated states and dependencies.

Antigua and Barbuda
Australia
Bahamas
Bangladesh
Barbados
Belize
Botswana
Brunei
Cameroon
Canada
Cyprus
Dominica
Fiji (suspended)
Gambia
Ghana
Grenada
Guyana
India
Jamaica
Kenya
Kiribati
Lesotho
Malawi
Malaysia
Maldives
Malta
Mauritius
Mozambique
Namibia
Nauru
New Zealand
Nigeria
Pakistan
Papua New Guinea
Rwanda
St Kitts and Nevis
St Lucia
St Vincent and the Grenadines
Samoa
Seychelles
Sierra Leone
Singapore
Solomon Islands
South Africa
Sri Lanka
Swaziland
Tanzania
Tonga
Trinidad and Tobago
Tuvalu
Uganda
United Kingdom
Vanuatu
Zambia

THE COMMONWEALTH OF AUSTRALIA

States and territories

State	*Capital*
New South Wales	Sydney
Northern Territory	Darwin
Queensland	Brisbane
South Australia	Adelaide
Tasmania	Hobart
Victoria	Melbourne
Western Australia	Perth
Australian Capital Territory	Canberra (*federal capital*)

CANADA

Federal capital: Ottawa

Provinces and territories

Province	*Postal abbr.*	*Capital*
Alberta	AB	Edmonton
British Columbia	BC	Victoria
Manitoba	MB	Winnipeg
New Brunswick	NB	Fredericton
Newfoundland and Labrador	NF	St John's
Nova Scotia	NS	Halifax
Ontario	ON	Toronto
Prince Edward Island	PE	Charlottetown
Quebec	QC	Quebec
Saskatchewan	SK	Regina
Northwest Territories	NT	Yellowknife
Nunavut	NU	Iqaluit
Yukon Territory	YT	Whitehorse

INDIA

States and Union Territories

State	*Capital*
Andhra Pradesh	Hyderabad
Arunachal Pradesh	Itanagar
Assam	Dispur
Bihar	Patna
Chhattisgarh	Raipur
Delhi	New Delhi
Goa	Panaji
Gujarat	Gandhinagar
Haryana	Chandigarh
Himachal Pradesh	Shimla
Jammu and Kashmir	Srinagar (summer), Jammu (winter)
Jharkand	Ranchi
Karnataka	Bangalore
Kerala	Thiruvananthapuram
Madhya Pradesh	Bhopal
Maharashtra	Mumbai (Bombay)
Manipur	Imphal
Meghalaya	Shillong
Mizoram	Aizawl
Nagaland	Kohima
Orissa	Bhubaneswar
Punjab	Chandigarh
Rajasthan	Jaipur
Sikkim	Gangtok
Tamil Nadu	Chennai (Madras)
Tripura	Agartala
Uttarakhand	Dehra Dun
Uttar Pradesh	Lucknow
West Bengal	Kolkata (Calcutta)
Union Territory	
Andaman and Nicobar Islands	Port Blair
Chandigarh	Chandigarh
Dadra and Nagar Haveli	Silvassa
Daman and Diu	Daman
Lakshadweep	Kavaratti
Puducherry	Puducherry

The European Union

Country	Date of joining	Country	Date of joining	Country	Date of joining	Country	Date of joining
Belgium	1957	Republic of Ireland	1973	Sweden	1995	Malta	2004
France	1957	United Kingdom	1973	Czech Republic	2004	Poland	2004
Italy	1957	Greece	1981	Cyprus	2004	Slovakia	2004
Luxembourg	1957	Spain	1986	Estonia	2004	Slovenia	2004
Netherlands	1957	Portugal	1986	Hungary	2004	Bulgaria	2007
West Germany	1957	Austria	1995	Latvia	2004	Romania	2007
Denmark	1973	Finland	1995	Lithuania	2004		

States of the United States of America

State	Postal abbr.	Capital	Informal name
Alabama	AL	Montgomery	Yellowhammer State, Heart of Dixie, Cotton State
Alaska	AK	Juneau	Great Land
Arizona	AZ	Phoenix	Grand Canyon State
Arkansas	AR	Little Rock	Land of Opportunity
California	CA	Sacramento	Golden State
Colorado	CO	Denver	Centennial State
Connecticut	CT	Hartford	Constitution State, Nutmeg State
Delaware	DE	Dover	First State, Diamond State
Florida	FL	Tallahassee	Sunshine State
Georgia	GA	Atlanta	Empire State of the South, Peach State
Hawaii	HI	Honolulu	Aloha State
Idaho	ID	Boise	Gem State
Illinois	IL	Springfield	Prairie State
Indiana	IN	Indianapolis	Hoosier State
Iowa	IA	Des Moines	Hawkeye State
Kansas	KS	Topeka	Sunflower State
Kentucky	KY	Frankfort	Bluegrass State
Louisiana	LA	Baton Rouge	Pelican State
Maine	ME	Augusta	Pine Tree State
Maryland	MD	Annapolis	Old Line State, Free State
Massachusetts	MA	Boston	Bay State, Old Colony
Michigan	MI	Lansing	Great Lake State, Wolverine State
Minnesota	MN	St Paul	North Star State, Gopher State
Mississippi	MS	Jackson	Magnolia State
Missouri	MO	Jefferson City	Show Me State
Montana	MT	Helena	Treasure State
Nebraska	NE	Lincoln	Cornhusker State
Nevada	NV	Carson City	Sagebrush State, Battleborn State, Silver State
New Hampshire	NH	Concord	Granite State
New Jersey	NJ	Trenton	Garden State
New Mexico	NM	Sante Fe	Land of Enchantment
New York	NY	Albany	Empire State
North Carolina	NC	Raleigh	Tar Heel State, Old North State
North Dakota	ND	Bismarck	Peace Garden State
Ohio	OH	Columbus	Buckeye State
Oklahoma	OK	Oklahoma City	Sooner State
Oregon	OR	Salem	Beaver State
Pennsylvania	PA	Harrisburg	Keystone State
Rhode Island	RI	Providence	Little Rhody, Ocean State
South Carolina	SC	Columbia	Palmetto State
South Dakota	SD	Pierre	Coyote State, Sunshine State
Tennessee	TN	Nashville	Volunteer State
Texas	TX	Austin	Lone Star State
Utah	UT	Salt Lake City	Beehive State
Vermont	VT	Montpelier	Green Mountain State
Virginia	VA	Richmond	Old Dominion
Washington	WA	Olympia	Evergreen State
West Virginia	WV	Charleston	Mountain State
Wisconsin	WI	Madison	Badger State
Wyoming	WY	Cheyenne	Equality State

Prime Ministers and Presidents

PRIME MINISTERS OF GREAT BRITAIN AND OF THE UNITED KINGDOM

[1721]–1742	Sir Robert Walpole	Whig
1742–1743	Earl of Wilmington	"
1743–1754	Henry Pelham	"
1754–1756	Duke of Newcastle	"
1756–1757	Duke of Devonshire	"
1757–1762	Duke of Newcastle	"
1762–1763	Earl of Bute	Tory
1763–1765	George Grenville	Whig
1765–1766	Marquess of Rockingham	"
1766–1768	William Pitt the Elder	"
1768–1770	Duke of Grafton	"
1770–1782	Lord North	Tory
1782	Marquess of Rockingham	Whig
1782–1783	Earl of Shelburne	"
1783	Duke of Portland	coalition
1783–1801	William Pitt the Younger	Tory
1801–1804	Henry Addington	"
1804–1806	William Pitt the Younger	"
1806–1807	Lord William Grenville	Whig
1807–1809	Duke of Portland	Tory
1809–1812	Spencer Perceval	"
1812–1827	Earl of Liverpool	"
1827	George Canning	"
1827–1828	Viscount Goderich	"
1828–1830	Duke of Wellington	"
1830–1834	Earl Grey	Whig
1834	Viscount Melbourne	"
1834	Duke of Wellington	Tory
1834–1835	Sir Robert Peel	Conservative
1835–1841	Viscount Melbourne	Whig
1841–1846	Sir Robert Peel	Conservative
1846–1852	Lord John Russell	Whig
1852	Earl of Derby	Conservative
1852–1855	Earl of Aberdeen	coalition
1855–1858	Viscount Palmerston	Whig
1858–1859	Earl of Derby	Conservative
1859–1865	Viscount Palmerston	Liberal
1865–1866	Earl Russell	Liberal
1866–1868	Earl of Derby	Conservative
1868	Benjamin Disraeli	"
1868–1874	William Ewart Gladstone	Liberal
1874–1880	Benjamin Disraeli	Conservative
1880–1885	William Ewart Gladstone	Liberal
1885–1886	Marquess of Salisbury	Conservative
1886	William Ewart Gladstone	Liberal
1886–1892	Marquess of Salisbury	Conservative
1892–1894	William Ewart Gladstone	Liberal
1894–1895	Earl of Rosebery	"
1895–1902	Marquess of Salisbury	Conservative
1902–1905	Arthur James Balfour	"
1905–1908	Sir Henry Campbell-Bannerman	Liberal
1908–1916	Herbert Henry Asquith	"
1916–1922	David Lloyd George	coalition
1922–1923	Andrew Bonar Law	Conservative
1923–1924	Stanley Baldwin	"
1924	James Ramsay MacDonald	Labour
1924–1929	Stanley Baldwin	Conservative
1929–1935	James Ramsay MacDonald	coalition
1935–1937	Stanley Baldwin	"
1937–1940	Neville Chamberlain	"
1940–1945	Winston Churchill	"
1945–1951	Clement Attlee	Labour
1951–1955	Sir Winston Churchill	Conservative
1955–1957	Sir Anthony Eden	"
1957–1963	Harold Macmillan	"
1963–1964	Sir Alec Douglas-Home	"
1964–1970	Harold Wilson	Labour
1970–1974	Edward Heath	Conservative
1974–1976	Harold Wilson	Labour
1976–1979	James Callaghan	"
1979–1990	Margaret Thatcher	Conservative
1990–1997	John Major	"
1997–2007	Tony Blair	Labour
2007–2010	Gordon Brown	"
2010–	David Cameron	Conservative (in coalition with the Liberal Democrats)

PRIME MINISTERS OF CANADA

1867–1873	John A. Macdonald	Conservative
1873–1878	Alexander Mackenzie	Liberal/Reform
1878–1891	John A. Macdonald	Conservative
1891–1892	John J. C. Abbott	Liberal-Conservative
1892–1894	John S. D. Thompson	Conservative
1894–1896	Mackenzie Bowell	"
1896	Charles Tupper	"
1896–1911	Wilfrid Laurier	Liberal
1911–1920	Robert L. Borden	Conservative
1920–1921	Arthur Meighen	Liberal
1921–1926	W. L. Mackenzie King	"
1926	Arthur Meighen	Conservative
1926–1930	W. L. Mackenzie King	Liberal
1930–1935	Richard B. Bennett	Conservative
1935–1948	W. L. Mackenzie King	Liberal
1948–1957	Louis Stephen St Laurent	"
1957–1963	John George Diefenbaker	Progressive Conservative
1963–1968	Lester B. Pearson	Liberal
1968–1979	Pierre Trudeau	"
1979–1980	Joseph Clark	Progressive Conservative
1980–1984	Pierre Trudeau	Liberal
1984	John Turner	"
1984–	Brian Mulroney	Progressive Conservative
1993	Kim Campbell	"
1993–2003	Jean Chrétien	Liberal
2003–2006	Paul Martin	"
2006–	Stephen Harper	Conservative

PRIME MINISTERS OF AUSTRALIA

1901–1903	Edmund Barton	—
1903–1904	Alfred Deakin	Liberal
1904	John C. Watson	Labor
1904–1905	George Houstoun Reid	Free Trade
1905–1908	Alfred Deakin	Liberal
1908–1909	Andrew Fisher	Labor
1909–1910	Alfred Deakin	Liberal
1910–1913	Andrew Fisher	Labor
1913–1914	Joseph Cook	Liberal
1914–1915	Andrew Fisher	Labor
1915–1923	William M. Hughes	Nationalist
1923–1929	Stanley M. Bruce	"
1929–1932	James H. Scullin	Labor
1932–1939	Joseph A. Lyons	United Australia Party
1939–1941	Robert Gordon Menzies	"
1941	Arthur William Fadden	Country Party
1941–1945	John Curtin	Labor
1945–1949	Joseph Benedict Chifley	Labor
1949–1966	Robert Gordon Menzies	Liberal
1966–1967	Harold Edward Holt	"
1967–1968	John McEwen	Country Party
1968–1971	John Grey Gorton	Liberal
1971–1972	William McMahon	"
1972–1975	Gough Whitlam	Labor
1975–1983	Malcolm Fraser	Liberal
1983–1991	Bob Hawke	Labor
1991–1996	Paul Keating	"
1996–2007	John Howard	Liberal
2007–2010	Kevin Rudd	Labor
2010–	Julia Gillard	"

PRIME MINISTERS OF NEW ZEALAND

(since the emergence of party government in 1891)

1891–1893	John Ballance	Liberal
1893–1906	Richard John Seddon	"
1906	William Hall-Jones	"
1906–1912	Joseph George Ward	"
1912	Thomas Mackenzie	"
1912–1925	William Ferguson Massey	Reform
1925	Francis Henry Dillon Bell	"
1925–1928	Joseph Gordon Coates	"
1928–1930	Joseph George Ward	Liberal
1930–1935	George William Forbes	"
1935–1940	Michael J. Savage	Labour
1940–1949	Peter Fraser	"
1949–1957	Sidney G. Holland	National Party
1957	Keith J. Holyoake	National Party
1957–1960	Walter Nash	Labour
1960–1972	Keith J. Holyoake	National Party
1972	John R. Marshall	"
1972–1974	Norman Kirk	Labour
1974–1975	Wallace Rowling	"
1975–1984	Robert D. Muldoon	National Party
1984–1989	David Lange	Labour
1989–1990	Geoffrey Palmer	"
1990	Mike Moore	"
1990–1997	James B. Bolger	National Party
1997–1999	Jenny Shipley	"
1999–2008	Helen Clark	Labour
2008–	John Key	National Party

PRESIDENTS OF THE UNITED STATES OF AMERICA

1789–1797	1. George Washington	Federalist
1797–1801	2. John Adams	"
1801–1809	3. Thomas Jefferson	Democratic Republican
1809–1817	4. James Madison	"
1817–1825	5. James Monroe	"
1825–1829	6. John Quincy Adams	Independent
1829–1837	7. Andrew Jackson	Democrat
1837–1841	8. Martin Van Buren	"
1841	9. William H. Harrison	Whig
1841–1845	10. John Tyler	Whig, then Democrat
1845–1849	11. James K. Polk	Democrat
1849–1850	12. Zachary Taylor	Whig
1850–1853	13. Millard Fillmore	"
1853–1857	14. Franklin Pierce	Democrat
1857–1861	15. James Buchanan	"
1861–1865	16. Abraham Lincoln	Republican
1865–1869	17. Andrew Johnson	Democrat
1869–1877	18. Ulysses S. Grant	Republican
1877–1881	19. Rutherford B. Hayes	"
1881	20. James A. Garfield	"
1881–1885	21. Chester A. Arthur	"
1885–1889	22. Grover Cleveland	Democrat
1889–1893	23. Benjamin Harrison	Republican
1893–1897	24. Grover Cleveland	Democrat
1897–1901	25. William McKinley	Republican
1901–1909	26. Theodore Roosevelt	"
1909–1913	27. William H. Taft	"
1913–1921	28. Woodrow Wilson	Democrat
1921–1923	29. Warren G. Harding	Republican
1923–1929	30. Calvin Coolidge	"
1929–1933	31. Herbert Hoover	"
1933–1945	32. Franklin D. Roosevelt	Democrat
1945–1953	33. Harry S. Truman	"
1953–1961	34. Dwight D. Eisenhower	Republican
1961–1963	35. John F. Kennedy	Democrat
1963–1969	36. Lyndon B. Johnson	"
1969–1974	37. Richard Nixon	Republican
1974–1977	38. Gerald Ford	"
1977–1981	39. Jimmy Carter	Democrat
1981–1989	40. Ronald Reagan	Republican
1989–1993	41. George Bush	"
1993–2001	42. Bill Clinton	Democrat
2001–2009	43. George W. Bush	Republican
2009–	44. Barack Obama	Democrat

Kings and Queens of England and the United Kingdom

Ruler	Dates of reign	Life
Saxon Line		
Edwy	955–957	died 959
Edgar	959–975	944–975
Edward the Martyr	975–978	*c.*963–978
Ethelred the Unready	978–1016	*c.*969–1016
Edmund Ironside	1016	*c.*980–1016
Danish Line		
Canute (Cnut)	1017–1035	*d.*1035
Harold I	1037–1040	*d.*1040
Hardecanute	1040–1042	*c.*1019–1042
Saxon Line		
Edward the Confessor	1042–1066	*c.*1003–1066
Harold II	1066	*c.*1019–1066
House of Normandy		
William I (the Conqueror)	1066–1087	*c.*1027–1087
William II	1087–1100	*c.*1060–1100
Henry I	1100–1135	1068–1135
Stephen	1135–1154	*c.*1097–1154
House of Plantagenet		
Henry II	1154–1189	1133–1189
Richard I	1189–1199	1157–1199
John	1199–1216	1165–1216
Henry III	1216–1272	1207–1272
Edward I	1272–1307	1239–1307
Edward II	1307–1327	1284–1327
Edward III	1327–1377	1312–1377
Richard II	1377–1399	1367–1400
House of Lancaster		
Henry IV	1399–1413	1367–1413
Henry V	1413–1422	1387–1422
Henry VI	1422–1461, 1470–1	1421–1471
House of York		
Edward IV	1461–1483	1442–1483
Edward V	1483	1470–*c.*1483
Richard III	1483–1485	1452–1485

Ruler	Dates of reign	Life
House of Tudor		
Henry VII	1485–1509	1457–1509
Henry VIII	1509–1547	1491–1547
Edward VI	1547–1553	1537–1553
Mary I	1553–1558	1516–1558
Elizabeth I	1558–1603	1533–1603
House of Stuart		
James I	1603–1625	1566–1625
Charles I	1625–1649	1600–1649
Commonwealth (declared 1649)		
Oliver Cromwell, Lord Protector	1653–1658	1599–1658
Richard Cromwell	1658–1659	1626–1712
House of Stuart		
Charles II	1660–1685	1630–1685
James II	1685–1688	1633–1701
William III and Mary II	1689–1702 (Mary *d.*1694)	William 1650–1702
Anne	1702–1714	1665–1714
House of Hanover		
George I	1714–1727	1660–1727
George II	1727–1760	1683–1760
George III	1760–1820	1738–1820
George IV	1820–1830	1762–1830
William IV	1830–1837	1765–1837
Victoria	1837–1901	1819–1901
House of Saxe-Coburg-Gotha		
Edward VII	1901–1910	1841–1910
House of Windsor		
George V	1910–1936	1865–1936
Edward VIII	1936	1894–1972
George VI	1936–1952	1895–1952
Elizabeth II	1952–	*b.*1926

Weights, Measures, and Notation

The conversion factors are not exact unless so marked. They are given only to the accuracy likely to be needed in everyday calculations.

1. BRITISH AND AMERICAN, WITH METRIC EQUIVALENTS

Linear measure

1 inch	= 25.4 millimetres exactly
1 foot = 12 inches	= 0.3048 metre exactly
1 yard = 3 feet	= 0.9144 metre exactly
1 (statute) mile = 1,760 yards	= 1.609 kilometres
1 nautical mile = 1.150779 miles	= 1.852 kilometres exactly

Square measure

1 square inch	= 6.45 sq. centimetres
1 square foot = 144 sq. inches	= 9.29 sq. decimetres
1 square yard = 9 sq. feet	= 0.836 sq. metre
1 acre = 4,840 sq. yards	= 0.405 hectare
1 square mile = 640 acres	= 259 hectares

Cubic measure

1 cubic inch	= 16.4 cu. centimetres
1 cubic foot = 1,728 cu. inches	= 0.0283 cu. metre
1 cubic yard = 27 cu. feet	= 0.765 cu. metre

Capacity measure

British

1 fluid ounce = 1.7339 cu. inches	= 0.0284 litre
1 gill = 5 fluid ounces	= 0.1421 litre
1 pint = 20 fluid ounces = 34.68 cu. inches	= 0.568 litre
1 quart = 2 pints	= 1.136 litres
1 gallon = 4 quarts	= 4.546 litres
1 peck = 2 gallons	= 9.092 litres
1 bushel = 4 pecks	= 36.4 litres
1 quarter = 8 bushels	= 291.2 litres

American dry

1 pint = 33.60 cu. inches	= 0.550 litre
1 quart = 2 pints	= 1.101 litres
1 peck = 8 quarts	= 8.81 litres
1 bushel = 4 pecks	= 35.3 litres

American liquid

1 pint = 16 fluid ounces = 28.88 cu. inches	= 0.473 litre
1 quart = 2 pints	= 0.946 litre
1 gallon = 4 quarts	= 3.785 litres

Avoirdupois weight

1 grain	= 0.065 gram
1 drachm	= 1.772 grams
1 ounce = 16 drams	= 28.35 grams
1 pound = 16 ounces = 7,000 grains	= 0.4536 kilogram (0.45359237 exactly)
1 stone = 14 pounds	= 6.35 kilograms
1 quarter = 2 stones	= 12.70 kilograms
1 hundredweight = 4 quarters	= 50.80 kilograms
1 (long) ton = 20 hundredweight	= 1.016 tonnes
1 short ton = 2,000 pounds	= 0.907 tonne

2. METRIC, WITH BRITISH EQUIVALENTS

Linear measure

1 millimetre	= 0.039 inch
1 centimetre = 10 mm	= 0.394 inch
1 decimetre = 10 cm	= 3.94 inches
1 metre = 100 cm	= 1.094 yards
1 decametre = 10 m	= 10.94 yards
1 hectometre = 100 m	= 109.4 yards
1 kilometre = 1,000 m	= 0.6214 mile

Square measure

1 square centimetre	= 0.155 sq. inch
1 square metre = 10,000 sq. centimetres	= 1.196 sq. yards
1 are = 100 sq. metres	= 119.6 sq. yards
1 hectare = 100 ares	= 2.471 acres
1 square kilometre = 100 hectares	= 0.386 sq. mile

Cubic measure

1 cubic centimetre	= 0.061 cu. inch
1 cubic metre = 1,000,000 cu. centimetres	= 1.308 cu. yards

Capacity measure

1 millilitre	= 0.002 pint (British)
1 centilitre = 10 millilitres	= 0.018 pint
1 decilitre = 100 millilitres	= 0.176 pint
1 litre = 1,000 millilitres	= 1.76 pints
1 decalitre = 10 litres	= 2.20 gallons
1 hectolitre = 100 litres	= 2.75 bushels
1 kilolitre = 1,000 litres	= 3.44 quarters

Weight

1 milligram	= 0.015 grain
1 centigram = 10 milligrams	= 0.154 grain
1 decigram = 100 milligrams	= 1.543 grain
1 gram = 1,000 milligrams	= 15.43 grain
1 decagram = 10 grams	= 5.64 drams
1 hectogram = 100 grams	= 3.527 ounces
1 kilogram = 1,000 grams	= 2.205 pounds
1 tonne (metric ton) = 1,000 kilograms	= 0.984 (long) ton

3. SI UNITS

Base units

Physical quantity	*Name*	*Abbreviation or symbol*
length	metre	m
mass	kilogram	kg
time	second	s
electric current	ampere	A
temperature	kelvin	K
amount of substance	mole	mol
luminous intensity	candela	cd

Supplementary units

Physical quantity	*Name*	*Abbreviation or symbol*
plane angle	radian	rad
solid angle	steradian	sr

Derived units with special names

Physical quantity	*Name*	*Abbreviation or symbol*
frequency	hertz	Hz
energy	joule	J
force	newton	N
power	watt	W
pressure	pascal	Pa
electric charge	coulomb	C
electromotive force	volt	V
electrical resistance	ohm	Ω
electrical conductance	siemens	S
electrical capacitance	farad	F
magnetic flux	weber	Wb
inductance	henry	H
magnetic flux density	tesla	T
luminous flux	lumen	lm
illumination	lux	lx

4. TEMPERATURE

Fahrenheit: water boils (under standard conditions) at 212° and freezes at 32°.

Celsius or Centigrade: water boils at 100° and freezes at 0°.

Kelvin: water boils at 373.15 kelvins and freezes at 273.15 kelvins.

Celsius	*Fahrenheit*
−17.8°	0°
−10°	14°
0°	32°
10°	50°
20°	68°
30°	86°
40°	104°
50°	122°
60°	140°
70°	158°
80°	176°
90°	194°
100°	212°

To convert Celsius into Fahrenheit: multiply by 9, divide by 5, and add 32.

To convert Fahrenheit into Celsius: subtract 32, multiply by 5, and divide by 9.

5. METRIC PREFIXES

	Abbreviation or symbol	*Factor*
deca-	da	10
hecto-	h	10^2
kilo-	k	10^3
mega-	M	10^6
giga-	G	10^9
tera-	T	10^{12}
peta-	P	10^{15}
exa-	E	10^{18}
deci-	d	10^{-1}
centi-	c	10^{-2}
milli-	m	10^{-3}
micro-	μ	10^{-6}
nano-	n	10^{-9}
pico-	p	10^{-12}
femto-	f	10^{-15}
atto-	a	10^{-18}

Pronunciations and derivations of these are given at their alphabetical places in the dictionary. They may be applied to any units of the metric system: hectogram (hg) = 100 grams; kilowatt (kW) = 1,000 watts; megahertz (MHz) = 1 million hertz; centimetre (cm) = one hundredth of a metre; microvolt (μV) = one millionth of a volt; picofarad (pF) = 10^{-12} farad. They are also sometimes applied to other units (megabit, microinch).

6. POWER NOTATION

This expresses concisely any power of ten (any number that is composed of factors of 10), and is sometimes used in the dictionary. 10^2 or ten squared = 10 x 10 = 100; 10^3 or ten cubed = 10 x 10 x 10 = 1,000. Similarly, 10^4 = 10,000, and 10^{10} = 1 followed by ten noughts = 10,000,000,000. Proceeding in the opposite direction, dividing by ten and subtracting one from the index, we have $10^2 = 100$, $10^1 = 10$, $10^0 = 1$, $10^{-1} = 1/10$, $10^{-2} = 1/100$, and so on; $10^{-10} = 1/10^{10} = 1/10{,}000{,}000{,}000$.

7. BINARY SYSTEM

Only two units (0 and 1) are used, and the position of each unit indicates a power of two.

One to ten written in binary form:

	eights (2^3)	*fours* (2^2)	*twos* (2^1)	*one*
1				1
2			1	0
3			1	1
4		1	0	0
5		1	0	1
6		1	1	0
7		1	1	1
8	1	0	0	0
9	1	0	0	1
10	1	0	1	0

i.e. ten is written as 1010 ($2^3 + 0 + 2^1 + 0$); one hundred is written as 1100100 ($2^6 + 2^5 + 0 + 0 + 2^2 + 0 + 0$).

Chemical Elements

Element	Symbol	Atomic no.	Element	Symbol	Atomic no.	Element	Symbol	Atomic no.	Element	Symbol	Atomic no.
actinium	Ac	89	einsteinium	Es	99	mendelevium	Md	101	rutherfordium	Rf	104
aluminium	Al	13	erbium	Er	68	mercury	Hg	80	samarium	Sm	62
americium	Am	95	europium	Eu	63	molybdenum	Mo	42	scandium	Sc	21
antimony	Sb	51	fermium	Fm	100	neodymium	Nd	60	seaborgium	Sg	106
argon	Ar	18	fluorine	F	9	neon	Ne	10	selenium	Se	34
arsenic	As	33	francium	Fr	87	neptunium	Np	93	silicon	Si	14
astatine	At	85	gadolinium	Gd	64	nickel	Ni	28	silver	Ag	47
barium	Ba	56	gallium	Ga	31	niobium	Nb	41	sodium	Na	11
berkelium	Bk	97	germanium	Ge	32	nitrogen	N	7	strontium	Sr	38
beryllium	Be	4	gold	Au	79	nobelium	No	102	sulphur	S	16
bismuth	Bi	83	hafnium	Hf	72	osmium	Os	76	tantalum	Ta	73
bohrium	Bh	107	hassium	Hs	108	oxygen	O	8	technetium	Tc	43
boron	B	5	helium	He	2	palladium	Pd	46	tellurium	Te	52
bromine	Br	35	holmium	Ho	67	phosphorus	P	15	terbium	Tb	65
cadmium	Cd	48	hydrogen	H	1	platinum	Pt	78	thallium	Tl	81
caesium	Cs	55	indium	In	49	plutonium	Pu	94	thorium	Th	90
calcium	Ca	20	iodine	I	53	polonium	Po	84	thulium	Tm	69
californium	Cf	98	iridium	Ir	77	potassium	K	19	tin	Sn	50
carbon	C	6	iron	Fe	26	praseodymium	Pr	59	titanium	Ti	22
cerium	Ce	58	krypton	Kr	36	promethium	Pm	61	tungsten	W	74
chlorine	Cl	17	lanthanum	La	57	protactinium	Pa	91	uranium	U	92
chromium	Cr	24	lawrencium	Lr	103	radium	Ra	88	vanadium	V	23
cobalt	Co	27	lead	Pb	82	radon	Rn	86	xenon	Xe	54
copper	Cu	29	lithium	Li	3	rhenium	Re	75	ytterbium	Yb	70
curium	Cm	96	lutetium	Lu	71	rhodium	Rh	45	yttrium	Y	39
darmstadtium	Ds	110	magnesium	Mg	12	roentgenium	Rg	111	zinc	Zn	30
dubnium	Db	105	manganese	Mn	25	rubidium	Rb	37	zirconium	Zr	40
dysprosium	Dy	66	meitnerium	Mt	109	ruthenium	Ru	44			

Pending agreement on their permanent names, newly discovered elements are given provisional names (IUPAC) based on the atomic number and formed systematically from the numerical roots *nil* (= 0), *un* (= 1), *bi* (= 2), etc. (*ununbium* = 112, *ununquadium* = 114, *ununhexium* = 116, *ununoctium* = 118).

The Periodic Table

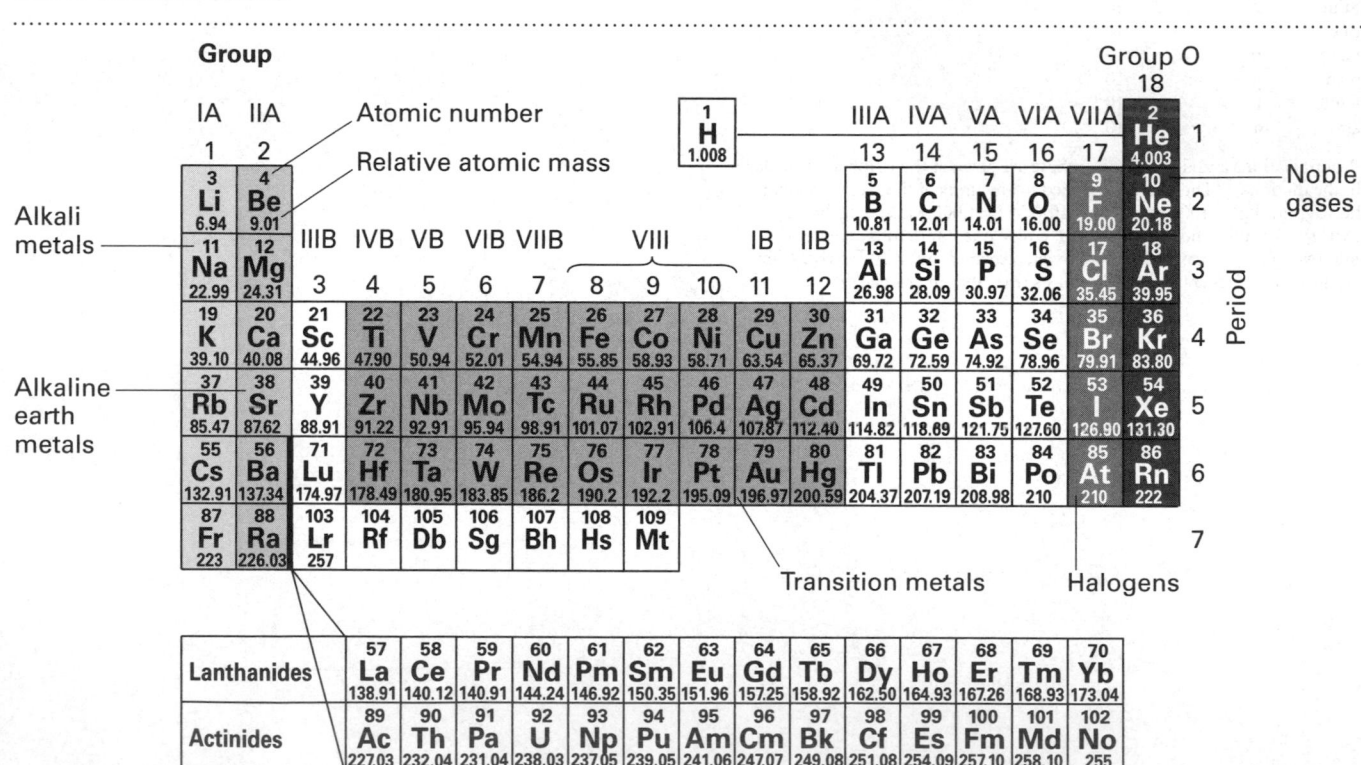

Group

Key: H — Atomic number 1; Relative atomic mass 1.008

Period	IA 1	IIA 2	IIIB 3	IVB 4	VB 5	VIB 6	VIIB 7	VIII 8	VIII 9	VIII 10	IB 11	IIB 12	IIIA 13	IVA 14	VA 15	VIA 16	VIIA 17	Group O 18
1	1 H 1.008																	2 He 4.003
2	3 Li 6.94	4 Be 9.01											5 B 10.81	6 C 12.01	7 N 14.01	8 O 16.00	9 F 19.00	10 Ne 20.18
3	11 Na 22.99	12 Mg 24.31											13 Al 26.98	14 Si 28.09	15 P 30.97	16 S 32.06	17 Cl 35.45	18 Ar 39.95
4	19 K 39.10	20 Ca 40.08	21 Sc 44.96	22 Ti 47.90	23 V 50.94	24 Cr 52.01	25 Mn 54.94	26 Fe 55.85	27 Co 58.93	28 Ni 58.71	29 Cu 63.54	30 Zn 65.37	31 Ga 69.72	32 Ge 72.59	33 As 74.92	34 Se 78.96	35 Br 79.91	36 Kr 83.80
5	37 Rb 85.47	38 Sr 87.62	39 Y 88.91	40 Zr 91.22	41 Nb 92.91	42 Mo 95.94	43 Tc 98.91	44 Ru 101.07	45 Rh 102.91	46 Pd 106.4	47 Ag 107.87	48 Cd 112.40	49 In 114.82	50 Sn 118.69	51 Sb 121.75	52 Te 127.60	53 I 126.90	54 Xe 131.30
6	55 Cs 132.91	56 Ba 137.34	71 Lu 174.97	72 Hf 178.49	73 Ta 180.95	74 W 183.85	75 Re 186.2	76 Os 190.2	77 Ir 192.2	78 Pt 195.09	79 Au 196.97	80 Hg 200.59	81 Tl 204.37	82 Pb 207.19	83 Bi 208.98	84 Po 210	85 At 210	86 Rn 222
7	87 Fr 223	88 Ra 226.03	103 Lr 257	104 Rf	105 Db	106 Sg	107 Bh	108 Hs	109 Mt									

Alkali metals (Group 1); Alkaline earth metals (Group 2); Transition metals; Halogens (Group 17); Noble gases (Group 18)

Lanthanides	57 La 138.91	58 Ce 140.12	59 Pr 140.91	60 Nd 144.24	61 Pm 146.92	62 Sm 150.35	63 Eu 151.96	64 Gd 157.25	65 Tb 158.92	66 Dy 162.50	67 Ho 164.93	68 Er 167.26	69 Tm 168.93	70 Yb 173.04
Actinides	89 Ac 227.03	90 Th 232.04	91 Pa 231.04	92 U 238.03	93 Np 237.05	94 Pu 239.05	95 Am 241.06	96 Cm 247.07	97 Bk 249.08	98 Cf 251.08	99 Es 254.09	100 Fm 257.10	101 Md 258.10	102 No 255

The Solar System

THE SUN AND PLANETS

Planet	*Mean distance from sun* (10^6 km)	*Equatorial diameter* (km)	*Mass* (earth = 1)	*Volume* (earth = 1)	*Orbital period or 'year'*	*Rotation period or 'day'*
Sun	–	1,400,000	330,000	1,300,000	–	25d*
Mercury	57.9	4,878	0.06	0.06	87.97d	58.65d
Venus	108.2	12,102	0.81	0.86	224.7d	243.0d(R)
Earth	149.6	12,756	1.00	1.00	365.3d	23.93h
Mars	227.9	6,786	0.11	0.15	687.0d	24.62h
Jupiter	778.3	142,980	318	1,323	11.86y	9.93h*
Saturn	1,427	120,540	95.2	752	29.46y	10.66h*
Uranus	2,871	51,120	14.5	64	84.01y	17.24h*(R)
Neptune	4,497	49,530	17.1	54	164.8y	16.11h*

*At equator. (R) retrograde.

PRINCIPAL PLANETARY SATELLITES

Planet	*Satellite*	*Year of discovery*	*Diameter* (km)	*Mean distance from centre of planet* (10^3 km)	*Orbital period* (d)
Earth	Moon	–	3,476	384.4	27.32
Mars	Phobos	1877	27*	9.4	0.319
	Deimos	1877	15*	23.5	1.262
Jupiter	Amalthea	1892	262*	181	0.498
	Io	1610	3,630	422	1.769
	Europa	1610	3,138	671	3.551
	Ganymede	1610	5,262	1,070	7.155
	Callisto	1610	4,800	1,883	16.69
Saturn	Mimas	1789	390	199	0.942
	Enceladus	1789	500	238	1.370
	Tethys	1684	1,050	295	1.888
	Dione	1684	1,120	377	2.737
	Rhea	1672	1,530	527	4.518
	Titan	1655	5,150	1,222	15.95
	Hyperion	1848	340*	1,481	21.28
	Iapetus	1671	1,440	3,561	79.33
	Phoebe	1898	220	12,952	550.5(R)
Uranus	Miranda	1948	480	130	1.414
	Ariel	1851	1,160	191	2.520
	Umbriel	1851	1,190	266	4.144
	Titania	1787	1,600	436	8.706
	Oberon	1787	1,550	583	13.46
Neptune	Proteus	1989	400	118	1.12
	Triton	1846	2,700	354	5.877(R)
	Nereid	1949	340	551	360.2

*Irregular: maximum dimension. (R) retrograde.

Many other small satellites are known for Jupiter, Saturn, Uranus, and Neptune.

Pluto was formerly regarded as the ninth planet, but in 2006 the International Astronomical Union declared it to be a dwarf planet rather than a planet proper.

Alphabets, Accents, and Symbols

Arabic

Alone	Final	Medial	Initial		
ا	ـا			'alif	'
ب	ـب	ـبـ	بـ	bā'	b
ت	ـت	ـتـ	تـ	tā'	t
ث	ـث	ـثـ	ثـ	thā'	th
ج	ـج	ـجـ	جـ	jīm	j
ح	ـح	ـحـ	حـ	ḥā'	ḥ
خ	ـخ	ـخـ	خـ	khā'	kh
د	ـد			dāl	d
ذ	ـذ			dhāl	dh
ر	ـر			rā'	r
ز	ـز			zāy	z
س	ـس	ـسـ	سـ	sīn	s
ش	ـش	ـشـ	شـ	shīn	sh
ص	ـص	ـصـ	صـ	ṣād	ṣ
ض	ـض	ـضـ	ضـ	ḍād	ḍ
ط	ـط	ـطـ	طـ	ṭā'	ṭ
ظ	ـظ	ـظـ	ظـ	ẓā'	ẓ
ع	ـع	ـعـ	عـ	'ayn	'
غ	ـغ	ـغـ	غـ	ghayn	gh
ف	ـف	ـفـ	فـ	fā'	f
ق	ـق	ـقـ	قـ	qāf	q
ك	ـك	ـكـ	كـ	kāf	k
ل	ـل	ـلـ	لـ	lām	l
م	ـم	ـمـ	مـ	mīm	m
ن	ـن	ـنـ	نـ	nūn	n
ه	ـه	ـهـ	هـ	hā'	h
و	ـو			wāw	w
ى	ـى	ـيـ	يـ	yā'	y

Hebrew

א	'aleph	'
ב	beth	b, bh
ג	gimel	g, gh
ד	daleth	d, dh
ה	he	h
ו	waw	w
ז	zayin	z
ח	ḥeth	ḥ
ט	ṭeth	ṭ
י	yodh	y
כ ך	kaph	k, kh
ל	lamedh	l
מ ם	mem	m
נ ן	nun	n
ס	samekh	s
ע	'ayin	'
פ ף	pe	p, ph
צ ץ	ṣadhe	ṣ
ק	qoph	q
ר	resh	r
שׂ	śin	ś
שׁ	shin	sh
ת	taw	t, th

Greek

Α α	alpha	a
Β β	beta	b
Γ γ	gamma	g
Δ δ	delta	d
Ε ε	epsilon	e
Ζ ζ	zeta	z
Η η	eta	ē
Θ θ	theta	th
Ι ι	iota	i
Κ κ	kappa	k
Λ λ	lambda	l
Μ μ	mu	m
Ν ν	nu	n
Ξ ξ	xi	x
Ο ο	omicron	o
Π π	pi	p
Ρ ρ	rho	r, rh
Σ σ ς	sigma	s
Τ τ	tau	t
Υ υ	upsilon	u
Φ φ	phi	ph
Χ χ	chi	kh
Ψ ψ	psi	ps
Ω ω	omega	ō

Russian

А а	a
Б б	b
В в	v
Г г	g
Д д	d
Е е	e, ye
Ё ё	yo
Ж ж	zh
З з	z
И и	i
Й й	ĭ
К к	k
Л л	l
М м	m
Н н	n
О о	o
П п	p
Р р	r
С с	s
Т т	t
У у	u
Ф ф	f
Х х	kh
Ц ц	ts
Ч ч	ch
Ш ш	sh
Щ щ	shch
Ъ ъ	″ ('hard sign')
Ы ы	y
Ь ь	′ ('soft sign')
Э э	e
Ю ю	yu
Я я	ya

DIACRITICS, ACCENTS, AND SPECIAL SORTS

á, é	acute
æ	ae ligature
&	ampersand
Æ, æ, ᚫ	Old English ash
Å, å	Scandinavian circled a
*	asterisk
⁂	asterism
@	at sign
ʿ	Arabic ayn, Hebrew ayin
\	backslash
( )	round brackets, parentheses
[ ]	square brackets
{ }	curly brackets, braces
< >	angle brackets
⟨ ⟩	narrow angle brackets
⟦ ⟧	double brackets
ă, ĕ	breve
^	caret
¢	cent sign
ç	cedilla
☧	chi-rho
â, î	circumflex
©	copyright
†	dagger/obelus
‡	double dagger
°	degree
₰	delete
ä, ü	diaeresis/umlaut
„	ditto mark
$	dollar sign
. . .	ellipsis/omission dots
—	em dash
–	en dash
ß	German *Eszett*
Ð, ᴆ, ð	Old English eth
€	euro sign
¡	Spanish inverted exclamation mark
♭	flat sign
/	forward slash/solidus
à, è	grave
᾿	Greek smooth breathing/lenis
῾	Greek rough breathing/ asper
«	opening guillemets
»	closing guillemets
ǎ, č	háček
ʾ	Arabic hamza, Hebrew aleph
#	hash
ę, ǫ	hook, ogonek
ᾳ, ῃ	Greek iota subscript
ſ	archaic long s
ā, ē	macron
Ø, ø	Scandinavian crossed o
œ	oe ligature
¶	paragraph mark
𝄐	pause mark
%	per cent
‰	per mille
£	pound sign
′	prime/minute
″	double prime/second
¿	Spanish inverted question mark
ə	schwa
§	section mark
♯	sharp sign
‐	sloping/soft hyphen
~	swung dash
Ꝥ, ꝥ, Ꝧ, Ꝧ	Old English thorn
ã, ñ	tilde
®	trademark
‖	tramlines
ü, ï	umlaut/diaeresis
Ƿ, ƿ	Old English wyn
¥	yen sign
Ȝ, ȝ	Old English yogh

MATHEMATICAL SYMBOLS

∞	infinity
$\int$	integral
$\sum$	summation
π	pi
$\prod$	product
$=$	equal to
$\neq$	not equal to
$\equiv$	identically equal to
$\not\equiv$	not identically equal to
$\approx$	approximately equal to
$\not\approx$	not approximately equal to
$\sim$	equivalent to, of the order of
$\not\sim$	not equivalent to, not of the order of
$\propto$	proportional to
$\rightarrow$	approaches
$>$	greater than
$\not>$	not greater than
$<$	less than
$\not<$	not less than
$\gg$	much greater than
$\ll$	much less than
$\geq$	greater than or equal to
$\leq$	less than or equal to
$\wedge$	vector product
$\emptyset$	the empty set
$+$	plus
$-$	minus
$\pm$	plus or minus
$\mp$	minus or plus
$p!$	factorial *p*
$'$	prime
$''$	double prime
$^\circ$	degree
$\angle$	angle
$:$	ratio
$::$	proportion
$\therefore$	therefore, hence
$\because$	because

The Beaufort Scale of Wind Force

Beaufort number	Knots	Kilometres per hour	Description of wind	Specifications for use at sea	Specifications for use on land
	Equivalent speed at 10 m above ground				
0	< 1	< 1	Calm	Sea like a mirror	Calm, smoke rises vertically
1	1–3	1–6	Light air	Ripples with the appearance of scales formed but without foam crests	Direction of wind shown by smoke drift, but not by wind vanes
2	4–6	7–12	Light breeze	Small wavelets, still short but more pronounced; crests have a glassy appearance and do not break	Wind felt on face; leaves rustle; ordinary vane moved by wind
3	7–10	13–19	Gentle breeze	Large wavelets; crests begin to break; foam of glassy appearance; perhaps scattered white horses	Leaves and small twigs in constant motion; wind extends light flag
4	11–16	20–30	Moderate breeze	Small waves, becoming longer; fairly frequent white horses	Raises dust and loose paper; small branches moved
5	17–21	31–39	Fresh breeze	Moderate waves, taking a more pronounced long form; many white horses are formed; chance of some spray	Small trees in leaf begin to sway; crested wavelets form on inland waters
6	22–27	40–50	Strong breeze	Large waves begin to form; the white foam crests are more extensive everywhere; probably some spray	Large branches in motion; whistling heard in telegraph wires; umbrellas used with difficulty
7	28–33	51–62	Near gale	Sea heaps up and white foam from breaking waves begins to be blown in streaks along the direction of the wind	Whole trees in motion; inconvenience felt when walking against wind
8	34–40	63–74	Gale	Moderately high waves of greater length; edges of crests begin to break into spindrift; the foam is blown in well-marked streaks along the direction of the wind	Breaks twigs off trees; generally impedes progress
9	41–47	75–87	Strong gale	High waves; dense streaks of foam along the direction of the wind; crests of waves begin to topple, tumble, and roll over; spray may affect visibility	Slight structural damage occurs (chimney pots and slates removed)
10	48–55	88–102	Storm	Very high waves with long overhanging crests; the resulting foam, in great patches, is blown in dense white streaks along the direction of the wind; on the whole, the surface of the sea takes a white appearance; the tumbling of the sea becomes heavy; visibility affected	Seldom experienced inland; trees uprooted; considerable structural damage occurs
11	56–63	103–117	Violent storm	Exceptionally high waves (small and medium-sized ships might be for a time lost to view behind the waves); the sea is completely covered with long white patches of foam lying along the direction of the wind; everywhere the edges of the wave crests are blown into froth; visibility affected	Very rarely experienced; accompanied by widespread damage
12	> 64	> 118	Hurricane	The air is filled with foam and spray; sea completely white with driving spray; visibility very seriously affected	–

Collective Nouns

Terms marked * belong to 15th-century lists of 'proper terms', notably that in the *Book of St Albans* attributed to Dame Juliana Barnes (1486). Many of these are fanciful or humorous terms which probably never had any real currency, but have been taken up by Joseph Strutt in *Sports and Pastimes of England* (1801) and by other antiquarian writers.

a *shrewdness of **apes**
a herd or *pace of **asses**
a *cete of **badgers**
a *sloth or *sleuth of **bears**
a hive of **bees**; a swarm, drift, or bike of **bees**
a flock, flight, (*dial.*) parcel, pod, *fleet, or *dissimulation of (small) **birds**; a volary of **birds** in an aviary
a sounder of **wild boar**
a *blush of **boys**
a herd or gang of **buffalo**
a *clowder or *glaring of **cats**; a *dowt (= ?do-out) or *destruction of **wild cats**
a herd, drove, (*dial.*) drift, or (*US* & *Austral.*) mob of **cattle**
a brood, (*dial.*) cletch or clutch, or *peep of **chickens**
a *chattering or *clattering of **choughs**
a *drunkship of **cobblers**
a *rag or *rake of **colts**
a *hastiness of **cooks**
a *covert of **coots**
a herd of **cranes**
a litter of **cubs**
a herd of **curlew**
a *cowardice of **curs**
a herd or mob of **deer**
a pack or kennel of **dogs**
a trip of **dotterel**
a flight, *dole, or *piteousness of **doves**
a raft, bunch, or *paddling of **ducks** on water; a team of **wild ducks** in flight
a fling of **dunlins**
a herd of **elephants**
a herd or (*US*) gang of **elk**
a *business of **ferrets**
a charm or *chirm of **finches**
a shoal of **fish**; a run of **fish** in motion
a cloud of **flies**
a *stalk of **foresters**
a *skulk of **foxes**
a gaggle or (in the air) a skein, team, or wedge of **geese**
a herd of **giraffes**
a flock, herd, or (*dial.*) trip of **goats**
a pack or covey of **grouse**
a *husk or *down of **hares**
a cast of **hawks** let fly
an *observance of **hermits**
a *siege of **herons**
a stud or *haras of (breeding) **horses**; (*dial.*) a team of **horses**
a kennel, pack, cry, or *mute of **hounds**
a flight or swarm of **insects**
a mob or troop of **kangaroos**
a kindle of **kittens**
a bevy of **ladies**
a *desert of **lapwing**
an *exaltation or bevy of **larks**
a *leap of **leopards**
a pride of **lions**
a *tiding of **magpies**
a *sord or *sute (= suit) of **mallard**
a *richesse of **martens**
a *faith of **merchants**
a *labour of **moles**
a troop of **monkeys**
a *barren of **mules**
a *watch of **nightingales**
a *superfluity of **nuns**
a covey of **partridges**
a *muster of **peacocks**
a *malapertness (= impertinence) of **pedlars**
a rookery of **penguins**
a head or (*dial.*) nye of **pheasants**
a kit of **pigeons** flying together
a herd of **pigs**
a stand, wing, or *congregation of **plovers**
a rush or flight of **pochards**
a herd, pod, or school of **porpoises**
a *pity of **prisoners**
a covey of **ptarmigan**
a litter of **pups**
a bevy or drift of **quail**
a string of **racehorses**
an *unkindness of **ravens**
a bevy of **roe deer**
a parliament or *building of **rooks**
a hill of **ruffs**
a herd or rookery of **seals**; a pod of **seals**
a flock, herd, (*dial.*) drift or trip, or (*Austral.*) mob of **sheep**
a *dopping of **sheldrake**
a wisp or *walk of **snipe**
a *host of **sparrows**
a *murmuration of **starlings**
a flight of **swallows**
a game or herd of **swans**; a wedge of **swans** in the air
a herd of **swine**; a *sounder of tame **swine**, a *drift of **wild swine**
a *glozing (= fawning) of **taverners**
a *spring of **teal**
a bunch or knob of **waterfowl**
a school, herd, or gam of **whales**; a pod of **whales**; a grind of **bottle-nosed whales**
a company or trip of **wigeon**
a bunch, trip, or plump of **wildfowl**; a knob (less than 30) of **wildfowl**
a pack or *rout of **wolves**
a gaggle of **women** (*derog.*)
a *fall of **woodcock**
a herd of **wrens**

M[1] (also **m**) ▸ **noun** (pl. **Ms** or **M's**) **1** the thirteenth letter of the alphabet. ■ denoting the next after L in a set of items, categories, etc.
2 the Roman numeral for 1,000. [from Latin *mille*.]

M[2] ▸ **abbreviation** ■ Cricket (on scorecards) maiden over(s). ■ male. ■ Malta (international vehicle registration). ■ medium (as a clothes size). ■ [in combination] (in units of measurement) mega-: *8 Mbytes of memory*. ■ Astronomy Messier (catalogue of nebulae): *the galaxy M33*. ■ Chemistry (with reference to solutions) molar. ■ Monsieur. ■ (in UK road designations) motorway: *the M25*. ■ used with following numeral in measures of money supply: *broad money, M3, grew by an annualized 9.7 per cent*.
▸ **symbol** Physics mutual inductance.

m ▸ **abbreviation** ■ mare. ■ married. ■ masculine. ■ (*m-*) [in combination] Chemistry meta-: *m-xylene*. ■ metre(s). ■ mile(s). ■ [in combination] (in units of measurement) milli-: *the generator operated at 40 kV and 100 mA*. ■ million(s): *£5 m*. ■ minute(s).
▸ **symbol** Physics mass: $E = mc^2$.

m' ▸ **possessive determiner** Brit. short for **MY** (representing the pronunciation used by lawyers in court to refer to or address the judge or a fellow barrister on the same side): *m'learned friend*.

'm[1] ▸ **abbreviation** informal am: *I'm a doctor*.

'm[2] ▸ **noun** informal madam: *yes'm*.

m- ▸ **prefix** denoting commercial activity conducted electronically by means of mobile phones: *m-commerce*.

MA ▸ **abbreviation** ■ Massachusetts (in official postal use). ■ Master of Arts: *David Jones, MA*. ■ Morocco (international vehicle registration). [from French *Maroc*.]

ma ▸ **noun** informal one's mother.
– ORIGIN early 19th cent.: abbreviation of **MAMA**.

ma'am ▸ **noun** a term of respectful or polite address used for: ■ Brit. female royalty. ■ Brit. a female officer in the police or armed forces who is senior to the speaker. ■ N. Amer. or archaic a woman.
– ORIGIN mid 17th cent.: contraction of **MADAM**.

maar /mɑː/ ▸ **noun** Geology a broad, shallow crater, typically filled by a lake, formed by a volcanic eruption with little lava.
– ORIGIN early 19th cent.: from German dialect, originally denoting a kind of crater lake in the Eifel district of Germany.

Maas /mɑːs/ Dutch name for **MEUSE**.

maas /mɑːs/ ▸ **noun** [mass noun] S. African thick, naturally soured milk.
– ORIGIN Afrikaans, from Zulu *amasi* (plural), denoting curdled milk.

Maasai ▸ **noun & adjective** variant spelling of **MASAI**.

maasbanker /mɑːs'baŋkə/ ▸ **noun** (pl. **same** or **maasbankers**) South African term for **HORSE MACKEREL**.
– ORIGIN from Dutch *marsbanker*.

Maastricht /'mɑːstrɪxt/ an industrial city in the Netherlands, capital of the province of Limburg, situated on the River Maas near the Belgian and German borders; pop. 118,004 (2008).

Maastricht Treaty a treaty on European economic and monetary union, agreed by the heads of government of the twelve member states of the European Community at a summit meeting in Maastricht in December 1991. Ratification was completed in October 1993.

Maat /mɑːt/ Egyptian Mythology the goddess of truth, justice, and cosmic order, daughter of the sun god Ra. She is depicted as a young and beautiful woman, standing or seated, with a feather on her head.

mabela /mə'biːlə/ (also **mabele**) ▸ **noun** [mass noun] S. African sorghum of a variety grown in southern Africa, used for making porridge and beer. ■ meal or porridge made from mabela.
– ORIGIN early 19th cent.: compare with Zulu and Xhosa *amabele*, plural of *ibele*.

Mabinogion /ˌmabɪ'nɒɡɪən, -'nəʊɡɪən/ a collection of Welsh prose tales of the 11th–13th centuries, dealing with Celtic legends and mythology.
– ORIGIN from Welsh *Mabinogi* 'instruction for young bards'.

Mabuse /mə'buːsə, mə'buːz/, Jan (*c*.1478–*c*.1533), Flemish painter; Flemish name *Jan Gossaert*. He was one of the first artists to disseminate the Italian style in the Netherlands.

Mac[1] ▸ **noun** trademark a type of personal computer.
– ORIGIN 1980s: from *Macintosh*, the brand name of a range of computers manufactured by Apple Computer Inc.; the range was named after a variety of dessert apple (see **MCINTOSH**).

Mac[2] ▸ **noun** N. Amer. informal a form of address for a man whose name is unknown to the speaker.
– ORIGIN early 17th cent. (originally a form of address to a Scotsman): from *Mac-*, a patronymic prefix in many Scots and Irish surnames.

mac (also **mack**) ▸ **noun** Brit. informal a mackintosh.
– ORIGIN early 20th cent.: abbreviation.

macabre /mə'kɑːbr(ə)/ ▸ **adjective** disturbing because concerned with or causing a fear of death: *a macabre series of murders*.
– ORIGIN late 19th cent.: from French *macabre*, from *Danse Macabre* 'dance of death', from Old French, perhaps from *Macabé* 'a Maccabee', with reference to a miracle play depicting the slaughter of the Maccabees.

macadam /mə'kadəm/ ▸ **noun** [mass noun] broken stone of even size, bound with tar or bitumen and used in successively compacted layers for surfacing roads and paths.
– DERIVATIVES **macadamed** adjective.
– ORIGIN early 19th cent.: named after John L. *McAdam* (1756–1836), the British surveyor who advocated using this material.

macadamia /ˌmakə'deɪmɪə/ ▸ **noun** an Australian rainforest tree with slender, glossy evergreen leaves and globular edible nuts. ● Genus *Macadamia*, family Proteaceae: several species, especially *M. integrifolia* and *M. tetraphylla*.
■ (also **macadamia nut**) the edible nut of the macadamia tree.
– ORIGIN modern Latin, named after John *Macadam* (1827–65), Australian chemist.

macadamized (also **macadamised**) ▸ **adjective** covered with macadam: *macadamized roads*.

macajuel /'makəwɛl/ ▸ **noun** West Indian term for **BOA CONSTRICTOR**.
– ORIGIN from an American Indian word.

McAleese /ˌmakə'liːs/, Mary (Patricia) (b.1951), Irish stateswoman, President since 1997.

MacAlpin /mə'kalpɪn/, Kenneth, see **KENNETH I**.

Macanese /ˌmakə'niːz/ ▸ **noun** (pl. **same**) **1** a native or inhabitant of Macao, especially one of mixed Chinese and Portuguese descent.
2 [mass noun] a Portuguese Creole formerly used in Macao.
▸ **adjective** relating to Macao or the Macanese.
– ORIGIN from **MACAO**, on the pattern of words such as *Japanese*.

Macao /mə'kaʊ/ a former Portuguese dependency on the SE coast of China, on the west side of the Pearl River estuary opposite Hong Kong; pop. 433,700 (est. 2006); official languages, Portuguese and Cantonese; capital, Macao City. Portuguese name **MACAU**.

> The area comprises the Macao peninsula and two nearby islands. Macao was developed by the Portuguese as a trading post, becoming in the 18th century the chief centre of trade between Europe and China. Under the terms of a 1987 agreement sovereignty passed to China in 1999.

Macapá /ˌmakə'pɑː/ a town in northern Brazil, on the Amazon delta, capital of the state of Amapá; pop. 344,153 (2007).

macaque /mə'kɑːk, -'kak/ ▸ **noun** a medium-sized, chiefly forest-dwelling Old World monkey which has a long face and cheek pouches for holding food. ● Genus *Macaca*, family Cercopithecidae: several species, including the rhesus monkey.
– ORIGIN late 17th cent.: via French and Portuguese; based on the Bantu morpheme *ma* (denoting a plural) + *kaku* 'monkey'.

Macarena /ˌmakə'raɪnə/ ▸ **noun** a dance performed with exaggerated hip motion to a fast Latin rhythm.
– ORIGIN apparently from the title of a song by the Spanish duo Los del Rio (1993).

Macaronesia /ˌmakərə(ʊ)'niːzɪə/ Botany a phytogeographical region comprising the Azores, Madeira, the Canary Islands, and the Cape Verde Islands in the eastern North Atlantic.
– DERIVATIVES **Macaronesian** adjective.
– ORIGIN from Greek *makarōn nēsoi* 'islands of the Blessed' (mythical islands later associated with the Canaries).

macaroni /ˌmakə'rəʊni/ ▸ **noun** (pl. **macaronies**) **1** [mass noun] pasta in the shape of narrow tubes.
2 an 18th-century British dandy who imitated continental fashions.
– ORIGIN early 16th cent.: from Italian *maccaroni* (now usually spelled *maccheroni*), plural of *maccarone*, from late Greek *makaria* 'food made from barley'.

macaronic /ˌmakə'rɒnɪk/ ▸ **adjective** denoting language, especially burlesque verse, containing words or inflections from one language introduced into the context of another.
▸ **noun** (**macaronics**) macaronic verse, especially that which mixes the vernacular with Latin.
– ORIGIN early 17th cent. (in the sense 'characteristic of a jumble or medley'): from modern Latin *macaronicus*, from obsolete Italian *macaronico*, a humorous formation from *macaroni* (see **MACARONI**).

macaroni cheese ▸ **noun** [mass noun] Brit. a savoury dish of macaroni in a cheese sauce.

macaroni penguin ▸ **noun** a penguin with an orange crest, breeding on islands in the Antarctic. ● *Eudyptes chrysolophus*, family Spheniscidae.

– ORIGIN early 19th cent.: so named because the orange crest was thought to resemble the hairstyle of dandies known as *macaronies* (see MACARONI).

macaroon /ˌmakəˈruːn/ ▸ **noun** a light biscuit made with egg white, sugar, and ground almonds or coconut.
– ORIGIN late 16th cent.: from French *macaron*, from Italian *maccarone* (see MACARONI).

MacArthur, Douglas (1880–1964), American general. Commander of US (later Allied) forces in the SW Pacific during the Second World War, he accepted Japan's surrender in 1945, and administered the ensuing Allied occupation.

Macassar /məˈkasə/ ▸ **noun 1** (also **Macassar oil**) [mass noun] a kind of oil formerly used by men to make their hair shine and lie flat.
2 variant spelling of **MAKASSAR**.
– ORIGIN mid 17th cent.: earlier form of **MAKASSAR**. The oil was originally represented as consisting of ingredients from Makassar.

Macau /məˈkau/ Portuguese name for **MACAO**.

Macaulay /məˈkɔːli/, Thomas Babington, 1st Baron (1800–59), English historian, essayist, and philanthropist. He was a civil servant in India before returning to Britain and devoting himself to literature and politics. Notable works: *The Lays of Ancient Rome* (1842) and *History of England* (1849–61).

macaw /məˈkɔː/ ▸ **noun** a large long-tailed parrot with brightly coloured plumage, native to Central and South America. ● *Ara* and related genera: family Psittacidae: several species.
– ORIGIN early 17th cent.: from obsolete Portuguese *macau*, of unknown origin.

Macbeth (*c.*1005–57), king of Scotland 1040–57. He came to the throne after killing his cousin Duncan I in battle, and was himself defeated and killed by Malcolm III. Shakespeare's tragedy *Macbeth* considerably embroiders the historical events.

Macc. ▸ **abbreviation** Maccabees (Apocrypha) (in biblical references).

Maccabaeus, Judas, see **JUDAS MACCABAEUS**.

M

Maccabees /ˈmakəbiːz/ ▸ **plural noun** historical the members or followers of the family of the Jewish leader Judas Maccabaeus. ■ (in full **the Books of the Maccabees**) four books of Jewish history and theology, of which the first and second are in the Apocrypha and feature Judas Maccabaeus.
– DERIVATIVES **Maccabean** /ˌmakəˈbiːən/ **adjective**.
– ORIGIN late Middle English: from Latin *Maccabaeus*, an epithet applied to Judas, perhaps from Hebrew *maqqeḇeṯ* 'hammer' (by association with the religious revolt led by Judas).

McCarthy[1], Joseph (Raymond) (1909–57), American Republican politician. Between 1950 and 1954 he was the instigator of widespread investigations into alleged communist infiltration in US public life.

McCarthy[2], Mary (Therese) (1912–89), American novelist and critic. Notable novels: *The Groves of Academe* (1952) and *The Group* (1963).

McCarthyism ▸ **noun** [mass noun] a vociferous campaign against alleged communists in the US government and other institutions carried out under Senator Joseph McCarthy in the period 1950–4. Many of the accused were blacklisted or lost their jobs, though most did not in fact belong to the Communist Party.
– DERIVATIVES **McCarthyite** (also **McCarthyist**) **adjective & noun**.

McCartney, Sir (James) Paul (b.1942), English pop and rock singer, songwriter, and bass guitarist. A founder member of the Beatles, he wrote most of their songs in collaboration with John Lennon. After the group broke up in 1970 he formed the band Wings.

macchiato /ˌmakɪˈɑːtəʊ/ ▸ **noun** (pl. **macchiatos**) a drink of espresso coffee with a dash of frothy steamed milk.
– ORIGIN from Italian (*caffè*) *macchiato*, literally 'stained, marked (coffee)', from *macchiare* 'mark, stain'.

McCoy ▸ **noun** (in phrase **the real McCoy**) informal the real thing; the genuine article: *the apparent fake turned out to be the real McCoy*.
– ORIGIN mid 19th cent.: first appears as *the real Mackay*, in which *real* may be a corruption of the name of the Reay branch of the Scottish Mackay family.

McCullers /məˈkʌləz/, (Lula) Carson (1917–67), American writer. Her work deals sensitively with loneliness and the plight of the eccentric. Notable works: *The Heart is a Lonely Hunter* (1940) and *The Ballad of The Sad Cafe* (1951).

MacDonald[1], Flora (1722–90), Scottish Jacobite heroine. She aided Charles Edward Stuart's escape from English pursuit, after his defeat at Culloden, by smuggling him from Benbecula to Skye in a small boat, disguised as her maid.

Macdonald[2], Sir John Alexander (1815–91), Scottish-born Canadian statesman, Prime Minister 1867–73 and 1878–91. He played a leading role in the confederation of the Canadian provinces, and was appointed first Prime Minister of the Dominion of Canada.

MacDonald[3], (James) Ramsay (1866–1937), British Labour statesman, Prime Minister 1924, 1929–31, and 1931–5. He served as Britain's first Labour Prime Minister.

MacDonnell Ranges a series of mountain ranges extending westwards from Alice Springs in Northern Territory, Australia. The highest peak is Mount Zeil, which rises to a height of 1,531 m (5,023 ft).
– ORIGIN named after Sir Richard *MacDonnell*, governor of South Australia when John McDouall Stuart explored the ranges in 1860.

Mace ▸ **noun** [mass noun] trademark an irritant chemical used in an aerosol to disable attackers.
▸ **verb** (also **mace**) [with obj.] spray (someone) with Mace.
– ORIGIN 1960s (originally US): probably from **MACE**[1].

mace[1] ▸ **noun 1** a staff of office, especially that which lies on the table in the House of Commons when the Speaker is in the chair, regarded as a symbol of the authority of the House.
2 historical a heavy club with a spiked metal head.
– ORIGIN Middle English: from Old French *masse* 'large hammer'.

mace[2] ▸ **noun** [mass noun] the reddish fleshy outer covering of the nutmeg, dried as a spice.
– ORIGIN Middle English *macis* (taken as plural), via Old French from Latin *macir*.

macédoine /ˈmasɪdwɑːn/ ▸ **noun** a mixture of vegetables or fruit cut into small pieces.
– ORIGIN French, literally 'Macedonia', with reference to the mixture of peoples in the Macedonian Empire of Alexander the Great.

Macedonia /ˌmasɪˈdəʊnɪə/ **1** a landlocked republic in the Balkans; pop. 2,066,700 (est. 2009); official language, Macedonian; capital, Skopje. Formerly a constituent republic of Yugoslavia, Macedonia became independent after a referendum in 1991. Also called **Former Yugoslav Republic of Macedonia**.
2 (also **Macedon** /ˈmasɪd(ə)n/) an ancient country in SE Europe, at the northern end of the Greek peninsula. In classical times it was a kingdom which under Philip II and Alexander the Great became a world power. The region is now divided between Greece, Bulgaria, and the republic of Macedonia.
3 a region in the north-east of modern Greece; capital, Thessaloníki.

Macedonian ▸ **noun 1** a native or inhabitant of the republic of Macedonia. ■ a native of ancient Macedonia. ■ a native or inhabitant of Macedonia in modern Greece.
2 [mass noun] the Southern Slavic language of the republic of Macedonia and adjacent parts of Bulgaria. ■ the language of ancient Macedonia, probably a dialect of Greek.
▸ **adjective** relating to Macedonia or Macedonian.

Macedonian Wars a series of four wars between Rome and Macedonia in the 3rd and 2nd centuries BC, which ended in the defeat of Macedonia and its annexation as a Roman province (148 BC).

Maceió /ˌmaseɪˈəʊ/ a port in eastern Brazil, on the Atlantic coast; pop. 896,965 (2007). It is the capital of the state of Alagoas.

McEnroe /ˈmakɪnrəʊ/, John (Patrick) (b.1959), American tennis player. He won seven Wimbledon titles (three for the singles: 1981, 1983–4) and four US Open singles championships (1979–84).

macer /ˈmeɪsə/ ▸ **noun** (in Scotland) an official who keeps order in a law court.
– ORIGIN Middle English: from Old French *massier*, from *masse* (see **MACE**[1]).

macerate /ˈmasəreɪt/ ▸ **verb 1** (especially with reference to food) soften or become softened by soaking in a liquid.
2 [with obj.] archaic cause to waste away by fasting.
– DERIVATIVES **maceration noun**, **macerator noun**.
– ORIGIN mid 16th cent.: from Latin *macerat-* 'made soft, soaked', from *macerare* 'to soften'.

macfarlane /məkˈfɑːlən/ ▸ **noun** dated a type of overcoat with a shoulder cape and slits for access to pockets in clothing worn underneath.
– ORIGIN 1920s: probably from the name of the designer or original manufacturer of the coat, which was first popular in France.

Macgillicuddy's Reeks /məˌgɪlɪˌkʌdɪz ˈriːks/ a range of hills in County Kerry in SW Ireland.
– ORIGIN apparently from the name of an Irish clan; *reek*, 'a hill or mountain', is from **RICK**[1] in a transferred sense 'heap, pile'.

McGonagall /məˈgɒnəg(ə)l/, William (1830–1902), Scottish poet. His poetry is naive yet entertaining doggerel which has won him a reputation as one of the worst poets in the world.

McGuffin /məˈgʌfɪn/ (also **MacGuffin**) ▸ **noun** an object or device in a film or a book which serves merely as a trigger for the plot.
– ORIGIN 1930s: a Scottish surname, coined in this sense by the English film director Alfred Hitchcock, allegedly from a humorous story involving such a pivotal factor.

Mach[1] /mɑːk, mak/, German /max/, Ernst (1838–1916), Austrian physicist and philosopher of science. He did important work on aerodynamics, while his writings inspired the logical positivist philosophers of the 1920s and influenced scientists such as Einstein and Niels Bohr.

Mach[2] /mɑːk, mak/ (also **Mach number**) ▸ **noun** the ratio of the speed of a body to the speed of sound in the surrounding medium. It is often used with a numeral (as **Mach 1**, **Mach 2**, etc.) to indicate the speed of sound, twice the speed of sound, etc.
– ORIGIN 1930s: named after E. *Mach* (see **MACH**[1]).

machair /ˈmakə, ˈmaxə/ ▸ **noun** [mass noun] (in Scotland, especially the Western Isles) low-lying arable or grazing land formed near the coast by the deposition of sand and shell fragments by the wind.
– ORIGIN late 17th cent.: from Scottish Gaelic.

machan /mʌˈtʃɑːn/ ▸ **noun** (in South Asia) a platform erected in a tree, used originally for hunting large animals and now for watching animals in wildlife reserves.
– ORIGIN via Hindi from Sanskrit *mañcaka*.

mache /mɑːʃ/ ▸ **noun** another term for **LAMB'S LETTUCE**.
– ORIGIN late 17th cent. (originally as the anglicized plural form *maches*): from French *mâche*.

macher /ˈmaxə/ ▸ **noun** US informal a person who gets things done. ■ derogatory an overbearing person.
– ORIGIN 1930s: from Yiddish *makher*, from Middle High German *Macher* 'doer, active person'.

machete /məˈtʃɛti, -ˈʃɛti/ (also **matchet**) ▸ **noun** a broad, heavy knife used as an implement or weapon, originating in Central America and the Caribbean.
– ORIGIN late 16th cent.: from Spanish, from *macho* 'hammer'.

Machiavel /ˈmakɪəvɛl/ ▸ **noun** archaic a person compared to Machiavelli for favouring expediency over morality.

Machiavelli /ˌmakɪəˈvɛli/, Niccolò di Bernardo dei (1469–1527), Italian statesman and political philosopher. His best-known work is *The Prince* (1532), which advises rulers that the acquisition and effective use of power may necessitate unethical methods. ■ (as noun **a Machiavelli**) a person perceived as prepared to use unethical means to gain an advantage.

Machiavellian /ˌmakɪəˈvɛlɪən/ ▸ **adjective** cunning, scheming, and unscrupulous, especially in politics.
▸ **noun** a person who schemes in a Machiavellian way.
– DERIVATIVES **Machiavellianism noun**.

machicolated /məˈtʃɪkəleɪtɪd/ ▸ **adjective** provided with machicolations: *a machicolated fortress*.
– ORIGIN late 18th cent.: from Anglo-Latin *machicollare*, based on Provençal *machacol*, from *macar* 'to crush' + *col* 'neck'.

machicolation ▸ **noun** (in medieval fortifications) an opening between the supporting corbels of a projecting parapet or the vault of a gate, through which stones or burning objects could be dropped on attackers. ■ a projecting structure containing a series of machicolations.

machinable /məˈʃiːnəb(ə)l/ ▸ **adjective** (of a material) able to be worked by a machine tool.
– DERIVATIVES **machinability noun**.

machinate /ˈmakɪneɪt, ˈmaʃ-/ ▸ **verb** [no obj.] engage in plots; scheme: *he machinated against other bishops*.
– DERIVATIVES **machinator noun**.

– ORIGIN early 16th cent.: from Latin *machinat-* 'contrived', from *machinari* 'contrive', from *machina* (see MACHINE).

machination /ˌmaʃɪˈneɪʃn/ ▸ noun (usu. **machinations**) a plot or scheme.
– ORIGIN late Middle English: from Old French, or Latin *machinatio-*, from *machinat-* 'contrived' (see MACHINATE).

machine ▸ noun an apparatus using mechanical power and having several parts, each with a definite function and together performing a particular task: *a fax machine.* ■ [with modifier] a coin-operated dispenser: *a cigarette machine.* ■ technical any device that transmits a force or directs its application. ■ an efficient and well-organized group of powerful people: *the party's fund-raising is helping it to build a formidable political machine.*
▸ verb [with obj.] make or operate on with a machine: (as adj. **machined**) *a decoratively machined brass rod.*
– ORIGIN mid 16th cent. (originally denoting a structure): from French, via Latin from Doric Greek *makhana* (Greek *mēkhanē*, from *mēkhos* 'contrivance').

machine code (also **machine language**) ▸ noun a computer programming language consisting of binary or hexadecimal instructions which a computer can respond to directly.

machine gun ▸ noun an automatic gun that fires bullets in rapid succession for as long as the trigger is pressed.
▸ verb (**machine-gun**) [with obj.] shoot with a machine gun.
– DERIVATIVES **machine-gunner** noun.

machine head ▸ noun each of the small pegs on the head of a guitar, used for tightening the strings.

machine instruction ▸ noun Computing an instruction in machine code.

machine-readable ▸ adjective (of data) in a form that a computer can process.

machinery ▸ noun [mass noun] machines collectively: *farm machinery.* ■ the components of a machine. ■ the organization or structure of something or for doing something: *the machinery of the state.*

machine screw ▸ noun a fastening device similar to a bolt but having a socket in its head which allows it to be turned with a screwdriver.

machine tool ▸ noun a fixed powered tool such as a lathe, for cutting or shaping metal, wood, or other material.
– DERIVATIVES **machine-tooled** adjective.

machine translation (also **automatic translation**) ▸ noun [mass noun] translation carried out by a computer.

machine washable ▸ adjective (of clothes or other fabric articles) able to be washed in a washing machine without damage.

machinima /məˈʃɪnɪmə/ ▸ noun [mass noun] the practice or technique of producing animated films through the manipulation of video game graphics.
– ORIGIN early 21st cent.: blend of MACHINE and CINEMA, probably influenced by ANIME.

machinist ▸ noun a person who operates a machine, especially a machine tool or a sewing machine. ■ a person who makes machinery.

machismo /məˈkɪzməʊ, -ˈtʃɪz-/ ▸ noun [mass noun] strong or aggressive masculine pride.
– ORIGIN 1940s: from Mexican Spanish, from *macho* 'male', from Latin *masculus*.

Machmeter /ˈmɑːkmiːtə, ˈmak-/ ▸ noun an instrument in an aircraft indicating airspeed as a Mach number.

Mach number ▸ noun see MACH[2].

MACHO ▸ noun Astronomy a relatively dark, dense object, such as a brown dwarf, a low-mass star, or a black hole, of a kind believed to occur in a halo around a galaxy and to contain a significant proportion of the galaxy's mass.
– ORIGIN 1990s: acronym from *Massive (Astrophysical) Compact Halo Object.*

macho /ˈmatʃəʊ/ ▸ adjective masculine in an overly assertive or aggressive way: *the big macho tough guy.*
▸ noun (pl. **machos**) a man who is aggressively proud of his masculinity. ■ [mass noun] machismo.
– ORIGIN 1920s: from Mexican Spanish, 'masculine or vigorous'.

Mach's principle ▸ noun Physics the hypothesis that a body's inertial mass results from its interaction with the rest of the matter in the universe.

Machtpolitik /ˈmɑːxtpɒlɪˌtiːk/ ▸ noun [mass noun] power politics.
– ORIGIN German.

Machu Picchu /ˌmɑːtʃuː ˈpiːtʃuː/ a fortified Inca town in the Andes in Peru, which the invading Spaniards never found. It is famous for its dramatic position, perched high on a steep sided ridge.

Machupo /məˈtʃuːpəʊ/ (also **Machupo virus**) ▸ noun [mass noun] Medicine a South American arenavirus carried by rodents, which causes a rare form of haemorrhagic fever in humans.
– ORIGIN 1960s: from the name of the River *Machupo* in Bolivia, where the disease was first recognized.

Macias Nguema /məˌsiːəs əŋˈgweɪmə/ former name (1973–9) for BIOKO.

McIntosh (also **McIntosh red**) ▸ noun a deep red dessert apple of a Canadian variety.
– ORIGIN late 19th cent.: named after John *McIntosh* (1777–1845 or 1846), the Canadian farmer on whose farm the wild apple was discovered.

macintosh ▸ noun variant spelling of MACKINTOSH.

McJob /məkˈdʒɒb/ ▸ noun a low-paid job with few prospects.

mack ▸ noun N. Amer. informal **1** a confident, successful man who has many sexual partners.
2 variant spelling of MAC.

Mackay /məˈkʌɪ/ a port in NE Australia, on the coast of Queensland; pop. 112,607 (2008).
– ORIGIN named after Captain John *MacKay*, who explored the region in 1860.

Mackenzie[1] /məˈkɛnzi/, Sir Alexander (1764–1820), Scottish explorer of Canada. He explored the Mackenzie River in 1789 and in 1793 became the first European to reach the Pacific Ocean by land along a northern route.

Mackenzie[2] /məˈkɛnzi/, William Lyon (1795–1861), Scottish-born Canadian politician and journalist, involved with the movement for political reform in Canada. In 1837 he led an unsuccessful rebellion in Toronto and fled to New York.

Mackenzie River the longest river in Canada, flowing 1,700 km (1,060 miles) north-westwards from the Great Slave Lake to the Beaufort Sea, a part of the Arctic Ocean.

mackerel ▸ noun (pl. **same** or **mackerels**) a predatory marine fish with a greenish-blue back, important as a food fish. ● *Scomber* and other genera, family Scombridae (the **mackerel family**): many species, in particular the **North Atlantic mackerel** (*S. scombrus*).
– ORIGIN Middle English: from Old French *maquerel*, of unknown origin.

mackerel shark ▸ noun another term for PORBEAGLE.

mackerel sky ▸ noun a sky dappled with rows of small white fleecy (typically cirrocumulus) clouds, like the pattern on a mackerel's back.

mackinaw /ˈmakɪnɔː/ (also **mackinaw coat** or **jacket**) ▸ noun N. Amer. a short coat or jacket made of a thick woollen cloth, typically with a plaid design.
– ORIGIN early 19th cent.: named after *Mackinaw* City, Michigan, formerly an important trading post.

McKinlay /məˈkɪnli/, John (1819–72), Scottish-born explorer. He led an expedition (1861) to search for the missing explorers Burke and Wills. He found only traces of their party, but carried out valuable exploratory work in the Australian interior.

McKinley /məˈkɪnli/, William (1843–1901), American Republican statesman, 25th President of the US 1897–1901. He was assassinated by an anarchist.

McKinley, Mount a mountain in south central Alaska. Rising to 6,194 m (20,321 ft), it is the highest mountain in North America. Also called DENALI.

Mackintosh, Charles Rennie (1868–1928), Scottish architect, designer, and painter. A leading exponent of art nouveau, he established a more severe and less floral interpretation of the style. Notable among his designs is the Glasgow School of Art (1898–1909).

mackintosh (also **macintosh**) ▸ noun Brit. a full-length waterproof coat. ■ [mass noun] [usu. as modifier] dated cloth waterproofed with rubber.
– ORIGIN mid 19th cent.: named after Charles *Macintosh* (1766–1843), the Scottish inventor who patented the cloth.

mackle /ˈmak(ə)l/ ▸ noun a blurred impression in printing.
– ORIGIN late 16th cent.: from French *macule*, from Latin *macula* 'stain'.

macle /ˈmak(ə)l/ ▸ noun **1** a diamond or other crystal that is twinned.
2 another term for CHIASTOLITE.
– ORIGIN early 19th cent.: from French, from Anglo-Latin *mascula* 'mesh'.

Maclean /məˈkleɪn/, Donald (Duart) (1913–83), British Foreign Office official and Soviet spy. After acting as a Soviet agent from the late 1930s he fled to the USSR with Guy Burgess in 1951.

Macleod /məˈklaʊd/, John James Rickard (1876–1935), Scottish physiologist. He directed the research on pancreatic extracts by F. G. Banting and C. H. Best which led to the discovery and isolation of insulin. Macleod shared the Nobel Prize for Physiology or Medicine with Banting in 1923.

McLuhan /məˈkluːən/, (Herbert) Marshall (1911–80), Canadian writer and thinker. He became famous in the 1960s for his phrase 'the medium is the message' and his argument that it is the characteristics of a particular medium rather than the information it disseminates which influence and control society.

McMansion /məkˈmanʃ(ə)n/ ▸ noun a large modern house that is considered ostentatious and lacking in architectural integrity.

Macmillan, (Maurice) Harold, 1st Earl of Stockton (1894–1986), British Conservative statesman, Prime Minister 1957–63. His term of office saw the signing of the Test-Ban Treaty (1963) with the US and the USSR. Macmillan resigned on grounds of ill health shortly after the scandal surrounding John Profumo.

McNaghten rules /məkˈnɔːt(ə)n/ (also **M'Naghten** or **McNaughten rules**) Brit. rules or criteria for judging criminal responsibility where there is a question of insanity.
– ORIGIN established by the House of Lords, following the case of Regina v McNaghten (1843).

MacNeice /məkˈniːs/, (Frederick) Louis (1907–63), Northern Irish poet. His work, such as *Collected Poems* (1966), is characterized by the use of assonance, internal rhymes, and ballad-like repetitions.

Macquarie /məˈkwɒri/, Lachlan (1762–1824), Scottish-born Australian colonial administrator, governor of New South Wales 1809–21.

Macquarie River a river in New South Wales, Australia, rising on the western slopes of the Great Dividing Range and flowing 960 km (600 miles) north-west to join the River Darling, of which it is a headwater.

macramé /məˈkrɑːmi, -meɪ/ ▸ noun [mass noun] the art of knotting string in patterns to make decorative articles. ■ [usu. as modifier] articles made using macramé.
– ORIGIN mid 19th cent.: French, from Turkish *makrama* 'tablecloth or towel', from Arabic *miqrama* 'bedspread'.

macro ▸ noun (pl. **macros**) **1** (also **macro instruction**) Computing a single instruction that expands automatically into a set of instructions to perform a particular task.
2 Photography a macro lens.
▸ adjective **1** large-scale; overall: *the analysis of social events at the macro level.*
2 Photography relating to macrophotography.

macro- ▸ combining form **1** large; large-scale: *macromolecule.* ■ (used in medical terms) large compared with the norm: *macrocephaly.*
2 long; over a long period: *macroevolution.*
– ORIGIN from Greek *makros* 'long, large'.

macrobiotic /ˌmakrə(ʊ)bʌɪˈɒtɪk/ ▸ adjective consisting of or relating to a diet of organic wholefoods which is based on Buddhist principles of the balance of yin and yang.
▸ plural noun (**macrobiotics**) [treated as sing.] the use or theory of a macrobiotic diet.

macrocarpa /ˌmakrə(ʊ)ˈkɑːpə/ ▸ noun a Californian cypress tree with a large spreading crown of horizontal branches and leaves that smell of lemon when crushed. Also called MONTEREY CYPRESS. ● *Cupressus macrocarpa*, family Cupressaceae.
– ORIGIN early 20th cent.: modern Latin, from MACRO- + Greek *karpos* 'fruit'.

macrocephalic /ˌmakrə(ʊ)sɪˈfalɪk, -kɛˈfalɪk-/ (also **macrocephalous**) ▸ adjective Anatomy having an unusually large head.
– DERIVATIVES **macrocephaly** noun.

macrocosm /ˈmakrə(ʊ)kɒz(ə)m/ ▸ noun the whole of a complex structure, especially the world or the universe, contrasted with a small or representative part of it. Contrasted with MICROCOSM.
– DERIVATIVES **macrocosmic** adjective, **macrocosmically** adverb.

macrocyclic /ˌmakrə(ʊ)ˈsʌɪklɪk, -ˈsɪk-/ ▸ **adjective** Chemistry relating to or denoting a ring composed of a relatively large number of atoms, such as occur in haem, chlorophyll, and several natural antibiotics.
– DERIVATIVES **macrocycle** noun.

macroeconomics ▸ **plural noun** [treated as sing.] the branch of economics concerned with large-scale or general economic factors, such as interest rates and national productivity.
– DERIVATIVES **macroeconomic** adjective.

macroeconomy ▸ **noun** a large-scale economic system.

macroevolution ▸ **noun** [mass noun] Biology major evolutionary change, especially with regard to the evolution of whole taxonomic groups over long periods of time.
– DERIVATIVES **macroevolutionary** adjective.

macrogamete ▸ **noun** Biology (especially in protozoans) the larger of a pair of conjugating gametes, usually regarded as female.

macro lens ▸ **noun** Photography a lens suitable for taking photographs unusually close to the subject.

macrolepidoptera /ˌmakrəʊlɛpɪˈdɒpt(ə)rə/ ▸ **plural noun** Entomology the families of butterflies and moths whose members are large enough to be of interest to the general collector.
– ORIGIN modern Latin (plural), from MACRO- + LEPIDOPTERA.

macromolecule ▸ **noun** Chemistry a molecule containing a very large number of atoms, such as a protein, nucleic acid, or synthetic polymer.
– DERIVATIVES **macromolecular** adjective.

macron /ˈmakrɒn/ ▸ **noun** a written or printed mark (¯) used to indicate a long vowel in some languages, or a stressed vowel in verse.
– ORIGIN mid 19th cent.: from Greek *makron*, neuter of *makros* 'long'.

macronutrient ▸ **noun** Biology **1** a type of food (e.g. fat, protein, carbohydrate) required in large amounts in the diet.
2 a chemical element (e.g. potassium, magnesium, calcium) required in large amounts for plant growth.

M

macrophage /ˈmakrə(ʊ)feɪdʒ/ ▸ **noun** Physiology a large phagocytic cell found in stationary form in the tissues or as a mobile white blood cell, especially at sites of infection.

macrophotography ▸ **noun** [mass noun] photography producing photographs of small items larger than life size.

macrophyte /ˈmakrə(ʊ)fʌɪt/ ▸ **noun** Botany an aquatic plant large enough to be seen by the naked eye.

macropod /ˈmakrə(ʊ)pɒd/ ▸ **noun** Zoology a plant-eating marsupial mammal of an Australasian family that comprises the kangaroos and wallabies. ● Family Macropodidae: *Macropus* and other genera.
– ORIGIN late 19th cent.: from modern Latin *Macropodidae* (plural), from MACRO- + Greek *pous, pod-* 'foot'.

macroscopic /ˌmakrə(ʊ)ˈskɒpɪk/ ▸ **adjective 1** visible to the naked eye; not microscopic.
2 relating to large-scale or general analysis.
– DERIVATIVES **macroscopically** adverb.

macrostructure ▸ **noun** the large-scale or overall structure of something, e.g. an organism, a mechanical construction, or a written text.
– DERIVATIVES **macrostructural** adjective.

macruran /məˈkruːərən/ ▸ **adjective** Zoology relating to or denoting those decapod crustaceans (such as lobsters and crayfish) which have a relatively long abdomen.
– DERIVATIVES **macrurous** adjective.
– ORIGIN mid 19th cent. (as a noun): from modern Latin *Macrura* (former suborder name), from Greek *makros* 'long' + *oura* 'tail', + -AN.

macula /ˈmakjʊlə/ ▸ **noun** (pl. **maculae** /-liː/) another term for MACULE. ■ (also **macula lutea** /ˈluːtɪə/) (pl. **maculae luteae** /-tiː/) Anatomy an oval yellowish area surrounding the fovea near the centre of the retina in the eye, which is the region of keenest vision.
– ORIGIN late Middle English: from Latin.

macular ▸ **adjective 1** relating to the macula of the eye.
2 Medicine consisting of a distinct spot or spots.

maculate /ˈmakjʊleɪt/ literary ▸ **adjective** spotted or stained.
▸ **verb** [with obj.] mark with a spot or spots; stain: *a dirty white T-shirt maculated with barbecue sauce.*
– DERIVATIVES **maculation** noun.
– ORIGIN late Middle English (as a verb): from Latin *maculat-* 'spotted', from *maculare* 'to spot', from *macula* 'spot'.

macule /ˈmakjuːl/ ▸ **noun** Medicine an area of skin discoloration.
– ORIGIN late 15th cent.: from French, or from Latin *macula* 'spot'.

macumba /məˈkʊmbə/ ▸ **noun** [mass noun] a religious cult practised among black people in Brazil, using sorcery, ritual dance, and fetishes.
– ORIGIN Portuguese.

macushla /məˈkʊʃlə/ ▸ **noun** Irish an affectionate form of address.
– ORIGIN from Irish *mo* 'my' + *cuisle* 'pulse' (see also ACUSHLA).

mad ▸ **adjective (madder, maddest) 1** chiefly Brit. mentally ill; insane: *he felt as if he were going mad.* ■ chiefly Brit. (of behaviour or an idea) extremely foolish; not sensible: *Antony's mother told him he was mad to be leaving Dublin.* ■ in a frenzied mental or physical state: *she pictured loved ones* ***mad with*** *anxiety about her | it was a mad dash to get ready.* ■ informal very angry: *don't be* ***mad at*** *me.* ■ (of a dog) rabid.
2 informal very enthusiastic about someone or something: *he's* ***mad about*** *football* | [in combination] *another myth is that Scorpios are sex-mad.* ■ Brit. very exciting.
▸ **verb (mads, madding, madded)** [with obj.] archaic make (someone) mad.
– PHRASES **go mad** informal allow oneself to get carried away by enthusiasm or excitement: *let's go mad and splash out.* **like mad** informal with great intensity, energy, or enthusiasm: *I run like mad.* **(as) mad as a hatter** informal completely insane. [with reference to Lewis Carroll's character the Mad Hatter in *Alice's Adventures in Wonderland* (1865), the allusion being to the effects of mercury poisoning from the use of mercurous nitrate in the manufacture of felt hats.] **mad keen** Brit. informal extremely enthusiastic.
– ORIGIN Old English *gemǣd(e)d* 'maddened', participial form related to *gemād* 'mad', of Germanic origin.

Madagascar /ˌmadəˈgaskə/ an island country in the Indian Ocean, off the east coast of Africa; pop. 20,653,600 (est. 2009); official languages, Malagasy and French; capital, Antananarivo.

> Settled by peoples of mixed Indo-Melanesian and African descent, Madagascar was visited by the Portuguese in 1500 but resisted colonization until the French established control in 1896. It regained its independence as the Malagasy Republic in 1960, changing its name back to Madagascar in 1975. Madagascar is the fourth-largest island in the world, and many of its plants and animals are not found elsewhere.

– DERIVATIVES **Madagascan** adjective & noun.

madam ▸ **noun 1** used to address or refer to a woman in a polite or respectful way: *Can I help you, madam?* ■ (**Madam**) used to address a woman at the start of a formal or business letter. ■ (**Madam**) used before a title to address or refer to a female holder of that position: *Madam President.*
2 Brit. informal a conceited or bossy girl or young woman: *she's a proper little madam.*
3 a woman who runs a brothel.
– ORIGIN Middle English: from Old French *ma dame* 'my lady'.

Madame /məˈdɑːm, ˈmadəm/, French /madam/ ▸ **noun** (pl. **Mesdames**) a title or form of address used of or to a French-speaking woman, corresponding to *Mrs*: *Madame Bovary.*
– ORIGIN French; compare with MADAM.

madcap ▸ **adjective** amusingly eccentric: *a surreal, madcap novel.* ■ done without considering the consequences; foolish or reckless: *a madcap scheme.*
▸ **noun** an eccentric or reckless person.

mad cow disease ▸ **noun** informal term for **BSE**.

madden ▸ **verb** [with obj.] drive (someone or something) insane: *the tribe say that millet was discovered by a woman maddened by famine.* ■ make (someone) extremely annoyed: *this is ridiculous, he told her, maddened by her reaction.*

maddening ▸ **adjective** extremely annoying: *she put the coins back with maddening slowness.*
– DERIVATIVES **maddeningly** adverb.

madder ▸ **noun** a Eurasian plant related to the bedstraws, with whorls of four to six leaves. ● Genera *Rubia* and *Sherardia*, family Rubiaceae: in particular *R. tinctorum*, formerly cultivated for its root which yields a red dye.
■ [mass noun] a red dye or pigment obtained from the root of the madder, or a synthetic dye resembling it.
– ORIGIN Old English *mædere*, of Germanic origin; obscurely related to Dutch *mede*, in the same sense.

madding ▸ **adjective** literary **1** acting madly; frenzied.
2 maddening.
– PHRASES **far from the madding crowd** private or secluded. [in allusion to Gray's *Elegy*, also to the title of one of Thomas Hardy's novels.]

made past and past participle of MAKE. ▸ **adjective** [in combination] made in a particular place or way: *a Japanese-made camera | handmade chocolates.*

Madeira[1] /məˈdɪərə/ **1** an island in the Atlantic Ocean off NW Africa, the largest of the Madeiras, a group of islands which constitutes an autonomous region of Portugal; pop. 247,161 (2007); capital, Funchal. Encountered by the Portuguese in 1419, the islands were occupied by the Spanish 1580–1640 and the British 1807–14.
2 a river in NW Brazil, which rises on the Bolivian border and flows about 1,450 km (900 miles) to meet the Amazon east of Manaus. It is navigable to large ocean-going vessels as far as Pôrto Velho.
– DERIVATIVES **Madeiran** adjective & noun.
– ORIGIN Portuguese, literally 'timber' (from Latin *materia* 'substance'), because of the island's dense woods.

Madeira[2] /məˈdɪərə/ (also **Madeira wine**) ▸ **noun** [mass noun] a fortified wine from the island of Madeira.

Madeira cake ▸ **noun** [mass noun] Brit. a close-textured, rich kind of sponge cake.
– ORIGIN so named because it was eaten as an accompaniment to a glass of Madeira.

madeleine /ˈmadleɪn, ˈmad(ə)lɛn/ ▸ **noun** a small rich sponge cake, baked in a fluted tin or mould and decorated with coconut and jam.
– ORIGIN French, probably named after *Madeleine* Paulmier, 19th-cent. French pastry cook.

made man ▸ **noun** N. Amer. a man whose success in life is assured. ■ a man who has been formally inducted as a full member of the Mafia.

Mademoiselle /ˌmad(ə)mwəˈzɛl/, French /madmwazɛl/ ▸ **noun** (pl. **Mesdemoiselles**) a title or form of address used of or to an unmarried French-speaking woman, corresponding to *Miss*: *Mademoiselle Rossignol.* ■ (**mademoiselle**) a young Frenchwoman. ■ (**mademoiselle**) a female French teacher in an English-speaking school.
– ORIGIN French, from *ma* 'my' + *demoiselle* 'damsel'.

maderization /ˌmadərʌɪˈzeɪʃ(ə)n/ (also **maderisation**) ▸ **noun** [mass noun] a form of oxidation which gives white wine a brownish colour and caramelized flavour like that of Madeira.
– DERIVATIVES **maderized** adjective.
– ORIGIN 1950s: from French *madérisation*, from *madériser*, from *Madère* 'Madeira'.

made road ▸ **noun** Brit. a road surfaced with a material such as asphalt.

made to measure ▸ **adjective** specially made to fit a particular person or thing: *a pair of made-to-measure curtains.*

made to order ▸ **adjective** specially made according to a customer's specifications.

made-up ▸ **adjective 1** wearing make-up: *a heavily made-up woman.*
2 invented; not true: *a made-up story.*
3 (of a meal or drink) prepared in advance of sale.
4 (of a road) surfaced with a material such as asphalt.

madhouse ▸ **noun** historical an institution for the care of mentally ill people. ■ informal a psychiatric hospital. ■ [in sing.] a scene of extreme confusion or uproar.

Madhya Pradesh /ˌmʌdjə prəˈdɛʃ/ a state in central India, formed in 1956; capital, Bhopal.

Madison[1] /ˈmadɪs(ə)n/ the state capital of Wisconsin; pop. 231,916 (est. 2008).
– ORIGIN named after President James *Madison* (see MADISON[2]).

Madison[2] /ˈmadɪs(ə)n/, James (1751–1836), American Democratic Republican statesman, 4th President of the US 1809–17. He played a leading part in drawing up the US Constitution (1787) and proposed the Bill of Rights (1791).

Madison[3] /ˈmadɪs(ə)n/ ▸ **noun** (**the Madison**) an energetic group dance popular in the 1960s.
– ORIGIN of unknown origin.

madison /ˈmadɪs(ə)n/ ▸ **noun** a cycle relay race for teams of two or more riders, typically held over several days.

– ORIGIN named after *Madison* Square Garden, New York, the site of the first such race in 1892.

Madison Avenue a street in New York City, centre of the American advertising business.

madly ▶ adverb in a mad, wild, or uncontrolled manner: *his eyes bulged madly.* ■ informal with extreme intensity: *the boys are all madly in love with you.*

madman ▶ noun (pl. **madmen**) a man who is mentally ill. ■ an extremely foolish or reckless person: *car got out of control—some madman going too fast.*

madness ▶ noun [mass noun] the state of having a serious mental illness. ■ extremely foolish behaviour: *it is madness to allow children to roam around after dark* | [count noun] *the new laws are a madness.* ■ a state of wild or chaotic activity: *at midnight it's absolute madness in here.*

mado /ˈmeɪdəʊ/ ▶ noun (pl. **mados**) a small yellowish marine fish with brown longitudinal streaks, occurring around eastern Australia and New Zealand. ● Genus *Atypichthys*, family Kyphosidae: two species.
– ORIGIN late 19th cent.: probably from an Aboriginal language of Queensland.

Madonna[1] ▶ noun (**the Madonna**) the Virgin Mary. ■ (**madonna**) a picture, statue, or medallion of the Madonna. ■ (**madonna**) an idealized virtuous and beautiful woman.
– ORIGIN late 16th cent. (as a respectful form of address to an Italian woman): Italian, from *ma* (old form of *mia* 'my') + *donna* 'lady' (from Latin *domina*).

Madonna[2] (b.1958), American pop singer and actress; born *Madonna Louise Ciccone*. Albums such as *Like a Virgin* (1984) and her image as a sex symbol brought her international stardom in the mid 1980s.

madonna lily ▶ noun a tall white-flowered lily of the eastern Mediterranean, often depicted in paintings of the Madonna. ● *Lilium candidum*, family Liliaceae.

Madras /məˈdrɑːs, -ˈdras/ **1** former name (until 1995) for **CHENNAI**.
2 former name (until 1968) for the state of **TAMIL NADU**.

madras /məˈdrɑːs, -ˈdras/ ▶ noun [mass noun] **1** a strong cotton fabric with colourful stripes or checks.
2 a dish of meat, fish, or vegetables in a hot curry sauce.
– ORIGIN mid 19th cent.: by association with **MADRAS**.

madrasa /məˈdrasə/ (also **madrasah** or **medrese**) ▶ noun a college for Islamic instruction.
– ORIGIN Arabic, from *darasa* 'to study'.

Madreporaria /ˌmadrɛpəˈrɛːrɪə/ ▶ plural noun Zoology another term for **SCLERACTINIA**.
– DERIVATIVES **madreporarian** noun & adjective, **madrepore** noun.
– ORIGIN modern Latin (plural), from *Madrepora* (genus name), from Italian, probably from *madre* 'mother', with reference to the prolific growth of the coral.

madreporite /maˈdrɛpərʌɪt, ˌmadrɪˈpɔːrʌɪt/ ▶ noun Zoology a perforated plate by which the entry of seawater into the vascular system of an echinoderm is controlled.
– ORIGIN early 19th cent.: from *madrepore* (see **MADREPORARIA**) + **-ITE**[1].

Madrid /məˈdrɪd/ the capital of Spain; pop. 3,213,271 (2008). Situated on a high plateau in the centre of the country, it replaced Valladolid as capital in 1561.

madrigal /ˈmadrɪɡ(ə)l/ ▶ noun a part-song for several voices, especially one of the Renaissance period, typically unaccompanied and arranged in elaborate counterpoint.
– DERIVATIVES **madrigalian** /-ˈɡeɪlɪən/ adjective, **madrigalist** noun.
– ORIGIN from Italian *madrigale* (from medieval Latin *carmen matricale* 'simple song'), from *matricalis* 'maternal or primitive', from *matrix* 'womb'.

madrilene /ˌmadrɪˈliːn, -ˈlɛn/ ▶ noun [mass noun] a clear soup flavoured with tomato and served cold.
– ORIGIN from French (*consommé à la*) *madrilène*, literally 'soup in the Madrid style'.

Madrilenian /ˌmadrɪˈlemɪən/ ▶ adjective relating to Madrid.
▶ noun a native or inhabitant of Madrid.
– ORIGIN from **MADRILEÑO** + **-IAN**.

Madrileño /ˌmadrɪˈlɛnjəʊ/ ▶ noun (pl. **Madrileños**) a native or inhabitant of Madrid.
– ORIGIN Spanish.

madroño /məˈdrəʊnjəʊ/ (also **madroña** /-njə/) ▶ noun (pl. **madroños**) an evergreen tree related to the strawberry tree, with white flowers, red berries, and glossy leaves, native to western North America. ● *Arbutus menziesii*, family Ericaceae.
– ORIGIN mid 19th cent.: from Spanish.

madtom ▶ noun a small North American freshwater catfish which has a venom gland at the base of the pectoral fin spines. ● Genus *Noturus*, family Ictaluridae: numerous species.

Madura /məˈdʊərə/ an island of Indonesia, off the NE coast of Java. Its chief town is Pamekasan.

Madurai /ˈmadjʊrʌɪ/ a city in Tamil Nadu in southern India; pop. 895,600 (est. 2009).

Madurese /ˌmadjʊˈriːz/ ▶ noun (pl. **same**) **1** a native or inhabitant of the island of Madura in Indonesia.
2 [mass noun] an Indonesian language spoken by over 12 million people in Madura and nearby parts of Java.
▶ adjective relating to the inhabitants of Madura or their language.

madwoman ▶ noun (pl. **madwomen**) a woman who is mentally ill.

Maeander /miːˈandə/ ancient name for **MENDERES**.

Maecenas /mʌɪˈsiːnəs/, Gaius (*c.*70–8 BC), Roman statesman. He was a trusted adviser of Augustus and a notable patron of poets such as Virgil and Horace.

maedi /ˈmeɪdi/ ▶ noun [mass noun] a form of progressive pneumonia in sheep, caused by a lentivirus. See also **VISNA**.
– ORIGIN 1950s: from Icelandic, literally 'shortness of breath'.

maelstrom /ˈmeɪlstrəm/ ▶ noun a powerful whirlpool in the sea or a river. ■ a situation or state of confused movement or violent turmoil: *the train station was a maelstrom of crowds.*
– ORIGIN late 17th cent.: from early modern Dutch (denoting a mythical whirlpool in the Arctic Ocean, west of Norway), from *maalen* 'grind, whirl' + *stroom* 'stream'.

Maelzel's metronome /ˈmɛlts(ə)lz/ ▶ noun see **MM**.

maenad /ˈmiːnad/ ▶ noun (in ancient Greece) a female follower of Bacchus, traditionally associated with divine possession and frenzied rites.
– DERIVATIVES **maenadic** adjective.
– ORIGIN late 16th cent.: via Latin from Greek *Mainas*, *Mainad-*, from *mainesthai* 'to rave'.

maestoso /mʌɪˈstəʊzəʊ, -səʊ/ Music ▶ adverb & adjective (especially as a direction) in a majestic manner.
▶ noun (pl. **maestosos**) a movement or passage marked to be performed in this way.
– ORIGIN Italian, 'majestic', based on Latin *majestas* 'majesty'.

maestro /ˈmʌɪstrəʊ/ ▶ noun (pl. **maestri** /-stri/ or **maestros**) a distinguished conductor or performer of classical music. ■ a distinguished figure in any sphere: *a Vietnam vet turned movie maestro.*
– ORIGIN early 18th cent.: Italian, 'master', from Latin *magister*.

Maeterlinck /ˈmeɪtəlɪŋk/, Count Maurice (1862–1949), Belgian poet, dramatist, and essayist. His prose dramas *La Princesse Maleine* (1889) and *Pelléas et Mélisande* (1892) established him as a leading figure in the symbolist movement. Nobel Prize for Literature (1911).

Mae West ▶ noun informal, dated an inflatable life jacket, originally as issued to RAF personnel during the Second World War.
– ORIGIN 1940s: from the name of the American film actress *Mae West* (see **WEST**[2]), noted for her large bust.

Mafeking /ˈmafɪkɪŋ/ a town in South Africa, capital of North West (as Mafikeng). In 1899–1900, during the Second Boer War, a small British force commanded by Lord Baden-Powell was besieged there for 215 days; its eventual relief was greeted in Britain with widespread celebration. Modern spelling (since 1980) **MAFIKENG**.

MAFF ▶ abbreviation (formerly in the UK) Ministry of Agriculture, Fisheries, and Food.

Mafia /ˈmafɪə/ ▶ noun (**the Mafia**) [treated as sing. or pl.] an organized international body of criminals, operating originally in Sicily and now especially in Italy and the US and having a complex and ruthless behavioural code. ■ (**mafia**) any organized group of criminals resembling the Mafia in its way of operating. ■ (**mafia**) a group regarded as exerting a hidden sinister influence: *the British literary mafia.*
– ORIGIN Italian (Sicilian dialect), originally in the sense 'bragging'.

mafic /ˈmafɪk/ ▶ adjective Geology relating to or denoting a group of dark-coloured, mainly ferromagnesian minerals such as pyroxene and olivine. Often contrasted with **FELSIC**.
– ORIGIN early 20th cent.: blend of **MAGNESIUM** and a contracted form of **FERRIC**.

Mafikeng modern spelling of **MAFEKING**.

Mafioso /ˌmafɪˈəʊzəʊ, -səʊ/ (also **mafioso**) ▶ noun (pl. **Mafiosi** /-zi, -si/) a member of the Mafia or a similar criminal organization.
– ORIGIN Italian.

mag[1] ▶ noun informal **1** a magazine (periodical).
2 a magazine (of ammunition).
3 [mass noun] magnesium or magnesium alloy.
4 a magneto.
5 magnitude (of stars or other celestial objects).

mag[2] Austral./NZ informal ▶ verb (**mags, magging, magged**) [no obj.] chatter incessantly.
▶ noun a gossip or chat.
– ORIGIN early 19th cent.: originally English dialect; related to **MAGPIE**.

maga /ˈmɑːɡə/ (also **marga**) ▶ adjective W. Indian (of a person or part of the body) very thin.
– ORIGIN compare with Dutch *mager* 'lean', French *maigre* 'thin'.

Magadha /ˈmʌɡədə/ an ancient kingdom situated in the valley of the River Ganges in NE India (modern Bihar) which was the centre of several empires, notably those of the Mauryan and Gupta dynasties, between the 6th century BC and the 8th century AD.

Magadi, Lake /məˈɡɑːdi/ a salt lake in the Great Rift Valley, in southern Kenya, with extensive deposits of sodium carbonate and other minerals.

Magahi /ˈmʌɡəhi/ ▶ noun [mass noun] one of the Bihari group of languages, spoken by some 12 million people in central Bihar and West Bengal.
– ORIGIN from Hindi *Magadhī* 'of Magadha'.

magalogue /ˈmaɡəlɒɡ/ ▶ noun a promotional catalogue designed to resemble a high-quality magazine.
– ORIGIN 1970s: blend of **MAGAZINE** and **CATALOGUE**.

magazine ▶ noun **1** a periodical publication containing articles and illustrations, often on a particular subject or aimed at a particular readership: *a women's weekly magazine.* ■ (also **magazine programme**) a regular television or radio programme comprising a variety of topical items.
2 a container or detachable receptacle for holding a supply of cartridges to be fed automatically to the breech of a gun. ■ a receptacle for storing and feeding film to a camera, CDs to a compact disc player, etc.
3 a store for arms, ammunition, and explosives for military use.
– ORIGIN late 16th cent.: from French *magasin*, from Italian *magazzino*, from Arabic *makzin*, *makzan* 'storehouse', from *kazana* 'store up'. The term originally meant 'store' and was often used from the mid 17th cent. in the title of books providing information useful to particular groups of people, whence sense 1 (mid 18th cent.). Sense 3, a contemporary specialization of the original meaning, gave rise to sense 2 in the mid 18th cent.

magdalen /ˈmaɡdəlɪn/ ▶ noun (**the Magdalen** or **the Magdalene**) St Mary Magdalene. ■ archaic a reformed prostitute. ■ archaic a home for reformed prostitutes.
– ORIGIN late Middle English: via ecclesiastical Latin from Greek (*Maria hē*) *Magdalēnē* '(Mary of) *Magdala*' (to whom Jesus appeared after his resurrection; John 20:1–18), formerly identified with the sinner of Luke 7:37.

Magdalena /ˌmaɡdəˈleɪnə/ the principal river of Colombia, rising in the Andes and flowing northwards for about 1,600 km (1,000 miles) to enter the Caribbean at Barranquilla.

Magdalenian /ˌmaɡdəˈliːnɪən/ ▶ adjective Archaeology relating to or denoting the final Palaeolithic culture in Europe, following the Solutrean and dated to about 17,000–11,500 years ago. It is characterized by a range of bone and horn tools, and by highly developed cave art. ■ (as noun **the Magdalenian**) the Magdalenian culture or period.
– ORIGIN late 19th cent.: from French *Magdalénien* 'from La Madeleine', a site of this culture in the Dordogne, France.

Magdeburg /ˈmaɡdəbəːɡ/, German /ˈmakdəbʊrk/ an industrial city in Germany, the capital of Saxony-Anhalt, situated on the River Elbe and linked to the Rhine and Ruhr by the Mittelland Canal; pop. 229,800 (est. 2006).

Magdeburg hemispheres ▶ plural noun a pair of copper or brass hemispheres joined to form a hollow globe from which the air can be extracted to

M

demonstrate the pressure of the atmosphere, which then prevents them from being pulled apart.
– ORIGIN early 19th cent.: named after the city of **MAGDEBURG**, home of the inventor, Otto von Guericke (1602–86).

mage /meɪdʒ/ ▸ **noun** archaic or literary a magician or learned person.
– ORIGIN late Middle English: anglicized form of Latin *magus* (see **MAGUS**).

Magellan[1] /məˈɡɛlən/, Ferdinand (*c.*1480–1521), Portuguese explorer; Portuguese name *Fernão Magalhães*. In 1519 he sailed from Spain, rounding South America through the strait which now bears his name, and reached the Philippines in 1521. He was killed in a skirmish on Cebu; the survivors sailed back to Spain round Africa, completing the first circumnavigation of the globe (1522).

Magellan[2] /məˈɡɛlən/ an American space probe launched in 1989 to map the surface of Venus, using radar to penetrate the dense cloud cover. The probe was deliberately burned up in Venus's atmosphere in 1994.

Magellan, Strait of a passage separating Tierra del Fuego and other islands from mainland South America, connecting the Atlantic and Pacific Oceans.

Magellanic Clouds /ˌmadʒɪˈlanɪk/ Astronomy two diffuse luminous patches in the southern sky, now known to be small irregular galaxies that are the closest to our own. The **Large Magellanic Cloud** is about 169,000 light years away and the **Small Magellanic Cloud** is about 210,000 light years.
– ORIGIN named after the Portuguese explorer *Magellan* (see **MAGELLAN**[1]).

Magen David /mɑːˌɡɛn dɑːˈviːd/ ▸ **noun** a hexagram used as a symbol of Judaism.
– ORIGIN early 20th cent.: Hebrew, literally 'shield of David', with reference to David, King of Israel (see **DAVID**[1]).

magenta /məˈdʒɛntə/ ▸ **noun** [mass noun] a light mauvish-crimson which is one of the primary subtractive colours, complementary to green. ■ the dye fuchsin.
– ORIGIN mid 19th cent.: named after *Magenta* in northern Italy, site of a battle (1859) fought shortly before the red dye was discovered.

M

maggid /ˈmɑːɡɪd/ ▸ **noun** (pl. **maggidim** /-ɪm/) an itinerant Jewish preacher.
– ORIGIN late 19th cent.: from Hebrew *maggīḏ* 'narrator'.

maggie ▸ **noun** (pl. **maggies**) **1** dialect term for **MAGPIE**.
2 Scottish term for **GUILLEMOT**.

Maggie's drawers ▸ **noun** US military slang a red flag used to indicate a miss in target practice.
– ORIGIN 1940s: said to be in reference to a song entitled *Those Old Red Flannel Drawers That Maggie Wore*.

Maggiore, Lake /maˈdʒɔːreɪ/ the second-largest of the lakes of northern Italy, extending into southern Switzerland.

maggot ▸ **noun 1** a soft-bodied legless larva of a fly or other insect, found in decaying matter.
2 archaic a whimsical or strange idea.
– PHRASES **act the maggot** Irish informal behave in a foolishly playful way.
– ORIGIN late Middle English: perhaps an alteration of dialect *maddock*, from Old Norse *mathkr*, of Germanic origin.

maggoty ▸ **adjective 1** full of maggots.
2 Austral./NZ informal angry or bad-tempered: *Scotty got a bit maggoty about all this.*

Maghrib /ˈmaɡrɪb, ˈmʌɡrəb/ (also **Maghreb**) a region of North and NW Africa between the Atlantic Ocean and Egypt, comprising the coastal plain and Atlas Mountains of Morocco, together with Algeria, Tunisia, and sometimes also Tripolitania. Compare with **BARBARY**.

Magi /ˈmeɪdʒʌɪ/ (**the Magi**) the 'wise men' from the East who brought gifts to the infant Jesus (Matt. 2:1), said in later tradition to be kings named Caspar, Melchior, and Balthasar who brought gifts of gold, frankincense, and myrrh.
– ORIGIN see **MAGUS**.

magi plural form of **MAGUS**.

Magian /ˈmeɪdʒɪən/ ▸ **adjective** relating to the magi of ancient Persia.
▸ **noun** a magus or one of the Magi.

magic ▸ **noun** [mass noun] the power of apparently influencing events by using mysterious or supernatural forces: *suddenly, as if by magic, the doors start to open.* ■ mysterious tricks, such as making things disappear and reappear, performed as entertainment. ■ a quality of being beautiful and delightful in a way that seems remote from daily life: *the magic of the theatre.* ■ informal exceptional skill or talent: *he's been working his magic on New Zealand movies for the past two decades.*
▸ **adjective 1** having or apparently having supernatural powers: *a magic wand.* ■ [attrib.] very effective in producing the desired results: *confidence is the magic ingredient needed to spark recovery.*
2 Brit. informal wonderful; exciting: *it was a great time, magic.*
▸ **verb** (**magics**, **magicking**, **magicked**) [with obj. and adverbial] move, change, or create by or as if by magic: *he must have been magicked out of the car at the precise second it exploded.*
– PHRASES **like magic** remarkably effectively or rapidly: *this method works like magic.*
– ORIGIN late Middle English: from Old French *magique*, from Latin *magicus* (adjective), late Latin *magica* (noun), from Greek *magikē* (*tekhnē*) '(art of) a magus': magi were regarded as magicians.

magical ▸ **adjective 1** relating to, using, or resembling magic: *magical healing powers.*
2 beautiful or delightful in a way that seems removed from everyday life: *it was a magical evening of pure nostalgia.*
– DERIVATIVES **magically** adverb.

magical realism ▸ **noun** another term for **MAGIC REALISM**.

magic bullet ▸ **noun** informal a medicine or other remedy with advanced or highly specific properties.

magic carpet ▸ **noun** (in stories set in Arabia) a mythical carpet that is able to transport people through the air.

magic circle ▸ **noun 1** a small group of people privileged to receive confidential information or make important decisions.
2 (**Magic Circle**) (in the UK) a society of conjurors.

magic eye ▸ **noun 1** informal a photoelectric cell or similar electrical device used for detection or measurement.
2 a small cathode ray tube in some radio receivers that displays a pattern which enables the radio to be accurately tuned.

magician ▸ **noun** a person with magical powers. ■ a conjuror. ■ informal a person with exceptional skill in a particular area.
– ORIGIN late Middle English: from Old French *magicien*, from late Latin *magica* (see **MAGIC**).

magick ▸ **noun** archaic spelling of **MAGIC**.
– DERIVATIVES **magickal** adjective.

magic lantern ▸ **noun** historical a simple form of image projector used for showing photographic slides.

Magic Marker ▸ **noun** trademark an indelible marker pen.

magic mushroom ▸ **noun** informal a toadstool with hallucinogenic properties, especially the liberty cap and its relatives. ● Genus *Psilocybe*, family Strophariaceae, class Hymenomycetes: several species.

magic number ▸ **noun** a figure regarded as significant in a particular context. ■ Baseball the number which, at a given stage in the season, signifies the combination of wins for the first-placed team and defeats for the second-placed team which will assure the former of finishing the season in first place in its division.

magic realism (also **magical realism**) ▸ **noun** [mass noun] a literary or artistic genre in which realistic narrative and naturalistic technique are combined with surreal elements of dream or fantasy.
– DERIVATIVES **magic realist** noun.

magic square ▸ **noun** a square divided into smaller squares each containing a number, such that the figures in each vertical, horizontal, and diagonal row add up to the same value.

magilp ▸ **noun** variant spelling of **MEGILP**.

Maginot Line /ˈmaʒɪnəʊ/ a system of fortifications constructed by the French along their eastern border during the 1930s, outflanked by German forces in 1940.
– ORIGIN named after André *Maginot* (1877–1932), a French minister of war.

magister /ˈmadʒɪstə, məˈdʒɪstə/ ▸ **noun** archaic a title or form of address given to scholars, especially those teaching in a medieval university.
– ORIGIN late Middle English: from Latin, 'master'.

magisterial /ˌmadʒɪˈstɪərɪəl/ ▸ **adjective 1** having or showing great authority: *a magisterial pronouncement.* ■ domineering; dictatorial: *he dropped his somewhat magisterial style of questioning.*
2 relating to a magistrate. ■ (of a person) holding the office of a magistrate.
– DERIVATIVES **magisterially** adverb.
– ORIGIN early 17th cent.: from medieval Latin *magisterialis*, from late Latin *magisterius*, from Latin *magister* 'master'.

magisterium /ˌmadʒɪˈstɪərɪəm/ ▸ **noun** [mass noun] the teaching authority of the Roman Catholic Church, especially as exercised by bishops or the Pope.
– ORIGIN mid 19th cent.: Latin, 'the office of master', from *magister* (see **MAGISTER**).

magistracy /ˈmadʒɪstrəsi/ ▸ **noun** (pl. **magistracies**) the office or authority of a magistrate. ■ (**the magistracy**) magistrates collectively.

magistral /ˈmadʒɪstr(ə)l, məˈdʒɪstr(ə)l/ ▸ **adjective** archaic relating to a master or masters.
– ORIGIN late 16th cent.: from French, or from Latin *magistralis*, from *magister* 'master'.

magistrate /ˈmadʒɪstrət, -streɪt/ ▸ **noun** a civil officer who administers the law, especially one who conducts a court that deals with minor offences and holds preliminary hearings for more serious ones.
– DERIVATIVES **magistrature** /-trətʃə/ **noun**.
– ORIGIN late Middle English: from Latin *magistratus* 'administrator', from *magister* 'master'.

Maglemosian /ˌmaɡləˈməʊsɪən, -z-/ ▸ **adjective** Archaeology relating to or denoting a northern European Mesolithic culture, dated to about 9,500–7,700 years ago. ■ (as noun **the Maglemosian**) the Maglemosian culture or period.
– ORIGIN 1920s: from *Maglemose*, a town in Denmark where objects from this culture were found, + **-IAN**.

maglev /ˈmaɡlɛv/ ▸ **noun** [mass noun] [usu. as modifier] a transport system in which trains glide above a track, supported by magnetic repulsion and propelled by a linear motor: *maglev trains.*
– ORIGIN 1970s: from *mag(netic) lev(itation)*.

magma /ˈmaɡmə/ ▸ **noun** (pl. **magmas** or **magmata** /-mətə/) [mass noun] hot fluid or semi-fluid material below or within the earth's crust from which lava and other igneous rock is formed on cooling.
– DERIVATIVES **magmatic** adjective.
– ORIGIN late Middle English (in the sense 'residue of dregs after evaporation or pressing of a semi-liquid substance'): via Latin from Greek *magma* (from *massein* 'knead').

magma chamber ▸ **noun** a reservoir of magma within the earth's crust beneath a volcano.

magmatism ▸ **noun** [mass noun] Geology the motion or activity of magma.

Magna Carta /ˌmaɡnə ˈkɑːtə/ a charter of liberty and political rights obtained from King John of England by his rebellious barons at Runnymede in 1215, which came to be seen as the seminal document of English constitutional practice. ■ (as noun **a Magna Carta**) a similar document of rights.
– ORIGIN from medieval Latin, 'great charter'.

magna cum laude /ˌmaɡnə kʌm ˈlɔːdi, ˌmaɡnɑː kʊm ˈlaʊdeɪ/ ▸ **adverb & adjective** N. Amer. with great distinction (with reference to university degrees and diplomas).
– ORIGIN Latin, literally 'with great praise'.

Magna Graecia /ˌmaɡnə ˈɡriːsɪə, ˈɡriːʃə/ the ancient Greek cities of southern Italy, founded from *c.*750 BC onwards by colonists from Euboea, Sparta, and elsewhere in Greece.
– ORIGIN Latin, literally 'Great Greece'.

magnanimity /maɡnəˈnɪmɪti/ ▸ **noun** [mass noun] the fact or condition of being magnanimous; generosity: *both sides will have to show magnanimity.*

magnanimous /maɡˈnanɪməs/ ▸ **adjective** generous or forgiving, especially towards a rival or less powerful person: *she should be magnanimous in victory.*
– DERIVATIVES **magnanimously** adverb.
– ORIGIN mid 16th cent.: from Latin *magnanimus* (from *magnus* 'great' + *animus* 'soul') + **-OUS**.

magnate /ˈmaɡneɪt/ ▸ **noun** a wealthy and influential businessman or businesswoman.
– ORIGIN late Middle English: from late Latin *magnas*, *magnat-* 'great man', from Latin *magnus* 'great'.

magnesia /maɡˈniːʒə, -zɪə, -ʃə/ ▸ **noun** [mass noun] Chemistry magnesium oxide. ● Chem. formula: MgO. ■ hydrated magnesium carbonate used as an antacid and laxative.

– ORIGIN late Middle English (referring to a mineral said to be an ingredient of the philosopher's stone): via medieval Latin from Greek *Magnēsia*, denoting a mineral from Magnesia in Asia Minor.

magnesian /mag'niːzɪən, -ʒ(ə)n/ ▶ **adjective** (of rocks and minerals) containing or relatively rich in magnesium.

magnesite /'magnɪsʌɪt/ ▶ **noun** [mass noun] a whitish mineral consisting of magnesium carbonate, used as a refractory lining in some furnaces.

magnesium /mag'niːzɪəm/ ▶ **noun** [mass noun] the chemical element of atomic number 12, a silver-white metal of the alkaline earth series. It is used to make strong lightweight alloys, and is also used in flash bulbs and pyrotechnics, as it burns with a brilliant white flame. (Symbol: **Mg**)

magnesium flare ▶ **noun** a brilliant white flare containing metallic magnesium wire or ribbon.

magnet ▶ **noun** a piece of iron or other material which has its component atoms so ordered that the material exhibits properties of magnetism, such as attracting other iron-containing objects or aligning itself in an external magnetic field. ■ a person or thing that has a powerful attraction: *the beautiful stretch of white sand is **a magnet for** sun-worshippers.* ■ archaic term for LODESTONE.

– ORIGIN late Middle English (denoting lodestone): from Latin *magnes, magnet-*, from Greek *magnēs lithos* 'lodestone', probably influenced by Anglo-Norman French *magnete* (from Latin *magnes, magnet-*).

magnetar ▶ **noun** Astronomy a neutron star with a much stronger magnetic field than ordinary neutron stars.

– ORIGIN 1990s: from MAGNETIC + *-ar* as in PULSAR and QUASAR.

magnetic ▶ **adjective 1** exhibiting or relating to magnetism: *the clock has a magnetic back to stick to the fridge.* ■ capable of being attracted by or acquiring the properties of a magnet: *steel is magnetic.*
2 (of a bearing in navigation) measured relative to magnetic north.
3 very attractive or alluring: *his magnetic personality.*

– DERIVATIVES **magnetically** adverb.

– ORIGIN early 17th cent.: from late Latin *magneticus*, from Latin *magneta* (see MAGNET).

magnetic compass ▶ **noun** another term for COMPASS (sense 1 of the noun).

magnetic disk ▶ **noun** see DISC (sense 1).

magnetic equator ▶ **noun** the irregular imaginary line, passing round the earth near the equator, on which a magnetic needle has no dip (see DIP (sense 4 of the noun)).

magnetic field ▶ **noun** a region around a magnetic material or a moving electric charge within which the force of magnetism acts.

magnetic induction ▶ **noun** [mass noun] **1** magnetic flux or flux density.
2 the process by which an object or material is magnetized by an external magnetic field.

magnetic mine ▶ **noun** a mine detonated by the proximity of a magnetized body such as a ship or tank.

magnetic moment ▶ **noun** Physics the property of a magnet that interacts with an applied field to give a mechanical moment.

magnetic needle ▶ **noun** a piece of magnetized steel used as an indicator on the dial of a compass and in magnetic and electrical apparatus.

magnetic north ▶ **noun** the direction in which the north end of a compass needle or other freely suspended magnet will point in response to the earth's magnetic field. It deviates from true north over time and from place to place because the earth's magnetic poles are not fixed in relation to its axis.

magnetic pole ▶ **noun** each of the points near the extremities of the axis of rotation of the earth or another celestial body where a magnetic needle dips vertically. ■ each of the two points or regions of a magnet to and from which the lines of magnetic force are directed.

magnetic resonance imaging (abbrev.: **MRI**) ▶ **noun** [mass noun] a technique for producing images of bodily organs by measuring the response of the atomic nuclei of body tissues to high-frequency radio waves when placed in a strong magnetic field.

magnetic storm ▶ **noun** a disturbance of the magnetic field of the earth (or other celestial body).

magnetic tape ▶ **noun** [mass noun] tape used in recording sound, pictures, or computer data.

magnetic termite ▶ **noun** a North Australian termite which builds tall flattened mounds that are aligned north–south. ● *Amitermes meridionalis*, family Termitidae.

magnetic variation ▶ **noun** see VARIATION (sense 1).

magnetism ▶ **noun** [mass noun] **1** a physical phenomenon produced by the motion of electric charge, which results in attractive and repulsive forces between objects.

> All magnetism is due to circulating electric currents. In magnetic materials the magnetism is produced by electrons orbiting within the atoms; in most substances the magnetic effects of different electrons cancel each other out, but in some, such as iron, a net magnetic field can be induced by aligning the atoms.

2 the ability to attract and charm people: *his personal magnetism attracted men to the brotherhood.*

– ORIGIN early 17th cent.: from modern Latin *magnetismus*, from Latin *magneta* (see MAGNET).

magnetite /'magnɪtʌɪt/ ▶ **noun** [mass noun] a grey-black magnetic mineral which consists of an oxide of iron and is an important form of iron ore.

– ORIGIN mid 19th cent.: from MAGNET + -ITE[1].

magnetize (also **magnetise**) ▶ **verb** [with obj.] give magnetic properties to.

– DERIVATIVES **magnetizable** adjective, **magnetization** noun, **magnetizer** noun.

magneto ▶ **noun** (pl. **magnetos**) a small electric generator containing a permanent magnet and used to provide high-voltage pulses, especially (formerly) in the ignition systems of internal-combustion engines.

– ORIGIN late 19th cent.: abbreviation of MAGNETO-ELECTRIC.

magneto- /mag'niːtəʊ/ ▶ **combining form** relating to a magnet or magnetism: *magneto-electric.*

magneto-electric ▶ **adjective** relating to the electric currents generated in a material by its motion in a magnetic field. ■ (of an electric generator) using permanent magnets.

– DERIVATIVES **magneto-electricity** noun.

magnetograph ▶ **noun** an instrument for recording measurements of magnetic forces.

magnetohydrodynamics /mag,niːtəʊ,hʌɪdrə(ʊ)dʌɪ'namɪks/ ▶ **plural noun** [treated as sing.] the branch of physics that studies the behaviour of an electrically conducting fluid (such as a plasma or molten metal) acted on by a magnetic field.

– DERIVATIVES **magnetohydrodynamic** adjective.

magnetometer /,magnɪ'tɒmɪtə/ ▶ **noun** an instrument used for measuring magnetic forces, especially the earth's magnetism.

– DERIVATIVES **magnetometry** noun.

magnetomotive force /mag,niːtə(ʊ)'məʊtɪv/ ▶ **noun** Physics a quantity representing the sum of the magnetizing forces along a circuit.

magneton /'magnɪtɒn/ ▶ **noun** a unit of magnetic moment in atomic and nuclear physics.

– ORIGIN early 20th cent.: from MAGNETIC + -ON.

magneto-optical ▶ **adjective** relating to or employing both optical and magnetic phenomena or technology.

magnetopause ▶ **noun** the outer limit of a magnetosphere.

magnetoresistance ▶ **noun** [mass noun] Physics the dependence of the electrical resistance of a body on an external magnetic field.

– DERIVATIVES **magnetoresistive** adjective.

magnetosphere ▶ **noun** the region surrounding the earth or another astronomical body in which its magnetic field is the predominant effective magnetic field.

– DERIVATIVES **magnetospheric** adjective.

magnetotail ▶ **noun** Astronomy the broad elongated extension of the earth's magnetosphere on the side away from the sun.

magnetron /'magnɪtrɒn/ ▶ **noun** an electron tube for amplifying or generating microwaves, with the flow of electrons controlled by an external magnetic field.

– ORIGIN 1920s: from MAGNETIC + *-tron* from ELECTRON.

magnet school ▶ **noun** a school designed to attract pupils from various areas or groups, especially one offering specialist tuition in a particular subject alongside the standard curriculum.

Magnificat /mag'nɪfɪkat/ ▶ **noun** the hymn of the Virgin Mary (Luke 1:46–55) used as a canticle in Christian liturgy, especially at vespers and evensong.

– ORIGIN Middle English: Latin, literally 'magnifies' (from the opening words, which translate as 'my soul magnifies the Lord').

magnification ▶ **noun** [mass noun] the action of magnifying something or the process of being magnified: *the lines are only visible under high magnification.* ■ [count noun] the degree to which something is or can be magnified: *at this magnification the pixels making up the image become visible.* ■ [count noun] the magnifying power of an instrument: *this microscope should give a magnification of about ×100.* ■ [count noun] a magnified reproduction of something.

magnificence ▶ **noun** [mass noun] the quality of being magnificent. ■ (**His/Your** etc. **Magnificence**) chiefly historical a title or form of address for a monarch or other distinguished person.

magnificent ▶ **adjective 1** extremely beautiful, elaborate, or impressive: *a dramatic landscape of magnificent mountains.*
2 very good; excellent: *she paid tribute to their magnificent efforts.*

– DERIVATIVES **magnificently** adverb.

– ORIGIN late Middle English: via Old French from Latin *magnificent-* 'making great', based on *magnus* 'great'.

magnifico /mag'nɪfɪkəʊ/ ▶ **noun** (pl. **magnificoes**) informal a very powerful, important, or eminent person.

– ORIGIN late 16th cent.: Italian, 'magnificent', originally used as a title for a Venetian magnate.

magnify ▶ **verb** (**magnifies, magnifying, magnified**) [with obj.] **1** make (something) appear larger than it is, especially with a lens or microscope: *the retinal image will be magnified.* ■ increase or exaggerate the importance or effect of: *you had problems before you went to Vietnam, and 'Nam magnified them.*
2 archaic praise highly; glorify: *praise the Lord and magnify Him.*

– DERIVATIVES **magnifier** noun.

– ORIGIN late Middle English (in the senses 'show honour to (God)' and 'make greater'): from Old French *magnifier* or Latin *magnificare*, based on Latin *magnus* 'great'. Sense 1 dates from the mid 17th cent.

M

magnifying glass ▶ **noun** a lens that produces an enlarged image, typically set in a frame with a handle and used to examine small or finely detailed things such as fingerprints and fine print.

magniloquence /mag'nɪləkwəns/ ▶ **noun** [mass noun] use of high-flown language: *there was no trace of magniloquence.*

magniloquent /mag'nɪləkwənt/ ▶ **adjective** using high-flown or bombastic language.

– DERIVATIVES **magniloquently** adverb.

– ORIGIN mid 17th cent.: from Latin *magniloquus* (from *magnus* 'great' + *-loquus* '-speaking') + -ENT.

Magnitogorsk /,magnɪːtə'gɔːsk/ an industrial city in southern Russia, on the Ural River close to the border with Kazakhstan; pop. 409,600 (est. 2009).

magnitude /'magnɪtjuːd/ ▶ **noun** [mass noun] **1** the great size or extent of something: *they may feel discouraged at the magnitude of the task before them.* ■ great importance: *events of tragic magnitude.*
2 size: *electorates of less than average magnitude.* ■ [count noun] a numerical quantity or value: *the magnitudes of all the economic variables could be determined.*
3 the degree of brightness of a star, as represented by a number on a logarithmic scale. ■ [count noun] the class into which a star falls by virtue of its brightness. ■ [count noun] a difference of one on a scale of brightness, treated as a unit of measurement.

– PHRASES **of the first magnitude** see FIRST.

– ORIGIN late Middle English (also in the sense 'greatness of character'): from Latin *magnitudo*, from *magnus* 'great'.

magnolia /mag'nəʊlɪə/ ▶ **noun** a tree or shrub with large, typically creamy-pink or -white, waxy flowers. ● Genus *Magnolia*, family Magnoliaceae. ■ [mass noun] a pale creamy-white colour like that of magnolia blossom.

– ORIGIN modern Latin, named after Pierre *Magnol* (1638–1715), French botanist.

Magnolia State informal name for MISSISSIPPI.

magnox /'magnɒks/ ▶ **noun** [mass noun] a magnesium-based alloy used to enclose uranium fuel elements in some nuclear reactors. ■ (**Magnox**) [as modifier] denoting the first widely used British design of nuclear power station, which used fuel clad with magnox.

– ORIGIN 1950s: from the phrase *mag(nesium) n(o) ox(idation)*.

magnum /ˈmagnəm/ ▶ **noun** (pl. **magnums**) **1** a wine bottle of twice the standard size, normally 1½ litres. **2** (trademark in the US) a gun designed to fire cartridges that are more powerful than its calibre would suggest.
– ORIGIN late 18th cent.: from Latin, neuter (used as a noun) of *magnus* 'great'.

magnum opus /ˌmagnəm ˈəʊpəs, ˈɒpəs/ ▶ **noun** (pl. **magnum opuses** or **magna opera** /ˌmagnə ˈəʊpərə, ˈɒpərə/) a work of art, music, or literature that is regarded as the most important or best work that an artist, composer, or writer has produced.
– ORIGIN late 18th cent.: from Latin, 'great work'.

Magnus effect /ˈmagnəs/ ▶ **noun** Physics the force exerted on a rapidly spinning cylinder or sphere moving through air or another fluid in a direction at an angle to the axis of spin. This force is responsible for the swerving of balls when hit or thrown with spin.
– ORIGIN 1920s: named after Heinrich G. *Magnus* (1802–70), German scientist.

Magog see **Gog and Magog**.

magpie ▶ **noun 1** a long-tailed crow with boldly marked (or green) plumage and a noisy call. ● Family Corvidae: five genera and several species, in particular the black-and-white (**black-billed**) **magpie** (*Pica pica*) of Eurasia and North America.
2 (also **bell magpie**) any bird of the Australasian butcher-bird family, having black-and-white plumage and musical calls. ● Family Cracticidae: several species.
3 used figuratively to refer to a person who obsessively collects things or who chatters idly.
4 the division of a circular target next to the outer one, or a shot which strikes this.
– ORIGIN late 16th cent.: probably shortening of dialect *maggot the pie, maggoty-pie*, from *Magot* (Middle English pet form of the given name *Marguerite*) + **pie[2]**.

magpie lark ▶ **noun** a common ground-dwelling Australian songbird with black-and-white plumage, long legs, and a loud piping call. Also called **peewee**. ● *Grallina cyanoleuca*, family Grallinidae.

M

magpie moth ▶ **noun** a white moth with black and yellow spots, the caterpillars of which are similarly coloured and can be pests of fruit bushes. ● Genus *Abraxas*, family Geometridae: *A. grossulariata* and other species.

magret /ˈmagreɪ/ ▶ **noun** a fillet of meat cut from a breast of duck.
– ORIGIN French, diminutive of Gascon dialect *magre* 'lean' (as the leanest meat is chosen), corresponding to standard French *maigre*.

Magritte /maˈgriːt/, French /magʀit/, René (François Ghislain) (1898–1967), Belgian surrealist painter. His paintings display startling or amusing juxtapositions of the ordinary, the strange, and the erotic, depicted in a realist manner.

magsman ▶ **noun** (pl. **magsmen**) Austral. informal, dated a confidence trickster. ■ a person who likes telling stories; a raconteur.
– ORIGIN early 19th cent.: from English dialect *mag* 'prattle' + **man**.

maguey /ˈmagweɪ/ ▶ **noun** an agave plant, especially one yielding pulque.
– ORIGIN mid 16th cent.: via Spanish from Taino.

magus /ˈmeɪgəs/ ▶ **noun** (pl. **magi** /ˈmeɪdʒʌɪ/) a member of a priestly caste of ancient Persia. ■ a sorcerer.
– ORIGIN Middle English: via Latin and Greek from Old Persian *maguš*.

mag wheel ▶ **noun** N. Amer. a motor-vehicle wheel made from lightweight magnesium steel, typically having a pattern of holes or spokes around the hub.

Magyar /ˈmagjɑː/ ▶ **noun 1** a member of a people who originated in the Urals and migrated westwards to settle in what is now Hungary in the 9th century AD.
2 [mass noun] the Uralic language of the Magyars; Hungarian.
▶ **adjective** relating to the Magyars or their language.
– ORIGIN the name in Hungarian.

Magyarország /ˈmɔ̃ɔrɔrˌsaːg/ Hungarian name for **Hungary**.

maha /ˈmʌhʌ/ ▶ **adjective** Indian very large or great: *the driver got a maha shock*.
– ORIGIN from Hindi *mahā*.

Mahabad /ˌmɑːhəˈbad/ a city in NW Iran, near the Iraqi border, with a chiefly Kurdish population; pop. 135,780 (2006). Between 1941 and 1946 it was the centre of a Soviet-supported Kurdish republic.

Mahabharata /ˌmɑːhəˈbɑːrətə/ one of the two great Sanskrit epics of the Hindus, existing in its present form since *c.*400 AD. It describes the civil war waged between the five Pandava brothers and their one hundred stepbrothers at Kuruksetra near modern Delhi.
– ORIGIN Sanskrit, literally 'great Bharata', i.e. the great epic of the Bharata dynasty.

mahajan /məˈhɑːdʒɑːn/ ▶ **noun** Indian a moneylender.
– ORIGIN via Hindi from Sanskrit *mahājana* 'head of a tribe or caste', from *mahā* 'great' + *jána* 'man'.

mahal /məˈhɑːl/ ▶ **noun** Indian **1** a mansion or palace: [in names] *the Taj Mahal*.
2 living quarters set aside for a particular group of people: *the whole servant mahal has been buzzing with the gossip*.
– ORIGIN early 17th cent.: from Urdu and Persian *maḥal(l)*, from Arabic *maḥall*, from *ḥall* 'stopping place, abode'.

Mahamad /ˈmahəmad/ ▶ **noun** the body of trustees ruling a Sephardic synagogue.
– ORIGIN Hebrew, from *'āmaḏ* 'to stand'.

mahant /məˈhʌnt/ ▶ **noun** Hinduism a chief priest of a temple or the head of a monastery.
– ORIGIN Hindi.

maharaja /ˌmɑː(h)əˈrɑːdʒə, ˌməhɑː-/ (also **maharajah**) ▶ **noun** historical an Indian prince.
– ORIGIN from Hindi *mahārājā*, from Sanskrit *mahā* 'great' + *rājan* 'raja'.

maharani /ˌmɑː(h)əˈrɑːni, ˌməhɑː-/ (also **maharanee**) ▶ **noun** a maharaja's wife or widow.
– ORIGIN from Hindi *mahārānī*, from Sanskrit *mahā* 'great' + *rājñī* 'rani'.

Maharashtra /ˌmɑːhəˈraʃtrə, -ˈrɑːʃtrə/ a large state in western India bordering on the Arabian Sea, formed in 1960 from the SE part of the former Bombay State; capital, Mumbai (Bombay).
– DERIVATIVES **Maharashtrian** adjective & noun.

Maharishi /ˌmɑː(h)əˈrɪʃi/ ▶ **noun** a great Hindu sage or spiritual leader.
– ORIGIN alteration of Sanskrit *maharṣi*, from *mahā* 'great' + *ṛṣi* 'rishi, sage, saint'.

mahatma /məˈhatmə, məˈhɑː-/ ▶ **noun** (in South Asia) a revered person regarded with love and respect; a holy person or sage. ■ (in some forms of theosophy) a person in India or Tibet said to have preternatural powers.
– ORIGIN from Sanskrit *mahātman*, from *mahā* 'great' + *ātman* 'soul'.

Mahaweli /ˌmɑːhəˈweɪli/ the largest river in Sri Lanka. Rising in the central highlands, it flows 330 km (206 miles) to the Bay of Bengal near Trincomalee.

Mahayana /ˌmɑː(h)əˈjɑːnə, ˌməhɑː-/ (also **Mahayana Buddhism**) ▶ **noun** [mass noun] one of the two major traditions of Buddhism, now practised especially in China, Tibet, Japan, and Korea. The tradition emerged around the 1st century AD and is typically concerned with personal spiritual practice and the ideal of the bodhisattva. Compare with **Theravada**.
– ORIGIN from Sanskrit, from *mahā* 'great' + *yāna* 'vehicle'.

Mahdi /ˈmɑːdi/ ▶ **noun** (pl. **Mahdis**) (in popular Muslim belief) a spiritual and temporal leader who will rule before the end of the world and restore religion and justice. ■ a person claiming to be the Mahdi, notably Muhammad Ahmad of Dongola in Sudan (1843–85), whose revolutionary movement captured Khartoum and overthrew the Egyptian regime. ■ (in Shiite belief) the twelfth imam, who is expected to return and triumph over injustice.
– DERIVATIVES **Mahdism** noun, **Mahdist** noun & adjective.
– ORIGIN from Arabic *(al-)mahdī* 'he who is guided in the right way', passive participle of *hadā* 'to guide'.

Mahican /ˈmahɪk(ə)n/ (also **Mohican**) ▶ **noun 1** a member of an American Indian people formerly inhabiting the Upper Hudson Valley in New York State. Compare with **Mohegan**.
2 [mass noun] the extinct Algonquian language of the Mahicans.
▶ **adjective** relating to the Mahicans or their language.
– ORIGIN the name in Mahican, said to mean 'wolf'.

Mahilyow /ˌmɑːhɪˈljəʊ/ an industrial city and railway centre in eastern Belarus, on the River Dnieper; pop. 372,000 (est. 2009). Russian name **Mogilyov**.

mahimahi /ˈmɑːhɪˌmɑːhi/ ▶ **noun** Hawaiian term for **dorado** (sense 1).

mah-jong /mɑːˈdʒɒŋ/ (also **mah-jongg**) ▶ **noun** a Chinese game played, usually by four people, with 136 or 144 rectangular pieces called tiles.
– ORIGIN from Chinese dialect *ma-tsiang*, literally 'sparrows'.

Mahler /ˈmɑːlə/, German /ˈmaːlɐ/, Gustav (1860–1911), Austrian composer, conductor, and pianist. Forming a link between romanticism and the experimentalism of Schoenberg, his works include nine complete symphonies (1888–1910) and the symphonic song cycle *Das Lied von der Erde* (1908).
– DERIVATIVES **Mahlerian** /-ˈlɪərɪən/ adjective.

mahlstick /ˈmɔːlstɪk/ (also **maulstick**) ▶ **noun** a light stick with a padded leather ball at one end, held against work by a painter or signwriter to support and steady the brush hand.
– ORIGIN mid 17th cent.: from Dutch *maalstok*, from *malen* 'to paint' + *stok* 'stick'.

mahoe[1] /məˈhəʊi/ ▶ **noun** a small bushy New Zealand tree of the violet family, with whitish bark and clusters of small greenish flowers. ● *Melicytus ramiflorus*, family Violaceae.
– ORIGIN early 19th cent.: from Maori.

mahoe[2] /məˈhəʊ/ ▶ **noun** W. Indian any of a number of tropical trees and shrubs yielding bast that is used to make cord. ● Several species, especially of the genus *Hibiscus* (family Malvaceae), in particular *H. tiliaceus* and the Caribbean *H. elatus*.
– ORIGIN from Arawak *maho*.

mahogany /məˈhɒgəni/ ▶ **noun 1** [mass noun] hard reddish-brown timber from a tropical tree, used for quality furniture. ■ a rich reddish-brown colour like that of mahogany wood.
2 the tropical tree which produces mahogany. ● *Swietenia mahagoni*, family Meliaceae (tropical America), and other species.
■ used in names of trees which yield timber similar to mahogany, e.g. **African mahogany**.
– ORIGIN mid 17th cent.: of unknown origin.

Mahon /məˈhɒn/ (also **Port Mahon**) the capital of the island of Minorca, a port on the SE coast; pop. 24,200 (est. 2002). Spanish name **Mahón**.

mahonia /məˈhəʊnɪə/ ▶ **noun** an evergreen shrub of the barberry family, which produces clusters of small fragrant yellow flowers followed by purple or black berries, native to eastern Asia and North and Central America. ● Genus *Mahonia*, family Berberidaceae.
– ORIGIN modern Latin, named after Bernard McMahon (*c.*1775–1816), American botanist.

Mahore /məˈhɔː/ another name for **Mayotte**.

mahout /məˈhaʊt/ ▶ **noun** (in South and SE Asia) a person who works with and rides an elephant.
– ORIGIN from Hindi *mahāvat*.

Mahratta ▶ **noun** variant spelling of **Maratha**.

Mahratti ▶ **noun** variant spelling of **Marathi**.

mahseer /ˈmɑːsɪə/ ▶ **noun** a large edible freshwater fish of the carp family, native to northern India and the Himalayan region. ● Genus *Tor*, family Cyprinidae: several species, especially the **Putitor mahseer** (*T. putitora*).
– ORIGIN via Hindi from Sanskrit *mahā* 'great' + *śaphara* 'carp'.

mahua /ˈmʌhʊə/ (also **mahwa** /ˈməʊwə/) ▶ **noun** an Indian tree which has fleshy edible flowers and yields oil-rich seeds. ● *Madhuca latifolia*, family Sapotaceae.
■ [mass noun] an alcoholic drink produced from the nectar-rich flowers of the mahua.
– ORIGIN late 17th cent.: via Hindi from Sanskrit *madhūka*, from *madhu* 'sweet'.

mahurat /məˈhuːrət/ ▶ **noun** Indian an auspicious time for an enterprise to begin or for a ceremony to take place: *the pandit selects the best mahurat for the wedding*. ■ an inauguration ceremony, especially one held to mark the start of the making of a film.
– ORIGIN from Hindi *mahūrat*, from Sanskrit *muhūrta* 'a division of time' (approximately 48 minutes, one thirtieth of a day).

Maia[1] /ˈmʌɪə/ Greek Mythology the daughter of Atlas and mother of Hermes.

Maia[2] /ˈmʌɪə/ Roman Mythology a goddess associated with Vulcan and also (by confusion with **Maia[1]**) with Mercury (Hermes). She was worshipped on 1 May and 15 May; that month is named after her.

maid ▶ **noun 1** a female domestic servant.
2 archaic an unmarried girl or young woman. ■ a virgin.
– ORIGIN Middle English: abbreviation of **maiden**.

maidan /mʌɪˈdɑːn/ ▸ **noun** (in South Asia) an open space in or near a town, used as a parade ground or for events such as public meetings.
– ORIGIN from Urdu and Persian *maidān*, from Arabic *maydān*.

maiden ▸ **noun 1** archaic an unmarried girl or young woman. ■ a virgin.
2 (also **maiden over**) Cricket an over in which no runs are scored.
▸ **adjective** [attrib.] **1** (of an older woman) unmarried: *a maiden aunt*. ■ (of a female animal) not having mated.
2 being or involving the first attempt or act of its kind: *the Titanic's maiden voyage*. ■ denoting a horse that has never won a race, or a race intended for such horses. ■ (of a tree or other fruiting plant) in its first year of growth.
– DERIVATIVES **maidenish adjective**.
– ORIGIN Old English *mægden*, from a Germanic diminutive meaning 'maid, virgin'; related to German *Mädchen*, diminutive of *Magd* 'maid', from an Indo-European root shared by Old Irish *mug* 'boy, servant'.

maidenhair (also **maidenhair fern**) ▸ **noun** a chiefly tropical fern having slender-stalked fronds with round or wedge-shaped divided lobes. ● Genus *Adiantum*, family Adiantaceae: several species, in particular *A. capillus-veneris* of Eurasia and North America.

maidenhair tree ▸ **noun** the ginkgo, whose leaves resemble those of the maidenhair fern.

Maidenhead a town in Berkshire, southern England to the west of London on the River Thames; pop. 53,900 (est. 2009).

maidenhead ▸ **noun** [mass noun] archaic virginity. ■ [count noun] the hymen.

maidenhood ▸ **noun** the fact or condition of being a young, unmarried woman. ■ a girl's virginity: *most brides wear white to symbolize maidenhood*.

maidenly ▸ **adjective** relating to or appropriate to a maiden; demure: *maidenly modesty*.

maiden name ▸ **noun** the surname that a married woman used before she was married and which she may still use when married, especially in her employment.

maiden over ▸ **noun** see MAIDEN (sense 2 of the noun).

Maid Marian (in English folklore) the lover of Robin Hood.

maid of honour ▸ **noun 1** an unmarried noblewoman attending a queen or princess. ■ N. Amer. a principal bridesmaid.
2 Brit. a small tart filled with flavoured milk curds.

maidservant ▸ **noun** dated a female domestic servant.

Maidstone a town in SE England, on the River Medway, the county town of Kent; pop. 91,200 (est. 2009).

maieutic /meɪˈjuːtɪk/ ▸ **adjective** of or denoting the Socratic mode of enquiry, which aims to bring a person's latent ideas into clear consciousness.
▸ **plural noun** (**maieutics**) [treated as sing.] the maieutic method.
– ORIGIN mid 17th cent.: from Greek *maieutikos*, from *maieuesthai* 'act as a midwife', from *maia* 'midwife'.

maigre /ˈmeɪgə/ ▸ **adjective** (in the Roman Catholic Church) denoting a day on which abstinence from meat is ordered. ■ (of food) suitable for eating on maigre days.
– ORIGIN late 17th cent.: from French, literally 'lean'.

Maikop /mʌɪˈkɒp/ a city in SW Russia, capital of the republic of Adygea; pop. 153,500 (est. 2008).

mail[1] ▸ **noun** [mass noun] letters and parcels sent by post. ■ (N. Amer. & W. Indian also **the mails**) the postal system: *you can order by mail*. ■ [in sing.] a single delivery or collection of mail: *I had a notice in by this morning's mail*. ■ email: *you've got mail*. ■ [count noun] dated a vehicle, such as a train, carrying mail. ■ [count noun] archaic a bag of letters to be sent by post. ■ [in names] used in titles of newspapers: *the Daily Mail*.
▸ **verb** [with obj.] send (a letter or parcel) by post: *three editions were mailed to our members*. ■ send (someone) email.
– DERIVATIVES **mailable adjective**.
– ORIGIN Middle English (in the sense 'travelling bag'): from Old French *male* 'wallet', of West Germanic origin. The notion 'by post' dates from the mid 17th cent.

mail[2] ▸ **noun** [mass noun] historical armour made of metal rings or plates joined together flexibly. ■ the protective shell or scales of certain animals.
▸ **verb** [with obj.] (often as adj. **mailed**) clothe or cover with mail: *a mailed gauntlet*.
– PHRASES **the mailed fist** the use of physical force to maintain control.
– ORIGIN Middle English (also denoting the individual metal elements composing mail armour): from Old French *maille*, from Latin *macula* 'spot or mesh'.

mailbag ▸ **noun** a large sack or bag for carrying mail. ■ the letters received by a person, especially a public figure such as a Member of Parliament.

mailboat ▸ **noun** a ship or boat that carries mail.

mail bomb ▸ **noun 1** US a letter bomb.
2 an overwhelming quantity of email messages sent to one address.
▸ **verb** (**mail-bomb**) [with obj.] send an overwhelming quantity of email messages to (someone).

mailbox ▸ **noun** N. Amer. a box into which mail is delivered, especially one mounted on a post at the entrance to a person's property. ■ N. Amer. a postbox. ■ a computer file in which email messages received by a particular user are stored.

mail cart ▸ **noun** Brit. historical a cart for carrying mail by road.

mail drop ▸ **noun 1** N. Amer. a receptacle for mail, especially one in which mail is kept until the addressee collects it.
2 Brit. a delivery of mail.

Mailer, Norman (1923–2007), American novelist and essayist. Notable novels: *The Naked and the Dead* (1948) and *The Presidential Papers* (1963).

mailer ▸ **noun 1** N. Amer. the sender of a letter or package by post. ■ a person employed to dispatch newspapers or periodicals by post. ■ a free advertising pamphlet or catalogue sent by post. ■ a container used for conveying items by post.
2 Computing a program that sends email messages.

mailing ▸ **noun** [mass noun] the action or process of sending something by mail. ■ [count noun] an item sent by mail, especially a piece of mass advertising.

mailing list ▸ **noun** a list of the names and addresses of people to whom advertising matter, information, or other material may be mailed regularly.

maillot /mʌɪˈjəʊ/ ▸ **noun** (pl. pronunc. **same**) **1** a pair of tights, especially as worn by ballet dancers and circus artistes.
2 N. Amer. a woman's swimsuit.
3 a jersey or top worn in cycle racing.
– ORIGIN French.

mailman ▸ **noun** (pl. **mailmen**) N. Amer. a postman.

mail merge ▸ **noun** [mass noun] Computing the automatic addition of names and addresses from a database to letters and envelopes in order to facilitate sending mail, especially advertising, to many addresses.

mail order ▸ **noun** [mass noun] the sale and ordering of goods by post, generally involving selection from a catalogue.

mail-out ▸ **noun** an instance of posting promotional material to a large number of people at one time.

mailshot Brit. ▸ **noun** a dispatch of mail, especially promotional material, to a large number of people. ■ an item sent in a mailshot.
▸ **verb** [with obj.] send promotional material to (a large number of people).

maim ▸ **verb** [with obj.] wound or injure (a person or animal) so that part of the body is permanently damaged: *100,000 soldiers were killed or maimed*.
– ORIGIN Middle English: from Old French *mahaignier*, of unknown origin.

Maimonides /mʌɪˈmɒnɪdiːz/ (1135–1204), Jewish philosopher and Rabbinic scholar, born in Spain; born *Moses ben Maimon*. His *Guide for the Perplexed* (1190) attempts to reconcile Talmudic scripture with the philosophy of Aristotle.

Main /mʌɪn/ a river of SW Germany which rises in northern Bavaria and flows 500 km (310 miles) westwards, through Frankfurt, to meet the Rhine at Mainz.

main[1] ▸ **adjective** [attrib.] chief in size or importance: *a main road | the main problem is one of resources*.
▸ **noun 1** a principal pipe carrying water or gas to buildings, or taking sewage from them. ■ a principal cable carrying electricity. ■ (**the mains**) Brit. the source of public water, gas, or electricity supply through pipes or cables.
2 (**the main**) archaic or literary the open ocean.
3 Nautical short for MAINSAIL or MAINMAST.
– PHRASES **by main force** through sheer strength. **in the main** on the whole.
– ORIGIN Middle English: from Old English *mægen* 'physical force', reinforced by Old Norse *meginn*, *megn* 'strong, powerful', both from a Germanic base meaning 'have power'.

main[2] ▸ **noun 1** (in the game of hazard) a number (5, 6, 7, 8, or 9) called by a player before dice are thrown.
2 historical a match between fighting cocks.
– ORIGIN late 16th cent.: probably from the phrase *main chance*.

main beam ▸ **noun 1** a principal beam which transmits a load directly to a column.
2 Brit. the full (rather than dipped) beam of the headlights of a motor vehicle.

mainboard ▸ **noun** another term for MOTHERBOARD.

main brace ▸ **noun** the brace attached to the main yard of a sailing ship.

main clause ▸ **noun** Grammar a clause that can form a complete sentence standing alone, having a subject and a predicate. Contrasted with SUBORDINATE CLAUSE.

main course ▸ **noun 1** the most substantial course of a meal.
2 the mainsail of a square-rigged sailing ship.

maincrop ▸ **adjective** Brit. denoting a vegetable produced as a principal crop of the season.

main drag ▸ **noun** (usu. **the main drag**) N. Amer. informal the main street of a town.

Maine a NE state of the US, on the Atlantic coast; pop. 1,316,456 (est. 2008); capital, Augusta. Visited by John Cabot in 1498 and colonized from England in the 17th and 18th centuries, it became the 23rd state of the US in 1820.
– DERIVATIVES **Mainer noun**.

Maine Coon (also **Maine Coon cat**) ▸ **noun** a large, powerful cat of a long-haired breed, originally from America.
– ORIGIN 1970s: so named because of partial resemblance to the raccoon.

mainframe ▸ **noun 1** a large high-speed computer, especially one supporting numerous workstations or peripherals.
2 the central processing unit and primary memory of a computer.

M

Mainland 1 the largest island in Orkney.
2 the largest island in Shetland.

mainland ▸ **noun** a large continuous extent of land that includes the greater part of a country or territory, as opposed to offshore islands and detached territories.
– DERIVATIVES **mainlander noun**.

main line ▸ **noun 1** a chief railway line: [as modifier] *a main-line station*. ■ N. Amer. a chief road or street.
2 informal a principal vein as a site for a drug injection.
▸ **verb** (**mainline**) [with obj.] informal inject (a drug) intravenously: *Mariella mainlines cocaine five times a day* | [no obj.] *he started mainlining on heroin*.
– DERIVATIVES **mainliner noun**.

mainly ▸ **adverb** more than anything else: *he is mainly concerned with fiction*. ■ for the most part: *the west will be mainly dry*.

main man ▸ **noun** informal, chiefly N. Amer. a close and trusted friend.

mainmast ▸ **noun** the principal mast of a ship, typically the second mast in a sailing ship of three or more masts.

mainplane ▸ **noun** a principal wing or other supporting surface of an aircraft, as opposed to a tailplane.

mainsail /ˈmeɪnseɪl, -s(ə)l/ ▸ **noun** the principal sail of a ship, especially the lowest sail on the mainmast in a square-rigged vessel. ■ the sail set on the after part of the mainmast in a fore-and-aft rigged vessel.

main sequence ▸ **noun** Astronomy a series of types to which most stars belong, represented on a Hertzsprung–Russell diagram as a continuous band extending from the upper left (hot, bright stars) to the lower right (cool, dim stars).

mainsheet ▸ **noun** a sheet used for controlling and trimming the mainsail of a sailing boat.

mainspring ▸ **noun 1** the main agent of motivation: *innovation is the mainspring of the new economy*.
2 the principal spring in a watch, clock, or other mechanism.

mainstay ▸ **noun** a stay which extends from the maintop to the foot of the foremast of a sailing ship. ■ someone or something on which something else is based or relies: *whitefish are the mainstay of the local industry.*

mainstream ▸ noun (**the mainstream**) the ideas, attitudes, or activities that are shared by most people and regarded as normal or conventional: *they withdrew from the mainstream of European politics.* ■ (also **mainstream jazz**) [mass noun] jazz that is neither traditional nor modern, based on the 1930s swing style and consisting especially of solo improvisation on chord sequences.
▸ adjective belonging to or characteristic of the mainstream: *mainstream pop music.* ■ (of a school or class) for pupils without special needs.
▸ verb [with obj.] bring into the mainstream: *vegetarianism has been mainstreamed.*

main street ▸ noun chiefly N. Amer. the principal street of a town, traditionally the site of shops, banks, and other businesses: *the money you save on a car can offset some of the higher prices on Main Street.* ■ (**Main Street**) US used in reference to the materialism, mediocrity, or parochialism regarded as typical of small-town life. [from the title of a novel (1920) by Sinclair Lewis.]

maintain ▸ verb [with obj.] **1** cause or enable (a condition or situation) to continue: *the need to maintain close links between industry and schools.* ■ keep (something) at the same level or rate: *agricultural prices will have to be maintained.* ■ keep (a building, machine, or road) in good condition by checking or repairing it regularly.
2 provide with necessities for life or existence: *the allowance covers the basic costs of maintaining a child.* ■ keep (a military unit) supplied with equipment and other requirements. ■ archaic give one's support to; uphold: *the king swears he will maintain the laws of God.*
3 [reporting verb] state something strongly to be the case; assert: [with obj.] *he has always maintained his innocence* | [with clause] *he had persistently maintained that he would not stand against his old friend.*
– DERIVATIVES **maintainability** noun, **maintainable** adjective.
– ORIGIN Middle English (also in the sense 'practise an action habitually'): from Old French *maintenir*, from Latin *manu tenere* 'hold in the hand'.

maintained ▸ adjective Brit. (of a school) financed with public money.

maintainer ▸ noun a person or thing that maintains something, in particular computer software.

maintenance ▸ noun [mass noun] **1** the process of preserving a condition or situation or the state of being preserved: *crucial conditions for the maintenance of democratic government.* ■ the process of keeping something in good condition: *car maintenance* | [as modifier] *essential maintenance work.*
2 the provision of financial support for a person's living expenses, or the support so provided. ■ Brit. a husband's or wife's provision for their spouse after separation or divorce.
3 Law the offence of aiding a party in a legal action without lawful cause.
– ORIGIN Middle English (in the sense 'aiding a party in a legal action without lawful cause'): from Old French, from *maintenir* (see MAINTAIN).

maintenance order ▸ noun Brit. a court order directing payment of a regular fixed sum for maintenance to be paid to a spouse after separation or divorce.

Maintenon /ˈmãtənɒ̃/, French /mɛ̃tnɔ̃/, Françoise d'Aubigné, Marquise de (1635–1719), mistress and later second wife of the French king Louis XIV.

maintop ▸ noun a platform around the head of the lower section of a sailing ship's mainmast.

maintopmast /meɪnˈtɒpməst/ ▸ noun the second section of a sailing ship's mainmast.

main verb ▸ noun Grammar **1** the verb in a main clause. **2** the head of a verb phrase, for example *eat* in *might have been going to eat it.*

Mainz /mʌɪnts/ a city in western Germany, capital of Rhineland-Palatinate, situated at the confluence of the Rhine and Main Rivers; pop. 196,400 (est. 2006).

maiolica /məˈjɒlɪkə, mʌɪˈɒlɪkə/ ▸ noun [mass noun] fine earthenware with coloured decoration on an opaque white tin glaze, originating in Italy during the Renaissance.
– ORIGIN mid 16th cent.: Italian, from *Maiolica* 'Majorca'.

maisonette /ˌmeɪzəˈnɛt/ ▸ noun a set of rooms for living in, typically on two storeys of a larger building and having a separate entrance.
– ORIGIN late 18th cent.: from French *maisonnette*, diminutive of *maison* 'house'.

maistry /ˈmeɪstri/ ▸ noun (pl. **maistries**) (in South Asia) a master workman; a foreman.
– ORIGIN from Portuguese *mestre* 'master'.

mai tai /ˈmʌɪ tʌɪ/ ▸ noun a cocktail based on light rum, curaçao, and fruit juices.
– ORIGIN Polynesian.

Maithili /ˈmʌɪtɪli/ ▸ noun [mass noun] one of the Bihari group of languages, spoken by some 25 million people in northern Bihar, elsewhere in India, and in Nepal.
– ORIGIN Sanskrit (as an adjective), from *Mithilā*, a place in northern Bihar.

maître d'hôtel /ˌmeɪtrə dəʊˈtɛl/, French /mɛtʀ dotɛl/ (also **maître d'** /ˌmeɪtrə ˈdiː/) ▸ noun (pl. **maîtres d'hôtel** pronunc. **same**, or **maître d's**) the head waiter of a restaurant. ■ the manager of a hotel.
– ORIGIN mid 16th cent.: French, literally 'master of (the) house'.

Maitreya /mʌɪˈtreɪjə/ Buddhism the Buddha who will appear in the future.
– ORIGIN Sanskrit, from *mitra* 'friend or friendship'.

maize ▸ noun [mass noun] Brit. a Central American cereal plant which yields large grains (corn or sweetcorn) set in rows on a cob. The many varieties include some used for stockfeed and corn oil. ● *Zea mays*, family Gramineae.
– ORIGIN mid 16th cent.: from Spanish *maíz*, from Taino *mahiz*.

Maj. ▸ abbreviation Major.

majestic ▸ adjective having or showing impressive beauty or scale: *the majestic Canadian Rockies.*
– DERIVATIVES **majestically** adverb.

majesty ▸ noun (pl. **majesties**) **1** impressive beauty, scale, or stateliness: *the majesty of Ben Nevis.*
2 royal power: *the majesty of the royal household.* ■ (**His**, **Your**, etc. **Majesty**) a title given to a sovereign or a sovereign's wife or widow.
– ORIGIN Middle English (in the sense 'greatness of God'): from Old French *majeste*, from Latin *majestas*, from a variant of *majus*, *major-* (see MAJOR).

majlis /ˈmadʒlɪs, madʒˈlɪs/ ▸ noun (pl. **same**) the parliament of various North African and Middle Eastern countries, especially Iran.
– ORIGIN Arabic, literally 'assembly'.

majolica /məˈjɒlɪkə, -ˈdʒɒl-/ ▸ noun [mass noun] a kind of earthenware made in imitation of Italian maiolica, especially in England during the 19th century.
– ORIGIN variant of MAIOLICA.

Major, Sir John (b.1943), British Conservative statesman, Prime Minister 1990–7.

major ▸ adjective **1** [attrib.] important, serious, or significant: *the use of drugs is a major problem.* ■ greater or more important; main: *he got the major share of the spoils.*
2 Music (of a scale) having intervals of a semitone between the third and fourth, and seventh and eighth degrees. Contrasted with MINOR. ■ (of an interval) equivalent to that between the tonic and another note of a major scale, and greater by a semitone than the corresponding minor interval. ■ [postpositive] (of a key) based on a major scale, tending to produce a bright or joyful effect: *Prelude in G Major.*
3 Brit. dated (appended to a surname in public schools) indicating the elder of two brothers.
4 Logic (of a term) occurring as the predicate in the conclusion of a categorical syllogism. ■ (of a premise) containing the major term in a categorical syllogism.
▸ noun **1** a rank of officer in the army and the US air force, above captain and below lieutenant colonel. [shortening of SERGEANT MAJOR, formerly a high rank.] ■ [with modifier] an officer in charge of a section of band instruments: *a trumpet major.*
2 Music a major key, interval, or scale. ■ Bell-ringing a system of change-ringing using eight bells.
3 a major organization or competition.
4 N. Amer. a student's principal subject or course. ■ [often with modifier] a student specializing in a specified subject: *a math major.*
5 Logic a major term or premise.
6 Bridge short for MAJOR SUIT.
7 Australian Rules a goal.
▸ verb [no obj.] (**major in**) N. Amer. & Austral./NZ specialize in (a particular subject) at college or university: *I was trying to decide if I should major in drama or English.*
– ORIGIN Middle English: from Latin, comparative of *magnus* 'great'; perhaps influenced by French *majeur*.

major arcana ▸ noun see ARCANA.

major axis ▸ noun Geometry the longer axis of an ellipse, passing through its foci.

Majorca /məˈjɔːkə/ the largest of the Balearic Islands; pop. 846,210 (2008); capital, Palma. Spanish name MALLORCA.
– DERIVATIVES **Majorcan** adjective & noun.

major-domo /ˌmeɪdʒəˈdəʊməʊ/ ▸ noun (pl. **major-domos**) the chief steward of a large household.
– ORIGIN late 16th cent.: via Spanish and Italian from medieval Latin *major domus* 'highest official of the household'.

majorette /ˌmeɪdʒəˈrɛt/ ▸ noun short for DRUM MAJORETTE.

major general ▸ noun a rank of officer in the army and the US air force, above brigadier or brigadier general and below lieutenant general.
– ORIGIN mid 17th cent.: shortening of *sergeant major general.*

majoritarian /məˌdʒɒrɪˈtɛːrɪən/ ▸ adjective governed by or believing in decision by a majority.
▸ noun a person who supports government by a majority.
– DERIVATIVES **majoritarianism** noun.

majority ▸ noun (pl. **majorities**) **1** the greater number: *in **the majority of** cases all will go smoothly* | [as modifier] *it was a majority decision.* ■ Brit. the number by which the votes cast for one party or candidate exceed those for the next: *Labour retained the seat with a majority of 9,830.* ■ a party or group receiving the greater number of votes. ■ US the number by which votes for one candidate are more than those for all other candidates together.
2 [mass noun] the age at which a person is legally a full adult, usually either 18 or 21.
3 the rank or office of a major.
– PHRASES **be in the majority** belong to or constitute the larger group or number.
– ORIGIN mid 16th cent. (denoting superiority): from French *majorité*, from medieval Latin *majoritas*, from Latin *major* (see MAJOR).

> **USAGE** Strictly speaking, **majority** should be used with countable nouns to mean 'the greater number', as in *the majority of cases*. Use with uncountable nouns to mean 'the greatest part', as in *I spent the majority of the day reading*, is not considered good standard English, although it is common in informal contexts.

majority rule ▸ noun [mass noun] the principle that the greater number should exercise greater power.

majority verdict ▸ noun English Law a verdict agreed by all but one or two of the members of a jury.

major league ▸ noun N. Amer. the highest-ranking league in a particular professional sport, especially baseball.
– DERIVATIVES **major-leaguer** noun.

majorly ▸ adverb [as submodifier] informal very; extremely: *I'm majorly depressed.*

major piece ▸ noun Chess a rook or queen.

major planet ▸ noun any of the eight main planets of the solar system, as distinct from an asteroid or moon.

major prophet ▸ noun any of the prophets after whom the longer prophetic books of the Bible are named; Isaiah, Jeremiah, or Ezekiel.

major suit ▸ noun Bridge spades or hearts.
– ORIGIN early 20th cent.: so named because of their higher scoring value.

major tranquillizer ▸ noun a tranquillizer of the kind used to treat psychotic states.

majuscule /ˈmadʒəskjuːl/ ▸ noun [mass noun] large lettering, either capital or uncial, in which all the letters are the same height. ■ [count noun] a large letter.
– ORIGIN early 18th cent.: from French, from Latin *majuscula (littera)* 'somewhat greater (letter)'.

makan /ˈmakan/ ▸ noun [mass noun] (in Malaysia and Singapore) food.
– ORIGIN Malay.

Makarios III /məˈkɑːrɪɒs/ (1913–77), Greek Cypriot archbishop and statesman, first President of the republic of Cyprus 1960–77; born *Mikhail Christodolou Mouskos*. He reorganized the movement for enosis (union of Cyprus with Greece) and was exiled 1956–9 by the British for allegedly supporting the EOKA terrorist campaign.

Makasarese /məˌkasəˈriːz/ (also **Makassarese**) ▸ **noun** (pl. **same**) **1** a native or inhabitant of Makassar (now Ujung Pandang) in Indonesia. **2** [mass noun] the Indonesian language of the Makasarese, with around 1.6 million speakers. ▸ **adjective** relating to the Makasarese or their language.

Makassar /məˈkasə/ (also **Macassar** or **Makasar**) former name (until 1973) for **Ujung Pandang**.

Makassar Strait a stretch of water separating the islands of Borneo and Sulawesi and linking the Celebes Sea in the north with the Java Sea in the south.

make ▸ **verb** (past and past participle **made**) [with obj.] **1** form (something) by putting parts together or combining substances; create: *my grandmother made a dress for me | cricket bats are **made of** willow.* ■ (**make something into**) alter something so that it forms (something else): *buffalo's milk can be made into cheese.* ■ compose or draw up (something written or abstract): *make a list of all the points you can think of.* ■ prepare (a dish, drink, or meal): *she was making lunch for Lucy and Francis* | [with two objs] *I'll make us both a cup of tea.* ■ arrange bedclothes tidily on (a bed) ready for use. ■ arrange and light materials for (a fire). ■ Electronics complete or close (a circuit). **2** cause (something) to exist or come about; bring about: *the drips had made a pool on the floor.* ■ [with obj. and complement or infinitive] cause to become or seem: *decorative features make brickwork more interesting | the best way to disarm your critics is to make them laugh.* ■ carry out, perform, or produce (a specified action or sound): *anyone can make a mistake.* ■ (in soccer) enable a teammate to score (a goal) by one's play. ■ communicate or express (an idea, request, or requirement): *there are two more points to make* | [with two objs] *make him an offer he can't refuse.* ■ archaic enter into a contract of (marriage). ■ [with obj. and complement] appoint or designate (someone) to a position: *he was made a fellow of the Royal Institute.* ■ [with obj. and complement] represent or cause to appear in a specified way: *the issue price makes them good value.* ■ cause to be successful: *the work which made Wordsworth's reputation.* **3** [with obj. and infinitive] compel (someone) to do something: *she bought me a brandy and made me drink it.* **4** constitute; amount to: *they made an unusual duo.* ■ be suitable for or likely to develop into: *this fern makes a good houseplant.* ■ consider to be; estimate as: *How many are there? I **make it** sixteen.* ■ agree or decide on (a specified arrangement): *let's **make it** 7.30.* **5** gain or earn (money or profit): *he'd made a lot of money out of hardware.* ■ Cricket score (a specified number of runs). **6** manage to arrive at (a place) within a specified time or catch (a train or other form of transport): *we've got a lot to do if you're going to make the shuttle | they didn't always **make it** on time.* ■ (**make it**) become successful: *he waited confidently for his band to make it.* ■ (**make it**) succeed in reaching safety or in surviving: *the pilot didn't make it—his neck's broken.* ■ achieve a place in: *Australia should make the final.* ■ achieve the rank of: *he wasn't going to make captain.* **7** [no obj., with adverbial of direction] prepare to go in a particular direction: *he struggled to his feet and **made towards** the car.* ■ [with infinitive] act as if one is about to perform an action: *she made as if to leave the room.* **8** N. Amer. informal induce (someone) to have sexual intercourse with one: *he had been trying to make Cynthia for two years now.* **9** (in bridge, whist, etc.) win (a trick). ■ win a trick with (a card). ■ win the number of tricks that fulfils (a contract). ■ shuffle (cards) for dealing. **10** [no obj.] Nautical (of the tide) begin to flow or ebb. ▸ **noun 1** the manufacturer or trade name of a product: *the make, model, and year of his car.* ■ the structure or composition of something. **2** the making of electrical contact.
– PHRASES **be made of money** [often with negative] informal be very rich. **be made up 1** N. English & Irish informal be delighted: *we're made up about the baby.* **2** Irish be assured of success; be lucky: *what with the high prices since the war started, we'll be made up if it lasts.* **have (got) it made** informal be in a position where success is certain. **make a day** (or **night**) **of it** devote a whole day (or night) to an activity. **make someone's day** make an otherwise ordinary or dull day pleasingly memorable for someone. **make a House** Brit. secure the presence of enough members for a quorum or support in the House of Commons. **make do** manage with the limited or inadequate means available: *Dad would have to make do with an old car.* **make like** N. Amer. informal pretend to be; imitate: *now make like my pants and split.* **make or break** be the factor which decides whether (something) will succeed or fail. **make sail** Sailing spread a sail or sails. ■ start a voyage. **make time 1** find an occasion when time is available to do something. **2** N. Amer. informal make sexual advances to someone: *I couldn't make time with Marilyn because she was already a senior.* **make up one's mind** make a decision; decide. **make way 1** allow room for someone or something else: *the land is due to be concreted over to **make way for** a car park.* **2** Nautical make progress; travel. **on the make** informal intent on gain, typically in an unscrupulous way. ■ looking for a sexual partner. **put the make on** N. Amer. informal make sexual advances to (someone).
– PHRASAL VERBS **make after** dated pursue (someone). **make away with** another way of saying **make off with**. ■ kill (someone). **make for 1** move or head towards (a place): *I made for the life raft and hung on for dear life.* ■ approach (someone) to attack them. **2** tend to result in or be received as (a particular thing): *job descriptions never make for exciting reading.* **3** (**be made for**) be eminently suited for (a particular function or person): *a man made for action.* **make something of** give a specified amount of attention or importance to: *he makes little of America's low investment rates.* ■ understand the meaning or character of: *he wasn't sure what to make of Sue.* **make off** leave hurriedly, especially in order to avoid duty or punishment: *they made off without paying.* **make off with** carry (something) away illicitly: *burglars made off with all their wedding presents.* **make out** informal **1** make progress; fare: *how are you making out, now that the summer's over?* **2** N. Amer. informal engage in sexual activity. **make someone/thing out 1** manage with some difficulty to see or hear something: *in the dim light it was difficult to make out the illustration.* ■ understand the character or motivation of. **2** [with infinitive or clause] assert; represent: *I'm not as bad as I'm **made out to be**.* ■ try to give a specified impression; pretend: *he made out he was leaving.* **3** draw up or write out a list or document: *send a cheque **made out to** Trinity College.* **make someone over** give someone a new image with hairstyling, make-up, or clothes. **make something over** transfer the possession of something to someone. **make up** be reconciled after a quarrel: *let's kiss and make up.* **make someone up** apply cosmetics to oneself or another. **make something up 1** (also **make up for**) compensate for something lost, missed, or deficient: *I'll make up the time tomorrow.* ■ (**make it up to**) compensate someone for negligent or unfair treatment. **2** (**make up**) (of parts) compose or constitute (a whole): *women make up 56 per cent of the student body.* ■ complete an amount or group: *he brought along a girl to make up a foursome.* **3** put together or prepare something from parts or ingredients: *make up the mortar to a consistency that can be moulded in the hands.* ■ get an amount or group together. ■ prepare a bed for use with fresh bedclothes. ■ Printing arrange text and illustrations into pages. **4** invent a story, lie, or plan. **make up to** Brit. informal attempt to win the favour of (someone) by being pleasant. **make with** US informal proceed to use or supply: *make with the feet, honey—you're embarrassing Jim.*
– DERIVATIVES **makeable** (also **makable**) adjective.
– ORIGIN Old English *macian*, of West Germanic origin, from a base meaning 'fitting'; related to **match**[1].

make-and-break ▸ **noun** a switch or other device in which electrical contact is automatically made and broken.

make-before-break ▸ **adjective** denoting a switch or other device in which a new electrical connection is made before the existing one is broken.

make-believe ▸ **noun** [mass noun] the action of pretending or imagining that things are better than they really are: *she's living in a world of make-believe.* ▸ **adjective** imitating something real: *he was firing a make-believe gun at the spy planes.* ▸ **verb** [no obj.] pretend; imagine.

make-do ▸ **adjective** [attrib.] makeshift; temporary: *make-do shelters dotted the landscape.*

makeover ▸ **noun** a complete transformation of the appearance of someone or something: *win one of our special pampering makeovers.*

maker ▸ **noun 1** [usu. in combination] a person or thing that makes or produces something: *film-makers | a cabinetmaker.* **2** (**our, the,** etc. **Maker**) God.
– PHRASES **meet one's Maker** chiefly humorous die.

makeshift ▸ **adjective** acting as an interim and temporary measure: *arranging a row of chairs to form a makeshift bed.* ▸ **noun** a temporary substitute or device.

make-up ▸ **noun** [mass noun] **1** cosmetics such as lipstick or powder applied to the face, used to enhance or alter the appearance. **2** the composition or constitution of something: *ozone damages the cellular make-up of plants and trees.* ■ the combination of qualities that form a person's temperament: *a curiously unexpected timidity in his make-up.* **3** Printing the arrangement of text, illustrations, etc. on a printed page: *page make-up.* **4** [count noun] N. Amer. a supplementary test or assignment given to a student who missed or failed the original one.

makeweight ▸ **noun** something put on a scale to make up the required weight. ■ an unimportant person or thing that is only added or included in order to complete something: *he has waited a long time to establish himself after two years as squad makeweight.*

make-work N. Amer. ▸ **adjective** denoting an activity that serves mainly to keep someone busy and is of little value in itself: *a make-work scheme for lawyers.* ▸ **noun** [mass noun] work or activity of this kind.

Makgadikgadi Pans /ˌmagəˈdiːgadi/ an extensive area of salt pans in central Botswana.

Makhachkala /ˌmaxətʃkəˈlɑː/ a port in SW Russia, on the Caspian Sea, capital of the autonomous republic of Dagestan; pop. 464,200 (est. 2008). Former name (until 1922) **Port Petrovsk**.

makhani /məˈkɑːni/ ▸ **adjective** [postpositive] denoting an Indian dish cooked in a rich sauce made with butter or ghee, onions, tomatoes, and cream: *chicken makhani.*
– ORIGIN Hindi *makkhani*, from *makkhan* 'butter'.

making ▸ **noun 1** [mass noun] the process of making or producing something: *the making of videos* | [in combination] *decision-making.* **2** (**makings**) the essential qualities needed for something: *she had the makings of a great teacher.* ■ (**makings**) N. Amer. & Austral./NZ informal paper and tobacco for rolling a cigarette. **3** (**makings**) informal, dated earnings or profit.
– PHRASES **be the making of someone** ensure someone's success or favourable development. **in the making** in the process of developing or being made: *a campaign that's been two years in the making.* **of one's (own) making** (of a difficulty) caused by oneself.

maki zushi /ˌmaki ˈzuːʃi/ (also **maki**) ▸ **noun** [mass noun] a Japanese dish consisting of sushi and raw vegetables wrapped in seaweed.
– ORIGIN 1970s: Japanese, from *maki-* (combining form of *maku* 'roll up') + *-zushi* **sushi**.

Makkah /ˈmakɑː/ Arabic name for **Mecca**.

mako[1] /ˈmɑːkəʊ, ˈmeɪkəʊ/ (also **mako shark**) ▸ **noun** (pl. **makos**) a large fast-moving oceanic shark with a deep blue back and white underparts. ● Genus *Isurus*, family Lamnidae: two species.
– ORIGIN mid 19th cent.: from Maori.

mako[2] /ˈmɑːkəʊ, ˈmakəʊ/ ▸ **noun** (pl. **makos**) a small New Zealand tree which bears large clusters of pink flowers followed by dark red berries. Also called **wineberry**. ● *Aristotelia racemosa*, family Elaeocarpaceae.
– ORIGIN mid 19th cent.: from Maori.

Makonde /məˈkɒndeɪ/ ▸ **noun** (pl. **same** or **Makondes**) **1** a member of a people inhabiting southern Tanzania and NE Mozambique. **2** [mass noun] the Bantu language of the Makonde, with about 1 million speakers. ▸ **adjective** relating to the Makonde or their language.
– ORIGIN the name in Makonde.

Makua /ˈmakuːə/ ▸ **noun** (pl. **same** or **Makuas**) **1** a member of a people inhabiting the border regions of Mozambique, Malawi, and Tanzania. **2** [mass noun] the Bantu language of the Makua, with around 3.5 million speakers.
– ORIGIN a local name.

makutu /məˈkuːtuː/ ▸ **noun** (pl. **same**) [mass noun] NZ sorcery; witchcraft. ■ [count noun] a magic spell.
– ORIGIN Maori.

MAL ▸ **abbreviation** Malaysia (international vehicle registration).

Mal. ▸ **abbreviation** Malachi (in biblical references).

mal- ▸ **combining form 1** in an unpleasant degree: *malodorous.*

M

2 in a faulty or inadequate manner: *malfunction* | *malnourishment*. ▪ in an improper manner: *malpractice*.
3 not: *maladroit*.
– ORIGIN from French *mal*, from Latin *male* 'badly'.

mala /ˈmɑːlɑː/ ▶ **noun** (in Hinduism and Sikhism) a string of prayer beads.
– ORIGIN from Hindi *mālā*.

Malabar Christians a group of Christians of SW India who trace their foundation to a mission of St Thomas the Apostle and have historically used a Syriac liturgy. Many now form a Uniate (Catholic) Church; others have links to the Syrian Orthodox or the Anglican Church.

Malabar Coast /ˈmaləbɑː/ the southern part of the west coast of India, including the coastal region of Karnataka and most of the state of Kerala.
– ORIGIN *Malabar* from *Malabars*, the name of an ancient Dravidian people.

Malabo /məˈlɑːbəʊ/ the capital of Equatorial Guinea, on the island of Bioko; pop. 96,000 (est. 2007).

malabsorption ▶ **noun** [mass noun] imperfect absorption of food material by the small intestine.

Malacca variant spelling of **MELAKA**.

malacca /məˈlakə/ ▶ **noun** [mass noun] brown cane that is used for walking sticks and umbrella handles.
• The cane is obtained from a Malaysian climbing palm (*Calamus scipionum*, family Palmae).
▪ [count noun] a walking stick of malacca cane.
– ORIGIN mid 19th cent.: from the place name **MALACCA**.

Malacca, Strait of the channel between the Malay Peninsula and the Indonesian island of Sumatra, an important sea passage linking the Indian Ocean to the South China Sea. The ports of Melaka and Singapore lie on this strait.

Malachi /ˈmaləkʌɪ/ a book of the Bible belonging to a period before Ezra and Nehemiah.
– ORIGIN from Hebrew *mal'ākī*, literally 'my messenger'; *Malachi* is probably not a personal name, though often taken as such.

M

malachite /ˈmaləkʌɪt/ ▶ **noun** [mass noun] a bright green mineral consisting of hydrated basic copper carbonate, which typically occurs in masses and fibrous aggregates.
– ORIGIN late Middle English: from Old French *melochite*, via Latin from Greek *molokhitis*, from *molokhē*, variant of *malakhē* 'mallow'.

malaco- /ˈmaləkəʊ/ ▶ **combining form** soft: *malacostracan*.
– ORIGIN from Greek *malakos* 'soft'.

malacology /ˌmaləˈkɒlədʒi/ ▶ **noun** [mass noun] the branch of zoology that deals with molluscs.
– DERIVATIVES **malacological** adjective, **malacologist** noun.

Malacostraca /ˌmaləˈkɒstrəkə/ ▶ **plural noun** Zoology a large class of crustaceans which includes crabs, shrimps, lobsters, isopods, and amphipods. They have compound eyes, which are typically on stalks.
– ORIGIN modern Latin (plural), from **MALACO-** 'soft' + Greek *ostrakon* 'shell'.

malacostracan Zoology ▶ **noun** a crustacean of the large class Malacostraca, such as a crab, shrimp, or lobster.
▶ **adjective** relating to or denoting malacostracans.

maladaptive ▶ **adjective** technical not adjusting adequately or appropriately to the environment or situation.
– DERIVATIVES **maladaptation** noun, **maladapted** adjective.

maladjusted ▶ **adjective** failing to cope with the demands of a normal social environment.
– DERIVATIVES **maladjustment** noun.

maladminister ▶ **verb** [with obj.] formal manage or administer inefficiently or dishonestly.

maladministration ▶ **noun** [mass noun] formal inefficient or dishonest administration; mismanagement: *I found no maladministration in the council's actions*.

maladroit /ˌmaləˈdrɔɪt/ ▶ **adjective** inefficient or inept; clumsy.
– DERIVATIVES **maladroitly** adverb, **maladroitness** noun.
– ORIGIN late 17th cent.: French.

malady ▶ **noun** (pl. **maladies**) literary a disease or ailment. ▪ a serious problem: *the nation's maladies*.
– ORIGIN Middle English: from Old French *maladie*, from *malade* 'sick', based on Latin *male* 'ill' + *habitus* 'having (as a condition)'.

mala fide /ˌmeɪlə ˈfʌɪdiː, ˌmalə ˈfiːdeɪ/ ▶ **adjective & adverb** Law in bad faith; with intent to deceive: [as adj.] *a mala fide abuse of position*.
– ORIGIN Latin, ablative of **MALA FIDES**.

mala fides /ˈfʌɪdiːz, malə ˈfiːdeɪz/ ▶ **noun** [mass noun] Law bad faith; intent to deceive.
– ORIGIN Latin.

Malaga[1] /ˈmaləgə/ a seaport on the Andalusian coast of southern Spain; pop. 566,447 (2008). Spanish name **Málaga** /ˈmalaɣa/.

Malaga[2] /ˈmaləgə/ ▶ **noun** [mass noun] a sweet fortified wine from Malaga.

Malagasy /ˌmaləˈgasi/ ▶ **noun** (pl. **same** or **Malagasies**) **1** a native or inhabitant of Madagascar.
2 [mass noun] the Austronesian language of Madagascar, a group of dialects spoken by some 10 million people.
▶ **adjective** relating to Madagascar or its people or language.
– ORIGIN variant of **MADAGASCAR**; earlier forms included *Malegass*, *Madegass*, because of dialect division between the sounds *-l-* and *-d-*.

Malagasy Republic former name (1960–75) for **MADAGASCAR**.

malagueña /ˌmaləˈgeɪnjə/ ▶ **noun** a Spanish dance similar to the fandango.
– ORIGIN mid 19th cent.: Spanish, lit. 'of Málaga'.

malaguetta /ˌmaləˈgɛtə/ (also **malagueta**) ▶ **noun** another term for **GRAINS OF PARADISE**.
– ORIGIN mid 16th cent.: probably from French *malaguette*, perhaps based on a diminutive of Italian *melica* 'millet'.

malaise /maˈleɪz/ ▶ **noun** [mass noun] a general feeling of discomfort, illness, or unease whose exact cause is difficult to identify: *a general air of malaise* | [in sing.] *a society afflicted by a deep cultural malaise*.
– ORIGIN mid 18th cent.: from French, from Old French *mal* 'bad' (from Latin *malus*) + *aise* 'ease'.

malamute /ˈmaləmjuːt/ (also **malemute**) ▶ **noun** a powerful dog of a breed with a thick, grey coat, bred by the Inuit and used to pull sledges.
– ORIGIN late 19th cent.: from Inuit *malimiut*, the name of a people of western Alaska, who developed the breed.

malanga /məˈlaŋgə/ ▶ **noun** another term for **TANNIA**.
– ORIGIN early 20th cent.: from American Spanish, probably from Kikongo, plural of *elanga* 'water lily'.

malapert /ˈmaləpəːt/ archaic ▶ **adjective** boldly disrespectful; impudent.
▶ **noun** an impudent person.
– ORIGIN Middle English: from **MAL-** 'improperly' + archaic *apert* 'insolent'.

malapropism /ˈmaləprɒˌpɪz(ə)m/ (US also **malaprop**) ▶ **noun** the mistaken use of a word in place of a similar-sounding one, often with an amusing effect (e.g. 'dance a *flamingo*' instead of *flamenco*).
– ORIGIN mid 19th cent.: from the name of the character Mrs *Malaprop* in Sheridan's play *The Rivals* (1775) + **-ISM**.

malapropos /ˌmalaprəˈpəʊ/ formal ▶ **adverb** in an inopportune or inappropriate way.
▶ **adjective** inopportune; inappropriate: *these terms applied to him seem to me malapropos*.
– ORIGIN mid 17th cent.: from French *mal à propos*, from *mal* 'ill' + *à* 'to' + *propos* 'purpose'.

malar /ˈmeɪlə/ ▶ **adjective** Anatomy & Medicine relating to the cheek.
▶ **noun** (also **malar bone**) another term for **ZYGOMATIC BONE**.
– ORIGIN late 18th cent.: from modern Latin *malaris*, from Latin *mala* 'jaw'.

Mälaren /ˈmɛlərɛn/ a lake in SE Sweden, extending inland from the Baltic Sea. The city of Stockholm is situated at its outlet.

malaria ▶ **noun** [mass noun] an intermittent and remittent fever caused by a protozoan parasite which invades the red blood cells and is transmitted by mosquitoes in many tropical and subtropical regions.
• The parasite belongs to the genus *Plasmodium* (phylum Sporozoa) and is transmitted by female mosquitoes of the genus *Anopheles*.
– DERIVATIVES **malarial** adjective, **malarious** adjective.
– ORIGIN mid 18th cent.: from Italian, from *mal'aria*, contracted form of *mala aria* 'bad air'. The term originally denoted the unwholesome atmosphere caused by the exhalations of marshes, to which the disease was formerly attributed.

malariology /məˌlɛːrɪˈɒlədʒi/ ▶ **noun** [mass noun] the scientific study of malaria.
– DERIVATIVES **malariologist** noun.

malarkey /məˈlɑːki/ ▶ **noun** [mass noun] informal meaningless talk; nonsense: *don't give me that malarkey*.
– ORIGIN 1920s: of unknown origin.

malate /ˈmeɪleɪt/ ▶ **noun** Chemistry a salt or ester of malic acid.

malathion /ˌmaləˈθʌɪən/ ▶ **noun** [mass noun] a synthetic organophosphorus compound which is used as an insecticide.
– ORIGIN 1950s: from *(diethyl) mal(eate)* (see **MALEIC ACID**) + **THIO-** + **-ON**.

Malawi /məˈlɑːwi/ a country of south central Africa, in the Great Rift Valley; pop. 15,028,800 (est. 2009); official languages, English and Nyanja; capital, Lilongwe.

> As Nyasaland Malawi was a British protectorate from 1891, and from 1953 to 1963 was a part of the Federation of Rhodesia and Nyasaland. It became an independent Commonwealth state under Hastings Banda in 1964 and a republic in 1966.

– DERIVATIVES **Malawian** adjective & noun.

Malawi, Lake another name for Lake Nyasa (see **NYASA, LAKE**).

Malay /məˈleɪ/ ▶ **noun 1** a member of a people inhabiting Malaysia and Indonesia. ▪ a person of Malay descent.
2 [mass noun] the Austronesian language of the Malays, closely related to Indonesian and spoken by about 20 million people.
▶ **adjective** relating to the Malays or their language.
– ORIGIN from Malay *Malayu* (now *Melayu*).

Malaya a former country in SE Asia, consisting of the southern part of the Malay Peninsula and some adjacent islands (originally including Singapore), now forming the western part of the federation of Malaysia and known as West Malaysia.

> The area was colonized by the Dutch, Portuguese, and the British, who eventually became dominant; the several Malay states federated under British control in 1896. The country became independent in 1957, the federation expanding into Malaysia in 1963.

Malayalam /ˌmaləˈjɑːləm/ ▶ **noun** [mass noun] a Dravidian language spoken in the southern Indian state of Kerala by about 35 million people. It is closely related to Tamil.
▶ **adjective** relating to Malayalam or its speakers.
– ORIGIN early 19th cent.: from Malayalam, from *mala* (Tamil *malai*) 'mountain' + *āḷ* 'man'.

Malayali /məˈlʌɪəli/ (also **Malayalee**) ▶ **noun** (pl. **Malayalis**) a member of a Malayalam-speaking people chiefly inhabiting the Indian state of Kerala.
▶ **adjective** relating to or characteristic of the Malayalis.
– ORIGIN mid 19th cent.: apparently irregularly from Malayalam *malayāḷam* **MALAYALAM** with substitution of **-I**[2] for the final syllable.

Malayan ▶ **noun** another term for **MALAY**.
▶ **adjective** relating to Malays, the Malay language, or Malaya (now part of Malaysia).

Malayan sun bear ▶ **noun** see **SUN BEAR**.

Malay Archipelago a very large group of islands, including Sumatra, Java, Borneo, the Philippines, and New Guinea, lying between the mainland of SE Asia and Australia. They constitute the bulk of the area formerly known as the East Indies.

Malayo- ▶ **combining form** Malay; Malay and ...: *Malayo-Polynesian*.

Malayo-Polynesian ▶ **noun** another term for **AUSTRONESIAN**.

Malay Peninsula a peninsula in SE Asia separating the Indian Ocean from the South China Sea. It extends approximately 1,100 km (700 miles) southwards from the Isthmus of Kra and comprises the southern part of Thailand and the whole of West Malaysia.

Malaysia /məˈleɪzɪə, -ˈleɪʒə/ a country in SE Asia; pop. 25,715,800 (est. 2009); official language, Malay; capital, Kuala Lumpur.

> Malaysia is a federation consisting of **East Malaysia** (the northern part of Borneo, including Sabah and Sarawak) and **West Malaysia** (the southern part of the Malay Peninsula, formerly Malaya). The two parts of Malaysia are separated from each other by 650 km (400 miles) of the South China Sea. Malaysia federated as an independent Commonwealth state in 1963; Singapore withdrew in 1965.

– DERIVATIVES **Malaysian** adjective & noun.

Malbec /ˈmalbɛk, ˈmɒlbɛk/ ▶ **noun** [mass noun] a variety of dark wine grape native to the Bordeaux region of France. ■ a red wine made from the Malbec grape.
– ORIGIN French *malbec*, *malbeck*, of unknown origin.

Malcolm the name of four kings of Scotland: ■ **Malcolm I** (d.954), reigned 943–54. ■ **Malcolm II** (*c*.954–1034), reigned 1005–34. ■ **Malcolm III** (*c*.1031–93), son of Duncan I, reigned 1058–93; known as **Malcolm Canmore** (from Gaelic *Ceann-mor* great head). He came to the throne after killing Macbeth in battle (1057), and helped to form Scotland into an organized kingdom. ■ **Malcolm IV** (1141–65), grandson of David I, reigned 1153–65; known as **Malcolm the Maiden**. His reign witnessed a progressive loss of power to Henry II of England; he died young and without an heir.

Malcolm X (1925–65), American political activist; born *Malcolm Little*. He joined the Nation of Islam in 1946 and became a vigorous campaigner for black rights, initially advocating the use of violence. In 1964 he converted to orthodox Islam and moderated his views on black separatism; he was assassinated the following year.

malcontent /ˈmalkəntɛnt/ ▶ **noun** a person who is dissatisfied and rebellious.
▶ **adjective** dissatisfied and complaining or rebellious.
– DERIVATIVES **malcontented** adjective.
– ORIGIN late 16th cent.: from French, from *mal* 'badly, ill' + *content* 'pleased'.

mal de mer /ˌmal dəˈmɛː/, French /mal də mɛʀ/ ▶ **noun** [mass noun] seasickness.
– ORIGIN French.

maldevelopment ▶ **noun** [mass noun] Medicine & Biology faulty or imperfect development.

maldistribution ▶ **noun** [mass noun] uneven, inefficient, or unfair distribution of something: *the maldistribution of wealth*.
– DERIVATIVES **maldistributed** adjective.

Maldives /ˈmɔːldʌɪvz, -diːv/ (also **Maldive Islands**) a country consisting of a chain of coral islands in the Indian Ocean south-west of Sri Lanka; pop. 396,300 (est. 2009); official language, Maldivian; capital, Male.

> The islands were probably first settled from southern India and Sri Lanka, but later came under Arab influence. A British protectorate from 1887, the Maldives became independent within the Commonwealth under the rule of a sultan in 1965 and then a republic in 1968.

Maldivian /mɔːlˈdɪvɪən/ ▶ **noun 1** a native or inhabitant of the Maldives.
2 [mass noun] the Indic language spoken in the Maldives, related to Sinhalese.
▶ **adjective** relating to the Maldives, their inhabitants, or their language.

mal du siècle /ˌmal d(j)uː ˈsjɛkl/, French /mal dy sjɛkl/ ▶ **noun** [mass noun] world-weariness.
– ORIGIN French, literally 'sickness of the century'.

Male /ˈmɑːleɪ/ the capital of the Maldives; pop. 111,000 (est. 2007).

male ▶ **adjective** of or denoting the sex that produces gametes, especially spermatozoa, with which a female may be fertilized or inseminated to produce offspring: *male children*. ■ relating to or characteristic of men or male animals: *a deep male voice*. ■ (of a plant or flower) bearing stamens but lacking functional pistils. ■ (of a fitting or part of machinery) manufactured to fit inside a corresponding female part.
▶ **noun** a male person, plant, or animal: *the audience consisted of adult males*.
– DERIVATIVES **maleness** noun.
– ORIGIN late Middle English: from Old French *masle*, from Latin *masculus*, from *mas* 'a male'.

maleate /məˈliːeɪt/ ▶ **noun** Chemistry a salt or ester of maleic acid.

male chauvinism ▶ **noun** [mass noun] male prejudice against women; the belief that men are superior in terms of ability, intelligence, etc.: *a bastion of male chauvinism*.
– DERIVATIVES **male chauvinist** noun & adjective.

male chauvinist pig ▶ **noun** informal a man who believes that men are superior to women.

malediction /ˌmalɪˈdɪkʃ(ə)n/ ▶ **noun** a magical word or phrase uttered with the intention of bringing about evil; a curse.
– DERIVATIVES **maledictive** adjective, **maledictory** adjective.
– ORIGIN late Middle English: from Latin *maledictio(n-)*, from *maledicere* 'speak evil of'.

malefactor /ˈmalɪˌfaktə/ ▶ **noun** formal a person who commits a crime or some other wrong.
– DERIVATIVES **malefaction** noun.
– ORIGIN late Middle English: from Latin, from *malefact-* 'done wrong', from the verb *malefacere*, from *male* 'ill' + *facere* 'do'.

male fern ▶ **noun** a fern with brown scales on the stalks of the fronds, found in woodland in both North America and Eurasia. ● Genus *Dryopteris*, family Dryopteridaceae. *D. filix-mas* and related species.

malefic /məˈlɛfɪk/ ▶ **adjective** literary causing harm or destruction, especially by supernatural means. ■ Astrology relating to the planets Saturn and Mars, traditionally considered to have an unfavourable influence.
– DERIVATIVES **maleficence** noun, **maleficent** adjective.
– ORIGIN mid 17th cent.: from Latin *maleficus*, from *male* 'ill' + *-ficus* 'doing'.

Malegaon /ˈmɑːləgaʊn/ a city in western India, in Maharashtra north-east of Mumbai (Bombay); pop. 461,300 (est. 2009).

maleic acid /məˈleɪɪk/ ▶ **noun** [mass noun] Chemistry a crystalline acid made by distilling malic acid, used in making synthetic resins. ● Chem. formula: HOOCCH=CHCOOH.
– ORIGIN mid 19th cent.: *maleic* from French *maléique*, alteration of *malique* (see **MALIC ACID**).

male menopause ▶ **noun** a stage in a middle-aged man's life supposedly corresponding to the menopause of a woman, associated with loss of vigour and a crisis of identity (not in technical use).

malemute ▶ **noun** variant spelling of **MALAMUTE**.

Malenkov /ˈmalɪnkɒf/, Georgi (Maksimilianovich) (1902–88), Soviet statesman, born in Russia. He became Prime Minister and First Secretary of the Soviet Communist Party in 1953, but was forced to resign in 1955 following internal party struggles.

Malesia /məˈliːzɪə/ Botany a phytogeographical region comprising Malaysia, Indonesia, New Guinea, the Philippines, and Brunei.
– DERIVATIVES **Malesian** adjective.

male sterility ▶ **noun** [mass noun] Genetics the situation whereby individuals of a normally hermaphrodite species produce only female gametes.

Malevich /ˈmaləvɪtʃ, maˈljɛrvɪtʃ/, Kazimir (Severinovich) (1878–1935), Russian painter and designer, founder of the suprematist movement. In his abstract works he used only basic geometrical shapes and a severely restricted range of colour.

malevolence /məˈlɛv(ə)l(ə)ns/ ▶ **noun** [mass noun] the state or condition of being malevolent; hostility: *his eyes were glowing with malevolence*.

malevolent /məˈlɛv(ə)l(ə)nt/ ▶ **adjective** having or showing a wish to do evil to others: *the glint of dark, malevolent eyes*.
– DERIVATIVES **malevolently** adverb.
– ORIGIN early 16th cent.: from Latin *malevolent-* 'wishing evil', from *male* 'ill' + *volent-* 'wishing' (from the verb *velle*).

malfatti /malˈfati/ ▶ **plural noun** dumplings or gnocchi made with spinach and ricotta.
– ORIGIN Italian, from *malfatto* 'badly made' (because they resemble ravioli without their pasta envelopes).

malfeasance /malˈfiːz(ə)ns/ ▶ **noun** [mass noun] Law wrongdoing, especially (US) by a public official.
– DERIVATIVES **malfeasant** noun & adjective.
– ORIGIN late 17th cent.: from Anglo-Norman French *malfaisance*, from *mal* 'evil' + Old French *faisance* 'activity'. Compare with **MISFEASANCE**.

malformation ▶ **noun** an abnormally formed part of the body. ■ [mass noun] abnormality of shape or form.

malformed ▶ **adjective** (of a person or part of the body) abnormally formed; misshapen: *her ribs are malformed*. ■ not conforming to a standard type: *malformed web pages*.

malfunction ▶ **verb** [no obj.] (of a piece of equipment or machinery) fail to function normally: *the unit is clearly malfunctioning*.
▶ **noun** a failure to function normally.

Malherbe /maˈlɛːb/, French /malɛʀb/, François de (1555–1628), French poet. An architect of classicism in poetic form and grammar, he criticized excess of emotion and ornamentation and the use of Latin and dialectal forms.

Mali /ˈmɑːli/ a landlocked country in West Africa, south of Algeria; pop. 13,443,200 (est. 2009); languages, French (official), other languages mainly of the Mande group; capital, Bamako. Former name (until 1958) **FRENCH SUDAN**.

> Conquered by the French in the late 19th century, Mali became part of French West Africa. It became a partner with Senegal in the Federation of Mali in 1959 and achieved full independence a year later, on the withdrawal of Senegal.

– DERIVATIVES **Malian** adjective & noun.

mali /ˈmɑːli/ ▶ **noun** (pl. **malis**) Indian a gardener.
– ORIGIN via Hindi from Sanskrit, from *mālā* 'garland'.

Malibu[1] /ˈmalɪbuː/ a resort on the Pacific coast of southern California, immediately to the west of Los Angeles.

Malibu[2] /ˈmalɪbuː/ (also **Malibu board**) ▶ **noun** (pl. **Malibus**) a kind of surfboard that is relatively long with a rounded front end.
– ORIGIN 1960s: named after *Malibu* beach (see **MALIBU**[1]).

malic acid /ˈmalɪk/ ▶ **noun** [mass noun] a crystalline acid present in unripe apples and other fruits. ● Chem. formula: $HOOCCH_2CH(OH)COOH$.
– ORIGIN late 18th cent.: *malic* from French *malique*, from Latin *malum* 'apple'.

malice ▶ **noun** [mass noun] the desire to harm someone; ill will: *I bear no malice towards anybody*. ■ Law wrongful intention, especially as increasing the guilt of certain offences.
– ORIGIN Middle English: via Old French from Latin *malitia*, from *malus* 'bad'.

malice aforethought ▶ **noun** [mass noun] Law the intention to kill or harm, which distinguishes murder from unlawful killing.

malicious ▶ **adjective** characterized by malice; intending or intended to do harm: *he was found guilty of malicious damage* | *the transmission of malicious software such as computer viruses*.
– DERIVATIVES **maliciously** adverb, **maliciousness** noun.
– ORIGIN Middle English: from Old French *malicios*, from Latin *malitiosus*, from *malitia* (see **MALICE**).

malign /məˈlʌɪn/ ▶ **adjective** evil in nature or effect: *she had a strong and malign influence*. ■ archaic (of a disease) malignant.
▶ **verb** [with obj.] speak about (someone) in a spitefully critical manner: *don't you dare malign her in my presence*.
– DERIVATIVES **malignity** /məˈlɪgnɪti/ noun, **malignly** adverb.
– ORIGIN Middle English: via Old French *maligne* (adjective), *malignier* (verb), based on Latin *malignus* 'tending to evil', from *malus* 'bad'.

malignancy /məˈlɪgnənsi/ ▶ **noun** (pl. **malignancies**) [mass noun] **1** the state or presence of a malignant tumour; cancer: *after biopsy, evidence of malignancy was found*. ■ [count noun] a cancerous growth. ■ [count noun] a form of cancer.
2 the quality of being malign: *her eyes sparkled with renewed malignancy*.

malignant ▶ **adjective 1** evil in nature or effect; malevolent: *in the hands of malignant fate*.
2 (of a disease) very virulent or infectious. ■ (of a tumour) tending to invade normal tissue or to recur after removal; cancerous. Contrasted with **BENIGN**.
– DERIVATIVES **malignantly** adverb.
– ORIGIN mid 16th cent. (also in the sense 'likely to rebel against God or authority'): from late Latin *malignant-* 'contriving maliciously', from the verb *malignare*. The term was used in its early sense to describe Royalist sympathizers during the English Civil War.

malignant pustule ▶ **noun** [mass noun] a form of anthrax causing severe skin ulceration.

malik /ˈmɑːlɪk/ ▶ **noun** (in parts of South Asia and the Middle East) the chief of a village or community.
– ORIGIN from Arabic, active participle of *malaka* 'possess or rule'.

malimbe /məˈlɪmbi/ ▶ **noun** a weaver bird of west and central Africa, having black plumage with red on the head or throat. ● Genus *Malimbus*, family Ploceidae.
– ORIGIN 1940s: named after the town of *Malimbe* in Angola.

Malines /malin/ French name for **MECHELEN**.

malinger /məˈlɪŋgə/ ▶ **verb** [no obj.] pretend to be ill in order to escape duty or work.
– ORIGIN early 19th cent.: back-formation from **MALINGERER**, apparently from French *malingre*, perhaps formed as *mal-* 'wrongly' + *haingre* 'weak', probably of Germanic origin.

M

malingerer ▸ **noun** a person who malingers; a shirker: *the doctor said my son was a malingerer*.

Malin Head /ˈmalɪn/ a point on the coast of County Donegal, the northernmost point of Ireland. The shipping forecast area **Malin** covers the Atlantic north of Ireland and west of the southern half of Scotland.

Malinke /məˈlɪŋkeɪ/ ▸ **noun** (pl. **same** or **Malinkes**) **1** a member of a West African people living mainly in Senegal, Mali, and Côte d'Ivoire (Ivory Coast). **2** [mass noun] the Mande language of the Malinke, with abut 800,000 speakers.
▸ **adjective** relating to the Malinke or their language.
– ORIGIN the name in Malinke.

malinvestment ▸ **noun** [mass noun] the action or fact of investing money in an ill-judged or wasteful way: *overgenerous credit and monetary policies contributed to massive malinvestment*.

malison /ˈmalɪz(ə)n, -s-/ ▸ **noun** archaic a curse.
– ORIGIN Middle English: from Old French.

mall /mal, mɔːl, mɒl/ ▸ **noun 1** (also **shopping mall**) chiefly N. Amer. a large enclosed shopping area from which traffic is excluded. **2** a sheltered walk or promenade. **3** historical another term for **PALL-MALL**. ■ an alley used for pall-mall.
– ORIGIN mid 17th cent. (in sense 3): probably a shortening of **PALL-MALL**. Sense 2 derives from *The Mall*, a tree-bordered walk in St James's Park, London, formerly the site of a pall-mall alley. Sense 1 dates from the 1960s.

mallam /ˈmaləm/ ▸ **noun** (in Nigeria and other parts of Africa) a learned man or scribe.
– ORIGIN from Hausa *mālam(i)*.

mallard ▸ **noun** (pl. **same** or **mallards**) the commonest duck of the northern hemisphere, the male having a dark green head and white collar. ● *Anas platyrhynchos*, family Anatidae.
– ORIGIN Middle English: from Old French, 'wild drake', from *masle* 'male'.

Mallarmé /ˌmalɑːˈmeɪ/, French /malaʀme/, Stéphane (1842–98), French poet. A symbolist, he experimented with rhythm and syntax by transposing words and omitting grammatical elements. Notable poems: 'Hérodiade' (*c*.1871) and 'L'Après-midi d'un faune' (1876).

M

Malle /mal/, Louis (1932–95), French film director. His films *Ascenseur pour l'échafaud* (1958) and *Les Amants* (1959) are seminal examples of the French *nouvelle vague*. Other notable films: *Pretty Baby* (1978) and *Au Revoir les enfants* (1987).

malleable /ˈmalɪəb(ə)l/ ▸ **adjective** (of a metal or other material) able to be hammered or pressed into shape without breaking or cracking. ■ easily influenced; pliable: *they are as malleable and easily led as sheep*.
– DERIVATIVES **malleability** noun, **malleably** adverb.
– ORIGIN late Middle English (in the sense 'able to be hammered'): via Old French from medieval Latin *malleabilis*, from Latin *malleus* 'a hammer'.

mallee /ˈmali/ ▸ **noun** a low-growing bushy Australian eucalyptus which has several slender stems. ● Genus *Eucalyptus*, family Myrtaceae: *E. dumosa* and other species. ■ [mass noun] scrub which is dominated by mallee, typical of some arid parts of Australia.
– ORIGIN mid 19th cent.: from Wuywurung (an Aboriginal language).

malleefowl (also **mallee hen**) ▸ **noun** (pl. **same**) a megapode (bird) found in the mallee scrub of southern Australia, with pale patterned plumage. ● *Leipoa ocellata*, family Megapodiidae.

malleolus /məˈliːələs/ ▸ **noun** (pl. **malleoli** /-lʌɪ/) Anatomy a bony projection with a shape likened to a hammer head, especially each of those on either side of the ankle.
– ORIGIN late 17th cent.: from Latin, diminutive of *malleus* 'hammer'.

mallet ▸ **noun** a hammer with a large, usually wooden head. ■ a long-handled wooden stick with a head like a hammer, used for hitting a croquet or polo ball. ■ a wooden stick with a padded head, used for hitting percussion instruments.
– ORIGIN late Middle English: from Old French *maillet*, from *mail* 'hammer', from Latin *malleus*.

malleus /ˈmalɪəs/ ▸ **noun** (pl. **mallei** /ˈmalɪʌɪ/) Anatomy a small bone in the middle ear which transmits vibrations of the eardrum to the incus.
– ORIGIN mid 17th cent.: from Latin, literally 'hammer'.

malling /ˈmɔːlɪŋ/ ▸ **noun** [mass noun] N. Amer. **1** the development of shopping malls. **2** the activity of passing time in a shopping mall: *Jessie had time to go malling*.

Mallophaga /məˈlɒfəgə/ ▸ **plural noun** Entomology an order of insects that comprises the biting lice. See also **PHTHIRAPTERA**.
– ORIGIN modern Latin (plural), from Greek *mallos* 'lock of wool' + *-phagos* 'eating'.

Mallorca /maˈjɔrka/ Spanish name for **MAJORCA**.

mallow ▸ **noun** a herbaceous plant with hairy stems, pink or purple flowers, and disc-shaped fruit. ● Genus *Malva*, family Malvaceae (the **mallow family**, which also contains hollyhocks, hibiscus, and abutilon): many species.
– ORIGIN Old English *meal(u)we*, from Latin *malva*; related to Greek *malakhē*; compare with **MAUVE**.

mall rat ▸ **noun** N. Amer. informal a young person who frequents shopping malls, usually for social purposes.

malm /mɑːm/ ▸ **noun** [mass noun] a soft, crumbly chalky rock, or the fertile loamy soil produced as it weathers. ■ (also **malm brick**) [count noun] a fine-quality brick made originally from malm, marl, or a similar chalky clay.
– ORIGIN Old English *mealm-*, of Germanic origin; related to **MEAL²**.

Malmö /ˈmɑːlməː/ a port and fortified city in SW Sweden, situated on the Øresund opposite Copenhagen; pop. 286,535 (2008).

malmsey /ˈmɑːmzi/ ▸ **noun** [mass noun] a fortified Madeira wine of the sweetest type. ■ historical a strong, sweet white wine imported from Greece and the eastern Mediterranean islands.
– ORIGIN late Middle English: from Middle Dutch *malemeseye*, via Old French from *Monemvasia*, a port in the Peloponnese, Greece. Compare with **MALVOISIE**.

malnourished ▸ **adjective** suffering from malnutrition.
– DERIVATIVES **malnourishment** noun.

malnutrition ▸ **noun** [mass noun] lack of proper nutrition, caused by not having enough to eat, not eating enough of the right things, or being unable to use the food that one does eat.

malocclusion ▸ **noun** [mass noun] Dentistry imperfect positioning of the teeth when the jaws are closed.

malodorous ▸ **adjective** smelling very unpleasant.

malodour ▸ **noun** a very unpleasant smell.

malolactic /ˌmalə(ʊ)ˈlaktɪk/ ▸ **adjective** of or denoting bacterial fermentation which converts malic acid to lactic acid, especially as a secondary process used to reduce the acidity of some wines.
▸ **noun** [mass noun] fermentation of this kind.

malonate /ˈmaləneɪt/ ▸ **noun** Chemistry a salt or ester of malonic acid.

malonic acid /məˈlɒnɪk/ ▸ **noun** [mass noun] Chemistry a crystalline acid obtained by the oxidation of malic acid. ● Chem. formula: $HOOCCH_2COOH$.
– ORIGIN mid 19th cent.: *malonic* from French *malonique*, alteration of *malique* 'malic'.

Malory /ˈmaləri/, Sir Thomas (d.1471), English writer. His major work, *Le Morte d'Arthur* (printed 1483), is a prose translation of a collection of the legends of King Arthur, selected from French and other sources.

maloti plural form of **LOTI**.

malperformance ▸ **noun** [mass noun] faulty or inadequate performance of a task.

Malpighi /malˈpiːgi/, Marcello (*c*.1628–94), Italian microscopist. He discovered the alveoli and capillaries in the lungs and the fibres and red cells of clotted blood, and demonstrated the pathway of blood from arteries to veins.
– DERIVATIVES **Malpighian** /maLˈpɪgɪən/ adjective.

Malpighian layer ▸ **noun** Zoology & Anatomy a layer in the epidermis in which skin cells are continually formed by division.

Malpighian tubule ▸ **noun** Zoology a tubular excretory organ, numbers of which open into the gut in insects and some other arthropods.

Malplaquet, Battle of /ˌmalplaˈkeɪ, ˈmalpləˌkeɪ/ a battle in 1709 during the War of the Spanish Succession, near the village of Malplaquet in northern France, on the border with Belgium. A force of allied British and Austrian troops under the Duke of Marlborough won a victory over the French.

malpractice ▸ **noun** [mass noun] improper, illegal, or negligent professional behaviour: *victims of medical malpractice* | [count noun] *investigations into malpractices and abuses of power*.

malpresentation ▸ **noun** [mass noun] Medicine abnormal positioning of a fetus at the time of delivery.

Malraux /malˈrəʊ/, French /malʀəo/, André (1901–76), French novelist, politician, and art critic. Involved in the Chinese communist uprising of 1927 and the Spanish Civil War, he was later appointed France's first Minister of Cultural Affairs (1959–69). Notable novels: *La Condition humaine* (1933).

malt /mɔːlt, mɒlt/ ▸ **noun** [mass noun] barley or other grain that has been steeped, germinated, and dried, used for brewing or distilling and vinegar-making. ■ short for **MALT WHISKY**. ■ N. Amer. short for **MALTED MILK**.
▸ **verb** [with obj.] convert (grain) into malt.
– DERIVATIVES **maltiness** noun, **malty** adjective (**maltier**, **maltiest**).
– ORIGIN Old English *m(e)alt*, of Germanic origin; related to **MELT**.

Malta /ˈmɔːltə, ˈmɒl-/ an island country in the central Mediterranean, about 100 km (60 miles) south of Sicily; pop. 405,200 (est. 2009); official languages, Maltese and English; capital, Valletta.

> Historically of great strategic importance, the island has been held in turn by invaders including the Greeks, Arabs, Normans, and Knights Hospitaller. It was annexed by Britain in 1814 and was an important naval base until independence within the Commonwealth in 1964. Besides Malta itself, the country includes two other inhabited islands, Gozo and Comino.

Malta fever ▸ **noun** another term for **UNDULANT FEVER**.
– ORIGIN mid 19th cent.: named after **MALTA**, where it was once prevalent.

maltase /ˈmɒlteɪz, ˈmɔːl-/ ▸ **noun** [mass noun] Biochemistry an enzyme, present in saliva and pancreatic juice, which catalyses the breakdown of maltose and similar sugars to form glucose.

malted ▸ **adjective** mixed with malt or a malt extract: *malted biscuits*.

malted milk ▸ **noun** [mass noun] a hot drink made from dried milk and a malt preparation.

Maltese /mɔːlˈtiːz, mɒl-/ ▸ **noun** (pl. **same**) **1** a native or inhabitant of Malta or a person of Maltese descent. **2** [mass noun] the national language of Malta, a Semitic language related to Arabic but much influenced by Italian, Spanish, and Norman French.
▸ **adjective** relating to Malta, its people, or their language.

Maltese cross ▸ **noun** a cross with arms of equal length which broaden from the centre and have their ends indented in a shallow V-shape.
– ORIGIN so named because the cross was formerly worn by the Knights Hospitaller, who were based in Malta 1530–1798.

Maltese dog (also **Maltese terrier**) ▸ **noun** a dog of a very small breed, with long white hair.

malthouse ▸ **noun** a building in which malt is prepared and stored.

Malthus /ˈmalθəs/, Thomas Robert (1766–1834), English economist and clergyman. In *Essay on Population* (1798) he argued that without the practice of 'moral restraint' the population tends to increase at a greater rate than its means of subsistence, resulting in the population checks of war, famine, and epidemic.
– DERIVATIVES **Malthusian** /malˈθjuːzɪən/ adjective & noun, **Malthusianism** noun.

maltings ▸ **noun** Brit. a malthouse.

malt liquor ▸ **noun** [mass noun] alcoholic drink made from malt by fermentation rather than distillation, for example beer.

maltodextrin ▸ **noun** [mass noun] dextrin containing maltose, used as a food additive.

maltose /ˈmɔːltəʊz, -s, mɒlt-/ ▸ **noun** [mass noun] Chemistry a sugar produced by the breakdown of starch, e.g. by enzymes found in malt and saliva. It is a disaccharide consisting of two linked glucose units.
– ORIGIN mid 19th cent.: from **MALT** + **-OSE²**.

maltreat ▸ **verb** [with obj.] treat (a person or animal) cruelly or with violence: *children die from neglect or are maltreated by their carers*.
– DERIVATIVES **maltreater** noun.
– ORIGIN early 18th cent.: from French *maltraiter*.

maltreatment ▸ **noun** [mass noun] cruel or violent treatment of a person or animal; mistreatment:

16 per cent of children experience serious maltreatment at the hands of their parents.

maltster ▸ noun a person whose occupation is making malt.

malt whisky ▸ noun [mass noun] whisky made only from malted barley and not blended with grain whisky.

Maluku /məˈluːkuː/ Indonesian name for **MOLUCCA ISLANDS**.

malvaceous /malˈveɪʃəs/ ▸ adjective Botany relating to or denoting plants of the mallow family (Malvaceae).
– ORIGIN late 17th cent.: from modern Latin *Malvaceae* (plural), based on Latin *malva* 'mallow', + **-OUS**.

Malvasia /ˌmalvəˈsiːə, -ˈziːə/ ▸ noun [mass noun] a variety of grape used to make white and red wines, especially in Italy.
– ORIGIN Italian form of the place name *Monemvasia*, in the Peloponnese (see **MALMSEY**).

Malvern Hills /ˈmɔːlv(ə)n/ (also **the Malverns**) a range of hills in western England, in Herefordshire and Worcestershire. The highest point is Worcestershire Beacon (425 m; 1,394 ft).

malversation /ˌmalvəˈseɪʃ(ə)n/ ▸ noun [mass noun] formal corrupt behaviour in a position of trust, especially in public office: *a charge of malversation*.
– ORIGIN mid 16th cent.: from French, from *malverser*, from Latin *male* 'badly' + *versari* 'behave'.

Malvinas, Islas /malˈviːnəs, ˈiːzlas/, Spanish /malˈβinas, ˈislas/ the name by which the Falkland Islands are known in Argentina.

malvoisie /ˈmalvɔɪzi, ˌmalvɔɪˈziː/, French /malvwazi/ ▸ noun [mass noun] (in French-speaking countries) any of several grape varieties used to make full-flavoured white wines.
– ORIGIN from Old French *malvesie*, from the French form of *Monemvasia* (see **MALMSEY**).

malware ▸ noun [mass noun] malicious software, such as a virus, which is specifically designed to disrupt or damage a computer system.

mam ▸ noun Brit. informal or dialect one's mother.
– ORIGIN late 16th cent.: perhaps imitative of a child's first syllables (see **MAMA**).

mama /ˈmamə, məˈmɑː/ (also **mamma**) ▸ noun **1** dated or N. Amer. one's mother (especially as a child's term). **2** US informal a mature woman: *the ultimate tough blues mama*.
– ORIGIN mid 16th cent.: imitative of a child's first syllables *ma, ma*.

mamaguy /ˈmaməɡʌɪ/ ▸ verb [with obj.] W. Indian try to deceive (someone), especially with flattery or untruths.
– ORIGIN from Spanish *mamar gallo* 'make a monkey of'.

mama-san /ˈmaməsan/ ▸ noun (in Japan and East Asia) a woman in a position of authority, especially one in charge of a geisha house or bar.
– ORIGIN Japanese, from *mama* 'mother' + **-SAN**.

mama's boy ▸ noun US term for **MUMMY'S BOY**.

mamba /ˈmambə/ ▸ noun a large, agile, highly venomous African snake. ● Genus *Dendroaspis*, family Elapidae: three species. See also **BLACK MAMBA**.
– ORIGIN mid 19th cent.: from Zulu *imamba*.

mambo /ˈmambəʊ/ ▸ noun (pl. **mambos**) **1** a Latin American dance similar in rhythm to the rumba. **2** a voodoo priestess.
▸ verb (**mamboes, mamboing, mamboed**) [no obj.] dance the mambo.
– ORIGIN 1940s: from American Spanish, probably from Haitian Creole, from Yoruba, literally 'to talk'.

mamee ▸ noun variant spelling of **MAMMEE**.

mamelon /ˈmamɪlɒn/ ▸ noun Biology a small rounded structure, e.g. the central knob of a tubercle on a sea urchin.
– ORIGIN mid 19th cent.: from French, 'nipple', from *mamelle* 'breast', from Latin *mamilla* 'little breast'.

Mameluke /ˈmaməluːk/ ▸ noun a member of a regime descended from Turkish, Mongol, and Circassian slaves which ruled Syria (1260–1516) and Egypt (1250–1517), and continued as a ruling military caste in Ottoman Egypt until massacred by the viceroy Muhammad Ali in 1811.
– ORIGIN from French *mameluk*, from Arabic *mamlūk* (passive participle used as a noun meaning 'slave'), from *malaka* 'possess'.

Mamet /ˈmamɪt/, David (b.1947), American dramatist, director, and screenwriter. Notable plays: *Glengarry Glen Ross* (Pulitzer Prize, 1984) and *Oleanna* (1992).

mamey ▸ noun variant spelling of **MAMMEE**.

mamilla /maˈmɪlə/ (also **mammilla**) ▸ noun (pl. **mamillae** /-liː/) Anatomy the nipple of a woman's breast. ■ the organ in any mammal corresponding to a woman's nipple. ■ a nipple-shaped structure.
– ORIGIN late 17th cent.: from Latin, diminutive of *mamma* 'breast' (see **MAMMA²**).

mamillary /ˈmamɪləri/ (also **mammillary**) ▸ adjective shaped like or resembling a breast or nipple. ■ (of a mineral) having several smoothly rounded convex surfaces. ■ Anatomy denoting two rounded bodies in the floor of the hypothalamus in the brain.
– ORIGIN early 17th cent.: from modern Latin *mamillaris*, from *mamilla* (see **MAMILLA**). The spelling variant of *-mm-* was due to association with **MAMMARY**.

mamillated /ˈmamɪleɪtɪd/ (also **mammillated**) ▸ adjective technical covered with rounded protuberances. ■ (of a mineral) mamillary.
– DERIVATIVES **mamillate** adjective.
– ORIGIN mid 18th cent.: from **MAMILLA** + the adjectival suffix *-ated*.

mamma¹ /ˈmamə, məˈmɑː/ ▸ noun variant spelling of **MAMA**.

mamma² /ˈmamə/ ▸ noun (pl. **mammae** /-miː/) technical a milk-secreting organ of female mammals (in humans, the breast). ■ a corresponding non-secretory structure in male mammals.
– DERIVATIVES **mammiform** adjective.
– ORIGIN Old English, from Latin, 'breast'.

mammal ▸ noun a warm-blooded vertebrate animal of a class that is distinguished by the possession of hair or fur, females that secrete milk for the nourishment of the young, and (typically) the birth of live young.

> The first small mammals evolved from reptiles about 200 million years ago, and the group diversified rapidly after the extinction of the dinosaurs to become the dominant form of land animal, with around 4,000 living species. Mammals belong to the class Mammalia, which contains the subclass Prototheria (monotremes) and the infraclasses Metatheria (marsupials) and Eutheria (placental mammals such as rodents, cats, whales, bats, and humans).

– DERIVATIVES **mammalian** adjective.
– ORIGIN early 19th cent.: anglicized form (first used in the plural) of modern Latin *mammalia*, neuter plural of Latin *mammalis* (adjective), from *mamma* 'breast' (see **MAMMA²**).

mammal-like reptile ▸ noun another term for **SYNAPSID**.

mammalogy /maˈmalədʒi/ ▸ noun [mass noun] the branch of zoology concerned with mammals.
– DERIVATIVES **mammalogist** noun.

mammary /ˈmaməri/ ▸ adjective denoting or relating to the human female breasts or the milk-secreting organs of other mammals.
▸ noun (pl. **mammaries**) informal a breast.
– ORIGIN late 17th cent.: from **MAMMA²** + **-ARY¹**.

mammary gland ▸ noun the milk-producing gland of women or other female mammals.

mammee /maˈmiː/ (also **mamee, mamey**) ▸ noun **1** (also **mammee apple**) a tropical American tree having large edible red fruit with sweet yellow flesh. ● *Mammea americana*, family Guttiferae. **2** (also **mammee sapote**) a Central American tree having edible russet fruit with spicy red flesh. [*sapote* from Spanish *zapote* 'sapodilla'.] ● *Pouteria sapota*, family Sapotaceae.
– ORIGIN late 16th cent.: from Spanish *mamei*, from Taino.

mammilla ▸ noun variant spelling of **MAMILLA**.

mammogram /ˈmaməɡram/ ▸ noun an image obtained by mammography.

mammography /maˈmɒɡrəfi/ ▸ noun [mass noun] Medicine a technique using X-rays to diagnose and locate tumours of the breasts.
– ORIGIN 1930s: from **MAMMA²** + **-GRAPHY**.

Mammon /ˈmamən/ ▸ noun [mass noun] wealth regarded as an evil influence or false object of worship and devotion.
– DERIVATIVES **Mammonism** noun.
– ORIGIN late Middle English: via late Latin from New Testament Greek *mamōnas* (see Matt. 6:24, Luke 16:9–13), from Aramaic *māmōn* 'riches'. The word was taken by medieval writers as the name of the devil of covetousness, and revived in this sense by Milton.

mammoth ▸ noun a large extinct elephant of the Pleistocene epoch, typically hairy with a sloping back and long curved tusks. ● Genus *Mammuthus*, family Elephantidae: several species. See **WOOLLY MAMMOTH**.
▸ adjective huge: *a mammoth corporation*.
– ORIGIN early 18th cent.: from Russian *mamo(n)t*, probably of Siberian origin.

Mammoth Cave National Park a national park in west central Kentucky, site of the largest known cave system in the world. It consists of over 480 km (300 miles) of charted passageways and contains some spectacular rock formations.

mammy ▸ noun (pl. **mammies**) informal a child's word for their mother: *he was screaming for his mammy*. ■ offensive (formerly in the southern United States) a black nursemaid or nanny in charge of white children.
– ORIGIN early 16th cent.: from **MAM** + **-Y²**; compare with **MOMMY** and **MUMMY¹**.

Mamoutzu /maˈmuːtsuː/ the capital (since 1977) of Mayotte; pop. 53,000 (est. 2007).

mampara /mamˈpɑːrə/ ▸ noun variant spelling of **MOMPARA**.

Mam'selle /mamˈzɛl/ ▸ noun short for **MADEMOISELLE**.

man ▸ noun (pl. **men**) **1** an adult human male. ■ a male member of a workforce, team, etc.: *over 700 men were made redundant*. ■ (**men**) ordinary members of the armed forces as distinct from the officers: *he had a platoon of forty men to prepare for battle*. ■ a husband or lover: *the two of them lived for a time as man and wife*. ■ [with modifier] a male person associated with a particular place, activity, or occupation: *a Cambridge man | I'm a solid Labour man*. ■ a person with the qualities associated with males, such as bravery, spirit, or toughness: *she was more of a man than any of them*. ■ a male pursued or sought by another, especially in connection with a crime: *Inspector Bull was sure they would find their man*. ■ dated a manservant or valet: *get me a cocktail, my man*. ■ historical a vassal. **2** a human being of either sex; a person: *God cares for all men*. ■ (also **Man**) [in sing.] human beings in general; the human race: *places untouched by the ravages of man*. ■ [in sing.] [with adj. or noun modifier] a type of prehistoric human named after the place where the remains were found: *Cro-Magnon man*. **3** (**the Man**) informal a group or person in a position of authority over others, such as a corporate employer or the police: *they've mastered their emotive grunge-pop without haggling with the Man*. ■ black slang white people collectively regarded as the controlling group in society: *he urged that black college athletes boycott the Man's Rose Bowl*. **4** a figure or token used in playing a board game.
▸ verb (**mans, manning, manned**) [with obj.] **1** (of personnel) work at, run, or operate (a place or piece of equipment) or defend (a fortification): *the firemen manned the pumps and fought the blaze*. ■ provide someone to fill (a post): *the chaplaincy was formerly manned by the cathedral*. **2** archaic fortify the spirits or courage of.
▸ exclamation informal, chiefly N. Amer. used, irrespective of the sex of the person addressed, to express surprise, admiration, delight, etc., or for emphasis: *wow, like cosmic, man*.
– PHRASES **as —— as the next man** as —— as the average person: *I'm as ambitious as the next man*. **as one man** with everyone acting together or in agreement: *the crowd rose to their feet as one man*. **be someone's** (or **the**) **man** be the person perfectly suited to a particular requirement or task: *if it's war you want, I'm your man*. **be man enough to do** (or **for**) be brave enough to do. **every man for himself and the Devil take the hindmost** proverb everyone should (or does) look after their own interests rather than considering those of others. [with allusion to a chase by the Devil, in which the slowest will be caught.] **make a man out of someone** (of an experience or person) turn a young man into a mature adult: *swimming will make a man out of you*. **man about town** a fashionable male socialite. **man and boy** from childhood: *I've been with this company man and boy*. **the man in the moon** the imagined likeness of a face seen on the surface of a full moon. **the man in** (or US **on**) **the street** the average man. **man of action** see **ACTION**. **man of the cloth** a clergyman. **man of God** a clergyman. ■ a holy man or saint. **man of honour** a man who adheres to what is right or to a high standard of conduct. **man of the house** the male head of a household. **man of letters** a male scholar or author. **man of the match** Brit. the team member who has given the most outstanding performance in a particular game. **man of the moment** a man of importance at a particular time. **man of**

straw (also **straw man**) **1** a person compared to a figure made of straw; a sham. **2** a person undertaking a financial commitment without adequate means. **man of the world** see WORLD. **the man on the Clapham omnibus** Brit. the average man, especially with regard to his opinions. **man's best friend** an affectionate or approving way of referring to dogs. **a man's man** a man who is more popular and at ease with other men than with women. **man to man 1** in a direct and frank way between two men: *he was able to talk man to man with the delegates.* **2** denoting a defensive tactic in soccer or other sport in which each player is responsible for marking one opponent: *the best man-to-man marker in the game.* **men in (grey) suits** powerful men within an organization who exercise their authority anonymously. **men in white coats** medical or laboratory staff, especially doctors. ■ humorous psychiatrists or psychiatric workers (used to imply that someone is mad): *I think the men in white coats will be calling soon.* **the men's** (or **the men's room**) a men's public toilet. **my** (or **my good** or **my dear**) **man** Brit. dated a patronizing form of address to a man. **separate** (or **sort out**) **the men from the boys** informal show or prove which people in a group are truly competent, brave, or mature. **to a man** without exception: *to a man, we all took a keen interest in the business.*

– PHRASAL VERBS **man up** US informal be brave or tough enough to deal with an unpleasant situation: *you just have to man up and take it.*
– DERIVATIVES **manless** adjective.
– ORIGIN Old English *man(n)*, (plural) *menn* (noun), *mannian* (verb), of Germanic origin; related to Dutch *man*, German *Mann*, and Sanskrit *manu* 'mankind'.

> **USAGE** Traditionally the word **man** has been used to refer not only to adult males but also to human beings in general, regardless of sex. There is a historical explanation for this: in Old English the principal sense of **man** was 'a human being', and the words **wer** and **wif** were used to refer specifically to 'a male person' and 'a female person' respectively. Subsequently, **man** replaced **wer** as the normal term for 'a male person', but at the same time the older sense 'a human being' remained in use.
> In the second half of the twentieth century the generic use of **man** to refer to 'human beings in general' (as in *reptiles were here long before man appeared on the earth*) became problematic; the use is now often regarded as sexist or at best old-fashioned. In some contexts, alternative terms such as **the human race** or **humankind** may be used. Fixed phrases and sayings such as *time and tide wait for no **man*** can be easily rephrased, e.g. *time and tide wait for **nobody**.* Alternatives for terms such as **manpower** or the verb **man** exist: for example, **staff** or **employees**, and **to staff** or **to operate**.

Man. ▶ abbreviation Manitoba.

-man ▶ combining form in nouns denoting: ■ a male of a specified nationality or origin: *Frenchman.* ■ a person, especially a man, belonging to a specified group or having a specified occupation or role: *chairman | layman.* ■ a ship of a specified kind: *merchantman.*

> **USAGE** Traditionally, the form **-man** was combined with other words to create a term denoting an occupation or role, as in **fireman, layman, chairman,** and **freshman.** As the role of women in society has changed, with the result that women are now more likely to be in roles previously held exclusively by men, many of these terms ending in **-man** have been challenged as sexist and out of date. As a result, there has been a gradual shift away from **-man** compounds except where referring to a specific male person. Alternative gender-neutral terms are used, for example **firefighter** and **fresher**, and new ones which only a few decades ago seemed odd or awkward today seem unexceptionable: **chair/chairperson, layperson,** and **sportsperson.**

Man, Isle of see ISLE OF MAN.

mana /ˈmɑːnə/ ▶ noun [mass noun] (in Polynesian, Melanesian, and Maori belief) an impersonal supernatural power which can be transmitted or inherited.
– ORIGIN Maori.

manacle /ˈmanək(ə)l/ ▶ noun (usu. **manacles**) one of two metal bands joined by a chain, for fastening a person's hands or ankles.
▶ verb [with obj.] confine (a person or part of the body) with manacles: *his hands were manacled behind his back.*
– ORIGIN Middle English: from Old French *manicle* 'handcuff', from Latin *manicula*, diminutive of *manus* 'hand'.

manage ▶ verb **1** [with obj.] be in charge of (a business, organization, or undertaking); run: *their elder son managed the farm.* ■ have the position of supervising (staff) at work. ■ be the manager of (a sports team or a performer): *he managed five or six bands in his career.* ■ use (money, time, or other resources) sensibly: *we manage our cash extremely well.* ■ maintain control over (a person or animal): *she manages horses better than anyone I know.* ■ control the use or exploitation of (land): *the forest is managed to achieve maximum growth.*
2 [no obj.] succeed in surviving or in achieving something despite difficult circumstances; cope: *Catherine managed on five hours' sleep a night.* ■ [with obj.] succeed in achieving or producing (something difficult): *she managed a brave but unconvincing smile* | [with infinitive] *Blanche finally managed to hail a cab.* ■ [with obj.] succeed in dealing with or withstanding (something): *there was more stress and anxiety than he could manage.* ■ [with obj.] be free to attend at (a certain time): *he could not manage 24 March after all.*
– ORIGIN mid 16th cent. (in the sense 'put (a horse) through the paces of the manège'): from Italian *maneggiare*, based on Latin *manus* 'hand'.

manageable ▶ adjective able to be controlled or dealt with without difficulty: *her long hair was black, wavy, and manageable.*
– DERIVATIVES **manageability** noun, **manageably** adverb.

managed care ▶ noun [mass noun] US a system of health care emphasizing preventative medicine and home treatment.

managed currency ▶ noun a currency whose exchange rate is regulated by the government.

managed economy ▶ noun an economy in which the framework and general policies are regulated by the government.

managed fund ▶ noun an investment fund run on behalf of an investor by an agent (typically, an insurance company).

management ▶ noun [mass noun] **1** the process of dealing with or controlling things or people: *the management of the economy | businesses were slow to adopt the key elements of environmental risk management.* ■ [treated as sing. or pl.] the people managing a company or organization, regarded collectively: *management were extremely cooperative.* ■ the responsibility for and control of a company or organization: *a successful career in management.* ■ Medicine & Psychiatry the treatment or control of diseases or disorders, or the care of patients who suffer them.
2 archaic trickery; deceit: *if there has been any management in the business, it has been concealed from me.*

management accounting ▶ noun [mass noun] the provision of financial data and advice to a company for use in the organization and development of its business.
– DERIVATIVES **management accountant** noun.

management buyout ▶ noun the purchase of a controlling share in a company by its executive directors and/or managers.

management company ▶ noun a company which is set up to manage a group of properties, a unit trust, an investment fund, etc.

manager ▶ noun **1** a person responsible for controlling or administering an organization or group of staff: *the manager of a bar.* ■ a person who controls the professional and business activities of a performer, sports player, group of musicians, etc. ■ a person in charge of the activities, tactics, and training of a sports team.
2 [with adj.] a person regarded in terms of their skill in managing resources, especially those of a household: *she was a good manager, and could make a meal out of nothing.*
3 [with modifier] Computing a program or system that controls or organizes a peripheral device or process: *a file manager.*
4 (in the Houses of Parliament and the US Senate) a member of a committee appointed by one house to confer with a similar committee of the other house.
– DERIVATIVES **managership** noun.

manageress ▶ noun Brit. a female manager of a shop, restaurant, etc.

managerial ▶ adjective relating to management or managers: *the division of managerial responsibilities.*
– DERIVATIVES **managerially** adverb.

managerialism ▶ noun [mass noun] belief in or reliance on the use of professional managers in administering or planning an activity.
– DERIVATIVES **managerialist** noun & adjective.

managing ▶ adjective [attrib.] **1** chiefly Brit. having executive control or authority: *the managing director.*
2 archaic economical.

Managua /məˈnɑːgwə/ the capital of Nicaragua; pop. 937,489 (2006). The city was almost completely destroyed by an earthquake in 1972.

manakin /ˈmanəkɪn/ ▶ noun a small brightly coloured tropical American bird with a large head and small bill. ● Family Pipridae (or Cotingidae, Tyrannidae): several genera and many species.
– ORIGIN early 17th cent.: variant of MANIKIN.

Manama /məˈnɑːmə/ the capital of Bahrain; pop. 157,000 (est. 2007).

mañana /manˈjɑːnə/ ▶ adverb tomorrow. ■ in the indefinite future.
– ORIGIN Spanish.

Mana Pools National Park /ˈmɑːnə/ a national park in northern Zimbabwe, in the Zambezi valley north-east of Lake Kariba, established in 1963.

Manasseh /məˈnasi, -ˈnasə/ (in the Bible) the elder son of Joseph, ancestor of the tribe of Manasseh (Gen. 48:19). ■ the tribe of Israel traditionally descended from Manasseh, which settled on both sides of the River Jordan.

Manasses, Prayer of see PRAYER OF MANASSES.

manat /ˈmanat/ ▶ noun (pl. **same**) the basic monetary unit of Azerbaijan and Turkmenistan, equal to 100 gopik in Azerbaijan and 100 tenesi in Turkmenistan.
– ORIGIN Azerbaijani and Turkmen.

man-at-arms ▶ noun (pl. **men-at-arms**) archaic a soldier, especially one heavily armed and on horseback.

manatee /ˌmanəˈtiː, ˈmanətiː/ ▶ noun a sea cow of tropical Atlantic coasts and estuaries, with a rounded tail flipper. ● Family Trichechidae and genus *Trichechus*: three species.
– ORIGIN mid 16th cent.: from Spanish *manatí*, from Carib *manáti*.

Manaus /məˈnaʊs/ a city in NW Brazil, capital of the state of Amazonas; pop. 1,646,602 (2007). It is the principal commercial centre of the upper Amazon region.

Manawatu /ˌmanəˈwɑːtuː/ **1** a river of the North Island, New Zealand, flowing into the sea near the town of Foxton.
2 a district in the south-west of the North Island, New Zealand, centred on Palmerston North.

manbag ▶ noun informal a man's handbag or shoulder bag.

Man Booker Prize see BOOKER PRIZE.

Manc /maŋk/ ▶ noun & adjective short for MANCUNIAN.

Manchego /manˈtʃeɪgəʊ/ ▶ noun [mass noun] a Spanish cheese traditionally made with sheep's milk.
– ORIGIN Spanish, from *La Mancha*, the name of the region of central Spain where the cheese originates.

Manchester an industrial city and metropolitan district in NW England; pop. 396,300 (est. 2009). Founded in Roman times, it developed in the 18th and 19th centuries as a centre of the English cotton industry.

manchester ▶ noun [mass noun] S. African & Austral./NZ household linen.

Manchester Ship Canal a waterway in NW England, which links Manchester with the estuary of the River Mersey and the Irish Sea. Opened in 1894, it is 57 km (36 miles) long.

Manchester terrier ▶ noun a small terrier of a breed with a short black-and-tan coat, formerly popular in the Manchester area of England.

manchet /ˈmantʃɪt/ ▶ noun historical a loaf of the finest kind of wheaten bread.
– ORIGIN late Middle English: perhaps from obsolete *maine* 'flour of the finest quality' + obsolete *cheat*, denoting a kind of wheaten bread.

man-child ▶ noun an immature man. ■ archaic a male child.

manchineel /ˌman(t)ʃɪˈniːl/ ▶ noun a Caribbean tree which has acrid apple-like fruit and poisonous milky sap which can cause temporary blindness. ● *Hippomane mancinella*, family Euphorbiaceae.
– ORIGIN mid 17th cent.: from French *mancenille*, from Spanish *manzanilla*, diminutive of *manzana* 'apple', based on Latin *matiana (poma)* (neuter plural), denoting a kind of apple.

Manchu /manˈtʃuː/ ▶ **noun 1** a member of a people originally living in Manchuria, who formed the last imperial dynasty of China (1644–1912).
2 [mass noun] the Tungusic language of the Manchus, still spoken by a few thousand people in Xinjiang, though most Manchus now speak Chinese.
▶ **adjective** relating to the Manchu people or their language.
– ORIGIN the name in Manchu, literally 'pure'.

Manchuria /manˈtʃʊərɪə/ a mountainous region forming the NE portion of China, now comprising the provinces of Jilin, Liaoning, and Heilongjiang. In 1932 it was declared an independent state by Japan and renamed Manchukuo; it was restored to China in 1945.
– DERIVATIVES **Manchurian** noun & adjective.

manciple /ˈmansɪp(ə)l/ ▶ **noun** chiefly archaic a person in charge of buying provisions for a college, an Inn of Court, or a monastery.
– ORIGIN Middle English: via Anglo-Norman French and Old French from Latin *mancipium* 'purchase', from *manceps* 'buyer', from *manus* 'hand' + *capere* 'take'.

Mancunian /manˈkjuːnɪən/ ▶ **noun** a native or inhabitant of Manchester.
▶ **adjective** relating to Manchester.
– ORIGIN early 20th cent.: from *Mancunium*, the Latin name of Manchester, + **-AN**.

-mancy ▶ **combining form** divination by a specified means: *geomancy*.
– DERIVATIVES **-mantic** combining form in corresponding adjectives.
– ORIGIN from Old French *-mancie*, via late Latin *-mantia* from Greek *manteia* 'divination'.

Mandaean /manˈdiːən/ (also **Mandean**) ▶ **noun 1** a member of a Gnostic sect of Iraq and SW Iran, who regard John the Baptist as the Messiah and stress salvation through knowledge of the divine origin of the soul.
2 [mass noun] the language of the Mandaeans, a form of Aramaic.
▶ **adjective** relating to the Mandaeans or their language.
– ORIGIN late 19th cent.: from Mandaean Aramaic *mandaia* 'Gnostics, those who have knowledge' (from *manda* 'knowledge') + **-AN**.

mandala /ˈmandələ, ˈmʌn-/ ▶ **noun** a circular figure representing the universe in Hindu and Buddhist symbolism.
– DERIVATIVES **mandalic** adjective.
– ORIGIN from Sanskrit *maṇḍala* 'disc'.

Mandalay /ˌmandəˈleɪ/ a port on the Irrawaddy River in central Burma (Myanmar); pop. 961,000 (est. 2007). Founded in 1857, it was the capital until 1885 of the Burmese kingdom. It is an important Buddhist religious centre.

mandamus /manˈdeɪməs/ ▶ **noun** [mass noun] Law a judicial writ issued as a command to an inferior court or ordering a person to perform a public or statutory duty.
– ORIGIN mid 16th cent.: from Latin, literally 'we command'.

Mandan /ˈmand(ə)n/ ▶ **noun** (pl. **same** or **Mandans**)
1 a member of an American Indian people formerly living along the northern reaches of the Missouri River.
2 [mass noun] the Siouan language of the Mandan, now virtually extinct.
▶ **adjective** relating to the Mandan or their language.
– ORIGIN from North American French *Mandane*, probably from Dakota Sioux *mawátāna*.

mandap /ˈmʌndəp/ (also **mandapam** /ˈmʌndəpʌm/)
▶ **noun** (in southern India) a temple porch. ■ a temporary platform set up for weddings and religious ceremonies.
– ORIGIN from Sanskrit *maṇḍapam*.

mandarin¹ /ˈmand(ə)rɪn/ ▶ **noun 1** (**Mandarin** or **Mandarin Chinese**) [mass noun] the standard literary and official form of Chinese, spoken by over 730 million people.
2 an official in any of the nine top grades of the former imperial Chinese civil service. ■ [as modifier] (of clothing) characteristic of a former Chinese mandarin: *a red-buttoned mandarin cap*. ■ a porcelain ornament consisting of a nodding figure in traditional Chinese costume.
3 a powerful official or senior bureaucrat, especially one perceived as reactionary and secretive: *a civil service mandarin*.
– DERIVATIVES **mandarinate** noun.
– ORIGIN late 16th cent. (denoting a Chinese official): from Portuguese *mandarim*, via Malay from Hindi *mantrī* 'counsellor'.

mandarin² /ˈmand(ə)rɪn/ (also **mandarine** /-riːn/, **mandarin orange**) ▶ **noun 1** a small flattish citrus fruit with a loose yellow-orange skin.
2 the citrus tree that yields the mandarin. ● *Citrus reticulata*, family Rutaceae.
– ORIGIN late 18th cent.: from French *mandarine*; perhaps related to **MANDARIN¹**, the colour of the fruit being likened to the official's yellow robes.

mandarin collar ▶ **noun** a small, close-fitting upright collar.

mandarin duck ▶ **noun** a small tree-nesting East Asian duck, the male of which has showy plumage with an orange ruff and orange sail-like feathers on each side of the body. ● *Aix galericulata*, family Anatidae.

mandarin jacket ▶ **noun** a straight jacket with a mandarin collar, typically of embroidered silk.

mandatary /ˈmandət(ə)ri/ (also **mandatory**) ▶ **noun** (pl. **mandataries**) historical a person or state receiving a mandate.
– ORIGIN late 15th cent. (denoting a person appointed by a papal mandate): from late Latin *mandatarius*, from *mandatum* (see **MANDATE**).

mandate ▶ **noun** /ˈmandeɪt/ **1** an official order or commission to do something: *a mandate to seek the release of political prisoners*. ■ Law a commission by which a party is entrusted to perform a service, especially without payment and with indemnity against loss by that party. ■ a written authorization enabling someone to carry out transactions on another's bank account. ■ historical a commission from the League of Nations to a member state to administer a territory: *the end of the British mandate in Palestine*.
2 the authority to carry out a policy, regarded as given by the electorate to a party or candidate that wins an election: *he called an election to seek a mandate for his policies*. ■ Canadian a period during which a government is in power.
▶ **verb** /manˈdeɪt/ [with obj.] **1** give (someone) authority to act in a certain way: *the rightful king was mandated and sanctioned by God*. ■ require (something) to be done; make mandatory: *the government began mandating better car safety*.
2 (**be mandated to**) historical (of territory) be assigned to (another power) under a mandate of the League of Nations.
– ORIGIN early 16th cent.: from Latin *mandatum* 'something commanded', neuter past participle of *mandare*, from *manus* 'hand' + *dare* 'give'. Sense 2 of the noun has been influenced by French *mandat*.

mandatory /ˈmandət(ə)ri/ ▶ **adjective** required by law or mandate; compulsory: *wearing helmets was made mandatory for pedal cyclists*.
▶ **noun** (pl. **mandatories**) variant spelling of **MANDATARY**.
– DERIVATIVES **mandatorily** adverb.
– ORIGIN late 15th cent.: from late Latin *mandatorius*, from Latin *mandatum* 'something commanded'.

man-day ▶ **noun** a day regarded in terms of the amount of work that can be done by one person within this period.

Mande /ˈmɑːndeɪ/ ▶ **noun** (pl. **same** or **Mandes**) **1** a member of any of a large group of peoples of West Africa.
2 [mass noun] the group of Niger–Congo languages spoken by the Mande. They include Malinke, Mende, and Bambara.
▶ **adjective** relating to the Mande or the Mande group of languages.
– ORIGIN the name in Mande.

Mandean ▶ **noun & adjective** variant spelling of **MANDAEAN**.

Mandela /manˈdɛlə/, Nelson (Rolihlahla) (b.1918), South African statesman, President 1994–9. He was sentenced to life imprisonment in 1964 as an activist for the African National Congress (ANC). Released in 1990, as leader of the ANC he engaged in talks on the introduction of majority rule with President F. W. de Klerk, with whom he shared the Nobel Peace Prize in 1993. He became the country's first democratically elected President in 1994.

Mandelbrot /ˈmand(ə)lbrɒt/, Benoit (b.1924), Polish-born French mathematician. Mandelbrot is known as the pioneer of fractal geometry.

Mandelbrot set ▶ **noun** Mathematics a particular set of complex numbers which has a highly convoluted fractal boundary when plotted.

Mandelstam /ˈmand(ə)lˌʃtam/ (also **Mandelshtam**), Osip (Emilevich) (1891–1938), Russian poet, a member of the Acmeist group. Sent into internal exile in 1934, he died in a prison camp. Notable works: *Stone* (1913) and *Tristia* (1922).

Mandeville /ˈmandəvɪl/, Sir John (14th century), English nobleman. He is remembered as the reputed author of a book of travels and travellers' tales which was actually compiled by an unknown hand from the works of several writers.

mandible /ˈmandɪb(ə)l/ ▶ **noun** Anatomy & Zoology the jaw or a jawbone, especially the lower jawbone in mammals and fishes. ■ either of the upper and lower parts of a bird's beak. ■ either half of the crushing organ in an arthropod's mouthparts.
– DERIVATIVES **mandibular** adjective, **mandibulate** adjective.
– ORIGIN late Middle English: from Old French, or from late Latin *mandibula*, from *mandere* 'to chew'.

Manding /ˈmandɪŋ/ (also **Mandingo** /manˈdɪŋgəʊ/)
▶ **noun & adjective** another term for **MANDE**.

Mandinka /mənˈdɪŋkə/ ▶ **noun** (pl. **same** or **Mandinkas**) **1** a member of a West African people living mainly in Senegal, Gambia, and Sierra Leone.
2 [mass noun] the Mande language of the Mandinka, with about 770,000 speakers.
▶ **adjective** relating to the Mandinka or their language.
– ORIGIN the name in Mandinka.

mandir /ˈmandɪə/ ▶ **noun** a Hindu temple.
– ORIGIN from Hindi and Sanskrit *mandira* 'dwelling place, temple'.

mandola /manˈdəʊlə/ ▶ **noun** a large tenor or bass mandolin, used in ensembles and folk groups. ■ (also **mandora** /-ˈdɔːrə/) historical an early stringed instrument of the mandolin or cittern type.
– ORIGIN early 18th cent.: from Italian.

mandolin ▶ **noun 1** a musical instrument resembling a lute, having paired metal strings plucked with a plectrum. It has a characteristic tremolo when sustaining long notes.
2 (also **mandoline**) a kitchen utensil consisting of a flat frame with adjustable blades, for slicing vegetables.
– DERIVATIVES **mandolinist** noun.
– ORIGIN early 18th cent.: from French *mandoline*, from Italian *mandolino*, diminutive of *mandola* (see **MANDOLA**).

M

mandorla /manˈdɔːlə/ ▶ **noun** another term for **VESICA PISCIS**.
– ORIGIN late 19th cent.: from Italian, literally 'almond'.

mandragora /manˈdragərə/ ▶ **noun** literary the mandrake, especially when used as a narcotic.
– ORIGIN Old English, via medieval Latin from Latin and Greek *mandragoras*.

mandrake ▶ **noun** a Mediterranean plant of the nightshade family, with a forked fleshy root which supposedly resembles the human form and which was formerly used in herbal medicine and magic; it was alleged to shriek when pulled from the ground. ● *Mandragora officinarum*, family Solanaceae.
– ORIGIN Middle English *mandrag(g)e*, from Middle Dutch *mandrag(r)e*, from medieval Latin *mandragora*; associated with **MAN** (because of the root) + *drake* in the Old English sense 'dragon'.

Mandrax /ˈmandraks/ ▶ **noun** [mass noun] trademark a sedative drug containing methaqualone and diphenhydramine hydrochloride.
– ORIGIN 1960s: of unknown origin.

mandrel /ˈmandr(ə)l/ ▶ **noun 1** a shaft or spindle in a lathe, to which work is fixed while being turned.
2 a rod round which metal or other material is forged or shaped.
3 Brit. a miner's pick.
– ORIGIN early 16th cent. (in sense 3): of unknown origin.

mandrill /ˈmandrɪl/ ▶ **noun** a large West African baboon with a red and blue face, the male having a blue rump. ● *Mandrillus sphinx*, family Cercopithecidae.
– ORIGIN mid 18th cent.: probably from **MAN** + **DRILL³**.

manducate /ˈmandjʊkeɪt/ ▶ **verb** [with obj.] formal chew or eat.
– DERIVATIVES **manducation** noun.
– ORIGIN early 17th cent. (earlier (early 16th cent.) as *manducation*): from Latin *manducat-* 'chewed', from the verb *manducare*, from *manduco* 'guzzler', from *mandere* 'to chew'.

mane ▶ **noun** a growth of long hair on the neck of a horse, lion, or other mammal. ■ a person's long flowing hair.
– DERIVATIVES **maned** adjective [in combination] *a black-maned lion*, **maneless** adjective.

– ORIGIN Old English *manu*, of Germanic origin; related to Dutch *manen*.

man-eater ▶ noun **1** an animal that has a propensity for killing and eating humans. ▪ another term for GREAT WHITE SHARK.
2 informal a dominant woman who has many sexual partners.
– DERIVATIVES **man-eating** adjective.

maneb /ˈmanɛb/ ▶ noun [mass noun] a white compound used as a fungicidal powder on vegetables and fruit. ● Chem. formula: $C_4H_6N_2S_4Mn$.
– ORIGIN from elements of the name *man(ganese) e(thylene) b(isdithiocarbamate)*.

maned wolf ▶ noun a large wild dog of South American grasslands, having a reddish coat with black hair across the shoulders and large erect ears. ● *Chrysocyon brachyurus*, family Canidae.

manège /maˈnɛʒ/ ▶ noun an enclosed area in which horses and riders are trained. ▪ [mass noun] the movements in which a horse is trained in a riding school. ▪ [mass noun] horsemanship.
– ORIGIN mid 17th cent.: French, from Italian (see MANAGE).

manes /ˈmɑːneɪz, ˈmeɪniːz/ ▶ plural noun (in Roman mythology) the souls of dead ancestors, worshipped as beneficent spirits.
– ORIGIN Latin.

Manet /ˈmaneɪ/, Édouard (1832–83), French painter. He adopted a realist approach which greatly influenced the Impressionists, using pure colour to give a direct unsentimental effect. Notable works: *Déjeuner sur l'herbe* (1863), *Olympia* (1865), and *A Bar at the Folies-Bergère* (1882).

Manetho /maˈnɛθəʊ/ (3rd century BC), Egyptian priest. He wrote a history of Egypt from mythical times to 323, in which he arbitrarily divided the succession of rulers known to him into thirty dynasties, an arrangement which is still followed.

maneuver ▶ noun & verb US spelling of MANOEUVRE.

man Friday ▶ noun a male personal assistant or servant.
– ORIGIN from *Friday*, a character in Defoe's novel *Robinson Crusoe* (1719), whom Crusoe often refers to as 'my man Friday'.

M

manful ▶ adjective brave and resolute, especially in a difficult situation: *a manful attempt to smile*.
– DERIVATIVES **manfulness** noun.

manfully ▶ adverb in a manful way; bravely: *his boys strove manfully to accomplish the task*.

manga /ˈmaŋgə/ ▶ noun [mass noun] a Japanese genre of cartoons, comic books, and animated films, having a science-fiction or fantasy theme and sometimes including violent or sexually explicit material.
– ORIGIN Japanese, from *man* 'indiscriminate' + *ga* 'picture'.

mangabey /ˈmaŋgəbeɪ/ ▶ noun a medium-sized long-tailed monkey native to the forests of West and central Africa. ● Genus *Cercocebus*, family Cercopithecidae: several species.
– ORIGIN late 18th cent.: by erroneous association with *Mangabey*, a region of Madagascar.

manganate /ˈmaŋgənət, -neɪt/ ▶ noun Chemistry a salt in which the anion contains both manganese and oxygen, especially one of the anion MnO_4^{2-}.

manganese /ˈmaŋgəniːz/ ▶ noun [mass noun] the chemical element of atomic number 25, a hard grey metal of the transition series. Manganese is an important component of special steels and magnetic alloys. (Symbol: **Mn**) ▪ the black dioxide of manganese as an industrial raw material or additive, especially in glass-making.
– ORIGIN late 17th cent.: via French from Italian *manganese*, alteration of medieval Latin *magnesia* (see MAGNESIA).

manganese bronze ▶ noun [mass noun] an alloy of copper and zinc with manganese.

manganese nodule ▶ noun a small concretion consisting of manganese and iron oxides, occurring in large numbers in ocean-floor sediment.

manganic /maŋˈganɪk/ ▶ adjective Chemistry of manganese with a higher valency, usually three. Compare with MANGANOUS.

Manganin /ˈmaŋgənɪn/ ▶ noun [mass noun] Brit. trademark an alloy of copper, manganese, and nickel, used chiefly in electrical devices.
– ORIGIN 1920s: from MANGANESE + -IN[1].

manganite /ˈmaŋgənʌɪt/ ▶ noun [mass noun] a mineral consisting of basic manganese oxide, typically occurring as steel-grey or black prisms.

manganous /ˈmaŋgənəs/ ▶ adjective Chemistry of manganese with a valency of two. Compare with MANGANIC.

mange /meɪn(d)ʒ/ ▶ noun [mass noun] a skin disease of mammals caused by parasitic mites and occasionally communicable to humans. It is characterized by severe itching, hair loss, and the formation of scabs and lesions.
– ORIGIN late Middle English: from Old French *mangeue*, from *mangier* 'eat', from Latin *manducare* 'to chew'.

mangel /ˈmaŋg(ə)l/ (also **mangel-wurzel** /-ˌwəːz(ə)l/) ▶ noun another term for MANGOLD.

manger ▶ noun a long trough from which horses or cattle feed.
– ORIGIN Middle English: from Old French *mangeure*, based on Latin *manducat-* 'chewed' (see MANDUCATE).

manger scene ▶ noun N. Amer. another term for NATIVITY SCENE.

mangetout /ˈmɒ̃ʒtuː, -ˈtuː/ ▶ noun (pl. **same** or **mangetouts** pronunc. **same**) Brit. a pea of a variety with an edible pod, eaten when the pod is young and flat.
– ORIGIN early 19th cent.: from French, literally 'eat all'.

mangey ▶ adjective variant spelling of MANGY.

mangle[1] ▶ noun a machine having two or more rollers turned by a handle, between which wet laundry is squeezed to remove excess moisture.
▶ verb [with obj.] press or squeeze with a mangle.
– ORIGIN late 17th cent.: from Dutch *mangel*, from *mangelen* 'to mangle', from medieval Latin *mango*, *manga*, from Greek *manganon* 'axis, engine of war'.

mangle[2] ▶ verb [with obj.] destroy or severely damage by tearing or crushing: *the car was mangled almost beyond recognition*. ▪ ruin or spoil (a text, piece of music, etc.): *he was mangling Bach on the piano*.
– DERIVATIVES **mangler** noun.
– ORIGIN late Middle English: from Anglo-Norman French *mahangler*, perhaps a frequentative of *mahaignier* 'maim'.

mango ▶ noun (pl. **mangoes** or **mangos**) **1** a fleshy, oval, yellowish-red tropical fruit which is eaten ripe or used green for pickles or chutneys.
2 (also **mango tree**) the evergreen tropical Indian tree which bears the mango. ● *Mangifera indica*, family Anacardiaceae.
3 a tropical American hummingbird that typically has green plumage with purple feathers on the wings, tail, or head. ● Genus *Anthracothorax*, family Trochilidae: several species.
– ORIGIN late 16th cent.: from Portuguese *manga*, from a Dravidian language.

mangold ▶ noun a beet of a variety with a large root, cultivated as stockfeed. Also called MANGEL, MANGEL-WURZEL. ● *Beta vulgaris crassa*, family Chenopodiaceae.
– ORIGIN mid 19th cent.: from German *Mangoldwurzel*, from *Mangold* 'beet' + *Wurzel* 'root'.

mangonel /ˈmaŋgən(ə)l/ ▶ noun historical a military device for throwing stones and other missiles.
– ORIGIN Middle English: from Old French *mangonel(le)*, from medieval Latin *manganellus*, diminutive of late Latin *manganum*, from Greek *manganon* 'axis, engine of war'.

mangosteen /ˈmaŋgəstiːn/ ▶ noun **1** a tropical fruit with sweet juicy white segments of flesh inside a thick reddish-brown rind.
2 the slow-growing Malaysian tree which bears the mangosteen. ● *Garcinia mangostana*, family Guttiferae.
– ORIGIN late 16th cent.: from Malay *manggustan*, dialect variant of *manggis*.

mangrove ▶ noun a tree or shrub which grows in tidal, chiefly tropical, coastal swamps, having numerous tangled roots that grow above ground and form dense thickets. ● Genera in several families, in particular *Rhizophora* and related genera (family Rhizophoraceae), and *Avicennia* (family Verbenaceae or Avicenniaceae).
▪ (also **mangrove swamp**) a tidal swamp which is dominated by mangroves.
– ORIGIN early 17th cent.: probably from Portuguese *mangue*, Spanish *mangle*, from Taino. The change in the ending was due to association with GROVE.

mangy (also **mangey**) ▶ adjective (**mangier**, **mangiest**) having mange. ▪ in poor condition; shabby: *a girl in a mangy fur coat*.
– DERIVATIVES **manginess** noun.

manhandle ▶ verb [with obj.] move (a heavy object) by hand with great effort: *men used to manhandle the piano down the stairs*. ▪ handle (someone) roughly by dragging or pushing.

Manhattan an island near the mouth of the Hudson River forming part of the city of New York. The site of the original Dutch settlement of New Amsterdam, it is now a borough containing the commercial and cultural centre of New York City.
– ORIGIN named after the Algonquin tribe from whom the Dutch settlers claimed to have bought the island in 1626.

manhattan ▶ noun a cocktail made of vermouth and whisky, sometimes with a dash of bitters.

Manhattan Project the code name for the American project set up in 1942 to develop an atom bomb. The project culminated in 1945 with the detonation of the first nuclear weapon, at White Sands in New Mexico.

manhole ▶ noun a small covered opening in a paved area allowing access beneath, especially one leading to a sewer.

manhood ▶ noun [mass noun] **1** the state or period of being a man rather than a child: *boys in the process of growing to manhood*. ▪ the qualities traditionally associated with men, such as courage, strength, and sexual potency: *we drank to prove our manhood*. ▪ the men of a country or society regarded collectively: *Germany had lost the best of her young manhood*. ▪ (**one's manhood**) informal used euphemistically to refer to a man's penis.
2 archaic the condition of being human.

man-hour ▶ noun an hour regarded in terms of the amount of work that can be done by one person within this period.

manhunt ▶ noun an organized search for a criminal, suspect, or escaped prisoner.

mania ▶ noun [mass noun] mental illness marked by periods of great excitement or euphoria, delusions, and overactivity. ▪ [count noun] an excessive enthusiasm or desire; an obsession: *he had **a mania for** automobiles*.
– ORIGIN late Middle English: via late Latin from Greek, literally 'madness', from *mainesthai* 'be mad'.

-mania ▶ combining form denoting a specified type of mental abnormality or obsession: *kleptomania*. ▪ denoting extreme enthusiasm or admiration: *Beatlemania*.
– DERIVATIVES **-maniac** combining form in corresponding nouns.

maniac /ˈmeɪnɪak/ ▶ noun a person exhibiting extremely wild or violent behaviour: *when he sits in front of a PlayStation he transforms into a karate-choppin' maniac*. ▪ [with adj. or noun modifier] informal an obsessive enthusiast: *a religious maniac*. ▪ Psychiatry, archaic a person suffering from mania.
– DERIVATIVES **maniacal** /məˈnʌɪək(ə)l/ adjective, **maniacally** /məˈnʌɪək(ə)li/ adverb.
– ORIGIN early 16th cent. (as an adjective): via late Latin from late Greek *maniakos*, from *mania* (see MANIA).

manic ▶ adjective (in psychiatry) relating to or affected by mania. ▪ showing wild, apparently deranged, excitement and energy: *a manic grin*. ▪ frantically busy; hectic: *the pace is utterly manic*.
– DERIVATIVES **manically** adverb.

Manicaland /məˈniːkəland/ a gold-mining province of eastern Zimbabwe; capital, Mutare.

manic depression ▶ noun another term for BIPOLAR DISORDER.
– DERIVATIVES **manic depressive** adjective & noun.

> **USAGE** The term **manic depression** is now felt to have negative connotations, and is being replaced by less loaded terms such as **bipolar disorder** or **bipolar affective disorder**. People with the condition can be referred to simply as **bipolar**, or as **having bipolar disorder**.

Manichaean /ˌmanɪˈkiːən/ (also **Manichean**) ▶ adjective chiefly historical relating to Manichaeism. ▪ Philosophy relating to dualism; dualistic.
▶ noun an adherent of Manichaeism.
– DERIVATIVES **Manichaeanism** noun.

Manichaeism /ˌmanɪˈkiːɪz(ə)m/ (also **Manicheism**) ▶ noun [mass noun] a dualistic religious system with Christian, Gnostic, and pagan elements, founded in Persia in the 3rd century by Manes (*c.*216–*c.*276) and based on a supposed primeval conflict between light and darkness. It was widespread in the Roman Empire and in Asia, and survived in Chinese Turkestan until the 13th century. ▪ religious or philosophical dualism.

– ORIGIN early 17th cent.: from late Latin *Manichaeus* (from the name *Manes*) + -ISM.

Manichee /ˌmanɪˈkiː/ ▸ noun & adjective archaic term for MANICHAEAN.
– ORIGIN Middle English: from late Latin *Manichaei*, plural of *Manichaeus* (see MANICHAEISM).

manicotti /ˌmanɪˈkɒti/ ▸ plural noun large tubular pasta shapes.
– ORIGIN Italian, plural of *manicotto* 'muff'.

manicou /ˈmanɪkuː/ ▸ noun W. Indian an opossum.
– ORIGIN from an American Indian word.

manicure ▸ noun a cosmetic treatment of the hands involving shaping and often painting of the nails, removal of the cuticles, and softening of the skin.
▸ verb [with obj.] give a manicure to. ■ (as adj. **manicured**) (of a lawn or garden) trimmed or neatly maintained.
– ORIGIN late 19th cent.: from French, from Latin *manus* 'hand' + *cura* 'care'.

manicurist ▸ noun a person who gives manicures professionally.

manifest[1] ▸ adjective clear or obvious to the eye or mind: *her manifest charm and proven ability*.
▸ verb [with obj.] show (a quality or feeling) by one's acts or appearance; demonstrate: *Lizzy manifested signs of severe depression*. ■ be evidence of; prove: *bad industrial relations are often manifested in strikes*. ■ [no obj.] (of an ailment) become apparent through the appearance of symptoms. ■ [no obj.] (of a ghost or spirit) appear: *one deity manifested in the form of a bird*.
– DERIVATIVES **manifestly** adverb.
– ORIGIN late Middle English: via Old French from Latin *manifestus*.

manifest[2] ▸ noun a document listing a ship's contents, cargo, passengers, and crew, for the use of customs officers. ■ a list of passengers or cargo in an aircraft. ■ a list of the wagons forming a freight train.
▸ verb [with obj.] record in a manifest: *every passenger is manifested at the point of departure*.
– ORIGIN mid 16th cent. (denoting a manifestation): from Italian *manifesto* (see MANIFESTO). The current sense dates from the early 17th cent.

manifestation ▸ noun an event, action, or object that clearly shows or embodies something abstract or theoretical: *the first obvious manifestations of global warming*. ■ [mass noun] the action or fact of showing something: *the manifestation of anxiety over disease*. ■ a symptom of an ailment. ■ a version or incarnation of something or someone: *the butterfly was one of the many manifestations of the Goddess*. ■ an appearance of a ghost or spirit.
– ORIGIN late Middle English: from late Latin *manifestatio(n-)*, from the verb *manifestare* 'make public'.

manifest destiny ▸ noun [mass noun] the 19th-century doctrine or belief that the expansion of the United States throughout the American continents was both justified and inevitable.

manifesto ▸ noun (pl. **manifestos**) a public declaration of policy and aims, especially one issued before an election by a political party or candidate.
– ORIGIN mid 17th cent.: from Italian, from *manifestare*, from Latin, 'make public', from *manifestus* 'obvious' (see MANIFEST[1]).

manifold /ˈmanɪfəʊld/ ▸ adjective formal or literary many and various: *the implications of this decision were manifold*. ■ having many different forms or elements: *the appeal of the crusade was manifold*.
▸ noun 1 a pipe or chamber branching into several openings. ■ (in an internal-combustion engine) the part conveying air and fuel from the carburettor to the cylinders or that leading from the cylinders to the exhaust pipe.
2 Mathematics a collection of points forming a certain kind of set, such as those of a topologically closed surface or an analogue of this in three or more dimensions.
– DERIVATIVES **manifoldly** adverb, **manifoldness** noun.
– ORIGIN Old English *manigfeald*; current noun senses date from the mid 19th cent.

manikin (also **mannikin**) ▸ noun 1 a very small man.
2 a jointed model of the human body, used in anatomy or as an artist's lay figure.
– ORIGIN mid 16th cent.: from Dutch *manneken*, diminutive of *man* 'man'.

Manila[1] /məˈnɪlə/ the capital and chief port of the Philippines, on the island of Luzon; pop. 1,660,700 (est. 2007).

Manila[2] /məˈnɪlə/ (also **Manilla**) ▸ noun 1 (also **Manila hemp**) [mass noun] the strong fibre of a Philippine plant, used for rope, matting, paper, etc. ● The plant is *Musa textilis*, family Musaceae.
■ (also **Manila paper**) strong brown paper, originally made from Manila hemp.
2 a cigar or cheroot made in Manila.
– ORIGIN late 17th cent. (as an adjective meaning 'from Manila'): from MANILA[1].

manilla /məˈnɪlə/ ▸ noun (in West Africa) a metal bracelet traditionally used as a medium of exchange.
– ORIGIN mid 16th cent.: from Spanish, based on Latin *manicula* (see MANACLE).

manioc /ˈmanɪɒk/ ▸ noun another term for CASSAVA.
– ORIGIN mid 16th cent.: from French, from Tupi *manioca*.

maniple /ˈmanɪp(ə)l/ ▸ noun 1 a subdivision of a Roman legion, containing either 120 or 60 men.
2 (in the Christian church) a vestment formerly worn by a priest celebrating the Eucharist, consisting of a strip hanging from the left arm.
– DERIVATIVES **manipular** adjective (sense 1).
– ORIGIN late Middle English (in sense 2): from Old French *maniple*, from Latin *manipulus* 'handful, troop', from *manus* 'hand' + the base of *plere* 'fill'.

manipulate /məˈnɪpjʊleɪt/ ▸ verb [with obj.] 1 handle or control (a tool, mechanism, information, etc.) in a skilful manner: *he manipulated the dials of the set*. ■ alter, edit, or move (text or data) on a computer. ■ examine or treat (a part of the body) by feeling or moving it with the hand.
2 control or influence (a person or situation) cleverly or unscrupulously: *the masses were deceived and manipulated by a tiny group*. ■ alter or present (data) so as to mislead.
– DERIVATIVES **manipulability** noun, **manipulable** adjective, **manipulatable** adjective.
– ORIGIN early 19th cent.: back-formation from MANIPULATION.

manipulation ▸ noun [mass noun] 1 the action of manipulating something in a skilful manner.
2 the action of manipulating someone in a clever or unscrupulous way.
– ORIGIN early 18th cent.: from French, from Latin *manipulus* 'handful'.

manipulative ▸ adjective 1 exercising unscrupulous control or influence over a person or situation: *she was sly, selfish, and manipulative*.
2 relating to manipulation of an object or part of the body.
– DERIVATIVES **manipulatively** adverb, **manipulativeness** noun.

manipulator ▸ noun 1 a person who controls or influences others in a clever or unscrupulous way.
2 a person who handles or controls something skilfully.
– DERIVATIVES **manipulatory** adjective.

Manipur /ˌmʌnɪˈpʊə/ a small state in the far east of India, east of Assam, on the border with Burma (Myanmar); capital, Imphal.

Manipuri /ˌmʌnɪˈpʊəri/ ▸ noun (pl. **same** or **Manipuris**) 1 a native or inhabitant of Manipur.
2 [mass noun] the official language of Manipur, which belongs to the Tibeto-Burman family.
▸ adjective relating to the people of Manipur or their language.

Manit. ▸ abbreviation Manitoba.

Manitoba /ˌmanɪˈtəʊbə/ a province of central Canada, with a coastline on Hudson Bay; pop. 1,148,401 (2006); capital, Winnipeg. The area was part of Rupert's Land from 1670 until it was transferred to Canada by the Hudson's Bay Company and became a province in 1870.
– DERIVATIVES **Manitoban** adjective & noun.

manitou /ˈmanɪtuː/ ▸ noun (among certain Algonquian North American Indians) a good or evil spirit as an object of reverence.
– ORIGIN late 17th cent.: via French from an Algonquian language.

mankind ▸ noun [mass noun] 1 human beings considered collectively; the human race: *research for the benefit of all mankind*.
2 archaic men, as distinct from women.

> **USAGE** On the use of mankind versus that of human-kind or the human race, see USAGE at MAN.

manky ▸ adjective (**mankier**, **mankiest**) Brit. informal 1 inferior; worthless: *he wanted recruits for his manky bee-keeping society*.
2 dirty and unpleasant: *the man in the manky mackintosh*.
– ORIGIN 1950s: probably from obsolete *mank* 'mutilated, defective', from Old French *manque*, from Latin *mancus* 'maimed'.

Manley, Michael (Norman) (1923–97), Jamaican statesman, Prime Minister 1972–80 and 1989–92.

manlike ▸ adjective 1 resembling a human being: *a manlike creature*.
2 (of a woman) having an appearance or qualities associated with men.

manliness ▸ noun [mass noun] the traditional male quality of being brave and strong: *men accustomed to proving their manliness on the streets*. ■ the fact of being typically male; masculinity: *the author's alleged lack of manliness*.

manly ▸ adjective (**manlier**, **manliest**) having or denoting those good qualities traditionally associated with men, such as courage, strength, and spirit: *a manly torso of perfect proportions*. ■ (of an activity) befitting a man: *honest, manly sports*.

man-made ▸ adjective made or caused by human beings (as opposed to occurring or being made naturally): *a man-made lake*.

Mann, Thomas (1875–1955), German novelist and essayist. The role and character of the artist in relation to society is a constant theme in his works. Notable works: *Buddenbrooks* (1901), *Death in Venice* (1912), and *Dr Faustus* (1947). Nobel Prize for Literature (1929).

manna ▸ noun [mass noun] 1 (in the Bible) the substance miraculously supplied as food to the Israelites in the wilderness (Exod. 16). ■ something beneficial that appears or is provided unexpectedly or opportunely: *a major aircraft accident is manna to lawyers*. ■ (in Christian contexts) spiritual nourishment, especially the Eucharist.
2 a sweet gum obtained from the manna ash or a similar plant, used as a mild laxative.
– ORIGIN Old English, via late Latin and Greek from Aramaic *mannā*, from Hebrew *mān*, corresponding to Arabic *mann*, denoting a product of the tamarisk *Tamarix mannifera*.

manna ash ▸ noun an ash tree which exudes a sweet edible gum (manna) from its branches when they are damaged, native to southern Europe and SW Asia.
● *Fraxinus ornus*, family Oleaceae.

Mannar /məˈnɑː/ an island off the NW coast of Sri Lanka, linked to India by the chain of coral islands and shoals known as Adam's Bridge. ■ a town on the island of Mannar; pop. 36,900 (est. 2009).

Mannar, Gulf of an inlet of the Indian Ocean lying between NW Sri Lanka and the southern tip of India. It lies to the south of Adam's Bridge, which separates it from the Palk Strait.

manned ▸ adjective (of an aircraft or spacecraft) having a human crew: *a manned mission to Mars*.

mannequin /ˈmanɪkɪn, -kwɪn/ ▸ noun a dummy used to display clothes in a shop window. ■ dated a person employed by a designer, costumier, etc., to model clothes.
– ORIGIN mid 18th cent.: from French (see MANIKIN).

manner ▸ noun 1 a way in which a thing is done or happens: *taking notes in an unobtrusive manner*. ■ a style in literature or art: *a dramatic poem in the manner of Goethe*. ■ [mass noun] Grammar a semantic category of adverbs and adverbials which answer the question 'how?': *an adverb of manner*. ■ (**manner of**) archaic a kind or sort: *what manner of man is he?*
2 a person's outward bearing or way of behaving towards others: *his arrogance and pompous manner*.
3 (**manners**) polite or well-bred social behaviour: *didn't your mother teach you any manners?* ■ social behaviour or habits: *Trevor apologized for his son's bad manners*.
– PHRASES **all manner of** many different kinds of: *echinacea is used by American Indians for all manner of ailments*. **by no manner of means** see MEANS. **in a manner of speaking** in some sense; so to speak. (**as if**) **to the manner born** naturally at ease in a specified job or situation. [with allusion to Shakespeare's *Hamlet* I. iv. 17.]
– DERIVATIVES **mannerless** adjective.
– ORIGIN Middle English: from Old French *maniere*, based on Latin *manuarius* 'of the hand', from *manus* 'hand'.

mannered ▸ adjective 1 [in combination] behaving in a specified way: *bad-mannered*.

M

2 (of behaviour, art, or a literary style) marked by idiosyncratic or exaggerated mannerisms; artificial: *inane dialogue and mannered acting.*

mannerism ▶ **noun 1** a habitual gesture or way of speaking or behaving: *learning the great man's speeches and studying his mannerisms.* ■ Psychiatry an ordinary gesture or expression that becomes abnormal through exaggeration or repetition.
2 [mass noun] excessive use of a distinctive style in art, literature, or music: *he seemed deliberately to be stripping his art of mannerism.*
3 (**Mannerism**) [mass noun] a style of 16th-century Italian art preceding the Baroque, characterized by distortions in scale and perspective and the use of bright, often lurid colours. It is particularly associated with the work of Parmigianino, Pontormo, Vasari, and the later Michelangelo.
– DERIVATIVES **mannerist** noun & adjective, **manneristic** adjective.

mannerly ▶ **adjective** well-mannered; polite.
– DERIVATIVES **mannerliness** noun.

Mannheim /ˈmanhʌɪm/ an industrial port at the confluence of the Rhine and the Neckar in Baden-Württemberg, SW Germany; pop. 307,900 (est. 2006).

mannie (also **manny**) ▶ **noun** (pl. **mannies**) informal, chiefly Scottish a boy.

mannikin ▶ **noun 1** a small waxbill of the Old World tropics, typically brown, black, and white and often kept as a cage bird. ● Genus *Lonchura*, family Estrildidae: many species.
2 variant spelling of **MANIKIN**.

Manning, Olivia (Mary) (1908–80), English novelist. Her experiences in Bucharest, Athens, and Egypt between 1939 and 1946 formed the basis for her Balkan and Levant trilogies, written 1960–1980.

mannish ▶ **adjective** derogatory (of a woman) having an appearance and qualities that are typically associated with men and considered unbecoming in a woman: *a mannish, sadistic matron.*
– DERIVATIVES **mannishly** adverb, **mannishness** noun.
– ORIGIN Old English *mennisc* 'human' (see **MAN**, **-ISH**[1]). The current sense dates from late Middle English.

mannitol /ˈmanɪtɒl/ ▶ **noun** [mass noun] Chemistry a colourless sweet-tasting crystalline alcohol which is found in many plants and is used in various foods and medical products. ● Chem. formula: $CH_2OH(CHOH)_4CH_2OH$.
– ORIGIN late 19th cent.: from *mannite* (from **MANNA** + **-ITE**[1]), in the same sense, + **-OL**.

mannose /ˈmanəʊz, -s/ ▶ **noun** [mass noun] Chemistry a sugar of the hexose class which occurs as a component of many natural polysaccharides. ● Chem. formula: $C_6H_{12}O_6$.
– ORIGIN late 19th cent.: from *mannite* 'mannitol' + **-OSE**[2].

manny ▶ **noun** variant spelling of **MANNIE**.

Mano /ˈmɑːnəʊ/ a river of West Africa. It rises in NW Liberia and flows to the Atlantic, forming for part of its length the boundary between Liberia and Sierra Leone.

mano-a-mano /ˌmɑːnəʊ ə ˈmɑːnəʊ, ˌmanəʊ a ˈmanəʊ/ US informal ▶ **adverb & adjective** head-to-head; one-to-one: [as adv.] *they want to settle this mano-a-mano.*
▶ **noun** (pl. **mano-a-manos**) an intense confrontation, contest, or fight between two adversaries: *a real courtroom mano-a-mano.*
– ORIGIN Spanish, literally 'hand-to-hand'.

manoeuvrable (US **maneuverable**) ▶ **adjective** (of a vehicle or ship) able to be manoeuvred easily while in motion.
– DERIVATIVES **manoeuvrability** noun.

manoeuvre /məˈnuːvə/ (US **maneuver**) ▶ **noun 1** a movement or series of moves requiring skill and care. ■ a carefully planned or cunning scheme or action: *shady financial manoeuvres.* ■ [mass noun] the fact or process of taking carefully planned or cunning action: *the economic policy provided no room for manoeuvre.*
2 (**manoeuvres**) a large-scale military exercise of troops, warships, and other forces: *the Russian vessel was on manoeuvres.*
▶ **verb** (**manoeuvres, manoeuvring, manoeuvred**)
1 move skilfully or carefully: [no obj.] *the lorry was unable to manoeuvre comfortably in the narrow street* | [with obj. and adverbial of direction] *she tried to manoeuvre her trolley round people.*
2 [with obj. and adverbial] carefully guide or manipulate (someone or something) in order to achieve an end: *they were manoeuvring him into betraying his friend.* ■ [no obj.] manipulate a situation to achieve an end; [with infinitive] *Rann was manoeuvring to elope with the girl.*
– DERIVATIVES **manoeuvrer** noun.
– ORIGIN mid 18th cent. (as a noun in the sense 'tactical movement'): from French *manœuvre* (noun), *manœuvrer* (verb), from medieval Latin *manuoperare* from Latin *manus* 'hand' + *operari* 'to work'.

man-of-war (also **man-o'-war**) ▶ **noun** (pl. **men-of-war** or **men-o'-war**) **1** historical an armed sailing ship.
2 (also **man-of-war bird**) another term for **FRIGATE BIRD**.

manoir /ˈmanwɑː/, French /manwaʀ/ ▶ **noun** a large country house or manor house in France.
– ORIGIN French.

manometer /məˈnɒmɪtə/ ▶ **noun** an instrument for measuring the pressure acting on a column of fluid, consisting of a U-shaped tube of liquid in which a difference in the pressures acting in the two arms of the tube causes the liquid to reach different heights in the two arms.
– DERIVATIVES **manometric** adjective.
– ORIGIN mid 18th cent.: from French *manomètre*, from Greek *manos* 'thin' + *-mètre* '(instrument) measuring'.

ma non troppo ▶ **adverb** Music but not too much: *allegro ma non troppo.*
– ORIGIN Italian.

manor ▶ **noun** Brit. **1** (also **manor house**) a large country house with lands. ■ chiefly historical (in England and Wales) a unit of land, originally a feudal lordship, consisting of a lord's demesne and lands rented to tenants.
2 (**one's manor**) informal the district covered by a police station. ■ one's own neighbourhood or area of operation.
– DERIVATIVES **manorial** adjective.
– ORIGIN Middle English: from Anglo-Norman French *maner* 'dwelling', from Latin *manere* 'remain'.

man orchid ▶ **noun** a European orchid of calcareous grassland with greenish-yellow flowers which have a lip resembling a human figure. ● *Aceras anthropophorum*, family Orchidaceae.

man page ▶ **noun** a document forming part of the documentation of a computer system.
– ORIGIN short for *manual page*.

manpower ▶ **noun** [mass noun] the number of people working or available for work or service: *the police had only limited manpower.*

manqué /ˈmɒ̃keɪ/ ▶ **adjective** [postpositive] having failed to become what one might have been: *he was a creature of suppressed passions, an artist manqué.*
– ORIGIN late 18th cent.: French, past participle of *manquer* 'to lack'.

Man Ray see **RAY**[2].

Mans, Le see **LE MANS**.

mansard /ˈmansɑːd, -səd/ ▶ **noun** (also **mansard roof**) a roof which has four sloping sides, each of which becomes steeper halfway down. ■ Brit. another term for **GAMBREL**. ■ a storey or apartment under a mansard roof.
– ORIGIN mid 18th cent.: from French *mansarde*, named after F. **MANSART**.

Mansart /ˈmɒ̃sɑː/, French /mɑ̃saʀ/, François (1598–1666), French architect. He rebuilt part of the château of Blois, which incorporated the type of roof now named after him.

manse /mans/ ▶ **noun** a house provided for a minister of certain Christian Churches, especially the Scottish Presbyterian Church. ■ US informal a person's house or home.
– PHRASES **son** (or **daughter**) **of the manse** the child of a minister, especially of the Scottish Presbyterian Church.
– ORIGIN late 15th cent. (denoting the principal house of an estate): from medieval Latin *mansus* 'house, dwelling', from *manere* 'remain'.

manservant ▶ **noun** (pl. **menservants**) a male servant.

Mansfield, Katherine (1888–1923), New Zealand short-story writer; pseudonym of *Kathleen Mansfield Beauchamp*. Her stories range from extended impressionistic evocations of family life to short sketches.

-manship ▶ **suffix** (forming nouns) denoting skill in a subject or activity: *marksmanship.*

mansion ▶ **noun** a large, impressive house. ■ (**mansion block**) Brit. a large block of flats. ■ [in names] a terrace or mansion block: *Carlyle Mansions.*
– ORIGIN late Middle English (denoting the chief residence of a lord): via Old French from Latin *mansio(n-)* 'place where someone stays', from *manere* 'remain'.

mansion house ▶ **noun** Brit. the house of a lord mayor or a landed proprietor. ■ (**the Mansion House**) the official residence of the Lord Mayor of London.

man-sized (also **man-size**) ▶ **adjective** large enough to clothe, suit, or satisfy a man: *chunky man-sized jumpers.*

manslaughter ▶ **noun** [mass noun] the crime of killing a human being without malice aforethought, or in circumstances not amounting to murder.

Manson, Charles (b.1934), American cult leader. He founded a commune based on free love and complete subordination to him. In 1969 its members carried out a series of murders, including that of the American actress Sharon Tate, for which he and some followers received the death sentence (later commuted to life imprisonment).

mansuetude /ˈmanswɪtjuːd/ ▶ **noun** [mass noun] archaic meekness; gentleness.
– ORIGIN late Middle English: from Old French, or from Latin *mansuetudo*, from *mansuetus* 'gentle, tame', from *manus* 'hand' + *suetus* 'accustomed'.

manta /ˈmantə/ ▶ **noun** a devil ray that occurs in tropical seas and may reach very great size. ● *Manta birostris*, family Mobulidae.
– ORIGIN late 17th cent.: from Latin American Spanish, literally 'large blanket'.

manteau /ˈmantəʊ/ ▶ **noun** a loose gown or cloak worn by women in the 17th and 18th centuries. ■ a long, loose coat or overshirt worn by Muslim women.
– ORIGIN late 17th cent.: from French; compare with **MANTUA**.

Mantegna /manˈtɛnjə/, Andrea (1431–1506), Italian painter and engraver. He is noted especially for his frescoes, which demonstrate his mastery of perspective and foreshortening.

mantel (also **mantle**) ▶ **noun** a mantelpiece or mantelshelf.
– ORIGIN mid 16th cent.: specialized use of **MANTLE**[1].

mantelletta /ˌmantɪˈlɛtə/ ▶ **noun** (pl. **mantellettas** or **mantellette** /-teɪ/) a sleeveless vestment reaching to the knees, worn by cardinals, bishops, and other high-ranking Catholic ecclesiastics.
– ORIGIN mid 19th cent.: from Italian, from a diminutive of Latin *mantellum* 'mantle'.

mantelpiece (also **mantlepiece**) ▶ **noun** a structure of wood, marble, or stone above and around a fireplace. ■ a mantelshelf.

mantelshelf (also **mantleshelf**) ▶ **noun** a shelf above a fireplace. ■ Climbing a projecting ledge of rock. ■ Climbing a move for climbing onto a projecting ledge of rock from below by pressing down on it with the hands to raise the upper body, enabling a foot or knee to reach the ledge.
▶ **verb** [no obj.] Climbing perform a mantelshelf move.

manteltree ▶ **noun** a beam or arch across the opening of a fireplace, supporting the masonry above.

mantic /ˈmantɪk/ ▶ **adjective** formal relating to divination or prophecy.
– ORIGIN mid 19th cent.: from Greek *mantikos*, from *mantis* 'prophet'.

manticore /ˈmantɪkɔː/ ▶ **noun** a mythical animal typically depicted as having the body of a lion, the head of a man, and the sting of a scorpion.
– ORIGIN late Middle English: from Old French, via Latin from Greek *mantikhōras*, corrupt reading in Aristotle for *martikhoras*, from an Old Persian word meaning 'maneater'.

mantid ▶ **noun** another term for **MANTIS**.

mantilla /manˈtɪlə/ ▶ **noun** (in Spain) a lace or silk scarf worn by women over the head and shoulders.
– ORIGIN Spanish, diminutive of *manta* 'mantle'.

mantis /ˈmantɪs/ (also **praying mantis**) ▶ **noun** (pl. **same** or **mantises**) a slender predatory insect with a triangular head, which waits motionless for prey with its large forelegs folded like hands in prayer. ● Suborder Mantodea, order Dictyoptera: Mantidae and other families, and many species, including *Mantis religiosa* of southern Europe.
– ORIGIN mid 17th cent.: modern Latin, from Greek, literally 'prophet'.

mantissa /manˈtɪsə/ ▶ **noun 1** Mathematics the part of a logarithm after the decimal point.
2 Computing the part of a floating-point number which represents the significant digits of that number.

– ORIGIN mid 17th cent.: from Latin, literally 'make-weight', perhaps from Etruscan.

mantis shrimp ▸ noun a predatory marine crustacean with a pair of large spined front legs that resemble those of a mantis and are used for capturing prey. ● Order Stomatopoda: many species.

mantle[1] ▸ noun 1 a loose sleeveless cloak or shawl, worn especially by women. ■ a covering of a specified sort: *the houses were covered with a thick mantle of snow*. ■ Ornithology a bird's back, scapulars, and wing coverts, especially when of a distinctive colour. ■ Zoology (in molluscs, cirripedes, and brachiopods) a fold of skin enclosing the viscera and secreting the shell.
2 an important role or responsibility that passes from one person to another: *the second son has now assumed his father's mantle*. [with allusion to the passing of Elijah's cloak (mantle) to Elisha (2 Kings 2:13).]
3 (also **gas mantle**) a mesh cover fixed round a gas jet to give an incandescent light when heated.
4 Geology the region of the earth's interior between the crust and the core, believed to consist of hot, dense silicate rocks (mainly peridotite). ■ the part of another planetary body corresponding to the earth's mantle: *the lunar mantle*.
▸ verb 1 [with obj.] literary cloak or envelop: *heavy mists mantled the forested slopes*. ■ [no obj.] archaic (of the face) glow with a blush: *her rich face mantling with emotion*. ■ [no obj.] archaic (of a liquid) become covered with a head or froth.
2 [no obj.] (of a bird of prey on the ground or on a perch) spread the wings and tail so as to cover captured prey.
– ORIGIN Old English *mentel*, from Latin *mantellum* 'cloak'; reinforced in Middle English by Old French *mantel*.

mantle[2] ▸ noun variant spelling of MANTEL.

mantlepiece ▸ noun variant spelling of MANTELPIECE.

mantle plume ▸ noun see PLUME.

mantleshelf ▸ noun variant spelling of MANTELSHELF.

mantlet ▸ noun 1 historical a woman's short, loose sleeveless cloak or shawl.
2 a bulletproof screen on a military vehicle. ■ historical a movable shelter or screen used to protect soldiers.
– ORIGIN late Middle English: from Old French *mantelet*, diminutive of *mantel* 'mantle'.

mantling ▸ noun Heraldry a piece of ornamental drapery depicted issuing from a helmet and surrounding a shield.
– ORIGIN late 16th cent.: from MANTLE[1] + -ING[1].

Mantoux test /ˈmɒ̃tuː, ˈmantuː/ ▸ noun Medicine a test for immunity to tuberculosis using intradermal injection of tuberculin.
– ORIGIN 1930s: named after Charles *Mantoux* (1877–1947), French physician.

mantra /ˈmantrə/ ▸ noun (originally in Hinduism and Buddhism) a word or sound repeated to aid concentration in meditation. ■ a Vedic hymn. ■ a statement or slogan repeated frequently: *the environmental mantra that energy has for too long been too cheap*.
– DERIVATIVES **mantric** adjective.
– ORIGIN late 18th cent.: Sanskrit, literally 'instrument of thought', from *man* 'think'.

mantrap ▸ noun a trap for catching people, especially trespassers or poachers.

Mantua /ˈmantjʊə/ a town in Lombardy, northern Italy, on the River Mincio; pop. 48,357 (2008). Italian name **Mantova** /ˈmantəʊvə/.
– DERIVATIVES **Mantuan** noun & adjective.

mantua /ˈmantjʊə/ ▸ noun a woman's loose gown of a kind fashionable during the 17th and 18th centuries.
– ORIGIN alteration of French *manteau*, influenced by MANTUA.

Manu /ˈmʌnuː/ the archetypal first man of Hindu mythology, survivor of the great flood and father of the human race. He is also the legendary author of one of the most famous codes of Hindu religious law, the *Manusmriti* (Laws of Manu), composed in Sanskrit and dating in its present form from the 1st century BC.

manual ▸ adjective relating to or done with the hands: *manual dexterity*. ■ (of a device) operated or controlled by hand, rather than automatically or electronically: *a manual typewriter*. ■ [attrib.] using or working with the hands: *a manual labourer*.
▸ noun 1 a book giving instructions or information: *a computer manual*. ■ historical (in the Christian Church) a book of the forms to be used by priests in the administration of the sacraments.
2 a vehicle with manual transmission.
3 an organ keyboard played with the hands not the feet.
– DERIVATIVES **manually** adverb.
– ORIGIN late Middle English: from Old French *manuel*, from (and later assimilated to) Latin *manualis*, from *manus* 'hand'.

manual alphabet ▸ noun another term for FINGER ALPHABET.

manubrium /məˈn(j)uːbrɪəm/ ▸ noun (pl. **manubria** or **manubriums**) Anatomy & Zoology a handle-shaped projection or part, in particular: ■ the broad upper part of the sternum of mammals, with which the clavicles and first ribs articulate. ■ the tube which bears the mouth of a coelenterate.
– DERIVATIVES **manubrial** adjective.
– ORIGIN mid 17th cent. (in the sense 'handle'): from Latin, 'haft'.

manucode /ˈmanjʊkəʊd/ ▸ noun a bird of paradise of which the male and female have similar blue-black plumage and breed as stable pairs. ● Genus *Manucodia*, family Paradisaeidae: five species.
– ORIGIN mid 19th cent.: from French, from modern Latin *manucodiata* (used in the same sense from the mid 16th to 18th cents), from Malay *manuk dewata* 'bird of the gods'.

Manueline /ˈmanjʊəlʌɪn/ ▸ adjective denoting an ornate style of Portuguese architecture developed during the reign of Manuel I (1495–1521) and characterized by elaborations of Gothic and Renaissance styles.

manufactory ▸ noun (pl. **manufactories**) archaic a factory.
– ORIGIN early 17th cent. (denoting a manufactured article): from MANUFACTURE, on the pattern of *factory*.

manufacture ▸ verb [with obj.] 1 make (something) on a large scale using machinery: *firms who manufacture ball bearings* | (as noun **manufacturing**) *even in manufacturing they no longer dominate*. ■ (of a living thing) produce (a substance) naturally. ■ make or produce (something abstract) in a merely mechanical way: (as adj. **manufactured**) *manufactured love songs*.
2 invent (evidence or a story): *claims that the entire row had been manufactured by the press*.
▸ noun [mass noun] the making of articles on a large scale using machinery: *the manufacture of armoured vehicles*. ■ [with modifier] a specified branch of industry: *the porcelain manufacture for which France became justly renowned*. ■ (**manufactures**) manufactured articles.
– DERIVATIVES **manufacturability** noun, **manufacturable** adjective.
– ORIGIN mid 16th cent. (as noun, denoting something made by hand): from French (re-formed by association with Latin *manu factum* 'made by hand'), from Italian *manifattura*. The verb dates from the mid 17th cent.

manufacturer ▸ noun a person or company that makes goods for sale: *the manufacturers supply the goods to the distribution centre*.

manuka /ˈmɑːnʊkə, məˈnuːkə/ ▸ noun a small tree with aromatic leaves which are sometimes used for tea, native to New Zealand and Tasmania. ● *Leptospermum scoparium*, family Myrtaceae.
– ORIGIN mid 19th cent.: from Maori.

manul /ˈmɑːnʊl/ ▸ noun another term for PALLAS'S CAT.
– ORIGIN late 18th cent.: apparently from Kyrgyz.

manumit /ˌmanjʊˈmɪt/ ▸ verb (**manumits**, **manumitting**, **manumitted**) [with obj.] historical release from slavery; set free.
– DERIVATIVES **manumission** noun, **manumitter** noun.
– ORIGIN late Middle English: from Latin *manumittere*, literally 'send forth from the hand', from *manus* 'hand' + *mittere* 'send'.

manure ▸ noun [mass noun] animal dung used for fertilizing land. ■ any compost or artificial fertilizer.
▸ verb [with obj.] apply manure to (land).
– ORIGIN late Middle English (as a verb in the sense 'cultivate (land)'): from Anglo-Norman French *mainoverer*, Old French *manouvrer* (see MANOEUVRE). The noun sense dates from the mid 16th cent.

manus /ˈmeɪnəs/ ▸ noun (pl. **same**) Zoology the terminal segment of a forelimb, corresponding to the hand and wrist in humans.
– ORIGIN early 19th cent.: from Latin, 'hand'.

manuscript ▸ noun a book, document, or piece of music written by hand rather than typed or printed: *an illuminated manuscript*. ■ an author's handwritten or typed text that has not yet been published.
– ORIGIN late 16th cent.: from medieval Latin *manuscriptus*, from *manu* 'by hand' + *scriptus* 'written' (past participle of *scribere*).

manuscript paper ▸ noun [mass noun] paper printed with staves for writing music on.

Manutius, Aldus, see ALDUS MANUTIUS.

Manx ▸ adjective relating to the Isle of Man.
▸ noun 1 [mass noun] the Celtic language formerly spoken in the Isle of Man.
2 (**the Manx**) Manx people collectively.
– DERIVATIVES **Manxman** noun (pl. **Manxmen**), **Manxwoman** noun (pl. **Manxwomen**).
– ORIGIN from Old Norse, from Old Irish *Manu* 'Isle of Man' + *-skr* (equivalent of -ISH[1]).

Manx cat ▸ noun a cat of a breed having no tail or an extremely short one.

Manx shearwater ▸ noun a dark-backed shearwater that nests on islands in the NE Atlantic and Mediterranean waters. ● *Puffinus puffinus*, family Procellariidae.

many ▸ determiner, pronoun, & adjective (**more**, **most**) a large number of: [as determiner] *many people agreed with her* | [as pronoun] *the solution to* **many of** *our problems* | *many think bungee jumping is a new craze* | [as adj.] *one of my many errors*.
▸ noun (as plural noun **the many**) the majority of people: *music for the many*.
– PHRASES **as many** the same number of: *changing his mind for the third time in as many months*. **a good** (or **great**) **many** a large number. **have one too many** informal become slightly drunk. **how many** used to ask what a particular quantity is. **many a** —— a large number of: *many a good man has been destroyed by booze* | *John and I have talked about it many a time*. **many's the** —— used to indicate that something happens often: *many's the time I've slept on her sofa*.
– ORIGIN Old English *manig*, of Germanic origin; related to Dutch *menig* and German *manch*.

manyatta /manˈjatə/ ▸ noun (among the Masai and some other African peoples) a group of huts forming a unit within a common fence.
– ORIGIN Masai.

M

manyfold ▸ adverb by many times: *the problems would be multiplied manyfold*.

many-sided ▸ adjective having many sides or aspects: *the reasons for poor collaboration are complex and many-sided*.
– DERIVATIVES **many-sidedness** noun.

manzanilla /ˌmanzəˈnɪlə, -ˈniːljə/ ▸ noun [mass noun] a pale, very dry Spanish sherry.
– ORIGIN Spanish, literally 'camomile' (because the flavour is reminiscent of that of camomile tea).

manzanita /ˌmanzəˈniːtə/ ▸ noun an evergreen Californian dwarf shrub related to the bearberry. ● Genus *Arctostaphylos*, family Ericaceae: several species.
– ORIGIN mid 19th cent.: from Spanish, diminutive of *manzana* 'apple'.

Manzoni /manˈzəʊni/, Alessandro (1785–1873), Italian novelist, dramatist, and poet. He is remembered chiefly as the author of the novel *I Promessi Sposi* (1825–42), a historical reconstruction of 17th-century Lombardy.

Mao /maʊ/ ▸ noun [as modifier] denoting a jacket or suit of a plain style with a mandarin collar, associated with communist China.
– ORIGIN 1960s: by association with MAO ZEDONG.

MAOI ▸ noun Medicine monoamine oxidase inhibitor, a type of antidepressant drug.

Maoism ▸ noun [mass noun] the communist doctrines of Mao Zedong as formerly practised in China, having as a central idea permanent revolution and stressing the importance of the peasantry, small-scale industry, and agricultural collectivization.
– DERIVATIVES **Maoist** noun & adjective.

Maori /ˈmaʊri/ ▸ noun (pl. **same** or **Maoris**) 1 a member of the aboriginal people of New Zealand.
2 [mass noun] the Polynesian language of the Maoris, with about 100,000 speakers.
▸ adjective relating to the Maoris or their language.

> The Maoris arrived in New Zealand as part of a series of waves of migration from Tahiti, probably from the 9th century onwards. They lost large amounts of land in the colonization of New Zealand by the British, and now number about 280,000.

– DERIVATIVES **Maoridom** noun.
– ORIGIN the name in Maori.

Maori bug ▸ noun NZ a large black wingless cockroach which emits an unpleasant smell when disturbed. ● *Platyzosteria novaeseelandiae*, suborder Blattodea.

Maori oven ▸ noun NZ another term for **HANGI**.

Maoritanga /ˌmaʊrɪˈtaŋə/ ▸ noun [mass noun] Maori culture, traditions, and way of life.
– ORIGIN Maori.

Maori Wars former name for **NEW ZEALAND WARS**.

mao-tai /maʊˈtʌɪ/ ▸ noun [mass noun] a strong sorghum-based alcoholic drink distilled in SW China.
– ORIGIN named after a town in SW China.

Mao Zedong /ˌmaʊ dziːˈdʊŋ/ (also **Mao Tse-tung** /tseɪˈtʊŋ/) (1893–1976), Chinese statesman, chairman of the Communist Party of the Chinese People's Republic 1949–76 and head of state 1949–59.

> A co-founder of the Chinese Communist Party in 1921 and its effective leader from the time of the Long March (1934–5), he eventually defeated both the occupying Japanese and rival Kuomintang nationalist forces to create the People's Republic of China in 1949, becoming its first head of state. At first Mao followed the Soviet Communist model, but from 1956 he introduced his own measures, such as the brief period of freedom of expression known as Hundred Flowers and the economically disastrous Great Leap Forward (1958–60). Despite having resigned as head of state Mao instigated the Cultural Revolution (1966–8), during which he became the focus of a personality cult.

map ▸ noun **1** a diagrammatic representation of an area of land or sea showing physical features, cities, roads, etc.: *a street map*. ■ a two-dimensional representation of the positions of stars or other astronomical objects. ■ a diagram or collection of data showing the spatial arrangement or distribution of something over an area: *an electron density map*. ■ Biology a representation of the sequence of genes on a chromosome or of bases in a DNA or RNA molecule. ■ Mathematics another term for **MAPPING**.
2 informal, dated a person's face.
▸ verb (**maps, mapping, mapped**) [with obj.] represent (an area) on a map; make a map of: *inaccessible parts will be mapped from the air*. ■ record in detail the spatial distribution of (something): *the project to map the human genome*. ■ chiefly Mathematics associate each element of (a set) with an element of another set. ■ [no obj.] (**map on to**) chiefly Mathematics be associated with or linked to.
– PHRASES **off the map** (of a place) very distant or remote. **put someone/thing on the map** bring someone or something to prominence: *one big international polo tournament could really put our club on the map*. **wipe something off the map** obliterate something totally.
– PHRASAL VERBS **map something out** plan a route or course of action in detail: *she mapped out a plan of action in ten minutes*.
– DERIVATIVES **mapless** adjective, **mappable** adjective, **mapper** noun.
– ORIGIN early 16th cent.: from medieval Latin *mappa mundi*, literally 'sheet of the world', from Latin *mappa* 'sheet, napkin' + *mundi* 'of the world' (genitive of *mundus*).

M

map butterfly ▸ noun a butterfly that has cream or brown wings crossed by narrow contrasting lines.
● Genera *Cyrestis* and *Araschnia*, subfamily Nymphalinae, family Nymphalidae.

mapepire /ˈmapəpɪə/ ▸ noun [usu. with modifier] W. Indian a snake.
– ORIGIN alteration of Carib *matapi*.

maple ▸ noun a tree or shrub with lobed leaves, winged fruits, and colourful autumn foliage, grown as an ornamental or for its timber or syrupy sap.
● Genus *Acer*, family Aceraceae: many species, including the common European **field maple** (*A. campestre*) and the North American **sugar maple** (*A. saccharum*).
– ORIGIN Old English *mapel* (as the first element of *mapeltrēow*, *mapulder* 'maple tree'); used as an independent word from Middle English.

maple leaf ▸ noun the leaf of the maple, used as an emblem of Canada.

maple sugar ▸ noun [mass noun] N. Amer. sugar produced by evaporating the sap of certain maples, especially the sugar maple.

maple syrup ▸ noun [mass noun] syrup produced from the sap of certain maples, especially the sugar maple.

map-maker ▸ noun a cartographer.
– DERIVATIVES **map-making** noun.

Mappa Mundi /ˌmapə ˈmʊndi/ a famous 13th-century map of the world, now in Hereford cathedral, England. The map is round and typical of similar maps of the time in that it depicts Jerusalem at its centre.
– ORIGIN from medieval Latin, literally 'sheet of the world'.

mappemonde /mapˈmɒnd/ ▸ noun a medieval map of the world.
– ORIGIN late Middle English: from Old French, from medieval Latin (see **MAPPA MUNDI**).

mapping ▸ noun Mathematics & Linguistics an operation that associates each element of a given set (the domain) with one or more elements of a second set (the range).

map projection ▸ noun see **PROJECTION** (sense 6).

map reference ▸ noun a set of numbers and letters specifying a location as represented on a map.

map turtle ▸ noun a small North American freshwater turtle with bold patterns on the shell and head.
● Genus *Graptemys*, family Emydidae: several species.

Mapuche /maˈpʊtʃi/ ▸ noun (pl. **same** or **Mapuches**) **1** a member of an American Indian people of central Chile and adjacent parts of Argentina.
2 [mass noun] the Araucanian language of the Mapuche, with about 400,000 speakers.
▸ adjective relating to the Mapuche or their language.
– ORIGIN the name in Mapuche, from *mapu* 'land' + *che* 'people'.

Maputo /məˈpuːtəʊ, -tuː/ the capital and chief port of Mozambique, on the Indian Ocean in the south of the country; pop. 1,099,102 (2007). Founded as a Portuguese fortress in the late 18th century, it became the capital of Mozambique in 1907. Former name (until 1976) **LOURENÇO MARQUES**.

maquette /maˈkɛt/ ▸ noun a sculptor's small preliminary model or sketch.
– ORIGIN early 20th cent.: from French, from Italian *machietta*, diminutive of *macchia* 'spot'.

maquila /məˈkiːlə/ ▸ noun another term for **MAQUILADORA**.

maquiladora /ˌmakɪləˈdɔːrə/ ▸ noun a factory in Mexico run by a foreign company and exporting its products to that company's country of origin.
– ORIGIN Mexican Spanish, from *maquilar* 'assemble'.

maquillage /ˌmakɪˈjɑːʒ/ ▸ noun [mass noun] make-up; cosmetics.
– ORIGIN French, from *maquiller* 'to make up', from Old French *masquiller* 'to stain'.

maquis /maˈkiː/, French /maki/ ▸ noun (pl. **same**) **1** (**the Maquis**) the French resistance movement during the German occupation (1940–5). ■ a member of the Maquis.
2 [mass noun] dense scrub vegetation consisting of hardy evergreen shrubs and small trees, characteristic of Mediterranean coastal regions.
– ORIGIN early 19th cent. (in sense 2): from French, 'brushwood', from Corsican Italian *macchia*.

maquisard /ˌmakɪˈzɑː/, French /makizaʀ/ ▸ noun a member of the Maquis.

mar ▸ verb (**mars, marring, marred**) [with obj.] impair the quality or appearance of; spoil: *violence marred a number of New Year celebrations*.
– ORIGIN Old English *merran* 'hinder, damage', of Germanic origin; probably related to Dutch *marren* 'loiter'.

Mar. ▸ abbreviation March.

mara /ˈmɑːrə/ ▸ noun a burrowing hare-like cavy with long hindlimbs and greyish fur, native to South America. ● Genus *Dolichotis*, family Caviidae: two species.
– ORIGIN mid 19th cent.: from American Spanish *mará*.

marabou /ˈmarəbuː/ ▸ noun **1** (also **marabou stork**) a large African stork with a massive bill and large neck pouch, which feeds mainly by scavenging.
● *Leptoptilos crumeniferus*, family Ciconiidae.
2 [mass noun] down from the wing or tail of the marabou used as a trimming for hats or clothing.
– ORIGIN early 19th cent.: from French, from Arabic *murābiṭ* 'holy man' (see also **MARABOUT**), the stork being regarded as holy.

marabout /ˈmarəbuːt/ ▸ noun a Muslim holy man or hermit, especially in North Africa. ■ a shrine marking the burial place of a Muslim holy man or hermit.
– ORIGIN early 17th cent.: via French and Portuguese from Arabic *murābiṭ* 'holy man'.

marabunta /ˌmarəˈbʌntə/ ▸ noun W. Indian a social wasp.
– ORIGIN late 19th cent.: a local word in Guyana.

maraca /məˈrakə/ ▸ noun (usu. **maracas**) a hollow gourd or gourd-shaped container filled with beans, pebbles, or similar objects, forming one of a pair and shaken as a percussion instrument in Latin American music.
– ORIGIN early 17th cent.: from Portuguese *maracá*, from Tupi.

Maracaibo /ˌmarəˈkʌɪbəʊ/ a city and port in NW Venezuela, situated on the channel linking the Gulf of Venezuela with Lake Maracaibo; pop. 1,891,800 (est. 2009).

Maracaibo, Lake a large lake in NW Venezuela, linked by a narrow channel to the Gulf of Venezuela and the Caribbean Sea.

Maradona /ˌmarəˈdɒnə/, Diego (Armando) (b.1960), Argentinian footballer. He captained the Argentina team that won the World Cup in 1986, arousing controversy when his apparent handball scored a goal in the quarter-final match against England.

marae /məˈrʌɪ/ ▸ noun (pl. **same**) the courtyard of a Maori meeting house, especially as a social or ceremonial forum.
– ORIGIN Polynesian, 'sacrificial altar, sacred enclosure'.

maraging steel /ˈmɑːreɪdʒɪŋ/ ▸ noun [mass noun] a steel alloy, containing up to 25 per cent nickel and other metals, strengthened by a process of slow cooling and age hardening.
– ORIGIN 1960s: *maraging* from *mar-* (abbreviation of **MARTENSITE**, because the process involves conversion of austenite to martensite) + *aging* from the verb **AGE**.

Maramba /məˈrambə/ a city in southern Zambia, about 5 km (3 miles) from the Zambezi River and the Victoria Falls; pop. 130,200 (est. 2009). Formerly called Livingstone in honour of the explorer David Livingstone, it was the capital of Northern Rhodesia from 1911 until Lusaka became capital in 1935.

Maranhão /ˌmarəˈnjaʊ/ a state of NE Brazil, on the Atlantic coast; capital, São Luís.

Marañón /ˌmarəˈnjɒn/ a river of northern Peru, which rises in the Andes and forms one of the principal headwaters of the Amazon.

maranta /məˈrantə/ ▸ noun a tropical American plant of a genus which includes the prayer plant and the arrowroot. ● Genus *Maranta*, family Marantaceae.
■ a calathea (plant).
– ORIGIN modern Latin, named after Bartolommeo *Maranta*, 16th-cent. Italian herbalist.

marari /maˈrariː/ ▸ noun the butterfish of New Zealand (*Odax pullus*).
– ORIGIN from Maori.

maraschino /ˌmarəˈskiːnəʊ, -ˈʃiːnəʊ/ ▸ noun (pl. **maraschinos**) [mass noun] a strong, sweet liqueur made from small black Dalmatian cherries. ■ [count noun] a maraschino cherry.
– ORIGIN Italian, from *marasca* (the name of the cherry), from *amaro* 'bitter', from Latin *amarus*.

maraschino cherry ▸ noun a cherry preserved in maraschino or maraschino-flavoured syrup.

marasmus /məˈrazməs/ ▸ noun [mass noun] Medicine undernourishment causing a child's weight to be significantly low for their age.
– DERIVATIVES **marasmic** adjective.
– ORIGIN mid 17th cent.: modern Latin, from Greek *marasmos* 'withering', from *marainein* 'wither'.

Marat /ˈmarɑː/, French /maʀa/, Jean Paul (1743–93), French revolutionary and journalist. A virulent critic of the moderate Girondists, he was instrumental (with Danton and Robespierre) in their fall from power in 1793.

Maratha /məˈrɑːtə, -ˈratə/ (also **Mahratta**) ▸ noun a member of the princely and military castes of the former Hindu kingdom of Maharashtra in central India. The Marathas rebelled against the Moguls and in 1674 established their own kingdom. They came to dominate southern and central India but were later subdued by the British.
– ORIGIN via Hindi from Sanskrit *Mahārāṣṭra* 'great kingdom'.

Marathi /məˈrɑːti, -ˈrati/ ▸ noun [mass noun] the Indic language spoken in the western Indian state of Maharashtra by about 68 million people.

marathon ▸ noun a long-distance running race, strictly one of 26 miles 385 yards (42.195 km). ■ a long-lasting or difficult task or activity: *the last leg of an interview marathon which began this summer* | [as modifier] *she's embarking on a marathon UK tour*.
– DERIVATIVES **marathoner** noun.
– ORIGIN late 19th cent.: from *Marathōn* in Greece, the scene of a victory over the Persians in 490 BC; the modern race is based on the tradition that a mes-

senger ran from Marathon to Athens (22 miles) with the news. The original account by Herodotus told of the messenger Pheidippides running 150 miles from Athens to Sparta before the battle, seeking help.

maraud /məˈrɔːd/ ▶ **verb** [no obj.] go about in search of things to steal or people to attack: *war parties crossed the river to maraud.* ■ [with obj.] raid and plunder (a place).
– ORIGIN late 17th cent.: from French *marauder*, from *maraud* 'rogue'.

marauder /məˈrɔːdə(r)/ ▶ **noun** a person who marauds; a raider: *a band of English marauders were surprised and overcome.*

marauding /məˈrɔːdɪŋ/ ▶ **adjective** going about in search of things to steal or people to attack: *marauding gangs of youths.*

maravedi /ˌmarəˈveɪdi/ ▶ **noun** (pl. **maravedis**) a medieval Spanish copper coin and monetary unit.
– ORIGIN Spanish, from Arabic *murābiṭīn* 'holy men', a name applied to the North African Berber rulers of Muslim Spain, from the late 11th cent. to 1145.

Marbella /mɑːˈbeɪjə/ a resort town on the Costa del Sol of southern Spain, in Andalusia; pop. 130,549 (2008).

marble ▶ **noun 1** [mass noun] a hard crystalline metamorphic form of limestone, typically white with coloured mottlings or streaks, which may be polished and is used in sculpture and architecture. ■ used figuratively to refer to something with the smoothness, hardness, or colour of marble: *her shoulders were as white as marble.* ■ [count noun] a marble sculpture.
2 a small ball of coloured glass or similar material used as a toy. ■ **(marbles)** [treated as sing.] a game in which such balls are rolled along the ground.
3 **(one's marbles)** informal one's mental faculties: *I thought she'd **lost her marbles**, asking a question like that.*
▶ **verb** [with obj.] stain or streak (something) so that it looks like marble: *the stone walls were marbled with moss and lichen.*
– DERIVATIVES **marbler** noun, **marbly** adjective.
– ORIGIN Middle English: via Old French (variant of *marbre*), from Latin *marmor*, from Greek *marmaros* 'shining stone', associated with *marmairein* 'to shine'.

Marble Arch a large arch with three gateways at the NE corner of Hyde Park in London. Designed by John Nash, it was erected in 1827 in front of Buckingham Palace and moved in 1851 to its present site.

marble cake ▶ **noun** a cake with a mottled appearance, made of light and dark sponge.

marbled ▶ **adjective** (especially of paper) having a streaked and patterned appearance like that of variegated marble. ■ (of meat) having the lean part streaked with thin layers of fat.

marbled white ▶ **noun** a white European butterfly with black markings which lives in rough grassland.
● Genus *Melanargia*, subfamily Satyrinae, family Nymphalidae: several species.

marble gall ▶ **noun** a hard spherical gall which forms on the common oak in response to the developing larva of a gall wasp. ● The wasp is *Andricus kollari*, family Cynipidae.

marbleize (also **marbleise**) ▶ **verb** [with obj.] (usu. as adj. **marbleized**) give a marble-like finish to (an object or material): *subtle marbleized flooring.*

marbling ▶ **noun** [mass noun] colouring or marking that resembles marble, especially as a decorative finish for interior walls. ■ streaks of fat in lean meat.

Marburg /ˈmɑːbəːɡ/, German /ˈmaːrbʊrk/ **1** a city in the state of Hesse in west central Germany; pop. 79,400 (est. 2006). It was the scene in 1529 of a debate between German and Swiss theologians, notably Martin Luther and Ulrich Zwingli, on the doctrine of consubstantiation.
2 German name for **MARIBOR**.

Marburg disease ▶ **noun** [mass noun] an acute, often fatal, form of haemorrhagic fever. It is caused by a filovirus (**Marburg virus**) which normally lives in African monkeys.

marc /mɑːk/ ▶ **noun** [mass noun] the refuse of grapes or other fruit that have been pressed for winemaking. ■ an alcoholic spirit distilled from marc.
– ORIGIN early 17th cent.: from French, from *marcher* in the early sense 'to trample'.

Marcan /ˈmɑːk(ə)n/ ▶ **adjective** relating to St Mark or the Gospel ascribed to him.

marcasite /ˈmɑːkəsʌɪt, -ziːt/ ▶ **noun** a semi-precious stone consisting of iron pyrites. ■ [mass noun] a bronze-yellow mineral consisting of iron disulphide but differing from pyrite in typically forming aggregates of tabular crystals. ■ a piece of polished steel or a similar metal cut as a gem.
– ORIGIN late Middle English: from medieval Latin *marcasita*, from Arabic *marqašīta*, from Persian.

marcato /mɑːˈkɑːtəʊ/ ▶ **adverb & adjective** Music (especially as a direction) played with emphasis.
– ORIGIN Italian, 'marked, accented', of Germanic origin.

Marceau /mɑːˈsəʊ/, French /maʀso/, Marcel (1923–2007), French mime artist. He is known for appearing as the white-faced Bip, a character he developed from the French Pierrot character.

marcel /mɑːˈsɛl/ dated ▶ **noun** (**marcel wave**) a deep artificial wave in the hair.
▶ **verb** (**marcels, marcelling, marcelled**) [with obj.] give a marcel wave to (hair).
– ORIGIN late 19th cent.: named after *Marcel* Grateau (1852–1936), the Parisian hairdresser who invented it.

marcescent /mɑːˈsɛs(ə)nt/ ▶ **adjective** Botany (of a leaf or frond) withering but remaining attached to the stem.
– ORIGIN early 18th cent.: from Latin *marcescent-* 'beginning to wither', from *marcere* 'wither'.

March ▶ **noun** the third month of the year, in the northern hemisphere usually considered the first month of spring: *the work was completed in March* | [as modifier] *the March issue of the magazine.*
– ORIGIN Middle English: from an Old French dialect variant of *marz*, from Latin *Martius* (*mensis*) '(month) of Mars'.

march¹ ▶ **verb** [no obj., usu. with adverbial of direction] walk in a military manner with a regular measured tread: *thousands marched behind the coffin.* ■ walk quickly and with determination: *without a word she marched from the room.* ■ [with obj. and adverbial of direction] force (someone) to walk somewhere quickly: *she gripped Rachel's arm and marched her through the door.* ■ walk along public roads in an organized procession as a form of protest: *unemployed workers marched from Jarrow to London* | *they planned to **march on** Baton Rouge.* ■ (of something abstract) proceed or advance inexorably: *time marches on.*
▶ **noun** an act or instance of marching: *the relieving force was more than a day's march away.* ■ a piece of music composed to accompany marching or with a rhythm suggestive of marching. ■ a procession organized as a protest: *a protest march.* ■ [in sing.] the steady and inevitable development or progress of something: *the march of history.*
– PHRASES **march to (the beat of) a different tune** (or **drummer**) informal consciously adopt a different approach or attitude to the majority of people. **on the march** marching. ■ making progress: *United are on the march again.*
– ORIGIN late Middle English: from French *marcher* 'to walk' (earlier 'to trample'), of uncertain origin.

march² ▶ **plural noun** (**Marches**) an area of land on the border between two countries or territories, especially between England and Wales or (formerly) England and Scotland: *the Welsh Marches.* ■ (**the Marches**) dated English name for **MARCHE**.
▶ **verb** [no obj.] (**march with**) (of a country, territory, or estate) have a common frontier with.
– ORIGIN Middle English: from Old French *marche* (noun), *marchir* (verb), of Germanic origin; related to **MARK¹**.

Marche /ˈmɑːkeɪ/ ▶ **noun** a region of east central Italy, between the Apennines and the Adriatic Sea; capital, Ancona. Italian name **Le Marche** /ˈmarke/.

marcher¹ ▶ **noun** a person taking part in a protest march.

marcher² ▶ **noun** historical an inhabitant of a frontier or border district.

marchesa /mɑːˈkeɪzə/, Italian /marˈkeza/ ▶ **noun** (pl. **marchese** /mɑːˈkeɪzeɪ/, Italian /marˈkeze/) an Italian marchioness.
– ORIGIN Italian, feminine of **MARCHESE**.

marchese /mɑːˈkeɪzeɪ/, Italian /marˈkeze/ ▶ **noun** (pl. **marchesi** /mɑːˈkeɪzi/, Italian /marˈkezi/) an Italian marquis.
– ORIGIN Italian.

March hare ▶ **noun** informal a brown hare in the breeding season, noted for its leaping, boxing, and chasing in circles.
– PHRASES **(as) mad as a March hare** (of a person) completely mad or irrational; crazy.

marching order ▶ **noun** [mass noun] Military equipment for marching.

marching orders ▶ **plural noun** orders for troops to depart. ■ informal a dismissal or sending-off: *the ref called me over and gave me my marching orders.*

marchioness /ˌmɑːʃəˈnɛs, ˈmɑːʃ(ə)nɪs/ ▶ **noun** the wife or widow of a marquess. ■ a woman holding the rank of marquess in her own right.
– ORIGIN late 16th cent.: from medieval Latin *marchionissa*, feminine of *marchio(n-)* 'ruler of a border territory', from *marcha* 'march' (see **MARCH²**).

marchpane /ˈmɑːtʃpeɪn/ ▶ **noun** archaic spelling of **MARZIPAN**.

march past ▶ **noun** [in sing.] a formal march by troops past a saluting point at a review.

Marciano /ˌmɑːsɪˈɑːnəʊ/, Rocky (1923–69), American boxer; born *Rocco Francis Marchegiano*. He became world heavyweight champion in 1952 and successfully defended his title six times until he retired, undefeated, in 1956.

Marconi /mɑːˈkəʊni/, Italian /marˈkɔːni/, Guglielmo (1874–1937), Italian electrical engineer, the founder of radio. In 1912 Marconi produced a continuously oscillating wave, essential for the transmission of sound. He went on to develop short-wave transmission over long distances. Nobel Prize for Physics (1909).

Marco Polo /ˌmɑːkəʊ ˈpəʊləʊ/ (c.1254–c.1324), Italian traveller. With his father and uncle he travelled to China and the court of Kublai Khan via central Asia (1271–5). He eventually returned home (1292–5) via Sumatra, India, and Persia.

Marcus Aurelius see **AURELIUS**.

Marcuse /mɑːˈkuːzə/, Herbert (1898–1979), German-born American philosopher. A member of the Frankfurt School, in *Soviet Marxism* (1958) he argued that revolutionary change can come only from alienated elites such as students.

Mar del Plata /ˌmɑː dɛl ˈplɑːtə/ a fishing port and resort in Argentina, on the Atlantic coast south of Buenos Aires; pop. 620,800 (est. 2008).

Mardi Gras /ˌmɑːdɪ ˈɡrɑː/, French /maʀdi ɡʀɑ/ ▶ **noun** a carnival held in some countries on Shrove Tuesday, most famously in New Orleans. ■ a carnival or fair held at any time.
– ORIGIN French, literally 'fat Tuesday', alluding to the last day of feasting before the fast of Lent.

Marduk /ˈmɑːdʊk/ Babylonian Mythology the chief god of Babylon, who became lord of the gods of heaven and earth after conquering Tiamat, the monster of primeval chaos.

mardy ▶ **adjective** (**mardier, mardiest**) N. English sulky; moody.
– ORIGIN early 20th cent.: from dialect *mard* 'spoilt' (describing a child), alteration of *marred* (see **MAR**).

Mare, Walter de la, see **DE LA MARE**.

mare¹ /mɛː/ ▶ **noun** the female of a horse or other equine animal. ■ Brit. informal, derogatory a woman.
– ORIGIN Old English *mearh* 'horse', *mere* 'mare', from a Germanic base with cognates in Celtic languages meaning 'stallion'.

mare² /ˈmɑːreɪ, -ri/ ▶ **noun** (pl. **maria** /ˈmɑːrɪə/) Astronomy a large, level basalt plain on the surface of the moon, appearing dark by contrast with highland areas.
– ORIGIN mid 19th cent.: special use of Latin *mare* 'sea'; these areas were once thought to be seas.

mare clausum /ˌmɑːreɪ ˈklaʊsʊm, ˈklɔːzəm/ ▶ **noun** (pl. **maria clausa** /ˌmɑːrɪə ˈklaʊsə, ˈklɔːzə/) Law the sea that is under the jurisdiction of a particular country.
– ORIGIN Latin, 'closed sea'.

Marek's disease /ˈmarɛks/ ▶ **noun** [mass noun] an infectious disease of poultry caused by a herpesvirus, which attacks nerves and causes paralysis or initiates widespread tumour formation.
– ORIGIN 1960s: named after Josef *Marek* (1868–1952), Hungarian veterinary surgeon.

mare liberum /ˌmɑːreɪ ˈliːbərʊm, ˈlʌɪbərəm/ ▶ **noun** (pl. **maria libera** /ˌmɑːrɪə ˈliːbərə, ˈlʌɪbərə/) Law the sea that is open to all nations.
– ORIGIN Latin, literally 'free sea'.

maremma /məˈrɛmə/ ▶ **noun** (pl. **maremme** /-mi/) (in Italy) an area of low, marshy land near a seashore.
– ORIGIN mid 19th cent.: Italian, from Latin *maritima*, feminine of *maritimus* (see **MARITIME**).

Marengo /məˈrɛŋɡəʊ/ ▶ **adjective** [postpositive] (of chicken or veal) sautéed in oil, served with a tomato

sauce, and traditionally garnished with eggs and crayfish: *chicken Marengo*.
– ORIGIN named after *Marengo*, a village in northern Italy and the site of a battle (1800) in which Napoleon defeated the Austrians, after which the dish is said to have been prepared for him.

Marengo, Battle of a decisive French victory of Napoleon's campaign in Italy in 1800, close to the village of Marengo, near Turin. Napoleon crossed the Alps to defeat and capture an Austrian army, a victory which led to Italy returning to French control.

mare's nest ▶ noun **1** a complex or confused situation; a muddle: *your desk's usually a mare's nest*.
2 an illusory discovery: *the mare's nest of perfect safety*.
– ORIGIN late 16th cent.: formerly in the phrase *to have found a mare's nest*, meaning 'to have discovered something amazing' (i.e. something that does not exist).

mare's tail ▶ noun **1** a widely distributed water plant with whorls of narrow leaves around a tall stout stem. ● *Hippuris vulgaris*, family Haloragaceae.
2 (**mare's tails**) long straight streaks of cirrus cloud.

Mareva injunction /məˈreɪvə, məˈriːvə/ ▶ noun English Law a court order freezing a debtor's assets to prevent them being taken abroad.
– ORIGIN named after *Mareva* Compania Naveria S.A., the first plaintiff to be granted such an injunction (1975).

Marfan's syndrome /ˈmɑːfãz/ ▶ noun [mass noun] Medicine a hereditary disorder of connective tissue, resulting in abnormally long and thin digits and also frequently in optical and cardiovascular defects.
– ORIGIN 1930s: named after Antonin B. J. *Marfan* (1858–1942), French paediatrician.

marg /mɑːg/ ▶ noun [usu. in place names] Indian a road or street: *Mahatma Gandhi Marg*.
– ORIGIN via Hindi from Sanskrit *mārga* 'way, road'.

marga ▶ adjective variant spelling of **MAGA**.

Margaret, Princess, Margaret Rose (1930–2002), only sister of Elizabeth II. In 1960 she married Antony Armstrong-Jones, who was later created Earl of Snowdon; the marriage was dissolved in 1978. Their two children are David, Viscount Linley and Lady Sarah Chatto.

M

Margaret, St (*c*.1046–93), Scottish queen, wife of Malcolm III. She exerted a strong influence over royal policy during her husband's reign, and was instrumental in the reform of the Scottish Church. Feast day, 16 November.

margarine /ˌmɑːdʒəˈriːn, ˈmɑːgəriːn/ ▶ noun [mass noun] a butter substitute made from vegetable oils or animal fats.
– ORIGIN late 19th cent.: from French, from Greek *margaron* 'pearl' (because of the lustre of the crystals of esters from which it was first made) + **-INE**[4].

Margarita /ˌmɑːgəˈriːtə/ an island in the Caribbean Sea, off the coast of Venezuela. Visited by Columbus in 1498, it was used as a base by Simón Bolívar in 1816 in the struggle for independence from Spanish rule.

margarita /ˌmɑːgəˈriːtə/ ▶ noun a cocktail made with tequila and citrus fruit juice.
– ORIGIN from the Spanish given name equivalent to *Margaret*.

margate /ˈmɑːgɪt/ ▶ noun a deep-bodied greyish fish which occurs in warm waters of the western Atlantic.
● Two species in the family Pomadasyidae.
– ORIGIN mid 18th cent.: of unknown origin.

margay /ˈmɑːgeɪ/ ▶ noun a small South American wild cat with large eyes and a yellowish coat with black spots and stripes. ● *Felis wiedii*, family Felidae.
– ORIGIN late 18th cent.: via French from Tupi *marakaya*.

marge[1] ▶ noun [mass noun] Brit. informal margarine.
– ORIGIN 1920s: abbreviation.

marge[2] ▶ noun literary a margin or edge.
– ORIGIN mid 16th cent.: from French, from Latin *margo* 'margin'.

margin ▶ noun **1** the edge or border of something: *the eastern margin of the Indian Ocean*. ■ the blank border on each side of the print on a page.
2 an amount by which something is won: *they won by a convincing 17-point margin*. ■ an amount of something included so as to be sure of success or safety: *there was no margin for error*. ■ the furthest limit of possibility, success, etc.: *the lighting is brighter than before but is still at the margins of acceptability*. ■ a profit margin. ■ Finance a sum deposited with a broker to cover the risk of loss on a transaction or account. ■ Austral./NZ an increment to a basic wage, paid for extra skill or responsibility.
▶ verb (**margins, margining, margined**) [with obj.]
1 provide with an edge or border: *the plant's leaves are margined with yellow*.
2 deposit an amount of money with a broker as security for (an account or transaction): (as adj. **margined**) *a margined transaction*.
3 archaic annotate or summarize (a text) in the margins.
– PHRASES **margin of error** a small amount that is allowed for in case of miscalculation or change of circumstances.
– DERIVATIVES **margined** adjective [in combination] *a wide-margined volume*.
– ORIGIN late Middle English: from Latin *margo, margin-* 'edge'.

marginal ▶ adjective **1** relating to or at the edge or margin: *marginal notes*. ■ relating to water adjacent to the land's edge or coast: *water lilies and marginal aquatics*.
2 minor and not important; not central: *it seems likely to make only a marginal difference | the cost is negligible, less than marginal*. ■ (of costs or benefits) relating to or resulting from small or unit changes. ■ (of taxation) relating to increases in income.
3 (of a decision or distinction) very narrow; borderline: *a marginal offside decision*. ■ Brit. (of a parliamentary or council seat) held by a small majority and therefore at risk in an election. ■ close to the limit of profitability, especially through difficulty of exploitation: *marginal farmland*.
▶ noun **1** Brit. a seat in a parliament or on a council that is held by a small majority and is at risk in an election.
2 a plant that grows in water close to the edge of land.
– DERIVATIVES **marginality** noun.
– ORIGIN late 16th cent.: from medieval Latin *marginalis*, from *margo, margin-* (see **MARGIN**).

marginal cost ▶ noun Economics the cost added by producing one extra item of a product.

marginalia /ˌmɑːdʒɪˈneɪlɪə/ ▶ plural noun notes written in the margins of a text.
– ORIGIN mid 19th cent.: from medieval Latin, neuter plural of *marginalis*, from *margo, margin-* (see **MARGIN**).

marginalize (also **marginalise**) ▶ verb [with obj.] treat (a person, group, or concept) as insignificant or peripheral: *by removing religion from the public space, we marginalize it* | (as adj. **marginalized**) *members of marginalized cultural groups*.
– DERIVATIVES **marginalization** noun.

marginally ▶ adverb to only a limited extent; slightly: *inflation is predicted to drop marginally* | [as submodifier] *he's marginally worse than he was*.

marginate Biology ▶ verb /ˈmɑːdʒɪneɪt/ [with obj.] provide with a margin or border; form a border to.
▶ adjective /ˈmɑːdʒɪnət/ having a distinct margin or border.
– DERIVATIVES **margination** noun.

margin call ▶ noun Finance a demand by a broker that an investor deposit further cash or securities to cover possible losses.

margin release ▶ noun a device on a typewriter allowing a word to be typed beyond the margin normally set.

margosa /mɑːˈgəʊsə/ ▶ noun another term for **NEEM**.
– ORIGIN Portuguese *amargosa*, feminine of *amargoso* 'bitter'.

margrave /ˈmɑːgreɪv/ ▶ noun historical the hereditary title of some princes of the Holy Roman Empire.
– DERIVATIVES **margravate** /ˈmɑːgrəvət/ noun.
– ORIGIN mid 16th cent., from Middle Dutch *markgrave* 'count of a border territory', from *marke* 'boundary' + *grave* 'count'.

margravine /ˈmɑːgrəviːn/ ▶ noun historical the wife of a margrave.
– ORIGIN late 17th cent.: from Dutch *markgravin*, feminine of *markgraaf*, earlier *markgrave* (see **MARGRAVE**).

marguerite /ˌmɑːgəˈriːt/ ▶ noun another term for **OX-EYE DAISY**.
– ORIGIN early 17th cent.: French equivalent of the given name Margaret.

Mari[1] /ˈmɑːri/ an ancient city on the west bank of the Euphrates, in Syria. Its period of greatest importance was from the late 19th to the mid 18th centuries BC; the vast palace of the last king, Zimri-Lim, has yielded an archive of 25,000 cuneiform tablets, which are the principal source for the history of northern Syria and Mesopotamia at that time.

Mari[2] /ˈmɑːriː/ ▶ noun (pl. **same** or **Maris**) **1** a member of a people of the central Volga valley in Russia.
2 [mass noun] the Uralic language of the Mari, which has two dialects with over 700,000 speakers in all. Formerly called **CHEREMIS**.
▶ adjective relating to the Mari or their language.
– ORIGIN the name in Mari.

maria plural form of **MARE**[2].

mariachi /ˌmarɪˈɑːtʃi/ ▶ noun (pl. **mariachis**) [as modifier] denoting a type of traditional Mexican folk music, performed by a small group of strolling musicians. ■ a musician in a group performing mariachi music.
– ORIGIN from Mexican Spanish *mariache, mariachi* 'street singer'.

Maria de' Medici see **MARIE DE MÉDICIS**.

mariage blanc /ˌmarɪɑːʒ ˈblɒ̃/, French /maʀjaʒ blɑ̃/ ▶ noun (pl. **mariages blancs** pronunc. **same**) an unconsummated marriage.
– ORIGIN French, literally 'white marriage'.

mariage de convenance /ˌmarɪɑːʒ də ˌkɒ̃vəˈnɒ̃s/, French /maʀjaʒ də kɔ̃vnɑ̃s/ ▶ noun (pl. **mariages de convenance** pronunc. **same**) French term for **MARRIAGE OF CONVENIENCE**.

Marian /ˈmɛːrɪən/ ▶ adjective **1** relating to the Virgin Mary.
2 relating to Queen Mary I of England.

Mariana Islands /ˌmarɪˈɑːnə/ (also **the Marianas**) a group of islands in the western Pacific, comprising Guam and the Northern Marianas.
– ORIGIN translating *Las Marianas*, the name given by Spanish colonists to the islands, in honour of *Maria Anna*, widow of Philip IV.

Mariana Trench an ocean trench to the south-east of the Mariana Islands in the western Pacific, with the greatest known ocean depth (11,034 m, 36,201 ft at the Challenger Deep).

Maria Theresa /məˌriːə təˈreɪzə/ (1717–80), Archduchess of Austria, queen of Hungary and Bohemia 1740–80. The daughter of the Emperor Charles VI, she succeeded to the Habsburg dominions in 1740 by virtue of the Pragmatic Sanction. Her accession triggered the War of the Austrian Succession, which in turn led to the Seven Years War.

Mari Autonomous Republic another name for **MARI EL**.

Maribor /ˈmarɪbɔː/ an industrial city in NE Slovenia, on the River Drava near the border with Austria; pop. 111,340 (2007). German name **MARBURG**.

mariculture /ˈmarɪˌkʌltʃə/ ▶ noun [mass noun] the cultivation of fish or other marine life for food.
– ORIGIN early 20th cent.: from Latin *mare, mari-* 'sea' + **CULTURE**, on the pattern of words such as *agriculture*.

Marie Antoinette /ˌmarɪ ˌɒ̃twəˈnɛt/, French /maʀi ɑ̃twanɛt/ (1755–93), French queen, wife of Louis XVI. A daughter of Maria Theresa, she married the future Louis XVI of France in 1770. Her extravagant lifestyle led to her widespread unpopularity and, like her husband, she was executed during the French Revolution.

Marie Byrd Land /ˌmɑːrɪ ˈbəːd/ a region of Antarctica bordering the Pacific, between Ellsworth Land and the Ross Sea.
– ORIGIN named after the wife of Richard E. *Byrd*, the American naval commander who explored the region in 1929.

Marie Celeste variant spelling of **MARY CELESTE**.

Marie de Médicis /məˌriː də ˌmeɪdɪˈsiːs/ (1573–1642), queen of France; Italian name *Maria de' Medici*. The second wife of Henry IV of France, she ruled as regent during the minority of her son Louis XIII (1610–17) and retained her influence after her son came to power.

Mari El /ˌmɑːriː ˈɛl/ an autonomous republic in European Russia, north of the Volga; pop. 700,900 (est. 2009); capital, Yoshkar-Ola. Also called **MARI AUTONOMOUS REPUBLIC**.

Marie Rose ▶ noun a cold sauce made from mayonnaise and tomato purée and served with seafood.

marigold ▶ noun a plant of the daisy family with yellow, orange, or copper-brown flowers, cultivated as an ornamental. ● Genera *Calendula* (the **common** (or **pot**) **marigold**) and *Tagetes* (the **French** and **African marigolds**), family Compositae.

■ used in names of plants with yellow flowers other than true marigolds, e.g. **corn marigold, marsh marigold**.
– ORIGIN late Middle English: from the given name *Mary* (probably referring to the Virgin) + dialect *gold*, denoting the corn or garden marigold in Old English.

marijuana /ˌmarɪˈhwɑːnə/ (also **marihuana**) ▶ **noun** [mass noun] cannabis, especially as smoked in cigarettes.
– ORIGIN late 19th cent.: from Latin American Spanish.

marimba /məˈrɪmbə/ ▶ **noun** a deep-toned xylophone of African origin.
– ORIGIN early 18th cent.: from Kimbundu, perhaps via Portuguese.

marina ▶ **noun** a specially designed harbour with moorings for pleasure yachts and small boats.
– ORIGIN early 19th cent.: from Italian or Spanish, feminine of *marino*, from Latin *marinus* (see MARINE).

marinade ▶ **noun** /ˌmarɪˈneɪd, ˈmarɪneɪd/ a mixture of oil, wine, spices, or similar ingredients, in which meat, fish, or other food is soaked before cooking in order to flavour or soften it.
▶ **verb** /ˈmarɪneɪd/ another term for MARINATE.
– ORIGIN late 17th cent. (as a verb): from French, from Spanish *marinada*, via *marinar* 'pickle in brine' from *marino* (see MARINA).

marinara /ˌmɑːrɪˈnɑːrə, ˈmar-/ ▶ **noun** [usu. as modifier] (in Italian cooking) a sauce made from tomatoes, onions, and herbs, served especially with pasta.
– ORIGIN from the Italian phrase *alla marinara* 'sailor-style'.

marinate /ˈmarɪneɪt/ ▶ **verb** [with obj.] soak (meat, fish, or other food) in a marinade: *the beef was marinated in red wine vinegar.* ■ [no obj.] (of food) undergo marination.
– DERIVATIVES **marination noun**.
– ORIGIN mid 17th cent.: from Italian *marinare* 'pickle in brine', or from French *mariner* (from *marine* 'brine').

marine /məˈriːn/ ▶ **adjective** relating to or found in the sea: *marine plants | marine biology.* ■ relating to shipping or naval matters: *marine insurance.* ■ (of artists or painting) depicting scenes at sea.
▶ **noun** a member of a body of troops trained to serve on land or sea, in particular (in the UK) a member of the Royal Marines or (in the US) a member of the Marine Corps.
– PHRASES **tell that to the marines** a scornful expression of disbelief. [from the saying *that will do for the marines but the sailors won't believe it*, referring to the *horse marines*, an imaginary corps of cavalrymen serving as marines (thus out of their element).]
– ORIGIN Middle English (as a noun in the sense 'seashore'): from Old French *marin, marine*, from Latin *marinus*, from *mare* 'sea'.

marine iguana ▶ **noun** a large lizard with webbed feet, native to the Galapagos Islands, which swims strongly and is the only marine lizard. ● *Amblyrhynchus cristatus*, family Iguanidae.

Mariner a series of American space probes launched in 1962–77 to investigate the planets Venus, Mars, and Mercury.

mariner ▶ **noun** a sailor.
– ORIGIN Middle English: from Old French *marinier*, from medieval Latin *marinarius*, from Latin *marinus* (see MARINE).

marine toad ▶ **noun** another term for CANE TOAD.

Marinetti /ˌmarɪˈnɛti/, Filippo Tommaso (1876–1944), Italian poet and dramatist. He launched the futurist movement with a manifesto (1909) which exalted technology, glorified war, and demanded revolution in the arts.

marinize /məˈriːnʌɪz/ (also **marinise**) ▶ **verb** [with obj.] modify or convert for marine use: (as adj. **marinized**) *a three-cylinder marinized 26 hp diesel engine.*

Mariolatry /ˌmɛːrɪˈɒlətri/ ▶ **noun** [mass noun] idolatrous worship of the Virgin Mary.
– ORIGIN early 17th cent.: from *Maria* (Latin equivalent of 'Mary') + -LATRY, on the pattern of *idolatry*.

Mariology /ˌmɛːrɪˈɒlədʒi/ ▶ **noun** [mass noun] the part of Christian theology dealing with the Virgin Mary.
– DERIVATIVES **Mariological adjective, Mariologist noun**.

marionette /ˌmarɪəˈnɛt/ ▶ **noun** a puppet worked by strings. ■ a person who is easily manipulated or controlled: *many officers dismissed him as the mayor's marionette.*
– ORIGIN early 17th cent.: from French *marionnette*, from *Marion*, diminutive of the given name *Marie*.

mariposa tulip /ˌmarɪˈpəʊsə/ (also **mariposa lily**) ▶ **noun** a North American lily with large brightly coloured cup-shaped flowers. ● Genus *Calochortus*, family Liliaceae.
– ORIGIN mid 19th cent.: *mariposa* from Spanish, literally 'butterfly'.

Maris Piper /ˈmarɪs/ ▶ **noun** a potato of a variety with creamy flesh and smooth oval tubers.
– ORIGIN 1970s: named after *Maris* Lane, original site of the Plant Breeding Institute; *Piper* was chosen arbitrarily as a word beginning with *p-* for *potato*.

Marist /ˈmɛːrɪst, ˈmarɪst/ ▶ **noun 1** (also **Marist Father**) a member of the Society of Mary, a Roman Catholic missionary and teaching order.
2 (also **Marist Brother**) a member of the Little Brothers of Mary, a Roman Catholic teaching order.
– ORIGIN late 19th cent.: from French *Mariste*, from the given name *Marie*, equivalent of *Mary*.

marital ▶ **adjective** relating to marriage or the relations between husband and wife: *she wanted to talk about their marital problems.*
– DERIVATIVES **maritally adverb**.
– ORIGIN early 16th cent.: from Latin *maritalis*, from *maritus* 'husband'.

marital status ▶ **noun** [mass noun] one's situation with regard to whether one is single, married, separated, divorced, or widowed.

maritime ▶ **adjective** connected with the sea, especially in relation to seaborne trade or naval matters: *a maritime museum | maritime law.* ■ living or found in or near the sea: *dolphins and other maritime mammals.* ■ bordering on the sea: *two species of Diptera occur in the maritime Antarctic.* ■ (of climate) moist and temperate owing to the influence of the sea.
– ORIGIN mid 16th cent.: from Latin *maritimus*, from *mare* 'sea'.

maritime pine ▶ **noun** a pine tree with long thick needles and clustered cones, native to the coasts of the Mediterranean and Iberia. Also called CLUSTER PINE. ● *Pinus pinaster*, family Pinaceae.

Maritime Provinces (also **the Maritimes**) the Canadian provinces of New Brunswick, Nova Scotia, and Prince Edward Island, with coastlines on the Gulf of St Lawrence and the Atlantic. Compare with ATLANTIC PROVINCES.

Maritsa /məˈrɪtsə/ a river of southern Europe, which rises in the Rila Mountains of SW Bulgaria and flows 480 km (300 miles) south to the Aegean Sea. It forms the border between Bulgaria and Greece and that between Greece and Turkey. Its ancient name is the Hebros or Hebrus. Turkish name MERIÇ; Greek name ÉVROS.

Mariupol /ˌmarɪˈuːpɒl/ an industrial port on the south coast of Ukraine, on the Sea of Azov; pop. 472,000 (est. 2009). Former name (1948–89) ZHDANOV.

Marius /ˈmarɪəs/, Gaius (*c*.157–86 BC), Roman general and politician. Elected consul in 107 BC, he defeated Jugurtha and invading Germanic tribes. After a power struggle with Sulla he was expelled from Italy, but returned to take Rome by force in 87 BC.

marjoram /ˈmɑːdʒ(ə)rəm/ ▶ **noun** (also **sweet marjoram**) [mass noun] an aromatic southern European plant of the mint family, the leaves of which are used as a culinary herb. ● *Origanum majorana*, family Labiatae.
■ (also **wild marjoram**) another term for OREGANO.
– ORIGIN late Middle English: from Old French *majorane*, from medieval Latin *majorana*, of unknown ultimate origin.

mark[1] ▶ **noun 1** a small area on a surface having a different colour from its surroundings, typically one caused by damage or dirt: *the blow left a red mark down one side of her face.* ■ a spot, area, or feature on a person's or animal's body by which they may be identified or recognized: *he was five feet nine, with no distinguishing marks.*
2 a line, figure, or symbol made as an indication or record of something. ■ a sign or indication of a quality or feeling: *the flag was at half mast as a mark of respect.* ■ a written symbol made on a document in place of a signature by someone who cannot write. ■ a competitor's starting point in a race. ■ Nautical a piece of material or a knot used to indicate a depth on a sounding line. ■ Telecommunications one of two possible states of a signal in certain systems. The opposite of SPACE. ■ a level or stage that is considered significant: *unemployment had passed the two million mark.* ■ Brit. a particular temperature level in a gas oven: *preheat the oven to Gas Mark 5.*
3 chiefly Brit. a point awarded for a correct answer or for proficiency in an examination or competition. ■ a figure or letter representing the total number of marks awarded in an examination or competition and signifying a person's score: *the highest mark was 98 per cent.* ■ (also **handicap mark**) Horse Racing an official assessment of a horse's form, expressed as a figure between 0 and 140 and used as the basis for calculating the weight the horse has to carry in a race. ■ (especially in athletics) a time or distance achieved by a competitor, especially one which represents a record or personal best.
4 (followed by a numeral) a particular model or type of a vehicle or machine: *a Mark 10 Jaguar.*
5 a target: *few bullets could have missed their mark.* ■ informal, chiefly US a person who is easily deceived or taken advantage of: *they figure I'm an easy mark.*
6 Rugby the act of cleanly catching the ball direct from a kick, knock-on, or forward throw by an opponent, on or behind one's own 22-metre line, and exclaiming 'Mark', after which a free kick can be taken by the catcher. ■ Australian Rules an act of catching a ball that has been kicked at least fifteen metres before it reaches the ground, or the spot from which the subsequent kick is taken.
▶ **verb** [with obj.] **1** make a visible impression or stain on: *he fingered the photograph gently, careful not to mark it.* ■ [no obj.] become stained: *they're made from a woven surface which doesn't mark or tear.*
2 write a word or symbol on (an object) in order to give information: *she marked all her possessions with her name.* ■ write or draw (a word, symbol, line, etc.) on an object: *she marked the date down on a card.* ■ (**mark something off**) put a line by or through something written or printed to indicate that it has passed or been dealt with: *he marked off their names in a ledger.*
3 indicate the position of: *the top of the pass marks the border between Alaska and the Yukon.* ■ separate or delineate (a particular section or area): *you need to* **mark out** *the part of the garden where the sun lingers longest.* ■ (of a particular quality or feature) distinguish (someone or something) from other people or things: *his sword* **marked** *him* **out** *as an officer.* ■ (**mark someone out for**) select or destine someone for (a particular role or fate): *the solicitor general marked him out for government office.* ■ (**mark someone down as**) judge someone to be (a particular type of person): *she had marked him down as a dangerous liberal.* ■ acknowledge or celebrate (an important event) with a particular action: *to mark its fiftieth birthday the charity held a fashion show.* ■ be an indication of (a significant event or stage): *a series of incidents which marked a new phase in the terrorist campaign.* ■ characterize as having a particular quality or feature: *the reaction to these developments has been marked by a note of hysteria.*
4 Brit. (of a teacher or examiner) assess the standard of (written work) by assigning points for proficiency or correct answers: *the examiner may have hundreds of scripts to mark.* ■ (**mark someone/thing down**) reduce the number of marks awarded to a person or their work.
5 notice or pay careful attention to: *he'll leave you, you mark my words!*
6 Brit. (of a player in a team game) stay close to (an opponent) in order to prevent them getting or passing the ball: *each central defender marks one attacker.* ■ Australian Rules catch (the ball) from a kick of at least ten metres.
– PHRASES **be quick** (or **slow**) **off the mark** be fast (or slow) in responding to a situation or understanding something. **get off the mark** get started. **leave its** (or **one's** or **a**) **mark** have a lasting or significant effect: *he left his mark on English football.* **make one's mark** attain recognition or distinction. **one's mark** Brit. something which is particularly typical of or suitable for someone: *'I took you out.' 'To a motel! That's just about your mark!'* **mark time** (of troops) march on the spot without moving forward. ■ pass one's time in routine activities until a more interesting opportunity presents itself. **mark you** chiefly Brit. used to emphasize a statement: *I was persuaded, against my better judgement, mark you, to vote for him.* **near** (or **close**) **to the mark** almost accurate: *to say he was their legal adviser would be nearer the mark.* **off** (or **wide of**) **the mark** incorrect or inaccurate. **of mark** dated having importance or distinction: *he had been a man of mark.* **on the mark** correct; accurate. **on your marks** used to instruct

M

competitors in a race to prepare themselves in the correct starting position. **up to the mark** up to the required standard. ■ [usu. with negative] (of a person) as healthy or as cheerful as usual.

– PHRASAL VERBS **mark something down** (of a retailer) reduce the indicated price of an item. **mark something up 1** (of a retailer) increase the indicated price of an item: *he marks up prized garments by at least 50 per cent.* **2** annotate or correct text for printing, keying, or typesetting.

– ORIGIN Old English *mearc, gemerce* (noun), *mearcian* (verb), of Germanic origin; from an Indo-European root shared by Latin *margo* 'margin'.

mark[2] ▶ **noun 1** (until the introduction of the euro in 2002) the basic monetary unit of Germany, equal to 100 pfennig; a Deutschmark.
2 a former English and Scottish money of account, equal to thirteen shillings and four pence in the currency of the day. ■ a denomination of weight for gold and silver, formerly used throughout western Europe and typically equal to 8 ounces (226.8 grams).
3 (also **marka**) the basic monetary unit of Bosnia and Herzegovina, equal to 100 fening.

– ORIGIN Old English *marc*, from Old Norse *mǫrk*; probably related to MARK[1].

Mark, St an Apostle, companion of St Peter and St Paul, traditional author of the second Gospel. Feast day, 25 April. ■ the second Gospel, the earliest in date (See GOSPEL (sense 2)).

marka /ˈmɑːkə/ ▶ **noun** (pl. **same** or **markas**) variant form of MARK[2] (sense 3).

– ORIGIN Bosnian.

Mark Antony see ANTONY.

markdown ▶ **noun** a reduction in price.

marked ▶ **adjective 1** having a visible mark or marking: *a houseplant with beautifully marked, dark green leaves.* ■ (of playing cards) having distinctive marks on their backs to assist cheating. ■ Linguistics (of words or forms) distinguished by a particular feature: *the word 'drake' is semantically marked as masculine.*
2 clearly noticeable: *a marked increase in UK sales.*

– DERIVATIVES **markedness** noun.

markedly ▶ **adverb** to an extent which is clearly noticeable; significantly: *new diagnoses have increased markedly since 1998* | [as submodifier] *this advice is markedly different to that last year.*

marked man ▶ **noun** a man who is singled out as a target for hostility or attack.

marker ▶ **noun 1** an object used to indicate a position, place, or route: *they erected a granite marker at the crash site.* ■ [in sing.] a distinctive feature or characteristic indicative of a particular quality or condition: *identification with one's own language has always been a marker of nationalism.* ■ a thing serving as a standard of comparison: *he has already **laid down a marker** by setting a fast time during practice.* ■ a radio beacon used to guide the pilot of an aircraft. ■ Genetics an allele used to identify a chromosome or to locate other genes on a genetic map.
2 (also **marker pen**) a felt-tip pen with a broad tip.
3 Brit. (in team games) a player who stays close to an opponent to prevent them from getting or passing the ball.
4 Brit. a person who assesses the standard of a test or examination. ■ a person who records the score in snooker, billiards, or squash.
5 N. Amer. informal a promissory note; an IOU.

market ▶ **noun 1** a regular gathering of people for the purchase and sale of provisions, livestock, and other commodities: *they wanted to browse around the street market.* ■ an open space or covered building where vendors convene to sell their goods.
2 an area or arena in which commercial dealings are conducted: *the UK market remained in recession* | *the labour market.* ■ a demand for a particular commodity or service: *there is **a market for** high-priced wine.* ■ the state of trade at a particular time or in a particular context: *the bottom's fallen out of the market.* ■ the free market: *future development cannot be left to the market* | [as modifier] *a market economy.* ■ a stock market.
▶ **verb** (**markets, marketing, marketed**) [with obj.] advertise or promote (something): *the product was marketed under the name 'aspirin'.* ■ offer for sale. ■ [no obj.] US go shopping for provisions: *then I have to go uptown and market.*

– PHRASES **be in the market for** wish to buy. **make a market** Finance take part in active dealing in particular shares or other assets. **on the market** available for sale: *she decided to put her flat on the market.*

– DERIVATIVES **marketer** noun.

– ORIGIN Middle English, via Anglo-Norman French from Latin *mercatus*, from *mercari* 'buy' (see also MERCHANT).

marketable ▶ **adjective** able or fit to be sold or marketed: *the flotation will make the shares marketable.* ■ attractive to potential employers or clients; in demand: *marketable skills.*

– DERIVATIVES **marketability** noun.

market basket ▶ **noun** a large basket, typically one with a lid, used to carry provisions. ■ Economics a selected list of food and household items chosen as a representative sample of common purchases and used to measure the cost of living.

market cross ▶ **noun** a stone cross situated in the marketplace of a British town.

market day ▶ **noun** a day on which a market is regularly held.

marketeer ▶ **noun** a person who sells goods or services in a market: *software marketeers.* ■ [with modifier] a person who works in or advocates a particular type of market: *in the US libertarians are free marketeers to the bone.*

market forces ▶ **plural noun** the economic factors affecting the price of, demand for, and availability of a commodity.

market garden ▶ **noun** Brit. a place where vegetables and fruit are grown for sale.

– DERIVATIVES **market gardener** noun, **market gardening** noun.

marketing ▶ **noun** [mass noun] the action or business of promoting and selling products or services, including market research and advertising.

marketization (also **marketisation**) ▶ **noun** [mass noun] the exposure of an industry or service to market forces. ■ the conversion of a national economy from a planned to a market economy.

– DERIVATIVES **marketize** (also **marketise**) verb.

market leader ▶ **noun** the company selling the largest quantity of a particular product. ■ a product which outsells its competitors.

market maker ▶ **noun** a dealer in securities or other assets who undertakes to buy or sell at specified prices at all times.

marketplace ▶ **noun** an open space where a market is or was formerly held. ■ the arena of commercial dealings: *the changing demands of the global marketplace.*

market research ▶ **noun** [mass noun] the action or activity of gathering information about consumers' needs and preferences.

– DERIVATIVES **market researcher** noun.

market share ▶ **noun** the portion of a market controlled by a particular company or product.

marketspace ▶ **noun 1** an arena within which commercial dealing takes place; a market.
2 [mass noun] commerce carried out by electronic means, especially via the Internet.

market town ▶ **noun** (in the UK) a town of moderate size where a regular market is held.

market value ▶ **noun** the amount for which something can be sold on a given market. Often contrasted with BOOK VALUE.

markhor /ˈmɑːkɔː/ ▶ **noun** a large wild goat with very long twisted horns, native to central Asia. ● *Capra falconeri*, family Bovidae.

– ORIGIN mid 19th cent.: from Persian *mār-ḵwār*, from *mār* 'serpent' + *ḵwār* '-eating'.

marking ▶ **noun** (usu. **markings**) a mark or set of marks: *the new outfits had luminous reflective markings.* ■ a mark or pattern of marks on an animal's fur, feathers, or skin: *a dun horse with black markings.* ■ Music a word or symbol on a score indicating the correct tempo, dynamic, or other aspect of performance.

markka /ˈmɑːkɑː, -kə/ ▶ **noun** (until the introduction of the euro in 2002) the basic monetary unit of Finland, equal to 100 penniä.

– ORIGIN Finnish.

Markova /mɑːˈkəʊvə, ˈmɑːkəvə/, Dame Alicia (1910–2004), English ballet dancer; born *Lilian Alicia Marks*. She founded the Markova–Dolin Ballet with Anton Dolin in 1935 and was prima ballerina with the London Festival Ballet 1950–2.

Markov model /ˈmɑːkɒf/ (also **Markov chain**) ▶ **noun** Statistics a stochastic model describing a sequence of possible events in which the probability of each event depends only on the state attained in the previous event.

– ORIGIN mid 20th cent.: named after Andrei A. *Markov* (1856–1922), Russian mathematician.

Marks, Simon, 1st Baron Marks of Broughton (1888–1964), English businessman. In 1907 he inherited the Marks and Spencer Penny Bazaars established by his father and Thomas Spencer. These formed the nucleus of the retail chain Marks & Spencer, created in 1926.

marksman ▶ **noun** (pl. **marksmen**) a person skilled in shooting. ■ informal a footballer skilled in scoring goals.

– DERIVATIVES **marksmanship** noun.

markswoman ▶ **noun** (pl. **markswomen**) a woman skilled in shooting.

mark-to-market ▶ **adjective** Finance denoting or relating to a system of valuing assets by the most recent market price.

markup ▶ **noun 1** the amount added to the cost price of goods to cover overheads and profit.
2 [mass noun] the process or result of correcting text in preparation for printing.
3 [mass noun] Computing a set of tags assigned to elements of a text to indicate their relation to the rest of the text or dictate how they should be displayed.

marl[1] ▶ **noun** [mass noun] an unconsolidated sedimentary rock or soil consisting of clay and lime, formerly used as fertilizer.
▶ **verb** [with obj.] apply marl to.

– DERIVATIVES **marly** adjective.

– ORIGIN Middle English: from Old French *marle*, from medieval Latin *margila*, from Latin *marga*, of Celtic origin.

marl[2] ▶ **noun** [mass noun] [usu. as modifier] a mottled yarn of differently coloured threads, or fabric made from this yarn: *blue marl leggings.*

– ORIGIN late 19th cent.: shortening of MARBLED.

Marlborough /ˈmɔːlb(ə)rə/, John Churchill, 1st Duke of (1650–1722), British general. He was commander of British and Dutch troops in the War of the Spanish Succession and won a series of victories (notably at Blenheim in 1704) over the French armies of Louis XIV, ending Louis's attempts to dominate Europe.

marled ▶ **adjective** (chiefly of yarn or fabric) mottled or streaked.

– ORIGIN early 16th cent.: perhaps a shortening of MARBLED.

Marley, Bob (1945–81), Jamaican reggae singer, guitarist, and songwriter; full name *Robert Nesta Marley*. Having formed the trio the Wailers in 1965, in the 1970s he was instrumental in popularizing reggae. His lyrics often reflected his commitment to Rastafarianism.

marlin /ˈmɑːlɪn/ ▶ **noun** a large edible billfish of warm seas, which is a highly prized game fish. ● Genera *Makaira* and *Tetrapterus*, family Istiophoridae: several species.

– ORIGIN early 20th cent.: from MARLINSPIKE (with reference to its pointed snout).

marline /ˈmɑːlɪn/ ▶ **noun** [mass noun] Nautical light rope made of two strands, used for binding larger ropes.

– ORIGIN late Middle English: from Middle Low German *marling*, with the ending influenced by LINE[1].

marlinspike ▶ **noun** a pointed metal tool used by sailors to separate strands of rope or wire.

– ORIGIN early 17th cent. (originally as *marling spike*): from *marling*, present participle of *marl* 'fasten with marline' (from Dutch *marlen* 'keep binding') + SPIKE[1].

Marlowe, Christopher (1564–93), English dramatist and poet. As a dramatist he brought a new strength and vitality to blank verse; his work influenced Shakespeare's early historical plays. Notable plays: *Doctor Faustus* (*c.*1590) and *The Jew of Malta* (1592).

– DERIVATIVES **Marlovian** adjective & noun.

marm ▶ **noun** N. Amer. variant spelling of MA'AM.

marmalade ▶ **noun** [mass noun] a preserve made from citrus fruit, especially bitter oranges.

– ORIGIN late 15th cent.: from Portuguese *marmelada* 'quince jam', from *marmelo* 'quince', based on Greek *melimēlon* (from *meli* 'honey' + *mēlon* 'apple').

marmalade cat ▶ **noun** a cat with orange fur and darker orange markings.

marmalize (also **marmalise**) ▶ **verb** [with obj.] Brit. informal beat (someone) up: *they're real aggro men who'll marmalize anybody for a few quid.* ■ defeat heavily: *we pulverized United, absolutely marmalized them.*

– ORIGIN 1960s: of uncertain origin; perhaps humorously from *marmal-* (in **MARMALADE**) + **-IZE** (perhaps after **PULVERIZE**).

Marmara, Sea of /ˈmɑːmərə/ a small sea in NW Turkey. Connected by the Bosporus to the Black Sea and by the Dardanelles to the Aegean, it separates European Turkey from Asian Turkey. In ancient times it was known as the Propontis.

Marmite /ˈmɑːmʌɪt/ ▸ **noun** [mass noun] Brit. trademark a dark savoury spread made from yeast extract and vegetable extract.

marmite /ˈmɑːmʌɪt, mɑːˈmiːt/ ▸ **noun** an earthenware cooking container.
– ORIGIN early 19th cent.: French, from Old French *marmite* 'hypocritical', with reference to the hidden contents of the lidded pot, from *marmotter* 'to mutter' + *mite* 'cat'.

marmoreal /mɑːˈmɔːrɪəl/ ▸ **adjective** literary made of or compared to marble: *the marmoreal skin took on the flush of colour*.
– DERIVATIVES **marmoreally** adverb.
– ORIGIN late 18th cent.: from Latin *marmoreus* (from *marmor* 'marble') + **-AL**.

marmoset /ˈmɑːməzɛt/ ▸ **noun** a small tropical American monkey with a silky coat and a long tail.
● Family Callitrichidae (or Callithricidae): genus *Callithrix* (three species), and the **pygmy marmoset** (*Cebuella pygmaea*).
– ORIGIN late Middle English (also in the sense 'grotesque figure'): from Old French *marmouset* 'grotesque image', of unknown ultimate origin.

marmot /ˈmɑːmət/ ▸ **noun** a heavily built, gregarious burrowing rodent of mountainous country in both Eurasia and North America. ● Genus *Marmota*, family Sciuridae: several species.
– ORIGIN early 17th cent.: from French *marmotte*, probably via Romansh *murmont* from late Latin *mus montanus* 'mountain mouse'.

Marne /mɑːn/, French /maʀn/ a river of east central France, which rises in the Langres plateau north of Dijon and flows 525 km (328 miles) north and west to join the Seine near Paris. Its valley was the scene of two important battles in the First World War. The first battle (September 1914) halted and repelled the German advance on Paris; the second (July 1918) ended the final German offensive.

marocain /ˌmarəˈkeɪn/ ▸ **noun** [mass noun] a dress fabric of ribbed crêpe, made of silk or wool or both.
– ORIGIN 1920s: from French, literally 'Moroccan', from *Maroc* 'Morocco'.

Maronite /ˈmarənʌɪt/ ▸ **noun** a member of a Christian sect of Syrian origin, living chiefly in Lebanon and in communion with the Roman Catholic Church.
▸ **adjective** relating to the Maronites.
– ORIGIN early 16th cent.: from medieval Latin *Maronita*, from the name of John *Maro*, a 5th-cent. Syrian religious leader, who may have been the first Maronite patriarch.

Maroon ▸ **noun** a member of any of various communities in parts of the Caribbean who were originally descended from escaped slaves. In the 18th century Jamaican Maroons fought two wars against the British, both of which ended with treaties affirming the independence of the Maroons.
– ORIGIN mid 17th cent.: from French *marron* 'feral', from Spanish *cimarrón* 'wild', (as a noun) 'runaway slave'.

maroon[1] ▸ **adjective** of a brownish-red colour.
▸ **noun 1** [mass noun] a brownish-red colour.
2 chiefly Brit. a firework that makes a loud bang, used as a signal or warning. [early 19th cent.: so named because the firework makes the noise of a chestnut (see below) bursting in the fire.]
– ORIGIN late 17th cent. (in the sense 'chestnut'): from French *marron* 'chestnut', via Italian from medieval Greek *maraon*. The sense relating to colour dates from the late 18th cent.

maroon[2] ▸ **verb** [with obj.] leave (someone) trapped and alone in an inaccessible place, especially an island: *a novel about schoolboys marooned on a desert island*.
– ORIGIN early 18th cent.: from **MAROON**, originally in the form *marooned* 'lost in the wilds'.

marque[1] /mɑːk/ ▸ **noun** a make of car, as distinct from a specific model.
– ORIGIN early 20th cent.: from French, back-formation from *marquer* 'to brand', of Scandinavian origin.

marque[2] /mɑːk/ ▸ **noun** see **LETTER OF MARQUE**.

marquee /mɑːˈkiː/ ▸ **noun 1** chiefly Brit. a large tent used for social or commercial functions.
2 N. Amer. a canopy projecting over the entrance to a theatre, hotel, or other building. ■ [as modifier] leading; pre-eminent: *a marquee player*. [with allusion to the practice of billing the name of an entertainer on the canopy over the entrance to a theatre.]
– ORIGIN late 17th cent.: from **MARQUISE**, taken as plural and assimilated to **-EE**.

marquesa /mɑːˈkeɪzə/ ▸ **noun** a Spanish marchioness.
– ORIGIN Spanish.

Marquesan /mɑːˈkeɪz(ə)n, -s(ə)n/ ▸ **noun 1** a native or inhabitant of the Marquesas Islands, especially a member of the aboriginal Polynesian people of these islands.
2 [mass noun] the Polynesian language of the Marquesans.
▸ **adjective** relating to the Marquesans or their language.

Marquesas Islands /mɑːˈkeɪzəs, -səs/ a group of volcanic islands in the South Pacific, forming part of French Polynesia; pop. 8,658 (2007). The islands were annexed by France in 1842. The largest island is Hiva Oa, on which the French painter Paul Gauguin spent the last two years of his life.

marquess /ˈmɑːkwɪs/ ▸ **noun** a British nobleman ranking above an earl and below a duke. Compare with **MARQUIS**.
– ORIGIN early 16th cent.: variant of **MARQUIS**.

marquessate /ˈmɑːkwɪsət/ ▸ **noun** variant spelling of **MARQUISATE**.

marquetry /ˈmɑːkɪtri/ ▸ **noun** [mass noun] inlaid work made from small pieces of coloured wood or other materials, used for the decoration of furniture.
– ORIGIN mid 16th cent.: from French *marqueterie*, from *marqueter* 'to variegate'.

Marquette /mɑːˈkɛt/, French /maʀkɛt/, Jacques (1637–75), French Jesuit missionary and explorer. Arriving in North America in 1666, he played a prominent part in the attempt to convert the American Indians to Christianity, and explored the Wisconsin and Mississippi Rivers.

Márquez, Gabriel García, see **GARCÍA MÁRQUEZ**.

marquis /ˈmɑːkwɪs/ ▸ **noun** (in some European countries) a nobleman ranking above a count and below a duke. Compare with **MARQUESS**. ■ another term for **MARQUESS**.
– ORIGIN Middle English: from Old French *marchis*, reinforced by Old French *marquis*, both from the base of **MARCH**[2].

marquisate /ˈmɑːkwɪsət/ (also **marquessate**) ▸ **noun** the rank of a marquess or marquis. ■ the territorial lordship or possessions of a marquis or margrave.
– ORIGIN early 16th cent.: from **MARQUIS**, on the pattern of French *marquisat*, Italian *marchesato*.

Marquis de Sade see **SADE**.

marquise /mɑːˈkiːz/ ▸ **noun 1** the wife or widow of a marquis. ■ a woman holding the rank of marquis in her own right.
2 a finger ring set with a pointed oval gem or cluster of gems.
3 archaic term for **MARQUEE**.
4 a chilled dessert similar to a chocolate mousse.
– ORIGIN early 17th cent.: French, feminine of **MARQUIS**.

marquisette /ˌmɑːkɪˈzɛt/ ▸ **noun** [mass noun] a fine light cotton, rayon, or silk gauze fabric, now used for net curtains.
– ORIGIN early 20th cent.: from French, diminutive of **MARQUISE**.

marra (also **marrer**) ▸ **noun** variant spelling of **MARROW**[2].

Marrakech /ˌmarəˈkɛʃ/ (also **Marrakesh**) a city in western Morocco, in the foothills of the High Atlas Mountains; pop. 1,070,838 (2004). It was founded in 1062 as the capital of the Almoravids.

marram grass /ˈmarəm/ (also **marram**) ▸ **noun** a coarse European grass of coastal sand dunes, binding the loose sand with its tough rhizomes. ● *Ammophila arenaria*, family Gramineae.
– ORIGIN mid 17th cent.: from Old Norse *marálmr*, from *marr* 'sea' + *hálmr* 'haulm'.

Marrano /məˈrɑːnəʊ/ ▸ **noun** (pl. **Marranos**) (in medieval Spain) a Jew or Moor who had converted to Christianity, especially one who professed conversion in order to avoid persecution.
– ORIGIN Spanish, of unknown origin.

marri /ˈmari/ ▸ **noun** (pl. **marris**) an Australian eucalyptus tree with rough grey-brown bark and ornamental flowers. ● *Eucalyptus calophylla*, family Myrtaceae.
– ORIGIN mid 19th cent.: from Nyungar.

marriage ▸ **noun 1** the formal union of a man and a woman, typically as recognized by law, by which they become husband and wife: *she has three children from a previous marriage*. ■ [mass noun] the state of being married: *women want equality in marriage*. ■ informal a similar union between partners of the same sex.
2 a combination or mixture of elements: *her music is a marriage of funk, jazz, and hip hop*.
– PHRASES **by marriage** as a result of a marriage. **in marriage** as husband or wife: *he asked my father for my hand in marriage*.
– ORIGIN Middle English: from Old French *mariage*, from *marier* 'marry'.

marriageable ▸ **adjective** fit or suitable for marriage, especially in being wealthy or of the right age.
– DERIVATIVES **marriageability** noun.

marriage broker ▸ **noun** (in a culture where arranged marriages are customary) a person who arranges marriages for a fee.

marriage bureau ▸ **noun** Brit. dated an establishment which arranges introductions between people who want to get married.

marriage certificate ▸ **noun** Brit. a copy of the record of a legal marriage, with details of names, date, etc.

marriage guidance ▸ **noun** [mass noun] (in the UK) counselling of married couples who have problems in their relationship.

marriage licence ▸ **noun** Brit. a licence which couples must obtain before getting married, except in civil marriage by certificate or church marriage authorized by the publication of banns. ■ US a marriage certificate.

marriage lines ▸ **plural noun** informal, chiefly Brit. a marriage certificate.

marriage of convenience ▸ **noun** a marriage that is arranged for practical, financial, or political reasons.

Marriage of the Adriatic a ceremony formerly held on Ascension Day in Venice to symbolize the city's sea power, during which the doge dropped a ring into the water from his official barge.

marriage portion ▸ **noun** see **PORTION**.

marriage settlement ▸ **noun** Brit. a legal arrangement by which property is given or secured when a couple get married.

married ▸ **adjective** (of two people) united in marriage. ■ (of a person) having a husband or wife: *a happily married man*. ■ relating to marriage: *married life*. ■ closely linked: *in the seventeenth century science was still **married to** religion*.
▸ **plural noun** (**marrieds**) married people: *we were young marrieds during World War Two*.

marron /ˈmarən/ ▸ **noun** (pl. **same** or **marrons**) a large Australian freshwater crayfish which lives on the sandy bottoms of rivers and streams. ● *Cherax tenuimanus*, infraorder Astacidea.
– ORIGIN 1940s: from Nyungar *marran*.

marron glacé /ˌmarɒ̃ ˈglaseɪ/ ▸ **noun** (pl. **marrons glacés** pronunc. **same**) a chestnut preserved in and coated with sugar.
– ORIGIN French, 'iced chestnut'.

marrow[1] ▸ **noun 1** (also **vegetable marrow**) Brit. a long white-fleshed gourd with green skin, which is eaten as a vegetable.
2 the plant of the gourd family which produces this. ● *Cucurbita pepo*, family Cucurbitaceae.
3 (also **bone marrow**) [mass noun] a soft fatty substance in the cavities of bones, in which blood cells are produced.
4 the essential part of something: *such men were the marrow of the organization*.
– PHRASES **to the marrow** to one's innermost being: *a sight which chilled me to the marrow*.
– DERIVATIVES **marrowy** adjective.
– ORIGIN Old English *mearg*, *mærg* (in sense 3), of Germanic origin; related to Dutch *merg* and German *Mark*. Sense 1 dates from the early 19th cent.

marrow[2] (also **marra**, **marrer**) ▸ **noun** N. English & Scottish **1** a friend, companion, or workmate (often used as a form of address): *come here, marrer, we need to talk*.
2 something that forms a pair with something else; a counterpart or twin.
– ORIGIN late Middle English: probably from Old Norse *margr* 'many', also 'friendly, communicative'.

marrowbone ▸ **noun** a bone containing edible marrow.

marrowfat pea ▸ **noun** a pea of a large variety which is processed and sold in cans.

marry[1] ▸ verb (**marries, marrying, married**) [with obj.] **1** join in marriage: *I was married in church | my sister got married to a Welshman.* ■ take (someone) as one's wife or husband in marriage: *Eric asked me to marry him.* ■ [no obj.] enter into marriage: *they had no plans to marry.* ■ [no obj.] (**marry into**) become a member of (a family) by marriage. ■ (of a parent or guardian) give (a son or daughter) in marriage, especially for reasons of expediency: *her parents married her to a wealthy landowner.*
2 join together; combine harmoniously: *the show **marries** poetry **with** art.* ■ [no obj.] blend or combine with something: *most Chardonnays don't **marry** well **with** salmon.* ■ Nautical splice (rope ends) together without increasing their girth.
– PHRASES **be the marrying kind** [with negative] be the type of person who is likely or inclined to marry. **marry in haste, repent at leisure** proverb those who rush impetuously into marriage may spend a long time regretting doing so. **marry money** informal marry a rich person.
– ORIGIN Middle English: from Old French *marier*, from Latin *maritare*, from *maritus*, literally 'married', (as a noun) 'husband'.

marry[2] ▸ exclamation archaic expressing surprise, indignation, or emphatic assertion.
– ORIGIN late Middle English: variant of **MARY**[1].

Marryat /ˈmarɪət/, Frederick (1792–1848), English novelist and naval officer; known as **Captain Marryat**. Notable works: *Peter Simple* (1833), *Mr Midshipman Easy* (1836), *The Children of the New Forest* (1847).

Mars 1 Roman Mythology the god of war and the most important Roman god after Jupiter. The month of March is named after him. Greek equivalent **ARES**.
2 Astronomy a small reddish planet which is the fourth in order from the sun and is periodically visible to the naked eye.

> Mars orbits between earth and Jupiter at an average distance of 228 million km from the sun, and has an equatorial diameter of 6,787 km. Its characteristic red colour arises from the iron-rich minerals covering its surface. There is a tenuous atmosphere of carbon dioxide and the seasonal polar caps are mainly of frozen carbon dioxide. Unambiguous evidence of life has yet to be found. There are two small satellites, Phobos and Deimos.

M

Marsala /mɑːˈsɑːlə/ ▸ noun [mass noun] a dark, sweet fortified dessert wine that resembles sherry, produced in Sicily.
– ORIGIN named after *Marsala*, a town in Sicily where it was originally made.

Marsanne /mɑːˈsan/ ▸ noun [mass noun] a variety of white wine grape originating in the northern Rhône area of France.
– ORIGIN the name of a town in southern France.

Marseillaise /ˌmɑːseɪˈjɛz, -s(ə)ˈleɪz/ the national anthem of France, written by Rouget de Lisle in 1792 and first sung in Paris by Marseilles patriots.
– ORIGIN French, feminine of *Marseillais* 'of Marseilles'.

Marseilles /mɑːˈseɪ, -ˈseɪlz/ a city and port on the Mediterranean coast of southern France; pop. 860,363 (2007). French name **Marseille** /marsɛj/.

Mars Global Surveyor see **GLOBAL SURVEYOR**.

Marsh, Dame Ngaio (Edith) (1899–1982), New Zealand writer of detective fiction. Her works include *Vintage Murder* (1937) and *Final Curtain* (1947).

marsh ▸ noun an area of low-lying land which is flooded in wet seasons or at high tide, and typically remains waterlogged at all times.
– ORIGIN Old English *mer(i)sc* (perhaps influenced by late Latin *mariscus* 'marsh'), of West Germanic origin.

marshal ▸ noun **1** an officer of the highest rank in the armed forces of some countries. ■ Brit. historical a high-ranking officer of state.
2 US a federal or municipal law-enforcement officer. ■ the head of a police department. ■ N. Amer. the head of a fire department.
3 an official responsible for supervising sports events, and for controlling crowds in other public events.
4 (in the UK) an official accompanying a judge on circuit to act as secretary and personal assistant.
▸ verb (**marshals, marshalling, marshalled**; US **marshals, marshaling, marshaled**) [with obj.] **1** assemble and arrange (a group of people, especially troops) in order: *the general marshalled his troops.* ■ bring together and arrange in order (facts, ideas, objects, etc.): *he paused for a moment, as if marshalling his thoughts.* ■ position (rolling stock) in the correct order. ■ direct the movement of (an aircraft) on the ground at an airport.
2 Heraldry combine (coats of arms) to indicate marriage, descent, or the bearing of office.
– DERIVATIVES **marshaller** noun, **marshalship** noun.
– ORIGIN Middle English (denoting a high-ranking officer of state): from Old French *mareschal* 'farrier, commander', from late Latin *mariscalcus*, from Germanic elements meaning 'horse' (compare with **MARE**[1]) and 'servant'.

Marshall, George C. (1880–1959), American general and statesman; full name *George Catlett Marshall*. As US Secretary of State (1947–9) he initiated the programme of economic aid to European countries known as the Marshall Plan. Nobel Peace Prize (1953).

Marshallese /ˌmɑːʃəˈliːz/ ▸ noun (pl. **same**) **1** a native or inhabitant of the Marshall Islands.
2 [mass noun] the Micronesian language of the Marshallese.
▸ adjective relating to the Marshall Islands, their inhabitants, or their language.

marshalling yard ▸ noun Brit. a large railway yard in which freight wagons are organized into trains.

Marshall Islands (also **the Marshalls**) a country consisting of two chains of islands in the NW Pacific; pop. 64,500 (est. 2009); languages, English (official), local Austronesian languages; capital, Majuro.

> The islands were made a German protectorate in 1885. After being under Japanese mandate following the First World War they were administered by the US as part of the Pacific Islands Trust Territory from 1947 until 1986, when they became a republic in free association with the US.

– ORIGIN named after John Marshall, an English adventurer who visited the islands in 1788.

Marshall Plan a programme of financial aid and other initiatives, sponsored by the US, designed to boost the economies of western European countries after the Second World War. It was originally advocated by Secretary of State George C. Marshall and passed by Congress in 1948. Official name **EUROPEAN RECOVERY PROGRAM**.

Marshal of the Royal Air Force ▸ noun the highest rank of officer in the RAF.

marshalsea /ˈmɑːʃ(ə)lsiː/ ▸ noun (in England) a court formerly held before the steward and the knight marshal of the royal household. It was abolished in 1849. ■ (**the Marshalsea**) a former prison in Southwark, London, under the control of the knight marshal.
– ORIGIN late Middle English (earlier *marchalcy*): from Anglo-Norman French *marschalcie*, from late Latin *mariscalcia*, from *mariscalcus* 'marshal'.

Marsh Arab ▸ noun a member of a semi-nomadic Arab people inhabiting marshland in southern Iraq, near the confluence of the Tigris and Euphrates Rivers.

marshbird ▸ noun a bird that frequents marshes and reed beds, in particular: ● a brown streaked Australian warbler (genus *Megalurus*, family Sylviidae). Also called **GRASSBIRD** ● a South American bird of the American blackbird family (genus *Pseudoleistes*, family Icteridae).

marsh fever ▸ noun [mass noun] archaic malaria, so called in reference to the marshes where the mosquitoes that transmit it breed.

marsh frog ▸ noun a large, gregarious European frog with warty skin and a loud laughing call. ● *Rana ridibunda*, family Ranidae.

marsh gas ▸ noun [mass noun] methane, especially as generated by decaying matter in marshes.

marsh harrier ▸ noun a dark-backed Old World harrier that frequents marshes and reed beds. ● Genus *Circus*, family Accipitridae: several species.

marsh hawk ▸ noun North American term for **HEN HARRIER**.

marshland ▸ noun [mass noun] (also **marshlands**) land consisting of marshes.

marshmallow ▸ noun [mass noun] a soft item of confectionery made from a mixture of sugar, albumen, and gelatin.

marsh mallow ▸ noun a tall pink-flowered European plant which grows in brackish marshes. The roots were formerly used to make marshmallow, and it is sometimes cultivated for medicinal use. ● *Althaea officinalis*, family Malvaceae.

marsh marigold ▸ noun a plant of the buttercup family which has large yellow flowers and grows in damp ground and shallow water, native to north temperate regions. Also called **KINGCUP**. ● *Caltha palustris*, family Ranunculaceae.

marsh tit ▸ noun a Eurasian woodland tit (songbird) with mainly grey-brown plumage, a shiny black cap, and white cheeks. ● *Parus palustris*, family Paridae.

marsh treader ▸ noun North American term for **WATER MEASURER**.

marshwort ▸ noun a white-flowered plant of the parsley family which grows beside streams and in boggy areas. ● Genus *Apium*, family Umbelliferae: several species.

marshy ▸ adjective (**marshier, marshiest**) characteristic of or resembling a marsh; waterlogged: *the marshy ground towards the sea.*
– DERIVATIVES **marshiness** noun.

Mars Pathfinder see **PATHFINDER**.

Marston Moor, Battle of a battle of the English Civil War, fought in 1644 on Marston Moor near York, in which the Royalist armies suffered a defeat which fatally weakened Charles I's cause.

marsupial /mɑːˈsuːpɪəl/ Zoology ▸ noun a mammal of an order whose members are born incompletely developed and are typically carried and suckled in a pouch on the mother's belly. Marsupials are found chiefly in Australia and New Guinea, and also in America. ● Order Marsupialia and infraclass Metatheria, subclass Theria.
▸ adjective relating to the marsupials.
– ORIGIN late 17th cent. (in the sense 'resembling a pouch'): from modern Latin *marsupialis*, via Latin from Greek *marsupion* 'pouch' (see **MARSUPIUM**).

marsupial cat ▸ noun a white-spotted catlike marsupial related to the quolls, native to New Guinea. ● *Dasyurus albopunctatus*, family Dasyuridae.

marsupial mole ▸ noun a mole-like burrowing Australian marsupial with yellow fur and a horny shield on the front of the head. ● *Notoryctes typhlops*, the only member of the family Notoryctidae.

marsupial mouse ▸ noun a carnivorous mouse-like marsupial native to Australia and New Guinea. ● Several genera and species, family Dasyuridae.

marsupium /mɑːˈsuːpɪəm/ ▸ noun (pl. **marsupia** /-pɪə/) Zoology a pouch that protects eggs, offspring, or reproductive structures, especially the pouch of a female marsupial mammal.
– ORIGIN mid 17th cent.: via Latin from Greek *marsupion*, diminutive of *marsipos* 'purse'.

Marsyas /ˈmɑːsɪəs/ Greek Mythology a satyr who challenged Apollo to a contest in flute playing and was flayed alive when he lost.

mart ▸ noun [usu. with modifier] a trade centre or market: *a liquor mart.*
– ORIGIN late Middle English: from Middle Dutch *mart*, variant of *marct* 'market'.

Martaban, Gulf of /ˌmɑːtəˈbɑːn/ an inlet of the Andaman Sea, a part of the Indian Ocean, on the coast of SE Burma (Myanmar) east of Rangoon.

martagon lily /ˈmɑːtəg(ə)n/ ▸ noun a Eurasian lily that has small purple flowers said to resemble turbans. Also called **TURK'S CAP LILY**. ● *Lilium martagon*, family Liliaceae.
– ORIGIN late Middle English (as *mortagon*): from medieval Latin *martagon*, of uncertain origin; cf. Ottoman Turkish *martagān*, denoting a kind of turban.

Martel, Charles, see **CHARLES MARTEL**.

Martello /mɑːˈtɛləʊ/ (also **Martello tower**) ▸ noun (pl. **Martellos**) any of numerous small circular forts that were erected for defence purposes along the coasts of Britain during the Napoleonic Wars.
– ORIGIN alteration (by association with Italian *martello* 'hammer') of Cape *Mortella* in Corsica, where such a tower proved difficult for the English to capture in 1794.

marten /ˈmɑːtɪn/ ▸ noun a semi-arboreal weasel-like mammal found in Eurasia and North America, hunted for its fur in some countries. ● Genus *Martes*, family Mustelidae: several species.
– ORIGIN Middle English: from Old French (*peau*) *martrine* 'marten (fur)', from *martre*, of West Germanic origin.

martensite /ˈmɑːtɪnzʌɪt/ ▸ noun [mass noun] Metallurgy a hard and very brittle solid solution of carbon in iron that is the main constituent of hardened steel.
– DERIVATIVES **martensitic** adjective.

– ORIGIN late 19th cent.: named after Adolf *Martens* (1850–1914), German metallurgist, + **-ITE[1]**.

Martha (in the New Testament) the sister of Lazarus and Mary and friend of Jesus (Luke 10:40). ■ (as noun **a Martha**) a woman who keeps herself very busy with domestic affairs.

Martha's Vineyard a resort island off the coast of Massachusetts, to the south of Cape Cod.

Martial /ˈmɑːʃ(ə)l/ (*c.*40–*c.*104 AD), Roman epigrammatist, born in Spain; Latin name *Marcus Valerius Martialis*. His fifteen books of epigrams, in a variety of metres, reflect all facets of Roman life.

martial /ˈmɑːʃ(ə)l/ ▸ **adjective** relating to fighting or war: *martial bravery*.
– DERIVATIVES **martially** adverb.
– ORIGIN late Middle English: from Old French, or from Latin *martialis*, from *Mars*, *Mart-* (see **MARS**).

martial arts ▸ **plural noun** various sports, which originated chiefly in Japan, Korea, and China as forms of self-defence or attack, such as judo, karate, and kendo.
– DERIVATIVES **martial artist** noun.

martial eagle ▸ **noun** a brown eagle with a brown-spotted white belly, which is Africa's largest eagle. ● *Polmaetus bellicosus*, family Accipitridae.

martial law ▸ **noun** [mass noun] military government, involving the suspension of ordinary law.

Martian ▸ **adjective** relating to the planet Mars or its supposed inhabitants.
▸ **noun** a hypothetical or fictional inhabitant of Mars.
– ORIGIN late Middle English (in the senses 'subject to Mars's influence' and 'martial'): from Latin *Mars*, *Mart-* (see **MARS**) + **-IAN**.

Martin[1], Dean (1917–95), American singer and actor; born *Dino Paul Crocetti*. He joined with Frank Sinatra and Sammy Davis Jr (1925–90) in a number of films, including *Bells are Ringing* (1960), and had his own television show from 1965.

Martin[2], Sir George (Leonard) (b.1926), English record producer. He was involved with most of the Beatles' recordings, producing the revolutionary *Revolver* (1966) and *Sergeant Pepper's Lonely Hearts Club Band* (1967).

Martin[3], Paul (Edgar Philippe) (b.1938), Canadian Liberal statesman, Prime Minister 2003–2006.

martin ▸ **noun** a swift-flying insectivorous songbird of the swallow family, typically having a less strongly forked tail than a swallow. ● Family Hirundinidae: several genera and numerous species, e.g. the **house martin**.
– ORIGIN late Middle English: probably a shortening of obsolete *martinet*, from French, probably from St *Martin* of Tours, celebrated at **MARTINMAS**.

Martin, St (d.397), French bishop (Bishop of Tours from 371), a patron saint of France. When giving half his cloak to a beggar he received a vision of Christ, after which he was baptized. Feast day, 11 November.

Martineau /ˈmɑːtɪnəʊ/, Harriet (1802–76), English writer. She wrote mainly on social, economic, and historical subjects, and is known for her twenty-five-volume series *Illustrations of Political Economy* (1832–4) and her translation of Auguste Comte's *Philosophie positive* (1853).

martinet /ˌmɑːtɪˈnɛt/ ▸ **noun** a person who demands complete obedience; a strict disciplinarian.
– ORIGIN late 17th cent. (denoting the system of drill invented by Martinet): named after Jean *Martinet*, 17th cent. French drill master.

martingale /ˈmɑːtɪŋɡeɪl/ ▸ **noun 1** a strap or set of straps running from the noseband or reins to the girth of a horse, used to prevent the horse from raising its head too high.
2 [mass noun] a gambling system of continually doubling the stakes in the hope of an eventual win that must yield a net profit.
– ORIGIN late 16th cent.: from French, from Spanish *almártaga*, from Arabic *al-marta'a* 'the fastening', influenced by *martingale*, from Occitan *martegal* 'inhabitant of Martigues (in Provence)'.

Martini[1] /mɑːˈtiːni/, Italian /marˈtini/, Simone (*c.*1284–1344), Italian painter. His work is characterized by strong outlines and the use of rich colour, as in *The Annunciation* (1333).

Martini[2] /mɑːˈtiːni/ ▸ **noun 1** [mass noun] trademark a type of vermouth produced in Italy.
2 a cocktail made from gin and dry vermouth.
– ORIGIN named after *Martini* and Rossi, an Italian firm selling vermouth.

Martinique /ˌmɑːtɪˈniːk/, French /maʀtinik/ an island in the Caribbean, in the Lesser Antilles group; pop. 399,000 (est. 2009); capital, Fort-de-France. It is an overseas department of France.
– DERIVATIVES **Martiniquan** (also **Martinican**) noun & adjective.

Martinist ▸ **noun** an adherent of a form of mystical pantheism developed by the French philosopher L. C. de Saint-Martin (1743–1803).
– DERIVATIVES **Martinism** noun.

Martinmas /ˈmɑːtɪnməs/ ▸ **noun** St Martin's Day, 11 November.

Martinware ▸ **noun** [mass noun] a type of brown salt-glazed pottery made by the Martin brothers in Southall, London, in the late 19th and early 20th centuries.

martlet /ˈmɑːtlɪt/ ▸ **noun** Heraldry a bird like a swallow without feet, borne as a charge or a mark of cadency for a fourth son. ■ literary a swift or house martin.
– ORIGIN late Middle English (denoting a swift): from Old French *merlet*, influenced by *martinet* (see **MARTIN**).

martyr ▸ **noun** a person who is killed because of their religious or other beliefs: *the first Christian martyr*. ■ a person who displays or exaggerates their discomfort or distress in order to obtain sympathy: *she wanted to play the martyr*. ■ (**martyr to**) a constant sufferer from (an ailment): *I'm a martyr to migraine!*
▸ **verb** [with obj.] kill (someone) because of their beliefs: *she was martyred for her faith*. ■ cause great pain or distress to: *there was no need to martyr themselves again*.
– DERIVATIVES **martyrization** (also **martyrisation**) noun.
– ORIGIN Old English *martir*, via ecclesiastical Latin from Greek *martur* 'witness' (in Christian use, 'martyr').

martyrdom ▸ **noun** [mass noun] the death or suffering of a martyr. ■ a display of pretended or exaggerated suffering to obtain sympathy.
– ORIGIN Old English *martyrdōm* (see **MARTYR**, **-DOM**).

martyred ▸ **adjective** (of a person) having been martyred. ■ (of an expression or manner) showing pretended or exaggerated suffering so as to obtain sympathy: *he got into the car with a martyred air*.

martyrology ▸ **noun** (pl. **martyrologies**) [mass noun] the branch of history that deals with the lives of martyrs. ■ [count noun] a list of martyrs.
– DERIVATIVES **martyrological** adjective, **martyrologist** noun.
– ORIGIN late 16th cent.: via medieval Latin from ecclesiastical Greek *marturologion*, from *martur* 'martyr' + *logos* 'account'.

martyry ▸ **noun** (pl. **martyries**) a shrine or church erected in honour of a martyr.
– ORIGIN Middle English (denoting martyrdom): via medieval Latin from Greek *marturion* 'martyrdom'.

Maruts /ˈmʌrʊts/ Hinduism the sons of Rudra. In the Rig Veda they are the storm gods, Indra's helpers. Also called **RUDRAS**.

marvel ▸ **verb** (**marvels**, **marvelling**, **marvelled**; US **marvels**, **marveling**, **marveled**) [no obj.] be filled with wonder or astonishment: *she* **marvelled at** *Geoffrey's composure* | [with direct speech] *'It looks huge,' marvelled Clare*.
▸ **noun** a wonderful or astonishing person or thing: *the marvels of technology*.
– DERIVATIVES **marveller** noun.
– ORIGIN Middle English (as a noun): from Old French *merveille*, from late Latin *mirabilia*, neuter plural of Latin *mirabilis* 'wonderful', from *mirari* 'wonder at'.

Marvell /mɑːˈvɛl, ˈmɑːv(ə)l/, Andrew (1621–78), English metaphysical poet. He was best known during his lifetime for his verse satires and pamphlets attacking the corruption of Charles II and his ministers; most of his poetry was published posthumously and was not recognized until the 20th century. Notable poems: 'To his Coy Mistress' and 'Bermudas'.

marvellous (US **marvelous**) ▸ **adjective** causing great wonder; extraordinary: *these marvellous technological toys are fun to play with*. ■ extremely good or pleasing; splendid: *you have done a marvellous job*.
– DERIVATIVES **marvellously** adverb, **marvellousness** noun.
– ORIGIN Middle English: from Old French *merveillus*, from *merveille* (see **MARVEL**).

marvel of Peru ▸ **noun** a tropical American herbaceous plant with fragrant trumpet-shaped flowers which open late in the afternoon. Also called **FOUR O'CLOCK PLANT**. ● *Mirabilis jalapa*, family Nyctaginaceae.

marvy ▸ **adjective** informal wonderful; marvellous.

Marwari /məˈwɑːri/ ▸ **noun** [mass noun] a native or inhabitant of Rajasthan in India. ■ the Indic language of Rajasthan, spoken by about 10 million people.
▸ **adjective** relating to the Marwari language or people.
– ORIGIN from Hindi *Mārvār*, from Sanskrit *maru* 'desert'.

Marx, Karl (Heinrich) (1818–83), German political philosopher and economist, resident in England from 1849. The founder of modern communism with Friedrich Engels, he collaborated with him in the writing of the *Communist Manifesto* (1848), and enlarged it into a series of books, most notably the three-volume *Das Kapital*.
– DERIVATIVES **Marxian** adjective & noun.

Marx Brothers a family of American comedians, consisting of the brothers **Chico** (Leonard, 1886–1961), **Harpo** (Adolph Arthur, 1888–1964), **Groucho** (Julius Henry, 1890–1977), and **Zeppo** (Herbert, 1901–79). Their films, which are characterized by their anarchic humour, include *Duck Soup* (1933) and *A Night at the Opera* (1935).

Marxism ▸ **noun** [mass noun] the political and economic theories of Karl Marx and Friedrich Engels, later developed by their followers to form the basis of communism.

> Central to Marxist theory is an explanation of social change in terms of economic factors, according to which the means of production provide the economic *base* which influences or determines the political and ideological *superstructure*. Marx and Engels predicted the revolutionary overthrow of capitalism by the proletariat and the eventual attainment of a classless communist society.

– DERIVATIVES **Marxist** noun & adjective.

Marxism–Leninism ▸ **noun** [mass noun] the doctrines of Marx as interpreted and put into effect by Lenin in the Soviet Union and (at first) by Mao Zedong in China.
– DERIVATIVES **Marxist–Leninist** noun & adjective.

Mary[1], mother of Jesus; known as **the (Blessed) Virgin Mary**, or **St Mary**, or **Our Lady**. According to the Gospels she was a virgin betrothed to Joseph and conceived Jesus by the power of the Holy Spirit. She is venerated by Catholic and Orthodox Churches. Feast days, 1 January (Roman Catholic Church), 25 March (Annunciation), 15 August (Assumption), 8 September (Nativity), 8 December (Immaculate Conception).

M

Mary[2] the name of two queens of England: ■ **Mary I** (1516–58), daughter of Henry VIII, reigned 1553–8; known as **Mary Tudor** or **Bloody Mary**. In an attempt to reverse the country's turn towards Protestantism she instigated the series of religious persecutions by which she earned her nickname. ■ **Mary II** (1662–94), daughter of James II, reigned 1689–94. Having been invited to replace her Catholic father on the throne after his deposition in 1689, she insisted that her husband, William of Orange, be crowned along with her.

Mary[3] ▸ **noun** (pl. **Maries**) Austral. offensive an Aboriginal woman.

Mary, Queen of Scots (1542–87), daughter of James V, queen of Scotland 1542–67; known as **Mary Stuart**. A devout Catholic, she was unable to control her Protestant lords, and fled to England in 1567. She became the focus of several Catholic plots against Elizabeth I and was eventually beheaded.

Mary, St see **MARY[1]**.

Mary Celeste /ˌmɛːri sɪˈlɛst/ (also **Marie Celeste**) an American brig that was found afloat in the North Atlantic in December 1872 in perfect condition but abandoned. The fate of the crew and the reason for the abandonment of the ship remain a mystery.

Mary Jane ▸ **noun 1** a flat, round-toed shoe for women and girls, with a single strap across the top.
2 [mass noun] informal marijuana.
– ORIGIN 1920s: from the female forename *Mary Jane*.

Maryland a state of the eastern US, on the Atlantic coast, surrounding Chesapeake Bay; pop. 5,633,597 (est. 2008); capital, Annapolis. Colonized from England in the 17th century, it was one of the original thirteen states of the Union (1788).
– DERIVATIVES **Marylander** noun.
– ORIGIN named after Queen Henrietta *Maria*, wife of Charles I.

Mary Magdalene, St /ˈmaɡdəliːn/ (also **Magdalen**) (in the New Testament) a woman of Magdala in Galilee. She was a follower of Jesus, who cured her of evil spirits (Luke 8:2); she is also traditionally identified with the 'sinner' of Luke 7:37. Feast day, 22 July.

Mary Rose a heavily armed ship, built for Henry VIII, that in 1545 sank with the loss of nearly all her company when going out to engage the French fleet off Portsmouth. The hull was raised in 1982.

Mary Stuart see MARY, QUEEN OF SCOTS.

Mary Tudor, Mary I of England (see MARY²).

marzipan /ˈmɑːzɪpan, ˌmɑːzɪˈpan/ ▸ noun [mass noun] a sweet yellow or white paste of ground almonds, sugar, and egg whites, used to coat cakes or to make confectionery. ■ [count noun] a sweet or small cake made of or coated with marzipan.
▸ verb [with obj.] (usu. as adj. **marzipanned**) cover with marzipan.
– ORIGIN late 15th cent. (as *marchpane*): from Italian *marzapane*, perhaps from Arabic. The form *marchpane* (influenced by MARCH and obsolete *pain* 'bread') was more usual until the late 19th cent., when *marzipan* (influenced by German *Marzipan*) displaced it.

mas /mɑːs/ ▸ noun [mass noun] W. Indian carnival celebrations.
– ORIGIN abbreviation of MASQUERADE.

masa /ˈmasa/ ▸ noun [mass noun] (in Latin American cuisine) dough made from maize flour and used to make tortillas, tamales, etc.
– ORIGIN Spanish.

Masaccio /maˈsatʃɪəʊ/, (1401–28), Italian painter; born *Tommaso Giovanni di Simone Guidi*. A pioneer in the application of the laws of perspective to painting, he is remembered particularly for his frescoes in the Brancacci Chapel in the church of Santa Maria del Carmine in Florence (1424–7).

Masada /məˈsɑːdə/ the site of the ruins of a palace and fortification built by Herod the Great on the SW shore of the Dead Sea in the 1st century BC. It was a Jewish stronghold in the Zealots' revolt against the Romans (AD 66–73) and was the scene in AD 73 of mass suicide by the Jewish defenders when the Romans breached the citadel after a siege of nearly two years.

M

Masai /ˈmɑːsʌɪ, məˈsʌɪ, mɑːˈsʌɪ/ (also **Maasai**) ▸ noun (pl. **same** or **Masais**) **1** a member of a pastoral people living in Tanzania and Kenya.
2 [mass noun] the Nilotic language of the Masai, with about 700,000 speakers.
▸ adjective relating to the Masai or their language.
– ORIGIN the name in Masai.

masala /məˈsɑːlə/ ▸ noun [mass noun] a mixture of ground spices used in Indian cookery. ■ a dish flavoured with masala: *chicken masala*. ■ someone or something that comprises a varied mixture of elements: *an Indian who grew up with a masala of influences in England, Jamaica, and Italy*.
– ORIGIN from Urdu *maṣālaḥ*, based on Arabic *maṣāliḥ* 'ingredients, materials'.

Masaryk /ˈmasərɪk/, Tomáš (Garrigue) (1850–1937), Czechoslovak statesman, President 1918–35. He became Czechoslovakia's first President when the country achieved independence in 1918.

Masbate /masˈbɑːti/ an island in the central Philippines; pop. 806,300 (est. 2009).

Mascagni /maˈskɑːnji/, Pietro (1863–1945), Italian composer and conductor. He is especially remembered for the opera *Cavalleria Rusticana* (1890).

mascara /maˈskɑːrə/ ▸ noun [mass noun] a cosmetic for darkening and thickening the eyelashes.
– DERIVATIVES **mascaraed** adjective.
– ORIGIN late 19th cent.: from Italian, literally 'mask', from Arabic *masḵara* 'buffoon'.

Mascarene Islands /ˌmaskəˈriːn/ (also **the Mascarenes**) a group of three islands in the western Indian Ocean, east of Madagascar, comprising Réunion, Mauritius, and Rodrigues.
– ORIGIN named after the 16th-cent. Portuguese navigator Pedro de *Mascarenhas*.

mascarpone /ˌmaskəˈpəʊneɪ, -ˈpəʊni/ ▸ noun [mass noun] a soft, mild Italian cream cheese.
– ORIGIN from Italian.

mascle /ˈmɑːsk(ə)l/ ▸ noun Heraldry a charge in the form of a lozenge with a central lozenge-shaped opening through which the field appears.
– ORIGIN late Middle English: from Anglo-Norman French, from Anglo-Latin *mascula* 'mesh'.

mascon /ˈmaskɒn/ ▸ noun a concentration of denser material below the surface of the moon or other body, causing a local increase in gravitational pull.
– ORIGIN 1960s: from *mas(s) con(centration)*.

mascot ▸ noun a person or thing that is supposed to bring good luck, especially one linked to a particular organization or event: *the team's dolphin mascot*.
– ORIGIN late 19th cent.: from French *mascotte*, from modern Provençal *mascotto*, feminine diminutive of *masco* 'witch'.

masculine ▸ adjective **1** having qualities or appearance traditionally associated with men: *he is outstandingly handsome and robust, very masculine*. ■ relating to men; male: *a masculine voice*.
2 Grammar of or denoting a gender of nouns and adjectives, conventionally regarded as male.
▸ noun (**the masculine**) the male sex or gender. ■ Grammar a masculine word or form.
– DERIVATIVES **masculinely** adverb.
– ORIGIN late Middle English (in grammatical use): via Old French from Latin *masculinus*, from *masculus* 'male'.

masculine rhyme ▸ noun Prosody a rhyme between final stressed syllables (e.g. *blow/flow, confess/redress*).

masculinist (also **masculist**) ▸ adjective characterized by or denoting attitudes or values held to be typical of men: *masculinist language*.
▸ noun an advocate of the rights or needs of men.

masculinity ▸ noun [mass noun] possession of the qualities traditionally associated with men: *a need for men to prove their masculinity through domination over women*.

masculinize (also **masculinise**) ▸ verb [with obj.] induce male physiological characteristics in. ■ make (someone or something) masculine in nature or appearance: *what feminism did was not to masculinize women but to ultra-feminize them*.
– DERIVATIVES **masculinization** noun.

Masefield /ˈmeɪsfiːld/, John (Edward) (1878–1967), English poet and novelist. He was appointed Poet Laureate in 1930. Notable works: *Salt-Water Ballads* (1902).

maser /ˈmeɪzə/ ▸ noun a device using the stimulated emission of radiation by excited atoms to amplify or generate coherent monochromatic electromagnetic radiation in the microwave range. Compare with LASER.
– ORIGIN 1950s: acronym from *microwave amplification by the stimulated emission of radiation*.

Maseru /məˈsɛːruː/ the capital of Lesotho, situated on the Caledon River near the border with the province of Free State in South Africa; pop. 211,000 (est. 2007).

mash ▸ verb [with obj.] **1** reduce (a food or other substance) to a pulpy mass by crushing it: *mash the beans to a paste* | (as adj. **mashed**) *mashed potato*. ■ crush or smash (something) to a pulp: *he almost had his head mashed by a slamming door*. ■ US & W. Indian informal press forcefully on (something): *the worst thing you can do is mash the brake pedal*. ■ US & W. Indian informal attack or assault: *they both got mashed up pretty bad*.
2 (in brewing) mix (powdered malt) with hot water to form wort.
3 N. English (with reference to tea) brew or infuse.
▸ noun a soft mass made by crushing a substance into a pulp, sometimes with the addition of liquid: *pound the garlic to a mash*. ■ [mass noun] Brit. informal boiled and mashed potatoes, with milk and butter added. ■ [mass noun] bran mixed with hot water, given as a warm food to horses and other animals. ■ [mass noun] (in brewing) a mixture of powdered malt and hot water, which is left to stand until the sugars dissolve to form the wort.
– ORIGIN Old English *māsc* (as a brewing term), of West Germanic origin; perhaps ultimately related to MIX.

masher¹ ▸ noun a utensil for mashing food.

masher² ▸ noun informal a dandy of late Victorian or Edwardian times. ■ N. Amer. informal a man who makes unwelcome sexual advances to women.
– ORIGIN late 19th cent.: probably a derivative of slang *mash* 'attract sexually', 'infatuation', perhaps from Romany *masherava* 'allure'.

Mashhad /maʃˈhad/ (also **Meshed**) a city in NE Iran, close to the border with Turkmenistan; pop. 2,427,316 (2006). The burial place in AD 809 of the Abbasid caliph Harun ar-Rashid and in 818 of the Shiite leader Ali ar-Rida, it is a holy city of the Shiite Muslims. It is the second-largest city in Iran.

mashie /ˈmaʃi/ ▸ noun Golf, dated an iron used for lofting or for medium distances.
– ORIGIN late 19th cent.: perhaps from French *massue* 'club'.

mash note ▸ noun N. Amer. informal a letter which expresses infatuation with or gushing admiration of someone.
– ORIGIN late 19th cent.: from slang *mash* (see MASHER²) + NOTE.

Mashona /məˈʃəʊnə/ ▸ noun [mass noun] the Shona people collectively, particularly those of Zimbabwe.
▸ adjective relating to the Shona people.
– ORIGIN the name in Shona.

Mashonaland an area of northern Zimbabwe, occupied by the Shona people. A former province of Rhodesia, it is now divided into the three provinces of Mashonaland East, West, and Central.

mash tun ▸ noun (in brewing) a vat in which malt is mashed.

mash-up ▸ noun a mixture or fusion of disparate elements, especially a musical track comprising the vocals of one recording placed over the instrumental backing of another.

masjid /ˈmʌsdʒɪd, ˈmas-/ ▸ noun a mosque.
– ORIGIN Arabic, 'place of worship or prostration in prayer', probably ultimately of Aramaic origin.

mask ▸ noun **1** a covering for all or part of the face, worn as a disguise, or to amuse or frighten others.
2 a covering made of fibre or gauze and fitting over the nose and mouth to protect against air pollutants, or made of sterile gauze and worn to prevent infection of the wearer or (in surgery) of the patient. ■ a protective covering fitting over the whole face, worn in fencing, ice hockey, and other sports. ■ a respirator used to filter inhaled air or to supply gas for inhalation. ■ a face pack.
3 a likeness of a person's face moulded or sculpted in clay or wax. ■ a person's face regarded as having set into a particular expression: *his face was a mask of rage*. ■ a hollow model of a human head worn by ancient Greek and Roman actors. ■ the face or head of a fox or other game animal, as a trophy.
4 a manner or expression that hides one's true character or feelings: *I let my mask of respectability slip*.
5 Photography a piece of material such as card used to cover a part of an image that is not required when exposing a print.
6 Electronics a patterned metal film used in the manufacture of microcircuits to allow selective modification of the underlying material.
7 Entomology the enlarged labium of a dragonfly larva, which can be extended to seize prey.
▸ verb [with obj.] **1** cover (the face) with a mask.
2 conceal (something) from view: *the poplars masked a factory*. ■ (of a taste, smell, etc.) prevent the perception of (another sensation): *brandy did not completely mask the bitter taste*.
3 cover (an object or surface) so as to protect it during painting.
– DERIVATIVES **masked** adjective.
– ORIGIN mid 16th cent.: from French *masque*, from Italian *maschera*, *mascara*, probably from medieval Latin *masca* 'witch, spectre', but influenced by Arabic *masḵara* 'buffoon'.

masked ball ▸ noun a ball at which participants wear masks to conceal their faces.

masker ▸ noun **1** a thing that masks or conceals something else.
2 (also **masquer**) a person taking part in a masquerade or masked ball.

masking tape ▸ noun [mass noun] adhesive tape used in painting to cover areas on which paint is not wanted.

maskinonge /ˈmaskɪnɒn(d)ʒ, -ˈnɒn(d)ʒi/ ▸ noun another term for MUSKELLUNGE.

masochism /ˈmasəkɪz(ə)m/ ▸ noun [mass noun] the tendency to derive sexual gratification from one's own pain or humiliation. ■ (in general use) the enjoyment of an activity that appears to be painful or tedious: *there's plenty to do when the weather turns moorland walks into exercises in masochism*.
– DERIVATIVES **masochist** noun, **masochistic** adjective, **masochistically** adverb.
– ORIGIN late 19th cent.: named after Leopold von Sacher-*Masoch* (1835–95), the Austrian novelist who described it, + -ISM.

Mason, James (Neville) (1909–84), English actor. He acted in more than a hundred films, notably *A Star is Born* (1954), *Lolita* (1962), and *Georgy Girl* (1966).

mason ▸ noun **1** a person skilled in cutting, dressing, and laying stone in buildings.
2 (**Mason**) a Freemason.

▶ **verb** [with obj.] build from or strengthen with stone. ■ cut or dress (stone).
– ORIGIN Middle English: from Old French *masson* (noun), *maçonner* (verb), probably of Germanic origin; perhaps related to **MAKE**.

mason bee ▶ **noun** a solitary bee which lays its eggs in cavities, constructing cells of sand and other particles glued together with saliva. ● *Osmia* and other genera, family Apidae.

Mason–Dixon Line ▶ **noun** (in the US) the boundary between Maryland and Pennsylvania, taken as the northern limit of the slave-owning states before the abolition of slavery.
– ORIGIN named after Charles *Mason* and Jeremiah *Dixon*, the 18th-cent. English astronomers who surveyed it in 1763–7.

Masonic /mə'sɒnɪk/ ▶ **adjective** relating to Freemasons.

Masonite ▶ **noun** [mass noun] N. Amer. trademark fibreboard made from wood fibre pulped under steam at high pressure.
– ORIGIN 1920s: from the name of the *Mason* Fibre Co., Mississippi, US, + **-ITE**[1].

Mason jar ▶ **noun** N. Amer. a wide-mouthed glass jar with an airtight screw top, used for preserving fruit and vegetables.
– ORIGIN late 19th cent.: named after John L. *Mason* (died 1902), American inventor.

masonry ▶ **noun** [mass noun] **1** stonework. ■ the occupation or work of a mason.
2 (**Masonry**) freemasonry.
– ORIGIN late Middle English: from Old French *maçonerie*, from *maçon* (see **MASON**).

mason's mark ▶ **noun** a distinctive device carved on stone by the mason who dressed it.

mason wasp ▶ **noun** a solitary wasp that lays its eggs in a cavity which it seals with mud or similar material. ● Several genera in the family Eumenidae.

masoor /mʌ'sʊə, mʌ'sɔː/ (also **masoor dahl**) ▶ **noun** a lentil of a small orange-red variety.
– ORIGIN from Hindi *masūr*.

Masorah /mə'sɔːrə/ (also **Massorah**) ▶ **noun** (**the Masorah**) the collection of information and comment on the text of the traditional Hebrew Bible by the Masoretes.
– ORIGIN from Hebrew *māsōrāh* based on *'āsar* 'to bind', later interpreted in the sense 'tradition' (as if from *māsar* 'hand down').

Masorete /'masəriːt/ ▶ **noun** any of the Jewish scholars of the 6th to 10th centuries AD who contributed to the establishment of a recognized text of the Hebrew Bible, and to the compilation of the Masorah.
– DERIVATIVES **Masoretic** /-'rɛtɪk/ **adjective**.
– ORIGIN from French *Massoret* and modern Latin *Massoreta*, from Hebrew *māsōreṯ*; related to *māsōrāh* (see **MASORAH**).

masque /mɑːsk/ ▶ **noun** a form of amateur dramatic entertainment, popular among the nobility in 16th- and 17th-century England, which consisted of dancing and acting performed by masked players.
– ORIGIN early 16th cent. (in the sense 'masquerade or masked ball'): probably a back-formation (influenced by French *masque* 'mask') from *masker*, from Italian *mascar* 'person wearing a mask'.

masquer ▶ **noun** variant spelling of **MASKER**.

masquerade /ˌmɑːskə'reɪd, ˌmas-/ ▶ **noun** a false show or pretence: *I doubt he could have kept up the masquerade for long*. ■ [mass noun] the wearing of disguise: *dressing up, role playing, and masquerade*. ■ chiefly N. Amer. a masked ball.
▶ **verb** [no obj.] pretend to be someone one is not: *a journalist* ***masquerading as*** *a man in distress*. ■ be disguised or passed off as something else: *idle gossip that masquerades as news*.
– DERIVATIVES **masquerader** noun.
– ORIGIN late 16th cent.: from French *mascarade*, from Italian *mascherata*, from *maschera* 'mask'.

Mass ▶ **noun** the celebration of the Christian Eucharist, especially in the Roman Catholic Church: *we went to Mass*. ■ a particular celebration of the Eucharist: *he pontificated at three Christmas Masses*. ■ a musical setting of parts of the liturgy used in the Mass.
– ORIGIN Old English *mæsse*, from ecclesiastical Latin *missa*, from Latin *miss-* 'dismissed', from *mittere*, perhaps from the last words of the service, *Ite, missa est* 'Go, it is the dismissal'.

mass ▶ **noun 1** a large body of matter with no definite shape: *the sun broke out from behind* ***a mass of*** *clouds*. ■ any of the main portions in a painting or drawing that each have some unity in colour, lighting, or some other quality.
2 a large number of people or objects crowded together: ***a mass of*** *cyclists*. ■ a large amount of material: ***a mass of*** *conflicting evidence*. ■ (**masses**) informal a large quantity or amount of something: *we get* ***masses of*** *homework*.
3 (**the mass of**) the majority of: *the mass of the people think that the problems are caused by government inefficiency*. ■ (**the masses**) the ordinary people.
4 [mass noun] Physics the quantity of matter which a body contains, as measured by its acceleration under a given force or by the force exerted on it by a gravitational field. ■ (in general use) weight.
▶ **adjective** [attrib.] involving or affecting large numbers of people or things: *the film has mass appeal* | *a mass exodus of refugees*.
▶ **verb** assemble or cause to assemble into a single body or mass: [with obj.] *both countries began massing troops in the region* | [no obj.] *clouds massed heavily on the horizon*.
– PHRASES **be a mass of** be completely covered with. **in mass** as a body. **in the mass** as a whole.
– DERIVATIVES **massless** adjective.
– ORIGIN late Middle English: from Old French *masse*, from Latin *massa*, from Greek *maza* 'barley cake'; perhaps related to *massein* 'knead'.

Mass. ▶ **abbreviation** Massachusetts.

massa /'masə/ ▶ **noun** (in representations of black speech) master: *Massa, I have some news for you*.

Massachusetts /ˌmasə'tʃuːsɪts/ a state in the north-eastern US, on the Atlantic coast; pop. 6,497,967 (est. 2008); capital, Boston. Settled by the Pilgrim Fathers in 1620, it was a centre of resistance to the British before becoming one of the original thirteen states of the Union (1788).

Massachusetts Institute of Technology (abbrev.: **MIT**) a US institute of higher education, famous for scientific and technical research, founded in 1861 in Cambridge, Massachusetts.

massacre ▶ **noun** an indiscriminate and brutal slaughter of many people: *reports of massacres by government troops*. ■ informal a heavy defeat of a sporting team or contestant.
▶ **verb** [with obj.] deliberately and brutally kill (many people). ■ informal inflict a heavy defeat on (a sporting opponent). ■ informal perform (a piece of music, a play, etc.) very ineptly: *the choir was massacring 'In the Bleak Midwinter'*.
– ORIGIN late 16th cent.: from French, of unknown origin.

Massacre of St Bartholomew the massacre of Huguenots throughout France ordered by Charles IX at the instigation of his mother, Catherine de' Medici, and begun without warning on 24 August (the feast of St Bartholomew) 1572.

massage /'masɑːʒ, mə'sɑːʒ, -dʒ/ ▶ **noun** [mass noun] the rubbing and kneading of muscles and joints of the body with the hands, especially to relieve tension or pain: *massage can ease tiredness* | [count noun] *a massage will help loosen you up*.
▶ **verb** [with obj.] **1** rub and knead (a person or part of the body) with the hands. ■ (**massage something in/into/on to**) rub a substance into (the skin or hair).
2 manipulate (facts or figures) to give a more acceptable result: *the accounts had been massaged to suit the government*.
– PHRASES **massage someone's ego** flatter someone.
– DERIVATIVES **massager** noun.
– ORIGIN late 19th cent.: from French, from *masser* 'knead, treat with massage', probably from Portuguese *amassar* 'knead', from *massa* 'dough'.

massage parlour ▶ **noun** an establishment providing massage. ■ euphemistic a brothel.

massasauga /ˌmasə'sɔːgə/ ▶ **noun** a small North American rattlesnake of variable colour which favours damp habitats. ● *Sistrurus catenatus*, family Viperidae.
– ORIGIN mid 19th cent.: formed irregularly from **MISSISSAUGA**.

Massawa /mə'sɑːwə/ (also **Mitsiwa**) the chief port of Eritrea, on the Red Sea; pop. 36,700 (est. 2004).

mass defect ▶ **noun** Physics the difference between the mass of an isotope and its mass number, representing binding energy.

massé /'maseɪ/ ▶ **noun** [usu. as modifier] Billiards & Snooker a stroke made with an inclined cue, imparting swerve to the ball: *a massé shot*.
– ORIGIN late 19th cent.: French, past participle of *masser* 'make a massé stroke'.

mass energy ▶ **noun** [mass noun] Physics the mass of a body regarded as energy, according to the laws of relativity.

masseter /ma'siːtə/ (also **masseter muscle**) ▶ **noun** Anatomy a muscle which runs through the rear part of the cheek from the temporal bone to the lower jaw on each side and closes the jaw in chewing.
– ORIGIN late 16th cent.: from Greek *masētēr*, from *masasthai* 'to chew'.

masseur /ma'səː/ ▶ **noun** a person who provides massage professionally.
– ORIGIN French, from *masser* 'to massage'.

masseuse /ma'səːz/ ▶ **noun** a female masseur.
– ORIGIN French.

massicot /'masɪkɒt/ ▶ **noun** [mass noun] a yellow form of lead monoxide, used as a pigment.
– ORIGIN late 15th cent.: from French (influenced by Italian *marzacotto* 'unguent'), ultimately from Arabic *martak*.

massif /'masɪf, ma'siːf/ ▶ **noun** a compact group of mountains.
– ORIGIN early 16th cent. (denoting a large building): French, 'massive', used as a noun. The current sense dates from the late 19th cent.

Massif Central /ˌmasiːf sɒ̃'trɑːl/, French /masif sɑ̃tʀal/ a mountainous plateau in south central France. Covering almost one sixth of the country, it rises to a height of 1,887 m (6,188 ft) at Puy de Sancy in the Auvergne.

Massine /ma'siːn/, Léonide Fédorovitch (1895–1979), Russian-born choreographer and ballet dancer, a French citizen from 1944; born *Leonid Fyodorovich Myasin*. He was the originator of the symphonic ballet, and danced in and choreographed the film *The Red Shoes* (1948).

Massinger /'masɪndʒə/, Philip (1583–1640), English dramatist. Notable works: *The Duke of Milan* (1621–2), *A New Way to Pay Old Debts* (1625–6), and *The City Madam* (1632).

massive ▶ **adjective 1** large and heavy or solid: *a massive rampart of stone*.
2 exceptionally large: *massive crowds are expected*. ■ very serious: *a massive heart attack*. ■ informal very successful or influential: *the band are going to be massive*.
3 Geology (of rocks or beds) having no discernible form or structure. ■ (of a mineral) not visibly crystalline.
▶ **noun** Brit. informal a group of young people from a particular area with a common interest in dance music: *the Bristol massive*.
– DERIVATIVES **massively** adverb [as submodifier] *a massively complicated network*, **massiveness** noun.
– ORIGIN late Middle English: from French *massif, -ive*, from Old French *massis*, based on Latin *massa* (see **MASS**).

massively parallel ▶ **adjective** Computing (of a computer) consisting of a great many parallel processing units, and so able to execute many different parts of a program at the same time.

mass-market ▶ **adjective** (of goods) produced in large quantities for many people: *standard mass-market aftershave*.
▶ **verb** [with obj.] market (a product) on a large scale.

mass media ▶ **plural noun** (**the mass media**) [treated as sing. or pl.] the media.

mass noun ▶ **noun** Grammar a noun denoting something which cannot be counted (e.g. a substance or quality), in English usually a noun which lacks a plural in ordinary usage and is not used with the indefinite article, e.g. *china, happiness*. Contrasted with **COUNT NOUN**. ■ a noun denoting something which normally cannot be counted but which may be countable when it refers to different units or types, e.g. *coffee* (*drank some coffee, ordered two coffees*).

mass number ▶ **noun** Physics the total number of protons and neutrons in a nucleus.

mass observation ▶ **noun** [mass noun] Brit., chiefly historical the study and recording of the social habits and opinions of ordinary people.

Masson /'masɒ̃/, André (1896–1987), French painter and graphic artist. He joined the surrealists in the mid 1920s and pioneered 'automatic' drawing, a form of fluid, spontaneous composition intended to express images emerging from the unconscious.

Massorah ▶ **noun** variant spelling of **MASORAH**.

mass-produce ▶ **verb** [with obj.] produce large quantities of (a standardized article) by an automated

M

mechanical process: (as adj. **mass-produced**) *cheap mass-produced goods.*
– DERIVATIVES **mass-producer** noun, **mass production** noun.

mass spectrograph ▶ noun a mass spectrometer in which the particles are detected photographically.

mass spectrometer ▶ noun an apparatus for measuring the masses of isotopes, molecules, and molecular fragments by ionizing them and determining their trajectories in electric and magnetic fields.

mass spectrum ▶ noun a distribution of ions shown by the use of a mass spectrograph or mass spectrometer.

mass transit ▶ noun [mass noun] N. Amer. public transport, especially in an urban area.

massy ▶ adjective literary consisting of a large mass; bulky; massive: *a round massy table.*

mast[1] ▶ noun a tall upright post, spar, or other structure on a ship or boat, in sailing vessels generally carrying a sail or sails. ■ a tall upright post on land, especially a flagpole or a television or radio transmitter.
– PHRASES **before the mast** historical serving as an ordinary seaman in a sailing ship (quartered in the forecastle). **nail** (or **pin**) **one's colours to the mast** declare one's beliefs or intentions openly: *they nailed their colours to the mast of youth revolt.*
– DERIVATIVES **masted** adjective [in combination] *a single-masted fishing boat.*
– ORIGIN Old English *mæst*, of West Germanic origin; related to Dutch *mast* and German *Mast*.

mast[2] ▶ noun [mass noun] the fruit of beech, oak, chestnut, and other forest trees, especially as food for pigs.
– ORIGIN Old English *mæst*, of West Germanic origin; probably related to **MEAT**.

mastaba /ˈmastəbə/ ▶ noun **1** Archaeology an ancient Egyptian tomb consisting of an underground burial chamber with rooms above it (at ground level) to store offerings.
2 (in Islamic countries) a stone or brick bench built into the wall of a house.
– ORIGIN from Arabic *maṣṭaba*.

M

mast cell ▶ noun a cell filled with basophil granules, found in numbers in connective tissue and releasing histamine and other substances during inflammatory and allergic reactions.
– ORIGIN late 19th cent.: *mast* from German *Mast* 'fattening, feeding'.

mastectomy /maˈstɛktəmi/ ▶ noun (pl. **mastectomies**) a surgical operation to remove a breast.
– ORIGIN 1920s: from Greek *mastos* 'breast' + **-ECTOMY**.

master[1] ▶ noun **1** chiefly historical a man who has people working for him, especially servants or slaves: *he acceded to his master's wishes.* ■ a person who has complete control of something: *he was master of the situation.* ■ dated a male head of a household. ■ the male owner of a dog, horse, or other domesticated animal. ■ a machine or device directly controlling another. Compare with **SLAVE**.
2 a man in charge of an organization or group, in particular: ■ Brit. a male schoolteacher: *the games master.* ■ the head of a college or school. ■ the presiding officer of a livery company or Masonic lodge. ■ the captain of a merchant ship. ■ the person in control of a pack of hounds. ■ (in England and Wales) an official of the Supreme Court.
3 a skilled practitioner of a particular art or activity: *I'm a master of disguise.* ■ a great artist or musician. ■ a very strong chess player, especially one who has qualified for the title at international tournaments. See also **GRAND MASTER**. ■ (**Masters**) [treated as sing.] (in some sports) a class for competitors over the usual age for the highest level of competition.
4 [usu. in titles] a person who holds a second or further degree: *a Master of Arts.*
5 used as a title prefixed to the name of a boy not old enough to be called 'Mr': *Master James Wishart.* ■ archaic a title for a man of high rank or learning. ■ the title of the heir apparent of a Scottish viscount or baron.
6 an original film, recording, or document from which copies can be made: [as modifier] *the master tape.*
▶ adjective [attrib.] **1** having or showing very great skill or proficiency: *a master painter.* ■ denoting a person skilled in a particular trade and able to teach others: *a master bricklayer.*
2 main; principal: *the master bedroom.*
▶ verb [with obj.] **1** acquire complete knowledge or skill in (a subject, technique, or art): *I never mastered Latin.*
2 gain control of; overcome: *I managed to master my fears.*
3 make a master copy of (a film or recording).
– PHRASES **be one's own master** be independent or free to do as one wishes.
– DERIVATIVES **masterdom** noun, **masterhood** noun, **masterless** adjective, **mastership** noun.
– ORIGIN Old English *mæg(i)ster* (later reinforced by Old French *maistre*), from Latin *magister*; probably related to *magis* 'more'.

master[2] ▶ noun [in combination] a ship or boat with a specified number of masts: *a three-master.*

Master Aircrew ▶ noun a generic RAF rank equivalent to warrant officer, only applied to members of an aircrew.

master-at-arms ▶ noun (pl. **masters-at-arms**) a warrant officer appointed to carry out or supervise police duties on board a ship.

masterclass ▶ noun a class, especially in music, given by an expert to highly talented students.

masterful ▶ adjective **1** powerful and able to control others: *he looked masculine and masterful.*
2 performed or performing very skilfully: *a masterful assessment of the difficulties.*
– DERIVATIVES **masterfully** adverb, **masterfulness** noun.

master key ▶ noun a key that opens several locks, each of which also has its own key.

masterly ▶ adjective showing great skill; very accomplished: *his masterly account of rural France.*
– DERIVATIVES **masterliness** noun.

master mariner ▶ noun a seaman qualified to be a captain, especially of a merchant ship.

master mason ▶ noun **1** a skilled mason, especially one who oversees the construction of buildings.
2 (**Master Mason**) a fully qualified Freemason.

mastermind ▶ noun a person with an outstanding intellect: *an eminent musical mastermind.* ■ a person who plans and directs an ingenious and complex scheme or enterprise: *McAvoy was the mastermind of the robbery.*
▶ verb [with obj.] plan and direct (an ingenious and complex scheme or enterprise).

master of ceremonies ▶ noun a person who presides over a formal event or entertainment and who introduces guests, speakers, or entertainers.

Master of the Rolls ▶ noun (in England and Wales) the judge who presides over the Court of Appeal (Civil Division) and who was formerly in charge of the Public Record Office.

masterpiece ▶ noun a work of outstanding artistry, skill, or workmanship: *a great literary masterpiece.* ■ historical a piece of work by a craftsman accepted as qualification for membership of a guild as an acknowledged master.

master plan ▶ noun a comprehensive plan of action.

master sergeant ▶ noun a high rank of non-commissioned officer in the US armed forces.

Masters Tournament a prestigious US golf competition, held in Augusta, Georgia, in which golfers (chiefly professionals) compete only by invitation on the basis of their past achievements.

master stroke ▶ noun a very skilful and opportune act.

master switch ▶ noun a switch controlling the supply of electricity or fuel to an entire system. ■ Biology a substance or gene that regulates gene expression or embryonic development, or initiates cancer.

masterwork ▶ noun a masterpiece.

masterwort ▶ noun a plant of the parsley family with white or pinkish flowers and lobed leaves, native to central and southern Europe. ● Genera *Peucedanum* and *Astrantia*, family Umbelliferae.

mastery ▶ noun [mass noun] **1** comprehensive knowledge or skill in a particular subject or activity: *she played with some mastery.* ■ the action of mastering a subject or skill: *a child's mastery of language.*
2 control or superiority over someone or something: *man's mastery over nature.*
– ORIGIN Middle English: from Old French *maistrie*, from *maistre* 'master'.

masthead ▶ noun **1** the highest part of a ship's mast or of the lower section of a mast.
2 the title of a newspaper or magazine at the head of the first or editorial page. ■ chiefly N. Amer. the listed details in a newspaper or magazine referring to ownership, editorial staff, advertising rates, etc.
▶ verb [with obj.] **1** historical send (a sailor) to the masthead as a punishment.
2 raise (a flag or sail) to the masthead.

mastic /ˈmastɪk/ ▶ noun **1** [mass noun] an aromatic gum or resin which exudes from the bark of a Mediterranean tree, used in making varnish and chewing gum and as a flavouring.
2 (also **mastic tree**) the bushy evergreen Mediterranean tree which yields mastic and has aromatic leaves and fruit, closely related to the pistachio. ● *Pistacia lentiscus*, family Anacardiaceae. ■ used in names of trees that are similar or related to the mastic tree, e.g. **American mastic**.
3 [mass noun] a putty-like waterproof filler and sealant used in building.
– ORIGIN late Middle English: via Old French and Latin from Greek *mastikhē* (perhaps from *mastikhan* 'masticate').

masticate /ˈmastɪkeɪt/ ▶ verb [with obj.] chew (food).
– DERIVATIVES **mastication** noun, **masticator** noun, **masticatory** adjective.
– ORIGIN mid 17th cent. (earlier (Middle English) as *mastication*): from late Latin *masticat-* 'chewed', from the verb *masticare*, from Greek *mastikhan* 'gnash the teeth' (related to *masasthai* 'to chew').

mastiff /ˈmastɪf, ˈmɑː-/ ▶ noun a dog of a large, strong breed with drooping ears and pendulous lips.
– ORIGIN Middle English: from Old French *mastin*, based on Latin *mansuetus* 'tame'.

mastiff bat ▶ noun a heavily built free-tailed bat with a broad muzzle, found mainly in America and Australasia. ● *Eumops*, *Molossus*, and other genera, family Molossidae: several species. ■ another term for **BULLDOG BAT**.

Mastigophora /ˌmastɪˈɡɒfərə/ ▶ plural noun Zoology a group of single-celled animals that includes the protozoal flagellates, which are now generally divided among several phyla of the kingdom Protista. ● Subphylum (or superclass) Mastigophora.
– ORIGIN modern Latin (plural), from Greek *mastigophoros*, from *mastix*, *mastig-* 'whip' + *-phoros* 'bearing'.

mastitis /maˈstʌɪtɪs/ ▶ noun [mass noun] inflammation of the mammary gland in the breast or udder, typically due to bacterial infection via a damaged nipple or teat.
– ORIGIN mid 19th cent.: from Greek *mastos* 'breast' + **-ITIS**.

mastodon /ˈmastədɒn/ ▶ noun a large extinct elephant-like mammal of the Miocene to Pleistocene epochs, having teeth of a relatively primitive form and number. ● Mammutidae and other families, order Proboscidea: many species.
– DERIVATIVES **mastodontic** /-ˈdɒntɪk/ adjective.
– ORIGIN early 19th cent.: modern Latin, from Greek *mastos* 'breast' + *odous*, *odont-* 'tooth' (with reference to nipple-shaped tubercles on the crowns of its molar teeth).

mastoid /ˈmastɔɪd/ ▶ adjective Anatomy relating to the mastoid process.
▶ noun Anatomy the mastoid process. ■ (**mastoids**) [treated as sing.] informal mastoiditis.
– ORIGIN mid 18th cent.: via French and modern Latin from Greek *mastoeidēs* 'breast-shaped', from *mastos* 'breast'.

mastoiditis /ˌmastɔɪˈdʌɪtɪs/ ▶ noun [mass noun] Medicine inflammation of the mastoid process.

mastoid process ▶ noun a conical prominence of the temporal bone behind the ear, to which neck muscles are attached, and which has air spaces linked to the middle ear.

masturbate /ˈmastəbeɪt/ ▶ verb [no obj.] stimulate one's genitals with one's hand for sexual pleasure. ■ [with obj.] stimulate the genitals of (someone) to give them sexual pleasure.
– DERIVATIVES **masturbation** noun, **masturbator** noun, **masturbatory** adjective.
– ORIGIN mid 19th cent.: from Latin *masturbat-* 'masturbated', from the verb *masturbari*, of unknown origin.

Masuria /məˈsjʊərɪə/ a low-lying region of NE Poland known for its forests and lakes. Formerly part of East Prussia, it was assigned to Poland after the Second World War. Also called **Masurian Lakes**.

mat[1] ▶ noun **1** a piece of coarse material placed on a floor for people to wipe their feet on. ■ a small rug. ■ a piece of thick or resilient material for lying on or for landing on in gymnastics, wrestling, or similar sports.
2 a small piece of cork, card, or fabric placed on a table or other surface to protect it from the heat or

moisture of an object placed on it. ■ (also **mouse mat**) Brit. a small piece of rigid or slightly resilient material on which a computer mouse is moved.
3 a thick, untidy layer of something hairy or woolly: *his chest was covered by a thick mat of soft fair hair.*
▸ **verb** (**mats, matting, matted**) [with obj.] tangle (something, especially hair) in a thick mass: *the fur on its flank was matted with blood.* ■ [no obj.] become tangled.
– PHRASES **go to the mat** informal vigorously engage in an argument, especially on behalf of another. **on the mat** informal being reprimanded by someone in authority. [with military reference to the orderly room mat, where an accused would stand before the commanding officer.]
– ORIGIN Old English *m(e)att(e)*, of West Germanic origin; related to Dutch *mat* and German *Matte*, from late Latin *matta*, from Phoenician.

mat[2] ▸ **noun** short for **MATRIX** (sense 3).

mat[3] ▸ **noun** US spelling of **MATT**.

Mata /ˈmɑːtəː/ ▸ **noun** Indian a mother (often used as a respectful form of address for a woman).
– ORIGIN via Hindi from Sanskrit *mātā* 'mother'.

Matabele /ˌmatəˈbiːli/ ▸ **noun** the Ndebele people collectively, particularly those of Zimbabwe.
– ORIGIN from Sotho *matebele*, singular *letebele*, the name given to this people.

Matabeleland a former province of Rhodesia, lying between the Limpopo and Zambezi rivers and occupied by the Matabele people. It is now divided into the two Zimbabwean provinces of Matabeleland North and South.

matador /ˈmatədɔː/ ▸ **noun 1** a bullfighter whose task is to kill the bull.
2 (in ombre, skat, and other card games) any of the highest trumps.
3 [mass noun] a domino game in which halves are matched so as to make a total of seven. ■ [count noun] any of the dominoes which have seven spots altogether, together with the double blank.
– ORIGIN Spanish, literally 'killer', from *matar* 'to kill', from Persian *māt* 'dead'; senses relating to games are extended uses, expressing a notion of 'dominance'.

Mata Hari /ˌmɑːtə ˈhɑːri/ (1876–1917), Dutch dancer and secret agent; born *Margaretha Geertruida Zelle*. She probably worked for both French and German intelligence services before being executed by the French in 1917. ■ (as noun **a Mata Hari**) a beautiful and seductive female spy.
– ORIGIN from Malay *mata* 'eye' and *hari* 'day', as a compound meaning 'sun'.

matai[1] /ˈmatʌɪ/ ▸ **noun** (pl. **matais**) a coniferous New Zealand tree which yields pale timber. ● *Prumnopitys taxifolia*, family Podocarpaceae.
– ORIGIN mid 19th cent.: from Maori.

matai[2] /ˈmatʌɪ/ ▸ **noun** (pl. **same**) (in a Samoan extended family or clan) the person who is chosen to succeed to a chief's or orator's title and honoured as the head of the family.
– ORIGIN Samoan.

matamata /ˌmatəˈmatə/ ▸ **noun** a South American freshwater turtle that has a broad flat head and neck with irregular projections of skin. ● *Chelus fimbriatus*, family Chelidae.
– ORIGIN mid 19th cent.: from Tupi *matamatá*.

matatu /məˈtatuː/ ▸ **noun** (in East Africa) a minibus or similar vehicle used as a taxi.
– ORIGIN Swahili, short for *mapeni matatu* 'thirty cents', a flat fare charged in the early 1960s.

match[1] ▸ **noun 1** a contest in which people or teams compete against each other in a particular sport: *a boxing match.*
2 a person or thing that is equal to another in quality or strength: *they were **no match for** the mercenaries.*
3 a person or thing that resembles or corresponds to another: *the child's identical twin would be a perfect match for organ donation.* ■ Computing a string that fulfils the specified conditions of a computer search. ■ a similar or complementary pair: *the headdresses and bouquet were a perfect match.* ■ the fact or appearance of corresponding: *stones of a perfect match and colour.*
4 a person viewed in regard to their eligibility for marriage, especially as regards class or wealth: *he was an unsuitable match for any of their girls.* ■ a marriage: *a dynastic match.*
▸ **verb 1** correspond or cause to correspond in some essential respect; make or be harmonious: [with obj.] *I thought we'd have primrose walls to match the bath* | [no obj.] *the jacket and trousers do not match.* ■ [with obj.] put (someone or something) together with someone or something else appropriate or harmonious: *she was trying to **match** the draperies **to** the couch.*
2 [with obj.] be equal to (something) in quality or strength: *his anger matched her own.* ■ succeed in reaching or equalling (a standard or quality): *he tried to match her nonchalance.* ■ equalize (two coupled electrical impedances) so as to bring about the maximum transfer of power from one to the other.
3 [with obj.] place (a person or group) in competition with another: *the big names were **matched against** nobodies* | (as adj., with submodifier **matched**) *evenly matched teams.*
– PHRASES **make a match** get married. **meet one's match** encounter one's equal in strength or ability. **to match** corresponding in some essential respect with something previously mentioned or chosen: *a new coat and a hat to match.*
– PHRASAL VERBS **match up to** be as good as or equal to: *she matches up to the challenges of the job.* **match someone with** archaic bring about the marriage of someone to.
– DERIVATIVES **matchable** adjective.
– ORIGIN Old English *gemæcca* 'mate, companion', of West Germanic origin; related to the base of **MAKE**.

match[2] ▸ **noun** a short, thin piece of wood or cardboard used to light a fire, being tipped with a composition that ignites when rubbed against a rough surface. ■ historical a piece of wick or cord designed to burn at a uniform rate, used for firing a cannon or lighting gunpowder.
– PHRASES **put a match to** set fire to.
– ORIGIN late Middle English (in the sense 'wick of a candle'): from Old French *meche*, perhaps from Latin *myxa* 'spout of a lamp', later 'lamp wick'.

matchboard ▸ **noun** [mass noun] interlocking boards joined together by a tongue cut along the edge of one board and fitting into a groove along the edge of another.

matchbook ▸ **noun** N. Amer. a small cardboard folder of matches with a striking surface on the back.

matchbox ▸ **noun** a small box in which matches are sold, with a striking surface on one side. ■ [as modifier] very small: *her matchbox apartment.*

matchet /ˈmatʃɪt/ ▸ **noun** variant spelling of **MACHETE**.

matching ▸ **adjective 1** corresponding in pattern, colour, or design; complementary: *a blue jacket and matching skirt.*
2 equal in number or amount; equivalent: *the college will provide matching funds to complete the project.*

matchless ▸ **adjective** so good as to be unequalled; incomparable: *the Parthenon has a matchless beauty.*
– DERIVATIVES **matchlessly** adverb.

matchlock ▸ **noun** historical a type of gun with a lock in which a piece of wick or cord was placed for igniting the powder.

matchmaker ▸ **noun** a person who arranges marriages or initiates romantic relationships between others. ■ a person or company that brings parties together for commercial purposes.
– DERIVATIVES **matchmaking** noun.

match play ▸ **noun** [mass noun] play in golf in which the score is reckoned by counting the holes won by each side. Compare with **STROKE PLAY**.
– DERIVATIVES **match player** noun.

match point ▸ **noun 1** (in tennis and other sports) a point which if won by one of the players or sides will also win them the match.
2 (in duplicate bridge) a unit of scoring in matches and tournaments.

matchstick ▸ **noun** the stem of a match. ■ something likened to a match in being long and thin: *cut the vegetables into matchsticks.* ■ [as modifier] Brit. (of a figure) drawn with short, thin straight lines: *matchstick men.*

matchup ▸ **noun** chiefly N. Amer. **1** a sporting contest between two players or teams.
2 a selected combination of people or things: *the matchups of flavours are ideal.*

matchwood ▸ **noun** [mass noun] very small pieces or splinters of wood: *the bomb reduced the flimsy huts to matchwood.* ■ light poor-quality wood.

matchy-matchy ▸ **adjective** informal very or excessively colour-coordinated: *the key to looking stylish is to avoid an outfit that's too matchy-matchy.*

mate[1] ▸ **noun 1** the sexual partner of a bird or other animal: *a male bird sings to court a mate.* ■ informal a person's husband, wife, or other sexual partner: *he couldn't satisfy his frisky young mate.* ■ informal one of a matched pair: *a sock without its mate.*
2 [in combination] a fellow member or joint occupant of a specified thing: *his table-mates.*
3 Brit. informal a friend or companion: *my best mate Steve.* ■ used as a friendly form of address between men or boys: *'See you then, mate.'*
4 chiefly Brit. an assistant or deputy in certain trades: *a plumber's mate.* ■ an officer on a merchant ship subordinate to the master. See also **FIRST MATE**.
▸ **verb 1** [no obj.] (of animals or birds) come together for breeding; copulate: *successful males may mate with many females* | (as noun **mating**) *ovulation occurs only if mating has taken place.* ■ [with obj.] bring (animals) together for breeding.
2 connect or be connected mechanically: [with obj.] *a four-cylinder engine **mated to** a five-speed gearbox.*
– DERIVATIVES **mateless** adjective.
– ORIGIN late Middle English: from Middle Low German *māt(e)* 'comrade', of West Germanic origin; related to **MEAT** (the underlying concept being that of eating together).

mate[2] ▸ **noun & verb** Chess short for **CHECKMATE**.
– PHRASES **fool's mate** a game in which White is mated by Black's queen on the second move. **scholar's mate** a game in which White mates Black on the fourth move with the queen, supported by the king's bishop.
– ORIGIN Middle English: the noun from Anglo-Norman French *mat* (from the phrase *eschec mat* 'checkmate'); the verb from Anglo-Norman French *mater* 'to checkmate'.

maté /ˈmateɪ/ ▸ **noun** [mass noun] **1** (also **maté tea**) a bitter infusion of the leaves of a South American shrub, which is high in caffeine. ■ the leaves of the maté shrub.
2 (also **yerba maté**) the South American shrub of the holly family which produces maté leaves. ● *Ilex paraguariensis*, family Aquifoliaceae.
– ORIGIN early 18th cent.: from Spanish *mate*, from Quechua *mati*.

matelassé /ˌmat(ə)ˈlaseɪ/ ▸ **noun** [mass noun] a silk or wool fabric woven so as to have a raised surface with a quilted appearance.
– ORIGIN late 19th cent.: French, literally 'quilted', past participle of *matelasser*, from *matelas* 'mattress'.

matelot /ˈmatləʊ/ ▸ **noun** Brit. informal a sailor.
– ORIGIN mid 19th cent. (nautical slang): from French, variant of *matenot*, from Middle Dutch *mattenoot* 'bed companion', because sailors had to share hammocks in twos.

matelote /ˈmat(ə)ləʊt/ ▸ **noun** [mass noun] a dish of fish in a sauce of wine and onions.
– ORIGIN French, from *à la matelote*, literally 'mariner-style', from *matelot* 'sailor' (see **MATELOT**).

mater /ˈmeɪtə/ ▸ **noun** Brit. informal, dated mother.
– ORIGIN Latin.

mater dolorosa /ˌmɑːtə ˌdɒləˈrəʊsə, ˌmeɪtə/ the Virgin Mary sorrowing for the death of Christ, especially as a representation in art.
– ORIGIN from medieval Latin, 'sorrowful mother'.

materfamilias /ˌmeɪtəfəˈmɪlɪas/ ▸ **noun** (pl. **matresfamilias** /ˌmeɪtriːz-/) the female head of a family or household. Compare with **PATERFAMILIAS**.
– ORIGIN Latin, from *mater* 'mother' + *familias*, old genitive form of *familia* 'family'.

material ▸ **noun** [mass noun] **1** the matter from which a thing is or can be made: *goats can eat more or less any plant material* | [count noun] *highly flammable materials.* ■ (**materials**) things needed for an activity: *cleaning materials.* ■ [with adj. or noun modifier] a person of a specified quality or suitability: *he's not really Olympic material.*
2 information or ideas for use in creating a book or other work: *his colonial experiences gave him material.* ■ items, such as songs or jokes, comprising a performer's act: *a watchable band playing original material.*
3 cloth or fabric: *a piece of dark material* | [count noun] *dress materials.*
▸ **adjective 1** [attrib.] denoting or consisting of physical objects rather than the mind or spirit: *the material world.* ■ concerned with money or possessions rather than the needs of the mind or spirit: *material living standards have risen.* ■ concerned with the matter of reasoning, not its form: *political conflict lacks mathematical or material certitude.*
2 significant; important: *the insects did not do any material damage to the crop.* ■ Law (of evidence or a fact) significant or relevant, especially to the extent of determining a cause or affecting a judgement: *information that could be **material to** a murder inquiry.*

M

– ORIGIN late Middle English (in the sense 'relating to matter'): from late Latin *materialis*, adjective from Latin *materia* 'matter'.

material cause ▶ noun Philosophy (in Aristotelian thought) the matter or substance which constitutes a thing.

materialism ▶ noun [mass noun] **1** a tendency to consider material possessions and physical comfort as more important than spiritual values.
2 Philosophy the theory or belief that nothing exists except matter and its movements and modifications. ■ the theory or belief that consciousness and will are wholly due to material agency. See also DIALECTICAL MATERIALISM.
– DERIVATIVES **materialist** noun & adjective.

materialistic ▶ adjective excessively concerned with material possessions; money-oriented: *we're living in a highly materialistic society*.
– DERIVATIVES **materialistically** adverb.

materiality ▶ noun (pl. **materialities**) [mass noun] the quality of being composed of matter. ■ Law the quality of being relevant or significant: *the applicant must establish materiality on the balance of probabilities*. ■ [count noun] a material quality or thing: *giving a materiality to space*.

materialize (also **materialise**) ▶ verb [no obj.] **1** become actual fact; happen: *the forecast rate of increase did not materialize*. ■ appear or be present when expected: *the train failed to materialize*.
2 (of a ghost, spirit, or similar entity) appear in bodily form. ■ [with obj.] represent or cause to appear in bodily or physical form.
– DERIVATIVES **materialization** noun.

materially ▶ adverb **1** [often as submodifier] in a significant way; considerably: *materially different circumstances*.
2 in terms of material possessions: *a materially and culturally rich area*.

material witness ▶ noun US Law a witness whose evidence is likely to be sufficiently important to influence the outcome of a trial.

M

materia medica /məˌtɪərɪə ˈmɛdɪkə/ ▶ noun [mass noun] the body of remedial substances used in the practice of medicine. ■ the study of the origin and properties of substances used in the practice of medicine.
– ORIGIN late 17th cent.: modern Latin, translation of Greek *hulē iatrikē* 'healing material' (the title of a work by Dioscorides).

materiel /məˌtɪərɪˈɛl/ ▶ noun [mass noun] military materials and equipment.
– ORIGIN early 19th cent.: from French *matériel*, adjective (used as a noun).

maternal ▶ adjective relating to a mother, especially during pregnancy or shortly after childbirth: *maternal care*. ■ (of feelings) typical of a caring mother; motherly: *a mother who radiated maternal concern*. ■ [attrib.] related through the mother's side of the family: *my maternal grandfather*.
– DERIVATIVES **maternalism** noun, **maternalistic** adjective, **maternally** adverb.
– ORIGIN late 15th cent.: from French *maternel*, from Latin *maternus*, from *mater* 'mother'.

maternity ▶ noun [mass noun] motherhood. ■ [usu. as modifier] the period during pregnancy and shortly after childbirth: *maternity leave*.
– ORIGIN early 17th cent.: from French *maternité*, from Latin *maternus*, from *mater* 'mother'.

mateship ▶ noun [mass noun] Austral./NZ informal companionship or friendship, especially between men.

matey (also **maty**) Brit. informal ▶ adjective (**matier**, **matiest**) familiar and friendly; sociable: *a matey grin*.
▶ noun used as a familiar form of address to a man: *shove off, matey, she's mine*.
– DERIVATIVES **mateyness** (also **matiness**) noun, **matily** adverb.

math ▶ noun [mass noun] N. Amer. mathematics.
– ORIGIN mid 19th cent.: abbreviation.

mathematical ▶ adjective relating to mathematics: *mathematical symbols*. ■ resembling mathematics in being rigorously precise: *mathematical thinking | he arranged the meal with mathematical precision on a plate*.
– DERIVATIVES **mathematically** adverb.
– ORIGIN late Middle English: from Latin *mathematicalis*, from Greek *mathēmatikos*, from *mathēma*, *mathēmat-* 'science', from the base of *manthanein* 'learn'.

mathematical induction ▶ noun see INDUCTION (sense 3).

mathematical logic ▶ noun [mass noun] logic that is mathematical in its method, manipulating symbols according to definite and explicit rules of derivation; symbolic logic.

mathematician ▶ noun an expert in or student of mathematics.
– ORIGIN late Middle English: from Old French *mathematicien*, from Latin *mathematicus* 'mathematical', from Greek *mathēmatikos* (see MATHEMATICAL).

mathematics ▶ plural noun [usu. treated as sing.] the abstract science of number, quantity, and space, either as abstract concepts (**pure mathematics**), or as applied to other disciplines such as physics and engineering (**applied mathematics**). ■ [often treated as pl.] the mathematical aspects of something: *James immerses himself in the mathematics of baseball*.
– ORIGIN late 16th cent.: plural of obsolete *mathematic* 'mathematics', from Old French *mathematique*, from Latin *(ars) mathematica* 'mathematical (art)', from Greek *mathēmatikē (tekhnē)*, from the base of *manthanein* 'learn'.

mathematize (also **mathematise**) ▶ verb [with obj.] regard or treat (a subject or problem) in mathematical terms.
– DERIVATIVES **mathematization** noun.

maths ▶ plural noun [treated as sing.] Brit. mathematics.
– ORIGIN early 20th cent.: abbreviation.

Matilda[1] (1102–67), English princess, daughter of Henry I and mother of Henry II; known as **the Empress Maud**. Henry's only legitimate child, she was named his heir, but her cousin Stephen seized the throne on Henry's death in 1135. She waged an unsuccessful civil war against Stephen until 1148.

Matilda[2] ▶ noun Austral./NZ informal, archaic a bushman's bundle.
– PHRASES **waltz** (or **walk**) **Matilda** carry such a bundle.
– ORIGIN late 19th cent.: from the given name *Matilda*.

matinal /ˈmatɪn(ə)l/ ▶ adjective literary or technical relating to or taking place in the morning.
– ORIGIN early 19th cent.: from French, from *matin* 'morning'.

matinee /ˈmatɪneɪ/ ▶ noun an afternoon performance in a theatre or cinema.
– ORIGIN mid 19th cent.: from French *matinée*, literally 'morning (as a period of activity)', from *matin* 'morning': performances were formerly also in the morning.

matinee coat ▶ noun Brit. a baby's short coat.

matinee idol ▶ noun informal, dated a handsome actor admired for his good looks.

mating ▶ noun the action of animals coming together to breed; copulation: *courtship and mating also occur on land*.

matins (also **mattins**) ▶ noun a Christian service of morning prayer, especially in the Anglican Church. ■ a service forming part of the traditional Divine Office of the Western Christian Church, originally said (or chanted) at or after midnight. ■ (also **matin**) literary the morning song of birds.
– ORIGIN Middle English: from Old French *matines*, plural (influenced by Church Latin *matutinae* 'morning prayers') of *matin* 'morning', from Latin *matutinum*, neuter of *matutinus* 'early in the morning', from *Matuta*, the name of the dawn goddess.

Matisse /maˈtiːs/, Henri (Emile Benoît) (1869–1954), French painter and sculptor. His use of non-naturalistic colour led him to be regarded as a leader of the Fauvists. His later painting and sculpture displays a trend towards formal simplification and abstraction, and includes large figure compositions and abstracts made from cut-out coloured paper.

Mato Grosso /ˌmatuː ˈɡrɒsəʊ/ a high plateau region of SW Brazil, forming a watershed between the Amazon and Plate River systems. The region is divided into two states, **Mato Grosso** (capital, Cuiabá) and **Mato Grosso do Sul** (capital, Campo Grande).
– ORIGIN Portuguese, literally 'dense forest'.

matriarch /ˈmeɪtrɪɑːk/ ▶ noun a woman who is the head of a family or tribe. ■ an older woman who is powerful within a family or organization.
– DERIVATIVES **matriarchal** /-ˈɑːk(ə)l/ adjective, **matriarchate** noun.
– ORIGIN early 17th cent.: from Latin *mater* 'mother', on the false analogy of *patriarch*.

matriarchy ▶ noun (pl. **matriarchies**) a system of society or government ruled by a woman or women. ■ a form of social organization in which descent and relationship are reckoned through the female line.

matric /məˈtrɪk/ ▶ noun [mass noun] informal, Brit. dated or S. African matriculation.
– ORIGIN late 19th cent.: abbreviation.

matrices plural form of MATRIX.

matricide /ˈmatrɪsʌɪd, ˈmeɪtrɪ-/ ▶ noun [mass noun] the killing of one's mother: *a man suspected of matricide*. ■ [count noun] a person who kills their mother.
– DERIVATIVES **matricidal** adjective.
– ORIGIN late 16th cent.: from Latin *matricidium*, from *mater*, *matr-* 'mother' + *-cidium* (see -CIDE).

matriculate /məˈtrɪkjʊleɪt/ ▶ verb **1** [no obj.] be enrolled at a college or university: *they had recently matriculated as undergraduates at Jesus College*. ■ [with obj.] admit (a student) to membership of a college or university. ■ S. African pass the final school-leaving examination.
2 [with obj.] Heraldry, Scottish record (arms) in an official register.
▶ noun /məˈtrɪkjʊlət/ chiefly Indian a person who has matriculated.
– DERIVATIVES **matriculant** noun (S. African).
– ORIGIN late 16th cent.: from medieval Latin *matriculat-* 'enrolled', from the verb *matriculare*, from late Latin *matricula* 'register', diminutive of Latin *matrix*.

matriculation ▶ noun [mass noun] **1** the action of matriculating at a college or university: [as modifier] *matriculation requirements*. ■ (also **matriculation examination**) [count noun] historical an examination to qualify for enrolment at a college or university. ■ (also **matriculation examination**) [count noun] (in South Africa) a school-leaving examination taken at the end of the twelfth year.
2 Heraldry, Scottish the registration of arms in an official register.

matrifocal ▶ adjective (of a society, culture, etc.) based on the mother as the head of the family or household.
– ORIGIN 1950s: from Latin *mater*, *matr-* 'mother' + FOCAL.

matrilineal ▶ adjective of or based on kinship with the mother or the female line.
– DERIVATIVES **matrilineally** adverb.
– ORIGIN early 20th cent.: from Latin *mater*, *matr-* 'mother' + LINEAL.

matrilocal ▶ adjective of or denoting a custom in marriage whereby the husband goes to live with the wife's community. Also called UXORILOCAL.
– DERIVATIVES **matrilocality** noun.
– ORIGIN early 20th cent.: from Latin *mater*, *matr-* 'mother' + LOCAL.

matrimonial ▶ adjective relating to marriage or married people: *the matrimonial home*.
– DERIVATIVES **matrimonially** adverb.
– ORIGIN late Middle English: via Old French from Latin *matrimonialis*, from *matrimonium* (see MATRIMONY).

matrimony /ˈmatrɪməni/ ▶ noun [mass noun] the state of being married; marriage: *the joys of matrimony*.
– ORIGIN late Middle English: via Old French from Latin *matrimonium*, based on *mater*, *matr-* 'mother'.

matrix /ˈmeɪtrɪks/ ▶ noun (pl. **matrices** /-siːz/ or **matrixes**) **1** the cultural, social, or political environment in which something develops: *Oxbridge was the matrix of the ideology*.
2 a mass of fine-grained rock in which gems, crystals, or fossils are embedded. ■ Biology the substance between cells or in which structures are embedded. ■ fine material used to bind together the coarser particles of a composite substance.
3 a mould in which something, such as a record or printing type, is cast or shaped.
4 Mathematics a rectangular array of quantities or expressions in rows and columns that is treated as a single entity and manipulated according to particular rules. ■ a grid-like arrangement of elements; a lattice.
5 an organizational structure in which two or more lines of command, responsibility, or communication may run through the same individual.
– ORIGIN late Middle English (in the sense 'womb'): from Latin, 'breeding female', later 'womb', from *mater*, *matr-* 'mother'.

matron ▶ noun **1** Brit. a woman in charge of domestic and medical arrangements at a boarding school or other institution. ■ Brit. the woman in charge of the nursing in a hospital (the official term is now **senior nursing officer**). ■ US a female prison officer.

2 an older married woman, especially one who is staid or dignified.
– DERIVATIVES **matronhood** noun.
– ORIGIN late Middle English (in sense 2): from Old French *matrone*, from Latin *matrona*, from *mater*, *matr-* 'mother'.

matronly ▸ adjective characteristic of an older married woman, especially in being staid or rather fat: *she was beginning to look matronly*.

matron of honour ▸ noun a married woman attending the bride at a wedding.

matronymic /ˌmatrəˈnɪmɪk/ ▸ noun a name derived from the name of a mother or female ancestor.
– ORIGIN late 18th cent.: from Latin *mater*, *matr-* 'mother', on the pattern of *patronymic*.

matryoshka /ˌmatrɪˈɒʃkə/ (also **matryoshka doll**) ▸ noun (pl. **matryoshki** /-ki/) another term for **RUSSIAN DOLL**.
– ORIGIN 1940s: from Russian *matrëshka*.

matsuri /matˈsuːri/ ▸ noun a solemn festival celebrated periodically at Shinto shrines in Japan.
– ORIGIN Japanese.

Matsuyama /ˌmatsuːˈjɑːmə/ a city in Japan, the capital and largest city of the island of Shikoku; pop. 513,902 (2007).

matt (also **matte** or US **mat**) ▸ adjective (of a surface or colour) dull and flat; without a shine: *prints are available on matt or glossy paper | a matt black*.
▸ noun **1** [mass noun] a matt paint or finish.
2 a sheet of cardboard placed on the back of a picture, either as a mount or to form a border.
▸ verb (**matts, matting, matted**) [with obj.] give a matt appearance to (something).
– ORIGIN early 17th cent. (as a verb): from French *mat*.

Matt. ▸ abbreviation Matthew (especially in biblical references).

mattar /ˈmʌtəː/ ▸ noun Indian term for **PEA**.
– ORIGIN from Hindi *maṭar*.

matte[1] /mat/ ▸ noun [mass noun] an impure product of the smelting of sulphide ores, especially those of copper or nickel.
– ORIGIN mid 19th cent.: from French (in Old French meaning 'curds'), feminine of *mat* (adjective) 'matt', used as a noun.

matte[2] /mat/ ▸ noun a mask used to obscure part of an image in a film and allow another image to be substituted, combining the two.
– ORIGIN mid 19th cent.: from French, perhaps from *mat* (see **MATT**).

matte[3] ▸ adjective, noun, & verb variant spelling of **MATT**.

matted ▸ adjective **1** (especially of hair, wool, or fur) tangled into a thick mass: *a cardigan of matted grey wool*.
2 covered or provided with mats: *the matted floor*.

matter ▸ noun **1** [mass noun] physical substance in general, as distinct from mind and spirit; (in physics) that which occupies space and possesses rest mass, especially as distinct from energy: *the structure and properties of matter*. ■ [usu. with adj.] a particular substance: *organic matter | faecal matter*. ■ written or printed material: *reading matter*. ■ Printing the body of a printed work, as distinct from titles, headings, etc.
2 a subject or situation under consideration: *a great deal of work was done on this matter | financial matters*. ■ Law something which is to be tried or proved in court; a case. ■ (**matters**) the present state of affairs: *we can do nothing to change matters*. ■ the substance or content of a text as distinct from its style or form. ■ Logic the particular content of a proposition, as distinct from its form.
3 [with negative or in questions] (**the matter**) the reason for distress or a problem: *what's the matter?*
▸ verb [no obj.] **1** [usu. with negative or in questions] be important or significant: *it doesn't matter what the guests wear | what did it matter to them?* ■ (of a person) be important or influential: *she was trying to get known by the people who matter*.
2 US (of a wound) secrete or discharge pus.
– PHRASES **for that matter** used to indicate that a subject, though mentioned second, is as relevant as the first. **in the matter of** as regards: *the British are given pre-eminence in the matter of tea*. **it is only a matter of time** there will not be long to wait. **a matter of 1** no more than (a specified period of time): *they were shown the door in a matter of minutes*. **2** a thing that involves or depends on: *it's a matter of working out how to get something done*. **3** (**a matter of/for**) something that evokes (a specified feeling): *it's a matter of complete indifference to me*. **a matter of course** the usual or expected thing: *the reports are published as a matter of course*. **a matter of form** a point of correct procedure. **a matter of record** see **RECORD**. **no matter 1** [with clause] regardless of: *no matter what the government calls them, they are cuts*. **2** it is of no importance: *no matter, I'll go myself*. **to make matters worse** with the result that a bad situation is made worse: *to make matters worse, free school meals have been withdrawn*. **what matter?** Brit. dated why should that worry us?: *They were in collusion. But what matter, since apparently he didn't care?*
– ORIGIN Middle English: via Old French from Latin *materia* 'timber, substance', also 'subject of discourse', from *mater* 'mother'.

Matterhorn /ˈmatəhɔːn/, German /ˈmatɐˌhɔrn/ a mountain in the Alps, on the border between Switzerland and Italy. Rising to 4,477 m (14,688 ft), it was first climbed in 1865 by the English mountaineer Edward Whymper. French name **MONT CERVIN**; Italian name **MONTE CERVINO**.

matter of fact ▸ noun a fact as distinct from an opinion or conjecture: *it's a matter of fact that they had a relationship*. ■ Law the part of a judicial inquiry concerned with the truth of alleged facts. Often contrasted with **MATTER OF LAW**.
▸ adjective (**matter-of-fact**) unemotional and practical: *she tried to keep her tone light and matter-of-fact*. ■ concerned only with factual content rather than style or expression: *the text is written in a breezy matter-of-fact manner*.
– PHRASES **as a matter of fact** in reality (used especially to correct a falsehood or misunderstanding): *as a matter of fact, I was talking to him this afternoon*.
– DERIVATIVES **matter-of-factly** adverb, **matter-of-factness** noun.

matter of law ▸ noun Law the part of a judicial inquiry concerned with the interpretation of the law. Often contrasted with **MATTER OF FACT**.

Matthew, St an Apostle, a tax-gatherer from Capernaum in Galilee, traditional author of the first Gospel. Feast day, 21 September. ■ the first Gospel, written after AD 70 and based largely on that of St Mark.

Matthew Paris (*c.*1199–1259), English chronicler and Benedictine monk, noted for his *Chronica Majora*, a history of the world from the Creation to the mid 13th century.

Matthews, Sir Stanley (1915–2000), English footballer. A winger famous for his dribbling skill, he played for Stoke City, Blackpool, and England and remained a professional player until he was 50.

Matthias, St /məˈθʌɪəs/ an Apostle, chosen by lot after the Ascension to replace Judas. Feast day (in the Western Church) 14 May; (in the Eastern Church) 9 August.

mattify /ˈmatɪfʌɪ/ ▸ verb (**mattifies, mattifying, mattified**) [with obj.] (of a cosmetic) reduce the shine or oiliness of (the complexion).

matting ▸ noun [mass noun] **1** coarse material woven from natural fibres, used for mats: *rush matting*.
2 the process of becoming matted.

mattins ▸ noun variant spelling of **MATINS**.

mattock ▸ noun an agricultural tool shaped like a pickaxe, with an adze and a chisel edge as the ends of the head.
– ORIGIN Old English *mattuc*, of uncertain origin.

mattress ▸ noun **1** a fabric case filled with soft, firm, or springy material, used for sleeping on.
2 Engineering a flat structure of concrete, brushwood, or other material, used as strengthening or support for foundations, embankments, etc.
– ORIGIN Middle English: via Old French and Italian from Arabic *maṭraḥ* 'carpet or cushion', from *ṭaraḥa* 'to throw'.

maturate /ˈmatjʊreɪt/ ▸ verb [no obj.] Medicine (of a boil, abscess, etc.) form pus.
– ORIGIN mid 16th cent.: from Latin *maturat-* 'ripened, hastened', from the verb *maturare*, from *maturus* (see **MATURE**).

maturation ▸ noun [mass noun] **1** the action or process of maturing: *sexual maturation*. ■ the process by which wine or other fermented drinks become ready for drinking. ■ the ripening of fruit: *pod maturation*. ■ Medicine the development of functional ova or sperm cells.
2 the formation of pus in a boil, abscess, etc.
– DERIVATIVES **maturational** adjective, **maturative** adjective.
– ORIGIN late Middle English (denoting the formation of pus): from medieval Latin *maturatio(n-)*, from Latin *maturare* (see **MATURE**).

mature ▸ adjective (**maturer, maturest**) **1** fully developed physically; full-grown: *she was now a mature woman | owls are sexually mature at one year*. ■ (especially of a young person) having reached a stage of mental or emotional development characteristic of an adult: *a young man mature beyond his years*. ■ (of thought or planning) careful and thorough: *on mature reflection he decided they should not go*. ■ used euphemistically to describe someone middle-aged or old: *Miss Walker was a mature lady when she married*.
2 having reached the most advanced stage in a process: *Van Gogh's mature work*. ■ (of certain foods or drinks) ready for consumption: *a rather nice mature Camembert*. ■ denoting an economy, industry, or market that has developed to a point where substantial expansion and investment no longer takes place.
3 (of a bill, bond, etc.) due for payment or repayment.
▸ verb [no obj.] **1** (of a person or thing) become fully grown or developed: *children mature at different ages | the trees take at least thirty years to mature*. ■ (of a person) reach an advanced stage of mental or emotional development: *he has matured and is ready to take on new responsibilities*. ■ (with reference to certain foods or drinks) become or cause to become ready for consumption: [no obj.] *leave the cheese to mature* | [with obj.] *the Scotch is matured for a minimum of three years*.
2 (of an insurance policy, security, etc.) reach the end of its term and hence become payable.
– DERIVATIVES **maturely** adverb.
– ORIGIN late Middle English: from Latin *maturus* 'timely, ripe'; perhaps related to **MATINS**.

mature student ▸ noun Brit. an adult student who attends college or university some years after leaving school.

maturity ▸ noun (pl. **maturities**) [mass noun] the state, fact, or period of being mature: *the progress of an ingénue from childhood to maturity | the fish takes 35 years to reach maturity*. ■ the time when an insurance policy, security, etc. matures. ■ [count noun] an insurance policy, security, etc. having a fixed maturity date.
– ORIGIN late Middle English: from Latin *maturitas*, from *maturus* (see **MATURE**).

matutinal /ˌmatjʊˈtʌɪn(ə)l, məˈtjuːtɪn(ə)l/ ▸ adjective formal of or occurring in the morning.
– ORIGIN mid 16th cent.: from late Latin *matutinalis*, from Latin *matutinus* 'early'.

maty ▸ adjective & noun variant spelling of **MATEY**.

matzo /ˈmatsə, ˈmatsəʊ/ (also **matzoh** or **matzah**) ▸ noun (pl. **matzos, matzohs,** or **matzoth** /-əʊt/) a crisp biscuit of unleavened bread, traditionally eaten by Jews during Passover.
– ORIGIN Yiddish, from Hebrew *maṣṣāh*.

matzo ball ▸ noun a small dumpling made of seasoned matzo meal bound together with egg and chicken fat, typically served in chicken soup.

matzo meal ▸ noun [mass noun] meal made from ground matzos.

mauby /ˈməʊbi/ ▸ noun [mass noun] a West Indian drink made from the bark of trees of the buckthorn family.
– ORIGIN from Carib *mabi*, denoting a drink made from sweet potatoes.

maud /mɔːd/ ▸ noun a grey-striped plaid cloak, formerly worn by shepherds in Scotland.
– ORIGIN late 18th cent.: of unknown origin.

maudlin /ˈmɔːdlɪn/ ▸ adjective self-pityingly or tearfully sentimental: *a bout of maudlin self-pity*. ■ (of a book, film, or song) highly sentimental: *a maudlin jukebox tune*.
– ORIGIN late Middle English (as a noun denoting Mary Magdalen): from Old French *Madeleine*, from Church Latin *Magdalena* (see **MAGDALEN**). The current sense derives from allusion to pictures of Mary Magdalen weeping.

Maugham /mɔːm/, (William) Somerset (1874–1965), British novelist, short-story writer, and dramatist, born in France. Notable works: *Of Human Bondage* (novel, 1915), *The Moon and Sixpence* (novel, 1919), *East of Suez* (play, 1922), and *Cakes and Ale* (novel, 1930).

Maui /ˈmaʊi/ the second-largest of the Hawaiian islands, lying to the north-west of Hawaii.

maul ▸ verb [with obj.] (of an animal) wound (a person or animal) by scratching and tearing: *a man was mauled by a lion at London Zoo*. ■ treat (something)

M

savagely or roughly. ■ handle (someone) roughly, especially for sexual gratification: *she hated being mauled by macho chauvinist pigs.* ■ informal defeat heavily in a game or match: *the team were mauled 4-0 by Manchester City.* ■ subject to fierce criticism: (as noun **mauling**) *he faces a mauling at next week's conference.* ■ [no obj.] Rugby take part in a maul.
▸ **noun 1** (in rugby union) a loose scrum formed around a player with the ball off the ground. Compare with **RUCK**[1].
2 another term for **BEETLE**[2] (sense 1 of the noun).
– ORIGIN Middle English (in the sense 'hammer or wooden club', also 'strike with a heavy weapon'): from Old French *mail*, from Latin *malleus* 'hammer'.

maulana /maʊˈlɑːnə/ ▸ **noun** [often as title] a Muslim man revered for his religious learning or piety.
– ORIGIN mid 19th cent.: from Arabic *mawlānā* 'our master'.

mauler ▸ **noun** (usu. **maulers**) informal a person's hand: *keep your rotten maulers off my things!*

maulstick /ˈmɔːlstɪk/ ▸ **noun** variant spelling of **MAHLSTICK**.

maulvi ▸ **noun** (pl. **maulvis**) variant spelling of **MOULVI**.

Mau Mau /ˈmaʊ maʊ/ an African secret society originating among the Kikuyu that in the 1950s used violence and terror to try to expel European settlers and end British rule in Kenya. The British eventually subdued the organization, but went on to institute political and social reforms which led to Kenya's independence in 1963. ■ (**mau-mau**) [as verb] [with obj.] US informal terrorize or threaten (someone).
– ORIGIN Kikuyu.

Mauna Kea /ˌmaʊnə ˈkeɪə/ an extinct volcano on the island of Hawaii, in the central Pacific. Rising to 4,205 m (13,796 ft), it is the highest peak in the Hawaiian islands. The summit area is the site of several large astronomical telescopes.

Mauna Loa /ˈləʊə/ an active volcano on the island of Hawaii, to the south of Mauna Kea, rising to 4,169 m (13,678 ft).

maund /mɔːnd/ ▸ **noun** Indian a woven basket. ■ a measure of capacity or of weight, equivalent to about 38 kilograms.
– ORIGIN Old English *mand*, reinforced by Old French *mande*, of Germanic origin; related to Dutch *mand*.

M

maunder /ˈmɔːndə/ ▸ **verb** [no obj.] talk in a rambling manner: *Dennis **maundered on about** the wine.* ■ [with adverbial] move or act in a dreamy or idle manner: *he maunders through the bank, composing his thoughts.*
– ORIGIN early 17th cent.: perhaps from obsolete *maunder* 'to beg'.

Maunder minimum /ˈmɔːndə/ a prolonged minimum in sunspot activity on the sun between about 1645 and 1715, which coincided with the Little Ice Age in the northern hemisphere.
– ORIGIN 1970s: named after Edward W. *Maunder* (1851–1928), English astronomer.

Maundy /ˈmɔːndi/ ▸ **noun** [mass noun] (in the UK) a public ceremony on the Thursday before Easter (**Maundy Thursday**) at which the monarch distributes specially minted coins. ■ (also **Royal Maundy**) Maundy money.
– ORIGIN Middle English: from Old French *mande*, from Latin *mandatum* 'mandate, commandment', from *mandatum novum* 'new commandment' (see John 13:34).

Maundy money ▸ **noun** [mass noun] specially minted silver coins distributed by the British sovereign on Maundy Thursday. The number of recipients and the face value in pence of the amount they each receive traditionally correspond to the number of years in the sovereign's age.

Maupassant /ˈməʊpasɒ̃/, French /mopasɑ̃/, (Henri René Albert) Guy de (1850–93), French novelist and short-story writer. He wrote about 300 short stories and six novels in a simple, direct narrative style. Notable novels: *Une Vie* (1883) and *Bel-Ami* (1885).

Mauretania /ˌmɒrɪˈteɪnɪə/ an ancient region of North Africa, corresponding to the northern part of Morocco and western and central Algeria.
– DERIVATIVES **Mauretanian** adjective & noun.
– ORIGIN based on Latin *Mauri* 'Moors', by whom the region was originally occupied.

Mauriac /ˈmɒrɪak/, French /mɔʀjak/, François (1885–1970), French novelist, dramatist, and critic. His stories show the conflicts of convention, religion, and human passions suffered by prosperous bourgeoisie. Notable works: *Thérèse Desqueyroux* (novel, 1927). Nobel Prize for Literature (1952).

Mauritania /ˌmɒrɪˈteɪnɪə/ a country in West Africa with a coastline on the Atlantic Ocean; pop. 3,129,500 (est. 2009); languages, Arabic (official), French; capital, Nouakchott.

> Mauritania was a centre of Berber power in the 11th and 12th centuries, at which time Islam became established in the region. Later, nomadic Arab tribes became dominant, while on the coast European nations, especially France, established trading posts. A French protectorate from 1902 and a colony from 1920, Mauritania achieved full independence in 1961.

– DERIVATIVES **Mauritanian** adjective & noun.

Mauritius /məˈrɪʃəs/ an island country in the Indian Ocean, about 850 km (550 miles) east of Madagascar; pop. 1,284,300 (est. 2009); languages, English (official), French Creole, Indian languages; capital, Port Louis.

> Previously uninhabited, Mauritius was discovered by the Portuguese in the early 16th century. It was held by the Dutch 1598–1710 and then by the French until 1810, when it was ceded to Britain. Mauritius became independent as a member of the Commonwealth in 1968.

– DERIVATIVES **Mauritian** adjective & noun.
– ORIGIN named by the Dutch in honour of Prince *Maurice* of Nassau, a stadtholder of the United Provinces.

Maury /ˈmɔːri/, Matthew Fontaine (1806–73), American oceanographer. He conducted the first systematic survey of oceanic winds and currents, and published charts of his findings.

Maurya /ˈmaʊrɪə/ a dynasty which ruled northern India 321–*c.*184 BC. It was founded by Chandragupta Maurya, who introduced a centralized government and uniform script. The oldest extant Indian art dates from this era.
– DERIVATIVES **Mauryan** adjective.

Mauser /ˈmaʊzə/ ▸ **noun** trademark a make of firearm, especially a repeating rifle or semi-automatic pistol.
– ORIGIN late 19th cent.: named after Paul von *Mauser* (1838–1914), German inventor.

mausoleum /ˌmɔːsəˈlɪəm, -z-/ ▸ **noun** (pl. **mausolea** /-ˈlɪə/ or **mausoleums**) a stately or impressive building housing a tomb or group of tombs.
– ORIGIN late 15th cent.: via Latin from Greek *Mausōleion*, from *Mausōlos*, the name of a king of Caria (4th cent. BC), to whose tomb in Halicarnassus the name was originally applied.

mauve /məʊv/ ▸ **adjective** of a pale purple colour: *blossoms with mauve and white petals.*
▸ **noun** [mass noun] **1** a pale purple colour: *a few pale streaks of mauve were all that remained of the sunset* | [count noun] *glowing with soft pastel mauves and pinks.*
2 historical a pale purple aniline dye prepared by William H. Perkin in 1856. It was the first synthetic dyestuff.
– DERIVATIVES **mauvish** adjective.
– ORIGIN mid 19th cent.: from French, literally 'mallow', from Latin *malva*.

mauveine /ˈməʊviːn/ ▸ **noun** another term for **MAUVE** (sense 2 of the noun).

maven /ˈmeɪv(ə)n/ ▸ **noun** [often with modifier] N. Amer. informal an expert or connoisseur: *fashion mavens call beige oatmeal.*
– ORIGIN 1960s: Yiddish.

maverick ▸ **noun 1** an unorthodox or independent-minded person: *he's the maverick of the senate.*
2 N. Amer. an unbranded calf or yearling.
▸ **adjective** unorthodox: *a maverick detective.*
– ORIGIN mid 19th cent.: from the name of Samuel A. *Maverick* (1803–70), a Texas rancher who did not brand his cattle.

mavis /ˈmeɪvɪs/ ▸ **noun** literary a song thrush.
– ORIGIN late Middle English: from Old French *mauvis*, of unknown origin.

maw ▸ **noun** the jaws or throat of a voracious animal: *a gigantic wolfhound with a fearful, gaping maw.* ■ informal the mouth or gullet of a greedy person.
– ORIGIN Old English *maga* (in the sense 'stomach'), of Germanic origin; related to Dutch *maag* and German *Magen* 'stomach'.

mawashi /məˈwɑːʃi/ ▸ **noun** a type of loincloth worn by a sumo wrestler.
– ORIGIN Japanese, from *mawasu* 'to put round'.

mawkish ▸ **adjective** sentimental in an exaggerated or false way: *a mawkish ode to parenthood.* ■ archaic or dialect having a faint sickly flavour: *the mawkish smell of warm beer.*
– DERIVATIVES **mawkishly** adverb, **mawkishness** noun.
– ORIGIN mid 17th cent. (in the sense 'inclined to sickness'): from obsolete *mawk* 'maggot', from Old Norse *mathkr*, of Germanic origin.

Mawlana /mɔːˈlɑːnə/ another name for **JALAL AD-DIN AR-RUMI**.

Mawlid /ˈmaʊlɪd/ (also **Milad** /ˈmiːlɑːd/) ▸ **noun** Islam the annual celebration of the prophet Muhammad's birthday.
– ORIGIN Arabic, 'birthday', 'celebration of a birth'.

max informal ▸ **noun** a maximum amount or setting: *the sound is distorted **to the max**.*
▸ **adverb** at the most: *the trip costs about 35p max.*
▸ **verb** N. Amer. informal reach or cause to reach the limit of capacity or ability: [no obj.] *job growth in high technology **will max out**.*

max. ▸ **abbreviation** maximum.

maxi ▸ **noun** (pl. **maxis**) **1** a skirt or coat reaching to the ankle.
2 (also **maxi yacht**) a racing yacht of between 15 and 20 metres in length.
– ORIGIN 1960s: abbreviation of **MAXIMUM**, on the pattern of *mini*.

maxi- ▸ **combining form** very large or long: *a maxi-farm.*
– ORIGIN from **MAXIMUM**.

maxilla /makˈsɪlə/ ▸ **noun** (pl. **maxillae** /-liː/) Anatomy & Zoology the jaw or jawbone, specifically the upper jaw in most vertebrates. In humans it also forms part of the nose and eye socket. ■ (in many arthropods) each of a pair of mouthparts used in chewing.
– ORIGIN late Middle English: from Latin, 'jaw'.

maxillary ▸ **adjective** Anatomy & Zoology of or attached to a jaw or jawbone, especially the upper jaw: *a maxillary fracture.* ■ relating to the maxillae of an arthropod.
– ORIGIN early 17th cent.: from **MAXILLA**, probably suggested by Latin *maxillaris*.

maxilliped /makˈsɪlɪpɛd/ ▸ **noun** Zoology (in crustaceans) an appendage modified for feeding, situated in pairs behind the maxillae.
– ORIGIN mid 19th cent.: from **MAXILLA** + Latin *pes, ped-* 'foot'.

maxillofacial /makˌsɪlə(ʊ)ˈfeɪʃ(ə)l, ˌmaksɪlə(ʊ)-/ ▸ **adjective** Anatomy relating to the jaws and face: *maxillofacial surgery.*
– ORIGIN late 19th cent.: from *maxillo-* (combining form of Latin *maxilla* 'jaw') + **FACIAL**.

maxim ▸ **noun** a short, pithy statement expressing a general truth or rule of conduct: *the maxim that actions speak louder than words.*
– ORIGIN late Middle English (denoting an axiom): from French *maxime*, from medieval Latin (*propositio*) *maxima* 'largest or most important (proposition)'.

maxima plural form of **MAXIMUM**.

maximal ▸ **adjective** of or constituting a maximum; as great or as large as possible: *the maximal speed.*
– DERIVATIVES **maximally** adverb.

maximalist ▸ **noun** (especially in politics) a person who holds extreme views and is not prepared to compromise.
▸ **adjective** of or denoting an extreme opinion: *the maximalist interpretation is more promising.*
– DERIVATIVES **maximalism** noun.
– ORIGIN early 20th cent.: from **MAXIMAL**, on the pattern of Russian *maksimalist.*

maximand /ˈmaksɪmand/ ▸ **noun** Economics a quantity or thing which is to be maximized.
– ORIGIN 1950s: from **MAXIMIZE** + **-AND**.

Maxim gun ▸ **noun** the first fully automatic water-cooled machine gun, designed in 1884 and used especially in the First World War.
– ORIGIN named after Sir Hiram S. *Maxim* (1840–1916), American-born British inventor.

Maximilian /ˌmaksɪˈmɪlɪən/ (1832–67), Austrian emperor of Mexico 1864–7; full name *Ferdinand Maximilian Joseph*. Brother of Franz Josef, Maximilian was established as emperor of Mexico under French auspices in 1864. He was executed by a popular uprising led by Benito Juárez.

maximin /ˈmaksɪmɪn/ ▸ **noun** Mathematics the highest of a set of minimum values. Compare with **MINIMAX**. ■ [as modifier] denoting a method or strategy in game theory that maximizes the smallest gain that can be relied on by a participant in a game or other situation of conflict.
– ORIGIN 1950s: blend of **MAXIMUM** and **MINIMUM**, on the pattern of *minimax*.

maximize (also **maximise**) ▶ **verb** [with obj.] make as large or great as possible: *the company was aiming to maximize profits.* ■ make the best use of: *a thriller that maximizes the potential of its locations.*
– DERIVATIVES **maximization** noun, **maximizer** noun.
– ORIGIN early 19th cent.: from Latin *maximus* (see **MAXIMUM**) + **-IZE**.

maximum ▶ **noun** (pl. **maxima** /-mə/ or **maximums**) the greatest amount, extent, or intensity possible, permitted, or recorded: *the school takes a maximum of 32 pupils | production levels are near their maximum.*
▶ **adjective** [attrib.] as great, high, or intense as possible or permitted: *the vehicle's maximum speed | a maximum penalty of ten years' imprisonment.*
– ORIGIN mid 17th cent. (as a noun): from modern Latin, neuter (used as a noun) of the Latin adjective *maximus*, superlative of *magnus* 'great'. The adjectival use dates from the early 19th cent.

maximum sustainable yield (abbrev.: **MSY**) ▶ **noun** [mass noun] (especially in forestry and fisheries) the maximum level at which a natural resource can be routinely exploited without long-term depletion.

maxixe /mak'siːks, mə'ʃiːʃə/ ▶ **noun** a Brazilian dance for couples, resembling the polka and the Brazilian tango.
– ORIGIN early 20th cent.: Portuguese.

Maxwell, James Clerk (1831–79), Scottish physicist. He extended the ideas of Faraday and Kelvin in his equations of electromagnetism and succeeded in unifying electricity and magnetism, identifying the electromagnetic nature of light, and postulating the existence of other electromagnetic radiation.

maxwell (abbrev.: **Mx**) ▶ **noun** Physics a unit of magnetic flux in the c.g.s. system, equal to that induced through one square centimetre by a perpendicular magnetic field of one gauss.
– ORIGIN early 20th cent.: named after J. C. *Maxwell* (see **MAXWELL**).

Maxwell–Boltzmann distribution ▶ **noun** Physics a formula describing the statistical distribution of particles in a system among different energy levels. The number of particles in a given energy level is proportional to $\exp(-E/kT)$, where E is the energy of the level, k is Boltzmann's constant, and T is the absolute temperature.
– ORIGIN 1920s: named after J. C. *Maxwell* (see **MAXWELL**) and L. **BOLTZMANN**.

Maxwell Davies, Sir Peter, see **DAVIES[1]**.

Maxwell's demon ▶ **noun** Physics a hypothetical being imagined as controlling a hole in a partition dividing a gas-filled container into two parts, and allowing only fast-moving molecules to pass in one direction, and slow-moving molecules in the other. This would result in one side of the container becoming warmer and the other colder, in violation of the second law of thermodynamics.
– ORIGIN late 19th cent.: named after J. C. *Maxwell* (see **MAXWELL**).

Maxwell's equations ▶ **plural noun** Physics a set of four linear partial differential equations which summarize the classical properties of the electromagnetic field.
– ORIGIN early 20th cent.: named after J. C. *Maxwell* (see **MAXWELL**).

May ▶ **noun** the fifth month of the year, in the northern hemisphere usually considered the last month of spring: *the new model makes its showroom debut in May | the full system was deployed last May.* ■ (**one's May**) literary one's bloom or prime: *others murmured that their May was passing.*
– ORIGIN late Old English, from Old French *mai*, from Latin *Maius (mensis)* '(month) of the goddess *Maia*'.

may[1] ▶ **modal verb** (3rd sing. present **may**; past **might** /mʌɪt/) **1** expressing possibility: *that may be true | he **may well** win.* ■ used when admitting that something is so before making another, more important point: *they may have been old-fashioned but they were excellent teachers.*
2 used to ask for or to give permission: *you may confirm my identity with your Case Officer, if you wish | may I ask a few questions?*
3 expressing a wish or hope: *may she rest in peace.*
– PHRASES **be that as it may** despite that; nevertheless. **may as well** another way of saying **MIGHT AS WELL** (see **MIGHT[1]**). **that is as may be** that may or may not be so (implying that this is not a significant consideration).
– ORIGIN Old English *mæg*, of Germanic origin, from a base meaning 'have power'; related to Dutch *mogen* and German *mögen*, also to **MAIN[1]** and **MIGHT[2]**.

> **USAGE** Traditionalists insist that one should distinguish between **may** (present tense) and **might** (past tense) in expressing possibility: *I may have some dessert if I'm still hungry; she might have known her killer*. However, this distinction is rarely observed today, and **may** and **might** are generally acceptable in either case: *she may have visited yesterday; I might go and have a cup of tea.*
> On the difference in use between **may** and **can**, see **USAGE** at **CAN[1]**.

may[2] ▶ **noun** [mass noun] the hawthorn or its blossom.
– ORIGIN late Middle English: from **MAY**.

Maya /'mʌɪ(j)ə, 'meɪ(j)ə/ ▶ **noun** (pl. **same** or **Mayas**) **1** a member of an American Indian people of Yucatán and elsewhere in Central America.
2 [mass noun] the language of the Maya, still spoken by about half a million people.
▶ **adjective** relating to the Maya or their language.

> The Maya civilization developed in southern Mexico, Guatemala, and Belize from the 2nd millennium BC, reaching its peak c.300–c.900 AD. Its remains include stone temples built on pyramids and ornamented with sculptures. The ancient Mayas used a system of hieroglyphic writing and an extremely accurate calendar system.

– ORIGIN the name in Maya.

maya /'mɑːjə/ ▶ **noun** [mass noun] Hinduism the supernatural power wielded by gods and demons. ■ Hinduism & Buddhism the power by which the universe becomes manifest; the illusion or appearance of the phenomenal world.
– ORIGIN from Sanskrit *māyā*, from *mā* 'create'.

Mayakovsky /ˌmʌɪə'kɒfski/, Vladimir (Vladimirovich) (1893–1930), Soviet poet and dramatist, born in Georgia. A fervent futurist, he wrote in a declamatory, aggressive avant-garde style, which he altered to have a comic mass appeal after the Bolshevik revolution.

Mayan /'mʌɪ(j)ən, 'meɪ(j)ən/ ▶ **noun** [mass noun] a large family of American Indian languages spoken in Central America and Mexico, of which the chief members are Maya, Quiché, and Tzeltal.
▶ **adjective** **1** denoting or relating to the Mayan family of languages.
2 relating to or denoting the Maya people.

mayapple ▶ **noun** an American herbaceous plant of the barberry family, which bears a yellow egg-shaped fruit in May. The plant has long been used medicinally. ● *Podophyllum peltatum*, family Berberidaceae.

maybe ▶ **adverb** perhaps; possibly: *maybe I won't go back | he was standing maybe 20 or 30 feet away.*
▶ **noun** a mere possibility or probability: *no ifs, buts, or maybes.*
– PHRASES **that's as maybe** used to admit the truth of a point in an argument before introducing another, more important point: *well, that's as maybe but it's not the way the BBC works.*
– ORIGIN late Middle English: from the phrase *it may be (that)*.

May bug ▶ **noun** another term for **COCKCHAFER**.

Mayday ▶ **noun** an international radio distress signal used by ships and aircraft.
– ORIGIN 1920s: representing a pronunciation of French *m'aider*, from *venez m'aider* 'come and help me'.

May Day ▶ **noun** 1 May, celebrated in many countries as a traditional springtime festival or as an international day honouring workers. ■ (in the UK) a public holiday on the first Monday in May.

Mayer /'meɪə/, Louis B. (1885–1957), Russian-born American film executive; full name *Louis Burt Mayer*; born *Eliezer Mayer*. In 1924 he formed Metro-Goldwyn-Mayer (MGM) with Samuel Goldwyn; he headed the company until 1951.

mayest /'meɪɪst/ archaic second person singular present of **MAY[1]**.

Mayfair a fashionable and wealthy district in the West End of London.
– ORIGIN originally the site of a fair held annually in May in the 17th and 18th cents.

Mayflower the ship in which the Pilgrim Fathers sailed from England to America.

mayflower ▶ **noun** the trailing arbutus.

mayfly ▶ **noun** (pl. **mayflies**) a short-lived slender insect with delicate transparent wings and two or three long filaments on the tail. It lives close to water, where the aquatic larvae develop. ● Order Ephemeroptera: several families.
■ an artificial fishing fly made to resemble a mayfly.

mayhap ▶ **adverb** archaic perhaps; possibly.
– ORIGIN mid 16th cent.: from *it may hap*.

mayhem ▶ **noun** [mass noun] violent or extreme disorder; chaos: *complete mayhem broke out.* ■ Law, historical the crime of maliciously injuring or maiming someone, originally so as to render them defenceless.
– ORIGIN early 16th cent.: from Old French *mayhem* (see **MAIM**). The sense 'disorder' (originally US) dates from the late 19th cent.

maying ▶ **noun** [mass noun] archaic the celebration of May Day.

Maynooth /meɪ'nuːθ/ a village in County Kildare in the Republic of Ireland; pop. 10,715 (2006). It is the site of St Patrick's College, a Roman Catholic seminary founded in 1795.

mayn't ▶ **contraction** may not.

Mayo a county in the Republic of Ireland, in the north-west in the province of Connacht; county town, Castlebar.

mayo ▶ **noun** informal short for **MAYONNAISE**.

mayonnaise ▶ **noun** [mass noun] a thick creamy dressing consisting of egg yolks beaten with oil and vinegar and seasoned. ■ [with modifier] Brit. a mixture of mayonnaise and a specified ingredient: *egg mayonnaise.*
– ORIGIN French, probably from the feminine of *mahonnais* 'of or from Port *Mahon*', the capital of Minorca.

mayor ▶ **noun** (in England, Wales, and Northern Ireland) the head of a town, borough, or county council, elected by council members and generally having purely ceremonial duties. ■ (in the US, Canada, and certain other countries) the head of a municipal corporation, elected by the public.
– DERIVATIVES **mayoral** adjective, **mayorship** noun.
– ORIGIN Middle English: from Old French *maire*, from the Latin adjective *major* 'greater', used as a noun in late Latin.

mayoralty /'mɛːr(ə)lti/ ▶ **noun** (pl. **mayoralties**) the office or position of mayor: *the party failed to win the mayoralty.* ■ a mayor's term of office.
– ORIGIN late Middle English: from Old French *mairalte*, from *maire* (see **MAYOR**).

mayoress /'mɛːrɪs, ˌmɛː'rɛs/ ▶ **noun** **1** the wife of a mayor.
2 a woman holding the office of mayor.

Mayotte /mɑː'jɒt/ an island to the east of the Comoros in the Indian Ocean; pop. 223,800 (est. 2009); languages, French (official), local Swahili dialect; capital, Mamoutzu. When the Comoros became independent in 1974, Mayotte remained an overseas territory of France. Also called **MAHORE**.

maypole ▶ **noun** a painted pole, decorated with flowers, round which people traditionally dance on May Day holding long ribbons attached to the top.

maypop ▶ **noun** the yellow edible fruit of a North American passion flower. ● The plant is *Passiflora incarnata*, family Passifloraceae.

May queen ▶ **noun** a pretty girl chosen and crowned in traditional celebrations of May Day.

mayst archaic second person singular present of **MAY[1]**.

mayweed ▶ **noun** [mass noun] a plant of the daisy family, typically found as a weed of arable land. ● Several species in the family Compositae, in particular **stinking mayweed** (*Anthemis cotula*) and **scentless mayweed** (*Tripleurospermum inodorum*).
– ORIGIN mid 16th cent.: from *maythe(n)*, an earlier name for this plant (in Old English *mægethe, magothe*), + **WEED**.

Mazar-e-Sharif /maˌzɑːriːʃə'riːf/ a city in northern Afghanistan; pop. 300,600 (est. 2006). The city, whose name means 'tomb of the saint', is the reputed burial place of Ali, son-in-law of Muhammad.

Mazarin /'mazərɪn, -rã/, French /mazarɛ̃/, Jules (1602–61), Italian-born French statesman; Italian name *Giulio Mazzarino*. Sent to Paris as the Italian papal legate (1634), he became a naturalized Frenchman; he was made a cardinal in 1641 and then chief minister of France (1642).

mazarine blue /ˌmazə'riːn, 'mazəriːn/ ▶ **noun** a migratory blue butterfly of Eurasian meadows. ● *Cyaniris semiargus*, family Lycaenidae.
– ORIGIN late 17th cent. (denoting a deep blue colour): apparently from the name of Cardinal **MAZARIN**, or of the Duchesse de *Mazarin* (died 1699), though the connection is unknown.

M

Mazatlán /ˌmazətˈlɑːn/ a seaport and resort in Mexico, on the Pacific coast in the state of Sinaloa; pop. 352,471 (2005). Founded in 1531, it developed as a centre of Spanish trade with the Philippines.

Mazdaism /ˈmazdəˌɪz(ə)m/ ▸ **noun** another term for **Zoroastrianism**.
– ORIGIN late 19th cent.: from Avestan *mazdā* (short for **Ahura Mazda**) + **-ism**.

mazdoor /mʌzˈdʊə, mʌzˈdɔː/ ▸ **noun** Indian an unskilled labourer.
– ORIGIN from Hindi *mazdūr*.

maze ▸ **noun** a network of paths and hedges designed as a puzzle through which one has to find a way. ■ a complex network of paths or passages: *they were trapped in a menacing **maze** of corridors.* ■ a confusing mass of information: ***a maze of** petty regulations.*
▸ **verb** (**be mazed**) archaic or dialect be dazed and confused: *she was still mazed with the drug she had taken.*
– ORIGIN Middle English (denoting delirium or delusion): probably from the base of **amaze**, of which the verb is a shortening.

mazel tov /ˈmaz(ə)l ˌtɔːv, ˌtɒf/ ▸ **exclamation** (among Jewish people) congratulations; good luck.
– ORIGIN from modern Hebrew *mazzāl ṭōḇ*, literally 'good star'.

mazer /ˈmeɪzə/ ▸ **noun** historical a hardwood drinking bowl.
– ORIGIN Middle English: from Old French *masere*, of Germanic origin.

mazuma /məˈzuːmə/ ▸ **noun** [mass noun] informal, chiefly US money; cash.
– ORIGIN early 20th cent.: Yiddish, from Hebrew *mĕzummān*, from *zimmēn* 'prepare'.

mazurka /məˈzəːkə, məˈzʊəkə/ ▸ **noun** a lively Polish dance in triple time.
– ORIGIN early 19th cent.: via German from Polish *mazurka*, accusative or genitive singular of *mazurek* 'folk dance from Mazovia', from *mazur*, denoting an inhabitant of the province Mazovia.

mazy ▸ **adjective** (**mazier**, **maziest**) **1** like a maze; labyrinthine: *the mazy old fishing quarter.*
2 N. English confused or dizzy.

M

mazzard /ˈmazəd/ ▸ **noun** another term for **gean**.
– ORIGIN late 16th cent.: perhaps a form of *mazard*, obsolete variant of **mazer**.

Mazzini /matˈsiːni/, Giuseppe (1805–72), Italian nationalist leader. He founded the patriotic movement Young Italy (1831) and was a leader of the Risorgimento. Following the country's unification as a monarchy in 1861, he continued to campaign for a republican Italy.

MB ▸ **abbreviation** ■ Bachelor of Medicine. [from Latin *Medicinae Baccalaureus*.] ■ Manitoba (in official postal use). ■ (also **Mb**) Computing megabyte(s).

MBA ▸ **abbreviation** Master of Business Administration.

Mbabane /ˌ(ə)mbɑːˈbɑːni/ the capital of Swaziland; pop. 78,000 (est. 2007).

mbalax /(ə)mˈbalaks/ ▸ **noun** [mass noun] a type of Senegalese popular music derived from a combination of traditional Wolof drumming patterns and Cuban popular music.
– ORIGIN Wolof, literally 'rhythm'.

mbaqanga /ˌ(ə)mbaˈkɑːŋɡə/ ▸ **noun** [mass noun] a rhythmical popular music style of southern Africa.
– ORIGIN from Zulu *umbaqanga*, literally 'steamed maize bread', with reference to the combined notion of the homely cultural sustenance of the townships and the musicians' 'daily bread'.

MBE ▸ **abbreviation** (in the UK) Member of the Order of the British Empire.

Mbeki /(ə)mˈbekɪ/, Thabo (b.1942), South African statesman, President 1999–2008.

mbira /(ə)mˈbɪərə/ ▸ **noun** (especially in southern Africa) another term for **thumb piano**.
– ORIGIN late 19th cent.: from Shona, probably an alteration of *rimba* 'a note'.

MBO ▸ **abbreviation** management buyout.

Mbps ▸ **abbreviation** Computing megabits per second.

Mbundu /(ə)mˈbʊnduː/ ▸ **noun** (pl. **same**) **1** a member of either of two peoples of western Angola.
2 [mass noun] either of the Bantu languages of the Mbundu peoples, often distinguished as **Umbundu** (related to Herero and spoken by around 3 million people) and **Kimbundu** (related to Kikongo and spoken by nearly 2 million people).
▸ **adjective** relating to the Mbundu or their languages.

Mbuti /(ə)mˈbuːti/ ▸ **noun** (pl. **same** or **Mbutis**) a member of a Pygmy people of western Uganda and adjacent areas of the Democratic Republic of the Congo (Zaire).
– ORIGIN the name in local languages.

Mbyte ▸ **abbreviation** megabyte(s).

MC ▸ **abbreviation** ■ (in the US) Member of Congress. ■ (in the UK) Military Cross. ■ Monaco (international vehicle registration). ■ music cassette.
▸ **noun** **1** short for **master of ceremonies**.
2 a person who provides entertainment at a club or party by instructing the DJ and performing rap music.
▸ **verb** (**MC's**, **MC'ing**, **MC'd**) [no obj.] perform as an MC: (as noun **MC'ing**) *a long bout of MC'ing.*

Mc ▸ **abbreviation** megacycle(s), a unit of frequency equal to one million cycles.

MCB ▸ **abbreviation** miniature circuit-breaker.

MCC Marylebone Cricket Club, founded in 1787, which has its headquarters at Lord's Cricket Ground in London. The tacitly accepted governing body of cricket until 1969, it continues to have primary responsibility for the game's laws.

McEwan /məˈkjuːən/, Ian (Russell) (b.1948), English novelist. Notable novels: *Black Dogs* (1992), *Amsterdam* (Booker Prize, 1998), and *Atonement* (2001).

mcg ▸ **abbreviation** microgram(s).

MCh (also **MChir**) ▸ **abbreviation** Master of Surgery.
– ORIGIN from Latin *Magister Chirurgiae*.

mCi ▸ **abbreviation** millicurie(s), a quantity of a radioactive substance having one thousandth of a curie of radioactivity.

MCom ▸ **abbreviation** Master of Commerce.

m-commerce (also **m-business**) ▸ **noun** [mass noun] commercial transactions conducted electronically by mobile phone.

MCP ▸ **abbreviation** informal male chauvinist pig.

MCR ▸ **abbreviation** Brit. Middle Common Room.

Mc/s ▸ **abbreviation** megacycles per second, a unit of frequency equal to one million cycles per second.

McTimoney /məkˈtɪməni/ ▸ **noun** [as modifier] denoting a gentle form of chiropractic treatment involving very light and swift movements of the practitioner's hands.
– ORIGIN 1970s: named after John *McTimoney* (1914–80), its British inventor.

MD ▸ **abbreviation** ■ Doctor of Medicine. [from Latin *Medicinae Doctor*.] ■ Brit. Managing Director. ■ Maryland (in official postal use). ■ musical director.

Md ▸ **symbol** the chemical element mendelevium.

Md. ▸ **abbreviation** Maryland.

MDF ▸ **abbreviation** medium density fibreboard.

MDMA ▸ **abbreviation** methylenedioxymethamphetamine, the drug Ecstasy.

MDT ▸ **abbreviation** Mountain Daylight Time (see **Mountain time**).

ME ▸ **abbreviation** ■ Maine (in official postal use). ■ US Medical Examiner. ■ Middle English. ■ Brit. myalgic encephalomyelitis or myalgic encephalopathy.

Me ▸ **abbreviation** ■ Maine. ■ Maître (title of a French advocate).

me¹ ▸ **pronoun** [first person singular] **1** used by a speaker to refer to himself or herself as the object of a verb or preposition: *do you understand me? | wait for me!* ■ used after the verb 'to be' and after 'than' or 'as': *hi, it's me | you have more than me.* ■ informal & W. Indian I or my: *I'll get me coat | me can come an go as me please.* ■ N. Amer. informal to or for myself: *I've got me a job.*
2 informal used in exclamations: *dear me!*
– PHRASES **me and mine** my relatives.
– ORIGIN Old English *mē*, accusative and dative of **I²**, of Germanic origin; related to Dutch *mij*, German *mir* (dative), from an Indo-European root shared by Latin *me*, Greek *(e)me*, and Sanskrit *mā*.

> **USAGE** **1** Traditional grammar teaches that it is correct to say *between you and **me*** and incorrect to say *between you and **I***. For details, see **usage** at **between**.
> **2** Which of the following is correct: *you have more than **me*** or *you have more than **I**?* See **usage** at **personal pronoun**.

me² (also **mi**) ▸ **noun** Music (in tonic sol-fa) the third note of a major scale. ■ the note E in the fixed-doh system.
– ORIGIN late Middle English *mi*, representing (as an arbitrary name for the note) the first syllable of *mira*, taken from a Latin hymn (see **solmization**).

mea culpa /ˌmeɪə ˈkʊlpə, ˌmiːə ˈkʌlpə/ ▸ **exclamation** used as an acknowledgement of one's fault or error: *'Well, whose fault was that?' 'Mea culpa!' Frank said.*
– ORIGIN Latin, 'by my fault'.

Mead, Margaret (1901–78), American anthropologist and social psychologist. She worked in Samoa and the New Guinea area and wrote a number of studies of primitive cultures.

mead¹ ▸ **noun** [mass noun] chiefly historical an alcoholic drink of fermented honey and water.
– ORIGIN Old English *me(o)du*, of Germanic origin; related to Dutch *mee* and German *Met*, from an Indo-European root shared by Sanskrit *madhu* 'sweet drink, honey' and Greek *methu* 'wine'.

mead² ▸ **noun** literary a meadow.
– ORIGIN Old English *mǣd*, of Germanic origin; related to **mow¹**.

meadow ▸ **noun** a piece of grassland, especially one used for hay. ■ a piece of low ground near a river.
– DERIVATIVES **meadowy** **adjective**.
– ORIGIN Old English *mǣdwe*, oblique case of *mǣd* (see **mead²**), from the Germanic base of **mow¹**.

meadow brown ▸ **noun** a common Eurasian butterfly that has brown and orange wings with small eyespots. ● *Maniola jurtina*, subfamily Satyrinae, family Nymphalidae.

meadow grass ▸ **noun** [mass noun] a perennial creeping grass which is used for fodder and lawns, and along roadside verges. Also called **bluegrass** in North America. ● Genus *Poa*, family Gramineae: many species.

meadowland ▸ **noun** [mass noun] (also **meadowlands**) land used for the cultivation of grass for hay.

meadowlark ▸ **noun** a ground-dwelling songbird of the American blackbird family, with a brown streaky back and yellow and black underparts. ● Genus *Sturnella*, family Icteridae: five species, in particular the **eastern meadowlark** (*S. magna*).

meadow pipit ▸ **noun** a common streaky brown pipit of open country, found in Europe and the Middle East. ● *Anthus pratensis*, family Motacillidae.

meadow rue ▸ **noun** a widely distributed plant of the buttercup family, with divided leaves and heads of small fluffy yellow flowers. ● Genus *Thalictrum*, family Ranunculaceae: many species.

meadow saffron ▸ **noun** a poisonous lilac-flowered autumn crocus of Europe and North Africa, a source of the drug colchicine. Also called **naked ladies**. ● *Colchicum autumnale*, family Liliaceae.

meadowsweet ▸ **noun** a tall Eurasian plant of the rose family, with heads of creamy-white sweet-smelling flowers, growing typically in damp meadows. ● *Filipendula ulmaria*, family Rosaceae.

meagre¹ (US **meager**) ▸ **adjective** (of something provided or available) lacking in quantity or quality: *they were forced to supplement their meagre earnings.* ■ (of a person, animal, or part of the body) lean; thin.
– DERIVATIVES **meagrely** **adverb**.
– ORIGIN Middle English (in the sense 'lean'): from Old French *maigre*, from Latin *macer*.

meagre² ▸ **noun** Brit. another term for **kabeljou**.
– ORIGIN mid 16th cent.: from French, noun use of *maigre* 'lean, thin'.

meagreness (US **meagerness**) ▸ **noun** [mass noun] lack of quantity or quality; inadequacy: *job satisfaction eclipses the meagreness of income.*

meal¹ ▸ **noun** any of the regular occasions in a day when a reasonably large amount of food is eaten: *the evening meal.* ■ the food eaten during a meal: *a bar serving light meals.*
– PHRASES **make a meal of** Brit. informal carry out (a task or action) with unnecessary effort or thoroughness, especially for effect. **meals on wheels** meals delivered to old people or invalids who cannot cook for themselves.
– ORIGIN Old English *mǣl* (also in the sense 'measure', surviving in words such as *piecemeal* 'measure taken at one time'), of Germanic origin. The early sense of *meal* involved a notion of 'fixed time'; compare with Dutch *maal* 'meal, (portion of) time' and German *Mal* 'time', *Mahl* 'meal', from an Indo-European root meaning 'to measure'.

meal² ▸ **noun** [mass noun] the edible part of any grain or pulse ground to powder. ■ Scottish oatmeal. ■ US maize flour. ■ any powdery substance made by grinding: *herring meal.*
– ORIGIN Old English *melu*, *meolo*, of Germanic origin; related to Dutch *meel* and German *Mehl*, from an Indo-European root shared by Latin *molere* 'to grind'.

meal beetle ▶ noun a dark brown beetle which is a pest of stored grain and cereal products. ● *Tenebrio molitor*, family Tenebrionidae.

mealie (also **mielie**) ▶ noun (usu. **mealies**) S. African a maize plant. ■ [mass noun] maize kernels; sweetcorn: [as modifier] *mealie pudding*. ■ a corncob.
– ORIGIN early 19th cent.: from Afrikaans *mielie*, from Portuguese *milho* 'maize, millet' from Latin *milium*.

mealie meal ▶ noun [mass noun] S. African maize meal, used especially for porridge.

mealiepap ▶ noun [mass noun] S. African porridge made of mealie meal.
– ORIGIN late 19th cent.: from MEALIE + Afrikaans *pap* 'porridge'.

mealie rice ▶ noun [mass noun] S. African crushed maize kernels, used as a substitute for rice.

meal moth ▶ noun a small moth which infests mills, granaries, and other places where grain is stored. The larvae spin silken webs. ● Several species in the family Pyralidae, in particular the **meal moth** (*Pyralis farinalis*).

meal ticket ▶ noun a person or thing that is exploited as a source of regular income: *the violin was going to be my meal ticket*.

mealtime ▶ noun the time at which a meal is eaten: *family life seemed to revolve around mealtimes*.

mealworm ▶ noun the larva of the meal beetle, which is used as food for cage birds and other insectivorous animals.

mealy ▶ adjective (**mealier**, **mealiest**) resembling or containing meal: *a mealy flavour* | *mealy puddings*. ■ (of a person's complexion, an animal's muzzle, or a bird's plumage) pale. ■ (of part of a plant or fungus) covered with granules resembling meal.
– DERIVATIVES **mealiness** noun.

mealy bug ▶ noun a small sap-sucking scale insect which is coated with a white powdery wax resembling meal and which can be a serious pest. ● Family Pseudococcidae, suborder Homoptera: *Pseudococcus* and other genera.

mealy-mouthed ▶ adjective afraid to speak frankly or straightforwardly: *mealy-mouthed excuses*.

mean¹ ▶ verb (past and past participle **meant**) [with obj.] **1** intend to convey or refer to (a particular thing); signify: *I don't know what you mean* | *he was asked to clarify what his remarks meant* | *I meant you, not Jones*. ■ (of a word) have (something) as its signification in the same language or its equivalent in another language: *its name means 'painted rock' in Cherokee*. ■ genuinely intend to express (something): *when she said that she meant it*. ■ (**mean something to**) be of a specified degree of importance to (someone): *animals have always meant more to him than people*.
2 intend (something) to occur or be the case: *they mean no harm* | [with infinitive] *it was meant to be a secret*. ■ (**be meant to do something**) be supposed to do something: *we were meant to go over yesterday*. ■ (often **be meant for**) design or destine for a particular purpose: *the jacket was meant for a much larger person*. ■ (**mean something by**) have something as a motive or explanation in saying or doing: *what do you mean by leaving me out here in the cold?* ■ (**be meant to be**) be generally considered to be: *this one's meant to be priceless*.
3 have as a consequence or result: *the proposals are likely to mean another hundred closures* | [with clause] *heavy rain meant that the pitch was waterlogged*. ■ necessarily or usually entail or involve: *coal stoves mean a lot of smoke*.
– PHRASES **I mean** used to explain or correct a statement: *I mean, it's not as if I owned property*. **mean business** be in earnest. **mean to say** [usu. in questions] used to emphasize a statement or to ask another if they really intend to say something: *do you mean to say you've uncovered something new?* **mean well** have good intentions, but not always the ability to carry them out.
– ORIGIN Old English *mænan*, of West Germanic origin; related to Dutch *meenen* and German *meinen*, from an Indo-European root shared by MIND.

mean² ▶ adjective **1** chiefly Brit. unwilling to give or share things, especially money; not generous: *she felt mean not giving a tip* | *they're not mean with the garlic*.
2 unkind, spiteful, or unfair: *I was mean to them over the festive season*. ■ N. Amer. vicious or aggressive in behaviour: *the dogs were considered mean, vicious, and a threat*.
3 (especially of a place) poor in quality and appearance; shabby: *her home was mean and small*. ■ (of a person's mental capacity or understanding) inferior: *it was obvious to even the meanest intelligence*. ■ dated of low birth or social class: *a muffler like that worn by the meanest of people*.
4 informal very skilful or effective; excellent: *he's a mean cook* | *she dances a mean tango*.
– PHRASES **mean streets** used in reference to a socially deprived area of a city, or one which is noted for violence and crime. **no mean ——** denoting something very good of its kind: *a profit that crossed the £100 million barrier was no mean achievement*.
– DERIVATIVES **meanly** adverb.
– ORIGIN Middle English, shortening of Old English *gemæne*, of Germanic origin, from an Indo-European root shared by Latin *communis* 'common'. The original sense was 'common to two or more people', later 'inferior in rank', leading to sense 3 and a sense 'ignoble, small-minded', from which sense 1 and sense 2 (which became common in the 19th cent.) arose.

mean³ ▶ noun **1** the quotient of the sum of several quantities and their number; an average: *acid output was calculated by taking the mean of all three samples*. See also ARITHMETIC MEAN, GEOMETRIC MEAN.
2 a condition, quality, or course of action equally removed from two opposite extremes: *the measure expresses a mean between saving and splashing out*.
▶ adjective [attrib.] **1** (of a quantity) calculated as a mean; average: *participants in the study had a mean age of 35 years*.
2 equally far from two extremes: *hope is the mean virtue between despair and presumption*.
– ORIGIN Middle English: from Old French *meien*, from Latin *medianus* 'middle' (see MEDIAN).

mean anomaly ▶ noun Astronomy the angle in an imaginary circular orbit corresponding to a planet's eccentric anomaly.

meander /mɪˈandə/ ▶ verb [no obj., with adverbial of direction] (of a river or road) follow a winding course: *a river that meandered gently through a meadow*. ■ wander at random: *kids meandered in and out*. ■ [no obj.] (of language, thought, etc.) proceed aimlessly or with little purpose: *a stylish offbeat thriller which occasionally meanders*.
▶ noun (usu. **meanders**) a winding curve or bend of a river or road: *the river flows in sweeping meanders*. ■ [in sing.] an indirect or aimless journey: *a leisurely meander round the twisting coastline road*. ■ an ornamental pattern of winding or interlocking lines.
– ORIGIN late 16th cent. (as a noun): from Latin *maeander*, from Greek *Maiandros*, the name of a river (see MENDERES).

meandering ▶ adjective following a winding course: *meandering rivers flow at vastly different rates*. ■ proceeding in a convoluted or undirected fashion: *a brilliant sample of meandering discourse* | *a florid and rather meandering melody*.
▶ noun (usu. **meanderings**) an act of following a winding course: *ox-bow lagoons left by the river's meanderings*. ■ an act of wandering in a leisurely or aimless manner: *in the course of his meanderings through the city*. ■ [mass noun] convoluted or undirected thought or language: *he has a penchant for obscure verbal meanderings*.

mean free path ▶ noun Physics the average distance travelled by a gas molecule or other particle between collisions with other particles.

meanie (also **meany**) ▶ noun (pl. **meanies**) informal a mean or small-minded person.

meaning ▶ noun what is meant by a word, text, concept, or action: *the meaning of the Hindu word is 'breakthrough, release'* | [mass noun] *the meaning of life*. ■ [mass noun] implied or explicit significance: *he gave me a look full of meaning*. ■ [mass noun] important or worthwhile quality; purpose: *this can lead to new meaning in the life of older people*.
▶ adjective [attrib.] intended to communicate something that is not directly expressed: *she gave Gabriel a meaning look*.
– PHRASES **not know the meaning of the word** informal behave as if unaware of the concept referred to: *Humanity? You don't know the meaning of the word!*
– DERIVATIVES **meaningly** adverb.
– ORIGIN late Middle English: verbal noun from MEAN¹.

meaningful ▶ adjective having meaning: *meaningful elements in a language* | *words likely to be meaningful to pupils*. ■ serious, important, or worthwhile: *the new structure would bring meaningful savings*. ■ communicating something that is not directly expressed: *meaningful glances and repressed passion*. ■ Logic having a recognizable function in a logical language or other sign system.
– DERIVATIVES **meaningfully** adverb, **meaningfulness** noun.

meaningless ▶ adjective having no meaning or significance: *the paragraph was a jumble of meaningless words*. ■ having no purpose or reason: *they'd rather live by begging than get a meaningless job* | *rules are meaningless to a child if they do not have a rationale*.
– DERIVATIVES **meaninglessly** adverb, **meaninglessness** noun.

meanness ▶ noun [mass noun] **1** chiefly Brit. lack of generosity; miserliness.
2 unkindness, spitefulness, or unfairness: *all the hatred and meanness, despair and sorrow surrounding us*. ■ N. Amer. aggressive character; viciousness: *he is also callous, with a streak of meanness*.
3 lack of quality or attractiveness; shabbiness: *the meanness of that existence*.

means ▶ plural noun **1** [treated as sing. or pl.] (often **means of/to do something**) an action or system by which a result is achieved; a method: *technology seen as a means to bring about emancipation* | *resolving disputes by peaceful means*.
2 financial resources; income: *a woman of modest but independent means*. ■ substantial resources; wealth: *a man of means*.
– PHRASES **beyond** (or **within**) **one's means** beyond (or within) one's budget or income. **by all means** of course; certainly (granting a permission): *'May I make a suggestion?' 'By all means.'* **by any means** [with negative] in any way; at all: *I'm not poor by any means*. **by means of** with the help of; by using: *supplying water to cities by means of aqueducts*. **by no means** (or **by no manner of means**) not at all; certainly not: *the outcome is by no means guaranteed*. **means of grace** Christian Theology the sacraments and other religious agencies viewed as the means by which divine grace is imparted to the soul, or by which growth in grace is promoted. **means of production** (in a political context) the facilities and resources for producing goods. **a means to an end** a thing that is not valued or important in itself but is useful in achieving an aim: *higher education was seen primarily as a means to an end*.
– ORIGIN late Middle English: plural of MEAN³, the early sense being 'intermediary'.

mean sea level ▶ noun the sea level halfway between the mean levels of high and low water.

mean solar day ▶ noun Astronomy the time between successive passages of the mean sun across the meridian.

mean solar time ▶ noun [mass noun] Astronomy time as calculated by the motion of the mean sun (such as is shown by an ordinary clock).

means test ▶ noun an official investigation into a person's financial circumstances to determine their eligibility for state assistance.
▶ verb (**means-test**) [with obj.] (usu. as adj. **means-tested**) make (a state benefit) conditional on a means test: *means-tested benefits*. ■ subject (someone) to a means test.

mean sun ▶ noun an imaginary sun conceived as moving through the sky throughout the year at a constant speed equal to the mean rate of the real sun, used in calculating solar time.

meant past and past participle of MEAN¹.

meantime ▶ adverb (also **in the meantime**) meanwhile: *in the meantime I'll make some enquiries of my own* | *Scotland, meantime, had her own monarchs*.
– ORIGIN Middle English (as a noun): from MEAN³ + TIME.

mean time ▶ noun another term for MEAN SOLAR TIME. See also GREENWICH MEAN TIME.

meanwhile ▶ adverb **1** (also **in the meanwhile**) in the intervening period of time: *meanwhile, I will give you a prescription for some pills*. ■ at the same time: *steam for a further five minutes; meanwhile, make a white sauce*.
2 on the other hand: *he has said little, meanwhile, about how he plans to live his life*.
– ORIGIN late Middle English: from MEAN³ + WHILE.

meany ▶ noun variant spelling of MEANIE.

measles ▶ plural noun [treated as sing.] an infectious viral disease causing fever and a red rash, typically occurring in childhood. ■ a disease of pigs and other animals caused by the larvae of the human tapeworm.
– ORIGIN Middle English *maseles*, probably from Middle Dutch *masel* 'pustule' (compare with modern Dutch *mazelen* 'measles'). The spelling change was due to association with Middle English *mesel* 'leprous, leprosy'.

M

measly ▸ adjective (**measlier**, **measliest**) informal ridiculously small or few: *three measly votes.*
– ORIGIN late 16th cent. (describing a pig or pork infected with measles): from **MEASLES** + **-Y**[1]. The current sense dates from the mid 19th cent.

measurable ▸ adjective able to be measured: *objectives should be measurable and achievable.* ■ large enough to be measured; noticeable: *a small but measurable improvement in behaviour.*
– DERIVATIVES **measurability** noun, **measurably** adverb [as submodifier] *the company's performance was measurably better.*
– ORIGIN Middle English (in the sense 'moderate'): from Old French *mesurable*, from late Latin *mensurabilis*, from Latin *mensurare* 'to measure'.

measure ▸ verb [with obj.] **1** ascertain the size, amount, or degree of (something) by using an instrument or device marked in standard units: *the amount of water collected is measured in pints* | (as adj. **measuring**) *measuring instruments.* ■ be of (a specified size or degree): *the fabric measures 137 cm wide.* ■ ascertain the size and proportions of (someone) in order to make or provide clothes for them: *he will be measured for his team blazer next week.* ■ (**measure something out**) take an exact quantity of something: *she helped to measure out the ingredients.*
2 assess the importance, effect, or value of (something): *it is hard to measure teaching ability.* ■ (**measure someone/thing against**) judge someone or something by comparison with (a certain standard): *she did not need to measure herself against some ideal.* ■ [no obj.] (**measure up**) reach the required or expected standard: *I'm afraid we didn't measure up to the standards they set.* ■ (**measure someone up**) scrutinize someone in order to form an assessment of them: *the two shook hands and silently measured each other up.*
3 archaic travel over (a certain distance or area): *we must measure twenty miles today.*
▸ noun **1** a plan or course of action taken to achieve a particular purpose: *cost-cutting measures* | *children were evacuated as a precautionary measure.* ■ a legislative bill: *the Senate passed the measure by a 48–30 vote.*
2 a standard unit used to express the size, amount, or degree of something: *a furlong is an obsolete measure of length* | *tables of weights and measures.* ■ [mass noun] a system or scale of units expressing size, amount, or degree of something: *the dimensions were in imperial measure.* ■ a standard quantity or amount: *heavy drinking may be five measures of spirits per day.* ■ a container of standard capacity used for taking fixed amounts of a substance. ■ a graduated rod or tape used for ascertaining the size of something.
3 a certain quantity or degree of something: *the states retain a large measure of independence.* ■ an indication of the degree, extent, or quality of something: *his resignation is a measure of how angry he is.*
4 the rhythm of a piece of poetry or a piece of music. ■ a particular metrical unit or group: *measures of two or three syllables are more frequent in English prose.* ■ N. Amer. a bar of music or the time of a piece of music. ■ archaic a dance, typically one that is stately: *now tread we a measure!*
5 (**measures**) [with modifier] a group of rock strata.
6 Mathematics a quantity contained in another an exact number of times; a divisor.
7 Printing the width of a full line of type or print, typically expressed in picas.
– PHRASES **beyond measure** to a very great extent. **for good measure** in addition to what has already been done or said: *he added a couple of chillies for good measure.* **get** (or **take** or **have**) **the measure of** assess or have assessed the character or abilities of (someone or something): *he's got her measure—she won't fool him.* **hard measure** archaic punishment or retribution inflicted on someone. **in —— measure** to the degree specified: *his style was rough and elegant in equal measure.* **measure one's length** dated (of a person) fall flat on the ground. **measure one's words** consider carefully what one says. **measure of capacity** a standard unit of volume used for containers, liquids, and substances such as grain. **take measures** take action to achieve a particular purpose: *they took measures to improve performance.*
– DERIVATIVES **measurer** noun.
– ORIGIN Middle English (as a noun in the senses 'moderation', 'instrument for measuring', 'unit of capacity'): from Old French *mesure*, from Latin *mensura*, from *mens-* 'measured', from the verb *metiri*.

measured ▸ adjective having a slow, regular rhythm: *she set off with measured tread.* ■ (of speech or writing) carefully considered and restrained.
– DERIVATIVES **measuredly** adverb.

measureless ▸ adjective having no bounds or limits; unlimited: *Otto had measureless charm.*
– DERIVATIVES **measurelessly** adverb.

measurement ▸ noun [mass noun] the action of measuring something: *accurate measurement is essential* | [count noun] *a telescope with which precise measurements can be made.* ■ [count noun] the size, length, or amount of something, as established by measuring: *his inside leg measurement.* ■ [count noun] a unit or system of measuring.

measuring jug (US **measuring cup**) ▸ noun Brit. a jug or cup marked up in graded amounts, used in cooking.

measuring tape ▸ noun another term for **TAPE MEASURE**.

measuring worm ▸ noun another term for **LOOPER**.

meat ▸ noun [mass noun] **1** the flesh of an animal or bird as food: *pieces of meat* | [as modifier] *meat pies* | [count noun] *cold meats.* ■ the flesh of a person's body: *this'll put meat on your bones!* ■ N. Amer. the edible part of fruits, nuts, or eggs. ■ (**the meat of**) the chief part of something: *he did the meat of the climb on the first day.*
2 archaic food of any kind. ■ a meal.
– PHRASES **be meat and drink to** Brit. **1** be a source of great pleasure to: *meat and drink to me, this life is!* **2** be a customary matter for. **easy meat** informal a person who is easily overcome or outwitted. **meat and potatoes** N. Amer. basic and essential aspects: *the club's meat and potatoes remains blues performers.* **meat and two veg** Brit. informal a man's genitals. **one man's meat is another man's poison** proverb things liked or enjoyed by one person may be distasteful to another.
– DERIVATIVES **meatless** adjective.
– ORIGIN Old English *mete* 'food' or 'article of food' (as in *sweetmeat*), of Germanic origin.

meat ant ▸ noun a carnivorous Australian ant, especially a large reddish-purple kind that builds mounds. ● Genus *Iridomyrmex*, family Formicidae: several species.

meat axe ▸ noun a butcher's cleaver.

meatball ▸ noun **1** a ball of minced or chopped meat.
2 N. Amer. informal a dull or stupid person.

meat grinder ▸ noun N. Amer. a machine for mincing meat. ■ a destructive action or process: *hockey was put through a meat grinder in the Barcelona preliminaries.*

Meath /miːθ/ a county in the eastern part of the Republic of Ireland, in the province of Leinster; county town, Navan.

meathead ▸ noun informal a stupid person.

meathook ▸ noun **1** a sharp metal hook of a kind used to hang meat carcasses and joints.
2 (**meathooks**) informal a person's hands or arms.

meat loaf ▸ noun [mass noun] a baked dish consisting of minced meat moulded into the shape of a loaf.

meat market ▸ noun informal a meeting place such as a bar or club for people seeking casual sexual partners.

meat safe ▸ noun Brit. historical a cupboard or cover of wire gauze or a similar material, used for storing meat.

meatspace ▸ noun [mass noun] informal the physical world, as opposed to cyberspace or a virtual environment.

meatus /mɪˈeɪtəs/ ▸ noun (pl. **same** or **meatuses**) Anatomy a passage or opening leading to the interior of the body: *the urethral meatus.* ■ (also **external auditory meatus**) the passage leading into the ear.
– ORIGIN late Middle English: from Latin, 'passage' from *meare* 'to flow, run'.

meat wagon ▸ noun informal an ambulance or hearse. ■ a police van.

meatworks ▸ plural noun Austral./NZ a slaughterhouse or place where meat is processed and packed.

meaty ▸ adjective (**meatier**, **meatiest**) full of or resembling meat: *a meaty flavour.* ■ fleshy; brawny: *the tall, meaty young man.* ■ full of substance or interest: *Lawrence has written a meaty, scholarly book.*
– DERIVATIVES **meatily** adverb, **meatiness** noun.

mebos /ˈmiːbɒs/ ▸ noun [mass noun] S. African a preserve made from dried apricots and other fruit, pulped or flattened.
– ORIGIN South African Dutch, probably from Japanese *umeboshi* 'plums pickled in salt and dried'.

Mecca a city in western Saudi Arabia, an oasis town in the Red Sea region of Hejaz, east of Jiddah, considered by Muslims to be the holiest city of Islam; pop. 1,385,000 (est. 2007). Arabic name **MAKKAH**. ■ (as noun **a Mecca**) a place which attracts people of a particular group or with a particular interest: *Holland is a Mecca for jazz enthusiasts.*

> The birthplace in AD 570 of the prophet Muhammad, it was the scene of his early teachings before his emigration to Medina in 622 (the Hegira). On Muhammad's return to Mecca in 630 it became the centre of the new Muslim faith. It is the site of the Great Mosque and the Kaaba, and is a centre of Islamic ritual, including the haj pilgrimage which leads thousands of visitors to the city each year.

– DERIVATIVES **Meccan** adjective & noun.

Meccano /mɪˈkɑːnəʊ/ ▸ noun [mass noun] trademark a children's toy consisting of a set of metal and plastic components for making mechanical models.
– ORIGIN early 20th cent.: an invented word suggested by *mechanic*.

mech ▸ noun informal **1** a mechanic.
2 the gear mechanism of a bicycle.
– ORIGIN mid 20th cent.: abbreviation.

mechanic ▸ noun **1** a skilled worker who repairs and maintains vehicle engines and other machinery.
2 archaic a manual labourer or artisan.
– ORIGIN late Middle English (as an adjective in the sense 'relating to manual labour'): via Old French or Latin from Greek *mēkhanikos*, from *mēkhanē* (see **MACHINE**).

mechanical ▸ adjective **1** operated by a machine or machinery: *a mechanical device.* ■ relating to machines or machinery: *the helicopters are prone to mechanical failure.*
2 (of an action) done without thought or spontaneity; automatic: *she stopped the mechanical brushing of her hair.*
3 relating to physical forces or motion; physical: *the smoothness was the result of mechanical abrasion.* ■ archaic (of a theory) explaining phenomena in terms only of physical processes. ■ archaic relating to mechanics as a science.
4 relating to the exclusive legal right to reproduce a particular recorded version of a song or piece of music: *mechanical copyright* | *mechanical royalties.*
▸ noun **1** (**mechanicals**) the working parts of a vehicle.
2 (usu. **mechanicals**) archaic a manual worker: *rude mechanicals.* [with allusion to Shakespeare's *A Midsummer Night's Dream*.]
– DERIVATIVES **mechanically** adverb, **mechanicalness** noun.
– ORIGIN late Middle English (describing an art or occupation concerned with the construction of machines): via Latin from Greek *mēkhanikos* (see **MECHANIC**) + **-AL**.

mechanical advantage ▸ noun the ratio of the force produced by a machine to the force applied to it, used in assessing the performance of a machine.

mechanical drawing ▸ noun a scale drawing of a mechanical or architectural structure done with precision instruments. ■ [mass noun] the action or process of making mechanical drawings.

mechanical engineering ▸ noun [mass noun] the branch of engineering dealing with the design, construction, and use of machines.
– DERIVATIVES **mechanical engineer** noun.

mechanician ▸ noun a person skilled in the design or construction of machinery.

mechanics ▸ plural noun **1** [treated as sing.] the branch of applied mathematics dealing with motion and forces producing motion.
2 the machinery or working parts of something: *he looks at the mechanics of a car before the bodywork.* ■ the practical study of machinery. ■ the way in which something is done or operated: *the mechanics of cello playing.*

mechanism ▸ noun **1** a system of parts working together in a machine; a piece of machinery: *a third motor powers the tape eject mechanism.*
2 a natural or established process by which something takes place or is brought about: *the immune system's mechanism for detecting pathogens.*
3 [mass noun] Philosophy the doctrine that all natural phenomena, including life and thought, can be explained with reference to mechanical or chemical processes.
– ORIGIN mid 17th cent.: from modern Latin *mechanismus*, from Greek *mēkhanē* (see **MACHINE**).

mechanist /ˈmɛk(ə)nɪst/ ▸ noun **1** Philosophy a person who believes in the doctrine of mechanism.

M

2 archaic a person skilled in the design or construction of machinery.

mechanistic ▸ adjective relating to theories which explain phenomena in purely physical or deterministic terms: *a mechanistic interpretation of nature.*
– DERIVATIVES **mechanistically** adverb.

mechanize (also **mechanise**) ▸ verb [with obj.] introduce machines or automatic devices into (a process or place): *the farm was mechanized in the 1950s.* ■ (usu. as adj. **mechanized**) equip (a military force) with modern weapons and vehicles: *the units comprised tanks and mechanized infantry.* ■ make mechanical in character: *public virtue cannot be mechanized or formulated.*
– DERIVATIVES **mechanization** noun.

mechano- /ˈmɛk(ə)nəʊ/ ▸ combining form relating to a mechanical source; mechanical: *mechanoreceptor.*
– ORIGIN from Greek *mēkhanē* 'machine'.

mechanoreceptor ▸ noun Zoology a sense organ or cell that responds to mechanical stimuli such as touch or sound.
– DERIVATIVES **mechanoreceptive** adjective.

mechatronics ▸ plural noun [treated as sing.] technology combining electronics and mechanical engineering.
– ORIGIN 1980s: blend of MECHANICS and ELECTRONICS.

Mechelen /ˈmɛxələn/ a city in northern Belgium, north of Brussels; pop. 79,503 (2008). It is noted for its cathedral, and for Mechlin lace. French name MALINES.

Mechlin /ˈmɛklɪn/ (also **Mechlin lace**) ▸ noun [mass noun] lace made at Mechelen (formerly known as Mechlin), characterized by patterns outlined in heavier thread.

Mecklenburg /ˈmɛklənbəːg/, German /ˈmeːklənbʊrk/ a former state of NE Germany, on the Baltic coast, now part of Mecklenburg-West Pomerania.

Mecklenburg-West Pomerania a state of NE Germany, on the coast of the Baltic Sea; capital, Schwerin. It consists of the former state of Mecklenburg and the western part of Pomerania.

MEcon ▸ abbreviation Master of Economics.

meconium /mɪˈkəʊnɪəm/ ▸ noun [mass noun] Medicine the dark green substance forming the first faeces of a newborn infant.
– ORIGIN early 18th cent.: from Latin, literally 'poppy juice', from Greek *mēkōnion*, from *mēkōn* 'poppy'.

meconopsis /ˌmiːkəˈnɒpsɪs, ˌmɛkə-/ ▸ noun (pl. **same** or **meconopses**) a Eurasian poppy which is often grown as an ornamental. ● Genus *Meconopsis*, family Papaveraceae: several species.
– ORIGIN modern Latin, from Greek *mēkōn* 'poppy' + *opsis* 'appearance'.

Mecoptera /mɪˈkɒptərə/ ▸ plural noun Entomology an order of insects that comprises the scorpion flies.
– DERIVATIVES **mecopteran** noun & adjective.
– ORIGIN modern Latin (plural), from Greek *mēkos* 'length' + *pteron* 'wing'.

MEd ▸ abbreviation Master of Education.

Med ▸ noun (**the Med**) informal, chiefly Brit. the Mediterranean Sea.
– ORIGIN 1940s: abbreviation.

med informal, chiefly N. Amer. ▸ adjective medical: *she's at med school.*
▸ plural noun (**meds**) medicine; medication: *he'd forgotten to take his meds.*

med. ▸ abbreviation medium.

médaillon /ˌmeɪdʌɪˈjɔ̃/ ▸ noun (pl. pronunc. **same**) a small flat round or oval cut of meat or fish: *veal médaillons.*
– ORIGIN French, literally 'medallion'.

medaka /məˈdɑːkə/ ▸ noun a small, slender freshwater fish with the dorsal fin set back near the tail, native to parts of SE Asia and Japan. ● Family Oryziatidae and genus *Oryzias*: several species.
– ORIGIN early 20th cent.: from Japanese *me(y)* 'eye' + *-daka* 'high'.

medal ▸ noun a metal disc typically of the size of a large coin and bearing an inscription or design, made to commemorate an event or awarded as a distinction to someone such as a soldier or athlete.
▸ verb (**medals, medalling, medalled**; US **medals, medaling, medaled**) 1 [no obj.] US win a medal in a sporting event: *Larsen medaled in 4th place in the 3,200 meter run.*
2 [with obj.] (often as adj. **medalled**) decorate or honour with a medal.
– DERIVATIVES **medallic** adjective.
– ORIGIN late 16th cent.: from French *médaille*, from Italian *medaglia*, from medieval Latin *medalia* 'half a denarius', from Latin *medialis* 'medial'.

medallion ▸ noun a piece of jewellery in the shape of a medal, worn as a pendant. ■ an oval or circular painting, panel, or design used to decorate a building or textile. ■ another term for MÉDAILLON.
– ORIGIN mid 17th cent.: from French *médaillon*, from Italian *medaglione*, augmentative of *medaglia* (see MEDAL).

medallist (US **medalist**) ▸ noun 1 an athlete or other person awarded a medal: *an Olympic gold medallist.*
2 an engraver or designer of medals.

medal play ▸ noun Golf another term for STROKE PLAY.

Medan /ˈmɛdɑːn/ a city in Indonesia, in NE Sumatra near the Strait of Malacca; pop. 1,772,800 (est. 2009). It was established as a trading post by the Dutch in 1682 and became a leading commercial centre.

meddle ▸ verb [no obj.] interfere in something that is not one's concern: *I don't want him* ***meddling in*** *our affairs* | (as noun **meddling**) *bureaucratic meddling.* ■ (**meddle with**) touch or handle (something) without permission: *you have no right to come in here meddling with my things.*
– DERIVATIVES **meddler** noun.
– ORIGIN Middle English (in the sense 'mingle, mix'): from Old French *medler*, variant of *mesler*, based on Latin *miscere* 'to mix'.

meddlesome ▸ adjective fond of meddling; interfering: *heaven rid him of meddlesome politicians!*
– DERIVATIVES **meddlesomely** adverb, **meddlesomeness** noun.

Mede /miːd/ ▸ noun a member of an Indo-European people who inhabited ancient Media, establishing an extensive empire during the 7th century BC.
– PHRASES **law of the Medes and Persians** something which cannot be altered. [with biblical allusion to Dan. vi. 12.]
– ORIGIN from Latin *Medi*, Greek *Mēdoi*, plural forms.

Medea /mɪˈdiːə/ Greek Mythology a sorceress, daughter of Aeetes king of Colchis, who helped Jason to obtain the Golden Fleece and then married him. When Jason deserted her for Creusa, the daughter of King Creon of Corinth, she took revenge by killing Creon, Creusa, and her own children, and fled to Athens.

Medellín /ˌmɛdeɪˈjiːn/ a city in eastern Colombia, the second-largest city in the country; pop. 2,219,861 (2005). A major centre of coffee production, it has in recent years gained a reputation as the hub of the Colombian drug trade.

medevac /ˈmɛdɪvak/ (also **medivac**) N. Amer. ▸ noun [mass noun] the evacuation of military or other casualties to hospital in a helicopter or aeroplane.
▸ verb (**medevacs, medevacking, medevacked**) [with obj.] transport (someone) to hospital in a helicopter or aeroplane: *I was medevacked out of Freetown.*
– ORIGIN 1960s: blend of MEDICAL and EVACUATION.

medfly ▸ noun (pl. **medflies**) chiefly N. Amer. another term for MEDITERRANEAN FRUIT FLY.

Media /ˈmiːdɪə/ an ancient region of Asia to the south-west of the Caspian Sea, corresponding approximately to present-day Azerbaijan, NW Iran, and NE Iraq. Originally inhabited by the Medes, the region was conquered in 550 BC by Cyrus the Great of Persia.
– DERIVATIVES **Median** adjective.

media[1] /ˈmiːdɪə/ ▸ noun 1 (**the media**) [treated as sing. or pl.] the main means of mass communication (television, radio, and newspapers) regarded collectively: *their demands were publicized by the media.*
2 plural form of MEDIUM.

> **USAGE** The word **media** comes from the Latin plural of **medium**. The traditional view is that it should therefore be treated as a plural noun in all its senses in English and be used with a plural rather than a singular verb: *the media* ***have*** *not followed the reports* (rather than 'has'). In practice, in the sense 'television, radio, and the press collectively', it behaves as a collective noun (like **staff** or **clergy**, for example), which means that it is now acceptable in standard English for it to take either a singular or a plural verb. The word is also increasingly used in the plural form **medias**, as if it had a conventional singular form **media**, especially when referring to different forms of new media, and in the sense 'the material or form used by an artist': *there were great efforts made by the medias of the involved countries* | *about 600 works in all genres and medias were submitted for review.*

media[2] /ˈmiːdɪə/ ▸ noun (pl. **mediae** /-dɪiː/) Anatomy an intermediate layer in the wall of a blood vessel or lymphatic vessel.
– ORIGIN late 19th cent.: shortening of modern Latin *tunica* (or *membrana*) *media* 'middle sheath (or layer)'.

mediacy ▸ noun [mass noun] the quality of being mediate.

mediaeval ▸ adjective variant spelling of MEDIEVAL.

media event ▸ noun an event staged primarily to attract publicity.

mediagenic /ˌmiːdɪəˈdʒɛnɪk/ ▸ adjective US creating a favourable impression when presented in the media.

medial ▸ adjective technical situated in the middle, in particular: ■ Anatomy & Zoology situated near the median plane of the body or the midline of an organ. The opposite of LATERAL. ■ Phonetics (of a speech sound) in the middle of a word. ■ Phonetics (of a vowel) pronounced in the middle of the mouth; central.
– DERIVATIVES **medially** adverb.
– ORIGIN late 16th cent. (in the sense 'relating to the mean or average'): from late Latin *medialis*, from Latin *medius* 'middle'.

median /ˈmiːdɪən/ ▸ adjective [attrib.] 1 denoting or relating to a value or quantity lying at the midpoint of a frequency distribution of observed values or quantities, such that there is an equal probability of falling above or below it: *the median duration of this treatment was four months.* ■ denoting the middle term (or mean of the middle two terms) of a series arranged in order of magnitude.
2 technical, chiefly Anatomy situated in the middle, especially of the body: *the median part of the sternum.*
▸ noun 1 the median value of a range of values: *acreages ranged from one to fifty-two with a median of twenty-four.*
2 (also **median strip**) North American term for CENTRAL RESERVATION.
3 Geometry a straight line drawn from any vertex of a triangle to the middle of the opposite side.
– DERIVATIVES **medianly** adverb.
– ORIGIN late Middle English (denoting a median vein or nerve): from medieval Latin *medianus*, from *medius* 'mid'.

mediant /ˈmiːdɪənt/ ▸ noun Music the third note of the diatonic scale of any key.
– ORIGIN mid 18th cent.: from French *médiante*, from Italian *mediante* 'coming between', present participle of obsolete *mediare* 'come between', from late Latin *mediare* 'be in the middle of'.

mediascape /ˈmiːdɪəskeɪp/ ▸ noun 1 communications media as a whole: *the rapidly changing mediascape in Belgium.*
2 [in sing.] the world as presented through, or perceived by, the mass media: *the vast, ubiquitous mediascape we inhabit today.*

mediastinum /ˌmiːdɪəˈstʌɪnəm/ ▸ noun (pl. **mediastina** /-nə/) Anatomy a membranous partition between two body cavities or two parts of an organ, especially that between the lungs.
– DERIVATIVES **mediastinal** adjective.
– ORIGIN late Middle English: neuter of medieval Latin *mediastinus* 'medial', based on Latin *medius* 'middle'.

media studies ▸ plural noun [usu. treated as sing.] the study of the mass media as an academic subject.

mediate ▸ verb /ˈmiːdɪeɪt/ 1 [no obj.] intervene in a dispute in order to bring about an agreement or reconciliation: *Wilson attempted to* ***mediate between*** *the powers to end the war.* ■ [with obj.] intervene in (a dispute) to bring about an agreement. ■ [with obj.] bring about (an agreement or solution) by intervening in a dispute: *efforts to mediate a peaceful resolution of the conflict.*
2 [with obj.] technical bring about (a result such as a physiological effect): *the right hemisphere plays an important role in mediating tactile perception of direction.* ■ be a means of conveying: *this important ministry of mediating the power of the word.* ■ form a link between: *structures which mediate gender divisions.*
▸ adjective /ˈmiːdɪət/ connected indirectly through another person or thing; involving an intermediate agency: *public law institutions are a type of mediate state administration.*
– DERIVATIVES **mediately** adverb.
– ORIGIN late Middle English (as an adjective in the sense 'interposed'): from late Latin *mediatus* 'placed in the middle', past participle of the verb *mediare*, from Latin *medius* 'middle'.

mediation /miːdɪˈeɪʃ(ə)n/ ▸ noun [mass noun] intervention in a dispute in order to resolve it; arbitration:

M

the parties have sought mediation and it has failed. ■ intervention in a process or relationship; intercession: *they are offering sacrifice and mediation between God and man.*
– DERIVATIVES **mediational** adjective.

mediator /ˈmiːdɪeɪtə/ ▸ noun a person who attempts to make people involved in a conflict come to an agreement; a go-between.
– DERIVATIVES **mediatory** /ˈmiːdɪət(ə)ri/ adjective.

medic /ˈmɛdɪk/ ▸ noun **1** informal, chiefly Brit. a medical practitioner or student.
2 US a paramedic in the armed forces.
– ORIGIN mid 17th cent.: from Latin *medicus* 'physician', from *mederi* 'heal'.

medicable ▸ adjective archaic able to be treated or cured medically.
– ORIGIN late 16th cent. (in the sense 'possessing medicinal properties'): from Latin *medicabilis*, from *medicari* 'administer remedies to' (see MEDICATE).

Medicaid (in the US) a federal system of health insurance for people requiring financial assistance.
– ORIGIN 1960s: from MEDICAL + AID.

medical ▸ adjective relating to the science or practice of medicine: *a medical centre | the medical profession.* ■ relating to medicine as distinguished from surgery, psychiatry, etc.: *a medical ward.*
▸ noun an examination to assess a person's state of physical health or fitness.
– DERIVATIVES **medically** adverb.
– ORIGIN mid 17th cent.: via French from medieval Latin *medicalis*, from Latin *medicus* 'physician'.

medical certificate ▸ noun a certificate from a doctor confirming the state of someone's health.

medical examination ▸ noun an examination to determine someone's physical health.

medical examiner ▸ noun N. Amer. an official whose duty is to investigate deaths occurring under suspicious or unusual circumstances, perform post-mortems, and initiate inquests.

medicalize (also **medicalise**) ▸ verb [with obj.] treat (something) as a medical problem, especially without justification.
– DERIVATIVES **medicalization** noun.

M

medical jurisprudence ▸ noun [mass noun] the branch of law relating to medicine.

medical officer ▸ noun a doctor in charge of the health services of a civilian or military authority or other organization.

medical practitioner ▸ noun a physician or surgeon.

medicament /mɪˈdɪkəm(ə)nt, ˈmɛdɪk-/ ▸ noun a substance used for medical treatment.
– ORIGIN late Middle English: via French from Latin *medicamentum*, from *medicari* (see MEDICATE).

Medicare (in the US) a federal system of health insurance for people over 65 years of age. ■ (in Canada and Australia) a national health-care scheme financed by taxation.
– ORIGIN 1960s: from MEDICAL + CARE.

medicate ▸ verb [with obj.] administer medicine or a drug to (someone): *both infants were heavily medicated to alleviate their seizures.* ■ treat (a condition) using medicine or a drug. ■ (usu. as adj. **medicated**) add a medicinal substance to (a dressing or product): *medicated shampoo.*
– ORIGIN early 17th cent.: from Latin *medicat-* 'treated', from the verb *medicari* 'administer remedies to', from *medicus* (see MEDIC).

medication ▸ noun [mass noun] a drug or other form of medicine that is used to treat or prevent disease: *he was given medication for pain* | [count noun] *certain medications can cause dizziness.* ■ treatment using drugs: *chronic gastrointestinal symptoms may require prolonged medication.*

Medicean /ˌmɛdɪˈtʃiːən, -ˈsiːən, mɛˈdiːtʃɪən/ ▸ adjective relating to the Medici family.

Medici /ˈmɛdɪtʃi, məˈdiːtʃi/ (also **de' Medici**) a powerful Italian family of bankers and merchants whose members effectively ruled Florence for much of the 15th century and from 1569 were grand dukes of Tuscany. **Cosimo** and **Lorenzo de' Medici** were notable rulers and patrons of the arts in Florence; the family also provided four popes (including **Leo X**) and two queens of France (**Catherine de' Medici** and **Marie de Médicis**).

medicinal ▸ adjective (of a substance or plant) having healing properties: *medicinal herbs.* ■ relating to medicines or drugs.
▸ noun a medicinal substance.
– DERIVATIVES **medicinally** adverb.
– ORIGIN late Middle English: from Latin *medicinalis*, from *medicina* (see MEDICINE).

medicinal leech ▸ noun a large European leech formerly used in medicine for bloodletting. After biting it secretes an anticoagulant to ensure the flow of blood. ● *Hirudo medicinalis*, family Hirudidae.

medicine ▸ noun [mass noun] **1** the science or practice of the diagnosis, treatment, and prevention of disease (in technical use often taken to exclude surgery).
2 a drug or other preparation for the treatment or prevention of disease: *give her some medicine* | [count noun] *your doctor will be able to prescribe medicines.*
3 (among North American Indians and some other peoples) a spell, charm, or fetish believed to have healing, protective, or other power: *Fleur was murdering him by use of* ***bad medicine****.*
– PHRASES **give someone a dose** (or **taste**) **of their own medicine** give someone the same bad treatment that they have given to others. **take one's medicine** submit to punishment as being deserved.
– ORIGIN Middle English: via Old French from Latin *medicina*, from *medicus* 'physician'.

medicine ball ▸ noun a large, heavy solid ball thrown and caught for exercise.

medicine cabinet (also **medicine chest**) ▸ noun a small cupboard or box containing medicines and first-aid items.

medicine man ▸ noun (among North American Indians and some other peoples) a person believed to have magical powers of healing; a shaman.

medicine wheel ▸ noun a stone circle built by North American Indians, believed to have religious, astronomical, territorial, or calendrical significance.

Médicis, Marie de, see MARIE DE MÉDICIS.

medick /ˈmiːdɪk/ ▸ noun a yellow-flowered Eurasian and African plant of the pea family related to alfalfa, some kinds of which are grown for fodder or green manure. ● Genus *Medicago*, family Leguminosae.
– ORIGIN late Middle English: from Latin *medica*, from Greek *Mēdikē* (*poa*) 'Median (grass)'.

medico ▸ noun (pl. **medicos**) informal a medical practitioner or student.
– ORIGIN late 17th cent.: via Italian from Latin *medicus* 'physician'.

medico- ▸ combining form relating to the field of medicine: *medico-social.*
– ORIGIN from Latin *medicus* 'physician'.

medieval /ˌmɛdɪˈiːv(ə)l, miː-/ (also **mediaeval**) ▸ adjective relating to the Middle Ages: *a medieval castle.* ■ informal resembling or likened to the Middle Ages, especially in being cruel, uncivilized, or primitive: *without other people around I would let my flat degenerate into medieval levels of squalor.*
– DERIVATIVES **medievalism** noun, **medievalist** noun, **medievalize** (also **medievalise**) verb, **medievally** adverb.
– ORIGIN early 19th cent.: from modern Latin *medium aevum* 'middle age' + -AL.

medieval history ▸ noun [mass noun] the history of the period from the 5th to the 15th centuries.

medieval Latin ▸ noun [mass noun] Latin of about AD 600–1500.

Medina /mɛˈdiːnə/ a city in western Saudi Arabia, around an oasis some 320 km (200 miles) north of Mecca; pop. 1,010,000 (est. 2007). Arabic name AL-MADINAH.

> Medina was the refuge of Muhammad's infant Muslim community from its removal from Mecca in AD 622 until its return there in 630. It is Muhammad's burial place and the site of the first Islamic mosque, constructed around his tomb. It is considered by Muslims to be the second most holy city after Mecca, and a visit to the prophet's tomb at Medina often forms a sequel to the formal pilgrimage to Mecca.

medina /mɛˈdiːnə/ ▸ noun the old walled part of a North African town.
– ORIGIN Arabic, literally 'town'.

mediocracy ▸ noun (pl. **mediocracies**) a dominant class consisting of mediocre people, or a system in which mediocrity is rewarded.

mediocre /ˌmiːdɪˈəʊkə/ ▸ adjective of only average quality; not very good: *he is an enthusiastic if mediocre painter.*
– DERIVATIVES **mediocrely** adverb.
– ORIGIN late 16th cent.: from French *médiocre*, from Latin *mediocris* 'of middle height or degree', literally 'somewhat mountainous', from *medius* 'middle' + *ocris* 'rugged mountain'.

mediocrity ▸ noun (pl. **mediocrities**) [mass noun] the quality or state of being mediocre: *the team suddenly came good after years of mediocrity.* ■ [count noun] a person of mediocre ability.

meditate ▸ verb [no obj.] focus one's mind for a period of time, in silence or with the aid of chanting, for religious or spiritual purposes or as a method of relaxation. ■ (**meditate on/upon**) think deeply about (something): *he went off to meditate on the new idea.* ■ [with obj.] plan mentally; consider: *they had suffered severely, and they began to meditate retreat.*
– DERIVATIVES **meditator** noun.
– ORIGIN mid 16th cent.: from Latin *meditat-* 'contemplated', from the verb *meditari*, from a base meaning 'measure'; related to METE[1].

meditation ▸ noun [mass noun] the action or practice of meditating: *a life of meditation.* ■ [count noun] a written or spoken discourse expressing considered thoughts on a subject: *this is not a mythopoetic meditation on manhood, it's a historical study.*
– ORIGIN Middle English: from Old French, from Latin *meditatio(n-)*, from *meditari* (see MEDITATE).

meditative /ˈmɛdɪtətɪv, -ˌteɪtɪv/ ▸ adjective relating to or absorbed in meditation or considered thought: *meditative techniques.*
– DERIVATIVES **meditatively** adverb, **meditativeness** noun.
– ORIGIN early 17th cent.: from MEDITATE + -IVE, reinforced by French *méditatif, -ive.*

Mediterranean /ˌmɛdɪtəˈreɪnɪən/ ▸ adjective of or characteristic of the Mediterranean Sea, the countries bordering it, or their inhabitants: *a leisurely Mediterranean cruise | our temperatures are Mediterranean.* ■ relating to or denoting a dark-complexioned human physical type found in some Mediterranean countries.
▸ noun **1** (**the Mediterranean**) the Mediterranean Sea or the countries bordering it.
2 a native of a Mediterranean country.
– ORIGIN mid 16th cent.: from Latin *mediterraneus* 'inland' (from *medius* 'middle' + *terra* 'land') + -AN.

Mediterranean climate ▸ noun a climate distinguished by warm, wet winters under prevailing westerly winds and calm, hot, dry summers, as is characteristic of the Mediterranean region and parts of California, Chile, South Africa, and SW Australia.

Mediterranean fruit fly ▸ noun a fruit fly whose larvae can be a serious pest of citrus and other fruits. Also called MEDFLY, chiefly in North America. ● *Ceratitis capitata*, family Tephritidae.

Mediterranean Sea an almost landlocked sea between southern Europe, the north coast of Africa, and SW Asia. It is connected with the Atlantic by the Strait of Gibraltar, with the Red Sea by the Suez Canal, and with the Black Sea by the Dardanelles, the Sea of Marmara, and the Bosporus.

medium ▸ noun (pl. **media** or **mediums**) **1** an agency or means of doing something: *using the latest technology as* ***a medium for*** *job creation | their primitive valuables acted as* ***a medium of*** *exchange.* ■ a means by which something is communicated or expressed: *here the Welsh language is the medium of instruction.*
2 the intervening substance through which sensory impressions are conveyed or physical forces are transmitted: *radio communication needs no physical medium between the two stations.* ■ the substance in which an organism lives or is cultured. ■ a liquid (e.g. oil or water) with which pigments are mixed, with a binder, to make paint.
3 a particular form of storage material for computer files, such as magnetic tape or discs.
4 the material or form used by an artist, composer, or writer: *oil paint is the most popular medium for glazing.*
5 (pl. **mediums**) a person claiming to be in contact with the spirits of the dead and to communicate between the dead and the living.
6 the middle quality or state between two extremes; a reasonable balance: *the song soon discovers* ***a happy medium between*** *thrash and catchy pop.*
▸ adjective halfway between two extremes of size, amount, length, etc.; average: *John is six feet tall, of medium build | plan for the medium term.* ■ Cricket (of bowling or a bowler) of a pace intermediate between fast and slow bowling.
– DERIVATIVES **mediumism** noun (sense 5 of the noun), **mediumistic** /-ˈmɪstɪk/ adjective (sense 5 of the noun), **mediumship** noun (sense 5 of the noun).

– ORIGIN late 16th cent. (originally denoting something intermediate in nature or degree): from Latin, literally 'middle', neuter of *medius*.

medium frequency ▶ **noun** a radio frequency between 300 kHz and 3 MHz.

medium-pacer ▶ **noun** Cricket a seam bowler who bowls at a medium pace. ■ a ball bowled at medium pace.

medium-range ▶ **adjective** (of an aircraft or missile) able to travel or operate over a medium distance.

medium-sized (also **medium-size**) ▶ **adjective** of average size: *a medium-sized car*.

medium wave ▶ **noun** chiefly Brit. a radio wave of a frequency between 300 kHz and 3 MHz. ■ [mass noun] broadcasting using a medium-wave frequency: *you can no longer get that station* ***on medium wave***.

medivac ▶ **noun & verb** variant spelling of MEDEVAC.

medlar ▶ **noun** a small bushy tree of the rose family. ● *Mespilus germanica*, family Rosaceae.
■ the small brown apple-like fruit of the medlar, which is only edible after it has begun to decay.
– ORIGIN late Middle English: from Old French *medler*, from *medle* 'medlar fruit', from Latin *mespila*, from Greek *mespilē*, *mespilon*.

medley ▶ **noun** (pl. **medleys**) a varied mixture of people or things: *an interesting medley of flavours*. ■ a collection of songs or other musical items performed as a continuous piece: *a medley of Beatles songs*. ■ a swimming race in which contestants swim sections in different strokes, either individually or in relay teams.
▶ **adjective** archaic mixed; motley: *a medley range of vague and variable impressions*.
▶ **verb** (past and past participle **medleyed** or **medlied**) [with obj.] archaic make a medley of; intermix.
– ORIGIN Middle English (denoting hand-to-hand combat, also cloth made of variegated wool): from Old French *medlee*, variant of *meslee* 'melee', based on medieval Latin *misculare* 'to mix'; compare with MEDDLE.

Médoc /meɪˈdɒk/, French /medɔk/ ▶ **noun** (pl. **same** or **Médocs**) [mass noun] a red wine produced in Médoc, the area along the left bank of the Gironde estuary in SW France.

medrese /mɛˈdrɛseɪ/ ▶ **noun** variant spelling of MADRASA.

medulla /mɛˈdʌlə/ ▶ **noun** Anatomy the inner region of an organ or tissue, especially when it is distinct from the outer region or cortex (as in a kidney, an adrenal gland, or hair). ■ short for MEDULLA OBLONGATA. ■ [mass noun] Botany the soft internal tissue or pith of a plant.
– DERIVATIVES **medullary** adjective.
– ORIGIN late Middle English (in the sense 'bone marrow'): from Latin, 'pith or marrow'.

medulla oblongata /ˌɒblɒŋˈɡɑːtə/ ▶ **noun** the continuation of the spinal cord within the skull, forming the lowest part of the brainstem and containing control centres for the heart and lungs.
– ORIGIN late 17th cent.: modern Latin, literally 'elongated medulla'.

Medusa /mɪˈdjuːzə/ Greek Mythology the only mortal gorgon, whom Perseus killed by cutting off her head.

medusa /mɪˈdjuːzə, -sə/ ▶ **noun** (pl. **medusae** /-ziː, -siː/ or **medusas**) Zoology a free-swimming sexual form of a coelenterate such as a jellyfish, typically having an umbrella-shaped body with stinging tentacles around the edge. In some species, medusae are a phase in the life cycle which alternates with a polypoid phase. Compare with POLYP. ■ a jellyfish.
– ORIGIN mid 18th cent.: named by association with MEDUSA.

medusa fish ▶ **noun** a fish of the cool temperate waters of the North Pacific, the young of which typically accompany jellyfishes and may feed on their tentacles. ● *Icichthys lockingtoni*, family Centrolophidae.

medusoid /mɪˈdjuːsɔɪd/ Zoology ▶ **adjective** relating to or resembling a medusa or jellyfish. ■ relating to or denoting the medusa phase in the life cycle of a coelenterate. Compare with POLYPOID (sense 1).
▶ **noun** a medusa or jellyfish. ■ a medusoid reproductive bud.

meed ▶ **noun** archaic a person's deserved share of praise, honour, etc.: *he must extract from her some meed of approbation*.
– ORIGIN Old English *mēd*, of Germanic origin; from an Indo-European root shared by Greek *misthos* 'reward'.

meeja /ˈmiːdʒə/ (also **meejah**) ▶ **plural noun** nonstandard spelling of MEDIA[1], used humorously in imitation of informal British speech.

meek ▶ **adjective** quiet, gentle, and easily imposed on; submissive: *she brought her meek little husband along*.
– DERIVATIVES **meekly** adverb.
– ORIGIN Middle English *me(o)c* (also in the sense 'courteous or indulgent'), from Old Norse *mjúkr* 'soft, gentle'.

meekness ▶ **noun** [mass noun] the fact or condition of being meek; submissiveness: *all his best friends make fun of him for his meekness*.

meerkat /ˈmɪəkat/ ▶ **noun** a small southern African mongoose, especially the suricate. ● *Suricata* and other genera, family Herpestidae: three species.
– ORIGIN early 18th cent.: from South African Dutch, from Dutch, 'long-tailed monkey', apparently from *meer* 'sea' + *kat* 'cat', but perhaps originally an alteration of an oriental word; compare with Hindi *markaṭ* 'ape'.

meerschaum /ˈmɪəʃɔːm, -ʃəm/ ▶ **noun** [mass noun] a soft white clay-like material consisting of hydrated magnesium silicate, found chiefly in Turkey. ■ (also **meerschaum pipe**) [count noun] a tobacco pipe with a bowl made from meerschaum.
– ORIGIN late 18th cent.: from German, literally 'sea foam', from *Meer* 'sea' + *Schaum* 'foam', translation of Persian *kef-i-daryā* (alluding to the frothy appearance of the silicate).

Meerut /ˈmɪərət/ a city in northern India, in Uttar Pradesh north-east of Delhi; pop. 1,365,100 (est. 2009). It was the scene in May 1857 of the first uprising against the British in the Indian Mutiny.

meet[1] ▶ **verb** (past and past participle **met**) [with obj.]
1 arrange or happen to come into the presence or company of (someone): *a week later I met him in the street* | [no obj.] *we met for lunch* | *they arranged to* ***meet up*** *that afternoon*. ■ make the acquaintance of (someone) for the first time: *she took Paul to meet her parents* | [no obj.] *we met at an office party*. ■ [no obj.] (of a group of people) assemble for a purpose: *the committee meets once a fortnight*. ■ [no obj.] (**meet with**) have a meeting with (someone): *he met with the president on September 16*. ■ go to a place and wait there for (a person or their means of transport) to arrive: *Stuart* ***met us off the boat***. ■ come together as opponents in a competition: *in the final group match, England will meet the Australians* | [no obj.] *the teams will meet in the European Cup final at Wembley*. ■ encounter or experience (a particular situation or attitude): *he met his death in 1946* | [no obj.] *we met with a slight setback*. ■ (**meet something with**) have (a particular reaction) to: *the announcement was met with widespread protests*. ■ [no obj.] (**meet with**) receive (a particular reaction): *I'm sorry if it doesn't meet with your approval*.
2 touch; join: *icebergs are created when glaciers meet the sea* | [no obj.] *the curtains failed to meet in the middle* | figurative *our eyes met across the table*.
3 fulfil or satisfy (a need, requirement, or condition): *this policy is doing nothing to meet the needs of women*. ■ pay (a financial claim or obligation): *all your household expenses will still have to be met*.
▶ **noun 1** Brit. a gathering of riders and hounds before a hunt begins.
2 an organized event at which a number of races or other athletic contests are held.
3 informal a meeting, typically one with an illicit purpose: *the meet with Frank is on for 10 o'clock*.
– PHRASES **make ends meet** see END. **meet the case** Brit. be adequate. **meet someone's eye** (or **eyes**) **1** be visible: *the sight that met his eyes was truly amazing*. **2** (also **meet someone's gaze**) look directly at someone. **meet someone halfway** make a compromise with someone: *I am prepared to meet him halfway by paying him a further £25,000*. **meet one's Maker** see MAKER. **meet one's match** see MATCH[1]. **there's more to someone** (or **something**) **than meets the eye** a person or situation is more complex or interesting than they appear.
– ORIGIN Old English *mētan* 'come upon', of Germanic origin; related to Dutch *moeten*, also to MOOT.

meet[2] ▶ **adjective** archaic suitable or proper: *it was not meet for us to see the king's dishonour*.
– DERIVATIVES **meetly** adverb, **meetness** noun.
– ORIGIN Middle English (in the sense 'made to fit'): shortening of Old English *gemǣte*, of Germanic origin; related to METE[1].

meet-and-greet ▶ **noun** an organized event during which a celebrity, politician, or other well-known figure meets and talks to the public.

meeting ▶ **noun 1** an assembly of people for a particular purpose, especially for formal discussion: *we held an urgent meeting to discuss the response to the epidemic*. ■ Christian Church a gathering of people, especially Quakers, for worship. ■ an organized event at which a number of races or other sporting contests are held: *an athletics meeting*.
2 a situation when two or more people meet, by chance or arrangement: *he intrigued her on their first meeting*.
– PHRASES **a meeting of minds** an understanding or agreement between people.

meeting ground ▶ **noun** [in sing.] an area of knowledge or interest held in common by two or more people or disciplines.

meeting house ▶ **noun** a Quaker place of worship. ■ N. Amer. historical a Protestant place of worship.

meetup ▶ **noun** chiefly US an informal meeting or gathering.

mefloquine /ˈmɛfləkwiːn/ ▶ **noun** [mass noun] Medicine an antimalarial drug consisting of a fluorinated derivative of quinoline.
– ORIGIN 1970s: from *me(thyl)* + *fl(uor)o* + *quin(olin)e*.

meg ▶ **noun** short for MEGABYTE.

mega informal ▶ **adjective 1** very large; huge: *he has signed a mega deal to make five movies*.
2 excellent: *it will be a mega film*.
▶ **adverb** [as submodifier] extremely: *they are mega rich*.
– ORIGIN 1980s: independent usage of MEGA-.

mega- ▶ **combining form 1** large: *megalith*.
2 (in units of measurement) denoting a factor of one million (10^6): *megahertz*.
3 Computing denoting a factor of 2^{20}.
– ORIGIN from Greek *megas* 'great'.

megabit ▶ **noun** Computing a unit of data size or (when expressed per second) network speed, equal to one million or (strictly) 1,048,576 bits.

megabucks ▶ **plural noun** informal a very large amount of money: *he has been earning megabucks for decades* | [as modifier] *megabuck salaries*.

megabyte (abbrev.: **Mb** or **MB**) ▶ **noun** Computing a unit of information equal to one million or (strictly) 1,048,576 bytes.

M

Megachiroptera /ˌmɛɡəkʌɪˈrɒpt(ə)rə/ ▶ **plural noun** Zoology a division of bats that comprises the fruit bats and flying foxes. ● Suborder Megachiroptera and family Pteropodidae, order Chiroptera.
– DERIVATIVES **megachiropteran** noun & adjective.
– ORIGIN modern Latin (plural), from MEGA- 'large' + CHIROPTERA.

megachurch ▶ **noun** US a church with an unusually large congregation, typically one preaching a conservative or evangelical form of Christianity.

megacity ▶ **noun** (pl. **megacities**) a very large city, typically one with a population of over ten million people.

megadeath ▶ **noun** a unit used in quantifying the casualties of nuclear war, equal to the deaths of one million people.

megadose ▶ **noun** a very large dose of a vitamin or drug.

Megaera /mɪˈdʒɪərə/ Greek Mythology one of the Furies.

megafauna ▶ **noun** [mass noun] the large mammals of a particular region, habitat, or geological period. ■ Ecology animals that are large enough to be seen with the naked eye.
– DERIVATIVES **megafaunal** adjective.

megaflop ▶ **noun** Computing a unit of computing speed equal to one million or (strictly) 1,048,576 floating-point operations per second.
– ORIGIN 1970s: back-formation from *megaflops* (see MEGA-, -FLOP).

megagamete ▶ **noun** another term for MACROGAMETE.

megahertz (abbrev.: **MHz**) ▶ **noun** (pl. **same**) a unit of frequency equal to one million hertz.

megalith ▶ **noun** Archaeology a large stone that forms a prehistoric monument (e.g. a standing stone) or part of one (e.g. a stone circle).
– ORIGIN mid 19th cent.: back-formation from MEGALITHIC.

megalithic ▶ **adjective** Archaeology relating to or denoting prehistoric monuments made of or containing megaliths. ■ (often **Megalithic**) relating to or denoting prehistoric cultures characterized by the erection of megalithic monuments.
– ORIGIN mid 19th cent.: from MEGA- 'large' + Greek *lithos* 'stone' + -IC.

megalitre (US **megaliter**) (abbrev. **Ml**) ▶ **noun** a metric unit of capacity equal to a million litres.

megalo- /ˈmɛɡələʊ/ ▶ **combining form** great: *megaloblast*.
– ORIGIN from Greek *megas, megal-* 'great'.

megaloblast /ˈmɛɡələ(ʊ)blast/ ▶ **noun** Medicine a large, abnormally developed red blood cell typical of certain forms of anaemia, associated with a deficiency of folic acid or of vitamin B_{12}.
– DERIVATIVES **megaloblastic** adjective.

Megaloceros /ˌmɛɡəˈlɒsərəs/ ▶ **noun** a very large extinct deer of the Pleistocene epoch, in particular the Irish elk.
– ORIGIN modern Latin, from Greek *megas, megalo-* 'great' + *keras* 'horn'.

megalomania ▶ **noun** [mass noun] obsession with the exercise of power. ■ delusion about one's own power or importance (typically as a symptom of manic or paranoid disorder).
– DERIVATIVES **megalomanic** adjective.

megalomaniac ▶ **noun** a person who has an obsessive desire for power. ■ a person who suffers delusions of their own power or importance.
▶ **adjective** exhibiting megalomania.
– DERIVATIVES **megalomaniacal** adjective.

megalopolis /ˌmɛɡəˈlɒp(ə)lɪs/ ▶ **noun** a very large, heavily populated city or urban complex.
– ORIGIN mid 19th cent.: from **MEGALO-** 'great' + Greek *polis* 'city'.

megalopolitan ▶ **adjective** of or denoting a very large city: *megalopolitan traffic*.
▶ **noun** an inhabitant of a very large city.
– ORIGIN mid 17th cent.: from **MEGALO-** 'great' + Greek *politēs* 'citizen' + **-AN**.

megalosaurus /ˌmɛɡ(ə)lə(ʊ)ˈsɔːrəs/ ▶ **noun** a large carnivorous bipedal dinosaur of the mid Jurassic period, whose remains have been found only in England. ● Genus *Megalosaurus*, suborder Theropoda, order Saurischia.
– ORIGIN modern Latin, from **MEGALO-** 'great' + Greek *sauros* 'lizard'.

M

megamouth (also **megamouth shark**) ▶ **noun** a rare shark with a very large wide mouth and tiny teeth, found in the Pacific Ocean. ● *Megachasma pelagios*, the only member of the family Megachasmidae.

megaphone ▶ **noun** a large funnel-shaped device for amplifying and directing the voice.
▶ **verb** [with obj.] utter through, or as if through, a megaphone: *the director stood around megaphoning orders*.
– DERIVATIVES **megaphonic** adjective.

megapixel (abbrev.: **MP**) ▶ **noun** Computing a unit of graphic resolution equivalent to 2^{20} or (strictly) 1,048,576 pixels.

megapode /ˈmɛɡəpəʊd/ ▶ **noun** a large ground-dwelling Australasian and SE Asian bird that builds a large mound of debris to incubate its eggs by the heat of decomposition. ● Family Megapodiidae (the **megapode family**), which comprises the scrubfowls, brush-turkeys, malleefowl, and maleo.
– ORIGIN mid 19th cent.: from modern Latin *Megapodius* (genus name), from **MEGA-** 'large' + Greek *pous, pod-* 'foot'.

megaron /ˈmɛɡər(ə)n/ ▶ **noun** Archaeology the central hall of a large Mycenaean house.
– ORIGIN Greek.

megaspore ▶ **noun** Botany the larger of the two kinds of spores produced by some ferns. Compare with **MICROSPORE**.

megastar ▶ **noun** informal a very famous person in the world of entertainment or sport.
– DERIVATIVES **megastardom** noun.

megastore ▶ **noun** a very large shop, typically one specializing in a particular type of product.

megastructure ▶ **noun** a massive construction or structure, especially a complex of many buildings.

megatherium /ˌmɛɡəˈθɪərɪəm/ ▶ **noun** (pl. **megatheriums** or **megatheria**) an extinct giant ground sloth of the Pliocene and Pleistocene epochs in America, reaching a height of 5 m (16 ft) when standing erect. ● Genus *Megatherium*, family Megatheriidae.
– ORIGIN modern Latin, from Greek *mega thērion* 'great animal'.

megaton (also **megatonne**) ▶ **noun** a unit of explosive power chiefly used for nuclear weapons, equivalent to one million tons of TNT.

megavolt (abbrev.: **MV**) ▶ **noun** a unit of electromotive force equal to one million volts.

megawatt (abbrev.: **MW**) ▶ **noun** a unit of power equal to one million watts, especially as a measure of the output of a power station.

me generation ▶ **noun** a generation of people characterized by selfish materialism.

Megger /ˈmɛɡə/ ▶ **noun** trademark an instrument for measuring the resistance of electrical insulation.
– ORIGIN early 20th cent.: perhaps from **MEGOHM**.

Meghalaya /meɪˈɡɑːləjə/ a small state in the extreme north-east of India, on the northern border of Bangladesh; capital, Shillong. It was created in 1970 from part of Assam.

Megiddo /məˈɡɪdəʊ/ an ancient city of NW Palestine, situated to the south-east of Haifa in present-day Israel. Its commanding location made the city the scene of many early battles, and from its name the word *Armageddon* ('hill of Megiddo') is derived. It was the scene in 1918 of the defeat of Turkish forces by the British under General Allenby.

Megillah /məˈɡɪlə/ a book of the Hebrew scriptures (the Song of Solomon, Ruth, Lamentations, Ecclesiastes, and Esther) appointed to be read on certain Jewish notable days, especially the Book of Esther, read at the festival of Purim. ■ (as noun **the whole megillah**) N. Amer. informal something in its entirety, especially a complicated set of arrangements or a long-winded story.
– ORIGIN from Hebrew *mĕgillāh*, literally 'scroll'.

megilp /məˈɡɪlp/ (also **magilp**) ▶ **noun** [mass noun] a mixture of mastic resin and linseed oil added to oil paints, widely used in the 19th century.
– ORIGIN mid 18th cent.: of unknown origin.

megohm /ˈmɛɡəʊm/ ▶ **noun** a unit of electrical resistance equal to one million ohms.
– ORIGIN mid 19th cent.: from **MEGA-** (as a unit of measurement) + **OHM**.

megrim[1] /ˈmiːɡrɪm/ ▶ **noun** archaic **1** (**megrims**) depression; low spirits: *exercise could banish most megrims*.
2 a whim or fancy.
– ORIGIN late Middle English: variant of **MIGRAINE**.

megrim[2] /ˈmiːɡrɪm/ ▶ **noun** a deep-water flatfish of the European Atlantic coast. Also called **SAIL-FLUKE, WHIFF**[2]. ● *Lepidorhombus whiffiagonis*, family Scophthalmidae (or Bothidae).
■ another term for **SCALDFISH**.
– ORIGIN mid 19th cent.: of unknown origin.

meh /mɛ/ informal ▶ **exclamation** expressing a lack of interest or enthusiasm: *meh, I'm not impressed so far*.
▶ **adjective** uninspiring; unexceptional: *a lot of his movies are ... meh*. ■ unenthusiastic; apathetic: *everyone else I talked to was kind of meh*.
– ORIGIN 1990s: apparently popularized by the US television show *The Simpsons*.

mehndi /ˈmɛndi/ (also **mehendi**) ▶ **noun** [mass noun] Indian the art or practice of applying temporary henna tattoos, especially as part of a bride or groom's preparations for a wedding. ■ [count noun] a temporary henna tattoo.
– ORIGIN early 19th cent. (originally denoting the henna plant): Hindi, from Sanskrit *mendhikā* 'henna plant'.

meibomian /mʌɪˈbəʊmɪən/ ▶ **adjective** Anatomy relating to or denoting large sebaceous glands of the human eyelid, whose infection results in inflammation and swelling.
– ORIGIN early 19th cent.: from the name of Heinrich *Meibom* (1638–1700), German anatomist, + **-IAN**.

Meiji /ˈmeɪdʒi/ ▶ **noun** [usu. as modifier] the period when Japan was ruled by the emperor Meiji Tenno, marked by the modernization and westernization of the country.
– ORIGIN Japanese, literally 'enlightened government'.

Meiji Tenno /ˌmeɪdʒi ˈtɛnəʊ/ (1852–1912), emperor of Japan 1868–1912; born *Mutsuhito*. He took the name Meiji Tenno when he became emperor. He encouraged Japan's modernization and political reform.

meiofauna /ˈmʌɪəʊˌfɔːnə/ ▶ **noun** [mass noun] Ecology minute interstitial animals living in soil and aquatic sediments.
– ORIGIN 1960s: from Greek *meiōn* 'less or smaller' + **FAUNA**.

meiosis /mʌɪˈəʊsɪs/ ▶ **noun** (pl. **meioses** /-siːz/) [mass noun] **1** Biology a type of cell division that results in four daughter cells each with half the number of chromosomes of the parent cell, as in the production of gametes and plant spores. Compare with **MITOSIS**.
2 another term for **LITOTES**.
– DERIVATIVES **meiotic** adjective, **meiotically** adverb.
– ORIGIN mid 16th cent. (in sense 2): modern Latin, from Greek *meiōsis*, from *meioun* 'lessen', from *meiōn* 'less'. Sense 1 dates from the early 20th cent.

Meir /meɪˈɪə/, Golda (1898–1978), Israeli stateswoman, Prime Minister 1969–74; born *Goldie Mabovich*. Born in Ukraine, she emigrated to the US in 1907 and in 1921 to Palestine. Following Israel's independence she served in ministerial posts from 1949 to 1966 before being elected Prime Minister.

Meissen[1] /ˈmʌɪs(ə)n/ a city in eastern Germany, in Saxony, on the River Elbe north-west of Dresden; pop. 28,100 (est. 2006). It is famous for its porcelain.

Meissen[2] /ˈmʌɪs(ə)n/ ▶ **noun** [mass noun] fine hard-paste porcelain produced in Meissen since 1710, in Britain often called Dresden china.

Meissner effect /ˈmʌɪsnə/ ▶ **noun** Physics the expulsion of magnetic flux when a material becomes superconducting in a magnetic field.
– ORIGIN 1930s; named after Fritz W. *Meissner* (1882–1974), German physicist.

Meissner's corpuscle ▶ **noun** Anatomy a sensory nerve ending that is sensitive to mechanical stimuli, found in the dermis in various parts of the body.
– ORIGIN late 19th cent.: named after Georg *Meissner* (1829–1905), German anatomist.

-meister /ˈmʌɪstə/ ▶ **combining form** denoting a person skilled or prominent in a specified area of activity: *funk-meister* | *gag-meister*.
– ORIGIN from German *Meister* 'master'.

Meistersinger /ˈmʌɪstəsɪŋə/ ▶ **noun** (pl. **same** or **Meistersingers**) a member of one of the guilds of German lyric poets and musicians which flourished from the 12th to 17th century, known for their elaborate technique.
– ORIGIN German, from *Meister* 'master' + *Singer* 'singer'.

Meitner /ˈmʌɪtnə/, Lise (1878–1968), Austrian-born Swedish physicist. She worked in the field of radiochemistry with Otto Hahn, discovering the element protactinium with him in 1917. She also formulated the concept of nuclear fission with her nephew Otto Frisch.

meitnerium /mʌɪtˈnɪərɪəm/ ▶ **noun** [mass noun] the chemical element of atomic number 109, a very unstable element made by high-energy atomic collisions. (Symbol: **Mt**)
– ORIGIN 1990s: modern Latin, from the name of L. **MEITNER**.

Mekele /mɪˈkeɪli/ a city in northern Ethiopia, the capital of Tigray province; pop. 175,000 (est. 2006).

Meknès /mɛkˈnɛs/ a city in northern Morocco, in the Middle Atlas mountains west of Fez; pop. 713,609 (2004). In the 17th century it was the residence of the Moroccan sultan.

Mekong /miːˈkɒŋ/ a river of SE Asia, which rises in Tibet and flows south-east and south for 4,180 km (2,600 miles) through southern China, Laos, Cambodia, and Vietnam to its extensive delta on the South China Sea. It forms the boundary between Laos and its western neighbours Burma and Thailand.

mela /ˈmeɪlɑː/ ▶ **noun** Indian a fair or Hindu festival.
– ORIGIN from Sanskrit *melā* 'assembly'.

melaena /mɪˈliːnə/ (also **melena**) ▶ **noun** [mass noun] Medicine the production of dark sticky faeces containing partly digested blood, as a result of internal bleeding or the swallowing of blood.
– ORIGIN early 19th cent.: modern Latin, from Greek *melaina*, feminine of *melas* 'black'.

Melaka /məˈlakə/ (also **Malacca**) a state of Malaysia, on the SW coast of the Malay Peninsula, on the Strait of Malacca. ■ its capital and chief port; pop. 194,400 (est. 2009). It was conquered by the Portuguese in 1511 and played an important role in the development of trade between Europe and the East, especially China.

melaleuca /ˌmɛləˈl(j)uːkə/ ▶ **noun** an Australian shrub or tree which bears spikes of bottlebrush-like flowers. Some kinds are a source of timber or medicinal oil. ● Genus *Melaleuca*, family Myrtaceae: many species.
– ORIGIN modern Latin: from Greek *melas* 'black' + *leukos* 'white' (because of the fire-blackened white bark of some Asian species).

melamine /ˈmɛləmiːn/ ▶ **noun** [mass noun] **1** Chemistry a white crystalline compound made by heating cyanamide and used in making plastics. ● A heterocyclic amine; chem. formula: $(CNH_2)_3N_3$.
2 a plastic used chiefly for laminated coatings, made by copolymerizing melamine with formaldehyde.

– ORIGIN mid 19th cent.: from German *melam* (an arbitrary formation), denoting an insoluble amorphous organic substance, + **AMINE**.

melancholia /ˌmɛlənˈkəʊlɪə/ ▶ **noun** [mass noun] a feeling of deep sadness; melancholy: *the haunting melancholia that dominates the album*. ■ dated severe depression.
– ORIGIN late Middle English (denoting black bile): from late Latin (see **MELANCHOLY**).

melancholy /ˈmɛlənkəli/ ▶ **noun** [mass noun] a feeling of pensive sadness, typically with no obvious cause: *an air of melancholy surrounded him*. ■ another term for **MELANCHOLIA** (as a mental condition). ■ historical another term for **BLACK BILE**.
▶ **adjective** having a feeling of melancholy; sad and pensive: *she felt a little melancholy* | *a dark, melancholy young man with deep-set eyes*. ■ causing or expressing sadness; depressing: *the melancholy tone of her writing*.
– DERIVATIVES **melancholic** adjective, **melancholically** adverb.
– ORIGIN Middle English: from Old French *melancolie*, via late Latin from Greek *melankholia*, from *melas*, *melan-* 'black' + *kholē* 'bile', an excess of which was formerly believed to cause depression.

Melanchthon /məˈlaŋkθɒn/, Philipp (1497–1560), German Protestant reformer; born *Philipp Schwarzerd*. He succeeded Luther as leader of the Reformation movement in Germany in 1521 and drew up the Augsburg Confession (1530).

Melanesia /ˌmɛləˈniːzɪə, -ˈniːʒə/ a region of the western Pacific to the south of Micronesia and west of Polynesia. It contains the Bismarck Archipelago, the Solomon Islands, Vanuatu, New Caledonia, Fiji, and the intervening islands.
– ORIGIN from Greek *melas* 'black' + *nēsos* 'island'.

Melanesian /ˌmɛləˈniːzɪ(ə)n, -ʒ(ə)n/ ▶ **noun 1** a native or inhabitant of any of the islands of Melanesia.
2 [mass noun] any of the languages of Melanesia, mostly Austronesian languages related to Malay but also including Neo-Melanesian (or Tok Pisin), an English-based pidgin.
▶ **adjective** relating to Melanesia, its peoples, or their languages.

melange /meɪˈlɒ̃ʒ/ ▶ **noun** a varied mixture: *a melange of tender vegetables and herbs*.
– ORIGIN from French *mélange*, from *mêler* 'to mix'.

melanin /ˈmɛlənɪn/ ▶ **noun** [mass noun] a dark brown to black pigment occurring in the hair, skin, and iris of the eye in people and animals. It is responsible for tanning of skin exposed to sunlight.
– ORIGIN mid 19th cent.: from Greek *melas*, *melan-* 'black' + **-IN**[1].

melanism /ˈmɛlənɪz(ə)m/ ▶ **noun** [mass noun] chiefly Zoology darkening of body tissues caused by excessive production of melanin, especially as a form of colour variation in animals.
– DERIVATIVES **melanic** /mɪˈlanɪk/ adjective.

melanite /ˈmɛlənʌɪt/ ▶ **noun** [mass noun] a black variety of andradite (garnet).
– ORIGIN early 19th cent.: from Greek *melas*, *melan-* 'black' + **-ITE**[1].

melanocyte /ˈmɛlənə(ʊ)ˌsʌɪt, mɪˈlanə(ʊ)-/ ▶ **noun** Physiology a mature melanin-forming cell, especially in the skin.

melanoid /ˈmɛlənɔɪd/ ▶ **adjective** (of a substance) resembling melanin.

melanoma /ˌmɛləˈnəʊmə/ ▶ **noun** Medicine a tumour of melanin-forming cells, especially a malignant tumour associated with skin cancer: *melanomas can appear anywhere on the body* | [mass noun] *the incidence of melanoma is rising steadily*.
– ORIGIN mid 19th cent.: from Greek *melas*, *melan-* 'black' + **-OMA**.

melanosis /ˌmɛləˈnəʊsɪs/ ▶ **noun** [mass noun] Medicine a condition of excessive production of melanin in the skin or other tissue.
– DERIVATIVES **melanotic** adjective.
– ORIGIN early 19th cent.: modern Latin, from Greek *melas*, *melan-* 'black' + **-OSIS**.

melatonin /ˌmɛləˈtəʊnɪn/ ▶ **noun** [mass noun] Biochemistry a hormone secreted by the pineal gland which inhibits melanin formation and is thought to be concerned with regulating the reproductive cycle.
– ORIGIN 1950s: from Greek *melas* 'black' + **SEROTONIN**.

Melba[1], Dame Nellie (1861–1931), Australian operatic soprano; born *Helen Porter Mitchell*. She was born near Melbourne, from which city she took her professional name. Melba gained worldwide fame with her coloratura singing.

Melba[2] ▶ **noun** (in phrase **do a Melba**) Austral. informal return from retirement, or make several farewell appearances.
– ORIGIN 1970s: from the name of the soprano Dame Nellie *Melba* (see **MELBA**[1]), who made repeated 'farewell' appearances.

Melba sauce ▶ **noun** [mass noun] a sauce made from puréed raspberries thickened with icing sugar.

Melba toast ▶ **noun** [mass noun] very thin crisp toast.

Melbourne[1] /ˈmɛlbən/ the capital of Victoria, SE Australia, on the Bass Strait opposite Tasmania; pop. 3,892,419 (2008). It became state capital in 1851 and was capital of Australia from 1901 until 1927. It is a major port and the second-largest city in Australia.

Melbourne[2] /ˈmɛlbən, -bɔːn/, William Lamb, 2nd Viscount (1779–1848), British Whig statesman, Prime Minister 1834 and 1835–41. He became chief political adviser to Queen Victoria after her accession in 1837.

Melchior /ˈmɛlkɪɔː/ the traditional name of one of the Magi, represented as a king of Nubia.

Melchizedek /mɛlˈkɪzɪdɛk/ (in the Bible) a priest and king of Salem (which is usually identified with Jerusalem). He was revered by Abraham, who paid tithes to him (Gen. 14:18).

meld[1] ▶ **verb** blend; combine: [with obj.] *Australia's winemakers have* **melded** *modern science* **with** *traditional art* | [no obj.] *the nylon bristles shrivel and* **meld together**.
▶ **noun** a thing formed by melding; a combination: *a meld of many contributions*.
– ORIGIN 1930s: perhaps a blend of **MELT** and **WELD**[1].

meld[2] ▶ **verb** [with obj.] (in rummy, canasta, and other card games) lay down or declare (a combination of cards) in order to score points.
▶ **noun** a completed set or run of cards in rummy, canasta, and other card games.
– ORIGIN late 19th cent. (originally US): from German *melden* 'announce'.

Meleager /ˌmɛlɪˈeɪɡə/ (*fl.* 1st century BC), Greek poet, best known as the compiler of *Stephanos*, one of the first large anthologies of epigrams.

melee /ˈmɛleɪ/ ▶ **noun** a confused fight or scuffle: *several people were hurt in the melee*. ■ a confused crowd of people: *the melee of people that were always thronging the streets*.
– ORIGIN mid 17th cent.: from French *mêlée*, from an Old French variant of *meslee* (see **MEDLEY**).

melena ▶ **noun** variant spelling of **MELAENA**.

melic /ˈmɛlɪk/ ▶ **adjective** (of an ancient Greek lyric poem) meant to be sung.
– ORIGIN late 17th cent.: via Latin from Greek *melikos*, from *melos* 'song'.

melick ▶ **noun** a grass with purplish florets, occurring in temperate woodland. ● Genus *Melica*, family Gramineae: many species.
– ORIGIN late 18th cent.: from modern Latin *melica*, perhaps from Italian *melica* 'sorghum'.

Melilla /mɛˈliːjə/ a Spanish enclave on the Mediterranean coast of Morocco; pop. 71,448 (2008). It was occupied by Spain in 1497.

melilot /ˈmɛlɪlɒt/ ▶ **noun** a fragrant herbaceous plant of the pea family, which is native to Eurasia and north Africa and is sometimes grown as forage or green manure. ● Genus *Melilotus*, family Leguminosae.
– ORIGIN Middle English: from Old French, via Latin from Greek *melilōtos* 'honey lotus'.

melioidosis /ˌmɛlɪɔɪˈdəʊsɪs/ ▶ **noun** [mass noun] an infectious disease of rodents, similar to glanders. It is occasionally transmitted to people, in whom it can cause pneumonia, multiple abscesses, and septicaemia. ● The agent is the bacterium *Pseudomonas pseudomallei*.
– ORIGIN 1920s: from Greek *mēlis*, denoting a disease (probably glanders) affecting asses, + **-OID** + **-OSIS**.

meliorate /ˈmiːlɪəreɪt/ ▶ **verb** formal another term for **AMELIORATE**.
– DERIVATIVES **melioration** noun, **meliorative** adjective.
– ORIGIN mid 16th cent.: from late Latin *meliorat-* 'improved' from the verb *meliorare*, based on *melior* 'better'.

meliorism /ˈmiːlɪərɪz(ə)m/ ▶ **noun** [mass noun] Philosophy the belief that the world can be made better by human effort.
– DERIVATIVES **meliorist** noun & adjective, **melioristic** adjective.
– ORIGIN late 19th cent.: from Latin *melior* 'better' + **-ISM**.

melisma /mɪˈlɪzmə/ ▶ **noun** (pl. **melismas** or **melismata** /-mətə/) Music a group of notes sung to one syllable of text.
– DERIVATIVES **melismatic** adjective.
– ORIGIN late 19th cent.: from Greek, literally 'melody'.

Melkite /ˈmɛlkʌɪt/ ▶ **noun** an Orthodox or Uniate Christian belonging to the patriarchate of Antioch, Jerusalem, or Alexandria. ■ historical an Eastern Christian adhering to the Orthodox faith as defined by the councils of Ephesus (AD 431) and Chalcedon (AD 451) and as accepted by the Byzantine emperor.
– ORIGIN early 17th cent.: via Church Latin from Byzantine Greek *Melkhitai*, plural representing Syriac *malkāyā* 'royalists' (i.e. expressing agreement with the Byzantine emperor), from *malkā* 'king'.

melliferous /mɛˈlɪf(ə)rəs/ ▶ **adjective** yielding or producing honey.
– ORIGIN mid 17th cent.: from Latin *mellifer* (from *mel* 'honey' + *-fer* 'bearing') + **-OUS**.

mellifluent /mɛˈlɪflʊənt/ ▶ **adjective** another term for **MELLIFLUOUS**.
– DERIVATIVES **mellifluence** noun.
– ORIGIN early 17th cent.: from late Latin *mellifluent-*, from Latin *mel*, *mell(i)-* 'honey' + *fluent-* 'flowing' (from the verb *fluere*).

mellifluous /mɛˈlɪflʊəs/ ▶ **adjective** (of a sound) pleasingly smooth and musical to hear: *her low mellifluous voice*.
– DERIVATIVES **mellifluously** adverb, **mellifluousness** noun.
– ORIGIN late 15th cent.: from late Latin *mellifluus* (from *mel* 'honey' + *fluere* 'to flow') + **-OUS**.

Mellon /ˈmɛlən/, Andrew (William) (1855–1937), American financier and philanthropist. He donated his art collection to establish the National Gallery of Art in Washington DC, opened in 1941.

mellophone /ˈmɛləfəʊn/ ▶ **noun** a brass instrument similar to the orchestral French horn, played in military and concert bands.
– ORIGIN 1920s: from **MELLOW** + **-PHONE**.

mellotron /ˈmɛlətrɒn/ ▶ **noun** an electronic keyboard instrument in which each key controls the playback of a single pre-recorded musical sound.
– ORIGIN 1960s: from **MELLOW** + *-tron*, element of **ELECTRONIC**.

mellow ▶ **adjective 1** (especially of a sound, flavour, or colour) pleasantly smooth or soft; free from harshness: *she was hypnotized by the mellow tone of his voice* | *slow cooking gives the dish a sweet, mellow flavour*. ■ (of wine) well-matured and smooth: *a mellow, richly flavoured Shiraz*. ■ archaic (of fruit) ripe, sweet, and juicy.
2 (of a person's character) tempered by maturity or experience: *a more mellow personality*. ■ relaxed and good-humoured: *Jean-Claude was feeling mellow*.
3 informal relaxed and cheerful through being slightly drunk: *everybody got very mellow and slept well*.
4 (of earth) rich and loamy.
▶ **verb** make or become mellow: [with obj.] *even a warm sun could not mellow the North Sea breeze* | [no obj.] *fuller-flavoured whiskies mellow with wood maturation*. ■ [no obj.] (**mellow out**) informal relax and enjoy oneself: *I need to mellow out, I need to calm down*.
– DERIVATIVES **mellowly** adverb, **mellowness** noun.
– ORIGIN late Middle English (in the sense 'ripe, sweet, and juicy'): perhaps from attributive use of Old English *melu*, *melw-* (see **MEAL**[2]). The verb dates from the late 16th cent.

melodeon /mɪˈləʊdɪən/ (also **melodion**) ▶ **noun 1** a small accordion of German origin, played especially by folk musicians. [mid 19th cent.: probably from **MELODY**, on the pattern of *accordion*.]
2 a small organ popular in the 19th century, similar to the harmonium. [alteration of earlier *melodium*.]

melodic ▶ **adjective** relating to or having melody: *melodic and rhythmic patterns*. ■ pleasant-sounding: *his voice was deep and melodic*.
– DERIVATIVES **melodically** adverb, **melodicism** /mɪˈlɒdɪsɪz(ə)m/ noun.
– ORIGIN early 19th cent.: from French *mélodique*, via late Latin from Greek *melōidikos*, from *melōidia* 'melody'.

melodica /məˈlɒdɪkə/ ▶ **noun** a wind instrument with a small keyboard controlling a row of reeds, and a mouthpiece at one end.
– ORIGIN 1960s: from **MELODY**, on the pattern of *harmonica*.

melodic minor ▶ **noun** Music a minor scale with the sixth and seventh degrees raised when ascending and lowered when descending.

M

melodious ▸ adjective relating to or characterized by melody: *the melodious chant of the monks.* ■ pleasant-sounding: *he heard a fruity melodious voice.*
– DERIVATIVES **melodiously** adverb, **melodiousness** noun.
– ORIGIN late Middle English: from Old French *melodieus*, from *melodie* (see MELODY).

melodist ▸ noun a composer of melodies. ■ archaic a singer.

melodize (also **melodise**) ▸ verb **1** [no obj.] play music. **2** [with obj.] make melodious.

melodrama ▸ noun **1** a sensational dramatic piece with exaggerated characters and exciting events intended to appeal to the emotions. ■ [mass noun] the genre of melodrama. ■ [mass noun] behaviour or events that resemble melodrama: *what little is known of his early life is cloaked in melodrama.*
2 historical a play interspersed with songs and orchestral music accompanying the action.
– DERIVATIVES **melodramatist** noun, **melodramatize** (also **melodramatise**) verb.
– ORIGIN early 19th cent.: from French *mélodrame*, from Greek *melos* 'music' + French *drame* 'drama'.

melodramatic ▸ adjective relating to melodrama. ■ characteristic of melodrama, especially in being exaggerated or overemotional: *he flung the door open with a melodramatic flourish.*
– DERIVATIVES **melodramatically** adverb.

melodramatics ▸ plural noun melodramatic behaviour.

melody ▸ noun (pl. **melodies**) a sequence of single notes that is musically satisfying; a tune: *he picked out an intricate melody on his guitar.* ■ [mass noun] the aspect of musical composition concerned with the arrangement of single notes to form a satisfying sequence. ■ the principal part in harmonized music: *we have the melody and bass of a song composed by Strozzi.* ■ [mass noun] sweet music; tunefulness.
– ORIGIN Middle English (also in the sense 'sweet music'): from Old French *melodie*, via late Latin from Greek *melōidia*, from *melos* 'song'.

melon ▸ noun **1** the large round fruit of a plant of the gourd family, with sweet pulpy flesh and many seeds. ■ (**melons**) informal a woman's breasts.
2 the Old World plant which yields the melon.
• *Cucumis melo* subsp. *melo*, family Cucurbitaceae: many varieties.
3 Zoology a waxy mass in the head of dolphins and other toothed whales, thought to focus acoustic signals.
– ORIGIN late Middle English: via Old French from late Latin *melo*, *melon-*, contraction of Latin *melopepo*, from Greek *mēlopepōn*, from *mēlon* 'apple' + *pepōn* 'gourd'.

melon hole ▸ noun Austral. another term for GILGAI.

Melos /ˈmiːlɒs/ a Greek island in the Aegean Sea, in the south-west of the Cyclades group. It was the centre of a flourishing civilization in the Bronze Age and is the site of the discovery in 1820 of a Hellenistic marble statue of Aphrodite, the Venus de Milo. Greek name MÍLOS.

Melpomene /mɛlˈpɒmɪni/ Greek & Roman Mythology the Muse of tragedy.
– ORIGIN Greek, literally 'singer'.

melt ▸ verb **1** make or become liquefied by heating: [with obj.] *the hot metal melted the wax* | (as adj. **melted**) *asparagus with melted butter* | [no obj.] *place under a hot grill until the cheese has melted.* ■ [with obj.] (**melt something down**) melt a metal article so as to reuse the raw material: *beautiful objects are being melted down and sold for scrap.* ■ [no obj.] dissolve in liquid: *add 400g sugar and boil until the sugar melts.* ■ [no obj.] informal (of a person) suffer extreme heat.
2 make or become more tender or loving: [with obj.] *Richard gave her a smile which* ***melted her heart*** | [no obj.] *she was so beautiful that I melted.*
3 [no obj., with adverbial] disappear or disperse: *the compromise was accepted and the opposition* ***melted away***. ■ (**melt into**) change or merge imperceptibly into (another form or state): *the cheers melted into gasps of admiration.*
▸ noun an act or period of melting: *the precipitation falls as snow and is released during the spring melt.* ■ [mass noun] metal or other material in a melted condition. ■ a quantity of metal melted at one operation. ■ [with modifier] N. Amer. a sandwich, hamburger, or other dish containing or topped with melted cheese: *a tuna melt.*
– PHRASES **melt in the mouth** (of food) be deliciously light or tender and need little chewing.
– PHRASAL VERBS **melt down 1** collapse or break down disastrously: *many expected him to melt down at the first sign of trouble.* **2** (of a nuclear reactor) undergo a catastrophic failure as a result of the fuel overheating.
– DERIVATIVES **meltable** adjective, **melter** noun, **meltingly** adverb.
– ORIGIN Old English *meltan*, *mieltan*, of Germanic origin; related to Old Norse *melta* 'to malt, digest', from an Indo-European root shared by Greek *meldein* 'to melt', Latin *mollis* 'soft', also by MALT.

meltdown ▸ noun **1** a disastrous collapse or breakdown: *the global financial system suffered a major meltdown.*
2 an accident in a nuclear reactor in which the fuel overheats and melts the reactor core or shielding.

> **WORD TRENDS** A **meltdown** was originally a catastrophic accident in a nuclear reactor, but this literal meaning has been swamped by the figurative sense of 'a disastrous collapse or breakdown'. This is a fairly recent coinage, first recorded in 1983, with the 'Black Monday' stock market crash of October 1987 labelled a *market meltdown*. The Oxford English Corpus shows a fairly steady use throughout the last decade, but in 2007 there was a massive leap in the number of examples. This reflects the beginning of the recession, with *financial*, *economic*, *global*, and *mortgage* becoming the word's most common collocates: *the global financial meltdown sent oil prices plummeting today.*

meltemi /mɛlˈtɛmi/ (also **meltemi wind**) ▸ noun a dry north-westerly wind which blows during the summer in the eastern Mediterranean.
– ORIGIN from modern Greek *meltémi*, Turkish *meltem*.

melting point ▸ noun the temperature at which a given solid will melt.

melting pot ▸ noun a pot in which metals or other materials are melted and mixed. ■ a place where different peoples, styles, theories, etc. are mixed together: *Toronto is a melting pot of different cultures.*
– PHRASES **in the melting pot** Brit. in a process of change and with an uncertain outcome: *the future of the railway is still in the melting pot.*

melton ▸ noun [mass noun] heavy woollen cloth with a close-cut nap, used for overcoats and jackets.
– ORIGIN early 19th cent.: named after *Melton Mowbray*, a town in central England, formerly a centre of cloth manufacture.

meltwater ▸ noun [mass noun] (also **meltwaters**) water formed by the melting of snow and ice, especially from a glacier.

Melville, Herman (1819–91), American novelist and short-story writer. His experiences on a whaling ship formed the basis of several novels, notably *Moby Dick* (1851). Other notable works: *Billy Budd* (first published in 1924).

member ▸ noun **1** a person, country, or organization that has joined a group, society, or team: *she's an active member of Greenpeace* | [as modifier] *the EU's member countries.* ■ a person, animal, or plant belonging to a particular group: *interest from members of the public.* ■ (**Member**) a person formally elected to certain legislative bodies: *Member of Parliament for Stretford.* ■ used in the title awarded to a person admitted to certain honours: *Member of the Order of the British Empire.*
2 a constituent piece of a complex structure, especially a component of a load-bearing structure: *the main member that joins the front and rear axles.* ■ a part of a sentence, equation, mathematical set, etc.
3 archaic a part of the body, especially a limb. ■ (also **male member**) used euphemistically to refer to the penis.
– DERIVATIVES **membered** adjective [in combination] (chiefly Chemistry) *a six-membered oxygen-containing ring*, **memberless** adjective.
– ORIGIN Middle English: via Old French from Latin *membrum* 'limb'.

membership ▸ noun [mass noun] the fact of being a member of a group: *countries seeking membership of the European Union* | [as modifier] *a membership card.* ■ [in sing.] the members or the number of members in a group: *our membership has grown by 600,000 in the past year.*

membrane ▸ noun Anatomy & Zoology a pliable sheet-like structure acting as a boundary, lining, or partition in an organism. ■ a thin pliable sheet of material forming a barrier or lining. ■ Biology a microscopic double layer of lipids and proteins forming the boundary of cells or organelles.
– DERIVATIVES **membranaceous** adjective, **membraneous** adjective, **membranous** adjective.
– ORIGIN late Middle English: from Latin *membrana*, from *membrum* 'limb'.

membranophone /mɛmˈbreɪnəfəʊn/ ▸ noun Music an instrument in which the sound is produced by a stretched membrane, such as a drum.

membranous labyrinth ▸ noun see LABYRINTH.

membrum virile /ˌmɛmbrəm vɪˈrʌɪli, vɪˈriːliː/ ▸ noun archaic a man's penis.
– ORIGIN Latin, literally 'male member'.

meme /miːm/ ▸ noun an element of a culture or system of behaviour passed from one individual to another by imitation or other non-genetic means. ■ an image, video, etc. that is passed electronically from one Internet user to another.
– DERIVATIVES **memetic** adjective.
– ORIGIN 1970s: from Greek *mimēma* 'that which is imitated', on the pattern of *gene*.

> **WORD TRENDS** When Richard Dawkins coined the word **meme** in his 1976 book *The Selfish Gene*, he wanted a word like **gene** that conveyed the way in which ideas and behaviour spread within society by non-genetic means. Since then the word has been picked up to describe a piece of information spread by email or via blogs and social networking sites. A **meme** can be almost anything—a joke, a video clip, a cartoon, a news story—and can also evolve as it spreads, with users editing the content or adding comments. Common collocates in the Oxford English Corpus are *spread*, *pass*, and *transmit*: as with the Internet sense of VIRAL, **meme** uses the metaphor of disease and infection.

Memel /ˈmɛːm(ə)l/ **1** German name for KLAIPEDA. ■ a former district of East Prussia, centred on the city of Memel (Klaipeda). It became an autonomous region of Lithuania in 1924. In 1938 it was taken by Germany, but it was restored to Lithuania by the Soviet Union in 1945.
2 the River Neman in its lower course (see NEMAN).

memento /mɪˈmɛntəʊ/ ▸ noun (pl. **mementos** or **mementoes**) an object kept as a reminder of a person or event: *you can purchase a memento of your visit.*
– ORIGIN late Middle English (denoting a prayer of commemoration): from Latin, literally 'remember!', imperative of *meminisse*.

memento mori /mɪˌmɛntəʊ ˈmɔːri, -rʌɪ/ ▸ noun (pl. **same**) an object kept as a reminder of the inevitability of death, such as a skull.
– ORIGIN Latin, literally 'remember (that you have) to die'.

Memnon /ˈmɛmnɒn/ Greek Mythology an Ethiopian king who went to Troy to help Priam, his uncle, and was killed.

memo ▸ noun (pl. **memos**) a memorandum.

memoir /ˈmɛmwɑː/ ▸ noun **1** a historical account or biography written from personal knowledge: *in 1924 she published a short memoir of her husband.* ■ (**memoirs**) an account written by a public figure of their life and experiences.
2 an essay on a learned subject. ■ (**memoirs**) the proceedings of a learned society.
– DERIVATIVES **memoirist** noun.
– ORIGIN late 15th cent. (denoting a memorandum or record): from French *mémoire* (masculine), a special use of *mémoire* (feminine) 'memory'.

memorabilia /ˌmɛm(ə)rəˈbɪlɪə/ ▸ plural noun [treated as sing. or pl.] objects kept or collected because of their associations with memorable people or events: *sixties memorabilia.* ■ archaic memorable or noteworthy observations or writings.
– ORIGIN late 18th cent.: from Latin, neuter plural of *memorabilis* 'memorable'.

memorable ▸ adjective worth remembering or easily remembered, especially because of being special or unusual: *he recalled memorable moments in his life.*
– DERIVATIVES **memorability** noun, **memorableness** noun, **memorably** adverb.
– ORIGIN late 15th cent.: from Latin *memorabilis*, from *memorare* 'bring to mind', from *memor* 'mindful'.

memorandum ▸ noun (pl. **memoranda** or **memorandums**) a written message in business or diplomacy: *he told them of his decision in a memorandum.* ■ a note recording something for future use: *the two countries signed a memorandum of understanding on economic cooperation.* ■ Law a document recording the terms of a contract or other legal details.
– ORIGIN late Middle English: from Latin, literally 'something to be brought to mind', gerundive of *memorare*. The original use was as an adjective, placed at the head of a note of a record made for future reference.

memorial ▸ **noun 1** a statue or structure established to remind people of a person or event: *a **memorial to** General Robert E. Lee.* ■ [as modifier] intended to commemorate someone or something: *a memorial service in the dead man's honour.*
2 chiefly historical a statement of facts, especially as the basis of a petition: *the Council sent a strongly worded memorial to the Chancellor of the Exchequer.* ■ a record or memoir.
– ORIGIN late Middle English: from late Latin *memoriale* 'record, memory, monument', from Latin *memorialis* 'serving as a reminder', from *memoria* 'memory'.

Memorial Day ▸ **noun** (in the US) a day on which those who died on active service are remembered, usually the last Monday in May.

memorialist ▸ **noun** a person who writes a memorial or memoir.

memorialize (also **memorialise**) ▸ **verb** [with obj.] preserve the memory of; commemorate: *the novel memorialized their childhood summers.*

memorize (also **memorise**) ▸ **verb** [with obj.] commit to memory; learn by heart: *he memorized thousands of verses.*
– DERIVATIVES **memorizable** adjective, **memorization** noun, **memorizer** noun.

memory ▸ **noun** (pl. **memories**) **1** the faculty by which the mind stores and remembers information: *I've a great **memory for** faces* | [mass noun] *the brain regions responsible for memory.* ■ the mind regarded as a store of things remembered: *he searched his memory frantically for an answer.*
2 something remembered from the past: *one of my earliest memories is of sitting on his knee* | [mass noun] *the mind can bury all memory of traumatic abuse.* ■ [mass noun] the remembering or commemoration of a dead person: *clubs devoted to the memory of Sherlock Holmes.* ■ [mass noun] the length of time over which a person or event continues to be remembered: *the worst slump in recent memory.*
3 the part of a computer in which data or program instructions can be stored for retrieval. ■ [mass noun] capacity for storing information in this way: *the module provides 16Mb of memory.*
– PHRASES **from memory** without reading or referring to notes: *each child was required to recite a verse from memory.* **in memory of** intended to honour and remind people of (a dead person). **take a trip** (or **walk**) **down memory lane** indulge in pleasant or sentimental memories.
– ORIGIN Middle English: from Old French *memorie*, from Latin *memoria*, from *memor* 'mindful, remembering'.

memory bank ▸ **noun** the memory device of a computer or other instrument.

memory board ▸ **noun** Computing a detachable board containing memory chips, which can be connected to a computer.

memory book ▸ **noun** US a scrapbook.

memory card ▸ **noun** a small, flat flash drive used especially in digital cameras and mobile phones.

memory cell ▸ **noun** Physiology a long-lived lymphocyte capable of responding to a particular antigen on its reintroduction, long after the exposure that prompted its production.

memory hole ▸ **noun** an imaginary place where inconvenient or unpleasant information is put and quickly forgotten.
– ORIGIN from George Orwell's *Nineteen Eighty-Four*, which described a slot where historical documents could be disposed of to allow for manipulation of memories of the past.

memory leak ▸ **noun** Computing a failure in a program to release discarded memory, causing impaired performance or failure.

memory mapping ▸ **noun** [mass noun] a technique in which a computer treats peripheral devices as if they were located in the main memory.

Memory Stick ▸ **noun** trademark a type of memory card. ■ (in general use) a flash drive.

memory trace ▸ **noun** a hypothetical permanent change in the nervous system brought about by memorizing something; an engram.

Memphis /ˈmɛmfɪs/ **1** an ancient city of Egypt, whose ruins are situated on the Nile about 15 km (nearly 10 miles) south of Cairo. It is thought to have been founded as the capital of the Old Kingdom of Egypt *c.*3100 BC and is the site of the pyramids of Saqqara and Giza and of the Sphinx.
2 a river port on the Mississippi in the extreme south-west of Tennessee; pop. 669,651 (est. 2008). Founded in 1819, it was the home in the late 19th century of blues music, the scene in 1968 of the assassination of Martin Luther King, and the childhood home and burial place of Elvis Presley.

MEMS ▸ **abbreviation** microelectromechanical systems.

memsahib /ˈmɛmsʌˌhiːb, ˈmɛmsɑːb/ ▸ **noun** Indian a married white or upper-class woman (often used as a respectful form of address by non-whites).
– ORIGIN from *mem* (representing an Indian pronunciation of MA'AM) + SAHIB.

men plural form of MAN.

menace ▸ **noun** a person or thing that is likely to cause harm; a threat or danger: *a new initiative aimed at beating the menace of drugs* | *the snakes are **a menace to** farm animals.* ■ [mass noun] a threatening quality or atmosphere: *he spoke the words with a hint of menace.* ■ (**menaces**) Brit. threatening words or actions: *a demand of money **with menaces**.*
▸ **verb** [with obj.] be a threat or possible danger to: *Africa's elephants are still menaced by poaching* | (as adj. **menacing**) *a menacing tone of voice.*
– ORIGIN Middle English: via Old French from late Latin *minacia*, from Latin *minax, minac-* 'threatening', from *minae* 'threats'.

menacing ▸ **adjective** suggesting the presence of danger; threatening: *our officers encountered menacing looks from teenagers.*
– DERIVATIVES **menacingly** adverb.

menadione /ˌmɛnəˈdʌɪəʊn/ ▸ **noun** [mass noun] Medicine a synthetic yellow compound related to menaquinone, used to treat haemorrhage. ● Chem. formula: $C_{11}H_8O_2$.
– ORIGIN 1940s: from *me(thyl)* + *na(phthalene)* + the suffix *-dione*, used in names of compounds containing two carbonyl groups.

ménage /meɪˈnɑːʒ/ ▸ **noun** the members of a household: *the Clelland ménage.*
– ORIGIN Middle English: from Old French *menage*, from *mainer* 'to stay', influenced by Old French *mesnie* 'household', both ultimately based on Latin *manere* 'remain'.

ménage à trois /meɪˌnɑːʒ ɑː ˈtrwʌ/ ▸ **noun** (pl. **ménages à trois** pronunc. **same**) an arrangement in which a married couple and the lover of one of them live together.
– ORIGIN French, 'household of three'.

menagerie /məˈnadʒ(ə)ri/ ▸ **noun** a collection of wild animals kept in captivity for exhibition.
– ORIGIN late 17th cent.: from French *ménagerie*, from *ménage* (see MÉNAGE).

Menai Strait /ˈmɛnʌɪ/ a channel separating Anglesey from the mainland of NW Wales. It is spanned by two bridges, a suspension bridge built by Thomas Telford 1819–26 and a second, built by Robert Stephenson 1846–50.

Menander /məˈnandə/ (*c.*342–292 BC), Greek dramatist. His comic plays deal with domestic situations and capture colloquial speech patterns. The sole complete extant play is *Dyskolos*.

Menapian /mɪˈnapɪən/ ▸ **adjective** Geology relating to or denoting a Middle Pleistocene glaciation in northern Europe, possibly corresponding to the Günz of the Alps. ■ (as noun **the Menapian**) the Menapian glaciation or the system of deposits laid down during it.
– ORIGIN 1950s: from Latin *Menapii*, a people of northern Gaul in Roman times, + -IAN.

menaquinone /ˌmɛnəˈkwɪnəʊn/ ▸ **noun** [mass noun] Biochemistry one of the K vitamins, a compound produced by bacteria in the large intestine and essential for the blood-clotting process. It is an isoprenoid derivative of menadione. Also called VITAMIN K_2.
– ORIGIN 1940s: from the chemical name *me(thyl)-na(phtho)quinone*.

menarche /mɛˈnɑːki/ ▸ **noun** the first occurrence of menstruation.
– ORIGIN late 19th cent.: modern Latin, from Greek *mēn* 'month' + *arkhē* 'beginning'.

Mencius /ˈmɛnʃɪəs/ (*c.*371–*c.*289 BC), Chinese philosopher; Latinized name of *Meng-tzu* or *Mengzi* ('Meng the Master'). Noted for developing Confucianism, he believed that rulers should provide for the welfare of the people and that human nature is intrinsically good. ■ one of the Four Books of Confucianism, containing the teachings of Mencius.

Mencken /ˈmɛŋkən/, H. L. (1880–1956), American journalist and literary critic; full name *Henry Louis Mencken*. In his book *The American Language* (1919) he opposed the dominance of European culture in America.

mend ▸ **verb** [with obj.] **1** repair (something that is broken or damaged): *workmen were mending faulty cabling.* ■ [no obj.] return to health; heal: *foot injuries can take months to mend.* ■ improve (an unpleasant situation): *quarrels could be mended by talking.*
2 add fuel to (a fire).
▸ **noun** a repair in a material: *the mend was barely visible.*
– PHRASES **mend (one's) fences** make peace with a person: *is it too late to mend fences with your ex-wife?* **mend one's manners** act more politely. **mend one's ways** improve one's habits or behaviour. **on the mend** improving in health or condition; recovering: *the economy is on the mend.* **mend one's pace** dated go faster; alter one's pace to match a companion.
– DERIVATIVES **mendable** adjective, **mender** noun.
– ORIGIN Middle English: shortening of AMEND.

mendacious /mɛnˈdeɪʃəs/ ▸ **adjective** not telling the truth; lying: *mendacious propaganda.*
– DERIVATIVES **mendaciously** adverb.
– ORIGIN early 17th cent.: from Latin *mendax, mendac-* 'lying' (related to *mendum* 'fault') + -IOUS.

mendacity ▸ **noun** [mass noun] untruthfulness: *people publicly castigated for past mendacity.*
– ORIGIN mid 17th cent.: from ecclesiastical Latin *mendacitas*, from *mendax, mendac-* 'lying' (see MENDACIOUS).

Mende /ˈmɛndi/ ▸ **noun** (pl. **same**) **1** a member of a people inhabiting Sierra Leone in West Africa.
2 [mass noun] the language of the Mende, belonging to the Mande group. It has over 1 million speakers.
▸ **adjective** relating to or denoting the Mende or their language.
– ORIGIN the name in Mende.

Mendel /ˈmɛnd(ə)l/, Gregor Johann (1822–84), Moravian monk, the father of genetics. From systematically breeding peas he demonstrated the transmission of characteristics in a predictable way by factors (genes) which remain intact and independent between generations and do not blend, though they may mask one another's effects.

M

Mendeleev /ˌmɛndəˈleɪɛf/, Dmitri (Ivanovich) (1834–1907), Russian chemist. He developed the periodic table and successfully predicted the discovery of several new elements.

mendelevium /ˌmɛndəˈliːvɪəm, -ˈleɪvɪəm/ ▸ **noun** [mass noun] the chemical element of atomic number 101, a radioactive metal of the actinide series. It does not occur naturally and was first made in 1955 by bombarding einsteinium with helium ions. (Symbol: **Md**)
– ORIGIN 1950s: modern Latin, from the name of D. MENDELEEV.

Mendelian /mɛnˈdiːlɪən/ ▸ **adjective** Biology relating to Mendel's theory of heredity: *Mendelian genetics.*
▸ **noun** a person who accepts or advocates Mendel's theory of heredity.

Mendelism /ˈmɛnd(ə)lɪz(ə)m/ ▸ **noun** [mass noun] Biology the theory of heredity as formulated by Mendel.

Mendelssohn /ˈmɛnd(ə)ls(ə)n/, German /ˈmɛndlzəːn/, Felix (1809–47), German composer and pianist; full name *Jakob Ludwig Felix Mendelssohn-Bartholdy*. His romantic music is elegant, light, and melodically inventive. Notable works include the oratorios *Fingal's Cave* (1830–2) and *Elijah* (1846) and eight volumes of *Lieder ohne Worte* (*Songs Without Words*) for piano.

Menderes /ˌmɛndəˈrɛs/ a river of SW Turkey. Rising in the Anatolian plateau, it flows for some 384 km (240 miles), entering the Aegean Sea south of the Greek island of Samos. Known in ancient times as the Maeander, and noted for its winding course, it gave its name to the verb *meander*.

mendicant /ˈmɛndɪk(ə)nt/ ▸ **adjective** given to begging. ■ of or denoting one of the religious orders who originally relied solely on alms: *a mendicant friar.*
▸ **noun** a beggar. ■ a member of a mendicant order.
– DERIVATIVES **mendicancy** noun.
– ORIGIN late Middle English: from Latin *mendicant-* 'begging', from the verb *mendicare*, from *mendicus* 'beggar', from *mendum* 'fault'.

mendicity /mɛnˈdɪsɪti/ ▸ **noun** [mass noun] the condition or activities of a beggar.
– ORIGIN late Middle English: from Old French *mendicite*, from Latin *mendicitas*, from *mendicus* 'beggar'.

mending ▸ **noun** [mass noun] things to be repaired by sewing or darning: *a muddle of books and mending.*

Mendip Hills (also **the Mendips**) a range of limestone hills in SW England.

Mendoza[1] /mɛnˈdəʊzə/, Spanish /menˈdoθa, -θa/ a city in western Argentina, situated in the foothills of the Andes at the centre of a wine-producing region; pop. 112,900 (est. 2008).

Mendoza[2] /mɛnˈdəʊzə/, Spanish /menˈdoθa, -θa/, Antonio de (*c.*1490–1552), Spanish colonial administrator, the first viceroy of New Spain (1535–50).

meneer /mɪˈnɪə/ ▸ **noun** S. African a title or form of address used of or to an Afrikaans man, corresponding to *Mr* or *sir*.
– ORIGIN South African Dutch, Afrikaans, from Dutch *mijnheer* 'sir, Mr, gentleman'.

Menelaus /ˌmɛnɪˈleɪəs/ Greek Mythology king of Sparta, husband of Helen and brother of Agamemnon. Helen was stolen from him by Paris, an event which provoked the Trojan War.

Menes /ˈmiːniːz/, Egyptian pharaoh, reigned *c.*3100 BC. He founded the first dynasty that ruled Egypt.

menfolk (US also **menfolks**) ▸ **plural noun** a group of men considered collectively, especially the men of a particular family or community.

Meng-tzu /mɛŋˈtsuː/ (also **Mengzi** /mɛŋˈziː/) Chinese name for **MENCIUS**.

menhaden /mɛnˈheɪd(ə)n/ ▸ **noun** a large deep-bodied fish of the herring family, which occurs along the east coast of North America. The oil-rich flesh is used to make fishmeal and fertilizer. ● Genus *Brevoortia*, family Clupeidae: several species.
– ORIGIN late 18th cent.: from Algonquian.

menhir /ˈmɛnhɪə/ ▸ **noun** a tall upright stone of a kind erected in prehistoric times in western Europe.
– ORIGIN mid 19th cent.: from Breton *men* 'stone' + *hir* 'long'.

menial /ˈmiːnɪəl/ ▸ **adjective** (of work) not requiring much skill and lacking prestige: *menial factory jobs.* ■ [attrib.] dated (of a servant) domestic.
▸ **noun** a person with a menial job. ■ dated a domestic servant.
– ORIGIN late Middle English (in the sense 'domestic'): from Old French, from *mesnee* 'household'.

M

Ménière's disease /mɛnˈjɛː/ (also **Ménière's syndrome**) ▸ **noun** [mass noun] a disease of unknown cause affecting the membranous labyrinth of the ear, causing progressive deafness and attacks of tinnitus and vertigo.
– ORIGIN late 19th cent.: named after Prosper *Ménière* (1799–1862), French physician.

meninges /mɪˈnɪndʒiːz/ ▸ **plural noun** (sing. **meninx**) Anatomy the three membranes (the dura mater, arachnoid, and pia mater) that line the skull and vertebral canal and enclose the brain and spinal cord.
– DERIVATIVES **meningeal** adjective.
– ORIGIN modern Latin, from Greek *mēninx, mēning-* 'membrane'.

meningioma /mɪˌnɪndʒɪˈəʊmə/ ▸ **noun** (pl. **meningiomas** or **meningiomata**) Medicine a tumour, usually benign, arising from meningeal tissue of the brain.

meningitis /ˌmɛnɪnˈdʒʌɪtɪs/ ▸ **noun** [mass noun] a serious disease in which there is inflammation of the meninges, caused by viral or bacterial infection, and marked by intense headache and fever, sensitivity to light, and muscular rigidity.
– DERIVATIVES **meningitic** adjective.

meningocele /mɪˈnɪŋgə(ʊ)siːl, -ˈnɪndʒə(ʊ)-/ ▸ **noun** Medicine a protrusion of the meninges through a gap in the spine due to a congenital defect.

meningococcus /mɪˌnɪŋgəʊˈkɒkəs, -ˌnɪndʒəʊ-/ ▸ **noun** (pl. **meningococci** /-ˈkɒk(s)ʌɪ, -ˈkɒk(s)iː/) a bacterium involved in some forms of meningitis and cerebrospinal infection. ● *Neisseria meningitidis.*
– DERIVATIVES **meningococcal** adjective.
– ORIGIN late 19th cent.: from **MENINGES** + **COCCUS**.

meningoencephalitis /mɪˈŋɪŋgəʊɛnˌsɛfəˈlʌɪtɪs, -ˈnɪndʒəʊ-, -ˌkɛf-/ ▸ **noun** [mass noun] Medicine inflammation of the membranes of the brain and the adjoining cerebral tissue.

meninx /ˈmiːnɪŋks/ singular form of **MENINGES**.

meniscectomy /ˌmɛnɪˈsɛktəmi/ ▸ **noun** [mass noun] surgical removal of a meniscus, especially that of the knee.

meniscus /mɪˈnɪskəs/ ▸ **noun** (pl. **menisci** /-sʌɪ/) Physics the curved upper surface of a liquid in a tube. ■ [usu. as modifier] a lens that is convex on one side and concave on the other. ■ Anatomy a thin fibrous cartilage between the surfaces of some joints, e.g. the knee.
– ORIGIN late 17th cent.: modern Latin, from Greek *mēniskos* 'crescent', diminutive of *mēnē* 'moon'.

Mennonite /ˈmɛnənʌɪt/ ▸ **noun** a member of a Protestant sect originating in Friesland in the 16th century and now mainly located in the US and Canada, emphasizing adult baptism and rejecting Church organization, military service, and public office.
– ORIGIN from the name of its founder, *Menno* Simons (1496–1561), + **-ITE[1]**.

meno /ˈmɛnəʊ/ ▸ **adverb** Music (in directions) less.
– ORIGIN Italian.

meno- ▸ **combining form** relating to menstruation: *menopause.*
– ORIGIN from Greek *mēn* 'month'.

menologion /ˌmɛnə(ʊ)ˈlɒgɪɒn, ˌmɛnə(ʊ)ˈləʊdʒɪən/ ▸ **noun** (pl. **menologia**) a calendar of the Greek Orthodox Church containing biographies of the saints.
– ORIGIN early 18th cent.: from ecclesiastical Greek *mēnologion*, from Greek *mēn* 'month' + *logos* 'account'.

Menominee /mɪˈnɒmɪniː/ (also **Menomini**) ▸ **noun** (pl. **same** or **Menominees**) **1** a member of an American Indian people of NE Wisconsin.
2 [mass noun] the extinct Algonquian language of the Menominee.
▸ **adjective** relating to or denoting the Menominee or their language.
– ORIGIN from Ojibwa *manōmini*, literally 'wild-rice person'.

meno mosso /ˌmɛnəʊ ˈmɒsəʊ/ ▸ **adverb & adjective** Music (especially as a direction) less quickly.
– ORIGIN Italian.

menopause /ˈmɛnəpɔːz/ ▸ **noun** the ceasing of menstruation. ■ the period in a woman's life (typically between the ages of 45 and 50) when menstruation ceases.
– DERIVATIVES **menopausal** adjective.
– ORIGIN late 19th cent.: from modern Latin *menopausis* (see **MENO-**, **PAUSE**).

menorah /mɪˈnɔːrə/ ▸ **noun** (**the Menorah**) a sacred candelabrum with seven branches used in the ancient temple in Jerusalem. ■ a candelabrum used in Jewish worship, typically with eight branches.
– ORIGIN Hebrew.

Menorca /meˈnɔrka/ Spanish name for **MINORCA**.

menorrhagia /ˌmɛnəˈreɪdʒɪə/ ▸ **noun** [mass noun] Medicine abnormally heavy bleeding at menstruation.
– ORIGIN late 18th cent.: modern Latin, from **MENO-** 'of menstruation' + *-rrhag-*, stem of Greek *rhēgnunai* 'to burst'.

menorrhoea /ˌmɛnəˈriːə/ ▸ **noun** [mass noun] Medicine the flow of blood at menstruation.
– ORIGIN mid 19th cent.: back-formation from **AMENORRHOEA**.

Mensa[1] /ˈmɛnsə/ Astronomy a small, faint southern constellation (the Table or Table Mountain), lying between Dorado and the south celestial pole. It contains part of the Large Magellanic Cloud.
– ORIGIN Latin.

Mensa[2] /ˈmɛnsə/ an international organization founded in England in 1945 whose members must achieve very high scores in IQ tests to be admitted.
– ORIGIN Latin, 'table', with allusion to a round table at which all members have equal status.

mensch /mɛnʃ/ (also **mensh**) ▸ **noun** N. Amer. informal a person of integrity and honour.
– ORIGIN 1930s: Yiddish *mensh*, from German *Mensch*, literally 'person'.

menses /ˈmɛnsiːz/ ▸ **plural noun** blood and other matter discharged from the uterus at menstruation. ■ [treated as sing.] the time of menstruation: *a late menses.*
– ORIGIN late 16th cent.: from Latin, plural of *mensis* 'month'.

Menshevik /ˈmɛnʃɪvɪk/ ▸ **noun** historical a member of the moderate non-Leninist wing of the Russian Social Democratic Workers' Party, opposed to the Bolsheviks and defeated by them after the overthrow of the tsar in 1917.
– ORIGIN from Russian *Men'shevik* 'a member of the minority', from *men'she* 'less'. Lenin coined the name at a time when the party was (untypically) in a temporary minority.

men's movement ▸ **noun** (chiefly in the US) a movement aimed at liberating men from traditional views about their character and role in society.

mens rea /ˌmɛnz ˈriːə/ ▸ **noun** [mass noun] Law the intention or knowledge of wrongdoing that constitutes part of a crime, as opposed to the action or conduct of the accused. Compare with **ACTUS REUS**.
– ORIGIN Latin, literally 'guilty mind'.

men's room ▸ **noun** chiefly N. Amer. a men's toilet in a public or institutional building.

menstrual ▸ **adjective** relating to the menses or menstruation: *menstrual blood.*
– ORIGIN late Middle English: from Latin *menstrualis*, from *menstruum* 'menses', from *mensis* 'month'.

menstrual cycle ▸ **noun** the process of ovulation and menstruation in women and other female primates.

menstrual period ▸ **noun** see **PERIOD** (sense 3 of the noun).

menstruate /ˈmɛnstrʊeɪt/ ▸ **verb** [no obj.] (of a woman) discharge blood and other material from the lining of the uterus as part of the menstrual cycle.
– ORIGIN mid 17th cent.: from late Latin *menstruat-* 'menstruated', from the verb *menstruare*, from Latin *menstrua* 'menses'.

menstruation ▸ **noun** [mass noun] the process in a woman of discharging blood and other material from the lining of the uterus at intervals of about one lunar month from puberty until the menopause, except during pregnancy.

menstruous ▸ **adjective** relating to or in the process of menstruation.
– ORIGIN late Middle English: from Old French *menstrueus*, from late Latin *menstruosus*, from *menstrua* 'menses'.

menstruum /ˈmɛnstrʊəm/ ▸ **noun** (pl. **menstrua** /-strʊə/) **1** [mass noun] menses.
2 archaic a solvent.
– ORIGIN late Middle English (in sense 1): from Latin, neuter of *menstruus* 'monthly', from *mensis* 'month'. Sense 2 is by analogy of the supposed agency of a solvent in the transmutation of metals into gold with the supposed action of menses on the ovum.

mensurable ▸ **adjective** able to be measured; having fixed limits. ■ Music another term for **MENSURAL**.
– ORIGIN late Middle English (in the sense 'moderate'): from late Latin *mensurabilis*, from *mensurare* 'to measure', from Latin *mensura* 'measure'.

mensural /ˈmɛnʃ(ə)r(ə)l, -sjə-/ ▸ **adjective** of or involving measuring: *mensural investigations.* ■ Music designating or relating to music in a definite metre.
– ORIGIN late 16th cent.: from Latin *mensuralis*, from *mensura* 'measure'.

mensuration ▸ **noun** [mass noun] measurement. ■ the part of geometry concerned with ascertaining lengths, areas, and volumes.
– ORIGIN late 16th cent. (denoting measurement in general): from late Latin *mensuratio(n-)*, from *mensurare* 'to measure'.

menswear ▸ **noun** [mass noun] clothes for men.

-ment ▸ **suffix 1** forming nouns expressing the means or result of an action: *curtailment | excitement.*
2 forming nouns from adjectives (such as *merriment* from *merry*).
– ORIGIN from French, or from Latin *-mentum*.

mental ▸ **adjective 1** relating to the mind: *mental faculties | mental phenomena.* ■ done by or occurring in the mind: *a quick mental calculation | she made a mental note to ring him later.*
2 of or relating to disorders or illnesses of the mind: *a mental hospital.* ■ [predic.] informal mad; insane: *I think he was a little worried that I might be mental.*
– PHRASES **go mental** informal lose one's self-control, typically as a result of anger or excitement: *the home crowd were going mental.*
– ORIGIN late Middle English: from late Latin *mentalis*, from Latin *mens, ment-* 'mind'.

> **USAGE** The use of **mental** in compounds such as **mental hospital** and **mental patient** was the normal accepted term in the first half of the 20th century. It is now, however, regarded as old-fashioned, sometimes even offensive, and has been largely replaced by the term **psychiatric** in both general and official use.

mental age ▸ **noun** a person's mental ability expressed as the age at which an average person reaches the same ability: *she was 65 but had a mental age of two.*

mental arithmetic ▸ **noun** [mass noun] arithmetical calculations performed in the mind, without writing figures down or using a calculator.

mental block ▸ noun an inability to recall something or to perform a mental action.

mental cruelty ▸ noun [mass noun] Law conduct that makes another person suffer but does not involve physical assault.

mental defective ▸ noun dated a person with a mental disability.

mental deficiency ▸ noun [mass noun] dated the condition of having a mental disability.

mental handicap ▸ noun a condition in which the intellectual capacity of a person is permanently lowered or underdeveloped to an extent which prevents normal function in society.

> **USAGE** The terms **mental handicap** and **mentally handicapped**, though widely used a few decades ago, have fallen out of favour in recent years and have been largely replaced in official contexts by terms such as **learning difficulties**. See **USAGE** at **LEARNING DIFFICULTIES**.

mental illness ▸ noun a condition which causes serious disorder in a person's behaviour or thinking.

mentalism ▸ noun [mass noun] Philosophy the theory that physical and psychological phenomena are ultimately explicable only in terms of a creative and interpretative mind.

mentalist[1] ▸ noun **1** a magician who performs feats that apparently demonstrate extraordinary mental powers, such as mind-reading.
2 Brit. informal an eccentric or mad person.

mentalist[2] Philosophy ▸ noun an adherent of mentalism.
▸ adjective relating to mentalists or mentalism.
– DERIVATIVES **mentalistic** adjective.

mentality ▸ noun (pl. **mentalities**) **1** often derogatory the characteristic way of thinking of a person or group: *I had inherited not only my father's blood but his bourgeois mentality as well.*
2 [mass noun] dated the capacity for intelligent thought.
– ORIGIN late 17th cent. (in the sense 'mental process'): from the adjective **MENTAL** + **-ITY**. Current senses date from the mid 19th cent.

mentally ▸ adverb in a manner relating to the mind: *soldiers become physically and mentally exhausted.*

mentally handicapped ▸ adjective (of a person) having very limited intellectual functions.

mentation ▸ noun [mass noun] technical mental activity.
– ORIGIN mid 19th cent.: from Latin *mens, ment-* 'mind' + **-ATION**.

mentee ▸ noun a person who is advised, trained, or counselled by a mentor.

menthol ▸ noun [mass noun] a crystalline alcohol with a minty taste and odour, found in peppermint and other natural oils. It is used as a flavouring and in decongestants and analgesics. ● Chem. formula: $C_{10}H_{19}OH$.
– ORIGIN late 19th cent.: from German, from Latin *mentha* 'mint' + **-OL**.

mentholated ▸ adjective treated with or containing menthol: *mentholated shaving creams.*

mention ▸ verb [with obj.] refer to (something) briefly and without going into detail: *I haven't **mentioned** it **to** William yet* | [with clause] *I mentioned that my father was meeting me later.* ■ [with obj.] refer to (someone) as being noteworthy, especially as a potential candidate for a post: *he is still regularly **mentioned as** a possible secretary of state.*
▸ noun a reference to someone or something: *their eyes light up at a mention of Sartre* | [mass noun] *she **made no mention of** her disastrous trip to Paris.* ■ a formal acknowledgement of something noteworthy: *he received a special mention and a prize of £100* | [mass noun] *two other points are worthy of mention.* ■ (in full **mention in dispatches**) Brit. an instance of being mentioned in dispatches.
– PHRASES **be mentioned in dispatches** Brit. be commended for one's actions by name in an official military report. **don't mention it** a polite expression used to indicate that thanks or an apology are not necessary. **mention someone in one's will** leave a legacy to someone. **not to mention** used to introduce an additional point which reinforces the point being made: *I'm amazed you find the time, not to mention the energy, to do any work at all.*
– DERIVATIVES **mentionable** adjective.
– ORIGIN Middle English (originally in *make mention of*): via Old French from Latin *mentio(n-)*; related to **MIND**.

mento ▸ noun (pl. **mentos**) [mass noun] a style of Jamaican folk music based on a traditional dance rhythm in duple time.
– ORIGIN early 20th cent.: of unknown origin.

mentor ▸ noun an experienced and trusted adviser: *he was her friend and mentor until his death.* ■ an experienced person in a company or educational institution who trains and counsels new employees or students.
▸ verb [with obj.] advise or train (someone, especially a younger colleague).
– ORIGIN mid 18th cent.: via French and Latin from Greek *Mentōr*, the name of the adviser of the young Telemachus in Homer's *Odyssey*.

mentum /ˈmɛntəm/ ▸ noun Entomology a part of the base of the labium in some insects.
– ORIGIN early 19th cent.: from Latin, literally 'chin'.

menu ▸ noun a list of dishes available in a restaurant: *the waiter handed her a menu* | figurative *politics and sport are **on the menu** tonight.* ■ the food available or to be served in a restaurant or at a meal: *a no-fuss dinner-party menu.* ■ Computing a list of commands or facilities displayed on screen.
– ORIGIN mid 19th cent.: from French, 'detailed list' (noun use of *menu* 'small, detailed'), from Latin *minutus* 'very small'.

menu bar ▸ noun Computing a horizontal bar, typically located at the top of the screen below the title bar, containing drop-down menus.

menudo /mɪˈnuːdəʊ/ ▸ noun (pl. **menudos**) [mass noun] a spicy Mexican soup made from tripe.
– ORIGIN noun use of a Mexican Spanish adjective meaning 'small'.

menu-driven ▸ adjective (of a program or computer) used by making selections from menus.

Menuhin /ˈmɛnjʊɪn/, Sir Yehudi (1916–99), American-born British violinist. He founded a school of music, named after him, in Surrey in 1962.

Menzies /ˈmɛnzɪz/, Sir Robert Gordon (1894–1978), Australian Liberal statesman, Prime Minister 1939–41 and 1949–66. He is Australia's longest-serving Prime Minister.

Meo /mɪˈəʊ/ ▸ noun (pl. **same** or **Meos**) & adjective another term for **HMONG**.

meow ▸ noun & verb variant spelling of **MIAOW**.

MEP ▸ noun a Member of the European Parliament.

mepacrine /ˈmɛpəkrɪn, -iːn/ ▸ noun another term for **QUINACRINE**.
– ORIGIN 1940s: from *me(thoxy-)* + *p(entane)* + *acr(id)ine*.

meperidine /mɛˈpɛrɪdiːn/ ▸ noun another term for **PETHIDINE**.
– ORIGIN 1940s: blend of **METHYL** and **PIPERIDINE**.

Mephistophelian /ˌmɛfɪstəˈfiːlɪən, mɪˌfɪstə-, ˌmɛfɪstɒfɪˈliːən/ (also **Mephistophelean**) ▸ adjective wicked; fiendish: *a Mephistophelian cackle.*
– ORIGIN mid 19th cent.: from *Mephistopheles*, an evil spirit to whom Faust, in the German legend, sold his soul.

mephitic /mɪˈfɪtɪk/ ▸ adjective literary (especially of a gas or vapour) foul-smelling; noxious.
– ORIGIN early 17th cent.: from late Latin *mephiticus*, from *mephitis* 'noxious exhalation'.

-mer ▸ combining form denoting polymers and related kinds of molecule: *elastomer.*
– ORIGIN from Greek *meros* 'part'.

meranti /məˈranti/ ▸ noun [mass noun] white, red, or yellow hardwood timber from Malaysia or Indonesia. ● This timber is obtained from trees of the genus *Shorea*, family Dipterocarpaceae.
– ORIGIN late 18th cent.: from Malay.

merbau /ˈməːbaʊ/ ▸ noun a tropical hardwood tree which yields valuable timber, native to Malaysia and Indonesia. ● Genus *Intsia*, family Leguminosae: three species.
– ORIGIN late 18th cent.: from Malay.

merbromin /məːˈbrəʊmɪn/ ▸ noun [mass noun] a greenish iridescent crystalline compound which dissolves in water to give a red solution used as an antiseptic. It is a fluorescein derivative containing bromine and mercury.
– ORIGIN 1940s: from **MERCURIC** + **BROMO-** + **-IN**[1].

Merc /məːk/ ▸ noun informal a Mercedes car.

merc /məːk/ ▸ noun informal a mercenary soldier.

mercado /məːˈkɑːdəʊ/ ▸ noun (pl. **mercados**) (in Spanish-speaking countries) a market.
– ORIGIN Spanish, from Latin *mercatus* 'market'.

Mercalli scale /məːˈkali/ ▸ noun a twelve-point scale for expressing the local intensity of an earthquake, ranging from I (virtually imperceptible) to XII (total destruction).
– ORIGIN 1920s: named after Giuseppe *Mercalli* (1850–1914), Italian geologist.

mercantile /ˈməːk(ə)ntʌɪl/ ▸ adjective relating to trade or commerce; commercial: *the shift of wealth to the mercantile classes.*
– ORIGIN mid 17th cent.: from French, from Italian, from *mercante* 'merchant'.

mercantile marine ▸ noun another term for **MERCHANT NAVY**.

mercantilism /ˈməːk(ə)ntʌɪˌlɪz(ə)m/ ▸ noun [mass noun] belief in the benefits of profitable trading. ■ historical the economic theory that trade generates wealth and is stimulated by the accumulation of profitable balances, which a government should encourage by means of protectionism.
– DERIVATIVES **mercantilist** noun & adjective.

mercaptan /məˈkapt(ə)n/ ▸ noun Chemistry another term for **THIOL**.
– ORIGIN mid 19th cent.: from modern Latin *mercurium captans*, literally 'capturing mercury'.

Mercator /məːˈkeɪtə/, Gerardus (1512–94), Flemish geographer and cartographer, resident in Germany from 1552; Latinized name of *Gerhard Kremer*. He invented the system of map projection that is named after him.

Mercator projection ▸ noun a projection of a map of the world on to a cylinder in such a way that all the parallels of latitude have the same length as the equator, used especially for marine charts and certain climatological maps.

mercenary /ˈməːsɪn(ə)ri/ ▸ adjective primarily concerned with making money at the expense of ethics: *she's nothing but a mercenary little gold-digger.*
▸ noun (pl. **mercenaries**) a professional soldier hired to serve in a foreign army. ■ a person primarily motivated by personal gain: *cricket's most infamous mercenary.*
– DERIVATIVES **mercenariness** noun.
– ORIGIN late Middle English (as a noun): from Latin *mercenarius* 'hireling', from *merces, merced-* 'reward'.

mercer ▸ noun Brit., chiefly historical a dealer in textile fabrics, especially silks, velvets, and other fine materials.
– DERIVATIVES **mercery** noun.
– ORIGIN Middle English: from Old French *mercier*, based on Latin *merx, merc-* 'goods'.

mercerize (also **mercerise**) ▸ verb [with obj.] (usu. as adj. **mercerized**) treat (cotton fabric or thread) under tension with caustic alkali to impart strength and lustre.
– ORIGIN mid 19th cent.: from the name of John *Mercer* (died 1866), said to have invented the process, + **-IZE**.

merchandise ▸ noun /ˈməːtʃ(ə)ndʌɪs, -z/ [mass noun] goods to be bought and sold: *shops which offered an astonishing range of merchandise.* ■ products used to promote a film, pop group, etc., or linked to a fictional character; merchandising.
▸ verb /ˈməːtʃ(ə)ndʌɪz/ (also **merchandize**) [with obj.] promote the sale of (goods), especially by their presentation in retail outlets: *a new breakfast food can easily be merchandised.* ■ promote or publicize (an idea or person): *they are merchandising 'niceness' to children.* ■ [no obj.] archaic engage in the business of a merchant.
– DERIVATIVES **merchandisable** adjective, **merchandiser** noun.
– ORIGIN late Middle English: from Old French *marchandise*, from *marchand* 'merchant'.

merchandising ▸ noun [mass noun] the activity of promoting the sale of goods, especially by their presentation in retail outlets: *problems rooted in poor merchandising.* ■ products used to promote a particular film, pop group, etc., or linked to a particular fictional character: *the characters are still popular and found on a wide variety of merchandising.*

Merchant, Ismail (1936–2005), Indian film producer. In 1961 he became a partner with James Ivory in Merchant Ivory Productions. Together they made a number of films, including *Howard's End* (1992) and *The Remains of the Day* (1993).

merchant ▸ noun **1** a person or company involved in wholesale trade, especially one dealing with foreign countries or supplying goods to a particular trade: *a builders' merchant* | *a tea merchant.* ■ chiefly N. Amer.

M

a retail trader: *the credit cards are accepted by 10 million merchants worldwide.* ■ a person who deals in something unpleasant: *a merchant of death.* ■ (in historical contexts) a person involved in trade or commerce.
2 [usu. with modifier] informal, derogatory a person who has a liking for a particular activity: *his driver was no speed merchant.*
▶ adjective [attrib.] (in historical contexts) relating to merchants or commerce: *the growth of the merchant classes.* ■ (of ships, sailors, or shipping activity) involved with commerce rather than military activity: *a merchant seaman.*
– ORIGIN Middle English: from Old French *marchant*, based on Latin *mercari* 'to trade', from *merx, merc-* 'merchandise'.

merchantable ▶ adjective suitable for sale: *goods must be of merchantable quality.*
– ORIGIN late 15th cent.: from the obsolete verb *merchant* 'haggle, trade as a merchant', from Old French *marchander*, from *marchand* 'merchant'.

Merchant Adventurers an English trading guild which was involved in trade overseas, principally with the Netherlands, during the period from the 15th to the 18th centuries.

merchant bank ▶ noun Brit. a bank dealing in commercial loans and investment.
– DERIVATIVES **merchant banker** noun, **merchant banking** noun.

merchantman ▶ noun (pl. **merchantmen**) a ship carrying merchandise.

merchant marine ▶ noun N. Amer. another term for MERCHANT NAVY.

merchant navy ▶ noun (often **the merchant navy**) Brit. a country's commercial shipping, as opposed to that involved in military activity.

merchant prince ▶ noun a person who has acquired sufficient wealth from trading to wield political influence.

Mercia /ˈməːʃɪə, ˈməːsɪə/ a former kingdom of central England. It was established by invading Angles in the 6th century AD in the border areas between the new Anglo-Saxon settlements in the east and the Celtic regions in the west. ■ used in names of modern organizations to refer to parts of the English midlands: *West Mercia Police.*
– DERIVATIVES **Mercian** adjective & noun.

M

merciful ▶ adjective showing or exercising mercy: *William did not believe in being merciful to those who fought against him.* ■ (of an event) coming as a mercy; bringing someone relief from something unpleasant: *her death was a merciful release.*
– DERIVATIVES **mercifulness** noun.

mercifully ▶ adverb 1 in a merciful manner.
2 [sentence adverb] to one's great relief; fortunately: *mercifully, the event passed off without incident.*

merciless ▶ adjective showing no mercy: *a merciless attack with a blunt instrument* | figurative *the merciless summer heat.*
– DERIVATIVES **mercilessly** adverb, **mercilessness** noun.

Merckx /məːks/, Eddy (b.1945), Belgian racing cyclist. During his professional career he won the Tour de France five times (1969–72 and 1974).

Mercosur /ˈməːkəʊsuːə/, Spanish /merkəʊˈsur/ a customs union between Argentina, Brazil, Paraguay, and Uruguay, which came into effect in January 1995. Bolivia and Chile joined as associate members in 1996.
– ORIGIN from elements of South American Spanish *mercado común del cono sur* 'Southern Cone Common Market' or *mercado común del sur* 'Southern Common Market'.

mercurial /məːˈkjʊərɪəl/ ▶ adjective 1 subject to sudden or unpredictable changes of mood or mind: *his mercurial temperament.*
2 of or containing the element mercury.
3 (**Mercurial**) of the planet Mercury.
▶ noun a drug or other compound containing mercury.
– DERIVATIVES **mercuriality** /-ˈalɪti/ noun, **mercurially** adverb.
– ORIGIN late Middle English (in sense 3 of the adjective): from Latin *mercurialis* 'relating to the god Mercury', from *Mercurius* 'Mercury'. Sense 1 of the adjective dates from the mid 17th cent.

mercuric /məːˈkjʊərɪk/ ▶ adjective Chemistry of mercury with a valency of two; of mercury(II). Compare with MERCUROUS.

mercuric chloride ▶ noun [mass noun] a toxic white crystalline compound, used as a fungicide. ● Chem. formula: $HgCl_2$.

Mercurochrome /məːˈkjʊərəkrəʊm/ ▶ noun US trademark for MERBROMIN.
– ORIGIN early 20th cent.: from MERCURY[1] + Greek *khrōma* 'colour'.

mercurous /ˈməːkjʊrəs/ ▶ adjective Chemistry of mercury with a valency of one; of mercury(I). Compare with MERCURIC.

Mercury 1 Roman Mythology the Roman god of eloquence, skill, trading, and thieving, herald and messenger of the gods, who was identified with Hermes. [from Latin *Mercurius*, from *merx, merc-* 'merchandise'.] ■ used in names of newspapers and journals: *the Leicester Mercury.*
2 Astronomy a small planet that is the closest to the sun in the solar system, sometimes visible to the naked eye just after sunset.

> Mercury orbits within the orbit of Venus at an average distance of 57.9 million km from the sun. With a diameter of 4,878 km it is only a third larger than earth's moon, which it resembles in having a heavily cratered surface. Its 'day' of 58.65 days is precisely two thirds the length of its 'year' of 87.97 days. Daytime temperatures average 170°C. There is no atmosphere and the planet has no satellites.

– DERIVATIVES **Mercurian** adjective.

mercury¹ ▶ noun [mass noun] the chemical element of atomic number 80, a heavy silvery-white metal which is liquid at ordinary temperatures. (Symbol: **Hg**) Also called QUICKSILVER. ■ the column of mercury in a thermometer or barometer, or its height as indicating atmospheric temperature or pressure: *coastal sunshine sends mercury soaring.* ■ historical mercury or one of its compounds used medicinally, especially to treat syphilis.
– ORIGIN Middle English: from Latin *Mercurius* (see MERCURY (sense 1)).

mercury² ▶ noun a plant of a genus which includes dog's mercury. ● Genus *Mercurialis*, family Euphorbiaceae.
– ORIGIN mid 16th cent.: from the genus name, from Latin *mercurialis* 'of the god Mercury'.

mercury tilt switch ▶ noun an electric switch in which the circuit is made by mercury flowing into a gap when the device tilts.

mercury vapour lamp ▶ noun a lamp in which light is produced by an electrical discharge through mercury vapour.

mercy ▶ noun (pl. **mercies**) [mass noun] compassion or forgiveness shown towards someone whom it is within one's power to punish or harm: *the boy was screaming and begging for mercy* | [count noun] *the mercies of God.* ■ [count noun] an event to be grateful for, because it prevents something unpleasant or provides relief from suffering: *his death was in a way a mercy.* ■ [as modifier] (especially of a journey or mission) performed out of a desire to relieve suffering: *mercy missions to refugees caught up in the fighting.*
▶ exclamation archaic used in expressions of surprise or fear: *'Mercy me!' uttered Mrs Diggory.*
– PHRASES **at the mercy of** completely in the power of: *consumers were at the mercy of every rogue in the marketplace.* **be thankful** (or **grateful**) **for small mercies** be relieved that an unpleasant situation is alleviated by minor advantages. **have mercy on** (or **upon**) show compassion or forgiveness to. **leave someone/thing to the mercy of** leave someone or something exposed to probable danger or harm: *the forest is left to the mercy of the loggers.* **throw oneself on someone's mercy** intentionally place oneself in someone's power in the expectation that they will behave mercifully towards one.
– ORIGIN Middle English: from Old French *merci* 'pity' or 'thanks', from Latin *merces, merced-* 'reward', in Christian Latin 'pity, favour, heavenly reward'.

mercy killing ▶ noun [mass noun] the killing of a patient suffering from an incurable and painful disease.

merde /mɛːd/, French /mɛʀd/ ▶ exclamation used as a mild, generally humorous substitute for 'shit': *Merde! What had she done!*
– ORIGIN French, from Latin *merda* 'excrement, dung'.

mere¹ /mɪə/ ▶ adjective [attrib.] used to emphasize how small or insignificant someone or something is: *questions that cannot be answered by mere mortals* | *the city is a mere 20 minutes from some stunning countryside.* ■ used to emphasize that the fact of something being present in a situation is enough to influence that situation: *his stomach rebelled at the mere thought of food.*
– ORIGIN late Middle English (in the senses 'pure' and 'sheer, downright'): from Latin *merus* 'undiluted'.

mere² /mɪə/ ▶ noun Brit., chiefly literary a lake or pond.
– ORIGIN Old English, of Germanic origin; related to Dutch *meer* 'lake' and German *Meer* 'sea', from an Indo-European root shared by Russian *more* and Latin *mare*.

mere³ /ˈmɛri/ ▶ noun a Maori war club, especially one made of greenstone.
– ORIGIN Maori.

Meredith /ˈmɛrədɪθ/, George (1828–1909), English novelist and poet. His semi-autobiographical verse collection *Modern Love* (1862) describes the disillusionment of married love. Other notable works: *The Egoist* (novel, 1871).

merely ▶ adverb just; only: *Gary, a silent boy, merely nodded.*

merengue /məˈrɛŋgeɪ/ (also **meringue**) ▶ noun [mass noun] a Caribbean style of dance music, typically in duple and triple time. ■ a style of dancing associated with merengue, with alternating long and short stiff-legged steps.
– ORIGIN late 19th cent.: probably American Spanish; compare with the sense 'upheaval, disorder', attested in Argentina, Paraguay, and Uruguay.

mereology /ˌmɛrɪˈɒlədʒi/ ▶ noun [mass noun] Philosophy the abstract study of the relations between parts and wholes.
– DERIVATIVES **mereological** adjective.
– ORIGIN 1940s: from French, formed irregularly from Greek *meros* 'part' + -LOGY.

mere right ▶ noun Law a right to property with no right to possession.

meretricious /ˌmɛrɪˈtrɪʃəs/ ▶ adjective 1 apparently attractive but having no real value: *meretricious souvenirs for the tourist trade.*
2 archaic relating to or characteristic of a prostitute.
– DERIVATIVES **meretriciously** adverb, **meretriciousness** noun.
– ORIGIN early 17th cent.: from Latin *meretricius* (adjective from *meretrix, meretric-* 'prostitute', from *mereri* 'be hired') + -OUS.

merganser /məːˈganzə, -sə/ ▶ noun a fish-eating diving duck with a long, thin serrated and hooked bill. Also called SAWBILL. ● Genus *Mergus*, family Anatidae: six species.
– ORIGIN mid 17th cent.: modern Latin, from Latin *mergus* 'diver' (from *mergere* 'to dive') + *anser* 'goose'.

merge ▶ verb combine or cause to combine to form a single entity: [no obj.] ***the merchant bank merged with another broker*** | [with obj.] ***he agreed to merge his broadcasting company with a multinational concern.*** ■ blend or cause to blend gradually into something else so as to become indistinguishable from it: [no obj.] *he crouched low and endeavoured to merge into the darkness of the forest* | [with obj.] *he placed a sheet of paper over the fresh paint to merge the colours.* ■ [with obj.] (usu. **merge something in**) Law absorb (a title or estate) in another.
– ORIGIN mid 17th cent. (in the sense 'immerse oneself'): from Latin *mergere* 'to dip, plunge'; the legal sense is from Anglo-Norman French *merger*.

merger ▶ noun a combination of two things, especially companies, into one: ***a merger between two supermarket chains*** | [mass noun] ***local companies ripe for merger or acquisition.*** ■ [mass noun] Law the merging of one estate or title in another.
– ORIGIN early 18th cent.: from Anglo-Norman French *merger* (verb used as a noun): see MERGE.

merguez /məːˈgɛz/ (also **merguez sausage**) ▶ noun (pl. **same**) a spicy beef and lamb sausage coloured with red peppers, originally made in parts of North Africa.
– ORIGIN French, from Arabic *mirkās, mirqās*.

Meriç /məˈriːtʃ/ Turkish name for MARITSA.

Mérida /ˈmɛrɪdə/ 1 a city in western Spain, on the Guadiana River, capital of Extremadura region; pop. 55,568 (2008).
2 a city in SE Mexico, capital of the state of Yucatán; pop. 734,153 (2005).

meridian /məˈrɪdɪən/ ▶ noun 1 a circle of constant longitude passing through a given place on the earth's surface and the terrestrial poles. ■ Astronomy a circle passing through the celestial poles and the zenith of a given place on the earth's surface.

2 (in acupuncture and Chinese medicine) each of a set of pathways in the body along which vital energy is said to flow.
▸ **adjective** [attrib.] relating to or situated at a meridian: *the meridian moon.*
– ORIGIN late Middle English: from Old French *meridien*, from Latin *meridianum* (neuter, used as a noun) 'noon', from *medius* 'middle' + *dies* 'day'. The use in astronomy is due to the fact that the sun crosses a meridian at noon.

meridian circle ▸ **noun** Astronomy a telescope mounted so as to move only on a North–South line, for observing the transit of celestial objects across the meridian.

meridional /məˈrɪdɪən(ə)l/ ▸ **adjective 1** of or in the south; southern: *the meridional leg of the journey.* ■ relating to or characteristic of the inhabitants of southern Europe, especially the South of France: *she was meridional in temperament.*
2 relating to a meridian. ■ Meteorology (of winds and air flow) aligned with lines of longitude.
▸ **noun** a native or inhabitant of southern Europe, especially the south of France.
– ORIGIN late Middle English: via Old French from late Latin *meridionalis*, formed irregularly from Latin *meridies* 'midday, south'.

meringue[1] /məˈraŋ/ ▸ **noun** an item of sweet food made from a mixture of egg whites and sugar baked until crisp: *chocolate meringues* | [mass noun] *cover the pudding with meringue.*
– ORIGIN from French, of unknown origin.

meringue[2] /məˈraŋ/ ▸ **noun** variant spelling of **MERENGUE**.

merino /məˈriːnəʊ/ ▸ **noun** (pl. **merinos**) (also **merino sheep**) a sheep of a breed with long, fine wool. ■ [mass noun] a soft woollen or wool-and-cotton material resembling cashmere, originally of merino wool. ■ [mass noun] a fine woollen yarn. ■ W. Indian an undershirt, originally one made of merino wool.
– ORIGIN late 18th cent.: from Spanish, of unknown origin.

Merionethshire /ˌmɛrɪˈɒnɪθʃɪə, -ʃə/ a former county of NW Wales. It became a part of Gwynedd in 1974.

meristem /ˈmɛrɪstɛm/ ▸ **noun** Botany a region of plant tissue, found chiefly at the growing tips of roots and shoots and in the cambium, consisting of actively dividing cells forming new tissue.
– DERIVATIVES **meristematic** /-stəˈmatɪk/ **adjective**.
– ORIGIN late 19th cent.: formed irregularly from Greek *meristos* 'divisible', from *merizein* 'divide into parts', from *meros* 'part'. The suffix *-em* is on the pattern of words such as *xylem*.

merit ▸ **noun** [mass noun] the quality of being particularly good or worthy, especially so as to deserve praise or reward: *composers of outstanding merit.* ■ [count noun] a good feature or point: *the relative merits of both approaches have to be considered.* ■ [count noun] a pass grade in an examination denoting above-average performance. Compare with **DISTINCTION**. ■ **(merits)** Law the intrinsic rights and wrongs of a case, outside of any other considerations. ■ **(merits)** Theology good deeds entitling someone to a future reward from God.
▸ **verb (merits, meriting, merited)** [with obj.] deserve or be worthy of (reward, punishment, or attention): *the results have been encouraging enough to merit further investigation.*
– PHRASES **judge** (or **consider**) **something on its merits** assess something solely with regard to its intrinsic quality rather than other external factors.
– ORIGIN Middle English (originally in the sense 'deserved reward or punishment'): via Old French from Latin *meritum* 'due reward', from *mereri* 'earn, deserve'.

merit good ▸ **noun** (Brit. usu. **merit goods**) a commodity or service, such as education, that is regarded by society or government as deserving public finance.

meritocracy /ˌmɛrɪˈtɒkrəsi/ ▸ **noun** (pl. **meritocracies**) [mass noun] government or the holding of power by people selected according to merit. ■ [count noun] a society governed by people selected according to merit. ■ [count noun] a ruling or influential class of educated or able people.
– DERIVATIVES **meritocrat noun, meritocratic** /-təˈkratɪk/ **adjective**.

Merit, Order of see **ORDER OF MERIT**.

meritorious /ˌmɛrɪˈtɔːrɪəs/ ▸ **adjective** deserving reward or praise: *a medal for meritorious conduct.* ■ Law, chiefly N. Amer. (of an action or claim) likely to succeed on the merits of the case.
– DERIVATIVES **meritoriously adverb, meritoriousness noun**.
– ORIGIN late Middle English (in the sense 'entitling a person to reward'): from late Latin *meritorius* (from *merit-* 'earned', from the verb *mereri*) + **-OUS**.

Merkel /ˈmɛːk(ə)l/, Angela (Dorothea) (b.1954), German Christian Democratic Union stateswoman, Chancellor of Germany since 2005.

merkin /ˈməːkɪn/ ▸ **noun** an artificial covering of hair for the pubic area.
– ORIGIN early 17th cent.: apparently a variant of dialect *malkin*, diminutive of *Malde* (early form of the given name *Maud*).

merle /məːl/ ▸ **noun** Scottish or archaic a blackbird.
– ORIGIN late Middle English: via Old French from Latin *merula*.

Merlin (in Arthurian legend) a magician who aided and supported King Arthur.

merlin ▸ **noun** a small dark falcon that hunts small birds, found throughout most of Eurasia and North America. ● *Falco columbarius*, family Falconidae.
– ORIGIN late Middle English: from Anglo-Norman French *merilun*, from Old French *esmerillon*, augmentative of *esmeril*, of Germanic origin; related to German *Schmerl*.

merlon /ˈməːlən/ ▸ **noun** the solid part of a crenellated parapet between two embrasures.
– ORIGIN early 18th cent.: from French, from Italian *merlone*, from *merlo* 'battlement'.

Merlot /ˈməːləʊ, -lɒt/ ▸ **noun** [mass noun] a variety of black wine grape originally from the Bordeaux region of France. ■ a red wine made from the Merlot grape.
– ORIGIN French.

mermaid ▸ **noun** a mythical sea creature with the head and trunk of a woman and the tail of a fish, conventionally depicted as beautiful and with long flowing golden hair.
– ORIGIN Middle English: from **MERE**[2] (in the obsolete sense 'sea') + **MAID**.

mermaid's purse ▸ **noun** the horny egg case of a skate, ray, or small shark.

merman ▸ **noun** (pl. **mermen**) the male equivalent of a mermaid.

mero- ▸ **combining form** partly; partial: *meronym.*
– ORIGIN from Greek *meros* 'part'.

Meroe /ˈmɛrəʊi/ an ancient city on the Nile, in present-day Sudan north-east of Khartoum. Founded in *c.*750 BC, it was the capital of the ancient kingdom of Cush from *c.*590 BC until it fell to the invading Aksumites in the early 4th century AD.
– DERIVATIVES **Meroitic adjective & noun**.

meronym /ˈmɛrənɪm/ ▸ **noun** Linguistics a term which denotes part of something but which is used to refer to the whole of it, e.g. *faces* when used to mean *people* in *I see several familiar faces present.*
– DERIVATIVES **meronymy** /məˈrɒnɪmi/ **noun**.
– ORIGIN from Greek *meros* 'part' + *onuma* 'name'.

-merous ▸ **combining form** Biology having a specified number of parts: *pentamerous.*
– ORIGIN on the pattern of words such as (*di*)*merous* (see also **-MER**).

Merovingian /ˌmɛrəˈvɪn(d)ʒɪən/ ▸ **adjective** relating to the Frankish dynasty founded by Clovis and reigning in Gaul and Germany *c.*500–750.
▸ **noun** a member of the Merovingian dynasty.
– ORIGIN from French *mérovingien*, from medieval Latin *Merovingi* 'descendants of Merovich' (Clovis' grandfather, semi-legendary 5th-cent. Frankish leader).

merrily ▸ **adverb 1** in a cheerful way. ■ in a brisk and lively way: *a fire burned merrily in the hearth.*
2 without consideration for the consequences: *marketers have been merrily debasing our language with non-words like 'infotainment'.*

merriment ▸ **noun** [mass noun] gaiety and fun: *her eyes sparkled with merriment.*

merry ▸ **adjective (merrier, merriest)** cheerful and lively: *the streets were dense with merry throngs of students.* ■ (of an occasion or season) characterized by festivity and enjoyment: *he wished me a merry Christmas.* ■ [predic.] informal slightly and good-humouredly drunk: *after the third beer he began to feel quite merry.*
– PHRASES **go on one's merry way** informal carry on with a course of action regardless of the consequences. **lead someone a merry dance** see **DANCE**. **make merry** enjoy oneself with others by dancing and drinking. **the more the merrier** the more people or things there are, the better a situation will be. **play merry hell with** see **HELL**.
– DERIVATIVES **merriness noun**.
– ORIGIN Old English *myrige* 'pleasing, delightful', of Germanic origin; related to **MIRTH**.

merry andrew ▸ **noun** archaic a person who entertains others by means of comic antics; a clown.

merry-go-round ▸ **noun** a revolving machine with model horses or cars on which people ride for amusement. ■ a continuous cycle of activities or events, especially when regarded as pointless: *the football management merry-go-round.* ■ [as modifier] Brit. denoting freight trains which deliver bulk loads of coal from collieries to power stations on a continuous cycle, loading and unloading automatically while moving.

merrymaking ▸ **noun** [mass noun] fun; festivity.
– DERIVATIVES **merrymaker noun**.

merrythought ▸ **noun** Brit. dated the wishbone of a bird.

Mersa Matruh /ˌməːsə məˈtruː/ a town on the Mediterranean coast of Egypt, 250 km (156 miles) west of Alexandria; pop. 120,500 (est. 2006).

Mersenne number /məːˈsɛn/ ▸ **noun** Mathematics a number of the form $2p-1$, where p is a prime number. Such a number which is itself prime is also called a **Mersenne prime**.
– ORIGIN late 19th cent.: named after Marin *Mersenne* (1588–1648), French mathematician.

Mersey /ˈməːzi/ a river in NW England, which rises in the Peak District of Derbyshire and flows 112 km (70 miles) to the Irish Sea near Liverpool.

Merseyside a former metropolitan county of NW England.

Mersin /məːˈsiːn/ an industrial port in southern Turkey, on the Mediterranean south-west of Adana; pop. 623,900 (est. 2007).

Merthyr Tydfil /ˌməːθə ˈtɪdvɪl/ a town in South Wales, traditionally a mining area; pop. 30,000 (est. 2009).

Meru /ˈmɛruː/ ▸ **noun** (pl. **same** or **Merus**) **1** a member of a people of central Kenya.
2 [mass noun] the Bantu language of the Meru, with over 1 million speakers.
▸ **adjective** relating to the Meru or their language.
– ORIGIN from the name of a town and district in central Kenya.

M

merveille du jour /mɛːˌveɪ d(j)uː ˈʒʊə/ ▸ **noun** a European moth with greyish-green coloration that camouflages it when at rest on lichen-covered bark. ● *Dichonia aprilina*, family Noctuidae.
– ORIGIN late 19th cent.: from French, literally 'wonder of the day'.

mesa /ˈmeɪsə/ ▸ **noun** an isolated flat-topped hill with steep sides, found in landscapes with horizontal strata.
– ORIGIN mid 18th cent.: Spanish, literally 'table', from Latin *mensa*.

mésalliance /meˈzalɪəns/ ▸ **noun** a marriage with a person thought to be unsuitable.
– ORIGIN French, from *més-* 'wrong, misdirected' + *alliance* (see **ALLIANCE**).

Mesa Verde /ˌmeɪsə ˈvəːdi/ a high plateau in southern Colorado, with the remains of many prehistoric Pueblo Indian dwellings.
– ORIGIN Spanish, literally 'green table(land)'.

mescal /ˈmɛskal, mɛˈskal/ ▸ **noun 1** another term for **MAGUEY**. ■ [mass noun] an alcoholic drink distilled from the sap of an agave.
2 another term for **PEYOTE**.
– ORIGIN early 18th cent.: from Spanish *mezcal*, from Nahuatl *mexcalli*.

mescal buttons ▸ **plural noun** another term for **PEYOTE BUTTONS**.

mescaline /ˈmɛskəlɪn, -iːn/ (also **mescalin** /-lɪn/) ▸ **noun** [mass noun] a hallucinogenic and intoxicating compound present in the peyote cactus. ● Chem. formula: $(CH_3O)_3C_6H_2CH_2CH_2NH_2$.

mesclun /ˈmɛsklən/ ▸ **noun** [mass noun] a Provençal green salad made from a mixture of edible leaves and flowers.
– ORIGIN Provençal, literally 'mixture', from *mesclar* 'mix thoroughly'.

Mesdames /meɪˈdɑːm, -ˈdam/ ▸ **plural noun 1** plural form of **MADAME**.
2 formal used as a title to refer to more than one woman simultaneously: *prizes were won by Mesdames Carter and Barnes.*

Mesdemoiselles /meɪd-/, French /med-/ plural form of **Mademoiselle**.

meself ▶ pronoun non-standard spelling of **myself**, used in representing informal speech.

mesembryanthemum /mɪˌzɛmbrɪˈanθɪməm/ ▶ noun a succulent South African plant with brightly coloured daisy-like flowers. ● *Mesembryanthemum* and related genera, family Aizoaceae.
– ORIGIN modern Latin, based on Greek *mesēmbria* 'noon' + *anthemon* 'flower'.

mesencephalon /ˌmɛsɛnˈsɛf(ə)lɒn, ˌmiːz-, -ˈkɛf-/ ▶ noun Anatomy another term for **midbrain**.
– DERIVATIVES **mesencephalic** adjective.
– ORIGIN mid 19th cent.: from Greek *mesos* 'middle' + **encephalon**.

mesenchyme /ˈmɛsəŋkʌɪm, ˈmiːz-/ ▶ noun [mass noun] Embryology a loosely organized, mainly mesodermal embryonic tissue which develops into connective and skeletal tissues, including blood and lymph.
– DERIVATIVES **mesenchymal** adjective.
– ORIGIN late 19th cent.: from Greek *mesos* 'middle' + *enkhuma* 'infusion'.

mesenteron /mɪˈsɛntərɒn/ ▶ noun Zoology the middle section of the intestine, especially in an embryo or arthropod.
– ORIGIN late 19th cent.: from Greek *mesos* 'middle' + *enteron* 'intestine'.

mesentery /ˈmɛs(ə)nt(ə)ri/ ▶ noun (pl. **mesenteries**) Anatomy a fold of the peritoneum which attaches the stomach, small intestine, pancreas, spleen, and other organs to the posterior wall of the abdomen.
– DERIVATIVES **mesenteric** adjective.
– ORIGIN late Middle English: via medieval Latin from Greek *mesenterion*, from *mesos* 'middle' + *enteron* 'intestine'.

mesh ▶ noun **1** [mass noun] material made of a network of wire or thread: *mesh for fishing nets* | [count noun] *finer wire meshes are used for smaller particles.* ■ the spacing of the strands of such material: *if the mesh is too big, small rabbits can squeeze through.* ■ [in sing.] used with reference to a complex or constricting situation: *you are just common people going about your lives caught in the common mesh of history.*
2 an interlaced structure: *cell fragments which agglutinate and form intricate meshes.* ■ Computing a set of finite elements used to represent a geometric object for modelling or analysis. ■ Computing a computer network in which each computer or processor is connected to a number of others, especially so as to form a multidimensional lattice.
▶ verb **1** [no obj.] (of the teeth of a gearwheel) be engaged with another gearwheel: *one gear meshes with the input gear.* ■ make or become entangled or entwined: [no obj.] *their fingers meshed* | [with obj.] *I don't want to get meshed in the weeds.* ■ be in or bring into harmony: [no obj.] *her memory of events doesn't mesh with the world around her.*
2 [with obj.] Computing represent a geometric object as a set of finite elements.
– ORIGIN late Middle English: probably from an unrecorded Old English word related to (and perhaps reinforced in Middle English by) Middle Dutch *maesche*, of Germanic origin.

Meshed /məˈʃɛd/ variant of **Mashhad**.

meshuga /mɪˈʃʊɡə/ (also **meshugga**) ▶ adjective N. Amer. informal (of a person) mad; crazy: *either a miracle is taking place, or we're all meshuga.*
– ORIGIN late 19th cent.: from Yiddish *meshuge*, from Hebrew.

meshugaas /mɪˈʃʊɡɑːs/ ▶ noun [mass noun] N. Amer. informal mad or foolish ideas or behaviour: *there's method in this man's meshugaas.*
– ORIGIN early 20th cent.: Yiddish, noun from **meshuga**.

meshuggener /mɪˈʃʊɡənə/ ▶ noun N. Amer. informal a mad or foolish person.
– ORIGIN early 20th cent. (as an adjective): variant of **meshuga**.

mesia /ˈmiːzɪə/ (also **silver-eared mesia**) ▶ noun a SE Asian bird of the babbler family, the male having red and yellow plumage with a black-and-white head. ● *Leiothrix argentauris*, family Timaliidae.
– ORIGIN modern Latin (former genus name).

mesial /ˈmiːzɪəl, ˈmɛsɪəl/ ▶ adjective Anatomy relating to or directed towards the middle line of a body.
– DERIVATIVES **mesially** adverb.
– ORIGIN early 19th cent.: formed irregularly from Greek *mesos* 'middle' + **-ial**.

mesic¹ /ˈmiːzɪk, ˈmɛzɪk/ ▶ adjective Ecology (of an environment or habitat) containing a moderate amount of moisture. Compare with **hydric** and **xeric**.
– ORIGIN 1920s: from Greek *mesos* 'middle' + **-ic**.

mesic² /ˈmiːzɪk, ˈmɛzɪk/ ▶ adjective Physics relating to a meson.

Mesmer /ˈmɛzmə/, Franz Anton (1734–1815), Austrian physician. Mesmer is chiefly remembered for introducing a therapeutic technique involving hypnotism; it was bound up with his ideas about 'animal magnetism', however, and steeped in sensationalism.

mesmeric /mɛzˈmɛrɪk/ ▶ adjective causing a person to become completely transfixed and unaware of their surroundings: *she found herself staring into his mesmeric gaze.* ■ archaic relating to or produced by mesmerism.
– DERIVATIVES **mesmerically** adverb.

mesmerism ▶ noun [mass noun] historical the therapeutic system of F. A. Mesmer. ■ (in general use) hypnotism.
– DERIVATIVES **mesmerist** noun.
– ORIGIN late 18th cent.: named after F. A. **Mesmer**.

mesmerize (also **mesmerise**) ▶ verb [with obj.] capture the complete attention of (someone); transfix: *they were mesmerized by his story* | (as adj. **mesmerizing**) *a mesmerizing stare.* ■ archaic hypnotize (someone).
– DERIVATIVES **mesmerization** noun, **mesmerizer** noun, **mesmerizingly** adverb.

mesne /miːn/ ▶ adjective Law intermediate or intervening.
– ORIGIN late Middle English (as adverb and noun): from legal French, variant of Anglo-Norman French *meen* 'middle' (see **mean³**).

mesne lord ▶ noun Brit. historical a lord holding an estate from a superior feudal lord.

mesne profits ▶ plural noun Law the profits of an estate received by a tenant in wrongful possession and recoverable by the landlord.

meso- /ˈmɛsəʊ, ˈmɛzəʊ, ˈmiːsəʊ, ˈmiːzəʊ/ ▶ combining form middle; intermediate: *mesoblast* | *mesomorph*.
– ORIGIN from Greek *mesos* 'middle'.

Meso-America the central region of America, from central Mexico to Nicaragua, especially as a region of ancient civilizations and native cultures before the arrival of the Spanish.
– DERIVATIVES **Meso-American** adjective & noun.

mesoblast /ˈmɛsə(ʊ)blast, ˈmɛz-, ˈmiːs-, ˈmiːz-/ ▶ noun Embryology the mesoderm of an embryo in its earliest stages.

mesocarp ▶ noun Botany the middle layer of the pericarp of a fruit, between the endocarp and the exocarp.

mesocephalic /ˌmɛsə(ʊ)sɪˈfalɪk, ˌmɛz-, ˌmiːs-, ˌmiːz-, -kɛ-/ ▶ adjective Anatomy having a head of medium proportions, not markedly brachycephalic or dolichocephalic.

mesoderm ▶ noun [mass noun] Embryology the middle layer of cells or tissues of an embryo, or the parts derived from this (e.g. cartilage, muscles, and bone).
– DERIVATIVES **mesodermal** adjective.
– ORIGIN late 19th cent.: from **meso-** 'middle' + Greek *derma* 'skin'.

mesofauna ▶ noun [mass noun] Ecology soil animals of intermediate size, such as earthworms, arthropods, nematodes, and molluscs.

mesogastrium ▶ noun (pl. **mesogastria**) Anatomy the middle region of the abdomen between the epigastrium and the hypogastrium.
– DERIVATIVES **mesogastric** adjective.
– ORIGIN mid 19th cent.: modern Latin, from **meso-** 'middle' + Greek *gastēr*, *gastr-* 'stomach'.

Mesolithic ▶ adjective Archaeology relating to or denoting the middle part of the Stone Age, between the Palaeolithic and Neolithic. ■ (as noun **the Mesolithic**) the Mesolithic period. Also called **Middle Stone Age**.

> In Europe, the Mesolithic falls between the end of the last glacial period (c.8500 BC) and the beginnings of agriculture. Mesolithic people lived by hunting, gathering, and fishing, and the period is characterized by the use of microliths and the first domestication of an animal (the dog).

– ORIGIN mid 19th cent.: from **meso-** 'middle' + Greek *lithos* 'stone' + **-ic**.

Mesolóngion /ˌmɛsɔˈlɔŋɡɪɔn/ Greek name for **Missolonghi**.

mesomerism /mɪˈsɒmərɪz(ə)m, mɪˈzɒm-/ ▶ noun Chemistry old-fashioned term for **resonance**.
– DERIVATIVES **mesomeric** adjective.

mesomorph ▶ noun Physiology a person whose build is compact and muscular. Compare with **ectomorph** and **endomorph**.
– DERIVATIVES **mesomorphic** adjective.
– ORIGIN 1920s: *meso-* from *mesodermal* (being the layer of the embryo giving rise to physical characteristics which predominate) + **-morph**.

meson /ˈmiːzɒn, ˈmɛzɒn/ ▶ noun Physics a subatomic particle which is intermediate in mass between an electron and a proton and transmits the strong interaction that binds nucleons together in the atomic nucleus.
– DERIVATIVES **mesonic** /mɪˈzɒnɪk/ adjective.
– ORIGIN 1930s: from **meso-** 'intermediate' + **-on**.

mesopause ▶ noun the boundary in the earth's atmosphere between the mesosphere and the thermosphere, at which the temperature stops decreasing with increasing height and begins to increase.

mesopelagic /ˌmɛsə(ʊ)pɪˈladʒɪk, ˌmɛz-, ˌmiːs-, ˌmiːz-/ ▶ adjective Biology (of fish and other organisms) inhabiting the intermediate depths of the sea, between about 200 and 1,000 metres (approximately 650 and 3,300 ft) down.

mesophyll ▶ noun [mass noun] Botany the inner tissue (parenchyma) of a leaf, containing many chloroplasts.
– ORIGIN mid 19th cent.: from **meso-** 'middle' + Greek *phullon* 'leaf'.

mesophyte ▶ noun Botany a plant needing only a moderate amount of water.
– DERIVATIVES **mesophytic** adjective.

Mesopotamia /ˌmɛsəpəˈteɪmɪə/ an ancient region of SW Asia in present-day Iraq, lying between the Rivers Tigris and Euphrates. Its alluvial plains were the site of the civilizations of Akkad, Sumer, Babylonia, and Assyria.
– DERIVATIVES **Mesopotamian** adjective & noun.
– ORIGIN from Greek *mesos* 'middle' + *potamos* 'river'.

mesosaur ▶ noun an extinct small aquatic reptile of the early Permian period, with an elongated body, flattened tail, and a long, narrow snout with numerous pointed teeth. ● Genus *Mesosaurus*, order Mesosauria, subclass Anapsida.
– ORIGIN 1950s: modern Latin, from Greek *mesos* 'middle' + *sauros* 'lizard'.

mesoscale ▶ noun Meteorology an intermediate scale between those of weather systems and of microclimates, on which storms and other phenomena occur.

mesosphere ▶ noun the region of the earth's atmosphere above the stratosphere and below the thermosphere, between about 50 and 80 km in altitude.

mesothelioma /ˌmɛsə(ʊ),θiːlɪˈəʊmə, ˌmɛz-, ˌmiːs-, ˌmiːz-/ ▶ noun [mass noun] Medicine a cancer of mesothelial tissue, associated especially with exposure to asbestos.

mesothelium /ˌmɛsə(ʊ)ˈθiːlɪəm, ˌmɛz-, ˌmiːs-, ˌmiːz-/ ▶ noun (pl. **mesothelia**) [mass noun] Anatomy the epithelium that lines the pleurae, peritoneum, and pericardium. ■ Embryology the surface layer of the embryonic mesoderm, from which the mesothelium is derived.
– DERIVATIVES **mesothelial** adjective.
– ORIGIN late 19th cent.: from **meso-** 'middle' + a shortened form of **epithelium**.

mesotherapy /ˌmɛsə(ʊ)ˈθɛrəpi, ˌmɛz-, ˌmiːs-, ˌmiːz-/ ▶ noun [mass noun] (in cosmetic surgery) a procedure in which multiple tiny injections of pharmaceuticals, vitamins, etc. are delivered into the mesodermal layer of tissue under the skin, to promote the loss of fat or cellulite.

mesothorax ▶ noun Entomology the middle segment of the thorax of an insect, bearing the forewings or elytra.
– DERIVATIVES **mesothoracic** adjective.

mesozoan /ˌmɛsəˈzəʊən, ˌmiːz-/ ▶ noun Zoology a minute worm which is an internal parasite of marine invertebrates. It lacks any internal organs other than reproductive cells, and dissolved nutrients are absorbed directly from the host's tissues. ● Phyla Orthonectida and Rhombozoa; formerly placed together in the phylum Mesozoa, which was thought to be intermediate between protozoans and metazoans.
– ORIGIN early 20th cent.: from modern Latin *Mesozoa* (from *mesos* 'intermediate' + *zōion* 'animal') + **-an**.

Mesozoic /ˌmɛsə(ʊ)ˈzəʊɪk, ˌmɛz-, ˌmiːs-, ˌmiːz-/ ▶ adjective Geology relating to or denoting the era between the Palaeozoic and Cenozoic eras, comprising the Triassic, Jurassic, and Cretaceous periods. ■ (as noun

the Mesozoic) the Mesozoic era or the system of rocks deposited during it.

> The Mesozoic lasted from about 245 to 65 million years ago. Large reptiles were dominant on land and sea and the first mammals, birds, and flowering plants appeared.

– ORIGIN mid 19th cent.: from **MESO-** 'intermediate' + Greek *zōion* 'animal' (referring to the appearance of the first mammals) + **-IC**.

mesquite /ˈmɛskiːt, mɛˈskiːt/ ▸ **noun** a spiny tree or shrub of the pea family, native to arid regions of south-western US and Mexico. It yields timber, tanbark, medicinal products, and edible pods. ● Genus *Prosopis*, family Leguminosae: several species.
– ORIGIN mid 18th cent.: from Mexican Spanish *mezquite*.

mesquite bean ▸ **noun** an edible pod from the mesquite, used especially to produce flour or as animal fodder.

mess ▸ **noun** [usu. in sing.] **1** a dirty or untidy state of things or of a place: *she made a mess of the kitchen* | *my hair was a mess*. ■ a thing or collection of things causing a dirty or untidy state: *she replaced the jug and mopped up the mess*. ■ a person who is dirty or untidy: *I look a mess*. ■ [with modifier] used euphemistically to refer to the excrement of a domestic animal: *dog mess*.
2 a situation that is confused and full of problems: *the economy is still in a terrible mess*. ■ a person whose life is confused and full of problems: *he needs treatment of some kind—he's a real mess*.
3 a portion of semi-liquid food: *a mess of mashed black beans and rice*.
4 a building or room providing meals and recreational facilities for members of the armed forces: *the sergeants' mess*.
5 (**a mess of**) N. Amer. informal a large amount or quantity of.
▸ **verb 1** [with obj.] make untidy or dirty: *you've messed up my beautiful carpet*. ■ [no obj.] (of a domestic animal) defecate. ■ make dirty by defecating: *he feared he would mess the bed*.
2 [no obj., with adverbial] have one's meals with a particular person, especially as a member of an armed forces' mess: *I messed at first with Harry, who became a lifelong friend*.
– PHRASES **mess with someone's head** US informal make someone feel frustrated, anxious, or upset.
– PHRASAL VERBS **mess about/around** behave in a silly or playful way. ■ spend time doing something in a pleasantly desultory way: *messing about in boats*. **mess about/around with** interfere with: *the minister messed around with health, and look at the state we are in*. ■ informal engage in an affair with (someone, especially the partner of another person). **mess someone about/around** Brit. informal cause someone problems, especially by acting unfairly or indecisively. **mess up** informal mishandle a situation: *I really messed up*. **mess someone up** informal cause someone emotional or psychological problems. ■ US inflict violence or injury on someone. **mess something up** informal spoil something by inept handling: *an error like that could easily mess up an entire day's work*. **mess with** informal meddle or interfere with: *stop messing with things you don't understand*.
– ORIGIN Middle English: from Old French *mes* 'portion of food', from late Latin *missum* 'something put on the table', past participle of *mittere* 'send, put'. The original sense was 'a serving of (semi-liquid) food', later 'liquid food for an animal'; this gave rise (early 19th cent.) to the senses 'unappetizing concoction' and 'predicament', on which sense 1 is based. In late Middle English the term also denoted any of the small groups into which the company at a banquet was divided (who were served from the same dishes); hence, 'a group who regularly eat together' (recorded in military use from the mid 16th cent.).

message ▸ **noun 1** a verbal, written, or recorded communication sent to or left for a recipient who cannot be contacted directly: *if I'm not there leave a message on the answerphone*. ■ (also **mail message**) an email or similar electronic communication. ■ an electronic communication generated automatically by a computer program and displayed on a screen: *an error message*. ■ a communication from a prophet or preacher, believed to be inspired by God. ■ US a television or radio advertisement.
2 a significant political, social, or moral point that is being conveyed by a film, speech, etc.: *a campaign to get the message about home security across*.
3 Scottish & Irish an errand: *he would run those interminable messages after school to the bookie*. ■ (**messages**) things bought on an errand; shopping.
▸ **verb** [with obj.] send a message to (someone), especially by email.
– PHRASES **get the message** informal understand what is implied by a remark or action. **send a message** make a significant statement, either implicitly or by one's actions: *it sends a message to potential foreign investors*.
– ORIGIN Middle English: from Old French, based on Latin *missus*, past participle of *mittere* 'send'.

message board ▸ **noun** an Internet site where users can post comments about a particular issue or topic and reply to other users' postings.

message box ▸ **noun** Computing a small box that appears on a computer screen, in which instructions to or from a user are displayed.

message stick ▸ **noun** (among Australian Aborigines) a piece of wood carved with symbolic patterns, used as a means of communication between communities.

message switching ▸ **noun** [mass noun] Computing & Telecommunications a mode of data transmission in which a message is sent as a complete unit and routed via a number of intermediate nodes at which it is stored and then forwarded.

Messalina /ˌmɛsəˈliːnə/ (also **Messallina**), Valeria (*c.*22–48 AD), Roman empress, third wife of Claudius. She became notorious in Rome for the murders she instigated in court and for her extramarital affairs, and was executed on Claudius' orders.

Messeigneurs plural form of **MONSEIGNEUR**.

messenger ▸ **noun** a person who carries a message or is employed to carry messages. ■ Biochemistry a substance that conveys information or a stimulus within the body.
▸ **verb** [with obj.] chiefly US send (a document or package) by messenger: *could you have it messengered over to me?*
– PHRASES **shoot** (or **kill**) **the messenger** treat the bearer of bad news as if they were to blame for it.
– ORIGIN Middle English: from Old Northern French *messanger*, variant of Old French *messager*, from Latin *missus* (see **MESSAGE**).

messenger bag ▸ **noun** a large bag with a long strap, worn across the body.

messenger RNA (abbrev.: **mRNA**) ▸ **noun** [mass noun] the form of RNA in which genetic information transcribed from DNA as a sequence of bases is transferred to a ribosome.

Messerschmidt /ˈmɛsəˌʃmɪt/, German /ˈmɛsɐˌʃmɪt/, Willy (1898–1978), German aircraft designer and industrialist; full name *Wilhelm Emil Messerschmidt*. He designed and constructed his first glider in 1915 and set up a company in 1923. The Messerschmidt 109 became the standard fighter of the Luftwaffe during the Second World War.

mess hall ▸ **noun** N. Amer. a room or building where people, especially soldiers, eat together.

Messiaen /ˈmɛsɪɑ̃/, French /mɛsjɑ̃/, Olivier (Eugène Prosper Charles) (1908–92), French composer. His music was influenced by Greek and Hindu rhythms, birdsong, Stravinsky and Debussy, and the composer's Roman Catholic faith. Notable works: *Quartet for the End of Time* (1941).

messiah /mɪˈsʌɪə/ ▸ **noun 1** (**the Messiah**) the promised deliverer of the Jewish nation prophesied in the Hebrew Bible. ■ Jesus regarded by Christians as the Messiah of the Hebrew prophecies and the saviour of humankind.
2 a leader regarded as the saviour of a particular country, group, or cause: *the club's supporters have been tempted to regard him as a messiah rather than a manager*.
– DERIVATIVES **messiahship** noun.
– ORIGIN Old English *Messias*: via late Latin and Greek from Hebrew *māšīaḥ* 'anointed'.

messianic /ˌmɛsɪˈanɪk/ ▸ **adjective 1** relating to the Messiah: *the messianic role of Jesus*. ■ inspired by hope or belief in a messiah: *the messianic expectations of that time*.
2 fervent or passionate: *an admirable messianic zeal*.
– DERIVATIVES **messianism** /mɪˈsʌɪənɪz(ə)m/ noun.
– ORIGIN mid 19th cent.: from French *messianique*, from *Messie* (see **MESSIAH**), on the pattern of *rabbinique* 'rabbinical'.

Messidor /ˈmɛsɪdɔː/, French /mɛsidɔʀ/ ▸ **noun** the tenth month of the French Republican calendar (1793–1805), originally running from 19 June to 18 July.
– ORIGIN French, from Latin *messis* 'harvest' + Greek *dōron* 'gift'.

Messier /ˈmɛsɪə/, French /mɛsje/, Charles (1730–1817), French astronomer. He discovered a number of nebulae, galaxies, and star clusters, which he designated by M numbers. Almost all of these designations, such as M1 (the Crab Nebula), are still in use today.

Messieurs plural form of **MONSIEUR**.

Messina /mɛˈsiːnə/ a city in NE Sicily; pop. 234,700 (est. 2009). Founded in 730 BC by the Greeks, it is situated on the Strait of Messina.

Messina, Strait of a channel separating the island of Sicily from the 'toe' of Italy. It forms a link between the Tyrrhenian and Ionian seas. The strait, which is 32 km (20 miles) in length, is noted for the strength of its currents.

mess jacket ▸ **noun** a short jacket worn by a military officer on formal occasions in the mess.

mess kit ▸ **noun 1** the uniform worn by a military officer on formal occasions in the mess.
2 a soldier's cooking and eating utensils.

messmate ▸ **noun** (in the navy) a person with whom one shares communal accommodation.

Messrs ▸ **plural noun** used as a title to refer formally to more than one man simultaneously, or in names of companies: *Messrs Sotheby*.
– ORIGIN late 18th cent.: abbreviation of **MESSIEURS**.

mess tin ▸ **noun** Brit. a rectangular metal dish with a folding handle, forming part of a soldier's mess kit.

messuage /ˈmɛswɪdʒ/ ▸ **noun** Law a dwelling house with outbuildings and land assigned to its use.
– ORIGIN late Middle English: from Anglo-Norman French, based on Latin *manere* 'dwell'.

messy ▸ **adjective** (**messier**, **messiest**) **1** untidy or dirty: *his messy hair*. ■ generating or involving mess: *stripping wallpaper can be a messy, time-consuming job*.
2 (of a situation) confused and difficult to deal with: *a messy divorce*.
– DERIVATIVES **messily** adverb, **messiness** noun.

mestizo /mɛˈstiːzəʊ/, Spanish /mesˈtiso, -ˈtiθo/ ▸ **noun** (fem. **mestiza** pl. **mestizos** or **mestizas**) (in Latin America) a person of mixed race, especially one having Spanish and American Indian parentage.
– ORIGIN Spanish, 'mixed', based on Latin *mixtus*.

M

Met ▸ **abbreviation** informal ■ meteorological: *a Met report*. ■ (also **the Met Office**) the Meteorological Office in the UK. ■ metropolitan. ■ (**the Met**) [treated as sing. or pl.] the Metropolitan Police in London. ■ (**the Met**) the Metropolitan Opera House in New York.

met past and past participle of **MEET**[1].

met- ▸ **combining form** variant spelling of **META-** shortened before a vowel or *h* (as in *metonym*).

meta /ˈmɛtə/ ▸ **noun** short for **META KEY**.
▸ **adjective** US (of a creative work) referring to itself or to the conventions of its genre; self-referential.
– ORIGIN 1980s: from **META-**.

meta- (also **met-** before a vowel or h) ▸ **combining form 1** denoting a change of position or condition: *metamorphosis*.
2 denoting position behind, after, or beyond: *metacarpus*.
3 denoting something of a higher or second-order kind: *metalanguage* | *metonym*.
4 Chemistry denoting substitution at two carbon atoms separated by one other in a benzene ring, e.g. in 1,3 positions: *metadichlorobenzene*. Compare with **ORTHO-** and **PARA-**[1] (sense 2).
5 Chemistry denoting a compound formed by dehydration: *metaphosphoric acid*.
– ORIGIN from Greek *meta* 'with, across, or after'.

metabolic pathway ▸ **noun** see **PATHWAY**.

metabolism /mɪˈtabəlɪz(ə)m/ ▸ **noun** [mass noun] the chemical processes that occur within a living organism in order to maintain life.

> Two kinds of metabolism are often distinguished: **constructive metabolism**, the synthesis of the proteins, carbohydrates, and fats which form tissue and store energy, and **destructive metabolism**, the breakdown of complex substances and the consequent production of energy and waste matter.

– DERIVATIVES **metabolic** /ˌmɛtəˈbɒlɪk/ adjective, **metabolically** adverb.
– ORIGIN late 19th cent.: from Greek *metabolē* 'change' (from *metaballein* 'to change') + **-ISM**.

metabolite /mɪˈtabəlʌɪt/ ▸ **noun** Biochemistry a substance formed in or necessary for metabolism.

metabolize (also **metabolise**) ▸ **verb** [with obj.] (of the body or an organ) process (a substance) by

metabolism. ■ [no obj.] (of a substance) undergo processing by metabolism: *the refined foods soon metabolize.*
– DERIVATIVES **metabolizable** adjective, **metabolizer** noun.

metacarpal ▶ noun any of the five bones of the hand. ■ any of the bones in an animal's forelimb equivalent to the metacarpals.
▶ adjective relating to these bones.

metacarpus ▶ noun (pl. **metacarpi**) the group of five bones of the hand between the wrist (carpus) and the fingers.
– ORIGIN late Middle English: modern Latin, alteration of Greek *metakarpion*.

metacentre (US **metacenter**) ▶ noun the point of intersection between an imaginary line drawn vertically through the centre of buoyancy of a floating vessel and a corresponding line through the new centre of buoyancy when the vessel is tilted.
– DERIVATIVES **metacentric** adjective.
– ORIGIN late 18th cent.: from French *métacentre* (see META-, CENTRE).

metachromasia /ˌmɛtəkrə(ʊ)ˈmeɪzɪə/ ▶ noun [mass noun] Biology the property of certain biological materials of staining a different colour from that of the stain used. ■ the property of certain stains of changing colour in the presence of certain biological materials.
– DERIVATIVES **metachromatic** adjective.
– ORIGIN early 20th cent.: modern Latin, from META- (expressing change) + Greek *khrōma* 'colour'.

metachrosis /ˌmɛtəˈkrəʊsɪs/ ▶ noun [mass noun] Zoology the ability of chameleons and some other animals to change colour.
– ORIGIN late 19th cent.: modern Latin, from META- (denoting a change of condition) + Greek *khrōsis* 'colouring'.

metacognition ▶ noun [mass noun] Psychology awareness and understanding of one's own thought processes.
– DERIVATIVES **metacognitive** adjective.

metadata ▶ noun [mass noun] a set of data that describes and gives information about other data.

M

metafiction ▶ noun [mass noun] fiction in which the author self-consciously alludes to the artificiality or literariness of a work by parodying or departing from novelistic conventions and traditional narrative techniques.
– DERIVATIVES **metafictional** adjective.

metafile ▶ noun Computing a piece of graphical information stored in a format that can be exchanged between different systems or software.

metage /ˈmiːtɪdʒ/ ▶ noun [mass noun] historical the duty paid for the official weighing of loads of coal, grain, or other material.
– ORIGIN early 16th cent.: from METE[1] + -AGE.

metagenesis /ˌmɛtəˈdʒɛnɪsɪs/ ▶ noun [mass noun] Biology the alternation of generations between sexual and asexual reproduction.
– DERIVATIVES **metagenetic** /-dʒɪˈnɛtɪk/ adjective.
– ORIGIN late 19th cent.: modern Latin.

meta key ▶ noun Computing a key on some keyboards which activates a particular function when held down simultaneously with another key.

metal ▶ noun [mass noun] **1** a solid material which is typically hard, shiny, malleable, fusible, and ductile, with good electrical and thermal conductivity (e.g. iron, gold, silver, and aluminium, and alloys such as steel): *an adjustable pole made of metal* | [count noun] *being a metal, aluminium readily conducts heat.* ■ (**metals**) the steel tracks of a railway. ■ Heraldry gold and silver (as tinctures in blazoning).
2 (also **road metal**) broken stone for use in road-making.
3 molten glass before it is blown or cast.
4 heavy metal or similar rock music.
▶ verb (**metals**, **metalling**, **metalled**; N. Amer. **metals**, **metaling**, **metaled**) [with obj.] **1** (as adj. **metalled**) made from or coated with metal.
2 (usu. as adj. **metalled**) Brit. make or mend (a road) with road metal.
– ORIGIN Middle English: from Old French *metal* or Latin *metallum*, from Greek *metallon* 'mine, quarry, or metal'.

metalanguage ▶ noun a form of language or set of terms used for the description or analysis of another language. Compare with OBJECT LANGUAGE (sense 1). ■ Logic a system of propositions about propositions.

metaldehyde /mɪˈtaldɪhʌɪd/ ▶ noun [mass noun] Chemistry a solid made by polymerizing acetaldehyde, used in slug pellets and as a fuel for portable stoves. ● Chem. formula: $C_4H_4O_4(CH_3)_4$.
– ORIGIN mid 19th cent.: from META- + ALDEHYDE.

metal detector ▶ noun an electronic device that gives an audible or other signal when it is close to metal, used for example to search for buried objects.

metalflake ▶ noun [mass noun] trademark a metallized film added to paint to increase protection against rust.

metalinguistics ▶ plural noun [treated as sing.] the branch of linguistics that deals with metalanguages.
– DERIVATIVES **metalinguistic** adjective.

metallic ▶ adjective relating to or resembling metal or metals: *metallic alloys* | *a curious metallic taste.* ■ (of sound) resembling that produced by metal objects striking each other; sharp and ringing: *the blade locked into place with a heavy metallic clunk.* ■ (of a person's voice) emanating via an electronic medium: *a metallic voice rasped tinnily from a speaker.* ■ having the lustre of metal; iridescent: *a beautiful metallic green sports car.*
▶ noun (usu. **metallics**) an article or substance made of or containing metal: *metallics can be recycled.* ■ a paint, fabric, or colour with a metallic sheen.
– DERIVATIVES **metallically** adverb.
– ORIGIN late Middle English: via Latin from Greek *metallikos*, from *metallon* (see METAL).

metallicity ▶ noun (pl. **metallicities**) [mass noun] the property of being metallic. ■ Astronomy the proportion of the material of a star or other celestial object that is an element other than hydrogen or helium.

metalliferous ▶ adjective (chiefly of deposits of minerals) containing or producing metal.
– ORIGIN mid 17th cent.: from Latin *metallifer* 'metal-bearing' + -OUS.

metalline /ˈmɛtəlʌɪn/ ▶ adjective archaic metallic.

metallize (also **metallise**, US also **metalize**) ▶ verb [with obj.] coat with a layer of metal. ■ make metallic in form or appearance.
– DERIVATIVES **metallization** noun.

metallogenic /mɪˌtalə(ʊ)ˈdʒɛnɪk, ˈmɛt(ə)lə(ʊ)-/ ▶ adjective Geology relating to the formation or occurrence of deposits of metals or their ores.

metallography /ˌmɛtəˈlɒɡrəfi/ ▶ noun [mass noun] the descriptive science of the structure and properties of metals.
– DERIVATIVES **metallographic** adjective **metallographically** adverb.

metalloid ▶ noun another term for SEMIMETAL.

metallophone /mɪˈtalə(ʊ)fəʊn, ˈmɛt(ə)lə(ʊ)-/ ▶ noun a musical instrument in which the sound is produced by striking metal bars of varying pitches.

metallurgy /mɪˈtalədʒi, ˈmɛt(ə)ˌləːdʒi/ ▶ noun [mass noun] the branch of science and technology concerned with the properties of metals and their production and purification.
– DERIVATIVES **metallurgic** /ˌmɛtəˈləːdʒɪk/ adjective, **metallurgical** adjective, **metallurgically** adverb, **metallurgist** noun.
– ORIGIN early 18th cent.: from Greek *metallon* 'metal' + *-ourgia* 'working'.

metalmark ▶ noun a butterfly with brilliant metallic markings on the wings, found chiefly in tropical America. ● Family Riodinidae: several genera.

metalware ▶ noun [mass noun] (also **metalwares**) utensils or other articles made of metal.

metalwork ▶ noun [mass noun] the skill of making things from metal. ■ metal objects collectively: *a wealth of fine metalwork, including a sword.* ■ the metal part of a construction: *engineers spotted cracks in the metalwork.*
– DERIVATIVES **metalworker** noun, **metalworking** noun.

metamathematics ▶ plural noun [treated as sing.] the field of study that deals with the structure and formal properties of mathematics and similar formal systems.
– DERIVATIVES **metamathematical** adjective, **metamathematician** noun.

metamere /ˈmɛtəmɪə/ ▶ noun Zoology another term for SOMITE.
– ORIGIN late 19th cent.: from META- 'together with' + Greek *meros* 'part'.

metameric /ˌmɛtəˈmɛrɪk/ ▶ adjective Zoology relating to or consisting of several similar segments or somites.
– DERIVATIVES **metamer** /ˈmɛtəmə/ noun, **metamerism** noun.

metamessage ▶ noun an underlying meaning or subtext.

metamorphic ▶ adjective **1** Geology denoting or relating to rock that has undergone transformation by heat, pressure, or other natural agencies, e.g. in the folding of strata or the nearby intrusion of igneous rocks.
2 of or marked by metamorphosis: *the supermodels' metamorphic ability to bend their looks.*
– ORIGIN early 19th cent.: from META- (denoting a change of condition) + Greek *morphē* 'form' + -IC.

metamorphism ▶ noun [mass noun] Geology alteration of the composition or structure of a rock by heat, pressure, or other natural agency.

metamorphose /ˌmɛtəˈmɔːfəʊz/ ▶ verb **1** [no obj.] (of an insect or amphibian) undergo metamorphosis, especially into the adult form: *feed the larvae to your fish before they **metamorphose into** adults.* ■ change or cause to change completely in form or nature: *overnight, family houses **metamorphose into** bed and breakfast as 7,000 visitors roll into town.*
2 [with obj.] Geology subject (rock) to metamorphism: (as adj. **metamorphosed**) *a metamorphosed sandstone.*
– ORIGIN late 16th cent.: from French *métamorphoser*, from *métamorphose* (see METAMORPHOSIS).

metamorphosis /ˌmɛtəˈmɔːfəsɪs, ˌmɛtəmɔːˈfəʊsɪs/ ▶ noun (pl. **metamorphoses** /-siːz/) [mass noun] Zoology (in an insect or amphibian) the process of transformation from an immature form to an adult form in two or more distinct stages. ■ a change of the form or nature of a thing or person into a completely different one: *his metamorphosis from presidential candidate to talk-show host.*
– ORIGIN late Middle English: via Latin from Greek *metamorphōsis*, from *metamorphoun* 'transform, change shape'.

metanoia /ˌmɛtəˈnɔɪə/ ▶ noun [mass noun] change in one's way of life resulting from penitence or spiritual conversion.
– ORIGIN late 19th cent.: from Greek, from *metanoein* 'change one's mind'.

metaphase ▶ noun [mass noun] Biology the second stage of cell division, between prophase and anaphase, during which the chromosomes become attached to the spindle fibres.

metaphor ▶ noun a figure of speech in which a word or phrase is applied to an object or action to which it is not literally applicable: *when we speak of gene maps and gene mapping, we use a cartographic metaphor* | [mass noun] *her poetry depends on suggestion and metaphor.* ■ a thing regarded as representative or symbolic of something else: *the amounts of money being lost by the company were enough to make it a **metaphor for** an industry that was teetering.*
– DERIVATIVES **metaphoric** adjective.
– ORIGIN late 15th cent.: from French *métaphore*, via Latin from Greek *metaphora*, from *metapherein* 'to transfer'.

metaphorical ▶ adjective characteristic of or relating to metaphor; figurative: *many of our metaphorical expressions develop from our perceptions of the body.*
– DERIVATIVES **metaphorically** adverb.

metaphosphate ▶ noun Chemistry a salt of metaphosphoric acid.

metaphosphoric acid ▶ noun [mass noun] Chemistry a glassy deliquescent solid obtained by heating orthophosphoric acid. ● A polymer; chem. formula $(HPO_3)_n$.

metaphrase ▶ noun a literal, word-for-word translation, as opposed to a paraphrase.
▶ verb [with obj.] alter the phrasing or language of.
– DERIVATIVES **metaphrastic** adjective.
– ORIGIN early 17th cent. (denoting a metrical translation): from Greek *metaphrazein*, literally 'word differently'.

metaphysic ▶ noun a system of metaphysics.

metaphysical ▶ adjective **1** relating to metaphysics: *the essentially metaphysical question of the nature of mind.* ■ based on abstract reasoning: *an empiricist rather than a metaphysical view of law.* ■ transcending physical matter or the laws of nature: *Good and Evil are inextricably linked in a metaphysical battle across space and time.*
2 of or characteristic of the metaphysical poets.
▶ noun (**the Metaphysicals**) the metaphysical poets.
– DERIVATIVES **metaphysically** adverb.

metaphysical poets a group of 17th-century poets whose work is characterized by the use of complex and elaborate images or conceits, typically using an intellectual form of argumentation to express emotional states. Members of the group include John Donne, George Herbert, Henry Vaughan, and Andrew Marvell.

metaphysics ▶ **plural noun** [usu. treated as sing.] the branch of philosophy that deals with the first principles of things, including abstract concepts such as being, knowing, identity, time, and space. ▪ abstract theory with no basis in reality: *his concept of society as an organic entity is, for market liberals, simply metaphysics.*

> Metaphysics has two main strands: that which holds that what exists lies beyond experience (as argued by Plato), and that which holds that objects of experience constitute the only reality (as argued by Kant, the logical positivists, and Hume).

– DERIVATIVES **metaphysician** noun.
– ORIGIN mid 16th cent.: representing medieval Latin *metaphysica* (neuter plural), based on Greek *ta meta ta phusika* 'the things after the Physics', referring to the sequence of Aristotle's works: the title came to denote the branch of study treated in the books, later interpreted as meaning 'the science of things transcending what is physical or natural'.

metaplasia /ˌmɛtəˈpleɪzɪə/ ▶ **noun** [mass noun] Physiology abnormal change in the nature of a tissue.
– DERIVATIVES **metaplastic** adjective.
– ORIGIN late 19th cent.: modern Latin, from German *Metaplase*, based on Greek *metaplassein* 'mould into a new form'.

metapsychology ▶ **noun** [mass noun] the study of mental processes and the mind–body relationship, beyond what can be studied experimentally.
– DERIVATIVES **metapsychological** adjective.

metasomatism /ˌmɛtəˈsəʊmətɪz(ə)m/ ▶ **noun** [mass noun] Geology change in the composition of a rock as a result of the introduction or removal of chemical constituents.
– DERIVATIVES **metasomatic** adjective.
– ORIGIN late 19th cent.: from **META-** (expressing change) + Greek *sōma, somat-* 'body' + **-ISM**.

metastable /ˌmɛtəˈsteɪb(ə)l/ ▶ **adjective** Physics (of a state of equilibrium) stable provided it is subjected to no more than small disturbances. ▪ (of a substance or particle) theoretically unstable but so long-lived as to be stable for practical purposes.
– DERIVATIVES **metastability** noun.

metastasis /mɪˈtastəsɪs/ ▶ **noun** (pl. **metastases** /-siːz/) [mass noun] Medicine the development of secondary malignant growths at a distance from a primary site of cancer. ▪ [count noun] a metastatic growth.
– DERIVATIVES **metastatic** adjective.
– ORIGIN late 16th cent. (as a rhetorical term, meaning 'rapid transition from one point to another'): from Greek, literally 'removal or change', from *methistanai* 'to change'.

metastasize (also **metastasise**) ▶ **verb** [no obj.] Medicine (of a cancer) spread to other sites in the body by metastasis.

metatarsal ▶ **noun** any of the bones of the foot. ▪ any of the bones in an animal's hindlimb equivalent to the metatarsals.

metatarsus ▶ **noun** (pl. **metatarsi**) the group of bones in the foot, between the ankle and the toes. ▪ the part of the foot between the ankle and the toes.
– ORIGIN late Middle English: modern Latin (see **META-**, **TARSUS**).

metate /məˈtɑːteɪ/ ▶ **noun** (in Central America) a flat or slightly hollowed oblong stone on which materials such as grain and cocoa are ground using a smaller stone.
– ORIGIN from American Spanish, from Nahuatl *métatl*.

Metatheria /ˌmɛtəˈθɪərɪə/ ▶ **plural noun** Zoology a group of mammals that comprises the marsupials. Compare with **EUTHERIA**. ● Infraclass Metatheria, subclass Theria.
– ORIGIN modern Latin (plural), from **META-** (expressing change) + Greek *thēria*, plural of *thērion* 'wild animal'.

metatherian Zoology ▶ **noun** a mammal of the group Metatheria; a marsupial.
▶ **adjective** relating to or denoting metatherians.

metathesis /mɪˈtaθɪsɪs/ ▶ **noun** (pl. **metatheses** /-siːz/) **1** [mass noun] Grammar the transposition of sounds or letters in a word.
2 (also **metathesis reaction**) Chemistry another term for **DOUBLE DECOMPOSITION**.
– DERIVATIVES **metathetic** /ˌmɛtəˈθɛtɪk/ adjective, **metathetical** adjective.
– ORIGIN late 16th cent.: from Greek, from *metatithenai* 'transpose, change the position of'.

metathorax ▶ **noun** Entomology the posterior segment of the thorax of an insect, bearing the hindwings.
– DERIVATIVES **metathoracic** adjective.

metaverse ▶ **noun** Computing a virtual-reality space in which users can interact with a computer-generated environment and other users.
– ORIGIN 1990s: blend of **META-** (sense 3) + and **UNIVERSE**.

Metazoa /ˌmɛtəˈzəʊə/ ▶ **plural noun** Zoology a major division of the animal kingdom that comprises all animals other than protozoans and sponges. They are multicellular animals with differentiated tissues. ● Subkingdom Metazoa, kingdom Animalia.
▪ (**metazoa**) animals of the Metazoa division.
– ORIGIN modern Latin (plural), from **META-** (expressing change) + Greek *zōia* (plural of *zōion* 'animal').

metazoan Zoology ▶ **noun** an animal of the Metazoa division.
▶ **adjective** relating to or denoting metazoans.

mete[1] /miːt/ ▶ **verb** [with obj.] (**mete something out**) dispense or allot justice, a punishment, or harsh treatment: *he denounced the maltreatment meted out to minorities.* ▪ (in biblical use) measure out: *with what measure ye mete, it shall be measured to you again.*
– ORIGIN Old English *metan* 'measure', of Germanic origin; related to Dutch *meten* and German *messen* 'to measure', from an Indo-European root shared by Latin *meditari* 'meditate', Greek *medesthai* 'care for', also by **MEET**[2].

mete[2] /miːt/ ▶ **noun** (usu. **metes and bounds**) historical a boundary or boundary stone.
– ORIGIN late Middle English: from Old French, from Latin *meta* 'boundary, goal'.

metempsychosis /ˌmɛtɛmsʌɪˈkəʊsɪs/ ▶ **noun** (pl. **metempsychoses** /-siːz/) [mass noun] the supposed transmigration at death of the soul of a human being or animal into a new body of the same or a different species.
– DERIVATIVES **metempsychotic** adjective, **metempsychotically** adverb.
– ORIGIN late 16th cent.: via late Latin from Greek *metempsukhōsis*, from *meta-* (expressing change) + *en* 'in' + *psukhē* 'soul'.

meteor ▶ **noun** a small body of matter from outer space that enters the earth's atmosphere, becoming incandescent as a result of friction and appearing as a streak of light.
– ORIGIN mid 16th cent. (denoting any atmospheric phenomenon): from modern Latin *meteorum*, from Greek *meteōron*, neuter (used as a noun) of *meteōros* 'lofty'.

Meteora /ˌmɛtɪˈɔːrə/ a group of monasteries in north central Greece, in the region of Thessaly. The monasteries, built between the 12th and the 16th centuries, are perched on the summits of curiously shaped rock formations.

meteoric ▶ **adjective** **1** relating to meteors or meteorites: *meteoric iron.* ▪ (of the development of something) very rapid: *her meteoric rise to the top of her profession.*
2 Geology relating to or denoting water derived from the atmosphere by precipitation or condensation.
– DERIVATIVES **meteorically** adverb.

meteorite ▶ **noun** a piece of rock or metal that has fallen to the earth's surface from outer space as a meteor. Over 90 per cent of meteorites are of rock while the remainder consist wholly or partly of iron and nickel.
– DERIVATIVES **meteoritic** adjective.

meteorograph /ˈmiːtɪərə(ʊ)grɑːf/ ▶ **noun** archaic an apparatus that records several meteorological phenomena at the same time.
– ORIGIN late 18th cent.: from French *météorographe* (see **METEOR**, **-GRAPH**).

meteoroid ▶ **noun** Astronomy a small body moving in the solar system that would become a meteor if it entered the earth's atmosphere.
– DERIVATIVES **meteoroidal** adjective.

Meteorological Office (in the UK) a government department providing weather forecasts.

meteorologist /ˌmiːtɪəˈrɒlədʒɪst/ ▶ **noun** an expert in or student of meteorology; a weather forecaster: *meteorologists predict rain for the rest of the week.*

meteorology /ˌmiːtɪəˈrɒlədʒi/ ▶ **noun** [mass noun] the branch of science concerned with the processes and phenomena of the atmosphere, especially as a means of forecasting the weather. ▪ the climate and weather of a region.
– DERIVATIVES **meteorological** adjective, **meteorologically** adverb.
– ORIGIN early 17th cent.: from Greek *meteōrologia*, from *meteōron* 'of the atmosphere' (see **METEOR**).

meteor shower ▶ **noun** a number of meteors that appear to radiate from one point in the sky at a particular date each year, due to the earth regularly passing through them at that position in its orbit.

meter[1] ▶ **noun** a device that measures and records the quantity, degree, or rate of something: *an electricity meter.*
▶ **verb** [with obj.] measure by means of a meter.
– ORIGIN Middle English (in the sense 'person who measures'): from **METE**[1] + **-ER**[1]. The current sense dates from the 19th cent.

meter[2] ▶ **noun** US spelling of **METRE**[1], **METRE**[2].

-meter ▶ **combining form** **1** in names of measuring instruments: *thermometer.*
2 Prosody in nouns denoting lines of poetry with a specified number of measures: *hexameter.*
– ORIGIN from Greek *metron* 'measure'.

meth ▶ **noun** [mass noun] informal **1** (also **crystal meth**) the drug methamphetamine.
2 short for **METHADONE**.
3 chiefly US another term for **METHS**.

methacrylate /mɪˈθakrɪleɪt/ ▶ **noun** Chemistry a salt or ester of methacrylic acid, especially any of these esters used in making resins by polymerization.

methacrylic acid ▶ **noun** [mass noun] Chemistry a colourless, low-melting solid which polymerizes when distilled and is used in the manufacture of synthetic resins. ● Chem. formula: $CH_2{=}C(CH_3)COOH$.

methadone /ˈmɛθədəʊn/ ▶ **noun** [mass noun] a powerful synthetic analgesic drug which is similar to morphine in its effects but less sedative and is used as a substitute drug in the treatment of morphine and heroin addiction.
– ORIGIN 1940s: from its chemical name, *(6-di)meth(yl)a(mino-4,4-)d(iphenyl-3-heptan)one.*

methaemoglobin /ˌmɛθiːməˈgləʊbɪn, mɛtˌhiː-/ (US **methemoglobin**) ▶ **noun** [mass noun] Biochemistry a stable oxidized form of haemoglobin which is unable to release oxygen to the tissues, produced in some inherited abnormalities and by oxidizing drugs.

methaemoglobinaemia /ˌmɛθiːməˌgləʊbɪˈniːmɪə, mɛtˌhiː-/ (US **methemoglobinemia**) ▶ **noun** [mass noun] Medicine the presence of methaemoglobin in the blood.

methamphetamine /ˌmɛθamˈfɛtəmiːn, -ɪn/ ▶ **noun** [mass noun] a synthetic drug with more rapid and lasting effects than amphetamine, used illegally as a stimulant. ● A methyl derivative of amphetamine; chem. formula $C_6H_5CH_2CH(CH_3)NH(CH_3)$.

methanal /ˈmɛθənal/ ▶ **noun** systematic chemical name for **FORMALDEHYDE**.
– ORIGIN late 19th cent.: blend of **METHANE** and **ALDEHYDE**.

methane /ˈmiːθeɪn, ˈmɛθeɪn/ ▶ **noun** [mass noun] Chemistry a colourless, odourless flammable gas which is the main constituent of natural gas. It is the simplest member of the alkane series of hydrocarbons.
● Chem. formula: CH_4.
– ORIGIN mid 19th cent.: from **METHYL** + **-ANE**[2].

methanogen /ˈmɛθənə(ʊ)dʒ(ə)n, mɛˈθanə(ʊ)-/ ▶ **noun** Biology a methane-producing bacterium, especially an archaean which reduces carbon dioxide to methane.
– DERIVATIVES **methanogenic** adjective.

methanogenesis /ˌmɛθənə(ʊ)ˈdʒɛnɪsɪs, mɛˈθanə(ʊ)-/ ▶ **noun** [mass noun] Biology the production of methane by bacteria or other living organisms.

methanoic acid /ˌmɛθəˈnəʊɪk/ ▶ **noun** systematic chemical name for **FORMIC ACID**.
– ORIGIN late 19th cent.: *methanoic*, from **METHANE** + *-oic* (perhaps on the pattern of *benzoic*).

methanol /ˈmɛθənɒl/ ▶ **noun** [mass noun] Chemistry a toxic, colourless, volatile flammable liquid alcohol, made chiefly by oxidizing methane. Also called **METHYL ALCOHOL**. ● Chem. formula: CH_3OH.
– ORIGIN late 19th cent.: from **METHANE** + **-OL**.

methaqualone /mɛˈθakwələʊn/ ▶ **noun** [mass noun] trademark a sedative and sleep-inducing drug. Also called **QUAALUDE** (trademark).
– ORIGIN 1960s: from elements of its chemical name *meth-* + *-a-* + *qu(inine)* + *a(zo-* + *-o)l* + **-ONE**.

methedrine /ˈmɛθədrɪn, -driːn/ ▶ **noun** (trademark in the UK) another term for **METHAMPHETAMINE**.
– ORIGIN 1930s: blend of **METHYL** and **BENZEDRINE**.

M

metheglin /mɪˈθɛɡlɪn, ˈmɛθəɡlɪn/ ▶ **noun** [mass noun] historical a spiced or medicated variety of mead, associated particularly with Wales.
– ORIGIN mid 16th cent.: from Welsh *meddyglyn*, from *meddyg* 'medicinal' (from Latin *medicus*) + *llyn* 'liquor'.

methemoglobinemia ▶ **noun** US spelling of METHAEMOGLOBINAEMIA.

methi /ˈmeɪti/ ▶ **noun** [mass noun] Indian fenugreek.
– ORIGIN Sanskrit, Hindi *methī*, from Dravidian.

methicillin /ˌmɛθɪˈsɪlɪn/ ▶ **noun** [mass noun] Medicine a semi-synthetic form of penicillin used against staphylococci which produce penicillinase.
– ORIGIN 1960s: from *meth(yl)* and *(pen)icillin*.

methinks ▶ **verb** (past **methought**) [no obj.] archaic or humorous it seems to me: *life has been rather hard on her, methinks*.
– ORIGIN Old English *mē thyncth*, from *mē* 'to me' + *thyncth* 'it seems' (from *thyncan* 'seem', related to THINK).

methiocarb /mɪˈθʌɪəkɑːb/ ▶ **noun** [mass noun] a synthetic compound used to kill garden pests. ● Chem. formula: $C_{11}H_{15}NO_2S$.
– ORIGIN 1960s: from *me(thyl)* + THIO- + *carb(amate)*.

methionine /mɪˈθʌɪəniːn/ ▶ **noun** [mass noun] Biochemistry a sulphur-containing amino acid which is a constituent of most proteins and is essential to the diet of vertebrates. ● Chem. formula: $CH_3S(CH_2)_2CH(NH_2)COOH$.
– ORIGIN 1920s: from METHYL + Greek *theion* 'sulphur'.

metho ▶ **noun** (pl. **methos**) [mass noun] Austral./NZ informal methylated spirit. ■ [count noun] a person addicted to drinking methylated spirit.
– ORIGIN 1930s: abbreviation.

method ▶ **noun** a particular procedure for accomplishing or approaching something, especially a systematic or established one: ***a method for** software maintenance* | *labour-intensive production methods*. ■ [mass noun] the quality of being well organized and systematic in thought or action: *historical study is the rigorous combination of knowledge and method*. ■ (usu. **Method**) short for METHOD ACTING.
– PHRASES **there is method in someone's madness** there is a sensible foundation for what appears to be foolish or strange behaviour. [from Shakespeare's *Hamlet* (II. ii. 211).]
– ORIGIN late Middle English (in the sense 'prescribed medical treatment for a disease'): via Latin from Greek *methodos* 'pursuit of knowledge', from *meta-* (expressing development) + *hodos* 'way'.

method acting ▶ **noun** [mass noun] a technique of acting in which an actor aspires to complete emotional identification with a part, based on the system evolved by Stanislavsky and brought into prominence in the US in the 1930s. Method acting was developed by Elia Kazan and Lee Strasberg in particular, and is associated with actors such as Marlon Brando and Dustin Hoffman.
– DERIVATIVES **method actor** noun.

méthode champenoise /meɪˌtəʊd ʃɒ̃pənˈwɑːz/ ▶ **noun** [mass noun] [often as modifier] a method of making sparkling wine by allowing the last stage of fermentation to take place in the bottle. ■ sparkling wine made by the méthode champenoise, especially a kind not made in the Champagne region of France.
– ORIGIN French, literally 'champagne method'.

methodical ▶ **adjective** done according to a systematic or established procedure: *a methodical approach to the evaluation of computer systems*. ■ (of a person) orderly or systematic in thought or behaviour.
– DERIVATIVES **methodic** adjective, **methodically** adverb.
– ORIGIN late 16th cent.: via late Latin from Greek *methodikos* (from *methodos*: see METHOD) + -AL.

Methodist ▶ **noun** a member of a Christian Protestant denomination originating in the 18th-century evangelistic movement of Charles and John Wesley and George Whitefield.

> The Methodist Church grew out of a religious society established within the Church of England, from which it formally separated in 1791. It is particularly strong in the US and now constitutes one of the largest Protestant denominations worldwide, with more than 30 million members. Methodism has a strong tradition of missionary work and concern with social welfare, and emphasizes the believer's personal relationship with God.

▶ **adjective** relating to Methodists or Methodism: *a Methodist chapel*.
– DERIVATIVES **Methodism** noun, **Methodistic** adjective.
– ORIGIN probably from the notion of following a specified 'method' of Bible study.

Methodius, St /mɪˈθəʊdɪəs/ the brother of St Cyril (see CYRIL, ST).

methodize (also **methodise**) ▶ **verb** [with obj.] rare arrange in an orderly or systematic manner.

methodology ▶ **noun** (pl. **methodologies**) a system of methods used in a particular area of study or activity: *a methodology for investigating the concept of focal points* | [mass noun] *courses in research methodology and practice*.
– DERIVATIVES **methodological** adjective, **methodologically** adverb, **methodologist** noun.
– ORIGIN early 19th cent.: from modern Latin *methodologia* or French *méthodologie*.

methotrexate /ˌmɛθəˈtrɛkseɪt, ˌmiːθə-/ ▶ **noun** [mass noun] Medicine a synthetic compound that interferes with cell growth and is used to treat leukaemia and other forms of cancer. ● Chem. formula: $C_{20}H_{22}N_8O_5$.
– ORIGIN 1950s: from *meth-* (denoting a substance containing methyl groups) + elements of unknown origin.

methought past of METHINKS.

meths ▶ **noun** [mass noun] Brit. informal methylated spirit.

Methuselah /mɪˈθ(j)uːz(ə)lə/ (in the Bible) a patriarch, the grandfather of Noah, who is said to have lived for 969 years (Gen. 5:27). ■ used to refer to a very old person: *I'm feeling older than Methuselah*.

methuselah ▶ **noun** a wine bottle of eight times the standard size.
– ORIGIN 1930s: from METHUSELAH.

methyl /ˈmiːθʌɪl, ˈmɛθ-, -θɪl/ ▶ **noun** [as modifier] Chemistry of or denoting the alkyl radical $-CH_3$, derived from methane and present in many organic compounds: *methyl bromide*.
– ORIGIN mid 19th cent.: from German *Methyl* or French *méthyle*, back-formations from German *Methylen* and French *méthylène* (see METHYLENE).

methyl alcohol ▶ **noun** another term for METHANOL.

methylate /ˈmɛθɪleɪt/ ▶ **verb** [with obj.] (often as adj. **methylated**) mix or impregnate with methanol or methylated spirit. ■ Chemistry introduce a methyl group into (a molecule or compound).
– DERIVATIVES **methylation** noun.

methylated spirit (also **methylated spirits**) ▶ **noun** [mass noun] alcohol for general use that has been made unfit for drinking by the addition of about 10 per cent methanol and typically also some pyridine and a violet dye.

methylbenzene ▶ **noun** systematic chemical name for TOLUENE.

methyl cyanide ▶ **noun** another term for ACETONITRILE.

methylene /ˈmɛθɪliːn/ ▶ **noun** [as modifier] Chemistry of or denoting the divalent radical or group $-CH_2-$, derived from methane by loss of two hydrogen atoms: *methylene chloride*.
– ORIGIN mid 19th cent.: from French *méthylène* (formed irregularly from Greek *methu* 'wine' + *hulē* 'wood') + -ENE.

methylphenidate /ˌmiːθʌɪlˈfɛnɪdeɪt, ˌmɛθ-, -θɪl-/ ▶ **noun** [mass noun] Medicine a synthetic drug that stimulates the sympathetic and central nervous systems, used chiefly to improve mental activity in attention deficit disorder. Also called RITALIN (trademark).

metic /ˈmɛtɪk/ ▶ **noun** a foreigner living in an ancient Greek city who had some of the privileges of citizenship.
– ORIGIN early 19th cent.: formed irregularly from Greek *metoikos*, from *meta-* (expressing change) + *oikos* 'dwelling'.

metical /ˌmɛtɪˈkal/ ▶ **noun** (pl. **meticais**) the basic monetary unit of Mozambique, equal to 100 centavos.
– ORIGIN Portuguese, based on Arabic *mitqāl*, from *ṯaqala* 'to weigh'.

meticulous /mɪˈtɪkjʊləs/ ▶ **adjective** showing great attention to detail; very careful and precise: *the designs are hand-glazed with meticulous care* | *he had always been so meticulous about his appearance*.
– DERIVATIVES **meticulously** adverb, **meticulousness** noun.
– ORIGIN mid 16th cent. (in the sense 'fearful or timid'): from Latin *meticulosus*, from *metus* 'fear'. The word came to mean 'overcareful about detail', hence the current sense (early 19th cent.).

métier /ˈmɛtjeɪ/ ▶ **noun** a profession or occupation: *the boy must begin to learn his métier as heir to the throne*. ■ an occupation or activity that one is good at: *television is rather more my métier*.
– ORIGIN late 18th cent.: French, based on Latin *ministerium* 'service'.

Metis /meɪˈtiːs/ ▶ **noun** (pl. **same**) (in Canada) a person of mixed race, especially one having white and American Indian parentage.
▶ **adjective** denoting or relating to people of mixed race in Canada.
– ORIGIN from French *métis*, from Latin *mixtus* 'mixed' (see also MESTIZO).

Met Office see MET.

metol /ˈmɛtɒl/ ▶ **noun** [mass noun] a soluble white compound used as a photographic developer. ● A sulphate of 4-methylaminophenol (chem. formula: $CH_3NHC_6H_4OH$).
– ORIGIN late 19th cent.: from German, arbitrarily named by the inventor.

Metonic cycle /mɪˈtɒnɪk/ ▶ **noun** a period of 19 years (235 lunar months), after which the new and full moons return to the same day of the year. It was the basis of the ancient Greek calendar, and is still used for calculating movable feasts such as Easter.
– ORIGIN named after *Metōn*, an Athenian astronomer of the 5th cent. BC.

metonym /ˈmɛtənɪm/ ▶ **noun** a word, name, or expression used as a substitute for something else with which it is closely associated. For example, *Washington* is a metonym for the US government.
– ORIGIN mid 19th cent.: back-formation from METONYMY.

metonymy /mɪˈtɒnɪmi/ ▶ **noun** (pl. **metonymies**) [mass noun] the substitution of the name of an attribute or adjunct for that of the thing meant, for example *suit* for *business executive*, or *the turf* for *horse racing*.
– DERIVATIVES **metonymic** adjective, **metonymical** adjective, **metonymically** adverb.
– ORIGIN mid 16th cent.: via Latin from Greek *metōnumia*, literally 'change of name'.

me-too ▶ **adjective** informal relating to the adoption or imitation of another person's views or policies, often for political advantage: *he has been a me-too liberal on many of the issues that matter most*. ■ (of a product) designed to emulate or rival another which has already been successful: *me-too drugs*.

metope /ˈmɛtəʊp, ˈmɛtəpi/ ▶ **noun** Architecture a square space between triglyphs in a Doric frieze.
– ORIGIN mid 16th cent.: via Latin from Greek *metopē*, from *meta* 'between' + *opē* 'hole for a beam end'.

metoprolol /mɪˈtɒprəlɒl/ ▶ **noun** [mass noun] Medicine a beta-blocking drug related to propranolol, used to treat hypertension and angina.
– ORIGIN 1970s: from *met-* (from METHYL) + *pro(prano)lol*.

metre[1] (US **meter**) (abbrev.: **m**) ▶ **noun** the fundamental unit of length in the metric system, equal to 100 centimetres or approximately 39.37 inches. ■ (**—— metres**) a race over a specified number of metres: *the 200 metres*.
– DERIVATIVES **metreage** noun.
– ORIGIN late 18th cent.: from French *mètre*, from Greek *metron* 'measure'.

metre[2] (US **meter**) ▶ **noun** the rhythm of a piece of poetry, determined by the number and length of feet in a line: *the Horatian ode has an intricate governing metre* | [mass noun] *unexpected changes of stress and metre*. ■ the basic rhythmic pattern of beats in a piece of music.
– ORIGIN Old English, reinforced in Middle English by Old French *metre*, from Latin *metrum*, from Greek *metron* 'measure'.

metre-kilogram-second (abbrev.: **mks**) ▶ **adjective** denoting a system of measure using the metre, kilogram, and second as the basic units of length, mass, and time.

metric[1] ▶ **adjective 1** relating to or based on the metre as a unit of length: *all measurements are given in metric form*. ■ relating to or using the metric system.
2 Mathematics & Physics relating to or denoting a metric.
▶ **noun 1** technical a system or standard of measurement. ■ (**metrics**) (in business) a set of figures or statistics that measure results. ■ Mathematics & Physics a binary function of a topological space which gives, for any two points of the space, a value equal to the distance between them, or to a value treated as analogous to distance for the purpose of analysis.
2 [mass noun] informal the metric system: *it's easier to work in metric*.

M

– ORIGIN mid 19th cent. (as an adjective relating to length): from French *métrique*, from *mètre* (see METRE[1]).

metric[2] ▸ adjective relating to or composed in a poetic metre.
▸ noun the metre of a poem.
– ORIGIN late 15th cent. (denoting the branch of study dealing with metre): via Latin from Greek *metrikos*, from *metron* (see METRE[2]).

-metric ▸ combining form in adjectives corresponding to nouns ending in *-meter* (such as *geometric* corresponding to *geometer* and *geometry*).
– DERIVATIVES **-metrically** combining form in corresponding adverbs.
– ORIGIN from French *-métrique*, from Latin (see METRIC[1]).

metrical ▸ adjective **1** relating to or composed in poetic metre: *metrical translations of the Psalms*.
2 of or involving measurement: *a metrical analysis of male and female scapulae*.
– DERIVATIVES **metrically** adverb.
– ORIGIN late Middle English: via Latin from Greek *metrikos* (from *metron*: see METRE[2]) + -AL.

-metrical ▸ combining form equivalent to -METRIC.

metricate ▸ verb [with obj.] convert to a metric system of measurement.
– DERIVATIVES **metrication** noun.

metric hundredweight ▸ noun see HUNDREDWEIGHT

metric mile ▸ noun a distance of 1,500 metres, or a race over this distance.

metric system ▸ noun the decimal measuring system based on the metre, litre, and gram as units of length, capacity, and weight or mass. The system was first proposed by the French astronomer and mathematician Gabriel Mouton (1618–94) in 1670 and was standardized in Republican France in the 1790s.

metric ton (also **metric tonne**) ▸ noun a unit of weight equal to 1,000 kilograms (2,205 lb).

metritis /mɪˈtrʌɪtɪs/ ▸ noun [mass noun] Medicine inflammation of the womb.
– ORIGIN mid 19th cent.: from Greek *mētra* 'womb' + -ITIS.

metro ▸ noun (pl. **metros**) an underground railway system in a city, especially Paris.
▸ adjective [attrib.] N. Amer. metropolitan: *the Detroit metro area*.
– ORIGIN early 20th cent.: from French *métro*, abbreviation of *métropolitain* (from *Chemin de Fer Métropolitain* 'Metropolitan Railway').

Metroland ▸ noun the area around London served by the underground railway.
– ORIGIN 1915: from METROPOLITAN + LAND.

metrology /mɪˈtrɒlədʒi/ ▸ noun [mass noun] the scientific study of measurement.
– DERIVATIVES **metrological** adjective.
– ORIGIN early 19th cent.: from Greek *metron* 'measure' + -LOGY.

metronidazole /ˌmɛtrəˈnʌɪdəzəʊl/ ▸ noun [mass noun] Medicine a synthetic drug used to treat trichomoniasis and some similar infections. ● Chem. formula: $C_6H_9N_3O_3$.
– ORIGIN 1960s: from *me(thyl)* + *(ni)tro-* + *(im)idazole*.

metronome /ˈmɛtrənəʊm/ ▸ noun a device used by musicians that marks time at a selected rate by giving a regular tick.
– DERIVATIVES **metronomic** adjective, **metronomically** adverb.
– ORIGIN early 19th cent.: from Greek *metron* 'measure' + *nomos* 'law'.

metronymic /ˌmɛtrəˈnɪmɪk/ ▸ adjective & noun variant spelling of MATRONYMIC.

metroplex ▸ noun chiefly N. Amer. a very large metropolitan area, especially one which is an aggregation of two or more cities.
– ORIGIN 1960s: blend of METROPOLITAN and COMPLEX.

metropole /ˈmɛtrəpəʊl/ ▸ noun the parent state of a colony.
– ORIGIN late 15th cent.: from Old French *metropole*, based on Greek *mētēr*, *mētr-* 'mother' + *polis* 'city' (see METROPOLIS).

metropolis /mɪˈtrɒp(ə)lɪs/ ▸ noun the capital or chief city of a country or region. ■ a very large and busy city.
– ORIGIN late Middle English (denoting the see of a metropolitan bishop): via late Latin from Greek *mētropolis* 'mother state', from *mētēr*, *mētr-* 'mother' + *polis* 'city'.

metropolitan ▸ adjective **1** relating to or denoting a metropolis: *the Boston metropolitan area*.
2 relating to or denoting the parent state of a colony.
3 Christian Church relating to or denoting a metropolitan or his see.
▸ noun **1** Christian Church a bishop having authority over the bishops of a province, in particular (in Orthodox Churches) one ranking above archbishop and below patriarch.
2 an inhabitant of a metropolis: *a sophisticated metropolitan*.
– DERIVATIVES **metropolitanate** noun (sense 1 of the noun), **metropolitanism** noun, **metropolitical** adjective (sense 1 of the noun).
– ORIGIN late Middle English (in the ecclesiastical sense): from late Latin *metropolitanus*, from Greek *mētropolitēs* 'citizen of a mother state', from *mētropolis* (see METROPOLIS).

metropolitan county ▸ noun (in England) each of six units of local government centred on a large urban area (in existence since 1974, although their councils were abolished in 1986).

metropolitan district ▸ noun (in England) an administrative unit consisting of a town or city and a borough.

metropolitan magistrate ▸ noun (in the UK) a stipendiary magistrate who sits in petty sessional courts in London.

Metropolitan Museum of Art a museum of art and archaeology in New York, founded in 1870.

metrorrhagia /ˌmiːtrəˈreɪdʒɪə/ ▸ noun [mass noun] abnormal bleeding from the womb.
– ORIGIN mid 19th cent.: modern Latin, from Greek *mētra* 'womb' + *-rrhag-*, stem of *rhēgnunai* 'to burst'.

metrosexual ▸ noun informal a heterosexual urban man who enjoys shopping, fashion, and similar interests traditionally associated with women or homosexual men.
– ORIGIN 1990s: blend of METROPOLITAN and HETEROSEXUAL.

-metry ▸ combining form in nouns denoting procedures and systems corresponding to names of instruments ending in *-meter* (such as *calorimetry* corresponding to *calorimeter*).
– ORIGIN from Greek *-metria*, from *-metrēs* 'measurer'.

metta /ˈmɛtə/ ▸ noun [mass noun] (in Theravada Buddhism) meditation focused on the development of unconditional love for all beings.
– ORIGIN from Pali *mettā* 'loving-kindness'.

Metternich /ˈmɛtənɪx/, German /ˈmɛtɐnɪç/, Klemens Wenzel Nepomuk Lothar, Prince of Metternich-Winneburg-Beilstein (1773–1859), Austrian statesman. As Foreign Minister (1809–48), he was one of the organizers of the Congress of Vienna (1814–15), which devised the settlement of Europe after the Napoleonic Wars.

mettle ▸ noun [mass noun] a person's ability to cope well with difficulties; spirit and resilience: *the team showed their true mettle in the second half*.
– PHRASES **be on one's mettle** be ready or forced to do one's best in a demanding situation. **put someone on their mettle** (of a demanding situation) test someone's ability to face difficulties.
– ORIGIN mid 16th cent.: specialized spelling (used for figurative senses) of METAL.

mettlesome ▸ adjective literary (of a person or animal) full of spirit and courage; lively: *their horses were beasts of burden, not mettlesome chargers*.

Metz /mɛts/ a city in Lorraine, NE France, on the Moselle River; pop. 126,706 (2006).

Meucci /meɪˈuːtʃi/, Antonio (1808–96), Italian engineer, now widely regarded as the inventor of the telephone. He demonstrated his device in 1860 and took out a patent caveat in 1871; however, the combined effects of poverty and mismanagement allowed credit for the invention to rest for many years with Alexander Graham Bell, who patented his own device in 1876.

meunière /məːnˈjɛː/ ▸ adjective [usu. postpositive] (especially of fish) cooked or served in lightly browned butter with lemon juice and parsley: *sole meunière*.
– ORIGIN from French *(à la) meunière* '(in the manner of) a miller's wife'.

Meursault /məːˈsəʊ, ˈməː-/ ▸ noun (pl. **same**) [mass noun] a burgundy wine, typically white, produced near Beaune.
– ORIGIN named after a commune in the Côte d'Or region of France.

Meuse /məːz/ a river of western Europe, which rises in NE France and flows 950 km (594 miles) through Belgium and the Netherlands to the North Sea south of Dordrecht. Flemish and Dutch name **MAAS**.

MeV ▸ abbreviation mega-electronvolt(s).

mew[1] ▸ verb [no obj.] (of a cat or gull) make a characteristic high-pitched crying noise: *cats mewing to be fed* | (as noun **mewing**) *he heard mewing somewhere near the house*.
▸ noun the high-pitched cry of a cat or gull.
– ORIGIN Middle English: imitative.

mew[2] Falconry ▸ noun (usu. **mews**) a cage or building for trained hawks, especially while they are moulting.
▸ verb **1** [no obj.] (of a trained hawk) moult.
2 [with obj.] confine (a trained hawk) to a cage or building while moulting. ■ confine (someone) in a restricting place or situation: *a lovely wife* ***mewed up*** *in an Oxfordshire farmhouse*.
– ORIGIN late Middle English: from Old French *mue*, from *muer* 'to moult', from Latin *mutare* 'to change'.

mew gull ▸ noun chiefly N. Amer. another term for COMMON GULL.
– ORIGIN mid 19th cent.: *mew* (in Old English *meau* 'mew gull'), of Germanic origin; related to Dutch *meeuw* and German *Möwe*.

mewl ▸ verb [no obj.] (often as adj. **mewling**) (especially of a baby) cry feebly or querulously; whimper: *dozens of mewling babies*. ■ (of a cat or gull) mew: *the mewling cry of a hawk*.
– ORIGIN late Middle English: imitative; compare with MIAUL.

mews ▸ noun (pl. **same**) Brit. a row or street of houses or flats that have been converted from stables or built to look like former stables: [as modifier] *a mews house*. ■ a group of stables, typically with rooms above, built round a yard or along an alley.
– ORIGIN late Middle English: plural of MEW[2], originally referring to the royal stables on the site of the hawk mews at Charing Cross, London. The sense 'converted dwellings' dates from the early 19th cent.

MEX ▸ abbreviation Mexico (international vehicle registration).

Mex ▸ adjective informal Mexican.

Mexicali /ˌmɛksɪˈkaːli/ the capital of the state of Baja California, in NW Mexico; pop. 653,046 (2005).

Mexican hairless ▸ noun a small dog of a breed lacking hair except for tufts on the head and tail.

Mexicano /ˌmɛksɪˈkaːnəʊ/ ▸ noun & adjective (pl. **Mexicanos**) US informal Mexican or a Mexican.
– ORIGIN Spanish.

Mexican wave ▸ noun an effect resembling a moving wave produced by successive sections of the crowd in a stadium standing up, raising their arms, lowering them, and sitting down again.
– ORIGIN so named because of the repeated practice of this movement at the 1986 soccer World Cup finals in Mexico City.

Mexico a country in North America, with extensive coastlines on the Gulf of Mexico and the Pacific Ocean, bordered by the US to the north; pop. 111,211,800 (est. 2009); official language, Spanish; capital, Mexico City. ■ a state of central Mexico, to the west of Mexico City; capital, Toluca de Lerdo.

> The centre of both Mayan and Aztec civilizations, Mexico was conquered and colonized by the Spanish in the early 16th century. It remained under Spanish rule until independence was achieved in 1821; a republic was established three years later. Texas rebelled and broke away in 1836, while all the remaining territory north of the Rio Grande was lost to the US in the Mexican War of 1846–8.

– DERIVATIVES **Mexican** adjective & noun.

Mexico, Gulf of a large extension of the western Atlantic Ocean. Bounded in a sweeping curve by the US to the north, by Mexico to the west and south, and by Cuba to the south-east, it is linked to the Atlantic by the Straits of Florida and to the Caribbean Sea by the Yucatán Channel.

Mexico City the capital of Mexico; pop. 8,720,916 (2005). Founded in about 1300 as the Aztec capital Tenochtitlán, it was destroyed in 1521 by the Spanish conquistador Cortés, who rebuilt it as the capital of New Spain.

Meyerbeer /ˈmʌɪəˌbɪə/, German /ˈmaɪɐbeːɐ/, Giacomo (1791–1864), German composer; born *Jakob Liebmann Beer*. He settled in Paris, establishing himself as a leading exponent of French grand opera with a series of works including *Les Huguenots* (1836).

M

meze /ˈmeɪzeɪ/ ▶ **noun** (pl. **same** or **mezes**) (in Turkish, Greek, and Middle Eastern cookery) a selection of hot and cold dishes, typically served as an hors d'oeuvre.
– ORIGIN from Turkish, literally 'appetizer', from Persian *maza* 'to relish'.

mezereon /mɪˈzɪərɪən/ ▶ **noun** a Eurasian shrub with fragrant purplish-red flowers and poisonous red berries, found chiefly in calcareous woodland. ● *Daphne mezereum*, family Thymelaeaceae.
– ORIGIN late 15th cent.: from medieval Latin, from Arabic *māzaryūn*.

mezuzah /mɛˈzuːzə/ ▶ **noun** (pl. **mezuzahs** or **mezuzoth** /-zəʊt/) a parchment inscribed with religious texts and attached in a case to the doorpost of a Jewish house as a sign of faith.
– ORIGIN mid 17th cent.: from Hebrew *mĕzūzāh* 'doorpost'.

mezzaluna /ˌmɛtsəˈluːnə/ ▶ **noun** a utensil for chopping herbs, vegetables, etc., with a semi-circular blade and a handle at each end.
– ORIGIN 1950s: from Italian, literally 'half moon'.

mezzanine /ˈmɛzəniːn, ˈmɛts-/ ▶ **noun** a low storey between two others in a building, typically between the ground and first floors. ■ N. Amer. the lowest balcony of a theatre, cinema, etc., or the front rows of the balcony.
▶ **adjective** [attrib.] Finance relating to or denoting unsecured, higher-yielding loans that are subordinate to bank loans and secured loans but rank above equity.
– ORIGIN early 18th cent.: from French, from Italian *mezzanino*, diminutive of *mezzano* 'middle', from Latin *medianus* 'median'.

mezza voce /ˌmɛtsə ˈvəʊtʃeɪ, ˈvɒtʃi/ Music ▶ **adverb & adjective** (especially as a direction) using about half the singer's vocal power.
▶ **noun** [mass noun] singing performed in this way.
– ORIGIN Italian, literally 'half voice'.

mezzo /ˈmɛtsəʊ/ ▶ **noun** (pl. **mezzos**) (also **mezzo-soprano**) a female singer with a voice pitched between soprano and contralto. ■ a singing voice of the mezzo type, or a part written for one.
– ORIGIN mid 18th cent.: Italian, from Latin *medius* 'middle'.

mezzo forte Music ▶ **adverb & adjective** (especially as a direction) moderately loud.
▶ **noun** [mass noun] a moderately high volume.

Mezzogiorno /ˌmɛtsəʊˈdʒɔːnəʊ/, Italian /meddzəʊˈdʒəɔrnəʊ/ the southern part of Italy, including Sicily and Sardinia.
– ORIGIN Italian, literally 'midday'; compare with **MIDI**.

mezzo piano Music ▶ **adverb & adjective** (especially as a direction) moderately soft.
▶ **noun** [mass noun] a moderately low volume.

mezzo-relievo /ˌmɛtsəʊrɪˈljiːvəʊ/ ▶ **noun** (pl. **mezzo-relievos**) Sculpture another term for **HALF RELIEF**.
– ORIGIN late 16th cent.: Italian *mezzo-rilievo*.

mezzotint /ˈmɛtsəʊtɪnt, ˈmɛzəʊ-/ ▶ **noun** a print made from an engraved copper or steel plate, the surface of which has been scraped and polished to give areas of shade and light respectively. The technique was much used in the 17th, 18th, and early 19th centuries for the reproduction of paintings. ■ [mass noun] the technique or process of making mezzotints.
▶ **verb** [with obj.] engrave (a picture) in mezzotint.
– ORIGIN from Italian *mezzotinto*, from *mezzo* 'half' + *tinto* 'tint'.

MF ▶ **abbreviation** medium frequency.

mf ▶ **abbreviation** mezzo forte.

MFH ▶ **abbreviation** Master of Foxhounds.

MFN ▶ **abbreviation** most favoured nation.

MG ▶ **abbreviation** ■ machine gun. ■ historical Morris Garages.

Mg ▶ **symbol** the chemical element magnesium.

mg ▶ **abbreviation** milligram(s): *100 mg paracetamol*.

MGM Metro-Goldwyn-Mayer, a film company formed in 1924 by Samuel Goldwyn and Louis B. Mayer.

MGR ▶ **abbreviation** Brit. merry-go-round (train).

Mgr ▶ **abbreviation** ■ (**mgr**) manager. ■ Monseigneur. ■ Monsignor: *Mgr O'Flaherty*.

MHK ▶ **abbreviation** (in the Isle of Man) Member of the House of Keys.

mho /məʊ/ ▶ **noun** (pl. **mhos**) the reciprocal of an ohm, a former unit of electrical conductance.
– ORIGIN late 19th cent.: the word **OHM** reversed.

MHR ▶ **abbreviation** (in the US and Australia) Member of the House of Representatives.

MHz ▶ **abbreviation** megahertz.

MI ▶ **abbreviation** ■ Michigan (in official postal use). ■ Brit. historical Military Intelligence: *MI5*.

mi ▶ **noun** variant spelling of **ME²**.

mi. ▶ **abbreviation** mile(s): *10 km/6 mi*.

MI5 (in the UK) the governmental agency responsible for dealing with internal security and counter-intelligence on British territory. Formed in 1909, the agency was officially named the Security Service in 1964, but the name MI5 remains in popular use.
– ORIGIN from *Military Intelligence section 5*.

MI6 (in the UK) the governmental agency responsible for dealing with matters of internal security and counter-intelligence overseas. Formed in 1912, the agency was officially named the Secret Intelligence Service in 1964, but the name MI6 remains in popular use.

MIA ▶ **abbreviation** N. Amer. ■ missing in action. ■ [as noun] a member of the armed forces who is missing in action.

Miami /mʌɪˈami/ a city and port on the coast of SE Florida; pop. 413,201 (est. 2008). Its subtropical climate and miles of beaches make this and the resort island of Miami Beach a year-round holiday resort.

mia-mia /ˈmʌɪəˌmʌɪə/ ▶ **noun** Austral. an Aboriginal hut or shelter.
– ORIGIN from Wathawurung (an extinct Aboriginal language) or Nyungar.

Miao /mɪˈaʊ/ ▶ **noun** (pl. **same**) & **adjective** another term for **HMONG**.
– ORIGIN from Chinese *Miáo*, literally 'tribes'.

miaow (also **meow**) ▶ **noun** the characteristic crying sound of a cat.
▶ **verb** [no obj.] (of a cat) make a miaow.
– ORIGIN early 17th cent.: imitative.

miasm /ˈmʌɪaz(ə)m/ ▶ **noun** (in homeopathy) a supposed predisposition to a particular disease, either inherited or acquired.
– ORIGIN mid 19th cent.: from German *Miasm*, from Greek *miasma* (see **MIASMA**).

miasma /mɪˈazmə, mʌɪ-/ ▶ **noun** (pl. **miasmas**) literary an unpleasant or unhealthy smell or vapour: ***a miasma of stale alcohol hung around him***. ■ an oppressive or unpleasant atmosphere which surrounds or emanates from something: ***a miasma of despair rose from the black workshops***.
– DERIVATIVES **miasmal** adjective, **miasmatic** adjective.
– ORIGIN mid 17th cent.: from Greek, literally 'defilement', from *miainein* 'pollute'.

miasmic ▶ **adjective** literary producing an unpleasant smell; noxious. ■ characterized by a mysterious and unpleasant atmosphere; oppressive: *we know the territory, its long and miasmic history*.

miaul /mɪˈɔːl/ ▶ **verb** [no obj.] rare (of a cat) miaow.
– ORIGIN mid 17th cent.: from French *miauler*, of imitative origin.

mic ▶ **noun** short for **MICROPHONE**.

Mic. ▶ **abbreviation** Micah (in biblical references).

mica /ˈmʌɪkə/ ▶ **noun** [mass noun] a shiny silicate mineral with a layered structure, found as minute scales in granite and other rocks, or as crystals. It is used as a thermal or electrical insulator.
– DERIVATIVES **micaceous** /mɪˈkeɪʃəs/ adjective.
– ORIGIN early 18th cent.: from Latin, literally 'crumb'.

Micah /ˈmʌɪkə/ (in the Bible) a Hebrew minor prophet. ■ a book of the Bible bearing his name, foretelling the destruction of Samaria and of Jerusalem.

mica schist ▶ **noun** [mass noun] a metamorphic rock containing quartz and mica which resembles slate in being easily split.

Micawber /mɪˈkɔːbə/, Wilkins, a character in Dickens's novel *David Copperfield* (1850), an eternal optimist who, despite evidence to the contrary, continues to have faith that 'something will turn up'.
– DERIVATIVES **Micawberish** adjective, **Micawberism** noun.

mice plural form of **MOUSE**.

micelle /mɪˈsɛl, mʌɪˈsɛl/ ▶ **noun** Chemistry an aggregate of molecules in a colloidal solution, such as those formed by detergents.
– DERIVATIVES **micellar** adjective.
– ORIGIN late 19th cent.: coined as a diminutive of Latin *mica* 'crumb'.

Mich. ▶ **abbreviation** Michigan.

Michael, St one of the archangels, typically represented slaying a dragon (see Rev. 12:7). Feast day, 29 September (Michaelmas Day).

Michaelis constant /mɪˈkeɪlɪs/ ▶ **noun** Biochemistry the concentration of a given substrate which catalyses the associated reaction at half the maximum rate.
– ORIGIN 1930s: named after Leonor *Michaelis* (1875–1949), German-born American chemist.

Michaelmas /ˈmɪk(ə)lməs/ ▶ **noun** the feast of St Michael, 29 September.
– ORIGIN Old English *Sanct Michaeles mæsse* 'Saint Michael's Mass', referring to the Archangel.

Michaelmas daisy ▶ **noun** a North American aster with numerous pinkish-lilac daisy-like flowers which bloom around Michaelmas. ● *Aster novi-belgii*, family Compositae.

Michaelmas term ▶ **noun** Brit. (in some universities) the autumn term.

Michelangelo /ˌmʌɪk(ə)lˈandʒələʊ, ˌmɪk(ə)ˈlandʒələʊ/ (1475–1564), Italian sculptor, painter, architect, and poet; full name *Michelangelo Buonarroti*.

> A leading figure of the High Renaissance, Michelangelo established his reputation with sculptures such as the *Pietà* (c.1497–1500) and *David* (1501–4). Under papal patronage he decorated the ceiling of the Sistine Chapel in Rome (1508–12) and painted the fresco *The Last Judgement* (1536–41), both important mannerist works. His architectural achievements include the completion of St Peter's in Rome (1546–64).

Michelin /ˈmɪtʃəlɪn/, French /miʃlɛ̃/, André (1853–1931) and Édouard (1859–1940), French industrialists. They founded the Michelin Tyre Company in 1888 and pioneered the use of pneumatic tyres on motor vehicles.

Michelin man ▶ **noun** informal a fat person.
– ORIGIN 1990s: from the name of a cartoon character with a body and limbs made up of pneumatic tyres.

Michelozzo /ˌmɪkɛˈlɒtsəʊ/ (1396–1472), Italian architect and sculptor; full name *Michelozzo di Bartolommeo*. In partnership with Ghiberti and Donatello he led a revival of interest in Roman architecture.

Michelson /ˈmʌɪk(ə)ls(ə)n/, Albert Abraham (1852–1931), American physicist. He specialized in precision measurement in experimental physics, and in 1907 became the first American to be awarded a Nobel Prize.

Michelson–Morley experiment Physics an experiment performed in 1887 which attempted to measure the relative motion of the earth and the ether by measuring the speed of light in directions parallel and perpendicular to the earth's motion. The result disproved the existence of the ether, which contradicted Newtonian physics but was explained by Einstein's special theory of relativity.
– ORIGIN named after A. A. **MICHELSON** and E. W. **MORLEY**.

Michigan /ˈmɪʃɪg(ə)n/ a state in the northern US, bordered on the west, north, and east by Lakes Michigan, Superior, Huron, and Erie; pop. 10,003,422 (est. 2008); capital, Lansing. It was acquired from Britain by the US in 1783, becoming the 26th state in 1837.
– DERIVATIVES **Michigander** /ˌmɪʃɪˈgandə/ noun.

Michigan, Lake one of the five Great Lakes of North America. Bordered by Michigan, Wisconsin, Illinois, and Indiana, it is the only one of the Great Lakes to lie wholly within the US.

Michoacán /ˌmiːtʃəʊəˈkɑːn/ a state of western Mexico, on the Pacific coast; capital, Morelia.

Mick ▶ **noun** informal, offensive **1** an Irishman (often as a form of address).
2 chiefly Austral. a Roman Catholic.
– ORIGIN mid 19th cent.: pet form of the given name *Michael*.

mick ▶ **noun** Austral./NZ informal (in the game of two-up) the reverse side of a coin.
– ORIGIN early 20th cent.: of unknown origin.

mickery (also **mickerie**) ▶ **noun** (pl. **mickeries**) Austral. a waterhole or excavated well, especially in a dry riverbed.
– ORIGIN from Wangganguru (an Aboriginal language) *migiri*.

mickey¹ (also **mick**, **micky**) ▶ **noun** (in phrase **take the mickey**) Brit. informal tease or ridicule someone.
– DERIVATIVES **mickey-taking** noun.
– ORIGIN 1950s: of unknown origin.

mickey[2] ▸ **noun** informal short for MICKEY FINN: *I bet some guy slipped me a mickey.*

mickey[3] ▸ **noun** Irish informal a man's penis.
– ORIGIN early 20th cent.: pet form of the given name *Michael*.

Mickey Finn ▸ **noun** informal a surreptitiously drugged or doctored drink given to someone so as to make them drunk or unconscious. ▪ a drug used in such a drink.
– ORIGIN 1920s: of unknown origin; sometimes said to be the name of a notorious Chicago saloon keeper (*c.*1896–1906).

Mickey Mouse a Walt Disney cartoon character, who first appeared as Mortimer Mouse in 1927, becoming Mickey in 1928. During the 1930s he became established as the central Disney character. ▪ [as modifier] informal of inferior quality: *people think you're a Mickey Mouse outfit if you work from home.*

mickle (also **muckle**) archaic or Scottish & N. English ▸ **noun** a large amount.
▸ **adjective** very large.
▸ **determiner & pronoun** much; a large amount.
– PHRASES **many a little makes a mickle** (also **many a mickle makes a muckle**) proverb many small amounts accumulate to make a large amount.
– ORIGIN Old English *micel* 'great, numerous, much', of Germanic origin; from an Indo-European root shared by Greek *megas, megal-*.

USAGE The original proverb **many a little makes a mickle** was misquoted (and first recorded in the writing of George Washington, 1793) as **many a mickle makes a muckle**. While **mickle** and **muckle** are, by origin, merely variants of the same (now dialect) word meaning 'a large amount', the misquotation spawned a misunderstanding that has now become widespread: that **mickle** means 'a small amount', and **muckle** means the opposite, 'a large amount'.

micky ▸ **noun** variant spelling of MICKEY[1].

Micmac /ˈmɪkmak/ (also **Mi'kmaq**) ▸ **noun** (pl. **same** or **Micmacs**) **1** a member of an American Indian people inhabiting the Maritime Provinces of Canada. **2** [mass noun] the Algonquian language of the Micmac, now with fewer than 8,000 speakers.
▸ **adjective** relating to the Micmac or their language.
– ORIGIN via French from Micmac.

micrite /ˈmɪkrʌɪt/ ▸ **noun** [mass noun] Geology microcrystalline calcite present in some types of limestone. ▪ limestone consisting chiefly of micrite.
– ORIGIN 1950s: from *micr(ocrystalline)* + -ITE[1].

micro ▸ **noun** (pl. **micros**) **1** a microcomputer. **2** a microprocessor. **3** a very short miniskirt or minidress.
▸ **adjective** extremely small: *a micro buffet area.* ▪ small-scale: *many people think on a micro level.*

micro- ▸ **combining form 1** small: *microcar*. ▪ of reduced or restricted size: *microdot*. **2** (used in units of measurement) denoting a factor of one millionth (10^{-6}): *microfarad*.
– ORIGIN from Greek *mikros* 'small'.

microaerophilic /ˌmʌɪkrəʊˌɛːrəˈfɪlɪk/ ▸ **adjective** Biology (of a microorganism) requiring little free oxygen, or oxygen at a lower partial pressure than that of atmospheric oxygen.

microanalyser (US also **microanalyzer**) ▸ **noun** Chemistry an instrument in which a beam of electrons or other radiation is focused on to a minute area of a sample and the resulting secondary radiation (usually X-ray fluorescence) is analysed to yield chemical information.

microanalysis ▸ **noun** [mass noun] the quantitative analysis of chemical compounds using a sample of a few milligrams.
– DERIVATIVES **microanalytical** adjective.

microarray ▸ **noun** Genetics a set of DNA sequences representing the entire set of genes of an organism, arranged in a grid pattern for use in genetic testing.

microbalance ▸ **noun** a balance for weighing masses of a fraction of a gram.

microbe /ˈmʌɪkrəʊb/ ▸ **noun** a microorganism, especially a bacterium causing disease or fermentation.
– DERIVATIVES **microbial** adjective, **microbic** adjective.
– ORIGIN late 19th cent.: from French, from Greek *mikros* 'small' + *bios* 'life'.

microbiology ▸ **noun** [mass noun] the branch of science that deals with microorganisms.
– DERIVATIVES **microbiological** adjective, **microbiologically** adverb, **microbiologist** noun.

microbiota /ˌmʌɪkrəʊbʌɪˈəʊtə/ ▸ **noun** [mass noun] the microorganisms of a particular site, habitat, or geological period.

microblogging ▸ **noun** [mass noun] the posting of very short entries or updates on a blog or social networking site, typically via a mobile phone.
– DERIVATIVES **microblog** noun.

microbrew ▸ **noun** chiefly N. Amer. a type of beer produced in a microbrewery.

microbrewery ▸ **noun** (pl. **microbreweries**) chiefly N. Amer. a brewery which produces limited quantities of beer, typically for consumption on its own premises.
– DERIVATIVES **microbrewer** noun.

microbrowser ▸ **noun** an Internet browser for use with mobile phones and other handheld devices with small screens.

microburst ▸ **noun** a sudden, powerful, localized air current, especially a downdraught.

microcapsule ▸ **noun** a minute capsule used to contain drugs, dyes, or other substances and render them temporarily inactive.

microcar ▸ **noun** a small and fuel-efficient car.

microcellular ▸ **adjective** containing or made up of minute cells. ▪ (of a mobile telephone system) having small cells, typically with a radius of five hundred metres.

microcephaly /ˌmʌɪkrəʊˈsɛfəli, -ˈkɛfəli/ ▸ **noun** [mass noun] Medicine abnormal smallness of the head, a congenital condition associated with incomplete brain development.
– DERIVATIVES **microcephalic** adjective & noun, **microcephalous** adjective.

microcheck ▸ **noun** [usu. as modifier] a pattern of very small squares.

microchemistry ▸ **noun** [mass noun] the branch of chemistry concerned with the reactions and properties of substances in minute quantities, e.g. in living tissue.

microchip ▸ **noun** a tiny wafer of semiconducting material used to make an integrated circuit.
▸ **verb** (**microchips, microchipping, microchipped**) [with obj.] implant a microchip under the skin of (a domestic animal) as a means of identification.

Microchiroptera /ˌmʌɪkrəʊkʌɪˈrɒpt(ə)rə/ ▸ **plural noun** Zoology a major division of bats which comprises all but the fruit bats. ● Suborder Microchiroptera, order Chiroptera: many families.
– DERIVATIVES **microchiropteran** noun & adjective.
– ORIGIN modern Latin (plural), from MICRO- 'small' + Greek *kheir* 'hand' + *pteron* 'wing'.

microcircuit ▸ **noun** a minute electric circuit, especially an integrated circuit.
– DERIVATIVES **microcircuitry** noun.

microcirculation ▸ **noun** [mass noun] circulation of the blood in the smallest blood vessels.
– DERIVATIVES **microcirculatory** adjective.

microclimate ▸ **noun** the climate of a very small or restricted area, especially when this differs from the climate of the surrounding area.
– DERIVATIVES **microclimatic** adjective, **microclimatically** adverb.

microcline /ˈmʌɪkrə(ʊ)klʌɪn/ ▸ **noun** [mass noun] a green, pink, or brown crystalline mineral consisting of potassium-rich feldspar, characteristic of granite and pegmatites.
– ORIGIN mid 19th cent.: from German *Mikroklin*, from Greek *mikros* 'small' + *klinein* 'to lean' (because its angle of cleavage differs only slightly from 90 degrees).

micrococcus /ˌmʌɪkrəʊˈkɒkəs/ ▸ **noun** (pl. **micrococci** /-ˈkɒk(s)ʌɪ, -(s)iː/) a spherical bacterium found on dead or decaying organic matter. ● Family Micrococcaceae of Gram-positive non-motile bacteria, in particular the genera *Micrococcus* and *Staphylococcus*.
– DERIVATIVES **micrococcal** adjective.

microcode ▸ **noun** [mass noun] Computing a very low-level instruction set which is stored permanently in a computer or peripheral controller and controls the operation of the device.

microcomputer ▸ **noun** a small computer that contains a microprocessor as its central processor.

microcontinent ▸ **noun** Geology an isolated fragment of continental crust forming part of a small crust plate.

microcontroller ▸ **noun** Computing a control device which incorporates a microprocessor.

microcopy ▸ **noun** (pl. **microcopies**) a copy of printed matter that has been reduced in size by microphotography.

microcosm /ˈmʌɪkrə(ʊ)kɒz(ə)m/ ▸ **noun** a community, place, or situation regarded as encapsulating in miniature the characteristics of something much larger: *the city is a microcosm of modern Malaysia.* ▪ humankind regarded as the representation in miniature of the universe.
– DERIVATIVES **microcosmic** /-ˈkɒzmɪk/ adjective, **microcosmically** /-ˈkɒzmɪk(ə)li/ adverb.
– ORIGIN Middle English: from Old French *microcosme* or medieval Latin *microcosmus*, from Greek *mikros kosmos* 'little world'.

microcosmic salt ▸ **noun** [mass noun] Chemistry a white crystalline salt obtained from human urine. ● Hydrated sodium ammonium hydrogen phosphate; chem. formula: $HNaNH_4PO_4.4H_2O$.
– ORIGIN late 18th cent.: translating Latin *sal microcosmicus*.

microcredit ▸ **noun** [mass noun] the lending of small amounts of money at low interest to new businesses in the developing world.

microcrystalline ▸ **adjective** (of a material) formed of microscopic crystals.

microcyte /ˈmʌɪkrə(ʊ)sʌɪt, ˈmɪ-/ ▸ **noun** Medicine an unusually small red blood cell, associated with certain anaemias.
– DERIVATIVES **microcytic** adjective.

microdensitometer ▸ **noun** a densitometer for measuring the density of very small areas of a photographic image.

microdermabrasion /mʌɪkrəʊˌdəːməˈbreɪʒ(ə)n/ ▸ **noun** [mass noun] a cosmetic treatment in which the face is sprayed with exfoliant crystals to remove dead epidermal cells.

microdot ▸ **noun 1** a microphotograph, especially of a document, that is only about 1 mm across. **2** a tablet of LSD.

microeconomics ▸ **plural noun** [treated as sing.] the part of economics concerned with single factors and the effects of individual decisions.
– DERIVATIVES **microeconomic** adjective.

microelectromechanical ▸ **adjective** containing or consisting of miniature electronic and mechanical components.

microelectronics ▸ **plural noun** [usu. treated as sing.] the design, manufacture, and use of microchips and microcircuits.
– DERIVATIVES **microelectronic** adjective.

microenterprise ▸ **noun** a business operating on a very small scale, especially one in the developing world that is supported by microcredit.

micro-environment ▸ **noun** Biology the immediate small-scale environment of an organism or a part of an organism, especially as a distinct part of a larger environment.

microevolution ▸ **noun** [mass noun] Biology evolutionary change within a species or small group of organisms, especially over a short period.
– DERIVATIVES **microevolutionary** adjective.

microfarad ▸ **noun** one millionth of a farad. (Symbol: **μF**).

microfauna ▸ **noun** [mass noun] Ecology microscopic interstitial animals living in the soil.

microfibre (US also **microfiber**) ▸ **noun** a very fine synthetic yarn.

microfibril ▸ **noun** Biology a small fibril in the cytoplasm or wall of a cell, visible only under an electron microscope, and typically aggregated into coarser fibrils or structures.

microfiche /ˈmʌɪkrə(ʊ)fiːʃ/ ▸ **noun** a flat piece of film containing microphotographs of the pages of a newspaper, catalogue, or other document.
▸ **verb** [with obj.] reproduce (a document) on microfilm.

microfilament ▸ **noun** Biology a small rod-like structure, about 4–7 nanometres in diameter, present in numbers in the cytoplasm of many eukaryotic cells.

microfilaria /ˌmʌɪkrəʊfɪˈlɛːrɪə/ ▸ **noun** (pl. **microfilariae**) Zoology the minute larva of a filaria.

microfilm ▸ **noun** [mass noun] film containing microphotographs of a newspaper, catalogue, or other document.
▸ **verb** [with obj.] reproduce (a document) on microfilm.

microfinance ▸ **noun** another term for MICROCREDIT.

M

microflora ▸ **noun** [mass noun] Biology bacteria and microscopic algae and fungi, esp. those living in a particular site or habitat.

microform ▸ **noun** [mass noun] microphotographic reproduction, on film or paper, of a manuscript, map, or other document.

microfossil ▸ **noun** a fossil or fossil fragment that can only be seen with a microscope.

microfungus ▸ **noun** (pl. **microfungi**) Biology a fungus in which no sexual process has been observed or in which the reproductive organs are microscopic.

microgamete ▸ **noun** Biology (especially in protozoans) the smaller of a pair of conjugating gametes, usually regarded as male.

microglia /ˌmʌɪkrə(ʊ)ˈglʌɪə, ˌmɪ-/ ▸ **plural noun** Anatomy glial cells derived from mesoderm that function as macrophages (scavengers) in the central nervous system and form part of the reticuloendothelial system.
– DERIVATIVES **microglial** adjective.

microgram ▸ **noun** one millionth of a gram. (Symbol: **μg**)

microgranite ▸ **noun** [mass noun] Geology granite that is recognizable as crystalline only under a microscope.

micrograph ▸ **noun** a photograph taken by means of a microscope.
– DERIVATIVES **micrographic** adjective, **micrography** noun.

microgravity ▸ **noun** [mass noun] very weak gravity, as in an orbiting spacecraft.

microgroove ▸ **noun** a very narrow groove on a long-playing record.

microhabitat ▸ **noun** Ecology a habitat which is of small or limited extent and which differs in character from some surrounding more extensive habitat.

microinject ▸ **verb** [with obj.] Biology inject (a substance) into a microscopic object.
– DERIVATIVES **microinjection** noun.

microinstruction ▸ **noun** Computing a single instruction in microcode.

microinvasive ▸ **adjective** **1** Pathology (of a cancerous growth) invasive at a microscopic level.
2 Surgery denoting or relating to techniques and procedures that minimize the extent of surgical intervention.

microkernel ▸ **noun** Computing a small modular part of an operating system kernel which implements its basic features.

microlending ▸ **noun** another term for **MICROCREDIT**.
– DERIVATIVES **microlender** noun.

microlepidoptera /ˌmʌɪkrə(ʊ)lɛpɪˈdɒpt(ə)rə/ ▸ **plural noun** Entomology the numerous small moths which are of interest only to the specialist collector.
– ORIGIN modern Latin (plural), from **MICRO-** 'small' + **LEPIDOPTERA**.

microlight ▸ **noun** chiefly Brit. a very small, light, one- or two-seater aircraft.

microlith ▸ **noun** Archaeology a minute shaped flint, typically part of a composite tool such as a spear.
– DERIVATIVES **microlithic** adjective.

microlitre (US also **microliter**) ▸ **noun** one millionth of a litre. (Symbol: **μl**).

micromanage ▸ **verb** [with obj.] N. Amer. control every part, however small, of (an enterprise or activity).
– DERIVATIVES **micromanagement** noun, **micromanager** noun.

micromesh ▸ **noun** [mass noun] a material, typically nylon, consisting of a very fine mesh.

micrometeorite ▸ **noun** a micrometeoroid that has entered the earth's atmosphere.

micrometeoroid ▸ **noun** a microscopic particle in space or of extraterrestrial origin which is small enough not to burn up in the earth's atmosphere but to drift to the surface instead.

micrometeorology ▸ **noun** [mass noun] the branch of meteorology concerned with small areas and with small-scale meteorological phenomena.
– DERIVATIVES **micrometeorological** adjective.

micrometer[1] /mʌɪˈkrɒmɪtə/ ▸ **noun** a gauge which measures small distances or thicknesses between its two faces, one of which can be moved away from or towards the other by turning a screw with a fine thread.
– DERIVATIVES **micrometry** noun.

micrometer[2] ▸ **noun** US spelling of **MICROMETRE**.

micrometre /ˈmʌɪkrə(ʊ)ˌmiːtə/ (US **micrometer**) ▸ **noun** one millionth of a metre. (Symbol: **μm**)

microminiaturization (also **microminiaturisation**) ▸ **noun** [mass noun] the manufacture of extremely small versions of electronic devices.

micron /ˈmʌɪkrɒn/ ▸ **noun** a unit of length equal to one millionth of a metre, used in many technological and scientific fields.
– ORIGIN late 19th cent.: from Greek *mikron*, neuter of *mikros* 'small'.

Micronesia /ˌmʌɪkrəʊˈniːzɪə, -ˈniːʒə/ **1** a region of the western Pacific to the north of Melanesia and north and west of Polynesia. It includes the Mariana, Caroline, and Marshall island groups and Kiribati.
2 a country in the western Pacific to the north of the equator, composed of hundreds of islands in the Caroline Islands group; pop. 107,400 (est. 2009); languages, English (official), Austronesian languages; capital, Palikir. The islands were administered by the US as part of the Pacific Islands Trust Territory from 1947 and entered into free association with the US as an independent state in 1986. Full name **FEDERATED STATES OF MICRONESIA**.
– ORIGIN from Greek *mikros* 'small' + *nēsos* 'island'.

Micronesian ▸ **adjective** relating to Micronesia, its people, or their languages.
▸ **noun 1** a native of Micronesia.
2 [mass noun] the group of Austronesian languages spoken in Micronesia.

micronize /ˈmʌɪkrənʌɪz/ (also **micronise**) ▸ **verb** [with obj.] break (a substance) into very fine particles.
– DERIVATIVES **micronization** noun.

micronutrient ▸ **noun** a chemical element or substance required in trace amounts for the normal growth and development of living organisms.

microorganism ▸ **noun** a microscopic organism, especially a bacterium, virus, or fungus.

micropayment ▸ **noun** a very small payment made each time a user accesses an Internet page or service.

microphage ▸ **noun** Physiology a small phagocytic blood cell, in particular a polymorphonuclear leucocyte.

microphagous /mʌɪˈkrɒfəgəs/ ▸ **adjective** Zoology (of an invertebrate) feeding on minute particles or microorganisms.

microphone ▸ **noun** an instrument for converting sound waves into electrical energy variations which may then be amplified, transmitted, or recorded.
– DERIVATIVES **microphonic** adjective.

microphotograph ▸ **noun** a photograph reduced to a very small size.
– DERIVATIVES **microphotographic** adjective, **microphotography** noun.

microphyll /ˈmʌɪkrə(ʊ)fɪl/ ▸ **noun** Botany a very short leaf, such as in a moss or clubmoss, with a single unbranched vein and no leaf gaps in the stele.

microphysics ▸ **plural noun** [treated as sing.] the branch of physics that deals with bodies and phenomena on a microscopic or smaller scale, especially with molecules, atoms, and subatomic particles.
– DERIVATIVES **microphysical** adjective.

micropipette ▸ **noun** a very fine pipette for measuring, transferring, or injecting very small quantities of liquid.

micropore ▸ **noun** a very narrow pore, especially in a material.
– DERIVATIVES **microporosity** noun, **microporous** adjective.

micropower ▸ **noun** [mass noun] [often as modifier] electrical power which is generated or utilized in relatively small quantities: *micropower generators*.

microprint ▸ **noun** [mass noun] printed text reduced by microphotography.
– DERIVATIVES **microprinting** noun.

microprism ▸ **noun** [usu. as modifier] an area of the focusing screen of some reflex cameras which is covered with a grid of tiny prisms and splits up the image when the subject is not in focus.

microprobe ▸ **noun** another term for **MICROANALYSER**.

microprocessor ▸ **noun** an integrated circuit that contains all the functions of a central processing unit of a computer.

microprogram ▸ **noun** a microinstruction program that controls the functions of a central processing unit or peripheral controller of a computer.

micropropagation ▸ **noun** [mass noun] Botany the propagation of plants by growing plantlets in tissue culture and then planting them out.

micropsia /mʌɪˈkrɒpsɪə/ ▸ **noun** [mass noun] a condition of the eyes in which objects appear smaller than normal.
– ORIGIN mid 19th cent.: from **MICRO-** 'small' + Greek *-opsia* 'seeing'.

micropterous /mʌɪˈkrɒpt(ə)rəs/ ▸ **adjective** Entomology having small or reduced wings.

micropyle /ˈmʌɪkrə(ʊ)pʌɪl/ ▸ **noun** Botany a small opening in the surface of an ovule, through which the pollen tube penetrates, often visible as a small pore in the ripe seed. ■ Zoology a small opening in the egg of a fish, insect, etc., through which spermatozoa can enter.
– ORIGIN early 19th cent.: from **MICRO-** 'small' + Greek *pulē* 'gate'.

microreader ▸ **noun** an apparatus for producing an enlarged readable image from a microfilm or microprint.

microsatellite ▸ **noun** Genetics a set of short repeated DNA sequences at a particular locus on a chromosome, which vary in number in different individuals and so can be used for genetic fingerprinting.

microscooter ▸ **noun** a small two-wheeled foldable aluminium scooter for both children and adults.

microscope ▸ **noun** an optical instrument used for viewing very small objects, such as mineral samples or animal or plant cells, typically magnified several hundred times.
– PHRASES **under the microscope** being subjected to critical examination or analysis.
– ORIGIN mid 17th cent.: from modern Latin *microscopium* (see **MICRO-**, **-SCOPE**).

microscopic ▸ **adjective 1** so small as to be visible only with a microscope: *microscopic algae*. ■ informal extremely small: *a microscopic skirt*. ■ concerned with minute detail: *such a vision is as microscopic as his is panoramic*.
2 relating to a microscope: *microscopic soil analysis*.
– DERIVATIVES **microscopical** adjective (sense 2), **microscopically** adverb.

Microscopium /ˌmʌɪkrəˈskəʊpɪəm/ a small and inconspicuous southern constellation (the Microscope), between Piscis Austrinus and Sagittarius.
– ORIGIN modern Latin.

microscopy /mʌɪˈkrɒskəpi/ ▸ **noun** [mass noun] the use of the microscope.
– DERIVATIVES **microscopist** noun.

microsecond ▸ **noun** one millionth of a second. (Symbol.: **μs**)

microseism /ˈmʌɪkrəʊˌsʌɪz(ə)m/ ▸ **noun** Geology a very small earthquake, less than 2 on the Richter scale.
– DERIVATIVES **microseismic** adjective.

microsite ▸ **noun 1** Ecology a small, distinct area or habitat within a particular ecosystem.
2 a small auxiliary website designed to function as a supplement to a primary website.

microsome /ˈmʌɪkrəsəʊm/ ▸ **noun** Biology a fragment of endoplasmic reticulum and attached ribosomes obtained by the centrifugation of homogenized cells.
– DERIVATIVES **microsomal** adjective.

microspecies ▸ **noun** (pl. **same**) Biology a species differing only in minor characteristics from others of its group, typically one of limited geographical range forming part of an aggregate species.

microsphere ▸ **noun** a microscopic hollow sphere, especially of a protein or synthetic polymer.

microsporangium /ˌmʌɪkrə(ʊ)spəˈrandʒɪəm/ ▸ **noun** (pl. **microsporangia** /-dʒɪə/) Botany a sporangium containing microspores.

microspore ▸ **noun** Botany the smaller of the two kinds of spore produced by some ferns. See also **MEGASPORE**.

microstructure ▸ **noun** the fine structure (in a metal or other material) which can be made visible and examined with a microscope.
– DERIVATIVES **microstructural** adjective.

microsurgery ▸ **noun** [mass noun] intricate surgery performed using miniaturized instruments and a microscope.
– DERIVATIVES **microsurgeon** noun, **microsurgical** adjective.

microswitch ▸ **noun** a very sensitive electric switch that can be operated rapidly by a small movement.

microtechnology ▸ **noun** [mass noun] technology that uses microelectronics.

microtome /ˈmʌɪkrə(ʊ)təʊm/ ▸ **noun** chiefly Biology an instrument for cutting extremely thin sections of material for examination under a microscope.

microtone ▶ noun Music an interval smaller than a semitone.
– DERIVATIVES **microtonal** adjective, **microtonality** noun, **microtonally** adverb.

microtubule ▶ noun Biology a microscopic tubular structure present in numbers in the cytoplasm of cells, sometimes aggregating to form more complex structures.

microvascular ▶ adjective relating to the smallest blood vessels.

microvillus ▶ noun (pl. **microvilli** /-lʌɪ, -liː/) Biology each of a large number of minute projections from the surface of some cells.
– DERIVATIVES **microvillar** adjective.

microwave ▶ noun an electromagnetic wave with a wavelength in the range 0.001–0.3 m, shorter than that of a normal radio wave but longer than those of infrared radiation. Microwaves are used in radar, in communications, and for heating in microwave ovens and in various industrial processes. ■ (also **microwave oven**) an oven that uses microwaves to cook or heat food.
▶ verb [with obj.] cook (food) in a microwave oven.
– DERIVATIVES **microwaveable** (also **microwavable**) adjective.

microwave background ▶ noun Astronomy a weak uniform microwave radiation which is detectable in nearly every direction of the sky. It is believed to be evidence of the Big Bang.

micrurgy /ˈmʌɪkrəːdʒi/ ▶ noun [mass noun] Biology the manipulation of individual cells under a microscope.
– ORIGIN 1920s: from MICRO- 'small' + Greek *-ourgia* 'work'.

micturate /ˈmɪktjʊreɪt/ ▶ verb [no obj.] formal urinate.
– DERIVATIVES **micturition** noun.
– ORIGIN mid 19th cent.: back-formation from *micturition*, from Latin *micturit-* 'urinated', from the verb *micturire*.

mid¹ ▶ adjective [attrib.] of or in the middle part or position of a range: *the mid 17th century* | [in combination] *mid-brown hair*. ■ Phonetics (of a vowel) pronounced with the tongue neither high nor low: *a mid central vowel*.

mid² ▶ preposition literary in the middle of. ■ in the course of.
– ORIGIN Shortening of AMID.

mid- ▶ combining form denoting the middle of: *midsection*. ■ in the middle; medium; half: *midway*.
– ORIGIN Old English *midd*, of Germanic origin; from an Indo-European root shared by Latin *medius* and Greek *mesos*.

mid-air ▶ noun a part or section of the air above ground level or above another surface: *the plane exploded in mid-air* | [as modifier] *a mid-air collision*.

Midas /ˈmʌɪdəs/ Greek Mythology a king of Phrygia, who, according to one story, was given by Dionysus the power of turning everything he touched into gold.
– PHRASES **the Midas touch** the ability to make money out of anything one undertakes.

mid-Atlantic ▶ adjective **1** situated or occurring in the middle of the Atlantic ocean: *the mid-Atlantic fault line*.
2 having characteristics of both Britain and America: *mid-Atlantic accents*.
3 relating to states in the middle of the Atlantic coast of the United States, including New York, Pennsylvania, New Jersey, West Virginia, Delaware, and Maryland.

Mid-Atlantic Ridge a submarine ridge system extending the length of the Atlantic Ocean from the Arctic to the Antarctic. It is seismically and (in places) volcanically active; the islands of Iceland, the Azores, Ascension, St Helena, and Tristan da Cunha are situated on it.

midbrain ▶ noun Anatomy a small central part of the brainstem, developing from the middle of the primitive or embryonic brain. Also called MESENCEPHALON.

midday ▶ noun the middle of the day; noon: *he awoke at midday* | [as modifier] *the midday sun*.
– ORIGIN Old English *middæg* (see MID-, DAY).

middelmannetjie /ˈmɛd(ə)l,manəki/ ▶ noun (pl. **middelmannetjies**) S. African a ridge between the wheel ruts of an unsurfaced road.
– ORIGIN Afrikaans, literally 'little man in the middle'.

midden /ˈmɪd(ə)n/ ▶ noun a dunghill or refuse heap. ■ short for KITCHEN MIDDEN.
– ORIGIN late Middle English *myddyng*, of Scandinavian origin; compare with Danish *mødding* 'muck heap'.

middle ▶ adjective [attrib.] **1** at an equal distance from the extremities of something; central: *the early and middle part of life* | *middle and eastern Europe*. ■ (of a member of a group or sequence) placed so as to have the same number of members on each side: *the woman was in her middle forties*. ■ intermediate in rank, quality, or ability: *there is a dearth of talent at middle level*. ■ (of a language) of the period between the old and modern forms: *Middle High German*.
2 Grammar denoting a voice of verbs in some languages, such as Greek, which expresses reciprocal or reflexive action. ■ denoting a transitive verb in English which does not have an equivalent passive, e.g. *had* in *he had an idea*.
▶ noun **1** [usu. in sing.] the point or position at an equal distance from the sides, edges, or ends of something: *she stood alone in the middle of the street*. ■ the point at or around the centre of a period of time, activity, etc.: *we were married in the middle of December*. ■ informal a person's waist and stomach: *he had a towel round his middle*.
2 Grammar the form or voice of a verb expressing reflexive or reciprocal action.
▶ verb [with obj.] (in cricket, tennis, etc.) strike (the ball) with the middle of the bat, racket, or club.
– PHRASES **down the middle** divided or dividing something equally into two parts. **in the middle of** in the process of doing (something). ■ involved in (something, typically something unpleasant): *he was caught in the middle of the emotional triangle*. **the middle of nowhere** informal a place that is very remote. **steer** (or **take**) **a middle course** adopt a policy which avoids extremes.
– ORIGIN Old English *middel*, of West Germanic origin; related to Dutch *middel* and German *Mittel*, also to MID¹.

middle age ▶ noun [mass noun] the period after early adulthood and before old age, about 45 to 65.
– DERIVATIVES **middle-aged** adjective.

middle-aged spread (also **middle-age spread**) ▶ noun [mass noun] the fat that may accumulate around the abdomen in middle age.

Middle Ages ▶ plural noun the period of European history from the fall of the Roman Empire in the West (5th century) to the fall of Constantinople (1453), or, more narrowly, from *c.*1000 to 1453.

> The earlier part of the period (c.500–c.1100) is sometimes distinguished as the Dark Ages, while the later part (c.1100–1453) is often thought of as the Middle Ages proper. The whole period is characterized by the emergence of separate kingdoms, the growth of trade and urban life, and the growth in power of monarchies and the Church. The growth of interest in classical models within art and scholarship in the 15th century is seen as marking the transition to the Renaissance period and the end of the Middle Ages.

Middle America ▶ noun [mass noun] **1** the middle class in the United States, regarded as a conservative political force. ■ the Midwest of the United States, regarded as the home of the conservative middle class.
2 Mexico and Central America.
– DERIVATIVES **Middle American** adjective & noun.

middlebrow often derogatory ▶ adjective demanding, involving, or having only a moderate degree of intellectual application: *middlebrow fiction*.
▶ noun a middlebrow person.

middle C ▶ noun Music the C near the middle of the piano keyboard, written on the first leger line below the treble stave or the first leger line above the bass stave.

middle class ▶ noun [treated as sing. or pl.] the social group between the upper and working classes, including professional and business people and their families.
▶ adjective relating to the middle class: *a middle-class suburb*. ■ characteristic of the middle class, especially in attaching importance to convention, security, and material comfort: *a rebellion against middle-class values*.
– DERIVATIVES **middle-classness** noun.

middle common room ▶ noun Brit. a common room for the use of postgraduate students in a university or college.

Middle Congo see CONGO (sense 2).

middle distance ▶ noun **1** (**the middle distance**) the part of a real or painted landscape between the foreground and the background.
2 [as modifier] Athletics denoting or relating to a race distance of between 800 and 5,000 metres: *middle-distance runners*.

Middle Dutch ▶ noun [mass noun] the Dutch language from *c.*1100–1500.

middle ear ▶ noun the air-filled central cavity of the ear, behind the eardrum.

Middle East an extensive area of SW Asia and northern Africa, stretching from the Mediterranean to Pakistan and including the Arabian peninsula.
– DERIVATIVES **Middle Eastern** adjective.

middle eight ▶ noun a short section (typically of eight bars) in the middle of a conventionally structured popular song, generally of a different character from the other parts of the song.

Middle England ▶ noun the middle classes in England outside London, especially as representative of conservative political views.
– DERIVATIVES **Middle Englander** noun.

Middle English ▶ noun [mass noun] the English language from *c.*1150 to *c.*1470.

Middle-European ▶ adjective relating to central Europe or its people.

middle finger ▶ noun the finger next to the forefinger.

middle game ▶ noun the phase of a chess game after the opening, when all or most of the pieces and pawns remain on the board.

middle ground ▶ noun (usu. **the middle ground**) **1** an intermediate position or area of compromise or possible agreement between two opposing views or groups: *each party wants to capture the votes of those occupying the middle ground*.
2 the middle distance of a painting or photograph.

Middle High German ▶ noun [mass noun] the language of southern Germany from *c.*1200–1500.

Middle Kingdom **1** a period of ancient Egyptian history (*c.*2040–1640 BC, 11th–14th dynasty).
2 historical China or its eighteen inner provinces.

middle life ▶ noun [mass noun] middle age.

Middle Low German ▶ noun [mass noun] the Low German language (spoken in northern Germany) from *c.*1200–1500.

M

middleman ▶ noun (pl. **middlemen**) a person who buys goods from producers and sells them to retailers or consumers: *we maintain value for money by cutting out the middleman and selling direct*. ■ a person who arranges business or political deals between other people.

middle management ▶ noun [mass noun] the managers in an organization at a level between senior and junior managers.
– DERIVATIVES **middle manager** noun.

middle name ▶ noun a person's name placed after the first name and before the surname. ■ a quality for which a person is notable: *optimism is my middle name*.

middle-of-the-road ▶ adjective avoiding extremes; moderate: *the paper reflected the views of its middle-of-the-road readers*. ■ (of music) tuneful but somewhat bland and unadventurous.

middle passage ▶ noun historical the sea journey undertaken by slave ships from West Africa to the West Indies.

Middle Persian ▶ noun [mass noun] the Persian language from *c.*300 BC to AD 800. See also PAHLAVI².

Middlesbrough /ˈmɪd(ə)lzbrə/ a port in NE England, on the estuary of the River Tees; pop. 140,200 (est. 2009).

middlescent /ˌmɪdəˈlɛs(ə)nt/ ▶ adjective middle-aged, but typically still maintaining the interests and activities of younger people.
– ORIGIN 1960s: blend of MIDDLE + ADOLESCENT.

middle school ▶ noun **1** (in the UK) a school for children from about 9 to 13 years old.
2 (in the US and Canada) a junior high school.

Middlesex a former county of SE England, situated to the north west of London. In 1965 it was divided between Hertfordshire, Surrey, and Greater London.

middle-sized ▶ adjective of medium size: *a middle-sized farm*.

Middle Stone Age the Mesolithic period.

Middle Temple one of the two Inns of Court on the site of the Temple in London, England. Compare with INNER TEMPLE.

middle term ▶ noun Logic the term common to both premises of a syllogism.

Middleton, Thomas (*c.*1570–1627), English dramatist. He is best known for the tragedies *The Changeling* (1622), written with the dramatist William Rowley, and *Women Beware Women* (1620–7).

middleveld /ˈmɪd(ə)lvɛlt/ ▶ noun [mass noun] a region of veld situated at an intermediate altitude, especially the region in north-eastern South Africa, between 900 and 1200 m (3000 and 4000 ft) above sea level.
– ORIGIN late 19th cent.: partial translation of Afrikaans *middelveld*.

middleware ▶ noun [mass noun] Computing software that acts as a bridge between an operating system or database and applications, especially on a network.

middle watch ▶ noun the period from midnight to 4 a.m. on board a ship.

middle way ▶ noun **1** a policy or course of action which avoids extremes: *there is no middle way between central planning and capitalism.*
2 (**the Middle Way**) the eightfold path of Buddhism between indulgence and asceticism.

middleweight ▶ noun [mass noun] a weight in boxing and other sports intermediate between welterweight and light heavyweight. In the amateur boxing scale it ranges from 71–5 kg. ■ [count noun] a middleweight boxer or other competitor.

Middle West another term for **MIDWEST**.

middle youth ▶ noun [mass noun] the time of life between early adulthood and middle age.

middling ▶ adjective moderate or average in size, amount, or rank: *people on middling incomes.* ■ neither very good nor very bad: *he had had a **good to middling** season.*
▶ noun (**middlings**) bulk goods of medium grade, especially flour of medium fineness.
▶ adverb [as submodifier] informal, dated fairly or moderately: *middling rich.*
– DERIVATIVES **middlingly** adverb.
– ORIGIN late Middle English (originally Scots): probably from **MID-** + the adverbial suffix *-ling*.

Middx ▶ abbreviation Middlesex.

M

middy[1] ▶ noun (pl. **middies**) **1** informal a midshipman.
2 (also **middy blouse**) chiefly historical a woman's or child's loose blouse with a sailor collar.

middy[2] ▶ noun (pl. **middies**) Austral. informal a beer glass containing half a pint (285 ml).
– ORIGIN so named because it is considered to be a medium-sized measure.

Mideast US term for **MIDDLE EAST**.

mid-engined ▶ adjective (of a car) having the engine located centrally between the front and rear axles.

mid-European ▶ adjective another term for **MIDDLE-EUROPEAN**.

midfield ▶ noun (chiefly in soccer) the central part of the field. ■ the players on a team who play in a central position between attack and defence.
– DERIVATIVES **midfielder** noun.

Midgard /ˈmɪdɡɑːd/ Scandinavian Mythology the region, encircled by the sea, in which human beings live; the earth.

Midgard's serpent Scandinavian Mythology a monstrous serpent that was the offspring of Loki and was thrown by Odin into the sea, where, with its tail in its mouth, it encircled the earth.

midge ▶ noun **1** a small or minute two-winged fly that forms swarms and breeds near water or marshy areas. ● The families Chironomidae (the **non-biting midges**), and Ceratopogonidae (see **BITING MIDGE**): numerous species.
■ [with modifier] used in names of other small flies whose larvae can be pests of plants, typically producing galls or damaging leaves.
2 informal a small person.
– ORIGIN Old English *mycg(e)*, of Germanic origin; related to Dutch *mug* and German *Mücke*, from an Indo-European root shared by Latin *musca* and Greek *muia* 'fly'.

midget ▶ noun a very small person or thing. ■ offensive a person affected by dwarfism.
▶ adjective very small: *a midget submarine.* ■ Canadian denoting a level of amateur sport typically involving children aged between sixteen and seventeen: *midget hockey.*
– ORIGIN mid 19th cent.: from **MIDGE** + **-ET**[1].

Mid Glamorgan a former county of South Wales formed in 1974 from parts of Breconshire, Glamorgan, and Monmouthshire and dissolved in 1996.

midgut ▶ noun Zoology the middle part of the alimentary canal, including (in vertebrates) the small intestine.

midheaven ▶ noun Astrology (on an astrological chart) the point where the ecliptic intersects the meridian.

MIDI ▶ noun [mass noun] [usu. as modifier] a widely used standard for interconnecting electronic musical instruments and computers: *a MIDI controller.*
– ORIGIN 1980s: acronym from *musical instrument digital interface.*

Midi /ˈmɪdi/ the south of France.
– ORIGIN French, literally 'midday'; compare with **MEZZOGIORNO**.

midi ▶ noun (pl. **midis**) a woman's calf-length skirt, dress, or coat.
– ORIGIN 1960s: from **MID**[1], on the pattern of *maxi* and *mini.*

midi- ▶ combining form medium-sized; of medium length: *midibus | midi-skirt.*
– ORIGIN from **MIDDLE**, on the pattern of *maxi-* and *mini-*.

midibus ▶ noun a bus seating up to about twenty-five passengers.

midinette /ˌmɪdɪˈnɛt/, French /midinɛt/ ▶ noun a seamstress or assistant in a Parisian fashion house.
– ORIGIN French, from *midi* 'midday' + *dînette* 'light dinner' (because only a short break was taken at lunchtime).

Midi-Pyrénées /ˌmɪdɪˌpɪrəˈneɪ/, French /midipiʀene/ a region of southern France, between the Pyrenees and the Massif Central, centred on Toulouse.

midiron ▶ noun Golf an iron with a medium degree of loft, such as a four-, five-, or six-iron.

midi system ▶ noun Brit. a set of compact stacking hi-fi equipment components.

midland ▶ noun the middle part of a country. ■ (**the Midlands**) the inland counties of central England. ■ (**Midland**) a part of the central United States, roughly bounded by Illinois, South Carolina, and Delaware.
▶ adjective of or in the middle part of a country. ■ (**Midland**) of or in the English Midlands. ■ (**Midland**) of or in the Midland of the United States.
– DERIVATIVES **midlander** noun.

midlife ▶ noun [mass noun] the central period of a person's life, between around 45 and 60 years old.

midlife crisis ▶ noun a loss of self-confidence and feeling of anxiety or disappointment that can occur in early middle age.

midline ▶ noun [often as modifier] a median line or plane of bilateral symmetry, especially that of the body: *the abdomen was opened by midline incision.*

Midlothian /mɪdˈləʊðɪən/ a council area and former county of central Scotland; administrative centre, Dalkeith.

midmost ▶ adjective & adverb literary in the very middle.

midnight ▶ noun twelve o'clock at night: *I left at midnight.* ■ [often as modifier] the middle period of the night: *the midnight hours.*
– ORIGIN Old English *midniht* (see **MID-**, **NIGHT**).

midnight blue ▶ noun [mass noun] a very dark blue.

midnight feast ▶ noun a meal eaten late at night, especially in secret by children.

midnight Mass ▶ noun a mass celebrated at or shortly before midnight, especially on Christmas Eve.

midnight sun ▶ noun the sun when seen at midnight during the summer in either the Arctic or Antarctic Circle.

mid-ocean ridge ▶ noun Geology a long, seismically active submarine ridge system situated in the middle of an ocean basin and marking the site of the upwelling of magma associated with sea-floor spreading. An example is the Mid-Atlantic Ridge.

mid-off ▶ noun Cricket a fielding position on the off side near the bowler. ■ a fielder at mid-off.

mid-on ▶ noun Cricket a fielding position on the on side near the bowler. ■ a fielder at mid-on.

midpoint ▶ noun the exact middle point: *the midpoint of each face of a cube.* ■ a point somewhere in the middle: *he would have been at the midpoint in his career.*

mid range ▶ noun **1** Statistics the arithmetic mean of the largest and the smallest values in a sample or other group.
2 the middle part of the range of audible frequencies.
▶ adjective (of a product) in the middle of a range of products with regard to size, quality, or price.

Midrash /ˈmɪdraʃ, -rʌʃ/ ▶ noun (pl. **Midrashim** /-ʃɪm/) an ancient commentary on part of the Hebrew scriptures, attached to the biblical text. The earliest Midrashim come from the 2nd century AD, although much of their content is older.
– ORIGIN from Hebrew *miḏrāš* 'commentary', from *dāraš* 'expound'.

midrib ▶ noun a large strengthened vein along the midline of a leaf.

midriff ▶ noun the region of the front of the body between the chest and the waist. ■ Anatomy, dated the diaphragm.
– ORIGIN Old English *midhrif*, from **MID**[1] + *hrif* 'belly'.

midsection ▶ noun the middle part of something. ■ the midriff.

midship ▶ noun [usu. as modifier] the middle part of a ship or boat: *her powerful midship section.*

midshipman ▶ noun (pl. **midshipmen**) **1** a rank of officer in the Royal Navy, above naval cadet and below sub lieutenant. [early 17th cent.: so named because the officer was stationed amidships.] ■ a naval cadet in the US navy.
2 an American toadfish with dorsal and anal fins that run most of the length of the body and rows of light organs on the underside. ● Genus *Porichthys*, family *Batrachoididae*: two or three species.

midships ▶ adverb & adjective another term for **AMIDSHIPS**.

mid shot ▶ noun Photography a shot taken at a medium distance.

midsize (also **midsized**) ▶ adjective chiefly N. Amer. of an average size; intermediate in size between large and small: *a midsize car.*

midsole ▶ noun a layer of material between the inner and outer soles of a shoe, for absorbing shock.

midst ▶ preposition archaic or literary in the middle of.
▶ noun the middle part or point: *he left his flat **in the midst of** a rainstorm.*
– PHRASES **in our** (or **your**, **their**, etc.) **midst** among us (or you or them).
– ORIGIN late Middle English: from *in middes* 'in the middle'.

midstream ▶ noun [mass noun] the middle of a stream or river: *the ferry was moving out **into midstream**.*
▶ adjective Medicine (of urine) passed in the middle part of an act of urinating.
– PHRASES **in midstream** part-way through the course of an activity, process, etc.: *our conversation was interrupted in midstream.*

midsummer ▶ noun the middle part of summer: *the plant blooms in midsummer.* ■ the summer solstice.
– ORIGIN Old English *midsumor* (see **MID-**, **SUMMER**[1]).

Midsummer Day (Brit. also **Midsummer's Day**) ▶ noun 24 June, a quarter day in England, Wales, and Ireland, originally coinciding with the summer solstice and in some countries marked by a summer festival.

midsummer madness ▶ noun [mass noun] foolish or reckless behaviour, considered to be at its height at midsummer.

midterm ▶ noun the middle of a period of office, an academic term, or a pregnancy: *Nixon resigned **in midterm** | [as modifier] midterm elections.* ■ N. Amer. an exam in the middle of an academic term.

midtown ▶ noun [usu. as modifier] N. Amer. the central part of a city between the downtown and uptown areas: *a huge midtown apartment.*

mid-Victorian ▶ adjective relating to the middle of the Victorian era.

midway ▶ adverb & adjective in or towards the middle of something: [as adv.] *Peter came to a halt midway down the street* | [as adj.] *midway profits soared from £130 m to £160 m.* ■ having some of the characteristics of one thing and some of another: [as adj.] *a midway path between the two factions* | [as adv.] *the leaves have a unique smell **midway between** eucalyptus and mint.*
▶ noun N. Amer. an area of sideshows or other amusements at a fair or exhibition.

Midway Islands two small islands with a surrounding coral atoll, in the central Pacific in the western part of the Hawaiian chain. The islands were annexed by the US in 1867 and remain a US territory and naval base. They were the scene in 1942 of the decisive Battle of Midway, in which the US navy repelled a Japanese invasion fleet.

midweek ▶ noun the middle of the week, usually regarded as being from Tuesday to Thursday: *he scored twice for the reserves* ***in midweek***.
▶ adjective & adverb in the middle of the week: [as adj.] *a special midweek reduction* | [as adv.] *we have opportunities to fish midweek.*

Midwest the region of northern states of the US from Ohio west to the Rocky Mountains. Formerly called **Far West**.
– DERIVATIVES **Midwestern** adjective, **Midwesterner** noun.

midwicket ▶ noun Cricket a fielding position on the leg side, level with the middle of the pitch. ■ a fielder at midwicket.

midwife ▶ noun (pl. **midwives**) a nurse (typically a woman) who is trained to assist women in childbirth. ■ a person who helps to create or develop something: *he survived to be one of the midwives of the Reformation.*
▶ verb [with obj.] assist (a woman) during childbirth. ■ help to bring about: *Gruber midwifed the deal.*
– DERIVATIVES **midwifery** /-'wɪf(ə)ri/ noun.
– ORIGIN Middle English: probably from the obsolete preposition *mid* 'with' + **wife** (in the archaic sense 'woman'), expressing the sense 'a woman who is with (the mother)'.

midwife toad ▶ noun a European toad, the male of which has a distinctive piping call in spring and carries the developing eggs wrapped around his hind legs. ● *Alytes obstetricans*, family Discoglossidae.

midwinter ▶ noun the middle part of winter: *in* ***midwinter*** *the track became a muddy morass.* ■ the winter solstice.
– ORIGIN Old English (see **mid-**, **winter**).

mielie ▶ noun variant spelling of **mealie**.

Mien /mjɛn/ ▶ noun another term for **Yao**².

mien /miːn/ ▶ noun a person's appearance or manner, especially as an indication of their character or mood: *he has a cautious, academic mien.*
– ORIGIN early 16th cent.: probably from French *mine* 'expression', influenced by obsolete *demean* 'bearing, demeanour' (from **demean**²).

Mies van der Rohe /ˌmiːz van də 'rəʊə/, German /ˌmiːs van deːɐ 'roːə/, Ludwig (1886–1969), German-born architect and designer. He designed the German pavilion at the 1929 International Exhibition at Barcelona and the Seagram Building in New York (1954–8), and was noted for his tubular steel furniture. He was director of the Bauhaus 1930–3.
– DERIVATIVES **Miesian** adjective.

mifepristone /ˌmɪfɛ'prɪstəʊn/ ▶ noun [mass noun] Medicine a synthetic steroid that inhibits the action of progesterone, given orally in early pregnancy to induce abortion. Also called **RU486** (trademark).
– ORIGIN 1980s: probably from Dutch *mifepriston*, from *mife-* (representing *aminophenol*) + *-pr-* (representing *propyl*) + *ist-* (representing **oestradiol**) + **-one**.

miff ▶ verb [with obj.] informal annoy: *I'll confess it miffed me slightly at the time.*
▶ noun archaic a petty quarrel or fit of pique.
– ORIGIN early 17th cent.: perhaps imitative; compare with early modern German *muff*, an exclamation of disgust.

miffed ▶ adjective informal somewhat annoyed; peeved: *she turned around, looking slightly miffed* | *she was* ***miffed at*** *not being invited.*

miffy ▶ adjective informal easily annoyed or irritated.

might¹ ▶ modal verb (3rd sing. present **might**) **1** past of **may**¹, used especially. ■ in reported speech, to express possibility or permission: *he said he might be late.* ■ expressing a possibility based on an unfulfilled condition: *we might have won if we'd played better.* ■ expressing annoyance about something that someone has not done: *you might have told me!* ■ expressing purpose: *he avoided social engagements so that he might work.*
2 used to tentatively ask permission or express a polite request: *might I just ask one question?* | *you might just call me Jane, if you don't mind.* ■ asking for information, especially condescendingly: *and who might you be?*
3 used to express possibility or make a suggestion: *this might be true* | *you might try pain relievers.*
– PHRASES **might as well 1** used to make an unenthusiastic suggestion: *I might as well begin.* **2** used to indicate that a situation is the same as if the hypothetical thing stated were true: *for readers seeking illumination, this book might as well have been written in Serbo-Croatian.* **might have known** (or **guessed**) used to express one's lack of surprise about something: *I might have known it was you.*

> **USAGE** On the distinction between **might** and **may**, see **usage** at **may**¹
> For a discussion of the use of **might of** instead of **might have**, see **usage** at **have**.

might² ▶ noun [mass noun] great and impressive power or strength, especially of a nation, large organization, or natural force: *a convincing display of military might.*
– PHRASES **might is right** those who are powerful can do what they wish unchallenged, even if their action is in fact unjustified. **with all one's might** using all one's power or strength. **with might and main** with all one's strength or power.
– ORIGIN Old English *miht*, *mieht*, of Germanic origin; related to **may**¹.

might-have-been ▶ noun informal an event or situation that could have happened or existed but did not.

mightily ▶ adverb **1** with a lot of force; fiercely: *Holly struggled mightily with her mother over doing her homework.*
2 to a great or impressive extent; enormously: *this little town has contributed mightily to the life of the nation* | [as submodifier] *I am mightily relieved that it is all over.*

mightn't ▶ contraction might not: *you mightn't believe it, but I saw him stop a fight.*

mighty ▶ adjective (**mightier**, **mightiest**) possessing great and impressive power or strength, especially because of size: *three mighty industrial countries* | *mighty beasts.* ■ (of an action) performed with or requiring great strength: *a mighty blow.* ■ informal very large: *a mighty £450.*
▶ adverb [as submodifier] informal, chiefly N. Amer. extremely: *my ears got cold mighty fast.*
– DERIVATIVES **mightiness** noun.
– ORIGIN Old English *mihtig* (see **might**², **-y**¹).

migmatite /'mɪgmətʌɪt/ ▶ noun Geology a rock composed of two intermingled but distinguishable components, typically a granitic rock within a metamorphic host rock.
– ORIGIN early 20th cent.: from Greek *migma*, *migmat-* 'mixture' + **-ite**¹.

mignonette /ˌmɪnjə'nɛt/ ▶ noun a herbaceous plant with spikes of small fragrant greenish flowers. ● Genus *Reseda*, family Resedaceae: several species, in particular the North African *R. odorata*, which is cultivated as an ornamental and for its essential oil, and the European **wild mignonette** (*R. lutea*).
– ORIGIN early 18th cent.: from French *mignonnette*, diminutive of *mignon* 'small and sweet'.

migraine /'miːgreɪn, 'mʌɪ-/ ▶ noun a recurrent throbbing headache that typically affects one side of the head and is often accompanied by nausea and disturbed vision.
– DERIVATIVES **migrainous** adjective.
– ORIGIN late Middle English: from French, via late Latin from Greek *hēmikrania*, from *hēmi-* 'half' + *kranion* 'skull'.

migraineur /ˌmiːgreɪ'nəː/ ▶ noun a person who suffers from migraine.

migrant ▶ noun **1** a person who moves from one place to another in order to find work or better living conditions.
2 an animal that migrates.
▶ adjective tending to migrate or having migrated: *migrant birds.*

migrant labour system ▶ noun chiefly historical (in South Africa) the laws and structures under which black contract labourers from rural areas, the homelands, or neighbouring states were recruited to work in the cities and mines.

migrate /mʌɪ'greɪt, 'mʌɪgreɪt/ ▶ verb [no obj.] **1** (of an animal, typically a bird or fish) move from one region or habitat to another according to the seasons: *as autumn arrives, the birds migrate south.* ■ (of a person) move to a new area or country in order to find work or better living conditions: *rural populations have* ***migrated to*** *urban areas.*
2 move from one part of something to another: *cells which can form pigment migrate beneath the skin.* ■ (with reference to computer users) change or cause to change from one system to another. ■ [with obj.] Computing transfer (programs or hardware) from one system to another.
– DERIVATIVES **migrator** noun.
– ORIGIN early 17th cent. (in the general sense 'move from one place to another'): from Latin *migrat-* 'moved, shifted', from the verb *migrare*.

migration /mʌɪ'greɪʃ(ə)n/ ▶ noun **1** seasonal movement of animals from one region to another: *this butterfly's annual migration across North America.* ■ movement of people to a new area or country in order to find work or better living conditions.
2 movement from one part of something to another: *there is virtually no cell migration in plants.*
– DERIVATIVES **migrational** adjective.

migratory /'mʌɪgrət(ə)ri, mʌɪ'greɪt(ə)ri/ ▶ adjective denoting an animal that migrates: *migratory birds.* ■ relating to animal migration: *the migratory route for whale sharks.*

Mihailović /mɪ'hʌɪləvɪtʃ/, Draža (1893–1946), Yugoslav soldier; full name *Dragoljub Mihailović*. Leader of the Chetniks during the Second World War, in 1941 he became Minister of War for the Yugoslav government in exile. After the war he was executed on the charge of collaboration with the Germans.

mihrab /'miːrɑːb/ ▶ noun a niche in the wall of a mosque, at the point nearest to Mecca, towards which the congregation faces to pray.
– ORIGIN from Arabic *miḥrāb* 'place for prayer'.

mikado /mɪ'kɑːdəʊ/ ▶ noun historical a title given to the emperor of Japan.
– ORIGIN Japanese, from *mi* 'august' + *kado* 'gate' (the gate of the Imperial palace being a place where the emperor traditionally held audiences). Compare with **Porte**.

Mike ▶ noun a code word representing the letter M, used in radio communication.

mike¹ informal ▶ noun a microphone.
▶ verb [with obj.] supply or equip with a microphone: *the minister was already* ***miked up*** *for the interview.*
– ORIGIN 1920s: abbreviation.

mike² Brit. informal, dated ▶ verb [no obj.] idle away one's time: *he thundered at anyone he thought was miking.*
▶ noun a period of idleness.
– ORIGIN early 19th cent.: of unknown origin.

Mi'kmaq ▶ noun & adjective variant spelling of **Micmac**.

Míkonos /'mikɒnɒs/ Greek name for **Mykonos**.

mikva /'mɪkvə/ ▶ noun a bath in which certain Jewish ritual purifications are performed.
– ORIGIN mid 19th cent.: from Yiddish *mikve*, from Hebrew *miqweh*, literally 'collection (usually of water)'.

mil¹ ▶ abbreviation informal ■ millimetres. ■ millilitres. ■ (used in sums of money) millions: *the insurance company coughed up five mil.*

mil² ▶ noun one thousandth of an inch.
– ORIGIN late 17th cent.: from Latin *millesimum* 'thousandth', from *mille* 'thousand'.

Milad ▶ noun variant form of **Mawlid**.

milady /mɪ'leɪdi/ ▶ noun (pl. **miladies**) historical or humorous used to address or refer to an English noblewoman or great lady: *I went off to milady's boudoir.*
– ORIGIN late 18th cent.: via French from English *my lady*; compare with **milord**.

milage ▶ noun variant spelling of **mileage**.

Milan /mɪ'lan/ a city in NW Italy, capital of Lombardy region; pop. 1,295,705 (2008). A powerful city in the past, particularly from the 13th to the 15th centuries, Milan is today a leading financial and commercial centre. Italian name **Milano** /mi'lanɔ/.
– DERIVATIVES **Milanese** adjective & noun.

Milan, Edict of an edict made by the Roman emperor Constantine in 313 which recognized Christianity and gave freedom of worship in the Roman Empire.

Milanese silk ▶ noun [mass noun] finely knitted silk or viscose.

milch /mɪltʃ/ ▶ adjective denoting a cow or other domestic mammal giving or kept for milk.
– ORIGIN Middle English: from Old English *-milce*, only in *thrimilce* 'May' (when cows could be milked three times a day), from the Germanic base of **milk**.

milch cow ▶ noun a person or organization that is a source of easy profit: *governments throughout the world are privatizing their milch cows.*

mild ▶ adjective **1** not severe, serious, or harsh: *mild criticism* | *mild flu-like symptoms.* ■ (of weather) moderately warm, especially less cold than expected: *mild winters.* ■ (of a feeling) not intense or extreme: *she looked at him in mild surprise.* ■ (of a medicine or cosmetic) acting gently. ■ (of food, drink, or

M

tobacco) not sharp, hot, or strong in flavour: *a mild Italian cheese.*
2 gentle and not easily provoked: *she was implacable, despite her mild exterior.*
▶ **noun** [mass noun] Brit. a kind of dark beer not strongly flavoured with hops.
– DERIVATIVES **mildish** adjective.
– ORIGIN Old English *milde* (originally in the sense 'gracious, not severe in command'), of Germanic origin; related to Dutch and German *mild*, from an Indo-European root shared by Latin *mollis* and Greek *malthakos* 'soft'.

mildew ▶ **noun** [mass noun] a thin whitish coating consisting of minute fungal hyphae, growing on plants or damp organic material such as paper.
▶ **verb** affect or be affected with mildew.
– DERIVATIVES **mildewed** adjective.
– ORIGIN Old English *mildēaw* 'honeydew', of Germanic origin. The first element is related to Latin *mel* and Greek *meli* 'honey'.

mildewy ▶ **adjective** affected by mildew; mouldy: *the first room had a mildewy smell to it.*

mildly ▶ **adverb** in a mild or gentle manner. ■ not seriously: *he had suffered mildly from the illness since he was 23.* ■ [as submodifier] to a slight extent: *he kept his voice mildly curious.*
– PHRASES **to put it mildly** (or **putting it mildly**) used to imply that the reality is more extreme, usually worse: *the proposals were, to put it mildly, unpopular.*

mild-mannered ▶ **adjective** (of a person) gentle and not given to extremes of emotion.

mildness ▶ **noun** [mass noun] **1** lack of intensity: *the tomatoes were sweet, compensating for the mildness of the cheese.*
2 lack of severity: *the mildness of her disease.* ■ relative warmth of weather.
3 a person's lack of aggressiveness: *the mildness of his manner and his desire to please everyone.*

mild steel ▶ **noun** [mass noun] steel which contains only a small percentage of carbon and is strong and easily worked but not readily tempered or hardened.

M

mile ▶ **noun 1** (also **statute mile**) a unit of linear measure equal to 1,760 yards (approximately 1.609 kilometres). ■ a race extending over a mile. ■ historical a Roman measure of 1,000 paces (approximately 1,620 yards).
2 (usu. **miles**) informal a very long way or a very great amount: *vistas which stretch for miles | this is my favourite film* ***by a mile.***
▶ **adverb** (as submodifier **miles**) informal by a great amount or a long way: *the second tape is miles better.*
– PHRASES **be miles away** informal be lost in thought and unaware of what is happening around one. **go the extra mile** make a special effort to achieve something. **a mile a minute** informal very quickly: *he talks a mile a minute.* **miles from anywhere** informal in a very isolated place. **the mile-high club** humorous used in reference to having sex on an aircraft: *she* ***joined the mile-high club*** *by making love on a flight between New York and LA.* **run a mile** informal used with reference to a situation regarded as frightening or alarming: *if someone proposed to me I'd probably run a mile.* **see** (or **tell** or **spot**) **something a mile off** informal recognize something very easily: *the baddies can be spotted a mile off.* **stand** (or **stick**) **out a mile** informal be very obvious.
– ORIGIN Old English *mīl*, based on Latin *mil(l)ia*, plural of *mille* 'thousand' (the original Roman unit of distance was *mille passus* 'a thousand paces').

mileage (also **milage**) ▶ **noun** [mass noun] **1** a number of miles travelled or covered: *the car is in good condition, considering its mileage.* ■ [usu. as modifier] travelling expenses paid according to the number of miles travelled: *the mileage rate will be 30p per mile.*
2 informal actual or potential benefit or use to be derived from a situation or event: *he was* ***getting a lot of mileage out of*** *the mix-up.*
– PHRASES **your mileage may vary** informal your experience may be different: *as with all holistic treatments you have to keep doing them, and your mileage may vary.*

mileometer ▶ **noun** variant spelling of **MILOMETER**.

milepost ▶ **noun** chiefly N. Amer. **1** a marker set up to indicate how distant a particular place is. ■ a post one mile from the finishing post of a race.
2 a significant stage or event in the development of something; a milestone: *they've recently passed mileposts in their careers.*

miler ▶ **noun** informal a person or horse trained specially to run a mile.
– DERIVATIVES **miling** noun.

miles gloriosus /ˌmiːleɪz ˌɡlɔːrɪˈəʊsəs, ˌmʌɪliːz/ ▶ **noun** (pl. **milites gloriosi** /ˌmɪlɪteɪz ˌɡlɔːrɪˈəʊsiː/) (in literature) a boastful soldier as a stock figure.
– ORIGIN Latin, from the title of a comedy by Plautus.

Milesian /mʌɪˈliːʃɪən, -ʃ(ə)n/ ▶ **noun** a native or inhabitant of ancient Miletus.
▶ **adjective** relating to Miletus or its inhabitants.
– ORIGIN mid 16th cent.: via Latin from Greek *Milēsios* + **-AN**.

milestone ▶ **noun 1** a stone set up beside a road to mark the distance in miles to a particular place.
2 a significant stage or event in the development of something: *the speech is being hailed as a milestone in race relations.*

Miletus /mʌɪˈliːtəs/ an ancient city of the Ionian Greeks in SW Asia Minor. In the 7th and 6th centuries BC it was a powerful port, from which more than sixty colonies were founded on the shores of the Black Sea and in Italy and Egypt.

MILF ▶ **noun** (pl. **MILFs**) informal a sexually attractive older woman, typically one who has children.
– ORIGIN 1990s: acronym from *mother I'd like to fuck.*

milfoil /ˈmɪlfɔɪl/ ▶ **noun 1** the common Eurasian yarrow.
2 (also **water milfoil**) a widely distributed aquatic plant with whorls of fine submerged leaves and wind-pollinated flowers. ● Genus *Myriophyllum*, family Haloragaceae.
– ORIGIN Middle English: via Old French from Latin *millefolium*, from *mille* 'thousand' + *folium* 'leaf'.

Milhaud /ˈmiːjəʊ/, Darius (1892–1974), French composer. A member of the group Les Six, he composed the music to Cocteau's ballet *Le Boeuf sur le toit* (1919). Much of his music was polytonal and influenced by jazz.

milia plural form of **MILIUM**.

miliaria /ˌmɪlɪˈɛːrɪə/ ▶ **noun** medical term for **PRICKLY HEAT**.
– ORIGIN early 19th cent.: modern Latin, from Latin *miliarius* (see **MILIARY**).

miliary /ˈmɪlɪəri/ ▶ **adjective** (of a disease) accompanied by a rash with lesions resembling millet seed: *miliary tuberculosis.*
– ORIGIN late 17th cent.: from Latin *miliarius*, from *milium* 'millet'.

milieu /ˈmiːljəː, mɪˈljəː/ ▶ **noun** (pl. **milieux** or **milieus** pronunc. **same** or /-ljəːz/) a person's social environment: *Gregory came from the same aristocratic milieu as Sidonius.*
– ORIGIN mid 19th cent.: French, from *mi* 'mid' + *lieu* 'place'.

militant ▶ **adjective** favouring confrontational or violent methods in support of a political or social cause: *the army are in conflict with militant groups.*
▶ **noun** a militant person.
– DERIVATIVES **militancy** noun, **militantly** adverb.
– ORIGIN late Middle English (in the sense 'engaged in warfare'): from Old French, or from Latin *militant-* 'serving as a soldier', from the verb *militare* (see **MILITATE**). The current sense dates from the early 20th cent.

WORD TRENDS See **FIGHTER**.

militaria /ˌmɪlɪˈtɛːrɪə/ ▶ **plural noun** military articles of historical interest, such as weapons, uniforms, and equipment.
– ORIGIN 1960s: from **MILITARY** + **-IA**².

militarism ▶ **noun** [mass noun] chiefly derogatory the belief that a country should maintain a strong military capability and be prepared to use it aggressively to defend or promote national interests.
– DERIVATIVES **militarist** noun & adjective.
– ORIGIN mid 19th cent.: from French *militarisme*, from *militaire* (see **MILITARY**).

militaristic ▶ **adjective** advocating or pursuing an aggressive military policy; hawkish: *the president and his militaristic administration.*
– DERIVATIVES **militaristically** adverb.

militarize (also **militarise**) ▶ **verb** [with obj.] (often as adj. **militarized**) give (something, especially an organization) a military character: *militarized police forces.* ■ equip or supply (a place) with soldiers and other military resources: *a militarized security zone.*
– DERIVATIVES **militarization** noun.

military ▶ **adjective** relating to or characteristic of soldiers or armed forces: *the build-up of military activity.*
▶ **noun** (**the military**) the armed forces of a country.
– DERIVATIVES **militarily** adverb.
– ORIGIN late Middle English: from French *militaire* or Latin *militaris*, from *miles, milit-* 'soldier'.

military attaché ▶ **noun** an army officer serving with an embassy or attached as an observer to a foreign army.

military band ▶ **noun** a group of musicians playing brass, woodwind, and percussion instruments, typically while marching.

Military Cross (abbrev.: **MC**) ▶ **noun** (in the UK and Commonwealth countries) a decoration awarded for distinguished active service on land, instituted in 1914 (originally for officers).

military honours ▶ **plural noun** ceremonies performed by troops as a mark of respect at the burial of a member of the armed forces: *he was buried with full military honours.*

military-industrial complex ▶ **noun** a country's military establishment and those industries producing arms or other military materials, regarded as a powerful vested interest.

military law ▶ **noun** [mass noun] the law governing an army, navy, or air force.

Military Medal (abbrev.: **MM**) ▶ **noun** (in the UK and Commonwealth countries) a decoration for distinguished active service on land, instituted in 1916 (originally for enlisted soldiers).

military police ▶ **noun** [treated as pl.] the corps responsible for police and disciplinary duties in an army.
– DERIVATIVES **military policeman** noun, **military policewoman** noun.

military tribune ▶ **noun** see **TRIBUNE**¹.

militate ▶ **verb** [no obj.] (**militate against**) (of a fact or circumstance) be a powerful or conclusive factor in preventing: *these fundamental differences will militate against the two communities coming together.*
– ORIGIN late 16th cent.: from Latin *militat-* 'served as a soldier', from the verb *militare*, from *miles, milit-* 'soldier'.

USAGE The verbs **militate** and **mitigate** are often confused. See **USAGE** at **MITIGATE**.

milites gloriosi plural form of **MILES GLORIOSUS**.

militia /mɪˈlɪʃə/ ▶ **noun** a military force that is raised from the civil population to supplement a regular army in an emergency. ■ a military force that engages in rebel or terrorist activities in opposition to a regular army. ■ (in the US) all able-bodied civilians eligible by law for military service.
– ORIGIN late 16th cent.: from Latin, literally 'military service', from *miles, milit-* 'soldier'.

militiaman ▶ **noun** (pl. **militiamen**) a member of a militia.

milium /ˈmɪlɪəm/ ▶ **noun** (pl. **milia** /ˈmɪlɪə/) Medicine a small, hard, pale keratinous nodule formed on the skin, typically by a blocked sebaceous gland.
– ORIGIN mid 19th cent.: from Latin, literally 'millet' (because of a resemblance to a millet seed).

milk ▶ **noun** [mass noun] an opaque white fluid rich in fat and protein, secreted by female mammals for the nourishment of their young. ■ the milk of cows (or occasionally goats or ewes) as a drink for humans: *a glass of milk.* ■ the white juice of certain plants: *coconut milk.* ■ a creamy-textured liquid with a particular ingredient or use: *cleansing milk.*
▶ **verb** [with obj.] **1** draw milk from (a cow or other animal), either by hand or mechanically. ■ [no obj.] (of an animal, especially a cow) produce milk: *the breed does seem to milk better in harder conditions.* ■ extract sap, venom, or other substances from.
2 exploit or defraud by taking small amounts of money over a period of time: *executives milked the health plan's funds for their personal use.* ■ get all possible advantage from (a situation): *the newspapers were milking the story for every possible drop of drama.* ■ elicit a favourable reaction from (an audience) and prolong it: *he milked the crowd for every last drop of applause.*
– PHRASES **in milk** (of an animal, especially a cow) producing milk. **it's no use crying over spilt** (or N. Amer. also **spilled**) **milk** proverb there is no point in regretting something which has already happened and cannot be changed or reversed. **milk and honey** prosperity and abundance. [with biblical allusion to the prosperity of the Promised Land (Exod. 3:8).] **milk of human kindness** care and compassion for others. [with allusion to Shakespeare's *Macbeth.*]
– ORIGIN Old English *milc, milcian*, of Germanic origin; related to Dutch *melk* and German *Milch*, from

an Indo-European root shared by Latin *mulgere* and Greek *amelgein* 'to milk'.

milk-and-water ▶ adjective [attrib.] lacking the will or ability to act effectively: *a milk-and-water government.*

milk bar ▶ noun **1** Brit. a snack bar that sells milk drinks and other refreshments.
2 Austral. a corner shop.

milk cap ▶ noun a large woodland toadstool with a concave cap, the flesh of which exudes a white or coloured milky fluid when cut. ● Genus *Lactarius*, family Russulaceae, class Hymenomycetes: several species, including the edible **saffron milk cap** (*L. deliciosus*).

milk chocolate ▶ noun [mass noun] light-brown chocolate made with milk.

milker ▶ noun **1** a cow or other animal that is kept for milk, especially one of a specified productivity: *the cows were no more than fair milkers.*
2 a person who milks cows.

milk fever ▶ noun [mass noun] **1** an acute illness in female cows, goats, etc. that have just produced young, caused by calcium deficiency.
2 a fever in women caused by infection after childbirth, formerly supposed to be due to the swelling of the breasts with milk.

milkfish ▶ noun (pl. **same** or **milkfishes**) a large active silvery fish of the Indo-Pacific region, farmed for food in SE Asia and the Philippines. ● *Chanos chanos*, the only member of the family Chanidae.

milk float ▶ noun Brit. an open-sided van, typically powered by electricity, that is used for delivering milk to houses.

milk-glass ▶ noun [mass noun] semi-translucent glass, whitened by the addition of various ingredients. Also called **OPALINE**.

milking parlour ▶ noun see **PARLOUR** (sense 4 of the noun).

milking stool ▶ noun a short three-legged stool, of a kind traditionally used while milking cows.

milk leg ▶ noun [mass noun] painful swelling of the leg after giving birth, caused by thrombophlebitis in the femoral vein.

milk loaf ▶ noun Brit. a loaf of bread made with milk instead of water.

milkmaid ▶ noun chiefly archaic a girl or woman who milks cows or does other work in a dairy.

milkman ▶ noun (pl. **milkmen**) a man who delivers and sells milk.

Milk of Magnesia ▶ noun [mass noun] Brit. trademark a white suspension of hydrated magnesium carbonate in water, used as an antacid or laxative.

milk powder ▶ noun [mass noun] milk dehydrated by evaporation.

milk pudding ▶ noun Brit. a baked pudding made of milk and rice or another grain such as sago or tapioca.

milk round ▶ noun Brit. a regular milk delivery along a fixed route. ■ a regular journey that includes calls at several places. ■ a series of visits to universities and colleges by recruiting staff from large companies.

milk run ▶ noun a routine, uneventful journey, especially by plane.

milkshake ▶ noun a cold drink made of milk, a sweet flavouring such as fruit or chocolate, and typically ice cream, whisked until it is frothy.

milk sickness ▶ noun [mass noun] a condition of cattle and sheep in the western US, caused by eating white snakeroot, which contains a toxic alcohol. It sometimes occurs in humans who have eaten meat or dairy produce from affected animals.

milk snake ▶ noun a harmless North American constrictor that is typically strongly marked with red and black on yellow or white. It was formerly supposed to suck milk from sleeping cows. ● Genus *Lampropeltis*, family Colubridae: several species, in particular *L. doliata*. Compare with **KINGSNAKE**.

milksop ▶ noun a man or boy who is indecisive and lacks courage.

milk stout ▶ noun [mass noun] a kind of sweet stout made with lactose.

milk sugar ▶ noun another term for **LACTOSE**.

milk thistle ▶ noun a European thistle with a solitary purple flower and glossy marbled leaves, naturalized in America and used in herbal medicine. ● *Silybum marianum*, family Compositae.
■ another term for **SOWTHISTLE**.

milk tooth ▶ noun any of a set of early, temporary (deciduous) teeth in children or young mammals which fall out as the permanent teeth emerge (in children between the ages of about six and twelve).

milk train ▶ noun a train that runs very early in the morning to transport milk but also carries passengers.

milk vetch ▶ noun a yellow-flowered Eurasian plant of the pea family, grown in some regions as a fodder plant. ● *Astragalus glycyphyllos*, family Leguminosae.

milkweed ▶ noun **1** [mass noun] a herbaceous American plant with milky sap, some kinds of which attract butterflies or yield a variety of useful products.
● Genus *Asclepias*, family Asclepiadaceae.
2 (also **milkweed butterfly**) another term for **MONARCH** (sense 2).

milk-white ▶ adjective of the opaque white colour of milk: *her milk-white skin.*

milkwort ▶ noun a small plant with blue, pink, or white flowers, which was formerly believed to increase the milk yield of cows and nursing mothers.
● Genus *Polygala*, family Polygalaceae: several species, including the European **common milkwort** (*P. vulgaris*).

milky ▶ adjective (**milkier**, **milkiest**) **1** containing or mixed with a large amount of milk: *a cup of sweet milky coffee.* ■ (of a cow) having a high milk yield.
2 resembling milk in colour: *not a blemish marred her milky skin.* ■ cloudy or opaque: *the old man's milky, uncomprehending eyes.*
3 informal, dated weak and compliant: *they just talk that way to make you turn milky.*
– DERIVATIVES **milkily** adverb, **milkiness** noun.

Milky Way a faint band of light crossing the night sky, made up of vast numbers of faint stars forming the bulk of the galaxy of which our solar system is a part.

Mill, John Stuart (1806–73), English philosopher and economist. Mill is best known for his political and moral works, especially *On Liberty* (1859), which argued for the importance of individuality, and *Utilitarianism* (1861), which extensively developed Bentham's theory.
– DERIVATIVES **Millian** adjective.

mill[1] ▶ noun **1** a building equipped with machinery for grinding grain into flour. ■ a piece of machinery for grinding grain. ■ a domestic device for grinding a solid substance to powder: *a pepper mill.*
2 a factory fitted with machinery for a particular manufacturing process: *a steel mill.* ■ a piece of manufacturing machinery.
3 informal an engine.
4 informal, dated a boxing match or a fist fight.
▶ verb [with obj.] **1** grind (something) in a mill: *hard wheats are easily milled into white flour* | (as adj., with submodifier **milled**) *freshly milled black pepper.*
2 cut or shape (metal) with a rotating tool. ■ (usu. as adj. **milled**) produce regular ribbed markings on the edge of (a coin) as a protection against illegal clipping.
3 [no obj.] (**mill about/around**) (of people or animals) move around in a confused mass: *tourists were milling about in the lobby* | (as adj. **milling**) *the milling crowds of guests.*
4 thicken (wool or another animal fibre) by fulling it.
– PHRASES **go** (or **put someone**) **through the mill** undergo (or cause someone to undergo) an unpleasant experience.
– DERIVATIVES **millable** adjective.
– ORIGIN Old English *mylen*, based on late Latin *molinum*, from Latin *mola* 'grindstone, mill', from *molere* 'to grind'.

mill[2] ▶ noun N. Amer. a monetary unit used only in calculations, worth one thousandth of a dollar.
– ORIGIN late 18th cent.: from Latin *millesimum* 'thousandth part'; compare with **CENT**.

Millais /ˈmɪleɪ/, Sir John Everett (1829–96), English painter. A founder member of the Pre-Raphaelite Brotherhood, he went on to produce lavishly painted portraits and landscapes. Notable works: *Christ in the House of his Parents* (1850) and *Bubbles* (1886).

millboard ▶ noun [mass noun] stiff grey pasteboard, used for the covers of books.

mill dam ▶ noun a dam built across a stream to raise the level of the water so that it will turn the wheel of a watermill.

Mille, Cecil B. de, see **DE MILLE**.

millefeuille /miːlˈfəːi/ ▶ noun a rich cake consisting of thin layers of puff pastry filled with jam and cream.
– ORIGIN French, literally 'thousand-leaf'.

millefiori /ˌmiːlɪfɪˈɔːri/ ▶ noun [mass noun] a kind of ornamental glass in which a number of glass rods of different sizes and colours are fused together and cut into sections which form various patterns, typically embedded in colourless transparent glass to make items such as paperweights.
– ORIGIN mid 19th cent.: from Italian *millefiore*, literally 'a thousand flowers'.

millefleurs /ˈmiːlflə:/ ▶ noun a pattern of flowers and leaves used in tapestry, on porcelain, or in other decorative items.
– ORIGIN mid 19th cent.: French, literally 'a thousand flowers'.

millenarian /ˌmɪlɪˈnɛːrɪən/ ▶ adjective relating to or believing in Christian millenarianism. ■ denoting a religious or political group believing in a millennium marking an era of radical change or the beginning of a utopian period.
▶ noun a person who believes in millenarianism.
– ORIGIN mid 17th cent.: from late Latin *millenarius* (see **MILLENARY**) + **-AN**.

millenarianism ▶ noun [mass noun] the doctrine of or belief in a future (and typically imminent) thousand-year age of blessedness, beginning with or culminating in the Second Coming of Christ. It is central to the teaching of groups such as Adventists, Mormons, and Jehovah's Witnesses. ■ belief in a future utopian period.
– DERIVATIVES **millenarianist** noun & adjective.

millenary /mɪˈlɛnəri, ˈmɪlməri/ ▶ noun (pl. **millenaries**) a period of a thousand years. Compare with **MILLENNIUM**. ■ a thousandth anniversary.
▶ adjective consisting of a thousand people, years, etc.
– ORIGIN mid 16th cent.: from late Latin *millenarius* 'having a thousand', based on Latin *mille* 'thousand'.

millennialism ▶ noun another term for **MILLENARIANISM**.
– DERIVATIVES **millennialist** noun & adjective.

millennium /mɪˈlɛnɪəm/ ▶ noun (pl. **millennia** /-nɪə/ or **millenniums**) **1** a period of a thousand years, especially when calculated from the traditional date of the birth of Christ. ■ (**the millennium**) Christian Theology the prophesied thousand-year reign of Christ at the end of the age (Rev. 20:1–5). ■ (**the millennium**) a utopian period of justice, peace, and prosperity.
2 an anniversary of a thousand years: *the millennium of the Russian Orthodox Church.* ■ (**the millennium**) the point at which one period of a thousand years ends and another begins.
– DERIVATIVES **millennial** adjective.
– ORIGIN mid 17th cent.: modern Latin, from Latin *mille* 'thousand', on the pattern of *biennium*.

> **USAGE** The correct spelling is **millennium** not **millenium**. The latter is a common error, formed by analogy with other similar words correctly spelled with only one **n**, such as **millenarian** and **millenary**. The differences in spelling are explained by different origins. **Millennium** was formed by analogy with words like **biennium**, while **millenary** and **millenarian** were formed from the Latin **milleni**.

millennium bug ▶ noun a problem with some computers arising from an inability of the software to deal correctly with dates of 1 January 2000 or later.

millepede ▶ noun variant spelling of **MILLIPEDE**

millepore /ˈmɪlɪpɔː/ ▶ noun Zoology a fire coral.
– ORIGIN mid 18th cent.: from French *millépore* or modern Latin *millepora*, from Latin *mille* 'thousand' + *porus* 'pore'.

Miller[1], Arthur (1915–2005), American dramatist. He established his reputation with *Death of a Salesman* (1949). *The Crucible* (1953) used the Salem witch trials of 1692 as an allegory for McCarthyism in America in the 1950s. Miller was married to Marilyn Monroe between 1955 and 1961.

Miller[2], (Alton) Glenn (1904–44), American jazz trombonist and bandleader. He led a celebrated swing big band, with whom he recorded his signature tune 'Moonlight Serenade'. He died when his aircraft disappeared over the English Channel.

Miller[3], Henry (Valentine) (1891–1980), American novelist. His autobiographical novels *Tropic of Cancer* (1934) and *Tropic of Capricorn* (1939) were banned in the US until the 1960s due to their frank depiction of sex and use of obscenities.

miller ▶ noun a person who owns or works in a corn mill.

millerite ▶ noun [mass noun] a mineral consisting of nickel sulphide and typically occurring as slender needle-shaped bronze crystals.

– ORIGIN mid 19th cent.: named after William H. *Miller* (1801–80), English scientist, + -ITE[1].

miller's thumb ▶ noun a small European freshwater fish of the sculpin family, having a broad flattened head and most active at night. Also called BULLHEAD. ● *Cottus gobio*, family Cottidae.

millesimal /mɪˈlɛsɪm(ə)l/ ▶ adjective consisting of thousandth parts; thousandth.
▶ noun a thousandth part.
– DERIVATIVES **millesimally** adverb.
– ORIGIN early 18th cent.: from Latin *millesimus* (from *mille* 'thousand') + -AL.

Millet /ˈmiːeɪ/, Jean (François) (1814–75), French painter. He was famous for the dignity he brought to the treatment of peasant subjects, on which he concentrated from 1850. Notable works: *The Gleaners* (1857).

millet ▶ noun [mass noun] a cereal grown in warm countries and regions with poor soils, bearing a large crop of small seeds which are chiefly used to make flour. ● Several species in the family Gramineae, in particular **common millet** (*Panicum miliaceum*), of temperate regions, the tropical **finger millet** (*Eleusine coracana*), which is a staple in parts of Africa and India, and **pearl millet**.
– ORIGIN late Middle English: from French, diminutive of dialect *mil*, from Latin *milium*.

millhand ▶ noun a worker in a mill or factory.

milli- ▶ combining form (used commonly in units of measurement) a thousand, chiefly denoting a factor of one thousandth: *milligram* | *millipede*.
– ORIGIN from Latin *mille* 'thousand'.

milliammeter /ˌmɪlɪˈamɪtə/ ▶ noun an instrument for measuring electric current in milliamperes.

milliamp ▶ noun short for MILLIAMPERE.

milliampere ▶ noun one thousandth of an ampere, a measure for small electric currents.

milliard /ˈmɪlɪɑːd/ ▶ noun Brit. one thousand million (a term now largely superseded by billion).
– ORIGIN late 18th cent.: French, from *mille* 'thousand'.

millibar ▶ noun one thousandth of a bar, the cgs unit of atmospheric pressure equivalent to 100 pascals.

millieme /ˌmiː(l)ˈjɛm/ ▶ noun a monetary unit of Egypt, equal to one thousandth of a pound.
– ORIGIN from French *millième* 'thousandth'.

milligram (also **milligramme**) (abbrev.: **mg**) ▶ noun one thousandth of a gram.

millilitre (US **milliliter**) (abbrev.: **ml**) ▶ noun one thousandth of a litre (0.002 pint).

millimetre (US **millimeter**) (abbrev.: **mm**) ▶ noun one thousandth of a metre (0.039 in.).

milliner ▶ noun a person who makes or sells women's hats.
– ORIGIN late Middle English (originally in the sense 'native of Milan', later 'a vendor of fancy goods from Milan'): from MILAN + -ER[1].

millinery ▶ noun (pl. **millineries**) [mass noun] women's hats. ■ the trade or business of a milliner.

million ▶ cardinal number (pl. **millions** or (with numeral or quantifying word) **same**) (**a**/**one million**) the number equivalent to the product of a thousand and a thousand; 1,000,000 or 10^6: *a million people will benefit* | *a population of half a million* | *a cost of more than £20 million*. ■ (**millions**) the numbers from a million to a billion. ■ (**millions**) several million things or people: *millions of TV viewers*. ■ informal an unspecified but very large number or amount of something: *I've got millions of beer bottles in my cellar* | *you're **one in a million**.* ■ a million pounds or dollars: *the author is set to make millions*.
– PHRASES **gone a million** Austral./NZ informal (of a person) completely defeated or finished. **look** (or **feel**) (**like**) **a million dollars** informal look or feel extremely good.
– DERIVATIVES **millionfold** adjective & adverb, **millionth** ordinal number.
– ORIGIN late Middle English: from Old French, probably from Italian *milione*, from *mille* 'thousand' + the augmentative suffix *-one*.

millionaire ▶ noun a person whose assets are worth one million pounds or dollars or more.
– ORIGIN early 19th cent.: from French *millionnaire*, from *million* (see MILLION).

millionairess ▶ noun a female millionaire.

millipede /ˈmɪlɪpiːd/ (also **millepede**) ▶ noun a myriapod invertebrate with an elongated body composed of many segments, most of which bear two pairs of legs. Most kinds are herbivorous and shun light, living in the soil or under stones and logs. ● Class Diplopoda: several orders.
– ORIGIN early 17th cent.: from Latin *millepeda* 'woodlouse', from *mille* 'thousand' + *pes*, *ped-* 'foot'.

millisecond ▶ noun one thousandth of a second.

millivolt ▶ noun one thousandth of a volt.

milliwatt (abbrev.: **mW**) ▶ noun a unit of power equal to one thousandth of a watt.

millpond ▶ noun the pool which is created by a dam to provide the head of water that powers a watermill. ■ a very calm stretch of water.

mill race ▶ noun the channel carrying the swift current of water that drives a mill wheel.

Mills and Boon ▶ noun [as modifier] trademark used to denote an idealized romantic situation of the kind associated with the fiction published by Mills & Boon Limited: *the Mills and Boon tall, dark stranger*.

Mills bomb ▶ noun historical an oval hand grenade.
– ORIGIN early 20th cent.: named after Sir William *Mills* (1856–1932), the English engineer who invented it.

millstone ▶ noun each of two circular stones used for grinding corn. ■ a heavy and inescapable responsibility: *she threatened to become **a millstone round his neck***.

millstone grit ▶ noun [mass noun] a coarse sandstone of the British Carboniferous, occurring immediately below the coal measures. ■ any hard siliceous rock suitable for making millstones.

millstream ▶ noun the flowing water that drives a mill wheel.

mill wheel ▶ noun a wheel used to drive a watermill.

millworker ▶ noun a worker in a mill or factory.

millwright ▶ noun a person who designs or builds corn mills or who maintains mill machinery.

Milne, A. A. (1882–1956), English writer for children; full name *Alan Alexander Milne*. He created the character of the toy bear Winnie-the-Pooh in stories written for his son Christopher Robin (1920–96), published in *Winnie-the-Pooh* (1926) and *The House at Pooh Corner* (1928).

milo /ˈmʌɪləʊ/ ▶ noun [mass noun] sorghum of a drought-resistant variety which is an important cereal in the central US.
– ORIGIN late 19th cent.: from Sesotho *maili*.

milometer /mʌɪˈlɒmɪtə/ (also **mileometer**) ▶ noun Brit. an instrument on a vehicle for measuring the number of miles travelled.

milonga /mɪˈlɒŋgə/ ▶ noun an Argentinian ballroom dance, the forerunner of the tango. ■ a piece of music written for or in the style of the milonga.
– ORIGIN South American Spanish, from Brazilian Portuguese *milonga*, 'angry or repetitive words, witchcraft', later referring to a lively dance; probably ultimately from a West African language.

milord ▶ noun historical or humorous used to address or refer to an English nobleman.
– ORIGIN early 17th cent.: via French from English *my lord*; compare with MILADY.

Mílos /ˈmiːlɒs/ Greek name for MELOS.

Milosevic /mɪˈlɒʃəvɪtʃ/, Slobodan (1941–2006), Serbian politician, President of Serbia 1989–97 and of Yugoslavia 1997–2000. His nationalist policies accelerated the break-up of Yugoslavia and led to war in Bosnia and Herzegovina, Croatia, and Kosovo. He was extradited to face war crimes charges at a UN tribunal in The Hague, but died before the trial ended.

milquetoast /ˈmɪlktəʊst/ ▶ noun chiefly N. Amer. a person who is timid or submissive: [as modifier] *a frail, milquetoast character*.
– ORIGIN 1930s: from the name of a cartoon character, Caspar *Milquetoast*, created by H. T. Webster in 1924.

milreis /ˈmɪlreɪs/ ▶ noun (pl. **same**) a former monetary unit of Portugal and Brazil equal to one thousand reals.
– ORIGIN Portuguese, from *mil* 'thousand' + *reis*, plural of *real* (see REAL[2]).

milt ▶ noun [mass noun] the semen of a male fish. ■ [count noun] a sperm-filled reproductive gland of a male fish.
– ORIGIN Old English *milte* 'spleen', of Germanic origin; perhaps related to MELT. The current sense dates from the late 15th cent.

milter ▶ noun a male fish during the spawning season.

Milton, John (1608–74), English poet. His three major works, completed after he had gone blind (1652), show his mastery of blank verse: they are the epic poems *Paradise Lost* (1667, revised 1674) and *Paradise Regained* (1671), and the verse drama *Samson Agonistes* (1671).
– DERIVATIVES **Miltonian** adjective, **Miltonic** adjective.

Milton Keynes /ˈkiːnz/ a town in Buckinghamshire, south central England; pop. 235,280 (est. 2009). It was established as a new town in the late 1960s, and is the site of the headquarters of the Open University.

Milwaukee /mɪlˈwɔːki/ an industrial port and city in SE Wisconsin, on the west shore of Lake Michigan; pop. 604,477 (est. 2008). It is noted for its brewing industry.

mim ▶ adjective Scottish affectedly modest or demure.
– ORIGIN late 16th cent.: imitative of pursing the lips.

Mimas /ˈmʌɪmas, -məs/ Astronomy a satellite of Saturn, the seventh closest to the planet, which has a crater a third of its whole diameter. It was discovered by William Herschel in 1789 (diameter 390 km).
– ORIGIN named after a giant in Greek mythology.

mimbar /ˈmɪmbɑː/ ▶ noun variant spelling of MINBAR.

mime ▶ noun **1** [mass noun] the theatrical technique of suggesting action, character, or emotion without words, using only gesture, expression, and movement. ■ [count noun] a theatrical performance using mime. ■ [count noun] an action or actions intended to convey another action, an idea, or an emotion: *he performed a brief mime of someone fencing*. ■ (also **mime artist**) [count noun] a practitioner of mime or a performer in a mime.
2 (in ancient Greece and Rome) a simple farcical drama including mimicry.
▶ verb **1** [with obj.] use only gesture and movement to act out (a play or role). ■ convey or represent (an action, idea, or emotion) by using only gesture and movement: *Eddie mimed an attack of nausea*.
2 [no obj.] pretend to sing or play an instrument as a recording is being played: *singers on television often **mime to** pre-recorded tape tracks*.
– DERIVATIVES **mimer** noun.
– ORIGIN early 17th cent. (also in the sense 'mimic or jester'): from Latin *mimus*, from Greek *mimos*.

mimeo /ˈmɪmɪəʊ/ ▶ noun short for MIMEOGRAPH.

mimeograph ▶ noun a duplicating machine which produces copies from a stencil, now superseded by the photocopier. ■ a copy produced on a mimeograph.
▶ verb [with obj.] make a copy of (a document) with a mimeograph.
– ORIGIN late 19th cent.: formed irregularly from Greek *mimeomai* 'I imitate' + -GRAPH.

mimesis /mɪˈmiːsɪs, mʌɪ-/ ▶ noun [mass noun] formal or technical imitation, in particular: ■ imitative representation of the real world in art and literature. ■ the deliberate imitation of the behaviour of one group of people by another as a factor in social change. ■ Zoology another term for MIMICRY.
– ORIGIN mid 16th cent.: from Greek *mimēsis*, from *mimeisthai* 'to imitate'.

mimetic /mɪˈmɛtɪk, mʌɪ-/ ▶ adjective formal or technical relating to, constituting, or habitually practising mimesis: *mimetic patterns in butterflies*.
– DERIVATIVES **mimetically** adverb.
– ORIGIN mid 17th cent.: from Greek *mimētikos* 'imitation', from *mimeisthai* 'to imitate'.

mimetite /ˈmɪmɪtʌɪt, ˈmʌɪ-/ ▶ noun [mass noun] a yellow or brown mineral consisting of a chloride and arsenate of lead, typically found as a crust or needle-like crystals in lead deposits.
– ORIGIN mid 19th cent.: from Greek *mimētēs* 'imitator' + -ITE[1].

mimic ▶ verb (**mimics**, **mimicking**, **mimicked**) [with obj.] imitate (someone or their actions or words), especially in order to entertain or ridicule: *she mimicked Eileen's pedantic voice*. ■ (of an animal or plant) resemble or imitate (another animal or plant) to deter predators or for camouflage. ■ (of a drug) replicate the physiological effects of (another substance). ■ (of a disease) exhibit symptoms that bear a deceptive resemblance to those of (another disease).
▶ noun a person skilled in imitating the voice or actions of others in an entertaining way. ■ an animal or plant that mimics another.
▶ adjective [attrib.] imitative of something: *they were waging mimic war*.
– DERIVATIVES **mimicker** noun.
– ORIGIN late 16th cent. (as noun and adjective): via Latin from Greek *mimikos*, from *mimos* 'mime'.

mimicry ▸ **noun** (pl. **mimicries**) [mass noun] the action or skill of imitating someone or something, especially in order to entertain or ridicule: *the word was spoken with gently teasing mimicry* | [count noun] *a playful mimicry of the techniques of realist writers.* ■ Biology the close external resemblance of an animal or plant (or part of one) to another animal, plant, or inanimate object.

mimosa /mɪˈməʊzə, -sə/ ▸ **noun 1** an Australian acacia tree with delicate fern-like leaves and yellow flowers. ● *Acacia dealbata*, family Leguminosae.
2 a plant of a genus that includes the sensitive plant. ● Genus *Mimosa*, family Leguminosae.
3 N. Amer. a drink of champagne and orange juice.
– ORIGIN modern Latin, apparently from Latin *mimus* 'mime' (because the plant seemingly mimics the sensitivity of an animal) + the feminine suffix *-osa*.

mimsy ▸ **adjective** rather feeble and prim or affected.
– ORIGIN late 19th cent.: probably from **MIM** + **-SY**.

mimulus /ˈmɪmjʊləs/ ▸ **noun** a plant of a genus which includes the musk plants and the monkey flower. ● Genus *Mimulus*, family Scrophulariaceae.
– ORIGIN modern Latin, apparently a diminutive of Latin *mimus* 'mime', perhaps with reference to its mask-like flowers.

Min ▸ **noun** [mass noun] a dialect of Chinese spoken by over 50 million people, mainly in Fujian province, Hainan, and Taiwan. It has two main forms, northern and southern.
– ORIGIN Chinese.

min. ▸ **abbreviation** ■ minim (fluid measure). ■ minimum. ■ minute(s).

minacious /mɪˈneɪʃəs/ ▸ **adjective** rare menacing; threatening.
– ORIGIN mid 17th cent.: from Latin *minax*, *minac-* 'threatening' (from *minari* 'threaten') + **-ous**.

Minamata disease /ˌmɪnəˈmɑːtə/ ▸ **noun** [mass noun] chronic poisoning by alkyl mercury compounds from industrial waste, characterized by (usually permanent) impairment of brain functions such as speech, sight, and muscular coordination.
– ORIGIN 1950s: named after *Minamata*, a town in Japan.

Minangkabau /ˌmiːnaŋkəˈbaʊ/ ▸ **noun** [mass noun] an Indonesian language spoken by over 6 million people in Sumatra and elsewhere.
– ORIGIN Malay and Indonesian.

minaret /ˈmɪnərɛt, ˌmɪnəˈrɛt/ ▸ **noun** a slender tower, typically part of a mosque, with a balcony from which a muezzin calls Muslims to prayer.
– DERIVATIVES **minareted** adjective.
– ORIGIN late 17th cent.: from French, or from Spanish *minarete*, Italian *minaretto*, via Turkish from Arabic *manār(a)* 'lighthouse, minaret', based on *nār* 'fire or light'.

Minas Gerais /ˌmiːnas ʒɛˈrʌɪs/ a state of SE Brazil; capital, Belo Horizonte. It has major deposits of iron ore, coal, gold, and diamonds.

minatory /ˈmɪnəˌt(ə)ri/ ▸ **adjective** formal expressing or conveying a threat: *he is unlikely to be deterred by minatory finger-wagging.*
– ORIGIN mid 16th cent.: from late Latin *minatorius*, from *minat-* 'threatened', from the verb *minari*.

minaudière /ˌmɪnəʊˈdjɛː/ ▸ **noun** a small, decorative handbag without handles or a strap.
– ORIGIN French, literally 'coquettish woman', from *minauder* 'simper'.

minbar /ˈmɪnbɑː/ (also **mimbar**) ▸ **noun** a short flight of steps used as a platform by a preacher in a mosque.
– ORIGIN from Arabic *minbar*.

mince ▸ **verb 1** [with obj.] (often as adj. **minced**) cut up (food, especially meat) into very small pieces, typically in a machine: *minced beef.*
2 [no obj.] walk with short quick steps in an affectedly dainty manner: *there were plenty of secretaries mincing about.*
▸ **noun** [mass noun] Brit. minced meat, especially beef.
– PHRASES **mince matters** [usu. with negative] dated use polite or moderate expressions to indicate disapproval. **not mince words** (or **one's words**) voice one's disapproval candidly and directly.
– DERIVATIVES **mincer** noun.
– ORIGIN late Middle English: from Old French *mincier*, based on Latin *minutia* 'smallness'.

mincemeat ▸ **noun** [mass noun] **1** chiefly Brit. a mixture of currants, raisins, sugar, apples, candied peel, spices, and suet, typically baked in pastry.
2 minced meat.
– PHRASES **make mincemeat of** informal defeat decisively in a fight, contest, or argument.

mince pie ▸ **noun** chiefly Brit. a small round pie or tart containing sweet mincemeat, typically eaten at Christmas.

Minch /mɪntʃ/ a channel of the Atlantic, between the mainland of Scotland and the Outer Hebrides. The northern stretch is called the **North Minch**, the southern stretch, north-west of Skye, is called the **Little Minch**. Also called **the Minches**.

mincing ▸ **adjective** (of a man) affectedly dainty in manner or gait; effeminate.
– DERIVATIVES **mincingly** adverb.

mind ▸ **noun 1** the element of a person that enables them to be aware of the world and their experiences, to think, and to feel; the faculty of consciousness and thought: *a lot of thoughts ran through my mind.*
2 a person's ability to think and reason; the intellect: *his keen mind.* ■ a person's memory: *the company's name **slips my mind**.* ■ a particular way of thinking, influenced by a person's profession or environment: *he had a deep contempt for the bureaucratic mind.* ■ a person identified with their intellectual faculties: *he was one of the greatest minds of his time.*
3 a person's attention: *employees should keep their minds on the job.* ■ a person's will or determination to achieve something: *anyone can slim if they set their mind to it.*
▸ **verb** [with obj.] **1** [often with negative] be distressed, annoyed, or worried by: *I don't mind the rain.* ■ object to: *what does that mean, if you don't mind my asking?* | [with clause] *do you mind if I have a cigarette?* ■ [with negative or in questions] (**mind doing something**) be reluctant to do something: *I don't mind admitting I was worried.* ■ (**would not mind something**) informal used to express one's strong enthusiasm for something: *I wouldn't mind some coaching from him!*
2 regard as important; feel concern about: *never mind the opinion polls* | [no obj.] *why should she **mind** about a few snubs from people she disliked?* ■ Scottish remember: *I mind the time when he lost his false teeth.*
3 [with clause, in imperative] used to urge someone to remember or take care to do something: *mind you look after the children.* ■ [in imperative] used to warn someone to avoid injury or an accident: *mind your head on that cupboard!* | [no obj.] chiefly Brit. *mind out—there's a step missing.* ■ [no obj., in imperative] informal used to emphasize a command: *be early to bed tonight, mind.* ■ [in imperative] be careful about the quality or nature of: *mind your manners!* ■ [with obj.] N. Amer. & Irish pay attention to; obey: *you think about how much Cal does for you, and you mind her, you hear?*
4 take care of temporarily: *we left our husbands to mind the children while we went out.*
5 [with infinitive] (**be minded**) be inclined to do something: *he was minded to reject the application.*
6 [no obj., in imperative] (also **mind you**) used to introduce a qualification to a previous statement: *we've got some decorations up—not a lot, mind you.*
– PHRASES **be in** (or N. Amer. **of**) **two minds** be unable to decide between alternatives. **be of one** (or **a different**) **mind** share the same (or hold a different) opinion. **close** (or **shut**) **one's mind to** (or **against**) refuse to consider or acknowledge. **come** (or **spring**) **to mind** (of a thought) occur to someone. **(I) don't mind if I do** informal used to accept an invitation: *'Have some breakfast.' 'Ta very much—don't mind if I do.'* **give someone a piece of one's mind** informal rebuke someone. **great minds think alike** humorous said when two people have the same opinion or make the same choice: *looks like me and Jackie were posting simultaneously; great minds think alike!* **have a** (or **a good** or **half a**) **mind to do something** be very much inclined to do something: *I've a good mind to write to the manager to complain.* **have someone/thing in mind** be thinking of someone or something. ■ intend to do something: *I **had it in mind** to ask you to work for me.* **have a mind of one's own** be capable of independent opinion or action. ■ (of an inanimate object) seem capable of thought and independent action: *the trolley had a mind of its own.* **in one's mind's eye** in one's imagination. **mind over matter** the use of willpower to overcome physical problems. **mind one's own business** refrain from prying or interfering. **mind one's Ps & Qs** be careful to behave well and avoid giving offence. [of unknown origin; said by some to refer to the care a young pupil must pay in differentiating the tailed letters *p* and *q*.] **mind the shop** Brit. informal have charge of something temporarily. **never mind 1** used to urge someone not to worry: *never mind—it's all right now.* **2** (also **never you mind**) used in refusing to answer a question: *never mind where I'm going.* **3** used to indicate that what has been said of one thing applies even more to another: *he found it hard to think, never mind talk.* **not pay someone any mind** N. Amer. not pay someone any attention. **on someone's mind** preoccupying someone. **open one's mind to** be receptive to: *she had opened her mind to new things.* **out of one's mind** having lost control of one's mental faculties. ■ informal suffering from a particular condition to a very high degree: *she was bored out of her mind.* **put someone in mind of** resemble and so remind someone of: *he was a small, well-dressed man who put her in mind of a jockey.* **put** (or **give** or **set**) **one's mind to** direct all one's attention to (achieving something): *she'd have made an excellent dancer, if she'd have put her mind to it.* **put someone/thing out of one's mind** deliberately forget someone or something. **to my mind** in my opinion: *this story is, to my mind, a masterpiece.*
– ORIGIN Old English *gemynd* 'memory, thought', of Germanic origin, from an Indo-European root meaning 'revolve in the mind, think', shared by Sanskrit *manas* and Latin *mens* 'mind'.

mind-altering ▸ **adjective** (of a hallucinogenic drug) producing mood changes or giving a sense of heightened awareness.

Mindanao /ˌmɪndəˈnaʊ/ the second-largest island in the Philippines, in the south-east of the group; pop. 19,874,000 (est. 2007). Its chief town is Davao.

mind-bending ▸ **adjective** informal (chiefly of a psychedelic drug) influencing or altering one's state of mind.
– DERIVATIVES **mind-bender** noun, **mind-bendingly** adverb.

mind-blowing ▸ **adjective** informal overwhelmingly impressive: *for a kid, Chicago was really mind-blowing.* ■ (of a drug) inducing hallucinations.
– DERIVATIVES **mind-blowingly** adverb.

mind-boggling ▸ **adjective** informal overwhelming; startling: *the implications are mind-boggling.*
– DERIVATIVES **mind-bogglingly** adverb.

minded ▸ **adjective** [in combination or with submodifier] inclined to think in a particular way: *liberal-minded scholars* | *I'm not scientifically minded.* ■ [in combination] interested in or enthusiastic about a particular thing: *conservation-minded citizens.*

Mindel /ˈmɪnd(ə)l/ ▸ **noun** [usu. as modifier] Geology a Pleistocene glaciation in the Alps preceding the Riss, possibly corresponding to the Elsterian of northern Europe. ■ the system of deposits laid down at the time of the Mindel glaciation.
– ORIGIN early 20th cent.: from the name of a river in southern Germany.

minder ▸ **noun** chiefly Brit. a person whose job it is to look after someone or something: [in combination] *a baby-minder.* ■ informal a bodyguard employed to protect a celebrity or criminal.

mind-expanding ▸ **adjective** (especially of a hallucinogenic drug) giving a sense of heightened or broader awareness.

mindful ▸ **adjective** [predic.] conscious or aware of something: *I arrived home for the summer, ever **mindful** of my obligations to my parents.* ■ [with infinitive] formal inclined or willing to do something: *the judge said that he was not mindful to postpone the eviction again.*
– DERIVATIVES **mindfully** adverb.

mindfulness ▸ **noun** [mass noun] **1** the quality or state of being conscious or aware of something: *their mindfulness of the wider cinematic tradition.*
2 a mental state achieved by focusing one's awareness on the present moment, while calmly acknowledging and accepting one's feelings, thoughts, and bodily sensations, used as a therapeutic technique.

mind game ▸ **noun** a course of psychologically manipulative behaviour intended to discomfit another person or gain an advantage over them.

mindless ▸ **adjective 1** acting or done without justification and with no concern for the consequences: *a generation of mindless vandals* | *mindless violence.* ■ (of an activity) so simple or repetitive as to be performed automatically.
2 (**mindless of**) not thinking of or concerned about: *mindless of the fact she was in her nightie, she rushed to the door.*
– DERIVATIVES **mindlessly** adverb, **mindlessness** noun.

mind-numbing ▸ **adjective** so extreme or intense as to prevent normal thought: *conversations of mind-numbing tedium.*
– DERIVATIVES **mind-numbingly** adverb.

M

Mindoro /mɪnˈdɔːrəʊ/ an island in the Philippines, situated to the south-west of Luzon; pop. 1,157,700 (est. 2007).

mind reader ▶ **noun** a person who can supposedly discern what another person is thinking.
– DERIVATIVES **mind reading** noun.

mindset ▶ **noun** [usu. in sing.] the established set of attitudes held by someone: *the region seems stuck in a medieval mindset.*

mindshare ▶ **noun** consumer awareness of a product or brand, typically as opposed to market share.

mind-your-own-business ▶ **noun** a creeping Mediterranean plant with masses of tiny pale green leaves, widely cultivated as a greenhouse or indoor plant. Also called MOTHER OF THOUSANDS. ● *Soleirolia soleirolii*, family Urticaceae.

mine[1] ▶ **possessive pronoun** used to refer to a thing or things belonging to or associated with the speaker: *you go your way and I'll go mine | some friends of* ***mine***.
▶ **possessive determiner** archaic (used before a vowel) my: *tears did fill mine eyes.*
– ORIGIN Old English *mīn*, of Germanic origin; related to ME[1] and to Dutch *mijn* and German *mein*.

mine[2] ▶ **noun 1** an excavation in the earth for extracting coal or other minerals: *a copper mine.* ■ [in sing.] an abundant source of something, especially information: *the text is* ***a mine of*** *information for biographers and historians.*
2 a type of bomb placed on or just below the surface of the ground or in the water, which detonates on contact with a person, vehicle, or ship. ■ historical a subterranean passage under the wall of a besieged fortress, especially one in which explosives were placed to blow up fortifications.
▶ **verb** [with obj.] **1** obtain (coal or other minerals) from a mine. ■ dig in (the earth) for coal or other minerals: *the hills were* ***mined for*** *copper oxide* | [no obj.] *many financiers obtained concessions to* ***mine for*** *silver.* ■ dig or burrow in (the earth). ■ exploit (a source of information or skill): *how do they manage to mine such a rich vein of talent?* ■ analyse (a database) to generate new information.
2 lay explosive mines on or just below the surface of (the ground or water): *the area was heavily mined.* ■ destroy by means of an explosive mine.
– DERIVATIVES **mineable** (also **minable**) adjective.
– ORIGIN late Middle English: from Old French *mine* (noun), *miner* (verb), perhaps of Celtic origin; compare with Welsh *mwyn* 'ore', earlier 'mine'.

mine detector ▶ **noun** an instrument used for detecting explosive mines.

minefield ▶ **noun** an area planted with explosive mines. ■ a subject or situation presenting unseen hazards: *tax is a minefield for the unwary.*

minehunter ▶ **noun** Brit. a ship or aircraft used for detecting explosive mines.
– DERIVATIVES **minehunting** noun & adjective.

minelayer ▶ **noun** a warship, aircraft, or land vehicle from which explosive mines are laid.
– DERIVATIVES **minelaying** noun.

miner[1] ▶ **noun 1** a person who works in a mine. ■ historical a person who dug tunnels in order to destroy an enemy position with explosives.
2 a small South American bird of the ovenbird family, which excavates a long burrow for breeding. ● Genus *Geositta*, family Furnariidae: several species.
3 short for LEAF MINER.
– ORIGIN Middle English: from Old French *minour*, from *miner* 'to mine' (see MINE[2]).

miner[2] ▶ **noun** an Australian bird of the honeyeater family, having a loud call. ● Genus *Manorina*, family Meliphagidae: five species, including the **bell miner** or bellbird (*M. melanophrys*), with greenish plumage and a bell-like call.
– ORIGIN early 19th cent.: variant of MYNAH.

mineral ▶ **noun 1** a solid, naturally occurring inorganic substance. ■ a substance obtained by mining. ■ an inorganic substance needed by the human body for good health.
2 (**minerals**) Brit. fizzy soft drinks.
▶ **adjective** of or denoting a mineral: *mineral ingredients such as zinc oxide.*
– ORIGIN late Middle English: from medieval Latin *minerale*, neuter (used as a noun) of *mineralis*, from *minera* 'ore'.

mineralize (also **mineralise**) ▶ **verb** [with obj.] convert (organic matter) wholly or partly into a mineral or inorganic material or structure. ■ impregnate (water or another liquid) with a mineral substance.
– DERIVATIVES **mineralization** noun.

mineralocorticoid /ˌmɪn(ə)rələ(ʊ)ˈkɔːtɪkɔɪd/ ▶ **noun** Biochemistry a corticosteroid which is involved with maintaining the salt balance in the body, such as aldosterone.

mineralogy ▶ **noun** [mass noun] the scientific study of minerals.
– DERIVATIVES **mineralogical** adjective, **mineralogically** adverb, **mineralogist** noun.

mineral oil ▶ **noun** [mass noun] petroleum. ■ a distillation product of petroleum.

mineral spirits ▶ **noun** North American term for WHITE SPIRIT.

mineral water ▶ **noun** [mass noun] water occurring in nature with some dissolved salts present, often bottled and sold as drinking water.

mineral wool ▶ **noun** [mass noun] a substance resembling matted wool and made from inorganic mineral material, used chiefly for packing or insulation.

miner's right ▶ **noun** Austral./NZ a licence to prospect and dig for gold or another mineral.

Minerva /mɪˈnəːvə/ Roman Mythology the goddess of handicrafts, widely worshipped and regularly identified with Athene, which led to her being regarded also as the goddess of war.

Minervois /ˌmɪnɛːˈvwʌ/, French /minɛʀvwa/ ▶ **noun** [mass noun] a wine produced in the district of Minervois, in the department of Aude in southern France.

mineshaft ▶ **noun** a deep narrow vertical hole, or sometimes a horizontal tunnel, that gives access to a mine.

minestrone /ˌmɪnɪˈstrəʊni/ ▶ **noun** [mass noun] a fairly thick soup containing vegetables and pasta.
– ORIGIN Italian.

minesweeper ▶ **noun** a ship or aircraft equipped for detecting and removing or destroying tethered explosive mines.
– DERIVATIVES **minesweeping** noun & adjective.

mineworker ▶ **noun** a person who works in a mine, especially a coal mine.

Ming ▶ **noun** the dynasty ruling China 1368–1644 founded by Zhu Yuanzhang (1328–98). ■ [mass noun] [usu. as modifier] Chinese porcelain made during the Ming dynasty, characterized by elaborate designs and vivid colours: *a priceless Ming vase.*
– ORIGIN Chinese, literally 'clear or bright'.

minge /mɪn(d)ʒ/ ▶ **noun** Brit. vulgar slang a woman's pubic hair or genitals.
– ORIGIN late 19th cent.: of unknown origin.

minger /ˈmɪŋə/ ▶ **noun** Brit. informal, derogatory an unattractive or unpleasant person or thing.
– ORIGIN 1990s: from MINGING.

minging /ˈmɪŋɪŋ/ ▶ **adjective** Brit. informal foul-smelling. ■ very bad or unpleasant: *the weather was minging.*
– ORIGIN 1970s: perhaps from Scots dialect *ming* 'excrement'.

mingle ▶ **verb** mix or cause to mix together: [no obj.] *the sound of voices* ***mingled with*** *a scraping of chairs* | [with obj.] *a smell which mingled disinfectant and soap.* ■ [no obj.] move among and engage with others at a social function: *a chance to* ***mingle with*** *celebs.*
– ORIGIN late Middle English: frequentative of obsolete *meng* 'mix or blend' (related to AMONG), perhaps influenced by Middle Dutch *mengelen*.

Mingus /ˈmɪŋgəs/, Charles (1922–79), American jazz bassist and composer. A leading figure of the 1940s jazz scene, he experimented with atonality and was influenced by gospel and blues. His compositions include 'Goodbye Porkpie Hat'.

mingy /ˈmɪn(d)ʒi/ ▶ **adjective** (**mingier**, **mingiest**) informal mean: *you've been too mingy with the sunscreen.* ■ undesirably small: *a mingy kitchenette.*
– DERIVATIVES **mingily** adverb.
– ORIGIN early 20th cent.: perhaps a blend of MEAN[2] and STINGY.

minhag /mɪnˈhɑːg/ ▶ **noun** (pl. **same** or **minhagim** /-gɪm/) Judaism a custom or practice, especially one which has taken on the force of law.
– ORIGIN Hebrew *minhāğ* 'custom, usage, conduct', from *nāhağ* 'to drive or lead'.

Minho /ˈmiɲu/ Portuguese name for MIÑO.

mini ▶ **adjective** denoting a miniature version of something: *a mini camera.*
▶ **noun** (pl. **minis**) **1** a very short skirt or dress.
2 short for MINICOMPUTER.
– ORIGIN 1960s: abbreviation.

mini- ▶ **combining form** very small or minor of its kind; miniature: *minicab* | *minicomputer.*
– ORIGIN from MINIATURE, reinforced by MINIMUM.

miniature ▶ **adjective** very small of its kind: *children dressed as miniature adults.*
▶ **noun** a thing that is much smaller than normal, especially a small replica or model. ■ a very small bottle of spirits. ■ a plant or animal that is a smaller version of an existing variety or breed. ■ a very small and highly detailed portrait or other painting. ■ a picture or decorated letter in an illuminated manuscript.
▶ **verb** [with obj.] literary represent on a smaller scale.
– PHRASES **in miniature** on a small scale: *a place that is Greece in miniature.*
– ORIGIN late 16th cent.: from Italian *miniatura*, via medieval Latin from Latin *miniare* 'rubricate, illuminate', from *minium* 'red lead, vermilion' (used to mark particular words in manuscripts).

miniaturist ▶ **noun** a painter of miniatures or an illuminator of manuscripts.

miniaturize (also **miniaturise**) ▶ **verb** [with obj.] (usu. as adj. **miniaturized**) make on a smaller or miniature scale.
– DERIVATIVES **miniaturization** noun.

minibar ▶ **noun** a refrigerator in a hotel room containing a selection of drinks which, if consumed, are charged to the occupant's bill.

minibeast ▶ **noun** Brit. informal a small invertebrate animal such as an insect or spider.

mini-break ▶ **noun** a short holiday, especially one lasting only two or three days.

minibus ▶ **noun** a small bus for about ten to fifteen passengers.

minicab ▶ **noun** Brit. a taxi which may be booked in advance but which is not licensed to pick up passengers who hail it in the street.

minicam ▶ **noun** a handheld video camera.

minicamp ▶ **noun** N. Amer. a session run by a professional sports team to train particular players, or to test potential new players, before its main preseason training.

minicom ▶ **noun** a small electronic typewriter and screen linked to a telephone system, enabling people with hearing or speech difficulties to send and receive messages.

minicomputer ▶ **noun** a computer of medium power, more than a microcomputer but less than a mainframe.

Minicoy Islands /ˈmɪnɪkɔɪ/ one of the groups of islands forming the Indian territory of Lakshadweep in the Indian Ocean.

minidisc ▶ **noun** a disc having a format similar to a small CD but able to record sound or data as well as play it back.

minidress ▶ **noun** a very short dress.

minifundium /ˌmɪnɪˈfʌndɪəm/ ▶ **noun** (pl. **minifundia** /-dɪə/) a small farm or property in Latin America, especially one that is too small to support a single family.
– ORIGIN 1950s: modern Latin, or from Spanish *minifundio* 'smallholding'.

minigolf ▶ **noun** [mass noun] an informal version of golf played on a short course consisting of a variety of obstacles.

minikin literary ▶ **adjective** small; insignificant.
▶ **noun** a small person or thing.
– ORIGIN mid 16th cent.: from Dutch *minneken*, from *minne* 'love' + *-ken* -KIN.

minim ▶ **noun 1** Music, Brit. a note having the time value of two crotchets or half a semibreve, represented by a ring with a stem. Also called HALF NOTE.
2 a small bronze or silver ancient Roman coin.
3 one sixtieth of a fluid drachm, about one drop of liquid.
4 (in calligraphy) a short vertical stroke, as in the letters *i*, *m*, *n*, *u*.
– ORIGIN late Middle English: from Latin *minima*, from *minimus* 'smallest'.

minima plural form of MINIMUM.

minimal ▶ **adjective 1** of a minimum amount, quantity, or degree; negligible: *the aircraft suffered minimal damage* | *production costs are minimal.*
2 Art characterized by the use of simple forms or structures, especially geometric or massive ones. ■ characterized by simplicity and lack of adornment or decoration: *minimal, simple evening dresses in luxurious fabrics.*
3 Music characterized by the repetition and gradual alteration of short phrases.

4 Linguistics (of a pair of forms) distinguished by only one feature.
– DERIVATIVES **minimally** adverb.
– ORIGIN mid 17th cent.: from Latin *minimus* 'smallest' + **-AL**.

minimalism ▶ noun [mass noun] **1** a movement in sculpture and painting which arose in the 1950s, characterized by the use of simple, massive forms.
2 an avant-garde movement in music characterized by the repetition of very short phrases which change gradually, producing a hypnotic effect.
3 deliberate lack of decoration or adornment in style or design: *his living room was a testament to minimalism.*

minimalist ▶ noun **1** a person who advocates or practises minimalism.
2 a person advocating moderate reform in politics.
▶ adjective (also **minimalistic**) **1** relating to minimalism. ■ lacking decoration or adornment; deliberately simple or basic in design or style: *his recently renovated minimalist Conran kitchen.*
2 advocating moderate political reform.
– ORIGIN early 20th cent.: first used with reference to the Russian Mensheviks. Usage in art and music dates from the 1960s.

mini-mall ▶ noun N. Amer. a shopping mall containing a relatively small number of retail outlets and with access to each shop from the outside rather than from an interior hallway.

minimart ▶ noun N. Amer. a convenience store.

minimax ▶ noun Mathematics the lowest of a set of maximum values. Compare with **MAXIMIN**. ■ [as modifier] (in game theory) denoting a strategy that minimizes the greatest risk to a participant. ■ [as modifier] denoting the theory that in a game with two players, a player's smallest possible maximum loss is equal to the same player's greatest possible minimum gain.
– ORIGIN 1940s: blend of **MINIMUM** and **MAXIMUM**.

mini-me ▶ noun informal a person closely resembling a smaller or younger version of another: *so far Eminem's mini-me has failed to get himself a money-making deal.*
– ORIGIN the name of a small cloned character in the film *Austin Powers: The Spy Who Shagged Me* (1999).

minimize (also **minimise**) ▶ verb [with obj.] reduce (something, especially something undesirable) to the smallest possible amount or degree: *the aim is to minimize costs.* ■ represent or estimate at less than the true value or importance: *they may minimize, or even overlook, the importance of such beliefs.*
– DERIVATIVES **minimization** noun, **minimizer** noun.

minimum ▶ noun (pl. **minima** or **minimums**) [usu. in sing.] the least or smallest amount or quantity possible, attainable, or required: ***keep costs to a minimum** | they checked visas with **the minimum of** fuss.* ■ the lowest or smallest amount of a varying quantity (e.g. temperature) allowed, attained, or recorded: *clients with a minimum of £500,000 to invest.*
▶ adjective [attrib.] smallest or lowest: *this can be done with the minimum amount of effort.*
– PHRASES **at a** (or **the**) **minimum** at the very least: *we zipped along at a minimum of 55 mph.*
– ORIGIN mid 17th cent.: from Latin, neuter of *minimus* 'least'.

minimum wage ▶ noun the lowest wage permitted by law or by a special agreement.

mining ▶ noun [mass noun] the process or industry of obtaining coal or other minerals from a mine.

mining bee ▶ noun a solitary bee that builds long underground tunnels containing nest chambers.
● *Andrena* and other genera, family Apidae.

minion /ˈmɪnjən/ ▶ noun a follower or underling of a powerful person, especially a servile or unimportant one.
– ORIGIN late 15th cent.: from French *mignon*, *mignonne*.

mini-pill ▶ noun a contraceptive pill containing a progestogen and not oestrogen.

mini-roundabout ▶ noun Brit. a small traffic roundabout, indicated by road markings or a very low island.

mini rugby ▶ noun [mass noun] a simplified version of rugby with only nine players in a team.

miniscule ▶ adjective see **MINUSCULE**.

miniseries ▶ noun (pl. **same**) a television drama shown in a small number of episodes, often on consecutive nights.

miniskirt ▶ noun a very short skirt.
– DERIVATIVES **miniskirted** adjective.

minister ▶ noun **1** (in certain countries) a head of a government department: *the Defence Minister.*
2 (also **minister of religion**) a member of the clergy, especially in the Presbyterian and Nonconformist Churches. ■ (also **minister general**) the superior of some religious orders.
3 a diplomatic agent, usually ranking below an ambassador, representing a state or sovereign in a foreign country.
▶ verb [no obj.] **1** (**minister to**) attend to the needs of (someone): *her doctor was busy ministering to the injured.*
2 act as a minister of religion. ■ [with obj.] administer (a sacrament).
– DERIVATIVES **ministership** noun.
– ORIGIN Middle English (in sense 2 of the noun); also in the sense 'a person acting under the authority of another'): from Old French *ministre* (noun), *ministrer* (verb), from Latin *minister* 'servant', from *minus* 'less'.

ministerial ▶ adjective **1** relating to a government minister or ministers: *a back-bencher who had never held ministerial office.*
2 relating to a minister of religion.
3 Law relating to or entrusted with the execution of the law or the commands of a superior.
– DERIVATIVES **ministerially** adverb.
– ORIGIN mid 16th cent.: from French *ministériel* or late Latin *ministerialis*, from Latin *ministerium* 'ministry'.

ministering angel ▶ noun often humorous a kind-hearted person, especially a woman, who nurses or comforts others.
– ORIGIN early 17th cent.: with biblical allusion to Mark 1:13.

Minister of State ▶ noun (in the UK) a minister ranking below a Secretary of State.

Minister of the Crown ▶ noun (in the UK and Canada) a member of the cabinet.

Minister without Portfolio ▶ noun (in the UK and some other countries) a government minister who has cabinet status, but is not in charge of a specific department of state.

ministration ▶ noun (usu. **ministrations**) **1** formal or humorous the provision of assistance or care: *a kitchen made spotless by **the ministrations of** a cleaning lady.*
2 the services of a minister of religion or of a religious institution. ■ [mass noun] the action of administering the sacrament.
– DERIVATIVES **ministrant** noun.
– ORIGIN late Middle English: from Latin *ministratio(n-)*, from *ministrare* 'wait upon', from *minister* (see **MINISTER**).

ministry ▶ noun (pl. **ministries**) **1** (in certain countries) a government department headed by a minister: *the Ministry of Defence.*
2 [usu. in sing.] the work or vocation of a minister of religion: *he is training for the ministry.* ■ the period of tenure of a minister of religion. ■ the spiritual work or service of a Christian or a group of Christians, especially evangelism.
3 (in certain countries) a period of government under one Prime Minister.
4 [mass noun] rare the action of ministering to someone.
– ORIGIN Middle English (in sense 2): from Latin *ministerium*, from *minister* (see **MINISTER**).

minitower ▶ noun a small vertical case for a computer, or a computer mounted in such a case.

minivan (also trademark **Mini Van**) ▶ noun a small van. ■ N. Amer. a people carrier.

miniver /ˈmɪnɪvə/ ▶ noun [mass noun] plain white fur used for lining or trimming clothes.
– ORIGIN Middle English: from Old French *menu vair* 'little vair', from *menu* 'little' + *vair* 'squirrel fur' (see **VAIR**).

minivet /ˈmɪnɪvɪt/ ▶ noun a boldly patterned Asian cuckoo-shrike (songbird), the male of which is typically red and black, and the female yellow and grey.
● Genus *Pericrocotus*, family Campephagidae: several species.
– ORIGIN mid 19th cent.: of unknown origin.

mink ▶ noun (pl. **same** or **minks**) a small semiaquatic stoat-like carnivore native to North America and Eurasia. The American mink is widely farmed for its fur, resulting in it becoming naturalized in many parts of Europe. ● Genus *Mustela*, family Mustelidae: the **American mink** (*M. vison*) and the smaller **European mink** (*M. lutreola*).
■ [mass noun] the thick brown fur of the mink. ■ a coat made of mink.
– ORIGIN late Middle English (denoting the animal's fur): from Swedish.

minke /ˈmɪŋkə, -ki/ (also **minke whale**) ▶ noun a small rorqual whale with a dark grey back, white underparts, and pale markings on the fins and behind the head. ● *Balaenoptera acutorostrata*, family Balaenopteridae.
– ORIGIN 1930s: probably from *Meincke*, the name of a Norwegian whaler.

min-min (also **min-min light**) ▶ noun Austral. a will-o'-the-wisp.
– ORIGIN possibly from a Queensland Aboriginal language.

Minn. ▶ abbreviation Minnesota.

Minneapolis /ˌmɪnɪˈapəlɪs/ an industrial city and port on the Mississippi in SE Minnesota; pop. 382,605 (est. 2008). It is a major agricultural centre of the upper Midwest.

minneola /ˌmɪnɪˈəʊlə/ ▶ noun a deep reddish tangelo (fruit) of a thin-skinned variety.
– ORIGIN mid 20th cent.: named after a town in Florida, US.

minnerichi /ˌmɪnəˈrɪtʃi/ (also **minnaritchi**) ▶ noun a small acacia of arid inland Australia, which typically has thin, peeling curls of reddish bark. ● *Acacia cyperophylla*, family Leguminosae.
– ORIGIN 1930s: an Aboriginal word.

Minnesinger /ˈmɪnəsɪŋə/ ▶ noun a German lyric poet and singer of the 12th–14th centuries, who performed songs of courtly love.
– ORIGIN early 19th cent.: from German *Minnesinger* 'love singer'.

Minnesota /ˌmɪnɪˈsəʊtə/ a state in the north central US, on the Canadian border; pop. 5,220,393 (est. 2008); capital, St Paul. It became the 32nd state of the US in 1858.
– DERIVATIVES **Minnesotan** noun & adjective.

minnow ▶ noun **1** a small freshwater Eurasian fish of the carp family, which typically forms large shoals.
● *Phoxinus phoxinus*, family Cyprinidae.
■ used in names of similar small freshwater fishes, e.g. **mudminnow**, **topminnow**. ■ Fishing an artificial lure imitating a minnow.
2 a small or insignificant person or organization: *the paper is a minnow in the national newspaper mass market.*
– ORIGIN late Middle English: probably related to Dutch *meun* and German *Münne*, influenced by Anglo-Norman French *menu* 'small, minnow'.

Miño /ˈmiːnjəʊ/ a river which rises in NW Spain and flows south to the Portuguese border, which it follows before entering the Atlantic north of Viana do Castelo. Portuguese name **MINHO**.

Minoan /mɪˈnəʊən/ ▶ adjective relating to or denoting a Bronze Age civilization centred on Crete (*c*.3000–1050 BC), its people, or its language.
▶ noun **1** an inhabitant of Minoan Crete or member of the Minoan people.
2 [mass noun] the language or scripts associated with the Minoans.

> The Minoan civilization had reached its zenith by the beginning of the late Bronze Age; impressive remains reveal the existence of large urban centres dominated by palaces. The civilization is also noted for its script (see **LINEAR A**) and distinctive art and architecture.

– ORIGIN named after the legendary Cretan king **MINOS**, to whom a palace excavated at Knossos was attributed.

minor ▶ adjective **1** lesser in importance, seriousness, or significance: *she requested a number of minor alterations.*
2 Music (of a scale) having intervals of a semitone between the second and third degrees, and (usually) the fifth and sixth, and the seventh and eighth. Contrasted with **MAJOR**. ■ (of an interval) characteristic of a minor scale and less by a semitone than the equivalent major interval. Compare with **DIMINISHED**. ■ [usu. postpositive] (of a key or mode) based on a minor scale and tending to produce a sad or pensive effect: *Concerto in A minor.*
3 Brit. dated (following a surname in public schools) indicating the younger of two brothers: *Smith minor.*
4 Logic (of a term) occurring as the subject of the conclusion of a categorical syllogism. ■ (of a premise) containing the minor term in a categorical syllogism.
▶ noun **1** a person under the age of full legal responsibility.
2 Music a minor key, interval, or scale. ■ Bell-ringing a system of change-ringing using six bells.

M

3 (**minors**) N. Amer. the minor leagues in baseball or American football: *Salinas was one of six teams in the minors*.
4 N. Amer. a student's subsidiary subject or course: *a minor in American Indian studies*.
5 Logic a minor term or premise.
6 Bridge short for **MINOR SUIT**.
7 a small drab moth which has purplish caterpillars that feed on grass. ● Genus *Oligia*, family Noctuidae.
▶ verb [no obj.] (**minor in**) N. Amer. study as or qualify in a subsidiary subject at college or university.
– ORIGIN Middle English: from Latin, 'smaller, less'; related to *minuere* 'lessen'. The term originally denoted a Franciscan friar, suggested by the Latin name *Fratres Minores* ('Lesser Brethren'), chosen by St Francis for the order.

minor arcana ▶ noun see **ARCANA**.

minor axis ▶ noun Geometry the shorter axis of an ellipse that is perpendicular to its major axis.

Minorca /mɪˈnɔːkə/ the most easterly and second-largest of the Balearic Islands; pop. 75,296 (2001); capital, Mahón. Spanish name **MENORCA**.
– DERIVATIVES **Minorcan** adjective & noun.

minor canon ▶ noun a member of the Christian clergy who assists in the daily services of a cathedral but is not a member of the chapter.

minor county ▶ noun Cricket, Brit. a county whose team does not take part in the County Championship.

Minorite /ˈmʌɪnərʌɪt/ ▶ noun a Franciscan friar or Friar Minor.

minority ▶ noun (pl. **minorities**) 1 the smaller number or part, especially a number or part representing less than half of the whole: *only **a minority of** properties are rented* | *those who acknowledge his influence are **in the minority*** | [as modifier] *a minority party*. ■ the number of votes cast for or by the smaller party in a legislative assembly: *a blocking minority of 23 votes*. ■ a small group of people within a community or country, differing from the main population in race, religion, language, or political persuasion: *ethnic minorities* | [as modifier] *minority rights*.
2 [mass noun] the state or period of being under the age of full legal responsibility.
– PHRASES **be** (or **find oneself**) **in a minority of one** often humorous be the sole person to hold a particular view.
– ORIGIN late 15th cent. (in sense 2): from French *minorité* or medieval Latin *minoritas*, from Latin *minor* 'smaller' (see **MINOR**).

minority government ▶ noun a government in which the governing party has most seats but still less than half the total.

minority report ▶ noun a separate report presented by members of a committee or other group who disagree with the majority.

minor league ▶ noun N. Amer. a league below the level of the major league in a professional sport, especially baseball. ■ [as modifier] insignificant; small-time: *a minor-league villain*.
– DERIVATIVES **minor-leaguer** noun.

minor orders ▶ plural noun chiefly historical the formal grades of Catholic or Orthodox clergy below the rank of deacon (most now discontinued).

minor piece ▶ noun Chess a bishop or knight.
– ORIGIN early 19th cent.: named in contrast to the rook or queen.

minor planet ▶ noun an asteroid. Often contrasted with **MAJOR PLANET**.

minor prophet ▶ noun any of the twelve prophets after whom the shorter prophetic books of the Bible, from Hosea to Malachi, are named.

minor suit ▶ noun Bridge diamonds or clubs.
– ORIGIN early 20th cent.: so named because of their lower scoring value.

minor tranquillizer ▶ noun a tranquillizer of the kind used to treat anxiety states, especially a benzodiazepine.

Minos /ˈmʌɪnɒs/ Greek Mythology a legendary king of Crete, son of Zeus and Europa. His wife Pasiphaë gave birth to the Minotaur; Minos later exacted tribute from Athens in the form of young people to be devoured by the monster.

Minos, Palace of a complex of buildings excavated and reconstructed by Sir Arthur Evans at Knossos in Crete, which yielded local coins portraying the labyrinth as the city's symbol and a Linear B religious tablet which refers to the 'lady of the labyrinth'.

Minotaur /ˈmɪnətɔː, ˈmʌɪ-/ Greek Mythology a creature who was half-man and half-bull, the offspring of Pasiphaë and a bull with which she fell in love. Confined in Crete in a labyrinth made by Daedalus and fed on human flesh, it was eventually slain by Theseus.
– ORIGIN from Old French, via Latin from Greek *Minōtauros*, from *Minōs* (see **MINOS**) + *tauros* 'bull'.

minotaur beetle ▶ noun a black Eurasian dung beetle with three horns on the thorax, living in sandy areas. ● *Typhaeus typhoeus*, family Geotrupidae.

minoxidil /mɪˈnɒksɪdɪl/ ▶ noun [mass noun] Medicine a synthetic drug which is used as a vasodilator in the treatment of hypertension, and is also used in lotions to promote hair growth.
– ORIGIN 1970s: from **AMINO** + **OXIDE** + *-dil* (perhaps representing **DILATE**).

Minsk /mɪnsk/ the capital of Belarus, an industrial city in the central region of the country; pop. 1,829,100 (est. 2009).

minster ▶ noun Brit. a large or important church, typically one of cathedral status in the north of England that was built as part of a monastery: *York Minster*.
– ORIGIN Old English *mynster*, via ecclesiastical Latin from Greek *monastērion* (see **MONASTERY**).

minstrel ▶ noun a medieval singer or musician, especially one who sang or recited lyric or heroic poetry to a musical accompaniment for the nobility. ■ chiefly historical a member of a band of entertainers with blackened faces who performed songs and music ostensibly of black American origin.
– ORIGIN Middle English: from Old French *menestral* 'entertainer, servant', via Provençal from late Latin *ministerialis* 'servant' (see **MINISTERIAL**).

minstrelsy ▶ noun [mass noun] the activity of performing as a minstrel or the occupation of a minstrel: *a long tradition of minstrelsy*.
– ORIGIN Middle English: from Old French *menestralsie*, from *menestrel* (see **MINSTREL**).

mint[1] ▶ noun 1 an aromatic plant native to temperate regions of the Old World, several kinds of which are used as culinary herbs. ● Genus *Mentha*, family Labiatae (or Lamiaceae; the **mint family**): several species and hybrids, in particular the widely cultivated **common mint** or **spearmint** (*M. spicata*) and **peppermint** (*M.* × *piperita*). The mint family, the members of which have distinctive two-lobed flowers and square stems, also includes the dead-nettles and many aromatic herbs.
■ [mass noun] the flavour of mint, especially peppermint.
2 a peppermint sweet.
– DERIVATIVES **minty** adjective (**mintier**, **mintiest**).
– ORIGIN Old English *minte*, of West Germanic origin; related to German *Minze*, ultimately via Latin from Greek *minthē*.

mint[2] ▶ noun a place where money is coined, especially under state authority. ■ (**a mint**) informal a large sum of money: *the curtains had **cost a mint*** | *the bank **made a mint** from the upheaval in the money markets*.
▶ adjective (of an object) in pristine condition; as new: *a pair of speakers, mint, £160*. ■ Brit. very good: *there was Dean, looking really mint in his new jacket*.
▶ verb [with obj.] make (a coin) by stamping metal. ■ (usu. as adj., with submodifier **minted**) produce for the first time: *an example of newly minted technology*.
– PHRASES **in mint condition** (of an object) new or as new.
– ORIGIN Old English *mynet* 'coin', of West Germanic origin; related to Dutch *munt* and German *Münze*, from Latin *moneta* 'money'. The adjective derives from an elliptical use of *in mint condition*.

mintage ▶ noun [mass noun] the minting of coins. ■ the number of copies issued of a particular coin.

minted ▶ adjective flavoured or seasoned with mint: *grilled lamb chops with minted potatoes*.

minter ▶ noun 1 a person who mints money.
2 Brit. informal a second-hand car in mint condition.

mint julep ▶ noun a long drink consisting of bourbon, crushed ice, sugar, and fresh mint and associated chiefly with the Southern states of the United States.

mint mark ▶ noun a mark on a coin indicating the mint at which it was struck.

mint master ▶ noun a superintendent at a mint.

Minton ▶ noun [mass noun] trademark pottery made at Stoke-on-Trent by Thomas Minton (1766–1836) or his factory. Minton's company popularized the willow pattern.

mint sauce ▶ noun [mass noun] chopped spearmint in vinegar and sugar, traditionally eaten with lamb.

minuend /ˈmɪnjʊend/ ▶ noun Mathematics a quantity or number from which another is to be subtracted.
– ORIGIN early 18th cent.: from Latin *minuendus*, gerundive of *minuere* 'diminish'.

minuet ▶ noun a slow, stately ballroom dance for two in triple time, popular especially in the 18th century. ■ a piece of music in triple time in the style of a minuet, typically as a movement in a suite, sonata, or symphony and frequently coupled with a trio.
▶ verb (**minuets, minueting, minueted**) [no obj.] dance a minuet.
– ORIGIN late 17th cent.: from French *menuet*, 'fine, delicate', diminutive (used as a noun) of *menu* 'small'.

minus ▶ preposition 1 with the subtraction of: *what's ninety three minus seven?* ■ informal lacking; deprived of: *he was minus a finger on each hand*.
2 (of temperature) below zero by: *minus 40 degrees centigrade*.
▶ adjective 1 (before a number) below zero; negative: *minus five*.
2 (after a grade) rather worse than: *C minus*.
3 having a negative electric charge.
▶ noun 1 short for **MINUS SIGN**.
2 a disadvantage: *for every plus with this equipment there can be a minus*.
– ORIGIN late 15th cent.: from Latin, neuter of *minor* 'less'.

minuscule /ˈmɪnəskjuːl/ (also **miniscule**) ▶ adjective 1 extremely small; tiny: *a minuscule fragment of DNA*. ■ informal so small as to be insignificant: *he believed the risk of infection was minuscule*.
2 of or in lower-case letters, as distinct from capitals or uncials. ■ of or in a small cursive script of the Roman alphabet, with ascenders and descenders, developed in the 7th century AD.
▶ noun [mass noun] minuscule script. ■ [count noun] a small or lower-case letter.
– ORIGIN early 18th cent.: from French, from Latin *minuscula* (*littera*) 'somewhat smaller (letter)'.

> **USAGE** The standard spelling is **minuscule** rather than **miniscule**. The latter form is a very common one (accounting for almost half of citations for the term in the Oxford English Corpus), and has been recorded since the late 19th century. It arose by analogy with other words beginning with **mini-**, where the meaning is similarly 'very small'. It is now so widely used that it can be considered as an acceptable variant, although it should be avoided in formal contexts.

minus sign ▶ noun the symbol –, indicating subtraction or a negative value.

minute[1] /ˈmɪnɪt/ ▶ noun 1 a period of time equal to sixty seconds or a sixtieth of an hour: *we waited for twenty minutes* | *I'll be there in ten minutes' time*. ■ the distance covered in this length of time by someone driving or walking: *the hotel is situated just ten minutes from the centre of the resort*. ■ informal a very short time: *come and sit down for a minute*. ■ a point in time: *she was laughing one minute and crying the next*.
2 (also **arc minute** or **minute of arc**) a sixtieth of a degree of angular measurement (symbol: ′).
– PHRASES **any minute** (or **at any minute**) very soon. **at the minute** Brit. informal at the present time. **by the minute** very rapidly: *matters grew worse by the minute*. **the minute** (or **the minute that**) as soon as. **not for a minute** not at all: *he didn't fool me for a minute*. **this minute** (or **this very minute**) informal 1 at once; immediately. 2 Brit. only a short while ago: *I've **just this minute** got back home*.
– ORIGIN late Middle English: via Old French from late Latin *minuta*, feminine (used as a noun) of *minutus* 'made small'. The senses 'period of sixty seconds' and 'sixtieth of a degree' derive from medieval Latin *pars minuta prima* 'first minute part'.

minute[2] /mʌɪˈnjuːt/ ▶ adjective (**minutest**) extremely small: *minute particles*. ■ so small as to be insignificant: *he will have no more than a minute chance of exercising influence*. ■ (of an investigation or account) taking the smallest points into consideration; precise and meticulous: *a minute examination of the islands*.
– DERIVATIVES **minuteness** noun.
– ORIGIN late Middle English (in the sense 'lesser', with reference to a tithe or tax): from Latin *minutus* 'lessened', past participle of *minuere*.

minute[3] /ˈmɪnɪt/ ▶ noun 1 (**minutes**) a summarized record of the proceedings at a meeting.
2 an official memorandum authorizing or recommending a course of action.
▶ verb [with obj.] 1 record (the proceedings of a meeting).

M

2 send a memorandum to (someone): *look up the case and minute me about it.*
– ORIGIN late Middle English (in the singular in the sense 'note or memorandum'): from French *minute*, from the notion of a rough copy in 'small writing' (Latin *scriptura minuta*) as distinct from the fair copy in book hand. The verb dates from the mid 16th cent.

minute gun ▶ noun a gun fired at intervals of a minute, especially at a funeral.

minute hand ▶ noun the hand on a watch or clock which indicates minutes.

minutely ▶ adverb with great attention to detail; meticulously: *systems of politics are examined minutely by academics* | [as submodifier] *minutely detailed descriptions covering every angle.*

minuteman /ˈmɪnɪtman/ ▶ noun (pl. **minutemen**) historical a member of a class of militiamen of the American revolutionary period who volunteered to be ready for service at a minute's notice.

minute steak ▶ noun a thin slice of steak cooked very quickly.

minutiae /mɪˈnjuːʃiː, mʌɪ-, -ʃɪʌɪ/ (also **minutia** /-ʃɪə/) ▶ plural noun the small, precise, or trivial details of something: *the minutiae of everyday life.*
– ORIGIN mid 18th cent.: Latin, literally 'trifles', from *minutia* 'smallness', from *minutus* (see **MINUTE**[2]).

minx ▶ noun humorous or derogatory an impudent, cunning, or boldly flirtatious girl or young woman.
– DERIVATIVES **minxish** adjective, **minxy** adjective.
– ORIGIN mid 16th cent. (denoting a pet dog): of unknown origin.

minyan /ˈmɪnjən/ ▶ noun (pl. **minyanim** /ˈmɪnjənɪm/) a quorum of ten men over the age of 13 required for traditional Jewish public worship.
– ORIGIN mid 18th cent.: from Hebrew *minyān*, literally 'reckoning'.

Miocene /ˈmʌɪə(ʊ)siːn/ ▶ adjective Geology relating to or denoting the fourth epoch of the Tertiary period, between the Oligocene and Pliocene epochs. ■ (as noun **the Miocene**) the Miocene epoch or the system of rocks deposited during it.

> The Miocene epoch lasted from 23.3 to 5.2 million years ago. During this time the Alps and Himalayas were being formed and there was diversification of the primates, including the first apes.

– ORIGIN mid 19th cent.: formed irregularly from Greek *meiōn* 'less' + *kainos* 'new'.

miosis /mʌɪˈəʊsɪs/ (also **myosis**) ▶ noun [mass noun] excessive constriction of the pupil of the eye.
– DERIVATIVES **miotic** adjective.
– ORIGIN early 19th cent.: from Greek *muein* 'shut the eyes' + **-OSIS**.

MIPS ▶ noun a unit of computing speed equivalent to a million instructions per second.
– ORIGIN 1970s: acronym.

Miquelet lock /ˈmɪkəlɪt/ ▶ noun historical a type of flintlock developed in Spain.
– ORIGIN late 17th cent.: via French from Spanish *miquelete*, from Catalan *Miquel*, equivalent of the given name Michael.

Miquelon see **ST PIERRE AND MIQUELON**.

Mir /mɪə/ a Soviet space station, launched in 1986 and designed to be permanently manned. It was deliberately brought down into the Pacific Ocean in 2001.

Mira /ˈmʌɪərə/ Astronomy a star in the constellation Cetus, regarded as the prototype of long-period variable stars.
– ORIGIN Latin, literally 'wonderful'.

Mirabeau /ˈmɪrəbəʊ/, French /miʀabəo/, Honoré Gabriel Riqueti, Comte de (1749–91), French revolutionary politician. Pressing for a form of constitutional monarchy, Mirabeau was prominent in the early days of the French Revolution.

mirabelle /ˈmɪrəbɛl/ ▶ noun a sweet yellow plum-like fruit that is a variety of the greengage. ■ the tree that bears mirabelles. ■ [mass noun] a liqueur distilled from mirabelles.
– ORIGIN early 18th cent.: from French.

mirabile dictu /mɪˌrɑːbɪleɪ ˈdɪktuː/ ▶ adverb wonderful to relate.
– ORIGIN Latin.

miracidium /ˌmʌɪrəˈsɪdɪəm/ ▶ noun (pl. **miracidia**) Zoology a free-swimming ciliated larval stage in which a parasitic fluke passes from the egg to its first host, typically a snail.
– ORIGIN late 19th cent.: from Greek *meirakidion*, diminutive of *meirakion* 'boy, stripling'.

miracle ▶ noun an extraordinary and welcome event that is not explicable by natural or scientific laws and is therefore attributed to a divine agency: *the miracle of rising from the grave.* ■ a remarkable event or development that brings very welcome consequences: *it was a miracle that more people hadn't been killed* | *industries at the heart of the economic miracle.* ■ an exceptional product or achievement, or an outstanding example of something: *a machine which was a miracle of design* | [as modifier] *a miracle drug.*
– ORIGIN Middle English: via Old French from Latin *miraculum* 'object of wonder', from *mirari* 'to wonder', from *mirus* 'wonderful'.

miracle play ▶ noun a mystery play.

miraculous ▶ adjective of the nature of a miracle or having the power to work miracles: *a miraculous cure.* ■ remarkable and bringing very welcome consequences: *I felt amazed and grateful for our miraculous escape.*
– DERIVATIVES **miraculously** adverb, **miraculousness** noun.
– ORIGIN late Middle English: from French *miraculeux* or medieval Latin *miraculosus*, from Latin *miraculum* (see **MIRACLE**).

mirador /ˌmɪrəˈdɔː, ˈmɪrədɔː/ ▶ noun a turret or tower attached to a building and providing an extensive view.
– ORIGIN late 17th cent.: from Spanish, from *mirar* 'to look'.

mirage /ˈmɪrɑːʒ, mɪˈrɑːʒ/ ▶ noun an optical illusion caused by atmospheric conditions, especially the appearance of a sheet of water in a desert or on a hot road caused by the refraction of light from the sky by heated air. ■ an unrealistic hope or wish that cannot be achieved: *the hope of sanctuary initially proved a mirage.*
– ORIGIN early 19th cent.: from French, from *se mirer* 'be reflected', from Latin *mirare* 'look at'.

Miranda[1] Astronomy a satellite of Uranus, the eleventh closest to the planet, having a complex terrain of cratered areas and tracts of grooves and ridges, discovered in 1948 (diameter 480 km).
– ORIGIN named after the daughter of Prospero in Shakespeare's *The Tempest*.

Miranda[2] ▶ adjective US Law denoting or relating to the duty of the police to inform a person taken into custody of their right to legal counsel and the right to remain silent under questioning: *the patrolman read Lee his Miranda rights.*
– ORIGIN 1960s: from *Miranda* versus Arizona, the case that led to this ruling by the Supreme Court.

MIRAS /ˈmʌɪrəs/ ▶ abbreviation (formerly in the UK) mortgage interest relief at source.

mirch /mɪətʃ/ ▶ noun Indian term for **CHILLI** or **CHILLI POWDER**.

mire ▶ noun **1** a stretch of swampy or boggy ground: *acres of land had been reduced to a mire.* ■ [mass noun] soft mud or dirt. ■ Ecology a wetland area or ecosystem based on peat.
2 a complicated or unpleasant situation from which it is difficult to extricate oneself: *the service is sinking in the mire of its own regulations.*
▶ verb [with obj.] cause to become stuck in mud. *sometimes a heavy truck gets mired down.* ■ cover or spatter with mud. ■ (**mire someone/thing in**) involve someone or something in (a difficult situation): *the economy is mired in its longest recession since the war.*
– ORIGIN Middle English: from Old Norse *mýrr*, of Germanic origin; related to **MOSS**.

mirepoix /ˈmɪəˌpwɑː/ ▶ noun a mixture of sautéed chopped vegetables used in various sauces.
– ORIGIN French, named after the Duc de *Mirepoix* (1699–1757), French general.

mirex /ˈmʌɪrɛks/ ▶ noun [mass noun] a synthetic insecticide of the organochlorine type used chiefly against ants.
– ORIGIN 1960s: of unknown origin.

mirid /ˈmɪrɪd, ˈmʌɪərɪd/ ▶ noun an active plant bug of a large family that includes numerous plant pests. Formerly called **CAPSID**[1]. ● Family Miridae (formerly Capsidae), suborder Heteroptera.
– ORIGIN 1940s: from modern Latin *Miridae*, from *mirus* 'wonderful'.

mirin /ˈmɪrɪn/ ▶ noun [mass noun] rice wine used as a flavouring in Japanese cookery.
– ORIGIN Japanese.

mirk ▶ noun & adjective archaic spelling of **MURK**.

mirky ▶ adjective archaic spelling of **MURKY**.

mirliton /ˈməːlɪtɒn/ ▶ noun **1** a musical instrument resembling a kazoo, with a nasal tone produced by a vibrating membrane.
2 US another term for **CHAYOTE** (sense 1).
– ORIGIN early 19th cent.: from French, 'reed pipe', of imitative origin.

miro /ˈmɪərəʊ/ (also **miro tree**) ▶ noun (pl. **miros**) an evergreen coniferous New Zealand tree which yields useful timber. ● *Prumnopitys ferruginea*, family Podocarpaceae.
– ORIGIN mid 19th cent.: from Maori.

Miró /mɪˈrəʊ/, Joan (1893–1983), Spanish painter. One of the most prominent figures of surrealism, he painted a brightly coloured fantasy world of variously spiky and amoebic calligraphic forms against plain backgrounds.

mirrnyong /ˈməːnjɒŋ/ (also **mirnyong**) ▶ noun Austral. a mound of shells, ashes, and other debris accumulated in a place used for cooking by Australian Aborigines.
– ORIGIN probably from an Aboriginal language of Victoria.

mirror ▶ noun a surface, typically of glass coated with a metal amalgam, which reflects a clear image. ■ a thing regarded as accurately representing something else: *the stage is supposed to be the mirror of life.* ■ (also **mirror site**) Computing a site on a network which stores the contents copied from another site.
▶ verb [with obj.] (of a surface) show a reflection of: *the clear water mirrored the sky.* ■ correspond to: *his own views mirrored those of his followers.* ■ Computing keep a copy of the contents of (a network site) at another site, typically in order to improve accessibility. ■ (usu. as noun **mirroring**) Computing store copies of data in (two or more hard disks) for protection.
– DERIVATIVES **mirrored** adjective.
– ORIGIN Middle English: from Old French *mirour*, based on Latin *mirare* 'look at'. Early senses also included 'a crystal used in magic' and 'a person deserving imitation'.

mirrorball ▶ noun a revolving ball covered with small mirrored facets, used to provide lighting effects at discos or dances.

mirror carp ▶ noun a common carp of an ornamental variety that has a row of large shiny plate-like scales along each side.

mirror finish ▶ noun a very smooth reflective finish produced on the surface of a metal.

mirror glass ▶ noun [mass noun] glass with a reflective metallic coating, as used for mirrors.

mirror image ▶ noun an image or object which is identical in form to another, but with the structure reversed, as in a mirror. ■ a person or thing that closely resembles another: *each shop is a mirror image of all the others.*

mirror symmetry ▶ noun [mass noun] symmetry about a plane, like that between an object and its reflection.

mirror writing ▶ noun [mass noun] reversed writing resembling ordinary writing reflected in a mirror.

mirth ▶ noun [mass noun] amusement, especially as expressed in laughter: *his six-foot frame shook with mirth.*
– ORIGIN Old English *myrgth*, of Germanic origin; related to **MERRY**.

mirthful ▶ adjective full of mirth; merry or amusing: *mirthful laughter.*
– DERIVATIVES **mirthfully** adverb.

mirthless ▶ adjective (of a smile or laugh) lacking real amusement and typically expressing irony.
– DERIVATIVES **mirthlessly** adverb, **mirthlessness** noun.

MIRV /məːv/ ▶ noun a type of intercontinental nuclear missile carrying several independent warheads.
– ORIGIN 1960s: acronym from *Multiple Independently targeted Re-entry Vehicle*.

miry /ˈmʌɪri/ ▶ adjective very muddy or boggy: *the roads were miry in winter.*

MIS ▶ abbreviation Computing management information systems.

mis-[1] ▶ prefix (added to verbs and their derivatives) wrongly: *misapply.* ■ badly: *mismanage.* ■ unsuitably: *misname.*
– ORIGIN Old English, of Germanic origin.

mis-[2] ▶ prefix occurring in a few words adopted from French expressing a sense with negative force: *misadventure* | *mischief.*

M

– ORIGIN from Old French *mes-* (based on Latin *minus*), assimilated to MIS-1.

misaddress ▶ verb [with obj.] address (a letter, parcel, email, etc.) wrongly.

misadventure ▶ noun **1** (also **death by misadventure**) [mass noun] English Law death caused by a person accidentally while performing a legal act without negligence or intent to harm.
2 an unfortunate incident; a mishap: *the petty misdemeanours and misadventures of childhood.*
– ORIGIN Middle English (in sense 2): from Old French *mesaventure*, from *mesavenir* 'turn out badly'.

misaligned ▶ adjective having an incorrect position or alignment: *misaligned headlights.*

misalignment ▶ noun [mass noun] the incorrect arrangement or position of something in relation to something else.

misalliance ▶ noun an unsuitable, unhappy, or unworkable alliance or marriage.
– ORIGIN mid 18th cent.: from MIS-1 'awry' + ALLIANCE, on the pattern of French *mésalliance*.

misallocate ▶ verb [with obj.] fail to allocate (something) efficiently or fairly.
– DERIVATIVES **misallocation** noun.

misandry /mɪ'sandri/ ▶ noun [mass noun] the hatred of men (i.e. the male sex specifically).
– DERIVATIVES **misandrist** noun.
– ORIGIN 1940s: from Greek *miso-* 'hating' + *anēr, andr-* 'man', on the pattern of *misogyny*.

misanthrope /'mɪz(ə)nθrəʊp, mɪs-/ (also **misanthropist** /mɪ'zanθrəpɪst, mɪ'san-/) ▶ noun a person who dislikes humankind and avoids human society.
– ORIGIN mid 16th cent.: from Greek *misanthrōpos*, from *misein* 'to hate' + *anthrōpos* 'man'.

misanthropic ▶ adjective having or showing a dislike of other people; unsociable: *a misanthropic drunken loner.*
– DERIVATIVES **misanthropical** adjective, **misanthropically** adverb.

misanthropy /mɪ'zanθrəpi, mɪ'san-/ ▶ noun [mass noun] a dislike of humankind.
– ORIGIN mid 17th cent.: from Greek *misanthrōpia*, from *miso-* 'hating' + *anthrōpos* 'man'.

misapply ▶ verb (**misapplies**, **misapplying**, **misapplied**) [with obj.] use (something) for the wrong purpose or in the wrong way.
– DERIVATIVES **misapplication** noun.

misapprehend ▶ verb [with obj.] fail to understand (a person or their words) correctly; misinterpret.

misapprehension ▶ noun a mistaken belief about or interpretation of something: *people tried to exchange the vouchers **under the misapprehension** that they were book tokens.*

misappropriate ▶ verb [with obj.] dishonestly or unfairly take (something, especially money, belonging to another) for one's own use: *the report revealed that department officials had misappropriated funds.*

misappropriation ▶ noun [mass noun] the action of misappropriating something; embezzlement: *an alleged misappropriation of funds.*

misattribute ▶ verb [with obj.] wrongly attribute: *the professor **misattributed** Robert Burn's famous line **to** Shakespeare.*
– DERIVATIVES **misattribution** noun.

misbegotten ▶ adjective badly conceived or planned: *someone's misbegotten idea of an English country house.* ■ contemptible (used as a term of abuse): *you misbegotten hound!* ■ archaic (of a child) illegitimate.

misbehave ▶ verb [no obj.] (of a person, especially a child) fail to conduct oneself in an acceptable way; behave badly. ■ (of a machine) fail to function correctly: *her regularly serviced car was misbehaving.*

misbehaviour (US **misbehavior**) ▶ noun [mass noun] the action of misbehaving; bad behaviour: *he had denied all sexual misbehaviour.*

misbelief ▶ noun a wrong or false belief or opinion: *the misbelief that alcohol problems require a specialist response.*
– DERIVATIVES **misbeliever** noun.

misc. ▶ abbreviation miscellaneous.

miscalculate ▶ verb [with obj.] calculate (an amount or measurement) wrongly. ■ assess (a situation) wrongly.

miscalculation ▶ noun an act of miscalculating; an error or misjudgement: *miscalculations were made in counting properties | it was a fatal miscalculation.*

miscall ▶ verb **1** [with obj. and complement] call (something) by a wrong or inappropriate name: *the agency is usually miscalled MI6 by the press.* ■ [with obj.] archaic or dialect insult (someone).
2 [with obj.] wrongly predict the result of (a future event, especially an election or a vote).

miscarriage ▶ noun **1** the spontaneous or unplanned expulsion of a fetus from the womb before it is able to survive independently: *his wife had a miscarriage* | [mass noun] *some pregnancies result in miscarriage.*
2 an unsuccessful outcome of something planned: *the miscarriage of the project.*

miscarriage of justice ▶ noun a failure of a court or judicial system to attain the ends of justice, especially one which results in the conviction of an innocent person.

miscarry ▶ verb (**miscarries**, **miscarrying**, **miscarried**) [no obj.] **1** (of a pregnant woman) experience a miscarriage: *Wendy miscarried after five weeks* | [with obj.] *she miscarried her first baby.*
2 (of a plan) fail to attain an intended outcome: *such a rash crime, and one so very likely to miscarry!* ■ dated (of a letter) fail to reach its intended destination.

miscast ▶ verb (past and past participle **miscast**) [with obj.] allot an unsuitable role to (an actor): *he is badly miscast in the romantic lead.* ■ allot the roles in (a play or film) to unsuitable actors.

miscegenation /ˌmɪsɪdʒɪ'neɪʃ(ə)n/ ▶ noun [mass noun] the interbreeding of people considered to be of different racial types.
– ORIGIN mid 19th cent.: formed irregularly from Latin *miscere* 'to mix' + *genus* 'race' + -ATION.

miscellanea /ˌmɪsə'leɪnɪə/ ▶ plural noun miscellaneous items, especially literary compositions, that have been collected together.
– ORIGIN late 16th cent.: from Latin, neuter plural of *miscellaneus* (see MISCELLANEOUS).

miscellaneous /ˌmɪsə'leɪnɪəs/ ▶ adjective (of items or people gathered or considered together) of various types or from different sources: *he picked up the miscellaneous papers in his in tray.* ■ (of a collection or group) composed of members or elements of different kinds: *a miscellaneous collection of well-known ne'er-do-wells.*
– DERIVATIVES **miscellaneously** adverb, **miscellaneousness** noun.
– ORIGIN early 17th cent.: from Latin *miscellaneus* (from *miscellus* 'mixed', from *miscere* 'to mix') + -OUS. In earlier use the word also described a person as 'having various qualities'.

miscellany /mɪ'sɛləni/ ▶ noun (pl. **miscellanies**) a group or collection of different items; a mixture: *a **miscellany of** houses.* ■ a book containing a collection of pieces of writing by different authors.
– DERIVATIVES **miscellanist** noun.
– ORIGIN late 16th cent.: from French *miscellanées* (feminine plural), from Latin *miscellanea* (see MISCELLANEA).

mischance ▶ noun [mass noun] bad luck: *by pure mischance the secret was revealed.* ■ [count noun] an unlucky occurrence: *innumerable mischances might ruin the enterprise.*
– ORIGIN Middle English: from Old French *mescheance*, from the verb *mescheoir*, from *mes-* 'adversely' + *cheoir* 'befall'.

mischief ▶ noun [mass noun] **1** playful misbehaviour, especially on the part of children: *she'll make sure Danny doesn't **get into mischief**.* ■ playfulness that is intended to tease or create trouble: *her eyes twinkled with irrepressible mischief.*
2 harm or trouble caused by someone or something: *she was bent on **making mischief**.* ■ [count noun] archaic a person responsible for harm or annoyance.
3 Law a wrong or hardship that a statute is designed to remove or for which the common law affords a remedy.
– PHRASES **do someone** (or **oneself**) **a mischief** Brit. informal injure someone or oneself.
– ORIGIN late Middle English (denoting misfortune or distress): from Old French *meschief*, from the verb *meschever*, from *mes-* 'adversely' + *chever* 'come to an end' (from *chef* 'head').

mischief-making ▶ noun [mass noun] the action of deliberately creating trouble for other people.
– DERIVATIVES **mischief-maker** noun.

mischievous /'mɪstʃɪvəs/ ▶ adjective **1** causing or showing a fondness for causing trouble in a playful way: *mischievous children | a mischievous grin.*
2 (of an action or statement) causing or intended to cause harm or trouble: *a mischievous allegation for which there is not a shred of evidence.*
– DERIVATIVES **mischievously** adverb, **mischievousness** noun.
– ORIGIN Middle English: from Anglo-Norman French *meschevous*, from Old French *meschever* 'come to an unfortunate end' (see MISCHIEF). The early sense was 'unfortunate or calamitous', later 'having harmful effects'; the sense 'playfully troublesome' dates from the late 17th cent.

> **USAGE** Mischievous is a three-syllable word; it should not be pronounced with four syllables, as if it were spelled **mischievious** /mɪs'tʃiːvɪəs/.

misch metal /mɪʃ/ ▶ noun [mass noun] an alloy of cerium, lanthanum, and other rare earth metals, used as an additive in various alloys, e.g. in flints for cigarette lighters.
– ORIGIN 1920s: from German *Mischmetall*, from *mischen* 'to mix' + *Metall* 'metal'.

miscible /'mɪsɪb(ə)l/ ▶ adjective (of liquids) forming a homogeneous mixture when added together: *sorbitol is miscible with glycerol.*
– DERIVATIVES **miscibility** noun.
– ORIGIN late 16th cent.: from medieval Latin *miscibilis*, from Latin *miscere* 'to mix'.

misclassify ▶ verb (**misclassifies**, **misclassifying**, **misclassified**) [with obj.] classify incorrectly; assign to the wrong category: *employees who were misclassified as temporary staff.*
– DERIVATIVES **misclassification** noun.

miscommunication ▶ noun [mass noun] failure to communicate adequately.

misconceive ▶ verb [with obj.] fail to understand (something) correctly: *some academic latinists did misconceive Pound's poem in that way.* ■ judge or plan badly, typically on the basis of faulty understanding: *criticism of the trade surplus in Washington is misconceived* | (as adj. **misconceived**) *this misconceived project.*

misconception ▶ noun a view or opinion that is incorrect because based on faulty thinking or understanding: ***public misconceptions about** AIDS remain high.*

misconduct ▶ noun /mɪs'kɒndʌkt/ [mass noun] **1** unacceptable or improper behaviour, especially by an employee or professional person: *she was found guilty of professional misconduct by a disciplinary tribunal and dismissed.* ■ [count noun] Ice Hockey a penalty assessed against a player for unsportsmanlike conduct.
2 mismanagement, especially culpable neglect of duties.
▶ verb /mɪskən'dʌkt/ **1** (**misconduct oneself**) behave in an improper manner.
2 [with obj.] mismanage (an activity).

misconfigure ▶ verb [with obj.] (often as adj. **misconfigured**) Computing configure (a system or part of it) incorrectly: *misconfigured Windows systems.*
– DERIVATIVES **misconfiguration** noun.

misconstruct ▶ verb [with obj.] rare misconstrue (something).

misconstruction ▶ noun [mass noun] the action of misconstruing words or actions; misinterpretation: *I used a phrase which may be open to misconstruction.*

misconstrue ▶ verb (**misconstrues**, **misconstruing**, **misconstrued**) [with obj.] interpret (a person's words or actions) wrongly: *my advice was deliberately misconstrued.*

miscopy ▶ verb (**miscopies**, **miscopying**, **miscopied**) [with obj.] copy (something) incorrectly.

miscount ▶ verb [with obj.] count (something) incorrectly.
▶ noun an incorrect reckoning: *a miscount necessitates a recount.*

miscreant /'mɪskrɪənt/ ▶ noun a person who has done something wrong or unlawful. ■ archaic a heretic.
▶ adjective (of a person) behaving badly or unlawfully: *her miscreant husband.* ■ archaic heretical.
– ORIGIN Middle English (as an adjective in the sense 'disbelieving'): from Old French *mescreant*, present participle of *mescreire* 'disbelieve', from *mes-* 'mis-' + *creire* 'believe' (from Latin *credere*).

miscue1 ▶ noun (in billiards and snooker) a shot in which the player fails to strike the ball properly with the cue. ■ (in other sports) a faulty strike, kick, or catch. ■ a mistake: *political miscues that led to resignations.*
▶ verb (**miscues**, **miscueing** or **miscuing**, **miscued**) [with obj.] (in snooker and other sports) fail to strike (the ball or a shot) properly.

miscue² ▶ **noun** Linguistics an error in reading, especially one caused by failure to respond correctly to a phonetic or contextual cue in the text.

misdate ▶ **verb** [with obj.] assign an incorrect date to (a document, event, or work of art).

misdeal ▶ **verb** (past and past participle **misdealt**) [no obj.] make a mistake when dealing cards.
▶ **noun** (in a card game) a hand dealt wrongly.

misdeclaration ▶ **noun** an incorrect declaration, especially in an official context.

misdeed ▶ **noun** a wicked or illegal act.
– ORIGIN Old English *misdǣd* (see **MIS-¹**, **DEED**).

misdelivery ▶ **noun** [mass noun] delivery to the wrong person or at the wrong time.

misdemeanant ▶ **noun** formal a person convicted of a misdemeanour or guilty of misconduct.
– ORIGIN early 19th cent.: from archaic *misdemean* 'misbehave' + **-ANT**.

misdemeanour (US **misdemeanor**) ▶ **noun** **1** a minor wrongdoing: *the player can expect a suspension for his latest misdemeanour.*
2 Law a non-indictable offence, regarded in the US (and formerly in the UK) as less serious than a felony.

misdescribe ▶ **verb** [with obj.] describe inaccurately or misleadingly: *he misdescribed the play as a tragedy.*
– DERIVATIVES **misdescription** noun.

misdiagnose ▶ **verb** [with obj.] make an incorrect diagnosis of (an illness): *the most common form of pneumonia is widely misdiagnosed.* ■ make an incorrect diagnosis of the illness from which (someone) is suffering: *the consultant misdiagnosed her as having cancer.*
– DERIVATIVES **misdiagnosis** noun.

misdial ▶ **verb** (**misdials**, **misdialling**, **misdialled**; US **misdials**, **misdialing**, **misdialed**) [no obj.] dial a telephone number incorrectly.
▶ **noun** an act of dialling a telephone number incorrectly.

misdirect ▶ **verb** [with obj.] **1** direct to the wrong place or in the wrong direction: *voters were misdirected to the wrong polling station.* ■ use or apply (something) wrongly or inappropriately: *their efforts have been largely misdirected.*
2 (of a judge) instruct (a jury) wrongly.
– DERIVATIVES **misdirection** noun.

misdoing ▶ **noun** a misdeed.

misdoubt ▶ **verb** [with obj.] **1** archaic or dialect have doubts about the truth, reality, or existence of: *he always misdoubted his own ability.*
2 fear or be suspicious about: *for I fear my father, and I misdoubt his hindrances.*

miseducate ▶ **verb** [with obj.] educate, teach, or inform (someone) wrongly.
– DERIVATIVES **miseducation** noun, **miseducative** adjective.

mise en place /ˌmiːz ɒ̃ ˈplas/, French /miz ɑ̃ plas/ ▶ **noun** [usu. in sing.] (in a professional kitchen) the preparation of dishes and ingredients before the beginning of service.
– ORIGIN French, literally 'putting in place'.

mise en scène /ˌmiːz ɒ̃ ˈsɛn/, French /miz ɑ̃ sɛn/ ▶ **noun** [usu. in sing.] the arrangement of scenery and stage properties in a play. ■ the setting or surroundings of an event.
– ORIGIN French, literally 'putting on stage'.

misemploy ▶ **verb** [with obj.] employ or use (something) wrongly or improperly.
– DERIVATIVES **misemployment** noun.

miser ▶ **noun** a person who hoards wealth and spends as little money as possible.
– ORIGIN late 15th cent. (as an adjective in the sense 'miserly'): from Latin, literally 'wretched'.

miserabilism ▶ **noun** [mass noun] gloomy pessimism or negativity: *the duo spent much of the eighties exploring the lonely outer reaches of miserabilism.*
– DERIVATIVES **miserabilist** noun & adjective.

miserable ▶ **adjective** **1** (of a person) wretchedly unhappy or uncomfortable: *their happiness made Anne feel even more miserable.* ■ causing unhappiness or discomfort: *horribly wet and miserable conditions.* ■ (of a person) habitually morose: *a miserable man in his late sixties.*
2 pitiably small or inadequate: *all they pay me is a miserable £8,000 a year.* ■ Austral./NZ & Scottish miserly: *a lousy dollar a day — could any government be more miserable?*
3 [attrib.] contemptible (used as a term of abuse or for emphasis): *you miserable old creep!*
– DERIVATIVES **miserableness** noun, **miserably** adverb.
– ORIGIN late Middle English: from French *misérable*, from Latin *miserabilis* 'pitiable', from *miserari* 'to pity', from *miser* 'wretched'.

misère /mɪˈzɛː/ ▶ **noun** (in solo whist) a bid by which a player undertakes to win no tricks.
ORIGIN early 19th cent.: French, literally 'poverty or misery'.

misère ouverte /mɪˌzɛː uːˈvɛːt/ ▶ **noun** (in solo whist) a bid by which a player undertakes to win no tricks, playing with all their cards exposed on the table.
– ORIGIN from **MISÈRE** + French *ouverte* (feminine) 'open (to view)'.

miserere /ˌmɪzəˈrɪəri, -ˈrɛː-/ ▶ **noun** **1** a psalm in which mercy is sought, especially Psalm 51 or the music written for it.
2 another term for **MISERICORD** (sense 1).
– ORIGIN Middle English: from Latin, 'have mercy!', imperative of *misereri*, from *miser* 'wretched'.

misericord /mɪˈzɛrɪkɔːd/ ▶ **noun** **1** a ledge projecting from the underside of a hinged seat in a choir stall which, when the seat is turned up, gives support to someone standing.
2 historical an apartment in a monastery in which some relaxations of the monastic rule were permitted.
3 historical a small dagger used to deliver a death stroke to a wounded enemy.
– ORIGIN Middle English (denoting pity): from Old French *misericorde*, from Latin *misericordia*, from *misericors* 'compassionate', from the stem of *misereri* 'to pity' + *cor*, *cord-* 'heart'.

miserliness ▶ **noun** [mass noun] excessive desire to save money; extreme meanness: *the party earned a damaging reputation for miserliness by cutting pensions.* ■ the quality of being small or inadequate; meagreness: *the relative miserliness of the prizes involved.*

miserly ▶ **adjective** of or characteristic of a miser: *his miserly great-uncle proved to be worth nearly £1 million.* ■ (of a quantity) pitiably small or inadequate: *the prize for the winner will be a miserly £3,500.*

misery ▶ **noun** (pl. **miseries**) [mass noun] a state or feeling of great physical or mental distress or discomfort: *a man who had brought her nothing but misery | the misery of the miner's existence.* ■ [count noun] (usu. **miseries**) a cause or source of great distress or discomfort: *the miseries of war.* ■ [count noun] Brit. informal a person who is constantly miserable or discontented: *have we really been such a bunch of miseries to work with?*
– PHRASES **make someone's life a misery** (or **make life a misery for someone**) cause someone severe distress by continued unpleasantness or harassment. **put someone/thing out of their misery** end the suffering of a person or animal in pain by killing them. ■ informal release someone from suspense or anxiety by telling them something they are anxious to know.
– ORIGIN late Middle English: from Old French *miserie*, from Latin *miseria*, from *miser* 'wretched'.

misestimate ▶ **verb** [with obj.] make an incorrect estimate of: *it became clear that we'd misestimated the difficulty of the project.*
– DERIVATIVES **misestimation** noun.

misfeasance /mɪsˈfiːz(ə)ns/ ▶ **noun** Law a transgression, especially the wrongful exercise of lawful authority.
– ORIGIN early 17th cent.: from Old French *mesfaisance*, from *mesfaire*, from *mes-* 'wrongly' + *faire* 'do' (from Latin *facere*). Compare with **MALFEASANCE**.

misfeed ▶ **noun** an instance of faulty feeding of something (typically paper) through a machine.

misfield ▶ **verb** [with obj.] (in cricket and rugby) field (a ball) badly or clumsily.
▶ **noun** (in cricket and rugby) a failure to field a ball correctly.

misfile ▶ **verb** [with obj.] file (a document) in the wrong place.

misfire ▶ **verb** [no obj.] **1** (of a gun or missile) fail to discharge or fire properly. ■ (of an internal-combustion engine) undergo failure of the fuel to ignite correctly or at all: *the car would misfire occasionally from the cold.* ■ (of a nerve cell) fail to transmit an electrical impulse at an appropriate moment.
2 (especially of a plan) fail to produce the intended result: *he didn't know that his plan had misfired.*
▶ **noun** a failure of a gun or missile to fire correctly. ■ a failure of fuel to ignite correctly in an internal-combustion engine.

misfit ▶ **noun** a person whose behaviour or attitude sets them apart from others in an uncomfortably conspicuous way: *a motley collection of social misfits.* ■ archaic something that does not fit or that fits badly.

misfit stream ▶ **noun** Geography a stream occupying a valley which is larger than would be predicted on the basis of the stream's present erosive power.

misfortune ▶ **noun** [mass noun] bad luck: *the project was dogged by misfortune.* ■ [count noun] an unfortunate condition or event: *never laugh at other people's misfortunes.*

misgive ▶ **verb** (past **misgave** ; past participle **misgiven**) [with obj.] literary (of a person's mind or heart) fill (that person) with doubt, apprehension, or foreboding: *my heart misgave me when I saw him.*

misgiving ▶ **noun** (usu. **misgivings**) a feeling of doubt or apprehension about the outcome or consequences of something: *we have* ***misgivings about*** *the way the campaign is being run* | [mass noun] *I felt a sense of misgiving at the prospect of retirement.*

misgovern ▶ **verb** [with obj.] govern (a state or country) unfairly or inefficiently.
– DERIVATIVES **misgovernment** noun.

misguide ▶ **verb** [with obj.] rare mislead: *a long survey that can only baffle and misguide the general reader.*
– DERIVATIVES **misguidance** noun.

misguided ▶ **adjective** having or showing faulty judgement or reasoning: *their misguided belief that they were defending the honour of their country.*
– DERIVATIVES **misguidedly** adverb, **misguidedness** noun.

mishandle ▶ **verb** [with obj.] **1** manage or deal with (something) wrongly or ineffectively: *the officer had mishandled the situation.*
2 manipulate roughly or carelessly: *the equipment could be dangerous if mishandled.*

mishap ▶ **noun** an unlucky accident: *although there were a few minor mishaps, none of the pancakes stuck to the ceiling* | [mass noun] *the event passed without mishap.*

mishear ▶ **verb** (past and past participle **misheard**) [with obj.] fail to hear (a person or their words) correctly.

mishit ▶ **verb** (**mishits**, **mishitting**, **mishit**) [with obj.] (in various sports) hit or kick (a ball) badly or in the wrong direction.
▶ **noun** an instance of hitting or kicking a ball badly or in the wrong direction.

mishmash ▶ **noun** [in sing.] a confused mixture: *a mishmash of outmoded ideas.*
– ORIGIN late 15th cent.: reduplication of **MASH**.

Mishnah /ˈmɪʃnə/ ▶ **noun** (**the Mishnah**) an authoritative collection of exegetical material embodying the oral tradition of Jewish law and forming the first part of the Talmud.
– DERIVATIVES **Mishnaic** /-ˈneɪɪk/ adjective.
– ORIGIN from Hebrew *mišnāh* '(teaching by) repetition'.

mishugas ▶ **noun** variant spelling of **MESHUGAAS**.

misidentify /mɪsʌɪˈdɛntɪfʌɪ/ ▶ **verb** (**misidentifies**, **misidentifying**, **misidentified**) [with obj.] identify (something or someone) incorrectly.
– DERIVATIVES **misidentification** /-fɪˈkeɪʃ(ə)n/ noun.

misinform ▶ **verb** [with obj.] give (someone) false or inaccurate information.

misinformation ▶ **noun** [mass noun] false or inaccurate information, especially that which is deliberately intended to deceive: *nuclear matters are often entangled in a web of secrecy and misinformation.*

misinterpret ▶ **verb** (**misinterprets**, **misinterpreting**, **misinterpreted**) [with obj.] interpret (something or someone) wrongly.
– DERIVATIVES **misinterpretation** noun, **misinterpreter** noun.

misjudge ▶ **verb** [with obj.] form a wrong opinion or conclusion about: *I've misjudged Doris—she hasn't told anyone.* ■ make an incorrect estimation or assessment of: *the horse misjudged the fence and Mrs Weaver was thrown off.*
– DERIVATIVES **misjudgement** (also **misjudgment**) noun.

miskey ▶ **verb** (**miskeys**, **miskeying**, **miskeyed**) [with obj.] key (a word or piece of data) into a computer or other machine incorrectly.

miskick ▶ **verb** [with obj.] kick (a ball) badly or wrongly.
▶ **noun** an instance of miskicking a ball.

Miskito /mɪˈskiːtəʊ/ (also **Mosquito**) ▸ noun (pl. same or **Miskitos**) **1** a member of an American Indian people of the Atlantic coast of Nicaragua and Honduras.
2 [mass noun] the language of the Miskito, possibly related to Chibchan.
▸ adjective relating to the Miskito or their language.
– ORIGIN the name in Miskito.

Miskolc /ˈmiːʃkɒlts/ a city in NE Hungary; pop. 170,234 (2009).

mislabel ▸ verb (**mislabels, mislabelling, mislabelled**) [with obj.] label incorrectly.

mislay ▸ verb (past and past participle **mislaid**) [with obj.] unintentionally put (an object) where it cannot readily be found and so lose it temporarily: *I seem to have mislaid my car keys.*

mislead ▸ verb (past and past participle **misled**) [with obj.] cause (someone) to have a wrong idea or impression: *the government misled the public about the road's environmental impact.*
– DERIVATIVES **misleader** noun.

misleading ▸ adjective giving the wrong idea or impression: *your article contains a number of misleading statements.*
– DERIVATIVES **misleadingly** adverb, **misleadingness** noun.

mislike archaic ▸ verb [with obj.] consider to be unpleasant.
▸ noun [mass noun] distaste; dislike.
– ORIGIN Old English *mislīcian* (see **MIS-**[1], **LIKE**[2]).

mismanage ▸ verb [with obj.] manage (something) badly or wrongly.
– DERIVATIVES **mismanagement** noun.

mismarriage ▸ noun an unsuitable marriage or alliance.

mismatch ▸ noun **1** a failure to correspond or match; a discrepancy: *a huge **mismatch between** supply and demand.*
2 an unequal or unfair sporting contest.
▸ verb [with obj.] (usu. as adj. **mismatched**) match (people or things) unsuitably or incorrectly: *a pair of mismatched cops.*

mismatch repair ▸ noun [mass noun] a DNA repair system whereby one member of a mismatched pair of bases is converted to the normally matched base.

mismate ▸ verb [with obj.] match unsuitably or wrongly; mismatch: (as adj. **mismated**) *a pair of mismated shoes.*

mismeasure ▸ verb [with obj.] measure or estimate incorrectly.
– DERIVATIVES **mismeasurement** noun.

misname ▸ verb [with obj.] give a wrong or inappropriate name to: *the place is misnamed—it's too well organized to be a wilderness.*

misnomer ▸ noun a wrong or inaccurate name or designation: *'King crab' is a misnomer—these creatures are not crustaceans at all.* ■ a wrong or inaccurate use of a name or term: *to call this 'neighbourhood policing' would be a misnomer.*
– ORIGIN late Middle English: from Anglo-Norman French, from the Old French verb *mesnommer*, from *mes-* 'wrongly' + *nommer* 'to name' (based on Latin *nomen* 'name').

misnumber ▸ verb [with obj.] number incorrectly.

miso /ˈmiːsəʊ/ ▸ noun [mass noun] paste made from fermented soya beans and barley or rice malt, used in Japanese cookery.
– ORIGIN Japanese.

misogamy /mɪˈsɒɡəmi, mʌɪ-/ ▸ noun [mass noun] rare the hatred of marriage.
– ORIGIN mid 17th cent.: from Greek *misos* 'hatred' + *gamos* 'marriage'.

misogynist /mɪˈsɒdʒ(ə)nɪst, mʌɪ-/ ▸ noun a man who hates women.
▸ adjective having or showing a hatred of women: *a misogynist attitude.*
– DERIVATIVES **misogynistic** adjective.

misogyny /mɪˈsɒdʒ(ə)ni, mʌɪ-/ ▸ noun [mass noun] the hatred of women by men: *she felt she was struggling against thinly disguised misogyny.*
– DERIVATIVES **misogynous** adjective.
– ORIGIN mid 17th cent.: from Greek *misos* 'hatred' + *gunē* 'woman'.

misperceive ▸ verb [with obj.] perceive wrongly or incorrectly.
– DERIVATIVES **misperception** noun.

mispickel /ˈmɪspɪk(ə)l/ ▸ noun another term for **ARSENOPYRITE**.
– ORIGIN late 17th cent.: from German.

misplace ▸ verb [with obj.] **1** put (an object) in the wrong place and so lose it temporarily: *I'm sure the jewellery has just been misplaced, and not stolen.*
2 position incorrectly: *Crewe came back into the game when Strachan misplaced a pass in the midfield.*
– DERIVATIVES **misplacement** noun.

misplaced ▸ adjective **1** incorrectly positioned: *a million dollars had been lost because of a misplaced comma.* ■ not appropriate or correct in the circumstances: *a telling sign of misplaced priorities.* ■ (of a feeling or emotion) directed unwisely or to an inappropriate object: *he began to wonder if his sympathy was misplaced.*
2 [attrib.] temporarily lost: *her misplaced keys.*

misplay ▸ verb [with obj.] play (a ball or card) wrongly, badly, or in contravention of the rules.
▸ noun an instance of misplaying a ball or card.

misprint ▸ noun an error in printed text: *Galway might be a misprint for Galloway.*
▸ verb [with obj.] print (something) incorrectly.

misprision[1] /mɪsˈprɪʒ(ə)n/ (also **misprision of treason** or **felony**) ▸ noun Law, chiefly historical the deliberate concealment of one's knowledge of a treasonable act or a felony.
– ORIGIN late Middle English: from Old French *mesprision* 'error', from *mesprendre*, from *mes-* 'wrongly' + *prendre* 'to take'.

misprision[2] /mɪsˈprɪʒ(ə)n/ ▸ noun [mass noun] rare failure to appreciate or recognize the value or identity of something: *he despised himself for his misprision.*
– ORIGIN late 16th cent.: from **MISPRIZE**, influenced by **MISPRISION**[1].

misprize ▸ verb [with obj.] rare fail to appreciate the value of (something); undervalue.
– ORIGIN late 15th cent.: from Old French *mesprisier*, from *mes-* 'wrongly' + *prisier* 'estimate the value of'.

mispronounce ▸ verb [with obj.] pronounce (a word) incorrectly: *she mispronounced my name.*
– DERIVATIVES **mispronunciation** noun.

misquote ▸ verb [with obj.] quote (a person or a piece of written or spoken text) inaccurately: *the government insisted that the official had been misquoted.*
▸ noun a passage or remark quoted inaccurately: *a misquote from a poem by Robert Burns.*
– DERIVATIVES **misquotation** noun.

misread ▸ verb (past and past participle **misread**) [with obj.] read (a piece of text) wrongly. ■ judge or interpret (a situation or a person's manner or behaviour) incorrectly: *had she been completely misreading his intentions?*

misrecognize (also **misrecognise**) ▸ verb [with obj.] mistake the identity of.
– DERIVATIVES **misrecognition** noun.

misremember ▸ verb [with obj.] remember imperfectly or incorrectly.

misreport ▸ verb [with obj.] give a false or inaccurate account of (something): *the press exaggerated and misreported the response to the film.*
▸ noun a false or incorrect report.

misrepresent ▸ verb [with obj.] give a false or misleading account of the nature of: *you are misrepresenting the views of the government.*
– DERIVATIVES **misrepresentative** adjective.

misrepresentation ▸ noun [mass noun] the action or offence of giving a false or misleading account of the nature of something: *she is seeking damages on allegations of misrepresentation* | [count noun] *a gross misrepresentation of the situation.*

misroute ▸ verb [with obj.] divert or direct to the wrong place or by the wrong route.

misrule ▸ noun [mass noun] **1** the unfair or inefficient conduct of the affairs of a country or state: *a country that is recovering from decades of misrule.*
2 the disruption of peace; disorder: *there was a tradition of misrule before, during, and after games.*
▸ verb [with obj.] govern (a country or state) badly.

miss[1] ▸ verb [with obj.] **1** fail to hit, reach, or come into contact with (something aimed at): *a laser-guided bomb had missed its target* | [no obj.] *he shot twice at the cashier, but missed both times.* ■ pass by without touching; chance not to hit: *the plane narrowly missed the control tower.* ■ fail to catch (something thrown or dropped).
2 fail to notice, hear, or understand: *the villa is impossible to miss—it's right by the road* | *these questions **miss the point**.* ■ fail to attend, participate in, or watch (something one is expected to do or habitually does): *Teague looks certain to miss England's match against Fiji.* ■ be too late to catch (a passenger vehicle or the post): *we'll miss the train if he doesn't hurry.* ■ fail to see or have a meeting with (someone): *'Potter's been here this morning?' 'You've just missed him.'* ■ not be able to experience or fail to take advantage of (an opportunity or chance): *don't miss the chance to visit the breathtaking Dolomites* | [no obj.] *he failed to recover from a leg injury and **missed out on** a trip to Barcelona.* ■ avoid; escape: *Christmas shoppers go out early to miss the crowds.* ■ (of a woman) fail to have (a monthly period).
3 (**miss someone/thing out**) Brit. fail to include someone or something; omit: *I'm sure Guy will fill in any bits I **missed out**.*
4 notice the loss or absence of: *he's rich—he won't miss the money* | *she slipped away when she thought she wouldn't be missed.* ■ feel regret or sadness at no longer being able to enjoy the presence of: *she misses all her old friends.* ■ feel regret or sadness at no longer being able to go to, do, or have: *I still miss France and I wish I could go back.*
5 [no obj.] (of an engine or motor vehicle) undergo failure of ignition in one or more cylinders.
▸ noun a failure to hit, catch, or reach something: *the penalty miss cost us the game.* ■ an unsuccessful record or film: *it is the public who decide whether a film is a hit or a miss.*
– PHRASES **give something a miss** Brit. informal decide not to do or have something: *we decided to give the popcorn a miss.* **miss a beat 1** (of the heart) temporarily fail or appear to fail to beat. **2** [usu. with negative] informal hesitate or falter, especially in demanding circumstances or when making a transition from one activity to another: *the Swiss handle metres of snow without missing a beat.* **miss the boat** (or **bus**) informal be too slow to take advantage of an opportunity: *people who've been holding off buying anything in case prices drop further could find they've missed the boat.* **a miss is as good as a mile** proverb the fact of failure or escape is not affected by the narrowness of the margin. **not miss a trick** informal never fail to take advantage of a situation.
– DERIVATIVES **missable** adjective.
– ORIGIN Old English *missan*, of Germanic origin; related to Dutch and German *missen*.

miss[2] ▸ noun **1** (**Miss**) a title prefixed to the name of an unmarried woman or girl, or to that of a married woman retaining her maiden name for professional purposes: *Miss Hazel Armstrong.* ■ used in the title of the winner in a beauty contest: *Miss World.* ■ used as a polite form of address to a young woman or to a waitress or female shop assistant. ■ Brit. used by children in addressing a female teacher: *please, Miss, can I be excused hockey?*
2 a girl or young woman, especially one regarded as silly or headstrong: *there was none of the country bumpkin about this young miss.*
– DERIVATIVES **missish** adjective (sense 2).
– ORIGIN mid 17th cent.: abbreviation of **MISTRESS**.

miss[3] ▸ noun informal a miscarriage.

Miss. ▸ abbreviation Mississippi.

missal /ˈmɪs(ə)l/ ▸ noun a book containing the texts used in the Catholic Mass throughout the year.
– ORIGIN Middle English: from medieval Latin *missale*, neuter of ecclesiastical Latin *missalis* 'relating to the Mass', from *missa* 'Mass'.

mis-sell ▸ verb [with obj.] (often as noun **mis-selling**) sell (something) to a customer on the basis of misleading advice.

missel thrush ▸ noun variant spelling of **MISTLE THRUSH**.

misshape ▸ noun a misshapen chocolate or other item of food, sold cheaply.
▸ verb [with obj.] give a bad or ugly shape or form to; deform.

misshapen ▸ adjective not having the normal or natural shape or form: *misshapen fruit.*
– DERIVATIVES **misshapenness** noun.

missile ▸ noun an object which is forcibly propelled at a target, either by hand or from a mechanical weapon. ■ a weapon that is self-propelled or directed by remote control, carrying conventional or nuclear explosive.
– ORIGIN early 17th cent. (as an adjective in the sense 'suitable for throwing (at a target)'): from Latin *missile*, neuter (used as a noun) of *missilis*, from *miss-* 'sent', from the verb *mittere*.

missilery /ˈmɪsʌɪlri/ ▸ noun [mass noun] **1** the study of the use and characteristics of missiles.
2 missiles collectively.

missing ▸ adjective (of a thing) not able to be found because it is not in its expected place: *a quantity of* *cash has gone missing.* ■ not present or included when expected or supposed to be: *you can fill in the missing details later.* ■ (of a person) absent from a place, especially their home, and of unknown whereabouts: *he has been reported as a missing person.* ■ (of a person) not yet traced or confirmed as alive, but not known to be dead, after an accident or during wartime.

missing link ▶ **noun** a thing that is needed in order to complete a series, provide continuity, or gain complete knowledge: *she is the missing link between the European ballad tradition and Anglo-American white soul.* ■ a hypothetical fossil form intermediate between two living forms, especially between humans and apes.

missiology ▶ **noun** [mass noun] the study of religious (typically Christian) missions and their methods and purposes.
– DERIVATIVES **missiological** **adjective**.
– ORIGIN 1930s: formed irregularly from MISSION + -LOGY.

mission ▶ **noun 1** an important assignment given to a person or group of people, typically involving travel abroad: *a fact-finding **mission to** the Czech Republic.* ■ [treated as sing. or pl.] a group of people sent on a mission: *by then, the mission had journeyed over 3,500 miles.* ■ an organization or institution involved in a long-term assignment abroad: *the head of the West German mission.* ■ an operation carried out by military aircraft: *a reconnaissance mission.* ■ an expedition into space.
2 the vocation or calling of a religious organization, especially a Christian one, to go out into the world and spread its faith: *the Christian mission* | [mass noun] *Gandhi's attitude to mission and conversion.* ■ a building or group of buildings used by a Christian mission.
3 a strongly felt aim, ambition, or calling: *his main mission in life has been to cut unemployment.*
– ORIGIN mid 16th cent. (denoting the sending of the Holy Spirit into the world): from Latin *missio(n-)*, from *mittere* 'send'.

missionary ▶ **noun** (pl. **missionaries**) a person sent on a religious mission, especially one sent to promote Christianity in a foreign country.
▶ **adjective** relating to or characteristic of a missionary or a religious mission: *missionary work* | *our taxi driver shared a sense of missionary zeal with us.*
– ORIGIN mid 17th cent.: from modern Latin *missionarius*, from Latin *missio* (see MISSION).

missionary position ▶ **noun** informal a position for sexual intercourse in which a couple lie face to face with the woman underneath the man.
– ORIGIN said to be so named because early missionaries advocated the position as 'proper' to primitive peoples, to whom the practice was unknown.

mission creep ▶ **noun** a gradual shift in objectives during the course of a military campaign, often resulting in an unplanned long-term commitment.

mission-critical ▶ **adjective** Computing (of hardware or software) vital to the functioning of an organization.

missioner ▶ **noun 1** a person in charge of a religious or charitable mission.
2 a missionary.

mission statement ▶ **noun** a formal summary of the aims and values of a company, organization, or individual.

missis /ˈmɪsɪs, -ɪz/ ▶ **noun** variant spelling of MISSUS.

Mississauga /ˌmɪsɪˈsɔːɡə/ a town in southern Ontario, Canada, on the western shores of Lake Ontario; pop. 668,549 (2006). It forms a southern suburb of Toronto.

Mississippi /ˌmɪsɪˈsɪpi/ **1** a major river of North America, which rises in Minnesota near the Canadian border and flows south to a delta on the Gulf of Mexico. With its chief tributary, the Missouri, it is 5,970 km (3,710 miles) long.
2 a state of the southern US, on the Gulf of Mexico, bounded to the west by the lower Mississippi River; pop. 2,938,618 (est. 2008); capital, Jackson. A French colony in the first half of the 18th century, it was ceded to Britain in 1763 and to the US in 1783, becoming the 20th state in 1817.

Mississippian ▶ **adjective 1** relating to the state of Mississippi.
2 Geology relating to or denoting the early part of the Carboniferous period in North America, following the Devonian and preceding the Pennsylvanian. This period corresponds to the Lower Carboniferous of Europe and lasted from about 363 to 323 million years ago. ■ Archaeology relating to or denoting a settled culture of the south-eastern US, dated to about AD 800–1300.
▶ **noun 1** a native or inhabitant of Mississippi.
2 (**the Mississippian**) Geology the Mississippian period or the system of rocks deposited during it. ■ Archaeology the Mississippian culture or period.

Mississippi mud pie ▶ **noun** a type of rich mousse-like chocolate cake.

missive ▶ **noun** often humorous a letter, especially a long or official one: *yet another missive from the Foreign Office.* ■ Scots Law a document in the form of a letter exchanged by the parties to a contract. See also CONCLUDE MISSIVES at CONCLUDE.
– ORIGIN late Middle English (as an adjective, originally in the phrase LETTER MISSIVE): from medieval Latin *missivus*, from Latin *mittere* 'send'. The current sense dates from the early 16th cent.

Missolonghi /ˌmɪsəˈlɒŋɡi/ a city in western Greece, on the north shore of the Gulf of Patras; pop. 12,800 (est. 2009). It is noted as the place where the poet Byron, who had joined the fight for Greek independence from the Turks, died of malaria in 1824. Greek name MESOLÓNGION.

Missouri /mɪˈzʊəri/ **1** a major river of North America, one of the main tributaries of the Mississippi. It rises in the Rocky Mountains in Montana and flows 3,736 km (2,315 miles) to meet the Mississippi just north of St Louis.
2 a state of the US, bounded on the east by the Mississippi River; pop. 5,911,605 (est. 2008); capital, Jefferson City. It was acquired as part of the Louisiana Purchase in 1803, becoming the 24th state of the US in 1821.
– DERIVATIVES **Missourian** **noun & adjective**.

misspeak ▶ **verb** (past **misspoke**; past participle **misspoken**) [no obj.] chiefly US express oneself in an insufficiently clear or accurate way.

misspell ▶ **verb** (past and past participle **misspelt** or **misspelled**) [with obj.] spell (a word) wrongly.

misspelling ▶ **noun** an incorrect spelling of a word.

misspend ▶ **verb** (past and past participle **misspent**) [with obj.] (usu. as adj. **misspent**) spend (one's time or money) foolishly, wrongly, or wastefully: *perhaps I am atoning for my misspent youth.*

misstate ▶ **verb** [with obj.] make wrong or inaccurate statements about.
– DERIVATIVES **misstatement** **noun**.

misstep ▶ **noun** a clumsy or badly judged step: *for a mountain goat one misstep could be fatal.* ■ N. Amer. a mistake or blunder.

missus /ˈmɪsəz/ (also **missis**) ▶ **noun** informal or humorous a man's wife: ***I promised the missus** I'd be home by eleven.* ■ Brit. informal used as a form of address to a woman whose name is not known: *sit down, missus.*
– ORIGIN late 18th cent.: representing an informal pronunciation of MISTRESS; compare with MRS.

missy ▶ **noun** (pl. **missies**) used as an affectionate or disparaging form of address to a young girl: *'Don't tell lies, missy,' he said sternly.*

mist ▶ **noun** [mass noun] a cloud of tiny water droplets suspended in the atmosphere at or near the earth's surface that limits visibility (to a lesser extent than fog, strictly, with visibility remaining above 1 km): *the peaks were shrouded in mist* | [in sing.] *a mist rose out of the river.* ■ [in sing.] a condensed vapour settling in fine droplets on a surface: *a breeze cooled the mist of perspiration that had dampened her temples.* ■ [in sing.] a haze or film over the eyes, especially caused by tears, and resulting in blurred vision: *Ruth saw most of the scene through a mist of tears.* ■ [count noun] used in reference to something that blurs one's perceptions or memory: *Sardinia's origins are lost in **the mists of time**.*
▶ **verb** cover or become covered with mist: [with obj.] *the windows of the car were **misted up** with condensation* | [no obj.] *the glass was beginning to **mist up**.* ■ [no obj.] (of a person's eyes) become covered with a film of tears causing blurred vision: *her eyes **misted over** with relief and joy.* ■ [with obj.] spray (something, especially a plant) with a fine cloud of water droplets.
– ORIGIN Old English, of Germanic origin; from an Indo-European root shared by Greek *omikhlē* 'mist, fog'.

mistake ▶ **noun** an act or judgement that is misguided or wrong: *coming here was a mistake* | *she **made the mistake of** thinking they were important.* ■ something, especially a word, figure, or fact, which is not correct; an inaccuracy: *a couple of spelling mistakes.*
▶ **verb** (past **mistook**; past participle **mistaken**) [with obj.] be wrong about: *because I was inexperienced I mistook the nature of our relationship.* ■ (**mistake someone/thing for**) wrongly identify someone or something as: *she thought he'd mistaken her for Diana.*
– PHRASES **and no mistake** informal without any doubt: *it's a bad business and no mistake.* **by mistake** accidentally; in error: *she'd left her purse at home by mistake.* **make no mistake (about it)** informal do not be deceived into thinking otherwise. **there is no mistaking ——** it is impossible not to recognize someone or something.
– DERIVATIVES **mistakable** (also **mistakeable**) **adjective**, **mistakably** (also **mistakeably**) **adverb**.
– ORIGIN late Middle English (as a verb): from Old Norse *mistaka* 'take in error', probably influenced in sense by Old French *mesprendre*.

mistaken ▶ **adjective** wrong in one's opinion or judgement: *she wondered whether she'd been mistaken about his intentions.* ■ based on or resulting from a misunderstanding or faulty judgement: *don't buy a hard bed in the mistaken belief that it is good for you* | *an unfortunate case of mistaken identity.*
– DERIVATIVES **mistakenness** **noun**.

mistakenly ▶ **adverb** in a mistaken way; wrongly: *they mistakenly believed her to be pregnant.* ■ by accident or oversight; accidentally: *warplanes mistakenly bombed a village.*

misteach ▶ **verb** (past and past participle **mistaught**) [with obj.] teach (someone) wrongly or incorrectly.

mister[1] ▶ **noun** variant form of MR, often used humorously or with offensive emphasis: *look here, mister know-all.* ■ informal used as a form of address to a man whose name is not known: *thanks, mister.*
– ORIGIN mid 16th cent.: weakened form of MASTER[1] in unstressed use before a name.

mister[2] ▶ **noun** a device with a nozzle for spraying a mist of water, especially on houseplants.

mistime ▶ **verb** [with obj.] choose a bad or inappropriate moment to do or say (something).
– ORIGIN Old English *mistīmian* 'happen unfortunately' (see MIS-[1], TIME).

mistimed ▶ **adjective** done at an inappropriate moment; badly timed: *her mistimed resignation from the government.*

M

mistitle ▶ **verb** [with obj.] give the wrong title or name to: *Mr Hammond mistitles his source.*

mistle thrush /ˈmɪs(ə)l/ (also **missel thrush**) ▶ **noun** a large Eurasian thrush with a spotted breast and harsh rattling call, with a fondness for mistletoe berries. ● *Turdus viscivorus*, family Turdidae.
– ORIGIN early 17th cent.: *mistle* from Old English *mistel* (see MISTLETOE).

mistletoe ▶ **noun** a leathery-leaved parasitic plant which grows on apple, oak, and other broadleaf trees and bears white glutinous berries in winter. ● Several species in the family Viscaceae, in particular the Eurasian *Viscum album* and the North American *Phoradendron flavescens*.
– ORIGIN Old English *misteltān*, from *mistel* 'mistletoe' (of Germanic origin, related to Dutch *mistel* and German *Mistel*) + *tān* 'twig'.

mistletoebird ▶ **noun** an Australian flowerpecker that feeds mainly on mistletoe berries, the male of which has a bright red breast. ● *Dicaeum hirundinaceum*, family Dicaeidae. Alternative name: **mistletoe flowerpecker**.

mistook past of MISTAKE.

mistral /ˈmɪstr(ə)l, mɪˈstrɑːl/ ▶ **noun** a strong cold north-westerly wind that blows through the Rhône valley and southern France towards the Mediterranean, mainly in winter.
– ORIGIN early 17th cent.: French, from Provençal, from Latin *magistralis (ventus)*, literally 'master wind'.

mistranslate ▶ **verb** [with obj.] translate (something) incorrectly.
– DERIVATIVES **mistranslation** **noun**.

mistreat ▶ **verb** [with obj.] treat (a person or animal) badly, cruelly, or unfairly.

mistreatment ▶ **noun** [mass noun] the action of mistreating or fact of being mistreated; ill-treatment: *the alleged mistreatment of the animals that perform in those shows.*

mistress ▶ **noun 1** a woman in a position of authority or control: *she is always **mistress of** the situation, coolly self-possessed.* ■ [with modifier] Brit. a female schoolteacher who teaches a particular subject: *a Geography mistress.* ■ a woman who is skilled in a particular subject or activity: *a **mistress of** the sound bite, she is famed for the acidity of her tongue.* ■ the

female owner of a dog, cat, or other domesticated animal. ■ archaic a female head of a household: *he asked for the mistress of the house.* ■ (especially formerly) a female employer of domestic staff.
2 a woman (other than the man's wife) having a sexual relationship with a married man. ■ archaic or literary a woman loved and courted by a man.
3 (**Mistress**) archaic or dialect used as a title prefixed to the name of a married woman; Mrs.
– ORIGIN Middle English: from Old French *maistresse*, from *maistre* 'master'.

Mistress of the Robes ▶ noun (in the English royal household) a woman of high rank in charge of the Queen's wardrobe.

mistrial ▶ noun a trial rendered invalid through an error in the proceedings. ■ US an inconclusive trial, such as one in which the jury cannot agree on a verdict.

mistrust ▶ verb [with obj.] be suspicious of; have no confidence in: *she had no cause to mistrust him.*
▶ noun [mass noun] lack of trust; suspicion: *the public mistrust of government.*

mistrustful ▶ adjective lacking in trust; suspicious: *he wondered if he had been unduly mistrustful of her.*
– DERIVATIVES **mistrustfully** adverb, **mistrustfulness** noun.

misty ▶ adjective (**mistier**, **mistiest**) full of, covered with, or accompanied by mist: *the evening was cold and misty | the misty air above the frozen river.* ■ (of a person's eyes) full of tears so as to blur the vision. ■ indistinct or dim in outline: *a misty out-of-focus silhouette* | figurative *a few misty memories.* ■ (of a colour) not bright; soft: *a misty pink.*
– DERIVATIVES **mistily** adverb, **mistiness** noun.
– ORIGIN Old English *mistig* (see **MIST**).

mistype ▶ verb [with obj.] make a mistake in typing (a word or letter).

misunderstand ▶ verb (past and past participle **misunderstood** /-ˈstʊd/) [with obj.] fail to interpret or understand (something) correctly: *he had misunderstood the police officer's hand signals* | [no obj.] *I must have misunderstood—I thought you were anxious to leave.* ■ fail to interpret or understand the words or actions of (someone) correctly: *don't misunderstand me—I'm not implying she should be working* | (as adj. **misunderstood**) *he is one of football's most misunderstood men.*

misunderstanding ▶ noun a failure to understand something correctly: *a misunderstanding of the government's plans* | [mass noun] *there must have been some kind of misunderstanding.* ■ a disagreement or quarrel: *he left the army after a slight misunderstanding with his commanding officer.*

misusage ▶ noun [mass noun] archaic unjust treatment: *they were determined to defend themselves from misusage.*

misuse ▶ verb [with obj.] use (something) in the wrong way or for the wrong purpose: *he was found guilty of misusing public funds.* ■ treat (someone or something) badly or unfairly.
▶ noun [mass noun] the wrong or improper use of something: *drugs of such potency that their misuse can have dire consequences* | [count noun] *a misuse of power.*
– DERIVATIVES **misuser** noun.

MIT ▶ abbreviation Massachusetts Institute of Technology.

mitch ▶ verb [no obj.] informal, chiefly Irish play truant from school: *we're looking for three young fellows who've* ***mitched from*** *school* | [with obj.] *he would mitch school and go down to the docks.*
– ORIGIN late Middle English (in the obsolete sense 'pilfer'): apparently from Old French *muchier* 'hide, lurk'; compare with **MOOCH**.

Mitchell[1], Joni (b.1943), Canadian singer and songwriter; born *Roberta Joan Anderson*. Starting to record in 1968, she moved from folk to a fusion of folk, jazz, and rock. Notable albums: *Blue* (1971) and *Hejira* (1976).

Mitchell[2], Margaret (1900–49), American novelist, famous as the author of the bestselling and Pulitzer Prize-winning novel *Gone with the Wind* (1936), set during the American Civil War.

Mitchell[3], R. J. (1895–1937), English aeronautical engineer; full name *Reginald Joseph Mitchell*. He designed the Spitfire fighter aircraft.

Mitchum /ˈmɪtʃəm/, Robert (1917–97), American actor. He was a professional boxer before rising to stardom in films such as *Out of the Past* (1947), *Night of the Hunter* (1955), and *Farewell My Lovely* (1975).

mite[1] ▶ noun a minute arachnid which has four pairs of legs when adult, related to the ticks. Many kinds live in the soil and a number are parasitic on plants or animals. ● Order (or subclass) Acari: numerous families.
– ORIGIN Old English *mīte*, of Germanic origin.

mite[2] ▶ noun **1** a small child or animal, especially when regarded as an object of sympathy: *the poor little mite looks half-starved.*
2 a very small amount: *his teacher thought he needed* ***a mite of*** *discipline.* ■ historical a small coin, in particular a small Flemish copper coin of very low face value. See also **WIDOW'S MITE**.
▶ adverb (**a mite**) informal a little; slightly: *I haven't eaten yet and I'm feeling a mite peckish.*
– ORIGIN late Middle English (denoting a small Flemish copper coin): from Middle Dutch *mīte*; probably from the same Germanic word as **MITE**[1].

miter ▶ noun & verb US spelling of **MITRE**.

Mitford /ˈmɪtfəd/, Nancy (Freeman) (1904–73) and her sister Jessica (Lucy) (1917–96), English writers. Nancy achieved fame with comic novels including *Love in a Cold Climate* (1949). Jessica became an American citizen in 1944, and is best known for her works on American culture, notably *The American Way of Death* (1963). Among their four sisters were **Unity** (1914–48), who was an admirer of Hitler, and **Diana** (1910–2003), who married Sir Oswald Mosley in 1936.

mithai /mɪˈtʌɪ/ ▶ noun [mass noun] Indian sweets, such as burfi or gulab jamun.
– ORIGIN from Hindi *miṭhai*.

mithan /ˈmɪθ(ə)n/ ▶ noun (pl. **same**) another term for **GAYAL**.
– ORIGIN mid 19th cent.: from Khasi (a Mon-Khmer language of NE India).

mither /ˈmʌɪðə/ ▶ verb [no obj.] dialect, chiefly N. English make a fuss; moan: *oh men—don't they mither?* ■ [with obj.] pester or irritate (someone).
– ORIGIN late 17th cent.: of unknown origin; compare with Welsh *moedrodd* 'to worry, bother'.

Mithraeum /mɪˈθriːəm/ ▶ noun (pl. **Mithraea** /-ˈθriːə/) a sanctuary or temple of the god Mithras.
– ORIGIN late Latin, from Latin *Mithras* (see **MITHRAS**).

Mithraism /ˈmɪθrəˌɪz(ə)m, ˈmɪθreɪ-/ ▶ noun [mass noun] the cult of the god Mithras, which became popular among Roman soldiers of the later empire, and was the main rival to Christianity in the first three centuries AD.
– DERIVATIVES **Mithraic** /-ˈθreɪɪk/ adjective, **Mithraist** noun.

Mithras /ˈmɪθras/ Mythology a god of light, truth, and honour, the central figure of the cult of Mithraism but probably of Persian origin. He was also associated with merchants and the protection of warriors.

Mithridates VI /ˌmɪθrɪˈdeɪtiːz/ (also **Mithradates VI**) (*c.*132–63 BC), king of Pontus 120–63; known as **Mithridates the Great**. His expansionist policies led to three wars with Rome (88–5; 83–2; 74–66). He was finally defeated by Pompey.

mitigate /ˈmɪtɪgeɪt/ ▶ verb [with obj.] make (something bad) less severe, serious, or painful: *drainage schemes have helped to mitigate this problem.* ■ lessen the gravity of (an offence or mistake): (as adj. **mitigating**) *he would have faced a prison sentence but for* ***mitigating circumstances.***
– DERIVATIVES **mitigable** adjective, **mitigator** noun, **mitigatory** adjective.
– ORIGIN late Middle English: from Latin *mitigat-* 'softened, alleviated', from the verb *mitigare*, from *mitis* 'mild'.

> **USAGE** The verbs **mitigate** and **militate** do not have the same meaning, although the similarity of the forms leads many people to confuse them. **Mitigate** means 'make (something bad) less severe', as in *drainage schemes have helped to* ***mitigate*** *this problem*, while **militate** is nearly always used in constructions with **against** to mean 'be a powerful factor in preventing', as in *these disagreements will* ***militate against*** *the two communities coming together.*

mitigation ▶ noun [mass noun] the action of reducing the severity, seriousness, or painfulness of something: *the identification and mitigation of pollution.*
– PHRASES **in mitigation** so as to make something, especially a crime, appear less serious and thus be punished more leniently: *in mitigation she said her client had been deeply depressed.*
– ORIGIN late Middle English: from Old French, or from Latin *mitigatio(n-)*, from the verb *mitigare* 'alleviate' (see **MITIGATE**).

Mitilíni /mitiˈlini/ Greek name for **MYTILENE**.

Mitla /ˈmiːtlə/ an ancient city in southern Mexico, to the east of the city of Oaxaca, now a noted archaeological site. Believed to have been established as a burial site by the Zapotecs, it was eventually overrun by the Mixtecs in about AD 1000.
– ORIGIN Nahuatl, literally 'place of the dead'.

mitochondrion /ˌmʌɪtə(ʊ)ˈkɒndrɪən/ ▶ noun (pl. **mitochondria** /-rɪə/) Biology an organelle found in large numbers in most cells, in which the biochemical processes of respiration and energy production occur. It has a double membrane, the inner part being folded inwards to form layers (cristae).
– DERIVATIVES **mitochondrial** adjective.
– ORIGIN early 20th cent.: modern Latin, from Greek *mitos* 'thread' + *khondrion* (diminutive of *khondros* 'granule').

mitogen /ˈmʌɪtədʒ(ə)n/ ▶ noun Physiology a substance that induces or stimulates mitosis.
– DERIVATIVES **mitogenic** adjective.
– ORIGIN 1960s: from **MITOSIS** + **-GEN**.

mitosis /mʌɪˈtəʊsɪs/ ▶ noun (pl. **mitoses**) [mass noun] Biology a type of cell division that results in two daughter cells each having the same number and kind of chromosomes as the parent nucleus, typical of ordinary tissue growth. Compare with **MEIOSIS**.
– DERIVATIVES **mitotic** adjective.
– ORIGIN late 19th cent.: modern Latin, from Greek *mitos* 'thread'.

mitral /ˈmʌɪtr(ə)l/ ▶ adjective denoting or relating to the mitral valve.
– ORIGIN early 17th cent.: from modern Latin *mitralis*, from Latin *mitra* 'belt or turban'.

mitral valve ▶ noun Anatomy the valve between the left atrium and the left ventricle of the heart, which has two tapered cusps.

mitre (US **miter**) ▶ noun **1** a tall headdress worn by bishops and senior abbots as a symbol of office, tapering to a point at front and back with a deep cleft between.
2 (also **mitre joint**) a joint made between two pieces of wood or other material at an angle of 90°, such that the line of junction bisects this angle. ■ a diagonal seam between two pieces of fabric that are sewn together at a corner.
3 (also **mitre shell**) a mollusc of warm seas which has a sharply pointed shell with a narrow aperture, supposedly resembling a bishop's mitre. ● Family Mitridae, class Gastropoda: *Mitra* and other genera.
▶ verb [with obj.] join by means of a mitre joint or seam.
– ORIGIN late Middle English: from Old French, via Latin from Greek *mitra* 'belt or turban'.

mitre box (also **mitre block** or **mitre board**) ▶ noun a guide to enable a saw to cut mitre joints at the desired angle.

mitred ▶ adjective **1** joined with a mitre joint or seam: *complete the sides with mitred corners.*
2 bearing, wearing, or entitled to wear a mitre: *the mitred abbot of Battle.*

mitre wheel ▶ noun each of a pair of bevelled cogwheels with teeth set at 45° and axes at right angles.

Mitsiwa /mɪˈtsiːwə/ variant spelling of **MASSAWA**.

mitt ▶ noun (usu. **mitts**) a mitten: *woolly mitts.* ■ a glove leaving the fingers and thumb-tip exposed. ■ (also **baseball mitt**) Baseball a large fingerless glove worn by the catcher or first baseman. ■ informal a person's hand: *it's essential to get your mitts on a pair of low-slung combat trousers.*
– ORIGIN mid 18th cent.: abbreviation of **MITTEN**.

Mitteleuropa /ˌmɪt(ə)ljʊˈrəʊpə/ ▶ noun [mass noun] central Europe regarded as a political or cultural entity.
– DERIVATIVES **Mitteleuropean** adjective & noun.
– ORIGIN early 20th cent.: German.

Mittelland Canal /ˈmɪt(ə)lˌland/, German /ˈmɪtlˌlant/ a canal in NW Germany, which was constructed between 1905 and 1930. It is part of an inland waterway network linking the Rivers Rhine and Elbe.

Mittelstand /ˈmɪt(ə)lstand/, German /ˈmɪtlʃtant/ ▶ noun the medium-sized companies in a country, viewed as an economic unit.
– ORIGIN German, literally 'middle group'.

mitten ▶ noun (usu. **mittens**) a glove with two sections, one for the thumb and the other for all four fingers. ■ (**mittens**) informal boxing gloves.
– DERIVATIVES **mittened** adjective.
– ORIGIN Middle English: from Old French *mitaine*, perhaps from *mite*, a pet name for a cat (because mittens were often made of fur).

mitten crab (also **Chinese mitten crab**) ▶ **noun** an olive-green Asian crab with hairy pincers that has been introduced into Europe, where it lives in fresh water and estuaries and can become a pest. ● *Eriocheir sinensis*, family Grapsidae.

Mitterrand /ˈmiːtərɒ̃/, French /mitɛʀɑ̃/, François (Maurice Marie) (1916–96), French statesman, President 1981–95. As President he initially moved to raise basic wages, increase social benefits, nationalize key industries, and decentralize government. The Socialist Party lost its majority vote in the 1986 general election and Mitterrand made the right-wing Jacques Chirac Prime Minister, resulting in a reversal of some policies.

mittimus /ˈmɪtɪməs/ ▶ **noun** a warrant committing a person to prison.
– ORIGIN Latin, literally 'we send', first used as the opening word of the writ which transferred records from one court to another (late Middle English to the early 18th cent.).

Mitty see **WALTER MITTY**.

mitumba /mɪˈtʊmbə/ ▶ **noun** [mass noun] (in eastern and central Africa) second-hand clothing, especially that donated by aid agencies in the West.
– ORIGIN Swahili, plural of *mtumba*, literally 'bale (of cloth)'.

mitzvah /ˈmɪtsvə/ ▶ **noun** (pl. **mitzvoth** /-vəʊt/) Judaism a precept or commandment. ■ a good deed done from religious duty.
– ORIGIN mid 17th cent.: from Hebrew *miṣwāh* 'commandment'.

mix ▶ **verb** [with obj.] **1** combine or put together to form one substance or mass: *peppercorns are sometimes **mixed with** other spices | these two chemicals, when **mixed together**, literally explode.* ■ [no obj.] [often with negative] (of different substances) be able to be combined to form one substance or mass: *oil and water don't mix.* ■ make or prepare by combining various ingredients: *mixing concrete is hard physical work.* ■ juxtapose or put together to form a whole whose constituent parts are still distinct: *he continues to mix an off-hand sense of humour **with** a sharp insight.*
2 [no obj.] (of a person) associate with others socially: *the people he **mixed with** were nothing to do with show business.*
3 (especially in sound recording) combine (two or more signals or soundtracks) into one: *up to eight tracks can be mixed simultaneously.* ■ produce (a sound signal or recording) by combining a number of separate signals or recorded soundtracks: *it was everyone's dream to mix their album in their front room.*
4 (**mix it**) informal be belligerent physically or verbally.
▶ **noun 1** [usu. in sing.] two or more different qualities, things, or people placed, combined, or considered together: *the decor is a fascinating mix of antique and modern.* ■ a group of people of different types within a particular society or community: *the school has a good social mix.* ■ the proportion of different people or other constituents that make up a mixture: *arriving at the correct mix of full-time to part-time staff | trousers made from a cotton and polyester mix.*
2 [often with modifier] a commercially prepared mixture of ingredients for making a particular type of food or a product such as concrete: *cake mixes have made cooking easier.*
3 [often with modifier] a version of a recording in which the component tracks are mixed in a different way from the original: *a dance mix version of 'This Charming Man'.* ■ an image or sound produced by the combination of two separate images or sounds.
– PHRASES **be** (or **get**) **mixed up in** be (or become) involved in (something regarded as dubious or dishonest): *Steve was mixed up in an insurance swindle.* **be** (or **get**) **mixed up with** be (or become) associated with (someone unsuitable or unreliable). **mix and match** select and combine different but complementary items, such as clothing or pieces of equipment, to form a coordinated set: *mix and match this season's colours for a combination that says 'winter'* | [as modifier] *a mix-and-match menu.* **mix one's drinks** drink different kinds of alcohol in close succession.
– PHRASAL VERBS **mix something up 1** spoil the order or arrangement of a collection of things: *disconnect all the cables, mix them up then try to reconnect them.* **2** (**mix someone/thing up**) confuse someone or something with another person or thing: *I'd got her **mixed up with** her sister.*
– DERIVATIVES **mixable** adjective.
– ORIGIN late Middle English: back-formation from **MIXED** (taken as a past participle).

mixed ▶ **adjective** consisting of different qualities or elements: *a mixed diet | beaches with mixed sand and shingle.* ■ (of an assessment of, reaction to, or feeling about something) containing a mixture of both favourable and negative elements: *the film opened last Friday to mixed reviews | I had mixed feelings about seeing Laura again.* ■ composed of different varieties of the same thing: *crab on a bed of mixed salad.* ■ (especially of an educational establishment or a sports team or competition) of or for members of both sexes: *the college's mixed hockey team.* ■ involving or showing a mixture of races or social classes: *people of mixed race.*
– ORIGIN late Middle English *mixt*: from Old French *mixte*, from Latin *mixtus*, past participle of *miscere* 'to mix'.

mixed bag (also **mixed bunch**) ▶ **noun** [in sing.] a diverse assortment of things or people: *we have a mixed bag of destinations and holiday choices for you.*

mixed blessing ▶ **noun** a thing that has disadvantages as well as advantages: *having children so early in their marriage was a mixed blessing.*

mixed company ▶ **noun** [mass noun] a gathering of people consisting of members of both sexes.

mixed crystal ▶ **noun** a crystal formed from more than one substance.

mixed doubles ▶ **plural noun** [treated as sing.] (especially in tennis and badminton) a game or competition involving sides each consisting of a man and a woman.

mixed economy ▶ **noun** an economic system combining private and state enterprise.

mixed farming ▶ **noun** [mass noun] a system of farming which involves the growing of crops as well as the raising of livestock.

mixed grill ▶ **noun** Brit. a dish consisting of various items of grilled food, typically bacon, sausages, tomatoes, and mushrooms.

mixed marriage ▶ **noun** a marriage between people of different races or religions.

mixed media ▶ **noun** [mass noun] a variety of media used in an entertainment or work of art.
▶ **adjective** (**mixed-media**) another term for **MULTIMEDIA**.

mixed metaphor ▶ **noun** a combination of two or more incompatible metaphors (e.g. *this tower of strength will forge ahead*).

mixed number ▶ **noun** a number consisting of an integer and a proper fraction.

mixed-race ▶ **adjective** denoting or relating to people whose parents or ancestors are from different ethnic backgrounds: *mixed-race children | a mixed-race neighbourhood.*

mixed spice ▶ **noun** [mass noun] a commercially prepared mixture of ground spices for cooking, typically including cinnamon, nutmeg, and cloves.

mixed up ▶ **adjective** informal (of a person) suffering from psychological or emotional problems: *a lonely mixed-up teenager.*

mixer ▶ **noun 1** a machine for mixing things, especially an electrical appliance for mixing foods: *a food mixer.*
2 [with adj.] a person considered in terms of their ability to mix socially with others: *media people need to be good mixers.* ■ N. Amer. a social gathering at which people can make new acquaintances.
3 a soft drink that can be mixed with alcohol. ■ [mass noun] a type of dry pet food which can be mixed with moist tinned food.
4 (in sound recording and cinematography) a device for merging input signals to produce a combined output in the form of sound or pictures. ■ a person who operates a signals mixer: *a sound mixer.*

mixer tap ▶ **noun** Brit. a tap through which both hot and cold water can be drawn at the same time by means of separate controls.

mixie ▶ **noun** Indian an electric food mixer or blender.

mixing desk ▶ **noun** a console where sound signals are mixed during recording or broadcasting.

Mixmaster ▶ **noun 1** US trademark a type of electric food processor.
2 (**mixmaster**) informal a sound-recording engineer or disc jockey who is an accomplished mixer of music, during recording or as a disc jockey.

mixologist ▶ **noun** informal a person who is skilled at mixing cocktails and other drinks.
– DERIVATIVES **mixology** noun.

Mixolydian mode /ˌmɪksəˈlɪdɪən/ ▶ **noun** Music the mode represented by the natural diatonic scale G–G (containing a minor 7th).
– ORIGIN late 16th cent.: *Mixolydian* from Greek *mixoludios* 'half-Lydian' + **-AN**.

mixtape ▶ **noun** a compilation of favourite pieces of music, typically by many different artists, recorded on to tape or another medium by an individual.

Mixtec /ˈmɪstɛk/ ▶ **noun** (pl. **same** or **Mixtecs**) **1** a member of an American Indian people of southern Mexico, noted for their skill in pottery and metallurgy.
2 the Otomanguean language of the Mixtec, spoken by about 250,000 people in several dialects.
▶ **adjective** relating to the Mixtec or their language.
– ORIGIN Spanish, from Nahuatl *mixtecah* 'person from a cloudy place'.

mixture ▶ **noun** a substance made by mixing other substances together: *form the mixture into a manageable dough | shandy is **a mixture of** beer and lemonade.* ■ [mass noun] the process of mixing or being mixed. ■ a combination of different things in which the component elements are individually distinct: *the old town is **a mixture of** narrow medieval streets and 18th-century architecture.* ■ Chemistry the product of the random distribution of one substance through another without any chemical reaction, as distinct from a compound. ■ the charge of gas or vapour mixed with air which is admitted to the cylinder of an internal-combustion engine, especially as regards the ratio of fuel to air: *newer pilots often leave their mixture rich during an entire flight.* ■ (also **mixture stop**) an organ stop in which each key sounds a group of small pipes of different pitches, giving a very bright tone.
– PHRASES **the mixture as before** Brit. the same treatment repeated. [used formerly as an instruction on a medicine bottle.]
– ORIGIN late Middle English: from French *mixture* or Latin *mixtura* (see **MIXED**).

mix-up ▶ **noun** informal **1** a confusion of one thing with another, or a misunderstanding or mistake that results in confusion: *there's a mix-up over the tickets.*
2 a combination of different things, especially one whose effect is inharmonious: *a ghastly mix-up of furniture styles.*

Mizo /ˈmiːzəʊ/ ▶ **noun** (pl. **same** or **Mizos**) **1** a member of a people inhabiting Mizoram.
2 [mass noun] the Tibeto-Burman language of the Mizo, with about 340,000 speakers. Also called **LUSHAI**.
▶ **adjective** relating to the Mizo or their language.
– ORIGIN the name in Mizo, literally 'highlander', from *mi-* 'person' + *zo* 'hill'.

Mizoram /ˈmɪzəʊram/ a state in the far north-east of India, lying between Bangladesh and Burma (Myanmar); capital, Aizawl. Separated from Assam in 1972, it was administered as a Union Territory in India until 1986, when it became a state.

mizuna /mɪˈzuːnə/ (also **mizuna greens**) ▶ **noun** [mass noun] oriental rape of a variety with finely cut leaves that are eaten in salads. ● *Brassica rapa* var. *nipposinica*, family Cruciferae.
– ORIGIN Japanese.

mizzen /ˈmɪz(ə)n/ (also **mizen**) ▶ **noun 1** (also **mizzenmast**) the mast aft of a ship's mainmast.
2 (also **mizzensail**) a sail on the mizzenmast of a ship, in particular the lowest sail on the mizzenmast of a square-rigged sailing ship.
– ORIGIN late Middle English: from Italian *mezzana* 'mizzensail', feminine (used as a noun) of *mezzano* 'middle', from Latin *medianus* (see **MEDIAN**).

mizzle[1] /ˈmɪz(ə)l/ chiefly dialect ▶ **noun** [mass noun] light rain; drizzle.
▶ **verb** [no obj.] (**it mizzles, it is mizzling**, etc.) rain lightly: *it was mizzling steadily.*
– DERIVATIVES **mizzly** adjective.
– ORIGIN late Middle English (as a verb): probably a frequentative from the base of **MIST**; compare with Low German *miseln* and Dutch dialect *miezelen*.

mizzle[2] /ˈmɪz(ə)l/ ▶ **verb** [no obj.] Brit. informal, dated go away suddenly; vanish: *he mizzled into the crowd.*
– ORIGIN late 18th cent.: of unknown origin.

Mk ▶ **abbreviation** ■ the German mark. ■ the Gospel of Mark (in biblical references). ■ (followed by a numeral) Mark, used to denote a design or model of car, aircraft, or other machine: *a VW Golf Mk III.*

mks ▶ **abbreviation** metre-kilogram-second.

Mkt ▶ **abbreviation** Market (in place names).

ml ▶ **abbreviation** ■ (**Ml**) megalitre(s). ■ mile(s). ■ millilitre(s).

M

MLA ▸ abbreviation ■ Member of the Legislative Assembly. ■ Modern Language Association (of America).

MLC ▸ abbreviation Member of the Legislative Council.

MLD ▸ abbreviation ■ minimum lethal dose. ■ moderate learning difficulties.

MLF ▸ abbreviation multilateral nuclear force.

MLitt ▸ abbreviation Master of Letters.
– ORIGIN from Latin *Magister Litterarum*.

Mlle ▸ abbreviation (pl. **Mlles**) Mademoiselle.

MLR ▸ abbreviation minimum lending rate.

MM ▸ abbreviation ■ Maelzel's metronome (an indication of tempo in music, given as the number of beats per minute). [with reference to the metronome invented by Johann N. *Maelzel* (died 1838).] ■ Messieurs. ■ (in the UK) Military Medal.

mm ▸ abbreviation millimetre(s).

Mmabatho /mə'bɑːtəʊ, ˌəmmə-/ a city in North West, South Africa, near the border with Botswana; pop. 74,200 (est. 2009).

Mme ▸ abbreviation (pl. **Mmes**) Madame.

m.m.f. ▸ abbreviation magnetomotive force.

MMOG ▸ noun (pl. **MMOGs**) an online video game which can be played by a very large number of people simultaneously.
– ORIGIN 1990s: from *massively multiplayer online game*.

MMORPG ▸ noun (pl. **MMORPGs**) an online role-playing video game in which a very large number of people participate simultaneously.
– ORIGIN 1990s: from *massively multiplayer online role-playing game*.

MMR ▸ abbreviation measles, mumps, and rubella, a vaccination given to small children.

MMS ▸ abbreviation Multimedia Messaging Service, a system that enables mobile phones to send and receive colour pictures and sound clips as well as text messages.

MMus ▸ abbreviation Master of Music.

M

MN ▸ abbreviation ■ (in the UK) Merchant Navy. ■ Minnesota (in official postal use).

Mn ▸ symbol the chemical element manganese.

MNA ▸ abbreviation (in Canada) Member of the National Assembly (of Quebec).

M'Naghten rules variant spelling of **McNaghten rules**.

mnemonic /nɪ'mɒnɪk/ ▸ noun a system such as a pattern of letters, ideas, or associations which assists in remembering something.
▸ adjective aiding or designed to aid the memory. ■ relating to the power of memory.
– DERIVATIVES **mnemonically** adverb, **mnemonist** /'niːmənɪst/ noun.
– ORIGIN mid 18th cent. (as an adjective): via medieval Latin from Greek *mnēmonikos*, from *mnēmōn* 'mindful'.

mnemonics ▸ plural noun [usu. treated as sing.] the study and development of systems for improving and assisting the memory.

Mnemosyne /niː'mɒzɪni/ Greek Mythology the mother of the Muses.
– ORIGIN from Greek *mnēmosunē*, literally 'memory'.

mnemotechnics /ˌniːmə(ʊ)'tɛknɪks/ ▸ plural noun another term for **mnemonics**.
– DERIVATIVES **mnemotechnic** adjective & noun.
– ORIGIN mid 19th cent.: from Greek *mnēmē* 'memory' + *-technics* (see **technic**).

MO ▸ abbreviation ■ Computing (of a disk or disk drive) magneto-optical. ■ Medical Officer. ■ Missouri (in official postal use). ■ modus operandi. ■ money order.

Mo ▸ symbol the chemical element molybdenum.

mo ▸ noun [in sing.] informal, chiefly Brit. a short period of time: *hang on a mo!*
– ORIGIN late 19th cent.: abbreviation of **moment**.

mo. ▸ abbreviation N. Amer. month.

-mo /məʊ/ ▸ suffix forming nouns denoting a book size by the number of leaves into which a sheet of paper has been folded: *twelvemo*.
– ORIGIN from the final syllable of Latin ordinal numbers such as *duodecimo* (masculine ablative singular).

moa /'məʊə/ ▸ noun a large extinct flightless bird resembling the emu, formerly found in New Zealand. ● Family Dinornithidae: several genera and species; *Dinornis maximus* is the tallest known bird at over 3 m, but *Megalapteryx didinus*, which may have survived until the early 19th century, was much smaller.
– ORIGIN mid 19th cent.: from Maori.

Moab /'məʊab/ the ancient kingdom of the Moabites, situated to the east of the Dead Sea.

Moabite /'məʊəbʌɪt/ ▸ noun a member of a Semitic people living in Moab in biblical times, traditionally descended from Lot.
▸ adjective relating to Moab or its people.

Moabite Stone a monument erected by Mesha, king of Moab, in *c.*850 BC which describes (in an early form of the Hebrew language) the campaign between Moab and ancient Israel (2 Kings 3), and bears an early example of an inscription in the Phoenician alphabet. It is now in the Louvre in Paris.

moan ▸ noun **1** a long, low sound made by a person expressing physical or mental suffering or sexual pleasure: *she gave a low moan of despair.* ■ a sound resembling a human moan: *the moan of the wind in the chimneys*.
2 informal a complaint which is perceived as trivial and not taken seriously by others: *there were moans about the car's feeble ventilation*.
▸ verb [no obj.] **1** make a long, low sound expressing physical or mental suffering or sexual pleasure: *just then their patient moaned and opened his eyes* | [with direct speech] *'Help me,' I moaned.* ■ make a sound resembling a human moan: *the foghorn moaned at intervals.* ■ literary lament.
2 [reporting verb] informal complain or grumble, typically about something trivial: [no obj.] *passengers moaned about overcrowded coaches* | [with clause] *my husband moans that I'm not as slim as when we first met.*
– DERIVATIVES **moaner** noun, **moanful** adjective.
– ORIGIN Middle English (in the sense 'complaint or lamentation'): of unknown origin.

moat ▸ noun a deep, wide ditch surrounding a castle, fort, or town, typically filled with water and intended as a defence against attack.
▸ verb [with obj.] (often as adj. **moated**) surround (a place) with a moat: *a moated castle*.
– ORIGIN late Middle English: from Old French *mote* 'mound'.

mob ▸ noun **1** a large crowd of people, especially one that is disorderly and intent on causing trouble or violence: *a mob of protesters.* ■ Brit. informal a group of people in the same place or with something in common: *he stood out from the rest of the mob with his silver hair and stacked shoes.* ■ (**the mob**) the ordinary people: *the age-old fear that the mob may organize to destroy the last vestiges of civilized life.*
2 (usu. **the Mob**) N. Amer. the Mafia or a similar criminal organization.
3 Austral./NZ a flock or herd of animals: *a mob of cattle.*
▸ verb (**mobs, mobbing, mobbed**) [with obj.] crowd round (someone) or into (a place) in an unruly way: *he was mobbed by autograph hunters.* ■ (of a group of birds or mammals) surround and attack (a predator or other source of threat) in order to drive it off.
– DERIVATIVES **mobber** noun.
– ORIGIN late 17th cent.: abbreviation of archaic *mobile*, short for Latin *mobile vulgus* 'excitable crowd'.

mob cap ▸ noun a large soft hat covering all of the hair and typically having a decorative frill, worn indoors by women in the 18th and early 19th centuries.
– ORIGIN mid 18th cent.: *mob*, variant of obsolete *mab* 'slut'. The word *mob* was first used in the sense 'prostitute' (mid to late 17th cent.), later denoting a negligee.

mobe (also **mobey**) ▸ noun informal a mobile phone.

mob-handed ▸ adverb Brit. informal in considerable numbers: *they came mob-handed.*

Mobile /məʊ'biːl/ an industrial city and port on the coast of southern Alabama; pop. 191,022 (est. 2008).

mobile /'məʊbʌɪl/ ▸ adjective **1** able to move or be moved freely or easily: *he has a weight problem and is not very mobile* | *highly mobile international capital.* ■ (of the face or its features) indicating feelings with fluid and expressive movements: *her mobile features worked overtime to register shock and disapproval.* ■ (of a shop, library, or other service) accommodated in a vehicle so as to travel around and serve various places. ■ (of a military or police unit) equipped and prepared to move quickly to any place it is needed.
2 relating to mobile phones, handheld computers, and similar technology: *the next generation of mobile networks* | *a mobile device.*
3 able or willing to move easily or freely between occupations, places of residence, or social classes: *an increasingly mobile society.*
▸ noun **1** a decorative structure that is suspended so as to turn freely in the air.
2 Brit. a mobile phone.
– PHRASES **upwardly** (or **downwardly**) **mobile** moving to a higher (or lower) social class; acquiring (or losing) wealth and status.
– ORIGIN late 15th cent.: via French from Latin *mobilis*, from *movere* 'to move'. The noun dates from the 1940s.

> **WORD TRENDS** People used to worry about being *upwardly* or *downwardly mobile*, but in the supposedly classless 21st century **mobile** primarily refers to mobile phones and other forms of technology that let us communicate and use the Internet on the move. In the Oxford English Corpus most of the words modified by **mobile** relate to technology, with *phone* followed by *operator*, *device*, *service*, and *network*—only the humble *mobile home* reminds us of a simpler low-tech world. Although *cell phone* is used in the US rather than *mobile phone*, **mobile** is still the adjective associated with it there.

-mobile /mə'biːl/ ▸ suffix forming nouns denoting vehicles of a particular type: *snowmobile*.
– ORIGIN from **automobile**.

mobile home ▸ noun a large caravan that is parked in one particular place and used as permanent living accommodation.

mobile phone ▸ noun Brit. a telephone with access to a cellular radio system so it can be used over a wide area, without a physical connection to a network.

mobility ▸ noun [mass noun] the ability to move or be moved freely and easily: *this exercise helps retain mobility in the damaged joints.* ■ the ability to move between different levels in society or employment: *industrialization would open up increasing chances of social mobility.*

mobility allowance ▸ noun Brit. a state benefit paid to disabled people to assist them in travelling for regular medical attention or other purposes.

mobilize (also **mobilise**) ▸ verb [with obj.] **1** (of a country or its government) prepare and organize (troops) for active service. ■ organize and encourage (a group of people) to take collective action in pursuit of a particular objective: *it would be hard for worker representatives to mobilize the workforce against the employers.* ■ bring (resources) into use for a particular purpose: *at sea we will mobilize any amount of resources to undertake a rescue.*
2 make (something) movable or capable of movement: *the physiotherapist might mobilize the patient's shoulder girdle.* ■ make (a substance) able to be transported by or as a liquid: *acid rain mobilizes the aluminium in forest soils.*
– DERIVATIVES **mobilizable** adjective, **mobilization** noun, **mobilizer** noun.
– ORIGIN mid 19th cent.: from French *mobiliser*, from *mobile* (see **mobile**).

Möbius strip /'məːbɪəs/ ▸ noun a surface with one continuous side formed by joining the ends of a rectangle after twisting one end through 180°.
– ORIGIN early 20th cent.: named after August F. *Möbius* (1790–1868), German mathematician.

moblog /'mɒblɒg/ ▸ noun a blog that consists of pictures and other content posted from a mobile phone.
– DERIVATIVES **moblogger** noun, **moblogging** noun.
– ORIGIN early 21st cent.: blend of **mobile** and **weblog**.

mobo ▸ noun (pl. **mobos**) Computing, informal a motherboard.

mobocracy ▸ noun (pl. **mobocracies**) [mass noun] rule or domination by the masses.

mob rule ▸ noun [mass noun] control of a political situation by those outside the conventional or lawful realm, typically involving violence and intimidation.

mobster ▸ noun informal a member of an organized group of violent criminals; a gangster.

Mobutu /mə'buːtuː/, Sese Seko (1930–97), African statesman, President of Zaire (now the Democratic Republic of the Congo) 1965–97; born *Joseph-Désiré Mobutu*. Seizing power in a military coup in 1965, he retained control despite opposition until 1997, when he was finally forced to stand down.

Mobutu Sese Seko, Lake /məˌbuːtuː ˌseɪseɪ 'seɪkəʊ/ the name in the Democratic Republic of the Congo (Zaire) for Lake Albert (see **Albert, Lake**).

moc /mɒk/ ▸ noun N. Amer. informal a moccasin.

moccasin ▸ noun **1** a soft leather slipper or shoe, strictly one without a separate heel, having the sole turned up on all sides and sewn to the upper in a simple gathered seam, in a style originating among North American Indians.
2 a venomous American pit viper. ● Genus *Agkistrodon*, family Viperidae: three species, in particular the **water** (or **cottonmouth**) **moccasin** (see COTTONMOUTH) and the **highland moccasin** (see COPPERHEAD).
– ORIGIN early 17th cent.: from Virginia Algonquian *mockasin*. The word is also found in other American Indian languages.

moccasin telegraph ▸ noun Canadian term for BUSH TELEGRAPH.

mocha /ˈmɒkə/ ▸ noun [mass noun] **1** a type of fine-quality coffee. ■ a drink or flavouring made with mocha, typically with chocolate added.
2 a soft kind of leather made from sheepskin.
– ORIGIN late 18th cent.: named after *Mocha*, a port in Yemen on the Red Sea, from where the coffee and leather were first shipped.

mochaccino /ˌmɒkəˈtʃiːnəʊ/ ▸ noun (pl. **mochaccinos**) cappuccino coffee containing chocolate syrup or chocolate flavouring.
– ORIGIN blend of MOCHA and CAPPUCCINO.

mock ▸ verb [with obj.] **1** tease or laugh at in a scornful or contemptuous manner: *opposition MPs mocked the government's decision.* ■ make (something) seem laughably unreal or impossible: *at Christmas, arguments and friction mock our pretence at peace.* ■ mimic (someone or something) scornfully or contemptuously.
2 (**mock something up**) make a replica or imitation of something.
▸ adjective [attrib.] not authentic or real, but without the intention to deceive: *a mock-Georgian red brick house | Jim threw up his hands in mock horror.* ■ (of an examination, battle, etc.) arranged for training or practice: *mock GCSEs.*
▸ noun **1** (**mocks**) Brit. informal mock examinations: *obtaining Grade A in mocks.*
2 dated an object of derision: *he has become the mock of all his contemporaries.*
– PHRASES **make (a) mock of** hold up to scorn or ridicule: *stop making a mock of other people's business.*
– DERIVATIVES **mockable** adjective.
– ORIGIN late Middle English: from Old French *mocquer* 'deride'.

mocker ▸ noun a person who mocks someone or something: *a mocker of authority.*
– PHRASES **put the mockers on** Brit. informal put an end to; thwart. ■ bring bad luck to: *someone has really put the mockers on the team.*

mockery ▸ noun (pl. **mockeries**) [mass noun] derision; ridicule: *stung by her mockery, Frankie hung his head.* ■ [in sing.] an absurd misrepresentation or imitation of something: *after **a mockery of** a trial in London, he was executed.* ■ archaic ludicrously futile action: *in her bitterness she felt that all rejoicing was mockery.*
– PHRASES **make a mockery of** make (something) seem foolish or absurd: *new technology is making a mockery of our outdated laws.*
– ORIGIN late Middle English: from Old French *moquerie*, from *mocquer* 'to deride'.

mock-heroic ▸ adjective (of a literary work or its style) imitating the style of heroic literature in order to satirize an unheroic subject.
▸ noun a burlesque imitation of the heroic character or literary style.

mocking ▸ adjective making fun of someone or something in a cruel way; derisive: *he got jeers and mocking laughter as he addressed the marchers.*
– DERIVATIVES **mockingly** adverb.

mockingbird ▸ noun a long-tailed thrush-like songbird with greyish plumage, found mainly in tropical America and noted for its mimicry of the calls and songs of other birds. ● Family Mimidae (the **mockingbird family**): three genera and several species, especially the **northern mockingbird** (*Mimus polyglottos*), of North America. The mockingbird family also includes the catbirds, thrashers, and tremblers.

mock moon ▸ noun Astronomy a paraselene.

mockney ▸ noun [mass noun] Brit. informal a form of speech regarded as an affected imitation of cockney in accent and vocabulary.

mock orange ▸ noun a bushy shrub of north temperate regions, which is cultivated for its strongly scented white flowers, the perfume of which resembles orange blossom. ● Genus *Philadelphus*, family Hydrangeaceae (formerly Philadelphaceae): several species and hybrids, in particular *P. coronarius*.

mock sun ▸ noun Astronomy a parhelion.

mocktail ▸ noun chiefly N. Amer. a non-alcoholic drink consisting of a mixture of fruit juices or other soft drinks.
– ORIGIN 1930s: blend of MOCK (adjective) and COCKTAIL.

mock turtle soup ▸ noun [mass noun] imitation turtle soup made from a calf's head.

mockumentary ▸ noun a television programme or film which takes the form of a serious documentary in order to satirize its subject.

mock-up ▸ noun a model or replica of a machine or structure, used for instructional or experimental purposes. ■ an arrangement of text and pictures to be printed: *a mock-up of the following day's front page.*

mocky US informal, dated, offensive ▸ noun (pl. **mockies**) a Jew.
▸ adjective Jewish.
– ORIGIN 1930s: perhaps from Yiddish *makeh* 'a plague'.

mocock /məʊˈkɒk/ ▸ noun N. Amer. a container resembling a basket made from birchbark.
– ORIGIN late 18th cent.: from an American Indian language.

MOD ▸ abbreviation (in the UK) Ministry of Defence.

Mod ▸ noun a Highland meeting for Gaelic literary and musical competitions.
– ORIGIN from Scottish Gaelic *mòd*.

mod[1] ▸ adjective informal modern.
▸ noun Brit. (especially in the early 1960s) a young person of a subculture characterized by a smart stylish appearance, the riding of motor scooters, and a liking for soul music.
– ORIGIN abbreviation of MODERN or MODERNIST.

mod[2] ▸ preposition Mathematics another term for MODULO.

mod[3] ▸ informal noun (usu. **mods**) a modification.
▸ verb (**mods, modding, modded**) [with obj.] make modifications to; modify: *both the single-player and multiplayer games can be modded.*
– DERIVATIVES **modder** noun.

modacrylic /ˌmɒdəˈkrɪlɪk/ ▸ adjective of or denoting a synthetic textile fibre which is a polymer containing a high proportion of units derived from acrylonitrile.
▸ noun [mass noun] a modacrylic textile fibre.
– ORIGIN 1950s: from *modified* (past participle of MODIFY) + ACRYLIC.

modal /ˈməʊd(ə)l/ ▸ adjective **1** relating to mode or form as opposed to substance.
2 Grammar of or denoting the mood of a verb. ■ relating to a modal verb.
3 Statistics relating to a value that occurs most frequently in a given set of data.
4 Music of or denoting music using melodies or harmonies based on modes other than the ordinary major and minor scales.
5 Logic (of a proposition) in which the predicate is affirmed of the subject with some qualification, or which involves the affirmation of possibility, impossibility, necessity, or contingency.
▸ noun Grammar a modal word or construction.
– DERIVATIVES **modally** adverb.
– ORIGIN mid 16th cent. (in sense 5 of the adjective): from medieval Latin *modalis*, from Latin *modus* (see MODE).

modalism ▸ noun [mass noun] **1** Theology the doctrine that the persons of the Trinity represent only three modes or aspects of the divine revelation, not distinct and coexisting parts of the divine nature.
2 Music the use of modal melodies and harmonies.
– DERIVATIVES **modalist** noun & adjective.

modality ▸ noun (pl. **modalities**) **1** [mass noun] modal quality: *the harmony had a touch of modality.*
2 a particular mode in which something exists or is experienced or expressed. ■ a particular method or procedure: *the modalities of troop withdrawals.* ■ a particular form of sensory perception: *the visual and auditory modalities.*
– ORIGIN early 17th cent.: from medieval Latin *modalitas*, from *modalis* (see MODAL).

modal verb ▸ noun Grammar an auxiliary verb that expresses necessity or possibility. English modal verbs include *must, shall, will, should, would, can, could, may*, and *might*.

mod cons ▸ plural noun Brit. informal the amenities and appliances characteristic of a well-equipped modern house that contribute to an easier and more comfortable way of life: *the property has **all mod cons**.*

mode ▸ noun **1** a way or manner in which something occurs or is experienced, expressed, or done: *his preferred mode of travel was a kayak.* ■ an option allowing a change in the method of operation of a device, especially a camera: *a camcorder **in automatic mode**.* ■ Computing a way of operating or using a system: *some computers provide several so-called processor modes.* ■ Physics any of the distinct kinds or patterns of vibration of an oscillating system. ■ Logic the character of a modal proposition (whether necessary, contingent, possible, or impossible). ■ Logic & Grammar another term for MOOD[2].
2 a fashion or style in clothes, art, literature, etc.: *in the Seventies the mode for active wear took hold.*
3 Statistics the value that occurs most frequently in a given set of data.
4 Music a set of musical notes forming a scale and from which melodies and harmonies are constructed.

> The modes of plainsong and later Western music (including the usual major and minor scales) correspond to the diatonic scales played on the white notes of a piano. They are named arbitrarily after ancient Greek modes: Ionian (or major), Dorian, Phrygian, Lydian, Mixolydian, Aeolian, and Locrian.

– ORIGIN late Middle English (in the musical and grammatical senses): from Latin *modus* 'measure', from an Indo-European root shared by METE[1]; compare with MOOD[2].

model ▸ noun **1** a three-dimensional representation of a person or thing or of a proposed structure, typically on a smaller scale than the original: *a model of St Paul's Cathedral* | [as modifier] *a model aeroplane.* ■ (in sculpture) a figure or object made in clay or wax, to be reproduced in another more durable material.
2 a thing used as an example to follow or imitate: *the project became a model for other schemes.* ■ a person or thing regarded as an excellent example of a specified quality: *as she grew older, she became **a model of** self-control* | [as modifier] *he was a model husband and father.* ■ an actual person or place on which a specified fictional character or location is based: *Preston was the model for Coketown in 'Hard Times'.* ■ (**the Model**) the plan for the reorganization of the Parliamentary army, passed by the House of Commons in 1644–5. See also NEW MODEL ARMY.
3 a simplified description, especially a mathematical one, of a system or process, to assist calculations and predictions: *a statistical model used for predicting the survival rates of endangered species.*
4 a person employed to display clothes by wearing them. ■ a person employed to pose for an artist, photographer, or sculptor: *an artist's model.*
5 a particular design or version of a product: *the company revealed their latest model at the Motor Show.* ■ a garment or a copy of a garment by a well-known designer.
▸ verb (**models, modelling, modelled**; US **models, modeling, modeled**) [with obj.] **1** fashion or shape (a three-dimensional figure or object) in a malleable material such as clay or wax: *use the icing to model a house.* ■ (in drawing or painting) represent so as to appear three-dimensional: *the body of the woman to the right is modelled in softer, riper forms.*
2 (**model something on/after**) use (a system, procedure, etc.) as an example to follow or imitate: *the research method will be modelled on previous work.* ■ (**model oneself on**) take (someone admired or respected) as an example to follow or imitate: *he models himself on rock legend Elvis Presley.* ■ devise a representation, especially a mathematical one, of (a phenomenon or system): *a computer program that can model the behaviour of smoke.*
3 display (clothes) by wearing them. ■ [no obj.] work as a model by displaying clothes or posing for an artist or sculptor.
– DERIVATIVES **modeller** noun.
– ORIGIN late 16th cent. (denoting a set of plans of a building): from French *modelle*, from Italian *modello*, from an alteration of Latin *modulus* (see MODULUS).

model home ▸ noun North American term for SHOW HOUSE.

modelling (US **modeling**) ▸ noun [mass noun] **1** the work of a fashion model.
2 the activity of making three-dimensional models.
3 [often with adj. or noun modifier] the devising or use of abstract or mathematical models: *macroeconomic modelling and policy analysis.*

model village ▸ noun **1** historical a village providing a high standard of housing, typically built by an employer for the workforce.
2 a small copy of a village or a collection of models of famous buildings arranged as a village, typically built as a tourist attraction.

M

modem /ˈməʊdɛm/ ▶ **noun** a combined device for modulation and demodulation, for example, between the digital data of a computer and the analogue signal of a telephone line.
▶ **verb** [with obj. and adverbial of direction] send (data) by modem.
– ORIGIN 1950s: blend of *modulator* and *demodulator*.

Modena /ˈmɒdɪnə/ a city in northern Italy, north-west of Bologna; pop. 181,807 (2008).

moderate ▶ **adjective** /ˈmɒd(ə)rət/ average in amount, intensity, quality, or degree: *we walked at a moderate pace.* ■ (of a person, party, or policy) not radical or excessively right- or left-wing: *a moderate reform programme.*
▶ **noun** /ˈmɒd(ə)rət/ a person who holds moderate views, especially in politics.
▶ **verb** /ˈmɒdəreɪt/ **1** make or become less extreme, intense, rigorous, or violent: [with obj.] *I shall not moderate my criticism* | [no obj.] *the weather has moderated considerably.*
2 [with obj.] Brit. review (examination papers, results, or candidates) in relation to an agreed standard so as to ensure consistency of marking.
3 [with obj.] (in academic and ecclesiastical contexts) preside over (a deliberative body) or at (a debate): *a panel moderated by a Harvard University law professor.* ■ [no obj.] (especially in the Presbyterian Church in Scotland) act as a moderator; preside.
4 monitor (an Internet message board or chat room) for inappropriate or offensive content.
5 [with obj.] Physics retard (neutrons) with a moderator.
– DERIVATIVES **moderatism** noun.
– ORIGIN late Middle English: from Latin *moderat-* 'reduced, controlled', from the verb *moderare*; related to MODEST.

moderate breeze ▶ **noun** a wind of force 4 on the Beaufort scale (11–16 knots or 20–30 kph).

moderate gale ▶ **noun** another term for NEAR GALE.

moderately ▶ **adverb** [as submodifier] to a certain extent; quite; fairly: *the event was moderately successful.* ■ within reasonable limits: *both hotels are moderately priced.*

moderation ▶ **noun** [mass noun] **1** the avoidance of excess or extremes, especially in one's behaviour or political opinions: *he urged the police to show moderation.* ■ the action of making something less extreme, intense, or violent: *the union's approach was based on increased dialogue and* ***the moderation of*** *demands.*
2 Brit. the action or process of moderating examination papers, results, or candidates. ■ **(Moderations)** the first public examination in some faculties for the BA degree at Oxford University.
3 Physics the retardation of neutrons by a moderator.
– PHRASES **in moderation** within reasonable limits; not to excess: *nuts can be eaten in moderation.*
– ORIGIN late Middle English: via Old French from Latin *moderatio(n-)*, from the verb *moderare* 'to control' (see MODERATE).

moderato /ˌmɒdəˈrɑːtəʊ/ Music ▶ **adverb & adjective** (especially as a direction) at a moderate pace: [postpositive] [as submodifier] *allegro moderato.*
▶ **noun** (pl. **moderatos**) a passage marked to be performed at a moderate pace.
– ORIGIN Italian, literally 'moderate'.

moderator ▶ **noun 1** an arbitrator or mediator: *Egypt managed to assert its role as a regional moderator.* ■ a presiding officer, especially a chairman of a debate. ■ a Presbyterian minister presiding over an ecclesiastical body.
2 Brit. a person who reviews examination papers to ensure consistency, or otherwise oversees an examination.
3 a person who moderates an Internet message board or chat room.
4 Physics a substance used in a nuclear reactor to retard neutrons.
– DERIVATIVES **moderatorship** noun.

modern ▶ **adjective** relating to the present or recent times as opposed to the remote past: *the pace of modern life* | *modern European history.* ■ characterized by or using the most up-to-date techniques, ideas, or equipment: *they do not have modern weapons.* ■ [attrib.] denoting the form of a language that is currently used, as opposed to any earlier form: *modern German.* ■ [attrib.] denoting a current or recent style or trend in art, architecture, or other cultural activity marked by a significant departure from traditional styles and values: *Matisse's contribution to modern art.*
▶ **noun** (usu. **moderns**) a person who advocates or practises a departure from traditional styles or values.
– DERIVATIVES **modernly** adverb, **modernness** noun.
– ORIGIN late Middle English: from late Latin *modernus*, from Latin *modo* 'just now'.

modern dance ▶ **noun** [mass noun] a free expressive style of dancing that developed in the early 20th century as a reaction to classical ballet. In recent years it has included elements not usually associated with dance, such as speech and film.

modern-day ▶ **adjective** in or relating to the present or recent times: *I bet you wish that I was a bank robber, some sort of modern-day Robin Hood.*

moderne /məˈdəːn/ ▶ **adjective** relating to a popularization of the art deco style marked by bright colours and geometric shapes. ■ often derogatory denoting an ultra-modern style.
– ORIGIN 1930s: French, 'modern'.

modern English ▶ **noun** [mass noun] the English language as it has been since about 1500.

Modern Greats ▶ **plural noun** (at Oxford University) the school of philosophy, politics, and economics.

modern history ▶ **noun** [mass noun] history up to the present day, from some arbitrary point taken to represent the end of the Middle Ages. In some contexts it may be contrasted with 'ancient' rather than 'medieval' history, and start (for example) from the fall of the Western Roman Empire.

modernism ▶ **noun** [mass noun] modern character or quality of thought, expression, or technique: *a strange mix of nostalgia and modernism.* ■ a style or movement in the arts that aims to depart significantly from classical and traditional forms. ■ a movement towards modifying traditional beliefs in accordance with modern ideas, especially in the Roman Catholic Church in the late 19th and early 20th centuries.

modernist ▶ **noun** a believer in or supporter of modernism, especially in the arts.
▶ **adjective** of or associated with modernism, especially in the arts.
– DERIVATIVES **modernistic** adjective.

modernity /məˈdəːnɪti/ ▶ **noun** [mass noun] the quality or condition of being modern: *an aura of technological modernity.* ■ a modern way of thinking, working, etc.; contemporariness: *Hobbes was the genius of modernity.*

modernize (also **modernise**) ▶ **verb** [with obj.] adapt (something) to modern needs or habits, typically by installing modern equipment or adopting modern ideas or methods: *he modernized the health service.*
– DERIVATIVES **modernization** noun, **modernizer** noun.

modern jazz ▶ **noun** [mass noun] jazz as developed in the 1940s and 1950s, especially bebop and the music that followed it.

modern languages ▶ **plural noun** European languages (especially French and German) as a subject of study, as contrasted with classical Latin and Greek.

modern Latin ▶ **noun** [mass noun] Latin as developed since 1500, used especially in scientific terminology.

modern pentathlon ▶ **noun** see PENTATHLON.

modest ▶ **adjective 1** unassuming in the estimation of one's abilities or achievements: *he was a very modest man, refusing to take any credit for the enterprise.*
2 (of an amount, rate, or level) relatively moderate, limited, or small: *drink modest amounts of alcohol* | *employment growth was relatively modest.* ■ not large, elaborate, or expensive: *a modest flat in Fulham* | *it was a nice wedding, necessarily modest.*
3 (of a woman) dressing or behaving so as to avoid impropriety or indecency, especially to avoid attracting sexual attention. ■ (of clothing) not revealing or emphasizing a person's figure.
– DERIVATIVES **modestly** adverb.
– ORIGIN mid 16th cent.: from French *modeste*, from Latin *modestus* 'keeping due measure', related to *modus* 'measure'.

modesty ▶ **noun** [mass noun] **1** the quality or state of being unassuming in the estimation of one's abilities: *with typical modesty he insisted on sharing the credit with others.*
2 the quality of being relatively moderate, limited, or small in amount, rate, or level: *the modesty of his political aspirations.*
3 behaviour, manner, or appearance intended to avoid impropriety or indecency: *modesty forbade her to undress in front of so many people.*

modicum /ˈmɒdɪkəm/ ▶ **noun** [in sing.] a small quantity of a particular thing, especially something desirable or valuable: *his statement had* ***a modicum of*** *truth.*
– ORIGIN late 15th cent.: from Latin, neuter of *modicus* 'moderate', from *modus* 'measure'.

modification ▶ **noun** [mass noun] the action of modifying something: *the parts supplied should fit with little or no modification.* ■ [count noun] a change made: *a number of modifications are being carried out to the engines.*
– ORIGIN late 15th cent. (in Scots law, denoting the assessment of a payment): from French, or from Latin *modificatio(n-)*, from *modificare* (see MODIFY).

modifier ▶ **noun** a person or thing that makes partial or minor changes to something. ■ Grammar a word, especially an adjective or noun used attributively, that restricts or adds to the sense of a head noun (e.g. *good* and *family* in *a good family house*). ■ Genetics a gene which modifies the phenotypic expression of a gene at another locus.

modify ▶ **verb** (**modifies**, **modifying**, **modified**) [with obj.] make partial or minor changes to (something): *she may be prepared to modify her views.* ■ Biology transform (a structure) from its original anatomical form during development or evolution. ■ Grammar (especially of an adjective) restrict or add to the sense of (a noun). ■ Phonetics pronounce (a speech sound) differently from the norm for that sound.
– DERIVATIVES **modifiable** adjective, **modificatory** adjective.
– ORIGIN late Middle English: from Old French *modifier*, from Latin *modificare*, from *modus* (see MODE).

Modigliani /ˌmɒdɪˈljɑːni/, Amedeo (1884–1920), Italian painter and sculptor, resident in France from 1906. His portraits and nudes are noted for their elongated forms, linear qualities, and earthy colours.

modillion /məˈdɪljən/ ▶ **noun** Architecture a projecting bracket under the corona of a cornice in the Corinthian and other orders.
– ORIGIN mid 16th cent.: from French *modillon*, from Italian *modiglione*, based on Latin *mutulus* 'mutule'.

modiolus /məˈdʌɪələs/ ▶ **noun** (pl. **modioli**) Anatomy the conical central axis of the cochlea of the ear.
– ORIGIN early 19th cent.: from Latin, literally 'nave of a wheel'.

modish /ˈməʊdɪʃ/ ▶ **adjective** often derogatory conforming to or following what is currently popular and fashionable: *it seems sad that such a scholar should feel compelled to use this modish jargon.*
– DERIVATIVES **modishly** adverb, **modishness** noun.

modiste /mɒˈdiːst/ ▶ **noun** dated a fashionable milliner or dressmaker.
– ORIGIN mid 19th cent.: French, from *mode* 'fashion'.

Mods ▶ **plural noun** informal the Moderations examination at Oxford University.

modular ▶ **adjective 1** employing or involving a module or modules as the basis of design or construction: *modular housing units.* ■ relating to an educational course designed as a series of independent units of study that can be combined in a number of ways.
2 Mathematics relating to a modulus.
– DERIVATIVES **modularity** noun.
– ORIGIN late 18th cent.: from modern Latin *modularis*, from Latin *modulus* (see MODULUS).

modulate /ˈmɒdjʊleɪt/ ▶ **verb** [with obj.] **1** exert a modifying or controlling influence on: *the state attempts to modulate private business's cash flow.*
2 vary the strength, tone, or pitch of (one's voice). ■ alter the amplitude or frequency of (an electromagnetic wave or other oscillation) in accordance with the variations of a second signal, typically one of a lower frequency. ■ [no obj.] Music change from one key to another. ■ [no obj.] **(modulate into)** change from one form or condition into (another): *the fraught silence would modulate into conciliatory monosyllables.*
– DERIVATIVES **modulation** noun, **modulator** noun.
– ORIGIN mid 16th cent. (in the sense 'intone a song'): from Latin *modulat-* 'measured, made melody', from the verb *modulari*, from *modulus* 'measure' (see MODULUS).

module ▶ **noun 1** each of a set of standardized parts or independent units that can be used to construct a more complex structure, such as an item of furniture or a building. ■ each of a set of independent units of study or training that can be combined in a number of ways to form a course at a college or university. ■ Computing any of a number of distinct but interrelated units from which a program may be built up or into which a complex activity may be analysed.
2 a detachable self-contained unit of a spacecraft.

– ORIGIN late 16th cent. (in the senses 'allotted scale' and 'plan, model'): from French, or from Latin *modulus* (see MODULUS). Current senses date from the 1950s.

modulo /ˈmɒdjʊləʊ/ ▶ **preposition** Mathematics (in number theory) with respect to or using a modulus of a specified number. Two numbers are congruent modulo a given number if they give the same remainder when divided by that number. ■ [as modifier] using moduli: *modulo operations*.
– ORIGIN late 19th cent.: from Latin, ablative of *modulus* (see MODULUS).

modulus /ˈmɒdjʊləs/ ▶ **noun** (pl. **moduli** /-lʌɪ, -liː/) Mathematics **1** another term for ABSOLUTE VALUE. ■ the positive square root of the sum of the squares of the real and imaginary parts of a complex number.
2 a constant factor or ratio. ■ a constant indicating the relation between a physical effect and the force producing it.
3 a number used as a divisor for considering numbers in sets, numbers being considered congruent when giving the same remainder when divided by a particular modulus.
– ORIGIN mid 16th cent. (denoting an architectural unit of length): from Latin, literally 'measure', diminutive of *modus*.

modus operandi /ˌməʊdəs ɒpəˈrandiː, -dʌɪ/ ▶ **noun** (pl. **modi operandi** /ˌməʊdi/) [usu. in sing.] a particular way or method of doing something: *every killer has his own special modus operandi*. ■ the way in which something operates or works.
– ORIGIN Latin, literally 'way of operating'.

modus ponens /ˌməʊdəs ˈpəʊnɛnz/ ▶ **noun** the rule of logic which states that if a conditional statement ('if *p* then *q*') is accepted, and the antecedent (*p*) holds, then the consequent (*q*) may be inferred. ■ an argument using the rule of modus ponens.
– ORIGIN Latin, literally 'mood that affirms'.

modus tollens /ˌməʊdəs ˈtɒlɛnz/ ▶ **noun** the rule of logic which states that if a conditional statement ('if *p* then *q*') is accepted, and the consequent does not hold (*not-q*) then the negation of the antecedent (*not-p*) can be inferred. ■ an argument using the rule of modus tollens.
– ORIGIN Latin, literally 'mood that denies'.

modus vivendi /ˌməʊdəs vɪˈvɛndiː, -dʌɪ/ ▶ **noun** (pl. **modi vivendi** /ˌməʊdi/) [usu. in sing.] an arrangement or agreement allowing conflicting parties to coexist peacefully, either indefinitely or until a final settlement is reached. ■ a way of living.
– ORIGIN Latin, literally 'way of living'.

Moeritherium /ˌmɪərɪˈθɪərɪəm/ ▶ **noun** a pig-like mammal of the late Eocene and Oligocene epochs, related to modern elephants.
– ORIGIN modern Latin, from the name of Lake *Moeris* in Egypt, where the first fossils were found, + Greek *thērion* 'wild beast'.

Moesia /ˈmiːsɪə, ˈmiːʃə/ an ancient country of southern Europe, corresponding to parts of modern Bulgaria and Serbia.

mofette /mɒˈfɛt/ ▶ **noun** archaic term for FUMAROLE.
– ORIGIN early 19th cent.: from French, from Neapolitan Italian *mofetta*.

moffie /ˈmɒfi/ ▶ **noun** (pl. **moffies**) S. African informal, derogatory a man regarded as effeminate. ■ a male homosexual.
– ORIGIN Afrikaans, perhaps an abbreviation of *moffiedaai*, dialect variant of *hermafrodiet* 'hermaphrodite'.

mofo ▶ **noun** (pl. **mofos**) vulgar slang short for MOTHERFUCKER.

mog ▶ **noun** Brit. informal another term for MOGGIE.

Mogadishu /ˌmɒgəˈdɪʃuː/ the capital of Somalia, a port on the Indian Ocean; pop. 1,100,000 (est. 2007). Also called MUQDISHO.

Mogadon /ˈmɒgədɒn/ ▶ **noun** trademark for NITRAZEPAM.

moggie (also **moggy**) ▶ **noun** (pl. **moggies**) Brit. informal a cat.
– ORIGIN late 17th cent.: variant of *Maggie*, pet form of the given name *Margaret*.

Moghlai (also **Moglai**) ▶ **adjective** variant spelling of MUGHLAI.

Mogilyov /magʲɪˈlʲɵf/ (also **Mogilev**) Russian name for MAHILYOW.

Mogul /ˈməʊg(ə)l/ (also **Moghul** or **Mughal**) ▶ **noun** a member of the Muslim dynasty of Mongol origin founded by the successors of Tamerlane, which ruled much of India from the 16th to the 19th century.
■ (often **the Great Mogul**) historical the Mogul emperor of Delhi.
– ORIGIN from Persian *muġul* 'Mongol'.

mogul¹ /ˈməʊg(ə)l/ ▶ **noun 1** informal an important or powerful person, especially in the film or media industry.
2 (**Mogul**) a steam locomotive of 2-6-0 wheel arrangement.
– ORIGIN late 17th cent.: figurative use of MOGUL.

mogul² /ˈməʊg(ə)l/ ▶ **noun** a bump on a ski slope formed by skiers turning.
– ORIGIN 1960s: probably from southern German dialect *Mugel, Mugl*.

MOH ▶ **abbreviation** ■ Ministry of Health. ■ Medical Officer of Health (chief health executive of a local authority).

Mohács /ˈməʊhɑːtʃ/ a river port and industrial town on the Danube in southern Hungary, close to the borders with Croatia and Serbia; pop. 19,129 (2009). It was the site of a battle in 1526 in which the Hungarians were defeated by a Turkish force, as a result of which Hungary became part of the Ottoman Empire.

mohair ▶ **noun** [mass noun] the hair of the angora goat. ■ a yarn or fabric made from mohair, typically mixed with wool: [as modifier] *a mohair sweater*.
– ORIGIN late 16th cent.: from Arabic *mukayyar* 'cloth made of goat's hair' (literally 'choice, select'). The change in ending was due to association with HAIR.

mohalla /məʊˈhʌlə:/ ▶ **noun** Indian an area of a town or village; a community.
– ORIGIN from Arabic *mohālla*.

Mohammed see MUHAMMAD.

Mohammerah /məˈhamərə/ former name (until 1924) for KHORRAMSHAHR.

Mohave Desert variant spelling of MOJAVE DESERT.

Mohawk ▶ **noun** (pl. **same** or **Mohawks**) **1** a member of an American Indian people, originally inhabiting parts of what is now upper New York State.
2 [mass noun] the Iroquoian language of the Mohawk.
3 chiefly N. Amer. a Mohican haircut.
4 Skating a step from either edge of the skate to the same edge on the other foot in the opposite direction.
▶ **adjective 1** relating to the Mohawk or their language.
2 chiefly N. Amer. denoting a Mohican haircut.
– ORIGIN Narragansett *mohowawog*, 'man-eaters'.

Mohegan /məʊˈhiːg(ə)n/ (also **Mohican**) ▶ **noun** (pl. **same** or **Mohegans**) **1** a member of an American Indian people formerly inhabiting the western parts of Connecticut and Massachusetts. Compare with MAHICAN.
2 [mass noun] the extinct Algonquian language of the Mohegan.
▶ **adjective** relating to the Mohegans or their language.
– ORIGIN from Mohegan, literally 'people of the tidal waters'.

mohel /ˈməʊ(h)(ə)l/ ▶ **noun** (pl. **mohels**, **mohelim**, or **mohalim**) a Jew who performs the rite of circumcision.
– ORIGIN mid 17th cent.: from Hebrew *mōhēl*.

Mohenjo-Daro /məˌhɛndʒəʊˈdɑːrəʊ/ an ancient city of the civilization of the Indus valley (*c*.2600–1700 BC), now a major archaeological site in Pakistan, south-west of Sukkur.

Mohican¹ /məʊˈhiːk(ə)n, ˈməʊɪk(ə)n/ ▶ **noun** a hairstyle with the head shaved except for a strip of hair from the middle of the forehead to the back of the neck, typically stiffened to stand erect or in spikes.
– ORIGIN 1960s: erroneously associated with the American Indian people (see HURON).

Mohican² /məʊˈhiːk(ə)n/ ▶ **adjective & noun** old-fashioned variant spelling of MAHICAN or MOHEGAN.

Moho /ˈməʊhəʊ/ ▶ **noun** Geology short for MOHOROVIČIĆ DISCONTINUITY.

Moholy-Nagy /ˌməʊhɔɪˈnɒdʒ/, László (1895–1946), Hungarian-born American painter, sculptor, and photographer. He pioneered the experimental use of plastic materials, light, photography, and film.

Mohorovičić discontinuity /ˌməʊhəˈrəʊvɪtʃɪtʃ/ ▶ **noun** Geology the boundary surface between the earth's crust and the mantle, lying at a depth of about 10–12 km under the ocean bed and 40–50 km under the continents.
– ORIGIN 1930s: named after Andrija *Mohorovičić* (1857–1936), Yugoslav seismologist.

Mohs' scale /məʊz/ ▶ **noun** a scale of hardness used in classifying minerals. It runs from 1 to 10 using a series of reference minerals, and position on the scale depends on ability to scratch minerals rated lower.
– ORIGIN late 19th cent.: named after Friedrich *Mohs*, (1773–1839), German mineralogist.

moi /mwɑː/ ▶ **exclamation** humorous me (used in questions when accused of something that one knows one is guilty of): *sarcastic, moi?*
– ORIGIN French, 'me'.

moidore /ˈmɔɪdɔː/ ▶ **noun** a Portuguese gold coin, current in England in the early 18th century and then worth about 27 shillings.
– ORIGIN from Portuguese *moeda d'ouro* 'money of gold'.

moiety /ˈmɔɪɪti/ ▶ **noun** (pl. **moieties**) formal or technical each of two parts into which a thing is or can be divided. ■ Anthropology each of two social or ritual groups into which a people is divided, especially among Australian Aborigines and some American Indians. ■ a part or portion, especially a lesser share. ■ Chemistry a distinct part of a large molecule.
– ORIGIN late Middle English: from Old French *moite*, from Latin *medietas* 'middle', from *medius* 'mid, middle'.

moil /mɔɪl/ archaic, dialect, or N. Amer. ▶ **verb** [no obj.] **1** work hard: *men who moiled for gold*.
2 move around in confusion or agitation: *a crowd of men and women moiled in the smoky haze*.
▶ **noun** [mass noun] **1** hard work; drudgery.
2 turmoil; confusion: *the moil of his intimate thoughts*.
– ORIGIN late Middle English (in the sense 'moisten or bedaub'): from Old French *moillier* 'paddle in mud, moisten', based on Latin *mollis* 'soft'. The sense 'work' dates from the mid 16th cent., often in the phrase *toil and moil*.

Moirai /ˈmɔɪrʌɪ/ Greek Mythology the Fates.

moire /mwɑː/ (also **moiré** /ˈmwɑːreɪ/) ▶ **noun** [mass noun] silk fabric that has been subjected to heat and pressure rollers after weaving to give it a rippled appearance.
▶ **adjective** (of silk) having a rippled, lustrous finish. ■ having a pattern of irregular wavy lines like that of moire.
– ORIGIN mid 17th cent.: French *moire* 'mohair' (the original fabric); the variant *moiré* 'given a watered appearance' (past participle of *moirer*, from *moire*).

M

moist ▶ **adjective 1** slightly wet: *the moist, fertile soil*. ■ (of the eyes) wet with tears: *her brother's eyes became moist*. ■ (of a climate) rainy.
2 Medicine marked by a fluid discharge.
– DERIVATIVES **moistly** adverb, **moistness** noun.
– ORIGIN late Middle English: from Old French *moiste*, based on Latin *mucidus* 'mouldy' (influenced by *musteus* 'fresh', from *mustum*: see MUST²).

moisten ▶ **verb** [with obj.] wet slightly: *she moistened her lips with the tip of her tongue*. ■ [no obj.] (of the eyes) fill with tears: *her eyes moistened*.

moisture ▶ **noun** [mass noun] water or other liquid diffused in a small quantity as vapour, within a solid, or condensed on a surface.
– DERIVATIVES **moistureless** adjective.
– ORIGIN late Middle English (denoting moistness): from Old French *moistour*, from *moiste* (see MOIST).

moisturize (also **moisturise**) ▶ **verb** [with obj.] make (something, especially the skin) less dry.

moisturizer (also **moisturiser**) ▶ **noun** a cosmetic preparation used to prevent dryness in the skin.

moisty ▶ **adjective** archaic or informal (especially of weather) moist or damp.

mojarra /məʊˈharə/ ▶ **noun** a small, typically silvery fish that lives in shallow coastal and brackish waters of tropical America. ● Family Gerreidae: several genera and numerous species.
– ORIGIN mid 19th cent.: from American Spanish.

Mojave Desert /məʊˈhɑːvi/ (also **Mohave**) a desert in southern California, to the south-east of the Sierra Nevada and north and east of Los Angeles.

mojito /mə(ʊ)ˈhiːtəʊ/ ▶ **noun** (pl. **mojitos**) a cocktail consisting of white rum, lime or lemon juice, sugar, mint, ice, and carbonated or soda water.
– ORIGIN 1930s: Cuban Spanish, from MOJO² + diminutive suffix *-ito*.

mojo¹ /ˈməʊdʒəʊ/ ▶ **noun** (pl. **mojos**) chiefly US a magic charm, talisman, or spell: *someone must have their mojo working over at the record company*. ■ [mass noun] influence, especially magic power.
– ORIGIN early 20th cent.: probably of African origin; compare with Gullah *moco* 'witchcraft'.

mojo² /ˈməʊdʒəʊ, ˈməʊhəʊ/ ▶ **noun** [mass noun] US a Cuban sauce or marinade containing garlic, olive oil, and sour oranges.

– ORIGIN probably from Spanish *mojo* 'wet' from *mojar* 'make wet'.

moke ▶ noun Brit. informal a donkey. ■ Austral./NZ a horse, typically one that is old or in poor condition.
– ORIGIN mid 19th cent.: of unknown origin.

moko /ˈməʊkəʊ/ ▶ noun (pl. **mokos**) NZ a traditional Maori tattoo, typically one on the face. ■ [mass noun] a pattern of moko tattoos: *a tall woman with moko on her chin*.
– ORIGIN Maori.

moksha /ˈmɒkʃə/ ▶ noun [mass noun] (in Hinduism and Jainism) release from the cycle of rebirth impelled by the law of karma. ■ the transcendent state attained by this release.
– ORIGIN from Sanskrit *mokṣa*.

mol /məʊl/ ▶ abbreviation Chemistry mole.

mola /ˈməʊlə/ ▶ noun (pl. **same** or **molas**) another term for SUNFISH (sense 1).
– ORIGIN late 16th cent.: from Latin, literally 'millstone', with reference to the shape.

molal /ˈməʊləl/ ▶ adjective Chemistry (of a solution) containing one mole of solute per kilogram of solvent.
– DERIVATIVES **molality** noun.

molar[1] (also **molar tooth**) ▶ noun a grinding tooth at the back of a mammal's mouth.
– ORIGIN late Middle English: from Latin *molaris*, from *mola* 'millstone'.

molar[2] ▶ adjective relating to mass; acting on or by means of large masses or units.
– ORIGIN mid 19th cent.: from Latin *moles* 'mass' + -AR[1].

molar[3] ▶ adjective Chemistry relating to one mole of a substance. ■ (of a solution) containing one mole of solute per litre of solvent.
– DERIVATIVES **molarity** noun.

molasses ▶ noun [mass noun] thick, dark brown juice obtained from raw sugar during the refining process. ■ N. Amer. a paler, sweeter version of this; golden syrup.
– ORIGIN mid 16th cent.: from Portuguese *melaço*, from late Latin *mellacium* 'must', based on *mel* 'honey'.

M

Mold /məʊld/ a town in NE Wales, administrative centre of Flintshire; pop. 10,500 (est. 2009).

mold ▶ noun & verb US spelling of MOULD[1], MOULD[2], and MOULD[3].

Moldau /ˈmɔldaʊ/ German name for VLTAVA.

Moldavia /mɒlˈdeɪvɪə/ **1** a former principality of SE Europe. Formerly a part of the Roman province of Dacia, the principality came under Turkish rule in the 16th century. In 1861 Moldavia united with Wallachia to form Romania.
2 another name for MOLDOVA.

Moldavian ▶ noun **1** a native or inhabitant of Moldavia.
2 [mass noun] the Romanian language as spoken and written (in the Cyrillic alphabet) in Moldavia.
▶ adjective relating to Moldavia, its inhabitants, or their language.

molder ▶ verb & noun US spelling of MOULDER[1].

molding ▶ noun US spelling of MOULDING.

Moldova /ˈmɒldəvə, mɒlˈdɒvə/ a landlocked country in SE Europe, between Romania and Ukraine; pop. 4,320,700 (est. 2009); languages, Moldavian (official), Russian; capital, Chişinău. Also called MOLDAVIA.

> A former constituent republic of the Soviet Union, Moldova was formed from territory ceded by Romania in 1940. It became independent as a member of the Commonwealth of Independent States in 1991.

– DERIVATIVES **Moldovan** adjective & noun.

moldy ▶ adjective US spelling of MOULDY.

mole[1] /məʊl/ ▶ noun **1** a small burrowing mammal with dark velvety fur, a long muzzle, and very small eyes, feeding mainly on worms, grubs, and other invertebrates. ● Family Talpidae: several genera and species, including the **European mole** (*Talpa europaea*).
2 a spy who gradually achieves an important position within the security defences of a country. ■ someone within an organization who anonymously betrays confidential information.
– ORIGIN late Middle English: from the Germanic base of Middle Dutch and Middle Low German *mol*.

mole[2] /məʊl/ ▶ noun a small, often slightly raised blemish on the skin made dark by a high concentration of melanin.
– ORIGIN Old English *māl* 'discoloured spot', of Germanic origin.

mole[3] /məʊl/ ▶ noun a large solid structure on a shore serving as a pier, breakwater, or causeway. ■ a harbour formed or protected by a mole.
– ORIGIN mid 16th cent.: from French *môle*, from Latin *moles* 'mass'.

mole[4] /məʊl/ (abbrev. **mol**) ▶ noun Chemistry the SI unit of amount of substance, equal to the quantity containing as many elementary units as there are atoms in 0.012 kg of carbon-12.
– ORIGIN early 20th cent.: from German *Mol*, from *Molekul*, from Latin (see MOLECULE).

mole[5] /məʊl/ ▶ noun Medicine an abnormal mass of tissue in the uterus. See also HYDATIDIFORM MOLE.
– ORIGIN late Middle English: from French *môle*, from Latin *mola* in the sense 'false conception'.

mole[6] /ˈməʊleɪ/ ▶ noun [mass noun] a highly spiced Mexican sauce made chiefly from chilli peppers and chocolate, served with meat.
– ORIGIN Mexican Spanish, from Nahuatl *molli* 'sauce, stew'.

mole cricket ▶ noun a large burrowing nocturnal cricket-like insect with broad forelegs, the female of which lays her eggs in an underground nest and guards the young. Very rare in Britain, it can be a pest in some other areas. ● Family Gryllotalpidae: several genera.

molecular /məˈlɛkjʊlə/ ▶ adjective relating to or consisting of molecules: *interactions between polymer and solvent at the molecular level* | *molecular oxygen*.
– DERIVATIVES **molecularity** noun, **molecularly** adverb.

molecular biology ▶ noun [mass noun] the branch of biology that deals with the structure and function of the macromolecules (e.g. proteins and nucleic acids) essential to life.

molecular electronics ▶ plural noun [treated as sing.] a branch of electronics in which individual molecules perform the same function as microelectronic devices such as diodes.

molecular gastronomy ▶ noun [mass noun] the application of scientific principles to the understanding and development of food preparation.

molecular sieve ▶ noun a crystalline substance (especially a zeolite) with pores of molecular dimensions which permit the passage of molecules below a certain size.

molecular weight ▶ noun another term for RELATIVE MOLECULAR MASS.

molecule /ˈmɒlɪkjuːl/ ▶ noun Chemistry a group of atoms bonded together, representing the smallest fundamental unit of a chemical compound that can take part in a chemical reaction.
– ORIGIN late 18th cent.: from French *molécule*, from modern Latin *molecula*, diminutive of Latin *moles* 'mass'.

molehill ▶ noun a small mound of earth thrown up by a mole burrowing near the surface.
– PHRASES **make a mountain out of a molehill** exaggerate the importance of something trivial.

mole plough ▶ noun a plough in which a pointed iron shoe attached to an upright support is drawn along beneath the surface, making a hollow drainage channel resembling a mole's burrow.

mole rat ▶ noun a herbivorous short-legged rat-like rodent that typically lives permanently underground, with long incisors that protrude from the mouth and are used in digging. ● Family Bathyergidae (African mole rats): several genera; also two subfamilies and three genera in the family Muridae (Eurasian blind mole rats and Asiatic mole rats).

mole salamander ▶ noun a stocky, broad-headed North American salamander which spends much of its life underground. ● Family Ambystomatidae: several genera, in particular *Ambystoma*, and numerous species, including *A. talpoideum*.

moleskin ▶ noun [mass noun] **1** the skin or prepared fur of a mole.
2 a thick, strong cotton fabric with a shaved pile surface: [as modifier] *moleskin trousers*.

molest ▶ verb [with obj.] **1** assault or abuse (a person, especially a woman or child) sexually.
2 dated pester or harass (someone) in an aggressive or persistent manner: *the crowd were shouting abuse and molesting the two police officers*.
– DERIVATIVES **molestation** noun, **molester** noun.
– ORIGIN late Middle English (in the sense 'cause trouble to, vex'): from Old French *molester* or Latin *molestare* 'annoy', from *molestus* 'troublesome'.

moletronics /ˌmɒlɪˈtrɒnɪks/ ▶ plural noun [treated as sing.] short for MOLECULAR ELECTRONICS.

Molière /ˈmɒlɪɛː/, French /mɔljɛʀ/ (1622–73), French dramatist; pseudonym of *Jean-Baptiste Poquelin*. He wrote more than twenty comic plays about contemporary France, developing stock characters from Italian commedia dell'arte. Notable works: *Tartuffe* (1664), *Le Misanthrope* (1666), and *Le Bourgeois gentilhomme* (1670).

moline /məˈlʌɪn/ ▶ adjective [postpositive] Heraldry (of a cross) having each extremity broadened, split, and curved back.
– ORIGIN mid 16th cent.: probably from Anglo-Norman French *moliné*, from *molin* 'mill', because of a resemblance to the iron support of a millstone.

Molise /mɒˈliːzeɪ/ a region of eastern Italy, on the Adriatic coast; capital, Campobasso.

moll ▶ noun informal **1** a gangster's female companion.
2 a prostitute.
– ORIGIN early 17th cent.: pet form of the given name *Mary*.

mollify /ˈmɒlɪfʌɪ/ ▶ verb (**mollifies**, **mollifying**, **mollified**) [with obj.] appease the anger or anxiety of (someone): *nature reserves were set up around the power stations to mollify local conservationists*. ■ rare reduce the severity of (something).
– DERIVATIVES **mollification** noun, **mollifier** noun.
– ORIGIN late Middle English (also in the sense 'make soft or supple'): from French *mollifier* or Latin *mollificare*, from *mollis* 'soft'.

mollisol /ˈmɒlɪsɒl/ ▶ noun Soil Science a soil of an order comprising temperate grassland soils with a dark, humus-rich surface layer containing high concentrations of calcium and magnesium.
– ORIGIN 1960s: from Latin *mollis* 'soft' + *solum* 'ground, soil'.

mollusc /ˈmɒləsk/ (US **mollusk**) ▶ noun an invertebrate of a large phylum which includes snails, slugs, mussels, and octopuses. They have a soft unsegmented body and live in aquatic or damp habitats, and most kinds have an external calcareous shell. ● Phylum Mollusca: several classes, in particular Gastropoda, Bivalvia, and Cephalopoda.
– DERIVATIVES **molluscan** /məˈlʌskən/ adjective.
– ORIGIN late 18th cent.: from modern Latin *mollusca*, neuter plural of Latin *molluscus*, from *mollis* 'soft'.

molluscum contagiosum /məˌlʌskəm kənˌteɪdʒɪˈəʊsəm/ ▶ noun [mass noun] Medicine a chronic viral disorder of the skin characterized by groups of small, smooth, painless pinkish nodules with a central depression, that yield a milky fluid when squeezed.
– ORIGIN early 19th cent.: from Latin *molluscum* (as a noun denoting a kind of fungus), neuter of *molluscus* + *contagiosum* (neuter of *contagiosus* 'contagious').

Mollweide projection /ˈmɒlvʌɪdə/ ▶ noun a projection of a map of the world on to an ellipse, with lines of latitude represented by straight lines (spaced more closely towards the poles) and meridians represented by equally spaced elliptical curves. This projection distorts shape but preserves relative area.
– ORIGIN early 20th cent.: named after Karl B. *Mollweide* (died 1825), German mathematician and astronomer.

molly (also **mollie**) ▶ noun (pl. **mollies**) a small livebearing killifish which is popular in aquaria and has been bred in many colours, especially black. ● Genus *Poecilia*, family Poeciliidae: several species, in particular *P. sphenops*. See also SAILFIN MOLLY.
– ORIGIN 1930s: from modern Latin *Mollienisia* (former genus name), from the name of Count *Mollien* (1758–1850), French statesman.

mollycoddle ▶ verb [with obj.] treat (someone) in an indulgent or overprotective way.
▶ noun an effeminate or ineffectual man or boy.
– ORIGIN mid 19th cent.: from *molly* 'girl or prostitute' (see MOLL) + CODDLE.

mollydooker /ˈmɒlɪˌduːkə/ ▶ noun Austral. informal a left-handed person.
– ORIGIN 1940s: from *Molly* (pet form of the given name *Mary*) or from the slang term *mauley* 'hand' + *-dook* representing a pronunciation of DUKE (sense 2 of the noun) + -ER[1].

mollymawk ▶ noun chiefly Austral./NZ an albatross. ● Genus *Diomedea*, family Diomedeidae: several species, excluding the wandering and royal albatrosses.

– ORIGIN late 17th cent.: from Dutch *mallemok*, from *mal* 'foolish' + *mok* 'gull'.

Moloch /ˈməʊlɒk/ a Canaanite idol to whom children were sacrificed. ■ (as noun **a Moloch**) a person or thing to which extreme or terrible sacrifices were made.
– ORIGIN via late Latin from Greek *Molokh*, from Hebrew *mōleḵ*.

moloch /ˈməʊlɒk/ ▸ **noun** a harmless spiny lizard of grotesque appearance which feeds chiefly on ants, found in arid inland Australia. Also called **MOUNTAIN DEVIL, THORNY DEVIL.** ● *Moloch horridus*, family Agamidae.
– ORIGIN from **MOLOCH**.

Molotov[1] /ˈmɒlətɒf/ former name (1940–57) for **PERM.**

Molotov[2] /ˈmɒlətɒf/, Vyacheslav (Mikhailovich) (1890–1986), Soviet statesman; born *Vyacheslav Mikhailovich Skryabin.* As Commissar (later Minister) for Foreign Affairs (1939–49; 1953–6), he negotiated the non-aggression pact with Nazi Germany (1939) and after 1945 represented the Soviet Union at meetings of the United Nations.

Molotov cocktail ▸ **noun** a crude incendiary device typically consisting of a bottle filled with flammable liquid and with a means of ignition.
– ORIGIN from the name of Vyacheslav *Molotov* (see **MOLOTOV[2]**), who led the Soviet campaign against Finland in 1939–40, when such weapons were used by the Finns.

molt ▸ **verb & noun** US spelling of **MOULT.**

molten /ˈməʊlt(ə)n/ ▸ **adjective** (especially of materials with a high melting point, such as metal and glass) liquefied by heat.
– ORIGIN Middle English: archaic past participle of **MELT.**

molto /ˈmɒltəʊ/ ▸ **adverb** Music (in directions) very: *molto maestoso* | [postpositive] [as submodifier] *allegro molto.*
– ORIGIN Italian, from Latin *multus* 'much'.

Molucca Islands /məˈlʌkə/ an island group in Indonesia, between Sulawesi and New Guinea; capital, Ambon. Settled by the Portuguese in the early 16th century, the islands were taken a century later by the Dutch. They were formerly known as the Spice Islands. Indonesian name **MALUKU.**
– DERIVATIVES **Moluccan** noun & adjective.

molvi ▸ **noun** variant form of **MOULVI.**

moly[1] /ˈməʊli/ ▸ **noun 1** a southern European plant related to the onions, with small yellow flowers.
● *Allium moly*, family Liliaceae (or Alliaceae).
2 a mythical herb with white flowers and black roots, endowed with magic properties.
– ORIGIN mid 16th cent. (in sense 2): via Latin from Greek *mōlu*.

moly[2] /ˈməʊli/ ▸ **noun** short for **MOLYBDENUM.**

molybdate /məˈlɪbdeɪt/ ▸ **noun** Chemistry a salt in which the anion contains both molybdenum and oxygen, especially one of the anion MoO_4^{2-}.
– ORIGIN late 18th cent.: from *molybdic (acid)*, a parent acid of molybdates, + **-ATE[1]**.

molybdenite /məˈlɪbdənʌɪt/ ▸ **noun** [mass noun] a blue-grey mineral, typically occurring as hexagonal crystals. It consists of molybdenum disulphide and is the most common ore of molybdenum.

molybdenum /məˈlɪbdənəm/ ▸ **noun** [mass noun] the chemical element of atomic number 42, a brittle silver-grey metal of the transition series, used in some alloy steels. (Symbol: **Mo**)
– ORIGIN early 19th cent.: modern Latin, earlier *molybdena* (originally denoting a salt of lead), from Greek *molubdaina* 'plummet', from *molubdos* 'lead'.

mom ▸ **noun** North American term for **MUM[1]**.

mom-and-pop ▸ **adjective** N. Amer. denoting a small shop of a type often run by a married couple: *a mom-and-pop store.*

Mombasa /mɒmˈbasə/ a seaport and industrial city in SE Kenya, on the Indian Ocean; pop. 862,100 (est. 2006). It is the leading port and second-largest city of Kenya.

moment ▸ **noun 1** a very brief period of time: *she was silent for a moment before replying* | *a few moments later he returned to the office.* ■ an exact point in time: *she would always remember the moment they met.* ■ an appropriate time for doing something; an opportunity: *I was waiting for the right moment to tell him.* ■ a particular stage in the development of something or in a course of events: *one of the great moments in aviation history.*
2 [mass noun] formal importance: *the issues were of little moment to the electorate.*
3 Physics a turning effect produced by a force acting at a distance on an object. ■ the magnitude of a turning effect produced by a force acting at a distance, expressed as the product of the force and the distance from its line of action to a given point.
4 Statistics a quantity that expresses the average or expected value of the first, second, third, or fourth power of the deviation of each component of a frequency distribution from a given value, typically mean or zero. The **first moment** is the mean, the **second moment** the variance, the **third moment** the skew, and the **fourth moment** the kurtosis.
– PHRASES **any moment** (or **at any moment**) very soon. **at the** (or **this**) **moment** at the present time; now. **for the moment** for now. **have one's** (or **its**) **moments** have short periods that are better or more impressive than others: *the LP may not be the best album of the year, but it has its moments.* **in a moment 1** very soon: *I'll be back in a moment.* **2** instantly: *the fugitive was captured in a moment.* **live for the moment** live or act without worrying about the future. **the moment —— as soon as ——:** *the heavens opened the moment we left the house.* **moment of truth** a time when a person or thing is tested, a decision has to be made, or a crisis has to be faced. [with allusion to the final sword thrust in a bullfight.] **not a moment too soon** almost too late. **not for a** (or **one**) **moment** not at all; never. **of the moment** currently popular, famous, or important: *the buzzword of the moment.* **one moment** (or **just a moment**) a request for someone to wait for a short period of time. **share a moment** informal experience a joint sensation of heightened emotion: *Alan and Bridget shared a moment yesterday after the memorial service.*
– ORIGIN late Middle English: from Latin *momentum* (see **MOMENTUM**).

momenta plural form of **MOMENTUM.**

momentarily ▸ **adverb 1** for a very short time: *as he passed Jenny's door, he paused momentarily.*
2 N. Amer. at any moment; very soon: *my husband will be here to pick me up momentarily.*

momentary ▸ **adjective** lasting for a very short time; brief: *a momentary lapse of concentration.*
– DERIVATIVES **momentariness** noun.
– ORIGIN late Middle English: from Latin *momentarius*, from *momentum* (see **MOMENT**).

momently ▸ **adverb** archaic or literary **1** from moment to moment; continually.
2 at any moment.
3 for a moment; briefly.

moment of inertia ▸ **noun** Physics a quantity expressing a body's tendency to resist angular acceleration, which is the sum of the products of the mass of each particle in the body with the square of its distance from the axis of rotation.

momentous ▸ **adjective** of great importance or significance, especially in having a bearing on future events: *a period of momentous changes in East–West relations* | *a momentous decision.*
– DERIVATIVES **momentously** adverb, **momentousness** noun.

momentum /məˈmɛntəm/ ▸ **noun** (pl. **momenta** /-tə/) [mass noun] **1** Physics the quantity of motion of a moving body, measured as a product of its mass and velocity.
2 the impetus gained by a moving object: *the vehicle gained momentum as the road dipped.* ■ the impetus and driving force gained by the development of a process or course of events: *the investigation gathered momentum in the spring.*
– ORIGIN late 17th cent.: from Latin, from *movimentum*, from *movere* 'to move'.

momism /ˈmɒmɪz(ə)m/ ▸ **noun** [mass noun] US informal excessive attachment to or domination by one's mother.

momma ▸ **noun** North American term for **MAMA.**

Mommsen /ˈmɒmz(ə)n/, Theodor (1817–1903), German historian. He is noted for his three-volume *History of Rome* (1854–6; 1885) and his treatises on Roman constitutional law (1871–88). Nobel Prize for Literature (1902).

mommy ▸ **noun** (pl. **mommies**) North American term for **MUMMY[1]**.

mommy track ▸ **noun** N. Amer. informal an interrupted or delayed career path followed by women as the result of bringing up a family.
– DERIVATIVES **mommy tracker** noun, **mommy tracking** noun.

mompara /mɒmˈpɑːrə/ (also **mampara**) ▸ **noun** S. African derogatory an unsophisticated country person.
– ORIGIN Fanakalo, literally 'a fool', also 'waste material'.

Mon /mɔːn/ ▸ **noun** (pl. **same** or **Mons**) **1** a member of a people now inhabiting parts of SE Burma (Myanmar) and western Thailand but having their ancient capital at Pegu in the south of Burma.
2 [mass noun] the language of the Mon, related to Khmer (Cambodian).
▸ **adjective** relating to the Mon or their language. See also **MON-KHMER.**
– ORIGIN the name in Mon.

Mon. ▸ **abbreviation** Monday.

mon- ▸ **combining form** variant spelling of **MONO-** shortened before a vowel (as in *monamine*).

Monaco /ˈmɒnəkəʊ/ a principality forming an enclave within French territory, on the Mediterranean coast near the Italian frontier; pop. 33,000 (est. 2009); official language, French.

> The smallest sovereign state in the world apart from the Vatican, Monaco was ruled by the Genoese from medieval times and by the Grimaldi family from 1297, becoming a constitutional monarchy in 1911. It includes the resort of Monte Carlo.

monad /ˈmɒnad, ˈməʊ-/ ▸ **noun** technical a single unit; the number one. ■ Philosophy (in the philosophy of Leibniz) an indivisible and hence ultimately simple entity, such as an atom or a person. ■ Biology, dated a single-celled organism, especially a flagellate protozoan, or a single cell.
– DERIVATIVES **monadic** adjective, **monadism** noun (Philosophy).
– ORIGIN early 17th cent.: via late Latin from Greek *monas, monad-* 'unit', from *monos* 'alone'.

monadelphous /ˌmɒnəˈdɛlfəs/ ▸ **adjective** Botany (of stamens) united by their filaments so as to form one group.
– ORIGIN early 19th cent.: from Greek *monos* 'one' + *adelphos* 'brother' + **-OUS.**

monadnock /məˈnadnɒk/ ▸ **noun** an isolated hill or ridge or erosion-resistant rock rising above a peneplain.
– ORIGIN late 19th cent.: named after Mount *Monadnock* in New Hampshire, US.

Monaghan /ˈmɒnəhən/ a county of the Republic of Ireland, part of the old province of Ulster. ■ the county town of Monaghan; pop. 6,221 (2006).

monal /mɒˈnɑːl/ (also **monal pheasant**) ▸ **noun** an Asian pheasant of mountainous wooded country, the male having dark plumage with colourful iridescence. ● Genus *Lophophorus*, family Phasianidae: three species, e.g. the crested **Himalayan monal** (*L. impeyanus*).
– ORIGIN mid 18th cent.: from Nepali *monāl*, from Hindi *munāl*.

Mona Lisa /ˌməʊnə ˈliːzə/ a painting (now in the Louvre in Paris) executed 1503–6 by Leonardo da Vinci. The sitter was the wife of Francesco del Giocondo; her enigmatic smile has become one of the most famous images in Western art. Also called **LA GIOCONDA.**

monamine ▸ **noun** variant spelling of **MONOAMINE.**

mona monkey /ˈməʊnə/ ▸ **noun** a West African guenon that has a bluish-grey face with a pink muzzle. The female has a distinctive moaning call.
● *Cercopithecus mona*, family Cercopithecidae.
– ORIGIN late 18th cent.: *mona* from Spanish and Portuguese *mona, mono*, Italian *monna*.

monandry /mɒˈnandri/ ▸ **noun** [mass noun] **1** Zoology a pattern of mating in which a female has only one mate at a time. ■ the custom of having only one husband at a time.
2 Botany the state of having a single stamen.
– DERIVATIVES **monandrous** adjective.
– ORIGIN mid 19th cent.: from **MONO-** 'single', on the pattern of words such as *polyandry*.

monarch /ˈmɒnək/ ▸ **noun 1** a sovereign head of state, especially a king, queen, or emperor.
2 (also **monarch butterfly**) a large migratory orange and black butterfly that occurs mainly in North America. The caterpillar feeds on milkweed, using the toxins in the plant to render both itself and the adult unpalatable to predators. Also called **MILKWEED.**
● *Danaus plexippus*, subfamily Danainae, family Nymphalidae.
3 (also **monarch flycatcher**) a flycatcher found in Africa, Asia, and Australasia, typically having boldly marked or colourful plumage. ● Family Monarchidae (the **monarch flycatcher family**): many genera and numerous species.

– DERIVATIVES **monarchal** adjective, **monarchial** adjective, **monarchic** adjective, **monarchical** adjective, **monarchically** adverb.
– ORIGIN late Middle English: from late Latin *monarcha*, from Greek *monarkhēs*, from *monos* 'alone' + *arkhein* 'to rule'.

Monarchian /mə'nɑːkɪən/ ▶ noun a member of a group of Christian heretics of the 2nd or 3rd century who denied the doctrine of the Trinity.
▶ adjective relating to the Monarchians or their beliefs.
– ORIGIN from late Latin *monarchiani* (plural), from *monarchia* (see MONARCHY).

monarchism ▶ noun [mass noun] support for the principle of having monarchs.
– DERIVATIVES **monarchist** noun & adjective.
– ORIGIN mid 19th cent.: from French *monarchisme*.

monarchy ▶ noun (pl. **monarchies**) [mass noun] a form of government with a monarch at the head. ■ [count noun] a state that has a monarch. ■ (**the monarchy**) the monarch and royal family of a country: *the monarchy is the focus of loyalty and service*.
– ORIGIN late Middle English: from Old French *monarchie*, via late Latin from Greek *monarkhia* 'the rule of one'.

monastery ▶ noun (pl. **monasteries**) a building or buildings occupied by a community of monks living under religious vows.
– ORIGIN late Middle English: via ecclesiastical Latin from ecclesiastical Greek *monastērion*, from *monazein* 'live alone', from *monos* 'alone'.

monastic ▶ adjective relating to monks, nuns, or others living under religious vows, or the buildings in which they live: *a monastic order*. ■ resembling or suggestive of monks or their way of life, especially in being austere, solitary, or celibate: *she set her things round the monastic student bedroom*.
▶ noun a monk or other follower of a monastic rule.
– DERIVATIVES **monastically** adverb, **monasticism** noun.
– ORIGIN late Middle English (in the sense 'anchoritic'): from late Latin *monasticus*, from Greek *monastikos*, from *monazein* 'live alone'.

M

Monastral /mɒ'nastr(ə)l/ ▶ noun trademark a synthetic pigment having exceptional fastness.
– ORIGIN 1930s: of unknown origin.

monatomic /ˌmɒnə'tɒmɪk/ ▶ adjective Chemistry consisting of one atom.

monaural /mɒn'ɔːr(ə)l/ ▶ adjective 1 of or involving one ear.
2 another term for MONOPHONIC (sense 1).
– DERIVATIVES **monaurally** adverb.

monazite /'mɒnəzʌɪt/ ▶ noun [mass noun] a brown crystalline mineral consisting of a phosphate of cerium, lanthanum, other rare earth elements, and thorium.
– ORIGIN mid 19th cent.: from German *Monazit*, from Greek *monazein* 'live alone' (because of its rare occurrence).

Monbazillac /mɒn'bazɪlak, mɔ̃'bazɪjak/ ▶ noun [mass noun] a sweet white French dessert wine, similar to Sauternes, produced at Monbazillac in the Dordogne.

Mönchengladbach /ˌmʊnʃ(ə)n'gladbax/, German /ˌmynçn'glatbax/ a city in NW Germany; pop. 261,000 (est. 2006). It is the site of the NATO headquarters for northern Europe.

Monck /mʌŋk/, George, 1st Duke of Albemarle (1608–70), English general. Initially a Royalist, he became a supporter of Oliver Cromwell and later suppressed the Royalists in Scotland (1651). Concerned at the growing unrest following Cromwell's death (1658), Monck negotiated the return of Charles II in 1660.

mondaine /mɒn'deɪn/, French /mɔ̃dɛn/ ▶ adjective belonging to fashionable society; worldly.
▶ noun dated a fashionable woman.
– ORIGIN French, feminine of *mondain* (see MUNDANE).

Monday ▶ noun the day of the week before Tuesday and following Sunday: *I saw him on Monday | the Monday before last | she's only in the office on Mondays*.
▶ adverb chiefly N. Amer. on Monday: *I'll ring you Monday*. ■ (**Mondays**) on Mondays; each Monday: *the restaurant is closed Mondays*.
– ORIGIN Old English *Mōnandæg* 'day of the moon', translation of late Latin *lunae dies*; compare with Dutch *maandag* and German *Montag*.

Monday morning quarterback ▶ noun N. Amer. informal a person who passes judgement on and criticizes something after the event.

mondegreen /'mɒndəgriːn/ ▶ noun a misunderstood or misinterpreted word or phrase resulting from a mishearing of the lyrics of a song.
– ORIGIN 1950s: from *Lady Mondegreen*, a misinterpretation of the phrase *laid him on the green*, from the traditional ballad 'The Bonny Earl of Murray'.

mondial /'mɒndɪəl/ ▶ adjective relating to, affecting, or involving the whole world; worldwide.
– ORIGIN early 20th cent.: French.

mondo /'mɒndəʊ/ ▶ adverb & adjective informal, chiefly US used in reference to something very striking or remarkable of its kind (often in conjunction with a pseudo-Italian noun or adjective): [as adv.] *I think it's going to be mondo weirdo this year, Andy*.
– ORIGIN from Italian *Mondo Cane*, literally 'dog's world', the title of a film (1961) depicting bizarre behaviour.

Mondrian /'mɒndrɪɑːn/, Piet (1872–1944), Dutch painter; born *Pieter Cornelis Mondriaan*. He was a co-founder of the De Stijl movement and the originator of neoplasticism, one of the earliest and strictest forms of geometrical abstract painting.

Monégasque /ˌmɒneɪ'gask/, French /mɔnegask/ ▶ noun a native or inhabitant of Monaco.
▶ adjective relating to Monaco or its inhabitants.
– ORIGIN French.

Monel /'məʊn(ə)l/ (also **Monel metal**) ▶ noun [mass noun] trademark a nickel-copper alloy with high tensile strength and resistance to corrosion.
– ORIGIN early 20th cent.: named after Ambrose *Monell* (died 1921), American businessman.

Monet /'mɒneɪ/, Claude (1840–1926), French painter. A founder member of the Impressionists, his fascination with the play of light on objects led him to produce series of paintings of single subjects painted at different times of the day and under different weather conditions, such as the *Water-lilies* sequence (1899–1906; 1916 onwards).

monetarism ▶ noun [mass noun] the theory or practice of controlling the supply of money as the chief method of stabilizing the economy.
– DERIVATIVES **monetarist** noun & adjective.

monetarize /'mʌnɪtərʌɪz/ (also **monetarise**) ▶ verb another term for MONETIZE.

monetary ▶ adjective relating to money or currency: *documents with little or no monetary value*.
– DERIVATIVES **monetarily** adverb.
– ORIGIN early 19th cent.: from French *monétaire* or late Latin *monetarius*, from Latin *moneta* 'money'.

monetary unit ▶ noun a standard unit of value of a country's coinage.

monetize /'mʌnɪtʌɪz/ (also **monetise**) ▶ verb [with obj.] convert into or express in the form of currency. ■ (usu. as adj. **monetized**) convert or adapt (a society, economy, etc.) to trade based on the exchange of money: *a fully monetized society*.
– DERIVATIVES **monetization** noun.
– ORIGIN late 19th cent.: from French *monétiser*, from Latin *moneta* 'money'.

money ▶ noun [mass noun] a current medium of exchange in the form of coins and banknotes; coins and banknotes collectively: *I counted the money before putting it in my wallet | he borrowed money to modernize the shop*. ■ (**moneys** or **monies**) formal sums of money: *a statement of all moneys paid into and out of the account*. ■ the assets, property, and resources owned by someone or something; wealth: *the college is very short of money*. ■ financial gain: *the main aim of a commercial organization is to make money*. ■ payment for work; wages: *she accepted the job at the bank since the money was better*.
– PHRASES **be in the money** informal have or win a lot of money. **for my money** in my opinion or judgement. **money for old rope** (or **money for jam**) Brit. informal money or reward earned for little or no effort. **(the love of) money is the root of all evil** proverb avarice gives rise to selfish or wicked actions. **money talks** proverb wealth gives power and influence to those who possess it. **one's money's worth** good value for one's money. **on the money** N. Amer. accurate; correct: *every criticism she made was right on the money*. **put money** (or **put one's money**) **on** place a bet on. ■ used to express one's confidence in the truth or success of something: *she won't have him back—I'd put money on it*. **put one's money where one's mouth is** informal take action to support one's statements or opinions. **see the colour of someone's money** receive some proof that someone has enough money to pay for something. **throw one's money about/around** spend one's money extravagantly or carelessly. **throw money at** try to solve (a problem) by recklessly spending money on it, without due consideration of what is required.
– DERIVATIVES **moneyless** adjective.
– ORIGIN Middle English: from Old French *moneie*, from Latin *moneta* 'mint, money', originally a title of the goddess Juno, in whose temple in Rome money was minted.

money-back ▶ adjective denoting an agreement or guarantee that provides for the customer's money to be refunded if they are not satisfied.

moneybags ▶ plural noun [usu. treated as sing.] informal a wealthy person.

money box ▶ noun Brit. a box used for saving money in, with a slit in the top through which the money is dropped.

money broker ▶ noun a person or company that negotiates loans between banks or other financial institutions.

money changer ▶ noun archaic a person whose business was the exchanging of one currency for another.

moneyed (also **monied**) ▶ adjective having much money; affluent: *the industrial revolution created a new moneyed class*. ■ characterized by affluence: *a moneyed lifestyle*.

moneyer ▶ noun archaic a person who mints money.

money-grubbing ▶ adjective informal overeager to make money; grasping: *money-grubbing speculators*.
– DERIVATIVES **money-grubber** noun.

money illusion ▶ noun [mass noun] Economics belief that money has a fixed value in terms of its purchasing power, so that, for example, changes in prices represent real gains and losses.

moneylender ▶ noun a person whose business is lending money to others who pay interest.
– DERIVATIVES **moneylending** noun & adjective.

moneymaker ▶ noun a person or thing that earns a lot of money: *the movie became one of the year's top moneymakers*.

moneymaking ▶ adjective producing a profit, especially with little effort; profitable: *he hit on an unusual moneymaking scheme*.
▶ noun [mass noun] the action of earning a lot of money: *this cynical exercise in moneymaking*.

money market ▶ noun the trade in short-term loans between banks and other financial institutions.

money of account ▶ noun see ACCOUNT.

money order ▶ noun a printed order for payment of a specified sum, issued by a bank or Post Office.

money spider ▶ noun a very small shiny black spider which is supposed to bring financial luck. ● Family Linyphiidae.

money-spinner ▶ noun chiefly Brit. a thing that brings in a profit.
– DERIVATIVES **money-spinning** adjective.

money supply ▶ noun the total amount of money in circulation or in existence in a country.

money tree ▶ noun US a source of easily obtained or unlimited money: *I knew how to **shake the money tree***. ■ a real or artificial tree to which people attach paper money, especially as a gift or donation.

money wages ▶ plural noun income expressed in terms of its monetary value, with no account taken of its purchasing power.

moneywort ▶ noun another term for CREEPING JENNY.

mong /mʌŋ/ ▶ noun Austral./NZ informal a mongrel.
– ORIGIN early 20th cent.: abbreviation.

-monger ▶ combining form denoting a dealer or trader in a specified commodity: *fishmonger | cheesemonger*. ■ denoting a person who promotes a specified activity, situation, or feeling, especially one that is undesirable or discreditable: *warmonger*.
– ORIGIN Old English *mangere*, from *mangian* 'to traffic', of Germanic origin, based on Latin *mango* 'dealer'.

mongo /'mɒŋgəʊ/ ▶ noun (pl. **same** or **mongos**) a monetary unit of Mongolia, equal to one hundredth of a tugrik.
– ORIGIN from Mongolian *möngö* 'silver'.

Mongol /'mɒŋg(ə)l/ ▶ noun 1 a native or inhabitant of Mongolia; a Mongolian.
2 [mass noun] the language of the Mongols; Mongolian.
3 (**mongol**) offensive a person with Down's syndrome.
▶ adjective relating to the people of Mongolia or their language.

> In the 13th century AD the Mongol empire under Genghis Khan extended across central Asia from Manchuria in the east to European Russia in the west. Under Kublai Khan China was conquered and the Mongol capital moved to Khanbaliq (modern Beijing). The Mongol empire collapsed after a series of defeats culminating in the destruction of the Golden Horde by the Muscovites in 1380.

– ORIGIN Mongolian, perhaps from *mong* 'brave'.

> **USAGE** The term **mongol** was adopted in the late 19th century to refer to a person with **Down's syndrome**, owing to the similarity of some of the physical symptoms of the disorder with the normal facial characteristics of East Asian people. In modern English this use is now unacceptable and considered offensive. It has been replaced in scientific as well as in most general contexts by the term **Down's syndrome** (first recorded in the early 1960s).

Mongolia /mɒŋˈɡəʊlɪə/ a large and sparsely populated country of East Asia, bordered by Siberian Russia and China; pop. 3,041,100 (est. 2009); official language, Mongolian; capital, Ulan Bator.

> The Gobi Desert occupies much of the southern half of the country. The centre of the medieval Mongol empire, Mongolia subsequently became a Chinese province, achieving de facto independence in 1911. In 1924 it became a communist state after the Soviet model; a new democratic constitution was introduced in 1992. The country was formerly known as Outer Mongolia to distinguish it from Inner Mongolia, which remains a province of China.

Mongolian ▶ noun 1 a native or inhabitant of Mongolia.
2 [mass noun] the language of Mongolia, a member of the Altaic family with an unusual vertical cursive script. It has some 2 million speakers, and related forms are spoken by over 3 million people in northern China.
▶ adjective relating to Mongolia, its people, or their language.

mongolism ▶ noun offensive another term for **DOWN'S SYNDROME**.

> **USAGE** See **USAGE** at **MONGOL**.

Mongoloid ▶ adjective 1 relating to the broad division of humankind including the indigenous peoples of East Asia, SE Asia, and the Arctic region of North America.
2 (**mongoloid**) offensive having Down's syndrome.
▶ noun 1 a person of a Mongoloid physical type.
2 offensive a person with Down's syndrome.

> **USAGE** The terms **Mongoloid**, **Negroid**, **Caucasoid**, and **Australoid** were introduced by 19th-century anthropologists such as Blumenbach attempting to classify human racial types, but today they are recognized as having very limited validity as scientific categories. Although occasionally used when making broad generalizations about the world's populations, in most modern contexts they are potentially offensive, especially when used of individuals. The names of specific peoples or nationalities should be used instead wherever possible.

mongoose ▶ noun (pl. **mongooses**) a small carnivorous mammal with a long body and tail and a grizzled or banded coat, native to Africa and Asia. ● Family Herpestidae (or Viverridae): several genera, in particular *Herpestes*, and many species.
– ORIGIN late 17th cent.: from Marathi *mangūs*.

mongrel ▶ noun a dog of no definable type or breed: [as modifier] *a mongrel bitch*. ■ any animal resulting from the crossing of different breeds or types. ■ offensive a person of mixed descent.
– DERIVATIVES **mongrelism** noun.
– ORIGIN late Middle English: of Germanic origin, apparently from a base meaning 'mix', and related to **MINGLE** and **AMONG**.

mongrelize (also **mongrelise**) ▶ verb [with obj.] cause to become mixed in race, composition, or character: (as adj. **mongrelized**) *a patois of mongrelized French*.
– DERIVATIVES **mongrelization** noun.

'mongst ▶ preposition literary short for **AMONGST** (see **AMONG**).

monial /ˈməʊnɪəl/ ▶ noun a mullion in a window.
– ORIGIN Middle English: from Old French *moinel* 'middle'.

monic /ˈmɒnɪk/ ▶ adjective Mathematics (of a polynomial) having the coefficient of the term of highest degree equal to one.
– ORIGIN 1930s: from **MONO-** + **-IC**.

Monica, St (332–*c*.387), mother of St Augustine of Hippo. She is often regarded as the model of Christian mothers for her patience with her son's spiritual crises, which ended with his conversion in 386. Feast day, 27 August (formerly 4 May).

monied ▶ adjective variant spelling of **MONEYED**.

monies plural form of **MONEY**, as used in financial contexts.

moniker /ˈmɒnɪkə/ (also **monicker**) ▶ noun informal a name.
– DERIVATIVES **monikered** adjective.
– ORIGIN mid 19th cent.: of unknown origin.

monilia /məˈnɪlɪə/ ▶ noun (pl. **same** or **moniliae** /-lɪʌɪ/) former term for **CANDIDA**.
– ORIGIN modern Latin, from Latin *monile* 'necklace' (with reference to the chains of spores).

moniliform /məˈnɪlɪfɔːm/ ▶ adjective Zoology & Botany resembling a string of beads.
– ORIGIN early 19th cent.: from French *moniliforme* or modern Latin *moniliformis*, from Latin *monile* 'necklace' + **-IFORM**.

monism /ˈmɒnɪz(ə)m, ˈməʊ-/ ▶ noun Philosophy & Theology a theory or doctrine that denies the existence of a distinction or duality in a particular sphere, such as that between matter and mind, or God and the world. ■ the doctrine that only one supreme being exists. Compare with **PLURALISM**.
– DERIVATIVES **monist** noun & adjective, **monistic** adjective.
– ORIGIN mid 19th cent.: from modern Latin *monismus*, from Greek *monos* 'single'.

monition /məˈnɪʃ(ə)n/ ▶ noun rare a warning of impending danger. ■ a formal notice from a bishop or ecclesiastical court admonishing a person not to do something specified.
– ORIGIN late Middle English: via Old French from Latin *monitio(n-)*, from *monere* 'warn'.

monitor ▶ noun 1 a device used for observing, checking, or keeping a continuous record of something: *a heart monitor*. ■ a person operating a monitor. ■ a person who observes a process or activity to check that it is carried out fairly or correctly, especially in an official capacity. ■ a person who listens to and reports on foreign radio broadcasts and signals.
2 a television receiver used in a studio to select or verify the picture being broadcast from a particular camera. ■ a screen which displays an image generated by a computer. ■ a loudspeaker used by performers on stage to hear themselves or in the studio to hear what has been recorded.
3 a school pupil with disciplinary or other special duties.
4 (also **monitor lizard**) a large tropical Old World lizard with a long neck, narrow head, forked tongue, strong claws, and a short body. Monitors were formerly believed to give warning of crocodiles. Called **GOANNA** in Australia. ● Family Varanidae and genus *Varanus*: many species. See also **KOMODO DRAGON**.
5 historical a shallow-draught warship mounting one or two heavy guns for bombardment.
▶ verb [with obj.] observe and check the progress or quality of (something) over a period of time; keep under systematic review: *equipment was installed to monitor air quality*. ■ maintain regular surveillance over: *he was a man of routine and it was easy for an enemy to monitor his movements*. ■ listen to and report on (a foreign radio broadcast or a telephone conversation). ■ check or regulate the technical quality of (a radio transmission or television signal).
– DERIVATIVES **monitorial** adjective, **monitorship** noun.
– ORIGIN early 16th cent. (in sense 3 of the noun): from Latin, from *monit-* 'warned', from the verb *monere*. Sense 1 of the noun dates from the 1930s.

monitory ▶ adjective rare giving or serving as a warning: *the chill, monitory wail of an air-raid siren*.
▶ noun (pl. **monitories**) (in church use) a letter of admonition from the Pope or a bishop.

Monk, Thelonious (Sphere) (1917–82), American jazz pianist and composer, one of the founders of the bebop style in the early 1940s. Notable compositions: 'Round Midnight', 'Straight, No Chaser', and 'Well, You Needn't'.

monk ▶ noun a member of a religious community of men typically living under vows of poverty, chastity, and obedience.
– DERIVATIVES **monkish** adjective, **monkishly** adverb, **monkishness** noun.
– ORIGIN Old English *munuc*, based on Greek *monakhos* 'solitary', from *monos* 'alone'.

monkery ▶ noun [mass noun] derogatory monasticism.

monkey ▶ noun (pl. **monkeys**) 1 a small to medium-sized primate that typically has a long tail, most kinds of which live in trees in tropical countries. ● Families Cebidae and Callitrichidae (or Callithricidae) (**New World monkeys**, often with prehensile tails), and Cercopithecidae (**Old World monkeys**, without prehensile tails). ■ (in general use) any primate. ■ a mischievous person, especially a child: *where have you been, you little monkey!* ■ a person who is dominated or controlled by another (with reference to the monkey traditionally kept by an organ-grinder).
2 Brit. informal a sum of £500.
3 (also **monkey engine**) a piledriving machine consisting of a heavy hammer or ram working vertically in a groove.
▶ verb (**monkeys, monkeying, monkeyed**) 1 [no obj.] (**monkey about/around**) behave in a silly or playful way. ■ (**monkey with**) tamper with: *don't monkey with that lock!*
2 [with obj.] archaic ape; mimic.
– PHRASES **as artful** (or **clever**) **as a wagonload** (or **cartload**) **of monkeys** Brit. informal extremely clever or mischievous. **make a monkey of** (or **out of**) **someone** humiliate someone by making them appear ridiculous. **a monkey on one's back** informal a burdensome problem. ■ a dependence on drugs. **not give a monkey's** Brit. informal be completely indifferent or unconcerned: *he doesn't give a monkey's what we think about him*.
– DERIVATIVES **monkeyish** adjective.
– ORIGIN mid 16th cent.: of unknown origin, perhaps from Low German.

monkey bars ▶ plural noun a piece of playground equipment consisting of a horizontally mounted overhead ladder, from which children may swing.

monkey business ▶ noun [mass noun] informal mischievous or deceitful behaviour.

monkey engine ▶ noun see **MONKEY** (sense 3 of the noun).

monkey flower ▶ noun a plant of boggy ground, having yellow or red flowers which resemble snapdragons. ● Genus *Mimulus*, family Scrophulariaceae: several species, in particular *M. guttatus*.

M

monkey jacket ▶ noun a short, close-fitting jacket worn by sailors or waiters or by officers in their mess.

monkey nut ▶ noun Brit. a peanut.

monkey orange ▶ noun S. African a small evergreen tree of warm climates, which bears a hard-shelled edible fruit with poisonous seeds. ● Genus *Strychnos*, family Loganiaceae: two species.

monkey puzzle (also **monkey puzzle tree**) ▶ noun an evergreen coniferous tree with branches covered in spirals of tough spiny leaf-like scales, native to Chile. ● *Araucaria araucana*, family Araucariaceae.
– ORIGIN mid 19th cent.: said to be so named in response to a remark that an attempt to climb the tree would puzzle a monkey.

monkey rope ▶ noun S. African a liana.

monkeyshines ▶ plural noun informal North American term for **MONKEY TRICKS**.

monkey suit ▶ noun informal a man's evening dress or formal suit.

monkey's wedding ▶ noun S. African informal simultaneous rain and sunshine.
– ORIGIN perhaps based on Portuguese *casamento de rapôsa* 'vixen's wedding', in the same sense.

monkey tricks ▶ plural noun Brit. informal mischievous behaviour.

monkey wrench ▶ noun an adjustable spanner with large jaws which has its adjusting screw located in the jaw that is fixed.
▶ verb (**monkey-wrench**) [with obj.] informal sabotage (something), especially as a form of protest.
– PHRASES **a monkey wrench in the works** see **WORK**.
– DERIVATIVES **monkey-wrencher** noun.

monkfish ▶ noun (pl. **same** or **monkfishes**) 1 a bottom-dwelling anglerfish of European waters. ● *Lophius piscatorius*, family Lophiidae.
2 see **ANGEL SHARK**.
3 [mass noun] the monkfish or angel shark as food.
– ORIGIN late 16th cent.: from **MONK** and **FISH**[1] (from the supposed resemblance of the head of the fish to that of a cowled monk).

Mon-Khmer /ˌməʊnˈkmɛː/ ▶ noun [mass noun] a family of languages spoken throughout SE Asia, of which the most important are Mon and Khmer. They are

distantly related to Munda, with which they form the Austro-Asiatic phylum or superfamily.
▶ adjective relating to or denoting the Mon-Khmer group of languages.
– ORIGIN late 19th cent.: from MON + KHMER.

monk seal ▶ noun a seal with a dark back and pale underside, occurring in warm waters of the northern hemisphere. ● Genus *Monachus*, family Phocidae: two or three species, including the endangered *M. monachus* of the Mediterranean and adjacent seas.

monkshood ▶ noun an aconite with blue or purple flowers. ● Genus *Aconitum*, family Ranunculaceae: several species, including the European *A. napellus* and the North American *A. uncinatum*.

Monmouth /ˈmɒnməθ/, James Scott, Duke of (1649–85), English claimant to the throne of England. The illegitimate son of Charles II, he became the focus for Whig supporters of a Protestant succession. In 1685 he led a rebellion against the Catholic James II, but was defeated at the Battle of Sedgemoor and executed.

Monmouthshire a county of SE Wales, on the border with England; administrative centre, Cwmbran. Most of the county was part of Gwent 1974–96.

mono ▶ adjective **1** monophonic.
2 monochrome.
▶ noun (pl. **monos**) **1** a monophonic recording. ■ [mass noun] monophonic reproduction.
2 a monochrome picture. ■ [mass noun] monochrome reproduction.
3 N. Amer. short for MONONUCLEOSIS.
4 N. Amer. short for MONOFILAMENT.

mono- (also **mon-** before a vowel) ▶ combining form
1 one; alone; single: *monocoque*.
2 Chemistry (forming names of compounds) containing one atom or group of a specified kind: *monoamine*.
– ORIGIN from Greek *monos* 'alone'.

monoacid ▶ adjective Chemistry (of a base) having one replaceable hydroxide ion.

monoamine /ˌmɒnəʊˈeɪmiːn/ (also **monamine**) ▶ noun Chemistry a compound having a single amine group in its molecule, especially one which is a neurotransmitter (e.g. serotonin, noradrenaline).

monoamine oxidase ▶ noun [mass noun] Biochemistry an enzyme (present in most tissues) which catalyses the oxidation and inactivation of monoamine neurotransmitters.

monoamine oxidase inhibitor ▶ noun Medicine any of a group of antidepressant drugs which inhibit the activity of monoamine oxidase (so allowing accumulation of serotonin and noradrenaline in the brain).

monobasic ▶ adjective Chemistry (of an acid) having one replaceable hydrogen atom.

monobloc ▶ adjective made as, contained in, or involving a single casting.
– ORIGIN early 20th cent.: from French, from *mono-* (from Greek *monos* 'alone') + *bloc* 'block'.

monobrow ▶ noun informal a pair of eyebrows that meet above the nose, giving the appearance of a single eyebrow.
– DERIVATIVES **monobrowed** adjective.

monocarpic /ˌmɒnə(ʊ)ˈkɑːpɪk/ ▶ adjective Botany (of a plant) flowering only once and then dying.
– ORIGIN mid 19th cent.: from MONO- 'single' + Greek *karpos* 'fruit' + -IC.

monocausal ▶ adjective in terms of a single cause: *the pitfalls of monocausal explanations*.

Monoceros /məˈnɒs(ə)rəs/ Astronomy an inconspicuous constellation (the Unicorn), lying on the celestial equator in the Milky Way between Canis Major and Canis Minor.
– ORIGIN via Latin from Greek.

monochasium /ˌmɒnə(ʊ)ˈkeɪzɪəm/ ▶ noun (pl. **monochasia**) Botany a cyme in which each flowering branch gives rise to one lateral branch, so that the inflorescence is helicoid or asymmetrical.
– ORIGIN late 19th cent.: modern Latin, from MONO- 'one' + Greek *khasis* 'separation'.

monochord ▶ noun an instrument for comparing musical pitches, using a taut wire whose vibrating length can be adjusted with a movable bridge.
– ORIGIN late Middle English: from Old French *monacorde*, via late Latin from Greek *monokhordon*, neuter (used as a noun) of *monokhordos* 'having a single string'.

monochromatic ▶ adjective containing or using only one colour: *monochromatic light*. ■ Physics (of light or other radiation) of a single wavelength or frequency.
– DERIVATIVES **monochromatically** adverb.

monochromatism ▶ noun [mass noun] complete colour blindness in which all colours appear as shades of one colour.

monochromator /ˈmɒnə(ʊ)krəˌmeɪtə, ˌmɒnə(ʊ)ˈkrɒmɪtə/ ▶ noun Physics a device used to select radiation of (or very close to) a single wavelength or energy.

monochrome ▶ noun a photograph or picture developed or executed in black and white or in varying tones of only one colour. ■ [mass noun] representation or reproduction in black and white or in varying tones of only one colour.
▶ adjective (of a photograph or picture, or a television screen) consisting of or displaying images in black and white or in varying tones of only one colour.
– DERIVATIVES **monochromic** adjective.
– ORIGIN mid 17th cent.: based on Greek *monokhrōmatos* 'of a single colour'.

monocle /ˈmɒnək(ə)l/ ▶ noun a single eyeglass, kept in position by the muscles around the eye.
– DERIVATIVES **monocled** adjective.
– ORIGIN mid 19th cent.: from French (earlier in the sense 'one-eyed'), from late Latin *monoculus* 'one-eyed'.

monocline /ˈmɒnə(ʊ)klʌɪn/ ▶ noun Geology a bend in rock strata that are otherwise uniformly dipping or horizontal.
– DERIVATIVES **monoclinal** adjective.
– ORIGIN late 19th cent.: from MONO- 'single' + Greek *klinein* 'to lean'.

monoclinic ▶ adjective of or denoting a crystal system or three-dimensional geometrical arrangement having three unequal axes of which one is at right angles to the other two.

monoclonal /ˌmɒnə(ʊ)ˈkləʊn(ə)l/ ▶ adjective Biology forming a clone which is derived asexually from a single individual or cell.

monoclonal antibody ▶ noun an antibody produced by a single clone of cells or cell line and consisting of identical antibody molecules.

monocoque /ˈmɒnə(ʊ)kɒk/ ▶ noun an aircraft or vehicle structure in which the chassis is integral with the body.
– ORIGIN early 20th cent.: from French, from *mono-* 'single' + *coque* 'shell'.

monocot ▶ noun Botany a monocotyledon.

monocotyledon /ˌmɒnə(ʊ)kɒtɪˈliːd(ə)n/ ▶ noun Botany a flowering plant with an embryo that bears a single cotyledon (seed leaf). Monocotyledons constitute the smaller of the two great divisions of flowering plants, and typically have elongated stalkless leaves with parallel veins (e.g. grasses, lilies, palms). Compare with DICOTYLEDON. ● Class Monocotyledoneae (or -donae, -dones; sometimes Liliopsida), subdivision Angiospermae.
– DERIVATIVES **monocotyledonous** adjective.

monocracy /məˈnɒkrəsi/ ▶ noun (pl. **monocracies**) [mass noun] a system of government by one person only.
– DERIVATIVES **monocrat** noun, **monocratic** adjective.

monocrystalline ▶ adjective consisting of a single crystal.

monocular /məˈnɒkjʊlə/ ▶ adjective with, for, or in one eye: *he had only monocular vision*.
▶ noun an optical instrument for viewing distant objects with one eye, resembling one half of a pair of binoculars.
– DERIVATIVES **monocularly** adverb.
– ORIGIN mid 17th cent.: from late Latin *monoculus* 'having one eye' + -AR^{1}.

monoculture ▶ noun [mass noun] the cultivation of a single crop in a given area.

monocycle ▶ noun another term for UNICYCLE.

monocyclic /ˌmɒnə(ʊ)ˈsʌɪklɪk, -ˈsɪk-/ ▶ adjective
1 Chemistry having one ring of atoms in its molecule.
2 relating to a single cycle of activity.

monocyte /ˈmɒnə(ʊ)sʌɪt/ ▶ noun Physiology a large phagocytic white blood cell with a simple oval nucleus and clear, greyish cytoplasm.

Monod /ˈmɒnəʊ/, Jacques Lucien (1910–76), French biochemist. Together with fellow French biochemist François Jacob (b.1920), with whom he was awarded a Nobel Prize in 1965, he formulated a theory to explain how genes are activated and in 1961 proposed the existence of messenger RNA.

monodactyly /ˌmɒnə(ʊ)ˈdaktɪli/ ▶ noun [mass noun] Medicine & Zoology a condition in which there is only one finger or toe on each hand or foot.
– DERIVATIVES **monodactyl** adjective.
– ORIGIN late 19th cent.: from *monodactyl* (from Greek *monodaktulos* 'one-fingered') + -Y^{3}.

monodisperse /ˌmɒnə(ʊ)ˈdɪspəːs/ ▶ adjective Chemistry (of a colloid) containing particles of uniform size.

monodrama ▶ noun a dramatic piece for one performer.

monody /ˈmɒnədi/ ▶ noun (pl. **monodies**) **1** an ode sung by a single actor in a Greek tragedy.
2 a poem lamenting a person's death.
3 [mass noun] music with only one melodic line.
– DERIVATIVES **monodic** adjective, **monodist** noun.
– ORIGIN early 17th cent.: via late Latin from Greek *monōidia*, from *monōidos* 'singing alone'.

monoecious /məˈniːʃəs/ ▶ adjective Biology (of a plant or invertebrate animal) having both the male and female reproductive organs in the same individual; hermaphrodite. Compare with DIOECIOUS.
– DERIVATIVES **monoecy** noun.
– ORIGIN mid 18th cent.: from modern Latin *Monoecia* (denoting a class of such plants in Linnaeus's system), from Greek *monos* 'single' + *oikos* 'house'.

monofilament (also **monofil**) ▶ noun a single strand of man-made fibre. ■ [mass noun] a type of fishing line using a monofilament.

monogamy /məˈnɒgəmi/ ▶ noun [mass noun] the practice of marrying or state of being married to one person at a time. ■ the practice or state of having a sexual relationship with only one partner. ■ Zoology the habit of having only one mate at a time.
– DERIVATIVES **monogamist** noun, **monogamous** adjective, **monogamously** adverb.
– ORIGIN early 17th cent.: from French *monogamie*, via ecclesiastical Latin from Greek *monogamia*, from *monos* 'single' + *gamos* 'marriage'.

monogenean /ˌmɒnə(ʊ)dʒɪˈniːən, mɒnə(ʊ)ˈdʒɛnɪən/ Zoology ▶ adjective relating to a group of flukes that are chiefly external or gill parasites of fish and only require a single host. Compare with DIGENEAN.
▶ noun a monogenean fluke. ● Class Monogenea, phylum Platyhelminthes; sometimes treated as a subclass of the class Trematoda.
– ORIGIN 1960s: from modern Latin *Monogenea* (from Greek *monos* 'single' + *genea* 'generation') + -AN.

monogenesis /ˌmɒnə(ʊ)ˈdʒɛnɪsɪs/ ▶ noun [mass noun] the theory that humans are all descended from a single pair of ancestors. Also called MONOGENY. ■ Linguistics the hypothetical origination of language or of a surname from a single source at a particular place and time.
– DERIVATIVES **monogenetic** adjective.

monogenic /ˌmɒnə(ʊ)ˈdʒɛnɪk/ ▶ adjective Genetics involving or controlled by a single gene.
– DERIVATIVES **monogenically** adverb.

monogeny /məˈnɒdʒəni/ ▶ noun another term for MONOGENESIS.
– DERIVATIVES **monogenism** noun, **monogenist** noun.

monoglot /ˈmɒnə(ʊ)glɒt/ ▶ adjective using or speaking only one language: *monoglot Irish-speakers*.
▶ noun a person who speaks only one language.
– ORIGIN mid 19th cent.: from Greek *monoglōttos*, from *monos* 'single' + *glōtta* 'tongue'.

monogram ▶ noun a motif of two or more interwoven letters, typically a person's initials, used to identify a personal possession or as a logo.
▶ verb (**monograms**, **monogramming**, **monogrammed**) [with obj.] decorate with a monogram.
– DERIVATIVES **monogrammatic** adjective.
– ORIGIN late 17th cent.: from French *monogramme*, from late Latin *monogramma*, from Greek.

monograph ▶ noun a detailed written study of a single specialized subject or an aspect of it.
▶ verb [with obj.] write a monograph on; treat in a monograph.
– ORIGIN early 19th cent. (earlier *monography*): from modern Latin *monographia*, from *monographus* 'writer on a single genus or species'.

monographic ▶ adjective relating to a monograph. ■ (of an art gallery or exhibition) showing the works of a single artist.

monogyne /ˈmɒnədʒʌɪn/ ▶ adjective Entomology (of a social insect) having only one egg-laying queen in each colony.
– ORIGIN from MONO- 'one' + Greek *gunē* 'woman, wife'.

monogyny /mə'nɒdʒɪni/ ▶ **noun** [mass noun] the custom of having only one wife at a time.
– ORIGIN late 19th cent.: from MONO- 'one' + Greek *gunē* 'woman, wife'.

monohull ▶ **noun** a boat with only one hull, as opposed to a catamaran or multihull.

monohybrid ▶ **noun** Genetics a hybrid that is heterozygous with respect to a specified gene.

monohydrate ▶ **noun** Chemistry a hydrate containing one mole of water per mole of the compound.

monohydric ▶ **adjective** Chemistry (of an alcohol) containing one hydroxyl group.

monokini ▶ **noun** a woman's one-piece beach garment equivalent to the lower half of a bikini.
– ORIGIN 1960s: from MONO- 'one' + a shortened form of BIKINI (the first syllable misinterpreted as *bi-* 'two').

monolatry /mə'nɒlətri/ ▶ **noun** [mass noun] the worship of one god without denial of the existence of other gods.
– DERIVATIVES **monolatrous** adjective.

monolayer ▶ **noun** Chemistry a layer one molecule thick. ■ Biology & Medicine a cell culture in a layer one cell thick.

monolingual ▶ **adjective** (of a person or society) speaking only one language: *monolingual families*. ■ (of a text or conversation) written or conducted in only one language: *monolingual and bilingual editions*.
▶ **noun** a person who speaks only one language.
– DERIVATIVES **monolingualism** noun, **monolingually** adverb.

monolith ▶ **noun 1** a large single upright block of stone, especially one shaped into or serving as a pillar or monument. ■ a very large and characterless building: *the 72-storey monolith overlooking the waterfront*. ■ a large block of concrete sunk in water, e.g. in the building of a dock.
2 a large, impersonal political, corporate, or social structure regarded as indivisible and slow to change: *independent voices have been crowded out by the media monoliths*.
– ORIGIN mid 19th cent.: from French *monolithe*, from Greek *monolithos*, from *monos* 'single' + *lithos* 'stone'.

monolithic ▶ **adjective 1** formed of a single large block of stone. ■ (of a building) very large and characterless.
2 (of an organization or system) large, powerful, indivisible, and slow to change: *rejecting any move towards a monolithic European superstate*.
3 Electronics (of a solid-state circuit) composed of active and passive components formed in a single chip.

monologue ▶ **noun** a long speech by one actor in a play or film, or as part of a theatrical or broadcast programme. ■ a long, tedious speech by one person during a conversation: *Fred carried on with his monologue as if I hadn't spoken*.
– DERIVATIVES **monologic** adjective, **monological** adjective, **monologist** (also **monologuist**) noun.
– ORIGIN mid 17th cent.: from French, from Greek *monologos* 'speaking alone'.

monomania ▶ **noun** [mass noun] exaggerated or obsessive enthusiasm for or preoccupation with one thing.
– DERIVATIVES **monomaniac** noun & adjective, **monomaniacal** adjective.

monomer /'mɒnəmə/ ▶ **noun** Chemistry a molecule that can be bonded to other identical molecules to form a polymer.
– DERIVATIVES **monomeric** adjective.

monometallic ▶ **adjective** consisting of one metal only. ■ historical relating to, involving, or using a standard of currency based on one metal.

monometer /mə'nɒmɪtə/ ▶ **noun** Prosody a line consisting of one metrical foot.

monomial /mə'nəʊmɪəl/ Mathematics ▶ **adjective** (of an algebraic expression) consisting of one term.
▶ **noun** an algebraic expression consisting of one term.
– ORIGIN early 18th cent.: from MONO- 'one', on the pattern of *binomial*.

monomolecular ▶ **adjective** Chemistry (of a layer) one molecule thick. ■ consisting of or involving one molecule.

monomorphemic /ˌmɒnə(ʊ)mɔː'fiːmɪk/ ▶ **adjective** Linguistics consisting of a single morpheme.

monomorphic /ˌmɒnə(ʊ)'mɔːfɪk/ ▶ **adjective** chiefly Biology having or existing in only one form, in particular: ■ (of a species or population) showing little or no variation in morphology or phenotype. ■ (of an animal species) having sexes that are similar in size and appearance.
– DERIVATIVES **monomorphism** noun, **monomorphous** adjective.
– ORIGIN late 19th cent.: from MONO- 'single' + Greek *morphē* 'form'.

mononuclear ▶ **adjective** Biology (of a cell) having one nucleus.

mononucleosis /ˌmɒnə(ʊ)njuːklɪ'əʊsɪs/ ▶ **noun** [mass noun] Medicine an abnormally high proportion of monocytes in the blood, especially associated with glandular fever.

monophagous /mə'nɒfəgəs/ ▶ **adjective** Zoology (of an animal) eating only one kind of food.

monophonic /ˌmɒnə(ʊ)'fɒnɪk/ ▶ **adjective 1** (of sound reproduction) using only one channel of transmission. Compare with STEREOPHONIC.
2 Music having a single melodic line without harmonies or melody in counterpoint. Compare with HOMOPHONIC and POLYPHONIC.
– DERIVATIVES **monophonically** adverb, **monophony** noun.
– ORIGIN early 19th cent.: from MONO- 'one' + Greek *phōnē* 'sound' + -IC.

monophthong /'mɒnəfθɒŋ, mə'nɒpθɒŋ/ ▶ **noun** Phonetics a vowel that has a single perceived auditory quality. Contrasted with DIPHTHONG, TRIPHTHONG.
– DERIVATIVES **monophthongal** adjective.
– ORIGIN early 17th cent.: from Greek *monophthongos*, from *monos* 'single' + *phthongos* 'sound'.

monophyletic /ˌmɒnə(ʊ)fʌɪ'lɛtɪk/ ▶ **adjective** Biology (of a group of organisms) descended from a common evolutionary ancestor or ancestral group, especially one not shared with any other group.

Monophysite /mə'nɒfɪsʌɪt/ ▶ **noun** Christian Theology a person who holds that there is only one inseparable nature (partly divine, partly and subordinately human) in the person of Christ.
– DERIVATIVES **Monophysitism** noun.
– ORIGIN late 17th cent.: via ecclesiastical Latin from ecclesiastical Greek *monophusitēs*, from *monos* 'single' + *phusis* 'nature'.

monoplane ▶ **noun** an aeroplane with one pair of wings. Often contrasted with BIPLANE, TRIPLANE.

monoplegia /ˌmɒnə(ʊ)'pliːdʒə/ ▶ **noun** [mass noun] paralysis restricted to one limb or region of the body. Compare with PARAPLEGIA.
– DERIVATIVES **monoplegic** adjective.

monoploid /'mɒnə(ʊ)plɔɪd/ ▶ **adjective** less common term for HAPLOID.

monopod ▶ **noun** a one-legged support for a camera or fishing rod.
– ORIGIN early 19th cent.: via Latin from Greek *monopodion*, from *monos* 'single' + *pous, pod-* 'foot'.

monopodium /ˌmɒnə(ʊ)'pəʊdɪəm/ ▶ **noun** (pl. **monopodia**) Botany a single continuous growth axis which extends at its apex and produces successive lateral shoots. Compare with SYMPODIUM.
– DERIVATIVES **monopodial** adjective.

monopole[1] ▶ **noun 1** Physics a single electric charge or magnetic pole, especially a hypothetical isolated magnetic pole.
2 a radio aerial or pylon consisting of a single pole or rod.
– DERIVATIVES **monopolar** adjective.

monopole[2] ▶ **noun** a champagne that is exclusive to one shipper.
– ORIGIN late 19th cent.: from French, 'monopoly'.

Monopolies and Mergers Commission a UK government body designed to investigate and report on activities relating to the setting up of trading monopolies, company mergers, and takeovers, in which the public has an interest.

monopolist ▶ **noun** a person or business that has a monopoly.
– DERIVATIVES **monopolistic** adjective, **monopolistically** adverb.

monopolistic competition ▶ **noun** another term for IMPERFECT COMPETITION.

monopolize (also **monopolise**) ▶ **verb** [with obj.] (of an organization or group) obtain exclusive possession or control of (a trade, commodity, or service). ■ have or take the greatest share of: *the bigger clubs monopolize the most profitable sponsorships and TV deals*. ■ get or keep exclusively to oneself: *Sophie monopolized the guest of honour for most of the evening*.
– DERIVATIVES **monopolization** noun, **monopolizer** noun.

monopoly ▶ **noun** (pl. **monopolies**) **1** the exclusive possession or control of the supply of or trade in a commodity or service: *the state's **monopoly of** radio and television broadcasting*. ■ a company or group having exclusive control over a commodity or service. ■ a commodity or service in the exclusive control of a company or group. ■ [usu. with negative] the exclusive possession, control, or exercise of something: *men don't have a **monopoly on** unrequited love*.
2 (**Monopoly**) trademark a board game in which players engage in simulated property and financial dealings using imitation money. It was invented in the US and the name was coined by Charles Darrow *c.*1935.
– ORIGIN mid 16th cent.: via Latin from Greek *monopōlion*, from *monos* 'single' + *pōlein* 'sell'.

monopoly capitalism ▶ **noun** [mass noun] Economics a capitalist system typified by trade monopolies in the hands of a few people.

Monopoly money ▶ **noun** [mass noun] informal money regarded as having no real existence or value: *the Monopoly money we'd won playing Internet stocks while dot-com fever swept the nation*.
– ORIGIN from the imitation money used in the game of *Monopoly* (see MONOPOLY (sense 2)).

monopropellant ▶ **noun** a substance used as rocket fuel without an additional oxidizing agent.
▶ **adjective** using a monopropellant.

monopsony /mə'nɒpsəni/ ▶ **noun** (pl. **monopsonies**) Economics a market situation in which there is only one buyer.
– ORIGIN 1930s: from MONO- 'one' + Greek *opsōnein* 'buy provisions' + -Y[3].

monopteros /mə'nɒptərɒs/ ▶ **noun** a classical temple consisting of a single circle of columns supporting a roof.
– ORIGIN late 17th cent.: from medieval Latin (adjective used as a noun), from Greek *monos* 'single' + *pteron* 'wing'.

monorail ▶ **noun** a railway in which the track consists of a single rail, typically elevated and with the trains suspended from it.

monorail camera ▶ **noun** a camera mounted on a rail which allows positional adjustment and may support additional components.

monorchid ▶ **adjective** (of a person or animal) having only one testicle.
▶ **noun** a person or animal having only one testicle.
– DERIVATIVES **monorchidism** noun.
– ORIGIN early 19th cent.: from modern Latin *monorchis, monorchid-*, from Greek *monos* 'single' + *orkhis* 'testicle'.

monosaccharide ▶ **noun** Chemistry any of the class of sugars (e.g. glucose) that cannot be hydrolysed to give a simpler sugar.

monosemy /'mɒnə(ʊ)ˌsiːmi/ ▶ **noun** [mass noun] Linguistics the property of having only one meaning.
– DERIVATIVES **monosemic** adjective, **monosemous** adjective.
– ORIGIN 1950s: from MONO- 'one' + Greek *sēma* 'sign' + -Y[3].

monoski ▶ **noun** a single broad ski attached to both feet.
– DERIVATIVES **monoskiing** noun.

monosodium glutamate ▶ **noun** a compound which occurs naturally as a breakdown product of proteins and is used as a flavour enhancer in food (although itself tasteless). A traditional ingredient in oriental cooking, it was originally obtained from seaweed but is now mainly made from bean and cereal protein. ● Chem. formula: $HOOC(CH_2)_2(NH_2)COONa$.

monosome /'mɒnə(ʊ)səʊm/ ▶ **noun** Biology an unpaired (usually X) chromosome in a diploid chromosome complement.

monosomy /ˌmɒnə(ʊ)'səʊmi/ ▶ **noun** [mass noun] Biology the condition of having a diploid chromosome complement in which one chromosome lacks its homologous partner.
– DERIVATIVES **monosomic** adjective.

monospecific ▶ **adjective** Biology relating to or consisting of only one species. ■ (of an antibody) specific to one antigen.

monostable Electronics ▶ **adjective** (of a circuit or device) having only one stable position or state.
▶ **noun** a device or circuit having only one stable position or state.

monostrophic /ˌmɒnə(ʊ)ˈstrɒfɪk, -ˈstrəʊf-/ ▸ adjective Prosody consisting of repetitions of the same strophic arrangement.

monosyllabic ▸ adjective (of a word or utterance) consisting of one syllable. ▪ (of a person) using brief or few words to signify reluctance to engage in conversation.
– DERIVATIVES **monosyllabically** adverb.

monosyllable ▸ noun a word consisting of only one syllable. ▪ (**monosyllables**) brief words, used when reluctant to engage in conversation: *if she spoke at all it was in monosyllables.*

monosynaptic /ˌmɒnə(ʊ)sɪˈnaptɪk/ ▸ adjective Physiology (of a reflex pathway) involving a single synapse.

monotechnic ▸ adjective (of a college) providing instruction in a single technical subject. Compare with POLYTECHNIC.

monotheism /ˈmɒnə(ʊ)ˌθiːɪz(ə)m/ ▸ noun [mass noun] the doctrine or belief that there is only one God.
– DERIVATIVES **monotheist** noun & adjective, **monotheistic** adjective, **monotheistically** adverb.
– ORIGIN mid 17th cent.: from MONO- 'one' + Greek *theos* 'god' + -ISM.

Monothelite /məˈnɒθəlʌɪt/ (also **Monothelete** /-liːt/) ▸ noun Christian Theology an adherent of the doctrine that Jesus had only one will, proposed in the 7th century to reconcile Monophysite and orthodox parties in the Byzantine Empire but condemned as heresy.
– ORIGIN late Middle English: via ecclesiastical Latin from ecclesiastical Greek *monothelētēs*, from *monos* 'single' + *thelētēs* (from *thelein* 'to will').

monotherapy ▸ noun [mass noun] the treatment of a disease with a single drug.

monotint ▸ noun archaic term for MONOCHROME.

monotone /ˈmɒnətəʊn/ ▸ noun [usu. in sing.] a continuing sound, especially of a person's voice, that is unchanging in pitch and without intonation: *he sat and answered the questions in a monotone.*
▸ adjective (of a voice or other sound) unchanging in pitch; without intonation or expressiveness: *his monotone reading of the two-hour report.* ▪ without colour or variety; dull: *the monotone housing estates of the big cities.*
– ORIGIN mid 17th cent.: from modern Latin *monotonus*, from late Greek *monotonos*.

M

monotonic ▸ adjective **1** Mathematics (of a function or quantity) varying in such a way that it either never decreases or never increases.
2 speaking or uttered with an unchanging pitch or tone: *her dour, monotonic husband.*
– DERIVATIVES **monotonically** adverb, **monotonicity** noun.

monotonous ▸ adjective dull, tedious, and repetitious; lacking in variety and interest: *the statistics that he quotes with monotonous regularity.* ▪ (of a sound or utterance) lacking in variation in tone or pitch: *her slurred monotonous speech.*
– DERIVATIVES **monotonously** adverb.

monotony ▸ noun [mass noun] lack of variety and interest; tedious repetition and routine: *you can become resigned to the monotony of captivity.* ▪ sameness of pitch or tone in a sound or utterance: *depression flattens the voice almost to monotony.*

monotreme /ˈmɒnə(ʊ)triːm/ ▸ noun Zoology a primitive mammal that lays large yolky eggs and has a common opening for the urogenital and digestive systems. Monotremes are now restricted to Australia and New Guinea, and comprise the platypus and the echidnas. ● Order Monotremata and subclass Prototheria: two families.
– ORIGIN mid 19th cent.: from MONO- 'single' + Greek *trēma* 'hole'.

monotropy /məˈnɒtrəpi/ ▸ noun [mass noun] Chemistry the existence of allotropes of an element, one of which is stable and the others metastable under all known conditions.
– DERIVATIVES **monotrope** noun.
– ORIGIN early 20th cent.: from MONO- 'one' + Greek *tropē* 'turning' + -Y³.

monotype ▸ noun **1** (**Monotype**) [usu. as modifier] Printing, trademark a typesetting machine, now little used, which casts type in metal, one character at a time: *Monotype machines.*
2 a single print taken from a design created in oil paint or printing ink on glass or metal.

monotypic /ˌmɒnə(ʊ)ˈtɪpɪk/ ▸ adjective chiefly Biology having only one type or representative, especially (of a genus) containing only one species.

monounsaturated ▸ adjective Chemistry (of an organic compound, especially a fat) saturated except for one multiple bond.

monovalent /ˌmɒnə(ʊ)ˈveɪl(ə)nt/ ▸ adjective Chemistry having a valency of one.

monoxide ▸ noun Chemistry an oxide containing one atom of oxygen in its molecule or empirical formula.

monozygotic /ˌmɒnə(ʊ)zʌɪˈgɒtɪk/ ▸ adjective (of twins) derived from a single ovum, and so identical.
– ORIGIN early 20th cent.: from MONO- 'single' + ZYGOTE + -IC.

monozygous /ˌmɒnə(ʊ)ˈzʌɪgəs/ ▸ adjective another term for MONOZYGOTIC.
– DERIVATIVES **monozygosity** noun.

Monroe¹ /mənˈrəʊ/, James (1758–1831), American Democratic Republican statesman, 5th President of the US 1817–25. In 1803, while minister to France under President Jefferson, he negotiated and ratified the Louisiana Purchase; he is chiefly remembered, however, as the originator of the Monroe Doctrine.

Monroe² /mənˈrəʊ/, Marilyn (1926–62), American actress; born *Norma Jean Mortenson*; later *Norma Jean Baker*. Her film roles, largely in comedies, made her the definitive Hollywood sex symbol. She is thought to have died of an overdose of sleeping pills. Notable films: *Gentlemen Prefer Blondes* (1953), *Some Like it Hot* (1959), and *The Misfits* (1961).

Monroe Doctrine a principle of US policy, originated by President James Monroe, that any intervention by external powers in the politics of the Americas is a potentially hostile act against the US.

Monrovia /mɒnˈrəʊvɪə/ the capital and chief port of Liberia; pop. 1,010,970 (2008).

Mons /mɒnz/ a town in southern Belgium, capital of the province of Hainaut; pop. 91,152 (2008). It was the scene in August 1914 of the first major battle of the First World War between British and German forces. Flemish name BERGEN.

mons /mɒnz/ ▸ noun short for MONS PUBIS.

Monseigneur /ˌmɒnseˈnjəː/, French /mɔ̃sɛɲœʀ/ ▸ noun (pl. **Messeigneurs** /ˌmesenˈjəː/, French /mesɛɲœʀ/) a title or form of address used of or to a French-speaking prince, cardinal, archbishop, or bishop.
– ORIGIN French, from *mon* 'my' + *seigneur* 'lord'.

Monsieur /məˈsjəː/, French /məsjø/ ▸ noun (pl. **Messieurs** /meˈsjəː/, French /mesjø/) a title or form of address used of or to a French-speaking man, corresponding to *Mr* or *sir*: *Monsieur Hulot.*
– ORIGIN French, from *mon* 'my' + *sieur* 'lord'.

Monsignor /mɒnˈsiːnjə, ˌmɒnsiːˈnjɔː/ ▸ noun (pl. **Monsignors** or **Monsignori** /-ˈnjɔːri/) the title of various senior Roman Catholic posts, such as a prelate or an officer of the papal court.
– ORIGIN Italian, on the pattern of French *Monseigneur*.

monsoon ▸ noun a seasonal prevailing wind in the region of South and South East Asia, blowing from the south-west between May and September and bringing rain (the **wet monsoon**), or from the north-east between October and April (the **dry monsoon**). ▪ the rainy season accompanying the wet monsoon.
– DERIVATIVES **monsoonal** adjective.
– ORIGIN late 16th cent.: from Portuguese *monção*, from Arabic *mawsim* 'season', from *wasama* 'to mark, brand'.

mons pubis /ˌmɒnz ˈpjuːbɪs/ ▸ noun the rounded mass of fatty tissue lying over the joint of the pubic bones, in women typically more prominent and also called the **mons Veneris**.
– ORIGIN late 19th cent.: Latin, 'mount of the pubes'.

monster ▸ noun **1** a large, ugly, and frightening imaginary creature. ▪ an inhumanly cruel or wicked person: *he was an unfeeling, treacherous monster.* ▪ humorous a rude or badly behaved person, typically a child: *he's only a year old, but already he is a little monster.*
2 a thing of extraordinary or daunting size: *this is a monster of a book, almost 500 pages* | [as modifier] *a monster 36lb carp.*
3 a congenitally malformed or mutant animal or plant.
▸ verb [with obj.] Brit. informal criticize or reprimand severely: *my mum used to monster me for coming home so late.*
– ORIGIN late Middle English: from Old French *monstre*, from Latin *monstrum* 'portent or monster', from *monere* 'warn'.

monstera /mɒnˈstɪərə/ ▸ noun a large tropical American climbing plant of the arum family, which typically has divided or perforated leaves and corky aerial roots. Several kinds are cultivated as indoor plants when young. ● Genus *Monstera*, family Araceae: several species, including the Swiss cheese plant.
– ORIGIN modern Latin, perhaps from Latin *monstrum* 'monster' (because of the unusual appearance of the leaves in some species).

monster truck ▸ noun an extremely large pickup truck with greatly oversized tyres.

monstrance /ˈmɒnstr(ə)ns/ ▸ noun (in the Roman Catholic Church) an open or transparent receptacle in which the consecrated Host is displayed for veneration.
– ORIGIN late Middle English (also in the sense 'demonstration or proof'): from medieval Latin *monstrantia*, from Latin *monstrare* 'to show'.

monstrosity ▸ noun (pl. **monstrosities**) **1** a thing, especially a building, which is very large and unsightly: *the shopping centre, a multi-storey monstrosity of raw concrete.* ▪ a grossly malformed animal or plant.
2 a thing which is outrageously evil or wrong: *how could anyone be capable of such monstrosities?*
3 [mass noun] the state or fact of being monstrous.
– ORIGIN mid 16th cent. (denoting an abnormality of growth): from late Latin *monstrositas*, from Latin *monstrosus* (see MONSTROUS).

monstrous ▸ adjective **1** having the ugly or frightening appearance of a monster: *monstrous, bug-eyed fish.*
2 inhumanly or outrageously evil or wrong: *he wasn't lovable, he was monstrous and violent* | *it is a monstrous waste of money.*
3 extraordinarily and dauntingly large: *the monstrous tidal wave swamped the surrounding countryside.*
– DERIVATIVES **monstrously** adverb, **monstrousness** noun.
– ORIGIN late Middle English (in the sense 'strange or unnatural'): from Old French *monstreux* or Latin *monstrosus*, from *monstrum* (see MONSTER). Current senses date from the 16th cent.

mons Veneris /ˌmɒnz ˈvɛnərɪs/ ▸ noun (in women) the mons pubis.
– ORIGIN late 17th cent.: Latin, 'mount of Venus'.

Mont. ▸ abbreviation Montana.

montage /mɒnˈtɑːʒ, ˈmɒntɑːʒ/ ▸ noun [mass noun] the technique of selecting, editing, and piecing together separate sections of film to form a continuous whole. ▪ [count noun] a sequence of film made using the technique of montage: *a montage of excerpts from the film.* ▪ the technique of producing a new composite whole from fragments of pictures, text, or music.
– ORIGIN early 20th cent.: French, from *monter* 'to mount'.

Montagna /mɒnˈtɑːnjə/, Bartolommeo Cincani (*c.*1450–1523), Italian painter. He is noted for his altarpiece *Sacra Conversazione* (1499).

Montagnais /ˌmɒntanˈjeɪ/ ▸ noun (pl. **same**) **1** a member of an American Indian people living in a vast area of Canada from north of the Gulf of St Lawrence to the southern shores of Hudson Bay.
2 [mass noun] the Algonquian language of the Montagnais, closely related to Cree. It has about 7,000 speakers.
▸ adjective relating to the Montagnais or their language.
– ORIGIN from French, literally 'of the mountains'.

Montagnard /ˌmɒntəˈnjɑː(d)/ ▸ noun & adjective former term for HMONG.
– ORIGIN French, from *montagne* 'mountain'.

Montagu's harrier /ˈmɒntəgjuːz/ ▸ noun a slender migratory Eurasian bird of prey, the male having pale grey plumage with black wing tips. ● *Circus pygargus*, family Accipitridae.
– ORIGIN mid 19th cent.: named after George Montagu (1751–1815), British naturalist.

Montaigne /mɒnˈteɪn/, French /mɔ̃tɛɲ/, Michel (Eyquem) de (1533–92), French essayist. Widely regarded as the originator of the modern essay, he wrote about prominent personalities and ideas of his age in his sceptical *Essays* (1580; 1588).

Montana /mɒnˈtanə/ a state in the western US, on the Canadian border to the east of the Rocky Mountains; pop. 967,440 (est. 2008); capital, Helena. Acquired from France as part of the Louisiana Purchase in 1803, it became the 41st state of the US in 1889.
– DERIVATIVES **Montanan** adjective & noun.

montane /ˈmɒnteɪn/ ▸ adjective of or inhabiting mountainous country: *montane grasslands*.
– ORIGIN mid 19th cent.: from Latin *montanus*, from *mons, mont-* 'mountain'.

Montanism /ˈmɒntənɪz(ə)m/ ▸ noun the tenets of a heretical millenarian and ascetic Christian sect that set great store by prophecy, founded in Phrygia by the priest Montanus in the middle of the 2nd century.
– DERIVATIVES **Montanist** noun & adjective.

Mont Blanc /ˌmɒ̃ ˈblɒ̃(k)/, French /mɔ̃ blɑ̃/ a peak in the Alps on the border between France and Italy, rising to 4,807 m (15,771 ft). It is the highest peak in the Alps and in western Europe.

montbretia /mɒn(t)ˈbriːʃə/ ▸ noun a plant of the iris family with bright orange-yellow trumpet-shaped flowers. ● *Crocosmia* × *crocosmiflora*, family Iridaceae.
– ORIGIN late 19th cent.: modern Latin, named after A. F. E. Coquebert de *Montbret* (1780–1801), French botanist.

Montcalm /mɒnˈkɑːm/, French /mɔ̃kalm/, Louis Joseph de Montcalm-Gozon, Marquis de (1712–59), French general. He defended Quebec against British troops under General Wolfe, but was defeated and fatally wounded in the battle on the Plains of Abraham.

Mont Cervin /mɔ̃ sɛʀvɛ̃/ French name for **MATTERHORN**.

monte /ˈmɒnti/ ▸ noun (usu. **three-card monte**) [mass noun] a game of Mexican origin played with three cards, similar to three-card trick.
– ORIGIN early 19th cent.: Spanish, literally 'mountain', also 'heap of cards left after dealing' (from an earlier game of chance played with forty-five cards).

Monte Albán /ˌmɒnteɪ alˈbɑːn/ an ancient city, now in ruins, in Oaxaca, southern Mexico. Occupied from the 8th century BC, it was a centre of the Zapotec culture from about the 1st century BC to the 8th century AD.

Monte Carlo /ˌmɒnti ˈkɑːləʊ/ a resort in Monaco, forming one of the four communes of the principality; pop. 14,600 (est. 2008). It is famous as a gambling resort and as the terminus of the annual Monte Carlo rally.

Monte Carlo method ▸ noun Statistics a technique in which a large quantity of randomly generated numbers are studied using a probabilistic model to find an approximate solution to a numerical problem that would be difficult to solve by other methods.
– ORIGIN 1940s: named after *Monte Carlo* (see **MONTE CARLO**), a resort famous for its gambling casino.

Monte Cassino /ˌmɒnteɪ kaˈsiːnəʊ/ a hill in central Italy near the town of Cassino, the site of the principal monastery of the Benedictines, founded by St Benedict *c.*529. The monastery and the town were destroyed in 1944 during bitter fighting between Allied and German forces, but have since been restored.

Monte Cervino /ˌmaonte tʃerˈvinao/ Italian name for **MATTERHORN**.

Montego Bay /mɒnˈtiːɡəʊ/ a free port and tourist resort on the north coast of Jamaica; pop. 80,400 (est. 2009).

Montenegro /ˌmɒntɪˈniːɡrəʊ/ a mountainous republic in the Balkans; pop. 672,200 (est. 2009); capital, Podgorica.

> Joined with Serbia before the Turkish conquest of 1355, Montenegro became independent in 1851. In 1918 it became part of Yugoslavia; on the break-up of the country it formed a federation with Serbia, but voted in 2006 to become independent.

– DERIVATIVES **Montenegrin** adjective & noun.

Montepulciano /ˌmɒnteɪpʊlˈtʃɑːnəʊ, ˌmɒntɪ-/ ▸ noun [mass noun] a red wine made in the region of Montepulciano, a town in Tuscany.

Monterey /ˌmɒntəˈreɪ/ a city and fishing port on the coast of California, founded by the Spanish in the 18th century; pop. 27,763 (est. 2008).

Monterey cypress ▸ noun another term for **MACROCARPA**.

Monterey Jack (also **Monterey cheese** or N. Amer. **Jack cheese**) ▸ noun [mass noun] a kind of cheese resembling Cheddar.
– ORIGIN from the name of *Monterey* County, California, where it was first made; the origin of *Jack* is unknown.

Monterrey /ˌmɒntəˈreɪ/ an industrial city in NE Mexico, capital of the state of Nuevo León; pop. 1,133,070 (2005).

Montespan /ˈmɒntɪspɒ̃/, French /mɔ̃tɛspɑ̃/, Françoise-Athénaïs de Rochechouart, Marquise de (1641–1707), French noblewoman. She was mistress of Louis XIV from 1667 to 1679, and had seven illegitimate children by him. She subsequently fell from favour when the king became attracted to the children's governess, Madame de Maintenon.

Montesquieu /ˈmɒntəskjəː, -sjkuː/, French /mɔ̃tɛskjø/, Charles Louis de Secondat, Baron de La Brède et de (1689–1755), French political philosopher. His reputation rests chiefly on *L'Esprit des lois* (1748), a comparative study of political systems in which he championed the separation of judicial, legislative, and executive powers as being most conducive to individual liberty.

Montessori[1] /ˌmɒntɪˈsɔːri/, Maria (1870–1952), Italian educationist. In her book *The Montessori Method* (1909) she advocated a child-centred approach to education, developed from her success with children with learning disabilities.

Montessori[2] /ˌmɒntɪˈsɔːri/ ▸ noun [usu. as modifier] a system of education for young children that seeks to develop natural interests and activities rather than use formal teaching methods: *a Montessori school*.

Monteverdi /ˌmɒntɪˈvɛːdi/, Claudio (1567–1643), Italian composer. His madrigals are noted for their use of harmonic dissonance; other important works include his opera *Orfeo* (1607) and his sacred *Vespers* (1610).

Montevideo /ˌmɒntɪvɪˈdeɪəʊ/, Spanish /maonteβiˈðeao/ the capital and chief port of Uruguay, on the River Plate; pop. 1,513,000 (est. 2007).

Montez /ˈmɒntɛz/, Lola (1818–61), Irish dancer; born *Marie Dolores Eliza Rosanna Gilbert*. She became the mistress of Ludwig I of Bavaria in 1846 and exercised great influence over him until banished the following year.

Montezuma II /ˌmɒntɪˈz(j)uːmə/ (1466–1520), Aztec emperor 1502–20. The last ruler of the Aztec empire in Mexico, he was defeated and imprisoned by the Spanish under Cortés in 1519. He was killed while trying to pacify some of his former subjects during an uprising against his captors.

Montezuma's revenge ▸ noun [mass noun] informal diarrhoea suffered by travellers, especially visitors to Mexico.

Montfort[1] /ˈmɒntfət/, Simon de (*c.*1165–1218), French soldier. From 1209 he led the Albigensian Crusade against the Cathars in southern France.

Montfort[2] /ˈmɒntfət/, Simon de, Earl of Leicester (*c.*1208–65), English soldier, born in Normandy. He was the son of Simon de Montfort. He led the baronial opposition to Henry III, defeating the king at Lewes in 1264 and summoning a Parliament (1265). He was defeated and killed by reorganized royal forces under Henry's son (later Edward I).

Montgolfier /mɒnˈɡɒlfɪeɪ, -fɪə/, French /mɔ̃ɡɔlfje/, Joseph Michel (1740–1810) and Jacques Étienne (1745–99), French inventors and pioneers in hot-air ballooning. In 1782 they built a large balloon from linen and paper and successfully lifted a number of animals; the first human ascents followed in 1783.

Montgomery[1] /mɒntˈɡʌməri, -ˈɡɒməri/ the state capital of Alabama; pop. 202,696 (est. 2008).

Montgomery[2] /mɒntˈɡʌməri, -ˈɡɒməri/, Bernard Law, 1st Viscount Montgomery of Alamein (1887–1976), British Field Marshal; known as **Monty**. His victory at El Alamein in 1942 proved the first significant Allied success in the Second World War. He commanded the Allied ground forces in the invasion of Normandy in 1944 and accepted the German surrender on 7 May, 1945.

Montgomery[3] /mɒntˈɡʌməri, -ˈɡɒməri/, L. M. (1874–1942), Canadian novelist; full name *Lucy Maud Montgomery*. She is noted for her bestselling first novel *Anne of Green Gables* (1908).

Montgomeryshire /mɒntˈɡʌmərɪʃɪə, -ˈɡɒm-, -ʃə/ a former county of central Wales. It became a part of Powys in 1974.

month ▸ noun (also **calendar month**) each of the twelve named periods into which a year is divided: *the first six months of 1992 | it was the end of the month*. ■ a period of time between the same dates in successive calendar months: *the president's rule was extended for six more months from March 3*. ■ a period of 28 days or four weeks.
– PHRASES **a month of Sundays** informal a very long period of time.
– ORIGIN Old English *mōnath*, of Germanic origin; related to Dutch *maand* and German *Monat*, also to **MOON**.

monthly ▸ adjective done, produced, or occurring once a month: *the Council held monthly meetings*.
▸ adverb once a month; every month: *most of us get paid monthly*.
▸ noun (pl. **monthlies**) **1** a magazine that is published once a month.
2 (**monthlies**) informal a menstrual period.

Montmartre /mɒnˈmɑːtr(ə)/, French /mɔ̃maʀtʀ/ a district in northern Paris, on a hill above the Seine, much frequented by artists in the late 19th and early 20th centuries when it was a separate village.

montmorillonite /ˌmɒntməˈrɪlənʌɪt/ ▸ noun [mass noun] an aluminium-rich clay mineral of the smectite group, containing some sodium and magnesium.
– ORIGIN mid 19th cent.: from *Montmorillon*, the name of a town in France, + **-ITE**[1].

Montonero /ˌmɒntəˈnɛːrəʊ/ ▸ noun (pl. **Montoneros**) a member of a left-wing Peronist guerrilla organization in Argentina.
– ORIGIN South American Spanish, literally 'guerrilla fighter', from Spanish *montón* 'crowd or mass': the term originally referred to a peasant rebel against imperial Spain.

Montparnasse /ˌmɒnpɑːˈnas/, French /mɔ̃paʀnas/ a district of Paris, on the left bank of the River Seine. Frequented in the late 19th century by writers and artists, it is traditionally associated with Parisian cultural life.

Montpelier /mɒntˈpiːljə/ the state capital of Vermont; pop. 7,760 (est. 2008).

Montpellier /mɒnˈpɛlɪeɪ/, French /mɔ̃pɛlje/ a city in southern France, near the Mediterranean coast, capital of Languedoc-Roussillon; pop. 254,974 (2006). A distinguished medical school and university, world-famous in medieval times, was founded there in 1221.

Montrachet /ˈmɒ̃traʃeɪ/ ▸ noun [mass noun] a white wine produced in the Montrachet region of France.

Montreal /ˌmɒntrɪˈɔːl/ a port on the St Lawrence in Quebec, SE Canada; pop. 1,162,693 (2006). Founded in 1642, Montreal was under French rule until 1763; almost two thirds of its present-day population are French-speaking. French name **Montréal** /mɔ̃ʀeal/.

Montreux /mɒ̃ˈtrəː/, French /mɔ̃tʀø/ a resort town in SW Switzerland, at the east end of Lake Geneva; pop. 23,800 (2007). Since the 1960s it has hosted annual festivals of both jazz and television.

Montrose /mɒnˈtrəʊz/, James Graham, 1st Marquis of (1612–50), Scottish general. Montrose supported Charles I in the English Civil War and inflicted a dramatic series of defeats on the stronger Covenanter forces in the north before being defeated. In 1650 he attempted to restore Charles II, but was betrayed to the Covenanters and hanged.

Mont St Michel /ˌmɒ̃ sã mɪˈʃɛl/, French /mɔ̃ sɛ̃ miʃɛl/ a rocky islet off the coast of Normandy, NW France. An island only at high tide, it is surrounded by sandbanks and linked to the mainland by a causeway. It is crowned by a medieval Benedictine abbey-fortress.

Montserrat /ˌmɒntsəˈrat, ˈmɒnsərat/ an island in the Caribbean, one of the Leeward Islands; pop. 5,100 (est. 2009); capital, Plymouth. It was colonized by Irish settlers in 1632 and is now a British overseas territory. Since 1995 it has been severely affected by the ongoing eruption of the Soufrière Hills volcano, causing the evacuation of the southern part of the island, including the now destroyed city of Plymouth.
– DERIVATIVES **Montserratian** adjective & noun /ˌmɒn(t)səˈraʃ(ə)n/.
– ORIGIN visited by Columbus in 1493, the island was named after a Benedictine monastery on the mountain of *Montserrat* in Catalonia, NE Spain.

montuno /mɒnˈtuːnəʊ/ ▸ noun (pl. **montunos**) **1** a traditional costume worn by men from Panama, consisting of short white cotton trousers and an embroidered shirt.
2 an improvised passage in a rumba.
– ORIGIN American Spanish, literally 'native to mountains, untamed'.

monty ▸ noun (in phrase **the full monty**) Brit. informal the full amount expected, desired, or possible: *they'll do the full monty for a few thousand each*.
– ORIGIN of unknown origin; the phrase is only recorded recently. Among various (unsubstantiated) theories, one cites the phrase *the full Montague Burton*, apparently meaning 'a complete three-piece

M

suit' (from the name of a tailor of made-to-measure clothing in the early 20th cent.); another recounts the possibility of a military usage, *the full monty* being 'the full cooked English breakfast' insisted upon by Field Marshal *Montgomery*.

monument ▸ noun a statue, building, or other structure erected to commemorate a notable person or event. ■ a statue or other structure placed over a grave in memory of the dead. ■ a building, structure, or site that is of historical importance or interest: *the amphitheatre is one of the many Greek monuments in Sicily.* ■ an enduring and memorable example of something: *recordings that are a **monument** to the art of playing the piano.*
– ORIGIN Middle English (denoting a burial place): via French from Latin *monumentum*, from *monere* 'remind'.

monumental ▸ adjective **1** great in importance, extent, or size: *it's been a monumental effort.*
2 of or serving as a monument: *additional details are found in monumental inscriptions.*
– DERIVATIVES **monumentality** noun, **monumentally** adverb.

monumentalism ▸ noun [mass noun] construction, especially of buildings, on a grand scale.

monumentalize (also **monumentalise**) ▸ verb [with obj.] make a permanent record of (something) by or as if by creating a monument: *the kind of ethic that monumentalizes the glory of a hero.*

monumental mason ▸ noun Brit. a person who makes tombstones and similar items.

-mony ▸ suffix forming nouns often denoting an action, state, or quality: *ceremony* | *harmony*.
– ORIGIN from Latin *-monia*, *-monium*.

monzonite /ˈmɒnzənʌɪt/ ▸ noun [mass noun] Geology a granular igneous rock with a composition intermediate between syenite and diorite, containing approximately equal amounts of orthoclase and plagioclase.
– DERIVATIVES **monzonitic** adjective.
– ORIGIN late 19th cent.: named after Mount *Monzoni* in the Tyrol, Italy, + **-ITE**[1].

M

moo ▸ verb (**moos, mooing, mooed**) [no obj.] make the characteristic deep resonant vocal sound of cattle.
▸ noun (pl. **moos**) **1** the characteristic sound of cattle.
2 Brit. informal an irritating or incompetent woman: *you silly old moo.*
– ORIGIN mid 16th cent.: imitative.

mooch ▸ verb informal **1** [no obj.] (**mooch about/around**) Brit. loiter in a bored or listless manner: *he just mooched about his bedsit.*
2 [with obj.] N. Amer. ask for or obtain (something) without paying for it: *a bunch of your friends will show up, mooching food* | [no obj.] *I'm **mooching off** you all the time.*
▸ noun **1** [in sing.] Brit. an instance of loitering in a bored or listless manner.
2 N. Amer. a beggar or scrounger.
– DERIVATIVES **moocher** noun.
– ORIGIN late Middle English (in the sense 'to hoard'): probably from Old French *muchier* (Anglo-Norman *muscher*) 'hide, skulk': compare with **MITCH**. Current senses date from the mid 19th cent.

moo-cow ▸ noun a child's name for a cow.

mood[1] ▸ noun **1** a temporary state of mind or feeling: *he appeared to be in a very good mood about something.* ■ the atmosphere or pervading tone of something: *a concept album which captures the mood of modern times.* ■ [as modifier] (especially of music) inducing or suggestive of a particular feeling or state of mind: *mood music.*
2 an angry, irritable, or sullen state of mind: *he was obviously in a mood.*
– PHRASES **in the** (or **in no**) **mood for/to do something** feeling (or not feeling) like doing or experiencing something: *she was in no mood for sightseeing.*
– ORIGIN Old English *mōd* (also in the senses 'mind' and 'fierce courage'), of Germanic origin; related to Dutch *moed* and German *Mut*.

mood[2] ▸ noun **1** Grammar a category or form which indicates whether a verb expresses fact (indicative mood), command (imperative mood), question (interrogative mood), wish (optative mood), or conditionality (subjunctive mood).
2 Logic any of the valid forms into which each of the figures of a categorical syllogism may occur.
– ORIGIN mid 16th cent.: variant of **MODE**, influenced by **MOOD**[1].

mood-altering ▸ adjective (of a drug) capable of inducing changes of mood.

mood swing ▸ noun an abrupt and unaccountable change of mood.

moody ▸ adjective (**moodier, moodiest**) (of a person) given to unpredictable changes of mood, especially sudden bouts of gloominess or sullenness: *his moody adolescent brother.* ■ giving an impression of melancholy or mystery: *grainy film which gives a soft, moody effect.*
– DERIVATIVES **moodily** adverb, **moodiness** noun.
– ORIGIN Old English *mōdig* 'brave or wilful' (see **MOOD**[1], **-Y**[1]).

mook /muːk/ ▸ noun US informal a stupid or incompetent person: *if you don't want to look like every other mook you need a sartorial trademark.*
– ORIGIN 1930s: of uncertain origin.

moolah /ˈmuːlə/ ▸ noun [mass noun] informal money.
– ORIGIN 1930s (originally US): of unknown origin.

mooli /ˈmuːli/ ▸ noun a radish of a variety with a large slender white root which is typically eaten cooked, especially in Eastern cuisine, and is also used for stockfeed.
– ORIGIN 1960s: from Hindi *mūlī*, from Sanskrit *mūla* 'root'.

moomba /ˈmuːmbə/ ▸ noun an annual pre-Lent festival held in Melbourne.
– ORIGIN an Aboriginal word.

Moon, Sun Myung (b.1920), Korean industrialist and religious leader. In 1954 he founded the Holy Spirit Association for the Unification of World Christianity, which became known as the Unification Church.

moon ▸ noun (also **Moon**) the natural satellite of the earth, visible (chiefly at night) by reflected light from the sun. ■ a natural satellite of any planet. ■ literary or humorous a month: *that wonderful night four moons ago* | *I got my first laser printer **many moons ago**.* ■ (**the moon**) anything that one could desire: *you must know he'd give you the moon.*

> The moon orbits the earth in a period of 27.32 days, going through a series of phases from new moon to full moon and back again during that time. Its average distance from the earth is some 384,000 km and it is 3,476 km in diameter. The bright and dark features which outline the face of 'the Man in the Moon' are highland and lowland regions, the former heavily pockmarked by craters due to the impact of meteorites. The moon has no atmosphere, and the same side is always presented to the earth.

▸ verb **1** [no obj., with adverbial] behave or move in a listless and aimless manner: *I don't want her **mooning about** in the morning.* ■ act in a dreamily infatuated manner: *Timothy's **mooning over** her like a schoolboy.*
2 [no obj.] informal expose one's buttocks to someone in order to insult or amuse them.
– PHRASES **over the moon** informal, chiefly Brit. extremely happy; delighted. [from *The Cow jumped over the Moon*, a line from a nursery rhyme.]
– DERIVATIVES **moonless** adjective, **moonlet** noun, **moonlike** adjective.
– ORIGIN Old English *mōna*, of Germanic origin; related to Dutch *maan* and German *Mond*, also to **MONTH**, from an Indo-European root shared by Latin *mensis* and Greek *mēn* 'month', and also Latin *metiri* 'to measure' (the moon being used to measure time).

moonbeam ▸ noun a ray of moonlight.

moon blindness ▸ noun [mass noun] **1** (in horses) a recurrent inflammatory disease of the eyes, causing intermittent blindness.
2 night blindness.
– DERIVATIVES **moon-blind** adjective.

moon boot ▸ noun a warm, thickly padded boot with an outer surface of fabric or plastic.

moon buggy ▸ noun informal term for **LUNAR ROVING VEHICLE**.

moon cake ▸ noun a round cake eaten during the Chinese Moon Festival.

mooncalf ▸ noun (pl. **mooncalves**) archaic a foolish person.

moon daisy ▸ noun another term for **OX-EYE DAISY**.

moon-eye ▸ noun a herring-like freshwater fish with large eyes, which lives in the south of the Great Lakes region of North America. ● *Hiodon tergisus*, family Hiodontidae.

moon-faced ▸ adjective having a round face.

Moon Festival ▸ noun a Chinese festival held in the middle of the autumn.

moonfish ▸ noun (pl. **same** or **moonfishes**) a deep-bodied laterally compressed marine fish, in particular: ● a silvery fish of the jack family (Carangidae), including *Selene setapinnis* of the Atlantic. ● an opah. ● a fingerfish.

moonflower ▸ noun a tropical American climbing plant of the convolvulus family, with sweet-smelling trumpet-shaped white flowers which open at dusk and close at midday. ● *Ipomoea alba*, family Convolvulaceae.

moong ▸ noun variant spelling of **MUNG**.

moon gate ▸ noun (in China) a circular opening forming a gateway in a wall.

Moonie ▸ noun [often as modifier] informal, often derogatory a member of the Unification Church.
– ORIGIN 1970s: from the name of its founder, Sun Myung *Moon* (see **MOON**).

moonlight ▸ noun [mass noun] the light of the moon: *the river glittered under the pale moonlight* | [as modifier] *a moonlight stroll.*
▸ verb (past and past participle **moonlighted**) [no obj.] informal have a second job, typically secretly and at night, in addition to one's regular employment.
– DERIVATIVES **moonlighter** noun.

moonlit ▸ adjective lit by the moon.

moon moth ▸ noun a large pale green silk moth with transparent eyespots on each wing and long tail-like projections on the hindwings. ● Several genera and species in the family Saturniidae. See also **LUNA MOTH**.

moon pool ▸ noun a shaft through the bottom of a drilling ship, oil rig, etc. for lowering and raising equipment into or from the water.

moonquake ▸ noun a tremor of the moon's surface.

moonraker ▸ noun **1** dialect a native of the county of Wiltshire. [with reference to the Wiltshire story of men caught raking a pond for kegs of smuggled brandy, who feigned madness to fool the revenue men, by saying they were raking out the moon.]
2 a small square sail set above a skysail on a sailing ship.

moonrat ▸ noun a shy insectivorous mammal of the hedgehog family, with a long snout and rat-like appearance, native to SE Asia and China. Also called **GYMNURE**. ● Subfamily Galericinae, family Erinaceidae: several genera and species, in particular *Echinosorex gymnurus*.

moonrise ▸ noun the rising or time of rising of the moon above the horizon: *it was actually about an hour after moonrise.*

moon roof ▸ noun US another term for **SUNROOF**.

moonscape ▸ noun a landscape resembling the surface of the moon, especially in being rocky and barren: *the pock-marked moonscape around the old colliery.*

moonseed ▸ noun a North American climbing plant with crescent-shaped seeds. ● *Menispermum canadense*, family Menispermaceae.

moonset ▸ noun the setting or time of setting of the moon below the horizon: *the best times to observe these meteors are after moonset.*

moon shell (also **moon snail**) ▸ noun a marine mollusc with a shiny, almost spherical, shell and a large foot. ● Family Naticidae, class Gastropoda: *Natica* and other genera.

moonshine ▸ noun [mass noun] **1** foolish talk or ideas: *whatever I said, it was moonshine.*
2 N. Amer. informal illicitly distilled or smuggled alcohol.
– DERIVATIVES **moonshiner** noun (sense 2).

moon shot ▸ noun the launching of a spacecraft to the moon.

moonstomp ▸ noun a dance to ska music characterized by heavy rhythmic stamping.
▸ verb [no obj.] perform a moonstomp.

moonstone ▸ noun a pearly white semi-precious stone, especially one consisting of alkali feldspar.

moonstruck ▸ adjective unable to think or act normally, especially as a result of being in love.

moonwalk ▸ noun **1** an act or period of walking on the surface of the moon.
2 a dance with a gliding motion, in which the dancer appears to be moving forward but in fact is moving backwards.
▸ verb [no obj.] **1** walk on the surface of the moon.
2 dance the moonwalk.
– DERIVATIVES **moonwalker** noun.

moonwort /ˈmuːnwəːt/ ▸ noun a widely distributed fern with a single small frond of fan-shaped lobes and a separate spike bearing the spore-producing organs, growing typically in grassy uplands and old meadows. ● Genus *Botrychium*, family Ophioglossaceae: several species, in particular *B. lunaria*.

moony ▸ adjective (**moonier, mooniest**) dreamy and unaware of one's surroundings, for example because one is in love: *little girls go moony over horses*.

Moor /mɔː, mʊə/ ▸ noun a member of a NW African Muslim people of mixed Berber and Arab descent. In the 8th century they conquered the Iberian peninsula, but were finally driven out of their last stronghold in Granada at the end of the 15th century.
– DERIVATIVES **Moorish** adjective.
– ORIGIN from Old French *More*, via Latin from Greek *Mauros* 'inhabitant of Mauretania'.

moor[1] /mɔː, mʊə/ ▸ noun chiefly Brit. a tract of open uncultivated upland, typically covered with heather. ■ a moor preserved for shooting: *a grouse moor*. ■ US or dialect a fen.
– ORIGIN Old English *mōr*, of Germanic origin.

moor[2] /mɔː, mʊə/ ▸ verb [with obj.] make fast (a boat) by attaching it by cable or rope to the shore or to an anchor: *twenty or so fishing boats were moored to the pierside* | [no obj.] *we moored alongside a jetty*.
– DERIVATIVES **moorage** noun.
– ORIGIN late 15th cent.: probably from the Germanic base of Dutch *meren*.

moorburn ▸ noun [mass noun] Scottish the seasonal burning of heather and other vegetation on a moor to make way for new growth.

moorcock ▸ noun Brit. a male red grouse.

Moore[1] /mɔː, mʊə/, Bobby (1941–93), English footballer; full name *Robert Frederick Moore*. A defender who spent most of his career with West Ham United, he captained the English team that won the World Cup in 1966.

Moore[2] /mɔː, mʊə/, Dudley (Stuart John) (1935–2002), English actor, comedian, and musician. He appeared with Peter Cook in the television shows *Beyond the Fringe* (1959–64) and *Not Only ... But Also* (1964–70). His films include *Arthur* (1981).

Moore[3] /mɔː, mʊə/, Francis (1657–*c*.1715), English physician, astrologer, and schoolmaster. His almanacs of meteorological and astrological predictions gave their name to the range of almanacs called 'Old Moore' that are available today.

Moore[4] /mɔː, mʊə/, George (Augustus) (1852–1933), Irish novelist. Notable works: *A Mummer's Wife* (1885) and *Esther Waters* (1894).

Moore[5] /mɔː, mʊə/, G. E. (1873–1958), English moral philosopher and member of the Bloomsbury Group; full name *George Edward Moore*. Notable works: *Principia Ethica* (1903).

Moore[6] /mɔː, mʊə/, Henry (Spencer) (1898–1986), English sculptor and draughtsman. His work is characterized by semi-abstract reclining forms, large upright figures, and family groups, which Moore intended to be viewed in the open air.

Moore[7] /mɔː, mʊə/, Sir John (1761–1809), British general. He commanded the British army during the Peninsular War and was killed at Corunna.

Moore[8] /mɔː, mʊə/, Thomas (1779–1852), Irish poet and musician. He wrote patriotic and nostalgic songs set to Irish tunes, notably 'The Harp that once through Tara's Halls' and 'The Minstrel Boy', and is also known for the oriental romance *Lalla Rookh* (1817).

Mooré /ˈmuːreɪ/ ▸ noun another term for **MORE**[2].

moorfowl ▸ noun (pl. **same**) Brit. another term for **RED GROUSE**.

moor grass ▸ noun [mass noun] either of two coarse upland grasses found in Eurasia: ● (**purple moor grass**) a purplish-green grass which grows in large tussocks, chiefly in wet and peaty areas (*Molinia caerulea*, family Gramineae). ● (**blue moor grass**) a wiry bluish-grey European grass which favours dry limestone soils (*Sesleria caerulea*, family Gramineae).

moorhen ▸ noun **1** a small aquatic rail with mainly blackish plumage. ● Family Rallidae: two genera and four species, in particular the widespread **common moorhen** or common gallinule (*Gallinula chloropus*), with a red and yellow bill.
2 Brit. a female red grouse.

mooring ▸ noun (often **moorings**) a place where a boat or ship is moored: *they tied up at Water Gypsy's permanent moorings*. ■ the ropes, chains, or anchors by or to which a boat, ship, or buoy is moored: *the great ship slipped her moorings and slid out into the Atlantic*.

Moorish idol ▸ noun a disc-shaped fish with bold vertical black-and-white bands and a very tall tapering dorsal fin, of coral reefs in the Indo-Pacific region. Also called **TOBY**. ● *Zanclus cornutus*, family Acanthuridae.

moorland ▸ noun [mass noun] (also **moorlands**) chiefly Brit. an extensive area of moor.

Moorpark ▸ noun an apricot of a large orange-fleshed variety.
– ORIGIN late 18th cent.: named after either of two houses in southern England, *Moor Park* in Sussex, the home of Sir William Temple (1628–99), or *Moor Park* in Hertfordshire, the home of George, Lord Anson (1697–1762). Both men are credited with first cultivating the fruit in England.

moose ▸ noun (pl. **same**) a large deer with palmate antlers and a growth of skin hanging from the neck, native to northern Eurasia and northern North America. Also called **ELK** in Britain. ● *Alces alces*, family Cervidae.
– ORIGIN early 17th cent.: from Abnaki *mos*.

moosewood ▸ noun a compact North American maple with large leaves and vertically striped bark. Moose often feed on the bark during severe winters. ● *Acer pensylvanicum*, family Aceraceae.

moo shi /ˌmuː ˈʃiː/ (also **moo shoo** /ˌmuː ˈʃuː/ or **moo shu roo** /ˌmuː ˌʃuː ˈruː/) ▸ noun [mass noun] a Chinese dish consisting of shredded pork with vegetables and seasonings, rolled in thin pancakes.
– ORIGIN Chinese *mùxu* 'dish containing scrambled egg'.

moot ▸ adjective **1** subject to debate, dispute, or uncertainty: *whether the temperature rise was mainly due to the greenhouse effect was a moot point*.
2 N. Amer. having little or no practical relevance: *the whole matter is becoming increasingly moot*.
▸ verb [with obj.] raise (a question or topic) for discussion; suggest (an idea or possibility): *the scheme was first mooted last October*.
▸ noun **1** historical an assembly held for debate, especially in Anglo-Saxon and medieval times. ■ a regular gathering of people having a common interest.
2 Law a mock judicial proceeding set up to examine a hypothetical case as an academic exercise.
– ORIGIN Old English *mōt* 'assembly or meeting' and *mōtian* 'to converse', of Germanic origin; related to **MEET**[1]. The adjective (originally an attributive noun use: see **MOOT COURT**) dates from the mid 16th cent.; the current verb sense dates from the mid 17th cent.

> **USAGE** Note that a question subject to debate or dispute is a **moot point**, not a **mute point**. As **moot** is a relatively uncommon word people sometimes interpret it as the more familiar word **mute**.

moot court ▸ noun N. Amer. a mock court at which law students argue imaginary cases for practice.

mop[1] ▸ noun **1** an implement consisting of a bundle of thick loose strings or a sponge attached to a handle, used for wiping floors or other surfaces. ■ [usu. in sing.] an act of wiping something clean: *the kitchen needed a quick mop*.
2 a thick mass of disordered hair: *her tousled mop of blonde hair*.
▸ verb (**mops, mopping, mopped**) [with obj.] clean or soak up liquid from (something) by wiping: *she mopped the floor and cleaned out two cupboards*. ■ [with obj. and adverbial] wipe (something) away from a surface: *a barmaid rushed forward to mop up the spilt beer*. ■ wipe sweat or tears from (one's face or eyes): *he pulled a handkerchief from his pocket to mop his brow*.
– PHRASAL VERBS **mop something up** (also **mop up**) complete the military conquest of an area by capturing or killing remaining enemy troops: *troops mopped up the last pockets of resistance*.
– DERIVATIVES **moppy** adjective.
– ORIGIN late 15th cent.: perhaps ultimately related to Latin *mappa* 'napkin'.

mop[2] (also **mop fair**) ▸ noun Brit. historical an autumn fair or gathering at which farmhands and servants were hired.
– ORIGIN late 17th cent.: probably from the practice at the fair whereby a mop was carried by a maidservant seeking employment.

mopane /mɒˈpɑːni/ (also **mopani**) ▸ noun a tree found in arid regions of southern Africa, with bitter-tasting leaves that are shaped like butterfly wings and fold together in intense heat. ● *Colophospermum mopane*, family Leguminosae.
– ORIGIN mid 19th cent.: from Setswana.

mopane worm ▸ noun the spotted caterpillar of a southern African moth, which feeds on mopane leaves and is a source of food for local people. ● *Gonimbrasia belina*, family Saturniidae.

mopboard ▸ noun US term for **SKIRTING**.

mope ▸ verb [no obj.] feel dejected and apathetic: *no use moping—things could be worse*. ■ (**mope around/about**) wander about listlessly and aimlessly because of unhappiness or boredom.
▸ noun a person given to prolonged spells of low spirits: *a bunch of totally depressed mopes*. ■ (**mopes**) dated low spirits; depression.
– DERIVATIVES **moper** noun, **mopey** (also **mopy**) adjective (**mopier, mopiest**) **mopish** adjective.
– ORIGIN mid 16th cent. (the early noun sense being 'fool or simpleton'): perhaps of Scandinavian origin; compare with Swedish dialect *mopa* 'to sulk'.

moped /ˈməʊpɛd/ ▸ noun a light motor cycle, especially one with an engine capacity of not more than 50 cc.
– ORIGIN 1950s: from Swedish, from (*trampcykel med*) *mo*(*tor och*) *ped*(*aler*) 'pedal cycle with motor and pedals'.

mopery ▸ noun [mass noun] **1** rare apathy and dejection.
2 US informal the action of committing a minor or petty offence such as loitering.

mop fair ▸ noun see **MOP**[2].

mophead ▸ noun informal a person with a full head of thick hair.

mopoke /ˈməʊpəʊk/ ▸ noun (also **morepork**) Austral. another term for **BOOBOOK**. ■ a tawny frogmouth (see **FROGMOUTH**).
– ORIGIN early 19th cent.: imitative of the bird's cry.

moppet ▸ noun informal a small endearingly sweet child.
– ORIGIN early 17th cent.: from obsolete *moppe* 'baby or rag doll' + **-ET**[1].

Mopti /ˈmɒpti/ a city in central Mali, at the junction of the Niger and Bani Rivers; pop. 103,400 (est. 2009).

moptop ▸ noun a man's hairstyle in the form of a long shaggy bob. ■ a person with such a hairstyle.

moquette /mɒˈkɛt/ ▸ noun [mass noun] a thick pile fabric used for carpets and upholstery.
– ORIGIN 1930s: from French, perhaps from obsolete Italian *mocaiardo* 'mohair'.

MOR ▸ abbreviation (of music) middle-of-the-road.

mor /mɔː/ ▸ noun [mass noun] Soil Science humus formed under acid conditions.
– ORIGIN 1930s: from Danish.

Moradabad /ˌmɔːrɑːdəˈbad/ a city and railway junction in northern India, in Uttar Pradesh; pop. 806,700 (est. 2009).

moraine /məˈreɪn/ ▸ noun Geology a mass of rocks and sediment carried down and deposited by a glacier, typically as ridges at its edges or extremity.
– DERIVATIVES **morainal** adjective, **morainic** adjective.
– ORIGIN late 18th cent.: from French, from Italian dialect *morena*, from French dialect *morre* 'snout'; related to **MORION**[1].

moral ▸ adjective **1** concerned with the principles of right and wrong behaviour: *the moral dimensions of medical intervention* | *a moral judgement*. ■ concerned with or derived from the code of behaviour that is considered right or acceptable in a particular society: *they have a moral obligation to pay the money back*. ■ [attrib.] examining the nature of ethics and the foundations of good and bad character and conduct: *moral philosophers*.
2 holding or manifesting high principles for proper conduct: *he prides himself on being a highly moral and ethical person*.
▸ noun **1** a lesson that can be derived from a story or experience: *the moral of this story was that one must see the beauty in what one has*.
2 (**morals**) standards of behaviour; principles of right and wrong: *the corruption of public morals* | *they believe addicts have no morals and cannot be trusted*.
– DERIVATIVES **morally** adverb.
– ORIGIN late Middle English: from Latin *moralis*, from *mos, mor-* 'custom', (plural) *mores* 'morals'. As a noun the word was first used to translate Latin *Moralia*, the title of St Gregory the Great's moral exposition of the Book of Job, and was subsequently applied to the works of various classical writers.

moral certainty ▸ noun [mass noun] probability so great as to allow no reasonable doubt.

M

morale /məˈrɑːl/ ▸ **noun** [mass noun] the confidence, enthusiasm, and discipline of a person or group at a particular time: *the team's morale was high*.
– ORIGIN mid 18th cent.: from French *moral*, respelled to preserve the final stress in pronunciation.

moral fibre ▸ **noun** see **FIBRE** (sense 1).

moral hazard ▸ **noun** [mass noun] Economics lack of incentive to guard against risk where one is protected from its consequences, e.g. by insurance.

moralism ▸ **noun** [mass noun] the practice of moralizing, especially the tendency to make judgements about others' morality.

moralist ▸ **noun** a person who teaches or promotes morality. ■ a person given to moralizing. ■ rare a person who behaves in a morally commendable way.

moralistic ▸ **adjective** overfond of making moral judgements about others' behaviour; too ready to moralize: *the media's homophobic and moralistic coverage of AIDS*.
– DERIVATIVES **moralistically** adverb.

morality ▸ **noun** (pl. **moralities**) [mass noun] principles concerning the distinction between right and wrong or good and bad behaviour: *the matter boiled down to simple morality: innocent prisoners ought to be freed*. ■ [count noun] a particular system of values and principles of conduct: *a bourgeois morality*. ■ the extent to which an action is right or wrong: *the issue of the morality of the possession of nuclear weapons*.
– ORIGIN late Middle English: from Old French *moralite* or late Latin *moralitas*, from Latin *moralis* (see **MORAL**).

morality play ▸ **noun** a kind of allegorical drama having personified abstract qualities as the main characters and presenting a lesson about good conduct and character, popular in the 15th and early 16th centuries.

moralize (also **moralise**) ▸ **verb 1** [no obj.] (often as noun **moralizing**) comment on issues of right and wrong, typically with an unfounded air of superiority: *the self-righteous moralizing of his aunt was ringing in his ears*.
2 [with obj.] reform the character and conduct of: *he endeavoured to moralize an immoral society*.
– DERIVATIVES **moralization** noun, **moralizer** noun.
– ORIGIN late Middle English (in the sense 'explain the moral meaning of'): from French *moraliser* or medieval Latin *moralizare*, from late Latin *moralis* (see **MORAL**).

moral law ▸ **noun** (in some systems of ethics) an absolute principle defining the criteria of right action (whether conceived as a divine ordinance or a truth of reason).

moral majority ▸ **noun** [treated as pl.] the majority of people, regarded as favouring firm moral standards: *smokers are often made to feel like social outcasts by the moral majority*.
– ORIGIN 1970s: originally as *Moral Majority*, the name of a right-wing movement in the US.

moral panic ▸ **noun** an instance of public anxiety or alarm in response to a problem regarded as threatening the moral standards of society: *the moral panic about 'the tide of filth' polluting our land*.

moral philosophy ▸ **noun** [mass noun] the branch of philosophy concerned with ethics.

Moral Rearmament an organization founded by the American Lutheran evangelist Frank Buchman (1878–1961) and first popularized in Oxford in the 1920s (hence until about 1938 called the **Oxford Group Movement**). It emphasizes personal integrity and confession of faults, cooperation, and mutual respect, especially as a basis for social transformation.

moral rights ▸ **plural noun** Law the right of an author or other creative artist to protect the integrity and ownership of their work.

moral science ▸ **noun** [mass noun] dated social sciences and/or philosophy.

moral sense ▸ **noun** [mass noun] the ability to distinguish between right and wrong.

moral support ▸ **noun** [mass noun] support or help whose effect is psychological rather than physical.

moral victory ▸ **noun** a defeat that can be interpreted as a victory on moral terms, for example because the defeated party defended their principles.

moran /ˈmɒr(ə)n/ ▸ **noun** (pl. **same**) a member of the warrior group of the Masai people of East Africa, which comprises the younger unmarried males.
– ORIGIN Masai.

Morar, Loch /ˈmɔːrə/ a loch in western Scotland. At 310 m (1,017 ft), it is Scotland's deepest loch.

morass /məˈras/ ▸ **noun 1** an area of muddy or boggy ground.
2 a complicated or confused situation: *she would become lost in a morass of lies and explanations*.
– ORIGIN late 15th cent.: from Dutch *moeras*, alteration (by assimilation to *moer* 'moor') of Middle Dutch *marasch*, from Old French *marais* 'marsh', from medieval Latin *mariscus*.

moratorium /ˌmɒrəˈtɔːrɪəm/ ▸ **noun** (pl. **moratoriums** or **moratoria** /-rɪə/) a temporary prohibition of an activity: ***a moratorium on** the use of drift nets*. ■ Law a legal authorization to debtors to postpone payment.
– ORIGIN late 19th cent.: modern Latin, neuter (used as a noun) of late Latin *moratorius* 'delaying', from Latin *morat-* 'delayed', from the verb *morari*, from *mora* 'delay'.

Moravia /məˈreɪvɪə/ a region of the Czech Republic, situated between Bohemia in the west and the Carpathians in the east; chief town, Brno. A province of Bohemia from the 11th century, it was made an Austrian province in 1848, becoming a part of Czechoslovakia in 1918.

Moravian ▸ **adjective** relating to Moravia or its people. ■ relating to or denoting a Protestant Church founded in Saxony by emigrants from Moravia holding views derived from the Hussites and accepting the Bible as the only source of faith.
▸ **noun** a native or inhabitant of Moravia. ■ a member of the Moravian Church.

Moray /ˈmʌri/ (also **Morayshire** /ˈmʌrɪʃɪə, -ʃə/) a council area and former county of northern Scotland, bordered on the north by the Moray Firth; administrative centre, Elgin.

moray /mɒˈreɪ, ˈmɒreɪ/ (also **moray eel**) ▸ **noun** a mainly nocturnal eel-like predatory fish of warm seas, which typically hides in crevices with just the head protruding. ● Family Muraenidae: several genera and numerous species, including *Muraena helena* of the East Atlantic and Mediterranean.
– ORIGIN early 17th cent.: from Portuguese *moréia*, via Latin from Greek *muraina*.

Moray Firth a deep inlet of the North Sea on the NE coast of Scotland.

morbid ▸ **adjective 1** characterized by an abnormal and unhealthy interest in disturbing and unpleasant subjects, especially death and disease: *his morbid fascination with the horrors of contemporary warfare*.
2 Medicine of the nature of or indicative of disease: *the treatment of morbid obesity*.
– DERIVATIVES **morbidity** noun, **morbidly** adverb, **morbidness** noun.
– ORIGIN mid 17th cent. (in the medical sense): from Latin *morbidus*, from *morbus* 'disease'.

morbid anatomy ▸ **noun** [mass noun] the anatomy of diseased organs and tissues.

morbific /mɔːˈbɪfɪk/ ▸ **adjective** dated causing disease.
– ORIGIN mid 17th cent.: from French *morbifique* or modern Latin *morbificus*, from Latin *morbus* 'disease'.

morbilli /mɔːˈbɪlʌɪ, -liː/ ▸ **plural noun** technical term for **MEASLES**.
– ORIGIN mid 16th cent.: Latin, plural of *morbillus* 'pustule', from *morbus* 'disease'.

morbillivirus /mɔːˈbɪlɪˌvʌɪrəs/ ▸ **noun** Medicine any of a group of paramyxoviruses which causes measles, rinderpest, and canine distemper.
– ORIGIN 1970s: from Latin *morbilli* (plural of *morbillus* 'pustule', from *morbus* 'disease') + **VIRUS**.

morceau /mɔːˈsəʊ/ ▸ **noun** (pl. **morceaux**) a short literary or musical composition.
– ORIGIN mid 18th cent.: French, literally 'morsel, piece'.

morcha /ˈmɔːtʃɑː/ ▸ **noun** Indian an organized march or rally.
– ORIGIN from Hindi *morcā*.

mordacious /mɔːˈdeɪʃəs/ ▸ **adjective** formal **1** denoting or using biting sarcasm or invective.
2 (of a person or animal) given to biting.
– ORIGIN mid 17th cent.: from Latin *mordax*, *mordac-* 'biting' + **-IOUS**.

mordant /ˈmɔːd(ə)nt/ ▸ **adjective** (especially of humour) having or showing a sharp or critical quality; biting: *a mordant sense of humour*.
▸ **noun 1** a substance, typically an inorganic oxide, that combines with a dye or stain and thereby fixes it in a material. ■ an adhesive compound for fixing gold leaf.
2 a corrosive liquid used to etch the lines on a printing plate.
▸ **verb** [with obj.] impregnate or treat (a fabric) with a mordant.
– DERIVATIVES **mordancy** noun, **mordantly** adverb.
– ORIGIN late 15th cent.: from French, present participle of *mordre* 'to bite', from Latin *mordere*.

mordent /ˈmɔːd(ə)nt/ ▸ **noun** Music a rapid alternation of a note with the note immediately below or above it in the scale (sometimes further distinguished as **lower mordent** and **upper mordent**). The term **inverted mordent** usually refers to the upper mordent.
– ORIGIN early 19th cent.: via German from Italian *mordente*, present participle of *mordere* 'to bite'.

Mordred /ˈmɔːdrɪd/ (in Arthurian legend) the nephew of King Arthur who abducted Guinevere and raised a rebellion against Arthur.

Mordvin /ˈmɔːdvɪn/ (also **Mordva** /ˈmɔːdvə/) ▸ **noun** (pl. **same**, **Mordvins**, or **Mordva**) **1** a member of a non-Russian people inhabiting Mordvinia.
2 [mass noun] the Finno-Ugric language of the Mordvin, which has two distinct dialects and over 1 million speakers altogether.
▸ **adjective** relating to the Mordvin or their language.

Mordvinia /mɔːdˈvɪnɪə/ an autonomous republic in European Russia, south-east of Nizhni Novgorod; pop. 835,400 (est. 2009); capital, Saransk. Also called **Mordvinian Autonomous Republic**.

More[1] /mɔː/, Sir Thomas (1478–1535), English scholar and statesman, Lord Chancellor 1529–32; canonized as **St Thomas More**. His *Utopia* (1516), describing an ideal city-state, established him as a leading humanist of the Renaissance. He was imprisoned in 1534 after opposing Henry's marriage to Anne Boleyn, and beheaded for opposing the Act of Supremacy. Feast day, 22 June.

More[2] /ˈmɔːri/ (also **Mooré**) ▸ **noun** [mass noun] the language of the Mossi people of Burkina Faso, a member of the Gur family of languages with about 4 million speakers.
– ORIGIN the name in More.

more ▸ **determiner & pronoun** a greater or additional amount or degree: [as determiner] *some more people arrived* | [as pronoun] *tell me more* | *they proved **more of** a hindrance than a help*.
▸ **adverb 1** forming the comparative of adjectives and adverbs, especially those of more than one syllable: *for them enthusiasm is more important than talent*.
2 to a greater extent: *in his experience females liked chocolate **more than** males did*. ■ **(more than)** extremely (used before an adjective conveying a positive feeling or attitude): *she is more than happy to oblige*.
3 again: *repeat **once more***.
4 moreover: *he was rich, and more, he was handsome*.
– PHRASES **more and more** at a continually increasing rate: *vacancies were becoming more and more rare*. **more like it** see **LIKE**[1]. **more or less** speaking imprecisely; to a certain extent: *they are more or less a waste of time*. ■ approximately: *more or less symmetrical*. **no more 1** nothing further: *there was no more to be said about it*. **2** no further: *you must have some hot soup, but no more wine*. **3 (be no more)** exist no longer. **4** never again: *mention his name no more to me*. **5** neither: *I had no complaints and no more did Tom*.
– ORIGIN Old English *māra*, of Germanic origin; related to Dutch *meer* and German *mehr*.

> **USAGE** It is incorrect to use **more** with an adjective that is already in a comparative form (*more hungrier, more better*); the correct usage is simply *hungrier* (or *more hungry*) or *better*.

Morecambe /ˈmɔːkəm/, Eric (1926–84), English comedian; born *John Eric Bartholomew*. In 1941 he formed a double act with comedian **Ernie Wise** (1925–99) that led to the enduringly popular TV series *The Morecambe and Wise Show* (1961–76).

Morecambe Bay an inlet of the Irish Sea, on the NW coast of England between Cumbria and Lancashire.

moreen /məˈriːn/ (also **morine**) ▸ **noun** [mass noun] a strong, ribbed cotton fabric, used chiefly for curtains.
– ORIGIN mid 17th cent.: perhaps a fanciful formation from **MOIRE**.

moreish ▸ **adjective** Brit. informal so pleasant to eat that one wants more: *a moreish aubergine dip*.

morel /mə'rɛl/ ▶ **noun** a widely distributed edible fungus which has a brown oval or pointed fruiting body with an irregular honeycombed surface bearing the spores. ● Genus *Morchella*, family Morchellaceae, subdivision Ascomycotina: several species, in particular the common *M. esculenta*.
– ORIGIN late 17th cent.: from French *morille*, from Dutch *morilje*; related to German *Morchel* 'fungus'.

Morelia /mɒ'reɪlɪə/ a city in central Mexico, capital of the state of Michoacán; pop. 608,049 (2005). Founded in 1541, it was known as Valladolid until 1828.
– ORIGIN renamed in honour of J. M. *Morelos* y Pavón (1765–1815), a key figure in Mexico's independence movement.

morello /mɒ'rɛləʊ/ ▶ **noun** (pl. **morellos**) a dark cherry of a sour kind used in cooking.
– ORIGIN mid 17th cent.: from Italian *morello* 'blackish', from medieval Latin *morellus*, diminutive of Latin *Maurus* 'Moor'.

Morelos /mə'reɪlɒs/ a state of central Mexico, to the west of Mexico City; capital, Cuernavaca.

moreover ▶ **adverb** as a further matter; besides: *moreover, statistics show that competition for places is growing.*

morepork /'mɔːpɔːk/ ▶ **noun** Austral./NZ another term for **BOOBOOK**.
– ORIGIN variant of **MOPOKE**.

mores /'mɔːreɪz, -riːz/ ▶ **plural noun** the essential or characteristic customs and conventions of a society or community.
– ORIGIN late 19th cent.: from Latin, plural of *mos*, *mor-* 'custom'.

Moresco /mə'rɛskəʊ/ ▶ **noun & adjective** variant spelling of **MORISCO**.

Moresque /mə'rɛsk, mɔː-/ ▶ **adjective** (of art or architecture) Moorish in style or design.
– ORIGIN late Middle English (as a noun denoting arabesque ornament): from French, from Italian *moresco*, from *Moro* 'Moor'.

Moreton Bay chestnut ▶ **noun** a large tree with red and yellow flowers and decorative timber, native to Queensland, Australia. Its heavy pods contain large poisonous seeds yielding an alkaloid that appears to inhibit the AIDS virus. Also called **BLACK BEAN**. ● *Castanospermum australe*, family Leguminosae.
– ORIGIN mid 19th cent.: so named because the tree was first found near *Moreton Bay*, Queensland.

Morgan[1], J. P. (1837–1913), American financier, philanthropist, and art collector; full name *John Pierpont Morgan*. He created General Electric (1891) and the United States Steel Corporation (1901). He bequeathed his large art collection to the Museum of Modern Art in New York.

Morgan[2], Thomas Hunt (1866–1945), American zoologist. His studies on inheritance using the fruit fly *Drosophila* showed that the genetic information was carried by genes arranged along the length of the chromosomes. Nobel Prize for Physiology or Medicine (1933).

Morgan[3] ▶ **noun** a horse of a light thickset breed developed in New England.
– ORIGIN mid 19th cent.: named after Justin *Morgan* (1747–98), American teacher and owner of the original sire of the breed.

morganatic /ˌmɔːgə'natɪk/ ▶ **adjective** relating to or denoting a marriage in which neither the spouse of lower rank, nor any children, have any claim to the possessions or title of the spouse of higher rank.
– DERIVATIVES **morganatically** adverb.
– ORIGIN early 18th cent.: from modern Latin *morganaticus*, from medieval Latin *matrimonium ad morganaticam* 'marriage with a morning gift' (because a morning gift, given by a husband to his wife on the morning after the marriage, was the wife's sole entitlement in a marriage of this kind).

morganite /'mɔːg(ə)nʌɪt/ ▶ **noun** [mass noun] a pink transparent variety of beryl, used as a gemstone.
– ORIGIN early 20th cent.: from the name of J. P. *Morgan* (see **MORGAN**[1]) + **-ITE**[1].

Morgan le Fay /ˌmɔːgən lə 'feɪ/ (in Arthurian legend) an enchantress, sister of King Arthur.

Morgannwg /mɔː'ganʊg/ Welsh name for **GLAMORGAN**.

morgen /'mɔːg(ə)n/ ▶ **noun 1** (in the Netherlands, South Africa, and parts of the US) a measure of land equal to about 0.8 hectare or two acres.
2 (in Norway, Denmark, and Germany) a measure of land now equal to about 0.3 hectare or two thirds of an acre.
– ORIGIN early 17th cent.: from Dutch, or from German *Morgen* 'morning', apparently from the notion of 'an area of land that can be ploughed in a morning'.

morgue /mɔːg/ ▶ **noun 1** a mortuary. ■ used in reference to a place that is quiet, gloomy, or cold: *she put us in that draughty morgue of a sitting room.*
2 informal a newspaper's collection of miscellaneous information for use in future obituaries.
– ORIGIN early 19th cent.: from French, originally the name of a building in Paris where bodies were kept until identified.

MORI /'mɒri/ (also **Mori**) ▶ **abbreviation** trademark Market and Opinion Research International, an organization which carries out opinion polls and other market research: [as modifier] *a MORI poll.*

moribund /'mɒrɪbʌnd/ ▶ **adjective** (of a person) at the point of death. ■ (of a thing) in terminal decline; lacking vitality or vigour: *the moribund commercial property market.*
– DERIVATIVES **moribundity** noun.
– ORIGIN early 18th cent.: from Latin *moribundus*, from *mori* 'to die'.

morine ▶ **noun** variant spelling of **MOREEN**.

morion[1] /'mɒrɪən/ ▶ **noun** a kind of helmet without beaver or visor, worn by soldiers in the 16th and 17th centuries.
– ORIGIN French, from Spanish *morrión*, from *morro* 'round object'.

morion[2] /'mɒrɪən/ ▶ **noun** [mass noun] a brown or black variety of quartz.
– ORIGIN mid 18th cent.: from French, from Latin *morion*, a misreading (in Pliny) for *mormorion*.

Morisco /mə'rɪskəʊ/ (also **Moresco**) ▶ **noun** (pl. **Moriscos** or **Moriscoes**) historical a Moor in Spain, especially one who had accepted Christian baptism.
– ORIGIN Spanish, from *Moro* 'Moor'.

Morisot /'mɒrɪzəʊ/, French /mɔʀizo/, Berthe (Marie Pauline) (1841–95), French painter, the first woman to join the Impressionists. Her works typically depict women and children and waterside scenes.

Morley /'mɔːli/, Edward Williams (1838–1923), American chemist. In 1887 he collaborated with Albert Michelson in an experiment to determine the speed of light, the result of which disproved the existence of the ether. See also **MICHELSON–MORLEY EXPERIMENT**.

Mormon /'mɔːmən/ ▶ **noun** a member of the Church of Jesus Christ of Latter-Day Saints, a religion founded in the US in 1830 by Joseph Smith Jr.

> Joseph Smith claimed to have found and translated *The Book of Mormon* by divine revelation. It tells the story of a group of Hebrews who migrated to America c.600 BC, and is taken as scriptural alongside the Bible. The Mormons came into conflict with the US government over their practice of polygamy (officially abandoned in 1890) and moved their headquarters from Illinois to Salt Lake City, Utah, in 1847 under Smith's successor, Brigham Young. Mormon doctrine emphasizes tithing, missionary work, and the Second Coming of Christ.

– DERIVATIVES **Mormonism** noun.
– ORIGIN the name of a prophet to whom Smith attributed *The Book of Mormon*.

morn ▶ **noun** literary term for **MORNING**.
– ORIGIN Old English *morgen*, of Germanic origin.

mornay /'mɔːneɪ/ ▶ **adjective** denoting or served in a cheese-flavoured white sauce: *mornay sauce* | [postpositive] *cauliflower mornay.*
– ORIGIN perhaps named after *Mornay*, the eldest son of the 19th-cent. French chef Joseph Voiron, who apparently invented the sauce.

morning ▶ **noun** the period of time between midnight and noon, especially from sunrise to noon: *I've got a meeting this morning* | *it was a beautiful sunny morning* | [as modifier] *the morning papers.* ■ sunrise: *a hint of steely light showed that morning was on its way.*
▶ **adverb** (**mornings**) informal every morning: *mornings, she'd sleep late.*
▶ **exclamation** informal short for **GOOD MORNING**.
– PHRASES **the morning after** (**the night before**) humorous the morning after an evening of drinking, when one has a hangover. **morning, noon, and night** all of the time.
– ORIGIN Middle English: from **MORN**, on the pattern of *evening*.

morning-after pill ▶ **noun** a contraceptive pill that is effective up to about seventy-two hours after intercourse.

morning coat ▶ **noun** Brit. a man's formal coat with a long back section cut into tails which curves up to join the waist at the front.

morning dress ▶ **noun** [mass noun] a man's morning coat and striped trousers, worn on formal occasions such as weddings, typically with a top hat.

morning glory ▶ **noun** a climbing plant of the convolvulus family, sometimes cultivated for its trumpet-shaped flowers. ● Genus *Ipomoea*, family Convolvulaceae: several species, in particular the purple-flowered *I. purpureus* of tropical America.

morning prayer ▶ **noun** (usu. **morning prayers**) a formal act of worship held in the morning. ■ (in the Anglican Church) the service of matins.

morning room ▶ **noun** chiefly historical a sitting room used in the morning.

morning sickness ▶ **noun** [mass noun] nausea in pregnancy, typically occurring in the first few months. Despite its name, the nausea can affect pregnant women at any time of day.

Morningside ▶ **adjective** Scottish (of a person's accent or manners) affected and refined.
– ORIGIN 1950s: from the name of a residential district in Edinburgh, Scotland.

morning star ▶ **noun 1** (**the morning star**) a planet, especially Venus, when visible in the east before sunrise.
2 historical a club with a heavy spiked head, sometimes attached to the handle by a chain. [translating German *Morgenstern*, comparing the weapon's spikes to rays of a star.]

morning watch ▶ **noun** the period from 4 to 8 a.m. on board a ship.

Moro /'mɔːrəʊ/ ▶ **noun** (pl. **Moros**) a Muslim inhabitant of the Philippines.
– ORIGIN Spanish, literally 'Moor'.

Morocco /mə'rɒkəʊ/ a country in NW Africa, with coastlines on the Mediterranean Sea and Atlantic Ocean; pop. 31,285,200 (est. 2009); languages, Arabic (official), Berber; capital, Rabat.

> Conquered by the Arabs in the 7th century, Morocco later fell under French and Spanish influence, each country establishing protectorates in the early 20th century. It became an independent monarchy after the withdrawal of the colonial powers in 1956, the sultan becoming king.

– DERIVATIVES **Moroccan** adjective & noun.

morocco ▶ **noun** (pl. **moroccos**) [mass noun] fine flexible leather made (originally in Morocco) from goatskins tanned with sumac, used especially for book covers and shoes.

morocoy /'mɒrəkɔɪ/ ▶ **noun** W. Indian a large tortoise. ● Genus *Geochelone*, family Testudinidae: two species.
– ORIGIN from Spanish *morrocoyo* 'land tortoise'.

moron ▶ **noun** informal a stupid person.
– ORIGIN early 20th cent. (as a medical term denoting an adult with a mental age of about 8–12): from Greek *mōron*, neuter of *mōros* 'foolish'.

Moroni /mə'rəʊni/ the capital of Comoros, on the island of Grande Comore; pop. 46,000 (est. 2007).

moronic ▶ **adjective** informal very foolish or stupid: *television's latest moronic soap opera.*
– DERIVATIVES **moronically** adverb.

morose ▶ **adjective** sullen and ill-tempered: *she was morose and silent when she got home.*
– DERIVATIVES **morosely** adverb, **moroseness** noun.
– ORIGIN mid 16th cent.: from Latin *morosus* 'peevish', from *mos*, *mor-* 'manner'.

Morpeth /'mɔːpəθ/ a town in NE England, the county town of Northumberland; pop. 13,700 (est. 2009).

morph[1] /mɔːf/ ▶ **verb** change smoothly from one image to another by small gradual steps using computer animation techniques: [with obj.] *the characters can be morphed on screen.* ■ undergo or cause to undergo a gradual process of transformation: [no obj.] *the cute moppet has* **morphed into** *the moody moll of the indie world.*
▶ **noun** an image that has been morphed. ■ an instance of morphing an image.
– ORIGIN 1990s: element from **METAMORPHOSIS**.

morph[2] /mɔːf/ ▶ **noun 1** Linguistics an actual linguistic form: *the present participle in English is always the morph '-ing'.*
2 Biology each of several variant forms of an animal or plant.
– ORIGIN 1940s: from Greek *morphē* 'form'.

M

-morph ▶ combining form denoting something having a specified form or character: *endomorph* | *polymorph*.
– ORIGIN from Greek *morphē* 'form'.

morphallaxis /ˌmɔːfəˈlaksɪs/ ▶ noun [mass noun] Zoology regeneration by the transformation of existing body tissues.
– DERIVATIVES **morphallactic** adjective.
– ORIGIN late 19th cent.: from Greek *morphē* 'form' + *allaxis* 'exchange'.

morpheme /ˈmɔːfiːm/ ▶ noun Linguistics a meaningful morphological unit of a language that cannot be further divided (e.g. *in, come, -ing*, forming *incoming*).
– DERIVATIVES **morphemic** adjective, **morphemically** adverb.
– ORIGIN late 19th cent.: from French *morphème*, from Greek *morphē* 'form', on the pattern of French *phonème* 'phoneme'.

morphemics /mɔːˈfiːmɪks/ ▶ plural noun [treated as sing.] Linguistics the study of word structure in terms of minimal meaningful units.

Morpheus /ˈmɔːfɪəs/ Roman Mythology the son of Somnus (god of sleep), the god of dreams and, in later writings, also god of sleep.

morphia /ˈmɔːfɪə/ ▶ noun old-fashioned term for **MORPHINE**.

morphic resonance ▶ noun [mass noun] (according to the theory developed by Rupert Sheldrake, British biologist b.1942) a paranormal influence by which a pattern of events or behaviour can facilitate subsequent occurrences of similar patterns.

morphine /ˈmɔːfiːn/ ▶ noun [mass noun] an analgesic and narcotic drug obtained from opium and used medicinally to relieve pain. ● An alkaloid; chem. formula: $C_{17}H_{19}NO_3$. Compare with **HEROIN**.
– ORIGIN early 19th cent.: from German *Morphin*, from the name of the Roman god *Morpheus* (see **MORPHEUS**).

morpho ▶ noun (pl. **morphos**) a large tropical butterfly, the male of which has bright blue iridescent wings. Native to the Central and South American rainforests, large numbers are caught each year for use in the jewellery trade. ● Genus *Morpho*, subfamily Morphinae, family Nymphalidae.
– ORIGIN modern Latin, from Greek *Morphō*, an epithet of Aphrodite.

M

morphogen /ˈmɔːfədʒ(ə)n/ ▶ noun Biology a chemical agent able to cause or determine morphogenesis.

morphogenesis /ˌmɔːfə(ʊ)ˈdʒɛnɪsɪs/ ▶ noun [mass noun] **1** Biology the origin and development of morphological characteristics.
2 Geology the formation of landforms or other structures.
– DERIVATIVES **morphogenetic** adjective, **morphogenic** adjective.
– ORIGIN late 19th cent.: modern Latin, from Greek *morphē* 'form' + **GENESIS**.

morpholine /ˈmɔːfəliːn/ ▶ noun [mass noun] Chemistry a synthetic compound used as a solvent for resins and dyes and (in the form of salts) as an ingredient of emulsifying soaps used in floor polishes. ● A cyclic amine; chem. formula: C_4H_9NO.
– ORIGIN late 19th cent.: from **MORPHINE**, with the insertion of the syllable *-ol-* (see **-OL**).

morphology /mɔːˈfɒlədʒi/ ▶ noun (pl. **morphologies**) **1** [mass noun] the study of the forms of things, in particular: ■ the branch of biology that deals with the form of living organisms, and with relationships between their structures. ■ Linguistics the study of the forms of words, in particular inflected forms.
2 a particular form, shape, or structure.
– DERIVATIVES **morphologic** adjective, **morphological** adjective, **morphologically** adverb, **morphologist** noun.
– ORIGIN mid 19th cent.: from Greek *morphē* 'form' + **-LOGY**.

morphometrics /ˌmɔːfə(ʊ)ˈmɛtrɪks/ ▶ plural noun [usu. treated as sing.] chiefly Biology morphometry, especially of living organisms.

morphometry /mɔːˈfɒmɪtri/ ▶ noun [mass noun] the process of measuring the external shape and dimensions of landforms, living organisms, or other objects.
– DERIVATIVES **morphometric** adjective, **morphometrically** adverb.

morphophoneme /ˌmɔːfə(ʊ)ˈfəʊniːm/ ▶ noun Phonetics a unit of sound from which all variants of a morpheme can be derived or predicted by rule.
– DERIVATIVES **morphophonemic** adjective.

morphophonemics ▶ noun another term for **MORPHOPHONOLOGY**.

morphophonology /ˌmɔːfə(ʊ)fəˈnɒlədʒi/ ▶ noun [mass noun] the branch of linguistics that deals with the phonological representation of morphemes.
– DERIVATIVES **morphophonological** adjective.

morphosyntactic /ˌmɔːfə(ʊ)sɪnˈtaktɪk/ ▶ adjective Linguistics involving both morphology and syntax.
– DERIVATIVES **morphosyntactically** adverb, **morphosyntax** noun.

Morris[1], William (1834–96), English designer, craftsman, poet, and writer. A leading figure in the Arts and Crafts Movement, in 1861 he established Morris & Company, an association of craftsmen whose members included Edward Burne-Jones and Dante Gabriel Rossetti, to produce handcrafted goods for the home. His many writings include *News from Nowhere* (1891), which portrays a socialist Utopia.

Morris[2], William Richard, see **NUFFIELD**.

Morris chair ▶ noun a type of easy chair with open padded arms and an adjustable back.
– ORIGIN late 19th cent.: named after William *Morris* (see **MORRIS**[1]).

morris dance ▶ noun a lively traditional English dance performed out of doors by groups known as 'sides'. Dancers wear a distinctive costume that is mainly black and white and has small bells attached, and often carry handkerchiefs or sticks.
– DERIVATIVES **morris dancer** noun, **morris dancing** noun.
– ORIGIN late Middle English: *morris* from *morys*, variant of *Moorish* (see **MOOR**); the association with the Moors remains unexplained.

Morrison[1], Jim (1943–71), American rock singer; full name *James Douglas Morrison*. Morrison was the lead singer of the Doors.

Morrison[2], Toni (b.1931), American novelist; full name *Chloe Anthony Morrison*. Her novels depict the black American experience and heritage. *Beloved* (1987) won the Pulitzer Prize, and Morrison became the first black woman writer to receive the Nobel Prize for Literature in 1993.

Morrison[3], Van (b.1945), Northern Irish singer, instrumentalist, and songwriter; full name *George Ivan Morrison*. He developed a distinctive personal style from a background of blues, soul, folk music, and rock. Notable albums: *Astral Weeks* (1968) and *Moondance* (1970).

Morrison shelter ▶ noun historical a movable air-raid shelter, shaped like a table and used indoors.
– ORIGIN named after Herbert S. *Morrison*, UK Secretary of State for Home Affairs and Home Security 1940–5, during which period the shelter was adopted.

morrow ▶ noun (**the morrow**) archaic or literary the following day: *on the morrow they attacked the city.* ■ the time following an event: *in the morrow of great victory.* ■ the near future: *the religious enthusiast who takes no thought for the morrow.*
– ORIGIN Middle English *morwe*, from Old English *morgen* (see **MORN**).

Morse ▶ noun (also **Morse code**) [mass noun] an alphabet or code in which letters are represented by combinations of long and short light or sound signals.
▶ verb [with obj.] signal (something) using Morse code.
– ORIGIN mid 19th cent.: named after Samuel F. B. *Morse* (1791–1872), American inventor.

morsel ▶ noun a small piece or amount of food; a mouthful: *Juliet pushed **a morsel of** toast into her mouth.* ■ a small piece or amount: *there was **a morsel of** consolation for the British team.*
– ORIGIN Middle English: from Old French, diminutive of *mors* 'a bite', from Latin *mors-* 'bitten', from the verb *mordere*.

Morse taper ▶ noun a taper on a shank or socket that is one of a standard series having specified dimensions and angles.
– ORIGIN late 19th cent.: probably named after the *Morse* Twist Drill Co., Massachusetts, US.

mort ▶ noun Hunting, archaic the note sounded on a horn when the quarry is killed.
– ORIGIN Middle English: via Old French from Latin *mors, mort-* 'death'.

mortadella /ˌmɔːtəˈdɛlə/ ▶ noun [mass noun] a type of light pink, smooth-textured Italian sausage containing pieces of fat, typically served in slices.
– ORIGIN Italian diminutive, formed irregularly from Latin *murtatum* '(sausage) seasoned with myrtle berries'.

mortal ▶ adjective **1** (of a living human being, often in contrast to a divine being) subject to death: *all men are mortal.* ■ relating to humans as subject to death: *the coffin held the mortal remains of her uncle.*
2 causing or liable to cause death; fatal: *a mortal disease* | figurative *the scandal appeared to have struck a mortal blow to the government.* ■ (of a battle) fought to the death: *the screams of men in mortal combat.* ■ (of an enemy or a state of hostility) admitting or allowing no reconciliation until death. ■ (of a feeling, especially fear) very intense: *parents live in mortal fear of children's diseases.*
3 informal conceivable or imaginable: *he knew every mortal thing you did.* ■ very great: *he was in a mortal hurry.* ■ dated long and tedious: *for three mortal days it rained.*
4 Christian Theology denoting a grave sin that is regarded as depriving the soul of divine grace. Often contrasted with **VENIAL**.
▶ noun a human being subject to death, as opposed to a divine being. ■ humorous a person contrasted with others regarded as being of higher status or ability: *an ambassador had to live in a style which was not expected of **lesser mortals**.*
– ORIGIN late Middle English: from Old French, or from Latin *mortalis*, from *mors, mort-* 'death'.

mortality ▶ noun (pl. **mortalities**) [mass noun] **1** the state of being subject to death: *the work is increasingly haunted by thoughts of mortality.*
2 death, especially on a large scale: *the causes of mortality among infants and young children.* ■ (also **mortality rate**) the number of deaths in a given area or period, or from a particular cause: *post-operative mortality was 90 per cent for some operations.*
– ORIGIN late Middle English: via Old French from Latin *mortalitas*, from *mortalis* (see **MORTAL**).

mortally ▶ adverb **1** in such a manner as to cause death: *the gunner was mortally wounded.*
2 very intensely or seriously: *I expected him to be mortally offended.*

mortar[1] ▶ noun **1** a short smooth-bore gun for firing shells (technically called bombs) at high angles. ■ a similar device used for firing a lifeline or firework.
2 a cup-shaped receptacle in which ingredients are crushed or ground, used in cooking or pharmacy: *a pestle and mortar.*
▶ verb [with obj.] attack or bombard with a mortar.
– ORIGIN late Old English (in sense 2 of the noun), from Old French *mortier*, from Latin *mortarium* (to which the English spelling was later assimilated).

mortar[2] ▶ noun [mass noun] a mixture of lime with cement, sand, and water, used in building to bond bricks or stones.
▶ verb [with obj.] fix or join using mortar: *the pipe can be mortared in place.*
– DERIVATIVES **mortarless** adjective.
– ORIGIN Middle English: from Old French *mortier*, from Latin *mortarium*, probably a transferred sense of the word denoting a container (see **MORTAR**[1]).

mortar board ▶ noun **1** an academic cap with a stiff, flat, square top and a tassel.
2 a small square board with a handle on the underside, used by bricklayers for holding mortar.

mortarium /mɔːˈtɛːrɪəm/ ▶ noun (pl. **mortaria**) Archaeology a Roman container for pounding or grinding.
– ORIGIN Latin.

mortgage /ˈmɔːɡɪdʒ/ ▶ noun a legal agreement by which a bank, building society, etc. lends money at interest in exchange for taking title of the debtor's property, with the condition that the conveyance of title becomes void upon the payment of the debt: *I put down a hundred thousand in cash and took out a mortgage for the rest.* ■ the amount of money borrowed in a mortgage: *a £60,000 mortgage.* ■ a deed effecting a mortgage.
▶ verb [with obj.] convey (a property) to a creditor as security on a loan. ■ expose to future risk or constraint for the sake of immediate advantage: *some people worry that selling off state assets mortgages the country's future.*
– DERIVATIVES **mortgageable** adjective.
– ORIGIN late Middle English: from Old French, literally 'dead pledge', from *mort* (from Latin *mortuus* 'dead') + *gage* 'pledge'.

mortgagee ▶ noun the lender in a mortgage, typically a bank, building society, or savings and loan association.

mortgage rate ▶ noun the rate of interest charged by a mortgage lender.

mortgagor /ˌmɔːɡɪˈdʒɔː/ ▶ noun the borrower in a mortgage, typically a homeowner.

mortice ▶ **noun & verb** variant spelling of MORTISE.

mortician /mɔːˈtɪʃ(ə)n/ ▶ **noun** N. Amer. an undertaker.
– ORIGIN late 19th cent.: from Latin *mors*, *mort-* 'death' + -ICIAN.

mortification ▶ **noun** [mass noun] **1** great embarrassment and shame: *they mistook my mortification for an admission of guilt.*
2 the action of subduing one's bodily desires: *mortification of the flesh has a long tradition in some religions.*

mortify /ˈmɔːtɪfʌɪ/ ▶ **verb** (**mortifies, mortifying, mortified**) [with obj.] **1** cause (someone) to feel very embarrassed or ashamed: *she was mortified to see her wrinkles in the mirror* | (as adj. **mortifying**) *how mortifying to find that he was right.*
2 subdue (the body or its needs and desires) by self-denial or discipline: *return to heaven by mortifying the flesh.*
3 [no obj.] (of flesh) be affected by gangrene or necrosis.
– DERIVATIVES **mortifyingly** adverb.
– ORIGIN late Middle English (in the senses 'put to death', 'deaden', and 'subdue by self-denial'): from Old French *mortifier*, from ecclesiastical Latin *mortificare* 'kill, subdue', from *mors*, *mort-* 'death'.

Mortimer, Roger de, 8th Baron of Wigmore and 1st Earl of March (*c.*1287–1330), English noble. In 1326 he invaded England with his lover Isabella of France, replacing her husband Edward II with her son, the future Edward III. When Edward III assumed royal power in 1330 he had Mortimer executed.

mortise /ˈmɔːtɪs/ (also **mortice**) ▶ **noun** a hole or recess cut into a part which is designed to receive a corresponding projection (a tenon) on another part so as to join or lock the parts together.
▶ **verb** [with obj.] join securely by using a mortise and tenon. ■ (often as adj. **mortised**) cut a mortise in or through: *the mortised ports.*
– DERIVATIVES **mortiser** noun.
– ORIGIN late Middle English: from Old French *mortaise*.

mortise lock ▶ **noun** a lock which is set within the body of a door in a recess or mortise, as opposed to one attached to the door surface.

mortmain /ˈmɔːtmeɪn/ ▶ **noun** [mass noun] Law the status of lands or tenements held inalienably by an ecclesiastical or other corporation.
– ORIGIN late Middle English: from Anglo-Norman French, Old French *mortemain*, from medieval Latin *mortua manus* 'dead hand' (probably alluding to impersonal ownership).

Morton[1], Jelly Roll (1885–1941), American jazz pianist, composer, and bandleader; born *Ferdinand Joseph La Menthe Morton*. He was one of the principal links between ragtime and New Orleans jazz.

Morton[2], John (*c.*1420–1500), English prelate and statesman. He was appointed Archbishop of Canterbury in 1486 and Chancellor under Henry VII a year later. The Crown's stringent taxation policies made the regime in general and Morton in particular widely unpopular.

Morton's Fork an argument used by John Morton in demanding gifts for the royal treasury: if a man lived well he was obviously rich and if he lived frugally then he must have savings. ■ a dilemma, especially one in which both choices are equally undesirable.

mortuary /ˈmɔːtjʊəri, -tʃʊ-/ ▶ **noun** (pl. **mortuaries**) a room or building in which dead bodies are kept, for hygienic storage or for examination, until burial or cremation.
▶ **adjective** relating to burial or tombs: *mortuary rituals* | *a mortuary temple.*
– ORIGIN late Middle English (denoting a gift claimed by a parish priest from a deceased person's estate): from Latin *mortuarius*, from *mortuus* 'dead'. The current noun sense dates from the mid 19th cent.

morula /ˈmɔːr(j)ʊlə/ ▶ **noun** (pl. **morulae** /-liː/) Embryology a solid ball of cells resulting from division of a fertilized ovum, and from which a blastula is formed.
– ORIGIN mid 19th cent.: modern Latin, diminutive of Latin *morum* 'mulberry'.

morwong /ˈmɔːwɒŋ/ ▶ **noun** a marine fish of Australian waters, typically brightly coloured and sometimes commercially fished. ● *Nemadactylus* and other genera, family Cheilodactylidae.
– ORIGIN late 19th cent.: probably from a New South Wales Aboriginal language.

Mosaic /məʊˈzeɪɪk/ ▶ **adjective** of or associated with Moses.
– ORIGIN mid 17th cent.: from French *mosaïque* or modern Latin *Mosaicus*.

mosaic /mə(ʊ)ˈzeɪɪk/ ▶ **noun 1** a picture or pattern produced by arranging together small pieces of stone, tile, glass, etc.: *mosaics on the interior depict scenes from the Old Testament* | [mass noun] *the walls and vaults are decorated by marble and mosaic.* ■ a colourful and variegated pattern: *the bird's plumage was a mosaic of slate-grey, blue, and brown.* ■ a combination of diverse elements forming a more or less coherent whole: *a cultural mosaic.* ■ an arrangement of photosensitive elements in a television camera.
2 Biology an individual (especially an animal) composed of cells of two genetically different types.
3 (also **mosaic disease**) a virus disease that results in leaf variegation in tobacco, maize, sugar cane, and other plants.
▶ **verb** (**mosaics, mosaicking, mosaicked**) [with obj.] decorate with a mosaic: (as adj. **mosaicked**) *the mosaicked swimming pool.* ■ combine (distinct or disparate elements) to form a picture or pattern.
▶ **adjective** Biology denoting an individual composed of cells of two genetically different types.
– DERIVATIVES **mosaicist** noun.
– ORIGIN late Middle English: from French *mosaïque*, based on Latin *musi(v)um* decoration with small square stones, perhaps ultimately from Greek *mousa* 'a muse'.

mosaic gold ▶ **noun** [mass noun] an imitation gold pigment consisting of tin disulphide.

mosaicism /məʊˈzeɪɪsɪz(ə)m/ ▶ **noun** [mass noun] Biology the property or state of being composed of cells of two genetically different types.

Mosaic Law ▶ **noun** another term for THE LAW OF MOSES (see LAW (sense 4)).

Mosander /mɒˈsandə/, Carl Gustaf (1797–1858), Swedish chemist. Mosander continued Berzelius's work on the rare earth elements and discovered the new elements lanthanum, erbium, and terbium, and the supposed element didymium.

mosasaur /ˈməʊzəsɔː/ ▶ **noun** a large fossil marine reptile of the late Cretaceous period, with large toothed jaws, paddle-like limbs, and a long flattened tail, related to the monitor lizards. ● Family Mosasauridae, suborder Lacertilia: several genera, including *Mosasaurus*.
– ORIGIN mid 19th cent.: from modern Latin *Mosasaurus*, from Latin *Mosa*, 'Meuse' (the river near which it was first discovered) + Greek *sauros* 'lizard'.

mosbolletjie /mɒsˈbɒləki/ ▶ **noun** (pl. **mosbolletjies**) S. African a semi-sweet bun eaten fresh or dried.
– ORIGIN Afrikaans, from Dutch *most* 'new wine' (because the yeast is of partially fermented grape juice) + *bolletje* 'little ball'.

moscato /mɒˈskɑːtəʊ/ ▶ **noun** [mass noun] a sweet Italian dessert wine.
– ORIGIN Italian; related to MUSCAT.

moschatel /ˌmɒskəˈtɛl/ ▶ **noun** a small plant of north temperate regions, with pale green musk-scented flowers which grow at right angles to each other, forming five sides of a cube. ● *Adoxa moschatellina*, family Adoxaceae.
– ORIGIN mid 18th cent.: from French *moscatelle*, from Italian *moscatella*, from *moscato* 'musk'.

Moscow /ˈmɒskəʊ/ the capital of Russia, situated at the centre of the vast plain of European Russia, on the River Moskva; pop. 10,470,300 (est. 2008). Russian name MOSKVA.

> Moscow became the capital when Ivan the Terrible proclaimed himself the first tsar of Russia in the 16th century. Peter the Great moved his capital to St Petersburg in 1712, but after the Bolshevik Revolution of 1917 Moscow was made the capital of the Soviet Union and seat of the new Soviet government, with its centre in the Kremlin.

Mosel /ˈməʊz(ə)l/ (also **Moselle**) a river of western Europe, which rises in the Vosges mountains of NE France and flows 550 km (346 miles) north-east through Luxembourg and Germany to meet the Rhine at Koblenz.

Moseley /ˈməʊzli/, Henry Gwyn Jeffreys (1887–1915), English physicist. He determined the atomic numbers of elements from their X-ray spectra, demonstrated that an element's chemical properties are determined by this number, and showed that there are only ninety-two naturally occurring elements.

Moselle /mə(ʊ)ˈzɛl/ (also **Mosel**) ▶ **noun** [mass noun] a light medium-dry white wine produced in the valley of the River Moselle (see MOSEL).

Moses[1] (*fl.* *c.*14th–13th centuries BC), Hebrew prophet and lawgiver, brother of Aaron. According to the biblical account, he was born in Egypt and led the Israelites away from servitude there, across the desert towards the Promised Land. During the journey he was inspired by God on Mount Sinai to write down the Ten Commandments on tablets of stone (Exod. 20).

Moses[2], Grandma (1860–1961), American painter; byname of *Anna Mary Robertson Moses*. She took up painting as a hobby when widowed in 1927, producing more than a thousand paintings in naive style, mostly of American rural life.

Moses basket ▶ **noun** a carrycot or small portable cot made of wickerwork.
– ORIGIN *Moses*, with allusion to the biblical story of Moses, left in a basket among the bulrushes as a baby (Exod. 2:3).

mosey informal ▶ **verb** (**mosey, moseying, moseyed**) [no obj., with adverbial of direction] walk or move in a leisurely manner: *we decided to mosey on up to Montgomery.*
▶ **noun** chiefly Brit. a leisurely walk or drive: *I'll just have a mosey round.*
– ORIGIN early 19th cent. (originally US): of unknown origin. The original sense was 'go away quickly'.

MOSFET ▶ **noun** Electronics a field-effect transistor in which there is a thin layer of silicon oxide between the gate and the channel.
– ORIGIN 1960s: acronym from *metal oxide semiconductor field-effect transistor*.

mosh /mɒʃ/ ▶ **verb** [no obj.] informal dance to rock music in a violent manner involving jumping up and down and deliberately colliding with other dancers.
– ORIGIN 1980s: perhaps from MASH or MUSH[1].

moshav /ˈməʊʃɑːv, məʊˈʃɑːv/ ▶ **noun** (pl. **moshavim**) a cooperative association of Israeli smallholders.
– ORIGIN from Hebrew *mōšāḇ*, literally 'dwelling'.

mosh pit ▶ **noun** informal an area in front of the stage at a rock concert, where moshing occurs.

Moskva /maˈskva/ Russian name for MOSCOW.

Moslem /ˈmɒzləm/ ▶ **noun & adjective** variant spelling of MUSLIM.

Mosley /ˈməʊzli/, Sir Oswald (Ernald), 6th Baronet (1896–1980), English Fascist leader. Successively a Conservative, Independent, and Labour MP, he founded the British Union of Fascists, also known as the Blackshirts, in 1932. The party was effectively destroyed by the Public Order Act of 1936. In 1948 Mosley founded the right-wing Union Movement.
– DERIVATIVES **Mosleyite** noun & adjective.

M

Mosotho /məˈsuːtuː/ singular form of BASOTHO.

mosque ▶ **noun** a Muslim place of worship.

> Mosques consist of an area reserved for communal prayers, frequently in a domed building with a minaret, and with a niche (mihrab) or other structure indicating the direction of Mecca. There may also be a platform for preaching (minbar), and an adjacent courtyard in which water is provided for the obligatory ablutions before prayer.

– ORIGIN late Middle English: from French *mosquée*, via Italian and Spanish from Egyptian Arabic *masgid*.

Mosquito ▶ **noun** (pl. **Mosquitos**) & **adjective** variant spelling of MISKITO.

mosquito ▶ **noun** (pl. **mosquitoes**) a slender long-legged fly with aquatic larvae. The bite of the blood-sucking female can transmit a number of serious diseases including malaria and elephantiasis. ● *Culex*, *Anopheles*, and other genera, family Culicidae.
– ORIGIN late 16th cent.: from Spanish and Portuguese, diminutive of *mosca*, from Latin *musca* 'fly'.

Mosquito Coast a sparsely populated coastal strip of swamp, lagoon, and tropical forest comprising the Caribbean coast of Nicaragua and NE Honduras, occupied by the Miskito people after whom it is named.

mosquito coil ▶ **noun** a spiral made from a dried paste of pyrethrum powder, which when lit burns slowly to produce a mosquito-repellent smoke.

mosquito fish ▶ **noun** another term for GAMBUSIA.

mosquito net ▶ **noun** a fine net hung across a door or window or around a bed to keep mosquitoes away.

Moss, Sir Stirling (b.1929), English motor-racing driver. He won various Grands Prix and other competitions in the 1950s, though the world championship eluded him.

moss ▶ **noun 1** [mass noun] a small flowerless green plant which lacks true roots, growing in low carpets or rounded cushions in damp habitats and reproducing

by means of spores released from stalked capsules. ● Class Musci, division Bryophyta.
■ used in names of algae, lichens, and higher plants resembling moss, e.g. **reindeer moss**, **Ceylon moss**, **Spanish moss**.
2 (also **moss green**) [mass noun] a green colour like that of moss.
3 Scottish & N. English a bog, especially a peat bog.
▶ **verb** [with obj.] (usu. as adj. **mossed**) cover with moss.
– DERIVATIVES **moss-like** adjective.
– ORIGIN Old English *mos* 'bog or moss', of Germanic origin; related to Dutch *mos* and German *Moos*.

Mossad /mɒˈsad/ **1** the Supreme Institution for Intelligence and Special Assignments, the principal secret intelligence service of the state of Israel, founded in 1951.
2 the Institution for the Second Immigration, an organization formed in 1938 for the purpose of bringing Jews from Europe to Palestine.
– ORIGIN from Hebrew *mōsāḏ* 'institution'.

moss agate ▶ **noun** [mass noun] agate with moss-like dendritic markings.

moss animal ▶ **noun** a sedentary colonial aquatic animal found chiefly in the sea, either encrusting rocks, seaweeds, or other surfaces, or forming stalked fronds. Each minute zooid filter-feeds by means of a crown of ciliated tentacles (lophophore). Also called **BRYOZOAN**, **POLYZOAN**, **ECTOPROCT**. ● Phylum Bryozoa (or Polyzoa, Ectoprocta).

mossback ▶ **noun** N. Amer. informal an old-fashioned or extremely conservative person.

Mössbauer effect /ˈmɜːsbaʊə/ ▶ **noun** Chemistry an effect in which certain atomic nuclei bound in a crystal emit gamma rays of sharply defined frequency which can be used as a probe of energy levels in other nuclei.
– ORIGIN 1960s: named after Rudolf L. *Mössbauer* (born 1929), German physicist.

moss campion ▶ **noun** an almost stemless campion with pink flowers, found on mountains and in arctic areas of both Eurasia and North America. ● *Silene acaulis*, family Caryophyllaceae.

M

moss-grown ▶ **adjective** overgrown with moss.

moss hag ▶ **noun** Scottish an area of broken ground or a hole from which peat has been taken.

Mossi /ˈmɒsi/ ▶ **noun** (pl. **same** or **Mossis**) a member of a people of Burkina Faso in West Africa. Their language is More.
▶ **adjective** relating to the Mossi.
– ORIGIN the name in More.

mossie ▶ **noun** (pl. **mossies**) **1** South African term for **CAPE SPARROW**. [Afrikaans, from Dutch *mosje* 'little sparrow'.]
2 variant spelling of **MOZZIE**.

mosso /ˈmɒsəʊ/ ▶ **adverb** Music (especially as a direction) fast and with animation.
– ORIGIN Italian, past participle of *muovere* 'move'.

moss stitch ▶ **noun** [mass noun] alternate plain and purl stitches in knitting.

mosstrooper ▶ **noun** a person who lived by plundering property in the Scottish Borders during the 17th century.

mossy ▶ **adjective** (**mossier**, **mossiest**) **1** covered in or resembling moss: *mossy tree trunks*.
2 US informal old-fashioned or extremely conservative.
– DERIVATIVES **mossiness** noun.

mossy cyphel ▶ **noun** another term for **CYPHEL**.

most ▶ **determiner & pronoun** greatest in amount or degree: [as determiner] *they've had the most success* | [as pronoun] *she had the most to lose*. ■ the majority of; nearly all of: [as determiner] *the two-pin sockets found in most European countries* | [as pronoun] *I spent most of the winter on the coast*.
▶ **adverb 1** forming the superlative of adjectives and adverbs, especially those of more than one syllable: *the most important event of my life* | *he was the most ambitious of all*.
2 to the greatest extent: *the things he most enjoyed* | *what she wanted most of all*.
3 extremely; very: *it was most kind of you* | *that is most probably correct*.
4 N. Amer. informal almost: *most everyone understood*.
– PHRASES **at (the) most** not more than: *the walk took four minutes at the most*. **be the most** informal be the best of all. **for the most part** in most cases; usually: *the older members, for the most part, shun him*. **make the most of** use to the best advantage: *he was eager to make the most of his visit*. ■ represent at its best: *how to make the most of your features*.
– ORIGIN Old English *māst*, of Germanic origin; related to Dutch *meest* and German *meist*.

-most ▶ **suffix** forming superlative adjectives and adverbs from prepositions and other words indicating relative position: *innermost* | *uppermost*.
– ORIGIN Old English *-mest*, assimilated to **MOST**.

Mostar /mɒsˈtɑː/ a largely Muslim city in Bosnia and Herzegovina south-west of Sarajevo, the chief town of Herzegovina; pop. 111,116 (2008). Its chief landmark, an old Turkish bridge across the River Neretva, was destroyed during the siege of the city by Croat forces in 1993; its rebuilding was completed in 2004.

mostest ▶ **pronoun** humorous most: *the winner is the person who can get there quickest with the mostest*.

most favoured nation ▶ **noun** a country which has been granted the most favourable trading terms available by another country.

Most Honourable ▶ **noun** (in the UK) a title given to marquesses, members of the Privy Council, and holders of the Order of the Bath.

mostly ▶ **adverb** as regards the greater part or number: *the culprits are mostly, but not exclusively, male*. ■ usually; generally: *I made some good friends, but mostly met closed-minded people*.

Most Reverend ▶ **noun** the title of an Anglican archbishop or an Irish Roman Catholic bishop.

most significant bit (abbrev.: **MSB**) ▶ **noun** Computing the bit in a binary number which is of the greatest numerical value.

Mosul /ˈməʊsʊl/ a city in northern Iraq, on the River Tigris, opposite the ruins of Nineveh; pop. 1,316,000 (est. 2007).

MOT ▶ **noun** (pl. **MOTs**) (also **MOT test**) (in the UK) a compulsory annual test for safety and exhaust emissions of motor vehicles of more than a specified age. ■ (also **MOT certificate**) a document certifying that a vehicle has passed the MOT test.
– ORIGIN abbreviation of *Ministry of Transport*, which introduced the original test.

mot¹ /məʊ/, French /mo/ ▶ **noun** (pl. pronunc. **same** or /məʊz/) short for **BON MOT**.

mot² /mɒt/ ▶ **noun** Irish informal a girl or young woman, especially a man's girlfriend.
– ORIGIN mid 16th cent.: of unknown origin.

mote ▶ **noun** a tiny piece of a substance; a speck: *the tiniest mote of dust*.
– PHRASES **a mote in someone's eye** a minor fault in a person observed by someone who ignores a greater fault in themselves. [with biblical allusion to Matt. 7:3.]
– ORIGIN Old English *mot*, related to Dutch *mot* 'dust, sawdust'.

motel ▶ **noun** a roadside hotel designed primarily for motorists, typically having the rooms arranged in low blocks with parking directly outside.
– ORIGIN 1920s: blend of **MOTOR** and **HOTEL**.

motet /məʊˈtɛt/ ▶ **noun** a short piece of sacred choral music.
– ORIGIN late Middle English: from Old French, diminutive of *mot* 'word'.

moth ▶ **noun** an insect with two pairs of broad wings covered in microscopic scales, typically drably coloured and held flat when at rest. Moths are chiefly nocturnal, and lack the clubbed antennae of butterflies. ● Most superfamilies of the order Lepidoptera. Formerly placed in a grouping known as the Heterocera.
■ informal a clothes moth.
– PHRASES **like a moth to the flame** with an irresistible attraction for someone or something: *he drew women to him like moths to the flame*.
– ORIGIN Old English *moththe*, of Germanic origin; related to Dutch *mot* and German *Motte*.

mothball ▶ **noun** (usu. **mothballs**) a small pellet of a pungent substance, typically naphthalene, put in among stored garments to keep away clothes moths.
▶ **verb** [with obj.] **1** store (clothes) with mothballs.
2 stop using (a piece of equipment or a building) but keep it in good condition so that it can readily be used again. ■ cancel or postpone work on (a plan or project): *plans to invest in four superstores have been mothballed*.
– PHRASES **in mothballs** unused but kept in good condition for future use.

moth-eaten ▶ **adjective** damaged or destroyed by clothes moths. ■ shabby, old, or in bad condition: *moth-eaten donkeys and horses*.

mother /ˈmʌðə/ ▶ **noun 1** a woman in relation to a child or children to whom she has given birth. ■ a female animal in relation to its offspring: [as modifier] *a mother penguin*. ■ archaic (especially as a form of address) an elderly woman. ■ [as modifier] denoting an institution or organization from which others of the same type derive: *the initiatives were based on the experience of the mother company*. ■ informal an extreme example or very large specimen of something: *I got stuck in the mother of all traffic jams*.
2 (**Mother**, **Mother Superior**, or **Reverend Mother**) (especially as a title or form of address) the head of a female religious community.
3 vulgar slang, chiefly N. Amer. short for **MOTHERFUCKER**.
▶ **verb** [with obj.] **1** (often as noun **mothering**) bring up (a child) with care and affection: *the art of mothering*. ■ look after (someone) kindly and protectively, sometimes excessively so: *she mothered her husband, insisting he should take cod liver oil in the winter*.
2 dated give birth to.
– DERIVATIVES **motherhood** noun, **motherless** adjective **mother-like** adjective & adverb.
– ORIGIN Old English *mōdor*, of Germanic origin; related to Dutch *moeder* and German *Mutter*, from an Indo-European root shared by Latin *mater* and Greek *mētēr*.

motherboard (also **mainboard**) ▶ **noun** Computing a printed circuit board containing the principal components of a computer or other device, with connectors for other circuit boards to be slotted into.

Mother Carey's chicken ▶ **noun** old-fashioned term for **STORM PETREL**.
– ORIGIN mid 18th cent.: of unknown origin.

mother country ▶ **noun** a country in relation to its colonies.

mothercraft ▶ **noun** [mass noun] archaic skill in or knowledge of looking after children as a mother.

Mother Earth ▶ **noun** the earth considered as the source of all its living beings and natural features.

mother figure ▶ **noun** an older woman who is regarded as a source of nurture and support.

motherfucker ▶ **noun** vulgar slang, chiefly N. Amer. a despicable or very unpleasant person or thing.
– DERIVATIVES **motherfucking** adjective.

mother goddess ▶ **noun** a mother-figure deity, a central figure of many early nature cults where maintenance of fertility was of prime religious importance. Examples of such goddesses include Isis, Astarte, Cybele, and Demeter.

mother hen ▶ **noun** informal a person who sees to the needs of others, especially in a fussy or interfering way.

mother house ▶ **noun** the founding house of a religious order.

Mother Hubbard ▶ **noun** chiefly US a woman's long, loose-fitting, shapeless dress or undergarment.
– ORIGIN so named from early illustrations of the nursery rhyme.

Mothering Sunday ▶ **noun** Brit. the fourth Sunday in Lent, traditionally a day for visiting or giving a present to one's mother.

mother-in-law ▶ **noun** (pl. **mothers-in-law**) the mother of one's husband or wife.

mother-in-law's tongue ▶ **noun** a West African plant of the agave family, which has long slender leaves with yellow marginal stripes. ● *Sansevieria trifasciata*, family Agavaceae.

motherland ▶ **noun** one's native country.

mother liquor ▶ **noun** [mass noun] Chemistry the liquid remaining after a substance has crystallized out.

mother lode ▶ **noun** Mining a principal vein of an ore or mineral. ■ a rich source of something: *your portfolio holds a mother lode of opportunities*.

motherly ▶ **adjective** of, resembling, or characteristic of a mother, especially in being caring, protective, and kind: *she held both her arms wide in a gesture of motherly love*.
– DERIVATIVES **motherliness** noun.
– ORIGIN Old English *mōdorlic* (see **MOTHER**, **-LY¹**).

mother-naked ▶ **adjective** completely naked.

Mother Nature ▶ **noun** nature personified as a creative and controlling force affecting the world and humans.

Mother of God a name given to the Virgin Mary (as mother of the divine Christ).

mother-of-pearl ▶ **noun** [mass noun] a smooth shining iridescent substance forming the inner layer of the shell of some molluscs, especially oysters and abalones, used in ornamentation.

mother of thousands ▶ **noun** any of a number of small-leaved prolific creeping plants, in particular: ● another term for **IVY-LEAVED TOADFLAX** (see **TOADFLAX**) ● another term for **MIND-YOUR-OWN-BUSINESS**.

Mother's Day ▶ **noun** a day of the year on which mothers are particularly honoured by their children. In North America and South Africa it is the second Sunday in May; in Britain it has become another term for Mothering Sunday.

mother's help ▶ **noun** a person who helps a mother, mainly by looking after children.

mother ship ▶ **noun** a large spacecraft or ship from which smaller craft are launched or maintained. ■ a place regarded as a base, source, or headquarters: *the Battersea Art Centre, the mother ship of experimental theatre.*

Mother Shipton ▶ **noun** a day-flying European moth with a marking on the wing that is said to resemble the crone-like profile of a legendary English seer. ● *Callistega mi*, family Noctuidae.

mother's milk ▶ **noun** [mass noun] something regarded as absolutely necessary or appropriate: *the bottom line is work and that is mother's milk to any performer.*

mother's ruin ▶ **noun** [mass noun] Brit. informal gin.

mother's son ▶ **noun** informal a man: *every mother's son personally knew his friendly local CIA agent.*

Mother Superior ▶ **noun** the head of a female religious community.

Mother Teresa see **TERESA, MOTHER**.

mother-to-be ▶ **noun** (pl. **mothers-to-be**) a woman who is expecting a baby.

mother tongue ▶ **noun** the language which a person has grown up speaking from early childhood.

mother wit ▶ **noun** [mass noun] natural ability to cope with everyday matters; common sense.

motherwort ▶ **noun** a tall strong-smelling European plant of the mint family. It is used in herbal medicine, especially in the treatment of gynaecological disorders. ● *Leonurus cardiaca*, family Labiatae.

mothproof ▶ **adjective** (of clothes or fabric) treated with a substance which repels moths.
▶ **verb** [with obj.] treat (clothes or fabric) with a substance which repels moths.

mothy ▶ **adjective** (**mothier**, **mothiest**) infested with or damaged by moths: *tattered mothy curtains.*

motif /məʊˈtiːf/ ▶ **noun 1** a decorative image or design, especially a repeated one forming a pattern: *the colourful hand-painted motifs which adorn narrowboats.* ■ a decorative device applied to a garment or textile.
2 a dominant or recurring idea in an artistic work: *superstition is a recurring motif in the book.* ■ Music a leitmotif or figure (see **FIGURE** (sense 5 of the noun)).
3 Biochemistry a distinctive sequence on a protein or DNA, having a three-dimensional structure that allows binding interactions to occur.
– ORIGIN mid 19th cent.: from French.

motile /ˈməʊtʌɪl/ ▶ **adjective 1** Zoology & Botany (of cells, gametes, and single-celled organisms) capable of motion.
2 Psychology relating to or characterized by responses that involve muscular rather than audiovisual sensations.
– DERIVATIVES **motility** noun.
– ORIGIN mid 19th cent.: from Latin *motus* 'motion', on the pattern of *mobile*.

Motion, Sir Andrew (b.1952), English poet. His first collection of lyrical poems *The Pleasure Steamers* (1978) was published to critical acclaim; later work includes *Love in a Life* (1991) and *Public Property* (2002). He was Poet Laureate 1999–2009.

motion ▶ **noun 1** [mass noun] the action or process of moving or being moved: *the laws of planetary motion | a cushioned shoe that doesn't restrict motion | flowing blonde hair that was constantly* ***in motion***. ■ [count noun] a gesture: *she made a motion with her free hand.* ■ [count noun] a piece of moving mechanism: *the earliest engines had the Gresley conjugated motion for the middle cylinder.*
2 a formal proposal put to a legislature or committee: *opposition parties* ***tabled a*** *no-confidence* ***motion***. ■ Law an application for a rule or order of court.
3 Brit. an evacuation of the bowels.
▶ **verb** [with obj. and adverbial of direction] direct or command (someone) with a movement of the hand or head: *he motions her towards the lift* | [with obj. and infinitive] *he motioned the young officer to sit down.*
– PHRASES **go through the motions 1** do something perfunctorily, without any enthusiasm or commitment. **2** simulate an action: *a child goes through the motions of washing up.* **set in motion** start something moving or working. ■ start or trigger a process or series of events: *plunging oil prices set in motion an economic collapse.*
– DERIVATIVES **motional** adjective.
– ORIGIN late Middle English: via Old French from Latin *motio(n-)*, from *movere* 'to move'.

motionless ▶ **adjective** not moving; stationary: *an eagle hung almost motionless close to the ground.*
– DERIVATIVES **motionlessly** adverb.

motion picture ▶ **noun** chiefly N. Amer. a cinema film: [as modifier] *the motion-picture industry.*

motion sickness ▶ **noun** [mass noun] nausea caused by motion, especially by travelling in a vehicle.

motivate ▶ **verb** [with obj.] **1** provide (someone) with a reason for doing something: *he was primarily motivated by the desire for profit.* ■ cause (someone) to have interest in or enthusiasm for something: *it is the teacher's job to motivate the child at school.*
2 S. African request (something) and present facts and arguments in support of one's request: *he said he would motivate funds to upgrade the food stalls.*
– DERIVATIVES **motivator** noun.

motivation ▶ **noun 1** a reason or reasons for acting or behaving in a particular way: *escape can be a strong motivation for travel.* ■ [mass noun] desire or willingness to do something; enthusiasm: *keep staff up to date and maintain interest and motivation.*
2 S. African a set of facts and arguments used in support of a proposal.
– DERIVATIVES **motivational** adjective, **motivationally** adverb.
– ORIGIN late 19th cent.: from **MOTIVE**, reinforced by **MOTIVATE**.

motive ▶ **noun 1** a reason for doing something: *police were unable to establish a motive for his murder.*
2 a motif in art, literature, or music.
▶ **adjective** [attrib.] **1** producing physical or mechanical motion: *the charge of gas is the motive force for every piston stroke.*
2 causing or being the reason for something: *the motive principle of a writer's work.*
– DERIVATIVES **motiveless** adjective **motivity** /-ˈtɪvɪti/ noun.
– ORIGIN late Middle English: from Old French *motif* (adjective used as a noun), from late Latin *motivus*, from *movere* 'to move'.

motive power ▶ **noun** [mass noun] the energy (in the form of steam, electricity, etc.) used to drive machinery. ■ the locomotives of a railway system collectively.

motivic /ˈməʊtɪvɪk/ ▶ **adjective** Music relating to a motif or motifs.

mot juste /məʊ ˈʒuːst/, French /mo ʒyst/ ▶ **noun** (pl. **mots justes** pronunc. **same**) (**the mot juste**) the exact, appropriate word.
– ORIGIN French.

Motlanthe /mɒtˈlanteɪ/, Kgalema (b.1949), South African statesman, President 2008–9.

motley /ˈmɒtli/ ▶ **adjective** (**motlier**, **motliest**)
1 incongruously varied in appearance or character; disparate: ***a motley crew*** *of discontents and zealots.*
2 archaic (of clothing) made up of a variety of colours.
▶ **noun 1** [usu. in sing.] an incongruous mixture: *a motley of interacting interest groups.*
2 [mass noun] historical the multicoloured costume of a jester: *life-size mannequins in full motley.*
– ORIGIN late Middle English: of unknown origin; perhaps ultimately related to **MOTE**.

motmot /ˈmɒtmɒt/ ▶ **noun** a tree-dwelling tropical American bird with colourful plumage, typically having two long racket-like tail feathers. ● Family Momotidae: several genera and species, in particular the widespread **blue-crowned motmot** (*Momotus momota*).
– ORIGIN mid 19th cent.: from Latin American Spanish, of imitative origin.

motocross ▶ **noun** [mass noun] cross-country racing on motorcycles.
– DERIVATIVES **motocrosser** noun.
– ORIGIN 1950s: abbreviation of **MOTOR** + **CROSS**.

motoneuron /ˌməʊtə(ʊ)ˈnjʊərɒn/ ▶ **noun** another term for **MOTOR NEURON**.

moto perpetuo /ˌməʊtəʊ pəˈpɛtjʊəʊ/ ▶ **noun** (pl. **moto perpetui**) a piece of fast-moving instrumental music consisting mainly of notes of equal length.
– ORIGIN Italian, literally 'perpetual motion'.

motor ▶ **noun 1** a machine, especially one powered by electricity or internal combustion, that supplies motive power for a vehicle or for another device with moving parts. ■ a source of power, energy, or motive force: *hormones are the motor of the sexual functions.*
2 Brit. informal a car.
▶ **adjective** [attrib.] **1** chiefly Brit. driven by a motor: *a motor van.* ■ relating to motor vehicles: *motor insurance.*
2 giving or producing motion or action: *demand is the principle motor force governing economic activity.* ■ Physiology relating to muscular movement or the nerves activating it: *the motor functions of each hand.*
▶ **verb** [no obj., with adverbial of direction] travel in a motor vehicle: *they motored north up the M6.* ■ informal run or move as fast as possible.
– ORIGIN late Middle English (denoting a person who imparts motion): from Latin, literally 'mover', based on *movere* 'to move'. The current sense of the noun dates from the mid 19th cent.

motorable ▶ **adjective** Brit. dated (of a road) able to be used by motor vehicles.

Motorail ▶ **noun** a rail service in which cars are transported together with their drivers and passengers.
– ORIGIN 1960s: blend of **MOTOR** and **RAIL**[1].

motor area ▶ **noun** Anatomy a part of the central nervous system concerned with muscular action, especially the motor cortex.

motorbike ▶ **noun** Brit. a motorcycle. ■ US a small, light motorcycle.

motor boat ▶ **noun** a boat powered by a motor.

motor bus ▶ **noun** dated a bus.

motorcade /ˈməʊtəkeɪd/ ▶ **noun** a procession of motor vehicles, typically carrying and escorting a prominent person.
– ORIGIN early 20th cent.: from **MOTOR**, on the pattern of *cavalcade*.

motor car ▶ **noun 1** Brit. a car.
2 US a self-propelled railway vehicle used to carry railway workers.

motor caravan ▶ **noun** Brit. a motorhome.

motor coach ▶ **noun 1** dated a coach.
2 a self-propelled railway passenger carriage.

motor cortex ▶ **noun** Anatomy the part of the cerebral cortex in the brain in which originate the nerve impulses that initiate voluntary muscular activity.

motorcycle ▶ **noun** a two-wheeled vehicle that is powered by a motor and has no pedals.
– DERIVATIVES **motorcycling** noun, **motorcyclist** noun.

motor drive ▶ **noun** a mechanical system that includes an electric motor and drives a machine. ■ a battery-driven motor in a camera used to wind the film rapidly between exposures.

motor generator ▶ **noun** a device consisting of a mechanically coupled electric motor and generator which may be used to control the voltage, frequency, or phase of an electrical supply.

motorhome ▶ **noun** a motor vehicle equipped like a caravan for living in.

motoric /məʊˈtɔːrɪk, -ˈtɒrɪk/ ▶ **adjective 1** Physiology relating to muscular movement: *the infants' motoric and linguistic capabilities.*
2 (usu. **motorik**) (of music) marked by a repetitive beat suggestive of mechanized action or movement.
– ORIGIN late 19th cent.: from **MOTOR** + **-IC**, after German *Motorik* 'motor functions'.

motorist ▶ **noun** the driver of a car.

motorize (also **motorise**) ▶ **verb** [with obj.] (usu. as adj. **motorized**) **1** equip (a vehicle or device) with a motor to operate or propel it: *a motorized wheelchair.*
2 equip (troops) with motor transport: *three motorized divisions.*
– DERIVATIVES **motorization** noun.

motor lodge (also **motor hotel**) ▶ **noun** a motel.

motorman ▶ **noun** (pl. **motormen**) the driver of a train or tram.

motormouth ▶ **noun** informal a person who talks quickly and incessantly.
– DERIVATIVES **motormouthed** adjective.

motor nerve ▶ **noun** a nerve carrying impulses from the brain or spinal cord to a muscle or gland.

motor neuron ▶ **noun** a nerve cell forming part of a pathway along which impulses pass from the brain or spinal cord to a muscle or gland.

M

motor neurone disease ▶ **noun** [mass noun] Brit. a progressive disease involving degeneration of the motor neurons and wasting of the muscles.

motor racing ▶ **noun** [mass noun] the sport of racing motor vehicles, especially cars.

motorsailer ▶ **noun** a boat equipped with both sails and an engine.

motor scooter ▶ **noun** see SCOOTER.

motor sport ▶ **noun** another term for MOTOR RACING.

motor vehicle ▶ **noun** a road vehicle powered by an internal-combustion engine.

motorway ▶ **noun** Brit. a dual-carriageway road designed for fast traffic, with relatively few places for joining or leaving. ■ informal a wide, fast, easy ski run.

motor wind /ˈməʊtə wʌɪnd/ ▶ **noun** a camera winding mechanism driven by a motor.

motor yacht ▶ **noun** a motor-driven boat equipped for cruising.

Motown /ˈməʊtaʊn/ ▶ **noun 1** (also trademark **Tamla Motown**) [mass noun] music released on or reminiscent of the US record label Tamla Motown. The first black-owned record company in the US, Tamla Motown was founded in Detroit in 1959 by Berry Gordy, and was important in popularizing soul music, producing artists such as the Supremes, Stevie Wonder, and Marvin Gaye.
2 informal name for DETROIT.
– ORIGIN 1960s: shortening of *Motor Town*, by association with the car manufacturing industry of Detroit.

motser /ˈmɒtsə/ (also **motza**) ▶ **noun** Austral. informal a large sum of money, especially as won in gambling.
– ORIGIN 1930s: probably from Yiddish *matse* 'bread'.

motte /mɒt/ ▶ **noun** historical a mound forming the site of a castle or camp.
– ORIGIN late 19th cent.: from French, 'mound', from Old French *mote* (see MOAT).

motte-and-bailey ▶ **adjective** denoting a castle consisting of a fort on a motte surrounded by a bailey.

mottle ▶ **verb** [with obj.] mark with spots or smears of colour: *green leaves that are heavily mottled with chocolate and maroon* | (as adj. **mottled**) *a bird with mottled brown plumage.*
▶ **noun** an irregular arrangement of spots or patches of colour. ■ a spot or patch forming part of such an arrangement: *a pale grey with lighter grey mottles.*
– ORIGIN late 18th cent.: probably a back-formation from MOTLEY.

motto ▶ **noun** (pl. **mottoes** or **mottos**) **1** a short sentence or phrase chosen as encapsulating the beliefs or ideals of an individual, family, or institution: *the family motto is 'Faithful though Unfortunate'.*
2 Music a phrase which recurs throughout a musical work and has some symbolical significance.
– ORIGIN late 16th cent.: from Italian, 'word'.

Motu /ˈməʊtuː/ ▶ **noun** (pl. **same**) **1** a member of a Melanesian people of Papua New Guinea inhabiting the area around Port Moresby.
2 [mass noun] the language of the Motu, the base of a pidgin known as **Hiri Motu** or (formerly) **Police Motu**, widely used as a lingua franca for administrative purposes.
▶ **adjective** relating to the Motu or their language.
– ORIGIN the name in Melanesian.

motu proprio /ˌməʊtuː ˈprəʊprɪəʊ/ ▶ **noun** (pl. **motu proprios**) an edict issued by the Pope personally to the Roman Catholic Church or to a part of it.
– ORIGIN Latin, literally 'of one's own volition'.

motza ▶ **noun** variant spelling of MOTSER.

moue /muː/ ▶ **noun** a pouting expression used to convey annoyance or distaste.
– ORIGIN mid 19th cent.: French, earlier having the sense 'lip'.

mouflon /ˈmuːflɒn/ (also **moufflon**) ▶ **noun** a small wild sheep with chestnut-brown wool, found in mountainous country from Iran to Asia Minor. It is the ancestor of the domestic sheep. ● *Ovis orientalis*, family Bovidae.
– ORIGIN late 18th cent.: from French, from Italian *muflone*.

mouillé /ˈmuːjeɪ/ ▶ **adjective** Phonetics (of a consonant) palatalized.
– ORIGIN French, 'wetted'.

moujik ▶ **noun** variant spelling of MUZHIK.

mould¹ (US **mold**) ▶ **noun 1** a hollow container used to give shape to molten or hot liquid material when it cools and hardens. ■ a pudding or savoury mousse made in a mould: *a lobster mould with a sauce of carrots and port.*
2 [in sing.] a distinctive and typical style, form, or character: *he's a superb striker* ***in the same mould as*** *Gary Lineker* | *he planned to conquer the world as a roving reporter* ***in the mould of*** *his hero.* ■ archaic form or shape, especially the features or physique of a person or the build of an animal.
3 a frame or template for producing mouldings.
▶ **verb** [with obj.] **1** form (an object) out of malleable material: *mould the figure from white fondant.* ■ give a shape to (malleable material): *take the marzipan and mould it into a cone shape.* ■ influence the formation or development of: *the professionals who were helping to mould US policy.*
2 (as adj. **moulded**) (of a column, ceiling, or other part of a building) having a decorative moulding: *a corridor with a moulded cornice.*
– PHRASES **break the mould** put an end to a restrictive pattern of events or behaviour by doing things in a markedly different way: *his work did much to break the mould of the old urban sociology.*
– DERIVATIVES **mouldable** adjective.
– ORIGIN Middle English: apparently from Old French *modle*, from Latin *modulus* (see MODULUS).

mould² (US **mold**) ▶ **noun** [mass noun] a furry growth of minute fungi occurring typically in moist warm conditions, especially on food or other organic matter. ● The fungi belong to the subdivision Deuteromycotina (or Ascomycotina).
– ORIGIN late Middle English: probably from obsolete *mould*, past participle of *moul* 'grow mouldy', of Scandinavian origin; compare with Old Norse *mygla* 'grow mouldy'.

mould³ (US **mold**) ▶ **noun** [mass noun] chiefly Brit. soft loose earth. See also LEAF MOULD. ■ the upper soil of cultivated land, especially when rich in organic matter.
– ORIGIN Old English *molde*, from a Germanic base meaning 'pulverize or grind'; related to MEAL².

mouldboard ▶ **noun** a board in a plough that turns the earth over.

moulder¹ (US **molder**) ▶ **verb** [no obj.] (often as adj. **mouldering**) slowly decay or disintegrate, especially because of neglect: *the smell of mouldering books* | figurative *I couldn't permit someone of your abilities to* ***moulder away*** *in a backwater.*
– ORIGIN mid 16th cent.: perhaps from MOULD³, but compare with Norwegian dialect *muldra* 'crumble'.

moulder² (US **molder**) ▶ **noun** a person or thing that moulds something: *a moulder of public opinion.*

moulding (US **molding**) ▶ **noun** a shaped strip of wood or other material fitted as a decorative architectural feature, especially in a cornice.

mouldwarp /ˈməʊldwɔːp/ (also **mouldywarp** or **mouldiwarp**) ▶ **noun** archaic or dialect a mole (animal).
– ORIGIN Middle English: probably from Middle Low German *moldewerp*, from the Germanic bases of MOULD³ and WARP; compare with Dutch *muldvarp*.

mouldy (US **moldy**) ▶ **adjective** (**mouldier**, **mouldiest**; US **moldier**, **moldiest**) **1** covered with a fungal growth which causes decay, due to age or damp conditions: *mouldy bread.*
2 informal tediously old-fashioned: *mouldy conventions.* ■ chiefly Brit. dull or depressing: *evenings filled with mouldy old shows.*
– DERIVATIVES **mouldiness** noun.

moules marinière /ˌmuːl marɪnˈjɛː/ (also **moules à la marinière**) ▶ **plural noun** mussels served in their shells and cooked in a wine and onion sauce.
– ORIGIN French, literally 'mussels in the marine style'.

Mouli /ˈmuːli/ ▶ **noun** trademark a type of kitchen utensil for grinding or puréeing food.
– ORIGIN 1930s: abbreviation of *moulinette*, from French *moulinet* 'little mill'.

moulin /ˈmuːlɪn/ ▶ **noun** a vertical or nearly vertical shaft in a glacier, formed by surface water percolating through a crack in the ice.
– ORIGIN mid 19th cent.: French, literally 'mill'.

Moulin Rouge /ˌmuːlã ˈruːʒ/, French /mulɛ̃ ʀuʒ/ a cabaret in Montmartre, Paris, a favourite resort of poets and artists around the end of the 19th century. Toulouse-Lautrec immortalized its dancers in his posters.
– ORIGIN French, literally 'red windmill'.

Moulmein /maʊlˈmeɪn/ a port in SE Burma (Myanmar); pop. 405,800 (est. 2004).

moult (US **molt**) ▶ **verb** [no obj.] (of an animal) shed old feathers, hair, or skin to make way for a new growth: *the adult birds were already moulting* | [with obj.] *the snake moults its skin.* ■ (of hair or feathers) fall out to make way for new growth: *the last of his juvenile plumage had moulted.*
▶ **noun** a loss of feathers, hair, or skin, especially as a regular feature of an animal's life cycle.
– ORIGIN Middle English *moute*, from an Old English verb based on Latin *mutare* 'to change'. For the intrusive *-l-*, compare with words such as *fault*.

moulvi /ˈmuːlvi/ (also **maulvi**, **molvi**) ▶ **noun** (pl. **moulvis**) (especially in South Asia) a Muslim doctor of the law.
– ORIGIN from Urdu *maulvī*, from Arabic *mawlawī* 'judicial' (adjective used as a noun), from *mawlā* 'mullah'.

mound¹ ▶ **noun 1** a rounded mass projecting above a surface. ■ a small hill. ■ a raised mass of earth and stones created for purposes of defence or burial. ■ Baseball a slight elevation from which the pitcher delivers the ball.
2 (**a mound of**/**mounds of**) a large pile or quantity of something: *a mound of dirty crockery.*
▶ **verb** [with obj.] **1** heap up into a rounded pile: *basmati rice was mounded on our plates.*
2 archaic enclose or fortify with an embankment.
– ORIGIN early 16th cent. (as a verb in the sense 'enclose with a fence or hedge'): of obscure origin. An early sense of the noun was 'boundary hedge or fence'.

mound² ▶ **noun** archaic a ball representing the earth, used as part of royal regalia, e.g. on top of a crown, typically of gold and surmounted by a cross.
– ORIGIN Middle English (denoting the world): from Old French *monde*, from Latin *mundus* 'world'.

mound-builder ▶ **noun** another term for MEGAPODE.

mount¹ ▶ **verb** [with obj.] **1** climb up (stairs, a hill, or other rising surface): *he mounted the steps.* ■ climb or move up on to (a raised surface): *the master of ceremonies mounted the platform.* ■ get up on (an animal or bicycle) in order to ride it. ■ set (someone) on horseback; provide with a horse: *she was mounted on a white horse.* ■ (of a male mammal or bird) assume a position on top of (a female) in order to copulate.
2 organize and initiate (a campaign or other course of action): *the company had successfully mounted takeover bids.* ■ establish; set up: *security forces mounted check points at every key road.* ■ produce (a play, exhibition, or other artistic event) for public viewing.
3 [no obj.] grow larger or more numerous: *the costs* ***mount up*** *when you buy a home.* ■ (of a feeling) become stronger or more intense: *his anxiety mounted as messages were left unanswered.* ■ (of blood) rise visibly into the cheeks: *feeling the blush mount in her cheeks, she looked down quickly.*
4 [with adverbial of place] place or fix (an object) on a support: *fluorescent lights are mounted on the ceiling* | *the engine is mounted behind the rear seats.* ■ set in or attach to a backing or setting: *the photographs will be mounted and framed.* ■ fix (an object for viewing) on a microscope slide. ■ Computing make (a disk or disk drive) available for use.
▶ **noun 1** a backing or setting on which a photograph, gem, or work of art is set for display. ■ a glass microscope slide for securing a specimen to be viewed. ■ a stamp hinge.
2 a support for a gun, camera, or similar piece of equipment.
3 a horse that is ridden or is available for riding: *he hung on to his mount's bridle.* ■ an opportunity to ride a horse, especially as a jockey: *the jockey's injuries forced him to give up the coveted mount on Cool Ground.*
– PHRASES **mount guard** keep watch.
– DERIVATIVES **mountable** adjective, **mounter** noun.
– ORIGIN Middle English: from Old French *munter*, based on Latin *mons*, *mont-* 'mountain'.

mount² ▶ **noun 1** a mountain or hill (archaic except in place names): *Mount Everest.*
2 any of several fleshy prominences on the palm of the hand regarded in palmistry as signifying the degree of influence of a particular planet: *the mount of Mars.*
– ORIGIN Old English *munt*, from Latin *mons*, *mont-* 'mountain', reinforced in Middle English by Old French *mont*.

mountain ▶ **noun 1** a large natural elevation of the earth's surface rising abruptly from the surrounding level; a large steep hill: *we set off down the mountain* | *they sought refuge in the mountains* | [as modifier] *a mountain peak.*

2 (**a mountain/mountains of**) a large pile or quantity of something: *a mountain of paperwork*. ■ [usu. with modifier] a large surplus stock of a commodity: *a butter mountain*.
– PHRASES **if the mountain won't come to Muhammad, Muhammad must go to the mountain** proverb if someone won't do as you wish or a situation can't be arranged to suit you, you must accept it and change your plans accordingly. [with allusion to a well-known story about Muhammad told by Bacon (*Essays* xii).] **make a mountain out of a molehill** see MOLEHILL. **move mountains 1** achieve spectacular and apparently impossible results: *faith can move mountains*. **2** make every possible effort: *his fans move mountains to catch as many of his performances as possible*.
– DERIVATIVES **mountainy** adjective.
– ORIGIN Middle English: from Old French *montaigne*, based on Latin *mons*, *mont-* 'mountain'.

mountain ash ▶ noun **1** a small deciduous tree of the rose family, with compound leaves, white flowers, and red berries. Compare with ROWAN. ● Genus *Sorbus*, family Rosaceae: several species, in particular the North American *S. americana*.
2 Austral. a eucalyptus tree that is grown for timber. ● Genus *Eucalyptus*, family Myrtaceae: several species, in particular the very tall *E. regnans*.

mountain avens ▶ noun a creeping arctic-alpine plant with white flowers and glossy leaves. See also DRYAS. ● *Dryas octopetala*, family Rosaceae.

mountain beaver ▶ noun a burrowing forest-dwelling rodent occurring only on the west coast of North America. Also called SEWELLEL. ● *Aplodontia rufa*, the only member of the family Aplodontidae.

mountain bike ▶ noun a bicycle with a light sturdy frame, broad deep-treaded tyres, and multiple gears, originally designed for riding on mountainous terrain.
– DERIVATIVES **mountain biker** noun, **mountain biking** noun.

mountainboard ▶ noun trademark a board resembling a skateboard with four wheels, used for riding down mountainsides.
▶ verb [no obj.] (often as noun **mountainboarding**) ride on a mountainboard.
– DERIVATIVES **mountainboarder** noun.

mountain devil ▶ noun another term for MOLOCH.

mountain dew ▶ noun [mass noun] informal illicitly distilled alcohol, especially whisky or rum.

mountaineer ▶ noun **1** a person who takes part in mountaineering.
2 rare a person living in a mountainous area.

mountaineering ▶ noun [mass noun] the sport or activity of climbing mountains.

mountain everlasting ▶ noun another term for CAT'S FOOT.

mountain gem ▶ noun a green hummingbird found in the upland forests of Central America. ● Genus *Lampornis*, family Trochilidae: several species.

mountain goat ▶ noun **1** (also **Rocky Mountain goat**) a goat-antelope with shaggy white hair and backward curving horns, living in the Rocky Mountains of North America. ● *Oreamnos americanus*, family Bovidae.
2 any goat that lives on mountains, proverbial for agility.

mountain hare ▶ noun a hare whose coat turns white in winter, found in upland and arctic areas of northern Eurasia. It is the only hare in Ireland. Also called BLUE HARE. ● *Lepus timidus*, family Leporidae.

mountain laurel ▶ noun a North American kalmia which bears clusters of bright pink flowers. ● *Kalmia latifolia*, family Ericaceae.

mountain lion ▶ noun North American term for PUMA.

mountainous ▶ adjective **1** (of a region) having many mountains.
2 very large; huge: *struggling under mountainous debts*.
– DERIVATIVES **mountainously** adverb.

mountain sheep ▶ noun see BIGHORN, WELSH MOUNTAIN SHEEP.

mountain sickness ▶ noun another term for ALTITUDE SICKNESS.

mountainside ▶ noun the sloping surface of a mountain.

Mountain State informal name for WEST VIRGINIA.

Mountain time the standard time in a zone including parts of Canada and the US in or near the Rocky Mountains, specifically: ● (**Mountain Standard Time** abbrev.: **MST**) standard time based on the mean solar time at the meridian 105° W., seven hours behind GMT. ● (**Mountain Daylight Time** abbrev.: **MDT**) Mountain time during daylight saving, six hours behind GMT.

mountaintop ▶ noun the area at the top of a mountain: *a snow-covered mountaintop* | [as modifier] *the mountaintop castle*.

mountant /ˈmaʊnt(ə)nt/ ▶ noun a substance used to mount photographs, microscope specimens, etc.
– ORIGIN late 19th cent.: from MOUNT[1], on the pattern of French *montant* 'mounting'.

Mount Ararat, Mount Carmel, etc. see ARARAT, MOUNT; CARMEL, MOUNT, etc.

Mountbatten /maʊntˈbat(ə)n/, Louis (Francis Albert Victor Nicholas), 1st Earl Mountbatten of Burma (1900–79), British admiral and administrator. He was supreme Allied commander in SE Asia (1943–5) and the last viceroy (1947) and first Governor General of India (1947–8). He was killed by an IRA bomb while on his yacht.

mountebank /ˈmaʊntɪbaŋk/ ▶ noun a person who deceives others, especially in order to trick them out of their money; a charlatan. ■ historical a person who sold patent medicines in public places.
– DERIVATIVES **mountebankery** noun.
– ORIGIN late 16th cent.: from Italian *montambanco*, from the imperative phrase *monta in banco!* 'climb on the bench!' (with allusion to the raised platform used to attract an audience).

mounted ▶ adjective riding an animal, typically a horse, especially for military or other duty: *mounted police controlled the crowd*.

Mountie ▶ noun informal a member of the Royal Canadian Mounted Police.

mounting ▶ noun **1** a backing, setting, or support for something: *he pulled the curtain rail from its mounting*.
2 [mass noun] the action of mounting something: *the mounting of rapid-fire guns*.

mounting block ▶ noun a block of stone or low wooden steps from which a rider mounts a horse.

Mount Isa /ˈʌɪzə/ a lead and silver-mining town in NE Australia, in western Queensland; pop. 21,570 (2008).

Mount of Olives the highest point in the range of hills to the east of Jerusalem. It is a holy place for both Judaism and Christianity and is frequently mentioned in the Bible. The Garden of Gethsemane is located nearby.

Mount Vernon /ˈvəːnən/ a property in NE Virginia, about 24 km (15 miles) from Washington DC, on a site overlooking the Potomac River. Built in 1743, it was the home of George Washington from 1747 until his death in 1799.

mourn ▶ verb [with obj.] feel or show sorrow for the death of (someone), typically by following conventions such as the wearing of black clothes: *Isobel mourned her husband* | [no obj.] *she mourned for her friends who died in the accident*. ■ feel regret or sadness about (the loss or disappearance of something): *publishers mourned declining sales of hardback fiction*.
– ORIGIN Old English *murnan*, of Germanic origin.

Mourne Mountains /mɔːn/ a range of hills in SE Northern Ireland, in County Down.

mourner ▶ noun **1** a person who attends a funeral as a relative or friend of the dead person. ■ historical a person hired to attend a funeral.
2 any of a number of drab-coloured South American tyrant flycatchers and related birds. ● Families Tyrannidae, Pipridae, and Cotingidae: four genera and several species; the classification is uncertain.

mournful ▶ adjective feeling, expressing, or inducing sadness, regret, or grief: *her large, mournful eyes* | *mournful music*.
– DERIVATIVES **mournfully** adverb, **mournfulness** noun.

mourning ▶ noun [mass noun] the expression of sorrow for someone's death: *she's still in mourning after the death of her husband*. ■ black clothes worn as an expression of sorrow when someone dies.

mourning band ▶ noun a strip of black crape or other material that is worn round a person's sleeve or hat as a mark of respect for someone who has recently died.

mourning cloak ▶ noun North American term for CAMBERWELL BEAUTY.

mourning dove ▶ noun a North and Central American dove with a long tail, a grey-brown back, and a plaintive call. ● *Zenaida macroura*, family Columbidae.

mourning ring ▶ noun historical a ring worn to remind the wearer of someone who has died.

mousaka variant spelling of MOUSSAKA.

Mousalla variant spelling of MUSALA, MOUNT.

mouse ▶ noun (pl. **mice**) **1** a small rodent that typically has a pointed snout, relatively large ears and eyes, and a long tail. ● Family Muridae: many genera and numerous species. Also, some species in the families Heteromyidae, Zapodidae, and Muscardinidae.
■ (in general use) any small mammal similar to a mouse, such as a shrew or vole. ■ a shy, timid, and quiet person. ■ [mass noun] a dull light brown colour reminiscent of a mouse's fur: *her flaxen hair dulled to mouse*.
2 (pl. **mice** or **mouses**) a small handheld device which is moved across a mat or flat surface to move the cursor on a computer screen.
3 informal a lump or bruise on or near the eye.
▶ verb also /maʊz/ [no obj.] **1** (of a cat or owl) hunt for or catch mice.
2 [with adverbial of direction] use a mouse to move a cursor on a computer screen: *simply mouse over any item on the list*.
– DERIVATIVES **mouse-like** adjective.
– ORIGIN Old English *mūs*, (plural) *mȳs*, of Germanic origin; related to Dutch *muis* and German *Maus*, from an Indo-European root shared by Latin and Greek *mus*.

> **USAGE** Is the plural of **mouse** in the computing sense **mice** or **mouses**? People often feel that this sense needs its own distinctive plural, but in fact the ordinary plural **mice** is commoner, and the first recorded use of the term in the plural (1984) is **mice**.

mousebird ▶ noun a small gregarious African bird with mainly drab plumage, a crest, and a long tail. ● Genera *Colius* and *Urocolius*, family Coliidae: six species.

mouse deer ▶ noun another term for CHEVROTAIN.

mouse-ear (also **mouse-ear chickweed**) ▶ noun a small white-flowered creeping chickweed with soft hairy leaves which supposedly resemble the ears of mice. ● Genus *Cerastium*, family Caryophyllaceae.

mouse-eared bat ▶ noun a myotis bat that has mouse-like ears and mainly brownish fur. ● Genus *Myotis*, family Vespertilionidae: several species, in particular the large *M. myotis*, found from SW Europe to Asia Minor.

mouse hare ▶ noun another term for PIKA.

mouse lemur ▶ noun a small nocturnal Madagascan lemur with large ears, close-set eyes, and a long tail. ● Genus *Microcebus*, family Cheirogaleidae: three species.

mouse mat ▶ noun see MAT[1] (sense 2 of the noun).

mouse opossum ▶ noun a mouse-like opossum with large ears and no marsupial pouch, native to Central and South America. ● Genus *Marmosa*, family Didelphidae: several species.

mouser ▶ noun an animal that catches mice, especially a cat.

mouse-tailed bat ▶ noun an insectivorous bat with a long mouse-like tail, native to Africa and Asia and often found in man-made structures. ● Family Rhinopomatidae and genus *Rhinopoma*: three species.

mousetrap ▶ noun a trap for catching and usually killing mice, especially one with a spring bar which snaps down on to the mouse when it touches a piece of cheese or other bait attached to the mechanism. ■ (also **mousetrap cheese**) [mass noun] Brit. informal cheese of poor quality.
▶ verb [with obj.] N. Amer. informal induce (someone) to do something by means of a trick: *the editor mousetrapped her into giving him an article*. ■ block (a user's) efforts to exit from a website, usually one to which they have been redirected.
– PHRASES **a better mousetrap** an improved version of a well-known article. [from 'If a man ... make a better mouse-trap than his neighbour ... the world will make a beaten path to his door', attributed to Ralph Waldo Emerson.]

mousey ▶ adjective variant spelling of MOUSY.

moussaka /muːˈsɑːkə, ˌmuːsəˈkɑː/ (also **mousaka**) ▶ noun [mass noun] a Greek dish made of minced lamb, aubergines, and tomatoes, with cheese sauce on top.
– ORIGIN from Turkish *musakka*, based on Arabic.

M

mousse ▶ **noun** [mass noun] **1** a sweet or savoury dish made as a smooth, light mass in which the main ingredient is whipped with cream and egg white: *sponge topped with chocolate mousse* | [count noun] *a salmon mousse.*
2 a soft, light, aerated gel such as a soap preparation: *fragrant shower mousse.* ■ a frothy preparation that is applied to the hair, enabling it to be styled more easily.
3 (also **chocolate mousse**) a frothy brown emulsion of oil and seawater formed by weathering of an oil slick.
▶ **verb** [with obj.] style (hair) using mousse.
– ORIGIN mid 19th cent.: from French, 'moss or froth'.

mousseline /ˈmuːsliːn/ ▶ **noun 1** [mass noun] a very fine, semi-opaque fabric similar to muslin.
2 a soft, light sweet or savoury mousse.
3 (also **sauce mousseline**) [mass noun] hollandaise sauce that has been made frothy with whipped cream or egg white, served mainly with fish or asparagus.
– ORIGIN late 17th cent.: from French (see **MUSLIN**).

mousseron /ˈmuːsərɒn/ ▶ **noun** an edible mushroom with a flattish white cap, pink gills, and a mealy smell. ● *Clitopilus prunulus*, family Agaricaceae, class Hymenomycetes.

mousseux /muːˈsəː/, French /musø/ ▶ **adjective** (of wine) sparkling: *vin mousseux.*
▶ **noun** (pl. **same**) [mass noun] sparkling wine.
– ORIGIN from French, from *mousse* 'froth'.

Moussorgsky variant spelling of **MUSSORGSKY**.

moustache (US also **mustache**) ▶ **noun** a strip of hair left to grow above the upper lip. ■ (**moustaches**) a long moustache. ■ a growth similar to a moustache, or a marking that resembles one, round the mouth of some animals.
– DERIVATIVES **moustached** adjective.
– ORIGIN late 16th cent.: from French, from Italian *mostaccio*, from Greek *mustax, mustak-*.

moustache cup ▶ **noun** a cup with a partial cover that protects the moustache of the person drinking from it.

M

Mousterian /muːˈstɪərɪən/ ▶ **adjective** Archaeology relating to or denoting the main culture of the Middle Palaeolithic period in Europe, between the Acheulian and Aurignacian periods (chiefly 80,000–35,000 years ago). It is associated with Neanderthal peoples and is typified by flints worked on one side only. See also **LEVALLOIS**. ■ (as noun **the Mousterian**) the Mousterian culture or period.
– ORIGIN late 19th cent.: from French *moustiérien*, from *Le Moustier*, a cave in SW France where objects from this culture were found.

mousy (also **mousey**) ▶ **adjective** (**mousier, mousiest**) of or like a mouse. ■ (of hair) of a dull light brown colour. ■ (of a person) shy, timid, and quiet: *he had a small mousy wife.*
– DERIVATIVES **mousiness** noun.

Moutan /ˈmuːt(ə)n/ (also **Moutan peony**) ▶ **noun** a tall shrubby peony with pink or white blotched flowers, native to China and Tibet and the parent of many garden varieties. ● *Paeonia suffruticosa*, family Paeoniaceae.
– ORIGIN early 19th cent.: from Chinese *mudan*.

mouth ▶ **noun** (pl. **mouths**) **1** the opening and cavity in the lower part of the human face, surrounded by the lips, through which food is taken in and vocal sounds are emitted. ■ the corresponding opening through which an animal takes in food. ■ [usu. with adj.] a horse's readiness to feel and obey the pressure of the bit in its mouth: *the horse had a hard mouth.* ■ the character or quality of a wine as judged by its feel or flavour in the mouth (rather than its aroma). ■ [mass noun] informal talkativeness or impudence: *you've got more mouth on you than any woman I've ever known.*
2 an opening or entrance to a hollow, concave, or enclosed structure: *the mouth of a cave.* ■ the opening for filling or emptying a container: *the mouth of the bottle.* ■ the muzzle of a gun. ■ the place where a river enters the sea. ■ the opening or entrance to a harbour or bay: *sand from the beach is silting up the harbour mouth.*
▶ **verb** [with obj.] **1** move the lips as if saying (something): *she mouthed a silent farewell* | [with direct speech] *'Come on,' he mouthed.* ■ say (something dull or unoriginal), especially in a pompous or affected way: *this clergyman mouths platitudes in breathy, soothing tones.* ■ utter very clearly and distinctly: *she would carefully mouth the right pronunciation.*
2 take in or touch with the mouth: *puppies may mouth each other's collars during play.* ■ train the mouth of (a horse) so that it responds to a bit.
– PHRASES **a mouth to feed** a person, typically a child, who has to be looked after and fed. **be all mouth (and no trousers)** informal tend to talk boastfully without any intention of acting on one's words. **give mouth** (of a dog) bark; bay. **keep one's mouth shut** informal not say anything, especially not reveal a secret: *would he keep his mouth shut under interrogation?* **open one's mouth** informal say something. **watch one's mouth** informal be careful about what one says.
– PHRASAL VERBS **mouth off** informal talk in an unpleasantly loud and boastful or opinionated way: *he was mouthing off about society in general.* ■ (**mouth off at**) loudly criticize or abuse: *yesterday an old tramp mouthed off at me outside the supermarket.*
– DERIVATIVES **mouthed** adjective [in combination] *wide-mouthed*, **mouther** /ˈmaʊðə/ noun, **mouthless** adjective.
– ORIGIN Old English *mūth*, of Germanic origin; related to Dutch *mond* and German *Mund*, from an Indo-European root shared by Latin *mentum* 'chin'.

mouth-breather ▶ **noun** informal a stupid person.
– DERIVATIVES **mouth-breathing** adjective.

mouthbrooder ▶ **noun** a freshwater cichlid fish which protects its eggs (and in some cases its young) by carrying them in its mouth. ● *Sarotherodon* and other genera, family Cichlidae.

mouthfeel ▶ **noun** the way an item of food or drink feels in the mouth, as distinct from its taste.

mouthful ▶ **noun** (pl. **mouthfuls**) **1** a quantity of food or drink that fills or can be put in the mouth: *he took a mouthful of beer.*
2 a long or complicated word or phrase that is difficult to say: *poliomyelitis is **a bit of a mouthful**.*
– PHRASES **give someone a mouthful** Brit. informal talk to or shout at someone in an angry or critical way. **say a mouthful** N. Amer. informal say something noteworthy.

mouth organ ▶ **noun** Brit. another term for **HARMONICA**.

mouthpart ▶ **noun** (usu. **mouthparts**) Zoology any of the appendages, typically found in pairs, surrounding the mouth of an insect or other arthropod and adapted for feeding.

mouthpiece ▶ **noun 1** the part of a musical instrument, telephone, etc. designed to be put in or against the mouth: *he shouted into the mouthpiece, but there was no response* | *the snorkel's mouthpiece.* ■ a gumshield.
2 chiefly derogatory a person or organization who speaks on behalf of another person or organization: *the media acts as a mouthpiece for the Party.* ■ N. Amer. informal a lawyer.

mouth-to-mouth ▶ **adjective** denoting a method of artificial respiration in which a person breathes into an unconscious patient's lungs through their mouth: *mouth-to-mouth resuscitation.*
▶ **noun** [mass noun] mouth-to-mouth respiration.

mouthwash ▶ **noun** [mass noun] a liquid used for rinsing the mouth or gargling with.

mouth-watering ▶ **adjective** smelling, looking, or sounding delicious: *a mouth-watering mixture of French and English cuisine.* ■ highly attractive or tempting: *mouth-watering views of the mountains.*
– DERIVATIVES **mouth-wateringly** adverb.

mouthy ▶ **adjective** (**mouthier, mouthiest**) informal inclined to talk a lot, especially in a cheeky way.

mouton /ˈmuːtɒn/ ▶ **noun** [mass noun] sheepskin cut and dyed to resemble beaver fur or sealskin.
– ORIGIN 1950s: from French, literally 'sheep'.

movable (also **moveable**) ▶ **adjective 1** capable of being moved: *they stripped the town of all movable objects and fled.* ■ (of a feast or festival) variable in date from year to year.
2 Law (of property) of the nature of a chattel, as distinct from land or buildings. Compare with **HERITABLE** (sense 2).
▶ **noun** (usu. **movables**) property or possessions not including land or buildings. ■ an article of furniture that may be removed from a house, as distinct from a fixture.
– DERIVATIVES **movability** noun, **movably** adverb.
– ORIGIN late Middle English: from Old French, from *moveir* 'to move'.

movable-doh ▶ **adjective** denoting a system of solmization (such as tonic sol-fa) in which doh is the keynote of any major scale. Compare with **FIXED-DOH**.

movable feast ▶ **noun** a religious feast day that does not occur on the same calendar date each year, in particular Easter Day and other Christian holy days whose dates are related to it.

movant /ˈmuːv(ə)nt/ ▶ **noun** US Law a person who applies to or petitions a court or judge for a ruling in their favour.
– ORIGIN late 19th cent.: from **MOVE** + **-ANT**.

move ▶ **verb 1** [no obj., usu. with adverbial of direction] go in a specified direction or manner; change position: *she moved to the door* | *I heard him moving about upstairs.* ■ [with obj.] change the place, position, or state of: *she moved the tray to a side table* | *can you move your car so I can get mine out?* ■ change one's place of residence or work: *his family moved to London when he was a child* | [with obj.] *they moved house four days after the baby was born.* ■ (of a player) change the position of a piece in a board game: *White has forced his opponent to move* | [with obj.] *if Black moves his bishop he loses a pawn.* ■ informal depart; start off: *let's move—it's time we started shopping.* ■ (in imperative **move it**) informal hurry up: *come on—move it!* ■ informal go quickly: *Kennings was really moving when he made contact with a tyre at the hairpin and flipped over.* ■ (with reference to merchandise) sell or be sold: [with obj.] *booksellers should easily be able to move this biography of Lincoln.*
2 [no obj.] make progress; develop in a particular manner or direction: *aircraft design had moved forward a long way* | *councillors are anxious to **get things moving** as soon as possible.* ■ change from one state, opinion, or activity to another: *the school moved over to the new course in 1987* | [with obj.] *she deftly moved the conversation to safer territory.* ■ (**move in/within**) spend one's time in (a particular sphere) or among (a particular group of people): *she moved in the pop and art worlds.*
3 [with obj. and infinitive] influence or prompt (someone) to do something: *his deep love of music moved him to take lessons with Dr Hill.* ■ [no obj.] take action: *hardliners may yet **move against** him, but their success might be limited.* ■ [with obj.] arouse a strong feeling, especially of sorrow or sympathy, in (someone): *she felt deeply moved by this picture of his plight.* ■ [with obj.] archaic stir up (an emotion) in someone: *he justly moves one's derision.*
4 [with obj.] propose for discussion and resolution at a meeting or legislative assembly: *she intends to move an amendment to the Bill* | [with clause] *I beg to move that this House deplores the government's economic policies.* ■ archaic apply formally to (a court or assembly) for something.
5 [with obj.] empty (the bowels).
▶ **noun** a change of place, position, or state: *she made a sudden move towards me* | *the country's move to independence* | *a career move.* ■ a change of house or business premises. ■ an act that initiates or advances a process or plan: *my next move is to talk to Matthew.* ■ a manoeuvre in a sport or game: *Robson began a move which saw Webb run from the halfway line down the right.* ■ a player's turn to change the position of a piece in a board game.
– PHRASES **get a move on** [often in imperative] informal hurry up. **get moving** [often in imperative] informal make a prompt start on a journey or task: *you're here to work, so get moving.* **make a move** take action: *each army was waiting for the other side to make a move.* ■ Brit. set off; leave somewhere: *I think I'd better be making a move.* **make a move on** (or **put the moves on**) informal make a proposition to (someone), especially of a sexual nature. **move the goalposts** see **GOALPOST**. **move heaven and earth** see **HEAVEN**. **move mountains** see **MOUNTAIN**. **move up a gear** see **GEAR**. **move with the times** keep abreast of current thinking or developments. **not move a muscle** see **MUSCLE**. **on the move** in the process of moving from one place or job to another: *it's difficult to contact her because she's always on the move.* ■ making progress: *the economy appeared to be on the move.*
– PHRASAL VERBS **move in 1** take possession of a new house. ■ (**move in with**) start to share accommodation with (an existing resident). **2** intervene, especially so as to attack or take control: *this riot could have been avoided had the police moved in earlier.* **move in on** approach, especially so as to take action: *the police moved in on him.* ■ become involved with so as to take control of or put pressure on: *the bank did not usually move in on doubtful institutions until they were almost bankrupt.* **move on** (or **move someone on**) **1** go or cause to leave somewhere: *the*

Mounties briskly ordered them to move on. **2** (**move on**) progress: *British cinema has moved on in the last decade.* **move over** (or **aside**) adjust one's position to make room for someone else: *Jo motioned to the girls on the couch to move over.* ■ relinquish a job or leading position through being superseded by someone or something else: *it's time for the film establishment to move over and make way for a new generation.*
– ORIGIN Middle English: from Old French *moveir*, from Latin *movere*.

moveable ▶ **adjective & noun** variant spelling of MOVABLE.

moveless ▶ **adjective** chiefly literary not moving or capable of moving or being moved.

movement ▶ **noun 1** an act of moving: *a slight movement of the body* | [mass noun] *the free movement of labour.* ■ an arrival or departure of an aircraft. ■ (**movements**) the activities and whereabouts of someone during a particular period of time: *your movements and telephone conversations are recorded.* ■ [mass noun] general activity or bustle: *the scene was almost devoid of movement.*
2 [often with modifier] a group of people working together to advance their shared political, social, or artistic ideas: *the labour movement.* ■ a campaign undertaken by such a group: *a movement to declare war on poverty.* ■ a change or development: *the movement towards greater sexual equality* | *movements in the underlying financial markets.*
3 Music a principal division of a longer musical work, self-sufficient in terms of key, tempo, and structure: *the slow movement of his violin concerto.*
4 the moving parts of a mechanism, especially a clock or watch.
5 (also **bowel movement**) an act of defecation.
– ORIGIN late Middle English: via Old French from medieval Latin *movimentum*, from Latin *movere* 'to move'.

mover ▶ **noun 1** a person or thing that moves: *she's a lovely mover* | *job movers.* ■ chiefly N. Amer. a person whose job is to remove and transport furniture from one house to another.
2 a person who makes a formal proposal at a meeting or in an assembly: *movers and seconders rise and give speeches.* ■ a person who instigates or organizes something: *she was the key mover in making this successful conference happen.*
– PHRASES **mover and shaker** a powerful person who initiates events and influences people. [from *movers and shakers*, a phrase from O'Shaughnessy's *Music & Moonlight* (1874).]

movie ▶ **noun** chiefly N. Amer. a cinema film. ■ (**the movies**) films generally or the film industry: *we decided to go the movies.*

moviegoer ▶ **noun** chiefly N. Amer. a person who goes to the cinema, especially regularly.
– DERIVATIVES **moviegoing noun & adjective.**

moviemaker ▶ **noun** chiefly N. Amer. a person who directs or produces cinema films.
– DERIVATIVES **moviemaking noun.**

movie theatre (also **movie house**) ▶ **noun** N. Amer. a cinema.

moving ▶ **adjective 1** [often with submodifier] in motion: *a fast-moving river.*
2 producing strong emotion, especially sadness or sympathy: *an unforgettable and moving book.*
– DERIVATIVES **movingly adverb** (sense 2).

moving average ▶ **noun** Statistics a succession of averages derived from successive segments (typically of constant size and overlapping) of a series of values.

moving-coil ▶ **adjective** (of an electrical device such as a voltmeter or microphone) containing a wire coil suspended in a magnetic field, so that the coil either moves in response to a current or produces a current when it is made to move.

moving pavement ▶ **noun** a mechanism resembling a conveyor belt for pedestrians in a place such as an airport.

moving picture ▶ **noun** dated a cinematographic film.

moving staircase ▶ **noun** Brit. another term for ESCALATOR.

moviola /ˌmuːvɪˈəʊlə/ ▶ **noun** trademark a device which reproduces the picture and sound of a film on a small scale, to allow checking and editing.
– ORIGIN 1920s: from MOVIE + *-ola* (probably from PIANOLA).

mow[1] ▶ **verb** (past participle **mowed** or **mown**) [with obj.] cut down (grass) with a machine: *Roger mowed the lawn* | (as adj. **mown**) *the delicious smell of newly mown grass.* ■ chiefly historical cut down (grass or a cereal crop) with a scythe.
– PHRASAL VERBS **mow someone down** kill someone with a fusillade of bullets or other missiles: *he was mown down in a hail of machine-gun bullets.* ■ recklessly knock down someone with a car or other vehicle: *a father-of-four was mown down and killed as he cycled home from work.*
– DERIVATIVES **mower noun.**
– ORIGIN Old English *māwan*, of Germanic origin; related to Dutch *maaien*, German *mähen* 'mow', also to MEAD[2].

mow[2] ▶ **noun** N. Amer. or dialect a stack of hay, corn, or other crop. ■ a place in a barn where a stack of hay, corn, etc. is put.
– ORIGIN Old English *mūga*; of unknown ultimate origin; compare with Swedish and Norwegian *muga* 'heap'.

mowing ▶ **noun 1** (**mowings**) loose pieces of grass resulting from mowing.
2 US a field of grass grown for hay.

MOX ▶ **noun** [mass noun] a type of nuclear fuel designed for use in breeder reactors, consisting of a blend of uranium and plutonium oxides.
– ORIGIN from *m(ixed) ox(ides)*.

moxa /ˈmɒksə/ ▶ **noun** [mass noun] a downy substance obtained from the dried leaves of an Asian plant related to mugwort. It is burnt on or near the skin in Eastern medicine as a counterirritant. ● The plant is *Crossostephium artemisioides*, family Compositae.
– ORIGIN late 17th cent.: from Japanese *mogusa*, from *moe kusa* 'burning herb'.

moxibustion /ˌmɒksɪˈbʌstʃ(ə)n/ ▶ **noun** [mass noun] (in Eastern medicine) the burning of moxa on or near a person's skin as a counterirritant.

moxie /ˈmɒksi/ ▶ **noun** [mass noun] N. Amer. informal force of character, determination, or nerve: *when you've got the moxie, you need the clothes to match.*
– ORIGIN 1930s: from *Moxie*, the proprietary name of a soft drink.

Moygashel /ˈmɔɪɡəʃ(ə)l/ ▶ **noun** trademark a type of Irish linen.
– ORIGIN 1930s: named after a village in Co. Tyrone, Northern Ireland.

Mozambique /ˌməʊzamˈbiːk/ a country on the east coast of southern Africa; pop. 21,669,300 (est. 2009); languages, Portuguese (official), Bantu languages; capital, Maputo.

> First visited by Vasco da Gama, Mozambique was colonized by the Portuguese in the early 16th century. It was a centre of the slave trade in the 17th and 18th centuries. Mozambique became an independent republic in 1975, after a ten-year armed struggle by the Frelimo liberation movement; civil war between the Frelimo government and the Renamo opposition followed until a peace agreement was signed in 1992. The country joined the Commonwealth in 1995.

– DERIVATIVES **Mozambican adjective & noun.**

Mozambique Channel an arm of the Indian Ocean separating the eastern coast of mainland Africa from the island of Madagascar.

Mozarabic /məʊˈzarəbɪk/ ▶ **adjective** historical relating to the Christian inhabitants of Spain under the Muslim Moorish kings.
– DERIVATIVES **Mozarab noun.**
– ORIGIN late 17th cent.: from Spanish *mozárabe* (from Arabic *mustaʿrib*, literally 'making oneself an Arab') + -IC.

Mozart /ˈməʊtsɑːt/, German /ˈmoːtsart/, (Johann Chrysostom) Wolfgang Amadeus (1756–91), Austrian composer.

> A child prodigy as a harpsichordist, pianist, and composer, he came to epitomize classical music in its purity of form and melody. A prolific composer, he wrote more than forty symphonies, nearly thirty piano concertos, over twenty string quartets, and sixteen operas, including *The Marriage of Figaro* (1786), *Don Giovanni* (1787), *Così fan tutte* (1790), and *The Magic Flute* (1791).

– DERIVATIVES **Mozartian adjective & noun.**

mozo /ˈməʊzəʊ/, Spanish /ˈmoθo, ˈmoso/ ▶ **noun** (pl. **mozos**) (in Spanish-speaking countries) a male servant or attendant.
– ORIGIN Spanish, literally 'boy'.

mozz ▶ **noun** (in phrase **put the mozz on**) Austral. informal exert a malign influence on (someone); jinx.
– ORIGIN 1920s: abbreviation of MOZZLE.

mozzarella /ˌmɒtsəˈrɛlə/ ▶ **noun** [mass noun] a firm white Italian cheese made from buffalo or cow's milk, used especially in pizzas and salads.
– ORIGIN Italian, diminutive of *mozza*, denoting a kind of cheese, from *mozzare* 'cut off'.

mozzetta /məʊˈzɛtə, məʊˈtsɛtə/ (also **mozetta**) ▶ **noun** (pl. **mozzette**) a short cape with a hood, worn by the Pope, cardinals, and some other ecclesiastics.
– ORIGIN late 18th cent.: Italian, shortened form of *almozzetta*, from medieval Latin *almucia* 'amice' + the diminutive suffix *-etta*.

mozzie (also **mossie**) ▶ **noun** (pl. **mozzies**) informal a mosquito.

mozzle ▶ **noun** [mass noun] Austral. informal luck; fortune.
– ORIGIN late 19th cent.: from Hebrew *mazzāl* 'star or luck'.

MP ▶ **noun** (pl. **MPs**) a Member of Parliament: *more than 80 MPs have signed the Commons motion.*
▶ **abbreviation** ■ megapixel. ■ military police. ■ military policeman.

mp ▶ **abbreviation** mezzo piano.

m.p. ▶ **abbreviation** melting point.

MP3 ▶ **noun** a means of compressing a sound sequence into a very small file, to enable digital storage and transmission. ■ a file in this format: [as modifier] *an MP3 player.*
– ORIGIN 1990s: from MPEG + *Audio Layer-3*.

MPC ▶ **abbreviation** multimedia personal computer.

MPD ▶ **abbreviation** multiple-personality disorder.

MPEG /ˈɛmpɛɡ/ ▶ **noun** [mass noun] Computing an international standard for encoding and compressing video images.
– ORIGIN 1980s: from *Motion Pictures Experts Group*.

mpg ▶ **abbreviation** miles per gallon (a measurement of a vehicle's rate of fuel consumption).

mph ▶ **abbreviation** miles per hour.

MPhil ▶ **abbreviation** Master of Philosophy.

mpingo /(ə)mˈpɪŋɡəʊ/ ▶ **noun** (pl. **mpingos**) an East African leguminous tree with dense black timber which is used for carvings and musical instruments. ● *Dalbergia melanoxylon*, family Leguminosae.
– ORIGIN from Kiswahili.

MPLA the Popular Movement for the Liberation of Angola, a Marxist organization founded in the 1950s that emerged as the ruling party in Angola after independence from Portugal in 1975. Once in power the MPLA fought UNITA and other rival groups for many years.
– ORIGIN abbreviation of Portuguese *Movimento Popular de Libertação de Angola*.

Mpumalanga /(ə)mˌpuːməˈlaŋɡə/ a province of NE South Africa, formerly part of Transvaal; capital, Nelspruit.

MPV ▶ **noun** (pl. **MPVs**) a large van-like car.
– ORIGIN abbreviation of *multipurpose vehicle*.

MR ▶ **abbreviation** Master of the Rolls.

Mr ▶ **noun** a title used before a surname or full name to address or refer to a man without a higher or honorific or professional title: *Mr Robert Smith.* ■ used before the name of an office to address a man who holds it: *Mr President.* ■ (in the UK) used before a surname to address or refer to a male surgeon. ■ used in the armed forces to address a senior warrant officer, officer cadet, or junior naval officer.
– ORIGIN late Middle English: originally an abbreviation of MASTER[1], compare with MISTER[1].

MRA ▶ **abbreviation** Moral Rearmament.

MRBM ▶ **abbreviation** medium-range ballistic missile.

MRC ▶ **abbreviation** (in the UK) Medical Research Council.

MRCP ▶ **abbreviation** Member of the Royal College of Physicians.

MRCVS ▶ **abbreviation** Member of the Royal College of Veterinary Surgeons.

MRE ▶ **abbreviation** meal ready to eat (a pre-cooked packaged meal used by US military personnel).

MRI ▶ **abbreviation** magnetic resonance imaging.

MRIA ▶ **abbreviation** Member of the Royal Irish Academy.

mridangam /mrɪˈdaŋəm/ ▶ **noun** a barrel-shaped double-headed drum with one head larger than the other, used in southern Indian music.
– ORIGIN late 19th cent.: Tamil alteration of Sanskrit *mṛdaṅga*.

M

MRM ▸ abbreviation mechanically recovered meat, meat that is left on a carcass after all the prime cuts have been removed and blasted off the bones using high pressure.

mRNA ▸ abbreviation Biology messenger RNA.

MRPhS ▸ abbreviation Member of the Royal Pharmaceutical Society.

Mr Right ▸ noun informal the ideal future husband: *I expect you're waiting for Mr Right.*

Mrs ▸ noun the title used before a surname or full name to address or refer to a married woman without a higher or honorific or professional title: *Mrs Sally Jones.*
– ORIGIN early 17th cent.: abbreviation of **MISTRESS**; compare with **MISSUS**.

MRSA ▸ abbreviation methicillin-resistant *Staphylococcus aureus*, a strain of antibiotic-resistant bacteria.

Mrs Grundy ▸ noun (pl. **Mrs Grundys**) a person with very conventional standards of propriety.
– ORIGIN early 19th cent.: a person repeatedly mentioned in T. Morton's comedy *Speed the Plough* (1798), often in the phrase 'What will Mrs Grundy say?', which became a popular catchphrase.

MS ▸ abbreviation ■ manuscript. ■ Master of Science. ■ Master of Surgery. ■ Master Seaman. ■ Mississippi (in official postal use). ■ multiple sclerosis. ■ motor ship.

Ms ▸ noun a title used before the surname or full name of any woman regardless of her marital status (a neutral alternative to **Mrs** or **Miss**): *Ms Sarah Brown.*
– ORIGIN 1950s: combination of **MRS** and **MISS²**.

msasa /(ə)m'sɑːsə/ ▸ noun a tree of central Africa (especially Zimbabwe), with fragrant white flowers and compound leaves which are crimson and bronze in spring. ● *Brachystegia spiciformis*, family Leguminosae.
– ORIGIN early 20th cent.: from Shona.

MSB ▸ abbreviation most significant bit.

MSC ▸ abbreviation (in the UK) Manpower Services Commission.

MSc ▸ abbreviation Master of Science.

MS-DOS ▸ abbreviation Computing, trademark Microsoft disk operating system.

M

MSG ▸ abbreviation monosodium glutamate.

msg ▸ abbreviation message: *he'd left his mobile at home so he didn't get the msg.*

Msgr ▸ abbreviation N. Amer. ■ Monseigneur. ■ Monsignor.

MSgt ▸ abbreviation Master Sergeant.

MSM ▸ abbreviation mainstream media (as opposed to the blogosphere).

MSN ▸ abbreviation trademark Microsoft Network.

MSP ▸ noun (pl. **MSPs**) a Member of the Scottish Parliament.

MSRP ▸ abbreviation N. Amer. manufacturer's suggested retail price.

MSS /ɛm'ɛsɪz/ ▸ abbreviation manuscripts.

MST ▸ abbreviation (in North America) Mountain Standard Time (see **MOUNTAIN TIME**).

MSY ▸ abbreviation maximum sustainable yield.

MT ▸ abbreviation ■ machine translation. ■ Montana (in official postal use).

Mt ▸ abbreviation ■ the Gospel of Matthew (in biblical references). ■ [in place names] Mount: *Mt Everest.*
▸ symbol the chemical element meitnerium.

MTB ▸ abbreviation ■ Brit. motor torpedo boat. ■ mountain bike.

MTBF ▸ abbreviation mean time between failures, a measure of the reliability of a device or system.

MTech ▸ abbreviation Master of Technology.

MTV trademark a cable and satellite television channel which broadcasts popular music and promotional music videos.
– ORIGIN 1980s: abbreviation of *music television.*

mu /mjuː/ ▸ noun the twelfth letter of the Greek alphabet (Μ, μ), transliterated as 'm'. ■ **(Mu)** [followed by Latin genitive] Astronomy the twelfth star in a constellation: *Mu Cassiopeiae.* ■ [as modifier] Physics relating to muons: *mu particle.*
▸ symbol ■ (μ) micron. ■ (μ) [in combination] 'micro-' in symbols for units: *the recommended daily amount is 750μg.* ■ (μ) permeability.
– ORIGIN Greek.

Mubarak /muː'bɑːrak/, (Muhammad) Hosni (Said) (b.1928), Egyptian statesman, President since 1981. He did much to establish closer links between Egypt and other Arab nations, though he aligned Egypt against Iraq in the Gulf War of 1991.

much ▸ determiner & pronoun (**more**, **most**) [often with negative or in questions] a large amount: [as determiner] *I didn't get much sleep that night* | *I did* **so much** *shopping* | [as pronoun] *he does not eat much* | *they must bear* **much of** *the blame.* ■ [as pronoun] [with negative] used to refer disparagingly to someone or something as being a poor specimen: *I'm* **not much of** *a gardener.*
▸ adverb to a great extent; a great deal: *did it hurt much?* | *thanks* **very much** | *they did not mind, much to my surprise* | [with comparative] *they look much better.* ■ [usu. with negative or in questions] for a large part of one's time; often: *I'm not there much.*
– PHRASES **as much** the same: *I am sure she would do as much for me.* **a bit much** informal somewhat excessive or unreasonable: *his earnestness can be a bit much.* **how much** used to ask what a particular amount or cost is. **make much of** flatter and praise someone: *Mr Smith was glad to be made much of.* **(as) much as** even though: *much as I had enjoyed my adventure it was good to be back.* **much less** see **LESS**. **not much in it** little difference between things being compared. **so much the better** (or **worse**) that is even better (or worse): *we want to hear your say, but if you make it short, so much the better.* **this much** the fact about to be stated: *I know this much, you would defy the world to get what you wanted.* **too much** an intolerable, impossible, or exhausting situation or experience: *the effort proved* **too much for** *her.*
– DERIVATIVES **muchly** adverb (humorous).
– ORIGIN Middle English: shortened from *muchel*, from Old English *micel* (see **MICKLE**).

Mucha /'muːkə/, Alphonse (1860–1939), Czech painter and designer; born *Alfons Maria.* He was a leading figure in the art nouveau movement, noted for his flowing poster designs, typically featuring the actress Sarah Bernhardt.

muchacho /muː'tʃatʃəʊ/ (or **muchacha** /muː'tʃatʃə/) ▸ noun (pl. **muchachos** or **muchachas**) (in Spanish-speaking countries) a young man (or woman). ■ a male (or female) servant.
– ORIGIN Spanish.

Muchinga Mountains /muː'tʃɪŋgə/ a range of mountains in eastern Zambia.

muchness ▸ noun [mass noun] greatness in quantity or degree.
– PHRASES **(much) of a muchness** informal very similar: *the polls looked much of a muchness but concealed politically crucial variations.*

mucho /'mʊtʃəʊ, 'mʌtʃəʊ/ informal, humorous ▸ determiner much or many: *that caused me mucho problems.*
▸ adverb [usu. as submodifier] very: *he was being mucho macho.*
– ORIGIN Spanish.

mucilage /'mjuːsɪlɪdʒ/ ▸ noun [mass noun] a viscous secretion or bodily fluid. ■ a polysaccharide substance extracted as a viscous or gelatinous solution from plant roots, seeds, etc., and used in medicines and adhesives. ■ N. Amer. an adhesive solution; gum or glue.
– DERIVATIVES **mucilaginous** /-'ladʒɪnəs/ adjective.
– ORIGIN late Middle English: via French from late Latin *mucilago* 'musty juice', from Latin *mucus* (see **MUCUS**).

mucin /'mjuːsɪn/ ▸ noun [mass noun] Biochemistry a glycoprotein constituent of mucus.
– ORIGIN mid 19th cent.: from **MUCUS** + **-IN¹**.

mucinous ▸ adjective relating to or covered with mucus.

muck ▸ noun [mass noun] dirt, rubbish, or waste matter: *I'll just clean the muck off the windscreen.* ■ farmyard manure, widely used as fertilizer. ■ informal something regarded as distasteful, unpleasant, or of poor quality: *why do you let her read this muck?*
▸ verb [with obj.] **1** (**muck something out**) chiefly Brit. remove manure and other dirt from a horse's stable or other animal's dwelling.
2 dialect spread manure on (land).
– PHRASES **as common as muck** Brit. informal of low social status. **make a muck of** Brit. informal handle (something) incompetently. **where there's muck there's brass** Brit. proverb dirty or unpleasant activities are also lucrative.
– PHRASAL VERBS **muck about/around** Brit. informal behave in a silly or aimless way: *we just muck around in training and have a laugh.* **muck about/around with** tinker with (something), typically so as to damage or spoil it: *have you been mucking about with the aerial?* **muck someone about/around** treat someone inconsiderately, typically by disrupting their plans. **muck in** Brit. informal share tasks or accommodation without expecting a privileged position: *she really enjoys* **mucking in with** *the lads.* **muck something up** informal do something badly or ineptly; mishandle something: *she had mucked up her first few weeks at college.*
– ORIGIN Middle English *muk*, probably of Scandinavian origin: compare with Old Norse *myki* 'dung', from a Germanic base meaning 'soft', shared by **MEEK**.

muckamuck /'mʌkəmʌk/ (also **mucky-muck**) ▸ noun N. Amer. informal a person of great importance or self-importance.
– ORIGIN mid 19th cent.: from Chinook Jargon, shortening of **HIGH MUCK-A-MUCK**.

mucker ▸ noun **1** a person who removes dirt and waste, especially from mines or stables.
2 Brit. informal a friend or companion.
3 US informal, dated a rough or coarse person.
– PHRASES **come a mucker** Brit. informal, dated another way of saying **COME A CROPPER** (see **CROPPER**).
– ORIGIN Middle English: from **MUCK** + **-ER¹**; sense 2 probably from the phrase *muck in.* Sense 3 is probably from German *Mucker* 'sulky person'.

muckle ▸ noun, adjective, determiner, & pronoun variant form of **MICKLE**.

> **USAGE** On the confused use of **muckle** and **mickle**, see **USAGE** at **MICKLE**.

muckraking ▸ noun [mass noun] the action of searching out and publicizing scandal about famous people: [as modifier] *a muckraking journalist.*
– DERIVATIVES **muckrake** verb, **muckraker** noun.
– ORIGIN coined by President Theodore Roosevelt in a speech (1906) alluding to Bunyan's *Pilgrim's Progress* and the man with the *muck rake.*

muck spreader ▸ noun Brit. a machine used to spread manure on fields.
– DERIVATIVES **muck-spreading** noun.

muck sweat ▸ noun informal a state of perspiring profusely: *I got there in a muck sweat.*

mucky ▸ adjective (**muckier**, **muckiest**) covered with dirt or filth: *he took off his mucky boots.* ■ informal corrupt or sordid: *a mucky mix of political wheeler-dealing and multinational corruption.* ■ Brit. informal mildly pornographic: *mucky books.*
– DERIVATIVES **muckiness** noun.

muco- ▸ combining form representing **MUCUS**.

mucoid /'mjuːkɔɪd/ ▸ adjective involving, resembling, or of the nature of mucus.

mucopolysaccharide /ˌmjuːkəʊpɒlɪ'sakərʌɪd/ ▸ noun Biochemistry any of a group of compounds occurring chiefly as components of connective tissue. They are complex polysaccharides containing amino groups.

mucosa /mjuː'kəʊsə/ ▸ noun (pl. **mucosae** /-siː/) a mucous membrane: *the intestinal mucosa.*
– DERIVATIVES **mucosal** adjective.
– ORIGIN late 19th cent.: modern Latin, feminine of *mucosus* (see **MUCOUS**).

mucous /'mjuːkəs/ ▸ adjective relating to, producing, covered with, or of the nature of mucus.
– ORIGIN mid 17th cent.: from Latin *mucosus* (see **MUCUS**).

mucous membrane ▸ noun an epithelial tissue which secretes mucus, and lines many body cavities and tubular organs including the gut and respiratory passages.

mucro /'mjuːkrəʊ/ ▸ noun (pl. **mucrones** /-'krəʊniːz/ or **mucros**) Botany & Zoology a short sharp point at the end of a part or organ.
– ORIGIN mid 17th cent.: from Latin, 'sharp point'.

mucronate /'mjuːkrənət/ ▸ adjective Botany & Zoology ending abruptly in a short sharp point or mucro.
– ORIGIN late 18th cent.: from Latin *mucronatus*, from *mucro, mucron-* 'point'.

mucuna /mjuː'kjuːnə/ ▸ noun a tropical climbing bean plant. ● Genus *Mucuna*, family Leguminosae: many species, especially the velvet bean, *M. deeringiana*, and *M. pruriens*, grown as a fodder plant and green manure.
– ORIGIN mid 19th cent.: via Portuguese from Tupi *mucunán.*

mucus /'mjuːkəs/ ▸ noun [mass noun] a slimy substance, typically not miscible with water, secreted by the mucous membranes and glands of animals for lubrication, protection, etc. ■ a gummy substance found in plants; mucilage.
– ORIGIN mid 17th cent.: from Latin.

MUD ▶ noun (pl. **MUDs**) a computer-based text or virtual reality game which several players play at the same time, interacting with each other as well as with characters controlled by the computer.
– ORIGIN 1980s: from *multi-user dungeon* or *multi-user dimension*.

mud ▶ noun **1** [mass noun] soft, sticky matter resulting from the mixing of earth and water.
2 information or allegations regarded as damaging or scandalous: *the two sides took over the local media to throw mud at each other*.
– PHRASES **drag someone/thing through the mud** slander or denigrate someone or something publicly. **here's mud in your eye!** informal expressing good wishes before drinking. **someone's name is mud** informal someone is in disgrace or unpopular: *if anything goes wrong, my name will be mud*.
– ORIGIN late Middle English: probably from Middle Low German *mudde*.

mudbank ▶ noun a bank of mud on the bed of a river or the bottom of the sea.

mudbath ▶ noun **1** a bath in the mud of mineral springs, taken to relieve rheumatic complaints.
2 a muddy place: *the pitch was a mudbath*.

mudbug ▶ noun N. Amer. a freshwater crayfish.

mud dauber ▶ noun a solitary wasp which builds a mud nest that typically consists of a series of tube-like cells on an exposed surface. ● Several genera in the family Sphecidae.

muddle ▶ verb [with obj.] **1** bring into a disordered or confusing state: *they were* ***muddling up*** *the cards*. ■ confuse (a person or their thoughts): *Paul was hopelessly muddled by the rates of exchange*. ■ [no obj., with adverbial] busy oneself in an aimless or ineffective way: *he was muddling about in the kitchen*.
2 mix (a drink) or stir (an ingredient) into a drink.
▶ noun [usu. in sing.] an untidy and disorganized state or collection: *the finances were* ***in a muddle*** | [mass noun] *she was able to cut through confusion and muddle*. ■ a mistake arising from or resulting in confusion: *a bureaucratic muddle*.
– PHRASAL VERBS **muddle through** (or Brit. **along**) cope more or less satisfactorily despite lack of expertise, planning, or equipment: *while the children were young, we managed to muddle through*. **muddle something up** confuse two or more things with each other: *the words seemed to have* ***got muddled up***.
– DERIVATIVES **muddling** adjective, **muddlingly** adverb, **muddly** adjective.
– ORIGIN late Middle English (in the sense 'wallow in mud'): perhaps from Middle Dutch *moddelen*, frequentative of *modden* 'dabble in mud'; compare with MUD. The sense 'confuse' was initially associated with alcoholic drink (late 17th cent.), giving rise to 'busy oneself in a confused way' and 'jumble up' (mid 19th cent.).

muddled ▶ adjective not arranged in order; untidy: *the muddled display of pictures has been taken down*. ■ not clear or coherent; confused: *such a view reflects muddled thinking*.

muddle-headed ▶ adjective mentally disorganized or confused: *a muddle-headed idealist*.
– DERIVATIVES **muddle-headedness** noun.

muddler ▶ noun **1** a person who creates muddles, especially because of a disorganized method of thinking or working.
2 (also **muddler minnow**) a type of fly used in trout-fishing.
3 a stick used to stir cocktails.

muddy ▶ adjective (**muddier, muddiest**) covered in or full of mud: *they changed their muddy boots*. ■ not bright or clear; dirty-looking: *the original colours were blurred into muddy pink and yellow*. ■ (of a sound, especially in music) not clearly defined: *an awful muddy sound that renders his vocals incoherent*. ■ confused, vague, or illogical: *some sentences are so muddy that their meaning can only be guessed*.
▶ verb (**muddies, muddying, muddied**) [with obj.] cover or fill (something) with mud. ■ make (something) hard or harder to understand: *the first year's results muddy rather than clarify the situation*.
– PHRASES **muddy the waters** make an issue or situation more confused or complicated.
– DERIVATIVES **muddily** adverb, **muddiness** noun.

Mudejar /muːˈdeɪhɑː/ ▶ adjective of or denoting a partly Gothic, partly Islamic style of architecture and art prevalent in Spain in the 12th to 15th centuries. ■ relating to Muslim subjects of Christian monarchs during the reconquest of the Iberian peninsula from the Moors (11th–15th centuries) who, until 1492, were allowed to retain Islamic laws and religion in return for loyalty to a Christian monarch.
▶ noun (pl. **Mudejares** /-reɪz/) a Mudejar Muslim during the Christian reconquest of the Iberian peninsula from the Moors.
– ORIGIN via Spanish from Arabic *mudajjan* 'allowed to stay'.

mud fever ▶ noun [mass noun] a bacterial skin infection which chiefly affects the lower legs of horses exposed to wet and muddy conditions, causing cracking and soreness of the skin and hair loss in the affected area. ● This condition is caused by the bacterium *Dermatophilus congolensis*.

mudfish ▶ noun (pl. **same** or **mudfishes**) **1** any of a number of elongated fish that are able to survive long periods of drought by burrowing in the mud:
● a New Zealand fish (genus *Neochanna*, family Galaxiidae).
● an African lungfish (*Protopterus annectens*, family Protopteridae).
2 another term for BOWFIN.

mudflap ▶ noun a flap that hangs behind the wheel of a vehicle and is designed to prevent water and stones thrown up from the road from hitting the bodywork or any following vehicles.

mudflat ▶ noun (usu. **mudflats**) a stretch of muddy land left uncovered at low tide.

mudflow ▶ noun a fluid or hardened stream or avalanche of mud.

mudguard ▶ noun a curved strip or cover over a wheel of a vehicle, especially a bicycle or motorcycle, designed to protect the vehicle and rider from water and dirt thrown up from the road.

mudlark (also **mudlarker**) ▶ noun a person who scavenges in river mud for objects of value. ■ historical a scruffy or dirty child who spent most of the time on the street.

mudminnow ▶ noun a small stout-bodied freshwater fish of both Eurasia and North America, able to survive low concentrations of oxygen and very low temperatures. ● Genus *Umbra*, family Umbridae: several species.

mud-nester ▶ noun a gregarious Australian bird of a family that comprises the apostlebird and the white-winged chough, which make nests of mud. ● Family Corcoracidae; sometimes placed with the magpie lark in the family Grallinidae.

mud pack ▶ noun a paste of fuller's earth or a similar substance, applied thickly to the face to improve the condition of the skin.

mud pie ▶ noun mud made into a pie shape by a child.

mud puppy ▶ noun a large aquatic salamander of the eastern US, reaching sexual maturity while retaining an immature body form with feathery external gills. ● *Necturus maculosus*, family Proteidae. Compare with WATERDOG.

mudra /ˈmʌdrə/ ▶ noun a symbolic hand gesture used in Hindu ceremonies and statuary, and in Indian dance. ■ a movement or pose in yoga.
– ORIGIN from Sanskrit *mudrā* 'sign or token'.

mudskipper ▶ noun a goby (fish) with its eyes on raised bumps on top of the head, found in mangrove swamps from East Africa to Australia. It moves about on land with great agility, often basking on mud or mangrove roots. ● *Periopthalmodon* and related genera, family Gobiidae: several species, including the common and widespread *P. schlosseri* (or *barbarus*).

mudslide ▶ noun a mass of mud and other earthy material that is falling or has fallen down a hillside or other slope.

mud-slinging ▶ noun [mass noun] informal the use of insults and accusations, especially unjust ones, with the aim of damaging the reputation of an opponent.
– DERIVATIVES **mud-sling** verb, **mud-slinger** noun.

mudstone ▶ noun [mass noun] a dark sedimentary rock formed from consolidated mud and lacking the laminations of shale.

mud turtle ▶ noun any of a number of drab-coloured freshwater turtles that often haul themselves out on to mudbanks, in particular: ● an American turtle with scent glands that produce an unpleasant odour (genus *Kinosternon*, family Kinosternidae). ● an African side-necked turtle (genus *Pelusios*, family Pelomedusidae). ● an Asian softshell (genera *Lissemys* and *Pelochelys*, family Trionychidae).

Mudville ▶ noun [mass noun] N. Amer. (in sport, especially baseball) used with reference to the emotions felt by fans or a team according to the outcome of a game: *there was joy in Mudville following the Vancouver Bar Association league 'A' division championship*.
– ORIGIN the name of a fictional town in E. L. Thayer's poem 'Casey at the Bat' (1888), which features the defeat of its baseball team.

mud volcano ▶ noun a small vent or fissure in the ground discharging hot mud.

mudwort ▶ noun a very small creeping plant that grows in mud and damp soils in north temperate regions. ● *Limosella aquatica*, family Scrophulariaceae.

muesli /ˈm(j)uːzli/ ▶ noun (pl. **mueslis**) [mass noun] chiefly Brit. a mixture of oats and other cereals, dried fruit, and nuts, eaten with milk at breakfast.
– ORIGIN Swiss German.

muezzin /muːˈɛzɪn/ ▶ noun a man who calls Muslims to prayer from the minaret of a mosque.
– ORIGIN late 16th cent.: dialect variant of Arabic *mu'addin*, active participle of *addana* 'proclaim'.

muff[1] ▶ noun **1** a tube made of fur or other warm material into which the hands are placed for warmth.
2 vulgar slang a woman's genitals.
– ORIGIN mid 16th cent.: from Dutch *mof*, Middle Dutch *muffel*, from medieval Latin *muff(u)la*, of unknown ultimate origin.

muff[2] informal ▶ verb [with obj.] handle (a situation, task, or opportunity) clumsily or badly: *the administration muffed several of its biggest projects*.
▶ noun a mistake or failure, especially a failure to catch or receive a ball cleanly in sport. ■ dated, chiefly Brit. a clumsy or incompetent person, especially in relation to a sport or manual skill.
– ORIGIN early 19th cent.: of unknown origin.

muff diver ▶ noun vulgar slang a person who performs cunnilingus.
– DERIVATIVES **muff diving** noun.

muffin ▶ noun **1** a small domed spongy cake made with eggs and baking powder: *blueberry muffins*.
2 (N. Amer. **English muffin**) a flat circular spongy bread roll made from yeast dough and eaten split, toasted, and buttered.
– ORIGIN early 18th cent.: of unknown origin.

muffin top ▶ noun informal a roll of fat visible above the top of a pair of women's tight-fitting low-waisted trousers.

muffle ▶ verb [with obj.] **1** wrap or cover for warmth: *everyone was* ***muffled up*** *in coats and scarves*.
2 cover or wrap up (a source of sound) to reduce its loudness: (as adj. **muffled**) *the soft beat of a muffled drum*. ■ make (a sound) quieter or less distinct: *his voice was muffled* | figurative *the trade unions fear their voice within the party is being muffled*.
▶ noun [usu. as modifier] a receptacle in a furnace or kiln in which things can be heated without contact with combustion products: *a muffle furnace*.
– ORIGIN late Middle English (as a verb): perhaps a shortening of Old French *enmoufler*; the noun (mid 17th cent.) from Old French *moufle* 'thick glove'.

muffled ▶ adjective (of a sound) not loud because of being obstructed in some way; muted: *they heard the sounds of muffled voices*.

muffler ▶ noun **1** a wrap or scarf worn around the neck and face for warmth.
2 a device used to deaden the sound of a drum, bell, piano, or other instrument. ■ N. Amer. a silencer for a motor vehicle exhaust.

mufti[1] /ˈmʌfti/ ▶ noun (pl. **muftis**) a Muslim legal expert who is empowered to give rulings on religious matters.
– ORIGIN late 16th cent.: from Arabic *muftī*, active participle of *'aftā* 'decide a point of law'.

mufti[2] /ˈmʌfti/ ▶ noun [mass noun] plain clothes worn by a person who wears a uniform for their job, such as a soldier or police officer: *a High Court judge in mufti*.
– ORIGIN early 19th cent.: perhaps humorously from MUFTI[1].

mug[1] ▶ noun **1** a large cup, typically cylindrical with a handle and used without a saucer. ■ the contents of a mug: *I drank a mug of tea*.
2 informal a person's face.
3 Brit. informal a stupid or gullible person.
4 US informal a hoodlum or thug.
▶ verb (**mugs, mugging, mugged**) informal **1** [with obj.] attack and rob (someone) in a public place: *he was mugged by three men who stole his bike*.
2 [no obj.] make faces, especially silly or exaggerated ones, before an audience or a camera: *he mugged for the camera*.
– PHRASES **a mug's game** informal an activity in which it is foolish to engage because it is likely to be unsuccessful or dangerous: *playing with drugs is a mug's game*.
– DERIVATIVES **mugful** noun (pl. **mugfuls**).

M

– ORIGIN early 16th cent. (originally Scots and northern English, denoting an earthenware bowl): probably of Scandinavian origin; compare with Norwegian *mugge*, Swedish *mugg* 'pitcher with a handle'.

mug[2] ▶ verb (**mugs, mugging, mugged**) [with obj.] (**mug something up**) Brit. informal learn or revise a subject as far as possible in a short time: *I'm constantly having to mug up things ahead of teaching them* | [no obj.] *we had* ***mugged up on*** *all things Venetian before the start of the course.*
– ORIGIN mid 19th cent.: of unknown origin.

Mugabe /mʊˈɡɑːbi/, Robert (Gabriel) (b.1924), Zimbabwean statesman, Prime Minister 1980–7 and President since 1987. He became Prime Minister in Zimbabwe's first post-independence elections. In 1987 his party ZANU merged with ZAPU and Mugabe became executive President of a one-party state.

Muganda /mʊˈɡandə/ ▶ noun singular form of **BAGANDA**.

mugger[1] ▶ noun a person who attacks and robs another in a public place.

mugger[2] ▶ noun a large Indian crocodile with a short snout. ● *Crocodylus palustris*, family Crocodylidae.
– ORIGIN mid 19th cent.: from Hindi *magar*, from Sanskrit *makara*, the name of a horned water beast represented in Hindu mythology.

mugging ▶ noun an act of attacking and robbing someone in a public place: *he was the victim of a brutal mugging.*

muggins ▶ noun (pl. **same** or **mugginses**) Brit. informal a foolish and gullible person (often used humorously to refer to oneself): *muggins has volunteered to do the catering.*
– ORIGIN mid 19th cent.: perhaps a use of the surname *Muggins*, with allusion to **MUG**[1].

muggle /ˈmʌɡ(ə)l/ ▶ noun informal a person who is not conversant with a particular activity or skill: *she's a muggle: no IT background, understanding, or aptitude at all.*
– ORIGIN 1990s: from **MUG**[1] + **-LE**[2]; used in the *Harry Potter* books by J. K. Rowling to mean 'a person without magical powers'.

Muggletonian /ˌmʌɡ(ə)lˈtəʊnɪən/ ▶ noun a member of a small Christian sect founded in England *c.*1651 by Lodowicke Muggleton (1609–98) and John Reeve (1608–58), who claimed to be the two witnesses mentioned in the book of Revelation (Rev. 11:3–6). Despite many eccentric doctrines, the sect survived into the late 19th century.
▶ adjective relating to the Muggletonians.

muggy ▶ adjective (**muggier, muggiest**) (of the weather) unpleasantly warm and humid.
– DERIVATIVES **mugginess** noun.
– ORIGIN mid 18th cent.: from dialect *mug* 'mist, drizzle', from Old Norse *mugga*.

Mughal /ˈmuːɡɑːl/ variant spelling of **MOGUL**.

Mughlai /ˈmʊɡlʌɪ, ˈmuːɡlʌɪ/ (also **Moghlai, Moglai**) ▶ adjective (of food or a dish) cooked in an Indian style involving one of a variety of rich, spicy sauces, typically containing butter, yogurt, or cream.
– ORIGIN Urdu *muġlai* 'in a Mughal style'.

mugshot ▶ noun informal a photograph of a person's face made for an official purpose, especially police records. ■ humorous any photograph of a person's face.

mugwort ▶ noun a plant of the daisy family, with aromatic divided leaves that are dark green above and whitish below, native to north temperate regions. ● Genus *Artemisia*, family Compositae: several species, in particular the common English hedgerow plant *A. vulgaris*, which has long been connected with magic and superstition.
– ORIGIN Old English *mucgwyrt* (see **MIDGE, WORT**).

mugwump /ˈmʌɡwʌmp/ ▶ noun N. Amer. a person who remains aloof or independent, especially from party politics.
– ORIGIN mid 19th cent.: from Algonquian *mugquomp* 'great chief'.

Muhammad /məˈhamɪd/ (also **Mohammed**) (*c.*570–632), Arab prophet and founder of Islam.

> In *c.*610 in Mecca Muhammad received the first of a series of revelations which, as the Koran, became the doctrinal and legislative basis of Islam. In the face of opposition to his preaching he and his small group of supporters were forced to flee to Medina in 622 (the Hegira). He then led his followers into a series of battles against the Meccans. In 630 Mecca capitulated, and by his death Muhammad had united most of Arabia.

Muhammad Ahmad /ˈɑːmad/ see **MAHDI**.

Muhammad Ali[1] /ˈɑːli, ɑːˈliː/ (1769–1849), Ottoman viceroy and pasha of Egypt 1805–49, possibly of Albanian descent. He modernized Egypt's infrastructure, making it the leading power in the eastern Mediterranean, and established a dynasty that survived until 1952.

Muhammad Ali[2] /ˈɑːli, ɑːˈliː/ (b.1942), American boxer; born *Cassius Marcellus Clay*. He won the world heavyweight title in 1964, 1974, and 1978, becoming the only boxer to be world champion three times.

Muhammadan /mʊˈhaməd(ə)n/ (also **Mohammedan**) ▶ noun & adjective archaic term for **MUSLIM** (not favoured by Muslims).
– DERIVATIVES **Muhammadanism** noun.
– ORIGIN late 17th cent.: from the name of the prophet *Muhammad* (see **MUHAMMAD**), + **-AN**.

> **USAGE** For a discussion of the terms **Muhammadan, Muslim**, and **Moslem**, see **USAGE** at **MUSLIM**.

Muharram /məˈhʌrəm/ ▶ noun the first month of the year in the Islamic calendar. ■ an annual celebration in the month of Muharram commemorating the death of Husayn, grandson of Muhammad, and his retinue.
– ORIGIN from Arabic *muḥarram* 'inviolable'.

Mühlhausen /ˈmyːlˌhaʊzn/ German name for **MULHOUSE**.

muishond /ˈmeɪs(h)ɒnt/ ▶ noun (pl. **same** or **muishonds** or **muishonde**) S. African any of a number of small carnivorous mammals, especially of the weasel or mongoose families.
– ORIGIN late 18th cent.: from South African Dutch, transferred use of Dutch *muishond* 'weasel'.

mujahideen /ˌmʊdʒahɪˈdiːn/ (also **mujahedin, mujahidin**) ▶ plural noun guerrilla fighters in Islamic countries, especially those who are fighting against non-Muslim forces.
– ORIGIN from Persian and Arabic *mujāhidīn*, colloquial plural of *mujāhid*, denoting a person who fights a jihad.

Mujibur Rahman /mʊˌdʒiːbʊə rəˈmɑːn/ (1920–75), Bangladeshi statesman, first Prime Minister of independent Bangladesh 1972–5 and President 1975; known as **Sheikh Mujib**. After failing to establish parliamentary democracy as Prime Minister, he assumed dictatorial powers in 1975. He and his family were assassinated in a military coup.

mujtahid /mʊdʒˈtɑːhɪd/ ▶ noun (pl. **mujtahids** or **mujtahidūn**) Islam a person accepted as an original authority in Islamic law. Such authorities continue to be recognized in the Shia tradition, but Sunni Muslims accord this status only to the great lawmakers of early Islam.
– ORIGIN Persian, from Arabic, active participle of *ijtahada* 'strive'.

Mukalla /mʊˈkalə/ a port on the south coast of Yemen, in the Gulf of Aden; pop. 182,500 (est. 2004).

Mukden /ˈmʊkdən/ former name for **SHENYANG**.

mukhtar /ˈmʊktɑː/ ▶ noun (in Turkey and some Arab countries) the head of local government of a town or village.
– ORIGIN from Arabic *muktār*, passive participle of *iktāra* 'choose'.

mukluk /ˈmʌklʌk/ ▶ noun N. Amer. a high, soft boot that is worn in the American Arctic and is traditionally made from sealskin.
– ORIGIN mid 19th cent.: from Yupik *maklak* 'bearded seal'.

mukti /ˈmʌkti, ˈmʊkti/ ▶ noun another term for **MOKSHA**.
– ORIGIN from Hindi, Sanskrit, literally 'release, deliverance'.

muktuk /ˈmʌktʌk/ ▶ noun [mass noun] the skin and blubber of a whale, typically the narwhal or the beluga, used as food by the Inuit.
– ORIGIN from Inuit *maktak*.

mulatto /m(j)uːˈlatəʊ/ dated, offensive ▶ noun (pl. **mulattoes** or **mulattos**) a person with one white and one black parent.
– ORIGIN late 16th cent.: from Spanish *mulato* 'young mule or mulatto', formed irregularly from *mulo* 'mule'.

mulberry ▶ noun (pl. **mulberries**) **1** (also **mulberry tree** or **bush**) a small deciduous tree with broad leaves, native to East Asia and long cultivated elsewhere. ● Genus *Morus*, family Moraceae, in particular the **white mulberry** (*M. alba*), originally grown for feeding silkworms, and the **black** (or **common**) **mulberry** (*M. nigra*), grown for its fruit. See also **PAPER MULBERRY**.
■ the dark red or white loganberry-like fruit of the mulberry.
2 [mass noun] a dark red or purple colour: [as modifier] *a mulberry carpet.*
– ORIGIN Old English *mōrberie*, from Latin *morum* + **BERRY**; related to Dutch *moerbezie* and German *Maulbeere*.

mulch /mʌl(t)ʃ/ ▶ noun [mass noun] material (such as decaying leaves, bark, or compost) spread around or over a plant to enrich or insulate the soil. ■ [count noun] an application of mulch: *regular mulches keep down annual weeds.*
▶ verb [with obj.] treat or cover with mulch.
– ORIGIN mid 17th cent.: probably from dialect *mulch* 'soft' used as a noun, from Old English *melsc, mylsc*.

mulct /mʌlkt/ formal ▶ verb [with obj.] extract money from (someone) by fine or taxation. ■ (**mulct something of**) take money or possessions from (someone) by fraudulent means: *a rapacious old woman who would never miss the few dollars mulcted of her.*
▶ noun a fine or compulsory payment.
– ORIGIN late 15th cent.: from Latin *mulctare, multare*, from *mulcta* 'a fine'.

Muldoon /mʌlˈduːn/, Sir Robert (David) (1921–92), New Zealand statesman, Prime Minister 1975–84. His Premiership was marked by domestic measures to tackle low economic growth and high inflation.

mule[1] ▶ noun **1** the offspring of a donkey and a horse (strictly, a male donkey and a female horse), typically sterile and used as a beast of burden. Compare with **HINNY**[1]. ■ an obstinate person. ■ informal a courier for illegal drugs.
2 a hybrid plant or animal, especially a sterile one. ■ any of several standard cross-bred varieties of sheep.
3 (also **spinning mule**) a kind of spinning machine producing yarn on spindles, invented by Samuel Crompton in 1779.
4 a small tractor or locomotive, typically one that is electrically powered.
5 a coin with the obverse and reverse of designs not originally intended to be used together.
– ORIGIN Old English *mūl*, probably of Germanic origin, from Latin *mulus, mula*; reinforced in Middle English by Old French *mule*.

mule[2] ▶ noun a woman's slipper or light shoe without a back.
– ORIGIN mid 16th cent.: from French, 'slipper'.

mule deer ▶ noun a North American deer with long ears and black markings on the tail. ● *Odocoileus hemionus*, family Cervidae.

mulesing /ˈmjuːlzɪŋ/ ▶ noun [mass noun] the process of removing folds of skin from the tail area of a sheep, intended to reduce fly strike.
– ORIGIN 1940s: from the name of John H. W. *Mules* (1876–1946), the Australian sheep farmer who developed the process, + **-ING**[1].

muleta /məˈleɪtə/ ▶ noun a red cloth fixed to a stick, brandished by a matador during a bullfight.
– ORIGIN Spanish.

muleteer /ˌmjuːlɪˈtɪə/ ▶ noun a person who drives mules.
– ORIGIN mid 16th cent.: from French *muletier*, from *mulet*, diminutive of Old French *mul* 'mule'.

muley[1] /ˈmjuːli/ ▶ adjective chiefly US (of cattle) hornless.
– ORIGIN late 16th cent. (as noun): perhaps from Irish *maol* or Welsh *moel*, literally 'bald', used in the sense 'hornless cow'. The adjective dates from the mid 19th cent.

muley[2] /ˈmjuːli/ (also **mulie**) ▶ noun (pl. **muleys** or **mulies**) US informal a mule deer.

mulga /ˈmʌlɡə/ ▶ noun (also **mulga tree** or **bush**) a small Australian acacia tree or shrub with greyish foliage, which forms dense scrubby growth and yields brown and yellow timber. ● Genus *Acacia*, family Leguminosae; several species, especially *Acacia aneura*.
■ [mass noun] an area of scrub or bush dominated by mulgas. ■ (**the mulga**) Austral. informal the outback.
– ORIGIN mid 19th cent.: from Kamilaroi, Yuwaalaraay, and other Aboriginal languages of New South Wales and South Australia.

mulgara /məlˈɡɑːrə/ ▶ noun a rat-sized carnivorous marsupial with a pointed snout, large eyes, and a short crested tail, native to central Australia. ● *Dasycercus cristicauda*, family Dasyuridae.
– ORIGIN 1940s: probably from Wangganguru (an Aboriginal language) *mardagura*.

Mulhacén /muːlə'sɛn/, Spanish /mula'θen, -sen/ a mountain in southern Spain, south-east of Granada, in the Sierra Nevada range. Rising to 3,482 m (11,424 ft), it is the highest mountain in the country.

Mülheim /'muːlhʌɪm/, German /'myːlhaɪm/ an industrial city in western Germany, in North Rhine-Westphalia south-west of Essen; pop. 169,400 (est. 2006). Full name **Mülheim an der Ruhr** /ˌan dɛː 'rʊə/, German /ˌan deːɐ 'ruːɐ/.

Mulhouse /mʊ'luːz/ an industrial city in NE France, in Alsace; pop. 112,260 (2006). It was a free imperial city until it joined the French Republic in 1798. In 1871, after the Franco-Prussian War, the city became part of the German Empire until it was reunited with France in 1918. German name **MÜHLHAUSEN**.

muliebrity /ˌmjuːlɪ'ɛbrɪti/ ▶ **noun** [mass noun] literary womanly qualities; womanliness.
– ORIGIN late 16th cent.: from late Latin *muliebritas*, from Latin *mulier* 'woman'.

mulish /'mjuːlɪʃ/ ▶ **adjective** resembling or likened to a mule in being stubborn: *a mulish expression*.
– DERIVATIVES **mulishly** adverb, **mulishness** noun.

Mull a large island of the Inner Hebrides; chief town, Tobermory. It is separated from the coast of Scotland near Oban by the Sound of Mull.

mull[1] ▶ **verb** [with obj.] think about (something) deeply and at length: *she began to **mull over** the various possibilities*.
– ORIGIN mid 19th cent.: of uncertain origin.

mull[2] ▶ **verb** [with obj.] (usu. as adj. **mulled**) warm (an alcoholic drink, especially wine or beer) and add sugar and spices to it: *a glass of mulled wine*.
– ORIGIN early 17th cent.: of unknown origin.

mull[3] ▶ **noun** [in place names] Scottish a promontory: *the Mull of Kintyre*.
– ORIGIN Middle English: compare with Scottish Gaelic *maol* and Icelandic *múli*.

mull[4] ▶ **noun** [mass noun] humus formed under non-acid conditions.
– ORIGIN 1920s: from Danish *muld* 'soil'.

mull[5] ▶ **noun** [mass noun] thin, soft, plain muslin, used in bookbinding for joining the spine of a book to its cover.
– ORIGIN late 17th cent.: abbreviation, from Hindi *malmal*.

mullah /'mʌlə, 'mʊlə/ ▶ **noun** a Muslim learned in Islamic theology and sacred law.
– ORIGIN early 17th cent.: from Persian, Turkish, and Urdu *mullā*, from Arabic *mawlā*.

mullein /'mʌlɪn/ ▶ **noun** a herbaceous Eurasian plant with woolly leaves and tall spikes of yellow flowers.
● Genus *Verbascum*, family Scrophulariaceae: several species, in particular the **common** (or **great**) **mullein** (*V. thapsus*).
– ORIGIN late Middle English: from Old French *moleine*, of Celtic origin; compare with Breton *melen*, Cornish and Welsh *melyn* 'yellow'.

Muller /'mʌlə/, Hermann Joseph (1890–1967), American geneticist. He discovered that X-rays induce mutations in the genetic material of the fruit fly *Drosophila* and thus recognized the danger of X-radiation to living things. Nobel Prize for Physiology or Medicine (1946).

muller[1] /'mʌlə/ ▶ **noun** a stone or other heavy weight used for grinding artists' pigments or other material on a slab.
– ORIGIN late Middle English: perhaps from Anglo-Norman French *moldre* 'to grind'.

muller[2] /'mʌlə/ ▶ **verb** [with obj.] Brit. informal wreck or destroy (something). ■ beat or defeat (an opponent) comprehensively: *we absolutely mullered Huddersfield in the second half*.
– ORIGIN 1990s: of unknown origin.

Müller[1] /'mʊlə/, German /'mylɐ/, (Friedrich) Max (1823–1900), German-born British philologist. He is remembered for his edition of the Sanskrit *Rig-veda* (1849–75).

Müller[2] /'mʊlə/, German /'mylɐ/, Johannes Peter (1801–58), German anatomist and zoologist. He was a pioneer of comparative and microscopical methods in biology.

mullered /'mʌləd/ ▶ **adjective** Brit. informal extremely drunk.

Müllerian mimicry /mʊ'lɪərɪən/ ▶ **noun** [mass noun] Zoology a form of mimicry in which two or more harmful or unpalatable animals develop similar appearances as a shared protective device.
– ORIGIN late 19th cent.: named after Johann F. T. *Müller* (1821–97), German zoologist.

Müller-Thurgau /ˌmʊlə'tʊəgaʊ/, German /ˌmylɐ'tuːɐgaʊ/ ▶ **noun** [mass noun] a variety of white grape used for making wine, developed as a cross between the Sylvaner and the Riesling vines. ■ a wine made from the Müller-Thurgau grape.
– ORIGIN named after Hermann *Müller* (1850–1927), Swiss viniculturist + *Thurgau*, the name of the Swiss canton where he was born.

mullet[1] ▶ **noun** any of various chiefly marine fish that are widely caught for food. ● Families Mullidae (see **RED MULLET**) and Mugilidae (see **GREY MULLET**).
– ORIGIN late Middle English: from Old French *mulet*, diminutive of Latin *mullus* 'red mullet', from Greek *mullos*.

mullet[2] ▶ **noun** Heraldry a star with five (or more) straight-edged points or rays, as a charge or a mark of cadency for a third son.
– ORIGIN late Middle English: from Old French *molette* 'rowel', diminutive of *meule* 'millstone', from Latin *mola* 'grindstone'.

mullet[3] /'mʌlɪt/ ▶ **noun** a man's hairstyle in which the hair is cut short at the front and sides and left long at the back.
– ORIGIN 1990s: of unknown origin.

mulligan /'mʌlɪg(ə)n/ ▶ **noun** informal, chiefly N. Amer. **1** a stew made from odds and ends of food.
2 (in informal golf) an extra stroke allowed after a poor shot, not counted on the scorecard.
– ORIGIN early 20th cent.: apparently from the surname *Mulligan*.

mulligatawny /ˌmʌlɪgə'tɔːni/ ▶ **noun** [mass noun] a spicy meat soup originally made in India.
– ORIGIN from Tamil *miḷaku-taṇṇi* 'pepper water'.

Mullingar /ˌmʌlɪŋ'gɑː/ the county town of Westmeath, in the Republic of Ireland; pop. 8,940 (2006).

mullion /'mʌljən/ ▶ **noun** a vertical bar between the panes of glass in a window. Compare with **TRANSOM**.
– DERIVATIVES **mullioned** adjective.
– ORIGIN mid 16th cent.: probably an altered form of **MONIAL**.

mullock /'mʌlək/ ▶ **noun** [mass noun] dialect worthless material; rubbish. ■ Austral./NZ rock which contains no gold or from which gold has been extracted. ■ Austral./NZ worthless information; nonsense.
– PHRASES **poke mullock at** Austral./NZ informal ridicule (someone).
– ORIGIN late Middle English: diminutive of earlier *mul* 'dust, rubbish', from Middle Dutch.

mulloway /'mʌləweɪ/ ▶ **noun** a large edible fast-swimming predatory fish of Australian coastal waters, which is popular with anglers. Also called **JEWFISH**. ● *Johnius antarctica*, family Sciaenidae.
– ORIGIN mid 19th cent.: from Yaralde (an Aboriginal language of South Australia).

Mulready /mʌl'riːdi/ ▶ **noun** a postage envelope with a design by the Irish painter William Mulready (1786–1863), the designer of the first penny postage envelope (1840).

Mulroney /mʌl'ruːni/, (Martin) Brian (b.1939), Canadian Progressive Conservative statesman, Prime Minister 1984–93.

Multan /mʊl'tɑːn/ a commercial city in Punjab province, east central Pakistan; pop. 1,566,900 (est. 2009).

multangular /mʌl'taŋgjʊlə/ ▶ **adjective** rare (of a polygon) having many angles.
– ORIGIN late 17th cent.: from medieval Latin *multangularis*.

multi- ▶ **combining form** more than one; many: *multicolour | multicultural*.
– ORIGIN from Latin *multus* 'much, many'.

multi-access ▶ **adjective** (of a computer system) allowing the simultaneous connection of a number of terminals.

multi-agency ▶ **adjective** involving cooperation between several organizations, especially in crime prevention, social welfare programmes, or research.

multiaxial ▶ **adjective** involving or possessing several or many axes.

multibillion ▶ **adjective** denoting something costing or valued at several billions of a currency: [in combination] *a multibillion-dollar industry*.

multibuy ▶ **noun** [usu. as modifier] a purchase of two or more articles at a special discount compared to the price when bought separately: *multibuy offers*.

multicast ▶ **verb** (past and past participle **multicast**) [with obj.] send (data) across a computer network to several users at the same time.
▶ **noun** a set of data sent across a computer network to many users at the same time.

multicellular ▶ **adjective** Biology (of an organism or part) having or consisting of many cells.
– DERIVATIVES **multicellularity** noun.

multichannel ▶ **adjective** employing or possessing many communication or television channels.

multicoloured (also **multicolour**, US **multicolored**) ▶ **adjective** having many colours.

multiculti /ˌmʌltɪ'kʌlti/ US informal ▶ **adjective** multicultural.
▶ **noun 1** [mass noun] popular music incorporating ethnically disparate elements.
2 an advocate of cultural diversity.
– ORIGIN 1990s: rhyming alteration of **MULTICULTURAL**.

multicultural ▶ **adjective** relating to or containing several cultural or ethnic groups within a society: *multicultural education*.
– DERIVATIVES **multiculturalism** noun, **multiculturalist** noun & adjective, **multiculturally** adverb.

multidimensional ▶ **adjective** of or involving several dimensions: *multidimensional space*.
– DERIVATIVES **multidimensionality** noun, **multidimensionally** adverb.

multidirectional ▶ **adjective** involving or operating in several directions: *a multidirectional antenna*.

multidisciplinary ▶ **adjective** combining or involving several academic disciplines or professional specializations in an approach to a topic or problem.

multi-ethnic ▶ **adjective** relating to or constituting several ethnic groups: *a multi-ethnic society*.

multifaceted ▶ **adjective 1** having many sides: *the diamond's multifaceted surface*.
2 having many different aspects or features: *his extraordinary and multifaceted career*.

multifactorial ▶ **adjective** involving or dependent on a number of factors, especially genetic or environmental factors.

multifaith ▶ **adjective** involving or characterized by a variety of religions: *the multifaith approach aims to develop an attitude of tolerance*.

multifarious /ˌmʌltɪ'fɛːrɪəs/ ▶ **adjective** many and of various types: *multifarious activities*. ■ having many varied parts or aspects: *a vast multifarious organization*.
– DERIVATIVES **multifariously** adverb, **multifariousness** noun.
– ORIGIN late 16th cent.: from Latin *multifarius* + **-OUS**.

multifilament ▶ **adjective** denoting a cord or yarn composed of a number of strands or filaments wound together.

multiflora (also **multiflora rose**) ▶ **noun** an East Asian shrubby or climbing rose which bears clusters of small single pink or white flowers. ● *Rosa multiflora*, family Rosaceae.
– ORIGIN early 19th cent.: from late Latin, feminine of *multiflorus* 'bearing many flowers'.

multifocal ▶ **adjective** chiefly Medicine & Optics having more than one focus.

multifoil ▶ **noun** Architecture an ornament consisting of more than five foils.

multifold ▶ **adjective** manifold.

multiform ▶ **adjective** existing in many forms or kinds: *a very complex, multiform illness like cancer*.
– DERIVATIVES **multiformity** noun.

multifunctional (also **multifunction**) ▶ **adjective** having or fulfilling several functions: *a multifunctional optical-disk drive*.

multigenerational ▶ **adjective** relating to several generations: *multigenerational families*.

multigrade ▶ **noun 1** an engine oil meeting the requirements of several standard grades.
2 (trademark in the US) a kind of photographic paper made with two emulsions of different sensitivities, from which prints with different levels of contrast can be made using colour filters.

multigrain ▶ **adjective** (of bread) made from more than one kind of grain.

multigravida /ˌmʌltɪ'gravɪdə/ ▶ **noun** (pl. **multigravidae** /-diː/) Medicine & Zoology a woman (or female animal) that is or has been pregnant for at least a second time.
– ORIGIN late 19th cent.: from **MULTI-** 'many', on the pattern of *primigravida*.

multigym ▶ noun an apparatus on which a number of weightlifting and other exercises can be performed to improve muscle tone.

multihull ▶ noun a boat with two or more, especially three, hulls.

multilateral ▶ adjective agreed upon or participated in by three or more parties, especially the governments of different countries: *multilateral negotiations | multilateral nuclear disarmament.* ■ having members or contributors from several groups, especially several different countries: *multilateral aid agencies.*
– DERIVATIVES **multilateralism** noun, **multilateralist** adjective & noun, **multilaterally** adverb.

multilayer chiefly technical ▶ adjective relating to or consisting of several or many layers: *a multilayer circuit board.*
▶ noun a coating or deposit consisting of several or many layers.

multilayered ▶ adjective having or involving several or many layers: *Updike's multilayered narratives.*

multilevel ▶ adjective relating to or involving many levels.

multilingual ▶ adjective in or using several languages: *a multilingual dictionary.*
– DERIVATIVES **multilingualism** noun, **multilingually** adverb.

multimedia ▶ adjective (of art, education, etc.) using more than one medium of expression or communication. ■ (of computer applications) incorporating audio and video, especially interactively.
▶ noun [mass noun] the use of a variety of artistic or communicative media. ■ an extension of hypertext allowing the provision of audio and video material cross-referenced to a computer text.

multimeter ▶ noun an instrument designed to measure electric current, voltage, and usually resistance, typically over several ranges of value.

multimillion ▶ adjective denoting something costing or involving several million of a currency: [in combination] *a multimillion-dollar advertising campaign.*

M

multimillionaire ▶ noun a person with assets worth several million pounds or dollars.

multimode (also **multimodal**) ▶ adjective **1** characterized by several different modes of activity or occurrence.
2 Statistics (of a frequency curve or distribution) having several modes or maxima. ■ (of a property) occurring with a multimode distribution.

multinational ▶ adjective including or involving several countries or individuals of several nationalities: *1,500 troops were sent to join the multinational force.* ■ (of a business organization) operating in several countries: *multinational corporations.*
▶ noun a company operating in several countries.
– DERIVATIVES **multinationally** adverb.

multinomial /ˌmʌltɪˈnəʊmɪəl/ ▶ adjective & noun Mathematics another term for **POLYNOMIAL**.
– ORIGIN early 17th cent.: from **MULTI-** 'many', on the pattern of *binomial.*

multi-occupy ▶ verb [with obj.] (usu. as adj. **multi-occupied**) occupy (a building) as one of a number of independent occupants or families of occupants, typically as tenants: *a multi-occupied house.*
– DERIVATIVES **multi-occupancy** noun, **multi-occupation** noun.

multipack ▶ noun a package containing a number of similar or identical products sold at a discount compared to the price when bought separately.

multipara /mʌlˈtɪp(ə)rə/ ▶ noun (pl. **multiparae** /-riː/) Medicine & Zoology a woman (or female animal) that has had more than one pregnancy resulting in viable offspring.
– ORIGIN mid 19th cent.: modern Latin, feminine of *multiparus* 'multiparous'.

multiparous /mʌlˈtɪp(ə)rəs/ ▶ adjective Medicine (of a woman) having borne more than one child. ■ chiefly Zoology producing more than one young at a birth.

multipartite /ˌmʌltɪˈpɑːtʌɪt/ ▶ adjective having or involving several or many parts or divisions.

multiparty ▶ adjective of or involving several political parties: *multiparty elections.*

multiphase ▶ adjective in or relating to more than one phase. ■ (of an electrical device or circuit) polyphase.

multiplatinum ▶ adjective denoting or relating to a musical recording that has sold more than two million copies.

multiplay ▶ adjective denoting a CD player which can be stacked with a number of discs before needing to be reloaded.

multiplayer ▶ noun **1** a CD player which can play a number of discs in succession.
2 a multimedia computer and home entertainment system that integrates a number of conventional and interactive audio and video functions with those of a computer.
▶ adjective denoting a computer game designed for or involving several players.

multiple ▶ adjective having or involving several parts, elements, or members: *multiple occupancy | a multiple pile-up | a multiple birth.* ■ numerous and often varied: *words with multiple meanings.* ■ (of a disease, injury, etc.) complex in its nature or effects; affecting several parts of the body: *a multiple fracture of the femur.*
▶ noun **1** a number that may be divided by another a certain number of times without a remainder: *15, 20, or any multiple of five.*
2 (also **multiple shop** or **store**) Brit. a shop with branches in many places, especially one selling a specific type of product.
– ORIGIN mid 17th cent.: from French, from late Latin *multiplus*, alteration of Latin *multiplex* (see **MULTIPLEX**).

multiple-choice ▶ adjective (of a question in an examination) accompanied by several possible answers from which the candidate must try to choose the correct one.

multiple fruit ▶ noun Botany a fruit formed from carpels derived from several flowers, such as a pineapple.

multiple-personality disorder ▶ noun Psychology a rare dissociative disorder in which two or more personalities with distinct memories and behaviour patterns apparently exist in one individual.

multiple sclerosis ▶ noun see **SCLEROSIS**.

multiple star ▶ noun a group of stars very close together as seen from the earth, especially one whose members are in fact close together and rotate around a common centre.

multiplet ▶ noun Physics a group of closely associated things, especially closely spaced spectral lines or atomic energy levels, or subatomic particles differing only in a single property (e.g. charge or strangeness).
– ORIGIN 1920s: from **MULTIPLE**, on the pattern of words such as *doublet* and *triplet.*

multiple unit ▶ noun a diesel or electric passenger train of two or more carriages powered by integral motors which drive a number of axles throughout the train.

multiplex ▶ adjective **1** involving or consisting of many elements in a complex relationship: *multiplex ties of work and friendship.* ■ involving simultaneous transmission of several messages along a single channel of communication.
2 (of a cinema) having several separate screens within one building.
▶ noun **1** a system or signal involving simultaneous transmission of several messages along a single channel of communication.
2 a cinema with several separate screens.
▶ verb [with obj.] incorporate into a multiplex signal or system.
– DERIVATIVES **multiplexer** (also **multiplexor**) noun.
– ORIGIN late Middle English in the mathematical sense 'multiple': from Latin.

multipliable ▶ adjective able to be multiplied.

multiplicable /ˈmʌltɪˌplɪkəb(ə)l/ ▶ adjective able to be multiplied.
– ORIGIN late 15th cent.: from Old French, from medieval Latin *multiplicabilis*, from Latin, from *multiplex, multiplic-* (see **MULTIPLEX**).

multiplicand /ˌmʌltɪplɪˈkand, ˈmʌltɪplɪˌkand/ ▶ noun a quantity which is to be multiplied by another (the multiplier).
– ORIGIN late 16th cent.: from medieval Latin *multiplicandus* 'to be multiplied', gerundive of Latin *multiplicare* (see **MULTIPLY[1]**).

multiplication ▶ noun [mass noun] the process or skill of multiplying. ■ Mathematics the process of combining matrices, vectors, or other quantities under specific rules to obtain their product.
– ORIGIN late Middle English: from Old French, or from Latin *multiplicatio(n-)*, from *multiplicare* (see **MULTIPLY[1]**).

multiplication sign ▶ noun the sign ×, used to indicate that one quantity is to be multiplied by another, as in $2 \times 3 = 6$.

multiplication table ▶ noun a list of multiples of a particular number, typically from 1 to 12.

multiplicative /ˈmʌltɪˌplɪkətɪv/ ▶ adjective subject to or of the nature of multiplication: *coronary risk factors are multiplicative.*

multiplicity ▶ noun (pl. **multiplicities**) a large number or variety: *the demand for higher education depends on a multiplicity of factors.*
– ORIGIN late Middle English: from late Latin *multiplicitas*, from Latin *multiplex* (see **MULTIPLEX**).

multiplier ▶ noun a person or thing that multiplies. ■ a quantity by which a given number (the multiplicand) is to be multiplied. ■ Economics a factor by which an increment of income exceeds the resulting increment of saving or investment. ■ a device for increasing by repetition the intensity of an electric current, force, etc. to a measurable level.

multiply[1] /ˈmʌltɪplʌɪ/ ▶ verb (**multiplies, multiplying, multiplied**) [with obj.] **1** obtain from (a number) another which contains the first number a specified number of times: *multiply fourteen by nineteen* | [no obj.] *we all know how to multiply by ten.*
2 increase or cause to increase greatly in number or quantity: [no obj.] *ever since I became a landlord my troubles have multiplied tenfold* | [with obj.] *cigarette smoking combines with other factors to multiply the risks of atherosclerosis.* ■ [no obj.] (of an animal or other organism) increase in number by reproducing. ■ [with obj.] propagate (plants).
– ORIGIN Middle English: from Old French *multiplier*, from Latin *multiplicare.*

multiply[2] /ˈmʌltɪpli/ ▶ adverb [often as submodifier] in several different ways or respects: *multiply injured patients.*

multipolar ▶ adjective **1** having many poles or extremities.
2 polarized in several ways or directions: *today's multipolar and multicultural world.*
– DERIVATIVES **multipolarity** noun, **multipole** adjective.

multiprocessing (also **multiprogramming**) ▶ noun Computing another term for **MULTITASKING**.

multiprocessor ▶ noun a computer with more than one central processor.

multipurpose ▶ adjective having several purposes or functions: *two tools may do a better job than one multipurpose tool.*

multiracial ▶ adjective made up of or relating to people of many races: *multiracial education.*
– DERIVATIVES **multiracialism** noun, **multiracialist** adjective & noun, **multiracially** adverb.

multirole ▶ adjective (chiefly of an aircraft) capable of performing several roles.

multisession ▶ adjective Computing denoting a format for recording digital information on to a CD-ROM disc over two or more separate sessions.

multispectral ▶ adjective operating in or involving several regions of the electromagnetic spectrum: *multispectral images from satellites.*

multistage ▶ adjective **1** consisting of, occurring in, or involving several stages or processes: *a multistage decision-making process.*
2 (of a rocket) having at least two sections which contain their own motor and are jettisoned as their fuel runs out.

multistorey ▶ adjective (of a building) having several storeys.
▶ noun Brit. a car park with several storeys.

multitalented ▶ adjective having many skills or talents: *a multitalented musician and songwriter.*

multitask ▶ verb [no obj.] (often as noun **multitasking**) **1** (of a person) deal with more than one task at the same time: *parenting skills such as multitasking and concentrating amid distractions are easily transferable to the workplace.*
2 (of a computer) execute more than one program or task simultaneously.
– DERIVATIVES **multitasker** noun.

multithreading ▶ noun [mass noun] Computing a technique by which a single set of code can be used by several processors at different stages of execution.
– DERIVATIVES **multithreaded** adjective.

multitrack ▶ adjective relating to or made by the mixing of several separately recorded tracks of sound: *the advent of multitrack recording facilities.*

▸ **noun** a recording made from the mixing of several separately recorded tracks.
▸ **verb** [with obj.] record using multitrack recording: (as adj. **multitracked**) *multitracked vocals.*

multituberculate /ˌmʌltɪtjuːˈbəːkjʊlət/ ▸ **noun** a small primitive fossil mammal of a mainly Cretaceous and Palaeocene order, distinguished by having molar teeth with several cusps arranged in two or three rows. ● Order Multituberculata, subclass Allotheria.
ORIGIN late 19th cent.: from modern Latin *Multituberculata*, from **multi-** 'many' + Latin *tuberculum* 'tubercle'.

multitude ▸ **noun** a large number of people or things: ***a multitude of** medical conditions are due to being overweight* | *Father Peter addressed **the multitude**.* ■ **(the multitude)** the mass of ordinary people without power or influence: *placing ultimate political power in the hands of the multitude.* ■ [mass noun] archaic the state of being numerous: *they would swarm over the river in their multitude.*
– PHRASES **a multitude of sins** a great number of problems or defects: *stucco could cover **a multitude of sins**, including poor brickwork.*
– ORIGIN Middle English: via Old French from Latin *multitudo*, from *multus* 'many'.

multitudinous /ˌmʌltɪˈtjuːdɪnəs/ ▸ **adjective 1** very numerous: *multitudinous rugs kept us warm.* ■ consisting of or containing many individuals or elements: *the multitudinous array of chemical substances that exist in the natural world.*
2 literary (of a body of water) vast.
– DERIVATIVES **multitudinously** adverb, **multitudinousness** noun.
– ORIGIN early 17th cent.: from Latin *multitudo* (see **multitude**) + **-ous**.

multi-user ▸ **adjective** denoting a computer system that is able to be used by a number of people simultaneously. ■ denoting a computer game in which several players participate simultaneously.

multi-utility ▸ **noun** a privatized utility which has extended or combined its business to offer its customers additional services (especially those of another privatized utility).

multivalent /ˌmʌltɪˈveɪl(ə)nt/ ▸ **adjective 1** having or susceptible of many applications, interpretations, meanings, or values: *visually complex and multivalent work.*
2 Medicine (of an antigen or antibody) having several sites at which attachment to an antibody or antigen can occur: *a multivalent antiserum.* Compare with **polyvalent**.
3 Chemistry another term for **polyvalent**.
– DERIVATIVES **multivalence** noun, **multivalency** noun.

multivalve ▸ **adjective** denoting an internal-combustion engine having more than two valves per cylinder, typically four (two inlet and two exhaust).

multivariate /ˌmʌltɪˈvɛːrɪət/ ▸ **adjective** Statistics involving two or more variable quantities.

multivendor ▸ **adjective** denoting or relating to computer hardware or software products or network services from more than one supplier.

multiverse ▸ **noun** the universe considered as lacking order or a single ruling and guiding power. ■ a hypothetical space or realm consisting of a number of universes, of which our own universe is only one.

multivibrator ▸ **noun** Electronics a device consisting of two amplifying transistors or valves, each with its output connected to the input of the other, which produces an oscillatory signal.

multivitamin ▸ **noun** a pill, tablet, etc. containing a variety of vitamins.

multiway ▸ **adjective** having several paths, routes, or channels: *a multiway switch.*

multum in parvo /ˌmʌltəm ɪn ˈpɑːvəʊ/ ▸ **noun** a great deal in a small space.
– ORIGIN Latin, literally 'much in little'.

multure /ˈmʌltʃə/ ▸ **noun** [mass noun] historical grain or flour due to a miller in return for grinding corn. ■ the right to collect multure.
– ORIGIN Middle English: from Old French *moulture*, from medieval Latin *molitura*, from *molit-* 'ground', from the verb *molere*.

mum¹ ▸ **noun** Brit. informal one's mother.
– ORIGIN mid 17th cent.: abbreviation of **mummy¹**.

mum² ▸ **adjective** [predic.] silent.
– PHRASES **keep mum** informal remain silent, especially so as not to reveal a secret: *he was keeping mum about a possible move to West Ham.* **mum's the word** informal (as a request or warning) say nothing; do not reveal a secret.
– ORIGIN late Middle English: imitative of a sound made with closed lips.

mum³ ▸ **verb (mums, mumming, mummed)** [no obj.] act in a traditional masked mime or a mummers' play.
– ORIGIN late Middle English: compare with **mum²** and Middle Low German *mummen*.

mum⁴ /mʌm/ ▸ **noun** informal a cultivated chrysanthemum.
– ORIGIN late 19th cent.: abbreviation.

Mumbai /mʊmˈbʌɪ/ a city and port on the west coast of India, capital of the state of Maharashtra; pop. 13,922,100 (est. 2009). Former name (until 1995) **Bombay**.

mumble ▸ **verb 1** [reporting verb] say something indistinctly and quietly, making it difficult for others to hear: [with obj.] *he mumbled something she didn't catch* | [with direct speech] *'Sorry,' she mumbled.*
2 [with obj.] bite or chew (something) with toothless gums or without making much use of the teeth.
▸ **noun** [usu. in sing.] a quiet and indistinct utterance: *Rosie had replied in a mumble.*
– DERIVATIVES **mumbler** noun, **mumbling** adjective, **mumblingly** adverb.
– ORIGIN Middle English: frequentative of **mum²**.

mumblety-peg /ˈmʌmb(ə)lti/ ▸ **noun** [mass noun] chiefly US a game in which each player in turn throws a knife or pointed stick from a series of positions, continuing until it fails to stick in the ground.
– ORIGIN early 17th cent.: also in the form *mumble the peg*, from **mumble** (sense 2 of the verb), from the requirement of the game that an unsuccessful player withdraw a peg from the ground using the mouth.

mumbo jumbo ▸ **noun** [mass noun] informal language or ritual causing or intended to cause confusion or bewilderment: *a maze of legal mumbo jumbo.*
– ORIGIN mid 18th cent. (as *Mumbo Jumbo*, denoting a supposed African idol): of unknown origin; the current sense dates from the late 19th cent.

mumchance /ˈmʌmtʃɑːns/ ▸ **adjective** archaic silent; tongue-tied.
– ORIGIN late 17th cent.: from Middle Low German *mummenschanze*, denoting a game of dice (also an early sense in English from the early 16th cent. to the mid 17th cent.).

mu-meson ▸ **noun** another term for **muon**.

mummer ▸ **noun** an actor in a traditional masked mime or a mummers' play. ■ archaic or derogatory an actor in the theatre.
– ORIGIN late Middle English: from Old French *momeur*, from *momer* 'act in a mime'; perhaps of Germanic origin.

Mummerset ▸ **noun** [mass noun] an imitation rustic West Country accent used by actors.
– ORIGIN 1950s: probably from **mummer**, on the pattern of *Somerset*.

mummers' play (also **mumming play**) ▸ **noun** a traditional English folk play, of a type often associated with Christmas and popular in the 18th and early 19th centuries. The plot typically features Saint George and involves the miraculous resurrection of a character.

mummery ▸ **noun** (pl. **mummeries**) a performance by mummers. ■ [mass noun] ridiculous or extravagant ceremonial procedures.
– ORIGIN mid 16th cent.: from Old French *momerie*, from *momer* (see **mummer**).

mummichog /ˈmʌmɪtʃɒg/ ▸ **noun** a small marine killifish which lives along the sheltered shores and estuaries of eastern North America. It is widely kept in aquaria and is also used as bait and for biological research. ● *Fundulus heteroclitus*, family Cyprinodontidae (or Fundulidae).
– ORIGIN late 18th cent.: from Narragansett *moamitteaug*.

mummify ▸ **verb (mummifies, mummifying mummified)** [with obj.] (usu. as adj. **mummified**) (especially in ancient Egypt) preserve (a body) by embalming and wrapping it in cloth. ■ dry up (a body) and so preserve it: *the bodies of prehistoric men, mummified by the effect of the acid in the bog water.*
– DERIVATIVES **mummification** noun.

mummy¹ ▸ **noun** (pl. **mummies**) Brit. informal one's mother.
– ORIGIN late 18th cent.: perhaps an alteration of earlier **mammy**.

mummy² ▸ **noun** (pl. **mummies**) (especially in ancient Egypt) a body of a human being or animal that has been ceremonially preserved by removal of the internal organs, treatment with natron and resin, and wrapping in bandages.
– ORIGIN late Middle English (denoting a substance taken from embalmed bodies and used in medicines): from French *momie*, from medieval Latin *mumia* and Arabic *mūmiyā* 'embalmed body', perhaps from Persian *mūm* 'wax'.

mummy's boy (US **mama's boy**) ▸ **noun** Brit. informal a boy or man who is excessively influenced by or attached to his mother.

mumpish ▸ **adjective** informal, dated sullen; sulky.
– ORIGIN early 18th cent.: from obsolete *mump* 'grimace, have a miserable expression' + **-ish¹**.

mumps ▸ **plural noun** [treated as sing.] a contagious and infectious viral disease causing swelling of the parotid salivary glands in the face, and a risk of sterility in adult males.
– ORIGIN late 16th cent.: from obsolete *mump* 'grimace, have a miserable expression'.

mumpsimus /ˈmʌmpsɪməs/ ▸ **noun** (pl. **mumpsimuses**) a traditional custom or idea adhered to although shown to be unreasonable. ■ a person who obstinately adheres to old customs or ideas in spite of evidence that they are wrong or unreasonable.
– ORIGIN mid 16th cent.: erroneously for Latin *sumpsimus* in *quod in ore sumpsimus* 'which we have taken into the mouth' (from the Eucharist), in allusion to the story of an illiterate priest who, when corrected for reading *quod in ore mumpsimus*, replied 'I will not change my old mumpsimus for your new sumpsimus'.

mumsy Brit. informal ▸ **adjective** giving an impression of dull domesticity; dowdy or unfashionable: *she wore a big mumsy dress.*
▸ **noun** [usu. as name] chiefly humorous one's mother.
– ORIGIN late 19th cent.: humorous variant of **mummy¹**.

mun /mʌn/ ▸ **modal verb** dialect form of **must¹**.
– ORIGIN Middle English: from Old Norse *muna*, from the Germanic base of **mind**.

Munch /mʊŋk/, Edvard (1863–1944), Norwegian painter and engraver. He infused his subjects with an intense emotionalism, exploring the use of vivid colour and linear distortion to express feelings about life and death. Notable works: the *Frieze of Life* sequence, incorporating *The Scream* (1893).

munch ▸ **verb** [with obj.] eat (something) steadily and often audibly: *Russell munched his breakfast toast.*
– DERIVATIVES **muncher** noun.
– ORIGIN late Middle English: imitative; compare with **crunch**.

Munchausen, Baron /ˈmʊn(t)ʃˌhaʊz(ə)n/, German /ˈmʏnçˌhaʊzn/ the hero of a book of fantastic travellers' tales (1785) written in English by a German, Rudolph Erich Raspe. The original Baron Munchausen is said to have lived 1720–97, to have served in the Russian army against the Turks, and to have related extravagant tales of his prowess.

Munchausen's syndrome /ˈmʌn(t)ʃˌaʊz(ə)nz/ ▸ **noun** [mass noun] Psychiatry a mental disorder in which a person repeatedly feigns severe illness so as to obtain hospital treatment. ■ **(Munchausen's syndrome by proxy)** a mental disorder in which a person seeks attention by inducing or feigning illness in another person, typically a child.

München /ˈmʏnçn/ German name for **Munich**.

munchies ▸ **plural noun** informal snacks or small items of food. ■ **(the munchies)** a sudden strong desire for food: *I bought a pork pie to stave off the munchies.*

munchkin ▸ **noun** N. Amer. informal a child or short person.
– ORIGIN from the *Munchkins*, depicted as a race of small childlike creatures, in L. Frank Baum's book *The Wonderful Wizard of Oz* (1900).

Munda /ˈmʊndə/ ▸ **noun** (pl. **same** or **Mundas**) **1** a member of a group of indigenous peoples living scattered in a region from east central India to Nepal and Bangladesh.
2 [mass noun] a family of languages spoken by the Munda, distantly related to the Mon-Khmer family, with which they are sometimes classified as Austro-Asiatic. They have over 5 million speakers altogether; the most widely spoken is Santali. ■ any language of the Munda family.
▸ **adjective** relating to or denoting the Munda or their languages.
– ORIGIN the name in Munda.

M

mundane /ˈmʌndeɪn, mʌnˈdeɪn/ ▶ **adjective** **1** lacking interest or excitement; dull: *his mundane, humdrum existence.*
2 of this earthly world rather than a heavenly or spiritual one.
– DERIVATIVES **mundanely** adverb, **mundaneness** noun, **mundanity** /-ˈdanɪti/ noun (pl. **mundanities**).
– ORIGIN late Middle English (in sense 2): from Old French *mondain*, from late Latin *mundanus*, from Latin *mundus* 'world'. Sense 1 dates from the late 19th cent.

mung /mʌŋ, muːŋ/ (also **moong** or **mung bean**) ▶ **noun** **1** a small round green bean.
2 the tropical Old World plant that yields mung beans, commonly grown as a source of bean sprouts. ● *Vigna radiata* (or *Phaseolus aureus*), family Leguminosae.
– ORIGIN early 19th cent.: from Hindi *mūng*.

mungo /ˈmʌŋgəʊ/ ▶ **noun** [mass noun] cloth made from recycled woven or felted material.
– ORIGIN mid 19th cent.: of unknown origin.

muni¹ /ˈmjuːni/ ▶ **noun** (pl. **munis**) US short for **MUNICIPAL BOND**.

muni² /ˈmʊni/ ▶ **noun** (pl. **munis**) (especially in India) an inspired holy person; an ascetic, hermit, or sage.
– ORIGIN from Sanskrit, literally 'silent', from *man* 'think'.

Munich /ˈmjuːnɪk/ a city in SE Germany, capital of Bavaria; pop. 1,294,600 (est. 2006). German name **MÜNCHEN**.

Munich Agreement an agreement between Britain, France, Germany, and Italy, signed at Munich on 29 September 1938, under which the Sudetenland was ceded to Germany.

municipal /mjʊˈnɪsɪp(ə)l/ ▶ **adjective** relating to a town or district or its governing body: *national and municipal elections | municipal offices.*
– DERIVATIVES **municipally** adverb.
– ORIGIN mid 16th cent. (originally relating to the internal affairs of a state as distinct from its foreign relations): from Latin *municipalis* (from *municipium* 'free city', from *municeps*, *municip-* 'citizen with privileges', from *munia* 'civic offices') + *capere* 'take'.

M

municipal bond ▶ **noun** (chiefly in the US) a security issued by or on behalf of a local authority.

municipality ▶ **noun** (pl. **municipalities**) a town or district that has local government. ■ the governing body of a municipality.
– ORIGIN late 18th cent.: from French *municipalité*, from *municipal* (see **MUNICIPAL**).

municipalize (also **municipalise**) ▶ **verb** [with obj.] bring under the control or ownership of the authorities of a town or district: *an expensive commitment to municipalize rented housing.*
– DERIVATIVES **municipalization** noun.

munificence /mjʊˈnɪfɪs(ə)ns/ ▶ **noun** [mass noun] the quality or action of being extremely generous: *we must be thankful for his munificence.*

munificent /mjʊˈnɪfɪs(ə)nt/ ▶ **adjective** characterized by or displaying great generosity: *a munificent bequest | a munificent patron of the arts.*
– DERIVATIVES **munificently** adverb.
– ORIGIN late 16th cent.: from Latin *munificent-* (stem of *munificentior*, comparative of *munificus* 'bountiful'), from *munus* 'gift'.

muniments /ˈmjuːnɪm(ə)nts/ ▶ **plural noun** chiefly Law title deeds or other documents proving a person's title to land.
– ORIGIN late Middle English: via Old French from Latin *munimentum* 'defence' (in medieval Latin 'title deed'), from *munire* 'fortify'.

munition /mjʊˈnɪʃ(ə)n/ ▶ **plural noun** (**munitions**) military weapons, ammunition, equipment, and stores.
▶ **verb** [with obj.] supply with munitions.
– ORIGIN late Middle English (denoting a granted right or privilege): from French, from Latin *munitio(n-)* 'fortification', from *munire* 'fortify or secure'.

Munro¹ /mənˈrəʊ/, H. H., see **SAKI**.

Munro² /mʌnˈrəʊ/ ▶ **noun** (pl. **Munros**) any of the 277 mountains in Scotland that are at least 3,000 feet high (approximately 914 metres).
– ORIGIN early 20th cent.: named after Sir Hugh Thomas *Munro* (1856–1919), who published a list of all such mountains in the Journal of the Scottish Mountaineering Club for 1891.

Munsell /ˈmʌns(ə)l/ ▶ **noun** [as modifier] denoting a system of classifying colours according to their hue, value (or lightness), and chroma (or intensity of colour).
– ORIGIN early 20th cent.: named after Albert H. *Munsell* (1858–1918), American painter.

munshi /ˈmuːnʃiː/ ▶ **noun** (pl. **munshis**) a secretary or language teacher in South Asia.
– ORIGIN Persian and Urdu *munšī* from Arabic *munšī* 'writer, author'.

Munsi /ˈmʊnsi/ ▶ **noun** see **DELAWARE²** (sense 2 of the noun).
– ORIGIN the name in Munsi.

munsif /ˈmuːnsɪf/ ▶ **noun** Indian a judge.
– ORIGIN Persian and Urdu, from Arabic *munṣif* 'just or honest'.

Munster /ˈmʌnstə/ a province of the Republic of Ireland, in the south-west of the country.

Münster /ˈmʊnstə/, German /ˈmʏnstɐ/ a city in NW Germany; pop. 272,100 (est. 2006). It was formerly the capital of Westphalia; the Treaty of Westphalia, ending the Thirty Years War, was signed simultaneously there and at Osnabrück in 1648.

muntin /ˈmʌntɪn/ ▶ **noun** US term for **GLAZING BAR**.
– DERIVATIVES **muntined** adjective.
– ORIGIN early 17th cent.: variant of obsolete *montant* (from French, literally 'rising').

muntjac /ˈmʌntdʒak/ ▶ **noun** a small SE Asian deer, the male of which has tusks, small antlers, and a dog-like bark. Also called **BARKING DEER**. ● Genus *Muntiacus*, family Cervidae: several species, including the **Chinese muntjac** (*M. reevesi*), which is naturalized in England and France.
– ORIGIN late 18th cent.: from Sundanese *minchek*.

Muntz metal /mʌnts/ ▶ **noun** [mass noun] a form of brass consisting of 60 per cent copper and 40 per cent zinc, used for casting and working at high temperatures.
– ORIGIN mid 19th cent.: named after George F. *Muntz* (1794–1857), English manufacturer.

munyeroo /ˌmʌnjəˈruː/ (also **munyeru**) ▶ **noun** Austral. a succulent plant whose seeds and leaves are used for food. ● *Portulaca oleracea* (or sometimes *Calandrinia balonensis*), family Portulacaceae.
– ORIGIN late 19th cent.: from Diyari (an Aboriginal language of South Australia).

muon /ˈmjuːɒn/ ▶ **noun** Physics an unstable subatomic particle of the same class as an electron (a lepton), but with a mass around 200 times greater. Muons make up much of the cosmic radiation reaching the earth's surface.
– DERIVATIVES **muonic** adjective.
– ORIGIN 1950s: contraction of **MU-MESON**; the particle, however, is no longer regarded as a meson.

muppet ▶ **noun** Brit. informal an incompetent or foolish person.
– ORIGIN 1990s: from *Muppet*, the generic name given to various puppets and marionettes created by Jim Henson (1936–90) for the children's television programmes *Sesame Street* and *The Muppet Show*.

Muqdisho /mʊkˈdɪʃəʊ/ another name for **MOGADISHU**.

murage /ˈmjʊərɪdʒ/ ▶ **noun** [mass noun] Brit. historical tax levied for building or repairing the walls of a town.
– ORIGIN late Middle English: from Old French from *mur* 'wall', from Latin *murus*.

mural /ˈmjʊər(ə)l/ ▶ **noun** a painting or other work of art executed directly on a wall.
▶ **adjective** [attrib.] **1** relating to or resembling a wall: *a mural escarpment.*
2 Medicine relating to or occurring in the wall of a body cavity or blood vessel: *mural thrombosis.*
– DERIVATIVES **muralist** noun.
– ORIGIN late Middle English: from French, from Latin *muralis*, from *murus* 'wall'. The adjective was first used in **MURAL CROWN**; later (mid 16th cent.) the sense 'placed or executed on a wall' arose, reflected in the current noun use (dating from the early 20th cent.).

mural crown ▶ **noun** **1** Heraldry a representation of a city wall in the form of a crown, borne above the shield in the arms of distinguished soldiers and of some civic authorities.
2 (in ancient Roman times) a crown or garland given to the soldier who was first to scale the wall of a besieged town.

Murano glass /mjʊˈrɑːnəʊ/ ▶ **noun** [mass noun] decorative glassware of a type associated with the island of Murano near Venice.

Murat /mjʊəˈrɑː/, French /myʀa/, Joachim (*c.*1767–1815), French general, king of Naples 1808–15. Murat made his name as a cavalry commander in Napoleon's Italian campaign (1800) and was made king of Naples. He attempted to become king of all Italy in 1815, but was captured in Calabria and executed.

Murchison Falls /ˈməːtʃɪs(ə)n/ former name for **KABALEGA FALLS**.

Murchison Rapids former name for **KAPACHIRA FALLS**.

Murcia /ˈmʊəsɪə/, Spanish /ˈmurθja, ˈmursja/ an autonomous region in SE Spain. In the Middle Ages, along with Albacete, it formed an ancient Moorish kingdom. ■ the capital city of Murcia; pop. 430,571 (2008).

murder ▶ **noun** **1** the unlawful premeditated killing of one human being by another: *the brutal murder of a German holidaymaker* | [mass noun] *he was put on trial for attempted murder.*
2 [mass noun] informal a very difficult or unpleasant task or experience: *the 40-mile-per-hour winds at the summit were murder.*
▶ **verb** [with obj.] **1** kill (someone) unlawfully and with premeditation: *he was accused of murdering his wife's lover.*
2 informal punish severely or be very angry with: *my father will murder me if I'm home late.* ■ conclusively defeat (an opponent) in a game or sport. ■ spoil by lack of skill or knowledge: *the only thing he had murdered was the English language.* ■ chiefly Brit. consume (food or drink) greedily or with relish: *I could murder some chips.*
– PHRASES **get away with (blue) murder** informal succeed in doing whatever one chooses without being punished or suffering any disadvantage. **murder one** (or **two**) N. Amer. informal first-degree (or second-degree) murder. **murder will out** murder cannot remain undetected. **scream** (or **yell**) **blue** (or N. Amer. **bloody**) **murder** informal make an extravagant and noisy protest: *if it gets into the papers, she'll be down here screaming blue murder.*
– ORIGIN Old English *morthor*, of Germanic origin; related to Dutch *moord* and German *Mord*, from an Indo-European root shared by Sanskrit *mará* 'death' and Latin *mors*; reinforced in Middle English by Old French *murdre*.

murderer ▶ **noun** a person who commits murder: *convicted murderers.*

murderess ▶ **noun** a female murderer.

murderous ▶ **adjective** **1** capable of or intending to murder; dangerously violent: *a brutal and murderous despot* | figurative *Mark gave him a murderous look.* ■ (of an action, event, or plan) involving murder or extreme violence: *murderous acts of terrorism.*
2 informal extremely arduous or unpleasant: *the team had a murderous schedule of four games in ten days.*
– DERIVATIVES **murderously** adverb, **murderousness** noun.

Murdoch¹ /ˈməːdɒk/, Dame (Jean) Iris (1919–99), British novelist and philosopher, born in Ireland. She is primarily known for her novels, many of which explore complex sexual relationships and spiritual life. Notable novels: *The Sandcastle* (1957) and *The Sea, The Sea* (Booker Prize, 1978).

Murdoch² /ˈməːdɒk/, (Keith) Rupert (b.1931), Australian-born American publisher and media entrepreneur. As the founder and head of the News International Communications empire he owns major newspapers in Australia, Britain, and the US, together with film and television companies and the publishing firm HarperCollins.

mure /mjʊə/ ▶ **verb** [with obj.] archaic imprison or shut up in an enclosed space: *they are not a little tired of being mured up in the cottage.*
– ORIGIN late Middle English: from Old French *murer*, from Latin *murare*, from *murus* 'wall'.

murex /ˈmjʊərɛks/ ▶ **noun** (pl. **murices** /-rɪsiːz/ or **murexes**) a predatory tropical marine mollusc, the shell of which bears spines and forms a long, narrow canal extending downwards from the aperture. ● Genus *Murex*, family Muricidae, class Gastropoda.
– ORIGIN late 16th cent.: from Latin; perhaps related to Greek *muax* 'sea mussel'.

murgh /mʊəg, mʊrg/ ▶ **noun** (in Indian cookery) chicken: [as modifier] *murgh kebabs.*
– ORIGIN from Urdu *murğ*, from Persian *murğ* 'bird, fowl'.

muriatic acid /ˌmjʊərɪˈatɪk/ ▶ **noun** archaic term for **HYDROCHLORIC ACID**.
– DERIVATIVES **muriate** noun.
– ORIGIN late 17th cent.: *muriatic* from Latin *muriaticus*, from *muria* 'brine'.

muricate /ˈmjʊərɪkət/ ▸ **adjective** Botany & Zoology studded with short rough points.
– ORIGIN mid 17th cent.: from Latin *muricatus* 'shaped like a murex'.

murid[1] /mjʊˈriːd, mʊ-/ ▸ **noun** a follower of a Muslim saint, especially a Sufi disciple. ■ (**Murid**) a member of any of several Muslim movements, especially one which advocated rebellion against the Russians in the Caucasus in the late 19th century.
– ORIGIN from Arabic *murīd*, literally 'he who desires'.

murid[2] /ˈmjʊərɪd/ ▸ **noun** Zoology a rodent of a very large family (Muridae) which includes most kinds of rats, mice, and voles.
– ORIGIN early 20th cent.: from modern Latin *Muridae* (plural), based on Latin *mus*, *mur-* 'mouse'.

Murillo /mʊˈriːjəʊ, -ˈriːljəʊ/, Bartolomé Esteban (*c.*1618–82), Spanish painter. He is noted for his genre scenes of urchins and peasants and for his devotional pictures.

murine /ˈmjʊəraɪn, -rɪn/ ▸ **adjective** Zoology relating to or affecting mice or related rodents. ● Murine rodents belong to the family Muridae, in particular the subfamily Murinae of the Old World.
– ORIGIN early 17th cent.: from Latin *murinus*, from *mus*, *mur-* 'mouse'.

muriqui /mjʊˈriːkwi/ ▸ **noun** (pl. **muriquis**) another term for **WOOLLY SPIDER MONKEY**.
– ORIGIN Portuguese, from Tupi.

murk ▸ **noun** [mass noun] darkness or thick mist that makes it difficult to see: *my eyes were straining to see through the murk of the rainy evening.*
▸ **adjective** archaic or Scottish murky; gloomy.
– ORIGIN Old English *mirce*, of Germanic origin; reinforced in Middle English by Old Norse *myrkr*.

murky ▸ **adjective** (**murkier**, **murkiest**) **1** dark and gloomy, especially due to thick mist: *the sky was murky and a thin drizzle was falling.* ■ (of liquid) dark and dirty; not clear: *the murky silt of a muddy pond.*
2 obscure or morally questionable: *a government minister with a murky past.*
– DERIVATIVES **murkily** adverb, **murkiness** noun.

Murmansk /mʊəˈmansk/ a port in NW Russia, on the northern coast of the Kola Peninsula, in the Barents Sea; pop. 314,700 (est. 2008). It is the largest city north of the Arctic Circle and its port is ice-free throughout the year.

murmur ▸ **noun 1** a low continuous background noise: *the distant murmur of traffic.*
2 a softly spoken or almost inaudible utterance: *a quiet murmur of thanks.* ■ the quiet or subdued expression of a particular feeling by a group of people: *there were murmurs of dissent from his colleagues.*
3 Medicine a recurring sound heard in the heart through a stethoscope that is usually a sign of disease or damage.
▸ **verb 1** [reporting verb] say something in a low or indistinct voice: [with obj.] *Nina murmured an excuse and hurried away* | [with direct speech] *'How interesting,' he murmured quietly.* ■ [no obj.] (**murmur against**) archaic express one's discontent about (someone or something) in a subdued manner.
2 [no obj.] make a low continuous sound: *the wind was murmuring through the trees.*
– PHRASES **without a murmur** without complaining.
– DERIVATIVES **murmurer** noun, **murmurous** adjective.
– ORIGIN late Middle English: from Old French *murmure*, from *murmurer* 'to murmur', from Latin *murmurare*, from *murmur* 'a murmur'.

murmuration ▸ **noun** literary **1** [mass noun] the action of murmuring: *the murmuration of a flock of warblers.*
2 rare a flock of starlings.
– ORIGIN late Middle English: from French, from Latin *murmuratio(n-)*, from *murmurare* 'to murmur'. The usage as a collective noun dates from the late 15th cent.

murmuring ▸ **noun 1** [mass noun] a low or indistinct continuous sound: *the murmuring of the River Derwent.*
2 (usu. **murmurings**) a subdued or private expression of discontent or dissatisfaction: *murmurings of discontent from the fans.*
– DERIVATIVES **murmuringly** adverb.

Murnau /ˈmʊənaʊ/, German /ˈmʊrnaʊ/, F. W. (1888–1931), German film director; born *Frederick Wilhelm Plumpe*. His revolutionary use of cinematic techniques to record and interpret human emotion paralleled the expressionist movement in art and drama. Notable films: *Nosferatu* (1922), *Der letzte Mann* (1924), and *Sunrise* (1927), which won three Oscars.

murphy ▸ **noun** (pl. **murphies**) informal a potato.
– ORIGIN early 19th cent.: from *Murphy*, an Irish surname.

Murphy's Law ▸ **noun** a supposed law of nature, expressed in various humorous popular sayings, to the effect that anything that can go wrong will go wrong.

murrain /ˈmʌrɪn/ ▸ **noun 1** [mass noun] redwater fever or a similar infectious disease affecting cattle or other animals.
2 archaic a plague, epidemic, or crop blight. ■ the potato blight during the Irish famine in the mid 19th century.
– ORIGIN late Middle English: from Old French *morine*, based on Latin *mori* 'to die'.

murram /ˈmʌrəm/ ▸ **noun** [mass noun] a form of laterite (clayey material) used for road surfaces in tropical Africa.
– ORIGIN 1920s: a local word.

Murray[1] /ˈmʌri/, (George) Gilbert (Aimé) (1866–1957), Australian-born British classical scholar. His translations of Greek dramatists helped to revive interest in Greek drama. He was also a founder of the League of Nations and later a joint president of the United Nations.

Murray[2] /ˈmʌri/, Sir James (Augustus Henry) (1837–1915), Scottish lexicographer. He was chief editor of the *Oxford English Dictionary*, but did not live to see the work completed.

Murray River the principal river of Australia, which rises in the Great Dividing Range in New South Wales and flows 2,590 km (1,610 miles) generally north-westwards, forming part of the border between the states of Victoria and New South Wales, before turning southwards in South Australia to empty into the Indian Ocean south-east of Adelaide.

murre /məː/ ▸ **noun** N. Amer. a guillemot with a white breast. ● Genus *Uria*, family Alcidae: two species.
– ORIGIN late 16th cent.: of unknown origin.

murrelet /ˈməːlɪt/ ▸ **noun** a small North Pacific auk (seabird), typically having a grey back and white underparts. ● Genera *Brachyramphus* and *Synthliboramphus*, family Alcidae: six species.

murrey /ˈmʌri/ ▸ **noun** [mass noun] archaic a deep purple-red cloth. ■ the deep purple-red colour of a mulberry. ■ Heraldry another term for **SANGUINE**.
– ORIGIN late Middle English: via Old French from medieval Latin *moratus*, from *morum* 'mulberry'.

murri /ˈmʌri/ ▸ **noun** (pl. **same** or **murris**) Austral. an Aborigine (used by some Aborigines to refer to themselves).
– ORIGIN from Kamilaroi (and other Aboriginal languages) *mari* 'the Aboriginal people', also 'people generally'.

Murrumbidgee /ˌmʌrəmˈbɪdʒiː/ a river of SE Australia, in New South Wales. Rising in the Great Dividing Range, it flows 1,759 km (1,099 miles) westwards to join the Murray, of which it is a major tributary.

murther /ˈməːðə/ ▸ **noun & verb** archaic spelling of **MURDER**.

Mururoa /ˌmʊərʊˈrəʊə/ a remote South Pacific atoll in the Tuamotu Archipelago, in French Polynesia, used as a nuclear testing site since 1966.

Musala, Mount /muːˈsɑːlə/ (also **Mousalla**) the highest peak in Bulgaria, in the Rila Mountains, rising to 2,925 m (9,596 ft).

musambi /mʊˈsambi/ ▸ **noun** an orange of a variety with green skin and yellow flesh
– ORIGIN alteration of **MOZAMBIQUE**.

MusB (also **Mus Bac**) ▸ **abbreviation** Bachelor of Music.
– ORIGIN from Latin *Musicae Baccalaureus*.

Musca /ˈmʌskə/ Astronomy a small southern constellation (the Fly), lying in the Milky Way between the Southern Cross and the south celestial pole.
– ORIGIN Latin.

muscadel /ˌmʌskəˈdɛl/ ▸ **noun** variant spelling of **MUSCATEL**.

Muscadelle /ˌmʌskəˈdɛl/ ▸ **noun** [mass noun] a variety of white grape grown mainly for sweet white wines in Bordeaux and Australia.
– ORIGIN French, variant of **MUSCATEL**.

Muscadet /ˈmʌskədeɪ, ˈmʊsk-/, French /myskadɛ/ ▸ **noun** [mass noun] a dry white wine from the part of the Loire region in France nearest the west coast.
– ORIGIN French, from *muscade* 'nutmeg', from *musc* 'musk'.

muscadine /ˈmʌskədɪn, -ʌɪn/ ▸ **noun** any of a group of species and varieties of wine grape native to Mexico and the south-eastern US, typically having thick skins and a musky flavour. ● Genus *Vitis* (section *Muscadinia*): several species, in particular *V. rotundifolia*.
– ORIGIN probably an alteration of **MUSCATEL**.

muscae volitantes /ˌmʌsiː ˌvɒlɪˈtantiːz/ ▸ **plural noun** Medicine dark specks appearing to float before the eyes, generally caused by particles in the vitreous humour of the eye.
– ORIGIN mid 18th cent.: Latin, literally 'flying flies'.

muscarine /ˈmʌskəriːn, -ɪn/ ▸ **noun** [mass noun] Chemistry a poisonous compound present in certain fungi, including the fly agaric. ● An alkaloid; chem. formula: $C_9H_{21}NO_3$.
– ORIGIN late 19th cent.: based on Latin *musca* 'fly'.

muscarinic /ˌmʌskəˈrɪnɪk/ ▸ **adjective** Physiology relating to a type of acetylcholine receptor in the nervous system which is capable of responding to muscarine.

Muscat /ˈmʌskat/ the capital of Oman, a port on the SE coast of the Arabian peninsula; pop. 620,000 (est. 2007).

muscat /ˈmʌskat/ ▸ **noun** [mass noun] a variety of white, red, or black grape with a musky scent, grown in warm climates for wine or raisins or as table grapes. ■ a wine made from muscat grapes, especially a sweet or fortified white wine.
– ORIGIN French, from Provençal, from *musc* 'musk'.

Muscat and Oman former name (until 1970) for **OMAN**.

muscatel /ˌmʌskəˈtɛl/ (also **muscadel**) ▸ **noun** a muscat grape, especially as grown for drying to make raisins. ■ a raisin made from a muscatel grape. ■ [mass noun] a wine made from muscatel grapes.
– ORIGIN via Old French from Provençal, diminutive of *muscat* (see **MUSCAT**).

Muscat Hamburg ▸ **noun** see **HAMBURG**[2] (sense 2).

Muschelkalk /ˈmʊʃ(ə)lkalk/ ▸ **noun** [mass noun] Geology a limestone or chalk deposit from the Middle Triassic in Europe, especially in Germany.
– ORIGIN mid 19th cent.: from German, literally 'mussel chalk'.

Musci /ˈmʌski/ ▸ **plural noun** Botany a class of lower plants that comprises the mosses.
– ORIGIN modern Latin, literally 'mosses'.

muscid /ˈmʌsɪd/ ▸ **noun** Entomology an insect of the housefly family (Muscidae).
– ORIGIN late 19th cent.: from modern Latin *Muscidae* (plural), from Latin *musca* 'fly'.

muscle ▸ **noun 1** a band or bundle of fibrous tissue in a human or animal body that has the ability to contract, producing movement in or maintaining the position of parts of the body: *the calf muscle* | [mass noun] *the sheet of muscle between the abdomen and chest.* ■ a muscle or muscles when well developed or prominently visible under the skin: *his muscles rippled beneath his tanned skin.*

> Muscles are formed of bands, sheets, or columns of elongated cells (or fibres) containing interlocking parallel arrays of the proteins actin and myosin. Projections on the myosin molecules respond to chemical signals by forming and reforming chemical bonds to the actin, so that the filaments move past each other and interlock more deeply. This converts chemical energy into the mechanical force of contraction, and also generates heat.

2 [mass noun] physical power; strength: *he had muscle but no brains.* ■ informal a man or men exhibiting physical power or strength, typically employed to use or threaten violence: *an ex-marine of enormous proportions who'd been brought along as muscle.* ■ power or influence, especially in a commercial or political sphere: *many companies lack the financial muscle to adopt a more hard-nosed relationship with buyers.*
▸ **verb** informal [with obj. and adverbial] chiefly N. Amer. move (an object) in a particular direction by using one's physical strength: *they were muscling baggage into the hold of the plane.* ■ coerce by violence or by economic or political pressure: *he was eventually muscled out of the market.*
– PHRASES **flex one's muscles** give a show of strength or power. **not move a muscle** not move at all.
– PHRASAL VERBS **muscle in/into** informal use one's power or influence to interfere with or become involved in (another's affairs): *the banks' attempts*

M

to muscle in on the insurance business. **muscle up** US informal build up one's muscles.
– DERIVATIVES **muscled** adjective [in combination] *hard-muscled*, **muscleless** adjective.
– ORIGIN late Middle English: from French, from Latin *musculus*, diminutive of *mus* 'mouse' (some muscles being thought to be mouse-like in form).

muscle-bound ▸ adjective having well-developed or overdeveloped muscles: *a muscle-bound hunk.*

muscleman ▸ noun (pl. **musclemen**) a large, strong man, especially one employed for protection or to intimidate people.

muscle Mary ▸ noun (pl. **muscle Marys**) informal a homosexual man who has prominent, well-developed muscles.

muscle tone ▸ noun see TONE (sense 6 of the noun).

muscly ▸ adjective (**musclier, muscliest**) muscular: *his muscly forearms.*

muscovado /ˌmʌskəˈvɑːdəʊ/ (also **muscovado sugar**) ▸ noun [mass noun] unrefined sugar made from the juice of sugar cane by evaporating it and draining off the molasses.
– ORIGIN early 17th cent.: from Portuguese *mascabado (açúcar)* '(sugar) of the lowest quality'.

Muscovite /ˈmʌskəvʌɪt/ ▸ noun a native or citizen of Moscow. ■ archaic a Russian.
▸ adjective relating to Moscow. ■ archaic relating to Russia.
– ORIGIN from modern Latin *Muscovita*, from *Muscovia* (see MUSCOVY).

muscovite /ˈmʌskəvʌɪt/ ▸ noun [mass noun] a silver-grey form of mica occurring in many rocks.
– ORIGIN mid 19th cent.: from obsolete *Muscovy glass* (in the same sense) + -ITE[1].

Muscovy /ˈmʌskəvi/ a medieval principality in west central Russia, centred on Moscow, which formed the nucleus of modern Russia. As Muscovy expanded, princes of Muscovy became the rulers of Russia; in 1472 Ivan III, grand duke of Muscovy, completed the unification of the country, and 1547 Ivan the Terrible became the first tsar of Russia.
■ archaic Russia.
– ORIGIN from obsolete French *Muscovie*, from modern Latin *Moscovia*, from Russian *Moskva* 'Moscow'.

M

Muscovy duck ▸ noun a large tropical American tree-nesting duck, having glossy greenish-black plumage in the wild but bred in a variety of colours as a domestic bird. ● *Cairina moschata*, family Anatidae.

muscular ▸ adjective relating to or affecting the muscles: *energy is needed for muscular activity.* ■ having well-developed muscles: *his legs were strong and muscular.* ■ vigorously robust: *a muscular economy.*
– DERIVATIVES **muscularity** noun, **muscularly** adverb.
– ORIGIN late 17th cent.: alteration of earlier *musculous*, in the same sense.

muscular Christianity ▸ noun [mass noun] a Christian life of brave and cheerful physical activity, especially as popularly associated with the writings of Charles Kingsley and with boys' public schools of the Victorian British Empire.
– DERIVATIVES **muscular Christian** noun.

muscular dystrophy ▸ noun [mass noun] a hereditary condition marked by progressive weakening and wasting of the muscles.

muscular rheumatism ▸ noun [mass noun] aching pain in the muscles and joints.

musculature /ˈmʌskjʊlətʃə/ ▸ noun [mass noun] the system or arrangement of muscles in a body, part of the body, or an organ.
– ORIGIN late 19th cent.: from French, from Latin *musculus* (see MUSCLE).

musculoskeletal /ˌmʌskjʊləʊˈskelɪt(ə)l/ ▸ adjective relating to or denoting the musculature and skeleton together.

MusD (also **Mus Doc**) ▸ abbreviation Doctor of Music.
– ORIGIN from Latin *Musicae Doctor*.

muse[1] ▸ noun **1** (**Muse**) (in Greek and Roman mythology) each of nine goddesses, the daughters of Zeus and Mnemosyne, who preside over the arts and sciences.

> The Muses are generally listed as Calliope (epic poetry), Clio (history), Euterpe (flute playing and lyric poetry), Terpsichore (choral dancing and song), Erato (lyre playing and lyric poetry), Melpomene (tragedy), Thalia (comedy and light verse), Polyhymnia (hymns, and later mime), and Urania (astronomy).

2 a woman, or a force personified as a woman, who is the source of inspiration for a creative artist.
– ORIGIN late Middle English: from Old French, or from Latin *musa*, from Greek *mousa*.

muse[2] ▸ verb [no obj.] be absorbed in thought: *he was musing on the problems he faced.* ■ say to oneself in a thoughtful manner: *'I think I've seen him somewhere before,' mused Rachel.* ■ (**muse on**) gaze thoughtfully at: *the sergeant stood, his eyes musing on the pretty police constable.*
▸ noun an instance or period of reflection.
– ORIGIN Middle English: from Old French *muser* 'meditate, waste time', perhaps from medieval Latin *musum* 'muzzle'.

museography /ˌmjuːzɪˈɒɡrəfi/ ▸ noun another term for MUSEOLOGY.
– DERIVATIVES **museographic** adjective, **museographical** adjective.

museology /ˌmjuːzɪˈɒlədʒi/ ▸ noun [mass noun] the science or practice of organizing, arranging, and managing museums.
– DERIVATIVES **museological** adjective, **museologist** noun.

musette /mjuːˈzɛt/ ▸ noun **1** a kind of small bagpipe played with bellows, common in the French court in the 17th–18th centuries and in later folk music. ■ a tune or piece of music imitating the sound of the musette, typically with a drone. ■ a dance to such a tune, especially in the 18th-century French court.
2 a small, simple variety of oboe, used chiefly in 19th-century France.
3 (also **musette bag**) US a small knapsack.
– ORIGIN late Middle English: from Old French, diminutive of *muse* 'bagpipe'.

museum ▸ noun a building in which objects of historical, scientific, artistic, or cultural interest are stored and exhibited.
– ORIGIN early 17th cent. (denoting a university building, specifically one erected at Alexandria by Ptolemy Soter): via Latin from Greek *mouseion* 'seat of the Muses', based on *mousa* 'muse'.

museum beetle ▸ noun a small dark beetle whose larvae can cause severe damage to carpets, stored goods, and zoological and entomological collections. ● *Anthrenus museorum* and related species, family Dermestidae.

museum piece ▸ noun an object that is worthy of display in a museum. ■ a person or thing regarded as old-fashioned, irrelevant, or no longer useful: *we're nothing but museum pieces—machines can do everything that we can do.*

Museveni /mʊˈsɛvəni/, Yoweri (Kaguta) (b.1944), Ugandan statesman, President since 1986. He came to power after ousting Milton Obote, and brought some stability to a country that had suffered under the dictatorial Obote and Idi Amin.

mush[1] /mʌʃ/ ▸ noun [mass noun] **1** a soft, wet, pulpy mass: *red lentils cook quickly and soon turn to mush* | [in sing.] *the flowers had been flattened into a sodden pink mush.*
2 feeble or cloying sentimentality: *the film's not just romantic mush.*
3 N. Amer. thick maize porridge.
▸ verb [with obj.] (usu. as adj. **mushed**) reduce (a substance) to a soft, wet, pulpy mass: *a cake combining layers of mushed prune and pastry.*
– ORIGIN late 17th cent. (in sense 3 of the noun): apparently a variant of MASH.

mush[2] /mʌʃ/ ▸ verb [no obj.] go on a journey across snow with a dog sled: *they got into the sleigh and mushed over the ice and snow.* ■ [with obj.] urge on (the dogs) during a journey with a dog sled.
▸ exclamation a command urging on dogs pulling a sled during a journey across snow.
▸ noun a journey across snow with a dog sled.
– ORIGIN mid 19th cent.: probably an alteration of French *marchez!* or *marchons!*, imperatives of *marcher* 'to advance'.

mush[3] /mʊʃ/ ▸ noun Brit. informal **1** a person's mouth or face.
2 used as a form of address: *what you doing round here, mush?*
– ORIGIN mid 19th cent.: probably from Romany, 'man'.

mushaira /mʊˈʃʌɪərə/ ▸ noun Indian an evening social gathering at which Urdu poetry is read, typically taking the form of a contest.
– ORIGIN from Urdu *mušā'ara*, via Persian from Arabic *mušaira* 'vying in poetry'.

Musharraf /mʊˈʃaraf/, Pervez (b.1943), Pakistani general and statesman, President of Pakistan 2001–8. He became head of state in 1999 following a bloodless coup d'état.

musher[1] ▸ noun the driver of a dog sled.

musher[2] ▸ noun Brit. informal a person who owns and drives a taxi cab.
– ORIGIN late 19th cent.: from slang *mush* 'owner-driver of a cab', from MUSHROOM, apparently referring to the increase in the number of vehicles owned as the business grows.

mushrat /ˈmʌʃrat/ ▸ noun North American term for MUSKRAT.

mushroom ▸ noun **1** a fungal growth that typically takes the form of a domed cap on a stalk, with gills on the underside of the cap. ■ a thing resembling a mushroom in shape: *a mushroom of smoke and flames.*

> Mushrooms are fruiting bodies that produce spores, growing from the hyphae of fungi concealed in soil or wood. Proverbial for rapid growth, many varieties are edible and toadstools are often called mushrooms when they are considered to be edible.

2 [mass noun] a pale pinkish-brown colour.
▸ verb [no obj.] **1** increase, spread, or develop rapidly: *environmental concern mushroomed in the 1960s.*
2 form a shape resembling that of a mushroom: *the grenade mushroomed into red fire as it hit the hillside.* ■ (of a bullet) expand and flatten on reaching its target.
3 (usu. as noun **mushrooming**) gather mushrooms.
– DERIVATIVES **mushroomy** adjective.
– ORIGIN late Middle English (originally denoting any fungus having a fleshy fruiting body): from Old French *mousseron*, from late Latin *mussirio(n-)*.

mushroom cloud ▸ noun a mushroom-shaped cloud of dust and debris formed after a nuclear explosion.

mushroom growth ▸ noun a sudden development or expansion: *a mushroom growth of new companies.*

mushy ▸ adjective (**mushier, mushiest**) **1** soft and pulpy: *mushy vegetables.*
2 informal excessively sentimental: *a mushy film.*
– DERIVATIVES **mushily** adverb, **mushiness** noun.

mushy peas ▸ plural noun Brit. marrowfat peas cooked until soft and served in their own juice.

music ▸ noun [mass noun] **1** the art or science of combining vocal or instrumental sounds (or both) to produce beauty of form, harmony, and expression of emotion: *he devoted his life to music.* ■ the vocal or instrumental sound produced in this way: *couples were dancing to the music* | *baroque music.* ■ a sound perceived as pleasingly harmonious: *the background music of softly lapping water.*
2 the written or printed signs representing vocal or instrumental sound: *Tony learned to **read music**.* ■ the score or scores of a musical composition or compositions: *the music was open on a stand.*
– PHRASES **music of the spheres** see SPHERE. **music to one's ears** something that is very pleasant or gratifying to hear or discover: *the commission's report was music to the ears of the government.*
– ORIGIN Middle English: from Old French *musique*, via Latin from Greek *mousikē (tekhnē)* '(art) of the Muses', from *mousa* 'muse'.

musica ficta /ˌmjuːzɪkə ˈfɪktə/ ▸ noun [mass noun] Music (in early contrapuntal music) the introduction by a performer of sharps, flats, or other accidentals to avoid unacceptable intervals.
– ORIGIN early 19th cent.: Latin, literally 'feigned music'.

musical ▸ adjective **1** relating to music: *they shared similar musical tastes.* ■ set to or accompanied by music: *an evening of musical entertainment.* ■ fond of or skilled in music: *Henry was very musical, but his wife was tone-deaf.*
2 having a pleasant sound; melodious or tuneful: *they burst out into rich, musical laughter.*
▸ noun a play or film in which singing and dancing play an essential part. Musicals developed from light opera in the early 20th century.
– DERIVATIVES **musicality** noun, **musically** adverb.
– ORIGIN late Middle English: from Old French, from medieval Latin *musicalis*, from Latin *musica* (see MUSIC).

musical box ▸ noun Brit. a small box which plays a tune when the lid is opened.

musical bumps ▸ noun [mass noun] Brit. a party game similar to musical chairs, in which the player who is last to sit on the floor when the music stops is eliminated in each round.

musical chairs ▶ noun [mass noun] a party game in which players compete for a decreasing number of chairs, the losers in successive rounds being those unable to find a chair to sit on when the accompanying music is stopped. ■ a situation in which people frequently exchange jobs or positions: *the management played musical chairs with the design team.*

musical comedy ▶ noun a light play or film with songs, dialogue, and dancing; a musical.

musical director ▶ noun the person responsible for the musical aspects of a performance or production, typically the conductor or leader of a music group.

musicale /ˌmjuːzɪˈkɑːl/ ▶ noun N. Amer. a musical gathering or concert.
– ORIGIN late 19th cent.: French, from *soirée musicale* 'evening of music'.

musical glasses ▶ plural noun a graduated series of glass bowls or tubes played as a musical instrument by rubbing them with the fingers.

musical instrument ▶ noun see INSTRUMENT (sense 3 of the noun).

musicalize (also **musicalise**) ▶ verb [with obj.] set (a novel, play, or poem) to music.

musical saw ▶ noun a saw, typically held between the knees and played with a bow like a cello, the note varying with the degree of bending of the blade.

musical sound ▶ noun see SOUND[1].

music box ▶ noun another term for MUSICAL BOX.

music centre ▶ noun Brit. a device that combines a radio and record or CD player.

music drama ▶ noun an opera whose structure is governed by considerations of dramatic effectiveness, rather than by the convention of having a series of formal arias.

music hall ▶ noun [mass noun] a form of variety entertainment popular in Britain from *c.*1850, consisting of singing, dancing, comedy, acrobatics, and novelty acts. Its popularity declined after the First World War with the rise of the cinema. ■ [count noun] a theatre where music-hall entertainment took place.

musician ▶ noun a person who plays a musical instrument, especially as a profession, or is musically talented.
– DERIVATIVES **musicianly** adjective, **musicianship** noun.
– ORIGIN late Middle English: from Old French *musicien*, from Latin *musica* (see MUSIC).

musicology ▶ noun [mass noun] the study of music as an academic subject, as distinct from training in performance or composition; scholarly research into music.
– DERIVATIVES **musicological** adjective, **musicologist** noun.
– ORIGIN early 20th cent.: from French *musicologie*.

music stand ▶ noun a rest or light frame on which sheet music or a score is supported.

music stool ▶ noun a stool for a pianist, typically adjustable in height and sometimes having a hinged top covering a storage space for musical scores.

music theatre ▶ noun [mass noun] a combination of music and drama in modern form distinct from traditional opera, typically for a small group of performers.

musing ▶ noun (usu. **musings**) a period of reflection or thought: *his musings were interrupted by the sound of the telephone.*
▶ adjective characterized by reflection or deep thought: *the sad musing gaze.*
– DERIVATIVES **musingly** adverb.

musique concrète /mjuːˌziːk kɔ̃ˈkrɛt/ ▶ noun [mass noun] music constructed by mixing recorded sounds, first developed by experimental composers in the 1940s.
– ORIGIN French, literally 'concrete music'.

musk ▶ noun 1 [mass noun] a strong-smelling reddish-brown substance which is secreted by the male musk deer for scent-marking and is an important ingredient in perfumery.
2 (also **musk plant**) a relative of the monkey flower, formerly cultivated for a musky fragrance which has been lost in the development of modern varieties.
● Genus *Mimulus*, family Scrophulariaceae: several species, in particular *M. moschatus*.
■ Austral. see MUSK TREE.
– ORIGIN late Middle English: from late Latin *muscus*, from Persian *mušk*, perhaps from Sanskrit *muṣka* 'scrotum' (because of the similarity in shape of the sac on the abdomen of a male musk deer in which musk is produced).

musk beetle ▶ noun a slender longhorn beetle that is dark metallic green and emits a musk-like scent.
● *Aromia moschata*, family Cerambycidae.

musk deer ▶ noun a small solitary deer-like East Asian mammal without antlers, the male having long protruding upper canine teeth. Musk is produced in a sac on the abdomen of the male. ● Family Moschidae and genus *Moschus*: several species.

musk duck ▶ noun an Australian stiff-tailed duck with dark grey plumage and a musky smell, the male having a large black lobe of skin hanging below the bill. ● *Biziura lobata*, family Anatidae.

muskeg /ˈmʌskɛg/ ▶ noun a swamp or bog in northern North America.
– ORIGIN early 19th cent.: from Cree.

muskellunge /ˈmʌskəˌlʌn(d)ʒ/ ▶ noun a large pike that occurs only in the Great Lakes region of North America. Also called MASKINONGE. ● *Esox masquinongy*, family Esocidae.
– ORIGIN late 18th cent.: based on Ojibwa, 'great fish'.

musket ▶ noun historical an infantryman's light gun with a long barrel, typically smooth-bored and fired from the shoulder.
– ORIGIN late 16th cent.: from French *mousquet*, from Italian *moschetto* 'crossbow bolt', from *mosca* 'a fly'.

musketeer ▶ noun historical 1 a soldier armed with a musket.
2 a member of the household troops of the French king in the 17th and 18th centuries.

musketry ▶ noun [mass noun] musket fire. ■ soldiers armed with muskets: *the Prussian musketry.* ■ the art or technique of handling a musket.

musk melon ▶ noun a yellow or green melon of a variety which has a raised network of markings on the skin.

Muskogean /ˌmʌskəˈgiːən, mʌˈskəʊgɪən/ ▶ noun a family of American Indian languages spoken in SE North America, including Creek and Choctaw.
▶ adjective relating to the Muskogean language family.
– ORIGIN from MUSKOGEE + -AN.

Muskogee /mʌˈskəʊgi/ ▶ noun (pl. **same** or **Muskogees**) 1 a member of an American Indian people of SE North America, who formed part of the Creek Indian confederacy.
2 [mass noun] the Muskogean language of the Muskogee, now all but extinct.
▶ adjective relating to the Muskogee or their language.
– ORIGIN from Creek *ma:skó:ki.*

musk ox ▶ noun a large heavily built goat-antelope with a thick shaggy coat and a horny protuberance on the head, native to the tundra of North America and Greenland. The male emits a musky odour during the breeding season. ● *Ovibos moschatus*, family Bovidae.

muskrat ▶ noun a large semiaquatic North American rodent with a musky smell, valued for its fur. ● *Ondatra zibethicus*, family Muridae.
■ [mass noun] the fur of the muskrat.

musk rose ▶ noun a rambling rose with large white musk-scented flowers. ● *Rosa moschata*, family Rosaceae.

musk thistle ▶ noun a thistle which has a solitary drooping flower with a musky fragrance. ● *Carduus nutans*, family Compositae.

musk tree ▶ noun either of two Australian trees with a musky smell. Also called MUSKWOOD. ● (also **musk**) a small tree or shrub that has musky leaves with silvery undersides (*Olearia argyrophylla*, family Compositae).
● a rainforest tree with musky timber (*Alangium villosum*, family Alangiaceae).

musk turtle ▶ noun a small drab-coloured American freshwater turtle which has scent glands that produce an unpleasant musky odour when the turtle is disturbed. ● Genus *Kinosternon* (or *Sternotherus*), family Kinosternidae: several species, including the stinkpot.

muskwood ▶ noun [mass noun] timber with a musky smell, especially that of a musk tree. ■ another term for MUSK TREE.

musky ▶ adjective (**muskier, muskiest**) having a smell or taste like that of musk.
– DERIVATIVES **muskiness** noun.

Muslim /ˈmʊzlɪm, ˈmʌz-, -s-/ (also **Moslem**) ▶ noun a follower of the religion of Islam.
▶ adjective relating to Muslims or their religion.
– ORIGIN early 17th cent.: from Arabic, active participle of *'aslama* (see ISLAM).

> **USAGE** **Muslim** is the preferred spelling for 'a follower of Islam', although the form **Moslem** is also used. The archaic term **Muhammadan** (or **Mohammedan**) is not favoured by Muslims and should be avoided.

Muslimah /ˈmʊzlɪmə, ˈmʌz-, -s-/ ▶ noun (especially among Muslims) a Muslim woman.
– ORIGIN Arabic *muslima*, feminine of MUSLIM.

Muslim Brotherhood an Islamic religious and political organization dedicated to the establishment of a nation based on Islamic principles. Founded in Egypt in 1928, it has become a radical underground force in Egypt and other Sunni countries, promoting strict moral discipline and opposing Western influence, often by violence.

Muslim League one of the main political parties in Pakistan. It was formed in 1906 in India to represent the rights of Indian Muslims; its demands from 1940 for an independent Muslim state led ultimately to the establishment of Pakistan.

muslin ▶ noun [mass noun] lightweight cotton cloth in a plain weave.
– ORIGIN early 17th cent.: from French *mousseline*, from Italian *mussolina*, from *Mussolo* 'Mosul' (see MOSUL, where it was first manufactured).

muso /ˈmjuːzəʊ/ ▶ noun (pl. **musos**) Brit. informal a musician, especially one over-concerned with technique.
■ a keen music fan.
– ORIGIN 1960s: abbreviation.

musquash /ˈmʌskwɒʃ/ ▶ noun another term for MUSKRAT. ■ [mass noun] Brit. the fur of the muskrat.
– ORIGIN early 17th cent.: from Abnaki *mòskwas*.

muss informal, chiefly N. Amer. ▶ verb [with obj.] make (someone's hair or clothes) untidy or messy: *the wind was mussing up his hair.*
▶ noun [usu. in sing.] a state of disorder.
– DERIVATIVES **mussy** adjective.
– ORIGIN mid 19th cent. (also as a noun in the sense 'disturbance or row'): apparently a variant of MESS.

mussel ▶ noun any of a number of bivalve molluscs with a brown or purplish-black shell: ● a marine bivalve which uses byssus threads to anchor to a firm surface (family Mytilidae, order Mytiloidea), including the **edible mussel** (*Mytilus edulis*). ● a freshwater bivalve which typically lies on the bed of a river, some species forming small pearls (family Unionidae, order Unionoida).
– ORIGIN Old English *mus(c)le*, superseded by forms from Middle Low German *mussel*, Middle Dutch *mosscele*; ultimately from late Latin *muscula*, from Latin *musculus* (see MUSCLE).

musselcracker ▶ noun S. African a large sea bream with powerful jaws, feeding on shellfish and crustaceans and popular with anglers. ● *Lithognathus* and other genera, family Sparidae: several species.

Mussolini /ˌmʊsəˈliːni/, Benito (Amilcare Andrea) (1883–1945), Italian Fascist statesman, Prime Minister 1922–43; known as **Il Duce** ('the leader'). He founded the Italian Fascist Party in 1919. He annexed Abyssinia in 1936 and entered the Second World War on Germany's side in 1940. Forced to resign after the Allied invasion of Sicily, he was rescued from imprisonment by German paratroopers, but was captured and executed by Italian communist partisans.

Mussorgsky /məˈsɔːgski/ (also **Moussorgsky**), Modest (Petrovich) (1839–81), Russian composer. His best-known works include the opera *Boris Godunov* (1874), *Songs and Dances of Death* (1875–7), and the piano suite *Pictures at an Exhibition* (1874)

Mussulman /ˈmʌs(ə)lmən/ ▶ noun (pl. **Mussulmans** or **Mussulmen**) & adjective archaic term for MUSLIM.
– ORIGIN late 16th cent.: from Persian *musulmān* (originally an adjective), from *muslim* (see MUSLIM).

must[1] ▶ modal verb (past **had to** or in reported speech **must**) 1 be obliged to; should (expressing necessity): *you must show your ID card | the essay mustn't be over 2,000 words | she said she must be going.* ■ expressing insistence: *you must try some of this fish | if you must smoke you could at least go in the living room.* ■ used in ironic questions expressing irritation: *Charlotte, must you put spanners in the works?*
2 expressing an opinion about something that is logically very likely: *there must be something wrong | you must be tired.*
▶ noun informal something that should not be overlooked or missed: *this video is a must for everyone.*
– PHRASES **I must say** see SAY. **must needs do something** see NEEDS.

M

– ORIGIN Old English *mōste*, past tense of *mōt* 'may', of Germanic origin; related to Dutch *moeten* and German *müssen*.

must[2] ▶ **noun** [mass noun] grape juice before or during fermentation.
– ORIGIN Old English, from Latin *mustum*, neuter (used as a noun) of *mustus* 'new'.

must[3] ▶ **noun** [mass noun] mustiness, dampness, or mould: *a pervasive smell of must*.
– ORIGIN early 17th cent.: back-formation from **MUSTY**.

must[4] (also **musth**) ▶ **noun** [mass noun] the frenzied state of certain male animals, especially elephants or camels, that is associated with the rutting season.
– ORIGIN late 19th cent.: via Urdu from Persian *mast* 'intoxicated'.

must- ▶ **combining form** used to form adjectives and nouns denoting things that are essential or highly recommended: *a must-visit destination* | *the new material on this disc makes it a must-buy*.

mustache ▶ **noun** US spelling of **MOUSTACHE**.

mustachios /məˈstɑːʃɪəʊz/ ▶ **plural noun** a long or elaborate moustache.
– DERIVATIVES **mustachioed** adjective.
– ORIGIN mid 16th cent.: from Spanish *mostacho* (singular), from Italian *mostaccio* (see **MOUSTACHE**).

mustang /ˈmʌstaŋ/ ▶ **noun** an American feral horse which is typically small and lightly built.
– ORIGIN early 19th cent.: from a blend of Spanish *mestengo* (from *mesta* 'company of graziers') and *mostrenco*, both meaning 'wild or masterless cattle'.

mustard ▶ **noun** [mass noun] **1** a hot-tasting yellow or brown paste made from the crushed seeds of certain plants, typically eaten with meat or used as a cooking ingredient.
2 the yellow-flowered Eurasian plant of the cabbage family whose seeds are used to make mustard.
● Genera *Brassica* and *Sinapis*, family Cruciferae: several species, in particular **black mustard** (*B. nigra*) and **white mustard** (*S. alba*), which is commonly eaten as a seedling in mustard and cress.
■ used in names of related plants, only some of which are used to produce mustard for the table, e.g. **hedge mustard**.
3 a brownish yellow colour.
– DERIVATIVES **mustardy** adjective.
– ORIGIN Middle English: from Old French *moustarde*, from Latin *mustum* 'must' (mustard being originally prepared with grape must).

M

mustard gas ▶ **noun** a colourless oily liquid whose vapour causes severe irritation and blistering of the skin, used in chemical weapons. ● Chem. formula: $(ClCH_2CH_2)_2S$.

mustard greens ▶ **plural noun** chiefly US the leaves of the mustard plant used in salads.

mustard plaster ▶ **noun** a poultice made with mustard.

mustelid /ˈmʌstɪlɪd, mʌˈstɛlɪd/ ▶ **noun** Zoology a mammal of the weasel family (Mustelidae), distinguished by having a long body, short legs, and musky scent glands under the tail.
– ORIGIN early 20th cent.: from modern Latin *Mustelidae* (plural), from Latin *mustela* 'weasel'.

muster ▶ **verb** [with obj.] **1** assemble (troops), especially for inspection or in preparation for battle: *17,000 men had been mustered on Haldon Hill*. ■ [no obj.] (of troops) gather for inspection or in preparation for battle: *the cavalrymen mustered beside the other regiments*. ■ [no obj.] (of a group of people) gather together: *reporters mustered outside her house*. ■ Austral./NZ round up (livestock).
2 collect or assemble (a number or amount): *he could fail to muster a majority*. ■ summon up (a feeling, attitude, or response): *he replied with as much dignity as he could muster*.
▶ **noun** a formal gathering of troops, especially for inspection, display, or exercise. ■ short for **MUSTER ROLL**. ■ Austral./NZ a rounding up of livestock. ■ Austral. informal the number of people attending a meeting.
– PHRASES **pass muster** be accepted as adequate or satisfactory: *this manifesto would not pass muster with the voters*.
– PHRASAL VERBS **muster someone in** (or **out**) US enrol someone into (or discharge someone from) military service.
– ORIGIN late Middle English: from Old French *moustrer* (verb), *moustre* (noun), from Latin *monstrare* 'to show'.

muster book ▶ **noun** historical a book in which military personnel were registered.

musterer ▶ **noun** Austral./NZ a person who rounds up livestock.

muster roll ▶ **noun** an official list of officers and men in a military unit or ship's company.

musth ▶ **noun** variant spelling of **MUST**[4].

must-have ▶ **adjective** essential or highly desirable: *the must-have blouse of the season*.
▶ **noun** an essential or highly desirable item: *this classic volume is a must-have for any collector*.

Mustique /mʌˈstiːk, mʊ-/ a small resort island in the northern Grenadines, in the Caribbean to the south of St Vincent.

mustn't ▶ **contraction** must not.

must-read ▶ **adjective** denoting a piece of writing that should or must be read: *his must-read article in the NY Times*.
▶ **noun** a compelling or particularly useful piece of writing: *it's a must-read for anyone interested in movies*.

must-see ▶ **adjective** highly recommended as worth seeing: *one of the must-see pieces at the exhibition*.
▶ **noun** a place, event, or entertainment that is highly recommended as worth seeing: *this sassy and superior suspense thriller is a must-see*.

musty ▶ **adjective** (**mustier**, **mustiest**) having a stale, mouldy, or damp smell: *a dark musty library*. ■ having a stale taste. ■ lacking freshness or vitality; old-fashioned: *the musty formalities of the occasion*.
– DERIVATIVES **mustily** adverb, **mustiness** noun.
– ORIGIN early 16th cent.: perhaps an alteration of *moisty* 'moist', influenced by **MUST**[2].

Mut /mʊt/ Egyptian Mythology a goddess who was the wife of Amun and mother of Khonsu.

mutable /ˈmjuːtəb(ə)l/ ▶ **adjective** liable to change: *the mutable nature of fashion*. ■ literary inconstant in one's affections: *youth is said to be fickle and mutable*.
– DERIVATIVES **mutability** noun.
– ORIGIN late Middle English: from Latin *mutabilis*, from *mutare* 'to change'.

mutagen /ˈmjuːtədʒ(ə)n/ ▶ **noun** an agent, such as radiation or a chemical substance, which causes genetic mutation.
– DERIVATIVES **mutagenesis** noun, **mutagenic** adjective, **mutagenicity** /-ˈnɪsɪti/ noun.
– ORIGIN 1940s: from **MUTATION** + **-GEN**.

mutagenize /ˈmjuːtədʒənʌɪz/ (also **mutagenise**) ▶ **verb** [with obj.] (usu. as adj. **mutagenized**) Biology treat (a cell, organism, etc.) with mutagenic agents: *mutagenized DNA*.

mutant ▶ **adjective** resulting from or showing the effect of mutation: *a mutant gene*.
▶ **noun** a mutant form.
– ORIGIN early 20th cent.: from Latin *mutant-* 'changing', from the verb *mutare*.

Mutare /muːˈtɑːri/ an industrial town in the eastern highlands of Zimbabwe; pop. 183,500 (est. 2009). Former name (until 1982) **UMTALI**.

mutate ▶ **verb** [no obj.] change in form or nature: *rhythm and blues mutated into rock and roll*. ■ Biology (with reference to a cell, DNA molecule, etc.) undergo or cause to undergo change in a gene or genes: [no obj.] *the virus is able to* **mutate into** *new forms that are immune to the vaccine* | [with obj.] *certain nucleotides were mutated*.
– DERIVATIVES **mutative** adjective, **mutator** noun.
– ORIGIN early 19th cent.: back-formation from **MUTATION**.

mutation ▶ **noun** [mass noun] **1** the action or process of mutating: *the mutation of punk's angry energy into something more thuggish and mindless* | [count noun] *his first novel went through several mutations*.
2 the changing of the structure of a gene, resulting in a variant form which may be transmitted to subsequent generations, caused by the alteration of single base units in DNA, or the deletion, insertion, or rearrangement of larger sections of genes or chromosomes. ■ [count noun] a distinct form resulting from genetic mutation.
3 Linguistics regular change of a sound when it occurs adjacent to another, in particular: ■ (in Celtic languages) change of an initial consonant in a word caused (historically) by the preceding word. See also **LENITION**. ■ (also **vowel mutation**) (in Germanic languages) the process by which the quality of a vowel was altered in certain phonetic contexts; umlaut.
– DERIVATIVES **mutational** adjective, **mutationally** adverb.
– ORIGIN late Middle English: from Latin *mutatio(n-)*, from *mutare* 'to change'.

mutatis mutandis /muːˌtɑːtɪs muːˈtandɪs, mjuː-, -iːs/ ▶ **adverb** (used when comparing two or more cases or situations) making necessary alterations while not affecting the main point at issue: *what is true of undergraduate teaching in England is equally true, mutatis mutandis, of American graduate schools*.
– ORIGIN Latin, literally 'things being changed that have to be changed'.

mutch ▶ **noun** chiefly historical a linen cap, especially one worn by older women or children.
– ORIGIN late Middle English (denoting a nightcap): from Middle Dutch *mutse*, from medieval Latin *almucia* 'amice'.

mutchkin ▶ **noun** a Scottish unit of capacity equal to a quarter of the old Scottish pint, or roughly three quarters of an imperial pint (0.43 litres).
– ORIGIN late Middle English: from early modern Dutch *mudsekin*, diminutive of *mud* 'hectolitre'.

mute /mjuːt/ ▶ **adjective 1** refraining from speech or temporarily speechless: *Harry sat mute, his cheeks burning resentfully*. ■ (of a person) lacking the faculty of speech. ■ not expressed in speech: *she gazed at him in mute appeal*. ■ characterized by an absence of sound; quiet: *the great church was mute and dark*. ■ (of hounds) not giving tongue while hunting.
2 (of a letter) not pronounced: *mute e is generally dropped before suffixes beginning with a vowel*.
▶ **noun 1** a person lacking the faculty of speech. ■ historical (in some Asian countries) a servant who was deprived of the power of speech. ■ historical an actor in a dumbshow. ■ historical a professional attendant or mourner at a funeral.
2 a clamp placed over the bridge of a stringed instrument to deaden the resonance without affecting the vibration of the strings. ■ a pad or cone placed in the opening of a brass or other wind instrument to soften the sound.
3 a device on a television, telephone, or other appliance that temporarily turns off the sound.
▶ **verb** [with obj.] deaden, muffle, or soften the sound of: *her footsteps were muted by the thick carpet*. ■ muffle the sound of (a musical instrument), especially by the use of a mute. ■ reduce the strength or intensity of: *police violence was always muted by the presence of the media*.
– DERIVATIVES **mutely** adverb, **muteness** noun.
– ORIGIN Middle English: from Old French *muet*, diminutive of *mu*, from Latin *mutus*.

USAGE 1 To describe a person without the power of speech as **mute** (especially as in **deaf mute**) is today likely to cause offence and the term is often regarded as outdated. Nevertheless, there is no directly equivalent term for **mute** in general use, apart from **speech-impaired**. **Profoundly deaf** may be used to imply that a person has not developed any spoken language skills.
2 Note that a question subject to debate or dispute is a **moot point**, not a **mute point**. See **USAGE** at **MOOT**.

mute button ▶ **noun** a device on a telephone that the caller can press to prevent themselves from being heard by the person to whom they are speaking.

muted ▶ **adjective** (of a sound or voice) quiet and soft: *the muted hum of the distant traffic*. ■ (of a musical instrument) having a muffled sound as a result of being fitted with a mute. ■ not expressed strongly or openly: *muted anger*. ■ (of colour or lighting) not bright; subdued: *a dress in muted tones of powder blue and dusty pink*.

mute swan ▶ **noun** the commonest Eurasian swan, having white plumage and an orange-red bill with a black knob at the base. ● *Cygnus olor*, family Anatidae.

mutha /ˈmʌðə/ ▶ **noun** chiefly US variant spelling of **MOTHER** (sense 3 of the noun).

muti /ˈmuːti/ ▶ **noun** [mass noun] S. African **1** traditional African medicine or magical charms.
2 informal medicine of any kind.
– ORIGIN from Zulu *umuthi* 'plant or medicine'.

mutilate ▶ **verb** [with obj.] inflict a violent and disfiguring injury on: *most of the prisoners had been mutilated*. ■ inflict serious damage on: *the fine carved screen was mutilated in the 18th century*.
– DERIVATIVES **mutilator** noun.
– ORIGIN early 16th cent.: from Latin *mutilat-* 'maimed, mutilated, lopped off', from the verb *mutilare*, from *mutilus* 'maimed'.

mutilation ▶ **noun** [mass noun] the action of mutilating or being mutilated: *a culture which found any mutilation of the body abhorrent* | [count noun] *there were fatalities and appalling mutilations*. ■ the infliction of serious damage on something: *the proposed mutilation of City Hall by our own councillors*.

mutineer ▶ noun a person, especially a soldier or sailor, who rebels or refuses to obey the orders of a person in authority.
– ORIGIN early 17th cent.: from French *mutinier*, from *mutin* 'rebellious', from *muete* 'movement', based on Latin *movere* 'to move'.

mutinous ▶ adjective (of a soldier or sailor) refusing to obey the orders of a person in authority. ■ wilful or disobedient: *Antoinette looked mutinous, but she obeyed.*
– DERIVATIVES **mutinously** adverb.
– ORIGIN late 16th cent.: from obsolete *mutine* 'rebellion' (see MUTINY) + -OUS.

mutiny ▶ noun (pl. **mutinies**) an open rebellion against the proper authorities, especially by soldiers or sailors against their officers: *a mutiny by those manning the weapons could trigger a global war* | [mass noun] *the crew were on the verge of mutiny.*
▶ verb (**mutinies, mutinying, mutinied**) [no obj.] refuse to obey the orders of a person in authority: *thousands of the soldiers mutinied over the non-payment of wages.*
– ORIGIN mid 16th cent.: from obsolete *mutine* 'rebellion', from French *mutin* 'mutineer', based on Latin *movere* 'to move'.

mutism /ˈmjuːtɪz(ə)m/ ▶ noun [mass noun] inability to speak, typically as a result of congenital deafness or brain damage. ■ (in full **elective mutism**) unwillingness or refusal to speak, arising from psychological causes such as depression or trauma.
– ORIGIN early 19th cent.: from French *mutisme*, from Latin *mutus* 'mute'.

muton /ˈmjuːtɒn/ ▶ noun Biology the smallest element of genetic material capable of undergoing a distinct mutation, usually identified as a single pair of nucleotides.

Mutsuhito /ˌmʊtsuːˈhiːtəʊ/ see MEIJI TENNO.

mutt ▶ noun informal **1** a dog, especially a mongrel.
2 a stupid or incompetent person: *he pitied the poor mutt who ever fell for her charms.*
– ORIGIN late 19th cent.: abbreviation of MUTTONHEAD.

mutter ▶ verb [reporting verb] say something in a low or barely audible voice, especially in dissatisfaction or irritation: [with obj.] *he muttered something under his breath* | [with direct speech] *'I knew she was a troublemaker,' Rebecca muttered.* ■ [no obj.] talk or grumble in secret or in private: *back-benchers were muttering about the next reshuffle.*
▶ noun a barely audible utterance, especially one expressing dissatisfaction or irritation: *a little mutter of disgust.*
– DERIVATIVES **mutterer** noun.
– ORIGIN late Middle English: imitative; compare with German dialect *muttern*.

muttering ▶ noun (usu. **mutterings**) a privately expressed complaint or expression of dissatisfaction: *there were disloyal mutterings about his leadership.*
– DERIVATIVES **mutteringly** adverb.

mutton ▶ noun [mass noun] the flesh of fully grown sheep used as food: *a leg of mutton.*
– PHRASES **(as) dead as mutton** quite dead. **mutton dressed as lamb** Brit. informal, derogatory a middle-aged or old woman dressed in a style suitable for a much younger woman.
– DERIVATIVES **muttony** adjective.
– ORIGIN Middle English: from Old French *moton*, from medieval Latin *multo(n-)*, probably of Celtic origin; compare with Scottish Gaelic *mult*, Welsh *mollt*, and Breton *maout*.

mutton bird ▶ noun a shearwater or petrel of the southern oceans. ● Family Procellariidae: several species, in particular (in Australia) the **short-tailed shearwater** (*Puffinus tenuirostris*), and (in New Zealand) the **sooty shearwater** (*P. griseus*).
– ORIGIN early 19th cent.: because when cooked, the flesh of some species resembles mutton in flavour.

mutton chops (also **mutton chop whiskers**) ▶ plural noun the whiskers on a man's cheek when shaped like a meat chop, narrow at the top and broad and rounded at the bottom.

muttonhead ▶ noun informal a stupid person.
– DERIVATIVES **muttonheaded** adjective.

mutual /ˈmjuːtʃʊəl, -tjʊəl/ ▶ adjective **1** (of a feeling or action) experienced or done by each of two or more parties towards the other or others: *a partnership based on mutual respect and understanding* | *my father hated him from the start and the feeling was mutual.* ■ (of two or more people) having the same specified relationship to each other: *they cooperated as potentially mutual beneficiaries of the settlement.*
2 held in common by two or more parties: *we were introduced by a mutual friend.*
3 denoting a building society or insurance company owned by its members and dividing some or all of its profits between them.
▶ noun a mutual building society or insurance company.
– ORIGIN late 15th cent.: from Old French *mutuel*, from Latin *mutuus* 'mutual, borrowed'; related to *mutare* 'to change'.
– DERIVATIVES **mutuality** noun.

mutual conductance ▶ noun Electronics another term for TRANSCONDUCTANCE.

mutual fund ▶ noun N. Amer. an investment programme funded by shareholders that trades in diversified holdings and is professionally managed.

mutual inductance ▶ noun Physics a measure or coefficient of mutual induction, usually expressed in henries. ■ the property of a circuit which permits mutual induction.

mutual induction ▶ noun [mass noun] Physics the production of an electromotive force in a circuit by a change in the current in an adjacent circuit which is linked to the first by the flux lines of a magnetic field.

mutualism ▶ noun [mass noun] **1** the doctrine that mutual dependence is necessary to social well-being.
2 Biology symbiosis which is beneficial to both organisms involved.
– DERIVATIVES **mutualist** noun & adjective, **mutualistic** adjective, **mutualistically** adverb.

mutualize (also **mutualise**) ▶ verb [with obj.] **1** organize (a company or business) on mutual principles.
2 share out (something) equally between involved parties.

mutually ▶ adverb with mutual action; in a mutual relationship: [as submodifier] *adoption and fostering are not necessarily mutually exclusive alternatives.*

mutuel /ˈmjuːtʃʊəl, -tjʊəl/ ▶ noun chiefly US (in betting) a totalizator or a pari-mutuel.
– ORIGIN early 20th cent.: shortening of PARI-MUTUEL.

mutule /ˈmjuːtjuːl/ ▶ noun Architecture a stone block projecting under a cornice in the Doric order.
– ORIGIN mid 17th cent.: from French, from Latin *mutulus*.

muumuu /ˈmuːmuː/ ▶ noun a woman's loose, brightly coloured dress, especially one traditionally worn in Hawaii.
– ORIGIN early 20th cent.: from Hawaiian *mu'u mu'u*, literally 'cut off'.

mux ▶ noun a multiplexer.
▶ verb short for MULTIPLEX.

Muzaffarabad /ˌmʊzəˌfarəˈbad/ a town in NE Pakistan, the administrative centre of Azad Kashmir; pop. 17,500 (est. 2009).

muzak /ˈmjuːzak/ ▶ noun [mass noun] trademark recorded light background music played through speakers in public places.
– ORIGIN 1930s: alteration of MUSIC.

muzhik /muːˈʒɪk, ˈmuːʒɪk/ (also **moujik**) ▶ noun historical a Russian peasant.
– ORIGIN Russian.

Muztag /muːsˈtɑːg/ a mountain in western China, on the north Tibetan border close to the Karamiran Shankou pass. Rising to 7,723 m (25,338 ft), it is the highest peak in the Kunlun Shan range.

muzz ▶ noun [mass noun] informal a muddle or state of confusion. ■ sounds or images lacking clarity or distinctness: *in the echoey hall, every other word is lost in the muzz.*
– ORIGIN mid 18th cent. (as a verb in the sense 'study intently'): of unknown origin; based partly perhaps on an alteration of MUSE[2].

muzzle ▶ noun **1** the projecting part of the face, including the nose and mouth, of an animal such as a dog or horse. ■ a guard, typically made of straps or wire, fitted over an animal's muzzle to stop it biting or feeding. ■ informal the part of a person's face including the nose, mouth, and chin.
2 the open end of the barrel of a firearm: *Devlin jammed the muzzle of the gun into the man's neck.*
▶ verb [with obj.] put a muzzle on (an animal). ■ prevent (a person or group) from expressing their opinions freely: *opposition leaders accused him of muzzling the news media.*
– ORIGIN late Middle English: from Old French *musel*, diminutive of medieval Latin *musum*, of unknown ultimate origin.

muzzle-loader ▶ noun historical a gun that is loaded through its muzzle.

muzzle velocity ▶ noun the velocity with which a bullet or shell leaves the muzzle of a gun.

muzzy ▶ adjective (**muzzier, muzziest**) **1** unable to think clearly; confused: *she was shivering and her head felt muzzy from sleep.* ■ not thought out clearly; vague: *society's muzzy notion of tolerance.*
2 blurred; indistinct: *a slightly muzzy picture.*
– DERIVATIVES **muzzily** adverb, **muzziness** noun.
– ORIGIN early 18th cent.: of unknown origin.

MV ▶ abbreviation ■ megavolt(s). ■ motor vessel: *on board the MV Alcinous.* ■ muzzle velocity.

MVD the Ministry of Internal Affairs, the secret police of the former Soviet Union from 1946 to 1953.
– ORIGIN abbreviation of Russian *Ministerstvo vnutrennikh del.*

MVO ▶ abbreviation Member of the Royal Victorian Order.

MVP ▶ abbreviation N. Amer. most valuable player (an award given in various sports to the best player in a team).

MW ▶ abbreviation ■ Malawi (international vehicle registration). ■ medium wave. ■ megawatt(s).

mW ▶ abbreviation milliwatt(s).

mwah /mwɑː/ ▶ interjection informal used to represent the sound of a kiss, typically one given in an exaggerated or theatrical way: *Mwah, mwah! How are you, dahling?*
– ORIGIN 1960s: imitative.

MWO ▶ abbreviation Master Warrant Officer.

Mx ▶ abbreviation ■ maxwell(s). ■ Middlesex.

MY ▶ abbreviation motor yacht.

my ▶ possessive determiner **1** belonging to or associated with the speaker: *my name is John* | *my friend.* ■ informal used with a name to refer to a member of the speaker's family: *my Johnny, see, he was smart.* ■ used with forms of address in affectionate, sympathetic, humorous, or patronizing contexts: *my dear boy* | *my poor baby.*
2 used in various expressions of surprise: *my goodness!* | *oh my!*
– PHRASES **My Lady** (or **Lord**) a polite form of address to certain titled people.
– ORIGIN Middle English *mi* (originally before words beginning with any consonant except *h*-), reduced from *min*, from Old English *mīn* (see MINE[1]).

my- ▶ combining form variant spelling of MYO- shortened before a vowel (as in *myalgia*).

myalgia /mʌɪˈaldʒə/ ▶ noun [mass noun] pain in a muscle or group of muscles.
– DERIVATIVES **myalgic** adjective.
– ORIGIN mid 19th cent.: modern Latin, from Greek *mus* 'muscle' + -ALGIA.

myalgic encephalomyelitis (also **myalgic encephalopathy**) (abbrev.: **ME**) ▶ noun another term for CHRONIC FATIGUE SYNDROME.

myalism /ˈmʌɪəlɪz(ə)m/ ▶ noun [mass noun] a Jamaican folk religion focused on the power of ancestors, typically involving drumming, dancing, spirit possession, ritual sacrifice, and herbalism.
– ORIGIN mid 19th cent.: from *myal*, in the same sense (perhaps from Hausa *mayl* 'sorcerer'), + -ISM.

myall /ˈmʌɪəl/ ▶ noun **1** an Australian acacia tree with silvery foliage sometimes used as fodder. ● Genus *Acacia*, family Leguminosae: several species, in particular *A. pendula*, which has violet-scented timber.
2 Austral. an Australian Aboriginal living in a traditional way.
– ORIGIN mid 19th cent. (in sense 1): sense 2 from Dharuk *myal*, *miyal* 'person from another tribe'; sense 1 is perhaps an unexplained transferred use of sense 2.

Myanmar /mjanˈmɑː, ˌmʌɪənˈmɑː/ see BURMA.

myasthenia /ˌmʌɪəsˈθiːnɪə/ ▶ noun [mass noun] a condition causing abnormal weakness of certain muscles. ■ (in full **myasthenia gravis** /ˈgrɑːvɪs, ˈgravɪs/) a rare chronic autoimmune disease marked by muscular weakness without atrophy, and caused by a defect in the action of acetylcholine at neuromuscular junctions.
– ORIGIN mid 19th cent.: modern Latin, from Greek *mus* 'muscle' + ASTHENIA.

mycelium /mʌɪˈsiːlɪəm/ ▶ noun (pl. **mycelia** /-lɪə/) Botany the vegetative part of a fungus, consisting of a network of fine white filaments (hyphae).
– DERIVATIVES **mycelial** adjective.
– ORIGIN mid 19th cent.: modern Latin, from Greek *mukēs* 'fungus', on the pattern of *epithelium*.

M

Mycenae /mʌɪˈsiːniː/ an ancient city in Greece, situated near the coast in the NE Peloponnese, the centre of the late Bronze Age Mycenaean civilization. The capital of King Agamemnon, it was at its most prosperous *c.*1400–1200 BC; systematic excavation of the site began in 1840.

Mycenaean /ˌmʌɪsɪˈniːən/ (also **Mycenean**) Archaeology ▶ **adjective** relating to or denoting a late Bronze Age civilization in Greece represented by finds at Mycenae and other ancient cities of the Peloponnese.
▶ **noun** an inhabitant of Mycenae or member of the Mycenaean people.

> The Mycenaeans controlled the Aegean after the fall of the Minoan civilization c.1400 BC, and built fortified citadels and impressive palaces. They spoke a form of Greek, written in a distinctive script (see **LINEAR B**), and their culture is identified with that portrayed in the Homeric poems. Their power declined during widespread upheavals at the end of the Mediterranean Bronze Age, around 1100 BC.

mycetoma /ˌmʌɪsɪˈtəʊmə/ ▶ **noun** [mass noun] Medicine chronic inflammation of the tissues caused by infection with a fungus or with certain bacteria.
– ORIGIN late 19th cent.: modern Latin, from Greek *mukēs*, *mukēt-* 'fungus' + **-OMA**.

-mycin ▶ **combining form** in names of antibiotic compounds derived from fungi: *streptomycin*.
– ORIGIN based on **MYCO-**.

myco- ▶ **combining form** relating to fungi: *mycoprotein*.
– ORIGIN formed irregularly from Greek *mukēs* 'fungus, mushroom'.

mycobacterium /ˌmʌɪkə(ʊ)bakˈtɪərɪəm/ ▶ **noun** (pl. **mycobacteria** /-rɪə/) a bacterium of a group which includes the causative agents of leprosy and tuberculosis. ● Genus *Mycobacterium* and family Mycobacteriaceae; Gram-positive aerobic acid-fast bacteria.
– DERIVATIVES **mycobacterial** adjective.

mycology /mʌɪˈkɒlədʒi/ ▶ **noun** [mass noun] the scientific study of fungi.
– DERIVATIVES **mycological** adjective, **mycologically** adverb, **mycologist** noun.

M

mycoplasma /ˌmʌɪkə(ʊ)ˈplazmə/ ▶ **noun** (pl. **mycoplasmas** or **mycoplasmata** /-mətə/) any of a group of small typically parasitic bacteria that lack cell walls and sometimes cause diseases. ● Class Mollicutes and order Mycoplasmatales.

mycoprotein ▶ **noun** [mass noun] protein derived from fungi, especially as produced for human consumption.

mycorrhiza /ˌmʌɪkə(ʊ)ˈrʌɪzə/ ▶ **noun** (pl. **mycorrhizae** /-ziː/) Botany a fungus which grows in association with the roots of a plant in a symbiotic or mildly pathogenic relationship.
– DERIVATIVES **mycorrhizal** adjective.
– ORIGIN late 19th cent.: modern Latin, from **MYCO-** 'of fungi' + Greek *rhiza* 'root'.

mycosis /mʌɪˈkəʊsɪs/ ▶ **noun** (pl. **mycoses** /-siːz/) a disease caused by infection with a fungus, such as ringworm or thrush.
– DERIVATIVES **mycotic** /-ˈkɒtɪk/ adjective.

mycotoxin ▶ **noun** any toxic substance produced by a fungus.

mycotrophic /ˌmʌɪkə(ʊ)ˈtrəʊfɪk, -ˈtrɒfɪk/ ▶ **adjective** Botany (of a plant) living in association with a mycorrhiza or another fungus which appears to improve the uptake of nutrients.
– ORIGIN 1920s: from **MYCO-** 'of fungi' + Greek *trophē* 'nourishment'.

mydriasis /ˌmɪdrɪˈeɪsɪs, mɪˈdrʌɪəsɪs/ ▶ **noun** [mass noun] Medicine dilation of the pupil of the eye.
– ORIGIN early 19th cent.: via Latin from Greek *mudriasis*.

myelin /ˈmʌɪəlɪn/ ▶ **noun** [mass noun] Anatomy & Physiology a mixture of proteins and phospholipids forming a whitish insulating sheath around many nerve fibres, which increases the speed at which impulses are conducted.
– DERIVATIVES **myelinated** adjective, **myelination** noun.
– ORIGIN late 19th cent.: from Greek *muelos* 'marrow' + **-IN**[1].

myelitis /ˌmʌɪəˈlʌɪtɪs/ ▶ **noun** [mass noun] Medicine inflammation of the spinal cord.
– ORIGIN mid 19th cent.: modern Latin, from Greek *muelos* 'marrow' + **-ITIS**.

myeloid /ˈmʌɪəlɔɪd/ ▶ **adjective 1** relating to bone marrow. ■ (of leukaemia) characterized by the proliferation of cells originating in the bone marrow. **2** relating to the spinal cord.
– ORIGIN mid 19th cent.: from Greek *muelos* 'marrow' + **-OID**.

myeloma /ˌmʌɪəˈləʊmə/ ▶ **noun** (pl. **myelomas** or **myelomata** /-mətə/) Medicine a malignant tumour of the bone marrow.
– ORIGIN mid 19th cent.: modern Latin, from Greek *muelos* 'marrow' + **-OMA**.

myelopathy /ˌmʌɪəˈlɒpəθi/ ▶ **noun** [mass noun] Medicine disease of the spinal cord.

myenteric /ˌmʌɪɛnˈtɛrɪk/ ▶ **adjective** Anatomy relating to or denoting a plexus of nerves of the sympathetic and parasympathetic systems situated between and supplying the two layers of muscle in the small intestine.

mygalomorph /ˈmɪɡ(ə)ləmɔːf/ ▶ **noun** Zoology a large spider of a group that includes the tarantulas, trapdoor spiders, and funnel-web spiders. Mygalomorphs have several primitive features, including fangs that stab downwards rather than towards one another. ● Suborder Mygalomorphae, order Araneae.
– ORIGIN 1920s: from modern Latin *Mygalomorphae*, from Greek *mugalē* 'shrew' + *morphē* 'form'.

Mykolayiv /ˌmɪkəˈlʌɪf/ an industrial city in southern Ukraine, on the Southern Bug River near the northern tip of the Black Sea; pop. 504,300 (est. 2009). Russian name **NIKOLAEV**.

Mykonos /ˈmɪkənɒs/ a Greek island in the Aegean, one of the Cyclades. Greek name **MÍKONOS**.

Mylar /ˈmʌɪlɑː/ ▶ **noun** [mass noun] trademark a form of polyester resin used to make heat-resistant plastic films and sheets. It is made by copolymerizing ethylene glycol and terephthalic acid.
– ORIGIN 1950s: an arbitrary formation.

mylodon /ˈmʌɪləd(ə)n/ ▶ **noun** an extinct giant ground sloth found in Pleistocene ice age deposits in South America. It died out only 11,000 years ago. ● Genus *Glossotherium* (formerly *Mylodon*), family Mylodontidae.
– ORIGIN mid 19th cent.: modern Latin, from Greek *mulē* 'mill, molar' + *odous*, *odont-* 'tooth'.

mylonite /ˈmʌɪlənʌɪt/ ▶ **noun** [mass noun] Geology a fine-grained metamorphic rock, typically banded, resulting from the grinding or crushing of other rocks.
– ORIGIN late 19th cent.: from Greek *mulōn* 'mill' + **-ITE**[1].

Mymensingh /ˌmʌɪmənˈsɪŋ/ a port on the Brahmaputra River in central Bangladesh; pop. 388,600 (est. 2009).

mynah /ˈmʌɪnə/ (also **mynah bird** or **myna**) ▶ **noun** an Asian and Australasian starling that typically has dark plumage, gregarious behaviour, and a loud call. ● Family Sturnidae: several genera and species, in particular the **hill mynah** or **southern grackle** (*Gracula religiosa*), which is popular as a cage bird because of its ability to mimic the human voice.
– ORIGIN mid 18th cent.: from Hindi *mainā*.

myo- (also **my-** before a vowel) ▶ **combining form** of muscle; relating to muscles: *myocardium* | *myometrium*.
– ORIGIN from Greek *mus*, *mu-* 'mouse or muscle'.

MYOB ▶ **abbreviation** informal mind your own business: *as for the identity of the mystery lady, I'm afraid it's strictly MYOB.*

myocardial infarction /ˌmʌɪə(ʊ)ˈkɑːdɪəl/ ▶ **noun** Medicine a heart attack.

myocarditis /ˌmʌɪəʊkɑːˈdʌɪtɪs/ ▶ **noun** [mass noun] Medicine inflammation of the heart muscle.

myocardium /ˌmʌɪə(ʊ)ˈkɑːdɪəm/ ▶ **noun** [mass noun] Anatomy the muscular tissue of the heart.
– DERIVATIVES **myocardial** adjective.
– ORIGIN late 19th cent.: modern Latin, from **MYO-** 'muscle' + Greek *kardia* 'heart'.

myoclonus /ˌmʌɪə(ʊ)ˈkləʊnəs/ ▶ **noun** [mass noun] Medicine spasmodic jerky contraction of groups of muscles.
– DERIVATIVES **myoclonic** adjective.

myofibril /ˌmʌɪə(ʊ)ˈfʌɪbrɪl/ ▶ **noun** any of the elongated contractile threads found in striated muscle cells.

myogenic /ˌmʌɪə(ʊ)ˈdʒɛnɪk/ ▶ **adjective** Physiology originating in muscle tissue (rather than from nerve impulses).

myoglobin /ˌmʌɪə(ʊ)ˈɡləʊbɪn/ ▶ **noun** [mass noun] Biochemistry a red protein containing haem, which carries and stores oxygen in muscle cells. It is structurally similar to a subunit of haemoglobin.

myology /mʌɪˈɒlədʒi/ ▶ **noun** [mass noun] the study of the structure, arrangement, and action of muscles.
– DERIVATIVES **myological** adjective.

myomere /ˈmʌɪə(ʊ)mɪə/ ▶ **noun** see **MYOTOME**.

myometrium /ˌmʌɪə(ʊ)ˈmiːtrɪəm/ ▶ **noun** [mass noun] Anatomy the smooth muscle tissue of the womb.
– ORIGIN early 20th cent.: modern Latin, from **MYO-** 'muscle' + Greek *mētra* 'womb'.

Myomorpha /ˈmʌɪə(ʊ),mɔːfə/ ▶ **plural noun** Zoology a major division of the rodents that includes the rats, mice, voles, hamsters, and their relatives. ● Suborder Myomorpha, order Rodentia.
– DERIVATIVES **myomorph** noun & adjective.
– ORIGIN modern Latin (plural), from Greek *mus*, *mu-* 'mouse' + *morphē* 'form'.

myopathy /mʌɪˈɒpəθi/ ▶ **noun** (pl. **myopathies**) Medicine a disease of muscle tissue.
– DERIVATIVES **myopathic** adjective.

myope /ˈmʌɪəʊp/ ▶ **noun** a short-sighted person.
– ORIGIN early 18th cent.: from French, via late Latin from Greek *muōps*, from *muein* 'to shut' + *ōps* 'eye'.

myopia /mʌɪˈəʊpɪə/ ▶ **noun** [mass noun] the quality of being short-sighted. ■ lack of foresight or intellectual insight: *the company's corporate myopia*.
– ORIGIN early 18th cent.: modern Latin, from late Greek *muōpia*, from Greek *muōps* (see **MYOPE**).

myopic /mʌɪˈɒpɪk/ ▶ **adjective** short-sighted. ■ lacking foresight or intellectual insight: *the government still has a myopic attitude to public spending.*
– DERIVATIVES **myopically** /-ˈɒpɪk(ə)li/ adverb.

myosin /ˈmʌɪə(ʊ)sɪn/ ▶ **noun** [mass noun] Biochemistry a fibrous protein which forms (together with actin) the contractile filaments of muscle cells and is also involved in motion in other types of cell.

myosis ▶ **noun** variant spelling of **MIOSIS**.

myositis /ˌmʌɪə(ʊ)ˈsʌɪtɪs/ ▶ **noun** [mass noun] Medicine inflammation and degeneration of muscle tissue.
– ORIGIN early 19th cent.: formed irregularly from Greek *mus*, *mu-* 'muscle' + **-ITIS**.

myosotis /ˌmʌɪə(ʊ)ˈsəʊtɪs/ ▶ **noun** a plant of a genus which includes the forget-me-nots. ● Genus *Myosotis*, family Boraginaceae.
– ORIGIN modern Latin, from Greek *muosōtis*, from *mus*, *mu-* 'mouse' + *ous*, *ōt-* 'ear'.

myotis /mʌɪˈəʊtɪs/ ▶ **noun** an insectivorous bat with a slender muzzle and with the flight membrane extending between the hind legs and the tip of the tail. ● Genus *Myotis*, family Vespertilionidae: numerous species.
– ORIGIN modern Latin, based on Greek *mus*, *mu-* 'mouse'.

myotome /ˈmʌɪətəʊm/ ▶ **noun** Embryology the dorsal part of each somite in a vertebrate embryo, giving rise to the skeletal musculature. Compare with **DERMATOME**, **SCLEROTOME**. ■ each of the muscle blocks along either side of the spine in vertebrates (especially fish and amphibians). Also called **MYOMERE**.

myotonia /ˌmʌɪə(ʊ)ˈtəʊnɪə/ ▶ **noun** [mass noun] Medicine inability to relax voluntary muscle after vigorous effort.
– DERIVATIVES **myotonic** adjective.
– ORIGIN late 19th cent.: from **MYO-** 'muscle' + Greek *tonos* 'tone'.

myotonic dystrophy ▶ **noun** [mass noun] a form of muscular dystrophy accompanied by myotonia.

myriad /ˈmɪrɪəd/ ▶ **noun 1** a countless or extremely great number of people or things: ***myriads of*** *insects danced around the light above my head.*
2 (chiefly in classical history) a unit of ten thousand.
▶ **adjective** countless or extremely great in number: *he gazed at the myriad lights of the city.* ■ having countless or very many elements or aspects: *the myriad political scene.*
– ORIGIN mid 16th cent. (in sense 2 of the noun): via late Latin from Greek *murias*, *muriad-*, from *murioi* '10,000'.

myriapod /ˈmɪrɪəpɒd/ ▶ **noun** Zoology an arthropod of a group that includes the centipedes, millipedes, and related animals. Myriapods have elongated bodies with numerous leg-bearing segments. ● Classes Chilopoda, Diplopoda, Pauropoda, and Symphyla; formerly placed together in the class Myriapoda.
– ORIGIN early 19th cent.: from modern Latin *Myriapoda*, from Greek *murias* (see **MYRIAD**) + *pous*, *pod-* 'foot'.

myringotomy /ˌmɪrɪnˈɡɒtəmi, -ˈɡɒtəmi/ ▶ **noun** [mass noun] surgical incision into the eardrum, to relieve pressure or drain fluid.
– ORIGIN late 19th cent.: from modern Latin *myringa* 'eardrum' + **-TOMY**.

myrmecology /ˌməːmɪˈkɒlədʒi/ ▶ **noun** [mass noun] the branch of entomology that deals with ants.
– DERIVATIVES **myrmecologist** noun.
– ORIGIN late 19th cent.: from Greek *murmēx*, *murmēk-* 'ant' + **-LOGY**.

myrmecophile /ˈməːmɪkə(ʊ)fʌɪl, məˈmiːkə(ʊ)-/ ▶ **noun** Biology an invertebrate or plant which has a symbiotic relationship with ants, such as being tended and protected by ants or living inside an ants' nest.
– DERIVATIVES **myrmecophilous** adjective, **myrmecophily** noun.
– ORIGIN late 19th cent.: from Greek *murmēx*, *murmēk-* 'ant' + **-PHILE**.

myrmidon /ˈməːmɪd(ə)n/ ▶ **noun** a follower or subordinate of a powerful person, typically one who is unscrupulous or carries out orders unquestioningly: *one of Hitler's myrmidons*.
– ORIGIN late Middle English: from Latin *Myrmidones* (plural), from Greek *Murmidones*, a warlike Thessalian people who accompanied Achilles to Troy.

myrobalan /mʌɪˈrɒbələn/ ▶ **noun 1** (also **myrobalan plum**) another term for **CHERRY PLUM**.
2 a tropical tree of a characteristic pagoda shape, which yields a number of useful items including dye, timber, and medicinal products. ● Genus *Terminalia*, family Combretaceae: several species, in particular *T. chebula*.
■ (also **myrobalan nut**) the fruit of the myrobalan tree, used especially for tanning leather.
– ORIGIN late Middle English: from French *myrobolan* or Latin *myrobalanum*, from Greek *murobalanos*, from *muron* 'unguent' + *balanos* 'acorn'.

Myron /ˈmʌɪ(ə)rən/ (*fl.* c.480–440 BC), Greek sculptor. None of his work is known to survive, but there are two certain copies, one being the *Discobolus* (c.450 BC), a figure of a man throwing the discus, which demonstrates a remarkable interest in symmetry and movement.

myrrh¹ /məː/ ▶ **noun** [mass noun] a fragrant gum resin obtained from certain trees and used, especially in the Near East, in perfumery, medicines, and incense. ● The trees belong to the genus *Commiphora*, family Burseraceae, in particular *C. myrrha*.
– ORIGIN Old English *myrra*, *myrre*, via Latin from Greek *murra*, of Semitic origin; compare with Arabic *murr* 'bitter'.

myrrh² /məː/ ▶ **noun** another term for **SWEET CICELY**.
– ORIGIN late 16th cent.: from Latin *myrris*, from Greek *murris*.

myrtaceous /məːˈteɪʃəs/ ▶ **adjective** Botany relating to or denoting plants of the myrtle family (Myrtaceae).
– ORIGIN mid 19th cent.: from modern Latin *Myrtaceae* (plural), from the genus name *Myrtus* (see **MYRTLE**), + **-OUS**.

myrtle ▶ **noun 1** an evergreen shrub which has glossy aromatic foliage and white flowers followed by purple-black oval berries. ● *Myrtus communis*, family Myrtaceae (the **myrtle family**). This family also includes several aromatic plants (clove, allspice) and many characteristic Australian plants (such as eucalyptus trees and bottlebrushes).
2 N. Amer. the lesser periwinkle. ● *Vinca minor*, family Apocynaceae. See **PERIWINKLE¹**.
– ORIGIN late Middle English: from medieval Latin *myrtilla*, *myrtillus*, diminutive of Latin *myrta*, *myrtus*, from Greek *murtos*.

myself ▶ **pronoun** [first person singular] **1** [reflexive] used by a speaker to refer to himself or herself as the object of a verb or preposition when he or she is the subject of the clause: *I hurt myself by accident* | *I strolled around, muttering to myself*.
2 [emphatic] I or me personally (used to emphasize the speaker): *I myself am unsure how this problem should be handled* | *I wrote it myself*.
3 literary used by a speaker to refer to himself or herself; I: *myself presented to him a bronze sword*.
– PHRASES **(not) be myself** see **BE ONESELF**, **NOT BE ONESELF** at **BE**. **by myself** see **BY ONESELF** at **BY**.
– ORIGIN Old English *me self*, from **ME¹** + **SELF** (used adjectivally); the change of *me* to *my* occurred in Middle English.

Mysia /ˈmɪsɪə/ an ancient region of NW Asia Minor, on the Mediterranean coast south of the Sea of Marmara.
– DERIVATIVES **Mysian** adjective & noun.

mysid /ˈmʌɪsɪd/ ▶ **noun** Zoology a crustacean of an order that comprises the opossum shrimps. ● Order Mysidacea, class Malacostraca.
– ORIGIN late 19th cent.: from modern Latin *Mysis* (genus name) + **-ID³**.

Mysore /mʌɪˈsɔː/ **1** a city in the Indian state of Karnataka; pop. 1,042,400 (est. 2009). It was the capital of the princely state of Mysore and is noted for the production of silk, incense, and sandalwood oil.
2 former name (until 1973) for **KARNATAKA**.

mystagogue /ˈmɪstəgɒg/ ▶ **noun** a teacher or propounder of mystical doctrines.
– DERIVATIVES **mystagogy** noun.
– ORIGIN mid 16th cent.: from French, or via Latin from Greek *mustagōgos*, from *mustēs* 'initiated person' + *agōgos* 'leading'.

mysterious ▶ **adjective** difficult or impossible to understand, explain, or identify: *his colleague had vanished in mysterious circumstances* | *a mysterious benefactor provided the money*. ■ (of a person) deliberately enigmatic: *she was mysterious about herself but said plenty about her husband*.
– DERIVATIVES **mysteriously** adverb, **mysteriousness** noun.
– ORIGIN late 16th cent.: from French *mystérieux*, from *mystère* 'mystery'.

mystery¹ ▶ **noun** (pl. **mysteries**) **1** something that is difficult or impossible to understand or explain: *the mysteries of outer space* | *what happened after he left home that day remains a mystery*. ■ [mass noun] secrecy or obscurity: *much of her past is shrouded in mystery*. ■ a person or thing whose identity or nature is puzzling or unknown: *'He's a bit of a mystery,' said Nina* | [as modifier] *a mystery guest*.
2 a novel, play, or film dealing with a puzzling crime, especially a murder.
3 (**mysteries**) the secret rites of Greek and Roman pagan religion, or of any ancient or tribal religion, to which only initiates are admitted. ■ the practices, skills, or lore peculiar to a particular trade or activity and regarded as baffling to those without specialized knowledge: *the mysteries of analytical psychology*. ■ archaic the Christian Eucharist.
4 chiefly Christian Theology a religious belief based on divine revelation, especially one regarded as beyond human understanding. ■ an incident in the life of Jesus or of a saint as a focus of devotion in the Roman Catholic Church, especially each of those commemorated during recitation of successive decades of the rosary.
– ORIGIN Middle English (in the sense 'mystic presence, hidden religious symbolism'): from Old French *mistere* or Latin *mysterium*, from Greek *mustērion*; related to **MYSTIC**.

mystery² ▶ **noun** (pl. **mysteries**) archaic a handicraft or trade, especially when referred to in indentures.
– ORIGIN late Middle English: from medieval Latin *misterium*, contraction of *ministerium* 'ministry', by association with *mysterium* (see **MYSTERY¹**).

mystery play ▶ **noun** a popular medieval play based on biblical stories or the lives of the saints. Also called **MIRACLE PLAY**.

> Mystery plays were performed by members of trade guilds in Europe from the 13th century, in churches or later on wagons or temporary stages along a route, frequently introducing apocryphal and satirical elements. Several cycles of plays survive in association with particular English cities and towns.

mystery religion ▶ **noun** a religion centred on secret or mystical rites for initiates, especially any of a number of cults popular during the late Roman Empire.

mystery shopper ▶ **noun** a person employed to visit a shop or restaurant incognito in order to assess the quality of the goods or services.

mystery tour ▶ **noun** Brit. a pleasure excursion to an unspecified destination.

mystic ▶ **noun** a person who seeks by contemplation and self-surrender to obtain unity with or absorption into the Deity or the absolute, or who believes in the spiritual apprehension of truths that are beyond the intellect.
▶ **adjective** another term for **MYSTICAL**.
– ORIGIN Middle English (in the sense 'mystical meaning'): from Old French *mystique*, or via Latin from Greek *mustikos*, from *mustēs* 'initiated person' from *muein* 'close the eyes or lips', also 'initiate'. The current sense of the noun dates from the late 17th cent.

mystical ▶ **adjective 1** relating to mystics or religious mysticism: *the mystical theology of Richard Rolle*. ■ having a spiritual symbolic or allegorical significance that transcends human understanding: *the mystical body of Christ*. ■ relating to ancient religious mysteries or other occult or esoteric rites: *the mystical practices of the Pythagoreans*. ■ of hidden or esoteric meaning: *a geometric figure of mystical significance*.
2 inspiring a sense of spiritual mystery, awe, and fascination: *the mystical city of Kathmandu*. ■ concerned with the soul or the spirit, rather than with material things: *the beliefs of a more mystical age*.
– DERIVATIVES **mystically** adverb.

Mysticeti /ˌmɪstɪˈsiːtiː/ ▶ **plural noun** Zoology a division of the whales that comprises the baleen whales.
● Suborder Mysticeti, order Cetacea.
– DERIVATIVES **mysticete** noun & adjective.
– ORIGIN modern Latin (plural), from Greek *mustikētos* representing (in old editions of Aristotle) the phrase *ho mus to kētos* 'the mouse, the whale so called'.

mysticism ▶ **noun** [mass noun] **1** belief that union with or absorption into the Deity or the absolute, or the spiritual apprehension of knowledge inaccessible to the intellect, may be attained through contemplation and self-surrender.
2 vague or ill-defined religious or spiritual belief, especially as associated with a belief in the occult.

mystify ▶ **verb** (**mystifies**, **mystifying**, **mystified**) [with obj.] utterly bewilder or perplex (someone): *I was completely mystified by his disappearance* | (as adj. **mystifying**) *a mystifying phenomenon*. ■ make obscure or mysterious: *lawyers who mystify the legal system so that laymen find it unintelligible*.
– DERIVATIVES **mystification** noun, **mystifier** noun, **mystifyingly** adverb.
– ORIGIN early 19th cent.: from French *mystifier*, formed irregularly from *mystique* 'mystic' or from *mystère* 'mystery'.

mystique ▶ **noun** [mass noun] a quality of mystery, glamour, or power associated with someone or something: *the mystique surrounding the monarchy*. ■ an air of secrecy surrounding a particular activity or subject that makes it impressive or baffling to those without specialized knowledge: *eliminating the mystique normally associated with computers*.
– ORIGIN late 19th cent.: from French, from Old French (see **MYSTIC**).

myth ▶ **noun 1** a traditional story, especially one concerning the early history of a people or explaining a natural or social phenomenon, and typically involving supernatural beings or events: *ancient Celtic myths* | [mass noun] *the heroes of Greek myth*.
2 a widely held but false belief or idea: *the belief that evening primrose oil helps to cure eczema is a myth, according to dermatologists*. ■ a fictitious or imaginary person or thing. ■ an exaggerated or idealized conception of a person or thing: *the book is a scholarly study of the Churchill myth*.
– ORIGIN mid 19th cent.: from modern Latin *mythus*, via late Latin from Greek *muthos*.

mythi plural form of **MYTHUS**.

mythic ▶ **adjective** mythical: *mythic creatures* | *a mythic land of plenty*. ■ exaggerated or idealized: *Scott of the Antarctic was a national hero of mythic proportions*.
– ORIGIN mid 17th cent.: via late Latin from Greek *muthikos*, from *muthos* 'myth'.

mythical ▶ **adjective** occurring in or characteristic of myths or folk tales: *one of Denmark's greatest mythical heroes*. ■ idealized, especially with reference to the past: *a mythical age of contentment and social order*. ■ fictitious: *a mythical customer whose name appears in brochures promoting the bank's services*.
– DERIVATIVES **mythically** adverb.

mythicize (also **mythicise**) ▶ **verb** [with obj.] make (someone or something) the subject of a myth or myths.
– DERIVATIVES **mythicism** noun, **mythicist** noun.

mythify ▶ **verb** another term for **MYTHICIZE**.
– DERIVATIVES **mythification** noun.

mytho- ▶ **combining form** relating to myth: *mythography*.
– ORIGIN from Greek *muthos*, or from **MYTH**.

mythography ▶ **noun** [mass noun] **1** the representation of myths in art.
2 the creation or collection of myths.
– DERIVATIVES **mythographer** noun.

mythological ▶ **adjective** relating to, based on, or appearing in myths or mythology: *the tree of life is one of the oldest of all mythological symbols*.
– DERIVATIVES **mythologic** adjective, **mythologically** adverb.

mythologize (also **mythologise**) ▶ **verb** [with obj.] convert into myth or mythology; make the subject of a myth: *there is a grave danger of mythologizing the past*. ■ create or promote an exaggerated or idealized

image of: *much of his life was devoted to mythologizing his own career.*
– DERIVATIVES **mythologizer** noun.

mythology ▶ noun (pl. **mythologies**) [mass noun] **1** a collection of myths, especially one belonging to a particular religious or cultural tradition: *tales from Greek mythology* | [count noun] *Jewish and Christian mythologies.* ■ a set of stories or beliefs about a particular person, institution, or situation, especially when exaggerated or fictitious: *we look for change in our thirties, not in our forties, as popular mythology has it.* **2** the study of myths.
– DERIVATIVES **mythologer** noun, **mythologist** noun.
– ORIGIN late Middle English: from French *mythologie*, or via late Latin from Greek *muthologia*, from *muthos* 'myth' + *-logia* (see **-LOGY**).

mythomania ▶ noun [mass noun] an abnormal or pathological tendency to exaggerate or tell lies.
– DERIVATIVES **mythomaniac** noun & adjective.

mythopoeia /ˌmɪθə(ʊ)ˈpiːə/ ▶ noun [mass noun] the making of a myth or myths.
– DERIVATIVES **mythopoeic** adjective, **mythopoetic** adjective.
– ORIGIN 1950s: from Greek *muthopoiia*, from *muthos* 'myth' + *poiein* 'make'.

mythos /ˈmʌɪθɒs, ˈmɪθɒs/ ▶ noun (pl. **mythoi** /-θɔɪ/) chiefly technical a myth or mythology: *the Arthurian mythos.* ■ a traditional or recurrent narrative theme or plot structure.
– ORIGIN mid 18th cent.: from Greek.

mythus /ˈmʌɪθəs, ˈmɪθəs/ ▶ noun (pl. **mythi** /-θʌɪ/) a myth or mythos.
– ORIGIN early 19th cent.: modern Latin.

Mytilene /ˌmɪtɪˈliːni/ the chief town of the Greek island of Lesbos; pop. 28,000 (est. 2009). Greek name **MITILÍNI**.

myxo- (also **myx-**) ▶ combining form relating to mucus: *myxodoema* | *myxovirus.*
– ORIGIN from Greek *muxa* 'slime, mucus'.

myxoedema /ˌmɪksɪˈdiːmə/ (US **myxedema**) ▶ noun [mass noun] Medicine swelling of the skin and underlying tissues giving a waxy consistency, typical of patients with underactive thyroid glands. ■ the more general condition associated with hypothyroidism, including weight gain, mental dullness, and sensitivity to cold.

myxoma /mɪkˈsəʊmə/ ▶ noun (pl. **myxomas** or **myxomata** /-mətə/) Medicine a benign tumour of connective tissue containing mucus or gelatinous material.
– DERIVATIVES **myxomatous** adjective.

myxomatosis /ˌmɪksəməˈtəʊsɪs/ ▶ noun [mass noun] a highly infectious and usually fatal viral disease of rabbits, causing swelling of the mucous membranes and inflammation and discharge around the eyes.

myxomycete /ˌmɪksə(ʊ)ˈmʌɪsiːt/ ▶ noun Biology a slime mould, especially an acellular one whose vegetative stage is a multinucleate plasmodium.
● Division Myxomycota, kingdom Fungi, in particular the class Myxomycetes; also treated as protozoan (phylum Gymnomyxa, kingdom Protista).
– ORIGIN late 19th cent.: from modern Latin *Myxomycetes*, from **MYXO-** 'slime' + Greek *mukētes* 'fungi'.

myxovirus /ˈmɪksə(ʊ)ˌvʌɪrəs/ ▶ noun any of a group of RNA viruses including the influenza virus.

mzee /(ə)mˈzeɪ/ ▶ noun (in East Africa) an older person; an elder.
– ORIGIN Kiswahili, 'ancestor, parent, old person'.

mzungu /(ə)mˈzʊŋgʊ/ ▶ noun (in East Africa) a white person: *there was a mzungu just off the Nyeri Road who was a teacher.*
– ORIGIN Swahili, from *m-* class prefix + *-zungu* 'European'.

M

N¹ (also **n**) ▸ **noun** (pl. **Ns** or **N's**) the fourteenth letter of the alphabet. See also **EN**. ▪ denoting the next after M in a set of items, categories, etc.

N² ▸ **abbreviation** ▪ (used in recording moves in chess) knight: *17.Na4?* [representing the pronunciation of *kn-*, since the initial letter *k-* represents 'king'.] ▪ (on a gear lever) neutral. ▪ (chiefly in place names) New: *N Zealand*. ▪ Physics newton(s). ▪ Chemistry (with reference to solutions) normal. ▪ North or Northern: *78° N* | *N Ireland*. ▪ Norway (international vehicle registration). ▪ nuclear.
▸ **symbol** the chemical element nitrogen.

n ▸ **abbreviation** [in combination] ▪ (in units of measurement) nano- (10^{-9}): *500 ng*. ▪ Grammar neuter. ▪ (*n-*) [in combination] Chemistry normal (denoting straight-chain hydrocarbons): *n-hexane*. ▪ note (used in a book's index to refer to a footnote): *450n*. ▪ Grammar noun.
▸ **symbol** an unspecified or variable number: *at the limit where n equals infinity*. See also **NTH**.

'n' (also **'n**) ▸ **contraction** and (conventionally used in informal contexts to coordinate two closely connected elements): *rock 'n' roll* | *fish 'n' chips*.

-n¹ ▸ **suffix** variant spelling of **-EN²**.

-n² ▸ **suffix** variant spelling of **-EN³**.

Na ▸ **symbol** the chemical element sodium.
– ORIGIN from modern Latin *natrium*.

na ▸ **adverb** Scottish form of **NOT**, used after an auxiliary verb: *we couldna speak to them*.

n/a ▸ **abbreviation** ▪ not applicable. ▪ not available.

NAACP ▸ **abbreviation** National Association for the Advancement of Colored People.

NAAFI /ˈnafi/ ▸ **abbreviation** ▪ Navy, Army, and Air Force Institutes, an organization running canteens and shops for British service personnel. ▪ [as noun] a canteen or shop run by the NAAFI.

naam /nɑːm/ ▸ **noun** Indian a name.
– ORIGIN from Urdu *nām*.

naan ▸ **noun** variant spelling of **NAN²**.

naartjie /ˈnɑːtʃi, ˈnɑːki/ ▸ **noun** (pl. **naartjies**) S. African a mandarin orange or tangerine.
– ORIGIN late 18th cent.: from Afrikaans, from Tamil *nārattai* 'citrus'.

Naas /neɪs/ the county town of Kildare in the Republic of Ireland; pop. 20,044 (2006).

nab ▸ **verb** (**nabs**, **nabbing**, **nabbed**) [with obj.] informal catch (someone) doing something wrong: *the Feds nabbed a suspected terrorist*. ▪ take, grab, or steal (something): *Dan nabbed the seat next to mine*.
– ORIGIN late 17th cent. (also as *napp*; compare with **KIDNAP**): of unknown origin.

Nabataean /ˌnabəˈtiːən/ (also **Nabatean**) ▸ **noun**
1 a member of an ancient Arabian people who from 312 BC formed an independent kingdom with its capital at Petra (now in Jordan). The kingdom was allied to the Roman Empire from 63 BC and incorporated as the province of Arabia in AD 106.
2 [mass noun] the extinct language of the Nabataeans, a form of Aramaic strongly influenced by Arabic.
▸ **adjective** relating to the Nabataeans or their language.
– ORIGIN from Latin *Nabat(h)aeus*, Greek *Nabat(h)aios* (compare with the Arabic adjective *Nabaṭī* 'relating to the Nabataeans') + **-AN**.

nabe ▸ **noun** US informal a neighbourhood. ▪ a local cinema. ▪ a neighbour.

Nabeul /naˈbəːl/ a resort town in NE Tunisia, on the Cape Bon peninsula; pop. 56,400 (est. 2004).

Nabi Group /ˈnɑːbi/ a group of late 19th-century French painters, largely symbolist in their approach and heavily indebted to Gauguin. Members of the group included Maurice Denis, Pierre Bonnard, and Édouard Vuillard.
– ORIGIN *Nabi* from Hebrew *nāḇī* 'prophet'.

Nablus /ˈnɑːbləs/ a town in the West Bank; pop. 190,600 (est. 2009).

nabob /ˈneɪbɒb/ ▸ **noun 1** historical a Muslim official or governor under the Mogul empire.
2 a person of conspicuous wealth or high status. ▪ historical a person who returned from India to Europe with a fortune.
– ORIGIN from Portuguese *nababo* or Spanish *nabab*, from Urdu; see also **NAWAB**.

Nabokov /ˈnabəkɒf/, Vladimir (Vladimirovich) (1899–1977), Russian-born American novelist and poet. He is best known for *Lolita* (1955), his novel about a middle-aged man's obsession with a twelve-year-old girl.

Nacala /nəˈkɑːlə/ a deep-water port on the east coast of Mozambique; pop. 104,828 (2007). It is linked by rail with landlocked Malawi.

nacelle /nəˈsɛl/ ▸ **noun** a streamlined casing on the outside of an aircraft or motor vehicle, especially one housing an aircraft engine. ▪ the passenger compartment of an airship.
– ORIGIN early 20th cent. (originally denoting the car of an airship): from French, from late Latin *navicella*, diminutive of Latin *navis* 'ship'.

naches /ˈnʌxəs/ (also **nachas** pronounced same) ▸ **noun** [mass noun] US pride or pleasure, especially at the achievements of one's children.
– ORIGIN early 20th cent.: from Yiddish *nakhes*, from Hebrew *naḥaṯ* 'contentment'.

nacho /ˈnatʃəʊ/ ▸ **noun** (pl. **nachos**) a small piece of tortilla, typically topped with melted cheese and spices.
– ORIGIN perhaps from Mexican Spanish *Nacho*, pet form of *Ignacio*, given name of the chef credited with creation of the dish. An alternative derivation is from Spanish *nacho* 'flat-nosed'.

NACODS /ˈneɪkɒds/ ▸ **abbreviation** (in the UK) National Association of Colliery Overmen, Deputies, and Shotfirers.

nacre /ˈneɪkə/ ▸ **noun** [mass noun] mother-of-pearl.
– DERIVATIVES **nacreous** adjective.
– ORIGIN late 16th cent.: from French, of unknown origin.

NAD ▸ **abbreviation** Biochemistry nicotinamide adenine dinucleotide, a coenzyme important in many biological oxidation reactions.

nada /ˈnɑːdə, ˈnadə/ ▸ **pronoun** N. Amer. informal nothing.
– ORIGIN Spanish.

Na-Dene /nɑːˈdeneɪ, -ni/ ▸ **adjective** denoting or belonging to a postulated phylum of North American Indian languages including the Athabaskan family, Tlingit, and (in some classifications) Haida.
▸ **noun** [mass noun] the Na-Dene language group.
– ORIGIN early 20th cent.: from Tlingit *naa* 'tribe' (related to Haida *náa* 'dwell') + North Athabaskan *dene* 'tribe'.

Nader /ˈneɪdə/, Ralph (b.1934), American lawyer and reformer. He campaigned on behalf of public safety and prompted legislation concerning car design, radiation hazards, food packaging, and insecticides.
– DERIVATIVES **Naderism** noun.

nadir /ˈneɪdɪə, ˈnadɪə/ ▸ **noun** [in sing.] **1** the lowest or most unsuccessful point in a situation: *asking that question was the nadir of my career*.
2 Astronomy the point on the celestial sphere directly below an observer. The opposite of **ZENITH**.
– ORIGIN late Middle English (in sense 2): via French from Arabic *naẓīr (as-samt)* 'opposite (to the zenith)'.

nads /nadz/ ▸ **plural noun** vulgar slang a man's testicles.
– ORIGIN 1960s: shortening of **GONAD**.

nae ▸ **determiner, exclamation, adverb, & noun** Scottish form of **NO**.
▸ **adverb & noun** Scottish form of **NOT**.

naevus /ˈniːvəs/ (US **nevus**) ▸ **noun** (pl. **naevi** /-vʌɪ, -viː/) a birthmark or a mole on the skin, especially a birthmark in the form of a raised red patch.
– ORIGIN mid 19th cent.: from Latin.

naff¹ ▸ **verb** [no obj.] (usu. in imperative **naff off**) Brit. informal go away: *she told press photographers to naff off*. ▪ (as adj. **naffing**) used to emphasize annoyance: *more naffing guidelines!*
– ORIGIN 1950s: euphemism for **FUCK**; compare with **EFF**.

naff² ▸ **adjective** Brit. informal lacking taste or style: *he always went for the most obvious melody he could get, no matter how naff it sounded*.
– DERIVATIVES **naffness** noun.
– ORIGIN 1960s: of unknown origin.

NAFTA (also **Nafta**) ▸ **abbreviation** North American Free Trade Agreement.

nag¹ ▸ **verb** (**nags**, **nagging**, **nagged**) [with obj.] harass (someone) constantly to do something that they are averse to: *she constantly **nags** her daughter **about** getting married* | [with infinitive] *she nagged him to do the housework* | [no obj.] *he's always **nagging at** her for staying out late*. ▪ [no obj.] be persistently painful or worrying to: *something nagged at the back of his mind*.
▸ **noun** a person who nags someone to do something. ▪ a persistent feeling of anxiety: *he felt a little nag of doubt*.
– DERIVATIVES **nagger** noun, **naggy** adjective.
– ORIGIN early 19th cent. (originally dialect in the sense 'gnaw'): perhaps of Scandinavian or Low German origin; compare with Norwegian and Swedish *nagga* 'gnaw, irritate' and Low German *(g)naggen* 'provoke'.

nag² ▸ **noun** informal, often derogatory a horse, especially one that is old or in poor health. ▪ archaic a horse suitable for riding rather than as a draught animal.
– ORIGIN Middle English: of unknown origin.

Naga /ˈnɑːgə/ ▸ **noun 1** a member of a group of peoples living in or near the Naga Hills of Burma (Myanmar) and NE India.
2 [mass noun] any of the Tibeto-Burman languages of the Nagas, with about 340,000 speakers altogether.
▸ **adjective** relating to the Nagas or their language.
– ORIGIN perhaps from Sanskrit *nagna* 'naked' or *naga* 'mountain'.

naga¹ /ˈnɑːgə/ ▸ **noun** (in Indian mythology) a member of a semi-divine race, part human, part cobra in

N

form, associated with water and sometimes with mystical initiation.
– ORIGIN from Sanskrit *nāga* 'serpent'.

naga[2] /ˈnɑːɡɑː/ ▸ **noun** (in some Hindu sects) a naked wandering ascetic, in particular one belonging to a sect whose members carry arms and serve as mercenaries.
– ORIGIN from Hindi *nāgā* 'naked'.

Nagaland /ˈnɑːɡəland/ a state in the far north-east of India, on the border with Burma (Myanmar); capital, Kohima. It was created in 1962 from parts of Assam.

nagana /nəˈɡɑːnə/ ▸ **noun** [mass noun] a disease of cattle, antelope, and other livestock in southern Africa, characterized by fever, lethargy, and oedema, and caused by trypanosome parasites transmitted by the tsetse fly.
– ORIGIN late 19th cent.: from Zulu *nakane*.

nagar /ˈnʌɡər/ ▸ **noun** Indian a town, city, or suburb.
– ORIGIN from Hindi.

Nagasaki /ˌnaɡəˈsɑːki/ a city and port in SW Japan, on the west coast of Kyushu island; pop. 452,064 (2007). It was the target of the second atom bomb, dropped by the United States on 9 August 1945.

nagging ▸ **adjective 1** (of a person) constantly harassing someone to do something: *a nagging wife*.
2 persistently painful or worrying: *a nagging pain* | *only a handful of nagging doubts remained*.
– DERIVATIVES **naggingly** adverb.

Nagorno-Karabakh /nəˌɡɔːnəʊˌkarəˈbax/ a region of Azerbaijan in the southern foothills of the Caucasus; pop. 134,900 (est. 2005); capital, Xankändi.

> Formerly a khanate, Nagorno-Karabakh was absorbed into the Russian empire in the 19th century, later becoming an autonomous region of the Soviet Union within Azerbaijan. Fighting between Azerbaijan and Armenia began in 1985, with the majority Armenian population desiring to be separated from Muslim Azerbaijan and united with Armenia; the region declared unilateral independence in 1991. A ceasefire was signed in 1994.

Nagoya /nəˈɡɔɪə/ a city in central Japan, on the south coast of the island of Honshu, capital of Chubu region; pop. 2,154,287 (2007).

Nagpur /naɡˈpʊə/ a city in central India, in the state of Maharashtra; pop. 2,403,200 (est. 2009).

N

nagware ▸ **noun** [mass noun] informal computer software which is free for a trial period and thereafter frequently reminds the user to pay for it.

Nagy /nɒdʒ/, Imre (1896–1958), Hungarian communist statesman, Prime Minister 1953–5 and 1956. In 1956 he withdrew Hungary from the Warsaw Pact, seeking neutral status for it. He was executed after the Red Army crushed the uprising later that year.

nah ▸ **determiner, exclamation, adverb, & noun** non-standard spelling of **NO**, used in representing southern English (especially cockney) speech.

Nah. ▸ **abbreviation** Nahum (in biblical references).

Naha /ˈnɑːhə/ a port in southern Japan, capital of Okinawa island; pop. 312,938 (2007).

Nahuatl /ˈnɑːwɑːt(ə)l, nɑːˈwɑːt(ə)l/ ▸ **noun** (pl. **same** or **Nahuatls**) **1** a member of a group of peoples native to southern Mexico and Central America, including the Aztecs.
2 [mass noun] the Uto-Aztecan language of the Nahuatl, which has over 1 million speakers.
▸ **adjective** relating to the Nahuatl or their language.
– ORIGIN via Spanish from Nahuatl.

Nahum /ˈneɪhəm/ (in the Bible) a Hebrew minor prophet. ■ a book of the Bible containing Nahum's prophecy of the fall of Nineveh (early 7th century BC).

nai /nʌɪ/ ▸ **noun** Indian a barber.
– ORIGIN from Hindi.

naiad /ˈnʌɪad/ ▸ **noun** (pl. **naiads** or **naiades** /ˈnʌɪəˌdiːz/) **1** (in classical mythology) a water nymph said to inhabit a river, spring, or waterfall.
2 the aquatic larva or nymph of a dragonfly, mayfly, or stonefly.
3 a submerged aquatic plant with narrow leaves and minute flowers. ● Genus *Najas*, family Najadaceae.
– ORIGIN via Latin from Greek *Naias*, *Naiad-*, from *naein* 'to flow'. Use as a term in entomology and botany dates from the early 20th cent.

naiant /ˈneɪənt/ ▸ **adjective** [postpositive] Heraldry (of a fish or marine creature) swimming horizontally.
– ORIGIN mid 16th cent.: from Anglo-Norman French, variant of Old French *noiant* 'swimming', present participle of *noier*, from Latin *natare* 'to swim'.

naïf /nʌɪˈiːf, nɑːˈiːf/ ▸ **adjective** naive or ingenuous.
▸ **noun** a naive or ingenuous person.
– ORIGIN French (see **NAIVE**).

nail ▸ **noun 1** a small metal spike with a broadened flat head, driven into wood to join things together or to serve as a hook.
2 a horny covering on the upper surface of the tip of the finger and toe in humans and other primates. ■ an animal's claw. ■ a hard growth on the upper mandible of some soft-billed birds.
3 a medieval measure of length for cloth, equal to $2^1/_4$ inches.
4 a medieval measure of wool, beef, or other commodity, roughly equal to 7 or 8 pounds.
▸ **verb** [with obj.] **1** [with adverbial of place] fasten with a nail or nails: *the strips are simply nailed to the roof*.
2 informal detect or catch (someone, especially a suspected criminal): *have you nailed the killer?* ■ expose (a lie or other deception).
3 informal (of a player) strike (a ball) forcefully and successfully: *she was stretched to the limit and failed to nail the smash*. ■ Baseball (of a fielder) put (a runner) out by throwing to a base. ■ chiefly N. Amer. (of a player) defeat or outwit (an opponent): *Navratilova tried to nail her on the backhand side*. ■ (of a player) secure (a victory) conclusively.
4 vulgar slang, chiefly US (of a man) have sexual intercourse with.
– PHRASES **fight tooth and nail** see **TOOTH**. **(as) hard as nails** (of a person) very tough or callous. **nail one's colours to the mast** see **MAST**[1]. **a nail in the coffin of** an action or event regarded as likely to have a detrimental or devastating effect on (a situation or person): *this was going to put the final nail in the coffin of his career*. **on the nail** (N. Amer. also **on the barrelhead**) informal (of payment) without delay.
– PHRASAL VERBS **nail someone down** elicit a firm commitment from someone: *I can't nail her down to a specific date*. **nail something down 1** identify something precisely: *something seems unexpected—I can't nail it down, but it makes me uneasy*. **2** secure an agreement: *the company has finally nailed down the agreement with its distributors*.
– DERIVATIVES **nailed** adjective [in combination] *dirty-nailed fingers*, **nailless** adjective.
– ORIGIN Old English *nægel* (noun), *næglan* (verb), of Germanic origin; related to Dutch *nagel* and German *Nagel*, from an Indo-European root shared by Latin *unguis* and Greek *onux*.

nail-biting ▸ **adjective** causing great anxiety or tension: *a nail-biting final game*.

nail brush ▸ **noun** a small brush designed for cleaning the fingernails and toenails.

nail enamel ▸ **noun** N. Amer. nail polish.

nailer ▸ **noun 1** chiefly historical a maker of nails.
2 a power tool for inserting nails.

nail file ▸ **noun** a strip of roughened metal or an emery board used for smoothing and shaping the fingernails and toenails.

nail head ▸ **noun** an ornament like the head of a nail, used chiefly in architecture and on clothing.

nail polish ▸ **noun** [mass noun] varnish applied to the fingernails or toenails to colour them or make them shiny.

nail punch (also **nail set**) ▸ **noun** a tool hit with a hammer to sink the head of a nail below a surface.

nail scissors ▸ **plural noun** small scissors for cutting the fingernails or toenails.

nail sickness ▸ **noun** [mass noun] the condition of a structure which is held together with corroded nails.

nailtail wallaby ▸ **noun** a brightly marked Australian wallaby with white stripes on the cheeks, hips, and behind the arms, and a small horny nail at the end of its long, slender tail. ● Genus *Onychogalea*, family Macropodidae: three species.

nail varnish ▸ **noun** [mass noun] Brit. nail polish.

nainsook /ˈneɪnsʊk/ ▸ **noun** [mass noun] a fine, soft cotton fabric, originally from South Asia.
– ORIGIN late 18th cent.: from Hindi *nainsukh*, from *nain* 'eye' + *sukh* 'pleasure'.

Naipaul /ˈnʌɪpɔːl/, V. S. (b.1932), Trinidadian writer, of Indian descent, resident in Britain since 1950; full name *Sir Vidiadhar Surajprasad Naipaul*. He is best known for his satirical novels, such as *A House for Mr Biswas* (1961); *In a Free State* (1971) won the Booker Prize. He was awarded the Nobel Prize for Literature in 2001.

naira /ˈnʌɪrə/ ▸ **noun** the basic monetary unit of Nigeria, equal to 100 kobo.
– ORIGIN contraction of **NIGERIA**.

Nairnshire /ˈnɛːnʃɪə, -ʃə/ a former county of NE Scotland, on the Moray Firth. It became a part of Highland region in 1975.

Nairobi /nʌɪˈrəʊbi/ the capital of Kenya; pop. 3,010,000 (est. 2007). It is situated on the central Kenyan plateau at an altitude of 1,680 m (5,500 ft).

naissant /ˈneɪs(ə)nt/ ▸ **adjective** Heraldry (of a charge, especially an animal) issuing from the middle of an ordinary, especially a fess.
– ORIGIN late 16th cent.: from French, literally 'being born', present participle of *naître*, from Latin *nasci* 'be born'.

naive /nʌɪˈiːv, nɑːˈiːv/ (also **naïve**) ▸ **adjective** (of a person or action) showing a lack of experience, wisdom, or judgement: *the rather naive young man had been totally misled*. ■ (of a person) natural and unaffected; innocent: *Andy had a sweet, naive look when he smiled*. ■ of or denoting art produced in a style which deliberately rejects sophisticated artistic techniques and has a bold directness resembling a child's work, typically in bright colours with little or no perspective.
– DERIVATIVES **naively** adverb, **naiveness** noun.
– ORIGIN mid 17th cent.: from French *naïve*, feminine of *naïf*, from Latin *nativus* 'native, natural'.

naivety /nʌɪˈiːvti, nɑːˈiːvti/ (also **naïvety**) ▸ **noun** (pl. **naiveties**) [mass noun] lack of experience, wisdom, or judgement: *his appalling naivety in going to the press*. ■ innocence or unsophistication: *the charm and naivety of the early to mid fifties*. ■ [count noun] a naive act.
– ORIGIN late 17th cent.: from French *naïveté*, from *naïf*, *-ive* (see **NAIVE**).

Najaf /ˈnadʒaf/ (also **an-Najaf**) a city in southern Iraq, on the Euphrates; pop. 500,000 (est. 2003). It contains the shrine of Ali, the prophet Muhammad's son-in-law, and is a holy city for the Shiite Muslims.

naked ▸ **adjective 1** (of a person or part of the body) without clothes: *he'd never seen a naked woman before* | *he was stripped naked*. ■ (of an object) without the usual covering or protection: *her room was lit by a single naked bulb*. ■ (of a tree, plant, or animal) without leaves, hairs, scales, etc.: *the naked branches of the trees*. ■ (**naked of**) devoid of. ■ exposed to harm; vulnerable: *John looked naked and defenceless without his spectacles*.
2 [attrib.] (especially of feelings or behaviour) expressed openly; undisguised: *naked fear made him tremble* | *the naked truth*.
– PHRASES **the naked eye** unassisted vision, without a telescope, microscope, or other device: *threadworm eggs are so small that they cannot be seen with the naked eye*.
– DERIVATIVES **nakedly** adverb.
– ORIGIN Old English *nacod*, of Germanic origin; related to Dutch *naakt* and German *nackt*, from an Indo-European root shared by Latin *nudus* and Sanskrit *nagna*.

naked ladies (also **naked boys**) ▸ **plural noun** the meadow saffron.

naked mole rat ▸ **noun** a blind and hairless mole rat living in large underground colonies in East Africa. The colony structure is similar to that of social insects, with only one pair breeding and most other individuals acting as workers. ● *Heterocephalus glaber*, family Bathyergidae.

nakedness ▸ **noun** [mass noun] the state or fact of being naked: *he made no attempt to conceal his nakedness*.

naker /ˈneɪkə/ ▸ **noun** historical a kettledrum.
– ORIGIN late Middle English: from Old French *nacaire*, from Arabic *naqqāra* 'drum'.

nakfa /ˈnakfə/ ▸ **noun** (pl. **same** or **nakfas**) the basic monetary unit of Eritrea, equal to one hundred cents.
– ORIGIN 1990s: from *Nak'fa*, the name of the town where the country's armed struggle against the Ethiopian regime was launched.

Nakhichevan /naxʲitʃiˈvan/ Russian name for **NAXÇIVAN**.

Nakuru /naˈkuːruː/ an industrial city in western Kenya; pop. 275,700 (est. 2009). Nearby is Lake Nakuru, famous for its spectacular flocks of flamingos.

nala ▸ **noun** another term for **NULLAH**.

Nalchik /ˈnaltʃɪk/ a city in the Caucasus, SW Russia, capital of the republic of Kabardino-Balkaria; pop. 269,600 (est. 2008).

nalidixic acid /ˌnalɪˈdɪksɪk/ ▸ **noun** [mass noun] Medicine a synthetic compound which inhibits the multiplication of bacteria, used chiefly to treat urinary

infections. ● A heterocyclic compound; chem. formula: $C_{12}H_{12}N_2O_3$.
– ORIGIN 1960s: *nalidixic* by rearrangement of elements from **NAPHTHALENE**, *carboxylic*, and **DI-**[1] (forming the systematic name).

naloxone /nəˈlɒksəʊn/ ▶ **noun** [mass noun] Medicine a synthetic drug, similar to morphine, which blocks opiate receptors in the nervous system.
– ORIGIN 1960s: contraction of *N-allylnoroxymorphone*.

naltrexone /nalˈtrɛksəʊn/ ▶ **noun** [mass noun] Medicine a synthetic drug, similar to morphine, which blocks opiate receptors in the nervous system and is used chiefly in the treatment of heroin addiction.
– ORIGIN 1970s: from a contraction of *N-al(lylnoroxymorph)one* (see **NALOXONE**), with the insertion of the arbitrary element *-trex-*.

Nam (also **'Nam**) informal name for **VIETNAM** in the context of the Vietnam War.

Nama /ˈnɑːmə/ ▶ **noun** (pl. **same** or **Namas**) **1** a member of one of the Khoikhoi peoples of South Africa and SW Namibia. Traditionally nomadic herders and hunter-gatherers, they were displaced from the region near the Cape by Dutch settlers.
2 [mass noun] the language of the Nama, which belongs to the Khoisan family and is the only language of the Khoikhoi peoples still spoken by a substantial number (over 100,000).
▶ **adjective** relating to the Nama or their language.
– ORIGIN the name in Nama.

namak /ˈnʌmək/ ▶ **noun** [mass noun] Indian salt.
– ORIGIN from Urdu.

Namangan /ˌnamənˈɡɑːn/ a city in eastern Uzbekistan, near the border with Kyrgyzstan; pop. 446,200 (est. 2007).

Namaqualand /nəˈmɑːkwəland/ a region of SW Africa, the homeland of the Nama people. **Little Namaqualand** lies immediately to the south of the Orange River and is in the South African province of Northern Cape, while **Great Namaqualand** lies to the north of the river, in Namibia.

Namaqualand daisy ▶ **noun** a widely cultivated annual African daisy. ● *Dimorphotheca sinuata*, family Compositae.

namaskar /ˌnʌmʌsˈkɑː/ ▶ **noun** a traditional Indian greeting or gesture of respect, made by bringing the palms together before the face or chest and bowing.
– ORIGIN via Hindi from Sanskrit *namaskāra*, from *namas* 'bowing' + *kāra* 'action'.

namaste /ˈnʌmasteɪ/ Indian ▶ **exclamation** a respectful greeting said when giving a namaskar.
▶ **noun** another term for **NAMASKAR**.
– ORIGIN via Hindi from Sanskrit *namas* 'bowing' + *te* 'to you'.

namaz /nəˈmɑːz/ ▶ **noun** [mass noun] the ritual prayers prescribed by Islam to be observed five times a day: *leave is given to perform namaz during office hours.*
– ORIGIN partly from Ottoman Turkish *namas* (Turkish *namaz*), partly from Urdu *namāz*, and partly from Persian *namāz*.

namby-pamby derogatory ▶ **adjective** lacking energy, strength, or courage; weak or ineffectual: *namby-pamby liberals.*
▶ **noun** (pl. **namby-pambies**) a weak or ineffectual person.
– ORIGIN mid 18th cent.: fanciful formation based on the given name of *Ambrose* Philips (died 1749), an English writer whose pastorals were ridiculed by Pope and others.

name ▶ **noun 1** a word or set of words by which a person or thing is known, addressed, or referred to: *my name is John Parsons* | *Köln is the German **name** for Cologne.*
2 a famous person: *the big race will lure the top names.* ■ [in sing.] a reputation, especially a good one: *the school has gained a name for excellence.*
3 (in the UK) an insurance underwriter belonging to a Lloyd's syndicate.
▶ **verb** [with obj.] **1** give a name to: *hundreds of diseases had not yet been isolated or named* | [with obj. and complement] *she decided to name the child Edward.* ■ identify correctly by name: *the dead man has been **named as** John Mackintosh.* ■ give a particular title or epithet to: *she was **named as** Student of the Year.* ■ mention by name: *the sea is as crystal clear as any spot in the Caribbean you might care to name.* ■ appoint (someone) to a particular position or task: *he was named to head a joint UN–OAS diplomatic effort.* ■ Brit. (of the Speaker) mention (a Member of Parliament) by name as disobedient to the chair and thereby subject to a ban from the House.
2 specify (a sum, time, or place) as something desired, suggested, or decided on: *the club have asked United to name their price for the striker.*
▶ **adjective** [attrib.] (of a person or product) having a well-known name: *specialized name brands geared to niche markets.*
– PHRASES **by name** using the name of someone or something: *ask for the street by name.* **by** (or **of**) **the name of** called: *a woman by the name of Smeeton.* **call someone names** insult someone verbally. **give someone/thing a bad name** damage the reputation of someone or something: *the gas guzzling machinery that gives the country such a bad name.* **give one's name to** invent, discover, or be the source of something which then becomes known by one's name: *the company's founder, Henry Ford, gave his name to Fordism.* **have someone's name on it** be destined or particularly suited for a particular person: *the bomb probably had my name on it.* **have to one's name** [often with negative] have in one's possession: *Jimmy hadn't a bean to his name.* **in all but name** existing in a particular state but not formally recognized as such: *these polytechnics had been universities in all but name for many years.* **in someone's name 1** formally registered as belonging to or reserved for someone: *the house was in her name.* **2** on behalf of someone: *he began to question what had been done in his name.* **in the name of** bearing or using the name of a specified person or organization. ■ for the sake of: *he withdrew his candidacy for the post in the name of party unity.* ■ by the authority of: *crimes committed in the name of religion.* ■ (**in the name of Christ/God/heaven** etc.) used for emphasis: *what in the name of God do you think you're doing?* **in name only** by description but not in reality: *a college in name only.* **make a name for oneself** become famous. **name the day** arrange a date for a specific occasion, especially a wedding. **one's name is mud** see **MUD**. **name names** mention specific names, especially of people accused of wrongdoing. **the name of the game** informal the main purpose or most important aspect of a situation. **no names, no pack drill** see **PACK DRILL**. **put down** (or **enter**) **one's** (or **someone's**) **name** apply to enter an educational institution, course, competition, etc.: *I put my name down for the course.* **put a name to** remember or decide what someone or something is called. **take someone's name in vain** see **VAIN**. **to name** (**but**) **a few** giving only these as examples, even though more could be cited: *the ingredients used are drawn from nature—avocado, lemon grass, and camomile to name a few.* **what's in a name?** used to say that names are arbitrary labels. **you name it** informal whatever you can think of (used to express the extent or variety of something): *easy-to-assemble kits of cars, lorries, ships ... you name it.*
– PHRASAL VERBS **name someone/thing after** (or N. Amer. also **for**) call someone or something by the same name as: *Nathaniel **was named after** his maternal grandfather.*
– DERIVATIVES **nameable** adjective.
– ORIGIN Old English *nama, noma* (noun), (*ge*)*namian* (verb), of Germanic origin; related to Dutch *naam* and German *Name*, from a root shared by Latin *nomen* and Greek *onoma*.

name-calling ▶ **noun** [mass noun] abusive language or insults.

namecheck ▶ **noun** a public mention or listing of the name of a person or thing, especially in acknowledgement or for publicity purposes.
▶ **verb** [with obj.] publicly mention or list the name of.

name-child ▶ **noun** archaic a person named after another.

name day ▶ **noun** the feast day of a saint after whom a person is named.

name-dropping ▶ **noun** [mass noun] the practice of casually mentioning the names of famous people one knows or claims to know in order to impress others.
– DERIVATIVES **name-drop** verb, **name-dropper** noun.

nameless ▶ **adjective 1** having no name or no known name. ■ deliberately not identified; anonymous: *the director of an organization which shall remain nameless.* ■ archaic (of a child) illegitimate.
2 (especially of an emotion) not easy to describe; indefinable: *a nameless yearning for transcendence.* ■ too horrific to be described: *the myths talk about nameless horrors infesting our universe.*
– DERIVATIVES **namelessly** adverb, **namelessness** noun.

namely ▶ **adverb** that is to say; to be specific (used to introduce detailed information or a specific example): *the menu makes good use of Scottish produce, namely game and seafood.*

Namen /ˈnɑːmə(n)/ Flemish name for **NAMUR**.

nameplate ▶ **noun 1** a plate or sign attached to something and bearing the name of the owner, occupier, maker, or the thing itself.
2 US the brand name or marque of a motor vehicle.

namesake ▶ **noun** a person or thing that has the same name as another.
– ORIGIN mid 17th cent.: from the phrase *for the name's sake*.

namespace ▶ **noun** Computing a class of elements (e.g. addresses, file locations, etc.) in which each element has a name unique to that class, although it may be shared with elements in other classes.

Namib Desert /ˈnɑːmɪb/ a desert of SW Africa. It extends for 1,900 km (1,200 miles) along the Atlantic coast, from the Curoca River in SW Angola through Namibia to the border between Namibia and South Africa.

Namibia /nəˈmɪbɪə/ a country in southern Africa, on the Atlantic Ocean; pop. 2,108,700 (est. 2009); languages, English (official), various Bantu languages, Khoisan languages, Afrikaans; capital, Windhoek.

> An arid country with large tracts of desert, Namibia was made the protectorate of German South West Africa in 1884. In 1920 it was mandated to South Africa by the League of Nations, becoming known as South West Africa. Despite international pressure South Africa continued to administer the country after the ending of the UN mandate in 1964, agreeing to withdraw only after several years of fighting by SWAPO guerrillas. Namibia became fully independent in 1990.

– DERIVATIVES **Namibian** adjective & noun.

namkin /nʌmˈkiːn/ ▶ **noun** [mass noun] Indian any savoury snack.
– ORIGIN from Hindi *namkīn*.

namma ▶ **noun** variant spelling of **GNAMMA**.

nam pla /nɑːm ˌplɑː, nam ˌplɑː/ ▶ **noun** [mass noun] (in Thai cuisine) a thin, pungent sauce made from fermented fish.
– ORIGIN Thai, from *nam* 'water' and *pla* 'fish'.

Namur /nəˈmʊə/ a province in central Belgium. It was the scene of the last German offensive in the Ardennes in 1945. Flemish name **NAMEN**. ■ the capital of Namur, at the junction of the Meuse and Sambre Rivers; pop. 107,939 (2008).

nan[1] /nan/ ▶ **noun** Brit. informal one's grandmother.
– ORIGIN 1940s: abbreviation of **NANNY**, or a child's pronunciation of **GRAN**.

nan[2] /nɑːn/ (also **naan**) ▶ **noun** (in Indian cookery) a type of leavened bread, typically of teardrop shape and traditionally cooked in a clay oven.
– ORIGIN from Urdu and Persian *nān*.

nana[1] /ˈnɑːnə/ ▶ **noun** Brit. informal a silly person; a fool (often as a general term of abuse): *I was made to look a right nana.*
– ORIGIN 1960s: perhaps a shortening of **BANANA**.

nana[2] /ˈnanə/ (Brit. also **nanna**) ▶ **noun** informal one's grandmother.
– ORIGIN mid 19th cent.: child's pronunciation of **NANNY** or **GRAN**.

Nanaimo /nəˈnʌɪməʊ/ a port on the east coast of Vancouver Island in British Columbia, Canada; pop. 78,692 (2006).

Nanak /ˈnɑːnʌk/ (1469–1539), Indian religious leader and founder of Sikhism; known as **Guru Nanak**. Not seeking to create a new religion, he preached that spiritual liberation could be achieved through meditating on the name of God. His teachings are contained in a number of hymns which form part of the Guru Granth Sahib.

nance ▶ **noun** another term for **NANCY**.

Nanchang /nanˈtʃaŋ/ a city in SE China, capital of Jiangxi province; pop. 1,613,200 (est. 2006).

Nancy /ˈnɒ̃si/ a city in NE France, chief town of Lorraine; pop. 107,434 (2006).

nancy informal, derogatory ▶ **noun** (pl. **nancies**) (also **nancy boy**) an effeminate or homosexual man.
▶ **adjective** effeminate.
– ORIGIN late 19th cent.: pet form of the given name *Ann*.

nancy story ▶ **noun** W. Indian a traditional African folk tale about Anancy the spider, who overcomes others by cunning. ■ an elaborate evasive story or lie: *the minister had left the country and so could not give his side of the nancy story.* ■ a superstitious belief.

N

– ORIGIN *nancy*, shortening of *Anancy*, from Akan *ananse* 'spider'.

NAND ▸ noun Electronics a Boolean operator which gives the value zero if and only if all the operands have a value of one, and otherwise has a value of one (equivalent to NOT AND). ■ (also **NAND gate**) a circuit which produces an output signal unless there are signals on all of its inputs.
– ORIGIN 1950s: from *n(ot) and*.

Nandi /ˈnʌndi/ Hinduism a bull which serves as the mount of Shiva and symbolizes fertility.
– ORIGIN Sanskrit.

nandina /nanˈdʌɪnə, -ˈdiːnə/ ▸ noun an evergreen East Asian shrub that resembles bamboo, cultivated for its foliage, which turns red or bronze in autumn. Also called CELESTIAL BAMBOO, SACRED BAMBOO. ● *Nandina domestica*, family Berberidaceae.
– ORIGIN mid 19th cent.: modern Latin (genus name), adapted from Japanese *nanten*.

nandrolone /ˈnandrələʊn/ ▸ noun [mass noun] an anabolic steroid with tissue-building properties, used unlawfully to enhance performance in sport.
– ORIGIN 1950s: shortened form of its chemical name *norandrostenolone*.

Nanga Parbat /ˌnʌŋgə ˈpɑːbʌt/ a mountain in northern Pakistan, in the western Himalayas. It rises to 8,126 m (26,660 ft).

Nanjing /nanˈdʒɪŋ/ (also **Nanking** /-ˈkɪŋ/) a city in eastern China, on the Yangtze River, capital of Jiangsu province; pop. 4,105,400 (est. 2006). It was the capital of various ruling dynasties and of China from 1368 until replaced by Beijing in 1421.

nankeen /naŋˈkiːn, nan-/ ▸ noun [mass noun] a yellowish cotton cloth. ■ (**nankeens**) historical trousers made of nankeen. ■ archaic the yellowish-buff colour of nankeen.
– ORIGIN mid 18th cent.: from the name of the city of *Nanking* (see NANJING), where it was first made.

nanna ▸ noun variant spelling of NANA².

Nanning /nanˈnɪŋ/ the capital of Guangxi Zhuang autonomous region in southern China; pop. 1,277,300 (est. 2006).

nannofossil (also **nanofossil**) ▸ noun the fossil of a minute planktonic organism, especially a calcareous unicellular alga.
– ORIGIN 1960s: from *nannoplankton* (variant of NANOPLANKTON) + FOSSIL.

N

nanny ▸ noun (pl. **nannies**) **1** a person, typically a woman, employed to look after a child in its own home. ■ a person or institution regarded as interfering and overprotective.
2 Brit. informal one's grandmother.
3 (in full **nanny goat**) a female goat.
▸ verb (**nannies, nannying, nannied**) (usu. as noun **nannying**) **1** [no obj.] work as a nanny.
2 [with obj.] be overprotective towards: *his well-intentioned nannying*.
– DERIVATIVES **nannyish** adjective.
– ORIGIN early 18th cent.: pet form of the given name *Ann*. The verb dates from the 1950s.

nannygai /ˈnanɪgʌɪ/ ▸ noun (pl. **nannygais**) the redfish of Australia. ● *Centroberyx affinis*, family Berycidae.
– ORIGIN late 19th cent.: from a New South Wales Aboriginal language.

nanny state ▸ noun chiefly Brit. the government regarded as overprotective or as interfering unduly with personal choice.

nano /ˈnanəʊ/ ▸ noun informal short for NANOTECHNOLOGY.

nano- /ˈnanəʊ/ ▸ combining form denoting a factor of 10^{-9} (used in units of measurement): *nanosecond*. ■ submicroscopic: *nanotube*.
– ORIGIN via Latin from Greek *nanos* 'dwarf'.

nanobacterium ▸ noun (pl. **nanobacteria**) a kind of microorganism about a tenth the size of the smallest normal bacteria, claimed to have been discovered in living tissue and in rock.

nanobe /ˈnanəʊb/ ▸ noun another term for NANOBACTERIUM.

nanobot ▸ noun a hypothetical very small (nanoscale) self-propelled machine, especially one that has some degree of autonomy and can reproduce.

nanocomposite ▸ adjective denoting a composite material that has a grain size measured in nanometres.
▸ noun a nanocomposite material.

nanogram (abbrev.: **ng**) ▸ noun one thousand-millionth of a gram.

nanomaterial ▸ noun a material having particles or constituents of nanoscale dimensions, or one that is produced by nanotechnology.

nanometre /ˈnanə(ʊ),miːtə/ (US **nanometer**) (abbrev.: **nm**) ▸ noun one thousand-millionth of a metre.

nanomole ▸ noun Chemistry one thousand-millionth of a mole.

nanoparticle ▸ noun a nanoscale particle.

nanoplankton ▸ noun [mass noun] Biology very small unicellular plankton, at the limits of resolution of light microscopy.
– ORIGIN early 20th cent.: from German, from Greek *nanos* 'dwarf' + PLANKTON.

nanorobot ▸ noun another term for NANOBOT.

nanoscale ▸ adjective on a scale of 10^{-9} metre; having or involving dimensions of less than 100 nanometres.

nanoscopic ▸ adjective another term for NANOSCALE. ■ extremely small: *his comment contains a nanoscopic grain of truth*.

nanosecond (abbrev.: **ns**) ▸ noun one thousand-millionth of a second. ■ informal a very short time; a moment: *she can flick between manic laughter and tears in a nanosecond*.

nanostructure ▸ noun a structure, especially a semiconductor device, that has dimensions of only a few nanometres.

nanotech ▸ noun short for NANOTECHNOLOGY.

nanotechnology ▸ noun [mass noun] the branch of technology that deals with dimensions and tolerances of less than 100 nanometres, especially the manipulation of individual atoms and molecules.
– DERIVATIVES **nanotechnological** adjective, **nanotechnologist** noun.

nanotube ▸ noun Chemistry a cylindrical molecule of a fullerene.

nanowire ▸ noun a wire with a thickness or diameter of only a few nanometres.

Nansen /ˈnans(ə)n/, Fridtjof (1861–1930), Norwegian Arctic explorer. In 1888 he led the first expedition to cross the Greenland ice fields, and five years later he sailed from Siberia for the North Pole, which he failed to reach, on board the *Fram*.

Nantes /nɒ̃t/ a city in western France, on the Loire, chief town of Pays de la Loire region; pop. 290,871 (2006).

Nantes, Edict of an edict of 1598 signed by Henry IV of France granting toleration to Protestants and ending the French Wars of Religion. It was revoked by Louis XIV in 1685.

Nantucket /nanˈtʌkɪt/ an island off the coast of Massachusetts, south of Cape Cod and east of Martha's Vineyard. It was an important whaling centre in the 18th and 19th centuries.

naos /ˈneɪɒs/ ▸ noun (pl. **naoi** /ˈneɪɔɪ/) the inner chamber or sanctuary of a Greek or other ancient temple. ■ the main body or nave of a Byzantine church.
– ORIGIN Greek, literally 'temple'.

nap¹ ▸ verb (**naps, napping, napped**) [no obj.] sleep lightly or briefly, especially during the day.
▸ noun a short sleep, especially during the day: *excuse me, I'll just take a little nap*.
– PHRASES **catch someone napping** Brit. informal find someone off guard and unprepared to respond: *the goalkeeper was caught napping by a shot from Carpenter*.
– ORIGIN Old English *hnappian*, probably of Germanic origin.

nap² ▸ noun **1** [in sing.] the raised hairs or threads on the surface of fabric or suede leather, in terms of the direction in which they naturally lie.
2 Austral. informal, dated a bedroll used for sleeping on in the open.
– DERIVATIVES **napless** adjective.
– ORIGIN late Middle English *noppe*, from Middle Dutch, Middle Low German *noppe* 'nap', *noppen* 'trim the nap from'. Sense 2 is probably from KNAPSACK.

nap³ ▸ noun **1** [mass noun] a card game resembling whist in which players declare the number of tricks they expect to take, up to five.
2 Brit. a tipster's prediction of the probable winner of a race.
▸ verb (**naps, napping, napped**) [with obj.] Brit. name (a horse or greyhound) as a probable winner of a race.
– PHRASES **go nap** attempt to take all five tricks in nap. ■ score or win five times: *Tranmere Rovers went nap to inflict a heavy 5–1 defeat on West Ham*. ■ risk everything in one attempt.
– ORIGIN early 19th cent.: abbreviation of NAPOLEON, the original name of the card game.

nap⁴ ▸ verb (**naps, napping, napped**) [no obj.] (of a horse) refuse, especially habitually, to go on at the rider's instruction; jib.
– ORIGIN 1950s: back-formation from *nappy*, an adjective first used to describe heady beer (late Middle English), later used in the sense 'intoxicated by drink' (early 18th cent.), and since the 1920s used to describe a disobedient horse.

napa ▸ noun variant spelling of NAPPA.

napa cabbage /ˈnapə/ ▸ noun chiefly N. Amer. a variety of Chinese leaf.
– ORIGIN *napa* fromJapanese *nappa* '(leaves of) brassica'.

napalm /ˈneɪpɑːm/ ▸ noun [mass noun] a highly flammable sticky jelly used in incendiary bombs and flame-throwers, consisting of petrol thickened with special soaps.
▸ verb [with obj.] attack with bombs containing napalm.
– ORIGIN 1940s: from *na(phthenic)* and *palm(itic acid)*.

nape ▸ noun (also **nape of the/one's neck**) the back of a person's neck.
– ORIGIN Middle English: of unknown origin.

napery /ˈneɪp(ə)ri/ ▸ noun [mass noun] household linen, especially tablecloths and napkins.
– ORIGIN Middle English: from Old French *naperie*, from *nape* 'tablecloth'.

nap hand ▸ noun informal a series of five winning points, victories, etc. in a game or sport.

Naphtali /ˈnaftəlʌɪ/ (in the Bible) a Hebrew patriarch, son of Jacob and Bilhah (Gen. 30:7–8). ■ the tribe of Israel traditionally descended from Naphtali.

naphtha /ˈnafθə/ ▸ noun [mass noun] Chemistry a flammable oil containing various hydrocarbons, obtained by the dry distillation of organic substances such as coal, shale, or petroleum.
– ORIGIN late Middle English *napte*, from Latin *naphtha* from Greek, of oriental origin; the Latin spelling was introduced in the late 16th cent.

naphthalene /ˈnafθəliːn/ ▸ noun [mass noun] Chemistry a volatile white crystalline compound produced by the distillation of coal tar, used in mothballs and as a raw material for chemical manufacture. ● A bicyclic aromatic hydrocarbon; chem. formula: $C_{10}H_8$.
– DERIVATIVES **naphthalic** adjective.
– ORIGIN early 19th cent.: from NAPHTHA + -ENE, with the insertion of *-l-* for ease of pronunciation.

naphthene /ˈnafθiːn/ ▸ noun Chemistry any of a group of cyclic aliphatic hydrocarbons (e.g. cyclohexane) obtained from petroleum.
– DERIVATIVES **naphthenic** adjective.

naphthol /ˈnafθɒl/ ▸ noun [mass noun] Chemistry a crystalline solid derived from naphthalene, used to make antiseptics and dyes. ● Chem. formula: $C_{10}H_7OH$; two isomers, especially naphthalen-2-ol (**β-naphthol**).

Napier¹ /ˈneɪpɪə/ a seaport on Hawke Bay, in the North Island, New Zealand; pop. 55,359 (2006). Originally a whaling port, the town was named after the British general and colonial administrator Sir Charles Napier (1809–54).

Napier² /ˈneɪpɪə/, John (1550–1617), Scottish mathematician. He was the inventor of logarithms.

Napierian logarithm /neɪˈpɪərɪən/ ▸ noun another term for NATURAL LOGARITHM.
– ORIGIN early 19th cent.: named after J. *Napier* (see NAPIER²).

Napier's bones ▸ plural noun Mathematics slips of ivory or other material divided into sections marked with digits, devised by John Napier and formerly used to facilitate multiplication and division.

napkin ▸ noun **1** (also **table napkin**) a square piece of cloth or paper used at a meal to wipe the fingers or lips and to protect garments.
2 Brit. dated a baby's nappy.
3 (also **sanitary napkin**) N. Amer. another term for SANITARY TOWEL.
– ORIGIN late Middle English: from Old French *nappe* 'tablecloth' (from Latin *mappa*: see MAP) + -KIN.

napkin ring ▸ noun a ring used to hold a person's table napkin when it is not in use.

Naples /ˈneɪp(ə)lz/ a city and port on the west coast of Italy, capital of Campania region; pop. 963,661 (2008). It was formerly the capital of the kingdom of Naples and Sicily (1816–60). Italian name **NAPOLI**.
– ORIGIN from Latin *Neapolis*, from Greek *neos* 'new' + *polis* 'city'.

Naples yellow ▶ **noun** [mass noun] a pale yellow pigment containing lead and antimony oxides. ■ the colour of the pigment Naples yellow.
– ORIGIN mid 18th cent.: named after **Naples**.

Napoleon /nəˈpəʊlɪən/ the name of three rulers of France: ■ **Napoleon I** (1769–1821), emperor 1804–14 and 1815; full name *Napoleon Bonaparte*; known as **Napoleon**. In 1799 Napoleon joined a conspiracy which overthrew the Directory, becoming the supreme ruler of France. He declared himself emperor in 1804, and established an empire stretching from Spain to Poland. After defeats at Trafalgar (1805) and in Russia (1812), he abdicated and was exiled to the island of Elba (1814). He returned to power in 1815, but was defeated at Waterloo and exiled to the island of St Helena. ■ **Napoleon II** (1811–1832), son of Napoleon I and Empress Marie-Louise; full name *Napoleon François Charles Joseph Bonaparte*. In 1814 Napoleon I abdicated on behalf of himself and Napoleon II, who had no active political role. ■ **Napoleon III** (1808–73), emperor 1852–70; full name *Charles Louis Napoleon Bonaparte*; known as **Louis-Napoleon**. A nephew of Napoleon I, Napoleon III was elected President of the Second Republic in 1848 and staged a coup in 1851. He abdicated in 1870 after defeat in the Franco-Prussian War.

napoleon ▶ **noun 1** historical a gold twenty-franc French coin minted in the reign of Napoleon I.
2 (also **napoleon boot**) historical a boot worn by men in the 19th century, reaching above the knee in front and with a piece cut out behind.
3 N. Amer. a flaky rectangular pastry with a sweet filling.

Napoleonic /nəpəʊlɪˈɒnɪk/ ▶ **adjective** relating to or characteristic of Napoleon I or his time.

Napoleonic Wars a series of campaigns (1800–15) of French armies under Napoleon against Austria, Russia, Great Britain, Portugal, Prussia, and other European powers. They ended with Napoleon's defeat at the Battle of Waterloo.

Napoli /ˈnapəli/ Italian name for **Naples**.

nappa /ˈnapə/ (also **napa**) ▶ **noun** [mass noun] a soft leather made by a special process from the skin of sheep or goats.
– ORIGIN late 19th cent.: from *Napa*, the name of a valley in California.

nappe /nap/ ▶ **noun** Geology a sheet of rock that has moved sideways over neighbouring strata as a result of an overthrust or folding.
– ORIGIN late 19th cent.: from French *nappe* 'tablecloth'.

napped[1] ▶ **adjective** [usu. in combination] (of a textile) having a nap, usually of a specified kind: *a long-napped paint roller*.

napped[2] ▶ **adjective** (of food) served in a sauce or other liquid: *mushrooms **napped with** melted butter*.
– ORIGIN 1970s: from French *napper* 'coat with (a sauce)', from *nappe* 'cloth', figuratively 'pool of liquid', + **-ed**[2].

napper ▶ **noun** Brit. informal a person's head: *a couple of shaven nappers*.
– ORIGIN late 18th cent.: from thieves' slang, of unknown origin.

nappy[1] ▶ **noun** (pl. **nappies**) Brit. a piece of towelling or other absorbent material wrapped round a baby's bottom and between its legs to absorb and retain urine and faeces.
– ORIGIN early 20th cent.: abbreviation of **napkin**.

nappy[2] ▶ **adjective** (**nappier**, **nappiest**) US informal (of a black person's hair) frizzy.
– ORIGIN late 15th cent. (in the sense 'shaggy'): from Middle Dutch *noppigh*, Middle Low German *noppich*, from *noppe* (see **nap**[2]). The current sense dates from the early 20th cent.

nappy rash ▶ **noun** [mass noun] Brit. inflammation of a baby's skin caused by prolonged contact with a damp nappy.

naproxen /naˈprɒksɛn/ ▶ **noun** [mass noun] Medicine a synthetic compound used as an anti-inflammatory drug, especially in the treatment of headache and arthritis. ● Chem. formula: $C_{14}H_{14}O_3$.
– ORIGIN 1970s: from *na(phthyl)* + *pr(opionic)* + *ox(y-)*, + *-en* on the pattern of words such as *tamoxifen*.

Nara /ˈnɑːrə/ a city in central Japan, on the island of Honshu; pop. 367,902 (2007). It was the first capital of Japan (710–84) and an important centre of Japanese Buddhism.

Narayan /nəˈrɑːjən, nʌˈrʌɪʌn/, R. K. (1906–2001), Indian novelist and short-story writer; full name *Rasipuram Krishnaswamy Narayan*. His best-known novels are set in an imaginary small Indian town, and portray its inhabitants in an affectionate yet ironic manner; they include *Swami and Friends* (1935) and *The Man-Eater of Malgudi* (1961).

Narayanganj /nəˈrɑːjənˌgʌndʒ/ a river port in Bangladesh, on the Ganges delta south-east of Dhaka; pop. 286,899 (2006).

Narbonne /nɑːˈbɒn/, French /naʀbɔn/ a city in southern France, in Languedoc-Roussillon, just inland from the Mediterranean; pop. 51,996 (2006). Founded by the Romans, it was capital of the province of Gallic Narbonensis. It was a prosperous port until its harbour silted up in the 14th century.

narc (also **nark**) ▶ **noun** informal, chiefly N. Amer. an official narcotics agent.
– ORIGIN 1960s: abbreviation of **narcotic**.

narcissism /ˈnɑːsɪsɪz(ə)m, nɑːˈsɪs-/ ▶ **noun** [mass noun] excessive interest in or admiration of oneself and one's physical appearance. ■ Psychology extreme selfishness, with a grandiose view of one's own talents and a craving for admiration, as characterizing a personality type. ■ Psychoanalysis self-centredness arising from failure to distinguish the self from external objects, either in very young babies or as a feature of mental disorder.
– DERIVATIVES **narcissist** noun.
– ORIGIN early 19th cent.: via Latin from the Greek name *Narkissos* (see **Narcissus**) + **-ism**.

narcissistic ▶ **adjective** having or showing an excessive interest in or admiration of oneself and one's physical appearance: *a narcissistic actress*. ■ relating to narcissism: *narcissistic personality disorder*.
– DERIVATIVES **narcissistically** adverb.

Narcissus /nɑːˈsɪsəs/ Greek Mythology a beautiful youth who rejected the nymph Echo and fell in love with his own reflection in a pool. He pined away and was changed into the flower that bears his name.

narcissus /nɑːˈsɪsəs/ ▶ **noun** (pl. **narcissi** /-sʌɪ/ or **narcissuses**) a bulbous Eurasian plant of a genus that includes the daffodil, especially (in gardening) one with flowers that have white or pale outer petals and a shallow orange or yellow cup in the centre. ● Genus *Narcissus*, family Liliaceae (or Amaryllidaceae): many species and varieties, in particular *N. poeticus*.
– ORIGIN via Latin from Greek *narkissos*, perhaps from *narkē* 'numbness', with reference to its narcotic effects.

narcissus fly ▶ **noun** another term for **bulb fly**.

narco ▶ **noun** (pl. **narcos**) US informal short for **narcotic**. ■ a drug trafficker or dealer.

narco- ▶ **combining form** relating to a state of insensibility: *narcolepsy*. ■ relating to narcotic drugs or their use: *narcoterrorism*.
– ORIGIN from Greek *narkē* 'numbness'.

narcolepsy /ˈnɑːkə(ʊ)lɛpsi/ ▶ **noun** [mass noun] Medicine a condition characterized by an extreme tendency to fall asleep whenever in relaxing surroundings.
– DERIVATIVES **narcoleptic** adjective & noun.
– ORIGIN late 19th cent.: from Greek *narkē* 'numbness', on the pattern of *epilepsy*.

narcosis /nɑːˈkəʊsɪs/ ▶ **noun** [mass noun] Medicine a state of stupor, drowsiness, or unconsciousness produced by drugs. See also **nitrogen narcosis**.
– ORIGIN late 17th cent.: from Greek *narkōsis*, from *narkoun* 'make numb'.

narcoterrorism ▶ **noun** [mass noun] terrorism associated with the trade in illicit drugs.
– DERIVATIVES **narcoterrorist** noun.

narcotic ▶ **noun** an addictive drug affecting mood or behaviour, especially an illegal one. ■ Medicine a drug which induces drowsiness, stupor, or insensibility, and relieves pain.
▶ **adjective** relating to or denoting narcotics or their effects or use: *the substance has a mild narcotic effect*.
– DERIVATIVES **narcotically** adverb, **narcotism** noun.
– ORIGIN late Middle English: from Old French *narcotique*, via medieval Latin from Greek *narkōtikos*, from *narkoun* 'make numb'.

narcotize (also **narcotise**) ▶ **verb** [with obj.] affect with or as if with a narcotic drug.
– DERIVATIVES **narcotization** noun.

nard ▶ **noun** the Himalayan spikenard (plant).
– ORIGIN late Old English, via Latin from Greek *nardos*; related to Sanskrit *nalada*, *narada*.

nardoo /nɑːˈduː, ˈnɑːduː/ ▶ **noun** an Australian fern with long stalks bearing either silvery-green clover-like lobes or woody globular cases containing spores, growing typically in water in areas of intermittent flooding. ● *Marsilea drummondii*, family Marsiliaceae. ■ [mass noun] a food made from the spores of the nardoo, traditionally eaten by Aborigines: [as modifier] *nardoo flour*.
– ORIGIN mid 19th cent.: from an Aboriginal language.

nares /ˈnɛːriːz/ ▶ **plural noun** (sing. **naris**) Anatomy & Zoology the nostrils.
– DERIVATIVES **narial** adjective.
– ORIGIN late 17th cent.: plural of Latin *naris* 'nostril, nose'.

narghile /ˈnɑːgɪleɪ, -li/ ▶ **noun** an oriental tobacco pipe with a long tube that draws the smoke through water; a hookah.
– ORIGIN mid 18th cent.: from Persian *nārgīl* 'coconut, hookah', from Sanskrit *nārikela* 'coconut'.

nariyal /ˈnɑːrɪəl/ ▶ **noun** Indian term for **coconut**.
– ORIGIN from Hindi *nāriyal*.

nark[1] informal ▶ **noun 1** Brit. a police informer: *I'm not a copper's nark*.
2 Austral./NZ an annoying person or thing.
▶ **verb** [with obj.] Brit. cause annoyance to: *women like her nark me*.
– PHRASES **nark it!** stop that!
– ORIGIN mid 19th cent.: from Romany *nāk* 'nose'.

nark[2] ▶ **noun** another term for **narc**.

narked ▶ **adjective** Brit. informal annoyed: *I was narked at being pushed around*.

narky ▶ **adjective** (**narkier**, **narkiest**) Brit. informal bad-tempered or irritable.

Narmada /ˈnəːmədə/ a river which rises in Madhya Pradesh, central India, and flows generally westwards for 1,245 km (778 miles) to the Gulf of Cambay. It is regarded by Hindus as sacred.

Narragansett /ˌnarəˈgansət/ (also **Narraganset**) ▶ **noun** (pl. **same** or **Narragansetts**) **1** a member of an American Indian people originally of Rhode Island, few of whom now remain.
2 [mass noun] the extinct Algonquian language of the Narragansett.
– ORIGIN the name in Narragansett, literally 'people of the promontory'.

narrate ▶ **verb** [with obj.] give a spoken or written account of: *the story is narrated by the heroine*. ■ deliver a commentary to accompany (a film, broadcast, piece of music, etc.).
– DERIVATIVES **narratable** adjective.
– ORIGIN mid 17th cent.: from Latin *narrat-* 'related, told', from the verb *narrare* (from *gnarus* 'knowing').

narration ▶ **noun** [mass noun] the action or process of narrating a story: *the style of narration in the novel*. ■ [count noun] a commentary delivered to accompany a film, broadcast, etc.: *Moore's narration is often sarcastic*.

narrative ▶ **noun** a spoken or written account of connected events; a story: *a gripping narrative*. ■ [mass noun] the narrated part of a literary work, as distinct from dialogue. ■ [mass noun] the practice or art of telling stories: *traditions of oral narrative*.
▶ **adjective** in the form of or concerned with narration: *a narrative poem* | *narrative technique*.
– DERIVATIVES **narratively** adverb.
– ORIGIN late Middle English (as an adjective): from French *narratif*, *-ive*, from late Latin *narrativus* 'telling a story', from the verb *narrare* (see **narrate**).

narrativity ▶ **noun** [mass noun] the quality or condition of presenting a narrative: *music has developed a narrativity which lends it the character of language*.
– ORIGIN 1970s: from French *narrativité*.

narrativize (also **narrativise**) ▶ **verb** [with obj.] present or interpret (experience, events, etc.) in the form of a narrative.

narratology ▶ **noun** [mass noun] the branch of knowledge or criticism that deals with the structure and function of narrative and its themes, conventions, and symbols.
– DERIVATIVES **narratological** adjective, **narratologist** noun.

narrator ▶ **noun** a person who narrates something, especially a character who recounts the events of a novel or narrative poem. ■ a person who delivers a commentary accompanying a film, broadcast, piece of music, etc.
– DERIVATIVES **narratorial** adjective.

narrow ▶ **adjective** (**narrower**, **narrowest**) **1** of small width in relation to length: *he made his way down the narrow road*.
2 limited in extent, amount, or scope: *they ate a narrow range of foods*. ■ (of a person's attitude or

N

beliefs) limited in range and unwilling or unable to appreciate alternative views: *companies fail through their narrow view of what contributes to profit.* ■ precise or strict in meaning: *the idea of nationalism in the narrowest sense of the word.* ■ (of a phonetic transcription) showing fine details of accent.
3 (especially of a victory, defeat, or escape) with only a small margin; barely achieved: *the home team just hung on for a narrow victory.*
4 Phonetics denoting a vowel pronounced with the root of the tongue drawn back so as to narrow the pharynx.
▶ **verb 1** become or make less wide: [no obj.] *the road narrowed and crossed an old bridge* | [with obj.] *the Victoria Embankment was built to narrow the river.* ■ almost close (one's eyes) so as to focus on something, or to indicate anger or other emotion: [with obj.] *she narrowed her eyes at him suspiciously* | [no obj.] *her eyes narrowed as she looked at him.*
2 become or make more limited in extent or scope: [no obj.] *the gap between the sexes is narrowing* | *the trade surplus* ***narrowed to*** *£70 m in January* | [with obj.] *the committee narrowed the selection to three designers.*
▶ **noun** (**narrows**) a narrow channel connecting two larger areas of water: *there was a car ferry across the narrows of Loch Long.*
– PHRASAL VERBS **narrow something down** reduce the number of possibilities or options: *the company has narrowed down the candidates for the job to two.*
– DERIVATIVES **narrowish** adjective, **narrowness** noun.
– ORIGIN Old English *nearu*, of Germanic origin; related to Dutch *naar* 'dismal, unpleasant' and German *Narbe* 'scar'. Early senses in English included 'constricted' and 'mean'.

narrowband ▶ **adjective** of or involving signals over a narrow range of frequencies.

narrowboat ▶ **noun** Brit. a canal boat less than 7 ft (2.1 metres) wide with a maximum length of 70 ft (21.3 metres) and steered with a tiller rather than a wheel.

narrowcast ▶ **verb** (past and past participle **narrowcast** or **narrowcasted**) [no obj.] transmit a television programme, especially by cable, or otherwise disseminate information, to a comparatively localized or specialist audience: (as noun **narrowcasting**) *we have moved from broadcasting to narrowcasting.*
▶ **noun** [mass noun] transmission by narrowcasting: [as modifier] *dozens of narrowcast niche channels.*
– DERIVATIVES **narrowcaster** noun.
– ORIGIN 1930s: back-formation from *narrowcasting*, on the pattern of *broadcasting*.

N

narrow circumstances ▶ **plural noun** poverty.

narrow gauge ▶ **noun** a railway gauge which is narrower than the standard gauge of 4 ft 8½ inches (1.435 m).

narrowly ▶ **adverb 1** only just; by only a small margin: *the party was narrowly defeated in the elections.*
2 closely or carefully: *he was looking at her narrowly.*
3 in a limited or restricted way: *narrowly defined tasks.*

narrow-minded ▶ **adjective** not willing to listen to or tolerate other people's views; prejudiced.
– DERIVATIVES **narrow-mindedly** adverb, **narrow-mindedness** noun.

narrow money ▶ **noun** [mass noun] Economics money in forms that can be used as a medium of exchange, generally notes, coins, and certain balances held by banks.

narrow seas ▶ **plural noun** archaic the English Channel and the Irish Sea.

narrow squeak ▶ **noun** [in sing.] Brit. informal an escape or victory that is narrowly achieved: *Hunt's championship was a narrow squeak, achieved in a car that was far from perfect.*

narthex /ˈnɑːθɛks/ ▶ **noun** an antechamber, porch, or distinct area at the western entrance of some early Christian churches, separated off by a railing. ■ an antechamber or large porch in a modern church.
– ORIGIN late 17th cent.: via Latin from Greek *narthēx*.

Narvik /ˈnɑːvɪk/ an ice-free port on the NW coast of Norway, north of the Arctic Circle; pop. 13,944 (2007).

narwhal /ˈnɑːw(ə)l/ ▶ **noun** a small Arctic whale, the male of which has a long forward-pointing spirally twisted tusk developed from one of its teeth. ● *Monodon monoceros*, family Monodontidae.
– ORIGIN mid 17th cent.: from Dutch *narwal*, Danish *narhval*, based on Old Norse *nár* 'corpse', with reference to skin colour.

nary /ˈnɛːri/ ▶ **adjective** informal or dialect form of NOT: *there was nary a murmur or complaint.*
– ORIGIN mid 18th cent.: from the phrase *ne'er a.*

NASA /ˈnasə/ ▶ **abbreviation** (in the US) National Aeronautics and Space Administration.

nasal /ˈneɪz(ə)l/ ▶ **adjective 1** relating to the nose: *the nasal passages* | *a nasal spray.*
2 Phonetics (of a speech sound) pronounced by the breath resonating in the nose, e.g. *m, n, ng*, or French *en, un*. Compare with **ORAL** (sense 2 of the adjective). ■ (of the voice or speech) produced or characterized by resonation in the nose as well as the mouth: *a drawling nasal voice.*
▶ **noun 1** a nasal speech sound.
2 historical a nosepiece on a helmet.
– DERIVATIVES **nasality** noun, **nasally** adverb.
– ORIGIN Middle English (in sense 2 of the noun): from medieval Latin *nasalis*, from Latin *nasus* 'nose'.

nasal concha ▶ **noun** see **CONCHA**.

nasalize (also **nasalise**) ▶ **verb** [with obj.] pronounce or utter (a speech sound) with the breath resonating in the nose: (as adj. **nasalized**) *a nasalized vowel.*
– DERIVATIVES **nasalization** noun.

NASCAR /ˈnaskɑː/ ▶ **abbreviation** (in the US) National Association for Stock Car Auto Racing.

nascent /ˈnas(ə)nt, ˈneɪ-/ ▶ **adjective** (especially of a process or organization) just coming into existence and beginning to display signs of future potential: *the nascent space industry.* ■ Chemistry (chiefly of hydrogen) freshly generated in a reactive form.
– DERIVATIVES **nascency** /ˈnas(ə)nsi, ˈneɪ-/ noun.
– ORIGIN early 17th cent.: from Latin *nascent-* 'being born', from the verb *nasci*.

NASDAQ /ˈnazdak/ ▶ **abbreviation** (in the US) National Association of Securities Dealers Automated Quotations, a computerized system for trading in securities.

naseberry /ˈneɪzb(ə)ri, -bɛri/ ▶ **noun** another term for **SAPODILLA** or **SAPODILLA PLUM**.
– ORIGIN late 17th cent.: from Spanish and Portuguese *néspera* 'medlar' + **BERRY**.

Naseby, Battle of /ˈneɪzbi/ a major battle of the English Civil War, which took place in 1645 near the village of Naseby in Northamptonshire. The Royalist army of Prince Rupert and King Charles I was decisively defeated by the New Model Army under General Fairfax and Oliver Cromwell.

Nash[1], (Frederic) Ogden (1902–71), American poet. His sophisticated light verse comprises puns, epigrams, and other verbal eccentricities.

Nash[2], John (1752–1835), English town planner and architect. He planned the layout of Regent's Park (1811–25), Trafalgar Square (1826–*c.*1835), and many other parts of London, and designed the Marble Arch.

Nash[3], Paul (1889–1946), English painter and designer. He was a war artist in both World Wars. Notable works: *Totes Meer* (1940–1).

Nash[4], Richard (1674–1762), Welsh dandy; known as **Beau Nash**. He was an arbiter of fashion and etiquette in the early Georgian age.

Nashe /naʃ/, Thomas (1567–1601), English pamphleteer, prose writer, and dramatist. Notable works: *The Unfortunate Traveller* (1594).

Nash equilibrium ▶ **noun** (in economics and game theory) a stable state of a system involving the interaction of different participants, in which no participant can gain by a unilateral change of strategy if the strategies of the others remain unchanged.

nashi /ˈnaʃiː/ (also **nashi pear**) ▶ **noun** the crisp apple-shaped fruit of a tree that is native to Japan and China and cultivated in Australia and New Zealand. Also called **ASIAN PEAR**. ● This fruit is obtained from varieties of *Pyrus pyrifolia*, family Rosaceae.
– ORIGIN 1960s: from Japanese, literally 'pear'.

Nashik /ˈnɑːsɪk/ (also **Nasik**) a city in western India, in Maharashtra, on the Godavari River north-east of Mumbai (Bombay); pop. 1,521,700 (est. 2009).

Nashville the state capital of Tennessee; pop. 626,144 (est. 2008). The city is noted for its music industry and the Country Music Hall of Fame.

Nasmyth /ˈneɪsmɪθ/, James (1808–90), Scottish engineer. He invented the steam hammer (1839).

naso- /ˈneɪzəʊ/ ▶ **combining form** relating to the nose: *nasogastric.*
– ORIGIN from Latin *nasus* 'nose'.

nasogastric ▶ **adjective** reaching or supplying the stomach via the nose: *she had to be fed by a nasogastric tube.*

nasopharynx ▶ **noun** Anatomy the upper part of the pharynx, connecting with the nasal cavity above the soft palate.
– DERIVATIVES **nasopharyngeal** adjective.

Nassau 1 /ˈnasaʊ/ a former duchy of western Germany, centred on the small town of Nassau, from which a branch of the House of Orange arose. It corresponds to parts of the present-day states of Hesse and Rhineland-Palatinate.
2 /ˈnasɔː/ a port on the island of New Providence, capital of the Bahamas; pop. 240,000 (est. 2007).

Nasser /ˈnɑːsə, ˈnas-/, Gamal Abdel (1918–70), Egyptian colonel and statesman, Prime Minister 1954–6 and President 1956–70. He deposed King Farouk in 1952 and President Muhammad Neguib in 1954. His nationalization of the Suez Canal brought war with Britain, France, and Israel in 1956; he also waged two unsuccessful wars against Israel (1956 and 1967).

Nasser, Lake a lake in SE Egypt created in the 1960s by the building of the two dams on the Nile at Aswan.

nastic /ˈnastɪk/ ▶ **adjective** Botany (of the movement of plant parts) caused by an external stimulus but unaffected in direction by it.
– ORIGIN early 20th cent.: from Greek *nastos* 'squeezed together' (from *nassein* 'to press') + **-IC**.

nastiness ▶ **noun** [mass noun] the state or quality of being nasty: *the nastiness of the campaign.*

nasturtium /nəˈstəːʃ(ə)m/ ▶ **noun** a South American trailing plant with round leaves and bright orange, yellow, or red flowers, which is widely grown as an ornamental. ● *Tropaeolum majus*, family Tropaeolaceae.
– ORIGIN Old English (originally denoting any cruciferous plant of the genus *Nasturtium*, including watercress): from Latin, apparently from *naris* 'nose' + *torquere* 'to twist'.

nasty ▶ **adjective** (**nastier**, **nastiest**) **1** very bad or unpleasant: *plastic bags burn with a nasty, acrid smell* | *dad's had a nasty accident.* ■ (of the weather) unpleasantly cold or wet: *it's a nasty old night.* ■ repugnant to the mind: *her stories are very nasty, full of murder and violence.*
2 behaving in an unpleasant or spiteful way: *Harry was a nasty, foul-mouthed old devil.*
3 annoying or unwelcome: *life has a nasty habit of repeating itself.*
4 damaging or harmful: *a nasty, vicious-looking hatchet.*
▶ **noun** (pl. **nasties**) informal an unpleasant or harmful person or thing: *a water conditioner to neutralize chlorine and other nasties.* ■ a horror video or film. See also **VIDEO NASTY**.
– PHRASES **a nasty piece** (or **bit**) **of work** Brit. informal an unpleasant or untrustworthy person. **a nasty taste in the mouth** see **TASTE**. **something nasty in the woodshed** see **WOODSHED**.
– DERIVATIVES **nastily** adverb.
– ORIGIN late Middle English: of unknown origin.

NASUWT ▶ **abbreviation** (in the UK) National Association of Schoolmasters and Union of Women Teachers.

Nat. ▶ **abbreviation** ■ national. ■ nationalist. ■ natural.

natak /ˈnɑːtək/ ▶ **noun** [mass noun] Indian drama or dramatic art.
– ORIGIN from Hindi.

Natal /nəˈtal, -ˈtɑːl/ **1** a former province of South Africa, situated on the east coast. Having been a Boer republic and then a British colony, Natal acquired internal self-government in 1893 and became a province of the Union of South Africa in 1910. It was renamed KwaZulu-Natal in 1994. [from Latin *Terra Natalis* 'land of the day of birth', a name given by Vasco da Gama in 1497, because he sighted the entrance to what is now Durban harbour on Christmas Day.]
2 a port on the Atlantic coast of NE Brazil, capital of the state of Rio Grande do Norte; pop. 774,230 (2007).

natal[1] /ˈneɪt(ə)l/ ▶ **adjective** relating to the place or time of one's birth: *he was living in the south, many miles from his natal city.*
– ORIGIN late Middle English: from Latin *natalis*, from *nat-* 'born', from the verb *nasci*.

natal[2] /ˈneɪt(ə)l/ ▶ **adjective** Anatomy relating to the buttocks: *the natal cleft.*
– ORIGIN late 19th cent.: from **NATES** + **-AL**.

natality /nəˈtalɪti/ ▸ **noun** [mass noun] the ratio of the number of births to the size of the population; birth rate: *in spite of falling natality, the population as a whole went up*.
– ORIGIN late 19th cent.: from French *natalité*, from *nat-* 'born', from the verb *nasci*.

natant /ˈneɪt(ə)nt/ ▸ **adjective** technical or literary swimming or floating.
– ORIGIN mid 18th cent.: from Latin *natant-* 'swimming', from the verb *natare*.

natation /nəˈteɪʃ(ə)n/ ▸ **noun** [mass noun] technical or literary swimming.
– DERIVATIVES **natatory** /ˈneɪtət(ə)ri, nəˈteɪt(ə)ri/ **adjective**.
– ORIGIN mid 16th cent.: from Latin *natatio(n-)*, from *natare* 'to swim'.

natatorium /ˌneɪtəˈtɔːrɪəm/ ▸ **noun** N. Amer. a swimming pool, especially one that is indoors.
– ORIGIN late 19th cent.: from late Latin, neuter (used as a noun) of *natatorius* 'relating to a swimmer', from *natare* 'to swim'.

natch ▸ **adverb** informal naturally; as may be expected.

nates /ˈneɪtiːz/ ▸ **plural noun** Anatomy the buttocks.
– ORIGIN late 17th cent.: Latin, plural of *natis* 'buttock, rump'.

NATFHE ▸ **abbreviation** (in the UK) National Association of Teachers in Further and Higher Education.

natheless /ˈneɪθlɪs/ (also **nathless**) ▸ **adverb** archaic nevertheless.
– ORIGIN Old English.

nation ▸ **noun** a large body of people united by common descent, history, culture, or language, inhabiting a particular state or territory: *the world's leading industrialized nations*. ▪ a North American Indian people or confederation of peoples.
– PHRASES **one nation** [often as modifier] a nation not divided by social inequality: *one-nation Tories*.
– DERIVATIVES **nationhood** **noun**.
– ORIGIN Middle English: via Old French from Latin *natio(n-)*, from *nat-* 'born', from the verb *nasci*.

national ▸ **adjective** relating to or characteristic of a nation; common to a whole nation: *this policy may have been in the national interest | a national newspaper*. ▪ owned, controlled, or financially supported by the state: *plans for a national art library*.
▸ **noun 1** a citizen of a particular country: *a German national*.
2 (usu. **nationals**) a national newspaper as opposed to a local one: *the inability of the local press to compete with the nationals | or news*.
3 (**the National**) another name for **GRAND NATIONAL**.
– DERIVATIVES **nationally** **adverb** [sentence adverb] *nationally, there has been a 2.5 per cent drop in car crime*.
– ORIGIN late 16th cent.: from French, from Latin *natio(n-)* 'birth, race of people' (see **NATION**).

national anthem ▸ **noun** see **ANTHEM** (sense 1).

National Assembly ▸ **noun** an elected legislature in various countries. ▪ the elected legislature in France during the first part of the Revolution, 1789–91.

National Assistance ▸ **noun** [mass noun] welfare payment made to people on low incomes in Britain between 1948 and 1965.

National Association for the Advancement of Colored People (abbrev.: **NAACP**) a US civil rights organization set up in 1909 to oppose racial segregation and discrimination by non-violent means.

national bank ▸ **noun** another term for **CENTRAL BANK**. ▪ (in the US) a commercial bank which is chartered under the federal government and is a member of the Federal Reserve System.

National Capital Territory of Delhi a territory in north central India containing the old city of Delhi and the capital New Delhi.

national convention ▸ **noun** US a convention of a major political party, especially one that nominates a candidate for the presidency.

national curriculum ▸ **noun** a common programme of study in schools that is designed to ensure nationwide uniformity of content and standards in education.

national debt ▸ **noun** the total amount of money which a country's government has borrowed.

National Front (abbrev.: **NF**) a right-wing UK political party, formed in 1967, with extreme reactionary views on immigration.

National Gallery an art gallery in Trafalgar Square, London, holding one of the chief national collections of pictures. The collection began in 1824, and the present main building was opened in 1838.

national government ▸ **noun** a coalition government, especially one subordinating party differences to the national interest in a time of crisis, as in Britain under Ramsay MacDonald in 1931–5.

national grid ▸ **noun** Brit. **1** the network of high-voltage power lines between major power stations.
2 the metric system of geographical coordinates used in maps of the British Isles.

National Guard ▸ **noun 1** (in the US) the primary reserve military force partly maintained by the states but also available for federal use. ▪ a member of the National Guard.
2 an armed force existing in France at various times between 1789 and 1871. ▪ historical a member of the French National Guard.

National Health Service (also **National Health**) (abbrev.: **NHS**) (in the UK) a system of national medical care paid for mainly by taxation and started by the Labour government in 1948.

National Hunt (also **National Hunt Committee**) ▸ **noun** the body controlling steeplechasing and hurdle racing in Great Britain.

national income ▸ **noun** the total amount of money earned within a country.

National Insurance (in the UK) the system of compulsory payments by employees and employers to provide state assistance for people who are sick, unemployed, or retired.

nationalism ▸ **noun** [mass noun] patriotic feeling, principles, or efforts. ▪ an extreme form of patriotism marked by a feeling of superiority over other countries: *playing with right-wing nationalism*. ▪ advocacy of political independence for a particular country: *Scottish nationalism*.

nationalist ▸ **noun** a person who advocates political independence for a country: *a Scottish nationalist*. ▪ a person with strong patriotic feelings, especially one who believes in the superiority of their country over others.
▸ **adjective** relating to nationalists or nationalism: *a nationalist movement*.

nationalistic ▸ **adjective** having strong patriotic feelings, especially a belief in the superiority of one's own country over others: *he was fiercely nationalistic*.
– DERIVATIVES **nationalistically** **adverb**.

nationality ▸ **noun** (pl. **nationalities**) **1** [mass noun] the status of belonging to a particular nation: *men of Spanish nationality* | [count noun] *the tapestry was created by women of all nationalities*. ▪ archaic distinctive national or ethnic character.
2 an ethnic group forming a part of one or more political nations: *all the main nationalities of Ethiopia*.

nationalize (also **nationalise**) ▸ **verb** [with obj.]
1 transfer (a major branch of industry or commerce) from private to state ownership or control.
2 give a national character to: *in the 13th and 14th centuries church designs were further nationalized*.
3 (usu. as adj. **nationalized**) archaic naturalize (a foreigner).
– DERIVATIVES **nationalization** **noun**, **nationalizer** **noun**.

national minority ▸ **noun** a minority group within a country felt to be distinct from the majority because of historical differences of language, religion, culture, etc.

national park ▸ **noun** an area of countryside, or occasionally sea or fresh water, protected by the state for the enjoyment of the general public or the preservation of wildlife.

National Party[1] an Australian political party established in 1914 (as the Country Party) to represent agricultural and rural interests.

National Party[2] a political party that held power in South Africa from 1948 until the country's first democratic elections in 1994. Formed in 1914 as an Afrikaner party, it favoured racial segregation and instituted apartheid. Now called the **NEW NATIONAL PARTY**.

National Portrait Gallery an art gallery in London holding the national collection of portraits of eminent or well-known British men and women. Founded in 1856, it moved to its present site next to the National Gallery in 1896.

national road ▸ **noun** (in South Africa) any of a network of major intercity roads.

National Security Agency (abbrev.: **NSA**) (in the US) a secret body established after the Second World War to gather intelligence, deal with coded communications from around the world, and safeguard US transmissions.

National Security Council (abbrev.: **NSC**) (in the US) a body created by Congress after the Second World War to advise the President (who chairs it) on issues relating to national security in domestic, foreign, and military policy.

national service ▸ **noun** [mass noun] a period of compulsory service in the armed forces during peacetime (phased out in the UK by 1963).

National Socialism ▸ **noun** [mass noun] historical the political doctrine of the Nazi Party of Germany.
– DERIVATIVES **National Socialist** **noun**.

national treasure ▸ **noun** an artefact, institution, or public figure regarded as being emblematic of a nation's cultural heritage or identity.

National Trust (abbrev.: **NT**) a trust for the preservation of places of historic interest or natural beauty in England, Wales, and Northern Ireland, founded in 1895 and supported by endowment and private subscription. The National Trust for Scotland was founded in 1931.

National Vocational Qualification (abbrev.: **NVQ**) ▸ **noun** (in the UK) a qualification in a vocational subject set at various levels and (at levels two and three) corresponding in standard to GCSE and GCE A levels.

Nation of Islam an exclusively black Islamic sect proposing a separate black nation, founded in Detroit *c.*1930. It came to prominence under the influence of Malcolm X.

nation state ▸ **noun** a sovereign state of which most of the citizens or subjects are united also by factors which define a nation, such as language or common descent.

nationwide ▸ **adjective & adverb** throughout the whole nation: [as adj.] *a nationwide hunt* | [as adverb] *the company employs 6,000 people nationwide*.

native ▸ **noun** a person born in a specified place or associated with a place by birth, whether subsequently resident there or not: *a **native of** Montreal*. ▪ a local inhabitant: *New York in the summer was too hot even for the natives*. ▪ dated, often offensive a non-white original inhabitant of a country, as regarded by European colonists or travellers. ▪ an animal or plant indigenous to a place: *the marigold is **a native of** southern Europe*. ▪ Brit. an oyster reared in British waters.
▸ **adjective 1** associated with the place or circumstances of a person's birth: *he's a native New Yorker | her native country*. ▪ of the indigenous inhabitants of a place: *a ceremonial native dance from Fiji*.
2 (of a plant or animal) of indigenous origin or growth: *eagle owls aren't **native to** Britain | Scotland's few remaining native pinewoods*. ▪ Austral./NZ used in names of animals or plants resembling others familiar elsewhere, e.g. **native bee**.
3 (of a quality) belonging to a person's character from birth; innate: *some last vestige of native wit prompted Guy to say nothing*.
4 (of a metal or other mineral) found in a pure or uncombined state.
5 Computing designed for or built into a given system, especially denoting the language associated with a given processor, computer, or compiler, and programs written in it.
– PHRASES **go native** humorous or derogatory (of a person living away from their own country or region) abandon one's own culture, customs, or way of life and adopt those of the country or region one is living in.
– DERIVATIVES **natively** **adverb**, **nativeness** **noun**.
– ORIGIN late Middle English: from Latin *nativus*, from *nat-* 'born', from the verb *nasci*.

USAGE In contexts such as *a **native** of Boston* or *New York in the summer was too hot even for the **natives*** the noun **native** is quite acceptable. But when it is used to mean 'a non-white original inhabitant of a country', as in *this dance is a favourite with the **natives***, it is more problematic. This meaning has an old-fashioned feel and, because of its associations with a colonial European outlook, it may cause offence.

N

Native American ▸ **noun** a member of any of the indigenous peoples of North and South America and the Caribbean Islands.
▸ **adjective** relating to Native Americans.

> **USAGE** In the US, **Native American** is now the current accepted term in many contexts. The term **American Indian** is still used elsewhere, by American Indians themselves, among others, and is the form used in this dictionary. See USAGE at AMERICAN INDIAN.

native bear ▸ **noun** Australian term for KOALA.

native cat ▸ **noun** Australian term for QUOLL.

native hen ▸ **noun** a moorhen found in Australia, with mainly dark plumage and a greenish bill. Also called WATERHEN or GALLINULE. ● Genus *Gallinula*, family Rallidae: *G. ventralis* of Australia and *G. mortierii* of Tasmania.

native rock ▸ **noun** [mass noun] rock in its original place, i.e. that has not been moved or quarried.

native speaker ▸ **noun** a person who has spoken the language in question from earliest childhood.

nativism /ˈneɪtɪvɪz(ə)m/ ▸ **noun** [mass noun] **1** the theory that concepts, mental capacities, and mental structures are innate rather than acquired by learning.
2 historical, chiefly US the policy of protecting the interests of native-born or established inhabitants against those of immigrants.
3 a return to or emphasis on indigenous customs, in opposition to outside influences.
– DERIVATIVES **nativist** noun & adjective, **nativistic** adjective.

nativity ▸ **noun** (pl. **nativities**) **1** the occasion of a person's birth: *the place of my nativity.* ■ Astrology, dated a horoscope relating to the time of birth; a birth chart.
2 (usu. **the Nativity**) the birth of Jesus Christ. ■ a picture, carving, or model representing Jesus Christ's birth. ■ the Christian festival of Christ's birth; Christmas.
– ORIGIN Middle English: from Old French *nativite*, from late Latin *nativitas*, from Latin *nativus* 'arisen by birth' (see NATIVE).

nativity play ▸ **noun** a play, typically performed by children at Christmas, based on the events surrounding the birth of Jesus Christ.

nativity scene ▸ **noun** a model or tableau representing the scene of Jesus Christ's birth, displayed in homes or public places at Christmas.

NATO (also **Nato**) ▸ **abbreviation** North Atlantic Treaty Organization.

natriuresis /ˌneɪtrɪjʊ(ə)ˈriːsɪs, ˌnat-/ ▸ **noun** [mass noun] Physiology excretion of sodium in the urine.
– DERIVATIVES **natriuretic** adjective.
– ORIGIN 1950s: from NATRON + Greek *ourēsis* 'urination'.

natron /ˈneɪtr(ə)n, ˈnat-/ ▸ **noun** [mass noun] a mineral salt found in dried lake beds, consisting of hydrated sodium carbonate.
– ORIGIN late 17th cent.: from French, from Spanish *natrón*, via Arabic from Greek *nitron* (see NITRE).

Natron, Lake /ˈneɪtrən/ a lake in northern Tanzania, on the border with Kenya, containing large deposits of salt and soda.

natter informal ▸ **verb** [no obj.] talk casually, especially on unimportant matters; chat: *they **nattered away** for hours.*
▸ **noun** [in sing.] a casual and leisurely conversation: *I could do with a drink and a natter.*
– DERIVATIVES **natterer** noun.
– ORIGIN early 19th cent. (in the dialect sense 'grumble, fret'): imitative.

natterjack (also **natterjack toad**) ▸ **noun** a small European toad which has a bright yellow stripe down its back and runs in short bursts. ● *Bufo calamita*, family Bufonidae.
– ORIGIN mid 18th cent.: perhaps from NATTER (because of its loud croak) + JACK[1].

Nattier blue /ˈnatjeɪ/ ▸ **noun** [mass noun] dated a soft shade of blue, especially in fine textiles.
– ORIGIN early 20th cent.: a colour much used by Jean-Marc *Nattier* (1685–1766), French painter.

natty[1] ▸ **adjective** (**nattier**, **nattiest**) informal (of a person or an article of clothing) smart and fashionable: *a natty blue blazer.* ■ well designed; clever: *a palmtop computer with many natty features.*
– DERIVATIVES **nattily** adverb, **nattiness** noun.
– ORIGIN late 18th cent. (originally slang): perhaps related to NEAT[1].

natty[2] ▸ **adjective** black English (among Rastafarians) denoting hair that is uncombed or matted, as in dreadlocks.
– ORIGIN variant of KNOTTY.

natty dread ▸ **noun** black English a Rastafarian, typically a man with dreadlocks.

Natufian /nɑːˈtuːfɪən/ ▸ **adjective** Archaeology relating to or denoting a late Mesolithic culture of the Middle East, dated to about 12,500–10,000 years ago. It provides evidence for the first settled villages, and is characterized by the use of microliths and of bone for implements. ■ (as noun **the Natufian**) the Natufian culture or period.
– ORIGIN 1930s: from Wadi *an-Natuf*, the type site (a cave north-west of Jerusalem), + -IAN.

natural ▸ **adjective 1** existing in or derived from nature; not made or caused by humankind: *carrots contain a natural antiseptic | natural disasters such as earthquakes.* ■ having had a minimum of processing or preservative treatment: *natural food | our nutritional products are completely natural.* ■ (of fabric) having a colour characteristic of the unbleached and undyed state; off-white.
2 in accordance with the nature of, or circumstances surrounding, someone or something: *sharks have no natural enemies.* ■ [attrib.] (of a person) having an innate skill or quality: *he was a natural entertainer.* ■ (of a skill or quality) coming instinctively to a person; innate: *Laura's natural adaptability enabled her to settle quickly.* ■ (of a person or their behaviour) relaxed and unaffected; spontaneous: *he replied with just a little too much nonchalance to sound natural.* ■ entirely to be expected: *Ken was a natural choice for chairman.* ■ [attrib.] (of law or justice) felt instinctively to be morally right and fair.
3 [attrib.] (of a parent or child) related by blood. ■ chiefly archaic (of a child) illegitimate.
4 Music (of a note) not sharp or flat: *the bassoon plays G natural instead of A flat.* ■ (of a brass instrument) having no valves and able to play only the notes of the harmonic series above a fundamental note. ■ relating to the notes and intervals of the harmonic series.
5 Christian Theology relating to earthly human or physical nature as distinct from the spiritual or supernatural realm.
6 Bridge (of a bid) straightforwardly reflecting one's holding of cards. Often contrasted with CONVENTIONAL or ARTIFICIAL.
▸ **noun 1** a person having an innate talent for a particular task or activity: *she was a **natural for** television work.*
2 Music a sign (♮) denoting a natural note when a previous sign or the key signature would otherwise demand a sharp or a flat. ■ a natural note. ■ any of the longer, lower keys on a keyboard instrument that are normally white.
3 [mass noun] an off-white colour.
4 a hand of cards, throw of dice, or other result which wins immediately, in particular: ■ a hand of two cards making 21 in the first deal in blackjack and similar games. ■ a first throw of 7 or 11 at craps.
5 Fishing an insect or other small creature used as bait, rather than an artificial imitation.
6 archaic a person born with a learning disability.
▸ **adverb** informal or dialect naturally: *keep walking—just act natural.*
– ORIGIN Middle English (in the sense 'having a certain status by birth'): from Old French, from Latin *naturalis*, from *natura* 'birth, nature, quality' (see NATURE).

natural-born ▸ **adjective** having a specified innate characteristic or ability: *Glen was a natural-born sailor.* ■ archaic having a particular position by birth: *a natural-born citizen.*

natural childbirth ▸ **noun** [mass noun] childbirth with minimal medical or technological intervention, usually involving special breathing and relaxation techniques.

natural classification ▸ **noun** a scientific classification according to features which are held to be objectively significant, rather than being selected for convenience.

natural frequency ▸ **noun** Physics the frequency at which a system oscillates when not subjected to a continuous or repeated external force.

natural gas ▸ **noun** [mass noun] flammable gas, consisting largely of methane and other hydrocarbons, occurring naturally underground (often in association with petroleum) and used as fuel.

natural history ▸ **noun** [mass noun] **1** the scientific study of animals or plants, especially as concerned with observation rather than experiment, and presented in popular form. ■ the study of the whole natural world, including mineralogy and palaeontology. ■ natural phenomena which are the subject of scientific observation: *the area has an abundance of wildlife and natural history.*
2 Medicine the usual course of development of a disease or condition, especially in the absence of treatment.
– DERIVATIVES **natural historian** noun.

Natural History Museum a museum of zoological, botanical, palaeontological, and mineralogical items in South Kensington, London.

naturalism ▸ **noun** [mass noun] **1** (in art and literature) a style and theory of representation based on the accurate depiction of detail.

> The name 'Naturalism' was given to a 19th-century artistic and literary movement, influenced by contemporary ideas of science and society, which rejected the idealization of experience and adopted an objective and often uncompromisingly realistic approach to art. Notable figures include the novelist Zola and the painter Courbet.

2 the philosophical belief that everything arises from natural properties and causes, and supernatural or spiritual explanations are excluded or discounted.
3 (in moral philosophy) the theory that ethical statements can be derived from non-ethical ones.

naturalist ▸ **noun 1** an expert in or student of natural history.
2 a person who practises naturalism in art or literature. ■ a person who adopts philosophical naturalism.
▸ **adjective** another term for NATURALISTIC.

naturalistic ▸ **adjective 1** derived from or closely imitating real life or nature: *a naturalistic rock garden.*
2 based on the theory of naturalism in art or literature: *naturalistic paintings of the city.* ■ of or according to the philosophy of naturalism.
– DERIVATIVES **naturalistically** adverb.

naturalize (also **naturalise**) ▸ **verb** [with obj.] **1** admit (a foreigner) to the citizenship of a country: *he was born in a foreign country and had never been naturalized* | (as adj. **naturalized**) *a naturalized US citizen born in Germany.* ■ [no obj.] (of a foreigner) be admitted to the citizenship of a country.
2 (usu. as adj. **naturalized**) Biology establish (a plant or animal) so that it lives wild in a region where it is not indigenous: *native and naturalized species | black mustard has become naturalized in Britain and America.* ■ (with reference to a cultivated plant) establish or become established in a natural situation: [with obj.] *this species of crocus **naturalizes itself** very easily.*
3 alter (an adopted foreign word) so that it conforms more closely to the phonology or orthography of the adopting language.
4 regard as or cause to appear natural: *although women do more childcare than men, feminists should beware of naturalizing that fact.* ■ explain (a phenomenon) in a naturalistic way.
– DERIVATIVES **naturalization** noun.
– ORIGIN mid 16th cent.: from French *naturaliser*, from Old French *natural* (see NATURAL).

natural killer cell ▸ **noun** Medicine a lymphocyte able to bind to certain tumour cells and virus-infected cells without the stimulation of antigens, and kill them by the insertion of granules containing perforin.

natural language ▸ **noun** a language that has developed naturally in use (as contrasted with an artificial language or computer code).

natural law ▸ **noun 1** [mass noun] a body of unchanging moral principles regarded as a basis for all human conduct.
2 an observable law relating to natural phenomena: *the natural laws of perspective.* ■ [mass noun] observable laws collectively.

natural life ▸ **noun** the expected span of a person's life or a thing's existence under normal circumstances: *the natural life of a hen is seven years.*

natural logarithm (abbrev.: **ln** or $\log_e$) ▸ **noun** Mathematics a logarithm to the base *e* (2.71828 ...).

naturally ▸ **adverb 1** without special intervention; in a natural manner: [as submodifier] *naturally curly hair.* ■ in a normal manner; without exaggeration or effort: *act naturally.* ■ [as submodifier] by nature: *a naturally bright pupil.* ■ as a logical result: *one leads naturally into the other.*
2 [sentence adverb] as may be expected: *naturally, I hoped for the best.*
– PHRASES **come naturally** (of an action or skill) be easily accomplished, without the need for teaching

or practice: *for some people creative writing may come naturally.*

natural magic ▶ noun [mass noun] (in the Middle Ages) magic practised for beneficial purposes, involving the making of images, healing, and the use of herbs.

naturalness ▶ noun [mass noun] the quality or state of being natural: *she demonstrates an ease and naturalness that many actors try hard to project.*

natural numbers ▶ plural noun the positive integers (whole numbers) 1, 2, 3, etc., and sometimes zero as well.

natural philosophy ▶ noun [mass noun] archaic natural science, especially physical science.
– DERIVATIVES **natural philosopher** noun.

natural religion ▶ noun [mass noun] religion based on reason rather than divine revelation, especially deism.

natural resources ▶ plural noun materials or substances occurring in nature which can be exploited for economic gain.

natural science ▶ noun (usu. **natural sciences**) a branch of science which deals with the physical world, e.g. physics, chemistry, geology, biology.
■ [mass noun] the branch of knowledge which deals with the study of the physical world.

natural selection ▶ noun [mass noun] Biology the process whereby organisms better adapted to their environment tend to survive and produce more offspring. The theory of its action was first fully expounded by Charles Darwin, and it is now regarded as the main process that brings about evolution. Compare with SURVIVAL OF THE FITTEST (see SURVIVAL).

natural theology ▶ noun [mass noun] theology or knowledge of God based on observed facts and experience apart from divine revelation.

natural virtues ▶ plural noun the traditional chief moral virtues of justice, prudence, temperance, and fortitude. Often contrasted with THEOLOGICAL VIRTUES.

natural wastage ▶ noun Brit. see WASTAGE (sense 2).

natural year ▶ noun the tropical or solar year. See YEAR (sense 1).

nature ▶ noun 1 [mass noun] the phenomena of the physical world collectively, including plants, animals, the landscape, and other features and products of the earth, as opposed to humans or human creations: *the breathtaking beauty of nature.* ■ the physical force regarded as causing and regulating the phenomena of the world: *it is impossible to change the laws of nature.* See also MOTHER NATURE.
2 the basic or inherent features, character, or qualities of something: *helping them to realize the nature of their problems | there are a lot of other documents of that nature.* ■ the innate or essential qualities or character of a person or animal: *it's not in her nature to listen to advice | I'm not violent **by nature**.* ■ [mass noun] inborn or hereditary characteristics as an influence on or determinant of personality. Often contrasted with NURTURE. ■ [with adj.] archaic a person of a specified character: *Emerson was so much more luminous a nature.*
– PHRASES **against nature** unnatural in a way perceived as immoral. **someone's better nature** a person's capacity for tolerance, generosity, or sympathy: *Charlotte planned to appeal to his better nature.* **the call of nature** used euphemistically to refer to a need to urinate or defecate. **from nature** (in art) using natural scenes or objects as models. **get** (or **go**) **back to nature** return to the type of life (regarded as being in tune with nature) that existed before the development of industrial societies. **in the nature of** having the characteristics of; similar to: *a week at home would be in the nature of a holiday.* **in the nature of things 1** inevitable. **2** inevitably: *in the nature of things, old people spend much more time indoors.* **in a state of nature 1** in a state unaffected by human intervention. **2** totally naked. **3** Christian Theology in a morally unregenerate condition, unredeemed by divine grace. **the nature of the beast** informal the inherent and unchangeable character of something.
– ORIGIN Middle English (denoting the physical power of a person): from Old French, from Latin *natura* 'birth, nature, quality', from *nat-* 'born', from the verb *nasci*.

nature cure ▶ noun another term for NATUROPATHY.

natured ▶ adjective [in combination] having a nature or disposition of a specified kind: *a good-natured man.*

nature printing ▶ noun [mass noun] a method of producing a print of a natural object (such as a leaf) or a textile by making an impression of it directly on to a soft metal printing plate under great pressure and then taking an inked impression on paper.

nature reserve ▶ noun a tract of land managed so as to preserve its flora, fauna, and physical features.

nature strip ▶ noun Austral. a piece of publicly owned land between the front boundary of a house or other building and the street, typically planted with grass.

nature study ▶ noun [mass noun] the practical study of plants, animals, and natural phenomena as a school subject.

nature trail ▶ noun a signposted path through the countryside designed to draw attention to natural features.

naturism ▶ noun [mass noun] **1** chiefly Brit. the practice of going naked in designated areas; nudism.
2 the worship of nature or natural objects.

naturist ▶ noun **1** chiefly Brit. a person who goes naked in designated areas; a nudist: *he is a dedicated naturist.*
2 a person who worships nature or natural objects.

naturopathy /ˌneɪtʃəˈrɒpəθi/ ▶ noun [mass noun] a system of alternative medicine based on the theory that diseases can be successfully treated or prevented without the use of drugs, by techniques such as control of diet, exercise, and massage.
– DERIVATIVES **naturopath** noun, **naturopathic** adjective.

Naugahyde /ˈnɔːgəhʌɪd/ ▶ noun [mass noun] N. Amer. (trademark in the US) an artificial material designed to resemble leather, made from fabric coated with rubber or vinyl resin.
– ORIGIN early 20th cent.: from *Nauga(tuck)*, the name of a town in Connecticut, US, where rubber is manufactured, + *-hyde* (alteration of HIDE²).

naught ▶ pronoun archaic nothing: *he's naught but a worthless fool.*
▶ noun N. Amer. variant spelling of NOUGHT.
– PHRASES **bring to naught** archaic ruin or foil. **come to naught** be ruined or foiled. **set at naught** archaic disregard or despise.
– ORIGIN Old English *nāwiht, -wuht*, from *nā* 'no' + *wiht* 'thing' (see WIGHT).

naughty ▶ adjective (**naughtier**, **naughtiest**) **1** (especially of a child) badly behaved; disobedient: *you've been a really naughty boy.*
2 informal mildly rude or indecent, typically because related to sex: *naughty goings-on.*
3 archaic wicked.
– PHRASES **the naughty step** Brit., informal a place where a child is sent after misbehaving in order to reflect on their actions. ■ a situation of public disgrace: *the bosses of the unions found themselves **on the naughty step**.*
– DERIVATIVES **naughtily** adverb, **naughtiness** noun.
– ORIGIN late Middle English: from NAUGHT + -Y¹. The earliest recorded sense was 'possessing nothing'; the sense 'wicked' also dates from late Middle English, and gave rise to the current senses.

naughty bits ▶ plural noun informal, humorous the parts of a person's body connected with sexual activity or attraction, especially their genitals.

naughty nineties ▶ plural noun the 1890s, regarded as a time of liberalism and permissiveness, especially in Britain and France.

nauplius /ˈnɔːplɪəs/ ▶ noun (pl. **nauplii** /-plɪʌɪ, -plɪiː/) Zoology the first larval stage of many crustaceans, having an unsegmented body and a single eye.
– ORIGIN mid 19th cent.: from Latin, denoting a kind of shellfish, or from the Greek name *Nauplios*, the son of Poseidon.

Nauru /nɑːˈuːruː/ an island country in the SW Pacific, near the equator; pop. 14,000 (est. 2009); official languages, Nauruan (an Austronesian language) and English; no official capital. Since 1968 it has been an independent republic with a limited form of membership of the Commonwealth. It has the world's richest deposits of phosphates.
– DERIVATIVES **Nauruan** adjective & noun.

nausea /ˈnɔːsɪə, -z-/ ▶ noun [mass noun] a feeling of sickness with an inclination to vomit. ■ a feeling of loathing or disgust: *the stories will launch a wave of public nausea and outrage.*
– ORIGIN late Middle English: via Latin from Greek *nausia*, from *naus* 'ship'.

nauseate ▶ verb [with obj.] affect with nausea: *the thought of food nauseated her.* ■ fill (someone) with disgust: *they were nauseated by the jingoism.*
– ORIGIN mid 17th cent.: from Latin *nauseat-* 'made to feel sick', from the verb *nauseare*, from *nausea* (see NAUSEA).

nauseating ▶ adjective causing or liable to cause a feeling of nausea or disgust; disgusting: *the stench was nauseating | some nauseating, sentimental ditty.*
– DERIVATIVES **nauseatingly** adverb [as submodifier] *Rafael looked nauseatingly smug.*

nauseous ▶ adjective **1** affected with nausea; feeling inclined to vomit: *a rancid odour that made him nauseous.*
2 causing nausea: *the smell was nauseous.* ■ disgusting or offensive: *this nauseous account of a court case.*
– DERIVATIVES **nauseously** adverb, **nauseousness** noun.
– ORIGIN early 17th cent.: from Latin *nauseosus* (from *nausea* 'seasickness').

nautch /nɔːtʃ/ ▶ noun (in South Asia) a traditional dance performed by professional dancing girls.
– ORIGIN from Hindi *nāc*, from Prakrit *nachcha*, from Sanskrit *nṛtya* 'dancing'.

nautical ▶ adjective of or concerning navigation, sailors, or the sea; maritime: *nautical charts.*
– DERIVATIVES **nautically** adverb.
– ORIGIN mid 16th cent.: from French *nautique*, or via Latin from Greek *nautikos*, from *nautēs* 'sailor', from *naus* 'ship'.

nautical almanac ▶ noun a yearbook containing astronomical and tidal information for navigators.

nautical mile ▶ noun a unit used in measuring distances at sea, equal to 1,852 metres (approximately 2,025 yards). Compare with SEA MILE.

nautiloid /ˈnɔːtɪlɔɪd/ ▶ noun Zoology a mollusc of a group of mainly extinct marine molluscs which includes the pearly nautilus. ● Subclass Nautiloidea, class Cephalopoda: *Nautilus* is the only surviving genus.
– ORIGIN mid 19th cent.: from the modern Latin genus name *Nautilus* (see NAUTILUS).

Nautilus /ˈnɔːtɪləs/ the first nuclear-powered submarine, launched in 1954. This US navy vessel made a historic journey (1–5 August 1958) under the ice of the North Pole.
– ORIGIN a name previously given to Robert Fulton's 'diving boat' (1800), also to the fictitious submarine in Jules Verne's *Twenty Thousand Leagues under the Sea*.

nautilus /ˈnɔːtɪləs/ ▶ noun (pl. **nautiluses** or **nautili** /-lʌɪ, -liː/) **1** a cephalopod mollusc with a light external spiral shell and numerous short tentacles around the mouth. ● Genus *Nautilus*, the only surviving genus of the subclass Nautiloidea: several species, in particular the **pearly nautilus**.
2 (also **paper nautilus**) another term for ARGONAUT.
– ORIGIN modern Latin, from Latin, from Greek *nautilos*, literally 'sailor'.

NAV ▶ abbreviation net asset value.

navaid /ˈnaveɪd/ ▶ noun a navigational device in an aircraft, ship, or other vehicle.
– ORIGIN 1950s: from *navigational aid*.

Navajo /ˈnavəhəʊ/ (also **Navaho**) ▶ noun (pl. **same** or **Navajos**) **1** a member of an American Indian people of New Mexico and Arizona.
2 [mass noun] the Athabaskan language of the Navajo, with about 130,000 speakers.
▶ adjective relating to the Navajo or their language.
– ORIGIN from Spanish *Apaches de Navajó* 'Apaches from Navajo', from Tewa *navahu:* 'fields adjoining an arroyo'.

naval ▶ adjective relating to a navy or navies: *a naval base | a naval officer.*
– DERIVATIVES **navally** adverb.
– ORIGIN late Middle English: from Latin *navalis*, from *navis* 'ship'.

naval architecture ▶ noun [mass noun] the activity or profession of designing ships.
– DERIVATIVES **naval architect** noun.

naval stores ▶ plural noun articles or materials used in shipping.

Navan /ˈnav(ə)n/ the county town of Meath, in the Republic of Ireland; pop. 3,710 (2006).

Navanagar /ˌnʌvəˈnʌgə/ a former princely state of NW India, centred on the city of Jamnagar. It is now part of the state of Gujarat.

Navaratri /ˌnʌvəˈrʌtri/ (also **Navaratra**) ▶ noun a Hindu autumn festival extending over the nine nights before Dussehra. It is associated with many local observances, especially the Bengali festival of Durga.

N

– ORIGIN Sanskrit, literally 'nine nights'.

navarin /'nav(ə)rın, -rā/ ▸ **noun** a casserole of lamb or mutton with vegetables.
– ORIGIN French.

Navarino, Battle of /ˌnavə'riːnəʊ/ a decisive naval battle in the Greek struggle for independence from the Ottoman Empire, fought in 1827 in the Bay of Navarino off Pylos in the Peloponnese. Britain, Russia, and France sent a combined fleet which destroyed the Egyptian and Turkish fleet.

Navarre /nə'vɑː/ an autonomous region of northern Spain, on the border with France; capital, Pamplona. It represents the southern part of the former kingdom of Navarre, which was conquered by Ferdinand in 1512 and attached to Spain, while the northern part passed to France in 1589 through inheritance by Henry IV. Spanish name **Navarra** /na'βarra/.

nave[1] ▸ **noun** the central part of a church building, intended to accommodate most of the congregation. In traditional Western churches it is rectangular, separated from the chancel by a step or rail, and from adjacent aisles by pillars.
– ORIGIN late 17th cent.: from Latin *navis* 'ship'.

nave[2] ▸ **noun** the hub of a wheel.
– ORIGIN Old English *nafu, nafa*, of Germanic origin; related to Dutch *naaf* and German *Nabe*, from an Indo-European root shared by Sanskrit *nābhis* 'nave, navel'. Compare with **NAVEL**.

navel ▸ **noun** a rounded knotty depression in the centre of a person's belly caused by the detachment of the umbilical cord after birth; the umbilicus. ■ the central point of a place: *the Incas saw Cuzco as the navel of the world.*
– PHRASES **contemplate one's navel** spend time complacently considering oneself or one's interests at the expense of a wider view.
– ORIGIN Old English *nafela*, of Germanic origin; related to Dutch *navel* and German *Nabel*, from an Indo-European root shared by Latin *umbo* 'boss of a shield', *umbilicus* 'navel', and Greek *omphalos* 'boss, navel'. Compare with **NAVE**[2].

navel-gazing ▸ **noun** [mass noun] complacent concentration on oneself or a single issue at the expense of a wider view.

navel orange ▸ **noun** a large seedless orange of a variety which has a navel-like depression at the top containing a small secondary fruit.

N

navelwort ▸ **noun** another term for **PENNYWORT**.

navicular /nə'vıkjʊlə/ ▸ **adjective** technical or archaic boat-shaped.
▸ **noun 1** (also **navicular bone**) a boat-shaped bone in the ankle or wrist, especially that in the ankle, between the talus and the cuneiform bones.
2 (also **navicular disease** or **navicular syndrome**) [mass noun] a chronic disorder of the navicular bone in horses, causing lameness in the front feet.
– ORIGIN late Middle English: from French *naviculaire* or late Latin *navicularis*, from Latin *navicula* 'little ship', diminutive of *navis*.

navigable ▸ **adjective** (of a waterway or sea) able to be sailed on by ships or boats. ■ (of a track or road) suitable for vehicles: *a good cart track, navigable by cars.* ■ Computing (of a website) easy to move around in.
– DERIVATIVES **navigability** noun.
– ORIGIN early 16th cent.: from French *navigable* or Latin *navigabilis*, from the verb *navigare* 'to sail' (see **NAVIGATE**).

navigate ▸ **verb 1** [no obj.] plan and direct the course of a ship, aircraft, or other form of transport, especially by using instruments or maps: *they navigated by the stars.* ■ [no obj., with adverbial of direction] travel on a desired course after planning a route: *he taught them how to navigate across the oceans.* ■ (of an animal or bird) find its way: *whales use their own inbuilt sonar system to navigate.* ■ (of a passenger in a vehicle) assist the driver by planning a route and map reading. ■ Computing move around a website, the Internet, etc.
2 [with obj.] sail or travel over (a stretch of water or terrain), especially carefully or with difficulty: *ships had been lost while navigating the narrows* | *the drivers skilfully navigated a muddy course.* ■ [no obj.] (of a ship or boat) sail; proceed: [with adverbial of direction] *we sailed out while navigating around large icebergs.* ■ guide (a vessel or vehicle) over a specified route or terrain: *she navigated the car safely through the traffic.* ■ informal guide or steer (someone).
– ORIGIN late 16th cent. (in the sense 'travel in a ship'): from Latin *navigat-* 'sailed', from the verb *navigare*, from *navis* 'ship' + *agere* 'drive'.

navigation ▸ **noun** [mass noun] **1** the process or activity of accurately ascertaining one's position and planning and following a route.
2 the passage of ships: *transporter bridges to span rivers without hindering navigation.* ■ [count noun] chiefly dialect a navigable inland waterway, especially a canal.
3 Computing the action of moving around a website, the Internet, etc.
– DERIVATIVES **navigational** adjective, **navigationally** adverb.
– ORIGIN early 16th cent. (denoting travel on water): from French, or from Latin *navigatio(n-)*, from the verb *navigare* (see **NAVIGATE**).

navigation lights ▸ **plural noun** a set of lights shown by a ship or aircraft at night to indicate its position and orientation.

navigator ▸ **noun** a person who navigates a ship, aircraft, etc. ■ historical a person who explores by sea. ■ an instrument or device which assists in navigating a vessel or aircraft. ■ Computing a browser program for accessing data on the Internet or another information system.

Navratilova /naˌvratı'ləʊvə/, Martina (b.1956), Czech-born American tennis player. Her major successes include nine Wimbledon singles titles (1978–9; 1982–7; 1990), two world championships (1980; 1984), and eight successive grand slam doubles titles.

navvy ▸ **noun** (pl. **navvies**) Brit. dated a labourer employed in the excavation and construction of a road, railway, or canal.
– ORIGIN early 19th cent.: abbreviation of **NAVIGATOR** (which was formerly also used in this sense).

navy ▸ **noun** (pl. **navies**) **1** (often **the navy**) the branch of the armed services of a state which conducts military operations at sea. ■ the ships of a navy: *we built their navy.* ■ literary a fleet of ships.
2 (also **navy blue**) [mass noun] a dark blue colour: [as modifier] *a navy-blue suit.*
– ORIGIN late Middle English (in the sense 'ships collectively, fleet'): from Old French *navie* 'ship, fleet', from popular Latin *navia* 'ship', from Latin *navis* 'ship'.

navy bean ▸ **noun** North American term for **HARICOT**.

Navy Department (in the US) the government department in charge of the navy.

Navy List (in the UK) an official list of the commissioned officers in the Royal Navy and the Royal Marines.

navy yard ▸ **noun** (in the US) a shipyard for the construction, repair, and equipping of naval vessels.

naw ▸ **determiner, exclamation, adverb, & noun** Scottish, N. English, & N. Amer. informal variant spelling of **NO**, representing a dialect or non-standard pronunciation.

nawab /nʌ'wɑːb/ ▸ **noun** Indian historical a native governor during the time of the Mogul empire: [as title] *Nawab Haider Beg.* ■ a Muslim nobleman or person of high status.
– ORIGIN from Urdu *nawwāb*, variant of Arabic *nuwwāb*, plural (used as singular) of *nā'ib* 'deputy'; compare with **NABOB**.

Naxalite /'naksəlʌıt/ ▸ **noun** (in South Asia) a member of an armed revolutionary group advocating Maoist communism.
– ORIGIN 1960s: from *Naxal(bari)*, the name of an area of West Bengal, India, + **-ITE**[1].

Naxçivan /ˌnaxtʃı'vɑːn/ a predominantly Muslim Azerbaijani autonomous republic, situated on the borders of Turkey and northern Iran and separated from the rest of Azerbaijan by a narrow strip of Armenia. Russian name **NAKHICHEVAN**. ■ the capital city of Naxçivan; pop. 71,200 (est. 2008).

> Persian from the 13th to the 19th century, Naxçivan became part of the Russian empire in 1828 and an autonomous republic of the Soviet Union in 1924. In 1990 it was the first Soviet territory to declare unilateral independence. It has a predominantly Azerbaijani population and, along with Nagorno-Karabakh, is a point of conflict between Armenia and Azerbaijan.

Naxos /'naksɒs/ a Greek island in the southern Aegean, the largest of the Cyclades.

nay ▸ **adverb 1** or rather (used to emphasize a more appropriate word than one just used): *permission to build the superstore will take months, nay years.*
2 archaic or dialect no: *nay, I must not think thus.*
▸ **noun** a negative answer: *the cabinet sits to give the final yea or nay to policies.*
– ORIGIN Middle English (in sense 2 of the adverb): from Old Norse *nei*, from *ne* 'not' + *ei* 'ever' (compare with **AYE**[2]).

nayaka /'neıjɑːkə/ ▸ **noun** Indian a lead male role in dance or a romantic hero in drama.
– ORIGIN from Sanskrit *nāyaka*, from *nī-* 'to lead'.

Nayarit /ˌnɑːjɑː'riːt/ a state of western Mexico, on the Pacific coast; capital, Tepic.

Naypyidaw /'neıpjiːˌdɔː/ (also **Nay Pyi Taw**) the capital of Burma (Myanmar); pop. 925,000 (est. 2007). Situated in a previously undeveloped area of relative isolation, the city was founded in 2005 to replace Rangoon as the nation's capital.

naysay ▸ **verb** (past and past participle **naysaid**) [with obj.] chiefly US say no to; deny or oppose: *I'm not going to naysay anything he does.*
– DERIVATIVES **naysayer** noun.

Nazarene /'nazəriːn, ˌnazə'riːn/ ▸ **noun 1** a native or inhabitant of Nazareth. ■ (**the Nazarene**) Jesus Christ. ■ (chiefly in Jewish or Muslim use) a Christian. ■ a member of an early sect of Jewish Christians, especially one in 4th-century Syria observing much of the Jewish law. ■ a member of the Church of the Nazarene, a Protestant denomination founded in California.
2 a member of a group of German painters formed in 1809, who sought to revive the art and techniques of medieval Germany and early Renaissance Italy.
▸ **adjective** relating to Nazareth or Nazarenes.
– ORIGIN via late Latin from Greek *Nazarēnos*, from *Nazaret* 'Nazareth'.

Nazareth /'nazərəθ/ a historic town in lower Galilee, in present-day northern Israel; pop. 66,400 (est. 2008). Mentioned in the Gospels as the home of Mary and Joseph, it is closely associated with the childhood of Jesus and is a centre of Christian pilgrimage.

Nazca Lines /'nazkə/ a group of huge abstract designs, including representations of birds and animals, and straight lines on the coastal plain north of Nazca in southern Peru, clearly visible from the air but almost indecipherable from ground level. Made by exposing the underlying sand, they belong to a pre-Inca culture, and their purpose is uncertain; some believe that the designs represent a vast calendar or astronomical information.

Nazi /'nɑːtsi/ ▸ **noun** (pl. **Nazis**) historical a member of the National Socialist German Workers' Party. ■ derogatory a person with extreme racist or authoritarian views. ■ a person who seeks to impose their views on others in a very autocratic or inflexible way: *I learned to be more open and not such a Nazi in the studio.*

> The Nazi Party was formed in Munich after the First World War. It advocated right-wing authoritarian nationalist government, and developed a racist ideology based on anti-Semitism and a belief in the superiority of 'Aryan' Germans. Its leader, Adolf Hitler, who was elected Chancellor in 1933, established a totalitarian dictatorship and precipitated the Second World War. The Nazi Party collapsed at the end of the War and was outlawed.

▸ **adjective** of or concerning the Nazis or Nazism.
– DERIVATIVES **Nazidom** noun, **Nazify** verb (**Nazifies, Nazifying, Nazified**), **Naziism** noun, **Nazism** noun.
– ORIGIN German, abbreviation representing the pronunciation of *Nati-* in *Nationalsozialist* 'national socialist', probably by analogy with *Sozi*, from *Sozialist* 'socialist'.

Nazirite /'nazərʌıt/ (also **Nazarite**) ▸ **noun** historical an Israelite who was consecrated to the service of God, under vows to abstain from alcohol, let the hair grow, and avoid defilement by contact with dead bodies (Num. 6).
– ORIGIN from Hebrew *nāzīr* 'consecrated one', from *nāzar* 'to separate or consecrate oneself', + **-ITE**[1].

Nazi salute ▸ **noun** a gesture or salute in which the right arm is inclined upwards, with the hand open and palm down.

NB ▸ **abbreviation** ■ New Brunswick (in official postal use). ■ nota bene; take special note. [Latin.]

Nb ▸ **symbol** the chemical element niobium.

nb ▸ **abbreviation** Cricket no-ball.

NBA ▸ **abbreviation** ■ (in North America) National Basketball Association. ■ (in the US) National Boxing Association. ■ net book agreement.

NBC ▸ **abbreviation** ■ (in the US) National Broadcasting Company. ■ (of weapons or warfare) nuclear, biological, and chemical.

NBG ▸ **abbreviation** informal no bloody good.

NC ▶ abbreviation ■ network computer. ■ North Carolina (in official postal use). ■ numerical control.

NC-17 ▶ symbol (in the US) films classified as suitable for adults only.
– ORIGIN representing *no children (under) 17*.

NCC ▶ abbreviation (in the UK) National Curriculum Council.

NCO ▶ abbreviation non-commissioned officer.

NCT ▶ abbreviation (in the UK) National Childbirth Trust.

ND ▶ abbreviation North Dakota (in official postal use).

Nd ▶ symbol the chemical element neodymium.

n.d. ▶ abbreviation no date (used especially in bibliographies).

-nd ▶ suffix variant spelling of **-AND, -END**.

N. Dak. ▶ abbreviation North Dakota.

Ndebele /ˌ(ə)ndəˈbiːli:/ ▶ noun (pl. **same** or **Ndebeles**) **1** a member of a people of Zimbabwe and NE South Africa. See also **MATABELE**.
2 [mass noun] the Bantu language of the Ndebele, with over 1 million speakers. Also called **SINDEBELE**.
▶ adjective relating to the Ndebele or their language.
– ORIGIN the name in the Nguni languages.

N'Djamena /ˌ(ə)ndʒaˈmeɪnə/ the capital of Chad; pop. 989,000 (est. 2007). Former name (1900–73) **FORT LAMY**.

Ndola /(ə)nˈdəʊlə/ a city in the Copperbelt region of central Zambia; pop. 482,300 (est. 2009).

NDP ▶ abbreviation (in Canada) New Democratic Party.

NE ▶ abbreviation ■ Nebraska (in official postal use). ■ New England. ■ north-east or north-eastern.

Ne ▶ symbol the chemical element neon.

né /neɪ/ ▶ adjective originally called; born (used before the name by which a man was originally known): *Al Kelly, né Kabish*.
– ORIGIN 1930s: French, literally 'born', masculine past participle of *naître*; compare with **NÉE**.

Neagh, Lough /neɪ/ a shallow lake in Northern Ireland, the largest freshwater lake in the United Kingdom.

Neanderthal /nɪˈandətɑːl/ ▶ noun (also **Neanderthal man**) an extinct species of human that was widely distributed in ice-age Europe between *c*.120,000 and 35,000 years ago, with a receding forehead and prominent brow ridges. The Neanderthals were associated with the Mousterian flint industry of the Middle Palaeolithic. ● *Homo neanderthalensis*; now usually regarded as a separate species from *H. sapiens* and probably at the end of a different evolutionary line.
■ an uncivilized, unintelligent, or uncouth man.
▶ adjective relating to Neanderthals. ■ (of a man) uncivilized, unintelligent, or uncouth: *they were pushed back by Neanderthal security guards*.
– ORIGIN mid 19th cent.: from *Neanderthal*, the name of a region in Germany (now *Neandertal*), where remains of Neanderthal man were found.

neap /niːp/ ▶ noun (also **neap tide**) a tide just after the first or third quarters of the moon when there is least difference between high and low water.
▶ verb (**be neaped**) (of a boat) be kept aground or in harbour by a neap tide.
– ORIGIN late Middle English, originally an adjective from Old English *nēp*, first element of *nēpflōd* 'neap flood', of unknown origin.

Neapolitan /nɪəˈpɒlɪt(ə)n/ ▶ noun a native or inhabitant of Naples.
▶ adjective relating to Naples.
– ORIGIN from Latin *Neapolitanus*, from Latin *Neapolis* 'Naples', from Greek *neos* 'new' + *polis* 'city'.

Neapolitan ice cream ▶ noun [mass noun] ice cream made in layers of different colours.

near ▶ adverb **1** at or to a short distance away; nearby: *a bomb exploded somewhere near* | [comparative] *she took a step nearer*.
2 a short time away in the future: *his retirement was drawing near*.
3 [as submodifier] almost: *a near perfect fit*.
4 archaic or dialect nearly: *I near fell out of the chair*.
▶ preposition (also **near to**) **1** at or to a short distance away from (a place): *the car park near the sawmill* | *do you live near here?* | [superlative] *the table nearest the door*.
2 a short period of time from: *near the end of the war* | [comparative] *details will be given nearer the date*.
3 close to (a state); verging on: *she gave a tiny smile, brave but near tears* | *she was near to death*. ■ a small amount below (another amount): *temperatures near 2 million degrees*.
4 similar to: *a shape near to the original*.
▶ adjective **1** located a short distance away: *a large house in the near distance* | [superlative] *I was a mile from the nearest village*.
2 only a short time ahead: *the conflict is unlikely to be resolved in the near future*.
3 similar: [superlative] *walking in these shoes is the nearest thing to floating on air*. ■ [attrib.] close to being (the thing mentioned): *his state of near despair* | *a near disaster*. ■ [attrib.] having a close family connection.
4 [attrib.] located on the nearside of a vehicle. *the near right-hand end window of the caravan*. Compare with **OFF** (sense 3 of the adjective).
5 archaic (of a person) mean; miserly.
▶ verb [with obj.] come near to; approach: *soon the cab would be nearing Oxford Street* | [no obj.] *lunchtime neared*.
– PHRASES **near at hand** close in distance or time: *help was near at hand*. **near enough** Brit. sufficiently close to being the case for all practical purposes: *this price was near enough the going rate for rent*. **one's nearest and dearest** one's close friends and relatives. **so near and yet so far** a rueful comment on a narrow failure to achieve an aim.
– DERIVATIVES **nearish** adjective.
– ORIGIN Middle English: from Old Norse *nær* 'nearer', comparative of *ná*, corresponding to Old English *nēah* 'nigh'.

nearby ▶ adjective not far away; close: *he slung his jacket over a nearby chair*.
▶ adverb (also **near by**) close by: *his four sisters live nearby*.

Nearctic /nɪˈɑːktɪk/ ▶ adjective Zoology relating to or denoting a zoogeographical region comprising North America as far south as northern Mexico, together with Greenland. Compare with **HOLARCTIC**. ■ (as noun **the Nearctic**) the Nearctic region.
– ORIGIN mid 19th cent.: from **NEO-** 'new' + **ARCTIC**.

near-death experience ▶ noun an unusual experience taking place on the brink of death and recounted by a person on recovery, typically an out-of-body experience or a vision of a tunnel of light.

Near East a term originally applied to the Balkan states of SE Europe, but now generally applied to the countries of SW Asia between the Mediterranean and India (including the Middle East), especially in historical contexts.
– DERIVATIVES **Near Eastern** adjective.

near gale ▶ noun a wind of force 7 on the Beaufort scale (28–33 knots or 51–62 kph).

near go ▶ noun Brit. dated informal term for **NEAR MISS**.

nearly ▶ adverb **1** very close to; almost: *David was nearly asleep* | *a rise of nearly 25 per cent*.
2 closely: *in the absence of anyone more nearly related, I was designated next of kin*.
– PHRASES **not nearly** nothing like; far from: *you're not nearly as clever as you think you are*.

nearly man ▶ noun Brit. informal someone who narrowly fails to achieve the success or position expected of them in their particular field.

near miss ▶ noun **1** a narrowly avoided collision or other accident.
2 a bomb or shot that just misses its target. ■ something almost achieved: *a victory in Houston and a near miss in the finals of the French Open*.

near money ▶ noun [mass noun] Finance assets which can readily be converted into cash, such as bills of exchange.

nearness ▶ noun [mass noun] the condition of being near; proximity: *the town's nearness to London*.

nearshore ▶ adjective relating to or denoting the region of the sea or seabed relatively close to a shore.

nearside ▶ noun (usu. **the nearside**) Brit. the side of a vehicle nearest the kerb (in Britain, the left). Compare with **OFFSIDE**. ■ the left side of a horse.

nearsighted ▶ adjective chiefly N. Amer. another term for **SHORT-SIGHTED**.
– DERIVATIVES **nearsightedly** adverb, **nearsightedness** noun.

near-term ▶ adjective **1** short-term.
2 (of a pregnant female or a fetus) close to the time of birth.

neat[1] ▶ adjective **1** arranged in a tidy way; in good order: *the books had been stacked up in neat piles*. ■ (of a person) habitually tidy, smart, or well organized: *her daughter was always neat and clean*. ■ having a pleasing appearance; well formed: *Alan noted down the orders in his neat, precise script*.
2 done with or demonstrating skill or efficiency: *a neat bit of deduction*. ■ tending to disregard specifics for the sake of convenience; facile: *this neat division does not take into account a host of associated factors*.
3 (of liquid, especially spirits) not diluted or mixed with anything else: *he drank neat Scotch*.
4 N. Amer. informal very good; excellent: *I took lessons in tracking from this really neat Indian guide*.
– ORIGIN late 15th cent. (in the sense 'clean, free from impurities'): from French *net*, from Latin *nitidus* 'shining', from *nitere* 'to shine'; related to **NET**[2]. The sense 'bright' (now obsolete) was recorded in English in the late 16th cent.

neat[2] ▶ noun archaic a bovine animal. ■ [mass noun] cattle.
– ORIGIN Old English, of Germanic origin; related to Dutch *noot*, also to the base of dialect *nait* meaning 'companion'.

neaten ▶ verb [with obj.] make (something) tidy.

Neath /niːθ/ an industrial town in South Wales on the River Neath; pop. 46,800 (est. 2009). Welsh name **CASTELL-NEDD**.

neath ▶ preposition chiefly literary beneath: *roaming around neath the trees*.

neatly ▶ adverb in a neat way: *neatly folded shirts* | *she neatly sidestepped the question*.

neatness ▶ noun [mass noun] the quality or condition of being neat: *his obsessive neatness*.

neat's-foot oil ▶ noun [mass noun] oil obtained by boiling the feet of cattle, used to dress leather.

NEB ▶ abbreviation ■ (in the UK) National Enterprise Board. ■ New English Bible.

neb ▶ noun Scottish & N. English a nose, snout, or bird's beak. ■ the peak of a cap.
– ORIGIN Old English *nebb*, of Germanic origin; related to Dutch *neb(be)*; compare with **NIB**.

Neb. ▶ abbreviation Nebraska.

Nebbiolo /ˌnɛbɪˈəʊləʊ/, Italian /nebˈbjɔləo/ ▶ noun [mass noun] a variety of black wine grape grown in Piedmont in northern Italy. ■ a red wine made from the Nebbiolo grape.
– ORIGIN Italian, from *nebbia* 'mist' (because the grape ripens in the autumn).

nebbish ▶ noun informal, chiefly N. Amer. a person, especially a man, who is regarded as pitifully ineffectual, timid, or submissive.
– DERIVATIVES **nebbishy** adjective.
– ORIGIN late 19th cent.: from Yiddish *nebekh* 'poor thing'.

Neblina, Pico da see **PICO DA NEBLINA**.

Nebr. ▶ abbreviation Nebraska.

Nebraska /nɪˈbraskə/ a state in the central US to the west of the Missouri River; pop. 1,783,432 (est. 2008); capital, Lincoln. It was acquired as part of the Louisiana Purchase in 1803 and became the 37th state of the US in 1867.
– DERIVATIVES **Nebraskan** adjective & noun.

nebuchadnezzar /ˌnɛbjʊkədˈnɛzə/ ▶ noun a very large wine bottle, equivalent in capacity to about twenty regular bottles.
– ORIGIN early 20th cent.: from *Nebuchadnezzar* (see **NEBUCHADNEZZAR II**).

Nebuchadnezzar II (*c*.630–562 BC), king of Babylon 605–562 BC. He rebuilt the city with massive walls, a huge temple, and a ziggurat, and extended his rule over neighbouring countries. In 586 BC he captured and destroyed Jerusalem and deported many Israelites in what is known as the Babylonian Captivity.

nebula /ˈnɛbjʊlə/ ▶ noun (pl. **nebulae** /-liː/ or **nebulas**) **1** Astronomy a cloud of gas and dust in outer space, visible in the night sky either as an indistinct bright patch or as a dark silhouette against other luminous matter. ■ dated a galaxy.
2 Medicine a clouded spot on the cornea causing defective vision.
– ORIGIN mid 17th cent. (as a medical term): from Latin, literally 'mist'.

nebular ▶ adjective relating to or denoting a nebula or nebulae: *a vast nebular cloud*.

nebular theory (also **nebular hypothesis**) ▶ noun the theory that the solar and stellar systems were developed from a primeval nebula.

nebulizer /ˈnɛbjʊlʌɪzə/ (also **nebuliser**) ▶ noun a device for producing a fine spray of liquid, used for example for inhaling a medicinal drug.
– DERIVATIVES **nebulize** (also **nebulise**) verb.
– ORIGIN late 19th cent.: from Latin *nebula* 'mist' + *-izer* (see **-IZE**).

nebulous /ˈnɛbjʊləs/ ▶ adjective **1** in the form of a cloud or haze; hazy: *a giant nebulous glow*. ■ another term for **NEBULAR**.

N

2 (of a concept) vague or ill-defined: *nebulous concepts like quality of life.*
– DERIVATIVES **nebulosity** noun, **nebulously** adverb, **nebulousness** noun.
– ORIGIN late Middle English (in the sense 'cloudy'): from French *nébuleux* or Latin *nebulosus*, from *nebula* 'mist'. Sense 2 dates from the early 19th cent.

nebulous star ▸ noun Astronomy a small cluster of indistinct stars, or a star in a luminous haze.

nebuly /ˈnɛbjʊli/ ▸ adjective Heraldry divided or edged with a line formed of deeply interlocking curves.
– ORIGIN mid 16th cent.: from French *nébulé*, from medieval Latin *nebulatus* 'clouded' (the curves being thought of as representing clouds), from Latin *nebula* 'mist'.

NEC ▸ abbreviation ■ National Executive Committee. ■ (in the UK) National Exhibition Centre.

nécessaire /ˌnɛsɛˈsɛː/ ▸ noun a small ornamental case for pencils, scissors, tweezers, and other small items.
– ORIGIN early 19th cent.: French, literally 'necessary (thing)'.

necessarian /ˌnɛsɪˈsɛːrɪən/ ▸ noun & adjective another term for NECESSITARIAN.

necessarily /ˈnɛsəs(ə)rɪli, ˌnɛsəˈsɛrɪli/ ▸ adverb as a necessary result; inevitably: *the prognosis can necessarily be only an educated guess.*
– PHRASES **not necessarily** (as a response) what has been said or suggested may not be true or unavoidable.

necessary ▸ adjective **1** needed to be done, achieved, or present; essential: *they granted the necessary planning permission | it's not* ***necessary for*** *you to be here.*
2 determined, existing, or happening by natural laws or predestination; inevitable: *a necessary consequence.* ■ Philosophy (of a concept, statement, etc.) inevitably resulting from the nature of things, so that the contrary is impossible. ■ Philosophy (of an agent) having no independent volition.
▸ noun (usu. **necessaries**) the basic requirements of life, such as food and warmth. ■ (**the necessary**) informal the action or item needed: *see when they need a tactful word of advice and* ***do the necessary.*** ■ (**the necessary**) Brit. informal the money needed.
– PHRASES **a necessary evil** something that is undesirable but must be accepted.
– ORIGIN late Middle English: from Latin *necessarius*, from *necesse* 'be needful'.

necessitarian /nəˌsɛsɪˈtɛːrɪən/ ▸ noun Philosophy another term for DETERMINIST (see DETERMINISM).
– DERIVATIVES **necessitarianism** noun.

necessitate ▸ verb [with obj.] make (something) necessary as a result or consequence: *a cut which necessitated eighteen stitches.* ■ [with obj. and present participle] make it necessary for (someone) to do something: *the late arrival had necessitated her getting out of bed.*
– ORIGIN early 17th cent.: from medieval Latin *necessitat-* 'compelled', from the verb *necessitare*, based on Latin *necesse* 'be needful'.

necessitous ▸ adjective (of a person) lacking the necessities of life; needy.
– ORIGIN early 17th cent.: from French *nécessiteux*, or from NECESSITY + -OUS.

necessity ▸ noun (pl. **necessities**) **1** [mass noun] the state or fact of being required: *the* ***necessity of*** *providing parental guidance.* ■ the state of being unavoidable: *the* ***necessity of*** *growing old.* ■ a situation enforcing a certain course of action: *political necessity induced him to consider it.*
2 an indispensable thing: *a good book is a necessity when travelling.*
3 [mass noun] Philosophy the principle according to which something must be so, by virtue either of logic or of natural law. ■ [count noun] a condition that cannot be otherwise, or a statement asserting this.
– PHRASES **necessity is the mother of invention** proverb when the need for something becomes essential, you are forced to find ways of getting or achieving it. **of necessity** unavoidably.
– ORIGIN late Middle English: from Old French *necessite*, from Latin *necessitas*, from *necesse* 'be needful'.

Nechtansmere, Battle of /ˈnɛktənzˌmɪə/ a battle which took place in 685 at Nechtansmere, near Forfar, Scotland, in which the Picts defeated the Northumbrians, stopping their expansion northward and forcing their withdrawal.

neck ▸ noun **1** the part of a person's or animal's body connecting the head to the rest of the body: *she had a silver crucifix around her neck.* ■ the part of a garment that is around or close to the neck: *her dress had three buttons at the neck undone | a round neck.* ■ [mass noun] meat from an animal's neck: *neck of lamb.* ■ a person's neck regarded as bearing a burden of responsibility or guilt: *he'll be stuck with a loan around his neck.*
2 a narrow connecting or end part of something, in particular: ■ the part of a bottle or other container near the mouth. ■ a narrow piece of land or sea, such as an isthmus or channel. ■ Anatomy a narrow part near one end of an organ, such as the uterus. ■ the part of a violin, guitar, or other similar instrument that bears the fingerboard. ■ (often **volcanic neck**) Geology a column of solidified lava or igneous rock formed in a volcanic vent, especially when exposed by erosion. ■ Botany a narrow supporting part in a plant, especially the terminal part of the fruiting body in a fern, bryophyte, or fungus.
3 the length of a horse's head and neck as a measure of its lead in a race: *Dolpour won by a neck from Wood Dancer.*
▸ verb **1** [no obj.] informal (of two people) kiss and caress amorously: *we started necking on the sofa.*
2 [with obj.] Brit. informal swallow (something, especially a drink): *after necking some beers, we left the bar.*
3 [no obj.] (often **neck down**) form a narrowed part at a particular point when subjected to tension.
– PHRASES **break one's neck to do something** informal exert oneself to the utmost to achieve something. **get** (or **catch**) **it in the neck** Brit. informal be severely criticized or punished. **have the neck to do something** informal have the impudence or nerve to do something. **neck and neck** level in a race or other competition. **neck of the woods** informal a particular area: *fancy seeing her in this neck of the woods!* **up to one's neck in** informal seriously or busily involved in: *they were up to their necks in debt.*
– DERIVATIVES **necked** adjective [in combination] *an open-necked shirt | a red-necked grebe*, **necker** noun, **neckless** adjective.
– ORIGIN Old English *hnecca* 'back of the neck', of Germanic origin; related to Dutch *nek* 'neck' and German *Nacken* 'nape'.

Neckar /ˈnɛkɑː/, German /ˈnɛkar/ a river of western Germany, which rises in the Black Forest and flows 367 km (228 miles) north and west through Stuttgart to meet the Rhine at Mannheim.

neckband ▸ noun a strip of material round the neck of a garment.

neckcloth ▸ noun a cravat.

Necker /ˈnɛkə/, French /nɛkɛr/, Jacques (1732–1804), Swiss-born banker and director general of French finances (1777–81; 1788–9). In 1789 he recommended summoning the States General and was dismissed, this being one of the factors which resulted in the storming of the Bastille.

neckerchief ▸ noun a square of cloth worn round the neck.

Necker cube ▸ noun a line drawing of a transparent cube, with opposite sides drawn parallel, so that the perspective is ambiguous.
– ORIGIN early 20th cent.: named after L. A. *Necker* (1786–1861), Swiss naturalist.

necking ▸ noun Architecture a short plain concave section between the capital and the shaft of a classical Doric or Tuscan column.

necklace ▸ noun **1** an ornamental chain or string of beads, jewels, or links worn round the neck.
2 (in South Africa) a tyre doused or filled with petrol, placed round a victim's neck and set alight.
▸ verb [with obj.] (in South Africa) kill (someone) with a tyre necklace.

necklet ▸ noun a fairly close-fitting and typically rigid ornament worn around the neck.

neckline ▸ noun the edge of a woman's garment at or below the neck, used with reference to its height or shape: *a sundress with a square neckline.*

necktie ▸ noun N. Amer. or dated another term for TIE (sense 4 of the noun).

necktie party ▸ noun N. Amer. informal a lynching or hanging.

neckwear ▸ noun [mass noun] items worn around the neck, such as collars or ties, collectively.

necro- ▸ combining form relating to a corpse or death: *necromancy.*
– ORIGIN from Greek *nekros* 'corpse'.

necrobiosis /ˌnɛkrə(ʊ)bʌɪˈəʊsɪs/ ▸ noun [mass noun] Medicine gradual degeneration and death of cells in the body tissues.
– DERIVATIVES **necrobiotic** /-ˈɒtɪk/ adjective.

necrologist /nɛˈkrɒlədʒɪst/ ▸ noun the author of an obituary notice.

necrology /nɛˈkrɒlədʒi/ ▸ noun (pl. **necrologies**) formal **1** an obituary notice.
2 a list of deaths.
– DERIVATIVES **necrological** adjective.

necromancer /ˈnɛkrə(ʊ)mansə/ ▸ noun a person who practises necromancy; a wizard or magician.

necromancy /ˈnɛkrə(ʊ)mansi/ ▸ noun [mass noun] the supposed practice of communicating with the dead, especially in order to predict the future. ■ witchcraft, sorcery, or black magic in general.
– DERIVATIVES **necromantic** adjective.
– ORIGIN Middle English *nigromancie*, via Old French from medieval Latin *nigromantia*, changed (by association with Latin *niger*, *nigr-* 'black') from late Latin *necromantia*, from Greek (see NECRO-, -MANCY). The spelling was changed in the 16th cent. to conform with the late Latin form.

necrophilia /ˌnɛkrə(ʊ)ˈfɪlɪə/ ▸ noun [mass noun] sexual intercourse with or attraction towards corpses.
– DERIVATIVES **necrophile** noun, **necrophiliac** noun, **necrophilic** adjective, **necrophilism** noun.

necrophobia ▸ noun [mass noun] extreme or irrational fear of death or dead bodies.

necropolis /nɛˈkrɒpəlɪs/ ▸ noun a cemetery, especially a large one belonging to an ancient city.
– ORIGIN early 19th cent.: from Greek, from *nekros* 'dead person' + *polis* 'city'.

necropsy /ˈnɛkrɒpsi, nɛˈkrɒpsi/ ▸ noun (pl. **necropsies**) another term for AUTOPSY.

necrosis /nɛˈkrəʊsɪs/ ▸ noun [mass noun] Medicine the death of most or all of the cells in an organ or tissue due to disease, injury, or failure of the blood supply.
– DERIVATIVES **necrotic** adjective.
– ORIGIN mid 17th cent.: modern Latin, from Greek *nekrōsis* (see NECRO-, -OSIS).

necrotizing /ˈnɛkrəˌtʌɪzɪŋ/ (also **necrotising**) ▸ adjective causing or accompanied by necrosis.
– DERIVATIVES **necrotized** adjective.

necrotizing fasciitis ▸ noun [mass noun] Medicine an acute disease in which inflammation of the fasciae of muscles or other organs results in rapid destruction of overlying tissues. ● This disease is caused by the bacterium *Streptococcus pyogenes.*

nectar ▸ noun [mass noun] **1** a sugary fluid secreted within flowers to encourage pollination by insects and other animals, collected by bees to make into honey.
2 (in Greek and Roman mythology) the drink of the gods. ■ a delicious drink: *the cold pint at the pub was nectar.* ■ N. Amer. a thick fruit juice.
– DERIVATIVES **nectarean** adjective, **nectarous** adjective.
– ORIGIN mid 16th cent. (in sense 2): via Latin from Greek *nektar.*

nectariferous /ˌnɛktəˈrɪf(ə)rəs/ ▸ adjective Botany (of a flower) producing nectar.

nectarine /ˈnɛktərɪn, -iːn/ ▸ noun a peach of a variety with smooth red and yellow skin and rich, firm flesh.
– ORIGIN early 17th cent. (also used as an adjective meaning 'nectar-like'): from NECTAR + -INE[4].

nectarivorous /ˌnɛktəˈrɪv(ə)rəs/ ▸ adjective Zoology (of an animal) feeding on nectar.

nectary ▸ noun (pl. **nectaries**) Botany a nectar-secreting glandular organ in a flower (floral) or on a leaf or stem (extrafloral).
– ORIGIN mid 18th cent.: from modern Latin *nectarium*, from *nectar* (see NECTAR).

ned ▸ noun Scottish informal a hooligan or petty criminal. ■ a stupid or loutish boy or man.
– ORIGIN early 19th cent.: perhaps from *Ned* (see NEDDY).

neddy ▸ noun (pl. **neddies**) informal **1** Brit. a child's word for a donkey.
2 Austral. a horse, especially a racehorse.
– ORIGIN mid 16th cent.: diminutive of *Ned*, pet form of the given name *Edward.*

Nederland /ˈneːdərlɑnt/ Dutch name for NETHERLANDS.

Ned Kelly ▸ noun Austral. informal **1** a person of reckless courage.
2 a person who shows a lack of scruples in business.
– PHRASES **as game as Ned Kelly** audaciously bold.
– ORIGIN late 19th cent.: from the name of *Ned Kelly* (see KELLY[1]).

née /neɪ/ ▸ adjective originally called; born (used in giving a married woman's maiden name after her surname): *Mary Toogood, née Johnson.*
– ORIGIN mid 18th cent.: French, literally 'born', feminine past participle of *naître*; compare with NÉ.

N

need ▸ verb [with obj.] **1** require (something) because it is essential or very important rather than just desirable: *I need help now* | [with present participle] *this shirt needs washing* | [with infinitive] *they need to win tomorrow.* ▪ **(not need something)** not want to be subjected to something: *I don't need your sarcasm.*
2 [as modal verb] [with negative or in questions] expressing necessity or obligation: *need I say more?* | *all you need bring are sheets.*
3 [no obj.] archaic be necessary.
▸ **noun 1** [mass noun] circumstances in which something is necessary; necessity: *the basic human* ***need for*** *food* | [with infinitive] *there's no need to cry.*
2 (often **needs**) a thing that is wanted or required: *his day-to-day needs.*
3 [mass noun] the state of requiring help, or of lacking basic necessities such as food: *help us in our hour of need* | *children in need.*
– PHRASES **at need** archaic when needed; in an emergency. **had need** archaic ought to. **have need of/to do something** formal need something: *Alida had need of company.* **if need be** if necessary. **in need of** needing (something): *he was in desperate need of medical care.*
– ORIGIN Old English *nēodian* (verb), *nēod, nēd* (noun), of Germanic origin; related to Dutch *nood* and German *Not* 'danger'.

USAGE 1 In modern English, there are two quite distinct uses for the verb **need**. In the first place it is used as a normal verb meaning 'require': *I* ***need*** *some money; I* ***need*** *to see her today.* Second, it is one of a small class of verbs called *modals* (like **can, could,** and **might**, for example), which cannot stand alone without another verb and do not take normal verb endings or normal negative constructions, e.g. *he* ***need not*** *worry*, not *he* ***needs not*** *worry; he* ***can't*** *swim*, not *he* ***doesn't can*** *swim.* Because of this dual grammatical status, it is sometimes called a *semi-modal.*
2 The two constructions in *that shirt* ***needs washing*** (verb + present participle) and *that shirt* ***needs to be washed*** (verb + infinitive and past participle) have more or less the same meaning. Both these constructions are acceptable in standard English, but a third construction, *that shirt* ***needs washed*** (verb + bare past participle), is restricted to certain dialects of Scotland and North America and is not considered acceptable in standard English.

need-blind ▸ adjective US of or denoting a university admissions policy in which applicants are judged solely on their own merits, irrespective of their ability to pay for tuition.

needful ▸ adjective **1** formal necessary; requisite: *a further word was needful.*
2 dated needy: *she gave her money away to needful people.*
▸ noun (**the needful**) what is necessary: *I call upon the authorities to do the needful.*
– DERIVATIVES **needfully** adverb, **needfulness** noun.

needle ▸ noun **1** a very fine slender piece of polished metal with a point at one end and a hole or eye for thread at the other, used in sewing. ▪ a similar, larger instrument used in crafts such as crochet, knitting, and lacemaking.
2 the pointed hollow end of a hypodermic syringe. ▪ a very fine metal spike used in acupuncture.
3 a thin pointer on a dial, compass, or other instrument.
4 something likened to a needle, in particular: ▪ a stylus used to play records. ▪ an etching tool. ▪ a steel pin exploding the cartridge of a breech-loading gun.
5 the sharp, stiff, slender leaf of a fir or pine tree.
6 a pointed rock or peak. ▪ (**the Needles**) a group of rocks in the sea off the western tip of the Isle of Wight in southern England. ▪ an obelisk: *Cleopatra's Needle.*
7 [mass noun] Brit. informal hostility or antagonism provoked by rivalry: *there is already a little bit of needle between the sides.*
8 a beam used as a temporary support during underpinning.
▸ verb [with obj.] **1** prick or pierce with or as if with a needle: *dust needled his eyes.*
2 informal provoke or annoy (someone) by continual criticism or questioning: *I just said that to Charlie to needle him.*
– PHRASES **the eye of a needle** a tiny aperture through which it would seem impossible to pass (especially with reference to Matt. 19:24). **give someone the needle** informal provoke or annoy someone. **a needle in a haystack** something that is almost impossible to find because it is hidden among so many other things.
– ORIGIN Old English *nǣdl*, of Germanic origin; related to Dutch *naald* and German *Nadel*, from an Indo-European root shared by Latin *nere* 'to spin' and Greek *nēma* 'thread'.

needlecord ▸ noun [mass noun] Brit. fine-ribbed corduroy fabric.

needlecraft ▸ noun [mass noun] needlework.

needlefish ▸ noun (pl. **same** or **needlefishes**) North American term for GARFISH.

needleful ▸ noun (pl. **needlefuls**) the length of thread put into a needle at one time.

needlelace ▸ noun another term for NEEDLEPOINT (sense 2 of the noun).

needlepoint ▸ noun [mass noun] **1** closely stitched embroidery worked over canvas.
2 (also **needlepoint lace**) lace made by hand using a needle rather than bobbins.
▸ verb [with obj.] embroider in needlepoint.

needless ▸ adjective (of something undesirable) not necessary because avoidable: *I deplore needless waste.*
– PHRASES **needless to say** of course.
– DERIVATIVES **needlessly** adverb, **needlessness** noun.

needletail (also **needle-tailed swift**) ▸ noun an Asian spine-tailed swift, believed to be the world's fastest flying bird. ● Genus *Hirundapus*, family Apodidae: four species.

needle time ▸ noun [mass noun] Brit. an agreed maximum allowance of time for broadcasting recorded music.
– ORIGIN 1960s: with reference to the 'needle' in the groove of a record.

needle valve ▸ noun a valve closed by a thin tapering part.

needlewoman ▸ noun (pl. **needlewomen**) a woman or girl who has particular sewing skills or who sews for a living.

needlework ▸ noun [mass noun] the art or practice of sewing or embroidery: *I took up needlework.* ▪ sewn or embroidered items collectively: *exhibits include Eastern needlework.*
– DERIVATIVES **needleworker** noun.

needn't ▸ contraction need not.

needs ▸ adverb archaic of necessity.
– PHRASES **must needs** (or **needs must**) **do something** cannot avoid or help doing something: *they must needs depart.* **needs must** it is or was necessary or unavoidable: *if needs must, they will eat any food.* **needs must when the Devil drives** proverb sometimes you have to do something you would rather not.
– ORIGIN Old English *nēdes* (see NEED, -S[3]).

needy ▸ adjective (**needier, neediest**) **1** (of a person) lacking the necessities of life; very poor. ▪ (of circumstances) characterized by poverty: *those from needy backgrounds.*
2 (of a person) needing emotional support; insecure.
– DERIVATIVES **neediness** noun.

neem /niːm/ ▸ noun a tropical Old World tree, which yields timber resembling mahogany, oil, medicinal products, and insecticide. ● *Azadirachta indica*, family Meliaceae.
– ORIGIN early 19th cent.: via Hindi from Sanskrit *nimba.*

neep ▸ noun Scottish & N. English a turnip.
– ORIGIN Old English *nǣp*, from Latin *napus.*

ne'er /nɛː/ literary or dialect ▸ contraction never.

ne'er-do-well ▸ noun a person who is lazy and irresponsible.
▸ adjective [attrib.] lazy and irresponsible.

NEET ▸ noun (pl. **NEETs**) Brit. a young person who is no longer in the education system and who is not working or being trained for work.
– ORIGIN early 21st cent.: acronym of *not in education, employment, or training.*

nef ▸ noun an elaborate table decoration in the shape of a ship for holding such things as table napkins and condiments.
– ORIGIN mid 19th cent.: from French, literally 'ship' (see NAVE[1]).

nefarious /nɪˈfɛːrɪəs/ ▸ adjective (typically of an action or activity) wicked or criminal: *the nefarious activities of the organized-crime syndicates.*
– DERIVATIVES **nefariously** adverb, **nefariousness** noun.
– ORIGIN early 17th cent.: from Latin *nefarius*, from *nefas, nefar-* 'wrong' (from *ne-* 'not' + *fas* 'divine law') + -OUS.

Nefertiti /ˌnɛfəˈtiːti/ (also **Nofretete**) (*fl.* 14th century BC), Egyptian queen, wife of Akhenaten. She is best known from the painted limestone bust of her, now in Berlin.

neg ▸ noun informal a photographic negative.
– ORIGIN late 19th cent.: abbreviation.

neg. ▸ abbreviation negative: *HIV neg.*

nega- ▸ combining form informal denoting the negative counterpart of a unit of measurement, in particular a unit of energy saved as a result of conservation measures: *negawatts.*
– ORIGIN abbreviation of NEGATIVE.

negate /nɪˈɡeɪt/ ▸ verb [with obj.] **1** make ineffective; nullify: *alcohol negates the effects of the drug.*
2 Logic & Grammar make (a clause, sentence, or proposition) negative in meaning.
3 deny the existence of: *negating the political nature of education.*
– ORIGIN early 17th cent. (in sense 1, sense 3): from Latin *negat-* 'denied', from the verb *negare.*

negation ▸ noun [mass noun] **1** the contradiction or denial of something: *there should be confirmation—or negation—of the findings.* ▪ Grammar denial of the truth of a clause or sentence, typically involving the use of a negative word (e.g. *not, no, never*) or a word or affix with negative force (e.g. *nothing, non-*). ▪ [count noun] Logic a proposition whose assertion specifically denies the truth of another proposition: *the negation of A is, briefly, 'not A'.* ▪ Mathematics inversion.
2 the absence or opposite of something actual or positive: *evil is not merely the negation of goodness.*
– DERIVATIVES **negatory** /nɪˈɡeɪt(ə)ri, ˈnɛɡət(ə)ri/ adjective.
– ORIGIN late Middle English: from Latin *negatio(n-)*, from the verb *negare* 'deny' (see NEGATE).

negative ▸ adjective **1** consisting in or characterized by the absence rather than the presence of distinguishing features. ▪ expressing or implying denial, disagreement, or refusal: *that, I take it, was a negative answer.* ▪ (of the results of a test or experiment) indicating that a certain substance or condition is not present or does not exist: *all the patients have tested negative for TB.* ▪ [in combination] (of a person or their blood) not having a specified substance or condition: *HIV-negative.* ▪ US informal denoting a complete lack of something: *they were described as having negative vulnerability to water entry.* ▪ Grammar & Logic (of a word, clause, or proposition) stating that something is not the case; expressing negation. Contrasted with AFFIRMATIVE and INTERROGATIVE. ▪ [as exclamation] no (usually used in a military context): *'Any snags, Captain?' 'Negative, she's running like clockwork.'*
2 (of a person, attitude, or situation) not desirable or optimistic: *the new tax was having a negative effect on car sales* | *I don't want to be negative, but I don't see how we could do it.*
3 (of a quantity) less than zero. ▪ denoting decrease or reversal: *the industry suffered negative growth in the 1990s.*
4 containing, producing, or denoting the kind of electric charge carried by electrons.
5 (of a photographic image) showing light and shade or colours reversed from those of the original.
6 Astrology relating to or denoting any of the earth or water signs, considered passive in nature.
7 Brit. (in Parliament) relating to or denoting proposed legislation which will come into force after a specified period unless explicitly rejected in a parliamentary vote.
▸ **noun 1** a word or statement that expresses denial, disagreement, or refusal: *she replied* ***in the negative.*** ▪ (usu. **the negative**) a bad or unwelcome quality or aspect of a situation: *confidence will not be instilled by harping solely on the negative.* ▪ Grammar a word, affix, or phrase expressing negation. ▪ Logic another term for NEGATION.
2 a negative photographic image made on film or specially prepared glass, from which positive prints may be made.
3 a result of a test or experiment indicating that a certain substance or condition is not present or does not exist: *the percentage of false negatives generated by a cancer test was of great concern.*
4 [mass noun] the part of an electric circuit that is at a lower electrical potential than another part designated as having zero electrical potential.
5 a number less than zero.
▸ verb [with obj.] **1** refuse to accept; reject: *the bill was negatived on second reading by 130 votes to 129.* ▪ prove to be untrue: *the insurer's main arguments were negatived by Lawrence.*

2 render ineffective; neutralize: *should criminal law allow consent to negative what would otherwise be a crime?*
– DERIVATIVES **negatively** adverb, **negativeness** noun.
– ORIGIN late Middle English: from late Latin *negativus*, from *negare* 'deny' (see NEGATE).

negative equity ▸ noun [mass noun] potential indebtedness arising when the market value of a property falls below the outstanding amount of a mortgage secured on it.

negative evidence ▸ noun [mass noun] evidence for a theory provided by the non-occurrence or absence of something.

negative feedback ▸ noun [mass noun] **1** chiefly Biology the diminution or counteraction of an effect by its own influence on the process giving rise to it, as when a high level of a particular hormone in the blood may inhibit further secretion of that hormone, or where the result of a certain action may inhibit further performance of that action.
2 Electronics the return of part of an output signal to the input, which is out of phase with it, so that amplifier gain is reduced and the output is improved.

negative geotropism ▸ noun [mass noun] the tendency of plant stems and other parts to grow upwards.

negative income tax ▸ noun [mass noun] money credited as allowances to a taxed income, and paid as benefit when it exceeds debited tax.

negative pole ▸ noun the south-seeking pole of a magnet.

negative sign ▸ noun another term for MINUS SIGN.

negativism ▸ noun [mass noun] the practice of being or tendency to be negative or sceptical in attitude while failing to offer positive suggestions or views.
– DERIVATIVES **negativist** noun & adjective, **negativistic** adjective.

negativity ▸ noun [mass noun] the expression of criticism of or pessimism about something: *he was taken aback by the negativity of the press.*

negator /nɪˈɡeɪtə/ ▸ noun Grammar a word expressing negation, especially (in English) the word *not*.

negentropic /ˌnɛɡɛnˈtrɒpɪk/ ▸ adjective Physics of or characterized by a reduction in entropy (and corresponding increase in order).
– DERIVATIVES **negentropy** noun.
– ORIGIN 1950s (as *negentropy*): from NEGATIVE + *entropic* (see ENTROPY).

N

Negev /ˈnɛɡɛv/ (**the Negev**) an arid region forming most of southern Israel, between Beersheba and the Gulf of Aqaba, on the Egyptian border. Large areas are irrigated for agriculture.

neglect ▸ verb [with obj.] fail to care for properly: *the old churchyard has been sadly neglected.* ■ not pay proper attention to; disregard: *you neglect our advice at your peril.* ■ [with infinitive] fail to do something: *he neglected to write to her.*
▸ noun [mass noun] the state of being uncared for: *the place had a hopeless air of neglect.* ■ the action of not taking proper care of someone or something: *she was accused of child neglect.* ■ failure to do something: *he was reported for **neglect of** duty.*
– ORIGIN early 16th cent.: from Latin *neglect-* 'disregarded', from the verb *neglegere*, from *neg-* 'not' + *legere* 'choose, pick up'.

neglected ▸ adjective suffering a lack of proper care: *some severely neglected children.* ■ not receiving proper attention; disregarded: *a neglected area of research.*

neglectful ▸ adjective not giving proper care or attention to someone or something: *you are being **neglectful of** our guests.*
– DERIVATIVES **neglectfully** adverb, **neglectfulness** noun.

negligee /ˈnɛɡlɪʒeɪ/ (also **négligée**) ▸ noun a woman's light dressing gown, typically made of a filmy fabric.
– ORIGIN mid 18th cent. (denoting a kind of loose gown worn by women): from French, literally 'given little thought or attention', feminine past participle of *négliger* 'to neglect'.

negligence ▸ noun [mass noun] failure to take proper care over something: *his injury was due to the negligence of his employers.* ■ Law breach of a duty of care which results in damage.
– ORIGIN Middle English: via Old French from Latin *negligentia*, from the verb *negligere* (variant of *neglegere* 'disregard, slight': see NEGLECT).

negligent ▸ adjective failing to take proper care over something: *the council had been negligent in its supervision of the children in care.*
– DERIVATIVES **negligently** adverb.

negligible ▸ adjective so small or unimportant as to be not worth considering; insignificant: *he said that the risks were negligible.*
– DERIVATIVES **negligibility** /-ˈbɪlɪti/ noun, **negligibly** adverb.
– ORIGIN early 19th cent.: from obsolete French, from *négliger* 'to neglect'.

Negombo /nɪˈɡɒmbəʊ/ a port and resort on the west coast of Sri Lanka; pop. 150,400 (est. 2007).

negotiable ▸ adjective **1** open to discussion or modification: *the price was not negotiable.* ■ (of a document) able to be transferred or assigned to the legal ownership of another person.
2 (of a route) able to be traversed; passable: *walkways must be accessible and negotiable for all users.*
– DERIVATIVES **negotiability** noun.

negotiate ▸ verb [with obj.] **1** obtain or bring about by discussion: *he negotiated a new contract with the sellers.* ■ [no obj.] try to reach an agreement or compromise by discussion: *they refused to **negotiate with** the rebels.*
2 find a way over or through (an obstacle or difficult route): *she cautiously negotiated the hairpin bend.*
3 transfer (a cheque, bill, or other document) to the legal ownership of another person, who thus becomes entitled to any benefit. ■ convert (a cheque) into cash or notes.
– DERIVATIVES **negotiant** noun (archaic).
– ORIGIN early 17th cent.: from Latin *negotiat-* 'done in the course of business', from the verb *negotiari*, from *negotium* 'business', from *neg-* 'not' + *otium* 'leisure'.

negotiation ▸ noun [mass noun] **1** (also **negotiations**) discussion aimed at reaching an agreement: *a worldwide ban is currently **under negotiation** | **negotiations between** unions and employers.*
2 the action or process of transferring legal ownership of a document.
– ORIGIN late 15th cent. (denoting an act of dealing with another person): from Latin *negotiatio(n-)*, from the verb *negotiari* (see NEGOTIATE).

negotiator ▸ noun a person who conducts negotiations: *US trade negotiators | a hostage negotiator.*

Negress /ˈniːɡrɪs, -ɡrɛs/ ▸ noun a woman or girl of black African origin. See usage at NEGRO.
– ORIGIN late 18th cent.: from French *négresse*, feminine of *nègre* 'negro'.

Negrillo /nɪˈɡrɪləʊ/ ▸ noun (pl. **Negrillos**) a member of a black people of short stature native to central and southern Africa.
– ORIGIN Spanish, diminutive of *negro* 'black' (see NEGRO); compare with NEGRITO.

Negri Sembilan /ˌnɛɡriː sɛmˈbiːlən/ a state of Malaysia, on the SW coast of the Malay Peninsula; capital, Seremban.

Negrito /nɪˈɡriːtəʊ/ ▸ noun (pl. **Negritos**) a member of a black people of short stature native to the Austronesian region.
– ORIGIN Spanish, diminutive of *negro* 'black' (see NEGRO); compare with NEGRILLO.

Negritude /ˈnɛɡrɪtjuːd/ ▸ noun [mass noun] the quality or fact of being of black African origin. ■ the affirmation or consciousness of the value of black or African culture and identity: *Negritude helped to guide Senegal into independence with pride.*
– ORIGIN 1940s: from French *négritude* 'blackness'.

Negro /ˈniːɡrəʊ/ ▸ noun (pl. **Negroes**) dated, often offensive a member of a dark-skinned group of peoples originally native to Africa south of the Sahara.
▸ adjective dated, often offensive relating to black people.
– ORIGIN via Spanish and Portuguese from Latin *niger, nigr-* 'black'.

> **USAGE** The word **Negro** was adopted from Spanish and Portuguese and first recorded from the mid 16th century. It remained the standard term throughout the 17th–19th centuries and was used by prominent black American campaigners such as W. E. B. DuBois and Booker T. Washington in the early 20th century. Since the Black Power movement of the 1960s, however, when the term **black** was favoured as the term to express racial pride, **Negro** (together with related words such as **Negress**) has dropped out of favour and now seems out of date or even offensive in both British and US English.

Negroid ▸ adjective relating to the division of humankind represented by the indigenous peoples of central and southern Africa.

> **USAGE** The term **Negroid** belongs to a set of terms introduced by 19th-century anthropologists attempting to categorize human races. Such terms are associated with outdated notions of racial types, and so are now potentially offensive and best avoided. See USAGE at MONGOLOID.

negroni /nɪˈɡrəʊni/ ▸ noun a cocktail made from gin, vermouth, and Campari.
– ORIGIN Italian.

Negrophobia ▸ noun [mass noun] intense or irrational dislike or fear of black people.
– DERIVATIVES **Negrophobe** noun.

Negros /ˈneɪɡrɒs/ an island, the fourth largest of the Philippines; pop. 3,602,200 (est. 2007); chief city, Bacolod.

Negro spiritual ▸ noun see SPIRITUAL.

Negus /ˈniːɡəs/ ▸ noun historical a ruler, or the supreme ruler, of Ethiopia.
– ORIGIN from Amharic *n'gus* 'king'.

negus /ˈniːɡəs/ ▸ noun historical a hot drink of port, sugar, lemon, and spice.
– ORIGIN mid 18th cent.: named after Colonel Francis *Negus* (died 1732), who created it.

Neh. ▸ abbreviation Nehemiah (in biblical references).

Nehemiah /niəˈmʌɪə/ (5th century BC) a Hebrew leader who supervised the rebuilding of the walls of Jerusalem (*c.*444 BC) and introduced moral and religious reforms (*c.*432 BC). ■ a book of the Bible telling of Nehemiah.

Nehru /ˈnɛːruː/, Jawaharlal (1889–1964), Indian statesman, Prime Minister 1947–64; known as **Pandit Nehru**. Nehru was elected leader of the Indian National Congress in 1929. He was imprisoned nine times by the British for his nationalist campaigns, but went on to become the first Prime Minister of independent India.

neigh /neɪ/ ▸ noun a characteristic high whinnying sound made by a horse.
▸ verb [no obj.] (of a horse) utter a neigh. ■ (of a person) make a sound similar to a neigh, especially when laughing: *they neighed dutifully at jokes they did not understand.*
– ORIGIN Old English *hnǣgan* (verb), of imitative origin; compare with Dutch dialect *neijen*.

neighbour (US **neighbor**) ▸ noun a person living next door to or very near to the speaker or person referred to: *our garden was the envy of the neighbours.* ■ a person or place in relation to others next or near to it: *I chatted with my neighbour on the flight to New York | matching our investment levels with those of our European neighbours.* ■ any person in need of one's help or kindness (after biblical use): *love thy neighbour as thyself.*
▸ verb [with obj.] (of a place or object) be situated next to or very near (another): *the square neighbours the old quarter of the town.*
– DERIVATIVES **neighbourless** adjective.
– ORIGIN Old English *nēahgebūr*, from *nēah* 'nigh, near' + *gebūr* 'inhabitant, peasant, farmer' (compare with BOOR).

neighbourhood (US **neighborhood**) ▸ noun **1** a district or community within a town or city: *she lived in a wealthy neighbourhood of Boston.* ■ the area surrounding a particular place, person, or object: *he was reluctant to leave the neighbourhood of London.* ■ [mass noun] neighbourly feeling or conduct: *the importance of neighbourhood to old people.*
2 Mathematics the set of points whose distance from a given point is less than (or less than or equal to) some value.
– PHRASES **in the neighbourhood of** approximately; about: *the cost would be in the neighbourhood of three billion dollars.*

neighbourhood watch ▸ noun a scheme of systematic local vigilance by householders to discourage crime, especially burglary.

neighbouring (US **neighboring**) ▸ adjective next to or very near another place; adjacent: *neighbouring countries | the neighbouring village.*

neighbourly (US **neighborly**) ▸ adjective characteristic of a good neighbour, especially in being helpful, friendly, or kind.
– DERIVATIVES **neighbourliness** noun.

Neisse /ˈnʌɪsə/ **1** a river in central Europe, which rises in the north of the Czech Republic and flows over 225 km (140 miles) generally northwards, forming the southern part of the border between

Germany and Poland (the Oder–Neisse Line) and joining the River Oder north-east of Cottbus. German name **Lausitzer Neisse**; Polish name **Nysa**.
2 a river of southern Poland, which rises near the border with the Czech Republic and flows 195 km (120 miles) generally north-eastwards, through the town of Nysa, joining the River Oder south-east of Wrocław. German name **Glatzer Neisse**.

neither /ˈnʌɪðə, ˈniː-/ ▶ **determiner & pronoun** not the one nor the other of two people or things; not either: [as determiner] *neither side of the brain is dominant over the other* | [as pronoun] *neither of us believes it*.
▶ **adverb 1** used before the first of two (or occasionally more) alternatives (the others being introduced by 'nor') to indicate that they are each untrue or each does not happen: *I am neither a liberal nor a conservative*.
2 used to introduce a further negative statement: *he didn't remember, and neither did I*.
– PHRASES **neither here nor there** see **here**. **neither one thing nor the other** not clearly either of two things: *Sam stands on the cusp, neither one thing nor the other*.
– ORIGIN Middle English: alteration (by association with **either**) of Old English *nawther*, contraction of *nāhwæther* (from *nā* 'no' + *hwæther* 'whether').

> **USAGE 1** The use of **neither** with another negative, as in *I* ***don't*** *like him* ***neither*** *or he's* ***not*** *much good at reading* ***neither*** is recorded from the 16th century onwards, but is not good English. This is because it is an example of a **double negative**, which, though standard in some other languages such as Spanish and found in many dialects of English, is not acceptable in standard English. In the sentences above, **either** should be used instead. For more information, see **usage** at **double negative**.
> **2** When **neither** is followed by **nor**, it is important in good English style that the two halves of the structure mirror each other: *she saw herself as* ***neither*** *wife* ***nor*** *mother* rather than *she* ***neither*** *saw herself as wife* ***nor*** *mother*. For more details, see **usage** at **either**.

Nejd /nɛdʒd/ an arid plateau region in central Saudi Arabia, north of the Rub' al-Khali desert, at an altitude of about 1,500 m (5,000 ft).

nek /nɛk/ ▶ **noun** S. African a mountain col.
– ORIGIN South African Dutch, literally 'neck'.

nekton /ˈnɛkt(ə)n, -tɒn/ ▶ **noun** [mass noun] Zoology aquatic animals that are able to swim and move independently of water currents. Often contrasted with **plankton**.
– DERIVATIVES **nektonic** adjective.
– ORIGIN late 19th cent.: via German from Greek *nēkton*, neuter of *nēktos* 'swimming', from *nēkhein* 'to swim'.

Nellore /nɛˈlɔː/ a city and river port in SE India, in Andhra Pradesh, on the River Penner; pop. 427,400 (est. 2009). Situated close to the mouth of the river, it is one of the chief ports of the Coromandel Coast.

nelly ▶ **noun** (pl. **nellies**) informal **1** a silly person.
2 derogatory an effeminate homosexual man.
– PHRASES **not on your nelly** Brit. certainly not. [originally as *not on your Nelly Duff*, rhyming slang for 'puff' (i.e. breath of life); modelled on the phrase *not on your life*.]
– ORIGIN 1930s: from the given name *Nelly*.

Nelson[1] a port in New Zealand, on the north coast of the South Island; pop. 42,888 (2006). It was founded in 1841 by the New Zealand Company and named after the British admiral Lord Nelson.

Nelson[2], Horatio, Viscount Nelson, Duke of Bronte (1758–1805), British admiral. Nelson became a national hero as a result of his victories at sea in the Napoleonic Wars, especially the Battle of Trafalgar, in which he was mortally wounded.

nelson ▶ **noun** a wrestling hold in which one arm is passed under the opponent's arm from behind and the hand is applied to the neck (**half nelson**), or both arms and hands are applied (**full nelson**).
– ORIGIN late 19th cent.: apparently from the surname *Nelson*, but the reference is unknown.

Nelson's Column a memorial to Lord Nelson in Trafalgar Square, London, consisting of a column 58 metres (170 feet) high surmounted by his statue.

Nelson touch ▶ **noun** (**the Nelson touch**) Brit. a masterly or sympathetic approach to a problem.
– ORIGIN early 19th cent.: with allusion to the skills of Admiral Horatio **Nelson**[2].

Nelspruit /ˈnɛlsprɔɪt/ a town in eastern South Africa, the capital of the province of Mpumalanga, situated on the Crocodile River to the west of Kruger National Park.

Neman /ˈnɛmən/ a river of eastern Europe, which rises south of Minsk in Belarus and flows 955 km (597 miles) west and north to the Baltic Sea. Its lower course, which forms the boundary between Lithuania and the Russian enclave of Kaliningrad, is called the Memel. Lithuanian name **Nemunas**; Belorussian name **Nyoman**.

nematic /nɪˈmatɪk/ ▶ **adjective** relating to or denoting a state of a liquid crystal in which the molecules are oriented in parallel but not arranged in well-defined planes. Compare with **smectic**.
▶ **noun** a nematic substance.
– ORIGIN early 20th cent.: from Greek *nēma*, *nēmat-* 'thread' + **-ic**.

nemato- /nɪˈmatəʊ, ˈnɛmətəʊ/ (also **nemat-** before a vowel) ▶ **combining form** denoting something thread-like in shape: *nematocyst*. ■ relating to Nematoda: *nematocide*.
– ORIGIN from Greek *nēma*, *nēmat-* 'thread'.

nematocide /nɪˈmatə(ʊ)sʌɪd, ˈnɛmətə(ʊ)-/ (also **nematicide** /nɪˈmatɪ-, ˈnɛmətɪ-/) ▶ **noun** a substance used to kill nematode worms.
– DERIVATIVES **nematocidal** adjective.

nematocyst /nɪˈmatə(ʊ)sɪst, ˈnɛmət-/ ▶ **noun** Zoology a specialized cell in the tentacles of a jellyfish or other coelenterate, containing a barbed or venomous coiled thread that can be projected in self-defence or to capture prey.

Nematoda /ˌnɛməˈtəʊdə/ ▶ **plural noun** Zoology a large phylum of worms with slender, unsegmented, cylindrical bodies, including the roundworms, threadworms, and eelworms. They are found abundantly in soil and water, and many are parasites.
– ORIGIN modern Latin (plural), from Greek *nēma*, *nēmat-* 'thread'.

nematode /ˈnɛmətəʊd/ ▶ **noun** Zoology a worm of the large phylum Nematoda, such as a roundworm or threadworm.

nematology /ˌnɛməˈtɒlədʒi/ ▶ **noun** [mass noun] the scientific study of nematode worms.
– DERIVATIVES **nematologist** noun.

Nematomorpha /nɛˌmatəˈmɔːfə/ ▶ **plural noun** Zoology a small phylum that comprises the horsehair worms.
– DERIVATIVES **nematomorph** noun.
– ORIGIN modern Latin (plural), from Greek *nēma*, *nēmat-* 'thread' + *morphē* 'form'.

Nembutal /ˈnɛmbjʊt(ə)l, -taːl/ ▶ **noun** (trademark in the US) the drug sodium pentobarbitone (see **pentobarbitone**).
– ORIGIN 1930s: from *N(a)* (symbol for sodium) + *e(thyl)*, *m(ethyl)*, *but(yl)*, elements of the systematic name, + **-al**.

nem. con. ▶ **adverb** with no one dissenting; unanimously: *the motions were carried nem. con.*
– ORIGIN from Latin *nemine contradicente*.

Nemertea /ˌnɛməˈtiːə, nɪˈməːtɪə/ ▶ **plural noun** Zoology a small phylum that comprises the ribbon worms.
ORIGIN modern Latin (plural), from Greek *Nēmertēs*, the name of a sea nymph.

nemertean (also **nemertine** /ˈnɛmətiːn, ˈnɛmətʌɪn/) Zoology ▶ **noun** a member of the small phylum Nemertea; a ribbon worm.
▶ **adjective** relating to or denoting nemerteans.

nemesia /nɪˈmiːʒə/ ▶ **noun** a plant related to the snapdragon, which is cultivated for its colourful funnel-shaped flowers. ● Genus *Nemesia*, family Scrophulariaceae: several species, in particular *N. strumosa* and its hybrids.
– ORIGIN modern Latin, from Greek *nemesion*, denoting various similar plants.

Nemesis /ˈnɛmɪsɪs/ Greek Mythology a goddess usually portrayed as the agent of divine punishment for wrongdoing or presumption (hubris).

nemesis /ˈnɛmɪsɪs/ ▶ **noun** (pl. **nemeses** /-siːz/) the inescapable agent of someone's or something's downfall: *injury, consistently his nemesis, struck him down during the match*. ■ a long-standing rival; an arch-enemy: *will Harry Potter finally defeat his nemesis, Voldemort?* ■ [mass noun] a downfall caused by an inescapable agent: *one risks nemesis by uttering such words*. ■ (often **Nemesis**) [mass noun] retributive justice: *Nemesis is notoriously slow*.
– ORIGIN late 16th cent.: Greek, literally 'retribution', from *nemein* 'give what is due'.

nemo dat /ˌniːməʊ ˈdat, ˈnɛməʊ/ (in full **nemo dat quod non habet**) ▶ **noun** Law the basic principle that a person who does not own property, especially a thief, cannot confer it on another except with the true owner's authority.
– ORIGIN Latin, literally 'no one gives (what he or she does not have)'.

Nemunas /ˈnjamʊnəs/ Lithuanian name for **Neman**.

nene /ˈneɪneɪ/ (also **ne-ne**) ▶ **noun** (pl. **same** or **nenes**) another term for **Hawaiian goose**.
– ORIGIN early 20th cent.: from Hawaiian.

Nenets /ˈnɛnɛts/ ▶ **noun** (pl. **same** or **Nentsy** or **Nentsi**) **1** a member of a nomadic people of Siberia, whose main traditional occupation is reindeer herding.
2 [mass noun] the language of the Nenets, the most widely used of the Samoyedic languages, with about 27,000 speakers.
– ORIGIN the name in Russian.

Nennius /ˈnɛnɪəs/ (*fl.* c.800), Welsh chronicler. He is traditionally credited with the compilation or revision of the *Historia Britonum*, which includes one of the earliest known accounts of King Arthur.

neo- /ˈniːəʊ/ ▶ **combining form 1** new: *neonate*.
2 a new or revived form of: *neo-Georgian*.
– ORIGIN from Greek *neos* 'new'.

neoclassical (also **neoclassic**) ▶ **adjective** relating to neoclassicism.

neoclassicism ▶ **noun** [mass noun] the revival of a classical style or treatment in art, literature, architecture, or music.

> As an aesthetic and artistic style neoclassicism originated in Rome in the mid 18th century, combining a reaction against the late baroque and rococo with a new interest in antiquity. In music, the term refers to a return by composers of the early 20th century to the forms and styles of the 17th and 18th centuries, as a reaction against 19th-century romanticism.

– DERIVATIVES **neoclassicist** noun & adjective.

neocolonialism ▶ **noun** [mass noun] the use of economic, political, cultural, or other pressures to control or influence other countries, especially former dependencies.
– DERIVATIVES **neocolonial** adjective, **neocolonialist** noun & adjective.

neocon chiefly N. Amer. ▶ **noun** (in politics) a person with neoconservative views.
▶ **adjective** neoconservative.

neo-Confucianism ▶ **noun** [mass noun] a movement in religious philosophy derived from Confucianism in China around AD 1000 in response to the ideas of Taoism and Buddhism.
– DERIVATIVES **neo-Confucian** adjective & noun.

neoconservative ▶ **adjective** relating to or denoting a return to a modified form of a traditional viewpoint, in particular a political ideology characterized by an emphasis on free-market capitalism and an interventionist foreign policy.
▶ **noun** a person with neoconservative views.
– DERIVATIVES **neoconservatism** noun.

neocortex ▶ **noun** (pl. **neocortices**) Anatomy a part of the cerebral cortex concerned with sight and hearing in mammals, regarded as the most recently evolved part of the cortex.
– DERIVATIVES **neocortical** adjective.

neo-Darwinian ▶ **adjective** relating to the modern version of Darwin's theory of evolution by natural selection, incorporating the findings of genetics.
– DERIVATIVES **neo-Darwinism** noun, **neo-Darwinist** noun & adjective.

neodymium /ˌniːə(ʊ)ˈdɪmɪəm/ ▶ **noun** [mass noun] the chemical element of atomic number 60, a silvery-white metal of the lanthanide series. Neodymium is a component of misch metal and some other alloys, and its compounds are used in colouring glass and ceramics. (Symbol: **Nd**)
– ORIGIN late 19th cent.: from **neo-** 'new' + a shortened form of **didymium**.

neo-fascist ▶ **noun** a member of an organization similar to the Italian Fascist movement of the early 20th century.
▶ **adjective** relating to neo-fascists or neo-fascism.
– DERIVATIVES **neo-fascism** noun.

Neogaea /ˌniːə(ʊ)ˈdʒiːə/ (US **Neogea**) Zoology a zoogeographical area comprising the Neotropical region.
– DERIVATIVES **Neogaean** adjective.
– ORIGIN modern Latin, from Greek *neos* 'new' + *gaia* 'earth'.

Neogene /ˈniːə(ʊ)dʒiːn/ ▶ **adjective** Geology relating to or denoting the later division of the Tertiary period, comprising the Miocene and Pliocene epochs. ■ (as noun **the Neogene**) the Neogene sub-period or the system of rocks deposited during it.

> The Neogene lasted from about 23 to 1.6 million years ago, during which time the mammals continued to evolve

> and eventually developed into the forms that are familiar today.

– ORIGIN late 19th cent.: from **NEO-** 'new' + Greek *-genēs* 'born, of a specified kind' (see **-GEN**).

neo-Georgian ▶ adjective relating to or imitative of a revival of a Georgian style in architecture.

neo-Gothic ▶ adjective of or in a style of art and architecture that originated in the 19th century, characterized by the revival of medieval Gothic forms. In architecture it is manifested in pointed arches, vaulted ceilings, and mock fortifications.
▶ noun [mass noun] the neo-Gothic style.

Neogrammarian /ˌniːə(ʊ)ɡrəˈmɛːrɪən/ ▶ noun a member of a group of 19th-century German scholars who, having noticed that sound changes in language are regular and that therefore lost word forms can be reconstructed, postulated the forms of entire lost languages such as Proto-Indo-European by the comparison of related forms in existing languages.
– ORIGIN translation of German *Junggrammatiker*.

neo-Impressionism ▶ noun [mass noun] a late 19th-century movement in French painting which sought to improve on Impressionism through a systematic approach to form and colour, particularly using pointillist technique. The movement's leading figures included Georges Seurat, Paul Signac, and Camille Pissarro.
– DERIVATIVES **neo-Impressionist** adjective & noun.

neo-Latin ▶ noun [mass noun] the Romance languages.

neo-liberal ▶ adjective relating to or denoting a modified form of liberalism tending to favour free-market capitalism.
▶ noun a person with neo-liberal views.
– DERIVATIVES **neo-liberalism** noun.

Neolithic /ˌniːə(ʊ)ˈlɪθɪk/ ▶ adjective Archaeology relating to or denoting the later part of the Stone Age, when ground or polished stone weapons and implements prevailed. ■ (as noun **the Neolithic**) the Neolithic period. Also called **NEW STONE AGE**.

> In the Neolithic period farm animals were first domesticated and agriculture was introduced: it began in the Near East by the 8th millennium BC and spread to northern Europe by the 4th millennium BC. Neolithic societies in NW Europe left such monuments as causewayed camps, henges, long barrows, and chambered tombs.

N

– ORIGIN mid 19th cent.: from **NEO-** 'new' + Greek *lithos* 'stone' + **-IC**.

neologism /nɪˈɒlədʒɪz(ə)m/ ▶ noun a newly coined word or expression. ■ [mass noun] the coining or use of new words.
– DERIVATIVES **neologist** noun, **neologize** (also **neologise**) verb.
– ORIGIN early 19th cent.: from French *néologisme*.

neo-Malthusianism /ˌniːəʊmalˈθjuːzɪənɪz(ə)m/ ▶ noun [mass noun] the view that the rate of increase of a population should be controlled.
– DERIVATIVES **neo-Malthusian** adjective & noun.

neo-Marxist ▶ adjective relating to forms of political philosophy which arise from the adaptation of Marxist thought to accommodate or confront modern issues such as the global economy, the capitalist welfare state, and the stability of liberal democracies.
▶ noun a person with neo-Marxist views.
– DERIVATIVES **neo-Marxism** noun.

Neo-Melanesian ▶ noun another term for **TOK PISIN**.

neomycin /ˌniːə(ʊ)ˈmʌɪsɪn/ ▶ noun [mass noun] Medicine an antibiotic related to streptomycin, active against a wide variety of bacterial infections. ● This antibiotic is obtained from the bacterium *Streptomyces fradiae*.

neon /ˈniːɒn/ ▶ noun [mass noun] the chemical element of atomic number 10, an inert gaseous element of the noble gas group. It is obtained by the distillation of liquid air and is used in fluorescent lamps and illuminated advertising signs. (Symbol: **Ne**) ■ fluorescent lighting or signs using neon or another gas: *the lobby of the hotel was bright with neon.* ■ [count noun] a small lamp containing neon. ■ [as modifier] very bright or fluorescent in colour: *she had recently dyed her hair neon pink.*
– ORIGIN late 19th cent.: from Greek, literally 'something new', neuter of the adjective *neos*.

neonatal /ˌniːə(ʊ)ˈneɪt(ə)l/ ▶ adjective relating to newborn children (or other mammals).
– DERIVATIVES **neonatally** adverb, **neonatologist** noun, **neonatology** noun.

neonate /ˈniːə(ʊ)neɪt/ ▶ noun a newborn child (or other mammal). ■ Medicine an infant less than four weeks old.
– ORIGIN 1930s: from modern Latin *neonatus*, from Greek *neos* 'new' + Latin *nat-* 'born' (from the verb *nasci*).

neo-Nazi ▶ noun (pl. **neo-Nazis**) a member of an organization similar to the German Nazi Party. ■ a person of extreme racist or nationalist views.
▶ adjective relating to neo-Nazis or neo-Nazism.
– DERIVATIVES **neo-Nazism** noun.

neon tetra ▶ noun a small Amazonian characin (fish) with a shining blue-green stripe along each side and a red band near the tail, popular in aquaria. ● *Paracheirodon innesi*, family Characidae.

neontology /ˌniːɒnˈtɒlədʒi/ ▶ noun [mass noun] the branch of zoology dealing with living forms as distinct from fossils. Often contrasted with **PALAEONTOLOGY**.
– DERIVATIVES **neontological** adjective.
– ORIGIN late 19th cent.: from **NEO-** 'new', on the pattern of *palaeontology*.

neopaganism ▶ noun [mass noun] a modern religious movement which seeks to incorporate beliefs or ritual practices from traditions outside the main world religions, especially those of pre-Christian Europe and North America.
– DERIVATIVES **neopagan** noun & adjective.

neophobia ▶ noun [mass noun] extreme or irrational fear or dislike of anything new or unfamiliar.
– DERIVATIVES **neophobic** adjective.

neophyte /ˈniːə(ʊ)fʌɪt/ ▶ noun **1** a person who is new to a subject or activity.
2 a new convert to a religion. ■ a novice in a religious order, or a newly ordained priest.
– ORIGIN late Middle English: via ecclesiastical Latin from Greek *neophutos*, literally 'newly planted' but first used in the sense 'new convert' by St Paul (1 Tim. 3:6), from *neos* 'new' + *phuton* 'plant'.

neoplasia /ˌniːə(ʊ)ˈpleɪzɪə/ ▶ noun [mass noun] Medicine the presence or formation of new, abnormal growth of tissue.
– ORIGIN late 19th cent.: from **NEO-** + Greek *plasis* 'formation'.

neoplasm ▶ noun a new and abnormal growth of tissue in a part of the body, especially as a characteristic of cancer.
– ORIGIN mid 19th cent.: from **NEO-** 'new' + Greek *plasma* 'formation' (see **PLASMA**).

neoplastic[1] ▶ adjective Medicine relating to a neoplasm or neoplasia.

neoplastic[2] ▶ adjective Art relating to neoplasticism.

neoplasticism ▶ noun [mass noun] a style of abstract painting developed by Piet Mondrian, using only vertical and horizontal lines and rectangular shapes in black, white, grey, and primary colours.
– ORIGIN 1920s: coined by Piet Mondrian.

Neoplatonism /ˌniːəʊˈpleɪt(ə)nɪz(ə)m/ ▶ noun [mass noun] a philosophical and religious system developed by the followers of Plotinus in the 3rd century AD.

> Neoplatonism combined ideas from Plato, Aristotle, Pythagoras, and the Stoics with oriental mysticism. Predominant in pagan Europe until the early 6th century, it was a major influence on early Christian writers, on later medieval and Renaissance thought, and on Islamic philosophy. It envisages the human soul rising above the imperfect material world through virtue and contemplation towards knowledge of the transcendent One.

– DERIVATIVES **Neoplatonic** adjective, **Neoplatonist** noun & adjective.

neoprene /ˈniːə(ʊ)priːn/ ▶ noun [mass noun] a synthetic polymer resembling rubber, resistant to oil, heat, and weathering.
– ORIGIN 1930s: from **NEO-** 'new' + *prene* (perhaps from **PROPYL** + **-ENE**), on the pattern of words such as *chloroprene*.

Neoptolemus /ˌniːɒpˈtɒlɪməs/ Greek Mythology the son of Achilles and killer of Priam after the fall of Troy.

neo-realism ▶ noun [mass noun] a movement or school in art or philosophy representing a modified form of realism. ■ a naturalistic movement in Italian literature and cinema that emerged in the 1940s. Important exponents include the writer Italo Calvino and the film director Federico Fellini.
– DERIVATIVES **neo-realist** noun & adjective.

neostigmine /ˌniːə(ʊ)ˈstɪɡmiːn/ ▶ noun [mass noun] Medicine a synthetic compound with the property of inhibiting cholinesterase, used to treat ileus, glaucoma, and myasthenia gravis.
– ORIGIN 1940s: from **NEO-** 'new', on the pattern of *physostigmine*.

neoteny /niːˈɒt(ə)ni/ ▶ noun [mass noun] Zoology the retention of juvenile features in the adult animal. Also called **PAEDOMORPHOSIS**. ■ the sexual maturity of an animal while it is still in a mainly larval state, as in the axolotl. Also called **PAEDOGENESIS**.
– DERIVATIVES **neotenic** adjective, **neotenous** adjective.
– ORIGIN late 19th cent.: from German *Neotenie*, from Greek *neos* 'new' (in the sense 'juvenile') + *teinein* 'extend'.

neoteric /ˌniːə(ʊ)ˈtɛrɪk/ ▶ adjective formal belonging to recent times; recent. ■ new or modern: *another effort by the White House to display its neoteric wizardry went awry.*
▶ noun a modern person; a person who advocates new ideas.
– ORIGIN late 16th cent.: via late Latin from Greek *neōterikos*, from *neōteros* 'newer', comparative of *neos*.

Neotropical ▶ adjective Zoology relating to or denoting a zoogeographical region comprising Central and South America, including the tropical southern part of Mexico and the Caribbean. Distinctive animals include edentates, opossums, marmosets, and tamarins. Compare with **NEOGAEA**. ■ Botany relating to or denoting a phytogeographical kingdom comprising Central and South America but excluding the southern parts of Chile and Argentina.
– DERIVATIVES **neotropics** plural noun.

NEPAD ▶ abbreviation New Partnership for Africa's Development, a development programme initiated by the African Union.

Nepal /nɪˈpɔːl/ a mountainous landlocked country in southern Asia, in the Himalayas (and including Mount Everest); pop. 28,563,400 (est. 2009); official language, Nepali; capital, Kathmandu.

> The country was conquered by the Gurkhas in the 18th century and has maintained its independence despite border defeats by the British in the 19th century. Nepal was for a long time an absolute monarchy, but in 1990 democratic elections were held under a new constitution. In 2001 the Crown Prince killed ten members of the royal family and took his own life.

– DERIVATIVES **Nepalese** adjective & noun.

Nepali /nɪˈpɔːli/ ▶ noun (pl. **same** or **Nepalis**) a native or inhabitant of Nepal. ■ [mass noun] the official language of Nepal, a member of the Indic branch of the Indo-European language family. It is also used in Sikkim and has about 8 million speakers in total. Also called **GURKHALI**.
▶ adjective relating to Nepal or its language or people.

nepenthes /nɪˈpɛnθiːz/ ▶ noun **1** (also **nepenthe**) [mass noun] literary a drug described in Homer's *Odyssey* as banishing grief or trouble from a person's mind. ■ a drug or potion bringing welcome forgetfulness.
2 a plant of a genus that comprises the Old World pitcher plants. ● Genus *Nepenthes* and family Nepenthaceae.
– ORIGIN via Latin from Greek *nēpenthēs* 'dispelling pain', from *nē-* 'not' + *penthos* 'grief'; sense 2 is from modern Latin.

neper /ˈniːpə, ˈneɪ-/ ▶ noun Physics a unit of measurement used in comparing voltages, currents, and power levels, especially in communication circuits. The difference between two values in nepers is equal to the natural logarithm of their ratio for voltages and currents or to half of this for power differences.
– ORIGIN early 20th cent.: from *Neperus*, Latinized form of *Napier* (see **NAPIER**[2]).

nepeta /nɪˈpiːtə/ ▶ noun a plant of a genus that includes catmint and several kinds cultivated for their spikes of blue or violet flowers. ● Genus *Nepeta*, family Labiatae.
– ORIGIN modern Latin, from Latin *nepeta* 'calamint' (formerly in this genus).

nepheline /ˈnɛf(ə)lɪn/ ▶ noun [mass noun] a colourless, greenish, or brownish mineral consisting of an aluminosilicate of sodium (often with potassium) and occurring as crystals and grains in igneous rocks.
– ORIGIN early 19th cent.: from French *néphéline*, from Greek *nephelē* 'cloud' (because its fragments are made cloudy on immersion in nitric acid) + **-INE**[2].

nepheline-syenite ▶ noun [mass noun] Geology a plutonic rock resembling syenite but containing nepheline and lacking quartz.

nephelinite /ˈnɛf(ə)lɪnʌɪt/ ▶ noun [mass noun] Geology a fine-grained basaltic rock containing nepheline in place of plagioclase feldspar.

nephelometer /ˌnɛfəˈlɒmɪtə/ ▶ noun an instrument for measuring the size and concentration of particles

suspended in a liquid or gas, especially by means of the light they scatter.
– ORIGIN late 19th cent.: from Greek *nephelē* 'cloud' + **-METER.**

nephew ▶ **noun** a son of one's brother or sister, or of one's brother-in-law or sister-in-law.
– ORIGIN Middle English: from Old French *neveu*, from Latin *nepos* 'grandson, nephew', from an Indo-European root shared by Dutch *neef* and German *Neffe*.

nephology /nɪˈfɒlədʒi/ ▶ **noun** [mass noun] rare the study or contemplation of clouds.
– ORIGIN late 19th cent.: from Greek *nephos* 'cloud' + **-LOGY.**

nephr- /nɪfr/ ▶ **combining form** variant spelling of **NEPHRO-** shortened before a vowel (as in *nephrectomy*).

nephrectomy /nɪˈfrɛktəmi/ ▶ **noun** (pl. **nephrectomies**) surgical removal of one or both of the kidneys.

nephridiopore /nɪˈfrɪdɪəpɔː/ ▶ **noun** Zoology the external opening of a nephridium.

nephridium /nɪˈfrɪdɪəm/ ▶ **noun** (pl. **nephridia**) Zoology (in many invertebrate animals) a tubule open to the exterior which acts as an organ of excretion or osmoregulation. It typically has ciliated or flagellated cells and absorptive walls.
– DERIVATIVES **nephridial** adjective.
– ORIGIN late 19th cent.: modern Latin, from Greek *nephrion* (diminutive of *nephros* 'kidney') + the diminutive ending *-idium*.

nephrite /ˈnɛfrʌɪt/ ▶ **noun** [mass noun] a hard, pale green or white mineral which is one of the forms of jade. It is a silicate of calcium and magnesium.
– ORIGIN late 18th cent.: from German *Nephrit*, from Greek *nephros* 'kidney' (with reference to its supposed efficacy in treating kidney disease).

nephritic /nɪˈfrɪtɪk/ ▶ **adjective** of or in the kidneys; renal. ■ relating to nephritis.
– ORIGIN early 19th cent.: via late Latin from Greek *nephritikos* 'of the kidneys' (see **NEPHRITIS**).

nephritis /nɪˈfrʌɪtɪs/ ▶ **noun** [mass noun] Medicine inflammation of the kidneys. Also called **BRIGHT'S DISEASE.**
– ORIGIN late 16th cent.: via late Latin from Greek, from *nephros* 'kidney'.

nephro- (also **nephr-** before a vowel) ▶ **combining form** of a kidney; relating to the kidneys: *nephrotoxic*.
– ORIGIN from Greek *nephros* 'kidney'.

nephrology /nɛˈfrɒlədʒi/ ▶ **noun** [mass noun] the branch of medicine that deals with the physiology and diseases of the kidneys.
– DERIVATIVES **nephrological** adjective, **nephrologist** noun.

nephron /ˈnɛfrɒn/ ▶ **noun** Anatomy each of the functional units in the kidney, consisting of a glomerulus and its associated tubule, through which the glomerular filtrate passes before emerging as urine.
– ORIGIN 1930s: via German from Greek *nephros* 'kidney'.

nephrosis /nɪˈfrəʊsɪs/ ▶ **noun** [mass noun] kidney disease, especially when characterized by oedema and the loss of protein from the plasma into the urine due to increased glomerular permeability (also called **nephrotic syndrome**).
– DERIVATIVES **nephrotic** adjective.

nephrotoxic /ˌnɛfrə(ʊ)ˈtɒksɪk/ ▶ **adjective** damaging or destructive to the kidneys.
– DERIVATIVES **nephrotoxicity** noun, **nephrotoxin** noun.

ne plus ultra /ˌneɪ plʊs ˈʊltrɑː/ ▶ **noun** (**the ne plus ultra**) the perfect or most extreme example of its kind; the ultimate: *he became the ne plus ultra of bebop trombonists*.
– ORIGIN Latin, literally 'not further beyond', the supposed inscription on the Pillars of Hercules prohibiting passage by ships.

nepotism /ˈnɛpətɪz(ə)m/ ▶ **noun** [mass noun] the practice among those with power or influence of favouring relatives or friends, especially by giving them jobs.
– DERIVATIVES **nepotist** noun, **nepotistic** adjective.
– ORIGIN mid 17th cent.: from French *népotisme*, from Italian *nepotismo*, from *nipote* 'nephew' (with reference to privileges bestowed on the 'nephews' of popes, who were in many cases their illegitimate sons).

Neptune 1 Roman Mythology the god of water and of the sea. Greek equivalent **POSEIDON.**
2 Astronomy a distant planet of the solar system, eighth in order from the sun, discovered in 1846.

> Neptune orbits between Uranus and Pluto at an average distance of 4,497 million km from the sun. It is the fourth-largest planet, with an equatorial diameter of 49,500 km, and the most remote of the gas giants. The planet is predominantly blue, with an upper atmosphere mainly of hydrogen and helium with some methane. There are at least eight satellites, the largest of which is Triton, and a faint ring system.

Neptunian ▶ **adjective 1** relating to the Roman sea god Neptune or to the sea.
2 relating to the planet Neptune.
3 Geology, historical advocating Neptunism.

neptunian dyke ▶ **noun** Geology a deposit of sand cutting through sedimentary strata in the manner of an igneous dyke, formed by the filling of an underwater fissure.

Neptunism ▶ **noun** [mass noun] Geology, historical the erroneous theory that rocks such as granite were formed by crystallization from the waters of a primeval ocean. The chief advocate of this theory was Abraham Gottlob Werner. Compare with **PLUTONISM.**
– DERIVATIVES **Neptunist** noun & adjective.

neptunium /nɛpˈtjuːnɪəm/ ▶ **noun** [mass noun] the chemical element of atomic number 93, a radioactive metal of the actinide series. Neptunium was discovered as a product of the bombardment of uranium with neutrons, and occurs only in trace amounts in nature. (Symbol: **Np**)
– ORIGIN late 19th cent.: from **NEPTUNE**, on the pattern of *uranium* (Neptune being the next planet beyond Uranus)

NERC ▶ **abbreviation** (in the UK) Natural Environment Research Council.

nerd (also **nurd**) ▶ **noun** informal a foolish or contemptible person who lacks social skills or is boringly studious: *I was a serious nerd until I discovered girls and cars*. ■ a single-minded expert in a particular technical field: *a computer nerd*.
– DERIVATIVES **nerdiness** noun, **nerdish** adjective, **nerdy** adjective (**nerdier, nerdiest**).
– ORIGIN 1950s (originally US): of unknown origin.

> **WORD TRENDS** See **GEEK**[1].

Nereid /ˈnɪərɪɪd/ **1** Greek Mythology any of the sea nymphs, daughters of Nereus. They include Thetis, mother of Achilles.
2 Astronomy a satellite of Neptune, the furthest from the planet, discovered in 1949. It has an irregular shape (with a diameter of about 340 km) and an eccentric orbit.

nereid ▶ **noun** Zoology a bristle worm of the ragworm family (Nereidae).
– ORIGIN mid 19th cent.: from modern Latin *Nereidae*, from the Greek name *Nēreus* (see **NEREID**).

Nereus /ˈnɪərɪəs/ Greek Mythology an old sea god, the father of the Nereids. Like Proteus he had the power of assuming various forms.

nerine /nɪˈrʌɪni, nəˈriːnə/ ▶ **noun** a bulbous South African plant with narrow strap-shaped petals that are typically crimped and twisted and appear when there are no leaves. ● Genus *Nerine*, family Liliaceae (or Amaryllidaceae).
– ORIGIN modern Latin, from Latin, 'Nereid'.

nerite /ˈnɪərʌɪt/ ▶ **noun** a chiefly tropical mollusc with a somewhat globe-shaped and brightly marked shell, typically found in water. ● Superfamily Neritacea, class Gastropoda: several genera and species, including the European freshwater snail *Theodoxus fluviatilis*.
– ORIGIN early 18th cent.: from Latin *nerita*, from Greek *nēritēs* 'sea mussel', from the name of the sea god **NEREUS.**

neritic /nɪˈrɪtɪk/ ▶ **adjective** Biology & Geology relating to or denoting the shallow part of the sea near a coast and overlying the continental shelf.
– ORIGIN late 19th cent.: from **NERITE** + **-IC.**

nerk ▶ **noun** Brit. informal a foolish, objectionable, or insignificant person: *you little nerk*.
– ORIGIN 1950s: of uncertain origin; compare with **NERD** and **JERK**[1].

Nernst /nɛːnst/, German /ˈnɛrnst/, Walther Hermann (1864–1941), German physical chemist. He is best known for his discovery of the third law of thermodynamics (also known as **Nernst's heat theorem**). Nobel Prize for Chemistry (1920).

Nero /ˈnɪərəʊ/ (AD 37–68), Roman emperor 54–68; full name *Nero Claudius Caesar Augustus Germanicus*. Infamous for his cruelty, he wantonly executed leading Romans. His reign witnessed a fire which destroyed half of Rome in 64.

neroli /ˈnɪərəli/ (also **neroli oil**) ▶ **noun** [mass noun] an essential oil distilled from the flowers of the Seville orange, used in perfumery.
– ORIGIN late 17th cent.: via French from Italian *neroli*, said to be from the name of an Italian princess.

Neruda /nəˈruːdə/, Pablo (1904–73), Chilean poet and diplomat; born *Ricardo Eliezer Neftalí Reyes*. He took his pseudonym from the Czech poet Jan Neruda. His *Canto General* (completed 1950) is an epic covering the history of the Americas.

Nerva /ˈnəːvə/, Marcus Cocceius (*c.*30–98 AD), Roman emperor 96–8. He returned to a liberal and constitutional form of rule after the autocracy of his predecessor, Domitian.

nervation ▶ **noun** [mass noun] Botany the arrangement of nerves in a leaf.
– ORIGIN early 18th cent.: from French, based on *nerf* 'nerve'.

nerve ▶ **noun 1** a whitish fibre or bundle of fibres in the body that transmits impulses of sensation to the brain or spinal cord, and impulses from these to the muscles and organs: *the optic nerve*.
2 (**one's nerve** or **one's nerves**) one's steadiness and courage in a demanding situation: *an amazing journey which tested her nerves to the full* | ***he kept his nerve*** *and won five games in a row*.
3 (**nerves**) feelings of nervousness: *his first-night nerves soon disappeared*.
4 [mass noun] informal impudence or audacity: ***he had the nerve*** *to insult my cooking* | [in sing.] ***she's got a nerve*** *wearing that short skirt with those legs*.
5 Botany a prominent unbranched rib in a leaf, especially in the midrib of the leaf of a moss.
▶ **verb** (**nerve oneself**) brace oneself mentally to face a demanding situation: *she nerved herself to enter the room*.
– PHRASES **a bag** (or **bundle**) **of nerves** informal someone who is extremely anxious or tense. **get on someone's nerves** informal irritate someone. **have nerves of steel** not be easily upset or frightened. **live on one's nerves** (or **one's nerve ends**) be extremely anxious or tense. **strain every nerve** make every possible effort. [from the earlier sense of *nerve* as 'tendon, sinew'.] **touch** (or **hit**) **a nerve** (or **a raw nerve**) provoke a reaction by referring to a sensitive topic. **war of nerves** a struggle in which opponents try to wear each other down by psychological means.
– DERIVATIVES **nerved** adjective [usu. in combination] *he was steely-nerved after the accident*.
– ORIGIN late Middle English (also in the sense 'tendon, sinew'): from Latin *nervus*; related to Greek *neuron* 'nerve' (see **NEURON**).

N

nerve block ▶ **noun** Medicine the production of insensibility in a part of the body by injecting an anaesthetic close to the nerves that supply it.

nerve cell ▶ **noun** a neuron.

nerve centre ▶ **noun 1** a group of closely connected nerve cells that perform a particular function; a ganglion.
2 the control centre of an organization or operation: *Frankfurt is the economic nerve centre of Germany*.

nerve cord ▶ **noun** Zoology the major cord of nerve fibres running the length of an animal's body, especially a ventral cord in invertebrates that connects segmental nerve ganglia.

nerve fibre ▶ **noun** the axon of a neuron. A nerve is formed of a bundle of many such fibres, with their sheaths.

nerve gas ▶ **noun** [mass noun] a poisonous vapour which has a rapid disabling or lethal effect by disrupting the transmission of nerve impulses.

nerve impulse ▶ **noun** a signal transmitted along a nerve fibre. It consists of a wave of electrical depolarization that reverses the potential difference across the nerve cell membranes.

nerveless ▶ **adjective 1** lacking vigour or feeling: *the knife dropped from Grant's nerveless fingers*.
2 not nervous; confident: *a nerveless lack of restraint*.
3 Anatomy & Biology lacking nerves or nervures.
– DERIVATIVES **nervelessly** adverb, **nervelessness** noun.

nerve net ▶ **noun** Zoology (in invertebrates such as coelenterates and flatworms) a diffuse network of neurons which conducts impulses in all directions from a point of stimulus.

nerve-racking (also **nerve-wracking**) ▶ **adjective** causing stress or anxiety: *his driving test was a nerve-racking ordeal*.

nervine /ˈnəːvʌɪn, -iːn/ ▶ adjective (of a medicine) used to calm the nerves.
▶ noun a nervine medicine.
– ORIGIN mid 17th cent.: from medieval Latin *nervinus* 'of the nerves or sinews', or suggested by French *nervin*.

nervous ▶ adjective **1** easily agitated or alarmed: *a sensitive, nervous person.* ■ anxious or apprehensive: *staying in the house on her own made her nervous* | *he's **nervous of** speaking in public.* ■ (of a feeling or reaction) resulting from anxiety or anticipation: *nervous energy.*
2 relating to or affecting the nerves: *a nervous disorder.*
– DERIVATIVES **nervously** adverb.
– ORIGIN late Middle English (in the senses 'containing nerves' and 'relating to the nerves'): from Latin *nervosus* 'sinewy, vigorous', from *nervus* 'sinew' (see NERVE). Sense 1 dates from the mid 18th cent.

nervous breakdown ▶ noun a period of mental illness resulting from severe depression, stress, or anxiety.

nervousness ▶ noun [mass noun] the quality or state of being nervous: *there was a trace of nervousness in his voice.*

nervous system ▶ noun the network of nerve cells and fibres which transmits nerve impulses between parts of the body. See also AUTONOMIC NERVOUS SYSTEM, CENTRAL NERVOUS SYSTEM, PERIPHERAL NERVOUS SYSTEM.

nervous wreck ▶ noun informal a person suffering from stress or emotional exhaustion: *by the end of the day I was a nervous wreck.*

nervure /ˈnəːvjʊə/ ▶ noun Entomology each of the hollow veins that form the framework of an insect's wing. ■ Botany the principal vein of a leaf.
– ORIGIN early 19th cent.: from French, from *nerf* 'nerve'.

nervy ▶ adjective (**nervier**, **nerviest**) **1** Brit. easily agitated or alarmed; nervous: *he was nervy and on edge.* ■ characterized or produced by apprehension or uncertainty: *they made a nervy start.*
2 N. Amer. informal bold or impudent: *it was kind of nervy for Billy to be telling him how to play.*
3 literary vigorous or strong.
– DERIVATIVES **nervily** adverb, **nerviness** noun.

N

Nesbit /ˈnɛzbɪt/, E. (1858–1924), English novelist; full name *Edith Nesbit*. She is best known for her children's books, including *Five Children and It* (1902) and *The Railway Children* (1906).

nescient /ˈnɛsɪənt/ ▶ adjective literary lacking knowledge; ignorant: *I ventured into the new Korean restaurant with some equally nescient companions.*
– DERIVATIVES **nescience** noun.
– ORIGIN late Middle English: from Latin *nescient-* 'not knowing', from the verb *nescire*, from *ne-* 'not' + *scire* 'know'.

nesh ▶ adjective dialect (especially of a person) weak and delicate; feeble: *it was nesh to go to school in a topcoat.*
– ORIGIN Old English *hnesce*, of Germanic origin; related to Dutch dialect *nes* 'soft or foolish'.

ness ▶ noun [usu. in place names] a headland or promontory: *Orford Ness.*
– ORIGIN Old English *næs*, perhaps reinforced in Middle English by Old Norse *nes*; related to Old English *nasu* 'nose'.

-ness ▶ suffix forming nouns chiefly from adjectives:
1 denoting a state or condition: *liveliness* | *sadness.* ■ an instance of a state or condition: *a kindness.*
2 something in a certain state: *wilderness.*
– ORIGIN Old English *-nes*, *-ness*, of Germanic origin.

Nessie informal name for LOCH NESS MONSTER.

Ness, Loch see LOCH NESS.

Nessus /ˈnɛsəs/ Greek Mythology a centaur who was killed by Hercules with a poisoned arrow. Hercules eventually died when he was given a shirt smeared with the centaur's blood, which poisoned him.

nest ▶ noun **1** a structure or place made or chosen by a bird for laying eggs and sheltering its young. ■ a place where an animal or insect breeds or shelters: *an ants' nest.* ■ something in the form of a bowl or layer, used to hold, protect, or support something: *potato nests filled with okra.* ■ a person's snug or secluded retreat.
2 a place filled with undesirable people, activities, or things: *a **nest of** spies.*
3 a set of similar objects of graduated sizes, made so that each smaller one fits into the next in size for storage: *a **nest of** tables.*
▶ verb **1** [no obj.] (of a bird or other animal) use or build a nest: *the owls often nest in barns* | (as adj. **nesting**) *do not disturb nesting birds.*
2 [with obj.] fit (an object or objects) inside a larger one: *the town is nested inside a large crater on the flanks of a volcano.* ■ [no obj.] (of a set of objects) fit inside one another: *Russian dolls that nest inside one another.* ■ (especially in computing and linguistics) place (an object or element) in a lower position in a hierarchy: (as adj. **nested**) *organisms classified in a series of nested sets.*
– DERIVATIVES **nestful** noun (pl. **nestfuls**), **nest-like** adjective.
– ORIGIN Old English, of Germanic origin; related to Latin *nidus*, from the Indo-European bases of NETHER (meaning 'down') and SIT.

nest box (also **nesting box**) ▶ noun a box provided for a bird to make its nest in.

nest egg ▶ noun **1** a sum of money saved for the future: *I worked hard to build up a nice little nest egg.*
2 a real or artificial egg left in a nest to induce hens to lay eggs there.

nester ▶ noun [usu. with adj. or noun modifier] a bird that nests in a specified manner or place: *a scarce nester in Britain* | *hole-nesters.* See also EMPTY NESTER.

nestle ▶ verb [no obj., with adverbial of place] settle or lie comfortably within or against something: *the baby nestled in her arms* | [with obj.] *she nestled her head against his shoulder.* ■ (of a place) be situated in a half-hidden or sheltered position: *picturesque villages nestle in the wooded hills.*
– ORIGIN Old English *nestlian*, from NEST; compare with Dutch *nestelen*.

nestling ▶ noun a bird that is too young to leave its nest.

Nestor /ˈnɛstə/ Greek Mythology a king of Pylos in the Peloponnese, who in old age led his subjects to the Trojan War. His wisdom was proverbial.

Nestorianism /nɛˈstɔːrɪənɪz(ə)m/ ▶ noun [mass noun] the Christian doctrine that there were two separate persons, one human and one divine, in the incarnate Christ. It is named after Nestorius, patriarch of Constantinople (428–31), and was maintained by some ancient Churches of the Middle East. A small Nestorian Church still exists in Iraq.
– DERIVATIVES **Nestorian** adjective & noun.

net¹ ▶ noun **1** a piece of open-meshed material made of twine, cord, or something similar, used typically for catching fish or other animals. ■ a piece of net supported by a frame at the end of a handle, used for catching fish or insects. ■ the total amount of fish caught in one session or expedition: *good nets of roach, chub, and perch.*
2 a structure consisting of a net supported on a frame, forming the goal in games such as football: *Wales did **find the net** in the 32nd minute.* ■ a net supported on a cord between two posts to divide the playing area in tennis, badminton, volleyball, etc. ■ Cricket a strip of ground enclosed by a net, for batting and bowling practice. ■ a safety net.
3 [mass noun] a fine fabric with a very open weave: [as modifier] *net curtains.* ■ (**nets**) Brit. informal net curtains.
4 a means of catching someone; a trap: *the search was delayed, allowing the murderers to escape the net.* ■ a means of selecting or securing someone or something: *he spread his net far and wide in his long search for success.*
5 a communications or broadcasting network, especially of maritime radio: *the radio net was brought to life with a mayday.* ■ a network of interconnected computers: *a computer news net.* ■ (**the Net**) the Internet.
▶ verb (**nets**, **netting**, **netted**) [with obj.] **1** catch (a fish or other animal) with a net. ■ fish with nets in (a river). ■ acquire or obtain in a skilful way: *customs officials have netted large caches of drugs.*
2 (in sport) hit (a ball) into the net; score (a goal): *Butler netted 14 goals.*
3 cover with a net: *we fenced off a rabbit-proof area for vegetables and netted the top.*
– PHRASES **slip** (or **fall**) **through the net** escape from or be missed by something intended to catch or deal with one: *the girl slipped through the net of all the care agencies.*
– DERIVATIVES **netful** noun (pl. **netfuls**), **netter** noun.
– ORIGIN Old English *net*, *nett*, of Germanic origin; related to Dutch *net* and German *Netz*.

net² (Brit. also **nett**) ▶ adjective **1** (of an amount, value, or price) remaining after the deduction of tax or other contributions: *net earnings per share rose* | *the camera will cost you, **net of** VAT, about £300.* Often contrasted with GROSS (sense 4 of the adjective). ■ (of a weight) excluding that of the packaging. ■ (of a score in golf) adjusted to take account of a player's handicap.
2 remaining after all factors have been taken into account; overall: *the net result is the same.*
▶ verb (**nets**, **netting**, **netted**) [with obj.] acquire (a sum of money) as clear profit: *he netted £2.45 million on the deal.* ■ [with two objs] return (profit or income) for (someone): *the land netted its owner a turnover of $800,000.* ■ (**net something down/off/out**) exclude a non-net amount, such as tax, when making a calculation, in order to reduce the amount left to a net sum: *the scrap value should be netted off against the original purchase price.*
– ORIGIN Middle English (in the senses 'clean' and 'smart'): from French *net* 'neat'; see NEAT¹. The sense 'free from deductions' is first recorded in late Middle English.

neta /ˈneɪtɑː/ ▶ noun Indian a politician or leader of an organization.
– ORIGIN via Bengali from Sanskrit *netā* 'leader'.

Netanyahu /ˌnɛt(ə)nˈjɑːhuː/, Benjamin (b.1949), Israeli Likud statesman, Prime Minister 1996–9 and since 2009. Leader of the right-wing Likud coalition 1993–9, he narrowly defeated Shimon Peres in the elections of 1996, but lost to the Labour statesman Ehud Barak in 1999.

netball ▶ noun [mass noun] a seven-a-side game in which goals are scored by throwing a ball so that it falls through a netted hoop. By contrast with basketball, a player receiving the ball must stand still until they have passed it to another player. ■ [count noun] the ball used in netball.

netbook ▶ noun a small laptop computer designed primarily for accessing Internet-based applications.
– ORIGIN early 21st cent.: blend of INTERNET and NOTEBOOK.

net current assets ▶ plural noun another term for WORKING CAPITAL.

nether /ˈnɛðə/ ▶ adjective lower in position: *the ballast is suspended from its nether end.*
– DERIVATIVES **nethermost** adjective.
– ORIGIN Old English *nithera*, *neothera*, of Germanic origin; related to Dutch *neder-* (found in compounds), *neer*, and German *nieder*, from an Indo-European root meaning 'down'.

Netherlands a country in western Europe, on the North Sea; pop. 16,716,000 (est. 2009); official language, Dutch; capital, Amsterdam; seat of government, The Hague. Dutch name NEDERLAND; also called HOLLAND. ■ historical the Low Countries.

> Following a struggle against the Spanish Habsburg empire, the northern (Dutch) part of the Low Countries won full independence in 1648 and became a leading imperial power. In 1814 north and south were united under a monarchy, but the south revolted in 1830 and became an independent kingdom, Belgium, in 1839. In 1948 the Netherlands formed the Benelux Customs Union with Belgium and Luxembourg, becoming a founder member of the EEC in 1957. The name **Holland** strictly refers only to the western coastal provinces of the country.

– DERIVATIVES **Netherlander** noun, **Netherlandish** adjective.

Netherlands Antilles two widely separated groups of Dutch islands in the Caribbean, in the Lesser Antilles; capital, Willemstad, on Curaçao; pop. 227,000 (est. 2009).

> The southernmost group, situated just off the north coast of Venezuela, comprises the islands of Bonaire and Curaçao. The northern group comprises the islands of St Eustatius, St Martin, and Saba. The islands were originally visited in the 16th century by the Spanish and were settled by the Dutch in the mid 17th century. In 1954 the islands were granted self-government and became an autonomous region of the Netherlands.

Netherlands Reformed Church the largest Protestant Church in the Netherlands, established in 1816 as the successor to the Dutch Reformed Church.

nether regions ▶ plural noun **1** (**the nether regions**) the lowest or furthest parts of a place, especially with allusion to hell or the underworld.
2 (**one's nether regions**) euphemistic one's genitals and bottom.

netherworld ▶ noun (**the netherworld**) the underworld; hell. ■ a hidden or illicit area of activity: *the narcotic netherworld thriving in post-war America.* ■ an ill-defined area of activity: *that cinematic netherworld between the multiplexes and the video stores.*

netiquette ▶ **noun** [mass noun] informal the correct or acceptable way of using the Internet.
– ORIGIN 1990s: blend of **NET**^{1} and **ETIQUETTE**.

netizen ▶ **noun** informal a user of the Internet, especially a habitual or keen one.
– ORIGIN 1990s: blend of **NET**^{1} and **CITIZEN**.

net national product (abbrev.: **NNP**) ▶ **noun** the total value of goods and services provided in a country during one year, after depreciation of capital goods has been allowed for.

net present value ▶ **noun** see **PRESENT VALUE**.

net profit ▶ **noun** the actual profit after working expenses not included in the calculation of gross profit have been paid.

netroots ▶ **plural noun** chiefly N. Amer. political activists and campaigners who communicate their message over the Internet, especially via blogs: *in the last election the netroots exerted their influence through prodigious fundraising*.
– ORIGIN early 21st cent.: blend of **INTERNET** and **GRASS ROOTS**.

netsuke /ˈnɛtski, ˈnɛtsʊki/ ▶ **noun** (pl. **same** or **netsukes**) a carved button-like ornament, especially of ivory or wood, formerly worn in Japan to suspend articles from the sash of a kimono.
– ORIGIN late 19th cent.: from Japanese.

nett ▶ **adjective & verb** Brit. variant spelling of **NET**^{2}.

netting ▶ **noun** [mass noun] open-meshed material made by knotting together twine, wire, rope, or thread.

nettle ▶ **noun** a herbaceous plant which has jagged leaves covered with stinging hairs. ● Genus *Urtica*, family Urticaceae: several species, in particular the Eurasian **stinging nettle** (*U. dioica*).
■ used in names of other plants with leaves of a similar appearance, e.g. **dead-nettle**.
▶ **verb** [with obj.] **1** irritate or annoy (someone).
2 archaic sting with nettles.
– PHRASES **grasp the nettle** see **GRASP**.
– ORIGIN Old English *netle*, *netele*, of Germanic origin; related to Dutch *netel* and German *Nessel*. The verb dates from late Middle English.

nettlerash ▶ **noun** another term for **URTICARIA** (from its resemblance to the sting of a nettle).

nettlesome ▶ **adjective** chiefly US causing annoyance or difficulty: *nettlesome regional disputes*.

nettle tree ▶ **noun** an Old World tree related to the hackberries, with a straight silvery-grey trunk and rough, toothed nettle-like leaves. ● Genus *Celtis*, family Ulmaceae: several species, in particular *C. australis*, which is a popular street and shade tree in Mediterranean countries.

net ton ▶ **noun** another term for **TON**^{1} (sense 2 of the noun).

netty ▶ **noun** (pl. **netties**) N. English a toilet, especially an earth closet.
– ORIGIN from Northumberland dialect.

network ▶ **noun 1** an arrangement of intersecting horizontal and vertical lines.
2 a group or system of interconnected people or things: *the company has a network of 326 branches | a trade network*. ■ a complex system of railways, roads, or other routes: *the railway network*. ■ a group of people who exchange information and contacts for professional or social purposes: *a support network*. ■ a group of broadcasting stations that connect for the simultaneous broadcast of a programme: [as modifier] *network television*. ■ a number of interconnected computers, machines, or operations. ■ a system of connected electrical conductors.
▶ **verb 1** [with obj.] connect as or operate with a network: *compared with the railways the canals were less effectively networked*. ■ Brit. broadcast (a programme) on a network: *the Spurs match which ITV had networked*. ■ link (computers or other machines) to operate interactively.
2 [no obj.] (often as noun **networking**) interact with others to exchange information and develop professional or social contacts.
– DERIVATIVES **networkable** adjective.

network analysis ▶ **noun** [mass noun] the mathematical analysis of complex working procedures in terms of a network of related activities. ■ calculation of the electric currents flowing in the various meshes of a network.

network appliance ▶ **noun** a relatively low-cost computer designed chiefly to provide Internet access and without the full capabilities of a standard computer.

networker ▶ **noun 1** a person who works from home or from an external office via a computer network.
2 a person who uses a network of professional or social contacts to further their career.

Neuchâtel, Lake /ˌnəːʃaˈtɛl/, French /nøʃɑtɛl/ the largest lake lying wholly within Switzerland, situated at the foot of the Jura Mountains in western Switzerland.

Neue Sachlichkeit /ˌnɔɪə ˈzaxlɪxkʌɪt/, German /ˌnɔyə ˈzaxlɪçkaɪt/ a movement in the fine arts, music, and literature, which developed in Germany during the 1920s and was characterized by realism and a deliberate rejection of romantic attitudes.
– ORIGIN German, literally 'new objectivity'.

Neufchâtel /nəːʃaˈtɛl/ ▶ **noun** [mass noun] a soft white French cheese, originally made in Neufchâtel-en-Bray, in Normandy.

Neumann /ˈnɔɪmən/, John von (1903–57), Hungarian-born American mathematician and computer pioneer. He pioneered game theory and the design and operation of electronic computers.

neume /njuːm/ (also **neum**) ▶ **noun** Music (in plainsong) a note or group of notes to be sung to a single syllable. ■ a sign indicating a neume.
– ORIGIN late Middle English: from Old French *neume*, from medieval Latin *neu(p)ma*, from Greek *pneuma* 'breath'.

neural ▶ **adjective** relating to a nerve or the nervous system: *patterns of neural activity*.
– DERIVATIVES **neurally** adverb.
– ORIGIN mid 19th cent.: from Greek *neuron* in the sense 'nerve' + **-AL**.

neural arch ▶ **noun** Anatomy the curved rear (dorsal) section of a vertebra, enclosing the canal through which the spinal cord passes.

neural computer ▶ **noun** a computer that uses neural networks.
– DERIVATIVES **neural computing** noun.

neuralgia /ˌnjʊəˈraldʒə/ ▶ **noun** [mass noun] intense, typically intermittent pain along the course of a nerve, especially in the head or face.
– DERIVATIVES **neuralgic** adjective.

neural network (also **neural net**) ▶ **noun** a computer system modelled on the human brain and nervous system.

neural tube ▶ **noun** Zoology & Medicine (in an embryo) a hollow structure from which the brain and spinal cord form. Defects in its development can result in congenital abnormalities such as spina bifida.

neuraminic acid /ˌnjʊərəˈmɪnɪk/ ▶ **noun** [mass noun] Biochemistry a crystalline compound of which derivatives occur in many animal substances, chiefly as sialic acids. ● A sugar with amino and acid groups; chem. formula: $C_9H_{17}NO_8$.
– ORIGIN 1940s: *neuraminic* from **NEURO-** (because it was originally isolated from brain tissue) + **AMINE** + **-IC**.

neuraminidase /ˌnjʊərəˈmɪnɪdeɪz/ ▶ **noun** [mass noun] Biochemistry an enzyme, present in many pathogenic or symbiotic microorganisms, which catalyses the breakdown of glycosides containing neuraminic acid.

neurasthenia /ˌnjʊərəsˈθiːnɪə/ ▶ **noun** [mass noun] chiefly dated an ill-defined medical condition characterized by lassitude, fatigue, headache, and irritability, associated chiefly with emotional disturbance.
– DERIVATIVES **neurasthenic** adjective & noun.

neurectomy /njʊəˈrɛktəmi/ ▶ **noun** [mass noun] Medicine surgical removal of all or part of a nerve.

neurilemma /ˌnjʊərɪˈlɛmə/ ▶ **noun** (pl. **neurilemmas** or **neurilemmata**) Anatomy the thin sheath around a nerve axon (including myelin where this is present).

neuritis /njʊəˈrʌɪtɪs/ ▶ **noun** [mass noun] Medicine inflammation of a peripheral nerve or nerves, usually causing pain and loss of function. ■ (in general use) neuropathy.
– DERIVATIVES **neuritic** adjective.

neuro- ▶ **combining form** relating to nerves or the nervous system: *neuroanatomy | neurohormone*.
– ORIGIN from Greek *neuron* 'nerve, sinew, tendon'.

neuroanatomy ▶ **noun** [mass noun] the anatomy of the nervous system.
– DERIVATIVES **neuroanatomical** adjective, **neuroanatomist** noun.

neurobics ▶ **plural noun** activities or mental tasks designed to stimulate the brain and help prevent memory loss.
– ORIGIN 1990s: on the pattern of **AEROBICS**.

neurobiology ▶ **noun** [mass noun] the biology of the nervous system.
– DERIVATIVES **neurobiological** adjective, **neurobiologist** noun.

neuroblast /ˈnjʊərə(ʊ)blast/ ▶ **noun** Embryology an embryonic cell from which nerve fibres originate.

neuroblastoma /ˌnjʊərə(ʊ)blaˈstəʊmə/ ▶ **noun** [mass noun] Medicine a malignant tumour composed of neuroblasts, most commonly in the adrenal gland.

neurochemistry ▶ **noun** [mass noun] the branch of biochemistry concerned with the processes occurring in nerve tissue and the nervous system.
– DERIVATIVES **neurochemist** noun, **neurochemical** adjective & noun.

neurocomputer ▶ **noun** another term for **NEURAL COMPUTER**.

neurodegenerative /ˌnjʊərə(ʊ)dɪˈdʒɛn(ə)rətɪv/ ▶ **adjective** resulting in or characterized by degeneration of the nervous system, especially the neurons in the brain.

neuroeconomics ▶ **plural noun** [treated as sing.] the combination of economics, neuroscience, and psychology to determine how individuals make economic decisions.

neuroepithelium /ˌnjʊərəʊˌɛpɪˈθiːlɪəm/ ▶ **noun** [mass noun] Anatomy **1** a type of epithelium containing sensory nerve endings and found in certain sense organs (e.g. the retina, the inner ear, the nasal membranes, and the taste buds).
2 (in embryology) ectoderm that develops into nerve tissue.
– DERIVATIVES **neuroepithelial** adjective.

neurofibril /ˌnjʊərə(ʊ)ˈfʌɪbrɪl/ ▶ **noun** Anatomy a fibril in the cytoplasm of a nerve cell, visible by light microscopy.
– DERIVATIVES **neurofibrillary** adjective.

neurofibroma /ˌnjʊərə(ʊ)fʌɪˈbrəʊmə/ ▶ **noun** (pl. **neurofibromas** or **neurofibromata** /-mətə/) Medicine a tumour formed on a nerve cell sheath, frequently symptomless but occasionally malignant.

neurofibromatosis /ˌnjʊərə(ʊ)fʌɪˌbrəʊməˈtəʊsɪs/ ▶ **noun** [mass noun] Medicine a disease in which neurofibromas form throughout the body. Also called **VON RECKLINGHAUSEN'S DISEASE**.

neurogenesis /ˌnjʊərə(ʊ)ˈdʒɛnɪsɪs/ ▶ **noun** [mass noun] Physiology the growth and development of nervous tissue.

neurogenic /ˌnjʊərə(ʊ)ˈdʒɛnɪk/ ▶ **adjective** Physiology caused or controlled by or arising in the nervous system.

neuroglia /ˌnjʊəˈrɒglɪə/ ▶ **noun** another term for **GLIA**.
– ORIGIN mid 19th cent.: from **NEURO-** 'of nerves' + Greek *glia* 'glue'.

neurohormone ▶ **noun** Physiology a hormone such as vasopressin or noradrenaline produced by nerve cells and secreted into the circulation.

neurohypophysis /ˌnjʊərəʊhʌɪˈpɒfɪsɪs/ ▶ **noun** (pl. **neurohypophyses** /-siːz/) Anatomy the posterior lobe of the hypophysis (pituitary gland), which stores and releases oxytocin and vasopressin produced in the hypothalamus.

neuroleptic /ˌnjʊərə(ʊ)ˈlɛptɪk/ Medicine ▶ **adjective** (of a drug) tending to reduce nervous tension by depressing nerve functions.
▶ **noun** a neuroleptic drug; a major tranquillizer.
– ORIGIN 1950s: from **NEURO-** 'relating to nerves' + *-leptic*, as in **ORGANOLEPTIC**.

neurolinguistic programming ▶ **noun** [mass noun] a system of alternative therapy intended to educate people in self-awareness and effective communication, and to model and change their patterns of mental and emotional behaviour.

neurolinguistics ▶ **plural noun** [treated as sing.] the branch of linguistics dealing with the relationship between language and the structure and functioning of the brain.
– DERIVATIVES **neurolinguistic** adjective.

neurology /ˌnjʊəˈrɒlədʒi/ ▶ **noun** [mass noun] the branch of medicine or biology that deals with the anatomy, functions, and organic disorders of nerves and the nervous system.
– DERIVATIVES **neurologic** adjective, **neurological** adjective, **neurologically** adverb, **neurologist** noun.
– ORIGIN late 17th cent.: from modern Latin *neurologia*, from **NEURO-** + **-LOGY**.

neuroma /ˌnjʊəˈrəʊmə/ ▶ **noun** (pl. **neuromas** or **neuromata** /-mətə/) another term for **NEUROFIBROMA**.

neuromast /ˈnjʊərə(ʊ)mast/ ▶ **noun** Zoology a sensory organ of fishes and larval or aquatic amphibians, typically forming part of the lateral line system.
– ORIGIN early 20th cent.: from **NEURO-** 'of nerves' + Greek *mastos* 'breast'.

N

neuromuscular ▸ adjective relating to nerves and muscles.

neuron /ˈnjʊərɒn/ (also **neurone** /-rəʊn/) ▸ noun a specialized cell transmitting nerve impulses; a nerve cell.
– DERIVATIVES **neuronal** /-ˈrəʊn(ə)l/ adjective, **neuronic** /-ˈrɒnɪk/ adjective.
– ORIGIN late 19th cent.: from Greek *neuron*, special use of the literal sense 'sinew, tendon'. See NERVE.

> **USAGE** In scientific sources the standard spelling is **neuron**. The spelling **neurone** is generally restricted to non-technical contexts, but note that it is usual in **motor neurone disease**.

neuropath /ˈnjʊərə(ʊ)paθ/ ▸ noun dated a person affected by nervous disease, or with an abnormally sensitive nervous system.

neuropathology ▸ noun [mass noun] the branch of medicine concerned with diseases of the nervous system.
– DERIVATIVES **neuropathological** adjective, **neuropathologist** noun.

neuropathy /ˌnjʊəˈrɒpəθi/ ▸ noun [mass noun] Medicine disease or dysfunction of one or more peripheral nerves, typically causing numbness or weakness.
– DERIVATIVES **neuropathic** adjective.

neuropeptide ▸ noun Biochemistry any of a group of compounds which act as neurotransmitters and are short-chain polypeptides.

neuropharmacology ▸ noun [mass noun] the branch of pharmacology that deals with the action of drugs on the nervous system.
– DERIVATIVES **neuropharmacological** adjective, **neuropharmacologist** noun.

neurophysiology ▸ noun [mass noun] the physiology of the nervous system.
– DERIVATIVES **neurophysiological** adjective, **neurophysiologist** noun.

neuropil /ˈnjʊərə(ʊ)pɪl/ (also **neuropile** /-pʌɪl/) ▸ noun Anatomy & Zoology a dense network of interwoven nerve fibres and their branches and synapses, together with glial filaments.
– ORIGIN late 19th cent.: probably an abbreviation of obsolete *neuropilema*, from Greek *neuron* 'nerve' + *pilēma* 'felt'.

N

neuropsychiatry ▸ noun [mass noun] psychiatry relating mental or emotional disturbance to disordered brain function.
– DERIVATIVES **neuropsychiatric** adjective, **neuropsychiatrist** noun.

neuropsychology ▸ noun [mass noun] the study of the relationship between behaviour, emotion, and cognition on the one hand, and brain function on the other.
– DERIVATIVES **neuropsychological** adjective, **neuropsychologist** noun.

Neuroptera /ˌnjʊəˈrɒpt(ə)rə/ ▸ plural noun Entomology an order of predatory flying insects that includes the lacewings, alderflies, snake flies, and ant lions. They have four finely veined membranous wings.
■ (**neuroptera**) insects of this order.
– ORIGIN modern Latin (plural), from NEURO- in the sense 'veined' + Greek *pteron* 'wing'.

neuropteran Entomology ▸ noun a predatory flying insect of the order Neuroptera, such as a lacewing or alderfly.
▸ adjective relating to or denoting neuropterans.

neuroscience ▸ noun any or all of the sciences, such as neurochemistry and experimental psychology, which deal with the structure or function of the nervous system and brain.
– DERIVATIVES **neuroscientist** noun.

neurosis /ˌnjʊəˈrəʊsɪs/ ▸ noun (pl. **neuroses** /-siːz/) Medicine a relatively mild mental illness that is not caused by organic disease, involving symptoms of stress (depression, anxiety, obsessive behaviour, hypochondria) but not a radical loss of touch with reality. Compare with PSYCHOSIS. ■ (in non-technical use) excessive and irrational anxiety or obsession: *too much neurosis about a child's progress is unproductive.*
– ORIGIN mid 18th cent.: modern Latin, from NEURO- 'of nerves' + -OSIS.

neurosurgery ▸ noun [mass noun] surgery performed on the nervous system, especially the brain and spinal cord.
– DERIVATIVES **neurosurgeon** noun, **neurosurgical** adjective.

neurosyphilis ▸ noun [mass noun] syphilis that involves the central nervous system.

neurotic ▸ adjective Medicine having, caused by, or relating to neurosis. ■ (in non-technical use) abnormally sensitive, obsessive, or anxious: *he seemed a neurotic, self-obsessed character.*
▸ noun a neurotic person.
– DERIVATIVES **neurotically** adverb, **neuroticism** noun.

neurotomy /ˌnjʊəˈrɒtəmi/ ▸ noun [mass noun] the surgical cutting of a nerve to produce sensory loss and relief of pain or to suppress involuntary movements.

neurotoxin /ˌnjʊərəʊˈtɒksɪn/ ▸ noun a poison which acts on the nervous system.
– DERIVATIVES **neurotoxic** adjective, **neurotoxicity** noun, **neurotoxicology** noun.

neurotransmitter ▸ noun Physiology a chemical substance which is released at the end of a nerve fibre by the arrival of a nerve impulse and, by diffusing across the synapse or junction, effects the transfer of the impulse to another nerve fibre, a muscle fibre, or some other structure.
– DERIVATIVES **neurotransmission** noun.

neurotrophic /ˌnjʊərə(ʊ)ˈtrəʊfɪk, -ˈtrɒfɪk/ ▸ adjective Physiology relating to the growth of nervous tissue.

neurotropic /ˌnjʊərə(ʊ)ˈtrəʊpɪk, -ˈtrɒpɪk/ ▸ adjective Medicine (of a virus, toxin, or chemical) tending to attack or affect the nervous system preferentially.
– DERIVATIVES **neurotropism** noun.

Neusiedler See /ˈnɔɪziːdlə ˌzeɪ/ a shallow lake in the steppe region between eastern Austria and NW Hungary. Hungarian name FERTŐ TÓ.

neuston /ˈnjuːstɒn/ ▸ noun [mass noun] Biology small aquatic organisms inhabiting the surface layer or moving on the surface film.
– ORIGIN early 20th cent.: via German from Greek, neuter of *neustos* 'swimming', on the pattern of *plankton*.

neuter ▸ adjective **1** of or denoting a gender of nouns in some languages, typically contrasting with masculine and feminine or common.
2 (of an animal) lacking developed sexual organs, or having had them removed. ■ (of a plant or flower) having neither functional pistils nor functional stamens. ■ (of a person) apparently having no sexual characteristics; asexual.
▸ noun **1** Grammar a neuter word. ■ (**the neuter**) the neuter gender.
2 a non-fertile caste of social insect, especially a worker bee or ant. ■ a castrated or spayed domestic animal. ■ an asexual person.
▸ verb [with obj.] **1** castrate or spay (a domestic animal).
2 make ineffective: *disarmament negotiations that will neuter their military power.*
– ORIGIN late Middle English: via Old French from Latin *neuter* 'neither', from *ne-* 'not' + *uter* 'either'.

neutral ▸ adjective **1** not supporting or helping either side in a conflict, disagreement, etc.; impartial: *neutral and non-aligned European nations.* ■ belonging to an impartial group or state: *the trial should be held on neutral ground.*
2 deliberately refraining from expressing or provoking strong feeling; dispassionate or inoffensive: *her tone was neutral, devoid of sentiment.*
3 of or denoting a pale grey, cream, or beige colour: *walls are painted in neutral tones.*
4 Chemistry neither acid nor alkaline; having a pH of about 7.
5 having neither a positive nor negative electrical charge.
▸ noun **1** an impartial or unbiased state or person: *Sweden and its fellow neutrals | I attended the Cup Final as a neutral.*
2 [mass noun] pale grey, cream, or beige.
3 [mass noun] a disengaged position of gears in which the engine is disconnected from the driven parts: *she slipped the gear into neutral.*
4 an electrically neutral point, terminal, conductor, or wire.
– DERIVATIVES **neutrally** adverb.
– ORIGIN late Middle English (as a noun): from Latin *neutralis* 'of neuter gender', from Latin *neuter* (see NEUTER).

neutral axis ▸ noun Engineering a line or plane through a beam or plate connecting points at which no extension or compression occurs when it is bent.

neutral density filter ▸ noun a photographic or optical filter that absorbs light of all wavelengths to the same extent, causing overall dimming but no change in colour.

neutralism ▸ noun [mass noun] a policy of political neutrality.
– DERIVATIVES **neutralist** noun & adjective.

neutrality ▸ noun [mass noun] **1** the state of not supporting or helping either side in a conflict, disagreement, etc.; impartiality: *during the war, Switzerland maintained its neutrality.*
2 absence of decided views, expression, or strong feeling: *the clinical neutrality of the description.*
3 the condition of being chemically or electrically neutral.

neutralize (also **neutralise**) ▸ verb [with obj.] make (something) ineffective by applying an opposite force or effect: *impatience at his frailty began to neutralize her fear.* ■ make (an acidic or alkaline substance) chemically neutral. ■ disarm (a bomb or similar weapon). ■ (in military or espionage contexts) used euphemistically to refer to killing or destruction.
– DERIVATIVES **neutralization** noun, **neutralizer** noun.
– ORIGIN mid 17th cent.: from French *neutraliser*, from medieval Latin *neutralizare*, from Latin *neutralis* (see NEUTRAL).

neutral zone ▸ noun the central area of an ice-hockey rink, lying between the two blue lines.

neutrino /njuːˈtriːnəʊ/ ▸ noun (pl. **neutrinos**) a neutral subatomic particle with a mass close to zero and half-integral spin, which rarely reacts with normal matter. Three kinds of neutrinos are known, associated with the electron, muon, and tau particle.
– ORIGIN 1930s: from Italian, diminutive of *neutro* 'neutral'.

neutron ▸ noun a subatomic particle of about the same mass as a proton but without an electric charge, present in all atomic nuclei except those of ordinary hydrogen.
– ORIGIN early 20th cent.: from NEUTRAL + -ON.

neutron bomb ▸ noun a nuclear weapon that produces large numbers of neutrons rather than heat or blast, and is consequently harmful to life but not destructive of property.

neutron star ▸ noun Astronomy a celestial object of very small radius (typically 30 km) and very high density, composed predominantly of closely packed neutrons. Neutron stars are thought to form by the gravitational collapse of the remnant of a massive star after a supernova explosion, provided that the star is insufficiently massive to produce a black hole.

neutropenia /ˌnjuːtrə(ʊ)ˈpiːniə/ ▸ noun [mass noun] Medicine the presence of abnormally few neutrophils in the blood, leading to increased susceptibility to infection.
– DERIVATIVES **neutropenic** adjective.
– ORIGIN 1930s: from NEUTRAL + Greek *penia* 'poverty, lack'.

neutrophil /ˈnjuːtrə(ʊ)fɪl/ ▸ noun Physiology a neutrophilic white blood cell.

neutrophilic ▸ adjective Physiology (of a cell or its contents) readily stained only by neutral dyes.
– ORIGIN late 19th cent.: from NEUTRAL + *-philic* (see -PHILIA).

Nev. ▸ abbreviation Nevada.

Neva /ˈniːvə, njɪˈvɑː/ a river in NW Russia which flows 74 km (46 miles) westwards from Lake Ladoga to the Gulf of Finland, passing through St Petersburg.

Nevada /nɪˈvɑːdə/ a state of the western US; pop. 2,600,167 (est. 2008); capital, Carson City. Acquired from Mexico in 1848, it became the 36th state of the US in 1864.
– DERIVATIVES **Nevadan** adjective & noun.

névé /ˈneveɪ/ ▸ noun another term for FIRN.
– ORIGIN mid 19th cent.: from Swiss French, literally 'glacier', based on Latin *nix, niv-* 'snow'.

never ▸ adverb **1** at no time in the past or future; not ever: *they had never been camping in their lives | I will never ever forget it.*
2 not at all: *he never turned up.* ■ [as exclamation] Brit. informal (expressing surprise) surely not: *What, you, Annabel? Never!*
– PHRASES **never fear** see FEAR. **never mind** see MIND. **never a one** not one: *there are no paintings, never a one.* **never say die** see DIE[1]. **well I never!** (or **well I never did!**) informal expressing surprise or indignation: *Well I never—that's not like you!*
– ORIGIN Old English *nǣfre*, from *ne* 'not' + *ǣfre* 'ever'.

never-ending ▸ adjective (especially of something unpleasant) having or seeming to have no end: *a never-ending series of disasters.*

nevermore ▸ adverb literary at no future time; never again: *I order you gone, nevermore to return.*

Never-Never 1 Austral. the unpopulated desert country of the interior of Australia; the remote outback. **2** (**Never-Never Land** (or **Country**)) a region of Northern Territory, Australia, south-east of Darwin; chief town, Katherine.
– ORIGIN mid 19th cent.: so named from the notion that one might never return from such remote country.

never-never ▸ **noun** (**the never-never**) Brit. informal hire purchase: *buying a telly on the never-never*.

never-never land ▸ **noun** an imaginary utopian place or situation: *a never-never land of unreal prices and easy bank loans.*
– ORIGIN early 20th cent.: often with allusion to the ideal country in J. M. Barrie's *Peter Pan*.

Nevers /nəˈvɛː/, French /nɛvɛʀ/ a city in central France, on the Loire; pop. 40,131 (2006). It was capital of the former province of Nivernais.

nevertheless ▸ **adverb** in spite of that; notwithstanding; all the same: *statements which, although literally true, are nevertheless misleading.*

Neville /ˈnɛvɪl/, Richard, see **WARWICK²**.

Nevis /ˈniːvɪs/ one of the Leeward Islands in the Caribbean, part of St Kitts and Nevis; capital, Charlestown.
– DERIVATIVES **Nevisian** /niːˈvɪsɪən/ **noun & adjective**.

Nevsky, Alexander, see **ALEXANDER NEVSKY**.

nevus ▸ **noun** (pl. **nevi**) US spelling of **NAEVUS**.

new ▸ **adjective 1** produced, introduced, or discovered recently or now for the first time; not existing before: *the new Madonna album | new crop varieties | this tendency is not new* | (as noun **the new**) *a fascinating mix of the old and the new.* ■ not previously used or owned: *a second-hand bus costs a fraction of a new one.* ■ of recent origin or arrival: *a new baby.* ■ (of vegetables) dug or harvested early in the season: *new potatoes.*
2 already existing but seen, experienced, or acquired recently or now for the first time: *her new bike | a new sensation.* ■ (**new to**) unfamiliar or strange to (someone): *a way of living that was new to me.* ■ (**new to/at**) inexperienced at or unaccustomed to (an activity): *I'm quite new to gardening.* ■ different from a recent previous one: *I have a new assistant | this would be her new home.* ■ in addition to another or others already existing: *looking for new business.* ■ [in place names] discovered or founded later than and named after: *New York.*
3 beginning anew and in a transformed way: *starting a new life | the new South Africa.* ■ (of a person) reinvigorated: *a bottle of pills would make him a new man.* ■ superseding and more advanced than another or others of the same kind: *the new architecture.* ■ reviving another or others of the same kind: *the New Bohemians.*
▸ **adverb** [usu. in combination] newly; recently: *new-mown hay | he was enjoying his new-found freedom.*
– PHRASES **a new one** informal an account, idea, or joke not previously encountered by someone: *somebody being too lazy to talk—that's a new one on me.* **what's new 1** (said on greeting someone) what's going on? how are you? **2** used to express the fact that a situation is entirely predictable: *United were unlucky ... so what's new?*
– DERIVATIVES **newish** adjective, **newness** noun.
– ORIGIN Old English *nīwe, nēowe*, of Germanic origin; related to Dutch *nieuw* and German *neu*, from an Indo-European root shared by Sanskrit *nava*, Latin *novus*, and Greek *neos* 'new'.

New Age ▸ **noun** [often as modifier] a broad movement characterized by alternative approaches to traditional Western culture, with an interest in spirituality, mysticism, holism, and environmentalism: *the New Age movement.*
– DERIVATIVES **New Ageism** noun, **New Ager** noun, **New Agey** adjective.

New Age music ▸ **noun** [mass noun] a style of chiefly instrumental music characterized by light melodic harmonies and sounds reproduced from the natural world, intended to promote serenity.

New Age traveller ▸ **noun** see **TRAVELLER**.

New Amsterdam former name for **NEW YORK**.

Newark /ˈnjuːək/ an industrial city in New Jersey; pop. 278,980 (est. 2008).

New Australian ▸ **noun** Austral. dated a recent immigrant to Australia, especially one from Europe.

newbie ▸ **noun** (pl. **newbies**) informal an inexperienced newcomer to a particular activity.

newborn ▸ **adjective** (of a child or animal) recently or just born.
▸ **noun** a recently born child or animal.

New Britain a mountainous island in the South Pacific, administratively part of Papua New Guinea, lying off the NE coast of New Guinea; pop. 404,600 (est. 2008); capital, Rabaul.

New Brunswick a maritime province on the SE coast of Canada; pop. 729,997 (2006); capital, Fredericton. It was first settled by the French and ceded to Britain in 1713. It became one of the original four provinces in the Dominion of Canada in 1867.

new build ▸ **noun** [mass noun] **1** the construction of new houses or other buildings: *prioritising refurbishment over new build* | [as modifier] *a two-bedroom new-build home.* ■ [count noun] a newly constructed house. **2** the construction of ships. ■ [count noun] a newly constructed ship.

New Caledonia an island in the South Pacific, east of Australia; pop. 227,400 (est. 2009); capital, Nouméa. Since 1946 the island has formed, with its dependencies, a French overseas territory; the French annexed the island in 1853. French name **NOUVELLE-CALÉDONIE**.
– DERIVATIVES **New Caledonian** noun & adjective.
– ORIGIN named, by Captain Cook in 1774, after the Roman name *Caledonia* 'Scotland'.

New Carthage see **CARTAGENA** (sense 1).

Newcastle¹ 1 an industrial city and metropolitan district in NE England, a port on the River Tyne; pop. 170,200 (est. 2009). Full name **Newcastle upon Tyne**. **2** an industrial town in Staffordshire, in England, just south-west of Stoke-on-Trent; pop. 77,500 (est. 2009). Full name **Newcastle-under-Lyme**. **3** an industrial port on the SE coast of Australia, in New South Wales; pop. 152,659 (2008).

Newcastle², Thomas Pelham-Holles, 1st Duke of (1693–1768), British Whig statesman, Prime Minister 1754–6 and 1757–62. During his second term in office he headed a coalition with William Pitt the Elder.

Newcastle disease ▸ **noun** [mass noun] an acute infectious viral fever affecting birds, especially poultry. Also called **FOWL PEST**.
– ORIGIN 1920s: so named because it was first recorded near Newcastle upon Tyne in 1927.

New Comedy ▸ **noun** [mass noun] a style of ancient Greek comedy associated with Menander, in which young lovers typically undergo endless vicissitudes in the company of stock fictional characters.

Newcomen /ˈnjuːˌkʌmən/, Thomas (1663–1729), English engineer, developer of the first practical steam engine. His beam engine to operate a pump for the removal of water from mines was first erected in Worcestershire in 1712.

newcomer ▸ **noun** a person who has recently arrived in a place: *she's a newcomer to the area.* ■ a novice in a particular activity or situation.

New Commonwealth those countries which have achieved self-government within the Commonwealth since 1945.

New Criticism an influential movement in literary criticism in the mid 20th century, which stressed the importance of focusing on the text itself rather than being concerned with external biographical or social considerations. Associated with the movement were John Crowe Ransom, who first used the term in 1941, I. A. Richards, and Cleanth Brooks.

New Deal the economic measures introduced by Franklin D. Roosevelt in 1933 to counteract the effects of the Great Depression. It involved a massive public works programme, complemented by the large-scale granting of loans, and succeeded in reducing unemployment by between 7 and 10 million.

New Delhi /ˈdɛli/ the capital of India, a city in north central India built 1912–29 to replace Calcutta (now Kolkata) as the capital of British India. With Delhi, it is part of the National Capital Territory of Delhi. Pop. (with Delhi) 12,259,200 (est. 2009).

newel /ˈnjuːəl/ ▸ **noun** the central supporting pillar of a spiral or winding staircase. ■ (also **newel post**) a post at the head or foot of a flight of stairs, supporting a handrail.
– ORIGIN late Middle English: from Old French *nouel* 'knob', from medieval Latin *nodellus*, diminutive of Latin *nodus* 'knot'.

New England an area on the NE coast of the US, comprising the states of Maine, New Hampshire, Vermont, Massachusetts, Rhode Island, and Connecticut.
– DERIVATIVES **New Englander** noun.

New English Bible (abbrev.: **NEB**) ▸ **noun** a modern English translation of the Bible, published in the UK in 1961–70 and revised (as the **Revised English Bible**) in 1989.

newfangled ▸ **adjective** derogatory different from what one is used to; objectionably new: *I've no time for such newfangled nonsense.*
– ORIGIN Middle English: from *newfangle* (now dialect) 'liking what is new', from the adverb **NEW** + a second element related to an Old English word meaning 'to take'.

new-fashioned ▸ **adjective** of a new type or style; up to date: *the development of a new-fashioned kind of language awareness.*

Newfie /ˈnjuːfi/ ▸ **noun** (pl. **Newfies**) Canadian informal a person from Newfoundland.

New Forest an area of heath and woodland in southern Hampshire. It has been reserved as Crown property since 1079, originally by William I as a royal hunting area, and is noted for its ponies.

Newfoundland¹ /ˌnjuːfəndˈland, ˈnjuːfən(d)lənd, -land, -ˈfaʊndlənd/ a large island off the east coast of Canada, at the mouth of the St Lawrence River. In 1949 it was united with Labrador (as Newfoundland and Labrador) to form a province of Canada.
– DERIVATIVES **Newfoundlander** noun.

Newfoundland² /ˈnjuːf(ə)n(d)lənd, -ˈfaʊndlənd/ (also **Newfoundland dog**) ▸ **noun** a dog of a very large breed with a thick coarse coat.

Newfoundland and Labrador a province of Canada, comprising the island of Newfoundland and the Labrador coast of eastern Canada; pop. 505,469 (2006); capital, St John's. It joined the confederation of Canada in 1949.

Newgate a former London prison whose unsanitary conditions became notorious in the 18th century before the building was burnt down in the Gordon Riots of 1780. A new edifice was erected on the same spot but was demolished in 1902 to make way for the Central Criminal Court.

New Georgia a group of islands in the Solomon Islands, north-west of Guadalcanal. ■ the largest of the New Georgia group of islands.

New Guinea an island in the western South Pacific, off the north coast of Australia, the second-largest island in the world (following Greenland). It is divided into two parts; the western half comprises the Indonesian provinces of Papua and West Papua, the eastern half forms part of Papua New Guinea.
– DERIVATIVES **New Guinean** noun & adjective.

New Hampshire a state in the north-eastern US, on the Atlantic coast; pop. 1,315,809 (est. 2008); capital, Concord. It was settled from England in the 17th century and was one of the original thirteen states of the Union (1788).
– DERIVATIVES **New Hampshirite** noun.

New Hebrides former name (until 1980) for **VANUATU**.

newie ▸ **noun** (pl. **newies**) informal, chiefly Brit. something or someone new, especially a newly released music record.

Ne Win /ˌneɪ ˈwɪn/ (1911–2002), Burmese general and socialist statesman, Prime Minister 1958–60, head of state 1962–74, and President 1974–81. After the military coup in 1962 he established a military dictatorship and formed a one-party state.

New International Version (abbrev.: **NIV**) ▸ **noun** a modern English translation of the Bible published in 1973–8.

New Ireland an island in the South Pacific, administratively part of Papua New Guinea, lying to the north of New Britain; pop. 145,700 (est. 2009); capital, Kavieng.

New Jersey a state in the north-eastern US, on the Atlantic coast; pop. 8,682,661 (est. 2008); capital, Trenton. Colonized by Dutch settlers and ceded to Britain in 1664, it became one of the original thirteen states of the Union (1787).
– DERIVATIVES **New Jerseyan** noun & adjective, **New Jerseyite** noun.

New Jerusalem Christian Theology the abode of the blessed in heaven (with reference to Rev. 21:2). ■ (as noun **a New Jerusalem**) an ideal place or situation.

New Jerusalem Church a Christian sect instituted by followers of Emanuel Swedenborg.

N

New Kingdom a period of ancient Egyptian history (*c.*1550–1070 BC, 18th–20th dynasty).

new-laid ▶ **adjective** (of an egg) recently laid.

Newlands, John Alexander Reina (1837–98), English industrial chemist. He proposed a form of periodic table shortly before Dmitri Mendeleev, based on a supposed **law of octaves** according to which similar chemical properties recurred in every eighth element.

New Look ▶ **noun** a style of women's clothing introduced in 1947 by Christian Dior, featuring calf-length full skirts and a generous use of material in contrast to wartime austerity.

newly ▶ **adverb 1** only just; recently: *a newly acquired hi-fi system*.
2 again; afresh: *social confidence for the newly single*.
■ in a new or different manner.

newly-wed ▶ **noun** (usu. **newly-weds**) a recently married person.

Newman[1], Barnett (1905–70), American painter. A seminal figure in colour-field painting, he juxtaposed large blocks of uniform colour with narrow marginal strips of contrasting colours.

Newman[2], John Henry (1801–90), English churchman and theologian. A founder of the Oxford Movement, in 1845 he turned to Roman Catholicism, becoming a cardinal in 1879.

Newman[3], Paul (1925–2008), American actor and film director. Among his many films are *Butch Cassidy and the Sundance Kid* (1969), *The Sting* (1973), *The Color of Money* (1987), for which he won an Oscar, and *The Glass Menagerie* (1987), which he also directed.

new man ▶ **noun** a man who rejects sexist attitudes and the traditional male role, especially in the context of domestic responsibilities and childcare.

Newman–Keuls test /kəːls/ ▶ **noun** Statistics a test for assessing the significance of differences between all possible pairs of different sets of observations, with a fixed error rate for the whole set of comparisons.
– ORIGIN 1950s: named after D. *Newman*, English statistician, and M. *Keuls*, Dutch horticulturalist.

Newmarket[1] a town in eastern England, in Suffolk; pop. 18,300 (est. 2009). It is a noted horse-racing centre and headquarters of the Jockey Club.

Newmarket[2] ▶ **noun 1** [mass noun] a card game in which the players put down cards in sequence, hoping to be the first to play all their cards and also to play certain special cards on which bets have been placed.
2 (also **Newmarket coat**) a close-fitting overcoat of a style originally worn for riding.

new maths (N. Amer. **new math**) ▶ **plural noun** [treated as sing.] a system of teaching mathematics to younger children, with emphasis on investigation and discovery by them and on set theory.

New Mexico a state in the south-western US, on the border with Mexico; pop. 1,984,356 (est. 2008); capital, Santa Fe. It was obtained from Mexico in 1848 and 1854, and in 1912 it became the 47th state of the US.
– DERIVATIVES **New Mexican adjective & noun.**

New Model Army an army created in 1645 by Oliver Cromwell to fight for the Parliamentary cause in the English Civil War. Led by Thomas Fairfax, it was a disciplined and well-trained army which later came to possess considerable political influence.

new moon ▶ **noun** the phase of the moon when it first appears as a slender crescent, shortly after its conjunction with the sun. ■ the time when the new moon appears. ■ Astronomy the time at which the moon is in conjunction with the sun, when it is not visible from the earth.

New National Party official name for **National Party**[2].

new order ▶ **noun** a new system, regime, or government: *a new economic order*. ■ (**New Order**) Hitler's planned reorganization of Europe under Nazi rule.

New Orleans /ˈɔːliːnz, ɔːˈliːnz/ a city and port in SE Louisiana, on the Mississippi; pop. 311,853 (est. 2008). It was founded by the French in 1718 and named after the Duc d'Orléans, regent of France. It is noted for its annual Mardi Gras celebrations and for its association with the development of blues and jazz.

New Plymouth a port in New Zealand, on the west coast of the North Island; pop. 68,902 (2006).

Newport a city in South Wales, on the Bristol Channel; pop. 119,600 (est. 2009). Welsh name **Casnewydd**.

Newport News a city in SE Virginia, at the mouth of the James River on the Hampton Roads estuary; pop. 179,614 (est. 2008).

New Red Sandstone ▶ **noun** a series of sedimentary rocks, chiefly soft red sandstones, belonging to the Permo-Triassic system of NW Europe.

New Revised Standard Version (abbrev.: **NRSV**) ▶ **noun** a modern English translation of the Bible, based on the Revised Standard Version and published in 1990.

New Romantic ▶ **adjective** denoting a style of popular music and fashion popular in Britain in the early 1980s in which both men and women wore make-up and dressed in flamboyant clothes.
▶ **noun** a performer or fan of New Romantic music.

Newry /ˈnjʊəri/ a city in the south-east of Northern Ireland, in County Down; pop. 28,100 (est. 2009).

news ▶ **noun** [mass noun] newly received or noteworthy information, especially about recent events: *I've got some good news for you*. ■ (**the news**) a broadcast or published report of news: *he was back in the news again*. ■ (**news to**) informal information not previously known to (someone): *this was hardly news to her*. ■ a person or thing considered interesting enough to be reported in the news: *Chanel became the hottest news in fashion*.
– PHRASES **be good** (or **bad**) **news** be commendable or admirable (or unpleasant or undesirable): *he's good news—I get very good vibes from him*. **no news is good news** proverb without information to the contrary you can assume that all is well.
– ORIGIN late Middle English: plural of **new**, translating Old French *noveles* or medieval Latin *nova* 'new things'.

news agency ▶ **noun** an organization that collects news items and distributes them to newspapers or broadcasters.

newsagent ▶ **noun** Brit. a person or shop selling newspapers, magazines, confectionery, etc.

newsboy ▶ **noun** a boy who sells or delivers newspapers.

news brief ▶ **noun** chiefly US a short news broadcast, especially on television; a newsflash.

news bulletin ▶ **noun** Brit. a short radio or television broadcast of news reports.

newscast ▶ **noun** N. Amer. a radio or television broadcast of news reports.

newscaster ▶ **noun** a newsreader.

news conference ▶ **noun** N. Amer. a press conference.

news crawl ▶ **noun** another term for **news ticker**.

news desk ▶ **noun** the department of a broadcasting organization or newspaper responsible for collecting and reporting the news.

newsfeed ▶ **noun 1** a service by which news is provided on a regular or continuous basis for onward distribution or broadcasting. ■ an item of information so provided.
2 a system by which data is transferred or exchanged between central computers to provide newsgroup access to networked users.

newsflash ▶ **noun** a single item of important news broadcast separately and often interrupting other programmes.

newsgathering ▶ **noun** [mass noun] the activity of researching news items for broadcast or publication.
– DERIVATIVES **newsgatherer noun.**

newsgroup ▶ **noun** a forum on the Usenet service for the discussion of a particular topic.

newshound ▶ **noun** informal a newspaper reporter.

newsie ▶ **noun** (pl. **newsies**) variant spelling of **newsy**.

newsletter ▶ **noun** a bulletin issued periodically to the members of a society or other organization.

newsmaker ▶ **noun** chiefly N. Amer. a newsworthy person or event.

newsman ▶ **noun** (pl. **newsmen**) a male reporter or journalist.

New South Wales a state of SE Australia; pop. 6,984,172 (2008); capital, Sydney. First colonized from Britain in 1788, it was federated with the other states of Australia in 1901.

New Spain a former Spanish viceroyalty established in Central and North America in 1535, centred on present-day Mexico City. It comprised all the land under Spanish control north of the Isthmus of Panama, including parts of the southern US. It also came to include the Spanish possessions in the Caribbean and the Philippines. The viceroyalty was abolished in 1821, when Mexico achieved independence.

newspaper ▶ **noun** a printed publication (usually issued daily or weekly) consisting of folded unstapled sheets and containing news, articles, advertisements, and correspondence.

newspaperman (or **newspaperwoman**) ▶ **noun** (pl. **newspapermen** or **newspaperwomen**) a newspaper journalist.

newspeak ▶ **noun** [mass noun] ambiguous euphemistic language used chiefly in political propaganda.
– ORIGIN 1949: the name of an artificial official language in George Orwell's *Nineteen Eighty-Four*.

newsprint ▶ **noun** [mass noun] cheap, low-quality absorbent printing paper made from coarse wood pulp and used chiefly for newspapers.

newsreader ▶ **noun 1** Brit. a person who reads out broadcast news bulletins.
2 a computer program for reading messages posted to newsgroups.

newsreel ▶ **noun** a short film of news and current affairs, formerly made for showing as part of the programme in a cinema.

newsroom ▶ **noun** the area in a newspaper or broadcasting office where news is processed.

news-sheet ▶ **noun** a simple form of newspaper.

news stand ▶ **noun** a stand or stall for the sale of newspapers.

news ticker ▶ **noun** a scrolling electronic display of news headlines on a building or along the bottom of a computer or television screen.

New Stone Age the Neolithic period.

New Style (abbrev.: **NS**) ▶ **noun** [mass noun] the method of calculating dates using the Gregorian calendar. It superseded the use of the Julian calendar in Scotland in 1600 and in England and Wales in 1752.

newsvendor ▶ **noun** Brit. a newspaper seller.

newswire ▶ **noun** a service transmitting the latest news stories via satellite, the Internet, etc.

newsworthy ▶ **adjective** noteworthy as news; topical: *a newsworthy event*.
– DERIVATIVES **newsworthiness noun.**

newsy informal ▶ **adjective** (**newsier**, **newsiest**) full of news, especially of a personal kind: *Susan's short, newsy letters*.
▶ **noun** (also **newsie**) (pl. **newsies**) US **1** a reporter.
2 a newsboy.

newt ▶ **noun** a small slender-bodied amphibian with lungs and a well-developed tail, typically spending its adult life on land and returning to water to breed.
● *Triturus* and other genera, family Salamandridae: numerous species.
– ORIGIN late Middle English: from *an ewt* (*ewt* from Old English *efeta*: see **eft**), interpreted (by wrong division) as *a newt*.

New Territories part of Hong Kong on the south coast of mainland China, lying to the north of the Kowloon peninsula and including the islands of Lantau, Tsing Yi, and Lamma.

New Testament ▶ **noun** the second part of the Christian Bible, written originally in Greek and recording the life and teachings of Christ and his earliest followers. It includes the four Gospels, the Acts of the Apostles, twenty-one Epistles by St Paul and others, and the book of Revelation.

Newton, Sir Isaac (1642–1727), English mathematician and physicist, considered the greatest single influence on theoretical physics until Einstein.

> In his *Principia Mathematica* (1687), Newton gave a mathematical description of the laws of mechanics and gravitation, and applied these to planetary motion. *Opticks* (1704) records his optical experiments and theories, including the discovery that white light is made up of a mixture of colours. His work in mathematics included the binomial theorem and differential calculus.

newton (abbrev.: **N**) ▶ **noun** Physics the SI unit of force. It is equal to the force that would give a mass of one kilogram an acceleration of one metre per second per second, and is equivalent to 100,000 dynes.
– ORIGIN early 20th cent.: named after Sir Isaac **Newton**.

Newtonian ▶ **adjective** relating to or arising from the work of Sir Isaac Newton. ■ formulated or behaving according to the principles of classical physics.

Newtonian mechanics ▸ **plural noun** [usu. treated as sing.] the system of mechanics which relies on Newton's laws of motion concerning the relations between forces acting and motions occurring.

Newtonian telescope ▸ **noun** Astronomy a reflecting telescope in which the light from the main mirror is deflected by a small flat secondary mirror set at 45°, sending it to a magnifying eyepiece in the side of the telescope.

Newton's laws of motion ▸ **plural noun** Physics three fundamental laws of classical physics. The first states that a body continues in a state of rest or uniform motion in a straight line unless it is acted on by an external force. The second states that the rate of change of momentum of a moving body is proportional to the force acting to produce the change. The third states that if one body exerts a force on another, there is an equal and opposite force (or reaction) exerted by the second body on the first.

Newton's rings ▸ **plural noun** Optics a set of concentric circular fringes seen around the point of contact when a convex lens is placed on a plane surface (or on another lens), caused by interference between light reflected from the upper and lower surfaces.

new town ▸ **noun** a planned urban centre created in an undeveloped or rural area, especially with government sponsorship.

new wave ▸ **noun** a group of people or artistic works introducing new styles or ideas, in particular: ■ [mass noun] a style of rock music popular in the late 1970s, deriving from punk but generally more poppy in sound and less aggressive in performance. ■ another term for NOUVELLE VAGUE.

New World North and South America regarded collectively in relation to Europe, especially after the early voyages of European explorers.

new year ▸ **noun** the calendar year just begun or about to begin: *Happy New Year!* ■ the first few days or weeks of a year: *the band is playing at Wembley in **the new year**.* ■ the period immediately before and after 31 December.
– PHRASES **New Year's** N. Amer. informal New Year's Eve or New Year's Day. **see the new year in** stay up until after midnight on 31 December to celebrate the start of a new year.

New Year's Day ▸ **noun** the first day of the year; in the modern Western calendar, 1 January.

New Year's Eve ▸ **noun** the last day of the year; in the modern Western calendar, 31 December. ■ the evening of 31 December.

Newyorican ▸ **noun** another term for NUYORICAN.

New York 1 a state in the north-eastern US; pop. 19,490,297 (est. 2008); capital, Albany. It stretches from the Canadian border and Lake Ontario in the north-west to the Atlantic in the east. Originally settled by the Dutch, it was surrendered to the British in 1664 and was one of the original thirteen states of the Union (1788).
2 a major city and port in the south-east of New York State, situated on the Atlantic coast at the mouth of the Hudson River; pop. 8,363,710 (est. 2008). The city is situated mainly on islands, linked by bridges, and comprises five boroughs: Manhattan, Brooklyn, the Bronx, Queens, and Staten Island. Manhattan is the economic and cultural heart of the city, containing the Stock Exchange in Wall Street and the headquarters of the United Nations. Former name (until 1664) NEW AMSTERDAM.
– DERIVATIVES **New Yorker** noun.

New York minute ▸ **noun** US informal a very short time; a moment.

New Zealand an island country in the South Pacific about 1,900 km (1,200 miles) east of Australia; pop. 4,213,400 (est. 2009); languages, English, Maori; capital, Wellington. Maori name AOTEAROA.

> New Zealand consists of two major islands (the North Island and the South Island) separated by Cook Strait, and several smaller islands. The original discoverers of the country were the Maoris. The first European to sight New Zealand was the Dutch navigator Abel Tasman in 1642; the islands were circumnavigated by Captain James Cook, and came under British sovereignty in 1840. Full dominion status was granted in 1907, and independence in 1931 within the Commonwealth.

– DERIVATIVES **New Zealander** noun.

New Zealand flatworm ▸ **noun** a speckled brown terrestrial flatworm up to 15 cm in length, accidentally introduced from New Zealand to Britain where it is destroying earthworm populations. ● *Artioposthia triangulata*, order Tricladida, class Turbellaria.

New Zealand flax ▸ **noun** another term for FLAX LILY.

New Zealand rug ▸ **noun** a strong waterproof rug for a horse, used during the winter.

New Zealand Wars a series of wars fought intermittently in 1845–8 and 1860–72 between Maoris and the colonial government of New Zealand over the enforced sale of Maori lands to Europeans, which was forbidden by the Treaty of Waitangi. Formerly called MAORI WARS.

next ▸ **adjective 1** (of a time) coming immediately after the time of writing or speaking: *we'll go to Corfu next year | next week's Cup Final.* ■ (of a day of the week) nearest (or the nearest but one) after the present: *not this Wednesday, next Wednesday |* [postpositive] *on Monday next.* ■ (of an event) occurring directly after the present one in time, without anything of the same kind intervening: *campaigning for the next election | next time I'll bring a hat.*
2 coming immediately after the present one in order, rank, or space: *the woman in the next room | the next chapter | building materials were next in importance.*
▸ **adverb 1** on the first or soonest occasion after the present; immediately afterwards: *he wondered what would happen next | next, I heard the sound of voices.*
2 [with superlative] following in the specified order: *Jo was the next oldest after Martin.*
▸ **noun** the next person or thing: *the week **after next**.*
▸ **determiner (a next)** W. Indian another: *every year sales down by a next ten per cent again.*
– PHRASES **next in line** immediately below the present holder of a position in order of succession: *he is **next in line to** the throne.* **next to 1** in or into a position immediately to one side of; beside. **2** following in order or importance: *next to buying a new wardrobe, nothing lifts the spirits like a new hairdo!* **3** almost: *I knew **next to nothing** about farming.* **4** in comparison with: *next to her I felt like a fraud.* **the next world** (according to some religious beliefs) the place where one goes after death. **what next** (or **whatever next**) used to express surprise or amazement.
– ORIGIN Old English *nēhsta* 'nearest', superlative of *nēah* 'nigh'; compare with Dutch *naast* and German *nächste*.

next best ▸ **adjective** second in order of preference: *the next best **thing to** flying is gliding.*

next door ▸ **adverb** in or to the next house or room: *the caretaker lives next door.*
▸ **adjective (next-door)** living or situated next door: *next-door neighbours.*
▸ **noun** [mass noun] the people, building, or room next door: *next door's dog | a man emerged from next door.*
– PHRASES **the boy** (or **girl**) **next door** a person perceived as familiar and dependable, typically in the context of a romantic relationship. **next door to** in the next house or room to. ■ informal almost; near to: *she thought George was next door to a saint.*

next of kin ▸ **noun** [treated as sing. or pl.] a person's closest living relative or relatives.

nexus /ˈnɛksəs/ ▸ **noun** (pl. **same** or **nexuses**) **1** a connection or series of connections linking two or more things: *the nexus between industry and political power.* ■ a connected group or series: *a nexus of ideas.*
2 a central or focal point: *the nexus of any government in this country is No. 10.*
– ORIGIN mid 17th cent.: from Latin, 'a binding together', from *nex-* 'bound', from the verb *nectere*.

Ney /neɪ/, Michel (1768–1815), French marshal. One of Napoleon's leading generals, he commanded the French cavalry at Waterloo (1815), but after Napoleon's overthrow was executed by the Bourbons.

Nez Percé /nɛz ˈpəːs, ˈpɛːseɪ/ ▸ **noun** (pl. **same** or **Nez Percés**) **1** a member of an American Indian people of central Idaho.
2 [mass noun] the Penutian language of the Nez Percé, now with few speakers.
▸ **adjective** relating to the Nez Percé or their language.
– ORIGIN French, literally 'pierced nose'.

NF ▸ **abbreviation** ■ National Front. ■ Newfoundland (in official postal use).

NFL ▸ **abbreviation** National Football League (the top professional league for American football in the US).

Nfld ▸ **abbreviation** Newfoundland.

NFU ▸ **abbreviation** National Farmers' Union.

ng ▸ **abbreviation** nanogram(s).

ngaio /ˈnʌɪəʊ/ ▸ **noun** (pl. **ngaios**) a small New Zealand tree with edible fruit and light white timber. ● *Myoporum laetum*, family Myoporaceae.
– ORIGIN mid 19th cent.: from Maori.

Ngaliema, Mount /(ə)ŋ,gɑːlɪˈeɪmə/ African name for Mount Stanley (see STANLEY, MOUNT).

Ngamiland /(ə)ŋˈgɑːmɪland/ a region in NW Botswana, north of the Kalahari Desert. It includes the Okavango marshes and Lake Ngami.

Ngata /ˈnɑːtə/, Sir Apirana Turupa (1874–1950), New Zealand Maori leader and politician. As Minister for Native Affairs he devoted much time to Maori resettlement, seeking to preserve the characteristic elements of Maori life and culture.

Ngbandi /(ə)ŋˈbandi/ ▸ **noun** [mass noun] a Bantu language of the northern Democratic Republic of the Congo (Zaire).
– ORIGIN the name in Ngbandi.

NGO ▸ **abbreviation** non-governmental organization.

ngoma /(ə)ŋˈgəʊmə/ ▸ **noun** (in East Africa) a dance; a night of dancing and music.
– ORIGIN Kiswahili, literally 'drum, dance, music'.

Ngoni /(ə)ŋˈgəʊni/ ▸ **noun** (pl. **same** or **Ngonis**) **1** a member of a people now living chiefly in Malawi.
2 (ngoni) a kind of traditional African drum.
▸ **adjective** relating to the Ngoni.
– ORIGIN a local name.

Ngorongoro /(ə)ŋ,gɔːr(ə)ŋˈgɔːrəʊ/ a huge extinct volcanic crater in the Great Rift Valley in NE Tanzania, 326 sq. km (126 sq. miles) in area.

ngultrum /(ə)ŋˈgʊltrəm/ ▸ **noun** (pl. **same**) the basic monetary unit of Bhutan, equal to 100 chetrum.
– ORIGIN Dzongkha.

Nguni /(ə)ŋˈguːni/ ▸ **noun** (pl. **same**) **1** a member of a group of Bantu-speaking peoples living mainly in southern Africa.
2 [mass noun] the group of closely related Bantu languages, including Xhosa, Zulu, Swazi, and Ndebele, spoken by the Nguni.
▸ **adjective** relating to the Nguni or their languages.
– ORIGIN from Zulu.

ngwee /(ə)ŋˈgweɪ/ ▸ **noun** (pl. **same**) a monetary unit of Zambia, equal to one hundredth of a kwacha.
– ORIGIN a local word.

NH ▸ **abbreviation** New Hampshire (in official postal use).

NHS ▸ **abbreviation** (in the UK) National Health Service.

Nhulunbuy /ˌnjuːlənˈbʌɪ/ a bauxite-mining centre on the NE coast of Arnhem Land in Northern Territory, Australia; pop. 4,112 (2008).

NI ▸ **abbreviation** ■ (in the UK) National Insurance. ■ Northern Ireland. ■ (in New Zealand) the North Island.

Ni ▸ **symbol** the chemical element nickel.

niacin /ˈnʌɪəsɪn/ ▸ **noun** another term for NICOTINIC ACID.

Niagara Falls /nʌɪˈag(ə)rə/ waterfalls on the Niagara River, consisting of two principal parts separated by Goat Island: the Horseshoe Falls adjoining the west (Canadian) bank, which fall 47 m (158 ft), and the American Falls adjoining the east (American) bank, which fall 50 m (167 ft). ■ a city in upper New York State situated on the right bank of the Niagara River beside the Falls; pop. 51,345 (est. 2008). ■ a city in Canada, in southern Ontario, situated on the left bank of the Niagara River beside the Falls, opposite the city of Niagara Falls, US, to which it is linked by bridges; pop. 82,184 (2006).

Niagara River a river of North America, flowing northwards for 56 km (35 miles) from Lake Erie to Lake Ontario, and forming part of the border between Canada and the US.

Niamey /njɑːˈmeɪ/ the capital of Niger, a port on the River Niger; pop. 915,000 (est. 2007).

nib ▸ **noun 1** the pointed end part of a pen, which distributes the ink on the writing surface. ■ a pointed or projecting part of an object.
2 (nibs) shelled and crushed coffee or cocoa beans.
3 a speck of solid matter in a coat of paint or varnish.
– DERIVATIVES **nibbed** adjective.
– ORIGIN late 16th cent. (in the sense 'beak, nose'): probably from Middle Dutch *nib* or Middle Low German *nibbe*, variant of *nebbe* 'beak' (see NEB).

nibbana /nɪˈbɑːnə/ ▸ **noun** Buddhism another term for NIRVANA.
– ORIGIN Pali *nibbāna*, from Sanskrit *nirvāṇa* (see NIRVANA).

N

nibble ▸ verb **1** [with obj.] take small bites out of: *he nibbled a biscuit* | [no obj.] *she nibbled at her food.* ■ [no obj.] eat frequently in small amounts. ■ gently bite at (a part of the body), especially amorously or nervously: *Sebastian was nibbling Gloria's ear.* ■ [no obj.] gradually erode or diminish: *inflation was **nibbling away** at spending power.*
2 [no obj.] informal show cautious interest in a commercial opportunity: *there's an American agent nibbling.*
▸ noun **1** an act or instance of nibbling. ■ a small piece of food bitten off. ■ (**nibbles**) informal small savoury snacks, typically eaten before a meal or with drinks.
2 informal a show of interest in a commercial opportunity.
– ORIGIN late 15th cent.: probably of Low German or Dutch origin; compare with Low German *nibbeln* 'gnaw'.

nibbler ▸ noun **1** a person who habitually nibbles at food.
2 a cutting tool in which a rapidly reciprocating punch knocks out a line of overlapping small holes from a metal sheet.

Nibelung /ˈniːbəlʊŋ/ ▸ noun (pl. **Nibelungs** or **Nibelungen** /-ˌlʊŋ(ə)n/) Germanic Mythology **1** a member of a Scandinavian race of dwarfs, owners of a hoard of gold and magic treasures, who were ruled by Nibelung, king of Nibelheim (land of mist).
2 (in the Nibelungenlied) a supporter of Siegfried, or one of the Burgundians who stole the hoard from him.
– ORIGIN Old High German, from *nibel* 'mist' + the patronymic ending *-ung*.

Nibelungenlied /ˈniːbəlʊŋən,liːd/, German /ˈniːbəlʊŋən,liːt/ a 13th-century German poem, embodying a story found in the (Poetic) Edda, telling of the life and death of Siegfried, a prince of the Netherlands. There have been many adaptations of the story, including Wagner's epic music drama *Der Ring des Nibelungen* (1847–74).
– ORIGIN German, from **NIBELUNG** + *Lied* 'song'.

niblet ▸ noun a small piece of food.
– ORIGIN late 19th cent.: from **NIBBLE** + **-LET**.

niblick /ˈnɪblɪk/ ▸ noun Golf, dated an iron with a heavy, lofted head, such as a nine-iron, used especially for playing out of bunkers.
– ORIGIN mid 19th cent.: of unknown origin.

nibs ▸ noun (**his nibs**) informal a mock title used to refer to a self-important man, especially one in authority.
– ORIGIN early 19th cent.: of unknown origin; compare with earlier *nabs*, used similarly with a possessive adjective as in *his nabs*, on the pattern of references to the aristocracy such as *his lordship*.

NIC ▸ abbreviation ■ (in the UK) National Insurance contribution. ■ newly industrialized country. ■ Nicaragua (international vehicle registration).

NiCad /ˈnʌɪkad/ (also US trademark **Nicad**) ▸ noun [usu. as modifier] a battery or cell with a nickel anode, a cadmium cathode, and a potassium hydroxide electrolyte. NiCads are used chiefly as a rechargeable power source for portable equipment.
– ORIGIN 1950s: blend of **NICKEL** and **CADMIUM**.

Nicaea /nʌɪˈsiːə/ an ancient city in Asia Minor, on the site of modern Iznik, which was important in Roman and Byzantine times. It was the site of two ecumenical councils of the early Christian Church (in 325 and 787). See also **NICENE CREED**.
– DERIVATIVES **Nicaean** adjective & noun.

Nicam /ˈnʌɪkam/ (also **NICAM**) ▸ noun [mass noun] a digital system used in British television to provide video signals with high quality stereo sound.
– ORIGIN 1980s: acronym from *near instantaneously companded audio multiplex*.

Nicaragua /ˌnɪkəˈragjʊə, -ˈragwə/ the largest country in Central America, with a coastline on both the Atlantic and the Pacific Ocean; pop. 5,891,200 (est. 2009); official language, Spanish; capital, Managua.

> Colonized by the Spaniards, Nicaragua broke away from Spain in 1821 and, after brief membership of the United Provinces of Central America, became an independent republic in 1838. In 1979 the dictator Anastasio Somoza was overthrown by a popular revolution; the new left-wing Sandinista regime then faced a counter-revolutionary guerrilla campaign by the US-backed Contras. In the 1990 election the Sandinistas lost power to an opposition coalition.

– DERIVATIVES **Nicaraguan** adjective & noun.

Nicaragua, Lake a lake near the west coast of Nicaragua, the largest lake in Central America.

Nice /niːs/ a resort city on the French Riviera, near the border with Italy; pop. 348,721 (2007).

nice ▸ adjective **1** giving pleasure or satisfaction; pleasant or attractive: *we had a very nice time.* ■ (of a person) good-natured; kind: *he's a nicer man than Mark* | *Joe had been very **nice to** her.* ■ ironic not good; unpleasant: *that's a nice way to come into my kitchen—no greeting!*
2 (especially of a difference) slight or subtle: *there is a nice distinction between self-sacrifice and martyrdom.* ■ requiring careful consideration: *a nice point.*
3 archaic fastidious; scrupulous.
– PHRASES **make nice** (or **nice-nice**) N. Amer. informal be pleasant or polite to someone, typically in a hypocritical way. **nice and ——** satisfactorily in terms of the quality described: *it's nice and warm in here.* **nice one** Brit. informal used to express approval. **nice to meet you** a polite formula used on being introduced to someone. **nice work** Brit. informal used to express approval of a task well done: *'You did a good job today—nice work, James.'* **nice work if you can get it** informal used to express envy of what is perceived to be another person's more favourable situation, which they seem to have attained with little effort.
– DERIVATIVES **niceish** adjective.
– ORIGIN Middle English (in the sense 'stupid'): from Old French, from Latin *nescius* 'ignorant', from *nescire* 'not know'. Other early senses included 'coy, reserved', giving rise to 'fastidious, scrupulous': this led both to the sense 'fine, subtle' (regarded by some as the 'correct' sense), and to the main current senses.

nicely ▸ adverb in a pleasant or attractive manner: *nicely dressed in flowered cotton.* ■ satisfactorily: *we're doing very nicely now.* ■ in a polite or friendly way.

Nicene Creed /nʌɪˈsiːn, ˈnʌɪ-/ a formal statement of Christian belief which is very widely used in Christian liturgies, based on that adopted at the first Council of Nicaea in 325.

niceness ▸ noun [mass noun] the quality of being nice; pleasantness: *her sheer niceness won her many friends.*

nicety /ˈnʌɪsɪti/ ▸ noun (pl. **niceties**) a fine or subtle detail or distinction: *legal niceties are wasted on him.* ■ [mass noun] accuracy or precision: *she prided herself on her nicety of pronunciation.* ■ a detail or aspect of polite social behaviour: *we were brought up to observe the niceties.*
– PHRASES **to a nicety** precisely.
– ORIGIN Middle English (in the sense 'foolish conduct'): from Old French *nicete*, based on Latin *nescius* 'ignorant' (see **NICE**).

niche /niːʃ, nɪtʃ/ ▸ noun **1** a shallow recess, especially one in a wall to display a statue or other ornament.
2 (**one's niche**) a comfortable or suitable position in life or employment. ■ Ecology a role taken by a type of organism within its community.
3 a specialized but profitable segment of the market: [as modifier] *a niche market for quality food.*
▸ verb [with obj.] place (something) in a niche.
– ORIGIN early 17th cent.: from French, literally 'recess', from *nicher* 'make a nest', based on Latin *nidus* 'nest'.

Nichiren /ˈnɪʃərən/ (also **Nichiren Buddhism**) ▸ noun [mass noun] a Japanese Buddhist sect founded by the religious teacher Nichiren (1222–82) with the Lotus Sutra as its central scripture. See also **SOKA GAKKAI**.

Nicholas the name of two tsars of Russia: ■ **Nicholas I** (1796–1855), brother of Alexander I, reigned 1825–55. At home he pursued rigidly conservative policies, while his expansionism in the Near East led to the Crimean War. ■ **Nicholas II** (1868–1918), son of Alexander III, reigned 1894–1917. Forced to abdicate after the Russian Revolution in 1917, he was shot along with his family a year later.

Nicholas, St (4th century), Christian prelate. Said to have been bishop of Myra in Lycia, he is patron saint of children, sailors, Greece, and Russia. The figure of Santa Claus (a corruption of St Nicholas) derives from the Dutch custom of giving gifts to children on his feast day (6 December).

Nicholson[1], Ben (1894–1982), English painter; full name *Benjamin Lauder Nicholson*. He was a pioneer of British abstract art, noted for his painted reliefs with circular and rectangular motifs.

Nicholson[2], Jack (b.1937), American actor. He won Oscars for *One Flew Over the Cuckoo's Nest* (1975) and *Terms of Endearment* (1983). Other films include *The Shining* (1980) and *Batman* (1989).

nichrome /ˈnʌɪkrəʊm/ ▸ noun [mass noun] trademark an alloy of nickel with chromium (10 to 20 per cent) and sometimes iron (up to 25 per cent), used chiefly in high-temperature applications such as electrical heating elements.
– ORIGIN early 20th cent.: blend of **NICKEL** and **CHROME**.

nick[1] ▸ noun **1** a small cut or notch.
2 (**the nick**) Brit. informal prison. ■ a police station: *he was being fingerprinted in the nick.*
3 the junction between the floor and side walls in a squash court or real tennis court.
▸ verb [with obj.] **1** make a nick or nicks in: *he had nicked himself while shaving.*
2 Brit. informal steal: *she nicked fivers from the till.* ■ (**nick someone for**) N. Amer. informal cheat someone of (a sum of money): *banks will be nicked for an extra $40 million.*
3 Brit. informal arrest (someone): *Stuart and Dan got nicked for burglary.*
– PHRASES **in —— nick** Brit. informal in a specified condition: *you've kept the car in good nick.* **in the nick of time** only just in time.
– ORIGIN late Middle English: of unknown origin.

nick[2] ▸ verb [no obj., with adverbial of direction] Austral./NZ informal go quickly or surreptitiously: *they nicked across the road.* ■ (**nick off**) depart; go away.
– ORIGIN late 19th cent.: probably a figurative use of **NICK**[1] in the sense 'to steal'.

nickel ▸ noun **1** [mass noun] a silvery-white metal, the chemical element of atomic number 28. (Symbol: **Ni**)

> Nickel occurs naturally in various minerals and the earth's core is believed to consist largely of metallic iron and nickel. Its chief use is in alloys, especially with iron, to which it imparts strength and resistance to corrosion, and with copper for coinage.

2 N. Amer. a five-cent coin; five cents.
▸ verb (**nickels, nickelling, nickelled**; US **nickels, nickeling, nickeled**) [with obj.] (usu. as adj. **nickelled**) coat with nickel.
– DERIVATIVES **nickelous** adjective.
– ORIGIN mid 18th cent.: shortening of German *Kupfernickel*, the copper-coloured ore from which nickel was first obtained, from *Kupfer* 'copper' + *Nickel* 'demon' (with reference to the ore's failure to yield copper).

nickel-and-dime N. Amer. informal ▸ verb [with obj.] harass (someone) by charging for many trivial items or services.
▸ adjective [attrib.] of little importance: *the only games this weekend are nickel-and-dime stuff.*
– ORIGIN 1930s: originally denoting a shop selling articles costing five or ten cents.

nickel brass ▸ noun [mass noun] an alloy of copper, zinc, and a small amount of nickel.

nickelodeon /ˌnɪkəˈləʊdɪən/ ▸ noun N. Amer. **1** informal, dated a jukebox, originally one operated by the insertion of a nickel coin.
2 historical a cinema with an admission fee of one nickel.
– ORIGIN early 20th cent.: from **NICKEL** + a shortened form of **MELODEON**.

nickel silver ▸ noun another term for **GERMAN SILVER**.

nickel steel ▸ noun [mass noun] a type of stainless steel containing chromium and nickel.

nicker[1] ▸ noun (pl. **same**) Brit. informal a pound sterling.
– ORIGIN early 20th cent.: of unknown origin.

nicker[2] ▸ verb [no obj.] (of a horse) give a soft breathy whinny.
▸ noun a nickering sound.
– ORIGIN late 16th cent.: imitative.

Nicklaus /ˈnɪklaʊs, -ləs/, Jack William (b.1940), American golfer. He won more than eighty tournaments during his professional career.

nick-nack ▸ noun variant spelling of **KNICK-KNACK**.

nickname ▸ noun a familiar or humorous name given to a person or thing instead of or as well as the real name.
▸ verb [with obj. and complement] give a nickname to: *an area nicknamed Sniper's Alley.*
– ORIGIN late Middle English: from *an eke-name* (*eke* meaning 'addition': see **EKE**[2]), misinterpreted, by wrong division, as *a neke name.*

Nicobarese /ˌnɪkəbəˈriːz/ ▸ noun (pl. **same**) **1** a native or inhabitant of the Nicobar Islands.
2 [mass noun] an ancient language spoken in the Nicobar Islands, distantly related to the Mon-Khmer and Munda families. It now has fewer than 20,000 speakers.

▶ **adjective** relating to the Nicobar Islands, their inhabitants, or their language.

Nicobar Islands see **ANDAMAN AND NICOBAR ISLANDS**.

Niçois /niːˈswɑː/ ▶ **noun** (fem. **Niçoise** /niːˈswɑːz/) a native or inhabitant of the city of Nice.
▶ **adjective** relating to Nice or its inhabitants: *the Niçois dialect*.
– ORIGIN French.

Nicol prism /ˈnɪk(ə)l/ ▶ **noun** a device for producing plane-polarized light, consisting of two pieces of optically clear calcite or Iceland spar cemented together with Canada balsam in the shape of a prism.
– ORIGIN mid 19th cent.: named after William *Nicol* (died 1851), the Scottish physicist who invented it.

Nicosia /ˌnɪkəˈsiːə/ the capital of Cyprus; pop. 233,000 (est. 2007). Since 1974 it has been divided into Greek and Turkish sectors.

nicotiana /ˌnɪkɒtɪˈɑːnə, -kəʊʃ-/ ▶ **noun** an ornamental plant related to tobacco, with tubular flowers that are particularly fragrant at night. Also called **TOBACCO PLANT**. ● Genus *Nicotiana*, family Solanaceae: several species, in particular *N. alata*.
– ORIGIN from modern Latin *nicotiana* (*herba*) 'tobacco (plant)', named after Jean *Nicot*, a 16th-cent. French diplomat who introduced tobacco to France in 1560.

nicotinamide /ˌnɪkəˈtɪnəmʌɪd/ ▶ **noun** [mass noun] Biochemistry a compound which is the form in which nicotinic acid often occurs in nature. ● The amide of nicotinic acid; chem. formula: $(C_5H_4N)CONH_2$.

nicotinamide adenine dinucleotide ▶ **noun** see **NAD**.

nicotinate /ˈnɪkətɪneɪt/ ▶ **noun** Chemistry a salt or ester of nicotinic acid.

nicotine /ˈnɪkətiːn/ ▶ **noun** [mass noun] a toxic colourless or yellowish oily liquid which is the chief active constituent of tobacco. It acts as a stimulant in small doses, but in larger amounts blocks the action of autonomic nerve and skeletal muscle cells. ● An alkaloid; chem. formula: $C_{10}H_{14}N_2$.
– ORIGIN early 19th cent.: from French, from **NICOTIANA** + **-INE**[4].

nicotine patch ▶ **noun** a patch impregnated with nicotine, which is worn on the skin by a person trying to give up smoking. Nicotine is gradually absorbed into the bloodstream, helping reduce the craving for cigarettes.

nicotinic acid /nɪkəˈtɪnɪk/ ▶ **noun** [mass noun] Biochemistry a vitamin of the B complex which is widely distributed in foods such as milk, wheat germ, and meat, and can be synthesized in the body from tryptophan. Its deficiency causes pellagra. Also called **NIACIN**. ● Alternative name: **3-pyridinecarboxylic acid**; chem. formula: $(C_5H_4N)COOH$.

nictation ▶ **noun** [mass noun] technical the action or process of blinking.
– ORIGIN late 18th cent.: from Latin *nictatio(n-)*, from the verb *nictare* 'to blink'.

nictitating membrane ▶ **noun** Zoology a whitish or translucent membrane that forms an inner eyelid in birds, reptiles, and some mammals. It can be drawn across the eye to protect it from dust and keep it moist. Also called **THIRD EYELID**.
– ORIGIN early 18th cent.: *nictitating* based on medieval Latin *nictitat* 'blinked', frequentative of *nictare*.

nidation /nʌɪˈdeɪʃ(ə)n/ ▶ **noun** another term for **IMPLANTATION**.
– ORIGIN late 19th cent.: from Latin *nidus* 'nest' + **-ATION**.

nide /nʌɪd/ ▶ **noun** archaic a brood or nest of pheasants.
– ORIGIN late 17th cent.: from French *nid* or Latin *nidus* 'nest'.

nidicolous /nɪˈdɪk(ə)ləs/ ▶ **adjective** another term for **ALTRICIAL**.
– ORIGIN early 20th cent.: from Latin *nidus* 'nest' + *-colus* 'inhabiting' (from the verb *colere* 'live in, cultivate').

nidification /ˌnɪdɪfɪˈkeɪʃ(ə)n/ ▶ **noun** [mass noun] Zoology nest-building.
– ORIGIN mid 17th cent.: from Latin *nidificat-* 'made into a nest' (from the verb *nidificare*, from *nidus* 'nest') + **-ATION**.

nidifugous /nɪˈdɪfjʊɡəs/ ▶ **adjective** another term for **PRECOCIAL**.
– ORIGIN early 20th cent.: from Latin *nidus* 'nest' + *fugere* 'flee' + **-OUS**.

nidus /ˈnʌɪdəs/ ▶ **noun** (pl. **nidi** /-dʌɪ/ or **niduses**) chiefly technical a place in which something is formed or deposited; a site of origin. ■ Medicine a place in which bacteria have multiplied or may multiply; a focus of infection.
– ORIGIN late 17th cent. (in the former sense 'place in which an insect deposits its eggs'): from Latin, literally 'nest'.

niece ▶ **noun** a daughter of one's brother or sister, or of one's brother-in-law or sister-in-law.
– ORIGIN Middle English: from Old French, based on Latin *neptis* 'granddaughter', feminine of *nepos* 'nephew, grandson' (see **NEPHEW**), from an Indo-European root shared by Dutch *nicht*, German *Nichte*.

Niederösterreich /ˈniːdɐˌøːstəraɪç/ German name for **LOWER AUSTRIA**.

Niedersachsen /ˈniːdɐˌzaksn/ German name for **LOWER SAXONY**.

niello /nɪˈɛləʊ/ ▶ **noun** [mass noun] a black compound of sulphur with silver, lead, or copper, used for filling in engraved designs in silver or other metals. ■ objects decorated with niello.
– DERIVATIVES **nielloed** adjective.
– ORIGIN early 19th cent.: from Italian, from Latin *nigellus*, diminutive of *niger* 'black'.

nielsbohrium /niːlzˈbɔːrɪəm/ ▶ **noun** [mass noun] a name proposed by the American Chemical Society for the chemical element of atomic number 107, now called **bohrium**.
– ORIGIN modern Latin, from the name of the scientist *Niels Bohr* (see **BOHR**). The term was originally proposed (*c.*1971) by Soviet scientists for element 105 (dubnium).

Niemeyer /ˈniːmʌɪə/, Oscar (b.1907), Brazilian architect. An early exponent of modernist architecture in Latin America, he designed the main public buildings of Brasilia (1950–60).

Niemöller /ˈniːməːlə/, German /ˈniːmœlɐ/, Martin (1892–1984), German Lutheran pastor. An outspoken opponent of Nazism, he was imprisoned in Sachsenhausen and Dachau concentration camps (1937–45).

niente /nɪˈɛnteɪ/ ▶ **adverb & adjective** Music (especially as a direction) with the sound or tone gradually fading to nothing.
– ORIGIN Italian, literally 'nothing'.

Niersteiner /ˈnɪəˌʃtʌɪnə/, German /ˈniːɐˌʃtaɪnɐ/ ▶ **noun** [mass noun] a white Rhine wine produced in the region around Nierstein, a town in Germany.

Nietzsche /ˈniːtʃə/, Friedrich Wilhelm (1844–1900), German philosopher. He is known for repudiating Christianity's compassion for the weak, exalting the 'will to power', and formulating the idea of the *Übermensch* (superman), who can rise above the restrictions of ordinary morality.
– DERIVATIVES **Nietzschean** adjective & noun, **Nietzscheanism** noun.

nifedipine /nʌɪˈfɛdɪpiːn/ ▶ **noun** [mass noun] Medicine a synthetic compound which acts as a calcium antagonist and is used as a coronary vasodilator in the treatment of cardiac and circulatory disorders.
– ORIGIN 1970s: from *ni(tro-)* + *fe* (alteration of **PHENYL**) + **DI-**[1] + *p(yrid)ine*, elements of the systematic name.

niff Brit. informal ▶ **noun** an unpleasant smell.
▶ **verb** [no obj.] have an unpleasant smell.
– DERIVATIVES **niffy** adjective (**niffier**, **niffiest**).
– ORIGIN early 20th cent. (originally dialect): perhaps from **SNIFF**.

Niflheim /ˈnɪv(ə)lˌheɪm, -ˌhʌɪm/ Scandinavian Mythology an underworld of eternal cold, darkness, and mist inhabited by those who died of old age or illness.
– ORIGIN from Old Norse *Niflheimr*, literally 'world of mist'.

nifty ▶ **adjective** (**niftier**, **niftiest**) informal particularly good, skilful, or effective: *nifty footwork*. ■ attractive or stylish: *a nifty black shirt*.
– DERIVATIVES **niftily** adverb, **niftiness** noun.
– ORIGIN mid 19th cent.: of unknown origin.

nigella /nʌɪˈdʒɛlə/ ▶ **noun** a plant of a genus which includes love-in-a-mist. ● Genus *Nigella*, family Ranunculaceae.
– ORIGIN modern Latin, feminine of Latin *nigellus*, diminutive of *niger* 'black'.

Niger 1 /ˈnʌɪdʒə/ a river in NW Africa, which rises on the NE border of Sierra Leone and flows in a great arc for 4,100 km (2,550 miles) north-east to Mali, then south-east through western Niger and Nigeria, before turning southwards into the Gulf of Guinea.
2 /niːˈʒɛː/ a landlocked country in West Africa, on the southern edge of the Sahara; pop. 15,306,300 (est. 2009): languages, French (official), Hausa, and other West African languages; capital, Niamey. Part of French West Africa from 1922, Niger became an autonomous republic within the French Community in 1958 and fully independent in 1960.
– DERIVATIVES **Nigerien** /niːˈʒɛːrɪən/ noun & adjective.

Niger–Congo ▶ **adjective** denoting or belonging to a large phylum of languages in Africa, named after the Rivers Niger and Congo. It comprises most of the languages spoken by the indigenous peoples of Africa south of the Sahara and includes the Bantu, Mande, Gur, and Kwa families.

Nigeria /nʌɪˈdʒɪərɪə/ a country on the coast of West Africa; pop. 149,229,100 (est. 2009); languages, English (official), Hausa, Igbo, Yoruba, and others; capital, Abuja.

> The site of highly developed kingdoms in the Middle Ages, the area came under British influence during the 19th century and was made into a single colony in 1914. Independence came in 1960 and the state became a federal republic in 1963, remaining a member of the Commonwealth. Oil was discovered in the 1960s and 1970s, since when Nigeria has emerged as one of the world's major exporters. The country was suspended from the Commonwealth 1995–9 following the execution of the writer and activist Ken Saro-Wiwa (b.1941) in 1995.

– DERIVATIVES **Nigerian** adjective & noun.

niggard /ˈnɪɡəd/ ▶ **noun** a mean or ungenerous person; a miser.
– ORIGIN late Middle English: alteration of earlier *nigon*, probably of Scandinavian origin.

niggardly ▶ **adjective** ungenerous with money, time, etc.; mean: *Madame's niggardly nature*. ■ meagre and given grudgingly: *niggardly allowances from the Treasury*.
▶ **adverb** archaic in a mean or meagre manner.
– DERIVATIVES **niggardliness** noun.
– ORIGIN mid 16th cent.: from **NIGGARD** + **-LY**[1].

> **USAGE** The word **niggardly** has no connection with the highly offensive term **nigger**, but because of the similarity of sound and its negative meaning of 'mean, ungenerous' many people are uncomfortable with using it for fear of causing offence, and in the US it is now widely avoided.

nigger ▶ **noun** offensive a contemptuous term for a black person.
– ORIGIN late 17th cent. (as an adjective): from earlier *neger*, from French *nègre*, from Spanish *negro* 'black' (see **NEGRO**).

> **USAGE** The word **nigger** was first used as an adjective denoting a black person in the 17th century, and has long had strong offensive connotations. Today it remains one of the most racially offensive words in the language. However, it has acquired a new strand of use in recent years: it is sometimes used by black people as a mildly disparaging way of referring to other black people, in much the same way that *queer* has been adopted by some gay people as a term of self-reference, acceptable only when used by those within the community.

niggle ▶ **verb** [no obj.] cause slight but persistent annoyance, discomfort, or anxiety: *Doreen wanted to discuss matters that* **niggled at** *her mind* | (as adj. **niggling**) *niggling aches and pains*. ■ [with obj.] criticize or annoy (someone) in a petty way: *people niggling me for doing too much work*.
▶ **noun** a trivial criticism, discomfort, or annoyance.
– DERIVATIVES **nigglingly** adverb, **niggly** adjective.
– ORIGIN early 17th cent. (in the sense 'do in an ineffectual way'): apparently of Scandinavian origin; compare with Norwegian *nigla*. Current senses date from the late 18th cent.

nigh ▶ **adverb, preposition, & adjective 1** archaic or literary near: [as adj.] *the end is nigh* | [as adv.] *they drew nigh unto the city*.
2 almost: [as adv.] *a car weighing* **nigh on** *two tons*.
– ORIGIN Old English *nēh*, *nēah*, of Germanic origin; related to Dutch *na*, German *nah*. Compare with **NEAR**.

night ▶ **noun 1** the period from sunset to sunrise in each twenty-four hours: *a moonless night* | *the door is always locked* **at night**. ■ the night as the interval between two days: *supplements per person per night*. ■ the darkness of night: *a line of watchfires stretched away* **into the night**. ■ literary nightfall.
2 the period between afternoon and bedtime; an evening: *he was not allowed to go out on weekday nights*. ■ an evening characterized by a particular event or activity: *a quiz night* | *wasn't it a great* **night out**?
▶ **exclamation** informal short for **GOODNIGHT**.

▸ adverb (**nights**) informal, chiefly N. Amer. during the night; at night: *investments that won't keep us awake nights with worry.*
– PHRASES **night and day** all the time; constantly.
– DERIVATIVES **nightless** adjective.
– ORIGIN Old English *neaht*, *niht*, of Germanic origin; related to Dutch *nacht* and German *Nacht*, from an Indo-European root shared by Latin *nox* and Greek *nux*.

night adder ▸ noun a venomous nocturnal African viper. ● Genus *Causus*, family Viperidae: several species, in particular the grey and black *C. rhombeatus*, common in southern Africa.
■ S. African any of a number of non-venomous nocturnal colubrid snakes.

nightbird ▸ noun another term for **NIGHT OWL**.

night blindness ▸ noun less technical term for **NYCTALOPIA**.

night-blooming cereus ▸ noun a tropical climbing cactus with aerial roots and heavily scented flowers that open only at night and are typically pollinated by bats. ● Genera *Hylocereus* and *Selenicereus*, family Cactaceae: several species, in particular *H. undatus*.

nightcap ▸ noun **1** historical a cap worn in bed.
2 a hot or alcoholic drink taken before bedtime.
3 Baseball the second game of a double-header.

nightclothes ▸ plural noun clothes worn in bed.

nightclub ▸ noun a club that is open from the evening until early morning, having facilities such as a bar and disco or other entertainment.
– DERIVATIVES **nightclubber** noun, **nightclubbing** noun.

night crawler ▸ noun N. Amer. **1** an earthworm that comes to the surface at night and is used as fishing bait.
2 informal a person who is socially active at night.

nightdress ▸ noun a light, loose garment worn by a woman or child in bed.

nightfall ▸ noun the onset of night; dusk.

nightgown ▸ noun **1** a nightdress.
2 archaic a dressing gown.

nighthawk ▸ noun **1** an American nightjar with sharply pointed wings. ● Family Caprimulgidae: four genera and several species, in particular the **common nighthawk** (*Chordeiles minor*) of North America.
2 North American term for **NIGHT OWL**.

N

night heron ▸ noun a small short-necked heron that is active mainly at night. ● Genus *Nycticorax*, family Ardeidae: several species.

nightie ▸ noun informal a nightdress.

Nightingale, Florence (1820–1910), English nurse and medical reformer. In 1854, during the Crimean War, she improved sanitation and medical procedures at the army hospital at Scutari, achieving a dramatic reduction in the mortality rate.

nightingale ▸ noun a small migratory thrush with drab brownish plumage, noted for its rich melodious song which can often be heard at night. ● *Luscinia megarhynchos*, family Turdidae.
– ORIGIN Old English *nihtegala*, of Germanic origin; related to Dutch *nachtegaal* and German *Nachtigall*, from the base of **NIGHT** and a base meaning 'sing'.

nightjar ▸ noun a nocturnal insectivorous bird with grey-brown camouflaged plumage, large eyes and gape, and a distinctive call. ● Family Caprimulgidae (the **nightjar family**): several genera, especially *Caprimulgus*, and many species, including the **European nightjar** (*C. europaeus*), which has a chirring call. The nightjar family also includes the nighthawks, pauraques, poorwills, whippoorwills, and chuck-will's-widow.

Night Journey (in Muslim tradition) the journey through the heavens made by Muhammad, guided by the archangel Gabriel. They flew first to Jerusalem, where Muhammad prayed with earlier prophets including Abraham, Moses, and Jesus, before entering the presence of Allah in heaven.

nightlife ▸ noun [mass noun] social activities or entertainment available at night in a town or city.

night light ▸ noun a lamp or candle providing a dim light during the night.

nightly ▸ adjective **1** happening or done every night: *his nightly TV talk show.*
2 happening, done, or existing in the night.
▸ adverb every night: *the hotel features live music nightly.*

nightmare ▸ noun **1** a frightening or unpleasant dream.
2 a very unpleasant or frightening experience or prospect: *the nightmare of racial hatred* | *developing thunderclouds are a balloonist's worst nightmare.* ■ a person or situation that is very difficult to deal with: *buying wine can be a nightmare if you don't know enough about it.*
– ORIGIN Middle English (denoting a female evil spirit thought to lie upon and suffocate sleepers): from **NIGHT** + Old English *mære* 'incubus'.

nightmarish ▸ adjective of the nature of a nightmare; very frightening or unpleasant: *a nightmarish vision of the future* | *a nightmarish eight-hour journey.*
– DERIVATIVES **nightmarishly** adverb.

night monkey ▸ noun another term for **DOUROUCOULI**.

night of the long knives ▸ noun a treacherous massacre or betrayal, especially the massacre of the Brownshirts on Hitler's orders in June 1934.

night owl ▸ noun informal a person who is habitually active or wakeful at night.

night safe ▸ noun Brit. a safe with access from the outer wall of a bank for the deposit of money or other valuables when the bank is closed.

night school ▸ noun an institution providing evening classes for those working during the day.

nightshade ▸ noun a plant related to the potato, typically having poisonous black or red berries. Several kinds of nightshade have been used in the production of herbal medicines. ● *Solanum* and other genera, family Solanaceae (the **nightshade family**): several species, including the European **woody nightshade** (*S. dulcamara*), a climber with purple flowers and red berries. The nightshade family includes many commercially important plants (potato, tomato, capsicum peppers, tobacco) as well as a number of highly poisonous ones (henbane, thorn apple). See also **DEADLY NIGHTSHADE**.
– ORIGIN Old English *nihtscada*, apparently from **NIGHT** + **SHADE**, probably with reference to the dark colour and poisonous properties of the berries. Compare with German *Nachtschatten*.

night shift ▸ noun a period of time worked at night in a factory, hospital, etc. ■ the employees who work during the night shift.

nightshirt ▸ noun a long shirt worn in bed especially by boys or men.

nightside ▸ noun **1** the side of a planet or moon facing away from the sun and therefore in darkness.
2 [mass noun] chiefly US activities that take place during the night.

night soil ▸ noun [mass noun] human excrement collected at night from buckets, cesspools, and privies and sometimes used as manure.

nightspot ▸ noun informal a nightclub.

nightstick ▸ noun N. Amer. a police officer's truncheon.

night table (also **nightstand**) ▸ noun N. Amer. a small low bedside table, typically having drawers.

night terrors ▸ plural noun feelings of great fear experienced on suddenly waking in the night.

night-time ▸ noun the time between evening and morning; the time of darkness: [as modifier] *they asked police for extra night-time patrols.*

night vision ▸ noun [mass noun] the faculty of seeing in the dark, especially when the eyes have become adapted to the low level of light. ■ [as modifier] denoting devices that enable the user to see in the dark.

nightwatchman ▸ noun (pl. **nightwatchmen**) **1** a person whose job is to guard a building at night.
2 Cricket an inferior batsman sent in to bat when a wicket falls just before the end of a day's play, to avoid the dismissal of a better one in adverse conditions.

nightwear ▸ noun [mass noun] clothing suitable for wearing in bed.

nigiri zushi /ˌnɪɡɪri ˈzuːʃi/ ▸ noun [mass noun] a type of sushi consisting of a small ball of rice, smeared with wasabi paste and topped with raw fish or other seafood.
– ORIGIN Japanese, from *nigiri-* (combining form of *nigiru* 'clasp, clench, roll in the hands') + *-zushi* **SUSHI**.

nigrescent /nɪˈɡrɛs(ə)nt, nʌɪ-/ ▸ adjective rare blackish.
– DERIVATIVES **nigrescence** noun.
– ORIGIN mid 18th cent.: from Latin *nigrescent-* 'growing black', from the verb *nigrescere*, from *niger*, *nigr-* 'black'.

nigritude /ˈnɪɡrɪtjuːd/ ▸ noun [mass noun] rare blackness.
– ORIGIN mid 17th cent.: from Latin *nigritudo* 'blackness', from *niger*, *nigr-* 'black'.

Nihang /ˈnɪhaŋ/ ▸ noun (in South Asia) a member of a militant fundamentalist Sikh movement.
– ORIGIN from Persian *nihang*, literally 'crocodile'.

nihilism /ˈnʌɪ(h)ɪlɪz(ə)m/ ▸ noun [mass noun] the rejection of all religious and moral principles, often in the belief that life is meaningless. ■ Philosophy the belief that nothing in the world has a real existence. ■ historical the doctrine of an extreme Russian revolutionary party *c.*1900 which found nothing to approve of in the established social order.
– DERIVATIVES **nihilist** noun.
– ORIGIN early 19th cent.: from Latin *nihil* 'nothing' + **-ISM**.

nihilistic /nʌɪ(h)ɪˈlɪstɪk/ ▸ adjective rejecting all religious and moral principles in the belief that life is meaningless: *an embittered, nihilistic teenager.*

nihility /nʌɪˈhɪlɪti, nɪ-/ ▸ noun [mass noun] rare nonexistence; nothingness.
– ORIGIN late 17th cent.: from medieval Latin *nihilitas*, from Latin *nihil* 'nothing'.

nihil obstat /ˌnʌɪhɪl ˈɒbstat, ˌnɪhɪl/ ▸ noun (in the Roman Catholic Church) a certificate that a book is not open to objection on doctrinal or moral grounds.
– ORIGIN Latin, literally 'nothing hinders'.

Niigata /ˌniːɪˈɡɑːtə/ an industrial port in central Japan, on the NW coast of the island of Honshu; pop. 803,791 (2007).

Nijinsky /nɪˈdʒɪnski/, Vaslav (Fomich) (1890–1950), Russian ballet dancer and choreographer. The leading dancer with Diaghilev's Ballets Russes from 1909, he went on to choreograph Debussy's *L'Après-midi d'un faune* (1912) and Stravinsky's *The Rite of Spring* (1913).

Nijmegen /ˈnʌɪmeɪɡ(ə)n/ an industrial town in the eastern Netherlands, south of Arnhem; pop. 161,251 (2008).

-nik ▸ suffix (forming nouns) denoting a person associated with a specified thing or quality: *beatnik* | *refusenik.*
– ORIGIN from Russian (on the pattern of *sputnik*) and Yiddish.

nikah /nɪˈkɑːhə/ ▸ noun a Muslim marriage.
– ORIGIN Urdu and Arabic.

Nike /ˈnʌɪki/ Greek Mythology the goddess of victory.
– ORIGIN Greek, literally 'victory'.

Nikkei index /ˈnɪkeɪ/ a figure indicating the relative price of representative shares on the Tokyo Stock Exchange. Also called **Nikkei average**.
– ORIGIN 1970s: *Nikkei*, abbreviation of *Ni(hon) Kei(zai Shimbun)* 'Japanese Economic Journal'.

Nikolaev /njikaˈlajif/ Russian name for **MYKOLAYIV**.

nil ▸ noun nothing, especially as the score in certain games; zero: *they beat us three-nil.*
▸ adjective non-existent: *his chance of survival was virtually nil.*
– ORIGIN mid 19th cent.: from Latin, contraction of *nihil* 'nothing'.

nil desperandum /ˌdɛspəˈrandəm/ ▸ exclamation do not despair; never despair.
– ORIGIN from Latin *nil desperandum Teucro duce* 'no need to despair with Teucer as your leader', from Horace's *Odes* 1.vii.27.

Nile a river in eastern Africa, the longest river in the world, which rises in east central Africa near Lake Victoria and flows 6,695 km (4,160 miles) generally northwards through Uganda, Sudan, and Egypt to empty through a large delta into the Mediterranean. See also **BLUE NILE**, **ALBERT NILE**, **VICTORIA NILE**, **WHITE NILE**.

Nile, Battle of the another name for **ABOUKIR BAY, BATTLE OF**.

Nile blue ▸ noun [mass noun] a pale greenish blue.
– ORIGIN late 19th cent.: suggested by French *eau de Nil*.

Nile crocodile ▸ noun a large crocodile with a long, narrow head, native to Africa and Madagascar. ● *Crocodilus niloticus*, family Crocodylidae.

Nile green ▸ noun [mass noun] a pale bluish green.

Nile monitor ▸ noun a large heavily built African lizard that has greyish-olive skin with yellow markings and is semiaquatic. ● *Varanus niloticus*, family Varanidae.

Nile perch ▸ noun a large predatory fish found in lakes and rivers in NE and central Africa, widely caught for food or sport. ● *Lates niloticus*, family Centropomidae.

nilgai /ˈnɪlɡʌɪ/ ▸ noun a large Indian antelope, the male of which has a blue-grey coat and short

horns, and the female a tawny coat and no horns. • *Boselaphus tragocamelus*, family Bovidae.
– ORIGIN late 18th cent.: from Hindi *nīlgāī*, from *nīl* 'blue' + *gāī* 'cow'.

Nilgiri Hills /ˈnɪlgɪri/ a range of hills in southern India, in western Tamil Nadu. They form a branch of the Western Ghats.

Nilo-Saharan /ˌnʌɪləʊsəˈhɑːrən/ ▶ **adjective** denoting or belonging to a phylum of languages that includes the Nilotic family together with certain other languages of northern and eastern Africa.
▶ **noun** [mass noun] the Nilo-Saharan phylum of languages.

Nilotic /nʌɪˈlɒtɪk/ ▶ **adjective 1** relating to the River Nile or to the Nile region of Africa.
2 denoting or belonging to a family of languages spoken in Egypt, Sudan, Kenya, and Tanzania. The western group includes Luo and Dinka; the eastern group includes Masai and Turkana.
– ORIGIN via Latin from Greek *Neilōtikos*, from *Neilos* 'Nile'.

nilpotent /nɪlˈpəʊt(ə)nt/ ▶ **adjective** Mathematics becoming zero when raised to some positive integral power.
– ORIGIN late 19th cent.: from NIL + Latin *potens, potent-* 'power'.

nim ▶ **noun** [mass noun] a game in which two players alternately take one or more objects from one of a number of heaps, each trying to take, or to compel the other to take, the last remaining object.
– ORIGIN early 20th cent.: apparently from archaic *nim* 'to take' or from German *nimm!* 'take!', imperative of *nehmen*.

nimble ▶ **adjective** (**nimbler**, **nimblest**) quick and light in movement or action; agile: *with a deft motion of her nimble fingers.* ■ (of the mind) able to think and understand quickly.
– ORIGIN Old English *nǣmel* 'quick to seize or comprehend', related to *niman* 'take', of Germanic origin. The *-b-* was added for ease of pronunciation.

nimbleness ▶ **noun** [mass noun] the quality of being nimble.

nimbly ▶ **adverb** in a nimble way: *the monkey leapt nimbly from rock to rock.*

nimbostratus /ˌnɪmbə(ʊ)ˈstrɑːtəs, -ˈstreɪtəs/ ▶ **noun** [mass noun] cloud forming a thick uniform grey layer at low altitude, from which rain or snow often falls (without any lightning or thunder).
– ORIGIN late 19th cent.: modern Latin, from NIMBUS + STRATUS.

nimbus /ˈnɪmbəs/ ▶ **noun** (pl. **nimbi** /-bʌɪ/ or **nimbuses**) **1** a luminous cloud or a halo surrounding a supernatural being or a saint. ■ a light, colour, etc., that surrounds someone or something.
2 a large grey rain cloud.
– ORIGIN early 17th cent.: from Latin, literally 'cloud, aureole'.

Nimby /ˈnɪmbi/ ▶ **noun** (pl. **Nimbys** or **Nimbies**) informal a person who objects to the siting of something perceived as unpleasant or hazardous in their own neighbourhood, especially while raising no such objections to similar developments elsewhere.
– DERIVATIVES **Nimbyism** noun.
– ORIGIN 1980s: acronym from *not in my back yard.*

Nîmes /niːm/ a city in southern France; pop. 147,114 (2006). It is noted for its many well-preserved Roman remains.

niminy-piminy ▶ **adjective** affectedly prim or refined: *she had a niminy-piminy ladylike air.*
– ORIGIN late 18th cent.: fanciful coinage; compare with NAMBY-PAMBY.

nimrod /ˈnɪmrɒd/ ▶ **noun 1** literary a skilful hunter.
2 N. Amer. informal an inept person.
– ORIGIN late 16th cent.: from Hebrew *Nimrōd*, the name of the great-grandson of Noah, known for his skill as a hunter (see Gen. 10:8-9).

Nimrud /ˈnɪmrʊd/ modern name of an ancient Mesopotamian city on the east bank of the Tigris south of Nineveh, near the modern city of Mosul. It was the capital of Assyria 879–722 BC. The city was known in biblical times as Calah (Gen. 10:11); the modern name arose through association in Islamic mythology with the biblical figure of Nimrod.

nincompoop /ˈnɪŋkəmpuːp/ ▶ **noun** a foolish or stupid person.
– ORIGIN late 17th cent.: perhaps from the given name *Nicholas* or from *Nicodemus* (by association with the Pharisee of this name, and his naive questioning of Christ; compare with French *nicodème* 'simpleton').

nine ▶ **cardinal number** equivalent to the product of three and three; one more than eight, or one less than ten; 9: *nine European countries | nine of the twelve members.* (Roman numeral: **ix** or **IX**) ■ a group of nine individuals. ■ nine years old: *I was only nine.* ■ nine o'clock: *it's ten to nine.* ■ a size of garment or other merchandise denoted by nine. ■ a playing card with nine pips. ■ (**the Nine**) Greek Mythology the nine Muses.
– PHRASES **to** (or Brit. **up to**) **the nines** to a great or elaborate extent: *the women were dressed to the nines.* **nine times out of ten** on nearly every occasion.
– ORIGIN Old English *nigon*, of Germanic origin; related to Dutch *negen* and German *neun*, from an Indo-European root shared by Sanskrit *nava*, Latin *novem*, and Greek *ennea*.

ninefold ▶ **adjective** nine times as great or as numerous: *a ninefold increase in the amount of traffic.* ■ having nine parts or elements.
▶ **adverb** by nine times; to nine times the number or amount: *consumption increased ninefold.*

ninepins ▶ **plural noun** [usu. treated as sing.] the traditional form of the game of skittles, using nine pins and played in an alley. ■ [treated as pl.] skittles used in the game of ninepins.
– PHRASES **go down** (or **drop** or **fall**) **like ninepins** Brit. succumb in large numbers or with little resistance.

nineteen ▶ **cardinal number** one more than eighteen; nine more than ten; 19: *nineteen of the interviewees had never worked.* (Roman numeral: **xix** or **XIX**) ■ nineteen years old: *she married at nineteen.* ■ a size of garment or other merchandise denoted by nineteen.
– PHRASES **talk nineteen to the dozen** see DOZEN.
– DERIVATIVES **nineteenth** ordinal number.
– ORIGIN Old English *nigontȳne*.

nineteenth hole ▶ **noun** humorous the bar in a golf clubhouse, as reached after a standard round of eighteen holes.

nine-to-five ▶ **adjective** used in reference to typical office hours, often to express an idea of predictable routine: *a nine-to-five job.*
▶ **noun** a nine-to-five job.
– DERIVATIVES **nine-to-fiver** noun.

ninety ▶ **cardinal number** (pl. **nineties**) equivalent to the product of nine and ten; ten less than one hundred; 90. (Roman numeral: **xc** or **XC**) ■ (**nineties**) the numbers from 90 to 99, especially the years of a century or of a person's life: *art in the nineties.* ■ ninety years old: *she is nearly ninety.* ■ ninety miles an hour: *we passed the junction doing about ninety.*
– DERIVATIVES **ninetieth** ordinal number, **ninetyfold** adjective & adverb.
– ORIGIN Old English *nigontig*.

ninety-nine (also **99**) ▶ **noun** Brit. a cone of ice cream with a stick of flaky chocolate in it.

Nineveh /ˈnɪnɪvə/ an ancient city located on the east bank of the Tigris, opposite the modern city of Mosul. It was the oldest city of the ancient Assyrian empire and its capital until it was destroyed by a coalition of Babylonians and Medes in 612 BC.

ning-nong ▶ **noun** Austral./NZ informal a fool.
– ORIGIN mid 19th cent.: of unknown origin.

Ningxia /nɪŋˈʃjɑː/ (also **Ningsia**) an autonomous region of north central China; capital, Yinchuan.

ninhydrin /nɪnˈhʌɪdrɪn/ ▶ **noun** [mass noun] Chemistry a synthetic crystalline compound which forms deeply coloured products with primary amines and is used in analytical tests for amino acids. • A ketone derivative of indene; chem. formula: $C_9H_6O_4$.
– ORIGIN early 20th cent.: from *nin-* (of unknown origin) + HYDRO- + -IN[1].

Ninian, St /ˈnɪnɪən/ (*c.*360–*c.*432), Scottish bishop and missionary. According to Bede he founded a church at Whithorn in SW Scotland (*c.*400) and from there evangelized the southern Picts.

ninja /ˈnɪndʒə/ ▶ **noun** a person skilled in ninjutsu.
– ORIGIN Japanese, literally 'spy'.

ninjutsu /nɪnˈdʒʌtsuː/ ▶ **noun** [mass noun] the traditional Japanese art of stealth, camouflage, and sabotage, developed in feudal times for espionage and now practised as a martial art.
– ORIGIN Japanese, from *nin* 'stealth' + *jutsu* 'art, science'.

ninny ▶ **noun** (pl. **ninnies**) informal a foolish and weak person.
– ORIGIN late 16th cent.: perhaps from INNOCENT.

ninon /ˈniːnɒn/ ▶ **noun** [mass noun] a lightweight silk dress fabric.
– ORIGIN early 20th cent.: from French.

ninth ▶ **ordinal number 1** constituting number nine in a sequence; 9th: *the ninth century | the ninth of March.* ■ the ninth finisher or position in a race or competition: *he came in ninth.* ■ Music an interval spanning nine consecutive notes in a diatonic scale. ■ Music the note which is higher by this interval than the tonic of a diatonic scale or root of a chord. ■ Music a chord in which the ninth note of the scale forms an important component.
2 each of nine equal parts into which something is or may be divided.
– DERIVATIVES **ninthly** adverb.

Niobe /ˈnʌɪəbi/ Greek Mythology the daughter of Tantalus. Apollo and Artemis, enraged because Niobe boasted herself superior to their mother Leto, killed her children and turned her into a stone.

niobium /nʌɪˈəʊbɪəm/ ▶ **noun** [mass noun] the chemical element of atomic number 41, a silver-grey metal of the transition series, used in superconducting alloys. (Symbol: **Nb**)
– ORIGIN mid 19th cent.: modern Latin, from NIOBE, by association with her father Tantalus (so named because the element was first found in TANTALITE).

Nip ▶ **noun** informal, offensive a Japanese person.
– ORIGIN 1940s: abbreviation of NIPPONESE.

nip[1] ▶ **verb** (**nips**, **nipping**, **nipped**) **1** [with obj.] bite or pinch sharply: *one of the dogs nipped him on the leg |* [no obj.] *his teeth **nipped at** her ear.* ■ (of the cold or frost) damage or hurt: *the vegetable garden, nipped now by frost.* ■ (**nip something off**) remove something by pinching or squeezing sharply: *he nipped off a length of wire with the cutters.*
2 [no obj., with adverbial of direction] Brit. informal go quickly: *I'm just nipping down to the Post Office.*
3 [with obj.] US informal steal or snatch (something).
▶ **noun** a sharp bite or pinch. ■ a feeling of biting cold: *a keen **nip in the air**.*
– PHRASES **in the nip** Irish informal in the nude; naked. **nip something in the bud** suppress or destroy something at an early stage.
– ORIGIN late Middle English: probably of Low German or Dutch origin.

nip[2] ▶ **noun** a small quantity or sip of spirits.
▶ **verb** (**nips**, **nipping**, **nipped**) [no obj.] take a sip or sips of spirits: *the men nipped from the bottle.*
– ORIGIN late 18th cent. (originally denoting a half-pint of ale): probably an abbreviation of the rare term *nipperkin* 'small measure'; compare with Low German and Dutch *nippen* 'to sip'.

nipa /ˈniːpə, ˈnʌɪpə/ (also **nipa palm**) ▶ **noun** a palm tree with creeping roots, characteristic of mangrove swamps in India and the Pacific islands. • *Nypa fruticans*, family Palmae.
ORIGIN late 16th cent. (denoting an alcoholic drink made from the sap of the tree): via Spanish or Portuguese from Malay *nipah*.

nip and tuck ▶ **adverb & adjective** neck and neck; closely contested: [as adv.] *it was nip and tuck to 7–7 until Best took the lead.*
▶ **noun** informal a cosmetic surgical operation.

nipped-in ▶ **adjective** (of a waist on a garment) narrow or tightly fitting: *a dress with a nipped-in waist.*

nipper ▶ **noun 1** informal a child.
2 (**nippers**) pliers, pincers, or a similar tool for gripping or cutting. ■ (usu. **nippers**) the grasping claw of a crab or lobster.
3 an insect or other creature that nips or bites.
4 Austral. a burrowing marine prawn used as fishing bait. Also called YABBY. • Infraorder Thalassinidea, order Decapoda.
5 Austral. a junior lifeguard.

nipple ▶ **noun 1** the small projection in which the mammary ducts of female mammals terminate and from which milk can be secreted. ■ the corresponding vestigial structure in a male. ■ N. Amer. the teat of a feeding bottle.
2 a small projection on a device, especially one from which oil or other fluid is dispensed. ■ a short section of pipe with a screw thread at each end for coupling.
– DERIVATIVES **nippled** adjective.
– ORIGIN mid 16th cent. (also as *neble, nible*): perhaps a diminutive of NEB.

nipplewort /ˈnɪp(ə)lwəːt/ ▶ **noun** a yellow-flowered European plant of the daisy family, growing in woods and waste places. • *Lapsana communis*, family Compositae.

N

Nippon /ˈnɪpɒn/ Japanese name for **JAPAN**.
– ORIGIN literally 'land where the sun rises or originates'.

Nipponese /ˌnɪpəˈniːz/ ▶ **noun & adjective** another term for **JAPANESE**.

nippy ▶ **adjective** (**nippier, nippiest**) informal **1** Brit. able to move quickly; nimble: *a very nippy scrum half*. ■ (of a motor vehicle) able to accelerate quickly.
2 (of the weather) chilly.
3 Scottish & Canadian (of food) sharp-tasting; tangy.
▶ **noun** (**Nippy**) (pl. **Nippies**) informal, historical a waitress in any of the restaurants of J. Lyons & Co. Ltd in London from about 1920 to 1950.
– DERIVATIVES **nippily** adverb, **nippiness** noun.

niqab /nɪˈkɑːb/ ▶ **noun** a veil worn by some Muslim women in public, covering all of the face apart from the eyes.
– ORIGIN Arabic *niqāb*.

NIREX /ˈnʌɪrɛks/ ▶ **abbreviation** (in the UK) Nuclear Industry Radioactive Waste Executive.

Niro, Robert De, see **DE NIRO**.

nirvana /nɪəˈvɑːnə/ ▶ **noun** [mass noun] (in Buddhism) a transcendent state in which there is neither suffering, desire, nor sense of self, and the subject is released from the effects of karma and the cycle of death and rebirth. It represents the final goal of Buddhism. ■ another term for **MOKSHA**. ■ an ideal or idyllic state or place: *the days of socialist nirvana in Europe are over*.
– ORIGIN from Sanskrit *nirvāṇa*, from *nirvā* 'be extinguished', from *nis* 'out' + *vā-* 'to blow'.

Nirvana principle ▶ **noun** Psychoanalysis yearning for a state of oblivion, as a manifestation of the death instinct.

Niš /niːʃ/ (also **Nish**) an industrial city in SE Serbia, on the Nišava River near its confluence with the Morava; pop. 172,900 (est. 2008).

Nisan /ˈnɪs(ə)n, ˈniːsɑːn/ ▶ **noun** (in the Jewish calendar) the seventh month of the civil and first of the religious year, usually coinciding with parts of March and April.
– ORIGIN from Hebrew *nīsān*.

nisei /ˈniːseɪ, niːˈseɪ/ ▶ **noun** (pl. **same** or **niseis**) N. Amer. an American or Canadian whose parents were immigrants from Japan. Compare with **ISSEI** and **SANSEI**.
– ORIGIN 1940s: from Japanese, literally 'second generation'.

N

Nish variant spelling of **NIŠ**.

nisi /ˈnʌɪsʌɪ/ ▶ **adjective** [postpositive] Law (of a decree, order, or rule) that takes effect or is valid only after certain conditions are met. See also **DECREE NISI**.
– ORIGIN mid 19th cent.: from Latin, literally 'unless'.

nisin /ˈnʌɪsɪn/ ▶ **noun** [mass noun] an antibiotic substance which is a mixture of related polypeptides and is used in some countries as a food preservative. ● This substance is produced by the bacterium *Streptococcus lactis*.
– ORIGIN 1940s: from (*Group*) *N i*(*nhibitory*) *s*(*ubstance*) + **-IN**[1].

Nissen hut /ˈnɪs(ə)n/ ▶ **noun** Brit. a tunnel-shaped hut made of corrugated iron with a cement floor.
– ORIGIN early 20th cent.: named after Peter N. *Nissen* (1871–1930), the British engineer who invented it.

nit[1] ▶ **noun** informal **1** the egg or young form of a louse or other parasitic insect, especially the egg of a human head louse attached to a hair.
2 Brit. a foolish person: *you stupid nit!*
– PHRASES **pick nits** chiefly N. Amer. look for and criticize trivial faults; nit-pick.
– DERIVATIVES **nitty** adjective.
– ORIGIN Old English *hnitu*, of West Germanic origin; related to Dutch *neet* and German *Nisse*.

nit[2] ▶ **exclamation** Austral. informal used as a warning that someone is approaching.
– PHRASES **keep nit** keep watch or act as a guard.
– ORIGIN late 19th cent.: probably from **NIX**[3].

nite ▶ **noun** informal non-standard spelling of **NIGHT**: *I didn't get much sleep last nite*.

niter ▶ **noun** US spelling of **NITRE**.

niterie /ˈnʌɪtəri/ ▶ **noun** (pl. **niteries**) informal a nightclub.

Niterói /ˌniːtəˈrɔɪ/ an industrial port on the coast of SE Brazil, on Guanabara Bay opposite the city of Rio de Janeiro; pop. 474,002 (2007).

nitinol /ˈnɪtɪnɒl/ ▶ **noun** [mass noun] an alloy of nickel and titanium.
– ORIGIN 1960s: from the chemical symbols **Ni** and **Ti** + the initial letters of *Naval Ordnance Laboratory* (in Maryland, US).

nitpicking ▶ **noun** [mass noun] informal fussy or pedantic fault-finding.
– DERIVATIVES **nitpick** verb, **nitpicker** noun, **nitpicky** adjective.

nitrate Chemistry ▶ **noun** /ˈnʌɪtreɪt/ a salt or ester of nitric acid, containing the anion NO_3^- or the group $-NO_3$.
▶ **verb** /nʌɪˈtreɪt/ [with obj.] treat (a substance) with nitric acid, especially so as to introduce nitro groups.
– DERIVATIVES **nitration** noun.
– ORIGIN late 18th cent.: from French (see **NITRE**, **-ATE**[1]).

nitrazepam /nʌɪˈtreɪzɪpam, -ˈtrazə-/ ▶ **noun** [mass noun] Medicine a short-acting hypnotic drug of the benzodiazepine group, used to treat insomnia.
– ORIGIN 1960s: from *nitr*(*o*) + *az*(*o*-) + *ep*(*ine*) + *am*(*ide*).

nitre /ˈnʌɪtə/ (US **niter**) ▶ **noun** another term for **SALTPETRE**.
– ORIGIN late Middle English: from Old French, from Latin *nitrum*, from Greek *nitron*.

nitric /ˈnʌɪtrɪk/ ▶ **adjective** Chemistry of or containing nitrogen with a higher valency, often five. Compare with **NITROUS**.
– ORIGIN late 18th cent.: from French (*acide*) *nitrique* (see **NITRE**, **-IC**).

nitric acid ▶ **noun** [mass noun] Chemistry a colourless or pale yellow corrosive poisonous liquid acid with strong oxidizing properties, made in the laboratory by distilling nitrates with sulphuric acid. ● Chem. formula: HNO_3.

nitric oxide ▶ **noun** another term for **NITROGEN MONOXIDE**.

nitride /ˈnʌɪtrʌɪd/ ▶ **noun** Chemistry a binary compound of nitrogen with a more electropositive element.
▶ **verb** [with obj.] (usu. as noun **nitriding**) Metallurgy heat (steel) in the presence of ammonia or other nitrogenous material so as to increase hardness and corrosion resistance.
– ORIGIN mid 19th cent.: from **NITRE** + **-IDE**.

nitrify /ˈnʌɪtrɪfʌɪ/ ▶ **verb** (**nitrifies, nitrifying, nitrified**) [with obj.] Chemistry convert (ammonia or another nitrogen compound) into nitrites or nitrates.
– DERIVATIVES **nitrification** noun.
– ORIGIN early 19th cent.: from French *nitrifier*.

nitrile /ˈnʌɪtrʌɪl/ ▶ **noun** an organic compound containing a cyanide group −CN bound to an alkyl group.
– ORIGIN mid 19th cent.: from **NITRE** + *-ile* (alteration of **-YL**).

nitrite /ˈnʌɪtrʌɪt/ ▶ **noun** Chemistry a salt or ester of nitrous acid, containing the anion NO_2^- or the group $-NO_2$.
– ORIGIN early 19th cent.: from **NITRE** + **-ITE**[1].

nitro ▶ **noun** short for **NITROGLYCERINE**.

nitro- /ˈnʌɪtrəʊ/ ▶ **combining form** of or containing nitric acid, nitrates, or nitrogen: *nitrogenous*. ■ Chemistry containing a nitro group: *nitromethane*.

nitrobenzene ▶ **noun** [mass noun] Chemistry a yellow oily liquid made by nitrating benzene, used in chemical synthesis. ● Chem. formula: $C_6H_5NO_2$.

nitroblue tetrazolium ▶ **noun** see **TETRAZOLIUM**.

nitrocellulose ▶ **noun** [mass noun] Chemistry a highly flammable material made by treating cellulose with concentrated nitric acid, used to make explosives (e.g. guncotton) and celluloid.

nitrochalk ▶ **noun** [mass noun] a mixture of chalk and ammonium nitrate, used as fertilizer.

nitrofurantoin /ˌnʌɪtrə(ʊ)fjʊˈrantəʊɪn/ ▶ **noun** [mass noun] a synthetic compound with antibacterial properties, used to treat urinary tract infections. ● A bicyclic furan derivative; chem. formula: $C_8H_6N_4O_5$.

nitrogen /ˈnʌɪtrədʒ(ə)n/ ▶ **noun** [mass noun] the chemical element of atomic number 7, a colourless, odourless unreactive gas that forms about 78 per cent of the earth's atmosphere. Liquid nitrogen (made by distilling liquid air) boils at 77.4 kelvins (−195.8°C) and is used as a coolant. (Symbol: **N**)
– ORIGIN late 18th cent.: from French *nitrogène* (see **NITRE**, **-GEN**).

nitrogen cycle ▶ **noun** Ecology the series of processes by which nitrogen and its compounds are interconverted in the environment and in living organisms, including nitrogen fixation and decomposition.

nitrogen dioxide ▶ **noun** [mass noun] Chemistry a reddish-brown poisonous gas formed when many metals dissolve in nitric acid. ● Chem. formula: NO_2. It usually exists in equilibrium with **dinitrogen tetroxide**, N_2O_4.

nitrogen fixation ▶ **noun** [mass noun] Biology the chemical processes by which atmospheric nitrogen is assimilated into organic compounds, especially by certain microorganisms as part of the nitrogen cycle.

nitrogen monoxide ▶ **noun** [mass noun] Chemistry a colourless toxic gas formed in many reactions in which nitric acid is reduced. It reacts immediately with oxygen to form nitrogen dioxide. Also called **NITRIC OXIDE**. ● Chem. formula: NO.

nitrogen mustard ▶ **noun** Chemistry any of a group of organic compounds containing the group $-N(CH_2CH_2Cl)_2$. They are powerful cytotoxic alkylating agents and some are used in chemotherapy to treat cancer.
– ORIGIN 1940s: *mustard* denoting a substance chemically similar to **MUSTARD GAS**.

nitrogen narcosis ▶ **noun** [mass noun] Medicine a drowsy state induced by breathing air under pressure, e.g. in deep-sea diving.

nitrogenous /nʌɪˈtrɒdʒɪnəs/ ▶ **adjective** containing nitrogen in chemical combination.

nitroglycerine (US also **nitroglycerin**) ▶ **noun** [mass noun] an explosive yellow liquid made by nitrating glycerol, used in explosives such as dynamite. ● Alternative name: **glyceryl trinitrate**; chem. formula: $CH_2(NO_3)CH(NO_3)CH_2(NO_3)$.

nitro group ▶ **noun** Chemistry a group $-NO_2$, attached to an organic group in a molecule.

nitromethane ▶ **noun** [mass noun] Chemistry an oily liquid which is used as a solvent and as rocket fuel. ● Chem. formula: CH_3NO_2.

nitrophilous /nʌɪˈtrɒfɪləs/ ▶ **adjective** Botany (of a plant) preferring soils rich in nitrogen.

nitrosamine /nʌɪˈtrəʊsəmiːn/ ▶ **noun** Chemistry a compound containing the group =NNO attached to two organic groups. Compounds of this kind are generally carcinogenic.
– ORIGIN late 19th cent.: from *nitroso-* (relating to nitric oxide in combination) + **AMINE**.

nitrous /ˈnʌɪtrəs/ ▶ **adjective** Chemistry of or containing nitrogen, especially in a state of low valency: *the effect of nitrous emissions on acid rain*. Compare with **NITRIC**.
– ORIGIN early 17th cent.: from Latin *nitrosus* 'nitrous'.

nitrous acid ▶ **noun** [mass noun] Chemistry an unstable, weak acid, existing only in solution and in the gas phase, made by the action of acids on nitrites. ● Chem. formula: HNO_2.

nitrous oxide ▶ **noun** [mass noun] a colourless gas with a sweetish odour, prepared by heating ammonium nitrate. It produces exhilaration or anaesthesia when inhaled and is used (mixed with oxygen) as an anaesthetic and as an aerosol propellant. ● Chem. formula: N_2O.

nitrox ▶ **noun** [mass noun] a mixture of oxygen and nitrogen used as a breathing gas by divers, especially a mixture containing a lower proportion of nitrogen than is normally present in air, to reduce the risk of decompression sickness.

nitty-gritty ▶ **noun** (**the nitty-gritty**) informal the most important aspects or practical details of a subject or situation.
– ORIGIN 1960s: of unknown origin.

nitwit ▶ **noun** informal a silly or foolish person (often as a general term of abuse).
– DERIVATIVES **nitwitted** adjective, **nitwittery** noun.
– ORIGIN early 20th cent.: apparently from **NIT**[1] + **WIT**[1].

Niue /nɪˈuːeɪ/ an island territory in the South Pacific to the east of Tonga; pop. 1,400 (est. 2009); languages, English (official), local Austronesian; capital, Alofi. Annexed by New Zealand in 1901, the island achieved self-government in free association with New Zealand in 1974. Niue is the world's largest coral island.

NIV ▶ **abbreviation** New International Version (of the Bible).

nival /ˈnʌɪv(ə)l/ ▶ **adjective** relating to or characteristic of a region of perpetual snow.
– ORIGIN mid 17th cent.: from Latin *nivalis*, from *nix*, *niv-* 'snow'.

nivas /ˈnɪvas/ ▶ **noun** Indian a place of residence; a house, block of flats, etc.
– ORIGIN from Hindi.

nivation /nʌɪˈveɪʃ(ə)n/ ▶ **noun** [mass noun] Geography erosion of the ground beneath and at the sides of a

snow bank, mainly as a result of alternate freezing and thawing.
– ORIGIN early 20th cent.: from Latin *nix, niv-* 'snow' + **-ATION**.

niveous /ˈnɪvɪəs/ ▶ **adjective** literary snowy or resembling snow.
– ORIGIN early 17th cent.: from Latin *niveus* (from *nix, niv-* 'snow') + **-OUS**.

Nivernais /ˌniːvəˈneɪ/, French /nivɛrnɛ/ a former duchy and province of central France. Its capital was the city of Nevers.

Nivose /niˈvəʊz/ (also **Nivôse** French /nivoz/) ▶ **noun** the fourth month of the French Republican calendar (1793–1805), originally running from 21 December to 19 January.
– ORIGIN French *Nivôse*, from Latin *nivosus* 'snowy', from *nix, niv-* 'snow'.

nix[1] informal ▶ **pronoun** nothing: *apart from that, nix.*
▶ **exclamation** expressing denial or refusal.
▶ **verb** [with obj.] chiefly N. Amer. put an end to; cancel: *he nixed the deal just before it was to be signed.*
– ORIGIN late 18th cent. (as a noun): from German, colloquial variant of *nichts* 'nothing'.

nix[2] ▶ **noun** (fem. **nixie**) rare a water sprite.
– ORIGIN mid 19th cent.: from German; related to the archaic English word *nicker*, denoting a water demon believed to live in the sea.

nix[3] ▶ **exclamation** Brit. informal, dated used as a signal or warning that a person in authority is approaching.
– ORIGIN mid 19th cent.: perhaps from the phrase *keep nix* 'to watch, guard' (see **NIX**[1]).

nixer ▶ **noun** Irish informal an extra or irregular job, the income from which is not declared for taxation purposes: *an RTE engineer* ***doing a nixer*** *installed the aerials.*
– ORIGIN from **NIX**[1] + **-ER**[1].

Nixon, Richard (Milhous) (1913–94), American Republican statesman, 37th President of the US 1969–74. His period of office was overshadowed by the Vietnam War. Re-elected in 1972, he became the first President to resign from office, owing to his involvement in the Watergate scandal.

Nizam /nɪˈzɑːm/ ▶ **noun** historical **1** the title of the hereditary ruler of Hyderabad.
2 (**the nizam**) the Turkish regular army.
– ORIGIN Sense 1 from Urdu *niẓām-al-mulk* 'administrator of the realm', sense 2 from Turkish *nizām askeri* 'regular soldier'; based on Arabic *niẓām* 'order, arrangement'.

Nizari /nɪˈzɑːri/ ▶ **noun** a member of a Muslim sect that split from the Ismaili branch in 1094 over disagreement about the succession to the caliphate. The majority of Nizaris now live in South Asia; their leader is the Aga Khan.

Nizhni Novgorod /ˌniːʒni ˈnɒvgərɒd/ a river port in European Russia on the Volga; pop. 1,274,700 (est. 2008). Between 1932 and 1991 it was named Gorky after the writer Maxim Gorky, who was born there.

Nizhni Tagil /ˌniːʒni təˈgiːl/ an industrial and metal-mining city in central Russia, in the Urals north of Yekaterinburg; pop. 375,700 (est. 2008).

NJ ▶ **abbreviation** New Jersey (in official postal use).

NK cell ▶ **abbreviation** natural killer cell.

Nkomo /(ə)ŋˈkəʊməʊ/, Joshua (Mqabuko Nyongolo) (1917–99), Zimbabwean statesman. He became leader of the ZAPU party in 1961; in 1976 he formed the Patriotic Front with Robert Mugabe, leader of ZANU, and he held a cabinet post in the first post-independence government. He was Vice-President 1990–9.

Nkrumah /(ə)ŋˈkruːmə/, Kwame (1909–72), Ghanaian statesman, Prime Minister 1957–60, President 1960–6. The first Prime Minister after independence, he became increasingly dictatorial and was finally overthrown in a military coup.

NKVD the secret police agency in the former Soviet Union which absorbed the functions of the former OGPU in 1934. It merged with the MVD in 1946.
– ORIGIN abbreviation of Russian *Narodnyĭ komissariat vnutrennikh del* 'People's Commissariat of Internal Affairs'.

NL ▶ **abbreviation** the Netherlands (international vehicle registration).

NLP ▶ **abbreviation** ■ natural language processing. ■ neurolinguistic programming.

NM ▶ **abbreviation** New Mexico (in official postal use).

nm ▶ **abbreviation** ■ nanometre. ■ (also **n.m.**) nautical mile.

N.Mex. ▶ **abbreviation** New Mexico.

NMR ▶ **abbreviation** Physics nuclear magnetic resonance.

NNE ▶ **abbreviation** north-north-east.

NNP ▶ **abbreviation** net national product.

NNW ▶ **abbreviation** north-north-west.

No[1] ▶ **symbol** the chemical element nobelium.

No[2] ▶ **noun** variant spelling of **NOH**.

no ▶ **determiner** not any: *there is no excuse | no two plants are alike.* ■ used to indicate that something is quite the opposite of what is being specified: *it was no easy task persuading her | Toby is no fool.* ■ hardly any: *you'll be back in no time.* ■ used in notices or slogans forbidding or rejecting something specified: *No Smoking signs | no nukes.*
▶ **exclamation** used to give a negative response: *'Is anything wrong?' 'No.'* ■ expressing disagreement or contradiction: *'This is boring.' 'No, it's not!'.* ■ expressing agreement with or affirmation of a negative statement: *they would never cause a fuss, oh no.* ■ expressing shock or disappointment: *oh no, look at this!*
▶ **adverb 1** [with comparative] not at all; to no extent: *they were no more able to perform the task than I was.*
2 Scottish not: *I'll no be a minute.*
▶ **noun** (pl. **noes**) a negative answer or decision, especially in voting.
– PHRASES **no can do** informal I am unable to do it. **the noes have it** the negative votes are in the majority. **no less** see **LESS**. **no longer** not now as formerly: *they no longer live here.* **no man** no person; no one. **no more** see **MORE**. **no place** N. Amer. nowhere. **no sooner —— than** see **SOON**. **no through road** an indication that passage along a street is blocked or prohibited. **not take no for an answer** persist in spite of refusals. **no two ways about it** used to convey that there can be no doubt about something. **no way** informal under no circumstances; not at all: *You think she's alone? No way.* **no worries** informal, chiefly Austral. all right; fine. **or no** or not: *she'd have ridden there, winter or no.* ■ (**—— or no ——**) regardless of the specified thing: *recession or no recession there is always going to be a shortage of good people.*
– ORIGIN Old English *nō, nā* (adverb), from *ne* 'not' + *ō, ā* 'ever'. The determiner arose in Middle English (originally before words beginning with any consonant except *h-*), reduced from *non*, from Old English *nān* (see **NONE**[1]).

No. ▶ **abbreviation** ■ US North. ■ (also **no.**) number: *No. 27.* [from Latin *numero*, ablative of *numerus* 'number'.]

n.o. ▶ **abbreviation** Cricket not out.

no-account N. Amer. informal ▶ **adjective** of little or no importance, value, or use; worthless.
▶ **noun** a worthless or unimportant person.

Noachian /nəʊˈeɪkɪən/ ▶ **adjective 1** relating to the biblical patriarch Noah or his time.
2 Astronomy relating to or denoting an early geological period on the planet Mars.

Noah /ˈnəʊə/ (in the Bible) a Hebrew patriarch represented as tenth in descent from Adam. According to a story in Genesis he made the ark which saved his family and specimens of every animal from the Flood.

noah ▶ **noun** Austral. informal a shark.
– ORIGIN 1940s: from rhyming slang *Noah's ark*.

Noah's ark ▶ **noun 1** the ship in which Noah, his family, and the animals were saved from the Flood, according to the biblical account (Genesis 6–8).
2 a small bivalve mollusc with a boat-shaped shell, found in the Mediterranean and off the Atlantic coasts of Africa and southern Europe. ● *Arca noae*, family Arcidae. See also **ARK SHELL**.

nob[1] ▶ **noun** Brit. informal a person of wealth or high social position.
– DERIVATIVES **nobby** adjective.
– ORIGIN late 17th cent. (originally Scots as *knab*): of unknown origin.

nob[2] ▶ **noun** informal a person's head.
– PHRASES **one for his nob** Cribbage a bonus point scored for holding the jack of the same suit as the card turned up by the dealer.
– ORIGIN late 17th cent.: apparently a variant of **KNOB**.

no-ball Cricket ▶ **noun** an unlawfully delivered ball, counting one as an extra to the batting side if not otherwise scored from.
▶ **verb** [with obj.] (of an umpire) declare (a bowler) to have bowled a no-ball; declare (a delivery) to be a no-ball.

nobble ▶ **verb** [with obj.] Brit. informal **1** try to influence or thwart by underhand or unfair methods: *an attempt to nobble the jury.* ■ tamper with (a racehorse or greyhound) to prevent it from winning a race, especially by giving it a drug.
2 obtain dishonestly; steal: *he intended to nobble Rose's money.* ■ seize or accost (someone): *they nobbled him and threw him on to the train | people always tried to nobble her at parties.*
– DERIVATIVES **nobbler** noun.
– ORIGIN mid 19th cent.: probably a variant of dialect *knobble, knubble* 'knock, strike with the knuckles'.

nobbut /ˈnɒbət/ ▶ **adverb** N. English nothing but; just: *he looked a lot like his uncle when he was nobbut a lad.*
– ORIGIN Middle English: from the adverb **NO** + the preposition **BUT**[1].

Nobel /nəʊˈbɛl/, Alfred Bernhard (1833–96), Swedish chemist and engineer. He invented dynamite (1866), gelignite, and other high explosives, making a large fortune which enabled him to endow the prizes that bear his name.

Nobelist /nəʊˈbɛlɪst/ ▶ **noun** chiefly N. Amer. a winner of a Nobel Prize.

nobelium /nə(ʊ)ˈbiːlɪəm, -ˈbɛl-/ ▶ **noun** [mass noun] the chemical element of atomic number 102, a radioactive metal of the actinide series. Nobelium does not occur naturally and was first produced by bombarding curium with carbon nuclei. (Symbol: **No**)
– ORIGIN 1950s: modern Latin, from the name **NOBEL** + **-IUM**.

Nobel Prize ▶ **noun** any of six international prizes awarded annually for outstanding work in physics, chemistry, physiology or medicine, literature, economics, and the promotion of peace. The Nobel Prizes, first awarded in 1901, are decided by members of Swedish learned societies or, in the case of the peace prize, the Norwegian Parliament.

nobiliary /nə(ʊ)ˈbɪljəri/ ▶ **adjective** rare relating to the nobility.
– ORIGIN mid 18th cent.: from French *nobiliaire*, based on Latin *nobilis* (see **NOBLE**).

nobiliary particle ▶ **noun** a preposition forming part of a title of the nobility (e.g. French *de*, German *von*).

nobility ▶ **noun** (pl. **nobilities**) [mass noun] **1** the quality of being noble in character: *a man of nobility and learning.*
2 the quality of belonging to the aristocracy. ■ (usu. **the nobility**) the group of people belonging to the highest social class in a country; the aristocracy: *a member of the English nobility.*
– ORIGIN late Middle English: from Old French *nobilite* or Latin *nobilitas*, from *nobilis* 'noted, high-born' (see **NOBLE**).

N

noble ▶ **adjective** (**nobler, noblest**) **1** belonging by rank, title, or birth to the aristocracy.
2 having or showing fine personal qualities or high moral principles: *the promotion of human rights was a noble aspiration.* ■ of imposing or magnificent size or appearance. ■ of excellent or superior quality.
▶ **noun 1** (especially in former times) a person of noble rank or birth.
2 historical a former English gold coin first issued in 1351.
– PHRASES **the noble art** (or **science**) (**of self-defence**) archaic boxing.
– DERIVATIVES **nobleness** noun, **nobly** adverb.
– ORIGIN Middle English: from Old French, from Latin *(g)nobilis* 'noted, high-born', from an Indo-European root shared by **KNOW**.

noble gas ▶ **noun** Chemistry any of the gaseous elements helium, neon, argon, krypton, xenon, and radon, occupying Group 0 (18) of the periodic table. They were long believed to be totally unreactive but compounds of xenon, krypton, and radon are now known.

nobleman ▶ **noun** (pl. **noblemen**) a man who belongs by rank, title, or birth to the aristocracy; a peer.

noble metal ▶ **noun** Chemistry a metal (e.g. gold, silver, or platinum) that resists chemical action, does not corrode, and is not easily attacked by acids.

noble rot ▶ **noun** [mass noun] a grey mould that is deliberately cultivated on grapes in order to perfect certain wines. ● The fungus is *Botrytis cinerea*, subdivision Deuteromycotina.
– ORIGIN 1930s: translation of French *pourriture noble*.

noble savage ▶ **noun** a representative of primitive mankind as idealized in Romantic literature, symbolizing the innate goodness of humanity when free from the corrupting influence of civilization.

noblesse /nəʊˈblɛs/ ▶ **noun** [mass noun] the nobility of a foreign country.
– PHRASES **noblesse oblige** /ɒˈbliːʒ/ privilege entails responsibility: *the notion of noblesse oblige was part of the ethic of the country gentleman.*
– ORIGIN French, literally 'nobility'.

noblewoman ▶ **noun** (pl. **noblewomen**) a woman who belongs by rank, title, or birth to the aristocracy; a peeress.

nobody ▶ **pronoun** no person; no one: *nobody was at home | nobody could predict how it might end.*
▶ **noun** (pl. **nobodies**) a person of no importance or authority: *they went from nobodies to superstars.*
– ORIGIN Middle English: originally as *no body*.

no-brainer ▶ **noun** N. Amer. informal something that requires or involves little or no mental effort.

nocebo /nəˈsiːbəʊ/ ▶ **noun** (pl. **nocebos**) a detrimental effect on health produced by psychological or psychosomatic factors such as negative expectations of treatment or prognosis.
– ORIGIN 1960s: from Latin, literally 'I shall cause harm', from *nocere* 'to harm', on the pattern of **PLACEBO**.

nociceptive /ˌnəʊsɪˈsɛptɪv/ ▶ **adjective** Physiology relating to or denoting pain arising from the stimulation of nerve cells (often as distinct from that arising from damage or disease in the nerves themselves).
– ORIGIN early 20th cent.: from Latin *nocere* 'to harm' + **RECEPTIVE**.

nociceptor /ˈnəʊsɪˌsɛptə/ ▶ **noun** Physiology a sensory receptor for painful stimuli.
– ORIGIN early 20th cent.: from Latin *nocere* 'to harm' + **RECEPTOR**.

nock ▶ **noun** Archery a notch at either end of a bow for holding the string. ■ a notch at the butt end of an arrow for receiving the bowstring.
▶ **verb** [with obj.] fit (an arrow) to the bowstring ready for shooting.
– ORIGIN late Middle English: perhaps from Middle Dutch *nocke* 'point, tip'.

no-claims bonus (also **no-claims discount**) ▶ **noun** Brit. a reduction in the premium charged for insurance when no claim has been made during an agreed preceding period.

N

noctambulist /nɒkˈtambjʊlɪst/ ▶ **noun** rare a sleepwalker.
– ORIGIN mid 18th cent.: from Latin *nox*, *noct-* 'night' + *ambulare* 'to walk' + **-IST**.

noctiluca /ˌnɒktɪˈluːkə/ ▶ **noun** (pl. **noctilucae** /-kiː/) a roughly spherical marine dinoflagellate which is strongly phosphorescent, especially when disturbed.
● Genus *Noctiluca*, division (or phylum) Dinophyta.
– ORIGIN modern Latin, from Latin, literally 'night light, lantern'.

noctilucent cloud /ˌnɒktɪˈluːs(ə)nt/ ▶ **noun** a luminous cloud of a kind occasionally seen at night in summer in high latitudes, at the altitude of the mesopause.
– ORIGIN late 19th cent.: from Latin *nox*, *noct-* 'night' + *lucere* 'to shine' + **-ENT**.

noctuid /ˈnɒktjʊɪd/ ▶ **noun** Entomology a moth of a large family (Noctuidae) whose members typically have dull forewings and pale or colourful hindwings. Also called **OWLET**.
– ORIGIN late 19th cent.: from modern Latin *Noctuidae* (plural), based on Latin *noctua* 'night owl'.

noctule /ˈnɒktjuːl/ ▶ **noun** a large golden-brown bat native to Eurasia and North Africa with long, slender wings, rounded ears, and a short muzzle. ● *Nyctalus noctula*, family Vespertilionidae.
– ORIGIN late 18th cent.: from French, from Italian *nottola* 'bat', literally 'small night creature'.

nocturn ▶ **noun** (in the Roman Catholic Church) a part of matins originally said at night.
– ORIGIN Middle English: from Old French *nocturne* or ecclesiastical Latin *nocturnum*, neuter of Latin *nocturnus* 'of the night'.

nocturnal ▶ **adjective** done, occurring, or active at night: *most owls are nocturnal.*
– DERIVATIVES **nocturnally** adverb.
– ORIGIN late 15th cent.: from late Latin *nocturnalis*, from Latin *nocturnus* 'of the night', from *nox*, *noct-* 'night'.

nocturnal emission ▶ **noun** an involuntary ejaculation of semen during sleep.

nocturne /ˈnɒktəːn/ ▶ **noun** **1** Music a short composition of a romantic nature, typically for piano.
2 Art a picture of a night scene.
– ORIGIN mid 19th cent.: French, from Latin *nocturnus* 'of the night'.

nocuous /ˈnɒkjʊəs/ ▶ **adjective** literary noxious, harmful, or poisonous.
– ORIGIN mid 17th cent.: from Latin *nocuus* (from *nocere* 'to hurt') + **-OUS**.

nod ▶ **verb** (**nods, nodding, nodded**) **1** [no obj.] lower and raise one's head slightly and briefly, especially in greeting, assent, or understanding, or to give someone a signal: *he looked around for support and everyone nodded* | [with obj.] *she nodded her head in agreement.* ■ [with obj.] signify or express (greeting, assent, or understanding) by nodding: *he nodded his consent.* ■ (**nod something through**) informal approve something by general agreement, without discussion: *the DTI nodded through the bid from Airtours.* ■ move one's head up and down repeatedly: *he shut his eyes, nodding to the beat* | figurative *foxgloves nodding by the path.*
2 [no obj.] let one's head fall forward when drowsy or asleep: *Anna nodded over her book.* ■ make a mistake due to a momentary lack of alertness or attention: *scientific reason, like Homer, sometimes nods.* [with allusion to Latin *dormitat Homerus* 'even Homer nods' (Horace *Ars Poet.* 359).]
3 [with obj. and adverbial of direction] Soccer head (the ball) without great force.
▶ **noun** an act of nodding the head: *at a nod from his father he left the room.* ■ (**a nod to**) a gesture of acknowledgement or concession to: *the device is a nod to the conventions of slapstick.*
– PHRASES **nodding acquaintance** a slight acquaintance with a person or knowledge of a subject: *students will need* ***a nodding acquaintance with*** *three other languages.* **be on nodding terms** know someone slightly. **get the nod 1** be selected or approved. **2** receive a signal or information. **give someone/thing the nod 1** select or approve someone or something: *they banned one book but gave the other the nod.* **2** give someone a signal. **a nod's as good as a wink to a blind horse** proverb used to convey that a hint or suggestion can be or has been understood without the need of further elaboration or explanation. **on the nod** informal **1** Brit. by general agreement and without discussion: *parliamentary approval of the treaty went through on the nod.* **2** dated on credit. **3** alternating between wakefulness and sleepiness on account of heroin use.
– PHRASAL VERBS **nod off** informal fall asleep, especially briefly or unintentionally: *he nodded off during the sermon.*
– ORIGIN late Middle English (as a verb): perhaps of Low German origin; compare with Middle High German *notten* 'move about, shake'. The noun dates from the mid 16th cent.

noddle[1] ▶ **noun** informal, dated a person's head.
– ORIGIN late Middle English (denoting the back of the head): of unknown origin.

noddle[2] ▶ **verb** [with obj.] archaic, informal nod or wag (one's head).
– ORIGIN mid 18th cent.: frequentative of the verb **NOD**.

Noddy a character in the writings of Enid Blyton, a toy figure of a boy whose head is fixed in such a way that he has to nod when he speaks.

noddy ▶ **noun** (pl. **noddies**) **1** dated a foolish person.
2 a tropical tern with mainly dark-coloured plumage. [perhaps from the nodding behaviour of the birds during courtship.] ● Genera *Anous* and *Procelsterna*, family Sternidae (or Laridae): four species.
3 informal a brief shot in a filmed interview in which the interviewer nods in agreement or acknowledgement.

node ▶ **noun** technical **1** a point in a network or diagram at which lines or pathways intersect or branch. ■ a piece of equipment, such as a computer or peripheral, attached to a network. ■ Mathematics a point at which a curve intersects itself. ■ Astronomy either of the two points at which a planet's orbit intersects the plane of the ecliptic or the celestial equator.
2 Botany the part of a plant stem from which one or more leaves emerge, often forming a slight swelling.
3 Anatomy a lymph node or other structure consisting of a small mass of differentiated tissue.
4 Physics & Mathematics a point at which the amplitude of vibration in a standing wave system is zero. ■ a point at which a harmonic function has the value zero, especially a point of zero electron density in an orbital. ■ a point of zero current or voltage.
– DERIVATIVES **nodal** adjective.
– ORIGIN late Middle English (denoting a knotty swelling or a protuberance): from Latin *nodus* 'knot'.

node of Ranvier /ˈrɑːnvɪeɪ/, French /rɑ̃vje/ (also **Ranvier's node**) ▶ **noun** Anatomy a gap in the myelin sheath of a nerve, between adjacent Schwann cells.
– ORIGIN late 19th cent.: named after Louis Antoine *Ranvier* (1835–1922), French histologist.

nodical ▶ **adjective** Astronomy relating to a node or the nodes of an orbit.

nodose /nəʊˈdəʊs/ ▶ **adjective** technical having or characterized by hard or tight lumps; knotty.
– DERIVATIVES **nodosity** noun.
– ORIGIN early 18th cent.: from Latin *nodosus*, from *nodus* 'knot'.

nodule ▶ **noun 1** a small swelling or aggregation of cells in the body, especially an abnormal one. ■ (usu. **root nodule**) a swelling on a root of a leguminous plant, containing nitrogen-fixing bacteria.
2 a small rounded lump of matter distinct from its surroundings, e.g. of flint in chalk, carbon in cast iron, or a mineral on the seabed.
– DERIVATIVES **nodular** adjective, **nodulated** adjective, **nodulation** noun.
– ORIGIN late Middle English: from Latin *nodulus*, diminutive of *nodus* 'knot'.

nodus /ˈnəʊdəs/ ▶ **noun** (pl. **nodi** /-dʌɪ/) rare a problem, difficulty, or complication.
– ORIGIN late Middle English (denoting a knotty swelling): from Latin, literally 'knot'.

Noel ▶ **noun** Christmas, especially as a refrain in carols and on Christmas cards.
– ORIGIN early 19th cent.: French *Noël*, based on Latin *natalis* (see **NATAL**[1]).

noetic /nəʊˈɛtɪk/ ▶ **adjective** formal relating to mental activity or the intellect.
– ORIGIN mid 17th cent.: from Greek *noētikos*, from *noētos* 'intellectual', from *noein* 'perceive'.

no-fault ▶ **adjective** denoting an insurance policy that is valid regardless of whether the policyholder was at fault. ■ denoting a form of divorce granted without requiring one party to prove the other is to blame for the breakdown of the marriage.

no-fly zone ▶ **noun** an area over which aircraft are forbidden to fly, especially during a conflict.

Nofretete /ˌnɒfrəˈtiːtiː/ variant of **NEFERTITI**.

no-frills ▶ **adjective** without unnecessary extras, especially ones for decoration or additional comfort: *cheap fast food in no-frills surroundings.*

nog[1] ▶ **noun** archaic a small block or peg of wood.
– ORIGIN early 17th cent.: of unknown origin.

nog[2] ▶ **noun** [mass noun] Brit. **1** archaic a kind of strong beer brewed in East Anglia.
2 short for **EGGNOG**.
– ORIGIN late 17th cent.: of unknown origin.

nogal /ˈnɒxal/ ▶ **adverb** S. African informal what is more; moreover: *the picture would be ready in three minutes and for free nogal.*
– ORIGIN Afrikaans, literally 'fairly, rather'.

noggin ▶ **noun** informal **1** a person's head.
2 a small quantity of alcoholic drink, typically a quarter of a pint.
– ORIGIN mid 17th cent. (in the sense 'small drinking cup'): of unknown origin.

nogging ▶ **noun** [mass noun] Building brickwork in a timber frame. ■ [count noun] a horizontal piece of wood fixed to a framework to strengthen it.
– ORIGIN early 19th cent.: from **NOG**[1] + **-ING**[1].

no go ▶ **adjective** informal impossible, hopeless, or forbidden: *I tried to start the engine again, but it was no go.*

no-go area ▶ **noun** Brit. an area to which entry is dangerous, impossible, or forbidden.

no-good ▶ **adjective** [attrib.] informal (of a person) contemptible; worthless: *a no-good layabout.*
▶ **noun** a worthless or contemptible person.

Noh /nəʊ/ (also **No**) ▶ **noun** [mass noun] traditional Japanese masked drama with dance and song, evolved from Shinto rites.

> Noh dates from the 14th and 15th centuries, and its subject matter is taken mainly from Japan's classical literature. Traditionally the players were all male, with the chorus playing a passive narrative role.

– ORIGIN Japanese.

no-hitter ▶ **noun** Baseball a game in which a pitcher yields no hits to the opposing team.

no-hoper ▶ **noun** informal a person who is not expected to be successful.

nohow ▶ adverb **1** US used, especially in uneducated speech, to emphasize a negative: *they never executes nobody nohow*.
2 archaic not attractive, well, or in good order.

noil /nɔɪl/ ▶ noun [mass noun] (also **noils**) short strands and knots combed out of wool fibre before spinning.
– ORIGIN early 17th cent.: probably from Old French *noel*, from medieval Latin *nodellus*, diminutive of Latin *nodus* 'knot'.

noir /nwɑː/ ▶ noun [mass noun] a genre of crime film or fiction characterized by cynicism, fatalism, and moral ambiguity: *his film proved that a Brit could do noir as darkly as any American*. ■ [count noun] a film or novel of this genre.
– DERIVATIVES **noirish** adjective.
– ORIGIN 1970s: from FILM NOIR.

noise ▶ noun **1** a sound, especially one that is loud or unpleasant or that causes disturbance: *making a noise like a pig | what's that rustling noise outside the door?* ■ [mass noun] a series or combination of loud, confused sounds, especially when causing disturbance: *she was dazed with the heat and noise | vibration and noise from traffic*. ■ (**noises**) conventional remarks made to express something: *the government made tough noises about defending sterling*.
2 [mass noun] technical irregular fluctuations that accompany a transmitted electrical signal but are not part of it and tend to obscure it. ■ random fluctuations that obscure or do not contain meaningful data or other information: *over half the magnitude of the differences came from noise in the data*.
▶ verb archaic **1** [with obj.] (usu. **be noised about**) talk about or make known publicly.
2 [no obj.] make much noise.
– PHRASES **make a noise** speak or act in a way designed to attract a lot of attention or publicity: *he knows how to make a noise and claim police harassment*. **noises off** sounds made offstage to be heard by the audience of a play.
– ORIGIN Middle English (also in the sense 'quarrelling'): from Old French, from Latin *nausea* 'seasickness' (see NAUSEA).

noiseless ▶ adjective **1** silent or very quiet: *the cycle is a noiseless form of transport*.
2 technical accompanied by or introducing no random fluctuations that obscure the real signal or data.
– DERIVATIVES **noiselessly** adverb, **noiselessness** noun.

noisemaker ▶ noun N. Amer. a device for making a loud noise at a festivity or sports match.

noise pollution ▶ noun [mass noun] harmful or annoying levels of noise.

noisette /nwʌˈzɛt/ ▶ noun **1** a small round piece of meat, especially lamb.
2 a chocolate made with hazelnuts.
– ORIGIN French, diminutive of *noix* 'nut'.

noisome /ˈnɔɪs(ə)m/ ▶ adjective literary having an extremely offensive smell: *noisome vapours from the smouldering waste*. ■ very disagreeable or unpleasant.
– DERIVATIVES **noisomeness** noun.
– ORIGIN late Middle English: from obsolete *noy* (shortened form of ANNOY) + -SOME[1].

noisy ▶ adjective (**noisier**, **noisiest**) **1** making or given to making a lot of noise: *a noisy, giggling group of children | diesel cars can be very noisy*. ■ full of or characterized by noise: *the pub was crowded and noisy*. ■ stridently seeking to attract attention to one's views: *noisy pressure groups*.
2 technical accompanied by or introducing random fluctuations that obscure the real signal or data.
– DERIVATIVES **noisily** adverb, **noisiness** noun.

noisy miner ▶ noun Austral. a grey and white honeyeater of eastern Australia. ● *Manorina melanocephala*, family Meliphagidae.

Nok /nɒk/ ▶ noun [usu. as modifier] Archaeology an ancient civilization of northern Nigeria, dated to the 5th–3rd centuries BC. It is characterized by the production of distinctive terracotta figurines and is significant for its development of iron-working.
– ORIGIN from the name of the site where remains of this culture were found.

no-knock ▶ adjective US denoting a search or raid by the police made without permission or warning: *a no-knock raid*.

Nolan /ˈnəʊlən/, Sir Sidney Robert (1917–93), Australian painter, known for his paintings of famous characters and events from Australian history.

nolens volens /ˌnəʊlɛnz ˈvəʊlɛnz/ ▶ adverb formal whether a person wants or likes something or not.
– ORIGIN Latin, from *nolens* 'not willing' and *volens* 'willing'.

noli me tangere /ˌnəʊlʌɪ miː ˈtan(d)ʒəri, ˌnəʊli meɪ ˈtaŋg(ə)ri/ ▶ noun **1** a warning or prohibition against meddling or interference. ■ a painting representing the appearance of Jesus to Mary Magdalen at the sepulchre (John 20:17).
2 another term for TOUCH-ME-NOT.
– ORIGIN Latin, literally 'do not touch me'.

nolle pros /ˌnɒlɪ ˈprɒs, ˈprəʊs/ ▶ verb (**prosses**, **prossing**, **prossed**) [with obj.] US Law abandon or dismiss (a suit) by issuing a nolle prosequi.

nolle prosequi /ˌnɒlɪ ˈprɒsɪkwʌɪ/ ▶ noun Law a formal notice of abandonment by a plaintiff or prosecutor of all or part of a suit. ■ (in the UK) the dismissal or termination of legal proceedings by the Attorney General.
– ORIGIN Latin, literally 'refuse to pursue'.

nollie ▶ noun (in skateboarding and snowboarding) a jump performed without the aid of a take-off ramp, executed by pressing the foot down on the nose of the board.
– ORIGIN 1990s: probably short for *nose ollie*: see OLLIE.

no-load ▶ adjective N. Amer. (of shares in a mutual fund) sold directly to a buyer by the mutual fund itself without a commission being charged.

nolo contendere /ˌnəʊləʊ kɒnˈtɛndəri/ ▶ noun [mass noun] US Law a plea by which a defendant in a criminal prosecution accepts conviction but does not plead or admit guilt. Also called NO CONTEST.
– ORIGIN Latin, literally 'I do not wish to contend'.

nom. ▶ abbreviation nominal.

nomad ▶ noun a member of a people that travels from place to place to find fresh pasture for its animals and has no permanent home. ■ a person who does not stay long in the same place; a wanderer.
– DERIVATIVES **nomadism** noun.
– ORIGIN late 16th cent.: from French *nomade*, via Latin from Greek *nomas*, *nomad-* 'roaming in search of pasture', from the base of *nemein* 'to pasture'.

nomadic ▶ adjective living the life of a nomad; wandering: *nomadic herdsmen*.
– DERIVATIVES **nomadically** adverb.

no-man's-land ▶ noun [mass noun] disputed ground between the front lines or trenches of two opposing armies: *enemy soldiers facing you across no-man's-land* | figurative *the no-man's-land between the two parties is where presidential contests are won and lost*. ■ [count noun] a piece of unowned land or wasteland.
– ORIGIN Middle English: originally the name of a plot of ground lying outside the north wall of the city of London, the site of a place of execution.

nomarch /ˈnɒmɑːk/ ▶ noun **1** the governor of an ancient Egyptian nome.
2 the senior administrator of a modern Greek nomarchy.
– ORIGIN mid 17th cent.: from Greek *nomarkhēs* or *nomarkhos*, from *nomos* 'nome' + *arkhēs* 'governor'.

nomarchy /ˈnɒmɑːki/ ▶ noun (pl. **nomarchies**) an administrative division of modern Greece (formerly a province, now a smaller unit).
– ORIGIN mid 17th cent.: from Greek *nomarkhia*, from *nomos* 'nome' + *arkhē* 'government'.

no-mark ▶ noun Brit. informal an unimportant, unsuccessful, or worthless person.
– ORIGIN 1980s: perhaps from the idea of performing badly at school.

nombril /ˈnɒmbrɪl/ ▶ noun Heraldry the point halfway between fess point and the base of the shield.
– ORIGIN mid 16th cent.: from French, literally 'navel'.

nom de guerre /ˌnɒm də ˈɡɛː/ ▶ noun (pl. **noms de guerre** pronunc. same) an assumed name under which a person engages in combat or some other activity or enterprise.
– ORIGIN French, literally 'war name'.

nom de plume /ˌnɒm də ˈpluːm/ ▶ noun (pl. **noms de plume** pronunc. same) an assumed name used by a writer instead of their real name; a pen-name.
– ORIGIN early 19th cent.: formed in English from French words, to render the sense 'pen name', on the pattern of *nom de guerre*.

Nome /nəʊm/ a city in western Alaska, on the south coast of the Seward Peninsula. Founded in 1896 as a gold-mining camp, it became a centre of the Alaskan gold rush at the turn of the century.

nome /nəʊm/ ▶ noun **1** each of the thirty-six territorial divisions of ancient Egypt.
2 an administrative division of modern Greece.
– ORIGIN early 18th cent.: from Greek *nomos* 'division', from *nemein* 'to divide'.

nomen /ˈnəʊmən/ ▶ noun Roman History the second personal name of a citizen of ancient Rome that indicates the gens to which he or she belonged, e.g. Marcus *Tullius* Cicero.
– ORIGIN Latin, literally 'name'.

nomenclature /nə(ʊ)ˈmɛŋklətʃə, ˈnəʊmənˌkleɪtʃə/ ▶ noun [mass noun] the devising or choosing of names for things, especially in a science or other discipline. ■ the body or system of such names in a particular field. ■ formal the term or terms applied to someone or something: *'customers' was preferred to the original nomenclature 'passengers'*.
– DERIVATIVES **nomenclator** noun, **nomenclatural** /-ˈklatʃ(ə)r(ə)l, -kləˈtʃʊər(ə)l/ adjective.
– ORIGIN early 17th cent.: from French, from Latin *nomenclatura*, from *nomen* 'name' + *clatura* 'calling, summoning' (from *calare* 'to call').

nomenklatura /nɒˌmɛnkləˈtjʊərə/ ▶ noun (in the former Soviet Union) the system whereby influential posts in government and industry were filled by Party appointees. ■ the holders of such posts collectively.
– ORIGIN Russian, from Latin *nomenclatura* (see NOMENCLATURE).

nominal ▶ adjective **1** (of a role or status) existing in name only: *Thailand retained nominal independence under Japanese military occupation*. ■ relating to or consisting of names.
2 (of a price or charge) very small; far below the real value or cost: *they charge a nominal fee for the service*.
3 (of a quantity or dimension) stated or expressed but not necessarily corresponding exactly to the real value: *EU legislation allowed variation around the nominal weight (that printed on each packet)*. ■ Economics expressed in terms of current prices or figures, without making allowance for changes over time: *the nominal exchange rate*.
4 Grammar relating to or functioning as a noun: *a nominal group*.
5 informal (chiefly in the context of space travel) functioning normally or acceptably.
– DERIVATIVES **nominally** adverb.
– ORIGIN late 15th cent. (as a term in grammar): from Latin *nominalis*, from *nomen*, *nomin-* 'name'.

nominal account ▶ noun Finance an account recording the financial transactions of a business in a particular category, rather than with a person or other organization.

nominal definition ▶ noun Logic a definition that describes something in terms of its properties, in order to distinguish it from other things, but without describing its underlying structure or 'essence'.

nominalism ▶ noun [mass noun] Philosophy the doctrine that universals or general ideas are mere names without any corresponding reality. Only particular objects exist, and properties, numbers, and sets are merely features of the way of considering the things that exist. Important in medieval scholastic thought, nominalism is associated particularly with William of Occam. Often contrasted with REALISM (sense 3).
– DERIVATIVES **nominalist** noun, **nominalistic** adjective.
– ORIGIN mid 19th cent.: from French *nominalisme*, from *nominal* 'relating to names' (see NOMINAL).

nominalize (also **nominalise**) ▶ verb [with obj.] Grammar form (a noun) from a verb or adjective, e.g. *output*, *truth*, from *put out*, *true*.
– DERIVATIVES **nominalization** noun.

nominal ledger ▶ noun Finance a ledger containing nominal accounts, or one containing both nominal and real accounts.

nominal value ▶ noun Economics the value that is stated on a coin or note; face value. ■ the price of a share, bond, or stock when it was issued, rather than its current market value.

nominate ▶ verb /ˈnɒmɪneɪt/ [with obj.] **1** propose or formally enter as a candidate for election or for an honour or award: *the film was nominated for several Oscars*. ■ appoint to a job or position: *the company nominated her as a delegate to the convention*.
2 specify (something) formally, typically the date or place for an event: *a day was nominated for the exchange of contracts*.
▶ adjective /ˈnɒmɪnət/ Zoology & Botany denoting a race or subspecies which is given the same epithet as the species to which it belongs, e.g. *Homo sapiens sapiens*.
– DERIVATIVES **nominator** noun.

N

– ORIGIN late Middle English (as an adjective in the sense 'named'): from Latin *nominat-* 'named', from the verb *nominare*, from *nomen, nomin-* 'a name'. The verb senses are first found in English in the 16th cent.

nomination ▶ noun [mass noun] the action of nominating or state of being nominated: *women's groups opposed the nomination of the judge* | [count noun] *the film received five nominations.* ■ [count noun] a person or thing nominated: *send your nominations in by 30th November.*

nominative /ˈnɒmɪnətɪv/ ▶ adjective **1** Grammar relating to or denoting a case of nouns, pronouns, and adjectives in Latin, Greek, and other inflected languages, used for the subject of a verb.
2 /ˈnɒmɪˌneɪtɪv/ of or appointed by nomination as distinct from election.
▶ noun Grammar a word in the nominative case. ■ (**the nominative**) the nominative case.
– ORIGIN late Middle English: from Latin *nominativus* 'relating to naming', translation of Greek *onomastikē (ptōsis)* 'naming (case)'.

nominee ▶ noun **1** a person who is nominated as a candidate for election or for an honour or award: *an Oscar nominee.*
2 a person or company, not the owner, in whose name a stock, bond, or company is registered.
– ORIGIN mid 17th cent.: from NOMINATE + -EE.

nomogram /ˈnɒməgram, ˈnəʊm-/ (also **nomograph**) ▶ noun a diagram representing the relations between three or more variable quantities by means of a number of scales, so arranged that the value of one variable can be found by a simple geometrical construction, e.g. by drawing a straight line intersecting the other scales at the appropriate values.
– DERIVATIVES **nomographic** adjective, **nomography** /nəˈmɒgrəfi/ noun.
– ORIGIN early 20th cent.: from Greek *nomos* 'law' + -GRAM[1].

nomological /ˌnɒməˈlɒdʒɪkəl/ ▶ adjective relating to or denoting principles that resemble laws, especially those laws of nature which are neither logically necessary nor theoretically explicable, but just are so. ■ another term for NOMOTHETIC.
– DERIVATIVES **nomologically** adverb.
– ORIGIN mid 19th cent.: from Greek *nomos* 'law' + *-logical* (see -LOGY).

N

nomothetic /ˌnɒməˈθɛtɪk, ˌnəʊm-/ ▶ adjective relating to the study or discovery of general scientific laws. Often contrasted with IDIOGRAPHIC.
– ORIGIN mid 17th cent.: from obsolete *nomothete* 'legislator' (from Greek *nomothetēs*) + -IC.

-nomy ▶ combining form denoting a specified area of knowledge or the laws governing it: *astronomy* | *gastronomy.*
– ORIGIN from Greek *-nomia*; related to *nomos* 'law' and *nemein* 'distribute'.

non- ▶ prefix **1** expressing negation or absence: *non-aggression* | *non-recognition.* ■ not of the kind or class described: *non-believer* | *nonconformist.* ■ not of the importance implied: *non-issue.*
2 (added to adverbs) not in the way described: *non-uniformly.*
3 (added to verbs to form adjectives) not causing or requiring: *non-skid* | *non-iron.*
4 expressing a neutral negative sense when a corresponding form beginning with *in-* or *un-* has a special connotation (such as *non-human* compared with *inhuman*).
– ORIGIN from Latin *non* 'not'.

USAGE The prefixes **non-** and **un-** both have the meaning 'not', but tend to be used with a difference of emphasis. See USAGE at UN-[1].

nona- /ˈnɒnə, ˈnəʊnə/ ▶ combining form nine; having nine: *nonagon.*
– ORIGIN from Latin *nonus* 'ninth'.

non-addictive ▶ adjective (of a drug or other substance) not causing addiction.

non-affective ▶ adjective Psychology denoting or relating to mental disorders which are not characterized by disturbance of mood.

nonage /ˈnəʊnɪdʒ, ˈnɒn-/ ▶ noun formal the period of a person's immaturity or youth.
– ORIGIN late Middle English: from Old French *nonage*, from *non-* 'non-' + *age* 'age'.

nonagenarian /ˌnɒnədʒɪˈnɛːrɪən, ˌnəʊn-/ ▶ noun a person who is between 90 and 99 years old.
– ORIGIN early 19th cent.: from Latin *nonagenarius* (based on *nonaginta* 'ninety') + -AN.

non-aggression ▶ noun [mass noun] absence of the desire or intention to be aggressive, especially on the part of nations or governments: [as modifier] *a non-aggression pact.*

nonagon /ˈnɒnəg(ə)n/ ▶ noun a plane figure with nine straight sides and nine angles.
– DERIVATIVES **nonagonal** adjective.
– ORIGIN mid 17th cent.: formed irregularly from Latin *nonus* 'ninth', on the pattern of words such as *hexagon.*

non-alcoholic ▶ adjective (of a drink) not containing alcohol.

non-aligned ▶ adjective not aligned with something else. ■ relating to a state in the Non-Aligned Movement.
– DERIVATIVES **non-alignment** noun.

Non-Aligned Movement a grouping of chiefly developing countries pursuing a policy of neutrality towards the superpowers (i.e. the US and formerly the USSR) in world politics.

non-allergenic ▶ adjective not causing an allergic reaction.

non-allergic ▶ adjective another term for NON-ALLERGENIC. ■ not having an allergy to something.

no-name chiefly N. Amer. ▶ adjective (of a product) having no brand name: *cheap, no-name cigarettes.* ■ (of a person) unknown, especially in a particular profession: *no-name, no-frills chefs.*
▶ noun a person who is unknown in a particular profession.

nonane /ˈnəʊneɪn, ˈnɒn-/ ▶ noun [mass noun] Chemistry a colourless liquid hydrocarbon of the alkane series, present in petroleum spirit. ● Chem. formula: C_9H_{20}; many isomers, especially the straight-chain isomer (*n*-**nonane**).
– ORIGIN mid 19th cent.: from NONA- (denoting nine carbon atoms) + -ANE[2].

non-appearance ▶ noun [mass noun] failure to appear or be present, especially at a gathering or engagement or in a court of law.

nonary /ˈnəʊnəri/ ▶ adjective rare relating to or based on the number nine.
– ORIGIN mid 17th cent. (as a noun): from Latin *nonus* 'ninth', on the pattern of words such as *denary.*

non-associative ▶ adjective **1** not characterized by association, especially of ideas.
2 Mathematics involving the condition that a group of quantities connected by operations gives a result dependent upon the order in which the operations are performed.

non-attendance ▶ noun [mass noun] failure to attend or be present at a place where you are expected to be: *pupils' non-attendance at school.*

non-attributable ▶ adjective not able to be attributed to a particular source or cause.
– DERIVATIVES **non-attributably** adverb.

non-availability ▶ noun [mass noun] the state of not being available, free, or able to be used.

non-being ▶ noun [mass noun] the state of not being; non-existence.

non-believer ▶ noun a person who does not believe in a particular thing, especially one who has no religious faith.

non-belligerent ▶ adjective not aggressive or engaged in a war or conflict.
▶ noun a nation or person that is not engaged in a war or conflict.
– DERIVATIVES **non-belligerence** noun.

non-biodegradable ▶ adjective not biodegradable: *non-biodegradable plastics.*

non-biological ▶ adjective not involving or derived from biology or living organisms. ■ (of a detergent) not containing enzymes.

non-capital ▶ adjective Law (of an offence) not punishable by death.

nonce[1] /nɒns/ ▶ adjective (of a word or expression) coined for one occasion: *a nonce word.*
– PHRASES **for the nonce** for the present; temporarily: *the room had been converted for the nonce into a nursery.*
– ORIGIN Middle English: from *then anes* 'the one (purpose)' (from *then*, obsolete oblique form of THE + *ane* 'one' + -S[3]), altered by wrong division; compare with NEWT and NICKNAME.

nonce[2] /nɒns/ ▶ noun Brit. informal a person convicted of a sexual offence, especially against a child.
– ORIGIN 1970s: of unknown origin.

nonchalance ▶ noun [mass noun] the state of being nonchalant: *an air of nonchalance.*

nonchalant /ˈnɒnʃ(ə)l(ə)nt/ ▶ adjective (of a person or manner) feeling or appearing casually calm and relaxed; not displaying anxiety, interest, or enthusiasm: *she gave a nonchalant shrug.*
– DERIVATIVES **nonchalantly** adverb.
– ORIGIN mid 18th cent.: from French, literally 'not being concerned', from the verb *nonchaloir.*

non-clerical ▶ adjective **1** not doing or involving routine clerical work in an office.
2 not relating to or belonging to the clergy.

non-clinical ▶ adjective not clinical. ■ not accompanied by directly observable symptoms.

non-coding ▶ adjective Biology (of a section of a nucleic acid molecule) not directing the production of a peptide sequence.

non-com ▶ noun Military, informal a non-commissioned officer.

non-combatant ▶ noun a person who is not engaged in fighting during a war, especially a civilian, army chaplain, or army doctor.

non-comedogenic ▶ adjective denoting a skincare product or cosmetic that is formulated so as not to cause blocked pores.

non-commercial ▶ adjective not having a commercial objective; not intended to make a profit: *a non-commercial radio station.*

non-commissioned ▶ adjective Military (of an officer in the army, navy, or air force) not holding a rank conferred by a commission.

non-committal ▶ adjective not expressing or revealing commitment to a definite opinion or course of action: *her tone was non-committal, and her face gave nothing away.*
– DERIVATIVES **non-committally** adverb.

non-communicant ▶ noun (in church use) a person who does not receive Holy Communion, especially regularly or at a particular service.

non-competitive ▶ adjective not involving competition; not competitive: *they joined in non-competitive activities like friendship week.*

non-compliance ▶ noun [mass noun] failure to act in accordance with a wish or command.

non-compliant ▶ adjective failing to act in accordance with a wish or command: *non-compliant companies face legal action* | *work which is non-compliant with building regulations.*

non compos mentis /ˌnɒn ˌkɒmpɒs ˈmɛntɪs/ (also **non compos**) ▶ adjective not sane or in one's right mind.
– ORIGIN Latin, literally 'not having control of one's mind'.

non-conductor ▶ noun a substance that does not conduct heat or electricity.
– DERIVATIVES **non-conducting** adjective.

nonconformist ▶ noun **1** (**Nonconformist**) a member of a Protestant Church which dissents from the established Church of England.
2 a person who does not conform to prevailing ideas or practices in their behaviour or views.
▶ adjective **1** (**Nonconformist**) relating to Nonconformists or their principles and practices.
2 characterized by behaviour or views that do not conform to prevailing ideas or practices.
– DERIVATIVES **nonconformism** noun.

nonconformity ▶ noun [mass noun] **1** (**Nonconformity**) Nonconformists as a body, especially Protestants dissenting from the Anglican Church. ■ the principles or practice of Nonconformists, especially Protestant dissent.
2 failure or refusal to conform to a prevailing rule or practice. ■ lack of similarity in form or type.

non-confrontational ▶ adjective tending to deal with situations calmly and diplomatically; not aggressive or hostile: *a non-confrontational approach to matrimonial disputes.*
– DERIVATIVES **non-confrontationally** adverb.

non-content ▶ noun a member of the British House of Lords who votes against a particular motion.

non-contentious ▶ adjective **1** not causing or likely to cause an argument.
2 Law not involving differences between contending parties.

non-contributory ▶ adjective (of a pension or pension scheme) funded by regular payments by the employer, not the employee. ■ (of a state benefit) paid to eligible people regardless of how much tax or other contributions they have made: *non-contributory invalidity benefits.*

non-controversial ▶ adjective not giving rise to disagreement; not controversial (tending to be less forceful in meaning than **uncontroversial**).

non-cooperation ▶ noun [mass noun] failure or refusal to cooperate, especially as a form of protest.

non-count ▶ adjective Grammar (of a noun) not countable.

nonda /ˈnɒndə/ ▶ noun a tropical Australian tree which bears an edible yellow plum-like fruit and grows in groves on sand ridges. ● *Parinari nonda*, family Chrysobalanaceae.
– ORIGIN mid 19th cent.: probably from a Queensland Aboriginal language.

non-dairy ▶ adjective containing no milk or milk products: *a non-dairy creamer.*

non-delivery ▶ noun [mass noun] chiefly Law failure to provide or deliver goods.

non-denominational ▶ adjective open or acceptable to people of any Christian denomination.

nondescript /ˈnɒndɪskrɪpt/ ▶ adjective lacking distinctive or interesting features or characteristics: *she lived in a nondescript suburban apartment block.*
▶ noun a nondescript person or thing.
– DERIVATIVES **nondescriptly** adverb, **nondescriptness** noun.
– ORIGIN late 17th cent. (in the sense 'not previously described or identified scientifically'): from **non-** + obsolete *descript* 'described, engraved' (from Latin *descriptus*).

non-destructive ▶ adjective technical not involving damage or destruction, especially of an object or material that is being tested.

non-directional ▶ adjective lacking directional properties. ■ (of sound, light, radio waves, etc.) equally sensitive, intense, etc., in every direction.

non-disjunction ▶ noun [mass noun] Genetics the failure of one or more pairs of homologous chromosomes or sister chromatids to separate normally during nuclear division, usually resulting in an abnormal distribution of chromosomes in the daughter nuclei.

non-dom ▶ noun Brit. a person who lives in a country but is not legally domiciled in it, sometimes obtaining tax advantages in the country of residence.

non-drinker ▶ noun a person who does not drink alcohol.

non-drip ▶ adjective (of paint) specially formulated so that it does not drip or run when wet.

non-driver ▶ noun a person who does not or cannot drive a motor vehicle.

none[1] /nʌn/ ▶ pronoun not any: *none of you want to work | don't use any more water, or there'll be none left for me.* ■ no person; no one: *none could match her looks.*
▶ adverb (**none the**) [with comparative] by no amount; not at all: *it is made none the easier by the differences in approach.*
– PHRASES **none the less** see **nonetheless**. **none other than** used to emphasize the surprising identity of a person or thing: *her first customer was none other than Henry du Pont.* **be none the wiser** see **wise**[1]. **none the worse for** see **worse**. **none too** see **too**. **will have** (or **want**) **none of something** refuse to accept a particular thing, especially a person's behaviour: *I will have none of it.*
– ORIGIN Old English *nān*, from *ne* 'not' + *ān* 'one', of Germanic origin; compare with German *nein* 'no!'.

> **USAGE** It is sometimes held that **none** can only take a singular verb, never a plural verb: ***none of them is coming tonight*** rather than ***none of them are coming tonight.*** There is little justification, historical or grammatical, for this view. **None** is descended from Old English **nān** meaning 'not one' and has been used for around a thousand years with both a singular and a plural verb, depending on the context and the emphasis needed.

none[2] /nəʊn/ (also **nones**) ▶ noun a service forming part of the Divine Office of the Western Christian Church, traditionally said (or chanted) at the ninth hour of the day (3 p.m.).
– ORIGIN mid 19th cent.: from French, from Latin *nona*, feminine singular of *nonus* 'ninth'. Compare with **noon**.

non-empty ▶ adjective Mathematics & Logic (of a set or class) not empty; having at least one element or member.

nonentity /nɒˈnɛntɪti/ ▶ noun (pl. **nonentities**)
1 a person or thing with no special or interesting qualities; an unimportant person or thing: *a political nonentity.* ■ [mass noun] the quality or condition of being uninteresting or unimportant.
2 [mass noun] non-existence: *asserting the nonentity of evil.*
– ORIGIN late 16th cent.: from medieval Latin *nonentitas* 'non-existence'.

nones /nəʊnz/ ▶ plural noun **1** in the ancient Roman calendar, the ninth day before the ides by inclusive reckoning, i.e. the 7th day of March, May, July, October, the 5th of other months.
2 another term for **none**[2].
– ORIGIN via Old French from Latin *nonas*, feminine accusative plural of *nonus* 'ninth'.

non-essential ▶ adjective not absolutely necessary (tending to be less forceful in meaning than **inessential**): *during the strike non-essential hospital services were halted.*
▶ noun (usu. **non-essentials**) a non-essential thing.

non est factum /ˌnɒn ɛst ˈfaktəm/ ▶ noun Law a plea that a written agreement is invalid because the defendant was mistaken about its character when signing it.
– ORIGIN Latin, literally 'it was not done'.

nonesuch /ˈnʌnsʌtʃ/ (also **nonsuch**) ▶ noun **1** archaic a person or thing regarded as excellent or perfect.
2 (usu. **nonsuch**) a small Eurasian medick which is widely grown as a constituent of grazing pasture. ● *Medicago lupulina*, family Leguminosae.
– ORIGIN early 17th cent.: coined on the pattern of *nonpareil*.

nonet /nəʊˈnɛt, nɒˈnɛt/ ▶ noun a group of nine people or things, especially musicians. ■ a musical composition for nine voices or instruments.
– ORIGIN mid 19th cent.: from Italian *nonetto*, from *nono* 'ninth', from Latin *nonus*.

nonetheless (also **none the less**) ▶ adverb in spite of that; nevertheless: *the rally, which the government had declared illegal, was nonetheless attended by some 6,000.*

non-Euclidean ▶ adjective Geometry denying or going beyond Euclidean principles in geometry, especially contravening the postulate that only one line through a given point can be parallel to a given line.

non-event ▶ noun an unexpectedly dull or insignificant event or occasion. ■ an event that did not happen.

non-executive Brit. ▶ adjective not having an executive function: *a non-executive chairman.*
▶ noun a person without executive responsibilities.

non-existent ▶ adjective not existing or not real or present: *she pretended to tie a non-existent shoelace.*
– DERIVATIVES **non-existence** noun.

non-factive ▶ adjective Linguistics denoting a verb that takes a clausal object which may or may not designate a true fact, e.g. *believe* as opposed to *know*. Contrasted with **contrafactive, factive**.

non-fat ▶ adjective (of food) containing little or no fat: *non-fat buttermilk.*

nonfeasance /nɒnˈfiːz(ə)ns/ ▶ noun [mass noun] Law failure to perform an act that is required by law.
– ORIGIN early 17th cent.: from **non-** + *feasance* (see **malfeasance**).

non-ferrous ▶ adjective relating to or denoting a metal other than iron or steel.

non-fiction ▶ noun [mass noun] prose writing that is informative or factual rather than fictional.
– DERIVATIVES **non-fictional** adjective.

non-figurative ▶ adjective not figurative. ■ (of art) abstract.

non-finite ▶ adjective not finite. ■ Grammar (of a verb form) not limited by tense, person, or number.

non-flam ▶ adjective short for **non-flammable**.

non-flammable ▶ adjective not catching fire easily.

> **USAGE** The adjectives **non-flammable** and **non-inflammable** have the same meaning: see **usage** at **flammable**.

non-fulfilment ▶ noun [mass noun] failure to fulfil or carry out something desired, planned, or promised.

non-functional ▶ adjective **1** not having any particular purpose or function.
2 not operating or in working order.

nong /nɒŋ/ ▶ noun Austral./NZ informal a foolish or stupid person (often as a general term of abuse).
– ORIGIN 1940s: of unknown origin.

non-governmental ▶ adjective (especially of an organization) not belonging to or associated with any government.

non-Hodgkin's lymphoma ▶ noun [mass noun] Medicine a form of malignant lymphoma distinguished from Hodgkin's disease only by the absence of binucleate giant cells.

non-human ▶ adjective not human: *non-human material objects.*
▶ noun a creature that is not a human being.

noni /ˈnəʊni/ ▶ noun **1** a tropical evergreen shrub native to southern and SE Asia and the Pacific islands. ● *Morinda citrifolia*, family Rubiaceae.
2 the fruit of the noni, used medicinally to stimulate the immune system and as a detoxifying agent.
– ORIGIN Tahitian.

non-infectious ▶ adjective (of a disease or disease-causing organism) not liable to be transmitted through the environment. ■ not liable to spread infection.

non-inflammable ▶ adjective not catching fire easily; not inflammable.

> **USAGE** The adjectives **non-inflammable** and **non-flammable** have the same meaning: see **usage** at **inflammable**.

non-inherent ▶ adjective (of an adjective) having the relevant meaning only when used attributively with reference to a particular individual; for example *poor* and *old* in *the poor old chap*, which is not equivalent to *the chap was poor and old.*

non-insulin-dependent ▶ adjective Medicine relating to or denoting a type of diabetes in which there is some insulin secretion. Such diabetes typically develops in adulthood and can frequently be managed by diet and hypoglycaemic agents.

non-interference ▶ noun [mass noun] failure or refusal to intervene without invitation or necessity, especially in political matters.

non-intervention ▶ noun [mass noun] the principle or practice of not becoming involved in the affairs of other countries.
– DERIVATIVES **non-interventionism** noun, **non-interventionist** adjective & noun.

non-invasive ▶ adjective **1** (of medical procedures) not involving the introduction of instruments into the body: *non-invasive techniques such as ultrasound.*
2 not tending to spread undesirably or harmfully: *non-invasive precancerous tissue.*

N

non-iron ▶ adjective not needing to be ironed.

non-ism ▶ noun [mass noun] US abstention from activities and substances regarded as damaging to one's health or well-being.

non-issue ▶ noun a topic of little or no importance.

nonjoinder ▶ noun Law the omission of a person who ought to be made a party to a lawsuit.

non-judgemental ▶ adjective not judgemental; avoiding moral judgements.

Nonjuror ▶ noun a member of the clergy who refused to take the oath of allegiance to William and Mary in 1689.

non-jury ▶ adjective Law denoting a trial or legal action not having or requiring a jury.

non-league ▶ adjective denoting or relating to a sports club that does not belong to one of a country's main professional leagues: *he's one of the best players in non-league football.*

non licet /nɒn ˈlɪsɛt/ ▶ adjective not lawful.
– ORIGIN Latin.

non-linear ▶ adjective **1** not arranged in a straight line. ■ Mathematics designating or involving an equation whose terms are not of the first degree. ■ Physics involving a lack of linearity between two related qualities such as input and output. ■ Mathematics involving measurement in more than one dimension.
2 not sequential or straightforward: *Joyce's stream-of-consciousness, non-linear narrative.*
3 of or denoting digital editing whereby a sequence of edits is stored on computer as opposed to videotape.
– PHRASES **go non-linear** informal become very excited or angry, especially about a particular obsession.
– DERIVATIVES **non-linearity** noun, **non-linearly** adverb.

non-logical ▶ adjective not derived from or according to the rules of logic or formal argument (less forceful in meaning than **illogical**).

non-magnetic ▶ adjective (of a substance) not magnetic.

non-malignant ▶ adjective (of a tumour) benign; not cancerous.

non-member ▶ noun a person, body, or country that is not a member of a particular organization.
– DERIVATIVES **non-membership** noun.

non-metal ▶ noun an element or substance that is not a metal.
– DERIVATIVES **non-metallic** adjective.

non-military ▶ adjective not belonging to, characteristic of, or involving the armed forces; civilian: *the widespread destruction of non-military targets.*

non-moral ▶ adjective not holding or manifesting moral principles: *non-moral value judgements.*

non-native ▶ adjective not indigenous or native to a particular place. ▪ not having spoken the language in question from earliest childhood: *native and non-native speakers alike.*

non-natural ▶ adjective not involving or manifesting natural means or processes. ▪ Philosophy existing but not part of the natural world (a term used by G.E. Moore of ethical properties).

non-negative ▶ adjective not negative. ▪ Mathematics either positive or equal to zero.

non-negotiable ▶ adjective not open to discussion or modification. ▪ (of a document) not able to be transferred or assigned to the legal ownership of another person.

non-net ▶ adjective (of an amount) including tax and other sums in addition to the net amount.

non-nuclear ▶ adjective **1** not possessing or involving nuclear energy or weapons.
2 Physics not involving or forming part of a nucleus or nuclei.

no-no ▶ noun (pl. **no-nos**) informal a thing that is not possible or acceptable: *perming highlighted hair used to be a definite no-no, but it's now possible.*

non-objective ▶ adjective **1** influenced by personal feeling or opinions in considering and representing facts.
2 (of art) abstract.

non-observance ▶ noun [mass noun] failure to fulfil or comply with an obligation, rule, or custom.

no-nonsense ▶ adjective simple and straightforward; sensible: *a no-nonsense approach.*

non-operational ▶ adjective not working or in use: *non-operational equipment.* ▪ not engaged in or involving active duties.

N

non-organic ▶ adjective **1** not relating to or derived from living matter.
2 (of food or farming methods) involving the use of chemical fertilizers and pesticides.

non-parametric ▶ adjective Statistics not involving any assumptions as to the form or parameters of a frequency distribution.

nonpareil /ˌnɒnpəˈreɪl/ ▶ adjective having no match or equal; unrivalled: *he is a nonpareil storyteller* | [postpositive] *a film critic nonpareil.*
▶ noun **1** an unrivalled or matchless person or thing.
2 US a flat round confection made of chocolate covered with white sugar sprinkles.
3 [mass noun] Printing an old type size equal to six points (larger than ruby).
– ORIGIN late Middle English: from French, from *non-* 'not' + *pareil* 'equal' (from popular Latin *pariculus*, diminutive of Latin *par* 'equal').

non-participating ▶ adjective **1** not taking part in an activity.
2 (of an insurance policy) not allowing the holder a share of the profits, typically in the form of a bonus, made by the company.

non-partisan ▶ adjective not biased or partisan, especially towards any particular political group.

non-party ▶ adjective independent of any political party.

non-payment ▶ noun [mass noun] failure to pay an amount of money that is owed: *homes repossessed for non-payment of mortgages.*

non-penetrative ▶ adjective (of sexual activity) in which penetration by the penis does not take place.

non-performance ▶ noun [mass noun] **1** failure or refusal to perform or fulfil a condition, promise, etc.: *the non-performance of his contractual obligations.*
2 the state or fact of not being performed: *the non-performance of the opera.*

non-person ▶ noun a person regarded as non-existent or unimportant, or as having no rights; an ignored or forgotten person: *these players were famous within their own communities, but non-persons outside them.* Compare with UNPERSON.

non-personal ▶ adjective not personal: *non-personal tax allowances.*

non-physical ▶ adjective **1** not relating to or concerning the body: *both physical and non-physical ill-treatment.*
2 not tangible or concrete: *non-physical digital money.*
– DERIVATIVES **non-physically** adverb.

non placet /nɒn ˈpleɪsɛt/ ▶ noun a negative vote in a Church or university assembly.
– ORIGIN Latin, literally 'it does not please'.

non-playing ▶ adjective (of a member of a team or club) not playing in a game or sport.

nonplus /nɒnˈplʌs/ ▶ verb (**nonplusses, nonplussing, nonplussed**) [with obj.] surprise and confuse (someone) so much that they are unsure how to react: *Diane was nonplussed by such an odd question.*
▶ noun a state of being very surprised and confused.
– ORIGIN late 16th cent.: from Latin *non plus* 'not more'. The noun originally meant 'a state in which no more can be said or done'.

nonplussed ▶ adjective **1** so surprised and confused that one is unsure how to react: *Henry looked completely nonplussed.*
2 N. Amer. informal not disconcerted; unperturbed.

> **USAGE** In standard use **nonplussed** means 'surprised and confused', as in *she was* **nonplussed** *at his eagerness to help out.* In North American English a new use has developed in recent years, meaning 'unperturbed'—more or less the opposite of its traditional meaning—as in *he was clearly trying to appear* **nonplussed**. This new use probably arose on the assumption that **non-** was the normal negative prefix and must therefore have a negative meaning. It is not considered part of standard English.

non-point source ▶ noun a source of pollution that issues from widely distributed or pervasive environmental elements. Compare with POINT SOURCE.

non-poisonous ▶ adjective not containing or using poison: *a non-poisonous snake.*

non-political ▶ adjective not relating to or motivated by politics: *non-political speeches.*

non-polluting ▶ adjective not releasing pollutants, especially carbon dioxide, into the atmosphere: *wind power is a non-polluting alternative to fossil fuels.*

non possumus /nɒn ˈpɒsjʊməs/ ▶ noun used as a statement expressing inability to act in a matter.
– ORIGIN Latin, literally 'we cannot'.

non-prescription ▶ adjective (of a medicine) available for sale without a prescription.

non-price competition ▶ noun [mass noun] Economics a form of competition in which two or more producers use such factors as packaging, delivery, or customer service rather than price to increase demand for their products.

non-productive ▶ adjective not producing or able to produce goods, crops, or economic benefit. ▪ achieving little.

non-professional ▶ adjective relating to or engaged in a paid occupation that does not require advanced education or training: *non-professional grades of staff.* ▪ relating to or engaged in an activity which is not one's main paid occupation: *non-professional actors.*
▶ noun a non-professional person.

non-profit (Brit. also **non-profit-making**) ▶ adjective not making or conducted primarily to make a profit: *charities and other non-profit organizations.*
▶ noun chiefly N. Amer. a non-profit organization: *I spent the next six years working for small non-profits.*

non-proliferation ▶ noun [mass noun] the prevention of an increase or spread of something, especially the number of countries possessing nuclear weapons: [as modifier] *a nuclear non-proliferation treaty.*

non-proprietary ▶ adjective not registered or protected as a trademark or brand name; generic. ▪ (especially of computer hardware or software) conforming to standards that are in the public domain or are widely licensed.

non-reader ▶ noun a person who cannot or does not read.

non-resident ▶ adjective not living or based in a particular place: *a non-resident caretaker.* ▪ Computing (of software) not kept permanently in memory but available to be loaded from a backing store or external device.
▶ noun a person not living in a particular place.
– DERIVATIVES **non-residence** noun.

non-resistance ▶ noun [mass noun] the practice or principle of not resisting authority, even when it is unjustly exercised.

non-restrictive ▶ adjective **1** not involving restrictions or limitations.
2 Grammar (of a relative clause or descriptive phrase) giving additional information about a noun phrase whose particular reference has already been specified.

> **USAGE** On the use of **restrictive** and **non-restrictive** relative clauses, see **USAGE** at **RESTRICTIVE**.

non-return ▶ adjective permitting the flow of air or liquid in one direction only: *a non-return valve.*

non-rhotic ▶ adjective Phonetics relating to or denoting a dialect of English (such as Standard British English) in which *r* is pronounced in prevocalic position only.

non-rigid ▶ adjective not rigid. ▪ denoting an airship whose shape is maintained solely by the pressure of the gas inside.

non-scene ▶ adjective informal (of a homosexual) not inclined to participate in the social environment frequented predominantly by other homosexuals.

non-scientific ▶ adjective not involving or relating to science or scientific methods.
– DERIVATIVES **non-scientist** noun.

non-secretor /ˌnɒnsɪˈkriːtə/ ▶ noun a person whose saliva and other secretions do not contain blood-group antigens.

non-sectarian ▶ adjective not involving or relating to different religious sects or political groups.

nonsense ▶ noun [mass noun] **1** spoken or written words that have no meaning or make no sense: *he was talking absolute nonsense.* ▪ [as exclamation] used to show strong disagreement: *'Nonsense! No one can do that.'* ▪ [as modifier] denoting verse or other writing intended to be amusing by virtue of its absurd or whimsical language: *nonsense poetry.*
2 foolish or unacceptable behaviour: *she's a strong woman who stands no nonsense.* ▪ [count noun] something ridiculously impractical or ill-advised: *the law is a nonsense* | *the proposal would* **make a nonsense** *of their plans.*

nonsense mutation ▶ noun Genetics a mutation in which a sense codon that corresponds to one of the twenty amino acids specified by the genetic code is changed to a chain-terminating codon.

nonsense word ▶ noun a word having no conventionally accepted meaning.

nonsensical /nɒnˈsɛnsɪk(ə)l/ ▶ adjective **1** having no meaning; making no sense: *a nonsensical argument* | *he dismissed the claim as nonsensical.*
2 ridiculously impractical or ill-advised: *a tax that everyone recognizes was nonsensical.*
– DERIVATIVES **nonsensicality** noun, **nonsensically** adverb.

non sequitur /nɒn ˈsɛkwɪtə/ ▶ noun a conclusion or statement that does not logically follow from the previous argument or statement.
– ORIGIN Latin, literally 'it does not follow'.

non-sexual ▶ adjective not involving or relating to sex or sexual reproduction.
– DERIVATIVES **non-sexually** adverb.

non-skid ▶ adjective designed to prevent sliding or skidding: *non-skid tyres.*

non-slip ▶ adjective designed to prevent slipping: *a non-slip bath mat.*

non-smoker ▶ noun a person who does not smoke tobacco.
– DERIVATIVES **non-smoking** adjective.

non-solid colour ▶ noun Computing a colour simulated by a pattern of dots of other colours, extending the range of colours available.

non-specialist ▶ noun a person who is not an expert or specialist in a particular subject.
▶ adjective not having or requiring specialist knowledge.

non-specific ▶ adjective not detailed or exact; general. ▪ Medicine not assignable to a particular cause, condition, or category.

non-specific urethritis (abbrev.: **NSU**) ▶ noun [mass noun] Medicine inflammation of the urethra due to infection by chlamydiae or other organisms (other than gonococci).

non-standard ▶ adjective not average or usual: *people working non-standard hours.* ▪ (of language) not of the form that is accepted as standard.

non-starter ▸ noun a person or animal that fails to take part in a race. ■ informal a person or plan that has no chance of succeeding or being effective.

non-state actor ▸ noun an individual or organization that has significant political influence but is not allied to any particular country or state.

non-stick ▸ adjective (of a pan or surface) covered with a substance that prevents food sticking to it during cooking: *a non-stick frying pan.*

non-stop ▸ adjective continuing without stopping or pausing: *we had two days of almost non-stop rain.* ■ (of a passenger vehicle or journey) not having or making stops at intermediate places on the way to its destination: *a non-stop flight to Los Angeles.* ■ oppressively constant; relentless; unremitting: *the show was axed after non-stop criticism.*
▸ adverb without stopping or pausing: *Stephen had been working non-stop.*

nonsuch ▸ noun variant spelling of **NONESUCH**.

nonsuit Law ▸ verb [with obj.] stop (a lawsuit or the plaintiff bringing it), either by voluntary withdrawal by the plaintiff, or by a finding by the judge that the plaintiff has failed to make a legal case or bring sufficient evidence.
▸ noun the stoppage of a suit on such grounds.
– ORIGIN late Middle English (as a noun): from Anglo-Norman French, literally 'not pursuing' (see **NON-**, **SUIT**).

non-swimmer ▸ noun a person who cannot or does not swim.

non-technical ▸ adjective not relating to or involving science or technology. ■ not having or requiring specialized or technical knowledge: *a non-technical account of the development of electronics.*

non-toxic ▸ adjective not poisonous or toxic: *non-toxic waste.*

non-transferable ▸ adjective not able to be transferred or made over to the possession of another person: *a special ticket which was non-transferable.*

non-treaty ▸ adjective N. Amer., chiefly historical relating to an American Indian person or people not subject to a treaty made with the government.

non-trivial ▸ adjective not trivial; significant. ■ Mathematics having some variables or terms that are not equal to zero or an identity.

non-tropical sprue ▸ noun see **SPRUE²**.

non-U ▸ adjective Brit. informal (of language or social behaviour) not characteristic of the upper social classes; not socially acceptable to certain people.
– ORIGIN 1950s: from **NON-** + **U³**.

non-uniform ▸ adjective not uniform, regular, or constant; varying.
– DERIVATIVES **non-uniformity** noun, **non-uniformly** adverb.

non-union ▸ adjective not belonging or relating to a trade union: *non-union agreements.*

non-unionized (also **non-unionised**) ▸ noun not belonging to or recognizing a trade union: *a non-unionized workforce.*

non-use (also **non-usage**) ▸ noun [mass noun] the refusal or failure to use something.
– DERIVATIVES **non-user** noun.

non-verbal ▸ adjective not involving or using words or speech: *forms of non-verbal communication.*
– DERIVATIVES **non-verbally** adverb.

non-vintage ▸ adjective denoting a wine that is not made from the crop of a single identified district in a good year.

non-violence ▸ noun [mass noun] the use of peaceful means, not force, to bring about political or social change.
– DERIVATIVES **non-violent** adjective.

non-volatile ▸ adjective not volatile. ■ Computing (of a computer's memory) retaining data even if there is a break in the power supply.

non-white ▸ adjective denoting or relating to a person whose origin is not predominantly European.
▸ noun a person whose origin is not predominantly European.

non-word ▸ noun a group of letters or speech sounds that looks or sounds like a word but that is not accepted as such by native speakers.

Nonya /ˈnɒnjə/ ▸ noun **1** a South East Asian woman of mixed ethnic descent, especially (in Singapore) a woman with a Malay mother and Chinese father.
2 [mass noun] (in Malaysia and Singapore) a spicy Singaporean cuisine consisting of a combination of Malay and Chinese ingredients and techniques.
– ORIGIN from Malay, Javanese *nyonya*, probably from Portuguese *senhora* 'lady' (see **SENHORA**).

nonyl /ˈnɒnʌɪl, -nɪl, ˈnəʊn-/ ▸ noun [as modifier] Chemistry of or denoting an alkyl radical $-C_9H_{19}$, derived from nonane.

non-zero ▸ adjective having a positive or negative value; not equal to zero.

noodle¹ ▸ noun a very thin, long strip of pasta or a similar flour paste, eaten with a sauce or in a soup.
– ORIGIN late 18th cent.: from German *Nudel*, of unknown origin.

noodle² ▸ noun informal **1** a stupid or silly person.
2 a person's head.
– ORIGIN mid 18th cent.: of unknown origin.

noodle³ /ˈnuːd(ə)l/ ▸ verb [no obj.] informal improvise or play casually on a musical instrument: *tapes of him noodling on his farfisa organ* | (as noun **noodling**) *ambient synthesizer noodling.*
– ORIGIN mid 19th cent.: of unknown origin.

noogie /ˈnʊgi/ ▸ noun N. Amer. informal a hard poke or grind with the knuckles, especially on a person's head.
– ORIGIN 1970s: perhaps a diminutive of **KNUCKLE**.

Noogoora burr /nʊˈguːrə/ ▸ noun Austral. a plant of the daisy family which has become naturalized in Australia, where it is considered a noxious weed because its hooked burrs become entangled in sheep's fleeces. ● *Xanthium occidentale*, family Compositae.
– ORIGIN late 19th cent.: *Noogoora* from the name of a sheep station in Queensland.

nook ▸ noun a corner or recess, especially one offering seclusion or security: *the nook beside the fire* | *the fish should be able to find* **nooks and crannies** *in which they will be safe.*
– PHRASES **every nook and cranny** every part or aspect of something: *the party reached into every nook and cranny of people's lives.*
– ORIGIN Middle English (denoting a corner or fragment): of unknown origin.

nooky (also **nookie**) ▸ noun [mass noun] informal sexual activity or intercourse.
– ORIGIN early 20th cent.: perhaps from **NOOK**.

noon ▸ noun twelve o'clock in the day; midday: *the service starts at* **twelve noon**.
– ORIGIN Old English *nōn* 'the ninth hour from sunrise, i.e. approximately 3 p.m', from Latin *nona (hora)* 'ninth hour'; compare with **NONE²**.

noonday ▸ noun the middle of the day: [as modifier] *the blinds were lowered to keep out the noonday sun.*

no one ▸ pronoun no person; not a single person: *no one came* | *she told no one she was going.*

nooner ▸ noun N. Amer. informal an event, especially an act of sexual intercourse, that occurs in the middle of the day.

noonoo ▸ noun (pl. **noonoos**) variant spelling of **NUNU**.

noontide (also **noontime**) ▸ noun literary noon.

noose ▸ noun a loop with a running knot, tightening as the rope or wire is pulled and used to trap animals or hang people. ■ (**the noose**) death by hanging: *he earned a reprieve from the noose.*
▸ verb [with obj.] put a noose on (someone). ■ catch (an animal) with a noose. ■ form (a rope) into a noose.
– PHRASES **put one's head in a noose** bring about one's own downfall.
– ORIGIN late Middle English: probably via Old French *no(u)s* from Latin *nodus* 'knot'.

noosphere /ˈnəʊəsfɪə/ ▸ noun a postulated sphere or stage of evolutionary development dominated by consciousness, the mind, and interpersonal relationships.
– ORIGIN 1940s: from French *noösphere*, based on Greek *noos* 'mind'.

Nootka /ˈnuːtkə, ˈnʊt-/ ▸ noun (pl. **same** or **Nootkas**) **1** a member of an American Indian people of Vancouver Island, Canada.
2 [mass noun] the Wakashan language of the Nootka, now with few speakers.
▸ adjective relating to the Nootka or their language.
– ORIGIN named after *Nootka* Sound, an inlet on the coast of Vancouver Island.

Nootka cypress ▸ noun a conical cypress whose foliage has an unpleasant turpentine smell when crushed, native to western North America and typically growing at high altitudes. ● *Chamaecyparis nootkatensis*, family Cupressaceae.

nootropic /ˌnəʊəˈtrəʊpɪk, -ˈtrɒpɪk/ ▸ adjective (of a drug) used to enhance memory or other cognitive functions.
▸ noun a nootropic drug.
– ORIGIN 1970s: from French *nootrope* (from Greek *noos* 'mind' + *tropē* 'turning') + **-IC**.

nopal /ˈnəʊp(ə)l, ˈnəʊpal/ ▸ noun a cactus which is a major food plant of the bugs from which cochineal is obtained. ● Genus *Nopalea*, family Cactaceae: several species, in particular *N. cochinellifera*.
■ (**nopales** /nəʊˈpɑːlɛz/) the edible fleshy pads of this cactus, used in Mexican cuisine.
– ORIGIN mid 18th cent.: via French and Spanish from Nahuatl *nopalli* 'cactus'.

nope ▸ exclamation informal variant of **NO**.

nor ▸ conjunction & adverb **1** used before the second or further of two or more alternatives (the first being introduced by a negative such as 'neither' or 'not') to indicate that they are each untrue or each do not happen: *they were neither cheap nor convenient* | *the sheets were never washed, nor the towels, nor his shirts.* ■ [as adv.] literary term for **NEITHER**: *nor God nor demon can undo the done.*
2 used to introduce a further negative statement: *'I don't see how.' 'Nor do I.'*
3 [conjunction or prep.] archaic or dialect than: *she thinks she knows better nor me.*
▸ noun (usu. **NOR**) Electronics a Boolean operator which gives the value one if and only if all operands have a value of zero and otherwise has a value of zero. ■ (also **NOR gate**) a circuit which produces an output signal only when there are no signals on any of the input connections.
– ORIGIN Middle English: contraction of Old English *nother* 'neither'.

nor' ▸ abbreviation (especially in compounds) north.

nor- ▸ prefix Chemistry denoting an organic compound derived from another, in particular by the shortening of a chain or ring by the removal of one methylene group or by the replacement of one or more methyl side chains by hydrogen atoms: *noradrenaline.*
– ORIGIN from *nor(mal)*, originally used to refer to a compound without methyl substituents.

NORAD /ˈnɔːrad/ ▸ abbreviation North American Aerospace Defence Command.

noradrenaline /ˌnɔːrəˈdrɛn(ə)lɪn/ ▸ noun [mass noun] Biochemistry a hormone which is released by the adrenal medulla and by the sympathetic nerves and functions as a neurotransmitter. It is also used as a drug to raise blood pressure. ● Chem. formula: $(HO)_2C_6H_3CHOHCH_2NH_2$.
– ORIGIN 1930s: from **NOR-** + **ADRENALIN**.

Norbertine /ˈnɔːbətɪn, -ʌɪn/ ▸ noun another term for **PREMONSTRATENSIAN**.
– ORIGIN late 17th cent.: named after St *Norbert* (c.1080–1134), founder of the order.

Nordic ▸ adjective relating to or denoting Scandinavia, Finland, and Iceland: *the Nordic countries.* ■ relating to or denoting a physical type of northern European peoples characterized by tall stature, a bony frame, light colouring, and a dolichocephalic head. ■ Skiing involving the disciplines of cross-country skiing or ski jumping. Often contrasted with **ALPINE**.
▸ noun a person from Scandinavia, Finland, or Iceland.
– ORIGIN from French *nordique*, from *nord* 'north'.

Nordic walking ▸ noun [mass noun] a sport or activity that involves walking across country with the aid of long poles resembling ski sticks.

Nordkapp /ˈnuːrkap/ Norwegian name for **NORTH CAPE**.

Nordkyn /ˈnʊətʃʊn/ a promontory on the north coast of Norway, to the east of North Cape. At 71° 8′ N, it is the northernmost point of the European mainland, North Cape being on an island.

Nord-Pas-de-Calais /ˌnɔːpɑːdəˈkaleɪ/, French /nɔʀpadəkalɛ/ a region of northern France, on the border with Belgium.

Nordrhein-Westfalen /ˌnɔrtraɪnvɛstˈfaːlən/ German name for **NORTH RHINE-WESTPHALIA**.

norepinephrine /ˌnɔːrɛpɪˈnɛfrɪn, -riːn/ ▸ noun another term for **NORADRENALINE**.
– ORIGIN 1940s: from **NOR-** + **EPINEPHRINE**.

Norfolk /ˈnɔːfək/ a county on the east coast of England, east of the Wash; county town, Norwich.

Norfolk Island an island in the Pacific Ocean, off the east coast of Australia, administered since 1913 as an external territory of Australia; pop. 2,100 (est. 2009). Discovered by Captain James Cook in 1774, it was occupied from 1788 to 1814 as a penal colony.

N

Norfolk Island pine (also **Norfolk pine**) ▸ noun an evergreen tree related to the monkey puzzle, having horizontal branches with upswept shoots bearing small scale-like leaves. Native to Norfolk Island, it is often grown in Mediterranean countries. ● *Araucaria heterophylla*, family Araucariaceae.

Norfolk jacket ▸ noun a loose belted jacket with box pleats, typically made of tweed.

Norfolk reed ▸ noun the common reed, which is cultivated in eastern England for use in thatching. ● *Phragmites australis*, family Gramineae.

Norfolk terrier ▸ noun a small thickset terrier of a breed with a rough red or black-and-tan coat and drop ears.

Norge /ˈnɒrgə/ Norwegian name for **Norway**.

nori /ˈnɔːri/ ▸ noun [mass noun] an edible seaweed eaten either fresh or dried, especially by the Japanese.
– ORIGIN Japanese.

noria /ˈnɔːrɪə/ ▸ noun a device for raising water from a stream or river, consisting of a chain of pots or buckets revolving round a wheel driven by the water current.
– ORIGIN via Spanish from Arabic *nāʿūra*.

norite /ˈnɔːrʌɪt/ ▸ noun [mass noun] Geology a coarse-grained plutonic rock similar to gabbro but containing hypersthene.
– ORIGIN late 19th cent.: from **Norway** + **-ite**[1].

nork ▸ noun (usu. **norks**) Austral. informal a woman's breast.
– ORIGIN 1960s: of unknown origin.

norm ▸ noun **1** (**the norm**) something that is usual, typical, or standard: *strikes were the norm*. ■ (usu. **norms**) a standard or pattern, especially of social behaviour, that is typical or expected: *the norms of good behaviour in the Civil Service*. ■ a required standard; a level to be complied with or reached: *the 7 per cent pay norm had been breached again*.
2 Mathematics the product of a complex number and its conjugate, equal to the sum of the squares of its real and imaginary components, or the positive square root of this sum. ■ an analogous quantity used to represent the magnitude of a vector.
▸ verb [with obj.] adjust (something) to conform to a norm.
– ORIGIN early 19th cent.: from Latin *norma* 'precept, rule, carpenter's square'.

N

Norma /ˈnɔːmə/ Astronomy a small and inconspicuous southern constellation (the Rule), lying partly in the Milky Way between Lupus and Ara.
– ORIGIN Latin, 'carpenter's square'.

normal ▸ adjective **1** conforming to a standard; usual, typical, or expected: *it's quite* ***normal for*** *puppies to bolt their food* | *normal working hours*. ■ (of a person) free from physical or mental disorders.
2 technical (of a line, ray, or other linear feature) intersecting a given line or surface at right angles.
3 Medicine (of a salt solution) containing the same salt concentration as the blood. ■ Chemistry, dated (of a solution) containing one gram-equivalent of solute per litre.
4 Geology denoting a fault or faulting in which a relative downward movement occurred in the strata situated on the upper side of the fault plane.
▸ noun **1** [mass noun] the usual, typical, or expected state or condition: *her temperature was* ***above normal*** | *the service will be* ***back to normal*** *next week*. ■ informal a person who is conventional or healthy.
2 technical a line at right angles to a given line or surface.
– ORIGIN mid 17th cent. (in the sense 'right-angled'): from Latin *normalis*, from *norma* 'carpenter's square' (see **norm**). Current senses date from the early 19th cent.

normal distribution ▸ noun Statistics a function that represents the distribution of many random variables as a symmetrical bell-shaped graph.

normal form ▸ noun **1** Computing a defined standard structure for relational databases in which a relation may not be nested within another relation.
2 Philosophy a standard structure or format in which all propositions in a (usually symbolic) language can be expressed.

normality (N. Amer. also **normalcy**) ▸ noun [mass noun] the condition of being normal; the state of being usual, typical, or expected: *the office gradually returned to a semblance of normality*.

normalize (also **normalise**) ▸ verb **1** bring or return to a normal or standard condition or state: [with obj.] *the two countries normalized diplomatic relations in 1995* | [no obj.] *the situation had normalized*.
2 [with obj.] Mathematics multiply (a series, function or item of data) by a factor that makes the norm or some associated quantity such as an integral equal to a desired value (usually 1). ■ Computing (in floating-point representation) express (a number) in the standard form as regards the position of the radix point, usually immediately following the first non-zero digit.
– DERIVATIVES **normalization** noun, **normalizer** noun.

normally ▸ adverb **1** [sentence adverb] under normal or usual conditions; as a rule: *normally, it takes three or four years to complete the training*.
2 in a normal manner: *try to breathe normally*.
3 technical at right angles to a given line or surface.

normally aspirated ▸ adjective (of an engine) not turbocharged or supercharged.

normal school ▸ noun (especially in North America and France) a school or college for the training of teachers.

Norman ▸ noun **1** a member of a people of mixed Frankish and Scandinavian origin who settled in Normandy from about AD 912 and became a dominant military power in western Europe and the Mediterranean in the 11th century. ■ any of the Normans who conquered England in 1066, or their descendants. ■ a native or inhabitant of modern Normandy.
2 [mass noun] the form of French spoken by the Normans.
▸ adjective relating to the Normans: *the Norman invasion*. ■ denoting or relating to the style of Romanesque architecture used in Britain under the Normans. ■ relating to modern Normandy.
– ORIGIN Middle English: from Old French *Normans*, plural of *Normant*, from Old Norse *Northmathr* 'Northman'.

Norman Conquest the conquest of England by William of Normandy (William the Conqueror) after the Battle of Hastings in 1066.

Normandy a former province of NW France with its coastline on the English Channel, now divided into the two regions of Lower Normandy (Basse-Normandie) and Upper Normandy (Haute-Normandie).

Norman French ▸ noun [mass noun] the northern form of Old French spoken by the Normans. ■ the variety of this used in English law courts from the 11th to 13th centuries; Anglo-Norman French. ■ the French dialect of modern Normandy.

normative ▸ adjective formal establishing, relating to, or deriving from a standard or norm, especially of behaviour: *negative sanctions to enforce normative behaviour*.
– DERIVATIVES **normatively** adverb, **normativeness** noun, **normativity** noun.
– ORIGIN late 19th cent.: from French *normatif, -ive*, from Latin *norma* 'carpenter's square' (see **norm**).

normoglycaemia /ˌnɔːmə(ʊ)glʌɪˈsiːmɪə/ (US **normoglycemia**) ▸ noun [mass noun] Medicine a normal concentration of sugar in the blood (as contrasted with hyper- or hypoglycaemia).
– DERIVATIVES **normoglycaemic** adjective.

normotensive /ˌnɔːmə(ʊ)ˈtɛnsɪv/ ▸ adjective Medicine having or denoting a normal blood pressure.

Norn /nɔːn/ ▸ noun [mass noun] a form of Norse formerly spoken in Orkney and Shetland but largely extinct by the 19th century.
▸ adjective relating to Norn.
– ORIGIN from Old Norse *norrœn* 'Norn, northern', from *northr* 'north'.

Norns /nɔːnz/ Scandinavian Mythology the three virgin goddesses of destiny (Urd or Urdar, Verdandi, and Skuld), who sit by the well of fate at the base of the ash tree Yggdrasil and spin the web of fate.
– ORIGIN from Old Norse, of unknown origin.

norovirus /ˈnɔːrəvʌɪrəs/ ▸ noun Medicine any of various single-stranded RNA viruses comprising the Norwalk virus. ● Genus *Norovirus*, family Caliciviridae.
– ORIGIN early 21st century: from *nor-* in **Norwalk virus** + *-o-* + **virus**.

Norplant ▸ noun [mass noun] trademark a contraceptive for women consisting of small rods implanted under the skin which gradually release the hormone levonorgestrel over a number of years.
– ORIGIN 1980s: from (*levo*)*nor*(*gestrel*) (*im*)*plant*.

Norrköping /ˈnɔːˌtʃəːpɪŋ/ an industrial city and seaport on an inlet of the Baltic Sea in SE Sweden; pop. 128,060 (2008).

Norroy /ˈnɒrɔɪ/ (in full **Norroy and Ulster**) ▸ noun Heraldry (in the UK) the title given to the third King of Arms, with jurisdiction north of the Trent and (since 1943) in Northern Ireland.
– ORIGIN late Middle English: from Old French *nord* 'north' + *roi* 'king'.

Norse /nɔːs/ ▸ noun **1** [mass noun] the Norwegian language, especially in an ancient or medieval form, or the Scandinavian language group.
2 (as plural noun **the Norse**) Norwegians or Scandinavians in ancient or medieval times.
▸ adjective relating to ancient or medieval Norway or Scandinavia.
– DERIVATIVES **Norseman** noun (pl. **Norsemen**).
– ORIGIN from Dutch *noor(d)sch*, from *noord* 'north'; compare with Swedish, Danish, and Norwegian *Norsk*.

norteño /nɔːˈtɛnjəʊ/ ▸ noun **1** (pl. **norteños** /-ɒs/) an inhabitant or native of northern Mexico.
2 (also **norteña** /nɔːˈtɛnjə/) [mass noun] a style of folk music, associated particularly with northern Mexico and Texas, typically featuring an accordion and using polkas and other rhythms found in the music of central European immigrants.
– ORIGIN Spanish, literally 'northerner'.

North, Frederick, Lord (1732–92), British Tory statesman, Prime Minister 1770–82. He sought to avoid the War of American Independence, but was regarded as responsible for the loss of the American colonies.

north ▸ noun (usu. **the north**) **1** the direction in which a compass needle normally points, towards the horizon on the left-hand side of a person facing east, or the part of the horizon lying in this direction: *a bitter wind blew from the north* | *Mount Kenya is* ***to the north of*** *Nairobi*. ■ the compass point corresponding to this. ■ a direction in space parallel to the earth's axis of rotation and towards the point on the celestial sphere around which the stars appear to turn anticlockwise.
2 the northern part of the world or of a specified country, region, or town: *there will be heavy wintry showers, particularly in the north*. ■ (usu. **the North**) the northern part of England. ■ (usu. **the North**) the NE states of the United States, especially those opposed to slavery during the Civil War. ■ (usu. **the North**) the industrialized and economically advanced nations of the world.
3 (**North**) [as name] Bridge the player occupying a designated position at the table, sitting opposite and partnering South.
▸ adjective [attrib.] **1** lying towards, near, or facing the north: *the north bank of the river* | *the north door*. ■ (of a wind) blowing from the north.
2 of or denoting the northern part of a specified country, region, or town: *North Wales* | *North African*.
▸ adverb **1** to or towards the north: *the town is twenty-five miles* ***north of*** *Newport* | *a north-facing wall*.
2 (**north of**) above (a particular amount, cost, etc.): *they expect to spend north of $6 million for this latest campaign*.
– PHRASES **north by east** (or **west**) between north and north-north-east (or north-north-west). **up north** informal to or in the north of a country: *he's taken a teaching job up north*.
– ORIGIN Old English, of Germanic origin; related to Dutch *noord* and German *nord*.

North Africa the northern part of the African continent, especially the countries bordering the Mediterranean and the Red Sea.

Northallerton /nɔːˈθalət(ə)n/ a town in the north of England, the administrative centre of North Yorkshire; pop. 17,600 (est. 2009).

North America a continent comprising the northern half of the American land mass, connected to South America by the Isthmus of Panama. It contains Canada, the United States, Mexico, and the countries of Central America.
– DERIVATIVES **North American** adjective & noun.

North American English ▸ noun [mass noun] the English language as spoken and written in Canada and the US. See also **American English**.

North American Free Trade Agreement (abbrev.: **NAFTA**) an agreement which came into effect in January 1994 between the US, Canada, and Mexico to remove barriers to trade between the three countries over a ten-year period.

Northampton /nɔːˈθampt(ə)n/ a town in SE central England, on the River Nene, the county town of Northamptonshire; pop. 185,600 (est. 2009).

Northamptonshire a county of central England; county town, Northampton.

Northants /nɔːˈθants/ ▸ **abbreviation** Northamptonshire.

North Atlantic Drift a continuation of the Gulf Stream across the Atlantic Ocean and along the coast of NW Europe, where it has a significant warming effect on the climate.

North Atlantic Ocean see **Atlantic Ocean**.

North Atlantic Treaty Organization (abbrev.: **NATO**) an association of European and North American states, formed in 1949 for the defence of Europe and the North Atlantic against the perceived threat of Soviet aggression. It includes most major Western powers, although France withdrew from the military side of the alliance in 1966.

northbound ▸ **adjective** travelling or leading towards the north: *northbound traffic*.

North Cape a promontory on Magerøya, an island off the north coast of Norway. North Cape is the northernmost point of the world accessible by road. Norwegian name **Nordkapp**.

North Carolina a state of the east central US, on the Atlantic coast; pop. 9,222,414 (est. 2008); capital, Raleigh. Originally settled by the English, it was one of the original thirteen states of the Union (1788).
– DERIVATIVES **North Carolinian** noun & adjective.
– ORIGIN *Carolina* from *Carolus*, the Latin name of Charles I.

North Channel the stretch of sea separating SW Scotland from Northern Ireland and connecting the Irish Sea to the Atlantic Ocean.

Northcliffe, Alfred Charles William Harmsworth, 1st Viscount (1865–1922), British newspaper proprietor. He built up a large newspaper empire, including *The Times*, the *Daily Mail*, and the *Daily Mirror*.

north country ▸ **noun** the northern part of a country, for example the part of England north of the River Humber.

North Dakota an agricultural state in the north central US, on the border with Canada; pop. 641,481 (est. 2008); capital, Bismarck. Acquired partly by the Louisiana Purchase in 1803 and partly from Britain by treaty in 1818, it became the 39th state of the US in 1889.
– DERIVATIVES **North Dakotan** noun & adjective.

north-east ▸ **noun 1** (usu. **the north-east**) the direction towards the point of the horizon midway between north and east: *I pointed to the north-east*. ■ the compass point corresponding to this.
2 the part of a country, region, or town lying to the north-east: *the north-east of Scotland*.
▸ **adjective 1** lying towards, near, or facing the north-east. ■ (of a wind) blowing from the north-east: *there was a strong north-east wind*.
2 of or denoting the north-eastern part of a specified country, region, or town: *north-east London*.
▸ **adverb** to or towards the north-east: *the ship sailed north-east | the north-east-facing slopes*.
– DERIVATIVES **north-eastern** adjective.

northeaster ▸ **noun** a wind blowing from the north-east.

north-easterly ▸ **adjective & adverb** another term for **north-east**.
▸ **noun** another term for **northeaster**.

North-East Passage a passage for ships along the northern coast of Europe and Asia, from the Atlantic to the Pacific via the Arctic Ocean, sought for many years as a possible trade route to the East. It was first navigated in 1878–9 by the Swedish Arctic explorer Baron Nordenskjöld (1832–1901).

north-eastward ▸ **adverb** (also **north-eastwards**) towards the north-east; in a north-east direction.
▸ **adjective** situated in, directed towards, or facing the north-east.

North Equatorial Current an ocean current that flows westwards across the North Atlantic Ocean just north of the equator.

norther ▸ **noun** US a strong cold north wind blowing in autumn and winter over Texas, Florida, and the Gulf of Mexico.

northerly /ˈnɔːðəli/ ▸ **adjective & adverb** in a northward position or direction: [as adj.] *he set off in a northerly direction*. ■ (of wind) blowing from the north: [as adj.] *a fresh northerly wind* | [as adv.] *the wind was gusting northerly*.
▸ **noun** (often **northerlies**) a wind blowing from the north.

northern /ˈnɔːð(ə)n/ ▸ **adjective 1** [attrib.] situated in the north, or directed towards or facing the north: *the northern slopes | northern Europe*. ■ (of a wind) blowing from the north.
2 living in or originating from the north: *northern breeds of cattle*. ■ relating to or characteristic of the north or its inhabitants: *she had a broad northern accent*.
– DERIVATIVES **northernmost** adjective.
– ORIGIN Old English *northerne* (see **north**, **-ern**).

Northern blot ▸ **noun** Biology an adaptation of the Southern blot procedure used to detect specific sequences of RNA by hybridization with complementary DNA.

Northern Cape a province of western South Africa, formerly part of Cape Province; capital, Kimberley.

Northern Circars /ˈsəːkɑːz/ a former name for the coastal region of eastern India between the Krishna River and Orissa, now in Andhra Pradesh.

northerner ▸ **noun** a native or inhabitant of the north, especially of northern England or the northern United States.

northern hemisphere the half of the earth that is north of the equator.

Northern Ireland a province of the United Kingdom occupying the NE part of Ireland; pop. 1,775,000 (est. 2008); capital, Belfast.

> Northern Ireland, which comprises six of the counties of Ulster, was established as a self-governing province in 1920. Northern Ireland has always been dominated by Unionist parties, which represent the Protestant majority. Many members of the Roman Catholic minority favour union with the Republic of Ireland. Discrimination against the latter group led to violent conflicts and (from 1969) the presence of British army units in an attempt to keep the peace. Terrorism and sectarian violence by the Provisional IRA and other paramilitary groups, both Republican and Loyalist, resulted in the imposition of direct rule from Westminster in 1972. Multiparty talks begun in 1996 led to an agreement between most political parties in 1998. In 1999 a devolved parliament was inaugurated, with representation from both Nationalist and Unionist groups.

Northern Lights another name for the aurora borealis. See **aurora**.

Northern Marianas a self-governing territory in the western Pacific, comprising the Mariana Islands with the exception of the southernmost, Guam; pop. 51,500 (est. 2009); languages, English (official), Austronesian languages; capital, Chalan Kanoa (on Saipan). The Northern Marianas are constituted as a self-governing commonwealth in union with the United States.

Northern Paiute ▸ **noun & adjective** see **Paiute**.

Northern Province former name (until 2002) for the province of **Limpopo** in South Africa.

Northern Rhodesia former name (until 1964) for **Zambia**.

Northern Territory a state of north central Australia; pop. 219,818 (2008); capital, Darwin. The territory was annexed by the state of South Australia in 1863, and administered by the Commonwealth of Australia from 1911. It became a self-governing territory in 1978.

North Frisian Islands see **Frisian Islands**.

North Germanic ▸ **noun** [mass noun] a subdivision of the Germanic group of languages, comprising the Scandinavian languages.
▸ **adjective** relating to North Germanic.

northing ▸ **noun** [mass noun] distance travelled or measured northward, especially at sea. ■ [count noun] a figure or line representing northward distance on a map (expressed by convention as the second part of a grid reference, after easting).

North Island the northernmost of the two main islands of New Zealand, separated from the South Island by Cook Strait.

North Korea a country in East Asia, occupying the northern part of the peninsula of Korea; pop. 22,665,300 (est. 2009); official language, Korean; capital, Pyongyang. Official name **Korea, Democratic People's Republic of**.

> North Korea was formed in 1948 when Korea was partitioned along the 38th parallel. In 1950 North Korean forces invaded the south, but in the war that followed were forced back to more or less the previous border (see **Korean War**). A communist state which was long dominated by the personality of Kim Il-sung, its leader from 1948 to 1994, North Korea has always sought Korean reunification.

– DERIVATIVES **North Korean** adjective & noun.

northland ▸ **noun** [mass noun] (also **northlands**) literary the northern part of a country or region.
– ORIGIN Old English (see **north**, **land**).

north light ▸ **noun** [mass noun] good natural light without direct sun, especially as desired by artists.

Northman ▸ **noun** (pl. **Northmen**) archaic a native or inhabitant of Scandinavia, especially of Norway.
– ORIGIN Old English (see **north**, **man**).

North Minch see **Minch**.

north-north-east ▸ **noun** the compass point or direction midway between north and north-east.

north-north-west ▸ **noun** the compass point or direction midway between north and north-west.

North Ossetia an autonomous republic of Russia, in the Caucasus on the border with Georgia; pop. 699,400 (est. 2009); capital, Vladikavkaz. See also **Ossetia**.

North Pole ▸ **noun** see **pole**[2].

North Rhine-Westphalia a state of western Germany; capital, Düsseldorf. German name **Nordrhein-Westfalen**.

North Sea an arm of the Atlantic Ocean lying between the mainland of Europe and the coast of Britain, important for its oil and gas deposits.

North Star Astronomy the Pole Star.

North Star State informal name for **Minnesota**.

North Uist see **Uist**.

Northumb. ▸ **abbreviation** Northumberland.

Northumberland /nɔːˈθʌmbələnd/ a county in NE England, on the Scottish border; county town, Morpeth.

Northumbria /nɔːˈθʌmbrɪə/ an area of NE England comprising Northumberland, Durham, and Tyne and Wear. ■ an ancient Anglo-Saxon kingdom in NE England extending from the Humber to the Forth.
– DERIVATIVES **Northumbrian** adjective & noun.
– ORIGIN from obsolete *Northumber*, denoting a person living beyond the Humber.

North Utsire see **Utsire**.

northward ▸ **adjective** lying towards, near, or facing the north.
▸ **adverb** (also **northwards**) towards the north.
▸ **noun** (**the northward**) the direction or region to the north.
– DERIVATIVES **northwardly** adjective & adverb.

North West a province of northern South Africa, formed in 1994 from the NE part of Cape Province and SW Transvaal; capital, Mafikeng.

north-west ▸ **noun** (usu. **the north-west**) **1** the direction towards the point of the horizon midway between north and west: *he pointed to the north-west*. ■ the compass point corresponding to this.
2 the north-western part of a country, region, or town: *the north-west of London*.
▸ **adjective 1** lying towards, near, or facing the north-west: *the north-west corner of the square*. ■ (of a wind) blowing from the north-west.
2 of or denoting the north-western part of a country, region, or towns: *north-west Europe*.
▸ **adverb** to or towards the north-west: *he turned on to the motorway and headed north-west*.
– DERIVATIVES **north-western** adjective.

northwester ▸ **noun** a wind blowing from the north-west.

north-westerly ▸ **adjective & adverb** another term for **north-west**.
▸ **noun** another term for **northwester**.

North-West Frontier Province a province of NW Pakistan, on the border with Afghanistan; capital, Peshawar.

North-West Passage a sea passage along the northern coast of the American continent, through the Canadian Arctic from the Atlantic to the Pacific. It was sought for many years as a possible trade route by explorers including Sebastian Cabot, Sir Francis Drake, and Martin Frobisher; it was first navigated in 1903–6 by Roald Amundsen.

Northwest Territories a territory of northern Canada extending northwards from the 60th parallel and westwards from Hudson Bay to the Rocky Mountains; pop. 41,464 (2006); capital, Yellowknife. From 1670 the southern part of this territory was part of Rupert's Land; the remainder was under nominal British rule until 1870, when both parts were ceded to Canada.

N

Northwest Territory a region and former territory of the US lying between the Mississippi and Ohio Rivers and the Great Lakes. It was acquired in 1783 after the War of American Independence and now forms the states of Indiana, Ohio, Michigan, Illinois, and Wisconsin.

north-westward ▶ adverb (also **north-westwards**) towards the north-west; in a north-west direction.
▶ adjective situated in, directed towards, or facing the north-west.

North Yorkshire a county in NE England; administrative centre, Northallerton. It was formed in 1974 from parts of the former North, East, and West Ridings of Yorkshire.

Norwalk virus /ˈnɔːwɔːk/ ▶ noun a virus which can cause epidemics of severe gastroenteritis.
– ORIGIN 1970s: from *Norwalk*, a town in Ohio where an outbreak of gastroenteritis occurred from which the virus was isolated.

Norway a mountainous European country on the northern and western coastline of Scandinavia; pop. 4,660,500 (est. 2009); official language, Norwegian; capital, Oslo. Norwegian name **Norge**.

> Norway was united with Denmark and Sweden by the Union of Kalmar in 1397, but after Sweden's withdrawal in 1523 became subject to Denmark. Ceded to Sweden in 1814, Norway emerged as an independent kingdom in 1905. An invitation to join the EC was rejected after a referendum in 1972; an application to join the European Union twenty years later was accepted by the European Parliament but failed to win approval in a referendum (1994).

Norway lobster ▶ noun a small, slender commercially important European lobster. Also called **Dublin Bay prawn**. ● *Nephrops norvegicus*, class Malacostraca.

Norway maple ▶ noun a Eurasian maple with yellow flowers that appear before the lobed leaves, widely planted as an ornamental. ● *Acer platanoides*, family Aceraceae.

Norway rat ▶ noun another term for **brown rat**.

Norway spruce ▶ noun a long-coned European spruce which is widely grown for timber and pulp. In Britain it is often used as a Christmas tree. ● *Picea abies*, family Pinaceae.

N

Norwegian /nɔːˈwiːdʒ(ə)n/ ▶ adjective relating to Norway or its people or language.
▶ noun 1 a native or inhabitant of Norway, or a person of Norwegian descent.
2 [mass noun] the language of Norway, a member of the Scandinavian language group.

> Norwegian today exists in two forms, *Bokmål*, the more widely used, a modified form of Danish, and *Nynorsk* ('new Norwegian'), a 19th-century literary form devised from the country dialects most closely descended from Old Norse, and considered to be a purer form of the language than *Bokmål*.

– ORIGIN from medieval Latin *Norvegia* 'Norway' (from Old Norse *Norvegr*, literally 'north way') + **-an**.

Norwegian Sea a sea which lies between Iceland and Norway and links the Arctic Ocean with the NE Atlantic.

nor'wester ▶ noun 1 short for **northwester**.
2 an oilskin jacket or sou'wester.

Norwich /ˈnɒrɪdʒ, -rɪtʃ/ a city in eastern England, the county town of Norfolk; pop. 171,500 (est. 2009).

Norwich School an English regional school of landscape painting associated with John Sell Cotman and John Crome.

Norwich terrier ▶ noun a small thickset terrier of a breed with a rough red or black-and-tan coat and pricked ears.

nos ▶ abbreviation numbers.
– ORIGIN plural of **No**.

no-score draw ▶ noun a goalless draw in soccer, especially as distinguished from a score draw in football pools.

nose ▶ noun 1 the part projecting above the mouth on the face of a person or animal, containing the nostrils and used for breathing and smelling. ■ [in sing.] the sense of smell, especially a dog's ability to track something by its scent: *a dog with a keen nose*. ■ [in sing.] an instinctive talent for detecting something: *he has a nose for a good script*. ■ the aroma of a particular substance, especially wine.
2 the front end of an aircraft, car, or other vehicle. ■ a projecting part of something: *the nose of the saddle*.
3 [in sing.] an act of looking around or prying: *she wanted a good nose round the house*. ■ informal a police informer.
▶ verb 1 [no obj., with adverbial of place] (of an animal) thrust its nose against or into something: *the pony nosed at the straw*. ■ [with obj.] smell or sniff (something).
2 [no obj.] look around or pry into something: *I was anxious to get inside and **nose around** her house* | *she's always **nosing into** my business*. ■ [with obj.] detect by diligent searching: *he **nosed out** the signs of trespass*.
3 [no obj., with adverbial of direction] (of a vehicle) move cautiously forward: *he turned left and nosed into an empty parking space*. ■ (of a competitor) manage to achieve a leading position by a small margin: *they nosed ahead by one point*.
– PHRASES **by a nose** (of a victory) by a very narrow margin. **cut off one's nose to spite one's face** disadvantage oneself through a wilful attempt to gain an advantage or assert oneself. **get one's nose in front** manage to achieve a winning or leading position. **get up someone's nose** Brit. informal irritate or annoy someone. **give someone a bloody nose** inflict a resounding defeat on someone. **have one's nose in a book** be reading studiously or intently. **keep one's nose clean** informal stay out of trouble. **keep one's nose out of** informal refrain from interfering in (someone else's affairs). **keep one's nose to the grindstone** see **grindstone**. **nose to tail** Brit. (of vehicles) moving or standing close behind one another, especially in heavy traffic. **not see further than one's** (or **the end of one's**) **nose** fail to consider different possibilities or to foresee the consequences of one's actions. **on the nose 1** to a person's sense of smell: *the wine is pungently smoky and peppery on the nose*. **2** informal, chiefly N. Amer. precisely: *at ten on the nose the van pulled up*. **3** Austral./NZ informal distasteful or offensive. **4** informal (of a bet) on a horse to win (as opposed to being placed). **put someone's nose out of joint** informal offend someone or hurt their pride. **turn one's nose up at** informal show distaste or contempt for: *he turned his nose up at the job*. **under someone's nose** informal directly in front of someone. ■ (of an action) committed openly and boldly but without anyone noticing: *he made a pass at John's wife, right under his nose and in his own house*. **with one's nose in the air** haughtily.
– DERIVATIVES **nosed** adjective [in combination] *snub-nosed*, **noseless** adjective.
– ORIGIN Old English *nosu*, of West Germanic origin; related to Dutch *neus*, and more remotely to German *Nase*, Latin *nasus*, and Sanskrit *nāsā*; also to **ness**.

nosebag ▶ noun a strong canvas or leather bag containing fodder, hung from a horse's head.

noseband ▶ noun the strap of a bridle or head collar, which passes over the horse's nose and under its chin.

nosebleed ▶ noun an instance of bleeding from the nose. ■ [as modifier] N. Amer. informal denoting cheap seating located in an extremely high position in a sports stadium, large theatre, or concert hall.

nose candy ▶ noun [mass noun] N. Amer. informal an illegal drug that is inhaled, in particular cocaine.

nose cone ▶ noun the cone-shaped nose of a rocket or aircraft.

nosedive ▶ noun a steep downward plunge by an aircraft. ■ a sudden dramatic deterioration: *the player's fortunes **took a nosedive***.
▶ verb [no obj.] (of an aircraft) make a nosedive. ■ deteriorate suddenly and dramatically: *massive strikes caused the economy to nosedive*.

no-see-um /nəʊˈsiːəm/ ▶ noun N. Amer. a minute bloodsucking insect, especially a biting midge.

nose flute ▶ noun a musical instrument of the flute type played by blowing through the nose rather than the mouth, associated especially with SE Asia and the Pacific islands.

nosegay ▶ noun literary a small bunch of flowers, typically one that is sweet-scented.
– ORIGIN late Middle English: from **nose** + **gay** in the obsolete sense 'ornament'.

nose guard ▶ noun American Football another term for **nose tackle**.

nose job ▶ noun informal an operation involving rhinoplasty or cosmetic surgery on a person's nose.

nose leaf ▶ noun a fleshy leaf-shaped structure on the nose of many bats, used for echolocation.

nosema /nəʊˈsiːmə/ ▶ noun a spore-forming parasitic protozoan that chiefly affects insects. ● Genus *Nosema*, phylum Microspora, kingdom Protista: several species, in particular *N. apis*, which causes infectious dysentery (**nosema disease**) in honeybees.
– ORIGIN modern Latin, from Greek *nosēma* 'disease'.

nosepiece ▶ noun 1 the part of a helmet or headdress that protects a person's nose. ■ chiefly N. Amer. another term for **noseband**. ■ the central part of a pair of glasses that fits over the bridge of the nose.
2 the part of a microscope to which the objective lenses are attached.

nose rag ▶ noun informal a handkerchief.

nose ring ▶ noun a ring fixed in the nose of a bull or other animal, for leading it. ■ a ring worn in a person's nose as a piece of jewellery.

nose tackle ▶ noun American Football a defensive lineman positioned opposite the offensive centre.

nose wheel ▶ noun a landing wheel under the nose of an aircraft.

nosey ▶ adjective & verb variant spelling of **nosy**.

nosh informal ▶ noun [mass noun] Brit. food: *filling the freezer with all kinds of nosh*. ■ [count noun] N. Amer. a snack or small item of food: *have plenty of noshes and nibbles conveniently placed*.
▶ verb [no obj.] eat food enthusiastically or greedily: *you can nosh to your heart's content* | [with obj.] *there I sat, noshing my favourite food*. ■ N. Amer. eat between meals.
– ORIGIN early 20th cent. (denoting a snack bar): Yiddish.

noshery ▶ noun (pl. **nosheries**) informal a restaurant or snack bar.

no-show ▶ noun a person who has made a reservation, booking, or appointment but neither keeps nor cancels it.

nosh-up ▶ noun Brit. informal a large meal: *the grand nosh-up after the ceremony*.

no side ▶ noun Rugby the end of a game.

nosing ▶ noun a rounded edge of a step or moulding. ■ a metal shield for such an edge.

nosocomial /ˌnɒsə(ʊ)ˈkəʊmɪəl/ ▶ adjective Medicine (of a disease) originating in a hospital.
– ORIGIN mid 19th cent.: from Greek *nosokomos* 'person who tends the sick' + **-ial**.

nosode /ˈnɒsəʊd/ ▶ noun (in homeopathy) a preparation of substances secreted in the course of a disease, used in the treatment of that disease.
– ORIGIN late 19th cent.: from Greek *nosos* 'disease' + **-ode**[1].

nosography /nɒˈsɒgrəfi/ ▶ noun [mass noun] the systematic description of diseases.
– DERIVATIVES **nosographic** adjective.
– ORIGIN mid 17th cent.: from Greek *nosos* 'disease' + **-graphy**.

nosology /nɒˈsɒlədʒi/ ▶ noun [mass noun] the branch of medical science dealing with the classification of diseases.
– DERIVATIVES **nosological** adjective, **nosologist** noun.
– ORIGIN early 18th cent.: from Greek *nosos* 'disease' + **-logy**.

nostalgia ▶ noun [mass noun] a sentimental longing or wistful affection for a period in the past: *I was overcome with acute nostalgia for my days at university*. ■ something done or presented in order to evoke such feelings: *an evening of TV nostalgia*.
– DERIVATIVES **nostalgist** noun.
– ORIGIN late 18th cent. (in the sense 'acute homesickness'): modern Latin (translating German *Heimweh* 'homesickness'), from Greek *nostos* 'return home' + *algos* 'pain'.

nostalgic ▶ adjective feeling, evoking, or characterized by nostalgia: *he remained nostalgic about the good old days* | *a nostalgic account of an idyllic childhood*.
▶ noun a nostalgic person.
– DERIVATIVES **nostalgically** adverb.

nostalgie de la boue /ˌnɒstal(d)ʒiː də la ˌbuː/ ▶ noun [mass noun] a desire for degradation and depravity.
– ORIGIN French, literally 'mud nostalgia'.

nostoc /ˈnɒstɒk/ ▶ noun Biology a microorganism composed of beaded filaments which aggregate to form a gelatinous mass, growing in water and damp places and able to fix nitrogen from the atmosphere. ● Genus *Nostoc*, division Cyanobacteria.
– ORIGIN early 17th cent.: name invented by Paracelsus.

Nostradamus /ˌnɒstrəˈdɑːməs, -ˈdeɪ-/ (1503–66), French astrologer and physician; Latinized name of *Michel de Nostredame*. His cryptic and apocalyptic predictions in rhyming quatrains appeared in two collections (1555; 1558). Their interpretation continues to be the subject of controversy.

Nostratic /nɒˈstratɪk/ ▶ **noun** [mass noun] a hypothetical phylum of languages of which the principal members are the Indo-European, Semitic, Altaic, and Dravidian families.
▶ **adjective** relating to Nostratic.
– ORIGIN 1960s: from German *nostratisch*, based on Latin *nostras, nostrat-* 'of our country'.

nostril ▶ **noun** either of two external openings of the nasal cavity in vertebrates that admit air to the lungs and smells to the olfactory nerves.
– DERIVATIVES **nostrilled adjective** [in combination].
– ORIGIN Old English *nosterl, nosthyrl*, from *nosu* 'nose' + *thӯr(e)l* 'hole'.

nostril fly ▶ **noun** a parasitic fly that lays its eggs in the nostrils of sheep, goats, and deer. The larvae develop in the nasal cavities before being sneezed out. ● The **sheep nostril fly** or sheep bot (*Oestrus ovis*) and the **deer nostril flies** (genus *Cephenemyia*), both in the family Oestridae.

nostro account /ˈnɒstrəʊ/ ▶ **noun** a bank account held by a UK bank with a foreign bank, usually in the currency of that country.
– ORIGIN *nostro* from Italian, 'our, ours'.

nostrum /ˈnɒstrəm/ ▶ **noun** a medicine prepared by an unqualified person, especially one that is not considered effective. ■ a scheme or remedy for bringing about some social or political reform or improvement: *right-wing nostrums such as a wage freeze and cutting public spending.*
– ORIGIN early 17th cent.: from Latin, used in the sense '(something) of our own making', neuter of *noster* 'our'.

nosy (also **nosey**) informal ▶ **adjective** (**nosier**, **nosiest**) showing too much curiosity about other people's affairs: *nosy neighbours | stop being so nosy!*
▶ **verb** (**nosies**, **nosying** or **noseying**, **nosied**) [no obj., with adverbial] pry into something: *they don't nosy into your business like some people.*
– DERIVATIVES **nosily** adverb, **nosiness** noun.

nosy parker ▶ **noun** Brit. informal an overly inquisitive person.
– ORIGIN early 20th cent.: from the postcard caption 'The Adventures of Nosey Parker', referring to a peeping Tom in Hyde Park.

not ▶ **adverb 1** (also **n't** joined to a preceding verb) used with an auxiliary verb or 'be' to form the negative: *he would not say | she isn't there | didn't you tell me?* ■ used in some constructions with other verbs: [with infinitive] *he has been warned not to touch | the pain of not knowing | she* **not only** *wrote the text* **but also** *researched the photographs.*
2 used as a short substitute for a negative clause: *maybe I'll regret it, but I hope not | 'Don't you keep in touch?' 'I'm afraid not' | they wouldn't know if I was telling the truth* **or not**.
3 used to express the negative of other words: *not a single attempt was made | treating the symptoms and not the cause | 'How was it?' 'Not so bad.'* ■ used with a quantifier to exclude a person or part of a group: *not all the poems are serious.* ■ no more than (used to indicate a surprisingly small quantity): *the brakes went on not ten feet from him.*
4 used in understatements to suggest that the opposite of a following word or phrase is true: *the not too distant future | not a million miles away.* ■ informal, humorous following and emphatically negating a statement: *that sounds like quality entertainment—not.* [late 19th cent.: popularized by the film *Wayne's World* (1992).]
▶ **noun** (often **NOT**) Electronics a Boolean operator with only one variable that has the value one when the variable is zero and vice versa. ■ (also **not gate**) a circuit which produces an output signal only when there is not a signal on its input.
▶ **adjective** (often **Not**) Art (of paper) not hot-pressed, and having a slightly textured surface.
– PHRASES **not at all 1** definitely not: *'You don't mind?' 'Not at all.'* **2** used as a polite response to thanks. **not but what** archaic nevertheless: *not but what the picture has its darker side.* **not half** see HALF. **not least** see LEAST. **not quite** see QUITE. **not that** it is not to be inferred that: *I'll never be allowed back—not that I'd want to go back.* **not a thing** nothing at all. **not very** see VERY.
– ORIGIN Middle English: contraction of the adverb NOUGHT.

nota bene /ˌnəʊtə ˈbɛneɪ/ ▶ **verb** [in imperative] formal (used in written text to draw attention to what follows) observe carefully or take special notice.
– ORIGIN Latin, literally 'note well!'.

notability ▶ **noun** (pl. **notabilities**) [mass noun] the fact or quality of being notable. ■ [count noun] dated a famous or important person: *a Fleet Street notability.*

notable ▶ **adjective** worthy of attention or notice; remarkable: *the gardens are* **notable for** *their collection of magnolias and camellias | the results, with one notable exception, have been superb.*
▶ **noun** (usu. **notables**) a famous or important person: *businessmen and local notables.*
– ORIGIN Middle English: from Old French, from Latin *notabilis* 'worthy of note', from the verb *notare* 'to note, mark'.

notably ▶ **adverb** especially; in particular: *a diet low in animal fat protects against potentially fatal diseases, notably diabetes.* ■ in a way that is striking or remarkable: [as submodifier] *such a statement is notably absent from the government's proposals.*

notam /ˈnəʊtəm/ ▶ **noun** a written notification issued to pilots before a flight, advising them of circumstances relating to the state of flying.
– ORIGIN 1940s: from *no(tice) t(o) a(ir)m(en).*

notaphily /nəʊˈtafɪli/ ▶ **noun** [mass noun] the collecting of banknotes as a hobby.
– DERIVATIVES **notaphilist** noun.

notarize (also **notarise**) ▶ **verb** [with obj.] have (the signature on a document) attested to by a notary.

notary /ˈnəʊt(ə)ri/ (in full **notary public**) ▶ **noun** (pl. **notaries**) a person authorized to perform certain legal formalities, especially to draw up or certify contracts, deeds, and other documents for use in other jurisdictions.
– DERIVATIVES **notarial** adjective.
– ORIGIN Middle English (in the sense 'clerk or secretary'): from Latin *notarius* 'secretary', from *nota* 'mark'.

notate ▶ **verb** [with obj.] write (something, typically music) in notation.
– DERIVATIVES **notator** noun.
– ORIGIN early 20th cent.: back-formation from NOTATION.

notation ▶ **noun 1** [mass noun] a series or system of written symbols used to represent numbers, amounts, or elements in something such as music or mathematics: *algebraic notation* | [count noun] *new terminologies and notations.*
2 a note or annotation: *he noticed the notations in the margin.*
3 short for SCALE OF NOTATION (see SCALE³).
– DERIVATIVES **notational** adjective, **notationally** adverb.
– ORIGIN late 16th cent.: from Latin *notatio(n-)*, from the verb *notare*, from *nota* 'mark'.

not-being ▶ **noun** [mass noun] non-existence.

notch ▶ **noun 1** an indentation or incision on an edge or surface: *there was a notch in the end of the arrow for the bowstring.* ■ each of a series of holes for the tongue of a buckle: *he tightened his belt an extra notch.* ■ a nick made on something in order to keep a score or record. ■ a point or degree in a scale: *her opinion of Nicole dropped a few notches.*
2 N. Amer. a deep, narrow mountain pass.
▶ **verb** [with obj.] **1** make notches in: (as adj. **notched**) *notched bamboo sticks.* ■ secure or insert by means of notches: *she notched her belt tighter.*
2 score or achieve (something): *he* **notched up** *fifteen years' service with the company.*
– DERIVATIVES **notcher** noun.
– ORIGIN mid 16th cent.: probably from Anglo-Norman French *noche*, variant of Old French *osche*, of unknown origin.

notchback ▶ **noun** a car with a back that extends approximately horizontally from the bottom of the rear window so as to make a distinct angle with it.

notch effect ▶ **noun** Engineering the increase in the susceptibility of a specimen to fracture caused by a notch.

notch filter ▶ **noun** Electronics a filter that attenuates signals within a very narrow band of frequencies.

notchy ▶ **adjective** (**notchier**, **notchiest**) (of a manual gear-changing mechanism) difficult to use because the lever has to be moved accurately (as if into a narrow notch).

note ▶ **noun 1** a brief record of points or ideas written down as an aid to memory: *I'll* **make a note** *in my diary | lecture notes.* ■ a short comment on or explanation of a word or passage in a book or article; an annotation: *see note iv above.*
2 a short informal letter or written message: *I left her a note explaining where I was going.* ■ a short official document certifying a particular thing: *you need a sick note from your doctor.* ■ an official letter sent from the representative of one government to another.
3 Brit. a banknote: *a ten-pound note.* ■ a written promise or notice of payment of various kinds: *a credit note.*
4 a single tone of definite pitch made by a musical instrument or the human voice: *the last notes of the symphony died away.* ■ a written sign representing the pitch and duration of such a sound. ■ a key of a piano or similar instrument: *black notes.* ■ a bird's song or call, or a single tone in this: *the tawny owl has a harsh flight note.*
5 [in sing.] a particular quality or tone that reflects or expresses a mood or attitude: *there was a note of scorn in her voice | the decade could have ended on an optimistic note.* ■ any of the basic components of a fragrance or flavour: *the fresh note of bergamot.*
▶ **verb** [with obj.] **1** notice or pay particular attention to (something): *he noted his mother's unusual gaiety* | [with clause] *please note that you will not receive a reminder that final payment is due.* ■ remark upon (something) in order to draw attention to it: *we noted earlier the difficulties inherent in this strategy.*
2 record (something) in writing: *he* **noted down** *her address on a piece of paper.*
– PHRASES **of note 1** worth paying attention to: *many of his comments are worthy of note.* **2** important; distinguished: *Roman historians of note include Livy, Tacitus, and Sallust.* **strike** (or **hit**) **a false note** appear insincere or inappropriate. **strike** (or **sound**) **a note of** express (a particular feeling or view) about something: *he sounded a note of caution about the trend towards health foods.* **strike** (or **hit**) **the right** (or **wrong**) **note** say or do something in a way that is very suitable (or unsuitable) for a particular audience or occasion. **take note** pay attention: *employers should* **take note of** *the needs of disabled people.*
– ORIGIN Middle English (in sense 4 of the noun and sense 1 of the verb): from Old French *note* (noun), *noter* (verb), from Latin *nota* 'a mark', *notare* 'to mark'.

notebook ▶ **noun** a small book with blank or ruled pages for writing notes in. ■ a laptop computer, especially a small, slim one.

notecard ▶ **noun** a decorative card with a blank space for a short message. ■ a small card used for making notes.

notecase ▶ **noun** Brit. dated a small flat folding case or wallet for holding banknotes.

note cluster ▶ **noun** Music a chord containing a number of closely adjacent notes. Also called TONE CLUSTER.

noted ▶ **adjective** well known; famous: *the restaurant is* **noted for** *its high standards of cuisine | a noted patron of the arts.*

notelet ▶ **noun** Brit. a small folded sheet of paper on which a note or informal letter may be written.

notepad ▶ **noun** a pad of blank or ruled pages for writing notes on. ■ a pocket-sized computer in which the user inputs text by writing with a stylus on the screen.

notepaper ▶ **noun** [mass noun] paper for writing letters on.

notes inégales /ˌnəʊts ɪneɪˈɡɑːl/ ▶ **plural noun** (in baroque music) notes performed by convention in an uneven rhythm though notated as equal in the score.
– ORIGIN French, literally 'unequal notes'.

noteworthy ▶ **adjective** worth paying attention to; interesting or significant: *noteworthy features* | [with clause] *it is noteworthy that no one at the Bank has accepted responsibility for the failure.*
– DERIVATIVES **noteworthiness** noun.

not-for-profit ▶ **adjective** another term for NON-PROFIT.

nothing ▶ **pronoun** not anything; no single thing: *I said nothing | there's nothing you can do | they found nothing wrong.* ■ something of no importance or concern: *'What are you laughing at?' 'Oh, nothing, sir' | they are nothing to him* | [as noun] *no longer could we be treated as nothings.* ■ (in calculations) no amount; nought.
▶ **adjective** [attrib.] informal having no prospect of progress; of no value: *he had a series of nothing jobs.*
▶ **adverb** not at all: *a man who cared nothing for her | he looks* **nothing like** *the others.* ■ [postpositive] N. Amer. informal used to contradict something emphatically: *'This is a surprise.' 'Surprise nothing.'*
– PHRASES **be nothing to do with** see DO¹. **for nothing 1** at no cost; without payment: *working for*

N

nothing is a luxury I can't afford. **2** to no purpose: *he died anyway, so it had all been for nothing.* **have nothing on someone** see HAVE. **have nothing to do with** see DO¹. **no nothing** informal (concluding a list of negatives) nothing at all: *how could you solve it with no clues, no witnesses, no nothing?* **not for nothing** for a very good reason: *not for nothing have I a brother-in-law who cooks professionally.* **nothing but** only: *nothing but the best will do.* **nothing daunted** see DAUNT. **nothing doing** informal **1** there is no prospect of success or agreement: *He wants to marry her. Nothing doing!* **2** nothing is happening: *there's nothing doing, and I've been waiting for weeks.* **nothing** (or **nothing else**) **for it** Brit. no alternative: *there was **nothing for it but to** follow.* **nothing less than** used to emphasize how great or extreme something is: *it was nothing less than sexual harassment.* **nothing much** not a great amount; nothing of importance. **there is nothing to it** there is no difficulty involved. **stop at nothing** see STOP. **sweet nothings** words of affection exchanged by lovers: *Ned appeared to be whispering sweet nothings in her ear.* **think nothing of it** do not apologize or feel bound to show gratitude (used as a polite response). **you ain't seen nothing yet** informal used to indicate that however extreme or impressive something may seem, it will be overshadowed by what is to come: *if you think that was muddy, you ain't seen nothing yet.*
– ORIGIN Old English *nān thing* (see NO, THING).

nothingness ▸ **noun** [mass noun] the absence or cessation of life or existence: *the fear of the total nothingness of death.* ■ worthlessness or insignificance: *the nothingness of it all overwhelmed him.*

nothosaur /ˈnəʊθəsɔː, ˈnəʊθ-/ ▸ **noun** a semiaquatic fossil carnivorous reptile of the Triassic period, having a slender body and long neck, related to the plesiosaurs. ● Infraorder Nothosauria, superorder Sauropterygia.
– ORIGIN 1930s: from modern Latin *Nothosauria*, from Greek *nothos* 'false' + *sauros* 'lizard'.

notice ▸ **noun 1** [mass noun] the fact of observing or paying attention to something: *their silence did not escape my notice | it has **come to our notice** that you have been missing school.*
2 [mass noun] notification or warning of something, especially to allow preparations to be made: *interest rates are subject to fluctuation without notice.* ■ a formal declaration of one's intention to end an agreement, typically one concerning employment or tenancy, at a specified time: *she handed in her notice | his employers gave him two weeks' notice.*
3 a displayed sheet or placard giving news or information: *the jobs were advertised in a notice posted in the common room.* ■ a small advertisement or announcement in a newspaper or magazine: *an obituary notice.*
4 (usu. **notices**) a short published review of a new film, play, or book: *she had good notices in her first film.*
▸ **verb** [with obj.] become aware of: *he noticed the youths behaving suspiciously* | [with clause] *I noticed that she was looking tired* | [no obj.] *they were too drunk to notice.* ■ treat (someone) as worthy of recognition or attention: *it was only last year that the singer really began to be noticed.* ■ archaic mention or remark on: *she looked so much better that Sir Charles noticed it to Lady Harriet.*
– PHRASES **at** (or N. Amer. **on**) **short** (or **a moment's**) **notice** with little warning or time for preparation: *tours may be cancelled at short notice.* **put someone on notice** (or **serve notice**) warn someone of something about or likely to occur, especially in a formal or threatening manner: *we're going to put foreign governments on notice that we want a change of trade policy.* **take no notice** pay no attention to someone or something: *he **took no notice of** her frantic gestures.* **take notice** pay attention; show signs of interest: *when the show was broadcast, he made TV viewers **sit up and take notice**.*
– ORIGIN late Middle English (in sense 2 of the noun): from Old French, from Latin *notitia* 'being known', from *notus* 'known' (see NOTION).

noticeable ▸ **adjective** easily seen or noticed; clear or apparent: *a noticeable increase in staff motivation | noticeable grey hairs.* ■ noteworthy: *the church is noticeable for the fresco above the door.*
– DERIVATIVES **noticeably** adverb.

noticeboard ▸ **noun** Brit. a board for displaying notices.

notifiable ▸ **adjective** denoting something, typically a serious infectious disease, that must be reported to the appropriate authorities.

notification ▸ **noun** [mass noun] the action of notifying someone or something: *we have yet to receive formal notification of the announcement.*

notify ▸ **verb** (**notifies, notifying, notified**) [with obj.] inform (someone) of something, typically in a formal or official manner: *you will be **notified of** our decision as soon as possible* | [with obj. and clause] *they were notified that John had been taken prisoner.* ■ give notice of or report (something) formally or officially: *births and deaths are required by law to be **notified to** the Registrar.*
– ORIGIN late Middle English: from Old French *notifier*, from Latin *notificare* 'make known', from *notus* 'known' (see NOTION) + *facere* 'make'.

notion ▸ **noun 1** a conception of or belief about something: *children have different notions about the roles of their parents | I had no notion of what her words meant.*
2 an impulse or desire, especially one of a whimsical kind: *she had a notion to ring her friend at work.*
3 (**notions**) chiefly N. Amer. items used in sewing, such as buttons, pins, and hooks.
– ORIGIN late Middle English: from Latin *notio(n-)* 'idea', from *notus* 'known', past participle of *noscere*.

notional ▸ **adjective 1** existing as or based on a suggestion, estimate, or theory; not existing in reality: *notional budgets for hospital and community health services.*
2 Linguistics denoting or relating to an approach to grammar which is dependent on the definition of terminology (e.g. 'a verb is a doing word') as opposed to identification of structures and processes.
– DERIVATIVES **notionally** adverb.
– ORIGIN late Middle English (in the Latin sense): from obsolete French, or from medieval Latin *notionalis* 'relating to an idea', from *notio(n-)* 'idea' (see NOTION).

notitia /nəʊˈtɪʃɪə/ ▸ **noun** a register or list of ecclesiastical sees or districts.
– ORIGIN early 18th cent.: from Latin, literally 'knowledge', later 'list or account', from *notus* 'known'.

notochord /ˈnəʊtə(ʊ)kɔːd/ ▸ **noun** Zoology a cartilaginous skeletal rod supporting the body in all embryonic and some adult chordate animals.
– ORIGIN mid 19th cent.: from Greek *nōton* 'back' + CHORD².

Notogaea /ˌnəʊtə(ʊ)ˈdʒiːə/ (US also **Notogea**) Zoology a zoogeographical area comprising the Australian region.
– DERIVATIVES **Notogaean** adjective.
– ORIGIN mid 19th cent.: modern Latin, from Greek *notos* 'south wind' + *gaia* 'earth'.

notoriety /nəʊtəˈrʌɪɪti/ ▸ **noun** [mass noun] the state of being famous or well known for some bad quality or deed: *the song has gained some notoriety in the press | she has a certain notoriety.*

notorious ▸ **adjective** famous or well known, typically for some bad quality or deed: *Los Angeles is **notorious for** its smog | he was a notorious drinker and womanizer.*
– DERIVATIVES **notoriously** adverb.
– ORIGIN late 15th cent. (in the sense 'generally known'): from medieval Latin *notorius* (from Latin *notus* 'known') + -OUS.

notornis /nə(ʊ)ˈtɔːnɪs/ ▸ **noun** another term for TAKAHE.
– ORIGIN mid 19th cent.: from Greek *notos* 'south' + *ornis* 'bird'.

notoungulate /ˌnəʊtəʊˈʌŋgjʊlət/ ▸ **noun** an extinct hoofed mammal of a large and varied group that lived in South America throughout the Tertiary period, finally dying out in the Pleistocene. ● Order Notoungulata: many families.
– ORIGIN early 20th cent.: from modern Latin *Notoungulata*, from Greek *notos* 'south' + Latin *ungula* 'nail'.

Notre Dame /ˌnɒtrə ˈdɑːm/, French /nɔtʀ(ə)dam/ a Gothic cathedral church in Paris, dedicated to the Virgin Mary, on the Île de la Cité (an island in the Seine). It was built between 1163 and 1250 and is especially noted for its innovatory flying buttresses and sculptured facade.
– ORIGIN French, literally 'our lady'.

no-trumper ▸ **noun** Bridge a hand on which a no-trump bid can suitably be made or has been made.

no trumps ▸ **noun** Bridge a situation in which no suit is designated as trumps.

Nottingham /ˈnɒtɪŋəm/ a city in east central England, the county town of Nottinghamshire; pop. 237,600 (est. 2009).

Nottingham lace ▸ **noun** [mass noun] a type of machine-made flat lace.

Nottinghamshire a county in central England; county town, Nottingham.

Notting Hill a district of NW central London, the scene of an annual street carnival.

Notts. ▸ **abbreviation** Nottinghamshire.

notum /ˈnəʊtəm/ ▸ **noun** (pl. **nota**) Entomology (in an insect) the tergum or dorsal exoskeleton of the thorax.
– DERIVATIVES **notal** adjective.
– ORIGIN late 19th cent.: from Greek *nōton* 'back'.

notwithstanding ▸ **preposition** in spite of: *notwithstanding the evidence, the consensus is that the jury will not reach a verdict* | [postpositive] *this small contretemps notwithstanding, they both had a good time.*
▸ **adverb** nevertheless; in spite of this: *she tells us she is an intellectual; notwithstanding, she is a beauty queen.*
▸ **conjunction** although; in spite of the fact that: ***notwithstanding that** the hall was packed with bullies, our champion played on steadily and patiently.*
– ORIGIN late Middle English: from NOT + *withstanding*, present participle of WITHSTAND, on the pattern of Old French *non obstant* 'not providing an obstacle to'.

Nouadhibou /ˌnwadɪˈbuː/ the principal port of Mauritania, on the Atlantic coast at the border with Western Sahara; pop. 113,500 (est. 2007). Former name PORT ÉTIENNE.

Nouakchott /nwakˈʃɒt/ the capital of Mauritania, situated on the Atlantic coast; pop. 673,000 (est. 2007).

nougat /ˈnuːgɑː, ˈnʌgət/ ▸ **noun** [mass noun] a sweet made from sugar or honey, nuts, and egg white.
– ORIGIN early 19th cent.: from French, from Provençal *nogat*, from *noga* 'nut'.

nougatine /ˌnuːgəˈtiːn/ ▸ **noun** [mass noun] nougat covered with chocolate.
– ORIGIN late 19th cent.: from NOUGAT + *-ine* 'resembling' (see -INE¹).

nought ▸ **noun** Brit. the digit 0.
▸ **pronoun** variant spelling of NAUGHT.
– DERIVATIVES **noughth** adjective.

noughties ▸ **plural noun** chiefly Brit. the decade from 2000 to 2009.
– ORIGIN 1990s: from NOUGHT, on the pattern of *twenties, thirties*, etc.

noughts and crosses ▸ **plural noun** [treated as sing.] Brit. a game in which two players seek to complete a row of either three noughts or three crosses drawn alternately in the spaces of a grid of nine squares.

Nouméa /nuːˈmeɪə/ the capital of the island of New Caledonia; pop. 91,386 (2004). Former name PORT DE FRANCE.

noumenon /ˈnuːmənɒn, ˈnaʊmənɒn/ ▸ **noun** (pl. **noumena**) (in Kantian philosophy) a thing as it is in itself, as distinct from a thing as it is knowable by the senses through phenomenal attributes.
– DERIVATIVES **noumenal** adjective.
– ORIGIN late 18th cent.: via German from Greek, literally '(something) conceived', from *noein* 'conceive, apprehend'.

noun ▸ **noun** Grammar a word (other than a pronoun) used to identify any of a class of people, places, or things (**common noun**), or to name a particular one of these (**proper noun**).
– DERIVATIVES **nounal** adjective.
– ORIGIN late Middle English: from Anglo-Norman French, from Latin *nomen* 'name'.

noun phrase ▸ **noun** Grammar a word or group of words containing a noun and functioning in a sentence as subject, object, or prepositional object.

nourish ▸ **verb** [with obj.] **1** provide with the food or other substances necessary for growth, health, and good condition: *I was doing everything I could to nourish and protect the baby* | figurative *spiritual resources which nourished her in her darkest hours.* ■ enhance the fertility of (soil): *a clay base nourished with plant detritus.*
2 keep (a feeling or belief) in one's mind, typically for a long time: *he has long nourished an ambition to bring the show to Broadway.*
– DERIVATIVES **nourisher** noun.
– ORIGIN Middle English: from Old French *noriss-*, lengthened stem of *norir*, from Latin *nutrire* 'feed, cherish'.

N

nourishing ▶ adjective (of food) containing substances necessary for growth, health, and good condition: *a simple but nourishing meal.*

nourishment ▶ noun [mass noun] the food necessary for growth, health, and good condition: *tubers from which plants obtain nourishment* | figurative *she was starved of emotional nourishment.* ■ the action of nourishing someone or something: *the nourishment of our bodies and of our minds.*

nous /naʊs/ ▶ noun [mass noun] **1** Brit. informal common sense; practical intelligence: *if he had any nous at all, he'd sell the film rights.*
2 Philosophy the mind or intellect.
– ORIGIN late 17th cent. (in sense 2): from Greek, 'mind, intelligence, intuitive apprehension'.

nouveau /'nuːvəʊ/, French /nuvo/ ▶ adjective informal
1 short for NOUVEAU RICHE.
2 modern or up to date.

nouveau riche /,nuːvəʊ 'riːʃ/, French /nuvo riʃ/ ▶ noun [treated as pl.] (usu. **the nouveau riche**) people who have recently acquired wealth, typically those perceived as ostentatious or lacking in good taste.
▶ adjective relating to or characteristic of such people: *nouveau-riche social climbers.*
– ORIGIN French, literally 'new rich'.

nouveau roman /,nuːvəʊ rəʊ'mɑːn/, French /nuvo ʀɔmɑ̃/ ▶ noun [mass noun] a style of avant-garde French novel that came to prominence in the 1950s. It rejected the plot, characters, and omniscient narrator central to the traditional novel in an attempt to reflect more faithfully the sometimes random nature of experience.
– ORIGIN French, literally 'new novel'.

nouvelle /nuː'vɛl/ ▶ adjective relating to or specializing in nouvelle cuisine: *nouvelle bistros.*

Nouvelle-Calédonie /nuvɛlkaledoni/ French name for NEW CALEDONIA.

nouvelle cuisine /nuː,vel kwɪ'ziːn/ ▶ noun [mass noun] a modern style of cookery that avoids rich, heavy foods and emphasizes the freshness of the ingredients and the presentation of the dishes.
– ORIGIN French, literally 'new cookery'.

nouvelle vague /nuː,vɛl 'vɑːg/, French /nuvɛl vag/ ▶ noun [mass noun] a grouping of French film directors in the late 1950s and 1960s who reacted against established French cinema and sought to make more individualistic and stylistically innovative films. Exponents included Claude Chabrol, Jean-Luc Godard, Alain Resnais, and François Truffaut.
– ORIGIN French, literally 'new wave'.

Nov. ▶ abbreviation November.

nova /'nəʊvə/ ▶ noun (pl. **novae** /-viː/ or **novas**) Astronomy a star showing a sudden large increase in brightness and then slowly returning to its original state over a few months. See also SUPERNOVA.
– ORIGIN late 19th cent.: from Latin, feminine of *novus* 'new' (because such stars were thought to be newly formed).

novaculite /nə(ʊ)'vakjʊlʌɪt/ ▶ noun [mass noun] Geology a hard, dense, fine-grained siliceous rock resembling chert, with a high content of microcrystalline quartz.
– ORIGIN late 18th cent.: from Latin *novacula* 'razor' + -ITE[1].

Nova Lisboa /,nəʊvə lɪz'bəʊə/ former name (until 1978) for HUAMBO.

Nova Scotia /,nəʊvə 'skəʊʃə/ **1** a peninsula on the SE coast of Canada, projecting into the Atlantic Ocean and separating the Bay of Fundy from the Gulf of St Lawrence.
2 a province of eastern Canada, comprising the peninsula of Nova Scotia and the adjoining Cape Breton Island; pop. 913,462 (2006); capital, Halifax. Settled by the French in the early 18th century as Acadia, it changed hands several times between the French and English before being awarded to Britain in 1713. It became one of the original four provinces in the Dominion of Canada in 1867.
– DERIVATIVES **Nova Scotian** adjective & noun.

novation /nə(ʊ)'veɪʃ(ə)n/ ▶ noun [mass noun] Law the substitution of a new contract in place of an old one.
– DERIVATIVES **novate** verb.
– ORIGIN early 16th cent.: from late Latin *novatio(n-)*, from the verb *novare* 'make new'.

Novaya Zemlya /,nəʊvəjə zɪm'ljɑː/ two large uninhabited islands in the Arctic Ocean off the north coast of Siberian Russia.

novel[1] ▶ noun a fictitious prose narrative of book length, typically representing character and action with some degree of realism: *the novels of Jane Austen* | *a paperback novel.* ■ (**the novel**) the literary genre represented or exemplified by novels: *the novel is the most adaptable of all literary forms.*
– ORIGIN mid 16th cent.: from Italian *novella (storia)* 'new (story)', feminine of *novello* 'new', from Latin *novellus*, from *novus* 'new'. The word is also found from late Middle English until the 18th cent. in the sense 'a novelty, a piece of news', from Old French *novelle* (see NOVEL[2]).

novel[2] ▶ adjective interestingly new or unusual: *he hit on a novel idea to solve his financial problems.*
– DERIVATIVES **novelly** adverb.
– ORIGIN late Middle English (in the sense 'recent'): from Old French, from Latin *novellus*, from *novus* 'new'.

novelese ▶ noun [mass noun] derogatory a style of writing supposedly characteristic of inferior novels.

novelette ▶ noun chiefly derogatory a short novel, typically one that is light and romantic or sentimental in character.
– DERIVATIVES **novelettish** adjective.

novelist ▶ noun a writer of novels.

novelistic ▶ adjective characteristic of or used in novels: *the novelistic detail of his film.*

novelize (also **novelise**) ▶ verb [with obj.] (usu. as adj. **novelized**) convert (a story, typically one in the form of a film or screenplay) into a novel.
– DERIVATIVES **novelization** noun.

novella /nə'vɛlə/ ▶ noun a short novel or long short story.
– ORIGIN early 20th cent.: from Italian, 'novel'.

Novello /nə'vɛləʊ/, Ivor (1893–1951), Welsh composer, songwriter, actor, and dramatist; born *David Ivor Davies*. His song 'Keep the Home Fires Burning' (1914) became one of the most popular songs of the First World War.

novelty ▶ noun (pl. **novelties**) **1** [mass noun] the quality of being new, original, or unusual: *the novelty of being a married woman wore off.* ■ [count noun] a new or unfamiliar thing or experience: *in 1914 air travel was still a novelty.* ■ [as modifier] denoting an object intended to be amusing as a result of its unusual design: *a novelty teapot.*
2 a small and inexpensive toy or ornament: *he bought chocolate novelties to decorate the Christmas tree.*
– ORIGIN late Middle English: from Old French *novelte*, from *novel* 'new, fresh' (see NOVEL[2]).

November ▶ noun **1** the eleventh month of the year, in the northern hemisphere usually considered the last month of autumn: *the shop opened in November* | *he hasn't played for England since last November.*
2 a code word representing the letter N, used in radio communication.
– ORIGIN Old English, from Latin, from *novem* 'nine' (being originally the ninth month of the Roman year).

novena /nə(ʊ)'viːnə/ ▶ noun (in the Roman Catholic Church) a form of worship consisting of special prayers or services on nine successive days.
– ORIGIN mid 19th cent.: from medieval Latin, from Latin *novem* 'nine'.

novennial /nə(ʊ)'vɛnɪəl/ ▶ adjective recurring every nine years. ■ lasting for or relating to a period of nine years.
– ORIGIN mid 17th cent.: from late Latin *novennis* 'nine years old' (from Latin *novem* 'nine') + -AL.

Noverre /nɒ'vɛː/, French /nɔvɛʀ/, Jean-Georges (1727–1810), French choreographer and dance theorist, who stressed the importance of dramatic motivation in ballet as opposed to technical virtuosity.

Novgorod /'nɒvgərɒd/ a city in NW Russia, on the Volkhov River at the northern tip of Lake Ilmen; pop. 214,400 (est. 2009). Russia's oldest city, it was settled by the Varangian chief Rurik in 862 and ruled by Alexander Nevsky between 1238 and 1263, when it was an important centre of medieval eastern Europe.

novice /'nɒvɪs/ ▶ noun **1** a person new to and inexperienced in a job or situation: *he was a complete novice in foreign affairs.* ■ an animal, especially a racehorse, that has not yet won a major prize or reached a sufficient level of performance to qualify for important events.
2 a person who has entered a religious order and is under probation, before taking vows.
– ORIGIN Middle English: from Old French, from late Latin *novicius*, from *novus* 'new'.

Novi Sad /,nəʊvɪ 'sad/ an industrial city in Serbia, on the River Danube, capital of the autonomous province of Vojvodina; pop. 197,900 (est. 2008).

novitiate /nə(ʊ)'vɪʃɪət, -ɪeɪt/ (also **noviciate**) ▶ noun the period or state of being a novice, especially in a religious order. ■ a novice, especially in a religious order. ■ a place housing religious novices.
– ORIGIN early 17th cent.: from ecclesiastical Latin *noviciatus*, from Latin *novicius* 'new' (see NOVICE).

novocaine /'nəʊvəkeɪn/ ▶ noun another term for PROCAINE.
– ORIGIN early 20th cent.: from Latin *novus* 'new' + *-caine* (from COCAINE).

Novokuznetsk /,nəʊvəkʊz'njɛtsk/ an industrial city in the Kuznets Basin in south central Siberian Russia; pop. 562,200 (est. 2008).

Novosibirsk /,nəʊvəsɪ'bɪəsk/ a city in central Siberian Russia, to the west of the Kuznets Basin, on the River Ob; pop. 1,390,500 (est. 2008).

Novotný /'nɒvɒt,niː/, Antonín (1904–75), Czechoslovak communist statesman, President 1957–68. A founder member of the Czechoslovak Communist Party (1921), he played a major part in the communist seizure of power in 1948. He was ousted by the reform movement in 1968.

now ▶ adverb **1** at the present time or moment: *where are you living now?* | *it's the most popular style of jazz* ***right now*** | *not now, I'm late* | *they should be back* ***by now.*** ■ at the time directly following the present moment; immediately: *if we leave now we can be home by ten* | *I'd rather do it now than leave it till later.* ■ under the present circumstances; as a result of something that has recently happened: *it is now clear that we should not pursue this policy* | *I didn't receive the letter, but it hardly matters now.* ■ on this further occasion, typically as the latest in a series of annoying situations or events: *what do you want now?* ■ used to emphasize a particular length of time: *they've been married four years now.* ■ (in a narrative or account of past events) at the time spoken of or referred to: *she was nineteen now, and she was alone.*
2 used, especially in conversation, to draw attention to a particular statement or point in a narrative: *now, my first impulse was to run away* | *I don't like Scotch. Now, if it had been Irish Whiskey you'd offered me.*
3 used in a request, instruction, or question, typically to give a slight emphasis to one's words: *we can hardly send her back, now can we?* | *run along now.* ■ used when pausing or considering one's next words: *let me see now, oh yes, I remember.*
4 used at the end of an ironic question echoing a previous statement: *'Mum says you might let me have some of your stamps.' 'Does she now?'.*
▶ conjunction as a consequence of the fact: *they spent a lot of time together* **now that** *he had retired* | *now you mention it, I haven't seen her around for ages.*
▶ adjective informal fashionable or up to date: *see more of what's now during our autumn catwalk show.*
– PHRASES **for now** until a later time: *that's all the news there is for now.* **now and again** (or **then**) from time to time. **now now** used as an expression of mild remonstrance: *now now, that's not the way to behave.* **now ——, now ——** at one moment ——, at the next ——: *a wind whipped about the house, now this way, now that.* **now or never** used to convey urgency: *it was now or never—I had to move fast.* **now then 1** used to get someone's attention or to invite a response: *now then, who's for a coffee?* **2** used as an expression of mild remonstrance or warning: *now then, Emily, I think Sarah has suffered enough.* **now you're talking** an expression of enthusiastic agreement or approval: *The Beatles! Now you're talking!*
– DERIVATIVES **nowness** noun.
– ORIGIN Old English *nū*, of Germanic origin; related to Dutch *nu*, German *nun*, from an Indo-European root shared by Latin *nunc* and Greek *nun*.

nowadays ▶ adverb at the present time, in contrast with the past: *the sort of clothes worn by almost all young people nowadays* | *nowadays, many people condemn hunting.*

noway (also **noways**) ▶ adverb chiefly archaic or N. Amer. not at all; by no means.

nowed /naʊd/ ▶ adjective [often postpositive] Heraldry knotted; (of a snake) depicted interlaced in a knot.
– ORIGIN late 16th cent.: from French *noué* 'knotted'.

Nowel (also **Nowell**) ▶ noun archaic spelling of NOEL.

nowhere ▶ adverb not in or to any place; not anywhere: *plants and animals found nowhere else in the world* | *the constable was nowhere to be seen.*
▶ pronoun **1** no place: *there was nowhere for her to sit* | *there's nowhere better to experience the wonders of the Pyrenees.*

N

2 a place that is remote, uninteresting, or nondescript: *a stretch of road between nowhere and nowhere*.
▶ adjective [attrib.] informal having no prospect of progress or success: *a nowhere job*.
– PHRASES **be** (or **come**) **nowhere** be badly beaten or completely unsuccessful in a race or competition. **from** (or **out of**) **nowhere** appearing or happening suddenly and unexpectedly: *they came from nowhere to win in the last three strokes of the race*. **get** (or **go**) **nowhere** make no progress: *he'll get nowhere with her, he's too young*. **get someone nowhere** be of no use or benefit to someone: *being angry would get her nowhere*. **nowhere near** not nearly: *he's nowhere near as popular as he used to be*. **a road to nowhere** a situation or course of action offering no prospects of progress or advancement.
– ORIGIN Old English *nāhwǣr* (see NO, WHERE).

nowheresville /ˈnəʊwɛːzvɪl/ ▶ noun US informal a place or situation of no significance, promise, or interest: *an unhappy girl stuck in industrial Nowheresville, UK*.

no-win ▶ adjective denoting a situation in which success or a favourable outcome is impossible.

nowise ▶ adverb archaic in no way or manner; not at all: *I can nowise accept the accusation*.

now-now ▶ adverb S. African informal used to refer to a time very shortly before or very soon after the moment of speaking: *I'll be back now-now*.

nowt /naʊt/ ▶ pronoun & adverb N. English nothing: *it's nowt to do with me*.

NOx ▶ noun [mass noun] oxides of nitrogen, especially as atmospheric pollutants.

noxious /ˈnɒkʃəs/ ▶ adjective harmful, poisonous, or very unpleasant: *they were overcome by the noxious fumes*.
– DERIVATIVES **noxiously** adverb, **noxiousness** noun.
– ORIGIN late 15th cent.: from Latin *noxius* (from *noxa* 'harm') + -OUS.

noyade /nwɑːˈjɑːd/ ▶ noun historical an execution carried out by drowning.
– ORIGIN early 19th cent. (referring especially to a mass execution by drowning, carried out in France in 1794): from French, literally 'drowning', from the verb *noyer*, from Latin *necare* 'kill without use of a weapon', later 'drown'.

N

noyau /nwʌˈjəʊ/ ▶ noun (pl. **noyaux** /-jəʊz/) [mass noun] a liqueur made of brandy flavoured with fruit kernels.
– ORIGIN French, literally 'kernel', based on Latin *nux, nuc-* 'nut'.

nozzle ▶ noun a cylindrical or round spout at the end of a pipe, hose, or tube used to control a jet of gas or liquid.
– ORIGIN early 17th cent.: from NOSE + -LE[2].

NP ▶ abbreviation notary public.

Np ▶ symbol the chemical element neptunium.

n.p. ▶ abbreviation ▪ new paragraph. ▪ no place of publication (used especially in book classification).

NPA ▶ abbreviation (in the UK) Newspaper Publishers' Association.

NPL ▶ abbreviation (in the UK) National Physical Laboratory.

NPN ▶ adjective Electronics denoting a semiconductor device in which a p-type region is sandwiched between two n-type regions.

NPV ▶ abbreviation net present value. See PRESENT VALUE.

nr ▶ abbreviation near.

NRA ▶ abbreviation ▪ (in the US) National Rifle Association. ▪ (in the UK) National Rivers Authority.

NRI ▶ abbreviation Indian non-resident Indian, denoting a person born in India who lives abroad.

NRSV ▶ abbreviation New Revised Standard Version (of the Bible).

NS ▶ abbreviation ▪ New Style. ▪ Nova Scotia (in official postal use).

ns ▶ abbreviation nanosecond.

n/s ▶ abbreviation non-smoker or non-smoking (used in personal advertisements).

NSA ▶ abbreviation (in the US) National Security Agency.

NSAID /ˈɛnsɛd/ ▶ abbreviation non-steroidal anti-inflammatory drug.

NSB ▶ abbreviation (in the UK) National Savings Bank.

NSC ▶ abbreviation (in the US) National Security Council.

NSF ▶ abbreviation (in the US) National Science Foundation.

NSPCC ▶ abbreviation (in the UK) National Society for the Prevention of Cruelty to Children.

NSU ▶ abbreviation Medicine non-specific urethritis.

NSW ▶ abbreviation New South Wales.

NT ▶ abbreviation ▪ National Trust. ▪ New Testament. ▪ Northern Territory. ▪ Northwest Territories (in official postal use). ▪ Bridge no trump(s).

-n't ▶ contraction not, used with auxiliary verbs (e.g. *can't, won't, didn't,* and *isn't*).

Nth ▶ abbreviation North.

nth ▶ adjective Mathematics denoting an unspecified member of a series of numbers or enumerated items: *systematic sampling by taking every nth name from the list*. ▪ (in general use) denoting an unspecified item or instance in a series, typically the last or latest in a long series: *he had just been booted out of his digs for the nth time*.
– PHRASES **to the nth degree** to the utmost: *the gullibility of the electorate was tested to the nth degree by such promises*.

NTP ▶ abbreviation Chemistry normal temperature and pressure.

NTSC ▶ noun [mass noun] the television broadcasting system used in North America and Japan.
– ORIGIN 1950s: acronym from *National Television System Committee*.

n-tuple ▶ noun Mathematics an ordered set with *n* elements.

n-type ▶ adjective Electronics denoting a region in a semiconductor in which electrical conduction is due chiefly to the movement of electrons. Often contrasted with P-TYPE.

NU ▶ abbreviation Nunavut (in official postal use).

nu /njuː/ ▶ noun the thirteenth letter of the Greek alphabet (Ν, ν), transliterated as 'n'. ▪ (**Nu**) [followed by Latin genitive] Astronomy the thirteenth star in a constellation: *Nu Draconis*.
▶ symbol (ν) frequency.
– ORIGIN Greek.

nu- ▶ combining form informal respelling of 'new', used especially in names of new or revived genres of popular music: *nu-metal bands | nu-disco*.

nuance /ˈnjuːɑːns/ ▶ noun a subtle difference in or shade of meaning, expression, or sound: *he was familiar with the nuances of the local dialect*.
▶ verb [with obj.] give nuances to: *the effect of the music is nuanced by the social situation of listeners*.
– ORIGIN late 18th cent.: from French, 'shade, subtlety', from *nuer* 'to shade', based on Latin *nubes* 'cloud'.

nub ▶ noun 1 (**the nub**) the crux or central point of a matter: *the nub of the problem lies elsewhere*.
2 a small lump or protuberance: *he pressed down on the two nubs on top of the phone*. ▪ a small chunk or nugget of metal or rock: *a nub of gold*.
– ORIGIN late 17th cent.: apparently a variant of dialect *knub* 'protuberance', from Middle Low German *knubbe, knobbe* 'knob'.

Nuba /ˈnuːbə/ ▶ noun (pl. **same** or **Nubas**) a member of a Nilotic people inhabiting southern Kordofan in Sudan.
▶ adjective relating to the Nuba.
– ORIGIN from Latin *Nubae* 'Nubians'.

nubbin /ˈnʌbɪn/ ▶ noun chiefly N. Amer. a small lump or residual part: *nubbins of bone or cartilage*.
– ORIGIN late 17th cent.: diminutive of NUB.

nubble ▶ noun a small knob or lump.
– DERIVATIVES **nubbled** adjective.
– ORIGIN early 19th cent.: diminutive of NUB; compare with KNOBBLE.

nubby (also **nubbly**) ▶ adjective chiefly US (of fabric) coarse or knobbly in texture: *nubby blue cotton*.
– ORIGIN early 19th cent. (as *nubbly*): derivative of NUBBLE.

Nubia /ˈnjuːbɪə/ an ancient region of southern Egypt and northern Sudan, including the Nile valley between Aswan and Khartoum and the surrounding area. Much of Nubia is now drowned by the waters of Lake Nasser, formed by the building of the two dams at Aswan. Nubians constitute an ethnic minority group in Egypt.

Nubian ▶ adjective relating to Nubia, its people, or their language.
▶ noun 1 a native or inhabitant of Nubia.
2 [mass noun] the Nilo-Saharan language spoken by the Nubians.
3 a goat of a short-haired breed with long pendant ears and long legs, originally from Africa.

nubile /ˈnjuːbʌɪl/ ▶ adjective 1 (of a girl or woman) sexually attractive: *he employed a procession of nubile young secretaries*.
2 (of a girl or young woman) sexually mature; old enough for marriage.
– DERIVATIVES **nubility** noun.
– ORIGIN mid 17th cent.: from Latin *nubilis* 'marriageable', from *nubere* 'cover or veil oneself for a bridegroom' (from *nubes* 'cloud').

nubuck /ˈnjuːbʌk/ ▶ noun [mass noun] cowhide leather which has been rubbed on the flesh side to give it a feel like that of suede.
– ORIGIN early 20th cent.: origin obscure, perhaps a respelling of NEW + BUCK[1].

nucellus /njuːˈsɛləs/ ▶ noun (pl. **nucelli** /-lʌɪ, -liː/) Botany the central part of an ovule, containing the embryo sac.
– DERIVATIVES **nucellar** adjective.
– ORIGIN late 19th cent.: modern Latin, apparently an irregular diminutive of NUCLEUS.

nuchal /ˈnjuːk(ə)l/ ▶ adjective Anatomy relating to the nape of the neck.
– ORIGIN mid 19th cent.: from obsolete *nucha* 'nape' (from medieval Latin *nucha* 'medulla oblongata', from Arabic *nukā'* 'spinal marrow') + -AL.

nuci- /ˈnjuːsi/ ▶ combining form of a nut or nuts: *nuciferous*.
– ORIGIN from Latin *nux, nuc-* 'nut'.

nuciferous /njuːˈsɪf(ə)rəs/ ▶ adjective Botany (of a tree or bush) bearing nuts.

nuclear ▶ adjective 1 relating to the nucleus of an atom. ▪ denoting, relating to, or powered by the energy released in nuclear fission or fusion: *nuclear submarines*. ▪ denoting, possessing, or involving weapons using nuclear energy: *a nuclear bomb | nuclear war*.
2 Biology relating to the nucleus of a cell: *nuclear DNA*.
– ORIGIN mid 19th cent.: from NUCLEUS + -AR[1].

nuclear club ▶ noun the nations which possess nuclear weapons.

nuclear energy ▶ noun [mass noun] the energy released during nuclear fission or fusion, especially when used to generate electricity.

nuclear family ▶ noun a couple and their dependent children, regarded as a basic social unit.

nuclear fission ▶ noun [mass noun] a nuclear reaction in which a heavy nucleus splits spontaneously or on impact with another particle, with the release of energy.

nuclear force ▶ noun Physics a strong attractive force between nucleons in the atomic nucleus that holds the nucleus together.

nuclear-free ▶ adjective (of a country or region) not having or allowing any nuclear weapons, materials, or power: *a nuclear-free zone*.

nuclear fuel ▶ noun a substance that will sustain a fission chain reaction so that it can be used as a source of nuclear energy.

nuclear fusion ▶ noun [mass noun] a nuclear reaction in which atomic nuclei of low atomic number fuse to form a heavier nucleus with the release of energy.

nuclear isomer ▶ noun another term for ISOMER (sense 2).

nuclear magnetic resonance (abbrev.: **NMR**) ▶ noun [mass noun] the absorption of electromagnetic radiation by a nucleus having a magnetic moment when in an external magnetic field, used mainly as an analytical technique and in diagnostic body imaging.

nuclear medicine ▶ noun [mass noun] the branch of medicine that deals with the use of radioactive substances in research, diagnosis, and treatment.

nuclear option ▶ noun the most drastic or extreme response possible to a particular situation: *extreme Eurosceptics championed the nuclear option of pulling out of Europe*.

nuclear physics ▶ plural noun [treated as sing.] the physics of atomic nuclei and their interactions, especially in the generation of nuclear energy.

nuclear power ▶ noun 1 [mass noun] electric or motive power generated by a nuclear reactor.
2 a country that has nuclear weapons.
– DERIVATIVES **nuclear-powered** adjective.

nuclear reactor ▶ noun see REACTOR.

nuclear threshold ▶ noun a point in a conflict at which nuclear weapons are or would be brought into use.

nuclear umbrella ▶ noun the supposed protection gained from an alliance with a country possessing nuclear weapons.

nuclear war ▶ noun a war in which nuclear weapons are used.

nuclear waste ▶ noun [mass noun] radioactive waste material, for example from the use or reprocessing of nuclear fuel.

nuclear winter ▶ noun a period of abnormal cold and darkness predicted to follow a nuclear war, caused by a layer of smoke and dust in the atmosphere blocking the sun's rays.

nuclease /ˈnjuːklɪeɪz/ ▶ noun Biochemistry an enzyme that cleaves the chains of nucleotides in nucleic acids into smaller units.

nucleate ▶ adjective /ˈnjuːklɪət/ chiefly Biology having a nucleus.
▶ verb /ˈnjuːklɪeɪt/ [no obj.] (usu. as adj. **nucleated**) form a nucleus. ■ form around a central area: *a nucleated village*.
– DERIVATIVES **nucleation** noun.

nuclei plural form of NUCLEUS.

nucleic acid /njuːˈkliːɪk, -ˈkleɪɪk/ ▶ noun Biochemistry a complex organic substance present in living cells, especially DNA or RNA, whose molecules consist of many nucleotides linked in a long chain.

nucleo- ▶ combining form representing NUCLEUS, NUCLEAR, or NUCLEIC ACID.

nucleocapsid /ˌnjuːklɪə(ʊ)ˈkapsɪd/ ▶ noun Biology the capsid of a virus with the enclosed nucleic acid.

nucleolus /ˌnjuːklɪˈəʊləs/ ▶ noun (pl. **nucleoli** /-lʌɪ/) Biology a small dense spherical structure in the nucleus of a cell during interphase.
– DERIVATIVES **nucleolar** adjective.
– ORIGIN mid 19th cent.: from late Latin, diminutive of Latin *nucleus* 'inner part, kernel' (see NUCLEUS).

nucleon /ˈnjuːklɪɒn/ ▶ noun Physics a proton or neutron.

nucleonics /ˌnjuːklɪˈɒnɪks/ ▶ plural noun [treated as sing.] the branch of science and technology concerned with atomic nuclei and nucleons, especially the exploitation of nuclear power.
– DERIVATIVES **nucleonic** adjective.
– ORIGIN 1940s: from NUCLEAR, on the pattern of *electronics*.

nucleophilic /ˌnjuːklɪə(ʊ)ˈfɪlɪk/ ▶ adjective Chemistry (of a molecule or group) having a tendency to donate electrons or react at electron-poor sites such as protons. Often contrasted with ELECTROPHILIC.
– DERIVATIVES **nucleophile** noun.

nucleoplasm ▶ noun [mass noun] Biology the substance of a cell nucleus, especially that not forming part of a nucleolus.

nucleoprotein ▶ noun Biochemistry a complex consisting of a nucleic acid bonded to a protein.

nucleoside ▶ noun Biochemistry a compound (e.g. adenosine or cytidine) consisting of a purine or pyrimidine base linked to a sugar.

nucleosome /ˈnjuːklɪə(ʊ)səʊm/ ▶ noun Biology a structural unit of a eukaryotic chromosome, consisting of a length of DNA coiled around a core of histones.
– DERIVATIVES **nucleosomal** adjective.

nucleosynthesis ▶ noun [mass noun] Astronomy the cosmic formation of atoms more complex than the hydrogen atom.
– DERIVATIVES **nucleosynthetic** adjective.

nucleotide ▶ noun Biochemistry a compound consisting of a nucleoside linked to a phosphate group. Nucleotides form the basic structural unit of nucleic acids such as DNA.

nucleus /ˈnjuːklɪəs/ ▶ noun (pl. **nuclei** /-lɪʌɪ/) **1** the central and most important part of an object, movement, or group, forming the basis for its activity and growth: *the nucleus of a British film-producing industry*.
2 Physics the positively charged central core of an atom that contains most of its mass.
3 Biology a dense organelle present in most eukaryotic cells, typically a single rounded structure bounded by a double membrane, containing the genetic material.
4 a discrete mass of grey matter in the central nervous system.
5 Astronomy the solid part of a comet's head.
– ORIGIN early 18th cent.: from Latin, literally 'kernel, inner part', diminutive of *nux*, *nuc-* 'nut'.

nuclide /ˈnjuːklʌɪd/ ▶ noun Physics a distinct kind of atom or nucleus characterized by a specific number of protons and neutrons.
– ORIGIN 1940s: from NUCLEUS + *-ide* (from Greek *eidos* 'form').

nuddy ▶ noun (in phrase **in the nuddy**) Brit. informal in the nude.
– ORIGIN 1950s: humorous alteration of NUDE.

nude ▶ adjective **1** wearing no clothes; naked: *a painting of a nude model*. ■ [attrib.] depicting or performed by naked people: *she won't do any nude scenes*.
2 of a pinkish-beige colour: *nude tights*.
▶ noun a naked human figure, typically as the subject of a painting, sculpture, or photograph: *a study of a kneeling nude*.
– PHRASES **in the nude** in an unclothed state: *I like to swim in the nude*.
– ORIGIN late Middle English (in the sense 'plain, explicit'): from Latin *nudus*. The current sense is first found in noun use in the early 18th cent.

nudge ▶ verb [with obj.] prod (someone) gently with one's elbow in order to attract attention: *people were nudging each other and pointing at me*. ■ touch or push (something) gently or gradually: *the canoe nudged a bank of reeds*. ■ coax or gently encourage (someone) to do something: *we have to **nudge** the politicians **in the right direction***. ■ approach (an age, figure, or level) very closely: *both men were nudging fifty*.
▶ noun a light touch or push: *he gave her shoulder a nudge* | figurative *she appreciated the nudge to her memory*.
– PHRASES **nudge nudge (wink wink)** used to draw attention to a sexual innuendo in the previous statement: *haven't seen much of the beach—we've been catching up on our sleep (nudge nudge)*. [a catchphrase from *Monty Python's Flying Circus*, a British television comedy programme.]
– DERIVATIVES **nudger** noun.
– ORIGIN late 17th cent. (as a verb): of unknown origin; compare with Norwegian dialect *nugga*, *nyggja* 'to push, rub'.

nudge bar ▶ noun another term for BULL BAR.

nudibranch /ˈnjuːdɪbraŋk/ ▶ noun Zoology a shell-less marine mollusc of the order Nudibranchia; a sea slug.

Nudibranchia /ˌnjuːdɪˈbraŋkɪə/ ▶ plural noun Zoology an order of shell-less marine molluscs which comprises the sea slugs. ● Order Nudibranchia, class Gastropoda.
– ORIGIN modern Latin (plural), from Latin *nudus* 'nude' + BRANCHIA.

nudie ▶ noun (pl. **nudies**) informal a publication, entertainment, or venue featuring nude performers or models: [as modifier] *a nudie calendar*.

nudist ▶ noun a person who engages in the practice of going naked wherever possible: [as modifier] *a nudist beach*.
– DERIVATIVES **nudism** noun.

nudity ▶ noun [mass noun] the state or fact of being naked: *scenes of full-frontal nudity*.

nudnik /ˈnʊdnɪk/ (also **nudnick**) ▶ noun N. Amer. informal a pestering, nagging, or irritating person; a bore.
– ORIGIN 1940s: Yiddish, from Russian *nudnyĭ* 'tedious'.

nuée ardente /ˌnjʊeɪ ɑːˈdɒ̃t/ ▶ noun Geology an incandescent cloud of gas, ash, and lava fragments ejected from a volcano, typically as part of a pyroclastic flow.
– ORIGIN French, literally 'burning cloud'.

Nuer /ˈnuːə/ ▶ noun (pl. **same** or **Nuers**) **1** a member of an African people of SE Sudan and Ethiopia, traditionally pastoralists and cattle-rearers.
2 [mass noun] the Nilotic language of the Nuer, with about 840,000 speakers.
▶ adjective relating to the Nuer or their language.
– ORIGIN the name in Dinka.

Nuevo León /ˌnweɪvəʊ leɪˈɒn/, Spanish /ˌnweβo leˈon/ a state of NE Mexico, on the border with the US; capital, Monterrey.

nuevo sol /ˌnweɪvəʊ ˈsɒl/, Spanish /ˌnweβo ˈsol/ ▶ noun another term for SOL³.
– ORIGIN Spanish, 'new sol'.

nuff ▶ determiner, pronoun, & adverb non-standard spelling of ENOUGH, representing informal speech: *The pen is mightier than the sword. Nuff said.* ■ [as determiner] black English much: *nuff respect goes out to Galliano*.

Nuffield /ˈnʌfiːld/, William Richard Morris, 1st Viscount (1877–1963), British motor manufacturer and philanthropist, who opened the first Morris automobile factory in Oxford in 1912. He endowed Nuffield College, Oxford (1937) and created the Nuffield Foundation (1943) for medical, social, and scientific research.

nuffin (also **nuffink**) ▶ pronoun, adjective, & adverb non-standard spelling of NOTHING, representing informal speech: *'There was nuffin in it,' Carrie retorted.*

nugacity /njuːˈgasɪti/ ▶ noun (pl. **nugacities**) [mass noun] rare triviality or frivolity. ■ [count noun] a trivial or frivolous thing or idea.
– ORIGIN late 16th cent.: from late Latin *nugacitas*, from Latin *nugax*, *nugac-* 'trifling, frivolous'.

nugatory /ˈnjuːgət(ə)ri, ˈnuː-/ ▶ adjective of no value or importance: *a nugatory and pointless observation*. ■ useless or futile: *the teacher shortages will render nugatory the hopes of implementing the new curriculum*.
– ORIGIN early 17th cent.: from Latin *nugatorius*, from *nugari* 'to trifle', from *nugae* 'jests'.

nugget ▶ noun a small lump of gold or other precious metal found ready-formed in the earth. ■ a small chunk or lump of another substance: *nuggets of meat*. ■ a valuable idea or fact: *nuggets of information*.
– ORIGIN mid 19th cent.: apparently from dialect *nug* 'lump', of unknown origin.

nuggety (also **nuggetty**) ▶ adjective chiefly Austral./NZ **1** occurring as nuggets: *nuggety gold*. ■ rich in nuggets: *nuggety gullies*.
2 (of a person) stocky or thickset.

nuisance ▶ noun a person or thing causing inconvenience or annoyance: *it's a nuisance having all those people clomping through the house* | *I hope you're not going to **make a nuisance of yourself***. ■ Law an act which is harmful or offensive to the public or a member of it and for which there is a legal remedy. See also PRIVATE NUISANCE, PUBLIC NUISANCE.
– ORIGIN late Middle English (in the sense 'injury, hurt'): from Old French, 'hurt', from the verb *nuire*, from Latin *nocere* 'to harm'.

nuisance call ▶ noun a telephone call made to threaten, annoy, or sexually harass its recipient.

nuisance grounds ▶ plural noun Canadian a rubbish dump.

nuisance value ▶ noun [mass noun] the significance of a person or thing arising from their capacity to cause inconvenience or annoyance.

nuit blanche /ˌnwiː ˈblɒ̃ʃ/ ▶ noun (pl. **nuits blanches** pronunc. **same**) a sleepless night.
– ORIGIN French, literally 'white night'.

Nuits-St-George /ˌnwiː sã ˈʒɔːʒ/, French /nɥi sɛ̃ ʒɔʀʒ/ ▶ noun [mass noun] a red burgundy wine produced in the district of Nuits-St-Georges, eastern France.

NUJ ▶ abbreviation (in the UK) National Union of Journalists.

nuke informal ▶ noun a nuclear weapon.
▶ verb [with obj.] attack or destroy with nuclear weapons. ■ chiefly N. Amer. cook or heat up (food) in a microwave oven: *I nuked a quick burger*.
– ORIGIN 1950s: abbreviation of NUCLEAR.

Nuku'alofa /ˌnuːkuːəˈləʊfə/ the capital of Tonga, situated on the island of Tongatapu; pop. 25,000 (est. 2007).

null ▶ adjective **1** [predic.] having no legal or binding force; invalid: *the establishment of a new interim government was declared **null and void***.
2 having or associated with the value zero. ■ Mathematics (of a set or matrix) having no elements, or only zeros as elements.
3 lacking distinctive qualities; having no positive substance or content: *his curiously null life*.
▶ noun **1** literary a zero.
2 a dummy letter in a cipher.
3 Electronics a condition of no signal. ■ a direction in which no electromagnetic radiation is detected or emitted.
▶ verb [with obj.] Electronics combine (a signal) with another in order to create a null; cancel out.
– ORIGIN late Middle English: from French *nul*, *nulle*, from Latin *nullus* 'none', from *ne* 'not' + *ullus* 'any'.

nullah /ˈnʌlə/ (also **nala** /ˈnɑːlə/) ▶ noun Indian a watercourse, riverbed, or ravine.
– ORIGIN late 18th cent.: from Hindi *nālā*.

nulla-nulla /ˈnʌlənʌlə/ (also **nulla**) ▶ noun a hardwood club used as a weapon by Australian Aborigines.
– ORIGIN from Dharuk *ngalla-ngalla*.

N

Nullarbor Plain /ˈnʌləbɔː/ a vast arid plain in SW Australia, stretching inland from the Great Australian Bight. It contains no surface water, has sparse vegetation, and is almost uninhabited.
– ORIGIN *Nullarbor* from Latin *nullus arbor* 'no tree'.

null character ▸ **noun** Computing a character denoting nothing, usually represented by a binary zero.

null hypothesis ▸ **noun** (in a statistical test) the hypothesis that there is no significant difference between specified populations, any observed difference being due to sampling or experimental error.

nullifidian /ˌnʌlɪˈfɪdɪən/ rare ▸ **noun** a person having no faith or religious belief.
▸ **adjective** having no faith or religious belief.
– ORIGIN mid 16th cent.: from medieval Latin *nullifidius* (from *nullus* 'no, none' + *fides* 'faith') + -AN.

nullify /ˈnʌlɪfʌɪ/ ▸ **verb** (**nullifies, nullifying, nullified**) [with obj.] make legally null and void; invalidate: *judges were unwilling to nullify government decisions.* ■ make of no use or value; cancel out: *insulin can block the release of the hormone and thereby nullify the effects of training.*
– DERIVATIVES **nullification** noun, **nullifier** noun.

null instrument (also **null indicator**) ▸ **noun** an instrument used to measure an electrical quantity by adjusting known quantities in the circuit until a reading of zero is obtained.

nullipara /nʌˈlɪp(ə)rə/ ▸ **noun** (pl. **nulliparae** /nʌˈlɪp(ə)riː/) Medicine & Zoology a woman (or female animal) that has never given birth. Compare with PRIMIPARA.
– DERIVATIVES **nulliparous** adjective.
– ORIGIN late 19th cent.: modern Latin, from Latin *nullus* 'none' + *-para* (feminine of *-parus*), from *parere* 'bear children'.

nullity ▸ **noun** (pl. **nullities**) **1** Law an act or thing that is legally void. ■ [mass noun] the state of being legally void or invalid, especially with reference to a marriage.
2 a thing of no importance or worth. ■ [mass noun] nothingness.
– ORIGIN mid 16th cent.: from French *nullité*, from medieval Latin *nullitas*, from Latin *nullus* 'none'.

null link ▸ **noun** Computing a reference incorporated into the last item in a list to indicate there are no further items in the list.

NUM ▸ **abbreviation** (in the UK) National Union of Mineworkers.

Num. ▸ **abbreviation** Numbers (in biblical references).

Numa Pompilius /ˌnjuːmə pɒmˈpɪlɪəs/ the legendary second king of Rome, successor to Romulus, revered by the ancient Romans as the founder of nearly all their religious institutions.

numb ▸ **adjective** (of a part of the body) deprived of the power of physical sensation: *my feet were numb with cold.* ■ unable to think, feel, or respond normally: *the tragic events left us shocked and numb.*
▸ **verb** [with obj.] deprive of feeling or responsiveness: *the cold had numbed her senses.* ■ cause (a sensation) to be felt less intensely; deaden: *vodka might numb the pain in my hand.*
– DERIVATIVES **numbly** adverb.
– ORIGIN late Middle English *nome(n)*, past participle of obsolete *nim* 'take'.

numbat /ˈnʌmbat/ ▸ **noun** a small termite-eating Australian marsupial with a black-and-white striped back and a bushy tail. Also called BANDED ANTEATER.
● *Myrmecobius fasciatus*, family Myrmecobiidae.
– ORIGIN early 20th cent.: from Nyungar.

number ▸ **noun 1** an arithmetical value, expressed by a word, symbol, or figure, representing a particular quantity and used in counting and making calculations: *think of a number from one to ten and multiply it by three | even numbers.* ■ a figure or group of figures used to identify someone or something: *she picked up the phone and dialled his home number.* ■ (**numbers**) dated arithmetic: *the boy was adept at numbers.*
2 a quantity or amount: *the company is seeking to increase the number of women on its staff | the exhibition attracted vast numbers of visitors.* ■ (**a number of**) several: *we have discussed the matter on a number of occasions.* ■ a group or company of people: *there were some distinguished names **among our number**.* ■ (**numbers**) a large quantity or amount, often in contrast to a smaller one; numerical preponderance: *the **weight of numbers** turned the battle against them.*
3 chiefly Brit. a single issue of a magazine: *the October number of 'Travel'.* ■ a song, dance, piece of music, etc., especially one of several in a performance: *they go from one melodious number to another.* ■ [usu. with adj. or noun modifier] informal an item of clothing of a particular type, regarded with approval or admiration: *Yvonne was wearing a little black number.*
4 [mass noun] a grammatical classification of words that consists typically of singular and plural, and, in Greek and certain other languages, dual.
▸ **verb** [with obj.] **1** amount to (a specified figure or quantity); comprise: *the demonstrators numbered more than 5,000.*
2 mark with a number or assign a number to, typically to indicate position in a series: *each document was numbered consecutively.* ■ count: *strategies like ours can be numbered on the fingers of one hand.*
3 include or classify as a member of a group: *the orchestra **numbers** Brahms **among** its past conductors.*
– PHRASES **any number of** any particular whole quantity of: *the game can involve any number of players.* ■ a large and unlimited quantity or amount of: *the results can be read any number of ways.* **by numbers** following simple instructions identified or as if identified by numbers: *painting by numbers.* **someone's** (or **something's**) **days are numbered** someone or something will not survive or remain in a position of power or advantage for much longer: *my days as director were numbered.* **do a number on** N. Amer. informal treat someone badly, typically by deceiving, humiliating, or criticizing them in a calculated way. **have someone's number** informal understand a person's real motives or character and thereby gain some advantage. **have someone's number on it** informal (of a bomb, bullet, or other missile) destined to find a specified person as its target. **someone's number is up** informal the time has come when someone is doomed to die or suffer some other disaster or setback. [with reference to a lottery number or a number by which one may be identified.] **without number** too many to count: *I began to write to you times without number.*
– ORIGIN Middle English: from Old French *nombre* (noun), *nombrer* (verb), from Latin *numerus*.

> **USAGE** The construction **the number of** + plural noun is used with a singular verb (as in ***the number of people** affected **remains** small*). Thus it is the noun **number** rather than the noun **people** which is taken to agree with the verb (and which is therefore functioning as the **head noun**). By contrast, the apparently similar construction **a number of** + plural noun is used with a plural verb (as in ***a number of people remain** to be contacted*). In this case it is the noun **people** which acts as the head noun and with which the verb agrees. In the latter case, **a number of** works as if it were a single word, such as **some** or **several**. See also USAGE at LOT.

number cruncher ▸ **noun** informal **1** a computer or program capable of performing rapid calculations with large amounts of data.
2 often derogatory a statistician, accountant, or other person whose job involves dealing with large amounts of numerical data.
– DERIVATIVES **number crunching** noun.

numbered account ▸ **noun** a bank account, especially in a Swiss bank, identified only by a number and not bearing the owner's name.

number eight ▸ **noun 1** (in rugby union) the forward at the back of the scrum.
2 [mass noun] NZ a wire of 4 mm gauge, used especially for fences.

numberless ▸ **adjective** too many to be counted; innumerable.

number line ▸ **noun** Mathematics a line on which numbers are marked at intervals, used to illustrate simple numerical operations.

number one informal ▸ **noun 1** a person or thing that is foremost or most important in an activity or area: *businesses that were number one in their markets.* ■ a record or book in a particular category that has sold the most copies in a particular time period: [as modifier] *the band's first number-one album.*
2 oneself: *you must **look after number one**.*
3 used euphemistically to refer to urine.
4 a first lieutenant in the navy.
▸ **adjective** most important or prevalent; foremost: *a number-one priority.*
– PHRASES **number one, number two, etc.** the shortest, or next shortest, etc., men's cropped haircut produced with electric hair clippers.

number opera ▸ **noun** an opera in which arias and other sections are clearly separable.

number plate ▸ **noun** Brit. a sign affixed to the front and rear of a vehicle displaying its registration number.

Numbers the fourth book of the Bible, relating the experiences of the Israelites in the wilderness after Moses led them out of Egypt.
– ORIGIN named in English from the book's accounts of a census; the title in Hebrew means 'in the wilderness'.

numbers game ▸ **noun 1** often derogatory the use or manipulation of statistics or figures, especially in support of an argument: *MPs were today playing the numbers game as the vote drew closer.*
2 (also **numbers pool** or **numbers racket**) N. Amer. a lottery based on the occurrence of unpredictable numbers in the results of races, a lottery, etc.

number sign ▸ **noun** N. Amer. the sign #, used to introduce a number (as in *question #2*).

Number Ten 10 Downing Street, the official London home of the British Prime Minister.

number theory ▸ **noun** [mass noun] the branch of mathematics that deals with the properties and relationships of numbers, especially the positive integers.

number two ▸ **noun** informal **1** a second in command: *he is currently number two at the Department of Employment.* ■ a person or thing ranked second in ability or size.
2 used euphemistically to refer to faeces.

number work ▸ **noun** [mass noun] simple arithmetic.

numbfish ▸ **noun** (pl. **same** or **numbfishes**) an electric ray, especially a heavy-bodied Australian ray that lies partly buried on sand flats and estuaries and can give a severe electric shock. ● Family Torpedinidae: many species, in particular *Hypnos monopterygium*.

numbing ▸ **adjective** depriving one of feeling or responsiveness: *the numbing effect of alcohol | a numbing defeat.*
– DERIVATIVES **numbingly** adverb.

numbles (also **umbles**) ▸ **plural noun** archaic the entrails of an animal, especially a deer, as used for food.
– ORIGIN Middle English (denoting the back and loins of a deer): from Old French, from Latin *lumbulus*, diminutive of *lumbus* 'loin'.

numbness ▸ **noun** [mass noun] the state of being numb: *tingling and numbness in the left arm.*

numbskull (also **numskull**) ▸ **noun** informal a stupid or foolish person.

numdah /ˈnʌmdə/ ▸ **noun** (in South Asia and the Middle East) an embroidered rug or carpet made of felt or coarse woollen cloth. ■ [mass noun] cloth of this type.
– ORIGIN from Urdu *namdā*, from Persian *namad* 'carpet'.

numen /ˈnjuːmən/ ▸ **noun** (pl. **numina** /-mɪnə/) the spirit or divine power presiding over a thing or place.
– ORIGIN early 17th cent.: from Latin.

numerable ▸ **adjective** able to be counted.
– ORIGIN mid 16th cent.: from Latin *numerabilis*, from *numerare* 'to number'.

numeracy ▸ **noun** [mass noun] the ability to understand and work with numbers.

numeraire /ˈnjuːmərɛː/ ▸ **noun** Economics an item or commodity acting as a measure of value or as a standard for currency exchange.
– ORIGIN 1960s: from French *numéraire*, from late Latin *numerarius*, from Latin *numerus* 'a number'.

numeral ▸ **noun** a figure, symbol, or group of figures or symbols denoting a number. ■ a word expressing a number.
▸ **adjective** of or denoting a number.
– ORIGIN late Middle English (as an adjective): from late Latin *numeralis*, adjective from Latin *numerus* 'a number' (see NUMBER).

numerate /ˈnjuːm(ə)rət/ ▸ **adjective** having a good basic knowledge of arithmetic; able to understand and work with numbers.
– ORIGIN 1950s: from Latin *numerus* 'a number', on the pattern of *literate*.

numeration ▸ **noun** [mass noun] the action or process of calculating or assigning a number to something. ■ [count noun] a method or process of numbering, counting, or computing.
– ORIGIN late Middle English: from Latin *numeratio(n-)* 'payment' (in late Latin 'numbering'), from the verb *numerare* 'to number'.

numerator ▶ noun the number above the line in a vulgar fraction showing how many of the parts indicated by the denominator are taken, for example, 2 in $^2/_3$.

numerical ▶ adjective relating to or expressed as a number or numbers: *the lists are in numerical order.*
– DERIVATIVES **numeric** adjective, **numerically** adverb.
– ORIGIN early 17th cent.: from medieval Latin *numericus* (from Latin *numerus* 'a number') + **-AL**.

numerical analysis ▶ noun [mass noun] the branch of mathematics that deals with the development and use of numerical methods for solving problems.

numerical control ▶ noun [mass noun] Engineering computer control of machine tools, where operations are directed by numerical data.

numerology /ˌnjuːməˈrɒlədʒi/ ▶ noun [mass noun] the branch of knowledge that deals with the occult significance of numbers.
– DERIVATIVES **numerological** adjective, **numerologist** noun.
– ORIGIN early 20th cent.: from Latin *numerus* 'a number' + **-LOGY**.

numero uno /ˌnjuːmərəʊ ˈuːnəʊ/ ▶ noun (pl. **numero unos**) informal the best or most important person or thing.
– ORIGIN Italian, literally 'number one'.

numerous ▶ adjective great in number; many: *she had complained to the council on numerous occasions.* ■ consisting of many members: *the orchestra and chorus were numerous.*
– DERIVATIVES **numerously** adverb, **numerousness** noun.
– ORIGIN late Middle English: from Latin *numerosus*, from *numerus* 'a number'.

numerus clausus /ˌnjuːmərəs ˈklaʊsəs/ ▶ noun a fixed maximum number of entrants admissible to an academic institution.
– ORIGIN Latin, literally 'closed number'.

Numidia /njuːˈmɪdɪə/ an ancient kingdom, later a Roman province, situated in North Africa in an area north of the Sahara corresponding roughly to present-day Algeria.
– DERIVATIVES **Numidian** adjective & noun.

numina plural form of **NUMEN**.

numinous /ˈnjuːmɪnəs/ ▶ adjective having a strong religious or spiritual quality; indicating or suggesting the presence of a divinity: *the strange, numinous beauty of this ancient landmark.*
– DERIVATIVES **numinosity** noun.
– ORIGIN mid 17th cent.: from Latin *numen, numin-* 'divine will' + **-OUS**.

numismatic /ˌnjuːmɪzˈmatɪk/ ▶ adjective relating to or consisting of coins or medals.
– ORIGIN late 18th cent.: from French *numismatique*, via Latin from Greek *nomisma, nomismat-* 'current coin', from *nomizein* 'use currently'.

numismatics ▶ plural noun [usu. treated as sing.] the study or collection of coins, banknotes, and medals.
– DERIVATIVES **numismatist** /njuːˈmɪzmətɪst/ noun.

numismatology /ˌnjuːmɪzməˈtɒlədʒi, njuːˌmɪz-/ ▶ noun [mass noun] numismatics.

nummular /ˈnʌmjʊlə/ ▶ adjective resembling a coin or coins.
– ORIGIN mid 18th cent.: from Latin *nummulus* (diminutive of *nummus* 'coin') + **-AR**[1].

nummulite /ˈnʌmjʊlʌɪt/ ▶ noun Palaeontology the flat disc-shaped calcareous shell of a foraminiferan, found commonly as a fossil up to 8 cm across in marine Tertiary deposits. ● Family Nummulitidae, order Foraminiferida: several genera, including *Nummulites*.
– ORIGIN early 19th cent.: from Latin *nummulus* (diminutive of *nummus* 'coin') + **-ITE**[1].

nummy ▶ adjective N. Amer. informal (of food) delicious.
– ORIGIN early 20th cent.: variant of **YUMMY**.

numnah /ˈnʌmnə/ ▶ noun a pad, typically made of sheepskin or foam, which is placed under a saddle.
– ORIGIN mid 19th cent.: from Urdu *namdā*.

num-num /nʊmˈnʊm/ ▶ noun S. African a white-flowered spiny southern African shrub or small tree which yields edible fruit. ● Genus *Carissa*, family Apocynaceae.
– ORIGIN early 19th cent.: from Afrikaans *noem-noem*, perhaps from Nama.

numpty ▶ noun (pl. **numpties**) Scottish informal a stupid or ineffectual person.
– ORIGIN 1980s: from obsolete *numps* 'a stupid person', of unknown origin.

numskull ▶ noun variant spelling of **NUMBSKULL**.

nun ▶ noun **1** a member of a religious community of women, typically one living under vows of poverty, chastity, and obedience.
2 any of a number of birds whose plumage resembles a nun's habit, especially an Asian mannikin. ■ a pigeon of a breed with a crest on its neck.
– DERIVATIVES **nunlike** adjective, **nunnish** adjective.
– ORIGIN Old English *nonne*, from ecclesiastical Latin *nonna*, feminine of *nonnus* 'monk', reinforced by Old French *nonne*.

nunatak /ˈnʌnətak/ ▶ noun an isolated peak of rock projecting above a surface of inland ice or snow.
– ORIGIN late 19th cent.: from Eskimo *nunataq*.

Nunavik /ˈnʊnəvɪk/ the Arctic region of northern Canada.
– ORIGIN Inuit, literally 'great land'.

Nunavummiut /ˌnʊnəˈvʊmɪət/ ▶ plural noun the people inhabiting the territory of Nunavut.
– ORIGIN from **NUNAVUT** and Inuktitut *-miut* 'people'.

Nunavut /ˈnʊnəvut/ a territory of northern Canada, created in 1999 as an Inuit territory from a part of Northwest Territories; capital, Iqaluit.
– ORIGIN Inuit, literally 'our land'.

nunbird ▶ noun a tropical American puffbird with mainly dark grey or blackish plumage. ● Genus *Monasa* (and *Hapaloptila*), family Bucconidae: five species.

nun buoy ▶ noun US a buoy which is circular in the middle and tapering to each end.
– ORIGIN early 18th cent.: from obsolete *nun* 'child's top' and **BUOY**.

Nunc Dimittis /ˌnʌŋk dɪˈmɪtɪs/ ▶ noun the Song of Simeon (Luke 2:29–32) used as a canticle in Christian liturgy, especially at compline and evensong.
– ORIGIN Latin, the opening words of the canticle, '(Lord) now you let (your servant) depart'.

nunchaku /nʌnˈtʃakuː/ (also **nunchuk** /ˈnʌntʃʌk/) ▶ noun (pl. **same** or **nunchakus**) a Japanese martial arts weapon consisting of two hardwood sticks joined together by a chain, rope, or thong.
– ORIGIN Japanese, from Okinawa dialect.

nunciature /ˈnʌnsɪəˌtjʊə, -ʃə-/ ▶ noun the office or tenure of a nuncio in the Roman Catholic Church.
– ORIGIN early 17th cent.: from Italian *nunziatura*, from *nunzio* 'message-bearer' (see **NUNCIO**).

nuncio /ˈnʌnsɪəʊ, ˈnʌnʃɪəʊ/ ▶ noun (pl. **nuncios**) (in the Roman Catholic Church) a papal ambassador to a foreign court or government.
– ORIGIN early 16th cent.: from Italian, from Latin *nuntius* 'messenger'.

nuncle ▶ noun archaic or dialect a person's uncle.
– ORIGIN late 16th cent.: by wrong division of *mine uncle*.

nuncupative /ˈnʌŋkjʊˌpətɪv/ ▶ adjective Law (of a will or testament) declared orally as opposed to in writing, especially by a mortally wounded soldier or sailor.
– ORIGIN mid 16th cent.: from late Latin *nuncupativus*, from Latin *nuncupat-* 'named, declared', from the verb *nuncupare*.

Nuneaton /nʌˈniːt(ə)n/ a town in north Warwickshire in central England, near Coventry; pop. 74,600 (est. 2009).

nunnery ▶ noun (pl. **nunneries**) a building or group of buildings in which nuns live as a religious community; a convent.

nunu /ˈnuːnuː/ (also **noonoo**) ▶ noun (pl. **nunus**) S. African informal an insect, spider, worm, or similar small creature.
– ORIGIN from Zulu *inunu* 'horrible object or animal'.

nuoc mam /nwɒk ˈmɑːm/ ▶ noun [mass noun] a spicy Vietnamese fish sauce.
– ORIGIN Vietnamese.

Nupe /ˈnuːpeɪ/ ▶ noun (pl. **same** or **Nupes**) **1** a member of a people of central Nigeria.
2 [mass noun] the Benue-Congo language of the Nupe, with over 1 million speakers.
▶ adjective relating to the Nupe or their language.
– ORIGIN the name of a former kingdom at the confluence of the Niger and Benue Rivers in West Africa.

nuptial /ˈnʌpʃ(ə)l/ ▶ adjective relating to marriage or weddings: *moments of nuptial bliss.* ■ Zoology denoting the characteristic breeding behaviour, coloration, or structures of some animals: *nuptial plumage.*
▶ noun (**nuptials**) a wedding: *the forthcoming nuptials between Richard and Jocelyn.*
– ORIGIN late 15th cent.: from Old French, or from Latin *nuptialis*, from *nuptiae* 'wedding', from *nubere* 'to wed'; related to **NUBILE**.

nuptiality ▶ noun [mass noun] the frequency or incidence of marriage within a population.

nuptial mass ▶ noun (in the Roman Catholic Church) a mass celebrated as part of a wedding ceremony.

nuptial pad ▶ noun Zoology a pigmented swelling on the inner side of the hand in some male frogs and toads, assisting grip during copulation.

nuragh /ˈnʊərag/ (also **nuraghe** /-gi/) ▶ noun (pl. **nuraghi** /-gi/) a type of large tower-shaped stone structure found in Sardinia, dating from the Bronze and Iron Ages.
– DERIVATIVES **nuraghic** adjective.
– ORIGIN Sardinian.

nurd ▶ noun variant spelling of **NERD**.

Nuremberg /ˈnjʊərəmbəːg/ a city in southern Germany, in Bavaria; pop. 500,900 (est. 2006). In the 1930s the Nazi Party congresses and annual rallies were held in the city and in 1945–6 it was the scene of the Nuremberg war trials, in which Nazi war criminals were tried by international military tribunal. German name **NÜRNBERG**.

Nureyev /nəˈreɪɛf, ˈnjʊərɪɛf/, Rudolf (1939–93), Russian-born ballet dancer and choreographer. He defected to the West in 1961, joining the Royal Ballet in London, where he began his noted partnership with Margot Fonteyn. He became a naturalized Austrian citizen in 1982.

Nürnberg /ˈnʏrnbɛrk/ German name for **NUREMBERG**.

Nurofen /ˈnjʊərəfɛn/ ▶ noun trademark for **IBUPROFEN**.

nurse[1] ▶ noun **1** a person trained to care for the sick or infirm, especially in a hospital. ■ dated a person employed or trained to take charge of young children: *her mother's old nurse.* ■ archaic a wet nurse.
2 Entomology a worker bee, ant, or other social insect, caring for a young brood. ■ [often as modifier] Forestry a tree or crop planted as a shelter to others.
▶ verb [with obj.] **1** give medical and other attention to (a sick person): *he was gradually nursed back to health.* ■ [no obj.] work as a nurse: *she nursed at the hospital for thirty years.* ■ try to cure or alleviate (an injury, injured part, or illness) by treating it carefully and protectively: *he has been nursing a cold* | figurative *he nursed his hurt pride.* ■ harbour (a belief or feeling), especially for a long time: *he still nursed a secret desire to try and make amends.* ■ take special care of, especially to promote development or well-being: *our political unity needs to be protected and nursed.*
2 feed (a baby) at the breast: (as adj. **nursing**) *nursing mothers.* ■ [no obj.] be fed at the breast: *the baby snuffled as he nursed.* ■ (**be nursed in**) dated be brought up in (a specified condition): *he was nursed in the lap of plenty.*
3 hold closely and carefully or caressingly: *he nursed his small case on his lap.* ■ hold (a drink), sipping it occasionally: *I nursed a double brandy.*
4 Billiards & Snooker try to play strokes which keep (the balls) close together.
– ORIGIN late Middle English: contraction of earlier *nourice*, from Old French, from late Latin *nutricia*, feminine of Latin *nutricius* '(person) that nourishes', from *nutrix, nutric-* 'nurse', from *nutrire* 'nourish'. The verb was originally a contraction of **NOURISH**, altered under the influence of the noun.

nurse[2] (also **grey nurse**) ▶ noun a greyish Australian shark of shallow inshore waters. Compare with **NURSE SHARK, NURSE HOUND**. ● *Odontaspis arenarius*, family Odontaspididae.
– ORIGIN late 15th cent.: originally as *nusse*, perhaps derived (by wrong division) from *an huss* (see **HUSS**).

nurse hound ▶ noun a large spotted dogfish of the NE Atlantic, which is caught for food. Also called **BULL HUSS** in Britain. ● *Scyliorhinus stellaris*, family Scyliorhinidae.

nurseling ▶ noun archaic spelling of **NURSLING**.

nursemaid ▶ noun dated a woman or girl employed to look after a young child or children.
▶ verb [with obj.] look after or be overprotective towards.

nurse practitioner ▶ noun a nurse who is qualified to treat certain medical conditions without the direct supervision of a doctor.

nursery ▶ noun (pl. **nurseries**) **1** a room in a house for the special use of young children. ■ (also **day nursery**) a place where young children are cared for during the working day; a nursery school. ■ an institution or environment in which certain types of people or qualities are fostered or bred: *that nursery of traitors.* ■ a place or natural habitat which breeds or supports animals. ■ [as modifier] denoting a race for two-year-old horses: *a six-furlong nursery handicap.*

N

2 a place where young plants and trees are grown for sale or for planting elsewhere.
– ORIGIN late Middle English: from Old French *nourice* 'nurse' (see **NURSE**[1]) + **-ERY**.

nursery cannon ▶ **noun** Billiards a cannon which keeps the balls close together.

nursery class ▶ **noun** a school class for the education of children mainly between the ages of three and five.

nurseryman ▶ **noun** (pl. **nurserymen**) a worker in or owner of a plant or tree nursery.

nursery nurse ▶ **noun** Brit. a person trained to look after young children and babies in a nursery or crèche.

nursery rhyme ▶ **noun** a simple traditional song or poem for children.

nursery school ▶ **noun** a school for young children, mainly between the ages of three and five.

nursery slope ▶ **noun** Skiing, Brit. a gentle slope suitable for beginners.

nurse shark ▶ **noun** a shark with barbels on the snout. ● Three species in the family Orectolobidae (or Ginglymostomatidae), in particular *Ginglymostoma cirratum*, a slow-swimming brownish shark of warm Atlantic waters.

nursey (also **nursie**) ▶ **noun** informal a nurse.

nursing ▶ **noun** [mass noun] the profession or practice of providing care for the sick and infirm.

nursing home ▶ **noun** a small private institution providing residential accommodation with health care, especially for elderly people.

nursing officer ▶ **noun** Brit. a senior nurse with administrative responsibility.

nursling ▶ **noun** a baby that is being breastfed.

nurturance ▶ **noun** [mass noun] emotional and physical nourishment and care given to someone. ■ the ability to provide such care.
– DERIVATIVES **nurturant** adjective.

nurture /ˈnəːtʃə/ ▶ **verb** [with obj.] care for and protect (someone or something) while they are growing: *Jarrett was nurtured by his parents in a close-knit family.* ■ help or encourage the development of: *my father nurtured my love of art.* ■ cherish (a hope, belief, or ambition): *for a long time she had nurtured the dream of buying a shop.*
▶ **noun** [mass noun] the action or process of nurturing someone or something: *the nurture of children.* ■ upbringing, education, and environment, contrasted with inborn characteristics as an influence on or determinant of personality. Often contrasted with **NATURE**.
– DERIVATIVES **nurturer** noun.
– ORIGIN Middle English: from Old French *noureture* 'nourishment', based on Latin *nutrire* 'feed, cherish'.

N

NUS ▶ **abbreviation** (in the UK) National Union of Students.

Nusselt number /ˈnʊs(ə)lt/ ▶ **noun** Physics a dimensionless parameter used in calculations of heat transfer between a moving fluid and a solid body. ● It is equal to *hD*/*k*, where *h* is the rate of heat loss per unit area per degree difference in temperature between the body and its surroundings, *D* is a characteristic length of the body, and *k* is the thermal conductivity of the fluid.
– ORIGIN 1930s: named after Ernst K. W. *Nusselt* (1882–1957), German engineer.

NUT ▶ **abbreviation** (in the UK) National Union of Teachers.

Nut /nʊt/ Egyptian Mythology the sky goddess, thought to swallow the sun at night and give birth to it in the morning.

nut ▶ **noun 1** a fruit consisting of a hard or tough shell around an edible kernel. ■ the hard kernel of such a fruit. ■ (usu. **nuts**) a small lump of something hard or solid, especially coal.
2 a small flat piece of metal or other material, typically square or hexagonal, with a threaded hole through it for screwing on to a bolt as a fastener. ■ the part at the lower end of the bow of a violin or similar instrument, with a screw for adjusting the tension of the hair.
3 informal a crazy or eccentric person. ■ [with adj. or noun modifier] a person who is excessively interested in or enthusiastic about a specified thing: *a football nut.*
4 informal a person's head.
5 (**nuts**) vulgar slang a man's testicles.
6 the fixed ridge on the neck of a stringed instrument over which the strings pass.
▶ **verb** (**nuts, nutting, nutted**) **1** [with obj.] Brit. informal butt (someone) with one's head.
2 [no obj.] (usu. as noun **nutting**) archaic gather nuts.
– PHRASES **do one's nut** Brit. informal become extremely angry or agitated. **nuts and bolts** informal the basic practical details: *the nuts and bolts of making a movie.* **off one's nut** informal out of one's mind; crazy. **a tough** (or **hard**) **nut** informal someone who is difficult to deal with; a formidable person. **a tough** (or **hard**) **nut to crack** informal a difficult problem or an opponent that is hard to beat. **use** (or **take**) **a sledgehammer to crack a nut** informal use disproportionately drastic measures to deal with a simple problem.
– DERIVATIVES **nut-like** adjective.
– ORIGIN Old English *hnutu*, of Germanic origin; related to Dutch *noot* and German *Nuss*.

nutation /njuːˈteɪʃ(ə)n/ ▶ **noun** [mass noun] **1** a periodic variation in the inclination of the axis of a rotating object. ■ Astronomy a periodic oscillation of the earth's axis which causes the precession of the poles to follow a wavy rather than a circular path.
2 Botany the circular swaying movement of the tip of a growing shoot.
– ORIGIN early 17th cent. (denoting nodding of the head): from Latin *nutatio(n-)*, from *nutare* 'to nod'.

nut-brown ▶ **adjective** of a rich dark brown colour: *a nut-brown face.*

nutcase ▶ **noun** informal a mad or foolish person.

nutcracker ▶ **noun 1** (usu. **nutcrackers**) a device for cracking nuts. ■ [as modifier] denoting a person's nose and chin with the points near each other, either naturally or as a result of the loss of teeth.
2 a crow that feeds on the seeds of conifers, found widely in Eurasia and in western North America. ● Genus *Nucifraga*, family Corvidae: the Eurasian **spotted nutcracker** (*N. caryocatactes*), with white-spotted brown plumage, and the North American **Clark's nutcracker** (*N. columbiana*), with pale grey and black plumage.

Nutcracker man ▶ **noun** the nickname of a fossil hominid with massive jaws and molar teeth, especially the original specimen found near Olduvai Gorge in 1959. ● *Australopithecus* (or *Zinjanthropus*) *boisei*, family Hominidae. See **AUSTRALOPITHECUS, PARANTHROPUS**.

nut cutlet ▶ **noun** Brit. a cutlet-shaped savoury cake made of chopped nuts, breadcrumbs, and other ingredients.

nutgall ▶ **noun 1** another term for **ALEPPO GALL**.
2 a gall which forms inside the buds of hazel bushes in response to the presence of mites, causing the buds to enlarge greatly. ● The mite is *Phytoptus avellanae*, family Eriophyidae.

nuthatch ▶ **noun** a small songbird with a stiffened tail, which climbs up and down tree trunks and feeds on nuts, seeds, and insects. ● Family Sittidae and genus *Sitta*: several species, including the widespread (**Eurasian**) **nuthatch** (*S. europaea*), with a grey back, black eyestripe, and white or buff underparts.
– ORIGIN Middle English: from **NUT** + obsolete *hatch* (related to **HACK**[1]), from the bird's habit of hacking with the beak at nuts wedged in a crevice.

nuthin ▶ **pronoun, adjective, & adverb** informal non-standard spelling of **NOTHING**, used to represent informal speech.

nuthouse ▶ **noun** informal a home or hospital for people with mental illnesses.

nutjob ▶ **noun** informal, chiefly N. Amer. a mad or crazy person.

nutlet ▶ **noun** Botany a small nut, especially an achene.

nut loaf ▶ **noun** a baked vegetarian dish made from ground or chopped nuts, vegetables, and herbs.

nutmeg ▶ **noun 1** the hard, aromatic, almost spherical seed of a tropical tree. ■ [mass noun] this seed grated and used as a spice.
2 the evergreen tree that bears nutmegs, native to the Moluccas. ● *Myristica fragrans*, family Myristicaceae.
3 Soccer, informal an instance of playing the ball through an opponent's legs. [extended use of obsolete *nutmegs* 'testicles'.]
▶ **verb** (**nutmegs, nutmegging, nutmegged**) [with obj.] Soccer, informal play the ball through the legs of (an opponent).
– ORIGIN late Middle English *notemuge*, partial translation of Old French *nois muguede*, based on Latin *nux* 'nut' + late Latin *muscus* 'musk'.

Nutmeg State informal name for **CONNECTICUT**.

nut oil ▶ **noun** [mass noun] oil obtained from the kernels of nuts and used in cooking and to make paints and varnishes.

nutraceutical /ˌnjuːtrəˈsuːtɪk(ə)l, -ˈsjuː-/ ▶ **noun** another term for **FUNCTIONAL FOOD**.
– ORIGIN 1990s: from Latin *nutrire* 'nourish' + **PHARMACEUTICAL**.

nutria /ˈnjuːtrɪə/ ▶ **noun** [mass noun] the skin or fur of the coypu.
– ORIGIN early 19th cent.: from Spanish, literally 'otter'.

nutrient ▶ **noun** a substance that provides nourishment essential for the maintenance of life and for growth: *fish is a source of many important nutrients, including protein, vitamins, and minerals.*
– ORIGIN mid 17th cent.: from Latin *nutrient-* 'nourishing', from the verb *nutrire*.

nutriment ▶ **noun** [mass noun] nourishment; sustenance.
– ORIGIN late Middle English: from Latin *nutrimentum*, from *nutrire* 'feed, nourish'.

nutrition ▶ **noun** [mass noun] the process of providing or obtaining the food necessary for health and growth: *a guide to good nutrition.* ■ food or nourishment: *a feeding tube gives her nutrition and water.* ■ the branch of science that deals with nutrients and nutrition, particularly in humans.
– DERIVATIVES **nutritional** adjective, **nutritionally** adverb.
– ORIGIN late Middle English: from late Latin *nutritio(n-)*, from *nutrire* 'feed, nourish'.

nutritionist (also **nutritionalist**) ▶ **noun** a person who studies or is an expert in nutrition.

nutritious ▶ **adjective** efficient as food; nourishing: *home-cooked burgers make a nutritious meal.*
– DERIVATIVES **nutritiously** adverb.
– ORIGIN mid 17th cent.: from Latin *nutritius* 'that nourishes' (from *nutrex* 'a nurse') + **-OUS**.

nutritive ▶ **adjective** relating to nutrition: *the food was low in nutritive value.* ■ providing nourishment; nutritious: *nutritive food.*
– ORIGIN late Middle English: from medieval Latin *nutritivus*, from *nutrire* 'feed, nourish'.

nut roast ▶ **noun** [mass noun] a baked vegetarian dish made from a mixture of ground or chopped nuts, vegetables, and herbs.

nuts informal ▶ **adjective** [predic.] mad: *the way he turns on the television as soon as he walks in drives me nuts.*
▶ **exclamation** (often **nuts to you** (or **him** etc.)) an expression of contempt or derision.
– PHRASES **be nuts about** (or Brit. **on**) like very much: *I was nuts about him.*

nutshell ▶ **noun 1** the hard woody covering around the kernel of a nut.
2 (**nut shell**) any of a number of bivalve molluscs occurring chiefly in cool seas, in particular: ● a small oval-shelled bivalve (genus *Nuculana*, family Nuculanidae). ● a bivalve with a rectangular shell which is rounded at the front and angled behind (genus *Nucula*, family Nuculidae).
– PHRASES **in a nutshell** in the fewest possible words: *she put the matter in a nutshell.*

nutso N. Amer. informal ▶ **adjective** mad.
▶ **noun** (pl. **nutsos**) a mad or eccentric person.

nutsy ▶ **adjective** (**nutsier, nutsiest**) N. Amer. informal mad.

nutter ▶ **noun** Brit. informal a mad or eccentric person.

nut tree ▶ **noun** a tree that bears nuts, especially the hazel.

nutty ▶ **adjective** (**nuttier, nuttiest**) **1** tasting like nuts: *wild rice has a very nutty flavour.* ■ containing a lot of nuts: *a nutty vegetable bake.*
2 informal mad: *he came up with a few nutty proposals.*
– PHRASES **be nutty about** informal like very much: *he is nutty about boats.* **(as) nutty as a fruitcake** informal completely mad.
– DERIVATIVES **nuttiness** noun.

Nuuk /nuːk/ the capital of Greenland, a port on the Davis Strait; pop. 15,000 (est. 2007). It was known by the Danish name Godthåb until 1979.

nux vomica /nʌks ˈvɒmɪkə/ ▶ **noun** [mass noun] a spiny southern Asian tree with berry-like fruit and toxic seeds that are a commercial source of strychnine. ● *Strychnos nux-vomica*, family Loganiaceae. ■ a homeopathic preparation of this plant used especially for the treatment of symptoms of overeating and overdrinking.
– ORIGIN late Middle English: from medieval Latin, from Latin *nux* 'nut' + *vomica* 'causing vomiting' (from *vomere* 'to vomit').

Nuyorican /ˌnjuːjəˈriːk(ə)n/ (also **Newyorican**) ▶ **noun** a Puerto Rican living in the United States, especially in New York City.

nuzzle ▶ **verb** [with obj.] rub or push against gently with the nose and mouth: *he nuzzled her hair* | [no obj.] *the*

foal nuzzled at its mother. ■ [no obj.] snuggle up to: *she nuzzled up against me.*
– ORIGIN late Middle English (in the sense 'grovel'): frequentative from NOSE, reinforced by Dutch *neuzelen* 'poke with the nose'.

NV ▸ abbreviation Nevada (in official postal use).

nvCJD ▸ abbreviation new variant Creutzfeldt–Jakob disease.

NVI ▸ abbreviation no value indicated, a postage stamp that does not bear a monetary value on it but instead shows which postal service it is valid for.

NVQ ▸ abbreviation (in the UK) National Vocational Qualification.

NW ▸ abbreviation ■ north-west. ■ north-western.

NWT ▸ abbreviation Northwest Territories (in Canada).

NY ▸ abbreviation New York (in official postal use).

nyaff /njaf/ ▸ noun Scottish informal a stupid, irritating, or insignificant person.
– ORIGIN mid 19th cent.: from Scots dialect *nyaff* 'yelp, complain'.

nyala /'njɑːlə/ ▸ noun (pl. **same**) a southern African antelope, which has a conspicuous crest on the neck and back and lyre-shaped horns. ● *Tragelaphus angasi*, family Bovidae.
– ORIGIN late 19th cent.: from Zulu.

nyam /'njam/ W. Indian ▸ verb [with obj.] eat: *whoever nyam dem left de empty box, nuttin' else!*
▸ noun [mass noun] food.
– ORIGIN from a West African language, probably related to YAM.

Nyamwezi /ˌnjam'weɪzi/ ▸ noun (pl. **same** or **Nyamwezis**) **1** a member of a people inhabiting western Tanzania.
2 [mass noun] the Bantu language of the Nyamwezi, related to Sukuma and having about 900,000 speakers.
▸ adjective relating to the Nyamwezi or their language.
– ORIGIN a local name.

Nyanja /'njandʒə/ ▸ noun (pl. **same** or **Nyanjas**) **1** a member of a people of Malawi and eastern and central Zambia.
2 [mass noun] the Bantu language of the Nyanja, with over 3 million speakers.
▸ adjective relating to the Nyanja or their language.
– ORIGIN a local name, literally 'lake'.

Nyasa, Lake /nʌɪ'asə/ a lake in east central Africa, the third-largest lake in Africa. About 580 km (360 miles) long, it forms most of the eastern border of Malawi with Mozambique and Tanzania. Also called MALAWI, LAKE.
– ORIGIN *Nyasa*, literally 'lake'.

Nyasaland /nʌɪ'asəland/ former name (until 1966) for MALAWI.

NYC ▸ abbreviation New York City.

nyctalopia /ˌnɪktə'ləʊpɪə/ ▸ noun [mass noun] Medicine a condition characterized by an abnormal inability to see in dim light or at night, typically caused by vitamin A deficiency.
– ORIGIN late 17th cent.: via late Latin from Greek *nuktalōps*, from *nux, nukt-* 'night' + *alaos* 'blind' + *ōps* 'eye'.

nyctinastic /ˌnɪktɪ'nastɪk/ ▸ adjective Botany (of the periodic movement of flowers or leaves) caused by nightly changes in light intensity or temperature.
– DERIVATIVES **nyctinasty** /'nɪktɪˌnasti/ noun.
– ORIGIN early 20th cent.: from Greek *nux, nukt-* 'night' + *nastos* 'pressed' + -IC.

nyctophobia /ˌnɪktə(ʊ)'fəʊbɪə/ ▸ noun [mass noun] extreme or irrational fear of the night or of darkness.
– ORIGIN early 20th cent.: from Greek *nux, nukt-* 'night' + PHOBIA.

Nyerere /njɛ'rɛːri/, Julius Kambarage (1922–99), Tanzanian statesman, President of Tanganyika 1962–4 and of Tanzania 1964–85. He led Tanganyika to independence in 1961 and in 1964 successfully negotiated a union with Zanzibar, creating the new state of Tanzania.

nylon ▸ noun [mass noun] a tough, lightweight, elastic synthetic polymer with a protein-like chemical structure, able to be produced as filaments, sheets, or moulded objects. ■ fabric or yarn made from nylon fibres. ■ (**nylons**) stockings or tights made of nylon.
– ORIGIN 1930s: an invented word, on the pattern of *cotton* and *rayon*.

nymph ▸ noun **1** a mythological spirit of nature imagined as a beautiful maiden inhabiting rivers, woods, or other locations. ■ chiefly literary a beautiful young woman.
2 an immature form of an insect that does not change greatly as it grows, e.g. a dragonfly, mayfly, or locust. Compare with LARVA. ■ an artificial fishing fly made to resemble the aquatic nymph of an insect.
3 a mainly brown butterfly that frequents woods and forest glades. ● Several genera in the subfamily Satyrinae, family Nymphalidae. See also WOOD NYMPH.
– DERIVATIVES **nymphal** adjective, **nymph-like** adjective.
– ORIGIN late Middle English: from Old French *nimphe*, from Latin *nympha*, from Greek *numphē* 'nymph, bride'; related to Latin *nubere* 'be the wife of'.

nymphaeum /nɪm'fiːəm/ ▸ noun (pl. **nymphaea**) a grotto or shrine dedicated to a nymph or nymphs.
– ORIGIN via Latin from Greek.

nymphalid /nɪm'falɪd/ ▸ noun Entomology an insect of a large family of strikingly marked butterflies which have small forelegs that are not used for walking, including many familiar butterflies of temperate regions. Compare with VANESSID. ● Family Nymphalidae (sometimes restricted to those that are now usually placed in the subfamily Nymphalinae).
– ORIGIN late 19th cent.: from modern Latin *Nymphalidae*, from Latin *nympha* 'nymph'.

nymphet /'nɪmfɛt, nɪm'fɛt/ (also **nymphette**) ▸ noun an attractive and sexually mature young girl.
– ORIGIN 1950s: from NYMPH + -ET[1].

nympho ▸ noun (pl. **nymphos**) informal a woman with strong sexual desires.
– ORIGIN 1930s: short for NYMPHOMANIAC.

nympholepsy /'nɪmfə(ʊ)ˌlɛpsi/ ▸ noun [mass noun] literary **1** passion aroused in men by beautiful young girls.
2 wild frenzy caused by desire for an unattainable ideal.
– ORIGIN late 18th cent.: from Greek *numpholēptos* 'caught by nymphs', from *numphē* 'nymph' and *lambanein* 'take hold of', on the pattern of EPILEPSY.

nympholept /'nɪmfə(ʊ)lɛpt/ ▸ noun a person affected by nympholepsy.
– DERIVATIVES **nympholeptic** adjective.
– ORIGIN early 19th cent.: from Greek *numpholēptos* 'caught by nymphs', from *numphē* 'nymph' + *lambanein* 'take'.

nymphomania ▸ noun [mass noun] uncontrollable or excessive sexual desire in a woman.
– DERIVATIVES **nymphomaniac** noun & adjective, **nymphomaniacal** adjective.
– ORIGIN late 18th cent.: modern Latin, from Latin *nympha* (see NYMPH) + -MANIA.

Nynorsk /'njuːnɔːsk/ ▸ noun [mass noun] a literary form of the Norwegian language, based on certain country dialects and constructed in the 19th century to serve as a national language more clearly distinct from Danish than Bokmål. See NORWEGIAN (sense 2 of the noun).
– ORIGIN Norwegian, from *ny* 'new' + *Norsk* 'Norwegian'.

Nyoman /'njɒmən/ Belorussian name for NEMAN.

Nyquist criterion /'nʌɪkwɪst/ ▸ noun Electronics a criterion for determining the stability or instability of a feedback system.
– ORIGIN 1930s: named after Harry *Nyquist* (1889–1976), Swedish-born American engineer.

Nyquist diagram (also **Nyquist plot**) ▸ noun Electronics a representation of the vector response of a feedback system (especially an amplifier) as a complex graphical plot showing the relationship between feedback and gain.

Nyquist frequency (also **Nyquist rate**) ▸ noun Electronics the minimum rate at which a signal can be sampled without introducing errors, which is twice the highest frequency present in the signal.

Nysa /'niːsa/ Polish name for NEISSE.

NYSE ▸ abbreviation New York Stock Exchange.

nystagmus /nɪ'stagməs/ ▸ noun [mass noun] rapid involuntary movements of the eyes.
– ORIGIN early 19th cent.: from Greek *nustagmos* 'nodding, drowsiness', from *nustazein* 'nod, be sleepy'.

nystatin /'nʌɪstətɪn, 'nɪs-/ ▸ noun [mass noun] an antibiotic used chiefly to treat fungal infections. ● This antibiotic is obtained from the bacterium *Streptomyces noursei*.
– ORIGIN 1950s: from *N(ew) Y(ork) Stat(e)* (where it was developed) + -IN[1].

Nyungar /'njʊŋə/ ▸ noun [mass noun] an Aboriginal language of SW Australia.
– ORIGIN the name in Nyungar, literally 'man'.

Nyx /nɪks/ Greek Mythology the female personification of the night, daughter of Chaos.

NZ ▸ abbreviation New Zealand.

Oo

O[1] (also **o**) ▶ **noun** (pl. **Os** or **O's**) **1** the fifteenth letter of the alphabet. ■ denoting the next after N in a set of items, categories, etc. ■ a human blood type (in the ABO system) lacking both the A and B antigens. In blood transfusion, a person with blood of this group is a potential universal donor.
2 (also **oh**) nought or zero (in a sequence of numerals, especially when spoken).
3 a shape like that of a capital O; a circle.

O[2] ▶ **abbreviation** ■ US Ohio. ■ Cricket (on scorecards) over(s).
▶ **symbol** the chemical element oxygen.

O[3] ▶ **exclamation 1** archaic spelling of **OH**[1].
2 archaic used before a name in the vocative: *give peace in our time, O Lord.*
– ORIGIN natural exclamation: first recorded in Middle English.

o ▶ **abbreviation** (*o-*) [in combination] Chemistry ortho-: *o-xylene.*

O' ▶ **prefix** in Irish patronymic names such as *O'Neill*.
– ORIGIN mid 18th cent.: from Irish *ó*, *ua* 'descendant'.

o' ▶ **preposition** short for **OF**, used to represent an informal pronunciation: *a cup o' coffee.*

-o ▶ **suffix** forming chiefly informal or slang variants or derivatives such as *beano*, *wino*.
– ORIGIN perhaps from **OH**[1], reinforced by abbreviated forms such as *hippo*, *photo*.

O

-o- ▶ **suffix** used as the terminal vowel of combining forms: *chemico-* | *Gallo-*.
– ORIGIN from Greek.

> **USAGE** The suffix **-o-** is often elided before a vowel, as in neuralgia.

oaf ▶ **noun** a man who is rough or clumsy and unintelligent.
– ORIGIN early 17th cent.: variant of obsolete *auf*, from Old Norse *álfr* 'elf'. The original meaning was 'elf's child, changeling', later 'idiot child' and 'half-wit', generalized in the current sense.

oafish ▶ **adjective** rough or clumsy and unintelligent: *oafish behaviour.*
– DERIVATIVES **oafishly adverb**, **oafishness noun**.

Oahu /əʊˈɑːhuː/ the third largest of the Hawaiian islands; pop. 836,207 (2000). Its principal town, Honolulu, is the state capital of Hawaii. The island is the site of the US naval base Pearl Harbor.

oak ▶ **noun 1** (also **oak tree**) a large tree which bears acorns and typically has lobed deciduous leaves. Oaks are dominant in many north temperate forests and are an important source of durable timber used in building, furniture, and (formerly) ships. ● Genus *Quercus*, family Fagaceae: many species, including the deciduous **common** (or **English**) **oak** (*Q. robur*), and the evergreen **holm oak**.
■ [mass noun] a smoky flavour or nose characteristic of wine aged in barrels made from oak wood. ■ chiefly Austral. used in names of other trees or plants that resemble the oaks in some way, e.g. **she-oak**, **silky oak**.
2 (**the Oaks**) an annual flat horse race for three-year-old fillies run on Epsom Downs, over the same course as the Derby. It was first run in 1779. [named after a nearby estate.] ■ [usu. with modifier] a flat horse race similar to that on Epsom Downs run on another course: *the Irish Oaks.*
– PHRASES **great oaks from little acorns grow** proverb something of small or modest proportions may grow into something very large or impressive. **sport the** (or **one's**) **oak** Brit. (in certain universities) shut the outer door of one's room as a sign that one does not wish to be disturbed. [such outer doors were formerly of oak.]
– DERIVATIVES **oaken adjective**, **oaky adjective** (**oakier**, **oakiest**).
– ORIGIN Old English *āc*, of Germanic origin; related to Dutch *eik* and German *Eiche*.

oak apple ▶ **noun** a spongy spherical gall which forms on oak trees in response to the developing larvae of a gall wasp. ● The wasp is *Biorhiza pallida* (in Europe) or *Amphibolips confluenta* (in America), family Cynipidae.

oaked ▶ **adjective** (of wine) matured in an oak barrel or other container.

oak fern ▶ **noun** a delicate fern of woods and damp places in the uplands of northern Eurasia and North America. ● Genus *Gymnocarpium* (formerly *Thelypteris*), family Woodsiaceae: two species, in particular *G. dryopteris*.

oak kermes ▶ **noun** see **KERMES** (sense 2).

Oakland an industrial port on the east side of San Francisco Bay in California; pop. 404,155 (est. 2008).

oak leaf (also **oak leaf lettuce**) ▶ **noun** [mass noun] a red or green variety of lettuce which has leaves with serrated edges and a slightly bitter taste.

oak leaf cluster ▶ **noun** (in the US) an attachment to a military decoration representing a twig with oak leaves and acorns, indicating distinguished action or a subsequent award of the same decoration.

Oakley, Annie (1860–1926), American markswoman; full name *Phoebe Anne Oakley Mozee*. In 1885 she joined Buffalo Bill's Wild West Show, of which she became a star attraction for the next seventeen years.

oakum ▶ **noun** [mass noun] chiefly historical loose fibre obtained by untwisting old rope, used especially in caulking wooden ships.
– ORIGIN Old English *ācumbe*, literally 'off-combings'. The current sense dates from Middle English.

oak wilt ▶ **noun** [mass noun] a fungal disease of oaks and other trees which makes the foliage wilt and eventually kills the tree. ● The fungus is *Ceratocystis fagacearum*, subdivision Ascomycotina.

OAM ▶ **abbreviation** Medal of the Order of Australia.

OAP ▶ **abbreviation** Brit. old-age pensioner.

OAPEC /əʊˈeɪpɛk/ ▶ **abbreviation** Organization of Arab Petroleum Exporting Countries.

oar ▶ **noun** a pole with a flat blade, used to row or steer a boat through the water. ■ an oarsman; a rower.
▶ **verb** [with obj.] propel with or as if with oars; row: *oaring the sea like madmen* | [no obj., with adverbial of direction] *oaring through the weeds.*
– PHRASES **put** (or **stick**) **one's oar in** informal, chiefly Brit. give an opinion without being asked.
– DERIVATIVES **oared adjective** [in combination] *four-oared sculls*, **oarless adjective**.
– ORIGIN Old English *ār*, of Germanic origin; related to Danish and Norwegian *åre*.

oarfish ▶ **noun** (pl. **same** or **oarfishes**) a very long, narrow silvery marine fish of deep water, with a deep red dorsal fin running the length of the body. Also called **RIBBONFISH**, **KING OF THE HERRINGS**. ● *Regalecus glesne*, family Regalecidae.

oarlock ▶ **noun** N. Amer. a rowlock.

oarsman (or **oarswoman**) ▶ **noun** (pl. **oarsmen** or **oarswomen**) a rower, especially as a member of a racing team.
– DERIVATIVES **oarsmanship noun**.

oarweed ▶ **noun** [mass noun] a large brown kelp with a long hard stalk and a large oar-shaped frond divided into ribbon-like strips, growing on rocky shores. Also called **TANGLE**[2]. ● Genus *Laminaria*, class Phaeophyceae, in particular *L. digitata*.

OAS ▶ **abbreviation** Organization of American States.

oasis /əʊˈeɪsɪs/ ▶ **noun** (pl. **oases** /-siːz/) **1** a fertile spot in a desert, where water is found. ■ a pleasant or peaceful area or period in the midst of a difficult or hectic place or situation: *the park is an oasis of calm in the centre of the city.*
2 (**Oasis**) [mass noun] trademark a type of rigid foam into which the stems of flowers can be secured in flower arranging.
– ORIGIN early 17th cent.: via late Latin from Greek, apparently of Egyptian origin.

oast /əʊst/ ▶ **noun** a kiln used for drying hops.
– ORIGIN Old English *āst* (originally denoting any kiln), of Germanic origin; related to Dutch *eest*, from an Indo-European root meaning 'burn'.

oast house ▶ **noun** a building containing an oast, typically built of brick in a conical shape with a cowl on top.

oat ▶ **noun 1** an Old World cereal plant with a loose, branched cluster of florets, cultivated in cool climates and widely used for animal feed. ● *Avena sativa*, family Gramineae.
■ (**oats**) the grain yielded by the oat plant, used as food. ■ used in names of wild grasses related to the cultivated oat, e.g. **wild oat**.
2 literary an oat stem used as a musical pipe by shepherds, especially in pastoral or bucolic poetry.
– PHRASES **feel one's oats** N. Amer. informal feel lively and energetic. **get one's oats** Brit. informal have sexual intercourse. **sow one's wild oats** go through a period of wild or promiscuous behaviour while young.
– DERIVATIVES **oaten adjective** (archaic), **oaty adjective** (**oatier**, **oatiest**).
– ORIGIN Old English *āte*, plural *ātan*, of unknown origin. Unlike other names of cereals (such as *wheat*, *barley*, etc.), *oat* is not a mass noun and may originally have denoted the individual grain, which may imply that oats were eaten in grains and not as meal.

oatcake ▶ **noun** a thin savoury oatmeal biscuit, traditionally made in Scotland.

oat cell ▶ **noun** Medicine a small oval cell with little cytoplasm and a densely staining nucleus, characteristic of carcinoma of the bronchus: [as modifier] *oat cell carcinoma.*

oater ▶ **noun** informal, chiefly US a western film.
– ORIGIN 1950s: from **OAT**, with allusion to horse feed; compare with the synonym **HORSE OPERA**.

Oates, Titus (1649–1705), English clergyman and conspirator, remembered as the fabricator of the Popish Plot. Convicted of perjury in 1685, Oates was imprisoned in the same year, but subsequently released and granted a pension.

oat grass ▶ **noun** [mass noun] a wild grass which resembles the oat. ● *Avenula* and other genera, family Gramineae.

oath ▶ **noun** (pl. **oaths**) **1** a solemn promise, often invoking a divine witness, regarding one's future

action or behaviour: *they took an oath of allegiance to the king.* ■ a sworn declaration, such as the promise to tell the truth, in a court of law.
2 a profane or offensive expression used to express anger or other strong emotions.
– PHRASES **my oath** Austral./NZ an exclamation of agreement or endorsement. **under** (or Brit. **on**) **oath** having sworn to tell the truth, especially in a court of law.
– ORIGIN Old English *āth*, of Germanic origin; related to Dutch *eed* and German *Eid*.

oatmeal ▶ **noun** [mass noun] **1** meal made from ground oats, used in porridge, oatcakes, or other food. ■ N. Amer. porridge made from oatmeal or rolled oats.
2 a greyish-fawn colour flecked with brown: [as modifier] *an oatmeal jacket.*
– ORIGIN late Middle English: from OAT and MEAL².

OAU ▶ **abbreviation** Organization of African Unity.

Oaxaca /wəˈhɑːkə/ a state of southern Mexico. ■ its capital city; pop. 265,006 (2005). Full name **Oaxaca de Juárez** /deɪ ˈhwɑːrɛz/.

OB ▶ **abbreviation** Brit. outside broadcast.

Ob /ɒb/ the principal river of the western Siberian lowlands and one of the largest rivers in Russia. Rising in the Altai Mountains, it flows generally north and west for 5,410 km (3,481 miles) before entering the Gulf of Ob (or Ob Bay), an inlet of the Kara Sea, a part of the Arctic Ocean.

ob. ▶ **abbreviation** he or she died: *ob. 1867.*
– ORIGIN from Latin *obiit*.

ob- ▶ **prefix 1** denoting exposure or openness: *obverse.* ■ expressing meeting or facing: *occasion.*
2 denoting opposition, hostility, or resistance: *opponent.* ■ denoting hindrance, blocking, or concealment: *obviate.*
3 denoting finality or completeness: *obsolete.*
4 (in modern technical words) in a direction or manner contrary to the usual; inversely: *obconical.*
– ORIGIN from Latin *ob* 'towards, against, in the way of'.

oba /ˈɒbə/ ▶ **noun** a local chief in Nigeria.
– ORIGIN Yoruba, originally the name of the absolute ruler of the ancient West African kingdom of Benin, now part of Nigeria.

Obad. ▶ **abbreviation** Obadiah (in biblical references).

Obadiah /ˌəʊbəˈdʌɪə/ (in the Bible) a Hebrew minor prophet. ■ the shortest book of the Bible, bearing his name.

Obama /əʊˈbɑːmə/, Barack (Hussein) (b.1961), American Democratic statesman, 44th President of the US since 2009. He is the first African American to be elected to the presidency. He was awarded the Nobel Peace Prize in 2009.

Oban /ˈəʊb(ə)n/ a port and tourist resort on the west coast of Scotland, in Argyll and Bute, opposite the island of Mull; pop. 9,500 (est. 2009).

obbligato /ˌɒblɪˈɡɑːtəʊ/ (US also **obligato**) ▶ **noun** (pl. **obbligatos** or **obbligati**) [usu. with or as modifier] an instrumental part, typically distinctive in effect, which is integral to a piece of music and should not be omitted in performance.
– ORIGIN Italian, literally 'obligatory', from Latin *obligatus*, past participle of *obligare* (see OBLIGE).

obconical /ɒbˈkɒnɪk(ə)l/ ▶ **adjective** Botany in the form of an inverted cone.

obcordate /ɒbˈkɔːdeɪt/ ▶ **adjective** Botany (of a leaf) in the shape of a heart with the pointed end at the base.

obduction ▶ **noun** [mass noun] Geology the sideways and upwards movement of the edge of a crustal plate over the margin of an adjacent plate.
– DERIVATIVES **obduct** verb.
– ORIGIN 1970s: from Latin *obduct-* 'covered over', from the verb *obducere*, from *ob-* 'against, towards' + *ducere* 'to lead'.

obdurate /ˈɒbdjʊrət/ ▶ **adjective** stubbornly refusing to change one's opinion or course of action: *I argued this point with him, but he was obdurate.*
– DERIVATIVES **obduracy** noun, **obdurately** adverb, **obdurateness** noun.
– ORIGIN late Middle English (originally in the sense 'hardened in sin, impenitent'): from Latin *obduratus*, past participle of *obdurare*, from *ob-* 'in opposition' + *durare* 'harden' (from *durus* 'hard').

OBE ▶ **abbreviation** Officer of the Order of the British Empire.

obeah /ˈəʊbɪə/ (also **obi**) ▶ **noun** [mass noun] a kind of sorcery practised especially in the Caribbean.
– ORIGIN Akan, from *bayi* 'sorcery'.

obeche /əʊˈbiːtʃi/ ▶ **noun** a tropical tree native to West and central Africa, grown for its pale timber which is used for plywood and veneers. ● *Triplochiton scleroxylon*, family Sterculiaceae.
– ORIGIN early 20th cent.: a term used in Nigeria.

obedience ▶ **noun** [mass noun] compliance with an order, request, or law or submission to another's authority: *children were taught to show their parents obedience* | *obedience to moral standards.* ■ observance of a monastic rule: *vows of poverty, chastity, and obedience.*
– PHRASES **in obedience to** in accordance with: *he was acting in obedience to his conscience.*
– ORIGIN Middle English: via Old French from Latin *oboedientia*, from the verb *oboedire* (see OBEY).

obedient ▶ **adjective** complying or willing to comply with an order or request; submissive to another's authority: *she was totally **obedient to** him.*
– PHRASES **your obedient servant** dated a formula used to end a letter.
– DERIVATIVES **obediently** adverb.
– ORIGIN Middle English: via Old French from Latin *oboedient-* 'obeying', from the verb *oboedire* (see OBEY).

obedientiary /ə(ʊ)ˌbiːdɪˈɛnʃ(ə)ri/ ▶ **noun** (pl. **obedientiaries**) the holder of a position of responsibility in a monastery or convent under a superior.
– ORIGIN mid 16th cent. (denoting a vassal): from medieval Latin *oboedientiarius*, from *oboedientia* (see OBEDIENCE).

obeisance /ə(ʊ)ˈbeɪs(ə)ns/ ▶ **noun** [mass noun] deferential respect: *they paid obeisance to the Prince.* ■ [count noun] a gesture expressing deferential respect, such as a bow or curtsy: *she made a deep obeisance.*
– DERIVATIVES **obeisant** adjective.
– ORIGIN late Middle English (in the sense 'obedience'): from Old French *obeissance*, from *obeissant* 'obeying', present participle of *obeir*.

obeli plural form of OBELUS.

obelia /ə(ʊ)ˈbiːlɪə/ ▶ **noun** Zoology a sedentary colonial coelenterate with upright branching stems bearing minute cups in which the polyps sit. ● Genus *Obelia*, class Hydrozoa.
– ORIGIN modern Latin, from Greek *obelos* 'pointed pillar'.

obelisk /ˈɒb(ə)lɪsk/ ▶ **noun 1** a tapering stone pillar, typically having a square or rectangular cross section, set up as a monument or landmark. ■ a mountain, tree, or other natural object resembling an obelisk in shape.
2 another term for OBELUS.
– ORIGIN mid 16th cent.: via Latin from Greek *obeliskos*, diminutive of *obelos* 'pointed pillar'.

obelize /ˈɒb(ə)lʌɪz/ (also **obelise**) ▶ **verb** [with obj.] mark (a word or passage) with an obelus to show that it is spurious, corrupt, or doubtful.
– ORIGIN mid 17th cent.: from Greek *obelizein*, in the same sense.

obelus /ˈɒb(ə)ləs/ ▶ **noun** (pl. **obeli** /-lʌɪ, -liː/) **1** a symbol (†) used as a reference mark in printed matter, or to indicate that a person is deceased.
2 a mark (– or ÷) used in ancient manuscripts to mark a word or passage as spurious, corrupt or doubtful.
– ORIGIN late Middle English: via Latin from Greek *obelos* 'pointed pillar', also 'critical mark'.

Oberammergau /ˌəʊbərˈaməɡaʊ/, German /ˌoːbɐˈamɐɡaʊ/ a village in the Bavarian Alps of SW Germany; pop. 5,400 (est. 2006). It is the site of the most famous of the few surviving passion plays, which has been performed by the villagers every tenth year (with few exceptions) from 1634 as a result of a vow made during an epidemic of plague.

Oberhausen /ˈəʊbəˌhaʊz(ə)n/, German /ˈoːbɐˌhaʊzn/ an industrial city in western Germany, in the Ruhr valley of North Rhine-Westphalia; pop. 218,200 (est. 2006).

Oberon /ˈəʊbərɒn/ Astronomy a satellite of Uranus, the furthest from the planet, which has a heavily cratered surface and was discovered by W. Herschel in 1787 (diameter 1,550 km).
– ORIGIN from the name of the king of the fairies in Shakespeare's *A Midsummer Night's Dream.*

Oberösterreich /ˈoːbɐˌøːstəraɪç/ German name for UPPER AUSTRIA.

obese ▶ **adjective** grossly fat or overweight.
– ORIGIN mid 17th cent.: from Latin *obesus* 'having eaten until fat', from *ob-* 'away, completely' + *esus* (past participle of *edere* 'eat').

obesity ▶ **noun** [mass noun] the state of being grossly fat or overweight: *the problem of obesity among children.*

obesogenic /ə(ʊ),biːsəˈdjɛnɪk/ ▶ **adjective** tending to cause obesity.

obey ▶ **verb** [with obj.] submit to the authority of (someone) or comply with (a law): *I always obey my father.* ■ carry out (a command or instruction): *the officer was convicted for refusing to obey orders* | [no obj.] *when the order was repeated, he refused to obey.* ■ behave in accordance with (a general principle, natural law, etc.): *the universe was complex but it obeyed certain rules.*
– DERIVATIVES **obeyer** noun.
– ORIGIN Middle English: from Old French *obeir*, from Latin *oboedire*, from *ob-* 'in the direction of' + *audire* 'hear'.

obfuscate /ˈɒbfʌskeɪt/ ▶ **verb** [with obj.] make obscure, unclear, or unintelligible: *the spelling changes will deform some familiar words and obfuscate their etymological origins.* ■ bewilder (someone): *the new rule is more likely to obfuscate people than enlighten them.*
– DERIVATIVES **obfuscation** noun, **obfuscatory** adjective.
– ORIGIN late Middle English: from late Latin *obfuscat-* 'darkened', from the verb *obfuscare*, based on Latin *fuscus* 'dark'.

ob-gyn /ɒbˈɡʌɪn/ ▶ **abbreviation** (in the US) obstetrics and gynaecology.

obi¹ /ˈəʊbi/ ▶ **noun** variant form of OBEAH.

obi² /ˈəʊbi/ ▶ **noun** (pl. **obis**) a broad sash worn round the waist of a Japanese kimono.
– ORIGIN Japanese, literally 'belt'.

obit /ˈɒbɪt, ˈəʊ-/ ▶ **noun** informal an obituary.
– ORIGIN late Middle English: now regarded as an abbreviation of OBITUARY, but originally also used in the senses 'death' and 'funeral service', from Latin *obitus* 'going down, death'.

obiter /ˈɒbɪtə/ ▶ **adverb & adjective** (chiefly in legal contexts) made or said in passing.
▶ **noun** short for OBITER DICTUM.
– ORIGIN Latin, originally as the phrase *ob itur* 'by the way'.

obiter dictum /ˈdɪktəm/ ▶ **noun** (pl. **obiter dicta** /ˈdɪktə/) Law a judge's expression of opinion uttered in court or in a written judgement, but not essential to the decision and therefore not legally binding as a precedent. ■ an incidental remark.
– ORIGIN Latin *obiter* 'in passing' + *dictum* 'something that is said'.

obituary /ə(ʊ)ˈbɪtʃʊəri, -tʃəri, -tjʊəri/ ▶ **noun** (pl. **obituaries**) a notice of a death, especially in a newspaper, typically including a brief biography of the deceased person.
– DERIVATIVES **obituarist** noun.
– ORIGIN early 18th cent.: from medieval Latin *obituarius*, from Latin *obitus* 'death', from *obit-* 'perished', from the verb *obire*.

object ▶ **noun** /ˈɒbdʒɪkt, -dʒɛkt/ **1** a material thing that can be seen and touched: *he was dragging a large object* | *small objects such as shells.* ■ Philosophy a thing external to the thinking mind or subject.
2 a person or thing to which a specified action or feeling is directed: *disease became the object of investigation* | *he hated being the object of public attention* ■ a goal or purpose: *the Institute was opened with the **object of** promoting scientific study.*
3 Grammar a noun or noun phrase governed by an active transitive verb or by a preposition.
4 Computing a data construct that provides a description of anything known to a computer (such as a processor or a piece of code) and defines its method of operation.
▶ **verb** /əbˈdʒɛkt/ [reporting verb] say something to express one's disapproval of or disagreement with something: [no obj.] ***residents object to** the volume of traffic* | [with clause] *the boy's father objected that the police had arrested him unlawfully* | [with direct speech] *'It doesn't seem natural,' she objected.* ■ [with obj.] archaic cite as a reason against something.
– PHRASES **no object** not influencing or restricting choices or decisions: *a tycoon for whom **money is no object**.* **the object of the exercise** the main purpose of an activity. **object of virtu** see VIRTU.
– DERIVATIVES **objectless** adjective, **objector** noun.
– ORIGIN late Middle English: from medieval Latin *objectum* 'thing presented to the mind', neuter past participle (used as a noun) of Latin *obicere*, from *ob-* 'in the way of' + *jacere* 'to throw'; the verb may also partly represent the Latin frequentative *objectare*.

object ball ▶ **noun** Billiards & Snooker the ball at which a player aims the cue ball.

O

object code ▸ noun [mass noun] Computing code produced by a compiler or assembler.

object glass ▸ noun old-fashioned term for OBJECTIVE (sense 3 of the noun).

objectify ▸ verb (**objectifies**, **objectifying**, **objectified**) [with obj.] **1** express (something abstract) in a concrete form: *good poetry objectifies feeling*.
2 degrade to the status of a mere object: *a deeply sexist attitude that objectifies women*.
– DERIVATIVES **objectification** noun.
– ORIGIN mid 19th cent.: from the noun OBJECT + -I- + -FY.

objection ▸ noun an expression or feeling of disapproval or opposition; a reason for disagreeing: *they have raised no objections to the latest plans*. ■ [mass noun] the action of challenging or disagreeing with something: *his view is open to objection*.
– ORIGIN late Middle English: from Old French, or from late Latin *objectio(n-)*, from the verb *obicere* (see OBJECT).

objectionable ▸ adjective arousing distaste or opposition; unpleasant or offensive: *I find his theory objectionable in its racist undertones*.
– DERIVATIVES **objectionableness** noun, **objectionably** adverb.

objective ▸ adjective **1** (of a person or their judgement) not influenced by personal feelings or opinions in considering and representing facts: *historians try to be objective and impartial*. Contrasted with SUBJECTIVE. ■ not dependent on the mind for existence; actual: *a matter of objective fact*.
2 [attrib.] Grammar relating to or denoting a case of nouns and pronouns serving as the object of a transitive verb or a preposition.
▸ noun **1** a thing aimed at or sought; a goal: *the system has achieved its objective*.
2 (**the objective**) Grammar the objective case.
3 (also **objective lens**) the lens in a telescope or microscope nearest to the object observed.
– DERIVATIVES **objectively** adverb, **objectiveness** noun, **objectivization** (also **objectivisation**) noun, **objectivize** (also **objectivise**) verb.
– ORIGIN early 17th cent.: from medieval Latin *objectivus*, from *objectum* (see OBJECT).

objective correlative ▸ noun the artistic and literary technique of representing or evoking a particular emotion by means of symbols which become indicative of that emotion and are associated with it.

objective danger ▸ noun Climbing a danger such as a rock fall that does not arise from a lack of skill on the part of the climber.

O

objective function ▸ noun Mathematics (in linear programming) the function that it is desired to maximize or minimize.

objectivism ▸ noun [mass noun] **1** the tendency to emphasize what is external to or independent of the mind.
2 Philosophy the belief that certain things, especially moral truths, exist independently of human knowledge or perception of them.
– DERIVATIVES **objectivist** noun & adjective, **objectivistic** adjective.

objectivity ▸ noun [mass noun] the quality of being objective: *the piece lacked any objectivity*.

object language ▸ noun **1** a language described by means of another language. Compare with METALANGUAGE, TARGET LANGUAGE.
2 Computing a language into which a program is translated by means of a compiler or assembler.

object lesson ▸ noun a striking practical example of a principle or ideal: *they responded to daily emergencies in a way that was an object lesson to us all*.

object-oriented ▸ adjective Computing (of a programming language) using a methodology which enables a system to be modelled as a set of objects which can be controlled and manipulated in a modular manner.

object program ▸ noun Computing a program into which another program is translated by an assembler or compiler.

objects clause ▸ noun Law a clause in a memorandum of association specifying the objects for which the company was established.

objet /ˈɒbʒeɪ/ ▸ noun an object displayed or intended for display as an ornament.
– ORIGIN French, literally 'object'.

objet d'art /ɒbʒeɪ ˈdɑː/ ▸ noun (pl. **objets d'art** pronunc. **same**) a small decorative or artistic object, typically when regarded as a collectable item.
– ORIGIN French, literally 'object of art'.

objet trouvé /ˈtruːveɪ/ ▸ noun (pl. **objets trouvés** pronunc. **same**) an object found by an artist and displayed with no, or minimal, alteration as a work of art.
– ORIGIN French, literally 'found object'.

objurgate /ˈɒbdʒəgeɪt/ ▸ verb [with obj.] rare rebuke severely; scold.
– DERIVATIVES **objurgation** noun, **objurgatory** -adjective.
– ORIGIN early 17th cent.: from Latin *objurgat-* 'chided, rebuked', from the verb *objurgare*, based on *jurgium* 'strife'.

oblanceolate /ɒbˈlɑːnsɪələt/ ▸ adjective technical (especially of leaves) lanceolate with the more pointed end at the base.
– ORIGIN mid 19th cent.: from OB- + LANCEOLATE.

oblast /ˈɒblast/ ▸ noun an administrative division or region in Russia and the former Soviet Union, and in some constituent republics of the former Soviet Union.
– ORIGIN Russian.

oblate[1] /ˈɒbleɪt/ ▸ noun a person who is dedicated to a religious life, but has typically not taken full monastic vows.
– ORIGIN late 17th cent.: from French, from medieval Latin *oblatus*, past participle (used as a noun) of Latin *offerre* 'to offer'.

oblate[2] /ˈɒbleɪt/ ▸ adjective Geometry (of a spheroid) flattened at the poles. Often contrasted with PROLATE.
– ORIGIN early 18th cent.: from modern Latin *oblatus* (from *ob-* 'inversely' + *-latus* 'carried'), on the pattern of Latin *prolatus* 'prolonged'.

oblation ▸ noun a thing presented or offered to God or a god. ■ [mass noun] Christian Church the presentation of bread and wine to God in the Eucharist.
– DERIVATIVES **oblatory** adjective.
– ORIGIN late Middle English: from Old French, or from late Latin *oblatio(n-)*, from Latin *offerre* 'to offer'.

obligate ▸ verb **1** [with obj. and infinitive] require or compel (someone) to undertake a legal or moral duty: *the medical establishment is obligated to take action in the best interest of the public*.
2 [with obj.] US commit (assets) as security: *the money must be obligated within 30 days*.
▸ adjective [attrib.] Biology restricted to a particular function or mode of life: *an obligate intracellular parasite*. Often contrasted with FACULTATIVE.
– ORIGIN late Middle English (as an adjective in the sense 'bound by law'): from Latin *obligatus*, past participle of *obligare* (see OBLIGE). The current adjectival use dates from the late 19th cent.

obligation ▸ noun an act or course of action to which a person is morally or legally bound; a duty or commitment: [with infinitive] *I have an obligation to look after her*. ■ [mass noun] the condition of being morally or legally bound to do something: *they are **under no obligation** to stick to the scheme*. ■ a debt of gratitude for a service or favour: *she didn't want to be under an obligation to him*. ■ Law a binding agreement committing a person to a payment or other action.
– PHRASES **day of obligation** (in the Roman Catholic Church) a day on which all are required to attend Mass.
– DERIVATIVES **obligational** adjective.
– ORIGIN Middle English (in the sense 'formal promise'): via Old French from Latin *obligatio(n-)*, from the verb *obligare* (see OBLIGE).

obligato ▸ noun US variant spelling of OBBLIGATO.

obligatory /əˈblɪgət(ə)ri/ ▸ adjective required by a legal, moral, or other rule; compulsory: *use of seat belts in cars is now obligatory*. ■ (of a ruling) having binding force: *a sovereign whose laws are obligatory*. ■ often humorous so customary or fashionable as to be expected of everyone or on every occasion: *it was a quiet little street with the obligatory pub at the end*.
– DERIVATIVES **obligatorily** adverb.
– ORIGIN late Middle English: from late Latin *obligatorius*, from Latin *obligat-* 'obliged', from the verb *obligare* (see OBLIGE).

oblige ▸ verb [with obj. and infinitive] make (someone) legally or morally bound to do something: *doctors are obliged by law to keep patients alive while there is a chance of recovery*. ■ [with obj.] do as (someone) asks or desires in order to help or please them: *oblige me by not being sorry for yourself* | [no obj.] *tell me what you want to know and I'll see if I can oblige*. ■ (**be obliged**) be indebted or grateful: *if you can give me a few minutes of your time I'll be much obliged*. ■ [with obj.] archaic bind (someone) by an oath, promise, or contract.
– DERIVATIVES **obliger** noun.
– ORIGIN Middle English (in the sense 'bind by oath'): from Old French *obliger*, from Latin *obligare*, from *ob-* 'towards' + *ligare* 'to bind'.

obligee /ˌɒblɪˈdʒiː/ ▸ noun Law a person to whom an obligation is owed under a contract or other legal procedure. Compare with OBLIGOR.

obligement ▸ noun chiefly Scottish a kindness; a favour.

obliging ▸ adjective willing to do a service or kindness; helpful.
– DERIVATIVES **obligingly** adverb, **obligingness** noun.

obligor /ˈɒblɪgɔː, ˌɒblɪˈgɔː/ ▸ noun Law a person who owes or undertakes an obligation to another by contract or other legal procedure. Compare with OBLIGEE.

oblique /əˈbliːk/ ▸ adjective **1** neither parallel nor at right angles to a specified or implied line; slanting: *we sat on the settee oblique to the fireplace*. ■ Geometry (of a line, plane figure, or surface) inclined at other than a right angle. ■ Geometry (of an angle) acute or obtuse. ■ Geometry (of a cone, cylinder, etc.) with an axis not perpendicular to the plane of its base. ■ Anatomy (especially of a muscle) neither parallel nor perpendicular to the long axis of a body or limb.
2 not expressed or done in a direct way: *he issued an oblique attack on the President*.
3 Grammar denoting any case other than the nominative or vocative.
▸ noun **1** Brit. another term for SLASH (sense 2 of the noun).
2 an oblique muscle.
– DERIVATIVES **obliqueness** noun, **obliquity** /əˈblɪkwɪti/ noun.
– ORIGIN late Middle English: from Latin *obliquus*.

obliquely ▸ adverb **1** not in a direct way; indirectly: *he referred only obliquely to current events*.
2 in an oblique direction; slantwise: *the strings of the instrument run obliquely away from the player*.

obliterate /əˈblɪtəreɪt/ ▸ verb [with obj.] destroy utterly; wipe out: *the memory was so painful that he obliterated it from his mind*. ■ make invisible or indistinct; conceal or cover: *clouds were darkening, obliterating the sun*. ■ cancel (something, especially a postage stamp) to prevent further use.
– DERIVATIVES **obliterative** /-rətɪv/ adjective, **obliterator** noun.
– ORIGIN mid 16th cent.: from Latin *obliterat-* 'struck out, erased', from the verb *obliterare*, based on *littera* 'letter, something written'.

obliteration ▸ noun [mass noun] the action or fact of obliterating or being obliterated; total destruction: *headlines about the obliteration of the green belt*.

oblivion ▸ noun [mass noun] **1** the state of being unaware or unconscious of what is happening around one: *they drank themselves into oblivion*. ■ the state of being forgotten, especially by the public: *his name will fade into oblivion*. ■ destruction or extinction: *only our armed forces stood between us and oblivion*.
2 Law, historical amnesty or pardon.
– ORIGIN late Middle English: via Old French from Latin *oblivio(n-)*, from *oblivisci* 'forget'.

oblivious ▸ adjective not aware of or concerned about what is happening around one: *she became absorbed, **oblivious to** the passage of time*.
– DERIVATIVES **obliviously** adverb, **obliviousness** noun.
– ORIGIN late Middle English: from Latin *obliviosus*, from *oblivio(n-)* (see OBLIVION).

oblong ▸ noun a rectangular object or flat figure with unequal adjacent sides.
▸ adjective having the shape of an oblong: *oblong tables*.
– ORIGIN late Middle English: from Latin *oblongus* 'longish'.

obloquy /ˈɒbləkwi/ ▸ noun [mass noun] strong public condemnation: *he endured years of contempt and obloquy*. ■ disgrace, especially that brought about by public condemnation.
– ORIGIN late Middle English: from late Latin *obloquium* 'contradiction', from Latin *obloqui*, from *ob-* 'against' + *loqui* 'speak'.

obnoxious /əbˈnɒkʃəs/ ▸ adjective extremely unpleasant: *obnoxious odours* | *he found her son somewhat obnoxious*.
– DERIVATIVES **obnoxiously** adverb, **obnoxiousness** noun.
– ORIGIN late 16th cent. (in the sense 'vulnerable to harm'): from Latin *obnoxiosus*, from *obnoxius* 'exposed to harm', from *ob-* 'towards' + *noxa* 'harm'. The current sense, influenced by NOXIOUS, dates from the late 17th cent.

obnubilate /ɒbˈnjuːbɪleɪt/ ▶ **verb** [with obj.] literary darken or cover with or as if with a cloud; obscure.
– DERIVATIVES **obnubilation** noun.
– ORIGIN late 16th cent.: from Latin *obnubilat-* 'covered with clouds or fog', from the verb *obnubilare*.

obo ▶ **abbreviation** N. Amer. or best offer: *$2,700 obo.*

oboe /ˈəʊbəʊ/ ▶ **noun** a woodwind instrument with a double-reed mouthpiece, a slender tubular body, and holes stopped by keys. ■ an organ stop resembling an oboe in tone.
– DERIVATIVES **oboist** noun.
– ORIGIN early 18th cent.: from Italian, or from French *hautbois*, from *haut* 'high' + *bois* 'wood'.

oboe d'amore /daˈmɔːreɪ/ ▶ **noun** a type of oboe with a bulbous bell, sounding a minor third lower than the ordinary oboe. It has a soft tone and is used in baroque music.
– ORIGIN late 19th cent.: from Italian, literally 'oboe of love'.

obol /ˈɒb(ə)l/ ▶ **noun** an ancient Greek coin worth one sixth of a drachma.
– ORIGIN via Latin from Greek *obolos*, variant of *obelos* (see OBELUS).

O-Bon /əʊˈbɒn/ ▶ **noun** another name for **BON**.

Obote /əˈbəʊteɪ, -ti/, (Apollo) Milton (1924–2005), Ugandan statesman, Prime Minister 1962–6, President 1966–71 and 1980–5. Overthrown by Idi Amin in 1971, he was re-elected President in 1980. He was removed in a second military coup in 1985.

obovate /ɒbˈəʊveɪt/ ▶ **adjective** Botany (of a leaf) ovate with the narrower end at the base.

O'Brien, Flann (1911–66), Irish novelist and journalist; pseudonym of *Brian O'Nolan*. Writing under the name of Myles na Gopaleen, he contributed a satirical column to the *Irish Times* for nearly twenty years. Notable novels: *At Swim-Two-Birds* (1939) and *The Third Policeman* (1967).

obscene ▶ **adjective** (of the portrayal or description of sexual matters) offensive or disgusting by accepted standards of morality and decency: *obscene jokes.* ■ offending against moral principles; repugnant: *using animals' skins for fur coats is obscene.*
– DERIVATIVES **obscenely** adverb.
– ORIGIN late 16th cent.: from French *obscène* or Latin *obscaenus* 'ill-omened or abominable'.

obscenity ▶ **noun** (pl. **obscenities**) [mass noun] the state or quality of being obscene: *the book was banned for obscenity.* ■ obscene behaviour, language, or images: *a stream of invective and obscenity.* ■ [count noun] an extremely offensive word or expression: *the men scowled and muttered obscenities.*
– ORIGIN late 16th cent.: from French *obscénité* or Latin *obscaenitas*, from *obscaenus* (see OBSCENE).

obscurantism /ˌɒbskjʊˈrantɪz(ə)m/ ▶ **noun** [mass noun] the practice of deliberately preventing the facts or full details of something from becoming known.
– DERIVATIVES **obscurant** noun & adjective, **obscurantist** noun & adjective.
– ORIGIN mid 19th cent.: from earlier *obscurant*, denoting a person who obscures something, via German from Latin *obscurant-* 'making dark', from the verb *obscurare*.

obscure ▶ **adjective** (**obscurer**, **obscurest**) **1** not discovered or known about; uncertain: *his origins and parentage are obscure.* ■ not important or well known: *a relatively obscure actor.*
2 not clearly expressed or easily understood: *obscure references to Proust.* ■ hard to make out or define; vague: *grey and obscure on the horizon rose a low island | I feel an obscure resentment.*
▶ **verb** [with obj.] keep from being seen; conceal: *grey clouds obscure the sun.* ■ make unclear and difficult to understand: *the debate has become obscured by conflicting ideological perspectives.* ■ keep from being known: *none of this should obscure the skill and perseverance of the workers.*
– DERIVATIVES **obscuration** noun, **obscurely** adverb.
– ORIGIN late Middle English: from Old French *obscur*, from Latin *obscurus* 'dark', from an Indo-European root meaning 'cover'.

obscurity ▶ **noun** (pl. **obscurities**) [mass noun] the state of being unknown, inconspicuous, or unimportant: *he is too good a player to slide into obscurity.* ■ the quality of being difficult to understand: *poems of impenetrable obscurity.* ■ [count noun] a thing that is unclear or difficult to understand: *the obscurities in his poems and plays.*
– ORIGIN late Middle English: from Old French *obscurite*, from Latin *obscuritas*, from *obscurus* 'dark'.

obsecration /ˌɒbsɪˈkreɪʃ(ə)n/ ▶ **noun** [mass noun] rare earnest pleading or supplication.
– ORIGIN late Middle English: from Latin *obsecratio(n-)*, from *obsecrare* 'entreat', based on *sacer, sacr-* 'sacred'.

obsequies /ˈɒbsɪkwɪz/ ▶ **plural noun** funeral rites.
– ORIGIN late Middle English: plural of obsolete *obsequy*, from Anglo-Norman French *obsequie*, from the medieval Latin plural *obsequiae* (from Latin *exsequiae* 'funeral rites', influenced by *obsequium* 'dutiful service').

obsequious /əbˈsiːkwɪəs/ ▶ **adjective** obedient or attentive to an excessive or servile degree: *they were served by obsequious waiters.*
– DERIVATIVES **obsequiously** adverb, **obsequiousness** noun.
– ORIGIN late 15th cent. (not depreciatory in sense in early use): from Latin *obsequiosus*, from *obsequium* 'compliance', from *obsequi* 'follow, comply with'.

observable ▶ **adjective** able to be noticed or perceived; discernible: *observable differences.*
– DERIVATIVES **observability** noun, **observably** adverb.

observance ▶ **noun** [mass noun] **1** the practice of observing the requirements of law, morality, or ritual: *strict observance of the rules | the decline in religious observance.* ■ [count noun] (usu. **observances**) an act performed for religious or ceremonial reasons: *official anniversary observances.* ■ [count noun] a rule to be followed by a religious order: *he drew up a body of monastic observances.*
2 the action of watching or noticing something: *the baby's motionless observance of me.*
3 archaic respect; deference: *the tramp gave them no observance.*
– ORIGIN Middle English: via Old French from Latin *observantia*, from *observant-* 'watching, paying attention to', from the verb *observare* (see OBSERVE).

observant ▶ **adjective 1** quick to notice things: *her observant eye took in every detail.*
2 adhering strictly to the rules of a particular religion, especially Judaism.
▶ **noun** (**Observant**) historical a member of a branch of the Franciscan order that followed a strict rule.
– ORIGIN late Middle English (as a noun): from French, literally 'watching', present participle of *observer* (see OBSERVE).

observation ▶ **noun 1** [mass noun] the action or process of closely observing or monitoring something or someone: *she was brought into hospital for observation | units kept enemy forces* ***under observation*** *for days* | [count noun] *detailed observations were carried out on the students' behaviour.* ■ the ability to notice things, especially significant details: *his powers of observation.* ■ the act of taking the altitude of the sun or another celestial body to find a latitude or longitude.
2 a statement based on something one has seen, heard, or noticed: *he made a telling observation about Hughie.*
– DERIVATIVES **observational** adjective, **observationally** adverb.
– ORIGIN late Middle English (in the sense 'respectful adherence to the requirements of rules or ritual'): from Latin *observatio(n-)*, from the verb *observare* (see OBSERVE).

observation car ▶ **noun** N. Amer. a railway carriage with large windows designed to provide a good view of passing scenery.

observation post ▶ **noun** Military a post for watching the movement of enemy forces or the effect of artillery fire.

observatory ▶ **noun** (pl. **observatories**) a room or building housing an astronomical telescope or other scientific equipment for the study of natural phenomena. ■ a position or building that gives an extensive view.
– ORIGIN late 17th cent.: from modern Latin *observatorium*, from Latin *observat-* 'watched', from the verb *observare* (see OBSERVE).

observe ▶ **verb** [with obj.] **1** notice or perceive (something) and register it as being significant: [with clause] *she observed that all the chairs were already occupied.* ■ watch (someone or something) carefully and attentively: *Rob stood in the hallway, from where he could observe the happenings on the street.* ■ take note of or detect (something) in the course of a scientific study: *the behaviour observed in groups of chimpanzees.*
2 [reporting verb] make a remark: [with direct speech] *'It's chilly,' she observed* | [with clause] *a stockbroker once observed that dealers live and work in hell.*
3 fulfil or comply with (a social, legal, ethical, or religious obligation): *a tribunal must observe the principles of natural justice.* ■ maintain (silence) in compliance with a rule or custom, or temporarily as a mark of respect: *a minute's silence will be observed.* ■ perform or take part in (a rite or ceremony): *relations gather to observe the funeral rites.* ■ celebrate or acknowledge (an anniversary): *they observed the one-year anniversary of the flood.*
– ORIGIN late Middle English (in sense 3): from Old French *observer*, from Latin *observare* 'to watch', from *ob-* 'towards' + *servare* 'attend to, look at'.

observer ▶ **noun** a person who watches or notices something: *to a casual observer, he was at peace.* ■ a person who follows events closely and comments publicly on them: *some observers expect interest rates to rise.* ■ a person posted in an official capacity to an area to monitor political or military events: *elections scrutinized by international observers.* ■ a person who attends a conference, inquiry, etc., to note the proceedings without participating in them: *he had been invited to attend the meeting as an observer.* ■ a person trained to spot and identify enemy aircraft or to reconnoitre enemy positions from the air.

obsess ▶ **verb** [with obj.] preoccupy or fill the mind of (someone) continually and to a troubling extent: *he was obsessed with the idea of revenge | I became more and more obsessed by him.* ■ [no obj.] be constantly talking or worrying about something: *her husband, who is obsessing about the wrong she has done him.*
– ORIGIN late Middle English (in the sense 'haunt, possess', referring to an evil spirit): from Latin *obsess-* 'besieged', from the verb *obsidere*, from *ob-* 'opposite' + *sedere* 'sit'. The current sense dates from the late 19th cent.

obsession ▶ **noun** [mass noun] the state of being obsessed with someone or something: *she cared for him with a devotion bordering on obsession.* ■ [count noun] an idea or thought that continually preoccupies or intrudes on a person's mind.
– DERIVATIVES **obsessional** adjective, **obsessionally** adverb.
– ORIGIN early 16th cent. (in the sense 'siege'): from Latin *obsessio(n-)*, from the verb *obsidere* (see OBSESS).

obsessive ▶ **adjective** of the nature of an obsession: *people dogged by obsessive jealousy.* ■ affected by an obsession: *she became obsessive about her school work.*
▶ **noun** a person who is affected by an obsession: *he's an obsessive, obsessed with having complete collections of things.*
– DERIVATIVES **obsessively** adverb, **obsessiveness** noun.

obsessive–compulsive ▶ **adjective** Psychiatry denoting or relating to an anxiety disorder in which a person feels compelled to perform certain stereotyped actions repeatedly to alleviate persistent fears or intrusive thoughts, typically resulting in severe disruption of daily life.

obsidian /əbˈsɪdɪən/ ▶ **noun** [mass noun] a hard, dark, glass-like volcanic rock formed by the rapid solidification of lava without crystallization.
– ORIGIN mid 17th cent.: from Latin *obsidianus*, error for *obsianus*, from *Obsius*, the name (in Pliny) of the discoverer of a similar stone.

obsolescent /ˌɒbsəˈlɛs(ə)nt/ ▶ **adjective** becoming obsolete: *obsolescent equipment | obsolescent slang.*
– DERIVATIVES **obsolesce** verb, **obsolescence** noun.
– ORIGIN mid 18th cent.: from Latin *obsolescent-* 'falling into disuse', from the verb *obsolescere*.

obsolete ▶ **adjective 1** no longer produced or used; out of date: *the disposal of old and obsolete machinery | the phrase was obsolete after 1625.*
2 Biology (of a part or characteristic of an organism) less developed than formerly or in a related species; rudimentary; vestigial.
▶ **verb** [with obj.] chiefly US cause (a product or idea) to become obsolete by replacing it with something new: *we're trying to stimulate the business by obsoleting last year's designs.*
– DERIVATIVES **obsoletely** adverb, **obsoleteness** noun, **obsoletism** noun.
– ORIGIN late 16th cent.: from Latin *obsoletus* 'grown old, worn out', past participle of *obsolescere* 'fall into disuse'.

obstacle ▶ **noun** a thing that blocks one's way or prevents or hinders progress: *the major* ***obstacle to*** *achieving that goal is money.*

O

– ORIGIN Middle English: via Old French from Latin *obstaculum*, from *obstare* 'impede', from *ob-* 'against' + *stare* 'stand'.

obstacle course ▶ noun an obstacle race. ■ an assault course. ■ a series of difficulties that have to be negotiated in order to achieve a particular aim: *the regulatory maze is an obstacle course for inexperienced would-be entrepreneurs.*

obstacle race ▶ noun a race in which various obstacles, such as fences, pits, and climbing nets, have to be negotiated.

obstetric ▶ adjective relating to childbirth and the processes associated with it.
– DERIVATIVES **obstetrical** adjective (chiefly N. Amer.), **obstetrically** adverb.
– ORIGIN mid 18th cent.: from modern Latin *obstetricus* from Latin *obstetricius* (based on *obstetrix* 'midwife'), from *obstare* 'be present'.

obstetrician /ˌɒbstəˈtrɪʃ(ə)n/ ▶ noun a physician or surgeon qualified to practise in obstetrics.

obstetrics ▶ plural noun [usu. treated as sing.] the branch of medicine and surgery concerned with childbirth and midwifery.

obstinacy ▶ noun [mass noun] the quality or condition of being obstinate; stubbornness: *his reputation for obstinacy.*

obstinate ▶ adjective stubbornly refusing to change one's opinion or chosen course of action, despite attempts to persuade one to do so: *her obstinate determination to pursue a career in radio.* ■ (of an unwelcome situation) very difficult to change or overcome: *the obstinate problem of unemployment.*
– DERIVATIVES **obstinately** adverb.
– ORIGIN Middle English: from Latin *obstinatus*, past participle of *obstinare* 'persist'.

obstipation /ˌɒbstɪˈpeɪʃ(ə)n/ ▶ noun [mass noun] Medicine severe or complete constipation.
– ORIGIN late 16th cent.: alteration of **CONSTIPATION**, by substitution of the prefix **OB-** for *con-*.

obstreperous /əbˈstrɛp(ə)rəs/ ▶ adjective noisy and difficult to control: *the boy is cocky and obstreperous.*
– DERIVATIVES **obstreperously** adverb, **obstreperousness** noun.
– ORIGIN late 16th cent. (in the sense 'clamorous, vociferous'): from Latin *obstreperus* (from *obstrepere*, from *ob-* 'against' + *strepere* 'make a noise') + **-OUS**.

O

obstruct ▶ verb [with obj.] block (an opening, path, road, etc.); be or get in the way of: *she was obstructing the entrance.* ■ prevent or hinder (movement or someone or something in motion): *they had to alter the course of the stream and obstruct the natural flow of the water.* ■ deliberately make (something) difficult: *fears that the regime would obstruct the distribution of food.* ■ Law commit the offence of intentionally hindering (a police officer). ■ (in various sports) impede (a player in the opposing team) in a manner which constitutes an offence.
– DERIVATIVES **obstructor** noun.
– ORIGIN late 16th cent.: from Latin *obstruct-* 'blocked up', from the verb *obstruere*, from *ob-* 'against' + *struere* 'build, pile up'.

obstruction ▶ noun [mass noun] the action of obstructing or the state of being obstructed: *walkers could proceed with the minimum of obstruction.* ■ [count noun] a thing that impedes or prevents passage or progress; an obstacle or blockage: *the tractor hit an obstruction.* ■ (in various sports) the action of unlawfully obstructing a player in the opposing team. ■ Medicine blockage of a bodily passage, especially the gut: *they presented with severe intestinal obstruction.* ■ Law the action of impeding the movement of traffic on a highway. ■ Law the action of deliberately hindering the police in their duties.
– ORIGIN mid 16th cent.: from Latin *obstructio(n-)*, from the verb *obstruere* (see **OBSTRUCT**).

obstructionism ▶ noun [mass noun] the practice of deliberately impeding or delaying the course of legal, legislative, or other procedures.
– DERIVATIVES **obstructionist** noun & adjective.

obstructive ▶ adjective **1** causing a blockage or obstruction: *all tubing should be cleared of obstructive algae and detritus.* ■ relating to obstruction of a passage in the body, especially the gut or the bronchi: *the child developed severe obstructive symptoms.* **2** causing or tending to cause deliberate difficulties and delays: *he denied the council had been obstructive.*
– DERIVATIVES **obstructively** adverb, **obstructiveness** noun.

obstructive jaundice ▶ noun [mass noun] Medicine jaundice resulting from blockage of the bile ducts or abnormal retention of bile in the liver.

obstruent /ˈɒbstrʊənt/ ▶ noun Phonetics a fricative or plosive speech sound.
– ORIGIN mid 17th cent.: from Latin *obstruent-* 'blocking up', from the verb *obstruere*.

obtain ▶ verb **1** [with obj.] get, acquire, or secure (something): *adequate insurance cover is difficult to obtain.* **2** [no obj.] formal be prevalent, customary, or established: *the price of silver fell to that obtaining elsewhere in the ancient world.*
– DERIVATIVES **obtainer** noun, **obtainment** noun.
– ORIGIN late Middle English: from Old French *obtenir*, from Latin *obtinere* 'obtain, gain'.

obtainable ▶ adjective able to be obtained: *customers' financial details are easily obtainable.*
– DERIVATIVES **obtainability** noun.

obtect (also **obtected**) ▶ adjective Entomology (of an insect pupa or chrysalis) covered in a hard case with the legs and wings attached immovably against the body.
– ORIGIN late 19th cent.: from Latin *obtectus*, past participle of *obtegere* 'cover over'.

obtention /əbˈtɛnʃ(ə)n/ ▶ noun the action of obtaining something.
– ORIGIN early 17th cent.: from French, or from late Latin *obtentio(n-)*, from *obtinere* 'obtain, gain'.

obtrude ▶ verb [no obj.] become noticeable in an unwelcome or intrusive way: *a sound from the reception hall obtruded into his thoughts.* ■ [with obj.] impose or force (something) on someone in an unwelcome or intrusive way: *I felt unable to obtrude my private sorrow upon anyone.*
– DERIVATIVES **obtrusion** noun.
– ORIGIN mid 16th cent.: from Latin *obtrudere*, from *ob-* 'towards' + *trudere* 'to push'.

obtrusive ▶ adjective noticeable or prominent in an unwelcome or intrusive way: *a large and obtrusive works where ammonia is produced.*
– DERIVATIVES **obtrusively** adverb, **obtrusiveness** noun.
– ORIGIN mid 17th cent.: from Latin *obtrus-* 'thrust forward', from the verb *obtrudere* (see **OBTRUDE**).

obtund /əbˈtʌnd/ ▶ verb [with obj.] dated, chiefly Medicine dull the sensitivity of; blunt; deaden.
– ORIGIN late Middle English: from Latin *obtundere*, from *ob-* 'against' + *tundere* 'to beat'.

obturator /ˈɒbtjʊəreɪtə/ ▶ noun Anatomy either of two muscles covering the outer front part of the pelvis on each side and involved in movements of the thigh and hip. ■ [as modifier] relating to the obturator or to the obturator foramen.
– ORIGIN early 18th cent.: from medieval Latin, literally 'obstructor', from *obturare* 'stop up'.

obturator foramen ▶ noun Anatomy a large opening in the hip bone between the pubis and the ischium.

obtuse ▶ adjective **1** annoyingly insensitive or slow to understand: *he wondered if the doctor was being deliberately obtuse.* ■ difficult to understand, especially deliberately so: *some of the lyrics are a bit obtuse.* **2** (of an angle) more than 90° and less than 180°. **3** not sharp-pointed or sharp-edged; blunt.
– DERIVATIVES **obtusely** adverb, **obtuseness** noun, **obtusity** noun.
– ORIGIN late Middle English (in sense 3): from Latin *obtusus*, past participle of *obtundere* 'beat against' (see **OBTUND**).

Ob-Ugrian /ɒbˈuːgrɪən, -ˈjuː-/ (also **Ob-Ugric**) ▶ adjective of or denoting a branch of the Finno-Ugric language family containing two languages of western Siberia, related to Hungarian.
▶ noun [mass noun] the Ob-Ugrian group of languages.
– ORIGIN 1930s: from the name of the Siberian river **OB** + **UGRIAN**.

obverse ▶ noun [usu. in sing.] **1** the side of a coin or medal bearing the head or principal design. ■ the design or inscription on the principal side of a coin. **2** the opposite or counterpart of a fact or truth: *true solitude is the obverse of true society.*
▶ adjective [attrib.] **1** of or denoting the obverse of a coin or medal. **2** corresponding to something else as its opposite or counterpart.
– DERIVATIVES **obversely** adverb.
– ORIGIN mid 17th cent. (in the sense 'turned towards the observer'): from Latin *obversus*, past participle of *obvertere* 'turn towards' (see **OBVERT**).

obvert ▶ verb [with obj.] Logic alter (a proposition) so as to infer another proposition with a contradictory predicate, e.g. *'no men are immortal'* to *'all men are mortal'*.
– DERIVATIVES **obversion** noun.
– ORIGIN early 17th cent. (in the sense 'turn something until it is facing'): from Latin *obvertere*, from *ob-* 'towards' + *vertere* 'to turn'.

obviate /ˈɒbvɪeɪt/ ▶ verb [with obj.] remove (a need or difficulty): *the presence of roller blinds obviated the need for curtains.* ■ avoid or prevent (something undesirable): *a parachute can be used to obviate disaster.*
– DERIVATIVES **obviation** noun.
– ORIGIN late 16th cent.: from late Latin *obviat-* 'prevented', from the verb *obviare*, based on Latin *via* 'way'.

obvious ▶ adjective easily perceived or understood; clear, self-evident, or apparent: *unemployment has been the most obvious cost of the recession* | [with clause] *it was obvious a storm was coming in.* ■ derogatory predictable and lacking in subtlety: *it was an obvious remark to make.*
– DERIVATIVES **obviousness** noun.
– ORIGIN late 16th cent. (in the sense 'frequently encountered'): from Latin *obvius* (from the phrase *ob viam* 'in the way') + **-OUS**.

obviously ▶ adverb in a way that is easily perceived or understood; clearly: *she was obviously unwell* | [sentence adverb] *obviously, everyone has to do what they think is right.*

OC ▶ abbreviation ■ Officer Commanding. ■ Officer of the Order of Canada.

oc- ▶ prefix variant spelling of **OB-** assimilated before *c* (as in *occasion, occlude*).

oca /ˈəʊkə/ ▶ noun a South American plant related to wood sorrel, long cultivated in Peru for its edible tubers. ● *Oxalis tuberosa*, family Oxalidaceae.
– ORIGIN early 17th cent.: from American Spanish, from Quechua *ócca*.

ocarina /ˌɒkəˈriːnə/ ▶ noun a small egg-shaped ceramic (especially terracotta) or metal wind instrument with holes for the fingers.
– ORIGIN late 19th cent.: from Italian, from *oca* 'goose' (from its shape).

OCAS ▶ abbreviation Organization of Central American States.

O'Casey, Sean (1880–1964), Irish dramatist. Notable plays: *The Shadow of a Gunman* (1923) and *Juno and the Paycock* (1924).

Occam /ˈɒkəm/ ▶ noun [mass noun] a computer programming language devised for use in parallel processing.
– ORIGIN 1980s: from the name of **WILLIAM OF OCCAM**.

Occam, William of see **WILLIAM OF OCCAM**.

Occam's razor (also **Ockham's razor**) the principle (attributed to William of Occam) that in explaining a thing no more assumptions should be made than are necessary. The principle is often invoked to defend reductionism or nominalism.

occasion ▶ noun **1** a particular event, or the time at which it takes place: *on one occasion I stayed up until two in the morning.* ■ a special or noteworthy event, ceremony, or celebration: *she was presented with a gold watch to mark the occasion* | [mass noun] *Sunday lunch has a suitable sense of occasion about it.* ■ a suitable or opportune time for doing something: *by-elections are traditionally an occasion for registering protest votes.* **2** [mass noun] formal reason; cause: [with infinitive] *it's the first time that I've had occasion to complain.*
▶ verb [with obj.] formal cause (something): *something vital must have occasioned this visit* | [with two objs] *his death occasioned her much grief.*
– PHRASES **on occasion** (or **occasions**) occasionally; from time to time: *on occasion, the state was asked to intervene.* **rise to the occasion** perform better than usual in response to a special situation or event. **take occasion** archaic make use of an opportunity to do something.
– ORIGIN late Middle English: from Latin *occasio(n-)* 'juncture, reason', from *occidere* 'go down, set', from *ob-* 'towards' + *cadere* 'to fall'.

occasional ▶ adjective occurring, appearing, or done infrequently and irregularly: *the occasional car went by but no taxis.* ■ (of furniture) made or adapted for use on a particular occasion or for infrequent use: *an occasional table.* ■ (of a literary composition, speech, religious service, etc.) produced on or intended for a special occasion: *he wrote occasional verse for patrons.* ■ dated employed for a particular occasion or on an irregular basis: *occasional freelancer seeks full-time position.*
– DERIVATIVES **occasionality** noun.

occasionalism ▶ **noun** [mass noun] Philosophy the doctrine ascribing the connection between mental and bodily events to the continuing intervention of God.

occasionally ▶ **adverb** at infrequent or irregular intervals; now and then: *we met up occasionally for a drink* | *very occasionally the condition can result in death.*

occasional table ▶ **noun** a small decorative table for infrequent and varied use.

Occident /ˈɒksɪd(ə)nt/ ▶ **noun** (**the Occident**) formal or literary the countries of the West, especially Europe and America.
– ORIGIN late Middle English: via Old French from Latin *occident-* 'going down, setting', from the verb *occidere.*

occidental ▶ **adjective** relating to the countries of the West.
▶ **noun** (**Occidental**) a native or inhabitant of the Occident.
– DERIVATIVES **occidentalism** noun, **occidentalize** (also **occidentalise**) verb.
– ORIGIN late Middle English: from Old French, or from Latin *occidentalis*, from *occident-* 'going down' (see **Occident**).

occipital bone /ɒkˈsɪpɪt(ə)l bəʊn/ ▶ **noun** Anatomy the bone which forms the back and base of the skull and encircles the spinal cord.

occipital condyle ▶ **noun** Anatomy each of two rounded knobs at the base of the skull which articulate with the first vertebra.

occipital lobe ▶ **noun** Anatomy the rearmost lobe in each cerebral hemisphere of the brain.

occipito- /ɒkˈsɪpɪtəʊ/ ▶ **combining form** relating to the occipital lobe or the occipital bone: *occipitotemporal.*
– ORIGIN from medieval Latin *occipitalis*, from Latin *caput, capit-* 'head'.

occipitotemporal /ɒkˌsɪpɪtə(ʊ)ˈtɛmp(ə)r(ə)l/ ▶ **adjective** Anatomy relating to the occipital and temporal bones.

occiput /ˈɒksɪpʌt/ ▶ **noun** Anatomy the back of the head.
– DERIVATIVES **occipital** adjective.
– ORIGIN late Middle English: from Latin *occiput*, from *ob-* 'against' + *caput* 'head'.

Occitan /ˈɒksɪt(ə)n/ ▶ **noun** [mass noun] the medieval or modern language of Languedoc, including literary Provençal of the 12th–14th centuries.
▶ **adjective** relating to Occitan.
– DERIVATIVES **Occitanian** noun & adjective.
– ORIGIN French (see also **langue d'oc**).

occlude /əˈkluːd/ ▶ **verb** [with obj.] formal or technical **1** stop, close up, or obstruct (an opening, orifice, or passage): *thick make-up can occlude the pores.* ■ shut in: *they were occluding the waterfront with a wall of buildings.* ■ cover (an eye) to prevent its use.
2 [no obj.] (of a tooth) come into contact with another tooth in the opposite jaw.
3 Chemistry (of a solid) absorb and retain (a gas or impurity).
– ORIGIN late 16th cent.: from Latin *occludere* 'shut up'.

occluded front ▶ **noun** Meteorology a composite front produced by occlusion.

occlusal ▶ **adjective** Dentistry relating to or involved in the occlusion of teeth. ■ denoting a surface of a tooth that comes into contact with a tooth in the other jaw.

occlusion ▶ **noun** [mass noun] **1** Medicine the blockage or closing of a blood vessel or hollow organ.
2 [count noun] Meteorology a process by which the cold front of a rotating low-pressure system catches up the warm front, so that the warm air between them is forced upwards off the earth's surface between wedges of cold air. ■ an occluded front.
3 Dentistry the position of the teeth when the jaws are closed.
– DERIVATIVES **occlusive** adjective.
– ORIGIN mid 17th cent.: from Latin *occlus-* 'shut up' (from the verb *occludere*) + **-ion**.

occult /ɒˈkʌlt, ˈɒkʌlt/ ▶ **noun** (**the occult**) mystical, supernatural, or magical powers, practices, or phenomena: *a secret society to study alchemy and the occult.*
▶ **adjective 1** involving or relating to mystical, supernatural, or magical powers, practices, or phenomena: *an occult ceremony* | *a weird occult sensation of having experienced the identical situation before.* ■ communicated only to the initiated; esoteric: *the typically occult language of the time.*
2 Medicine (of a disease or process) not accompanied by readily discernible signs or symptoms. ■ (of blood) abnormally present, e.g. in faeces, but detectable only chemically or microscopically.
▶ **verb** /ɒˈkʌlt/ [with obj.] cut off from view by interposing something: *a wooden screen designed to occult the competitors.* ■ Astronomy (of a celestial body) conceal (an apparently smaller body) from view by passing or being in front of it.
– DERIVATIVES **occultation** noun, **occultism** noun, **occultist** noun, **occultly** adverb.
– ORIGIN late 15th cent. (as a verb): from Latin *occultare* 'secrete', frequentative of *occulere* 'conceal', based on *celare* 'to hide'; the adjective and noun from *occult-* 'covered over', from the verb *occulere.*

occulting light ▶ **noun** a light in a lighthouse or buoy which shines for a longer period than that for which it is cut off.

occupance ▶ **noun** another term for **occupancy**.
■ Geography the inhabiting and modification of an area by humans.
– ORIGIN early 19th cent.: from **occupant** + **-ance**.

occupancy ▶ **noun** (pl. **occupancies**) [mass noun] the action or fact of occupying a place: *the palace proved unready for occupancy.* ■ the proportion of hotel or office accommodation occupied or used: *70 per cent occupancy is needed to give a profit* | [count noun] *average daily room occupancies.*

occupant ▶ **noun** a person who resides or is present in a house, vehicle, seat, etc., at a given time: *the previous occupant of her room* | figurative *occupants of the moral high ground.* ■ the holder of a position or office: *the first occupant of the Chair of Botany.* ■ Law a person in actual possession of property, especially land. ■ Law a person who establishes a title by taking possession of something that previously did not have an established owner.
– ORIGIN late 16th cent. (in the legal sense 'person who establishes a title'): from French, or from Latin *occupant-* 'seizing', from the verb *occupare.*

occupation ▶ **noun 1** a job or profession: *people in professional occupations.* ■ a way of spending time: *a game of cards is a pretty harmless occupation.*
2 [mass noun] the action, state, or period of occupying or being occupied by military force: *the Roman occupation of Britain.* ■ the action of entering and taking control of a building: *the workers remained in **occupation** until 16 October.*
3 [mass noun] the action of living in or using a building or other place: *a property suitable for occupation by older people.*
▶ **adjective** Brit. for the sole use of the occupiers of the land concerned.
– ORIGIN Middle English: via Old French from Latin *occupatio(n-)*, from the verb *occupare* (see **occupy**). Sense 2 of the noun dates from the mid 16th cent.

occupational ▶ **adjective** relating to a job or profession: *an occupational pension scheme.*
– DERIVATIVES **occupationally** adverb.

occupational hazard (also **occupational risk**) ▶ **noun** a risk accepted as a consequence of a particular occupation.

occupational psychology ▶ **noun** [mass noun] the study of human behaviour at work, including methods of selecting personnel, improving productivity, and coping with stress.
– DERIVATIVES **occupational psychologist** noun.

occupational therapy ▶ **noun** [mass noun] the use of particular activities as an aid to recuperation from physical or mental illness.
– DERIVATIVES **occupational therapist** noun.

occupied ▶ **adjective 1** (of a building, seat, etc.) being used by someone: *only the ground floor is fully occupied.*
2 busy and active: *tasks which kept her occupied for the day.*
3 (of a place, especially a country) taken control of by military conquest or settlement: *the occupied territories.*

occupier ▶ **noun 1** Brit. a person or company residing in or using a property as its owner or tenant, or (illegally) as a squatter.
2 a member of a group that takes possession of a country by force.

occupy ▶ **verb** (**occupies, occupying, occupied**) [with obj.] **1** reside or have one's place of business in (a building): *the rented flat she occupies in Hampstead.*
2 fill or take up (a space or time): *two long windows occupied almost the whole of the end wall.* ■ be situated in or at (a position in a system or hierarchy): *the Bank of England occupies a central position in the UK financial system.* ■ hold (a position or job).
3 fill or preoccupy (the mind): *her mind was occupied with alarming questions.* ■ keep (someone) busy and active: *Sarah **occupied herself** taking the coffee cups over to the sink.*
4 take control of (a place, especially a country) by military conquest or settlement: *Syria was occupied by France under a League of Nations mandate.* ■ enter and stay in (a building) without authority and often forcibly, especially as a form of protest: *the workers occupied the factory.*
– ORIGIN Middle English: formed irregularly from Old French *occuper*, from Latin *occupare* 'seize'. A now obsolete vulgar sense 'have sexual relations with' seems to have led to the general avoidance of the word in the 17th and most of the 18th cent.

occur ▶ **verb** (**occurs, occurring, occurred**) [no obj., with adverbial] happen; take place: *the accident occurred at about 3.30 p.m.* ■ exist or be found to be present in a place or under a particular set of conditions: *radon occurs naturally in rocks such as granite.* ■ (**occur to**) (of a thought or idea) come into the mind of: [with clause] *it occurred to him that he hadn't eaten.*
– ORIGIN late 15th cent.: from Latin *occurrere* 'go to meet, present itself', from *ob-* 'against' + *currere* 'to run'.

occurrence /əˈkʌr(ə)ns/ ▶ **noun** an incident or event: *vandalism used to be a rare occurrence.* ■ [mass noun] the fact or frequency of something happening: *the occurrence of cancer increases with age.* ■ [mass noun] the fact of something existing or being found in a place or under a particular set of conditions: *the occurrence of natural gas fields.*
– ORIGIN mid 16th cent.: probably from the plural of archaic *occurrent*, in the same sense, via French from Latin *occurrent-* 'befalling', from the verb *occurrere* (see **occur**).

occurrent ▶ **adjective** actually occurring or observable, not potential or hypothetical.
– ORIGIN late 15th cent.: from French, or from Latin *occurrent-* 'befalling', from the verb *occurrere.*

OCD ▶ **abbreviation** obsessive–compulsive disorder.

ocean ▶ **noun** a very large expanse of sea, in particular each of the main areas into which the sea is divided geographically: *the Atlantic Ocean.* ■ (**the ocean**) N. Amer. the sea: *they scramble across the beach to the ocean and plunge into the surf.* ■ (**an ocean of/ oceans of**) informal a very large expanse or quantity: *she had oceans of energy.*
– DERIVATIVES **oceanward** (also **oceanwards**) adverb & adjective.
– ORIGIN Middle English: from Old French *occean*, via Latin from Greek *ōkeanos* 'great stream encircling the earth's disc'. 'The ocean' originally denoted the whole body of water regarded as encompassing the earth's single land mass.

O

oceanarium /ˌəʊʃəˈnɛːrɪəm/ ▶ **noun** (pl. **oceanariums** or **oceanaria** /-rɪə/) a large seawater aquarium in which marine animals are kept for study and public entertainment.
– ORIGIN 1940s: from **ocean**, on the pattern of *aquarium.*

ocean basin ▶ **noun** a depression of the earth's surface in which an ocean lies.

oceanfront ▶ **noun** chiefly N. Amer. the land that borders an ocean.

ocean-going ▶ **adjective** (of a ship) designed to cross oceans.

Oceania /ˌəʊsɪˈɑːnɪə, -ʃɪ-/ the islands of the Pacific Ocean and adjacent seas.
– DERIVATIVES **Oceanian** adjective & noun.
– ORIGIN modern Latin, from French *Océanie.*

oceanic /ˌəʊsɪˈanɪk, -ʃɪ-/ ▶ **adjective 1** relating to the ocean: *oceanic atolls.* ■ of or inhabiting the part of the ocean beyond the edge of a continental shelf: *stocks of oceanic fish.* ■ (of a climate) governed by the proximity of the ocean. ■ of enormous size or extent; huge; vast: *an oceanic failure.*
2 (**Oceanic**) relating to Oceania: *a gallery specializing in Oceanic art.*

oceanic bonito ▶ **noun** another term for **skipjack** (sense 1).

oceanic crust ▶ **noun** Geology the relatively thin part of the earth's crust which underlies the ocean basins. It is geologically young compared with the continental crust and consists of basaltic rock overlain by sediments.

oceanic ridge ▶ **noun** another term for **mid-ocean ridge**.

Oceanid /əʊ'si:ənɪd, 'əʊʃ(ə)nɪd/ ▸ **noun** (pl. **Oceanids** or **Oceanides** /ˌəʊsɪ'anɪdi:z, ˌəʊʃɪ-/) Greek Mythology a sea nymph.
– ORIGIN from French *Océanide*, from Greek *ōkeanis*, *ōkeanid-*.

Ocean Island another name for **Banaba**.

ocean liner ▸ **noun** see **liner**[1] (sense 1).

oceanography ▸ **noun** [mass noun] the branch of science that deals with the physical and biological properties and phenomena of the sea.
– DERIVATIVES **oceanographer** noun, **oceanographic** adjective, **oceanographical** adjective.

oceanology ▸ **noun** another term for **oceanography**. ■ the branch of technology and economics dealing with human use of the sea.
– DERIVATIVES **oceanological** adjective, **oceanologist** noun.

oceanside ▸ **noun** N. Amer. a place or area of land by the sea: [as modifier] *an oceanside resort.*

Ocean State informal name for **Rhode Island**.

ocean trench ▸ **noun** see **trench**.

Oceanus /əʊ'si:ənəs, ˌəʊsɪ'em-, ˌəʊsɪ'ɑ:n-/ Greek Mythology the son of Uranus (Heaven) and Gaia (Earth), the personification of the great river believed to encircle the whole world.

ocellated /'ɒsɪleɪtɪd/ ▸ **adjective** (of an animal) having eye-like markings.

ocellus /ə'sɛləs/ ▸ **noun** (pl. **ocelli** /-lʌɪ, -li:/) Zoology
1 another term for **simple eye**.
2 another term for **eyespot** (sense 1, sense 2).
– DERIVATIVES **ocellar** adjective.
– ORIGIN early 19th cent.: from Latin, diminutive of *oculus* 'eye'.

ocelot /'ɒsɪlɒt, 'əʊs-/ ▸ **noun** a medium-sized wild cat that has an orange-yellow coat marked with black stripes and spots, native to South and Central America. ● *Felis pardalis*, family Felidae.
■ [mass noun] the fur of the ocelot.
– ORIGIN late 18th cent.: from French, from Nahuatl *tlatlocelotl*, literally 'field tiger'.

och /ɒk, ɒx/ ▸ **exclamation** Scottish & Irish used to express a range of emotions, typically surprise, regret, or disbelief: *Och, you're kidding.*

oche /'ɒki/ (also **hockey**) ▸ **noun** Brit. the line behind which darts players stand when throwing.
– ORIGIN 1930s: perhaps related to Old French *ocher* 'cut a deep notch in'.

O

ocher ▸ **noun** US spelling of **ochre**.

ochlocracy /ɒk'lɒkrəsi/ ▸ **noun** [mass noun] government by the populace; mob rule.
– DERIVATIVES **ochlocratic** adjective.
– ORIGIN late 16th cent.: via French from Greek *okhlokratia*, from *okhlos* 'mob' + *-kratia* 'power'.

ochone /əʊ'həʊn, ɒ'xəʊn/ (also **ohone**) ▸ **exclamation** Irish & Scottish literary used to express regret or sorrow.
– ORIGIN from Scottish Gaelic *ochòin*, Irish *ochón*.

ochre /'əʊkə/ (US also **ocher**) ▸ **noun** [mass noun] an earthy pigment containing ferric oxide, typically with clay, varying from light yellow to brown or red. ■ a pale brownish yellow colour.
– DERIVATIVES **ochreous** /'əʊkrɪəs/ adjective, **ochry** adjective.
– ORIGIN Middle English: from Old French *ocre*, via Latin from Greek *ōkhra* 'yellow ochre'.

ochrea /'ɒkrɪə/ ▸ **noun** (pl. **ochreas** or **ochreae** /'ɒkrii:/) Botany a dry sheath round a stem formed by the cohesion of two or more stipules, characteristic of the dock family.
– ORIGIN mid 19th cent.: from Latin, literally 'protective legging'.

-ock ▸ **suffix** forming nouns originally with diminutive sense: *haddock* | *pollock*. ■ also occasionally forming words from other sources: *bannock* | *hassock*.
– ORIGIN Old English *-uc*, *-oc*.

ocker ▸ **noun** Austral. informal a rough and uncultivated Australian man: [as modifier] *an ocker sports writer.*
– ORIGIN alteration of *Oscar*, popularized by the name of a character in an Australian television series (1965–68).

Ockham's razor variant spelling of **Occam's razor**.

Ockham, William of see **William of Occam**.

o'clock ▸ **adverb** used to specify the hour when telling the time: *the gates will open at eight o'clock.* ■ used following a numeral to indicate direction or bearing with reference to an imaginary clock face, 12 o'clock being thought of as directly in front or overhead.

O'Connell, Daniel (1775–1847), Irish nationalist leader and social reformer; known as **the Liberator**. His election to Parliament in 1828 forced the British government to grant Catholic Emancipation in order to enable him to take his seat in the House of Commons. In 1839 he established the Repeal Association to abolish the union with Britain.

O'Connor, (Mary) Flannery (1925–64), American novelist and short-story writer. Notable novels: *Wise Blood* (1952) and *The Violent Bear It Away* (1960).

ocotillo /ˌəʊkə'ti:jəʊ/ ▸ **noun** (pl. **ocotillos**) chiefly US a spiny scarlet-flowered desert shrub of the southwestern US and Mexico, which is sometimes planted as a hedge. ● *Fouquieria splendens*, family Fouquieriaceae.
– ORIGIN mid 19th cent.: via American Spanish (diminutive form) from Nahuatl *ocotl* 'torch'.

OCR ▸ **abbreviation** optical character recognition.

-ocracy ▸ **combining form** see **-cracy**.

Oct. ▸ **abbreviation** October.

oct. ▸ **abbreviation** octavo.

oct- ▸ **combining form** variant spelling of **octa-** and **octo-** assimilated before a vowel (as in *octennial*).

octa- (also **oct-** before a vowel) ▸ **combining form** eight; having eight: *octahedron*.
– ORIGIN from Greek *oktō* 'eight'.

octad /'ɒktad/ ▸ **noun** technical a group or set of eight.
– ORIGIN mid 19th cent.: via late Latin from Greek *oktas*, *oktad-*, from *oktō* 'eight'.

octagon ▸ **noun** a plane figure with eight straight sides and eight angles. ■ an object or building with an octagonal plan or cross section.
– DERIVATIVES **octagonal** /-'tag(ə)n(ə)l/ adjective.
– ORIGIN late 16th cent.: via Latin from Greek *octagōnos* 'eight-angled'.

octahedron /ˌɒktə'hi:drən, -'hɛd-/ ▸ **noun** (pl. **octahedra** /-drə/ or **octahedrons**) a three-dimensional shape having eight plane faces, especially a regular solid figure with eight equal triangular faces. ■ a body, especially a crystal, in the form of a regular octahedron.
– DERIVATIVES **octahedral** adjective.
– ORIGIN late 16th cent.: from Greek *oktaedron*, neuter (used as a noun) of *oktaedros* 'eight-faced'.

octal /'ɒkt(ə)l/ ▸ **adjective** relating to or using a system of numerical notation that has 8 rather than 10 as a base.
▸ **noun** [mass noun] the octal system; octal notation.

octamerous /ɒk'tam(ə)rəs/ ▸ **adjective** Botany & Zoology having parts arranged in groups of eight. ■ consisting of eight joints or parts.

octameter /ɒk'tamɪtə/ ▸ **noun** Prosody a line of verse consisting of eight metrical feet.

octane ▸ **noun** [mass noun] Chemistry a colourless flammable hydrocarbon of the alkane series, present in petroleum spirit. ● Chem. formula: C_8H_{18}; many isomers, especially the straight-chain isomer (***n*-octane**). See also **isooctane**.
– ORIGIN late 19th cent.: from **octo-** 'eight' (denoting eight carbon atoms) + **-ane**[2].

octane number (also **octane rating**) ▸ **noun** a figure indicating the anti-knock properties of a fuel, based on a comparison with a mixture of isooctane and heptane.

octangular ▸ **adjective** having eight angles.

Octans /'ɒktanz/ Astronomy a faint southern constellation (the Octant), containing the south celestial pole.
– ORIGIN Latin.

octant /'ɒkt(ə)nt/ ▸ **noun** an arc of a circle equal to one eighth of its circumference, or the area enclosed by such an arc with two radii of the circle. ■ each of eight parts into which a space or solid body is divided by three planes which intersect (especially at right angles) at a single point. ■ an obsolete instrument in the form of a graduated eighth of a circle, used in astronomy and navigation.
– ORIGIN late 17th cent.: from Latin *octans*, *octant-* 'half-quadrant', from *octo* 'eight'.

octaroon ▸ **noun** variant spelling of **octoroon**.

octastyle ▸ **adjective** (of a building or portico) having eight columns at the end or in front.
▸ **noun** an octastyle portico or building.
– ORIGIN early 18th cent.: via Latin from Greek *oktastulos*, from *okta-* 'eight' + *stulos* 'pillar'.

octavalent /ˌɒktə'veɪl(ə)nt/ ▸ **adjective** Chemistry having a valency of eight.

octave /'ɒktɪv/ ▸ **noun 1** Music a series of eight notes occupying the interval between (and including) two notes, one having twice or half the frequency of vibration of the other. ■ the interval between the two notes at the extremes of an octave. ■ each of the two notes at the extremes of an octave. ■ the two notes at the extremes of an octave sounding together.
2 a group or stanza of eight lines; an octet.
3 the seventh day after a Church festival. ■ a period of eight days beginning with the day of a Church festival.
4 Fencing the last of eight parrying positions.
5 Brit. a wine cask holding an eighth of a pipe.
– PHRASES **law of octaves** see **Newlands**.
– ORIGIN Middle English (in sense 3): via Old French from Latin *octava dies* 'eighth day'.

octave coupler ▸ **noun** another term for **coupler**.

Octavian /ɒk'teɪvɪən/ see **Augustus**.

octavo /ɒk'tɑ:vəʊ, -'teɪ-/ (abbrev.: **8vo**) ▸ **noun** (pl. **octavos**) a size of book page that results from folding each printed sheet into eight leaves (sixteen pages). ■ a book of octavo size.
– ORIGIN late 16th cent.: from Latin *in octavo* 'in an eighth', from *octavus* 'eighth'.

octennial ▸ **adjective** recurring every eight years. ■ lasting for or relating to a period of eight years.
– ORIGIN mid 17th cent.: from late Latin *octennium* 'period of eight years' + **-al**.

octet /ɒk'tɛt/ ▸ **noun** a group of eight people or things, in particular: ■ a group of eight musicians. ■ a musical composition for eight voices or instruments. ■ the first eight lines of a sonnet. ■ Chemistry a stable group of eight electrons occupying a single shell in an atom.
– ORIGIN mid 19th cent.: from Italian *ottetto* or German *Oktett*, on the pattern of *duet* and *quartet*.

octo- (also **oct-** before a vowel) ▸ **combining form** eight; having eight: *octosyllabic*.
– ORIGIN from Latin *octo* or Greek *oktō* 'eight'.

October ▸ **noun** the tenth month of the year, in the northern hemisphere usually considered the second month of autumn: *the project started in October* | *one of the wettest Octobers on record.*
– ORIGIN late Old English, from Latin, from *octo* 'eight' (being originally the eighth month of the Roman year).

October Revolution ▸ **noun** see **Russian Revolution**.

October War Arab name for **Yom Kippur War**.

Octobrist /ɒk'təʊbrɪst/ ▸ **noun** historical a member of the moderate party in the Russian Duma, which supported Tsar Nicholas II's reforming manifesto of 30 October 1905.
– ORIGIN suggested by Russian *oktyabrist*.

octocentenary ▸ **noun** (pl. **octocentenaries**) the eight-hundredth anniversary of a significant event.

octodecimo /ˌɒktəʊ'dɛsɪməʊ/ ▸ **noun** (pl. **octodecimos**) a size of book page resulting from folding each printed sheet into eighteen leaves (36 pages). ■ a book of octodecimo size.
– ORIGIN mid 19th cent.: from Latin *in octodecimo* 'in an eighteenth', from *octodecimus* 'eighteenth'.

octofoil ▸ **adjective** having or consisting of eight leaves or lobes.
▸ **noun** an octofoil ornamental or heraldic figure.
– ORIGIN mid 19th cent.: from **octo-** 'eight', on the pattern of words such as *trefoil*.

octogenarian /ˌɒktə(ʊ)dʒɪ'nɛ:rɪən/ ▸ **noun** a person who is between 80 and 89 years old.
– ORIGIN early 19th cent.: from Latin *octogenarius* (based on *octoginta* 'eighty') + **-an**.

octonary /'ɒktə(ʊ)n(ə)ri/ ▸ **adjective** rare relating to or based on the number eight.

octopamine /ɒk'təʊpəmi:n/ ▸ **noun** [mass noun] Biochemistry a compound which can accumulate in nerves as a result of the use of monoamine oxidase inhibitors and cause a rise in blood pressure.
● An amine related to noradrenaline; chem. formula: $HOC_6H_4CHOHCH_2NH_2$.
– ORIGIN 1940s: from **octopus** (from which it was first extracted) + **amine**.

octopod ▸ **noun** Zoology a cephalopod mollusc of the order Octopoda; an octopus.

Octopoda /ˌɒktə'pəʊdə/ ▸ **plural noun** Zoology an order of cephalopod molluscs that comprises the octopuses.
– ORIGIN modern Latin (plural), from Greek *oktōpous*, *oktōpod-*, from *oktō* 'eight' + *pous*, *pod-* 'foot'.

octopus ▸ **noun** (pl. **octopuses**) a cephalopod mollusc with eight sucker-bearing arms, a soft sac-like body,

strong beak-like jaws, and no internal shell. ● Order Octopoda, class Cephalopoda: *Octopus* and other genera.
– DERIVATIVES **octopoid** adjective.
– ORIGIN mid 18th cent.: modern Latin, from Greek *oktōpous* (see **OCTOPODA**).

USAGE The standard plural in English of **octopus** is **octopuses**. However, the word **octopus** comes from Greek and the Greek plural form **octopodes** is still occasionally used. The plural form **octopi**, formed according to rules for some Latin plurals, is incorrect.

octoroon /ˌɒktəˈruːn/ (also **octaroon**) ▶ **noun** dated a person who is one-eighth black by descent.
– ORIGIN mid 19th cent.: from **OCTO-** 'eight', on the pattern of *quadroon*.

octosyllable ▶ **noun** a word or line of verse with eight syllables.
– DERIVATIVES **octosyllabic** adjective.

octothorp /ˈɒktə(ʊ)θɔːp/ (also **octothorpe**) ▶ **noun** chiefly N. Amer. another term for the symbol #.
– ORIGIN 1970s: of uncertain origin; probably from **OCTO-** (referring to the eight points on the symbol) + the surname *Thorpe*.

octroi /ˈɒktrwɑː/ ▶ **noun** (pl. **octrois**) a duty levied in some countries on various goods entering a town or city.
– ORIGIN late 16th cent.: from French *octroyer* 'to grant', based on medieval Latin *auctorizare* (see **AUTHORIZE**). Current senses date from the early 18th cent.

octuple /ˈɒktjʊp(ə)l, ɒkˈtjuːp(ə)l/ ▶ **adjective** [attrib.] consisting of eight parts or things. ■ eight times as many or as much.
▶ **verb** make or become eight times as numerous or as large.
– ORIGIN early 17th cent.: from French *octuple* or Latin *octuplus* (both adjectives), from *octo* 'eight' + *-plus* (as in *duplus* 'double').

octuplet ▶ **noun** (usu. **octuplets**) each of eight children born at one birth.

octyl /ˈɒktʌɪl, -tɪl/ ▶ **noun** [as modifier] Chemistry of or denoting an alkyl radical $-C_8H_{17}$, derived from octane.

ocular /ˈɒkjʊlə/ ▶ **adjective** Medicine of or connected with the eyes or vision: *ocular trauma*.
▶ **noun** another term for **EYEPIECE**.
– DERIVATIVES **ocularly** adverb.
– ORIGIN late 16th cent.: from late Latin *ocularis*, from Latin *oculus* 'eye'.

ocular dominance ▶ **noun** the priority of one eye over the other as regards preference of use or acuity of vision.

ocularist ▶ **noun** a person who makes artificial eyes.
– ORIGIN mid 19th cent.: from French *oculariste*, from late Latin *ocularis* (see **OCULAR**).

oculist /ˈɒkjʊlɪst/ ▶ **noun** dated a person who specializes in the medical treatment of diseases or defects of the eye; an ophthalmologist. ■ US an optician.
– ORIGIN late 16th cent.: from French *oculiste*, from Latin *oculus* 'eye'.

oculo- /ˈɒkjʊləʊ/ ▶ **combining form** relating to the eye or the sense of vision: *oculomotor*.
– ORIGIN from Latin *oculus* 'eye'.

oculomotor /ˈɒkjʊlə(ʊ),məʊtə/ ▶ **adjective** relating to the motion of the eye.

oculomotor nerve ▶ **noun** Anatomy each of the third pair of cranial nerves, supplying most of the muscles around and within the eyeballs.

oculus /ˈɒkjʊləs/ ▶ **noun** (pl. **oculi** /-lʌɪ, -liː/) Architecture a round or eye-like opening or design, in particular: ■ a circular window. ■ the central boss of a volute. ■ an opening at the apex of a dome.
– ORIGIN mid 19th cent.: from Latin, literally 'eye'.

OD[1] ▶ **abbreviation** ordnance datum.

OD[2] informal ▶ **verb** (**OD's, OD'ing, OD'd**) [no obj.] take an overdose of a drug: *Spike had OD'd on barbiturates*. ■ humorous have too much of something: *I almost OD'd on mushroom salad*.
▶ **noun** an overdose of a narcotic drug.

od[1] ▶ **noun** [mass noun] historical a hypothetical power once thought to pervade nature and account for various scientific phenomena.
– ORIGIN mid 19th cent.: arbitrary term coined in German by Baron von Reichenbach (1788–1869), German scientist.

od[2] ▶ **noun** an archaic euphemism for God, used in exclamations: *ods blood!*

odalisque /ˈəʊd(ə)lɪsk/ ▶ **noun** historical a female slave or concubine in a harem, especially one in the seraglio of the Sultan of Turkey. ■ an exotic, sexually attractive woman.
– ORIGIN late 17th cent.: from French, from Turkish *odalik*, from *oda* 'chamber' + *lik* 'function'.

odd ▶ **adjective 1** different to what is usual or expected; strange: *the neighbours thought him very odd* | [with clause] *it's odd that she didn't recognize me*.
2 (of whole numbers such as 3 and 5) having one left over as a remainder when divided by two. ■ [in combination] in the region of or somewhat more than a particular number or quantity: *she looked younger than her fifty-odd years*. ■ denoting a single goal by which one side defeats another, especially where each side scores at least once: *they lost a close-fought game by the odd goal in five*.
3 [attrib.] happening or occurring infrequently and irregularly; occasional: *we have the odd drink together*. ■ spare; unoccupied: *when you've got an odd five minutes, could I have a word?*
4 separated from a usual pair or set and therefore out of place or mismatched: *he's wearing odd socks*.
– PHRASES **odd one** (or **man**) **out** a person or thing differing from all other members of a particular group or set in some way.
– DERIVATIVES **oddish** adjective (sense 1), **oddly** adverb (sense 1): [sentence adverb] *oddly enough, I didn't feel nervous* | [as submodifier] *she felt oddly guilty*, **oddness** noun.
– ORIGIN Middle English (in sense 2): from Old Norse *odda-*, found in combinations such as *odda-mathr* 'third or odd man', from *oddi* 'angle'.

oddball informal ▶ **noun** a strange or eccentric person.
▶ **adjective** strange; bizarre: *oddball training methods*.

odd bod ▶ **noun** Brit. informal a strange or eccentric person.

Oddfellow ▶ **noun** (usu. **Oddfellows**) a member of a fraternity similar to the Freemasons.

oddity ▶ **noun** (pl. **oddities**) a strange or peculiar person or thing: *she was regarded as a bit of an oddity*. ■ [mass noun] the quality of being strange or peculiar: *realizing the oddity of the remark, he retracted it*.

odd job ▶ **noun** (usu. **odd jobs**) a casual or isolated piece of work, especially one of a routine domestic or manual nature.
– DERIVATIVES **odd-jobbing** noun.

odd-job man (also **odd-jobber**) ▶ **noun** Brit. a man who does odd jobs.

odd lot ▶ **noun** an incomplete set or random mixture of things. ■ US Finance a transaction involving an unusually small number of shares.

oddment ▶ **noun** (usu. **oddments**) an item or piece of something, typically one left over from a larger piece or set: *a quilt made from oddments of silk*.

odds ▶ **plural noun** the ratio between the amounts staked by the parties to a bet, based on the expected probability either way: *Nicer is starting **at odds of** 8-1* | *it is possible for the race to be won **at very long odds***. ■ (usu. **the odds**) the chances or likelihood of something happening or being the case: ***the odds are** that he is no longer alive* | ***the odds against** this ever happening are high*. ■ (usu. **the odds**) the balance of advantage; superiority in strength, power, or resources: *she clung to the lead **against all the odds*** | ***the odds were** overwhelmingly **in favour of** the banks rather than the customer*.
– PHRASES **at odds** in conflict or at variance: *his behaviour is **at odds with** the interests of the company*. **by all odds** N. Amer. certainly. **it makes no odds** informal, chiefly Brit. it does not matter. [from an earlier use of *odds* in the sense 'difference in advantage or effect'.] **lay** (or **give**) **odds** offer a bet with odds favourable to the other better. ■ be very sure about something: *I'd lay odds that the person responsible is an insider*. **over the odds** Brit. above what is generally considered acceptable, especially for a price: *you could be paying over the odds for perfume*. **take odds** offer a bet with odds unfavourable to the other better. **what's the odds?** informal what does it matter? [from an earlier sense of *odds*; compare with *it makes no odds*.]
– ORIGIN early 16th cent.: apparently the plural of the obsolete noun *odd* 'odd number or odd person'.

odds and ends ▶ **plural noun** miscellaneous articles or remnants.

odds and sods ▶ **plural noun** Brit. informal miscellaneous people or articles.

oddsmaker ▶ **noun** N. Amer. a person who works for a bookmaker by predicting a future event, such as the outcome of a race, and setting the odds for betting on it.

odds-on ▶ **adjective** (especially of a horse) rated as more likely than evens to win: *the odds-on favourite*. ■ very likely to happen or succeed: *it seemed odds-on that Jones would add another century to his 157*.

odd-toed ungulate ▶ **noun** a hoofed mammal of an order which includes horses, rhinoceroses, and tapirs. Mammals of this group have either one or three toes on each foot. Compare with **EVEN-TOED UNGULATE**. ● Order Perissodactyla: three families.

ode ▶ **noun** a lyric poem, typically one in the form of an address to a particular subject, written in varied or irregular metre. ■ a classical poem of a kind originally meant to be sung.
– ORIGIN late 16th cent.: from French, from late Latin *oda*, from Greek *ōidē*, Attic form of *aoidē* 'song', from *aeidein* 'sing'.

-ode[1] ▶ **combining form** of the nature of a specified thing: *geode*.
– ORIGIN from Greek adjectival ending *-ōdēs*.

-ode[2] ▶ **combining form** in names of electrodes, or devices having them: *diode*.
– ORIGIN from Greek *hodos* 'way'.

Odense /ˈəʊd(ə)nsə/ a port in eastern Denmark, on the island of Fyn; pop. 158,678 (2009).

odeon /ˈəʊdɪən/ ▶ **noun 1** variant spelling of **ODEUM**.
2 (**Odeon**) a cinema. [from the name of a chain built in the 1930s.]
– ORIGIN from Greek *ōideion*, from *ōidē* 'song' (see **ODE**).

Oder /ˈəʊdə/ a river of central Europe which rises in the mountains in the east of the Czech Republic and flows northwards through western Poland to meet the River Neisse, then continues northwards forming the northern part of the border between Poland and Germany before flowing into the Baltic Sea. Czech and Polish name **ODRA**.

Odessa /əʊˈdɛsə/ a city and port on the south coast of Ukraine, on the Black Sea; pop. 1,008,600 (est. 2009). Ukrainian name **Odesa** /ɔˈdɛsa/.

odeum /ˈəʊdɪəm/ (also **odeon** /ˈəʊdɪən/) ▶ **noun** (pl. **odeums** or **odea** /-dɪə/) (especially in ancient Greece or Rome) a building used for musical performances.
– ORIGIN from French *odéum* or Latin *odeum*, from Greek *ōideion* (see **ODE**).

ODI ▶ **abbreviation** Cricket one-day international.

odiferous /əʊˈdɪf(ə)rəs/ ▶ **adjective** variant spelling of **ODORIFEROUS**.

Odin /ˈəʊdɪn/ (also **Woden** or **Wotan**) Scandinavian Mythology the supreme god and creator, god of victory and the dead. Wednesday is named after him.

odious ▶ **adjective** extremely unpleasant; repulsive: *a pretty odious character* | *odious hypocrisy*.
– DERIVATIVES **odiously** adverb, **odiousness** noun.
– ORIGIN late Middle English: from Old French *odieus*, from Latin *odiosus*, from *odium* 'hatred'.

odium /ˈəʊdɪəm/ ▶ **noun** [mass noun] general or widespread hatred or disgust incurred by someone as a result of their actions: *he incurred widespread odium for military failures and government corruption*.
– ORIGIN early 17th cent.: from Latin, 'hatred', from the verb stem *od-* 'hate'.

odometer /əʊˈdɒmɪtə/ ▶ **noun** an instrument for measuring the distance travelled by a wheeled vehicle.
– ORIGIN late 18th cent.: from French *odomètre*, from Greek *hodos* 'way' + **-METER**.

Odonata /ˌəʊdəˈnɑːtə/ ▶ **plural noun** Entomology an order of predatory insects that comprises the dragonflies and damselflies. They have long, slender bodies, two pairs of membranous wings, large compound eyes, and aquatic larvae. ■ (**odonata**) insects of this order; dragonflies and damselflies.
– ORIGIN modern Latin (plural), formed irregularly from Greek *odōn* (variant of *odous*) 'tooth', with reference to the insect's mandibles.

odonate Entomology ▶ **noun** a predatory insect of the order Odonata; a dragonfly or damselfly.
▶ **adjective** relating to or denoting odonates.

odontalgia /ˌɒdɒnˈtaldʒə/ ▶ **noun** [mass noun] technical toothache.

odonto- ▶ **combining form** relating to a tooth or teeth: *odontology* | *odontophore*.
– ORIGIN from Greek *odous, odont-* 'tooth'.

odontoblast /ɒˈdɒntə(ʊ)blast/ ▶ **noun** Anatomy a cell in the pulp of a tooth that produces dentine.

Odontoceti /əʊˌdɒntə(ʊ)ˈsiːtiː/ ▶ **plural noun** Zoology a division of the whales that comprises the toothed whales. ● Suborder Odontoceti, order Cetacea.
– DERIVATIVES **odontocete** noun & adjective.

O

– ORIGIN modern Latin (plural), from Greek *odous, odont-* 'tooth' + *ceti* 'of a whale' (genitive of *cetus*, from Greek *kētos* 'whale').

odontoglossum /ə(ʊ),dɒntə(ʊ)'glɒsəm/ ▶ **noun** an orchid bearing flowers with jagged edges like tooth marks.
– ORIGIN mid 18th cent.: modern Latin, from **ODONTO-** 'of teeth' + Greek *glōssa* 'tongue'.

odontoid /ə(ʊ)'dɒntɔɪd/ (also **odontoid process**) ▶ **noun** Anatomy a projection from the second cervical vertebra (axis) on which the first (atlas) can pivot: [as modifier] *the anterior odontoid joint*.
– ORIGIN early 19th cent.: from Greek *odontoeidēs*, from *odous, odont-* 'tooth' + *eidos* 'form'.

odontology /,ɒdɒn'tɒlədʒi, ,əʊdɒn-/ ▶ **noun** [mass noun] the scientific study of the structure and diseases of teeth.
– DERIVATIVES **odontological** adjective, **odontologist** noun.

odontophore /ə'dɒntə(ʊ)fɔː/ ▶ **noun** Zoology a cartilaginous projection in the mouth of a mollusc, on which the radula is supported.
– DERIVATIVES **odontophoral** adjective.

odor ▶ **noun** US spelling of **ODOUR**.

odorant ▶ **noun** a substance used to give a particular odour to a product.
– ORIGIN late Middle English (as an adjective in the sense 'odorous'): from Old French, present participle of *odorer*, from Latin *odorare* 'give an odour to'. The current sense dates from the 1940s.

odoriferous /,əʊdə'rɪf(ə)rəs/ ▶ **adjective** having or giving off a smell, especially an unpleasant one: *an odoriferous pile of fish*.
– ORIGIN late Middle English: from Latin *odorifer* 'odour-bearing' + **-OUS**.

odorize (also **odorise**) ▶ **verb** [with obj.] give an odour or scent to.
– ORIGIN late 19th cent.: from Latin *odor* 'odour' + **-IZE**.

odorous ▶ **adjective** having or giving off an odour: *a dark and odorous cave*.
– DERIVATIVES **odorously** adverb.
– ORIGIN late Middle English: from Latin *odorus* 'fragrant' (from *odor* 'odour') + **-OUS**.

odour (US **odor**) ▶ **noun 1** a distinctive smell, especially an unpleasant one: *the odour of cigarette smoke*. **2** a lingering quality or impression attaching to something: *an odour of suspicion*. ■ [mass noun] [with adj.] the state of being held in a specified regard: *a decade of bad odour between Britain and the European Community*.
– PHRASES **be in good** (or **bad**) **odour with** informal be in (or out of) favour with (someone). **odour of sanctity** a sweet odour reputedly emitted by the bodies of saints at or near death. ■ a state of holiness.
– ORIGIN Middle English: from Anglo-Norman French, from Latin *odor* 'smell, scent'.

odourless (US **odorless**) ▶ **adjective** having no odour: *an odourless gas*.

Odra /'ɒdra/ Polish name for **ODER**.

Odysseus /ə'dɪsɪəs/ Greek Mythology the king of Ithaca and central figure of the *Odyssey*, renowned for his cunning and resourcefulness. Roman name **ULYSSES**.

Odyssey /'ɒdɪsi/ a Greek hexameter epic poem traditionally ascribed to Homer, describing the travels of Odysseus during his ten years of wandering after the sack of Troy. He eventually returned home to Ithaca and killed the suitors who had plagued his wife Penelope during his absence. ■ (**odyssey**) a long and eventful or adventurous journey or experience: *his odyssey from military man to politician*.
– DERIVATIVES **Odyssean** /ə'dɪsɪən/ adjective.

OE ▶ **abbreviation** Old English.

Oe ▶ **abbreviation** oersted(s).

Oea /'iːə/ ancient name for **TRIPOLI** (sense 1).

OECD ▶ **abbreviation** Organization for Economic Cooperation and Development.

OED ▶ **abbreviation** Oxford English Dictionary.

oedema /ɪ'diːmə/ (US **edema**) ▶ **noun** [mass noun] a condition characterized by an excess of watery fluid collecting in the cavities or tissues of the body. Also called **DROPSY**¹.
– DERIVATIVES **oedematous** adjective.
– ORIGIN late Middle English: modern Latin, from Greek *oidēma*, from *oidein* 'to swell'.

Oedipus /'iːdɪpəs/ Greek Mythology the son of Jocasta and of Laius, king of Thebes.

> Left to die on a mountain by Laius, who had been told by an oracle that he would be killed by his own son, the infant Oedipus was saved by a shepherd. Returning eventually to Thebes, Oedipus solved the riddle of the sphinx, but unwittingly killed his father and married Jocasta. On discovering what he had done he put out his own eyes in a fit of madness, and Jocasta hanged herself.

Oedipus complex ▶ **noun** Psychoanalysis (in Freudian theory) the complex of emotions aroused in a young child, typically around the age of four, by an unconscious sexual desire for the parent of the opposite sex and wish to exclude the parent of the same sex. (The term was originally applied to boys, the equivalent in girls being called the **Electra complex**.)
– DERIVATIVES **Oedipal** adjective, **Oedipally** adverb.
– ORIGIN early 20th cent.: by association with **OEDIPUS**.

OEEC ▶ **abbreviation** Organization for European Economic Cooperation.

oeil-de-boeuf /,əːɪdə'bəːf/ ▶ **noun** (pl. **oeils-de-boeuf** pronunc. **same**) a small round window.
– ORIGIN mid 18th cent.: French, literally 'ox-eye'.

OEM ▶ **abbreviation** original equipment manufacturer, an organization that makes devices from component parts bought from other organizations.

oenology /iː'nɒlədʒi/ (US also **enology**) ▶ **noun** [mass noun] the study of wines.
– DERIVATIVES **oenological** adjective, **oenologist** noun.
– ORIGIN early 19th cent.: from Greek *oinos* 'wine' + **-LOGY**.

Oenone /iː'nəʊni/ Greek Mythology a nymph of Mount Ida and lover of Paris, who deserted her for Helen.

oenophile /'iːnə(ʊ)fʌɪl/ (US also **enophile**) ▶ **noun** a connoisseur of wines.
– DERIVATIVES **oenophilist** /iː'nɒfɪlɪst/ noun.
– ORIGIN 1930s: from Greek *oinos* 'wine' + **-PHILE**.

o'er ▶ **adverb & preposition** archaic or literary term of **OVER**.

Oersted /'əːstɛd/, Hans Christian (1777–1851), Danish physicist, discoverer of the magnetic effect of an electric current. He also worked on the compressibility of gases and liquids, and on diamagnetism.

oersted (abbrev.: **Oe**) ▶ **noun** Physics a unit of magnetic field strength equivalent to 79.58 amperes per metre.
– ORIGIN late 19th cent.: named after H. C. **OERSTED**.

oesophagitis /ɪ,sɒfəgə'dʒʌɪtɪs/ (US **esophagitis**) ▶ **noun** [mass noun] Medicine inflammation of the oesophagus.

oesophagoscope /ɪ'sɒfəgə,skəʊp/ (US **esophagoscope**) ▶ **noun** an instrument for the inspection or treatment of the oesophagus.

oesophagus /ɪ'sɒfəgəs/ (US **esophagus**) ▶ **noun** (pl. **oesophagi** /-dʒʌɪ/ or **oesophaguses**) the part of the alimentary canal which connects the throat to the stomach. In humans and other vertebrates it is a muscular tube lined with mucous membrane.
– DERIVATIVES **oesophageal** /ɪ,sɒfə'dʒiːəl, ,iːsə'fadʒɪəl/ adjective.
– ORIGIN late Middle English: modern Latin, from Greek *oisophagos*.

oestradiol /,iːstrə'dʌɪɒl, ,ɛstrə-/ (US **estradiol**) ▶ **noun** [mass noun] Biochemistry a major oestrogen produced in the ovaries.
– ORIGIN 1930s: from **OESTRUS** + **DI-**¹ + **-OL**.

oestriol /'iːstrɪɒl, 'ɛstrɪɒl/ (US **estriol**) ▶ **noun** [mass noun] Biochemistry an oestrogen which is one of the metabolic products of oestradiol.
– ORIGIN 1930s: from *oestrane* (the parent molecule of most oestrogens) + **TRI-** + **-OL**.

oestrogen /'iːstrədʒ(ə)n, 'ɛstrə-/ (US **estrogen**) ▶ **noun** any of a group of steroid hormones which promote the development and maintenance of female characteristics of the body. Such hormones are also produced artificially for use in oral contraceptives or to treat menopausal and menstrual disorders.
– DERIVATIVES **oestrogenic** adjective.
– ORIGIN 1920s: from **OESTRUS** + **-GEN**.

oestrone /'iːstrəʊn, 'ɛstrəʊn/ (US **estrone**) ▶ **noun** [mass noun] Biochemistry an oestrogen similar to but less potent than oestradiol.
– ORIGIN 1930s: from *oestrane* (parent molecule of most oestrogens) + **-ONE**.

oestrus /'iːstrəs, 'ɛstrəs/ (US **estrus**) ▶ **noun** [mass noun] a recurring period of sexual receptivity and fertility in many female mammals; heat: *a mare in oestrus*.
– DERIVATIVES **oestrous** adjective.
– ORIGIN late 17th cent.: from Greek *oistros* 'gadfly or frenzy'.

oeuvre /'əːvr(ə)/ ▶ **noun** the body of work of a painter, composer, or author: *the complete oeuvre of Mozart*. ■ a work of art, music, or literature: *an early oeuvre*.
– ORIGIN late 19th cent.: French, literally 'work'.

of ▶ **preposition 1** expressing the relationship between a part and a whole: ■ with the word denoting the part functioning as the head of the phrase: *the sleeve of his coat | in the back of the car | the days of the week*. ■ after a number, quantifier, or partitive noun, with the word denoting the whole functioning as the head of the phrase: *nine of the children came to the show | a series of programmes* | [with mass noun] *a piece of cake*.
2 expressing the relationship between a scale or measure and a value: *an increase of 5% | a height of 10 metres*. ■ expressing an age: *a boy of 15*.
3 indicating an association between two entities, typically one of belonging, in which the first is the head of the phrase and the second is something associated with it: *the son of a friend | the government of India | a photograph of the bride* | [with a possessive] *a former colleague of John's*. ■ expressing the relationship between an author, artist, or composer and their works collectively: *the plays of Shakespeare | the paintings of Rembrandt*.
4 expressing the relationship between a direction and a point of reference: *north of Watford*.
5 expressing the relationship between a general category or type and the thing being specified which belongs to such a category: *the city of Prague | the idea of a just society | the population of interbreeding individuals | this type of book*.
6 expressing the relationship between an abstract concept having a verb-like meaning and a noun denoting the subject of the underlying verb: *the opinion of the directors | the decision of the County Council*. ■ where the second noun denotes the object of the underlying verb: *the murder of two boys | payment of his debts | an admirer of Dickens*. ■ where the head of the phrase is a predicative adjective: *it was kind of you to ask | I am certain of that*.
7 indicating the relationship between a verb and an indirect object: ■ with a verb expressing a mental state: *I don't know of anything that would be suitable*. ■ expressing a cause: *he died of cancer*.
8 indicating the material or substance constituting something: *the house was built of bricks | walls of stone*.
9 N. Amer. expressing time in relation to the following hour: *it would be just a quarter of three in New York*.
– PHRASES **be of** possess intrinsically; give rise to: *this work is of great interest and value*. **of all** denoting the least likely or expected example: *Jordan, of all people, committed a flagrant foul*. **of all the nerve** (or Brit. **cheek**) an expression of indignation. **of an evening** (or **morning** etc.) informal **1** on most evenings (or mornings etc.). **2** at some time in the evenings (or mornings etc.).
– ORIGIN Old English, of Germanic origin; related to Dutch *af* and German *ab*, from an Indo-European root shared by Latin *ab* and Greek *apo*.

> **USAGE** It is a mistake to use **of** instead of **have** in constructions such as *you should **have** asked* (not *you should **of** asked*). For more information, see **USAGE** at **HAVE**.

of- ▶ **prefix** variant spelling of **OB-** assimilated before *f* (as in *offend*).

ofay /'əʊfeɪ/ ▶ **noun** US informal a derogatory term for a white person used by black people.
– ORIGIN early 20th cent. (as an adjective): from French *au fait* 'socially proper, genteel'.

Ofcom ▶ **abbreviation** (in the UK) Office of Communications, a regulatory body supervising the communications industry.

off ▶ **adverb 1** away from the place in question; to or at a distance: *the man ran off | she dashed off to her room | we must be off now*. ■ away from the main route: *turning off for Ripon*.
2 so as to be removed or separated: *he whipped off his coat | a section of the runway had been cordoned off*. ■ absent; away from work: *take a day off | he is off on sick leave*.
3 starting a journey or race; leaving: *we're off on holiday tomorrow | the gunmen made off on foot | they're off!*
4 so as to bring to an end or be discontinued: *the Christmas party rounded off a hugely successful year | she broke off her reading to look at her husband*. ■ cancelled: *tell them the wedding's off*. ■ Brit. informal (of an item on a menu) temporarily unavailable: *strawberries are off*.
5 (of an electrical appliance or power supply) not functioning or so as to cease to function: *switch the TV off | the electricity was off for four days*.

6 having access to or possession of material goods or wealth to the extent specified: *we'd been rather* ***badly off*** *for books | how are you off for money?*
7 chiefly Brit. (with preceding numeral) denoting a quantity produced at one time.
▶ **preposition 1** moving away and often down from: *he rolled off the bed | the coat slipped off his arms | trying to get us off the stage.*
2 situated or leading in a direction away from (a main route or intersection): *single wires leading off the main lines | in a little street off Whitehall.* ■ out at sea from (a place on the coast): *anchoring off Blue Bay | six miles off Dunkirk.*
3 so as to be removed or separated from: *threatening to tear the door off its hinges | they knocked $2,000 off the price |* figurative *it's a huge burden off my shoulders.* ■ absent from: *I took a couple of days off work.* ■ informal abstaining from: *he managed to stay off alcohol.*
4 informal having a temporary dislike of: *he's running a temperature and he's off his food.*
▶ **adjective 1** [attrib.] characterized by performing or feeling worse than usual; unsatisfactory or inadequate: *even the greatest athletes have* ***off days.*** ■ [predic.] Brit. informal unwell: *I felt decidedly off.*
2 [predic.] (of food) no longer fresh: *the fish was a bit off.*
3 [attrib.] located on the side of a vehicle that is normally furthest from the kerb; offside. Compare with **NEAR** (sense 4 of the adjective).
4 [predic.] Brit. informal annoying or unfair: *His boss deducted the money from his pay. That was a bit off.*
5 [predic.] Brit. informal unfriendly or hostile: *there's no one there except the barmaid, and she's a bit off.*
▶ **noun 1** (also **off side**) Cricket the half of the field (as divided lengthways through the pitch) towards which the batsman's feet are pointed when standing to receive the ball. The opposite of **LEG**.
2 Brit. informal the start of a race, journey, or experience: *now Ian is* ***ready for the off.***
▶ **verb** informal **1** [no obj.] leave: *supposedly loyal workers suddenly* ***upped and offed*** *to the new firms.*
2 [with obj.] N. Amer. kill; murder: *she might off a cop, but she wouldn't shoot her boyfriend.*
– PHRASES **off and on** intermittently; now and then. **off limits** see **LIMIT**.
– ORIGIN Old English, originally a variant of **OF** (which combined the senses of 'of' and 'off').

> **USAGE** *Off of* is often used in place of the preposition **off** in contexts such as *she picked it up off of the floor* (compared with *she picked it up* **off** *the floor*). Although **off of** is recorded from the 16th century (it was used by Shakespeare) and is logically parallel to the standard **out of**, it is regarded as incorrect in standard modern English.

Off. ▶ **abbreviation** ■ Office. ■ Officer.
Offa /ˈɒfə/ (d.796), king of Mercia 757–96. He organized the construction of Offa's Dyke.
off-air ▶ **adjective & adverb** not being broadcast on radio or television: [as adj.] *an off-air interview |* [as adv.] *journalists can talk to the control room off-air.*
offal ▶ **noun** [mass noun] the entrails and internal organs of an animal used as food. ■ waste material. ■ decomposing animal flesh.
– ORIGIN late Middle English (in the sense 'refuse from a process'): probably suggested by Middle Dutch *afval*, from *af* 'off' + *vallen* 'to fall'.
Offaly /ˈɒfəli/ a county in the central part of the Republic of Ireland, in the province of Leinster; county town, Tullamore.
Offa's Dyke a series of earthworks marking the traditional boundary between England and Wales, running from near the mouth of the Wye to near the mouth of the Dee, originally constructed by Offa in the second half of the 8th century to mark the boundary established by his wars with the Welsh.
offbeat ▶ **adjective 1** Music not coinciding with the beat.
2 informal unconventional; unusual: *she's a little offbeat but she's a wonderful actress.*
▶ **noun** Music any of the normally unaccented beats in a bar.
off-board ▶ **adjective** relating to or denoting hardware or software that does not form an integral part of a computer.
off-brand ▶ **noun** [usu. as modifier] chiefly N. Amer. an unknown, unpopular, or inferior brand of retail product: *with cheaper or off-brand inks you are likely to get less quality.*
off break ▶ **noun** Cricket a ball which deviates from the off side towards the leg side after pitching.
off-Broadway ▶ **adjective** (of a theatre, play, or performer) located in or associated with an area of New York other than Broadway, typically with reference to experimental productions.
off-centre ▶ **adjective & adverb** not quite in the centre of something: [as adj.] *the main axes of the quadrangle are off-centre |* [as adv.] *if the ball's struck off-centre, it will wobble.* ■ unconventional or unusual: *an off-centre comedy sketch show.*
off colour ▶ **adjective 1** Brit. slightly unwell: *I'm feeling a bit off colour.*
2 slightly indecent or obscene: *off-colour jokes.*
offcomer ▶ **noun** dialect an outsider or newcomer to a district.
offcut ▶ **noun** Brit. a piece of waste material that is left behind after cutting a larger piece.
off-cutter ▶ **noun** Cricket a fast off break.
off-diagonal ▶ **adjective** Mathematics denoting an element of a square matrix that is not on the diagonal running from the upper left to the lower right.
off drive Cricket ▶ **noun** a drive to the off side.
▶ **verb** [with obj.] (**off-drive**) drive (the ball) to the off side; drive a ball from (a bowler) to the off side.
off-dry ▶ **adjective** (of wine) having an almost dry flavour, with just a trace of sweetness.
Offenbach /ˈɒf(ə)nbɑːx/, Jacques (1819–80), German composer, resident in France from 1833; born *Jacob Offenbach*. He is associated with the rise of the operetta, whose style is typified by his *Orpheus in the Underworld* (1858). Other notable works: *The Tales of Hoffmann* (1881).
offence /əˈfɛns/ (US **offense**) ▶ **noun 1** a breach of a law or rule; an illegal act: *the new offence of obtaining property by deception.* ■ a thing that constitutes a violation of what is judged to be right or natural: *the outcome is an offence to basic justice.*
2 [mass noun] annoyance or resentment brought about by a perceived insult to or disregard for oneself: *he made it clear he'd* ***taken offence*** *| I didn't intend to* ***give offence.***
3 [mass noun] the action of attacking someone or something. ■ (**offense**) /ˈɒfɛns, ˈɑː-/ N. Amer. the attacking team or players in a sport, especially in American football.
– PHRASES **no offence** informal do not be offended.
– ORIGIN late Middle English: from Old French *offens* 'misdeed', from Latin *offensus* 'annoyance', reinforced by French *offense*, from Latin *offensa* 'a striking against, a hurt, or displeasure'; based on Latin *offendere* 'strike against'.
offend ▶ **verb 1** [with obj.] cause to feel upset, annoyed, or resentful: *17 per cent of viewers said they had been offended by bad language.* ■ be displeasing or cause problems to: *the smell of ash offended him |* (as adj. **offending**) *she eliminated the offending foods from her diet.*
2 [no obj.] commit an illegal act: *a small hard core of young criminals who offend again and again.* ■ break a commonly accepted rule or principle: *those activities which* ***offend against*** *public order and decency.*
– ORIGIN late Middle English: from Old French *offendre*, from Latin *offendere* 'strike against'.
offended ▶ **adjective** resentful or annoyed, typically as a result of a perceived insult: *he sounded rather offended.*
– DERIVATIVES **offendedly** adverb.
offender ▶ **noun 1** a person who commits an illegal act: *an institution for young offenders.*
2 a person or thing that does something wrong or causes problems: *you can't get away from sex these days, and the TV is the worst offender.*
offense ▶ **noun** US spelling of **OFFENCE**.
offensive ▶ **adjective 1** causing someone to feel resentful, upset, or annoyed: *the allegations made are deeply offensive to us | offensive language.* ■ (of a sight or smell) disgusting; repulsive: *an offensive odour.*
2 [attrib.] actively aggressive; attacking: *offensive operations against the insurgents.* ■ (of a weapon) meant for use in attack. ■ chiefly N. Amer. relating to the team in possession of the ball or puck in a game.
▶ **noun** an attacking military campaign: *an impending military offensive against the guerrillas.* ■ an organized and forceful campaign to achieve something, typically a political or social end: *the need to* ***launch an offensive*** *against crime.*
– PHRASES **be on the offensive** act or be ready to act aggressively. **go on (to) the offensive** (or **take the offensive**) take the initiative by beginning to attack or act aggressively: *security forces took the offensive ten days ago.*
– DERIVATIVES **offensively** adverb, **offensiveness** noun.
– ORIGIN mid 16th cent.: from French *offensif, -ive* or medieval Latin *offensivus*, from Latin *offens-* 'struck against', from the verb *offendere* (see **OFFEND**).
offer ▶ **verb 1** [with two objs] present or proffer (something) for (someone) to accept or reject as desired: *may I offer you a drink? | I was offered a job on the spot.* ■ [reporting verb] express readiness to do something for or on behalf of someone: [with infinitive] *he offered to fix the gate |* [with direct speech] *'Can I help you, dear?' a kindly voice offered.* ■ [with obj.] make available for sale: *the product is offered at a very competitive price.* ■ [with obj.] (also **offer something up**) present (a prayer or sacrifice) to a deity.
2 [with obj.] provide (access or an opportunity): *the Coast Road offers easy access to the Nine Glens of Antrim | the opportunities which the economic recovery will offer.* ■ make an attempt at or show one's readiness for (violence or resistance): *he had to offer some resistance to her tirade.* ■ archaic give an opportunity for (battle) to an enemy: *Darius was about to meet him and to offer battle.*
3 [with obj.] (**offer something up**) technical put something in place to assess its appearance or fit: *the infill panels are offered up and bolted in position.*
▶ **noun** an expression of readiness to do or give something if desired: *sympathetic offers of help |* [with infinitive] *he had accepted Mallory's offer to buy him a drink.* ■ an amount of money that someone is willing to pay for something: *the prospective purchaser who made the highest offer.* ■ a specially reduced price: *the offer runs right up until Christmas Eve.* ■ a proposal of marriage.
– PHRASES **have something to offer** have something available to be used or appreciated. **offer one's hand** extend one's hand to be shaken as a sign of friendship. **on offer** available: *the number of permanent jobs on offer is relatively small.* ■ (also **on special offer**) Brit. available for sale at a reduced price: *the fruit cocktail trifle is on offer at 99p.* **open to offers** willing to sell something or do a job for a reasonable price.
– DERIVATIVES **offerer** (or **offeror**) noun.
– ORIGIN Old English *offrian* 'sacrifice something to a deity', of Germanic origin, from Latin *offerre* 'bestow, present' (in ecclesiastical Latin 'offer to God'), reinforced by French *offrir* (which continued to express the primary sense). The noun (late Middle English) is from French *offre*.
offer document ▶ **noun** a document containing details of a takeover bid which is sent to the shareholders of the target company.
offering ▶ **noun** a thing offered, especially as a gift or contribution: *everyone transported their offerings to the bring-and-buy stall.* ■ a thing produced for entertainment or sale: *the latest offerings from the garage showrooms.* ■ a contribution, especially of money, to a Church. ■ a thing offered as a religious sacrifice or token of devotion.
offer price ▶ **noun** the price at which a market-maker or institution is prepared to sell securities or other assets. Compare with **BID PRICE**.
offertory /ˈɒfət(ə)ri/ ▶ **noun** (pl. **offertories**) Christian Church **1** the offering of the bread and wine at the Eucharist. ■ an anthem accompanying this.
2 an offering or collection of money made at a religious service.
– ORIGIN late Middle English: from ecclesiastical Latin *offertorium* 'offering', from late Latin *offert-* (which replaced Latin *oblat-*) 'offered', from the verb *offerre* (see **OFFER**).
off-gas ▶ **noun** a gas which is given off, especially one emitted as the by-product of a chemical process.
▶ **verb** [no obj.] give off a chemical, especially a harmful one, in the form of a gas.
off-glide ▶ **noun** Phonetics a glide terminating the articulation of a speech sound, when the vocal organs either return to a neutral position or adopt a position anticipating the formation of the next sound. Compare with **ON-GLIDE**.
off-grid ▶ **adjective & adverb** not using or depending on public utilities, especially the supply of electricity: [as adj.] *off-grid housing.*
offhand ▶ **adjective** ungraciously or offensively nonchalant or cool in manner: *you were a bit offhand with her this afternoon.*
▶ **adverb** without previous thought or consideration: *I can't think of a better answer offhand.*

O

– DERIVATIVES **offhanded** adjective, **offhandedly** adverb, **offhandedness** noun.

off-hours ▶ plural noun N. Amer. the time when one is not at work; one's leisure time.

office ▶ noun **1** a room, set of rooms, or building used as a place of business for non-manual work: [as modifier] *an office job.* ▪ the local centre of a large business: *a company which has four US and four European offices.* ▪ a room, department, or building used to provide a particular service: *a ticket office | a Post Office.* ▪ N. Amer. the consulting room of a professional person.
2 a position of authority or service, typically one of a public nature: *the office of chief constable.* ▪ [mass noun] tenure of an official position, especially that of a Minister of State or of the party forming the government: *a year ago, when the President **took office** | he was ejected from office in 1988.* ▪ (**Office**) the quarters, staff, or collective authority of a particular government department or agency: *the Foreign Office.*
3 (usu. **offices**) a service done for another or others: *rescued **through the good offices of** the Italian Ambassador, he was returned safely to England.* ▪ dated a duty attaching to one's position: *the offices of a nurse.*
4 (also **Divine Office**) Christian Church the series of services of prayers and psalms said (or chanted) daily by Catholic priests, members of religious orders, and other clergy. ▪ a service conducted daily as part of the office: *the noon office.*
5 (**offices**) Brit. dated the parts of a house given over to household work or to storage. ▪ (usu. **usual offices**) euphemistic a toilet.
– ORIGIN Middle English: via Old French from Latin *officium* 'performance of a task' (in medieval Latin also 'office, divine service'), based on *opus* 'work' + *facere* 'do'.

office-bearer ▶ noun a person holding a position of authority in an organization.

office block ▶ noun Brit. a large multistorey building containing the offices of one or more companies.

office boy (or **office girl**) ▶ noun a young person employed to do routine tasks in a business office.

office holder ▶ noun a person who holds a position of authority or service, especially within a government or government organization.

office hours ▶ plural noun the hours during which business is normally conducted.

office lady ▶ noun (in Japan) a woman working in an office.

O

office of arms ▶ noun Heraldry the College of Arms, or a similar body in another country.

officer ▶ noun **1** a person holding a position of authority, especially one with a commission, in the armed services, the mercantile marine, or on a passenger ship. ▪ a policeman or policewoman. ▪ a bailiff.
2 a holder of a public, civil, or ecclesiastical office: *a probation officer | the Chief Medical Officer.* ▪ a holder of a senior post in a society, company, or other organization: *a chief executive officer.*
3 a member of a certain grade in some honorary orders, such as the grade next below commander in the Order of the British Empire.
▶ verb [with obj.] provide with military officers: *the aristocracy wielded considerable power, **officering** the army.* ▪ act as the commander of (a unit): *foreign mercenaries were hired to officer new regiments.*
– ORIGIN Middle English: via Anglo-Norman French from medieval Latin *officiarius*, from Latin *officium* (see OFFICE).

officer of arms ▶ noun Heraldry a heraldic official; a herald or pursuivant.

official ▶ adjective relating to an authority or public body and its activities and responsibilities: *the prime minister's official engagements.* ▪ having the approval or authorization of an authority or public body: *members would know when industrial action is official | official statistics.* ▪ employed by an authority or public body in a position of authority: *an official spokesman.*
▶ noun a person holding public office or having official duties, especially as a representative of an organization or government department: *a union official.* ▪ (also **official principal**) Brit. the presiding officer or judge of an archbishop's, bishop's, or archdeacon's court.
– DERIVATIVES **officialdom** noun, **officialism** noun, **officialize** (also **officialise**) verb.
– ORIGIN Middle English (originally as a noun): via Old French from Latin *officialis*, from *officium* (see OFFICE).

official assignee ▶ noun New Zealand term for OFFICIAL RECEIVER.

official birthday ▶ noun (in the UK) a day in June chosen for observing the sovereign's birthday.

officialese ▶ noun [mass noun] the formal and typically verbose style of writing considered to be characteristic of official documents, especially when it is difficult to understand.

officially ▶ adverb in a formal and public way: *on June 24 the election campaign will officially begin.* ▪ with the authority of the government or other organization: *it was officially acknowledged that the economy was in recession.* ▪ in public and for official purposes but not necessarily so in reality: [sentence adverb] *there is a possibility he was murdered—officially, he died in a car smash.*

official receiver ▶ noun Brit. another term for RECEIVER (sense 3).

official secret ▶ noun Brit. a piece of confidential information that is important for national security.

Official Secrets Act (in the UK) the legislation that controls access to confidential information important for national security.

Official Solicitor ▶ noun (in the UK) an officer of the Supreme Court who intervenes to protect the interests of children or those with a disability.

officiant /əˈfɪʃɪənt, -ʃ(ə)nt/ ▶ noun a person, typically a priest or minister, who performs a religious service or ceremony.
– ORIGIN mid 19th cent.: from medieval Latin *officiant-* 'performing divine service', from the verb *officiare*.

officiate /əˈfɪʃɪeɪt/ ▶ verb [no obj.] act as an official in charge of something, especially a sporting event: *three judges will officiate at the two Grands Prix.* ▪ perform a religious service or ceremony: *he baptized children and officiated at weddings.*
– DERIVATIVES **officiation** noun, **officiator** noun.
– ORIGIN mid 17th cent.: from medieval Latin *officiare* 'perform divine service', from *officium* (see OFFICE).

officinal /əˈfɪsɪn(ə)l, ɒfɪˈsiːn(ə)l/ ▶ adjective chiefly historical (of a herb or drug) standardly used in medicine.
– ORIGIN late 17th cent. (as a noun denoting an officinal medicine): from medieval Latin *officinalis* 'storeroom for medicines', from Latin *officina* 'workshop'.

officious ▶ adjective assertive of authority in a domineering way, especially with regard to trivial matters: *the security people were very officious.* ▪ intrusively enthusiastic in offering help or advice; interfering: *an officious bystander.*
– DERIVATIVES **officiously** adverb, **officiousness** noun.
– ORIGIN late 15th cent.: from Latin *officiosus* 'obliging', from *officium* (see OFFICE). The original sense was 'performing its function, efficacious', whence 'ready to help or please' (mid 16th cent.), later becoming depreciatory (late 16th cent.).

offie (also **offy**) ▶ noun (pl. **offies**) Brit. informal an off-licence.
– ORIGIN 1970s: abbreviation.

offing ▶ noun the more distant part of the sea in view.
– PHRASES **in the offing** likely to happen or appear soon: *there are several initiatives in the offing.*
– ORIGIN early 17th cent.: perhaps from OFF + -ING[1].

offish ▶ adjective informal aloof or distant in manner; not friendly: *he was being offish with her.*
– DERIVATIVES **offishness** noun.

off-key ▶ adjective & adverb (of music) not having the correct pitch; out of tune. ▪ not in accordance with what is appropriate or correct in the circumstances: [as adv.] *some of the cinematic effects are distractingly off-key.*

off-kilter ▶ adjective & adverb not aligned or balanced. ▪ [as adj.] unconventional or eccentric: *an off-kilter comedy about living in mud.*

off-label ▶ adjective relating to the prescription of a drug for a condition other than that for which it has been officially approved: *the off-label use of potent antipsychotic medications.*

off-licence ▶ noun Brit. a shop selling alcoholic drink for consumption elsewhere.

offline ▶ adjective not controlled by or directly connected to a computer or the Internet.
▶ adverb while not directly controlled by or connected to a computer or the Internet. ▪ with a delay between the production of computer data and its processing.

offload ▶ verb [with obj.] unload (a cargo): *a delivery could be offloaded immediately on arrival.* ▪ rid oneself of (something) by selling or passing it on to someone else: *a dealer offloaded 5,000 of these shares on a client.* ▪ relieve oneself of (a problem or worry) by talking to someone else: *it would be nice to have been able to offload your worries on to someone.* ▪ Computing move (data or a task) from one processor to another in order to free the first processor for other tasks: *a system designed to offload the text on to a host computer.*

off-message ▶ adjective (of a politician) departing from the official party line.

off-patent ▶ adjective & adverb out of patent restrictions.

off-peak ▶ adjective & adverb at a time when demand is less: [as adj.] *off-peak travel.*

off-piste ▶ adjective & adverb Skiing away from prepared ski runs: [as adj.] *off-piste slopes* | [as adv.] *heli-skiing is an expensive way of skiing off-piste.*

off-pitch ▶ adjective Music not of the correct pitch.

off-plan ▶ adverb & adjective (of the selling or purchasing of property) before the property is built and with only the plans available for inspection.

off-price N. Amer. ▶ noun [mass noun] a method of retailing in which branded goods (especially clothing) are sold for less than the usual retail price: [as modifier] *an off-price store.*
▶ adverb using this method: *selling goods off-price.*

offprint ▶ noun a printed copy of an article that originally appeared as part of a larger publication.

off-putting ▶ adjective unpleasant, disconcerting, or repellent: *his scar is somewhat off-putting.*
– DERIVATIVES **off-puttingly** adverb.

off-ramp ▶ noun N. Amer. a sloping one-way road leading off a main highway.

off-road ▶ adverb away from the road; on rough terrain.
▶ adjective denoting a vehicle or bicycle for use over rough terrain.

off-roading ▶ noun [mass noun] the sport or activity of driving a motor vehicle over rough terrain.
– DERIVATIVES **off-roader** noun.

off-sale ▶ noun [mass noun] the sale of alcoholic drink for consumption elsewhere than at the place of sale.

off-sales ▶ noun (in South Africa) a retail outlet attached to a hotel, where alcohol is sold for consumption off the premises.

offscourings ▶ plural noun rubbish or dregs.

off-screen ▶ adjective not appearing on a cinema, television, or computer screen: *he drawls to an off-screen interrogator.* ▪ [attrib.] happening in reality rather than fictionally on-screen: *they were off-screen lovers.*
▶ adverb outside what can be seen on a television or cinema screen: *the girl is looking off-screen to the right.* ▪ in real life rather than fictionally in a film or on television: *happy endings rarely happen off-screen.*

off season ▶ noun a time of year when a particular activity, typically a sport, is not engaged in. ▪ a time of year when business in a particular sphere is slack.

offset ▶ noun **1** a consideration or amount that diminishes or balances the effect of an opposite one: *widow's bereavement allowance is an offset against income.*
2 the amount or distance by which something is out of line: *these wheels have an offset of four inches.* ▪ Surveying a short distance measured perpendicularly from the main line of measurement. ▪ Electronics a small deviation or bias in a voltage or current.
3 a side shoot from a plant serving for propagation. ▪ a spur in a mountain range.
4 Architecture a sloping ledge in a wall or other feature where the thickness of the part above is diminished.
5 a bend in a pipe to carry it past an obstacle.
6 [mass noun] [often as modifier] a method of printing in which ink is transferred from a plate or stone to a uniform rubber surface and from that to the paper.
▶ verb (**offsets**, **offsetting**; past and past participle **offset**)
1 [with obj.] counteract (something) by having an equal and opposite force or effect: *donations to charities can be **offset against** tax | his unfortunate appearance was offset by a compelling personality.*
2 [with obj.] place out of line: *several places where the ridge was offset at right angles to its length.*
3 [no obj.] (of ink or a freshly printed page) transfer an impression to the next leaf or sheet.

off-shears ▸ adjective Austral./NZ (of a sheep) recently shorn.

offshoot ▸ noun a side shoot or branch on a plant. ■ a thing that develops from something else: *commercial offshoots of universities*.

offshore ▸ adjective & adverb **1** situated at sea some distance from the shore: [as adj.] *offshore islands* | [as adv.] *we dropped anchor offshore*. ■ (of the wind) blowing towards the sea from the land. ■ relating to the business of extracting oil or gas from the seabed. **2** made, situated, or registered abroad, especially in order to take advantage of lower taxes or costs or less stringent regulation: [as adj.] *offshore accounts*. ■ of or derived from a foreign country: [as adj.] *American offshore politics*.
▸ verb [with obj.] move (some of a company's processes or services) overseas: *he predicts that 750,000 UK jobs will be offshored in the next 10 years*.

offshoring ▸ noun [mass noun] the practice of basing some of a company's processes or services overseas, so as to take advantage of lower costs.

offside ▸ adjective & adverb (of a player, especially in soccer, rugby, or hockey) occupying a position on the field where playing the ball or puck is not allowed, generally through being between the ball and the opponents' goal: [as adv.] *the attacker looked offside by several yards* | figurative *his radicalism caught him offside with the law*.
▸ noun **1** the fact or an instance of being offside in soccer, rugby, etc.: *the goal was disallowed for offside*. **2** (usu. **the off side**) Brit. the side of a vehicle furthest from the kerb (in Britain, the right). Compare with **NEARSIDE**. See also **OFF SIDE** at **OFF** (sense 1 of the noun). ■ the right side of a horse.

offsider ▸ noun Austral./NZ informal a partner, assistant, or deputy.

offside trap ▸ noun Soccer a manoeuvre in which players on the defending team push upfield in order to put one or more opposing players into an offside position.

off spin ▸ noun [mass noun] Cricket a type of spin bowling that causes the ball to deviate from the off side towards the leg side after pitching; off breaks.
– DERIVATIVES **off-spinner** noun.

offspring ▸ noun (pl. **same**) a person's child or children: *the offspring of middle-class parents*. ■ an animal's young. ■ the product or result of something: *German nationalism was the offspring of military ambition*.
– ORIGIN Old English *ofspring* (see **OFF**, **SPRING**).

offstage ▸ adjective & adverb (in a theatre) not on the stage and so not visible to the audience.

off-street ▸ adjective (of parking facilities) not on a public road.

off stump ▸ noun Cricket the stump on the off side of a wicket.

off-tackle ▸ adjective American Football of, directed towards, or occurring in a part of the offensive line immediately to the outside of either of the tackles.

offtake ▸ noun [mass noun] the removal of oil from a reservoir or supply.

off the ball ▸ adjective & adverb Soccer not in contact with or playing the ball.

off the shoulder ▸ adjective (especially of a dress or blouse) not covering the shoulders.

off-topic ▸ adjective & adverb (especially of posts on an Internet message board) not relevant to the subject in question: [as adj.] *his second comment is entirely off-topic* | [as adv.] *you're drifting off-topic*.

off-track ▸ adjective N. Amer. situated or taking place away from a racetrack.

off-trade ▸ noun [mass noun] the part of the market in alcoholic drinks which is made up of off-sales.

off-white ▸ noun [mass noun] a white colour with a grey or yellowish tinge.

off-width ▸ adjective Climbing (of a crack in the rock) considered too wide to be a jam and too narrow to be a chimney.

offy ▸ noun (pl. **offies**) variant spelling of **OFFIE**.

off year ▸ noun US **1** a year in which there is no major election, especially one in which there is a Congressional election but no Presidential election. **2** a year that is inferior or substandard compared to previous ones: *he roared back last season from an off year during which he was plagued by injuries*.

Oflag /ˈɒflag/ ▸ noun historical a German prison camp for captured enemy officers. Compare with **STALAG**.
– ORIGIN German, contraction of *Offizier(s)lager* 'officers' camp'.

Ofsted /ˈɒfstɛd/ ▸ abbreviation (in the UK) Office for Standards in Education, an organization monitoring standards in schools by regular inspections.

OFT ▸ abbreviation (in the UK) Office of Fair Trading.

oft ▸ adverb archaic or literary form of **OFTEN**: [in combination] *an oft-quoted tenet*.
– ORIGIN Old English, of Germanic origin; related to German *oft*.

often /ˈɒf(ə)n, ˈɒft(ə)n/ ▸ adverb (**oftener**, **oftenest**) frequently; many times: *he often goes for long walks by himself* | *how often do you have your hair cut?* ■ in many instances: *vocabulary often reflects social standing*.
– PHRASES **as often as not** quite frequently or commonly: *I had two homes really, because as often as not I was down at her house*. **more often than not** usually: *food is scarce and more often than not they go hungry*.
– ORIGIN Middle English: extended form of **OFT**, probably influenced by *selden* 'seldom'. Early examples appear to be northern English; the word became general in the 16th cent.

oftentimes ▸ adverb archaic or North American form of **OFTEN**.
– ORIGIN late Middle English: extended form of **OFT-TIMES**, influenced by **OFTEN**.

oft-times ▸ adverb archaic or literary form of **OFTEN**.

Ofwat /ˈɒfwɒt/ ▸ abbreviation (in the UK) Office of Water Services, a regulatory body supervising the operation of the water industry.

Ogaden /ˌɒgəˈdɛn/ (**the Ogaden**) a desert region in SE Ethiopia, largely inhabited by Somali nomads. It has been claimed by successive governments of neighbouring Somalia.

ogam ▸ noun variant spelling of **OGHAM**.

Ogbomosho /ˌɒgbəˈməʊʃəʊ/ a city and agricultural market in SW Nigeria, north of Ibadan; pop. 951,000 (est. 2007).

ogdoad /ˈɒgdəʊad/ ▸ noun rare a group or set of eight.
– ORIGIN early 17th cent.: via late Latin from Greek *ogdoas, ogdoad-*, from *ogdoos* 'eighth', from *oktō* 'eight'.

ogee /ˈəʊdʒiː, əʊˈdʒiː/ Architecture ▸ adjective showing in section a double continuous S-shaped curve.
▸ noun an S-shaped line or moulding.
– DERIVATIVES **ogeed** adjective.
– ORIGIN late Middle English: apparently from **OGIVE** (with which it was originally synonymous). The current sense arose in the late 17th cent.

ogee arch ▸ noun Architecture an arch with two ogee curves meeting at the apex.

Ogen /ˈəʊgɛn/ (also **Ogen melon**) ▸ noun a small melon with pale green flesh and an orange skin ribbed with green.
– ORIGIN 1960s: from the name of a kibbutz in Israel.

ogham /ˈɒgəm/ (also **ogam**) ▸ noun [mass noun] an ancient British and Irish alphabet, consisting of twenty characters formed by parallel strokes on either side of or across a continuous line. ■ [count noun] an inscription in or character from the ogham alphabet.
– ORIGIN early 18th cent.: from Irish *ogam*, connected with *Ogma*, the name of its mythical inventor.

ogive /ˈəʊdʒʌɪv, əʊˈdʒʌɪv/ ▸ noun **1** Architecture a pointed or Gothic arch. ■ one of the diagonal groins or ribs of a vault. ■ a thing having the profile of an ogive, especially the head of a projectile or the nose cone of a rocket. **2** Statistics a cumulative frequency graph.
– DERIVATIVES **ogival** adjective.
– ORIGIN late Middle English: from French, of unknown origin.

ogle ▸ verb [with obj.] stare at in a lecherous manner: *he was ogling her breasts*.
▸ noun a lecherous look.
– DERIVATIVES **ogler** noun.
– ORIGIN late 17th cent.: probably from Low German or Dutch; compare with Low German *oegeln*, frequentative of *oegen* 'look at'.

ogonek /ɒˈgɒnɛk/ ▸ noun a diacritic mark (˛) placed beneath a letter, typically to indicate nasalization of a vowel in Polish and other languages.
– ORIGIN Polish, literally 'little hook'.

OGPU (also **Ogpu**) an organization for investigating and combating counter-revolutionary activities in the former Soviet Union, existing from 1922 (1922–3 as the GPU) to 1934 and replacing the Cheka. It was absorbed into the NKVD in 1934.
– ORIGIN acronym from Russian *Ob"edinënnoe gosudarstvennoe politicheskoe upravlenie* 'United State Political Directorate'.

O grade ▸ noun short for **ORDINARY GRADE**.

ogre ▸ noun (in folklore) a man-eating giant. ■ a cruel or terrifying person.
– DERIVATIVES **ogreish** (also **ogrish**) adjective.
– ORIGIN early 18th cent.: from French, first used by the French writer Perrault in 1697.

ogress ▸ noun a female ogre.

OH ▸ abbreviation Ohio (in official postal use).

oh[1] ▸ exclamation used to express a range of emotions including surprise, anger, disappointment, or joy, or when reacting to a remark: *'Oh no,' said Daisy, appalled* | *Me? Oh, I'm fine* | *oh, shut up*.
– PHRASES **oh yeah?** used to express disbelief.
– ORIGIN mid 16th cent.: variant of **O**[3].

oh[2] ▸ noun variant spelling of **O**[1] (sense 2).

OHC ▸ abbreviation overhead camshaft.

O'Higgins, Bernardo (*c.*1778–1842), Chilean revolutionary leader and statesman, head of state 1817–23. With the help of José de San Martín he led the army which defeated Spanish forces in 1817 and paved the way for Chilean independence the following year.

Ohio /əʊˈhʌɪəʊ/ a state in the north-eastern US, bordering on Lake Erie; pop. 11,485,910 (est. 2008); capital, Columbus. Acquired by Britain from France in 1763 and by the US in 1783, it became the 17th state of the US in 1803.
– DERIVATIVES **Ohioan** adjective & noun.

Ohm /əʊm/, Georg Simon (1789–1854), German physicist. The units ohm and mho are named after him, as is Ohm's law on electricity.

ohm ▸ noun the SI unit of electrical resistance, transmitting a current of one ampere when subjected to a potential difference of one volt. (Symbol: Ω)
– DERIVATIVES **ohmic** adjective.
– ORIGIN mid 19th cent.: named after G. S. **OHM**.

ohmmeter /ˈəʊmˌmiːtə/ ▸ noun an instrument for measuring electrical resistance.

OHMS ▸ abbreviation on Her (or His) Majesty's Service.

Ohm's law ▸ noun Physics a law stating that electric current is proportional to voltage and inversely proportional to resistance.

oho ▸ exclamation used to express pleased surprise or recognition.
– ORIGIN Middle English: from **O**[3] + **HO**[1].

-oholic ▸ suffix variant spelling of **-AHOLIC**.

ohone ▸ exclamation variant spelling of **OCHONE**.

OHP ▸ abbreviation Brit. overhead projector.

Ohrid, Lake /ˈɒxrɪd/ a lake in SE Europe, on the border between Macedonia and Albania.

oh-so ▸ adverb informal extremely: *their oh-so-ordinary lives*.

ohu /ˈəʊhuː/ ▸ noun (pl. **same** or **ohus**) NZ a working party.
– ORIGIN Maori.

OHV ▸ abbreviation overhead valve.

oi ▸ exclamation (also **oy**) Brit. informal used to attract someone's attention, especially in a rough or angry way.
– ORIGIN variant of **HOY**[1]: first recorded in the 1930s.

-oid ▸ suffix forming adjectives and nouns: **1** Zoology denoting an animal belonging to a higher taxon with a name ending in *-oidea*: *hominoid* | *percoid*. **2** denoting form or resemblance: *asteroid* | *rhomboid*.
– DERIVATIVES **-oidal** suffix forming corresponding adjectives, **-oidally** suffix forming corresponding adverbs.
– ORIGIN from modern Latin *-oides*, from Greek *-oeidēs*; related to *eidos* 'form'.

oidium /əʊˈɪdɪəm/ ▸ noun (pl. **oidia** /-dɪə/) **1** Botany a type of fungal spore (conidium) formed by the breaking up of fungal hyphae into cells, especially as produced by powdery mildews. **2** [mass noun] a fungal disease affecting vines, caused by a powdery mildew. ● The fungus is *Uncinula necator* (formerly *Oidium tuckeri*), family Erysiphaceae, subdivision Ascomycotina.
– ORIGIN mid 19th cent.: modern Latin, from Greek *ōion* 'egg' + the diminutive suffix *-idion*.

OIEO ▸ abbreviation Brit. offers in excess of (used in advertisements).

oik (also **oick**) ▸ noun Brit. informal an uncouth or obnoxious person.
– ORIGIN 1930s: of unknown origin.

oil ▸ noun [mass noun] **1** a viscous liquid derived from petroleum, especially for use as a fuel or lubricant. ■ petroleum. ■ [with modifier] any of various viscous liquids which are insoluble in water but soluble in organic solvents and are obtained from animals or plants: *potatoes fried in vegetable oil*. ■ a liquid preparation used on the hair or skin as a cosmetic: *suntan oil*. ■ [count noun] Chemistry any of a group of natural esters of glycerol and various fatty acids, which are liquid at room temperature. Compare with FAT.
2 (often **oils**) oil paint: *a portrait in oils*. ■ [count noun] an oil painting.
3 Austral./NZ informal information or facts: *Young had some good oil on the Adelaide races*.
▸ verb [with obj.] (often as adj. **oiled**) **1** lubricate, coat, or impregnate with oil: *a lightly oiled baking tray*.
2 supply with oil as fuel: *attempts should not be made to oil individual tanks too rapidly*.
– PHRASES **oil and water** used to refer to two elements, factors, or people that are incompatible or do not blend together. **oil the wheels** Brit. help something go smoothly: *compliments oil the wheels of life*.
– ORIGIN Middle English: from Old Northern French *olie*, Old French *oile*, from Latin *oleum* '(olive) oil'; compare with *olea* 'olive'.

oil bath ▸ noun a receptacle containing oil, used for cooling, heating, lubricating, or insulating equipment immersed in it.

oil beetle ▸ noun a slow-moving flightless beetle that releases a foul-smelling oily secretion when disturbed. The larvae develop as parasites in the nests of solitary bees. ● *Meloe* and other genera, family Meloidae.

oilbird ▸ noun a large nocturnal fruit-eating bird that resembles a nightjar, living in caves in Central and South America. Called GUACHARO in America. ● *Steatornis caripensis*, the only member of the family Steatornithidae.

oilcake ▸ noun a mass of compressed linseed or other plant material left after oil has been extracted, used as fodder or fertilizer.

oilcan ▸ noun a can containing oil, especially one with a long nozzle for oiling machinery.

oilcloth ▸ noun [mass noun] cotton fabric treated on one side with oil to make it waterproof. ■ [count noun] a canvas coated with linseed or other oil and used to cover a table or floor.

O

oil colour ▸ noun another term for OIL PAINT.

oil drum ▸ noun a metal drum used for transporting oil.

oiled silk ▸ noun [mass noun] silk treated on one side with oil to make it waterproof.

oil engine ▸ noun an internal-combustion engine in which the fuel enters the cylinder as a liquid.

oiler ▸ noun **1** a thing that holds or supplies oil, in particular: ■ an oil tanker. ■ an oilcan. ■ N. Amer. informal an oil well.
2 (**oilers**) N. Amer. informal oilskin garments.

oilfield ▸ noun an area of land or seabed underlain by strata yielding mineral oil, especially in amounts that justify commercial exploitation.

oil-fired ▸ adjective (especially of a heating system or power station) using oil as fuel.

oilfish ▸ noun (pl. **same** or **oilfishes**) a large violet or purple-brown escolar, the flesh of which is oily and unpalatable. ● *Ruvettus pretiosus*, family Gempylidae.

oil gas ▸ noun [mass noun] a gaseous mixture derived from mineral oils by destructive distillation.

oil gland ▸ noun Botany & Zoology a gland which secretes oil. ■ Ornithology another term for PREEN GLAND.

oil lamp ▸ noun a lamp using oil as fuel.

oilman ▸ noun (pl. **oilmen**) an owner or employee of an oil company.

oil meal ▸ noun [mass noun] ground oilcake.

oil mill ▸ noun a machine or a factory in which seeds, fruits, or other plant parts are crushed or pressed to extract oil.

oil of cloves ▸ noun see CLOVE[1] (sense 1).

oil of turpentine ▸ noun see TURPENTINE (sense 1 of the noun).

oil of vitriol ▸ noun archaic term for SULPHURIC ACID.

oil paint ▸ noun a thick paint made with ground pigment and a drying oil such as linseed oil, used chiefly by artists.

oil painting ▸ noun [mass noun] the art of painting in oils. ■ [count noun] a picture painted in oils.
– PHRASES **be no oil painting** Brit. informal (of a person) be unattractive.

oil palm ▸ noun a tropical West African palm which is the chief source of palm oil. ● *Elaeis guineensis*, family Palmae: several cultivars.

oil pan ▸ noun N. Amer. an engine sump.

oil paper ▸ noun [mass noun] paper made transparent or waterproof by soaking in oil.

oil platform ▸ noun a structure designed to stand on the seabed to provide a stable base above water for the drilling and regulation of oil wells.

oil press ▸ noun an apparatus for pressing oil from seeds, fruits, etc.

oil rig ▸ noun a structure with equipment for drilling an oil well; an oil platform.

oil sand ▸ noun (often **oil sands**) a deposit of loose sand or partially consolidated sandstone containing bitumen.

oilseed ▸ noun [mass noun] any of a number of seeds from cultivated crops yielding oil, e.g. rape, peanut, or cotton.

oilseed rape ▸ noun see RAPE[2].

oil shale ▸ noun [mass noun] fine-grained sedimentary rock from which oil can be extracted.

oilskin ▸ noun [mass noun] heavy cotton cloth waterproofed with oil. ■ (**oilskins**) garments made of oilskin.

oil slick ▸ noun a film or layer of oil floating on an expanse of water.

oil spot ▸ noun a silvery marking on brown Chinese porcelain (especially of the Song period) caused by precipitation of iron in firing.

oilstone ▸ noun a fine-grained flat stone used with oil for sharpening chisels, planes, or other tools.

oil tanker ▸ noun a ship designed to carry oil in bulk.

oil well ▸ noun an artificially made well or shaft in rock from which mineral oil is drawn.

oily ▸ adjective (**oilier**, **oiliest**) **1** containing oil: *taramasalata and hummus are both oily and rich*. ■ covered or soaked with oil: *an oily rag*. ■ resembling oil in appearance or behaviour: *the oily swell of the river*.
2 (of a person or their behaviour) unpleasantly smooth and ingratiating: *his oily smile*.
– DERIVATIVES **oilily** adverb, **oiliness** noun.

oink ▸ noun the characteristic grunting sound of a pig.
▸ verb [no obj.] make an oink.
– ORIGIN 1940s: imitative.

ointment ▸ noun [mass noun] a smooth oily substance that is rubbed on the skin for medicinal purposes or as a cosmetic.
– ORIGIN Middle English: alteration of Old French *oignement*, from a popular Latin form of Latin *unguentum* (see UNGUENT); influenced by obsolete *oint* 'anoint' (from Old French, past participle of *oindre* 'anoint').

Oireachtas /ˈɛrəktəs/, Irish /ˈəɾʲəxtəs/ the legislature of the Republic of Ireland: the President, Dáil, and Seanad.
– ORIGIN Irish, literally 'assembly, convocation'.

OIRO ▸ abbreviation Brit. offers in the region of (used in advertisements).

Oirot-Tura /ˌɔɪrɒtˈtuːrə/ former name (1932–48) for GORNO-ALTAISK.

Oisin /ˈəʊʃiːn/ another name for OSSIAN.

OJ ▸ noun [mass noun] informal orange juice.
– ORIGIN 1940s: abbreviation.

Ojibwa /ə(ʊ)ˈdʒɪbweɪ/ ▸ noun (pl. **same** or **Ojibwas**)
1 a member of an American Indian people inhabiting a wide area around Lake Superior. Also called CHIPPEWA.
2 [mass noun] the Algonquian language of the Ojibwa.
▸ adjective relating to the Ojibwa or their language.
– ORIGIN from Ojibwa *ojibwe*, said to mean 'puckered', with reference to their moccasins.

OK[1] (also **okay**) informal ▸ exclamation used to express agreement or acceptance: *OK, I'll pass on your message | OK, OK, I give in*. ■ used to introduce an utterance: *'OK, let's go'*.
▸ adjective [predic.] satisfactory but not especially good: *the flight was OK*. ■ in a satisfactory physical or mental state: *are you okay, Ben?* ■ permissible; allowable: *it's not OK to say that to a teacher*.
▸ adverb in a satisfactory manner or to a satisfactory extent: *the computer continues to work OK*.
▸ noun [in sing.] an authorization or approval: *the officer gave me the OK*.
▸ verb (**OK's**, **OK'ing**, **OK'd**) [with obj.] give approval to: *despite objections, the committee ok'd the construction*.
– ORIGIN mid 19th cent. (originally US): probably an abbreviation of *orl korrect*, humorous form of *all correct*, popularized as a slogan during President Van Buren's re-election campaign of 1840 in the US; his nickname *Old Kinderhook* (derived from his birthplace) provided the initials.

OK[2] ▸ abbreviation Oklahoma (in official postal use).

Oka /ˈəʊkə/ ▸ noun [mass noun] a variety of cured Canadian cheese, made by Trappist monks.
– ORIGIN named after a town in southern Quebec, where the cheese is made.

oka /ˈɒkə/ (also **oke**) ▸ noun **1** an Egyptian and former Turkish unit of weight, variable but now usually equal to approximately 1.3 kg ($2\frac{3}{4}$ lb).
2 an Egyptian and former Turkish unit of capacity equal to approximately 0.2 litre ($\frac{1}{3}$ pint).
– ORIGIN early 17th cent.: via Italian and French *oque* from Turkish *okka*, from Arabic *ūqīya*, based on Latin *uncia* 'ounce'.

okapi /ə(ʊ)ˈkɑːpi/ ▸ noun (pl. **same** or **okapis**) a large browsing mammal of the giraffe family that lives in the rainforests of northern Democratic Republic of the Congo (Zaire). It has a dark chestnut coat with stripes on the hindquarters and upper legs. ● *Okapia johnstoni*, family Giraffidae.
– ORIGIN early 20th cent.: a local word.

Okara /əʊˈkɑːrə/ a commercial city in NE Pakistan, in Punjab province; pop. 232,400 (est. 2009).

Okavango /ˌəʊkəˈvaŋgəʊ/ a river of SW Africa which rises in central Angola and flows 1,600 km (1,000 miles) south-eastwards to Namibia, where it turns eastwards to form part of the border between Angola and Namibia before entering Botswana, where it drains into the extensive Okavango marshes of Ngamiland. Also called CUBANGO.

okay ▸ exclamation, adjective, adverb, noun, & verb variant spelling of OK[1].

Okayama /ˌəʊkəˈjɑːmə/ an industrial city and major railway junction in SW Japan, on the SW coast of the island of Honshu; pop. 683,258 (2007).

oke[1] ▸ noun variant spelling of OKA.

oke[2] (also **okie**) ▸ noun (pl. **okes** or **okies**) S. African informal a man: *who's that oke talking to your sister?* ■ (**okie**) used to refer to or address a boy or, patronizingly, a man.
– ORIGIN shortened form of *okie*, anglicized form of Afrikaans *outjie* 'little chap'.

Okeechobee, Lake /ˌəʊkəˈtʃəʊbiː/ a lake in southern Florida. It forms part of the Okeechobee Waterway, which crosses the Florida peninsula from west to east, linking the Gulf of Mexico with the Atlantic.

O'Keeffe /əʊˈkiːf/, Georgia (1887–1986), American painter. Her best-known paintings depict enlarged studies, particularly of flowers, and are often regarded as being sexually symbolic (for example *Black Iris*, 1926).

Okefenokee Swamp /ˌəʊkəfəˈnəʊkiː/ an area of swampland in SE Georgia and NE Florida.

okey-dokey (also **okey-doke**) ▸ exclamation, adjective, & adverb another term for OK[1].

Okhotsk, Sea of /əʊˈxɒtsk/ an inlet of the northern Pacific Ocean on the east coast of Russia, between the Kamchatka peninsula and the Kuril Islands.

Okie ▸ noun (pl. **Okies**) US informal a native or inhabitant of Oklahoma. ■ historical, derogatory a migrant agricultural worker from Oklahoma who had been forced to leave a farm during the depression of the 1930s.

Okinawa /ˌəʊkɪˈnɑːwə/ a region in southern Japan, in the southern Ryukyu Islands; capital, Naha.

Okla ▸ abbreviation Oklahoma.

Oklahoma /ˌəʊkləˈhəʊmə/ a state in the south central US, north of Texas; pop. 3,642,361 (est. 2008); capital, Oklahoma City. In 1803 it was acquired from the French as part of the Louisiana Purchase. It became the 46th state of the US in 1907.
– DERIVATIVES **Oklahoman** noun & adjective.

Oklahoma City the state capital of Oklahoma; pop. 551,789 (est. 2008).

okra /ˈɒkrə, ˈəʊkrə/ ▸ noun [mass noun] a plant of the mallow family with long ridged seed pods, native to the Old World tropics. ● *Abelmoschus esculentus*, family Malvaceae.

■ the immature seed pods of the okra plant, eaten as a vegetable. Also called **BHINDI**, **GUMBO**, or **LADIES' FINGERS**.
– ORIGIN early 18th cent.: a West African word, perhaps from the root *nkru*; compare with *nkran*, the name of the town Europeanized as *Accra*.

okrug /ˈɒkrʊg/ ▸ noun (in Russia and Bulgaria) a territorial division for administrative and other purposes.
– ORIGIN Russian *okrug*, Bulgarian *okrăg*.

okta /ˈɒktə/ ▸ noun (pl. **same** or **oktas**) Meteorology a unit used in expressing the extent of cloud cover, equal to one eighth of the sky.
– ORIGIN 1950s: alteration of **OCTA-**.

-ol ▸ suffix Chemistry forming names of organic compounds: **1** denoting alcohols and phenols: *glycerol* | *retinol*.
2 denoting oils and oil-derived compounds: *benzol*.
– ORIGIN Sense 1 from (*alcoh*)*ol*; sense 2 from Latin *oleum* 'oil'. See also **-OLE**.

Olaf /ˈəʊlaf/ the name of five kings of Norway:
■ **Olaf I Tryggvason** (969–1000), reigned 995–1000.
■ **Olaf II Haraldsson** (*c*.995–1030), reigned 1016–30; canonized as **St Olaf** for his attempts to spread Christianity in his kingdom. He is the patron saint of Norway. Feast day, 29 July. ■ **Olaf III Haraldsson** (d.1093), reigned 1066–93. ■ **Olaf IV Haakonson** (1370–87), reigned 1380–7. ■ **Olaf V** (1903–91), reigned 1957–91; full name *Olaf Alexander Edmund Christian Frederik*.

Öland /ˈəːland/ a narrow island in the Baltic Sea off the SE coast of Sweden, separated from the mainland by Kalmar Sound.

Olbers' Paradox /ˈɒlbəz/ ▸ noun Astronomy the apparent paradox that if stars are distributed evenly throughout an infinite universe, the sky should be as bright by night as by day, since more distant stars would be fainter but more numerous. This is not the case because the universe is of finite age, and the light from the more distant stars is dimmed because they are receding from the observer as the universe expands.
– ORIGIN 1950s: named after Heinrich W. M. *Olbers* (1758–1840), the German astronomer who propounded it in 1826.

old ▸ adjective (**older**, **oldest**) **1** having lived for a long time; no longer young: *the old man lay propped up on cushions*. See also **ELDER**[1], **ELDEST**. ■ made or built long ago: *the old quarter of the town*. ■ possessed or used for a long time: *he gave his old clothes away*.
2 [attrib.] belonging to the past; former: *valuation under the old rating system was inexact*. ■ used to refer to a thing which has been replaced by something similar: *we moved back into our old house*. ■ dating from far back; long-established or known: *we greeted each other like old friends* | *I get sick of the **same old** routine*. ■ denoting someone who formerly attended a specified school: *an old Etonian*. ■ (of a form of a language) as used in former or earliest times.
3 [in combination] of a specified age: *he was fourteen years old* | *a seven-month-old baby*. ■ [as noun] [in combination] a person or animal of the age specified: *a nineteen-year-old*.
4 [attrib.] informal used to express affection, familiarity, or contempt: *good old Mum* | *I didn't like playing with silly old dolls*.
– PHRASES **any old** any item of a specified type (used to show that no particular individual is in question): *any old room would have done*. **any old how** in no particular order: *they've dropped things just any old how*. **as old as the hills** very old (often used in exaggerated statements). **be old enough to be someone's father** (or **mother**) informal be much older than someone (used to suggest that a romantic or sexual relationship between the people concerned is inappropriate). **for old times' sake** see **SAKE**[1]. **of old 1** in or belonging to the past: *he was more reticent than of old*. **2** for a long time: *they knew him of old*. **the old days** a period in the past, typically regarded as significantly better or worse than the present: *it was easier in the old days* | *we are less confident than in the good old days*. **the Old Firm** informal (in Scotland) a name for Celtic and Rangers Football Clubs, either singly or collectively: [as modifier] *an Old Firm match*. **you can't put an old head on young shoulders** proverb you can't expect a young person to have the wisdom or maturity associated with older people.
– DERIVATIVES **oldish** adjective, **oldness** noun.
– ORIGIN Old English *ald*, of West Germanic origin; related to Dutch *oud* and German *alt*, from an Indo-European root meaning 'adult', shared by Latin *alere* 'nourish'.

old age ▸ noun [mass noun] the later part of normal life: *loneliness affects many people **in old age***. ■ the state of being old: *old age itself is not a disease*.

old-age pension ▸ noun Brit. another term for **RETIREMENT PENSION**.

old-age pensioner ▸ noun Brit. an old person, especially one receiving an old-age pension.

Old Bailey the Central Criminal Court in London, formerly standing in an ancient bailey of the London city wall. The present court was built in 1903–6 on the site of Newgate Prison.

old bean ▸ noun see **BEAN**.

Old Believer ▸ noun a member of a Russian Orthodox group which refused to accept the liturgical reforms of the patriarch Nikon (1605–81).

Old Bill ▸ noun see **BILL**.

old boy ▸ noun **1** Brit. a former male student of a school or college. ■ a former male member of a sports team or company.
2 informal an elderly man. ■ chiefly Brit. an affectionate form of address to a boy or man.

old boy network (also **old boys' network**) ▸ noun an informal system through which men are thought to use their positions of influence to help others who went to the same school or university as they did, or who share a similar social background.

Old Catholic ▸ noun a member of a religious group which separated from the Roman Catholic Church after the time of the Reformation, especially the Church of Utrecht (which broke with Rome in 1724), and a number of German-speaking Churches which refused to accept papal infallibility after the First Vatican Council.

Old Church Slavonic ▸ noun [mass noun] the oldest recorded Slavic language, as used by the apostles Cyril and Methodius and surviving in texts from the 9th–12th centuries. It is related particularly to the Southern Slavic languages. See also **CHURCH SLAVONIC**.

Old Colony informal name for **MASSACHUSETTS**.

Old Contemptibles the veterans of the British Expeditionary Force sent to France in the First World War (1914), so named because of a supposed German reference to the 'contemptible little army' facing them.

old country ▸ noun (**the old country**) the native country of a person who has gone to live abroad.

Old Dart ▸ noun Austral./NZ informal England.
– ORIGIN *Dart* as a figurative use representing a pronunciation of *dirt*, from **PAY DIRT**.

old dear ▸ noun informal a patronizing term for an elderly woman.

Old Delhi see **DELHI**.

Old Dominion informal name for **VIRGINIA**[1].

olde /əʊld, ˈəʊldi/ ▸ adjective [attrib.] pseudo-archaic in or relating to an old-fashioned style that is intended to be quaint and attractive: *Ye Olde Tea Shoppe*.

olden ▸ adjective [attrib.] archaic relating to former times: *the olden days*.

Old English ▸ noun [mass noun] the language of the Anglo-Saxons (up to about 1150), an inflected language with a Germanic vocabulary, very different from modern English. Also called **ANGLO-SAXON**.

Old English sheepdog ▸ noun a large sheepdog of a breed with a shaggy blue-grey and white coat.

olde worlde /əʊldi ˈwəːldi/ ▸ adjective Brit. pseudo-archaic in or relating to an old-fashioned style that is intended to be quaint and attractive (often used to suggest a lack of authenticity): *olde worlde inns*.

old-fangled ▸ adjective old-fashioned.

old-fashioned ▸ adjective in or according to styles or types no longer current; not modern: *an old-fashioned kitchen range*. ■ favouring traditional or conservative ideas or customs: *she's stuffy and old-fashioned*. ■ (of a facial expression) disapproving: *Jonas gave her an old-fashioned look*.
▸ noun N. Amer. a cocktail consisting chiefly of whisky, bitters, water, and sugar.
– DERIVATIVES **old-fashionedness** noun.

old-fashioned rose ▸ noun another term for **OLD ROSE** (sense 1).

old-fashioned waltz ▸ noun a waltz played in quick time.

Old French ▸ noun [mass noun] the French language up to *c*.1400.

Old Frisian ▸ noun [mass noun] the Frisian language up to *c*.1400, closely related to both Old English and Old Saxon.

old fruit ▸ noun Brit. informal, dated a friendly form of address to a man.

old girl ▸ noun **1** Brit. a former female student of a school or college. ■ a former female member of a sports team or company.
2 informal, chiefly Brit. an elderly woman. ■ an affectionate form of address to a girl or woman.

Old Glory US an informal name for the US national flag.

old gold ▸ noun [mass noun] a dull brownish-gold colour.

old-growth ▸ adjective (of a tree, forest, etc.) never felled; mature.

old guard ▸ noun the original or long-standing members of a group, regarded as unwilling to accept change or new ideas: *the ageing right-wing old guard*.

Oldham /ˈəʊldəm/ an industrial town in NW England, near Manchester; pop. 105,100 (est. 2009).

old hand ▸ noun a person with a lot of experience in something: *the examiner is an old hand at the game*.

old hat ▸ noun [mass noun] informal something tediously familiar or outdated: *last year's electronics are already old hat*.

Old High German ▸ noun [mass noun] the language of southern Germany up to *c*.1200, from which modern standard German is derived. See **GERMAN**.

Old Icelandic ▸ noun [mass noun] Icelandic up to the 16th century, a form of Old Norse in which the medieval sagas were composed.

old identity ▸ noun Austral./NZ a person long resident or well known in a place.

oldie ▸ noun informal an old song, film, or television programme that is still well known or popular. ■ an older person.

Old Irish ▸ noun [mass noun] the Irish Gaelic language up to *c*.1000, from which modern Irish and Scottish Gaelic are derived.

Old Kingdom a period of ancient Egyptian history (*c*.2575–2134 BC, 4th–8th dynasty).

old lady ▸ noun **1** an elderly woman. ■ (**one's old lady**) informal a person's mother or a man's wife or girlfriend.
2 a brownish European moth with a creamy pattern on the wings. ● *Mormo maura*, family Noctuidae.

Old Lady of Threadneedle Street the nickname of the Bank of England, which stands in this street.

O

Old Latin ▸ noun [mass noun] Latin before about 100 BC.

old-line ▸ adjective N. Amer. **1** holding conservative views.
2 well established.
DERIVATIVES **old-liner** noun.

Old Line State informal name for **MARYLAND**.

Old Low German ▸ noun [mass noun] the language of northern Germany and the Netherlands up to *c*.1200, from which modern Dutch and modern Low German are derived.

old maid ▸ noun **1** derogatory a single woman regarded as too old for marriage. ■ a prim and fussy person: *he said John was an old maid*.
2 [mass noun] a card game in which players collect pairs and try not to be left with an odd penalty card, typically a queen.
3 chiefly W. Indian another term for **PERIWINKLE**[1].
– DERIVATIVES **old-maidish** adjective.

old man ▸ noun **1** an elderly male person. ■ (**one's old man**) informal a person's father or a woman's husband or boyfriend. ■ (**the old man**) informal a man in authority over others, especially an employer or commanding officer. ■ Brit. informal an affectionate form of address between men or boys: *are you all right, old man?* ■ informal used with a surname instead of Mr: *old man Roberts*.
2 another term for **SOUTHERNWOOD**.

old man's beard ▸ noun [mass noun] **1** a wild clematis which has grey fluffy hairs around the seeds. ● Genus *Clematis*, family Ranunculaceae: several species, in particular (in Britain) traveller's joy.
2 a large lichen that forms shaggy greyish beard-like growths on the branches of trees. ● *Usnea barbata* and related species, order Parmeliales.

old master ▸ noun a great artist of former times, especially of the 13th–17th century in Europe. ■ a painting by a great artist of former times: *a large collection of old masters*.

old moon ▸ noun the phase of the moon in its last quarter, before the new moon. ■ [mass noun] the time when the old moon occurs.

Old Nick an informal name for the Devil.
– ORIGIN mid 17th cent.: probably from a pet form of the given name *Nicholas*.

Old Norse ▸ noun [mass noun] the North Germanic language of medieval Norway, Iceland, Denmark, and Sweden up to the 14th century, from which the modern Scandinavian languages are derived. See also **OLD ICELANDIC**.

Old North State informal name for **NORTH CAROLINA**.

Oldowan /ˈɒldə(ʊ)wən/ ▸ adjective Archaeology relating to or denoting an early Lower Palaeolithic culture of Africa, dated to about 2.0–1.5 million years ago. It is characterized by primitive stone tools that are associated chiefly with *Homo habilis*. ■ (as noun **the Oldowan**) the Oldowan culture or period.
– ORIGIN 1930s: from *Oldoway*, alteration of **OLDUVAI GORGE**, Tanzania, + **-AN**.

Old Pals Act ▸ noun Brit. informal used humorously to imply that someone is using a position of influence to help their friends.

Old Persian ▸ noun [mass noun] the Persian language up to the 3rd century BC, used in the ancient Persian empire and written in cuneiform.

Old Pretender see **STUART²**.

Old Prussian ▸ noun [mass noun] a Baltic language, related to Lithuanian, spoken in Prussia until the 17th century.

Old Red Sandstone ▸ noun [mass noun] Geology a series of sedimentary rocks, chiefly red sandstones, belonging to the Devonian system of NW Europe.

old religion ▸ noun a religion replaced by another, in particular paganism or Roman Catholicism.

old rose ▸ noun 1 a double-flowered rose of a variety or hybrid evolved before the development of the hybrid tea rose.
2 [mass noun] a shade of deep pink.

Old Sarum a hill in southern England 3 km (2 miles) north of Salisbury, the site of an ancient Iron Age settlement and hill fort, and later of a Norman castle and town. The settlement fell into decline after the new cathedral and town of Salisbury were established in 1220, and the site was deserted.

Old Saxon ▸ noun 1 a member of the Saxon peoples who remained in Germany, as opposed to an Anglo-Saxon.
2 [mass noun] the dialect of Old Low German spoken in Saxony up to *c.*1200.
▸ adjective relating to the Old Saxons or their language.

O

old school ▸ noun used, usually approvingly, to refer to someone or something that is old-fashioned or traditional: *he was one of the old school of English gentlemen*.
▸ adjective having or adhering to old-fashioned values or ways: *the restaurant is an old-school brasserie of the Parisian model*. ■ denoting or relating to a style or genre of popular music, especially rap or hip hop, regarded as traditional or relatively uninfluenced by newer styles.

old school tie ▸ noun Brit. a necktie with a characteristic pattern worn by the former pupils of a particular school, especially a public school. ■ used to refer to the group loyalty, social class, and traditional attitudes associated with people who attended public schools: *appointments based on social class and the old school tie*.

Old Slavonic ▸ noun another name for **CHURCH SLAVONIC**.

old soldier ▸ noun a male ex-soldier.
– PHRASES **come** (or **play**) **the old soldier** informal use one's greater age or experience of life to deceive someone or to shirk a duty.

Old South ▸ noun (**the Old South**) the Southern states of the US before the civil war of 1861–5.

old Spanish custom (also **Spanish practice**) ▸ noun informal a long-standing practice in a company which is unauthorized or otherwise irregular.

oldspeak ▸ noun [mass noun] chiefly humorous normal English usage as opposed to technical or propagandist language.
– ORIGIN 1949: from George Orwell's *Nineteen Eighty-Four* (see **NEWSPEAK**).

oldsquaw ▸ noun North American term for **LONG-TAILED DUCK**.

old stager ▸ noun a very experienced or long-serving person: *the changes aroused the hostility of the old stagers*.

oldster ▸ noun informal, chiefly N. Amer. an older person.
– ORIGIN early 19th cent.: from **OLD**, on the pattern of *youngster*.

Old Stone Age the Palaeolithic period.

Old Style (abbrev.: **OS**) ▸ noun [mass noun] [often as modifier] the method of calculating dates using the Julian calendar.

old sweat ▸ noun informal a veteran soldier.

old talk W. Indian ▸ noun [mass noun] small talk; chatter: *they would start big old talk with the travellers*. ■ empty or insincere talk: *the old talk and empty promises by the politicians*.
▸ verb (**old-talk**) [no obj.] engage in chatter or insincere talk.

Old Testament ▸ noun the first part of the Christian Bible, comprising thirty-nine books and corresponding approximately to the Hebrew Bible. Most of the books were written in Hebrew, some in Aramaic, between about 1200 and 100 BC. They comprise the chief texts of the law, history, prophecy, and wisdom literature of the ancient people of Israel.

old thing ▸ noun informal a familiar form of address: *sorry if I woke you, old thing*.

old-time ▸ adjective [attrib.] relating to or characteristic of the past; long-standing: *the charm of old-time steam engines*. ■ US denoting traditional or folk styles of American popular music, such as gospel or bluegrass. ■ denoting ballroom dances in which a sequence of dance steps is repeated throughout, as opposed to modern dancing in which steps may be varied.

old-timer ▸ noun informal a very experienced or long-serving person. ■ N. Amer. an old person.

Olduvai Gorge /ˈɒldʊvʌɪ/ a gorge in northern Tanzania, 48 km (30 miles) long and up to 90 metres (300 ft) deep. The exposed strata contain numerous fossils (especially hominids) spanning the full range of the Pleistocene period.

Old Vic the popular name of the Royal Victoria Theatre in London. Under the management of Lilian Baylis from 1912 it gained an enduring reputation for its Shakespearean productions.

Old Welsh ▸ noun [mass noun] the Welsh language up to *c.*1150.

old wife ▸ noun any of a number of deep-bodied edible marine fishes, in particular: ● a brightly patterned tropical Atlantic triggerfish (*Balistes vetula*, family Balistidae). ● a small brightly patterned Australian fish (*Enoplosus armatus*, the only member of the family Enoplosidae). ● the black sea bream of European Atlantic waters (*Spondyliosoma cantharus*, family Sparidae).

old witch grass ▸ noun see **WITCH GRASS**.

old wives' tale ▸ noun a widely held traditional belief that is now thought to be unscientific or incorrect.

old woman ▸ noun an elderly female person. ■ (**one's old woman**) informal a person's mother or a man's wife or girlfriend. ■ derogatory a fussy or timid person, especially a man: *he's always telling me I'm an old woman about security*.
– DERIVATIVES **old-womanish** adjective.

Old World Europe, Asia, and Africa, regarded collectively as the part of the world known before the discovery of the Americas.

old-world ▸ adjective belonging to or associated with former times, especially when considered quaint and attractive: *medieval towns which still retain old-world charm*.

old year ▸ noun the year just ended or just about to end.

OLE ▸ abbreviation Computing object linking and embedding, denoting a set of techniques for transferring an object from one application to another.

ole ▸ adjective US informal old.
– ORIGIN mid 19th cent.: representing a pronunciation.

olé /əʊˈleɪ/ ▸ exclamation bravo.
– ORIGIN Spanish.

-ole ▸ combining form in names of organic compounds, especially heterocyclic compounds: *thiazole*.
– ORIGIN from Latin *oleum* 'oil' (compare with **-OL**).

oleaceous /ˌəʊlɪˈeɪʃəs/ ▸ adjective Botany relating to or denoting plants of the olive family (Oleaceae).
– ORIGIN mid 19th cent.: from modern Latin *Oleaceae* (plural), based on Latin *olea* 'olive tree', + **-OUS**.

oleaginous /ˌəʊlɪˈadʒɪnəs/ ▸ adjective 1 rich in, covered with, or producing oil; oily.
2 exaggeratedly and distastefully complimentary; obsequious: *candidates made oleaginous speeches praising government policies*.
– ORIGIN late Middle English: from French *oléagineux*, from Latin *oleaginus* 'of the olive tree', from *oleum* 'oil'.

oleander /ˌəʊlɪˈandə/ ▸ noun a poisonous evergreen Old World shrub grown in warm countries for its clusters of white, pink, or red flowers. ● *Nerium oleander*, family Apocynaceae.
– ORIGIN early 16th cent.: from medieval Latin, of unknown ultimate origin.

oleaster /ˌəʊlɪˈastə/ ▸ noun a Eurasian shrub or small tree cultivated as an ornamental. ● Genus *Elaeagnus*, family Elaeagnaceae: several species, in particular *E. angustifolia*, which bears edible yellow olive-shaped fruit (also called **RUSSIAN OLIVE** in North America).
– ORIGIN late Middle English: from Latin, from *olea* 'olive tree'.

oleate /ˈəʊlɪeɪt/ ▸ noun Chemistry a salt or ester of oleic acid.

olecranon /əʊˈlɛkrənɒn, ˌəʊlɪˈkreɪnən/ ▸ noun Anatomy a bony prominence at the elbow, on the upper end of the ulna.
– ORIGIN early 18th cent.: from Greek *ōle(no)kranon*, from *ōlenē* 'elbow' + *kranion* 'head'.

olefin /ˈəʊlɪfɪn/ (also **olefine**) ▸ noun Chemistry another term for **ALKENE**.
– DERIVATIVES **olefinic** adjective.
– ORIGIN mid 19th cent.: from French *oléfiant* 'oil-forming' (with reference to oily ethylene dichloride).

oleic acid /əʊˈliːɪk/ ▸ noun [mass noun] Chemistry an unsaturated fatty acid present in many fats and soaps. ● Chem. formula: $CH_3(CH_2)_7CH{-}CH(CH_2)_7COOH$.
– ORIGIN early 19th cent.: *oleic* from Latin *oleum* 'oil'.

oleiferous /ˌəʊlɪˈɪf(ə)rəs/ ▸ adjective Botany (of seeds, glands, etc.) producing oil.
– ORIGIN early 19th cent.: from Latin *oleum* 'oil' + **-FEROUS**.

oleo- /ˈəʊlɪəʊ, ˈɒlɪəʊ/ ▸ combining form relating to or containing oil: *oleomargarine* | *oleoresin*.
– ORIGIN from Latin *oleum* 'oil'.

oleochemical /ˌəʊlɪəʊˈkɛmɪk(ə)l, ˌɒlɪəʊ-/ ▸ noun a chemical compound derived industrially from animal or vegetable oils or fats.

oleograph ▸ noun a print textured to resemble an oil painting.

oleomargarine ▸ noun [mass noun] a fatty substance extracted from beef fat and used in the manufacture of margarine. ■ N. Amer. old-fashioned term for **MARGARINE**.

oleoresin ▸ noun a natural or artificial mixture of essential oils and a resin, e.g. balsam.
– DERIVATIVES **oleoresinous** adjective.

Olestra /ɒˈlɛstrə/ ▸ noun [mass noun] trademark a synthetic compound used as a calorie-free substitute for fat in various foods because of its ability to pass through the body without being absorbed. It is a polyester derived from sucrose.
– ORIGIN 1980s: from *(p)ol(y)est(e)r* + the suffix *-a*.

oleum /ˈəʊlɪəm/ ▸ noun [mass noun] a dense, corrosive liquid consisting of concentrated sulphuric acid containing excess sulphur trioxide in solution.
– ORIGIN early 20th cent.: from Latin, literally 'oil'.

O level ▸ noun short for **ORDINARY LEVEL**. ■ an O-level exam or pass.

olfaction /ɒlˈfakʃ(ə)n/ ▸ noun [mass noun] technical the action or capacity of smelling; the sense of smell.
– DERIVATIVES **olfactive** adjective.
– ORIGIN mid 19th cent.: from Latin *olfactus* 'a smell' (from *olere* 'to smell' + *fact-* 'made', from the verb *facere*) + **-ION**.

olfactometer /ˌɒlfakˈtɒmɪtə/ ▸ noun an instrument for measuring the intensity of an odour or the sensitivity of someone or something to an odour.
– DERIVATIVES **olfactometry** noun.

olfactory /ɒlˈfakt(ə)ri/ ▸ adjective relating to the sense of smell: *the olfactory organs*.
– ORIGIN mid 17th cent.: from Latin *olfactare* (frequentative of *olfacere* 'to smell') + **-ORY²**.

olfactory nerve ▸ noun Anatomy each of the first pair of cranial nerves, supplying the smell receptors in the mucous membrane of the nose.

olibanum /ɒˈlɪbənəm/ ▸ noun frankincense.
– ORIGIN late Middle English: from medieval Latin, from late Latin *libanus*, from Greek *libanos* 'frankincense'.

oligaemia /ˌɒlɪˈɡiːmɪə/ (US **oligemia**) ▶ **noun** another term for **HYPOVOLAEMIA**.
– ORIGIN mid 19th cent.: from French *oligaimie*, from Greek *oligaimia*.

oligarch /ˈɒlɪɡɑːk/ ▶ **noun 1** a ruler in an oligarchy.
2 (especially in Russia) a very rich businessman with a great deal of political influence.
– ORIGIN late 19th cent.: from Greek *oligarkhēs*, from *oligoi* 'few' + *arkhein* 'to rule'.

WORD TRENDS If it's true that money is power, then **oligarch** is the perfect name for the new breed of ultra-rich businessmen. Originally, an **oligarch** was one of a very small group of leaders of a country. Most of today's **oligarchs** gained their fortunes very quickly after the fall of the former Soviet republics, and though they do not have any official political power their massive fortunes can mean they have influence over governments and politicians. Unsurprisingly, the word **oligarch** has acquired some negative associations, reflected in the examples seen in the Oxford English Corpus—*corrupt*, *exiled*, and *jailed* are all common collocates, as is *so-called*, a sign of anger at the assumption of political influence the name **oligarch** implies: *millions of citizens revile the so-called oligarchs*. See also **TSAR**.

oligarchy ▶ **noun** (pl. **oligarchies**) a small group of people having control of a country or organization: *the ruling oligarchy of military men around the president*. ■ a country governed by an oligarchy. ■ [mass noun] government by an oligarchy.
– DERIVATIVES **oligarchic** adjective, **oligarchical** adjective.
– ORIGIN late 15th cent.: from Greek *oligarkhia*, from *oligoi* 'few' and *arkhein* 'to rule'.

oligo ▶ **noun** (pl. **oligos**) Biochemistry short for **OLIGONUCLEOTIDE**.

oligo- ▶ **combining form** having few; containing a relatively small number of units: *oligopoly* | *oligosaccharide*.
– ORIGIN from Greek *oligos* 'small', *oligoi* 'few'.

Oligocene /ˈɒlɪɡə(ʊ)siːn/ ▶ **adjective** Geology relating to or denoting the third epoch of the Tertiary period, between the Eocene and Miocene epochs. ■ (as noun **the Oligocene**) the Oligocene epoch or the system of rocks deposited during it.

The Oligocene epoch lasted from 35.4 to 23.3 million years ago. It was a time of falling temperatures, with evidence of the first primates.

– ORIGIN mid 19th cent.: from **OLIGO-** 'few' + Greek *kainos* 'new'.

Oligochaeta /ˌɒlɪɡə(ʊ)ˈkiːtə/ ▶ **plural noun** Zoology a class of annelid worms which includes the earthworms. They have simple setae projecting from each segment and a small head lacking sensory appendages.
– ORIGIN modern Latin (plural), from **OLIGO-** 'few' + Greek *khaitē* 'long hair' (taken to mean 'bristle'), because they have fewer setae than polychaetes.

oligochaete ▶ **noun** Zoology an annelid worm of the class Oligochaeta, such as an earthworm.

oligoclase /ˈɒlɪɡə(ʊ)kleɪz/ ▶ **noun** [mass noun] a feldspar mineral common in siliceous igneous rocks, consisting of a sodium-rich plagioclase (with more calcium than albite).
– ORIGIN mid 19th cent.: from **OLIGO-** 'relatively little' + Greek *klasis* 'breaking' (because thought to have a less perfect cleavage than albite).

oligodendrocyte /ˌɒlɪɡə(ʊ)ˈdɛndrəsʌɪt/ ▶ **noun** Anatomy a glial cell similar to an astrocyte but with fewer protuberances, concerned with the production of myelin in the central nervous system.
– ORIGIN 1930s: from **OLIGODENDROGLIA** + **-CYTE**.

oligodendroglia /ˌɒlɪɡə(ʊ)dɛndrəˈɡlʌɪə/ ▶ **plural noun** Anatomy oligodendrocytes collectively.
– DERIVATIVES **oligodendroglial** adjective.
– ORIGIN 1920s: from **OLIGO-** 'few' + **DENDRO-** 'branching' + a shortened form of **NEUROGLIA**.

oligodendroglioma /ˌɒlɪɡə(ʊ)ˌdɛndrə(ʊ)ɡlɪˈəʊmə/ ▶ **noun** (pl. **oligodendrogliomas** or **oligodendrogliomata** /-mətə/) Medicine a tumour derived from oligodendroglia.

oligomer /əˈlɪɡəmə, ˈɒlɪɡ-/ ▶ **noun** Chemistry a polymer whose molecules consist of relatively few repeating units.

oligomerize /əˈlɪɡəmərʌɪz/ (also **oligomerise**) ▶ **verb** [with obj.] Chemistry join a number of molecules of (a monomer) together to form an oligomer.
– DERIVATIVES **oligomerization** noun.

oligomerous /ˌɒlɪˈɡɒmərəs/ ▶ **adjective** Biology having a small number of segments or parts.

oligonucleotide /ˌɒlɪɡə(ʊ)ˈnjuːklɪətʌɪd/ ▶ **noun** Biochemistry a polynucleotide whose molecules contain a relatively small number of nucleotides.

oligopeptide /ˌɒlɪɡə(ʊ)ˈpɛptʌɪd/ ▶ **noun** Biochemistry a peptide whose molecules contain a relatively small number of amino-acid residues.

oligopoly /ˌɒlɪˈɡɒp(ə)li/ ▶ **noun** (pl. **oligopolies**) a state of limited competition, in which a market is shared by a small number of producers or sellers.
– DERIVATIVES **oligopolist** noun, **oligopolistic** adjective.
– ORIGIN late 19th cent.: from **OLIGO-** 'small number', on the pattern of *monopoly*.

oligopsony /ˌɒlɪˈɡɒps(ə)ni/ ▶ **noun** (pl. **oligopsonies**) a state of the market in which only a small number of buyers exists for a product.
– DERIVATIVES **oligopsonistic** adjective.
– ORIGIN 1940s: from **OLIGO-** 'small number' + Greek *opsōnein* 'buy provisions', on the pattern of *monopsony*.

oligosaccharide /ˌɒlɪɡə(ʊ)ˈsakərʌɪd/ ▶ **noun** Biochemistry a carbohydrate whose molecules are composed of a relatively small number of monosaccharide units.

oligospermia /ˌɒlɪɡə(ʊ)ˈspəːmɪə/ ▶ **noun** [mass noun] Medicine deficiency of sperm cells in the semen.

oligotrophic /ˌɒlɪɡə(ʊ)ˈtrəʊfɪk, -ˈtrɒfɪk/ ▶ **adjective** Ecology (especially of a lake) relatively poor in plant nutrients and containing abundant oxygen in the deeper parts. Compare with **DYSTROPHIC**, **EUTROPHIC**.
– DERIVATIVES **oligotrophy** noun.

oliguria /ɒlɪˈɡjʊərɪə/ ▶ **noun** [mass noun] Medicine the production of abnormally small amounts of urine.
– DERIVATIVES **oliguric** adjective.

olingo /ɒˈlɪŋɡəʊ/ ▶ **noun** (pl. **olingos**) a small nocturnal mammal resembling the kinkajou but with a long muzzle and a bushy non-prehensile tail, living in tropical American rainforests. ● Genus *Bassaricyon*, family Procyonidae: between one and five species.
– ORIGIN 1920s: via American Spanish from Mayan.

olio /ˈəʊlɪəʊ/ ▶ **noun** (pl. **olios**) **1** a highly spiced stew of various meats and vegetables originating from Spain and Portugal.
2 a miscellaneous collection of things. ■ a variety act or show.
– ORIGIN mid 17th cent.: from Spanish *olla* 'stew', from Latin *olla* 'cooking pot'.

olivaceous /ˌɒlɪˈveɪʃəs/ ▶ **adjective** technical of a dusky yellowish green colour; olive green.

olivary /ˈɒlɪv(ə)ri/ ▶ **adjective** Anatomy relating to or denoting the nucleus situated in the olive of the medulla oblongata in the brain.
– ORIGIN late Middle English: from Latin *olivarius* 'relating to olives', from *oliva* (see **OLIVE**).

olive ▶ **noun 1** a small oval fruit with a hard stone and bitter flesh, green when unripe and bluish black when ripe, used as food and as a source of oil.
2 (also **olive tree**) the small evergreen tree which produces olives and which has narrow leaves with silvery undersides, native to warm regions of the Old World. ● *Olea europaea*, family Oleaceae (the **olive family**). This family also includes the ash, lilac, jasmine, and privet. ■ used in names of other trees which are related to the olive, resemble it, or bear similar fruit, e.g. **Russian olive**.
3 (also **olive green**) [mass noun] a greyish-green colour like that of an unripe olive.
4 a slice of beef or veal made into a roll with stuffing inside and stewed.
5 (also **olive shell**) a marine mollusc with a smooth, roughly cylindrical shell which is typically brightly coloured. ● Genus *Oliva*, family Olividae, class Gastropoda.
6 Anatomy each of a pair of smooth, oval swellings in the medulla oblongata.
7 a metal ring or fitting which is tightened under a threaded nut to form a seal, as in a compression joint.
▶ **adjective** greyish-green: *a small figure in olive fatigues*. ■ (of the complexion) yellowish-brown; sallow.
– ORIGIN Middle English: via Old French from Latin *oliva*, from Greek *elaia*, from *elaion* 'oil'.

olive branch ▶ **noun** an offer of reconciliation: *the government is **holding out an olive branch** to the demonstrators*.
– ORIGIN in allusion to the story of Noah in Gen. 8:1, in which a dove returns with an olive branch after the Flood, taken as a symbol of peace after God's punishment of mankind.

olive brown ▶ **noun** [mass noun] a dull shade of yellowish brown.

olive drab ▶ **noun** [mass noun] a dull olive-green colour, used in some military uniforms.

olive oil ▶ **noun** [mass noun] an oil obtained from olives, used in cookery and salad dressings.

Oliver the companion of Roland in the *Chanson de Roland* (see **ROLAND**).

Olives, Mount of see **MOUNT OF OLIVES**.

olivette /ɒlɪˈvɛt/ ▶ **noun** a small oval weight threaded on a fishing line.
– ORIGIN early 19th cent. (in the sense 'an oval button or bead').

Olivier /əˈlɪvɪeɪ/, Laurence (Kerr), Baron Olivier of Brighton (1907–89), English actor and director. Following his professional debut in 1924, he performed all the major Shakespearean roles; he was also director of the National Theatre (1963–73). His films include *Rebecca* (1940), *Henry V* (1944), and *Hamlet* (1948).

olivine /ˈɒlɪviːn, -ʌɪn/ ▶ **noun** [mass noun] an olive-green, grey-green, or brown mineral occurring widely in basalt, peridotite, and other basic igneous rocks. It is a silicate containing varying proportions of magnesium, iron, and other elements.
– ORIGIN late 18th cent.: from Latin *oliva* (see **OLIVE**) + **-INE**[1].

olla podrida /ˌɒlə pə(ʊ)ˈdriːdə/, Spanish /ˌoja pəɔˈðriða/ ▶ **noun** another term for **OLIO**.
– ORIGIN Spanish, literally 'rotten pot', from Latin *olla* 'jar' + *putridus* 'rotten'.

ollie ▶ **noun** (pl. **ollies**) (in skateboarding and snowboarding) a jump performed without the aid of a take-off ramp, executed by pressing the foot down on the tail of the board to rebound the deck off the ground.
▶ **verb** (**ollies**, **ollieing**, **ollied**) [no obj.] perform an ollie.
– ORIGIN 1980s: of unknown origin.

ollycrock /ˈɒlɪkrɒk/ ▶ **noun** S. African a periwinkle-like mollusc which is eaten as seafood and used as bait. ● *Turbo sarmaticus*, family Turbinidae, class Gastropoda.
– ORIGIN anglicized form of Afrikaans *alikreukel*.

olm /əʊlm, ɒlm/ ▶ **noun** a pale-skinned blind salamander with external gills which lives in limestone caves in SE Europe. ● *Proteus anguinus*, family Proteidae.
– ORIGIN late 19th cent.: from German.

Olmec /ˈɒlmɛk/ ▶ **noun** (pl. **same** or **Olmecs**) **1** a member of a prehistoric people inhabiting the coast of Veracruz and western Tabasco on the Gulf of Mexico (*c.*1200–400 BC), who established what was probably the first developed civilization of Meso-America.
2 a people living in the same general area during the 15th and 16th centuries.
– ORIGIN from Nahuatl *Olmecatl*, (plural) *Olmeca*, literally 'inhabitants of the rubber country'.

Olmos /ˈɒlmɒs/ a small town on the eastern edge of the Sechura Desert in NW Peru, which gave its name to a major irrigation project initiated in 1926.

ology ▶ **noun** (pl. **ologies**) informal, humorous a subject of study; a branch of knowledge.
– DERIVATIVES **ologist** noun.

-ology ▶ **combining form** common form of **-LOGY**.

Olomouc /ˈɒləməʊts/ an industrial city on the Morava River in northern Moravia in the Czech Republic; pop. 99,996 (2007).

oloroso /ˌɒləˈrəʊsəʊ/ ▶ **noun** (pl. **olorosos**) [mass noun] a heavy, dark, medium-sweet sherry. ■ sherry which does not have a covering of flor (yeast) during production, used to make oloroso and cream sherries. Compare with **FINO**.
– ORIGIN Spanish, literally 'fragrant'.

Olsztyn /ˈɒlʃtɪn/ a city in northern Poland, in the area of Masuria; pop. 175,098 (2007). Founded in 1348 by the Teutonic Knights, it was a part of Prussia between 1772 and 1945. German name **ALLENSTEIN**.

Olympia 1 a plain in Greece, in the western Peloponnese. In ancient Greece it was the site of the chief sanctuary of the god Zeus, the place where the original Olympic Games were held, after which the site is named.
2 the capital of the state of Washington, a port on Puget Sound; pop. 45,322 (est. 2008).

Olympiad /əˈlɪmpɪad/ ▶ **noun** an occasion when the ancient or modern Olympic Games were or are held. ■ a period of four years between Olympic Games, used by the ancient Greeks in dating events. ■ a major international contest in a particular game, sport, or scientific subject.
– ORIGIN via French or Latin from Greek *Olumpias Olumpiad-*, from *Olumpios* (see also **OLYMPIAN** and **OLYMPIC**).

Olympian ▶ adjective **1** associated with Mount Olympus in NE Greece, or with the Greek gods whose home was traditionally held to be there: *a temple of Olympian Zeus.* ■ resembling or appropriate to a god, especially in superiority and aloofness: *the court is capable of an Olympian impartiality.*
2 [attrib.] relating to the ancient or modern Olympic Games: *an Olympian champion.*
▶ noun **1** any of the pantheon of twelve Greek gods regarded as living on Olympus. ■ a person of great attainments or exalted position.
2 a competitor in the Olympic Games.
– ORIGIN late 15th cent.: sense 1 of the adjective from Latin *Olympus* (see **OLYMPUS**) + **-IAN**; sense 2 of the adjective from *Olympia* (see **OLYMPIA**) + **-AN**.

Olympic ▶ adjective [attrib.] relating to ancient Olympia or the Olympic Games: *an Olympic champion.*
▶ noun (**the Olympics**) the Olympic Games.
– ORIGIN late 16th cent.: via Latin from Greek *Olumpikos* 'of Olympus or Olympia'.

Olympic Games (also **the Olympics**) a sports festival held every four years in different venues, instigated by the Frenchman Baron de Coubertin (1863–1937) in 1896. Athletes representing more than 200 countries compete for gold, silver, and bronze medals in more than twenty sports. ■ an ancient Greek festival with athletic, literary, and musical competitions held at Olympia every four years, traditionally from 776 BC until abolished by the Roman emperor Theodosius I in AD 393.

Olympic-sized (also **Olympic-size**) ▶ adjective (of a swimming pool or other sports venue) of the dimensions prescribed for modern Olympic competitions.

Olympus Greek Mythology the home of the twelve greater gods, identified in later antiquity with Mount Olympus in Greece.

Olympus, Mount 1 a mountain in northern Greece, at the eastern end of the range dividing Thessaly from Macedonia; height 2,917 m (9,570 ft).
2 a mountain in Cyprus, in the Troodos range. Rising to 1,951 m (6,400 ft), it is the highest peak on the island.

OM ▶ abbreviation (in the UK) Order of Merit.

om /əʊm, ɒm/ ▶ noun a mystic syllable, considered the most sacred mantra in Hinduism and Tibetan Buddhism. It appears at the beginning and end of most Sanskrit recitations, prayers, and texts.
– ORIGIN Sanskrit, sometimes regarded as three sounds, *a-u-m*, symbolic of the three major Hindu deities.

O

-oma ▶ suffix (forming nouns) denoting tumours and other abnormal growths: *carcinoma.*
– DERIVATIVES **-omatous** suffix forming corresponding adjectives.
– ORIGIN modern Latin, from a Greek suffix denoting the result of verbal action.

omadhaun /ˈɒmədɔːn/ ▶ noun Irish a foolish person.
– ORIGIN early 19th cent.: from Irish *amadán.*

Omagh /əʊˈmɑː, ˈəʊmə/ a town in Northern Ireland, principal town of County Tyrone; pop. 22,500 (est. 2009).

Omaha[1] /ˈəʊməhɑː/ a city in eastern Nebraska, on the Missouri River; pop. 438,646 (est. 2008).

Omaha[2] /ˈəʊməhɑː/ ▶ noun (pl. **same** or **Omahas**)
1 a member of an American Indian people of NE Nebraska.
2 [mass noun] the Siouan language of the Omaha, now all but extinct.
▶ adjective relating to the Omaha or their language.
– ORIGIN from Omaha *umonhon* 'upstream people'.

Oman /əʊˈmɑːn/ a country at the eastern corner of the Arabian peninsula; pop. 3,418,100 (est. 2009); official language, Arabic; capital, Muscat.

> An independent sultanate, known as Muscat and Oman until 1970, Oman was the most influential power in the region in the 19th century, controlling Zanzibar and other territory. Since the late 19th century Oman has had strong links with Britain. The economy is dependent on oil, discovered in 1964.

– DERIVATIVES **Omani** adjective & noun.

Oman, Gulf of an inlet of the Arabian Sea, connected by the Strait of Hormuz to the Persian Gulf.

Omar I /ˈəʊmɑː/ (*c.*581–644), Muslim caliph 634–44. He conquered Syria, Palestine, and Egypt.

Omar Khayyám /kʌɪˈɑːm/ (d.1123), Persian poet, mathematician, and astronomer. His *rubáiyát* (quatrains), found in *The Rubáiyát of Omar Khayyám* (translation published 1859), are meditations on the mysteries of existence and celebrations of worldly pleasures.

omasum /əʊˈmeɪsəm/ ▶ noun (pl. **omasa** /-sə/) Zoology the muscular third stomach of a ruminant animal, between the reticulum and the abomasum. Also called **PSALTERIUM**.
– ORIGIN early 18th cent.: from Latin, literally 'bullock's tripe'.

Omayyad /əʊˈmʌɪjad/ variant spelling of **UMAYYAD**.

ombre /ˈɒmbə, ˈɒmbreɪ/ ▶ noun [mass noun] a trick-taking card game for three people using a pack of forty cards, popular in Europe in the 17th–18th centuries.
– ORIGIN from Spanish *hombre* 'man', with reference to one player seeking to win the pool.

ombré /ˈɒmbreɪ/ ▶ adjective (of a fabric) having a dyed, printed, or woven design in which the colour is graduated from light to dark.
– ORIGIN French, past participle of *ombrer* 'to shade'.

ombro- ▶ combining form relating to rain: *ombrotrophic.*
– ORIGIN from Greek *ombros* 'rain shower'.

ombrogenous /ɒmˈbrɒdʒɪnəs/ ▶ adjective Ecology (of a bog or peat) dependent on rain for its formation.

ombrotrophic /ˌɒmbrə(ʊ)ˈtrəʊfɪk, -ˈtrɒfɪk/ ▶ adjective Ecology (of a bog or its vegetation) dependent on atmospheric moisture for its nutrients.

ombudsman /ˈɒmbʊdzmən/ ▶ noun (pl. **ombudsmen**) an official appointed to investigate individuals' complaints against a company or organization, especially a public authority. ■ (**the Ombudsman**) Brit. informal term for **PARLIAMENTARY COMMISSIONER FOR ADMINISTRATION**.
– ORIGIN 1950s: from Swedish, 'legal representative'.

ombudsperson ▶ noun (pl. **ombudspersons**) N. Amer. a person acting as an ombudsman (used as a neutral alternative).

Omdurman /ˌɒmdəːˈmɑːn/ a city in central Sudan, on the Nile opposite Khartoum; pop. 3,151,600 (est. 2007). In 1898 it was the site of a battle which marked the final British defeat of the Mahdist forces.

-ome ▶ suffix chiefly Biology forming nouns denoting objects or parts having a specified nature: *rhizome | trichome.*
– ORIGIN variant form of **-OMA**.

omega /ˈəʊmɪgə/ ▶ noun the last letter of the Greek alphabet (Ω, ω), transliterated as 'o' or 'ō'. ■ [usu. as modifier] the last of a series: *the omega point.* ■ (**Omega**) [followed by Latin genitive] Astronomy the twenty-fourth star in a constellation: *Omega Scorpii.*
▶ symbol ■ (Ω) ohm(s). ■ (ω) angular frequency.
– ORIGIN from Greek *ō mega* 'the great O'.

omega-3 fatty acid ▶ noun an unsaturated fatty acid of a kind occurring chiefly in fish oils, with double bonds between the carbon atoms that are third and second from the end of the hydrocarbon chain.

omelette (US also **omelet**) ▶ noun a dish of beaten eggs cooked in a frying pan and served plain or with a savoury or sweet topping or filling.
– PHRASES **one can't make an omelette without breaking eggs** proverb one cannot accomplish something without adverse effects elsewhere. [translating French *On ne saurait faire une omelette sans casser des oeufs*.]
– ORIGIN French, earlier *amelette* (alteration of *alumette*), variant of *alumelle*, from *lemele* 'knife blade', from Latin *lamella* (see **LAMELLA**). The association with 'knife blade' is probably because of the thin flat shape of an omelette.

omen ▶ noun an event regarded as a portent of good or evil: *the ghost's appearance was an ill omen | a rise in imports might be an omen of recovery.* ■ [mass noun] prophetic significance: *the raven seemed a bird of evil omen.*
– ORIGIN late 16th cent.: from Latin.

omentum /əʊˈmɛntəm/ ▶ noun (pl. **omenta** /-tə/) Anatomy a fold of peritoneum connecting the stomach with other abdominal organs.
– DERIVATIVES **omental** adjective.
– ORIGIN late Middle English: from Latin.

omer /ˈəʊmə/ ▶ noun **1** an ancient Hebrew dry measure, the tenth part of an ephah.
2 (**Omer**) Judaism a sheaf of corn or omer of grain presented as an offering on the second day of Passover. ■ the period of 49 days between the second day of Passover and Pentecost.
– ORIGIN from Hebrew *ʿōmer.*

omertà /ˌəʊmɛːˈtɑː/, Italian /omerˈta/ ▶ noun [mass noun] (among the Mafia) a code of silence about criminal activity and a refusal to give evidence to the police.
– ORIGIN Italian dialect, variant of *umiltà* 'humility'.

-ometer /ˈɒmətə/ ▶ combining form forming nouns denoting an instrument for measuring something: *milometer.* ■ informal forming nouns denoting a measure of a quality, emotion, etc.: *stressometer | drunkometer.*

OMG ▶ abbreviation informal oh my God!: *OMG! If my parents find out they will go mad!*

omicron /ə(ʊ)ˈmʌɪkrɒn/ ▶ noun the fifteenth letter of the Greek alphabet (Ο, ο), transliterated as 'o'. ■ (**Omicron**) [followed by Latin genitive] Astronomy the fifteenth star in a constellation: *Omicron Piscium.*
– ORIGIN from Greek *o mikron* 'small o'.

omigod /ˌəʊmʌɪˈgɒd/ ▶ exclamation informal used to express shock or disbelief: *omigod, omigod, I'm going to be famous!*
– ORIGIN 1960s: altered spelling of *oh my God.*

ominous ▶ adjective giving the worrying impression that something bad is going to happen; threateningly inauspicious: *there were ominous dark clouds gathering overhead.*
– DERIVATIVES **ominously** adverb, **ominousness** noun.
– ORIGIN late 16th cent.: from Latin *ominosus*, from *omen, omin-* 'omen'.

omission ▶ noun someone or something that has been left out or excluded: *there are glaring omissions in the report.* ■ [mass noun] the action of excluding or leaving out someone or something: *the omission of recent publications from his bibliography.* ■ a failure to fulfil a moral or legal obligation: *to pay compensation for a wrongful act or omission.*
– DERIVATIVES **omissive** adjective.
– ORIGIN late Middle English: from late Latin *omissio(n-)*, from the verb *omittere* (see **OMIT**).

omit ▶ verb (**omits, omitting, omitted**) [with obj.] leave out or exclude (someone or something), either intentionally or forgetfully: *he was **omitted from** the second Test.* ■ [with infinitive] fail or neglect to do: *he modestly omits to mention that he was a pole-vault champion.*
– DERIVATIVES **omissible** adjective, **omittable** adjective.
– ORIGIN late Middle English: from Latin *omittere*, from *ob-* 'down' + *mittere* 'let go'.

ommatidium /ˌɒməˈtɪdɪəm/ ▶ noun (pl. **ommatidia** /-dɪə/) Entomology each of the optical units that make up the compound eye of an insect.
– ORIGIN late 19th cent.: modern Latin, from Greek *ommatidion*, diminutive of *omma, ommat-* 'eye'.

ommatophore /ˈɒmətəfɔː/ ▶ noun Zoology a part of an invertebrate animal, especially a tentacle, which bears an eye.
– ORIGIN late 19th cent.: from Greek *omma, ommat-* 'eye' + **-PHORE**.

omni- ▶ combining form all; of all things: *omniscient | omnifarious.* ■ in all ways or places: *omnicompetent | omnipresent.*
– ORIGIN from Latin *omnis* 'all'.

omnibus ▶ noun **1** a volume containing several books previously published separately: *an omnibus of her first trilogy.* ■ Brit. a single edition of two or more consecutive television or radio programmes previously broadcast separately.
2 dated a bus.
▶ adjective comprising several items: *omnibus editions of novels.*
– ORIGIN early 19th cent.: via French from Latin, literally 'for all', dative plural of *omnis.*

omnicompetent ▶ adjective able to deal with all matters. ■ (of a legislative body) having powers to legislate on all matters.
– DERIVATIVES **omnicompetence** noun.

omnidirectional ▶ adjective Telecommunications receiving signals from or transmitting in all directions.

omnifarious /ˌɒmnɪˈfɛːrɪəs/ ▶ adjective formal comprising or relating to all sorts or varieties.
– ORIGIN mid 17th cent.: from late Latin *omnifarius* + **-OUS**; compare with **MULTIFARIOUS**.

Omnimax /ˈɒmnɪmaks/ ▶ noun [mass noun] trademark a technique of widescreen cinematography in which 70 mm film is projected through a fisheye lens on to a hemispherical screen.
– ORIGIN 1970s: from **OMNI-** 'everywhere' + **MAXIMUM**.

omnipotence ▶ noun [mass noun] the quality of having unlimited or very great power: *God's omnipotence.*

omnipotent /ɒmˈnɪpət(ə)nt/ ▶ adjective (of a deity) having unlimited power. ■ having great power and influence: *an omnipotent sovereign.*
– DERIVATIVES **omnipotently** adverb.
– ORIGIN Middle English (as a divine attribute): via Old French from Latin *omnipotent-* 'all-powerful'.

omnipresent ▶ adjective (of God) present everywhere at the same time. ■ widely or constantly encountered; widespread: *the omnipresent threat of natural disasters.*
– DERIVATIVES **omnipresence** noun.
– ORIGIN early 17th cent.: from medieval Latin *omnipraesent-*.

omnirange ▶ noun a navigation system in which short-range omnidirectional VHF transmitters serve as radio beacons.

omniscient /ɒmˈnɪsɪənt/ ▶ adjective knowing everything: *a third-person omniscient narrator.*
– DERIVATIVES **omniscience** noun, **omnisciently** adverb.
– ORIGIN early 17th cent.: from medieval Latin *omniscient-* 'all-knowing', based on *scire* 'to know'.

omnisexual ▶ adjective involving, related to, or characterized by a diverse sexual propensity.
– DERIVATIVES **omnisexuality** noun.

omnium gatherum /ˌɒmnɪəm ˈɡaðərəm/ ▶ noun a collection of miscellaneous people or things.
– ORIGIN early 16th cent.: mock Latin, from Latin *omnium* 'of all' and GATHER + the Latin suffix *-um*.

omnivore /ˈɒmnɪvɔː/ ▶ noun an animal or person that eats a variety of food of both plant and animal origin.
– ORIGIN late 19th cent.: from French, from Latin *omnivorus* 'omnivorous'.

omnivorous /ɒmˈnɪv(ə)rəs/ ▶ adjective **1** (of an animal or person) feeding on a variety of food of both plant and animal origin.
2 indiscriminate in taking in or using whatever is available: *an omnivorous reader.*
– DERIVATIVES **omnivorously** adverb, **omnivorousness** noun.
– ORIGIN mid 17th cent.: from Latin *omnivorus* + **-OUS**.

omophagy /ə(ʊ)ˈmɒfədʒi/ (also **omophagia**) ▶ noun [mass noun] the eating of raw food, especially raw meat.
– DERIVATIVES **omophagic** adjective.
– ORIGIN early 18th cent.: from Greek *ōmophagia*, from *ōmos* 'raw' + *-phagia* (from *phagein* 'eat').

Omotic /əʊˈmɒtɪk/ ▶ noun [mass noun] a subfamily of Afro-Asiatic languages spoken in Ethiopia, with over thirty members, all having comparatively few speakers.
▶ adjective denoting or belonging to Omotic.
– ORIGIN 1970s: from *Omo*, the name of a river in SW Ethiopia, + **-OTIC**.

omphalo- /ˈɒmfələʊ/ ▶ combining form relating to the navel: *omphalocele.*
– ORIGIN from Greek *omphalos* 'navel'.

omphalocele /ˈɒmfələʊˌsiːl/ ▶ noun Medicine a hernia in which abdominal organs protrude into a baby's umbilical cord.

omphalos /ˈɒmfəlɒs/ ▶ noun (pl. **omphaloi** /-lɔɪ/)
1 literary the centre or hub of something: *this was the omphalos of confusion.*
2 (in ancient Greece) a conical stone (especially that at Delphi) representing the navel of the earth. ■ a boss on an ancient Greek shield.
– ORIGIN Greek, literally 'navel, boss'.

Omsk /ɒmsk/ a city in south central Russia, on the Irtysh River; pop. 1,131,100 (est. 2008).

ON¹ ▶ abbreviation Ontario (in official postal use).

ON² ▶ abbreviation Old Norse.

on ▶ preposition **1** physically in contact with and supported by (a surface): *on the table was a water jug | she was lying on the floor | a sign on the front gate.* ■ located somewhere in the general surface area of (a place): *an internment camp on the island | the house on the corner.* ■ as a result of accidental physical contact with: *he banged his head on a beam.* ■ supported by (a part of the body): *he was lying on his back.* ■ on to: *put it on the table.* ■ in the possession of; being carried by: *she only had a few pounds on her.*
2 forming a distinctive or marked part of the surface of: *a scratch on her arm | a smile on her face.*
3 having (the thing mentioned) as a topic; about: *a book on careers.* ■ having (the thing mentioned) as a basis: *a constitution modelled on America's.*
4 as a member of (a committee, jury, or other body): *they would be allowed to serve on committees.*
5 having (the thing mentioned) as a target, aim, or focus: *five air raids on Schweinfurt | thousands marching on Washington | her eyes were fixed on his dark profile.*
6 (often followed by a noun without a determiner) having (the thing mentioned) as a medium for transmitting or storing information: *put your ideas down on paper | stored on the client's own computer.* ■ being broadcast by (a radio or television channel): *a new twelve-part TV series on Channel 4.*
7 in the course of (a journey): *he was on his way to see his mother.* ■ while travelling in (a public vehicle): *John got some sleep on the plane.* ■ on to (a public vehicle) with the intention of travelling in it: *we got on the train.*
8 indicating the day or part of a day during which an event takes place: *reported on September 26 | on a very hot evening in July.* ■ at the time of: *she was booed on arriving home.*
9 engaged in: *his attendant was out on errands.*
10 regularly taking (a drug or medicine): *he is on morphine to relieve the pain.*
11 paid for by: *the drinks are on me.*
12 added to: *a few pence on the electricity bill is nothing compared with your security.*
▶ adverb **1** physically in contact with and supported by a surface: *make sure the lid is on.* ■ (of clothing) being worn by a person: *sitting with her coat on.*
2 indicating continuation of a movement or action: *she burbled on | he drove on | and so on.* ■ further forward; in an advanced state: *I'll see you later on | time's getting on.*
3 (of an event) taking place or being presented: *what's on at the May Festival | there's a good film on this afternoon.* ■ due to take place as planned: *the match is still on.*
4 (of an electrical appliance or power supply) functioning: *they always left the lights on.*
5 (of an actor) on stage. ■ (of an employee) working; on duty.
▶ noun (also **on side**) Cricket the leg side.
– PHRASES **be on about** Brit. informal talk about tediously and at length: *she's always on about doing one's duty.* **be on at someone** Brit. informal nag or grumble at someone. **be on to someone** informal be close to discovering the truth about an illegal or undesirable activity that someone is engaging in. **be on to something** informal have an idea or information that is likely to lead to an important discovery. **it's not on** informal it's impractical or unacceptable. **on and off** intermittently: *it rained on and off most of the afternoon.* **on and on** continually; at tedious length: *he went on and on about his grandad's trombone.* **on it** Austral./NZ informal drinking heavily. **on to 1** moving to a location on the surface of: *they went up on to the ridge.* **2** moving aboard (a public service vehicle) with the intention of travelling in it. **what are you on?** informal said to express incredulity at someone's behaviour, with the implication that they must be under the influence of drugs. **you're on** informal said by way of accepting a challenge or bet.
– ORIGIN Old English *on, an*, of Germanic origin; related to Dutch *aan* and German *an*, from an Indo-European root shared by Greek *ana*.

-on ▶ suffix Physics, Biochemistry, & Chemistry forming nouns:
1 denoting subatomic particles or quanta: *neutron | photon.*
2 denoting molecular units: *codon.*
3 denoting substances: *interferon.*
– ORIGIN Sense 1 originally in *electron*, from **ION**, influenced (as in sense 2) by Greek *on* 'being'; sense 3 is on the pattern of words such as *cotton* or from German *-on*.

onager /ˈɒnəɡə/ ▶ noun an animal of a race of the Asian wild ass native to northern Iran. ● *Equus hemionus onager*, family Equidae. Compare with **KIANG**, **KULAN**.
– ORIGIN Middle English: via Latin from Greek *onagros*, from *onos* 'ass' + *agrios* 'wild'.

on-air ▶ adjective & adverb being broadcast on radio or television: [as adj.] *live, on-air interviews* | [as adv.] *he apologized on-air for the comment.*

onanism /ˈəʊnənɪz(ə)m/ ▶ noun [mass noun] formal
1 masturbation.
2 coitus interruptus.
– DERIVATIVES **onanist** noun, **onanistic** adjective.
– ORIGIN early 18th cent.: from French *onanisme* or modern Latin *onanismus*, from the name *Onan* (Gen. 38:9), who practised coitus interruptus.

Onassis¹ /əʊˈnasɪs/, Aristotle (Socrates) (1906–75), Greek shipping magnate and international businessman. He owned a substantial shipping empire and founded the Greek national airline, Olympic Airways (1957).

Onassis² /əʊˈnasɪs/, Jacqueline Lee Bouvier Kennedy (1929–94), American First Lady; known as **Jackie O**. She married John F. Kennedy in 1953. After he was assassinated she married Aristotle Onassis in 1968.

on-board ▶ adjective [attrib.] **1** available or situated on board a ship, aircraft, or other vehicle.
2 (**onboard**) denoting or controlled from a facility or feature incorporated into the main circuit board of a computer or computerized device.

ONC ▶ abbreviation historical (in the UK) Ordinary National Certificate (a technical qualification).

once ▶ adverb **1** on one occasion or for one time only: *they deliver once a week* | (as noun **the once**) informal *he'd only met her the once.* ■ (usu. with negative or **if**) on even one occasion; at all (used for emphasis): *he never once complained | if she once got an idea in her head you'd never move it.*
2 at some time in the past; formerly: *Gran had once been a famous singer.*
3 multiplied by one: *once two is two.*
▶ conjunction as soon as; when: *once the grapes were pressed, the juice was put into barrels.*
– PHRASES **all at once 1** suddenly: *all at once the noise stopped.* **2** all at the same time. **at once 1** immediately: *I fell asleep at once.* **2** at the same time; simultaneously: *computers that can do many things at once.* **for once** (or **this once**) on this occasion only, as an exception: *I hope you'll forgive me this once.* **once a ——, always a ——** proverb a person cannot change their fundamental nature: *once a whinger, always a whinger.* **once again** (or **more**) one more time. **once and for all** (or **once for all**) now and for the last time; finally. **once bitten, twice shy** see **BITE**. **once** (or **every once**) **in a while** from time to time; occasionally. **once or twice** a few times. **once upon a time** at some time in the past (used as a conventional opening of a story). ■ formerly: *once upon a time she would have been jealous, but no longer.*
– ORIGIN Middle English *ones*, genitive of **ONE**. The spelling change in the 16th cent. was in order to retain the unvoiced sound of the final consonant.

once-over ▶ noun informal a rapid search or inspection: *some doctor came and gave us a once-over.* ■ a piece of work that is done quickly.

oncer ▶ noun informal **1** Brit. historical a one-pound note.
2 Brit. a person who does a particular thing only once.
3 Austral. an MP regarded as likely to serve only one term.

on-chip ▶ adjective Electronics denoting or relating to circuitry included in a single integrated circuit or in the same integrated circuit as a given device.

onchocerciasis /ˌɒŋkəʊsəːˈsʌɪəsɪs, -ˈkʌɪəsɪs/ ▶ noun technical term for **RIVER BLINDNESS**.
– ORIGIN early 20th cent.: from modern Latin *Onchocerca* (from Greek *onkos* 'barb' + *kerkos* 'tail') + **-IASIS**.

onco- ▶ combining form relating to tumours: *oncology.*
– ORIGIN from Greek *onkos* 'mass'.

oncogene /ˈɒŋkə(ʊ)dʒiːn/ ▶ noun Medicine a gene which in certain circumstances can transform a cell into a tumour cell.

oncogenic /ˌɒŋkə(ʊ)ˈdʒɛnɪk/ ▶ adjective Medicine causing development of a tumour or tumours.
– DERIVATIVES **oncogenesis** noun, **oncogenicity** noun.

oncology /ɒŋˈkɒlədʒi/ ▶ noun [mass noun] Medicine the study and treatment of tumours.
– DERIVATIVES **oncological** adjective, **oncologist** noun.

oncoming ▶ adjective [attrib.] approaching from the front; moving towards one: *she walked into the path of an oncoming car.* ■ due to happen soon: *the oncoming winter.*
▶ noun [mass noun] the approach or onset of something: *the oncoming of age.*

oncost ▶ noun Brit. an overhead expense.

OND ▶ abbreviation historical (in the UK) Ordinary National Diploma (a qualification in technical subjects).

Ondaatje /ɒnˈdɑːtjə/, (Philip) Michael (b.1943), Sri Lankan-born Canadian writer. Notable works: *Running in the Family* (autobiography, 1982) and *The English Patient* (novel; Booker Prize, 1992).

ondes martenot /ɔ̃d ˈmɑːt(ə)nəʊ/, French /ɔ̃d maʀtəno/ ▶ noun (pl. **same**) Music an electronic keyboard producing one note of variable pitch.
– ORIGIN 1950s: from French *ondes musicales*, literally 'musical waves' (the original name of the

instrument) and the name of Maurice *Martenot* (1898–1980), its French inventor.

on dit /ɔ̃ 'diː/ ▶ noun (pl. **on dits** pronunc. **same**) a piece of gossip; a rumour.
– ORIGIN early 19th cent.: from French, literally 'they say'.

on drive Cricket ▶ noun a drive to the on side.
▶ verb (**on-drive**) [with obj.] drive a ball delivered by (a bowler) to the on side.

one ▶ cardinal number **1** the lowest cardinal number; half of two; 1: *there's only room for one person | two could live as cheaply as one | one hundred miles | a one-bedroom flat.* (Roman numeral: **i, I**) ■ a single person or thing: *they would straggle home in ones and twos.* ■ just one as opposed to any more or to none at all; single (used for emphasis): *her one concern is to save her daughter.* ■ denoting a particular item of a pair or number of items: *electronics is one of his hobbies | a glass tube closed at one end.* ■ denoting a particular but unspecified occasion or period: *one afternoon in late October.* ■ used before a name to denote a person who is not known to the reader or hearer; a certain: *he worked as a clerk for one Mr Ming.* ■ informal, chiefly N. Amer. a noteworthy example of (used for emphasis): *the actor was one smart-mouthed troublemaker | he was **one hell of a** snappy dresser.* ■ one year old. ■ one o'clock: *I'll be there at one.* ■ a size of garment or other merchandise denoted by one. ■ a domino or dice with one spot.
2 the same; identical: *all types of training meet one common standard.*
3 informal a joke or story: *the one about the Englishman, the Irishman, and the Yank.*
4 informal an alcoholic drink: *a cool one after a day on the water.*
5 W. Indian alone. [a use recorded in Old English, becoming obsolete in standard use in the mid 16th cent.]
▶ pronoun **1** referring to a person or thing previously mentioned or easily identified: *her mood changed from one of moroseness to one of joy | her best apron, the white one | do you want one?*
2 a person of a specified kind: *you're the one who ruined her life | my friends and **loved ones**.* ■ a person who is remarkable in some way: *you never saw **such a one** for figures.*
3 [third person singular] used to refer to the speaker, or any person, as representing people in general: *one must admire him for his willingness | one gets the impression that he is ahead.*
– PHRASES **at one** in agreement or harmony: *they were completely **at one with** their environment.* **for one** used to stress that the person named holds the specified view, even if no one else does: *I for one am getting a little sick of writing about it.* **get it in one** informal understand or succeed in guessing something immediately. **have one over the eight** see EIGHT. **one after another** (or **the other**) following each other in quick succession: *one after another the buses drew up.* **one and all** everyone. **one and only** unique; single (used for emphasis or as a designation of a celebrity): *the title of his one and only book | the one and only Muhammad Ali.* **one another** each other. **one by one** separately and in succession; singly. **one day** at a particular but unspecified time in the past or future: *he would one day be a great President.* **one for one** denoting or referring to a situation in which one thing corresponds to or is exchanged for another: *these donations would be matched on a one-for-one basis with public revenues.* **one of a kind** see KIND[1]. **one or another** (or **the other**) denoting or referring to a particular but unspecified one out of a set of items: *not all instances fall neatly into one or another of these categories.* **one or two** informal a few: *there are one or two signs worth watching for.* **one thing and another** informal used to cover various unspecified matters or events: ***what with one thing and another** she hadn't had much sleep recently.*
– ORIGIN Old English *ān*, of Germanic origin; related to Dutch *een* and German *ein*, from an Indo-European root shared by Latin *unus*. The initial *w* sound developed before the 15th cent. and was occasionally represented in the spelling; it was not accepted into standard English until the late 17th cent.

> **USAGE** In modern English the use of **one** as a pronoun to mean 'anyone' or 'me and people in general', as in ***one** must try **one's** best*, is generally restricted to formal contexts, outside which it is likely to be regarded as rather pompous or old-fashioned. In informal and spoken contexts the normal alternative is **you**, as in ***you** have to do what **you** can, don't **you**?*

-one ▶ suffix Chemistry forming nouns denoting various compounds, especially ketones: *acetone | quinone.*
– ORIGIN from Greek patronymic *-ōnē*.

one-armed bandit ▶ noun informal a fruit machine operated by pulling a long handle at the side.

one-design ▶ noun a yacht built from a standard design: [as modifier] *one-design racing.*

one-dimensional ▶ adjective having or relating to a single dimension: *one-dimensional curves.* ■ lacking depth; superficial: *the supporting roles are alarmingly one-dimensional creations.*
– DERIVATIVES **one-dimensionality** noun.

onefold ▶ adjective consisting of only one part or element.

Onega, Lake /ə'njɛɪgə/ a lake in NW Russia, near the border with Finland, the second-largest European lake.

one-hit wonder ▶ noun informal a group or singer that has only one hit record before returning to obscurity.

one-horse ▶ adjective drawn by or using a single horse.
– PHRASES **one-horse race** a contest in which one candidate or competitor is clearly superior to all the others and seems certain to win. **one-horse town** informal a small town with few and poor facilities.

Oneida /əʊ'nʌɪdə/ ▶ noun (pl. **same** or **Oneidas**) **1** a member of an American Indian people formerly inhabiting upper New York State, one of the five peoples comprising the original Iroquois confederacy.
2 [mass noun] the extinct Iroquoian language of the Oneida.
▶ adjective relating to the Oneida or their language.
– ORIGIN from a local word meaning 'erected stone', the name of successive principal Oneida settlements, near which, by tradition, a large syenite boulder was erected.

Oneida Community a religious community, founded in New York State in 1848 and originally embracing primitive Christian beliefs and radical social and economic ideas, later relaxed. It became a joint-stock company in 1881.

O'Neill, Eugene (Gladstone) (1888–1953), American dramatist. He was awarded the Pulitzer Prize for his first full-length play, *Beyond the Horizon* (1920). Other notable works: *The Iceman Cometh* (1946) and *Long Day's Journey into Night* (1956, posthumously).

oneiric /ə(ʊ)'nʌɪrɪk/ ▶ adjective formal relating to dreams or dreaming.
– ORIGIN mid 19th cent.: from Greek *oneiros* 'dream' + **-IC**.

oneiro- /ə(ʊ)'nʌɪrəʊ/ ▶ combining form relating to dreams or dreaming: *oneiromancy.*
– ORIGIN from Greek *oneiros* 'dream'.

oneiromancy /ə'nʌɪrə(ʊ),mansi/ ▶ noun [mass noun] the interpretation of dreams in order to foretell the future.

one-liner ▶ noun informal a short joke or witty remark.

one-man ▶ adjective involving, done, or operated by only one person: *a one-man show.*

one-man band ▶ noun a street entertainer who plays many instruments at the same time. ■ a person who runs a business alone.

oneness ▶ noun [mass noun] **1** the fact or state of being unified or whole, though comprised of two or more parts: *the oneness of all suffering people.* ■ the state of being in harmony with someone or something: *a strong sense of oneness is felt with all things.*
2 the fact or state of being one in number: *holding to the oneness of God the Father as the only God.*

one-nighter ▶ noun a one-night stand.

one-night stand ▶ noun **1** informal a sexual relationship lasting only one night. ■ a person with whom one has a one-night stand.
2 a single performance of a play or show in a particular place.

one-off informal, chiefly Brit. ▶ adjective done, made, or happening only once: *a one-off benefit show.*
▶ noun something done, made, or happening only once: *the meeting is a one-off.* ■ a unique or remarkable person: *he's a one-off, no one else has his skills.*

one-piece ▶ adjective (especially of an article of clothing) made or consisting of a single piece.
▶ noun an article of clothing made or consisting of a single piece: *I was wearing a tight black one-piece.*

oner ▶ noun Brit. informal **1** something denoted or characterized by the number one: *I did the last drink in a oner.* ■ one pound or one hundred pounds sterling.
2 archaic a remarkable person or thing.

onerous /'əʊn(ə)rəs, 'ɒn-/ ▶ adjective (of a task or responsibility) involving a great deal of effort, trouble, or difficulty: *he found his duties increasingly onerous.* ■ Law involving heavy obligations: *an onerous lease.*
– DERIVATIVES **onerously** adverb, **onerousness** noun.
– ORIGIN late Middle English: from Old French *onereus*, from Latin *onerosus*, from *onus, oner-* 'burden'.

oneself ▶ pronoun [third person singular] **1** [reflexive] used as the object of a verb or preposition when this is the same as the subject of the clause and the subject is stated or understood as 'one': *it is difficult to wrest oneself away | resolutions that one makes to oneself.*
2 [emphatic] used to emphasize that one does something individually or unaided: *the idea of publishing a book oneself.*
3 in one's normal and individual state of body or mind; not influenced by others: *freedom to be oneself.*
– PHRASES **by oneself** see BY.

one-shot ▶ adjective informal, chiefly N. Amer. achieved with a single attempt or action: *there is no one-shot solution to the problem.* ■ done, produced, or occurring only once: *a one-shot deal.*

one-sided ▶ adjective **1** unfairly giving or dealing with only one side of a contentious issue; biased: *one-sided agitprop that devalues the causes it promotes.* ■ (of a contest or conflict) having a marked inequality of strength or ability between the participants. ■ (of a relationship or conversation) having all the effort coming from one participant.
2 having or occurring on one side of something only: *one-sided documents.*
– DERIVATIVES **one-sidedly** adverb, **one-sidedness** noun.

one-size-fits-all ▶ adjective informal suitable for or used in all circumstances: *people want greater choice—the end of a one-size-fits-all approach.*
– ORIGIN 1970s (originally denoting a garment designed to fit people of all sizes).

one-star ▶ adjective having one star in a grading system (especially of accommodation) in which this denotes the lowest standard: *a good one-star hotel.* ■ having or denoting the fifth-highest military rank, distinguished in the US armed forces by one star on the uniform: *a one-star general.*

one-step ▶ noun a vigorous kind of foxtrot in duple time.
▶ adjective (of a process or procedure) consisting of only one stage; straightforward: *a one-step self-help programme.*

one-stop ▶ adjective informal denoting a business capable of supplying all of a customer's needs within a particular range of goods or services: *the **one-stop shop** serves local residents seeking advice on council services.*

one-tailed ▶ adjective Statistics denoting a test for deviation from the null hypothesis in one direction only.

one-time ▶ adjective **1** former: *a one-time actor.*
2 relating to a single occasion: *a one-time charge.*
▶ adverb (**one time**) W. Indian all at once; immediately: *he does eat six roti one time.*

one-time pad ▶ noun a pad of keys for a cipher, each page being destroyed after one use, so that each message is sent using a different key.

one-to-one (also chiefly N. Amer. **one-on-one**)
▶ adjective & adverb denoting or referring to a situation in which two parties come into direct contact, opposition, or correspondence: [as adj.] *you can be treated by a therapist on a one-to-one basis.* ■ Mathematics in which each member of one set is associated with one member of another.
▶ noun informal a face-to-face encounter.

one-touch ▶ adjective **1** (of an electrical device or facility) able to be operated simply at or as though at the touch of a button.
2 Soccer denoting fast-moving play in which players manage to control and pass the ball with the first touch of the foot.

one-track mind ▶ noun used in reference to a person whose thoughts are preoccupied with one subject or interest.

one-trick pony ▶ noun a person or thing with only one special feature, talent, or area of expertise.

one-two ▶ noun **1** a pair of punches delivered in quick succession with alternate hands.
2 chiefly Soccer a move in which a player plays a short pass to a teammate and moves forward to receive an immediate return pass.

O

one up informal ▶ **adjective** having an advantage over someone: *you're always trying to be **one up on** whoever you're with.*
▶ **verb** (**one-up**) [with obj.] gain an advantage over.

one-upmanship ▶ **noun** [mass noun] informal the technique or practice of gaining an advantage or feeling of superiority over another person.

one-way ▶ **adjective** moving or allowing movement in one direction only: *a one-way valve* | *a one-way street.* ■ (of a ticket) allowing a person to travel to a place but not back again; single. ■ denoting a mirror or glass that acts as a reflective surface on one side but that is transparent from the other. ■ denoting a relationship in which all the input comes from only one member: *interaction between the organism and the environment is not a one-way process.*

one-woman ▶ **adjective** involving, done, or operated by only one woman.

one-world ▶ **adjective** relating to or holding the view that the world's inhabitants are interdependent and should behave accordingly.
– DERIVATIVES **one-worlder** noun, **one-worldism** noun.

onflow ▶ **noun** [mass noun] the action or process of flowing or moving steadily onward.

onglaze ▶ **adjective** (of painting or decoration) done on a glazed surface.

on-glide ▶ **noun** Phonetics a glide produced at the beginning of articulating a speech sound. Compare with **OFF-GLIDE**.

ongoing ▶ **adjective** continuing; still in progress: *ongoing negotiations.*
– DERIVATIVES **ongoingness** noun.

onion ▶ **noun 1** a swollen edible bulb used as a vegetable, having a pungent taste and smell and composed of several concentric layers.
2 the plant that produces the onion, with long rolled or strap-like leaves and spherical heads of greenish-white flowers. ● *Allium cepa*, family Liliaceae (or Alliaceae).
– PHRASES **know one's onions** informal be very knowledgeable about something.
– DERIVATIVES **oniony** adjective.
– ORIGIN Middle English: from Old French *oignon*, based on Latin *unio(n-)*, denoting a kind of onion.

onion bag ▶ **noun** Soccer, informal a goal net (used especially in the context of scoring a goal).

onion dome ▶ **noun** a dome which bulges in the middle and rises to a point, used especially in Russian church architecture.
– DERIVATIVES **onion-domed** adjective.

onion fly ▶ **noun** a small fly whose larvae are a pest of onions. ● The European *Delia antiqua* (family Anthomyiidae), and the American *Tritoxa flexa* (family Otitidae), which also attacks garlic.

onion hoe ▶ **noun** a small hoe with a curved neck, used for weeding between onions and other closely grown plants.

onion set ▶ **noun** a small onion bulb planted instead of seed to yield a mature bulb.

onion-skin paper ▶ **noun** [mass noun] very fine smooth translucent paper.

onkus /ˈɒŋkəs/ ▶ **adjective** Austral./NZ informal, dated unpleasant or inferior.
– ORIGIN early 20th cent.: of unknown origin.

on-lend ▶ **verb** [with obj.] lend (borrowed money) to a third party.

onliest ▶ **adjective** black English superlative of **ONLY**: *you're the onliest man I've seen who has everything.*

online ▶ **adjective** controlled by or connected to a computer. ■ (of an activity or service) available on or performed using the Internet or other computer network: *online banking.*
▶ **adverb 1** while connected to a computer or under computer control. ■ by means of the Internet or other computer network. ■ with processing of computer data carried out simultaneously with its production.
2 in or into operation or existence: *the new power plant will go online this month.*

onlooker ▶ **noun** a non-participating observer; a spectator: *a crowd of fascinated onlookers.*
– DERIVATIVES **onlooking** adjective.

only ▶ **adverb 1** and no one or nothing more besides; solely: *there are only a limited number of tickets available* | *only their faith sustained them.* ■ no more than (implying that more was expected); merely: *deaths from heart disease have only declined by 10 per cent* | *she was still only in her mid thirties.*
2 no longer ago than: *genes that were discovered only last year.* ■ not until: *a final report reached him only on January 15.*
3 [with infinitive] with the negative or unfortunate result that: *she turned into the car park, only to find her way blocked.* ■ [with modal] in an inevitable but undesirable way: *rebellion **will only** bring more unhappiness.*
▶ **adjective** [attrib.] alone of its or their kind; single or solitary: *the only medal we had ever won* | *he was an only child.* ■ alone deserving consideration: *it's simply the only place to be seen these days.*
▶ **conjunction** informal except that; but: *he is still a young man, only he seems older because of his careworn expression* | *the place was like school, only better.*
– PHRASES **only just** by a very small margin; almost not: *the building survived the earthquake, but only just.* ■ very recently. **only too ——** used to emphasize that something is the case to an extreme or regrettable extent: *you should be only too glad to be rid of him.*
– ORIGIN Old English *ānlic* (adjective) (see **ONE**, **-LY**[1]).

> **USAGE** The traditional view is that the adverb **only** should be placed next to the word or words whose meaning it restricts: *I have seen him **only once*** rather than *I have **only** seen him **once***. The argument for this, a topic which has occupied grammarians for more than 200 years, is that if **only** is not placed correctly the scope or emphasis is wrong, and could even result in ambiguity. But in normal, everyday English, the impulse is to state **only** as early as possible in the sentence, generally just before the verb. The result is, in fact, hardly ever ambiguous: few native speakers would be confused by the sentence *I have **only** seen him **once***, and the supposed 'logical' sense often emerges only with further clarification, as in *I've **only** seen him once, but I've heard him many times.*

only-begotten ▶ **adjective** literary used to denote an only child.

on-message ▶ **adjective** (of a politician) stating the official party line.

Ono /ˈəʊnəʊ/, Yoko (b.1933), American musician and artist, born in Japan. She married John Lennon in 1969 and collaborated with him on various experimental recordings.

o.n.o. ▶ **abbreviation** Brit. or nearest offer (used in advertisements): *beginner's guitar £150 o.n.o.*

on–off ▶ **adjective 1** (of a switch) having two positions, 'on' and 'off'.
2 (of a relationship) not continuous or steady.

onomasiology /ˌɒnə(ʊ)meɪsɪˈɒlədʒi/ ▶ **noun** [mass noun] the branch of knowledge that deals with terminology, in particular contrasting terms for similar concepts, as in a thesaurus. Compare with **SEMASIOLOGY**.
– DERIVATIVES **onomasiological** adjective.
– ORIGIN early 20th cent.: from Greek *onomasia* 'term' + **-LOGY**.

onomast /ˈɒnəmast/ ▶ **noun** a person who studies proper names, especially personal names.
– ORIGIN 1980s: back-formation from **ONOMASTIC**.

onomastic /ɒnəˈmastɪk/ ▶ **adjective** relating to the study of the history and origin of proper names.
– ORIGIN late 16th cent. (as a noun in the sense 'alphabetical list of proper nouns', later also 'lexicographer'): from Greek *onomastikos*, from *onoma* 'name'. The adjective dates from the early 18th cent.

onomastics ▶ **plural noun** [usu. treated as sing.] the study of the history and origin of proper names, especially personal names.

onomatopoeia /ˌɒnə(ʊ)matəˈpiːə/ ▶ **noun** [mass noun] the formation of a word from a sound associated with what is named (e.g. *cuckoo, sizzle*). ■ the use of onomatopoeia for literary effect.
– ORIGIN late 16th cent.: via late Latin from Greek *onomatopoiia* 'word-making', from *onoma, onomat-* 'name' + *-poios* 'making' (from *poiein* 'to make').

onomatopoeic /ˌɒnə(ʊ)matəˈpiːɪk/ ▶ **adjective** using or relating to onomatopoeia: *onomatopoeic words like 'bang' and 'coo'.*
– DERIVATIVES **onomatopoeically** adverb.

Onondaga /ˌɒnənˈdɑːɡə/ ▶ **noun** (pl. **same** or **Onondagas**) **1** a member of an Iroquois people, one of the five comprising the original Iroquois confederacy, formerly inhabiting an area near Syracuse, New York.
2 [mass noun] the extinct Iroquoian language of the Onondaga.
▶ **adjective** relating to the Onondaga or their language.
– ORIGIN from the Iroquoian name of their main settlement, literally 'on the hill'.

on-road ▶ **adjective** denoting or relating to events or conditions on a road, especially a vehicle's performance.

onrush ▶ **noun** a surging rush forward: *the mesmerizing onrush of the sea.*
– DERIVATIVES **onrushing** adjective.

on-screen ▶ **adjective & adverb** shown or appearing in a film or television programme: [as adj.] *on-screen violence.* ■ making use of or performed with the aid of a computer screen: [as adj.] *on-screen editing facilities* | [as adv.] *graphics can be edited on screen.*

onsen /ˈɒnsɛn/ ▶ **noun** (in Japan) a hot spring, or a resort that has developed around a hot spring.
– ORIGIN Japanese.

onset ▶ **noun** the beginning of something, especially something unpleasant: *the onset of winter* | [as modifier, in combination] *early-onset Alzheimer's disease.* ■ archaic a military attack.

on-set ▶ **adjective** taking place during or relating to the rehearsing of a play or the making of a film.

onshore ▶ **adjective & adverb** situated or occurring on land (often used in relation to the oil and gas industry): [as adj.] *an onshore oilfield.* ■ (especially of the wind) from the sea towards the land.

onside ▶ **adjective & adverb 1** (of a player, especially in soccer, rugby, or hockey) occupying a position where playing the ball or puck is allowed; not offside.
2 informal in or into a position of agreement: [as adv.] *the assurances helped bring officials onside.*

onside kick (also **onsides kick**) ▶ **noun** American Football an intentionally short kick-off that travels forward only slightly further than the legally required distance of 10 yards, and which the kicking team attempts to recover.

on-site ▶ **adjective & adverb** taking place or available on a particular site or premises.

onslaught ▶ **noun** a fierce or destructive attack: *a series of **onslaughts on** the citadel.* ■ an overwhelmingly large number of people or things: *in some parks the onslaught of cars and people far exceeds capacity.*
– ORIGIN early 17th cent. (also in the form *anslaight*): from Middle Dutch *aenslag*, from *aen* 'on' + *slag* 'blow'. The change in the ending was due to association with (now obsolete) *slaught* 'slaughter'.

onstage ▶ **adjective & adverb** (in a theatre) on the stage and so visible to the audience.

on-street ▶ **adjective** (of parking facilities) at the side of a public road.

Ont. ▶ **abbreviation** Ontario.

-ont ▶ **combining form** Biology denoting an individual or cell of a specified type: *schizont.*
– ORIGIN from Greek *ont-* 'being', present participle of *eimi* 'be'.

on-target ▶ **adjective & adverb** hitting a target or achieving an aim.

Ontario /ɒnˈtɛːrɪəʊ/ a province of eastern Canada, between Hudson Bay and the Great Lakes; pop. 12,160,282 (2006); capital, Toronto. It was settled by the French and English in the 17th century, ceded to Britain in 1763, and became one of the original four provinces in the Dominion of Canada in 1867.
– DERIVATIVES **Ontarian** adjective & noun.

Ontario, Lake the smallest and most easterly of the Great Lakes, lying on the US–Canadian border between Ontario and New York State.

ontic /ˈɒntɪk/ ▶ **adjective** Philosophy relating to entities and the facts about them; relating to real as opposed to phenomenal existence.
– ORIGIN 1940s: from Greek *ōn, ont-* 'being' + **-IC**.

onto ▶ **preposition 1** variant form of **ON TO** (see **ON**).
2 Mathematics expressing the relationship of a set to its image under a mapping when every element of the image set has an inverse image in the first set: [as modifier] *an onto mapping.*

> **USAGE** The preposition **onto** written as one word (instead of **on to**) is recorded from the early 18th century and has been widely used ever since, but is still not wholly accepted as part of standard British English (unlike **into**, for example). Many style guides still advise writing it as two words, and that is the practice followed in this dictionary. However, **onto** is more or less the standard form in US English and in the specialized mathematics sense. Nevertheless, it is important to maintain a distinction between the preposition **onto** or **on to** and the use of the adverb **on** followed by the preposition **to**: *she climbed **on to** (or **onto**) the roof* but *let's go **on to** (not **onto**) the next point.*

O

ontogenesis /ˌɒntə(ʊ)ˈdʒɛnɪsɪs/ ▸ **noun** [mass noun] Biology the development of an individual organism or anatomical or behavioural feature from the earliest stage to maturity. Compare with **PHYLOGENESIS**.
– DERIVATIVES **ontogenetic** adjective, **ontogenetically** adverb.
– ORIGIN late 19th cent.: from Greek *ōn, ont-* 'being' + *genesis* 'birth'.

ontogeny /ɒnˈtɒdʒəni/ ▸ **noun** [mass noun] the branch of biology that deals with ontogenesis. Compare with **PHYLOGENY**. ■ another term for **ONTOGENESIS**.
– DERIVATIVES **ontogenic** adjective.
– ORIGIN late 19th cent.: from Greek *ōn, ont-* 'being' + **-GENY**.

ontological argument ▸ **noun** Philosophy the argument that God, being defined as most great or perfect, must exist, since a God who exists is greater than a God who does not. Compare with **COSMOLOGICAL ARGUMENT** and **TELEOLOGICAL ARGUMENT**.

ontology /ɒnˈtɒlədʒi/ ▸ **noun** [mass noun] the branch of metaphysics dealing with the nature of being.
– DERIVATIVES **ontological** adjective, **ontologically** adverb, **ontologist** noun.
– ORIGIN early 18th cent.: from modern Latin *ontologia*, from Greek *ōn, ont-* 'being' + **-LOGY**.

on-topic ▸ **adjective & adverb** (especially of posts on an Internet message board) relevant to the subject in question: [as adj.] *on-topic contributions to the discussion* | [as adv.] *I'll do my best to stay on-topic.*

on-trend ▸ **adjective** very fashionable: *her fitted jacket is bang on-trend.*

onus /ˈəʊnəs/ ▸ **noun** (**the onus**) something that is one's duty or responsibility: ***the onus is on** you to show that you have suffered loss.*
– ORIGIN mid 17th cent.: from Latin, literally 'load or burden'.

onward ▸ **adverb** (Brit. also **onwards**) in a continuing forward direction; ahead: *she stumbled onward.* ■ forward in time: *the period **from 1969 onward**.* ■ so as to make progress or become more successful: *the business moved **onward and upward**.*
▸ **adjective** (of a journey) continuing or moving forward: *informing passengers where to change for their onward journey* | figurative *the onward march of history.*

Onychophora /ˌɒnɪˈkɒf(ə)rə/ ▸ **plural noun** Zoology a small phylum of terrestrial invertebrates which comprises the velvet worms such as peripatus. They share characteristics with the arthropods and annelids, having a long, soft segmented body with stubby legs (lobopods).
– ORIGIN modern Latin (plural), from Greek *onux, onukh-* 'nail, claw' + *-phoros* 'bearing'.

O

onychophoran Zoology ▸ **noun** a terrestrial invertebrate of the small phylum Onychophora, which comprises the velvet worms.
▸ **adjective** relating to or denoting onychophorans.

-onym ▸ **combining form** forming nouns: **1** denoting a type of name: *pseudonym.*
2 denoting a word having a specified relationship to another: *antonym.*
– ORIGIN from Greek *-ōnumon*, neuter of *-ōnumos*, combining form of *onoma* 'name'.

onymous /ˈɒnɪməs/ ▸ **adjective** rare having a name; named.
– ORIGIN late 18th cent.: shortening of **ANONYMOUS**.

onyx /ˈɒnɪks, ˈəʊnɪks/ ▸ **noun** [mass noun] a semi-precious variety of agate with different colours in layers.
– ORIGIN Middle English: from Old French *oniche, onix*, via Latin from Greek *onux* 'fingernail or onyx'.

onyx marble ▸ **noun** [mass noun] banded calcite or other stone used as a decorative material.

oo- /ˈəʊə/ ▸ **combining form** Biology relating to or denoting an egg or ovum.
– ORIGIN from Greek *ōion* 'egg'.

o-o /ˈəʊəʊ/ (also **oo**) ▸ **noun** (pl. **o-os**) a honeyeater (bird) found in Hawaii, now probably extinct, which had a thin curved bill and climbed about on tree trunks. Compare with **OU²**. ● Genus *Moho*, family Meliphagidae.
– ORIGIN late 19th cent.: from Hawaiian.

oocyst /ˈəʊəsɪst/ ▸ **noun** Zoology a cyst containing a zygote formed by a parasitic protozoan such as the malaria parasite.

oocyte /ˈəʊəsʌɪt/ ▸ **noun** Biology a cell in an ovary which may undergo meiotic division to form an ovum.

oodles ▸ **plural noun** informal a very great number or amount of something: *if only I had **oodles of** cash.*
– ORIGIN mid 19th cent. (originally US): of unknown origin.

oo-er ▸ **exclamation** expressing surprise or alarm.
– ORIGIN early 20th cent.: from the interjections **OOH** and **ER**.

oof¹ ▸ **exclamation** expressing alarm, annoyance, or relief.
– ORIGIN natural exclamation: first recorded in English in the mid 19th cent.

oof² ▸ **noun** [mass noun] informal money; cash.
– ORIGIN late 19th cent.: from Yiddish *oyf* 'on', *tish* 'table', i.e. 'on the table' (referring to money in gambling).

oofy ▸ **adjective** (**oofier**, **oofiest**) informal rich; wealthy.
– ORIGIN late 19th cent.: from **OOF²** + **-Y¹**.

oogamous /əʊˈɒɡəməs/ ▸ **adjective** Biology relating to or denoting reproduction by the union of mobile male and immobile female gametes.
– DERIVATIVES **oogamously** adverb, **oogamy** noun.

oogenesis /əʊəˈdʒɛnɪsɪs/ ▸ **noun** [mass noun] Biology the production or development of an ovum.

oogonium /ˌəʊəˈɡəʊnɪəm/ ▸ **noun** (pl. **oogonia**)
1 Botany the female sex organ of certain algae and fungi, typically a rounded cell or sac containing one or more oospheres.
2 Biology an immature female reproductive cell that gives rise to primary oocytes by mitosis.
– ORIGIN mid 19th cent.: from **oo-** 'of an egg' + Greek *gonos* 'generation' + **-IUM**.

ooh ▸ **exclamation** used to express a range of emotions including surprise, delight, or pain: *ooh, this is fun* | *ooh, my feet!*
▸ **noun** an utterance of 'ooh'.
▸ **verb** (**oohs**, **oohing**, **oohed**) [no obj.] utter an 'ooh': *visitors **oohed and aahed** at the Christmas tree.*
– ORIGIN natural exclamation: first recorded in English in the early 20th cent.

ooh la la /uː lɑː ˈlɑː/ ▸ **interjection** humorous (especially in contexts stereotypically associated with France or the French) used to express surprise or excitement: *ooh la la, the traffic!* ■ used to convey a sexual innuendo: *the Britney Spears commercial? Ooh la la!* | [as adj.] *ooh-la-la satin French knickers.*
– ORIGIN French.

oojah /ˈuːdʒɑː/ (also **oojamaflip** /ˈuːdʒəməflɪp/) ▸ **noun** informal used when one cannot think of or does not wish to use the name of something.
– ORIGIN early 20th cent.: of unknown origin.

ooky /ˈʊki/ ▸ **adjective** informal unpleasant or repellent.
– ORIGIN 1960s: symbolic.

oolite /ˈəʊəlʌɪt/ ▸ **noun** [mass noun] Geology limestone consisting of a mass of rounded grains (ooliths) made up of concentric layers. ■ [count noun] another term for **OOLITH**.
– DERIVATIVES **oolitic** /-ˈlɪtɪk/ adjective.
– ORIGIN early 19th cent.: from French *oölithe*, modern Latin *oolites* (see **OO-**, **-LITE**).

oolith /ˈəʊəlɪθ/ ▸ **noun** Geology any of the rounded grains making up oolite.

oology /əʊˈɒlədʒi/ ▸ **noun** [mass noun] the study or collecting of birds' eggs.
– DERIVATIVES **oological** adjective, **oologist** noun.

oolong /ˈuːlɒŋ/ ▸ **noun** [mass noun] a kind of dark-coloured China tea made by fermenting the withered leaves to about half the degree usual for black teas.
– ORIGIN mid 19th cent.: from Chinese *wūlóng*, literally 'black dragon'.

oom /ʊəm/ ▸ **noun** S. African a man, especially an older one. ■ used as a respectful and affectionate form of address to an older man.
– ORIGIN Afrikaans, literally 'uncle', from Dutch.

oompah (also **oompah-pah**) informal ▸ **noun** [mass noun] the rhythmical sound of deep-toned brass instruments in a band.
▸ **verb** (**oompahs**, **oompahing**, **oompahed**) [no obj.] make an 'oompah'.
– ORIGIN late 19th cent.: imitative.

oomph (also **umph**) ▸ **noun** [mass noun] informal the quality of being exciting, energetic, or sexually attractive: *he showed entrepreneurial oomph.*
– ORIGIN 1930s: perhaps imitative.

-oon ▸ **suffix** forming nouns, originally from French words having the final stressed syllable *-on*: *balloon* | *buffoon.*
– ORIGIN representing French *-on*, from Latin *-onis*, sometimes via Italian *-one*.

oophorectomy /ˌəʊəfəˈrɛktəmi/ ▸ **noun** (pl. **oophorectomies**) [mass noun] surgical removal of one or both ovaries; ovariectomy.
– ORIGIN late 19th cent.: from modern Latin *oophoron* 'ovary' (from Greek *ōophoros* 'egg-bearing') + **-ECTOMY**.

oophoritis /ˌəʊəfəˈrʌɪtɪs/ ▸ **noun** [mass noun] Medicine inflammation of an ovary.

oops ▸ **exclamation** informal used to show recognition of a mistake or minor accident, often as part of an apology: *Oops! I'm sorry. I just made you miss your bus!*
– ORIGIN natural exclamation: first recorded in English in the 1930s.

oops-a-daisy ▸ **exclamation** variant spelling of **UPSY-DAISY**.

Oort /ɔːt/, Jan Hendrik (1900–92), Dutch astronomer. He proved that the Galaxy is rotating, and determined the position and orbital period of the sun within it.

Oort cloud /ɔːt, ʊət/ Astronomy a spherical cloud of small rocky and icy bodies postulated to orbit the sun beyond the orbit of Pluto and up to 1.5 light years from the sun, and to act as a reservoir of comets. Its existence was proposed by J. H. Oort.

oosphere /ˈəʊəsfɪə/ ▸ **noun** Botany the female reproductive cell of certain algae or fungi, which is formed in the oogonium and when fertilized becomes the oospore.

oospore /ˈəʊəspɔː/ ▸ **noun** Botany the thick-walled zygote of certain algae and fungi, formed by fertilization of an oosphere. Compare with **ZYGOSPORE**.

Oostende /əʊstˈɛndə/ Flemish name for **OSTEND**.

ootheca /ˌəʊəˈθiːkə/ ▸ **noun** (pl. **oothecae** /-kiː/) Entomology the egg case of cockroaches, mantises, and related insects.
– ORIGIN mid 19th cent.: from **OO-** 'of an egg' + Greek *thēkē* 'receptacle'.

ootid /ˈəʊətɪd/ ▸ **noun** Biology a haploid cell formed by the meiotic division of a secondary oocyte, especially the ovum, as distinct from the polar bodies.
– ORIGIN early 20th cent.: from **OO-** 'egg', on the pattern of *spermatid*.

ooze¹ ▸ **verb 1** [no obj., with adverbial of direction] (of a fluid) slowly trickle or seep out of something: *blood was oozing from a wound in his scalp* | *honey oozed out of the comb.* ■ [no obj.] slowly exude or discharge a viscous fluid: *her mosquito bites were oozing and itching like mad.*
2 [with obj.] give a powerful impression of (a quality): *she oozes a raunchy sex appeal.*
▸ **noun 1** [mass noun] the sluggish flow of a fluid.
2 an infusion of oak bark or other vegetable matter, used in tanning.
– DERIVATIVES **oozy** adjective (**oozier**, **ooziest**).
– ORIGIN Old English *wōs* 'juice or sap'; the verb dates from late Middle English.

ooze² ▸ **noun** [mass noun] wet mud or slime, especially that found at the bottom of a river, lake, or sea. ■ Geology a deposit of white or grey calcareous matter largely composed of foraminiferan remains, covering extensive areas of the ocean floor.
– DERIVATIVES **oozy** adjective (**oozier**, **ooziest**).
– ORIGIN Old English *wāse*; related to Old Norse *veisa* 'stagnant pool'. In Middle English and the 16th cent. the spelling was *wose* (rhyming with *repose*), but from 1550 spellings imply a change in pronunciation and influence by **OOZE¹**.

OP ▸ **abbreviation** ■ observation post. ■ (in the theatre) opposite prompt. ■ organophosphate(s). ■ (in the Roman Catholic Church) Order of Preachers (Dominican). [Latin *Ordo Praedicatorum*.]

op ▸ **noun** informal **1** a surgical operation: *a minor op.* ■ (**ops**) military operations.
2 a radio or telephone operator.

Op. (also **op.**) ▸ **abbreviation** Music opus (before a number given to each work of a particular composer, usually indicating the order of publication).

o.p. ▸ **abbreviation** ■ (of a book) out of print. ■ (of alcohol) overproof.

op- ▸ **prefix** variant spelling of **OB-** assimilated before *p* (as in *oppress*, *oppugn*).

opacify /ə(ʊ)ˈpasɪfʌɪ/ ▸ **verb** (**opacifies**, **opacifying**, **opacified**) technical make or become opaque.
– DERIVATIVES **opacifier** noun.

opacity /ə(ʊ)ˈpasɪti/ ▸ **noun** [mass noun] the quality of lacking transparency or translucence: *thinner paints need black added to increase opacity.* ■ the quality of being obscure in meaning: *the difficulty and opacity in Barthes' texts.*

– ORIGIN mid 16th cent.: from French *opacité*, from Latin *opacitas*, from *opacus* 'darkened'.

opah /'əʊpə/ ▶ noun a large deep-bodied fish with a deep blue back, silvery belly, and crimson fins, which lives in deep oceanic waters. Also called MOONFISH.
• *Lampris guttatus*, family Lampridae.
– ORIGIN mid 18th cent.: a West African word.

opal ▶ noun a gemstone consisting of a quartz-like form of hydrated silica, typically semi-transparent and showing many small points of shifting colour against a pale or dark ground.
– ORIGIN late 16th cent.: from French *opale* or Latin *opalus*, probably based on Sanskrit *upala* 'precious stone' (having been first brought from India).

opalescent ▶ adjective showing many small points of shifting colour against a pale or dark ground.
– DERIVATIVES **opalescence** noun.

opal glass ▶ noun [mass noun] a type of semi-translucent white glass.

opaline /'əʊp(ə)lʌɪn, -lɪn/ ▶ adjective opalescent.
▶ noun another term for MILK-GLASS. ■ translucent glass of a colour other than white.

op-amp ▶ abbreviation operational amplifier.

opanka /ɒ'pankə/ ▶ noun (pl. **opankas** or **opanci**) a kind of Serbian shoe made of soft leather and fastened with straps, similar in style to a moccasin.
– ORIGIN early 19th cent.: from Serbian and Croatian *opanak*.

opaque /ə(ʊ)'peɪk/ ▶ adjective (**opaquer**, **opaquest**) not able to be seen through; not transparent: *bottles filled with a pale opaque liquid*. ■ (especially of language) hard or impossible to understand: *technical jargon that was* ***opaque to*** *her*.
▶ noun an opaque thing. ■ [mass noun] Photography a substance for producing opaque areas on negatives.
– DERIVATIVES **opaquely** adverb, **opaqueness** noun.
– ORIGIN late Middle English *opake*, from Latin *opacus* 'darkened'. The current spelling (rare before the 19th cent.) has been influenced by the French form.

op art (also **optical art**) ▶ noun [mass noun] a form of abstract art that gives the illusion of movement by the precise use of pattern and colour, or in which conflicting patterns emerge and overlap. Bridget Riley and Victor Vasarely are its most famous exponents.
– ORIGIN 1960s: on the pattern of *pop art*.

op. cit. ▶ adverb in the work already cited.
– ORIGIN from Latin *opere citato*.

opcode ▶ noun Computing short for OPERATION CODE.

ope ▶ adjective & verb literary or archaic form of OPEN.

OPEC ▶ abbreviation Organization of the Petroleum Exporting Countries.

op-ed ▶ noun N. Amer. a newspaper page opposite the editorial page, devoted to personal comment, feature articles, etc.

Opel /'əʊp(ə)l/, Wilhelm von (1871–1948), German motor manufacturer. His company was the first in Germany to introduce assembly-line production, selling over one million cars.

open ▶ adjective **1** allowing access, passage, or a view through an empty space; not closed or blocked: *he climbed through the open window | she was put in a cubicle with the curtains left open | the pass is kept open by snowploughs*. ■ (of a container) not fastened or sealed: *the case burst open and its contents flew all over the place*. ■ (of a garment or its fastenings) not done up: *his tie was knotted below the open collar of his shirt*. ■ (of the mouth or eyes) with lips or lids parted: *his eyes were open but he could see nothing |* [as complement] *the boy's mouth dropped open in shock*. ■ (of the bowels) not constipated.
2 [attrib.] exposed to the air or to view; not covered: *an open fire burned in the grate | he crossed the ocean in an open boat*. ■ (of land) not covered with buildings or trees: *the plans allow increasing numbers of new houses in open countryside*. ■ [as complement] damaged by a deep cut in the surface: *he had his arm slashed open*. ■ (**open to**) likely to suffer from or be affected by; vulnerable or subject to: *the system is open to abuse*. ■ (of a goalmouth or other object of attack in a game) unprotected by defenders. ■ (of a town or city) officially declared to be undefended, and so immune under international law from bombardment.
3 with the outer edges or sides drawn away from each other; unfolded or spread out: *the trees had buds and a few open flowers*. ■ (of a book or file) with the covers parted allowing it to be read: *she was copying verses from an open Bible*. ■ (of a hand) not clenched into a fist. ■ (of a game or style of play) characterized by action which is spread out over the field.
4 [predic.] (of a business, place of entertainment, etc.) admitting customers or visitors; available for business: *the shop stays open until 9 p.m | parts of the castle are* ***open to*** *the public*. ■ (of a bank account) available for transactions. ■ (of a telephone line) ready to take calls.
5 freely available or accessible; unrestricted: *the service is open to all students*. ■ (of an offer or opportunity) still available: *the offer is open while stocks last | we need to consider what options are left open*. ■ (also **Open**) with no restrictions on those allowed to participate: *open discussion meetings | each horse had won two open races*. ■ (also **Open**) (of a victor) having won an open competition. ■ (of a ticket) not restricted as to day of travel. ■ Brit. (of a cheque) not crossed. ■ Mathematics (of a set) not containing any of its limit points.
6 not concealing one's thoughts or feelings; frank and communicative: *she behaved in an open and cheerful manner | I was quite open about my views*. ■ not concealed: *his eyes showed open admiration as they swept over her*. ■ [attrib.] (of conflict) fully developed and unconcealed: *the dispute erupted into open war*. ■ welcoming public discussion, criticism, and enquiry: *the party's commitment to open government*.
7 (of a matter or decision) not finally settled; still admitting of debate: *students' choice of degree can be kept open until the second year*. ■ (of the mind) accessible to new ideas: *I'm keeping an open mind about my future*. ■ (**open to**) receptive to: *the union was open to suggestions for improvements*. ■ (**open to**) admitting of; making possible: *the message is open to different interpretations*.
8 Phonetics (of a vowel) produced with a relatively wide opening of the mouth and the tongue kept low. ■ (of a syllable) ending in a vowel.
9 Music (of a string) allowed to vibrate along its whole length. ■ (of a pipe) unstopped at each end. ■ (of a note) sounded from an open string or pipe.
10 (of an electric circuit) having a break in the conducting path.
11 (of a fabric) loosely knitted or woven.
▶ verb [with obj.] **1** move (a door or window) so as to leave a space allowing access and vision: *she opened the door and went in |* [no obj., in imperative] *'Open up!' he said*. ■ [no obj.] (of a door or window) be moved to leave a space allowing access: *the door opened and a man came out*. ■ undo or remove the lid, cover, or fastening of (a container, package, letter, etc.) to get access to the contents: *he opened a bottle inexpertly, spilling some of the wine | can we open the presents now?* ■ part the lips or lids of (one's mouth or eye). ■ [no obj.] (of the mouth or eyes) have the lips or lids parted: *her eyes slowly opened*. ■ [no obj.] come apart; lose or lack its protective covering: *old wounds opened and I bled a little bit*. ■ [no obj.] (**open on to**/**into**) (of a room, door, or window) give access to: *the kitchen opened into a pleasant sitting room*. ■ cause evacuation of (the bowels).
2 unfold or be unfolded; spread out: [with obj.] *the eagle opened its wings and circled up into the air | the tail looks like a fan when it is* ***opened out*** *fully |* [no obj.] *the flowers only open during bright weather*. ■ [with obj.] part the covers of (a book or file) to read it: *she opened her book at the prologue*. ■ [no obj.] (**open out**) become wider: *the path opened out into a glade*. ■ [no obj., with adverbial] (of a prospect) extend into view: *stop to marvel at the views that* ***open out*** *below*. ■ [with obj.] Nautical achieve a clear view of (a place) by sailing past a headland or other obstruction: *we shall open Torbay shortly*.
3 make or become formally ready for customers, visitors, or business: [with obj.] *she raised $731 by opening her home and selling coffee and tea |* [no obj.] *the shops didn't open until 10*. ■ [with obj.] ceremonially declare (a building, road, etc.) to be completed and ready for use: *the Queen opened the power plant on 17 October 1956*. ■ [with obj.] make possible access to or passage through: *the President announced that his government would open the border*.
4 formally establish or begin (a new business, movement, or enterprise): *she began to teach and opened her own school | we* ***opened up*** *a branch in Madrid*. ■ [no obj.] (of an enterprise, meeting, or event) begin or be formally established: *two new restaurants open this week*. ■ take the action required to begin using: *they have the £10 necessary to open a savings account | click twice to open a file for the software selected*. ■ [no obj.] (of a piece of writing or music) begin: *the chapter opens with a discussion of Anglo-Irish relations*. ■ [no obj.] (**open up**) (of a process) start to develop: *a new and dramatic phase was opening up*. ■ (of a counsel in a law court) make a preliminary statement in (a case) before calling witnesses. ■ Cricket another term for OPEN THE BATTING below. ■ Bridge make (the first bid) in the auction.
5 make available or more widely known: *new technologies* ***open up*** *thousands of different opportunities*. ■ [no obj.] (**open out**/**up**) become more communicative or confiding: *he was very reserved and only opened out to her slowly*. ■ make (one's mind) more receptive or sympathetic: ***open your mind to*** *what is going on around you*. ■ (**open someone to**/**up to**) make someone vulnerable to: *the process is going to open them to a legal threat*.
6 break the conducting path of (an electric circuit). ■ [no obj.] (of an electric circuit or device) suffer a break in its conducting path.
▶ noun **1** [mass noun] (**the open**) outdoors or in the countryside: *guests were sitting in the open on the terrace*. ■ (**in**/**into the open**) not subject to concealment; made public: *we have never let our dislike for him come into the open*.
2 (**Open**) a championship or competition with no restrictions on who may compete: *his victory in the 2003 Australian Open*.
3 an accidental break in the conducting path for an electric current.
– PHRASES **be open with** speak frankly to: *I had always been completely open with my mother*. **an open book** a person or thing that is easy to understand or about which everything is known: *her mind was an open book to him*. **in open court** in a court of law, before the judge and the public. **open-and-shut** (of a case or argument) admitting no doubt or dispute; straightforward. **open the batting** Cricket play as one of the pair of batsmen who begin a side's innings. **open the door to** see DOOR. **open someone's eyes** see EYE. **open fire** begin to shoot. **with one's eyes open** (or **with open eyes**) fully aware of the implications of an action or situation: *I went into the job with my eyes open—everyone knows what happens to an unsuccessful manager*. **with open arms** see ARM[1].
– PHRASAL VERBS **open up** begin shooting: *the enemy artillery had opened up*. **open something up 1** informal accelerate a motor vehicle: *Sam took me back on the motorway to open her up*. **2** (of a player or team) create an advantage for one's side: *he opened up a lead of 14–8*.
– DERIVATIVES **openable** adjective, **openness** noun.
– ORIGIN Old English *open* (adjective), *openian* (verb), of Germanic origin; related to Dutch *open* and German *offen*, from the root of the adverb UP.

open access ▶ noun [mass noun] availability to all: *open access to scientific and technological information*. ■ a system where users of a library have direct access to bookshelves.

open air ▶ noun a free or unenclosed space outdoors: *getting out* ***in the open air***.
▶ adjective located or taking place out of doors: *an open-air swimming pool*.

open bar ▶ noun a bar at a special function at which the drinks have been paid for by the host or are prepaid through the admission fee.

open bite ▶ noun [mass noun] Dentistry lack of occlusion of the front teeth when the jaw is closed normally.

Open Brethren one of the two principal divisions of the Plymouth Brethren (the other is the Exclusive Brethren), formed in 1849 as a result of doctrinal and other differences. The Open Brethren are less rigorous and less exclusive in matters such as conditions for membership and contact with outsiders than the Exclusive Brethren.

opencast Brit. ▶ adjective denoting a method of mining in which coal or ore is extracted at or from a level near the earth's surface, rather than from shafts.
▶ noun [mass noun] the activity of opencast mining.

open chain ▶ noun Chemistry a molecular structure consisting of a chain of atoms with no closed rings.

open-circuit ▶ adjective consisting of or containing an open electric circuit.
– DERIVATIVES **open-circuited** adjective.

open cluster ▶ noun Astronomy a loose grouping of stars.

Open College ▶ noun (in the UK) an organization established to provide retraining opportunities, chiefly by arranging managerial and technical courses for company staff.

open communion ▶ noun [mass noun] Christian Church communion administered to any Christian believer.

open-concept ▶ adjective Canadian another term for OPEN-PLAN.

open date ▸ noun US a future available date for which no sports fixture has yet been arranged.

open day ▸ noun Brit. a day when members of the public may visit a place or institution to which they do not usually have access.

open door ▸ noun [in sing.] an unrestricted means of admission or access: *being homeless is not an open door to decent housing.* ■ [usu. as modifier] the policy or practice by which a country allows the free admission of immigrants or foreign imports: *an open-door immigration policy.*

open-ended (also **open-end**) ▸ adjective having no predetermined limit or boundary. ■ (of a question) allowing the formulation of any answer, rather than a selection from a set of possible answers.
– DERIVATIVES **open-endedness** noun.

opener ▸ noun **1** [usu. with modifier] a device for opening something, especially a container: *a tin opener | a letter opener.*
2 informal the first in a series of events, games, or actions: *Denver stuffed Buffalo 22–7 in the season opener.* ■ the first goal in a match. ■ a remark used as an excuse to initiate a conversation: *we blurted out the obvious opener.* ■ Cricket a batsman who opens the batting. ■ Bridge the player who makes the first bid in the auction.
– PHRASES **for openers** informal to start with; first of all: *for openers we chose lobster.*

open-faced ▸ adjective **1** having a frank or ingenuous expression.
2 (of a watch) having no cover other than the glass.
3 (also **open-face**) N. Amer. (of a sandwich or pie) without an upper layer of bread or pastry.

open-field system ▸ noun the traditional medieval system of farming in England, in which land was divided into strips and managed by an individual only in the growing season, being available to the community for grazing animals during the rest of the year.

open go ▸ noun Austral. informal a fair chance.

open-handed ▸ adjective **1** (of a blow) delivered with the palm of the hand.
2 giving freely; generous: *open-handed philanthropy.*
– DERIVATIVES **open-handedness** noun.

open-hearted ▸ adjective freely expressing or displaying one's warm and kindly feelings: *Betty's open-hearted goodwill.*
– DERIVATIVES **open-heartedness** noun.

O

open-hearth process ▸ noun a steel-making process in which scrap iron or steel, limestone, and pig iron are melted together in a shallow reverberatory furnace, the mixture being heated from above using gaseous fuel and air which oxidizes impurities in the iron.

open-heart surgery ▸ noun [mass noun] surgery in which the heart is exposed and the blood made to bypass it.

open house ▸ noun a place or situation in which all visitors are welcome: *our basement is an open house for other kids* | [mass noun] *they **kept open house**, entertaining a wide variety of writers.* ■ N. Amer. an open day. ■ N. Amer. & Austral./NZ an occasion during which a dwelling that is for sale may be viewed by prospective buyers without an appointment.

open ice ▸ noun [mass noun] ice-covered water through which navigation is possible.

opening ▸ noun **1** a space or gap that allows passage or access: *an opening in the roof would get rid of the smoke.*
2 a beginning; an initial part: *Maya started tapping out the opening of her story.* ■ a ceremony or celebratory gathering at which a building, show, etc. is declared to be open. ■ Chess a recognized sequence of moves at the beginning of a game. ■ a counsel's preliminary statement of a case in a law court.
3 an opportunity to achieve something: *they seem to have exploited fully the openings offered.* ■ an available job: *there are few openings for the ex-footballer.*
▸ adjective [attrib.] coming at the beginning of something; initial: *she stole the show with her opening remark.*

opening gambit ▸ noun an introductory remark or stratagem, especially one designed to make social contact or secure one's own position.

opening hours ▸ plural noun the times during which a shop, bank, etc. is open for business.

opening night ▸ noun the first night of a theatrical play or other entertainment.

opening time ▸ noun Brit. the time at which public houses may legally open for custom.

open interest ▸ noun [mass noun] Finance the number of contracts or commitments outstanding in futures and options trading on an official exchange at any one time.

open-jaw ▸ adjective denoting or relating to a trip in which an airline passenger flies in to one destination and returns from another.

open learning ▸ noun [mass noun] learning based on independent study or initiative rather than formal classroom instruction.

open letter ▸ noun a letter addressed to a particular person or group of people but intended for publication in a newspaper or journal.

open line ▸ noun a telephone line on which conversations can be overheard or intercepted by others.
▸ adjective Canadian denoting a phone-in radio or television programme.

openly ▸ adverb without concealment, deception, or prevarication, especially where these might be expected; frankly or honestly: *a lecturer who had openly criticized the government.*
– ORIGIN Old English *openlīce* (see **OPEN**, **-LY²**).

open market ▸ noun (often **the open market**) an unrestricted market with free access by and competition of buyers and sellers.

open marriage (also **open relationship**) ▸ noun a marriage or relationship in which both partners agree that each may have sexual relations with others.

open mike ▸ noun [often as modifier] a session in a club where anyone is welcome to sing or perform stand-up comedy.

open-minded ▸ adjective willing to consider new ideas; unprejudiced: *a serious and open-minded newspaper.*
– DERIVATIVES **open-mindedly** adverb, **open-mindedness** noun.

open-mouthed ▸ adjective with the mouth open, especially in surprise or excitement.

open-necked ▸ adjective (of a shirt) worn with the collar unbuttoned and without a tie.

open outcry ▸ noun [mass noun] a system of financial trading in which dealers shout their bids and contracts aloud.

open-pit ▸ adjective North American term for **OPENCAST**.

open-plan ▸ adjective (of a room or building) having large rooms with few or no internal dividing walls.

open primary ▸ noun US a primary election open to all registered voters.

open prison ▸ noun Brit. a prison with the minimum of restrictions on prisoners' movements and activities.

open question ▸ noun a matter that is not yet decided or is unable to be decided.

open range ▸ noun N. Amer. a tract of land without fences or other barriers.

open-reel ▸ adjective (of a tape recorder) having reels of tape requiring individual threading, as distinct from a cassette.

open road ▸ noun (**the open road**) a main road, especially one outside an urban area where progress is unimpeded: *we hit the open road and raced along.*

open sandwich ▸ noun a sandwich without a top slice of bread.

open sea ▸ noun (usu. **the open sea**) an expanse of sea away from land.

open season ▸ noun [in sing.] the annual period when restrictions on the killing of certain types of wildlife, especially for sport, are lifted. ■ a period when all restrictions on an activity, especially on criticizing a particular group, are abandoned: *it's **open season on** public figures.*

open secret ▸ noun a supposed secret that is in fact known to many people.

open sesame ▸ noun see **SESAME**.

open shop ▸ noun a system whereby employees in a place of work do not have to join a trade union. ■ a place of work following an open-shop system.

open side ▸ noun [in sing.] Rugby the side of the scrum on which the main line of the opponents' backs is ranged.

open society ▸ noun a society characterized by a flexible structure, freedom of belief, and wide dissemination of information.

open-source ▸ adjective Computing denoting software for which the original source code is made freely available and may be redistributed and modified.

open system ▸ noun **1** Computing a system in which the components and protocols conform to standards independent of a particular supplier.
2 Physics a material system in which mass or energy can be lost to or gained from the environment.

open texture ▸ noun chiefly Philosophy the inability of certain concepts to be fully or precisely defined or of regulations to be exhaustive and leave no room for interpretation.

open-toed ▸ adjective (of a shoe) having an upper that does not cover the toes.

open-top (also **open-topped**) ▸ adjective (of a vehicle) not having a roof or having a folding or detachable roof.

Open University (in the UK) a university that teaches mainly by broadcasting, correspondence, and summer schools, and is open to those without formal academic qualifications.

open verdict ▸ noun Law a verdict of a coroner's jury affirming the occurrence of a suspicious death but not specifying the cause.

open water ▸ noun [mass noun] a stretch of water which is not enclosed by land, ice, or other barriers. ■ Canadian the melting of ice on rivers and lakes in spring.

openwork ▸ noun [mass noun] [usu. as modifier] ornamental work in cloth, metal, leather, or other material with regular patterns of openings and holes.

opepe /əʊˈpiːpi/ ▸ noun a tropical West African tree which yields timber that is used in harbour work because of its resistance to marine borers. ● *Nauclea diderichii*, family Rubiaceae.
– ORIGIN late 19th cent.: from Yoruba.

opera¹ ▸ noun a dramatic work in one or more acts, set to music for singers and instrumentalists. ■ [mass noun] operas as a genre of classical music. ■ a building for the performance of opera.
– ORIGIN mid 17th cent.: from Italian, from Latin, literally 'labour, work'.

opera² plural form of **OPUS**.

operable ▸ adjective **1** able to be used: *less than half the rail network was operable.*
2 able to be treated by means of a surgical operation: *operable breast cancer.*
– DERIVATIVES **operability** noun.
– ORIGIN mid 17th cent.: from late Latin *operabilis*, from Latin *operari* 'expend labour on' (see **OPERATE**).

opéra bouffe /ˌɒp(ə)rə ˈbuːf/, French /ɔpeʀa buf/ ▸ noun (pl. **opéras bouffes**) a French comic opera, with dialogue in recitative and characters drawn from everyday life.
– ORIGIN French, from Italian (see **OPERA BUFFA**).

opera buffa /ˌɒp(ə)rə ˈbuːfə/ ▸ noun a comic opera (usually in Italian), especially one with characters drawn from everyday life.
– ORIGIN Italian, from *opera* 'opera' + *buffa* 'jest'.

opera cloak ▸ noun a cloak of rich material worn over evening clothes, especially by women.

opéra comique /ˌɒp(ə)rə kɒˈmiːk/, French /ɔpeʀa kɔmik/ ▸ noun an opera (usually in French) on a light-hearted theme, with spoken dialogue.
– ORIGIN French.

opera glasses ▸ plural noun small binoculars for use at the opera or theatre.

opera hat ▸ noun a collapsible top hat.

opera house ▸ noun a theatre designed for the performance of opera.

operand /ˈɒpərand/ ▸ noun Mathematics the quantity on which an operation is to be done.
– ORIGIN late 19th cent.: from Latin *operandum*, neuter gerundive of *operari* 'expend labour on' (see **OPERATE**).

operant /ˈɒp(ə)r(ə)nt/ Psychology ▸ noun an item of behaviour that is not a response to a prior stimulus but something which is initially spontaneous, which may reinforce or inhibit recurrence of that behaviour.
▸ adjective involving the modification of behaviour by the reinforcing or inhibiting effect of its own consequences.
– ORIGIN late Middle English: from Latin *operant-* 'being at work', from the verb *operari*.

opera seria /ˈsɪərɪə/ ▸ noun an opera (especially one of the 18th century in Italian) on a serious, usually classical or mythological theme.
– ORIGIN Italian, literally 'serious opera'.

operate ▸ **verb 1** [with obj.] (of a person) control the functioning of (a machine, process, or system): *the Prime Minister operates a system of divide and rule.* ■ [no obj., with adverbial] (of a machine, process, or system) function in a specified manner: *market forces were allowed to operate freely.* ■ manage (a business): *many foreign companies operate factories in the United States.* ■ [no obj., with adverbial] (of an organization) be managed in a specified way or from a specified place: *neither company had operated within the terms of its constitution.* ■ [no obj., with adverbial] (of an armed force) conduct military activities in a specified area.
2 [no obj.] be in effect: *there is a powerful law which operates in politics.*
3 [no obj.] perform a surgical operation: *my brother had to be* **operated on** *last week.*
– ORIGIN early 17th cent.: from Latin *operat-* 'done by labour', from the verb *operari*, from *opus*, *oper-* 'work'.

operatic ▸ **adjective** relating to or characteristic of opera: *operatic arias.* ■ extravagantly theatrical; histrionic: *she wrung her hands in operatic despair.*
– DERIVATIVES **operatically** adverb.

operatics ▸ **plural noun** [often treated as sing.] **1** the production or performance of operas.
2 theatrically exaggerated or overemotional behaviour.

operating profit ▸ **noun** a gross profit before deduction of expenses.

operating system ▸ **noun** the low-level software that supports a computer's basic functions, such as scheduling tasks and controlling peripherals.

operating table ▸ **noun** a table on which a patient is placed during a surgical operation.

operating theatre (N. Amer. **operating room**) ▸ **noun** a room in a hospital in which surgical operations are performed.

operation ▸ **noun 1** [mass noun] the action of functioning or the fact of being active or in effect: *restrictions on the operation of market forces | the company's first hotel is now* **in operation**. ■ [count noun] an active process; a discharge of a function: *the operations of the mind.*
2 an act of surgery performed on a patient.
3 [often with adj. or noun modifier] an organized activity involving a number of people: *a rescue operation.* ■ a business organization; a company: *he reopened his operation under a different name.* ■ an activity in which a business is involved: *the company is selling most of its commercial banking operations.*
4 Mathematics a process in which a number, quantity, expression, etc., is altered or manipulated according to set formal rules, such as those of addition, multiplication, and differentiation.
ORIGIN late Middle English: via Old French from Latin *operatio(n-)*, from the verb *operari* 'expend labour on' (see OPERATE).

operational ▸ **adjective 1** in or ready for use: *the new laboratory is fully operational.* ■ relating to the routine functioning and activities of an organization: *the coffee bar's initial operational costs.* ■ relating to active operations of the armed forces, police, or emergency services: *an operational fighter squadron.*
2 Philosophy relating to or in accordance with operationalism.
– DERIVATIVES **operationally** adverb.

operational amplifier ▸ **noun** Electronics an amplifier with high gain and high input impedance (usually with external feedback), used especially in circuits for performing mathematical operations on an input voltage.

operationalism ▸ **noun** [mass noun] Philosophy a form of positivism which defines scientific concepts in terms of the operations used to determine or prove them.
– DERIVATIVES **operationalist** noun & adjective.

operationalize (also **operationalise**) ▸ **verb** [with obj.] **1** put into operation or use.
2 Philosophy express or define (something) in terms of the operations used to determine or prove it.

operational research (also **operations research**) ▸ **noun** [mass noun] a method of mathematically based analysis for providing a quantitive basis for management decisions.

operation code ▸ **noun** Computing the part of a machine code instruction that defines the operation to be performed.

operations room ▸ **noun** a room from which military or police operations are directed.

operative ▸ **adjective 1** functioning or having effect: *the transmitter is operative | the mining ban would remain operative.* ■ [attrib.] (of a word) having the most significance in a phrase or sentence: *I was madly—the operative word—in love.*
2 [attrib.] relating to surgery: *wounds needing operative treatment.*
▸ **noun 1** a worker, especially one in a manufacturing industry.
2 chiefly N. Amer. a secret agent or private detective.
– DERIVATIVES **operatively** adverb.
– ORIGIN late Middle English: from late Latin *operativus*, from Latin *operat-* 'done by labour', from the verb *operari* (see OPERATE).

operator ▸ **noun 1** [often with modifier] a person who operates equipment or a machine: *a radio operator.* ■ a person who works at the switchboard of a telephone exchange.
2 [usu. with modifier] a person or company that runs a business: *a tour operator.*
3 [with adj.] informal a person who acts in a shrewd or manipulative way: *her reputation as a cool, clever operator.*
4 Mathematics a symbol or function denoting an operation (e.g. ×, +).

operatorship ▸ **noun** (in the oil and gas industries) the right to operate a well, field, or other oil source.

opera window ▸ **noun** N. Amer. a small fixed window on a car, usually behind a rear side window.

operculum /ə(ʊ)ˈpəːkjʊləm/ ▸ **noun** (pl. **opercula** /-lə/) Zoology & Botany a structure that closes or covers an aperture, in particular: ■ technical term for GILL COVER. ■ a secreted plate that closes the aperture of a gastropod mollusc's shell when the animal is retracted. ■ a lid-like structure of the spore-containing capsule of a moss.
– DERIVATIVES **opercular** adjective, **operculate** adjective, **operculi-** combining form.
– ORIGIN early 18th cent.: from Latin, literally 'lid, covering', from *operire* 'to cover'.

operetta ▸ **noun** a short opera, usually on a light or humorous theme and typically having spoken dialogue. Notable composers of operettas include Offenbach, Johan Strauss, Franz Lehár, and Gilbert and Sullivan.
– ORIGIN late 18th cent.: from Italian, diminutive of *opera* (see OPERA[1]).

operon /ˈɒpərɒn/ ▸ **noun** Biology a unit made up of linked genes which is thought to regulate other genes responsible for protein synthesis.
– ORIGIN 1960s: from French *opérer* 'to effect, work' + -ON.

operose /ˈɒpərəʊs/ ▸ **adjective** rare involving or displaying much industry or effort.
– ORIGIN late 17th cent.: from Latin *operosus*, from *opus* 'work'.

ophicleide /ˈɒfɪklʌɪd/ ▸ **noun** an obsolete bass brass instrument with keys, used in bands in the 19th century but superseded by the tuba.
– ORIGIN mid 19th cent.: from French *ophicléide*, from Greek *ophis* 'serpent' + *kleis, kleid-* 'key'.

Ophidia /ɒˈfɪdɪə/ ▸ **plural noun** Zoology a group of reptiles which comprises the snakes. Also called SERPENTES. ● Suborder Ophidia, order Squamata.
– ORIGIN modern Latin (plural), from Greek *ophis, ophid-* 'snake'.

ophidian Zoology ▸ **noun** a reptile of the group Ophidia; a snake.
▸ **adjective** relating to or denoting snakes.

ophiolite /ˈɒfɪəlʌɪt/ ▸ **noun** [mass noun] Geology an igneous rock consisting largely of serpentine, believed to have been formed from the submarine eruption of oceanic crustal and upper mantle material.
– DERIVATIVES **ophiolitic** adjective.
– ORIGIN mid 19th cent.: from Greek *ophis* 'snake' + -LITE.

Ophir /ˈəʊfə/ (in the Bible) an unidentified region, perhaps in SE Arabia, famous for its fine gold and precious stones.

ophitic /əˈfɪtɪk/ ▸ **adjective** Geology relating to or denoting a poikilitic rock texture in which crystals of feldspar are interposed between plates of augite.
– ORIGIN late 19th cent.: via Latin from Greek *ophitēs* 'serpentine stone' (from *ophis* 'snake') + -IC.

Ophiuchus /ɒˈfjuːkəs/ Astronomy a large constellation (the Serpent Bearer or Holder), said to represent a man in the coils of a snake. Both the celestial equator and the ecliptic pass through it, but it is not counted among the signs of the zodiac.
– ORIGIN via Latin from Greek *Ophioukos*.

ophiuroid Zoology ▸ **noun** an echinoderm of the class Ophiuroidea, which comprises the brittlestars.
▸ **adjective** relating to or denoting ophiuroids.

Ophiuroidea /ˌɒfɪ(j)ʊəˈrɔɪdɪə/ ▸ **plural noun** Zoology a class of echinoderms that comprises the brittlestars.
– ORIGIN modern Latin (plural), based on the genus name *Ophiura*, from Greek *ophis* 'snake' + *oura* 'tail'.

ophthalmia /ɒfˈθalmɪə, ɒpˈθalmɪə/ ▸ **noun** [mass noun] Medicine inflammation of the eye, especially conjunctivitis.
– ORIGIN late Middle English: via late Latin from Greek, from *ophthalmos* 'eye'.

ophthalmic ▸ **adjective** [attrib.] relating to the eye and its diseases.
– ORIGIN early 17th cent.: via Latin from Greek *ophthalmikos*, from *ophthalmos* 'eye'.

ophthalmic optician ▸ **noun** Brit. an optician qualified to prescribe and dispense glasses and contact lenses and to detect eye diseases.

ophthalmitis /ˌɒfθalˈmʌɪtɪs, ˌɒpθalˈmʌɪtɪs/ ▸ **noun** [mass noun] Medicine inflammation of the eye.

ophthalmo- ▸ **combining form** Medicine relating to the eyes: *ophthalmoscope.*
– ORIGIN from Greek *ophthalmos* 'eye'.

ophthalmology /ˌɒfθalˈmɒlədʒi, ˌɒpθalˈmɒlədʒi/ ▸ **noun** [mass noun] the branch of medicine concerned with the study and treatment of disorders and diseases of the eye.
– DERIVATIVES **ophthalmological** adjective, **ophthalmologist** noun.

ophthalmoplegia /ɒfˌθalmə(ʊ)ˈpliːdʒə, ɒpˌθalmə(ʊ)ˈpliːdʒə/ ▸ **noun** [mass noun] Medicine paralysis of the muscles within or surrounding the eye.
– DERIVATIVES **ophthalmoplegic** adjective.

ophthalmoscope /ɒfˈθalməskəʊp, ɒpˈθalməskəʊp/ ▸ **noun** an instrument for inspecting the retina and other parts of the eye.
– DERIVATIVES **ophthalmoscopic** adjective, **ophthalmoscopy** noun.

-opia ▸ **combining form** denoting a visual disorder: *myopia.*
– ORIGIN from Greek *ōps, ōp-* 'eye, face'.

opiate ▸ **adjective** /ˈəʊpɪət/ relating to, resembling, or containing opium.
▸ **noun** /ˈəʊpɪət/ a drug derived from or related to opium. ■ a thing which soothes or stupefies: *the capacity to use books as an opiate.*
▸ **verb** /ˈəʊpɪeɪt/ [with obj.] (usu. as adj. **opiated**) impregnate with opium. ■ dull the senses of (someone) with or as if with opium: *she is not opiated with resignation.*
– ORIGIN late Middle English (as a noun): from medieval Latin *opiatus* (adjective), *opiatus* (noun), based on Latin *opium* (see OPIUM).

Opie /ˈəʊpi/, John (1761–1807), English painter. His work includes portraits and history paintings such as *The Murder of Rizzio* (1787).

opine ▸ **verb** [reporting verb] formal hold and state as one's opinion: [with direct speech] *'The man is a genius,' he opined* | [with clause] *the headmistress opined that the outing would make a nice change for Flora.*
– ORIGIN late Middle English: from Latin *opinari* 'think, believe'.

opinion ▸ **noun 1** a view or judgement formed about something, not necessarily based on fact or knowledge: *that,* **in my opinion**, *is right | the area's residents share vociferous opinions about the future.* ■ [mass noun] the beliefs or views of a group or majority of people: *the changing climate of opinion.* ■ an estimation of the quality or worth of someone or something: *I had a higher opinion of myself than I deserved.*
2 a statement of advice by an expert on a professional matter: *if in doubt, get a second opinion.* ■ Law a barrister's advice on the merits of a case. ■ Law a formal statement of reasons for a judgement given.
– PHRASES **be of the opinion that** believe or maintain that. **difference of opinion** a disagreement or mild quarrel: *there was a* **difference of opinion** *between myself and the chief planner.* **a matter of opinion** something not capable of being proven either way.
– ORIGIN Middle English: via Old French from Latin *opinio(n-)*, from the stem of *opinari* 'think, believe'.

opinionated ▸ **adjective** characterized by conceited assertiveness and dogmatism: *an arrogant and opinionated man.*
– ORIGIN early 17th cent.: from the (rare) verb *opinionate* 'hold the opinion (that)', from OPINION.

O

opinion poll ▶ noun an assessment of public opinion by questioning a representative sample, especially as the basis for forecasting the results of voting.

opioid /ˈəʊpɪɔɪd/ Biochemistry ▶ noun a compound resembling opium in addictive properties or physiological effects.
▶ adjective relating to or denoting opioids.
– ORIGIN 1950s: from **OPIUM** + **-OID**.

opistho- /əˈpɪsθəʊ/ ▶ prefix behind; to the rear: *opisthosoma*.
– ORIGIN from Greek *opisthen* 'behind'.

Opisthobranchia /əˌpɪsθə(ʊ)ˈbraŋkɪə/ ▶ plural noun Zoology a group of molluscs which includes the sea slugs and sea hares. They have a small or absent shell and are typically brightly coloured with conspicuous external gills. ● Subclass Opisthobranchia, class Gastropoda.
– DERIVATIVES **opisthobranch** /əˈpɪsθə(ʊ)braŋk/ noun.
– ORIGIN modern Latin (plural), from **OPISTHO-** 'to the rear' + *brankhia* 'gills'.

opisthosoma /əˌpɪsθəˈsəʊmə/ ▶ noun Zoology the abdomen of a spider or other arachnid.

opisthotonos /ˌɒpɪsˈθɒt(ə)nəs/ (also **opisthotonus**) ▶ noun [mass noun] Medicine spasm of the muscles causing backward arching of the head, neck, and spine, as in severe tetanus, some kinds of meningitis, and strychnine poisoning.
– ORIGIN mid 17th cent.: via late Latin from Greek *opisthotonos* 'drawn backwards'.

opium ▶ noun [mass noun] a reddish-brown heavy-scented addictive drug prepared from the juice of the opium poppy, used illicitly as a narcotic and occasionally in medicine as an analgesic.
– PHRASES **the opium of the people** (or **masses**) something regarded as inducing a false and unrealistic sense of contentment among people. [translating the German phrase *Opium des Volks*, used by Marx in reference to religion (1844).]
– ORIGIN late Middle English: via Latin from Greek *opion* 'poppy juice', from *opos* 'juice', from an Indo-European root meaning 'water'.

opium den ▶ noun a public room where opium is sold and smoked.

opium poppy ▶ noun a Eurasian poppy with ornamental white, red, pink, or purple flowers. Its immature capsules yield a latex from which opium is obtained. ● *Papaver somniferum*, family Papaveraceae.

Opium Wars two wars in which China was involved, regarding the question of commercial rights.

> That between Britain and China (1839–42) followed China's attempt to prohibit the illegal importation of opium from British India into China. The second, involving Britain and France against China (1856–60), followed Chinese restrictions on foreign trade. Defeat of the Chinese resulted in the ceding of Hong Kong to Britain and the opening of five 'treaty ports' to traders.

opopanax /ə(ʊ)ˈpɒpənaks/ (also **opoponax**) ▶ noun
1 an acacia tree with violet-scented flowers that yield an essential oil used in perfumery, native to warm regions of America and cultivated elsewhere. ● *Acacia farnesiana*, family Leguminosae.
2 a yellow-flowered Mediterranean plant of the parsley family. ● *Opopanax chironium*, family Umbelliferae. ■ (also **gum opopanax**) [mass noun] a fetid gum resin obtained from the roots of the Mediterranean opopanax, used in perfumery.
3 [mass noun] a fragrant gum resin which is used in perfumery. ● This resin is obtained from the tree *Commiphora kataf*, family Burseraceae.
– ORIGIN late Middle English: via Latin from Greek, from *opos* 'juice' + *panax* 'all-healing'; compare with **PANACEA**.

Oporto /əʊˈpɔːtuː/ the principal city and port of northern Portugal, near the mouth of the River Douro, famous for port wine; pop. 221,800 (2007). Portuguese name **Porto**.

opossum /əˈpɒs(ə)m/ ▶ noun an American marsupial which has a naked prehensile tail and hind feet with an opposable thumb. ● Family Didelphidae: several genera and numerous species. See also **VIRGINIA OPOSSUM**. ■ Austral./NZ a possum.
– ORIGIN early 17th cent.: from Virginia Algonquian *opassom*, from *op* 'white' + *assom* 'dog'.

opossum shrimp ▶ noun a small shrimp-like crustacean which has a long abdomen and conspicuous eyes and is typically transparent. The eggs and young are carried in a ventral brood pouch. ● Order Mysidacea: *Praunus* and other genera. See also **MYSID**.

opp. ▶ abbreviation opposite.

Oppenheimer /ˈɒp(ə)nˌhʌɪmə/, Julius Robert (1904–67), American theoretical physicist. He was director of the laboratory at Los Alamos during the development of the first atom bomb, but opposed the development of the hydrogen bomb after the Second World War.

oppidum /ˈɒpɪdəm/ ▶ noun (pl. **oppida**) an ancient Celtic fortified town, especially one under Roman rule.
– ORIGIN Latin, 'town'.

oppo ▶ noun (pl. **oppos**) Brit. informal a colleague or friend.
– ORIGIN 1930s: abbreviation of *opposite number*.

opponens /əˈpəʊnənz/ ▶ noun Anatomy another term for **OPPONENT MUSCLE**.
– ORIGIN late 18th cent.: from Latin, literally 'setting against'.

opponent ▶ noun someone who competes with or opposes another in a contest, game, or argument: *he beat his Republican opponent by a landslide margin.* ■ a person who disagrees with or resists a proposal or practice: *an* ***opponent of*** *the economic reforms.*
– ORIGIN late 16th cent. (denoting a person opening an academic debate by proposing objections to a philosophical or religious thesis): from Latin *opponent-* 'setting against', from the verb *opponere*, from *ob-* 'against' + *ponere* 'place'.

opponent muscle ▶ noun Anatomy any of several muscles enabling the thumb to be placed front to front against a finger of the same hand.

opportune /ˈɒpətjuːn, ˌɒpəˈtjuːn/ ▶ adjective (of a time) especially convenient or appropriate for a particular action or event: *he couldn't have arrived at a less opportune moment.* ■ done or occurring at a favourable time; well timed: *the opportune use of humour to lower tension.*
– DERIVATIVES **opportunely** adverb, **opportuneness** noun.
– ORIGIN late Middle English: from Old French *opportun(e)*, from Latin *opportunus*, from *ob-* 'in the direction of' + *portus* 'harbour', originally describing the wind driving towards the harbour, hence 'seasonable'.

opportunism ▶ noun [mass noun] the taking of opportunities as and when they arise, regardless of planning or principle: *he was accused of political opportunism.*

opportunist ▶ noun a person who takes advantage of opportunities as and when they arise, regardless of planning or principle: *most burglaries are committed by casual opportunists.*
▶ adjective opportunistic: *the calculating and opportunist politician.*
– ORIGIN late 19th cent.: from **OPPORTUNE** + **-IST**.

opportunistic ▶ adjective exploiting immediate opportunities, especially regardless of planning or principle: *an opportunistic political lightweight.* ■ Ecology (of a plant or animal) able to spread quickly in a previously unexploited habitat. ■ Medicine (of a microorganism or an infection caused by it) affecting patients only or chiefly when the immune system is depressed.
– DERIVATIVES **opportunistically** adverb.

opportunity ▶ noun (pl. **opportunities**) a time or set of circumstances that makes it possible to do something: *increased* ***opportunities for*** *export | the night drive gave us the opportunity of spotting rhinos.* ■ a chance for employment or promotion: *career opportunities in our New York headquarters.*
– PHRASES **opportunity knocks** a chance of success occurs.
– ORIGIN late Middle English: from Old French *opportunite*, from Latin *opportunitas*, from *opportunus* (see **OPPORTUNE**).

opportunity cost ▶ noun Economics the loss of other alternatives when one alternative is chosen.

opportunity shop ▶ noun Austral./NZ a charity shop.

opposable ▶ adjective Zoology (of the thumb of a primate) capable of facing and touching the other digits on the same hand.

oppose ▶ verb [with obj.] disagree with and attempt to prevent, especially by argument: *a majority of the electorate opposed EC membership.* ■ actively resist (a person or system): *a workers' movement opposed the regime.* ■ compete with (someone): *a candidate to oppose the leader in the presidential contest.*
– DERIVATIVES **opposer** noun.
– ORIGIN late Middle English: from Old French *opposer*, from Latin *opponere* (see **OPPONENT**), but influenced by Latin *oppositus* 'set or placed against' and Old French *poser* 'to place'.

opposed ▶ adjective 1 (**opposed to**) anxious to prevent or put an end to; disagreeing with: *he was opposed to discrimination.* ■ in conflict with or hostile to: *parties opposed to the ruling party.*
2 (of two or more things) contrasting or conflicting with each other: *the agency is being asked to do two diametrically opposed things.*
– PHRASES **as opposed to** distinguished from or in contrast with: *an approach that is theoretical as opposed to practical.*

opposing ▶ adjective 1 in conflict or competition with someone or something: *the opposing team.* ■ (of two or more subjects) differing from or in conflict with each other: *the brothers fought on opposing sides in the war.*
2 facing; opposite: *on the opposing page there were two addresses.*

opposite ▶ adjective 1 [attrib.] situated on the other or further side when seen from a specified or implicit viewpoint; facing: *a crowd gathered on the opposite side of the street.* ■ (of angles) between opposite sides of the intersection of two lines. ■ Botany (of leaves or shoots) arising in pairs at the same level on opposite sides of the stem.
2 completely different; of a contrary kind: *a word that is* ***opposite in meaning to another*** *| currents flowing in* ***opposite directions.*** ■ [attrib.] being the other of a contrasted pair: *the opposite ends of the price range.*
▶ noun a person or thing that is totally different from or the reverse of someone or something else: *we were opposites in temperament | the literal is* ***the opposite of*** *the figurative.*
▶ adverb in a position facing a specified or implied subject: *she was sitting almost opposite | he went into the shop opposite.*
▶ preposition 1 in a position on the other side of a specific area from; facing: *they sat opposite one another.*
2 (of a leading actor) in a complementary role to (another).
– PHRASES **the opposite sex** women in relation to men or vice versa.
– DERIVATIVES **oppositely** adverb, **oppositeness** noun.
– ORIGIN late Middle English: via Old French from Latin *oppositus*, past participle of *opponere* 'set against'.

opposite number ▶ noun (**one's opposite number**) a person whose position in another group, organization, or country is equivalent to that held by someone already mentioned.

opposite prompt ▶ noun Brit. the offstage area of a theatre stage to the right of an actor facing the audience.

opposition ▶ noun 1 [mass noun] resistance or dissent, expressed in action or argument: *there was considerable* ***opposition to*** *the proposal.* ■ (often **the opposition**) a group of opponents, especially in sport, business, or politics. ■ (**the Opposition**) Brit. the principal parliamentary party opposed to that in office. ■ Astronomy & Astrology the apparent position of two celestial objects that are directly opposite each other in the sky, especially the position of a planet when opposite the sun.
2 a contrast or antithesis: *a nature–culture opposition* | [mass noun] *the opposition between practical and poetic language.*
– PHRASES **in opposition** in contrast or conflict: *they found themselves* ***in opposition to*** *state policy.* ■ (of a major political party) not forming the government.
– DERIVATIVES **oppositional** adjective.
– ORIGIN late Middle English: from Latin *oppositio(n-)*, from *opponere* 'set against'.

oppositionist ▶ noun (typically in a political context) a person who opposes someone or something: *a prominent oppositionist who criticized the party line.*
▶ adjective relating to opposition or oppositionists: *oppositionist union leaders.*

oppress ▶ verb [with obj.] 1 keep (someone) in subjection and hardship, especially by the unjust exercise of authority: *a system which oppressed working people.* ■ cause distress or anxiety to: *he was oppressed by some secret worry.*
2 Heraldry another term for **DEBRUISE**.
– ORIGIN late Middle English: from Old French *oppresser*, from medieval Latin *oppressare*, from Latin *oppress-* 'pressed against', from the verb *opprimere*.

oppressed ▶ adjective subject to harsh and authoritarian treatment: *oppressed racial minorities* | (as plural noun **the oppressed**) *his sympathies were with the oppressed.*

oppression ▶ **noun** [mass noun] prolonged cruel or unjust treatment or exercise of authority: *a region shattered by oppression and killing.* ■ the state of being subject to oppressive treatment: *a response to collective poverty and oppression.* ■ mental pressure or distress: *Beatrice's mood had initially been alarm and a sense of oppression.*
– ORIGIN Middle English: from Old French, from Latin *oppressio(n-)*, from the verb *opprimere* (see OPPRESS).

oppressive ▶ **adjective 1** inflicting harsh and authoritarian treatment: *an oppressive dictatorship.* ■ weighing heavily on the mind or spirits: *the offices present an oppressive atmosphere.*
2 (of weather) close and sultry.
– DERIVATIVES **oppressively** adverb, **oppressiveness** noun.
– ORIGIN late 16th cent.: from medieval Latin *oppressivus*, from *oppress-* 'pressed against', from the verb *opprimere* (see OPPRESS).

oppressor ▶ **noun** a person or group that oppresses people: *they overthrew their colonial oppressors.*

opprobrious /əˈprəʊbrɪəs/ ▶ **adjective** (of language) expressing scorn or criticism.
– DERIVATIVES **opprobriously** adverb.
– ORIGIN late Middle English: from late Latin *opprobriosus*, from *opprobrium* (see OPPROBRIUM).

opprobrium /əˈprəʊbrɪəm/ ▶ **noun** [mass noun] harsh criticism or censure: *the critical opprobrium generated by his films.* ■ public disgrace arising from shameful conduct: *the opprobrium of being closely associated with gangsters.* ■ [count noun] archaic an occasion or cause of reproach or disgrace.
– ORIGIN mid 17th cent.: from Latin, literally 'infamy', from *opprobrum*, from *ob-* 'against' + *probrum* 'disgraceful act'.

oppugn /əˈpjuːn/ ▶ **verb** [with obj.] formal question the truth or validity of.
– ORIGIN late Middle English (in the sense 'fight against'): from Latin *oppugnare* 'attack, besiege', from *ob-* 'against' + *pugnare* 'to fight'.

oppugnant /əˈpʌɡnənt/ ▶ **adjective** formal opposing; antagonistic.
– DERIVATIVES **oppugnancy** noun.
– ORIGIN early 16th cent.: from Latin *oppugnant-* 'fighting against', from the verb *oppugnare* (see OPPUGN).

op shop (also **opp shop**) ▶ **noun** Austral./NZ short for OPPORTUNITY SHOP.

opsimath /ˈɒpsɪmaθ/ ▶ **noun** rare a person who begins to learn or study only late in life.
– ORIGIN late 19th cent.: from Greek *opsimathēs*, from *opse* 'late' + the stem *math-* 'learn'.

opsin /ˈɒpsɪn/ ▶ **noun** [mass noun] Biochemistry a protein which forms part of the visual pigment rhodopsin and is released by the action of light.
– ORIGIN 1950s: shortening of RHODOPSIN.

opsonin /ˈɒpsənɪn/ ▶ **noun** Biochemistry an antibody or other substance which binds to foreign microorganisms or cells making them more susceptible to phagocytosis.
– DERIVATIVES **opsonic** adjective.
– ORIGIN early 20th cent.: from Latin *opsonare* 'buy provisions' (from Greek *opsōnein*) + -IN[1].

opsonize (also **opsonise**) ▶ **verb** [with obj.] Medicine make (a foreign cell) more susceptible to phagocytosis.
– DERIVATIVES **opsonization** noun.

opt ▶ **verb** [no obj.] make a choice from a range of possibilities: *consumers will **opt for** low-priced goods* | [with infinitive] *pupils opting to continue with physics.*
– PHRASAL VERBS **opt in** choose to participate in something: *the database would not include a person's name unless he opted in.* **opt out** choose not to participate in something: *you can **opt out of** the state pension scheme.* ■ Brit. (of a school or hospital) decide to withdraw from local authority control.
– ORIGIN late 19th cent.: from French *opter*, from Latin *optare* 'choose, wish'.

optant ▶ **noun** a person who chooses or has chosen. ■ a person who may choose one of two nationalities.
– ORIGIN early 20th cent.: via German and Danish from Latin *optant-* 'choosing', from the verb *optare*.

optative /ˈɒptətɪv, ɒpˈteɪtɪv/ Grammar ▶ **adjective** relating to or denoting a mood of verbs in Greek and certain other languages, expressing a wish, equivalent in meaning to English *let's* or *if only*.
▶ **noun** a verb in the optative mood. ■ (**the optative**) the optative mood.
– ORIGIN mid 16th cent.: from French *optatif, -ive*, from late Latin *optativus*, from *optat-* 'chosen', from the verb *optare* (see OPT).

optic ▶ **adjective** relating to the eye or vision.
▶ **noun 1** a lens or other optical component in an optical instrument.
2 archaic or humorous the eye.
3 Brit. trademark a device fastened to the neck of an inverted bottle for measuring out spirits.
– ORIGIN late Middle English: from French *optique* or medieval Latin *opticus*, from Greek *optikos*, from *optos* 'seen'.

optical ▶ **adjective 1** relating to sight, especially in relation to the action of light: *optical illusions.* ■ constructed to assist sight: *an optical aid.* ■ relating to the science of optics.
2 Physics operating in or employing the visible part of the electromagnetic spectrum: *optical telescopes.* ■ Electronics (of a device) requiring electromagnetic radiation for its operation: *integrated optical circuits.*
▶ **noun** (**opticals**) Indian a pair of glasses: *he pushed his opticals on to the bridge of his nose.*
– DERIVATIVES **optically** adverb.

optical activity ▶ **noun** [mass noun] Chemistry the property (displayed by solutions of some compounds, notably many sugars) of rotating the plane of polarization of plane-polarized light.

optical art ▶ **noun** another term for OP ART.

optical axis ▶ **noun 1** a line passing through the centre of curvature of a lens or spherical mirror and parallel to the axis of symmetry.
2 Crystallography a direction in a doubly refracting crystal along which a light ray does not undergo double refraction.

optical bench ▶ **noun** a straight rigid bar, typically marked with a scale, to which supports for lenses, light sources, and other optical components can be attached.

optical brightener ▶ **noun** a fluorescent substance added to detergents in order to produce a whitening effect on laundry.

optical character recognition ▶ **noun** [mass noun] the identification of printed characters using photoelectric devices and computer software.

optical density ▶ **noun** Physics the degree to which a refractive medium retards transmitted rays of light.

optical disk ▶ **noun** see DISC (sense 1).

optical double ▶ **noun** Astronomy a group of two stars which appear to constitute a double star due to their being in the same line of sight as seen from the earth, but are actually at different distances.

optical fibre ▶ **noun** a thin glass fibre through which light can be transmitted.

optical glass ▶ **noun** [mass noun] a very pure kind of glass used for lenses.

optical illusion ▶ **noun** something that deceives the eye by appearing to be other than it is. ■ an experience of seeming to see something which does not exist or is other than it appears.

optical indicatrix ▶ **noun** see INDICATRIX.

optical isomer ▶ **noun** Chemistry each of two or more forms of a compound which have the same structure but are mirror images of each other and typically differ in optical activity.
– DERIVATIVES **optical isomerism** noun.

optical microscope ▶ **noun** a microscope using visible light, typically viewed directly by the eye.

optical path ▶ **noun** Physics the distance which in a vacuum would contain the same number of wavelengths as the actual path taken by a ray of light.

optical rotation ▶ **noun** [mass noun] Chemistry the rotation of the plane of polarization of plane-polarized light by an optically active substance.

optical scanner ▶ **noun** Electronics a device which performs optical character recognition and produces coded signals corresponding to the characters identified.

optic angle ▶ **noun 1** the angle formed by notional lines from the extremities of an object to the eye, or by lines from the eyes to a given point.
2 Crystallography the angle between the optic axes of a biaxial doubly refracting crystal.

optic axis ▶ **noun** another term for OPTICAL AXIS.

optic chiasma ▶ **noun** see CHIASMA (sense 1).

optic cup ▶ **noun** Anatomy a cup-like outgrowth of the brain of an embryo which develops into the retina.

optic disc ▶ **noun** Anatomy the raised disc on the retina at the point of entry of the optic nerve, lacking visual receptors and so creating a blind spot.

optician ▶ **noun** Brit. a person qualified to prescribe and dispense glasses and contact lenses, and to detect eye diseases (**ophthalmic optician**) or to make and supply glasses and contact lenses (**dispensing optician**). ■ US a dispensing optician.
– ORIGIN late 17th cent.: from French *opticien*, from medieval Latin *optica* 'optics'.

optic lobe ▶ **noun** Anatomy a lobe in the midbrain from which the optic nerve partly arises.

optic nerve ▶ **noun** Anatomy each of the second pair of cranial nerves, transmitting impulses to the brain from the retina at the back of the eye.

optic neuritis ▶ **noun** [mass noun] Medicine inflammation of an optic nerve, causing blurred vision.

optics ▶ **plural noun** [usu. treated as sing.] the scientific study of sight and the behaviour of light, or the properties of transmission and deflection of other forms of radiation.

optic tectum ▶ **noun** see TECTUM.

optic tract ▶ **noun** Anatomy the pathway between the optic chiasma and the brain.

optima plural form of OPTIMUM.

optimal ▶ **adjective** best or most favourable; optimum: *seeking the optimal solution.*
– DERIVATIVES **optimality** noun, **optimally** adverb.
– ORIGIN late 19th cent.: from Latin *optimus* 'best' + -AL.

optimific /ˌɒptɪˈmɪfɪk/ ▶ **adjective** Philosophy producing the maximum good consequences.
– ORIGIN 1930s: from Latin *optimus* 'best' + -IFIC.

optimism ▶ **noun** [mass noun] **1** hopefulness and confidence about the future or the success of something: *the talks had been amicable and there were grounds for optimism.*
2 Philosophy the doctrine, especially as set forth by Leibniz, that this world is the best of all possible worlds. ■ the belief that good must ultimately prevail over evil in the universe.
– DERIVATIVES **optimist** noun.
– ORIGIN mid 18th cent.: from French *optimisme*, from Latin *optimum* 'best thing' (see OPTIMUM).

optimistic ▶ **adjective** hopeful and confident about the future: *the optimistic mood of the Sixties* | *the government was **optimistic that** reform would take place.* ■ (of an estimate) unrealistically high: *previous estimates of whale numbers may be wildly optimistic.*
– DERIVATIVES **optimistically** adverb.

optimize (also **optimise**) ▶ **verb** [with obj.] make the best or most effective use of (a situation or resource): *we manage our time so that we optimize our productivity.* ■ Computing rearrange or rewrite (data, software, etc.) to improve efficiency of retrieval or processing.
– DERIVATIVES **optimization** noun, **optimizer** noun.
– ORIGIN early 19th cent.: from Latin *optimus* 'best' + -IZE.

optimum ▶ **adjective** most conducive to a favourable outcome; best: *the optimum childbearing age.*
▶ **noun** (pl. **optima** or **optimums**) the most favourable situation or level for growth, reproduction, or success.
– ORIGIN late 19th cent.: from Latin, neuter (used as a noun) of *optimus* 'best'.

option ▶ **noun** a thing that is or may be chosen: *choose the cheapest options for supplying energy.* ■ [in sing.] the freedom or right to choose something: *she was given the option of resigning or being dismissed* | *he **has no option but** to pay up.* ■ a right to buy or sell a particular thing at a specified price within a set time: *Columbia Pictures **has an option on** the script.*
▶ **verb** [with obj.] buy or sell an option on.
– PHRASES **keep** (or **leave**) **one's options open** not commit oneself. **not be an option** not be feasible.
– ORIGIN mid 16th cent.: from French, or from Latin *optio(n-)*, from the stem of *optare* 'choose'. The verb dates from the 1930s.

optional ▶ **adjective** available to be chosen but not obligatory: *a wide range of optional excursions is offered.*
– DERIVATIVES **optionality** noun, **optionally** adverb.

optional extra ▶ **noun** a non-essential additional item which is available for purchase.

option card ▶ **noun 1** Computing an expansion card.

O

2 a credit card issued for use in a particular store or chain of stores.

optocoupler ▸ **noun** Electronics a device containing light-emitting and light-sensitive components, used to couple isolated circuits.

optoelectronics ▸ **plural noun** [treated as sing.] the branch of technology concerned with the combined use of electronics and light.
– DERIVATIVES **optoelectronic** adjective.

optometer /ɒp'tɒmɪtə/ ▸ **noun** an instrument for testing the refractive power of the eye.
– ORIGIN mid 18th cent.: from Greek *optos* 'seen' + **-METER.**

optometrist ▸ **noun** a person who practises optometry.

optometry ▸ **noun** [mass noun] the occupation of measuring eyesight, prescribing corrective lenses, and detecting eye disease.
– DERIVATIVES **optometric** adjective.

opt-out ▸ **noun** an instance of choosing not to participate in something: *opt-outs from key parts of the treaty.* ■ Brit. an instance of a school or hospital withdrawing from local authority control.

optronics ▸ **plural noun** [treated as sing.] short for **OPTOELECTRONICS.**
– DERIVATIVES **optronic** adjective.

opulence ▸ **noun** [mass noun] great wealth or luxuriousness: *rooms of spectacular opulence.*

opulent ▸ **adjective** ostentatiously costly and luxurious: *the opulent comfort of a limousine.* ■ wealthy: *his more opulent tenants.*
– DERIVATIVES **opulently** adverb.
– ORIGIN mid 16th cent. (in the sense 'wealthy'): from Latin *opulent-* 'wealthy, splendid', from *opes* 'wealth'.

opuntia /ɒ'pʌnʃɪə, ə(ʊ)-/ ▸ **noun** a cactus of a genus that comprises the prickly pears. ● Genus *Opuntia*, family Cactaceae.
– ORIGIN early 17th cent.: from Latin, a name given to a plant growing around *Opus* (stem *Opunt-*), a city in Locris in ancient Greece. The term was later used as a genus name.

opus /'əʊpəs, 'ɒp-/ ▸ **noun** (pl. **opuses** or **opera** /'ɒp(ə)rə/) **1** Music a separate composition or set of compositions. See also **OP.**
2 an artistic work, especially one on a large scale.
– ORIGIN early 18th cent.: from Latin, literally 'work'.

opuscule /ə'pʌskjuːl/ (also **opusculum** /ə'pʌskjʊləm/) ▸ **noun** (pl. **opuscules** or **opuscula** /-lə/) rare a small or minor literary or musical work.
– ORIGIN mid 17th cent.: from French, from Latin *opusculum*, diminutive of *opus* 'work'.

opus Dei /ˌəʊpəs 'deɪiː, 'ɒpəs/ ▸ **noun** **1** [mass noun] Christian Church liturgical worship regarded as humankind's primary duty to God.
2 (**Opus Dei**) trademark a Roman Catholic organization of laymen and priests founded in Spain in 1928 with the aim of re-establishing Christian ideals in society.
– ORIGIN late 19th cent.: from medieval Latin, literally 'work of God'.

OR ▸ **abbreviation** ■ operational research. ■ Oregon (in official postal use). ■ Military, Brit. other ranks (as opposed to commissioned officers).

or¹ ▸ **conjunction** **1** used to link alternatives: *a cup of tea or coffee* | *are you coming* ***or not?*** | *I* ***either*** *take taxis* ***or*** *walk everywhere* | *it doesn't matter* ***whether*** *the theory is right* ***or*** *wrong.*
2 introducing a synonym or explanation of a preceding word or phrase: *yoga is a series of postures, or asanas.*
3 otherwise (used to introduce the consequences of something not being done or not being the case): *hurry up, or you'll miss it all.*
4 introducing an afterthought, usually in the form of a question: *John's indifference—or was it?—left her unsettled.*
5 archaic either: *to love is the one way to know* ***or*** *God* ***or*** *man.*
▸ **noun** (**OR**) a logical operation which gives the value one if at least one operand has the value one, and otherwise gives a value of zero. ■ [as modifier] Electronics denoting a gate circuit which produces an output if there is a signal on any of its inputs.
– PHRASES **or else** see **ELSE. or so** (after a quantity) approximately: *a dozen or so people.*
– ORIGIN Middle English: a reduced form of the obsolete conjunction *other* (which superseded Old English *oththe* 'or'), of uncertain ultimate origin.

> **USAGE** **1** Where a verb follows a list separated by **or**, the traditional rule is that the verb should be singular, as long as the things in the list are individually singular, as in *a sandwich* ***or*** *other snack* ***is*** *included in the price* (rather than *a sandwich* ***or*** *other snack* ***are*** *included in the price*). The argument is that each of the elements agrees separately with the verb. The opposite rule applies when the elements are joined by **and**: here, the verb should be plural: *a sandwich* ***and*** *a cup of coffee* ***are*** *included in the price.* These traditional rules are observed in good English writing style but are often disregarded in speech.
> **2** On the use of **either ... or**, see **USAGE** at **EITHER.**

or² ▸ **noun** [mass noun] gold or yellow, as a heraldic tincture.
– ORIGIN early 16th cent.: from French, from Latin *aurum* 'gold'.

-or¹ ▸ **suffix** (forming nouns) denoting a person or thing performing the action of a verb, or denoting another agent: *escalator* | *governor* | *resistor.*
– ORIGIN from Latin, sometimes via Anglo-Norman French *-eour* or Old French *-eor* (see also **-ATOR**).

-or² ▸ **suffix** forming nouns denoting a state or condition: *error* | *pallor* | *terror.*
– ORIGIN from Latin, sometimes via Old French *-or, -ur.*

-or³ ▸ **suffix** forming adjectives expressing a comparative sense: *junior* | *major.*
– ORIGIN via Anglo-Norman French from Latin.

-or⁴ ▸ **suffix** US form of **-OUR¹.**

ora plural form of **OS².**

orache /'ɒrətʃ/ (also **orach**) ▸ **noun** a plant of the goosefoot family with leaves that are sometimes covered in a white mealy substance. Several kinds are edible and can be used as a substitute for spinach or sorrel. ● Genus *Atriplex*, family Chenopodiaceae: several species, in particular the **common orache** (*A. hortensis*), which is cultivated in some areas.
– ORIGIN Middle English *orage*, from Anglo-Norman French *arasche*, from Latin *atriplex*, from Greek *atraphaxus.*

oracle ▸ **noun** **1** a priest or priestess acting as a medium through whom advice or prophecy was sought from the gods in classical antiquity. ■ a place at which divine advice or prophecy was sought. ■ a person or thing regarded as an infallible authority on something: *he reigned supreme as the Colonial Office's oracle on Africa.*
2 archaic a response or message given by an oracle, especially an ambiguous one.
– ORIGIN late Middle English: via Old French from Latin *oraculum*, from *orare* 'speak'.

oracle bones ▸ **plural noun** bones used in ancient China for divination.

oracular /ɒ'rakjʊlə/ ▸ **adjective** relating to an oracle. ■ (of an utterance, advice, etc.) hard to interpret; enigmatic: *an ambiguous, oracular remark.* ■ holding or claiming the authority of an oracle: *he holds forth in oracular fashion.*
– DERIVATIVES **oracularity** noun, **oracularly** adverb.
– ORIGIN mid 17th cent.: from Latin *oraculum* (see **ORACLE**) + **-AR¹.**

oracy /'ɔːrəsi/ ▸ **noun** [mass noun] Brit. the ability to express oneself fluently and grammatically in speech.
– ORIGIN 1960s: from Latin *os, or-* 'mouth', on the pattern of *literacy.*

Oradea /ɒ'rɑːdɪə/ an industrial city in western Romania, near the border with Hungary; pop. 205,956 (2006).

oral ▸ **adjective** **1** spoken rather than written; verbal: *they had reached an oral agreement.* ■ relating to the transmission of information or literature by word of mouth. ■ (of a society) not having reached the stage of literacy.
2 relating to the mouth: *oral hygiene.* ■ done or taken by the mouth: *oral contraceptives.* ■ Phonetics (of a speech sound) pronounced by the voice resonating in the mouth, as the vowels in English. Compare with **NASAL** (sense 2 of the adjective). ■ Psychoanalysis (in Freudian theory) relating to or denoting a stage of infantile psychosexual development in which the mouth is the main source of pleasure and the centre of experience.
▸ **noun** a spoken examination or test: *a French oral.*
– DERIVATIVES **orally** adverb.
– ORIGIN early 17th cent.: from late Latin *oralis*, from Latin *os, or-* 'mouth'.

oral-formulaic ▸ **adjective** relating to or denoting poetry belonging to an early spoken tradition characterized by the use of poetic formulae.

oral history ▸ **noun** [mass noun] the collection and study of historical information using tape recordings of interviews with people having personal knowledge of past events.

oralism ▸ **noun** [mass noun] the system of teaching profoundly deaf people to communicate by the use of speech and lip-reading rather than sign language.

oralist ▸ **adjective** relating to or advocating oralism.
▸ **noun** a profoundly deaf person who uses speech and lip-reading to communicate, rather than sign language.

orality ▸ **noun** [mass noun] **1** the quality of being verbally communicated. ■ preference for or tendency to use spoken forms of language.
2 Psychoanalysis the focusing of sexual energy and feeling on the mouth.

Oral Law ▸ **noun** [mass noun] Judaism the part of Jewish religious law believed to have been passed down by oral tradition before being collected in the Mishnah.

oral sex ▸ **noun** [mass noun] sexual activity in which the genitals of one partner are stimulated by the mouth of the other; fellatio or cunnilingus.

Oran /ɔː'rɑːn/ a port on the Mediterranean coast of Algeria; pop. 679,900 (est. 2009).

orang /ɔː'raŋ, ə'raŋ/ ▸ **noun** short for **ORANG-UTAN.**

Orang Asli /ˌɒrəŋ 'azli/ ▸ **noun** [treated as pl.] a collective term for the indigenous peoples of Malaysia.
– ORIGIN Malay, from *orang* 'person' and *as(a)li* 'of ancient origin' (from *asal* 'source or origin').

Orange¹ a town in southern France, on the Rhône, home of the ancestors of the Dutch royal house. See **ORANGE, HOUSE OF.**

Orange² ▸ **adjective** relating to the Orange Order.
– DERIVATIVES **Orangeism** noun.

orange ▸ **noun** **1** a large round juicy citrus fruit with a tough bright reddish-yellow rind. ■ [mass noun] chiefly Brit. a drink made from or flavoured with oranges: *a vodka and orange.*
2 (also **orange tree**) the leathery-leaved evergreen tree which produces oranges, native to warm regions of south and SE Asia. ● Genus *Citrus*, family Rutaceae: several species, in particular the **sweet orange** (*C. sinensis*) and the **Seville orange.**
■ used in names of other plants with similar fruit or flowers, e.g. **mock orange.**
3 [mass noun] a bright reddish-yellow colour like that of the skin of a ripe orange.
4 [with modifier] a butterfly with mainly or partly orange wings. ● Several species in the family Pieridae, in particular American species in the genera *Colias* and *Eurema*.
▸ **adjective** reddish yellow: *an orange glow in the sky.*
– DERIVATIVES **orangey** (also **orangy**) adjective, **orangish** adjective.
– ORIGIN late Middle English: from Old French *orenge* (in the phrase *pomme d'orenge*), based on Arabic *nāranj*, from Persian *nārang.*

Orange, House of the Dutch royal house, originally a princely dynasty of the principality centred on the town of Orange in the 16th century.

> Members of the family held the position of stadtholder or magistrate from the mid 16th until the late 18th century. In 1689 William of Orange became King William III of Great Britain and Ireland and the son of the last stadtholder became King William I of the United Netherlands in 1815.

Orange, William of William III of Great Britain and Ireland (see **WILLIAM**).

orangeade ▸ **noun** [mass noun] Brit. a fizzy non-alcoholic drink flavoured with orange.

orange flower water ▸ **noun** [mass noun] a solution of neroli in water, used in perfumery and as a food flavouring.

Orange Free State an area and former province in central South Africa, situated to the north of the Orange River. An area inhabited by Bantu-speaking farmers, it was first settled by Boers after the Great Trek. It became a province of the Union of South Africa in 1910 and in 1994 became one of the new provinces of South Africa. It was named **FREE STATE** (sense 2) in 1995.

Orange Lodge another name for **ORANGE ORDER.**

Orangeman ▸ **noun** (pl. **Orangemen**) a member of the Orange Order.

Orange Order a Protestant political society in Ireland, especially in Northern Ireland.

The Orange Order was formed in 1795 (as the Association of Orangemen) for the defence of Protestantism and maintenance of Protestant ascendancy in Ireland. It was probably named from the wearing of orange badges as a symbol of adherence to William III (William of Orange). In the early 20th century it was strengthened in the north of Ireland in its campaign to resist the Home Rule bill and has continued to form a core of Protestant Unionist opinion since.

orange peel ▸ **noun** [mass noun] the skin of an orange. ▪ [as modifier] denoting skin dimpled like that of an orange, especially when resulting from subcutaneous fat deposits.

orange pekoe ▸ **noun** [mass noun] a type of black tea made from young leaves.

orangequit /ˈɒrɪn(d)ʒkwɪt/ ▸ **noun** a Jamaican tanager (songbird), the male of which has grey-blue plumage with a reddish throat. ● *Euneornios campestris*, family Emberizidae (subfamily Thraupinae).
– ORIGIN mid 19th cent.: from **ORANGE** (because it feeds on oranges) + **QUIT**[2].

Orange River the longest river in South Africa, which rises in the Drakensberg Mountains in NE Lesotho and flows generally westward for 1,859 km (1,155 miles) to the Atlantic, forming the border between Namibia and South Africa in its lower course.

orangery ▸ **noun** (pl. **orangeries**) a building like a large conservatory where orange trees are grown.

orange stick ▸ **noun** a thin stick, pointed at one end and typically made of orange wood, used for manicuring the fingernails.

orange tip ▸ **noun** a cream-coloured butterfly of both Eurasia and North America, the male (and sometimes the female) of which has orange tips to the forewings. ● *Anthocharis* and other genera, family Pieridae: several species.

orang-utan /ɔːˌraŋuːˈtan, əˈraŋuːtan/ (also **orang-utang** /-uːˈtaŋ/) ▸ **noun** a large mainly solitary arboreal ape with long red hair, long arms, and hooked hands and feet, native to Borneo and Sumatra. ● *Pongo pygmaeus*, family Pongidae.
– ORIGIN late 17th cent.: from Malay *orang utan* 'forest person'.

Oranjestad /ˈɒranjəˌstɑːt/ the capital of the Dutch island of Aruba in the Caribbean; pop. 32,000 (est. 2007).

Oraşul Stalin /ˌɒraʃʊl ˈstɑːlɪn/ former name for **BRAŞOV**.

orate /ɔːˈreɪt, ɒˈreɪt/ ▸ **verb** [no obj.] make a speech, especially pompously or at length.
– ORIGIN early 17th cent.: back-formation from **ORATION**.

oration ▸ **noun** a formal speech, especially one given on a ceremonial occasion. ▪ [mass noun] the style or manner in which an oration is given: *there is nothing quite like his messianic oration.*
– ORIGIN late Middle English (denoting a prayer): from Latin *oratio(n-)* 'discourse, prayer', from *orare* 'speak, pray'.

orator ▸ **noun** a public speaker, especially one who is eloquent or skilled. ▪ (also **public orator**) an official speaking for a university on ceremonial occasions.
– DERIVATIVES **oratorial** adjective.
– ORIGIN late Middle English: from Anglo-Norman French *oratour*, from Latin *orator* 'speaker, pleader'.

oratorical /ɒrəˈtɒrɪk(ə)l/ ▸ **adjective** relating to the art or practice of public speaking: *oratorical skills.*
– DERIVATIVES **oratorically** adverb.

oratorio /ˌɒrəˈtɔːrɪəʊ/ ▸ **noun** (pl. **oratorios**) a large-scale, usually narrative musical work for orchestra and voices, typically on a sacred theme, performed without costume, scenery, or action. Well-known examples include Bach's *Christmas Oratorio*, Handel's *Messiah*, and Haydn's *The Creation*.
– ORIGIN Italian, from ecclesiastical Latin *oratorium* 'oratory', from the musical services held in the church of the Oratory of St Philip Neri in Rome.

oratory[1] /ˈɒrət(ə)ri/ ▸ **noun** (pl. **oratories**) **1** a small chapel, especially for private worship.
2 (**Oratory**) (in the Roman Catholic Church) a religious society of secular priests founded in Rome in 1564 to provide plain preaching and popular services and established in various countries.
– DERIVATIVES **Oratorian** noun & adjective (sense 2).
– ORIGIN Middle English: from Anglo-Norman French *oratorie*, from ecclesiastical Latin *oratorium*, based on Latin *orare* 'pray, speak'; sense 2 is from *Congregation of the Fathers of the Oratory*.

oratory[2] ▸ **noun** [mass noun] the art or practice of formal speaking in public. ▪ eloquent or rhetorical language: *learned discussions degenerated into pompous oratory.*
– ORIGIN early 16th cent.: from Latin *oratoria*, feminine (used as a noun) of *oratorius* 'relating to an orator'.

orb ▸ **noun** a spherical object or shape. ▪ a golden globe surmounted by a cross, forming part of the regalia of a monarch. ▪ literary a celestial body. ▪ (usu. **orbs**) literary an eye. ▪ Astrology a circle of up to 10° radius around the position of a celestial object: *within an orb of 1° of Mars.*
– ORIGIN late Middle English (denoting a circle): from Latin *orbis* 'ring'.

orbat ▸ **noun** Military short for **ORDER OF BATTLE** (see **ORDER**).

orbicular /ɔːˈbɪkjʊlə/ ▸ **adjective** technical **1** having the shape of a flat ring or disc.
2 having a spherical or rounded shape. ▪ Geology (of a rock) containing spheroidal igneous inclusions.
– DERIVATIVES **orbicularity** noun.
– ORIGIN late Middle English: from late Latin *orbicularis*, from Latin *orbiculus*, diminutive of *orbis* 'ring'.

Orbison /ˈɔːbɪs(ə)n/, Roy (1936–88), American singer and composer. Notable songs: 'Only the Lonely' (1960) and 'Oh, Pretty Woman' (1964).

orbit ▸ **noun 1** the regularly repeated elliptical course of a celestial object or spacecraft about a star or planet. ▪ one complete circuit round an orbited body. ▪ [mass noun] the state of moving in an orbit: *the earth is in orbit around the sun.* ▪ the path of an electron round an atomic nucleus.
2 an area of activity, interest, or influence: *audiences drawn largely from outside the Party orbit.*
3 Anatomy the cavity in the skull of a vertebrate that contains the eye; the eye socket. ▪ the area around the eye of a bird or other animal.
▸ **verb** (**orbits**, **orbiting**, **orbited**) [with obj.] (of a celestial object or spacecraft) move in orbit round (a star or planet): *Mercury orbits the Sun.* ▪ [no obj.] move in a circle: *the discs spun and orbited slowly.* ▪ put (a satellite) into orbit.
– PHRASES **into orbit** informal into a state of heightened activity, anger, or excitement: *his goal sent the fans into orbit.*
– ORIGIN mid 16th cent. (in sense 3 of the noun): from Latin *orbita* 'course, track' (in medieval Latin 'eye socket'), feminine of *orbitus* 'circular', from *orbis* 'ring'.

orbital ▸ **adjective** relating to an orbit or orbits. ▪ Brit. (of a road) passing round the outside of a town.
▸ **noun 1** Brit. an orbital road.
2 Physics each of the actual or potential patterns of electron density which may be formed in an atom or molecule by one or more electrons, and can be represented as a wave function.
– DERIVATIVES **orbitally** adverb.
– ORIGIN mid 16th cent. (referring to the eye socket): probably from medieval Latin *orbitalis*, from Latin *orbita* (see **ORBIT**).

orbital sander ▸ **noun** a sander in which the sanding surface has a minute circular motion without rotating relative to the workpiece.

orbiter ▸ **noun** a spacecraft designed to go into orbit, especially one that does not subsequently land. Compare with **LANDER**.

orbitofrontal cortex ▸ **noun** Anatomy the area of the cerebral cortex located at the base of the frontal lobes above the orbits (or eye sockets), involved especially in social and emotional behaviour.

orbitosphenoid (also **orbitosphenoid bone**) ▸ **noun** Anatomy & Zoology a bone in the floor of the mammalian cranium, in the region of the optic nerve. In the human skull it is represented by the lesser wings of the sphenoid bone.

orb web ▸ **noun** a circular vertical spider's web formed of threads radiating from a central point, crossed by radial links that spiral in from the edge.

orb-web spider ▸ **noun** a spider of a kind that builds orb webs. Many species are large and brightly coloured, and wait either in the centre of the web or in a retreat at the edge.

orc ▸ **noun** (in fantasy literature and games) a member of an imaginary race of human-like creatures, characterized as ugly, warlike, and malevolent.
– DERIVATIVES **orcish** /ˈɔːkɪʃ/ adjective.
– ORIGIN late 16th cent. (denoting an ogre): perhaps from Latin *orcus* 'hell' or Italian *orco* 'demon, monster', influenced by obsolete *orc* 'ferocious sea creature' and by Old English *orcneas* 'monsters'. The current sense is due to the use of the word in Tolkien's fantasy adventures.

orca /ˈɔːkə/ ▸ **noun** another term for **KILLER WHALE**.
– ORIGIN late 17th cent.: from Latin, denoting a kind of whale.

Orcadian /ɔːˈkeɪdɪən/ ▸ **adjective** relating to the Orkney Islands or their inhabitants.
▸ **noun** a native or inhabitant of the Orkney Islands.
– ORIGIN from *Orcades*, the Latin name for the Orkney Islands, + **-IAN**.

Orcagna /ɔːˈkɑːnjə/ (*c.*1308–68), Italian painter, sculptor, and architect; born *Andrea di Cione*. His paintings include frescoes and an altarpiece in the church of Santa Maria Novella, Florence (1357).

orcein /ˈɔːsiːɪn/ ▸ **noun** [mass noun] Chemistry a red dye obtained from orchil, used as a microscopic stain.
– ORIGIN mid 19th cent.: alteration of *orcin*, another name for **ORCINOL**.

orch. ▸ **abbreviation** ▪ orchestra. ▪ orchestrated by.

orchard ▸ **noun** a piece of enclosed land planted with fruit trees.
– DERIVATIVES **orchardist** noun.
– ORIGIN Old English *ortgeard*; the first element from Latin *hortus* 'garden', the second representing **YARD**[2].

orchard grass ▸ **noun** North American term for **COCKSFOOT**.

orchestra ▸ **noun 1** [treated as sing. or pl.] a group of instrumentalists, especially one combining string, woodwind, brass, and percussion sections and playing classical music.
2 (also **orchestra pit**) the part of a theatre where the orchestra plays, typically in front of the stage and on a lower level. ▪ N. Amer. the stalls in a theatre.
3 the semicircular space in front of an ancient Greek theatre stage where the chorus danced and sang.
– ORIGIN early 17th cent.: via Latin from Greek *orkhēstra*, from *orkheisthai* 'to dance'.

orchestral ▸ **adjective** written for an orchestra to play: *orchestral music.* ▪ relating to an orchestra: *an orchestral conductor.*
– DERIVATIVES **orchestrally** adverb.

orchestra stalls ▸ **plural noun** Brit. the front part of the stalls in a theatre.

orchestrate ▸ **verb** [with obj.] **1** arrange or score (music) for orchestral performance.
2 plan or coordinate the elements of (a situation) to produce a desired effect, especially surreptitiously: *the situation has been orchestrated by a tiny minority.*
– DERIVATIVES **orchestration** noun, **orchestrator** noun.
– ORIGIN late 19th cent.: from **ORCHESTRA**, perhaps suggested by French *orchestrer*.

orchestrion /ɔːˈkɛstrɪən/ (also **orchestrina** /ˌɔːkɪˈstriːnə/) ▸ **noun** a large mechanical musical instrument designed to imitate the sound of an orchestra.
– ORIGIN mid 19th cent.: from **ORCHESTRA**, on the pattern of *accordion*.

orchid ▸ **noun** a plant with complex flowers that are often showy or bizarrely shaped, having a large specialized lip (labellum) and frequently a spur. Orchids occur worldwide, especially as epiphytes in tropical forests, and are valuable hothouse plants. ● Family Orchidaceae: numerous genera and species.
– DERIVATIVES **orchidology** /-ˈdɒlədʒi/ noun.
– ORIGIN mid 19th cent.: from modern Latin *Orchid(ac)eae*, formed irregularly from Latin *orchis* (see **ORCHIS**).

orchidaceous ▸ **adjective** Botany relating to or denoting plants of the orchid family (Orchidaceae).
– ORIGIN mid 19th cent.: from modern Latin *Orchidaceae* (plural) + **-OUS**.

orchidectomy ▸ **noun** [mass noun] surgical removal of one or both testicles.
– ORIGIN late 19th cent.: from modern Latin *orchido-* (from a Latinized stem of Greek *orkhis* 'testicle') + **-ECTOMY**.

orchil /ˈɔːtʃɪl/ ▸ **noun 1** [mass noun] a red or violet dye obtained from certain lichens, used as a source of litmus, orcinol, and other pigments.
2 a lichen with flattened fronds from which orchil is produced. ● *Roccella* (order Graphidiales) and other genera: several species, including the Mediterranean *R. tinctoria*, used for dyeing, and the Madagascan *R. montagnei*, used for litmus.
– ORIGIN late 15th cent.: from Old French *orcheil*, related to Spanish *urchilla*; of uncertain origin.

O

orchis /ˈɔːkɪs/ ▶ **noun** an orchid of (or formerly of) a genus native to north temperate regions, characterized by a tuberous root and an erect fleshy stem bearing a spike of typically purple or pinkish flowers.
● Genus *Orchis* (or *Dactylorhiza*), family Orchidaceae.
– ORIGIN modern Latin, based on Greek *orkhis*, literally 'testicle' (with reference to the shape of its tuber).

orchitis /ɔːˈkʌɪtɪs/ ▶ **noun** [mass noun] Medicine inflammation of one or both of the testicles.
– ORIGIN late 18th cent.: modern Latin, from Greek *orkhis* 'testicle' + **-ITIS**.

orcinol /ˈɔːsɪnɒl/ ▶ **noun** [mass noun] Chemistry a crystalline compound extracted from certain lichens and used to make dyes. ● Alternative name: **2-hydroxyphenylmethanol**; chem. formula: $C_7H_8O_2$.
– ORIGIN mid 19th cent.: from modern Latin *orcina*, from Italian *orcello* 'orchil'.

Orczy /ˈɔːtsi/, Baroness Emmusca (1865–1947), Hungarian-born British novelist. Her best-known novel is *The Scarlet Pimpernel* (1905).

ord. ▶ **abbreviation** ■ order. ■ ordinary.

ordain ▶ **verb** [with obj.] **1** make (someone) a priest or minister; confer holy orders on.
2 order (something) officially: *equal punishment was ordained for the two crimes* | [with clause] *the king ordained that these courts should be revived.* ■ (of God or fate) decide (something) in advance: *the path ordained by God.*
– DERIVATIVES **ordainer** noun, **ordainment** noun.
– ORIGIN Middle English (also in the sense 'put in order'): from Anglo-Norman French *ordeiner*, from Latin *ordinare*, from *ordo, ordin-* (see **ORDER**).

ordeal ▶ **noun 1** a very unpleasant and prolonged experience: *the* **ordeal of** *having to give evidence.*
2 historical an ancient test of guilt or innocence by subjection of the accused to severe pain, survival of which was taken as divine proof of innocence.
– ORIGIN Old English *ordāl, ordēl*, of Germanic origin; related to German *urteilen* 'give judgement', from a base meaning 'share out'. The word is not found in Middle English (except once in Chaucer's *Troilus*); modern use of sense 2 began in the late 16th cent., whence sense 1 (mid 17th cent.).

order ▶ **noun 1** [mass noun] the arrangement or disposition of people or things in relation to each other according to a particular sequence, pattern, or method: *I filed the cards in alphabetical order.* ■ a state in which everything is in its correct or appropriate place: *she tried to put her shattered thoughts into some semblance of order.* ■ a state in which the laws and rules regulating public behaviour are observed and authority is obeyed: *the army was deployed to keep order.* ■ the prescribed or established procedure followed by a meeting, legislative assembly, debate, or court of law: *the meeting was* **called to order**. ■ a stated form of liturgical service, or of administration of a rite, prescribed by ecclesiastical authority.
2 an authoritative command or instruction: *he was not going to take orders from a mere administrator* | [with infinitive] *the skipper gave the order to abandon ship.* ■ a verbal or written request for something to be made, supplied, or served: *the firm has won an order for six tankers.* ■ a thing made, supplied, or served as a result of an order: *he would deliver special orders for the Sunday dinner.* ■ a written direction of a court or judge: *she was admitted to hospital under a guardianship order.* ■ a written direction to pay money or deliver property.
3 a particular social, political, or economic system: *they were dedicated to overthrowing the established order.* ■ (often **orders**) a social class: *the upper social orders.* ■ a rank in the Christian ministry, especially that of bishop, priest, or deacon. ■ (**orders**) the rank of a member of the clergy or an ordained minister of the Church: *he took priest's orders.* See also **HOLY ORDERS**. ■ Theology any of the nine grades of angelic beings in the celestial hierarchy as formulated by Pseudo-Dionysius.
4 (also **Order**) a society of monks, nuns, or friars living under the same religious, moral, and social regulations and discipline: *the Franciscan Order.* ■ historical a society of knights bound by a common rule of life and having a combined military and monastic character. ■ an institution founded by a monarch along the lines of a medieval crusading monastic order for the purpose of honouring meritorious conduct. ■ the insignia worn by members of an order of honour or merit. ■ a Masonic or similar fraternity.
5 [in sing.] the quality or nature of something: *poetry of the highest* **order**. ■ [with adj.] the overall state or condition of something: *the house had only just been vacated and was in good order.*
6 Biology a principal taxonomic category that ranks below class and above family.
7 any of the five classical styles of architecture (Doric, Ionic, Corinthian, Tuscan, and Composite) based on the proportions of columns and the style of their decoration. ■ any style of architecture subject to uniform established proportions.
8 [mass noun] [with modifier] Military equipment or uniform for a specified purpose or of a specified type: *the platoon changed from drill order into PT kit.* ■ (**the order**) the position in which a rifle is held after ordering arms. See **ORDER ARMS** below.
9 Mathematics the degree of complexity of an equation, expression, etc., as denoted by an ordinal number. ■ the number of differentiations required to reach the highest derivative in a differential equation. ■ the number of elements in a finite group. ■ the number of rows or columns in a square matrix.
▶ **verb 1** [reporting verb] give an authoritative instruction to do something: [with obj. and infinitive] *she ordered me to leave* | [with direct speech] *'Stop frowning,' he ordered* | [with clause] *he ordered that the ship be abandoned* | [with obj.] *the judge ordered a retrial.* ■ [with obj.] (**order someone about/around**) continually tell someone to do things in an overbearing way. ■ [with obj. and complement] N. Amer. command (something) to be done or (someone) to be treated in a particular way: *he ordered the anchor dropped.*
2 [with obj.] request (something) to be made, supplied, or served: *my mate ordered the tickets last week* | [with two objs] *I asked the security guard to order me a taxi* | [no obj.] *are you ready to order, sir?*
3 [with obj.] arrange (something) in a methodical way: *all entries are ordered by date* | (as adj., in combination **-ordered**) *her normally well-ordered life.*
– PHRASES **by order** according to directions given by the proper authority. **in order 1** according to a particular sequence. **2** in the correct condition for operation or use. **3** in accordance with the rules of procedure at a meeting, legislative assembly, etc. ■ appropriate in the circumstances: *a little bit of flattery was now in order.* **in order for** (or **that**) so that: *staff must be committed to the change in order for it to succeed.* **in order to do something** with the purpose of doing something: *he slouched into his seat in order to avoid drawing attention to himself.* **of the order of** chiefly Brit. **1** approximately: *sales increases are of the order of 20%.* **2** Mathematics having the order of magnitude specified by. **on order** (of goods) requested but not yet received from the supplier or manufacturer. **on the order of** chiefly N. Amer. **1** approximately. **2** similar to: *singers on the order of Janis Joplin.* **Order!** (or **Order! Order!**) a call for silence or the observance of the prescribed procedures by someone in charge of a meeting, legislative assembly, etc. **order arms** Military hold a rifle with its butt on the ground close to one's right side. **order of battle** the units, formations, and equipment of a military force. **the order of the day 1** the prevailing custom or state of affairs: *on Sundays, a black suit was the order of the day* | *confusion would seem to be the order of the day.* **2** (in a legislature) the business to be considered on a particular day. **orders are orders** commands must be obeyed, however much one may disagree with them. **order to view** Brit. an estate agent's request to an occupier to allow inspection of their premises by a client. **out of order 1** (of a device) not working properly or at all. **2** not in the correct sequence. **3** not according to the rules of a meeting, legislative assembly, etc. ■ Brit. informal (of a person or their behaviour) unacceptable or wrong: *Chris was well out of order.* **to order** according to a customer's particular requirements: *the jumpers are knitted to order.*
– ORIGIN Middle English: from Old French *ordre*, from Latin *ordo, ordin-* 'row, series, rank'.

order book ▶ **noun** chiefly Brit. a book in which orders are entered as they are received by a business, especially regarded as a measure of the organization's success.

ordered pair ▶ **noun** Mathematics a pair of elements *a, b* having the property that $(a, b) = (u, v)$ if and only if $a = u$, $b = v$.

order form ▶ **noun** a printed form on which a customer writes the details of a product or service they wish to order.

Order in Council ▶ **noun** Brit. a sovereign's order on an administrative matter, given on the advice of the Privy Council.

orderly ▶ **adjective 1** neatly and methodically arranged: *an orderly arrangement of objects.* ■ (of a person or group) well behaved.
2 [attrib.] Military charged with the conveyance or execution of orders: *the orderly sergeant.*
▶ **noun** (pl. **orderlies**) **1** an attendant in a hospital responsible for the non-medical care of patients and the maintenance of order and cleanliness.
2 a soldier who carries orders or performs minor tasks for an officer.
– DERIVATIVES **orderliness** noun.

orderly book ▶ **noun** Brit. Military a regimental or company book in which orders are entered.

orderly officer ▶ **noun** Brit. Military the officer who is in charge of the security and administration of a unit or establishment for a day at a time.

orderly room ▶ **noun** Military the room in a barracks used for regimental or company business.

Order of Australia an order instituted in 1975 to honour Australians for outstanding achievement and divided into four classes: Companion (AC), Officer (AO), Member (AM), and Medal of the Order of Australia (OAM). A fifth class of Knight or Dame, above Companion, was abolished in 1986.

Order of Canada an order instituted in 1967 to honour Canadians for outstanding achievement and divided into three classes: Companion (CC), Officer (OC), and Member (CM).

order of magnitude ▶ **noun** a class in a system of classification determined by size, typically in powers of ten. ■ size or quantity: *the new problems were of a different order of magnitude.*

Order of Merit (in the UK) an order founded in 1902, for distinguished achievement, with membership limited to twenty-four people.

Order of St Michael and St George (in the UK) an order of knighthood instituted in 1818, divided into three classes: Knight or Dame Grand Cross of the Order of St Michael and St George (GCMG), Knight or Dame Commander (KCMG/DCMG), and Companion (CMG).

Order of the Bath (in the UK) an order of knighthood, so called from the ceremonial bath which originally preceded installation. It has four classes of membership, which are: Knight or Dame Grand Cross of the Order of the Bath (GCB), Knight or Dame Commander (KCB/DCB), and Companion (CB).

Order of the British Empire (in the UK) an order of knighthood instituted in 1917 and divided into five classes, each with military and civilian divisions. The classes are: Knight or Dame Grand Cross of the Order of the British Empire (GBE), Knight or Dame Commander (KBE/DBE), Commander (CBE), Officer (OBE), and Member (MBE). The two highest classes entail the awarding of a knighthood.

Order of the Garter the highest order of English knighthood, founded by Edward III *c.*1344. According to tradition, the garter was that of the Countess of Salisbury, which the king placed on his own leg after it fell off while she was dancing with him. The king's comment to those present, 'Honi soit qui mal y pense' (shame be to him who thinks evil of it), was adopted as the motto of the order.

Order of the Thistle a Scottish order of knighthood instituted in 1687 by James II.

Order Paper ▶ **noun** Brit. & Canadian a paper on which the day's business for a legislative assembly is entered.
– PHRASES **die on the Order Paper** Canadian (of a bill) fail to be voted on before the end of a legislative session.

ordinal ▶ **noun 1** short for **ORDINAL NUMBER**.
2 Christian Church, historical a service book, especially one with the forms of service used at ordinations.
▶ **adjective 1** relating to the order of something in a series: *ordinal scales.* ■ relating to an ordinal number.
2 Biology relating to a taxonomic order.
– ORIGIN Middle English (in sense 2 of the noun): the noun from medieval Latin *ordinale* (neuter); the adjective from late Latin *ordinalis* 'relating to order in a series', from Latin *ordo, ordin-* (see **ORDER**).

ordinal number ▶ **noun** a number defining the position of something in a series, such as 'first', 'second', or 'third'. Ordinal numbers are used as adjectives, nouns, and pronouns. Compare with **CARDINAL NUMBER**.

ordinance ▶ **noun** formal **1** an authoritative order. ■ N. Amer. a municipal by-law.

2 a religious rite.
3 archaic term for **ORDONNANCE**.
– ORIGIN Middle English (also in the sense 'arrangement in ranks'): from Old French *ordenance*, from medieval Latin *ordinantia*, from Latin *ordinare* 'put in order' (see **ORDAIN**).

ordinand /ˈɔːdɪnand/ ▶ **noun** a person who is training to be ordained as a priest or minister.
– ORIGIN mid 19th cent.: from Latin *ordinandus*, gerundive of *ordinare* 'put in order' (see **ORDAIN**).

ordinarily /ˈɔːd(ə)n(ə)rɪli, ˌɔːdɪˈnɛrɪli/ ▶ **adverb**
1 [sentence adverb] usually: *a person who is ordinarily resident in the United Kingdom*.
2 in a normal way: *an effort to behave ordinarily*.

ordinary ▶ **adjective 1** with no special or distinctive features; normal: *he sets out to depict ordinary people | it was just an ordinary evening*. ■ not interesting or exceptional; commonplace: *she seemed very ordinary*.
2 (especially of a judge or bishop) exercising authority by virtue of office and not by deputation.
▶ **noun** (pl. **ordinaries**) **1** (**the ordinary**) what is commonplace or standard: *their* **clichés** *were vested with enough emotion to elevate them above the ordinary*.
2 Law, Brit. a judge who exercises authority by virtue of office and not by deputation.
3 (**the Ordinary**) a clergyman, such as an archbishop in a province or a bishop in a diocese, with immediate jurisdiction.
4 (**Ordinary**) those parts of a Roman Catholic service, especially the Mass, which do not vary from day to day. ■ a rule or book laying down the order of divine service.
5 Heraldry any of the simplest principal charges used in coats of arms (especially chief, pale, bend, fess, bar, chevron, cross, saltire).
6 short for **ORDINARY SHARE**.
7 archaic a meal provided at a fixed time and price at an inn. ■ an inn providing a meal at a fixed time and price.
8 historical, chiefly N. Amer. a penny-farthing bicycle.
– PHRASES **in ordinary** Brit. (in titles) by permanent appointment, especially to the royal household: *painter in ordinary to Her Majesty*. **in the ordinary way** Brit. if the circumstances are or were not exceptional; normally. **out of the ordinary** unusual: *nothing out of the ordinary happened*.
– DERIVATIVES **ordinariness** noun.
– ORIGIN late Middle English: the noun partly via Old French; the adjective from Latin *ordinarius* 'orderly' (reinforced by French *ordinaire*), from *ordo, ordin-* 'order'.

ordinary grade ▶ **noun** (in Scotland) the lower of the two main levels of the Scottish Certificate of Education examination. Compare with **HIGHER**.

ordinary level ▶ **noun** [mass noun] historical (in the UK except Scotland) the lower of the two main levels of the GCE examination. Compare with **ADVANCED LEVEL**.

ordinary ray ▶ **noun** Optics (in double refraction) the ray that obeys the ordinary laws of refraction.

ordinary seaman ▶ **noun** the lowest rank of sailor in the Royal Navy, below able seaman.

ordinary share ▶ **noun** Brit. a share entitling its holder to dividends which vary in amount and may even be missed, depending on the fortunes of the company. Compare with **PREFERENCE SHARE**.

ordinate /ˈɔːdɪnət/ ▶ **noun** Mathematics a straight line from any point drawn parallel to one coordinate axis and meeting the other, especially a coordinate measured parallel to the vertical. Compare with **ABSCISSA**.
– ORIGIN late 17th cent.: from Latin *linea ordinata applicata* 'line applied parallel', from *ordinare* 'put in order'.

ordination ▶ **noun** [mass noun] **1** the action of ordaining someone in holy orders. ■ [count noun] a ceremony in which someone is ordained.
2 [count noun] chiefly Ecology a statistical technique in which data from a large number of sites or populations are represented as points in a multidimensional space.
3 literary the action of decreeing or ordaining.
– ORIGIN late Middle English (in the general sense 'arrangement in order'): from Latin *ordinatio(n-)*, from Latin *ordinare* 'put in order' (see **ORDAIN**).

ordnance /ˈɔːdnəns/ ▶ **noun** [mass noun] **1** mounted guns; artillery. ■ US munitions.
2 a branch of government service dealing especially with military stores and materials.
– ORIGIN late Middle English: variant of **ORDINANCE**.

ordnance datum ▶ **noun** Brit. the mean sea level as defined for Ordnance Survey.

Ordnance Survey (in the UK) an official survey organization, originally under the Master of the Ordnance, preparing large-scale detailed maps of the whole country.

ordonnance /ˈɔːdənəns/ ▶ **noun** [mass noun] the systematic or orderly arrangement of parts, especially in art and architecture.
– ORIGIN mid 17th cent.: from French, alteration of Old French *ordenance* (see **ORDINANCE**).

Ordovician /ˌɔːdəˈvɪʃɪən/ ▶ **adjective** Geology relating to or denoting the second period of the Palaeozoic era, between the Cambrian and Silurian periods. ■ (as noun **the Ordovician**) the Ordovician period or the system of rocks deposited during it.

> The Ordovician lasted from about 510 to 439 million years ago. It saw the diversification of many invertebrate groups and the appearance of the first vertebrates (jawless fish).

– ORIGIN late 19th cent.: from *Ordovices*, the Latin name of an ancient British tribe in North Wales, + **-IAN**.

ordure /ˈɔːdjʊə/ ▶ **noun** [mass noun] excrement; dung. ■ something regarded as vile or abhorrent: *can you give credence to this ordure?*
– ORIGIN Middle English: from Old French, from *ord* 'foul', from Latin *horridus* (see **HORRID**).

Ordzhonikidze /ˌɔːdʒɒnəˈkɪdzi/ former name (1931–44 and 1954–93) for **VLADIKAVKAZ**.

ore ▶ **noun** a naturally occurring solid material from which a metal or valuable mineral can be extracted profitably.
– ORIGIN Old English *ōra* 'unwrought metal', of West Germanic origin; influenced in form by Old English *ār* 'bronze' (related to Latin *aes* 'crude metal, bronze').

Ore. ▶ **abbreviation** Oregon.

øre /ˈəːrə/ ▶ **noun** (pl. **same**) a monetary unit of Denmark and Norway, equal to one hundredth of a krone.
– ORIGIN Danish and Norwegian.

öre /ˈəːrə/ ▶ **noun** (pl. **same**) a monetary unit of Sweden, equal to one hundredth of a krona.
– ORIGIN Swedish.

oread /ˈɔːrɪad/ ▶ **noun** Greek & Roman Mythology a nymph believed to inhabit mountains.
– ORIGIN from Latin *Oreas, Oread-*, from Greek *Oreias*, from *oros* 'mountain'.

orebody ▶ **noun** a connected mass of ore in a mine or suitable for mining.

Örebro /ˌəːrəˈbruː/ an industrial city in south central Sweden; pop. 132,277 (2008).

orecchiette /ˌɒrɛkɪˈɛtɪ/ ▶ **plural noun** small pieces of ear-shaped pasta.
– ORIGIN Italian, literally 'little ears'.

orectic /ɒˈrɛktɪk/ ▶ **adjective** technical of or concerning desire or appetite.
– ORIGIN late 17th cent. (as a noun in the sense 'stimulant for the appetite'): from Greek *orektikos*, from *oregein* 'stretch out, reach for'. The current sense dates from the late 18th cent.

Oreg. ▶ **abbreviation** Oregon.

oregano /ˌɒrɪˈɡɑːnəʊ, əˈrɛɡənəʊ/ ▶ **noun** [mass noun] an aromatic Eurasian plant related to marjoram, with small purple flowers and leaves used as a culinary herb. ● *Origanum vulgare*, family Labiatae.
– ORIGIN late 18th cent.: from Spanish, variant of **ORIGANUM**.

Oregon /ˈɒrɪɡ(ə)n/ a state in the north-western US, on the Pacific coast; pop. 3,790,060 (est. 2008); capital, Salem. British claims to Oregon were formally ceded to the US in 1846 and it became the 33rd state in 1859.
– DERIVATIVES **Oregonian** adjective & noun.

Oregon grape ▶ **noun** a North American mahonia which forms a spreading bush with spiny leaves. ● *Mahonia aquifolium*, family Berberidaceae.

Oregon pine ▶ **noun** another term for **DOUGLAS FIR**.

Oregon Trail a route across the central US, from the Missouri to Oregon, some 3,000 km (2,000 miles) in length. It was used chiefly in the 1840s by settlers moving west.

Orel /ɒˈrɛl/ an industrial city in SW Russia; pop. 320,800 (est. 2008).

Ore Mountains another name for the **ERZGEBIRGE**.

Orenburg /ˈɒrənbəːɡ/ a city in southern Russia, on the Ural River; pop. 526,400 (est. 2008). Former name (1938–57) **CHKALOV**.

orenda /ɒˈrɛndə/ ▶ **noun** [mass noun] invisible magic power believed by the Iroquois to pervade all natural objects as a spiritual energy.
– ORIGIN early 20th cent.: coined in English as the supposed Huron form of a Mohawk word.

Oreo /ˈɔːrɪəʊ/ ▶ **noun** (pl. **Oreos**) US trademark a chocolate biscuit with a white cream filling. ■ informal, derogatory a black American who is seen, especially by other black people, as wishing to be part of the white establishment.
– ORIGIN early 20th cent.: invented name.

Orestes /ɒˈrɛstiːz/ Greek Mythology the son of Agamemnon and Clytemnestra. He killed his mother and her lover Aegisthus to avenge his father's murder.

Øresund /ˌəːrəˈsʊnd/ a narrow channel between Sweden and the Danish island of Zealand. Also called **THE SOUND**.

orf ▶ **noun** [mass noun] an infectious disease of sheep and goats caused by a poxvirus, characterized by skin lesions and secondary bacterial infection.
– ORIGIN mid 19th cent.: probably from Old Norse *hrufa*.

orfe /ɔːf/ ▶ **noun** a silvery freshwater fish of the carp family, which is fished commercially in eastern Europe. Also called **IDE**. ● *Leuciscus idus*, family Cyprinidae. See also **GOLDEN ORFE**.
– ORIGIN late 19th cent.: from German; perhaps related to French *orphe*, Latin *orphus*, and Greek *orphos* 'sea perch'.

Orff /ɔːf/, Carl (1895–1982), German composer. He is best known for his secular cantata *Carmina Burana* (1937), based on a collection of characteristically bawdy medieval Latin poems.

organ ▶ **noun 1** a part of an organism which is typically self-contained and has a specific vital function: *the internal organs*. ■ used euphemistically to refer to the penis. ■ archaic a region of the brain formerly held to be the seat of a particular faculty.
2 a large musical instrument having rows of pipes supplied with air from bellows (now usually electrically powered), and played using a keyboard or by an automatic mechanism. The pipes are generally arranged in ranks of a particular type, each controlled by a stop, and often into larger sets linked to separate keyboards. ■ a smaller instrument without pipes, producing similar sounds electronically. See also **REED ORGAN**.
3 a department or organization that performs a specified function: *the organs of local government*.
4 a newspaper or periodical which promotes the views of a political party or movement: *he repositioned the journal as a leading organ of neoconservatism*.
– ORIGIN late Old English, via Latin from Greek *organon* 'tool, instrument, sense organ', reinforced in Middle English by Old French *organe*.

organ-blower ▶ **noun** a person or mechanism working the bellows of an organ.

organdie /ˈɔːɡ(ə)ndi, ɔːˈɡandi/ (US also **organdy**) ▶ **noun** (pl. **organdies**) [mass noun] a fine translucent cotton muslin that is usually stiffened and is used for women's clothing.
– ORIGIN early 19th cent.: from French *organdi*, of unknown origin.

organelle /ˌɔːɡəˈnɛl/ ▶ **noun** Biology any of a number of organized or specialized structures within a living cell.
– ORIGIN early 20th cent.: from modern Latin *organella*, diminutive of *organum* 'instrument, tool' (see **ORGAN**).

organ grinder ▶ **noun** a street musician who plays a barrel organ. ■ a person in control of another. [with reference to the tradition of an organ grinder's keeping a monkey trained to collect money.]

organic ▶ **adjective 1** relating to or derived from living matter: *organic soils*. ■ Chemistry relating to or denoting compounds containing carbon (other than simple binary compounds and salts) and chiefly or ultimately of biological origin. Compare with **INORGANIC**.
2 (of food or farming methods) produced or involving production without the use of chemical fertilizers, pesticides, or other artificial chemicals.
3 Physiology relating to a bodily organ or organs. ■ Medicine (of a disease) affecting the structure of an organ.
4 denoting or characterized by a harmonious relationship between the elements of a whole: *the organic unity of the integral work of art*. ■ characterized by gradual or natural development: *the organic growth of community projects*.

O

▸ noun (usu. **organics**) **1** a food produced by organic farming.
2 an organic chemical compound.
– DERIVATIVES **organically** adverb.
– ORIGIN late Middle English: via Latin from Greek *organikos* 'relating to an organ or instrument'.

organic chemistry ▸ noun [mass noun] the branch of chemistry that deals with carbon compounds (other than simple salts such as carbonates, oxides, and carbides).

organicism ▸ noun [mass noun] **1** the doctrine that everything in nature has an organic basis or is part of an organic whole.
2 the use or advocacy of literary or artistic forms in which the parts are connected or coordinated in the whole.
– DERIVATIVES **organicist** adjective & noun.
– ORIGIN mid 19th cent.: from French *organicisme*.

organic law ▸ noun a law stating the formal constitution of a nation.

organigram /ɔːˈɡanɪɡram/ (also **organogram**) ▸ noun another term for ORGANIZATION CHART.
– ORIGIN 1960s: from ORGANIZATION + -GRAM[1].

organism ▸ noun an individual animal, plant, or single-celled life form. ▪ the material structure of an organism. ▪ a system or organization consisting of interdependent parts, compared to a living being: *the Church is a divinely constituted organism*.
– DERIVATIVES **organismal** adjective, **organismic** adjective.
– ORIGIN early 18th cent. (in the sense 'organization', from ORGANIZE): current senses derive from French *organisme*.

organist ▸ noun a person who plays the organ.

organization (also **organisation**) ▸ noun **1** an organized group of people with a particular purpose, such as a business or government department: *a research organization*.
2 [mass noun] the action of organizing something: *the organization of conferences*. ▪ the quality of being systematic and efficient: *his lack of organization*.
3 [mass noun] the way in which the elements of a whole are arranged: *the spatial organization of the cells*.
– DERIVATIVES **organizational** adjective, **organizationally** adverb.

organization chart ▸ noun a graphic representation of the structure of an organization showing the relationships of the positions or jobs within it.

Organization for Economic Cooperation and Development (abbrev.: **OECD**) an organization formed in 1961 to assist the economy of its member nations and to promote world trade. Its members include the industrialized countries of western Europe together with Australia, Japan, New Zealand, and the US. Its headquarters are in Paris.

Organization for European Economic Cooperation (abbrev.: **OEEC**) an organization established in 1948 by sixteen western European countries to promote trade and stability. It was replaced by the Organization for Economic Cooperation and Development in 1961.

organization man ▸ noun derogatory a man who lets his individuality and personal life be dominated by the organization he serves.

Organization of African Unity (abbrev.: **OAU**) an association of African states founded in 1963 for mutual cooperation and the elimination of colonialism in Africa. In 2002 it was reconstituted as the African Union.

Organization of American States (abbrev.: **OAS**) an association including most of the countries of North and South America, originally founded in 1890 for largely commercial purposes. From 1948 it has aimed to work for peace and prosperity in the region and to uphold the sovereignty of member nations. Its headquarters are in Washington DC.

Organization of Arab Petroleum Exporting Countries (abbrev.: **OAPEC**) an association of Arab countries, founded in 1968 to promote economic cooperation and safeguard its members' interests and to ensure the supply of oil to consumer markets. Its headquarters are in Safat, Kuwait.

Organization of Central American States (abbrev.: **OCAS**) an association of Guatemala, Honduras, El Salvador, and Costa Rica founded in 1951 for economic and political cooperation.

Organization of the Petroleum Exporting Countries (abbrev.: **OPEC**) an association of the thirteen major oil-producing countries, founded in 1960 to coordinate policies. Its headquarters are in Vienna.

organize (also **organise**) ▸ verb [with obj.] **1** arrange systematically; order: *organize lessons in a planned way*. ▪ coordinate the activities of (a person or group) efficiently: *she was unsuited to anything where she had to organize herself*. ▪ form (a number of people) into a trade union or other political group: *we all believed in the need to organize women*.
2 make arrangements or preparations for (an event or activity): *social programmes are organized by the school*. ▪ take responsibility for providing or arranging: *Julie organized food and drink for the band*.
3 archaic arrange or form into a living being or tissue.
– DERIVATIVES **organizable** adjective.
– ORIGIN late Middle English: from medieval Latin *organizare*, from Latin *organum* 'instrument, tool' (see ORGAN).

organized (also **organised**) ▸ adjective arranged in a systematic way, especially on a large scale: *organized crime*. ▪ able to plan one's activities efficiently: *she used to be so organized*. ▪ having formed a trade union or other political group: *a repressive regime which crushed organized labour*.

organizer (also **organiser**) ▸ noun **1** a person who arranges an event or activity.
2 a thing used for organizing. See also PERSONAL ORGANIZER.

organ loft ▸ noun a gallery in a church or concert hall for an organ.

organo- /ˈɔːɡ(ə)nəʊ, ɔːˈɡanəʊ/ ▸ combining form **1** chiefly Biology relating to bodily organs: *organogenesis*.
2 Chemistry (forming names of classes of organic compounds containing a particular element or group) organic: *organochlorine | organophosphate*.
– ORIGIN from Greek *organon* 'organ'; sense 2 from ORGANIC.

organochlorine ▸ noun [often as modifier] any of a large group of pesticides and other synthetic organic compounds with chlorinated aromatic molecules.

organ of Corti ▸ noun Anatomy a structure in the cochlea of the inner ear which produces nerve impulses in response to sound vibrations.
– ORIGIN late 19th cent.: named after Alfonso *Corti* (1822–76), Italian anatomist.

organogenesis /ˌɔːɡ(ə)nə(ʊ)ˈdʒɛnɪsɪs, ɔːˌɡan(ə)-/ ▸ noun [mass noun] Biology the production and development of the organs of an animal or plant.

organogram ▸ noun variant spelling of ORGANIGRAM.

organoleptic /ˌɔːɡ(ə)nə(ʊ)ˈlɛptɪk/ ▸ adjective acting on, or involving the use of, the sense organs.
– ORIGIN mid 19th cent.: from French *organoleptique*, from Greek *organon* 'organ' + *lēptikos* 'disposed to take' (from *lambanein* 'take').

organometallic ▸ adjective Chemistry (of a compound) containing a metal atom bonded to an organic group or groups.

organon /ˈɔːɡ(ə)nɒn/ ▸ noun an instrument of thought, especially a means of reasoning or a system of logic.
– ORIGIN late 16th cent. (denoting a bodily organ): from Greek, literally 'instrument, organ'. *Organon* was the title of Aristotle's logical treatises.

organophosphate /ɔːˌɡanəʊˈfɒsfeɪt/ ▸ noun any organic compound whose molecule contains one or more phosphate ester groups, especially a pesticide of this kind.

organophosphorus /ˌɔːɡ(ə)nəʊˈfɒsf(ə)rəs/ ▸ noun [as modifier] denoting synthetic organic compounds containing phosphorus, especially pesticides and nerve gases of this kind.

organotherapy ▸ noun [mass noun] the treatment of disease with extracts from animal organs, especially glands.

organ pipe cactus ▸ noun a large cactus native to the south-western US, having columnar stems or branches and typically flowering at night. ● Several species in the family Cactaceae, including *Lemaireocereus marginatus* and *Cereus thurberi*.

organ-pipe coral ▸ noun a tropical coral which forms narrow parallel calcareous tubes linked by transverse plates. ● Genus *Tubipora*, order Stolonifera.

organ screen ▸ noun an ornamental screen above which the organ is placed in some cathedrals and large churches, typically between the choir and the nave.

organ stop ▸ noun a set of pipes of a similar tone in an organ. ▪ the handle of the mechanism that brings an organ stop into action.

organum /ˈɔːɡ(ə)nəm/ ▸ noun (pl. **organa** /-nə/) an early type of polyphonic music based on plainsong with an accompaniment sung below or above the melody. ▪ a part sung as an accompaniment below or above a melody.
– ORIGIN Latin, from Greek *organon*, literally 'instrument, organ'.

organza /ɔːˈɡanzə/ ▸ noun [mass noun] a thin, stiff, transparent dress fabric made of silk or a synthetic yarn.
– ORIGIN early 19th cent.: probably from French *organsin* (see ORGANZINE).

organzine /ˈɔːɡ(ə)nziːn, -ˈɡanziːn/ ▸ noun [mass noun] a silk thread made of strands twisted together in the contrary direction to that of each individual strand.
– ORIGIN late 17th cent.: from French *organsin*, from Italian *organzino*, of unknown ultimate origin.

orgasm ▸ noun the climax of sexual excitement, characterized by intensely pleasurable feelings centred in the genitals and (in men) experienced as an accompaniment to ejaculation.
▸ verb [no obj.] have an orgasm.
– ORIGIN late 17th cent.: from French *orgasme*, or from modern Latin *orgasmus*, from Greek *orgasmos*, from *organ* 'swell or be excited'.

orgasmic ▸ adjective relating to orgasm. ▪ (of a person) able to achieve orgasm. ▪ informal very enjoyable: *an orgasmic new drink*.
– DERIVATIVES **orgasmically** adverb, **orgastic** adjective, **orgastically** adverb.

OR gate ▸ noun see OR[1].

orgeat /ˈɔːdʒɪət/ ▸ noun [mass noun] a cooling drink made from orange flower water and either barley or almonds.
– ORIGIN French, from Provençal *orjat*, from *ordi* 'barley', from Latin *hordeum* 'barley'.

orgiastic ▸ adjective of or resembling an orgy: *orgiastic dancing*.
– DERIVATIVES **orgiastically** adverb.
– ORIGIN late 17th cent.: from Greek *orgiastikos*, from *orgiastēs*, agent noun from *orgiazein* 'hold an orgy'.

orgone /ˈɔːɡəʊn/ ▸ noun [mass noun] a supposed excess sexual energy or life force distributed throughout the universe which can be collected and stored for subsequent therapeutic use.
– ORIGIN 1940s: coined by the Austrian-born psychoanalyst Wilhelm Reich (1897–1957), from ORGANISM or ORGANIC + *-one*, on the pattern of HORMONE.

orgulous /ˈɔːɡjʊləs/ ▸ adjective literary haughty.
– ORIGIN Middle English: from Old French *orguillus*, from *orguill* 'pride'. The word was rare from the 16th cent. until used by Robert Southey and Sir Walter Scott as a historical archaism and affected by 19th-cent. journalists.

orgy ▸ noun (pl. **orgies**) **1** a wild party characterized by excessive drinking and indiscriminate sexual activity. ▪ an instance of excessive indulgence in a specified activity: *an orgy of buying*.
2 (**orgies**) historical secret rites used in the worship of Bacchus, Dionysus, and other Greek and Roman deities, celebrated with dancing, drunkenness, and singing.
– ORIGIN early 16th cent.: originally plural, from French *orgies*, via Latin from Greek *orgia* 'secret rites or revels'.

oribi /ˈɒrɪbi/ ▸ noun (pl. **same** or **oribis**) a small antelope of the African savannah, having a reddish-fawn back, white underparts, and short vertical horns. ● *Ourebia ourebi*, family Bovidae.
– ORIGIN late 18th cent.: from Afrikaans, from Khoikhoi.

orichalc /ˈɒrɪkalk/ (also **orichalcum**) ▸ noun [mass noun] a yellow metal prized in ancient times, probably a form of brass or a similar alloy.
– ORIGIN late Middle English: via Latin from Greek *oreikhalkon*, literally 'mountain copper'.

oriel /ˈɔːrɪəl/ ▸ noun a large upper-storey bay with a window, supported by brackets or on corbels. ▪ (also **oriel window**) a window in an oriel.
– ORIGIN late Middle English: from Old French *oriol* 'gallery', of unknown origin; compare with medieval Latin *oriolum* 'upper chamber'.

orient ▸ noun /ˈɔːrɪənt, ˈɒr-/ **1** (**the Orient**) literary the countries of the East, especially East Asia.
2 [mass noun] the special lustre of a pearl of the finest quality (with reference to fine pearls from the East). ▪ [count noun] a pearl of the finest quality.
▸ adjective /ˈɔːrɪənt, ˈɒr-/ **1** literary situated in or belonging to the east; oriental.
2 (especially of precious stones) lustrous.

▸ **verb** /ˈɔːrɪɛnt, ˈɒr-/ [with obj. and adverbial] **1** align or position (something) relative to the points of a compass or other specified positions: *the fires are oriented in direct line with the midsummer sunset.* ■ **(orient oneself)** find one's position in relation to unfamiliar surroundings: *there were no street names to enable her to orient herself.* ■ guide (someone) in a specified direction.
2 tailor or adapt (something) to specified circumstances: *magazines oriented to the business community* | (as adj., in combination **-oriented**) *market-oriented economic reforms.*
– ORIGIN late Middle English: via Old French from Latin *orient-* 'rising or east', from *oriri* 'to rise'.

oriental (also **Oriental**) ▸ **adjective 1** of, from, or characteristic of Asia, especially East Asia: *oriental countries.* ■ **(Oriental)** Zoology relating to or denoting a zoogeographical region comprising Asia south of the Himalayas and Indonesia west of Wallace's line. Distinctive animals include pandas, gibbons, tree shrews, tarsiers, and moonrats.
2 (of a pearl or other jewel) orient.
▸ **noun** often offensive a person of Asian, especially East Asian, descent.
– DERIVATIVES **orientalize** (also **orientalise**) verb, **orientally** adverb.
– ORIGIN late Middle English: from Old French, or from Latin *orientalis*, from *orient-* (see **ORIENT**).

> **USAGE** The term **oriental** has an out-of-date feel as a term denoting people from Asia; it tends to be associated with a rather offensive stereotype of the people and their customs as inscrutable and exotic. In US English **Asian** is the standard accepted term in modern use; in British English, where **Asian** tends to denote people from the Indian subcontinent, specific terms such as **Chinese** or **Japanese** are more likely to be used.

orientalia /ˌɔːrɪɛnˈteɪlɪə, ɒr-/ ▸ **plural noun** books and other items relating to or characteristic of the Orient.
– ORIGIN early 20th cent.: from Latin, neuter plural of *orientalis* 'oriental'.

orientalism ▸ **noun** [mass noun] style, artefacts, or traits considered characteristic of the peoples and cultures of Asia. ■ the representation of Asia in a stereotyped way that is regarded as embodying a colonialist attitude.
– DERIVATIVES **orientalist** noun & adjective.

oriental poppy ▸ **noun** a SW Asian poppy with coarse deeply cut hairy leaves and large scarlet flowers with a black mark at the base of each petal, widely grown as a garden perennial. ● *Papaver orientale*, family Papaveraceae.

oriental sore ▸ **noun** [mass noun] Medicine a form of leishmaniasis occurring in Asia and Africa, causing open ulcers.

oriental topaz ▸ **noun** a yellow sapphire.

orientate ▸ **verb** another term for **ORIENT**.
– ORIGIN mid 19th cent.: probably a back-formation from **ORIENTATION**.

orientation ▸ **noun** [mass noun] **1** the action of orienting someone or something relative to the points of a compass or other specified positions: *studies of locational awareness and orientation in young children.* ■ [count noun] the relative position or direction of something: *using the orientation of a building to capture energy from the sun.* ■ Zoology the faculty by which birds and other animals find their way back to a place after going or being taken to a place distant from it.
2 a person's basic attitude, beliefs, or feelings in relation to a particular subject or issue: *his book is well worth reading, regardless of your political orientation.*
3 familiarization with something: *many judges give instructions to assist jury orientation.*
– DERIVATIVES **orientational** adjective.
– ORIGIN mid 19th cent.: apparently from **ORIENT**.

orientation course ▸ **noun** chiefly N. Amer. a course giving information to newcomers to a university or other institution.

orienteer ▸ **noun** a person who takes part in orienteering.
▸ **verb** [no obj.] take part in orienteering.

orienteering ▸ **noun** [mass noun] a competitive sport in which runners have to find their way across rough country with the aid of a map and compass.
– ORIGIN 1940s: from Swedish *orientering*.

Orient Express a train which ran between Paris and Istanbul and other Balkan cities, via Vienna, from 1883 to 1961. Since 1961 the name has been used for various trains running over parts of the old route.

orifice /ˈɒrɪfɪs/ ▸ **noun** an opening, particularly one in the body such as a nostril or the anus.
– ORIGIN late Middle English: from French, from late Latin *orificium*, from *os, or-* 'mouth' + *facere* 'make'.

oriflamme /ˈɒrɪflam/ ▸ **noun** historical the sacred scarlet banner of St Denis, given to early French kings by the abbot of St Denis on setting out for war. ■ literary a bright, conspicuous object: *her hair is swept up to a glossy oriflamme.*
– ORIGIN late Middle English: from Old French, from Latin *aurum* 'gold' + *flamma* 'flame'.

origami /ˌɒrɪˈɡɑːmi/ ▸ **noun** [mass noun] the Japanese art of folding paper into decorative shapes and figures.
– ORIGIN Japanese, from *oru, -ori* 'fold' + *kami* 'paper'.

origanum /ɒˈrɪɡ(ə)nəm/ ▸ **noun** an aromatic plant of a genus that includes marjoram and oregano. ● Genus *Origanum*, family Labiatae.
– ORIGIN Latin, from Greek *origanon*, perhaps from *oros* 'mountain' + *ganos* 'brightness'.

Origen /ˈɒrɪdʒ(ə)n/ (*c.*185–*c.*254), Christian scholar and theologian, probably born in Alexandria. His most famous work was the *Hexapla*, an edition of the Old Testament with six or more parallel versions. His Neoplatonist theology was ultimately rejected by Church orthodoxy.

origin ▸ **noun 1** (also **origins**) the point or place where something begins, arises, or is derived: *his theory of the origin of life* | *the name is Norse in origin* | *the terminology has its origins in America.* ■ a person's social background or ancestry: *a family of peasant origin* | *a voice that betrays his Welsh origins.*
2 Anatomy the more fixed end or attachment of a muscle.
3 Mathematics a fixed point from which coordinates are measured.
– ORIGIN early 16th cent.: from French *origine*, from Latin *origo, origin-*, from *oriri* 'to rise'.

original ▸ **adjective 1** present or existing from the beginning; first or earliest: *the original owner of the house* | *the plasterwork is probably original.*
2 created personally by a particular artist, writer, musician, etc.; not a copy: *original Rembrandts.*
3 not dependent on other people's ideas; inventive or novel: *a subtle and original thinker.*
▸ **noun 1** the earliest form of something, from which copies may be made: *the portrait may be a copy of the original* | *one set of originals and four photocopies.* ■ **(the original)** the language in which something was first written: *the study of Russian texts in the original.* ■ **(the original of)** a person or place on which a character or location in a literary work is based: *the house is reputed to be the original of Mansfield Park.* ■ a book or recording that has not been previously made available in a different form: *paperback originals.* ■ a garment made to order from a design specially prepared for a fashion collection.
2 an eccentric or unusual person: *he was one of the true originals.*
– ORIGIN Middle English (the earliest use being in the phrase *original sin*): from Old French, or from Latin *originalis*, from *origin-* (see **ORIGIN**).

original gravity ▸ **noun** [mass noun] the relative density of the wort before it is fermented to produce beer, being chiefly dependent on the quantity of fermentable sugars in solution. It is regarded as a guide to the alcoholic strength of the finished beer.

original instrument ▸ **noun** a musical instrument, or a copy of one, dating from the time the music played on it was composed.

originalism ▸ **noun** [mass noun] the principle or belief that the original intent of an author should be adhered to in later interpretations of a work. ■ US the judicial interpretation of the constitution which aims to follow closely the original intentions of those who drafted it.

originality ▸ **noun** [mass noun] the ability to think independently and creatively: *she's a writer of great originality.* ■ the quality of being novel or unusual: *he congratulated her on the originality of her costume.*

originally ▸ **adverb 1** from or in the beginning; at first: *potatoes originally came from South America.*
2 in a novel and inventive way: *the suggestions so originally and persuasively outlined.*

original print ▸ **noun** Art a print made directly from an artist's own woodcut, etching, or other original production, and printed under the artist's supervision.

original sin ▸ **noun** [mass noun] Christian Theology the tendency to evil supposedly innate in all human beings, held to be inherited from Adam in consequence of the Fall. The concept of original sin was established by the writings of St Augustine.

originate ▸ **verb** [no obj., with adverbial] have a specified beginning: *the word originated as a marketing term.* ■ [with obj.] create or initiate (something): *he is responsible for originating this particular cliché.*
– DERIVATIVES **origination** noun, **originative** adjective.
– ORIGIN mid 17th cent.: from medieval Latin *originat-* 'caused to begin', from Latin *origo, origin-* 'source, origin'.

origination fee ▸ **noun** Finance a fee charged by a lender on entering into a loan agreement to cover the cost of processing the loan.

originator ▸ **noun** a person who creates or initiates something: *Wegener was the originator of the theory of continental drift.*

Orimulsion /ˌɒrɪˈmʌlʃ(ə)n/ ▸ **noun** [mass noun] trademark a fuel consisting of an emulsion of bitumen in water.
– ORIGIN 1980s: blend of *Orinoco* (the name of an oil belt in Venezuela, where the bitumen was originally extracted) and **EMULSION**.

O-ring ▸ **noun** a gasket or seal in the form of a ring with a circular cross section, typically made of rubber and used especially in swivelling joints.

Orinoco /ˌɒrɪˈnəʊkəʊ/ a river in northern South America, which rises in SE Venezuela and flows 2,060 km (1,280 miles), entering the Atlantic Ocean through a vast delta. For part of its length it forms the border between Colombia and Venezuela.

oriole /ˈɔːrɪəʊl, ˈɔːrɪəl/ ▸ **noun 1** a tree-dwelling Old World bird of which the male typically has bright yellow and black plumage. ● Family Oriolidae and genus *Oriolus*: many species, including the **golden oriole**.
2 a New World bird of the American blackbird family, with black and orange or yellow plumage. ● Genus *Icterus*, family Icteridae (sometimes called the **American oriole family**): many species.
– ORIGIN late 18th cent.: from medieval Latin *oriolus* (in Old French *oriol*), from Latin *aureolus*, diminutive of *aureus* 'golden', from *aurum* 'gold'.

Orion /əˈrʌɪən/ **1** Greek Mythology a giant and hunter who was changed into a constellation at his death.
2 Astronomy a conspicuous constellation (the Hunter), said to represent a hunter holding a club and shield. It lies on the celestial equator and contains many bright stars, including Rigel, Betelgeuse, and a line of three that form **Orion's Belt**.
– ORIGIN via Latin from Greek.

Orisha /əˈrɪʃə/ ▸ **noun** (pl. **same** or **Orishas**) (in southern Nigeria) any of several minor gods. The term is also used in various black religious cults of South America and the Caribbean.
– ORIGIN Yoruba.

orison /ˈɒrɪz(ə)n, -s(ə)n/ ▸ **noun** (usu. **orisons**) archaic a prayer.
– ORIGIN Middle English: from Old French *oreison*, from Latin *oratio(n-)* 'speech' (see **ORATION**).

Orissa /əˈrɪsə/ a state in eastern India, on the Bay of Bengal; capital, Bhubaneswar.

-orium ▸ **suffix** forming nouns denoting a place for a particular function: *auditorium* | *sanatorium.*
– ORIGIN from Latin; compare with **-ORY**[1].

Oriya /ɒˈriːjə/ ▸ **adjective** relating to Orissa, its people, or their language.
▸ **noun** (pl. **same** or **Oriyas**) **1** a native or inhabitant of Orissa.
2 [mass noun] the language of the Oriya, an Indic language spoken by more than 31 million people.
– ORIGIN from Hindi *Uṛiyā*.

Orkney Islands /ˈɔːkni/ (also **Orkney** or **the Orkneys**) a group of more than seventy islands off the NE tip of Scotland, constituting a council area of Scotland; pop. 20,100 (est. 2009); chief town, Kirkwall. They came into Scottish possession in 1472, having previously been ruled by Norway and Denmark.

Orlando /ɔːˈlandəʊ/ a city and tourist resort in central Florida; pop. 230,519 (est. 2008).

orle /ɔːl/ ▸ **noun** Heraldry a narrow border inset from the edge of a shield. ■ a series of charges placed in orle.
– PHRASES **in orle** (of a series of charges) arranged around the edge of a shield.
– ORIGIN late 16th cent.: from French *ourle*, from *ourler* 'to hem', based on Latin *ora* 'edge'.

Orleanist /ˈɔːlɪənɪst, ɔːˈliːənɪst/ ▸ **noun** historical a person supporting the claim to the French throne of the descendants of the Duke of Orleans (1640–1701),

younger brother of Louis XIV, especially Louis Philippe (King of France, 1830–48).
– ORIGIN from French *Orléaniste*, from *Orléans*.

Orleans /ɔːˈliːənz/ a city in central France, on the Loire; pop. 116,256 (2006). In 1429 it was the scene of Joan of Arc's first victory over the English during the Hundred Years War. French name **Orléans** /ɔrleɑ̃/.

Orlon /ˈɔːlɒn/ ▶ **noun** [mass noun] trademark a synthetic acrylic fibre used for textiles and knitwear, or a fabric made from it.
– ORIGIN 1950s: invented word, on the pattern of *nylon*.

orlop /ˈɔːlɒp/ (also **orlop deck**) ▶ **noun** the lowest deck of a wooden sailing ship with three or more decks.
– ORIGIN late Middle English: from Dutch *overloop* 'covering', from *overlopen* 'run over'.

Ormazd /ˈɔːməzd/ another name for **AHURA MAZDA**.

ormer /ˈɔːmə/ ▶ **noun** an abalone (mollusc), especially one used as food in the Channel Islands. ● Genus *Haliotis*, in particular *H. tuberculata*.
– ORIGIN mid 17th cent.: Channel Islands French, from French *ormier*, from Latin *auris maris* 'ear of the sea' (because of its ear-like shape).

ormolu /ˈɔːməluː/ ▶ **noun** [mass noun] a gold-coloured alloy of copper, zinc, and tin used in decoration and making ornaments.
– ORIGIN mid 18th cent.: from French *or moulu* 'powdered gold' (used in gilding).

Ormuz /ˈɔːmʊz, ɔːˈmuːz/ variant spelling of **HORMUZ**.

ornament ▶ **noun** /ˈɔːnəm(ə)nt/ **1** a thing used or serving to make something look more attractive but usually having no practical purpose, especially a small object such as a figurine: *tables covered with ornaments and books*. ■ [mass noun] decoration added to embellish something: *Gothic buildings notable for their finely detailed ornament*. ■ a quality or person adding grace, beauty, or honour to something: *sense of humour is an ornament to character*. ■ (**ornaments**) Music embellishments made to a melody.
2 (usu. **ornaments**) Christian Church the accessories of worship, such as the altar, chalice, and sacred vessels.
▶ **verb** /ˈɔːnəmɛnt/ [with obj.] make (something) look more attractive by adding decorative items: *a jewel to ornament your wife's lovely throat*.
– ORIGIN Middle English (also in the sense 'accessory'): from Old French *ournement*, from Latin *ornamentum* 'equipment, ornament', from *ornare* 'adorn'. The verb dates from the early 18th cent.

O

ornamental ▶ **adjective** serving or intended as an ornament; decorative: *an ornamental fountain*.
▶ **noun** a plant grown for its attractive appearance.
– DERIVATIVES **ornamentalism** noun, **ornamentalist** noun, **ornamentally** adverb.

ornamentation ▶ **noun** [mass noun] decorative elements added to something to enhance its appearance: *a baroque chandelier with plasterwork ornamentation*. ■ the action of decorating something or making it more elaborate: *the rhetorical ornamentation of text*.

ornate ▶ **adjective** elaborately or highly decorated: *an ornate wrought-iron railing*. ■ (of literary style) using unusual words and complex constructions: *peculiarly ornate and metaphorical language*.
– DERIVATIVES **ornately** adverb, **ornateness** noun.
– ORIGIN late Middle English: from Latin *ornatus* 'adorned', past participle of *ornare*.

ornery /ˈɔːnəri/ ▶ **adjective** N. Amer. informal bad-tempered or difficult to deal with: *an ornery old military man*.
– DERIVATIVES **orneriness** noun.
– ORIGIN early 19th cent.: variant of **ORDINARY**, representing a dialect pronunciation.

ornithine /ˈɔːnɪθiːn/ ▶ **noun** [mass noun] Biochemistry an amino acid which is produced by the body and is important in protein metabolism. ● Chem. formula: $NH_2(CH_2)_3CH(NH_2)COOH$.
– ORIGIN late 19th cent.: from **ORNITHO-** (with reference to a constituent found in bird excrement) + **-INE**[4].

ornithischian /ˌɔːnɪˈθɪskɪən, -ˈθɪʃɪən/ Palaeontology ▶ **adjective** relating to or denoting herbivorous dinosaurs of an order distinguished by having a pelvic structure resembling that of birds. Compare with **SAURISCHIAN**.
▶ **noun** an ornithischian dinosaur. ● Order Ornithischia, superorder Dinosauria; comprises the stegosaurs, ankylosaurs, ornithopods, pachycephalosaurs, and ceratopsians.
– ORIGIN early 20th cent.: from modern Latin *Ornithiscia*, from Greek *ornis*, *ornith-* 'bird' + *iskhion* 'hip joint'.

ornitho- ▶ **combining form** relating to or resembling a bird or birds: *ornithology* | *ornithopod*.
– ORIGIN from Greek *ornis*, *ornith-* 'bird'.

ornithology /ˌɔːnɪˈθɒlədʒi/ ▶ **noun** [mass noun] the scientific study of birds.
– DERIVATIVES **ornithological** adjective, **ornithologically** adverb, **ornithologist** noun.
– ORIGIN late 17th cent.: from modern Latin *ornithologia*, from Greek *ornithologos* 'treating of birds'.

ornithomimosaur /ˌɔːnɪθə(ʊ)ˈmʌɪməsɔː/ ▶ **noun** technical term for **OSTRICH DINOSAUR**.
– ORIGIN 1980s: from modern Latin *Ornithomimosauria*, from Greek *ornis*, *ornith-* 'bird' + *mimos* 'mime' + *sauros* 'lizard'.

ornithopod /ˈɔːnɪθəˌpɒd/ ▶ **noun** a mainly bipedal herbivorous dinosaur. ● Infraorder Ornithopoda, order Ornithischia; includes the hadrosaurs, iguanodon, hypsilophodon, etc.
– ORIGIN late 19th cent.: from modern Latin *Ornithopoda*, from Greek *ornis*, *ornith-* 'bird' + *pous*, *pod-* 'foot'.

ornithopter /ˈɔːnɪˌθɒptə/ ▶ **noun** chiefly historical a machine designed to achieve flight by means of flapping wings.
– ORIGIN early 20th cent.: coined in French as *ornithoptère*.

ornithosis /ˌɔːnɪˈθəʊsɪs/ ▶ **noun** another term for **PSITTACOSIS**.

oro- ▶ **combining form** relating to mountains: *orogeny*.
– ORIGIN from Greek *oros* 'mountain'.

orogen /ˈɒrədʒ(ə)n/ ▶ **noun** Geology a belt of the earth's crust involved in the formation of mountains.
– ORIGIN 1920s: from Greek *oros* 'mountain' + **-GEN**.

orogeny /ɒˈrɒdʒəni/ ▶ **noun** [mass noun] Geology a process in which a section of the earth's crust is folded and deformed by lateral compression to form a mountain range.
– DERIVATIVES **orogenesis** noun, **orogenic** adjective.

orographic /ˌɒrəˈgrafɪk/ ▶ **adjective** relating to mountains, especially as regards their position and form. ■ (of clouds or rainfall) resulting from the effects of mountains in forcing moist air to rise.

orography /ɒˈrɒgrəfi/ ▶ **noun** [mass noun] the branch of physical geography dealing with the formation and features of mountains.

Oromo /ˈɒrəməʊ/ ▶ **noun** (pl. **same** or **Oromos**) **1** a member of an East African people, the largest ethnic group in Ethiopia.
2 [mass noun] the Cushitic language of the Oromo, spoken by some 17 million people in several different dialects.
▶ **adjective** relating to the Oromo or their language.
– ORIGIN the name in Oromo. An earlier term was *Galla*, which remains in use but is not favoured by the Oromo themselves.

Orontes /əˈrɒntiːz/ a river in SW Asia which rises near Baalbek in northern Lebanon and flows 571 km (355 miles) through western and northern Syria before turning west through southern Turkey to enter the Mediterranean. It is an important source of water for irrigation, especially in Syria.

oropendola /ˌɒrəˈpɛndələ/ ▶ **noun** a large gregarious tropical American bird of the American blackbird family, which has brown or black plumage with yellow outer tail feathers, and constructs a pendulous nest. ● Genus *Psarocolius*, family Icteridae: several species.
– ORIGIN late 19th cent.: from Spanish, literally 'golden oriole'.

oropharynx /ˌɔːrə(ʊ)ˈfarɪŋks/ ▶ **noun** (pl. **oropharynges** or **oropharynxes**) Anatomy the part of the pharynx that lies between the soft palate and the hyoid bone.
– DERIVATIVES **oropharyngeal** adjective.
– ORIGIN late 19th cent.: formed irregularly from Latin *os*, *-or* 'mouth' + **PHARYNX**.

orotund /ˈɒrə(ʊ)tʌnd, ˈɔː-/ ▶ **adjective** (of a person's voice) resonant and imposing. ■ (of writing, style, or expression) pompous or pretentious.
– DERIVATIVES **orotundity** noun.
– ORIGIN late 18th cent.: from Latin *ore rotundo* 'with rounded mouth'.

orphan ▶ **noun 1** a child whose parents are dead.
2 Printing the first line of a paragraph set as the last line of a page or column, considered undesirable.
▶ **verb** [with obj.] make (a child) an orphan: *John was orphaned at 12*.
– DERIVATIVES **orphanhood** noun.
– ORIGIN late Middle English: via late Latin from Greek *orphanos* 'bereaved'.

orphanage ▶ **noun 1** a residential institution for the care and education of orphans.
2 [mass noun] archaic the state or condition of being an orphan.

orphan drug ▶ **noun** a synthetic pharmaceutical which remains commercially undeveloped.

orpharion /ɔːˈfarɪən/ ▶ **noun** Music a stringed instrument of the 16th and 17th centuries, resembling a bandora but tuned like an ordinary lute.
– ORIGIN late 16th cent.: blend of the names *Orpheus* (see **ORPHEUS**) and *Arion*, musicians in Greek mythology.

Orpheus /ˈɔːfɪəs/ Greek Mythology a poet who could entrance wild beasts with the beauty of his singing and lyre playing. He went to the underworld after the death of his wife Eurydice and secured her release from the dead, but lost her because he failed to obey the condition that he must not look back at her until they had reached the world of the living.
– DERIVATIVES **Orphean** adjective.

Orphic ▶ **adjective** of or relating to Orpheus or Orphism.
– ORIGIN late 17th cent.: via Latin from Greek *Orphikos*, from *Orpheus* (see **ORPHEUS**).

Orphism /ˈɔːfɪz(ə)m/ ▶ **noun** [mass noun] **1** a mystic religion of ancient Greece, originating in the 7th or 6th century BC and based on poems (now lost) attributed to Orpheus, emphasizing the necessity for individuals to rid themselves of the evil part of their nature by ritual and moral purification throughout a series of reincarnations.
2 a short-lived art movement (*c*.1912) within cubism, pioneered by a group of French painters (including Robert Delaunay, Sonia Delaunay-Terk, and Fernand Léger) and emphasizing the lyrical use of colour rather than the austere intellectual cubism of Picasso, Braque, and Gris.

orphrey /ˈɔːfri/ ▶ **noun** (pl. **orphreys**) an ornamental stripe or border, especially one on an ecclesiastical vestment such as a chasuble.
– ORIGIN Middle English: from Old French *orfreis*, from a medieval Latin alteration of *auriphrygium*, from Latin *aurum* 'gold' + *Phrygius* 'Phrygian' (also used in the sense 'embroidered').

orpiment /ˈɔːpɪm(ə)nt/ ▶ **noun** [mass noun] a bright yellow mineral consisting of arsenic trisulphide, formerly used as a dye and artist's pigment.
– ORIGIN late Middle English: via Old French from Latin *auripigmentum*, from *aurum* 'gold' + *pigmentum* 'pigment'.

orpine /ˈɔːpɪn/ (also **orpin**) ▶ **noun** a purple-flowered Eurasian stonecrop. ● *Sedum telephium*, family Crassulaceae.
– ORIGIN Middle English: from Old French *orpine*, probably an alteration of **ORPIMENT**, originally applied to a yellow-flowered sedum.

Orpington /ˈɔːpɪŋt(ə)n/ ▶ **noun 1** a chicken of a buff, white, or black breed.
2 a duck of a buff or white breed, kept for its meat.
– ORIGIN late 19th cent.: from *Orpington*, the name of a town in Kent.

orra /ˈɒrə/ ▶ **adjective** Scottish **1** separated from a usual pair or set; odd.
2 used irregularly or only occasionally; extra.
– ORIGIN late 16th cent.: of unknown origin.

orrery /ˈɒrəri/ ▶ **noun** (pl. **orreries**) a clockwork model of the solar system, or of just the sun, earth, and moon.
– ORIGIN early 18th cent.: named after the fourth Earl of *Orrery*, for whom one was made.

orris /ˈɒrɪs/ (also **orris root**) ▶ **noun** [mass noun] a preparation of the fragrant rootstock of an iris, used in perfumery and formerly in medicine. ● The root is usually taken from *Iris* × *germanica* var. 'Florentina'.
– ORIGIN mid 16th cent.: apparently an unexplained alteration of **IRIS**.

Orsk /ɔːsk/ a city in southern Russia, in the Urals on the Ural River near the border with Kazakhstan; pop. 245,500 (est. 2008).

ortanique /ˌɔːtəˈniːk/ ▶ **noun** a citrus fruit which is a cross between an orange and a tangerine, developed in Jamaica in the 1920s. ● *Citrus sinensis* × *reticulata*, family Rutaceae.
– ORIGIN blend of **ORANGE**, **TANGERINE**, and **UNIQUE**.

Ortega /ɔːˈteɪgə/, Daniel (1945), Nicaraguan statesman, President 1985–90 and since 2007; full name *Daniel Ortega Saavedra*. He became the leader of the

Sandinista National Liberation Front (FSLN) in 1966 and first served as President after the Sandinista election victory in 1984. He was re-elected President in 2007.

Ortega y Gasset /ɔːˌteɪgə iː gaˈsɛt/, José (1883–1955), Spanish philosopher. His works include *The Revolt of the Masses* (1930), in which he proposed leadership by an intellectual elite.

ortho- ▶ **combining form 1** straight; rectangular; upright: *orthodontics*. ■ right; correct: *orthoepy*.
2 Chemistry denoting substitution at two adjacent carbon atoms in a benzene ring, e.g. in 1,2 positions: *orthodichlorobenzene*. Compare with **META-** and **PARA-**[1].
3 Chemistry denoting a compound from which a *meta*-compound is formed by dehydration: *orthophosphoric acid*.
– ORIGIN from Greek *orthos* 'straight, right'.

orthochromatic ▶ **adjective** (of black-and-white photographic film) sensitive to all visible light except red. Orthochromatic film can therefore be handled in red light in the darkroom but does not produce black-and-white tones that correspond very closely to the colours seen by the eye. Often contrasted with **PANCHROMATIC**.

orthoclase /ˈɔːθəkleɪz/ ▶ **noun** [mass noun] a common rock-forming mineral occurring typically as white or pink crystals. It is a potassium-rich alkali feldspar and is used in ceramics and glass-making.
– ORIGIN mid 19th cent.: from **ORTHO-** 'straight' + Greek *klasis* 'breaking' (because of the characteristic two cleavages at right angles).

orthocone /ˈɔːθəkəʊn/ ▶ **noun** Palaeontology the straight shell typical of early nautiloid cephalopods. ■ a fossil cephalopod with such a shell.
– DERIVATIVES **orthoconic** adjective.

orthodontics /ˌɔːθəˈdɒntɪks/ (also **orthodontia** /-ˈdɒntɪə/) ▶ **plural noun** [treated as sing.] the treatment of irregularities in the teeth and jaws.
– DERIVATIVES **orthodontic** adjective, **orthodontically** adverb, **orthodontist** noun.
– ORIGIN early 20th cent.: from **ORTHO-** 'straight' + Greek *odous, odont-* 'tooth'.

orthodox ▶ **adjective 1** following or conforming to the traditional or generally accepted rules or beliefs of a religion, philosophy, or practice: *Burke's views were orthodox in his time | orthodox medical treatment | orthodox Hindus*. ■ (of a person) not independent-minded; conventional and unoriginal: *a relatively orthodox artist*.
2 of the ordinary or usual type; normal: *they avoided orthodox jazz venues*.
3 (usu. **Orthodox**) relating to Orthodox Judaism.
4 (usu. **Orthodox**) relating to the Orthodox Church.
– DERIVATIVES **orthodoxly** adverb.
– ORIGIN late Middle English: from Greek *orthodoxos* (probably via ecclesiastical Latin), from *orthos* 'straight or right' + *doxa* 'opinion'.

Orthodox Church a Christian Church or federation of Churches originating in the Greek-speaking Church of the Byzantine Empire, not accepting the authority of the Pope of Rome, and using elaborate and archaic forms of service.

> The chief Orthodox Churches (often known collectively as the **Eastern Orthodox Church**) include the national Churches of Greece, Russia, Bulgaria, Romania, and Serbia. The term is also used by other ancient Churches, mainly of African or Asian origin, e.g. the Coptic, Syrian, and Ethiopian Churches.

Orthodox Judaism a major branch within Judaism which teaches strict adherence to rabbinical interpretation of Jewish law and its traditional observances. There are more than 600 rules governing religious and everyday life.

orthodoxy ▶ **noun** (pl. **orthodoxies**) [mass noun]
1 authorized or generally accepted theory, doctrine, or practice: *monetarist orthodoxy* | [count noun] *he challenged many of the established orthodoxies*.
■ the quality of conforming to orthodox theories, doctrines, or practices: *writings of unimpeachable orthodoxy*.
2 the whole community of Orthodox Jews or Orthodox Christians.
– ORIGIN mid 17th cent.: via late Latin from late Greek *orthodoxia* 'sound doctrine', from *orthodoxos* (see **ORTHODOX**).

orthodromic /ˌɔːθəˈdrəʊmɪk/ ▶ **adjective** Physiology (of an impulse) travelling in the normal direction in a nerve fibre. The opposite of **ANTIDROMIC**.
– ORIGIN 1940s: from **ORTHO-** 'right, correct' + Greek *dromos* 'running' + **-IC**.

orthoepy /ˈɔːθəʊɛpi, -iːpi, ɔːˈθəʊɪpi/ ▶ **noun** [mass noun] the correct or accepted pronunciation of words. ■ the study of correct or accepted pronunciation.
– DERIVATIVES **orthoepist** noun.
– ORIGIN mid 17th cent.: from Greek *orthoepeia* 'correct speech', from *orthos* 'right or straight' + *epos, epe-* 'word'.

orthogenesis /ˌɔːθə(ʊ)ˈdʒɛnɪsɪs/ ▶ **noun** [mass noun] Biology, chiefly historical evolution in which variations follow a particular direction and are not merely sporadic and fortuitous.
– DERIVATIVES **orthogenetic** adjective.

orthognathous /ˌɔːθəgˈneɪθəs, ɔːˈθɒgnəθəs/ ▶ **adjective** Anatomy (especially of a person) having a jaw which does not project forwards and a facial angle approaching a right angle.
– ORIGIN mid 19th cent.: from **ORTHO-** 'straight' + Greek *gnathos* 'jaw' + **-OUS**.

orthogonal /ɔːˈθɒg(ə)n(ə)l/ ▶ **adjective 1** of or involving right angles; at right angles.
2 Statistics (of variates) statistically independent. ■ (of an experiment) having variates which can be treated as statistically independent.
– DERIVATIVES **orthogonality** noun, **orthogonally** adverb.
– ORIGIN late 16th cent.: from French, based on Greek *orthogōnios* 'right-angled'.

orthogonal projection ▶ **noun** [mass noun] Engineering a system of making engineering drawings showing several different views of an object at right angles to each other on a single drawing.

orthographic projection ▶ **noun** [mass noun] Engineering a method of projection in which an object is depicted using parallel lines to project its outline on to a plane.

orthography /ɔːˈθɒgrəfi/ ▶ **noun** (pl. **orthographies**)
1 the conventional spelling system of a language.
■ [mass noun] the study of spelling and how letters combine to represent sounds and form words.
2 another term for **ORTHOGRAPHIC PROJECTION**.
– DERIVATIVES **orthographic** adjective, **orthographical** adjective, **orthographically** adverb.
– ORIGIN late Middle English: via Old French and Latin from Greek *orthographia*, from *orthos* 'correct' + *-graphia* 'writing'.

orthomolecular ▶ **adjective** (in complementary medicine) denoting or relating to a form of treatment that seeks to achieve an optimal biochemical balance in the body, typically by the use of large doses of supplementary vitamins and minerals.

orthomorphic /ˌɔːθəˈmɔːfɪk/ ▶ **adjective** Geography (of a map projection) preserving the correct shape of small areas.

Orthonectida /ˌɔːθə(ʊ)ˈnɛktɪdə/ ▶ **plural noun** Zoology a minor phylum of mesozoan worms which are internal parasites of a range of marine invertebrates.
– ORIGIN modern Latin (plural), from Greek *orthos* 'straight' + *nektos* 'swimming' (see **NEKTON**).

orthonormal ▶ **adjective** Mathematics both orthogonal and normalized.
– DERIVATIVES **orthonormality** noun, **orthonormalization** noun.

orthopaedics /ˌɔːθəˈpiːdɪks/ (US **orthopedics**) ▶ **plural noun** [treated as sing.] the branch of medicine dealing with the correction of deformities of bones or muscles.
– DERIVATIVES **orthopaedic** adjective, **orthopaedically** adverb, **orthopaedist** noun.
– ORIGIN mid 19th cent. (originally relating specifically to children): from French *orthopédie*, from Greek *orthos* 'right or straight' + *paideia* 'rearing of children'.

orthophosphoric acid /ˌɔːθə(ʊ)fɒsˈfɒrɪk/ ▶ **noun** another term for **PHOSPHORIC ACID**.
– DERIVATIVES **orthophosphate** noun.

orthopsychiatry ▶ **noun** [mass noun] the branch of psychiatry concerned with the prevention of mental or behavioural disorders, especially by studying borderline cases.

orthopter /ɔːˈθɒptə/ ▶ **noun** another term for **ORNITHOPTER**.

Orthoptera /ɔːˈθɒpt(ə)rə/ ▶ **plural noun** Entomology an order of insects that comprises the grasshoppers, crickets, and their relatives. They have a saddle-shaped thorax, hind legs that are typically long and modified for jumping, and a characteristic song which the male produces by stridulation.
■ (**orthoptera**) insects of this order.
– ORIGIN modern Latin (plural), from **ORTHO-** 'straight' + Greek *pteros* 'wing'.

orthopteran Entomology ▶ **noun** an insect of the order Orthoptera, such as a grasshopper or cricket.
▶ **adjective** relating to or denoting orthopterans.
– DERIVATIVES **orthopterous** adjective.

orthopteroid /ɔːˈθɒptərɔɪd/ ▶ **adjective** Entomology relating to a group of insect orders that are related to the grasshoppers and crickets, including also the stoneflies, stick insects, earwigs, cockroaches, mantises, and termites.

orthoptics ▶ **plural noun** [treated as sing.] the study or treatment of irregularities of the eyes, especially those of the eye muscles that prevent normal binocular vision.
– DERIVATIVES **orthoptic** adjective, **orthoptist** noun.
– ORIGIN late 19th cent.: from **ORTHO-** 'correct' + Greek *optikos* (see **OPTIC**).

orthopyroxene /ˌɔːθə(ʊ)pʌɪˈrɒksiːn/ ▶ **noun** [mass noun] a mineral of the pyroxene group crystallizing in the orthorhombic system.

orthorexia /ˌɔːθəˈrɛksɪə/ ▶ **noun** [mass noun] an obsession with eating foods that one considers healthy.
■ (also **orthorexia nervosa**) a medical condition in which the sufferer systematically avoids specific foods that they believe to be harmful.
– DERIVATIVES **orthorexic** adjective & noun.
– ORIGIN 1990s: from **ORTHO-** + Greek *orexia* 'appetite', after **ANOREXIA**.

orthorhombic /ˌɔːθə(ʊ)ˈrɒmbɪk/ ▶ **adjective** of or denoting a crystal system or three-dimensional geometrical arrangement having three unequal axes at right angles.

orthosis /ɔːˈθəʊsɪs/ ▶ **noun** (pl. **orthoses** /-siːz/) Medicine a brace, splint, or other artificial external device serving to support the limbs or spine or to prevent or assist relative movement.
– ORIGIN 1950s: from Greek *orthōsis* 'making straight', from *orthoun* 'set straight'.

orthostat /ˈɔːθə(ʊ)stat/ ▶ **noun** Archaeology an upright stone or slab forming part of a structure or set in the ground.
– ORIGIN early 20th cent.: from Greek *orthostatēs*, from *orthos* 'right or straight' + *statos* 'standing'.

orthostatic ▶ **adjective 1** Medicine relating to or caused by an upright posture.
2 Archaeology (of a stone) set on end. ■ (of a structure) built of upright stones.

orthostichy /ɔːˈθɒstɪki/ ▶ **noun** (pl. **orthostichies**) Botany (in phyllotaxis) a vertical row of leaves arranged one directly above another. Contrasted with **PARASTICHY**.
– ORIGIN late 19th cent.: from **ORTHO-** 'upright, straight' + Greek *stikhos* 'row, rank'.

orthotic ▶ **adjective** relating to orthotics.
▶ **noun** an artificial support or brace for the limbs or spine.

orthotics /ɔːˈθɒtɪkz/ ▶ **plural noun** [treated as sing.] the branch of medicine that deals with the provision and use of artificial devices such as splints and braces.
– DERIVATIVES **orthotist** noun.

orthotropic /ˌɔːθə(ʊ)ˈtrəʊpɪk, -ˈtrɒpɪk/ ▶ **adjective**
1 Botany (of a shoot, stem, or axis) growing vertically.
2 Engineering having three mutually perpendicular planes of elastic symmetry at each point.

ortolan /ˈɔːt(ə)lən/ (also **ortolan bunting**) ▶ **noun** a small Eurasian songbird that was formerly eaten as a delicacy, the male having an olive-green head and yellow throat. ● *Emberiza hortulana*, family Emberizidae (subfamily Emberizinae).
– ORIGIN early 16th cent.: from French, from Provençal, literally 'gardener', based on a diminutive of Latin *hortus* 'garden'.

Orton[1], Arthur (1834–98), English butcher; known as **the Tichborne claimant**. In 1866 he returned to England from Australia claiming to be the heir to the valuable Tichborne estate. He lost his claim and was tried and imprisoned for perjury.

Orton[2], Joe (1933–67), English dramatist; born *John Kingsley Orton*. He wrote a number of unconventional black comedies, examining corruption, sexuality, and violence; they include *Entertaining Mr Sloane* (1964) and *Loot* (1965). Orton was murdered by his homosexual lover, who then committed suicide.
– DERIVATIVES **Ortonesque** adjective.

orts /ɔːts/ ▶ **plural noun** archaic or dialect scraps; remains.
– ORIGIN late Middle English: from Middle Low German *orte* 'food remains', originally a compound the second element of which is related to **EAT**.

O

Oruro /ə'rʊərəʊ/ a city in western Bolivia; pop. 216,714 (2009). It is the centre of an important mining region, with rich deposits of tin, zinc, silver, copper, and gold.

Orvieto[1] /ɔː'vjeɪtəʊ/, Italian /əɔr'vjetɔ/ a town in Umbria, central Italy; pop. 21,059 (2008). It lies at the centre of a wine-producing area.

Orvieto[2] /ˌɔːvɪ'eɪtəʊ/ ▶ **noun** [mass noun] a white wine made near Orvieto.

Orwell, George (1903–50), British novelist and essayist, born in India; pseudonym of *Eric Arthur Blair*. Orwell's work is characterized by his concern for social injustice. His most famous works are *Animal Farm* (1945), a satire on Communism as it developed under Stalin, and *Nineteen Eighty-Four* (1949), a dystopian account of a future state in which every aspect of life is controlled by Big Brother.
– DERIVATIVES **Orwellian** adjective.

-ory[1] ▶ **suffix** (forming nouns) denoting a place for a particular function: *dormitory* | *repository*.
– DERIVATIVES **-orial** suffix forming corresponding adjectives.
– ORIGIN from Latin *-oria*, *-orium*, sometimes via Anglo-Norman French *-orie*, Old French *-oire*.

-ory[2] ▶ **suffix** forming adjectives (and occasionally nouns) relating to or involving a verbal action: *compulsory* | *directory* | *mandatory*.
– ORIGIN from Latin *-orius*, sometimes via Anglo-Norman French *-ori(e)*.

oryx /'ɒrɪks/ ▶ **noun** a large antelope living in arid regions of Africa and Arabia, having dark markings on the face and long horns. ● Genus *Oryx*, family Bovidae: three species, including the **Arabian oryx** (*O. leucoryx*). See also BEISA, SCIMITAR ORYX.
– ORIGIN late Middle English: via Latin from Greek *orux* 'stonemason's pickaxe' (because of its pointed horns).

orzo /'ɔːtsəʊ/ ▶ **noun** [mass noun] small pieces of pasta, shaped like grains of barley or rice.
– ORIGIN Italian, literally 'barley'.

OS ▶ **abbreviation** ■ (in calculating dates) Old Style. ■ Computing open-source. ■ Computing operating system. ■ Ordinary Seaman. ■ (in the UK) Ordnance Survey. ■ (as a size of clothing) outsize. ■ out of stock. ■ overseas.

Os ▶ **symbol** the chemical element osmium.

os[1] /ɒs/ ▶ **noun** (pl. **ossa** /'ɒsə/) Anatomy a bone (used chiefly in Latin names of individual bones, e.g. *os trapezium*).
– ORIGIN Latin.

os[2] /ɒs/ ▶ **noun** (pl. **ora** /'ɔːrə/) Anatomy an opening or entrance to a passage, especially one at either end of the cervix of the womb.
– ORIGIN mid 18th cent.: from Latin, 'mouth'.

Osage /əʊ'seɪdʒ, 'əʊseɪdʒ/ ▶ **noun** (pl. **same** or **Osages**) **1** a member of an American Indian people formerly inhabiting the Osage River valley in Missouri.
2 [mass noun] the Siouan language of the Osage, now virtually extinct.
▶ **adjective** relating to the Osage or their language.
– ORIGIN alteration of Osage *Wazhazhe*, the name of one of the three groups that compose this people.

Osage orange ▶ **noun** a small spiny North American deciduous tree which bears inedible green orange-like fruit. Its durable orange-coloured timber was formerly used by American Indians for bows and other weapons. ● *Maclura pomifera*, family Moraceae.

Osaka /əʊ'sɑːkə/ a port and commercial city in central Japan, on the island of Honshu, capital of Kinki region; pop. 2,510,459 (2007).

Osborne, John (James) (1929–94), English dramatist. His first play, *Look Back in Anger* (1956), ushered in a new era of kitchen-sink drama; its hero Jimmy Porter personified contemporary disillusioned youth, the so-called 'angry young man'.

Oscan /'ɒsk(ə)n/ ▶ **noun** [mass noun] an extinct Italic language of southern Italy, related to Umbrian and surviving in inscriptions mainly of the 4th to 1st centuries BC.
▶ **adjective** relating to Oscan.
– ORIGIN late 16th cent.: from Latin *Oscus* 'Oscan' + -AN.

Oscar[1] ▶ **noun 1** (trademark in the US) the nickname for a gold statuette given as an Academy Award. [one of the several speculative stories of its origin claims that the statuette reminded Margaret Herrick, an executive director of the Academy of Motion Picture Arts and Sciences, of her uncle Oscar.]
2 a code word representing the letter O, used in radio communication.

Oscar[2] ▶ **noun** [mass noun] Austral./NZ informal, dated money.
– ORIGIN early 20th cent.: from the name *Oscar Asche* (1871–1936), Australian actor, used as rhyming slang for 'cash'.

oscar (also **oscar cichlid**) ▶ **noun** a South American cichlid fish with velvety brown young and multi-coloured adults, popular in aquaria. ● *Astronotus ocellatus*, family Cichlidae. Alternative name: **velvet cichlid**.

oscillate /'ɒsɪleɪt/ ▶ **verb** [no obj.] **1** move or swing back and forth in a regular rhythm: *the grain pan near the front of the combine oscillates back and forth.* ■ [with adverbial] vary or fluctuate between two states, limits, opinions, etc.: ***he was oscillating between fear and bravery.***
2 Physics vary in magnitude or position in a regular manner about a central point. ■ (of a circuit or device) cause the electric current or voltage running through it to behave in this way.
– DERIVATIVES **oscillatory** /ɒ'sɪlət(ə)ri, 'ɒsɪləˌt(ə)ri/ adjective.
– ORIGIN early 18th cent.: from Latin *oscillat-* 'swung', from the verb *oscillare*.

oscillation ▶ **noun** [mass noun] **1** movement back and forth in a regular rhythm: *the natural oscillation of a spring* | [count noun] *the oscillations of a pendulum*. ■ variation or fluctuation between two states, limits, opinions, etc.: *the plot's oscillation between bleak and comic elements*.
2 Physics regular variation in magnitude or position about a central point, especially of an electric current or voltage.

oscillator ▶ **noun** a device for generating oscillatory electric currents or voltages by non-mechanical means.

oscillo- /ə'sɪləʊ/ ▶ **combining form** relating to oscillation, especially of electric current: *oscilloscope*.

oscillogram ▶ **noun** a record produced by an oscillograph.

oscillograph ▶ **noun** a device for recording oscillations, especially those of an electric current.
– DERIVATIVES **oscillographic** adjective.

oscilloscope ▶ **noun** a device for viewing oscillations by a display on the screen of a cathode ray tube.
– DERIVATIVES **oscilloscopic** adjective.

oscine /'ɒsʌɪn, -sɪn/ Ornithology ▶ **adjective** relating to or denoting passerine birds of a large division that includes the songbirds. Compare with SUBOSCINE. ● Suborder Oscines, order Passeriformes.
▶ **noun** a bird of this division.
– ORIGIN late 19th cent.: from Latin *oscen*, *oscin-* 'songbird' + -INE[1].

Osco-Umbrian ▶ **noun 1** [mass noun] a group of ancient Italic languages including Oscan and Umbrian, spoken in Italy in the 1st millennium BC, before the emergence of Latin as a standard language.
2 a member of any of the peoples who spoke a language in the Osco-Umbrian group.
▶ **adjective** relating to the Osco-Umbrians or their languages.

oscula plural form of OSCULUM.

oscular /'ɒskjʊlə/ ▶ **adjective 1** humorous relating to kissing.
2 Zoology relating to an osculum.
– ORIGIN early 19th cent.: from Latin *osculum* 'mouth, kiss' (diminutive of *os* 'mouth') + -AR[1].

osculate /'ɒskjʊleɪt/ ▶ **verb** [with obj.] **1** Mathematics (of a curve or surface) touch (another curve or surface) so as to have a common tangent at the point of contact.
2 formal or humorous kiss.
– DERIVATIVES **osculant** adjective, **osculation** noun, **osculatory** adjective.
– ORIGIN mid 17th cent.: from Latin *osculat-* 'kissed', from the verb *osculari*, from *osculum* 'little mouth or kiss'.

osculum /'ɒskjʊləm/ ▶ **noun** (pl. **oscula** /-lə/) Zoology a large aperture in a sponge through which water is expelled.
– ORIGIN early 17th cent.: from Latin 'little mouth'.

-ose[1] ▶ **suffix** (forming adjectives) having a specified quality: *bellicose* | *comatose* | *verbose*.
– DERIVATIVES **-osely** suffix forming corresponding adverbs, **-oseness** suffix forming corresponding nouns. Compare with -OSITY.
– ORIGIN from Latin *-osus*.

-ose[2] ▶ **suffix** Chemistry forming names of sugars and other carbohydrates: *cellulose* | *glucose*.
– ORIGIN on the pattern of *(gluc)ose*.

Osh /ɒʃ/ a city in western Kyrgyzstan, near the border with Uzbekistan; pop. 300,000 (est. 2009). It was, until the 15th century, an important post on an ancient trade route to China and India.

OSHA ▶ **abbreviation** (in the US) Occupational Safety and Health Administration.

Oshawa /'ɒʃəwə/ a city in Ontario, on the northern shores of Lake Ontario east of Toronto; pop. 141,590 (2006).

oshi /'ɒʃi/ ▶ **noun** (pl. **same**) (in sumo wrestling) a move in which an opponent is pushed backwards or down.
– ORIGIN Japanese.

osier /'əʊzɪə/ ▶ **noun** a small Eurasian willow which grows mostly in wet habitats. It is usually coppiced, being a major source of the long flexible shoots (withies) used in basketwork. ● *Salix viminalis*, family Salicaceae.
■ a shoot of a willow. ■ dated any willow tree.
– ORIGIN late Middle English: from Old French; compare with medieval Latin *auseria* 'osier bed'.

Osijek /'ɒsɪjɛk/ a city in eastern Croatia, on the River Drava; pop. 85,800 (est. 2009).

Osiris /ə(ʊ)'sʌɪrɪs/ Egyptian Mythology a god originally connected with fertility, husband of Isis and father of Horus. He is known chiefly through the story of his death at the hands of his brother Seth and his subsequent restoration to a new life as ruler of the afterlife.
– DERIVATIVES **Osirian** adjective.

-osis ▶ **suffix** (pl. **-oses**) denoting a process or condition: *metamorphosis*. ■ denoting a pathological state: *neurosis* | *thrombosis*.
– ORIGIN via Latin from Greek *-ōsis*, verbal noun ending.

-osity ▶ **suffix** forming nouns from adjectives ending in *-ose* (such as *verbosity* from *verbose*) and from adjectives ending in *-ous* (such as *pomposity* from *pompous*).
– ORIGIN from French *-osité* or Latin *-ositas*.

Oslo /'ɒzləʊ/ the capital and chief port of Norway, on the south coast at the head of Oslofjord; pop. 839,423 (2007). Founded in the 11th century, it was known as Christiania (or Kristiania) from 1624 until 1924 in honour of Christian IV of Norway and Denmark (1577–1648).

Osman I /'ɒzmən/ (also **Othman**) (1259–1326), Turkish conqueror, founder of the Ottoman (Osmanli) dynasty and empire. Osman reigned as sultan of the Seljuk Turks from 1288, conquering NW Asia Minor. He assumed the title of emir in 1299.

Osmanli /ɒz'manli/ ▶ **adjective & noun** (pl. **same** or **Osmanlis**) old-fashioned term for OTTOMAN.
– ORIGIN Turkish, from the name *Osman*, from Arabic *'uṯmān* (see OTTOMAN), + the adjectival suffix *-li*.

osmic /'ɒzmɪk/ ▶ **adjective** relating to odours or the sense of smell.
– ORIGIN 1930s: from Greek *osmē* 'smell, odour' + -IC.

osmic acid ▶ **noun** [mass noun] Chemistry a solution of osmium tetroxide.
– ORIGIN mid 19th cent.: *osmic* from OSMIUM + -IC.

osmium /'ɒzmɪəm/ ▶ **noun** [mass noun] the chemical element of atomic number 76, a hard, dense silvery-white metal of the transition series. (Symbol: **Os**)
– ORIGIN early 19th cent.: modern Latin, from Greek *osmē* 'smell' (from the pungent smell of its tetroxide).

osmium tetroxide ▶ **noun** [mass noun] a poisonous pale yellow solid with a distinctive pungent smell, used in solution as a biological stain (especially for lipids) and fixative. ● Chem. formula: OsO_4.

osmo- ▶ **combining form** representing OSMOSIS.

osmolality /ˌɒzmə(ʊ)'lalɪti/ ▶ **noun** Chemistry the concentration of a solution expressed as the total number of solute particles per kilogram.
– ORIGIN 1950s: blend of *osmotic* (see OSMOSIS) and MOLAL, + -ITY.

osmolarity /ˌɒzmə(ʊ)'larɪti/ ▶ **noun** Chemistry the concentration of a solution expressed as the total number of solute particles per litre.
– ORIGIN 1950s: blend of *osmotic* (see OSMOSIS) and MOLAR[3], + -ITY.

osmometer /ɒz'mɒmɪtə/ ▶ **noun** an instrument for demonstrating or measuring osmotic pressure.
– DERIVATIVES **osmometry** noun.

osmoregulation ▶ **noun** [mass noun] Biology the maintenance of constant osmotic pressure in the

O

fluids of an organism by the control of water and salt concentrations.
– DERIVATIVES **osmoregulatory** adjective.

osmose /ˈɒzməʊs/ ▶ verb [no obj.] literary pass by or as if by osmosis.
– ORIGIN mid 19th cent. (as a noun in the sense 'osmosis'): from the element common to *endosmose* and *exosmose*.

osmosis /ɒzˈməʊsɪs/ ▶ noun [mass noun] **1** Biology & Chemistry a process by which molecules of a solvent tend to pass through a semipermeable membrane from a less concentrated solution into a more concentrated one. **2** the process of gradual or unconscious assimilation of ideas, knowledge, etc.: *by some strange political osmosis, private reputations became public.*
– DERIVATIVES **osmotic** adjective, **osmotically** adverb.
– ORIGIN mid 19th cent.: Latinized form of earlier *osmose*, from Greek *ōsmos* 'a push'.

osmotic pressure /ɒzˈmɒtɪk/ ▶ noun Chemistry the pressure that would have to be applied to a pure solvent to prevent it from passing into a given solution by osmosis, often used to express the concentration of the solution.

osmunda /ɒzˈmʌndə/ ▶ noun a plant of a genus that includes the royal and cinnamon ferns. ● Genus *Osmunda*, family Osmundaceae.
– ORIGIN Anglo-Latin, from Anglo-Norman French *osmunde*, of unknown origin.

Osnabrück /ˈɒznəbrʊk/, German /ˌɔsnaˈbrʏk/ a city in NW Germany, in Lower Saxony; pop. 163,000 (est. 2006). In 1648 the Treaty of Westphalia, ending the Thirty Years War, was signed there and in Münster.

osnaburg /ˈɒznəbəːɡ/ ▶ noun [mass noun] a kind of coarse linen or cotton used for such items as furnishings and sacks.
– ORIGIN late Middle English: alteration of OSNABRÜCK, where the cloth was originally produced.

os penis ▶ noun Zoology a bone in the penis of carnivores and some other mammals. Also called BACULUM.

osprey /ˈɒspri, -preɪ/ ▶ noun (pl. **ospreys**) a large fish-eating bird of prey with long, narrow wings and a white underside and crown, found throughout the world. Also called FISH HAWK. ● *Pandion haliaetus*, the only member of the family Pandionidae.
– ORIGIN late Middle English: from Old French *ospres*, apparently based on Latin *ossifraga* (mentioned by Pliny and identified with the lammergeier), from *os* 'bone' + *frangere* 'to break', probably because of the lammergeier's habit of dropping bones from a height to break them and reach the marrow.

OSS ▶ abbreviation (in the US) Office of Strategic Services, an intelligence organization.

ossa plural form of **os**[1].

Ossa, Mount /ˈɒsə/ **1** a mountain in Thessaly, NE Greece, south of Mount Olympus, rising to a height of 1,978 m (6,489 ft). In Greek mythology the giants were said to have piled Mount Ossa on to Mount Pelion, and vice versa, in an attempt to reach heaven and destroy the gods.
2 the highest mountain on the island of Tasmania, rising to a height of 1,617 m (5,305 ft).

ossein /ˈɒsɪɪn/ ▶ noun [mass noun] Biochemistry the collagen of bones.
– ORIGIN mid 19th cent.: from Latin *osseus* 'bony' + -IN[1].

osseous /ˈɒsɪəs/ ▶ adjective chiefly Zoology & Medicine consisting of or turned into bone; ossified.
– ORIGIN late Middle English: from Latin *osseus* 'bony' + -OUS.

Ossete /ˈɒsiːt/ ▶ noun **1** a native or inhabitant of Ossetia.
2 another term for OSSETIAN (the language).
▶ adjective relating to Ossetia or the Ossetes.
– DERIVATIVES **Ossetic** adjective & noun.
– ORIGIN from Russian *osetin*, from Georgian.

Ossetia /ɒˈsetɪə/ a region of the central Caucasus. It is divided by the boundary between Russia and Georgia into two parts, North Ossetia and South Ossetia, and between 1989 and 1992 was the scene of ethnic conflict.

Ossetian ▶ noun **1** [mass noun] the language of the Ossetes, belonging to the Iranian group.
2 a native or inhabitant of Ossetia.
▶ adjective relating to the Ossetes or their language.

Ossi /ˈɒsi/ ▶ noun (pl. **Ossies** or **Ossis**) informal, often derogatory (in Germany) a citizen of the former German Democratic Republic.
– ORIGIN German, probably an abbreviation of *Ostdeutsche* 'East German'.

Ossian /ˈɒʃɪən, ˈɒsɪ-/ a legendary Irish warrior and bard, whose name became well known in 1760–3 when the Scottish poet James Macpherson (1736–96) published his own verse as an alleged translation of 3rd-century Gaelic tales. Irish name OISIN.

ossicle /ˈɒsɪk(ə)l/ ▶ noun Anatomy & Zoology a very small bone, especially one of those in the middle ear.
■ Zoology a small piece of calcified material forming part of the skeleton of an invertebrate animal such as an echinoderm.
– ORIGIN late 16th cent.: from Latin *ossiculum*, diminutive of *os* 'bone'.

Ossie ▶ noun variant spelling of AUSSIE.

ossify /ˈɒsɪfʌɪ/ ▶ verb (**ossifies**, **ossifying**, **ossified**) [no obj.] **1** turn into bone or bony tissue: *these tracheal cartilages may ossify.*
2 (often as adj. **ossified**) cease developing; stagnate: *ossified political institutions.*
– DERIVATIVES **ossification** noun.
– ORIGIN early 18th cent.: from French *ossifier*, from Latin *os*, *oss-* 'bone'.

Ossining Correctional Facility official name for SING SING.

osso buco /ˌɒsəʊ ˈbuːkəʊ/ ▶ noun [mass noun] an Italian dish made of shin of veal containing marrowbone, stewed in wine with vegetables.
– ORIGIN Italian, literally 'marrowbone'.

ossuary /ˈɒsjʊəri/ ▶ noun (pl. **ossuaries**) a container or room in which the bones of dead people are placed.
– ORIGIN mid 17th cent.: from late Latin *ossuarium*, formed irregularly from Latin *os*, *oss-* 'bone'.

OST ▶ abbreviation original soundtrack.

Ostade /ɒˈstɑːdə/, Adriaen van (1610–85), Dutch painter and engraver. His work chiefly depicts lively genre scenes of peasants carousing or brawling in crowded taverns or barns.

Osteichthyes /ˌɒstɪˈɪkθɪiːz/ ▶ plural noun Zoology a class of fishes that includes those with a bony skeleton. Compare with CHONDRICHTHYES.
– ORIGIN modern Latin (plural), from Greek *osteon* 'bone' + *ikhthus* 'fish'.

osteitis /ˌɒstɪˈʌɪtɪs/ ▶ noun [mass noun] Medicine inflammation of the substance of a bone. ■ (**osteitis fibrosa cystica** /fʌɪˌbrəʊsə ˈsɪstɪkə/) another term for VON RECKLINGHAUSEN'S DISEASE (sense 2). ■ (**osteitis deformans** /dɪˈfɔːmanz/) another term for PAGET'S DISEASE (sense 1).
– ORIGIN mid 19th cent.: from Greek *osteon* 'bone' + -ITIS.

Ostend /ɒˈstɛnd/ a port on the North Sea coast of NW Belgium, in West Flanders; pop. 69,175 (2008). It is a major ferry port with links to Dover. French name **Ostende** /ɔstɑ̃d/. Flemish name OOSTENDE.

ostensible /ɒˈstɛnsɪb(ə)l/ ▶ adjective [attrib.] stated or appearing to be true, but not necessarily so: *the real dispute which lay behind the ostensible complaint.*
– ORIGIN mid 18th cent.: from French, from medieval Latin *ostensibilis* from Latin *ostens-* 'stretched out to view', from the verb *ostendere*, from *ob-* 'in view of' + *tendere* 'to stretch'.

ostensibly ▶ adverb as appears or is stated to be true, though not necessarily so; apparently: [sentence adverb] *the party secretary resigned, ostensibly from ill health.*

ostensive ▶ adjective directly demonstrative.
■ Linguistics denoting a way of defining by direct demonstration, e.g. pointing.
– DERIVATIVES **ostensively** adverb.
– ORIGIN mid 16th cent.: from late Latin *ostensivus*, from *ostens-* 'stretched out to view' (see OSTENSIBLE).

ostensory /ɒˈstɛns(ə)ri/ ▶ noun (pl. **ostensories**) another term for MONSTRANCE.
– ORIGIN early 18th cent.: from medieval Latin *ostensorium*, from *ostens-* 'stretched out to view' (see OSTENSIBLE).

ostentation ▶ noun [mass noun] the pretentious or showy display of wealth and luxury, designed to impress.
– ORIGIN late Middle English: via Old French from Latin *ostentatio(n-)*, from the verb *ostentare*, frequentative of *ostendere* 'stretch out to view'.

ostentatious /ˌɒstɛnˈteɪʃəs/ ▶ adjective characterized by pretentious or showy display; designed to impress: *a simple design that is glamorous without being ostentatious.*
– DERIVATIVES **ostentatiously** adverb, **ostentatiousness** noun.

osteo- ▶ combining form relating to the bones: *osteoporosis.*
– ORIGIN from Greek *osteon* 'bone'.

osteoarthritis ▶ noun [mass noun] Medicine degeneration of joint cartilage and the underlying bone, most common from middle age onward. It causes pain and stiffness, especially in the hip, knee, and thumb joints. Compare with RHEUMATOID ARTHRITIS.
– DERIVATIVES **osteoarthritic** adjective.

osteoblast /ˈɒstɪə(ʊ)blast/ ▶ noun Physiology a cell which secretes the substance of bone.
– DERIVATIVES **osteoblastic** adjective.

osteoclast /ˈɒstɪə(ʊ)klast/ ▶ noun Physiology a large multinucleate bone cell which absorbs bone tissue during growth and healing.
– DERIVATIVES **osteoclastic** adjective.
– ORIGIN late 19th cent.: from OSTEO- 'bone' + Greek *klastēs* 'breaker'.

osteocyte /ˈɒstɪə(ʊ)sʌɪt/ ▶ noun Physiology a bone cell, formed when an osteoblast becomes embedded in the material it has secreted.

osteogenesis /ˌɒstɪə(ʊ)ˈdʒɛnɪsɪs/ ▶ noun [mass noun] Physiology the formation of bone.
– DERIVATIVES **osteogenic** adjective.

osteogenesis imperfecta /ˌɪmpəːˈfɛktə/ ▶ noun [mass noun] Medicine an inherited disorder characterized by extreme fragility of the bones.
– ORIGIN modern Latin, from OSTEOGENESIS + Latin *imperfecta* 'imperfect' (feminine of *imperfectus*).

osteoid /ˈɒstɪɔɪd/ Physiology & Medicine ▶ adjective resembling bone in appearance or structure.
▶ noun [mass noun] the unmineralized organic component of bone.

osteology /ˌɒstɪˈɒlədʒi/ ▶ noun [mass noun] the study of the structure and function of the skeleton and bony structures.
– DERIVATIVES **osteological** adjective, **osteologically** adverb, **osteologist** noun.

osteolysis /ˌɒstɪˈɒlɪsɪs/ ▶ noun [mass noun] Medicine the pathological destruction or disappearance of bone tissue.
– DERIVATIVES **osteolytic** adjective.

osteomalacia /ˌɒstɪəʊməˈleɪʃɪə/ ▶ noun [mass noun] Medicine softening of the bones, typically through a deficiency of vitamin D or calcium.
– DERIVATIVES **osteomalacic** /-ˈlasɪk/ adjective.
– ORIGIN early 19th cent.: modern Latin, from OSTEO- 'bone' + Greek *malakos* 'soft'.

osteomyelitis /ˌɒstɪəʊmʌɪˈlʌɪtɪs/ ▶ noun [mass noun] Medicine inflammation of bone or bone marrow, usually due to infection.

osteonecrosis /ˌɒstɪəʊnɛˈkrəʊsɪs/ ▶ noun [mass noun] Medicine the death of bone tissue.

osteopathy /ˌɒstɪˈɒpəθi/ ▶ noun [mass noun] a system of complementary medicine involving the treatment of medical disorders through the manipulation and massage of the skeleton and musculature.
– DERIVATIVES **osteopath** noun, **osteopathic** adjective.

osteopenia /ˌɒstɪəʊˈpiːnɪə/ ▶ noun [mass noun] a medical condition in which the protein and mineral content of bone tissue is reduced, but less severely than in osteoporosis.
– ORIGIN 1960s: from OSTEO- and Greek *penia* 'poverty'.

osteophyte /ˈɒstɪə(ʊ)fʌɪt/ ▶ noun Medicine a bony projection associated with the degeneration of cartilage at joints.
– DERIVATIVES **osteophytic** adjective.

osteoporosis /ˌɒstɪəʊpəˈrəʊsɪs/ ▶ noun [mass noun] a medical condition in which the bones become brittle and fragile from loss of tissue, typically as a result of hormonal changes, or deficiency of calcium or vitamin D.
– DERIVATIVES **osteoporotic** adjective.
– ORIGIN mid 19th cent.: from OSTEO- 'bone' + Greek *poros* 'passage, pore' + -OSIS.

osteosarcoma /ˌɒstɪəʊsɑːˈkəʊmə/ ▶ noun (pl. **osteosarcomas** or **osteosarcomata** /-mətə/) Medicine a malignant tumour of bone in which there is a proliferation of osteoblasts.

osteospermum /ɒstɪəʊˈspəːməm/ ▶ noun (pl. **osteospermums**) a plant or shrub of the daisy family, native to Africa and the Middle East, some varieties of which are cultivated for their yellow, violet, pink, or white flowers. ● Genus *Osteospermum*, family Compositae.
– ORIGIN mid 19th cent.: modern Latin, from OSTEO- + Greek *sperma* 'seed'.

osteotome /ˈɒstɪətəʊm/ ▶ noun a surgical instrument for cutting bone, typically resembling a chisel.

O

osteotomy /ˌɒstɪˈɒtəmi/ ▶ **noun** (pl. **osteotomies**) [mass noun] the surgical cutting of a bone, especially to allow realignment.

osteria /ɒstəˈriːə/ ▶ **noun** an Italian restaurant, typically a simple or inexpensive one.
– ORIGIN Italian, 'inn, hotel'.

Österreich /ˈøːstəˌrʌɪç/ German name for **AUSTRIA**.

Ostia /ˈɒstɪə/ an ancient city and harbour which was situated on the western coast of Italy at the mouth of the River Tiber. It was the first colony founded by ancient Rome and was a major port and commercial centre.

ostinato /ˌɒstɪˈnɑːtəʊ/ ▶ **noun** (pl. **ostinatos** or **ostinati** /-ti/) a continually repeated musical phrase or rhythm.
– ORIGIN Italian, literally 'obstinate'.

ostiole /ˈɒstɪəʊl/ ▶ **noun** Botany (in some small algae and fungi) a small pore through which spores are discharged.
– ORIGIN mid 19th cent.: from Latin *ostiolum*, diminutive of *ostium* 'opening'.

ostium /ˈɒstɪəm/ ▶ **noun** (pl. **ostia** /ˈɒstɪə/) Anatomy & Zoology an opening into a vessel or cavity of the body. ■ Zoology each of a number of pores in the wall of a sponge, through which water is drawn in.
– ORIGIN early 17th cent.: from Latin, 'door, opening'.

ostler /ˈɒslə/ (also **hostler**) ▶ **noun** historical a man employed to look after the horses of people staying at an inn.
– ORIGIN late Middle English: from Old French *hostelier* 'innkeeper', from *hostel* (see **HOSTEL**).

Ostmark /ˈɒstmɑːk/ ▶ **noun** historical the basic monetary unit of the former German Democratic Republic, equal to 100 pfennig.
– ORIGIN German, literally 'east mark' (see **MARK²**).

ostomy /ˈɒstəmi/ ▶ **noun** (pl. **ostomies**) Medicine an artificial opening in an organ of the body, created during an operation such as a colostomy, ileostomy, or gastrostomy; a stoma.
– ORIGIN 1950s: from **COLOSTOMY**, **ILEOSTOMY**, etc.

Ostpolitik /ˈɒstpɒlɪˌtiːk/ ▶ **noun** [mass noun] historical the foreign policy of western European countries of détente with reference to the former communist bloc, especially the opening of relations with the Eastern bloc by the Federal Republic of Germany (West Germany) in the 1960s.
– ORIGIN German, from *Ost* 'east' + *Politik* 'politics'.

ostracism /ˈɒstrəsɪz(ə)m/ ▶ **noun** [mass noun] **1** exclusion from a society or group: *the family suffered social ostracism.*
2 (in ancient Greece) temporary banishment from a city by popular vote.

O

ostracize /ˈɒstrəsʌɪz/ (also **ostracise**) ▶ **verb 1** [with obj.] exclude from a society or group: *she was declared a witch and ostracized by the villagers.*
2 (in ancient Greece) banish (an unpopular or overly powerful citizen) from a city for five or ten years by popular vote.
– ORIGIN mid 17th cent.: from Greek *ostrakizein*, from *ostrakon* 'shell or potsherd' (on which names were written in voting to banish unpopular citizens).

ostracod /ˈɒstrəkɒd/ (also **ostracode**) ▶ **noun** Zoology a minute aquatic crustacean of the class Ostracoda.

Ostracoda /ˌɒstrəˈkəʊdə/ ▶ **plural noun** Zoology a class of minute aquatic crustaceans that have a hinged shell from which the antennae protrude, and a reduced number of appendages.
– ORIGIN modern Latin (plural), from Greek *ostrakōdēs* 'testaceous', from *ostrakon* 'shell'.

ostracoderm /ɒˈstrakədəːm/ ▶ **noun** an early jawless fossil fish of the Cambrian to Devonian periods, having a heavily armoured body. ● Class Agnatha: several orders.
– ORIGIN late 19th cent.: from modern Latin *Ostracodermi* (former taxonomic name), from Greek *ostrakon* 'shell' + *derma* 'skin'.

ostracon /ˈɒstrəkɒn/ (also **ostrakon**) ▶ **noun** (pl. **ostraca** or **ostraka**) historical a potsherd used as a writing surface.
– ORIGIN Greek, 'hard shell or potsherd'.

Ostrava /ˈɒstrəvə/ an industrial city in the Moravian lowlands of the NE Czech Republic; pop. 308,832 (2007). It is situated in the coal-mining region of Silesia.

ostrich ▶ **noun 1** a flightless swift-running African bird with a long neck, long legs, and two toes on each foot. It is the largest living bird, with males reaching a height of up to 2.75 m. ● *Struthio camelus*, the only member of the family Struthionidae.
2 a person who refuses to face reality or accept facts. [from the popular belief that ostriches bury their heads in the sand if pursued.]
– ORIGIN Middle English: from Old French *ostriche*, from Latin *avis* 'bird' + late Latin *struthio* (from Greek *strouthiōn* 'ostrich', from *strouthos* 'sparrow or ostrich').

ostrich dinosaur ▶ **noun** a lightly built toothless bipedal dinosaur of the late Cretaceous period, adapted for running and somewhat resembling an ostrich. Also called **ORNITHOMIMOSAUR**. ● Infraorder Ornithomimisauria, suborder Theropoda, order Saurischia: several genera, including *Gallimimus*, *Ornithomimus*, and *Struthiomimus*.

Ostrogoth /ˈɒstrəgɒθ/ ▶ **noun** a member of the eastern branch of the Goths, who conquered Italy in the 5th–6th centuries AD.
– DERIVATIVES **Ostrogothic** adjective.
– ORIGIN from late Latin *Ostrogothi* (plural), from the Germanic base of **EAST** + late Latin *Gothi* 'Goths'.

Oswald, Lee Harvey (1939–63), American alleged assassin of John F. Kennedy. He denied the charge of assassinating the president, but was murdered before he could be brought to trial.

Oswald of York, St (d.992), English prelate and Benedictine monk. As Archbishop of York, he founded several monasteries and, with St Dunstan, revived the Church and learning in 10th-century England. Feast day, 28 February.

oswego tea /ɒˈzwiːgəʊ/ ▶ **noun** another term for **SWEET BERGAMOT** (see **BERGAMOT¹** (sense 3)).
– ORIGIN mid 18th cent.: named after a river and town in the northern part of the state of New York.

OT ▶ **abbreviation** ■ occupational therapist. ■ occupational therapy. ■ Old Testament.

-ot¹ ▶ **suffix** forming nouns which were originally diminutives: *ballot* | *parrot*.
– ORIGIN from French.

-ot² ▶ **suffix** (forming nouns) denoting a person of a particular type: *harlot* | *idiot*. ■ denoting a native of a place: *Cypriot*.
– ORIGIN via French and Latin from Greek *ōtēs*.

Otago /ɒˈtɑːgəʊ/ a region of New Zealand, on the SE coast of the South Island.

otaku /əʊˈtɑːkuː/ ▶ **noun** (pl. **same**) (in Japan) a young person who is obsessed with computers or particular aspects of popular culture to the detriment of their social skills.
– ORIGIN Japanese, literally 'your house', alluding to the reluctance of such young people to leave the house.

otalgia /əʊˈtaldʒə/ ▶ **noun** [mass noun] Medicine earache.
– ORIGIN mid 17th cent.: from Greek *ōtalgia*, from *ous*, *ōt-* 'ear' + *algos* 'pain'.

OTC ▶ **abbreviation** ■ (in the UK) Officers' Training Corps. ■ over the counter.

OTE ▶ **abbreviation** on-target earnings, as used to indicate the expected salary of a salesperson, with bonuses and commission.

other ▶ **adjective & pronoun 1** used to refer to a person or thing that is different or distinct from one already mentioned or known about: [as adj.] *stick the camera on a tripod or* ***some other*** *means of support* | *other people found her difficult* | [as pronoun] *a language unrelated to any other.* ■ alternative of two: [as adj.] *the other side of the street* | [as pronoun] *she flung up first one arm and then the other* | ***one or other*** *of his parents.* ■ those remaining in a group; those not already mentioned: [as adj.] *they took the other three away in an ambulance* | [as pronoun] *Freddie set off and* ***the others*** *followed.*
2 further; additional: [as adj.] *one other word of advice* | [as pronoun] *Labour would have 49 MPs plus ten others.*
3 [pronoun] (**the other**) Brit. informal used euphemistically to refer to sexual intercourse: *a bit of the other.*
4 [pronoun] (**the other**) Philosophy & Sociology that which is distinct from, different from, or opposite to something or oneself.
▶ **verb** [with obj.] view or treat (a person or group of people) as intrinsically different from and alien to oneself: *a critique of the ways in which the elderly are othered by society.*
– PHRASES **how the other half lives** used to express or allude to the way of life of a different group in society, especially a wealthier one. **no other** archaic nothing else: *we can do no other.* **other than** [with negative or in questions] apart from; except: *he claims not to own anything other than his home.* ■ differently or different from; otherwise than: *there is no suggestion that we are to take this other than literally.* **on the other hand** see **HAND**. **the other day** (or **night**, **week**, etc.) a few days (or nights, weeks, etc.) ago. **the other thing** Brit., chiefly humorous an unexpressed alternative: *if you keep a lot of rules I'll reward you, and if you don't I'll do the other thing.* **someone** (or **something** or **somehow** etc.) **or other** some unspecified or unknown person, thing, manner, etc.: *they were protesting about something or other.*
– ORIGIN Old English *ōther*, of Germanic origin; related to Dutch and German *ander*, from an Indo-European root meaning 'different'.

other-directed ▶ **adjective** Psychology (of a person or their behaviour) governed by external circumstances and the behaviour and standards of others.

other half ▶ **noun** (**one's other half**) Brit. informal one's wife, husband, or partner.

otherness ▶ **noun** [mass noun] the quality or fact of being different: *the developed world has been celebrating African music while altogether denying its otherness.*

other place ▶ **noun** (**the other place**) Brit. humorous hell, as opposed to heaven. ■ Oxford University as regarded by Cambridge, and vice versa. ■ the House of Lords as regarded by the House of Commons, and vice versa.

other ranks ▶ **plural noun** Brit. (in the armed forces) all those who are not commissioned officers.

otherwhere ▶ **adverb & pronoun** archaic or literary elsewhere.

otherwise ▶ **adverb 1** in circumstances different from those present or considered; or else: *the collection is a good draw that brings visitors who might not come otherwise* | *I'm not motivated by money, otherwise I would have quit.*
2 in other respects; apart from that: *an otherwise totally black cat with a single white whisker.*
3 in a different way: *he means mischief—it's no good pretending otherwise* | *all the staff were* ***otherwise engaged.*** ■ as an alternative: *the Cosa Nostra,* ***otherwise known as*** *the Brotherhood.*
▶ **adjective** [predic.] in a different state or situation: *I would that it were otherwise.*
– PHRASES **or** (or **and**) **otherwise** indicating the opposite of or a contrast to something stated: *we don't want a president, elected or otherwise.*
– ORIGIN Old English *on ōthre wīsan* (see **OTHER**, **WISE²**).

other woman ▶ **noun** (**the other woman**) the lover of a married or similarly attached man.

other world ▶ **noun** (**the other world**) the spiritual world or afterlife.

other-worldly ▶ **adjective 1** relating to an imaginary or spiritual world: *music of an almost other-worldly beauty.*
2 unworldly: *celibate clerics with a very other-worldly outlook.*
– DERIVATIVES **other-worldliness** noun.

Othman /ˈɒθmən/ variant form of **OSMAN I**.

Otho /ˈəʊθəʊ/, Marcus Salvius (AD 32–69), Roman emperor January–April 69. He was proclaimed emperor after he had procured the death of Galba in a conspiracy of the praetorian guard, but the German legions, led by their imperial candidate, Vitellius, defeated his troops and Otho committed suicide.

otic /ˈəʊtɪk, ˈɒtɪk/ ▶ **adjective** Anatomy relating to the ear.
– ORIGIN mid 17th cent.: from Greek *ōtikos*, from *ous*, *ōt-* 'ear'.

-otic ▶ **suffix** forming adjectives and nouns corresponding to nouns ending in *-osis* (such as *neurotic* corresponding to *neurosis*).
– DERIVATIVES **-otically** suffix forming corresponding adverbs.
– ORIGIN from French *-otique*, via Latin from the Greek adjectival ending *-ōtikos*.

otiose /ˈəʊtɪəʊs, ˈəʊʃɪ-, -z/ ▶ **adjective 1** serving no practical purpose or result.
2 archaic indolent or idle.
– ORIGIN late 18th cent.: from Latin *otiosus*, from *otium* 'leisure'.

Otis /ˈəʊtɪs/, Elisha Graves (1811–61), American inventor and manufacturer. He produced the first efficient elevator with a safety device in 1852.

otitis /ə(ʊ)ˈtʌɪtɪs/ ▶ **noun** [mass noun] Medicine inflammation of the ear, usually distinguished as **otitis externa** (of the passage of the outer ear), **otitis media** (of the middle ear), and **otitis interna** (of the inner ear; labyrinthitis).
– ORIGIN late 18th cent.: modern Latin, from Greek *ous*, *ōt-* 'ear' + **-ITIS**.

oto- /ˈəʊtəʊ/ ▸ **combining form** (used chiefly in medical terms) of or relating to the ears: *otoscope*.
– ORIGIN from Greek *ous, ōt-* 'ear'.

otocyst ▸ **noun** another term for **STATOCYST**.

otolaryngology /ˌəʊtə(ʊ)larɪŋˈɡɒlədʒi/ ▸ **noun** [mass noun] the study of diseases of the ear and throat.
– DERIVATIVES **otolaryngological** adjective, **otolaryngologist** noun.

otolith ▸ **noun** Zoology each of three small oval calcareous bodies in the inner ear of vertebrates, involved in sensing gravity and movement.
– DERIVATIVES **otolithic** adjective.

otology /əʊˈtɒlədʒi/ ▸ **noun** [mass noun] the study of the anatomy and diseases of the ear.
– DERIVATIVES **otological** adjective, **otologist** noun.

Otomanguean /ˌəʊtə(ʊ)ˈmaŋɡiən, -ˈmaŋɡwiən/ ▸ **adjective** relating to or denoting a family of American Indian languages of central and southern Mexico, including Mixtec, Otomi, and Zapotec.
– ORIGIN 1940s: from **OTOMI** + *Mangue* (an extinct language of Costa Rica) + **-AN**.

Otomi /ˌəʊtəˈmiː/ ▸ **noun** (pl. **same**) **1** a member of an American Indian people inhabiting parts of central Mexico.
2 [mass noun] the Otomanguean language of the Otomi.
▸ **adjective** relating to the Otomi or their language.
– ORIGIN via American Spanish from Nahuatl *otomih*, literally 'unknown'.

otoplasty /ˈəʊtə(ʊ)ˌplasti/ ▸ **noun** (pl. **otoplasties**) Medicine a surgical operation to restore or enhance the appearance of an ear or the ears.

otorhinolaryngology /ˌəʊtə(ʊ)ˌrʌɪnəʊˌlarɪŋˈɡɒlədʒi/ ▸ **noun** [mass noun] the study of diseases of the ear, nose, and throat.
– DERIVATIVES **otorhinolaryngologist** noun.

otosclerosis ▸ **noun** [mass noun] Medicine a hereditary disorder causing progressive deafness due to overgrowth of bone in the inner ear.

otoscope ▸ **noun** an instrument designed for visual examination of the eardrum and the passage of the outer ear, typically having a light and a set of lenses. Also called **AURISCOPE**.
– DERIVATIVES **otoscopic** adjective, **otoscopically** adverb.

ototoxic ▸ **adjective** Medicine having a toxic effect on the ear or its nerve supply.
– DERIVATIVES **ototoxicity** noun.

Otranto, Strait of /ɒˈtrantəʊ/ a channel linking the Adriatic Sea with the Ionian Sea and separating the 'heel' of Italy from Albania.

OTT ▸ **abbreviation** Brit. informal over the top: *presenting him as a goalscoring Superman seems a bit OTT*.

ottava rima /ɒˌtɑːvə ˈriːmə/ ▸ **noun** [mass noun] a form of poetry consisting of stanzas of eight lines of ten or eleven syllables, rhyming *abababcc*.
– ORIGIN late 18th cent.: from Italian, literally 'eighth rhyme'.

Ottawa /ˈɒtəwə, -wɑː/ the federal capital of Canada, on the Ottawa River (a tributary of the St Lawrence); pop. 812,129 (2006). Founded in 1827, it was named Bytown until 1854 after Colonel John By (1779–1836).

otter ▸ **noun** **1** a semiaquatic fish-eating mammal of the weasel family, with an elongated body, dense fur, and webbed feet. ● *Lutra* and other genera, family Mustelidae: several species, including the **European otter** (*L. lutra*). See also **SEA OTTER**.
2 a piece of board used to carry fishing bait in water.
– ORIGIN Old English *otr, ot(t)or*, of Germanic origin; related to Greek *hudros* 'water snake'.

otter board ▸ **noun** either of a pair of boards or metal plates, attached to each side of the mouth of a trawl net at an angle which keeps the net open as it is pulled through the water.

otter dog (also **otter hound**) ▸ **noun** a large hound of a breed with a long rough coat, used in otter hunting.

otter shell ▸ **noun** a burrowing marine bivalve mollusc with a relatively thin elliptical shell. ● Genus *Lutraria*, family Mactridae: numerous species.

otter shrew ▸ **noun** a semiaquatic mammal of the tenrec family, with a sleek body and long tail, native to central and West Africa. ● Genera *Potamogale* and *Micropotamogale*, family Tenrecidae: three species, including the **giant otter shrew** (*P. velox*), which resembles an otter.

otter trawl ▸ **noun** a trawl net fitted with an otter board.

Otto, Nikolaus August (1832–91), German engineer, whose name is given to the four-stroke cycle on which most internal-combustion engines work.

otto ▸ **noun** another term for **ATTAR**.

ottocento /ˌɒtə(ʊ)ˈtʃɛntəʊ/ ▸ **adjective** relating to the 19th century in Italy.
– ORIGIN Italian, literally '800' (shortened from *milottocento* '1800'), used with reference to the years 1800–99.

Otto I (912–73), king of the Germans 936–73, Holy Roman emperor 962–73; known as **Otto the Great**. As king of the Germans he carried out a policy of eastward expansion and as Holy Roman emperor he established a presence in Italy to rival that of the papacy.

Ottoman /ˈɒtəmən/ ▸ **adjective** historical **1** relating to the Turkish dynasty of Osman I (Othman I). ■ relating to the branch of the Turks to which Osman I belonged.
2 relating to the Ottoman Empire.
3 Turkish.
▸ **noun** (pl. **Ottomans**) a Turk, especially of the period of the Ottoman Empire.
– ORIGIN based on Arabic *ʿuṯmānī* (adjective), from *ʿUṯmān* 'Othman'.

ottoman ▸ **noun** (pl. **ottomans**) **1** a low upholstered seat without a back or arms that typically serves also as a box, with the seat hinged to form a lid.
2 [mass noun] a heavy ribbed fabric made from silk and either cotton or wool.
– ORIGIN early 19th cent.: from French *ottomane*, feminine of *ottoman* 'Ottoman'.

Ottoman Empire the Turkish empire, established in northern Anatolia by Osman I at the end of the 13th century and expanded by his successors to include all of Asia Minor and much of SE Europe. After setbacks caused by the invasion of the Mongol ruler Tamerlane in 1402, Constantinople was captured in 1453. The empire reached its zenith under Suleiman in the mid 16th century; it had greatly declined by the 19th century and collapsed after the First World War.

Ottoman Porte see **PORTE**.

Otto the Great see **OTTO I**.

Otway, Thomas (1652–85), English dramatist. He is chiefly remembered for his two blank verse tragedies, *The Orphan* (1680) and *Venice Preserved* (1682).

OU ▸ **abbreviation** (in the UK) Open University.

ou[1] /əʊ/ ▸ **noun** (pl. **ouens** /ˈəʊənz/ or **ous**) S. African informal a man.
– ORIGIN Afrikaans, probably from Dutch *ouwe* 'old man'.

ou[2] /ˈəʊuː/ ▸ **noun** a fruit-eating Hawaiian honeycreeper (bird) with a stout bill and green and yellow plumage. Compare with **O-O**. ● *Psittirostra psittacea*, family Drepanididae.
– ORIGIN late 19th cent.: the name in Hawaiian.

ouabain /ˈuːəbeɪn/ ▸ **noun** [mass noun] Chemistry a toxic compound obtained from certain trees, used as a very rapid cardiac stimulant. It is a polycyclic glycoside.
– ORIGIN late 19th cent.: via French from Somali *wabayo*, denoting a tree that yields poison (used on arrow points) containing ouabain.

Ouagadougou /ˌwɑːɡəˈduːɡuː/ the capital of Burkina Faso; pop. 1,149,000 (est. 2007).

ouananiche /ˌwanəˈniːʃ/ ▸ **noun** (pl. **same**) Canadian an Atlantic salmon of landlocked populations living in lakes in Labrador and Newfoundland.
– ORIGIN late 19th cent.: via Canadian French from Algonquian.

oubaas /ˈəʊbɑːs/ ▸ **noun** S. African a head of a family. ■ an elderly man.
– ORIGIN Afrikaans, from Dutch *oud* 'old' + **BAAS**.

oubliette /ˌuːblɪˈɛt/ ▸ **noun** a secret dungeon with access only through a trapdoor in its ceiling.
– ORIGIN late 18th cent.: from French, from *oublier* 'forget'.

ouboet /ˈəʊbʊt/ ▸ **noun** S. African informal used as an affectionate way of addressing or referring to an older brother or male friend.
– ORIGIN Afrikaans, from *ou* 'old' + *boet* 'mate' (from Dutch dialect *boet* 'youngster').

ouch ▸ **exclamation** used to express pain.
– ORIGIN natural exclamation: first recorded in English in the mid 17th cent.

oud /uːd/ ▸ **noun** a form of lute or mandolin played principally in Arab countries.
– ORIGIN mid 18th cent.: from Arabic *al-ʿūd*.

Oudenarde, Battle of /ˈuːdənɑːd/ a battle which took place in 1708 during the War of the Spanish Succession, near the town of Oudenarde in eastern Flanders, Belgium. A force of allied British and Austrian troops defeated the French.

Oudh /aʊd/ (also **Audh** or **Awadh**) a region of northern India. In 1877 it joined with Agra and in 1902 it formed the United Provinces of Agra and Oudh. This was renamed Uttar Pradesh in 1950.

ouens plural form of **OU**[1].

ought[1] ▸ **modal verb** (3rd sing. present and past **ought**) [with infinitive] **1** used to indicate duty or correctness, typically when criticizing someone's actions: *they ought to respect the law* | *thanks for your letter which I ought to have answered sooner*. ■ used to indicate a desirable or expected state: *he ought to be able to take the initiative*. ■ used to give or ask for advice: *you ought to go* | *what ought I to do?*
2 used to indicate something that is probable: *five minutes ought to be enough time*.
– ORIGIN Old English *āhte*, past tense of *āgan* 'owe' (see **OWE**).

> **USAGE** The verb **ought** is a modal verb and this means that, grammatically, it does not behave like ordinary verbs. In particular, the negative is formed with the word **not** alone and not also with auxiliary verbs such as **do** or **have**. Thus the standard construction for the negative is *he* ***ought not*** *to have gone*. The alternative forms *he* ***didn't ought*** *to have gone* and *he* ***hadn't ought*** *to have gone*, formed as if **ought** were an ordinary verb rather than a modal verb, are found in dialect from the 19th century but are not acceptable in standard modern English.

ought[2] (also **aught**) ▸ **noun** archaic term for **NOUGHT**.
– ORIGIN mid 19th cent.: perhaps from *an ought*, by wrong division of *a nought*; compare with **ADDER**[1].

ought[3] ▸ **pronoun** variant spelling of **AUGHT**[1].

oughtn't ▸ **contraction** ought not.

ouguiya /uːˈɡiːjə/ (also **ougiya**) ▸ **noun** the basic monetary unit of Mauritania, equal to five khoums.
– ORIGIN via French from Mauritanian Arabic, from Arabic *ʾūqīya*, from Greek *ounkia*, from Latin *uncia* 'ounce'.

Ouija board /ˈwiːdʒə/ ▸ **noun** trademark a board with letters, numbers, and other signs around its edge, to which a planchette, movable pointer, or upturned glass moves, supposedly in answer to questions from people at a seance.
– ORIGIN late 19th cent.: *Ouija* from French *oui* 'yes' + German *ja* 'yes'.

O

ouklip /ˈəʊklɪp/ ▸ **noun** [mass noun] S. African an iron-rich lateritic conglomerate formed from the decomposition of underlying rocks by subsurface chemical weathering.
– ORIGIN late 19th cent.: from Afrikaans, from *ou* 'old' + *klip* 'rock, stone'.

Oulu /ˈaʊluː/ a city in central Finland, on the west coast, capital of a province of the same name; pop. 137,454 (2009). Swedish name **ULEÅBORG**.

ouma /ˈəʊmə/ ▸ **noun** S. African used as a respectful or affectionate form of address for a grandmother or elderly woman.
– ORIGIN Afrikaans, 'grandmother'.

ounce[1] ▸ **noun** **1** (abbrev.: **oz**) a unit of weight of one sixteenth of a pound avoirdupois (approximately 28 grams). ■ a unit of one twelfth of a pound troy or apothecaries' measure, equal to 480 grains (approximately 31 grams).
2 a very small amount of something: *Robyn summoned up every ounce of strength*.
– ORIGIN Middle English: from Old French *unce*, from Latin *uncia* 'twelfth part (of a pound or foot)'; compare with **INCH**[1].

ounce[2] ▸ **noun** another term for **SNOW LEOPARD**.
– ORIGIN Middle English: from Old French *once*, earlier *lonce* (the *l-* being misinterpreted as the definite article), based on Latin *lynx, lync-* (see **LYNX**).

oupa /ˈəʊpə/ ▸ **noun** S. African used as a respectful or affectionate form of address for a grandfather or elderly man.
– ORIGIN Afrikaans, 'grandfather'.

our ▸ **possessive determiner** **1** belonging to or associated with the speaker and one or more other people previously mentioned or easily identified: *Jo and I had our hair cut*. ■ belonging to or associated with people in

general: *when we hear a sound, our brains identify the source quickly.*
2 used in formal contexts by a royal person or a writer or editor to refer to something belonging to or associated with himself or herself: *we want to know what you, our readers, think.*
3 informal, chiefly N. English used with a name to refer to a relative, friend, or colleague of the speaker: *really, she is a one, our Gillian.*
– ORIGIN Old English *ūre*, of Germanic origin; related to **us** and German *unser*.

-our¹ ▶ suffix variant spelling of **-OR²** surviving in some nouns such as *ardour, colour*.

-our² ▶ suffix variant spelling of **-OR¹** (as in *saviour*).

Our Father used as a title for God. ▪ a name for the Lord's Prayer.

Our Lady used as a title for the Virgin Mary.

ouroboros /jʊərəʊˈbɒrəs/ ▶ noun variant spelling of **UROBOROS**.

ours ▶ possessive pronoun used to refer to a thing or things belonging to or associated with the speaker and one or more other people previously mentioned or easily identified: *ours was the ugliest house on the block* | *this chat* **of ours** *is strictly between us.*

USAGE There is no need for an apostrophe: the spelling should be **ours** not **our's**.

ourself ▶ pronoun [first person plural] **1** used instead of 'ourselves' typically when 'we' refers to people in general rather than a definite group of people: [reflexive] *we must choose which aspects of ourself to express to the world* | [emphatic] *this is our affair—we deal with it ourself.*
2 archaic used instead of 'myself' by a sovereign or other person in authority.

USAGE The standard reflexive form corresponding to **we** and **us** is **ourselves**, as in *we can only blame* **ourselves**. The singular form **ourself**, first recorded in the 15th century, is sometimes used in modern English, typically where 'we' refers to people in general. This use, though logical, is uncommon and not widely accepted in standard English.

ourselves ▶ pronoun [first person plural] **1** [reflexive] used as the object of a verb or preposition when this is the same as the subject of the clause and the subject is the speaker and one or more other people considered together: *since we're here, we might as well enjoy ourselves.*
2 [emphatic] we or us personally (used to emphasize the speaker and one or more other people considered together): *we invented it ourselves.*
– PHRASES **(not) be ourselves** see **BE ONESELF, NOT BE ONESELF** at **BE**. **by ourselves** see **BY ONESELF** at **BY**.

-ous ▶ suffix forming adjectives: **1** characterized by; of the nature of: *dangerous* | *mountainous*.
2 Chemistry denoting an element in a lower valency: *ferrous* | *sulphurous*. Compare with **-IC**.
– DERIVATIVES **-ously suffix** forming corresponding adverbs, **-ousness suffix** forming corresponding nouns.
– ORIGIN from Anglo-Norman French, or Old French *-eus*, from Latin *-osus*.

Ouse /uːz/ **1** (also **Great Ouse**) a river of eastern England, which rises in Northamptonshire and flows 257 km (160 miles) eastwards then northwards through East Anglia to the Wash near King's Lynn.
2 a river of NE England, formed at the confluence of the Ure and Swale in North Yorkshire and flowing 92 km (57 miles) south-eastwards through York to the Humber estuary.
3 a river of SE England, which rises in the Weald of West Sussex and flows 48 km (30 miles) south-eastwards to the English Channel.
4 (also **Little Ouse**) a river of East Anglia, which forms a tributary of the Great Ouse.

ousel ▶ noun variant spelling of **OUZEL**.

oust /aʊst/ ▶ verb [with obj.] drive out or expel (someone) from a position or place: *the reformists were* **ousted from** *power.* ▪ Law deprive of or exclude from possession of something. ▪ Law take away (a court's jurisdiction) in a matter.
– ORIGIN late Middle English (as a legal term): from Anglo-Norman French *ouster* 'take away', from Latin *obstare* 'oppose, hinder'.

ouster ▶ noun [mass noun] **1** Law ejection from a property, especially wrongful ejection; deprivation of an inheritance. ▪ removal from the jurisdiction of the courts. ▪ [count noun] a clause that is or is claimed to be outside the jurisdiction of the courts.
2 N. Amer. dismissal or expulsion from a position: *the junta's ouster of the Emperor.*

out ▶ adverb **1** moving or appearing to move away from a particular place, especially one that is enclosed or hidden: *he walked out into the street* | *watch the stars come out.* ▪ situated or operating in the open air, away from buildings: *the search-and-rescue team have been out looking for you.* ▪ no longer detained in prison: *they would be out on bail in no time.*
2 situated far or at a particular distance from somewhere: *an old farmhouse right out in the middle of nowhere* | *they lived eight miles* **out of** *town* | *a cold front hundreds of miles out in the Atlantic.* ▪ to sea, away from the land: *the Persian fleet put out from Cyprus.* ▪ (of the tide) falling or at its lowest level: *the tide was going out.* ▪ indicating a specified distance away from the goal line or finishing line: *he scored from 70 metres out.*
3 away from home: *he's gone out.* ▪ in or to a public place for purposes of pleasure or entertainment: *an evening out at a restaurant.*
4 so as to be revealed or known: *find out what you can.* ▪ aloud; so as to be heard: *Miss Beard cried out in horror.*
5 at or to an end: *the romance fizzled out.* ▪ so as to be finished or complete: *I'll leave them to fight it out* | *I typed out the poem.* ▪ in various other completive uses: *the crowd had thinned out* | *he crossed out a word.*
6 (of a light or fire) so as to be extinguished or no longer burning: *at ten o'clock the lights went out.* ▪ (of a stain or mark) no longer visible; removed: *try and get the stain out.*
7 no longer involved in a situation, competition, or activity: *Oxford United are* **out of** *the FA Cup.*
▶ preposition non-standard contraction of *out of*: *he ran out the door.*
▶ adjective [predic.] **1** not at home or at one's place of work: *if he called, she'd pretend to be out.*
2 revealed or made public: *the secret was soon out.* ▪ published: *the book should be out before the end of the month.* ▪ informal in existence or use: *it works as well as any system that's out.* ▪ (of a jury) considering its verdict in secrecy. ▪ dated (of a young upper-class woman) introduced into society. ▪ open about one's homosexuality: *I had been out since I was 17.*
3 no longer alight; extinguished: *the fire was nearly out.*
4 at an end: *school was out for the summer.* ▪ informal no longer in fashion: *grunge is out.*
5 not possible or worth considering: *a trip to the seaside is out for a start.*
6 in a state of unconsciousness. ▪ Boxing unable to rise from the floor.
7 mistaken; in error: *he was slightly out in his calculations.*
8 (of the ball in tennis and similar games) outside the designated playing area.
9 Cricket & Baseball no longer batting or at bat; having had one's innings or at bat ended by the fielding side: *England were all out for 159.*
10 (of a flower) in bloom; open.
▶ noun **1** informal a way of escaping from a problem or dilemma: *he was desperately looking for an out.*
2 Baseball an act of putting a player out.
3 (**the outs**) the political party not in office.
▶ verb [with obj.] **1** knock (someone) out.
2 informal reveal the homosexuality of (a prominent person).
3 W. Indian extinguish: *out the lamp when you're ready.*
4 dated expel, reject, or dismiss: *they had outed Asquith quite easily.*
– PHRASES **at outs** (N. Amer. **on the outs**) in dispute: *you were* **at outs with** *my uncle Ned.* **not out** Cricket (of a side or batsman) having begun an innings and not been dismissed. **out and about** engaging in normal activity after an illness. **out for** intent on having: *he was out for a good time.* **out of 1** indicating the source or derivation of something; from: *a bench fashioned out of a fallen tree trunk* | *I get a lot of enjoyment out of teaching.* ▪ having (the thing mentioned) as a motivation: *he was acting out of spite.* **2** indicating the dam of a pedigree animal, especially a horse. **3** from among (a number): *nine times out of ten, companies are the source of such information.* **4** not having (a particular thing): *they had run out of cash* | *you're out of luck, mate, there's none left.* **out of it** informal **1** not included; rejected: *I hate feeling out of it.* **2** unaware of what is happening as a result of being uninformed. ▪ unable to think or react properly, especially as a result of taking drugs or drinking too much alcohol. **out to do something** keenly striving to do something: *they were out to impress.* **out with it** say what you are thinking.
– ORIGIN Old English *ūt* (adverb), *ūtian* (verb), of Germanic origin; related to Dutch *uit* and German *aus*.

USAGE The use of **out** as a preposition (rather than the standard prepositional phrase **out of**), as in *he threw it out the window*, is common in informal contexts, and is standard in American, Australian, and New Zealand English. Traditionalists do not accept it as part of standard British English, however.

out- ▶ prefix **1** to the point of surpassing or exceeding: *outfight* | *outperform*.
2 external; separate; from outside: *outbuildings* | *outpatient*.
3 away from; outward: *outbound* | *outpost*.

outa ▶ preposition variant spelling of **OUTTA**.

outact ▶ verb [with obj.] surpass (someone) in acting or performing something.

outage /ˈaʊtɪdʒ/ ▶ noun a period when a power supply or other service is not available or when equipment is closed down.

out and out ▶ adjective [attrib.] in every respect; absolute: *an out-and-out rogue.*
▶ adverb completely: *he was induced to part out and out with all the money.*

out-and-outer ▶ noun archaic, informal an out-and-out possessor of a particular quality.

outback ▶ noun (**the outback**) the remote and usually uninhabited inland districts of Australia. ▪ any remote or sparsely populated inland region.
– DERIVATIVES **outbacker** noun.

outbalance ▶ verb [with obj.] be more valuable, important, or influential than: *the advantages far outbalanced the drawbacks.*

outbid ▶ verb (**outbids, outbidding**; past and past participle **outbid**) [with obj.] offer to pay a higher price for something than (another person): *residential builders could always outbid any farmer for the land round London.*

outboard ▶ adjective & adverb **1** on, towards, or near the outside of a ship or aircraft: [as adj.] *the outboard wing panels* | [as adv.] *the chart table faces outboard.* ▪ [as adj.] (of a motor) portable and attachable to the outside of the stern of a boat.
2 [as adj.] (of an electronic accessory) in a separate container from the device with which it is used.
▶ noun an outboard motor. ▪ a boat with an outboard motor.
– PHRASES **outboard of** to the outside or on the far side of: *the controls are placed just outboard of the wheel.*

outbound ▶ adjective & adverb travelling away from a particular place, especially on the first leg of a return journey: [as adj.] *an outbound flight* | [as adv.] *flying outbound.*

outbox ▶ noun N. Amer. an out tray. ▪ a folder in which emails written by an individual are held before being sent.
▶ verb [with obj.] Boxing defeat (an opponent) by superior boxing ability.

outbrave ▶ verb [with obj.] archaic outdo in bravery: *I would outbrave the hart most daring on the earth.* ▪ face (something) with a show of brave defiance: *the Duke sat outfacing his accusers, and outbraving their accusations.*

outbreak ▶ noun a sudden occurrence of something unwelcome, such as war or disease: *the outbreak of World War II.*

outbreed ▶ verb (past and past participle **outbred**) [with obj.] (usu. as noun **outbreeding**) breed from parents not closely related: *many specific genetic factors are known which regulate the degree of outbreeding.*

outbuilding ▶ noun a smaller separate building such as a shed or barn that belongs to a main building, such as a house or farm.

outburst ▶ noun a sudden release of strong emotion: *an angry outburst from the prime minister.* ▪ a sudden occurrence of a particular activity: *a wild outburst of applause.* ▪ Physics a sudden emission of energy or particles: *a very dramatic outburst of neutrons.*

outcall ▶ noun a house call made by a prostitute.

outcast ▶ noun a person who has been rejected or ostracized by their society or social group.
▶ adjective (of a person) rejected or ostracized: *they can be made to feel outcast and inadequate.*

O

outcaste ▶ noun (in Hindu society) a person who has no caste or a person who is expelled from their caste.
▶ verb [with obj.] cause (someone) to lose their caste.

outclass ▶ verb [with obj.] be far superior to: *Villa totally outclassed us in the first half.*

outcome ▶ noun the way a thing turns out; a consequence: *it is the outcome of the vote that counts.*

outcompete ▶ verb [with obj.] surpass in a competitive situation: *they were outcompeted by their foreign rivals.* ■ Biology displace (another species) in the competition for space, food, or other resources.

outcrop ▶ noun a rock formation that is visible on the surface: *dramatic limestone outcrops.*
▶ verb (**outcrops**, **outcropping**, **outcropped**) [no obj.] appear as an outcrop.
– DERIVATIVES **outcropping** noun.

outcross ▶ verb [with obj.] breed (an animal or plant) with one not closely related.
▶ noun an animal or plant produced as the result of outcrossing.

outcry ▶ noun (pl. **outcries**) an exclamation or shout: *an outcry of spontaneous passion.* ■ a strong expression of public disapproval or anger: *the public outcry over the bombing.*

outcurve ▶ noun Baseball a ball pitched so as to curve away from the batter.

outdance ▶ verb [with obj.] dance better than (someone else).

outdated ▶ adjective out of date; obsolete: *outdated equipment.*
– DERIVATIVES **outdate** verb, **outdatedness** noun.

outdistance ▶ verb [with obj.] leave (a competitor or pursuer) far behind: *she could maintain a fast enough pace to outdistance any pursuers.*

outdo ▶ verb (**outdoes**, **outdoing**; past **outdid**; past participle **outdone**) [with obj.] be superior to in action or performance: *the men tried to outdo each other in their generosity* | ***not to be outdone****, Vicky and Laura reached the same standard.*

outdoor ▶ adjective [attrib.] done, situated, or used out of doors: *a huge outdoor concert.* ■ fond of the open air or open-air activities: *a rugged, outdoor type.*

outdoor pursuits ▶ plural noun Brit. open-air sporting or leisure activities, such as orienteering, mountaineering, and canoeing.

outdoors ▶ adverb in or into the open air; outside a building or shelter: *it was warm enough to eat outdoors.*
▶ noun (usu. **the outdoors**) any area outside buildings or shelter, typically that far away from human habitation: *a lover of the great outdoors.*

outdoorsman ▶ noun (pl. **outdoorsmen**) a man who spends a lot of time outdoors or doing outdoor activities.

outdoorsy ▶ adjective informal, chiefly N. Amer. of, associated with, or fond of the outdoors: *Bill is such an outdoorsy kind of guy.*

outdraw ▶ verb (past **outdrew**; past participle **outdrawn**) [with obj.] (of a person or event) attract a larger crowd than (another person or event).

outdrink ▶ verb (past **outdrank**; past participle **outdrunk**) [with obj.] drink more than.

outdrive ▶ verb (past **outdrove**; past participle **outdriven**) [with obj.] **1** drive a golf ball further than (another player): *Buck outdrove him by forty yards.*
2 drive a vehicle better or faster than (someone else): *he knew he couldn't outdrive the police.*
▶ noun (on a motor boat) an inboard motor connected to an outboard unit containing the gears, shaft, and propeller.

outer ▶ adjective [attrib.] **1** outside; external: *the outer layer of the skin* | *the outer door.* ■ further from the centre or inside: *the outer city bypass.* ■ (especially in place names) more remote: *Outer Mongolia.*
2 objective or physical; not subjective.
▶ noun Brit. **1** an outer garment or part of one: *boots with stiff leather outers.*
2 the division of a target furthest from the bullseye. ■ a shot that strikes this.
3 a container in which packaged objects are placed for transport or display.
4 Austral. informal the part of a racecourse outside the enclosure.
– ORIGIN late Middle English: from OUT + -ER[2], replacing earlier UTTER[1].

outer bar ▶ noun (**the outer bar**) (in the UK) a collective term for barristers who are not Queen's or King's Counsels.

outer belt ▶ noun US a ring road.

Outer Hebrides see HEBRIDES.

Outer House (in full **the Outer House of the Court of Session**) (in Scotland) a law court that hears cases in the first instance, presided over by a single judge (a Lord Ordinary).

Outer Mongolia see MONGOLIA.

outermost ▶ adjective [attrib.] furthest from the centre: *the outermost layer of the earth.*
▶ pronoun the one that is furthest from the centre: *the orbit of the outermost of these eight planets.*

outer planet ▶ noun a planet whose orbit lies outside the asteroid belt, i.e. Jupiter, Saturn, Uranus, or Neptune.

outer space ▶ noun [mass noun] the physical universe beyond the earth's atmosphere.

outerwear ▶ noun [mass noun] clothing worn over other clothes, especially outdoors.

outface ▶ verb [with obj.] disconcert or defeat (an opponent) by confronting them boldly: *these achievements were based on outfacing militant unions.*

outfall ▶ noun the place where a river, drain, or sewer empties into the sea, a river, or a lake.

outfield ▶ noun **1** Cricket the part of the field furthest from the wicket. ■ Baseball the grassy area beyond the infield. ■ [treated as sing. or pl.] the players stationed in the outfield, regarded collectively.
2 the outlying land of a farm.
– DERIVATIVES **outfielder** noun.

outfight ▶ verb (past and past participle **outfought**) [with obj.] fight better than and beat (an opponent).

outfit ▶ noun **1** a set of clothes worn together, especially for a particular occasion or purpose: *her wedding outfit.* ■ a complete set of equipment needed for a particular purpose: *a first-aid outfit.*
2 informal a group of people undertaking a particular activity together, especially a group of musicians, a team, or a business concern: *an obscure 1970s country rock outfit.*
▶ verb (**outfits**, **outfitting**, **outfitted**) [with obj.] provide with a set of clothes: *warders outfitted in special suits.* ■ provide with equipment: *planes outfitted with sophisticated electronic gear.*

outfitter (also **outfitters**) ▶ noun **1** Brit. dated a shop selling men's clothing.
2 N. Amer. a shop selling equipment, typically for outdoor pursuits: *a canoe outfitter.*

outflank ▶ verb [with obj.] move round the side of (an enemy) so as to outmanoeuvre them: *the Germans had sought to outflank them from the north-east.* ■ outwit: *an attempt to outflank the opposition.*

outflow ▶ noun a large amount of money, liquid, or people that moves or is transferred out of a place: *an outflow of foreign currency* | [mass noun] *capital outflow took place on a very large scale.*

outflung ▶ adjective (especially of a person's arm) thrown out to one side: *he turned, one arm outflung.*

outfly ▶ verb (**outflies**, **outflying**; past **outflew**; past participle **outflown**) [with obj.] fly faster, further, or with more agility than: *a high-powered combat aircraft that can outfly anything.*

outfox ▶ verb [with obj.] informal defeat (someone) by being more clever or cunning than them.

outgas ▶ verb (**outgases**, **outgassing**, **outgassed**) [with obj.] release or give off (a substance) as a gas or vapour.

outgeneral ▶ verb (**outgenerals**, **outgeneralling**, **outgeneralled**; US **outgenerals**, **outgeneraling**, **outgeneraled**) [with obj.] get the better of by superior strategy or tactics: *he had outgeneraled a few Indians at the battle.*

outgo archaic ▶ verb (**outgoes**, **outgoing**; past **outwent**; past participle **outgone**) [with obj.] go faster than: *he on horseback outgoes him on foot.*
▶ noun [mass noun] the outlay of money: *the secret of success lies in the relation of income to outgo.*

outgoing ▶ adjective **1** friendly and socially confident: *she's always been very outgoing and she's got heaps of friends.*
2 [attrib.] leaving an office or position: *the outgoing Prime Minister.* ■ going out or away from a particular place: *incoming and outgoing calls.*
▶ noun Brit. **1** (**outgoings**) a person's regular expenditure.
2 an instance of going out: *the inward deliveries and outgoings of raw materials.*

outgross ▶ verb [with obj.] surpass in gross takings or profit: *the film has outgrossed all other movie comedies.*

out-group ▶ noun **1** Sociology those people who do not belong to a specific in-group.
2 Biology a group of organisms not belonging to the group whose evolutionary relationships are being investigated. Such a group is used for comparison, to assess which characteristics of the group being studied are more widely distributed and may therefore be older in origin.

outgrow ▶ verb (past **outgrew**; past participle **outgrown**) [with obj.] grow too big for: *the cradle which Patrick had outgrown.* ■ stop doing or having an interest in (something) as one matures: *by this time, I had outgrown my adolescent appetite for being shocked.* ■ grow faster or taller than: *the more vigorous plants outgrow their weaker neighbours.*
– PHRASES **outgrow one's strength** Brit. become lanky and weak through excessively rapid growth.

outgrowth ▶ noun something that grows out of something else: *the eye first appears as an outgrowth from the brain.* ■ [mass noun] the process of growing out: *with further outgrowth the radius and ulna develop.* ■ a natural development or result of something: *the book is an imaginative outgrowth of practical criticism.*

outguess ▶ verb [with obj.] outwit (someone) by guessing correctly what they intend to do: *a brilliant military commander outguesses the enemy.*

outgun ▶ verb (**outguns**, **outgunning**, **outgunned**) [with obj.] have better or more weaponry than: *the gangs have carved up the city and easily outgun the police.* ■ shoot better than: *the correspondents proudly outgunned the army sharpshooters.* ■ surpass in power or strength: *the team were outgunned by the joint title favourites.*

out-half ▶ noun Rugby another term for STAND-OFF HALF.

outhaul ▶ noun Sailing a rope used to haul out the clew of a sail.

outhit ▶ verb (**outhits**, **outhitting**; past and past participle **outhit**) [with obj.] surpass (someone) in hitting; hit a higher score than.

outhouse ▶ noun a building such as a shed or barn that is built on to or in the grounds of a house. ■ chiefly N. Amer. an outside toilet.
▶ verb [with obj.] store or accommodate away from the main storage or accommodation area: *books outhoused in the annex take longer to deliver.*

outie /'aʊti/ ▶ noun (pl. **outies**) S. African informal a homeless person.

outing ▶ noun **1** a trip taken for pleasure, especially one lasting a day or less: *a family outing to Weston-super-Mare.* ■ a brief journey from home: *her daily outing to the shops.* ■ informal an appearance in something, especially a sporting event or film: *Madonna's first screen outing in three years.*
2 [mass noun] the practice of revealing the homosexuality of a prominent person.
– ORIGIN late Middle English (in the sense 'the action of going out or of expelling'): from the verb OUT + -ING[1].

outing flannel ▶ noun [mass noun] US a type of flannelette with a short nap on both sides.

out island ▶ noun an island situated away from the mainland.

outjie /'əʊki, -tʃi/ ▶ noun (pl. **outjies**) S. African informal a young boy.
– ORIGIN Afrikaans, from *ou* 'old' + the diminutive suffix *-jie*.

outjump ▶ verb [with obj.] jump higher or further than (a competitor in a sporting event).

outlander ▶ noun N. Amer. a foreigner or a stranger.

outlandish ▶ adjective **1** looking or sounding bizarre or unfamiliar: *outlandish, brightly coloured clothes.*
2 archaic foreign or alien: *three wise, outlandish kings.*
– DERIVATIVES **outlandishly** adverb, **outlandishness** noun.
– ORIGIN Old English *ūtlendisc* 'not native', from *ūtland* 'foreign country'.

outlast ▶ verb [with obj.] live or last longer than: *the kind of beauty that will outlast youth.*

outlaw ▶ noun a person who has broken the law, especially one who remains at large or is a fugitive. ■ historical a person deprived of the benefit and protection of the law.
▶ verb [with obj.] ban or make illegal: *secondary picketing has been outlawed* | (as adj. **outlawed**) *the outlawed*

O

terrorist group. ■ historical deprive (someone) of the benefit and protection of the law.
– DERIVATIVES **outlawry** noun.
– ORIGIN late Old English *ūtlaga* (noun), *ūtlagian* (verb), from Old Norse *útlagi*, noun from *útlagr* 'outlawed or banished'.

outlay ▸ noun an amount of money spent on something: *a modest outlay on local advertising* | [mass noun] *comparatively little financial outlay*.

outlet ▸ noun **1** a pipe or hole through which water or gas may escape. ■ the mouth of a river. ■ an output socket in an electrical device.
2 a point from which goods are sold or distributed: *a fast-food outlet*. ■ a market for goods: *the state system provided an outlet for farm produce*. ■ a shop that sells goods made by a particular manufacturer at discounted prices: *a designer outlet* | [as modifier] *an outlet store*.
3 a means of expressing one's talents, energy, or emotions: *writing became the main outlet for his energies*.
– ORIGIN Middle English: from OUT- + the verb LET[1].

outlet box ▸ noun a box giving access to connections to electric wiring where it is led out of conduits.

outlet pass ▸ noun Basketball a pass from a player who has just taken a rebound to a teammate who can initiate an offensive break.

outlier /ˈaʊtlʌɪə/ ▸ noun a person or thing situated away or detached from the main body or system: *a western outlier in the Andaman archipelago*. ■ Geology a younger rock formation isolated among older rocks. ■ Statistics a data point on a graph or in a set of results that is very much bigger or smaller than the next nearest data point.

outline ▸ noun **1** a line or set of lines enclosing or indicating the shape of an object in a sketch or diagram. ■ the contours or bounds of an object: *the outlines of dockside warehouses standing sharp on the skyline*. ■ a representation of a word in shorthand.
2 a general description or plan showing the essential features of something but not the detail: *an outline of parliamentary procedure* | [as modifier] *an outline proposal*.
▸ verb [with obj.] **1** draw, trace, or define the outer edge or shape of: *her eyes were darkly outlined with kohl*.
2 give a summary of: *she outlined the case briefly*.
– PHRASES **in outline** in broad terms: *the plan has been agreed in outline*.

outliner ▸ noun a computer program, or part of a program, which allows its user to create and edit a hierarchically arranged outline of the logical structure of a document.

outlive ▸ verb [with obj.] (of a person) live longer than (another person): *women generally outlive men*. ■ survive or last beyond (a specified period or expected lifespan): *the organization had largely **outlived its usefulness***. ■ archaic live through (an experience): *the world has outlived much*.

outlook ▸ noun **1** a person's point of view or general attitude to life: *he had a practical **outlook on** life*.
2 a view: *the pleasant outlook from the club window*. ■ a place from which a view is possible; a vantage point. ■ the prospect for the future: *the deteriorating economic outlook* | *the outlook for tomorrow is dry and cold*.

outlying ▸ adjective [attrib.] situated far from a centre; remote: *an outlying village*.

outman ▸ verb (**outmans**, **outmanning**, **outmanned**) [with obj.] (often as adj. **outmanned**) outnumber: *outgunned and outmanned armies*.

outmanoeuvre ▸ verb [with obj.] evade (an opponent) by moving faster or with greater agility: *the YF-22 can outmanoeuvre any fighter flying today*. ■ use skill and cunning to gain an advantage over: *he hoped he would be able to outmanoeuvre his critics*.

outmatch ▸ verb [with obj.] be superior to (an opponent or rival).

outmeasure ▸ verb [with obj.] archaic exceed in quantity or extent: *there are some days that might outmeasure years*.

outmigrant ▸ noun a person who has migrated from one place to another, especially within a country.
– DERIVATIVES **outmigration** noun.

outmoded ▸ adjective old-fashioned: *an outmoded Victorian building*.
– DERIVATIVES **outmodedness** noun.

outmost ▸ adjective chiefly archaic furthest away: *the outmost reaches of the empire*.
– ORIGIN Middle English: variant of *utmest* 'utmost'.

outmuscle /aʊtˈmʌs(ə)l/ ▸ verb [with obj.] dominate or defeat by means of superior strength or force.

outnumber ▸ verb [with obj.] be more numerous than: *women outnumbered men by three to one*.

out-of-area ▸ adjective (of a military operation) conducted away from the place of origin or expected place of action of the force concerned.

out-of-body experience ▸ noun a sensation of being outside one's body, typically of floating and being able to observe oneself from a distance.

out-of-court ▸ adjective (of a settlement) made or done without a court's involvement.

out of date ▸ adjective old-fashioned: *everything in her wardrobe must be hopelessly out of date*. ■ no longer valid or relevant: *an out-of-date passport*.

out-of-town ▸ adjective situated, originating from, or taking place outside a town: *an out-of-town hypermarket*.

outpace ▸ verb [with obj.] go, rise, or improve faster than: *he outpaced all six defenders* | *import growth outpaced export growth in the second quarter*.

outpatient ▸ noun a patient who attends a hospital for treatment without staying there overnight: [as modifier] *an outpatient clinic*.

outperform ▸ verb [with obj.] perform better than: *an experienced employee will outperform the novice*. ■ (of an investment) be more profitable than: *Georgian silver has outperformed the stock market*.
– DERIVATIVES **outperformance** noun.

outplacement ▸ noun [mass noun] the provision of assistance to redundant employees in finding new employment, either as a benefit provided by the employer directly, or through a specialist service.

outplay ▸ verb [with obj.] play better than: *we were absolutely and totally outplayed*.

outpoint ▸ verb [with obj.] Boxing defeat (an opponent) on points: *Berbick outpointed him easily*.

outpoll /aʊtˈpəʊl/ ▸ verb [with obj.] receive more votes than: *the Labour Party outpolled the Conservatives in the region by nearly two to one*.

outport ▸ noun **1** a subsidiary port built near an existing one. ■ Brit. any British port other than London.
2 Canadian (especially in Newfoundland) a small remote fishing village.

outpost ▸ noun **1** a small military camp or position at some distance from the main army, used especially as a guard against surprise attack.
2 a remote part of a country or empire. ■ an isolated or remote branch of something: *the community is the last outpost of civilization in the far north*.

outpouring ▸ noun something that streams out rapidly: *a massive outpouring of high-energy gamma rays*. ■ (often **outpourings**) an outburst of strong emotion: *outpourings of nationalist discontent*.

outpunch ▸ verb [with obj.] surpass (an opponent) in punching ability.

output ▸ noun **1** [mass noun] the amount of something produced by a person, machine, or industry: *output from the mine ceased in May* | [count noun] *efficiency can lead to higher outputs*. ■ the action or process of producing something: *the output of certain hormones under stress*. ■ the power, energy, or other results supplied by a device or system.
2 Electronics a place where power or information leaves a system.
▸ verb (**outputs**, **outputting**; past and past participle **output** or **outputted**) [with obj.] (of a computer or other device) produce, deliver, or supply (data): *you can output the image directly to a video recording system*.
– DERIVATIVES **outputter** noun.

output gap ▸ noun Economics the amount by which the actual output of an economy falls short of its potential output.

outrace ▸ verb [with obj.] exceed in speed, amount, or extent: *demand for trained clergy is outracing the supply*.

outrage ▸ noun [mass noun] an extremely strong reaction of anger, shock, or indignation: *her voice trembled with outrage*. ■ [count noun] an action or event causing outrage: *some of the worst terrorist outrages*.
▸ verb [with obj.] arouse fierce anger, shock, or indignation in (someone): *the public were outraged at the brutality involved*. ■ flagrantly violate or infringe (a principle, law, etc.): *their behaviour outraged all civilized standards*.
– ORIGIN Middle English (in the senses 'lack of moderation' and 'violent behaviour'): from Old French *ou(l)trage*, based on Latin *ultra* 'beyond'. Sense development has been affected by the belief that the word is a compound of OUT and RAGE.

outrageous ▸ adjective **1** shockingly bad or excessive: *an outrageous act of bribery*. ■ wildly exaggerated or improbable: *the outrageous claims made by the previous government*.
2 very bold and unusual and rather shocking: *her outrageous leotards and sexy routines*.
– DERIVATIVES **outrageously** adverb, **outrageousness** noun.
– ORIGIN late Middle English: from Old French *outrageus*, from *outrage* 'excess' (see OUTRAGE).

outran past of OUTRUN.

outrange ▸ verb [with obj.] (of a gun or similar weapon) have a greater range than.

outrank ▸ verb [with obj.] have a higher rank than (someone else). ■ be better or more important than: *surveys show the firm outranking the others in food quality*.

outré /ˈuːtreɪ/ ▸ adjective unusual and typically rather shocking: *the composer's more outré harmonies*.
– ORIGIN French, literally 'exceeded', past participle of *outrer* (see OUTRAGE).

outreach ▸ verb /aʊtˈriːtʃ/ [with obj.] reach further than: *their pack outreached and outwitted the Welsh team*. ■ [no obj.] literary stretch out one's arms.
▸ noun /ˈaʊtriːtʃ/ [mass noun] the extent or length of reaching out: *the loving outreach of God to the world*. ■ an organization's involvement with or influence in the community, especially in the context of religion or social welfare: *the growth of evangelistic outreach* | [as modifier] *outreach centres*.

out relief ▸ noun [mass noun] Brit. historical assistance given to very poor people not living in a workhouse.

Outremer /ˈuːtrəmɛː/ a name applied to the medieval French crusader states, including Armenia, Antioch, Tripoli, and Jerusalem.
– ORIGIN from French *outremer* (adverb) 'overseas', from *outre* 'beyond' + *mer* 'sea'.

outride ▸ verb (past **outrode**; past participle **outridden**) [with obj.] **1** ride better, faster, or further than.
2 archaic (of a ship) come safely through (a storm).

outrider ▸ noun a person in a motor vehicle or on horseback who goes in front of or beside a vehicle as an escort or guard. ■ US a mounted official who escorts racehorses to the starting post. ■ US a mounted herdsman who prevents cattle from straying beyond a certain limit.
– DERIVATIVES **outriding** noun.

outrigger ▸ noun a beam, spar, or framework projecting from or over a boat's side. ■ a float or secondary hull fixed parallel to a canoe or small boat to stabilize it. ■ a boat fitted with such a structure. ■ a projecting support similar to an outrigger in another structure or vehicle.
– DERIVATIVES **outrigged** adjective.
– ORIGIN mid 18th cent.: perhaps influenced by the obsolete nautical term *outligger*, in the same sense.

outright ▸ adverb **1** wholly and completely: *logging has been banned outright*. ■ directly or openly: *she couldn't ask him outright*.
2 immediately or instantly: *the impact killed four horses outright*. ■ not by degrees or instalments: *they decided to buy the company outright*.
▸ adjective [attrib.] open and direct: *an outright refusal*. ■ total: *the outright abolition of the death penalty*. ■ clear and undisputed: *an outright victory*.

outrival ▸ verb (**outrivals**, **outrivalling**, **outrivalled**; US **outrivals**, **outrivaling**, **outrivaled**) [with obj.] archaic surpass in competition or comparison.

outro ▸ noun (pl. **outros**) informal the concluding section of a piece of music or a radio or television programme.
– ORIGIN 1970s: from OUT, on the pattern of *intro*.

outrode past of OUTRIDE.

outrun ▸ verb (**outruns**, **outrunning**; past **outran**; past participle **outrun**) [with obj.] run or travel faster or further than. ■ escape from: *it's harder than anyone imagines to outrun destiny*. ■ go beyond or exceed: *his courage outran his prudence*.

outrush ▸ verb [with obj.] American Football surpass in rushing.

outsail ▸ verb [with obj.] sail better or faster than (a competitor).

outscore ▸ verb [with obj.] score more than (an opponent) in a game.

outsell ▶ verb (past and past participle **outsold**) [with obj.] sell or be sold in greater quantities than: *some experts predict that diesels will outsell petrol cars.*

outsert ▶ noun a piece of promotional material which is placed on the outside of a package, publication, or other product.
– ORIGIN 1960s: from OUT + INSERT.

outset ▶ noun [in sing.] the start or beginning of something: *the project was flawed **from the outset**.*

outshine ▶ verb (past and past participle **outshone**) [with obj.] shine more brightly than. ▪ be much better than (someone) in a particular area: *it is a shame when a mother outshines a daughter.*

outshoot ▶ verb (past and past participle **outshot**) [with obj.] shoot better than (someone else).

outshop ▶ verb (**outshops**, **outshopping**, **outshopped**) [with obj.] Brit. send (a railway vehicle) out from a workshop or factory after construction or overhaul.

outshout ▶ verb [with obj.] shout louder than: *each team tried to outshout the other.*

outside ▶ noun the external side or surface of something: *record the date on the outside of the file.* ▪ the part of a path nearer to a road or further from a wall. ▪ the side of a bend or curve where the edge or surface is longer in extent. ▪ (**outsides**) the outer sheets of a ream of paper. ▪ the external appearance of someone or something: *was he as straight as he appeared **on the outside**?*
▶ adjective [attrib.] **1** situated on or near the exterior or external surface of something: *Anne put the outside lights on.* ▪ (in hockey, soccer, and other sports) denoting positions nearer to the sides of the field: *he played at outside left.*
2 not belonging to or coming from within a particular group: *the use of outside contractors will speed up the process.* ▪ beyond one's own immediate personal concerns: *I was able to face the outside world again.*
▶ preposition & adverb **1** situated or moving beyond the confines or boundaries of: [as prep.] *there was a boy outside the door* | *I stepped outside the marquee for a breather* | [as adv.] *the dog was still barking outside* | *we ran outside.* ▪ not being a member of (a particular group): [as prep.] *critics outside the government.* ▪ (in soccer, rugby, and other sports) closer to the side of the field than (another player): [as prep.] *Swift appeared outside him with the powerful Fallon overlapping on his left.*
2 [prep.] beyond the limits or scope of: *the switchboard is not staffed outside normal office hours.*
– PHRASES **at the outside** (of an estimate) at the most: *every minute, or at the outside, every ninety seconds.* **get outside of** informal eat or drink: *we'll get outside of a feed of bacon and egg.* **on the outside** away from or not belonging to a particular group or institution. **on the outside looking in** excluded from a group or activity. **an outside chance** a remote possibility. **outside of** chiefly N. Amer. beyond the boundaries of: *a village 20 miles outside of New York.* ▪ apart from: *outside of an unfortunate sermon, he never put a foot wrong.*

> **USAGE** Outside and outside of: is there any difference between *the books have been distributed **outside** Europe* and *the books have been distributed **outside of** Europe*? Broadly speaking, both have the same meaning, but the use of **outside of** is much commoner and better established in North American than in British English.

outside broadcast ▶ noun Brit. a radio or television programme that is recorded or broadcast live on location and not in a studio.

outside director ▶ noun a director of a company who is not employed by that company, typically an employee of an associated company.

outside interest ▶ noun an interest not connected with one's work or studies.

outside line ▶ noun a telephone connection with an external exchange.

outside loop ▶ noun a looping movement made by an aircraft in which the back of the aircraft is on the outside of the curve.

outside money ▶ noun [mass noun] Economics money held in a form such as gold which is an asset for the holder and does not represent a corresponding liability for someone else.

outsider ▶ noun **1** a person who does not belong to a particular organization or profession. ▪ a person who is not accepted by or who isolates themselves from society.
2 a competitor, applicant, etc. thought to have little chance of success: *the winner was Beech Road, a fifty-to-one outsider* | *he started as a rank outsider.*

outsider art ▶ noun [mass noun] art produced by untrained artists, for example children or mentally ill people.
– DERIVATIVES **outsider artist** noun.

outside track ▶ noun the outer, longer side of a racecourse or running track.

outsing ▶ verb (past **outsang**; past participle **outsung**) [with obj.] sing better or louder than (someone else).

outsit ▶ verb (**outsits**, **outsitting**, **outsat**) [with obj.] sit longer than (someone or something).

outsize ▶ adjective (also **outsized**) exceptionally large: *an outsize bed* | *her outsized glasses.*
▶ noun an exceptionally large person or thing, especially a garment.

outskirts ▶ plural noun the outer parts of a town or city.

outsmart ▶ verb [with obj.] defeat or get the better of (someone) by being clever or cunning: *the hero is invariably outsmarted by the heroine.*

outsold past and past participle of OUTSELL.

outsole ▶ noun the outer sole of a boot or shoe, especially a sports shoe.

outsource ▶ verb [with obj.] obtain (goods or a service) by contract from an outside supplier: *there can be no question of outsourcing components **from** other countries.* ▪ contract (work) out: *you may choose to outsource this function **to** another company or do it yourself.*

outspan S. African ▶ verb (**outspans**, **outspanning**, **outspanned**) [with obj.] unharness (an animal) from a wagon. ▪ [no obj.] rest or camp at the side of the road while travelling by wagon.
▶ noun a place for grazing or camping on a wagon journey.
– ORIGIN early 19th cent.: from Dutch *uitspannen* 'unyoke'.

outspend ▶ verb (past and past participle **outspent**) [with obj.] spend more than (someone else).

outspoken ▶ adjective frank in stating one's opinions, especially if they are shocking or controversial: *he has been outspoken in his criticism.*
– DERIVATIVES **outspokenly** adverb, **outspokenness** noun.

outspread ▶ adjective fully extended or expanded: *outspread hands.*
▶ verb (past and past participle **outspread**) [with obj.] literary spread out: *that eagle outspreading his wings for flight.*

outsprint ▶ verb [with obj.] sprint faster than (someone).

outstanding ▶ adjective **1** exceptionally good: *the team's outstanding performance.* ▪ clearly noticeable: *works of outstanding banality.*
2 not yet paid, resolved, or dealt with: *much of the work is still outstanding* | *Julian's outstanding debts.*

outstandingly ▶ adverb [usu. as submodifier] exceptionally: *outstandingly beautiful gardens.*

outstare ▶ verb [with obj.] stare at (someone) for longer than they can stare back in order to intimidate or disconcert them.

outstation ▶ noun a branch of an organization situated at some distance from its headquarters. ▪ [as modifier] Indian working in a place where one does not live: *an outstation journalist.* ▪ Austral./NZ a part of a farming estate that is separate from the main estate. ▪ Austral. an autonomous Aboriginal community situated at some distance from a centre on which it depends.

outstation cheque ▶ noun Indian a cheque issued at one place but cashed elsewhere.

outstay ▶ verb [with obj.] **1** stay beyond the limit of (one's expected or permitted time): *employees who had outstayed their coffee break.*
2 endure or last longer than (another competitor): *his mount tenaciously outstayed Melody for second place.*
– PHRASES **outstay one's welcome** see WELCOME.

outstep ▶ verb (**outsteps**, **outstepping**, **outstepped**) [with obj.] rare exceed.

outstretch ▶ verb [with obj.] (usu. as adj. **outstretched**) extend or stretch out (something, especially a hand or arm): *I walked with my arms outstretched.* ▪ go beyond the limit of: *their good intentions far outstretched their capacity to offer help.*

outstrip ▶ verb (**outstrips**, **outstripping**, **outstripped**) [with obj.] move faster than and overtake (someone else). ▪ exceed: *supply far outstripped demand.*

outswinger ▶ noun Cricket a ball bowled with a swerve or swing from the leg to the off side.
– DERIVATIVES **outswing** noun, **outswinging** adjective.

outta (also **outa**) ▶ preposition a non-standard contraction of 'out of', used in representing informal speech: *we'd better get outta here.*

out-take ▶ noun a scene, sequence, or song filmed or recorded for a film, programme, or record album but not included in the final version.

out-talk ▶ verb [with obj.] outdo or overcome in talking: *he was out-talked by his mother.*

out-think ▶ verb [with obj.] outdo in thinking; outwit: *machines that can out-think humans.*

out-thrust ▶ adjective extended outward: *with his out-thrust foot he sent the man keeling over.*

out-top ▶ verb [with obj.] rare surpass in number, amount, height, or extent: *Nellie out-topped him by three inches.*

out tray ▶ noun a tray on a person's desk for letters and documents that have been dealt with.

out-turn ▶ noun the amount of something produced, especially money: *the financial out-turn.* ▪ the result of a process or sequence of events: *an entirely implausible out-turn.*

outvalue ▶ verb (**outvalues**, **outvaluing**, **outvalued**) [with obj.] chiefly archaic be of greater value than: *a ray of beauty outvalues all the utilities of the world.*

outvote ▶ verb [with obj.] defeat by gaining more votes.

outwait ▶ verb [with obj.] wait longer than (someone else).

outwalk ▶ verb [with obj.] walk faster or farther than (someone else).

outward ▶ adjective [attrib.] **1** of, on, or from the outside: *outward pressure.* ▪ relating to the external appearance of something rather than its true nature: *an outward display of friendliness.* ▪ archaic outer: *the outward physical body.*
2 going out or away from a place: *the outward voyage.*
▶ adverb outwards.
– DERIVATIVES **outwardness** noun.
– ORIGIN Old English *ūtweard* (see OUT-, -WARD).

outward bound ▶ adjective (of a ship or passenger) going away from home: *they were outward bound for the Great Barrier Reef.*
▶ noun (**Outward Bound**) [usu. as modifier] trademark an organization that provides naval and adventure training and other outdoor activities for young people.

outward investment ▶ noun [mass noun] investment whereby the property or company invested in is based in a country other than that from which the capital originates and to which the profit or income returns.

outwardly ▶ adverb [often as submodifier] on the surface: *an outwardly normal life* | [sentence adverb] *outwardly she seemed no different.* ▪ on or from the outside: *outwardly featureless modern offices* | [sentence adverb] *outwardly it's not a bad-looking car.*

outwards ▶ adverb chiefly Brit. away from the centre or a particular point; towards the outside: *a window that opens outwards.*

outwash ▶ noun [mass noun] material carried away from a glacier by meltwater and deposited beyond the moraine.

outwatch ▶ verb [with obj.] archaic watch (something) until it disappears. ▪ keep awake beyond the end of.

outwear ▶ verb (past **outwore**; past participle **outworn**) [with obj.] last longer than: *a material that will outwear any other waterproof sheeting.*

outweigh ▶ verb [with obj.] be heavier, greater, or more significant than: *the advantages greatly outweigh the disadvantages.*

outwent past of OUTGO.

outwit ▶ verb (**outwits**, **outwitting**, **outwitted**) [with obj.] deceive by greater ingenuity: *Ray had outwitted many an opponent.*

outwith ▶ preposition Scottish outside; beyond: *he has lived outwith Scotland for only five years.*

outwore past of OUTWEAR.

outwork ▶ noun **1** a section of a fortification or system of defence which is in front of the main part.

O

2 [mass noun] Brit. work done outside the factory or office which provides it.
▸ **verb** [with obj.] work harder than (someone else).
– DERIVATIVES **outworker** noun (sense 2 of the noun).

outworking ▸ **noun** [mass noun] **1** the action or process by which something is brought to completion: *the practical outworking of EU legislation.*
2 Brit. the action or process of doing outwork.

outworld ▸ **noun** (in science fiction) an outlying or alien planet.

outworn past participle of **OUTWEAR** ▸ **adjective** out of date: *outworn prejudices.* ■ no longer usable or serviceable because of excessive wear: *outworn lead flashings.*

ouzel /ˈuːz(ə)l/ (also **ousel**) ▸ **noun** a bird that resembles the blackbird, especially the ring ouzel. See also **WATER OUZEL**.
– ORIGIN Old English *ōsle* 'blackbird', of Germanic origin; related to German *Amsel* 'blackbird'.

ouzo /ˈuːzəʊ/ ▸ **noun** (pl. **ouzos**) [mass noun] a Greek aniseed-flavoured spirit.
– ORIGIN modern Greek.

ova plural form of **OVUM**.

oval ▸ **adjective** having a rounded and slightly elongated outline or shape like that of an egg: *her smooth oval face.*
▸ **noun** a body, object, or design with an oval shape or outline: *cut out two small ovals from the felt.* ■ an oval sports field or racing track. ■ Austral. a ground for Australian Rules football.
– DERIVATIVES **ovality** noun, **ovalness** noun.
– ORIGIN mid 16th cent.: from French, or modern Latin *ovalis*, from Latin *ovum* 'egg'.

ovalbumin /əʊˈvalbjʊmɪn/ ▸ **noun** [mass noun] Biochemistry albumin derived from the white of eggs.
– ORIGIN mid 19th cent.: from Latin *ovi albumen* 'albumen of egg', altered on the pattern of *albumin*.

Oval Office the office of the US President in the White House.

oval window ▸ **noun** informal term for **FENESTRA OVALIS** (see **FENESTRA**).

Ovambo /əʊˈvambəʊ/ ▸ **noun** (pl. **same** or **Ovambos**)
1 a member of a people of northern Namibia.
2 [mass noun] the Bantu language of the Ovambo.
▸ **adjective** relating to the Ovambo or their language.
– ORIGIN a local name, from *ova-* (prefix denoting a plural) + *ambo* 'man of leisure'.

Ovamboland a semi-arid region of northern Namibia, the homeland of the Ovambo people.

ovarian /əʊˈvɛːrɪən/ ▸ **adjective** relating to an ovary or the ovaries: *an ovarian cyst.*

ovarian follicle ▸ **noun** another term for **GRAAFIAN FOLLICLE**.

ovariectomy /ˌəʊvərɪˈɛktəmi/ ▸ **noun** (pl. **ovariectomies**) [mass noun] surgical removal of one or both ovaries; oophorectomy.

ovariotomy /əʊvɛːrɪˈɒtəmi/ ▸ **noun** (pl. **ovariotomies**) another term for **OVARIECTOMY**.

ovaritis /ˌəʊvəˈrʌɪtəs/ ▸ **noun** another term for **OOPHORITIS**.

ovary /ˈəʊv(ə)ri/ ▸ **noun** (pl. **ovaries**) a female reproductive organ in which ova or eggs are produced, present in humans and other vertebrates as a pair. ■ Botany the hollow base of the carpel of a flower, containing one or more ovules.
– ORIGIN mid 17th cent.: from modern Latin *ovarium*, from Latin *ovum* 'egg'.

ovate¹ /ˈəʊveɪt/ ▸ **adjective** chiefly Biology having an oval outline or ovoid shape, like an egg.
– ORIGIN mid 18th cent.: from Latin *ovatus* 'egg-shaped'.

ovate² /ˈɒvət/ ▸ **noun** a member of an order of Welsh bards recognized at an Eisteddfod. ■ historical a Celtic priest or natural philosopher.
– ORIGIN early 18th cent.: from the Greek plural *ouateis* 'soothsayers'.

ovation ▸ **noun 1** a sustained and enthusiastic show of appreciation from an audience, especially by means of applause.
2 Roman History a processional entrance into Rome by a victorious commander, of lesser honour than a triumph.
– ORIGIN early 16th cent. (in sense 2): from Latin *ovatio(n-)*, from *ovare* 'exult'. The word had the sense 'exultation' from the mid 17th to early 19th cent.

oven ▸ **noun 1** an enclosed compartment, usually part of a cooker, for cooking and heating food: *bake the dish in a preheated oven* | figurative *the house was like an oven when I came in.* ■ a small furnace or kiln.
2 a cremation chamber in a Nazi concentration camp.
– ORIGIN Old English *ofen*, of Germanic origin; related to Dutch *oven*, German *Ofen*, from an Indo-European root shared by Greek *ipnos*.

ovenbird ▸ **noun 1** a small, drab tropical American bird belonging to a diverse family, many members of which make domed oven-like nests of mud.
● Family Furnariidae (the **ovenbird family**): many genera and numerous species. The ovenbird family comprises the horneros, miners, spinetails, and many others.
2 a migratory brown North American warbler that builds a domed oven-like nest of vegetation on the ground. ● *Seiurus aurocapillus*, family Parulidae.

oven glove ▸ **noun** a padded glove for handling dishes in or from a hot oven.

ovenproof ▸ **adjective** (of cookware) suitable for use in an oven; heat-resistant.

oven-ready ▸ **adjective** (of food) prepared before sale so as to be ready for cooking in an oven.

ovenware ▸ **noun** [mass noun] dishes that can be used for cooking food in the oven.

over ▸ **preposition 1** extending directly upwards from: *I saw flames over Berlin* | *cook the sauce over a moderate heat.* ■ above so as to cover or protect: *an oxygen tent over the bed* | *ladle this sauce over fresh pasta.* ■ extending above (an area) from a vantage point: *views over Hyde Park.*
2 at a higher level or layer than: *his flat was over the shop.* ■ higher in rank than: *over him is the financial director.* ■ expressing authority or control: *editorial control over what is included.* ■ expressing preference: *I'd choose the well-known brand over that one.* ■ expressing majority: *there was a slight predominance of boys over girls.* ■ higher in volume or pitch than: *he shouted over the noise of the taxis.*
3 higher or more than (a specified number or quantity): *over 40 degrees C* | *they've been married for over a year.*
4 expressing passage or trajectory across: *she trudged over the lawn.* ■ beyond and falling or hanging from: *he toppled over the side of the boat.* ■ at the other side of; beyond: *over the hill is a small village.*
5 expressing duration: *you've given us a lot of heartache over the years* | *she told me over coffee.*
6 expressing the medium by which something is done; by means of: *a voice came over the loudspeaker.*
7 on the subject of: *a long and heated debate over unemployment.*
▸ **adverb 1** expressing passage or trajectory across an area: *he leant over and tapped me on the hand.* ■ in or to the place indicated: *I'm over here.*
2 beyond and falling or hanging from a point: *she knocked the jug over.*
3 used to express action and result: *the car flipped over* | *hand the money over.* ■ finished: *the match is over* | *message understood, over and out.*
4 used to express repetition of a process: *the jukebox plays every song twice over* | *the sums will have to be done over again.*
▸ **noun** Cricket a sequence of six balls bowled by a bowler from one end of the pitch, after which another bowler takes over from the other end.
– PHRASES **be over** no longer be affected by: *we were over the worst.* **get something over with** do or undergo something unpleasant or difficult, so as to be rid of it. **over against 1** adjacent to: *over against the wall.* **2** in contrast with: *over against heaven is hell.* **over and above** in addition to: *exceptional service over and above what normally might be expected.* **over and done with** completely finished. **over and over** again and again: *doing the same thing over and over again.*
– ORIGIN Old English *ofer*, of Germanic origin; related to Dutch *over* and German *über*, from an Indo-European word (originally a comparative of the element represented by *-ove* in *above*) which is also the base of Latin *super* and Greek *huper*.

over- ▸ **prefix 1** excessively; to an unwanted degree: *overambitious* | *overcareful.* ■ completely; utterly: *overawe* | *overjoyed.*
2 upper; outer; extra: *overcoat* | *overtime.* ■ over; above: *overcast* | *overhang.*

over-abundant ▸ **adjective** excessive in quantity: *over-abundant microbial growth.*
– DERIVATIVES **over-abundance** noun, **over-abundantly** adverb.

overachieve ▸ **verb** [no obj.] do better than is expected, especially in schoolwork: *David continued to overachieve all through high school.* ■ (often as adj. **overachieving**) be excessively dedicated to achieving success in one's work: *overachieving geeks.*
– DERIVATIVES **overachievement** noun, **overachiever** noun.

overact ▸ **verb** [no obj.] (of an actor or actress) act a role in an exaggerated manner: *a weepy actress with a strong tendency to overact* | (as noun **overacting**) *there was a certain amount of overacting.*

overactive ▸ **adjective** excessively active: *the product of an overactive imagination.*
– DERIVATIVES **overactivity** noun.

overage¹ (also **overaged**) ▸ **adjective** over a certain age limit: *they were banned after fielding overage players.*

overage² ▸ **noun** an excess or surplus, especially the amount by which a sum of money is greater than a previous estimate.

overall ▸ **adjective** [attrib.] taking everything into account: *the governors and head have overall responsibility for managing the school* | *the overall effect is impressive.*
▸ **adverb** [sentence adverb] taken as a whole; in all: *overall, 10,000 jobs will go.*
▸ **noun** (usu. **overalls**) Brit. a loose-fitting coat or one-piece garment worn, typically over ordinary clothes, for protection against dirt or heavy wear. ■ (**overalls**) Brit. close-fitting trousers formerly worn as part of an army uniform, now only on ceremonial or formal occasions. ■ N. Amer. dungarees.
– DERIVATIVES **overalled** adjective.

overambitious ▸ **adjective** excessively ambitious.
– DERIVATIVES **overambition** noun, **overambitiously** adverb.

overanalyse (US **overanalyze**) ▸ **verb** [with obj.] analyse (something) in too much detail: *his movies have been overanalysed* | [no obj.] *I do tend to overanalyse.*
– DERIVATIVES **overanalysis** noun.

overanxious ▸ **adjective** excessively anxious.
– DERIVATIVES **overanxiety** noun, **overanxiously** adverb.

overarch ▸ **verb** [with obj.] form an arch over: *an old dirt road, overarched by forest.*

overarching ▸ **adjective** comprehensive or all-embracing: *a single overarching principle.*
– DERIVATIVES **overarchingly** adverb.

overarm ▸ **adjective & adverb** chiefly Brit. (of a throw or a stroke with a racket) made with the hand or arm passing above the level of the shoulder: [as adj.] *the bowler was happy to demonstrate his overarm technique* | [as adv.] *competitors can throw overarm or underarm.*

overate past of **OVEREAT**.

overawe ▸ **verb** [with obj.] impress (someone) so much that they are silent or inhibited: *the eleven-year-old was overawed by the atmosphere.*

overbalance ▸ **verb** chiefly Brit. fall or cause to fall over from loss of balance: [no obj.] *he overbalanced and fell against the wall* | [with obj.] *their combined weight had overbalanced them.* ■ [with obj.] outweigh: *the days of unhappiness were far overbalanced by days of wild expressions of love.*
▸ **noun** archaic an excess of weight, value, or amount: *an overbalance of propriety.*

overbear ▸ **verb** (past **overbore**; past participle **overborne**) [with obj.] overcome by emotional pressure or physical force: *his will had not been overborne by another's influence.*

overbearing ▸ **adjective** unpleasantly overpowering: *an overbearing, ill-tempered brute.*
– DERIVATIVES **overbearingly** adverb, **overbearingness** noun.

overbid ▸ **verb** (**overbids**, **overbidding**; past and past participle **overbid**) [no obj.] **1** (in an auction) make a higher bid than a previous bid.
2 (in competitive tendering, the auction at bridge, etc.) bid more than is warranted or manageable.
▸ **noun** a bid that is higher than another or higher than is justified.
– DERIVATIVES **overbidder** noun.

overbite ▸ **noun** [mass noun] Dentistry the overlapping of the lower teeth by the upper.

overblouse ▸ **noun** a blouse designed to be worn without being tucked into a skirt or trousers.

overblowing ▸ **noun** [mass noun] a technique for playing high notes on a wind instrument by producing harmonics.

overblown ▸ **adjective 1** made to seem more impressive or important than is the case; exaggerated

or pretentious: *his most rhetorically overblown screenplay.*
2 (of a flower) past its prime: *an overblown rose.*

overboard ▶ adverb from a ship into the water: *the severe storm washed a man overboard.*
– PHRASES **go overboard 1** be very enthusiastic: *Garry went overboard for you.* **2** react in an immoderate way: *Chris has a bit of a temper and can sometimes go overboard.* **throw something overboard** abandon or discard something.

overbold ▶ adjective excessively bold.
– DERIVATIVES **overboldly** adverb, **overboldness** noun.

overbook ▶ verb [with obj.] accept more reservations for (a flight or hotel) than there is room for: *airlines deliberately overbook some scheduled flights.*

overboot ▶ noun a boot worn over another boot or shoe to protect it or to provide extra warmth.

overbore past of OVERBEAR.

overborne past participle of OVERBEAR.

overbought past and past participle of OVERBUY.
▶ adjective Stock Market overvalued owing to excessive buying at unjustifiably high prices.

overbreathe ▶ verb another term for HYPERVENTILATE.

overbreed ▶ verb (past and past participle **overbred**) breed or cause to breed to excess: (as adj. **overbred**) *the cats are overbred and their immune system is too weak to fight infections.*

overbridge ▶ noun a bridge over a railway or road.

overbrim ▶ verb [with obj.] archaic flow over the brim of: *the liquor that o'erbrims the cup.* ■ [no obj.] (of a container or liquid) overflow at the brim.

overbrimming ▶ adjective abundant, especially excessively so: *overbrimming confidence.*

overbuild ▶ verb (past and past participle **overbuilt**) [with obj.] **1** put up too many buildings in (an area): *investors overbuilt the Atlantic and Mediterranean coasts.* ■ build too elaborately or expensively.
2 (often as noun **overbuilding**) build on top of.

overburden ▶ verb [with obj.] load (someone) with too many things to carry. ■ give (someone) more work or pressure than they can deal with: *ministers are overburdened with engagements.*
▶ noun **1** [mass noun] rock or soil overlying a mineral deposit, archaeological site, or other underground feature.
2 an excessive burden: *an overburden of costs.*
– DERIVATIVES **overburdensome** adjective.

overbusy ▶ adjective excessively busy: *their overbusy lives.*

overbuy ▶ verb (past and past participle **overbought**) [with obj.] buy more of (something) than one needs.

overcall Bridge ▶ verb [no obj.] make a higher bid than an opponent's bid.
▶ noun an act or instance of overcalling.

overcame past of OVERCOME.

overcapacity ▶ noun [mass noun] the situation in which an industry or factory cannot sell as much as its plant is designed to produce.

overcapitalize (also **overcapitalise**) ▶ verb [with obj.] (usu. as adj. **overcapitalized**) provide (a company) with more capital than is advisable or necessary: *a bleak time for the overcapitalized firm.* ■ estimate the capital value of (a company) at too high an amount.
– DERIVATIVES **overcapitalization** noun.

overcareful ▶ adjective excessively careful.
– DERIVATIVES **overcarefully** adverb.

overcast ▶ adjective **1** (of the sky or weather) marked by a covering of grey cloud; dull: *a chilly, overcast day.*
2 (of the edge of a piece of fabric) sewn with long slanting stitches to prevent fraying.
▶ noun [mass noun] cloud covering a large part of the sky.
▶ verb (past and past participle **overcast**) [with obj.] **1** cover with clouds or shade: *the pebbled beach, overcast with the shadows of the high cliffs.*
2 stitch over (a raw edge) to prevent fraying.

overcautious ▶ adjective excessively cautious.
– DERIVATIVES **overcaution** noun, **overcautiously** adverb, **overcautiousness** noun.

overcharge ▶ verb [with obj.] **1** charge (someone) too high a price for goods or a service: *send your bill to the Law Society if you think you've been overcharged.* ■ charge someone (a sum) beyond the correct amount: [with two objs] *customers have been overcharged £12 million in the last year.*
2 put too much electric charge into (a battery).
▶ noun an excessive charge for goods or a service.

overcheck[1] ▶ noun a check pattern superimposed on a colour or design.

overcheck[2] ▶ noun a strap passing over a horse's head between the ears, to pull up on the bit and make breathing easier.

overclass ▶ noun a privileged, wealthy, or powerful section of society.

overclock ▶ verb [with obj.] (often as noun **overclocking**) run (the processor of one's computer) at a speed higher than that intended by the manufacturers.
– DERIVATIVES **overclocker** noun.

overcloud ▶ verb [with obj.] make dark, gloomy, or obscure.

overcoat ▶ noun **1** a long warm coat.
2 a top, final layer of paint or a similar covering.

overcome ▶ verb (past **overcame**; past participle **overcome**) [with obj.] succeed in dealing with (a problem or difficulty): *he overcame his pain for a time.* ■ defeat (an opponent): *an experienced England side overcame the determined home team.* ■ (of a feeling or emotion) overpower or overwhelm: *she was obviously **overcome with** excitement.*
– ORIGIN Old English *ofercuman* (see OVER-, COME).

overcommit ▶ verb (**overcommits**, **overcommitting**, **overcommitted**) [with obj.] oblige (someone) to do more than they are capable of, especially to repay a loan they cannot afford: *multiple borrowers who may be overcommitting themselves.* ■ allocate more (resources) to a purpose than can be provided: *they could easily overcommit their budgets.*
– DERIVATIVES **overcommitment** noun.

overcompensate ▶ verb [no obj.] take excessive measures in attempting to correct or make amends for an error, weakness, or problem: *he was **overcompensating for** fears about the future.*
– DERIVATIVES **overcompensatingly** adverb, **overcompensation** noun, **overcompensatory** adjective.

overcomplicate ▶ verb [with obj.] make (something) more complicated than necessary: *the basic idea is quite simple but some people tend to overcomplicate it.*

overconfident ▶ adjective excessively confident.
– DERIVATIVES **overconfidence** noun, **overconfidently** adverb.

overconsumption ▶ noun [mass noun] the action or fact of consuming something to excess: *the overconsumption of alcohol | the environmental cost of overconsumption.*

overcook ▶ verb cook too much or for too long: [with obj.] *don't overcook the vegetables* | [no obj.] *ensure that the food doesn't overcook during reheating.*

overcritical ▶ adjective inclined to find fault too readily.

overcrop ▶ verb (**overcrops**, **overcropping**, **overcropped**) [with obj.] (usu. as noun **overcropping**) exhaust (land) by growing crops continuously on it.

overcrowd ▶ verb [with obj.] (often as adj. **overcrowded**) fill (accommodation or a space) beyond what is usual or comfortable: *overcrowded conditions* | (as noun **overcrowding**) *severe overcrowding at a football match.*

overcurious ▶ adjective excessively eager to know or learn something.
– DERIVATIVES **overcuriosity** noun.

overdamp ▶ verb [with obj.] Physics damp (a system) to a greater extent than the minimum needed to prevent oscillations.

overdelicate ▶ adjective excessively delicate.
– DERIVATIVES **overdelicacy** noun.

overdependence ▶ noun dependence to an excessive degree: *overdependence on the tourism sector.*
– DERIVATIVES **overdependent** adjective.

overdetermine ▶ verb [with obj.] technical determine, account for, or cause (something) in more than one way or with more conditions than are necessary: *direct control overdetermines prices.*
– DERIVATIVES **overdetermination** noun.

overdevelop ▶ verb (**overdevelops**, **overdeveloping**, **overdeveloped**) [with obj.] develop too much or to excess: *cycling may overdevelop the calf muscles* | (as adj. **overdeveloped**) *Majorca's overdeveloped coastline.* ■ Photography treat with developer for too long.
– DERIVATIVES **overdevelopment** noun.

overdo ▶ verb (**overdoes**, **overdoing**; past **overdid**; past participle **overdone**) [with obj.] do, use, or carry to excess; exaggerate: *she rather overdoes the early cockney scenes | I'd overdone the garlic in the curry.* ■ (**overdo it/things**) exhaust oneself by overwork or overexertion: *I'd simply overdone it in the gym.* ■ overcook.
– ORIGIN Old English *oferdōn* (see OVER-, DO[1]).

overdog ▶ noun informal a person who is successful or dominant in their field.

overdone ▶ adjective **1** (of food) overcooked: *he sat there chewing his overdone steak.*
2 done to excess; exaggerated: *an overdone show of camaraderie.*

overdose ▶ noun an excessive and dangerous dose of a drug: *a fatal overdose of painkillers.*
▶ verb [no obj.] take an overdose of a drug: *he was admitted to hospital after **overdosing on** cocaine.* ■ [with obj.] give an overdose to.
– DERIVATIVES **overdosage** /əʊvəˈdəʊsɪdʒ/ noun.

overdraft ▶ noun a deficit in a bank account caused by drawing more money than the account holds.

overdramatize (also **overdramatise**) ▶ verb [with obj.] react to or portray (something) in an excessively dramatic manner.
– DERIVATIVES **overdramatic** adjective.

overdraw ▶ verb (past **overdrew**; past participle **overdrawn**) [with obj.] **1** draw money from (one's bank account) in excess of what the account holds: *you only pay interest if your account is overdrawn.* ■ (**be overdrawn**) (of a person) have taken money out of an account in excess of what it holds: *I'm already overdrawn this month.*
2 exaggerate in describing or depicting (someone or something): *some of the characters were overdrawn.*

overdress ▶ verb [no obj.] (also **be overdressed**) dress too elaborately or formally: *she felt wildly overdressed in her velvet suit.*

overdrink ▶ verb (past **overdrank**; past participle **overdrunk**) [no obj.] (usu. as noun **overdrinking**) drink too much alcohol.

overdrive ▶ noun **1** a gear in a motor vehicle providing a gear ratio higher than that of direct drive (the usual top gear), so that the engine speed can be reduced at high road speeds to lessen fuel consumption or to allow further acceleration. ■ a mechanism which permits the exceeding of some normal operating level in a piece of equipment, especially the amplifier of an electric guitar.
2 [mass noun] a state of great or excessive activity: *the city's worried public relations group **went into overdrive**.*
▶ verb [with obj.] (usu. as adj. **overdriven**) **1** drive or work to exhaustion: *an overdriven mother of ten children.*
2 give (an electric guitar) a distorted sound.

O

overdry ▶ verb (**overdries**, **overdrying**, **overdried**) [with obj.] make too dry.

overdub ▶ verb (**overdubs**, **overdubbing**, **overdubbed**) [with obj.] record (additional sounds) on an existing recording: *he overdubbed vocals in the US.*
▶ noun an instance of overdubbing: *a guitar overdub.*

overdue ▶ adjective **1** not having arrived, happened, or been done by the expected time: *the rent was nearly three months overdue | overdue bills.* ■ (of a woman) not having had a menstrual period at the expected time: *I was already a week-and-a-half overdue.* ■ (of a baby) not having been born by the expected time: *our daughter was six days overdue.* ■ (of a library book) retained longer than the period allowed.
2 having been needed for some time: *reform is now overdue | critics say action is **long overdue**.* ■ having deserved or needed something for some time: *she **was overdue for** some leave.*

overdye ▶ verb (**overdyes**, **overdyeing**, **overdyed**) [with obj.] (often as adj. **overdyed**) dye (something that is already dyed) with a second dye.

overeager ▶ adjective excessively eager.
– DERIVATIVES **overeagerly** adverb, **overeagerness** noun.

over easy ▶ adjective N. Amer. (of a fried egg) turned over when almost cooked and fried lightly on the other side, so that the yolk remains slightly liquid.

overeat ▶ verb (past **overate**; past participle **overeaten**) [no obj.] (usu. as noun **overeating**) eat too much: *the effect of overeating is weight gain.*
– DERIVATIVES **overeater** noun.

overeducated ▶ adjective having been educated to a higher academic level than is necessary: *an overeducated music snob.*

over-egg ▶ verb (in phrase **over-egg the pudding**) go too far in embellishing, exaggerating, or doing something.

over-elaborate ▶ adjective excessively elaborate.
▶ verb [with obj.] explain or treat in excessive detail: *if they don't over-elaborate the story I don't question it.*
– DERIVATIVES **over-elaborately** adverb **over-elaboration** noun.

overemotional ▶ adjective having feelings that are too easily excited and displayed: *we're not an overemotional family.*
– DERIVATIVES **overemotionally** adverb.

overemphasis ▶ noun [mass noun] excessive emphasis.

overemphasize (also **overemphasise**) ▶ verb [with obj.] place excessive emphasis on: *the importance of adequate preparation cannot be overemphasized.*

overenthusiasm ▶ noun [mass noun] excessive enthusiasm.
– DERIVATIVES **overenthusiastic** adjective, **overenthusiastically** adverb.

overestimate ▶ verb [with obj.] form too high or favourable an estimate of: *his influence cannot be overestimated.*
▶ noun an excessively high estimate.
– DERIVATIVES **overestimation** noun.

overexcite ▶ verb [with obj.] (often as adj. **overexcited**) excite excessively: *an overexcited schoolgirl at a party.*
– DERIVATIVES **overexcitable** adjective, **overexcitement** noun.

over-exercise ▶ verb [no obj.] take too much exercise.

overexert ▶ verb (**overexert oneself**) engage in too much or too strenuous exertion.
– DERIVATIVES **overexertion** noun.

overexpose ▶ verb [with obj.] expose too much, especially to the public eye or to risk: *many UK banks were overexposed to overseas lending risks.* ■ Photography expose (film or a part of an image) for too long a time.
– DERIVATIVES **overexposure** noun.

overextend ▶ verb [with obj.] **1** make (something) too long: *at nine minutes plus the song is somewhat overextended.*
2 impose an excessive burden of work or commitments on (someone): *he should not overextend himself on the mortgage.*
– DERIVATIVES **overextension** noun.

overfall ▶ noun a turbulent stretch of open water caused by a strong current or tide over a submarine ridge, or by a meeting of currents. ■ a place where surplus water overflows from a dam, weir, or pool.

O

overfamiliar ▶ adjective too well known: *the overfamiliar teacher's voice.* ■ (**overfamiliar with**) too well acquainted with: *the researcher is overfamiliar with the community.* ■ behaving or speaking in an inappropriately informal way: *her trainer was dismissed for being overfamiliar with her.*
– DERIVATIVES **overfamiliarity** noun.

overfatigue ▶ noun [mass noun] excessive fatigue.

overfeed ▶ verb (past and past participle **overfed**) [with obj.] give too much food to: *the general view was that you cannot overfeed a baby.*

overfill ▶ verb [with obj.] put more into (a container) than it either should or can contain.

overfine ▶ adjective excessively or extremely fine: *the distinction may seem overfine to westerners.*

overfish ▶ verb [with obj.] deplete the stock of fish in (a body of water) by excessive fishing: *this part of the Mediterranean is terribly overfished.* ■ deplete the stock of (a fish): *yellowfin tuna has been overfished.*

overflow ▶ verb [no obj.] (especially of a liquid) flow over the brim of a receptacle: *chemicals overflowed from a storage tank* | [with obj.] *the river overflowed its banks.* ■ (of a container) be so full that the contents go over the sides: *boxes **overflowing with** bright flowers* | (as adj. **overflowing**) *an overflowing ashtray.* ■ (of a space) be so crowded that people spill out: *the waiting area was overflowing.* ■ [with obj.] flood or flow over (a surface or area): *her hair overflowed her shoulders.* ■ (**overflow with**) be very full of (an emotion or quality): *her heart overflowed with joy.*
▶ noun **1** [mass noun] the flowing over of a liquid: *there was some overflow after heavy rainfall* | [count noun] *an overflow of sewage.* ■ [in sing.] the excess or surplus not able to be accommodated by an available space: *to accommodate the overflow five more offices have been built.*
2 (also **overflow pipe**) (in a bath or sink) an outlet for excess water.
3 [mass noun] Computing the generation of a number or other data item which is too large for the assigned location or memory space.
– PHRASES **full to overflowing** completely full.
– ORIGIN Old English *oferflōwan* (see OVER-, FLOW).

overfly ▶ verb (**overflies**, **overflying**; past **overflew**; past participle **overflown**) [with obj.] fly over (a place): *Nato is sending a surveillance plane to overfly the city.* ■ fly beyond (a place or object): *overfly the radio beacon by approximately 15 seconds.*
– DERIVATIVES **overflight** noun.

overfold ▶ noun a part of something which is folded over another part: *the tunic is belted over a long overfold.* ■ Geology a fold in which both the limbs dip in the same direction so that strata in the middle part are upside down.

overfond ▶ adjective having too great an affection or liking for someone or something: *he's been getting **overfond of** this Pinot Grigio.*
– DERIVATIVES **overfondly** adverb, **overfondness** noun.

overfulfil (US **overfulfill**) ▶ verb (**overfulfils**, **overfulfilling**, **overfulfilled**) [with obj.] fulfil (a contract or quota) earlier or in greater quantity than required: *he overfulfilled the quota by forty per cent.*
– DERIVATIVES **overfulfilment** noun.

overfull ▶ adjective containing an excessive amount of something: *an overfull cup of tea.*

overfund ▶ verb [with obj.] provide more funding for (something) than is necessary or permitted.

overgarment ▶ noun a garment that is worn over others.

overgeneralize (also **overgeneralise**) ▶ verb [with obj.] draw a conclusion or make a statement about (something) that is more general than is justified: *children overgeneralize simple rules.*
– DERIVATIVES **overgeneralization** noun.

overgenerous ▶ adjective excessively generous: *she was not overgenerous with praise.*
– DERIVATIVES **overgenerosity** noun, **overgenerously** adverb.

overglaze ▶ noun [mass noun] decoration or a second glaze applied to glazed ceramic ware: [as modifier] *overglaze enamel.*

overgraze ▶ verb [with obj.] graze (grassland) so heavily that the vegetation is damaged and the ground becomes liable to erosion: *their own pastures were overgrazed and arid* | (as noun **overgrazing**) *the failure of the rains led to overgrazing and deforestation.*

overground ▶ adverb & adjective **1** on or above the ground: [as adv.] *it has suggested that a new line be built overground* | [as adj.] *overground stations.*
2 [as adj.] not subversive or illicit: *they devised plans for using overground political processes.*

overgrow ▶ verb (past **overgrew**; past participle **overgrown**) [with obj.] grow or spread over (something) so as to choke or stifle it.

overgrown ▶ adjective **1** covered with plants that have been allowed to grow wild: *the garden was overgrown and deserted.*
2 grown too large or beyond its normal size: *the town is only an overgrown village.* ■ derogatory used to describe an adult behaving in a childish manner: *a pair of overgrown schoolboys.*

overgrowth ▶ noun [mass noun] excessive growth: *intestinal bacterial overgrowth.*

overhand ▶ adjective & adverb **1** chiefly N. Amer. another term for OVERARM.
2 with the palm of the hand downward or inward: [as adj.] *an overhand grip.*

overhand knot ▶ noun a simple knot made by forming a loop and passing a free end round the standing part and through the loop.

overhang ▶ verb (past and past participle **overhung**) [with obj.] hang or extend outwards over: *a concrete path overhung by jacaranda trees* | (as adj. **overhanging**) *overhanging branches.*
▶ noun **1** a part of something that extends or hangs over something else: *he crouched beneath an overhang of bushes.*
2 a quantity of securities or commodities large enough to make prices fall if offered for sale.

overhasty ▶ adjective excessively hasty.
– DERIVATIVES **overhastily** adverb.

overhaul ▶ verb [with obj.] **1** take apart (a piece of machinery or equipment) in order to examine it and repair it if necessary: *the steering box was recently overhauled.* ■ analyse and improve (a system).
2 Brit. overtake (someone), especially in a sporting event: *Jodami overhauled his chief rival.*
▶ noun a thorough examination of machinery or a system, with repairs or changes made if necessary: *a major overhaul of environmental policies.*
– ORIGIN early 17th cent. (originally in nautical use in the sense 'release rope tackle by slackening'): from OVER- + HAUL.

overhead ▶ adverb above the level of the head; in the sky: *a helicopter buzzed overhead.*
▶ adjective **1** situated above the level of the head: *the sun was directly overhead.*
2 (of a driving mechanism) above the object driven: *an overhead cam four-cylinder engine.*
3 [attrib.] (of a cost or expense) incurred in the upkeep or running of a plant, premises, or business and not attributable to individual products or items.
▶ noun **1** (usu. **overheads**) an overhead cost or expense.
2 a transparency designed for use with an overhead projector.
3 an overhead compartment, especially on an aircraft.

overhead projector ▶ noun a device that projects an enlarged image of an acetate or other transparency placed on it on to a wall or screen by means of an overhead mirror.

overhear ▶ verb (past and past participle **overheard**) [with obj.] hear (someone or something) without meaning to or without the knowledge of the speaker: *I couldn't help overhearing your conversation.*

overheat ▶ verb **1** make or become too hot: [no obj.] *her car started to overheat* | [with obj.] *it's vital not to overheat the liquid.* ■ make or become too excited: (as adj. **overheated**) *his overheated imagination.*
2 [no obj.] (of a country's economy) show marked inflation when increased demand results in rising prices rather than increased output: *in 1987 the Treasury had allowed the economy to overheat.*

overhit ▶ verb (**overhits**, **overhitting**; past and past participle **overhit**) [with obj.] (in sporting contexts) hit (a ball) too strongly or too far.

overhype ▶ verb [with obj.] make exaggerated claims about (a product, idea, or event); publicize or promote excessively.
▶ noun [mass noun] excessive publicity or promotion.

Overijssel /ˌəʊvərˈʌɪs(ə)l/ a province of the east central Netherlands, north of the IJssel River, on the border with Germany; capital, Zwolle.

overindulge ▶ verb [no obj.] have too much of something enjoyable, especially food or drink: *it is easy to **overindulge in** these kinds of food.* ■ [with obj.] gratify the wishes of (someone) to an excessive extent: *his mother had overindulged him.*

overindulgence ▶ noun [mass noun] **1** the action or fact of having too much of something enjoyable: *her alleged **overindulgence in** alcohol.*
2 excessive gratification of a person's wishes: *his overindulgence of her whims.*
– DERIVATIVES **overindulgent** adjective.

overinflated ▶ adjective **1** (of a price or value) excessive: *overinflated land values.* ■ exaggerated: *there were many overinflated claims.*
2 filled with too much air: *an overinflated balloon.*
– DERIVATIVES **overinflation** noun.

overinsured ▶ adjective having excessive insurance cover.
– DERIVATIVES **overinsurance** noun.

overissue ▶ verb (**overissues**, **overissuing**, **overissued**) [with obj.] issue (banknotes, shares, etc.) beyond the authorized amount or the issuer's ability to pay them on demand.
▶ noun [mass noun] the action of overissuing banknotes, shares, etc.

overjoyed ▶ adjective extremely happy: *all of them were overjoyed at my success.*

overkeen ▶ adjective excessively keen or enthusiastic: *I'm not overkeen on clubbing.*

overkill ▶ noun [mass noun] **1** excessive use, treatment, or action: *animators now face a dilemma of technology overkill.*
2 the amount by which destruction or the capacity for destruction exceeds what is necessary: *the existing nuclear overkill.*

overladen ▶ adjective having too large or too heavy a load: *an overladen trolley* | figurative *the film is overladen with tear-jerking moments.*

overlaid past and past participle of OVERLAY[1].

overlain past participle of OVERLIE.

overland ▶ adjective & adverb by land: [as adj.] *an overland trade route* | [as adv.] *she journeyed overland.*

▶ verb [no obj., with adverbial of direction] travel a long distance over land: *they left the ship and overlanded to Coolgardie.* ■ [with obj. and adverbial of direction] Austral./NZ historical drive (livestock) over a long distance.
– DERIVATIVES **overlander** noun.

overlap ▶ verb (**overlaps**, **overlapping**, **overlapped**) [with obj.] extend over so as to cover partly: *the canopy overlaps the house roof at one end* | [no obj.] *the curtains overlap at the centre when closed.* ■ [no obj.] cover part of the same area of interest, responsibility, etc.: *the union's commitments* ***overlapped with*** *those of NATO.* ■ [no obj.] partly coincide in time: *two new series overlapped.*
▶ noun a part or amount which overlaps: *an overlap of about half an inch.* ■ a common area of interest, responsibility, etc.: *there are many overlaps between the approaches* | [mass noun] *there is some overlap in requirements.* ■ a period of time in which two events or activities happen together.

overlarge ▶ adjective too large: *an overlarge meal.*

overlay[1] ▶ verb (past and past participle **overlaid**) [with obj.] (often **be overlaid with**) **1** cover the surface of (something) with a coating: *their fingernails were overlaid with silver or gold.* ■ lie on top of: *a third screen which will overlay the others.*
2 (of a quality or feeling) become more prominent than (a previous quality or feeling): *his openness had been overlaid by his new self-confidence.*
▶ noun **1** something laid as a covering over something else: *a durable, cost-effective floor overlay.* ■ a transparent sheet placed over artwork or something such as a map, giving additional information or detail.
2 [mass noun] Computing the process of transferring a block of program code or other data into internal memory, replacing what is already stored. ■ [count noun] a block of code or other data transferred in such a way.

overlay[2] past of OVERLIE.

overlayer ▶ noun a top or covering layer.

overleaf ▶ adverb on the other side of the page: *an information sheet is printed overleaf.*

overleap ▶ verb (past and past participle **overleaped** or **overleapt**) [with obj.] archaic jump over or across. ■ omit or ignore: *whatever objection made by us, he finds too heavy to remove, he overleaps it.*
– ORIGIN Old English *oferhlēapan* (see OVER, LEAP).

overleveraged ▶ adjective Finance (of a company) having taken on too much debt.

overlie ▶ verb (**overlies**, **overlying**; past **overlay**; past participle **overlain**) [with obj.] lie on top of: *soft clays overlie the basalt* | figurative *the national situation was overlain by sharp regional differences.*

overload ▶ verb [with obj.] load with too great a burden or cargo: *both boats were overloaded and low in the water* | (as adj. **overloaded**) *overloaded vehicles.* ■ give excessive work, responsibility, or information to: *the staff are heavily overloaded with casework.* ■ put too great a demand on (an electrical system).
▶ noun [in sing.] an excessive amount of something: *an overload of stress.*

overlock ▶ verb [with obj.] strengthen and prevent fraying of (an edge of cloth) by oversewing it.
– DERIVATIVES **overlocker** noun.

overlong ▶ adjective & adverb too long: [as adj.] *an overlong sermon* | [as adv.] *the pass was delayed overlong.*

overlook ▶ verb [with obj.] **1** fail to notice: *he seems to have overlooked one important fact.* ■ ignore or disregard (something, especially a fault or offence): *she was more than ready to overlook his faults.* ■ pass over (someone) in favour of another: *he was overlooked by the Nobel committee.*
2 have a view of from above: *the chateau overlooks fields of corn and olive trees.* ■ (**be overlooked**) (of a place) be open to view and so lack privacy: *it's better if the property isn't overlooked.*
3 archaic supervise: *he was overlooking his harvest men.*
4 archaic bewitch with the evil eye.
▶ noun N. Amer. a commanding position or view: *the overlook to the townsite.*

overlooker ▶ noun a person whose job it is to supervise the work of others.

overlord ▶ noun a ruler, especially a feudal lord. ■ a person of great power or authority: *the undisputed overlord of the crime family.*
– DERIVATIVES **overlordship** noun.

overloud ▶ adjective excessively noisy or loud.

overly ▶ adverb [as submodifier] excessively: *she was a jealous and overly possessive woman.*

overlying present participle of OVERLIE.

overman ▶ verb (**overmans**, **overmanning**, **overmanned**) [with obj.] provide with more staff than necessary: *the company was vastly overmanned.*
▶ noun (pl. **overmen**) **1** an overseer in a colliery.
2 Philosophy another term for SUPERMAN. [translation of Nietzsche's *Übermensch*.]

overmantel ▶ noun an ornamental structure over a mantelpiece, typically of plaster or carved wood and sometimes including a mirror.

overmaster ▶ verb [with obj.] literary overcome; conquer: *he was overmastered by events* | (as adj. **overmastering**) *an overmastering force of bombers.*

overmatch ▶ verb [with obj.] (usu. as adj. **overmatched**) chiefly N. Amer. be stronger, better armed, or more skilful than: *the city's overmatched police.*

overmighty ▶ adjective Brit. excessively powerful.

overmuch ▶ adverb, determiner, & pronoun too much: [as adv.] *I would not worry overmuch* | [as determiner] *the police may have overmuch regard for public order considerations* | [as pronoun] *she was requiring overmuch from him.*

overnice ▶ adjective dated excessively fussy or fastidious: *Mildred was overnice in regard to their father.*

overnight ▶ adverb for the duration of a night: *they refused to stay overnight.* ■ during the course of a night: *you can recharge the battery overnight.* ■ instantly or very quickly: *the picture made Wallis famous overnight.*
▶ adjective [attrib.] done, happening, or for use overnight: *an overnight stay* | *an overnight bag.* ■ instant: *Tom became an overnight celebrity.*
▶ verb [no obj., with adverbial of place] stay for the night in a particular place: *I overnighted at the Beverly Wilshire.* ■ [with obj.] N. Amer. convey (goods) at night, so that they arrive the next day: *Forster overnighted the sample to headquarters by courier.*
▶ noun a stop or stay lasting one night.

overnighter ▶ noun a person who stops at a place overnight. ■ N. Amer. an overnight trip or stay.

over-optimistic ▶ adjective unjustifiably optimistic.
– DERIVATIVES **over-optimism** noun, **over-optimistically** adverb.

overpack ▶ verb [with obj.] pack too many items into (a container).

overpaid past and past participle of OVERPAY.

overpaint ▶ verb [with obj.] cover with a layer of paint.

overparted ▶ adjective chiefly Brit. (of an actor or singer) having too difficult a part or role or too many parts or roles to play: *a sadly overparted soprano.*

over-particular ▶ adjective fussy: *passengers who were not over-particular about their time of arrival.*

overpass ▶ noun a bridge by which a road or railway line passes over another.
▶ verb [with obj.] rare surpass: *did not its sublimity overpass a little the bounds of the ridiculous?*

overpay ▶ verb (past and past participle **overpaid**) [with obj.] pay too highly: *many fans think our top players are overpaid.* ■ pay (money) in excess of what is due: (as adj. **overpaid**) *the recovery of overpaid tax.*
– DERIVATIVES **overpayment** noun.

overpitch ▶ verb [with obj.] Cricket bowl (a ball) so that it pitches or would pitch too far up the pitch.

overplay ▶ verb [with obj.] give undue importance to; overemphasize: *he thinks the idea of a special relationship between sitter and artist is much overplayed.* ■ exaggerate the performance of (a dramatic role): *the uncontrollable urge of ham actors to overplay their parts.*
– PHRASES **overplay one's hand 1** (in a card game) play or bet on one's hand with a mistaken optimism. **2** spoil one's chance of success through excessive confidence in one's position.

overplus ▶ noun dated a surplus or excess: *an overplus of one ingredient.*
– ORIGIN late Middle English: partial translation of French *surplus* or medieval Latin *superplus*.

overpopulate ▶ verb [with obj.] (often as adj. **overpopulated**) populate (an area) in excessively large numbers: *an overpopulated country.*
– DERIVATIVES **overpopulation** noun.

overpower ▶ verb [with obj.] defeat or overcome with superior strength. ■ be too intense for; overwhelm: *they were overpowered by the fumes.*

overpowering ▶ adjective extremely strong or intense; overwhelming: *a feeling of overpowering sadness.*
– DERIVATIVES **overpoweringly** adverb [as submodifier] *he found the weather overpoweringly hot.*

overpraise ▶ verb [with obj.] praise more highly than is warranted: *the island's tourist publications tend to overpraise their restaurants.*

overprescribe ▶ verb [with obj.] prescribe (a drug or treatment) in greater amounts or on more occasions than necessary: *doctors have been overprescribing antibiotics for decades.*
– DERIVATIVES **overprescription** noun.

overprice ▶ verb [with obj.] (often as adj. **overpriced**) charge too high a price for: *overpriced hotels.*

overprint ▶ verb [with obj.] **1** print additional matter on (a stamp or other surface already bearing print): *menus will be* ***overprinted with*** *company logos.*
2 print too many copies of.
3 Photography make (a print or other positive) darker than intended.
▶ noun [mass noun] words or other matter printed on to something already bearing print. ■ [count noun] an overprinted postage stamp.

overproduce ▶ verb [with obj.] **1** produce more of (a product or commodity) than is wanted or needed: *our unplanned manufacturing system continually overproduces consumer products.*
2 (often as adj. **overproduced**) record or produce (a song or film) in such an elaborate way that the spontaneity or artistry of the original material is lost: *a series of overproduced albums.*
– DERIVATIVES **overproduction** noun.

overproof ▶ adjective containing more alcohol than proof spirit does: *overproof rum.*

overprotective ▶ adjective having a tendency to protect someone, especially a child, excessively.
– DERIVATIVES **overprotect** verb, **overprotection** noun, **overprotectiveness** noun.

overqualified ▶ adjective too highly qualified for a particular job.

overran past of OVERRUN.

overrate ▶ verb [with obj.] (often as adj. **overrated**) have a higher opinion of (someone or something) than is deserved: *an overrated player.*

overreach ▶ verb **1** [no obj.] reach out too far: *never lean sideways from a ladder or overreach.* ■ (**overreach oneself**) try to do more than is possible: *the Church overreached itself in securing a territory that would prove impossible to hold.* ■ (of a horse or dog) bring the hind feet so far forward that they fall alongside or strike the forefeet.
2 [with obj.] get the better of by cunning; outwit: *Faustus's lunacy in thinking he can overreach the devil.*
– DERIVATIVES **overreacher** noun.

overreact ▶ verb [no obj.] respond more emotionally or forcibly than is justified: *the Authority are urging people not to overreact to the problem.*
– DERIVATIVES **overreaction** noun.

over-refine ▶ verb [with obj.] refine (something, especially food) too much.
– DERIVATIVES **over-refinement** noun.

over-refreshed ▶ adjective Brit. humorous drunk.

over-report ▶ verb [with obj.] report (an event or instance of something) with disproportionately great frequency or emphasis: *newspapers over-reported sexual offences.*

over-represent ▶ verb [with obj.] include a disproportionately large number of (a particular category). ■ (**be over-represented**) form a disproportionately large percentage: *women are over-represented in fields such as education, English, and psychology.*
– DERIVATIVES **over-representation** noun.

override ▶ verb (past **overrode**; past participle **overridden**) [with obj.] **1** use one's authority to reject or cancel (a decision, view, etc.): *the courts will ultimately override any objections.* ■ be more important than: *this commitment should override all other considerations.*
2 interrupt the action of (an automatic device), typically in order to take manual control: *you can override the cut-out by releasing the switch.*
3 technical extend over; overlap.
4 travel or move over.
▶ noun **1** a device for suspending an automatic function on a machine.
2 an excess or increase on a budget, salary, or cost.
3 chiefly US a cancellation of a decision by exertion of authority or winning of votes.

overrider ▶ noun Brit. either of a pair of projecting pieces on the bumper of a car.

O

overriding ▸ adjective **1** more important than any other considerations: *the overriding concern of the organizers was the financial crisis.*
2 technical extending or moving over something, especially while remaining in close contact.

overripe ▸ adjective too ripe; past its best: *overripe tomatoes.* ■ (especially of an artistic work) exaggerated or overblown: *an overripe melodrama.*

overrode past of OVERRIDE.

overruff ▸ verb [no obj.] (in bridge, whist, and similar card games) play a trump that is higher than one already played in the same trick.
▸ noun an act of overruffing.

overrule ▸ verb [with obj.] reject or disallow by exercising one's superior authority: *Chief Judge Moran overruled the government's objections.* ■ reject the decision or opinion of: *welfare staff overruled an experienced detective.*

overrun ▸ verb (**overruns**, **overrunning**; past **overran**; past participle **overrun**) **1** [with obj.] spread over or occupy (a place) in large numbers: *the Mediterranean has been overrun by tourists* | *the northern frontier was overrun by invaders.* ■ move or extend over or beyond: *let the text overrun the right-hand margin.* ■ run over or beyond: *Rufus overran third base.* ■ rotate faster than (another part of a machine).
2 [no obj.] continue beyond or above an expected or allowed time or cost: *he allowed the match to overrun by 2 minutes* | [with obj.] *he mustn't overrun his budget.*
▸ noun **1** an instance of something exceeding an expected or allowed time or cost: *the cost overrun caused the company's share price to fall.*
2 [mass noun] the movement or extension of something beyond an expected or allotted position. ■ [count noun] a clear area beyond the end of a runway.
3 [mass noun] the movement of a vehicle at a speed greater than is imparted by the engine.
– ORIGIN Old English *oferyrnan* (see OVER-, RUN).

oversail ▸ verb [with obj.] (of a part of a building) project beyond (a lower part): *a sloping stone coping oversailing a gutter.*
– ORIGIN late 17th cent. (originally Scots): from OVER + French *saillir* 'jut out'.

oversampling ▸ noun [mass noun] Electronics the technique of increasing the apparent sampling frequency of a digital signal by repeating each digit a number of times, in order to facilitate the subsequent filtering of unwanted noise.

oversaw past of OVERSEE.

O

overscan ▸ noun [mass noun] the facility on some computer screens or televisions to adjust the picture size so that the picture is bigger but the edges of the picture are lost.

overscrupulous ▸ adjective excessively scrupulous.
– DERIVATIVES **overscrupulousness** noun.

overseas (Brit. also **oversea**) ▸ adverb in or to a foreign country, especially one across the sea: *he spent quite a lot of time working overseas.*
▸ adjective [attrib.] from, to, or relating to a foreign country: *overseas trips.*
– PHRASES **from overseas** from abroad.

oversee ▸ verb (**oversees**, **overseeing**; past **oversaw**; past participle **overseen**) [with obj.] supervise (a person or their work), especially in an official capacity: *the Home Secretary oversees the police service.*
– ORIGIN Old English *oferséon* 'look at from above' (see OVER-, SEE[1]).

overseer ▸ noun a person who supervises others, especially workers.
– ORIGIN late Middle English (also denoting a person appointed by a testator to assist the executor of a will): from OVERSEE.

overseer of the poor ▸ noun Brit. historical a parish official who administered funds to the poor.

oversell ▸ verb (past and past participle **oversold**) [with obj.] sell more of (something) than exists or can be delivered. ■ exaggerate the merits of: *computer-aided software engineering has been oversold.*

oversensitive ▸ adjective (especially of a person or an instrument) excessively sensitive: *Bentley was oversensitive to criticism.*
– DERIVATIVES **oversensitiveness** noun, **oversensitivity** noun.

overset ▸ verb (**oversets**, **oversetting**; past and past participle **overset**) [with obj.] dated **1** overturn: *he overset the primus stove while cooking his supper.*
2 upset emotionally: *the small kindness nearly overset her again.*

oversew ▸ verb (past participle **oversewn** or **oversewed**) [with obj.] sew (the edges of something) with every stitch passing over the join.

oversexed ▸ adjective having unusually strong sexual desires.

overshadow ▸ verb [with obj.] **1** tower above and cast a shadow over: *an enormous oak tree stood overshadowing the cottage.* ■ cast gloom over: *it is easy to let this feeling of tragedy overshadow his story.*
2 appear more prominent or important than: *his competitive nature often overshadows the other qualities.* ■ be more impressive or successful than (another person): *he was always overshadowed by his brilliant elder brother.*
– ORIGIN Old English *ofersceadwian* (see OVER-, SHADOW).

overshirt ▸ noun a loose shirt worn over other garments.

overshoe ▸ noun a shoe worn over a normal shoe, typically made either of rubber to protect the normal shoe or of felt to protect a floor surface.

overshoot ▸ verb (past and past participle **overshot**) [with obj.] go past (an intended stopping or turning point) inadvertently: *they overshot their intended destination* | [no obj.] *he had overshot by fifty yards but backed up to the junction.* ■ exceed (a financial target or limit): *the department may overshoot its cash limit.*
▸ noun an act of overshooting something.
– PHRASES **overshoot the mark** go beyond what is intended or acceptable.

overshot past and past participle of OVERSHOOT
▸ adjective **1** (of a waterwheel) turned by water falling on to it from a channel.
2 denoting an upper jaw which projects beyond the lower jaw.

overside ▸ adverb over the side of a ship: *we saw him dumped unceremoniously overside by the guards.*

oversight ▸ noun **1** an unintentional failure to notice or do something: *he had simply missed Parsons out by an oversight* | [mass noun] *was the mistake due to oversight?*
2 [mass noun] the action of overseeing something: *effective oversight of the financial reporting process.*

oversimplify ▸ verb (**oversimplifies**, **oversimplifying**, **oversimplified**) [with obj.] (often as adj. **oversimplified**) simplify (something) so much that a distorted impression of it is given: *an oversimplified view of human personality.*
– DERIVATIVES **oversimplification** noun.

oversite ▸ noun a layer of concrete used to seal the earth under the ground floor of a house.

oversized (also **oversize**) ▸ adjective bigger than the usual size: *an oversized T-shirt.*

overskirt ▸ noun an outer skirt, worn over the skirt of a dress.

overslaugh /ˈəʊvəslɔː/ ▸ verb [with obj.] US pass over (someone) in favour of another: *during the war officers were often overslaughed.*
– ORIGIN mid 18th cent.: from Dutch *overslag* (noun), from *overslaan* 'pass over'.

oversleep ▸ verb (past and past participle **overslept**) [no obj.] sleep longer or later than one intended: *we talked until the early hours and consequently I overslept.*

oversleeve ▸ noun a protective sleeve covering an ordinary sleeve.

oversold past and past participle of OVERSELL.
▸ adjective Stock Market sold at a price below its true value: *technology stocks remain oversold and are considered ripe for buying.*

oversolicitous ▸ adjective showing excessive concern for another person's welfare or interests.
– DERIVATIVES **oversolicitude** noun.

oversoul ▸ noun [in sing.] (especially in Transcendentalism) a divine spirit supposed to pervade the universe and to encompass all human souls.

overspecialize (also **overspecialise**) ▸ verb [no obj.] concentrate too much on one aspect or area of something: (as adj. **overspecialized**) *overspecialized medicine.*
– DERIVATIVES **overspecialization** noun.

overspend ▸ verb (past and past participle **overspent**) [no obj.] spend more than the expected or allotted amount: *she overspent on her husband's funeral* | [with obj.] *the department is going to overspend its budget.*
▸ noun an act of overspending.

overspill ▸ noun [mass noun] the action or result of spilling over or spreading into another area. ■ Brit. a surplus population moving or forced to move from an overcrowded area to a less heavily populated one: *organizing arrangements for overspill from the cities.*

overspin ▸ noun [mass noun] a rotating motion given to a ball when throwing or hitting it, used to give it extra speed or distance or to make it bounce awkwardly.

overspray ▸ noun [mass noun] excess paint or other liquid which spreads or blows beyond an area being sprayed.

overspread ▸ verb (past and past participle **overspread**) [with obj.] cover the surface of; spread over: *a giant bramble had overspread the path.*
– ORIGIN Old English *ofersprǣdan* (see OVER-, SPREAD).

overstaffed ▸ adjective having more members of staff than are necessary: *government departments are always overstaffed.*
– DERIVATIVES **overstaffing** noun.

overstate ▸ verb [with obj.] state too strongly; exaggerate: *I overstated my case to make my point.*

overstatement ▸ noun [mass noun] the action of stating something too strongly; exaggeration: *a classic piece of overstatement* | [count noun] *to describe the show as a success would be an overstatement.*

overstay ▸ verb [with obj.] stay longer than the time, limits, or duration of: *he was arrested for overstaying his visa.*
– PHRASES **overstay one's welcome** see WELCOME.
– DERIVATIVES **overstayer** noun.

oversteer ▸ verb [no obj.] (of a motor vehicle) have a tendency to turn more sharply than intended.
▸ noun [mass noun] the tendency of a vehicle to turn more sharply than intended.

overstep ▸ verb (**oversteps**, **overstepping**, **overstepped**) pass beyond or exceed (a limit or standard): *you must not overstep your borrowing limit* | *he has overstepped the bounds of acceptable discipline.*
– PHRASES **overstep the mark** behave in an unacceptable way.

overstimulate ▸ verb [with obj.] stimulate physiologically or mentally to an excessive degree: *hot water overstimulates the sebaceous glands.*
– DERIVATIVES **overstimulation** noun.

overstitch ▸ noun a stitch made over an edge or over another stitch.
▸ verb [with obj.] sew with an overstitch.

overstock ▸ verb [with obj.] supply with more of something than is necessary or required: *do not overstock the kitchen with food.* ■ put more animals in (an area) than it is capable of supporting.
▸ noun [mass noun] a supply or quantity in excess of demand or requirement: *factory overstock* | [count noun] *publishers' overstocks and remainders.*

overstorey ▸ noun (pl. **overstoreys**) Ecology the uppermost canopy level of a forest, formed by the tallest trees.

overstrain ▸ verb [with obj.] subject to an excessive demand on strength, resources, or abilities: *there was a risk he might overstrain his heart.*
▸ noun [mass noun] the action or result of overstraining: *overstrain had brought on tuberculosis.*

overstress ▸ verb [with obj.] subject to too much physical or mental stress: *they are prone to nervous breakdowns if overstressed.* ■ lay too much emphasis on: *the value of good legal assistance cannot be overstressed.*
▸ noun [mass noun] excessive stress.

overstretch ▸ verb [with obj.] (often as adj. **overstretched**) **1** stretch too much: *the aches and pains of overstretched muscles.*
2 make excessive demands on: *classes are very large and facilities are overstretched.*

overstrike ▸ noun [mass noun] the superimposing of one printed character or one coin design on another. ■ [count noun] a coin showing one design superimposed on another.
– DERIVATIVES **overstriking** noun.

overstrung ▸ adjective **1** /ˈəʊvəstrʌŋ/ (of a piano) having strings in sets crossing each other obliquely.
2 /əʊvəˈstrʌŋ/ dated (of a person) extremely nervous or tense.

overstudy ▸ verb (**overstudies**, **overstudying**, **overstudied**) study excessively.
▸ noun [mass noun] excessive study.

overstuff ▸ verb [with obj.] (usu. as adj. **overstuffed**) **1** force too much into (a container): *an overstuffed briefcase.*
2 cover (furniture) completely with upholstery: *an overstuffed armchair.*

oversubscribed ▸ adjective (of something for sale) applied for in greater quantities than are available: *shares on sale in Europe were oversubscribed.* ■ (of a course or institution) having more applications than available places.

oversubtle ▸ adjective making excessively fine distinctions: *an oversubtle argument.*

oversupply ▸ noun (pl. **oversupplies**) an excessive supply: *an oversupply of teachers* | [mass noun] *oversupply causes prices to fall.*
▸ verb (**oversupplies, oversupplying, oversupplied**) [with obj.] supply with too much or too many: *the country was oversupplied with lawyers.*

oversusceptible ▸ adjective too susceptible or vulnerable.

oversweet ▸ adjective excessively sweet in taste.

overt /əʊˈvəːt, ˈəʊvət/ ▸ adjective done or shown openly; plainly apparent: *an overt act of aggression* | *people with HIV progressing to overt AIDS.*
– DERIVATIVES **overtly** adverb, **overtness** noun.
– ORIGIN Middle English: from Old French, past participle of *ovrir* 'to open', from Latin *aperire.*

overtake ▸ verb (past **overtook**; past participle **overtaken**) [with obj.] **1** chiefly Brit. catch up with and pass while travelling in the same direction: *the driver overtook a line of vehicles* | [no obj.] *he overtook in the face of oncoming traffic.* ■ become greater or more successful than: *Germany rapidly overtook Britain in industrial output.*
2 (especially of misfortune) come suddenly or unexpectedly upon: *disaster overtook the town in* AD *296.* ■ (of a feeling) affect (someone) suddenly and powerfully: *weariness overtook him and he retired to bed.*

overtask ▸ verb [with obj.] impose too much work on: (as adj. **overtasked**) *an overtasked school system.*

overtax ▸ verb [with obj.] **1** require to pay too much tax: *the UK is not overtaxed compared to other countries.*
2 make excessive demands on (a person's strength, abilities, etc.): *do athletes overtax their hearts?*
– DERIVATIVES **overtaxation** noun (sense 1).

overthink ▸ verb [with obj.] think about (something) too much or for too long: *I often wonder if women tend to overthink situations* | [no obj.] *he doesn't make snap decisions, but he doesn't overthink either.*

overthrow ▸ verb (past **overthrew**; past participle **overthrown**) [with obj.] **1** remove forcibly from power: *military coups which had attempted to overthrow the King.* ■ put an end to (something) by the use of force: *their subversive activities are calculated to overthrow parliamentary democracy.* ■ archaic knock or throw to the ground.
2 throw (a ball) further than the intended distance. ■ chiefly N. Amer. throw a ball beyond (a receiving player): *Dodge overthrew a receiver in the end zone.*
▸ noun **1** [in sing.] a removal from power: *plotting the overthrow of the government.*
2 (in cricket, baseball, and other games) a throw which sends a ball past its intended recipient or target. ■ a score made because the ball has been overthrown: *his throw missed the stumps and went for four overthrows.*
3 a panel of decorated wrought-iron work above an arch or gateway.

overthrust Geology ▸ noun [mass noun] the thrust of one series of rock strata over another, especially along a fault line at a shallow angle to the horizontal.
▸ verb (past and past participle **overthrust**) [with obj.] force (a body of rock) over another.

overtime ▸ noun [mass noun] **1** time worked in addition to one's normal working hours: *fewer opportunities for overtime.* ■ payment for overtime.
2 N. Amer. extra time played at the end of a game that is tied at the end of the regulation time: *they lost in overtime.*
▸ adverb in addition to normal working hours: *we worked overtime to fulfil a big order* | figurative *his brain was working overtime.*

overtip ▸ verb [with obj.] give an excessively generous tip to: *the food was so cheap that I overtipped the waitress.*

overtire ▸ verb [with obj.] exhaust (someone): *walk at a pace that does not overtire you.*
– DERIVATIVES **overtired** adjective.

overtone ▸ noun **1** a musical tone which is a part of the harmonic series above a fundamental note, and may be heard with it. ■ Physics a component of any oscillation whose frequency is an integral multiple of the fundamental frequency.
2 (often **overtones**) a subtle or subsidiary quality, implication, or connotation: *the decision may have political overtones.*
– ORIGIN mid 19th cent.: from OVER- + TONE, suggested by German *Oberton.*

overtop ▸ verb (**overtops, overtopping, overtopped**) [with obj.] exceed in height: *no building is allowed to overtop the cathedral.* ■ (especially of water) rise over the top of (a barrier): *the old sea wall is regularly overtopped by high tides.* ■ archaic be superior to: *none can overtop him in goodness.*
▸ adverb & preposition chiefly Canadian over: [as prep.] *sprinkle the mixture overtop the batter.*

overtrade ▸ verb [no obj.] engage in more business than can be supported by the market or by the funds or resources available.

overtrain ▸ verb (especially with reference to an athlete) train or cause to train excessively.

overtrick ▸ noun Bridge a trick taken by the declarer in excess of the contract.

overtrousers ▸ plural noun waterproof trousers, typically worn over other trousers.

overtrump ▸ verb another term for OVERRUFF.

overture ▸ noun **1** an orchestral piece at the beginning of an opera, play, etc. ■ an independent orchestral composition in one movement.
2 an introduction to something more substantial: *the talks were no more than an overture to a long debate.*
3 (usu. **overtures**) an approach or proposal made to someone with the aim of opening negotiations or establishing a relationship: *he began* ***making overtures to*** *British merchant banks.*
– ORIGIN late Middle English (in the sense 'aperture'): from Old French, from Latin *apertura* 'aperture'.

overturn ▸ verb [with obj.] **1** tip (something) over so that it is on its side or upside down: *the crowd proceeded to overturn cars and set them on fire.* ■ [no obj.] turn over and come to rest upside down: *a coach hit a car and overturned.*
2 abolish, invalidate, or reverse (a previous system, decision, situation, etc.): *the results overturned previous findings* | *he fought for eight years to overturn a conviction for armed robbery.*
▸ noun rare an act of overturning something. ■ [mass noun] Ecology the occasional (typically twice yearly) mixing of the water of a thermally stratified lake.

overtype ▸ verb [with obj.] type over (another character) on a computer screen.

overuse ▸ verb [with obj.] use too much: *young children sometimes overuse 'and' in their writing.*
▸ noun [mass noun] excessive use: *overuse of natural resources.*

overvalue ▸ verb (**overvalues, overvaluing, overvalued**) [with obj.] overestimate the importance of: *intelligence can be overvalued.* ■ fix the value of (something, especially a currency) at too high a level: *sterling was overvalued against the dollar.*
– DERIVATIVES **overvaluation** noun.

overview ▸ noun a general review or summary of a subject: *a brief overview of the survey.*
▸ verb [with obj.] give a general review or summary of: *the report overviews the needs of the community.*

overwater ▸ verb [with obj.] water (a plant, sports field, etc.) too much: *your cutting needs some water, but make sure you don't overwater it.*

overwear ▸ noun [mass noun] outer clothing.

overweening ▸ adjective showing excessive confidence or pride: *overweening ambition.*
– DERIVATIVES **overweeningly** adverb.

overweight ▸ adjective above a weight considered normal or desirable: *she was a stone overweight.* ■ above an allowed weight: *an overweight lorry.*
▸ noun [mass noun] excessive or extra weight.
▸ verb [with obj.] (usu. as adj. **overweighted**) put too much weight on; overload.

overwhelm ▸ verb [with obj.] **1** bury or drown beneath a huge mass of something, especially water: *floodwaters overwhelmed hundreds of houses.* ■ give too much of something to; inundate: *they were overwhelmed by farewell messages.*
2 have a strong emotional effect on: *I was overwhelmed with guilt.*
3 defeat completely: [with obj. and complement] *the Irish side was overwhelmed 15–3 by Scotland.* ■ be too strong for; overpower: *the Stilton doesn't overwhelm the flavour of the trout.*

overwhelming ▸ adjective very great in amount: *his party won overwhelming support.* ■ (especially of an emotion) very strong: *she felt an overwhelming desire to giggle.*
– DERIVATIVES **overwhelmingly** adverb [as submodifier] *friends have been overwhelmingly generous,* **overwhelmingness** noun.

overwind ▸ verb (past and past participle **overwound**) [with obj.] wind (a mechanism, especially a watch) beyond the proper stopping point.

overwinter ▸ verb [no obj.] **1** [with adverbial of place] spend the winter: *many birds overwinter in equatorial regions.*
2 (of an insect, plant, etc.) live through the winter: *the germinated seeds will overwinter.*

overwork ▸ verb [with obj.] (often as adj. **overworked**) exhaust with too much work: *tired, overworked, demoralized staff.* ■ [no obj.] work too hard: *the doctor advised a complete rest because he had been overworking.* ■ make excessive use of: *our lifts are overworked.* ■ use (a word or idea) too much and so make it weaker in meaning or effect: *'Breathtaking' is an overworked brochure cliché.*
▸ noun [mass noun] excessive work: *his health broke down under the strain of overwork.*

overwound past and past participle of OVERWIND.

overwrap ▸ verb (**overwraps, overwrapping, overwrapped**) [with obj.] cover with a wrapping: *when the food is cold, overwrap it tightly with foil.*
▸ noun an outer wrapping: *a cellophane overwrap.*

overwrite ▸ verb (past **overwrote**; past participle **overwritten**) [with obj.] **1** write on top of (other writing): *many names had been scratched out or overwritten.* ■ Computing destroy (data) by entering new data in its place. ■ another term for OVERTYPE.
2 write too elaborately or ornately: *there is a tendency to overwrite their parts and fall into cliché.*
3 [no obj.] (usu. as noun **overwriting**) (in insurance) accept more risk than the premium income limits allow.

overwrought ▸ adjective **1** in a state of nervous excitement or anxiety: *she was too overwrought to listen to reason.*
2 (of a piece of writing or a work of art) too elaborate or complicated in design or construction.
– ORIGIN late Middle English: archaic past participle of OVERWORK.

overzealous ▸ adjective too zealous in one's attitude or behaviour: *he's been overzealous in handing out parking tickets.*

ovi- ▸ combining form chiefly Zoology relating to eggs or ova: *oviparous.*
– ORIGIN from Latin *ovum* 'egg'.

O

Ovid /ˈɒvɪd/ (43 BC–*c.*17 AD), Roman poet; full name *Publius Ovidius Naso.* He is particularly known for his elegiac love poems (such as the *Amores* and the *Ars Amatoria*) and for the *Metamorphoses,* a hexametric epic which retells Greek and Roman myths.
– DERIVATIVES **Ovidian** adjective.

oviduct /ˈəʊvɪdʌkt/ ▸ noun Anatomy & Zoology the tube through which an ovum or egg passes from an ovary.
– DERIVATIVES **oviducal** /-ˈdjuːk(ə)l/ adjective, **oviductal** adjective.

Oviedo /ˌɒvɪˈeɪdəʊ/, Spanish /əˈβjeðəʊ/ a city in NW Spain, capital of Asturias; pop. 220,644 (2008).

oviform /ˈəʊvɪfɔːm/ ▸ adjective egg-shaped.

Ovimbundu see MBUNDU.

ovine /ˈəʊvʌɪn/ ▸ adjective relating to or resembling sheep: *the ovine immune system.*
– ORIGIN early 19th cent.: from late Latin *ovinus,* from Latin *ovis* 'sheep'.

oviparous /əʊˈvɪp(ə)rəs/ ▸ adjective Zoology (of an animal) producing young by means of eggs which are hatched after they have been laid by the parent, as in birds. Compare with VIVIPAROUS and OVOVIVIPAROUS.
– DERIVATIVES **oviparity** noun.

oviposit /ˌəʊvɪˈpɒzɪt/ ▸ verb (**oviposits, ovipositing, oviposited**) [no obj.] Zoology (especially of an insect) lay an egg or eggs: *larger females have the potential to oviposit on a greater number of hosts.*
– DERIVATIVES **oviposition** noun.
– ORIGIN early 19th cent.: from **ovi-** 'egg' + Latin *posit-* 'placed' (from the verb *ponere*).

ovipositor /ˌəʊvɪˈpɒzɪtə/ ▸ noun Zoology a tubular organ through which a female insect or fish deposits eggs.

oviraptor /ˌəʊvɪˈraptə/ ▸ noun a bipedal dinosaur of the late Cretaceous period, having a toothless jaw and long forelimbs with clawed fingers. ● Genus *Oviraptor,* family Oviraptoridae, suborder Theropoda.

– ORIGIN 1920s: from **ovi-** (from Latin *ovum* 'egg') + **RAPTOR**, the original supposition being that it fed on the eggs of other dinosaurs.

ovoid /ˈəʊvɔɪd/ ▸ **adjective** (of a solid or a three-dimensional surface) more or less egg-shaped. ■ (of a plane figure) oval, especially with one end more pointed than the other.
▸ **noun** an ovoid body or surface.
– ORIGIN early 19th cent.: from French *ovoïde*, from modern Latin *ovoides*, from Latin *ovum* 'egg'.

ovolo /ˈəʊvələʊ/ ▸ **noun** (pl. **ovoli** /-liː/) Architecture a rounded convex moulding.
– ORIGIN mid 17th cent.: from Italian, diminutive of *ovo* 'egg', from Latin *ovum*.

ovotestis /ˌəʊvəʊˈtɛstɪs/ ▸ **noun** (pl. **ovotestes** /-tiːz/) Zoology an organ producing both ova and spermatozoa, especially in some gastropod molluscs.
– ORIGIN late 19th cent.: from **OVUM** + **TESTIS**.

ovoviviparous /ˌəʊvəʊvɪˈvɪp(ə)rəs/ ▸ **adjective** Zoology (of an animal) producing young by means of eggs which are hatched within the body of the parent, as in some snakes. Compare with **OVIPAROUS** and **VIVIPAROUS**.
– DERIVATIVES **ovoviviparity** noun.

ovulate /ˈɒvjʊleɪt/ ▸ **verb** [no obj.] discharge ova or ovules from the ovary: *women who ovulate but cannot conceive* | [with obj.] *all the eggs that will be ovulated are present at birth.*
– DERIVATIVES **ovulation** noun, **ovulatory** adjective.
– ORIGIN late 19th cent.: back-formation from *ovulation*, or from medieval Latin *ovulum* 'little egg' (see **OVULE**) + **-ATE**[3].

ovule /ˈɒvjuːl, ˈəʊ-/ ▸ **noun** Botany the part of the ovary of seed plants that contains the female germ cell and after fertilization becomes the seed.
– DERIVATIVES **ovular** adjective.
– ORIGIN early 19th cent.: from French, from medieval Latin *ovulum*, diminutive of **OVUM**.

ovum /ˈəʊvəm/ ▸ **noun** (pl. **ova** /ˈəʊvə/) Biology a mature female reproductive cell, especially of a human or other animal, which can divide to give rise to an embryo usually only after fertilization by a male cell.
– ORIGIN early 18th cent.: from Latin, literally 'egg'.

ow ▸ **exclamation** used to express sudden pain: *Ow! You're hurting me!*
– ORIGIN natural exclamation: first recorded in English in the mid 19th cent.

O

owe ▸ **verb** [with obj.] have an obligation to pay or repay (something, especially money) in return for something received: *they have denied they **owe** money **to** the company* | [with two objs] *you owe me £19.50 for the electricity bill.* ■ owe something, especially money, to: *I owe you for the taxi.* ■ be under a moral obligation to give someone (gratitude, respect, etc.): *I owe it to him to explain what's happened* | [with two objs] *I owe you an apology.* ■ **(owe something to)** have something because of: *champagne houses owe their success to brand image* | *I owe my life to you.*
– PHRASES **owe it to oneself** (**to do something**) need to do something to protect one's own interests: *you owe it to yourself to take care of your body.* **owe someone one** informal feel indebted to someone: *thanks, I owe you one for this.* —— **owes one a living** used to express disapproval of someone who expects to receive financial support or other benefits without doing any work: *they think the world owes them a living.*
– ORIGIN Old English *āgan* 'own, have it as an obligation', of Germanic origin; from an Indo-European root shared by Sanskrit *īś* 'possess, own'. Compare with **OUGHT**[1].

Owen[1], Sir Richard (1804–92), English anatomist and palaeontologist. Owen made important contributions to evolution, taxonomy, and palaeontology and coined the word *dinosaur* in 1841. He was a strong opponent of Darwinism.

Owen[2], Robert (1771–1858), Welsh social reformer and industrialist. A pioneer socialist thinker, he founded a model industrial community in Scotland, organized on principles of mutual cooperation, the first of a series of cooperative communities.

Owen[3], Wilfred (1893–1918), English poet. His experiences of fighting in the First World War inspired his best-known works, such as 'Anthem for Doomed Youth'.

Owens, Jesse (1913–80), American athlete; born *James Cleveland Owens*. In 1935 he equalled or broke six world records in 45 minutes, and in 1936 won four gold medals at the Olympic Games in Berlin. The success at the games of Owens, as a black man, outraged Hitler.

owing ▸ **adjective** [predic.] chiefly Brit. (of money) yet to be paid: *no rent was owing.*
– PHRASES **owing to** because of or on account of: *his reading was hesitant owing to a stammer.*

> **USAGE** For an explanation of the difference between **owing to** and **due to**, see **USAGE** at **DUE**.

owl ▸ **noun** a nocturnal bird of prey with large eyes, a facial disc, a hooked beak, and typically a loud hooting call. ● Order Strigiformes: families Strigidae (**typical owls** such as tawny owls and eagle owls) and Tytonidae (**barn owls** and their relatives).
■ informal a person who habitually goes to bed late and feels energetic in the evening. Often contrasted with **LARK**[1].
– DERIVATIVES **owl-like** adjective.
– ORIGIN Old English *ūle*, of Germanic origin; related to Dutch *uil* and German *Eule*, from a base imitative of the bird's call.

owl butterfly ▸ **noun** a very large South American butterfly which flies at dusk, with a large eye-like marking on the underside of each hindwing. ● Genus *Caligo*, subfamily Brassolinae, family Nymphalidae.

owlet ▸ **noun 1** a small owl found chiefly in Asia and Africa. ● Genus *Glaucidium* and *Athene*, family Strigidae: several species.
■ a young owl of any kind.
2 another term for **NOCTUID**.

owlet-nightjar ▸ **noun** a nocturnal Australasian bird resembling a small nightjar, with an owl-like face and a large gape. ● Family Aegothelidae and genus *Aegotheles*: several species.

owlish ▸ **adjective** like an owl, especially in appearing to be solemn or wise: *he had an owlish and solemn air.* ■ (of glasses) resembling the large round eyes of an owl.
– DERIVATIVES **owlishly** adverb.

owl light ▸ **noun** dusk; twilight.

owl monkey ▸ **noun** another term for **DOUROUCOULI**.

owl parrot ▸ **noun** another term for **KAKAPO**.

own ▸ **adjective & pronoun** used with a possessive to emphasize that someone or something belongs or relates to the person mentioned: [as adj.] *they can't handle their own children* | *I was an outcast among my own kind* | [as pronoun] *the Church would look after its own.* ■ done or produced by and for the person mentioned: [as adj.] *I used to design all my own clothes* | [as pronoun] *they claimed the work as their own.* ■ particular to the person or thing mentioned; individual: [as adj.] *the style had its own charm* | [as pronoun] *the film had a quality all its own.*
▸ **verb 1** [with obj.] have (something) as one's own; possess: *his father owns a restaurant* | (as adj., in combination **-owned**) *a state-owned company.*
2 [no obj.] formal admit or acknowledge that something is the case or that one feels a certain way: *she **owned to** a feeling of profound jealousy* | [with clause] *he was reluctant to own that he was indebted.* ■ [with obj.] take or acknowledge full responsibility for (something): *I emphasize the importance of owning our anger and finding ways to control it.* ■ [with obj.] archaic acknowledge paternity, authorship, or possession of: *he has published little, trivial things which he will not own.*
3 [with obj.] US informal utterly defeat or humiliate: *yeah right, she totally owned you, man.*
– PHRASES **as if** (or **like**) **one owns the place** informal in an overbearing or self-important manner. **be one's own man** (or **woman**) **1** act independently and with confidence. **2** archaic be in full possession of one's faculties. **come into its** (or **one's**) **own** become fully effective, used, or recognized: *the two folk languages will at last come into their own.* **hold one's own** retain a position of strength in a challenging situation. **of one's own** belonging to oneself alone: *at last I've got a place of my own.* **on one's own** unaccompanied by others; alone or unaided.
– PHRASAL VERBS **own up** admit to having done something wrong or embarrassing: *he **owns up to** few mistakes.*
– ORIGIN Old English *āgen* (adjective and pronoun) 'owned, possessed', past participle of *āgan* 'owe'; the verb (Old English *āgnian* 'possess', also 'make own's own') was originally from the adjective, later probably reintroduced from **OWNER**.

own affair ▸ **noun** historical (in South Africa) a matter defined as being specific to a particular ethnic group, and controlled by that group through a chamber of the tricameral parliament.

own brand ▸ **noun** Brit. a product manufactured specially for a retailer and bearing the retailer's name: *my dogs eat the supermarket's own brand* | [as modifier] *own-brand products.*

owner ▸ **noun** a person who owns something: *the proud owner of a huge Dalmatian* | *restaurant owners.*
– DERIVATIVES **ownerless** adjective.

owner-occupier ▸ **noun** Brit. a person who owns the house, flat, etc. in which they live.
– DERIVATIVES **owner-occupied** adjective.

ownership ▸ **noun** the act, state, or right of possessing something: *the ownership of land* | *the rise in car ownership.*

own goal ▸ **noun** (in soccer) a goal scored when a player inadvertently strikes or deflects the ball into their own team's goal. ■ Brit. informal an act that unintentionally harms one's own interests: *government scores own goal by assisting organized crime in London.*

own-label ▸ **noun** Brit. another term for **OWN BRAND**.

owt /aʊt/ ▸ **pronoun** N. English anything: *I didn't say owt.*
– ORIGIN mid 19th cent.: variant of **AUGHT**[1].

ox ▸ **noun** (pl. **oxen** /ˈɒks(ə)n/) a domesticated bovine animal kept for milk or meat; a cow or bull. See **CATTLE**. ■ a castrated bull used as a draught animal: [as modifier] *an ox cart.* ■ used in names of wild animals related to or resembling a domesticated ox, e.g. **musk ox**.
– ORIGIN Old English *oxa*, of Germanic origin; related to Dutch *os* and German *Ochse*, from an Indo-European root shared by Sanskrit *ukṣán* 'bull'.

ox- ▸ **combining form** variant spelling of **OXY-**[2] reduced before a vowel (as in *oxazole*).

oxacillin /ˌɒksəˈsɪlɪn/ ▸ **noun** [mass noun] Medicine an antibiotic drug made by chemical modification of penicillin and used to treat bacterial infections.
– ORIGIN 1960s: blend of **OXAZOLE** and **PENICILLIN**.

oxalate /ˈɒksəleɪt/ ▸ **noun** Chemistry a salt or ester of oxalic acid.

oxalic acid /ɒkˈsalɪk/ ▸ **noun** [mass noun] Chemistry a poisonous crystalline acid with a sour taste, present in rhubarb leaves, wood sorrel, and other plants. ● Alternative name: **ethanedioic acid**; chem. formula: $(COOH)_2$.
– ORIGIN late 18th cent.: *oxalic* from French *oxalique*, via Latin from Greek *oxalis* 'wood sorrel'.

oxalis /ˈɒksəlɪs, ɒkˈsɑːlɪs/ ▸ **noun** a plant of a genus which includes the wood sorrel, typically having three-lobed leaves and white, yellow, or pink flowers. ● Genus *Oxalis*, family Oxalidaceae.
– ORIGIN early 17th cent.: via Latin from Greek, from *oxus* 'sour' (because of its sharp-tasting leaves).

oxazole /ˈɒksəzəʊl/ ▸ **noun** [mass noun] Chemistry a volatile liquid with weakly basic properties, whose molecule contains a five-membered ring important as the basis of a number of medicinal drugs. ● A heterocyclic compound; chem. formula: C_3H_3NO.
– ORIGIN late 19th cent.: from **ox-** 'oxygen' + **AZO-** + **-OLE**.

oxbow /ˈɒksbəʊ/ ▸ **noun 1** a loop formed by a horseshoe bend in a river. ■ short for **OXBOW LAKE**.
2 a U-shaped collar of an ox-yoke.

oxbow lake ▸ **noun** a curved lake formed from a horseshoe bend in a river where the main stream has cut across the narrow end and no longer flows around the loop of the bend.

Oxbridge ▸ **noun** Oxford and Cambridge universities regarded together: [as modifier] *Oxbridge colleges.*
– ORIGIN mid 19th cent.: blend of **OXFORD** and **CAMBRIDGE**.

oxen plural form of **OX**.

oxer ▸ **noun** an ox fence. ■ (in showjumping) a jump consisting of a brush fence with a guard rail on one or both sides.

ox-eye ▸ **noun** a yellow-flowered North American plant of the daisy family. ● *Heliopsis helianthoides*, family Compositae.

ox-eye daisy ▸ **noun** a Eurasian daisy which has large white flowers with yellow centres. Also called **MOON DAISY** or **MARGUERITE**. ● *Leucanthemum vulgare*, family Compositae.

Oxf. ▸ **abbreviation** Oxford.

Oxfam a British charity founded in Oxford in 1942, dedicated to helping victims of famine and natural disasters as well as raising living standards in developing countries.
– ORIGIN from *Ox(ford Committee for) Fam(ine Relief).*

ox fence ▶ noun a strong fence for confining cattle, consisting of a hedge with a strong guard rail on one side, and usually a ditch on the other.

Oxford a city in central England, on the River Thames, the county town of Oxfordshire; pop. 146,100 (est. 2009). Oxford University is located there.

oxford ▶ noun **1** (also **oxford cloth**) [mass noun] a thick cotton fabric chiefly used to make shirts: [as modifier] *an oxford shirt*.
2 (also **oxford shoe**) a type of lace-up shoe with a low heel.

Oxford bags ▶ plural noun Brit. wide baggy trousers.

Oxford blue ▶ noun Brit. **1** [mass noun] a dark blue, typically with a purple tinge.
2 a person who has represented Oxford University at a particular sport in a match against Cambridge University.

Oxford comma ▶ noun another term for SERIAL COMMA.
– ORIGIN a characteristic of the house style of *Oxford* University Press.

Oxford English Dictionary (abbrev.: **OED**) the largest dictionary of the English language, prepared in Oxford and originally issued in instalments between 1884 and 1928.

Oxford Group a Christian movement popularized in Oxford in the late 1920s, advocating discussion of personal problems by groups. Later known as MORAL REARMAMENT.

Oxfordian ▶ adjective **1** Geology relating to or denoting an age in the Upper Jurassic period, lasting from about 157 to 155 million years ago. Also called CORALLIAN.
2 relating to or denoting the theory that Edward de Vere (1550–1604), Earl of Oxford, wrote the plays attributed to Shakespeare.
▶ noun **1** (**the Oxfordian**) Geology the Oxfordian age or the system of rocks (chiefly coral-derived limestones) deposited during it.
2 a supporter of the Oxfordian theory.

Oxford Movement a Christian movement started in Oxford in 1833, seeking to restore traditional Catholic teachings and ceremonial within the Church of England. Its leaders were John Keble, Edward Pusey, and (until he became a Roman Catholic) John Henry Newman. It formed the basis of the present Anglo-Catholic (or High Church) tradition. Also called TRACTARIANISM.

Oxfordshire a county of south central England; county town, Oxford.

Oxford University the oldest English university, comprising a federation of thirty-nine colleges, the first of which, University College, was formally founded in 1249. The university was established at Oxford soon after 1167.

oxherd ▶ noun archaic a cowherd.
– ORIGIN Old English, from **ox** + obsolete *herd* 'herdsman'.

oxhide ▶ noun [mass noun] leather made from the hide of an ox.

oxic /'ɒksɪk/ ▶ adjective (of a process or environment) in which oxygen is involved or present.
– ORIGIN 1960s: from *ox(ide)* or *ox(ygen)* + -IC.

oxidant /'ɒksɪd(ə)nt/ ▶ noun an oxidizing agent.
– ORIGIN late 19th cent.: from French (modern French *oxydant*), present participle of *oxider* 'oxidize'.

oxidase /'ɒksɪdeɪz/ ▶ noun Biochemistry an enzyme which promotes the transfer of a hydrogen atom from a particular substrate to an oxygen molecule, forming water or hydrogen peroxide.
– ORIGIN late 19th cent.: from French *oxydase*, from *oxyde* 'oxide'.

oxidation ▶ noun [mass noun] Chemistry the process or result of oxidizing or being oxidized.
– DERIVATIVES **oxidational** adjective, **oxidative** adjective.
– ORIGIN late 18th cent.: from French (modern French *oxydation*), from *oxider* 'oxidize'.

oxidation number (also **oxidation state**) ▶ noun Chemistry a number assigned to an element in chemical combination which represents the number of electrons lost (or gained, if the number is negative), by an atom of that element in the compound.

oxide /'ɒksʌɪd/ ▶ noun a binary compound of oxygen with another element or group: *nitrogen oxide*.
– ORIGIN late 18th cent.: from French, from *oxygène* 'oxygen' + *-ide* (as in *acide* 'acid').

oxidize /'ɒksɪdʌɪz/ (also **oxidise**) ▶ verb combine chemically with oxygen: [with obj.] *when coal is burnt any sulphur is oxidized to sulphur dioxide* | [no obj.] *the fats in the food will oxidize, turning it rancid*.
■ Chemistry undergo or cause to undergo a reaction in which electrons are lost to another species. The opposite of REDUCE.
– DERIVATIVES **oxidizable** adjective, **oxidization** noun, **oxidizer** noun.

oxidizing agent ▶ noun Chemistry a substance that tends to bring about oxidation by being reduced and gaining electrons.

oximeter /ɒk'sɪmɪtə/ ▶ noun an instrument for measuring the proportion of oxygenated haemoglobin in the blood.
– DERIVATIVES **oximetry** noun.

oxisol /'ɒksɪsɒl/ ▶ noun Soil Science a soil of an order comprising stable, highly weathered, tropical mineral soils with highly oxidized subsurface horizons.
– ORIGIN 1960s: from OXIC + -SOL.

oxlip ▶ noun a woodland Eurasian primula with yellow flowers that hang down one side of the stem.
● *Primula elatior*, family Primulaceae.
■ (also **false oxlip**) a natural hybrid between a primrose and a cowslip.
– ORIGIN Old English *oxanslyppe*, from *oxa* 'ox' + *slyppe* 'slime'; compare with COWSLIP.

Oxon /'ɒks(ə)n, -sɒn/ ▶ abbreviation ■ Oxfordshire.
■ (in degree titles) of Oxford University: *BA, Oxon*.
– ORIGIN from medieval Latin *Oxoniensis*, from *Oxonia* (see OXONIAN).

Oxonian /ɒk'səʊnɪən/ ▶ adjective relating to Oxford or Oxford University.
▶ noun a native or inhabitant of Oxford. ■ a member of Oxford University.
– ORIGIN mid 16th cent.: from *Oxonia* (Latinized name of Oxford, from its old form *Oxenford*) + -AN.

oxpecker ▶ noun a brown African bird related to the starlings, feeding on parasites that infest the skins of large grazing mammals. ● Genus *Buphagus*, family Sturnidae (or Buphagidae): two species.

oxtail ▶ noun [mass noun] meat from the tail of a cow, used for making soup: [as modifier] *oxtail soup*.

oxter /'ɒkstə/ ▶ noun Scottish & N. English a person's armpit.
– ORIGIN Old English *ōhsta*, *ōxta*.

ox tongue ▶ noun **1** [mass noun] meat from the tongue of a cow.
2 an Old World plant of the daisy family with yellow dandelion-like flowers and prickly hairs on the stem and leaves. ● Genus *Picris*, family Compositae.

Oxus /'ɒksəs/ ancient name for AMU DARYA.

ox wagon ▶ noun a heavy wagon drawn by oxen, used by settlers and pioneers in South Africa.

oxy-[1] ▶ combining form denoting sharpness: *oxytone*.
– ORIGIN from Greek *oxus* 'sharp'.

oxy-[2] (also **ox-**) ▶ combining form Chemistry representing OXYGEN.

oxyacetylene ▶ adjective of or denoting welding or cutting techniques using a very hot flame produced by mixing acetylene and oxygen.

oxyacid ▶ noun an inorganic acid whose molecules contain oxygen, such as sulphuric acid.

oxyanion /ˌɒksɪ'anʌɪən/ ▶ noun Chemistry an anion containing one or more oxygen atoms bonded to another element (as in the sulphate and carbonate ions).

oxycodone /ˌɒksɪ'kəʊdəʊn/ (also trademark **OxyContin**) ▶ noun [mass noun] a synthetic analgesic drug which is similar to morphine in its effects.
– ORIGIN 1970s: from OXY-[2] + *co-* in CODEINE.

oxygen ▶ noun [mass noun] a colourless, odourless reactive gas, the chemical element of atomic number 8 and the life-supporting component of the air. (Symbol: **O**)

> Oxygen is essential to plant and animal life and is a constituent of most organic compounds. It forms about 20 per cent of the earth's atmosphere, and is the most abundant element in the earth's crust, mainly in the form of oxides, silicates, and carbonates.

– DERIVATIVES **oxygenic** adjective.
– ORIGIN late 18th cent.: from French (*principe*) *oxygène* 'acidifying constituent' (because at first it was held to be the essential component in the formation of acids).

oxygenate /'ɒksɪdʒəneɪt, ɒk'sɪdʒ-/ ▶ verb [with obj.] supply, treat, charge, or enrich with oxygen: (as adj. **oxygenated**) *a good supply of oxygenated blood*.
– DERIVATIVES **oxygenation** noun.
– ORIGIN late 18th cent.: from French *oxygéner* 'supply with oxygen' + -ATE[3].

oxygenator ▶ noun a medical apparatus for oxygenating the blood. ■ an aquatic plant which enriches the surrounding water with oxygen.

oxygen bar ▶ noun an establishment where people pay to inhale pure oxygen for its reputedly therapeutic effects.

oxygen debt ▶ noun [mass noun] a temporary oxygen shortage in the body tissues arising from exercise.

oxygenize (also **oxygenise**) ▶ verb rare term for OXYGENATE.

oxygen mask ▶ noun a mask placed over the nose and mouth and connected to a supply of oxygen, used when the body is not able to gain enough oxygen by breathing air, for example at high altitudes, or because of a medical condition.

oxygen tent ▶ noun a tent-like enclosure within which the air supply can be enriched with oxygen to aid a patient's breathing.

oxyhaemoglobin (US **oxyhemoglobin**) ▶ noun [mass noun] Biochemistry a bright red substance formed by the combination of haemoglobin with oxygen, present in oxygenated blood.

oxymoron /ˌɒksɪ'mɔːrɒn/ ▶ noun a figure of speech in which apparently contradictory terms appear in conjunction (e.g. *faith unfaithful kept him falsely true*).
– DERIVATIVES **oxymoronic** adjective.
– ORIGIN mid 17th cent.: from Greek *oxumōron*, neuter (used as a noun) of *oxumōros* 'pointedly foolish', from *oxus* 'sharp' + *mōros* 'foolish'.

oxyntic /ɒk'sɪntɪk/ ▶ adjective of or denoting the secretory cells which produce hydrochloric acid in the main part of the stomach, or the glands which they compose.
– ORIGIN late 19th cent.: from Greek *oxunteos* (verbal noun from *oxunein* 'sharpen') + -IC.

oxytetracycline /ˌɒksɪtɛtrə'sʌɪkliːn/ ▶ noun [mass noun] Medicine an antibiotic related to tetracycline, used to treat a variety of bacterial infections.

oxytocin /ˌɒksɪ'təʊsɪn/ ▶ noun [mass noun] Biochemistry a hormone released by the pituitary gland that causes increased contraction of the womb during labour and stimulates the ejection of milk into the ducts of the breasts.
– DERIVATIVES **oxytocic** adjective.
– ORIGIN 1920s: from Greek *oxutokia* 'sudden delivery' (from *oxus* 'sharp' + *tokos* 'childbirth') + -IN[1].

oxytone /'ɒksɪtəʊn/ ▶ adjective (especially in ancient Greek) having an acute accent on the last syllable. Compare with PAROXYTONE.
▶ noun a word having an acute accent on the last syllable.
– ORIGIN mid 18th cent.: from Greek *oxutonos*, from *oxus* 'sharp' + *tonos* 'tone'.

oy ▶ exclamation **1** variant spelling of OI.
2 see OY VEY.

oyer and terminer /ˌɔɪə(r) ən(d) 'təːmɪnə/ ▶ noun historical a commission issued to judges on a circuit to hold courts: *a court of oyer and terminer*.
– ORIGIN late Middle English: from Anglo-Norman French *oyer et terminer* 'hear and determine'.

oyez /əʊ'jɛs, -'jɛz, -'jeɪ/ (also **oyes**) ▶ exclamation a call given, typically three times, by a public crier or a court officer to command silence and attention before an announcement.
– ORIGIN late Middle English: from Old French *oiez!*, *oyez!* 'hear!', imperative plural of *oir*, from Latin *audire* 'hear'.

oyster ▶ noun **1** any of a number of bivalve molluscs with rough irregular shells. Several kinds are eaten (especially raw) as a delicacy and may be farmed for food or pearls: ● a true oyster (family Ostreidae), in particular the edible **common European oyster** (*Ostrea edulis*) and **American oyster** (*Crassostrea virginica*). ● [with modifier] a similar bivalve of another family, in particular the **thorny oysters** (Spondylidae), **wing oysters** (Pteriidae), and **saddle oysters** (Anomiidae).
2 (also **oyster white**) [mass noun] a shade of greyish white.
3 an oyster-shaped morsel of meat on each side of the backbone in poultry.
▶ verb [no obj.] (usu. as noun **oystering**) raise, dredge, or gather oysters: *oystering is still the lifeblood of this town*.
– PHRASES **the world is your oyster** you are in a position to take the opportunities that life has to offer. [from Shakespeare's *Merry Wives of Windsor* (II. ii. 5).]

– ORIGIN Middle English: from Old French *oistre*, via Latin from Greek *ostreon*; related to *osteon* 'bone' and *ostrakon* 'shell or tile'.

oyster bar ▶ **noun 1** a hotel bar or small restaurant where oysters are served.
2 (especially in the south-eastern US) an oyster bed.

oystercatcher ▶ **noun** a wading bird with black-and-white or all-black plumage and a strong orange-red bill, typically found on the coast and feeding chiefly on shellfish. ● Family Haematopodidae and genus *Haematopus*: several species, e.g. the black and white *H. ostralegus* of Eurasia.

oyster farm ▶ **noun** an area of the seabed used for breeding oysters.

oyster mushroom ▶ **noun** a widely distributed edible fungus with a greyish-brown oyster-shaped cap and a very short or absent stem, growing on the wood of broadleaved trees and causing rot. ● *Pleurotus ostreatus*, family Pleurotaceae, class Hymenomycetes.

oyster plant ▶ **noun 1** another term for SALSIFY.
2 a blue-flowered thick-leaved creeping plant of the borage family, native to northern Europe and growing chiefly on stony beaches. ● *Mertensia maritima*, family Boraginaceae.

oyster sauce ▶ **noun** [mass noun] a sauce made with oysters and soy sauce, used especially in oriental cookery.

oyster white ▶ **noun** see OYSTER (sense 2 of the noun).

oy vey /ɔɪ 'veɪ/ (also **oy** or **oy veh**) ▶ **exclamation** indicating dismay or grief (used mainly by Yiddish-speakers).
– ORIGIN late 19th cent.: Yiddish, literally 'oh woe'.

Oz Austral./NZ informal ▶ **adjective** Australian: *Oz hospitality*.
▶ **noun** Australia. ■ a person from Australia.
– ORIGIN 1940s: representing a pronunciation of an abbreviation of AUSTRALIA.

oz ▶ **abbreviation** ounce(s).
– ORIGIN from Italian *onza* 'ounce'.

Ozalid /'əʊzəlɪd, 'ɒz-/ ▶ **noun** trademark a photocopy made by a process in which a diazonium salt and coupler are present in the paper coating, so that the image develops in the presence of ammonia.
– ORIGIN 1920s: by reversal of DIAZO and insertion of *-l*.

Ozark Mountains /'əʊzɑːk/ (also **the Ozarks**) a heavily forested highland plateau dissected by rivers, valleys, and streams, lying between the Missouri and Arkansas Rivers and within the states of Missouri, Arkansas, Oklahoma, Kansas, and Illinois.

ozokerite /əʊ'zəʊkərʌɪt, -sərʌɪt, ˌəʊzə(ʊ)'sɪərʌɪt/ ▶ **noun** [mass noun] a brown or black paraffin wax occurring naturally in some shales and sandstones and formerly used in candles, polishes, and electrical insulation.
– ORIGIN mid 19th cent.: from German *Ozokerit*, from Greek *ozein* 'to smell' + *kēros* 'wax'.

ozone ▶ **noun** [mass noun] **1** a colourless unstable toxic gas with a pungent odour and powerful oxidizing properties, formed from oxygen by electrical discharges or ultraviolet light. It differs from normal oxygen (O_2) in having three atoms in its molecule (O_3). ■ short for OZONE LAYER.
2 Brit. informal fresh invigorating air, especially that blowing on to the shore from the sea.
– DERIVATIVES **ozonic** adjective.
– ORIGIN mid 19th cent.: from German *Ozon*, from Greek *ozein* 'to smell'.

ozone-friendly ▶ **adjective** (of manufactured products) not containing chemicals that are destructive to the ozone layer.

ozone hole ▶ **noun** a region of marked thinning of the ozone layer in high latitudes, chiefly in winter, attributed to the chemical action of CFCs and other atmospheric pollutants. The resulting increase in ultraviolet light at ground level gives rise to an increased risk of skin cancer.

ozone layer ▶ **noun** a layer in the earth's stratosphere at an altitude of about 10 km (6.2 miles) containing a high concentration of ozone, which absorbs most of the ultraviolet radiation reaching the earth from the sun.

ozonide /'əʊzənʌɪd/ ▶ **noun** Chemistry any of a class of unstable cyclic compounds formed by the addition of ozone to a carbon–carbon double bond. ■ a salt of the anion O_3^-, derived from ozone.

ozonize /'əʊzənʌɪz/ (also **ozonise**) ▶ **verb** [with obj.] (often as adj. **ozonized**) convert (oxygen) into ozone. ■ enrich or treat with ozone: *ozonized air*.
– DERIVATIVES **ozonization** noun, **ozonizer** noun.

ozonosphere /əʊ'zəʊnəsfɪə/ ▶ **noun** technical term for OZONE LAYER.

Ozzie ▶ **noun** variant spelling of AUSSIE.

O

Pp

P[1] (also **p**) ▸ **noun** (pl. **Ps** or **P's**) the sixteenth letter of the alphabet. ■ denoting the next after O (or N if O is omitted) in a set of items, categories, etc.

P[2] ▸ **abbreviation** ■ (in tables of sports results) games played. ■ (on an automatic gear shift) park. ■ (on road signs and street plans) parking. ■ [in combination] (in units of measurement) peta- (10^{15}): *27 PBq of radioactive material.* ■ Physics poise (unit of viscosity). ■ Portugal (international vehicle registration). ■ proprietary.
▸ **symbol** the chemical element phosphorus.

p ▸ **abbreviation** ■ page. ■ (*p-*) [in combination] Chemistry para-: *p-xylene.* ■ Brit. penny or pence. ■ Music piano (softly). ■ [in combination] (in units of measurement) pico- (10^{-12}): *a 220 pf capacitor.* ■ Chemistry denoting electrons and orbitals possessing one unit of angular momentum. [from *principal*, originally applied to lines in atomic spectra.]
▸ **symbol** ■ Physics pressure. ■ Statistics probability.

p. & h. ▸ **abbreviation** N. Amer. postage and handling.

P & L ▸ **abbreviation** profit and loss account.

P & O ▸ **abbreviation** Peninsular and Oriental Shipping Company (or Line).

p. & p. ▸ **abbreviation** Brit. postage and packing.

P45 ▸ **noun** (in the UK and the Republic of Ireland) a certificate given to an employee at the end of a period of employment, providing details of their tax code, gross pay, and the tax paid for that year, to be passed to a subsequent employer or benefit agency.

PA ▸ **abbreviation** ■ Panama (international vehicle registration). ■ Pennsylvania (in official postal use). ■ Brit. personal assistant. ■ Press Association. ■ public address.

Pa ▸ **abbreviation** pascal(s).
▸ **symbol** the chemical element protactinium.

pa ▸ **noun** informal father: [as name] *Pa is busy on the telephone.*
– ORIGIN early 19th cent.: abbreviation of **PAPA**.

p.a. ▸ **abbreviation** per annum.

paan /pɑːn/ (also **pan**) ▸ **noun** [mass noun] Indian betel leaves prepared and used as a stimulant.
– ORIGIN via Hindi from Sanskrit *parṇa* 'feather, leaf'.

pa'anga /pɑːˈɑːŋɡə/ ▸ **noun** (pl. **same**) the basic monetary unit of Tonga, equal to 100 seniti.
– ORIGIN Tongan.

Paarl /pɑːl/ a town in SW South Africa, in the province of Western Cape, north-east of Cape Town; pop. 191,000 (est. 2009). It is at the centre of a noted wine-producing region.

pabulum /ˈpabjʊləm/ (also **pablum**) ▸ **noun** [mass noun] literary bland or insipid intellectual matter, entertainment, etc.
– ORIGIN mid 17th cent. (in the sense 'food'): from Latin, from the stem of *pascere* 'to feed'.

PABX ▸ **abbreviation** private automatic branch exchange, a private telephone switchboard.

PAC ▸ **abbreviation** Pan-Africanist Congress.

paca /ˈpakə/ ▸ **noun** a large nocturnal South American rodent that has a reddish-brown coat patterned with white spots and is hunted for its meat. ● Genus *Cuniculus*, family Dasyproctidae: two species.
– ORIGIN mid 17th cent.: via Spanish and Portuguese from Tupi.

pacamac /ˈpakəmak/ ▸ **noun** variant spelling of **PAKAMAC**.

pacarana /ˌpakəˈrɑːnə/ ▸ **noun** a slow-moving South American cavy-like rodent that has coarse dark hair with white stripes along the back, and a short furry tail. ● *Dinomys branickii*, the only member of the family Dinomyidae.
– ORIGIN from Tupi, literally 'false paca'.

PACE ▸ **abbreviation** Brit. Police and Criminal Evidence Act.

pace[1] /peɪs/ ▸ **noun 1** a single step taken when walking or running. ■ a unit of length representing the distance between two successive steps in walking. ■ a gait of a horse or other animal, especially one of the recognized trained gaits of a horse. ■ [mass noun] literary a person's manner of walking or running: *I steal with quiet pace.*
2 [mass noun] speed in walking, running, or moving: *he's an aggressive player with plenty of pace* | [in sing.] *the ring road allows traffic to flow at a remarkably fast pace.* ■ the speed or rate at which something happens or develops: *the industrial boom **gathered pace*** | [in sing.] *the story rips along at a cracking pace.* ■ Cricket the state of a wicket as affecting the speed of the ball.
▸ **verb 1** [no obj., with adverbial of direction] walk at a steady speed, especially without a particular destination and as an expression of anxiety or annoyance: *we paced up and down in exasperation* | [with obj.] *she had been pacing the room.* ■ [with obj.] measure (a distance) by walking it and counting the number of steps taken: *I **paced out** the dimensions of my new home.* ■ [no obj.] (of a trained horse) move in a distinctive lateral gait in which both legs on the same side are lifted together.
2 [with obj. and adverbial] move or develop (something) at a particular rate or speed: *the action is paced to the beat of a perky march* | (as adj., in combination **-paced**) *our fast-paced daily lives.* ■ lead (another runner in a race) in order to establish a competitive speed: *McKenna paced us for four miles.* ■ (**pace oneself**) do something at a slow and steady rate in order to avoid overexertion: *Frank was pacing himself for the long night ahead.*
– PHRASES **change of pace** chiefly N. Amer. a change from what one is used to: *the magenta is a change of pace from traditional red.* **keep pace with** move or progress at the same speed or rate as: *fees have been raised to keep pace with inflation.* **off the pace** behind the leader or leading group in a race or contest. **put someone** (or **something**) **through their** (or **its**) **paces** make someone (or something) demonstrate their (or its) abilities. **set the pace** be the fastest runner in the early part of a race. ■ lead the way in doing something: *space movies have set the pace for the development of special effects.* **stand** (or **stay**) **the pace** be able to keep up with another or others.
– ORIGIN Middle English: from Old French *pas*, from Latin *passus* 'stretch (of the leg)', from *pandere* 'to stretch'.

pace[2] /ˈpɑːtʃeɪ, ˈpeɪsi/ ▸ **preposition** with due respect to (someone or their opinion), used to express polite disagreement or contradiction: *narrative history, pace some theorists, is by no means dead.*
– ORIGIN Latin, literally 'in peace', ablative of *pax*, as in *pace tua* 'by your leave'.

pace bowler ▸ **noun** Cricket a fast bowler.

pace car ▸ **noun** Motor Racing a car that sets the pace for the warm-up lap before a race but does not take part in it, or one that controls the pace in temporarily hazardous conditions.

pacemaker ▸ **noun 1** a person or animal who sets the pace at the beginning of a race, sometimes in order to help a runner break a record. ■ a person who sets standards of achievement for others.
2 a device for stimulating the heart muscle and regulating its contractions. ■ the part of the heart muscle (the sino-atrial node) which normally regulates contractions. ■ the part of an organ or of the body which controls rhythmic physiological activity.
– DERIVATIVES **pacemaking adjective & noun.**

paceman ▸ **noun** (pl. **pacemen**) Cricket a fast bowler.

pacer ▸ **noun 1** a pacemaker.
2 chiefly US a horse bred or trained to pace, used in some types of racing.

pacesetter ▸ **noun** chiefly N. Amer. another term for **PACEMAKER** (sense 1).
– DERIVATIVES **pacesetting adjective & noun.**

pacey ▸ **adjective** variant spelling of **PACY**.

pacha ▸ **noun** variant spelling of **PASHA** (sense 1).

Pachelbel /ˈpax(ə)lbɛl/, Johann (1653–1706), German composer and organist. His compositions include seventy-eight chorale preludes, thirteen settings of the Magnificat, and the Canon and Gigue in D for three violins and continuo.

pachinko /pəˈtʃɪŋkəʊ/ ▸ **noun** [mass noun] a Japanese form of pinball.
– ORIGIN Japanese.

pachisi /pəˈtʃiːzi/ (also US trademark **parcheesi**) ▸ **noun** a four-handed Indian board game in which six cowries are used like dice.
– ORIGIN from Hindi *paccīsī*, literally '(throw) of 25' (the highest of the game).

Pachuca de Soto /pəˌtʃuːkə deɪ ˈsəʊtəʊ/ (also **Pachuca**) a city in Mexico, capital of the state of Hidalgo; pop. 267,751 (2005).

pachuco /pəˈtʃuːkəʊ/ ▸ **noun** (pl. **pachucos** /-əʊz/) chiefly US, dated a member of a gang of young Mexican-Americans.
– ORIGIN Mexican Spanish, literally 'flashily dressed'.

pachycephalosaur /ˌpakɪˈsɛfələsɔː, -ˈkɛf-/ ▸ **noun** a bipedal herbivorous dinosaur of the late Cretaceous period, with a thick domed skull. ● Infraorder Pachycephalosauria, order Ornithischia: several genera, including *Pachycephalosaurus*.
– ORIGIN from Greek *pakhus* 'thick' + *kephalē* 'head' + *sauros* 'lizard'.

pachyderm /ˈpakɪdəːm/ ▸ **noun** a very large mammal with thick skin, especially an elephant, rhinoceros, or hippopotamus.
– DERIVATIVES **pachydermal adjective, pachydermatous** /ˌpakɪˈdəːmətəs/ **adjective, pachydermic adjective.**
– ORIGIN mid 19th cent.: from French *pachyderme*, from Greek *pakhudermos*, from *pakhus* 'thick' + *derma* 'skin'.

pachysandra /ˌpakɪˈsandrə/ ▸ **noun** an evergreen creeping shrubby plant of the box family. ● Genus *Pachysandra*, family Buxaceae: several species, in particular the Japanese *P. terminalis*.

P

– ORIGIN formed irregularly from Greek *pakhus* 'thick' + *anēr*, *andr-* 'male' (with reference to the thick stamens).

pachytene /ˈpakɪtiːn/ ▶ noun [mass noun] Biology the third stage of the prophase of meiosis, following zygotene, during which the paired chromosomes shorten and thicken, the two chromatids of each separate, and exchange of segments between chromatids may occur.
– ORIGIN early 20th cent.: from Greek *pakhus* 'thick' + *tainia* 'band'.

pacific ▶ adjective **1** peaceful in character or intent: *a pacific gesture.*
2 (**Pacific**) relating to the Pacific Ocean: *the Pacific War.*
▶ noun (**Pacific**) **1** (**the Pacific**) short for PACIFIC OCEAN.
2 a steam locomotive of 4-6-2 wheel arrangement.
– DERIVATIVES **pacifically** adverb.
– ORIGIN mid 16th cent.: from French *pacifique* or Latin *pacificus* 'peacemaking', from *pax, pac-* 'peace'.

Pacific islander ▶ noun a native or inhabitant of any of the islands in the South Pacific, especially an aboriginal of Polynesia.

Pacific Ocean the largest of the world's oceans, lying between America to the east and Asia and Australasia to the west.

Pacific Rim the countries and regions bordering the Pacific Ocean, especially the small nations of East Asia.

Pacific Security Treaty another name for ANZUS.

Pacific time the standard time in a zone including the Pacific coastal region of Canada and the US, specifically: ● (**Pacific Standard Time**, abbrev.: **PST**) standard time based on the mean solar time at longitude 120° W, eight hours behind GMT. ● (**Pacific Daylight Time**, abbrev.: **PDT**) Pacific time during daylight saving, seven hours behind GMT.

pacifier ▶ noun a person or thing that pacifies someone or something. ■ N. Amer. a baby's dummy.

pacifism ▶ noun [mass noun] the belief that war and violence are unjustifiable and that all disputes should be settled by peaceful means.
– ORIGIN early 20th cent.: from French *pacifisme*, from *pacifier* 'pacify'.

pacifist ▶ noun a person who believes that war and violence are unjustifiable: *she was a committed pacifist all her life.*
▶ adjective holding the belief that war and violence are unjustifiable.

pacify ▶ verb (**pacifies**, **pacifying**, **pacified**) [with obj.] quell the anger, agitation, or excitement of: *he had to pacify angry spectators.* ■ bring peace to (a country or warring factions), especially by the use or threat of military force: *the general pacified northern Italy.*
– DERIVATIVES **pacification** noun, **pacificatory** adjective.
– ORIGIN late 15th cent. (earlier (late Middle English) as *pacification*): from Old French *pacefier*, from Latin *pacificare*, based on *pax, pac-* 'peace'.

Pacinian corpuscle /pəˈsɪnɪən/ ▶ noun Anatomy an encapsulated ending of a sensory nerve that acts as a receptor for pressure and vibration.
– ORIGIN late 19th cent.: named after Filippo *Pacini* (1812–83), Italian anatomist.

Pacino /pəˈtʃiːnəʊ/, Al (b.1940), American film actor; full name *Alfredo James Pacino*. He achieved recognition with *The Godfather* (1972) and went on to receive eight Oscar nominations, winning one for *Scent of a Woman* (1992).

pack¹ ▶ noun **1** a small cardboard or paper container and the items contained within it: ***a pack of** cigarettes.* ■ (often **the pack**) a quantity of fish, fruit, or other foods packed or canned in a particular season.
2 a group of similar things or people, especially one regarded as unpleasant: *the reports were **a pack of** lies.* ■ Brit. a set of playing cards. ■ a collection of related documents: *an information pack.* ■ (**Pack**) an organized group of Cub Scouts or Brownies. ■ Rugby a team's forwards considered as a group. ■ (**the pack**) the main body of competitors following the leader or leaders in a race or competition: *Price broke from the pack to pursue him* | figurative *Japanese cars are ahead of the pack in this category.*
3 a group of wild animals, especially wolves, living and hunting together. ■ a group of hounds kept and used for hunting.
4 a rucksack.
5 (also **ice pack**) an expanse of large pieces of floating ice driven together into a nearly continuous mass, as occurs in polar seas.
6 a hot or cold pad of absorbent material, especially as used for treating an injury.
▶ verb [with obj.] **1** fill (a suitcase or bag) with clothes and other items needed for travel: *I packed a bag and left* | [no obj.] *she had packed and checked out of the hotel.* ■ place (something) in a container for transport, storage, or sale: *I **packed up** my stuff and drove to Detroit.* ■ [no obj.] be capable of being folded up for transport or storage: *a pneumatic igloo tent that packs away compactly.* ■ store (something perishable) in a specified substance in order to preserve it: *the organs were **packed in** ice.*
2 cram a large number of things into: *it was a large room, packed with beds jammed side by side.* ■ (often as adj. **packed**) (of a large number of people) crowd into and fill (a place): *a packed Merseyside pub.* ■ cover, surround, or fill (something): *if you have a nosebleed, try packing the nostrils with cotton wool.*
3 [no obj.] Rugby (of players) form a scrum: *we often **packed down** with only seven men.*
4 informal carry (a gun).
– PHRASES **go to the pack** Austral./NZ informal deteriorate; go to pieces. **pack one's bags** prepare for one's imminent departure. **pack heat** N. Amer. informal carry a gun. **pack it in** informal stop what one is doing. **pack a punch** be capable of hitting with skill or force. ■ have a powerful effect: *the Spanish wine packed quite a punch.* **packed out** Brit. informal (of a place) very crowded. **send someone packing** informal make someone leave in an abrupt or peremptory way.
– PHRASAL VERBS **pack something in** informal give up an activity or job. **pack someone off** informal send someone somewhere without much warning or notice: *I was packed off to hospital for surgery.* **pack something out** N. Amer. pack something up and take it away. **pack up** (or **in**) Brit. informal (of a machine) break down.
– DERIVATIVES **packable** adjective.
– ORIGIN Middle English: from Middle Dutch, Middle Low German *pak* (noun), *pakken* (verb). The verb appears early in Anglo-Latin and Anglo-Norman French in connection with the wool trade; trade in English wool was chiefly with the Low Countries.

pack² ▶ verb [with obj.] fill (a jury, committee, etc.) with people likely to support a particular verdict or decision: *his efforts to **pack** the Supreme Court **with** men who shared his ideology.*
– ORIGIN early 16th cent. (in the sense 'enter into a private agreement'): probably from the obsolete verb *pact* 'enter into an agreement with', the final *-t* being interpreted as an inflection of the past tense.

package ▶ noun **1** an object or group of objects wrapped in paper or packed in a box. ■ N. Amer. a packet: *a package of peanuts.*
2 (also **package deal**) a set of proposals or terms offered or agreed as a whole: *a package of measures announced by the government.* ■ informal a package holiday.
3 Computing a collection of programs or subroutines with related functionality.
▶ verb [with obj.] **1** put into a box or wrapping for sale or transport: *choose products which are packaged in recyclable materials* | (as adj. **packaged**) *packaged foods.* ■ combine (various products) for sale as one unit: *films would be packaged with the pictures of a production company.* ■ commission and produce (a book, typically a highly illustrated one) to sell as a complete product to publishers.
2 present (someone or something) in an attractive or advantageous way: *school science is packaged to appeal to boys, not girls* | (as adj., with submodifier **packaged**) *everything became a carefully packaged photo opportunity.*
– DERIVATIVES **packager** noun.
– ORIGIN mid 16th cent. (as a noun denoting the action or mode of packing goods): from the verb PACK¹ + -AGE; compare with Anglo-Latin *paccagium*. The verb dates from the 1920s.

package holiday (also **package tour**) ▶ noun a holiday organized by a travel agent, with arrangements for transport, accommodation, etc., made at an inclusive price.

packaging ▶ noun [mass noun] materials used to wrap or protect goods. ■ the business or process of packing goods. ■ the presentation of a person or thing in an advantageous way: *diplomatic packaging of the key provisions will make a confrontation unlikely.*

pack animal ▶ noun **1** an animal used to carry loads.
2 an animal that lives and hunts in a pack.

packcloth ▶ noun [mass noun] a strong coarse cloth used for packing.

pack drill ▶ noun a military punishment of marching up and down carrying full equipment.
– PHRASES **no names, no pack drill** punishment will be prevented if names and details are not mentioned.

packed lunch ▶ noun Brit. a cold lunch carried in a bag or box to work or school or on an excursion.

packer ▶ noun a person or machine that packs something, especially someone who prepares and packs food for transportation and sale.

packet ▶ noun **1** a paper or cardboard container, typically one in which goods are sold: ***a packet of** crisps.*
2 [in sing.] informal, chiefly Brit. a large sum of money: *a hectic social life could **cost a packet**.*
3 (also **packet boat**) dated a ship travelling at regular intervals between two ports, originally for the conveyance of mail.
4 Computing a block of data transmitted across a network.
▶ verb (**packets**, **packeting**, **packeted**) [with obj.] (often as adj. **packeted**) wrap up in a packet: *packeted fruit pies.*
– ORIGIN mid 16th cent.: diminutive of PACK¹, perhaps from Anglo-Norman French; compare with Anglo-Latin *paccettum*.

packetize (also **packetise**) ▶ verb [with obj.] Computing partition or separate (data) into units for transmission in a packet-switching network.

packet radio ▶ noun [mass noun] a method of broadcasting that makes use of radio signals carrying packets of data.

packet sniffer ▶ noun Computing a sniffer program which targets packets of data transmitted over the Internet.

packet switching ▶ noun [mass noun] Computing & Telecommunications a mode of data transmission in which a message is broken into a number of parts which are sent independently, over whatever route is optimum for each packet, and reassembled at the destination. Compare with MESSAGE SWITCHING.

packframe ▶ noun a frame into which a knapsack or other pack is fitted to make it easier to carry.

packhorse ▶ noun a horse used to carry loads.

pack ice ▶ noun [mass noun] a mass of ice floating in the sea, formed by smaller pieces freezing together.

packing ▶ noun [mass noun] the action or process of packing something: *she finished her packing.* ■ a charge made when delivering goods to cover the cost of packing them. ■ material used to protect fragile goods in transit: *polystyrene packing.* ■ material used to seal a join or assist in lubricating an axle.

packing case ▶ noun a large strong box, typically a wooden one, in which goods are packed for transportation or storage.

packing density ▶ noun see DENSITY.

packing station ▶ noun an official depot where goods are graded and packed.

packman ▶ noun (pl. **packmen**) archaic a pedlar.

pack rat ▶ noun **1** another term for WOODRAT.
2 N. Amer. derogatory a person who hoards things.

packsack ▶ noun N. Amer. a rucksack.

packsaddle ▶ noun chiefly N. Amer. a horse's saddle adapted for supporting loads.

pack shot ▶ noun (in advertising) a close-up picture of the advertised product in its packaging.

packthread ▶ noun [mass noun] strong thread for sewing or tying up packs.

Pac-Man trademark an electronic computer game in which a player attempts to guide a voracious, blob-shaped character through a maze while eluding attacks from opposing images which it may in turn devour. It is also the name of the blob-shaped character itself.
– ORIGIN 1980s: *Pac*, probably a respelling of PACK¹ (from the character's action of 'packing away' (i.e. eating) obstacles in its path) + MAN.

pact ▶ noun a formal agreement between individuals or parties: *the country negotiated a trade pact with the US.*
– ORIGIN late Middle English: from Old French, from Latin *pactum* 'something agreed', neuter past participle (used as a noun) of *paciscere* 'agree'.

pacu /paˈkuː, ˈpakuː/ ▶ noun (pl. **same**) a deep-bodied herbivorous freshwater fish native to northern South America, which has been introduced into the Old World. ● *Colossoma nigripinnis*, family Characidae.
– ORIGIN early 19th cent.: from Tupi *pacú*.

P

pacy (also **pacey**) ▶ adjective (**pacier**, **paciest**) moving or progressing quickly: *a pacy thriller*.

pad¹ ▶ noun **1** a thick piece of soft material, typically used to protect or shape something, or to absorb liquid: *a pad of cotton wool*. ■ a protective guard worn by a sports player to protect a part of the body.
2 the fleshy underpart of an animal's foot or of a human finger.
3 a number of sheets of blank paper fastened together at one edge, used for writing or drawing.
4 a flat-topped structure or area used for helicopter take-off and landing or for rocket-launching.
5 informal a person's home: *the police raided my pad*.
6 Electronics a flat area on a track of a printed circuit or on the edge of an integrated circuit to which wires or component leads can be attached to make an electrical connection.
▶ verb (**pads**, **padding**, **padded**) [with obj.] **1** (often as adj. **padded**) fill or cover (something) with a soft material in order to protect or shape it or to make it more comfortable: *a padded envelope*.
2 (**pad something out**) lengthen a speech or piece of writing with unnecessary material.
3 N. Amer. defraud by adding false items to (an expenses claim or bill).
4 [no obj.] (**pad up**) put on protective pads in order to play a sport, especially cricket. ■ Cricket (of a batsman) deliberately use one's pads to block a ball.
– ORIGIN mid 16th cent. (in the sense 'bundle of straw to lie on'): the senses may not be of common origin; the meaning 'underpart of an animal's foot' is perhaps related to Low German *pad* 'sole of the foot'; the history remains obscure.

pad² ▶ verb (**pads**, **padding**, **padded**) [no obj., with adverbial of direction] walk with steady steps making a soft dull sound: *she padded along the corridor*. ■ [with obj.] tramp along (a road or route) on foot: *he was padding the streets*.
▶ noun [in sing.] the soft dull sound of steady steps: *he heard the pad of feet*.
– ORIGIN mid 16th cent.: from Low German *padden* 'to tread, go along a path', partly imitative.

Padang /pəˈdaŋ/ a seaport of Indonesia, the largest city on the west coast of Sumatra; pop. 686,900 (est. 2005).

padauk /pəˈdaʊk/ (also **padouk**) ▶ noun **1** [mass noun] timber from a tropical tree, resembling rosewood.
2 the large tree of the pea family which produces padauk, native to the Old World tropics. ● Genus *Pterocarpus*, family Leguminosae: three species, in particular **African padauk** (*P. soyauxii*).
– ORIGIN mid 19th cent.: from Burmese.

padded cell ▶ noun a room in a psychiatric hospital with padding on the walls to prevent violent patients from injuring themselves.

padding ▶ noun [mass noun] soft material such as foam or cloth used to pad or stuff something. ■ superfluous material in a book, speech, etc., introduced in order to make it reach a desired length.

paddle¹ ▶ noun **1** a short pole with a broad blade at one or both ends, used without a rowlock to move a small boat or canoe through the water. ■ an act of paddling a boat: *a gentle paddle on sluggish water*. ■ a paddle-shaped instrument used for mixing food, or stirring or mixing in industrial processes. ■ N. Amer. a short-handled bat used in table tennis. ■ N. Amer. informal a paddle-shaped instrument used to administer corporal punishment. ■ each of the boards fitted round the circumference of a paddle wheel or mill wheel. ■ the fin or flipper of an aquatic mammal or bird.
2 a flat array of solar cells projecting from a spacecraft.
3 Medicine a plastic-covered electrode used in cardiac stimulation.
▶ verb **1** [no obj., with adverbial of direction] move through the water in a boat using a paddle or paddles: *she paddled along the coast* | [with obj.] *he was teaching trainees to paddle canoes*. ■ [with obj.] propel a boat along (a stretch of water) using paddles: *a legal right to paddle Scottish rivers*. ■ (of bird or other animal) swim with short fast strokes: *the swan paddled away*.
2 [with obj.] informal, chiefly N. Amer. beat (someone) with a paddle as a punishment.
– PHRASES **paddle one's own canoe** informal be independent and self-sufficient.
– DERIVATIVES **paddler** noun.
– ORIGIN late Middle English (denoting a small spade-like implement): of unknown origin. Current senses date from the 17th cent.

paddle² ▶ verb [no obj.] walk with bare feet in shallow water: *the children paddled at the water's edge*. ■ dabble the feet or hands in water: *Peter paddled idly in the water with his fingers*.
▶ noun [in sing.] chiefly Brit. an act of walking with bare feet in shallow water.
– DERIVATIVES **paddler** noun.
– ORIGIN mid 16th cent.: of obscure origin; compare with Low German *paddeln* 'tramp about'; the association with water remains unexplained.

paddleball ▶ noun [mass noun] a game played with a light ball and wooden bat in a four-walled handball court.

paddlefish ▶ noun (pl. **same** or **paddlefishes**) a large mainly freshwater fish related to the sturgeon, with an elongated snout. ● The plankton-feeding *Polyodon spathula* of the Mississippi basin, and the fish-eating *Psephurus gladius* of the Yangtze River, the only surviving members of the family Polyodontidae.

paddle steamer (also **paddle boat**) ▶ noun a boat powered by steam and propelled by paddle wheels.

paddle tennis ▶ noun [mass noun] a type of tennis played in a small court with a sponge-rubber ball and wooden or plastic bat.

paddle wheel ▶ noun a large steam-driven wheel with boards round its circumference, situated at the stern or side of a ship so as to propel the ship through the water by its rotation.

paddling pool ▶ noun Brit. a shallow artificial pool for children to paddle in.

paddock ▶ noun a small field or enclosure where horses are kept or exercised. ■ an enclosure adjoining a racecourse or track where horses or cars are gathered and displayed before a race. ■ Austral./NZ a field or plot of land enclosed by fencing or defined by natural boundaries.
▶ verb [with obj.] keep (a horse) in a paddock: *horses paddocked on a hillside*.
– ORIGIN early 17th cent.: apparently a variant of dialect *parrock*, of unknown ultimate origin.

Paddy ▶ noun (pl. **Paddies**) informal, usu. offensive an Irishman (often as a form of address).
– ORIGIN late 18th cent.: pet form of the Irish given name *Padraig*.

paddy¹ ▶ noun (pl. **paddies**) **1** (also **paddy field**) a field where rice is grown.
2 [mass noun] rice before threshing or in the husk.
– ORIGIN early 17th cent.: from Malay *pādī*.

paddy² ▶ noun (pl. **paddies**) [in sing.] Brit. informal a fit of temper: *John drove off in a paddy*.
– ORIGIN late 19th cent.: from PADDY, associated with obsolete *paddywhack* 'Irishman (given to brawling)'.

paddymelon¹ ▶ noun Austral. a plant of the gourd family, especially a trailing or climbing annual that has become naturalized in inland Australia. ● Several species in the family Cucurbitaceae, in particular *Cucumis myriocarpus*, which has bristly melon-like fruits and is native to Africa.
– ORIGIN late 19th cent.: probably by erroneous association with PADDYMELON².

paddymelon² ▶ noun variant spelling of PADEMELON.

paddy wagon ▶ noun N. Amer. informal a police van.
– ORIGIN 1930s: *paddy* from PADDY, perhaps because formerly many American police officers were of Irish descent.

pademelon /ˈpadɪˌmɛlən/ (also **paddymelon**) ▶ noun a small wallaby inhabiting the coastal scrub of Australia and New Guinea. Also called SCRUB WALLABY. ● Genus *Thylogale*, family Macropodidae: three species.
– ORIGIN early 19th cent. (earlier as *paddymelon*): probably an alteration of Dharuk *badimalion*.

Paderewski /ˌpadəˈrɛfski/, Ignacy Jan (1860–1941), Polish pianist, composer, and statesman, Prime Minister 1919. He was the first Prime Minister of independent Poland, but resigned after only ten months in office and resumed his musical career.

pad eye ▶ noun a flat metal plate with a projecting loop or ring, made all in one piece.

padkos /ˈpatkɒs/ ▶ noun [mass noun] S. African food taken to eat on a journey.
– ORIGIN Afrikaans, from *pad* 'road' + *kos* 'food'.

padlock ▶ noun a detachable lock hanging by a pivoted hook on the object fastened.
▶ verb [with obj.] secure with a padlock: *his father had padlocked the gate*.
– ORIGIN late 15th cent.: from *pad-* (of unknown origin) + the noun LOCK¹.

padloper /ˈpatˌlʊəpə/ ▶ noun S. African a small tortoise native to southern Africa, often seen on roads and paths. ● Genus *Homopus*, family Testudinidae: several species.
– ORIGIN Afrikaans, literally 'vagabond', from *pad* 'path' + *loper* 'runner'.

Padma /ˈpadmə/ a river of southern Bangladesh, formed by the confluence of the Ganges and the Brahmaputra near Rajbari.

padouk /pəˈduːk/ ▶ noun variant spelling of PADAUK.

Padova /ˈpadəʊva/ Italian name for PADUA.

padre /ˈpɑːdreɪ, -dri/ ▶ noun the title of a priest or chaplain in some countries. ■ informal a chaplain in the armed services. ■ (also **padri**) Indian a Christian priest.
– ORIGIN late 16th cent.: from Italian, Spanish, and Portuguese, literally 'father, priest', from Latin *pater*, *patr-* 'father'.

padrino /pəˈdriːnəʊ/ ▶ noun (pl. **padrinos**) (in Spanish-speaking countries) a godfather; a patron. ■ a best man at a wedding.
– ORIGIN Spanish.

padrona /pəˈdrəʊnə/ ▶ noun (pl. **padronas**) (in Italian-speaking countries) a female boss or proprietess.
– ORIGIN Italian.

padrone /pəˈdrəʊneɪ, -ni/ ▶ noun (pl. **padrones**) a patron or master, in particular: ■ a Mafia boss. ■ US informal an employer, especially one who exploits immigrant workers. ■ (in Italy) the proprietor of a hotel.
– ORIGIN Italian.

padsaw ▶ noun a small saw with a narrow blade, for cutting curves.

pad thai /pad ˈtʌɪ/ ▶ noun [mass noun] a Thai dish based on rice noodles.
– ORIGIN Thai.

Padua /ˈpadjʊə/ a city in NE Italy; pop. 211,936 (2008). It was the birthplace of Livy, and Galileo taught at its university from 1592 to 1610. Italian name PADOVA.
– DERIVATIVES **Paduan** adjective.

paduasoy /ˈpadjʊəˌsɔɪ/ ▶ noun [mass noun] a heavy, rich corded or embossed silk fabric, popular in the 18th century.
– ORIGIN late 16th cent. (as *poudesoy*), from French *pou-de-soie*, of unknown origin; altered by association with *Padua say*, denoting a cloth resembling serge.

paean /ˈpiːən/ ▶ noun a song of praise or triumph. ■ a creative work expressing enthusiastic praise: *he's created a filmic paean to his hero*.
– ORIGIN late 16th cent.: via Latin from Greek *paian* 'hymn of thanksgiving to Apollo' (invoked by the name *Paian*, originally the Homeric name for the physician of the gods).

P

paederast ▶ noun variant spelling of PEDERAST.

paederasty ▶ noun variant spelling of PEDERASTY.

paediatrician /ˌpiːdɪəˈtrɪʃ(ə)n/ (US **pediatrician**) ▶ noun a medical practitioner specializing in children and their diseases.

paediatrics /ˌpiːdɪˈatrɪks/ (US **pediatrics**) ▶ plural noun [treated as sing.] the branch of medicine dealing with children and their diseases.
– DERIVATIVES **paediatric** adjective.
– ORIGIN late 19th cent.: from PAEDO- 'of children' + Greek *iatros* 'physician' + -ICS.

paedo- (US **pedo-**) ▶ combining form of a child; relating to children: *paedophile*.
– ORIGIN from Greek *pais*, *paid-* 'child, boy'.

paedodontics /ˌpiːdəˈdɒntɪks/ (US **pedodontics**) ▶ plural noun [treated as sing.] the branch of dentistry that deals with children's teeth.

paedogenesis /ˌpiːdə(ʊ)ˈdʒɛnɪsɪs/ ▶ noun Zoology see NEOTENY.

paedomorphosis /ˌpiːdə(ʊ)ˈmɔːfəsɪs, -mɔːˈfəʊsɪs/ ▶ noun Zoology see NEOTENY.
– DERIVATIVES **paedomorphic** adjective.

paedophile (US **pedophile**) ▶ noun a person who is sexually attracted to children.

paedophilia (US **pedophilia**) ▶ noun [mass noun] sexual feelings directed towards children.
– DERIVATIVES **paedophiliac** noun & adjective.

paella /pʌɪˈɛlə/ ▶ noun [mass noun] a Spanish dish of rice, saffron, chicken, seafood, etc., cooked and served in a large shallow pan.
– ORIGIN Catalan, from Old French *paele*, from Latin *patella* (see PATELLA).

paeon /ˈpiːən/ ▶ noun a metrical foot of one long syllable and three short syllables in any order.
– DERIVATIVES **paeonic** /piːˈɒnɪk/ adjective.

– ORIGIN early 17th cent.: via Latin from Greek *paiōn*, the Attic form of *paian* 'hymn of thanksgiving to Apollo' (see PAEAN).

paeony ▸ noun variant spelling of PEONY.

Pagalu /ˌpɑːɡəˈluː/ former name (1973–9) for ANNOBÓN.

Pagan /pəˈɡɑːn/ a town in Burma, situated on the Irrawaddy south-east of Mandalay. It is the site of an ancient city, founded in about AD 849, which was the capital of a powerful Buddhist dynasty from the 11th to the end of the 13th centuries.

pagan /ˈpeɪɡ(ə)n/ ▸ noun a person holding religious beliefs other than those of the main world religions. ■ dated, derogatory a non-Christian. ■ a member of a modern religious movement which seeks to incorporate beliefs or practices from outside the main world religions, especially nature worship.
▸ adjective relating to pagans or their beliefs: *a pagan god*.
– DERIVATIVES **paganish** adjective, **paganism** noun.
– ORIGIN late Middle English: from Latin *paganus* 'villager, rustic', from *pagus* 'country district'. Latin *paganus* also meant 'civilian', becoming, in Christian Latin, 'heathen' (i.e. one not enrolled in the army of Christ).

Paganini /ˌpaɡəˈniːni/, Niccolò (1782–1840), Italian violinist and composer. His virtuoso violin recitals, including widespread use of pizzicato and harmonics, established him as a major figure of the romantic movement.

Page, Sir Frederick Handley (1885–1962), English aircraft designer. He is noted for designing the first twin-engined bomber (1915), as well as the Halifax heavy bombers of the Second World War.

page[1] ▸ noun one or both sides of a sheet of paper in a book, magazine, newspaper, or other collection of bound sheets. ■ the material written or printed on a page: *she silently read several pages*. ■ [with modifier] a page of a newspaper or magazine set aside for a particular topic: *the Letters Page*. ■ Computing a section of stored data, especially that which can be displayed on a screen at one time. ■ a significant event or period considered as a part of a longer history: *the vote will form a page in the world's history*.
▸ verb 1 [no obj.] (**page through**) look through the pages of (a book, magazine, etc.): *she was paging through a pile of Sunday newspapers*. ■ Computing move through and display (text) one page at a time.
2 [with obj.] (usu. as noun **paging**) Computing divide (a piece of software or data) into sections, keeping the most frequently accessed in main memory and storing the rest in virtual memory.
3 [with obj.] assign numbers to the pages in (a book or periodical); paginate.
– PHRASES **on the same page** US in agreement.
– DERIVATIVES **paged** adjective [in combination] *a many-paged volume*.
– ORIGIN late 16th cent.: from French, from Latin *pagina*, from *pangere* 'fasten'.

page[2] ▸ noun a boy or young man, usually in uniform, employed in a hotel or club to run errands, open doors, etc. ■ a young boy attending a bride at a wedding. ■ historical a boy in training for knighthood, ranking next below a squire in the personal service of a knight. ■ historical a man or boy employed as the personal attendant of a person of rank.
▸ verb [with obj.] summon (someone) over a public address system, so as to pass on a message: *no need to interrupt the background music just to page the concierge*. ■ (often as noun **paging**) contact by means of a pager.
– ORIGIN Middle English (in the sense 'youth, uncouth male'): from Old French, perhaps from Italian *paggio*, from Greek *paidion*, diminutive of *pais*, *paid-* 'boy'. Early use of the verb (mid 16th cent.) was in the sense 'follow as or like a page'; its current sense dates from the early 20th cent.

pageant /ˈpadʒ(ə)nt/ ▸ noun 1 a public entertainment consisting of a procession of people in elaborate, colourful costumes, or an outdoor performance of a historical scene. ■ something regarded as a series of interesting and varied events: *it's all part of life's rich pageant*. ■ historical a scene erected on a fixed stage or moving vehicle as a public show.
2 (also **beauty pageant**) N. Amer. a beauty contest.
– ORIGIN late Middle English *pagyn*, of unknown origin.

pageantry ▸ noun [mass noun] elaborate display or ceremony: *the pageantry of George V's jubilee*.

pageboy ▸ noun 1 a page in a hotel or attending a bride at a wedding.
2 a woman's hairstyle consisting of a shoulder-length bob with the ends rolled under.

page-one ▸ adjective N. Amer. worthy of being featured on the front page of a newspaper or magazine: *page-one news*.

page proof ▸ noun a printer's proof of a page to be published.

pager ▸ noun a small radio device, activated from a central point, which emits a series of bleeps or vibrates to inform the wearer that someone wishes to contact them or that it has received a short text message.

Page Three ▸ noun Brit. trademark a feature which appears daily on page three of the *Sun* newspaper, comprising a picture of a topless young woman.

Paget's disease /ˈpadʒɪts/ ▸ noun [mass noun] 1 a chronic disease of elderly people characterized by alteration of bone tissue, especially in the spine, skull, or pelvis, sometimes causing severe pain; osteitis deformans.
2 an inflammation of the nipple associated with breast cancer.
– ORIGIN late 19th cent.: named after Sir James *Paget* (1814–99), English surgeon.

page-turner ▸ noun informal an exciting book.
– DERIVATIVES **page-turning** adjective.

paginal /ˈpadʒɪn(ə)l/ ▸ adjective relating to the pages of a book or periodical.
– ORIGIN mid 17th cent.: from late Latin *paginalis*, from *pagina* (see PAGE[1]).

pagination /ˌpadʒɪˈneɪʃ(ə)n/ ▸ noun [mass noun] the sequence of numbers assigned to pages in a book or periodical.
– DERIVATIVES **paginate** verb.
– ORIGIN mid 19th cent.: noun of action from *paginate*, from French *paginer*, based on Latin *pagina* 'a page' (see PAGE[1]).

Pagnol /paˈnjɒl/, Marcel (1895–1974), French dramatist, film director, and writer. As a director Pagnol is best known for the humorous film trilogy *Marius* (1931), *Fanny* (1932), and *César* (1936). His novels include *La Gloire de mon père* (1957) and *Le Chateau de ma mère* (1958).

pagoda /pəˈɡəʊdə/ ▸ noun (in India and East Asia) a Hindu or Buddhist temple, typically in the form of a many-tiered tower. ■ an ornamental imitation of a Hindu or Buddhist pagoda.
– ORIGIN late 16th cent.: from Portuguese *pagode*, perhaps based on Persian *butkada* 'temple of idols', influenced by Prakrit *bhagodī* 'divine'.

pagoda sleeve ▸ noun a funnel-shaped outer sleeve turned back to expose an inner sleeve and lining.

pagoda tree ▸ noun a SE Asian tree of the pea family, which has hanging clusters of cream flowers and is cultivated as an ornamental. ● *Sophora japonica*, family Leguminosae.

pagri /ˈpʌɡriː/ ▸ noun (pl. **pagris**) (in South Asia) a turban worn by employees of exclusive establishments or by people in the north of the region.
– ORIGIN from Hindi *pagṛī* 'turban'.

pah ▸ exclamation used to express disgust or contempt: *'Pah! They know nothing.'*
– ORIGIN natural utterance: first recorded in English in the late 16th cent.

Pahang /pəˈhaŋ/ a mountainous forested state of Malaysia, on the east coast of the Malay Peninsula; capital, Kuantan.

Pahlavi[1] /ˈpɑːləvɪ/ the name of two shahs of Iran:
■ **Reza** (1878–1944), ruled 1925–41; born *Reza Khan*. An army officer, he took control of the Persian government after a coup in 1921. He was elected Shah in 1925 but abdicated following the occupation of Iran by British and Soviet forces. ■ **Muhammad Reza** (1919–80), ruled 1941–79, son of Reza Pahlavi; also known as **Reza Shah**. Opposition to his regime culminated in the Islamic revolution of 1979 under Ayatollah Khomeini; Reza Shah was forced into exile and died in Egypt.

Pahlavi[2] /ˈpɑːləvi/ (also **Pehlevi**) ▸ noun [mass noun] an Aramaic-based writing system used in Persia from the 2nd century BC to the advent of Islam in the 7th century AD. It was also used for the recording of ancient Avestan sacred texts. ■ the form of the Middle Persian language written in Pahlavi, used in the Sassanian empire.
– ORIGIN from Persian *pahlawī*, from *pahlav*, from *parthava* 'Parthia'.

pahoehoe /pəˈhəʊɪhəʊi/ ▸ noun [mass noun] Geology basaltic lava forming smooth undulating or ropy masses. Often contrasted with AA.
– ORIGIN mid 19th cent.: from Hawaiian.

paid past and past participle of PAY[1] ▸ adjective (of work or leave) for or during which one receives pay: *five weeks paid holiday a year*. ■ [attrib.] (of a person in a specified occupation) in receipt of pay: *a paid informer*.
– PHRASES **put paid to** informal stop abruptly; destroy: *Denmark's victory put paid to our hopes of qualifying*.

paideia /pʌɪˈdʌɪə/ ▸ noun [mass noun] (in ancient Greece) a system of broad cultural education. ■ formal the culture of a society.
– ORIGIN Greek.

paid-up ▸ adjective [attrib.] 1 (of a member of an organization) having paid all the necessary subscriptions in full. ■ firmly committed to an organization or cause: *a fully paid-up Green*.
2 denoting the part of the subscribed capital of an undertaking which has actually been paid.

Paignton /ˈpeɪnt(ə)n/ a resort town in SW England, on the south coast of Devon; pop. 50,600 (est. 2009).

pail ▸ noun a bucket.
– DERIVATIVES **pailful** noun (pl. **pailfuls**).
– ORIGIN Middle English: origin uncertain; compare with Old English *pægel* 'gill, small measure' and Old French *paelle* 'pan, liquid measure, brazier'.

Pailin /ˈpeɪlɪn/ a ruby-mining town in western Cambodia, close to the border with Thailand.

paillasse ▸ noun variant spelling of PALLIASSE.

paillette /palˈjɛt, pʌɪˈjɛt/ ▸ noun a piece of glittering material used to decorate clothing; a spangle. ■ a piece of bright metal used in enamel painting.
– ORIGIN mid 19th cent.: from French, diminutive of *paille*, from Latin *palea* 'straw, chaff'.

pain ▸ noun [mass noun] 1 highly unpleasant physical sensation caused by illness or injury: *she's **in** great **pain*** | [count noun] *chest pains*. ■ (also **pain in the neck** or vulgar slang **arse**) informal an annoying or tedious person or thing: *she's a pain*.
2 mental suffering or distress: *the pain of loss*.
3 (**pains**) great care or trouble: *she **took pains** to see that everyone ate well*.
▸ verb [with obj.] cause mental or physical pain to: *it pains me to say this* | *her legs had been paining her*. ■ [no obj.] chiefly N. Amer. (of a part of the body) hurt: *sometimes my right hand would pain*.
– PHRASES **for one's pains** informal as an unfairly bad return for one's efforts: *he was sued for his pains*. **no pain, no gain** suffering is necessary in order to achieve something. [originally used as a slogan in fitness classes.] **on** (or **under**) **pain of** the penalty for disobedience or shortcoming being: *they proscribed all such practices on pain of death*.
– ORIGIN Middle English (in the sense 'suffering inflicted as punishment for an offence'): from Old French *peine*, from Latin *poena* 'penalty', later 'pain'.

pain barrier ▸ noun the state of greatest pain, especially during physical exertion, beyond which the pain diminishes: *marathon runners go through the pain barrier*.

Paine, Thomas (1737–1809), English political writer. His pamphlet *Common Sense* (1776) called for American independence, and *The Rights of Man* (1791) defended the French Revolution. His radical views prompted the British government to indict him for treason and he fled to France. Other notable works: *The Age of Reason* (1794).

pained ▸ adjective affected with pain, especially mental pain; hurt or troubled: *a pained expression came over his face* | *Susan looked pained*.

Paine Towers /ˈpʌɪni, -neɪ/ a group of spectacular granite peaks in southern Chile, rising to a height of 2,668 m (8,755 ft).

painful ▸ adjective (of a part of the body) affected with pain: *her ankle was very painful*. ■ causing physical pain: *a painful knock*. ■ causing distress or trouble: *a painful experience*. ■ informal very bad: *their attempts at reggae are painful*.
– DERIVATIVES **painfulness** noun.

painfully ▸ adverb in a painful manner or to a painful degree: *she coughed painfully*. ■ [as submodifier] (with reference to something undesirable) exceedingly: *progress was painfully slow*.

painkiller ▸ noun a drug or a medicine for relieving pain.
– DERIVATIVES **painkilling** adjective.

P

painless ▸ adjective not causing or suffering physical pain: *a painless death.* ■ involving little effort or stress: *a painless way to travel.*
– DERIVATIVES **painlessly** adverb, **painlessness** noun.

painstaking ▸ adjective done with or employing great care and thoroughness: *painstaking attention to detail | he is a gentle, painstaking man.*
– DERIVATIVES **painstakingly** adverb, **painstakingness** noun.

paint ▸ noun **1** [mass noun] a coloured substance which is spread over a surface and dries to leave a thin decorative or protective coating: *a tin of paint |* [count noun] *bituminous paints.* ■ [count noun] an act of painting something: *the house looked in need of a good paint.* ■ informal cosmetic make-up: *one has false curls, another too much paint.* ■ Computing the function or capability of producing graphics, especially those that mimic the effect of real paint: [as modifier] *a paint program.*
2 N. Amer. a piebald horse: [as modifier] *a paint mare.*
3 [in sing.] Basketball the rectangular area marked near the basket at each end of the court: *the two players jostled* ***in the paint.***
▸ verb [with obj.] **1** cover the surface of (something) with paint: [with obj. and complement] *the ceiling was painted dark grey |* (as adj., with submodifier **painted**) *a brightly painted caravan.* ■ apply cosmetics to (the skin). ■ apply (a liquid) to a surface with a brush. ■ (**paint something out**) obliterate something with paint: *the markings on the plane were hurriedly painted out.*
2 depict (someone or something) or produce (a picture) with paint: *I painted a woman sitting next to a table lamp | he paints landscapes and portraits.* ■ give a description of: *the city is not as bad as it is painted.* ■ Computing create (a graphic or screen display) using a paint program.
3 display a mark representing (an aircraft or vehicle) on a radar screen.
– PHRASES **like watching paint dry** (of an activity or experience) extremely boring. **paint a picture of** describe (someone or something) in a particular way: *the president painted a grim picture of life in the next century.* **paint oneself into a corner** leave oneself no means of escape or room to manoeuvre. **paint the town red** informal go out and enjoy oneself flamboyantly.
– DERIVATIVES **paintable** adjective, **painty** adjective.
– ORIGIN Middle English: from *peint* 'painted', past participle of Old French *peindre*, from Latin *pingere* 'to paint'.

paintball ▸ noun [mass noun] a game in which participants simulate military combat using airguns to shoot capsules of paint at each other. ■ [count noun] a capsule of paint used in paintball.
– DERIVATIVES **paintballer** noun, **paintballing** noun.

paintbox ▸ noun a box holding dry paints for painting pictures. ■ (**Paintbox**) trademark an electronic system used to create video graphics by storing filmed material on disk and manipulating it using a graphics tablet.

paintbrush ▸ noun **1** a brush for applying paint.
2 [with modifier] a North American plant which bears brightly coloured brush-like flowering spikes. See also DEVIL'S PAINTBRUSH. ● Genus *Castilleja*, family Scrophulariaceae: several species, including the **Indian paintbrush** (*C. coccinea*).

paint-by-numbers ▸ adjective (of a child's picture) marked out in advance into sections which are numbered according to the colour to be used. ■ denoting something mechanical or formulaic rather than imaginative or natural: *a paint-by-numbers way to feel or act.*

paint chip ▸ noun **1** a small area on a painted surface where the paint has been chipped away.
2 N. Amer. a card showing a colour or a range of related colours available in a type of paint.

painted lady ▸ noun **1** a migratory butterfly with predominantly orange-brown wings and darker markings. ● Genus *Cynthia*, subfamily Nymphalinae, family Nymphalidae: the widely distributed *C. cardui*, with black-and-white markings, and the **American painted lady** (*C. virginiensis*), with markings resembling eyes on the undersides of the wings.
2 South African term for GLADIOLUS.

painted snipe ▸ noun a small long-billed wading bird which has brown plumage with bold and colourful markings. ● Family Rostratulidae: two species, in particular *Rostratula benghalensis* of the Old World.

painter¹ ▸ noun **1** an artist who paints pictures: *a German landscape painter.*
2 a person whose job is painting buildings.
– ORIGIN Middle English: from Anglo-Norman French *peintour*, based on Latin *pictor*, from the verb *pingere* 'to paint'.

painter² ▸ noun a rope attached to the bow of a boat for tying it to a quay.
– ORIGIN Middle English: of uncertain origin; compare with Old French *pentoir* 'something from which to hang things'.

painterly ▸ adjective of or appropriate to a painter; artistic: *she has a painterly eye.* ■ (of a painting or its style) characterized by qualities of colour, stroke, and texture rather than of line.
– DERIVATIVES **painterliness** noun.

paint gun ▸ noun a gun-shaped tool for applying paint. ■ an airgun firing capsules of paint, used in the game of paintball.

pain threshold ▸ noun the point beyond which a stimulus causes pain.

painting ▸ noun [mass noun] the action or skill of using paint, either in a picture or as decoration. ■ [count noun] a painted picture: *an oil painting.*

paint kettle ▸ noun a container with a handle used to hold paint during use.

paint shop ▸ noun the part of a factory where goods are painted, typically by spraying.

paintstick ▸ noun a stick of water-soluble paint used like a crayon.

paintwork ▸ noun [mass noun] chiefly Brit. painted surfaces in a building or on a vehicle.

pair ▸ noun **1** a set of two things used together or regarded as a unit: *a pair of gloves | three pairs of shoes.* ■ two playing cards of the same denomination. ■ two people related in some way or considered together: *a company run by a pair of brothers | get out,* ***the pair of you.*** ■ the second member of a pair in relation to the first: *each course member tries to persuade his pair of the merits of his model.* ■ a mated couple of animals: *76 pairs of red kites.* ■ two horses harnessed side by side. ■ either or both of two members of a legislative assembly on opposite sides who absent themselves from voting by mutual arrangement, leaving the relative position of the parties unaffected.
2 an article consisting of two joined or corresponding parts not used separately: *a pair of jeans | a pair of scissors.*
▸ verb [with obj.] put together or join to form a pair: *a cardigan* ***paired with*** *a matching skirt.* ■ [no obj.] (of animals) form a pair for breeding purposes: *killer whales pair for life.* ■ [no obj.] (**pair off/up**) form a romantic or sexual relationship: *my friends had paired off and I was the only one playing the field.* ■ give (a member of a legislative assembly) another member as a pair, to allow both to absent themselves from a vote without affecting the result.
– PHRASES **pair of hands** used in reference to a person seen in terms of their participation in a task: *we can always do with an extra pair of hands.*
– DERIVATIVES **pairwise** adjective & adverb.
– ORIGIN Middle English: from Old French *paire*, from Latin *paria* 'equal things', neuter plural of *par* 'equal'. Formerly phrases such as *a pair of gloves* were expressed without *of*, as in *a pair gloves* (compare with German *ein Paar Handschuhe*).

pair-bond ▸ verb [no obj.] (of an animal or person) form a close relationship through courtship and sexual activity with one other animal or person.
▸ noun (**pair bond**) a relationship formed by pair-bonding.

paired ▸ adjective occurring in pairs or as a pair: *a characteristic arrangement of paired fins.*

pairing ▸ noun an arrangement or match resulting from forming people or things into pairs: *the dancers made a fine pairing.* ■ [mass noun] the action of pairing things or people: *the pairing of food and wine.*

pair production ▸ noun [mass noun] Physics the conversion of a radiation quantum into an electron and a positron.

paisa /ˈpʌɪsɑː, -sə/ ▸ noun (pl. **paise** /-seɪ/ or /-sə/) a monetary unit of India, Pakistan, and Nepal, equal to one hundredth of a rupee.
– ORIGIN Hindi *paisā*.

paisan /pʌɪˈzɑːn/ ▸ noun US informal (among people of Italian or Spanish descent) a fellow countryman or friend (often as a term of address).
– ORIGIN from Italian *paisano* 'peasant, rustic'.

paisano /pʌɪˈsɑːnəʊ, -ˈzɑː-/ ▸ noun (pl. **paisanos** /-əʊz/) US a peasant of Spanish or Italian ethnic origin.
– ORIGIN Spanish.

Paisley¹ /ˈpeɪzli/ a town in central Scotland, to the west of Glasgow, administrative centre of Renfrewshire; pop. 71,700 (est. 2009).

Paisley² /ˈpeɪzli/, Ian (Richard Kyle) (b.1926), Northern Irish clergyman and politician, First Minister of Northern Ireland 2007–8. MP for North Antrim since 1970 and co-founder of the Ulster Democratic Unionist Party (1972), he has been an outspoken defender of the Protestant Unionist position.

paisley /ˈpeɪzli/ ▸ noun [mass noun] [usu. as modifier] a distinctive intricate pattern of curved feather-shaped figures based on an Indian pine-cone design: *a paisley silk tie.*
– ORIGIN early 19th cent.: named after the town of *Paisley* (see PAISLEY¹), the original place of manufacture.

Paiute /ˈpʌɪuːt/ ▸ noun (pl. **same** or **Paiutes**) **1** a member of either of two culturally similar but geographically separate and linguistically distinct American Indian peoples (the **Southern Paiute** and the **Northern Paiute**) of the western US.
2 [mass noun] either of the Uto-Aztecan languages of the Paiute, now with few speakers.
▸ adjective relating to the Paiute or their languages.
– ORIGIN from Spanish *Payuchi*, *Payuta*, influenced by UTE.

pajamas ▸ plural noun US spelling of PYJAMAS.

Pak ▸ abbreviation Pakistan or Pakistani.

pakamac /ˈpakəmak/ (also **pacamac**) ▸ noun Brit. a kind of lightweight plastic mackintosh that can be folded up into a small pack when not required.
– ORIGIN 1950s: phonetic respelling of *pack a mac.*

pak choi /pak ˈtʃɔɪ/ (N. Amer. also **bok choy**) ▸ noun [mass noun] a Chinese cabbage of a variety with smooth-edged tapering leaves. ● *Brassica rapa* var. *chinensis*, family Cruciferae.
– ORIGIN from Chinese (Cantonese dialect) *paâk ts'oì* 'white vegetable'.

Pakeha /ˈpɑːkɪhɑː/ ▸ noun NZ a white New Zealander as opposed to a Maori: [as modifier] *Pakeha influences.*
– ORIGIN Maori.

Pakhtun ▸ noun variant form of PASHTUN.

Paki ▸ noun (pl. **Pakis**) Brit. informal, offensive a person from Pakistan or South Asia by birth or descent, especially one living in Britain.
– ORIGIN 1960s: abbreviation.

Pakistan /ˌpɑːkɪˈstɑːn, ˌpakɪ-, -ˈstan/ a country in South Asia; pop. 174,578,600 (est. 2009); languages, Urdu (official), Punjabi, Sindhi, Pashto; capital, Islamabad.

> Pakistan was created as a separate country in 1947, following the British withdrawal from India. It originally comprised two territories, respectively to the east and west of India, in which the population was predominantly Muslim. Civil war in East Pakistan led to the establishment of the independent state of Bangladesh in 1972. Pakistan withdrew from the Commonwealth in 1972 as a protest against international recognition of Bangladesh, but rejoined in 1989; it was suspended 1999–2004 following a military coup.

– DERIVATIVES **Pakistani** adjective & noun.
– ORIGIN from Punjab, Afghan Frontier, Kashmir, Baluchi*stan*, lands where Muslims predominated.

Pakistan People's Party (abbrev.: **PPP**) one of the main political parties in Pakistan. It was founded in 1967 by Zulfikar Ali Bhutto, and was led 1984–2007 by his daughter Benazir Bhutto.

pakora /pəˈkɔːrə/ ▸ noun (in Indian cookery) a piece of vegetable or meat, coated in seasoned batter and deep-fried.
– ORIGIN from Hindi *pakoṛā*, denoting a dish of vegetables in gram flour.

pa kua /pɑːˈkwɑː/ ▸ noun variant spelling of BA GUA.

PAL ▸ noun [mass noun] the television broadcasting system used in most of Europe.
– ORIGIN acronym from *Phase Alternate Line* (so named because the colour information in alternate lines is inverted in phase).

pal informal ▸ noun a friend. ■ used as a form of address, especially to indicate anger or aggression: *back off, pal.*
▸ verb (**pals, palling, palled**) [no obj.] (**pal up**) form a friendship: *she* ***palled up with*** *some English chaps.* ■ (**pal around**) spend time with a friend: *we got acquainted but we never really palled around.*
– ORIGIN late 17th cent.: from Romany, 'brother, mate', based on Sanskrit *bhrātṛ* 'brother'.

P

palace ▶ noun a large and impressive building forming the official residence of a ruler, pope, archbishop, etc. ■ informal a large, splendid house or place of entertainment.
– ORIGIN Middle English: from Old French *paleis*, from Latin *Palatium*, the name of the Palatine hill in Rome, where the house of the emperor was situated.

Palace of Westminster see WESTMINSTER, PALACE OF.

palace revolution (also **palace coup**) ▶ noun the non-violent overthrow of a sovereign or government by senior officials within the ruling group.

paladin /ˈpalədɪn/ ▶ noun historical any of the twelve peers of Charlemagne's court, of whom the Count Palatine was the chief. ■ a knight renowned for heroism and chivalry.
– ORIGIN late 16th cent.: from French *paladin*, from Italian *paladino*, from Latin *palatinus* '(officer) of the palace' (see PALATINE[1]).

Palaearctic /ˌpalɪˈɑːktɪk, ˌpeɪ-/ (also chiefly US **Palearctic**) ▶ adjective Zoology relating to or denoting a zoogeographical region comprising Eurasia north of the Himalayas, together with North Africa and the temperate part of the Arabian peninsula. The fauna is closely related to that of the Nearctic region. Compare with HOLARCTIC. ■ (as noun **the Palaearctic**) the Palaearctic region.

palaeo- /ˈpalɪəʊ, ˈpeɪlɪəʊ/ (US **paleo-**) ▶ combining form older or ancient, especially relating to the geological past: *Palaeolithic* | *palaeomagnetism*.
– ORIGIN from Greek *palaios* 'ancient'.

palaeoanthropology (US **paleoanthropology**) ▶ noun the branch of anthropology concerned with fossil hominids.
– DERIVATIVES **palaeoanthropological** adjective, **palaeoanthropologist** noun.

palaeobiology (US **paleobiology**) ▶ noun [mass noun] the biology of fossil animals and plants.
– DERIVATIVES **palaeobiological** adjective, **palaeobiologist** noun.

palaeobotany (US **paleobotany**) ▶ noun [mass noun] the study of fossil plants.
– DERIVATIVES **palaeobotanical** adjective, **palaeobotanist** noun.

Palaeocene /ˈpalɪə(ʊ)siːn, ˈpeɪ-/ (US **Paleocene**) ▶ adjective Geology relating to or denoting the earliest epoch of the Tertiary period, between the Cretaceous period and the Eocene epoch. ■ (as noun **the Palaeocene**) the Palaeocene epoch or the system of rocks deposited during it.

> The Paleocene epoch lasted from 65.0 to 56.5 million years ago. It was a time of sudden diversification among the mammals, probably as a result of the mass extinctions (notably of the dinosaurs) which occurred at the end of the Cretaceous period (see CRETACEOUS–TERTIARY BOUNDARY).

– ORIGIN late 19th cent.: from PALAEO- + Greek *kainos* 'new'.

palaeoclimate (US **paleoclimate**) ▶ noun a climate prevalent at a particular time in the geological past.
– DERIVATIVES **palaeoclimatic** adjective, **palaeoclimatologist** noun, **palaeoclimatology** noun.

palaeocurrent (US **paleocurrent**) ▶ noun a current which existed at some time in the geological past, as inferred from the features of sedimentary rocks.

palaeodemography (US **paleodemography**) ▶ noun [mass noun] the branch of knowledge that deals with the demographic features of past populations and cultures.

palaeoecology (US **paleoecology**) ▶ noun [mass noun] the ecology of fossil animals and plants.
– DERIVATIVES **palaeoecological** adjective, **palaeoecologist** noun.

palaeoenvironment (US **paleoenvironment**) ▶ noun an environment at a period in the geological past.
– DERIVATIVES **palaeoenvironmental** adjective.

Palaeo-Eskimo (US **Paleo-Eskimo**) ▶ noun a member of the earliest prehistoric Inuit people, inhabiting the Arctic from Greenland to Siberia.
▶ adjective relating to the Palaeo-Eskimos.

palaeoethnobotany (US **paleoethnobotany**) ▶ noun [mass noun] the branch of ethnobotany that deals archaeologically with the remains of plants cultivated or used by human beings.
– DERIVATIVES **palaeoethnobotanical** adjective.

Palaeogene /ˈpalɪə(ʊ)dʒiːn, ˈpeɪ-/ (US **Paleogene**) ▶ adjective Geology relating to or denoting the earlier division of the Tertiary period, comprising the Palaeocene, Eocene, and Oligocene epochs. Compare with NEOGENE. ■ (as noun **the Palaeogene**) the Palaeogene sub-period or the system of rocks deposited during it.

> The Palaeogene lasted from about 65 to 23 million years ago. The mammals diversified following the demise of the dinosaurs, and many bizarre and gigantic forms appeared.

– ORIGIN late 19th cent.: from PALAEO- + Greek *genēs* 'of a specified kind' (see -GEN).

palaeogeography (US **paleogeography**) ▶ noun [mass noun] the study of geographical features at periods in the geological past.
– DERIVATIVES **palaeogeographer** noun, **palaeogeographical** adjective.

palaeography /ˌpalɪˈɒɡrəfi, peɪ-/ (US **paleography**) ▶ noun [mass noun] the study of ancient writing systems and the deciphering and dating of historical manuscripts.
– DERIVATIVES **palaeographic** adjective, **palaeographical** /-əˈɡrafɪk(ə)l/ adjective, **palaeographically** adverb.

Palaeo-Indian ▶ adjective relating to or denoting the earliest human inhabitants of the Americas, to *c.*5000 BC. The date of their first arrival in America is debated (possibly up to 30,000 or 40,000 years ago, but artefacts do not become numerous until the Clovis period).
▶ noun **1** (**the Palaeo-Indian**) the Palaeo-Indian culture or period.
2 a member of the Palaeo-Indian peoples.

palaeolatitude (US **paleolatitude**) ▶ noun the latitude of a place at some time in the past, measured relative to the earth's magnetic poles in the same period. Differences between this and the present latitude are caused by continental drift and movement of the earth's magnetic poles.

Palaeolithic /ˌpalɪə(ʊ)ˈlɪθɪk, ˌpeɪ-/ (US **Paleolithic**) ▶ adjective Archaeology relating to or denoting the early phase of the Stone Age, lasting about 2.5 million years, when primitive stone implements were used. ■ (as noun **the Palaeolithic**) the Palaeolithic period. Also called OLD STONE AGE.

> The Palaeolithic period extends from the first appearance of artefacts to the end of the last ice age (about 8,500 years BC). The period has been divided into the **Lower Palaeolithic**, with the earliest forms of humankind and the emergence of hand-axe industries (ending about 120,000 years ago), the **Middle Palaeolithic**, the era of Neanderthal man (ending about 35,000 years ago), and the **Upper Palaeolithic**, during which only modern *Homo sapiens* is known to have existed.

– ORIGIN mid 19th cent.: from PALAEO- + Greek *lithos* 'stone' + -IC.

palaeomagnetism (US **paleomagnetism**) ▶ noun [mass noun] the branch of geophysics concerned with the magnetism in rocks that was induced by the earth's magnetic field at the time of their formation.
– DERIVATIVES **palaeomagnetic** adjective.

palaeontology /ˌpalɪɒnˈtɒlədʒi, ˌpeɪ-/ (US **paleontology**) ▶ noun [mass noun] the branch of science concerned with fossil animals and plants.
– DERIVATIVES **palaeontological** adjective, **palaeontologist** noun.
– ORIGIN mid 19th cent.: from PALAEO- + Greek *onta* 'beings' (neuter plural of *ōn*, present participle of *einai* 'be') + -LOGY.

palaeopathology (US **paleopathology**) ▶ noun [mass noun] the branch of science concerned with the pathological conditions found in ancient human and animal remains.
– DERIVATIVES **palaeopathological** adjective.

palaeopole (US **paleopole**) ▶ noun a magnetic pole of the earth as it was situated at a time in the distant past.

Palaeo-Siberian ▶ adjective denoting or belonging to a group of languages spoken in eastern Siberia, formerly thought to constitute a phylum or superfamily. The most important is Chukchi.

palaeosol /ˈpalɪə(ʊ)sɒl, ˈpeɪ-/ (US **paleosol**) ▶ noun Geology a stratum or soil horizon which was formed as a soil in a past geological age.

palaeotemperature (US **paleotemperature**) ▶ noun Geology the temperature or mean temperature of a locality at a time in the geological past.

Palaeotropical (US **Paleotropical**) ▶ adjective Botany relating to or denoting a phytogeographical kingdom comprising Africa, tropical Asia, New Guinea, and many Pacific islands (excluding Australia and New Zealand). ■ Zoology relating to or denoting a zoogeographical region comprising the tropical parts of the Old World.

Palaeozoic /ˌpalɪə(ʊ)ˈzəʊɪk, ˌpeɪ-/ (US **Paleozoic**) ▶ adjective Geology relating to or denoting the era between the Precambrian aeon and the Mesozoic era. Formerly called PRIMARY. ■ (as noun **the Palaeozoic**) the Palaeozoic era or the system of rocks deposited during it.

> The Palaeozoic lasted from about 570 to 245 million years ago, its end being marked by mass extinctions. The **Lower Palaeozoic** sub-era comprises the Cambrian, Ordovician, and Silurian periods, and the **Upper Palaeozoic** sub-era comprises the Devonian, Carboniferous, and Permian periods. The era began with the first invertebrates with hard external skeletons, notably trilobites, and ended with the rise to dominance of the reptiles.

– ORIGIN mid 19th cent.: from PALAEO- + Greek *zōē* 'life' + -IC.

palaestra /pəˈliːstrə, -ˈlʌɪstrə/ (also **palestra**) ▶ noun (in ancient Greece and Rome) a wrestling school or gymnasium.
– ORIGIN via Latin from Greek *palaistra*, from *palaiein* 'wrestle'.

palagi /ˈpɑːləŋi/ (also **papalagi**) ▶ noun (pl. **same**) (in Samoa) a white or non-Samoan person.
– ORIGIN from Samoan *papālagi*.

palais /ˈpaleɪ/ ▶ noun [often in names] Brit. a public hall for dancing: *Hammersmith Palais*.
– ORIGIN early 20th cent.: from French *palais (de danse)* '(dancing) hall'.

palais de danse /ˌpaleɪ də ˈdɒ̃s/, French /palɛ də dɑ̃s/ ▶ noun (pl. **same**) a dance hall.
– ORIGIN early 20th cent.: from French.

Palais de l'Elysée /palɛ də lelize/ French name for ELYSÉE PALACE.

palak /ˈpɑːlak/ ▶ noun Indian spinach: *lamb palak*.
– ORIGIN Hindi *pālak* from Sanskrit *pālakyā* 'green vegetables'.

palampore /ˈpaləmpɔː/ ▶ noun [mass noun] Indian a type of chintz cloth used, especially formerly, for bedspreads, wall hangings, etc. ■ [count noun] a palampore bedspread.
– ORIGIN late 17th cent.: origin uncertain; perhaps from Portuguese *palangapuz(es)* plural, from Urdu, Persian *palangpoš* 'bedcover', or perhaps from *Pālanpur*, a town in Gujarat, India.

palanquin /ˌpalənˈkiːn/ (also **palankeen**) ▶ noun (in India and the East) a covered litter for one passenger, consisting of a large box carried on two horizontal poles by four or six bearers.
– ORIGIN late 16th cent.: from Portuguese *palanquim*, from Oriya *pālaṅki*, based on Sanskrit *palyanka* 'bed, couch'.

palapa /pəˈlapə/ ▶ noun a traditional Mexican shelter roofed with palm leaves or branches.
– ORIGIN Mexican Spanish, denoting the palm *Orbignya cohune*.

Palari (also **Palare**) ▶ noun variant spelling of POLARI.

Palashi /pəˈlasi/ modern name of PLASSEY.

palatable /ˈpalətəb(ə)l/ ▶ adjective (of food or drink) pleasant to taste: *a very palatable local red wine*. ■ (of an action or proposal) acceptable or satisfactory: *a device that made increased taxation more palatable*.
– DERIVATIVES **palatability** noun, **palatableness** noun, **palatably** adverb.

palatal /ˈpalət(ə)l/ ▶ adjective technical relating to the palate: *a palatal lesion*. ■ Phonetics (of a speech sound) made by placing the blade of the tongue against or near the hard palate (e.g. *y* in *yes*).
▶ noun Phonetics a palatal sound.
– DERIVATIVES **palatally** adverb.
– ORIGIN early 18th cent.: from French, from Latin *palatum* (see PALATE).

palatalize (also **palatalise**) ▶ verb [with obj.] Phonetics make (a speech sound) palatal, especially by changing a velar to a palatal by moving the point of contact between tongue and palate further forward in the mouth.
– DERIVATIVES **palatalization** noun.

palate ▶ noun **1** the roof of the mouth, separating the cavities of the mouth and nose in vertebrates.
2 a person's ability to distinguish between and appreciate different flavours: *a fine range of drink for sophisticated palates* | figurative *the suggestions may not suit everyone's palate*. ■ the flavour of wine or beer: *a wine with a zingy, peachy palate*.
– ORIGIN late Middle English: from Latin *palatum*.

P

palatial ▶ **adjective** resembling a palace in being spacious and splendid: *her palatial apartment in Mayfair*.
– DERIVATIVES **palatially** adverb.
– ORIGIN mid 18th cent.: from Latin *palatium* 'palace' (see PALACE) + -AL.

palatinate /pəˈlatɪnət/ ▶ **noun** historical a territory under the jurisdiction of a count palatine. ■ (**the Palatinate**) the territory of the German Empire ruled by the Count Palatine of the Rhine.

palatine[1] /ˈpalətʌɪn, -tɪn/ ▶ **adjective** [usu. postpositive] chiefly historical (of an official or feudal lord) having local authority that elsewhere belongs only to a sovereign. ■ (of a territory) subject to palatine authority.
– ORIGIN late Middle English: from French *palatin(e)*, from Latin *palatinus* 'of the palace'.

palatine[2] /ˈpalətʌɪn, -tɪn/ Anatomy ▶ **adjective** relating to the palate or the palatine bone.
▶ **noun** (also **palatine bone**) each of two bones within the skull forming parts of the eye socket, the nasal cavity, and the hard palate.
– ORIGIN mid 17th cent.: from French *palatin(e)*, from Latin *palatum* 'palate'.

palatine uvula ▶ **noun** see UVULA.

Palau /pəˈlaʊ/ (also **Belau**) a group of islands in the western Pacific Ocean, an independent republic since 1990, pop. 20,800 (est. 2009); capital, Melekeok. It was part of the Pacific Islands Trust Territory administered by the US 1947–80.

Palaung /pəˈlaʊŋ/ ▶ **noun** (pl. **same** or **Palaungs**) **1** a member of an indigenous people of the northern Shan states of Burma (Myanmar).
2 [mass noun] the Mon-Khmer language of the Palaung.
▶ **adjective** relating to the Palaung or their language.
– ORIGIN the name in Palaung.

palaver /pəˈlɑːvə/ informal ▶ **noun** [mass noun] prolonged and tedious fuss or discussion: *mucking around with finances and all that palaver*. ■ [count noun] (in Africa) a parley or improvised conference between two sides.
▶ **verb** [no obj.] talk unnecessarily and at length: *it's too hot for palavering*.
– ORIGIN mid 18th cent. (in the sense 'a talk between tribespeople and traders'): from Portuguese *palavra* 'word', from Latin *parabola* 'comparison' (see PARABLE).

Palawan /pəˈlɑːwən/ a long, narrow island in the western Philippines, separating the Sulu Sea from the South China Sea; pop. 1,010,000 (est. 2009); chief town, Puerto Princesa.

palazzo /pəˈlatsəʊ/ ▶ **noun** (pl. **palazzos** or **palazzi** /-tsi/) a palatial building, especially in Italy.
– ORIGIN Italian, 'palace'.

palazzo pants ▶ **plural noun** women's loose wide-legged trousers.

pale[1] ▶ **adjective 1** light in colour or shade; containing little colour or pigment: *choose pale floral patterns for walls*. ■ (of a person or their complexion) having less colour than usual, typically as a result of shock, fear, or ill health: *she looked pale and drawn*. ■ [usu. attrib.] (of a light) not strong or bright: *a pale dawn*.
2 inferior or unimpressive: *the new cheese is a pale imitation of continental cheeses*.
▶ **verb** [no obj.] **1** become pale in one's face from shock or fear: *I paled at the thought of what she might say*.
2 seem or become less important: *all else pales by comparison*.
– DERIVATIVES **palely** adverb, **paleness** noun, **palish** adjective.
– ORIGIN Middle English: from Old French *pale*, from Latin *pallidus*; the verb is from Old French *palir*.

pale[2] ▶ **noun 1** a wooden stake or post used with others to form a fence. ■ a conceptual boundary: *bring these things back within the pale of decency*.
2 historical an area within determined bounds, or subject to a particular jurisdiction. ■ (**the Pale**) another term for ENGLISH PALE. ■ the areas of Russia to which Jewish residence was formerly restricted.
3 Heraldry a broad vertical stripe down the middle of a shield.
– PHRASES **beyond the pale** outside the bounds of acceptable behaviour: *the language my father used was beyond the pale*. **in pale** Heraldry arranged vertically. **per pale** Heraldry divided by a vertical line.
– ORIGIN Middle English: from Old French *pal*, from Latin *palus* 'stake'.

palea /ˈpeɪlɪə/ ▶ **noun** (pl. **paleae** /-lɪiː/) Botany the upper bract of the floret of a grass. Compare with LEMMA[2].
– ORIGIN mid 18th cent.: from Latin, literally 'chaff'.

Palearctic etc. ▶ **adjective** US spelling of PALAEARCTIC etc.

paleface ▶ **noun** a name supposedly used by the North American Indians for a white person.

Palekh /ˈpɑːlɛk/ ▶ **adjective** denoting a type of Russian iconography or a style of miniature painting on boxes, trays, and other small items.
– ORIGIN from the name of a town north-east of Moscow renowned for this type of work.

Palembang /ˌpɑːləmˈbɑːŋ, pɑːˈlɛmbɑːŋ/ a city in Indonesia, in the SE part of the island of Sumatra, a river port on the Musi River; pop. 1,323,200 (est. 2005).

Palenque /pəˈlɛŋkeɪ/ the site of a former Mayan city in SE Mexico, south-east of present-day Villahermosa. The well-preserved ruins of the city, which existed from about AD 300 to 900, include notable examples of Mayan architecture and extensive hieroglyphic texts.

paleo- ▶ **combining form** US spelling of PALAEO-.

paleo-conservative ▶ **noun** N. Amer. a person who advocates traditional forms of conservatism; an extremely right-wing conservative.

Palermo /pəˈlɛːməʊ/, Italian /paˈlɛrmo/ the capital of the Italian island of Sicily, a port on the north coast; pop. 659,433 (2008).

Palestine /ˈpalɪstʌɪn/ a territory in the Middle East on the eastern coast of the Mediterranean Sea.

> In biblical times Palestine comprised the kingdoms of Israel and Judah. The land was controlled at various times by the Egyptian, Assyrian, Persian, and Roman empires before being conquered by the Arabs in AD 634. It was part of the Ottoman Empire from 1516 to 1918. The name Palestine was used as the official political title for the land west of the Jordan mandated to Britain in 1920; in 1948 the state of Israel was established in what was traditionally Palestine, but the name continued to be used in the context of the struggle for territory and political rights of displaced Palestinian Arabs. The first Palestinian intifada or uprising against Israeli occupation of the West Bank and Gaza Strip broke out in 1987; in 1993 an agreement was signed between Israel and the Palestine Liberation Organization giving some autonomy to the Gaza Strip and the West Bank and setting up the Palestine National Authority, but this proved unsuccessful in bringing the conflict to a resolution.

– ORIGIN from Greek *Palaistinē* (used in early Christian writing), from Latin *(Syria) Palaestina* (the name of a Roman province), from *Philistia* 'land of the Philistines'.

Palestine Liberation Organization (abbrev.: **PLO**) a political and military organization formed in 1964 to unite various Palestinian Arab groups and ultimately to bring about an independent state of Palestine. It was led by Yasser Arafat from 1968 until 2004.

Palestinian /ˌpalɪˈstɪnɪən/ ▶ **adjective** relating to Palestine or its peoples.
▶ **noun** a member of the native Arab population of the region of Palestine (including the modern state of Israel).

palestra /pəˈlɛstrə/ ▶ **noun** variant spelling of PALAESTRA.

Palestrina /ˌpaləˈstriːnə/, Giovanni Pierluigi da (*c.*1525–94), Italian composer. Palestrina is chiefly known for his sacred music, including 105 masses, over 250 motets, and the *Missa Papae Marcelli* (1567).

palette /ˈpalɪt/ ▶ **noun** a thin board or slab on which an artist lays and mixes colours. ■ the range of colours used by a particular artist or in a particular picture: *Pollock's hard, bright palette*. ■ the range or variety of tonal or instrumental colour in a musical piece: *he commands the sort of tonal palette which this music needs*. ■ (in computer graphics) the range of colours or shapes available to the user.
– ORIGIN late 18th cent.: from French, diminutive of *pale* 'shovel', from Latin *pala* 'spade'.

palette knife ▶ **noun 1** a thin steel blade with a handle for mixing colours or applying or removing paint.
2 Brit. a kitchen knife or spatula with a long, flexible round-ended blade.

palfrey /ˈpɔːlfri, ˈpal-/ ▶ **noun** (pl. **palfreys**) archaic a docile horse used for ordinary riding, especially by women.
– ORIGIN Middle English: from Old French *palefrei*, from medieval Latin *palefredus*, alteration of late Latin *paraveredus*, from Greek *para* 'beside, extra' + Latin *veredus* 'light horse'.

Palgrave /ˈpalgreɪv, ˈpɔːl-/, Francis Turner (1824–97), English critic and poet, known for his anthology *The Golden Treasury of Songs and Lyrical Poems in the English Language* (1861).

Pali /ˈpɑːliː/ ▶ **noun** [mass noun] an Indic language, closely related to Sanskrit, in which the sacred texts of southern Buddhism are written. Pali developed in northern India in the 5th–2nd centuries BC.
▶ **adjective** relating to Pali.
– ORIGIN from Pali *pāli(-bhāsā)* 'canonical texts'.

pali /ˈpɑːliː/ ▶ **noun** (pl. **same** or **palis**) (in Hawaii) a cliff.
– ORIGIN Hawaiian.

palilalia /ˌpalɪˈleɪlɪə/ ▶ **noun** [mass noun] Medicine a speech disorder characterized by involuntary repetition of words, phrases, or sentences.
– ORIGIN early 20th cent.: from French *palilalie*, from Greek *palin* 'again' + *lalia* 'speech, chatter'.

palimony /ˈpalɪməni/ ▶ **noun** [mass noun] informal, chiefly N. Amer. compensation made by one member of an unmarried couple to the other after separation.
– ORIGIN 1970s: from PAL + a shortened form of ALIMONY.

palimpsest /ˈpalɪm(p)sɛst/ ▶ **noun** a manuscript or piece of writing material on which later writing has been superimposed on effaced earlier writing. ■ something reused or altered but still bearing visible traces of its earlier form: *Sutton Place is a palimpsest of the taste of successive owners*.
– DERIVATIVES **palimpsestic** adjective.
– ORIGIN mid 17th cent.: via Latin from Greek *palimpsēstos*, from *palin* 'again' + *psēstos* 'rubbed smooth'.

palindrome /ˈpalɪndrəʊm/ ▶ **noun** a word, phrase, or sequence that reads the same backwards as forwards, e.g. *madam* or *nurses run*.
– DERIVATIVES **palindromic** /-ˈdrɒmɪk/ adjective, **palindromist** noun.
– ORIGIN early 17th cent.: from Greek *palindromos* 'running back again', from *palin* 'again' + *drom-* (from *dramein* 'to run').

paling /ˈpeɪlɪŋ/ ▶ **noun** a fence made from pointed wooden or metal posts. ■ a post used in such a fence.

palingenesis /ˌpalɪnˈdʒɛnɪsɪs/ ▶ **noun** [mass noun] Biology the exact reproduction of ancestral characteristics in ontogenesis.
– DERIVATIVES **palingenetic** adjective.
– ORIGIN early 19th cent.: from Greek *palin* 'again' + *genesis* 'birth'.

palinode /ˈpalɪnəʊd/ ▶ **noun** a poem in which the poet retracts a view or sentiment expressed in a former poem. ■ a retraction of a statement.
– ORIGIN late 16th cent.: via Latin from Greek *palinōidia*, from *palin* 'again' + *ōidē* 'song'.

Palio /ˈpalɪəʊ/, Italian /ˈpaljo/ (pl. **Palii** /-ɪiː/, Italian /-ii/) a traditional horse race held in Siena twice a year, in July and August.
– ORIGIN Italian, from Latin *pallium* 'covering' (with reference to the cloth given as a prize).

palisade /ˌpalɪˈseɪd/ ▶ **noun 1** a fence of wooden stakes or iron railings fixed in the ground, forming an enclosure or defence. ■ historical a strong pointed wooden stake fixed in the ground with others in a close row, used as a defence.
2 (**palisades**) US a line of high cliffs.
▶ **verb** [with obj.] (usu. as adj. **palisaded**) enclose or provide (a building or place) with a palisade.
– ORIGIN early 17th cent.: from French *palissade*, from Provençal *palissada*, from *palissa* 'paling', based on Latin *palus* 'stake'.

palisade layer ▶ **noun** Botany a layer of parallel elongated cells below the epidermis of a leaf.

Palissy /ˈpalɪsi/, Bernard (*c.*1510–90), French potter, known for his richly coloured earthenware decorated with reliefs of plants and animals.

Palk Strait /pɔːlk/ an inlet of the Bay of Bengal separating northern Sri Lanka from the coast of Tamil Nadu in India. It lies to the north of Adam's Bridge, which separates it from the Gulf of Mannar.

pall[1] /pɔːl/ ▶ **noun 1** a cloth spread over a coffin, hearse, or tomb.
2 a dark cloud of smoke, dust, etc.: *a pall of black smoke hung over the quarry*. ■ something regarded as enveloping a situation with an air of gloom or fear:

P

torture and murder have cast a pall of terror over the villages.
3 an ecclesiastical pallium. ▪ Heraldry a Y-shaped charge representing the front of an ecclesiastical pallium.
– ORIGIN Old English *pæll* 'rich (purple) cloth', 'cloth cover for a chalice', from Latin *pallium* 'covering, cloak'.

pall[2] /pɔːl/ ▶ **verb** [no obj.] become less appealing or interesting through familiarity: *the novelty of the quiet life palled.*
– ORIGIN late Middle English: shortening of **APPAL**.

palladia plural form of **PALLADIUM**[2].

Palladian /pəˈleɪdɪən/ ▶ **adjective** Architecture relating to or denoting the neoclassical style of Andrea Palladio, in particular with reference to the phase of English architecture from *c.*1715, when there was a revival of interest in Palladio and his English follower, Inigo Jones, and a reaction against the baroque.
– DERIVATIVES **Palladianism** noun.

Palladian window ▶ **noun** chiefly US a large window consisting of a central arched section flanked by two narrow rectangular sections.

Palladio /pəˈlɑːdɪəʊ/, Andrea (1508–80), Italian architect. He led a revival of classical architecture, in particular promoting the Roman ideals of harmonic proportions and symmetrical planning. A notable example of his many villas, palaces, and churches is the church of San Giorgio Maggiore in Venice.

palladium[1] /pəˈleɪdɪəm/ ▶ **noun** [mass noun] the chemical element of atomic number 46, a rare silvery-white metal resembling platinum. (Symbol: **Pd**)
– ORIGIN early 19th cent.: modern Latin, from *Pallas*, the name given to an asteroid discovered just before the element (see **PALLAS**).

palladium[2] /pəˈleɪdɪəm/ ▶ **noun** (pl. **palladia** /-dɪə/) archaic a safeguard or source of protection.
– ORIGIN late Middle English (in the Greek sense): via Latin from Greek *palladion*, denoting an image of the goddess Pallas (Athene), on which the safety of Troy was believed to depend.

Pallas /ˈpaləs/ **1** Greek Mythology (also **Pallas Athene**) one of the names (of unknown meaning) of **ATHENE**.
2 Astronomy asteroid 2, discovered in 1802. It is the second largest (diameter 523 km).

pallasite /ˈpaləsʌɪt/ ▶ **noun** a meteorite consisting of roughly equal proportions of iron and olivine.
– ORIGIN mid 19th cent.: from the name of Peter S. *Pallas* (1741–1811), German naturalist, + **-ITE**[1].

Pallas's cat /ˈpaləsɪz/ ▶ **noun** a small wild cat that has a long orange-grey coat with black-and-white head markings, occurring in the mountains of central Asia. Also called **MANUL**. ● *Felis manul*, family Felidae.
– ORIGIN mid 19th cent.: named after Peter S. *Pallas* (1741–1811), German naturalist.

pall-bearer ▶ **noun** a person helping to carry or officially escorting a coffin at a funeral.

pallet[1] ▶ **noun** a straw mattress. ▪ a crude or makeshift bed.
– ORIGIN Middle English: from Anglo-Norman French *paillete*, from *paille* 'straw', from Latin *palea*.

pallet[2] ▶ **noun 1** a portable platform on which goods can be stacked, stored, and moved.
2 a flat wooden blade with a handle, used to shape clay or plaster.
3 a projection on a machine part, serving to change the mode of motion of a wheel. ▪ (in a clock or watch) a projection transmitting motion from an escapement to a pendulum or balance wheel.
– DERIVATIVES **palleted** adjective.
– ORIGIN late Middle English (in sense 2): from French *palette* 'little blade', from Latin *pala* 'spade' (related to *palus* 'stake').

pallet[3] ▶ **noun** Heraldry the diminutive of the pale, a narrow vertical strip, usually borne in groups of two or three.
– ORIGIN late 15th cent.: diminutive of the noun **PALE**[2].

palletize (also **palletise**) ▶ **verb** [with obj.] (usu. as adj. **palletized**) place, stack, or transport (goods) on a pallet or pallets.

pallia plural form of **PALLIUM**.

palliasse /ˈpalɪas/ (also **paillasse**) ▶ **noun** a straw mattress.
– ORIGIN early 16th cent. (originally Scots): from French *paillasse*, based on Latin *palea* 'straw'.

palliate /ˈpalɪeɪt/ ▶ **verb 1** [with obj.] make (a disease or its symptoms) less severe without removing the cause.
2 disguise the seriousness of (an offence): *there is no way to excuse or palliate his dirty deed.* ▪ allay or moderate (fears or suspicions).
– DERIVATIVES **palliation** noun, **palliator** noun.
– ORIGIN late Middle English: from late Latin *palliat-* 'cloaked', from the verb *palliare*, from *pallium* 'cloak'.

palliative /ˈpalɪətɪv/ ▶ **adjective** (of a medicine or medical care) relieving pain without dealing with the cause of the condition. ▪ (of an action) intended to alleviate a problem without addressing the underlying cause: *short-term palliative measures had been taken.*
▶ **noun** a palliative medicine, measure, etc.
– DERIVATIVES **palliatively** adverb.
– ORIGIN late Middle English (as an adjective): from French *palliatif, -ive* or medieval Latin *palliativus*, from the verb *palliare* 'to cloak' (see **PALLIATE**).

palliative care ▶ **noun** [mass noun] care for the terminally ill and their families, especially that provided by an organized health service.

pallid ▶ **adjective 1** (of a person's face) pale, typically because of poor health.
2 lacking vigour or intensity; insipid: *a pallid ray of winter sun | pallid liberalism.*
– DERIVATIVES **pallidity** /-ˈlɪdɪti/ noun, **pallidly** adverb.
– ORIGIN late 16th cent.: from Latin *pallidus* 'pale' (related to *pallere* 'be pale').

pallium /ˈpalɪəm/ ▶ **noun** (pl. **pallia** /-lɪə/ or **palliums**)
1 a woollen vestment conferred by the Pope on an archbishop, consisting of a narrow circular band placed round the shoulders with a short lappet hanging from front and back.
2 historical a man's large rectangular cloak, especially as worn by Greek philosophical and religious teachers.
3 Zoology the mantle of a mollusc or brachiopod.
4 Anatomy the outer wall of the mammalian cerebrum, corresponding to the cerebral cortex.
– DERIVATIVES **pallial** adjective (sense 3, sense 4).
– ORIGIN Middle English: from Latin, literally 'covering'.

pall-mall /palˈmal/ ▶ **noun** [mass noun] historical a 16th- and 17th-century game in which a boxwood ball was driven through an iron ring suspended at the end of a long alley. The street Pall Mall in London was on the site of a pall-mall alley.
– ORIGIN from obsolete French *pallemaille*, from Italian *pallamaglio*, from *palla* 'ball' + *maglio* 'mallet'.

pallor ▶ **noun** [in sing.] an unhealthy pale appearance.
– ORIGIN late Middle English: from Latin, from *pallere* 'be pale'.

pally ▶ **adjective** (**pallier**, **palliest**) [predic.] informal having a close, friendly relationship: *I see you're getting quite pally with Carlos.*

palm[1] ▶ **noun** (also **palm tree**) an unbranched evergreen tree of tropical and warm regions, with a crown of very long feathered or fan-shaped leaves, and typically having old leaf scars forming a regular pattern on the trunk. ● Family Palmae (or Arecaceae): numerous genera and species, some of which are of great commercial importance, e.g. the **oil palm**, **date palm**, and coconut.
▪ a leaf of a palm tree awarded as a prize or viewed as a symbol of victory: *the consensus was that the palm should go to Doerner.*
– ORIGIN Old English *palm(a)*, of Germanic origin; related to Dutch *palm* and German *Palme*, from Latin *palma* 'palm (of a hand)', its leaf being likened to a spread hand.

palm[2] ▶ **noun 1** the inner surface of the hand between the wrist and fingers. ▪ a part of a glove that covers the palm. ▪ a hard shield worn on the hand by sailmakers to protect the palm.
2 the palmate part of a deer's antler.
▶ **verb 1** [with obj.] conceal (a small object) in the hand, especially as part of a trick or theft.
2 [with obj. and adverbial of direction] (of a goalkeeper) deflect (the ball) with the palm of the hand.
– PHRASES **have** (or **hold**) **someone in the palm of one's hand** have someone under one's control or influence: *she had the audience in the palm of her hand.* **read someone's palm** tell someone's fortune by looking at the lines on their palm.
– PHRASAL VERBS **palm someone off** informal persuade someone to accept something by deception: *most sellers are palmed off with a fraction of what something is worth.* **palm something off** sell or dispose of something by misrepresentation or fraud: *unscrupulous businessmen may palm off their property to the buyers without proper papers.*
– DERIVATIVES **palmar** /ˈpalmə/ adjective, **palmed** adjective [in combination] *sweaty-palmed*, **palmful** noun.
– ORIGIN Middle English: from Old French *paume*, from Latin *palma*. Current senses of the verb date from the late 17th cent.

Palma /ˈpɑːmə, ˈpalmə/ the capital of the Balearic Islands, an industrial port and resort on the island of Majorca; pop. 396,570 (est. 2008). Full name **Palma de Mallorca** /ˌpalma ðe maˈjəɔrka/.

palmarosa /ˌpalməˈrəʊsə/ ▶ **noun** [mass noun] a fragrant tropical Indian grass related to citronella and lemon grass. ● *Cymbopogon martinii*, family Gramineae.
▪ (also **palmarosa oil**) the essential oil obtained from palmarosa, used in perfumery and aromatherapy.
– ORIGIN late 19th cent.: from Italian, literally 'rose palm'.

Palmas /ˈpalmas/ a town in central Brazil, on the Tocantins River, capital of the state of Tocantins; pop. 178,386 (2007).

palmate /ˈpalmeɪt/ ▶ **adjective 1** Botany (of a leaf) having five or more lobes whose midribs all radiate from one point.
2 Zoology (of an antler) in which the angles between the tines are partly filled in to form a broad flat surface, as in fallow deer and moose.
– DERIVATIVES **palmated** adjective.
– ORIGIN mid 18th cent.: from Latin *palmatus*, from *palma* 'palm' (see **PALM**[2]).

palmate newt ▶ **noun** a small olive-brown smooth-skinned newt native to western Europe, with partially webbed feet. ● *Triturus helveticus*, family Salamandridae.

palm ball ▶ **noun** a baseball pitch in which the ball is released from the palm and thumb rather than the fingers.

Palm Beach a resort town in SE Florida, situated on an island just off the coast; pop. 9,535 (est. 2008).

palm civet ▶ **noun** a mainly arboreal civet that typically has pale spots or stripes on a dark coat, and powerful curved claws, native to Africa and Asia. It is often a pest of banana plantations. ● *Paradoxurus* and other genera, family Viverridae: several species, including the **common palm civet** or toddy cat (*P. hermaphroditus*) of Asia.

palmcorder ▶ **noun** a small handheld camcorder.
– ORIGIN 1980s: blend of **PALM**[2] and **RECORDER**.

Palmer[1] /ˈpɑːmə/, Arnold (Daniel) (b.1929), American golfer. His many championship victories include the Masters (1958; 1960; 1962; 1964), the US Open (1960), and the British Open (1961–2).

Palmer[2], Samuel (1805–91), English painter and etcher. His friendship with William Blake resulted in the mystical, visionary landscape paintings, such as *Repose of the Holy Family* (1824), for which he is best known. He was leader of a group of artists called The Ancients.

palmer ▶ **noun 1** historical a pilgrim, especially one who had returned from the Holy Land with a palm branch or leaf as a sign of having undertaken the pilgrimage. ▪ an itinerant monk travelling from shrine to shrine under a vow of poverty.
2 a hairy artificial fly used in angling.
– ORIGIN Middle English: from Anglo-Norman French, from medieval Latin *palmarius* 'pilgrim', from Latin *palma* 'palm'.

Palmerston /ˈpɑːməst(ə)n/, Henry John Temple, 3rd Viscount (1784–1865), British Whig statesman, Prime Minister 1855–8 and 1859–65. Palmerston declared the second Opium War against China in 1856, and oversaw the successful conclusion of the Crimean War in 1856 and the suppression of the Indian Mutiny in 1858.

Palmerston North a city in the SW part of the North Island, New Zealand; pop. 75,540 (2006).

palmette /palˈmɛt/ ▶ **noun** Archaeology an ornament of radiating petals like a palm leaf.
– ORIGIN mid 19th cent.: from French, literally 'small palm', diminutive of *palme*.

palmetto /palˈmɛtəʊ/ ▶ **noun** (pl. **palmettos**) a fan palm, especially one of a number occurring from the southern US to northern South America. ● *Sabal* and other genera, family Palmae: several species, in particular the **cabbage palmetto** (*S. palmetto*), which is the state tree of Florida.
– ORIGIN mid 16th cent.: from Spanish *palmito*, literally 'small palm', diminutive of *palma*, assimilated to Italian words ending in *-etto*.

Palmetto State informal name for **South Carolina**.

palmier /ˈpalmɪeɪ/ ▶ **noun** (pl. pronunc. **same**) a sweet crisp pastry shaped like a palm leaf.
– ORIGIN French, literally 'palm tree'.

palmist ▶ **noun** a person who practises palmistry; a palm-reader.

palmistry ▶ **noun** [mass noun] the art or practice of supposedly interpreting a person's character or predicting their future by examining the lines and other features of the hand, especially the palm and fingers.
– ORIGIN late Middle English: from **palm**[2] + *-estry* (of unknown origin), later altered to *-istry*, perhaps on the pattern of *sophistry*.

palmitate /ˈpalmɪteɪt/ ▶ **noun** Chemistry a salt or ester of palmitic acid.

palmitic acid /palˈmɪtɪk/ ▶ **noun** Chemistry a solid saturated fatty acid obtained from palm oil and other vegetable and animal fats. ● Chem. formula: $CH_3(CH_2)_{14}COOH$.
– ORIGIN mid 19th cent.: *palmitic* from French *palmitique*, from *palme* (see **palm**[1]).

palm oil ▶ **noun** [mass noun] oil from the fruit of certain palms, especially the West African oil palm.

Palm Springs a resort city in the desert area of southern California, east of Los Angeles, noted for its hot mineral springs; pop. 47,952 (est. 2008).

palm squirrel ▶ **noun** an Old World squirrel that frequents palm trees, especially a tree squirrel with a striped back and a shrill bird-like call. ● Genus *Funambulus* and other genera, family Sciuridae: several species, in particular *F. pennanti* of northern India.

Palm Sunday ▶ **noun** the Sunday before Easter, on which Christ's entry into Jerusalem is celebrated in many Christian churches by processions in which branches of palms are carried.

palmtop ▶ **noun** a computer small and light enough to be held in one hand.

palm wine ▶ **noun** [mass noun] an alcoholic drink made from fermented palm sap.

palmy ▶ **adjective** (**palmier**, **palmiest**) **1** (especially of a previous period) flourishing or successful: *the palmy days of the 1970s*.
2 covered with palms.

Palmyra /palˈmʌɪrə/ an ancient city of Syria, an oasis in the Syrian desert north-east of Damascus on the site of present-day Tadmur.
– ORIGIN Greek form of the city's modern and ancient pre-Semitic name Tadmur or Tadmor, meaning 'city of palms'.

palmyra ▶ **noun** an Asian fan palm which yields a wide range of useful products, including timber, fibre, and fruit. ● *Borassus flabellifer*, family Palmae.
– ORIGIN late 17th cent.: from Portuguese *palmeira* 'palm tree'. The change in the ending was due to association with the name of the city of **Palmyra**.

Palo Alto /ˌpaləʊ ˈaltəʊ/ a city in western California, south of San Francisco; pop. 59,395 (est. 2008). It is a noted centre for electronics and computer technology, and the site of Stanford University.

palolo worm /pəˈləʊləʊ/ ▶ **noun** a marine bristle worm which swarms in response to changes in light intensity, particularly that of the moon. The worm's posterior segments detach themselves and swim to the surface where the reproductive cells are released into the sea. ● Several species in Eunicidae and other families, in particular the **Samoan palolo worm** (*Palola* (or *Eunice*) *viridis*), which occurs on South Pacific reefs.
– ORIGIN late 19th cent.: *palolo* from Samoan or Tongan.

Palomar, Mount /ˈpaləmɑː/ a mountain in southern California, north-east of San Diego, rising to a height of 1,867 m (6,126 ft). It is the site of an astronomical observatory.
– ORIGIN Spanish *Palomar*, literally 'place of the pigeon'.

palomino /ˌpaləˈmiːnəʊ/ ▶ **noun 1** (pl. **palominos**) a pale golden or tan-coloured horse or pony with a white mane and tail, originally bred in the south-western US. ■ [mass noun] a pale golden-brown colour.
2 [mass noun] a variety of white grape used to make sherry and fortified wines.
– ORIGIN early 20th cent.: from Latin American Spanish, from Spanish *palomino* 'young pigeon', from Latin *palumbinus* 'resembling a dove'.

palooka /pəˈluːkə/ ▶ **noun** N. Amer. informal a stupid, uncouth person; a lout. ■ US dated an inferior or average prizefighter.
– ORIGIN 1920s: of unknown origin.

Palookaville /pəˈluːkəvɪl/ ▶ **noun** N. Amer. informal a state of obscurity: *defeat would have meant a one-way trip to Palookaville*.

Palouse /pəˈluːz/ ▶ **noun** (pl. **same** or **Palouses**) a member of an American Indian people inhabiting the Palouse River valley in SW Washington and NW Idaho.
▶ **adjective** relating to the Palouse.
– ORIGIN the name in their own language.

paloverde /ˌpaləʊˈvəːdi/ ▶ **noun** a thorny yellow-flowered tree that grows along water courses in the warm desert areas of America. ● Genus *Cercidium*, family Leguminosae.
– ORIGIN early 19th cent.: from Latin American Spanish, literally 'green tree'.

palp /palp/ (also **palpus**) ▶ **noun** (pl. **palps** or **palpi** /-pʌɪ, -piː/) Zoology each of a pair of elongated segmented appendages near the mouth of an arthropod, usually concerned with the senses of touch and taste.
– DERIVATIVES **palpal** **adjective**.
– ORIGIN mid 19th cent.: from Latin *palpus*, from *palpare* 'to feel'.

palpable /ˈpalpəb(ə)l/ ▶ **adjective** able to be touched or felt: *the palpable bump at the bridge of the nose*. ■ (of a feeling or atmosphere) so intense as to seem almost tangible: *a palpable sense of loss*. ■ plain to see or comprehend: *to talk of dawn raids in the circumstances is palpable nonsense*.
– DERIVATIVES **palpability** **noun**, **palpably** **adverb**.
– ORIGIN late Middle English: from late Latin *palpabilis*, from Latin *palpare* 'feel, touch gently'.

palpate /palˈpeɪt/ ▶ **verb** [with obj.] examine (a part of the body) by touch, especially for medical purposes.
– DERIVATIVES **palpation** **noun**.
– ORIGIN mid 19th cent. (earlier (late 15th cent.) as *palpation*): from Latin *palpat-* 'touched gently', from the verb *palpare*.

palpebral /ˈpalpɪbr(ə)l/ ▶ **adjective** Anatomy relating to the eyelids.
– ORIGIN mid 19th cent.: from late Latin *palpebralis*, from Latin *palpebra* 'eyelid'.

palpitant ▶ **adjective** literary palpitating.
– ORIGIN mid 19th cent.: from French, present participle of *palpiter*, from Latin *palpitare* 'continue to pat'.

palpitate /ˈpalpɪteɪt/ ▶ **verb 1** [no obj.] (often as adj. **palpitating**) (of the heart) beat rapidly, strongly, or irregularly.
2 shake; tremble: *she was palpitating with terror*.
– ORIGIN early 17th cent.: from Latin *palpitat-* 'patted', from the verb *palpitare*, frequentative of *palpare* 'touch gently'.

palpitation ▶ **noun** (usu. **palpitations**) a noticeably rapid, strong, or irregular heartbeat due to agitation, exertion, or illness.
– ORIGIN late Middle English: from Latin *palpitatio(n-)*, from the verb *palpitare* (see **palpitate**).

palpus /ˈpalpəs/ ▶ **noun** another term for **palp**.
– ORIGIN early 19th cent.: from Latin, literally 'feeler'.

palsgrave /ˈpɔːlzgreɪv/ ▶ **noun** historical a count palatine.
– ORIGIN mid 16th cent.: from early modern Dutch *paltsgrave*, from *palts* 'palatinate' + *grave* 'count'.

palstave /ˈpɔːlsteɪv/ ▶ **noun** Archaeology a type of chisel, typically made of bronze, which is shaped to fit into a split handle rather than having a socket for the handle.
– ORIGIN mid 19th cent.: from Danish *paalstav*, from Old Norse *pálstavr*, from *páll* 'hoe' (compare with Latin *palus* 'stake') + *stafr* 'staff'.

palsy /ˈpɔːlzi, ˈpɒl-/ ▶ **noun** (pl. **palsies**) [mass noun] dated paralysis, especially that which is accompanied by involuntary tremors: *a kind of palsy had seized him*. ■ archaic a condition of incapacity or helplessness.
▶ **verb** (**palsies**, **palsying**, **palsied**) [with obj.] affect with paralysis and involuntary tremors.
– ORIGIN Middle English: from Old French *paralisie*, from an alteration of Latin *paralysis* (see **paralysis**).

palsy-walsy ▶ **adjective** informal very friendly or intimate.
– ORIGIN 1930s (as a noun in the sense 'friend'): from the noun **pal** + **-sy**, by reduplication.

palter /ˈpɔːltə, ˈpɒl-/ ▶ **verb** [no obj.] archaic **1** equivocate or prevaricate in action or speech.
2 (**palter with**) trifle with: *this great work should not be paltered with*.
– ORIGIN mid 16th cent. (in the sense 'mumble or babble'): of unknown origin.

paltry ▶ **adjective** (**paltrier**, **paltriest**) (of an amount) very small or meagre: *she would earn a paltry £33 more a month*. ■ petty; trivial: *naval glory struck him as paltry*.
– DERIVATIVES **paltriness** **noun**.
– ORIGIN mid 16th cent.: apparently based on dialect *pelt* 'rubbish, especially rags'; compare with Low German *paltrig* 'ragged'.

paludal /pəˈl(j)uːd(ə)l, ˈpal(j)ʊd(ə)l/ ▶ **adjective** Ecology (of a plant, animal, or soil) living or occurring in a marshy habitat.
– ORIGIN early 19th cent.: from Latin *palus, palud-* 'marsh' + **-al**.

Paludrine /ˈpal(j)ʊdrɪn, -iːn/ ▶ **noun** trademark for **proguanil**.
– ORIGIN 1940s: from Latin *palus, palud-* 'marsh' + *-rine*, on the pattern of *Atabrine* and *mepacrine*.

paly /ˈpeɪli/ ▶ **adjective** Heraldry divided into equal vertical stripes: *paly of six, argent and gules*.
– ORIGIN late Middle English: from Old French *pale* 'divided by stakes', from *pal* 'pale, stake'.

palynology /ˌpalɪˈnɒlədʒi/ ▶ **noun** [mass noun] the study of pollen grains and other spores, especially as found in archaeological or geological deposits. Pollen extracted from such deposits may be used for radiocarbon dating and for studying past climates and environments by identifying plants then growing.
– DERIVATIVES **palynological** **adjective**, **palynologist** **noun**.
– ORIGIN 1940s: from Greek *palunein* 'sprinkle' + **-logy**.

Pama-Nyungan /ˌpɑːməˈnjʌŋgən/ ▶ **adjective** relating to or denoting the main family of Australian Aboriginal languages, covering much of the continent except for a northern fringe. Most have become extinct during the 20th century.
▶ **noun** [mass noun] the Pama-Nyungan family of languages.

Pamir Mountains /pəˈmɪə/ (also **the Pamirs**) a mountain system of central Asia, centred in Tajikistan and extending into Kyrgyzstan, Afghanistan, Pakistan, and western China. The highest peak in the Pamirs, Ismail Samani Peak in Tajikistan, rises to 7,495 m (24,590 ft).

pampas /ˈpampəs, -z/ ▶ **noun** [treated as sing. or pl.] large treeless plains in South America.
– ORIGIN early 18th cent.: via Spanish from Quechua *pampa* 'plain'.

pampas grass ▶ **noun** [mass noun] a tall South American grass with silky flowering plumes, widely grown as a specimen lawn plant. ● *Cortaderia selloana*, family Gramineae.

pampelmoes /ˌpamp(ə)lˈmuːs/ ▶ **noun** South African term for **pomelo**.
– ORIGIN Afrikaans.

pamper ▶ **verb** [with obj.] indulge with every attention, comfort, and kindness; spoil: *famous people just love being pampered*.
– ORIGIN late Middle English (in the sense 'cram with food'): probably of Low German or Dutch origin; compare with German dialect *pampfen* 'cram, gorge'; perhaps related to **pap**[1].

pampero /pamˈpɛːrəʊ/ ▶ **noun** (pl. **pamperos**) a strong, cold south westerly wind in South America, blowing from the Andes across the pampas towards the Atlantic.
– ORIGIN late 18th cent.: from Spanish *pampas* 'plain'.

pamphlet /ˈpamflɪt/ ▶ **noun** a small booklet or leaflet containing information or arguments about a single subject.
▶ **verb** (**pamphlets**, **pamphleting**, **pamphleted**) [with obj.] distribute pamphlets to.
– ORIGIN late Middle English: from *Pamphilet*, the familiar name of the 12th-cent. Latin love poem *Pamphilus, seu de Amore*.

pamphleteer ▶ **noun** a writer of pamphlets, especially ones of a political and controversial nature.
▶ **verb** [no obj.] (usu. as noun **pamphleteering**) write and issue political pamphlets.

Pamphylia /pamˈfɪlɪə/ an ancient coastal region of southern Asia Minor, between Lycia and Cilicia, to the east of the modern port of Antalya.
– DERIVATIVES **Pamphylian** **adjective & noun**.

Pamplona /pamˈpləʊnə/ a city in northern Spain, capital of the former kingdom and modern region of Navarre; pop. 197,275 (2008). It is noted for the fiesta of San Fermin, held there in July, which is celebrated with the running of bulls through the streets of the city.

P

Pan Greek Mythology a god of flocks and herds, typically represented with the horns, ears, and legs of a goat on a man's body. His sudden appearance was supposed to cause terror similar to that of a frightened and stampeding herd, and the word *panic* is derived from his name.
– ORIGIN probably originally in the sense 'the feeder' (i.e. herdsman), although the name was regularly associated with Greek *pas* or *pan* (= 'all'), giving rise to his identification as a god of nature or the universe.

pan[1] /pan/ ▸ **noun 1** a metal container used for cooking food in. ■ an amount of something contained in a pan: *a pan of hot water*.
2 a bowl or other container, in particular: ■ a bowl fitted at either end of a pair of scales. ■ Brit. the bowl of a toilet. ■ a large container used in a technical or manufacturing process for subjecting a material to heat or a mechanical or chemical process. ■ a steel drum. ■ a shallow bowl in which gold is separated from gravel and mud by agitation and washing. ■ a part of the lock that held the priming in old types of gun.
3 a hard stratum of compacted soil.
4 a hollow in the ground in which water may collect or in which a deposit of salt remains after water has evaporated.
5 US informal a person's face.
▸ **verb** (**pans, panning, panned**) [with obj.] **1** informal criticize severely: *the movie was panned by the critics.*
2 wash gravel in a pan to separate out (gold). ■ [no obj.] (**pan out**) (of gravel) yield gold.
– PHRASES **go down the pan** Brit. informal fail utterly: *the company went down the pan last year.*
– PHRASAL VERBS **pan out** end up; conclude: *he's happy with the way the deal panned out.* ■ turn out well: *Harold's idea had been a good one even if it hadn't panned out.*
– DERIVATIVES **panful** noun (pl. **panfuls**), **pan-like** adjective.
– ORIGIN Old English *panne*, of West Germanic origin; related to Dutch *pan*, German *Pfanne*, perhaps based on Latin *patina* 'dish'.

pan[2] /pan/ ▸ **verb** (**pans, panning, panned**) [with obj. and adverbial of direction] swing (a video or film camera) in a horizontal or vertical plane, typically to give a panoramic effect or follow a subject. ■ [no obj., with adverbial of direction] (of a camera) be swung in a horizontal or vertical plane: *the camera panned to the dead dictator.*
▸ **noun** a panning movement: *that slow pan over London.*
– PHRASES **pan and scan** a technique for narrowing the aspect ratio of a widescreen film to fit the squarer shape of a television screen by continuously selecting the most significant portion of the original picture, rather than just the middle portion.
– ORIGIN early 20th cent.: abbreviation of PANORAMA.

pan[3] /pɑːn/ ▸ **noun** variant spelling of PAAN.

pan- ▸ **combining form** all-inclusive, especially in relation to the whole of a continent, racial group, religion, etc.: *pan-African* | *pansexual*.
– ORIGIN from Greek *pan*, neuter of *pas* 'all'.

panacea /ˌpanəˈsiːə/ ▸ **noun** a solution or remedy for all difficulties or diseases: *the panacea for all corporate ills* | *the time-honoured panacea, cod liver oil.*
– DERIVATIVES **panacean** adjective.
– ORIGIN mid 16th cent.: via Latin from Greek *panakeia*, from *panakēs* 'all-healing', from *pan* 'all' + *akos* 'remedy'.

panache /pəˈnaʃ/ ▸ **noun 1** [mass noun] flamboyant confidence of style or manner: *he entertained London society with great panache.*
2 historical a tuft or plume of feathers, especially as a headdress or on a helmet.
– ORIGIN mid 16th cent.: from French, from Italian *pennacchio*, from late Latin *pinnaculum*, diminutive of *pinna* 'feather'.

panada /pəˈnɑːdə/ ▸ **noun** [mass noun] a simple dish consisting of bread boiled to a pulp and flavoured.
– ORIGIN late 16th cent.: from Spanish and Portuguese, based on Latin *panis* 'bread'.

Panadol ▸ **noun** trademark for PARACETAMOL.
– ORIGIN 1950s: of unknown origin.

pan-African ▸ **adjective** relating to all people of African birth or descent.

pan-Africanism ▸ **noun** [mass noun] the principle or advocacy of the political union of all the indigenous inhabitants of Africa.
– DERIVATIVES **pan-Africanist** noun.

Pan-Africanist Congress (in full **Pan-Africanist Congress of Azania**) (abbrev.: **PAC**) a South African political movement formed in 1959 as a militant offshoot of the African National Congress. It was outlawed in 1960 after the Sharpeville massacre, but continued its armed opposition to the South African government until it was legalized in 1990.

Panaji /ˈpʌnədʒi/ (also **Panjim**) a city in western India, a port on the Arabian Sea; pop. 59,200 (est. 2009). It is the capital of the state of Goa.

Panama /ˈpanəmɑː, ˌpanəˈmɑː/ a country in Central America; pop. 3,360,500 (est. 2009); official language, Spanish; capital, Panama City.

> Panama occupies the isthmus connecting North and South America. Colonized by Spain in the early 16th century, Panama was freed from imperial control in 1821, becoming a Colombian province. It gained full independence in 1903, although the construction of the Panama Canal and the leasing of the zone around it to the US (until 1979) split the country in two; the canal itself was ceded to Panama in 1999.

– DERIVATIVES **Panamanian** adjective & noun.

panama (also **panama hat**) ▸ **noun** a man's wide-brimmed hat of straw-like material, originally made from the leaves of a particular tropical palm tree.
– ORIGIN mid 19th cent.: named after the country of PANAMA.

Panama Canal a canal about 80 km (50 miles) long, across the Isthmus of Panama, connecting the Atlantic and Pacific Oceans. Its construction, begun by Ferdinand de Lesseps in 1881 but abandoned in 1889, was completed by the US between 1904 and 1914. Control of the canal remained with the US until 1999, at which date it was ceded to Panama.

Panama City the capital of Panama, situated on the Pacific coast close to the Panama Canal; pop. 425,600 (est. 2009).

Panama disease ▸ **noun** [mass noun] a fungal disease of bananas producing yellowing and wilting of the leaves. ● The fungus is *Fusarium oxysporum* (f. sp. *cubense*), subdivision Deuteromycotina.

Panamax ▸ **adjective** denoting a ship with a deadweight tonnage of not more than 69,000, the maximum size for a ship navigating the Panama canal.
– ORIGIN 1980s: blend of PANAMA and the adjective MAXIMUM.

pan-American ▸ **adjective** relating to, representing, or involving all the countries of North and South America.

pan-Americanism ▸ **noun** [mass noun] the principle or advocacy of political or commercial and cultural cooperation among all the countries of North and South America.

pan-and-tilt ▸ **adjective** denoting a stand, tripod, or other item of mounting equipment that allows a camera to move in both horizontal and vertical planes.

pan-Arabism ▸ **noun** [mass noun] the principle or advocacy of political alliance or union of all the Arab states.
– DERIVATIVES **pan-Arab** adjective.

panatella /ˌpanəˈtɛlə/ ▸ **noun** a long thin cigar.
– ORIGIN mid 19th cent.: from Latin American Spanish *panatela*, denoting a long thin biscuit, from Italian *panatello* 'small loaf', diminutive of *panata*.

Panay /pəˈnʌɪ/ an island in the central Philippines; pop. 3,403,900 (est. 2007); chief town, Iloilo.

pancake ▸ **noun 1** a thin, flat cake of batter, fried on both sides in a pan and typically rolled up with a sweet or savoury filling.
2 (also **pancake make-up**) [mass noun] make-up consisting of a flat solid layer of compressed powder, used especially in the theatre.
▸ **verb 1** (with reference to an aircraft) make or cause to make a pancake landing: [no obj.] *the plane landed, pancaking down on the runway.*
2 informal flatten or become flattened: [with obj.] *Hurley's car was pancaked.*
– PHRASES **(as) flat as a pancake** completely flat.
– ORIGIN late Middle English: from PAN[1] + CAKE.

Pancake Day ▸ **noun** Shrove Tuesday, when pancakes are traditionally eaten.

pancake landing ▸ **noun** an emergency landing in which an aircraft levels out close to the ground and drops vertically with its undercarriage still retracted.

pancake race ▸ **noun** a race in which each competitor must toss a pancake from a pan as they run, traditionally held in some places on Shrove Tuesday.

pancetta /panˈ(t)ʃɛtə/ ▸ **noun** [mass noun] Italian cured belly of pork.
– ORIGIN Italian, diminutive of *pancio* 'belly'.

panchakarma /ˌpʌntʃəˈkɑːmə/ ▸ **noun** (in Ayurvedic medicine) a fivefold detoxification treatment involving massage, herbal therapy, and other procedures.
– ORIGIN from Sanskrit *panca* 'five' + *karma* 'action'.

panchayat /pʌnˈtʃʌɪjət/ ▸ **noun** Indian a village council.
– ORIGIN from Hindi (originally denoting a council consisting of five members), from Sanskrit *panca* 'five' + *āyatta* 'depending upon'.

Panchen Lama /ˌpantʃ(ə)n ˈlɑːmə/ ▸ **noun** a Tibetan lama ranking next after the Dalai Lama.
– ORIGIN Tibetan *panchen*, abbreviation of *pandi-tachen-po* 'great learned one'; compare with PUNDIT.

panchromatic ▸ **adjective** Photography (of photographic film) sensitive to all visible colours of the spectrum. Often contrasted with ORTHOCHROMATIC.

pancreas /ˈpaŋkrɪəs/ ▸ **noun** (pl. **pancreases**) a large gland behind the stomach which secretes digestive enzymes into the duodenum. Embedded in the pancreas are the islets of Langerhans, which secrete into the blood the hormones insulin and glucagon.
– DERIVATIVES **pancreatic** adjective.
– ORIGIN late 16th cent.: modern Latin, from Greek *pankreas*, from *pan* 'all' + *kreas* 'flesh'.

pancreatectomy /ˌpaŋkrɪəˈtɛktəmi/ ▸ **noun** (pl. **pancreatectomies**) [mass noun] surgical removal of the pancreas.

pancreatic juice ▸ **noun** [mass noun] the clear alkaline digestive fluid secreted by the pancreas.

pancreatin /ˈpaŋkrɪətɪn/ ▸ **noun** [mass noun] a mixture of enzymes obtained from animal pancreases, given as a medicine to aid digestion.

pancreatitis /ˌpaŋkrɪəˈtʌɪtɪs/ ▸ **noun** [mass noun] Medicine inflammation of the pancreas.

pancreozymin /ˌpaŋkrɪə(ʊ)ˈzʌɪmɪn/ ▸ **noun** [mass noun] Biochemistry a hormone which stimulates the production of enzymes by the pancreas.

pancytopenia /ˌpansʌɪtə(ʊ)ˈpiːnɪə/ ▸ **noun** [mass noun] Medicine deficiency of all three cellular components of the blood (red cells, white cells, and platelets).
– ORIGIN 1940s: from PAN- 'all' + CYTO- 'cell' + Greek *penia* 'poverty, lack'.

panda[1] /ˈpandə/ (also **giant panda**) ▸ **noun** a large bear-like mammal with characteristic black-and-white markings, native to certain mountain forests in China. It feeds almost entirely on bamboo and has become increasingly rare. See also RED PANDA.
● *Ailuropoda melanoleuca*; it is now usually placed with the bears (family Ursidae), but was formerly thought to belong with the raccoons (family Procyonidae).
– ORIGIN mid 19th cent.: from Nepali.

panda[2] /ˈpʌndə/ ▸ **noun** a Brahmin expert in genealogy, who provides religious guidance and acts as a family priest.
– ORIGIN via Hindi from Sanskrit *paṇḍita* 'learned, wise'.

panda car ▸ **noun** Brit. informal a small police patrol car (originally black and white or blue and white).

pandal /ˈpand(ə)l, panˈdɑːl/ ▸ **noun** Indian a marquee.
– ORIGIN from Tamil *pantal*.

pandanus /panˈdeɪnəs, -ˈdan-/ (also **pandan**) ▸ **noun** a tropical tree or shrub with a twisted and branched stem, stilt roots, spiral tufts of long, narrow spiny leaves, and fibrous edible fruit. Also called SCREW PINE. ● Genus *Pandanus*, family Pandanaceae.
■ [mass noun] fibre from the leaves of the pandanus, often woven into a material for roofing, mats, etc.
– ORIGIN modern Latin, from Malay *pandan*.

Pandarus /ˈpandərəs/ Greek Mythology a Lycian fighting on the side of the Trojans, described in the *Iliad* as breaking the truce with the Greeks by wounding Menelaus with an arrow. The role as the lovers' go-between that he plays in Chaucer's (and later Shakespeare's) story of Troilus and Cressida originated with Boccaccio and is also the origin of the word *pander*.

pandect /ˈpandɛkt/ ▸ **noun** chiefly historical a complete body of the laws of a country. ■ (usu. **the Pandects**) a compendium in 50 books of the Roman civil law made by order of Justinian in the 6th century.
– ORIGIN mid 16th cent.: from French *pandecte*, from Latin *pandecta*, from Greek *pandektēs* 'all-receiver', from *pan* 'all' + *dektēs* (from *dekhesthai* 'receive').

pandemic /panˈdɛmɪk/ ▸ **adjective** (of a disease) prevalent over a whole country or the world.
▸ **noun** an outbreak of a pandemic disease.
– ORIGIN mid 17th cent.: from Greek *pandēmos* (from *pan* 'all' + *dēmos* 'people') + -IC.

P

pandemonium /ˌpandɪˈməʊnɪəm/ ▶ **noun** [mass noun] wild and noisy disorder or confusion; uproar: *there was complete pandemonium—everyone just panicked.*
– ORIGIN mid 17th cent.: modern Latin (denoting the place of all demons, in Milton's *Paradise Lost*), from **PAN-** 'all' + Greek *daimōn* 'demon'.

pander ▶ **verb** [no obj.] (**pander to**) gratify or indulge (an immoral or distasteful desire or taste or a person with such a desire or taste): *newspapers are pandering to people's baser instincts.*
▶ **noun** dated a pimp. ■ archaic a person who assists the immoral desires or evil designs of others: *the lowest panders of a venal press.*
– ORIGIN late Middle English (as a noun): from *Pandare*, the name of a character in Chaucer's *Troilus and Criseyde* (see **PANDARUS**). The verb dates from the early 17th cent.

Pandit /ˈpʌndɪt/, Vijaya (Lakshmi) (1900–90), Indian politician and diplomat, sister of Jawaharlal Nehru. Having been imprisoned three times by the British for nationalist activities, after independence she became the first woman to serve as president of the UN General Assembly (1953–4).

pandit (also **pundit**) ▶ **noun** a Hindu scholar learned in Sanskrit and Hindu philosophy and religion, typically also a practising priest. ■ Indian a wise man or teacher. ■ Indian a talented musician (used as a respectful title or form of address).

Pandora Greek Mythology the first mortal woman. In one story she was created by Zeus and sent to earth with a jar or box of evils in revenge for Prometheus' having brought the gift of fire back to the world. She let out all the evils from the container to infect the earth; hope alone remained to assuage the lot of humankind.
– ORIGIN from the Greek name *Pandōra* 'all-gifted' (from *pan* 'all' + *dōron* 'gift').

pandora (also **pandora shell** or **Pandora's box shell**) ▶ **noun** a burrowing bivalve mollusc with a fragile shell, the unequal valves of which form a 'box' with a lid. ● Genus *Pandora*, family Pandoridae.
– ORIGIN modern Latin, from Greek *pandoura* 'three-stringed lute' (because of the shell's resemblance to the soundbox of a stringed instrument).

Pandora's box ▶ **noun** a process that once begun generates many complicated problems: *these policies might open a Pandora's box of inflationary wage claims.*

pandowdy /panˈdaʊdi/ ▶ **noun** (pl. **pandowdies**) N. Amer. a kind of spiced apple pudding baked in a deep dish.
– ORIGIN mid 19th cent.: of unknown origin.

pane ▶ **noun 1** a single sheet of glass in a window or door. ■ Computing a separate defined area within a window for the display of, or interaction with, a specified part of that window's application or output.
2 a sheet or page of stamps.
– ORIGIN late Middle English (originally denoting a piece of something, such as a fence or strip of cloth): from Old French *pan*, from Latin *pannus* 'piece of cloth'.

paneer /pəˈnɪə/ (also **panir**) ▶ **noun** [mass noun] a type of milk curd cheese used in Indian, Iranian, and Afghan cooking.
– ORIGIN from Hindi or Persian *panīr* 'cheese'.

panegyric /ˌpanɪˈdʒɪrɪk/ ▶ **noun** a public speech or published text in praise of someone or something: *a panegyric on the pleasures of malt whisky.*
– DERIVATIVES **panegyrical** adjective.
– ORIGIN early 17th cent.: from French *panégyrique*, via Latin from Greek *panēgurikos* 'of public assembly', from *pan* 'all' + *aguris* 'agora, assembly'.

panegyrize /ˈpanɪdʒɪrʌɪz/ (also **panegyrise**) ▶ **verb** [with obj.] archaic speak or write in praise of; eulogize.
– DERIVATIVES **panegyrist** noun.

panel ▶ **noun 1** a typically rectangular piece of wood or glass forming or set into the surface of a door, wall, or ceiling. ■ a thin piece of metal forming part of the outer shell of a vehicle: *body panels for the car trade.* ■ a piece of material forming part of a garment. ■ a decorated area within a larger design containing a separate subject: *the central panel depicts the Crucifixion.* ■ one of several drawings making up a cartoon strip.
2 a flat board on which instruments or controls are fixed: *a control panel.*
3 a small group of people brought together to investigate or decide on a particular matter: *an interview panel.* ■ Brit. a list of medical practitioners registered in a district as accepting patients under the National Health Service or, formerly, the National Insurance Act. ■ chiefly N. Amer. a list of available jurors or a jury.
4 Scots Law a person or people charged with an offence.
▶ **verb** (**panels**, **panelling**, **panelled**; US **panels**, **paneling**, **paneled**) [with obj.] (usu. as adj. **panelled**) cover (a wall or other surface) with panels: *panelled rooms.*
– ORIGIN Middle English: from Old French, literally 'piece of cloth', based on Latin *pannus* '(piece of) cloth'. The early sense 'piece of parchment' was extended to mean 'list', whence the notion 'advisory group'. Sense 1 of the noun derives from the late Middle English sense 'distinct section of a surface'.

panel beater ▶ **noun** Brit. a person whose job is to beat out the bodywork of motor vehicles.

panel game ▶ **noun** Brit. a broadcast quiz played by a panel or team of people.

panel heating ▶ **noun** [mass noun] a system of heating rooms by panels in the walls and ceiling that contain hot-water pipes or another source of heat.

panelling (US **paneling**) ▶ **noun** [mass noun] panels collectively, when used to decorate a wall.

panellist (US **panelist**) ▶ **noun** a member of a panel, especially in a broadcast game or discussion.

panel pin ▶ **noun** Brit. a light, thin nail with a very small head.

panel saw ▶ **noun** Brit. a light saw with small teeth, for cutting thin wood.

panel study ▶ **noun** an investigation of attitude changes using a constant set of people and comparing each individual's opinions at different times.

panel truck ▶ **noun** N. Amer. a small enclosed delivery truck.

panel van ▶ **noun** Austral./NZ & S. African a small van, especially one without windows and passenger seats.

panentheism /panˈɛnθiːɪz(ə)m/ ▶ **noun** [mass noun] the belief or doctrine that God is greater than the universe and includes and interpenetrates it.
– DERIVATIVES **panentheistic** adjective.

panettone /ˌpanɪˈtəʊneɪ, -ni/ ▶ **noun** (pl. **panettoni** /ˌpanɪˈtəʊni/) a rich Italian bread made with eggs, fruit, and butter and typically eaten at Christmas.
– ORIGIN Italian, from *panetto* 'cake', diminutive of *pane* 'bread' (from Latin *panis* 'bread').

panfish N. Amer. ▶ **noun** (pl. **same** or **panfishes**) a fish suitable for frying whole in a pan, especially one caught by an angler rather than bought.
▶ **verb** [no obj.] (often as noun **panfishing**) fish for panfish.

panforte /panˈfɔːteɪ, -ti/, Italian /panˈfɔorte/ ▶ **noun** [mass noun] a hard, spicy Sienese cake containing nuts, candied peel, and honey.
– ORIGIN Italian, from *pane* 'bread' + *forte* 'strong'.

pan-fry ▶ **verb** [with obj.] (often as adj. **pan-fried**) fry in a pan in shallow fat: *pan-fried trout.*

pang ▶ **noun** a sudden sharp pain or painful emotion: *Lindsey experienced a sharp pang of guilt | the snack bar will keep those hunger pangs at bay.*
– ORIGIN late 15th cent.: perhaps an alteration of **PRONG**.

panga /ˈpaŋgə/ ▶ **noun** a bladed African tool like a machete.
– ORIGIN Kiswahili.

Pangaea /panˈdʒiːə/ a vast continental area or supercontinent comprising all the continental crust of the earth, which is postulated to have existed in late Palaeozoic and Mesozoic times before breaking up into Gondwana and Laurasia.
– ORIGIN early 20th cent.: from **PAN-** 'all' + Greek *gaia* 'earth'.

pan-German ▶ **adjective** relating to or advocating pan-Germanism.
– DERIVATIVES **pan-Germanic** adjective.

pan-Germanism ▶ **noun** [mass noun] the idea or principle of a political unification of all Europeans speaking German or a Germanic language.

Pangloss /ˈpaŋglɒs/ ▶ **noun** a person who is optimistic regardless of the circumstances.
– DERIVATIVES **Panglossian** adjective.
– ORIGIN mid 19th cent.: from the name of the tutor and philosopher in Voltaire's *Candide* (1759).

pangolin /paŋˈgəʊlɪn/ ▶ **noun** an African and Asian mammal that has a body covered with horny overlapping scales, a small head with an elongated snout, a long sticky tongue for catching ants and termites, and a tapering tail. Also called **SCALY ANTEATER**. ● Family Manidae and order Pholidota: genera *Manis* (three species in Asia) and *Phataginus* (four species in Africa).
– ORIGIN late 18th cent.: from Malay *peng-guling*, literally 'roller' (from its habit of rolling into a ball).

pangram /ˈpangram/ ▶ **noun** a sentence containing every letter of the alphabet.
– ORIGIN late 19th cent.: from **PAN-** + **-GRAM**[1], after **ANAGRAM**.

panhandle N. Amer. ▶ **noun** [often in place names] a narrow strip of territory projecting from the main territory of one state into another: *the Oklahoma Panhandle.*
▶ **verb** [no obj.] informal beg in the street. ■ [with obj.] beg for something from (someone) in the street.
– DERIVATIVES **panhandler** noun.

Panhellenic /ˌpanhɛˈlɛnɪk, -hɛˈliː-/ ▶ **adjective** of or representing all people of Greek origin or ancestry. ■ relating to, advocating, or denoting the idea of a political union of all Greeks.

panic[1] ▶ **noun** [mass noun] sudden uncontrollable fear or anxiety, often causing wildly unthinking behaviour: *she hit him in panic* | [in sing.] *he ran to the library in a blind panic.* ■ [count noun] a state of widespread financial alarm provoking hasty action: *he caused an economic panic by his sudden resignation* | [as modifier] *panic selling.* ■ [count noun] informal a frenzied hurry to do something.
▶ **verb** (**panics**, **panicking**, **panicked**) feel or cause to feel panic: [no obj.] *the crowd panicked and stampeded for the exit* | [with obj.] *talk of love panicked her.* ■ [with obj.] (**panic someone into**) drive someone through panic into (hasty action): *we are not going to be panicked into a decision.*
– PHRASES **panic stations** Brit. informal a state of alarm or emergency: *many people were at panic stations because of popular unrest.*
– DERIVATIVES **panicky** adjective.
– ORIGIN early 17th cent.: from French *panique*, from modern Latin *panicus*, from Greek *panikos*, from the name of the god **PAN**, noted for causing terror, to whom woodland noises were attributed.

panic[2] (also **panic grass**) ▶ **noun** [mass noun] a cereal and fodder grass of a group including millet. ● *Panicum* and related genera, family Gramineae.
– ORIGIN late Middle English: from Latin *panicum*, from *panus* 'ear of millet' (literally 'thread wound on a bobbin'), based on Greek *pēnos* 'web', *pēnion* 'bobbin'.

panic attack ▶ **noun** a sudden overwhelming feeling of acute and disabling anxiety.

panic button ▶ **noun** a button for summoning help in an emergency.
– PHRASES **press** (or **push** or **hit**) **the panic button** informal respond to a situation by panicking or taking emergency measures.

panicle /ˈpanɪk(ə)l/ ▶ **noun** Botany a loose branching cluster of flowers, as in oats.
– DERIVATIVES **panicled** adjective.
– ORIGIN late 16th cent.: from Latin *panicula*, diminutive of *panus* 'ear of millet' (see **PANIC**[2]).

panic-monger ▶ **noun** a person who fosters a panic.
– DERIVATIVES **panic-mongering** noun.

panic room ▶ **noun** a secret room in a house or other building that is designed to be invulnerable to attack or intrusion.

panic-stricken (also **panic-struck**) ▶ **adjective** affected with panic; very frightened: *the panic-stricken victims rushed out of their blazing homes.*

pan-Indian ▶ **adjective 1** relating to the whole of India, or to all its ethnic, religious, or linguistic groups.
2 denoting or relating to a cultural movement or religious practice participated in by many or all American Indian peoples.

Panini /ˈpɑːnɪni/, Indian grammarian. Sources vary as to when he lived, with dates ranging from the 4th to the 7th century BC. He is noted as the author of the *Ashtadhyayi*, a grammar of Sanskrit.

panini /pəˈniːni/ (also **panino** /-nəʊ/) ▶ **noun** (pl. **same** or **paninis** /-niːz/) a sandwich made with Italian bread, usually toasted.
– ORIGIN Italian *panino*, literally 'bread roll'.

pani puri /ˈpɑːniː ˌpuːri/ ▶ **plural noun** (in Indian cookery) fried puff-pastry balls filled with spiced mashed potato, spiced water, and tamarind juice.
– ORIGIN from Hindi *pānī* 'water' and *pūrī* from Sanskrit *pūrikā* 'small, fried wheaten cake'.

panir ▶ **noun** variant spelling of **PANEER**.

Panjabi ▶ **noun** (pl. **Panjabis**) & **adjective** variant spelling of **PUNJABI**.

P

panjandrum /panˈdʒandrəm/ ▶ **noun** a person who has or claims to have a great deal of authority or influence.
– ORIGIN late 19th cent.: from *Grand Panjandrum*, an invented phrase in a nonsense verse (1755) by S. Foote.

Panjim /ˈpʌnʒɪm/ another name for **PANAJI**.

Pankhurst /ˈpaŋkhəːst/, Mrs Emmeline (1858–1928), Christabel (1880–1958), and (Estelle) Sylvia (1882–1960), English suffragettes. In 1903 Emmeline and her daughters founded the Women's Social and Political Union, with the motto 'Votes for Women'. Following the imprisonment of Christabel in 1905, Emmeline initiated the militant suffragette campaign which continued until the outbreak of the First World War.

pan loaf ▶ **noun** Scottish & Irish a loaf baked in a pan or tin.

panmixia /panˈmɪksɪə/ ▶ **noun** [mass noun] Zoology random mating within a breeding population.
– DERIVATIVES **panmictic adjective**.
– ORIGIN late 19th cent.: modern Latin, from German *Panmixie*, from Greek *pan* 'all' + *mixis* 'mixing'.

panna cotta /ˌpanə ˈkɒtə/ ▶ **noun** a cold Italian dessert made with double cream, often served with caramel syrup.
– ORIGIN Italian, literally 'cooked cream'.

pannage /ˈpanɪdʒ/ ▶ **noun** [mass noun] chiefly historical the right of feeding pigs or other animals in a wood. ■ pasturage for pigs in woodland.
– ORIGIN late Middle English: from Old French *pasnage*, from medieval Latin *pastionaticum*, from *pastio(n-)* 'pasturing', from the verb *pascere* 'to feed'.

panne /pan/ (also **panne velvet**) ▶ **noun** [mass noun] a glossy fabric resembling velvet, made of silk or rayon and having a flattened pile.
– ORIGIN late 18th cent.: from French, of unknown origin.

pannier ▶ **noun 1** a basket, especially one of a pair carried by a beast of burden. ■ each of a pair of bags or boxes fitted on either side of the rear wheel of a bicycle or motorcycle.
2 historical part of a skirt looped up round the hips. ■ a frame supporting a pannier of a skirt.
– ORIGIN Middle English: from Old French *panier*, from Latin *panarium* 'bread basket', from *panis* 'bread'.

pannier tank ▶ **noun** a small steam locomotive with an overhanging rectilinear water tank along each side of the boiler.

pannikin ▶ **noun** a small metal drinking cup.
– ORIGIN early 19th cent.: from **PAN**[1], on the pattern of *cannikin*.

pannikin boss ▶ **noun** Austral./NZ informal a minor overseer or foreman.

pannist ▶ **noun** W. Indian a person who plays a pan (steel drum) in a steel band.

Pannonia /pəˈnəʊnɪə/ an ancient country and former province of the Roman Empire lying south and west of the Danube, in present-day Austria, Hungary, Slovenia, and Croatia. It lost its separate identity after the Romans withdrew at the end of the 4th century.
– DERIVATIVES **Pannonian noun & adjective**.

pannus /ˈpanəs/ ▶ **noun** [mass noun] Medicine a condition in which a layer of vascular fibrous tissue extends over the surface of an organ or other specialized anatomical structure, especially the cornea.
– ORIGIN late Middle English: perhaps from Latin, literally 'cloth'.

panoply /ˈpanəpli/ ▶ **noun** an extensive or impressive collection: *a deliciously inventive panoply of insults*. ■ a splendid display: *I leaned forward to take in the full panoply of tourist London*. ■ historical or literary a complete suit of armour.
– DERIVATIVES **panoplied adjective**.
– ORIGIN late 16th cent. (in the sense 'complete protection for spiritual warfare', often with biblical allusion to Eph. 6:11, 13): from French *panoplie* or modern Latin *panoplia* 'full armour', from Greek, from *pan* 'all' + *hopla* 'arms'.

panoptic /panˈɒptɪk/ ▶ **adjective** showing or seeing the whole at one view: *a panoptic aerial view*.
– ORIGIN early 19th cent.: from Greek *panoptos* 'seen by all', from *panoptēs* 'all-seeing' + **-IC**.

panopticon /panˈɒptɪk(ə)n/ ▶ **noun** historical a circular prison with cells arranged around a central well, from which prisoners could at all times be observed.
– ORIGIN mid 18th cent.: from **PAN-** 'all' + Greek *optikon*, neuter of *optikos* 'optic'.

panorama ▶ **noun** an unbroken view of the whole region surrounding an observer: *the tower offers a wonderful panorama of Prague*. ■ a picture or photograph containing a wide view. ■ a complete survey or presentation of a subject.
– ORIGIN late 18th cent.: from **PAN-** 'all' + Greek *horama* 'view' (from *horan* 'see').

panoramic ▶ **adjective** (of a view or picture) with a wide view surrounding the observer; sweeping: *on a clear day there are panoramic views*. ■ including all aspects of a subject; wide-ranging: *his panoramic vision of post-World War I peace*.
– DERIVATIVES **panoramically adverb**.

pan-pan ▶ **noun** an international radio distress signal, of less urgency than a mayday signal.
– ORIGIN 1920s: *pan* from French *panne* 'breakdown'.

pan pipes ▶ **plural noun** a musical instrument made from a row of short pipes of varying length fixed together and played by blowing across the top.
– ORIGIN originally associated with the Greek rural god **PAN**.

panpsychism /panˈsʌɪkɪz(ə)m/ ▶ **noun** [mass noun] the doctrine or belief that everything material, however small, has an element of individual consciousness.
– DERIVATIVES **panpsychist adjective & noun**.

pansexual ▶ **adjective** not limited or inhibited in sexual choice with regard to gender or activity.
▶ **noun** a pansexual person.
– DERIVATIVES **pansexuality noun**.

pansified /ˈpanzɪfʌɪd/ ▶ **adjective** informal, derogatory markedly effeminate or affected.

pan-Slavism /panˈslɑːvɪz(ə)m/ ▶ **noun** [mass noun] the principle or advocacy of the union of all Slavs or all Slavic peoples in one political organization.
– DERIVATIVES **pan-Slavist adjective & noun**.

panspermia /panˈspəːmɪə/ ▶ **noun** [mass noun] the theory that life on the earth originated from microorganisms or chemical precursors of life present in outer space and able to initiate life on reaching a suitable environment.
– ORIGIN mid 19th cent.: from Greek, from *panspermos* 'containing all kinds of seed'.

panstick ▶ **noun** [mass noun] a kind of matt cosmetic foundation in stick form, widely used in theatrical make-up.
– ORIGIN 1940s: from **PANCAKE** + **STICK**[1].

pansy ▶ **noun** (pl. **pansies**) **1** a cultivated variety of viola with brightly coloured flowers. ● Genus *Viola*, family Violaceae: several species and hybrids, in particular *V.* × *wittrockiana*.
2 informal, derogatory an effeminate or homosexual man.
3 S. African a sand dollar with a flower-like purple marking on the shell. ● *Echinodiscus bisperforatus*, class Echinoidea.
– ORIGIN late Middle English: from French *pensée* 'thought, pansy', from *penser* 'think', from Latin *pensare*, frequentative of *pendere* 'weigh, consider'.

pant ▶ **verb** [no obj.] **1** breathe with short, quick breaths, typically from exertion or excitement: *he was panting when he reached the top*. ■ [with direct speech] say something breathlessly: *'We'll never have time,' she panted*.
2 long for or to do something: *the opening song makes you* **pant for** *more*. ■ literary (of the heart or chest) throb or heave from strong emotions.
▶ **noun 1** a short, quick breath.
2 literary a throb or heave of a person's heart or chest.
– ORIGIN Middle English: related to Old French *pantaisier* 'be agitated, gasp', based on Greek *phantasioun* 'cause to imagine', from *phantasia* (see **FANTASY**).

Pantagruelian /ˌpantəgruːˈɛlɪən/ ▶ **adjective** rare enormous: *a Pantagruelian banquet*.
– ORIGIN late 17th cent.: from *Pantagruel* (the name of an enormous giant in Rabelais's novel *Pantagruel* (1532)) + **-IAN**.

pantalettes (N. Amer. also **pantalets**) ▶ **plural noun** long underpants with a frill at the bottom of each leg, worn by women and girls in the 19th century.

pantaloon ▶ **noun 1** (**pantaloons**) women's baggy trousers gathered at the ankles. ■ historical men's close-fitting breeches fastened below the calf or at the foot.
2 (**Pantaloon**) a Venetian character in Italian commedia dell'arte represented as a foolish old man wearing pantaloons.
– ORIGIN late 16th cent. (in sense 2): from French *pantalon*, from the Italian name *Pantalone* 'Pantaloon'.

Pantanal /ˌpantəˈnɑːl/ a vast region of tropical swampland in the upper reaches of the Paraguay River in SW Brazil.

pantec (also **pantech**) ▶ **noun** Austral./NZ informal a container trailer forming the rear part of an articulated lorry.
– ORIGIN 1970s: abbreviation of **PANTECHNICON**.

pantechnicon /panˈtɛknɪk(ə)n/ ▶ **noun** Brit. a large van for transporting furniture.
– ORIGIN mid 19th cent.: from **PAN-** 'all' + *tekhnikon* 'piece of art', originally the name of a bazaar in London for all kinds of artistic work, later converted into a furniture warehouse.

Pantelleria /ˌpantɛləˈrɪə/ a volcanic Italian island in the Mediterranean, situated between Sicily and the coast of Tunisia. It was used as a place of exile by the ancient Romans, who called it Cossyra.

Panthalassa /ˌpanθəˈlasə/ a universal sea or single ocean, such as would have surrounded the postulated supercontinent of Pangaea.
– ORIGIN late 19th cent.: from **PAN-** 'all' + Greek *thalassa* 'sea'.

pantheism /ˈpanθiːɪz(ə)m/ ▶ **noun** [mass noun] **1** a doctrine which identifies God with the universe, or regards the universe as a manifestation of God.
2 the worship or tolerance of many gods.
– DERIVATIVES **pantheist noun**, **pantheistic adjective**, **pantheistically adverb**.
– ORIGIN mid 18th cent.: from **PAN-** 'all' + Greek *theos* 'god' + **-ISM**.

pantheon /ˈpanθɪən/ ▶ **noun 1** all the gods of a people or religion collectively: *the deities of the Hindu pantheon*. ■ (especially in ancient Greece and Rome) a temple dedicated to all the gods.
2 a group of famous or important people: *the pantheon of the all-time greats*. ■ a building in which the illustrious dead of a nation are buried or honoured.
– ORIGIN late Middle English (referring especially to the Pantheon, a large circular temple in Rome): via Latin from Greek *pantheion*, from *pan* 'all' + *theion* 'holy' (from *theos* 'god').

panther ▶ **noun** a leopard, especially a black one. ■ N. Amer. a puma or a jaguar.
– ORIGIN Middle English: from Old French *pantere*, from Latin *panthera*, from Greek *panthēr*. In Latin, *pardus* 'leopard' also existed; the two terms led to confusion: until the mid 19th cent. many taxonomists regarded the panther and the leopard as separate species.

panther cap ▶ **noun** a poisonous toadstool which has a brownish-grey cap with fluffy white spots and white gills, found in woodland in both Eurasia and North America. ● *Amanita pantherina*, family Amanitaceae, class Hymenomycetes.

panties ▶ **plural noun** informal legless underpants worn by women and girls; knickers.

pantihose ▶ **plural noun** variant spelling of **PANTYHOSE**.

pantile /ˈpantʌɪl/ ▶ **noun** a roof tile curved to form an S-shaped section, fitted to overlap its neighbour.
– DERIVATIVES **pantiled adjective**.
– ORIGIN mid 17th cent.: from **PAN**[1] + **TILE**, probably suggested by Dutch *dakpan*, literally 'roof pan'.

panting ▶ **adjective** breathing with short, quick breaths; out of breath: *a panting dog*.
– DERIVATIVES **pantingly adverb**.

Pantisocracy /ˌpantɪˈsɒkrəsi/ ▶ **noun** [mass noun] a form of utopian social organization in which all are equal in social position and responsibility.
– DERIVATIVES **Pantisocratic adjective**.
ORIGIN late 18th cent.: from **PANTO-** 'all' + Greek *isokratia* 'equality of power'.

panto ▶ **noun** (pl. **pantos**) Brit. informal short for **PANTOMIME** (sense 1 of the noun).

panto- ▶ **combining form** all; universal: *pantograph* | *pantomime*.
– ORIGIN from Greek *pas*, *pant-* 'all'.

Pantocrator /panˈtɒkrətə/ ▶ **noun** a title of Christ represented as the ruler of the universe, especially in Byzantine church decoration.
– ORIGIN late 19th cent.: via Latin from Greek, 'ruler over all'.

pantograph ▶ **noun 1** an instrument for copying a plan or drawing on a different scale by a system of hinged and jointed rods.
2 a jointed framework conveying a current to a train, tram, or other electric vehicle from overhead wires.
– DERIVATIVES **pantographic adjective**.
– ORIGIN early 18th cent.: from **PANTO-** 'all, universal' + Greek *-graphos* 'writing'.

pantomime ▶ noun **1** Brit. a theatrical entertainment, mainly for children, which involves music, topical jokes, and slapstick comedy and is based on a fairy tale or nursery story, usually produced around Christmas.
2 a dramatic entertainment, originating in Roman mime, in which performers express meaning through gestures accompanied by music.
3 an absurdly exaggerated piece of behaviour: *he made a pantomime of checking his watch.* ■ an absurd or confused situation: *the drive to town was a pantomime.*
▶ verb [with obj.] express or represent by exaggerated mime: *they pantomimed picking up dropped food.*
– DERIVATIVES **pantomimic** adjective.
– ORIGIN late 16th cent. (first used in the Latin form and denoting an actor using mime): from French *pantomime* or Latin *pantomimus*, from Greek *pantomimos* 'imitator of all' (see PANTO-, MIME).

pantomime dame ▶ noun Brit. see DAME.

pantomime horse ▶ noun Brit. a comic character in the form of a horse, played by two actors in one costume, one providing the front legs and operating the head, the other providing the back legs.

Pantone ▶ noun [usu. as modifier] trademark a system for matching colours, used in specifying printing inks: *Pantone colours.*
– ORIGIN 1960s: an invented name.

pantothenate /ˌpantə(ʊ)ˈθɛneɪt/ ▶ noun Chemistry a salt or ester of pantothenic acid.

pantothenic acid /ˌpantəˈθɛnɪk/ ▶ noun [mass noun] Biochemistry a vitamin of the B complex, found in rice, bran, and many other foods, and essential for the oxidation of fats and carbohydrates.
– ORIGIN 1930s: *pantothenic* from Greek *pantothen* 'from every side' (with allusion to its widespread occurrence).

pantoum /panˈtuːm/ (also **pantun**) ▶ noun a Malay verse form, also imitated in French and English, with a rhyme scheme *abab*.
– ORIGIN late 18th cent.: Malay *pantun*.

pantry ▶ noun (pl. **pantries**) a small room or cupboard in which food, crockery, and cutlery are kept.
– ORIGIN Middle English: from Anglo-Norman French *panterie*, from *paneter* 'baker', based on late Latin *panarius* 'bread seller', from Latin *panis* 'bread'.

pantryman ▶ noun (pl. **pantrymen**) a butler or a butler's assistant.

pants ▶ plural noun **1** Brit. underpants or knickers.
2 chiefly N. Amer. trousers: *corduroy pants* | (as modifier **pant**) *wide pant legs.*
3 Brit. informal rubbish; nonsense: *he thought we were going to be absolute pants.*
– PHRASES **catch someone with their pants** (or **trousers**) **down** informal catch someone in an embarrassingly unprepared state. **fly** (or **drive**) **by the seat of one's pants** informal rely on instinct rather than logic or knowledge. **scare** (or **bore** etc.) **the pants off someone** informal make someone extremely scared (or bored etc.).
– ORIGIN mid 19th cent.: abbreviation of *pantaloons* (see PANTALOON).

pantsuit (also **pants suit**) ▶ noun N. Amer. a trouser suit.

pantsula /pantˈsuːlə/ ▶ noun (pl. **pantsulas** or **mapantsula**) S. African informal **1** a fashionable young urban black person, especially a man.
2 [mass noun] a dance style in which each person performs a solo turn within a circle of dancers doing a repetitive, shuffling step.
– ORIGIN perhaps related to Zulu *p(h)ansula* 'strike sharply (with a whip)', with reference to elements of the dance style.

pantun /panˈtuːn/ ▶ noun variant spelling of PANTOUM.

panty girdle (also **pantie girdle**) ▶ noun a woman's control undergarment with a crotch shaped like pants.

pantyhose (also **pantihose**) ▶ plural noun N. Amer. women's thin nylon tights.

pantywaist N. Amer. informal ▶ noun a feeble or effeminate man.
▶ adjective [attrib.] effeminate or feeble.
– ORIGIN 1930s: extended use of the term's literal sense 'child's garment consisting of panties attached to a bodice'.

panzanella /ˌpanzəˈnɛlə, ˌpantsə-/ ▶ noun [mass noun] a type of Tuscan salad made with anchovies, chopped salad vegetables, and bread soaked in dressing.
– ORIGIN Italian, from *pane* 'bread' + *zanella* 'small basket'.

panzer /ˈpanzə/ ▶ noun [usu. as modifier] a German armoured unit: *panzer divisions.*
– ORIGIN from German *Panzer*, literally 'coat of mail'.

pap¹ ▶ noun [mass noun] **1** bland soft or semi-liquid food such as that suitable for babies or invalids: *a trayful of tasteless pap.* ■ (in Africa and the Caribbean) porridge, usually made with maize meal.
2 worthless or trivial reading matter or entertainment: *limitless channels serving up an undemanding diet of pap.*
▶ adjective S. African (of food) lacking flavour and firmness. ■ (of a person) lacking physical or emotional strength; feeble. ■ (of an inflatable object) underinflated; flat.
– ORIGIN late Middle English: probably from Middle Low German, Middle Dutch *pappe*, probably based on Latin *pappare* 'eat'.

pap² ▶ noun archaic or dialect a woman's breast or nipple.
– ORIGIN Middle English: probably of Scandinavian origin, from a base imitative of the sound of sucking.

pap³ informal ▶ noun a paparazzo.
▶ verb (**paps, papping, papped**) [with obj.] take a photograph of (a celebrity) without permission: *she can't go to the gym or pop to the shops without being papped.*

papa /pəˈpɑː, ˈpɑːpə/ ▶ noun **1** N. Amer. or dated one's father.
2 a code word representing the letter P, used in radio communication.
– ORIGIN late 17th cent.: from French, via late Latin from Greek *papas*.

papabile /pəˈpɑːbɪleɪ, -li/ ▶ adjective worthy of being or eligible to be pope.
– ORIGIN Italian, from Latin *papa* 'pope'.

papacy /ˈpeɪpəsi/ ▶ noun (pl. **papacies**) [usu. in sing.] the office or authority of the Pope. ■ the tenure of office of a pope: *during the papacy of Pope John.*
– ORIGIN late Middle English: from medieval Latin *papatia*, from *papa* 'pope'.

papad /ˈpapəd/ ▶ noun Indian a poppadom.
– ORIGIN Hindi *pāpaṛ* from Tamil *pappaḍam* POPPADOM.

Papago /ˈpapəɡəʊ, ˈpɑː-/ ▶ noun (pl. **same** or **Papagos**) **1** a member of an American Indian people of the south-western US and northern Mexico.
2 [mass noun] the Uto-Aztecan language of the Papago, a form of Pima with around 10,000 speakers.
▶ adjective relating to the Papago or their language.
– ORIGIN via Spanish from an American Indian word.

papain /pəˈpeɪn, pəˈpʌɪn/ ▶ noun [mass noun] a protein-digesting enzyme obtained from unripe papaya fruit, used to tenderize meat and as a food supplement to aid digestion.
– ORIGIN late 19th cent.: from PAPAYA + -IN¹.

papal /ˈpeɪp(ə)l/ ▶ adjective relating to a pope or to the papacy: *a papal visit.*
– DERIVATIVES **papally** adverb.
– ORIGIN late Middle English: from Old French, from medieval Latin *papalis*, from ecclesiastical Latin *papa* 'bishop (of Rome)'.

papalagi /paˈpɑːləŋi/ ▶ noun (pl. **same**) another term for PALAGI.
– ORIGIN from Samoan *papālagi*.

papal infallibility ▶ noun see INFALLIBILITY.

papalist ▶ noun historical a supporter of the papacy, especially an advocate of papal supremacy.

Papal States historical the temporal dominions belonging to the Pope, especially in central Italy.

paparazzo /ˌpapəˈratsəʊ/ ▶ noun (pl. **paparazzi** /-tsi/) (usu. **paparazzi**) a freelance photographer who pursues celebrities to get photographs of them.
– ORIGIN 1960s: from Italian, from the name of a character in Fellini's film *La Dolce Vita* (1960).

papaveraceous /pəˌpeɪvəˈreɪʃəs, -ˌpav-/ ▶ adjective Botany relating to or denoting plants of the poppy family (Papaveraceae).
– ORIGIN mid 19th cent.: from modern Latin *Papaveraceae* (plural), based on Latin *papaver* 'poppy', + -OUS.

papaverine /pəˈpeɪvərʌɪn, -ˈpav-, -iːn/ ▶ noun [mass noun] Chemistry a compound present in opium used medicinally to alleviate muscle spasm and asthma.
● An alkaloid; chem. formula: $C_{20}H_{21}NO_4$.
– ORIGIN mid 19th cent.: from Latin *papaver* 'poppy' + -INE⁴.

papaw /pəˈpɔː/ ▶ noun variant spelling of PAWPAW.

papaya /pəˈpʌɪə/ ▶ noun **1** a tropical fruit shaped like an elongated melon, with edible orange flesh and small black seeds. Also called PAPAW or PAWPAW.
2 (also **papaya tree**) the fast-growing tree which bears the papaya, native to warm regions of America. It is widely cultivated for its fruit, both for eating and for papain production. ● *Carica papaya*, family Caricaceae.
– ORIGIN late 16th cent.: from Spanish and Portuguese (see PAWPAW).

pap boat ▶ noun historical a boat-shaped container for holding soft food for feeding babies.

Papeete /ˌpɑːpɪˈeɪti, ˈiːti/ the capital of French Polynesia, situated on the NW coast of Tahiti; pop. 26,000 (est. 2009).

paper ▶ noun **1** [mass noun] material manufactured in thin sheets from the pulp of wood or other fibrous substances, used for writing, drawing, or printing on, or as wrapping material: *a sheet of paper* | [as modifier] *a paper napkin* | [count noun] *toffee papers.* ■ wallpaper.
2 (usu. **papers**) a sheet of paper with something written or printed on it: *he riffled through the papers on his desk.* ■ a newspaper. ■ (**papers**) personal documents. ■ (**papers**) documents attesting identity; credentials: *two men stopped us and asked us for our papers.* ■ a government report or policy document: *a recently leaked cabinet paper.* ■ [as modifier] denoting something that is officially documented but has no real existence: *a paper profit.*
3 Brit. a set of examination questions to be answered at one session: *we had to sit a three-hour paper.* ■ the written answers to examination questions.
4 an essay or dissertation, especially one read at an academic lecture or seminar or published in an academic journal.
5 [mass noun] theatrical slang free passes of admission to a theatre or other entertainment.
▶ verb [with obj.] **1** apply wallpaper to (a wall or room): *the walls were papered in a Regency stripe.* ■ (**paper something over**) cover a hole or blemish with wallpaper. ■ (**paper something over**) disguise an awkward problem instead of resolving it: *the unions tried to paper over their differences.*
2 theatrical slang fill (a theatre) by giving out free tickets.
– PHRASES **be not worth the paper it is written on** be of no value or validity despite having been written down. **make the papers** be written about in newspapers and thus become famous. **on paper** in writing. ■ in theory rather than in reality: *the combatants were, on paper at least, evenly matched.*
– DERIVATIVES **paperless** adjective.
– ORIGIN Middle English: from Anglo-Norman French *papir*, from Latin *papyrus* 'paper-reed' (see PAPYRUS). The verb dates from the late 16th cent.

paperback ▶ noun a book bound in stiff paper or flexible card.
– PHRASES **in paperback** in an edition bound in stiff paper or flexible card.

paper bag ▶ noun a small bag made of paper.
– PHRASES **be unable to punch one's way out of a paper bag** informal be completely ineffectual or inept.

paperbark ▶ noun a cajuput tree. ■ used in names of other trees which have a peeling papery bark, e.g. **paperbark maple**.

paper birch (also **paperbark birch**) ▶ noun a North American birch with large leaves and peeling white bark. ● *Betula papyrifera*, family Betulaceae.

paperboard ▶ noun [mass noun] cardboard or pasteboard.

paper boy (or **girl**) ▶ noun a boy (or girl) who delivers newspapers to people's homes.

paper chain ▶ noun a chain made of paper links and used for decorating a room, especially at Christmas.

paperchase ▶ noun **1** Brit. a cross-country race in which the runners follow a trail marked by torn-up paper.
2 informal an administration characterized by excessive bureaucracy.

paper clip ▶ noun a piece of bent wire or plastic used for holding several sheets of paper together.

paper cup ▶ noun a disposable cup made of thin cardboard.

paper feed ▶ noun a device for inserting sheets of paper into a typewriter, printer, or similar machine.

paperhanger ▶ noun a person who decorates with wallpaper, especially professionally.

paperknife ▶ noun (pl. **paperknives**) a blunt knife used for cutting paper, such as when opening envelopes or slitting the uncut pages of books.

papermaking ▶ noun [mass noun] the manufacture of paper.
– DERIVATIVES **papermaker** noun.

P

paper mill ▸ noun a factory in which paper is manufactured.

paper money ▸ noun [mass noun] money in the form of banknotes.

paper mulberry ▸ noun a small tree of the mulberry family, the inner bark of which is used for making paper and tapa cloth, occurring from eastern Asia to Polynesia. ● *Broussonetia papyrifera*, family Moraceae.

paper nautilus ▸ noun another term for ARGONAUT.

paper plate ▸ noun a disposable plate made of cardboard.

paper-pusher ▸ noun N. Amer. informal a bureaucrat or menial clerical worker.
– DERIVATIVES **paper-pushing** noun & adjective.

paper round (N. Amer. **paper route**) ▸ noun a job of regularly delivering newspapers.

paper taffeta ▸ noun [mass noun] a lightweight taffeta with a crisp papery finish.

paper tape ▸ noun [mass noun] paper in the form of a long, narrow strip. ■ paper tape with holes punched in it, used in older computer systems for conveying data or instructions.

paper-thin ▸ adjective very thin or insubstantial: *paper-thin pancakes | her sophistication was paper-thin.*

paper tiger ▸ noun a person or thing that appears threatening but is ineffectual.

paper trail ▸ noun chiefly N. Amer. the total amount of written evidence of someone's activities.

paper wasp ▸ noun a social wasp that forms a small umbrella-shaped nest made from wood pulp. ● Genus *Polistes*, family Vespidae.

paperweight ▸ noun a small, heavy object for keeping loose papers in place.

paperwork ▸ noun [mass noun] routine work involving written documents such as reports or letters: *I need to catch up on some paperwork.* ■ written documents.

papery ▸ adjective thin and dry like paper: *papery onion skins.*

Paphlagonia /ˌpaflə'ɡəʊnɪə/ an ancient region of northern Asia Minor, on the Black Sea coast between Bithynia and Pontus, to the north of Galatia.
– DERIVATIVES **Paphlagonian** adjective & noun.

Papiementu /ˌpapɪə'mɛntuː/ (also **Papiemento** /-'mɛntəʊ/) ▸ noun [mass noun] the Creole language of the Caribbean islands of Aruba, Bonaire, and Curaçao, based on Spanish, Portuguese, and Dutch, and influenced by African languages.
– ORIGIN from Spanish *Papiamento*.

P

papier collé /ˌpapɪeɪ 'kɒleɪ/ ▸ noun (pl. **papiers collés** pronunc. **same**) [mass noun] the technique of using paper for collage. ■ [count noun] a collage made from paper.
– ORIGIN French, literally 'glued paper'.

papier mâché /papɪeɪ 'maʃeɪ/ ▸ noun [mass noun] a malleable mixture of paper and glue, or paper, flour, and water, that becomes hard when dry, used to make boxes, trays, or ornaments.
– ORIGIN French, literally 'chewed paper'.

papilionaceous /pəˌpɪlɪə'neɪʃəs/ ▸ adjective Botany relating to or denoting leguminous plants of a group (subfamily Papilionoideae or family Papilionaceae) with flowers that resemble a butterfly.
– ORIGIN mid 17th cent.: from modern Latin *Papilionaceae* (plural), based on Latin *papilio* 'butterfly', + -OUS.

papilionid /pəˌpɪlɪ'əʊnɪd/ ▸ noun Entomology a butterfly of a family (Papilionidae) which includes the swallowtails, birdwings, and apollos. They are typically large and boldly marked, and most kinds have tail-like projections on the hindwings.
– ORIGIN late 19th cent.: from modern Latin *Papilionidae* (plural), from Latin *papilio(n-)* 'butterfly'.

papilla /pə'pɪlə/ ▸ noun (pl. **papillae** /-liː/) a small rounded protuberance on a part or organ of the body. ■ a small fleshy projection on a plant.
– DERIVATIVES **papillary** adjective, **papillate** /'papɪleɪt, pə'pɪlət/ adjective, **papillose** /'papɪləʊs/ adjective.
– ORIGIN late 17th cent.: from Latin, literally 'nipple', diminutive of *papula* 'small protuberance'.

papilloma /ˌpapɪ'ləʊmə/ ▸ noun (pl. **papillomas** or **papillomata** /-mətə/) Medicine a small wart-like growth on the skin or on a mucous membrane, derived from the epidermis and usually benign.
– ORIGIN mid 19th cent.: from PAPILLA + -OMA.

papillomavirus /ˌpapɪ'ləʊməˌvʌɪrəs/ ▸ noun Medicine any of a group of DNA viruses that cause the formation of papillomas or warts.

papillon /'papɪlɒn, 'papɪjɔ̃/ ▸ noun a dog of a toy breed with ears suggesting the form of a butterfly.
– ORIGIN early 20th cent.: from French, literally 'butterfly', from Latin *papilio(n-)*.

papist /'peɪpɪst/ chiefly derogatory ▸ noun a Roman Catholic. ■ another term for PAPALIST.
▸ adjective relating to or associated with the Roman Catholic Church.
– DERIVATIVES **papism** noun, **papistical** adjective (archaic), **papistry** noun.
– ORIGIN mid 16th cent.: from French *papiste* or modern Latin *papista*, from ecclesiastical Latin *papa* 'bishop (of Rome)'.

papoose /pə'puːs/ ▸ noun **1** offensive a young North American Indian child.
2 a type of bag used to carry a child on one's back.
– ORIGIN mid 17th cent.: from Algonquian *papoos*.

papovavirus /pə'pəʊvəˌvʌɪrəs/ ▸ noun Medicine any of a group of small DNA viruses, most of which infect mammals and can cause sarcoma and warts.
– ORIGIN 1960s: from *pa(pilloma)* + *po(lyoma)* + *va(cuolating)* + VIRUS.

pappardelle /ˌpapɑː'dɛleɪ/, Italian /ˌpappar'delle/ ▸ plural noun pasta in the form of broad flat ribbons, usually served with a meat sauce.
– ORIGIN Italian, from *pappare* 'eat hungrily'.

Pappus /'papəs/ (*fl.* c.300–350 AD), Greek mathematician; known as **Pappus of Alexandria**. Little is known of his life, but his *Collection* of six books (another two are missing) is the principal source of knowledge of the mathematics of his predecessors.

pappus /'papəs/ ▸ noun (pl. **pappi** /-pʌɪ, -piː/) Botany the tuft of hairs on each seed of thistles, dandelions, and similar plants, which assists dispersal by the wind.
– ORIGIN early 18th cent.: via Latin from Greek *pappos*.

pappy[1] ▸ noun (pl. **pappies**) [usu. as name] a child's word for father: *Pappy was always busy.*
– ORIGIN mid 18th cent.: from PAPA + -Y[2].

pappy[2] ▸ adjective of the nature or consistency of pap: *pappy desserts.*

pappyshow ▸ noun [in sing.] W. Indian a person or thing that is a parody or mockery of something else: *he is merely making a pappyshow of the volunteer litter wardens.*
– ORIGIN variant of *puppet show*.

paprika /'paprɪkə, pə'priːkə/ ▸ noun [mass noun] a powdered spice with a deep orange-red colour and a mildly pungent flavour, made from the dried and ground fruits of certain varieties of sweet pepper. ■ a deep orange-red colour.
– ORIGIN late 19th cent.: from Hungarian.

Pap test /pap/ ▸ noun a test carried out on a cervical smear to detect cancer of the cervix or womb.
– ORIGIN 1960s: named after George N. *Papanicolaou* (1883–1962), Greek-born American scientist.

Papua /'papwə, pa'puːə, 'papjʊə/ **1** a province of Indonesia comprising most of the western part of the island of New Guinea, with some offshore islands; capital, Jayapura. Until its incorporation into Indonesia in 1963 it was known as Dutch New Guinea. Formerly called IRIAN JAYA, WEST IRIAN.
2 a name for the island of New Guinea. See also PAPUA NEW GUINEA.
– ORIGIN named by a Portuguese navigator who visited it in 1526–7, from a Malay word meaning 'woolly-haired'.

Papuan ▸ noun **1** a native or inhabitant of Papua, or of Papua New Guinea.
2 [mass noun] a heterogeneous group of around 750 languages spoken by some 3 million people in Papua New Guinea and neighbouring islands.
▸ adjective relating to Papua or its people or their languages.

Papua New Guinea a country in the western Pacific comprising the eastern half of the island of New Guinea together with some neighbouring islands; pop. 5,940,800 (est. 2009); languages, English (official), Tok Pisin, and several hundred native Austronesian and Papuan languages; capital, Port Moresby.

> Papua New Guinea was formed from the administrative union, in 1949, of Papua, an Australian Territory since 1906, and the Trust Territory of New Guinea (NE New Guinea), formerly under German control and an Australian trusteeship since 1921. In 1975 Papua New Guinea became an independent state within the Commonwealth.

– DERIVATIVES **Papua New Guinean** adjective & noun.

papule /'papjuːl/ (also **papula** /-jʊlə/) ▸ noun (pl. **papules** or **papulae** /-jʊliː/) Medicine a small pimple or swelling on the skin, often forming part of a rash.
– DERIVATIVES **papular** adjective.
– ORIGIN early 18th cent.: from Latin *papula*.

papyrology /ˌpapɪ'rɒlədʒi/ ▸ noun [mass noun] the branch of study that deals with ancient papyri.
– DERIVATIVES **papyrological** adjective, **papyrologist** noun.

papyrus /pə'pʌɪrəs/ ▸ noun (pl. **papyri** /-rʌɪ, -riː/ or **papyruses**) **1** [mass noun] a material prepared in ancient Egypt from the pithy stem of a water plant, used in sheets throughout the ancient Mediterranean world for writing or painting on and also for making articles such as rope. ■ [count noun] a document written on papyrus.
2 the tall aquatic sedge from which papyrus is obtained, native to central Africa and the Nile valley. ● *Cyperus papyrus*, family Cyperaceae.
– ORIGIN late Middle English (in sense 2): via Latin from Greek *papuros*. Sense 1 dates from the early 18th cent.

par[1] ▸ noun **1** Golf the number of strokes a first-class player should normally require for a particular hole or course: *Woosnam had advanced from his overnight position of three* **under par** *| the sixteenth is a par five.* ■ a score of this number of strokes at a hole.
2 Stock Exchange the face value of a share or other security, as distinct from its market value. ■ (also **par of exchange**) the recognized value of one country's currency in terms of another's.
▸ verb (**pars, parring, parred**) [with obj.] Golf play (a hole) in par.
– PHRASES **above** (or **below** or **under**) **par** better (or worse) than is usual or expected: *poor nutrition can leave you feeling below par.* **on a par with** equal in importance or quality to: *this home cooking is on a par with the best in the world.* **par for the course** what is normal or expected in any given circumstances: *looking gorgeous is par for the course with her.* **up to par** at an expected or usual quality.
– ORIGIN late 16th cent. (in the sense 'equality of value or standing'): from Latin, 'equal', also 'equality'. The golf term dates from the late 19th cent.

par[2] ▸ noun informal a paragraph.
– ORIGIN mid 19th cent.: abbreviation.

par. (also **para.**) ▸ abbreviation paragraph.

par- ▸ combining form variant spelling of PARA-[1] shortened before a vowel or *h* (as in *paraldehyde, parody, parhelion*).

para[1] /'parə/ informal ▸ noun **1** a paratrooper.
2 a paragraph.

para[2] /'pɑːrə/ ▸ noun (pl. **same** or **paras**) a monetary unit of Serbia, equal to one hundredth of a dinar.
– ORIGIN Turkish, from Persian *pāra* 'piece, portion'.

para-[1] (also **par-**) ▸ prefix **1** beside; adjacent to: *parataxis | parathyroid.* ■ beyond or distinct from, but analogous to: *paramilitary | paratyphoid.*
2 Chemistry denoting substitution at diametrically opposite carbon atoms in a benzene ring, e.g. in 1,4 positions: *paradichlorobenzene.* Compare with META- and ORTHO-.
– ORIGIN from Greek *para* 'beside'; in combinations often meaning 'amiss, irregular' and denoting alteration or modification.

para-[2] ▸ combining form denoting something that protects or wards off: *parachute | parasol.*
– ORIGIN from French, from the Italian imperative singular of *parare* 'defend, shield' (originally meaning 'prepare', from Latin *parare*).

Pará /pə'rɑː/ a state in northern Brazil, on the Atlantic coast at the delta of the Amazon; capital, Belém. It is a region of dense rainforest.

para-aminobenzoic acid /ˌparəəˌmiːnəʊbɛn'zəʊɪk, -ə'mʌɪnəʊ-/ ▸ noun [mass noun] Biochemistry a crystalline acid which is widely distributed in plant and animal tissue, and has been used to treat rickettsial infections. ● Chem. formula: $NH_2C_6H_4COOH$.

parabasis /pə'rabəsɪs/ ▸ noun (pl. **parabases** /-siːz/) (in ancient Greek comedy) a direct address to the audience, sung or chanted by the chorus on behalf of the author. ■ a digression in a fictional work in which the author addresses the reader.
– ORIGIN early 19th cent.: from Greek, from *parabainein* 'go aside'.

paraben /ˈparəbɛn/ ▶ **noun** Chemistry any of a group of compounds used as preservatives in pharmaceutical and cosmetic products and in the food industry.
– ORIGIN 1950s: from PARA-¹ + *(hydroxy)ben(zoic)*.

parabiosis /ˌparəbʌɪˈəʊsɪs/ ▶ **noun** [mass noun] Biology the anatomical joining of two individuals, especially artificially in physiological research.
– DERIVATIVES **parabiotic** adjective.
– ORIGIN early 20th cent.: modern Latin, from PARA-¹ 'beside, distinct from' + Greek *biōsis* 'mode of life' (from *bios* 'life').

parable ▶ **noun** a simple story used to illustrate a moral or spiritual lesson, as told by Jesus in the Gospels.
– ORIGIN Middle English: from Old French *parabole*, from an ecclesiastical Latin sense 'discourse, allegory' of Latin *parabola* 'comparison', from Greek *parabolē* (see PARABOLA).

parabola /pəˈrab(ə)lə/ ▶ **noun** (pl. **parabolas** or **parabolae** /-liː/) a symmetrical open plane curve formed by the intersection of a cone with a plane parallel to its side. The path of a projectile under the influence of gravity follows a curve of this shape.
– ORIGIN late 16th cent.: modern Latin, from Greek *parabolē* 'placing side by side, application', from *para-* 'beside' + *bolē* 'a throw' (from the verb *ballein*).

parabolic /ˌparəˈbɒlɪk/ ▶ **adjective 1** of or like a parabola or part of one.
2 of or expressed in parables: *parabolic teaching*.
– DERIVATIVES **parabolically** adverb.
– ORIGIN late Middle English: via late Latin from Greek *parabolikos*, from *parabolē* 'application' (see PARABOLA).

paraboloid /pəˈrab(ə)lɔɪd/ ▶ **noun 1** (also **paraboloid of revolution**) a solid generated by the rotation of a parabola about its axis of symmetry.
2 a solid having two or more non-parallel parabolic cross sections.
– DERIVATIVES **paraboloidal** adjective.

Paracel Islands /ˌparəˈsɛl/ (also **the Paracels**) a group of about 130 small barren coral islands and reefs in the South China Sea to the south-east of the Chinese island of Hainan. The islands are claimed by both China and Vietnam.

paracellular ▶ **adjective** Biology passing or situated beside or between cells.

Paracelsus /ˌparəˈsɛlsəs/ (*c*.1493–1541), Swiss physician: born *Theophrastus Phillipus Aureolus Bombastus von Hohenheim*. He developed a new approach to medicine and philosophy based on observation and experience. He saw illness as having a specific external cause (rather than resulting from an imbalance of the bodily humours), and introduced chemical remedies to replace traditional ones.

paracentesis /ˌparəsɛnˈtiːsɪs/ ▶ **noun** (pl. **paracenteses** /-siːz/) [mass noun] Medicine the perforation of a cavity of the body or of a cyst or similar outgrowth, especially with a hollow needle to remove fluid or gas.
– ORIGIN late 16th cent.: via Latin from Greek *parakentēsis*, from *parakentein* 'pierce at the side'.

paracentric inversion ▶ **noun** Genetics a reversal of the normal order of genes in a chromosome segment involving only the part of a chromosome at one side of the centromere.

paracetamol /ˌparəˈsiːtəmɒl, -ˈsɛt-/ ▶ **noun** (pl. **same** or **paracetamols**) [mass noun] Brit. a synthetic compound used as a drug to relieve and reduce fever, usually taken in tablet form. ● Alternative name: **para-acetylaminophenol**; chem. formula: $C_8H_9NO_2$. Compare with ACETAMINOPHEN.
– ORIGIN 1950s: from *par(a-)acet(yl)am(inophen)ol*.

parachute ▶ **noun** a cloth canopy which fills with air and allows a person or heavy object attached to it to descend slowly when dropped from an aircraft, or which is released from the rear of an aircraft on landing to act as a brake.
▶ **verb 1** drop from an aircraft by parachute: [no obj.] *airborne units **parachuted in** to secure the airport* | [with obj.] *an air operation to **parachute** relief supplies into Bosnia*.
2 appoint or be appointed in an emergency or from outside the existing hierarchy: [with obj.] *the former Conservative minister was controversially **parachuted into** the safe seat*.
– DERIVATIVES **parachutist** noun.
– ORIGIN late 18th cent.: from French *para-* 'protection against' + *chute* 'fall'.

Paraclete /ˈparəkliːt/ ▶ **noun** (in Christian theology) the Holy Spirit as advocate or counsellor (John 14:16, 26).
– ORIGIN via late Latin from Greek *paraklētos* 'called in aid', from *para-* 'alongside' + *klētos* (from *kalein* 'to call').

paraclinical ▶ **adjective** relating to the branches of medicine, especially the laboratory sciences, that provide a service for patients without direct involvement in care.

paracrine /ˈparəkrʌɪn/ ▶ **adjective** Physiology relating to or denoting a hormone which has effect only in the vicinity of the gland secreting it.
– ORIGIN 1970s: from PARA-¹ 'beside' + *krinein* 'to separate'.

paracrystal ▶ **noun** Chemistry a piece of a substance that is not a true crystal but has some degree of order in its structure.
– DERIVATIVES **paracrystalline** adjective.

parade ▶ **noun 1** a public procession, especially one celebrating a special day or event. ■ a formal march or gathering of troops for inspection or display: *a military parade* | [mass noun] *the men massed for parade*. ■ a series of people or things appearing or being displayed one after the other: *the parade of Hollywood celebrities who troop on to his show*. ■ a boastful or ostentatious display: *a pompous parade of erudition*.
2 Brit. a public square or promenade. ■ a row of shops: *a shopping parade*.
3 a parade ground.
▶ **verb 1** [no obj.] (of troops) assemble for a formal inspection or ceremonial occasion. ■ walk or march through a public place in a formal procession or in an ostentatious way: *officers will parade through the town centre* | [with obj.] *carefree young men were parading the streets*.
2 [with obj.] display (someone or something) while marching or moving around a place: *they paraded national flags*. ■ display (something) in order to impress or attract attention: *he paraded his knowledge*. ■ [no obj.] (**parade as**) appear falsely as; masquerade as: *these untruths parading as history*.
– PHRASES **on parade** taking part in a parade. ■ on public display: *politicians are always on parade*.
– DERIVATIVES **parader** noun.
– ORIGIN mid 17th cent.: from French, literally 'a showing', from Spanish *parada* and Italian *parata*, based on Latin *parare* 'prepare, furnish'.

parade ground ▶ **noun** a place where troops gather for parade.

parade ring ▶ **noun** a circuit at a racecourse round which horses can be walked to warm up before a race.

paradiddle /ˈparəˌdɪd(ə)l/ ▶ **noun** Music one of the basic patterns (rudiments) of drumming, consisting of four even strokes played in the order 'left right left left' or 'right left right right'.
– ORIGIN 1920s: imitative.

paradigm /ˈparədʌɪm/ ▶ **noun 1** a typical example or pattern of something; a pattern or model: *society's paradigm of the 'ideal woman'*. ■ a world view underlying the theories and methodology of a particular scientific subject.
2 Linguistics a set of linguistic items that form mutually exclusive choices in particular syntactic roles. Often contrasted with SYNTAGM.
3 (in the traditional grammar of Latin, Greek, and other inflected languages) a table of all the inflected forms of a particular verb, noun, or adjective, serving as a model for other words of the same conjugation or declension.
– ORIGIN late 15th cent.: via late Latin from Greek *paradeigma*, from *paradeiknunai* 'show side by side', from *para-* 'beside' + *deiknunai* 'to show'.

paradigmatic /ˌparədɪɡˈmatɪk/ ▶ **adjective** of or denoting the relationship between a set of linguistic items that form mutually exclusive choices in particular syntactic roles. Contrasted with SYNTAGMATIC.
– DERIVATIVES **paradigmatically** adverb.

paradigm shift ▶ **noun** a fundamental change in approach or underlying assumptions.
– ORIGIN 1970s: term used in the writings of Thomas S. Kuhn (1922–96), philosopher of science.

paradisal /parəˈdʌɪs(ə)l/ ▶ **adjective** (of a place or state) ideal or idyllic; heavenly: *she told me tales of her paradisal childhood*.

paradise /ˈparədʌɪs/ ▶ **noun** (in some religions) heaven as the ultimate abode of the just. ■ (**Paradise**) the abode of Adam and Eve before the Fall in the biblical account of the Creation; the Garden of Eden. ■ an ideal or idyllic place or state: *the surrounding countryside is a walker's paradise* | *my idea of paradise is to relax on the seafront*.
– DERIVATIVES **paradisiacal** /-dɪˈsʌɪək(ə)l/ (also **paradisaical** /-dɪˈseɪɪk(ə)l/ or **paradisical** /-ˈdɪsɪk(ə)l/) adjective.
– ORIGIN Middle English: from Old French *paradis*, via ecclesiastical Latin from Greek *paradeisos* 'royal (enclosed) park', from Avestan *pairidaēza* 'enclosure, park'.

paradise fish ▶ **noun** a small colourful labyrinth fish that is native to SE Asia and popular in aquaria.
● Genus *Macropodus*, family Belontiidae: several species, including *M. opercularis*.

paradise flycatcher ▶ **noun** a tropical monarch flycatcher with brown, black, and white plumage, the male having very long central tail feathers. ● Genus *Terpsiphone*, family Monarchidae: several species.

parador /ˈparədɔː, ˌparəˈdɔː/ ▶ **noun** (pl. **paradors** or **paradores** /-ˈdɔːreɪz/) a hotel in Spain owned and administered by the Spanish government.
– ORIGIN Spanish.

parados /ˈparədɒs/ ▶ **noun** an elevation of earth behind a fortified place as a protection against attack from the rear, especially a mound along the back of a trench.
– ORIGIN mid 19th cent.: from French, from *para-* 'protection against' + *dos* 'back' (from Latin *dorsum*).

paradox ▶ **noun** a seemingly absurd or contradictory statement or proposition which when investigated may prove to be well founded or true. ■ a statement or proposition which, despite sound (or apparently sound) reasoning from acceptable premises, leads to a conclusion that seems logically unacceptable or self-contradictory. ■ a person or thing that combines contradictory features or qualities: *cathedrals face the paradox of having enormous wealth in treasures but huge annual expenses*.
– ORIGIN mid 16th cent. (originally denoting a statement contrary to accepted opinion): via late Latin from Greek *paradoxon* 'contrary (opinion)', neuter adjective used as a noun, from *para-* 'distinct from' + *doxa* 'opinion'.

paradoxical ▶ **adjective** seemingly absurd or self-contradictory: *by glorifying the acts of violence they achieve the paradoxical effect of making them trivial*.
– DERIVATIVES **paradoxically** adverb [sentence adverb] *paradoxically, the more fuel a star starts off with, the sooner it runs out*.

paradrop ▶ **noun** a descent or delivery by parachute.
▶ **verb** (**paradrops**, **paradropping**, **paradropped**) [with obj.] drop by parachute.

paraesthesia /ˌparɪsˈθiːzɪə/ (US **paresthesia**) ▶ **noun** (pl. **paraesthesiae** /-zɪiː/ or **paraesthesias**) [mass noun] Medicine an abnormal sensation, typically tingling or pricking ('pins and needles'), caused chiefly by pressure on or damage to peripheral nerves.
– ORIGIN late 19th cent.: from PARA-¹ 'alongside, irregular' + Greek *aisthēsis* 'sensation' + -IA¹.

paraffin ▶ **noun** (also **paraffin wax**) [mass noun] chiefly Brit. a flammable, whitish, translucent, waxy solid consisting of a mixture of saturated hydrocarbons, obtained by distillation from petroleum or shale and used in candles, cosmetics, polishes, and sealing and waterproofing compounds. ■ (also **paraffin oil** or **liquid paraffin**) a colourless, flammable, oily liquid similarly obtained and used as fuel, especially kerosene. ■ [count noun] Chemistry old-fashioned term for ALKANE.
– ORIGIN mid 19th cent.: from German, from Latin *parum* 'little' + *affinis* 'related' (from its low reactivity).

paragenesis /ˌparəˈdʒɛnɪsɪs/ ▶ **noun** (pl. **parageneses** /-siːz/) Geology a set of minerals which were formed together, especially in a rock, or with a specified mineral.
– DERIVATIVES **paragenetic** /-dʒɪˈnɛtɪk/ adjective.

paraglider ▶ **noun** a wide canopy resembling a parachute that is attached to a person's body by a harness in order to allow them to glide through the air after jumping from or being hauled to a height. ■ a person flying a paraglider.
– DERIVATIVES **paraglide** verb, **paragliding** noun.

paragoge /ˌparəˈɡəʊdʒi/ ▶ **noun** Linguistics the addition of a letter or syllable to a word in particular contexts (e.g. *n* in *an*) or as a language develops (e.g. *t* in *peasant*).
– ORIGIN mid 16th cent.: via late Latin from Greek *paragōgē* 'addition, derivation', from *para-* 'alongside' + *agōgē* 'carrying'.

P

paragon ▶ **noun** a person or thing regarded as a perfect example of a particular quality: *it would have taken a paragon of virtue not to feel viciously jealous.* ▪ a person or thing viewed as a model of excellence: *your cook is a paragon.* ▪ a perfect diamond of 100 carats or more.
– ORIGIN mid 16th cent.: from obsolete French, from Italian *paragone* 'touchstone to try good (gold) from bad', from medieval Greek *parakonē* 'whetstone'.

paragrammatism /ˌparəˈgramətɪz(ə)m/ ▶ **noun** [mass noun] Psychiatry confused or incomplete use of grammatical structures, found in certain forms of speech disturbance.

paragraph ▶ **noun** a distinct section of a piece of writing, usually dealing with a single theme and indicated by a new line, indentation, or numbering.
▶ **verb** [with obj.] arrange (a piece of writing) in paragraphs.
– DERIVATIVES **paragraphic** adjective.
– ORIGIN late 15th cent.: from French *paragraphe*, via medieval Latin from Greek *paragraphos* 'short stroke marking a break in sense', from *para-* 'beside' + *graphein* 'write'.

paragraph mark (also **paragraph symbol**) ▶ **noun** a symbol (usually ¶) used in printed text to mark a new paragraph or as a reference mark.

Paraguay /ˈparəgwʌɪ/, Spanish /paraˈɣwaj/ a landlocked country in central South America; pop. 6,995,700 (est. 2009); languages, Spanish (official), Guarani; capital, Asunción.

> The territory was occupied by semi-nomadic Guarani peoples before Spanish rule was established in the 16th century. Paraguay achieved independence in 1811. It was devastated, losing more than half of its population, in war against Brazil, Argentina, and Uruguay in 1865–70, but gained land in the Chaco War with Bolivia in 1932–5. The country was ruled by the military dictator Alfredo Stroessner (b.1912) from 1954 to 1989.

– DERIVATIVES **Paraguayan** adjective & noun.

Paraíba /ˌparaˈiːbə/ a state of eastern Brazil, on the Atlantic coast; capital, João Pessoa.

parainfluenza ▶ **noun** [mass noun] Medicine a disease caused by any of a group of viruses which resemble the influenza viruses.

parakeet /ˈparəkiːt/ (also **parrakeet**) ▶ **noun** a small parrot with predominantly green plumage and a long tail. • Family Psittacidae: five genera, e.g. *Psittacula* of Asia and Africa and *Cyanoramphus* of Australasia, and many species.
– ORIGIN mid 16th cent.: from Old French *paroquet*, Italian *parrocchetto*, and Spanish *periquito*; origin uncertain, perhaps (via Italian) based on a diminutive meaning 'little wig', referring to head plumage, or (via Spanish) based on a diminutive of the given name *Pedro*.

P

paralanguage ▶ **noun** [mass noun] the non-lexical component of communication by speech, for example intonation, pitch and speed of speaking, hesitation noises, gesture, and facial expression.

paraldehyde /pəˈraldɪhʌɪd/ ▶ **noun** [mass noun] Chemistry a liquid made by treating acetaldehyde with acid, used medicinally as a sedative, hypnotic, and anticonvulsant. • A cyclic trimer of acetaldehyde; chem. formula: $(CH_3CHO)_3$.

paralegal N. Amer. ▶ **adjective** relating to auxiliary aspects of the law.
▶ **noun** a person trained in subsidiary legal matters but not fully qualified as a lawyer.

paralinguistic ▶ **adjective** relating to or denoting paralanguage or the non-lexical elements of communication by speech.

paralipomena /ˌparəlɪˈpɒmɪnə/ (also **paraleipomena** /-lʌɪ-/) ▶ **plural noun** (sing. **paralipomenon**) formal things omitted from a work and added as a supplement. ▪ (usu. **Paralipomenon**) archaic (in the Vulgate Bible and some other versions) the name of the books of Chronicles, regarded as supplementary to the books of Kings.
– ORIGIN late Middle English: via ecclesiastical Latin from Greek *paraleipomena*, from *paraleipein* 'omit', from *para-* 'to one side' + *leipein* 'to leave'.

paralipsis /ˌparəˈlɪpsɪs/ ▶ **noun** [mass noun] Rhetoric the device of giving emphasis by professing to say little or nothing of a subject, as in *not to mention their unpaid debts of several millions*.
– ORIGIN late 16th cent.: via late Latin from Greek *paraleipsis* 'passing over', from *paraleipein* 'omit', from *para-* 'aside' + *leipein* 'to leave'.

parallax /ˈparəlaks/ ▶ **noun** [mass noun] the effect whereby the position or direction of an object appears to differ when viewed from different positions, e.g. through the viewfinder and the lens of a camera. ▪ [count noun] the angular amount of this in a particular case, especially that of a star viewed from different points in the earth's orbit.
– DERIVATIVES **parallactic** adjective.
– ORIGIN late 16th cent. (also in the general sense 'fact of seeing wrongly'): from French *parallaxe*, from Greek *parallaxis* 'a change', from *parallassein* 'to alternate', based on *allassein* 'to exchange' (from *allos* 'other').

parallel ▶ **adjective 1** (of lines, planes, or surfaces) side by side and having the same distance continuously between them: *parallel lines never meet* | *the road* ***runs parallel to*** *the Ottawa River.*
2 occurring or existing at the same time or in a similar way; corresponding: *a parallel universe* | *they shared a flat in London while establishing parallel careers.*
3 of or denoting electrical components or circuits connected to common points at each end, rather than one to another in sequence. The opposite of SERIES.
4 Computing involving the simultaneous performance of operations.
▶ **noun 1** a person or thing that is similar or analogous to another: *a challenge which has no parallel in peacetime this century.* ▪ a similarity or comparison: *she* ***draws a parallel between*** *personal destiny and social forces.*
2 (also **parallel of latitude**) each of the imaginary parallel circles of constant latitude on the earth's surface.
3 Printing two parallel lines (‖) as a reference mark.
▶ **verb** (**parallels**, **paralleling**, **paralleled**) [with obj.] **1** be side by side with (something extending in a line), always keeping the same distance; run or lie parallel to: *a big concrete gutter that paralleled the road.*
2 be similar or corresponding to: *the increase in the quality of wines has paralleled the rise of interest in food.*
– PHRASES **in parallel** occurring at the same time and having some connection. ▪ (of electrical components or circuits) connected to common points at each end; not in series.
– ORIGIN mid 16th cent.: from French *parallèle*, via Latin from Greek *parallēlos*, from *para-* 'alongside' + *allēlos* 'one another'.

parallel bars ▶ **plural noun** a pair of parallel rails on posts used in gymnastics.

parallel cousin ▶ **noun** the offspring of a parent's sibling; a first cousin.

parallel distributed processing (abbrev.: **PDP**) ▶ **noun** another term for CONNECTIONISM.

parallelepiped /ˌparəlɛləˈpʌɪpɛd, ˌparəlɛˈlɛpɪpɛd/ ▶ **noun** Geometry a solid body of which each face is a parallelogram.
– ORIGIN late 16th cent.: from Greek *parallēlepipedon*, from *parallēlos* 'beside another' + *epipedon* 'plane surface'.

parallel imports ▶ **plural noun** goods imported by unlicensed distributors for sale at less than the manufacturer's official retail price.
– DERIVATIVES **parallel importing** noun.

parallelism ▶ **noun** [mass noun] the state of being parallel or of corresponding in some way. ▪ the use of successive verbal constructions in poetry or prose which correspond in grammatical structure, sound, metre, meaning, etc. ▪ Computing the use of parallel processing.
– DERIVATIVES **parallelistic** adjective.

parallelize /ˈparəlɛlʌɪz/ (also **parallelise**) ▶ **verb** [with obj.] Computing adapt (a program) to be suitable for running on a parallel processing system.
– DERIVATIVES **parallelization** noun.

parallel market ▶ **noun** an unofficial market in goods or currencies, especially in a country with a controlled economy.

parallel-medium ▶ **adjective** S. African relating to or denoting schools in which two languages are used in separate classes.

parallelogram /ˌparəˈlɛləgram/ ▶ **noun** a four-sided plane rectilinear figure with opposite sides parallel.
– PHRASES **parallelogram of forces** a parallelogram illustrating the theorem that if two forces acting at a point are represented in magnitude and direction by two sides of a parallelogram meeting at that point, their resultant is represented by the diagonal drawn from that point.
– ORIGIN late 16th cent.: from French *parallélogramme*, via late Latin from Greek *parallēlogrammon*, from *parallēlos* 'alongside another' + *grammē* 'line'.

parallel parking ▶ **noun** [mass noun] the action of parking a vehicle parallel and close to the roadside.

parallel port ▶ **noun** Computing a connector for a device that sends or receives several bits of data simultaneously by using more than one wire.

parallel processing ▶ **noun** [mass noun] Computing a mode of operation in which a process is split into parts, which are executed simultaneously on different processors attached to the same computer.

parallel ruler ▶ **noun** an instrument for drawing parallel lines, consisting of two or more rulers connected by jointed crosspieces so as to be always parallel, at whatever distance they are set.

parallel turn ▶ **noun** Skiing a turn with the skis kept parallel to each other.

paralogical ▶ **adjective** relating to a form of reasoning which does not conform to the rules of logic.

paralogism /pəˈralədʒɪz(ə)m/ ▶ **noun** Logic a piece of illogical or fallacious reasoning, especially one which appears superficially logical or which the reasoner believes to be logical.
– DERIVATIVES **paralogist** noun.
– ORIGIN mid 16th cent.: from French *paralogisme*, via late Latin from Greek *paralogismos*, from *paralogizesthai* 'reason falsely'.

paralogous /pəˈraləgəs/ ▶ **adjective** Genetics relating to genes that are descended from the same ancestral gene by gene duplication in the course of evolution, especially when present in different species which have diverged after the duplication.

paralogy /pəˈralədʒi/ ▶ **noun** [mass noun] **1** Genetics the state of being paralogous.
2 paralogical reasoning.

Paralympian /ˌparəˈlɪmpɪən/ ▶ **noun** a competitor in the Paraylmpic Games.

Paralympics ▶ **plural noun** an international athletic competition for disabled athletes.
– DERIVATIVES **Paralympic** adjective.
– ORIGIN 1950s: blend of *paraplegic* (see PARAPLEGIA) and *Olympics* (plural of OLYMPIC).

paralyse (chiefly US also **paralyze**) ▶ **verb** [with obj.] cause (a person or part of the body) to become partly or wholly incapable of movement: *Mrs Burrows had been paralysed by a stroke.* ▪ make (someone) unable to think or act normally, especially through panic or fear: *some people are paralysed by the thought of failure* | (as adj. **paralysing**) *her paralysing shyness.* ▪ stop (a system, place, or organization) from operating by causing disruption: *the regional capital was paralysed by a general strike.*
– DERIVATIVES **paralysingly** adverb.
– ORIGIN early 19th cent.: from French *paralyser*, from *paralysie* 'paralysis'.

paralysed (chiefly US also **paralyzed**) ▶ **adjective** (of a person or part of the body) partly or wholly incapable of movement; disabled: *he became partially paralysed.*

paralysis /pəˈralɪsɪs/ ▶ **noun** (pl. **paralyses** /-siːz/) [mass noun] the loss of the ability to move (and sometimes to feel anything) in part or most of the body, typically as a result of illness, poison, or injury. ▪ inability to act or function properly: *the paralysis gripping the country.*
– ORIGIN late Old English, via Latin from Greek *paralusis*, from *paraluesthai* 'be disabled at the side', from *para* 'beside' + *luein* 'loosen'.

paralysis agitans /ˈadʒɪtanz/ ▶ **noun** less common term for PARKINSON'S DISEASE.
– ORIGIN Latin, literally 'shaking paralysis'.

paralytic ▶ **adjective 1** relating to paralysis: *the incidence of paralytic disease.*
2 [predic.] Brit. informal extremely drunk: *a leaving party which left everyone paralytic.*
▶ **noun** a person affected by paralysis.
– DERIVATIVES **paralytically** adverb.
– ORIGIN late Middle English: from Old French *paralytique*, via Latin from Greek *paralutikos* 'relating to paralysis' (see PARALYSIS).

paramagnetic ▶ **adjective** (of a substance or body) very weakly attracted by the poles of a magnet, but not retaining any permanent magnetism.
– DERIVATIVES **paramagnetism** noun.

Paramaribo /ˌparəˈmarɪbəʊ/ the capital of Suriname, a port on the Atlantic coast; pop. 252,000 (est. 2007).

paramatta ▶ **noun** variant spelling of PARRAMATTA.

paramecium /ˌparəˈmiːsɪəm/ ▶ **noun** (pl. **paramecia**) Zoology a single-celled freshwater animal which has a characteristic slipper-like shape and is covered with cilia. ● Genus *Paramecium*, phylum Ciliophora, kingdom Protista.
– ORIGIN mid 18th cent.: modern Latin, from Greek *paramēkēs* 'oval' from *para-* 'against' + *mēkos* 'length'.

paramedic ▶ **noun** a person who is trained to do medical work, especially emergency first aid, but is not a fully qualified doctor.

paramedical ▶ **adjective** relating to services and professions which supplement and support medical work but do not require a fully qualified doctor (such as nursing, radiography, emergency first aid, physiotherapy, and dietetics).

parameter /pəˈramɪtə/ ▶ **noun 1** technical a numerical or other measurable factor forming one of a set that defines a system or sets the conditions of its operation. ■ Mathematics a quantity whose value is selected for the particular circumstances and in relation to which other variable quantities may be expressed. ■ Statistics a numerical characteristic of a population, as distinct from a statistic of a sample.
2 a limit or boundary which defines the scope of a particular process or activity: *the parameters within which the media work*.
– ORIGIN mid 17th cent.: modern Latin, from Greek *para-* 'beside' + *metron* 'measure'.

parameterize /pəˈramɪt(ə)rʌɪz/ (also **parametrize** /pəˈramɪtrʌɪz/) ▶ **verb** [with obj.] technical describe or represent in terms of a parameter or parameters.
– DERIVATIVES **parameterization** noun.

parametric ▶ **adjective** relating to or expressed in terms of a parameter or parameters. ■ Statistics assuming the value of a parameter for the purpose of analysis. ■ Electronics relating to or denoting a process in which amplification or frequency conversion is obtained using a device modulated by a pumping frequency, which enables power to be transferred from the pumping frequency to the signal.
– DERIVATIVES **parametrically** adverb.

parametric equalizer ▶ **noun** an electronic device or computer program which allows any specific part of the frequency range of a signal to be selected and altered in strength.

paramilitary ▶ **adjective** organized similarly to a military force: *illegal paramilitary groups* | *paramilitary police*.
▶ **noun** (pl. **paramilitaries**) a member of a paramilitary organization.

paramnesia /ˌparəmˈniːzɪə/ ▶ **noun** [mass noun] Psychiatry a condition or phenomenon involving distorted memory or confusions of fact and fantasy, such as confabulation or déjà vu.

paramo /ˈparəməʊ/ ▶ **noun** (pl. **paramos**) a high treeless plateau in tropical South America.
– ORIGIN Spanish and Portuguese, from Latin *paramus*.

paramoecium ▶ **noun** old-fashioned spelling of PARAMECIUM.

paramotor ▶ **noun** (trademark in the US) a motorized steerable parachute, powered by a motor and propeller strapped to the pilot's back.
– DERIVATIVES **paramotoring** noun.

Paramount a US film production and distribution company established in 1914. A major studio of the silent era, Paramount acted as an outlet for many of the films of Cecil B. de Mille and helped to create stars such as Mary Pickford and Rudolf Valentino.

paramount ▶ **adjective 1** more important than anything else; supreme: *the interests of the child are of paramount importance*.
2 [attrib.] having supreme power: *a paramount chief*.
– DERIVATIVES **paramountcy** noun, **paramountly** adverb.
– ORIGIN mid 16th cent. (in the sense 'highest in jurisdiction' in the phrases *lord paramount* and *paramount chief*): from Anglo-Norman French *paramont*, from Old French *par* 'by' + *amont* 'above'.

paramour ▶ **noun** archaic a lover, especially the illicit partner of a married person.
– ORIGIN Middle English: from Old French *par amour* 'by love'; in English the phrase was written from an early date as one word and came to be treated as a noun.

paramyxovirus /ˌparəˈmɪksə(ʊ)ˌvʌɪrəs/ ▶ **noun** Medicine any of a group of RNA viruses similar to the myxoviruses but larger and haemolytic, including those causing mumps, measles, distemper, rinderpest, and various respiratory infections (parainfluenza).

Paraná /ˌparəˈnɑː/ **1** a river of South America, which rises in SE Brazil and flows some 3,300 km (2,060 miles) southwards to the River Plate estuary in Argentina. For part of its length it forms the SE border of Paraguay.
2 a river port in eastern Argentina, on the Paraná River; pop. 249,500 (est. 2005).
3 a state of southern Brazil, on the Atlantic coast; capital, Curitiba.

parang[1] /ˈpɑːraŋ, ˈpa-/ ▶ **noun** a Malayan machete.
– ORIGIN Malay.

parang[2] /ˈparaŋ/ ▶ **noun** [mass noun] a variety of Trinidadian folk music, traditionally played at Christmas by groups which travel from house to house.
– ORIGIN Spanish creole, based on Spanish *parranda* 'spree, binge'.

paranoia /ˌparəˈnɔɪə/ ▶ **noun** [mass noun] a mental condition characterized by delusions of persecution, unwarranted jealousy, or exaggerated self-importance, typically worked into an organized system. It may be an aspect of chronic personality disorder, of drug abuse, or of a serious condition such as schizophrenia in which the person loses touch with reality. ■ unjustified suspicion and mistrust of other people.
– DERIVATIVES **paranoiac** adjective & noun, **paranoiacally** adverb, **paranoic** /-ˈnɔɪɪk/ adjective, **paranoically** /-ˈnɔɪɪk(ə)li/ adverb.
– ORIGIN early 19th cent.: modern Latin, from Greek, from *paranoos* 'distracted', from *para* 'irregular' + *noos* 'mind'.

paranoid ▶ **adjective** characterized by or suffering from the mental condition of paranoia: *paranoid schizophrenia*. ■ unreasonably or obsessively anxious, suspicious, or mistrustful: *you think I'm paranoid but I tell you there is something going on*.
▶ **noun** a person who is paranoid.

paranormal ▶ **adjective** denoting events or phenomena such as telekinesis or clairvoyance that are beyond the scope of normal scientific understanding: *a mystic who can prove he has paranormal powers* | (as noun **the paranormal**) *an investigator of the paranormal*.
– DERIVATIVES **paranormally** adverb.

Paranthropus /pəˈranθrəpəs/ ▶ **noun** a genus name often applied to robust fossil hominids first found in South Africa in 1938. ● *Australopithecus robustus* and *A.* (or *Zinjanthropus*) *boisei*, family Hominidae. See AUSTRALOPITHECUS.
– ORIGIN modern Latin, from Greek *para-* (expressing relationship) + *anthrōpos* 'man'.

paranumismatica /ˌparənjuːmɪzˈmatɪkə/ ▶ **plural noun** Brit. collectable items that are similar to coins and medals, such as tokens and medallions.

paraparesis /ˌparəpəˈriːsɪs/ ▶ **noun** [mass noun] partial paralysis of the lower limbs.

parapente /ˈparəpɒnt/ ▶ **noun** [mass noun] the activity of gliding by means of an aerofoil parachute launched from high ground. ■ [count noun] a parachute used for parapenting.
▶ **verb** [no obj.] glide using an aerofoil parachute.
– ORIGIN 1980s: from French, from *para(chute)* + *pente* 'slope'.

parapet /ˈparəpɪt/ ▶ **noun** a low protective wall along the edge of a roof, bridge, or balcony. ■ a protective wall or earth defence along the top of a trench or other place of concealment for troops.
– DERIVATIVES **parapeted** adjective.
– ORIGIN late 16th cent.: from French, or from Italian *parapetto* 'chest-high wall', from *para-* 'protecting' + *petto* 'chest' (from Latin *pectus*).

paraph /ˈparaf/ ▶ **noun** a flourish after a signature, originally as a precaution against forgery.
– ORIGIN late Middle English (denoting a paragraph): from French *paraphe*, from medieval Latin *paraphus* (contraction of *paragraphus* 'short horizontal stroke').

paraphasia /ˌparəˈfeɪzɪə/ ▶ **noun** [mass noun] Psychology speech disturbance resulting from brain damage in which words are jumbled and sentences meaningless.

paraphernalia /ˌparəfəˈneɪlɪə/ ▶ **noun** [treated as sing. or pl.] miscellaneous articles, especially the equipment needed for a particular activity. ■ trappings associated with a particular institution or activity that are regarded as superfluous: *the rituals and paraphernalia of government*.
– ORIGIN mid 17th cent. (denoting property owned by a married woman): from medieval Latin, based on Greek *parapherna* 'property apart from a dowry', from *para* 'distinct from' + *pherna* (from *phernē* 'dower').

paraphilia /ˌparəˈfɪlɪə/ ▶ **noun** [mass noun] Psychiatry a condition characterized by abnormal sexual desires, typically involving extreme or dangerous activities.
– DERIVATIVES **paraphiliac** adjective & noun.

paraphrase ▶ **verb** [with obj.] express the meaning of (something written or spoken) using different words, especially to achieve greater clarity: *you can either quote or paraphrase literary texts*.
▶ **noun** a rewording of something written or spoken.
– DERIVATIVES **paraphrasable** adjective, **paraphrastic** adjective.
– ORIGIN mid 16th cent. (as a noun): via Latin from Greek *paraphrasis*, from *paraphrazein*, from *para-* (expressing modification) + *phrazein* 'tell'.

paraphyletic /ˌparəfʌɪˈlɛtɪk/ ▶ **adjective** Biology (of a group of organisms) descended from a common evolutionary ancestor or ancestral group, but not including all the descendant groups.

paraphysis /pəˈrafɪsɪs/ ▶ **noun** (pl. **paraphyses** /-siːz/) Botany a sterile hair-like filament present among the reproductive organs in many lower plants, especially bryophytes, algae, and fungi.
– ORIGIN mid 19th cent.: modern Latin, from Greek *para-* 'beside, subsidiary' + *phusis* 'growth'.

paraplegia /ˌparəˈpliːdʒə/ ▶ **noun** [mass noun] paralysis of the legs and lower body, typically caused by spinal injury or disease.
– DERIVATIVES **paraplegic** adjective & noun.
– ORIGIN mid 17th cent.: modern Latin, from Greek *paraplēgia*, from *paraplēssein* 'strike at the side', from *para* 'beside' + *plēssein* 'to strike'.

parapodium /ˌparəˈpəʊdɪəm/ ▶ **noun** (pl. **parapodia** /-ɪə/) Zoology (in a polychaete worm) each of a number of paired muscular bristle-bearing appendages used in locomotion, sensation, or respiration. ■ (in a sea slug or other mollusc) a lateral extension of the foot used as an undulating fin for swimming.
– DERIVATIVES **parapodial** adjective.
– ORIGIN late 19th cent.: modern Latin, from Greek *para-* 'subsidiary' + *pous, pod-* 'foot'.

paraprofessional chiefly N. Amer. ▶ **noun** a person to whom a particular aspect of a professional task is delegated but who is not licensed to practise as a fully qualified professional.
▶ **adjective** relating to or denoting a paraprofessional.

paraprotein ▶ **noun** Medicine a protein found in the blood only as a result of cancer or other disease.

parapsychic ▶ **adjective** relating to or denoting mental phenomena for which no adequate scientific explanation exists.

parapsychology ▶ **noun** [mass noun] the study of mental phenomena which are excluded from or inexplicable by orthodox scientific psychology (such as hypnosis, telepathy, etc.). P
– DERIVATIVES **parapsychological** adjective, **parapsychologically** adverb, **parapsychologist** noun.

paraquat /ˈparəkwɒt, -kwat/ ▶ **noun** [mass noun] a toxic fast-acting herbicide, which becomes deactivated in the soil.
– ORIGIN 1960s: from PARA-[1] (sense 2) + QUATERNARY (it is a quaternary ammonium salt containing pyridine rings linked at the para-position).

pararhyme ▶ **noun** [mass noun] partial rhyme between words with the same pattern of consonants but different vowels.

parasagittal /ˌparəˈsadʒɪt(ə)l/ ▶ **adjective** Anatomy relating to or situated in a plane adjacent or parallel to the plane which divides the body into right and left halves.
– DERIVATIVES **parasagittally** adverb.

parasail ▶ **verb** [no obj.] (often as noun **parasailing**) glide through the air wearing an open parachute while being towed by a motor boat.
▶ **noun** a parachute designed for parasailing.

parascending ▶ **noun** [mass noun] Brit. the sport or activity of paragliding or parasailing.
– DERIVATIVES **parascend** verb, **parascender** noun.

paraselene /ˌparəsɪˈliːni/ ▶ **noun** (pl. **paraselenae** /-niː/) a bright spot in the sky similar to a parhelion but formed by moonlight.
– ORIGIN mid 17th cent.: modern Latin, from Greek *para-* 'beside' + *selēnē* 'moon'.

parasitaemia /ˌparəsɪˈtiːmɪə/ (US **parasitemia**) ▶ **noun** [mass noun] Medicine the demonstrable presence of parasites in the blood.

parasite ▸ **noun 1** an organism which lives in or on another organism (its host) and benefits by deriving nutrients at the other's expense.

> Parasites exist in huge variety and include animals, plants, and micro-organisms. They may live as ectoparasites on the surface of the host (e.g. arthropods such as ticks, mites, lice, fleas, and many insects infesting plants) or as endoparasites in the gut or tissues (e.g. many kinds of worm), and cause varying degrees of damage or disease to the host.

2 derogatory a person who habitually relies on or exploits others and gives nothing in return.
– ORIGIN mid 16th cent.: via Latin from Greek *parasitos* '(person) eating at another's table', from *para-* 'alongside' + *sitos* 'food'.

parasitic ▸ **adjective 1** (of an organism) living as a parasite: *mistletoe is* ***parasitic on*** *trees.* ■ resulting from infestation by a parasite: *mortality from parasitic diseases.*
2 derogatory habitually relying on or exploiting others: *attacks on the parasitic existence of Party functionaries.*
3 Phonetics (of a speech sound) inserted without etymological justification (e.g. the *b* in *thimble*); epenthetic.
– DERIVATIVES **parasitical** adjective, **parasitically** adverb, **parasitism** noun.
– ORIGIN early 17th cent.: via Latin from Greek *parasitikos*, from *parasitos* '(person) eating at another's table'.

parasitic bronchitis ▸ **noun** technical term for HUSK[2] (sense 1 of the noun).

parasiticide /ˌparəˈsɪtɪsʌɪd/ ▸ **noun** a substance used in medicine and veterinary medicine to kill parasites (especially those other than bacteria or fungi).

parasitize /ˈparəsʌɪtʌɪz, -sɪ-/ (also **parasitise**) ▸ **verb** [with obj.] infest or exploit (an organism or part) as a parasite.
– DERIVATIVES **parasitization** noun.

parasitoid /ˈparəsɪtɔɪd/ ▸ **noun** Entomology an insect whose larvae live as parasites which eventually kill their hosts, e.g. an ichneumon wasp.

parasitology /ˌparəsɪˈtɒlədʒi/ ▸ **noun** [mass noun] the branch of biology or medicine concerned with the study of parasitic organisms.
– DERIVATIVES **parasitological** adjective, **parasitologically** adverb, **parasitologist** noun.

parasol ▸ **noun 1** a light umbrella used to give shade from the sun.
2 (also **parasol mushroom**) a widely distributed large mushroom with a broad scaly greyish-brown cap and a tall, slender stalk. ● Genus *Lepiota*, family Lepiotaceae, class Hymenomycetes: numerous species, especially the edible *L. procera*.
– ORIGIN early 17th cent.: from French, from Italian *parasole*, from *para-* 'protecting against' + *sole* 'sun' (from Latin *sol*).

P

parastatal /ˌparəˈsteɪt(ə)l/ ▸ **adjective** (of an organization or industry, especially in some African countries) having some political authority and serving the state indirectly.
▸ **noun** a parastatal organization.

parasternal /ˌparəˈstəːnəl/ ▸ **adjective** Anatomy situated beside the sternum.

parastichy /pəˈrastɪki/ ▸ **noun** (pl. **parastichies**) Botany (in phyllotaxis) an oblique row of leaves arranged in a secondary spiral. Contrasted with ORTHOSTICHY.
– ORIGIN late 19th cent.: from PARA-[1] 'adjacent' + Greek *stikhos* 'row, rank'.

parasuicide ▸ **noun** [mass noun] Psychiatry apparent attempted suicide without the actual intention of killing oneself.

parasympathetic ▸ **adjective** Physiology relating to the part of the autonomic nervous system which balances the action of the sympathetic nerves. It consists of nerves arising from the brain and the lower end of the spinal cord and supplying the internal organs, blood vessels, and glands.
– ORIGIN early 20th cent.: from PARA-[1] 'alongside' + SYMPATHETIC, because some of these nerves run alongside sympathetic nerves.

parasynthesis ▸ **noun** [mass noun] Linguistics a process by which a term is formed by adding a bound morpheme (e.g. *-ed*) to a combination of existing words (e.g. *black-eyed* from *black eye(s)* + *-ed*).
– DERIVATIVES **parasynthetic** adjective, **parasynthetically** adverb.
– ORIGIN mid 19th cent.: from Greek *parasunthesis*, from *para-* 'subsidiary' + SYNTHESIS.

parataxis /ˌparəˈtaksɪs/ ▸ **noun** [mass noun] Grammar the placing of clauses or phrases one after another, without words to indicate coordination or subordination, as in *Tell me, how are you?* Contrasted with HYPOTAXIS.
– DERIVATIVES **paratactic** adjective, **paratactically** adverb.
– ORIGIN mid 19th cent.: from Greek *parataxis*, from *para-* 'beside' + *taxis* 'arrangement' (from *tassein* 'arrange').

paratha /pəˈrɑːtə/ ▸ **noun** (in Indian cookery) a flat, thick piece of unleavened bread fried on a griddle.
– ORIGIN from Hindi *parāṭhā*.

parathion /ˌparəˈθʌɪən/ ▸ **noun** [mass noun] a highly toxic synthetic organophosphorus compound containing phosphorus and sulphur, used as an agricultural insecticide.
– ORIGIN 1940s: from PARA-[1] (sense 2) + THIO- + -ON.

parathormone /ˌparəˈθɔːməʊn/ ▸ **noun** [mass noun] Physiology parathyroid hormone.

parathyroid ▸ **noun** Anatomy a gland next to the thyroid which secretes a hormone (**parathyroid hormone**) that regulates calcium levels in a person's body: [as modifier] *parathyroid tissue.*

paratrooper ▸ **noun** a member of a paratroop regiment or airborne unit.

paratroops ▸ **plural noun** troops trained and equipped to be dropped by parachute from aircraft: (as modifier usu. **paratroop**) *a paratroop regiment.*
– ORIGIN 1940s: from an abbreviation of PARACHUTE + *troops* (plural of TROOP).

paratyphoid (also **paratyphoid fever**) ▸ **noun** [mass noun] a fever resembling typhoid but caused by different (though related) bacteria. ● The bacteria are species of the genus *Salmonella*, in particular (in humans) *S. paratyphi*.

paravane ▸ **noun** a device towed behind a boat at a depth regulated by its vanes or planes, so that the cable to which it is attached can cut the moorings of submerged mines.
– ORIGIN early 20th cent.: from PARA-[2] 'protecting' + VANE.

paraventricular /ˌparəvɛnˈtrɪkjələ/ ▸ **adjective** Anatomy situated next to a ventricle of the brain.

par avion /pɑː(r) aˈvjɒ̃/, French /paʀ avjɔ̃/ ▸ **adverb** by airmail (written on a letter or parcel to indicate how it is to reach its destination).
– ORIGIN French, literally 'by aeroplane'.

parawing ▸ **noun** a type of parachute or kite having a flattened shape like a wing, to give greater manoeuvrability.

paraxial /pəˈraksɪəl/ ▸ **adjective** Anatomy & Zoology situated alongside, or on each side of, an axis, especially the central axis of the body.

parboil ▸ **verb** [with obj.] partly cook (food) by boiling.
– ORIGIN late Middle English: from Old French *parbouillir*, from late Latin *perbullire* 'boil thoroughly', from Latin *per-* 'through, thoroughly' (later confused with PART) + *bullire* 'to boil'.

Parcae /ˈpɑːkʌɪ, ˈpɑːsiː/ Roman Mythology the Fates.

parcel ▸ **noun 1** an object or collection of objects wrapped in paper in order to be carried or sent by post.
2 a quantity or amount of something, especially as dealt with in one commercial transaction: *a parcel of shares.* ■ a piece of land, especially one considered as part of an estate. ■ archaic, derogatory a group of people of a specified sort: *a parcel of rogues.*
▸ **verb** (**parcels, parcelling, parcelled**; US **parcels, parceling, parceled**) [with obj.] **1** make (something) into a parcel by wrapping it: *he* ***parcelled up*** *his only winter suit to take to the pawnbroker.* ■ (**parcel something out**) divide into portions and then distribute: *the farmers argue that parcelling out commercial farmland in small plots will reduce productivity.*
2 Nautical wrap (rope) with strips of tarred canvas, before binding it with yarn as part of a traditional technique to reduce chafing.
– PHRASES **pass the parcel** a children's game in which a parcel is passed around to the accompaniment of music, the child holding the parcel when the music stops being allowed to unwrap a layer.
– ORIGIN late Middle English (chiefly in the sense 'small portion'): from Old French *parcelle*, from Latin *particula* 'small part'.

parcel bomb ▸ **noun** an explosive device hidden in a package and sent with the intention of causing death or injury to the recipient.

parcel-gilt ▸ **adjective** (of an item of furniture, silverware, or similar) partly gilded, especially on the inner surface only.
– ORIGIN from PARCEL in the technical adjectival sense 'partial' + GILT[1].

parcel post ▸ **noun** the branch of the postal service dealing with parcels.

parcel shelf ▸ **noun** a shelf in a motor vehicle behind the rear seat.

parch ▸ **verb 1** make or become dry through intense heat: [with obj.] *a piece of grassland parched by the sun* | [no obj.] *his crops parched during the last two summers* | (as adj. **parching**) *a fierce parching heat has set in.* ■ [with obj.] roast (corn, peas, etc.) lightly.
2 (as adj. **parched**) informal extremely thirsty: *I'm parched—I'll die without a drink.*
– ORIGIN late Middle English: of unknown origin.

parcheesi ▸ **noun** variant spelling of PACHISI.

parchment ▸ **noun** [mass noun] a stiff, flat, thin material made from the prepared skin of an animal, usually a sheep or goat, and used as a durable writing surface in ancient and medieval times. ■ [count noun] a manuscript written on parchment: *a large collection of ancient parchments.* ■ (also **parchment paper**) a type of stiff translucent paper treated to resemble parchment and used for lampshades, as a writing surface, and in baking. ■ [count noun] informal a diploma or other formal document.
– ORIGIN Middle English: from Old French *parchemin*, from a blend of late Latin *pergamina* 'writing material from Pergamum' and *Parthica pellis* 'Parthian skin' (a kind of scarlet leather).

parclose /ˈpɑːkləʊz/ ▸ **noun** a screen or railing in a church enclosing a tomb or altar or separating off a side chapel.
– ORIGIN Middle English: from Old French *parclos(e)* 'enclosed', past participle of *parclore* (from Latin *per-* 'thoroughly' + *claudere* 'to close').

pard ▸ **noun** archaic or literary a leopard.
– ORIGIN late Middle English: from Old French, via Latin from Greek *pardos*.

pardalote /ˈpɑːdələʊt/ ▸ **noun** a small short-billed Australian songbird related to the flowerpeckers, typically having white spots or streaks on the dark wings and crown. Also called DIAMOND-BIRD in Australia. ● Genus *Pardalotus*, family Dicaeidae (or Pardalotidae): several species.
– ORIGIN mid 19th cent.: from modern Latin *Pardalotus*, from Greek *pardalōtos* 'spotted like a leopard', based on *pardos* (see PARD).

pardner ▸ **noun** US dated or humorous variant spelling of PARTNER, used to represent US dialect speech: *you and me, pardner, against the world.*

pardon ▸ **noun** [mass noun] the action of forgiving or being forgiven for an error or offence: *he obtained pardon for his sins.* ■ [count noun] a cancellation of the legal consequences of an offence or conviction: *he offered a full pardon to five convicted men.* ■ [count noun] Christian Church an indulgence, as widely sold in medieval Europe.
▸ **verb** [with obj.] forgive or excuse (a person, error, or offence). ■ release (an offender) from the legal consequences of an offence or conviction, and often implicitly from blame: *he was pardoned for his treason.* ■ (**be pardoned**) used to indicate that someone is justified in doing or thinking a particular thing given the circumstances: *one can be pardoned the suspicion that some of his errors were deliberate.*
▸ **exclamation** a request to a speaker to repeat something because one did not hear or understand it: *'Pardon?' I said, cupping a hand to my ear.*
– PHRASES **I beg your pardon** (or N. Amer. **pardon me**) used to express polite apology: *I beg your pardon for intruding.* ■ used to indicate that one has not heard or understood something. ■ used to express one's anger or indignation at what someone has just said. **if you'll pardon the expression** used to apologize for having used or being about to use coarse or offensive expressions. **pardon me for ——** used to express in a sarcastic way one's indignation at being criticized for doing something: *'Well, pardon me for breathing!'*.
– ORIGIN Middle English: from Old French *pardun* (noun), *pardoner* (verb), from medieval Latin *perdonare* 'concede, remit', from *per-* 'completely' + *donare* 'give'.

pardonable ▸ **adjective** able to be forgiven; excusable: *no mistake, even a tiny one, is pardonable.*
– DERIVATIVES **pardonably** adverb.

pardoner ▸ **noun** historical a person licensed to sell papal pardons or indulgences.
– ORIGIN Middle English: from Anglo-Norman French.

pare ▶ verb [with obj.] trim (something) by cutting away its outer edges. ■ cut off (the outer skin) of something: *pare off the rind using a peeler*. ■ reduce (something) in size, extent, or quantity in a number of small successive stages: *union leaders publicly pared down their demands | we pared costs by doing our own cleaning*.
– DERIVATIVES **parer** noun.
ORIGIN Middle English: from Old French *parer* 'adorn, prepare', also 'peel, trim', from Latin *parare* 'prepare'.

paregoric /ˌparɪˈɡɒrɪk/ ▶ noun [mass noun] historical a medicine consisting of opium flavoured with camphor, aniseed, and benzoic acid, formerly used to treat diarrhoea and coughing in children.
– ORIGIN late 17th cent.: via late Latin from Greek *parēgorikos* 'soothing', from the verb *parēgorein*, literally 'speak in the assembly', hence 'soothe, console'.

pareira /pəˈrɛːrə/ ▶ noun [mass noun] a drug obtained from the root of a Brazilian climbing plant, used as a homeopathic diuretic, especially after abdominal surgery. ● This drug is obtained from *Chondrodendron tomentosum*, family Menispermaceae.
– ORIGIN early 18th cent.: from Portuguese *parreira* 'vine trained against a wall'.

paren /pəˈrɛn/ ▶ noun (usu. **parens**) Printing a round bracket.
– ORIGIN early 20th cent.: abbreviation of PARENTHESIS.

parenchyma /pəˈrɛŋkɪmə/ ▶ noun [mass noun] Anatomy the functional tissue of an organ as distinguished from the connective and supporting tissue. ■ Botany the cellular tissue, typically soft and succulent, found chiefly in the softer parts of leaves, pulp of fruits, bark and pith of stems, etc. ■ Zoology cellular tissue lying between the body wall and the organs of invertebrate animals lacking a coelom, such as flatworms.
– DERIVATIVES **parenchymal** adjective (chiefly Anatomy), **parenchymatous** adjective (chiefly Botany).
– ORIGIN mid 17th cent.: from Greek *parenkhuma* 'something poured in besides', from *para-* 'beside' + *enkhuma* 'infusion'.

parens patriae /ˌparɛnz ˈpatrɪiː/ ▶ noun Law the monarch, or any other authority, regarded as the legal protector of citizens unable to protect themselves. ■ [mass noun] the principle that political authority carries with it the responsibility for such protection.
– ORIGIN modern Latin, literally 'parent of the country'.

parent ▶ noun a person's father or mother: *the parents of the bride | his adoptive parents*. ■ archaic a forefather or ancestor. ■ an animal or plant from which new ones are derived. ■ a source or origin of a smaller or less important part. ■ [often as modifier] an organization or company which owns or controls a number of subsidiaries: *policy considerations were determined largely by the parent company*.
▶ verb [with obj.] (often as noun **parenting**) be or act as a mother or father to (someone).
– DERIVATIVES **parental** /pəˈrɛnt(ə)l/ adjective, **parentally** adverb, **parentless** adjective.
– ORIGIN late Middle English: from Old French, from Latin *parent-* 'bringing forth', from the verb *parere*. The verb dates from the mid 17th cent.

parentage ▶ noun [mass noun] the identity and origins of one's parents: *a boy of Jamaican parentage*. ■ the origin of something: *this ice cream boasts American parentage*.
– ORIGIN late 15th cent.: from Old French.

parentcraft ▶ noun [mass noun] the combination of skills and knowledge that facilitate the rearing of children.

parenteral /pəˈrɛnt(ə)r(ə)l/ ▶ adjective Medicine administered or occurring elsewhere in the body than the mouth and alimentary canal: *parenteral nutrition*. Often contrasted with ENTERAL.
– DERIVATIVES **parenterally** adverb.
– ORIGIN early 20th cent.: from PARA-[1] 'beside' + Greek *enteron* 'intestine' + -AL.

parenthesis /pəˈrɛnθɪsɪs/ ▶ noun (pl. **parentheses** /-siːz/) **1** a word or phrase inserted as an explanation or afterthought into a passage which is grammatically complete without it, in writing usually marked off by brackets, dashes, or commas. ■ (**parentheses**) a pair of round brackets ( ) used to include such a word or phrase.
2 an interlude or interval: *the three months of coalition government were a lamentable political parenthesis*.
– PHRASES **in parenthesis** as a digression or afterthought.
– ORIGIN mid 16th cent.: via late Latin from Greek, from *parentithenai* 'put in beside'.

parenthesize (also **parenthesise**) ▶ verb [with obj.] (usu. as adj. **parenthesized**) put (a word or phrase) into brackets: *parenthesized clauses*. ■ add as a parenthesis.

parenthetical /ˌpar(ə)nˈθɛtɪk(ə)l/ ▶ adjective relating to or inserted as a parenthesis: *parenthetical remarks*.
– DERIVATIVES **parenthetic** adjective, **parenthetically** adverb.
– ORIGIN late 18th cent.: from PARENTHESIS, on the pattern of pairs such as *synthesis, synthetic*.

parenthood ▶ noun [mass noun] the state of being a parent and the responsibilities involved: *high rates of single parenthood*.

parent–teacher association ▶ noun Brit. a local organization of parents and teachers for promoting closer relations and improving educational facilities at a school.

parergon /pəˈrəːɡɒn/ ▶ noun (pl. **parerga** /-ɡə/) formal a piece of work that is supplementary to or a by-product of a larger work. ■ archaic work that is subsidiary to one's ordinary employment: *he pursued astronomy as a parergon*.
– ORIGIN early 17th cent.: via Latin from Greek *parergon*, from *para-* 'beside, additional' + *ergon* 'work'.

paresis /pəˈriːsɪs, ˈparɪsɪs/ ▶ noun (pl. **pareses** /-siːz/) [mass noun] Medicine a condition of muscular weakness caused by nerve damage or disease; partial paralysis. ■ (also **general paresis**) inflammation of the brain in the later stages of syphilis, causing progressive dementia and paralysis.
– DERIVATIVES **paretic** adjective.
– ORIGIN late 17th cent.: modern Latin, from Greek *parienai* 'let go', from *para-* 'alongside' + *hienai* 'let go'.

paresthesia ▶ noun US spelling of PARAESTHESIA.

Pareto /pəˈreɪtəʊ, -ˈriːtəʊ/ ▶ adjective denoting or involving the theories and methods of the Italian economist and sociologist Vilfredo Pareto (1848–1923), especially a formula used to express the income distribution of a society.

Pareto-optimal ▶ adjective Economics relating to or denoting a distribution of wealth such that any redistribution or other change beneficial to one individual is detrimental to one or more others.
– DERIVATIVES **Pareto-optimality** noun.

pareu /ˈpɑːreɪuː/ (also **pareo**) ▶ noun a kind of sarong made of a single straight piece of printed cotton cloth, worn in Polynesia or as a fashion garment elsewhere.
– ORIGIN Tahitian.

pareve /ˈpɑːrəvə/ (also **parev** /ˈpɑːrəv/) ▶ adjective Judaism designating or relating to a foodstuff made without milk, meat, or their derivatives, and therefore permissible to be eaten with both meat and dairy dishes according to dietary laws.
– ORIGIN 1930s: from Yiddish *parev* 'neutral'.

par excellence /pɑːr ˈɛks(ə)l(ə)ns/, French /paʀ ɛksɛlɑ̃s/ ▶ adjective [postpositive] better or more than all others of the same kind: *Nash is, to many, the Regency architect par excellence*.
– ORIGIN French, literally 'by excellence'.

parfait /ˈpɑːfeɪ/ ▶ noun [mass noun] **1** a rich cold dessert made with whipped cream, eggs, and fruit. ■ a dessert consisting of layers of ice cream, meringue, and fruit, served in a tall glass.
2 a rich pâté with a very smooth consistency.
– ORIGIN from the French adjective *parfait*, literally 'perfect'.

parfleche /ˈpɑːflɛʃ/ ▶ noun (in American Indian culture) a hide, especially a buffalo's hide, with the hair removed, dried by being stretched on a frame. ■ an article, especially a bag, made from parfleche.
– ORIGIN from Canadian French *parflèche*, from French *parer* 'ward off' + *flèche* 'arrow'.

parfumerie /pɑːˈfjuːm(ə)ri/ ▶ noun (pl. **parfumeries**) a place where perfume is sold or made.
– ORIGIN French.

parfumier /pɑːˈf(j)uːmɪə/ ▶ noun a person who manufactures or retails perfume.
– ORIGIN French, from *parfum* PERFUME.

pargana /pəˈɡʌnə/ ▶ noun a group of villages or a subdivision of a district in India.
– ORIGIN Urdu, literally 'district'.

parget /ˈpɑːdʒɪt/ (also **parge** /pɑːdʒ/) ▶ verb (**pargets**, **pargeting**, **pargeted**) [with obj.] cover (a part of a building) with plaster or mortar that typically bears an ornamental pattern.
▶ noun another term for PARGETING.
– ORIGIN late Middle English: from Old French *parjeter*, from *par-* 'all over' + *jeter* 'to throw'.

pargeting (also **parging**) ▶ noun [mass noun] plaster or mortar applied over part of a building, typically with an ornamental pattern.

parhelion /pɑːˈhiːlɪən/ ▶ noun (pl. **parhelia** /-lɪə/) a bright spot in the sky appearing on either side of the sun, formed by refraction of sunlight through ice crystals high in the atmosphere. Also called MOCK SUN, SUN DOG.
– ORIGIN mid 17th cent.: from Latin *parelion*, from Greek *para-* 'beside' + *hēlios* 'sun'.

pariah /pəˈrʌɪə/ ▶ noun **1** an outcast: *they were treated as social pariahs*.
2 historical a member of an indigenous people of southern India originally functioning as ceremonial drummers but later having a low caste.
– ORIGIN early 17th cent.: from Tamil *paṟaiyar*, plural of *paṟaiyan* '(hereditary) drummer', from *paṟai* 'a drum'.

pariah dog ▶ noun another term for PYE-DOG.

Parian /ˈpɛːrɪən/ ▶ adjective relating to the Greek island of Paros or the fine white marble for which it is renowned. ■ denoting a form of fine white unglazed hard paste porcelain likened to Parian marble.
▶ noun **1** a native or inhabitant of Paros.
2 [mass noun] Parian ware (porcelain).

parietal /pəˈrʌɪɪt(ə)l/ ▶ adjective **1** Anatomy & Biology relating to or denoting the wall of the body or of a body cavity or hollow structure. ■ of the parietal lobe: *the parietal cortex*.
2 N. Amer. relating to residence within a college and especially to visits from members of the opposite sex: *parietal rules*.
3 Archaeology denoting prehistoric art found on rock walls.
▶ noun Anatomy & Zoology a parietal structure. ■ short for PARIETAL BONE.
– ORIGIN late Middle English: from late Latin *parietalis*, from Latin *paries, pariet-* 'wall'.

parietal bone ▶ noun a bone forming the central side and upper back part of each side of the skull.

parietal cell ▶ noun an oxyntic (acid-secreting) cell of the stomach wall.

parietal lobe ▶ noun either of the paired lobes of the brain at the top of the head, including areas concerned with the reception and correlation of sensory information.

pari-mutuel /ˌpɑːrɪˈmjuːtʃʊəl, -ˈtjʊəl/ ▶ noun [often as modifier] a form of betting in which those backing the first three places divide the losers' stakes (less the operator's commission): *pari-mutuel betting*.
– ORIGIN French, literally 'mutual stake'.

parings ▶ plural noun thin strips that have been pared off from something: *fingernail parings*.

pari passu /ˌpɑːrɪ ˈpasuː, ˌparɪ/ ▶ adverb side by side; at the same rate or on an equal footing: *early opera developed **pari passu with** solo song*.
– ORIGIN Latin, literally 'with equal step'.

Paris[1] /ˈparɪs/, French /paʀi/ the capital of France, on the River Seine; pop. 2,203,817 (2006).

> Paris was held by the Romans, who called it Lutetia, and the Franks, and was established as the capital in 987 under Hugh Capet. It was organized into three parts, the Île de la Cité (an island in the Seine), the Right Bank, and the Left Bank, during the reign of Philippe-Auguste (1180–1223). The city's neoclassical architecture dates from the modernization of the Napoleonic era; this continued under Napoleon III, when the bridges and boulevards of the modern city were built.

– ORIGIN named after the *Parisii*, a Gallic people who settled on the Île de la Cité.

Paris[2] /ˈparɪs/ Greek Mythology a Trojan prince, the son of Priam and Hecuba. Appointed by the gods to decide who among the three goddesses Hera, Athene, and Aphrodite should win a prize for beauty, he awarded it to Aphrodite, who promised him the most beautiful woman in the world—Helen, wife of Menelaus king of Sparta. He abducted Helen, bringing about the Trojan War, in which he killed Achilles but was later himself killed.

Paris[3], Matthew, see MATTHEW PARIS.

Paris club a group of the major creditor nations of the International Monetary Fund, meeting

P

informally in Paris to discuss the financial relations of the IMF member nations.

Paris Commune ▸ noun see COMMUNE[1] (sense 3).

Paris green ▸ noun [mass noun] a vivid green toxic crystalline salt of copper and arsenic, used as a preservative, pigment, and insecticide.

parish ▸ noun (in the Christian Church) a small administrative district typically having its own church and a priest or pastor: [as modifier] *a parish church.* ■ (also **civil parish**) Brit. the smallest unit of local government, constituted only in rural areas. ■ US (in Louisiana) a territorial division corresponding to a county in other states.
– ORIGIN Middle English: from Anglo-Norman French and Old French *paroche*, from late Latin *parochia*, from Greek *paroikia* 'sojourning', based on *para-* 'beside, subsidiary' + *oikos* 'dwelling'.

parishad /ˈpʌrɪʃʌd/ ▸ noun Indian a council or assembly.
– ORIGIN from Sanskrit, from *pari* 'around' + *sad-* 'sit'.

parish clerk ▸ noun an official performing various mainly administrative duties concerned with the Church or with a civil parish.

parish council ▸ noun Brit. the administrative body in a civil parish.

parishioner ▸ noun an inhabitant of a particular church parish, especially one who is a regular churchgoer.

parish-pump ▸ adjective [attrib.] Brit. of local importance or interest only; parochial: *I looked down on parish-pump politics.*

parish register ▸ noun a book recording christenings, marriages, and burials at a parish church.

Parisian /pəˈrɪzɪən/ ▸ adjective relating to Paris.
▸ noun a native or inhabitant of Paris.
– ORIGIN late Middle English: from French *parisien*.

Parisienne /pəˌrɪzɪˈɛn/, French /paʀizjɛn/ ▸ noun a Parisian girl or woman.
– ORIGIN mid 17th cent.: French, feminine of *parisien* 'Parisian'.

parison /ˈparɪs(ə)n/ ▸ noun a rounded mass of glass formed by rolling the substance immediately after removal from the furnace.
– ORIGIN early 19th cent.: from French *paraison*, from *parer* 'prepare', from Latin *parare*.

parity[1] /ˈparɪti/ ▸ noun [mass noun] **1** the state or condition of being equal, especially as regards status or pay: *parity of incomes between rural workers and those in industrial occupations.* ■ equivalent value of one currency in terms of another at an established exchange rate.
2 Mathematics (of a number) the fact of being even or odd. ■ Physics the property of a spatial wave equation that either remains the same (**even parity**) or changes sign (**odd parity**) under a given transformation. ■ Physics the value of a quantum number corresponding to this property. ■ Computing a function whose being even (or odd) provides a check on a set of binary values.
– ORIGIN late 16th cent.: from late Latin *paritas*, from *par* 'equal'.

parity[2] /ˈparɪti/ ▸ noun [mass noun] Medicine the fact or condition of having borne children. ■ the number of children previously borne: *very high parity (six children or more).*
– ORIGIN late 19th cent.: from *parous* 'having borne offspring' (back-formation from adjectives ending in -PAROUS) + -ITY.

parity bit ▸ noun Computing a bit which acts as a check on a set of binary values, calculated in such a way that the number of 1s in the set plus the parity bit should always be even (or occasionally, should always be odd).

Park, Mungo (1771–1806), Scottish explorer. He undertook a series of explorations in West Africa (1795–7), among them the navigation of the Niger. He drowned on a second expedition to the Niger (1805–6).

park ▸ noun **1** a large public garden or area of land used for recreation: *a walk round the park | a country park.* ■ a large enclosed piece of ground attached to a country house: *the house is set in its own park.* ■ (also **wildlife park**) a large enclosed area of land used to accommodate wild animals in captivity. ■ (**the park**) Brit. informal (in soccer) the pitch: *he was the liveliest player on the park.* ■ N. Amer. an enclosed sports ground.
2 [with adj. or noun modifier] an area devoted to a specified purpose: *an industrial park.* ■ [with modifier] chiefly Brit. an area for motor vehicles to be left in: *a coach park.*
3 [mass noun] (in a car with automatic transmission) the position of the gear selector in which the gears are locked, preventing the vehicle's movement.
▸ verb [with obj.] bring (a vehicle that one is driving) to a halt and leave it temporarily, typically in a car park or by the side of the road: *he parked his car outside her house* | [no obj.] *he couldn't find anywhere to park.* ■ [with obj. and adverbial of place] informal leave (something) in a convenient place until required: *come on in, and park your bag by the door.* ■ (**park oneself**) informal sit down: *after dinner, we parked ourselves on a pair of couches.*
– ORIGIN Middle English: from Old French *parc*, from medieval Latin *parricus*, of Germanic origin; related to German *Pferch* 'pen, fold', also to PADDOCK. The word was originally a legal term designating land held by royal grant for keeping game animals: this was enclosed and therefore distinct from a *forest* or *chase*, and (also unlike a *forest*) had no special laws or officers. A military sense 'space occupied by artillery, wagons, stores, etc., in an encampment' (late 17th cent.) is the origin of the verb sense (mid 19th cent.) and of sense 2 of the noun (early 20th cent.).

parka ▸ noun a large windproof jacket with a hood, designed to be worn in cold weather. ■ a hooded jacket made of animal skin, worn by the Inuit.
– ORIGIN late 18th cent.: via Aleut from Russian.

parkade ▸ noun Canadian a multistorey car park.
– ORIGIN 1950s: from PARK, on the pattern of *arcade*.

park-and-ride ▸ noun [often as modifier] a system for reducing urban traffic congestion, in which drivers leave their cars in car parks on the outskirts of a city and travel to the city centre on public transport.

park cattle (also **white park cattle**) ▸ plural noun animals of a breed of primitive cattle that are maintained in a semi-wild state in several parks in Britain. They are typically white in colour with dark ears and muzzles.

Park Chung-hee /ˌpɑːk tʃʊŋˈhiː/ (1917–79), South Korean statesman, President 1963–79. After staging a coup in 1961 he was elected President, assuming dictatorial powers in 1971. Under Park's presidency South Korea emerged as a leading industrial nation.

Parker[1], Charlie (1920–55), American saxophonist; full name *Charles Christopher Parker*; known as **Bird** or **Yardbird**. From 1944 he played with Thelonious Monk and Dizzy Gillespie, and became one of the key figures of the bebop movement.

Parker[2], Dorothy (Rothschild) (1893–1967), American humorist, literary critic, and writer. From 1927 Parker wrote book reviews and short stories for the *New Yorker* magazine, becoming one of its legendary wits.

parkerizing (also **parkerising**) ▸ noun [mass noun] a process for rustproofing iron or steel by brief immersion in a hot acidic solution of a metal phosphate.
– DERIVATIVES **parkerized** adjective.
– ORIGIN 1920s: from *Parker* Rust-Proof Company of America (which introduced the process) + -IZE + -ING[1].

park home ▸ noun a prefabricated building occupied as a permanent home, located with others in a dedicated area of ground.

parkie (also **parky**) ▸ noun (pl. **parkies**) Brit. informal a park-keeper.

parkin ▸ noun [mass noun] Brit. a kind of dark gingerbread, typically with a soft, dry texture, made with oatmeal and treacle or molasses, especially in Yorkshire around Bonfire Night.
– ORIGIN early 19th cent.: perhaps from the family name *Parkin*, diminutive of *Per* 'Peter'.

parking light ▸ noun a small light on the side of a vehicle, for use when parking the vehicle at night.

parking lot ▸ noun see LOT (sense 5 of the noun).

parking meter ▸ noun a machine next to a parking space in a street, into which the driver puts money so as to be authorized to park the vehicle for a particular length of time.

parking ticket ▸ noun a notice telling a driver of a fine imposed on them for parking illegally, typically written by a traffic warden and attached to a car windscreen.

parkinsonism ▸ noun another term for PARKINSON'S DISEASE.

Parkinson's disease ▸ noun [mass noun] a progressive disease of the nervous system marked by tremor, muscular rigidity, and slow, imprecise movement, chiefly affecting middle-aged and elderly people. It is associated with degeneration of the basal ganglia of the brain and a deficiency of the neurotransmitter dopamine.
– DERIVATIVES **Parkinsonian** adjective.
– ORIGIN late 19th cent.: named after James *Parkinson* (1755–1824), English surgeon.

Parkinson's law ▸ noun the notion that work expands so as to fill the time available for its completion.
– ORIGIN 1950s: named after Cyril Northcote *Parkinson* (1909–93), English writer.

parkland ▸ noun [mass noun] (also **parklands**) open grassy land with scattered groups of trees.

parkour /pɑːˈkʊə/ (also **parcour**) ▸ noun [mass noun] the activity or sport of running through an area, typically in an urban environment, using acrobatic techniques to negotiate obstacles.
– ORIGIN early 21st cent.: French, alteration of *parcours* 'route, course'.

parkway ▸ noun **1** N. Amer. an open landscaped highway.
2 [in names] Brit. a railway station with extensive parking facilities: *Didcot Parkway.*

parky[1] ▸ adjective (**parkier**, **parkiest**) Brit. informal chilly: *it was parky on Bradfield Moors last week.*
– ORIGIN late 19th cent.: of unknown origin.

parky[2] ▸ noun variant spelling of PARKIE.

Parl. ▸ abbreviation Brit. ■ Parliament. ■ Parliamentary.

parlance /ˈpɑːl(ə)ns/ ▸ noun [mass noun] a particular way of speaking or using words, especially a way common to those with a particular job or interest: *dated terms that were once in common parlance | medical parlance.*
– ORIGIN late 16th cent. (denoting speech or debate): from Old French, from *parler* 'speak', from Latin *parabola* 'comparison' (in late Latin 'speech').

parlando /pɑːˈlandəʊ/ Music ▸ adverb & adjective (with reference to singing) expressive or declamatory in the manner of speech.
▸ noun [mass noun] composition or performance in a parlando manner.
– ORIGIN Italian, literally 'speaking'.

parlay /ˈpɑːleɪ/ N. Amer. ▸ verb [with obj.] (**parlay something into**) turn an initial stake or winnings from a previous bet into (a greater amount) by gambling: *parlaying a small bankroll into big winnings.*
▸ noun a cumulative series of bets in which winnings accruing from each transaction are used as a stake for a further bet.
– ORIGIN late 19th cent.: from French *paroli*, from Italian, from *paro* 'like', from Latin *par* 'equal'.

parley /ˈpɑːli/ ▸ noun (pl. **parleys**) a conference between opposing sides in a dispute, especially a discussion of terms for an armistice.
▸ verb (**parleys**, **parleying**, **parleyed**) [no obj.] hold a conference with the opposing side to discuss terms: *they disagreed over whether to parley with the enemy.*
– ORIGIN late Middle English (denoting speech or debate): perhaps from Old French *parlee* 'spoken', feminine past participle of the verb *parler*.

parliament /ˈpɑːləm(ə)nt/ ▸ noun (**Parliament**) (in the UK) the highest legislature, consisting of the Sovereign, the House of Lords, and the House of Commons: *the Secretary of State will lay proposals before Parliament | an Act of Parliament.* ■ the members of Parliament between one dissolution and the next: *the act was passed by the last parliament of the reign.* ■ a similar legislature in other nations and states: *the Russian parliament.*
– ORIGIN Middle English: from Old French *parlement* 'speaking', from the verb *parler*.

parliamentarian ▸ noun **1** a member of a parliament, especially one well versed in its procedure and experienced in debate.
2 historical a supporter of Parliament in the English Civil War; a Roundhead.
▸ adjective **1** relating to a parliament or its members: *parliamentarian committees.*
2 historical relating to the Roundheads.
– DERIVATIVES **parliamentarianism** noun.

parliamentary ▸ adjective relating to, enacted by, or suitable for a parliament: *a parliamentary candidate | parliamentary legislation.*

Parliamentary Commissioner for Administration ▸ noun (in the UK) an official appointed to investigate complaints by individuals against public authorities. Also called THE OMBUDSMAN.

Parliamentary Counsel ▸ noun (in the UK) a group of barristers employed as civil servants to draft government bills and amendments.

parliamentary party ▸ noun the members of a political party who are in parliament, as distinguished from the party in the country as a whole.

parliamentary private secretary ▸ noun (in the UK) a Member of Parliament assisting a government minister.

parliamentary undersecretary ▸ noun (in the UK) a Member of Parliament in a department of state, ranking below a minister.

parlour (US **parlor**) ▸ noun **1** dated a sitting room in a private house.
2 a room in a public building for receiving guests: *the mayor's parlour*. ■ a room in a monastery or convent that is set aside for conversation.
3 [usu. with modifier] chiefly N. Amer. a shop or business providing specified goods or services: *an ice-cream parlour | a funeral parlour*.
4 (also **milking parlour**) a room or building equipped for milking cows.
▸ adjective [attrib.] derogatory denoting a person who professes belief in but does not actively support a specified (especially radical) political view: *the parlour Socialists of the late Victorian period*.
– ORIGIN Middle English: from Anglo-Norman French *parlur* 'place for speaking', from Latin *parlare* 'speak'.

parlour car ▸ noun N. Amer. a luxuriously fitted railway carriage, typically with individually reserved seats.

parlour game ▸ noun an indoor game, especially a word game.

parlourmaid ▸ noun historical a maid employed to wait at table.

parlour palm ▸ noun a small Central American palm which is grown as a popular pot plant. ● *Chamaedorea elegans*, family Palmae.

parlous /ˈpɑːləs/ ▸ adjective archaic or humorous full of danger or uncertainty; precarious: *the parlous state of the economy | the General's position was parlous*.
▸ adverb archaic greatly or excessively: *she is parlous handsome*.
– DERIVATIVES **parlously** adverb, **parlousness** noun.
– ORIGIN late Middle English: contraction of PERILOUS.

Parma /ˈpɑːmə/, Italian /ˈparma/ a province of northern Italy, south of the River Po in Emilia-Romagna. ■ the capital of Parma; pop. 182,389 (2008). Founded by the Romans in 183 BC, it became a bishopric in the 9th century AD and capital of the duchy of Parma and Piacenza in about 1547.

Parma ham ▸ noun [mass noun] a strongly flavoured Italian cured ham, eaten uncooked and thinly sliced.

Parma violet ▸ noun a sweet violet of a variety with a heavy scent and lavender-coloured flowers which are often crystallized and used for food decoration.

parma wallaby ▸ noun a small dark brown Australian wallaby, restricted to the rainforests of New South Wales. ● *Macropus parma*, family Macropodidae.
– ORIGIN mid 19th cent.: *parma* (probably from a New South Wales Aboriginal language) was applied by George Robert Waterhouse (1810–88), English naturalist.

Parmenides /pɑːˈmɛnɪdiːz/ (*fl.* 5th century BC), Greek philosopher. Born in Elea in SW Italy, he founded the Eleatic school of philosophers. In his work *On Nature*, written in hexameter verse, he maintained that the apparent motion and changing forms of the universe are in fact manifestations of an unchanging and indivisible reality.

Parmentier /ˈpɑːmɒ̃tɪeɪ/ ▸ adjective [postpositive] (of a dish) made with or accompanied by potatoes: *potage Parmentier*.
– ORIGIN from the name of Antoine A. *Parmentier* (1737–1813), the French agriculturalist who popularized the potato in France.

Parmesan /pɑːmɪˈzan/ ▸ noun [mass noun] a hard, dry cheese used chiefly in grated form, especially on Italian dishes.
– ORIGIN early 16th cent.: from French, from Italian *parmigiano* 'of *Parma*', where it was originally made.

Parmigiana /ˌpɑːmɪˈdʒɑːnə/, Italian /ˌparmiˈdʒana/ ▸ adjective [postpositive] (of a dish) cooked or served with Parmesan cheese: *veal Parmigiana*.
– ORIGIN Italian, feminine of *Parmigiano* 'of Parma'.

Parmigianino /ˌpɑːmɪdʒɑːˈniːnəʊ/, Italian /ˌparmidʒaˈninoː/ (also **Parmigiano** /-ˈdʒɑːnəʊ/, Italian /-ˈdʒanoː/) (1503–40), Italian painter; born *Girolano Francesco Maria Mazzola*. He made an important contribution to early Mannerism, and is noted for the elongated and graceful forms of his figures, as in *Madonna with the Long Neck* (1534).

Parnassian /pɑːˈnasɪən/ ▸ adjective **1** literary relating to poetry; poetic.
2 denoting a group of French poets of the late 19th century who emphasized strictness of form, named from the anthology *Le Parnasse contemporain* (1866).
▸ noun a member of the Parnassian group of poets.

Parnassus, grass of ▸ noun see GRASS OF PARNASSUS.

Parnassus, Mount /pɑːˈnasəs/ a mountain in central Greece, just north of Delphi, rising to a height of 2,457 m (8,064 ft). Held to be sacred by the ancient Greeks, as was the spring of Castalia on its southern slopes, it was associated with Apollo and the Muses and regarded as a symbol of poetry. Greek name **Parnassós** /ˌparnaˈsɔs/.

Parnell /pɑːˈnɛl/, Charles Stewart (1846–91), Irish nationalist leader. Parnell became leader of the Irish Home Rule faction in 1880 and raised the profile of Irish affairs through obstructive parliamentary tactics. He was forced to retire from public life in 1890 after the exposure of his adultery with Mrs Katherine ('Kitty') O'Shea.
– DERIVATIVES **Parnellite** adjective & noun.

parochial /pəˈrəʊkɪəl/ ▸ adjective **1** relating to a Church parish: *the parochial church council*.
2 having a limited or narrow outlook or scope: *parochial attitudes | their interests are too parochial*.
– DERIVATIVES **parochiality** noun, **parochially** adverb.
– ORIGIN late Middle English: from Old French, from ecclesiastical Latin *parochialis* 'relating to an ecclesiastical district', from *parochia* (see PARISH).

parochialism /pəˈrəʊkɪəlɪz(ə)m/ ▸ noun [mass noun] a limited or narrow outlook, especially focused on a local area; narrow-mindedness: *accusations of parochialism*.

parochial school ▸ noun North American term for CHURCH SCHOOL.

parody ▸ noun (pl. **parodies**) an imitation of the style of a particular writer, artist, or genre with deliberate exaggeration for comic effect: *the film is a parody of the horror genre* | [mass noun] *his provocative use of parody*. ■ an imitation or version of something that falls far short of the real thing; a travesty: *he gave her a parody of a smile*.
▸ verb (**parodies**, **parodying**, **parodied**) [with obj.] produce a humorously exaggerated imitation of (a writer, artist, or genre). ■ mimic humorously: *he parodied his friend's voice*.
– DERIVATIVES **parodic** adjective, **parodically** adjective, **parodist** noun.
– ORIGIN late 16th cent.: via late Latin from Greek *parōidia* 'burlesque poem', from *para-* 'beside' (expressing alteration) + *ōidē* 'ode'.

par of exchange ▸ noun see PAR[1] (sense 2 of the noun).

parol /pəˈrəʊl, ˈpar(ə)l/ ▸ adjective Law given or expressed orally: *the parol evidence*. ■ (of a document) agreed orally, or in writing but not under seal: *there was a parol agreement*.
– PHRASES **by parol** by oral declaration.
– ORIGIN late 15th cent. (as a noun): from Old French *parole* 'word' (see PAROLE).

parole ▸ noun [mass noun] **1** the temporary or permanent release of a prisoner before the expiry of a sentence, on the promise of good behaviour: *he committed a burglary while on parole*. ■ [count noun] historical a promise or undertaking given by a prisoner of war to return to custody or act as a non-belligerent if released.
2 Linguistics the actual linguistic behaviour or performance of individuals, in contrast to the linguistic system of a community. Contrasted with LANGUE.
▸ verb [with obj.] release (a prisoner) on parole: *he was paroled after serving nine months of a two-year sentence*.
– DERIVATIVES **parolee** noun.
– ORIGIN late 15th cent.: from Old French, literally 'word', also 'formal promise', from ecclesiastical Latin *parabola* 'speech'; compare with PAROL.

paronomasia /ˌparənəˈmeɪzɪə/ ▸ noun a play on words; a pun.
– ORIGIN late 16th cent.: via Latin from Greek *paronomasia*, from *para-* 'beside' (expressing alteration) + *onomasia* 'naming' (from *onomazein* 'to name', from *onoma* 'a name').

paronym /ˈparənɪm/ ▸ noun Linguistics a word which is a derivative of another and has a related meaning: *'wisdom' is a paronym of 'wise'*. ■ a word formed by adaptation of a foreign word. Contrasted with HETERONYM.
– DERIVATIVES **paronymy** noun.
– ORIGIN mid 19th cent.: from Greek *parōnumon*, neuter (used as a noun) of *parōnumos* 'naming by modification', from *para-* 'beside' + *onuma* 'a name'.

Paros /ˈparɒs, ˈpɛːrɒs/ a Greek island in the southern Aegean, in the Cyclades. It is noted for the translucent white Parian marble which has been quarried there since the 6th century BC.

parotid /pəˈrɒtɪd/ Anatomy ▸ adjective relating to, situated near, or affecting a parotid gland.
▸ noun short for PAROTID GLAND.
– ORIGIN late 17th cent.: via Latin from Greek *parōtis*, *parōtid-*, from *para-* 'beside' + *ous*, *ōt-* 'ear'.

parotid gland ▸ noun Anatomy either of a pair of large salivary glands situated just in front of each ear.

parotitis /ˌparəˈtʌɪtɪs/ ▸ noun [mass noun] Medicine inflammation of a parotid gland, especially (**infectious parotitis**) mumps.

-parous ▸ combining form Biology bearing offspring of a specified number or reproducing in a specified manner: *multiparous | viviparous*.
– ORIGIN from Latin *-parus* '-bearing' (from *parere* 'bring forth, produce') + **-ous**.

Parousia /pəˈruːzɪə/ ▸ noun Christian Theology another term for SECOND COMING.
– ORIGIN Greek, literally 'being present'.

paroxysm /ˈparəksɪz(ə)m/ ▸ noun a sudden attack or outburst of a particular emotion or activity: ***a paroxysm of weeping***. ■ Medicine a sudden recurrence or attack of a disease.
– DERIVATIVES **paroxysmal** adjective.
– ORIGIN late Middle English: from French *paroxysme*, via medieval Latin from Greek *paroxusmos*, from *paroxunein* 'exasperate', from *para-* 'beyond' + *oxunein* 'sharpen' (from *oxus* 'sharp').

paroxytone /pəˈrɒksɪtəʊn/ ▸ adjective (especially in ancient Greek) having an acute accent on the last syllable but one. Compare with OXYTONE.
▸ noun a word with a paroxytone accent.
– ORIGIN mid 18th cent.: from modern Latin *paroxytonus*, from Greek *paroxutonos*, from *para-* 'alongside' + *oxutonos* 'sharp pitch'.

parp informal ▸ noun a honking sound produced by, or like that produced by, a car horn.
▸ verb [no obj.] make a honking sound.
– ORIGIN 1950s: imitative.

parpen /ˈpɑːp(ə)n/ ▸ noun a stone passing through a wall from side to side, with two smooth vertical faces.
– ORIGIN Middle English: from Old French *parpain* 'length of a stone', probably based on Latin *perpes* 'continuous'.

parquet /ˈpɑːkɪ, ˈpɑːkeɪ/ ▸ noun **1** (also **parquet flooring**) [mass noun] flooring composed of wooden blocks arranged in a geometric pattern.
2 N. Amer. the ground floor of a theatre or auditorium, especially the orchestra pit.
3 (**the Parquet**) (in France and French-speaking countries) the branch of the administration of the law that deals with the prosecution of crime.
DERIVATIVES **parqueted** adjective.
– ORIGIN late 17th cent. (as a verb): from French, literally 'small park (i.e. delineated area)'. The noun dates from the early 19th cent.

parquetry /ˈpɑːkɪtri/ ▸ noun [mass noun] inlaid work of blocks of various woods arranged in a geometric pattern, especially for flooring or furniture.

Parr, Katherine (1512–48), sixth and last wife of Henry VIII. Having married the king in 1543, she influenced his decision to restore the succession to his daughters Mary and Elizabeth (later Mary I and Elizabeth I respectively).

parr ▸ noun (pl. **same**) a young salmon (or trout) between the stages of fry and smolt, distinguished by dark rounded patches evenly spaced along its sides.
– ORIGIN early 18th cent.: of unknown origin.

parrakeet ▸ noun variant spelling of PARAKEET.

parramatta /ˌparəˈmatə/ (also **paramatta**) ▸ noun [mass noun] a fine-quality twill fabric with a weft of worsted and a warp of cotton or silk, used originally as a dress material and now particularly in the making of rubber-proofed garments.
– ORIGIN early 19th cent.: named after *Parramatta*, a city in New South Wales, Australia, which was the site of a prison whose inmates manufactured the

cloth for clothing supplied to the convict servants of settlers.

parricide /ˈparɪsʌɪd/ ▸ **noun** [mass noun] the killing of a parent or other near relative. ■ [count noun] a person who commits parricide.
– DERIVATIVES **parricidal** adjective.
– ORIGIN late 16th cent.: from French, from Latin *parricidium* 'murder of a parent', with first element of unknown origin, but for long associated with Latin *pater* 'father' and *parens* 'parent'.

parrot ▸ **noun** a bird, often vividly coloured, with a short downcurved hooked bill, grasping feet, and a raucous voice, found especially in the tropics and feeding on fruits and seeds. Many are popular as cage birds, and some are able to mimic the human voice. ● Order Psittaciformes: numerous species, sometimes all placed in the family Psittacidae. The order also contains the cockatoos, lories, lovebirds, macaws, conures, and budgerigar.
▸ **verb** (**parrots**, **parroting**, **parroted**) [with obj.] repeat mechanically: *encouraging students to parrot back information*.
– ORIGIN early 16th cent.: probably from dialect French *perrot*, diminutive of the male given name *Pierre* 'Peter'. Compare with PARAKEET.

parrotbill ▸ **noun** a tit-like Asian songbird with brown and grey plumage and a short arched bill. ● Family Panuridae (or Paradoxornithidae): two genera and several species, including the bearded tit or reedling.

parrot-fashion ▸ **adverb** Brit. without thought or understanding; mechanically: *she repeated the phrase parrot-fashion*.

parrot fever ▸ **noun** less formal term for PSITTACOSIS.

parrotfish ▸ **noun** (pl. **same** or **parrotfishes**) **1** any of a number of brightly coloured marine fish with a parrot-like beak, which they use to scrape food from coral and other hard surfaces: ● a widespread fish of warm seas which may secrete a mucous cocoon to deter predators (family Scaridae: *Scarus* and other genera). ● an edible fish of the southern Indian ocean (*Oplegnathus conwayi*, family Oplegnathidae).
2 Austral./NZ a brightly coloured marine fish, especially one of the wrasse family. ● Several species in the family Labridae.

parrotlet ▸ **noun** a tiny tropical American parrot with mainly green plumage and a short tail. ● Family Psittacidae: three genera, in particular *Forpus* and *Touit*, and several species.

parrot tulip ▸ **noun** a cultivated tulip of a variety which has irregularly fringed or wavy petals, typically of two colours.

Parry, Sir (Charles) Hubert (Hastings) (1848–1918), English composer. Parry's best-known work is his setting of William Blake's poem 'Jerusalem' (1916), which has acquired the status of a national song.

P

parry ▸ **verb** (**parries**, **parrying**, **parried**) [with obj.] ward off (a weapon or attack) with a countermove: *he parried the blow by holding his sword vertically*. ■ answer (a question or accusation) evasively: *he parried questions from reporters outside the building*.
▸ **noun** (pl. **parries**) an act of parrying something.
– ORIGIN late 17th cent.: probably representing French *parez!* 'ward off!', imperative of *parer*, from Italian *parare* 'ward off'.

parse /pɑːz/ ▸ **verb** [with obj.] resolve (a sentence) into its component parts and describe their syntactic roles. ■ Computing analyse (a string or text) into logical syntactic components.
▸ **noun** Computing an act of parsing a string or a text.
– ORIGIN mid 16th cent.: perhaps from Middle English *pars* 'parts of speech', from Old French *pars* 'parts' (influenced by Latin *pars* 'part').

parsec /ˈpɑːsɛk/ ▸ **noun** a unit of distance used in astronomy, equal to about 3.25 light years (3.08×10^{16} metres). One parsec corresponds to the distance at which the mean radius of the earth's orbit subtends an angle of one second of arc.
– ORIGIN early 20th cent.: blend of PARALLAX and SECOND².

Parsee /pɑːˈsiː, ˈpɑːsiː/ ▸ **noun** an adherent of Zoroastrianism, especially a descendant of those Zoroastrians who fled to India from Muslim persecution in Persia during the 7th–8th centuries.
– ORIGIN from Persian *pārsī* 'Persian', from *pārs* 'Persia'.

parser ▸ **noun** Computing a program for parsing.

parse tree ▸ **noun** Linguistics a diagrammatic representation of the parsed structure of a sentence or string.

Parsifal /ˈpɑːsɪf(ə)l/ another name for PERCEVAL¹.

parsimonious /ˌpɑːsɪˈməʊnɪəs/ ▸ **adjective** very unwilling to spend money or use resources: *even the parsimonious Joe paid for drinks all round*.
– DERIVATIVES **parsimoniously** adverb, **parsimoniousness** noun.

parsimony /ˈpɑːsɪməni/ ▸ **noun** [mass noun] extreme unwillingness to spend money or use resources: *a great tradition of public design has been shattered by government parsimony*.
– PHRASES **principle** (or **law**) **of parsimony** the scientific principle that things are usually connected or behave in the simplest or most economical way, especially with reference to alternative evolutionary pathways. Compare with OCCAM'S RAZOR.
– ORIGIN late Middle English: from Latin *parsimonia*, *parcimonia*, from *parcere* 'be sparing'.

parsley ▸ **noun** [mass noun] a biennial plant with white flowers and aromatic leaves which are either crinkly or flat and are used as a culinary herb and for garnishing food. ● *Petroselinum crispum*, family Umbelliferae (or Apiaceae; the **parsley family**). Members of this family have their flowers arranged in umbels and are known as umbellifers; typical members include hogweed and hemlock as well as many food plants and herbs (carrot, parsnip, celery, fennel, anise).
– ORIGIN Old English *petersilie*, via late Latin based on Greek *petroselinon*, from *petra* 'rock' + *selinon* 'parsley', influenced in Middle English by Old French *peresil*, of the same origin.

parsley fern ▸ **noun** a fern with finely divided fronds resembling parsley leaves, found typically on rocky ground in mountainous and boreal areas. ● Genus *Cryptogramma*, family Adiantaceae: several species.

parsley piert /ˌpɑːslɪ ˈpɪət/ ▸ **noun** a small hairy European plant with divided leaves, growing as a weed of fields and waste places. ● *Aphanes arvensis*, family Rosaceae.
– ORIGIN late 16th cent.: probably an altered form of French *perce-pierre*, literally 'pierce stone', used to denote various plants living in rock or wall crevices.

parsnip ▸ **noun 1** a long tapering cream-coloured root vegetable with a sweet flavour.
2 the Eurasian plant of the parsley family which yields parsnips. ● *Pastinaca sativa*, family Umbelliferae.
– ORIGIN late Middle English: from Old French *pasnaie*, from Latin *pastinaca* (related to *pastinare* 'dig and trench the ground'). The change in the ending was due to association with NEEP.

parson ▸ **noun** a beneficed member of the clergy; a rector or a vicar. ■ informal any member of the clergy, especially a Protestant one.
– DERIVATIVES **parsonical** adjective.
– ORIGIN Middle English: from Old French *persone*, from Latin *persona* 'person' (in medieval Latin 'rector').

parsonage ▸ **noun** a church house provided for a member of the clergy.

parson-bird ▸ **noun** NZ another term for TUI.

parson's nose ▸ **noun** informal the fatty extremity of the rump of a cooked fowl.

pars pro toto /ˌpɑːz prəʊ ˈtəʊtəʊ/ ▸ **noun** formal a part or aspect of something taken as representative of the whole.
– ORIGIN Latin, literally 'part on behalf of the whole'.

part ▸ **noun 1** an amount or section which, when combined with others, makes up the whole of something: *divide the circle into three equal parts* | *the early part of 1999* | *body parts*. ■ an element or constituent that is essential to the nature of something: *I was part of the family*. ■ a manufactured object assembled with others to make a machine; a component: *the production of aircraft parts*. ■ a division of a book, periodical, or broadcast serial. ■ a measure allowing comparison between the amounts of different ingredients used in a mixture: *use a mix of one part cement to five parts ballast*.
2 some but not all of something: *the painting tells only part of the story*. ■ a point on or area of something: *hold the furthest part of your leg that you can reach*. ■ (**parts**) informal a region, especially one not clearly specified or delimited: *those of you who jet off to foreign parts for your holidays*.
3 a role played by an actor or actress: *she played a lot of leading parts* | *he took the part of Prospero*. ■ the words and directions to be learned and performed by an actor in a role: *she was memorizing a part*. ■ Music a melody or other constituent of harmony assigned to a particular voice or instrument in a musical work: *he coped well with the percussion part*.
4 the contribution made by someone or something to an action or situation: *he **played a key part in** ending the revolt* | *he may be jailed for his part in the robbery*. ■ (**one's part**) the appropriate or expected behaviour in a particular role or situation; one's duty: *in such a place his part is to make good*.
5 (**parts**) archaic abilities.
6 N. Amer. a parting in the hair.
▸ **verb 1** [no obj.] (of two things) move away from each other: *his lips parted in a smile*. ■ divide to leave a central space: [no obj.] *at that moment the mist parted* | [with obj.] *she parted the ferns and looked between them*.
2 [no obj.] (also **be parted**) leave someone's company: *there was a good deal of kissing before we parted* | *she can't bear to **be parted from** her daughter again*.
3 [no obj.] (**part with**) give up possession of; hand over: *even quite small companies parted with large sums*.
4 [with obj.] separate (the hair of the head on either side of the parting) with a comb.
▸ **adverb** to some extent; partly (often used to contrast different parts of something): *the city is now part slum, part consumer paradise*.
– PHRASES **be part and parcel of** be an essential feature or element of: *it's best to accept that some inconveniences are part and parcel of travel*. [*parcel* here is in archaic sense 'part, portion'.] **for my** (or **his**, **her**, etc.) **part** as far as I am (or he, she, etc., is) concerned: *I for my part find the story less than convincing*. **in part** to some extent though not entirely: *the cause of the illness is at least in part psychological*. **look the part** have an appearance or style of dress appropriate to one's role or situation. **a man of** (**many**) **parts** a man with great ability in many different areas. **on the part of** (or **on my**, **their**, etc., **part**) used to ascribe responsibility for something to someone: *there was a series of errors on my part*. **part company** (of two or more people) cease to be together; go in different directions: *they parted company outside the Red Lion*. ■ (of two or more parties) cease to associate with each other, especially as the result of a disagreement: *the chairman has **parted company with** the club*. **take part** join in an activity; be involved: *we have come here to **take part in** a major game* | *they ran away and **took no part in** the battle*. **take the part of** Brit. give support and encouragement to (someone) in a dispute.
– ORIGIN Old English (denoting a part of speech), from Latin *pars*, *part-*. The verb (originally in Middle English in the sense 'divide into parts') is from Old French *partir*, from Latin *partire*, *partiri* 'divide, share'.

partake ▸ **verb** (past **partook**; past participle **partaken**) [no obj.] formal **1** (**partake of**) eat or drink (something): *he partook of a well-earned drink*.
2 (**partake in**) join in (an activity): *visitors can partake in golfing or clay pigeon shooting*.
3 (**partake of**) be characterized by (a quality): *the birth of twins became an event which partook of the mythic*.
– DERIVATIVES **partaker** noun.
– ORIGIN mid 16th cent.: back-formation from earlier *partaker* 'person who takes a part'.

parter ▸ **noun** [in combination] a broadcast or published work with a specified number of parts: *the first in a six-parter*.

parterre /pɑːˈtɛː/ ▸ **noun 1** a level space in a garden occupied by an ornamental arrangement of flower beds.
2 N. Amer. the part of the ground floor of a theatre auditorium behind the orchestra pit, especially the part beneath the balconies.
– ORIGIN early 17th cent.: from French, from *par terre* 'on the ground'.

part exchange Brit. ▸ **noun** [mass noun] a method of buying something in which one gives an article that one owns as part of the payment for another, more expensive, article: *he sold the car **in part exchange** for another vehicle*.
▸ **verb** (**part-exchange**) [with obj.] give or take (an article) in part exchange.

parthenocarpy /ˈpɑːθɪnə(ʊ)ˌkɑːpi/ ▸ **noun** [mass noun] Botany the development of a fruit without prior fertilization.
– DERIVATIVES **parthenocarpic** adjective.
– ORIGIN early 20th cent.: from German *Parthenocarpie*, from Greek *parthenos* 'virgin' + *karpos* 'fruit'.

parthenogenesis /ˌpɑːθɪnə(ʊ)ˈdʒɛnɪsɪs/ ▸ **noun** [mass noun] Biology reproduction from an ovum without fertilization, especially as a normal process in some invertebrates and lower plants.
– DERIVATIVES **parthenogenetic** adjective, **parthenogenetically** adverb.

– ORIGIN mid 19th cent.: modern Latin, from Greek *parthenos* 'virgin' + *genesis* 'creation'.

Parthenon /ˈpɑːθɪnən/ the temple of Athene Parthenos, built on the Acropolis in 447–432 BC by Pericles to honour Athens' patron goddess and to commemorate the recent Greek victory over the Persians. It was designed by Ictinus and Callicrates with sculptures by Phidias.
– ORIGIN from Greek *parthenos* 'virgin'.

parthenote /ˈpɑːθənəʊt/ ▶ **noun** Biology an organism produced from an unfertilized ovum, which is incapable of developing beyond the early embryonic stages.
– ORIGIN 1930s: from **PARTHENOGENESIS** and **ZYGOTE**.

Parthia /ˈpɑːθɪə/ an ancient kingdom which lay south-east of the Caspian Sea in present-day Iran. From *c.*250 BC to *c.*230 AD the Parthians ruled an empire stretching from the Euphrates to the Indus.
– DERIVATIVES **Parthian** noun & adjective.

Parthian shot ▶ **noun** another term for **PARTING SHOT**.
– ORIGIN late 19th cent.: so named because of the trick used by Parthians of shooting arrows backwards while in real or pretended flight.

partial ▶ **adjective 1** existing only in part; incomplete: *a question to which we have only partial answers.*
2 favouring one side in a dispute above the other; biased: *the paper gave a distorted and very partial view of the situation.*
3 (**partial to**) having a liking for: *you know I'm very partial to bacon and eggs.*
▶ **noun** Music a component of a musical sound; an overtone or harmonic.
– ORIGIN late Middle English (in sense 2 of the adjective): from Old French *parcial* (sense 2 of the adjective), French *partiel* (sense 1 of the adjective), from late Latin *partialis*, from *pars*, *part-* 'part'.

partial derivative ▶ **noun** Mathematics a derivative of a function of two or more variables with respect to one variable, the other(s) being treated as constant.

partial differential equation ▶ **noun** Mathematics an equation containing one or more partial derivatives.

partial eclipse ▶ **noun** an eclipse of a celestial body in which only part of the luminary is obscured or darkened.

partial fraction ▶ **noun** Mathematics each of two or more fractions into which a more complex fraction can be decomposed as a sum.

partiality ▶ **noun 1** [mass noun] unfair bias in favour of one person or thing; favouritism: *an attack on the partiality of judges.*
2 [count noun] a particular liking or fondness for something: *Miller's **partiality for** flowering shrubs is evident.*
– ORIGIN late Middle English: from Old French *parcialite*, from medieval Latin *partialitas*, based on Latin *pars*, *part-* 'part'.

partially ▶ **adverb** only in part; to a limited extent: *the work partially fulfills the function of a historical memoir* | [as submodifier] *a partially open door.*

partially sighted ▶ **adjective** having a visual impairment: *a partially sighted child.*

partial order (also **partial ordering**) ▶ **noun** Mathematics a transitive antisymmetric relation among the elements of a set, which does not necessarily apply to each pair of elements.

partial pressure ▶ **noun** Chemistry the pressure that would be exerted by one of the gases in a mixture if it occupied the same volume on its own.

partial product ▶ **noun** Mathematics the product of one term of a multiplicand and one term of its multiplier. ■ the product of the first *n* terms of a large or infinite series, where *n* is a finite integer (including 1).

partible ▶ **adjective** Law (of a property interest) divisible. ■ involving or denoting a system of inheritance in which a deceased person's estate is divided equally among the heirs.
– DERIVATIVES **partibility** noun.
– ORIGIN late Middle English (in the sense 'able to be parted'): from late Latin *partibilis*, from Latin *partiri* 'divide into parts'.

participant ▶ **noun** a person who takes part in something: *staff are to be active **participants in** the decision-making process.*
– ORIGIN late Middle English: from Latin *participant-*, literally 'sharing in', from the verb *participare* (see **PARTICIPATE**).

participate ▶ **verb** [no obj.] **1** be involved; take part: *thousands **participated in** a nationwide strike.*
2 (**participate of**) archaic have or possess (a particular quality): *both members participate of harmony.*
– DERIVATIVES **participative** adjective, **participator** noun, **participatory** adjective.
– ORIGIN late 15th cent.: from Latin *participat-* 'shared in', from the verb *participare*, based on *pars*, *part-* 'part' + *capere* 'take'.

participation ▶ **noun** [mass noun] the action of taking part in something: ***participation in** chapel activities* | *the scheme is based on employer participation.*
– ORIGIN late Middle English: from Old French, from Latin *participatio(n-)*, from *participat-* (see **PARTICIPATE**).

participial adjective ▶ **noun** Grammar an adjective that is a participle in origin and form, such as *burnt*, *cutting*, *engaged*.

participle /ˈpɑːtɪsɪp(ə)l/ ▶ **noun** Grammar a word formed from a verb (e.g. *going, gone, being, been*) and used as an adjective (e.g. *working woman, burnt toast*) or a noun (e.g. *good breeding*). In English participles are also used to make compound verb forms (e.g. *is going, has been*). Compare with **GERUND**.
– DERIVATIVES **participial** /-ˈsɪpɪəl/ adjective.
– ORIGIN late Middle English: from Old French, by-form of *participe*, from Latin *participium* ('verbal form) sharing (the functions of a noun'), from *participare* 'share in'.

particle ▶ **noun 1** a minute portion of matter: *tiny particles of dust.* ■ (also **subatomic** or **elementary particle**) Physics any of numerous subatomic constituents of the physical world that interact with each other, including electrons, neutrinos, photons, and alpha particles. ■ Mathematics a hypothetical object having mass but no physical size.
2 [with negative] the least possible amount: *he agrees without hearing the least **particle of** evidence.*
3 Grammar (in English) any of the class of words such as *in, up, off, over*, used with verbs to make phrasal verbs. ■ (in ancient Greek) any of a class of words used for contrast and emphasis, such as *de* and *ge*.
– ORIGIN late Middle English: from Latin *particula* 'little part', diminutive of *pars, part-*.

particle accelerator ▶ **noun** an apparatus for accelerating subatomic particles to high velocities by means of electric or electromagnetic fields. The accelerated particles are generally made to collide with other particles, either as a research technique or for the generation of high-energy X-rays and gamma rays.

particle board ▶ **noun** another term for **CHIPBOARD**.

particle physics ▶ **plural noun** [treated as sing.] the branch of physics that deals with the properties, relationships, and interactions of subatomic particles.

particoloured (US **particolored**) ▶ **adjective** having or consisting of two or more different colours: *particoloured Devon cattle.*
– ORIGIN early 16th cent.: from the adjective **PARTY**[2] + **COLOURED**.

particular ▶ **adjective 1** [attrib.] used to single out an individual member of a specified group or class: *the action seems to discriminate against a particular group of companies.* ■ Logic denoting a proposition in which something is asserted of some but not all of a class. Contrasted with **UNIVERSAL**.
2 [attrib.] especially great or intense: *when handling or checking cash the cashier should exercise particular care.*
3 insisting that something should be correct or suitable in every detail; fastidious: *she is very particular about cleanliness.*
▶ **noun 1** a detail: *he is wrong **in every particular**.* ■ (**particulars**) detailed information about someone or something: *a clerk took the woman's particulars.*
2 Philosophy an individual item, as contrasted with a universal quality.
– PHRASES **in particular** especially (used to show that a statement applies to one person or thing more than any other): *he socialized with the other young people, one boy in particular.*
– ORIGIN late Middle English: from Old French *particuler*, from Latin *particularis* 'concerning a small part', from *particula* 'small part'.

Particular Baptist ▶ **noun** a member of a Baptist denomination holding the doctrine of the election and redemption of some but not all people.

particular integral ▶ **noun** Mathematics another term for **PARTICULAR SOLUTION**.

particular intention ▶ **noun** another term for **SPECIAL INTENTION**.

particularism ▶ **noun** [mass noun] **1** exclusive attachment to one's own group, party, or nation. ■ the principle of leaving each state in an empire or federation free to promote its own interests, without reference to those of the whole.
2 Theology the doctrine that some but not all people are elected and redeemed.
– DERIVATIVES **particularist** noun & adjective, **particularistic** adjective.
– ORIGIN early 19th cent.: from French *particularisme*, modern Latin *particularismus*, and German *Partikularismus*, based on Latin *particularis* 'concerning a small part'.

particularity ▶ **noun** (pl. **particularities**) [mass noun] **1** the quality of being individual. ■ fullness or minuteness of detail in the treatment of something: *parties must present their case with some degree of accuracy and particularity.* ■ (**particularities**) small details: *the tedious particularities of daily life.*
2 Christian Theology the doctrine of God's incarnation as Jesus as a particular person at a particular time and place.
– ORIGIN early 16th cent. (as *particularities* 'details'): from Old French *particularite* or late Latin *particularitas*, from Latin *particularis* 'concerning a small part'.

particularize (also **particularise**) ▶ **verb** [with obj.] formal treat individually or in detail: *he was the first to particularize themes in the poetry.*
– DERIVATIVES **particularization** noun.

particularly ▶ **adverb 1** to a higher degree than is usual or average: *I don't particularly want to be reminded of that time* | [as submodifier] *particularly able students.* ■ used to single out a subject to which a statement is especially applicable: *the team's defence is excellent, particularly their two centre backs.*
2 so as to give special emphasis to a point; specifically: *he particularly asked that I should help you.*

particular solution ▶ **noun** Mathematics a form of the solution of a differential equation with specific values assigned to the arbitrary constants.

particulate /pɑːˈtɪkjʊlət, -eɪt, pə-/ ▶ **adjective** relating to or in the form of minute separate particles: *particulate pollution.*
▶ **noun** (**particulates**) matter in the form of minute separate particles.
– ORIGIN late 19th cent.: from Latin *particula* 'particle' + **-ATE**[2].

parting ▶ **noun** [mass noun] **1** the action of leaving or being separated from someone: *they exchanged a few words on parting* | [count noun] *the wrench of her parting from Stephen.*
2 the action of dividing something into parts: *the parting of the Red Sea.*
3 Brit. a line of scalp revealed in a person's hair by combing the hair away in opposite directions on either side: *his hair was dark, with a side parting.*
– PHRASES **parting of the ways** a point at which two people must separate or at which a decision must be taken: *the best course is to seek an amicable parting of the ways.*

parting shot ▶ **noun** a final remark, typically a cutting one, made by someone at the moment of departure: *as her parting shot she told me never to phone her again.*

parti pris /ˌpɑːtɪ ˈpriː/ ▶ **noun** (pl. **partis pris** pronunc. **same**) a preconceived view; a bias.
▶ **adjective** prejudiced; biased.
– ORIGIN French, literally 'side taken'.

partisan /ˈpɑːtɪzan, ˌpɑːtɪˈzan/ ▶ **noun 1** a strong supporter of a party, cause, or person.
2 a member of an armed group formed to fight secretly against an occupying force, in particular one operating in German-occupied Yugoslavia, Italy, and parts of eastern Europe in the Second World War.
▶ **adjective** prejudiced in favour of a particular cause: *newspapers have become increasingly partisan.*
– ORIGIN mid 16th cent.: from French, via Italian dialect from Italian *partigiano*, from *parte* 'part' (from Latin *pars, part-*).

partisanship /ˈpɑːtɪz(ə)nʃɪp/ ▶ **noun** [mass noun] prejudice in favour of a particular cause; bias: *an act of blatant political partisanship.*

partita /pɑːˈtiːtə/ ▶ **noun** (pl. **partitas** or **partite** /-teɪ, -tiː/) Music a suite, typically for a solo instrument or chamber ensemble.
– ORIGIN late 19th cent.: from Italian, literally 'divided off', feminine past participle of *partire*.

partite /ˈpɑːtʌɪt/ ▶ **adjective** [usu. in combination] divided into parts: *multipartite.* ■ Botany & Zoology (especially

P

of a leaf or an insect's wing) divided to or nearly to the base.
– ORIGIN late 16th cent.: from Latin *partitus* 'divided up', past participle of *partiri*.

partition ▸ noun **1** [mass noun] (especially with reference to a country with separate areas of government) the action or state of dividing or being divided into parts: *the country's partition into separate states.* ■ Chemistry the distribution of a solute between two immiscible or slightly miscible solvents in contact with one another, in accordance with its differing solubility in each.
2 a structure dividing a space into two parts, especially a light interior wall. ■ Computing each of a number of portions into which some operating systems divide memory or storage.
▸ verb [with obj.] divide into parts: *an agreement was reached to partition the country.* ■ divide (a room) into smaller rooms or areas by erecting partitions: *the hall was partitioned to contain the noise of the computers* | **partition off** *part of a large bedroom to create a small bathroom.*
– DERIVATIVES **partitioner** noun, **partitionist** noun.
– ORIGIN late Middle English: from Latin *partitio(n-)*, from *partiri* 'divide into parts'.

partition coefficient ▸ noun Chemistry the ratio of the concentrations of a solute in two immiscible or slightly miscible liquids, or in two solids, when it is in equilibrium across the interface between them.

partitive /ˈpɑːtɪtɪv/ Grammar ▸ adjective denoting a grammatical construction used to indicate that only a part of a whole is referred to, for example *a slice of bacon, a series of accidents, some of the children.*
▸ noun a partitive construction. ■ a noun or pronoun used as the first term in a partitive construction.
– DERIVATIVES **partitively** adverb.

partitive genitive ▸ noun Grammar a genitive used to indicate a whole divided into or regarded in parts, expressed in English by *of* as in *most of us.*

partizan ▸ noun & adjective old-fashioned spelling of PARTISAN.

partly ▸ adverb to some extent; not completely: *the result is partly a matter of skill and partly of chance* | *you're only partly right.*

partner ▸ noun a person who takes part in an undertaking with another or others, especially in a business or firm with shared risks and profits. ■ either of two people dancing together or playing a game or sport on the same side. ■ either member of a married couple or of an established unmarried couple: *she lived with her partner.* ■ a person with whom one has sex; a lover. ■ US dated or dialect a friendly form of address by one man to another: *how you doing, partner?*
▸ verb [with obj.] be the partner of: *young farmers who partnered Isabel to the village dance.* ■ [no obj.] N. Amer. associate as partners: *I never expected to* **partner with** *a man like you.*
– DERIVATIVES **partnerless** adjective.
– ORIGIN Middle English: alteration of *parcener* 'partner, joint heir', from Anglo-Norman French *parcener*, based on Latin *partitio(n-)* 'partition'. The change in the first syllable was due to association with PART.

partners' desk (also **partnership desk**) ▸ noun a large flat-topped pedestal desk with space for two people to sit opposite each other.

partnership ▸ noun **1** [mass noun] the state of being a partner or partners: *we should go on working together* **in partnership**.
2 an association of two or more people as partners: *an increase in partnerships with housing associations.* ■ a business or firm owned and run by two or more partners. ■ a position as one of the partners in a business or firm. ■ Cricket the number of runs added by a pair of batsmen before one of them is dismissed or the innings ends.

part of speech ▸ noun a category to which a word is assigned in accordance with its syntactic functions. In English the main parts of speech are noun, pronoun, adjective, determiner, verb, adverb, preposition, conjunction, and interjection. Also called WORD CLASS.

Parton, Dolly (Rebecca) (b.1946), American country music singer and songwriter; her hits include 'Jolene' (1974).

partook past of PARTAKE.

part-own ▸ verb [with obj.] own (something) jointly with another or others: *he part-owns a nightclub out in Essex.*
– DERIVATIVES **part-owner** noun.

partridge ▸ noun (pl. **same** or **partridges**) a short-tailed game bird with mainly brown plumage, found chiefly in Europe and Asia. ● Family Phasianidae: several genera and many species, in particular the European **grey partridge** (*Perdix perdix*) and **red-legged partridge** (*Alectoris rufa*).
– ORIGIN Middle English *partrich*, from Old French *pertriz, perdriz*, from Latin *perdix*.

partridgeberry ▸ noun (pl. **partridgeberries**) either of two North American plants with edible red berries that are eaten by game birds. ● *Mitchella repens*, family Rubiaceae. ● the cowberry.
■ the fruit of either of these plants.

partridge pea ▸ noun **1** a field pea of a variety with speckled seeds.
2 US a yellow-flowered plant of the pea family with sensitive leaves. ● *Cassia fasciculata*, family Leguminosae.

part-song ▸ noun a secular song with three or more voice parts, typically unaccompanied, and homophonic rather than contrapuntal in style.

part-time ▸ adjective & adverb for only part of the usual working day or week: [as adj.] *part-time jobs* | *a part-time teacher* | [as adv.] *he only worked part-time.*
– DERIVATIVES **part-timer** noun.

parturient /pɑːˈtjʊərɪənt/ technical ▸ adjective (of a woman or female mammal) about to give birth; in labour.
▸ noun a parturient woman.
– ORIGIN late 16th cent.: from Latin *parturient-* 'being in labour', from the verb *parturire*, inceptive of *parere* 'bring forth'.

parturition /ˌpɑːtjʊˈrɪʃ(ə)n/ ▸ noun [mass noun] formal or technical the action of giving birth to young; childbirth: *the weeks following parturition.*
– ORIGIN mid 17th cent.: from late Latin *parturit-io(n-)*, from *parturire* 'be in labour' (see PARTURIENT).

part way ▸ adverb part of the way: *part way along the corridor he stopped.*

part-work ▸ noun Brit. a publication appearing in several parts over a period of time.

party¹ ▸ noun (pl. **parties**) **1** a social gathering of invited guests, typically involving eating, drinking, and entertainment: *an engagement party.*
2 a formally constituted political group that contests elections and attempts to form or take part in a government: *draft the party's election manifesto.* ■ a group of people taking part in a particular activity or trip.
3 a person or people forming one side in an agreement or dispute: *a contract between two parties.* ■ informal a person, especially one with specified characteristics: *an old party has been coming in to clean.*
▸ verb (**parties, partying, partied**) [no obj.] informal enjoy oneself at a party or other lively gathering, typically with drinking and music: *put on your glad rags and party!*
– PHRASES **be party** (or **a party**) **to** be involved in: *he was party to some very shady deals.* **bring something to the party** see BRING.
– DERIVATIVES **partier** noun (informal).
– ORIGIN Middle English (denoting a body of people united in opposition to others, also in sense 2 of the noun): from Old French *partie*, based on Latin *partiri* 'divide into parts'. Sense 1 of the noun dates from the early 18th cent.

party² ▸ adjective Heraldry divided into parts of different tinctures: *party per fess, or, and azure.*
– ORIGIN Middle English (in the sense 'parti-coloured'): from Old French *parti* 'parted', based on Latin *partitus* 'divided into parts' (from the verb *partiri*).

partygoer ▸ noun a person attending a party: *I was an avid partygoer—I liked the good life.*

party line ▸ noun **1** a policy, or the policies collectively, officially adopted by a political party: *they rarely fail to toe the party line.*
2 a telephone line or circuit shared by two or more subscribers.

party list ▸ noun an electoral system of proportional representation in which people vote for a party rather than a candidate and seats are filled from lists of candidates according to each party's share of the vote.

party piece ▸ noun Brit. a poem, song, or trick regularly performed by someone in order to entertain others.

party political ▸ adjective chiefly Brit. relating to or involved in party politics: *thinly disguised party political propaganda.*

party political broadcast ▸ noun Brit. a television or radio programme on which a representative of a political party presents material intended to foster support for it.

party politics ▸ plural noun [also treated as sing.] politics that relate to political parties rather than to the good of the general public.

party pooper ▸ noun informal a person who throws gloom over social enjoyment: *I hate to be a party pooper, but I've got to catch the last train.*
– DERIVATIVES **party-pooping** noun & adjective.

party popper ▸ noun a device used as an amusement at parties, which explodes when a string is pulled, ejecting thin paper streamers.

party wall ▸ noun a wall common to two adjoining buildings or rooms.

parure /pəˈrʊə/ ▸ noun a set of jewels intended to be worn together.
– ORIGIN early 19th cent.: from French, from *parer* 'adorn'.

Parvati /ˈpɑːvəti/ Hinduism a benevolent goddess, wife of Shiva, mother of Ganesha and Skanda, often identified in her malevolent aspect with Durga and Kali.
– ORIGIN from Sanskrit *Pārvatī*, literally 'daughter of the mountain'.

parvenu /ˈpɑːvənuː, -njuː/ ▸ noun often derogatory a person of humble origin who has gained wealth, influence, or celebrity: *the political inexperience of a parvenu* | [as modifier] *cynical parvenu bureaucrats.*
– ORIGIN early 19th cent.: from French, literally 'arrived', past participle of *parvenir*, from Latin *pervenire* 'come to, reach'.

parvis /ˈpɑːvɪs/ (also **parvise**) ▸ noun an enclosed area in front of a cathedral or church, typically surrounded with colonnades or porticoes.
– ORIGIN late Middle English: from Old French, based on late Latin *paradisus* 'paradise', in the Middle Ages denoting a court in front of St Peter's, Rome.

parvovirus /ˈpɑːvəʊˌvʌɪrəs/ ▸ noun Medicine any of a class of very small viruses chiefly affecting animals, especially one (**canine parvovirus**) which causes contagious disease in dogs.
– ORIGIN 1960s: from Latin *parvus* 'small' + VIRUS.

PAS ▸ abbreviation power-assisted steering.

pas /pɑː/ ▸ noun (pl. **same**) a step in dancing, especially in classical ballet.
– ORIGIN French.

Pasadena /ˌpasəˈdiːnə/ a city in California, in the San Gabriel Mountains on the NE side of the Los Angeles conurbation; pop. 143,080 (est. 2008). It is the site of the Rose Bowl stadium, venue for the American Football Super Bowl.

pasanda /pəˈsandə/ ▸ noun a north Indian dish consisting of sliced meat cooked in a sauce made with tomatoes, yogurt, cream, and spices.
– ORIGIN Urdu *pasandā*, from Persian *pasanda* 'pleasing'.

Pascal¹ /pasˈkɑːl/, French /paskal/, Blaise (1623–62), French mathematician, physicist, and religious philosopher. He founded the theory of probabilities and developed a forerunner of integral calculus, but is best known for deriving the principle that the pressure of a fluid at rest is transmitted equally in all directions. His *Lettres Provinciales* (1656–7) and *Pensées* (1670) argue for his Jansenist Christianity.

Pascal² /ˈpask(ə)l/ (also **PASCAL**) ▸ noun [mass noun] a high-level structured computer programming language used for teaching and general programming.
– ORIGIN 1970s: named after B. Pascal (see PASCAL¹) because he built a calculating machine.

pascal /ˈpask(ə)l/ (abbrev.: **Pa**) ▸ noun the SI unit of pressure, equal to one newton per square metre (approximately 0.000145 pounds per square inch, or 9.9×10^{-6} atmospheres).
– ORIGIN 1950s: named after B. Pascal (see PASCAL¹).

Pascal's triangle ▸ noun Mathematics a triangular array of numbers in which those at the ends of the rows are 1 and each of the others is the sum of the nearest two numbers in the row above (the apex, 1, being at the top).

Pascal's wager ▸ noun [in sing.] Philosophy the argument that it is in one's own best interest to behave as if God exists, since the possibility of eternal punishment in hell outweighs any advantage in believing otherwise.

paschal /ˈpask(ə)l, ˈpɑːs-/ ▸ adjective formal **1** relating to Easter.
2 relating to the Jewish Passover.

– ORIGIN late Middle English: from Old French, from ecclesiastical Latin *paschalis*, from *pascha* 'feast of Passover', via Greek and Aramaic from Hebrew *Pesaḥ* 'Passover'.

paschal candle ▶ **noun** Christian Church a large candle blessed and lit on Holy Saturday and placed by the altar until Pentecost.

paschal lamb ▶ **noun** a lamb sacrificed at Passover. ■ (**the Paschal Lamb**) Christ.

Paschen series /ˈpaʃ(ə)n/ Physics a series of lines in the infrared spectrum of atomic hydrogen, between 1.88 and 0.82 micrometres.
– ORIGIN 1920s: named after L. C. H. Friedrich *Paschen* (1865–1947), German physicist.

pas de basque /ˌpɑː də ˈbask, ˈbɑːsk/ ▶ **noun** (pl. **same**) a ballet step in three beats, with a circular movement of the right leg on the second beat. ■ (especially in jigs and reels) a step in three beats with one long and two short movements, transferring weight from one foot to the other on the spot.
– ORIGIN French, literally 'step of a Basque'.

pas de bourrée /ˌpɑː də ˈbʊəreɪ/ ▶ **noun** Ballet a sideways step in which one foot crosses behind or in front of the other.
– ORIGIN French, literally 'bourrée step'.

pas de chat /ˌpɑː də ˈʃa/ ▶ **noun** (pl. **same**) Ballet a jump in which each foot in turn is raised to the opposite knee.
– ORIGIN French, literally 'step of a cat'.

pas de deux /ˌpɑː də ˈdəː/ ▶ **noun** (pl. **same**) a dance for two people, typically a man and a woman.
– ORIGIN French, literally 'step of two'.

pas de quatre /ˌpɑː də ˈkatr(ə)/ ▶ **noun** (pl. **same**) a dance for four people.
– ORIGIN French, literally 'step of four'.

pas de trois /ˌpɑː də ˈtrwʌ/ ▶ **noun** (pl. **same**) a dance for three people.
– ORIGIN French, literally 'step of three'.

paseo /paˈseɪəʊ/ ▶ **noun** (pl. **paseos** /-əʊz/) (in Spain or Spanish-speaking parts of the south-western US) a leisurely walk or stroll, especially one taken in the evening in which young people may socialize with each other.
– ORIGIN Spanish, literally 'step'.

pash informal ▶ **noun** dated a brief infatuation: *Kath's got a pash on him.*
▶ **verb** [no obj.] Austral./NZ kiss and caress amorously.
– ORIGIN early 20th cent.: abbreviation of PASSION.

pasha /ˈpaʃə/ ▶ **noun 1** (also **pacha**) historical the title of a Turkish officer of high rank.
2 (**two-tailed pasha**) a large orange-brown butterfly with two tails on each hindwing and complex patterns on the underwings, occurring around the Mediterranean and in Africa. ● *Charaxes jasius*, subfamily Nymphalinae, family Nymphalidae.
– ORIGIN mid 17th cent.: from Turkish *paşa*, from Pahlavi *pati* 'lord' + *šāh* 'shah'.

pashm /ˈpaʃ(ə)m/ ▶ **noun** [mass noun] fine, soft wool from the underfur of some Tibetan goats and sheep.
– ORIGIN late 19th cent.: from Persian *pašm* 'wool'.

pashmina /pʌʃˈmiːnə/ ▶ **noun** a shawl made from fine-quality goat's wool. ■ another term for PASHM.
– ORIGIN Persian, from *pašm* 'wool'.

Pashto /ˈpʌʃtəʊ/ ▶ **noun** [mass noun] the language of the Pashtuns, which belongs to the Iranian group. It is the official language of Afghanistan and is also spoken in northern areas of Pakistan.
– ORIGIN the name in Pashto.

Pashtun /pəʃˈtuːn/ (also **Pakhtun** /pəkˈtuːn/) ▶ **noun** a member of a Pashto-speaking people inhabiting NW Pakistan and SE Afghanistan. Also called PATHAN.
– ORIGIN from Pashto *paštūn*.

Pašić /ˈpaʃɪtʃ/, Nikola (1845–1926), Serbian statesman, Prime Minister of Serbia five times between 1891 and 1918, and of the Kingdom of Serbs, Croats, and Slovenes 1921–4 and 1924–6. He was a party to the formation of the Kingdom of Serbs, Croats, and Slovenes (called Yugoslavia from 1929) in 1918.

Pasiphaë /pəˈsɪfiː/ Greek Mythology the wife of Minos and mother of the Minotaur.

paskha /ˈpaskə/ ▶ **noun** [mass noun] a rich Russian dessert made with curd cheese, dried fruit, nuts, and spices and traditionally eaten at Easter.
– ORIGIN Russian, literally 'Easter'.

paso doble /ˌpasə(ʊ) ˈdəʊbleɪ/ ▶ **noun** (pl. **paso dobles**) a fast-paced ballroom dance based on a Latin American style of marching. ■ a piece of music for the paso doble, typically in duple time.
– ORIGIN 1920s: from Spanish, literally 'double step'.

Pasolini /ˌpasəˈliːni/, Pier Paolo (1922–75), Italian film director and novelist. A Marxist, he drew on his experiences in the slums of Rome for his work, but became recognized for his controversial, bawdy literary adaptations, such as *The Gospel According to St Matthew* (1964) and *The Canterbury Tales* (1973).

pas op /pas ˈɒp/ ▶ **exclamation** S. African informal look out!
– ORIGIN Afrikaans, imperative of Dutch *oppassen* 'be on guard'.

paspalum /ˈpasp(ə)ləm/ ▶ **noun** [mass noun] a grass of warm and tropical regions, which is grown for fodder, erosion control, and as a pasture grass. ● Genus *Paspalum*, family Gramineae.
– ORIGIN modern Latin, from Greek *paspalos*, denoting a kind of millet.

pasque flower /pask, pɑːsk/ ▶ **noun** a spring-flowering European plant related to the anemones, with purple flowers and fern-like foliage. ● *Pulsatilla vulgaris*, family Ranunculaceae.
– ORIGIN late 16th cent. (as *passeflower*): from French *passe-fleur*. The change in spelling of the first word was due to association with archaic *pasque* 'Easter' (because of the plant's early flowering).

pasquinade /ˌpaskwɪˈneɪd/ ▶ **noun** a satire or lampoon, originally one displayed or delivered in a public place.
– ORIGIN late 16th cent.: from Italian *pasquinata*, from *Pasquino*, the name of a statue in Rome on which abusive Latin verses were posted annually.

pass[1] ▶ **verb 1** move or cause to move in a specified direction: [no obj., with adverbial of direction] *he passed through towns and villages | a plane was passing lazily overhead* | [with obj. and adverbial of direction] *he passed a weary hand across his forehead | pass an electric current through it.* ■ [no obj., with adverbial of direction] change from one state or condition to another: *homes which have passed from public to private ownership.* ■ [no obj.] euphemistic, chiefly N. Amer. die: *I was with him the night he passed.*
2 [with obj.] go past or across; leave behind or on one side in proceeding: *on the way to the station she passed a cinema | the two vehicles had no room to pass each other* | [no obj.] *we will not let you pass.* ■ go beyond the limits of; surpass or exceed: *the Portuguese trade passed its peak in the 1760s | this item has passed its sell-by date.* ■ Tennis hit a winning shot past (an opponent).
3 [no obj.] (of time) elapse; go by: *the day and night passed slowly.* ■ [with obj.] spend or use up (a period of time): *this was how they passed the time.* ■ come to an end: *the danger had passed.* ■ happen; be done or said: *not another word **passed between** them* | [with complement] *this fact has passed almost unnoticed.*
4 [with obj. and usu. with adverbial of direction] transfer (something) to someone, especially by handing or bequeathing it to the next person in a series: *your letter has been passed to Mr Rich for action | pass the milk | the poem was passed from generation to generation* | [with two objs] *he passed her a cup.* ■ [no obj., with adverbial] be transferred from one person or place to another, especially by inheritance: *if Ann remarried the estate would pass to her new husband.* ■ (in soccer, rugby, and other games) kick, hit, or throw (the ball) to another player of one's own side: *his intent was to pass the ball forward rather than knock it back.* ■ put (something, especially money) into circulation: *persons who have passed bad cheques.* ■ [no obj.] (especially of money) circulate; be current.
5 [with obj.] (of a candidate) be successful in (an examination, test, or course): *she passed her driving test.* ■ judge the performance or standard of (someone or something) to be satisfactory: [with obj. and complement] *he was passed fit by army doctors.* ■ [no obj.] (**pass as/for**) be accepted as or taken for: *he could pass for a native of Sweden.* ■ [no obj.] be accepted as adequate; go unremarked: *she couldn't agree, but **let it pass**.*
6 (of a legislative or other official body) approve or put into effect (a proposal or law) by voting on it: *the bill was passed despite fierce opposition.* ■ [no obj.] (of a proposal) be approved by a legislative or other official body: *the Bill passed by 164 votes to 107.*
7 [with obj.] pronounce (a judgement or judicial sentence): ***passing judgement on** these crucial issues | it is now my duty to **pass sentence upon** you.* ■ utter (something, especially criticism): *she would pass remarks about the Peebles in their own house.* ■ [no obj.] (**pass on/upon**) archaic adjudicate or give a judgement on.
8 [with obj.] discharge (something, especially urine or faeces) from the body.
9 [no obj.] forgo one's turn in a game or an offered opportunity to do or have something: *we pass on pudding and have coffee.* ■ [as exclamation] said when one does not know the answer to a question, for example in a quiz: *to the enigmatic question we answered 'Pass'.* ■ [with obj.] (of a company) not declare or pay (a dividend). ■ Bridge make no bid when it is one's turn during an auction.
▶ **noun 1** an act or instance of moving past or through something: *repeated passes with the swipe card | an unmarked plane had been making passes over his house.* ■ an act of passing the hands over something, as in conjuring or hypnotism. ■ a thrust in fencing. ■ a juggling trick. ■ Computing a single scan through a set of data or a program.
2 a success in an examination, test, or course: *an A-level pass in Music* | [as modifier] *a 100 per cent pass rate.* ■ Brit. an achievement of a university degree without honours: [as modifier] *a pass degree.*
3 a card, ticket, or permit giving authorization for the holder to enter or have access to a place, form of transport, or event: *a bus pass | you could only get in with a pass.* ■ historical (in South Africa) an identity book which black people had to carry between 1952 and 1986, used to limit the movement of black people to urban areas.
4 (in soccer, rugby, and other games) an act of kicking, hitting, or throwing the ball to another player on the same side.
5 informal an amorous or sexual advance made to someone: *she **made a pass at** Stephen.*
6 a state or situation of a specified, usually undesirable, nature: *if this was what was being taught these days in colleges things had **come to a pretty pass**.*
7 Bridge an act of refraining from bidding during the auction.
– PHRASES **pass the baton** see BATON. **pass the buck** see BUCK[3]. **pass one's eye over** read (a document) cursorily. **pass go** successfully complete the first stage of an undertaking: *home builders can't actually pass go unless they sell the houses.* [from a manoeuvre in the board game Monopoly.] **pass the hat** (**round**) see HAT. **pass one's lips** see LIP. **pass muster** see MUSTER. **pass the parcel** see PARCEL. **pass the time of day** see TIME. **pass water** urinate.
– PHRASAL VERBS **pass away** euphemistic die: *she passed away in her sleep.* **pass someone by** happen without being noticed or fully experienced by someone: *sometimes I feel that life is passing me by.* **pass off** Brit. (of proceedings) happen or be concluded in a specified, usually satisfactory way: *the weekend had passed off entirely without incident.* **pass something off 1** evade or lightly dismiss an awkward remark: *he made a light joke and passed it off.* **2** Basketball throw the ball to a teammate who is unmarked. **pass someone/thing off as** falsely represent a person or thing as (something else): *the drink was packaged in champagne bottles and was being passed off as the real stuff.* **pass on** euphemistic die: *his wife passed on twelve years ago.* **pass out 1** become unconscious: *he consumed enough alcohol to make him pass out.* **2** Brit. complete one's initial training in the armed forces. **pass over** euphemistic die: *by the time I reached the hospital she had passed over.* **pass someone over** ignore the claims of someone to promotion or advancement: *he was passed over for a cabinet job.* **pass something over** avoid mentioning or considering something: *I shall pass over the matter of the transitional period.* **pass something up** refrain from taking up an opportunity: *he passed up a career in pro baseball.*
– DERIVATIVES **passer** noun.
– ORIGIN Middle English: from Old French *passer*, based on Latin *passus* 'pace'.

pass[2] ▶ **noun** a route over or through mountains: *the pass over the mountain was open again after the snows* | [in place names] *the Khyber Pass.* ■ a passage for fish over or past a weir or dam.
– PHRASES **head** (or **cut**) **someone/thing off at the pass** forestall someone or something: *he came up with this story at the last minute, just to cut me off at the pass.* **sell the pass** Brit. betray a cause: *he is merciless to other poets whom he considers to have sold the pass.*
– ORIGIN Middle English (in the sense 'division of a text, passage through'): variant of PACE[1], influenced by PASS[1] and French *pas*.

passable ▶ **adjective 1** just good enough to be acceptable; satisfactory: *he spoke passable English.*
2 (of a route or road) clear of obstacles and able to be travelled on: *the road was passable with care.*
– ORIGIN late Middle English: from Old French, from *passer* 'to pass'.

passably ▶ adverb in a way that is just good enough; reasonably: [as submodifier] *he was passably attractive.*

passacaglia /ˌpasəˈkɑːlɪə/ ▶ noun Music a composition similar to a chaconne, typically in slow triple time with variations over a ground bass.
– ORIGIN Italian, from Spanish *pasacalle*, from *pasar* 'to pass' + *calle* 'street' (because originally it was a dance often played in the streets).

passade /pəˈseɪd/ ▶ noun a movement performed in advanced dressage and classical riding, in which the horse performs a 180° turn, with its forelegs describing a large circle and its hind legs a smaller one.
– ORIGIN mid 17th cent.: French, from Italian *passata* or Provençal *passada*, from medieval Latin *passare* 'to pass'.

passage[1] /ˈpasɪdʒ/ ▶ noun **1** [mass noun] the action or process of moving through or past somewhere on the way from one place to another: *there were moorings for boats wanting passage through the lock.* ■ the action or process of moving forward: *despite the passage of time she still loved him.* ■ the right to pass through somewhere: *we obtained a permit for safe passage from the embassy.* ■ [count noun] a journey by sea or air: *I booked a passage on the next ship.* ■ Ornithology (of a migrating bird) the action of passing through a place en route to its final destination: *the species occurs regularly* ***on passage*** | [as modifier] *a passage migrant.*
2 a narrow way allowing access between buildings or to different rooms within a building; a passageway. ■ a duct, vessel, or other channel in the body.
3 [mass noun] the process of transition from one state to another: *an allegory on the theme of the passage from ignorance to knowledge.* ■ the passing of a bill into law: *a catalyst for the unrest was the passage of a privatization law.*
4 a short extract from a book or other printed material: *he picked up the newspaper and read the passage again.* ■ a section of a piece of music: *an orchestral passage.* ■ an episode in a spell of longer activity such as a sporting event: *a neat passage of midfield play.*
5 Medicine & Biology /paˈsɑːʒ/ the propagation of microorganisms or cells in a series of host organisms or culture media, so as to maintain them or modify their virulence.
▶ verb /paˈsɑːʒ/ [with obj.] Medicine & Biology subject (a strain of microorganisms or cells) to a passage.
– PHRASES **passage of** (or **at**) **arms** archaic a fight or dispute. **work one's passage** work in return for a free place on a voyage: *he worked his passage home as a steward.*
– ORIGIN Middle English: from Old French, based on Latin *passus* 'pace'.

P

passage[2] /paˈsɑːʒ/ ▶ noun a movement performed in advanced dressage and classical riding, in which the horse executes a slow elevated trot, giving the impression of dancing.
– ORIGIN early 18th cent.: from French, from an alteration of Italian *passeggiare* 'to walk, pace', based on Latin *passus* 'pace'.

passage grave ▶ noun Archaeology a prehistoric megalithic burial chamber of a type found chiefly in western Europe, with a passage leading to the exterior. Passage graves were originally covered by a mound, which in many cases has disappeared, and most date from the Neolithic period.

passage hawk ▶ noun a hawk caught for training while on migration, especially as an immature bird of less than twelve months. Compare with HAGGARD.

passageway ▶ noun a long, narrow way, typically having walls either side, that allows access between buildings or to different rooms within a building.

passagework ▶ noun [mass noun] music notable chiefly for the scope it affords for virtuoso playing: *some of the passagework in early Beethoven is very awkward.*

Passamaquoddy /ˌpasəməˈkwɒdi/ ▶ noun (pl. **same** or **Passamaquoddies**) **1** a member of an American Indian people inhabiting parts of SE Maine and, formerly, SW New Brunswick.
2 [mass noun] the Algonquian language of the Passamaquoddy, now with few speakers.
▶ adjective relating to the Passamaquoddy or their language.
– ORIGIN from a Micmac name for *Passamaquoddy* Bay, literally 'place where pollack are plentiful'.

passant /ˈpas(ə)nt/ ▶ adjective [usu. postpositive] Heraldry (of an animal) represented as walking, with the right front foot raised. The animal is depicted in profile facing the dexter side with the tail raised, unless otherwise specified (e.g. as 'passant guardant').
– ORIGIN late Middle English: from Old French, literally 'proceeding', present participle of *passer*.

passata /pəˈsɑːtə/ ▶ noun [mass noun] a thick paste made from sieved tomatoes and used especially in Italian cooking.
– ORIGIN Italian.

passband ▶ noun a frequency band within which signals are transmitted by a filter without attenuation.

passbook ▶ noun **1** a book issued by a bank or building society to an account holder, recording sums deposited and withdrawn.
2 historical (in South Africa under apartheid) a black person's pass.

Passchendaele, Battle of /ˈpaʃ(ə)ndeɪl/ (also **Passendale**) a prolonged episode of trench warfare involving appalling loss of life during the First World War in 1917, near the village of Passchendaele in western Belgium. It is also known as the third Battle of Ypres.

pass door ▶ noun a door in a theatre connecting the backstage area and the auditorium.

passé /ˈpaseɪ/ ▶ adjective [predic.] no longer fashionable; out of date: *minis are passé—the best skirts are knee-length.* ■ archaic (especially of a woman) past one's prime.
– ORIGIN French, literally 'gone by', past participle of *passer*.

passed pawn ▶ noun Chess a pawn that no enemy pawn can stop from queening.

passeggiata /ˌpasɛˈdʒɑːtə/ ▶ noun (pl. **passeggiate** /-teɪ/) (especially in Italy or Italian-speaking areas) a leisurely walk or stroll, especially one taken in the evening for the purpose of socializing.
– ORIGIN Italian.

passel /ˈpas(ə)l/ ▶ noun informal, chiefly US a large group of people or things: ***a passel of** journalists.*
– ORIGIN mid 19th cent.: representing a pronunciation of PARCEL.

passementerie /ˈpasm(ə)ntri/ ▶ noun [mass noun] decorative textile trimming consisting of gold or silver lace, gimp, or braid.
– ORIGIN early 17th cent.: from French, from *passement* 'gold lace'.

Passendale, Battle of /ˈpas(ə)ndeɪl/ variant spelling of PASSCHENDAELE, BATTLE OF.

passenger ▶ noun a traveller on a public or private conveyance other than the driver, pilot, or crew. ■ chiefly Brit. a member of a team or group who does far less effective work than the other members.
– ORIGIN Middle English: from the Old French adjective *passager* 'passing, transitory', used as a noun, from *passage* (see PASSAGE[1]).

passenger mile ▶ noun one mile travelled by one passenger, as a unit of traffic.

passenger pigeon ▶ noun an extinct long-tailed North American pigeon, noted for its long migrations in huge flocks. It was relentlessly hunted, the last individual dying in captivity in 1914. ● *Ectopistes migratorius*, family Columbidae.

passepartout /ˌpaspɑːˈtuː, ˌpɑːs-/ ▶ noun **1** (also **passepartout frame**) a picture or photograph mounted between a piece of glass and a sheet of card (or two pieces of glass) stuck together at the edges with adhesive tape. ■ [mass noun] adhesive tape or paper used in making a passepartout frame.
2 archaic a master key.
– ORIGIN late 17th cent.: from French, literally 'passes everywhere'.

passepied /ˌpasˈpɪeɪ/ ▶ noun a Breton dance similar to a quick minuet, popular in the 17th and 18th centuries.
– ORIGIN French, from *passer* 'to pass' + *pied* 'foot'.

passer-by ▶ noun (pl. **passers-by**) a person who happens to be going past something, especially on foot.

passerine /ˈpasərʌɪn, -riːn/ Ornithology ▶ adjective relating to or denoting birds of a large order distinguished by having feet that are adapted for perching, including all songbirds.
▶ noun a passerine bird; a perching bird.

> The order Passeriformes comprises more than half of all bird species, the remainder being known informally as the **non-passerines**. All passerines in Europe belong to the suborder Oscines (the **oscine passerines**), so that the term is effectively synonymous with 'songbird' there (see SONGBIRD). Those of the suborder Deutero-Oscines (the **suboscine passerines**) are found mainly in America.

– ORIGIN late 18th cent.: from Latin *passer* 'sparrow' + -INE[1].

pas seul /pɑː ˈsəːl/ ▶ noun a dance for one person.
– ORIGIN French, literally 'single step'.

passible /ˈpasɪb(ə)l/ ▶ adjective Christian Theology capable of feeling or suffering; susceptible to sensation or emotion: *only the humanity of Jesus is regarded as passible.*
– DERIVATIVES **passibility** noun.
– ORIGIN late Middle English: from Old French, from late Latin *passibilis*, from Latin *pass-* 'suffered', from the verb *pati*.

passim /ˈpasɪm/ ▶ adverb (of allusions or references in a published work) to be found at various places throughout the text.
– ORIGIN Latin, from *passus* 'scattered', from the verb *pandere*.

passing ▶ adjective [attrib.] **1** going past: *passing cars.*
2 (of a period of time) going by: *she detested him more with every passing second.* ■ carried out quickly and lightly: *a passing glance.*
3 (of a resemblance or similarity) slight.
▶ noun [mass noun] **1** the passage of something, especially time: *with the passing of the years she had become a little eccentric.*
2 (in sport) the action of passing a ball to another team member: *his play showed good passing and control.*
3 the end of something: *the passing of the Cold War.* ■ euphemistic a person's death: *her passing will be felt deeply by many people.*
– PHRASES **in passing** briefly and casually: *the research was mentioned only in passing.*
– DERIVATIVES **passingly** adverb.

passing bell ▶ noun chiefly historical a bell rung immediately after a death as a signal for prayers.

passing note ▶ noun Music a note not belonging to the harmony but interposed to secure a smooth transition.

passing shot ▶ noun Tennis a shot aiming the ball beyond and out of reach of one's opponent.

passion ▶ noun **1** [mass noun] strong and barely controllable emotion: *a man of impetuous passion.* ■ [in sing.] a state or outburst of strong emotion: *oratory in which he gradually works himself up into a passion.* ■ intense sexual love: *their all-consuming passion for each other* | [in sing.] *she nurses a passion for Thomas.* ■ [in sing.] an intense desire or enthusiasm for something: *the English have **a passion for** gardens.* ■ [count noun] a thing arousing great enthusiasm: *modern furniture is a particular passion of Bill's.*
2 (**the Passion**) the suffering and death of Jesus. ■ a narrative of this from any of the Gospels. ■ a musical setting of any of these narratives: *an aria from Bach's St Matthew Passion.*
– ORIGIN Middle English: from Old French, from late Latin *passio(n-)* (chiefly a term in Christian theology), from Latin *pati* 'suffer'.

passional ▶ adjective literary relating to or marked by passion: *a current of passional electric energy.*
▶ noun Christian Church a book about the sufferings of saints and martyrs, for reading on their feast days.

passionate ▶ adjective having, showing, or caused by strong feelings or beliefs: *passionate pleas for help* | *he's passionate about football.* ■ arising from intense feelings of sexual love: *a passionate kiss.*
– DERIVATIVES **passionately** adverb, **passionateness** noun.
– ORIGIN late Middle English (also in the senses 'easily moved to passion' and 'enraged'): from medieval Latin *passionatus* 'full of passion', from *passio* (see PASSION).

passion flower ▶ noun an evergreen climbing plant of warm regions, which bears distinctive flowers with parts that supposedly resemble instruments of the Crucifixion. ● Genus *Passiflora*, family Passifloraceae.

passion fruit ▶ noun the edible purple fruit of a kind of passion flower that is grown commercially, especially in tropical America and the Caribbean. Also called GRANADILLA. ● This fruit is obtained from *Passiflora edulis*, family Passifloraceae.

passionless ▶ adjective lacking strong emotion; unemotional: *the voice is passionless, monotone.*

Passion play ▶ noun a dramatic performance representing Christ's Passion from the Last Supper to the Crucifixion.

Passion Sunday ▶ noun the fifth Sunday in Lent.

Passiontide ▶ noun the last two weeks of Lent.

Passion Week ▶ noun **1** the week between Passion Sunday and Palm Sunday.
2 older name for HOLY WEEK.

passivate /ˈpasɪveɪt/ ▶ **verb** [with obj.] (usu. as adj. **passivated**) make (a metal or other substance) unreactive by altering the surface layer or coating the surface with a thin inert layer. ■ Electronics coat (a semiconductor) with inert material to protect it from contamination.
– DERIVATIVES **passivation** noun.

passive ▶ **adjective 1** accepting or allowing what happens or what others do, without active response or resistance: *the women were portrayed as passive victims*.
2 Grammar denoting a voice of verbs in which the subject undergoes the action of the verb (e.g. *they were killed* as opposed to the active form *he killed them*). The opposite of ACTIVE.
3 (of a circuit or device) containing no source of electromotive force. ■ (of radar or a satellite) receiving or reflecting radiation from a transmitter or target rather than generating its own signal. ■ (of a heating system) making use of incident sunlight as an energy source.
4 Chemistry (of a metal) made unreactive by a thin inert surface layer of oxide.
▶ **noun** Grammar a passive form of a verb. ■ (**the passive**) the passive voice.
– DERIVATIVES **passively** adverb, **passiveness** noun, **passivity** noun.
– ORIGIN late Middle English (in sense 2 of the adjective, also in the sense '(exposed to) suffering, acted on by an external agency'): from Latin *passivus*, from *pass-* 'suffered', from the verb *pati*.

passive-aggressive ▶ **adjective** of or denoting a type of behaviour or personality characterized by indirect resistance to the demands of others and an avoidance of direct confrontation.

passive immunity ▶ **noun** [mass noun] Physiology the short-term immunity which results from the introduction of antibodies from another person or animal. Compare with ACTIVE IMMUNITY.

passive matrix ▶ **noun** Electronics a display system in which individual pixels are selected using two control voltages for the row and column.

passive resistance ▶ **noun** [mass noun] non-violent opposition to authority, especially a refusal to cooperate with legal requirements.

passive smoking ▶ **noun** [mass noun] the involuntary inhaling of smoke from other people's cigarettes, cigars, or pipes.

passivize (also **passivise**) ▶ **verb** [with obj.] Grammar convert (a verb or clause) into the passive form.
– DERIVATIVES **passivization** noun.

pass key ▶ **noun 1** a key to the door of a restricted area, given only to those who are officially allowed access.
2 a master key.

pass laws ▶ **plural noun** historical a body of laws in operation in South Africa under apartheid, controlling the rights of black people to residence and travel and implemented by means of identity documents compulsorily carried.

pass mark ▶ **noun** the minimum mark needed to pass an examination.

Passos, John Dos, see DOS PASSOS.

Passover ▶ **noun** the major Jewish spring festival which commemorates the liberation of the Israelites from Egyptian slavery, lasting seven or eight days from the 15th day of Nisan.
– ORIGIN from *pass over* 'pass without touching', with reference to the exemption of the Israelites from the death of their firstborn (Exod. 12).

passport ▶ **noun** an official document issued by a government, certifying the holder's identity and citizenship and entitling them to travel under its protection to and from foreign countries. ■ [in sing.] a thing that ensures admission to or the achievement of something: *good qualifications are a passport to success*.
– ORIGIN late 15th cent. (denoting authorization to depart from a port): from French *passeport*, from *passer* 'to pass' + *port* 'seaport'.

passus /ˈpasəs/ ▶ **noun** (pl. **same**) a section, division, or canto of a story or poem, especially a medieval one.
– ORIGIN late 16th cent.: from Latin, literally 'step, pace', in medieval Latin 'passage of a book'.

password ▶ **noun** a secret word or phrase that must be used to gain admission to a place. ■ a string of characters that allows access to a computer, interface, or system.

past ▶ **adjective** gone by in time and no longer existing: *the danger is now past*. ■ [attrib.] belonging to a former time: *they made a study of the reasons why past attempts had failed* | *he is a past chairman of the society*. ■ [attrib.] (of a specified period of time) occurring before and leading up to the time of speaking or writing: *the band has changed over the past twelve months*. ■ [attrib.] Grammar (of a tense) expressing an action that has happened or a state that previously existed.
▶ **noun 1** (usu. **the past**) the time before the moment of speaking or writing: *she found it hard to make ends meet in the past* | *the war-damaged church is preserved as a reminder of the past*. ■ the history of a person or place: *the monuments act as guidelines through the country's colourful past*. ■ informal a part of a person's history that is considered to be shameful: *the heroine was a lady with a past*.
2 Grammar a past tense or form of a verb: *a simple past of the first conjugation*.
▶ **preposition 1** to or on the further side of: *he rode on past the crossroads*. ■ in front of or from one side to the other of: *he began to drive slowly past the houses*.
2 beyond in time; later than: *by this time it was past 3.30* | *my watch said twenty past twelve*.
3 no longer capable of: *he is past giving the best advice*. ■ beyond the limits or scope of: *I was long past caring and immediately fell asleep on the bed*.
▶ **adverb 1** so as to pass from one side of something to the other: *a flotilla of glossy limousines swept past*.
2 used to indicate the lapse of time: *a week went past and nothing changed*.
– PHRASES **not put it past someone** believe someone to be capable of doing a particular wrong or rash thing: *I wouldn't put it past him to slip something into the drinks*. **past it** Brit. informal too old to be of any use or any good at anything.
– DERIVATIVES **pastness** noun.
– ORIGIN Middle English: variant of *passed*, past participle of PASS[1].

pasta ▶ **noun** [mass noun] a dish originally from Italy consisting of dough made from durum wheat and water, extruded or stamped into various shapes and typically cooked in boiling water.
– ORIGIN late 19th cent.: from Italian, literally 'paste'.

paste ▶ **noun** [mass noun] a thick, soft, moist substance typically produced by mixing dry ingredients with a liquid: *blend onions, sugar, and oil to a paste*. ■ a paste used as an adhesive, especially for sticking paper: *wallpaper paste*. ■ a savoury spread: *salmon paste*. ■ a mixture consisting mainly of clay and water that is used in making ceramic ware, especially a mixture of low plasticity based on kaolin for making porcelain. ■ a hard vitreous composition used in making imitation gems: [as modifier] *paste brooches*.
▶ **verb** [with obj.] **1** coat with paste: *when coating walls with fabric, paste the wall, not the fabric*. ■ [with obj. and adverbial of place] fasten or stick (something) with paste: *the posters were pasted up on to street noticeboards*. ■ Computing insert (a piece of text or other data copied from elsewhere).
2 informal beat or defeat severely: *he pasted the guy and tied his ankles together*.
– ORIGIN late Middle English: from Old French, from late Latin *pasta* 'medicinal preparation in the shape of a small square', probably from Greek *pastē*, (plural) *pasta* 'barley porridge', from *pastos* 'sprinkled'.

pasteboard ▶ **noun** [mass noun] a type of thin board made by pasting together sheets of paper.

paste-down ▶ **noun** (in bookbinding) the part of an endpaper which is pasted to the inside of the cover.

pastel ▶ **noun 1** a crayon made of powdered pigments bound with gum or resin. ■ a work of art created with pastels: *a pastel entitled 'Girl braiding her hair'*.
2 a soft and delicate shade of a colour: *the subtlest of pastels and creams*.
▶ **adjective** of a soft and delicate shade of colour: *pastel blue curtains*.
– DERIVATIVES **pastellist** (also **pastelist**) noun.
– ORIGIN mid 17th cent.: via French from Italian *pastello*, diminutive of *pasta* 'paste'.

pastern /ˈpast(ə)n/ ▶ **noun** the sloping part of a horse's foot between the fetlock and the hoof. ■ a corresponding part in some other domestic animals.
– ORIGIN Middle English: from Old French *pasturon*, from *pasture* 'strap for hobbling a horse', transferred in sense to the joint of the foot.

Pasternak /ˈpastənak/, Boris (Leonidovich) (1890–1960), Russian poet, novelist, and translator. His best-known novel, *Doctor Zhivago* (1957), describes the experience of the Russian intelligentsia during the Revolution; it was banned in the Soviet Union.

paste-up ▶ **noun** a document prepared for copying or printing by combining and pasting various sections on a backing.

Pasteur /paˈstəː/, French /pastœʀ/, Louis (1822–95), French chemist and bacteriologist. He introduced pasteurization and made pioneering studies in vaccination techniques.

pasteurellosis /ˌpɑːstərɛˈləʊsɪs, ˌpastərɛˈləʊsɪs/ ▶ **noun** [mass noun] a bacterial infection commonly affecting animals and sometimes transferred to humans through bites and scratches. ● The causative bacteria are Gram-negative rods of the genus *Pasteurella*, in particular *P. multocida*.
– ORIGIN early 20th cent.: from French *pasteurellose* (from the name of L. PASTEUR) + -OSIS.

pasteurize /ˈpɑːstʃərʌɪz, -stjə-, ˈpas-/ (also **pasteurise**) ▶ **verb** [with obj.] (often as adj. **pasteurized**) subject (milk, wine, or other products) to a process of partial sterilization, especially one involving heat treatment or irradiation, thus making the product safe for consumption and improving its keeping quality: *pasteurized milk*.
– DERIVATIVES **pasteurization** noun, **pasteurizer** noun.
– ORIGIN late 19th cent.: from the name of L. PASTEUR + -IZE.

Pasteur pipette ▶ **noun** a simple glass pipette drawn into a capillary tube at one end, used with a rubber teat fitted to the other.

pasticcio /paˈstɪtʃəʊ/ ▶ **noun** (pl. **pasticcios**) another term for PASTICHE.
– ORIGIN Italian.

pastiche /paˈstiːʃ/ ▶ **noun** an artistic work in a style that imitates that of another work, artist, or period: *the operetta is a pastiche of 18th century style* | [mass noun] *the songs amount to much more than blatant pastiche*. ■ an artistic work consisting of a medley of pieces imitating various sources.
▶ **verb** [with obj.] imitate the style of (an artist or work): *Gauguin took himself to a Pacific island and pastiched the primitive art he found there*.
– ORIGIN late 19th cent.: from French, from Italian *pasticcio*, based on late Latin *pasta* 'paste'.

pasticheur /ˌpastiːˈʃəː/ ▶ **noun** an artist who imitates the style of another: *the early paintings reveal him as merely a pasticheur with panache*.

pastie ▶ **noun** (pl. **pasties**) **1** /ˈpeɪsti/ informal a decorative covering for the nipple worn by a stripper.
2 /ˈpasti/ variant spelling of PASTY[1].

pastilla /paˈstiːjə/ ▶ **noun** a type of Moroccan meat pie, typically filled with spiced pigeon meat and apricots and having a sugared crust.
– ORIGIN Spanish, or Moroccan Arabic *bestila*, from Spanish *pastel* pie.

pastille /ˈpast(ə)l, -tɪl/ ▶ **noun 1** chiefly Brit. a small sweet or lozenge.
2 a small pellet of aromatic paste burnt as a perfume or deodorizer.
– ORIGIN mid 17th cent.: from French, from Latin *pastillus* 'little loaf, lozenge', from *panis* 'loaf'.

pastime ▶ **noun** an activity that someone does regularly for enjoyment rather than work; a hobby: *his favourite pastimes were shooting and golf*.
– ORIGIN late 15th cent.: from the verb PASS[1] + TIME, translating French *passe-temps*.

pasting /ˈpeɪstɪŋ/ ▶ **noun** informal a severe beating or defeat: *another pasting for England's bowlers*.

pastis /ˈpastɪs, paˈstiːs/ ▶ **noun** (pl. **same**) [mass noun] an aniseed-flavoured aperitif.
– ORIGIN French.

past master ▶ **noun 1** a person who is particularly skilled at a specified activity or art: *he's a past master at keeping his whereabouts secret*.
2 a person who has held the position of master in an organization: *he was a past master of the City Company of Grocers*.

pastor /ˈpɑːstə/ ▶ **noun 1** a minister in charge of a Christian church or congregation, especially in some non-episcopal churches.
2 (also **rosy pastor**) another term for ROSE-COLOURED STARLING.
▶ **verb** [with obj.] be pastor of (a church or congregation).
– DERIVATIVES **pastorate** noun, **pastorship** noun.
– ORIGIN late Middle English: from Anglo-Norman French *pastour*, from Latin *pastor* 'shepherd', from *past-* 'fed, grazed', from the verb *pascere*.

pastoral /ˈpɑːst(ə)r(ə)l/ ▶ **adjective 1** (of land) used for the keeping or grazing of sheep or cattle: *scattered pastoral farms*. ■ associated with country life:

P

the view was pastoral, with rolling fields and grazing sheep. ■ (of a work of art) portraying or evoking country life, typically in a romanticized or idealized form.
2 (in the Christian Church) concerning or appropriate to the giving of spiritual guidance: *pastoral and doctrinal issues | clergy doing pastoral work.* ■ relating to or denoting a teacher's responsibility for the general well-being of pupils or students: *the pastoral care of boarders.*
▸ **noun** a work of literature portraying an idealized version of country life.
– DERIVATIVES **pastoralism** noun, **pastorally** adverb.
– ORIGIN late Middle English: from Latin *pastoralis* 'relating to a shepherd', from *pastor* 'shepherd' (see PASTOR).

pastorale /ˌpastəˈrɑːl/ ▸ **noun** (pl. **pastorales** or **pastorali** /-liː/) **1** Music a slow instrumental composition in compound time, usually with drone notes in the bass.
2 a simple musical play with a rural subject.
– ORIGIN early 18th cent.: from Italian, literally 'pastoral' (adjective used as a noun).

Pastoral Epistles the books of the New Testament comprising the two letters of Paul to Timothy and the one to Titus.

pastoralist ▸ **noun 1** (especially in Australia) a sheep or cattle farmer.
2 archaic a writer of pastorals.

pastoral letter ▸ **noun** an official letter from a bishop to all the clergy or members of the diocese.

pastoral staff ▸ **noun** a bishop's crozier.

pastoral theology ▸ **noun** [mass noun] Christian theology that considers religious truth in relation to spiritual needs.

pastorie /ˌpastʊˈri/ ▸ **noun** (in South Africa) the residence of a minister of one of the Dutch Reformed Churches.
– ORIGIN Afrikaans, from medieval Latin *pastoria* 'place belonging to a shepherd'.

pastourelle /ˌpastʊˈrɛl/ (also **pastorela** /ˌpastəˈrɛlə/) ▸ **noun** (pl. **same** or **pastourelles** or **pastorelas**) a medieval lyric whose theme is love for a shepherdess.
– ORIGIN French, feminine of *pastoureau* 'shepherd'.

past participle ▸ **noun** Grammar the form of a verb, typically ending in *-ed* in English, which is used in forming perfect and passive tenses and sometimes as an adjective, e.g. *looked* in *have you looked?*, *lost* in *lost property.*

past perfect ▸ **adjective & noun** another term for PLUPERFECT.

P

pastrami /paˈstrɑːmi/ ▸ **noun** [mass noun] highly seasoned smoked beef, typically served in thin slices.
– ORIGIN Yiddish.

pastry ▸ **noun** (pl. **pastries**) [mass noun] a dough of flour, fat, and water, used as a base and covering in baked dishes such as pies. ■ [count noun] an item of food consisting of sweet pastry with a cream, jam, or fruit filling.
– ORIGIN late Middle English (as a collective term): from PASTE, influenced by Old French *pastaierie.*

pastry cook ▸ **noun** a professional cook who specializes in making pastry.

pastry cream ▸ **noun** [mass noun] a thick, creamy custard used as a filling for cakes or flans.

pasturage ▸ **noun** [mass noun] land used for pasture. ■ the occupation or process of pasturing cattle, sheep, or other grazing animals: *the human species has only engaged in pasturage for 12,000 to 15,000 years.*
– ORIGIN early 16th cent.: from Old French, from *pasture* (see PASTURE).

pasture ▸ **noun 1** [mass noun] land covered with grass and other low plants suitable for grazing animals, especially cattle or sheep.
2 (**pastures**) used to refer to a person's situation in life: *she left the office for* ***pastures new.*** [suggested by 'Tomorrow to fresh woods and pastures new' (Milton's *Lycidas*).]
▸ **verb** [with obj.] put (animals) to graze in a pasture: *they pastured their cows in the water meadow.* ■ [no obj.] (of animals) graze.
– PHRASES **put someone out to pasture** force someone to retire.
– ORIGIN Middle English: from Old French, from late Latin *pastura* 'grazing', from *past-* 'grazed', from the verb *pascere.*

pastureland ▸ **noun** land used as pasture.

pasty[1] /ˈpasti/ (also **pastie**) ▸ **noun** (pl. **pasties**) Brit. a folded pastry case filled with seasoned meat and vegetables.
– ORIGIN Middle English: from Old French *paste(e)*, based on late Latin *pasta* 'paste'.

pasty[2] /ˈpeɪsti/ ▸ **adjective** (**pastier**, **pastiest**) **1** (of a person's face) unhealthily pale: *a pasty complexion.*
2 of or like paste: *a pasty mixture.*
– DERIVATIVES **pastiness** noun.

Pat ▸ **noun** Brit. informal, often offensive a nickname for an Irishman.
– ORIGIN early 19th cent.: abbreviation of the male given name *Patrick.*

pat[1] ▸ **verb** (**pats**, **patting**, **patted**) [with obj.] touch quickly and gently with the flat of the hand: *he patted him consolingly on the shoulder.* ■ draw attention to (something) by tapping it gently: *he patted the bench beside him and I sat down.* ■ [with obj. and adverbial] mould into shape or put in position with gentle taps: *she patted down the earth in each pot.*
▸ **noun 1** a quick, light touch with the hand: *giving him a friendly pat on the arm, she went off to join the others.*
2 a compact mass of soft material: ***a pat of** butter.*
– PHRASES **a pat on the back** an expression of approval or congratulation: *they deserve a pat on the back for a job well done.* **pat someone on the back** express approval of or admiration for someone.
– ORIGIN late Middle English (as a noun denoting a blow with something flat): probably imitative. The verb dates from the mid 16th cent.

pat[2] ▸ **adjective** simple and somewhat glib or unconvincing: *there are no pat answers to these questions.*
▸ **adverb** at exactly the right moment or in the right way; very conveniently or opportunely: *the happy ending came rather pat.*
– PHRASES **have something off** (or **down**) **pat** have something memorized perfectly: *she has her answer off pat.* **stand pat** chiefly N. Amer. **1** stick stubbornly to one's opinion or decision: *many ranchers stood pat with the old strains of cattle.* **2** (in poker and blackjack) retain one's hand as dealt, without drawing other cards.
– DERIVATIVES **patly** adverb, **patness** noun.
– ORIGIN late 16th cent.: related to PAT[1]; apparently originally symbolic: a frequently found early use was *hit pat* (i.e. hit as if with flat blow).

Pat. ▸ **abbreviation** Patent.

pataca /pəˈtɑːkə/ ▸ **noun** the basic monetary unit of Macao, equivalent to 100 avos.
– ORIGIN Spanish and Portuguese.

pat-a-cake ▸ **noun** [mass noun] a children's game in which participants gently clap their hands in time to the words of a rhyme.

patagium /ˌpatəˈdʒʌɪəm/ ▸ **noun** (pl. **patagia** /-ˈdʒʌɪə/) Zoology a membrane or fold of skin between the forelimbs and hindlimbs on each side of a bat or gliding mammal. ■ Entomology a lobe that covers the wing joint in many moths.
– ORIGIN early 19th cent.: from Latin, denoting gold edging on a Roman lady's tunic, from Greek *patageion.*

Patagonia /ˌpatəˈɡəʊnɪə/ a region of South America, in southern Argentina and Chile. Consisting largely of a dry barren plateau, it extends from the Colorado River in central Argentina to the Strait of Magellan and from the Andes to the Atlantic coast.
– DERIVATIVES **Patagonian** adjective & noun.
– ORIGIN from obsolete *Patagon*, denoting a member of a native people alleged by travellers of the 17th and 18th cents to be the tallest known.

Patagonian cavy (also **Patagonian hare**) ▸ **noun** another term for MARA.

Patagonian toothfish ▸ **noun** see TOOTHFISH.

Pataliputra /ˌpɑːtlɪˈpʊtrə/ ancient name for PATNA.

pata-pata /ˌpɑːtaˈpɑːta/ ▸ **noun** [mass noun] S. African a sexually suggestive dance style in which pairs of dancers touch each other's bodies. ■ kwela music arranged to suit this style of dance. ■ informal sexual intercourse.
– ORIGIN from Xhosa and Zulu *phatha* 'to touch, feel'.

pataphysics /ˌpatəˈfɪzɪks/ ▸ **plural noun** [usu. treated as sing.] the branch of philosophy that deals with an imaginary realm additional to metaphysics.
– ORIGIN 1940s: from Greek *ta epi ta metaphusika*, literally 'the (works) imposed on the Metaphysics'. The concept was introduced by Alfred Jarry (1873–1907), French writer of the Absurd.

patas monkey /pəˈtɑː/ ▸ **noun** a central African guenon with reddish-brown fur, a black face, and a white moustache. ● *Erythrocebus patas*, family Cercopithecidae.
– ORIGIN mid 18th cent.: *patas* from Senegalese French, from Wolof *pata.*

Patau's syndrome /ˈpataʊz/ ▸ **noun** [mass noun] Medicine a congenital disorder in which there are three copies of chromosome 13, 14, or 15 instead of the usual two. This results in brain, heart, and kidney defects which are usually fatal soon after birth.
– ORIGIN 1960s: named after Klaus *Patau*, 20th-cent. German physician.

Patavium /pəˈteɪvɪəm/ Latin name for PADUA.

patball ▸ **noun** [mass noun] Brit. a simple game in which a ball is hit back and forth between two players.

patch ▸ **noun 1** a piece of cloth or other material used to mend or strengthen a torn or weak point. ■ a pad or shield worn over a sightless or injured eye. ■ a piece of cloth sewn on to clothing as a badge or distinguishing mark. ■ an adhesive piece of drug-impregnated material worn on the skin so that the drug may be absorbed gradually over a period of time. ■ historical a small disc of black silk worn attached to the face for adornment by women in the 17th and 18th centuries.
2 a part of something marked out from the rest by a particular characteristic: *his hair was combed forward to hide a growing bald patch | the bird has a bright red patch under its wing.* ■ a small area or amount of something: *patches of bluebells in the grass.*
3 a small piece of ground, especially one used for gardening: *they spent Sundays digging their vegetable patch.* ■ Brit. informal an area for which someone is responsible or in which they operate: *we didn't want any secret organizations on our patch.*
4 Brit. informal a particular period of time: *he may have been going through a bad patch.*
5 a temporary electrical or telephone connection. ■ a preset configuration or sound data file in an electronic musical instrument, especially a synthesizer.
6 Computing a small piece of code inserted into a program to improve its functioning or to correct a fault.
▸ **verb** [with obj.] **1** mend or strengthen (fabric or clothing) with a patch: *her jeans were neatly patched.* ■ cover small areas of (a surface) with something different, causing it to appear variegated: *the grass was patched with sandy stretches.*
2 (**patch someone/thing up**) informal treat someone's injuries or repair the damage to something in an improvised way: *they did their best to patch up the gaping wounds.* ■ (**patch something together**) construct something hastily from unsuitable components: *lean-tos patched together from aluminium siding and planks.* ■ (**patch something up**) restore peaceful or friendly relations after a quarrel or dispute: *any ill feeling could be patched up with a phone call | they sent him home to* ***patch things up with*** *his wife.*
3 [with obj. and adverbial] connect by a temporary electrical, radio, or telephonic connection: ***patch me through** to number nine.*
4 Computing improve or correct (a routine or program) by inserting a patch.
– PHRASES **not a patch on** Brit. informal greatly inferior to: *he no longer looked so handsome—he wasn't a patch on Peter.*
– DERIVATIVES **patcher** noun.
– ORIGIN late Middle English: perhaps from a variant of Old French *pieche*, dialect variant of *piece* 'piece'.

patchboard (also **patch panel**) ▸ **noun** a board in a switchboard, computer, or other device with a number of electric sockets that may be connected in various combinations.

patch cord (also **patch lead**) ▸ **noun** an insulated lead with a plug at each end, for use with a patchboard.

patchouli /ˈpatʃʊli, pəˈtʃuːli/ ▸ **noun** [mass noun] **1** an aromatic oil obtained from a SE Asian shrub, which is used in perfumery, insecticides, and medicine.
2 the strongly scented shrub of the mint family from which patchouli is obtained. ● *Pogostemon cablin*, family Labiatae.
– ORIGIN mid 19th cent.: from Tamil *paccuḷi.*

patch pocket ▸ **noun** a pocket made of a separate piece of cloth sewn on to the outside of a garment.

patch reef ▸ **noun** a small isolated platform of coral.

patch test ▸ **noun** a test to discover whether a person is allergic to any of a range of substances which are applied to the skin in light scratches or under a plaster.

patchwork ▸ **noun** [mass noun] needlework in which small pieces of cloth in different designs, colours, or textures are sewn together: *a piece of patchwork* | [as modifier] *a patchwork bedspread*. ■ [count noun] a thing composed of many different elements so as to appear variegated: *a patchwork of stone walls and green fields*.
– DERIVATIVES **patchworked** adjective.

patchy ▸ adjective (**patchier, patchiest**) existing or happening in small, isolated areas: *patchy fog*. ■ not of the same quality throughout; inconsistent: *your coursework was patchy* | *my knowledge of Egyptology is patchy*.
– DERIVATIVES **patchily** adverb, **patchiness** noun.

pate /peɪt/ ▸ **noun** archaic or humorous a person's head: *he scratched his balding pate*.
– ORIGIN Middle English: of unknown origin.

pâte /pɑːt/ ▸ **noun** [mass noun] the paste of which porcelain is made.
– ORIGIN mid 19th cent.: French, literally 'paste'.

pâté /ˈpateɪ/ ▸ **noun** [mass noun] a rich, savoury paste made from finely minced or mashed ingredients, typically seasoned meat or fish.
– ORIGIN French, from Old French *paste* 'pie of seasoned meat'.

pâté de campagne /də kɒmˈpɑːnjə/ ▸ **noun** [mass noun] coarse pork and liver pâté.
– ORIGIN French, literally 'country pâté'.

pâté de foie gras /ˌpateɪ də fwɑː ˈgrɑː/ ▸ **noun** [mass noun] a smooth rich paste made from fatted goose or duck liver.
– ORIGIN French.

patée ▸ adjective variant spelling of PATTÉE.

patella /pəˈtɛlə/ ▸ **noun** (pl. **patellae** /-liː/) Anatomy the kneecap.
– DERIVATIVES **patellar** adjective, **patellate** /-lət/ adjective.
– ORIGIN late 16th cent.: from Latin, diminutive of *patina* 'shallow dish', from Greek *patanē* (see PATEN).

paten /ˈpat(ə)n/ ▸ **noun** a plate, typically made of gold or silver, used for holding the bread during the Eucharist and sometimes as a cover for the chalice. ■ a shallow metal plate or dish.
– ORIGIN Middle English: from Old French *patene*, from Latin *patina* 'shallow dish', from Greek *patanē* 'a plate'.

patency /ˈpeɪt(ə)nsi/ ▸ **noun** [mass noun] Medicine the condition of being open or unobstructed. ■ the condition of showing detectable parasite infection.

patent /ˈpat(ə)nt, ˈpeɪt(ə)nt/ ▸ **noun** a government authority or licence conferring a right or title for a set period, especially the sole right to make, use, or sell an invention: *he **took out a patent** for an improved steam hammer*.
▸ adjective **1** /ˈpeɪt(ə)nt/ easily recognizable; obvious: *she was smiling with patent insincerity*.
2 Medicine (of a vessel, duct, or aperture) open and unobstructed; failing to close. ■ (of a parasitic infection) showing detectable parasites in the tissues or faeces.
3 made and marketed under a patent; proprietary: *patent milk powder*.
▸ verb [with obj.] obtain a patent for (an invention): *an invention is not your own until it is patented*.
– DERIVATIVES **patentability** noun, **patentable** adjective, **patentor** noun.
– ORIGIN late Middle English: from Old French, from Latin *patent-* 'lying open', from the verb *patere*. The noun sense is from LETTERS PATENT.

patentee /ˌpeɪt(ə)nˈtiː, ˌpat-/ ▸ **noun** a person or organization that obtains or holds a patent for something.

patent leather ▸ **noun** [mass noun] leather with a glossy varnished surface, used chiefly for shoes, belts, and handbags.

patent log ▸ **noun** a mechanical device towed in the water behind a boat to measure its speed and distance travelled.

patently /ˈpeɪt(ə)ntli/ ▸ **adverb** [often as submodifier] clearly; without doubt: *these claims were patently false* | *the Government's approach had patently failed to address the problem*.

patent medicine ▸ **noun** a proprietary medicine made and marketed under a patent and available without prescription.

patent office ▸ **noun** an office from which patents are issued.

patent right ▸ **noun** the exclusive right conferred by a patent.

Patent Roll ▸ **noun** historical (in the UK) a parchment roll listing the patents issued in a particular year.

Pater /ˈpeɪtə/, Walter (Horatio) (1839–94), English essayist and critic. His *Studies in the History of the Renaissance* (1873) had a major impact on the development of the Aesthetic Movement.

pater /ˈpeɪtə/ ▸ **noun 1** Brit. informal, dated father: *the pater gives her fifty pounds a year as a dress allowance*.
2 Anthropology a person's legal father. Often contrasted with GENITOR.
– ORIGIN Latin.

patera /ˈpat(ə)rə/ ▸ **noun** (pl. **paterae** /-riː/) **1** a broad, shallow dish used in ancient Rome for pouring libations. ■ Architecture a flat round ornament resembling a shallow dish.
2 a broad, shallow bowl-shaped feature on the surface of a planet.
– ORIGIN Latin, from *patere* 'be or lie open'.

paterfamilias /ˌpeɪtəfəˈmɪlɪas, ˌpatə-/ ▸ **noun** (pl. **patresfamilias** /ˌpeɪtriːz-, ˌpatriːz-/) the male head of a family or household. Compare with MATERFAMILIAS.
– ORIGIN Latin, literally 'father of the family'.

paternal ▸ adjective **1** of or appropriate to a father: *he reasserted his paternal authority*. ■ showing a kindness and care associated with a father; fatherly: *my elders in the newsroom kept a paternal eye on me*.
2 [attrib.] related through the father: *his father and paternal grandfather were porcelain painters*.
– DERIVATIVES **paternally** adverb.
– ORIGIN late Middle English: from late Latin *paternalis*, from Latin *paternus* 'fatherly, belonging to a father', from *pater* 'father'.

paternalism ▸ **noun** [mass noun] the policy or practice on the part of people in authority of restricting the freedom and responsibilities of those subordinate to or otherwise dependent on them in their supposed interest: *attitudes in society reinforce a degree of paternalism among doctors*.
– DERIVATIVES **paternalist** noun & adjective, **paternalistic** adjective, **paternalistically** adverb.

paternity ▸ **noun** [mass noun] **1** (especially in legal contexts) the state of being someone's father: *he refused to admit paternity of the child*.
2 paternal origin: *his enemies made great play of the supposed dubiety of his paternity*.
– ORIGIN late Middle English: from Old French *paternité*, from late Latin *paternitas*, from *paternus* 'relating to a father'.

paternity suit ▸ **noun** chiefly N. Amer. a court case held to establish formally the identity of a child's father.

paternity test ▸ **noun** a medical test, typically a blood test, to determine whether a man is the father of a particular child.

paternoster /ˌpatəˈnɒstə/ ▸ **noun 1** (in the Roman Catholic Church) the Lord's Prayer, especially in Latin. ■ any of a number of special beads occurring at regular intervals in a rosary, indicating that the Lord's Prayer is to be recited.
2 (also **paternoster lift**) a lift consisting of a series of linked compartments moving continuously on an endless belt.
3 (also **paternoster line**) a fishing line to which hooks or weights are attached at intervals.
– ORIGIN Old English, from Latin *pater noster* 'our father', the first words of the Lord's Prayer.

path ▸ **noun** (pl. **paths**) a way or track laid down for walking or made by continual treading. ■ the course or direction in which a person or thing is moving: *the missile traced a fiery path in the sky*. ■ a course of action or way of achieving something: *a chosen career path* | *a vegetarian diet could be the path to a longer life*. ■ a schedule available for allocation to an individual railway train over a given route. ■ Computing a definition of the order in which an operating system or program searches for a file or executable program.
▸ verb [no obj.] (usu. as noun **pathing**) (chiefly in computing and railway contexts) allocate a path.
– PHRASES **the path of least resistance** see RESISTANCE.
– DERIVATIVES **pathless** adjective.
– ORIGIN Old English *pæth*, of West Germanic origin; related to Dutch *pad*, German *Pfad*, of unknown ultimate origin.

-path ▸ combining form **1** denoting a practitioner of curative treatment: *homeopath*.
2 denoting a person who suffers from a disease: *psychopath*.
– ORIGIN back-formation from -PATHY, or from Greek *-pathēs* '-sufferer'.

Pathan /pəˈtɑːn/ ▸ **noun** another term for PASHTUN.
– ORIGIN from Hindi *Paṭhān*.

path-breaking ▸ adjective pioneering; innovative: *their path-breaking work opened up a new era in cancer research*.
– DERIVATIVES **path-breaker** noun.

Pathé /ˈpaθeɪ/, Charles (1863–1957), French film pioneer. In 1896 he and his brothers founded a company which came to dominate the production and distribution of films. It became internationally known for its newsreels, first introduced in France in 1909.

pathetic ▸ adjective **1** arousing pity, especially through vulnerability or sadness: *she looked so pathetic that I bent down to comfort her*.
2 informal miserably inadequate: *he's a pathetic excuse for a man*.
3 archaic relating to the emotions.
– DERIVATIVES **pathetically** adverb.
– ORIGIN late 16th cent. (in the sense 'affecting the emotions'): via late Latin from Greek *pathētikos* 'sensitive', based on *pathos* 'suffering'.

pathetic fallacy ▸ **noun** [mass noun] the attribution of human feelings and responses to inanimate things or animals, especially in art and literature.

Pathfinder (in full **Mars Pathfinder**) an unmanned American spacecraft which landed on Mars in 1997, deploying a small robotic rover (Sojourner) to explore the surface and examine the rocks.

pathfinder ▸ **noun** a person who goes ahead and discovers or shows others a path or way. ■ an aircraft sent ahead to locate and mark the target area for bombing. ■ [usu. as modifier] an experimental plan or forecast: *a pathfinder prospectus*.

path length ▸ **noun** Physics the overall length of the path followed by a light ray or sound wave.

pathname ▸ **noun** Computing a description of where a file or other item is to be found in a hierarchy of directories.

patho- ▸ combining form relating to disease: *pathogenesis* | *pathology*.
– ORIGIN from Greek *pathos* 'suffering, disease'.

pathogen /ˈpaθədʒ(ə)n/ ▸ **noun** Medicine a bacterium, virus, or other microorganism that can cause disease.
– DERIVATIVES **pathogenic** adjective, **pathogenicity** noun, **pathogenous** /-ˈθɒdʒɪnəs/ adjective.

pathogenesis /ˌpaθə(ʊ)ˈdʒɛnɪsɪs/ ▸ **noun** Medicine the manner of development of a disease.
– DERIVATIVES **pathogenetic** adjective.

pathogenicity island ▸ **noun** Genetics a series of contiguous genes in a pathogenic microorganism including one or more that determines virulence, acquired by horizontal gene transfer.

pathognomonic /ˌpaθəgnə(ʊ)ˈmɒnɪk/ ▸ adjective Medicine (of a sign or symptom) specifically characteristic or indicative of a particular disease or condition.
– ORIGIN early 17th cent.: from Greek *pathognōmonikos* 'skilled in diagnosis', from *pathos* 'suffering' + *gnōmōn* 'judge'.

pathography /pəˈθɒgrəfi/ ▸ **noun** (pl. **pathographies**) [mass noun] the study of the life of an individual or the history of a community with regard to the influence of a particular disease or psychological disorder.

pathological (N. Amer. also **pathologic**) ▸ adjective **1** relating to pathology: *the interpretation of pathological studies*.
2 involving or caused by a physical or mental disease: *glands with a pathological abnormality*.
3 informal compulsive; obsessive: *a pathological gambler*.
– DERIVATIVES **pathologically** adverb.

pathologize (also **pathologise**) ▸ verb [with obj.] regard or treat as psychologically abnormal: *most of the older theories pathologize same-sex attraction*.
– DERIVATIVES **pathologization** noun.

pathology ▸ **noun** [mass noun] the science of the causes and effects of diseases, especially the branch of medicine that deals with the laboratory examination of samples of body tissue for diagnostic or forensic purposes: *research people skilled in experimental pathology*. ■ Medicine pathological features considered collectively; the typical behaviour of a disease: *the pathology of Huntington's disease*. ■ Medicine a pathological condition: *the dominant pathology is multiple sclerosis*. ■ [usu. with modifier] mental, social, or linguistic abnormality or malfunction: *the city's inability to cope with the pathology of a burgeoning underclass*.
– DERIVATIVES **pathologist** noun.

P

– ORIGIN early 17th cent.: from modern or medieval Latin *pathologia* (see **PATHO-**, **-LOGY**).

pathophysiology ▶ **noun** [mass noun] Medicine the disordered physiological processes associated with disease or injury.
– DERIVATIVES **pathophysiologic** adjective, **pathophysiological** adjective, **pathophysiologically** adverb.

pathos /ˈpeɪθɒs/ ▶ **noun** [mass noun] a quality that evokes pity or sadness: *the actor injects his customary humour and pathos into the role.*
– ORIGIN mid 17th cent.: from Greek *pathos* 'suffering'; related to *paskhein* 'suffer' and *penthos* 'grief'.

pathway ▶ **noun** a way that constitutes or serves as a path. ■ Physiology a route, formed by a chain of nerve cells, along which impulses of a particular kind usually travel. ■ (also **metabolic pathway**) Biochemistry a sequence of chemical reactions undergone by a compound or class of compounds in a living organism.

-pathy ▶ **combining form 1** denoting feelings: *telepathy.*
2 denoting disorder in a particular part of the body: *neuropathy.*
3 relating to curative treatment of a specified kind: *hydropathy.*
– ORIGIN from Greek *patheia* 'suffering, feeling'.

patience ▶ **noun** [mass noun] **1** the capacity to accept or tolerate delay, problems, or suffering without becoming annoyed or anxious: *you can find bargains if you have the patience to sift through the rubbish | I have* ***run out of patience with*** *her.*
2 Brit. any of various forms of card game for one player, the object of which is to use up all one's cards by forming particular arrangements and sequences.
– PHRASES **lose patience** (or **lose one's patience**) become unable to keep one's temper: *even Laurence finally* ***lost patience with*** *him.*
– ORIGIN Middle English: from Old French, from Latin *patientia*, from *patient-* 'suffering', from the verb *pati*.

patient ▶ **adjective** able to accept or tolerate delays, problems, or suffering without becoming annoyed or anxious: *be patient, your time will come | a patient and painstaking approach.*
▶ **noun 1** a person receiving or registered to receive medical treatment.
2 Linguistics the semantic role of a noun phrase denoting something that is affected or acted upon by the action of a verb.
– DERIVATIVES **patiently** adverb.
– ORIGIN Middle English: from Old French, from Latin *patient-* 'suffering', from the verb *pati*.

patient Lucy ▶ **noun** North American term for **BUSY LIZZIE**.

P

patina /ˈpatɪnə/ ▶ **noun** a green or brown film on the surface of bronze or similar metals, produced by oxidation over a long period. ■ a gloss or sheen on wooden furniture produced by age and polishing. ■ the impression or appearance of something: *he carries the patina of old money and good breeding.*
– DERIVATIVES **patinated** adjective, **patination** noun.
– ORIGIN mid 18th cent.: from Italian, from Latin *patina* 'shallow dish'.

patio ▶ **noun** (pl. **patios**) a paved outdoor area adjoining a house. ■ a roofless inner courtyard in a Spanish or Spanish-American house.
– ORIGIN early 19th cent.: from Spanish, denoting an inner courtyard.

patio door ▶ **noun** a large glass sliding door leading to a patio, garden, or balcony.

patio rose ▶ **noun** a miniature floribunda rose.

patisserie /pəˈtiːs(ə)ri, -ˈtɪs-/ ▶ **noun** a shop where pastries and cakes are sold. ■ [mass noun] pastries and cakes collectively: *cream cakes and French patisserie.*
– ORIGIN late 16th cent.: from French *pâtisserie*, from medieval Latin *pasticium* 'pastry', from *pasta* 'paste'.

patissier /pəˈtɪsɪeɪ/ ▶ **noun** (pl. pronunc. **same**) a maker or seller of pastries and cakes.
– ORIGIN mid 19th cent.: French.

patka /ˈpʌtkɑː, -kə/ ▶ **noun** a man's head covering consisting of a small piece of cloth wrapped around the head, worn especially by Sikh boys or young men.
– ORIGIN Punjabi *paṭkā* from Sanskrit *paṭṭikā* 'turban cloth'.

Pat Malone ▶ **noun** (in phrase **on one's Pat Malone** or **pat**) Austral./NZ informal on one's own.
– ORIGIN early 20th cent.: rhyming slang.

Patmore, Coventry (Kersey Dighton) (1823–96), English poet. His most important work is *The Angel in the House* (1854–63), a sequence of poems in praise of married love.

Patmos /ˈpatmɒs/ a Greek island in the Aegean Sea, one of the Dodecanese group. It is believed that St John was living there in exile (from AD 95) when he had the visions described in Revelation.

Patna /ˈpatnə/ a city in NE India, on the Ganges, capital of the state of Bihar; pop. 1,814,000 (est. 2009). An important city in ancient times, it had become deserted by the 7th century but was refounded in 1541 by the Moguls and became a viceregal capital. Former name **PATALIPUTRA**.

Patna rice ▶ **noun** [mass noun] rice of a variety with long firm grains, which was originally produced at Patna.

patois /ˈpatwɑː/ ▶ **noun** (pl. **same** /-wɑːz/) the dialect of a particular region, especially one with low status in relation to the standard language of the country: *the nurse talked to me in a patois that even Italians would have had difficulty in understanding.* ■ the jargon or informal speech used by a particular social group: *the raunchy patois of inner-city kids.*
– ORIGIN mid 17th cent.: French, literally 'rough speech', perhaps from Old French *patoier* 'treat roughly', from *patte* 'paw'.

Paton /ˈpeɪt(ə)n/, Alan (Stewart) (1903–88), South African writer and politician. He is best known for his novel *Cry, the Beloved Country* (1948), a passionate indictment of the apartheid system.

patonce /pəˈtɒns/ ▶ **adjective** [postpositive] Heraldry (of a cross) with limbs which broaden from the centre and end in three pointed lobes: *a cross patonce.*
– ORIGIN mid 16th cent.: probably related to French *potencé*, a heraldic term denoting T-shaped endings to each limb of a cross, based on medieval Latin *potentia* 'crutch'.

patootie /pəˈtuːti/ ▶ **noun** (pl. **patooties**) N. Amer. informal **1** dated a girlfriend or a pretty girl.
2 a person's or animal's buttocks.
– ORIGIN 1920s: perhaps an alteration of **POTATO**.

Patras /pəˈtras, ˈpatrəs/ an industrial port in the NW Peloponnese, on the Gulf of Patras; pop. 167,400 (est. 2009). Taken by the Turks in the 18th century, it was the site in 1821 of the outbreak of the Greek war of independence. It was finally freed in 1828. Greek name **Pátrai** /ˈpatrɛ/.

patresfamilias plural form of **PATERFAMILIAS**.

patria /ˈpatrɪə, ˈpeɪtrɪə/ ▶ **noun** literary one's native country or homeland.
– ORIGIN Latin.

patrial /ˈpeɪtrɪəl/ ▶ **noun** Brit. a person with the right to live in the UK through the British birth of a parent or grandparent.
– DERIVATIVES **patriality** /-ˈalɪti/ **noun**.
– ORIGIN early 17th cent.: from French, or from medieval Latin *patrialis*, from Latin *patria* 'fatherland', from *pater* 'father'.

patriarch /ˈpeɪtrɪɑːk/ ▶ **noun 1** the male head of a family or tribe. ■ an older man who is powerful within an organization: *Hollywood's reigning patriarch rose to speak.* ■ the male founder of something: *he's the patriarch of all spin doctors.*
2 any of those biblical figures regarded as fathers of the human race, especially Abraham, Isaac, and Jacob, and their forefathers, or the sons of Jacob.
3 a bishop of one of the most ancient Christian sees (Alexandria, Antioch, Constantinople, Jerusalem, and formerly Rome). ■ the head of an autocephalous or independent Orthodox Church. ■ a Roman Catholic bishop ranking above primates and metropolitans and immediately below the Pope, often the head of a Uniate community.
– ORIGIN Middle English: from Old French *patriarche*, via ecclesiastical Latin from Greek *patriarkhēs*, from *patria* 'family' + *arkhēs* 'ruling'.

patriarchal ▶ **adjective 1** relating to a patriarch.
2 relating to or denoting a system of society or government controlled by men: *patriarchal values.*
– DERIVATIVES **patriarchally** adverb.

patriarchate ▶ **noun** the office, see, or residence of an ecclesiastical patriarch.

patriarchy ▶ **noun** (pl. **patriarchies**) [mass noun] a system of society or government in which the father or eldest male is head of the family and descent is reckoned through the male line. ■ a system of society or government in which men hold the power and women are largely excluded from it. ■ [count noun] a society or community organized on patriarchal lines.
– ORIGIN mid 17th cent.: via medieval Latin from Greek *patriarkhia*, from *patriarkhēs* 'ruling father' (see **PATRIARCH**).

patriate /ˈpatrɪeɪt, ˈpeɪtrɪeɪt/ ▶ **verb** [with obj.] transfer control over (a constitution) from a mother country to its former dependency: *the Canadian government moved to patriate the constitution from Great Britain.*

patrician /pəˈtrɪʃ(ə)n/ ▶ **noun** an aristocrat or nobleman. ■ N. Amer. a member of a long-established wealthy family. ■ a member of a noble family or class in ancient Rome.
▶ **adjective** belonging to or characteristic of the aristocracy: *a proud, patrician face.* ■ N. Amer. belonging to or characteristic of a long-established and wealthy family. ■ belonging to the nobility of ancient Rome.
– ORIGIN late Middle English: from Old French *patricien*, from Latin *patricius* 'having a noble father', from *pater, patr-* 'father'.

patriciate ▶ **noun** a noble order or class: *the Venetian merchants became a great hereditary patriciate.* ■ the position or rank of patrician in ancient Rome.

patricide /ˈpatrɪsʌɪd/ ▶ **noun** [mass noun] the killing of one's father. ■ [count noun] a person who kills their father.
– DERIVATIVES **patricidal** adjective.
– ORIGIN early 17th cent.: from late Latin *patricidium*, alteration of Latin *parricidium* (see **PARRICIDE**).

Patrick, St (5th century), Apostle and patron saint of Ireland. Of Romano-British parentage, he was taken as a slave to Ireland, where he experienced a religious conversion. He founded the archiepiscopal see of Armagh in about 454. Feast day, 17 March.

patrilineal ▶ **adjective** relating to or based on relationship to the father or descent through the male line: *in Polynesia inheritance of land was predominantly patrilineal.*
– ORIGIN early 20th cent.: from Latin *pater, patr-* 'father' + **LINEAL**.

patrilocal ▶ **adjective** relating to a pattern of marriage in which the couple settles in the husband's home or community: *the residence pattern is patrilocal.* Also called **VIRILOCAL**.
– DERIVATIVES **patrilocality** noun.
– ORIGIN early 20th cent.: from Latin *pater, patr-* 'father' + **LOCAL**.

patrimony /ˈpatrɪməni/ ▶ **noun** (pl. **patrimonies**) [mass noun] property inherited from one's father or male ancestor. ■ valued things passed down from previous generations; heritage: *an organization that saves the world's cultural patrimony by restoring historic buildings.* ■ chiefly historical the estate or property belonging by ancient endowment or right to a church or other institution.
– DERIVATIVES **patrimonial** /-ˈməʊnɪəl/ **adjective**.
– ORIGIN Middle English: from Old French *patrimoine*, from Latin *patrimonium*, from *pater, patr-* 'father'.

patriot /ˈpatrɪət, ˈpeɪt-/ ▶ **noun** a person who vigorously supports their country and is prepared to defend it against enemies or detractors.
– ORIGIN late 16th cent. (in the late Latin sense): from French *patriote*, from late Latin *patriota* 'fellow countryman', from Greek *patriōtēs*, from *patrios* 'of one's fathers', from *patris* 'fatherland'.

patriotic ▶ **adjective** having or expressing devotion to and vigorous support for one's country: *today's game will be played before a fiercely patriotic crowd.*
– DERIVATIVES **patriotically** adverb.
– ORIGIN mid 17th cent.: via late Latin from Greek *patriōtikos* 'relating to a fellow countryman' (see **PATRIOT**).

patriotic front ▶ **noun** a militant nationalist political organization.

patriotism ▶ **noun** [mass noun] the quality of being patriotic; vigorous support for one's country.

patristic /pəˈtrɪstɪk/ ▶ **adjective** relating to the early Christian theologians or to patristics.
– ORIGIN mid 19th cent.: from German *patristisch*, from Latin *pater, patr-* 'father'.

patristics ▶ **plural noun** [treated as sing.] the branch of Christian theology that deals with the lives, writings, and doctrines of the early Christian theologians.

Patroclus /pəˈtrɒkləs/ Greek Mythology a Greek hero of the Trojan War, the close friend of Achilles.

patrol ▶ **noun 1** an expedition to keep watch over an area, especially by guards or police walking or driving around at regular intervals: *we were ordered to investigate on a night patrol.* ■ a person or group of people sent to keep watch over an area: *a police patrol stopped the man and searched him.* ■ [mass noun] the action of keeping watch over an area: *the police were* ***on patrol*** *when they were ordered to investigate the incident.* ■ a routine operational voyage of a ship

or aircraft: *a submarine patrol.* ■ Brit. an official who controls traffic where children cross the road: *there were two schools but no crossing patrol.*
2 a unit of six to eight Scouts or Guides forming part of a troop.
▸ verb (**patrols, patrolling, patrolled**) [with obj.] keep watch over (an area) by regularly walking or travelling around it: *the garrison had to patrol the streets to maintain order* | [no obj.] *pairs of men were patrolling on each side of the thoroughfare.*
– DERIVATIVES **patroller** noun.
– ORIGIN mid 17th cent. (as a noun): from German *Patrolle*, from French *patrouille*, from *patrouiller* 'paddle in mud', from *patte* 'paw' + dialect (*gad*) *rouille* 'dirty water'.

patrol car ▸ noun a police car used used for patrolling the streets: *the thieves were spotted by police in a patrol car.*

patrolman ▸ noun (pl. **patrolmen**) N. Amer. a patrolling police officer.

patrology /pəˈtrɒlədʒi/ ▸ noun another term for **PATRISTICS**.
– ORIGIN early 17th cent.: from Greek *patēr, patr-* 'father' + **-LOGY**.

patron ▸ noun **1** a person who gives financial or other support to a person, organization, or cause: *a celebrated patron of the arts.* ■ a distinguished person who takes an honorary position in a charity: *the Mental Health Foundation, of which Her Royal Highness is Patron.*
2 a customer of a shop, restaurant, etc., especially a regular one: *we surveyed the plushness of the hotel and its sleek, well-dressed patrons.*
3 Roman History a patrician in relation to a client. ■ the former owner and (frequently) protector of a freed slave.
4 Brit., chiefly historical a person or institution with the right to grant a benefice to a member of the clergy.
– ORIGIN Middle English: from Old French, from Latin *patronus* 'protector of clients, defender', from *pater, patr-* 'father'.

patronage /ˈpatr(ə)nɪdʒ, ˈpeɪt-/ ▸ noun [mass noun] **1** the support given by a patron: *the arts could no longer depend on private patronage.*
2 the power to control appointments to office or the right to privileges: *recruits are selected on merit, not through political patronage.*
3 a patronizing or condescending manner: *a twang of self-satisfaction—even patronage—about him.*
4 the regular custom attracted by a shop, restaurant, etc.: *the direct train link was ending because of poor patronage.*
5 Roman History the rights and duties or position of a patron.
– ORIGIN late Middle English: from Old French, from *patron* 'protector, advocate' (see **PATRON**).

patronal /pəˈtrəʊn(ə)l/ ▸ adjective relating to a patron saint: *the patronal festival of the parish church of St Peter.*

patroness ▸ noun a female patron.

patronize (also **patronise**) ▸ verb [with obj.] **1** (often as adj. **patronizing**) treat with an apparent kindness which betrays a feeling of superiority: *'She's a good-hearted girl,' he said in a patronizing voice.*
2 frequent (a shop, restaurant, or other establishment) as a customer: *he's a denizen of flashy pubs patronized by the underworld.*
3 give financial or other support to (a person, organization, or cause).
– DERIVATIVES **patronization** noun, **patronizer** noun, **patronizingly** adverb.

patronne /paˈtrɒn/ ▸ noun (especially in France) a woman who is the owner, or the wife of the owner, of a business, especially a cafe, hotel, or restaurant.
– ORIGIN French, feminine of *patron*.

patron saint ▸ noun the protecting or guiding saint of a person or place.

patronymic /ˌpatrəˈnɪmɪk/ ▸ noun a name derived from the name of a father or ancestor, e.g. *Johnson, O'Brien, Ivanovich.*
– ORIGIN early 17th cent.: via late Latin from Greek *patrōnumikos*, from *patrōnumos*, from *patēr, patr-* 'father' + *onuma* 'name'.

patroon /pəˈtruːn/ ▸ noun US historical a person given land and granted certain manorial privileges under the former Dutch governments of New York and New Jersey.
– ORIGIN mid 17th cent.: from Dutch.

patsy ▸ noun (pl. **patsies**) informal, chiefly N. Amer. a person who is easily taken advantage of, especially by being cheated or blamed for something.
– ORIGIN early 20th cent.: of unknown origin.

patta /ˈpʌtə/ ▸ noun Indian a title deed to a property.
– ORIGIN Hindi, perhaps from Sanskrit *pattra* 'document'.

Pattaya /paˈtʌɪə/ a resort on the coast of southern Thailand, south-east of Bangkok.

pattée /ˈpateɪ, -ti/ (also **patée**) ▸ adjective [postpositive] Heraldry (of a cross) having almost triangular arms, very narrow at the centre and broadening to squared ends: *a cross pattée.*
– ORIGIN late 15th cent.: from French, from *patte* 'paw'.

Patten, Christopher (Francis), Baron Patten of Barnes (b.1944), English politician, an EU commissioner since 1999 and Chancellor of Oxford University since 2003. He was a Conservative MP 1979–92 and governor of Hong Kong 1992–7.

patten /ˈpat(ə)n/ ▸ noun historical a shoe or clog with a raised sole or set on an iron ring, worn to raise one's feet above wet or muddy ground when walking outdoors.
– ORIGIN late Middle English: from Old French *patin*, perhaps from *patte* 'paw'.

patter[1] ▸ verb [no obj.] make a repeated light tapping sound: *a flurry of rain pattered against the window.* ■ [no obj., with adverbial of direction] run with quick light steps: *he quickly pattered down the stairs.*
▸ noun [in sing.] a repeated light tapping: *the plashing patter of steady rain.*
– PHRASES **the patter of tiny feet** humorous used in reference to the presence or imminent birth of a child: *I had given up hope of* ***hearing the patter of tiny feet.***
– ORIGIN early 17th cent.: frequentative of **PAT**[1].

patter[2] ▸ noun [mass noun] rapid continuous talk, such as that used by a comedian or salesperson: *take a friend with you to deflect the sales patter.* ■ the jargon of a profession or social group: *he picked up the patter from watching his dad.* ■ rapid speech included in a song, especially for comic effect: [as modifier] *a patter song of invective.*
▸ verb [no obj.] talk at length without saying anything significant: *she pattered on incessantly.*
– ORIGIN late Middle English (as a verb in the sense 'recite (a prayer, charm, etc.) rapidly'): from **PATERNOSTER**. The noun dates from the mid 18th cent.

pattern ▸ noun **1** a repeated decorative design: *a neat blue herringbone pattern.* ■ an arrangement or design regularly found in comparable objects: *the house had been built on the usual pattern.*
2 a regular and intelligible form or sequence discernible in the way in which something happens or is done: *a complicating factor is the change in working patterns.*
3 a model or design used as a guide in needlework and other crafts. ■ a set of instructions to be followed in making a sewn or knitted item. ■ a wooden or metal model from which a mould is made for a casting. ■ a sample of cloth or wallpaper.
4 an excellent example for others to follow: *he set the pattern for subsequent study.*
▸ verb [with obj.] **1** (usu. as adj. **patterned**) decorate with a recurring design: *rosebud patterned wallpapers.*
2 give a regular or intelligible form to: *the brain not only receives information, but interprets and patterns it.* ■ (**pattern something on/after**) give something a form based on that of (something else): *the clothing is patterned on athletes' wear.*
– ORIGIN Middle English *patron* 'something serving as a model', from Old French (see **PATRON**). The change in sense is from the idea of a patron giving an example to be copied. Metathesis in the second syllable occurred in the 16th cent. By 1700 *patron* ceased to be used of things, and the two forms became differentiated in sense.

pattern baldness ▸ noun [mass noun] genetically determined baldness in which hair is gradually lost according to a characteristic pattern.

pattern book ▸ noun a book containing samples of patterns and designs of cloth or wallpaper.

pattern drill ▸ noun another term for **PATTERN PRACTICE**.

patterned ground ▸ noun [mass noun] Geology ground showing a pattern of stones, fissures, and vegetation, typically forming polygons, rings, or stripes caused by repeated freezing and thawing.

patternless ▸ adjective having no pattern; plain and undecorated: *patternless wallpaper.* ■ forming no discernible pattern: *phenomena that are completely patternless and disorganized.*

pattern practice ▸ noun [mass noun] the intensive repetition of the distinctive constructions and patterns of a foreign language as a means of learning.

pattern welding ▸ noun [mass noun] Archaeology a technique in which metal bars and strips of different type and colour were welded together and hammered out to give a patterned artefact.

pattress /ˈpatrɪs/ ▸ noun a wooden or plastic block fixed to a wall or ceiling to receive an electric light switch, ceiling rose, etc.
– ORIGIN late 19th cent.: alteration of *pateras*, plural of **PATERA**.

patty ▸ noun (pl. **patties**) **1** a small flat cake of minced food, especially meat. ■ a small pie or pasty.
2 N. Amer. a thin circular chocolate-covered peppermint sweet.
– ORIGIN mid 17th cent.: alteration of French *pâté*, by association with **PASTY**[1].

pattypan (also **pattypan squash**) ▸ noun chiefly US a squash of a saucer-shaped variety with a scalloped rim and creamy white flesh.
– ORIGIN so named from the resemblance in shape to a pan for baking a patty.

patulous /ˈpatjʊləs/ ▸ adjective literary (especially of the branches of a tree) spreading. ■ technical open; expanded.
– ORIGIN early 17th cent.: from Latin *patulus* (from *patere* 'be or lie open') + **-OUS**.

patwari /pʌtˈwɑːri/ ▸ noun (pl. **patwaris**) Indian a government official who keeps records regarding the ownership of land.
– ORIGIN from Hindi *paṭwārī*, from Sanskrit *paṭṭa* 'document' + *pāla* 'keeper'.

patzer /ˈpɑːtsə, ˈpat-/ ▸ noun informal a poor player at chess.
– ORIGIN 1940s: perhaps related to German *patzen* 'to bungle'.

paua /ˈpɑːwə/ ▸ noun NZ a large edible abalone (mollusc). ■ the shell of the paua, used to make jewellery, ornaments, etc.
– ORIGIN mid 19th cent.: from Maori.

paucity /ˈpɔːsɪti/ ▸ noun [in sing.] the presence of something in only small or insufficient quantities or amounts: *a* ***paucity of*** *information.*
– ORIGIN late Middle English: from Old French *paucite* or Latin *paucitas*, from *paucus* 'few'.

Paul, Les (1915–2009), American jazz guitarist and guitar designer; born *Lester Polfus*. In the 1940s he pioneered the development of the solid-body electric guitar.

Paul III (1468–1549), Italian pope 1534–49; born *Alessandro Farnese*. He excommunicated Henry VIII of England in 1538, instituted the order of the Jesuits in 1540, and initiated the Council of Trent in 1545.

Paul, St (died *c.*64), missionary of Jewish descent; known as **Paul the Apostle**, or **Saul of Tarsus**, or **the Apostle of the Gentiles**. He first opposed the followers of Jesus, assisting at the martyrdom of St Stephen. On a mission to Damascus he was converted to Christianity after a vision and became one of the first major Christian missionaries and theologians. His epistles form part of the New Testament. Feast day, 29 June.

Paul–Bunnell test ▸ noun Medicine a test in which an antibody reaction to sheep red blood cells confirms a diagnosis of infectious mononucleosis (glandular fever).
– ORIGIN 1930s: named after John R. *Paul* (1893–1936) and Walls W. *Bunnell* (1902–65), American physicians.

Pauli /ˈpaʊli/, Wolfgang (1900–58), Austrian-born American physicist. He made a major contribution to quantum theory with the Pauli exclusion principle. In 1931 he postulated the existence of the neutrino, later discovered by Enrico Fermi. Nobel Prize for Physics (1945).

Paulician /pɔːˈlɪʃ(ə)n/ ▸ noun a member of a religious sect which arose in Armenia in the 7th century AD, professing a modified form of Manichaeism.
– ORIGIN from medieval Latin *Pauliciani*, Greek *Paulikianoi*, of unknown origin.

Pauli exclusion principle (also **Pauli's exclusion principle**) ▸ noun Physics the assertion that no two fermions can have the same quantum number.
– ORIGIN 1920s: named after W. **PAULI**.

P

Pauline /ˈpɔːlʌɪn/ ▶ **adjective** Christian Theology relating to or characteristic of St Paul, his writings, or his doctrines. ■ (in the Roman Catholic Church) relating to Pope Paul VI, or the liturgical and doctrinal reforms pursued during his pontificate (1963–78) as a result of the Second Vatican Council.

Pauling /ˈpɔːlɪŋ/, Linus Carl (1901–94), American chemist. He is renowned for his study of molecular structure and chemical bonding, for which he received the 1954 Nobel Prize for Chemistry. His suggestion of a helical structure for proteins formed the foundation for the elucidation of the structure of DNA.

Paul Jones ▶ **noun** a ballroom dance in which the dancers change partners after circling in concentric rings of men and women.
– ORIGIN 1920s: named after John *Paul Jones* (see JONES[4]).

paulownia /pɔːˈləʊnɪə, -ˈlɒvnɪə/ ▶ **noun** a small SE Asian tree with heart-shaped leaves and fragrant lilac flowers. ● Genus *Paulownia*, family Scrophulariaceae.
– ORIGIN modern Latin, named after Anna *Pavlovna* (1795–1865), a Russian princess.

Paul Pry ▶ **noun** informal, dated an inquisitive person.
– ORIGIN from the name of a character in a US song of 1820.

paunch ▶ **noun 1** a large or protruding belly.
2 Nautical, archaic a thick strong mat used to give protection from chafing on a mast or spar.
▶ **verb** [with obj.] disembowel (an animal).
– DERIVATIVES **paunchiness** noun, **paunchy** adjective (**paunchier**, **paunchiest**).
– ORIGIN late Middle English: from Anglo-Norman French *pa(u)nche*, based on Latin *pantex*, *pantic-*, usually in the plural in the sense 'intestines'.

pauper ▶ **noun** a very poor person: *he died a pauper*. ■ historical a recipient of relief under the provisions of the Poor Law or of public charity. ■ US Law a poor person who may bring a legal action without payment of costs.
– DERIVATIVES **pauperdom** noun, **pauperism** noun, **pauperization** noun, **pauperize** (also **pauperise**) verb.
– ORIGIN late 15th cent.: from Latin, literally 'poor'. The word's use in English originated in the Latin legal phrase *in forma pauperis*, literally 'in the form of a poor person' (allowing non-payment of costs).

paupiette /pɔːˈpjɛt/ ▶ **noun** a long, thin slice of fish or meat, rolled and stuffed with a filling.
– ORIGIN French, probably from Italian *polpetta*, from Latin *pulpa* 'pulp'.

pauraque /paʊˈrɑːkeɪ/ ▶ **noun** a long-tailed nightjar found mainly in Central and South America. ● Family Caprimulgidae: two genera and species, in particular the **common pauraque** (*Nyctidromus albicollis*).
– ORIGIN probably a Hispanicized form of a local word.

P

Pauropoda /ˈpɔːrəpɒdə/ ▶ **plural noun** Zoology a small class of myriapod invertebrates which resemble the centipedes. They are small soft-bodied animals with one pair of legs per segment, living chiefly in forest litter.
– ORIGIN modern Latin (plural), from Greek *pauros* 'small' + *pous*, *pod-* 'foot'.

Pausanias /pɔːˈseɪnɪəs/ (2nd century), Greek geographer and historian. His *Description of Greece* (also called the *Itinerary of Greece*) is a guide to the topography and remains of ancient Greece and is still considered an invaluable source of information.

pause ▶ **verb** [no obj.] interrupt action or speech briefly: *she paused, at a loss for words*. ■ [with obj.] temporarily interrupt the operation of (a process or device): *she had paused a tape on the VCR*.
▶ **noun** a temporary stop in action or speech: *she dropped me outside during a brief pause in the rain* | [mass noun] *he chattered away without pause*. ■ Music a mark (𝄐) over a note or rest that is to be lengthened by an unspecified amount. ■ (also **pause button**) a control allowing the temporary interruption of recording, playback, or other process.
– PHRASES **give pause to someone** (or **give someone pause for thought**) cause someone to think carefully or hesitate before doing something: *the sight of these gives any would-be attacker pause for thought*.
– ORIGIN late Middle English: from Old French, from Latin *pausa*, from Greek *pausis*, from *pausein* 'to stop'.

pavage /ˈpeɪvɪdʒ/ ▶ **noun** [mass noun] historical a tax or toll to cover the cost of the paving of streets.
– ORIGIN late Middle English: from Old French, from *paver* 'to pave'.

pavane /pəˈvan, -ˈvɑːn/ (also **pavan** /ˈpav(ə)n/) ▶ **noun** a stately dance in slow duple time, popular in the 16th and 17th centuries and performed in elaborate clothing. ■ a piece of music for a pavane.
– ORIGIN mid 16th cent.: from French *pavane*, from Italian *pavana*, feminine adjective from *Pavo*, dialect name of PADUA.

Pavarotti /ˌpavəˈrɒti/, Luciano (1935–2007), Italian operatic tenor. He made his debut as Rodolfo in Puccini's *La Bohème* in 1961 and gained international acclaim and popularity for his bel canto singing.

pave ▶ **verb** [with obj.] cover (a piece of ground) with flat stones or bricks; lay paving over: *the yard at the front was paved with flagstones* | (as adj. **paved**) *a paved area*.
– PHRASES **pave the way for** create the circumstances to enable (something) to happen or be done: *the proposals will pave the way for a resolution to the problem*. **the streets are paved with gold** used to suggest that it is easy to become rich and successful in a particular place: *few people now imagine that the streets of New York, Paris, or London are paved with gold*.
– ORIGIN Middle English: from Old French *paver* 'pave'.

pavé /ˈpaveɪ/ ▶ **noun 1** a setting of precious stones placed so closely together that no metal shows: *a solid diamond pavé*.
2 a paved street, road, or path.
– ORIGIN French, literally 'paved', past participle of *paver*.

pavement ▶ **noun** Brit. a raised paved or asphalted path for pedestrians at the side of a road. ■ any paved area or surface. ■ [mass noun] N. Amer. the hard surface of a road or street. ■ Geology a horizontal expanse of bare rock or cemented fragments.
– ORIGIN Middle English: from Old French, from Latin *pavimentum* 'trodden down floor', from *pavire* 'beat, tread down'.

pavement artist ▶ **noun** Brit. an artist who draws with coloured chalks on paving stones or paper laid on a pavement to earn money from passers-by.

paver ▶ **noun 1** a paving stone.
2 a person who lays paving or paving stones.

Pavese /paˈveɪzeɪ, -zi/, Cesare (1908–50), Italian novelist, poet, and translator. He is best known for his last novel *La Luna e i falò* (1950), in which he portrays isolation and the failure of communication as a general human predicament.

pavilion ▶ **noun** a building or similar structure used for a specific purpose, in particular: ■ Brit. a building at a cricket ground or other sports ground, used for changing and taking refreshments. ■ a summer house or other decorative building used as a shelter in a park or large garden. ■ used in the names of buildings used for theatrical or other entertainments: *the resort's Spa Pavilion*. ■ a detached or semi-detached block at a hospital or other building complex. ■ a large tent with a peak and crenellated decorations, used at a show or fair. ■ a temporary building, stand, or other structure in which items are displayed at a trade exhibition.
– ORIGIN Middle English (denoting a large decorated tent): from Old French *pavillon*, from Latin *papilio(n-)* 'butterfly or tent'.

paving ▶ **noun** [mass noun] a surface made up of flat stones laid in a pattern. ■ the stones used for a paved surface.

paving stone ▶ **noun** a large, flat piece of stone or similar material, used in paving.

paviour /ˈpeɪvɪə/ (also **pavior**) ▶ **noun** a paving stone. ■ archaic a person who lays paving stones.
– ORIGIN Middle English: from Old French *paveur*, from *paver* 'pave'.

Pavlov /ˈpavlɒf/, Ivan (Petrovich) (1849–1936), Russian physiologist. He was awarded a Nobel Prize in 1904 for his work on digestion, but is best known for his studies on the conditioned reflex. He showed by experiment with dogs how the secretion of saliva can be stimulated not only by food but also by the sound of a bell associated with the presentation of food.

Pavlova /pavˈləʊvə/, Anna (Pavlovna) (1881–1931), Russian dancer, resident in Britain from 1912. Her highly acclaimed solo dance *The Dying Swan* was created for her by Michel Fokine in 1905. On settling in Britain she formed her own company.

pavlova ▶ **noun** a dessert consisting of a meringue base or shell filled with whipped cream and fruit.
– ORIGIN named after A. PAVLOVA.

Pavlovian /pavˈləʊvɪən/ ▶ **adjective** relating to classical conditioning as described by I. P. Pavlov: *the sound of the tea trolley created a Pavlovian reaction among the men*.

Pavo /ˈpɑːvəʊ/ Astronomy a southern constellation (the Peacock), between Grus and Triangulum Australe. Its brightest star is itself sometimes called 'the Peacock'.
– ORIGIN Latin.

pavonine /ˈpavənʌɪn/ ▶ **adjective** rare of or like a peacock.
– ORIGIN mid 17th cent.: from Latin *pavoninus*, from *pavo*, *pavon-* 'peacock'.

paw ▶ **noun** an animal's foot having claws and pads. ■ informal a person's hand: *the Internet is the easiest way to get your paws on mucky pictures*.
▶ **verb** [with obj.] (of an animal) feel or scrape with a paw or hoof: *the horse rose up, its forelegs pawing the air* | [no obj.] *young dogs may paw at the floor and whine*. ■ informal (of a person) touch or handle clumsily or lasciviously: *some overweight Casanova had tried to paw her*.
– ORIGIN Middle English: from Old French *poue*, probably of Germanic origin and related to Dutch *poot*.

pawky ▶ **adjective** (**pawkier**, **pawkiest**) chiefly Scottish & N. English having or showing a sardonic sense of humour: *a gentle man with a pawky wit*.
– DERIVATIVES **pawkily** adverb, **pawkiness** noun.
– ORIGIN mid 17th cent.: from Scots and northern English *pawk* 'trick', of unknown origin.

pawl /pɔːl/ ▶ **noun** a pivoted curved bar or lever whose free end engages with the teeth of a cogwheel or ratchet so that the wheel or ratchet can only turn or move one way. ■ each of a set of short bars that engage with the whelps and prevent a capstan, windlass, or winch from recoiling.
– ORIGIN early 17th cent.: perhaps from Low German and Dutch *pal* (related to *pal* 'fixed').

pawn[1] ▶ **noun** a chess piece of the smallest size and value, that moves one square forwards along its file if unobstructed (or two on the first move), or one square diagonally forwards when making a capture. Each player begins with eight pawns on the second rank, and can promote a pawn to become any other piece (typically a queen) if it reaches the opponent's end of the board. ■ a person used by others for their own purposes: *he was a pawn in the game of power politics*.
– ORIGIN late Middle English: from Anglo-Norman French *poun*, from medieval Latin *pedo*, *pedon-* 'foot soldier', from Latin *pes*, *ped-* 'foot'. Compare with PEON.

pawn[2] ▶ **verb** [with obj.] deposit (an object) with a pawnbroker as security for money lent: *I pawned the necklace to cover the loan*.
▶ **noun** archaic an object left as security for money lent.
– PHRASES **in pawn** (of an object) held as security by a pawnbroker.
– PHRASAL VERBS **pawn someone/thing off** pass off someone or something unwanted: *newly industrialized economies are racing to* ***pawn off*** *old processes* ***on*** *poorer countries*.
– ORIGIN late 15th cent. (as a noun): from Old French *pan* 'pledge, security', of West Germanic origin; related to Dutch *pand* and German *Pfand*.

pawnbroker ▶ **noun** a person who lends money at interest on the security of an article pawned.
– DERIVATIVES **pawnbroking** noun.

Pawnee /pɔːˈniː/ ▶ **noun** (pl. **same** or **Pawnees**) **1** a member of an American Indian confederacy formerly living in Nebraska, and now mainly in Oklahoma.
2 [mass noun] the language of the Pawnee, belonging to the Caddoan family and now almost extinct.
▶ **adjective** relating to the Pawnee or their language.
– ORIGIN from Canadian French *Pani*, from a North American Indian language.

pawnshop ▶ **noun** a pawnbroker's shop.

pawn ticket ▶ **noun** a ticket issued by a pawnbroker in exchange for an article pawned, bearing particulars of the loan.

pawpaw /ˈpɔːpɔː/ (also **papaw**) ▶ **noun 1** another term for PAPAYA.
2 (also **pawpaw tree**) a North American tree of the custard apple family, with purple flowers and edible oblong yellow fruit with sweet pulp. ● *Asimina triloba*, family Annonaceae.
■ the fruit of the pawpaw tree.

– ORIGIN early 17th cent.: from Spanish and Portuguese *papaya*, of Carib origin. The change in spelling is unexplained.

Pax Roman Mythology the goddess of peace. Greek equivalent **EIRENE**.

pax[1] ▶ **noun 1** [as exclamation] Brit. informal, dated a call for a truce, used especially by schoolchildren when playing: *Pax! No offence meant, honest old chum.*
2 chiefly historical (in the Christian Church) the kissing by all the participants at a mass of a tablet depicting the Crucifixion or other sacred object; the kiss of peace.
– ORIGIN Latin, literally 'peace'.

pax[2] ▶ **noun** (pl. **same**) (chiefly in commercial use) a person or persons: *the buffet costs $53 per pax* | *two pilots and four pax on board.*
– ORIGIN 1970s: apparently an alteration of *pass-* (from **PASSENGER**).

Pax Americana /ˌpaks əmɛrɪˈkɑːnə/ (also **Pax Britannica** /brɪˈtanɪkə/) ▶ **noun** [mass noun] a state of relative international peace regarded as overseen by the US (or the UK).
– ORIGIN late 19th cent.: Latin, literally 'American peace', after **PAX ROMANA**.

Pax Romana /ˌpaks rəʊˈmɑːnə/ ▶ **noun** [mass noun] the peace which existed between nationalities within the Roman Empire.
– ORIGIN mid 19th cent.: Latin, literally 'Roman peace'.

Paxton, Sir Joseph (1801–65), English gardener and architect. He became head gardener at Chatsworth House in Derbyshire in 1826 and designed a series of glass-and-iron greenhouses. He later reworked these in his design for the Crystal Palace (1851).

pay[1] ▶ **verb** (past and past participle **paid**) **1** [with obj.] give (someone) money that is due for work done, goods received, or a debt incurred: [with obj. and infinitive] *the traveller paid a guide to show him across* | [no obj.] *I'll pay for your ticket.* ■ give (a sum of money) in exchange for goods or work done or to settle a debt: *the company was rumoured to have paid 450p a share* | [with two objs] *they paid him an annual retainer.* ■ hand over or transfer the amount due of (a debt, wages, etc.) to someone: *I always prefer to pay all my bills by cheque.* ■ (of work, an investment, etc.) provide someone with (a sum of money): *jobs that pay £5 an hour.* ■ [no obj.] (of a business, activity, or an attitude) be profitable or advantageous: *crime doesn't pay* | [with infinitive] *it pays to choose varieties carefully.*
2 [no obj.] suffer a misfortune as a consequence of an action: *the destroyer would have to pay with his life.*
3 [with two objs] give (attention, respect, or a compliment) to (someone): *no one paid them any attention.* ■ make (a visit or call) to (someone): *she has been prevailed upon to pay us a visit.* ■ [with obj.] give what is due or deserved to: *it was his way of* ***paying out*** *Maguire for giving him the push.*
▶ **noun** [mass noun] the money paid to someone for regular work: *an entitlement to sickness pay.*
– PHRASES **he who pays the piper calls the tune** proverb the person who provides the money for something has the right to determine how it's spent. **in the pay of** employed by. **pay attention** see **ATTENTION**. **pay one's compliments** see **COMPLIMENT**. **pay court to** see **COURT**. **pay dearly** obtain something at a high cost or great effort. ■ suffer for a misdemeanour or failure: *they paid dearly for wasting goal-scoring opportunities.* **pay one's dues** see **DUE**. **pay for itself** (of a thing) earn or save enough money to cover the cost of its purchase. **pay its** (or **one's**) **way** (of an enterprise or person) earn enough to cover its or one's costs. **pay one's last respects** show respect towards a dead person by attending their funeral. **pay one's respects** make a polite visit to someone: *we went to pay our respects to the head lama.* **pay through the nose** informal pay much more than a fair price. **you pays your money and you takes your choice** informal used to convey that there is little to choose between one alternative and another.
– PHRASAL VERBS **pay someone back** repay a loan to someone. ■ take revenge on someone: *he had left him out to* ***pay him back for*** *stealing his wife.* **pay something back** repay a loan to someone. **pay something in** pay money into a bank account. **pay off** informal (of a course of action) yield good results; succeed: *all the hard work I had done over the summer paid off.* **pay someone off** dismiss someone with a final payment: *when directors are fired, they should not be lavishly paid off.* **pay something off** pay a debt in full. **pay something out** (or **pay out**) **1** pay a large sum of money from funds under one's control. **2** let out (a rope) by slackening it: *I began paying out the nylon line.* **pay up** (or **pay something up**) pay a debt in full: *you've got ninety days to pay up the principal.*
– DERIVATIVES **payer** noun.
– ORIGIN Middle English (in the sense 'pacify'): from Old French *paie* (noun), *payer* (verb), from Latin *pacare* 'appease', from *pax, pac-* 'peace'. The notion of 'payment' arose from the sense of 'pacifying' a creditor.

pay[2] ▶ **verb** (past and past participle **payed**) [with obj.] Nautical seal (the deck or seams of a wooden ship) with pitch or tar to prevent leakage.
– ORIGIN early 17th cent.: from Old Northern French *peier*, from Latin *picare*, from *pix, pic-* 'pitch'.

payable ▶ **adjective** [predic.] **1** (of money) required to be paid; due: *interest is payable on the money owing.*
2 able to be paid: *it costs just $195, payable in five monthly instalments.*
▶ **noun** (**payables**) debts owed by a business; liabilities.

pay and display ▶ **noun** [mass noun] [usu. as modifier] a parking system in which a motorist buys a temporary permit from a coin-operated machine and displays it in the window of the vehicle.

pay as you earn (abbrev.: **PAYE**) ▶ **noun** [mass noun] (in the UK and South Africa) a system by which an employer deducts income tax from an employee's wages before paying them to the employee and sends the deduction to the government.

pay as you go ▶ **noun** [mass noun] a system of meeting costs as they arise or paying for a service before it is used.

payback ▶ **noun 1** [mass noun] profit from an investment equal to the initial outlay.
2 an act of revenge or retaliation.

payback period ▶ **noun** the length of time required for an investment to recover its initial outlay in terms of profits or savings.

pay bed ▶ **noun** (in the UK) a hospital bed for private patients in a National Health Service hospital.

pay cable ▶ **noun** [mass noun] US a cable television service available on a subscription basis.

pay channel ▶ **noun** a television channel for which viewers pay a subscription fee additional to that already paid for the basic provision of a cable or satellite television service.

pay cheque (US **paycheck**) ▶ **noun** a salary or wages cheque made out to an employee. ■ N. Amer. a salary or income.

pay day ▶ **noun** a day on which someone is paid their wages. ■ informal an amount of money won or available to be won, especially in a sporting contest: *the win landed him the biggest pay day of his career—£20,000.*

pay dirt ▶ **noun** [mass noun] N. Amer. ground containing ore in sufficient quantity to be profitably extracted. ■ informal profit; success: *the gig pays three hundred bucks a week—looks like I just* ***hit pay dirt****.*

PAYE ▶ **abbreviation** chiefly Brit. pay as you earn.

payee ▶ **noun** a person to whom money is paid or is to be paid, especially the person to whom a cheque is made payable.

pay envelope ▶ **noun** North American term for **PAY PACKET**.

payess /ˈpeɪɛs/ ▶ **plural noun** chiefly N. Amer. uncut sideburns worn by male Orthodox Jews.
– ORIGIN Yiddish *peyes*, from Hebrew *pē'ōṯ* 'corners' (see Lev. 19:27).

paying guest ▶ **noun** a person who lives in someone else's house and pays for food and accommodation; a lodger.

payload ▶ **noun** the part of a vehicle's load, especially an aircraft's, from which revenue is derived; passengers and cargo. ■ an explosive warhead carried by an aircraft or missile. ■ equipment, personnel, or satellites carried by a spacecraft.

paymaster ▶ **noun 1** a person or organization that pays another to do something and therefore controls them: *both political parties were beholden to their corporate paymasters.*
2 an official who pays troops or workers. ■ (in full **Paymaster General**) Brit. the minister at the head of the Treasury department responsible for payments.

payment ▶ **noun 1** [mass noun] the action or process of paying someone or something or of being paid: *ask for a discount for payment by cash* | [count noun] *three interest-free monthly payments.*
2 an amount paid or payable: *a compensation payment of £2500.* ■ [mass noun] something given as a reward or in recompense for something done: *a suit with a velvet collar that I got as payment for being in the show.*
– ORIGIN late Middle English: from Old French *paiement*, from *payer* 'to pay'.

Payne's grey ▶ **noun** [mass noun] Printing a composite pigment composed of blue, red, black, and white permanent pigments, used especially for watercolours.
– ORIGIN mid 19th cent.: named after William *Payne* (*fl.* 1800), English artist.

paynim /ˈpeɪnɪm/ ▶ **noun** archaic a non-Christian, especially a Muslim.
– ORIGIN Middle English: from Old French *paienime*, from ecclesiastical Latin *paganismus* 'heathenism', from *paganus* 'heathen' (see **PAGAN**).

pay-off ▶ **noun** informal a payment made to someone, especially as a bribe or on leaving a job: *he left the company with an £800,000 pay-off.* ■ the return on investment or on a bet. ■ a final outcome or result: *the restructuring of the last few years was supposed to have a big pay-off.*

payola /peɪˈəʊlə/ ▶ **noun** [mass noun] chiefly N. Amer. the practice of bribing someone in return for the unofficial promotion of a product in the media: *if a record company spends enough money on payola, it can make any record a hit.*
– ORIGIN 1930s: from **PAY**[1] + *-ola* as in *Victrola*, the name of a make of gramophone.

payout ▶ **noun** a large payment of money, especially as compensation or a dividend: *an insurance payout.*

pay packet ▶ **noun** Brit. an envelope containing an employee's wages. ■ a salary or income: *she was looking for other jobs to supplement her pay packet.*

pay-per-view ▶ **noun** [mass noun] a television service in which viewers are required to pay a fee in order to watch a specific programme.

payphone ▶ **noun** a public telephone that is operated by coins or by a credit or prepaid card.

payroll ▶ **noun** a list of a company's employees and the amount of money they are to be paid: *there are just three employees* ***on the payroll****.* ■ the total amount of wages paid by a company: *small employers with a payroll of less than £45,000.*

paysage /peɪˈzɑːʒ/ ▶ **noun** a landscape, especially as depicted in art.
– ORIGIN French, literally 'countryside', from *pays* 'country'.

paysan /peɪˈzɒ̃/, French /peizɑ̃/ ▶ **noun** a peasant or countryman, especially in France.
– ORIGIN French.

Pays Basque /pei bask/ French name for **BASQUE COUNTRY**.

Pays de la Loire /ˌpeɪ də la ˈlwɑː/, French /pei də la lwaʀ/ a region of western France centred on the Loire valley.

payslip ▶ **noun** chiefly Brit. a note given to an employee when they have been paid, detailing the amount of pay given, and the tax and insurance deducted.

pay spine ▶ **noun** see **SPINE** (sense 4).

pay station ▶ **noun** US term for **PAYPHONE**.

pay TV (also **pay television**) ▶ **noun** [mass noun] television broadcasting in which viewers pay by subscription to watch a particular channel.

paywall ▶ **noun** (on a website) an arrangement whereby access is restricted to users who have paid to subscribe to the site.

Paz /paz/, Octavio (1914–98), Mexican poet and essayist. His poems reflect a preoccupation with Aztec mythology. He is also noted for his essays written in response to the brutal suppression of student demonstrations in 1968. Nobel Prize for Literature (1990).

pazazz ▶ **noun** variant spelling of **PIZZAZZ**.

Pb ▶ **abbreviation** (also **PB**) petabyte(s).
▶ **symbol** the chemical element lead. [from Latin *plumbum*.]

pb ▶ **abbreviation** paperback: *hb £16.99, pb £7.99.*

PBS ▶ **abbreviation** (in the US) Public Broadcasting System (or Service).

PBX ▶ **abbreviation** private branch exchange, a private telephone switchboard.

PC ▶ **noun** a personal computer: *you can download the software on to your PC.*
▶ **abbreviation** ■ Brit. a police constable. ■ (also **pc**) politically correct; political correctness: *PC language.* ■ Privy Counsellor.

p.c. ▶ **abbreviation** per cent.

P

PCAS ▸ abbreviation historical (in the UK) Polytechnics Central Admissions System (incorporated into UCAS in the 1993–4 academic year).

PCB ▸ abbreviation ■ Electronics printed circuit board. ■ Chemistry polychlorinated biphenyl.

PC card ▸ noun a printed circuit board for a personal computer, especially one built to the PCMCIA standard.

P-Celtic ▸ noun & adjective another term for BRYTHONIC.
– ORIGIN *P*, from the development of the Indo-European *kw* sound into *p* in this group of languages.

PCI ▸ noun [mass noun] a standard for connecting computers and their peripherals.
– ORIGIN 1990s: abbreviation of *Peripheral Component Interconnect*.

PCM ▸ abbreviation pulse code modulation.

PCMCIA ▸ abbreviation Personal Computer Memory Card International Association, denoting a standard specification for memory cards and interfaces in personal computers.

PCN ▸ abbreviation personal communications network, a digital mobile telephony system.

p-code ▸ noun another term for PSEUDOCODE.

PCP ▸ abbreviation ■ pentachlorophenol. ■ phencyclidine. ■ pneumocystis carinii pneumonia.

PC Plod ▸ noun see PLOD (sense 2 of the noun).

PCR ▸ abbreviation Biochemistry polymerase chain reaction.

PCS ▸ abbreviation personal communications services, a digital mobile telephony system.

PCSO ▸ abbreviation (in the UK) police community support officer.

PCT ▸ abbreviation (in the UK) Primary Care Trust, a National Health Service body responsible for the provision of community health services in a particular area.

pct. ▸ abbreviation N. Amer. per cent.

PCV ▸ abbreviation Brit. passenger-carrying vehicle.

PD ▸ abbreviation ■ US Police Department: *the Chicago PD*. ■ public domain: *PD software*.

Pd ▸ symbol the chemical element palladium.

pd ▸ abbreviation paid.

PDA ▸ noun a palmtop computer that functions as a personal organizer but also provides email and Internet access.
– ORIGIN 1990s: abbreviation of *personal digital assistant*.

PDC ▸ abbreviation programme delivery control, a system for broadcasting a coded signal at the beginning and end of a television programme which can be recognized by a video recorder and used to begin and end recording.

P

PDF ▸ noun [mass noun] Computing a file format for capturing and sending electronic documents in exactly the intended format: [as modifier] *PDF files*.
– ORIGIN 1990s: abbreviation of *Portable Document Format*.

PDP ▸ abbreviation parallel distributed processing.

p.d.q. ▸ abbreviation informal pretty damn quick.

PDSA ▸ abbreviation (in the UK) People's Dispensary for Sick Animals.

PDT ▸ abbreviation Pacific Daylight Time (see PACIFIC TIME).

PE ▸ abbreviation ■ Peru (international vehicle registration). ■ physical education. ■ Prince Edward Island (in official postal use).

pea ▸ noun **1** a spherical green seed which is eaten as a vegetable. ■ W. Indian any legume, including peas, beans, or lentils, eaten as a vegetable.
2 the hardy Eurasian climbing plant which yields pods containing peas. ● *Pisum sativum*, family Leguminosae (or Fabaceae; the **pea family**). The members of this family (known as legumes) are sometimes divided among three smaller families: Papilionaceae (peas, beans, clovers, vetches, brooms, laburnums, etc.), Mimosaceae (mimosas, acacias), and Caesalpiniaceae (cassia, carob, and many tropical timber trees).
3 [with modifier] used in names of similar or related plants or seeds, e.g. **chickpea**, **sweet pea**.
– PHRASES **like peas (or two peas) in a pod** so similar as to be indistinguishable or nearly so.
– DERIVATIVES **pea-like** adjective.
– ORIGIN mid 17th cent.: back-formation from PEASE (interpreted as plural).

pea bean ▸ noun a variety of kidney bean with small rounded seeds.

peaberry ▸ noun (pl. **peaberries**) a coffee berry containing one rounded seed instead of the usual two, through non-fertilization of one ovule or subsequent abortion. Such beans are esteemed for their fine strong flavour.

pea-brain ▸ noun informal a stupid person.
– DERIVATIVES **pea-brained** adjective.

peace ▸ noun [mass noun] **1** freedom from disturbance; tranquillity: *he just wanted to drink a few beers in peace*. ■ mental or emotional calm: *the **peace of mind** this insurance gives you*.
2 a state or period in which there is no war or a war has ended: *the Straits were to be open to warships in time of peace* | [in sing.] *the peace didn't last*. ■ [in sing.] a treaty agreeing peace between warring states: *support for a negotiated peace*. ■ the state of being free from civil disorder: *police action to restore peace*. ■ the state of being free from dissension: *the 8.8 per cent offer promises peace with the union*.
3 (**the peace**) a ceremonial handshake or kiss exchanged during a service in some Churches (now usually only in the Eucharist), symbolizing Christian love and unity. See also KISS OF PEACE at KISS.
– PHRASES **at peace 1** euphemistic free from anxiety or distress. ■ dead and therefore free from the difficulties of life. **2** in a state of friendliness: *a man at peace with the world*. **hold one's peace** remain silent about something. **keep the peace** refrain or prevent others from disturbing civil order. **make (one's) peace** re-establish friendly relations: *he returned to the village to make peace with his mother*. **no peace for the wicked** see NO REST FOR THE WICKED at WICKED.
– ORIGIN Middle English: from Old French *pais*, from Latin *pax*, *pac-* 'peace'.

peaceable ▸ adjective inclined to avoid conflict or dissent: *an industrious, peaceable people*. ■ free from conflict or dissent; peaceful: *peaceable demonstrations for democratic reform*.
– DERIVATIVES **peaceableness** noun, **peaceably** adverb.
– ORIGIN Middle English: from Old French *peisible*, alteration of *plaisible*, from late Latin *placibilis* 'pleasing', from Latin *placere* 'to please'.

peace camp ▸ noun an informal encampment set up as a public protest against a military establishment or an aspect of military policy.

Peace Corps an organization sending young people to work as volunteers in developing countries.

peace dividend ▸ noun a sum of public money which becomes available for other purposes when spending on defence is reduced.

peaceful ▸ adjective **1** free from disturbance; tranquil: *his peaceful mood vanished*.
2 not involving war or violence: *a soldier was shot at an otherwise peaceful demonstration*. ■ (of a person) inclined to avoid conflict: *Dad was a peaceful, law-abiding citizen*.
– DERIVATIVES **peacefulness** noun.

peacefully ▸ adverb **1** without disturbance; tranquilly: *the baby slept peacefully in its cradle*. ■ (of death) without pain: *she died peacefully in her sleep*.
2 without war or violence: *the siege ended peacefully*.

Peace Garden State informal name for NORTH DAKOTA.

peacekeeping ▸ noun [usu. as modifier] the active maintenance of a truce between nations or communities, especially by an international military force: *the 2,300-strong UN peacekeeping force*.
– DERIVATIVES **peacekeeper** noun.

peacemaker ▸ noun a person who brings about peace, especially by reconciling adversaries.
– DERIVATIVES **peacemaking** noun & adjective.

peace movement ▸ noun a broad movement opposed to preparations for war, especially a movement in Britain and western Europe attempting since the 1950s to bring about a reduction in or elimination of nuclear weapons.

peacenik ▸ noun informal, often derogatory a member of a pacifist movement.
– ORIGIN 1960s: from PEACE + -NIK.

peace offering ▸ noun **1** a propitiatory or conciliatory gift: *he took the flowers to Jean as a peace offering*.
2 (in biblical use) an offering presented as a thanksgiving to God.

peace officer ▸ noun chiefly N. Amer. a civil officer appointed to preserve law and order, such as a sheriff or police officer.

peace pipe ▸ noun a tobacco pipe offered and smoked as a token of peace among North American Indians.

Peace Pledge Union (abbrev.: **PPU**) a pacifist organization formed in 1936 and supported by a number of socialist writers and intellectuals including Bertrand Russell, Siegfried Sassoon, and Aldous Huxley.

peace sign ▸ noun **1** a sign of peace made by holding up the hand with palm out-turned and the first two fingers extended in a V-shape.
2 a figure representing peace, in the form of a circle with one line bisecting it from top to bottom and two shorter lines radiating downward on either side.

peacetime ▸ noun [mass noun] a period when a country is not at war.

peach¹ ▸ noun **1** a round stone fruit with juicy yellow flesh and downy pinkish-yellow skin. ■ [mass noun] a pinkish-yellow colour like that of a peach.
2 (also **peach tree**) the Chinese tree which bears peaches. ● *Prunus persica*, family Rosaceae: many cultivars, including the nectarine.
3 [in sing.] informal an exceptionally good or attractive person or thing: *it was **another peach of a day***.
– PHRASES **peaches and cream** (of a person's complexion) of a cream colour with downy pink cheeks.
– ORIGIN late Middle English: from Old French *pesche*, from medieval Latin *persica*, from Latin *persicum (malum)*, literally 'Persian apple'.

peach² ▸ verb [no obj.] (**peach on**) informal inform on: *the other members of the gang would not hesitate to peach on him*.
– ORIGIN late Middle English: shortening of archaic *appeach*, from Old French *empechier* 'impede' (see IMPEACH).

peach-bloom ▸ noun [mass noun] a matte glaze of reddish pink, mottled with green and brown, used on fine Chinese porcelain since around 1700. ■ a delicate purplish-pink colour.
– ORIGIN early 19th cent.: applied to the porcelain glaze from the 1880s.

peach blossom ▸ noun a European woodland moth that has brownish wings with pink markings. ● *Thyatira batis*, family Geometridae.

peach-blow ▸ noun [mass noun] **1** another term for PEACH-BLOOM.
2 a type of late 19th-century American coloured glass.
– ORIGIN early 19th cent.: from PEACH¹ + BLOW³.

peach fuzz ▸ noun [mass noun] N. Amer. informal the down on the chin of an adolescent boy whose beard has not yet developed.

peachick ▸ noun a young peafowl.

peach Melba ▸ noun a dish of ice cream and peaches with Melba sauce.
– ORIGIN named after Dame Nellie *Melba* (see MELBA¹).

Peach State informal name for the US state of GEORGIA.

peachy ▸ adjective (**peachier**, **peachiest**) **1** of the nature or appearance of a peach.
2 (also **peachy-keen**) informal, chiefly N. Amer. attractive; excellent: *everything is just peachy*.
– DERIVATIVES **peachiness** noun.

pea coat ▸ noun another term for PEA JACKET.

Peacock, Thomas Love (1785–1866), English novelist and poet. He is chiefly remembered for his prose satires, including *Nightmare Abbey* (1818) and *Crotchet Castle* (1831), lampooning the romantic poets.

peacock ▸ noun a male peafowl, which has very long tail feathers with eye-like markings that can be erected and fanned out in display.
– ORIGIN Middle English: from Old English *pēa* (from Latin *pavo*) 'peacock' + COCK¹.

peacock blue ▸ noun [mass noun] a greenish-blue colour like that of a peacock's neck.

peacock butterfly ▸ noun a brightly coloured Eurasian butterfly with conspicuous eyespots on its wings. ● *Inachis io*, subfamily Nymphalinae, family Nymphalidae.

peacock ore ▸ noun another term for BORNITE.

peacock worm ▸ noun a colourful European fan worm of shallow waters. ● *Sabella pavonina*, class Polychaeta.

pea crab ▸ noun a minute soft-bodied crab that lives inside the shell of a bivalve mollusc, where it filters food particles from the water drawn into the shell by its host. ● Family Pinnotheridae: *Pinnotheres* and other genera.

pea flower ▸ noun a flower that is characteristic of many leguminous plants and typified by that of the pea. See PAPILIONACEOUS.

peafowl ▸ noun a large crested pheasant found mainly in Asia. See PEACOCK, PEAHEN. ● Two genera and three species in the family Phasianidae, in particular the widely introduced **common peafowl** (*Pavo cristatus*).

pea green ▸ noun [mass noun] a bright green colour like that of a pea.

peahen ▸ noun a female peafowl, which has drabber colours and a shorter tail than the male.

pea jacket (also **pea coat**) ▸ noun a short double-breasted overcoat of coarse woollen cloth, formerly worn by sailors.
– ORIGIN early 18th cent.: probably from Dutch *pij-jakker*, from *pij* 'coat of coarse cloth' + *jekker* 'jacket'. The change in the ending was due to association with JACKET.

peak[1] ▸ noun **1** the pointed top of a mountain. ■ a mountain with a pointed top.
2 a projecting pointed part or shape: *whisk two egg whites to stiff peaks.* ■ Brit. a stiff brim at the front of a cap. ■ the narrow part of a ship's hold at the bow or stern. ■ the upper, outer corner of a sail extended by a gaff.
3 the point of highest activity, quality, or achievement: *he was at his peak as a cricketer | package holiday sales hit a peak of around 12 million.* ■ a point in a curve or on a graph, or a value of a physical quantity, higher than those around it.
▸ verb [no obj., with adverbial] reach a highest point, either of a specified value or at a specified time: *the disease peaked in summer.*
▸ adjective [attrib.] at the highest level; maximum: *the canal was restored to peak condition.* ■ characterized by maximum activity or demand: *traffic speeds are reduced at peak hours.*
– DERIVATIVES **peakless** adjective.
– ORIGIN mid 16th cent.: probably a back-formation from *peaked*, variant of dialect *picked* 'pointed'.

> **USAGE** The word meaning 'look quickly or furtively' and 'a quick or furtive look' is **peek**, not **peak**. See USAGE at PEEK.

peak[2] ▸ verb [no obj.] archaic decline in health and spirits; waste away.
– ORIGIN early 17th cent.: of unknown origin.

peak cap ▸ noun a flat cap with a peak at the front.

Peak District a hilly area in Derbyshire, at the southern end of the Pennines, rising to 636 m (2,088 ft) at Kinder Scout.

peaked[1] ▸ adjective having a peak.

peaked[2] ▸ adjective [predic.] chiefly N. Amer. gaunt and pale from illness or fatigue: *you do look a little peaked.*

peak flow meter ▸ noun Medicine a calibrated instrument used to measure lung capacity in monitoring breathing disorders such as asthma.

peak load ▸ noun the maximum of electrical power demand.

peak oil ▸ noun [in sing.] the point in time when the global production of oil will reach its maximum rate, after which production will gradually decline.

peak-to-peak ▸ adjective & adverb measured between the greatest peaks of a periodically varying quantity.

peaky ▸ adjective (**peakier**, **peakiest**) Brit. pale from illness or fatigue; sickly: *you're looking a bit peaky—a change of scene would do you good.*
– ORIGIN early 19th cent.: from PEAK[2] + -Y[1].

peal ▸ noun **1** a loud ringing of a bell or bells. ■ Bell-ringing a series of changes (strictly, at least five thousand) rung on a set of bells. ■ a set of bells.
2 a loud repeated or reverberating sound of thunder or laughter.
▸ verb [no obj.] (of a bell or bells) ring loudly or in a peal: *all the bells of the city began to peal.* ■ (of laughter or thunder) sound in a peal. ■ [with obj.] convey by the ringing of bells: *the carillon **pealed out** the news to the waiting city.*
– ORIGIN late Middle English: shortening of APPEAL.

pean /piːn/ ▸ noun [mass noun] Heraldry fur resembling ermine but with gold spots on a black ground.
– ORIGIN mid 16th cent.: of unknown origin.

Peano axioms /peɪˈɑːnəʊ/ ▸ plural noun Mathematics a set of axioms from which the properties of the natural numbers may be deduced.
– ORIGIN early 20th cent.: named after Giuseppe *Peano* (1858–1932), Italian mathematician.

peanut ▸ noun **1** the oval seed of a tropical South American plant, often roasted and salted and eaten as a snack or used to make oil or animal feed.
2 the plant of the pea family that bears peanuts, which develop in pods that ripen underground.
● *Arachis hypogaea*, family Leguminosae.
3 (**peanuts**) informal a very small or inadequate sum of money: *he pays peanuts.*
4 (**peanuts**) small pieces of styrofoam used as packing material.

peanut butter ▸ noun [mass noun] a paste of ground roasted peanuts, usually eaten spread on bread.

peanut gallery ▸ noun N. Amer. informal the top gallery in a theatre where the cheaper seats are located.

peanut oil ▸ noun [mass noun] oil produced from peanuts and used mainly for culinary purposes, but also in some soaps and pharmaceuticals. Also called ARACHIS OIL.

peanut worm ▸ noun an unsegmented burrowing marine worm with a stout body and a slender retractable anterior part bearing a terminal mouth surrounded by tentacles. ● Phylum Sipuncula.

pear ▸ noun **1** a sweet yellowish- or brownish-green edible fruit which is narrow at the stalk and wider towards the base.
2 (also **pear tree**) the Eurasian tree which bears the pear. ● Genus *Pyrus*, family Rosaceae: several species and hybrids, in particular *P. communis*.
– ORIGIN Old English *pere*, *peru*, of West Germanic origin; related to Dutch *peer*, from Latin *pirum*.

pear drop ▸ noun a small boiled sweet in the shape of a pear, with a pungently sweet flavour.

pearl[1] ▸ noun **1** a hard, lustrous spherical mass, typically white or bluish-grey, formed within the shell of a pearl oyster or other bivalve mollusc and highly prized as a gem. ■ an artificial imitation of a pearl. ■ (**pearls**) a necklace of pearls. ■ something resembling a pearl: *the sweat stood in pearls along his forehead.* ■ short for MOTHER-OF-PEARL. ■ [mass noun] a very pale bluish grey or white colour like that of a pearl.
2 a person or thing of great worth: *he has some **pearls of wisdom** to offer.*
▸ verb [no obj.] **1** literary form pearl-like drops: *the juice on the blade pearled into droplets.* ■ [with obj.] make bluish-grey: *sunset pearling the sky above the hills.*
2 (usu. as noun **pearling**) dive or fish for pearl oysters.
– PHRASES **cast pearls before swine** offer valuable things to people who do not appreciate them. [with biblical allusion to Matt. 7:6.]
– DERIVATIVES **pearler** noun.
– ORIGIN late Middle English: from Old French *perle*, perhaps based on Latin *perna* 'leg', extended to denote a leg-of-mutton-shaped bivalve.

pearl[2] ▸ noun Brit. another term for PICOT.

pearl ash ▸ noun [mass noun] archaic commercial potassium carbonate.

pearl barley ▸ noun [mass noun] barley reduced to small round grains by grinding.

pearl bulb ▸ noun Brit. an electric light bulb with translucent glass.

pearl button ▸ noun a button made of real or imitation mother-of-pearl.

pearl diver ▸ noun a person who dives for pearl oysters.

pearled ▸ adjective **1** literary adorned with pearls: *we saw her pearled like the Queen.* ■ bluish-grey, like a pearl.
2 formed into drops or grains: *pearled barley.*

pearlescent ▸ adjective having a lustre resembling that of mother-of-pearl: *pearlescent colours.*

pearl everlasting ▸ noun variant of PEARLY EVERLASTING.

pearleye ▸ noun a long-bodied fish of open oceans, with tubular eyes which are directed upward and bear a glistening white spot that may be a light organ. ● Family Scopelarchidae: several genera and species.

pearlfish ▸ noun (pl. **same** or **pearlfishes**) **1** a long slender fish found chiefly in warmer seas, which lives inside the shells of bivalve molluscs or the body cavities of sea cucumbers and other invertebrates.
● Family Carapidae: several genera and species.
2 a small Argentinian killifish, popular in aquaria.
● *Cynolebius belotti*, family Cyprinodontidae.

Pearl Harbor a harbour on the island of Oahu, in Hawaii, the site of a major American naval base, where a surprise attack on 7 December 1941 by Japanese carrier-borne aircraft inflicted heavy damage and brought the US into the Second World War.

pearlite ▸ noun [mass noun] Metallurgy a finely laminated mixture of ferrite and cementite present in cast iron and steel, formed by the cooling of austenite.
– ORIGIN late 19th cent.: from PEARL[1] + -ITE[1].

pearlized (also **pearlised**) ▸ adjective made to have or give a lustre like that of mother-of-pearl.

pearl millet ▸ noun a tall tropical cereal with long cylindrical ears, cultivated as a food crop in the driest areas of Africa and South Asia. ● *Pennisetum glaucum* (or *typhoides*), family Gramineae.

pearl mussel ▸ noun an elongated freshwater bivalve mollusc which occasionally produces small pearls, found in large rivers of the northern hemisphere. ● *Margaritifera margaritifera*, family Margaritiferidae.

pearl onion ▸ noun a very small onion used for pickling.

pearl oyster ▸ noun a tropical marine bivalve mollusc with a ridged scaly shell, which produces pearls.
● Genus *Pinctada*, family Pteriidae: several species, in particular *P. margaritifera*, a major source of commercial pearls.

Pearl River a river of southern China, flowing from Guangzhou (Canton) southwards to the South China Sea and forming part of the delta of the Xi River. Its lower reaches widen to form the Pearl River estuary, the inlet between Hong Kong and Macao.

pearlware ▸ noun [mass noun] fine glazed earthenware pottery, typically white, of a type introduced by Josiah Wedgwood in 1779.

pearlwort ▸ noun a small plant of the pink family, with inconspicuous white flowers, native to north temperate regions. ● Genus *Sagina*, family Caryophyllaceae.

pearly ▸ adjective (**pearlier**, **pearliest**) resembling a pearl in lustre or colour: *nice pearly teeth.* ■ made of or adorned with pearls or mother-of-pearl.
▸ noun (pl. **pearlies**) (**pearlies**) **1** Brit. pearly kings and queens. ■ a pearly king's or queen's clothes or pearl buttons.
2 (also **pearly whites**) informal a person's teeth.

pearly everlasting (also **pearl everlasting**) ▸ noun an ornamental North American plant with grey-green foliage and pearly white flower heads, used in dry flower arrangements. ● *Anaphalis margaritacea*, family Compositae.

Pearly Gates ▸ plural noun informal the gates of heaven: *I am getting less fond of poems about old age as I near the Pearly Gates.*
– ORIGIN with biblical allusion to Revelation 21:21.

pearly king (also **pearly queen**) ▸ noun a London costermonger wearing traditional ceremonial clothes covered with pearl buttons.

pearly nautilus ▸ noun a common nautilus of the Indo-Pacific, with a light spiral shell that is white with brownish bands on the outside and lined with mother-of-pearl on the inside. ● *Nautilus pompilius*, subclass Nautiloidea.

Pearmain /ˈpɛːmeɪn, ˈpəːmeɪn, pəˈmeɪn/ ▸ noun a pear-shaped dessert apple of a variety with firm white flesh.
– ORIGIN Middle English (denoting an old variety of baking pear): from Old French *parmain*, probably based on Latin *parmensis* 'of Parma'.

Pears /pɪəz/, Sir Peter (1910–86), English operatic tenor. In his lifelong partnership with Benjamin Britten he performed the title roles in all Britten's operas and with Britten co-founded the Aldeburgh Festival in 1948.

pear-shaped ▸ adjective tapering towards the top, like a pear. ■ (of a person) having hips that are disproportionately wide in relation to the upper part of the body.
– PHRASES **go pear-shaped** Brit. informal go wrong: *everything went pear-shaped.* [originally RAF slang.]

Pearson[1], Karl (1857–1936), English mathematician, the principal founder of 20th-century statistics. He defined the concept of standard deviation and devised the chi-square test.

Pearson[2], Lester Bowles (1897–1972), Canadian diplomat and Liberal statesman, Prime Minister 1963–8. As Secretary of State for External Affairs (1948–57) he acted as a mediator in the resolution of the Suez crisis (1956). Nobel Peace Prize (1957).

P

Pearson's correlation coefficient (also **Pearson's product-moment correlation coefficient**) ▶ noun Statistics a statistic measuring the linear interdependence between two variables or two sets of data.
– ORIGIN early 20th cent.: named after K. *Pearson* (see PEARSON[1]).

peart /pɪət, pjəːt/ ▶ adjective US dialect lively; cheerful.
– ORIGIN late 15th cent.: variant of PERT.

Peary /ˈpɪəri/, Robert Edwin (1856–1920), American explorer of the Arctic. He is generally credited with being the first person to reach the North Pole, on 6 April 1909, although his achievement is now doubted.

Peary Land a mountainous region on the Arctic coast of northern Greenland.

peasant ▶ noun a poor smallholder or agricultural labourer of low social status (chiefly in historical use or with reference to subsistence farming in poorer countries). ■ informal an ignorant, rude, or unsophisticated person.
– DERIVATIVES **peasantry** noun, **peasanty** adjective.
– ORIGIN late Middle English: from Old French *paisent* 'country dweller', from *pais* 'country', based on Latin *pagus* 'country district'.

peasant economy ▶ noun an agricultural economy in which the family is the basic unit of production.

Peasants' Revolt an uprising in 1381 among the peasant and artisan classes in England, particularly in Kent and Essex. The rebels marched on London, occupying the city and executing unpopular ministers, but after the death of their leader, Wat Tyler, they were persuaded to disperse by Richard II.

pease /piːz/ ▶ plural noun archaic peas.
– ORIGIN Old English *pise* 'pea', (plural) *pisan*, via Latin from Greek *pison*. Compare with PEA.

pease pudding ▶ noun [mass noun] chiefly Brit. a dish of split peas boiled with onion and carrot and mashed to a pulp.

pea-shooter ▶ noun a toy weapon consisting of a small tube out of which dried peas are blown.

pea soup ▶ noun [mass noun] soup made from peas, especially a thick, yellow soup made from dried split peas.

pea-souper ▶ noun Brit. informal a very thick yellowish fog.

peat ▶ noun [mass noun] a brown material consisting of partly decomposed vegetable matter forming a deposit on acidic, boggy, ground, which is dried for use in gardening and as fuel. ■ [count noun] (usu. **peats**) a cut piece of peat.
– DERIVATIVES **peaty** adjective (**peatier**, **peatiest**).
– ORIGIN Middle English: from Anglo-Latin *peta*, perhaps of Celtic origin.

P

peat hag ▶ noun another term for HAG[2] (sense 1).

peatland ▶ noun [mass noun] (also **peatlands**) land consisting largely of peat or peat bogs.

peat moss ▶ noun **1** [mass noun] a large absorbent moss which grows in dense masses on boggy ground, where the lower parts decay slowly to form peat deposits. ● Genus *Sphagnum*, family Sphagnaceae: many species.
2 a lowland peat bog.

pea tree ▶ noun a shrub or small tree with yellow pea-like flowers, native to Siberia and grown as an ornamental. ● *Caragana arborescens*, family Leguminosae.

peau de soie /ˌpəʊdəˈswɑː/ ▶ noun [mass noun] a smooth, finely ribbed satin fabric of silk or rayon.
– ORIGIN mid 19th cent.: French, literally 'skin of silk'.

peau d'orange /ˌpəʊ dɒˈrɒ̃ʒ/ ▶ noun [mass noun] a pitted or dimpled appearance of the skin, especially as characteristic of some cases of breast cancer or due to cellulite.
– ORIGIN French, literally 'orange skin'.

peavey /ˈpiːvi/ (also **peavy**) ▶ noun (pl. **peaveys** or **peavies**) N. Amer. a lumberer's cant hook with a spike at the end.
– ORIGIN late 19th cent.: from the surname of the inventor.

peavine /ˈpiːvʌɪn/ ▶ noun a North American meadow vetch. ● *Vicia americana*, family Leguminosae.

pebble ▶ noun a small stone made smooth and round by the action of water or sand.
▶ adjective [attrib.] informal (of a spectacle lens) very thick and convex: *pebble glasses*.
– PHRASES **not the only pebble on the beach** (especially of a former lover) not unique or irreplaceable.
– DERIVATIVES **pebbled** adjective, **pebbly** adjective (**pebblier**, **pebbliest**).
– ORIGIN late Old English, recorded as the first element of *papel-stān* 'pebble-stone', *pyppelrīpig* 'pebble-stream', of unknown origin. The word is recorded in place names from the early 12th cent. onwards.

pebble-dash ▶ noun [mass noun] Brit. mortar with pebbles in it, used as a coating for external walls.
– DERIVATIVES **pebble-dashed** adjective.

pebble-grained ▶ adjective (of leather) having a rough and indented surface as a result of treatment with a patterned roller.

pec ▶ noun (usu. **pecs**) informal a pectoral muscle (especially with reference to the development of these muscles in bodybuilding).

pecan /ˈpiːk(ə)n, pɪˈkan, pɪˈkɑːn/ ▶ noun a smooth pinkish-brown nut with an edible kernel similar to a walnut. ● This nut is obtained from a hickory tree (*Carya illinoensis*, family Juglandaceae), native to the southern US.
– ORIGIN late 18th cent.: from French *pacane*, from Illinois (an American Indian language).

peccable /ˈpɛkəb(ə)l/ ▶ adjective formal capable of sinning: *we hold all mankind to be peccable.*
– DERIVATIVES **peccability** noun.
– ORIGIN early 17th cent.: from French, from medieval Latin *peccabilis*, from Latin *peccare* 'to sin'.

peccadillo /ˌpɛkəˈdɪləʊ/ ▶ noun (pl. **peccadilloes** or **peccadillos**) a relatively minor fault or sin: *the sexual peccadilloes of celebrities aren't necessarily news.*
– ORIGIN late 16th cent.: from Spanish *pecadillo*, diminutive of *pecado* 'sin', from Latin *peccare* 'to sin'.

peccant /ˈpɛk(ə)nt/ ▶ adjective archaic **1** having committed a fault or sin.
2 diseased or causing disease.
– DERIVATIVES **peccancy** noun.
– ORIGIN late 16th cent. (in sense 2): from Latin *peccant-* 'sinning', from the verb *peccare*.

peccary /ˈpɛk(ə)ri/ ▶ noun (pl. **peccaries**) a gregarious piglike mammal that is found from the southwestern US to Paraguay. ● Family Tayassuidae: two genera and three species, in particular the **collared peccary** (*Tayassu tajacu*).
– ORIGIN early 17th cent.: from Carib *pakira*.

peccavi /pɛˈkɑːviː/ ▶ exclamation archaic used to express one's guilt.
– ORIGIN Latin, literally 'I have sinned'.

pech /pɛx/ ▶ verb [no obj.] Scottish, Irish, & N. English breathe hard or with difficulty; pant: *by the time he reached the second floor, he was peching.*
▶ noun a gasping or laboured breath; a pant.

Pechenga /ˈpɛtʃɪŋgə/ a region of NW Russia, lying west of Murmansk on the border with Finland. Formerly part of Finland, it was ceded to the Soviet Union in 1940. It was known by its Finnish name, Petsamo, from 1920 until 1944.

Pechora /pɪˈtʃɔːrə/ a river of northern Russia, which rises in the Urals and flows some 1,800 km (1,125 miles) north and east to the Barents Sea.

Peck, (Eldred) Gregory (1916–2003), American actor. His many films range from the thriller *Spellbound* (1945) to the western *The Big Country* (1958); he won an Oscar for his role in *To Kill a Mockingbird* (1962).

peck[1] ▶ verb **1** [no obj.] (of a bird) strike or bite something with its beak: *two geese were **pecking at** some grain* | [with obj.] *vultures **pecked out** the calf's eyes.* ■ [with obj.] make (a hole) by striking with the beak. ■ (**peck at**) informal (of a person) eat (food) listlessly or daintily: *don't peck at your food, eat a whole mouthful.*
2 [with obj.] kiss (someone) lightly or perfunctorily: *she **pecked him on the cheek**.*
3 [with obj.] type (something) laboriously: *Paul was **pecking out** letters with two fingers on his typewriter.*
4 [with obj.] archaic strike with a pick or other tool.
▶ noun **1** a stroke or bite by a bird with its beak.
2 a light or perfunctory kiss: *a fatherly **peck on the cheek**.*
3 [mass noun] archaic, informal food: *he wants a little more peck.*
– ORIGIN late Middle English: of unknown origin; compare with Middle Low German *pekken* 'peck (with the beak)'.

peck[2] ▶ noun a measure of capacity for dry goods, equal to a quarter of a bushel (2 imperial gallons = 9.092 l, or 8 US quarts = 8.81 l). ■ archaic a large number or amount of something: *a peck of dirt.*
– ORIGIN Middle English (used especially as a measure of oats for horses): from Anglo-Norman French *pek*, of unknown origin.

peck[3] /pɛk/ ▶ verb [no obj.] (of a horse) pitch forward or stumble as a result of striking the ground with the front rather than the flat of the hoof.
– ORIGIN variant of obsolete *pick* 'fix (something pointed) in the ground'.

pecker ▶ noun N. Amer. vulgar slang a man's penis.
– PHRASES **keep your pecker up** Brit. informal remain cheerful. [*pecker* probably in the sense 'beak, bill'.]

peckerhead ▶ noun N. Amer. vulgar slang an aggressive, objectionable person.

peckerwood ▶ noun US informal, often derogatory a white person, especially a poor one.
– ORIGIN 1920s: from a reversal of the elements of *woodpecker*, originally a dialect word for the bird, used commonly in Mississippi and Tennessee.

pecking order (also **peck order**) ▶ noun a hierarchy of status seen among members of a group of people or animals, originally as observed among hens.

peckish ▶ adjective [predic.] informal, chiefly Brit. hungry: *I hadn't eaten and was quite peckish.*

Pecksniffian /pɛkˈsnɪfɪən/ ▶ adjective affecting benevolence or high moral principles.
– ORIGIN mid 19th cent.: from Mr *Pecksniff*, the name of a character in Dickens's *Martin Chuzzlewit*, + -IAN.

pecorino /ˌpɛkəˈriːnəʊ/ ▶ noun (pl. **pecorinos**) [mass noun] an Italian cheese made from ewes' milk.
– ORIGIN Italian, from *pecorino* 'of ewes', from *pecora* 'sheep'.

Pécs /peɪtʃ/ an industrial city in SW Hungary; pop. 156,974 (2009). It was formerly the capital of the southern part of the Roman province of Pannonia.

pecten /ˈpɛktɛn/ ▶ noun (pl. **pectens** or **pectines** /-tɪniːz/) Zoology **1** any of a number of comb-like structures occurring in animal bodies, in particular: ■ a pigmented vascular projection from the choroid in the eye of a bird. ■ an appendage of an insect consisting of or bearing a row of bristles or chitinous teeth. ■ a sensory appendage on the underside of a scorpion.
2 a scallop. ● Genus *Pecten*, family Pectinidae.
– DERIVATIVES **pectinate** /-nət/ adjective, **pectinated** adjective.
– ORIGIN late Middle English (denoting the metacarpus): from Latin *pecten*, *pectin-* 'a comb, rake'.

pectin ▶ noun [mass noun] a soluble gelatinous polysaccharide which is present in ripe fruits and is used as a setting agent in jams and jellies.
– DERIVATIVES **pectic** adjective.
– ORIGIN mid 19th cent.: from Greek *pektos* 'congealed' (from *pēgnuein* 'make solid') + -IN[1].

pectoral /ˈpɛkt(ə)r(ə)l/ ▶ adjective relating to the breast or chest: *pectoral development.* ■ worn on the chest: *a pectoral shield.*
▶ noun **1** (usu. **pectorals**) a pectoral muscle. ■ a pectoral fin.
2 an ornamental breastplate.
– ORIGIN late Middle English (in the sense 'breastplate'): from Latin *pectorale* 'breastplate', *pectoralis* 'of the breast', from *pectus*, *pector-* 'breast, chest'.

pectoral cross ▶ noun Christian Church a cross or crucifix worn on a long chain around the neck so that it rests on the chest, worn especially by bishops, abbots, and priests.

pectoral fin ▶ noun Zoology each of a pair of fins situated on either side just behind a fish's head, helping to control the direction of movement during locomotion. They correspond to the forelimbs of other vertebrates.

pectoral girdle ▶ noun (in vertebrates) the skeletal framework which provides attachment for the forelimbs or pectoral fins, usually consisting of the scapulas and clavicles.

pectoral muscle ▶ noun (usu. **pectoral muscles**) each of the four large paired muscles which cover the front of the ribcage and serve to draw the forelimbs towards the chest.

pectoral sandpiper ▶ noun a migratory sandpiper with dark streaks on the breast and a white belly, breeding chiefly in Arctic Canada. ● *Calidris melanotos*, family Scolopacidae.

peculate /ˈpɛkjʊleɪt/ ▶ verb [with obj.] formal embezzle or steal (money, especially public funds).
– DERIVATIVES **peculation** noun, **peculator** noun.
– ORIGIN mid 18th cent.: from Latin *peculat-* 'embezzled', from the verb *peculari* (related to *peculium* 'property').

peculiar ▶ adjective **1** different to what is normal or expected; strange: *he gave her some very peculiar looks* | *Stella thought the play peculiar.* ■ [predic.] informal slightly and indefinably unwell: *I felt a little peculiar for a while.*
2 particular; special: *any attempt to explicate the theme is bound to run into peculiar difficulties.*
■ (**peculiar to**) belonging exclusively to: *some languages are peculiar to one region.*
▶ noun chiefly Brit. a parish or church exempt from the jurisdiction of the diocese in which it lies, and subject to the direct jurisdiction of the monarch or an archbishop.
– ORIGIN late Middle English (in the sense 'particular'): from Latin *peculiaris* 'of private property', from *peculium* 'property', from *pecu* 'cattle' (cattle being private property). The sense 'strange' dates from the early 17th cent.

peculiarity ▶ noun (pl. **peculiarities**) a strange or unusual feature or habit: *for all his peculiarities, she finds him quite endearing.* ■ a characteristic that is distinctive of a particular person or place: *his essays characterized decency as a British peculiarity.* ■ [mass noun] the quality of being peculiar: *the peculiarity of their upbringing.*

peculiarly ▶ adverb **1** [as submodifier] more than usually; especially: *some patients were peculiarly difficult to cure.*
2 in an unusual way; oddly.
3 used to emphasize restriction to an individual or group: [as submodifier] *the peculiarly British hobby of brass rubbing.*

pecuniary /pɪˈkjuːnɪəri/ ▶ adjective formal relating to or consisting of money: *he admitted obtaining a pecuniary advantage by deception.*
– DERIVATIVES **pecuniarily** adverb.
– ORIGIN early 16th cent.: from Latin *pecuniarius*, from *pecunia* 'money', from *pecu* 'cattle, money'.

pedagogic /ˌpɛdəˈɡɒdʒɪk, -ˈɡɒɡ-/ ▶ adjective relating to teaching: *they show great pedagogic skills.* ■ rare of or characteristic of a pedagogue.
▶ plural noun (**pedagogics**) [treated as sing.] old-fashioned term for PEDAGOGY.
– DERIVATIVES **pedagogical** adjective, **pedagogically** adverb.
– ORIGIN late 18th cent.: from French *pédagogique*, from Greek *paidagōgikos*.

pedagogue /ˈpɛdəɡɒɡ/ ▶ noun formal or humorous a teacher, especially a strict or pedantic one.
– ORIGIN late Middle English: via Latin from Greek *paidagōgos*, denoting a slave who accompanied a child to school (from *pais, paid-* 'boy' + *agōgos* 'guide').

pedagogy /ˈpɛdəɡɒdʒi, -ɡɒɡi/ ▶ noun (pl. **pedagogies**) [mass noun] the method and practice of teaching, especially as an academic subject or theoretical concept: *the relationship between applied linguistics and language pedagogy* | [count noun] *subject-based pedagogies.*
– ORIGIN late 16th cent.: from French *pédagogie*, from Greek *paidagōgia* 'office of a pedagogue', from *paidagōgos* (see PEDAGOGUE).

pedal[1] /ˈpɛd(ə)l/ ▶ noun **1** each of a pair of foot-operated levers used for powering a bicycle or other vehicle propelled by the legs.
2 a foot-operated throttle, brake, or clutch control in a motor vehicle.
3 each of a set of two or three levers on a piano, particularly (also **sustaining pedal**) one which, when depressed, prevents the dampers from stopping the sound when the keys are released. The second is the **soft pedal**; a third, if present, produces either selective sustaining or complete muffling of the tone. ■ a foot-operated lever on other musical instruments, such as an organ. ■ a foot-operated device for producing a sound effect on an electric guitar.
■ short for PEDAL NOTE.
▶ verb (**pedals, pedalling, pedalled**; US **pedals, pedaling, pedaled**) **1** [no obj., with adverbial of direction] move by working the pedals of a bicycle: *they pedalled along the canal towpath.* ■ [with obj. and adverbial of direction] move (a bicycle) by working its pedals. ■ [no obj.] work the pedals of a bicycle: *he was coming down the path on his bike, pedalling hard.*
2 [no obj.] use the pedals of a piano, organ, etc., especially in a particular style: (as noun **pedalling**) *Chopin gave no indications of pedalling in his manuscript.*
– PHRASES **with the pedal to the metal** N. Amer. informal at full speed (with reference to pressing the accelerator of a car to the floor).
– DERIVATIVES **pedaller** (US **pedaler**) noun.
– ORIGIN early 17th cent. (denoting a foot-operated lever of an organ): from French *pédale*, from Italian *pedale*, from Latin *pedalis* 'a foot in length', from *pes, ped-* 'foot'.

USAGE People often confuse the words **pedal** and **peddle**. **Pedal** is a noun referring to a foot-operated lever, as on a bicycle, and a verb chiefly meaning 'move by working the pedals of a bicycle' (*they pedalled along the road*). **Peddle**, on the other hand, is a verb meaning 'sell goods or promote an idea' (*he peddled printing materials around the country* | *she peddled a ludicrously Utopian view of the past*). The related words **pedlar** and **pedaller** are also confused. A **pedlar** (also spelled **peddler**, especially in the US) is a person who goes from place to place selling goods, while a **pedaller** (or, in the US, a **pedaler**) is someone who rides a bike.

pedal[2] /ˈpɛd(ə)l, ˈpiːd(ə)l/ ▶ adjective chiefly Medicine & Zoology relating to the foot or feet.
– ORIGIN early 17th cent.: from Latin *pedalis*, from *pes, ped-* 'foot'.

pedal bin ▶ noun Brit. a rubbish bin with a lid opened by means of a pedal.

pedalboard ▶ noun the keyboard of pedals on an organ.

pedal boat ▶ noun a small pleasure boat driven by pedals.

pedal car ▶ noun a child's pedal-operated car.

pedal cycle ▶ noun a bicycle.

pedal note ▶ noun Music **1** the lowest or fundamental note of a harmonic series in some brass and wind instruments.
2 (also **pedal point**) a note sustained in one part (usually the bass) through successive harmonies, some of which are independent of it.

pedalo /ˈpɛdələʊ/ ▶ noun (pl. **pedalos** or **pedaloes**) Brit. a small pedal-operated pleasure boat.
– ORIGIN 1950s: from PEDAL[1] + -O.

pedal power ▶ noun [mass noun] informal cycling as a means of transport.

pedal pusher ▶ noun **1** (**pedal pushers**) women's calf-length trousers.
2 informal a cyclist.

pedal steel (also **pedal steel guitar**) ▶ noun a musical instrument played like the Hawaiian guitar, but set on a stand with pedals to adjust the tension of the strings.

pedant /ˈpɛd(ə)nt/ ▶ noun a person who is excessively concerned with minor details and rules or with displaying academic learning.
– ORIGIN late 16th cent.: from French *pédant*, from Italian *pedante*, perhaps from the first element of Latin *paedogogus* (see PEDAGOGUE).

pedantic ▶ adjective excessively concerned with minor details or rules; overscrupulous: *his analyses are careful and even painstaking, but never pedantic.*
– DERIVATIVES **pedantically** adverb.

pedantry /ˈpɛd(ə)ntri/ ▶ noun [mass noun] excessive concern with minor details and rules: *to object to this is not mere pedantry.*

peddle ▶ verb [with obj.] try to sell (something, especially small goods) by going from place to place: *he peddled printing materials around the country.* ■ sell (an illegal drug or stolen item): (as noun **peddling**) *youths involved in drug peddling.* ■ promote (an idea or view) persistently or widely: *the giant con that has been peddled in the Conservative press.*
– ORIGIN early 16th cent.: back-formation from PEDLAR.

USAGE On the confusion of **peddle** and **pedal**, see USAGE at PEDAL[1].

peddler ▶ noun variant spelling of PEDLAR.

pederast /ˈpɛdərast/ (also **paederast**) ▶ noun a man who indulges in pederasty.
– ORIGIN mid 17th cent.: from Greek *paiderastēs*.

pederasty (also **paederasty**) ▶ noun [mass noun] sexual activity involving a man and a boy.
– DERIVATIVES **pederastic** adjective.
– ORIGIN early 17th cent.: from modern Latin *paederastia*, from Greek *paiderastia*, from *pais, paid-* 'boy' + *erastēs* 'lover'.

pedes plural form of PES.

pedestal ▶ noun **1** the base or support on which a statue, obelisk, or column is mounted. ■ each of the two supports of a kneehole desk or table. ■ the supporting column or base of a washbasin or toilet pan.
2 a position in which someone is greatly or uncritically admired: *It's as if I'm on a pedestal and he worships me – I hate that.*
▶ verb (**pedestals, pedestalling, pedestalled**; US **pedestals, pedestaling, pedestaled**) [with obj.] (often as adj. **pedestalled**) set or support on a pedestal.
– PHRASES **put** (or **place**) **someone on a pedestal** give someone uncritical respect or admiration; treat someone as an ideal rather than a real person: *if you idolize a girl and put her on a pedestal, she will sense it instantly.*
– ORIGIN mid 16th cent.: from French *piédestal*, from Italian *piedestallo*, from *piè* 'foot' (from Latin *pes, ped-*, which later influenced the spelling) + *di* 'of' + *stallo* 'stall'.

pedestal table ▶ noun a table with a single central support.

pedestrian ▶ noun a person walking rather than travelling in a vehicle.
▶ adjective lacking inspiration or excitement; dull: *disenchantment with their pedestrian lives.*
– DERIVATIVES **pedestrianly** adverb.
– ORIGIN early 18th cent.: from French *pédestre* or Latin *pedester* 'going on foot', also 'written in prose' + -IAN. Early use in English was in the description of writing as 'prosaic'.

pedestrian crossing ▶ noun Brit. a specified part of a road where pedestrians have right of way to cross.

pedestrianize (also **pedestrianise**) ▶ verb [with obj.] close (a street or area) to traffic, making it accessible only to pedestrians: *the ancient centre of the town was pedestrianized.*
– DERIVATIVES **pedestrianization** noun.

pedestrian precinct ▶ noun Brit. an area of a town restricted to pedestrians.

Pedi /ˈpɛdi/ ▶ noun (pl. **same** or **Pedis**) **1** a member of a people traditionally inhabiting the northern region of South Africa.
2 another term for SEPEDI.
▶ adjective relating to the Pedi or their language.
– ORIGIN from Sotho *Mopedi*, denoting a member of this people.

pediatrics ▶ plural noun US spelling of PAEDIATRICS.

pedicab /ˈpɛdɪkab/ ▶ noun a small pedal-operated vehicle, serving as a taxi in some countries.

pedicel /ˈpɛdɪs(ə)l/ ▶ noun Botany a small stalk bearing an individual flower in an inflorescence. Compare with PEDUNCLE. ■ Anatomy & Zoology another term for PEDICLE.
– DERIVATIVES **pedicellate** /-ˈdɪs(ə)leɪt/ adjective.
– ORIGIN late 17th cent.: from modern Latin *pedicellus* 'small foot', diminutive of *pes, ped-* 'foot'.

pedicellaria /ˌpɛdɪsəˈlɛːrɪə/ ▶ noun (pl. **pedicellariae** /-rɪiː/) Zoology a defensive organ like a minute pincer present in large numbers on an echinoderm.
– ORIGIN late 19th cent.: modern Latin, from Latin *pediculus* 'small foot' (see PEDICEL).

pedicle /ˈpɛdɪk(ə)l/ ▶ noun Anatomy & Zoology a small stalk-like structure connecting an organ or other part to the human or animal body. Compare with PEDICEL.
■ Medicine part of a graft, especially a skin graft, left temporarily attached to its original site.
– ORIGIN early 17th cent.: from Latin *pediculus* 'small foot', diminutive of *pes, ped-*.

pediculicide /ˌpɛdɪˈkjuːlɪsʌɪd/ ▶ noun a chemical used to kill lice.
– ORIGIN early 20th cent.: from Latin *pediculus* 'louse' + -CIDE.

pediculosis /pɪˌdɪkjʊˈləʊsɪs/ ▶ noun [mass noun] Medicine infestation with lice.
– ORIGIN early 19th cent.: from Latin *pediculus* 'louse' + -OSIS.

pedicure ▶ noun a cosmetic treatment of the feet and toenails.
▶ verb [with obj.] (usu. as adj. **pedicured**) give a pedicure to (the feet).
– DERIVATIVES **pedicurist** noun.
– ORIGIN mid 19th cent.: from French *pédicure*, from Latin *pes, ped-* 'foot' + *curare* 'attend to'.

pedigree ▶ noun **1** the record of descent of an animal, showing it to be pure-bred. ■ informal a pure-bred animal.
2 the recorded ancestry or lineage of a person or family. ■ the history or provenance of a person or thing, especially as conferring distinction: *the scheme has a long pedigree.* ■ a genealogical table.
▶ adjective Brit. (of an animal) pure-bred: *pedigree cats.*
– DERIVATIVES **pedigreed** adjective.

P

– ORIGIN late Middle English: from Anglo-Norman French *pé de grue* 'crane's foot', a mark used to denote succession in pedigrees.

pediment ▶ noun **1** the triangular upper part of the front of a classical building, typically surmounting a portico. ■ a triangular feature surmounting a door, window, or other part of a non-classical building. **2** Geology a broad, gently sloping expanse of rock debris extending outwards from the foot of a mountain slope, especially in a desert.
– DERIVATIVES **pedimental** adjective, **pedimented** adjective.
– ORIGIN late 16th cent. (as *periment*): perhaps an alteration of PYRAMID.

pedipalp /ˈpɛdɪpalp, ˈpiːdɪpalp/ ▶ noun Zoology each of the second pair of appendages attached to the cephalothorax of most arachnids. They are variously specialized as pincers in scorpions, sensory organs in spiders, and locomotory organs in horseshoe crabs.
– ORIGIN early 19th cent.: from modern Latin *pedipalpi* (plural), from Latin *pes*, *ped-* 'foot' + *palpus* 'palp'.

pediplain /ˈpɛdɪpleɪn/ ▶ noun Geology an extensive plain formed in a desert by the coalescence of neighbouring pediments.
– ORIGIN 1930s: from PEDIMENT + PLAIN[1].

pediplanation /ˌpɛdɪpləˈneɪʃ(ə)n/ ▶ noun [mass noun] Geology the formation of pediplains by coalescence of pediments.

pedlar (chiefly US also **peddler**) ▶ noun a person who goes from place to place selling small goods. ■ a person who sells illegal drugs or stolen goods: *a drug pedlar*. ■ a person who promotes an idea or view persistently or widely: *pedlars of dangerous Utopianism*.
– DERIVATIVES **pedlary** noun (archaic).
– ORIGIN Middle English: perhaps an alteration of synonymous dialect *pedder*, apparently from dialect *ped* 'pannier'.

USAGE See USAGE at PEDAL[1].

pedo-[1] ▶ combining form US spelling of PAEDO-.

pedo-[2] /ˈpɛdəʊ/ ▶ combining form relating to soil or soil types: *pedogenic*.
– ORIGIN from Greek *pedon* 'ground'.

pedogenic /ˌpɛdə(ʊ)ˈdʒɛnɪk/ ▶ adjective relating to or denoting processes occurring in soil or leading to the formation of soil.

pedology /pɪˈdɒlədʒi, pɛ-/ ▶ noun another term for SOIL SCIENCE.
– DERIVATIVES **pedological** /ˌpɛdəˈlɒdʒɪk(ə)l/ adjective, **pedologist** noun.

pedometer /pɪˈdɒmɪtə, pɛ-/ ▶ noun an instrument for estimating the distance travelled on foot by recording the number of steps taken.
– ORIGIN early 18th cent.: from French *pédomètre*, from Latin *pes*, *ped-* 'foot'.

Pedro Ximenez /ˌpɛdrəʊ hɪˈmeɪnɛz/ ▶ noun [mass noun] a variety of sweet white Spanish grape used in making sherry and sweet wine. ■ a sweet white wine made from the Pedro Ximenez grape.
– ORIGIN from the name of the grape's Spanish originator.

peduncle /pɪˈdʌŋk(ə)l/ ▶ noun Botany the stalk bearing a flower or fruit, or the main stalk of an inflorescence. Compare with PEDICEL. ■ Zoology a stalk-like part by which an organ is attached to an animal's body, or by which a barnacle or other sedentary animal is attached to a substrate.
– DERIVATIVES **peduncular** /pɪˈdʌŋkjʊlə/ adjective.
– ORIGIN mid 18th cent.: from modern Latin *pedunculus*, from Latin *pes*, *ped-* 'foot'.

pedunculate /pɪˈdʌŋkjʊlət/ ▶ adjective Botany & Zoology having a peduncle.

pedunculate oak ▶ noun the common or English oak.

pedway ▶ noun chiefly N. Amer. a footway built for pedestrians in an urban area.
– ORIGIN 1960s: from PEDESTRIAN + WAY.

pee informal ▶ verb (**pees, peeing, peed**) [no obj.] urinate. ■ [with obj.] (**pee oneself/one's pants**) urinate involuntarily (often used to suggest loss of self-control through fear or hilarity): *Mom just about peed herself laughing*.
▶ noun [in sing.] an act of urinating. ■ [mass noun] urine.
– PHRASES **peed off** annoyed; irritated.
– ORIGIN late 18th cent.: euphemistic use of the initial letter of PISS.

Peeblesshire /ˈpiːb(ə)lzʃɪə, -ʃə/ a former county of southern Scotland. It became a part of Borders region (now Scottish Borders) in 1975.

peedie /ˈpiːdi/ ▶ adjective Scottish little; small: *a schoolteacher much loved by all her peedie bairns*.
– ORIGIN 1920s: alteration of PEERIE.

peek ▶ verb [no obj., with adverbial] look quickly or furtively: *faces peeked from behind twitched curtains*. ■ protrude slightly so as to be just visible: *his socks were so full of holes his toes peeked through*.
▶ noun a quick or furtive look: *she sneaked a peek at the map*.
– ORIGIN late Middle English *pike*, *pyke*, of unknown origin.

USAGE The word meaning 'look quickly or furtively' and 'a quick or furtive look' is **peek**, not **peak**: *the sun peeks out only intermittently, a sneak peek at what's in store*. In some contexts this error is very common: for example, almost a third of citations for the expression **a sneak peek** in the Oxford English Corpus are for the incorrect spelling.

peekaboo (also **peek-a-boo**) ▶ noun [mass noun] a game played with a young child, which involves hiding and suddenly reappearing, saying 'peekaboo'.
▶ adjective [attrib.] (of a garment) made of transparent fabric or having a pattern of small holes: *a black lace peekaboo dress*. ■ (of a hairstyle) concealing one eye with a fringe or wave.
– ORIGIN late 16th cent.: from PEEK + BOO[1].

Peel, Sir Robert (1788–1850), British Conservative statesman, Prime Minister 1834–5 and 1841–6. As Home Secretary (1828–30) he established the Metropolitan Police (hence the nicknames *bobby* and *peeler*). His repeal of the Corn Laws in 1846 split the Conservatives and forced his resignation.

peel[1] ▶ verb **1** [with obj.] remove the outer covering or skin from (a fruit, vegetable, or prawn). ■ remove (the outer covering or skin) from a fruit or vegetable: ***peel off** the skins and thickly slice the potatoes*. ■ [no obj.] (of a fruit or vegetable) have a skin that can be removed: *oranges that peel easily*. **2** [with obj.] (**peel something away/off**) remove a thin outer covering or part: *I peeled off the tissue paper*. ■ (**peel something off**) remove a garment: *Suzy peeled off her white pullover*. **3** [no obj.] (of a surface or object) lose parts of its outer layer or covering in small strips or pieces: *the walls are peeling*. ■ [with adverbial] (of an outer layer) come off in strips or small pieces.
▶ noun **1** [mass noun] the outer covering or rind of a fruit or vegetable: *pieces of potato peel*. **2** an act of exfoliating dead skin in the cosmetic treatment of microdermabrasion.
– PHRASAL VERBS **peel off** leave a formation or group by veering away: *the pace was much too hot for Beris, and he peeled off after five laps*. **peel out** N. Amer. informal leave quickly: *he peeled out down the street*.
– DERIVATIVES **peelable** adjective.
– ORIGIN Middle English (in the sense 'to plunder'): variant of dialect *pill*, from Latin *pilare* 'to strip hair from', from *pilus* 'hair'. The differentiation of *peel* and *pill* may have been by association with the French verbs *peler* 'to peel' and *piller* 'to pillage'.

peel[2] ▶ noun archaic a shovel, especially a baker's shovel for carrying loaves into or out of an oven.
– ORIGIN late Middle English: from Old French *pele*, from Latin *pala*, from the base of *pangere* 'fasten'.

peel[3] (also **pele** or **peel tower**) ▶ noun a small square defensive tower of a kind built in the 16th century in the border counties of England and Scotland.
– ORIGIN probably short for synonymous *peel-house*: *peel* from Anglo-Norman French *pel* 'stake, palisade', from Latin *palus* 'stake'.

peel[4] ▶ verb [with obj.] Croquet send (another player's ball) through a hoop: *the better players are capable of peeling a ball through two or three hoops*.
– ORIGIN late 19th cent.: from the name of Walter H. Peel, founder of the All England Croquet Association, a leading exponent of the practice.

peeler[1] ▶ noun [usu. with modifier] a knife or device for removing the skin from fruit and vegetables: *a potato peeler*.

peeler[2] ▶ noun Brit. informal, archaic a police officer.
– ORIGIN early 19th cent. (originally denoting a member of the Irish constabulary): from the name of Sir Robert PEEL.

peelings (US also **peels**) ▶ plural noun [usu. with modifier] strips of the outer skin of a vegetable or fruit: *potato peelings*.

Peelite ▶ noun historical a Conservative supporting Sir Robert Peel, especially with reference to his repeal of the Corn Laws (1846).

peely-wally /ˈpiːlɪwɒli, ˌpiːlɪˈwali/ (also **peely-wallie**) ▶ adjective Scottish pale and sickly in appearance: *his face assumes a peely-wally hue*.
– ORIGIN mid 19th cent.: probably imitative of a whining sound.

peen /piːn/ (also **pein**) ▶ noun the end of a hammer head opposite the face, typically wedge-shaped, curved, or spherical.
▶ verb [with obj.] strike with a hammer or the peen of a hammer. ■ another term for SHOT-PEEN.
– ORIGIN early 16th cent. (as a verb): probably of Scandinavian origin; compare with Swedish dialect *pena (ut)*, Danish dialect *pene (ud)* 'beat (out)'.

Peenemunde /ˌpeɪnəˈmʊndə/ a village in NE Germany, on a small island just off the Baltic coast. During the Second World War it was the chief site of German rocket research and testing.

peep[1] ▶ verb [no obj.] look quickly and furtively at something, especially through a narrow opening: *his door was ajar and she couldn't resist peeping in*. ■ (**peep out**) come gradually or partially into view: *the sun began to peep out*.
▶ noun [usu. in sing.] a quick or furtive look: *Jonathan took a little peep at his watch*. ■ a momentary or partial view of something: *black curls and a peep of gold earring*.
– ORIGIN late 15th cent.: symbolic; compare with PEEK.

peep[2] ▶ noun **1** a feeble, high-pitched sound made by a young bird or mammal. ■ [with negative] a slight sound, utterance, or complaint: *not a peep out of them since shortly after eight*. ■ a brief, high-pitched electronic sound: *the phone gives three sharp peeps*. **2** N. Amer. informal a small sandpiper or similar wading bird.
▶ verb [no obj.] make a brief, high-pitched sound.
– ORIGIN late Middle English: imitative; compare with CHEEP.

peep-bo ▶ noun British term for PEEKABOO.

pee-pee ▶ noun N. Amer. informal a child's word for an act of urinating. ■ [mass noun] urine. ■ a penis.

peeper[1] ▶ noun **1** a person who peeps at someone or something, especially in a voyeuristic way. **2** (**peepers**) informal a person's eyes: *keep your peepers peeled for a familiar face*.

peeper[2] (also **spring peeper**) ▶ noun a small North American tree frog with a dark cross on the back, the males of which sing in early spring. ● *Hyla crucifer*, family Hylidae.

peephole ▶ noun a small hole that may be looked through, especially one in a door through which callers may be identified before the door is opened.

peeping Tom ▶ noun a person who derives sexual pleasure from secretly watching people undressing or engaging in sexual activity.
– ORIGIN from the name of the person said to have watched Lady GODIVA ride naked through Coventry.

peep show ▶ noun a sequence of pictures viewed through a lens or hole set into a box, formerly offered as a public entertainment. ■ an erotic or pornographic film viewed from a coin-operated booth.

peep sight ▶ noun a backsight for rifles with a circular hole through which the foresight is brought into line with the object aimed at.

peep-toe ▶ adjective Brit. (of a shoe) having the tip cut away to leave the large toe partially exposed.

peepul /ˈpiːpʌl/ (also **pipal**) ▶ noun another term for BO TREE.
– ORIGIN late 18th cent.: via Hindi from Sanskrit *pippala*.

peer[1] ▶ verb [no obj., with adverbial] look with difficulty or concentration at someone or something: *Faye peered at her with suspicion*. ■ be just visible: *the towers peer over the roofs*. ■ [no obj.] archaic come into view; appear.
– ORIGIN late 16th cent.: perhaps a variant of dialect *pire* or perhaps partly from a shortening of APPEAR.

peer[2] ▶ noun **1** a member of the nobility in Britain or Ireland, comprising the ranks of duke, marquess, earl, viscount, and baron.

In the British peerage, earldoms and baronies were the earliest to be conferred; dukes were created from 1337, marquesses from the end of the 14th century, and viscounts from 1440. Such peerages are hereditary, although since 1958 there have also been non-hereditary life peerages. All peers were entitled to a seat in the House of Lords until 1999, when their number was restricted to 92 as an interim reform measure.

2 a person of the same age, status, or ability as another specified person: *he has incurred much criticism from his academic peers.*
▸ **verb** archaic make or become equal with.
– PHRASES **without peer** unrivalled: *he is a goalkeeper without peer.*
– ORIGIN Middle English: from Old French *peer*, from Latin *par* 'equal'.

peerage ▸ **noun** the title and rank of peer or peeress: *on his retirement as cabinet secretary, he was given a peerage.* ■ (**the peerage**) peers as a class: *he was elevated to the peerage two years ago.* ■ a book containing a list of peers and peeresses, with their genealogy and history.

peeress /ˈpɪərɪs, -rɛs/ ▸ **noun** a woman holding the rank of a peer in her own right. ■ the wife or widow of a peer.

peer group ▸ **noun** a group of people of approximately the same age, status, and interests.

peerie /ˈpiːri/ ▸ **adjective** Scottish tiny; insubstantial.
– ORIGIN early 19th cent.: of unknown origin.

peering ▸ **noun** [mass noun] Computing the exchange of data directly between Internet service providers, rather than via the Internet.
– ORIGIN 1980s: from PEER² + -ING¹.

peerless ▸ **adjective** unequalled; unrivalled: *a peerless cartoonist.*
– DERIVATIVES **peerlessly** adverb.

peer of the realm ▸ **noun** a member of the class of peers who has the right to sit in the House of Lords.

peer pressure ▸ **noun** [mass noun] influence from members of one's peer group: *his behaviour was affected by drink and peer pressure.*

peer review ▸ **noun** [mass noun] evaluation of scientific, academic, or professional work by others working in the same field.
▸ **verb** [with obj.] (**peer-review**) subject to a peer review.

peer-to-peer ▸ **adjective** Computing denoting networks in which each computer can act as a server for the others, allowing shared access to files and peripherals without the need for a central server.

peery /ˈpɪəri/ ▸ **noun** (pl. **peeries**) Scottish & N. English a child's spinning top.
– ORIGIN mid 17th cent.: from *peer* (Scots spelling of PEAR) + -Y¹.

peeve informal ▸ **verb** [with obj.] (usu. as adj. **peeved**) make (someone) rather annoyed; irritate: *he was peeved at being excluded from the meeting.*
▸ **noun** a cause of annoyance: *someone lying to me is my pet peeve.*
– ORIGIN early 20th cent.: back-formation from PEEVISH.

peever ▸ **noun** (often **peevers**) Scottish term for HOPSCOTCH.
– ORIGIN mid 19th cent. (denoting the stone or piece of pottery used in the game): of unknown origin.

peevish ▸ **adjective** having or showing an irritable disposition: *a thin peevish voice.*
– DERIVATIVES **peevishly** adverb, **peevishness** noun.
– ORIGIN late Middle English (in the sense 'perverse, coy'): of unknown origin.

peewee ▸ **noun 1** any of a number of birds with a call that resembles the word 'peewee': ■ Austral. another term for MAGPIE LARK. ■ Scottish the northern lapwing. ■ N. Amer. variant of PEWEE.
2 [usu. as modifier] N. Amer. a level of amateur sport, involving children aged eight or nine (in the US) or twelve or thirteen (in Canada): *a peewee baseball team.* ■ a player at a peewee level of sport.
3 a small marble.
– ORIGIN mid 19th cent. (in sense 3); sense 1 is imitative; sense 2, sense 3 are from WEE¹, by reduplication.

peewit ▸ **noun** Brit. the northern lapwing.
– ORIGIN early 16th cent.: imitative of the bird's call.

PEG ▸ **abbreviation** polyethylene glycol.

peg ▸ **noun 1** a short pin or bolt, typically tapered at one end, that is used for securing something in place, hanging things on, or marking a position: *she put her mack on a peg in the hall.* ■ (also **tent peg**) a pin or bolt driven into the ground to hold one of the ropes or corners of a tent in position. ■ Brit. short for CLOTHES PEG. ■ a bung for stoppering a cask. ■ informal a footrest on a motorbike.
2 a point or limit on a scale, especially of exchange rates.
3 chiefly Indian a measure of spirits: *have a peg of whisky.*
4 a place marked by a peg and allotted to a competitor to fish or shoot from.
5 informal a person's leg.
6 chiefly Baseball a strong throw.
▸ **verb** (**pegs, pegging, pegged**) **1** [with obj. and adverbial] fix, secure, or mark with a peg or pegs: *drape plants with nets, **pegging down** the edges.* ■ hang (washing) on a line with clothes pegs: *clothes were **pegged out** on a line.* ■ allot a specified place to (a competitor) in a fishing or shooting competition by means of a marker: *we've been pegged next to the winning team.*
2 [with obj.] fix (a price, rate, or amount) at a particular level: *the dividend was **pegged at** 23.59p.* ■ informal, chiefly N. Amer. form a fixed opinion of; categorize: *the officer probably **has us pegged as** anarchists.*
3 chiefly Baseball throw (a ball) hard and low.
– PHRASES **off the peg** Brit. (of clothes) ready-made: [as modifier] *budget off-the-peg outfits.* **a peg to hang a matter on** something used as a pretext or occasion for the treatment of a wider subject. **a square peg in a round hole** a person in a situation unsuited to their abilities or character. **take** (or **bring**) **someone down a peg or two** make someone realize that they are less talented or important than they think they are.
– PHRASAL VERBS **peg away** informal work hard at or try to achieve something over a long period. **peg someone back** reduce or eradicate the lead of an opponent in a contest. **peg out 1** informal, chiefly Brit. die. **2** score the winning point at cribbage. **3** Croquet hit the peg with the ball as the final stroke in a game. **peg something out** mark the boundaries of an area of land.
– ORIGIN late Middle English: probably of Low German origin; compare with Dutch dialect *peg* 'plug, peg'. The verb dates from the mid 16th cent.

Pegasus /ˈpɛɡəsəs/ **1** Greek Mythology a winged horse which sprang from the blood of Medusa when Perseus cut off her head.
2 Astronomy a large northern constellation, said to represent a winged horse. The three brightest stars, together with one star of Andromeda, form the prominent **Square of Pegasus**.
– ORIGIN via Latin from Greek.

pegboard ▸ **noun** a board having a regular pattern of small holes for pegs, used chiefly for games or the display of information.

pegbox ▸ **noun** a structure at the head of a stringed instrument where the strings are attached to the tuning pegs.

pegged ▸ **adjective** North American term for PEGTOP.

peggy ▸ **noun** (pl. **peggies**) Nautical slang a steward in a ship's mess (often used as a form of address).
– ORIGIN early 20th cent. (earlier denoting a man of feminine habits): alteration of *Meggy*, pet form of the given name *Margaret*.

peg leg ▸ **noun** informal an artificial leg, especially a wooden one.

pegmatite /ˈpɛɡmətʌɪt/ ▸ **noun** Geology a coarsely crystalline granite or other igneous rock with crystals several centimetres in length.
– ORIGIN mid 19th cent.: from Greek *pēgma, pēgmat-* 'thing joined together' + -ITE¹.

pego /ˈpiːɡəʊ/ ▸ **noun** (pl. **pegos**) vulgar slang a penis.
– ORIGIN late 17th cent.: of unknown origin.

pegtop ▸ **noun** a pear-shaped spinning top with a metal pin or peg forming the point.
▸ **adjective** dated (of a garment) wide at the top and narrow at the bottom: *pegtop trousers.*

Pegu /pɛˈɡuː/ a city and river port of southern Burma (Myanmar), on the Pegu River north-east of Rangoon; pop. 200,900 (est. 2004). Founded in 825 as the capital of the Mon kingdom, it is a centre of Buddhist culture.

Pehlevi /ˈpeɪləvi/ ▸ **noun** variant spelling of PAHLAVI².

PEI ▸ **abbreviation** Prince Edward Island.

Pei /peɪ/, I. M. (b.1917), American architect, born in China; full name *Ieoh Ming Pei*. Notable works include the John F. Kennedy Memorial Library at Harvard University (1964) and the glass and steel pyramid in the forecourt of the Louvre (1989).

Peigan /ˈpiːɡ(ə)n/ (also **Piegan**) ▸ **noun** (pl. **same** or **Peigans**) a member of a North American Indian people of the Blackfoot confederacy.
– ORIGIN from Blackfoot *Piikániwa*.

peignoir /ˈpeɪnwɑː/ ▸ **noun** a woman's light dressing gown or negligee.
– ORIGIN French, from *peigner* 'to comb' (the garment was originally worn while combing the hair).

pein ▸ **noun & verb** variant spelling of PEEN.

peine forte et dure /pɛn ˌfɔːt eɪ ˈd(j)ʊə/ ▸ **noun** [mass noun] a medieval form of torture in which the body was pressed with heavy weights.
– ORIGIN French, literally 'strong and hard suffering'.

Peirce /pɪəs/, Charles Sanders (1839–1914), American philosopher and logician. A founder of American pragmatism, he argued that the meaning of a belief is to be understood by the actions and uses to which it gives rise.

Peisistratus variant spelling of PISISTRATUS.

pejorative /pɪˈdʒɒrətɪv/ ▸ **adjective** expressing contempt or disapproval: *permissiveness is used almost universally as a pejorative term.*
▸ **noun** a word expressing contempt or disapproval.
– DERIVATIVES **pejoratively** adverb.
– ORIGIN late 19th cent.: from French *péjoratif, -ive*, from late Latin *pejorare* 'make worse', from Latin *pejor* 'worse'.

pekan /ˈpɛk(ə)n/ ▸ **noun** North American term for FISHER.
– ORIGIN mid 18th cent.: from Canadian French, from Algonquian.

peke ▸ **noun** informal a Pekinese dog.
– ORIGIN early 20th cent.: abbreviation.

Pekinese /ˌpiːkɪˈniːz/ (also **Pekingese**) ▸ **noun** (pl. **same**) a lapdog of a short-legged breed with long hair and a snub nose, originally brought to Europe from the Summer Palace at Beijing (Peking) in 1860.
▸ **adjective** relating to Beijing, its citizens, or their culture or cuisine.

Peking /piːˈkɪŋ/ variant of BEIJING.

Peking duck ▸ **noun** [mass noun] a Chinese dish consisting of strips of roast duck served with shredded vegetables and a sweet sauce.

Peking man ▸ **noun** a fossil hominid of the middle Pleistocene period, identified from remains found near Beijing in 1926. ● A late form of *Homo erectus* (formerly *Sinanthropus pekinensis*), family Hominidae.

Peking opera ▸ **noun** [mass noun] a stylized Chinese form of opera dating from the late 18th century, in which speech, singing, mime, and acrobatics are performed to an instrumental accompaniment.

Pekin robin ▸ **noun** another term for LEIOTHRIX.

pekoe /ˈpiːkəʊ, ˈpɛ-/ ▸ **noun** [mass noun] a high-quality black tea made from young leaves.
– ORIGIN early 18th cent.: from Chinese dialect *pekho*, from *pek* 'white' + *ho* 'down' (the leaves being picked young when covered with down).

pelage /ˈpɛlɪdʒ/ ▸ **noun** [mass noun] Zoology the fur, hair, or wool of a mammal.
– ORIGIN early 19th cent.: from French, from Old French *pel* 'hair'.

pelagic /pɪˈladʒɪk/ ▸ **adjective** technical relating to the open sea: *the kittiwakes return from their pelagic winter wanderings.* ■ (chiefly of fish) inhabiting the upper layers of the open sea. Often contrasted with DEMERSAL. ■ (of a bird) inhabiting the open sea and returning to the shore only to breed.
▸ **noun** a pelagic fish or bird.
– ORIGIN mid 17th cent.: via Latin from Greek *pelagikos*, from *pelagios* 'of the sea' (from *pelagos* 'level surface of the sea').

P

Pelagius /pɪˈleɪdʒɪəs/ (c.360–c.420), British or Irish monk. He denied the doctrines of original sin and predestination, defending innate human goodness and free will. His beliefs were opposed by St Augustine of Hippo and condemned as heretical by the Synod of Carthage in about 418.
– DERIVATIVES **Pelagian** adjective & noun, **Pelagianism** noun.

pelargonium /ˌpɛləˈɡəʊnɪəm/ ▸ **noun** a tender shrubby plant which is widely cultivated for its red, pink, or white flowers. Some kinds have fragrant leaves which yield an essential oil. See also GERANIUM. ● Genus *Pelargonium*, family Geraniaceae: many species and several hybrid groups, including the **zonal pelargoniums** (*P. × hortorum*), with rounded leaves bearing coloured zones, and the trailing **ivy-leaved pelargoniums** (*P. peltatum*).
– ORIGIN modern Latin, from Greek *pelargos* 'stork', apparently on the pattern of *geranium* (based on Greek *geranos* 'crane').

Pelasgian /pɪˈlazɡɪən/ ▸ **adjective** relating to or denoting an ancient people inhabiting the coasts and islands of the Aegean Sea and eastern Mediterranean before the arrival of Greek-speaking peoples in the Bronze Age (12th century BC).
▸ **noun** a member of the Pelasgian people.
– ORIGIN late 15th cent.: via Latin from Greek *Pelasgos* + -IAN.

pelau /pəˈlaʊ/ ▸ **noun** [mass noun] a spicy West Indian dish consisting of meat, rice, and pigeon peas.
– ORIGIN from French Creole *pêlao*.

pele ▸ **noun** variant spelling of PEEL^{3}.

Pelé /ˈpɛleɪ/ (b.1940), Brazilian footballer; born *Edson Arantes do Nascimento*. Regarded as one of the greatest footballers of all time, he appeared 111 times for Brazil and is credited with over 1,200 goals in first-class soccer.

pelecypod /pɪˈlɛsɪpɒd/ ▸ **noun** another term for BIVALVE.
– ORIGIN late 19th cent.: from modern Latin *Pelecypoda* (alternative class name), from Greek *pelekus* 'hatchet' + *-podos* 'footed'.

Pelée, Mount /pəˈleɪ/ a volcano on the island of Martinique, in the Caribbean. Its eruption in 1902 destroyed the island's then capital St Pierre, killing its population of some 30,000.

pelerine /ˈpɛlərɪn, ˈpɛləriːn/ ▸ **noun** historical a woman's cape of lace or silk with pointed ends at the centre front, popular in the 19th century.
– ORIGIN mid 18th cent.: from French *pèlerine*, the sense being a transferred use of the feminine of *pèlerin* 'pilgrim'.

Pele's hair /ˈpɛleɪz/ ▸ **noun** [mass noun] fine threads of volcanic glass, formed when a spray of lava droplets cools rapidly in the air.
– ORIGIN mid 19th cent.: translating Hawaiian *lauohu o Pele*, Pele being the goddess of volcanoes in Hawaiian mythology.

Peleus /ˈpiːlɪəs/ Greek Mythology a king of Phthia in Thessaly, who was given as his wife the sea nymph Thetis; their child was Achilles.

pelf ▸ **noun** [mass noun] archaic money, especially when gained in a dishonest or dishonourable way.
– ORIGIN late Middle English (in the sense 'booty, pilfered property'): from a variant of Old French *pelfre* 'spoils', of unknown origin. Compare with PILFER.

Pelham /ˈpɛləm/, Henry (1696–1754), British Whig statesman, Prime Minister 1743–54. He introduced a period of peace and prosperity by bringing to an end the War of the Austrian Succession (1740–8).

pelham ▸ **noun** a horse's bit which combines the action of a curb bit and a snaffle.
– ORIGIN mid 19th cent.: from the surname *Pelham*.

pelican ▸ **noun** a large gregarious waterbird with a long bill, an extensible throat pouch for scooping up fish, and mainly white or grey plumage. ● Family Pelecanidae and genus *Pelecanus*: several species.
– ORIGIN late Old English *pellicane*, via late Latin from Greek *pelekan*, probably based on *pelekus* 'axe' (with reference to its bill).

P

pelican crossing ▸ **noun** (in the UK) a pedestrian crossing with traffic lights operated by pedestrians.
– ORIGIN 1960s: *pelican* from *pe(destrian) li(ght) con(trolled)*, altered to conform with the bird's name.

Pelican State informal name for LOUISIANA.

pelike /ˈpɛlɪki, pɛˈliːki/ ▸ **noun** (pl. **pelikai** /ˈpɛlɪkʌɪ/) a wide-mouthed amphora with a broad base, used in ancient Greece for holding wine or water.
– ORIGIN from Greek *pelika*.

Pelion /ˈpiːlɪən/ a wooded mountain in Greece, near the coast of SE Thessaly, rising to 1,548 m (5,079 ft). It was held in Greek mythology to be the home of the centaurs, and the giants were said to have piled Mounts Olympus and Ossa on its summit in their attempt to reach heaven and destroy the gods.
– PHRASES **pile** (or **heap**) **Pelion on Ossa** add an extra difficulty to something which is already onerous.

pelisse /pɪˈliːs/ ▸ **noun** historical a woman's ankle-length cloak with armholes or sleeves. ▪ a fur-lined cloak, especially as part of a hussar's uniform.
– ORIGIN early 18th cent.: from French, from medieval Latin *pellicia (vestis)* '(garment) of fur', from *pellis* 'skin'.

pelite /ˈpiːlʌɪt/ ▸ **noun** Geology a sediment or sedimentary rock composed of very fine clay or mud particles.
– ORIGIN late 19th cent.: from Greek *pēlos* 'clay, mud' + -ITE^{1}.

pellagra /pɛˈlagrə, -ˈleɪgrə/ ▸ **noun** [mass noun] a deficiency disease caused by a lack of nicotinic acid or its precursor tryptophan in the diet. It is characterized by dermatitis, diarrhoea, and mental disturbance, and is often linked to over-dependence on maize as a staple food.
– ORIGIN early 19th cent.: from Italian, from *pelle* 'skin', on the pattern of *podagra*.

pellet ▸ **noun** a small, rounded, compressed mass of a substance: *fish food pellets*. ▪ a piece of small shot or other lightweight bullet. ▪ a small mass of bones and feathers regurgitated by a bird of prey. ▪ a small round piece of animal faeces, especially from a rabbit or rodent.
▸ **verb** (**pellets**, **pelleting**, **pelleted**) [with obj.] **1** form (a substance) into pellets.
2 hit with or as if with pellets: *the last drops of rain were pelleting the windshield*.
– ORIGIN late Middle English: from Old French *pelote* 'metal ball', from a diminutive of Latin *pila* 'ball'.

pelletize (also **pelletise**) ▸ **verb** [with obj.] form or shape (a substance) into pellets.

pellicle /ˈpɛlɪk(ə)l/ ▸ **noun** technical a thin skin, cuticle, membrane, or film.
– ORIGIN late Middle English: from French *pellicule*, from Latin *pellicula* 'small piece of skin', diminutive of *pellis*.

pellitory /ˈpɛlɪtəri/ (also **pellitory of the wall**) ▸ **noun** a European plant of the nettle family with greenish flowers, which grows on or at the foot of walls or in stony places. ● *Parietaria judaica*, family Urticaceae.
– ORIGIN late Middle English: alteration of obsolete *parietary*, from Old French *paritaire*, based on Latin *paries, pariet-* 'wall'.

pell-mell ▸ **adverb** in a confused, rushed, or disorderly manner: *they rushed pell-mell up the hill*.
▸ **adjective** hasty or disorganized: *steps to slow the pell-mell pace of deforestation*.
▸ **noun** [in sing.] a disorderly situation or collection of things: *the pell-mell of ascending gables and roof tiles*.
– ORIGIN late 16th cent.: from French *pêle-mêle*, from earlier *pesle mesle, mesle pesle*, reduplication from *mesler* 'to mix'.

pellucid /pɪˈluːsɪd, pɛ-, -ˈljuːsɪd/ ▸ **adjective** literary translucently clear: *mountains reflected in the pellucid waters*. ▪ easily understood; lucid: *he writes, as always, in pellucid prose*. ▪ (of music or other sound) clear and pure in tone: *his pellucid singing tone*.
– DERIVATIVES **pellucidity** /-ˈsɪdɪti/ **noun**, **pellucidly** **adverb**.
– ORIGIN early 17th cent.: from Latin *pellucidus*, from *perlucere* 'shine through'.

Pelmanism /ˈpɛlmənɪz(ə)m/ ▸ **noun** [mass noun] a system of memory training originally devised by the Pelman Institute for the Scientific Development of Mind, Memory, and Personality in London. ▪ a card game in which matching pairs must be selected from memory from cards laid face down.

pelmet ▸ **noun** a narrow border of cloth or wood, fitted across the top of a door or window to conceal the curtain fittings. ▪ Brit. informal a very short skirt.
– ORIGIN early 20th cent.: probably an alteration of French *palmette*, literally 'small palm' (see PALMETTE).

Peloponnese /ˌpɛləpəˈniːz/ (**the Peloponnese**) the mountainous southern peninsula of Greece, connected to central Greece by the Isthmus of Corinth. Greek name **Pelopónnisos** /ˌpɛlɔˈpɔnisɔs/, also called **Peloponnesus** /-ˈniːsəs/.
– ORIGIN from Greek, literally 'island of Pelops'.

Peloponnesian War /ˌpɛləpəˈniːʃ(ə)n, -ˈniːʒ(ə)n/ the war of 431–404 BC fought between Athens and Sparta with their respective allies, occasioned largely by Spartan opposition to the Delian League. It ended in the total defeat of Athens and the transfer, for a brief period, of the leadership of Greece to Sparta.

Pelops /ˈpiːlɒps/ Greek Mythology son of Tantalus, brother of Niobe, and father of Atreus. He was killed by his father and served up as food to the gods, but only one shoulder was eaten, and he was restored to life with an ivory shoulder replacing the one that was missing.

pelorus /pɪˈlɔːrəs/ ▸ **noun** (pl. **peloruses**) a sighting device on a ship for taking the relative bearings of a distant object.
– ORIGIN mid 19th cent.: perhaps from *Pelorus*, said to be the name of Hannibal's pilot.

pelota /pɪˈlɒtə, -ˈləʊtə/ ▸ **noun** [mass noun] a Basque or Spanish game played in a walled court with a ball and basket-like rackets attached to the hand. ▪ [count noun] the ball used in pelota.
– ORIGIN Spanish, literally 'ball', augmentative of *pella*, from Latin *pila* 'ball'.

peloton /ˈpɛlətɒn/ ▸ **noun** the main field or group of cyclists in a race.
– ORIGIN French, literally 'small ball' (because of the concentrated grouping of the pack).

pelt^{1} ▸ **verb 1** [with obj.] hurl missiles repeatedly at: *two boys pelted him with rotten apples*. ▪ hurl (something) at someone or something: *she spotted four boys pelting stones at ducks*. ▪ [no obj.] (**pelt down**) (of rain, hail, or snow) fall quickly and very heavily: *the rain was pelting down*.
2 [no obj., with adverbial of direction] informal run somewhere very quickly: *I pelted across the road*.
▸ **noun** archaic an act of hurling something at someone.
– PHRASES **(at) full pelt** as fast as possible: *I ran downstairs at full pelt*.
– ORIGIN late 15th cent.: of unknown origin.

pelt^{2} ▸ **noun** the skin of an animal with the fur, wool, or hair still on it. ▪ an animal's coat of fur or hair. ▪ the raw skin of a sheep or goat, stripped and ready for tanning. ▪ informal a person's hair.
– PHRASES **in one's pelt** Irish informal naked.
– ORIGIN Middle English: either from obsolete *pellet* 'skin', from an Old French diminutive of *pel* 'skin', from Latin *pellis* 'skin', or a back-formation from PELTRY.

pelta /ˈpɛltə/ ▸ **noun** (pl. **peltae** /-tiː/) a small light shield, as used by the ancient Greeks and Romans. ▪ an ornamental motif resembling a shield.
– ORIGIN from Latin, from Greek *peltē*.

peltate /ˈpɛlteɪt/ ▸ **adjective** chiefly Botany shield-shaped. ▪ (of a leaf) more or less circular, with the stalk attached at a point on the underside.

Peltier effect /ˈpɛltɪeɪ/ ▸ **noun** Physics an effect whereby heat is given out or absorbed when an electric current passes across a junction between two materials.
– ORIGIN mid 19th cent.: named after Jean C. A. *Peltier* (1785–1845), French amateur scientist.

peltry ▸ **noun** [mass noun] (also **peltries**) animal pelts collectively.
– ORIGIN late Middle English: from Anglo-Norman French *pelterie*, based on Old French *pel* 'skin', from Latin *pellis*.

pelvic ▸ **adjective** relating to or situated within the bony pelvis. ▪ relating to the renal pelvis.

pelvic fin ▸ **noun** Zoology each of a pair of fins on the underside of a fish's body, attached to the pelvic girdle and helping to control direction. Also called VENTRAL FIN.

pelvic floor ▸ **noun** the muscular base of the abdomen, attached to the bony pelvis.

pelvic girdle ▸ **noun** (in vertebrates) the enclosing structure formed by the bony pelvis, providing attachment for the hindlimbs or pelvic fins.

pelvic inflammatory disease (abbrev.: **PID**) ▸ **noun** [mass noun] inflammation of the female genital tract, accompanied by fever and lower abdominal pain.

pelvimetry /pɛlˈvɪmɪtri/ ▸ **noun** [mass noun] Medicine measurement of the dimensions of the bony pelvis, undertaken chiefly to help determine whether a woman can give birth normally or will require a caesarean section.

pelvis ▸ **noun** (pl. **pelvises** or **pelves** /-viːz/) **1** the large bony frame near the base of the spine to which the hindlimbs or legs are attached in humans and many other vertebrates. ▪ the part of the abdomen including or enclosed by the pelvis.
2 (also **renal pelvis**) the broadened top part of the ureter into which the kidney tubules drain.
– ORIGIN early 17th cent.: from Latin, literally 'basin'.

pelycosaur /ˈpɛlɪkəsɔː/ ▸ **noun** a large fossil reptile of the late Carboniferous and Permian periods, typically having a line of long bony spines along the back supporting a sail-like crest. ● Order Pelycosauria, subclass Synapsida: several families and genera, including *Dimetrodon* and *Edaphosaurus*.
– ORIGIN early 20th cent.: from Greek *pelux, peluk-* 'bowl' + *sauros* 'lizard'.

Pemba /ˈpɛmbə/ **1** a seaport in northern Mozambique, on the Indian Ocean; pop. 141,316 (2007).
2 an island off the coast of Tanzania, in the western Indian Ocean north of Zanzibar.

Pembroke /ˈpɛmbrʊk/ a port in SW Wales, in Pembrokeshire; pop. 7,700 (est. 2009). It was a Norman stronghold from the 11th century. Welsh name PENFRO.

Pembrokeshire a county of SW Wales; administrative centre, Haverfordwest. It was part of Dyfed from 1974 to 1996.

Pembroke table ▶ noun a small table with fixed legs and a drop-leaf on each side.

Pembs. ▶ abbreviation Pembrokeshire.

pemmican /ˈpɛmɪk(ə)n/ ▶ noun [mass noun] a pressed cake of pounded dried meat mixed to a paste with melted fat and other ingredients, originally made by North American Indians and later adapted by Arctic explorers.
– ORIGIN from Cree *pimecan*, from *pime* 'fat'.

pemphigoid /ˈpɛmfɪgɔɪd/ ▶ noun [mass noun] Medicine a skin disease resembling pemphigus, chiefly affecting elderly people.

pemphigus /ˈpɛmfɪgəs/ ▶ noun [mass noun] Medicine a skin disease in which watery blisters form on the skin.
– ORIGIN late 18th cent.: modern Latin, from Greek *pemphix*, *pemphig-* 'bubble'.

PEN ▶ abbreviation International Association of Poets, Playwrights, Editors, Essayists, and Novelists.

pen[1] ▶ noun **1** an instrument for writing or drawing with ink, typically consisting of a metal nib or ball, or a nylon tip, fitted into a metal or plastic holder. ■ **(the pen)** the occupation of writing: *she was forced to support herself by the pen.* ■ an electronic pen-like device used in conjunction with a writing surface to enter commands or data into a computer.
2 Zoology the tapering cartilaginous internal shell of a squid.
▶ verb **(pens, penning, penned)** [with obj.] write or compose: *Olivia penned award-winning poetry.*
– PHRASES **pen and ink** Brit. rhyming slang a stink. **the pen is mightier than the sword** proverb writing is more effective than military power or violence. **put** (or **set**) **pen to paper** write or begin to write something.
– ORIGIN Middle English (originally denoting a feather with a sharpened quill): from Old French *penne*, from Latin *penna* 'feather' (in late Latin 'pen').

pen[2] ▶ noun **1** a small enclosure in which sheep, pigs, or other farm animals are kept. ■ a number of animals in or sufficient to fill a pen: ***a pen of** twenty-five Cheviots.* ■ any small enclosure in which someone or something can be confined. ■ a covered dock for a submarine or other warship.
2 (in the West Indies) a farm or plantation.
▶ verb **(pens, penning, penned)** [with obj.] put or keep (an animal) in a pen. ■ **(pen someone up/in)** confine someone in a restricted space: *they had been penned up day and night in the house.*
– ORIGIN Old English *penn*, of unknown origin.

pen[3] ▶ noun a female swan.
– ORIGIN mid 16th cent.: of unknown origin.

pen[4] ▶ noun N. Amer. informal short for **PENITENTIARY** (sense 1).

Pen. ▶ abbreviation Peninsula.

penal ▶ adjective relating to, used for, or prescribing the punishment of offenders under the legal system: *the campaign for penal reform | penal institutions.* ■ (of an act or offence) punishable by law. ■ (especially of taxation or interest rates) extremely severe.
– DERIVATIVES **penally** adverb.
– ORIGIN late Middle English: from Old French *penal*, from Latin *poenalis*, from *poena* 'pain, penalty'.

penalize (also **penalise**) ▶ verb [with obj.] **1** subject to a penalty or punishment: *high-spending councils will be penalized.* ■ (in various sports) punish (a player or team) for a breach of the rules by awarding an advantage to the opposition. ■ Law make or declare (an act or offence) legally punishable: *section twenty penalizes possession of a firearm when trespassing.*
2 put at an unfair disadvantage: *if the bill is not amended genuine claimants will be penalized.*
– DERIVATIVES **penalization** noun.

Penal Laws ▶ plural noun various statutes passed in Britain and Ireland during the 16th and 17th centuries that imposed harsh restrictions on Roman Catholics. The laws were repealed by various Acts between 1791 and 1926. See also **CATHOLIC EMANCIPATION**, **TEST ACT**.

penal servitude ▶ noun [mass noun] imprisonment with hard labour.

penalty ▶ noun (pl. **penalties**) **1** a punishment imposed for breaking a law, rule, or contract: *the charge carries a maximum penalty of ten years' imprisonment.*
2 (in sports and games) a handicap imposed on a player or team for infringement of rules. ■ a kick or shot awarded to a team because of an infringement of the rules by an opponent. ■ Bridge points won by the defenders when a declarer fails to make the contract.
3 a disadvantage suffered as the result of an action or situation: *the cold never leaves my bones these days—one of the penalties of age.*
– PHRASES **under** (or **on**) **penalty of** under the threat of: *he ordered enterprises to fulfil contracts under penalty of strict fines.*
– ORIGIN early 16th cent.: probably via Anglo-Norman French, from medieval Latin *poenalitas*, based on *poena* 'pain'.

penalty area ▶ noun Soccer the rectangular area marked out in front of each goal, within which a foul by a defender involves the award of a penalty kick and outside which the goalkeeper is not allowed to handle the ball.

penalty box ▶ noun **1** Soccer another term for **PENALTY AREA**.
2 Ice Hockey an area beside the rink reserved for penalized players and an official who records penalties.

penalty double ▶ noun Bridge another term for **BUSINESS DOUBLE**.

penalty kick ▶ noun **1** Soccer a free kick at the goal from the penalty spot (which only the goalkeeper is allowed to defend), awarded to the attacking team after a foul within the penalty area by an opponent.
2 Rugby a place kick awarded to a team after an offence by an opponent.

penalty killer ▶ noun Ice Hockey a player who plays while their own team is reduced through a penalty, especially one skilled at preventing the opposing team from scoring.
– DERIVATIVES **penalty killing** noun.

penalty point ▶ noun a punishment awarded by the courts for a driving offence and recorded cumulatively on a person's driving licence.

penalty rate ▶ noun Austral./NZ historical an increased rate of pay for overtime or for work performed under abnormal conditions.

penalty shoot-out ▶ noun see **SHOOT-OUT**.

penalty spot ▶ noun Soccer the point within the penalty area from which penalty kicks are taken.

penalty try ▶ noun Rugby a try awarded to a side by the referee when a touchdown is prevented by an offence by the opposition.

penance ▶ noun [mass noun] **1** punishment inflicted on oneself as an outward expression of repentance for wrongdoing: *he had **done** public **penance for** those hasty words.*
2 a sacrament in which a member of the Church confesses sins to a priest and is given absolution. In the Roman Catholic Church often called **SACRAMENT OF RECONCILIATION**. ■ a religious observance or other duty required of a person by a priest as part of this sacrament to indicate repentance.
▶ verb [with obj.] archaic impose a penance on.
– ORIGIN Middle English: from Old French, from Latin *paenitentia* 'repentance', from the verb *paenitere* 'be sorry'.

Penang /pɪˈnaŋ/ (also **Pinang**) an island of Malaysia, situated off the west coast of the Malay Peninsula. In 1786 it was ceded to the East India Company as a British colony by the sultan of Kedah. Known as Prince of Wales Island until 1867, it united with Malacca and Singapore in a union of 1826, which in 1867 became the British colony called the Straits Settlements. It joined the federation of Malaya in 1948. ■ a state of Malaysia, consisting of the island of Penang and a coastal strip on the mainland; capital, George Town (on Penang island). The mainland strip was united with the island in 1798 as part of the British colony. ■ another name for **GEORGE TOWN** (sense 2).

penannular /pɛˈnanjʊlə/ ▶ adjective Archaeology in the form of a ring but with a small part of the circumference missing: *penannular neck ornaments.*
– ORIGIN mid 19th cent.: from Latin *paene* 'almost' + **ANNULAR**.

penates /pɪˈnɑːtiːz, -ˈneɪt-/ ▶ plural noun household gods worshipped in conjunction with Vesta and the lares by the ancient Romans.
– ORIGIN Latin, from *penus* 'provision of food'; related to *penes* 'within'.

pence Brit. plural form of **PENNY**.

> **USAGE** Both **pence** and **pennies** have existed as plural forms of **penny** since at least the 16th century. The two forms now tend to be used for different purposes: **pence** refers to sums of money (*five pounds and sixty-nine **pence***) while **pennies** refers to the coins themselves (*I left two **pennies** on the table*). The use of **pence** rather than **penny** as a singular (*the chancellor will put **one pence** on income tax*) is not regarded as correct in standard English.

penchant /ˈpɒ̃ʃɒ̃/ ▶ noun [usu. in sing.] a strong or habitual liking for something or tendency to do something: *he has a **penchant for** adopting stray dogs.*
– ORIGIN late 17th cent.: from French, 'leaning, inclining', present participle of the verb *pencher*.

pencil ▶ noun **1** an instrument for writing or drawing, consisting of a thin stick of graphite or a similar substance enclosed in a long thin piece of wood or fixed in a cylindrical case. ■ [mass noun] graphite or a similar substance used as a medium for writing or drawing: *the words were scribbled in pencil.* ■ [usu. with modifier] a cosmetic in a long thin stick: *an eyebrow pencil.* ■ something with the shape of a pencil: *a pencil of light* | [as modifier] *a pencil torch.*
2 Physics & Geometry a set of light rays, lines, etc. converging to or diverging narrowly from a single point.
▶ verb **(pencils, pencilling, pencilled**; US **pencils, penciling, penciled)** [with obj.] write, draw, or colour with a pencil: *a previous owner has pencilled their name inside the cover* | (as adj. **pencilled**) *a pencilled note.*
– PHRASAL VERBS **pencil something in** arrange, forecast, or note down something provisionally: *May 15 was pencilled in as the date for the meeting.* **pencil someone in** make a provisional arrangement with or for someone: *he was pencilled in for surgery at the end of the month.*
– DERIVATIVES **penciller** noun.
– ORIGIN Middle English (denoting a fine paintbrush): from Old French *pincel*, from a diminutive of Latin *peniculus* 'brush', diminutive of *penis* 'tail'. The verb was originally (early 16th cent.) in the sense 'paint with a fine brush'.

pencil case ▶ noun a small container for pencils, pens, and other writing equipment.

pencil moustache ▶ noun a very thin moustache.

pencil pusher ▶ noun N. Amer. another term for **PEN-PUSHER**.

pencil sharpener ▶ noun a device for sharpening a pencil by rotating it against a cutting edge.

pencil skirt ▶ noun a very narrow straight skirt.

pendant ▶ noun **1** a piece of jewellery that hangs from a chain worn round the neck. ■ a necklace with a pendant.
2 a light designed to hang from the ceiling.
3 the part of a pocket watch by which it is suspended. ■ a short rope hanging from the head of a ship's mast, yardarm, or clew of a sail, used for attaching tackles.
4 /ˈpɛnd(ə)nt, ˈpɒdɒ̃/ an artistic, literary, or musical composition intended to match or complement another: *the triptych's pendant will occupy the corresponding wall in the south transept.*
5 Nautical a tapering flag.
▶ adjective hanging downwards; pendent: *pendant flowers on frail stems.*
– ORIGIN Middle English (denoting an architectural decoration projecting downwards): from Old French, literally 'hanging', present participle of the verb *pendre*, from Latin *pendere*.

pendent ▶ adjective **1** hanging down or overhanging: *pendent catkins.*
2 remaining undecided; pending: *the use of jurisdiction to decide pendent claims.*
– DERIVATIVES **pendency** noun.

pendente lite /pɛnˌdɛnteɪ ˈlʌɪti, -ˌdɛnti/ ▶ adverb Law during litigation. ■ depending on the outcome of litigation.
– ORIGIN Latin, literally 'with the lawsuit pending'.

pendentive /pɛnˈdɛntɪv/ ▶ noun Architecture a curved triangle of vaulting formed by the intersection of a dome with its supporting arches.
– ORIGIN early 18th cent.: from the French adjective *pendentif, -ive*, from Latin *pendent-* 'hanging down', from the verb *pendere*.

Penderecki /ˌpɛndəˈrɛtski/, Krzysztof (b.1933), Polish composer. His music frequently features sounds drawn from extramusical sources and note clusters, as in his *Threnody for the Victims of Hiroshima* (1960) for fifty-two strings. Notable religious works: *Stabat Mater* (1962) and *Polish Requiem* (1980–4).

pending ▶ adjective awaiting decision or settlement: *nine cases were still pending.* ■ about to happen; imminent: *the pending lay-off of fifty staff.*
▶ preposition until (something) happens: *they were released on bail pending an appeal.*
– ORIGIN mid 17th cent.: anglicized spelling of French *pendant* 'hanging'.

P

Pendragon /pɛnˈdrag(ə)n/ ▸ **noun** a title given to an ancient British or Welsh prince holding or claiming supreme power.
– ORIGIN Welsh, literally 'chief war-leader', from *pen* 'head' + *dragon* 'standard'.

penduline tit /ˈpɛndjʊlʌɪn/ ▸ **noun** a small tit-like Old World songbird that builds a nest suspended from a branch. ● Family Remizidae: genera *Anthoscopus* (several species in Africa) and *Remiz* (*R. pendulinus* of Eurasia).
– ORIGIN early 19th cent. (as *penduline titmouse*): *penduline* from French or modern Latin *pendulinus*, from Latin *pendulus* 'hanging down'.

pendulous /ˈpɛndjʊləs/ ▸ **adjective** hanging down loosely: *pendulous branches*.
– DERIVATIVES **pendulously** adverb.
– ORIGIN early 17th cent.: from Latin *pendulus* 'hanging down' (from *pendere* 'hang') + **-ous**.

pendulum /ˈpɛndjʊləm/ ▸ **noun** a weight hung from a fixed point so that it can swing freely, especially a rod with a weight at the end that regulates the mechanism of a clock. ■ used to refer to the tendency of a situation to oscillate between one extreme and another: *the pendulum of fashion*.

> The use of the pendulum for regulating clocks depends on the principle, discovered by Galileo c.1602, that for small amplitudes the time of oscillation of a pendulum depends only on its length. A freely suspended pendulum resists changes in its plane of oscillation, a fact employed by Jean Foucault in 1851 to demonstrate the earth's rotation.

– DERIVATIVES **pendular** adjective.
– ORIGIN mid 17th cent.: from Latin, neuter (used as a noun) of *pendulus* 'hanging down'.

penecontemporaneous /ˌpiːnɪkənˌtɛmpəˈreɪnɪəs/ ▸ **adjective** Geology (of a process) occurring immediately after deposition of a particular stratum.
– ORIGIN early 20th cent.: from Latin *paene* 'almost' + CONTEMPORANEOUS.

penectomy /pɛˈnɛktəmi/ ▸ **noun** [mass noun] surgical amputation of the penis.

Penelope /pəˈnɛləpi/ Greek Mythology the wife of Odysseus, who was beset by suitors when her husband did not return after the fall of Troy. She put them off by saying that she would marry only when she had finished the piece of weaving on which she was engaged, and every night unravelled the work she had done during the day.

peneplain /ˈpiːnɪpleɪn/ ▸ **noun** Geology a more or less level land surface produced by erosion over a long period, undisturbed by crustal movement.
– ORIGIN late 19th cent.: from Latin *paene* 'almost' + PLAIN[1].

penetrable ▸ **adjective 1** allowing things to pass through; permeable: *the outer membrane is penetrable*.
2 possible to understand; understandable: *the translation makes the original text penetrable*.
– DERIVATIVES **penetrability** noun.

penetralia /ˌpɛnɪˈtreɪlɪə/ ▸ **plural noun** literary the innermost parts of a building; a secret or hidden place.
– ORIGIN mid 17th cent.: from Latin, literally 'innermost things', neuter plural of *penetralis* 'interior'.

penetrance /ˈpɛnɪtr(ə)ns/ ▸ **noun** [mass noun] Genetics the extent to which a particular gene or set of genes is expressed in the phenotypes of individuals carrying it, measured by the proportion of carriers showing the characteristic phenotype.
– ORIGIN 1930s: from German *Penetranz*.

penetrant /ˈpɛnɪtr(ə)nt/ ▸ **adjective** Genetics (of a gene or group of genes) producing characteristic effects in the phenotypes of individuals possessing it.
▸ **noun** a coloured or fluorescent liquid used to penetrate cracks, pores, and other surface defects to facilitate their detection.

penetrate ▸ **verb** [with obj.] **1** go into or through (something), especially with force or effort: *the shrapnel had penetrated his head* | [no obj.] *tunnels that penetrate deep into the earth's core*. ■ (of a man) insert the penis into the vagina or anus of (a sexual partner).
2 gain access to (an organization, place, or system), especially when this is difficult to do: *M15 had been penetrated by Russian intelligence*. ■ (of a company) begin to sell its products in (a particular market or area): *the company has succeeded in penetrating Western motorcycle markets*.
3 succeed in understanding or gaining insight into (something complex or mysterious): *I could never penetrate his thoughts*. ■ [no obj.] be fully understood or realized by someone: *as his words penetrated, she saw a mental picture of him with Dawn*.
– ORIGIN mid 16th cent.: from Latin *penetrat-* 'placed or gone into', from the verb *penetrare*; related to *penitus* 'inner'.

penetrating ▸ **adjective** able to make a way through or into something: *the problem of penetrating damp*. ■ (of a sound) clearly heard through or above other sounds: *her scream was sudden and penetrating*. ■ (of a person's eyes or expression) reflecting an apparent ability to see into another's mind; intense: *her penetrating gaze*. ■ having or showing clear insight: *the students asked some penetrating questions*.
– DERIVATIVES **penetratingly** adverb.

penetration ▸ **noun** [mass noun] **1** the action or process of penetrating something: *the zip has a Velcro-secured flap to minimize rain penetration*. ■ the insertion by a man of his penis into the vagina or anus of a sexual partner.
2 the selling of a company's products in a particular market or area. ■ the extent to which a product is recognized and bought by customers in a particular market: *the software has attained a high degree of market penetration*.
3 the perceptive understanding of complex matters: *the survey shows subtlety and penetration*.
– ORIGIN late Middle English: from Latin *penetratio(n-)*, from the verb *penetrare* 'place within or enter'.

penetrative ▸ **adjective 1** able to make a way into or through something: *the gunpowder weapons have extra penetrative power*. ■ (of sexual activity) in which a man inserts his penis into the vagina or anus of a sexual partner.
2 having or showing clear insight: *a thorough and penetrative survey*.

penetrator ▸ **noun** a person or thing that penetrates something. ■ a missile containing a hard alloy rod, designed to penetrate the armour of tanks or fortifications.

penetrometer /ˌpɛnɪˈtrɒmɪtə/ ▸ **noun** an instrument for determining the consistency or hardness of a substance by measuring the depth or rate of penetration of a rod or needle driven into it by a known force.

penfriend ▸ **noun** Brit. a person with whom one becomes friendly by exchanging letters, especially someone in a foreign country whom one has never met.

Penfro /ˈpɛnvrəʊ/ Welsh name for PEMBROKE.

penghulu /pəŋˈhuːluː/ ▸ **noun** (in Malaysia and Indonesia) a village headman or chief.
– ORIGIN Malay.

pengö /ˈpɛŋgə, -gəʊ/ ▸ **noun** (pl. **same** or **pengös**) the basic monetary unit of Hungary from 1927 until 1946, when it was replaced by the forint.
– ORIGIN Hungarian, literally 'ringing'.

penguin ▸ **noun** a large flightless seabird of the southern hemisphere, with black upper parts and white underparts and wings developed into flippers for swimming under water. ● Family Spheniscidae: six genera and several species.
– ORIGIN late 16th cent. (originally denoting the great auk): of unknown origin.

penguin suit ▸ **noun** informal a black dinner jacket worn with a white shirt.

penicillate /ˈpɛnɪsɪlət, -ˈsɪlət/ ▸ **adjective** Biology having, forming, or resembling a small tuft or tufts of hair.
– ORIGIN early 19th cent.: from Latin *penicillus* 'paintbrush' + -ATE[2].

penicillin ▸ **noun** [mass noun] **1** an antibiotic or group of antibiotics produced naturally by certain blue moulds, now usually prepared synthetically. Penicillin was discovered in 1928 and during the Second World War became the first antibiotic to be used by doctors.
2 a blue mould of a type that produces penicillin. ● Genus *Penicillium*, subdivision Deuteromycotina.
– ORIGIN from the modern Latin genus name *Penicillium* (see PENICILLIUM) + -IN[1].

penicillinase /ˌpɛnɪˈsɪlɪneɪz/ ▸ **noun** [mass noun] Biochemistry an enzyme which can inactivate penicillin, produced by certain bacteria.

penicillium /ˌpɛnɪˈsɪlɪəm/ ▸ **noun** (pl. **penicillia**) a blue mould that is common on food, being added to some cheeses and used sometimes to produce penicillin.
– ORIGIN mid 19th cent.: modern Latin, from Latin *penicillus* 'paintbrush' (because of the brush-like fruiting bodies).

penile /ˈpiːnʌɪl/ ▸ **adjective** [attrib.] chiefly technical relating to or affecting the penis.
– ORIGIN mid 19th cent.: from modern Latin *penilis*, from *penis* 'tail, penis'.

penillion /pɛˈnɪ(θ)lɪən/ (also **pennillion**) ▸ **plural noun** improvised verses in Welsh sung to the accompaniment of a harp, especially in contest at an eisteddfod.
– ORIGIN Welsh, literally 'stanzas', from *pen* 'head'.

peninsula /pɪˈnɪnsjʊlə/ ▸ **noun** a piece of land almost surrounded by water or projecting out into a body of water.
– DERIVATIVES **peninsular** adjective.
– ORIGIN mid 16th cent.: from Latin *paeninsula*, from *paene* 'almost' + *insula* 'island'.

> **USAGE** The spelling of the noun as **peninsular** instead of **peninsula** is a common mistake. The spelling **peninsula** should be used when a noun is intended (*the end of the Cape Peninsula*), whereas **peninsular** is the spelling of the adjective (*the peninsular part of Malaysia*).

Peninsular War a campaign waged on the Iberian peninsula between the French and the British, the latter assisted by Spanish and Portuguese forces, from 1808 to 1814 during the Napoleonic Wars. The French were finally driven back over the Pyrenees in an expedition led by Wellington.

penis /ˈpiːnɪs/ ▸ **noun** (pl. **penises** or **penes** /-niːz/) the male genital organ of higher vertebrates, carrying the duct for the transfer of sperm during copulation. In humans and most other mammals it consists largely of erectile tissue and is used also for urination. ■ Zoology a type of male copulatory organ present in some invertebrates, such as gastropod molluscs.
– ORIGIN late 17th cent.: from Latin, 'tail, penis'.

penis envy ▸ **noun** [mass noun] Psychoanalysis supposed envy of the male's possession of a penis, postulated by Freud to account for some aspects of female behaviour (notably the castration complex) but controversial among modern theorists.

penistone /ˈpɛnɪstən/ ▸ **noun** [mass noun] a kind of coarse woollen cloth formerly used for making clothes.
– ORIGIN mid 16th cent.: from the name of a town in south Yorkshire, where the cloth was made.

penitence ▸ **noun** [mass noun] the action of feeling or showing sorrow and regret for having done wrong; repentance: *a public display of penitence*.

penitent ▸ **adjective** feeling or showing sorrow and regret for having done wrong; repentant: *a penitent expression*.
▸ **noun** a person who repents their sins and (in the Christian Church) seeks forgiveness from God. ■ (in the Roman Catholic Church) a person who confesses their sins to a priest and submits to the penance that he imposes.
– DERIVATIVES **penitently** adverb.
– ORIGIN Middle English: from Old French, from Latin *paenitent-* 'repenting', from the verb *paenitere*.

penitential ▸ **adjective** relating to or expressing penitence or penance: *penitential tears*.
– DERIVATIVES **penitentially** adverb.
– ORIGIN late 15th cent.: from late Latin *paenitentialis*, from Latin *paenitentia* 'repentance'.

Penitential Psalms ▸ **plural noun** seven psalms (6, 32, 38, 51, 102, 130, 143) which express penitence.

penitentiary /ˌpɛnɪˈtɛnʃ(ə)ri/ ▸ **noun** (pl. **penitentiaries**) **1** N. Amer. a prison for people convicted of serious crimes.
2 (in the Roman Catholic Church) a priest appointed to administer penance. ■ an office in the papal court forming a tribunal for deciding on questions relating to penance, dispensations, and absolution.
– ORIGIN late Middle English (as a term in ecclesiastical law): from medieval Latin *paenitentiarius*, from Latin *paenitentia* 'repentance'. The North American usage dates from the early 19th cent.

penknife ▸ **noun** (pl. **penknives**) a small knife with a blade which folds into the handle.

penlight ▸ **noun** a small electric torch shaped like a fountain pen.

penman ▸ **noun** (pl. **penmen**) **1** historical a person, such as a clerk, who was employed to write by hand on behalf of others.
2 a person who writes with a specified degree of skill: *this talented penman's work*. ■ an author.

penmanship ▸ **noun** [mass noun] the art or skill of writing by hand. ■ a person's handwriting.

Penn, William (1644–1718), English Quaker, founder of Pennsylvania. Having been imprisoned in 1668 for his Quaker writings, he was granted a charter to land in North America by Charles II. He founded the colony of Pennsylvania as a sanctuary for Quakers and other Nonconformists in 1682.

Penn. (also **Penna.**) ▶ **abbreviation** Pennsylvania.

pen name ▶ **noun** an assumed name used by a writer instead of their real name.

pennant ▶ **noun 1** a tapering flag on a ship, especially one flown at the masthead of a vessel in commission. ■ a long triangular or swallow-tailed flag, especially as the military ensign of lancer regiments. ■ N. Amer. a flag denoting a sports championship or identifying a team.
2 Nautical a short rope hanging from the head of a ship's mast; a pendant.
– ORIGIN early 17th cent.: blend of PENDANT and PENNON.

pennate /ˈpɛnət/ ▶ **adjective** Botany (of a diatom) bilaterally symmetrical. Compare with CENTRIC.
– ORIGIN mid 19th cent.: from Latin *pennatus* 'feathered, winged', from *penna* 'feather'.

penne /ˈpɛneɪ, ˈpɛni/ ▶ **plural noun** pasta in the form of short wide tubes.
– ORIGIN Italian, plural of *penna* 'quill'.

penni /ˈpɛni/ ▶ **noun** (pl. **penniä** /ˈpɛnɪɑː/) (until the introduction of the euro in 2002) a monetary unit of Finland, equal to one hundredth of a markka.
– ORIGIN Finnish.

penniless ▶ **adjective** (of a person) having no money; very poor: *a penniless young student*.
– DERIVATIVES **pennilessness** noun.

pennillion ▶ **plural noun** variant spelling of PENILLION.

Pennine Hills /ˈpɛnʌɪn/ (also **Pennine Chain** or **the Pennines**) a range of hills in northern England, extending from the Scottish border southwards to the Peak District in Derbyshire. Its highest peak is Cross Fell in Cumbria, which rises to 893 m (2,930 ft).

pennon /ˈpɛnən/ ▶ **noun** less common term for PENNANT.
– DERIVATIVES **pennoned** adjective.
– ORIGIN late Middle English: from Old French, from a derivative of Latin *penna* 'feather'.

penn'orth /ˈpɛnəθ/ ▶ **noun** Brit. variant spelling of PENNYWORTH.

Pennsylvania /ˌpɛnsɪlˈveɪnɪə/ a state of the north-eastern US; pop. 12,448,279 (est. 2008); capital, Harrisburg. Founded in 1682 by William Penn, it became one of the original thirteen states of the Union in 1787.

Pennsylvania Dutch (also **Pennsylvania German**) ▶ **noun** [mass noun] a dialect of High German spoken in parts of Pennsylvania, chiefly by descendants of 17th- and 18th-century Protestant immigrants.
– ORIGIN *Dutch* from German *Deutsch* 'German'.

Pennsylvanian ▶ **adjective 1** relating to the state of Pennsylvania.
2 Geology relating to or denoting the later part of the Carboniferous period in North America, following the Mississippian and preceding the Permian, and corresponding to the Upper Carboniferous of Europe. This period lasted from about 323 to 290 million years ago.
▶ **noun 1** a native or inhabitant of Pennsylvania.
2 (**the Pennsylvanian**) Geology the Pennsylvanian period or the system of rocks deposited during it.

penny ▶ **noun** (pl. for separate coins **pennies**, for a sum of money **pence**) **1** (abbrev.: **p**) a British bronze coin and monetary unit equal to one hundredth of a pound. ■ (abbrev.: **d**) a former British coin and monetary unit equal to one twelfth of a shilling and 240th of a pound. ■ N. Amer. informal a one-cent coin. ■ (in biblical use) a denarius.
2 (**pennies**) a small sum of money: *any chance to save a few pennies is welcome*. ■ [with negative] (**a penny**) used for emphasis to denote no money at all: *we didn't get paid a penny*.
– PHRASES **a bad penny always turns up** proverb someone or something unwelcome will always reappear or return. **be two** (or **ten**) **a penny** chiefly Brit. be plentiful and consequently of little value. **count** (or **watch** or US **pinch**) **the** (or **your**) **pennies** be careful about how much one spends. **in for a penny, in for a pound** used to express someone's intention to see an undertaking through, however much time, effort, or money this entails. **look after the pennies and the pounds will look after themselves** proverb if you concentrate on saving small amounts of money, you'll soon amass a large amount. **pennies from heaven** unexpected benefits, especially financial ones. **the penny dropped** informal, chiefly Brit. used to indicate that someone has finally realized something. **a penny for your thoughts** used to ask someone what they are thinking about.
– ORIGIN Old English *penig, penning* of Germanic origin; related to Dutch *penning*, German *Pfennig*, perhaps also to PAWN[2] and (with reference to shape) PAN[1].

> **USAGE** On the different uses of the plural forms **pence** and **pennies**, see **USAGE** at **PENCE**.

-penny ▶ **combining form** Brit. (especially in pre-decimal currency) costing a specified number of pence: *threepenny*.
– ORIGIN from PENNY.

penny ante ▶ **noun** [mass noun] chiefly N. Amer. poker played for very small stakes. ■ [as modifier] informal petty; contemptible: *a penny-ante scandal of little substance*.

penny arcade ▶ **noun** chiefly N. Amer. another term for AMUSEMENT ARCADE.

penny black ▶ **noun** the world's first adhesive postage stamp, issued in Britain in 1840. It was printed in black with an effigy of Queen Victoria, and had a value of one penny.

penny bun ▶ **noun** another term for CEP.

pennycress ▶ **noun** a European weed with flat round pods, which has become naturalized in North America. ● *Thlaspi arvense*, family Cruciferae.

penny dreadful ▶ **noun** a cheap, sensational comic or storybook.
– ORIGIN late 19th cent.: so named because the original cost was one penny.

penny-farthing ▶ **noun** historical an early type of bicycle, made in Britain, with a very large front wheel and a small rear wheel.

penny loafer ▶ **noun** a casual leather shoe with a decorative slotted leather strip over the upper, in which a coin may be placed.

penny-pinching ▶ **adjective** unwilling to spend money; miserly: *penny-pinching governments with a utilitarian approach to the arts*.
▶ **noun** [mass noun] unwillingness to spend money.
– DERIVATIVES **penny-pincher** noun.

penny plain ▶ **adjective** Brit. plain and simple: *a penny plain version that takes away some of the character from the piece*.
– ORIGIN mid 19th cent.: with reference to prints of characters sold for toy theatres, costing one penny for black-and-white ones, and two pennies for coloured ones.

penny post ▶ **noun** [in sing.] historical a system of carrying letters at a charge of one penny, in particular the system established in the UK in 1840 at the instigation of Sir Rowland Hill.

pennyroyal ▶ **noun** either of two small-leaved plants of the mint family, used in herbal medicine. ● A creeping Eurasian plant (*Mentha pulegium*), and **American pennyroyal** (*Hedeoma pulegioides*), family Labiatae.
– ORIGIN mid 16th cent.: from Anglo-Norman French *puliol* (based on Latin *pulegium* 'thyme') + *real* 'royal'.

penny stock ▶ **noun** N. Amer. a common stock valued at less than one dollar, and therefore highly speculative.

pennyweight ▶ **noun** a unit of weight, 24 grains or one twentieth of an ounce troy.

penny whistle ▶ **noun** another term for TIN WHISTLE. ■ [as modifier] S. African used to denote kwela music or the musicians playing it.

penny wise ▶ **adjective** extremely careful about the way one spends even small amounts of money.
– PHRASES **penny wise and pound foolish** careful and economical in small matters while being wasteful or extravagant in large ones.

pennywort /ˈpɛnɪwəːt/ ▶ **noun** any of a number of plants with rounded leaves, in particular: ● (**wall pennywort**) a small Eurasian plant that grows in crevices (*Umbilicus rupestris*, family Crassulaceae). Also called COTYLEDON or NAVELWORT. ● (**marsh** or **water pennywort**) a small creeping or floating plant of marshy places (*Hydrocotyle vulgaris*, family Umbelliferae). Also called NAVELWORT.

pennyworth (also **penn'orth**) ▶ **noun** Brit. **1** an amount of something that may be bought for a penny: ***a pennyworth of chips***. ■ archaic value for one's money.
2 (**one's pennyworth**) a person's contribution to a discussion: *Bob would have to **put his two pennyworth in first***.

Penobscot /pɛˈnɒbskɒt/ ▶ **noun** (pl. **same**) **1** a member of an American Indian people of the Penobscot River valley in Maine.
2 [mass noun] the extinct Algonquian language of the Penobscot, a dialect of Eastern Abnaki.
▶ **adjective** relating to the Penobscot or their language.
– ORIGIN the name in Abnaki.

penology /piːˈnɒlədʒi, pɪ-/ ▶ **noun** [mass noun] the study of the punishment of crime and of prison management.
– DERIVATIVES **penological** adjective, **penologist** noun.
– ORIGIN mid 19th cent.: from Latin *poena* 'penalty' + -LOGY.

pen pal ▶ **noun** a penfriend.

pen-pusher ▶ **noun** informal a person with a clerical job involving a lot of tedious and repetitive paperwork.

Penrose tile ▶ **noun** Mathematics any of a finite number of shapes that are components of a spatially non-periodic two- or three-dimensional tiling.
– ORIGIN 1970s: named after Roger *Penrose* (born 1931), British mathematical physicist.

pensée /pɒ̃ˈseɪ/, French /pɑ̃se/ ▶ **noun** a thought or reflection put into literary form; an aphorism.
– ORIGIN French.

pen shell ▶ **noun** a large wedge-shaped bivalve mollusc of warm seas which burrows into the seabed where it attaches itself by strong byssus threads. ● Family Pinnidae: *Pinna* and other genera.

pensile /ˈpɛnsʌɪl/ ▶ **adjective** hanging down; pendulous: *pensile nests*.
– ORIGIN early 17th cent.: from Latin *pensilis*, from the verb *pendere* 'hang'.

pension[1] /ˈpɛnʃ(ə)n/ ▶ **noun** (Brit. also **state pension**) a regular payment made by the state to people of or above the official retirement age and to some widows and disabled people. ■ a regular payment made during a person's retirement from an investment fund to which that person or their employer has contributed during their working life. ■ chiefly historical a regular payment made to a royal favourite or to an artist or scholar to enable them to carry on work of public interest or value.
▶ **verb** [with obj.] (**pension someone off**) dismiss someone from employment, typically because of age or ill health, and pay them a pension. ■ (**pension something off**) discard something because it is too old or no longer wanted: *garden sheds were raided to **bring out machines long since pensioned off***.
– DERIVATIVES **pensionless** adjective.
– ORIGIN late Middle English (in the sense 'payment, tax, regular sum paid to retain allegiance'): from Old French, from Latin *pensio(n-)* 'payment', from *pendere* 'to pay'. The current verb sense dates from the mid 19th cent.

pension[2] /pɒ̃ˈsjɒ̃/, French /pɑ̃sjɔ̃/ ▶ **noun** a small hotel or boarding house in France and other European countries.
– ORIGIN French.

pensionable ▶ **adjective** entitling to or qualifying for a pension: *women over **pensionable age***.
– DERIVATIVES **pensionability** noun.

pension book ▶ **noun** Brit. a book of vouchers supplied by the government for the weekly payment of a person's pension.

pensione /ˌpɛnsɪˈəʊneɪ/ ▶ **noun** (pl. **pensioni** /-ni/) a small hotel or boarding house in Italy.
– ORIGIN Italian.

pensioner ▶ **noun** a person who receives a pension, especially the retirement pension.

pension fund ▶ **noun** a fund from which pensions are paid, accumulated from contributions from employers, employees, or both.

pension mortgage ▶ **noun** a mortgage in which the borrower repays interest only and also contributes to a pension plan designed to provide an eventual tax-free lump sum, part of which is used to repay the capital at the end of the mortgage period and the rest to provide a pension for the borrower's retirement.

pensionnat /ˌpɒ̃sjɒˈnɑː/, French /pɑ̃sjɔna/ ▶ **noun** (pl. pronunc. **same**) (in France and other European countries) a boarding school.
– ORIGIN French.

P

pension pot ▸ noun Brit. informal the total fund of money that constitutes the basis of someone's retirement pension.

pensive ▸ adjective engaged in, involving, or reflecting deep or serious thought: *a pensive mood.*
– DERIVATIVES **pensively** adverb, **pensiveness** noun.
– ORIGIN late Middle English: from Old French *pensif, -ive*, from *penser* 'think', from Latin *pensare* 'ponder', frequentative of *pendere* 'weigh'.

penstemon /ˈpɛnstəmən, pɛnˈstiːmən/ (also **pentstemon**) ▸ noun a North American plant with stems of showy flowers resembling snapdragons. ● Genus *Penstemon*, family Scrophulariaceae.
– ORIGIN modern Latin, formed irregularly from PENTA- 'five' + Greek *stēmōn* 'warp', used to mean 'stamen'.

penstock ▸ noun a sluice for controlling or directing the flow of water. ■ a channel or pipe for conveying water to a hydroelectric station or waterwheel.
– ORIGIN early 17th cent.: from PEN² (in the sense 'mill dam') + STOCK.

pent ▸ adjective chiefly literary another term for PENT-UP: *with pent breath she waited out the meeting.*

penta- ▸ combining form five; having five: *pentagram* | *pentadactyl.*
– ORIGIN from Greek *pente* 'five'.

pentachlorophenol /ˌpɛntəˌklɔːrəʊˈfiːnɒl/ ▸ noun [mass noun] Chemistry a colourless crystalline synthetic compound used in insecticides, fungicides, weedkillers, and wood preservatives. ● Chem. formula: C_6Cl_5OH.

pentachord ▸ noun **1** a musical instrument with five strings.
2 a series of five musical notes.

pentacle /ˈpɛntək(ə)l/ ▸ noun a talisman or magical object, typically disc-shaped and inscribed with a pentagram, used as a symbol of the element of earth. ■ a pentagram. ■ (**pentacles**) one of the suits in some tarot packs, corresponding to coins in others.
– ORIGIN late 16th cent.: from medieval Latin *pentaculum*, apparently based on Greek *penta-* 'five'.

pentad /ˈpɛntad/ ▸ noun technical a group or set of five.
– ORIGIN mid 17th cent.: from Greek *pentas, pentad-*, from *pente* 'five'.

pentadactyl /ˌpɛntəˈdaktɪl/ ▸ adjective Zoology (of a vertebrate limb) having five toes or fingers, or derived from such a form, as characteristic of all tetrapods.
– DERIVATIVES **pentadactyly** /-ˈdaktɪli/ noun.
– ORIGIN early 19th cent.: from PENTA- 'five' + Greek *daktulos* 'finger'.

pentagastrin /ˌpɛntəˈgastrɪn/ ▸ noun [mass noun] Biochemistry a synthetic peptide which has the same action as the hormone gastrin. It is used to promote gastric secretions prior to sampling them for tests.

P

Pentagon (**the Pentagon**) the pentagonal building serving as the headquarters of the US Department of Defense, near Washington DC. Part of the building was badly damaged in the terrorist attacks of 11 September 2001. ■ the US Department of Defense: *the Pentagon said that ten soldiers had been killed.*

pentagon ▸ noun a plane figure with five straight sides and five angles.
– DERIVATIVES **pentagonal** adjective.
– ORIGIN late 16th cent.: via Latin from Greek *pentagōnon*, neuter (used as a noun) of *pentagōnos* 'five-angled'.

Pentagonese /ˌpɛntəgəˈniːz/ ▸ noun [mass noun] US informal the euphemistic or cryptic language supposedly used among high-ranking US military personnel.
– ORIGIN 1950s: from PENTAGON + -ESE.

pentagram ▸ noun a five-pointed star that is formed by drawing a continuous line in five straight segments, often used as a mystic and magical symbol. Compare with PENTACLE.
– ORIGIN mid 19th cent.: from Greek *pentagrammon* (see PENTA-, -GRAM¹).

pentahedron /ˌpɛntəˈhiːdr(ə)n, -ˈhɛd-/ ▸ noun (pl. **pentahedra** /-drə/ or **pentahedrons**) a solid figure with five plane faces.
– DERIVATIVES **pentahedral** adjective.
– ORIGIN late 18th cent.: from PENTA- 'five' + -HEDRON, on the pattern of words such as *polyhedron.*

pentamer /ˈpɛntəmə/ ▸ noun Chemistry a polymer comprising five monomer units.
– DERIVATIVES **pentameric** /ˌpɛntəˈmɛrɪk/ adjective.

pentameral /pɛnˈtamərəl/ ▸ adjective Zoology (of symmetry) fivefold, as typical of many echinoderms. Compare with PENTAMEROUS.
– DERIVATIVES **pentamerally** adverb, **pentamery** noun.

pentamerous /pɛnˈtam(ə)rəs/ ▸ adjective Botany & Zoology having parts arranged in groups of five. ■ consisting of five joints or parts. Compare with PENTAMERAL.

pentameter /pɛnˈtamɪtə/ ▸ noun Prosody a line of verse consisting of five metrical feet, or (in Greek and Latin verse) of two halves each of two feet and a long syllable.
– ORIGIN early 16th cent.: via Latin from Greek *pentametros* (see PENTA-, -METER).

pentamidine /pɛnˈtamɪdiːn/ ▸ noun [mass noun] Medicine a synthetic antibiotic drug used chiefly in the treatment of PCP infection.
– ORIGIN 1940s: from PENTANE + AMIDE + -INE⁴.

pentane /ˈpɛnteɪn/ ▸ noun [mass noun] Chemistry a volatile liquid hydrocarbon of the alkane series, present in petroleum spirit. ● Chem. formula: C_5H_{12}; three isomers, especially the straight-chain isomer (*n*-**pentane**).
– ORIGIN late 19th cent.: from Greek *pente* 'five' (denoting five carbon atoms) + a shortened form of ALKANE.

pentangle ▸ noun another term for PENTAGRAM.
– ORIGIN late Middle English: perhaps from medieval Latin *pentaculum* 'pentacle' (*-aculum* assimilated to Latin *angulus* 'an angle').

pentanoate /ˈpɛnteɪnəʊət, ˈpɛnteɪnəʊeɪt/ ▸ noun Chemistry a salt or ester of pentanoic acid.

pentanoic acid /ˌpɛntəˈnəʊɪk/ ▸ noun [mass noun] Chemistry a colourless liquid fatty acid present in various plant oils, used in making perfumes. ● Chem. formula: $CH_3(CH_2)_3COOH$.
– ORIGIN 1920s: *pentanoic* from PENTANE.

pentaploid /ˈpɛntəplɔɪd/ Genetics ▸ adjective (of a cell or nucleus) containing five homologous sets of chromosomes. ■ (of an organism or species) composed of pentaploid cells.
▸ noun a pentaploid organism, variety, or species.

pentaprism ▸ noun a prism having a five-sided cross section with two silvered surfaces, giving a constant deviation of all rays of light through 90°, used chiefly in the viewfinders of single-lens reflex cameras.

Pentateuch /ˈpɛntətjuːk/ the first five books of the Old Testament (Genesis, Exodus, Leviticus, Numbers, and Deuteronomy). Traditionally ascribed to Moses, it is now held by scholars to be a compilation from texts of the 9th to 5th centuries BC. Jewish name TORAH.
– DERIVATIVES **Pentateuchal** adjective.
– ORIGIN via ecclesiastical Latin from ecclesiastical Greek *pentateukhos*, from *penta-* 'five' + *teukhos* 'implement, book'.

pentathlon ▸ noun an athletic event comprising five different events for each competitor, in particular (also **modern pentathlon**) an event involving fencing, shooting, swimming, riding, and cross-country running.
– DERIVATIVES **pentathlete** noun.
– ORIGIN early 17th cent. (denoting the original five events of leaping, running, discus-throwing, spear-throwing, and wrestling): from Greek, from *pente* 'five' + *athlon* 'contest'.

pentathol ▸ noun variant spelling of PENTOTHAL, regarded as a misspelling in technical use.

pentatonic /ˌpɛntəˈtɒnɪk/ ▸ adjective Music relating to, based on, or denoting a scale of five notes, especially one without semitones equivalent to an ordinary major scale with the fourth and seventh omitted.
– DERIVATIVES **pentatonicism** noun.

pentavalent /ˌpɛntəˈveɪl(ə)nt/ ▸ adjective Chemistry having a valency of five.

pentazocine /pɛnˈtazə(ʊ)siːn/ ▸ noun [mass noun] Medicine a synthetic compound that is a potent non-addictive analgesic, often given during childbirth. ● A tricyclic compound; chem. formula: $C_{19}H_{27}NO$.
– ORIGIN 1960s: from PENTANE + AZO- + OCTA- + -INE⁴.

Pentecost /ˈpɛntɪkɒst/ ▸ noun **1** the Christian festival celebrating the descent of the Holy Spirit on the disciples of Jesus after his Ascension, held on the seventh Sunday after Easter. ■ the day on which the festival of Pentecost is held; Whit Sunday.
2 the Jewish festival of Shavuoth.
– ORIGIN Old English *pentecosten*, via ecclesiastical Latin from Greek *pentēkostē* (*hēmera*) 'fiftieth (day)' (because the Jewish festival is held on the fiftieth day after the second day of Passover).

Pentecostal ▸ adjective **1** relating to Pentecost.
2 relating to or denoting any of a number of Christian sects emphasizing baptism in the Holy Spirit, evidenced by 'speaking in tongues', prophecy, healing, and exorcism. [with reference to the baptism in the Holy Spirit at the first Pentecost (Acts 2:9-11).]
▸ noun a member of a Pentecostal sect.
– DERIVATIVES **Pentecostalism** noun, **Pentecostalist** adjective & noun.

Pentelic marble /pɛnˈtɛlɪk/ ▸ noun [mass noun] a white marble quarried on Mount Pentelicus near Athens.

Penthesilea /ˌpɛnθɛsɪˈliːə/ Greek Mythology the queen of the Amazons, who came to the help of Troy after the death of Hector and was killed by Achilles.

penthouse ▸ noun **1** a flat on the top floor of a tall building, typically one that is luxuriously fitted.
2 archaic an outhouse or shelter with a sloping roof, built on to the side of a building.
– ORIGIN Middle English *pentis* (in sense 2), shortening of Old French *apentis*, based on late Latin *appendicium* 'appendage', from Latin *appendere* 'hang on'. The change of form in the 16th cent. was by association with French *pente* 'slope' and HOUSE.

pentimento /ˌpɛntɪˈmɛntəʊ/ ▸ noun (pl. **pentimenti** /-tiː/) a visible trace of earlier painting beneath a layer or layers of paint on a canvas.
– ORIGIN early 20th cent.: from Italian, literally 'repentance'.

Pentland Firth a channel separating the Orkney Islands from the northern tip of mainland Scotland. It links the North Sea with the Atlantic.

pentlandite /ˈpɛntləndʌɪt/ ▸ noun [mass noun] a bronze-yellow mineral which consists of a sulphide of iron and nickel and is the principal ore of nickel.
– ORIGIN mid 19th cent.: from the name of Joseph B. *Pentland* (1797–1873), Irish traveller, + -ITE¹.

pentobarbitone /ˌpɛntə(ʊ)ˈbɑːbɪtəʊn/ (US **pentobarbital**) ▸ noun [mass noun] Medicine a narcotic and sedative barbiturate drug formerly used to relieve insomnia. ● Alternative name: **5-ethyl-5-(1-methylbutyl)-barbituric acid**; often used as the sodium salt (**sodium pentobarbitone**, Nembutal).
– ORIGIN 1930s: from PENTANE + BARBITONE (or BARBITAL).

pentode /ˈpɛntəʊd/ ▸ noun Electronics a thermionic valve having five electrodes.
– ORIGIN early 20th cent.: from Greek *pente* 'five' + *hodos* 'way'.

pentose /ˈpɛntəʊz, -s/ ▸ noun Chemistry any of the class of simple sugars whose molecules contain five carbon atoms, such as ribose and xylose. They generally have the chemical formula $C_5H_{10}O_5$.
– ORIGIN late 19th cent.: from PENTA- 'five' + -OSE².

Pentothal /ˈpɛntəθal/ ▸ noun trademark for THIOPENTONE.

pentoxide /pɛnˈtɒksʌɪd/ ▸ noun Chemistry an oxide containing five atoms of oxygen in its molecule or empirical formula.

pent roof ▸ noun a roof consisting of a single sloping surface.
– ORIGIN mid 19th cent.: from PENTHOUSE + ROOF.

pentstemon ▸ noun variant spelling of PENSTEMON.

pent-up ▸ adjective **1** (of emotions, energy, etc.) unable to be expressed or released: *pent-up frustrations.*
2 closely confined or held back: *a surge of pent-up water.*
– ORIGIN late 16th cent.: *pent*, obsolete past participle of PEN² (verb).

pentyl /ˈpɛntʌɪl, -tɪl/ ▸ noun [as modifier] Chemistry of or denoting an alkyl radical $-C_5H_{11}$, derived from pentane. Compare with AMYL.

penult /pɪˈnʌlt, ˈpɛnʌlt/ ▸ noun Linguistics the penultimate syllable of a word.
▸ adjective archaic term for PENULTIMATE.

penultimate ▸ adjective [attrib.] last but one in a series of things; second last: *the penultimate chapter of the book.*
– ORIGIN late 17th cent.: from Latin *paenultimus*, from *paene* 'almost' + *ultimus* 'last', on the pattern of *ultimate.*

penumbra /pɪˈnʌmbrə/ ▸ noun (pl. **penumbrae** /-briː/ or **penumbras**) **1** the partially shaded outer region of the shadow cast by an opaque object. ■ Astronomy the shadow cast by the earth or moon over an area experiencing a partial eclipse. ■ Astronomy the less dark outer part of a sunspot, surrounding the core.
2 a peripheral or indeterminate area or group: *an immense penumbra of theory surrounds any observation.*
– DERIVATIVES **penumbral** adjective.

– ORIGIN mid 17th cent.: modern Latin, from Latin *paene* 'almost' + *umbra* 'shadow'.

penurious /pɪˈnjʊərɪəs/ ▸ **adjective** formal **1** extremely poor; poverty-stricken: *a penurious old tramp.* ■ characterized by poverty: *penurious years.*
2 unwilling to spend money; mean: *his stingy and penurious wife.*
– DERIVATIVES **penuriously** adverb, **penuriousness** noun.
– ORIGIN late 16th cent.: from medieval Latin *penuriosus*, from Latin *penuria* 'need, scarcity' (see **PENURY**).

penury /ˈpɛnjʊri/ ▸ **noun** [mass noun] the state of being very poor; extreme poverty: *he couldn't face another year of penury.*
– ORIGIN late Middle English: from Latin *penuria* 'need, scarcity'; perhaps related to *paene* 'almost'.

Penutian /pəˈnuːʃ(ə)n, -ˈnuːtɪən/ ▸ **noun** [mass noun] a proposed superfamily or phylum of American Indian languages, most of which are now extinct or nearly so. Some scholars include certain living languages of Central and South America, principally Mayan and Mapuche, in this group.
▸ **adjective** relating to or denoting these languages or any of the peoples speaking them.
– ORIGIN from *pen* and *uti*, words for 'two' in two groups of Penutian languages + **-AN**.

Penza /ˈpjɛnzə/ a city in south central Russia; pop. 507,800 (est. 2008). Situated on the River Sura, a tributary of the Volga, it is an industrial and transportation centre.

Penzance /pɛnˈzans/ a resort town in SW England, on the south coast of Cornwall near Land's End; pop. 21,500 (est. 2009).

peon /ˈpiːən/ ▸ **noun 1** also /peɪˈɒn/ a Spanish-American day labourer or unskilled farm worker. ■ N. Amer. a person who does menial work: *racing drivers aren't exactly nine-to-five peons.* ■ historical a debtor held in servitude by a creditor, especially in the southern US and Mexico.
2 also /pjuːn/ (in South and SE Asia) a low-ranking soldier or worker.
3 (pl. **peones** /peɪˈəʊneɪz/) another term for **BANDERILLERO**.
– DERIVATIVES **peonage** noun.
– ORIGIN from Portuguese *peão* and Spanish *peón*, from medieval Latin *pedo, pedon-* 'walker, foot soldier', from Latin *pes, ped-* 'foot'. Compare with **PAWN**[1].

peony /ˈpiːəni/ (also **paeony**) ▸ **noun** a herbaceous or shrubby plant of north temperate regions, which has long been cultivated for its showy flowers. ● Genus *Paeonia*, family Paeoniaceae.
– ORIGIN Old English *peonie*, via Latin from Greek *paiōnia*, from *Paiōn*, the name of the physician of the gods.

people ▸ **plural noun 1** human beings in general or considered collectively: *the earthquake killed 30,000 people | people think I'm mad.* ■ (**the people**) the citizens of a country, especially when considered in relation to those who govern them: *his reforms no longer have the support of the people.* ■ (**the people**) the members of a society without special rank or position: *he is very much a man of the people.* ■ (**the People**) US the state prosecution in a trial: *pre-trial statements made by the People's witnesses.*
2 (pl. **peoples**) [treated as sing. or pl.] the members of a particular nation, community, or ethnic group: *the native peoples of Canada.*
3 (**one's people**) one's supporters or employees: *I've had my people watching the house for some time now.*
4 (**one's people**) dated one's parents or relatives: *my people live in Warwickshire.*
▸ **verb** [with obj.] (of a group of people) inhabit (a place): *an arid mountain region peopled by warring clans.* ■ fill or be present in (a place or domain): *in her imagination the flat was suddenly peopled with ghosts.* ■ fill (a place) with inhabitants: *it was his intention to people the town with English colonists.*
– DERIVATIVES **peoplehood** noun.
– ORIGIN Middle English: from Anglo-Norman French *poeple*, from Latin *populus* 'populace'.

people carrier ▸ **noun** Brit. a motor vehicle with three rows of seats, enabling the transport of more passengers than the average car.

people meter ▸ **noun** (in North America) an electronic device used to record the television viewing habits of a household so that the information obtained can be used to compile ratings.

people mover ▸ **noun** informal a means of transport, in particular an automated system for carrying large numbers of people over short distances.

People of the Book ▸ **plural noun** see **BOOK**.

people person ▸ **noun** informal a person who enjoys or is particularly good at interacting with others.

people's court ▸ **noun 1** an unofficial court set up by a revolutionary or vigilante group.
2 an official court in a communist country.

people's democracy ▸ **noun** a political system in which power is regarded as being invested in the people.

People's Liberation Army (abbrev.: **PLA**) the armed forces of the People's Republic of China, including all its land, sea, and air forces. The PLA traces its origins to an unsuccessful uprising by communist-led troops against pro-Nationalist forces in Jiangxi province on 1 August 1927, a date celebrated annually as its anniversary.

Peoples of the Sea another term for **SEA PEOPLES**.

People's Republic of China official name (since 1949) of **CHINA**.

Peoria /piːˈɔːrɪə/ a river port and industrial city in central Illinois, on the Illinois River; pop. 114,114 (est. 2008). The city developed around a fort built by the French in 1680.
– ORIGIN named after the American Indians who occupied the area when the French arrived.

PEP ▸ **abbreviation** Brit. ■ personal equity plan. ■ Political and Economic Planning.

pep informal ▸ **verb** (**peps, pepping, pepped**) [with obj.] (**pep someone/thing up**) make someone or something more lively or interesting: *measures to pep up the economy.*
▸ **noun** [mass noun] energy and high spirits; liveliness: *he was an enthusiastic player, full of pep.*
– ORIGIN early 20th cent.: abbreviation of **PEPPER**.

peperino /ˌpɛpəˈriːnəʊ/ ▸ **noun** [mass noun] a light porous (especially brown) volcanic rock formed of small grains of sand, cinders, etc.
– ORIGIN 17th cent.: Italian, from *pepere* 'pepper' on account of its grainy appearance.

peperomia /ˌpɛpəˈrəʊmɪə/ ▸ **noun** a small fleshy-leaved tropical plant of the pepper family. Many are grown as houseplants, chiefly for their decorative foliage. ● Genus *Peperomia*, family Piperaceae.
– ORIGIN modern Latin, from Greek *peperi*.

peperoni ▸ **noun** variant spelling of **PEPPERONI**.

pepino /pɛˈpiːnəʊ/ ▸ **noun** (pl. **pepinos**) a spiny plant of the nightshade family, with edible purple-streaked yellow fruit, native to the Andes. ● *Solanum muricatum*, family Solanaceae.
– ORIGIN mid 19th cent.: from Spanish, literally 'cucumber' (because of the elongated shape of the fruit).

peplos /ˈpɛplɒs/ ▸ **noun** (pl. **peploses** or **peplos**) a rich outer robe or shawl worn by women in ancient Greece, hanging in loose folds and sometimes drawn over the head.
– ORIGIN Greek.

peplum /ˈpɛpləm/ ▸ **noun 1** a short gathered or pleated strip of fabric attached at the waist of a woman's jacket, dress, or blouse to create a hanging frill or flounce.
2 (in ancient Greece) a woman's loose outer tunic or shawl.
– ORIGIN late 17th cent.: via Latin from Greek *peplos*.

pepo /ˈpiːpəʊ/ ▸ **noun** (pl. **pepos**) any fleshy watery fruit of the melon or cucumber type, with numerous seeds and a firm rind.
– ORIGIN mid 19th cent.: from Latin, literally 'pumpkin', from Greek *pepōn* (from *pepōn sikuos* 'ripe gourd').

pepper ▸ **noun 1** [mass noun] a pungent hot-tasting powder prepared from dried and ground peppercorns, used as a spice or condiment to flavour food. ■ a reddish hot-tasting spice prepared from various forms of capsicum.
2 a capsicum, especially a sweet pepper.
3 a climbing vine with berries that are dried as black or white peppercorns. ● *Piper nigrum*, family Piperaceae. ■ used in names of other plants which are related or similar to this, e.g. **Jamaica pepper**, **water pepper**.
4 Baseball a practice game in which a fielder throws at close range to a batter who hits back to the fielder.
▸ **verb** [with obj.] **1** (usu. as adj. **peppered**) sprinkle or season (food) with pepper: *peppered beef.*
2 (usu. **be peppered with**) cover or fill with a liberal amount of scattered items: *the script is peppered with four-letter words.* ■ hit repeatedly with small missiles or gunshot: *another burst of enemy bullets peppered his defenceless body.* ■ archaic inflict severe punishment or suffering upon.
– ORIGIN Old English *piper, pipor*, of West Germanic origin; related to Dutch *peper* and German *Pfeffer*; via Latin from Greek *peperi*, from Sanskrit *pippali* 'berry, peppercorn'.

pepper-and-salt ▸ **adjective** flecked or speckled with intermingled dark and light shades: *his pepper-and-salt beard.*

pepperbox ▸ **noun 1** a gun or piece of artillery with a revolving set of barrels.
2 archaic a pepper pot.

peppercorn ▸ **noun** the dried berry of a climbing vine, used whole as a spice or ground to make pepper. ■ (**peppercorns**) S. African hair growing in tight curly tufts, characteristic of the Khoikhoi and San peoples.

peppercorn rent ▸ **noun** Brit. a very low or nominal rent.
– ORIGIN from the (formerly common) practice of stipulating the payment of a peppercorn as a nominal rent.

pepper dulse ▸ **noun** a dark red seaweed with branching fronds, growing on rocks. ● *Laurencia pinnatifida*, division Rhodophyta.

peppered moth ▸ **noun** a European moth of woods and gardens, which is typically white with black speckling. In industrial areas sooty brown forms predominate as a result of industrial melanism. ● *Biston betularia*, family Geometridae.

peppergrass ▸ **noun** US term for **PEPPERWORT**.

pepperidge ▸ **noun** a deciduous North American tree with colourful autumn foliage. Also called **TUPELO**. ● *Nyssa sylvatica*, family Nyssaceae.
– ORIGIN late 17th cent.: alteration of dialect *pipperidge*, denoting the barberry and its fruit, of unknown origin.

peppermint ▸ **noun 1** [mass noun] the aromatic leaves of a plant of the mint family, or an essential oil obtained from them, used as a flavouring in food. ■ [count noun] a sweet flavoured with peppermint oil.
2 [mass noun] the cultivated Old World plant which yields peppermint leaves or oil. ● *Mentha × piperita*, family Labiatae.
3 Austral. any of a number of trees or shrubs with peppermint-scented foliage, in particular: ● a gum tree with leaves that yield an aromatic essential oil (genus *Eucalyptus*, family Myrtaceae). ● a myrtle grown as an ornamental tree or shrub (genus *Agonis*, family Myrtaceae).
– DERIVATIVES **pepperminty** adjective.

pepperoni /ˌpɛpəˈrəʊni/ (also **peperoni**) ▸ **noun** [mass noun] beef and pork sausage seasoned with pepper.
– ORIGIN from Italian *peperone* 'chilli'.

pepper pot ▸ **noun 1** (N. Amer. **pepper shaker**) a container with a perforated top for sprinkling pepper.
2 a West Indian dish consisting of stewed meat or fish with vegetables, typically flavoured with cassareep.

pepper-shrike ▸ **noun** a tropical American songbird with mainly green and yellow plumage and a heavy bill like that of a shrike. ● Genus *Cyclarhis*, now in the family Vireonidae: two species.

pepper spray ▸ **noun** an aerosol spray containing oils derived from cayenne pepper, irritant to the eyes and respiratory passages and used as a disabling weapon.

pepper tree ▸ **noun** any of a number of shrubs or trees which have aromatic leaves or fruit with a pepper-like smell, in particular: ● an evergreen Peruvian tree, grown as a shade tree in hot countries (*Schinus molle*, family Anacardiaceae). ● another term for **KAWA-KAWA**.

pepperwort ▸ **noun** a wild cress, particularly one with pungent leaves. ● Genus *Lepidium*, family Cruciferae.

peppery ▸ **adjective 1** strongly flavoured with pepper or other hot spices: *a hot, peppery dish.* ■ having a flavour or scent like that of pepper.
2 (of a person) irritable and sharp-tongued: *retired generals are expected to be peppery.*
– DERIVATIVES **pepperiness** noun.

pep pill ▸ **noun** informal a pill containing a stimulant drug.

peppy ▸ **adjective** (**peppier, peppiest**) informal, chiefly N. Amer. lively and high-spirited: *a peppy and energetic woman.*
– DERIVATIVES **peppily** adverb, **peppiness** noun.

P

pep rally ▸ **noun** N. Amer. informal a meeting aimed at inspiring enthusiasm, especially one held before a sporting event.

pepsin ▸ **noun** [mass noun] Biochemistry the chief digestive enzyme in the stomach, which breaks down proteins into polypeptides.
– ORIGIN mid 19th cent.: from Greek *pepsis* 'digestion' + **-IN**[1].

pepsinogen /pɛpˈsɪnədʒ(ə)n/ ▸ **noun** [mass noun] Biochemistry a substance which is secreted by the stomach wall and converted into the enzyme pepsin by gastric acid.

pep talk ▸ **noun** informal a talk intended to make someone feel more courageous or enthusiastic.

peptic ▸ **adjective** relating to digestion, especially that in which pepsin is concerned.
– ORIGIN mid 17th cent.: from Greek *peptikos* 'able to digest'.

peptic gland ▸ **noun** Anatomy a gland that secretes the gastric juice containing pepsin.

peptic ulcer ▸ **noun** a lesion in the lining (mucosa) of the digestive tract, typically in the stomach or duodenum, caused by the digestive action of pepsin and stomach acid.

peptidase /ˈpɛptɪdeɪz/ ▸ **noun** Biochemistry an enzyme which breaks down peptides into amino acids.

peptide /ˈpɛptʌɪd/ ▸ **noun** Biochemistry a compound consisting of two or more amino acids linked in a chain, the carboxyl group of each acid being joined to the amino group of the next by a bond of the type –OC–NH–.
– ORIGIN early 20th cent.: from German *Peptid*, back-formation from *Polypeptid* 'polypeptide'.

peptidoglycan /pɛpˌtʌɪdə(ʊ)ˈglʌɪkan/ ▸ **noun** [mass noun] Biochemistry a substance forming the cell walls of many bacteria, consisting of glycosaminoglycan chains interlinked with short peptides.

peptone /ˈpɛptəʊn/ ▸ **noun** [mass noun] Biochemistry a soluble protein formed in the early stage of protein breakdown during digestion. ■ (also **peptone water**) a solution of peptone in saline, used as a liquid medium for growing bacteria.
– ORIGIN mid 19th cent.: from German *Pepton*, from Greek *pepton*, neuter of *peptos* 'cooked, digested'.

Pepys /piːps/, Samuel (1633–1703), English diarist and naval administrator. He is particularly remembered for his *Diary* (1660–9), which describes events such as the Great Plague and the Fire of London.

Péquiste /peɪˈkiːst/ ▸ **noun** Canadian a member or supporter of the Parti Québecois, a political party originally advocating independent rule for Quebec.
– ORIGIN from the French pronunciation of the abbreviation *PQ* + the noun suffix *-iste*.

P

Pequot /ˈpiːkwɒt/ ▸ **noun** (pl. **same** or **Pequots**) **1** a member of an American Indian people of southern New England.
2 [mass noun] the extinct Algonquian language of the Pequot.
▸ **adjective** relating to the Pequot or their language.
– ORIGIN from Narragansett *paquatanog* 'destroyers'.

per ▸ **preposition 1** for each (used with units to express a rate): *he charges £2 per square yard.*
2 archaic by means of: *send it per express.*
3 Heraldry divided by a line in the direction of: *per saltire.*
– PHRASES **as per** in accordance with: *made as per instructions.* **as per usual** as usual.
– ORIGIN Latin, 'through, by means of'; partly via Old French.

per- ▸ **prefix 1** through; all over: *perforation | pervade.* ■ completely; very: *perfect | perturb.* ■ to destruction; to ill effect: *perdition | pervert.*
2 Chemistry having the maximum proportion of some element in combination: *peroxide | permanganate.*
– ORIGIN from Latin (see **PER**).

peracute ▸ **adjective** chiefly Veterinary Medicine (of a disease) very severe and of very short duration, generally proving quickly fatal.
– ORIGIN late Middle English: from Latin *peracutus* 'very sharp'.

peradventure archaic or humorous ▸ **adverb** perhaps: *peradventure I'm not as wealthy as he is.*
▸ **noun** [mass noun] uncertainty or doubt as to whether something is the case: *that shows beyond peradventure the strength of the economy.*
– ORIGIN Middle English: from Old French *per* (or *par*) *auenture* 'by chance'.

Perak /ˈpɛːrə, pɛˈrak/ a state of Malaysia, on the west side of the Malay Peninsula; capital, Ipoh. It is a major tin-mining centre.

peralkaline ▸ **adjective** Geology (of an igneous rock) containing a higher proportion (taken together) of sodium and potassium than of aluminium.

peraluminous ▸ **adjective** Geology (of an igneous rock) containing a higher proportion of aluminium than of sodium and potassium (taken together).

perambulate /pəˈrambjʊleɪt/ ▸ **verb** [no obj.] formal or humorous walk or travel through or round a place: *the locals perambulate up and down the thoroughfare* | [with obj.] *she perambulated the square.* ■ [with obj.] Brit. historical walk round (a parish, forest, etc.) in order to officially assert and record its boundaries.
– DERIVATIVES **perambulation** noun, **perambulatory** adjective.
– ORIGIN late Middle English: from Latin *perambulat-* 'walked about', from the verb *perambulare*, from *per-* 'all over' + *ambulare* 'to walk'.

perambulator ▸ **noun** old-fashioned term for **PRAM**[1].

per annum ▸ **adverb** for each year (used in financial contexts): *an average growth rate of 2 per cent per annum.*
– ORIGIN early 17th cent.: Latin.

p/e ratio ▸ **abbreviation** price–earnings ratio.

perborate /pəˈbɔːreɪt/ ▸ **noun** Chemistry a salt which is an oxidized borate containing a peroxide linkage, especially a sodium salt of this kind used as a bleach.

percale /pəˈkeɪl/ ▸ **noun** [mass noun] a closely woven fine cotton fabric.
– ORIGIN early 17th cent.: from French, of unknown origin.

per capita /pəː ˈkapɪtə/ (also **per caput** /ˈkapʊt/) ▸ **adverb & adjective** for each person; in relation to people taken individually: [as adv.] *the state had fewer banks per capita than elsewhere | lower than average per capita spending.*
– ORIGIN late 17th cent.: Latin, literally 'by heads'.

perceive ▸ **verb** [with obj.] **1** become aware or conscious of (something); come to realize or understand: *his mouth fell open as he perceived the truth* | [with clause] *he was quick to perceive that there was little future in such arguments.* ■ become aware of (something) by the use of one of the senses, especially that of sight: *he perceived the faintest of flushes creeping up her neck.*
2 interpret or regard (someone or something) in a particular way: *if Guy does not perceive himself as disabled, nobody else should* | [with obj. and infinitive] *some geographers perceive hydrology to be a separate field of scientific enquiry.*
– DERIVATIVES **perceivable** adjective, **perceiver** noun.
– ORIGIN Middle English: from a variant of Old French *perçoivre*, from Latin *percipere* 'seize, understand', from *per-* 'entirely' + *capere* 'take'.

per cent (also US **percent**) ▸ **adverb** by a specified amount in or for every hundred: *new car sales may be down nineteen per cent | staff rejected a 1.8 per cent increase.*
▸ **noun** one part in every hundred: *a reduction of half a per cent or so in price.* ■ the rate, number, or amount in each hundred.
– ORIGIN mid 16th cent.: from **PER** + **CENT**, perhaps an abbreviation of pseudo-Latin *per centum*.

percentage ▸ **noun** a rate, number, or amount in each hundred: *the percentage of Caesareans at the hospital was three per cent higher than the national average* | [as modifier] *a large percentage increase.* ■ any proportion or share in relation to a whole: *only a tiny percentage of the day trippers are aware of the village's gastronomic distinction.* ■ an amount, such as an allowance or commission, that is a proportion of a larger sum of money: *I hope to be on a percentage.* ■ [mass noun] informal personal benefit or advantage: *I don't see the percentage in selling perfectly good furniture.*
– PHRASES **play the percentages** (or **the percentage game**) informal choose a safe and methodical course of action when calculating the odds in favour of success. [referring to the calculated percentage of success from statistics.]

percentage point ▸ **noun** a unit of one per cent: *interest rates rose by 1.75 percentage points.*

-percenter ▸ **combining form 1** denoting a member of a group forming a specified and usually small percentage of the population: *he was a one-percenter, riding outside of the law.*
2 denoting a person who takes commission at a specified rate: [as modifier] *ten-percenter agents.* ■ denoting something whose value is estimated as a specified percentage: [as modifier] *five-percenter Treasury bonds.*

percentile /pəˈsɛntʌɪl/ ▸ **noun** Statistics each of the 100 equal groups into which a population can be divided according to the distribution of values of a particular variable. ■ each of the 99 intermediate values of a random variable which divide a frequency distribution into 100 such groups.

percept /ˈpəːsɛpt/ ▸ **noun** Philosophy an object of perception; something that is perceived. ■ a mental concept that is developed as a consequence of the process of perception.
– ORIGIN mid 19th cent.: from Latin *perceptum* 'something perceived', neuter past participle of *percipere* 'seize, understand', on the pattern of *concept*.

perceptible ▸ **adjective** (especially of a slight movement or change of state) able to be seen or noticed: *a perceptible decline in public confidence.*
– DERIVATIVES **perceptibility** noun, **perceptibly** adverb.
– ORIGIN late Middle English: from late Latin *perceptibilis*, from Latin *percipere* 'seize, understand' (see **PERCEIVE**).

perception ▸ **noun** [mass noun] **1** the ability to see, hear, or become aware of something through the senses: *the normal limits to human perception.* ■ awareness of something through the senses: *the perception of pain.* ■ Psychology & Zoology the neurophysiological processes, including memory, by which an organism becomes aware of and interprets external stimuli.
2 the way in which something is regarded, understood, or interpreted: *Hollywood's perception of the tastes of the American public* | [count noun] *we need to challenge many popular perceptions of old age.* ■ intuitive understanding and insight: *'He wouldn't have accepted,' said my mother with unusual perception.*
– DERIVATIVES **perceptional** adjective.
– ORIGIN late Middle English: from Latin *perceptio(n-)*, from the verb *percipere* 'seize, understand' (see **PERCEIVE**).

perceptive ▸ **adjective** having or showing sensitive insight: *an extraordinarily perceptive account of their relationship.*
– DERIVATIVES **perceptively** adverb, **perceptiveness** noun, **perceptivity** /-ˈtɪvɪti/ noun.

perceptron /pəˈsɛptrɒn/ ▸ **noun** a computer model or computerized machine devised to represent or simulate the ability of the brain to recognize and discriminate.

perceptual ▸ **adjective** relating to the ability to interpret or become aware of something through the senses: *a patient with perceptual problems who cannot judge distances.*
– DERIVATIVES **perceptually** adverb.

Perceval[1] /ˈpəːsɪv(ə)l/ a legendary figure dating back to ancient times, found in French, German, and English poetry from the late 12th century onwards. He is the father of Lohengrin and the hero of a number of legends, some of which are associated with the Holy Grail. Also called **PARSIFAL**.

Perceval[2] /ˈpəːsɪv(ə)l/, Spencer (1762–1812), British Tory statesman, Prime Minister 1809–12. He was shot dead in the lobby of the House of Commons by a bankrupt merchant who blamed the government for his insolvency.

perch[1] ▸ **noun** an object on which a bird alights or roosts, typically a branch or horizontal bar. ■ a place where someone or something rests or sits, especially one that is high or precarious: *Marian looked down from her perch in a beech tree above the road.*
▸ **verb** [no obj., with adverbial of place] (of a bird) alight or rest on something: *a herring gull perched on the rails.* ■ (of a person) sit on something high or narrow: *Eve perched on the side of the armchair.* ■ (**be perched**) (of a building) be situated above or on the edge of something: *the fortress is perched on a crag in the mountains.* ■ [with obj.] (**perch someone/thing on**) set or balance someone or something on: *Peter perched a pair of gold-rimmed spectacles on his nose.*
– PHRASES **knock someone off their perch** informal cause someone to lose a position of superiority or pre-eminence: *will this knock London off its perch as Europe's leading financial centre?*
– DERIVATIVES **percher** noun.
– ORIGIN late Middle English: the noun from **PERCH**[3]; the verb from Old French *percher*.

perch[2] ▸ **noun** (pl. **same** or **perches**) an edible freshwater fish with a high spiny dorsal fin, dark vertical bars on the body, and orange lower fins. ● Genus *Perca*, family Percidae (the **perch family**): three species, in particular

P. fluviatilis of Europe (also called **BASS**[2]), and the almost identical **yellow perch** (*P. flavescens*) of North America. The perch family also includes the pikeperches, ruffe, and darters. ■ used in names of other freshwater and marine fishes resembling or related to the perch, e.g. **climbing perch, pikeperch, sea perch, surfperch**.
– ORIGIN late Middle English: from Old French *perche*, via Latin from Greek *perkē*.

perch[3] ▶ **noun** historical, chiefly Brit. **1** a measure of length, especially for land, equal to a quarter of a chain or 5½ yards (approximately 5.029 m). Also called **POLE**[1], **ROD**.
2 (also **square perch**) a measure of area, especially for land, equal to 160th of an acre or 30¼ square yards (approximately 25.29 sq. metres). Also called **POLE**[1], **ROD, SQUARE POLE, SQUARE ROD**.
– ORIGIN Middle English (in the general sense 'pole, stick'): from Old French *perche*, from Latin *pertica* 'measuring rod, pole'.

perchance ▶ **adverb** archaic or literary by some chance; perhaps: *we dare not go ashore lest perchance we should fall into some snare*.
– ORIGIN Middle English: from Old French *par cheance* 'by chance'.

percheron /ˈpəːʃ(ə)rɒn/ ▶ **noun** a powerful draught horse of a grey or black breed, originally from France.
– ORIGIN late 19th cent.: from French, originally bred in le *Perche*, the name of a district of northern France.

perchlorate /pəˈklɔːreɪt/ ▶ **noun** Chemistry a salt or ester of perchloric acid.

perchloric acid /pəˈklɔːrɪk/ ▶ **noun** [mass noun] Chemistry a fuming toxic liquid with powerful oxidizing properties. ● Chem. formula: $HClO_4$.

perchloroethylene /pə,klɔːrəʊˈɛθɪliːn/ ▶ **noun** [mass noun] a toxic colourless volatile solvent used commonly as a dry-cleaning fluid. Also called **TETRACHLOROETHYLENE**. ● Chem. formula: $Cl_2C{=}CCl_2$.

percid /ˈpəːkɪd/ ▶ **noun** Zoology a fish of the perch family (Percidae).
– ORIGIN late 19th cent.: from modern Latin *Percidae* (plural), from Latin *perca* 'perch'.

perciform /ˈpəːsɪfɔːm/ ▶ **adjective** Zoology relating to fishes of an order (Perciformes) that comprises those resembling the perches. This is the largest vertebrate order and includes nearly half of all bony fishes.
▶ **noun** a perciform fish.
– ORIGIN late 19th cent.: from modern Latin *Perciformes* (plural), from Latin *perca* 'perch' + *forma* 'shape'.

percipience /pəˈsɪpɪəns/ ▶ **noun** [mass noun] the quality of having sensitive insight or understanding; perceptiveness.

percipient /pəˈsɪpɪənt/ ▶ **adjective** having good insight or understanding; perceptive: *he is a percipient interpreter of the public mood*.
▶ **noun** (especially in philosophy or with reference to psychic phenomena) a person who is able to perceive things.
– DERIVATIVES **percipiently** adverb.
– ORIGIN mid 17th cent.: from Latin *percipient-* 'seizing, understanding', from the verb *percipere*.

percoid /ˈpəːkɔɪd/ Zoology ▶ **noun** a fish of a large group that includes the perches, basses, jacks, snappers, grunts, sea breams, and drums. ● Superfamily Percoidea: many families.
▶ **adjective** relating to or denoting fish of this group.
– ORIGIN mid 19th cent.: from modern Latin *Percoïdes* (plural), from Latin *perca* 'perch'.

percolate ▶ **verb 1** [no obj., with adverbial of direction] (of a liquid or gas) filter gradually through a porous surface or substance: *the water percolating through the soil may leach out minerals*. ■ spread gradually through an area or group of people: *continental ideas on art, science, and architecture percolated from Venice to London*.
2 [no obj.] (of coffee) be prepared in a percolator: *he put some coffee on to percolate*. ■ [with obj.] prepare (coffee) in a percolator: (as adj. **percolated**) *freshly percolated coffee*. ■ [no obj.] US be or become full of lively activity or excitement: *the night was percolating with an expectant energy*.
– DERIVATIVES **percolation** noun.
– ORIGIN early 17th cent.: from Latin *percolat-* 'strained through', from the verb *percolare*, from *per-* 'through' + *colare* 'to strain' (from *colum* 'strainer').

percolator ▶ **noun** a machine for making coffee, consisting of a pot in which boiling water is circulated through a small chamber that holds the ground beans.

per contra /pəː ˈkɒntrə/ ▶ **adverb** formal on the other hand: *he had worked very hard on the place; she, per contra, had little to do*.
▶ **noun** the opposite side of an account or an assessment.
– ORIGIN mid 16th cent.: from Italian.

per curiam /ˈkjʊərɪam/ Law ▶ **adverb & adjective** by or denoting decision of an appellate court in unanimous agreement, written anonymously.
▶ **noun** a decision taken per curiam.
– ORIGIN Latin, literally 'by a court'.

percuss /pəˈkʌs/ ▶ **verb** [with obj.] Medicine gently tap (a part of the body) with a finger or an instrument as part of a diagnosis: *the bladder was percussed*.
– ORIGIN mid 16th cent. (in the general sense 'give a blow to'): from Latin *percuss-* 'struck forcibly', from the verb *percutere*, from *per-* 'through' + *quatere* 'to shake, strike'.

percussion ▶ **noun** [mass noun] **1** musical instruments played by striking with the hand or with a stick or beater, or by shaking, including drums, cymbals, xylophones, gongs, bells, and rattles: [as modifier] *percussion instruments*.
2 the striking of one solid object with or against another with some degree of force: *the clattering percussion of objects striking the walls and the shutters*. ■ Medicine the action of tapping a part of the body as part of a diagnosis.
– DERIVATIVES **percussionist** noun (sense 1).
– ORIGIN late Middle English: from Latin *percussio(n-)*, from the verb *percutere* 'to strike forcibly' (see **PERCUSS**).

percussion cap ▶ **noun** a small amount of explosive powder contained in metal or paper and exploded by striking, used in toy guns and formerly in firearms.

percussion drill ▶ **noun** another term for **HAMMER DRILL**.

percussive ▶ **adjective** relating to or produced by percussion: *percussive sounds*.
– DERIVATIVES **percussively** adverb, **percussiveness** noun.

percutaneous /,pəːkjʊˈteɪnɪəs/ ▶ **adjective** Medicine made, done, or effected through the skin.
– DERIVATIVES **percutaneously** adverb.
– ORIGIN late 19th cent.: from Latin *per cutem* 'through the skin' + **-ANEOUS**.

Percy, Sir Henry (1364–1403), English soldier; known as **Hotspur** or **Harry Hotspur**. Son of the 1st Earl of Northumberland, he was killed at the battle of Shrewsbury during his father's revolt against Henry IV.

per diem /pəː ˈdiːɛm, ˈdʌɪɛm/ ▶ **adverb & adjective** for each day (used in financial contexts): [as adv.] *he agreed to pay at certain specified rates per diem* | [as adj.] *they are now demanding a per diem rate*.
▶ **noun** an allowance or payment made for each day.
– ORIGIN early 16th cent.: Latin.

perdition /pəˈdɪʃ(ə)n/ ▶ **noun** [mass noun] (in Christian theology) a state of eternal punishment and damnation into which a sinful and unrepentant person passes after death. ■ complete and utter ruin: *she used her last banknote to buy herself a square meal before perdition*.
– ORIGIN late Middle English: from Old French *perdiciun*, from ecclesiastical Latin *perditio(n-)*, from Latin *perdere* 'destroy', from *per-* 'completely, to destruction' + the base of *dare* 'put'.

perdurable /pəˈdjʊərəb(ə)l/ ▶ **adjective** formal enduring continuously; imperishable.
– DERIVATIVES **perdurability** noun, **perdurably** adverb.
– ORIGIN late Middle English: via Old French from late Latin *perdurabilis*, from Latin *perdurare* 'endure'.

perdure /pəˈdjʊə/ ▶ **verb** [no obj.] formal, chiefly US remain in existence; endure.
– DERIVATIVES **perdurance** noun.
– ORIGIN late 15th cent.: from Old French *perdurer*, from Latin *perdurare* 'endure', from *per-* 'through' + *durare* 'to last'.

père /pɛː/ ▶ **noun** used after a surname to distinguish a father from a son of the same name: *Alexandre Dumas père*. Compare with **FILS**[2].
– ORIGIN French, literally 'father'.

Père David's deer ▶ **noun** a large deer with a red summer coat that turns dark grey in winter, and long antlers with backward pointing tines. Formerly a native of China, it is now found only in captivity. ● *Elaphurus davidianus*, family Cervidae.
– ORIGIN late 19th cent.: named after Father Armand *David* (1826–1900), French missionary and naturalist.

peregrinate /ˈpɛrɪgrɪ,neɪt/ ▶ **verb** [no obj., with adverbial] archaic or humorous travel or wander from place to place.
– DERIVATIVES **peregrinator** noun.
– ORIGIN late 16th cent. (earlier (Middle English) as *peregrination*): from Latin *peregrinat-* 'travelled abroad', from the verb *peregrinari*, from *peregrinus* 'foreign, travelling'.

peregrination ▶ **noun** literary or humorous a journey, especially a long or meandering one: *she kept Aunt Ilsa company on her peregrinations*.

peregrine /ˈpɛrɪgrɪn/ ▶ **noun** (also **peregrine falcon**) a powerful falcon found on most continents, breeding chiefly on mountains and coastal cliffs and much used for falconry. ● *Falco peregrinus*, family Falconidae.
▶ **adjective** archaic coming from another country; foreign or outlandish: *peregrine species of grass*.
– ORIGIN late Middle English: from Latin *peregrinus* 'foreign', from *peregre* 'abroad', from *per-* 'through' + *ager* 'field'. The falcon's name is a translation of the modern Latin taxonomic name, literally 'pilgrim falcon', because falconers' birds were caught fully grown on migration, not taken from the nest.

pereiopod /pəˈrʌɪəpɒd, -ˈrɪː-/ ▶ **noun** Zoology each of the eight walking limbs of a crustacean such as a crab or lobster, growing from the thorax.
– ORIGIN late 19th cent.: from Greek *peraioōn* 'transporting' (present participle of *peraioun*) + *pous, pod-* 'foot'.

Perelman /ˈpɛrəlmən/, S. J. (1904–79), American humorist and writer; full name *Sidney Joseph Perelman*. In the early 1930s he worked in Hollywood as a scriptwriter, and from 1934 his name is linked with the *New Yorker* magazine, for whom he wrote most of his short stories and sketches.

peremptory /pəˈrɛm(p)t(ə)ri, ˈpɛrɪm-/ ▶ **adjective** insisting on immediate attention or obedience, especially in a brusquely imperious way: *'Just do it!' came the peremptory reply*. ■ Law not open to appeal or challenge; final: *a peremptory order of the court*.
– DERIVATIVES **peremptorily** adverb, **peremptoriness** noun.
– ORIGIN late Middle English (as a legal term): via Anglo-Norman French from Latin *peremptorius* 'deadly, decisive', from *perempt-* 'destroyed, cut off', from the verb *perimere*, from *per-* 'completely' + *emere* 'take, buy'.

peremptory challenge ▶ **noun** Law a defendant's or lawyer's objection to a proposed juror, made without needing to give a reason.

perennate /ˈpɛrəneɪt/ ▶ **verb** [no obj.] (usu. as adj. **perennating**) Botany (of a plant or part of a plant) live through a number of years, usually with an annual quiescent period.
– DERIVATIVES **perennation** noun.
– ORIGIN early 17th cent.: from Latin *perennat-* 'continued for many years' (from the verb *perennare*) + **-ATE**[3].

perennial ▶ **adjective 1** lasting or existing for a long or apparently infinite time; enduring or continually recurring: *his perennial distrust of the media* | *perennial manifestations of urban crisis*. ■ [attrib.] apparently permanently engaged in a specified role or way of life: *he's a perennial student*.
2 (of a plant) living for several years: *cow parsley is perennial*. Compare with **ANNUAL, BIENNIAL**.
3 (of a stream or spring) flowing throughout the year.
▶ **noun** a perennial plant.
– DERIVATIVES **perennially** adverb.
– ORIGIN mid 17th cent. (in the sense 'remaining leafy throughout the year, evergreen'): from Latin *perennis* 'lasting the year through' + **-IAL**.

perentie /pəˈrɛnti, ˈprɛnti/ (also **perenty**) ▶ **noun** (pl. **perenties**) a large brown and yellow monitor lizard which lives in arid regions of Australia. ● *Varanus giganteus*, family Varanidae.
– ORIGIN early 20th cent.: probably from Diyara *pirindi*.

Peres /ˈpɛrɛz/, Shimon (b.1923), Polish-born Israeli statesman, Prime Minister 1984–6 and 1995–6; President since 2007; Polish name *Szymon Perski*. As Foreign Minister under Yitzhak Rabin he played a major role in negotiating the PLO–Israeli peace accord (1993). Nobel Peace Prize (1994), shared with Rabin and Yasser Arafat.

P

perestroika /ˌperɪˈstrɔɪkə/ ▶ **noun** [mass noun] (in the former Soviet Union) the policy or practice of restructuring or reforming the economic and political system. First proposed by Leonid Brezhnev in 1979 and actively promoted by Mikhail Gorbachev, perestroika originally referred to increased automation and labour efficiency, but came to entail greater awareness of economic markets and the ending of central planning. See also **GLASNOST**.
– ORIGIN Russian, literally 'restructuring'.

Pérez de Cuéllar /ˌperɛz də ˈkweɪjɑː/, Spanish /ˌperes de ˈkwejar, ˌpereθ/, Javier (b.1920), Peruvian diplomat, Secretary General of the United Nations 1982–91.

perfect ▶ **adjective** /ˈpəːfɪkt/ **1** having all the required or desirable elements, qualities, or characteristics; as good as it is possible to be: *she strove to be the perfect wife* | *life certainly isn't perfect at the moment.* ■ free from any flaw or defect in condition or quality; faultless: *the equipment was in perfect condition.* ■ precisely accurate; exact: *a perfect circle.* ■ highly suitable for someone or something; exactly right: *Giles was perfect for her—ten years older and with his own career.* ■ dated thoroughly trained in or conversant with: *she was* **perfect in** *French.*
2 [attrib.] absolute; complete (used for emphasis): *a perfect stranger* | *all that Joseph said made perfect sense to me.*
3 Mathematics (of a number) equal to the sum of its positive divisors, e.g. the number 6, whose divisors (1, 2, 3) also add up to 6.
4 Grammar (of a tense) denoting a completed action or a state or habitual action which began in the past. The perfect tense is formed in English with *have* or *has* and the past participle, as in *they have eaten* and *they have been eating* (**present perfect**), *they had eaten* (**past perfect**), and *they will have eaten* (**future perfect**).
5 Botany (of a flower) having both stamens and carpels present and functional. ■ Entomology (of an insect) fully adult and (typically) winged.
6 Botany denoting the stage or state of a fungus in which the sexually produced spores are formed.
▶ **verb** /pəˈfɛkt/ [with obj.] make (something) completely free from faults or defects; make as good as possible: *he's busy perfecting his bowling technique.* ■ archaic bring to completion; finish. ■ complete (a printed sheet of paper) by printing the second side. ■ Law satisfy the necessary conditions or requirements for the transfer of (a gift, title, etc.).
▶ **noun** /ˈpəːfɪkt/ (**the perfect**) Grammar the perfect tense.
– DERIVATIVES **perfecter** noun, **perfectibility** noun, **perfectible** adjective, **perfectness** noun.
– ORIGIN Middle English: from Old French *perfet*, from Latin *perfectus* 'completed', from the verb *perficere*, from *per-* 'through, completely' + *facere* 'do'.

P

perfecta /pəˈfɛktə/ ▶ **noun** N. Amer. a bet in which the first two places in a race must be predicted in the correct order. Compare with **QUINELLA**.
– ORIGIN 1970s: from Latin American Spanish *quiniela perfecta* 'perfect quinella'.

perfect binding ▶ **noun** [mass noun] a form of bookbinding in which the leaves are bound by gluing rather than sewing.

perfect cadence ▶ **noun** Music a cadence in which the chord of the dominant immediately precedes that of the tonic.

perfect competition ▶ **noun** [mass noun] the situation prevailing in a market in which buyers and sellers are so numerous and well informed that all elements of monopoly are absent and the market price of a commodity is beyond the control of individual buyers and sellers.

perfect fifth ▶ **noun** Music see **FIFTH**.

perfect fourth ▶ **noun** Music see **FOURTH**.

perfect gas ▶ **noun** another term for **IDEAL GAS**.

perfection ▶ **noun** [mass noun] the state or quality of being perfect: *the satiny perfection of her skin* | *his pursuit of golfing perfection.* ■ a person or thing perceived as the embodiment of such a state or quality: *I am told that she is perfection itself.* ■ the action or process of improving something until it is faultless: *among the key tasks was the perfection of new mechanisms of economic management.*
– PHRASES **to perfection** in a way that could not be better; perfectly: *a blue suit that showed off her blonde hair to perfection.*
– ORIGIN Middle English (in the sense 'completeness'): via Old French from Latin *perfectio(n-)*, from *perficere* 'to complete' (see **PERFECT**).

perfectionism ▶ **noun** [mass noun] refusal to accept any standard short of perfection. ■ Philosophy a doctrine holding that perfection is attainable, especially the theory that human moral or spiritual perfection should be or has been attained.

perfectionist ▶ **noun** a person who refuses to accept any standard short of perfection: *he was a perfectionist who worked slowly.*
▶ **adjective** refusing to accept any standard short of perfection.
– DERIVATIVES **perfectionistic** adjective.

perfective Grammar ▶ **adjective** denoting or relating to an aspect of verbs in Slavic languages that expresses completed action. The opposite of **IMPERFECTIVE**.
▶ **noun** (**the perfective**) the perfective aspect.

perfectly ▶ **adverb** in a manner or way that could not be better: *the ring fitted perfectly* | [as submodifier] *perfectly clean glass bottles.* ■ [as submodifier] used for emphasis, especially in order to assert something that has been challenged or doubted: *you know perfectly well I can't stay.*

perfecto ▶ **noun** (pl. **perfectos**) a type of cigar that is thick in the centre and tapered at each end.
– ORIGIN late 19th cent.: Spanish, literally 'perfect'.

perfect pitch ▶ **noun** [mass noun] the ability to recognize the pitch of a note or produce any given note; a sense of absolute pitch.

perfect square ▶ **noun** another term for **SQUARE NUMBER**.

perfect storm ▶ **noun** a particularly violent storm arising from a rare combination of adverse meteorological factors. ■ an especially bad situation caused by a combination of unfavourable circumstances: *the past two years have been a perfect storm for the travel industry.*

perfervid /pəˈfəːvɪd/ ▶ **adjective** literary intense and impassioned: *perfervid nationalism.*
– ORIGIN mid 19th cent.: from modern Latin *perfervidus*, from Latin *per-* 'utterly' + *fervidus* 'glowing hot, fiery'.

perfidious /pəˈfɪdɪəs/ ▶ **adjective** literary deceitful and untrustworthy: *a perfidious lover.*
– DERIVATIVES **perfidiously** adverb, **perfidiousness** noun.
– ORIGIN late 16th cent.: from Latin *perfidiosus*, from *perfidia* 'treachery'.

perfidy /ˈpəːfɪdi/ ▶ **noun** [mass noun] literary the state of being deceitful and untrustworthy.
– ORIGIN late 16th cent.: via French from Latin *perfidia*, from *perfidus* 'treacherous', based on *per-* 'to ill effect' + *fides* 'faith'.

perfin /ˈpəːfɪn/ ▶ **noun** Philately a postage stamp perforated with the initials or insignia of an organization, especially to prevent misuse.
– ORIGIN 1950s: from *perf(orated) in(itials)*.

perfoliate /pəˈfəʊlɪət/ ▶ **adjective** Botany (of a stalkless leaf or bract) extended at the base to encircle the node, so that the stem apparently passes through it. ■ (of a plant) having perfoliate leaves.
– ORIGIN late 17th cent.: from modern Latin *perfoliatus*, from Latin *per-* 'through' + *foliatus* 'leaved'.

perforate ▶ **verb** /ˈpəːfəreɪt/ [with obj.] (often as adj. **perforated**) pierce and make a hole or holes in: *a perforated appendix.* ■ make a row of small holes in (paper) so that a part may be torn off easily.
▶ **adjective** /ˈpəːf(ə)rət/ Biology & Medicine perforated: *a perforate shell.*
– DERIVATIVES **perforator** /ˈpəːfəreɪtə/ noun.
– ORIGIN late Middle English (as an adjective): from Latin *perforat-* 'pierced through', from the verb *perforare*, from *per-* 'through' + *forare* 'pierce'.

perforation ▶ **noun** a hole made by boring or piercing: *the perforations allow water to enter the well.* ■ a small hole or row of small holes punched in a sheet of paper, e.g. of postage stamps, so that a part can be torn off easily. ■ [mass noun] the action or state of perforating or being perforated: *there was evidence of intestinal perforation.*
– ORIGIN late Middle English: from medieval Latin *perforatio(n-)*, from the verb *perforare* (see **PERFORATE**).

perforce ▶ **adverb** formal used to express necessity or inevitability: *amateurs, perforce, have to settle for less expensive solutions.*
– ORIGIN Middle English: from Old French *par force* 'by force'.

perforin /ˈpəːfərɪn/ ▶ **noun** [mass noun] Biochemistry a protein, released by killer cells of the immune system, which destroys targeted cells by creating lesions like pores in their membranes.
– ORIGIN 1980s: from the verb **PERFORATE** + **-IN**[1].

perform ▶ **verb** [with obj.] **1** carry out, accomplish, or fulfil (an action, task, or function): *I have my duties to perform.* ■ [no obj., usu. with adverbial] work, function, or do something well or to a specified standard: *the car performs well at low speeds* | *our £120 million investment in the company is not performing at present.* ■ [no obj.] informal have successful or satisfactory sexual intercourse with someone.
2 present (a form of entertainment) to an audience: *the play has already been performed in Britain.* ■ [no obj.] entertain an audience, typically by acting, singing, or dancing on stage: *the band will be performing live in Hyde Park.*
– DERIVATIVES **performability** noun, **performable** adjective.
– ORIGIN Middle English: from Anglo-Norman French *parfourmer*, alteration (by association with *forme* 'form') of Old French *parfournir*, from *par* 'through, to completion' + *fournir* 'furnish, provide'.

performance ▶ **noun 1** an act of presenting a play, concert, or other form of entertainment: *Don Giovanni had its first performance in 1787.* ■ an act of performing a dramatic role, song, or piece of music: *Bailey gives a sound performance as the doctor.* ■ informal, chiefly Brit. a display of exaggerated behaviour or a process involving a great deal of unnecessary time and effort; a fuss: *he stopped to fasten his shoelace and seemed to be making quite a performance of it.*
2 [mass noun] the action or process of performing a task or function: *the continual performance of a single task reduces a man to the level of a machine.* ■ a task or operation seen in terms of how successfully it is performed: *pay increases are now being linked more closely to performance* | [count noun] *it was a tremendous all-round performance by Wigan.* ■ the capabilities of a machine, product, or vehicle: *the hardware is put through tests which assess the performance of the processor* | [as modifier] *a performance car.* ■ (also **linguistic performance**) Linguistics an individual's use of a language, i.e. what a speaker actually says, including hesitations, false starts, and errors. Often contrasted with **COMPETENCE**.

performance art ▶ **noun** [mass noun] an art form that combines visual art with dramatic performance.
– DERIVATIVES **performance artist** noun.

performance bond ▶ **noun** a bond issued by a bank or other financial institution, guaranteeing the fulfilment of a particular contract.

performance poetry ▶ **noun** [mass noun] a form of poetry intended to be performed as a dramatic monologue or exchange and frequently involving extemporization.
– DERIVATIVES **performance poet** noun.

performative Linguistics & Philosophy ▶ **adjective** relating to or denoting an utterance by means of which the speaker performs a particular act (e.g. *I bet, I apologize, I promise*). Often contrasted with **CONSTATIVE**.
▶ **noun** a performative utterance.

performer ▶ **noun** a person who entertains an audience: *a circus performer.*

performing arts ▶ **plural noun** forms of creative activity that are performed in front of an audience, such as drama, music, and dance.

perfume /ˈpəːfjuːm/ ▶ **noun** [mass noun] a fragrant liquid typically made from essential oils extracted from flowers and spices, used to give a pleasant smell to one's body. ■ a pleasant smell: *the heady perfume of lilacs.*
▶ **verb** also /pəˈfjuːm/ [with obj.] give a pleasant smell to: *just one bloom of jasmine has the power to perfume a whole room.* ■ impregnate with perfume or a sweet-smelling substance: *the cream is perfumed with rosemary and iris extracts.* ■ apply perfume to: *her hair was oiled and perfumed.*
– DERIVATIVES **perfumy** adjective.
– ORIGIN mid 16th cent. (originally denoting pleasant-smelling smoke from a burning substance, especially one used in fumigation): from French *parfum* (noun), *parfumer* (verb), from obsolete Italian *parfumare*, literally 'to smoke through'.

perfumed /ˈpəːfjuːmd/ ▶ **adjective** naturally having or producing a sweet, pleasant smell: *perfumed soap.* ■ impregnated or scented with a sweet-smelling substance: *perfumed soap.*

perfumer ▶ **noun** a producer or seller of perfumes.

perfumery ▶ **noun** (pl. **perfumeries**) [mass noun] the action or business of producing or selling perfumes: *an oil used in perfumery.* ■ [count noun] a shop that sells perfumes.

perfunctory /pəˈfʌŋ(k)t(ə)ri/ ▶ **adjective** (of an action) carried out without real interest, feeling, or effort: *he gave a perfunctory nod.*
– DERIVATIVES **perfunctorily** adverb, **perfunctoriness** noun.
– ORIGIN late 16th cent.: from late Latin *perfunctorius* 'careless', from Latin *perfunct-* 'done with, discharged', from the verb *perfungi*.

perfusate /pəˈfjuːzeɪt/ ▶ **noun** Medicine a fluid used in perfusion.

perfuse ▶ **verb** [with obj.] permeate or suffuse with a liquid, colour, or quality: *the yellow light is perfused with white.* ■ Medicine supply (an organ or tissue) with a fluid by circulating it through blood vessels or other natural channels.
– DERIVATIVES **perfusion** noun, **perfusionist** noun.
– ORIGIN late Middle English (in the sense 'cause to flow through or away'): from Latin *perfus-* 'poured through', from the verb *perfundere*, from *per-* 'through' + *fundere* 'pour'.

Pergamum /ˈpəːɡəməm/ a city in ancient Mysia, in western Asia Minor, situated to the north of Izmir on a rocky hill close to the Aegean coast. The capital in the 3rd and 2nd centuries BC of the Attalid dynasty, it was one of the greatest and most beautiful of the Hellenistic cities and was famed for its cultural institutions, especially its library, which was second only to that at Alexandria.
– DERIVATIVES **Pergamene** /-ˌmiːn/ adjective & noun.

pergana ▶ **noun** variant spelling of **PARGANA**.

pergola /ˈpəːɡələ/ ▶ **noun** an arched structure in a garden or park consisting of a framework covered with climbing or trailing plants.
– ORIGIN mid 17th cent.: from Italian, from Latin *pergula* 'projecting roof', from *pergere* 'come or go forward'.

perhaps ▶ **adverb** used to express uncertainty or possibility: *perhaps I should have been frank with him.* ■ used when one does not wish to be too definite or assertive in the expression of an opinion: *perhaps not surprisingly, he was cautious about committing himself.* ■ used when making a polite request, offer, or suggestion: *would you perhaps consent to act as our guide?*
– ORIGIN late 15th cent.: from **PER** + **HAP**.

peri /ˈpɪəri/ ▶ **noun** (pl. **peris**) (in Persian mythology) a mythical superhuman being, originally represented as evil but subsequently as a good or graceful genie or fairy.
– ORIGIN from Persian *perī*.

peri- ▶ **prefix 1** round; about: *pericardium* | *peristyle*.
2 Astronomy denoting the point nearest to a specified celestial body: *perihelion* | *perilune*. Compare with **APO-**.
– ORIGIN from Greek *peri* 'about, around'.

perianal /ˌpɛrɪˈeɪnəl/ ▶ **adjective** Medicine situated in or affecting the area around the anus.

perianth /ˈpɛrɪanθ/ ▶ **noun** Botany the outer part of a flower, consisting of the calyx (sepals) and corolla (petals).
– ORIGIN early 18th cent.: from French *périanthe*, from modern Latin *perianthium*, from Greek *peri* 'around' + *anthos* 'flower'.

periapsis /ˌpɛrɪˈapsɪs/ ▶ **noun** (pl. **periapses** /-siːz/) Astronomy the point in the path of an orbiting body at which it is nearest to the body that it orbits.

periapt /ˈpɛrɪapt/ ▶ **noun** archaic an item worn as a charm or amulet.
– ORIGIN late 16th cent.: from French *périapte*, from Greek *periapton*, from *peri* 'around' + *haptein* 'fasten'.

periarticular /ˌpɛrɪɑːˈtɪkjʊlə/ ▶ **adjective** Medicine situated or occurring around a joint of the body.

periastron /ˌpɛrɪˈastrən/ ▶ **noun** Astronomy the point nearest to a star in the path of a body orbiting that star.
– ORIGIN mid 19th cent.: from **PERI-** 'around' + Greek *astron* 'star', on the pattern of *perigee* and *perihelion*.

pericarditis /ˌpɛrɪkɑːˈdʌɪtɪs/ ▶ **noun** [mass noun] Medicine inflammation of the pericardium.

pericardium /ˌpɛrɪˈkɑːdɪəm/ ▶ **noun** (pl. **pericardia** /-dɪə/) Anatomy the membrane enclosing the heart, consisting of an outer fibrous layer and an inner double layer of serous membrane.
– DERIVATIVES **pericardial** adjective.
– ORIGIN late Middle English: modern Latin, from Greek *perikardion*, from *peri* 'around' + *kardia* 'heart'.

pericarp ▶ **noun** Botany the part of a fruit formed from the wall of the ripened ovary.
– ORIGIN late 17th cent.: from French *péricarpe*, from Greek *perikarpion* 'pod, shell', from *peri-* 'around' + *karpos* 'fruit'.

pericentric inversion /ˌpɛrɪˈsɛntrɪk/ ▶ **noun** [mass noun] Genetics a reversal of the normal order of genes in a chromosome segment involving parts of a chromosome at both sides of the centromere.

perichondrium /ˌpɛrɪˈkɒndrɪəm/ ▶ **noun** Anatomy the connective tissue that envelops cartilage where it is not at a joint.
– ORIGIN mid 18th cent.: modern Latin, from **PERI-** 'around' + Greek *khondros* 'cartilage'.

periclase /ˈpɛrɪkleɪz, -s/ ▶ **noun** [mass noun] a colourless mineral consisting of magnesium oxide, occurring chiefly in marble and limestone.
– ORIGIN mid 19th cent.: from modern Latin *periclasia*, erroneously from Greek *peri* 'utterly' + *klasis* 'breaking' (because it cleaves perfectly).

Pericles /ˈpɛrɪkliːz/ (*c.*495–429 BC), Athenian statesman and general. A champion of Athenian democracy, he pursued an imperialist policy and masterminded Athenian strategy in the Peloponnesian War. He commissioned the building of the Parthenon in 447 and promoted a flourishing of Athenian culture.
– DERIVATIVES **Periclean** adjective.

periclinal /ˌpɛrɪˈklʌɪn(ə)l/ ▶ **adjective** Botany (of a cell wall) parallel to the surface of the meristem. ■ (of cell division) taking place by the formation of periclinal walls.
– DERIVATIVES **periclinally** adverb.
– ORIGIN late 19th cent.: from Greek *periklinēs* 'sloping on all sides', from *peri-* 'around' + *klinēs* 'sloping' (from the verb *klinein*).

pericope /pəˈrɪkəpi/ ▶ **noun** an extract from a text, especially a passage from the Bible.
– ORIGIN mid 17th cent.: via late Latin from Greek *perikopē* 'section', from *peri-* 'around' + *kopē* 'cutting' (from *koptein* 'to cut').

pericranium ▶ **noun** Anatomy the periosteum (vascular connective tissue) enveloping the skull.
– ORIGIN late Middle English: modern Latin, from Greek *peri-* 'around' + *kranion* 'skull'.

pericycle ▶ **noun** Botany a thin layer of plant tissue between the endodermis and the phloem.
– ORIGIN late 19th cent.: from Greek *perikuklos* 'spherical', from *perikukloun* 'encircle'.

pericyclic /ˌpɛrɪˈsʌɪklɪk, -ˈsɪk-/ ▶ **adjective 1** Chemistry relating to or denoting a reaction that involves a concerted rearrangement of bonding in which all the bonds broken or formed in the reaction lie on a closed ring, whether or not a cyclic molecule is involved.
2 Botany relating to a pericycle.

periderm ▶ **noun** [mass noun] Botany the corky outer layer of a plant stem formed in secondary thickening or as a response to injury or infection.
– DERIVATIVES **peridermal** adjective.
– ORIGIN mid 19th cent.: from **PERI-** 'around' + Greek *derma* 'skin'.

peridium /pɪˈrɪdɪəm/ ▶ **noun** (pl. **peridia** /-dɪə/) Botany the outer skin of a sporangium or other fruiting body of a fungus.
– ORIGIN early 19th cent.: from Greek *pēridion*, literally 'small wallet', diminutive of *pēra*.

peridot /ˈpɛrɪdɒt/ ▶ **noun** [mass noun] a green semi-precious variety of forsterite (olivine).
– ORIGIN early 18th cent.: from French, from Old French *peritot*, of unknown origin.

peridotite /ˈpɛrɪdɒtʌɪt/ ▶ **noun** [mass noun] Geology a dense, coarse-grained plutonic rock containing a large amount of olivine, believed to be the main constituent of the earth's mantle.
– DERIVATIVES **peridotitic** adjective.

perigee /ˈpɛrɪdʒiː/ ▶ **noun** Astronomy the point in the orbit of the moon or a satellite at which it is nearest to the earth. The opposite of **APOGEE**.
– ORIGIN late 16th cent.: from French *périgée*, via modern Latin from Greek *perigeion* 'close round the earth', from *peri-* 'around' + *gē* 'earth'.

periglacial ▶ **adjective** Geology relating to or denoting an area adjacent to a glacier or ice sheet or otherwise subject to repeated freezing and thawing.

Périgord /ˈpɛrɪɡɔː/, French /peʀiɡɔʀ/ an area of SW France, in the SW Massif Central. A former countship, it became a part of Navarre in 1470, becoming united with France in 1670.

perigynous /pəˈrɪdʒɪnəs/ ▶ **adjective** Botany (of a plant or flower) having the stamens and other floral parts at the same level as the carpels. Compare with **EPIGYNOUS**, **HYPOGYNOUS**.
– ORIGIN early 19th cent.: from modern Latin *perigynus* (from Greek *peri-* 'around' + *gunē* 'woman') + **-OUS**.

perihelion /ˌpɛrɪˈhiːlɪən/ ▶ **noun** (pl. **perihelia** /-lɪə/) Astronomy the point in the orbit of a planet, asteroid, or comet at which it is closest to the sun. The opposite of **APHELION**.
– ORIGIN mid 17th cent.: alteration of modern Latin *perihelium* (by substitution of the Greek inflection *-on*), from Greek *peri-* 'around' + *hēlios* 'sun'.

perikaryon /ˌpɛrɪˈkarɪən/ ▶ **noun** (pl. **perikarya** /-ˈkarɪə/) Physiology the cell body of a neuron, containing the nucleus.
– DERIVATIVES **perikaryal** adjective.

peril ▶ **noun** [mass noun] serious and immediate danger: *you could well place us both in peril* | *the movement is **in peril of** dying* | [count noun] *a setback to the state could present a peril to the regime.* ■ (**perils**) the risks or difficulties that arise from a particular situation or activity: *she first witnessed the perils of pop stardom a decade ago.*
▶ **verb** (**perils**, **perilling**, **perilled**; US **perils**, **periling**, **periled**) [with obj.] archaic expose to danger; threaten: *Jonathon perilled his life for love of David*
– PHRASES **at one's peril** at one's own risk (used in warnings): *neglect our advice at your peril.*
– ORIGIN Middle English: from Old French, from Latin *peric(u)lum* 'danger', from the base of *experiri* 'to try'.

perilous ▶ **adjective** full of danger or risk: *a perilous journey south.* ■ exposed to imminent risk of disaster or ruin: *the economy is in a perilous state.*
– DERIVATIVES **perilously** adverb, **perilousness** noun.
– ORIGIN Middle English: from Old French *perillous*, from Latin *periculosus*, from *periculum* 'danger' (see **PERIL**).

perilune /ˈpɛrɪluːn/ ▶ **noun** [mass noun] the point at which a spacecraft in lunar orbit is closest to the moon. The opposite of **APOLUNE**.
– ORIGIN 1960s: from **PERI-** 'around' + Latin *luna* 'moon', on the pattern of *perigee*.

perilymph ▶ **noun** [mass noun] Anatomy the fluid between the membraneous labyrinth of the ear and the bone which encloses it.
– DERIVATIVES **perilymphatic** adjective.

perimenopause ▶ **noun** the period of a woman's life shortly before the occurrence of the menopause.
– DERIVATIVES **perimenopausal** adjective.

perimeter ▶ **noun 1** the continuous line forming the boundary of a closed geometrical figure: *the perimeter of a rectangle.* ■ the outermost parts or boundary of an area or object: *the perimeter of the garden* | [as modifier] *a perimeter fence.* ■ Basketball an area away from the basket, beyond the reach of the defensive team.
2 an instrument for measuring the extent and characteristics of a person's field of vision.
– DERIVATIVES **perimetric** adjective.
– ORIGIN late Middle English: via Latin from Greek *perimetros*, based on *peri-* 'around' + *metron* 'measure'.

perimetry ▶ **noun** [mass noun] measurement of a person's field of vision.

perimysium /ˌpɛrɪˈmɪsɪəm/ ▶ **noun** [mass noun] Anatomy the sheath of connective tissue surrounding a bundle of muscle fibres.
– DERIVATIVES **perimysial** adjective.
– ORIGIN mid 19th cent.: modern Latin, from Greek *peri-* 'around' + *mus* 'muscle'.

perinatal ▶ **adjective** Medicine relating to the time, usually a number of weeks, immediately before and after birth.
– DERIVATIVES **perinatally** adverb.

perinatology /ˌpɛrɪneɪˈtɒlədʒi/ ▶ **noun** [mass noun] Medicine the branch of obstetrics dealing with the period around childbirth.
– DERIVATIVES **perinatologist** noun.

per incuriam /ˌpə(r) ɪnˈkjʊərɪam/ ▶ **adverb & adjective** Law through or characterized by lack of due regard to the law or the facts: [as adv.] *the decision was made per incuriam.*
– ORIGIN Latin, literally 'through lack of care'.

perineum /ˌpɛrɪˈniːəm/ ▶ **noun** (pl. **perinea**) Anatomy the area between the anus and the scrotum or vulva.
– DERIVATIVES **perineal** adjective.

– ORIGIN late Middle English: from late Latin, from Greek *perinaion*.

perineurium /ˌpɛrɪˈnjʊərɪəm/ ▶ **noun** [mass noun] Anatomy the sheath of connective tissue surrounding a bundle (fascicle) of nerve fibres within a nerve.
– DERIVATIVES **perineural** adjective.
– ORIGIN mid 19th cent.: modern Latin, from Greek *peri-* 'around' + *neuron* 'sinew'.

perinuclear /ˌpɛrɪˈnjuːklɪə/ ▶ **adjective** Biology situated or occurring around the nucleus of a cell.

period ▶ **noun 1** a length or portion of time: *he had long periods of depression* | *the period 1977–85* | *the training period is between 16 and 18 months.* ■ a portion of time in the life of a nation, civilization, etc. characterized by the same prevalent features or conditions: *the early medieval period.* ■ a major division of geological time that is a subdivision of an era and is itself subdivided into epochs: *the Cretaceous period.* ■ each of the set divisions of the day in a school allocated to a lesson or other activity. ■ each of the divisions of the playing time of a sporting event.
2 Physics the interval of time between successive occurrences of the same state in an oscillatory or cyclic phenomenon, such as a mechanical vibration, an alternating current, a variable star, or an electromagnetic wave. ■ Astronomy the time taken by a celestial object to rotate about its axis, or to make one circuit of its orbit. ■ Mathematics the interval between successive equal values of a periodic function.
3 (also **menstrual period**) a flow of blood and other material from the lining of the uterus, lasting for a few days and occurring in sexually mature women who are not pregnant at intervals of about one lunar month until the menopause.
4 N. Amer. a full stop. ■ informal, chiefly N. Amer. added to the end of a statement to indicate that no further discussion is possible or desirable: *he is the sole owner of the trademark, period.*
5 Chemistry a set of elements occupying a horizontal row in the periodic table.
6 Rhetoric a complex sentence, especially one consisting of several clauses, constructed as part of a formal speech or oration. ■ Music a complete idea, typically consisting of two or four phrases.
▶ **adjective** [attrib.] belonging to or characteristic of a past historical time, especially in style or design: *a splendid selection of period furniture.*
– PHRASES **put a period to** dated put an end to: *in dry climates, the onset of summer drought may put a period to plant activity.*
– ORIGIN late Middle English (denoting the time during which something, especially a disease, runs its course): from Old French *periode*, via Latin from Greek *periodos* 'orbit, recurrence, course', from *peri-* 'around' + *hodos* 'way, course'. The sense 'portion of time' dates from the early 17th cent.

P

periodate /pəːˈrʌɪədeɪt/ ▶ **noun** Chemistry a salt or ester of periodic acid.

periodic /ˌpɪərɪˈɒdɪk/ ▶ **adjective 1** appearing or occurring at intervals: *the periodic visits she made to her father.*
2 Chemistry relating to the periodic table of the elements.
3 relating to a rhetorical period.
– ORIGIN mid 17th cent.: from French *périodique*, or via Latin from Greek *periodikos* 'coming round at intervals', from *periodos* (see **PERIOD**).

periodic acid /ˌpəːrʌɪˈɒdɪk/ ▶ **noun** [mass noun] Chemistry a hygroscopic solid acid with strong oxidizing properties. ● Chem. formula: H_5IO_6.
– ORIGIN mid 19th cent.: from **PER-** (sense 2) + **IODIC ACID**.

periodical ▶ **noun** a magazine or newspaper published at regular intervals.
▶ **adjective** [attrib.] occurring or appearing at intervals; occasional: *she took periodical gulps of her tea.* ■ (of a magazine or newspaper) published at regular intervals: *Britain's best periodical art magazine.*
– DERIVATIVES **periodically** adverb.

periodical cicada ▶ **noun** an American cicada whose nymphs emerge in large numbers in a seventeen-year (or, in the south, a thirteen-year) cycle.
● *Magicicada septendecim*, family Cicadidae, suborder Homoptera. Alternative name: **seventeen-year cicada**.

periodic function ▶ **noun** Mathematics a function returning to the same value at regular intervals.

periodicity /ˌpɪərɪəˈdɪsɪti/ ▶ **noun** [mass noun] chiefly technical the quality or character of being periodic; the tendency to recur at intervals: *the periodicity of the sunspot cycle.*

periodic law ▶ **noun** Chemistry a law stating that the elements, when listed in order of their atomic numbers, fall into recurring groups, so that elements with similar properties occur at regular intervals.

periodic table ▶ **noun** Chemistry a table of the chemical elements arranged in order of atomic number, usually in rows, so that elements with similar atomic structure (and hence similar chemical properties) appear in vertical columns.

periodize (also **periodise**) ▶ **verb** [with obj.] formal divide (a portion of time) into periods.
– DERIVATIVES **periodization** noun.

periodontics /ˌpɛrɪəˈdɒntɪks/ ▶ **plural noun** [treated as sing.] the branch of dentistry concerned with the structures surrounding and supporting the teeth.
– DERIVATIVES **periodontal** adjective, **periodontist** noun.
– ORIGIN 1940s: from **PERI-** 'around' + Greek *odous, odont-* 'tooth' + **-ICS**.

periodontitis /ˌpɛrɪədɒnˈtʌɪtɪs/ ▶ **noun** [mass noun] Medicine inflammation of the tissue around the teeth, often causing shrinkage of the gums and loosening of the teeth.

periodontology /ˌpɛrɪədɒnˈtɒlədʒi/ ▶ **noun** another term for **PERIODONTICS**.

period piece ▶ **noun** an object or work that is set in or reminiscent of an earlier historical period.

perioperative ▶ **adjective** Medicine (of a process or treatment) occurring or performed at or around the time of an operation.

periosteum /ˌpɛrɪˈɒstɪəm/ ▶ **noun** (pl. **periostea** /-tɪə/) Anatomy a dense layer of vascular connective tissue enveloping the bones except at the surfaces of the joints.
– DERIVATIVES **periosteal** adjective.
– ORIGIN late 16th cent.: modern Latin, from Greek *periosteon*, from *peri-* 'around' + *osteon* 'bone'.

periostitis /ˌpɛrɪɒˈstʌɪtɪs/ ▶ **noun** [mass noun] Medicine inflammation of the membrane enveloping a bone.

peripatetic /ˌpɛrɪpəˈtɛtɪk/ ▶ **adjective 1** travelling from place to place, in particular working or based in various places for relatively short periods: *the peripatetic nature of military life.* ■ (of a teacher) working in more than one school or college: *a peripatetic music teacher.*
2 (**Peripatetic**) Aristotelian. [with reference to Aristotle's practice of walking to and fro while teaching.]
▶ **noun 1** a person who travels from place to place, especially a teacher who works in more than one school or college.
2 (**Peripatetic**) an Aristotelian philosopher.
– DERIVATIVES **peripatetically** adverb, **peripateticism** noun.
– ORIGIN late Middle English (denoting an Aristotelian philosopher): from Old French *peripatetique*, via Latin from Greek *peripatētikos* 'walking up and down', from the verb *peripatein*.

peripatus /pəˈrɪpətəs/ ▶ **noun** (pl. **peripatuses**) Zoology a tropical terrestrial invertebrate with a soft worm-like body and stumpy legs. See **ONYCHOPHORA**. ● Genus *Peripatus*, phylum Onychophora.
– ORIGIN modern Latin, from Greek *peripatos* 'that walks about'.

peri-peri /ˌpɛrɪˈpɛri/ ▶ **noun** South African term for **PIRI-PIRI**.

peripeteia /ˌpɛrɪpɪˈtʌɪə, -ˈtiːə/ ▶ **noun** formal a sudden reversal of fortune or change in circumstances, especially in reference to fictional narrative.
– ORIGIN late 16th cent.: from Greek *peripeteia* 'sudden change', from *peri-* 'around' + the stem of *piptein* 'to fall'.

peripheral ▶ **adjective 1** relating to or situated on the edge or periphery of something: *the peripheral areas of Europe.* ■ of secondary or minor importance; marginal: *she will see their problems as peripheral to her own.* ■ Anatomy near the surface of the body, with special reference to the circulation and nervous system: *lymphocytes from peripheral blood.*
2 (of a device) able to be attached to and used with a computer, though not an integral part of it.
▶ **noun** Computing a peripheral device.
– DERIVATIVES **peripherality** noun, **peripheralization** (also **peripheralisation**) noun, **peripheralize** (also **peripheralise**) verb, **peripherally** adverb.

peripheral nervous system ▶ **noun** Anatomy the nervous system outside the brain and spinal cord.

periphery /pəˈrɪf(ə)ri/ ▶ **noun** (pl. **peripheries**) the outer limits or edge of an area or object: *new buildings on the periphery of the hospital site.* ■ a marginal or secondary position in, or aspect of, a group, subject, or sphere of activity: *a shift in power from the centre to the periphery.*
– ORIGIN late 16th cent. (denoting a line that forms the boundary of something): via late Latin from Greek *periphereia* 'circumference', from *peripherēs* 'revolving around', from *peri-* 'around' + *pherein* 'to bear'.

periphrasis /pəˈrɪfrəsɪs/ ▶ **noun** (pl. **periphrases** /-siːz/) [mass noun] the use of indirect and circumlocutory speech or writing. ■ [count noun] an indirect and circumlocutory phrase. ■ Grammar the use of separate words to express a grammatical relationship that is otherwise expressed by inflection, e.g. *did go* as opposed to *went* and *more intelligent* as opposed to *cleverer*.
– ORIGIN mid 16th cent.: via Latin from Greek, from *periphrazein*, from *peri-* 'around' + *phrazein* 'declare'.

periphrastic /ˌpɛrɪˈfrastɪk/ ▶ **adjective** (of speech or writing) indirect and circumlocutory: *the periphrastic nature of legal syntax.* ■ Grammar (of a case or tense) formed by a combination of words rather than by inflection (such as *did go* and *of the people* rather than *went* and *the people's*).
– DERIVATIVES **periphrastically** adverb.
– ORIGIN early 19th cent.: from Greek *periphrastikos*, from *periphrazein* 'declare in a roundabout way'.

periphyton /pəˈrɪfɪtɒn/ ▶ **noun** [mass noun] Ecology freshwater organisms attached or clinging to plants and other objects projecting above the bottom sediments.
– DERIVATIVES **periphytic** adjective.
– ORIGIN 1960s: from Greek *peri-* 'around' + *phuton* 'plant'.

peripteral /pəˈrɪpt(ə)r(ə)l/ ▶ **adjective** Architecture (of a building) having a single row of pillars on all sides in the style of the temples of ancient Greece.
– ORIGIN early 19th cent.: from Greek *peripteron* (from *peri-* 'around' + *pteron* 'wing') + **-AL**.

perique /pɛˈriːk/ ▶ **noun** [mass noun] a strong dark tobacco from Louisiana.
– ORIGIN late 19th cent.: Louisiana French, apparently from the nickname of Pierre Chenet, who first grew it.

periscope ▶ **noun** an apparatus consisting of a tube attached to a set of mirrors or prisms, by which an observer (typically in a submerged submarine or behind a high obstacle) can see things that are otherwise out of sight.

periscopic ▶ **adjective** relating to a periscope. ■ (of a lens or an optical instrument) giving a wide field of view: *a periscopic sextant.*

perish ▶ **verb** [no obj.] **1** literary die, especially in a violent or sudden way: *a great part of his army perished of hunger and disease.* ■ suffer complete ruin or destruction: *must these noble hopes perish so soon?*
2 (of rubber, food, etc.) lose its normal qualities; rot or decay: *an abandoned tyre whose rubber had perished.*
3 (**be perished**) Brit. informal be suffering from extreme cold: *I was perished with cold before the end of the day.*
– PHRASES **perish the thought** informal used, often ironically, to show that one finds a suggestion or idea completely ridiculous or unwelcome: *he wasn't out to get drunk—perish the thought!*
– ORIGIN Middle English: from Old French *periss-*, lengthened stem of *perir*, from Latin *perire* 'pass away', from *per-* 'through, completely' + *ire* 'go'.

perishable ▶ **adjective** (especially of food) likely to decay or go bad quickly. ■ (of something abstract) having a brief life or significance; transitory: *ballet is the most perishable of arts.*
▶ **noun** (**perishables**) things, especially foodstuffs, likely to decay or go bad quickly.
– DERIVATIVES **perishability** noun.

perisher ▶ **noun** Brit. informal a mischievous or awkward person, especially a child: *some pushy little perisher.*

perishing ▶ **adjective** Brit. informal **1** dated used for emphasis or to express annoyance: *I could murder that perishing kid!* | [as submodifier] *you've been a perishing long time with that coffee!*
2 [predic.] extremely cold: *it's perishing in the tent.*
– DERIVATIVES **perishingly** adverb.

perisperm ▶ **noun** Botany (in some seeds) a mass of nutritive material outside the embryo sac.
– ORIGIN early 19th cent.: from **PERI-** 'around' + Greek *sperma* 'seed'.

perissodactyl /pɪˌrɪsə(ʊ)ˈdakt(ɪ)l/ Zoology ▶ **noun** a mammal of the order Perissodactyla, such as a horse or rhinoceros.
▶ **adjective** relating to or denoting perissodactyls.

Perissodactyla /ˌpərɪsə(ʊ)'daktɪlə/ ▸ **plural noun** Zoology an order of mammals that comprises the odd-toed ungulates. Compare with **ARTIODACTYLA**.
– ORIGIN modern Latin (plural), from Greek *perissos* 'uneven' + *daktulos* 'finger, toe'.

peristalsis /ˌpɛrɪ'stalsɪs/ ▸ **noun** [mass noun] Physiology the involuntary constriction and relaxation of the muscles of the intestine or another canal, creating wave-like movements which push the contents of the canal forward.
– DERIVATIVES **peristaltic** adjective, **peristaltically** adverb.
– ORIGIN mid 19th cent.: modern Latin, from Greek *peristallein* 'wrap around', from *peri-* 'around' + *stallein* 'to place'.

peristaltic pump ▸ **noun** a mechanical pump in which pressure is provided by the movement of a constriction along a tube, similar to biological peristalsis.

peristome /'pɛrɪstəʊm/ ▸ **noun 1** Zoology the parts surrounding the mouth of various invertebrates.
2 Botany a fringe of small projections around the mouth of a capsule in mosses and certain fungi.
– ORIGIN late 18th cent.: from modern Latin *peristoma*, from Greek *peri-* 'around' + *stoma* 'mouth'.

peristyle ▸ **noun** Architecture a row of columns surrounding a space within a building such as a court or internal garden or edging a veranda or porch. ■ a space such as a court or porch that is surrounded or edged by a peristyle.
– ORIGIN early 17th cent.: from French *péristyle*, from Latin *peristylum*, from Greek *peristulon*, from *peri-* 'around' + *stulos* 'pillar'.

perithecium /ˌpɛrɪ'θiːsɪəm/ ▸ **noun** (pl. **perithecia** /-sɪə/) Botany (in some fungi) a round or flask-shaped fruiting body with a pore through which the spores are discharged.
– ORIGIN mid 19th cent.: modern Latin, from **PERI-** 'around' + Greek *thēkē* 'case'.

peritoneum /ˌpɛrɪtə'niːəm/ ▸ **noun** (pl. **peritoneums** or **peritonea** /-'niːə/) Anatomy the serous membrane lining the cavity of the abdomen and covering the abdominal organs.
– DERIVATIVES **peritoneal** adjective.
– ORIGIN late Middle English: via late Latin from Greek *peritonaion*, from *peritonos* 'stretched round', from *peri-* 'around' + *-tonos* 'stretched'.

peritonitis /ˌpɛrɪtə'nʌɪtɪs/ ▸ **noun** [mass noun] Medicine inflammation of the peritoneum, typically caused by bacterial infection either via the blood or after rupture of an abdominal organ.

peri-track ▸ **noun** another term for **TAXIWAY**.
– ORIGIN contraction of *perimeter track*.

peritus /pə'rʌɪtəs/ ▸ **noun** (pl. **periti** /-tʌɪ, -tiː/) a theological adviser or consultant to a council of the Roman Catholic Church.
– ORIGIN 1960s: from Latin; related to *expertus* 'expert'.

perivascular ▸ **adjective** Medicine situated or occurring around a blood vessel.

periventricular /ˌpɛrɪvɛn'trɪkjʊlə/ ▸ **noun** Anatomy & Medicine situated or occurring around a ventricle, especially a ventricle of the brain.

periwig ▸ **noun** archaic a wig. ■ a highly styled wig worn formerly as a fashionable headdress by both women and men and retained by judges and barristers as part of their professional dress.
– DERIVATIVES **periwigged** adjective.
– ORIGIN early 16th cent.: alteration of **PERUKE**, with *-wi-* representing the French *-u-* sound.

periwinkle¹ ▸ **noun** an Old World plant with flat five-petalled flowers and glossy leaves. Some kinds are grown as ornamentals and some contain alkaloids used in medicine. ● Genera *Vinca* and *Catharanthus*, family Apocynaceae.
– ORIGIN late Old English *peruince*, from late Latin *pervinca*, reinforced in Middle English by Anglo-Norman French *pervenke*. The change of *-v-* to *-w-* and the addition of *-le* seem to have occurred before the appearance of **PERIWINKLE²**.

periwinkle² ▸ **noun** another term for **WINKLE**.
– ORIGIN mid 16th cent.: of unknown origin.

perjure ▸ **verb** (**perjure oneself** or **be perjured**) Law wilfully tell an untruth or make a misrepresentation under oath; commit perjury: *she admitted that she had perjured herself*. ■ (as adj. **perjured**) (of evidence) involving wilfully told untruths.
– DERIVATIVES **perjurer** noun.
– ORIGIN late Middle English (as *perjured* in the sense 'guilty of perjury'): from Old French *parjurer*, from Latin *perjurare* 'swear falsely', from *per-* 'to ill effect' + *jurare* 'swear'.

perjury /'pəːdʒ(ə)ri/ ▸ **noun** (pl. **perjuries**) [mass noun] Law the offence of wilfully telling an untruth or making a misrepresentation under oath.
– DERIVATIVES **perjurious** /-'dʒʊərɪəs/ adjective.
– ORIGIN late Middle English: from Anglo-Norman French *perjurie*, from Latin *perjurium* 'false oath', from the verb *perjurare* (see **PERJURE**).

perk¹ ▸ **verb** (**perk up** or **perk someone/thing up**) become or make more cheerful, lively, or interesting: [no obj.] *she'd been depressed, but she seemed to perk up last week* | [with obj.] *the coffee had perked him up long enough to tackle the reviews*.
– ORIGIN late Middle English (in the senses 'perch' and 'be lively'): perhaps from an Old French dialect variant of *percher* 'to perch'.

perk² ▸ **noun** (usu. **perks**) informal a benefit to which one is entitled because of one's job: *many agencies are helping to keep personnel at their jobs by providing perks*. ■ an advantage or benefit arising from a particular situation: *they were busy discovering the perks of town life*.
– ORIGIN early 19th cent.: abbreviation of **PERQUISITE**.

perk³ informal ▸ **verb** (with reference to coffee) percolate: [no obj.] *while the coffee perks, head out for the morning paper* | [with obj.] *she showed us how to perk the coffee*.
▸ **noun** a coffee percolator.
– ORIGIN 1930s: abbreviation of **PERCOLATE**.

Perkin, Sir William Henry (1838–1907), English chemist and pioneer of the synthetic organic chemical industry. He prepared and manufactured the first synthetic dyestuff, mauve, from aniline.

perky ▸ **adjective** (**perkier**, **perkiest**) cheerful and lively: *she certainly looked less than her usual perky self*. ■ cheeky: *don't be perky, miss!*
– DERIVATIVES **perkily** adverb, **perkiness** noun.

Perl ▸ **noun** [mass noun] Computing a high-level general-purpose programming language used especially for developing Web applications.
– ORIGIN 1980s: respelling of **PEARL¹**, arbitrarily chosen for its positive connotations.

perlé /pəː'leɪ/ ▸ **noun** [mass noun] a semi-sweet, slightly sparkling wine produced in South Africa.
– ORIGIN French, literally 'beaded', perhaps from an abbreviation of German *Perlwein*, denoting a slightly sparkling wine, from *Perle* 'pearl, bubble' + *Wein* 'wine'.

perlemoen /ˌpəːlə'mʊn/ ▸ **noun** (pl. **same**) S. African an abalone.
– ORIGIN Afrikaans, from obsolete *perlemoer* 'mother of pearl' (referring to the pearlized layer inside the shell).

Perlis /'pəːlɪs/ the smallest state of Malaysia and the most northerly of those on the Malay Peninsula; capital, Kangar.

perlite /'pəːlʌɪt/ ▸ **noun** [mass noun] a form of obsidian consisting of glassy globules, used as insulation or in plant growth media.
– ORIGIN mid 19th cent.: from French, from *perle* 'pearl'.

perlocution ▸ **noun** Philosophy & Linguistics an act of speaking or writing which has an action as its aim but which in itself does not effect or constitute the action, for example persuading or convincing. Compare with **ILLOCUTION**.
– DERIVATIVES **perlocutionary** adjective.
– ORIGIN 1950s: from modern Latin *perlocutio(n-)*, from *per-* 'throughout' + *locutio(n-)* 'speaking'.

Perm /pəːm/ an industrial city in Russia, in the western foothills of the Ural Mountains; pop. 987,200 (est. 2008). Former name (1940–57) **MOLOTOV¹**.

perm¹ ▸ **noun** (also **permanent wave**) a method of setting the hair in waves or curls and then treating it with chemicals so that the style lasts for several months.
▸ **verb** [with obj.] set (the hair) in a perm: *her hair was permed and then set*.
– ORIGIN 1920s: abbreviation of **PERMANENT**.

perm² Brit. informal ▸ **noun** a permutation, especially a selection of a specified number of matches in a football pool: *a full perm of 8 from 11*.
▸ **verb** [with obj.] make a selection of (so many) from a larger number: *one of the teams was to perm any 11 from 20*.
– ORIGIN 1950s: abbreviation of **PERMUTATION**.

perma- ▸ **combining form** permanent or permanently: *women on perma-diets* | *a perma-tanned steward*.

permaculture ▸ **noun** [mass noun] the development of agricultural ecosystems intended to be sustainable and self-sufficient.
– ORIGIN 1970s: blend of **PERMANENT** and **AGRICULTURE**.

permafrost ▸ **noun** [mass noun] a thick subsurface layer of soil that remains below freezing point throughout the year, occurring chiefly in polar regions.
– ORIGIN 1940s: from **PERMANENT** + **FROST**.

permalloy /'pəːmalɔɪ/ ▸ **noun** [mass noun] an alloy of nickel and iron that is easily magnetized and demagnetized, used in electrical equipment.
– ORIGIN 1920s: from **PERMEABLE** + **ALLOY**.

permanence ▸ **noun** [mass noun] the state or quality of lasting or remaining unchanged indefinitely: *the clarity and permanence of the dyes*.
– DERIVATIVES **permanency** noun.
– ORIGIN late Middle English: from medieval Latin *permanentia* (perhaps via French), from *permanent-* 'remaining to the end', from the verb *permanere*.

permanent ▸ **adjective** lasting or intended to last or remain unchanged indefinitely: *a permanent ban on the dumping of radioactive waste at sea* | *damage was not thought to be permanent* | *some temporary workers did not want a permanent job*. ■ lasting or continuing without interruption: *he's in a permanent state of rage*.
▸ **noun** N. Amer. a perm for the hair.
– ORIGIN late Middle English: from Latin *permanent-* 'remaining to the end' (perhaps via Old French), from *per-* 'through' + *manere* 'remain'.

permanent hardness ▸ **noun** [mass noun] the presence in water of mineral salts (chiefly calcium sulphate) that are not removed by boiling.

permanently ▸ **adverb** in a way that lasts or remains unchanged indefinitely; for all time: *his lungs are permanently damaged*. ■ in a way that lasts or continues without interruption; continually: *we need to be permanently vigilant*.

permanent magnet ▸ **noun** a magnet that retains its magnetic properties in the absence of an inducing field or current.

permanent revolution ▸ **noun** [mass noun] the state or condition, envisaged by Leon Trotsky, of a country's continuing revolutionary progress being dependent on a continuing process of revolution in other countries.

permanent set ▸ **noun** an irreversible deformation that remains in a structure or material after it has been subjected to stress.

permanent tooth ▸ **noun** a tooth in a mammal that replaces a temporary milk tooth and lasts for most of the mammal's life.

Permanent Undersecretary (also **Permanent Secretary**) ▸ **noun** (in the UK) a senior civil servant who is a permanent adviser to a Secretary of State.

P

permanent wave ▸ **noun** see **PERM¹**.

permanent way ▸ **noun** Brit. the finished trackbed of a railway together with the track and other permanent equipment.

permanganate /pə'maŋgənət, -eɪt/ ▸ **noun** Chemistry a salt containing the anion MnO_4^-, typically deep purplish-red and with strong oxidizing properties.

permeability ▸ **noun** [mass noun] **1** the state or quality of being permeable.
2 Physics a quantity measuring the influence of a substance on the magnetic flux in the region it occupies.

permeabilize /'pəːmɪəbɪˌlʌɪz/ (also **permeabilise**) ▸ **verb** [with obj.] (often as adj. **permeabilized**) technical make permeable.
– DERIVATIVES **permeabilization** noun.

permeable ▸ **adjective** (of a material or membrane) allowing liquids or gases to pass through it: *a frog's skin is **permeable to** water* | *permeable sandy soils*.
– ORIGIN late Middle English: from Latin *permeabilis*, from *permeare* 'pass through' (see **PERMEATE**).

permeance /'pəːmɪəns/ ▸ **noun** Physics the property of allowing the passage of lines of magnetic flux.

permeate ▸ **verb** [with obj.] spread throughout (something); pervade: *the aroma of soup permeated the air* | [no obj.] *his personality has begun to **permeate through** the whole organization*.
– DERIVATIVES **permeation** noun.
– ORIGIN mid 17th cent.: from Latin *permeat-* 'passed through', from the verb *permeare*, from *per-* 'through' + *meare* 'pass, go'.

permethrin /pə'miːθrɪn/ ▸ **noun** [mass noun] a synthetic insecticide of the pyrethroid class, used chiefly against disease-carrying insects.

– ORIGIN 1970s: from **PER-** (sense 2) + *(res)methrin*, denoting a synthetic pyrethroid.

Permian /ˈpəːmɪən/ ▶ **adjective** Geology relating to or denoting the last period of the Palaeozoic era, between the Carboniferous and Triassic periods. See also **PERMO–TRIASSIC**. ■ (as noun **the Permian**) the Permian period or the system of rocks deposited during it.

The Permian lasted from about 290 to 245 million years ago. The climate was hot and dry in many parts of the world during this period, which saw the extinction of many marine animals, including trilobites, and the proliferation of reptiles.

– ORIGIN late 16th cent.: from the name of the Russian province **PERM**, from the extensive development of such strata there.

per mille /pəː ˈmɪleɪ, ˈmɪli/ (also **per mil** /mɪl/) ▶ **adverb** by a specified amount in every thousand: *foreign holidays account for 30 per mille of the cost of living*.
– ORIGIN late 17th cent.: Latin.

permineralized (also **permineralised**) ▶ **adjective** Geology (of organic material) fossilized through the precipitation of dissolved minerals in the interstices of hard tissue.
– DERIVATIVES **permineralization** noun.

permissible ▶ **adjective** permitted; allowed: *it is permissible to edit and rephrase the statement*.
– DERIVATIVES **permissibility** noun, **permissibly** adverb.
– ORIGIN late Middle English: from medieval Latin *permissibilis*, from *permiss-* 'allowed', from the verb *permittere* (see **PERMIT**[1]).

permission ▶ **noun** [mass noun] the action of officially allowing someone to do a particular thing; consent or authorization: *they had entered the country without permission* | [with infinitive] *he received permission to go to Brussels*. ■ [count noun] an official document giving authorization: *permissions to reproduce copyright material*.
– ORIGIN late Middle English: from Latin *permissio(n-)*, from the verb *permittere* 'allow' (see **PERMIT**[1]).

permissive ▶ **adjective 1** allowing or characterized by great or excessive freedom of behaviour: *a permissive parent* | *the permissive society of the 60s and 70s*.
2 Law allowed but not obligatory; optional: *the Hague Convention was permissive, not mandatory*. ■ denoting a path available for public use by the landowner's consent, not as a legal right of way.
3 Biology allowing a biological or biochemical process to occur: *the mutants grow well at the permissive temperature*.
– DERIVATIVES **permissively** adverb, **permissiveness** noun.
– ORIGIN late 15th cent. (in the sense 'tolerated, allowed'): from Old French, or from medieval Latin *permissivus*, from *permiss-* 'allowed', from the verb *permittere* (see **PERMIT**[1]).

P

permit[1] ▶ **verb** /pəˈmɪt/ (**permits, permitting, permitted**) [with obj. and infinitive] officially allow (someone) to do something: *the law permits councils to monitor any factory emitting smoke* | [with two objs] *he would not permit anybody access to the library*. ■ [with obj.] authorize or allow (something): *the country is not ready to permit any rice imports*. ■ [with obj.] provide an opportunity or scope for (something) to take place; make possible: *the car park was too rutted and stony to permit ball games* | [no obj.] *weather permitting, guests can dine outside on the veranda*. ■ [no obj.] (**permit of**) formal allow for; admit of: *the camp permits of no really successful defence*.
▶ **noun** /ˈpəːmɪt/ [often with modifier] an official document giving someone authorization to do something: *he is only in Britain on a work permit*.
– DERIVATIVES **permittee** noun.
– ORIGIN late Middle English (originally in the sense 'commit, hand over'): from Latin *permittere*, from *per-* 'through' + *mittere* 'send, let go'.

permit[2] /ˈpəːmɪt/ ▶ **noun** a deep-bodied fish of the jack family, found in warm waters of the western Atlantic and Caribbean and caught for food and sport.
● *Trachinotus falcatus*, family Carangidae.
– ORIGIN alteration of Spanish *palometa* 'little dove'.

permittivity /ˌpəːmɪˈtɪvɪti/ ▶ **noun** Physics the ability of a substance to store electrical energy in an electric field.

Permo–Carboniferous /ˈpəːməʊ/ ▶ **adjective** Geology relating to or linking the Permian and Carboniferous periods or rock systems together.

Permo–Triassic ▶ **adjective** Geology relating to or denoting the boundary of the Permian and Triassic periods, about 245 million years ago. Mass extinctions occurred at this time, marking the end of the Palaeozoic era. ■ (as noun **the Permo–Triassic** or **Permo–Trias**) the Permian and Triassic periods together or the system of rocks deposited during them.

permutate /ˈpəːmjʊteɪt/ ▶ **verb** [with obj.] change the order or arrangement of: *statistics may be sorted and permutated according to requirements*.
– ORIGIN late 19th cent.: regarded as a back-formation from **PERMUTATION**.

permutation ▶ **noun** each of several possible ways in which a set or number of things can be ordered or arranged: *his thoughts raced ahead to fifty different permutations of what he must do*. ■ [mass noun] Mathematics the action of changing the arrangement, especially the linear order, of a set of items. ■ Brit. a selection of a specified number of matches in a football pool.
– DERIVATIVES **permutational** adjective.
– ORIGIN late Middle English (in the sense 'exchange, barter'): via Old French from Latin *permutatio(n-)*, from the verb *permutare* 'change completely' (see **PERMUTE**).

permute ▶ **verb** [with obj.] technical submit to a process of alteration, rearrangement, or permutation: *we wish to permute the order of the bytes*.
– ORIGIN late Middle English (also in the sense 'interchange'): from Latin *permutare* 'change completely', from *per-* 'through, completely' + *mutare* 'to change'.

Pernambuco /ˌpəːnamˈbuːkuː/ a state of eastern Brazil, on the Atlantic coast; capital, Recife. ■ former name for **RECIFE**.

pernambuco (also **pernambuco wood**) ▶ **noun** [mass noun] the hard reddish timber of a Brazilian tree, used for making violin bows and as a source of red dye.
● The tree is *Caesalpinia echinata*, family Leguminosae.
– ORIGIN late 16th cent.: from the name of the Brazilian state **PERNAMBUCO**.

pernicious /pəˈnɪʃəs/ ▶ **adjective** having a harmful effect, especially in a gradual or subtle way: *the pernicious influences of the mass media*.
– DERIVATIVES **perniciously** adverb, **perniciousness** noun.
– ORIGIN late Middle English: from Latin *perniciosus* 'destructive', from *pernicies* 'ruin', based on *nex, nec-* 'death'.

pernicious anaemia ▶ **noun** [mass noun] a deficiency in the production of red blood cells through a lack of vitamin B_{12}.

pernickety ▶ **adjective** Brit. informal placing too much emphasis on trivial or minor details; fussy: *she's very pernickety about her food*. ■ requiring a particularly precise or careful approach: *the system does not encourage additional enquiries on detailed and pernickety points*.
– ORIGIN early 19th cent. (originally Scots): of unknown origin.

pernoctate /ˈpəːnɒkteɪt, pəˈnɒkteɪt/ ▶ **verb** [no obj.] formal pass the night somewhere.
– DERIVATIVES **pernoctation** noun.
– ORIGIN early 17th cent.: from Latin *pernoctat-* 'spent the night', from the verb *pernoctare*, from *per-* 'through' + *nox, noct-* 'night'.

Pernod /ˈpəːnəʊ/ ▶ **noun** [mass noun] trademark an aniseed-flavoured aperitif.
– ORIGIN named after the manufacturing firm *Pernod Fils*.

peroba /pəˈrəʊbə/ ▶ **noun** [mass noun] the timber of certain Brazilian hardwood trees: ● (**white peroba**) timber used for furniture and storage vats, from the tree *Paratecoma peroba* (family Bignoniaceae). ● (**red peroba**) similar but less versatile timber from trees of the genus *Aspidosperma* (family Apocynaceae).
– ORIGIN early 19th cent.: via Portuguese from Tupi *iperoba*, literally 'bitter bark'.

perogi ▶ **noun** variant spelling of **PIEROGI**.

Perón[1] /pεˈrɒn/, Eva (1919–52), Argentinian politician, second wife of Juan Perón; full name *María Eva Duarte de Perón*; known as **Evita**. A former actress, after her marriage in 1945 she became de facto Minister of Health and of Labour until her death from cancer; her social reforms earned her great popularity with the poor.

Perón[2] /pεˈrɒn/, Juan Domingo (1895–1974), Argentinian soldier and statesman, President 1946–55 and 1973–4. He participated in the 1943 military coup, and was later elected President, winning popular support with his social reforms. The faltering economy and conflict with the Church led to his removal and exile.
– DERIVATIVES **Peronism** /ˈpεrəˌnɪz(ə)m/ noun, **Peronist** adjective & noun.

peroneal /ˌpεrəˈniːəl/ ▶ **adjective** Anatomy relating to or situated in the outer side of the calf of the leg.
– ORIGIN mid 19th cent.: from modern Latin *peronaeus* 'peroneal muscle' (based on Greek *peronē* 'pin, fibula') + **-AL**.

perorate /ˈpεrəreɪt/ ▶ **verb** [no obj.] formal speak at length: *he perorated against his colleague*. ■ archaic sum up and conclude a speech.
– ORIGIN early 17th cent.: from Latin *perorat-* 'spoken at length', from the verb *perorare*, from *per-* 'through' + *orare* 'speak'.

peroration ▶ **noun** the concluding part of a speech, typically intended to inspire enthusiasm in the audience.
– ORIGIN late Middle English: from Latin *peroratio(n-)*, from *perorare* 'speak at length' (see **PERORATE**).

perovskite /pəˈrɒfskʌɪt/ ▶ **noun** [mass noun] a yellow, brown, or black mineral consisting largely of calcium titanate. ■ [count noun] any of a group of related minerals and ceramics having the same crystal structure as perovskite.
– ORIGIN mid 19th cent.: from the name of L. A. *Perovsky* (1792–1856), Russian mineralogist, + **-ITE**[1].

peroxidase /pəˈrɒksɪdeɪz/ ▶ **noun** Biochemistry an enzyme that catalyses the oxidation of a particular substrate by hydrogen peroxide.

peroxide ▶ **noun** Chemistry a compound containing two oxygen atoms bonded together in its molecule or as the anion O_2^{2-}. ■ [mass noun] hydrogen peroxide, especially as used as a bleach for the hair: [as modifier] *a peroxide blonde*.
▶ **verb** [with obj.] bleach (hair) with peroxide.
– ORIGIN early 19th cent.: from **PER-** (sense 2) + **OXIDE**.

peroxisome /pəˈrɒksɪsəʊm/ ▶ **noun** Biology a small organelle present in the cytoplasm of many cells, which contains the reducing enzyme catalase and usually some oxidases.
– DERIVATIVES **peroxisomal** adjective.
– ORIGIN 1960s: from **PEROXIDE** + **-SOME**[3].

perp ▶ **noun** N. Amer. informal the perpetrator of a crime.
– ORIGIN 1980s: abbreviation.

perpend /ˈpəːpεnd/ ▶ **noun** a vertical layer of mortar between two bricks.

perpendicular /ˌpəːp(ə)nˈdɪkjʊlə/ ▶ **adjective 1** at an angle of 90° to a given line, plane, or surface or to the ground: *dormers and gables that extend perpendicular to the main roofline*. ■ at an angle of 90° to the ground; vertical: *the perpendicular cliff*. ■ so steep as to be almost vertical: *houses seem to cling by blind faith to the perpendicular hillside*.
2 (**Perpendicular**) denoting the latest stage of English Gothic church architecture, prevalent from the late 14th to mid 16th centuries and characterized by broad arches, elaborate fan vaulting, and large windows with vertical tracery.
▶ **noun** a straight line at an angle of 90° to a given line, plane, or surface. ■ [mass noun] (usu. **the perpendicular**) perpendicular position or direction: *the wall declines from the perpendicular a little inward*.
– DERIVATIVES **perpendicularity** noun, **perpendicularly** adverb.
– ORIGIN late Middle English (as an adverb meaning 'at right angles'): via Old French from Latin *perpendicularis*, from *perpendiculum* 'plumb line', from *per-* 'through' + *pendere* 'to hang'.

perpetrate /ˈpəːpɪtreɪt/ ▶ **verb** [with obj.] carry out or commit (a harmful, illegal, or immoral action): *a crime has been perpetrated against a sovereign state*.
– DERIVATIVES **perpetration** noun, **perpetrator** noun.
– ORIGIN mid 16th cent.: from Latin *perpetrat-* 'performed', from the verb *perpetrare*, from *per-* 'to completion' + *patrare* 'bring about'. In Latin the act perpetrated might be good or bad; in English the verb was first used in the statutes referring to crime, hence the negative association.

USAGE The words **perpetrate** and **perpetuate** are sometimes confused. **Perpetrate** means 'commit a harmful, illegal, or immoral action', as in *a crime has been perpetrated against a sovereign state*, whereas **perpetuate** means 'make something continue indefinitely', as in *a monument to perpetuate the memory of those killed in the war*.

perpetual /pəˈpɛtʃʊəl, -tjʊəl/ ▶ **adjective 1** never ending or changing: *deep caves in perpetual darkness.* ■ [attrib.] denoting or having a position, job, or trophy held for life: *a perpetual secretary of the society.* ■ (of an investment) having no fixed maturity date; irredeemable: *a perpetual bond.*
2 occurring repeatedly; so frequent as to seem endless and uninterrupted: *their perpetual money worries.*
3 (of a plant) blooming or fruiting several times in one season.
– DERIVATIVES **perpetually** adverb.
– ORIGIN Middle English: from Old French *perpetuel*, from Latin *perpetualis*, from *perpetuus* 'continuing throughout', from *perpes*, *perpet-* 'continuous'.

perpetual calendar ▶ **noun** a calendar in which the day, the month, and the date are adjusted independently to show any combination of the three.

perpetual check ▶ **noun** [mass noun] Chess the situation of play when a draw is obtained by repeated checking of the king.

perpetual motion ▶ **noun** [mass noun] a state in which movement or action is or appears to be continuous and unceasing. ■ the motion of a hypothetical machine which, once activated, would run forever unless subject to an external force or to wear.

perpetual spinach ▶ **noun** another term for **SPINACH BEET**.

perpetuate /pəˈpɛtʃʊeɪt, -tjʊ-/ ▶ **verb** [with obj.] make (something) continue indefinitely: *the confusion was perpetuated through inadvertence | a monument to perpetuate the memory of those killed in the war.*
– DERIVATIVES **perpetuation** noun, **perpetuator** noun.
– ORIGIN early 16th cent.: from Latin *perpetuat-* 'made permanent', from the verb *perpetuare*, from *perpetuus* 'continuing throughout' (see **PERPETUAL**).

> **USAGE** On the difference between **perpetuate** and **perpetrate**, see **USAGE** at **PERPETRATE**.

perpetuity ▶ **noun** (pl. **perpetuities**) **1** [mass noun] the state or quality of lasting forever: *he did not believe in the perpetuity of military rule.*
2 a bond or other security with no fixed maturity date.
3 Law a restriction making an interest in land inalienable perpetually or for a period beyond certain limits fixed by law.
– PHRASES **in** (or **for**) **perpetuity** forever: *all the Bonapartes were banished from France in perpetuity.*
– ORIGIN late Middle English: from Old French *perpetuite*, from Latin *perpetuitas*, from *perpetuus* 'continuing throughout' (see **PERPETUAL**).

perpetuum mobile /pəːˌpɛtjʊəm ˈməʊbɪleɪ, ˈməʊbɪli/ ▶ **noun 1** another term for **PERPETUAL MOTION**.
2 Music another term for **MOTO PERPETUO**.
– ORIGIN Latin, literally 'continuously moving (thing)', on the pattern of *primum mobile*.

Perpignan /ˈpəːpɪnjɒn/, French /pɛʀpiɲɑ̃/ a city in southern France, in the NE foothills of the Pyrenees, close to the border with Spain; pop. 117,500 (2006). A former fortress town, it was the capital of the old province of Roussillon.

perplex ▶ **verb** [with obj.] make (someone) feel completely baffled: *she was perplexed by her husband's moodiness.* ■ dated complicate or confuse (a matter): *they were perplexing a subject plain in itself.*
– ORIGIN late 15th cent. (as the adjective *perplexed*): from the obsolete adjective *perplex* 'bewildered', from Latin *perplexus* 'entangled', based on *plexus* 'interwoven', from the verb *plectere*.

perplexed ▶ **adjective** completely baffled; very puzzled: *she gave him a perplexed look.*
– DERIVATIVES **perplexedly** adverb.

perplexing ▶ **adjective** completely baffling; very puzzling: *a perplexing problem.*
– DERIVATIVES **perplexingly** adverb.

perplexity ▶ **noun** (pl. **perplexities**) [mass noun]
1 inability to deal with or understand something: *she paused in perplexity.* ■ [count noun] (usu. **perplexities**) a complicated or baffling situation or thing: *the perplexities of international relations.*
2 archaic an entangled state: *the dense perplexity of dwarf palm, garlanded creepers, glossy undergrowth.*
– ORIGIN Middle English: from Old French *perplexite* or late Latin *perplexitas*, from Latin *perplexus* 'entangled, confused' (see **PERPLEX**).

per pro. /pəː ˈprəʊ/ ▶ **abbreviation** per procurationem (used when signing a letter on behalf of someone else; now usually abbreviated to **pp**). See usage at **PP**.
– ORIGIN Latin.

perquisite /ˈpəːkwɪzɪt/ ▶ **noun** formal a benefit which one enjoys or is entitled to on account of one's job or position: *the wife of a president has all the perquisites of stardom.* ■ historical a thing which has served its primary use and to which a subordinate or employee has a customary right.
– ORIGIN late Middle English: from medieval Latin *perquisitum* 'acquisition', from Latin *perquirere* 'search diligently for', from *per-* 'thoroughly' + *quaerere* 'seek'.

Perrault /pɛˈrəʊ/, French /pɛʀəo/, Charles (1628–1703), French writer. He is remembered for his *Mother Goose Tales* (1697), containing such fairy tales as 'Sleeping Beauty', 'Little Red Riding Hood', 'Puss in Boots', and 'Cinderella'.

perron /ˈpɛrən/ ▶ **noun** Architecture an exterior set of steps and a platform at the main entrance to a large building such as a church or mansion.
– ORIGIN late Middle English: from Old French, literally 'large stone', from Latin *petra* 'stone'.

Perry, Fred (1909–95), British-born American tennis player; full name *Frederick John Perry*. His record of winning three consecutive singles titles at Wimbledon (1934–6) was unequalled until 1978.

perry ▶ **noun** (pl. **perries**) [mass noun] an alcoholic drink made from the fermented juice of pears.
– ORIGIN Middle English: from Old French *pere*, from an alteration of Latin *pirum* 'pear'.

per se /pəː ˈseɪ/ ▶ **adverb** by or in itself or themselves; intrinsically: *it is not these facts per se that are important.*
– ORIGIN Latin.

persecute ▶ **verb** [with obj.] subject (someone) to hostility and ill-treatment, especially because of their race or political or religious beliefs: *his followers were persecuted by the authorities.* ■ harass or annoy (someone) persistently: *Hilda was persecuted by some of the other girls.*
– DERIVATIVES **persecutor** noun, **persecutory** adjective.
– ORIGIN late Middle English: from Old French *persecuter*, from Latin *persecut-* 'followed with hostility', from the verb *persequi*, from *per-* 'through, utterly' + *sequi* 'follow, pursue'.

persecution ▶ **noun** [mass noun] hostility and ill-treatment, especially because of race or political or religious beliefs; oppression: *her family fled religious persecution.* ■ persistent annoyance or harassment: *his persecution at the hands of other students.*

persecution complex ▶ **noun** an irrational and obsessive feeling or fear that one is the object of collective hostility or ill-treatment on the part of others.

Perseids /ˈpəːsɪɪdz/ Astronomy an annual meteor shower with a radiant in the constellation Perseus, reaching a peak about 12 August.

Persephone /pəˈsɛfəni/ Greek Mythology a goddess, the daughter of Zeus and Demeter. Roman name **PROSERPINA**.

> Persephone was carried off by Hades and made queen of the underworld. Demeter refused to let the earth produce its fruits until her daughter was restored to her, but because Persephone had eaten some pomegranate seeds in the other world, she was obliged to spend part of every year there. Her story symbolizes the return of spring and the life and growth of corn.

Persepolis /pəˈsɛpəlɪs/ a city in ancient Persia, situated to the north-east of Shiraz. It was founded in the late 6th century BC by Darius I as the ceremonial capital of Persia under the Achaemenid dynasty. The city's impressive ruins include functional and ceremonial buildings and cuneiform inscriptions in Old Persian, Elamite, and Akkadian.

Perseus /ˈpəːsɪəs, -sjuːs/ **1** Greek Mythology the son of Zeus and Danae, a hero celebrated for many achievements. He cut off the head of the gorgon Medusa and gave it to Athene; he also rescued and married Andromeda, and became king of the ancient city of Tiryns in Greece.
2 Astronomy a large northern constellation which includes a dense part of the Milky Way. It contains several star clusters and the variable star Algol.

perseverance ▶ **noun** [mass noun] persistence in doing something despite difficulty or delay in achieving success: *medicine is a field which requires dedication and perseverance.*
– ORIGIN Middle English: from Old French, from Latin *perseverantia*, from *perseverant-* 'abiding by strictly', from the verb *perseverare* (see **PERSEVERE**).

perseverate /pəˈsɛvəreɪt/ ▶ **verb** [no obj.] Psychology repeat or prolong an action, thought, or utterance after the stimulus that prompted it has ceased.
– DERIVATIVES **perseveration** noun.
– ORIGIN early 20th cent.: from Latin *perseverat-* 'strictly abided by', from the verb *perseverare* (see **PERSEVERE**).

persevere ▶ **verb** [no obj.] continue in a course of action even in the face of difficulty or with little or no indication of success: *his family **persevered with** his treatment* | (as adj. **persevering**) *she has been a remarkably steadfast, persevering, and dutiful woman.*
– DERIVATIVES **perseveringly** adverb.
– ORIGIN late Middle English: from Old French *perseverer*, from Latin *perseverare* 'abide by strictly', from *perseverus* 'very strict', from *per-* 'thoroughly' + *severus* 'severe'.

Persia /ˈpəːʃə, ˈpəːʒə/ a former country of SW Asia, now called Iran.

> Under Cyrus the Great in the 6th century BC Persia became the centre of a powerful empire which included all of western Asia, Egypt, and parts of eastern Europe; it was eventually overthrown by Alexander the Great in 330 BC. The country was conquered by the Muslim Arabs between AD 633 and 651. It was renamed Iran in 1935.

Persian ▶ **noun 1** a native or inhabitant of ancient or modern Persia (or Iran), or a person of Persian descent. ■ (also **Persian cat**) a long-haired domestic cat of a breed originating in Persia, having a broad round head, stocky body, and short thick legs. ■ a sheep of a breed common in South Africa.
2 [mass noun] the language of modern Iran, an Indo-European language written in Arabic script. Also called **FARSI**. ■ an earlier form of Persian spoken in ancient or medieval Persia.
▶ **adjective** relating to ancient Persia or modern Iran or its people or language.

> Persian (or Farsi) is spoken by over 30 million people in Iran, by about 5 million in Afghanistan (as Dari), and by another 2.2 million in Tajikistan (as Tajik). Old Persian, written in cuneiform and attested from the 6th century BC, was the language of the Persian empire, which once spread from the Mediterranean to India. In the 2nd century BC the Persians created their own alphabet (Pahlavi), which was used until the Islamic conquest in the 7th century.

– ORIGIN Middle English: from Old French *persien*, from Latin *Persia*, via Greek from Old Persian *pārsa* 'Persia' (modern Persian *pārs*, Arabic *fārs*).

Persian blue ▶ **noun** [mass noun] a shade of bright pale blue.

Persian carpet (also **Persian rug**) ▶ **noun** a carpet or rug woven in Iran in a traditional design incorporating stylized symbolic imagery, or made elsewhere in such a style.

Persian cat ▶ **noun** see **PERSIAN** (sense 1 of the noun).

Persian Gulf an arm of the Arabian Sea, to which it is connected by the Strait of Hormuz and the Gulf of Oman. It extends north-westwards between the Arabian peninsula and the coast of SW Iran. Also called **ARABIAN GULF** and informally **THE GULF**.

Persian lamb ▶ **noun** [mass noun] a silky, tightly curled fur made from or resembling the fleece of a young karakul, used to make clothing.

Persian Wars the wars fought between Greece and Persia in the 5th century BC, in which the Persians sought to extend their territory over the Greek world.

> The Persian Wars began in 490 BC when Darius I sent an expedition to punish the Greeks for having supported the Ionian cities in their unsuccessful revolt against Persian rule; the Persians were defeated by a small force of Athenians at Marathon. Ten years later Darius' son Xerxes I attempted an invasion. He devastated Attica, but Persian forces were defeated on land at Plataea and in a sea battle at Salamis (480 BC), and retreated. Intermittent war continued in various areas until peace was signed in 449 BC.

persiflage /ˈpəːsɪflɑːʒ/ ▶ **noun** [mass noun] formal light and slightly contemptuous mockery or banter.
– ORIGIN mid 18th cent.: from French *persifler* 'to banter', based on *siffler* 'to whistle'.

persimmon /pəˈsɪmən/ ▶ **noun 1** an edible fruit that resembles a large tomato and has very sweet flesh.
2 the tree which yields the persimmon, related to ebony. ● Genus *Diospyros*, family Ebenaceae: the evergreen American *D. virginiana*, with dark red fruit, and the **Japanese persimmon** (*D. kaki*), cultivated for its orange fruit.

P

– ORIGIN early 17th cent.: alteration of Algonquian *pessemmins*.

persist ▶ verb [no obj.] continue in an opinion or course of action in spite of difficulty or opposition: *the minority of drivers who* **persist in** *drinking* | *we are* **persisting with** *policies that will create jobs for the future.* ■ continue to exist; be prolonged: *if the symptoms persist for more than a few days, then contact your doctor.*
– ORIGIN mid 16th cent.: from Latin *persistere*, from *per-* 'through, steadfastly' + *sistere* 'to stand'.

persistence ▶ noun [mass noun] the fact of continuing in an opinion or course of action in spite of difficulty or opposition: *Cardiff's persistence was rewarded with a try.* ■ the continued or prolonged existence of something: *the persistence of huge environmental problems.*
– DERIVATIVES **persistency** noun.
– ORIGIN mid 16th cent.: from French *persistance*, from the verb *persister*; influenced in spelling by Latin *persistent-* 'continuing steadfastly'.

persistent ▶ adjective **1** continuing firmly or obstinately in an opinion or course of action in spite of difficulty or opposition: *one of the government's most persistent critics* | *an attempt to stop persistent drink-drivers.*
2 continuing to exist or occur over a prolonged period: *persistent rain will affect many areas* | *persistent reports of human rights abuses by the military.* ■ (of chemicals or radioactivity) remaining within the environment for a long time after introduction: *PCBs are persistent environmental contaminants.*
3 Botany & Zoology (of a part of an animal or plant, such as a horn, leaf, etc.) remaining attached instead of falling off in the normal manner.
– DERIVATIVES **persistently** adverb.

persistent organic pollutant ▶ noun a hazardous organic chemical compound that is resistant to biodegradation and thus remains in the environment for a long period of time.

persistent vegetative state ▶ noun a condition in which a medical patient is completely unresponsive to psychological and physical stimuli and displays no sign of higher brain function, being kept alive only by medical intervention.

persnickety ▶ adjective North American term for PERNICKETY.

person ▶ noun (pl. **people** or **persons**) **1** a human being regarded as an individual: *the porter was the last person to see her prior to her disappearance* | *she is a person of astonishing energy.* ■ (in legal or formal contexts) an unspecified individual: *each of the persons using unlawful violence is guilty of riot* | *the entrance fee is £2.00 per person.* ■ [with modifier] an individual characterized by a preference or liking for a specified thing: *she's not a cat person.* ■ a character in a play or story: *his previous roles in the person of a fallible cop.* ■ an individual's body: *I would have publicity photographs* **on my person** *at all times.* ■ dated (especially in legal contexts) used euphemistically to refer to a man's genitals.
2 Grammar a category used in the classification of pronouns, possessive determiners, and verb forms, according to whether they indicate the speaker (**first person**), the addressee (**second person**), or a third party (**third person**).
3 Christian Theology each of the three modes of being of God, namely the Father, the Son, or the Holy Ghost, who together constitute the Trinity.
– PHRASES **be one's own person** do or be what one wishes or in accordance with one's own character rather than as influenced by others. **in one's own person** archaic oneself; in person (used for emphasis). **in person** with the personal presence or action of the individual specified: *he had to pick up his welfare cheque in person.* **in the person of** in the physical form of: *trouble arrived in the person of a short, moustached Berliner.*
– ORIGIN Middle English: from Old French *persone*, from Latin *persona* 'actor's mask, character in a play', later 'human being'.

> **USAGE** The words **people** and **persons** can both be used as the plural of **person**, but they have slightly different connotations. **People** is by far the commoner of the two words and is used in most ordinary contexts: *a group of* ***people***; *there were only about ten* ***people***; *several thousand* ***people*** *have been rehoused.* **Persons**, on the other hand, tends now to be restricted to official or formal contexts, as in *this vehicle is authorized to carry twenty* ***persons***; *no* ***persons*** *admitted without a pass.*

-person ▶ combining form used as a neutral alternative to *-man* in nouns denoting professional status, a position of authority, etc.: *chairperson* | *salesperson* | *sportsperson.*

persona /pəˈsəʊnə, pəː-/ ▶ noun (pl. **personas** or **personae** /-niː/) the aspect of someone's character that is presented to or perceived by others: *her public persona.* In psychology, often contrasted with ANIMA. ■ a role or character adopted by an author or an actor.
– ORIGIN early 20th cent.: Latin, literally 'mask, character played by an actor'.

personable ▶ adjective (of a person) having a pleasant appearance and manner.
– DERIVATIVES **personableness** noun, **personably** adverb.

personage ▶ noun a person (used to express importance or elevated status): *it was no less a personage than the bishop.* ■ a character in a play or other work.
– ORIGIN late Middle English: from Old French, reinforced by medieval Latin *personagium* 'effigy'. In early use the word was qualified by words such as *honourable*, *eminent*, but since the 19th cent. the notion 'significant, notable' has been implied in the word itself.

persona grata /pəˌsəʊnə ˈɡrɑːtə, pəː-/ ▶ noun (pl. **personae gratae** /-niː, -tiː/) a person, especially a diplomat, acceptable to certain others.
– ORIGIN Latin, from *persona* (see PERSONA) + *grata*, feminine of *gratus* 'pleasing'.

personal ▶ adjective **1** [attrib.] belonging to or affecting a particular person rather than anyone else: *her personal fortune was recently estimated at £37 million.* ■ done or made by a particular person; involving the actual presence or action of a particular individual: *the President and his wife made personal appearances for the re-election of the state governor.*
2 of or concerning one's private life, relationships, and emotions rather than one's career or public life: *the book describes his sporting career and gives little information about his personal life.* ■ referring to an individual's character, appearance, or private life in an inappropriate or offensive way: *he had the cheek to make personal remarks.*
3 relating to a person's body: *personal hygiene.*
4 Grammar of or denoting one of the three persons. See PERSON (sense 2).
5 Theology existing as a self-aware entity, not as an abstraction or an impersonal force: *he rejected the notion of a personal God.*
▶ noun (usu. **personals**) chiefly N. Amer. an advertisement or message in the personal column of a newspaper.
– ORIGIN late Middle English: from Old French, from Latin *personalis* 'of a person', from *persona* (see PERSON).

personal action ▶ noun Law an action brought for compensation or damages for loss of a thing from the person responsible, rather than for recovery of the thing itself.

personal advertisement (also informal **personal ad**) ▶ noun a private advertisement or message placed in a newspaper, especially one from someone seeking a sexual or romantic partner.

personal assistant ▶ noun a secretary or administrative assistant working exclusively for one particular person.

personal column ▶ noun a section of a newspaper devoted to personal advertisements.

personal computer (abbrev.: **PC**) ▶ noun a computer designed for use by one person at a time.

personal equity plan (abbrev.: **PEP**) ▶ noun (in the UK) an investment scheme whereby personal investors may invest a limited sum each year in shares or unit trusts in British companies without liability for tax on dividends or capital gains (closed to new subscriptions in 1999, when replaced by the ISA).

personal estate ▶ noun Law another term for PERSONAL PROPERTY.

personal identification number (abbrev.: **PIN**) ▶ noun a number allocated to an individual and used to validate electronic transactions.

personal information manager ▶ noun a computer program functioning as an address book, organizer, diary, etc.

personal injury ▶ noun [mass noun] Law physical injury inflicted to a person's body, as opposed to damage to property or reputation.

personalism ▶ noun [mass noun] the quality of being personal. ■ a theory or system based on subjective ideas or applications. ■ allegiance to a particular political leader rather than to a party or ideology.
– DERIVATIVES **personalist** noun, **personalistic** adjective.

personality ▶ noun (pl. **personalities**) **1** the combination of characteristics or qualities that form an individual's distinctive character: *she had a sunny personality that was very engaging* | [mass noun] *she has triumphed by sheer force of personality.* ■ [mass noun] lively, engaging qualities: *she's always had loads of personality.*
2 a celebrity or famous person: *an official opening by a famous personality.*
3 [mass noun] archaic the quality or fact of being a person as distinct from a thing or animal.
4 (**personalities**) archaic disparaging remarks about an individual.
– ORIGIN late Middle English (in sense 3): from Old French *personalite*, from medieval Latin *personalitas*, from Latin *personalis* 'of a person' (see PERSONAL). Sense 1 dates from the late 18th cent.

personality cult ▶ noun excessive public admiration for or devotion to a famous person, especially a political leader.

personality disorder ▶ noun Psychiatry a deeply ingrained and maladaptive pattern of behaviour of a specified kind, typically apparent by the time of adolescence, causing long-term difficulties in personal relationships or in functioning in society.

personality inventory ▶ noun a type of questionnaire designed to reveal the respondent's personality traits.

personality type ▶ noun Psychology a collection of personality traits which are thought to occur together consistently, especially as determined by a certain pattern of responses to a personality inventory.

personalize (also **personalise**) ▶ verb [with obj.] **1** design or produce (something) to meet someone's individual requirements: *the wedding invitations will be personalized to your exact requirements.* ■ make (something) identifiable as belonging to a particular person, especially by marking it with their name or initials: (as adj. **personalized**) *a personalized number plate.*
2 cause (an issue, argument, etc.) to become concerned with personalities or feelings rather than with general or abstract matters: *the mass media's tendency to personalize politics.*
3 personify (something, especially a deity or spirit): *evil spirits personalized in Satan.*
– DERIVATIVES **personalization** noun.

personally ▶ adverb **1** with the personal presence or action of the individual specified; in person: *she stayed to thank O'Brien personally.* ■ as an individual rather than indirectly: *every pupil is known personally* | *he never forgave his father, holding him personally responsible for this betrayal.*
2 from one's personal standpoint; subjectively rather than objectively: *he had spoken personally and emotionally* | [sentence adverb] *personally, I think he made a very sensible move.* ■ in a private rather than public or professional capacity: *nothing had gone well personally or politically.*
– PHRASES **take something personally** interpret a remark or action as directed against oneself and be upset or offended by it: *at first I took it personally when he yelled at me.*

personal organizer ▶ noun a loose-leaf notebook with sections including a diary and pages for recording addresses and telephone numbers. ■ a handheld computer having the function of a personal organizer.

personal pension ▶ noun a pension scheme that is independent of the contributor's employer.

personal pronoun ▶ noun each of the pronouns in English (*I, you, he, she, it, we, they, me, him, her, us,* and *them*) comprising a set that shows contrasts of person, gender, number, and case.

> **USAGE** The correct use of personal pronouns is one of the most debated areas of English usage. **I, we, they, he,** and **she** are **subjective** personal pronouns, which means they are used as the subject of the sentence, often coming before the verb (***she*** *lives in Paris;* ***we*** *are leaving*). **Me, us, them, him,** and **her**, on the other hand, are **objective** personal pronouns, which means that they are used as the object of a verb or preposition (*John hates* ***me***; *his father left* ***him***; *I did it for* ***her***). This explains why it is not correct to say *John and* **me** *went to the shops*: the personal pronoun is in subject position, so it must be **I** not **me**. Using the pronoun alone makes the incorrect use obvious: ***me*** *went*

to the shops is clearly not acceptable. This analysis also explains why it is not correct to say *he came with you and I*: the personal pronoun is governed by a preposition (**with**) and is therefore objective, so it must be **me** not **I**. Again, a simple test for correctness is to use the pronoun alone: *he came with I* is clearly not acceptable. (See also **USAGE** at **BETWEEN**.)

Where a personal pronoun is used alone without the context of a verb or a preposition, however, the traditional analysis starts to break down. Traditionalists sometimes argue, for example, that *she's younger than* **me** and *I've not been here as long as* **her** are incorrect and that the correct forms are *she's younger than* **I** and *I've not been here as long as* **she**. This is based on the assumption that **than** and **as** are conjunctions and so the personal pronoun is still subjective even though there is no verb (in full form it would be *she's younger than* **I am**). Yet for most native speakers the supposed 'correct' form does not sound natural at all and is almost never used in speech. It would perhaps be more accurate to say that, in modern English, those personal pronouns listed above as being **objective** are used neutrally—i.e. they are used in all cases where the pronoun is not explicitly **subjective**. From this it follows that, despite the objections of prescriptive grammarians (whose arguments are based on Latin rather than English), it is standard accepted English to use any of the following: *Who is it? It's* **me**!; *she's taller than* **him**; *I didn't do as well as* **her**.

personal property ▸ **noun** [mass noun] Law all of someone's property except land and those interests in land that pass to their heirs. Compare with **REAL PROPERTY**.

personal representative ▸ **noun** Law an executor or administrator of the estate of a deceased person.

personal services ▸ **plural noun** commercial services such as catering and cleaning that supply the personal needs of customers.

personal shopper ▸ **noun** an individual who is paid to assist another to purchase goods, either by accompanying them while shopping or by shopping on their behalf.

personal space ▸ **noun** [mass noun] the physical space immediately surrounding someone, into which encroachment can feel threatening or uncomfortable: *he was invading her personal space*.

personal stereo ▸ **noun** a small portable audio player, used with lightweight headphones.

personal touch ▸ **noun** an element or feature contributed by someone to make something less impersonal: *all the rooms are simple but each has a personal touch to make you feel at home*.

personalty /ˈpəːs(ə)n(ə)lti/ ▸ **noun** [mass noun] Law a person's personal property. Compare with **REALTY**.
– ORIGIN mid 16th cent. (in the legal phrase *in the personalty* 'for damages'): from Anglo-Norman French *personaltie*, from medieval Latin *personalitas* (see **PERSONALITY**).

personal video recorder ▸ **noun** a device that records television programmes on to a hard disk and allows manipulation of programmes while they are being transmitted.

personal watercraft ▸ **noun** another term for **JET SKI**.

persona non grata ▸ **noun** (pl. **personae non gratae**) an unacceptable or unwelcome person: *Nabokov was persona non grata with the regime*.
– ORIGIN Latin, from *persona* (see **PERSONA**) + *non* 'not' + *grata*, feminine of *gratus* 'pleasing'.

personate ▸ **verb** [with obj.] formal play the part of (a character in a drama). ■ pretend to be (someone else), especially for fraudulent purposes such as casting a vote in another person's name.
– DERIVATIVES **personation** noun.
– ORIGIN late 16th cent.: from late Latin *personat-* 'represented by acting', from Latin *persona* 'mask' (see **PERSON**).

personhood ▸ **noun** [mass noun] the quality or condition of being an individual person.

personification ▸ **noun 1** [mass noun] the attribution of a personal nature or human characteristics to something non-human, or the representation of an abstract quality in human form.
2 a figure intended to represent an abstract quality: *the knight is accompanied by two feminine personifications of vice*. ■ a person or thing regarded as embodying a quality, concept, etc.: *he was the very personification of British pluck and diplomacy*.

personify ▸ **verb** (**personifies**, **personifying**, **personified**) [with obj.] represent (a quality or concept) by a figure in human form: *public pageants and dramas in which virtues and vices were personified*. ■ attribute a personal nature or human characteristics to (something non-human): *in the poem the oak trees are personified*. ■ represent or embody (a quality, concept, etc.) in a physical form: *the car personified motoring fun for two decades*.
– DERIVATIVES **personifier** noun.
– ORIGIN early 18th cent.: from French *personnifier*, from *personne* 'person'.

personnel ▸ **plural noun** people employed in an organization or engaged in an organized undertaking such as military service: *many of the personnel involved require training* | *sales personnel*. ■ short for **PERSONNEL DEPARTMENT**.
– ORIGIN early 19th cent.: from French (adjective used as a noun), contrasted with *matériel* 'equipment or materials used in an organization or undertaking'.

personnel carrier ▸ **noun** an armoured vehicle for transporting troops.

personnel department ▸ **noun** the part of an organization concerned with the appointment, training, and welfare of employees.

person of colour ▸ **noun** a person who is not white or of European parentage.

USAGE The term **person of colour** is first recorded at the end of the 18th century. It was revived in the 1990s as the recommended term to use in some official contexts, especially in US English, to refer to a person who is not white. The term is not common in general use, however, where terms such as **non-white** are still used.

person-to-person ▸ **adjective & adverb** taking place directly between individuals: [as adj.] *person-to-person transmission of the disease* | [as adv.] *making contact with him person to person*. ■ (in the US) denoting a phone call booked through the operator to a specified person.

perspective ▸ **noun 1** [mass noun] the art of representing three-dimensional objects on a two-dimensional surface so as to give the right impression of their height, width, depth, and position in relation to each other. ■ the appearance of viewed objects with regard to their relative position, distance from the viewer, etc.: *a trick of perspective*. ■ [count noun] a view or prospect. ■ Geometry the relation of two figures in the same plane, such that pairs of corresponding points lie on concurrent lines, and corresponding lines meet in collinear points.
2 a particular attitude towards or way of regarding something; a point of view: *most guidebook history is written from the editor's perspective*. ■ [mass noun] true understanding of the relative importance of things; a sense of proportion: *we must keep a sense of perspective about what he's done* | *though these figures shock, they need to be* **put into perspective**.
3 an apparent spatial distribution in perceived sound.
– DERIVATIVES **perspectival** adjective, **perspectively** adverb.
– ORIGIN late Middle English (in the sense 'optics'): from medieval Latin *perspectiva (ars)* '(science of) optics', from *perspect-* 'looked at closely', from the verb *perspicere*, from *per-* 'through' + *specere* 'to look'.

perspectivism ▸ **noun** [mass noun] **1** Philosophy the theory that knowledge of a subject is inevitably partial and limited by the individual perspective from which it is viewed.
2 the practice of regarding and analysing a situation or work of art from different points of view.
– DERIVATIVES **perspectivist** noun.

perspex ▸ **noun** [mass noun] trademark solid transparent plastic made of polymethyl methacrylate (the same material as plexiglas or lucite).
– ORIGIN 1930s: formed irregularly from Latin *perspicere* 'look through', from *per-* 'through' + *specere* 'to look'.

perspicacious /ˌpəːspɪˈkeɪʃəs/ ▸ **adjective** having a ready insight into and understanding of things: *it offers quite a few facts to the perspicacious reporter*.
– DERIVATIVES **perspicaciously** adverb.
– ORIGIN early 17th cent.: from Latin *perspicax, perspicac-* 'seeing clearly' + **-ACIOUS**.

perspicacity /ˌpəːspɪˈkasɪti/ ▸ **noun** [mass noun] the quality of having a ready insight into things; shrewdness: *the perspicacity of her remarks*.

perspicuous /pəˈspɪkjʊəs/ ▸ **adjective** formal clearly expressed and easily understood; lucid: *it provides simpler and more perspicuous explanations than its rivals*. ■ able to give an account or express an idea clearly.
– DERIVATIVES **perspicuity** noun, **perspicuously** adverb.
– ORIGIN late 15th cent. (in the sense 'transparent'): from Latin *perspicuus* 'transparent, clear' (from the verb *perspicere* 'look at closely') + **-OUS**.

perspiration ▸ **noun** [mass noun] the process of sweating: *exercise causes perspiration and a speeded-up heartbeat*. ■ sweat: *perspiration ran down his forehead*.
– DERIVATIVES **perspiratory** adjective.
– ORIGIN early 17th cent.: from French, from *perspirer* (see **PERSPIRE**).

perspire ▸ **verb** [no obj.] give out sweat through the pores of the skin as a result of heat, physical exertion, or stress: *Will was perspiring heavily*.
– ORIGIN mid 17th cent.: from French *perspirer*, from Latin *perspirare*, from *per-* 'through' + *spirare* 'breathe'.

persuadable ▸ **adjective** easily persuaded; amenable: *they need to identify the most persuadable voters*.
– DERIVATIVES **persuadability** noun.

persuade ▸ **verb** [with obj. and infinitive] induce (someone) to do something through reasoning or argument: *it wasn't easy, but I persuaded him to do the right thing*. ■ [with obj.] cause (someone) to believe something, especially after a sustained effort; convince: *health boards were finally* **persuaded of** *the desirability of psychiatric units* | [with obj. and clause] *he did everything he could to persuade the police that he was the robber*. ■ (of a situation or event) provide a sound reason for (someone) to do something: *the cost of the manor's restoration persuaded them to take in guests*.
– ORIGIN late 15th cent.: from Latin *persuadere*, from *per-* 'through, to completion' + *suadere* 'advise'.

USAGE For a discussion of the difference between **persuade** and **convince**, see **USAGE** at **CONVINCE**.

persuader ▸ **noun** a person who persuades someone to do something. ■ informal a gun or other weapon used to compel submission or obedience.

persuasion ▸ **noun 1** [mass noun] the action or process of persuading someone or of being persuaded to do or believe something: *Monica needed plenty of persuasion before she actually left*.
2 a belief or set of beliefs, especially religious or political ones: *writers of all political persuasions*. ■ a group or sect holding a particular religious belief: *the village had two chapels for those of the Primitive Methodist persuasion*. ■ humorous sort, kind, or nature: *half a dozen gents of British persuasion*.
– ORIGIN late Middle English: from Latin *persuasio(n-)*, from the verb *persuadere* (see **PERSUADE**).

P

persuasive ▸ **adjective** good at persuading someone to do or believe something through reasoning or the use of temptation: *an informative and persuasive speech*.
– DERIVATIVES **persuasively** adverb, **persuasiveness** noun.
– ORIGIN late 15th cent.: from French *persuasif, -ive* or medieval Latin *persuasivus*, from *persuas-* 'convinced by reasoning', from the verb *persuadere* (see **PERSUADE**).

PERT ▸ **abbreviation** programme evaluation and review technique.

pert ▸ **adjective 1** (of a girl or young woman) attractively lively or cheeky: *a pert, slightly plump girl called Rose*. ■ impudent or cheeky: *no need to be pert, miss*.
2 (of a bodily feature or garment) attractively small and well shaped: *she had a pert nose and deep blue eyes*.
– DERIVATIVES **pertly** adverb.
– ORIGIN Middle English (in the sense 'manifest'): from Old French *apert*, from Latin *apertus* 'opened', past participle of *aperire*, reinforced by Old French *aspert*, from Latin *expertus* (see **EXPERT**).

pertain ▸ **verb** [no obj.] **1** (**pertain to**) be appropriate, related, or applicable to: *matters pertaining to the organization of government*. ■ chiefly Law belong to something as a part, appendage, or accessory: *the shop premises and stock and all assets pertaining to the business*.
2 formal be in effect or existence in a specified place or at a specified time: *their economic circumstances are vastly different from those which pertained in their land of origin*.

– ORIGIN late Middle English: from Old French *partenir*, from Latin *pertinere* 'extend to, have reference to', from *per-* 'through' + *tenere* 'to hold'.

Pertex /ˈpəːtɛks/ ▶ **noun** [mass noun] trademark a lightweight breathable fabric used to make clothing and equipment for camping, climbing, and other outdoor pursuits.

Perth 1 a town in eastern Scotland, at the head of the Tay estuary; pop. 44,200 (est. 2009). The administrative centre of Perth and Kinross, it was the capital of Scotland from 1210 until 1452.
2 the capital of the state of Western Australia, on the Indian Ocean; pop. 1,602,559 (2008). Founded by the British in 1829, it developed rapidly after the discovery in 1890 of gold in the region and the opening in 1897 of the harbour at Fremantle.

Perth and Kinross a council area of central Scotland; administrative centre, Perth.

Perthshire a former county of central Scotland. It became a part of Tayside region in 1975 and of Perth and Kinross in 1996.

pertinacious /ˌpəːtɪˈneɪʃəs/ ▶ **adjective** formal holding firmly to an opinion or a course of action: *he worked with a pertinacious resistance to interruptions.*
– DERIVATIVES **pertinaciously** adverb, **pertinacity** noun.
– ORIGIN early 17th cent.: from Latin *pertinax, pertinac-* 'holding fast' + **-OUS**.

pertinent ▶ **adjective** relevant or applicable to a particular matter; apposite: *she asked me a lot of very pertinent questions | practitioners must consider all factors **pertinent to** a situation.*
– DERIVATIVES **pertinence** noun, **pertinency** noun, **pertinently** adverb.
– ORIGIN late Middle English: from Old French, or from Latin *pertinent-* 'having reference to', from the verb *pertinere* (see **PERTAIN**).

pertness ▶ **noun** [mass noun] **1** the quality of being attractively small and well shaped.
2 impudence; cheek.

perturb ▶ **verb** [with obj.] **1** make (someone) anxious or unsettled: *they were perturbed by her capricious behaviour* | [with obj. and clause] *he was perturbed that his bleeper wouldn't work.*
2 subject (a system, moving object, or process) to an influence tending to alter its normal or regular state or path: *nuclear weapons could be used to perturb the orbit of an asteroid.*
– DERIVATIVES **perturbable** adjective, **perturbative** /pəˈtəːbətɪv, ˈpəːtəbeɪtɪv/ adjective (sense 2).
– ORIGIN late Middle English: from Old French *pertourber*, from Latin *perturbare*, from *per-* 'completely' + *turbare* 'disturb'.

P

perturbation ▶ **noun 1** [mass noun] anxiety; mental uneasiness: *she sensed her friend's perturbation.* ■ [count noun] a cause of anxiety or uneasiness: *Frank's atheism was more than a perturbation to Michael.*
2 a deviation of a system, moving object, or process from its regular or normal state or path, caused by an outside influence. ■ Astronomy a minor deviation in the course of a celestial body, caused by the attraction of a neighbouring body.
– ORIGIN late Middle English: from Latin *perturbatio(n-)*, from the verb *perturbare* 'disturb greatly' (see **PERTURB**).

perturbed ▶ **adjective** anxious or unsettled; upset: *she didn't seem perturbed about the noises around her.*

pertussis /pəˈtʌsɪs/ ▶ **noun** medical term for **WHOOPING COUGH**.
– ORIGIN late 18th cent.: modern Latin, from **PER-** 'away, extremely' + Latin *tussis* 'a cough'.

Peru /pəˈruː/ a country in South America on the Pacific coast, traversed throughout its length by the Andes; pop. 29,547,000 (est. 2009); official languages, Spanish and Quechua; capital, Lima.

> The centre of the Inca empire, Peru was conquered by the Spanish conquistador Pizarro in 1532. Peru was liberated by Simón Bolívar and José de San Martín in 1820–4, and a republic established. It lost territory in the south in a war with Chile (1879–83) and also had border disputes with Colombia and Ecuador in the 1930s and 1940s.

– DERIVATIVES **Peruvian** adjective & noun.

Perugia /pəˈruːdʒə/ a city in central Italy, the capital of Umbria; pop. 165,207 (2008). It flourished in the 15th century as a centre of the Umbrian school of painting. A papal possession from 1540, it became a part of united Italy in 1860.
– DERIVATIVES **Perugian** noun & adjective.

peruke /pəˈruːk/ ▶ **noun** archaic a wig or periwig.
– ORIGIN mid 16th cent. (denoting a natural head of hair): from French *perruque*, from Italian *perrucca*, of unknown origin.

perusal ▶ **noun** [mass noun] formal the action of reading or examining something: *I continued my perusal of the instructions* | [count noun] *a quick perusal of the index to the book reveals an interesting fact.*

peruse /pəˈruːz/ ▶ **verb** [with obj.] formal read (something), typically in a thorough or careful way: *he has spent countless hours in libraries perusing art history books and catalogues.* ■ examine carefully or at length: *Laura perused a Caravaggio.*
– DERIVATIVES **peruser** noun.
– ORIGIN late 15th cent. (in the sense 'use up, wear out'): perhaps from **PER-** 'thoroughly' + **USE**, but compare with Anglo-Norman French *peruser* 'examine'.

> **USAGE** Note that **peruse** means 'read', typically with an implication of thoroughness and care. It does not mean 'read through quickly; glance over', as in *documents will be **perused** rather than analysed thoroughly*.

Peruvian bark ▶ **noun** [mass noun] cinchona bark.

Peruvian Current a cold ocean current that moves northwards from the Southern Ocean along the Pacific coast of Chile and Peru before turning westwards into the South Equatorial Current.

perv (also **perve**) informal ▶ **noun 1** a sexual pervert.
2 [in sing.] Austral./NZ a lustful or lecherous look: *come out here for a perv.*
▶ **verb** [no obj.] Austral./NZ gaze lustfully or lecherously: *we **perved on** them from a distance.*
– DERIVATIVES **pervy** adjective (**pervier**, **perviest**).
– ORIGIN 1940s: abbreviation of the noun **PERVERT**.

pervade ▶ **verb** [with obj.] (especially of a smell) spread through and be perceived in every part of: *a smell of stale cabbage pervaded the air.* ■ be present and apparent throughout: *the sense of crisis which pervaded Europe in the 1930s.*
– DERIVATIVES **pervader** noun, **pervasion** noun.
– ORIGIN mid 17th cent. (also in the sense 'traverse'): from Latin *pervadere*, from *per-* 'throughout' + *vadere* 'go'.

pervasive ▶ **adjective** (especially of an unwelcome influence or physical effect) spreading widely throughout an area or a group of people: *ageism is pervasive and entrenched in our society.*
– DERIVATIVES **pervasively** adverb, **pervasiveness** noun.
– ORIGIN mid 18th cent.: from Latin *pervas-* 'passed through' (from the verb *pervadere*) + **-IVE**.

perverse ▶ **adjective 1** showing a deliberate and obstinate desire to behave in a way that is unreasonable or unacceptable: *Kate's perverse decision not to cooperate held good.*
2 contrary to the accepted or expected standard or practice: *in two general elections the outcome was quite perverse.* ■ Law (of a verdict) against the weight of evidence or the direction of the judge on a point of law.
3 sexually perverted.
– DERIVATIVES **perversely** adverb [sentence adverb] *perversely, she felt nearer to tears now than at any other moment in the conversation*, **perverseness** noun.
– ORIGIN late Middle English (in the sense 'turned away from what is right or good'): from Old French *pervers(e)*, from Latin *perversus* 'turned about', from the verb *pervertere* (see **PERVERT**).

perversion ▶ **noun** [mass noun] **1** distortion or corruption of the original course, meaning, or state of something: *the thing which most disturbed him was the perversion of language and truth* | [count noun] *a scandalous perversion of the law.*
2 sexual behaviour that is considered abnormal and unacceptable.
– ORIGIN late Middle English: from Latin *perversio(n-)*, from the verb *pervertere* 'turn about' (see **PERVERT**).

perversity ▶ **noun** (pl. **perversities**) **1** a deliberate desire to behave in an unreasonable or unacceptable way; contrariness: *they responded with typical perversity.*
2 the quality of being contrary to accepted standards or practice; unreasonableness: *the perversity of being able to carry a gun but not purchase a drink.*
3 the quality of being sexually perverted.

pervert ▶ **verb** [with obj.] **1** distort or corrupt the original course, meaning, or state of (something): *he was charged with conspiring to pervert the course of justice.*
2 lead (someone) away from what is considered natural or acceptable: *Hector is a man who is simply perverted by his time.* ■ (as adj. **perverted**) sexually abnormal and unacceptable: *he whispered perverted obscenities.*
▶ **noun** a person whose sexual behaviour is regarded as abnormal and unacceptable.
– DERIVATIVES **pervertedly** adverb, **perverter** noun.
– ORIGIN late Middle English (as a verb): from Old French *pervertir*, from Latin *pervertere*, from *per-* 'thoroughly, to ill effect' + *vertere* 'to turn'. The current noun sense dates from the late 19th cent.

pervious /ˈpəːvɪəs/ ▶ **adjective** (of a substance) allowing water to pass through; permeable: *pervious rocks.*
– ORIGIN early 17th cent.: from Latin *pervius* 'having a passage through' (based on *via* 'way') + **-OUS**.

pes /peɪz, piːz/ ▶ **noun** (pl. **pedes** /ˈpɛdeɪz, ˈpɛdiːz/) technical the human foot, or the corresponding terminal segment of the hindlimb of a vertebrate animal.
– ORIGIN mid 19th cent.: from Latin, 'foot'.

Pesach /ˈpeɪsɑːx/ ▶ **noun** Jewish term for the Passover festival.
– ORIGIN from Hebrew *Pesaḥ*.

pescatarian /ˌpɛskəˈtɛːrɪən/ ▶ **noun** a person who does not eat meat but does eat fish.
– ORIGIN 1990s: from Italian *pesce* 'fish', on the pattern of *vegetarian*.

pes cavus /ˈkeɪvəs, ˈkɑːvəs/ ▶ **noun** technical term for **CLAW FOOT** (sense 2).
– ORIGIN Latin.

peseta /pəˈseɪtə/ ▶ **noun** (until the introduction of the euro in 2002) the basic monetary unit of Spain, equal to 100 centimos.
– ORIGIN Spanish, diminutive of *pesa* 'weight', from Latin *pensa* 'things weighed', from the verb *pendere* 'weigh'.

pesewa /pɛˈsiːwə/ ▶ **noun** a monetary unit of Ghana, equal to one hundredth of a cedi.
– ORIGIN Akan, literally 'penny'.

Peshawar /pəˈʃɑːwə/ the capital of North-West Frontier Province, in Pakistan; pop. 1,390,900 (est. 2009). Mentioned in early Sanskrit literature, it is one of Pakistan's oldest cities. Under Sikh rule from 1834, it was occupied by the British between 1849 and 1947. Situated near the Khyber Pass on the border with Afghanistan, it is of strategic and military importance.

Peshitta /pəˈʃiːtə/ ▶ **noun** the ancient Syriac version of the Bible, used in Syriac-speaking Christian countries from the early 5th century and still the official Bible of the Syrian Christian Churches.
– ORIGIN Syriac, literally 'simple, plain'.

peshmerga /pɛʃˈməːɡə/ ▶ **noun** (pl. **same** or **peshmergas**) a member of a Kurdish nationalist guerrilla organization.
– ORIGIN from Kurdish *pêshmerge*, from *pêsh* 'before' + *merg* 'death'.

pesky ▶ **adjective** (**peskier**, **peskiest**) informal, chiefly N. Amer. causing trouble; annoying: *a pesky younger brother.*
– DERIVATIVES **peskily** adverb, **peskiness** noun.
– ORIGIN late 18th cent.: perhaps related to **PEST**.

peso /ˈpeɪsəʊ/ ▶ **noun** (pl. **pesos**) the basic monetary unit of several Latin American countries and of the Philippines, equal to 100 centésimos in Uruguay and 100 centavos elsewhere.
– ORIGIN Spanish, literally 'weight', from Latin *pensum* 'something weighed', from the verb *pendere* 'weigh'.

pes planus /ˈpleɪnəs, ˈplɑːnəs/ ▶ **noun** technical term for **FLAT FOOT**.
– ORIGIN Latin.

pessary /ˈpɛs(ə)ri/ ▶ **noun** (pl. **pessaries**) a small soluble block that is inserted into the vagina to treat infection or as a contraceptive. ■ an elastic or rigid device that is inserted into the vagina to support the uterus.
– ORIGIN late Middle English: from late Latin *pessarium*, based on Greek *pessos* 'oval stone' (used in board games).

pessimism ▶ **noun** [mass noun] **1** a tendency to see the worst aspect of things or believe that the worst will happen: *the dispute cast an air of deep pessimism over the future of the peace talks.*
2 Philosophy a belief that this world is as bad as it could be or that evil will ultimately prevail over good.
– DERIVATIVES **pessimist** noun.
– ORIGIN late 18th cent.: from Latin *pessimus* 'worst', on the pattern of *optimism*.

pessimistic ▶ adjective tending to see the worst aspect of things or believe that the worst will happen: *he was pessimistic about the prospects.*
– DERIVATIVES **pessimistically** adverb.

pest ▶ noun a destructive insect or other animal that attacks crops, food, livestock, etc. ■ informal an annoying person or thing; a nuisance: *he was a real pest.* ■ **(the pest)** archaic bubonic plague.
– ORIGIN late 15th cent. (denoting the bubonic plague): from French *peste* or Latin *pestis* 'plague'.

Pestalozzi /ˌpɛstəˈlɒtsi/, Johann Heinrich (1746–1827), Swiss educational reformer. He pioneered education for poor children and had a major impact on the development of primary education.

pester ▶ verb [with obj.] trouble or annoy (someone) with frequent or persistent requests or interruptions: *she constantly pestered him with telephone calls.*
– ORIGIN mid 16th cent. (in the senses 'overcrowd (a place)' and 'impede (a person)'): from French *empestrer* 'encumber', influenced by **PEST**. The current sense is an extension of an earlier use, 'infest', referring to vermin.

pester power ▶ noun [mass noun] informal the ability of children to pressurize their parents into buying them products, especially items advertised in the media.

pesthouse ▶ noun historical a hospital for people suffering from infectious diseases, especially the plague.

pesticide ▶ noun a substance used for destroying insects or other organisms harmful to cultivated plants or to animals.
– DERIVATIVES **pesticidal** adjective.

pestiferous ▶ adjective literary harbouring infection and disease: *the pestiferous area around the prison.* ■ humorous constituting a nuisance; very annoying: *that pestiferous nephew of yours.*
– ORIGIN late Middle English (in the sense 'morally corrupting'): from Latin *pestifer* 'bringing pestilence' + **-OUS**.

pestilence ▶ noun archaic a fatal epidemic disease, especially bubonic plague.
– ORIGIN Middle English (also denoting something morally corrupting): from Old French, from Latin *pestilentia*, based on *pestis* 'a plague'.

pestilent ▶ adjective destructive to life; deadly: *pestilent diseases.* ■ informal, dated causing annoyance; troublesome: *he regarded journalists as a whole as a pestilent race.* ■ archaic harmful or dangerous to morals or public order; pernicious: *the pestilent sect of Luther.*
– DERIVATIVES **pestilently** adverb.
– ORIGIN late Middle English: from Latin *pestilens*, *pestilent-* 'unhealthy, destructive', from *pestis* 'plague'.

pestilential ▶ adjective relating to or tending to cause infectious diseases: *pestilential fever.* ■ very widespread and troublesome: *a pestilential weed.* ■ informal annoying: *what a pestilential man!*

pestle /ˈpɛs(ə)l/ ▶ noun a heavy tool with a rounded end, used for crushing and grinding substances such as spices or drugs, typically in a mortar. ■ a mechanical device for grinding, pounding, or stamping something.
▶ verb [with obj.] crush or grind with a pestle.
– ORIGIN Middle English: from Old French *pestel*, from Latin *pistillum*, from *pist-* 'pounded', from the verb *pinsere*.

pesto /ˈpɛstəʊ/ ▶ noun [mass noun] a sauce of crushed basil leaves, pine nuts, garlic, Parmesan cheese, and olive oil, typically served with pasta.
– ORIGIN Italian, from *pestare* 'pound, crush'.

PET ▶ abbreviation ■ polyethylene terephthalate. ■ positron emission tomography, a form of tomography used especially for brain scans.

pet¹ ▶ noun a domestic or tamed animal or bird kept for companionship or pleasure: *the pony was a family pet* | [as modifier] *a pet cat* | *pet food.* ■ a person treated with special favour or affection: *she is the pet of the family* | [as modifier] *I found the chairs at my pet antiques dealer in Cannes.* ■ [as modifier] treated with special attention or evoking particularly strong feelings: *another of her pet projects was the arts centre* | *my pet hate is woodwork.* ■ Brit. used as an affectionate form of address: *don't cry, pet, it's all right.*
▶ verb **(pets, petting, petted)** [with obj.] stroke or pat (an animal) affectionately: *the cats came to be petted.* ■ treat (someone) with affection or favouritism; pamper: *I was cosseted and petted and never shouted at.* ■ [no obj.] engage in sexually stimulating caressing and touching: *couples necking and petting in cars.*
– DERIVATIVES **petter** noun.
– ORIGIN early 16th cent. (as a noun; originally Scots and northern English): of unknown origin.

pet² ▶ noun [in sing.] a fit of sulking or ill humour: *Mother's in a pet.*
– ORIGIN late 16th cent.: of unknown origin.

Pet. ▶ abbreviation Peter (in biblical references).

peta- /ˈpɛtə/ ▶ combining form (used in units of measurement) denoting a factor of 10^{15}: *petabytes.*
– ORIGIN from *pe(n)ta-* (see **PENTA-**), based on the supposed analogy of *tera-* and *tetra-*.

petabyte (abbrev.: **Pb** or **PB**) ▶ noun Computing a unit of information equal to one thousand million million (10^{15}) or strictly 2^{50} bytes.

Pétain /peɪˈtã/, French /petɛ̃/, (Henri) Philippe (Omer) (1856–1951), French general and statesman, head of state 1940–4. He concluded an armistice with Nazi Germany in 1940 and established the French government at Vichy (effectively a puppet regime for the Third Reich) until 1944.

petal ▶ noun each of the segments of the corolla of a flower, which are modified leaves and are typically coloured.
– ORIGIN early 18th cent.: from modern Latin *petalum* (in late Latin 'metal plate'), from Greek *petalon* 'leaf', neuter (used as a noun) of *petalos* 'outspread'.

pétanque /pəˈtaŋk/, French /petɑ̃k/ ▶ noun [mass noun] a game similar to boules played chiefly in Provence.
– ORIGIN French, from Provençal *pèd tanco*, literally 'foot fixed (to the ground)', describing the start position.

petard /pɪˈtɑːd/ ▶ noun historical a small bomb made of a metal or wooden box filled with powder, used to blast down a door or to make a hole in a wall. ■ a kind of firework that explodes with a sharp report.
– PHRASES **be hoist with** (or **by**) **one's own petard** have one's plans to cause trouble for others backfire on one. [from Shakespeare's *Hamlet* (III. iv. 207); *hoist* is in the sense 'lifted and removed', past participle of dialect *hoise* (see **HOIST**).]
– ORIGIN mid 16th cent.: from French *pétard*, from *péter* 'break wind'.

petasus /ˈpɛtəsəs/ ▶ noun a hat with a low crown and broad brim, worn in ancient Greece. ■ Greek Mythology a winged petasus worn by Hermes.
– ORIGIN via Latin from Greek *petasos*.

petcock ▶ noun a small valve positioned in the pipe of a steam boiler or cylinder of a steam engine for drainage or testing.

petechia /pɪˈtiːkɪə/ ▶ noun (pl. **petechiae** /-kiː/) Medicine a small red or purple spot caused by bleeding into the skin.
– DERIVATIVES **petechial** adjective.
– ORIGIN late 18th cent.: modern Latin, from Italian *petecchia*, denoting a freckle or spot on the face, from Latin *petigo* 'scab, eruption'.

peter¹ ▶ verb [no obj.] decrease or fade gradually before coming to an end: *the storm had petered out.*
– ORIGIN early 19th cent.: of unknown origin.

peter² ▶ noun informal **1** a man's penis.
2 Austral./NZ a prison cell.
3 a safe or trunk.
– ORIGIN late Middle English: from the given name *Peter*, applied in many transferred uses. Current senses date from the 19th cent.

peter³ ▶ noun & verb Bridge another term for **ECHO**.
– ORIGIN late 19th cent.: from **BLUE PETER** (the invitation to one's partner to play a further lead in the suit being likened to the raising of this flag).

Peter I (1672–1725), tsar of Russia 1682–1725; known as **Peter the Great**. Peter modernized his armed forces before waging the Great Northern War (1700–21) and expanding his territory in the Baltic. His extensive administrative reforms were instrumental in transforming Russia into a significant European power. In 1703 he made the new city of St Petersburg his capital.

Peter, St an Apostle; born *Simon*. Peter ('stone') is the name given him by Jesus, signifying the rock on which he would establish his Church. He is regarded by Roman Catholics as the first bishop of the Church at Rome, where he is said to have been martyred in about AD 67. He is often represented as the keeper of the door of heaven. Feast day, 29 June. ■ either of the two epistles in the New Testament ascribed to St Peter.

Peterborough /ˈpiːtəˌbərə, -ˌbʌrə/ an industrial city in east central England; pop. 153,000 (est. 2009). An old city with a 12th-century cathedral, it has been developed as a planned urban centre since the late 1960s.

Peterborough ware ▶ noun [mass noun] Archaeology prehistoric pottery of the mid to late Neolithic in Britain (*c.*3400–2500 BC), characterized by a round base and decorated with the impressions of twisted cord and bird bones. Unlike the contemporary grooved ware, it is not associated with henge monuments.
– ORIGIN named after **PETERBOROUGH**, where certain Neolithic sites were located.

Peterloo massacre an attack by Manchester yeomanry on 16 August 1819 against a large but peaceable crowd. Sent to arrest the speaker at a rally of supporters of political reform in St Peter's Field, Manchester, the local yeomanry charged the crowd, killing 11 civilians and injuring more than 500.
– ORIGIN so named in ironical reference to the Battle of Waterloo.

peterman ▶ noun (pl. **petermen**) archaic a thief or safe-breaker.
– ORIGIN early 19th cent.: from slang *peter* 'a trunk or safe' + **MAN**.

Peter Pan the hero of J. M. Barrie's play of the same name (1904), a boy with magical powers who never grew up. ■ (as noun **a Peter Pan**) a person who retains youthful features or childlike characteristics.

Peter Pan collar ▶ noun a flat collar with rounded points.

Peter Principle ▶ noun the principle that members of a hierarchy are promoted until they reach the level at which they are no longer competent.
– ORIGIN 1960s: named after Laurence J. Peter (1919–90), the Canadian educationalist who put forward the theory.

petersham ▶ noun [mass noun] a corded tape used in dressmaking and millinery for stiffening.
– ORIGIN early 19th cent.: named after Lord *Petersham* (1790–1851), English army officer.

Peterson, Oscar (Emmanuel) (1925–2007), Canadian jazz pianist and composer. He became internationally famous in the 1960s, when he often appeared with Ella Fitzgerald.

Peter's pence ▶ plural noun **1** historical an annual tax of one penny from every householder having land of a certain value, paid to the papal see at Rome from Anglo-Saxon times until discontinued in 1534 after Henry VIII's break with Rome.
2 a voluntary payment by Roman Catholics to the papal treasury, made since 1860.
– ORIGIN named after St Peter, the first Pope (see **PETER, ST**).

P

Peters projection ▶ noun a world map projection in which areas are shown in correct proportion at the expense of distorted shape, using a rectangular decimal grid to replace latitude and longitude. It was devised in 1973 to be a fairer representation of equatorial (i.e. mainly developing) countries, whose area is under-represented by the usual projections such as Mercator's.
– ORIGIN named after Arno Peters (1916–2002), German historian.

Peter the Hermit (*c.*1050–1115), French monk. His preaching on the First Crusade was a rallying cry for thousands of peasants throughout Europe to journey to the Holy Land; most were massacred by the Turks in Asia Minor. Peter later became prior of an Augustinian monastery in Flanders.

pet form ▶ noun an altered form of a name used to express affection or familiarity.

pethidine /ˈpɛθɪdiːn/ ▶ noun [mass noun] Medicine a synthetic compound used as a painkilling drug, especially for women in labour.
– ORIGIN 1940s: from *p(iper)idine* (from which the drug is derived), with the insertion of *eth(yl)*.

pétillant /ˈpɛtɪjɒ̃/ ▶ adjective (of wine) slightly sparkling.
– ORIGIN French.

petiole /ˈpɛtɪəʊl/ ▶ noun **1** Botany the stalk that joins a leaf to a stem.
2 Zoology a slender stalk between two structures, especially that between the abdomen and thorax of a wasp or ant.
– DERIVATIVES **petiolar** adjective, **petiolate** /-lət/ adjective.
– ORIGIN mid 18th cent.: from French *pétiole*, from Latin *petiolus* 'little foot, stalk'.

Petipa /'pɛtɪpɑː/, Marius (Ivanovich) (1818–1910), French ballet dancer and choreographer, resident in Russia from 1847. Petipa choreographed more than fifty ballets, working with Tchaikovsky on *Sleeping Beauty* (1890) and *The Nutcracker* (1892).

petit /'pɛti/ ▸ **adjective** Law (of a crime) petty: *petit larceny.*
– ORIGIN late Middle English (in the sense 'small or insignificant'): from Old French, 'small'; the same word as PETTY, with retention of the French spelling.

petit battement ▸ **noun** Ballet a movement in which one leg is extended and lightly moved forwards and backwards from the ankle of the supporting leg.

petit beurre /,pɛtɪ 'bəː/ (also **petit beurre biscuit**) ▸ **noun** (pl. **petits beurres** pronunc. **same**) a sweet butter biscuit.
– ORIGIN French, literally 'little butter'.

petit bourgeois ▸ **adjective** of or characteristic of the lower middle class, especially with reference to a perceived conventionalism and conservatism: *the frail facade of petit bourgeois respectability.*
▸ **noun** (pl. **petits bourgeois** pronunc. **same**) a member of the lower middle class, especially when perceived as conventional and conservative.
– ORIGIN French, literally 'little citizen'.

petite ▸ **adjective** (of a woman) attractively small and dainty: *she was petite and vivacious.*
– ORIGIN late 18th cent.: French, feminine of *petit* 'small'.

petite bourgeoisie (also **petit bourgeoisie**) ▸ **noun** (**the petite bourgeoisie**) [treated as sing. or pl.] the lower middle class.
– ORIGIN French, literally 'little townsfolk'.

petite marmite /pə,tiːt mɑː'miːt/ ▸ **noun** [mass noun] soup served in an earthenware pot.
– ORIGIN French, literally 'little earthenware pot'.

petit four /,pɛtɪ 'fɔː, ,pɛtɪ/ ▸ **noun** (pl. **petits fours** /'fɔːz/) a very small fancy cake, biscuit, or sweet, typically made with marzipan and traditionally served after a meal.
– ORIGIN French, literally 'little oven'.

petitgrain /'pɛtɪgreɪn/ ▸ **noun** [mass noun] an essential oil with a floral scent distilled from the leaves and bark of the orange tree and from other citrus plants, used in perfumery.
– ORIGIN from French *petit grain* 'little grain' (from the small green fruits originally used).

petition ▸ **noun** a formal written request, typically one signed by many people, appealing to authority in respect of a particular cause: *she was asked to sign a petition against plans to build on the local playing fields.* ■ an appeal or request to a deity or a superior. ■ Law an application to a court for a writ, judicial action in a suit, etc.: *a divorce petition.*
▸ **verb** [with obj.] (often **petition someone/thing for**) present a petition to (an authority) in respect of a particular cause: *the organization is petitioning the EU for a moratorium on the patent* | [with obj. and infinitive] *the islanders petitioned the government to help them leave St Kilda.* ■ make an appeal to (a deity or superior): *a Highland chief petitioned her father for her hand in marriage.* ■ Law make a formal application to (a court) for a writ, judicial action in a suit, etc.: *the custodial parent petitioned the court for payment of the arrears* | [no obj.] *the Act allowed couples to petition for divorce after one year of marriage.*
– DERIVATIVES **petitionary** adjective, **petitioner** noun.
– ORIGIN Middle English: from Latin *petitio(n-)*, from *petit-* 'aimed at, sought, laid claim to', from the verb *petere*.

Petition of Right ▸ **noun 1** Brit. historical a parliamentary declaration of rights and liberties of the people assented to by Charles I in 1628.
2 English Law, chiefly historical a common-law remedy against the Crown for the recovery of property.

petitio principii /pɪ,tɪʃɪəʊ prɪn'sɪpɪʌɪ, prɪŋ'kɪp-/ ▸ **noun** Logic a fallacy in which a conclusion is taken for granted in the premises; begging the question.
– ORIGIN Latin, literally 'laying claim to a principle'.

petit jeté ▸ **noun** Ballet a jump in which a dancer brushes one leg out to the side in the air then brings it back in again and lands on it with the other leg lifted and bent behind the body.

petit-maître /,pətɪ'meɪtr(ə)/, French /p(ə)timɛtʀ/ ▸ **noun 1** a dandy or fop.
2 a minor musician, writer, or other artist.
– ORIGIN French, literally 'little master'.

petit mal /mal/ ▸ **noun** [mass noun] a mild form of epilepsy characterized by brief spells of unconsciousness without loss of posture. Compare with GRAND MAL. ■ [count noun] a petit mal fit.
– ORIGIN late 19th cent.: from French, literally 'little sickness'.

petit pain /,pətɪ 'pã/ ▸ **noun** (pl. **petits pains**) a small bread roll.
– ORIGIN French, literally 'little loaf'.

petit point /pɔɪnt, pwã/ ▸ **noun** [mass noun] a type of embroidery on a canvas ground, consisting of small, diagonal, adjacent stitches.
– ORIGIN late 19th cent.: from French, literally 'little stitch'.

petits pois /,pətɪ 'pwɑː/ ▸ **plural noun** young peas that are picked before they are grown to full size.
– ORIGIN French, literally 'small peas'.

pet name ▸ **noun** a name that is used instead of someone's usual first name to express fondness or familiarity.

Petra /'pɛtrə/ an ancient city of SW Asia, in present-day Jordan. The city, which lies in a hollow surrounded by cliffs, is accessible only through narrow gorges. Its extensive ruins include temples and tombs hewn from the rose-red sandstone cliffs.

Petrarch /'pɛtrɑːk/ (1304–74), Italian poet; Italian name *Francesco Petrarca*. His reputation is chiefly based on the *Canzoniere* (*c.*1351–3), a sonnet sequence in praise of a woman he calls Laura.

Petrarchan /pɪ'trɑːk(ə)n/ ▸ **adjective** denoting a sonnet of the kind used by the Italian poet Petrarch, with an octave rhyming *abbaabba*, and a sestet typically rhyming *cdcdcd* or *cdecde*.

petrel /'pɛtr(ə)l/ ▸ **noun** a seabird related to the shearwaters, typically flying far from land. ● Order Procellariiformes, in particular the families Procellariidae (e.g. the **giant petrel** and **pintado petrel**) or Hydrobatidae (the **storm petrels**).
– ORIGIN early 17th cent.: associated with St Peter, from the bird's habit of flying low with legs dangling, giving the appearance of walking on the water (see Matt. 14:30).

Petri dish /'pɛtri, 'piːtri/ ▸ **noun** a shallow, circular, transparent dish with a flat lid, used for the culture of microorganisms.
– ORIGIN late 19th cent.: named after Julius R. *Petri* (1852–1922), German bacteriologist.

Petrie /'piːtri/, Sir (William Matthew) Flinders (1853–1942), English archaeologist and Egyptologist. He began excavating the Great Pyramid in 1880. Petrie was the first to establish the system of sequence dating, now standard archaeological practice, by which sites are excavated layer by layer and historical chronology determined by the dating of artefacts found *in situ*.

petrification ▸ **noun** [mass noun] **1** (also **petrifaction**) the process by which organic matter exposed to minerals over a long period is turned into a stony substance. ■ [count noun] an organic object which has been turned to stone.
2 a state of such extreme fear that one is unable to move: *his heavy footfalls served to spur Paul out of his petrification.*

petrified ▸ **adjective 1** so frightened that one is unable to move; terrified: *the petrified child clung to her mother.*
2 (of organic matter) changed into a stony substance; ossified: *petrified wood.*

petrify ▸ **verb** (**petrifies**, **petrifying**, **petrified**) [with obj.] **1** change (organic matter) into a stony substance by encrusting or replacing it with a calcareous, siliceous, or other mineral deposit.
2 make (someone) so frightened that they are unable to move: *his icy controlled quietness petrified her.*
– ORIGIN late Middle English: from French *pétrifier*, from medieval Latin *petrificare*, from Latin *petra* 'rock', from Greek.

Petrine /'piːtrʌɪn/ ▸ **adjective 1** Christian Theology relating to St Peter or his writings or teachings. ■ relating to the authority of the Pope over the Church, in his role as the successor of St Peter.
2 relating to Peter I of Russia: *the Petrine reforms of the early 18th century.*

petrissage /pɛtrɪ'sɑːʒ/ ▸ **noun** [mass noun] a massage technique that involves kneading the body.
– ORIGIN late 19th cent.: French *pétrissage*, from *pétrir* 'to knead'.

petro- /'pɛtrəʊ/ ▸ **combining form 1** of rock; relating to rocks: *petrography.*
2 relating to petroleum: *petrodollar.*
– ORIGIN Sense 1 from Greek *petros* 'stone', *petra* 'rock'; sense 2 from PETROLEUM.

petrochemical ▸ **adjective** relating to or denoting substances obtained by the refining and processing of petroleum or natural gas: *a huge petrochemical works producing plastics.* ■ relating to petrochemistry.
▸ **noun** (usu. **petrochemicals**) a chemical obtained from petroleum and natural gas.

petrochemistry ▸ **noun** [mass noun] **1** the branch of chemistry concerned with the composition and formation of rocks (as distinct from minerals and ore deposits).
2 the branch of chemistry concerned with petroleum and natural gas, and with their refining and processing.

petrodollar ▸ **noun** a notional unit of currency earned by a country from the export of petroleum: *petrodollars were pouring into the kingdom.*

petrogenesis ▸ **noun** [mass noun] Geology the formation of rocks, especially igneous and metamorphic rocks.
– DERIVATIVES **petrogenetic** adjective.

petroglyph /'pɛtrə(ʊ)glɪf/ ▸ **noun** a rock carving, especially a prehistoric one.
– ORIGIN late 19th cent.: from PETRO- 'rock' + Greek *glyphē* 'carving'.

Petrograd /'pɛtrə(ʊ)grad/ former name (1914–24) for ST PETERSBURG.

petrography /pɛ'trɒgrəfi/ ▸ **noun** [mass noun] the branch of science concerned with the composition and properties of rocks.
– DERIVATIVES **petrographer** noun, **petrographic** adjective, **petrographical** adjective.

petrol ▸ **noun** [mass noun] Brit. **1** a light fuel oil that is obtained by distilling petroleum and used in internal-combustion engines.
2 (also **petrol blue**) a shade of greenish or greyish blue.
– ORIGIN late 19th cent.: from French *pétrole*, from medieval Latin *petroleum* (see PETROLEUM).

petrolatum /,pɛtrə'leɪtəm/ ▸ **noun** North American term for PETROLEUM JELLY.
– ORIGIN late 19th cent.: modern Latin, from PETROL + the Latin suffix *-atum*.

petrol bomb ▸ **noun** Brit. a crude bomb consisting of a bottle containing petrol and an improvised cloth wick that is ignited just before the bottle is thrown at the target.

petroleum ▸ **noun** [mass noun] a liquid mixture of hydrocarbons which is present in suitable rock strata and can be extracted and refined to produce fuels including petrol, paraffin, and diesel oil; oil.
– ORIGIN late Middle English: from medieval Latin, from Latin *petra* 'rock' (from Greek) + Latin *oleum* 'oil'.

petroleum coke ▸ **noun** [mass noun] the solid non-volatile carbon residue left after the distillation and cracking of petroleum.

petroleum ether ▸ **noun** [mass noun] a volatile liquid distilled from petroleum, consisting of a mixture of hydrocarbons.

petroleum jelly ▸ **noun** [mass noun] a translucent jelly consisting of a mixture of hydrocarbons, used as a lubricant or ointment.

petrolhead ▸ **noun** Brit. informal a car fanatic.

petroliferous /,pɛtrə'lɪf(ə)rəs/ ▸ **adjective** (of rock) yielding or containing petroleum.

petrology /pɪ'trɒlədʒi/ ▸ **noun** [mass noun] the branch of science concerned with the origin, structure, and composition of rocks. Compare with LITHOLOGY.
– DERIVATIVES **petrologic** adjective, **petrological** adjective, **petrologist** noun.

petrol station ▸ **noun** Brit. an establishment selling petrol and oil (and sometimes also other supplies and services) for motor vehicles.

Petronius /pɪ'trəʊnɪəs/, Gaius (d. AD 66), Roman writer; known as **Petronius Arbiter**. Petronius is generally accepted as the author of the *Satyricon*, a work in prose and verse satirizing the excesses of Roman society.

Petropavlovsk /,pɛtrə'pavlɒfsk/ **1** a Russian fishing port and naval base on the east coast of the Kamchatka peninsula in eastern Siberia; pop. 190,100 (est. 2006). Full name **Petropavlovsk-Kamchatsky** /,pɛtrə,pavlɒfsk,kam'tʃatski/.
2 a city in northern Kazakhstan; pop. 190,100 (est. 2006).

P

petrophysics ▸ plural noun [treated as sing.] the branch of geology concerned with the physical properties and behaviour of rocks.
– DERIVATIVES **petrophysical** adjective, **petrophysicist** noun.

petrosal /pɪˈtrəʊs(ə)l/ Anatomy ▸ noun the dense part of the temporal bone at the base of the skull, surrounding the inner ear.
▸ adjective relating to or denoting this part of the temporal bone, or the nerves which pass through it.
– ORIGIN mid 18th cent.: from Latin *petrosus* 'stony, rocky' (from *petra* 'rock') + **-AL**.

petrotectonics /ˌpɛtrəʊtɛkˈtɒnɪks/ ▸ plural noun [treated as sing.] the branch of geology concerned with the structure of rocks, especially as a guide to their past movements.
– DERIVATIVES **petrotectonic** adjective.

petrous /ˈpɛtrəs/ ▸ adjective Anatomy another term for **PETROSAL**.
– ORIGIN late Middle English: from Latin *petrosus* 'stony, rocky', from *petra* 'rock', from Greek.

Petrozavodsk /ˌpɛtrəzaˈvɒdsk/ a city in NW Russia, on Lake Onega, capital of the republic of Karelia; pop. 268,800 (est. 2008).

pe tsai /peɪ ˈtsʌɪ/ ▸ noun [mass noun] Chinese leaf of a variety which resembles lettuce.
– ORIGIN late 18th cent.: from Chinese (Cantonese dialect) *báicài*, literally 'white vegetable'.

Petsamo /ˈpɛtsəməʊ/ former name (1920–44) for **PECHENGA**.

petticoat ▸ noun a woman's light, loose undergarment hanging from the shoulders or the waist, worn under a skirt or dress. ■ [as modifier] informal, often derogatory used to denote female control of something regarded as more commonly dominated by men: *he was in danger of succumbing to the petticoat government of Mary and Sarah*.
– DERIVATIVES **petticoated** adjective.
– ORIGIN late Middle English: from *petty coat*, literally 'small coat': the word originally referred to a garment worn by men under a coat or doublet. The second sense derives from a later use to mean 'skirt'.

pettifog ▸ verb (**pettifogs**, **pettifogging**, **pettifogged**) [no obj.] archaic quibble about petty points.
■ practise legal deception or trickery.
– DERIVATIVES **pettifoggery** noun.
– ORIGIN early 17th cent.: back-formation from **PETTIFOGGER**.

pettifogger ▸ noun archaic an inferior legal practitioner, especially one who deals with petty cases or employs dubious practices.
– ORIGIN mid 16th cent.: from **PETTY** + obsolete *fogger* 'underhand dealer', probably from *Fugger*, the name of a family of merchants in Augsburg in the 15th and 16th cents.

pettifogging ▸ adjective placing undue emphasis on petty details; petty or trivial: *pettifogging attorneys were the bane of civil society*.

petting zoo ▸ noun N. Amer. a zoo at which visitors, especially children, may handle and feed the animals.

pettish ▸ adjective (of a person or their behaviour) childishly bad-tempered and petulant: *he comes across in his journal entries as spoiled and pettish*.
– DERIVATIVES **pettishly** adverb, **pettishness** noun.

petty ▸ adjective (**pettier**, **pettiest**) **1** of little importance; trivial: *the petty divisions of party politics*.
■ unduly concerned with trivial matters, especially in a small-minded or spiteful way: *she thought readers were being petty in writing to complain about blocked paths*.
2 [attrib.] of secondary or lesser importance, rank, or scale; minor: *a petty official*. ■ Law (of a crime) of lesser importance: *petty theft*. Compare with **GRAND**.
– DERIVATIVES **pettily** adverb, **pettiness** noun.
– ORIGIN late Middle English (in the sense 'small in size'): from a phonetic spelling of the pronunciation of French *petit* 'small'. Compare with **PETIT**.

petty bourgeois ▸ noun another term for **PETIT BOURGEOIS**.

petty bourgeoisie ▸ noun another term for **PETITE BOURGEOISIE**.

petty cash ▸ noun [mass noun] an accessible store of money kept by an organization for expenditure on small items.

petty larceny ▸ noun [mass noun] Law (in many US states and formerly in Britain) theft of personal property having a value less than a legally specified amount.

petty officer ▸ noun a rank of non-commissioned officer in the navy, above leading seaman or seaman and below chief petty officer.

petty serjeanty ▸ noun see **SERJEANTY**.

petty sessions ▸ noun (in the UK) a magistrates' court for the summary trial of certain offences.

petty treason ▸ noun see **TREASON**.

petty whin ▸ noun a small spiny European broom (shrub) of heath and moorland. ● *Genista anglica*, family Leguminosae.
– ORIGIN mid 16th cent.: from **PETTY** + **WHIN**[1].

petulance /ˈpɛtʃʊl(ə)ns/ ▸ noun [mass noun] the quality of being childishly sulky or bad-tempered: *a slight degree of petulance had crept into his voice*.

petulant /ˈpɛtjʊl(ə)nt/ ▸ adjective (of a person or their manner) childishly sulky or bad-tempered: *he was moody and petulant* | *a petulant shake of the head*.
– DERIVATIVES **petulantly** adverb.
– ORIGIN late 16th cent. (in the sense 'immodest'): from French *pétulant*, from Latin *petulant-* 'impudent' (related to *petere* 'aim at, seek'). The current sense (mid 18th cent.) is influenced by **PETTISH**.

petunia ▸ noun a South American plant of the nightshade family which has white, purple, or red funnel-shaped flowers, with many ornamental varieties.
● *Petunia* × *hybrida*, family Solanaceae.
– ORIGIN modern Latin, from French *petun*, from Guarani *petȳ* 'tobacco' (to which these plants are related).

petuntse /peɪˈtʊntsə, pɪˈtʌntsə/ ▸ noun [mass noun] a type of fine china stone used to make Chinese porcelain.
– ORIGIN early 18th cent.: from Chinese (Mandarin dialect) *báidūnzi*, from *bái* 'white' + *dūn* 'stone' + the suffix *-zi*.

Pevsner[1] /ˈpɛvznə/, Antoine (1886–1962), Russian-born French sculptor and painter, brother of Naum Gabo. With his brother he was a founder of Russian constructivism; the theoretical basis of the movement was put forward in their *Realistic Manifesto* (1920).

Pevsner[2] /ˈpɛvznə/, Sir Nikolaus (1902–83), German-born British art historian. He is best known for *The Buildings of England* (1951–74), a county-by-county guide to British architecture in 46 volumes which he edited and largely wrote.

pew ▸ noun a long bench with a back, placed in rows in the main part of some churches to seat the congregation. ■ Brit. informal a seat: *'Take a pew. What'll you have?'*
– ORIGIN late Middle English (originally denoting a raised, enclosed place in a church, provided for particular worshippers): from Old French *puye* 'balcony', from Latin *podia*, plural of *podium* 'elevated place'.

pewee /ˈpiːwiː/ (also **peewee**) ▸ noun a North American tyrant flycatcher with dark olive-grey plumage.
● Genus *Contopus*, family Tyrannidae: several species.
– ORIGIN late 18th cent.: imitative.

pewter ▸ noun [mass noun] a grey alloy of tin with copper and antimony (formerly, tin and lead). ■ utensils made of pewter: *the kitchen pewter*. ■ a shade of bluish or silver grey: [as modifier] *a pewter sky*.
– DERIVATIVES **pewterer** noun.
– ORIGIN Middle English: from Old French *peutre*, of unknown origin.

Peyer's patches /ˈpʌɪəz/ ▸ plural noun Anatomy the numerous areas of lymphoid tissue in the wall of the small intestine which are involved in the development of immunity to antigens present there.
– ORIGIN mid 19th cent.: named after Johann K. Peyer (1653–1712), Swiss anatomist.

peyote /peɪˈəʊti/ ▸ noun a small soft blue-green spineless cactus, native to Mexico and the southern US. Also called **MESCAL**. ● *Lophophora williamsii*, family Cactaceae.
■ [mass noun] a hallucinogenic drug prepared from the peyote cactus, containing mescaline.
– ORIGIN mid 19th cent.: from Latin American Spanish, from Nahuatl *peyotl*.

peyote buttons ▸ plural noun the disc-shaped dried tops of the peyote cactus, eaten or chewed for their hallucinogenic effects.

Peyronie's disease /ˈpɛrəniːz/ ▸ noun [mass noun] a condition in which a fibrous region forms in the erectile tissue of the penis, causing pain and curvature during erection.
– ORIGIN early 20th cent.: named after F. de la *Peyronie* (1678–1747), French physician.

Pf. ▸ abbreviation pfennig.

PFA ▸ abbreviation (in the UK) Professional Footballers' Association.

Pfc. ▸ abbreviation Private First Class.

PFD ▸ abbreviation personal flotation device, a life jacket or similar buoyancy aid.

pfennig /ˈ(p)fɛnɪg/ ▸ noun (pl. **same** or **pfennigs**) (until the introduction of the euro in 2002) a monetary unit of Germany, equal to one hundredth of a mark.
– ORIGIN from German *Pfennig*; related to **PENNY**.

PFI ▸ abbreviation (in the UK) private finance initiative, a scheme whereby public services such as the National Health Service raise funds for capital projects from commercial organizations.

pfui /ˈ(p)fuːi/ ▸ exclamation US variant spelling of **PHOOEY**.
– ORIGIN mid 19th cent.: from German.

PG ▸ abbreviation ■ parental guidance, a film classification indicating that some parents may find the film unsuitable for their children. ■ paying guest.

PGA ▸ abbreviation Professional Golfers' Association.

PGCE ▸ abbreviation Brit. Postgraduate Certificate of Education.

PGP ▸ noun Computing an email encryption program.
– ORIGIN 1990s: from the initial letters of *Pretty Good Privacy*.

pH ▸ noun Chemistry a figure expressing the acidity or alkalinity of a solution on a logarithmic scale on which 7 is neutral, lower values are more acid and higher values more alkaline. The pH is equal to $-\log_{10} c$, where *c* is the hydrogen ion concentration in moles per litre.
– ORIGIN early 20th cent.: from *p* representing German *Potenz* 'power' + **H**[2], the symbol for hydrogen.

phacelia /fəˈsiːlɪə/ ▸ noun a herbaceous American plant with clustered blue, violet, or white flowers.
● Genus *Phacelia*, family Hydrophyllaceae.
– ORIGIN modern Latin, from Greek *phakelos* 'cluster'.

Phaeacian /fiːˈeɪʃ(ə)n/ ▸ noun (in the *Odyssey*) an inhabitant of Scheria (Corfu), whose people were noted for their hedonism.
– ORIGIN from Latin *Phaeacia*, Greek *Phaiakia*, the name of the island of Scheria, + **-AN**.

Phaedra /ˈfeɪdrə, ˈfiːdrə/ Greek Mythology the wife of Theseus. She fell in love with her stepson Hippolytus, who rejected her, whereupon she hanged herself, leaving behind a letter which accused him of raping her. Theseus would not believe his son's protestations of innocence and banished him.

Phaeophyceae /ˌfʌɪə(ʊ)ˈfʌɪsiː/ ▸ plural noun Botany a class of lower plants that comprises the brown algae.
● Class Phaeophyceae, division Heterokontophyta (or phylum Heterokonta, kingdom Protista); formerly division Phaeophyta.
– ORIGIN modern Latin (plural), from Greek *phaios* 'dusky' + *phukos* 'seaweed'.

Phaethon /ˈfeɪəθən/ Greek Mythology the son of Helios the sun god. He asked to drive his father's solar chariot for a day, but could not control the immortal horses and the chariot plunged too near to the earth until Zeus killed Phaethon with a thunderbolt in order to save the earth from destruction.

phaeton /ˈfeɪt(ə)n/ ▸ noun historical a light, open four-wheeled horse-drawn carriage. ■ US a vintage touring car.
– ORIGIN mid 18th cent.: from French *phaéton*, via Latin from the Greek name *Phaethōn* (see **PHAETHON**).

phage /feɪdʒ/ ▸ noun short for **BACTERIOPHAGE**.

phage display ▸ noun [mass noun] Biochemistry a technique for the production and screening of novel proteins and polypeptides by inserting a gene fragment into a gene responsible for the surface protein of a bacteriophage. The new protein appears in the surface coating of the phage, in which it can be manipulated and tested for biological activity.

phagocyte /ˈfagə(ʊ)sʌɪt/ ▸ noun Physiology a type of cell within the body capable of engulfing and absorbing bacteria and other small cells and particles.
– DERIVATIVES **phagocytic** adjective.
– ORIGIN late 19th cent.: from Greek *phago-* 'eating' (from the verb *phagein*) + **-CYTE**.

phagocytosis /ˌfagə(ʊ)sʌɪˈtəʊsɪs/ ▸ noun [mass noun] Biology the ingestion of bacteria or other material by phagocytes and amoeboid protozoans.
– DERIVATIVES **phagocytize** /ˈfagəsʌɪtʌɪz/ (also **phagocytise**) verb, **phagocytose** verb.

P

phagosome /ˈfagə(ʊ)səʊm/ ▶ **noun** Biology a vacuole in the cytoplasm of a cell, containing a phagocytosed particle enclosed within a part of the cell membrane.
– DERIVATIVES **phagosomal** adjective.

-phagous ▶ **combining form** feeding or subsisting on a specified food: *coprophagous*.
– ORIGIN from Latin *-phagus*, Greek *-phagos* (from *phagein* 'eat') + **-OUS**.

-phagy ▶ **combining form** denoting the practice of eating a specified food: *anthropophagy*.
– ORIGIN from Greek *-phagia*, from *phagein* 'eat'.

phalange /ˈfalan(d)ʒ/ ▶ **noun 1** Anatomy another term for **PHALANX** (sense 2).
2 (**Phalange**) a right-wing Maronite party in Lebanon founded in 1936 by Pierre Gemayel.
– DERIVATIVES **Phalangist** noun & adjective (sense 2).
– ORIGIN mid 19th cent.: back-formation from *phalanges*, plural of **PHALANX**. Sense 2 is a shortening of French *Phalanges Libanaises* 'Lebanese phalanxes'.

phalangeal ▶ **adjective** Anatomy relating to a phalanx or the phalanges.

phalanger ▶ **noun** a lemur-like tree-dwelling marsupial native to Australia and New Guinea. ● Family Phalangeridae: several genera, in particular *Phalanger* and *Spilocuscus*, and including the cuscuses; the **common phalanger** is either the spotted cuscus or the grey cuscus. See also **FLYING PHALANGER**.
– ORIGIN late 18th cent.: from French, from Greek *phalangion* 'spider's web' (because of the webbed toes of their hind feet).

phalanges plural form of **PHALANX** (sense 2).

phalanstery /ˈfalanˌst(ə)ri/ ▶ **noun** (pl. **phalansteries**) a group of people living together in a community and holding property in common.
– ORIGIN mid 19th cent.: from French *phalanstère* (used by Charles Fourier in his socialist scheme for the reorganization of society), blend of Latin *phalanx* 'band (of soldiers), group' and French *monastère* 'monastery'.

phalanx /ˈfalaŋks/ ▶ **noun 1** (pl. **phalanxes**) a body of troops or police officers standing or moving in close formation: *six hundred marchers set off, led by a phalanx of police*. ■ a group of people or things of a similar type forming a compact body: *he headed past the phalanx of waiting reporters to the line of limos*. ■ (in ancient Greece) a body of Macedonian infantry drawn up in close order with shields touching and long spears overlapping.
2 (pl. **phalanges** /fəˈlan(d)ʒiːz/) Anatomy a bone of the finger or toe.
– ORIGIN mid 16th cent. (denoting a body of Macedonian infantry): via Latin from Greek.

P

phalarope /ˈfalərəʊp/ ▶ **noun** a small wading or swimming bird with a straight bill and lobed feet, unusual in that the female is more brightly coloured than the male. ● Genus *Phalaropus*, family Scolopacidae (subfamily Phalaropodinae): three species.
– ORIGIN late 18th cent.: from French, from modern Latin *Phalaropus*, formed irregularly from Greek *phalaris* 'coot' + *pous, pod-* 'foot'.

phalera /ˈfalərə/ ▶ **noun** (pl. **phalerae** /ˈfaləriː/) (in ancient Greece and Rome) a bright metal disc worn on the chest as an ornament by men, or used to adorn the harness of horses.
– ORIGIN Latin, from the Greek plural *phalara*.

phalli plural form of **PHALLUS**.

phallic ▶ **adjective** relating to or resembling a phallus or erect penis: *a phallic symbol*. ■ Psychoanalysis of or denoting the genital phase of psychosexual development, especially in males.
– DERIVATIVES **phallically** adverb.
– ORIGIN late 18th cent.: from French *phallique*, from Greek *phallikos*, from *phallos* (see **PHALLUS**).

phallocentric /ˌfalə(ʊ)ˈsɛntrɪk/ ▶ **adjective** focused on or concerned with the phallus or penis as a symbol of male dominance: *the apartment block was an architectural monument to a phallocentric world*.
– DERIVATIVES **phallocentricity** noun, **phallocentrism** noun.

phallocracy /faˈlɒkrəsi/ ▶ **noun** (pl. **phallocracies**) a society or system which is dominated by men and in which the male sex is thought superior.
– DERIVATIVES **phallocratic** adjective.
– ORIGIN 1970s: from Greek *phallos* 'phallus' + **-CRACY**.

phalloidin /faˈlɔɪdɪn/ ▶ **noun** [mass noun] Chemistry the toxin present in the death cap toadstool. It is a peptide with seven amino acids in a ring structure bridged by a sulphur atom.
– ORIGIN 1930s: from modern Latin *phalloides*, specific epithet of the death cap toadstool *Amanita phalloides* (based on Greek *phallos* 'phallus') + **-IN**[1].

phalloplasty /ˈfalə(ʊ)ˌplasti/ ▶ **noun** [mass noun] Medicine plastic surgery performed to construct, repair, or enlarge the penis.
– ORIGIN late 19th cent.: from Greek *phallos* 'phallus' + **-PLASTY**.

phallus /ˈfaləs/ ▶ **noun** (pl. **phalli** /-lʌɪ, -liː/ or **phalluses**) a penis, especially when erect (typically used with reference to male potency or dominance). ■ an image or representation of an erect penis, typically symbolizing fertility or potency.
– DERIVATIVES **phallicism** noun, **phallism** noun.
– ORIGIN early 17th cent.: via late Latin from Greek *phallos*.

Phanariot /fəˈnarɪət/ ▶ **noun** a Greek official in Constantinople under the Ottoman Empire.
– ORIGIN modern Greek *phanariōtēs*, from *Phanar*, chief Greek quarter of Istanbul, from Greek *phanarion* 'lighthouse' (one being situated in this area).

phanerogam /ˈfan(ə)rə(ʊ)gam/ ▶ **noun** Botany old-fashioned term for **SPERMATOPHYTE**.
– ORIGIN mid 19th cent.: from French *phanérogame*, from Greek *phaneros* 'visible' + *gamos* 'marriage'.

Phanerozoic /ˌfan(ə)rə(ʊ)ˈzəʊɪk/ ▶ **adjective** Geology relating to or denoting the aeon covering the whole of time since the beginning of the Cambrian period, and comprising the Palaeozoic, Mesozoic, and Cenozoic eras. Compare with **CRYPTOZOIC**. ■ (as noun **the Phanerozoic**) the Phanerozoic aeon or the system of rocks deposited during it.

> The Phanerozoic began about 570 million years ago, and covers the period in which rocks contain evidence of abundant life in the form of obvious mineralized fossils.

– ORIGIN late 19th cent.: from Greek *phaneros* 'visible, evident' + *zōion* 'animal' + **-IC**.

phantasize (also **phantasise**) ▶ **verb** variant spelling of **FANTASIZE** (restricted to archaic uses or, in modern use, to the fields of psychology and psychiatry).

phantasm /ˈfantaz(ə)m/ ▶ **noun** literary an illusion, apparition, or ghost: *the cart seemed to glide like a terrible phantasm*. ■ archaic an illusory likeness of something: *every phantasm of a hope was quickly nullified*.
– DERIVATIVES **phantasmal** adjective, **phantasmic** adjective.
– ORIGIN Middle English (in the sense 'deceptive appearance'): from Old French *fantasme*, via Latin from Greek *phantasma*, from *phantazein* 'make visible', from *phainein* 'to show'. The change from *f-* to *ph-* in the 16th cent. was influenced by the Latin spelling.

phantasmagoria /ˌfantazməˈgɔːrɪə, -ˈgɒrɪə/ ▶ **noun** a sequence of real or imaginary images like that seen in a dream: *what happened next was a phantasmagoria of horror and mystery*.
– DERIVATIVES **phantasmagoric** adjective, **phantasmagorical** adjective.
– ORIGIN early 19th cent. (originally the name of a London exhibition (1802) of optical illusions produced chiefly by magic lantern): probably from French *fantasmagorie*, from *fantasme* 'phantasm' + a fanciful suffix.

phantast ▶ **noun** variant spelling of **FANTAST**.

phantasy ▶ **noun** variant spelling of **FANTASY** (restricted to archaic uses or, in modern use, to the fields of psychology and psychiatry).

phantom ▶ **noun** a ghost: *a phantom who haunts lonely roads* | [as modifier] *a phantom ship*. ■ a figment of the imagination: *he tried to clear the phantoms from his head and grasp reality*. ■ [as modifier] not real; illusory: *a phantom conspiracy* | *the women suffered from phantom pain that no physician could ever find*. ■ [as modifier] denoting a financial arrangement or transaction which has been invented for fraudulent purposes: *he diverted an estimated £1,500,000 into 'phantom' bank accounts*.
– ORIGIN Middle English (also in the sense 'illusion, delusion'): from Old French *fantosme*, based on Greek *phantasma* (see **PHANTASM**).

phantom circuit ▶ **noun** an arrangement of telegraph or other electric wires equivalent to an extra circuit.

phantom limb ▶ **noun** a sensation experienced by someone who has had a limb amputated that the limb is still there.

phantom pregnancy ▶ **noun** Medicine an abnormal condition in which signs of pregnancy such as amenorrhoea, nausea, and abdominal swelling are present in a woman who is not pregnant.

pharaoh /ˈfɛːrəʊ/ ▶ **noun** a ruler in ancient Egypt.
– DERIVATIVES **pharaonic** /ˌfɛːreɪˈɒnɪk/ adjective.
– ORIGIN Middle English: via ecclesiastical Latin from Greek *Pharaō*, from Hebrew *par'ōh*, from Egyptian *pr-'o* 'great house'.

pharaoh ant (also **pharaoh's ant**) ▶ **noun** a small yellowish African ant that has established itself worldwide, living as a pest in heated buildings. ● *Monomorium pharaonis*, family Formicidae.
– ORIGIN so named because such ants were believed to be one of the plagues of ancient Egypt.

Pharaoh hound ▶ **noun** a hunting dog of a short-coated tan-coloured breed with large, pointed ears.
– ORIGIN 1960s: so named because the breed is said to have been first introduced to Gozo and Malta by Phoenician sailors.

Pharaoh's serpent ▶ **noun** an indoor firework that produces ash in a coiled, serpentine form as it burns.
– ORIGIN named by association with Aaron's staff which turned into a serpent before the Pharaoh (Exod. 7:9).

Pharisee /ˈfarɪsiː/ ▶ **noun** a member of an ancient Jewish sect, distinguished by strict observance of the traditional and written law, and commonly held to have pretensions to superior sanctity. ■ a self-righteous or hypocritical person.

> The Pharisees are mentioned only by Josephus and in the New Testament. Unlike the Sadducees, who tried to apply Mosaic law strictly, the Pharisees allowed some freedom of interpretation. Although in the Gospels they are represented as the chief opponents of Christ they seem to have been less hostile than the Sadducees to the nascent Church, with which they shared belief in the Resurrection.

– DERIVATIVES **Pharisaic** /ˌfarɪˈseɪɪk/ adjective, **Pharisaical** adjective, **Pharisaism** /ˈfarɪseɪˌɪz(ə)m/ noun.
– ORIGIN Old English *fariseus*, via ecclesiastical Latin from Greek *Pharisaios*, from Aramaic *prīšayyā* 'separated ones' (related to Hebrew *pārūš* 'separated').

pharma /ˈfɑːmə/ ▶ **noun 1** [mass noun] (often in phrase **big pharma**) pharmaceutical companies collectively as a sector of industry.
2 a pharmaceutical company.

pharmaceutical /ˌfɑːməˈsuːtɪk(ə)l, -ˈsjuː-/ ▶ **adjective** relating to medicinal drugs, or their preparation, use, or sale.
▶ **noun** (usu. **pharmaceuticals**) a compound manufactured for use as a medicinal drug. ■ (**pharmaceuticals**) shares in companies manufacturing medicinal drugs.
– DERIVATIVES **pharmaceutically** adverb, **pharmaceutics** plural noun.
– ORIGIN mid 17th cent.: via late Latin from Greek *pharmakeutikos* (from *pharmakeutēs* 'druggist', from *pharmakon* 'drug') + **-AL**.

pharmacist ▶ **noun** a person who is professionally qualified to prepare and dispense medicinal drugs.

pharmaco- /ˈfɑːməkəʊ/ ▶ **combining form** relating to drugs: *pharmacogenetics*.
– ORIGIN from Greek *pharmakon* 'drug, medicine'.

pharmacodynamics ▶ **plural noun** [treated as sing.] the branch of pharmacology concerned with the effects of drugs and the mechanism of their action.
– DERIVATIVES **pharmacodynamic** adjective.

pharmacogenetics ▶ **plural noun** [treated as sing.] the branch of pharmacology concerned with the effect of genetic factors on reactions to drugs.
– DERIVATIVES **pharmacogenetic** adjective.

pharmacogenomics /ˌfɑːməkəʊdʒɛˈnɒmɪks/ ▶ **plural noun** [treated as sing.] the branch of genetics concerned with determining the likely response of an individual to therapeutic drugs.

pharmacognosy /ˌfɑːməˈkɒgnəsi/ ▶ **noun** [mass noun] the branch of knowledge concerned with medicinal drugs obtained from plants or other natural sources.
– DERIVATIVES **pharmacognosist** noun.
– ORIGIN mid 19th cent.: from **PHARMACO-** 'of drugs' + *gnōsis* 'knowledge'.

pharmacokinetics /ˌfɑːməkəʊkɪˈnɛtɪks, -kʌɪ-/ ▶ **plural noun** [treated as sing.] the branch of pharmacology concerned with the movement of drugs within the body.
– DERIVATIVES **pharmacokinetic** adjective.

pharmacology /ˌfɑːməˈkɒlədʒi/ ▶ **noun** [mass noun] the branch of medicine concerned with the uses, effects, and modes of action of drugs.

– DERIVATIVES **pharmacologic** adjective, **pharmacological** adjective, **pharmacologically** adverb, **pharmacologist** noun.
– ORIGIN early 18th cent.: from modern Latin *pharmacologia*, from Greek *pharmakon* 'drug'.

pharmacophore /ˈfɑːməkəˌfɔː/ ▸ **noun** a part of a molecular structure that is responsible for a particular biological or pharmacological interaction that it undergoes.

pharmacopoeia /ˌfɑːməkəˈpiːə/ (US also **pharmacopeia**) ▸ **noun** an official publication containing a list of medicinal drugs with their effects and directions for their use. ■ a stock of medicinal drugs.
– DERIVATIVES **pharmacopoeial** adjective.
– ORIGIN early 17th cent.: modern Latin, from Greek *pharmakopoiia* 'art of preparing drugs', based on *pharmakon* 'drug' + *-poios* 'making'.

pharmacotherapy ▸ **noun** [mass noun] medical treatment by means of drugs.

pharmacy ▸ **noun** (pl. **pharmacies**) a shop or hospital dispensary where medicinal drugs are prepared or sold. ■ [mass noun] the science or practice of the preparation and dispensing of medicinal drugs.
– ORIGIN late Middle English (denoting the administration of drugs): from Old French *farmacie*, via medieval Latin from Greek *pharmakeia* 'practice of the druggist', based on *pharmakon* 'drug'.

pharming ▸ **noun** [mass noun] **1** the process of genetically modifying plants and animals so that they produce substances which may be used as pharmaceuticals.
2 the fraudulent practice of directing Internet users to a bogus website that mimics the appearance of a legitimate one, in order to obtain personal information such as passwords, account numbers, etc.
– ORIGIN 1990s: sense 1 punningly after **FARMING**; sense 2 patterned on **PHISHING**.

Pharos /ˈfɛːrɒs/ a lighthouse, often considered one of the Seven Wonders of the World, erected by Ptolemy II (308–246 BC) in *c.*280 BC on the island of Pharos, off the coast of Alexandria. ■ (as noun **a pharos**) a lighthouse or beacon to guide sailors.

pharyngeal /fəˈrɪn(d)ʒɪəl, ˌfarɪnˈdʒiːəl/ (also **pharyngal** /fəˈrɪŋɡl/) ▸ **adjective** relating to the pharynx. ■ Phonetics (of a speech sound) produced by articulating the root of the tongue with the pharynx, a feature of certain consonants in Arabic, for example.
▸ **noun** Phonetics a pharyngeal consonant.
– ORIGIN early 19th cent.: from modern Latin *pharyngeus* (from Greek *pharunx*, *pharung-* 'throat') + **-AL**.

pharyngealize /fəˈrɪn(d)ʒɪəlʌɪz/ (also **pharyngealise**) ▸ **verb** [with obj.] Phonetics articulate (a speech sound) with constriction of the pharynx.

pharyngitis /ˌfarɪnˈdʒʌɪtɪs/ ▸ **noun** [mass noun] Medicine inflammation of the pharynx, causing a sore throat.

pharyngo- /fəˈrɪŋɡəʊ/ ▸ **combining form** relating to the pharynx: *pharyngotomy*.
– ORIGIN from modern Latin *pharynx*, *pharyng-*.

pharyngotomy /ˌfarɪŋˈɡɒtəmi/ ▸ **noun** (pl. **pharyngotomies**) a surgical incision into the pharynx.

pharynx /ˈfarɪŋks/ ▸ **noun** (pl. **pharynges** /fəˈrɪn(d)ʒiːz/) Anatomy & Zoology the membrane-lined cavity behind the nose and mouth, connecting them to the oesophagus. ■ Zoology the part of the alimentary canal immediately behind the mouth in invertebrates.
– ORIGIN late 17th cent.: modern Latin, from Greek *pharunx*, *pharung-*.

phascogale /faˈskɒɡəliː/ ▸ **noun** a small arboreal flesh- and nectar-eating Australian marsupial with a pointed snout, large eyes and ears, and a bushy tail. ● Genus *Phascogale*, family Dasyuridae: two species.
– ORIGIN modern Latin, from Greek *phaskōlos* 'purse' + *galē* 'weasel'.

phase /feɪz/ ▸ **noun 1** a distinct period or stage in a process of change or forming part of something's development: *the final phases of the war* | [as modifier] *phase two of the development*. ■ a stage in a person's psychological development, especially a period of temporary difficulty during adolescence or a particular stage during childhood: *most of your fans are going through a phase*. ■ a stage in the life cycle or annual cycle of an animal.
2 each of the aspects of the moon or a planet, according to the amount of its illumination, especially the new moon, the first quarter, the full moon, and the last quarter.
3 Zoology a genetic or seasonal variety of an animal's coloration.
4 Chemistry a distinct and homogeneous form of matter (i.e. a particular solid, liquid, or gas) separated by its surface from other forms.
5 Physics the relationship in time between the successive states or cycles of an oscillating or repeating system (such as an alternating electric current or a light or sound wave) and either a fixed reference point or the states or cycles of another system with which it may or may not be in synchrony. ■ each of the electrical windings or connections of a polyphase machine or circuit.
6 Linguistics (in systemic grammar) the relationship between a catenative verb and the verb that follows it, as in *she hoped to succeed* and *I like swimming*. ■ a structure containing two verbs in a phase.
▸ **verb** [with obj.] **1** carry out (something) in gradual stages: *the work is being phased over a number of years* | (as adj. **phased**) *a phased withdrawal of troops*. ■ (**phase something in/out**) introduce something into (or withdraw something from) use in gradual stages: *the changes will be phased in over 10 years*.
2 Physics adjust the phase of (something), especially so as to synchronize it with something else.
– PHRASES **in** (or **out of**) **phase 1** being or happening in (or out of) synchrony or harmony: *the cabling work should be carried out* ***in phase with*** *the building work*. **2** Physics having or in the same (or different) phase or stage of variation.
– ORIGIN early 19th cent. (in sense 2 of the noun): from French *phase*, based on Greek *phasis* 'appearance', from the base of *phainein* 'to show'.

USAGE See **USAGE** at **FAZE**.

phase angle ▸ **noun** Physics a phase difference expressed as an angle, 360 degrees (2π radians) corresponding to one complete cycle. ■ Astronomy the angle between the lines joining a given planet to the sun and to the earth.

phase contrast ▸ **noun** [mass noun] the technique in microscopy of introducing a phase difference between parts of the light supplied by the condenser so as to enhance the outlines of the sample, or the boundaries between parts differing in optical density.

phase diagram ▸ **noun** Chemistry a diagram representing the limits of stability of the various phases in a chemical system at equilibrium, with respect to variables such as composition and temperature.

phase-lock ▸ **verb** [with obj.] Electronics fix the frequency of (an oscillator or a laser) relative to a stable oscillator of lower frequency by a method that utilizes a correction signal derived from the phase difference generated by any shift in the frequency.

phase modulation ▸ **noun** [mass noun] Electronics variation of the phase of a radio or other wave as a means of carrying information such as an audio signal.

phaser ▸ **noun 1** a device that alters a sound signal by phasing it.
2 (in science fiction) a weapon that delivers a beam that can stun or annihilate.

phase rule ▸ **noun** Chemistry a rule relating the possible numbers of phases, constituents, and degrees of freedom in a chemical system.

phase shift ▸ **noun** Physics a change in the phase of a waveform.

phase space ▸ **noun** Physics a multidimensional space in which each axis corresponds to one of the coordinates required to specify the state of a physical system, all the coordinates being thus represented so that a point in the space corresponds to a state of the system.

phase velocity ▸ **noun** Physics the speed of propagation of a sine wave or a sinusoidal component of a complex wave, equal to the product of its wavelength and frequency.

phasic /ˈfeɪzɪk/ ▸ **adjective** relating to a phase or phases. ■ chiefly Physiology occurring in phases rather than continuously: *phasic and tonic stretch reflexes*.

phasing ▸ **noun** [mass noun] the action of dividing a large task or process into phases: *the phasing of the overall project*. ■ the relationship between the timing of two or more events: *graphical techniques were used to investigate the phasing of traffic lights*. ■ the modification of the sound signal from an electric guitar or other electronic instrument by introducing a phase shift into either of two copies of it and then recombining them.

Phasmida /ˈfazmɪdə/ ▸ **plural noun 1** Entomology an order of insects that comprises the stick insects and leaf insects. They have very long bodies that resemble twigs or leaves.
2 Zoology a class of nematodes that includes the parasitic hookworms and roundworms. Also called **SECERNENTEA**.
– DERIVATIVES **phasmid** noun & adjective.
– ORIGIN modern Latin (plural), from Latin *phasma* 'apparition', from Greek.

phasor /ˈfeɪzə/ ▸ **noun** Physics a line used to represent a complex electrical quantity as a vector.
– ORIGIN 1940s: from **PHASE**, on the pattern of *vector*.

phat /fat/ ▸ **adjective** black slang excellent: *a London crew with a really phat funk sound*.
– ORIGIN 1970s (originally used to describe a woman, in the sense 'sexy, attractive'): of uncertain origin.

phatic /ˈfatɪk/ ▸ **adjective** denoting or relating to language used for general purposes of social interaction, rather than to convey information or ask questions. Utterances such as *hello, how are you?* and *nice morning, isn't it?* are phatic.
– ORIGIN 1920s: from Greek *phatos* 'spoken' or *phatikos* 'affirming'.

PhD ▸ **abbreviation** Doctor of Philosophy.
– ORIGIN from Latin *philosophiae doctor*.

pheasant ▸ **noun** a large long-tailed game bird native to Asia, the male of which typically has very showy plumage. ● Family Phasianidae: several genera and many species, in particular the **common pheasant** (*Phasianus colchicus*), which has been widely introduced for shooting.
– ORIGIN Middle English: from Old French *fesan*, via Latin from Greek *phasianos* '(bird) of Phasis', the name of a river in the Caucasus, from which the bird is said to have spread westwards.

pheasantry ▸ **noun** (pl. **pheasantries**) a place where pheasants are reared or kept.

pheasant's eye ▸ **noun** a plant of the buttercup family which has scarlet flowers with dark centres, native to southern Europe and SW Asia. ● *Adonis annua*, family Ranunculaceae.

pheasant shell ▸ **noun** a small marine mollusc which has a glossy white shell with red-brown markings. The foot bears a conspicuous white operculum. ● Family Phasianellidae, class Gastropoda: *Phasianella*, *Tricolia*, and other genera, including the European *T. pullus*.

Pheidippides /fʌɪˈdɪpɪdiːz/ (5th century BC), Athenian messenger. He was sent to Sparta to ask for help after the Persian landing at Marathon in 490 and is said to have covered the 250 km (150 miles) in two days on foot.

phen- ▸ **combining form** variant spelling of **PHENO-** shortened before a vowel (as in *phenelzine*).

phenacetin /fɪˈnasɪtɪn/ ▸ **noun** [mass noun] Medicine a synthetic compound used as a painkilling and antipyretic drug.
– ORIGIN late 19th cent.: from **PHENO-** + *acet(yl)* + **-IN**[1].

phenanthrene /fɪˈnanθriːn/ ▸ **noun** [mass noun] Chemistry a crystalline hydrocarbon present in coal tar. ● A tricyclic compound; chem. formula: $C_{14}H_{10}$.

phenanthridine /fɪˈnanθrɪdiːn/ ▸ **noun** [mass noun] Chemistry a white crystalline compound used in the treatment of trypanosome blood infection. ● A tricyclic compound; chem. formula: $C_{13}H_9N$.
– ORIGIN late 19th cent.: from **PHEN-** + *anthr(acene)* + **-IDE** + **-INE**[4].

phencyclidine /fɛnˈsʌɪklɪdiːn/ (abbrev.: **PCP**) ▸ **noun** [mass noun] a synthetic compound derived from piperidine, used as a veterinary anaesthetic and in hallucinogenic drugs such as angel dust.
– ORIGIN 1950s: from **PHENO-** + **CYCLO-** + a shortened form of **PIPERIDINE**.

phenelzine /fəˈnɛlziːn/ ▸ **noun** [mass noun] Medicine a synthetic compound used as a monoamine oxidase inhibitor.
– ORIGIN 1950s: from **PHENO-** + *e(thy)l* + *(hydra)zine*.

pheno- (also **phen-** before a vowel) ▸ **combining form**
1 Chemistry derived from benzene: *phenobarbitone*.
2 showing: *phenotype*.
– ORIGIN Sense 1 from French *phényle* 'phenyl', from Greek *phaino-* 'shining'; both senses from Greek *phainein* 'to show'.

phenobarbital /ˌfiːnə(ʊ)ˈbɑːbɪt(ə)l, ˌfɛnə(ʊ)ˈbɑːbɪt(ə)l/ ▸ **noun** US term for **PHENOBARBITONE**.

phenobarbitone /ˌfiːnə(ʊ)ˈbɑːbɪtəʊn, ˌfɛnə(ʊ)ˈbɑːbɪtəʊn/ ▸ **noun** [mass noun] Medicine a narcotic and sedative barbiturate drug used chiefly to treat epilepsy.

phenocopy /ˈfiːnə(ʊ)kɒpi/ ▸ **noun** (pl. **phenocopies**) Genetics an individual showing features characteristic

P

of a genotype other than its own, but produced environmentally rather than genetically.

phenocryst /ˈfiːnə(ʊ)krɪst, ˈfɛnə(ʊ)krɪst/ ▶ **noun** Geology a large or conspicuous crystal in a porphyritic rock, distinct from the groundmass.
– ORIGIN late 19th cent.: from French *phénocryste*, from Greek *phainein* 'to show' + *krustallos* 'crystal'.

phenol /ˈfiːnɒl/ ▶ **noun** [mass noun] Chemistry a mildly acidic toxic white crystalline solid obtained from coal tar and used in chemical manufacture, and in dilute form (under the name **carbolic**) as a disinfectant. • Chem. formula: C_6H_5OH.
■ [count noun] any compound with a hydroxyl group linked directly to a benzene ring.
– DERIVATIVES **phenolic** adjective.
– ORIGIN mid 19th cent.: from French *phénole*, based on *phène* 'benzene'.

phenology /fɪˈnɒlədʒi/ ▶ **noun** [mass noun] the study of cyclic and seasonal natural phenomena, especially in relation to climate and plant and animal life.
– DERIVATIVES **phenological** adjective.
– ORIGIN late 19th cent.: from PHENOMENON + -LOGY.

phenolphthalein /ˌfiːnɒlˈ(f)θaliːn, -ˈ(f)θeɪl-/ ▶ **noun** [mass noun] Chemistry a colourless crystalline solid (pink in alkaline solution) used as an acid–base indicator and medicinally as a laxative. • Chem. formula: $C_{20}H_{14}O_4$.
– ORIGIN late 19th cent.: from PHENOL + *-phthal-* (from NAPHTHALENE) + -IN[1].

phenol red ▶ **noun** [mass noun] Chemistry a red dye which is used as a pH indicator and (in medicine) injected in testing kidney function.

phenom ▶ **noun** N. Amer. informal a person who is outstandingly talented or admired; a star.
– ORIGIN late 19th cent.: abbreviation of PHENOMENON.

phenomena plural form of PHENOMENON.

phenomenal ▶ **adjective 1** remarkable or exceptional, especially exceptionally good: *the town expanded at a phenomenal rate*.
2 perceptible by the senses or through immediate experience: *the phenomenal world*.
– DERIVATIVES **phenomenally** adverb.

phenomenalism ▶ **noun** [mass noun] Philosophy the doctrine that human knowledge is confined to or founded on the realities or appearances presented to the senses.
– DERIVATIVES **phenomenalist** noun & adjective, **phenomenalistic** adjective.

phenomenology /fɪˌnɒmɪˈnɒlədʒi/ ▶ **noun** [mass noun] Philosophy the science of phenomena as distinct from that of the nature of being. ■ an approach that concentrates on the study of consciousness and the objects of direct experience.
– DERIVATIVES **phenomenological** adjective, **phenomenologically** adverb, **phenomenologist** noun.

P

phenomenon ▶ **noun** (pl. **phenomena**) **1** a fact or situation that is observed to exist or happen, especially one whose cause or explanation is in question: *glaciers are interesting natural phenomena*.
2 Philosophy the object of a person's perception.
3 a remarkable person or thing.
– ORIGIN late 16th cent.: via late Latin from Greek *phainomenon* 'thing appearing to view', based on *phainein* 'to show'.

> **USAGE** The word **phenomenon** comes from Greek, and its plural form is **phenomena**, as in *these phenomena are not fully understood*. It is a mistake to treat **phenomena** as if it were a singular form, as in *this is a strange phenomena*.

phenothiazine /ˌfiːnəʊˈθʌɪəziːn, ˌfɛnəʊ-/ ▶ **noun** [mass noun] Chemistry a synthetic compound which is used in veterinary medicine to treat parasitic infestations of animals. • A heterocyclic compound; chem. formula: $C_{12}H_9NS$.
■ [count noun] Psychiatry any of a group of derivatives of phenothiazine with tranquillizing properties, used in the treatment of mental illness.

phenotype /ˈfiːnə(ʊ)tʌɪp/ ▶ **noun** Biology the set of observable characteristics of an individual resulting from the interaction of its genotype with the environment.
– DERIVATIVES **phenotypic** adjective, **phenotypical** adjective, **phenotypically** adverb.
– ORIGIN early 20th cent.: from German *Phaenotypus* (see PHENO-, TYPE).

phentolamine /fɛnˈtɒləmiːn/ ▶ **noun** [mass noun] Medicine a synthetic compound used as a vasodilator, especially in certain cases of hypertension.
– ORIGIN 1950s: from PHEN- + *tol(yl)* (an isomeric cyclic radical derived from toluene) + AMINE.

phenyl /ˈfiːnʌɪl, ˈfɛnɪl/ ▶ **noun** [as modifier] Chemistry of or denoting the radical $-C_6H_5$, derived from benzene by removal of a hydrogen atom: *a phenyl group*.
– ORIGIN mid 19th cent.: from French *phényle*, from Greek *phaino-* 'shining' (because first used in names of compounds denoting by-products of the manufacture of gas used for illumination).

phenylalanine /ˌfiːnʌɪlˈalәniːn, ˌfɛnɪl-/ ▶ **noun** [mass noun] Biochemistry an amino acid widely distributed in plant proteins. It is an essential nutrient in the diet of vertebrates. • Chem. formula: $C_6H_5CH_2CH(NH_2)COOH$.

phenylbutazone /ˌfiːnʌɪlˈbjuːtəzəʊn, ˌfɛnɪl-/ ▶ **noun** [mass noun] a synthetic compound used as an analgesic drug in veterinary medicine.
– ORIGIN 1950s: from PHENYL + *but(yl)* + AZO- + -ONE.

phenylephrine /ˌfiːnʌɪlˈɛfrɪn, ˌfɛnɪl-, -ˈɛfriːn/ ▶ **noun** [mass noun] Medicine a synthetic compound related to adrenalin, used as a vasoconstrictor and nasal decongestant.
– ORIGIN 1940s: from PHENYL + a contraction of EPINEPHRINE.

phenylketonuria /ˌfiːnʌɪlˌkiːtə(ʊ)ˈnjʊərɪə, ˌfɛnɪl-/ (abbrev.: **PKU**) ▶ **noun** [mass noun] Medicine an inherited inability to metabolize phenylalanine which, if untreated, causes brain and nerve damage.

phenytoin /fɛˈnɪtəʊɪn/ ▶ **noun** [mass noun] Medicine a synthetic compound related to hydantoin, used as an anticonvulsant in the treatment of epilepsy.
– ORIGIN 1940s: blend of PHENYL and HYDANTOIN.

pheromone /ˈfɛrəməʊn/ ▶ **noun** Zoology a chemical substance produced and released into the environment by an animal, especially a mammal or an insect, affecting the behaviour or physiology of others of its species.
– DERIVATIVES **pheromonal** adjective.
– ORIGIN 1950s: from Greek *pherein* 'convey' + HORMONE.

phew ▶ **exclamation** informal expressing a strong reaction of relief, or of disgust at a smell: *phew, what a year!*
– ORIGIN early 17th cent.: imitative of puffing.

phi /fʌɪ/ ▶ **noun** the twenty-first letter of the Greek alphabet (Φ, φ), transliterated as 'ph' or (in modern Greek) 'f'. ■ (**Phi**) [followed by Latin genitive] Astronomy the twenty-first star in a constellation: *Phi Eridani*.
▶ **symbol** ■ (φ) a plane angle. ■ (φ) a polar coordinate. Often coupled with θ (theta).
– ORIGIN Greek.

phial /ˈfʌɪəl/ ▶ **noun** a small cylindrical glass bottle, typically used for medical samples or for potions or medicines: ***a phial of blood***.
– ORIGIN Middle English: from Old French *fiole*, via Latin from Greek *phialē*, denoting a broad flat container. Compare with VIAL.

Phi Beta Kappa /ˌfʌɪ ˌbiːtə ˈkapə/ ▶ **noun** (in the US) an honorary society of undergraduates and some graduates to which members are elected on the basis of high academic achievement. ■ a member of a Phi Beta Kappa society.
– ORIGIN from the initial letters of a Greek motto *philosophia biou kubernētēs* 'philosophy is the guide to life'.

Phidias /ˈfɪdɪas, ˈfʌɪd-/ (5th century BC), Athenian sculptor. He directed the carving of the Elgin Marbles and other sculptures at the Parthenon (447–432 BC); he is noted also for his vast statue of Zeus at Olympia (*c*.430), which was one of the Seven Wonders of the World.

Phil. ▶ **abbreviation** ■ Epistle to the Philippians (in biblical references). ■ Philadelphia. ■ Philharmonic. ■ Philosophy.

phil- ▶ **combining form** variant spelling of PHILO- shortened before a vowel or *h* (as in *philanthrope*, *philharmonic*).

-phil ▶ **combining form** having a chemical affinity for a substance: *acidophil* | *neutrophil*.
– ORIGIN see -PHILE.

Philadelphia /ˌfɪləˈdɛlfɪə/ the chief city of Pennsylvania, on the Delaware River; pop. 1,447,395 (est. 2008). Established as a Quaker colony by William Penn and others in 1681, it was the site in 1776 of the signing of the Declaration of Independence and in 1787 of the adoption of the Constitution of the United States.
– DERIVATIVES **Philadelphian** noun & adjective.
– ORIGIN from Greek *philadelphia* 'brotherly love'.

Philadelphia chromosome ▶ **noun** Genetics an abnormal small chromosome sometimes found in the leucocytes of leukaemia patients.

Philadelphia lawyer ▶ **noun** informal a very shrewd lawyer expert in the exploitation of legal technicalities.
– ORIGIN with reference to Andrew Hamilton of Philadelphia, who successfully defended John Zenger (1735), an American journalist and publisher, from libel charges.

philadelphus /ˌfɪləˈdɛlfəs/ ▶ **noun** a mock orange.
– ORIGIN late 18th cent.: modern Latin (adopted by Linnaeus as a genus name), from Greek *philadelphos* 'loving one's brother'.

philander /fɪˈlandə/ ▶ **verb** [no obj.] (of a man) readily or frequently enter into casual sexual relationships with women: *they accepted that their husbands would philander with other women*.
– ORIGIN mid 18th cent.: from the earlier noun *philander* 'man, husband', often used in literature as the given name of a lover, from Greek *philandros* 'fond of men', from *philein* 'to love' + *anēr* 'man'.

philanderer /fɪˈland(ə)rə/ ▶ **noun** a man who readily or frequently enters into casual sexual relationships with women; a womanizer: *he was known as a philanderer*.

philanthrope /ˈfɪlənˌθrəʊp/ ▶ **noun** archaic term for PHILANTHROPIST.
– ORIGIN mid 18th cent.: from Greek *philanthrōpos*, from *philein* 'to love' + *anthrōpos* 'human being'.

philanthropic /ˌfɪlənˈθrɒpɪk/ ▶ **adjective** (of a person or organization) seeking to promote the welfare of others; generous and benevolent: *they receive financial support from philanthropic bodies*.
– DERIVATIVES **philanthropically** adverb.
– ORIGIN late 18th cent.: from French *philanthropique*, from Greek *philanthrōpos* 'man-loving' (see PHILANTHROPE).

philanthropist ▶ **noun** a person who seeks to promote the welfare of others, especially by the generous donation of money to good causes.

philanthropy /fɪˈlanθrəpi/ ▶ **noun** [mass noun] the desire to promote the welfare of others, expressed especially by the generous donation of money to good causes. ■ [count noun] N. Amer. a philanthropic institution; a charity.
– DERIVATIVES **philanthropism** noun.
– ORIGIN early 17th cent.: via late Latin from Greek *philanthrōpia*, from *philanthrōpos* 'man-loving' (see PHILANTHROPE).

philately /fɪˈlat(ə)li/ ▶ **noun** [mass noun] the collection and study of postage stamps.
– DERIVATIVES **philatelic** adjective, **philatelically** adverb, **philatelist** noun.
– ORIGIN mid 19th cent.: from French *philatélie*, from *philo-* 'loving' + Greek *ateleia* 'exemption from payment' (from *a-* 'not' + *telos* 'toll, tax'), used to mean a franking mark or postage stamp exempting the recipient from payment.

Philby /ˈfɪlbi/, Kim (1912–88), British Foreign Office official and spy; born *Harold Adrian Russell Philby*. While working at the British Embassy in Washington DC (1949–51), Philby was asked to resign on suspicion of being a Soviet agent, although there was no firm evidence to this effect. He defected to the USSR in 1963 and was officially revealed to have spied for the Soviets from 1933.

-phile ▶ **combining form** denoting a person or thing having a fondness for a specified thing: *bibliophile* | *Francophile*.
– ORIGIN from Greek *philos* 'loving'.

Philem. ▶ **abbreviation** Philemon (in biblical references).

Philemon /fɪˈliːmən/ Greek Mythology a good old countryman living with his wife Baucis in Phrygia who offered hospitality to Zeus and Hermes when the two gods came to earth, without revealing their identities, to test people's piety. Philemon and Baucis were subsequently saved from a flood which covered the district.

Philemon, Epistle to a book of the New Testament, an epistle of St Paul to a well-to-do Christian living probably at Colossae in Phrygia.

philharmonic ▶ **adjective** devoted to music (chiefly used in the names of orchestras): *the Boston Philharmonic Orchestra*.
– ORIGIN mid 18th cent.: from French *philharmonique*, from Italian *filarmonico* 'loving harmony' (see PHIL-, HARMONIC).

philhellene /ˈfɪlhɛliːn, fɪlˈhɛliːn/ ▶ **noun** a lover of Greece and Greek culture: *a romantic philhellene*.
■ historical a supporter of Greek independence.

– DERIVATIVES **philhellenic** adjective, **philhellenism** noun.
– ORIGIN early 19th cent.: from Greek *philellēn* 'loving the Greeks' (see PHIL-, HELLENE).

-philia ▸ combining form denoting fondness, especially an abnormal love for a specified thing: *paedophilia.* ■ denoting undue inclination: *spasmophilia.*
– DERIVATIVES **-philiac** combining form in corresponding nouns and adjectives, **-philic** combining form in corresponding adjectives, **-philous** combining form in corresponding adjectives.
– ORIGIN from Greek *philia* 'fondness'.

philibeg /'fɪləbɛg/ ▸ noun variant spelling of FILIBEG.

Philip[1] the name of five kings of ancient Macedonia, notably: ■ **Philip II** (382–336 BC), father of Alexander the Great, reigned 359–336; known as **Philip II of Macedon**. He unified and expanded ancient Macedonia as well as carrying out a number of army reforms. His victory over Athens and Thebes at the battle of Chaeronea in 338 established his hegemony over Greece. ■ **Philip V** (238–179 BC), reigned 221–179. His expansionist policies led to a series of confrontations with Rome, culminating in his defeat and his resultant loss of control over Greece.

Philip[2] the name of six kings of France: ■ **Philip I** (1052–1108), reigned 1059–1108. ■ **Philip II** (1165–1223), son of Louis VII, reigned 1180–1223; known as **Philip Augustus**. After mounting a series of campaigns against the English kings Henry II, Richard I, and John, Philip succeeded in regaining Normandy (1204), Anjou (1204), and most of Poitou (1204–5). ■ **Philip III** (1245–85), reigned 1270–85; known as **Philip the Bold**. ■ **Philip IV** (1268–1314), son of Philip III, reigned 1285–1314; known as **Philip the Fair**. He continued to extend French dominions, waging wars with England (1294–1303) and Flanders (1302–5). ■ **Philip V** (1293–1322), reigned 1316–22; known as **Philip the Tall**. ■ **Philip VI** (1293–1350), reigned 1328–50; known as **Philip of Valois**. The founder of the Valois dynasty, Philip came to the throne on the death of Charles IV, whose only child was a girl and barred from ruling. His claim was challenged by Edward III of England; the dispute developed into the Hundred Years War.

Philip[3] the name of five kings of Spain: ■ **Philip I** (1478–1506), reigned 1504–6; known as **Philip the Handsome**. Son of the Holy Roman emperor Maximilian I, in 1496 Philip married the infanta Joanna, daughter of Ferdinand of Aragon and Isabella of Castile. After Isabella's death he ruled Castile jointly with Joanna, establishing the Habsburgs as the ruling dynasty in Spain. ■ **Philip II** (1527–98), son of Charles I, reigned 1556–98. Philip came to the throne following his father's abdication. His reign was dominated by an anti-Protestant crusade which exhausted the Spanish economy. His Armada against England (1588) ended in defeat. ■ **Philip III** (1578–1621), reigned 1598–1621. ■ **Philip IV** (1605–65), reigned 1621–65. ■ **Philip V** (1683–1746), grandson of Louis XIV, reigned 1700–24 and 1724–46. His selection as successor to Charles II, and Louis XIV's insistence that he remain an heir to the French throne, gave rise to the War of the Spanish Succession (1701–14). In 1724 Philip abdicated in favour of his son Louis I, but returned to the throne following Louis's death.

Philip, Prince, Duke of Edinburgh (b.1921), husband of Elizabeth II. The son of Prince Andrew of Greece and Denmark, he married Princess Elizabeth in 1947; on the eve of his marriage he was created Duke of Edinburgh.

Philip, St[1] an Apostle. He is commemorated with St James the Less on 1 May.

Philip, St[2], deacon of the early Christian Church; known as **St Philip the Evangelist**. He was one of seven deacons appointed to superintend the secular business of the Church at Jerusalem (Acts 6:5–6). Feast day, 6 June.

Philip II of Macedon /'masɪdɒn, -d(ə)n/, Philip II of Macedonia (see PHILIP[1]).

Philip Augustus, Philip II of France (see PHILIP[2]).

Philip of Valois, Philip VI of France (see PHILIP[2]).

Philippi /'fɪlɪpʌɪ, fɪ'lɪpʌɪ/ a city in ancient Macedonia, the scene in 42 BC of two battles in which Mark Antony and Octavian defeated Brutus and Cassius. The ruins lie close to the Aegean coast in NE Greece, near the port of Kavála (ancient Neapolis). Greek name FILIPPOI.

Philippians, Epistle to the /fɪ'lɪpɪənz/ a book of the New Testament, an epistle of St Paul to the Church at Philippi in Macedonia.

philippic /fɪ'lɪpɪk/ ▸ noun literary a bitter attack or denunciation, especially a verbal one.
– ORIGIN late 16th cent.: via Latin from Greek *philippikos*, the name given to Demosthenes' speeches against Philip II of Macedon, also to those of Cicero against Mark Antony.

Philippine /'fɪlɪpiːn/ ▸ adjective relating to the Philippines. See also FILIPINO.

Philippines /'fɪlɪpiːnz/ a country in SE Asia consisting of an archipelago of over 7,000 islands separated from the Asian mainland by the South China Sea; pop. 97,976,600 (est. 2009); official languages, Filipino and English; capital, Manila.

> The main islands of the Philippines are Luzon, Mindanao, Mindoro, Leyte, Samar, Negros, and Panay. Conquered by Spain in 1565, the islands were ceded to the US following the Spanish-American War in 1898. The Philippines achieved full independence as a republic in 1946. From 1965 the country was under the increasingly dictatorial rule of President Ferdinand Marcos (1917–89); he was driven from power in 1986 and replaced by Corazón Aquino (b.1933), President 1986–92.

Philippopolis /ˌfɪlɪ'pɒpəlɪs/ ancient Greek name for PLOVDIV.

Philip the Bold, Philip III of France (see PHILIP[2]).

Philip the Fair, Philip IV of France (see PHILIP[2]).

Philip the Handsome, Philip I of Spain (see PHILIP[3]).

Philip the Tall, Philip V of France (see PHILIP[2]).

Philistine /'fɪlɪstʌɪn/ ▸ noun **1** a member of a non-Semitic people of ancient southern Palestine, who came into conflict with the Israelites during the 12th and 11th centuries BC.

> The Philistines, from whom the country of Palestine took its name, were one of the Sea Peoples who, according to the Bible, came from Crete and settled the southern coastal plain of Canaan in the 12th century BC.

2 (**philistine**) a person who is hostile or indifferent to culture and the arts: [as modifier] *a philistine government.*
– DERIVATIVES **philistinism** /-stɪnɪz(ə)m/ noun.
– ORIGIN from French *Philistin*, via late Latin from Greek *Philistinos*, from Hebrew *pĕlištī*. Sense 2 arose as a result of a confrontation between town and gown in Jena, Germany, in the late 17th cent.; a sermon on the conflict quoted: 'the Philistines are upon you' (Judges 16), which led to an association between the townspeople and those hostile to culture.

Phillips ▸ adjective trademark denoting a screw with a cross-shaped slot for turning, or a corresponding screwdriver.
– ORIGIN 1930s: from the name of Henry F. *Phillips* (died 1958), the original American manufacturer.

Phillips curve ▸ noun Economics a supposed inverse relationship between the level of unemployment and the rate of inflation.
– ORIGIN 1960s: named after Alban W. H. *Phillips* (1914–75), New Zealand economist.

phillumenist /fɪ'luːmənɪst/ ▸ noun a collector of matchbox or matchbook labels.
– DERIVATIVES **phillumeny** noun.
– ORIGIN 1940s: from PHIL- 'loving' + Latin *lumen* 'light' + -IST.

Philly ▸ noun US informal Philadelphia.

philo- (also **phil-** before a vowel or *h*) ▸ combining form denoting a liking for a specified thing: *philogynist.*
– ORIGIN from Greek *philein* 'to love' or *philos* 'loving'.

philodendron /ˌfɪlə'dɛndrən/ ▸ noun (pl. **philodendrons** or **philodendra** /-drə/) a tropical American climbing plant which is widely grown as a greenhouse or indoor plant. ● Genus *Philodendron*, family Araceae.
– ORIGIN late 19th cent.: from PHILO- 'loving' + Greek *dendron* 'tree'.

philogynist /fɪ'lɒdʒɪnɪst/ ▸ noun formal a person who likes or admires women.
– DERIVATIVES **philogyny** noun.
– ORIGIN mid 19th cent.: from PHILO- 'loving' + Greek *gunē* 'woman' + -IST.

Philo Judaeus /ˌfʌɪləʊ dʒuː'diːəs/ (*c*.15 BC–*c*.50 AD), Jewish philosopher of Alexandria. He is particularly known for his commentaries on the Pentateuch (written in Greek), which he interpreted allegorically in the light of Platonic and Aristotelian philosophy.

philology ▸ noun [mass noun] the branch of knowledge that deals with the structure, historical development, and relationships of a language or languages. ■ chiefly N. Amer. literary or classical scholarship.
– DERIVATIVES **philologian** noun, **philological** adjective, **philologically** adverb, **philologist** noun.
– ORIGIN late Middle English (in the Greek sense): current usage (late 17th cent.) from French *philologie*, via Latin from Greek *philologia* 'love of learning' (see PHILO-, -LOGY).

Philomel /'fɪləmɛl/ (also **Philomela** /ˌfɪlə'miːlə/) Greek Mythology the daughter of Pandion, king of Athens. She was turned into a swallow and her sister Procne into a nightingale (or, in Latin versions, into a nightingale with Procne the swallow) when they were being pursued by the cruel Tereus, who had married Procne and raped Philomel.

philopatric /ˌfɪlə(ʊ)'patrɪk/ ▸ adjective Zoology (of an animal or species) tending to return to or remain near a particular site or area.
– DERIVATIVES **philopatry** noun.
– ORIGIN 1940s: from PHILO- 'liking' + Greek *patra* 'fatherland' + -IC.

philoprogenitive /ˌfɪlə(ʊ)prə(ʊ)'dʒɛnɪtɪv/ ▸ adjective formal having many offspring: *a philoprogenitive ill-paid artisan.* ■ showing love towards one's offspring.
– DERIVATIVES **philoprogenitiveness** noun.

philosopher ▸ noun a person engaged or learned in philosophy, especially as an academic discipline.
– ORIGIN Middle English: from a variant of Old French *philosophe*, via Latin from Greek *philosophos* 'lover of wisdom', from *philein* 'to love' + *sophos* 'wise'.

philosopher's stone ▸ noun (**the philosopher's stone**) a mythical substance supposed to change any metal into gold or silver and, according to some, to cure all diseases and prolong life indefinitely. Its discovery was the supreme object of alchemy.

philosophia perennis /fɪləˌsɒfɪə pə'rɛnɪs/ ▸ noun Philosophy a core of philosophical truths which is hypothesized to exist independently of and unaffected by time or place.
– ORIGIN mid 19th cent.: Latin, literally 'perennial philosophy'.

philosophical ▸ adjective **1** relating or devoted to the study of the fundamental nature of knowledge, reality, and existence: *philosophical discussions about free will | the Cambridge Philosophical Society.*
2 having or showing a calm attitude towards disappointments or difficulties: *he was **philosophical** about losing the contract.*
– DERIVATIVES **philosophic** adjective, **philosophically** adverb.

P

philosophical analysis ▸ noun [mass noun] the branch of philosophy that deals with the clarification of existing concepts and knowledge.

philosophize (also **philosophise**) ▸ verb [no obj.] speculate or theorize about fundamental or serious issues, especially in a tedious or pompous way: *he paused for a while to philosophize on racial equality.* ■ [with obj.] explain or argue (an idea) in terms of one's philosophical theories.
– DERIVATIVES **philosophizer** noun.

philosophy ▸ noun (pl. **philosophies**) **1** [mass noun] the study of the fundamental nature of knowledge, reality, and existence, especially when considered as an academic discipline. See also NATURAL PHILOSOPHY. ■ [count noun] a particular system of philosophical thought: *the philosophies of Plato and Aristotle.* ■ the study of the theoretical basis of a particular branch of knowledge or experience: *the philosophy of science.*
2 a theory or attitude that acts as a guiding principle for behaviour: *don't expect anything and you won't be disappointed, that's my philosophy.*
– ORIGIN Middle English: from Old French *philosophie*, via Latin from Greek *philosophia* 'love of wisdom'.

philtre /'fɪltə/ (US **philter**) ▸ noun a drink supposed to excite sexual love in the drinker; a love potion.
– ORIGIN late 16th cent.: from French *philtre*, via Latin from Greek *philtron*, from *philein* 'to love'.

-phily ▸ combining form equivalent to -PHILIA.

phimosis /fʌɪ'məʊsɪs/ ▸ noun [mass noun] Medicine a congenital narrowing of the opening of the foreskin so that it cannot be retracted.
– DERIVATIVES **phimotic** adjective.

– ORIGIN late 17th cent.: modern Latin, from Greek, literally 'muzzling'.

Phintias /ˈfɪntɪas/ see **DAMON**.

phishing /ˈfɪʃɪŋ/ ▸ **noun** [mass noun] the fraudulent practice of sending emails purporting to be from reputable companies in order to induce individuals to reveal personal information, such as passwords and credit card numbers, online.
– DERIVATIVES **phisher** noun.
– ORIGIN 1990s: respelling of **FISHING**, on the pattern of **PHREAKING**.

Phiz /fɪz/ (1815–82), English illustrator; pseudonym of *Hablot Knight Browne*. He illustrated many of Dickens's works, including *Martin Chuzzlewit*, *Pickwick Papers*, and *Bleak House*. He took his pseudonym to complement Dickens's 'Boz'.

phiz /fɪz/ (also **phizog**, **fizzog** /ˈfɪzɒg/) ▸ **noun** Brit. informal a person's face or expression.
– ORIGIN late 17th cent.: abbreviation of **PHYSIOGNOMY**.

phlebitis /flɪˈbʌɪtɪs/ ▸ **noun** [mass noun] Medicine inflammation of the walls of a vein.
– DERIVATIVES **phlebitic** adjective.
– ORIGIN early 19th cent.: modern Latin, from Greek, from *phleps*, *phleb-* 'vein'.

phlebography /flɪˈbɒgrəfi/ ▸ **noun** another term for **VENOGRAPHY**.

phlebotomy /flɪˈbɒtəmi/ ▸ **noun** (pl. **phlebotomies**) [mass noun] the surgical opening or puncture of a vein in order to withdraw blood, to introduce a fluid, or (historically) when letting blood.
– DERIVATIVES **phlebotomist** noun.
– ORIGIN late Middle English: via Old French from late Latin *phlebotomia* from Greek, from *phleps*, *phleb-* 'vein' + *-tomia* 'cutting'.

phlegm /flɛm/ ▸ **noun** [mass noun] the thick viscous substance secreted by the mucous membranes of the respiratory passages, especially when produced in excessive quantities during a cold. ■ (in medieval science and medicine) one of the four bodily humours, believed to be associated with a calm, stolid, or apathetic temperament. ■ calmness of temperament: *phlegm and determination carried them through many difficult situations*.
– DERIVATIVES **phlegmy** adjective.
– ORIGIN Middle English *fleem*, *fleume*, from Old French *fleume*, from late Latin *phlegma* 'clammy moisture (of the body)', from Greek *phlegma* 'inflammation', from *phlegein* 'to burn'. The spelling change in the 16th cent. was due to association with the Latin and Greek.

phlegmatic /flɛgˈmatɪk/ ▸ **adjective** (of a person) having an unemotional and stolidly calm disposition: *the phlegmatic British character*.
– DERIVATIVES **phlegmatically** adverb.
– ORIGIN Middle English (in the sense 'relating to the humour phlegm'): from Old French *fleumatique*, via Latin from Greek *phlegmatikos*, from *phlegma* 'inflammation' (see **PHLEGM**).

P

phloem /ˈfləʊɛm/ ▸ **noun** [mass noun] Botany the vascular tissue in plants which conducts sugars and other metabolic products downwards from the leaves.
– ORIGIN late 19th cent.: from Greek *phloos* 'bark' + the passive suffix *-ēma*.

phlogiston /fləˈdʒɪst(ə)n, -ˈgɪst-/ ▸ **noun** [mass noun] a substance supposed by 18th-century chemists to exist in all combustible bodies, and to be released in combustion.
– ORIGIN mid 18th cent.: modern Latin, from Greek *phlogizein* 'set on fire', from *phlox*, *phlog-* 'flame', from the base of *phlegein* 'to burn'.

phlogopite /ˈflɒgəpʌɪt/ ▸ **noun** [mass noun] a brown micaceous mineral which occurs chiefly in metamorphosed limestone and magnesium-rich igneous rocks.
– ORIGIN mid 19th cent.: from Greek *phlogōpos* 'fiery' (from the base of *phlegein* 'to burn') + *ōps*, *ōp-* 'face' + **-ITE**[1].

phlox /flɒks/ ▸ **noun** a North American plant that typically has dense clusters of colourful scented flowers, widely grown as an alpine or border plant. ● Genus *Phlox*, family Polemoniaceae.
– ORIGIN modern Latin, from Latin, denoting a flame-coloured flower, from Greek, literally 'flame'.

Phnom Penh /nɒm ˈpɛn/ the capital of Cambodia, a port at the junction of the Mekong and Tonlé Sap Rivers; pop. 1,438,300 (est. 2009). It became the capital of a Khmer kingdom in the mid 15th century. Between 1975 and 1979 the Khmer Rouge forced a great many of its population (then 2.5 million) to leave the city and resettle in the country.

pho /fəː/ ▸ **noun** [mass noun] a type of Vietnamese soup, typically made from beef stock and spices to which noodles and thinly sliced beef or chicken are added.
– ORIGIN Vietnamese, perhaps from French *feu* (in **POT-AU-FEU**).

-phobe ▸ **combining form** denoting a person having a fear or dislike of what is specified: *homophobe* | *xenophobe*.
– ORIGIN from French, via Latin *-phobus* from Greek *-phobos* 'fearing', from *phobos* 'fear'.

phobia /ˈfəʊbɪə/ ▸ **noun** an extreme or irrational fear of or aversion to something: *she suffered from a phobia about birds*.
– DERIVATIVES **phobic** adjective & noun.
– ORIGIN late 18th cent.: independent usage of **-PHOBIA**.

-phobia ▸ **combining form** extreme or irrational fear or dislike of a specified thing or group: *arachnophobia* | *Russophobia*.
– DERIVATIVES **-phobic** combining form in corresponding adjectives.
– ORIGIN via Latin from Greek.

Phobos /ˈfəʊbɒs/ Astronomy the inner of the two small satellites of Mars, discovered in 1877 (27 km long and 22 km across).
– ORIGIN named after one of the sons of the Greek war god **ARES**.

phocine /ˈfəʊsʌɪn/ ▸ **adjective** Zoology relating to or affecting the true (earless) seals.
– ORIGIN mid 19th cent.: from modern Latin *Phocinae* (subfamily name), from Greek *phōkē* 'seal'.

phocomelia /ˌfəʊkə(ʊ)ˈmiːlɪə/ ▸ **noun** [mass noun] Medicine a rare congenital deformity in which the hands or feet are attached close to the trunk, the limbs being grossly underdeveloped or absent. This condition was a side effect of the drug thalidomide taken during early pregnancy.
– ORIGIN late 19th cent.: modern Latin, from Greek *phōkē* 'seal' + *melos* 'limb'.

Phoebe /ˈfiːbi/ **1** Greek Mythology a Titaness, daughter of Uranus (Heaven) and Gaia (Earth). She became the mother of Leto and thus the grandmother of Apollo and Artemis. In later Greek writing her name was often used for Selene (Moon).
2 Astronomy a satellite of Saturn, the furthest from the planet and with an eccentric retrograde orbit, discovered in 1898 (average diameter 220 km).
– ORIGIN from Greek *Phoibē*, literally 'bright one'.

phoebe ▸ **noun** an American tyrant flycatcher with mainly grey-brown or blackish plumage. ● Genus *Sayornis*, family Tyrannidae: three species.
– ORIGIN early 18th cent.: imitative; influenced by the name **PHOEBE**.

Phoebus /ˈfiːbəs/ Greek Mythology an epithet of Apollo, used in contexts where the god was identified with the sun.
– ORIGIN from Greek *Phoibos*, literally 'bright one'.

Phoenicia /fəˈniːʃə/ an ancient country on the shores of the eastern Mediterranean, corresponding to modern Lebanon and the coastal plains of Syria. It consisted of a number of city-states, including Tyre and Sidon, and was a flourishing centre of Mediterranean trade and colonization during the early part of the 1st millennium BC.
– ORIGIN from Latin, from Greek *Phoinikē*.

Phoenician /fəˈnɪʃ(ə)n, -ˈniː-/ ▸ **noun** **1** a member of a Semitic people inhabiting ancient Phoenicia and its colonies. The Phoenicians prospered from trade and manufacturing until the capital, Tyre, was sacked by Alexander the Great in 332 BC.
2 [mass noun] the Semitic language of the Phoenicians, written in an alphabet that was the ancestor of the Greek and Roman alphabets.
▸ **adjective** relating to Phoenicia, its people, or its language.

Phoenix[1] /ˈfiːnɪks/ Astronomy a southern constellation (the Phoenix), west of Grus.
– ORIGIN Latin.

Phoenix[2] /ˈfiːnɪks/ the state capital of Arizona; pop. 1,567,924 (est. 2008). Its dry climate makes it a popular winter resort.

phoenix ▸ **noun** (in classical mythology) a unique bird that lived for five or six centuries in the Arabian desert, after this time burning itself on a funeral pyre and rising from the ashes with renewed youth to live through another cycle. ■ a person or thing regarded as uniquely remarkable in some respect.
– PHRASES **rise like a phoenix from the ashes** emerge renewed after apparent disaster or destruction.
– ORIGIN from Old French *fenix*, via Latin from Greek *phoinix* 'Phoenician, reddish purple, or phoenix'. The relationship between the Greek senses is obscure: it could not be 'the Phoenician bird' because the legend centres on the temple at Heliopolis in Egypt, where the phoenix is said to have burnt itself on the altar. Perhaps the basic sense is 'purple', symbolic of fire and possibly the primary sense of *Phoenicia* as the purple land (or land of the sunrise).

Phoenix Islands a group of eight islands lying just south of the equator in the western Pacific. They form a part of Kiribati.

pholas /ˈfəʊləs/ ▸ **noun** the common piddock (mollusc). ● *Pholas dactylus*, family Pholadidae.
– ORIGIN mid 17th cent.: modern Latin (later adopted as a genus name), from Greek *phōlas* 'that lurks in a hole', from *phōleos* 'hole'.

Pholidota /ˌfɒlɪˈdəʊtə/ ▸ **plural noun** Zoology a small order of mammals that comprises the pangolins.
– ORIGIN modern Latin (plural), from Greek *pholidōtos* 'scaly', from *pholis*, *pholid-* 'scale'.

phon /fɒn/ ▸ **noun** a unit of the perceived loudness of sounds.
– ORIGIN 1930s: from Greek *phōnē* 'sound'.

phonation /fə(ʊ)ˈneɪʃ(ə)n/ ▸ **noun** [mass noun] Phonetics the production or utterance of speech sounds.
– DERIVATIVES **phonate** /fə(ʊ)ˈneɪt/ verb, **phonatory** /ˈfəʊnət(ə)ri/ adjective.
– ORIGIN mid 19th cent.: from Greek *phōnē* 'sound, voice' + **-ATION**.

phone[1] ▸ **noun** **1** a telephone: *a few seconds later the phone rang* | *a receptionist answered the phone* | [as modifier] *a phone number*.
2 (**phones**) informal headphones or earphones.
▸ **verb** (also **phone up** or **phone someone up**) call someone on the telephone: [with obj.] *he phoned her at work* | [no obj.] *she phoned about twenty minutes ago*. ■ (**phone it in**) US informal work or perform in a desultory fashion.

phone[2] ▸ **noun** Phonetics a speech sound; the smallest discrete segment of sound in a stream of speech.
– ORIGIN mid 19th cent.: from Greek *phōnē* 'sound, voice'.

-phone ▸ **combining form** **1** denoting an instrument using or connected with sound: *megaphone*.
2 denoting a person who uses a specified language: *francophone*.
– DERIVATIVES **-phonic** combining form in corresponding adjectives, **-phony** combining form in corresponding nouns.
– ORIGIN from Greek *phōnē* 'sound, voice'.

phone bank ▸ **noun** US a battery of telephones.

phone book ▸ **noun** a telephone directory.

phonecard ▸ **noun** chiefly Brit. a prepaid card which allows the user to make telephone calls up to a specified number of units using a cardphone.

phone-in ▸ **noun** chiefly Brit. a radio or television programme during which the listeners or viewers telephone the studio and participate. ■ [as modifier] denoting something conducted by people leaving answers or messages by telephone: *a phone-in contest*.

phonematic /ˌfəʊnɪˈmatɪk, ˌfɒn-/ ▸ **adjective** (in prosodic analysis) denoting a segmental element of vowel or consonant features which combines with other elements such as intonation or stress.
– ORIGIN 1930s: from Greek *phōnēma*, *phōnēmatik-* 'relating to a sound'.

phoneme /ˈfəʊniːm/ ▸ **noun** Phonetics any of the perceptually distinct units of sound in a specified language that distinguish one word from another, for example *p*, *b*, *d*, and *t* in the English words *pad*, *pat*, *bad*, and *bat*. Compare with **ALLOPHONE**[1].
– DERIVATIVES **phonemic** /-ˈniːmɪk/ adjective, **phonemics** plural noun.
– ORIGIN late 19th cent.: from French *phonème*, from Greek *phōnēma* 'sound, speech', from *phōnein* 'speak'.

phone sex ▸ **noun** [mass noun] sexually explicit telephone conversation engaged in for sexual gratification.

phonetic /fəˈnɛtɪk/ ▸ **adjective** Phonetics relating to speech sounds: *detailed phonetic information*. ■ (of a system of writing) having a direct correspondence between symbols and sounds: *a phonetic alphabet*. ■ relating to phonetics: *phonetic training*.
– DERIVATIVES **phonetically** adverb, **phoneticism** noun, **phoneticist** noun, **phoneticize** (also **phoneticise**) verb.

– ORIGIN early 19th cent.: from modern Latin *phoneticus*, from Greek *phōnētikos*, from *phōnein* 'speak'.

phonetics ▶ **plural noun** [treated as sing.] the study and classification of speech sounds.
– DERIVATIVES **phonetician** noun.

phoney (chiefly N. Amer. also **phony**) informal ▶ **adjective** (**phonier**, **phoniest**) not genuine; fraudulent: *phoney cruise-ship job offers*.
▶ **noun** (pl. **phoneys** or **phonies**) a fraudulent person or thing.
– DERIVATIVES **phonily** adverb, **phoniness** noun.
– ORIGIN late 19th cent.: of unknown origin.

phoney war the period of comparative inaction at the beginning of the Second World War between the German invasions of Poland (September 1939) and of Norway (April 1940).

phonic /ˈfəʊnɪk, ˈfɒnɪk/ ▶ **adjective** relating to speech sounds. ■ relating to phonics: *the English language presents difficulties if a purely phonic approach is attempted*.
– DERIVATIVES **phonically** adverb.
– ORIGIN early 19th cent.: from Greek *phōnē* 'voice' + **-IC**.

phonics ▶ **plural noun** [treated as sing.] a method of teaching people to read by correlating sounds with symbols in an alphabetic writing system.

phono ▶ **adjective** [usu. attrib.] denoting a type of plug, and the corresponding socket, used with audio and video equipment, in which one conductor is cylindrical and the other is a central prong that extends beyond it.
– ORIGIN 1940s: abbreviation of **PHONOGRAPH**.

phono- /ˈfəʊnəʊ, ˈfɒn-/ ▶ **combining form** relating to sound: *phonograph*.
– ORIGIN from Greek *phōnē* 'sound, voice'.

phonocardiogram ▶ **noun** Medicine a chart or record of the sounds made by the heart.

phonogram ▶ **noun** Phonetics a symbol representing a vocal sound.

phonograph ▶ **noun** Brit. an early form of gramophone using cylinders and able to record as well as reproduce sound. ■ N. Amer. a record player.
– DERIVATIVES **phonographic** adjective.

phonograph record ▶ **noun** N. Amer. fuller form of **RECORD** (sense 4 of the noun).

phonolite /ˈfəʊnəlʌɪt/ ▶ **noun** [mass noun] Geology a fine-grained volcanic igneous rock composed of alkali feldspars and nepheline.
– ORIGIN early 19th cent.: from **PHONO-** 'relating to sound' (because of its resonance when struck) + **-ITE**[1].

phonology /fəˈnɒlədʒi/ ▶ **noun** [mass noun] the system of contrastive relationships among the speech sounds that constitute the fundamental components of a language. ■ the study of phonological relationships within a language or between different languages.
– DERIVATIVES **phonological** adjective, **phonologically** adverb, **phonologist** noun.

phonon /ˈfəʊnɒn/ ▶ **noun** Physics a quantum of energy or a quasiparticle associated with a compressional wave such as sound or a vibration of a crystal lattice.
– ORIGIN 1930s: from Greek *phōnē* 'sound', on the pattern of *photon*.

phonotactics /ˌfəʊnə(ʊ)ˈtaktɪks/ ▶ **plural noun** [treated as sing.] the study of the rules governing the possible phoneme sequences in a language.
– DERIVATIVES **phonotactic** adjective.

phony ▶ **adjective & noun** variant spelling of **PHONEY**.

phooey informal ▶ **exclamation** (US also **pfui**) used to express disdain or disbelief: *so phooey to sophistication*.
▶ **noun** [mass noun] nonsense: *they dismiss it all as movie phooey*.
– ORIGIN 1920s: imitative.

phorbol /ˈfɔːbɒl/ ▶ **noun** [mass noun] Chemistry a compound present (in the form of highly carcinogenic esters) in croton oil. ● A tetracyclic alcohol; chem. formula: $C_{20}H_{28}O_6$.
– ORIGIN 1930s: from Greek *phorbē* 'fodder' (from *pherbein* 'to feed') + **-OL**.

-phore ▶ **combining form** denoting an agent or bearer of a specified thing: *ionophore | semaphore*.
– DERIVATIVES **-phorous** combining form in corresponding adjectives.
– ORIGIN from modern Latin *-phorus*, from Greek *-phoros*, *-phoron* 'bearing, bearer', from *pherein* 'to bear'.

phoresy /fəˈriːsi, ˈfɒrəsi/ ▶ **noun** [mass noun] Zoology an association between two organisms in which one (e.g. a mite) travels on the body of another, without being a parasite.
– DERIVATIVES **phoretic** /fəˈrɛtɪk/ **adjective**.
– ORIGIN 1920s: from French *phorésie*, from Greek *phorēsis* 'being carried'.

phormium /ˈfɔːmɪəm/ ▶ **noun** the flax-lily of New Zealand.
– ORIGIN early 19th cent.: modern Latin, from Greek *phormion* 'small basket' (with reference to the use made of the fibres).

Phoronida /fəˈrɒnɪdə/ ▶ **plural noun** Zoology a small phylum of worm-like invertebrates that comprises the horseshoe worms.
– DERIVATIVES **phoronid** noun.
– ORIGIN modern Latin (plural), from Latin *Phoronis*, *Phoronid-*, the name of a character in Greek mythology.

phosgene /ˈfɒzdʒiːn/ ▶ **noun** [mass noun] Chemistry a colourless poisonous gas made by the reaction of chlorine and carbon dioxide. It was used as a poison gas, notably in the First World War. ● Alternative name: **carbonyl chloride**; chem. formula: $COCl_2$.
– ORIGIN early 19th cent.: from Greek *phōs* 'light' + **-GEN**, with reference to its original production by the action of sunlight on chlorine and carbon monoxide.

phosphatase /ˈfɒsfəteɪz/ ▶ **noun** [mass noun] Biochemistry an enzyme that catalyses the hydrolysis of organic phosphates in a specified (acid or alkaline) environment.

phosphate /ˈfɒsfeɪt/ ▶ **noun** Chemistry a salt or ester of phosphoric acid, containing PO_4^{3-} or a related anion or a group such as $-OPO(OH)_2$.
– ORIGIN late 18th cent.: from French, from *phosphore* 'phosphorus'.

phosphatic /fɒsˈfatɪk/ ▶ **adjective** (chiefly of rocks and fertilizer) containing or consisting of phosphates.

phosphatide /ˈfɒsfətʌɪd/ ▶ **noun** Biochemistry any of a class of compounds which are fatty acid esters of glycerol phosphate with a nitrogen base linked to the phosphate group.

phosphatidylcholine /fɒsˌfatɪdʌɪlˈkəʊliːn/ ▶ **noun** [mass noun] Biochemistry a substance widely distributed in animal tissues, egg yolk, and some higher plants, consisting of phospholipids linked to choline.

phosphene /ˈfɒsfiːn/ ▶ **noun** a sensation of a ring or spot of light produced by pressure on the eyeball or direct stimulation of the visual system other than by light.
– ORIGIN late 19th cent.: formed irregularly from Greek *phōs* 'light' + *phainein* 'to show'.

phosphide /ˈfɒsfʌɪd/ ▶ **noun** Chemistry a binary compound of phosphorus with another element or group.

phosphine /ˈfɒsfiːn/ ▶ **noun** [mass noun] Chemistry a colourless foul-smelling gaseous compound of phosphorus and hydrogen, analogous to ammonia. ● Chem. formula: PH_3. It forms salts containing the **phosphonium** ion, PH_4^+.
– ORIGIN late 19th cent.: from **PHOSPHO-** 'relating to phosphorus' + **-INE**[4], on the pattern of *amine*.

phosphite /ˈfɒsfʌɪt/ ▶ **noun** Chemistry old-fashioned term for **PHOSPHONATE**.

phospho- ▶ **combining form** representing **PHOSPHORUS**.

phosphocreatine /ˌfɒsfə(ʊ)ˈkriːətiːn/ ▶ **noun** [mass noun] Biochemistry a phosphate ester of creatine found in vertebrate muscle, where it serves to store phosphates to provide energy for muscular contraction.

phosphodiesterase /ˌfɒsfə(ʊ)dʌɪˈɛstəreɪz/ ▶ **noun** [mass noun] Biochemistry an enzyme which breaks a phosphodiester bond in an oligonucleotide.

phosphodiester bond /ˌfɒsfə(ʊ)dʌɪˈɛstə/ ▶ **noun** Biochemistry a chemical bond of the kind joining successive sugar molecules in a polynucleotide.

phospholipase /ˌfɒsfə(ʊ)ˈlɪpeɪz, -ˈlʌɪpeɪz/ ▶ **noun** Biochemistry an enzyme which hydrolyses phosphatidylcholine or a similar phospholipid.

phospholipid /ˌfɒsfə(ʊ)ˈlɪpɪd/ ▶ **noun** Biochemistry a lipid containing a phosphate group in its molecule, e.g. phosphatidylcholine.

phosphonate /ˈfɒsfəneɪt/ ▶ **noun** Chemistry a salt or ester of phosphonic acid.

phosphonic acid /fɒsˈfɒnɪk/ ▶ **noun** [mass noun] Chemistry a crystalline acid obtained by the reaction of phosphorus trioxide with water. ● A dibasic acid; chem. formula: $HPO(OH)_2$.
– ORIGIN late 19th cent.: *phosphonic* from **PHOSPHO-** 'relating to phosphorus', on the pattern of *sulphonic*.

phosphonium /fɒsˈfəʊnɪəm/ ▶ **noun** see **PHOSPHINE**.
– ORIGIN late 19th cent.: blend of **PHOSPHORUS** and **AMMONIUM**.

phosphoprotein ▶ **noun** Biochemistry a protein that contains phosphorus (other than in a nucleic acid or a phospholipid).

phosphor /ˈfɒsfə/ ▶ **noun** [mass noun] a synthetic fluorescent or phosphorescent substance, especially one used to coat the screen of a cathode ray tube. ■ old-fashioned term for **PHOSPHORUS**.
– ORIGIN early 17th cent.: from Latin *phosphorus* (see **PHOSPHORUS**).

phosphorated ▶ **adjective** combined or impregnated with phosphorus.

phosphor bronze ▶ **noun** [mass noun] a tough, hard form of bronze containing a small amount of phosphorus, used especially for bearings.

phosphoresce /ˌfɒsfəˈrɛs/ ▶ **verb** [no obj.] emit light or radiation by phosphorescence.

phosphorescence ▶ **noun** [mass noun] light emitted by a substance without combustion or perceptible heat: *the stones overhead gleamed with phosphorescence*. ■ Physics the emission of radiation in a similar manner to fluorescence but on a longer timescale, so that emission continues after excitation ceases.
– DERIVATIVES **phosphorescent** adjective.

phosphoric /fɒsˈfɒrɪk/ ▶ **adjective** relating to or containing phosphorus. ■ Chemistry of phosphorus with a valency of five. Compare with **PHOSPHOROUS**.
– ORIGIN late 18th cent.: from French *phosphorique*, from *phosphore* 'phosphorus'.

phosphoric acid ▶ **noun** [mass noun] Chemistry a crystalline acid obtained e.g. by treating phosphates with sulphuric acid, used in fertilizer and soap manufacture and food processing. ● A tribasic acid; chem. formula: H_3PO_4.

phosphorite /ˈfɒsfərʌɪt/ ▶ **noun** [mass noun] a sedimentary rock containing a high proportion of calcium phosphate.
– ORIGIN late 18th cent.: from **PHOSPHORUS** + **-ITE**[1].

phosphorous /ˈfɒsf(ə)rəs/ ▶ **adjective** relating to or containing phosphorus. Compare with **PHOSPHORIC**. ■ Chemistry of phosphorus with a valency of three. ■ phosphorescent.

> **USAGE** The correct spelling for the noun denoting the chemical element is **phosphorus**, while the adjective meaning 'relating to or containing phosphorus' is spelled **phosphorous**. A common mistake is to use the spelling **phosphorous** for the noun as well as the adjective.

P

phosphorous acid ▶ **noun** another term for **PHOSPHONIC ACID**.

phosphorus /ˈfɒsf(ə)rəs/ ▶ **noun** [mass noun] the chemical element of atomic number 15, a poisonous, combustible non-metal which exists in two common allotropic forms, **white phosphorus**, a yellowish waxy solid which ignites spontaneously in air and glows in the dark, and **red phosphorus**, a less reactive form used in making matches. (Symbol: **P**)
– ORIGIN late 17th cent.: from Latin, from Greek *phōsphoros*, from *phōs* 'light' + *-phoros* '-bringing'.

phosphoryl /ˈfɒsfərʌɪl, -rɪl/ ▶ **noun** [as modifier] Chemistry denoting the trivalent group ≡PO. ■ Biochemistry denoting the monovalent phosphate group $-PO(OH)_2$.
– ORIGIN late 19th cent.: from **PHOSPHORUS** + **-YL**.

phosphorylase /fɒsˈfɒrɪleɪz/ ▶ **noun** [mass noun] Biochemistry an enzyme which introduces a phosphate group into an organic molecule, notably glucose.

phosphorylate /fɒsˈfɒrɪleɪt/ ▶ **verb** [with obj.] chiefly Biochemistry introduce a phosphate group into (a molecule or compound).
– DERIVATIVES **phosphorylation** noun.

phossy jaw /ˈfɒsi/ ▶ **noun** [mass noun] historical, informal gangrene of the jawbone caused by phosphorus poisoning.
– ORIGIN late 19th cent.: *phossy* by abbreviation of *phosphorus necrosis*, denoting gangrene of the jaw.

phot /fəʊt/ ▶ **noun** a unit of illumination equal to one lumen per square centimetre.
– ORIGIN early 20th cent.: from Greek *phōs*, *phōt-* 'light'.

photic ▶ **adjective** technical relating to light, especially as an agent of chemical change or physiological response. ■ Ecology denoting the layers of the ocean reached by sufficient sunlight to allow plant growth.

photino /fə(ʊ)'tiːnəʊ/ ▸ **noun** (pl. **photinos**) Physics the hypothetical supersymmetric counterpart of the photon, with spin $-^{1}/_{2}$.
– ORIGIN 1970s: from **PHOTON** + *-ino* from **NEUTRINO**.

photism /'fəʊtɪz(ə)m/ ▸ **noun** Psychology a hallucinatory sensation or vision of light.
– ORIGIN late 19th cent.: from Greek *phōtismos*, from *phōtizein* 'to shine', from *phōs*, *phōt-* 'light'.

Photius /'fəʊtɪəs/ (*c.*820–*c.*891), Byzantine scholar and patriarch of Constantinople. His most important work is the *Bibliotheca*, a critical account of 280 earlier prose works and an invaluable source of information about many works now lost.

photo ▸ **noun** (pl. **photos**) a photograph. ■ informal a photo finish.
▸ **verb** (**photoes**, **photoing**, **photoed**) [with obj.] informal take a photograph of.

photo- /'fəʊtəʊ/ ▸ **combining form 1** relating to light: *photochemical*.
2 relating to photography: *photofit*.
– ORIGIN Sense 1 from Greek *phōs*, *phōt-* 'light'; sense 2, abbreviation of **PHOTOGRAPHY**.

photoactive ▸ **adjective** (of a substance) capable of a chemical or physical change in response to illumination.

photobiology ▸ **noun** [mass noun] the study of the effects of light on living organisms.

photobleaching ▸ **noun** [mass noun] Biochemistry loss of colour by a pigment (such as chlorophyll or rhodopsin) when illuminated.

photocall ▸ **noun** Brit. an occasion on which famous people pose for photographers by arrangement.

photocatalysis /ˌfəʊtə(ʊ)kə'talɪsɪs/ ▸ **noun** [mass noun] Chemistry the acceleration of a chemical reaction by light.
– DERIVATIVES **photocatalytic** adjective.

photocathode ▸ **noun** a cathode which emits electrons when illuminated, causing an electric current.

photo CD ▸ **noun** a CD on which still photographs may be stored.

photocell ▸ **noun** short for **PHOTOELECTRIC CELL**.

photochemical ▸ **adjective** relating to or caused by the chemical action of light. ■ relating to photochemistry.
– DERIVATIVES **photochemically** adverb.

photochemical smog ▸ **noun** [mass noun] haze in the atmosphere accompanied by high levels of ozone and nitrogen oxides, caused by the action of sunlight on pollutants.

photochemistry ▸ **noun** [mass noun] the branch of chemistry concerned with the chemical effects of light.

photochromic ▸ **adjective** (of a substance) undergoing a reversible change in colour or shade when exposed to light of a particular frequency or intensity: *photochromic sunglasses*.
– DERIVATIVES **photochromism** noun.
– ORIGIN 1950s: from **PHOTO-** 'relating to light' + Greek *khrōma* 'colour' + **-IC**.

photocoagulation /ˌfəʊtə(ʊ)kəʊˌagjʊ'leɪʃ(ə)n/ ▸ **noun** [mass noun] Medicine the use of a laser beam or other intense light source to coagulate and destroy or fuse small areas of tissue, especially in the retina.

photocomposition ▸ **noun** another term for **FILMSETTING**.

photoconductivity /ˌfəʊtə(ʊ)kɒndʌk'tɪvɪti/ ▸ **noun** [mass noun] increased electrical conductivity caused by the presence of light.
– DERIVATIVES **photoconductive** adjective, **photoconductor** noun.

photocopier ▸ **noun** a machine for making photocopies.

photocopy ▸ **noun** (pl. **photocopies**) a photographic copy of printed or written material produced by a process involving the action of light on a specially prepared surface.
▸ **verb** (**photocopies**, **photocopying**, **photocopied**) [with obj.] make a photocopy of.
– DERIVATIVES **photocopiable** adjective.

photocurrent ▸ **noun** an electric current induced by the action of light.

photodegradable ▸ **adjective** capable of being decomposed by the action of light, especially sunlight: *photodegradable plastic*.

photodetector ▸ **noun** a device that detects or responds to incident light by using the electrical effect of individual photons.

photodiode ▸ **noun** a semiconductor diode which, when exposed to light, generates a potential difference or changes its electrical resistance.

photodissociation ▸ **noun** [mass noun] Chemistry dissociation of a chemical compound by the action of light.

photodynamic ▸ **adjective** Medicine denoting treatment for cancer involving the injection of a cytotoxic compound which is relatively inactive until activated by a laser beam after collecting in the tumour.

photoelectric ▸ **adjective** characterized by or involving the emission of electrons from a surface by the action of light.
– DERIVATIVES **photoelectricity** noun.

photoelectric cell ▸ **noun** a device using a photoelectric effect to generate current.

photoelectron ▸ **noun** an electron emitted from an atom by interaction with a photon, especially an electron emitted from a solid surface by the action of light.
– DERIVATIVES **photoelectronic** adjective.

photoemission ▸ **noun** [mass noun] the emission of electrons from a surface caused by the action of light striking it.
– DERIVATIVES **photoemissive** adjective, **photoemitter** noun.

photoessay ▸ **noun** an account of something told predominantly through photographs, with some accompanying text.

photo finish ▸ **noun** a close finish of a race in which the winner is identifiable only from a photograph taken as the competitors cross the line.

photofinishing ▸ **noun** [mass noun] the commercial development and printing of film.

photofit ▸ **noun** Brit. a reconstructed picture of a person, especially one sought by the police, made from composite photographs of facial features.

photogenic /ˌfəʊtə(ʊ)'dʒɛnɪk, -'dʒiːn-/ ▸ **adjective 1** (especially of a person) looking attractive in photographs or on film: *a photogenic child*.
2 Biology (of an organism or tissue) producing or emitting light.
– DERIVATIVES **photogenically** adverb.

photogeology ▸ **noun** [mass noun] the field of study concerned with the geological interpretation of aerial photographs.
– DERIVATIVES **photogeological** adjective, **photogeologist** noun.

photogram ▸ **noun** a picture produced with photographic materials, such as light-sensitive paper, but without a camera. ■ archaic a photograph.

photogrammetry /ˌfəʊtə(ʊ)'gramɪtri/ ▸ **noun** [mass noun] the use of photography in surveying and mapping to ascertain measurements between objects.
– DERIVATIVES **photogrammetric** adjective, **photogrammetrist** noun.

photograph ▸ **noun** a picture made using a camera, in which an image is focused on to light-sensitive material and then made visible and permanent by chemical treatment, or stored digitally.
▸ **verb** [with obj.] take a photograph of. ■ [no obj., with adverbial] appear in a particular way when in a photograph: *that cityscape photographs well*.
– DERIVATIVES **photographable** adjective.

photographer ▸ **noun** a person who takes photographs, especially as a job: *a freelance press photographer*.

photographic ▸ **adjective** relating to or resembling photographs: *high-tech digital photographic equipment*.
– DERIVATIVES **photographically** adverb.

photographic memory ▸ **noun** the ability to remember information or visual images in great detail.

photography ▸ **noun** [mass noun] the art or practice of taking and processing photographs.

photogravure /ˌfəʊtə(ʊ)grə'vjʊə/ ▸ **noun** an image produced from a photographic negative transferred to a metal plate and etched in. ■ [mass noun] the production of photogravure images.
– ORIGIN late 19th cent.: from French, from *photo-* 'relating to light' + *gravure* 'engraving'.

photoionization /ˌfəʊtəʊˌʌɪənʌɪ'zeɪʃ(ə)n/ (also **photoionisation**) ▸ **noun** [mass noun] Physics ionization produced in a medium by the action of electromagnetic radiation.

photojournalism ▸ **noun** [mass noun] the practice of communicating news by photographs, especially in magazines.
– DERIVATIVES **photojournalist** noun.

photolithography (also **photolitho**) ▸ **noun** [mass noun] lithography using plates made photographically.
– DERIVATIVES **photolithographic** adjective, **photolithographically** adverb.

photolysis /fə(ʊ)'tɒlɪsɪs/ ▸ **noun** [mass noun] Chemistry the decomposition or separation of molecules by the action of light.
– DERIVATIVES **photolytic** adjective.

photomap ▸ **noun** a map made from or drawn on photographs of the area concerned.

photomask ▸ **noun** Electronics a photographic pattern used in making microcircuits, ultraviolet light being shone through the mask on to a photoresist in order to transfer the pattern.

photomechanical ▸ **adjective** relating to or denoting processes in which photography is involved in the making of a printing plate.
– DERIVATIVES **photomechanically** adverb.

photometer /fə(ʊ)'tɒmɪtə/ ▸ **noun** an instrument for measuring the intensity of light.
– DERIVATIVES **photometric** adjective, **photometrically** adverb, **photometry** noun.

photomicrograph ▸ **noun** a photograph of a microscopic object, taken with the aid of a microscope.
– DERIVATIVES **photomicrographer** noun, **photomicrography** noun.

photomontage /ˌfəʊtəʊmɒn'tɑːʒ/ ▸ **noun** a montage constructed from photographic images. ■ [mass noun] the technique of constructing a photomontage.

photomorphogenesis /ˌfəʊtə(ʊ)mɔːfə'dʒɛnɪsɪs/ ▸ **noun** [mass noun] Botany development of form and structure in plants which is affected by light, other than that occurring for photosynthesis.

photomosaic ▸ **noun** a large-scale detailed picture or map built up by combining photographs of small areas.

photomultiplier ▸ **noun** an instrument containing a photoelectric cell and a series of electrodes, used to detect and amplify the light from very faint sources.

photon /'fəʊtɒn/ ▸ **noun** Physics a particle representing a quantum of light or other electromagnetic radiation. A photon carries energy proportional to the radiation frequency but has zero rest mass.
– DERIVATIVES **photonic** adjective.
– ORIGIN early 20th cent.: from Greek *phōs*, *phōt-* 'light', on the pattern of *electron*.

photonegative ▸ **adjective 1** Biology (of an organism) tending to move away from light.
2 Physics (of a substance) exhibiting a decrease in electrical conductivity under illumination.

photonics /fəʊ'tɒnɪks/ ▸ **plural noun** [treated as sing.] the branch of technology concerned with the properties and transmission of photons, for example in fibre optics.

photo-offset ▸ **noun** [mass noun] offset printing using plates made photographically.

photo op ▸ **noun** chiefly N. Amer. informal term for **PHOTO OPPORTUNITY**.

photo opportunity ▸ **noun** another term for **PHOTOCALL**.

photo-oxidation ▸ **noun** [mass noun] Chemistry oxidation caused by the action of light.

photoperiod ▸ **noun** Botany & Zoology the period of time each day during which an organism receives illumination; day length.
– DERIVATIVES **photoperiodic** adjective.

photoperiodism ▸ **noun** [mass noun] Botany & Zoology the response of an organism to seasonal changes in day length.

photophobia ▸ **noun** [mass noun] extreme sensitivity to light.
– DERIVATIVES **photophobic** adjective.

photophore /'fəʊtə(ʊ)fɔː/ ▸ **noun** Zoology a light-producing organ in certain fishes and other animals.
– ORIGIN late 19th cent.: from Greek *phōtophoros* 'light-bearing'.

photopic /fəʊ'tɒpɪk, fəʊ'təʊpɪk/ ▸ **adjective** Physiology relating to or denoting vision in daylight or other bright light, believed to involve chiefly the cones of the retina. Often contrasted with **SCOTOPIC**.
– ORIGIN early 20th cent.: from **PHOTO-** 'light' + **-OPIA** + **-IC**.

photopigment ▸ noun a pigment whose chemical state depends on its degree of illumination, such as those in the retina of the eye.

photopolarimeter /ˌfəʊtəʊpəʊləˈrɪmɪtə/ ▸ noun a telescopic apparatus for photographing stars, galaxies, etc., and measuring the polarization of light from them.

photopolymer ▸ noun a light-sensitive polymeric material, especially one used in printing plates or microfilms.

photopositive ▸ adjective **1** Biology (of an organism) tending to move towards light.
2 Physics (of a substance) exhibiting an increase in electrical conductivity under illumination.

photoproduct ▸ noun a product of a photochemical reaction.

photoprotein ▸ noun Biochemistry a protein active in the emission of light by a living creature.

photorealism ▸ noun [mass noun] a style of art and sculpture characterized by the highly detailed depiction of ordinary life with the impersonality of a photograph.
– DERIVATIVES **photorealist** noun & adjective, **photorealistic** adjective.

photoreceptor ▸ noun a structure in a living organism, especially a sensory cell or sense organ, that responds to light falling on it.
– DERIVATIVES **photoreceptive** adjective.

photoreconnaissance ▸ noun [mass noun] military reconnaissance carried out by means of aerial photography.

photoresist ▸ noun a photosensitive resist which, when exposed to light, loses its resistance or its susceptibility to attack by an etchant or solvent. Such materials are used in making microcircuits.

photorespiration ▸ noun [mass noun] Botany a respiratory process in many higher plants by which they take up oxygen in the light and give out some carbon dioxide, contrary to the general pattern of photosynthesis.

photoresponse ▸ noun Biology a response of a plant or other organism to light, mediated otherwise than through photosynthesis.

photosensitive ▸ adjective having a chemical, electrical, or other response to light: *photosensitive cells* | *photosensitive drugs*.
– DERIVATIVES **photosensitivity** noun.

photo session ▸ noun a prearranged session in which a photographer takes photographs of someone for publication.

photosetter ▸ noun a machine for filmsetting.

photosetting ▸ noun another term for FILMSETTING.
– DERIVATIVES **photoset** verb (past and past participle **photoset**).

photo shoot ▸ noun another term for PHOTO SESSION.

photoshop ▸ verb (**photoshops, photoshopping, photoshopped**) [with obj.] alter (a photographic image) digitally using computer software: *the pictures have obviously been photoshopped*.
– ORIGIN 1990s: from *Adobe Photoshop*, the proprietary name of such a software package.

photosphere ▸ noun Astronomy the luminous envelope of a star from which its light and heat radiate.
– DERIVATIVES **photospheric** adjective.

photostat /ˈfəʊtə(ʊ)stat/ ▸ noun trademark a type of machine for making photocopies on special paper.
■ a copy made by a photostat.
▸ verb (**photostats, photostatting, photostatted**) [with obj.] copy (a document) with a photostat.
– DERIVATIVES **photostatic** adjective.

photostory ▸ noun a strip cartoon with photographs in place of drawings.

photosynthate /ˌfəʊtəʊˈsɪnθeɪt/ ▸ noun Biochemistry a sugar or other substance made by photosynthesis.

photosynthesis ▸ noun [mass noun] the process by which green plants and some other organisms use sunlight to synthesize nutrients from carbon dioxide and water. Photosynthesis in plants generally involves the green pigment chlorophyll and generates oxygen as a by-product.
– DERIVATIVES **photosynthetic** adjective, **photosynthetically** adverb.

photosynthesize (also **photosynthesise**) ▸ verb [no obj.] (of a plant) synthesize sugars or other substances by means of photosynthesis.

photosystem ▸ noun a biochemical mechanism in plants by which chlorophyll absorbs light energy for photosynthesis. There are two such mechanisms (**photosystems I** and **II**) involving different chlorophyll–protein complexes.

phototaxis /ˌfəʊtəʊˈtaksɪs/ ▸ noun (pl. **phototaxes**) [mass noun] Biology the bodily movement of a motile organism in response to light, either towards the source of light (**positive phototaxis**) or away from it (**negative phototaxis**). Compare with PHOTOTROPISM.
– DERIVATIVES **phototactic** adjective.

phototherapy ▸ noun [mass noun] the use of light in the treatment of physical or mental illness.

phototransistor ▸ noun a transistor that responds to light striking it by generating and amplifying an electric current.

phototroph /ˈfəʊtə(ʊ)trəʊf/ ▸ noun Biology an organism that uses energy from sunlight to synthesize organic compounds for nutrition.
– DERIVATIVES **phototrophic** adjective.

phototropism /ˌfəʊtə(ʊ)ˈtrəʊpɪz(ə)m, fəʊˈtɒtrəˌpɪz(ə)m/ ▸ noun [mass noun] Biology the orientation of a plant or other organism in response to light, either towards the source of light (**positive phototropism**) or away from it (**negative phototropism**). Compare with HELIOTROPISM, PHOTOTAXIS.
– DERIVATIVES **phototropic** adjective.

phototube ▸ noun Electronics a photocell in the form of an electron tube with a photoemissive cathode.

phototypesetter ▸ noun a machine for filmsetting.
– DERIVATIVES **phototypeset** adjective, **phototypesetting** noun.

photovoltaic /ˌfəʊtəʊvɒlˈteɪɪk/ ▸ adjective relating to the production of electric current at the junction of two substances exposed to light.

photovoltaics ▸ plural noun [treated as sing.] the branch of technology concerned with the production of electric current at the junction of two substances.
■ [treated as pl.] devices having a photovoltaic junction.

phragmites /fragˈmʌɪtiːz/ ▸ noun [mass noun] a common and invasive tall reed. ● Genus *Phragmites*, family Gramineae: several species, in particular the common or Norfolk reed.
– ORIGIN modern Latin, from Greek *phragmitēs* 'growing in hedges', from *phragma* 'hedge'.

phrasal ▸ adjective [attrib.] Grammar consisting of a phrase or phrases: *the text fragments itself into phrasal units*.

phrasal verb ▸ noun Grammar an idiomatic phrase consisting of a verb and another element, typically either an adverb, as in *break down*, or a preposition, for example *see to*, or a combination of both, such as *look down on*.

phrase ▸ noun a small group of words standing together as a conceptual unit, typically forming a component of a clause. ■ an idiomatic or short pithy expression: *his favourite phrase is 'it's a pleasure'*.
■ Music a group of notes forming a distinct unit within a longer passage. ■ Ballet a group of steps within a longer sequence or dance.
▸ verb [with obj. and adverbial] put into a particular form of words: *it's important to phrase the question correctly*. ■ (often as noun **phrasing**) divide (music) into phrases in a particular way, especially in performance: *original phrasing brought out unexpected aspects of the music*.
– PHRASES **turn of phrase** a person's particular or characteristic manner of expression: *a vituperative turn of phrase*.
– ORIGIN mid 16th cent. (in the sense 'style or manner of expression'): via late Latin from Greek *phrasis*, from *phrazein* 'declare, tell'.

phrase book ▸ noun a book for people visiting a foreign country, listing useful expressions in the language of the country together with their equivalent in the visitor's own language.

phraseology /ˌfreɪzɪˈɒlədʒi/ ▸ noun (pl. **phraseologies**) a particular mode of expression, especially one characteristic of a particular speaker or subject area: *legal phraseology*.
– DERIVATIVES **phraseological** adjective.
– ORIGIN mid 17th cent.: from modern Latin *phraseologia*, from Greek *phraseōn*, genitive plural of *phrasis* 'a phrase' + *-logia* (see -LOGY).

phratry /ˈfreɪtri/ ▸ noun (pl. **phratries**) Anthropology a descent group or kinship group in some tribal societies.
– ORIGIN mid 19th cent.: from Greek *phratria*, from *phratēr* 'clansman'.

phreaking ▸ noun [mass noun] informal, chiefly N. Amer. the action of hacking into telecommunications systems, especially to obtain free calls.
– DERIVATIVES **phreak** noun, **phreaker** noun.
– ORIGIN 1970s: alteration of *freaking* (see FREAK). The change from *f-* to *ph-* was due to association with PHONE[1].

phreatic /frɪˈatɪk/ ▸ adjective Geology relating to or denoting underground water in the zone of saturation (beneath the water table). Compare with VADOSE. ■ (of a volcanic eruption) caused by the heating and expansion of groundwater.
– ORIGIN late 19th cent.: from Greek *phrear, phreat-* 'a well' + -IC.

phreatomagmatic /frɪˌatə(ʊ)magˈmatɪk/ ▸ adjective Geology (of a volcanic eruption) in which both magmatic gases and steam from groundwater are expelled.
– ORIGIN mid 20th cent.: from Greek *phrear, phreat-* 'a well' + *magmatic* (see MAGMA).

phreatophyte /frɪˈatəfʌɪt/ ▸ noun Botany a plant with a deep root system that draws its water supply from near the water table.
– DERIVATIVES **phreatophytic** adjective.
– ORIGIN 1920s: from Greek *phrear, phreat-* 'a well' + -PHYTE.

phrenic /ˈfrɛnɪk/ ▸ adjective [attrib.] Anatomy relating to the diaphragm: *the phrenic nerves*.
– ORIGIN early 18th cent.: from French *phrénique*, from Greek *phrēn, phren-* 'diaphragm, mind' (because the mind was once thought to lie in the diaphragm).

phrenology /frɪˈnɒlədʒi/ ▸ noun [mass noun] chiefly historical the detailed study of the shape and size of the cranium as a supposed indication of character and mental abilities.
– DERIVATIVES **phrenological** adjective, **phrenologist** noun.
– ORIGIN early 19th cent.: from Greek *phrēn, phren-* 'mind' + -LOGY.

Phrygia /ˈfrɪdʒɪə/ an ancient region of west central Asia Minor, to the south of Bithynia. Centred on the city of Gordium, it dominated Asia Minor after the decline of the Hittites in the 12th century BC, reaching the peak of its power in the 8th century under King Midas. It was eventually absorbed into the kingdom of Lydia in the 6th century BC.

Phrygian ▸ adjective relating to Phrygia, its people, or their language.
▸ noun **1** a native or inhabitant of ancient Phrygia.
2 [mass noun] the language of the ancient Phrygians, of which only a few inscriptions survive. It is generally classified as an Indo-European language, with affinities to Greek and Armenian.

Phrygian bonnet (also **Phrygian cap**) ▸ noun a conical cap with the top bent forwards, worn in ancient times and now identified with the CAP OF LIBERTY.

Phrygian mode ▸ noun Music the mode represented by the natural diatonic scale E–E (containing a minor 2nd, 3rd, 6th, and 7th).

phthalate /ˈ(f)θaleɪt/ ▸ noun Chemistry a salt or ester of phthalic acid.

phthalic acid /ˈ(f)θalɪk/ ▸ noun Chemistry a crystalline acid derived from benzene, with two carboxylic acid groups attached to the benzene ring. ● Chem. formula: $C_6H_4(COOH)_2$; three isomers.
– ORIGIN mid 19th cent.: *phthalic*, shortening of *naphthalic* (see NAPHTHALENE).

phthalic anhydride ▸ noun [mass noun] Chemistry a crystalline compound made by oxidizing naphthalene, used as an intermediate in the manufacture of plastics, resins, and dyes. ● A bicyclic anhydride; chem. formula: $C_6H_4(CO)_2O$.
– ORIGIN mid 19th cent.: *phthalic*, shortening of *naphthalic* (see NAPHTHALENE).

phthalocyanine /ˌ(f)θaləʊˈsʌɪəniːn/ ▸ noun [mass noun] Chemistry a greenish-blue crystalline dye of the porphyrin group. ● Chem. formula: $C_{32}H_{18}N_8$.
■ [count noun] any of a large class of green or blue pigments and dyes which are chelate complexes of phthalocyanine or one of its derivatives with a metal (in particular, copper).
– ORIGIN 1930s: from *phthalic* (see PHTHALIC ACID) + Greek *kuan(e)os* 'dark blue' + -INE[4].

Phthiraptera /(f)θɪˈraptərə/ ▸ plural noun Entomology an order of insects that is sometimes applied, comprising both the sucking lice and the biting lice.
– ORIGIN modern Latin (plural), from Greek *phtheir* 'louse' + *pteron* 'wing'.

P

phthisis /ˈ(f)θʌɪsɪs, ˈtʌɪ-/ ▸ **noun** [mass noun] Medicine, archaic pulmonary tuberculosis or a similar progressive wasting disease.
– ORIGIN mid 16th cent.: via Latin from Greek, from *phthinein* 'to decay'.

Phuket /puːˈkɛt/ **1** an island of Thailand, situated at the head of the Strait of Malacca off the west coast of the Malay Peninsula.
2 a port at the south end of Phuket island, a major resort and outlet to the Indian Ocean.

phulkari /pʊlˈkɑːri/ ▸ **noun** (pl. **phulkaris**) (in South Asia) an ornamental cloth or shawl embroidered with silk flowers. ■ [mass noun] the style of embroidery used on a phulkari.
– ORIGIN from Hindi *phūlkārī*, based on *phūl* 'flower'.

phut ▸ **exclamation** used to represent a dull abrupt sound as of a slight impact or explosion.
– PHRASES **go phut** informal fail to work properly or at all.
– ORIGIN late 19th cent.: perhaps from Hindi *phaṭnā* 'to burst'.

phwoah /ˈfwɔːə/ (also **phwoar**) ▸ **exclamation** Brit. informal used to express sexual desire.
– ORIGIN 1980s: imitative.

phyco- ▸ **combining form** relating to seaweed: *phycology*.
– ORIGIN from Greek *phukos* 'seaweed'.

phycobilin /ˌfʌɪkə(ʊ)ˈbʌɪlɪn/ ▸ **noun** Biochemistry any of a group of red or blue photosynthetic pigments present in some algae.

phycocyanin /ˌfʌɪkəʊˈsʌɪənɪn/ ▸ **noun** Biochemistry any of a group of blue photosynthetic pigments present in cyanobacteria.

phycoerythrin /ˌfʌɪkəʊˈɛrɪθrɪn/ ▸ **noun** Biochemistry any of a group of red photosynthetic pigments present in red algae and some cyanobacteria.

phycology /fʌɪˈkɒlədʒi/ ▸ **noun** [mass noun] the branch of botany concerned with seaweeds and other algae.
– DERIVATIVES **phycological** adjective, **phycologist** noun.

phycomycete /ˌfʌɪkəʊˈmʌɪsiːt/ ▸ **noun** Botany any of the lower fungi, which typically form a non-septate mycelium. ● Subdivisions Mastigomycotina and Zygomycotina; formerly placed in a class Phycomycetes.

phycomycosis /ˌfʌɪkəʊmʌɪˈkəʊsɪs/ ▸ **noun** [mass noun] Medicine & Veterinary Medicine infection with a parasitic fungus which affects the sinuses and the tissues of the lungs, skin, and nerves. ● The fungus is typically a phycomycete, especially of the genera *Rhizopus*, *Absidia*, or *Mucor*.

phyla plural form of **PHYLUM**.

P

phylactery /fɪˈlakt(ə)ri/ ▸ **noun** (pl. **phylacteries**) a small leather box containing Hebrew texts on vellum, worn by Jewish men at morning prayer as a reminder to keep the law.
– ORIGIN late Middle English: via late Latin from Greek *phulaktērion* 'amulet', from *phulassein* 'to guard'.

phyletic /fʌɪˈlɛtɪk/ ▸ **adjective** Biology relating to or denoting the evolutionary development of a species or other group.
– DERIVATIVES **phyletically** adverb.
– ORIGIN late 19th cent.: from Greek *phuletikos*, from *phuletēs* 'tribesman', from *phulē* 'tribe'.

phyllite /ˈfɪlʌɪt/ ▸ **noun** [mass noun] Geology a fine-grained metamorphic rock with a well-developed laminar structure, intermediate between slate and schist.
– ORIGIN late 19th cent.: from Greek *phullon* 'leaf' + **-ITE**[1].

phyllo ▸ **noun** variant spelling of **FILO**.

phyllo- ▸ **combining form** of a leaf; relating to leaves: *phyllotaxis*.
– ORIGIN from Greek *phullon* 'leaf'.

phylloclade /ˈfɪlə(ʊ)kleɪd/ ▸ **noun** Botany a flattened branch or stem-joint resembling and functioning as a leaf.
– ORIGIN mid 19th cent.: from modern Latin *phyllocladium*, from Greek *phullōdēs* 'leaf-like', from *phullon* 'leaf'.

phyllode /ˈfɪləʊd/ ▸ **noun** Botany a winged leaf stalk which functions as a leaf.
– ORIGIN mid 19th cent.: from modern Latin *phyllodium*, from Greek *phullōdēs* 'leaf-like', from *phullon* 'leaf'.

phyllopod /ˈfɪlə(ʊ)pɒd/ ▸ **noun** Zoology, dated a branchiopod crustacean.
– ORIGIN from modern Latin *Phyllopoda* (former class name), from Greek *phullon* 'leaf' + *pous*, *pod-* 'foot'.

phylloquinone /ˌfɪlə(ʊ)ˈkwɪnəʊn/ ▸ **noun** [mass noun] Biochemistry one of the K vitamins, found in cabbage, spinach, and other leafy green vegetables, and essential for the blood-clotting process. Also called **VITAMIN** K_1.

phyllotaxis /ˌfɪlə(ʊ)ˈtaksɪs/ (also **phyllotaxy** /-ˈtaksi/) ▸ **noun** [mass noun] Botany the arrangement of leaves on an axis or stem.
– DERIVATIVES **phyllotactic** adjective.

phylloxera /ˌfɪlɒkˈsɪərə, fɪˈlɒksərə/ ▸ **noun** a plant louse that is a pest of vines. ● *Phylloxera vitifoliae*, family Phylloxeridae, suborder Homoptera.
– ORIGIN mid 19th cent.: modern Latin, from Greek *phullon* 'leaf' + *xēros* 'dry'.

phylogenesis /ˌfʌɪlə(ʊ)ˈdʒɛnɪsɪs/ ▸ **noun** [mass noun] Biology the evolutionary development and diversification of a species or group of organisms, or of a particular feature of an organism. Compare with **ONTOGENESIS**.
– DERIVATIVES **phylogenetic** adjective, **phylogenetically** adverb.
– ORIGIN late 19th cent.: from Greek *phulon*, *phulē* 'race, tribe' + **GENESIS**.

phylogeny /fʌɪˈlɒdʒ(ə)ni/ ▸ **noun** [mass noun] the branch of biology that deals with phylogenesis. Compare with **ONTOGENY**. ■ another term for **PHYLOGENESIS**.
– DERIVATIVES **phylogenic** adjective, **phylogenically** adverb.
– ORIGIN late 19th cent.: from Greek *phulon*, *phulē* 'race, tribe' + **-GENY**.

phylum /ˈfʌɪləm/ ▸ **noun** (pl. **phyla** /-lə/) **1** Zoology a principal taxonomic category that ranks above class and below kingdom, equivalent to the division in botany.
2 Linguistics a group of languages related to each other less closely than those forming a family, especially one in which the relationships are unclear.
– ORIGIN late 19th cent.: modern Latin from Greek, *phulon* 'race'.

physalis /ˈfʌɪsəlɪs, ˈfɪs-, fʌɪˈseɪlɪs/ ▸ **noun** a plant of a genus that includes the Cape gooseberry and Chinese lantern, which has an inflated lantern-like calyx. ● Genus *Physalis*, family Solanaceae: many species.
– ORIGIN modern Latin, from Greek *phusallis* 'bladder' (because of the inflated calyx).

Physeptone /fʌɪˈsɛptəʊn/ ▸ **noun** trademark for **METHADONE**.
– ORIGIN 1940s: of unknown origin.

physiatrics /ˌfɪzɪˈatrɪks/ ▸ **plural noun** [treated as sing.] North American term for **PHYSIOTHERAPY**.
– DERIVATIVES **physiatrist** noun.

physic archaic ▸ **noun** [mass noun] medicinal drugs. ■ the art of healing.
▸ **verb** (**physics**, **physicking**, **physicked**) [with obj.] treat with a medicine.
– ORIGIN Middle English: from Old French *fisique* 'medicine', from Latin *physica*, from Greek *phusikē* (*epistēmē*) '(knowledge) of nature'.

physical ▸ **adjective 1** relating to the body as opposed to the mind: *a range of physical and mental challenges*. ■ involving bodily contact or activity: *less physical sports such as bowls | a physical relationship*.
2 relating to things perceived through the senses as opposed to the mind; tangible or concrete: *the physical world*.
3 relating to physics or the operation of natural forces generally: *physical laws*.
▸ **noun 1** (also **physical examination**) a medical examination to determine a person's bodily fitness.
2 (**physicals**) Stock Exchange stocks held in actual commodities for immediate exchange, for example as opposed to futures.
– PHRASES **get physical 1** informal become aggressive or violent. **2** become sexually intimate with someone.
– DERIVATIVES **physicality** /-ˈkalɪti/ noun, **physically** adverb, **physicalness** noun.
– ORIGIN late Middle English (in the sense 'relating to medicine'): from medieval Latin *physicalis*, from Latin *physica* 'things relating to nature' (see **PHYSIC**). Sense 2 dates from the late 16th cent. and sense 1 from the late 18th cent.

physical anthropology ▸ **noun** see **ANTHROPOLOGY**.

physical chemistry ▸ **noun** [mass noun] the branch of chemistry concerned with the application of the techniques and theories of physics to the study of chemical systems.

physical culture ▸ **noun** [mass noun] dated the development of the body by exercise.

physical education ▸ **noun** [mass noun] instruction in physical exercise and games, especially in schools.

physical geography ▸ **noun** [mass noun] the branch of geography dealing with natural features.

physicalism ▸ **noun** [mass noun] Philosophy the doctrine that the real world consists simply of the physical world.
– DERIVATIVES **physicalist** noun & adjective, **physicalistic** adjective.

physicalize (also **physicalise**) ▸ **verb** [with obj.] express or represent by physical means or in physical terms: *physicalizing your anger can help release tension*.
– DERIVATIVES **physicalization** noun.

physical jerks ▸ **plural noun** Brit. informal energetic exercises done as part of a fitness routine.

physical sciences ▸ **plural noun** the sciences concerned with the study of inanimate natural objects, including physics, chemistry, astronomy, and related subjects. Often contrasted with **LIFE SCIENCES**.

physical theatre ▸ **noun** [mass noun] a form of theatre which emphasizes the use of physical movement, as in dance and mime, for expression.

physical therapy ▸ **noun** US term for **PHYSIOTHERAPY**.
– DERIVATIVES **physical therapist** noun.

physical training ▸ **noun** [mass noun] the systematic use of exercises to promote bodily fitness and strength.

physic garden ▸ **noun** a garden for cultivating medicinal herbs.

physician ▸ **noun** a person qualified to practise medicine, especially one who specializes in diagnosis and medical treatment as distinct from surgery.
– PHRASES **physician, heal thyself** proverb before attempting to correct others, make sure that you aren't guilty of the same faults yourself. [with biblical allusion to Luke 4:23.]
– ORIGIN Middle English: from Old French *fisicien*, based on Latin *physica* 'things relating to nature' (see **PHYSIC**).

physicist ▸ **noun** an expert in or student of physics.

physico- ▸ **combining form** physical; physical and ...: *physico-mental*.
– ORIGIN from **PHYSICS**.

physico-chemical ▸ **adjective** relating to physics and chemistry or to physical chemistry.

physics ▸ **plural noun** [treated as sing.] the branch of science concerned with the nature and properties of matter and energy. The subject matter of physics includes mechanics, heat, light and other radiation, sound, electricity, magnetism, and the structure of atoms. ■ the physical properties and phenomena of something: *the physics of plasmas*.
– ORIGIN late 15th cent. (denoting natural science in general, especially the Aristotelian system): plural of obsolete *physic* 'physical (thing)', suggested by Latin *physica*, Greek *phusika* 'natural things' from *phusis* 'nature'.

physio ▸ **noun** (pl. **physios**) Brit. informal a physiotherapist. ■ [mass noun] physiotherapy.

physio- ▸ **combining form 1** relating to nature and natural phenomena: *physiography*.
2 representing **PHYSIOLOGY**.
– ORIGIN from Greek *phusis* 'nature'.

physiochemical ▸ **adjective** relating to physiological chemistry.

physiocrat ▸ **noun** a member of an 18th-century group of French economists who believed that agriculture was the source of all wealth and that agricultural products should be highly priced. Advocating adherence to a supposed natural order of social institutions, they also stressed the necessity of free trade.
– DERIVATIVES **physiocracy** noun, **physiocratic** adjective.
– ORIGIN late 18th cent.: from French *physiocrate*, from *physiocratie* 'physiocracy' (see **PHYSIO-**, **-CRACY**).

physiognomist ▸ **noun** a person supposedly able to judge character (or, formerly, to predict the future) from facial characteristics.
– ORIGIN late 16th cent.: from Old French *physionomiste*.

physiognomy /ˌfɪzɪˈɒ(g)nəmi/ ▸ **noun** (pl. **physiognomies**) a person's facial features or expression, especially when regarded as indicative of character or ethnic origin. ■ [mass noun] the supposed art of judging character from facial characteristics. ■ the general form or appearance of something: *the physiognomy of the landscape*.
– DERIVATIVES **physiognomic** adjective, **physiognomical** adjective, **physiognomically** adverb.

– ORIGIN late Middle English: from Old French *phisonomie*, via medieval Latin from Greek *phusiognōmonia* 'judging of a man's nature (by his features)', based on *gnōmōn* 'a judge, interpreter'.

physiography ▸ noun another term for PHYSICAL GEOGRAPHY.
– DERIVATIVES **physiographer** noun, **physiographic** adjective, **physiographical** adjective, **physiographically** adverb.
– ORIGIN early 19th cent.: from French *physiographie* (see PHYSIO-, -GRAPHY).

physiological saline ▸ noun a solution of salts that is isotonic with the body fluids.

physiology ▸ noun [mass noun] the branch of biology that deals with the normal functions of living organisms and their parts. ▪ the way in which a living organism or bodily part functions: *the physiology of the brain*.
– DERIVATIVES **physiologic** adjective, **physiological** adjective, **physiologically** adverb, **physiologist** noun.
– ORIGIN early 17th cent.: from Latin *physiologia* (perhaps via French), from Greek *phusiologia* 'natural philosophy' (see PHYSIO-, -LOGY).

physiotherapy (US **physical therapy**) ▸ noun [mass noun] the treatment of disease, injury, or deformity by physical methods such as massage, heat treatment, and exercise rather than by drugs or surgery.
– DERIVATIVES **physiotherapist** noun.

physique /fɪˈziːk/ ▸ noun the form, size, and development of a person's body: *a sturdy, muscular physique* | [mass noun] *they were much alike in physique*.
– ORIGIN early 19th cent.: from French, literally 'physical' (used as a noun).

physostigmine /ˌfʌɪsəʊˈstɪgmiːn/ ▸ noun [mass noun] Chemistry a compound which is the active ingredient of the Calabar bean and is used medicinally in eye drops on account of its anticholinesterase activity.
● A tricyclic alkaloid; chem. formula: $C_{15}H_{21}N_3O_2$.
– ORIGIN mid 19th cent.: from the modern Latin genus name *Physostigma* (to which the Calabar bean belongs) + -INE[4].

-phyte ▸ combining form denoting a plant or plant-like organism: *epiphyte*.
– DERIVATIVES **-phytic** combining form in corresponding adjectives.
– ORIGIN from Greek *phuton* 'a plant', from *phuein* 'come into being'.

phyto- ▸ combining form of a plant; relating to plants: *phytogeography*.
– ORIGIN from Greek *phuton* 'a plant', from *phuein* 'come into being'.

phytoalexin /ˌfʌɪtəʊəˈlɛksɪn/ ▸ noun Botany a substance that is produced by plant tissues in response to contact with a parasite and specifically inhibits the growth of that parasite.
– ORIGIN 1940s: from PHYTO- 'of plants' + *alexin*, a name for a class of substances found in blood serum, able to destroy bacteria.

phytochemical /fʌɪtəʊˈkɛmɪk(ə)l/ ▸ noun any of various biologically active compounds found in plants.
▸ adjective relating to phytochemistry or phytochemicals.

phytochemistry ▸ noun [mass noun] the branch of chemistry concerned with plants and plant products.

phytochrome ▸ noun [mass noun] Biochemistry a blue-green pigment found in many plants, in which it regulates various developmental processes.
– ORIGIN late 19th cent.: from PHYTO- 'relating to plants' + Greek *khrōma* 'colour'.

phytoestrogen /ˌfʌɪtəʊˈiːstrədʒ(ə)n/ ▸ noun Biochemistry a substance found in certain plants which can produce effects like that of the hormone oestrogen when ingested into the body.

phytogenetic ▸ adjective Botany relating to the origin and evolution of plants.

phytogeographical kingdom ▸ noun Botany each of a number of major areas of the earth distinguished on the basis of the characteristic plants present. They usually include the Boreal, Palaeotropical, Neotropical, Australian, South African, and Antarctic kingdoms. Also called FLORAL KINGDOM.

phytogeography ▸ noun [mass noun] the branch of botany that deals with the geographical distribution of plants. Also called PLANT GEOGRAPHY.
– DERIVATIVES **phytogeographic** adjective, **phytogeographical** adjective.

phytohaemagglutinin /ˌfʌɪtə(ʊ)hiːməˈgluːtɪnɪn/ (US **phytohemagglutinin**) ▸ noun [mass noun] Biochemistry a plant protein, especially that extracted from the French bean, that causes red blood cells to clump together.

phytolith /ˈfʌɪtə(ʊ)lɪθ/ ▸ noun Botany a minute mineral particle formed inside a plant. ▪ Palaeontology a fossilized particle of plant tissue.

phytonutrient ▸ noun a substance found in certain plants which is believed to be beneficial to human health and help prevent various diseases.

phytopathology ▸ noun [mass noun] the study of plant diseases.
– DERIVATIVES **phytopathological** adjective.

phytophagous /fʌɪˈtɒfəgəs/ ▸ adjective Zoology (especially of an insect or other invertebrate) feeding on plants.

phytoplankton /ˈfʌɪtəʊˌplaŋ(k)t(ə)n/ ▸ noun [mass noun] Biology plankton consisting of microscopic plants.

phytosanitary ▸ adjective relating to the health of plants, especially with respect to the requirements of international trade.

phytotoxic ▸ adjective Botany poisonous to plants.
– DERIVATIVES **phytotoxicity** noun.

phytotoxin ▸ noun Botany a poisonous substance derived from a plant. ▪ a substance that is phytotoxic, especially one produced by a parasite.

pi[1] /pʌɪ/ ▸ noun the sixteenth letter of the Greek alphabet (Π, π), transliterated as 'p'. ▪ the numerical value of the ratio of the circumference of a circle to its diameter (approximately 3.14159). [from the initial letter of Greek *periphereia* 'circumference'.] ▪ **(Pi)** [followed by Latin genitive] Astronomy the sixteenth star in a constellation: *Pi Herculis*. ▪ [as modifier] Chemistry & Physics relating to or denoting an electron or orbital with one unit of angular momentum about an internuclear axis.
▸ symbol ▪ (π) the numerical value of pi. ▪ (Π) osmotic pressure. ▪ (Π) mathematical product.
– ORIGIN Greek.

pi[2] /pʌɪ/ ▸ adjective Brit. informal short for PIOUS.

pia /ˈpʌɪə, ˈpiːə/ (in full **pia mater**) ▸ noun [mass noun] Anatomy the delicate innermost membrane enveloping the brain and spinal cord. See also MENINGES.
– DERIVATIVES **pial** adjective.
– ORIGIN late 19th cent.: from medieval Latin, in full literally 'tender mother', translating Arabic *al-'umm ar-raqīqa*.

piacular /pʌɪˈakjʊlə/ ▸ adjective rare making or requiring atonement.
– ORIGIN early 17th cent.: from Latin *piacularis*, from *piaculum* 'expiation', from *piare* 'appease'.

Piaf /ˈpiːaf/, Edith (1915–63), French singer; born *Edith Giovanna Gassion*. She became known as a cabaret and music-hall singer in the late 1930s. Her songs included 'La Vie en rose' and 'Je ne regrette rien'.

piaffe /pɪˈaf/ ▸ noun (also **piaffer** /pɪˈafə/) a movement performed in advanced dressage and classical riding, in which the horse executes a slow elevated trot without moving forward.
▸ verb [no obj.] (of a horse) perform a piaffe.
– ORIGIN mid 18th cent.: from French *piaffer* 'to strut'.

Piaget /pɪˈaʒeɪ/, Jean (1896–1980), Swiss psychologist. Piaget's work on the intellectual and logical abilities of children provided the single biggest impact on the study of the development of human thought processes. He described the mind as proceeding through a series of fixed stages of cognitive development, each being a prerequisite for the next.

pia mater /ˌpʌɪə ˈmeɪtə, ˌpiːə ˈmɑːtə/ ▸ noun see PIA.

piani plural form of PIANO[2].

pianism /ˈpɪənɪz(ə)m/ ▸ noun [mass noun] technical skill or artistry in playing the piano, or in composing piano music.
– DERIVATIVES **pianistic** adjective, **pianistically** adverb.

pianissimo /ˌpɪəˈnɪsɪməʊ/ Music ▸ adverb & adjective (especially as a direction) very soft or softly.
▸ noun (pl. **pianissimos** or **pianissimi** /ˌpɪəˈnɪsɪmi/) a passage performed or marked to be performed very softly.
– ORIGIN Italian, superlative of *piano* (see PIANO[2]).

pianist ▸ noun a person who plays the piano, especially professionally.
– ORIGIN mid 19th cent.: from French *pianiste*, from *piano* (see PIANO[1]).

piano[1] /pɪˈanəʊ/ ▸ noun (pl. **pianos**) a large keyboard musical instrument with a wooden case enclosing a soundboard and metal strings, which are struck by hammers when the keys are depressed. The strings' vibration is stopped by dampers when the keys are released and can be regulated for length and volume by two or three pedals.
– ORIGIN early 19th cent.: from Italian, abbreviation of PIANOFORTE.

piano[2] /ˈpjɑːnəʊ/ Music ▸ adverb & adjective (especially as a direction) soft or softly.
▸ noun (pl. **pianos** or **piani** /ˈpjɑːni/) a passage performed or marked to be performed softly.
– ORIGIN Italian, literally 'soft'.

piano accordion ▸ noun an accordion with the melody played on a small vertical keyboard like that of a piano.

pianoforte /pɪˌanəʊˈfɔːteɪ, pɪˌanəʊˈfɔːti/ ▸ noun formal term for PIANO[1].
– ORIGIN mid 18th cent.: from Italian, earlier *piano e forte* 'soft and loud', expressing the gradation in tone.

pianola /ˌpɪəˈnəʊlə/ ▸ noun trademark a piano equipped to be played automatically using a piano roll.
– ORIGIN late 19th cent.: apparently a diminutive of PIANO[1].

piano nobile /ˌpjɑːnəʊ ˈnəʊbɪleɪ/ ▸ noun Architecture the first floor of a large Palladian or Georgian house, containing the principal rooms.
– ORIGIN Italian, literally 'noble floor'.

piano organ ▸ noun a mechanical piano constructed like a barrel organ.

piano roll ▸ noun a roll of perforated paper which controls the movement of the keys in a pianola or similar instrument, so producing a particular melody.

piano trio ▸ noun a trio for piano and two stringed instruments, usually violin and cello.

piano wire ▸ noun [mass noun] strong steel wire used for piano strings.

piapiac /ˈpɪəpɪak/ ▸ noun a black long-tailed African crow that often feeds gregariously among grazing mammals. ● *Ptilostomus afer*, family Corvidae.
– ORIGIN probably imitative.

piassava /ˌpiːəˈsɑːvə/ ▸ noun [mass noun] a stout fibre obtained from the leaf stalks of a number of South American and African palm trees. ▪ [count noun] a palm tree producing piassava.
– ORIGIN mid 19th cent.: via Portuguese from Tupi *piaçába*.

piastre /pɪˈastə/ (US also **piaster**) ▸ noun a monetary unit of several Middle Eastern countries, equal to one hundredth of a pound.
– ORIGIN from French, from Italian *piastra (d'argento)* 'plate (of silver)'.

Piauí /pjaʊˈiː/ a state of NE Brazil, on the Atlantic coast; capital, Teresina.

P

piazza /pɪˈatsə/ ▸ noun 1 a public square or marketplace, especially in an Italian town.
2 US archaic the veranda of a house.
– ORIGIN late 16th cent.: Italian.

pibroch /ˈpiːbrɒk, ˈpiːbrɒx/ ▸ noun [mass noun] a form of music for the Scottish bagpipes involving elaborate variations on a theme, typically of a martial or funerary character. ▪ [count noun] a piece of pibroch music.
– ORIGIN early 18th cent.: from Scottish Gaelic *piobaireachd* 'art of piping', from *piobair* 'piper', from *piob*, from English PIPE.

pic ▸ noun informal a photograph or cinema film.
– ORIGIN late 19th cent.: abbreviation of PICTURE.

pica[1] /ˈpʌɪkə/ ▸ noun Printing a unit of type size and line length equal to 12 points (about $^1/_6$ inch or 4.2 mm). ▪ [mass noun] a size of letter in typewriting, with 10 characters to the inch (about 3.9 to the centimetre).
– ORIGIN late 16th cent.: from Anglo-Latin *pica* (literally 'magpie'), commonly identified with a 15th-cent. book of rules about Church feasts, but no edition of such a *pica* printed in 'pica' type is known.

pica[2] /ˈpʌɪkə/ ▸ noun [mass noun] Medicine a tendency or craving to eat substances other than normal food (such as clay, plaster, or ashes), occurring during childhood or pregnancy, or as a symptom of disease.
– ORIGIN mid 16th cent.: modern Latin, from Latin, literally 'magpie', probably translating Greek *kissa* 'magpie', also 'false appetite'.

picador /ˈpɪkədɔː/ ▸ noun (in bullfighting) a person on horseback who goads the bull with a lance.
– ORIGIN Spanish, from *picar* 'to prick'.

picante /pɪˈkanteɪ/ ▸ adjective (of food) spicy.
– ORIGIN Spanish, literally 'pricking, biting'.

Picard /ˈpɪkɑːd/, French /pikaʀ/ ▶ **noun 1** a native or inhabitant of Picardy.
2 the dialect of French spoken in Picardy.
▶ **adjective** relating to Picardy, its inhabitants, or their dialect.

Picardy /ˈpɪkədi/ a region and former province of northern France, centred on the city of Amiens. It was the scene of heavy fighting in the First World War. French name **Picardie** /pikaʀdi/.

picaresque /ˌpɪkəˈrɛsk/ ▶ **adjective** relating to an episodic style of fiction dealing with the adventures of a rough and dishonest but appealing hero.
– ORIGIN early 19th cent.: from French, from Spanish *picaresco*, from *pícaro* 'rogue'.

picaro /ˈpɪkərəʊ/ ▶ **noun** (pl. **picaros**) a rogue.
– ORIGIN early 17th cent.: from Spanish.

picaroon /ˌpɪkəˈruːn/ ▶ **noun** archaic a rogue or scoundrel. ■ historical a pirate or privateer.
– ORIGIN early 17th cent.: from Spanish *picarón*, augmentative of *picaro* 'rogue'.

Picasso /pɪˈkasəʊ/, Pablo (1881–1973), Spanish painter, sculptor, and graphic artist, resident in France from 1904.

> Picasso's prolific inventiveness and technical versatility made him the dominant figure in avant-garde art in the first half of the 20th century. Following his Blue Period (1901–4) and Rose Period (1905–6), *Les Demoiselles d'Avignon* (1907) signalled his development of cubism (1908–14). In the 1920s and 1930s he adopted a neoclassical figurative style and produced semi-surrealist paintings using increasingly violent imagery, notably *The Three Dancers* (1935) and *Guernica* (1937).

– DERIVATIVES **Picassoesque** adjective.

picayune /ˌpɪkəˈjuːn/ N. Amer. ▶ **adjective** informal of little value or significance; petty: *the picayune squabbling of party politicians*.
▶ **noun** dated a small coin of little value, especially a 5-cent piece. ■ informal an insignificant person or thing.
– ORIGIN early 19th cent.: from French *picaillon*, denoting a Piedmontese copper coin, also used to mean 'cash', from Provençal *picaioun*, of unknown ultimate origin.

Piccadilly /ˌpɪkəˈdɪli/ a street in central London, extending from Hyde Park eastwards to Piccadilly Circus, noted for its fashionable shops, hotels, and restaurants.

piccalilli /ˌpɪkəˈlɪli/ ▶ **noun** (pl. **piccalillies** or **piccalillis**) [mass noun] a pickle of chopped vegetables, mustard, and hot spices.
– ORIGIN mid 18th cent.: probably from a blend of PICKLE and CHILLI.

piccaninny /ˈpɪkənɪni, ˌpɪkəˈnɪni/ (US **pickaninny**) ▶ **noun** (pl. **piccaninnies**) offensive a small black child.
▶ **adjective** archaic very small.
– ORIGIN mid 17th cent.: from West Indian creole, from Spanish *pequeño* or Portuguese *pequeno* 'little', *pequenino* 'tiny'.

piccolo ▶ **noun** (pl. **piccolos**) a small flute sounding an octave higher than the ordinary one.
– ORIGIN mid 19th cent.: from Italian, 'small (flute)'.

piccy ▶ **noun** (pl. **piccies**) informal a picture.
– ORIGIN mid 19th cent.: abbreviation.

pice /pʌɪs/ ▶ **noun** (pl. **same**) a former monetary unit of India and Pakistan, equal to one quarter of an anna.
– ORIGIN from Hindi *paisā*.

pichi /ˈpɪtʃi/ ▶ **noun** a small armadillo living in open pampas country in southern South America. ● *Zaedyus pichiy*, family Dasypodidae.
– ORIGIN early 19th cent.: via American Spanish from Araucanian, literally 'small'.

pick[1] ▶ **verb 1** [with obj.] take hold of and remove (a flower, fruit, or vegetable) from where it is growing: *I went to pick some flowers for Jenny's room*. ■ [with obj. and adverbial] take hold of and lift or move: *he picked a match out of the ashtray* | ***picking her up**, he carried her from the room*. ■ [no obj.] (**pick up**) Golf take hold of and lift up one's ball, especially when conceding a hole.
2 [with obj.] choose (someone or something) from a number of alternatives: *maybe I picked the wrong career* | *he was picked for the England squad* | [no obj.] *Maggie **picked on** a nice reliable chap*. ■ (**pick one's way**) [with adverbial of direction] walk slowly and carefully, selecting the best places to put one's feet: *he picked his way along the track, avoiding the potholes*.
3 [no obj.] repeatedly pull at something with one's fingers: *the old woman was picking at the sheet*. ■ eat food in small amounts or without much appetite: *she **picked at** her breakfast*. ■ [with obj.] remove unwanted matter from (one's nose or teeth) by using one's finger or a pointed instrument. ■ criticize someone in a petty way: *don't start **picking at** Ruth*.
4 [with obj.] pluck the strings of (a guitar or banjo).
▶ **noun 1** [in sing.] an act or the right of selecting something from a number of alternatives: *take your pick from our extensive menu* | *Laura should have first pick*. ■ (**the pick of**) informal the person or thing perceived as the best in a group: *he was the pick of the bunch*. ■ someone or something that has been selected: *the club made him their first pick*.
2 Basketball an act of blocking or screening a defensive player from the ball handler.
– PHRASES **pick and choose** select only the best from a number of alternatives. **pick someone's brains** (or **brain**) informal obtain information by questioning someone who is better informed about a subject than oneself. **pick something clean** completely remove the flesh from a bone or carcass. **pick one's feet up** raise one's feet clear of the ground when walking. **pick a fight** (or **quarrel**) talk or behave in such a way as to provoke a fight or argument. **pick holes in** find fault with. **pick a lock** open a lock with an instrument other than the proper key. **pick someone's pockets** steal something surreptitiously from someone's pocket. **pick someone/thing to pieces** (or **apart**) criticize someone or something severely. **pick up the pieces** restore one's life or a situation to a more normal state after a shock or disaster. **pick up** (or **get up**) **speed** (or **steam**) (of a vehicle) go faster; accelerate. **pick up the threads** resume something that has been interrupted.
– PHRASAL VERBS **pick someone/thing off** shoot a member of a group, aiming carefully from a distance. ■ Baseball put out a runner by throwing the ball to a base. **pick on** repeatedly single (someone) out for criticism or unkind treatment in a way perceived to be unfair. **pick someone/thing out 1** distinguish someone or something from a group: *Lester picked out two familiar voices*. ■ (of a light) illuminate an object by shining directly on it. ■ highlight or accentuate something from its surroundings by painting or fashioning it in a contrasting colour or medium: *the initials are picked out in diamonds*. **2** play a tune on a musical instrument slowly or with difficulty: *she began to pick out a rough melody on the guitar*. **pick something over** (or **pick through**) sort through a number of items carefully: *they picked through the charred remains of their home*. **pick up 1** become better; improve: *my luck's picked up*. ■ become stronger; increase: *the wind has picked up*. **2** answer a telephone call. **pick someone up 1** go somewhere to collect someone, typically in one's car. ■ stop for someone to board a train, boat, etc. ■ informal arrest someone. **2** informal casually strike up a relationship with a stranger as a sexual overture. **3** return to a point made by someone in order to criticize it: *she **picked him up on** one niggling point*. **4** make someone feel more energetic and cheerful: *songs to pick you up and make you feel good*. **pick something up 1** collect something that has been left elsewhere: *Wanda came over to pick up her things*. **2** obtain, acquire, or learn something, especially in an informal way: *he had picked up a little Russian from his father*. ■ catch an illness or infection. **3** detect or receive a signal or sound, especially by means of electronic apparatus. ■ (also **pick up on**) become aware of or sensitive to something: *women are very quick to pick up emotional atmospheres*. **4** (also **pick up**) resume something: *they picked up their friendship without the slightest difficulty*. ■ (also **pick up on**) refer to or develop a point mentioned earlier: *Dawson picked up her earlier remark*. **5** informal pay the bill for something. **6** find and take a particular road or route. **7** N. Amer. tidy a room or building. **pick up after** chiefly US tidy up things left strewn around by (someone).
– DERIVATIVES **pickable** adjective, **picker** noun.
– ORIGIN Middle English (earlier as *pike*, which continues in dialect use): of unknown origin. Compare with Dutch *pikken* 'pick, peck', and German *picken* 'peck, puncture', also with French *piquer* 'to prick'.

pick[2] ▶ **noun 1** a tool consisting of a long handle set at right angles in the middle of a curved iron or steel bar with a point at one end and a chisel edge or point at the other, used for breaking up hard ground or rock.
2 an instrument for picking: *an ebony hair pick*. ■ informal a plectrum.
– ORIGIN Middle English: variant of PIKE[2].

pickaback ▶ **noun, adverb, & verb** old-fashioned term for PIGGYBACK.

pick-and-mix (also **pick 'n' mix**) ▶ **adjective** Brit. denoting a method of assembling something by choosing items from among a large variety of different possibilities: *enjoy the freedom and choice of our pick-and-mix holidays*.

pickaninny ▶ **noun** US spelling of PICCANINNY.

pickaxe (US also **pickax**) ▶ **noun** another term for PICK[2] (sense 1).
▶ **verb** [with obj.] break or strike with a pickaxe.
– ORIGIN Middle English *pikoys*, from Old French *picois*; related to PIKE[2]. The change in the ending was due to association with AXE.

pickelhaube /ˈpɪk(ə)l,(h)aʊbə/ ▶ **noun** historical a spiked helmet worn by German soldiers.
– ORIGIN German.

pickerel /ˈpɪk(ə)r(ə)l/ ▶ **noun** (pl. **same** or **pickerels**) a small pike occurring in North America. ● Genus *Esox*, family Esocidae: several species, including the **redfin** (or **grass**) **pickerel** (*E. americanus*).
■ a young pike.
– ORIGIN Middle English: diminutive of PIKE[1].

pickerelweed ▶ **noun** [mass noun] either of two broadleaved freshwater plants which were formerly believed to give rise to, or provide food for, young pike. ● a North American plant with spikes of blue flowers (*Pontederia cordata*, family Pontederiaceae). ● Brit. dialect term for PONDWEED.

Pickering, William Hayward (1910–2004), New Zealand-born American engineer, director of the Jet Propulsion Laboratory at the California Institute of Technology 1954–76. During his directorate the laboratory launched America's first satellite, Explorer I (1958), and several unmanned probes to the moon and planets.

picket ▶ **noun 1** a person or group of people who stand outside a workplace or other venue as a protest or to try to persuade others not to enter during a strike.
■ a blockade of a workplace or other venue staged by a picket.
2 (also **picquet**) a soldier or small group of soldiers performing a particular duty, especially one sent out to watch for the enemy.
3 [usu. as modifier] a pointed wooden stake driven into the ground, typically to form a fence or to tether a horse.
▶ **verb** (**pickets, picketing, picketed**) [with obj.] act as a picket outside (a workplace or other venue): *strikers picketed the newspaper's main building*.
– DERIVATIVES **picketer** noun.
– ORIGIN late 17th cent. (denoting a pointed stake, on which a soldier was required to stand on one foot as a military punishment): from French *piquet* 'pointed stake', from *piquer* 'to prick', from *pic* 'pike'.

picket fence ▶ **noun** a wooden fence made of spaced uprights connected by two or more horizontal rails.
■ N. Amer. a picket fence as a symbol of middle-class domesticity and contentment: *we'd get a house with a white picket fence, and a dog, and have two kids*.

picket line ▶ **noun** a boundary established by workers on strike, especially at the entrance to the place of work, which others are asked not to cross.

Pickford, Mary (1893–1979), Canadian-born American actress; born *Gladys Mary Smith*. She was a star of silent films such as *Pollyanna* (1920). She also co-founded United Artists (1919).

pickings ▶ **plural noun 1** profits or gains that are made effortlessly or dishonestly: *thieves found **easy pickings** in the underprotected bedsits*.
2 remaining scraps or leftovers.

pickle ▶ **noun 1** [mass noun] a relish consisting of vegetables or fruit preserved in vinegar or brine. ■ [count noun] N. Amer. a pickled cucumber. ■ liquid used to preserve food or other perishable items.
2 [in sing.] informal a difficult situation: *I am **in a pickle***.
3 [in sing.] Brit. informal, dated used as an affectionate form of address to a mischievous child.
4 an acid solution for cleaning metal objects.
▶ **verb** [with obj.] **1** preserve (food or other perishable items) in vinegar or brine: *fish **pickled in** brine*.
2 immerse (a metal object) in an acid or other chemical solution for cleaning.
– ORIGIN late Middle English (denoting a spicy sauce served with meat): from Middle Dutch, Middle Low German *pekel*, of unknown ultimate origin.

pickled ▶ **adjective 1** (of food) preserved in vinegar or brine: *pickled onions*.
2 [predic.] informal drunk.

pickled fish ▶ **noun** [mass noun] a traditional South African dish of fish prepared with onions in a vinegar sauce and flavoured with curry powder, turmeric, and other spices.

pickler ▸ noun a vegetable or fruit suitable for pickling.

pickling ▸ adjective (of food) suitable for being pickled or used in making pickles: *pickling onions*.

picklock ▸ noun a person who picks locks. ▪ an instrument for picking locks.

pick-me-up ▸ noun informal a thing that makes one feel more energetic or cheerful: *ginseng has long been used as a pick-me-up*.

pickney /ˈpɪkni/ ▸ noun black English a child: *me and the pickney have to survive some way*.
– ORIGIN contraction of PICCANINNY.

pick 'n' mix ▸ adjective variant of PICK-AND-MIX.

pickoff ▸ noun **1** Baseball an act of catching a runner off base, involving a sudden throw of the ball to that base by the pitcher or catcher.
2 a device in the control or guidance system of an aircraft or boat which emits or alters an electrical, optical, or pneumatic output in response to a change in motion.

pickpocket ▸ noun a person who steals from people's pockets.
▸ verb [with obj.] steal from the pockets of (someone): *I think someone pickpocketed me in Brighton on my way to the station* | (as noun **pickpocketing**) *crimes such as pickpocketing*.

Pick's disease ▸ noun [mass noun] a rare form of progressive dementia, typically in late middle age and often familial, involving localized atrophy of the brain.
– ORIGIN early 20th cent.: named after Arnold *Pick* (1851–1924), Bohemian neurologist.

pickup ▸ noun **1** (also **pickup truck**) a small van or truck with low sides.
2 an act of collecting a person or goods, especially in a vehicle.
3 informal a casual encounter with a stranger with a view to having sexual intercourse. ▪ a person encountered with a view to having sexual intercourse.
4 an improvement, especially in an economy: *a pickup in demand*.
5 a device that produces an electrical signal in response to some other kind of signal or change, in particular: ▪ the cartridge of a record player, carrying the stylus. ▪ a device on an electric guitar which converts sound vibrations into electrical signals for amplification.
6 [mass noun] the reception of signals, especially interference or noise, by electrical apparatus.
7 Music a series of introductory notes leading into the opening part of a tune.
8 Fishing a semicircular loop of metal for guiding the line back on to the spool as it is reeled in.
▸ adjective [attrib.] N. Amer. informal informal and spontaneous: *a pickup basketball game*.

Pickwickian /pɪkˈwɪkɪən/ ▸ adjective of or like Mr Pickwick in Dickens's *Pickwick Papers*, especially in being jovial, plump, or generous. ▪ (of words) misunderstood or misused, especially to avoid offence.

picky ▸ adjective (**pickier**, **pickiest**) informal fussy and hard to please: *they are becoming increasingly picky about where they stay*.
– DERIVATIVES **pickiness** noun.

pick-your-own ▸ adjective relating to a system in which commercially grown fruit or vegetables are dug or picked by the customer for purchase at the place of production.

picnic ▸ noun an occasion when a packed meal is eaten outdoors, especially during an outing to the countryside. ▪ a packed meal eaten outdoors.
▸ verb (**picnics**, **picnicking**, **picnicked**) [no obj.] have or take part in a picnic.
– PHRASES **be no picnic** informal be difficult or unpleasant: *being a freelance was no picnic*.
– DERIVATIVES **picnicker** noun, **picnicky** adjective.
– ORIGIN mid 18th cent. (denoting a social event at which each guest contributes a share of the food): from French *pique-nique*, of unknown origin.

picnic races ▸ plural noun Austral./NZ a race meeting for amateurs held in a rural area.

pico- /ˈpiːkəʊ, ˈpʌɪkəʊ/ ▸ combining form (used in units of measurement) denoting a factor of 10^{-12}: *picosecond*. ▪ very small: *picornavirus*.
– ORIGIN from Spanish *pico*, literally 'beak, peak, little bit'.

Pico da Neblina /ˌpiːkuː dɑː nɛˈbliːnə/ a mountain in NW Brazil, close to the border with Venezuela. Rising to 3,014 m (9,888 ft), it is the highest peak in Brazil.

Pico de Orizaba /ˌpikəʊ ðe əʊriˈθaβa, -ˈsaβa/ Spanish name for CITLALTÉPETL.

picong /ˈpiːkɒŋ/ ▸ noun [mass noun] W. Indian taunting or ridicule: *the boys might start to give Frederick picong*.
– ORIGIN from Spanish *picón*.

picornavirus /pɪˈkɔːnəˌvʌɪrəs/ ▸ noun any of a group of very small RNA viruses which includes enteroviruses, rhinoviruses, and the virus of foot-and-mouth disease.
– ORIGIN 1960s: from PICO- + **RNA** + VIRUS.

picot /ˈpiːkəʊ/ ▸ noun [often as modifier] a small loop or series of small loops of twisted thread in lace or embroidery, typically decorating the border of a fabric.
– ORIGIN early 17th cent.: from French, literally 'small peak or point', diminutive of *pic*.

picotee /ˌpɪkəˈtiː/ ▸ noun a type of carnation of which the flowers have a light ground and dark-edged petals.
– ORIGIN early 18th cent.: from French *picoté(e)* 'marked with points', past participle of *picoter* 'to prick'.

picquet ▸ noun variant of PICKET (sense 2 of the noun).

picrate /ˈpɪkreɪt/ ▸ noun Chemistry a salt or ester of picric acid.

picric acid /ˈpɪkrɪk/ ▸ noun [mass noun] Chemistry a bitter yellow compound obtained by nitrating phenol, used as a dye and in the manufacture of explosives.
● Alternative name: **2,4,6-trinitrophenol**; chem. formula: $C_6H_2(NO_2)_3OH$.
– ORIGIN mid 19th cent.: *picric* from Greek *pikros* 'bitter' + -IC.

picrite /ˈpɪkrʌɪt/ ▸ noun [mass noun] Geology a dark basaltic igneous rock rich in olivine.
– DERIVATIVES **picritic** /pɪˈkrɪtɪk/ adjective.
– ORIGIN early 19th cent.: from Greek *pikros* 'bitter' + -ITE[1].

picrotoxin /ˌpɪkrə(ʊ)ˈtɒksɪn/ ▸ noun [mass noun] Medicine a bitter compound used to stimulate the respiratory and nervous system, especially in treating barbiturate poisoning. ● This toxin is obtained from the seeds of the shrub *Anamirta cocculus* (family Menispermaceae).
– ORIGIN mid 19th cent.: from Greek *pikros* 'bitter' + TOXIN.

Pict ▸ noun a member of an ancient people inhabiting northern Scotland in Roman times.

> Roman writings of around 300 AD apply the term *Picti* to the hostile tribes of the area north of the Antonine Wall. Their origins are uncertain, but they may have been a loose confederation of Celtic tribes.

– DERIVATIVES **Pictish** adjective & noun
– ORIGIN from late Latin *Picti*, perhaps from *pict-* 'painted, tattooed' (from *pingere* 'to paint'), or perhaps influenced by a local name.

pictograph (also **pictogram**) ▸ noun a pictorial symbol for a word or phrase. Pictographs were used as the earliest known form of writing, examples having been discovered in Egypt and Mesopotamia from before 3000 BC. ▪ a pictorial representation of statistics on a chart, graph, or computer screen.
– DERIVATIVES **pictographic** adjective, **pictography** noun.
– ORIGIN mid 19th cent.: from Latin *pict-* 'painted' (from the verb *pingere*) + -GRAPH.

Pictor /ˈpɪktə/ Astronomy an inconspicuous southern constellation (the Easel or Painter), close to the star Canopus in Puppis.
– ORIGIN Latin.

pictorial ▸ adjective of or expressed in pictures; illustrated: *feelings presented in a pictorial form*.
▸ noun [usu. in names] a newspaper or periodical with pictures as a main feature.
– DERIVATIVES **pictorially** adverb.
– ORIGIN mid 17th cent.: from late Latin *pictorius* (from Latin *pictor* 'painter', from the verb *pingere* 'to paint') + -AL.

picture ▸ noun **1** a painting or drawing: *draw a picture of a tree*. ▪ a photograph: *we were warned not to take pictures*. ▪ a portrait: *she had her picture painted*. ▪ an image on a television screen. ▪ a cinema film: *the movie took five honours including best picture*. ▪ (**the pictures**) the cinema: *I'm going to the pictures with my mates*.
2 an impression of something formed from a description: *a full picture of the disaster had not yet emerged*.
3 archaic a person or thing resembling another closely.
▸ verb [with obj.] represent in a photograph or picture: *he is pictured with party guests*. ▪ describe in a certain way: *biographers have pictured him as a St Francis*. ▪ form a mental image of: *she pictured Benjamin waiting*.
– PHRASES **be in pictures** chiefly N. Amer. act in films or work for the film industry. **be** (or **look**) **a picture** be very pleasing to look at. **the big** (or **bigger** or **larger**) **picture** informal the situation as a whole: *he's so involved in the minutiae that he often overlooks the big picture*. **get the picture** informal understand a situation. **in the picture** fully informed about something. **out of the picture** so as to be no longer involved in a situation: *hostages were better left out of the picture*. **a** (or **the**) **picture of ——** the embodiment of a specified state or emotion: *she looked a picture of health*. **(as) pretty as a picture** very pretty.
– ORIGIN late Middle English: from Latin *pictura*, from *pict-* 'painted' (from the verb *pingere*).

picture book ▸ noun a book containing many illustrations, especially one for children.

picture card ▸ noun an illustrated card used in games or as a teaching aid. ▪ another term for COURT CARD.

picture hat ▸ noun a woman's highly decorated hat with a wide brim, as shown in pictures by 18th-century English painters such as Reynolds and Gainsborough.

picture messaging ▸ noun [mass noun] a system that enables digital photos and animated graphics to be sent and received by mobile phone.

picture palace ▸ noun Brit. dated a cinema.

picture-perfect ▸ adjective N. Amer. completely lacking in defects or flaws; ideal: *a picture-perfect summer day*.

picture plane ▸ noun (in perspective painting or drawing) the imaginary plane corresponding to the surface of a picture, perpendicular to the viewer's line of sight.

picture postcard ▸ noun a postcard with a picture on one side. ▪ [as modifier] prettily picturesque, like the scenes typically shown on picture postcards.

picture rail ▸ noun a horizontal strip of wood on a wall from which pictures can be hung.

picture space ▸ noun [mass noun] the apparent space behind the picture plane of a painting, created by perspective and other techniques.

picturesque ▸ adjective (of a place or building) visually attractive, especially in a quaint or charming way: *ruined abbeys and picturesque villages*. ▪ (of language) unusual and vivid: *the salad has no regional or picturesque name*.
– DERIVATIVES **picturesquely** adverb, **picturesqueness** noun.
– ORIGIN early 18th cent.: from French *pittoresque*, from Italian *pittoresco*, from *pittore* 'painter' (from Latin *pictor*). The change from *-tt-* to *-ct-* was due to association with PICTURE.

picture tube ▸ noun Electronics the cathode ray tube of a television set designed for the reproduction of television pictures.

picture window ▸ noun a large window consisting of one pane of glass, typically facing an attractive view.

picture writing ▸ noun [mass noun] a mode of recording events by pictorial symbols; pictography.

picturize (also **picturise**) ▸ verb [with obj.] adapt (a story or screenplay) into a film.
– DERIVATIVES **picturization** noun.

piculet /ˈpɪkjʊlɪt/ ▸ noun a tiny tropical woodpecker with a short tail, found chiefly in Central and South America. ● *Picumnus* and other genera, family Picidae: numerous species.
– ORIGIN mid 19th cent.: apparently a double diminutive of Latin *picus* 'woodpecker'.

PID ▸ abbreviation pelvic inflammatory disease.

piddle informal ▸ verb [no obj.] urinate.
▸ noun [in sing.] an act of urinating. ▪ [mass noun] urine.
– PHRASAL VERBS **piddle about/around** spend time in trifling activities; potter: *I piddled around the house all day*.
– DERIVATIVES **piddler** noun.
– ORIGIN mid 16th cent.: probably from a blend of PISS and PUDDLE.

piddling (also **piddly**) ▸ adjective informal pathetically trivial; trifling: *piddling little questions*.

piddock /ˈpɪdək/ ▸ noun a bivalve mollusc which bores into soft rock or other firm surfaces. The

valves of the shell have a conspicuous gap between them and rough frontal ridges to aid in boring.
● *Pholas* and other genera, family Pholadidae.
– ORIGIN mid 19th cent.: of unknown origin.

pidgin /ˈpɪdʒɪn/ ▶ **noun** [often as modifier] a grammatically simplified form of a language, typically English, Dutch, or Portuguese, some elements of which are taken from local languages, used for communication between people not sharing a common language.
■ (**Pidgin**) another term for **TOK PISIN**. ■ [as modifier] denoting a simplified form of a language, especially as used by a non-native speaker: *we exchanged greetings, communicating in pidgin Spanish.*
– ORIGIN late 19th cent.: Chinese alteration of English *business*.

pidgin English ▶ **noun** [mass noun] a pidgin in which the chief language is English, used originally between Chinese people and Europeans.

pi-dog ▶ **noun** variant spelling of **PYE-DOG**.

pie[1] ▶ **noun** a baked dish of fruit, or meat and vegetables, typically with a top and base of pastry.
– PHRASES (**as**) —— **as pie** informal very ——: *using the camera was as easy as pie.* (**as**) **nice** (or **sweet**) **as pie** extremely pleasant or polite. **a piece** (or **slice**) **of the pie** a share of an amount of money or business available to be claimed or distributed: *orchestras have seen cultural rivals get a bigger piece of the pie.* **pie in the sky** informal used to describe or refer to something that is pleasant to contemplate but is very unlikely to be realized.
– ORIGIN Middle English: probably the same word as **PIE**[2], the various combinations of ingredients being compared to objects randomly collected by a magpie.

pie[2] ▶ **noun** used in names of birds that resemble the magpie, especially in having black-and-white plumage, e.g. **tree pie**.
– ORIGIN Middle English: from Old French, from Latin *pica* 'magpie' (related to *picus* 'green woodpecker').

pie[3] ▶ **noun** a former monetary unit of India and Pakistan, equal to one twelfth of an anna.
– ORIGIN from Hindi *pā'ī*, from Sanskrit *pada, padī* 'quarter'.

piebald ▶ **adjective** (of a horse) having irregular patches of two colours, typically black and white.
▶ **noun** a piebald horse.
– ORIGIN late 16th cent.: from **PIE**[2] (because of the magpie's black-and-white plumage) + **BALD** (in the obsolete sense 'streaked with white').

piece ▶ **noun 1** a portion of an object or of material, produced by cutting, tearing, or breaking the whole: ***a piece of** cheese* | *the dish lay **in pieces** on the floor.*
■ an item used in constructing something: *take a car **to pieces**.* ■ an item forming part of a set: ***a piece of** luggage.* ■ a financial share: *each employee owns a piece of the company.*
2 a written, musical, or artistic creation: *a haunting piece of music.*
3 an instance or example: *a crucial piece of evidence.*
4 [with modifier] a coin of specified value: *a 10p piece.*
5 a figure or token used to make moves in a board game. ■ Chess a king, queen, bishop, knight, or rook, as opposed to a pawn.
6 informal, chiefly N. Amer. a firearm.
7 informal, offensive a woman.
8 Scottish a sandwich or other item of food taken as a snack.
▶ **verb** [with obj.] **1** (**piece something together**) assemble something from parts or pieces: *the dinosaur was pieced together from 119 bones.* ■ slowly make sense of something from separate pieces of evidence: *Daniel had pieced the story together from the radio.*
2 (**piece something out**) archaic extend something.
3 archaic patch (something).
– PHRASES **a piece of ass** (or **tail**) vulgar slang a woman regarded as sexually attractive. **a piece of cake** see **CAKE**. **a piece** (or **slice**) **of the action** informal a share in an exciting or profitable enterprise. **come** (or **fall**) **to pieces** break into parts or become damaged: *it splintered loudly and fell to pieces under his weight.* **go to pieces** become so upset or nervous that one is unable to function normally. **in one piece** unharmed or undamaged, especially after a dangerous experience. (**all**) **of a piece** (entirely) consistent. **piece by piece** in gradual stages. **piece of water** a small lake or pond. **piece of work** informal a person of a specified kind, especially an unpleasant one: *he's a nasty piece of work.* **say one's piece** give one's opinion or make a prepared statement. **tear** (or **pull**) **someone/thing to pieces** criticize someone or something harshly.
– ORIGIN Middle English: from Old French *piece* (compare with medieval Latin *pecia, petium*), of obscure ultimate origin.

pièce de résistance /ˌpjɛs də reɪˈzɪstɒ̃s/, French /pjɛs də ʀezistɑ̃s/ ▶ **noun** [in sing.] (especially with reference to creative work) the most important or remarkable feature: *the pièce de résistance of the meal was flaming ice cream.*
– ORIGIN French, literally 'piece (i.e. means) of resistance'.

piece-dyed ▶ **adjective** (of fabric) dyed after being woven.

piece goods ▶ **plural noun** fabrics woven in standard lengths for sale.

piecemeal ▶ **adjective & adverb** characterized by unsystematic partial measures taken over a period of time: [as adj.] *the village is slowly being killed off by piecemeal development* | [as adv.] *many organizations have been built up piecemeal.*
– ORIGIN Middle English: from the noun **PIECE** + *-meal* from Old English *mǣlum*, in the sense 'measure, quantity taken at one time'.

piece of eight ▶ **noun** historical a Spanish dollar, equivalent to 8 reals.

piecer ▶ **noun** a person who pieces something together or patches something up. ■ historical a person, often a child, employed in a spinning mill to join the ends of broken threads.

piece rate ▶ **noun** a rate of payment for piecework.

piecework ▶ **noun** [mass noun] work paid for according to the amount produced.
– DERIVATIVES **pieceworker** noun.

pie chart ▶ **noun** a type of graph in which a circle is divided into sectors that each represent a proportion of the whole.
– ORIGIN 1920s: because of the resemblance of the graph to a pie divided into portions.

pie crust ▶ **noun** the baked pastry crust of a pie.
■ [mass noun] N. Amer. shortcrust pastry.

piecrust table ▶ **noun** a table with an indented edge like a piecrust.

pied /pʌɪd/ ▶ **adjective** having two or more different colours: *the pied flycatcher.*
– ORIGIN Middle English (originally in the sense 'black and white like a magpie'): from **PIE**[2] + **-ED**[1].

pied-à-terre /ˌpjeɪdɑːˈtɛː/, French /pjetatɛʀ/ ▶ **noun** (pl. **pieds-à-terre** pronunc. **same**) a small flat, house, or room kept for occasional use.
– ORIGIN early 19th cent.: French, literally 'foot to earth'.

Piedfort /ˈpjeɪfɔːt/ ▶ **noun** a coin that is thicker than a normal issue, made as a collector's item.
– ORIGIN from French *pied* 'foot' + *fort* 'strong'.

Piedmont /ˈpiːdmɒnt/ **1** a region of NW Italy, in the foothills of the Alps; capital, Turin. Dominated by Savoy from 1400, it became a part of the kingdom of Sardinia in 1720. It was the centre of the movement for a united Italy in the 19th century. Italian name **PIEMONTE**.
2 a hilly region of the eastern US, between the Appalachians and the coastal plain.
– DERIVATIVES **Piedmontese** noun & adjective.
– ORIGIN from Italian *piemonte* 'mountain foot'.

piedmont ▶ **noun** a gentle slope leading from the foot of mountains to a region of flat land.
– ORIGIN mid 19th cent.: from Italian *piemonte* 'mountain foot' (see **PIEDMONT**).

pied noir /pjeɪ ˈnwɑː/, French /pje nwaʀ/ ▶ **noun** (pl. **pieds noirs** pronunc. **same**) a person of European origin who lived in Algeria during French rule, especially one who returned to Europe after Algeria was granted independence.
– ORIGIN French, literally 'black foot', so named because of the western-style black leather shoes worn by the first colonists.

pie-dog ▶ **noun** variant spelling of **PYE-DOG**.

Pied Piper the hero of *The Pied Piper of Hamelin*, a poem by Robert Browning (1842), based on an old German legend. The piper, dressed in particoloured costume, rid the town of Hamelin (Hameln) in Brunswick of rats by enticing them away with his music, and when refused the promised payment he lured away the town's children in the same manner.
■ (as noun **a Pied Piper**) a person who entices people to follow them in a particular course of action.

pied wagtail ▶ **noun** a bird of a black-and-white race of the white wagtail, found in the British Isles, Spain, and Morocco. ● *Motacilla alba yarrelli*, family Motacillidae.

pie-eyed ▶ **adjective** informal very drunk.

pie-faced ▶ **adjective** informal having a roundish face and typically a blank or stupid expression.

Piegan ▶ **noun** (pl. **same** or **Piegans**) & **adjective** variant spelling of **PEIGAN**.

pieman ▶ **noun** (pl. **piemen**) archaic a pie seller.

Piemonte /pjeˈmɔnte/ Italian name for **PIEDMONT**.

piemontite /ˈpiːmɒntʌɪt/ ▶ **noun** [mass noun] a brown or black mineral consisting of a silicate of calcium, aluminium, iron, and manganese.
– ORIGIN late 19th cent.: from Italian *Piemonte* (see **PIEDMONT**) + **-ITE**[1].

pie plate (also **pie pan**) ▶ **noun** a shallow metal or glass dish with sloping sides in which pies are baked.

pier ▶ **noun 1** a platform on pillars projecting from the shore into the sea, typically incorporating entertainment arcades and places to eat. ■ a structure projecting from the shore into a river, lake, or the sea, used as a landing stage for boats. ■ a breakwater or mole.
2 Brit. a long, narrow structure projecting from an airport terminal, giving passengers access to an aircraft.
3 a solid support designed to sustain vertical pressure, in particular: ■ the pillar of an arch or supporting a bridge. ■ a wall between windows or other adjacent openings.
– ORIGIN Middle English: from medieval Latin *pera*, of unknown origin.

Pierce, Franklin (1804–69), American Democratic statesman, 14th President of the US 1853–7.

pierce ▶ **verb** [with obj.] **1** (of a sharp pointed object) go into or through (something): *a splinter had pierced the skin.* ■ make (a hole) with a sharp instrument.
■ make a hole in (the ears or other part of the body) so as to wear jewellery in them: (as adj. **pierced**) *a punk with a pierced nose.* ■ make an opening in or bore a tunnel through: *the dividing wall is pierced by arches.*
2 force a way through; penetrate: *they were seeking to pierce the anti-ballistic-missile defences* | *a shrill voice pierced the air.*
– DERIVATIVES **piercer** noun.
– ORIGIN Middle English: from Old French *percer*, based on Latin *pertus-* 'bored through', from the verb *pertundere*, from *per* 'through' + *tundere* 'thrust'.

piercing ▶ **adjective** having or showing shrewdness or keen intelligence: *her piercing analysis* | *a tall blonde with piercing eyes.* ■ (of a sound) extremely high or loud: *she let out a piercing scream.* ■ (of wind or extreme cold) seeming to cut through one. ■ (of a feeling) intense, typically in a distressing way.
▶ **noun** (usu. **piercings**) holes in parts of the body, typically other than the ears, made so as to wear rings, studs, or other jewellery in them.
– DERIVATIVES **piercingly** adverb.

pier glass ▶ **noun** a large mirror, used originally to fill wall space between windows.

pierid /ˈpʌɪərɪd/ ▶ **noun** Entomology a butterfly of a family (Pieridae) which includes the whites, brimstones, and sulphurs.
– ORIGIN late 19th cent.: from modern Latin *Pieridae* (plural), from Latin *pieris* 'Muse'.

pieris /ˈpɪərɪs, ˈpʌɪ-/ ▶ **noun** an evergreen shrub of the heather family, typically having pink or red young leaves and loose clusters of waxy white bell-shaped flowers. It is native to North America and Asia.
● Genus *Pieris*, family Ericaceae.
– ORIGIN modern Latin, from Latin, literally 'Muse', from *Pieria*, the name of a district in northern Thessaly, said to be the home of the Muses.

Piero della Francesca /ˌpjɛːrəʊ ˌdɛlə franˈtʃɛskə/ (1416–92), Italian painter. He used perspective, proportion, and geometrical relationships to create ordered and harmonious pictures in which the figures appear to inhabit real space. He is best known for his frescoes, notably a cycle in Arezzo depicting the story of the True Cross (begun 1452).

pierogi /pɪəˈrəʊgi/ (also **perogi**, **pirogi**, or **pierogies**) ▶ **plural noun** N. Amer. dough dumplings stuffed with a filling such as potato or cheese, typically served with onions or sour cream.
– ORIGIN from Polish *pieróg* or Ukrainian *pyrih*.

Pierre /pɪə/ the state capital of South Dakota, situated on the Missouri River; pop. 13,899 (est. 2008).

Pierrot /ˈpɪərəʊ, ˈpjɛrəʊ/ ▶ **noun** a stock male character in French pantomime, with a sad white-painted face, a loose white costume, and a pointed hat.

– ORIGIN French, diminutive of the male given name *Pierre* 'Peter'.

pier table ▶ noun a low table or bracket in the space between two windows, typically placed under a pier glass.

Piesporter /ˈpiːz,pɔːtə/ ▶ noun [mass noun] a white Moselle wine produced in the Piesport region of Germany.

pietà /pjeɪˈtɑː/ ▶ noun a picture or sculpture of the Virgin Mary holding the dead body of Christ on her lap or in her arms.
– ORIGIN Italian, from Latin *pietas* 'dutifulness'.

pietas /ˈpʌɪətɑːs, piːˈeɪtɑːs/ ▶ noun [mass noun] respect due to an ancestor, country, institution, etc.
– ORIGIN Latin, literally 'dutifulness'.

Pietermaritzburg /,piːtəˈmarɪtsbəːg/ a city in eastern South Africa, the capital of KwaZulu-Natal; pop. 891,600 (est. 2009).

Pietersburg /ˈpiːtəzbəːg/ former name (until 2002) for **POLOKWANE**.

pietism /ˈpʌɪətɪz(ə)m/ ▶ noun [mass noun] pious sentiment, especially of an exaggerated or affected nature. ■ (usu. **Pietism**) a 17th-century movement for the revival of piety in the Lutheran Church.
– DERIVATIVES **pietist** noun, **pietistic** adjective, **pietistical** adjective.
– ORIGIN late 17th cent.: from German *Pietismus*, from modern Latin, based on Latin *pietas* (see **PIETY**).

piet-my-vrou /ˈpɪtmɔɪ,frəʊ/ ▶ noun S. African an African cuckoo which has a russet band on the upper part of the breast. ● *Cuculus solitarius*, family Cuculidae. Alternative name: **red-chested cuckoo**.
– ORIGIN mid 18th cent.: from South African Dutch, imitative of the bird's three-note call.

pietra dura /,pjɛtrə ˈduːrə/ ▶ noun [mass noun] pictorial mosaic work using semi-precious stones, typically for table tops and other furniture.
– ORIGIN early 19th cent.: from Italian (plural *pietre dure*), literally 'hard stone'.

piety /ˈpʌɪəti/ ▶ noun (pl. **pieties**) [mass noun] the quality of being religious or reverent: *acts of piety and charity*. ■ [count noun] a belief which is accepted with unthinking conventional reverence: *the accepted pieties of our time*.
– ORIGIN early 16th cent. (in the sense 'devotion to religious observances'): from Old French *piete*, from Latin *pietas* 'dutifulness', from *pius* (see **PIOUS**).

piezo /pʌɪˈiːzəʊ, ˈpiːzəʊ/ ▶ adjective piezoelectric.

piezoelectricity ▶ noun [mass noun] electric polarization in a substance (especially certain crystals) resulting from the application of mechanical stress.

> Piezoelectric substances are able to convert mechanical signals (such as sound waves) into electrical signals, and vice versa. They are therefore widely used in microphones, gramophone pickups, and earphones, and also to generate a spark for lighting gas.

– DERIVATIVES **piezoelectric** adjective, **piezoelectrically** adverb.
– ORIGIN late 19th cent.: from Greek *piezein* 'press, squeeze' + **ELECTRICITY**.

piezometer /,pʌɪɪˈzɒmɪtə/ ▶ noun an instrument for measuring the pressure of a liquid or gas, or something related to pressure (such as the compressibility of liquid). Piezometers are often placed in boreholes to monitor the pressure or depth of groundwater.
– ORIGIN early 19th cent.: from Greek *piezein* 'press, squeeze' + **-METER**.

piffle ▶ noun [mass noun] informal nonsense.
– ORIGIN mid 19th cent.: diminutive of imitative *piff-*.

piffling ▶ adjective informal trivial; unimportant.

pig ▶ noun **1** an omnivorous domesticated hoofed mammal with sparse bristly hair and a flat snout for rooting in the soil, kept for its meat. ● *Sus domesticus*, family Suidae (the **pig family**), descended from the wild boar and domesticated over 8,000 years ago. The pig family also includes the warthog and babirusa.
■ a wild animal of the pig family; a hog. ■ N. Amer. a young pig; a piglet. ■ [mass noun] the flesh of a pig as food.
2 informal a greedy, dirty, or unpleasant person: *I bet he's scoffed them all, greedy pig*.
3 derogatory a police officer.
4 an oblong mass of iron or lead from a smelting furnace. See also **PIG IRON**.
5 a device which fits snugly inside an oil or gas pipeline and is sent through it to clean or test the inside, or to act as a barrier.
▶ verb (**pigs, pigging, pigged**) [no obj.] **1** informal gorge oneself with food: *lovesick people **pig out on** chocolate*.
2 informal crowd together with other people in disorderly or dirty conditions: *he didn't approve of the proposal **to pig it** in the studio*.
3 (of a sow) give birth to piglets; farrow.
4 operate a pig within an oil or gas pipeline.
– PHRASES **in pig** (of a sow) pregnant. **in a pig's eye** informal, chiefly N. Amer. expressing scornful disbelief at a statement. **make a pig of oneself** informal overeat. **make a pig's ear of** Brit. informal handle ineptly. **on the pig's back** Irish informal living a life of ease and luxury; in a very fortunate situation. **pig in the middle** see **PIGGY IN THE MIDDLE** at **PIGGY**. **a pig in a poke** something that is bought or accepted without first being seen or assessed. **a pig of a ——** Brit. informal used to describe something unpleasant or difficult: *it's **a pig of a** job*. **pigs might** (or **can**) **fly** Brit. used ironically to express disbelief. **sweat like a pig** informal sweat profusely.
– DERIVATIVES **piglike** adjective, **pigling** noun.
– ORIGIN Middle English: probably from the first element of Old English *picbrēd* 'acorn', literally 'pig bread' (i.e. food for pigs).

pigeon¹ ▶ noun **1** a stout seed- or fruit-eating bird with a small head, short legs, and a cooing voice, typically having grey and white plumage. See also **DOVE¹** (sense 1). ● Family Columbidae: numerous genera and species.
■ (also **domestic** or **feral pigeon**) a pigeon descended from the wild rock dove, kept for racing, showing, and carrying messages, and common as a feral bird in towns.
2 informal, chiefly N. Amer. a gullible person, especially someone swindled in gambling or the victim of a confidence trick.
3 military slang an aircraft from one's own side.
– ORIGIN late Middle English: from Old French *pijon*, denoting a young bird, especially a young dove, from an alteration of late Latin *pipio(n-)*, 'young cheeping bird' of imitative origin.

pigeon² ▶ noun **1** archaic spelling of **PIDGIN**.
2 (**one's pigeon**) Brit. informal a person's particular responsibility or business: *Hermia will have to tell them first, it's her pigeon*.

pigeon breast (also **pigeon chest**) ▶ noun a deformed human chest with a projecting breastbone.
– DERIVATIVES **pigeon-breasted** (also **pigeon-chested**) adjective.

pigeon fancier ▶ noun a person who keeps and breeds pigeons.
– DERIVATIVES **pigeon-fancying** noun.

pigeon-hearted ▶ adjective timid; cowardly.

pigeonhole ▶ noun **1** a small recess for a domestic pigeon to nest in.
2 each of a set of small open-fronted compartments in a workplace or other organization where letters or messages may be left for individuals. ■ a compartment built into a desk for keeping documents in.
3 a category, typically an overly restrictive one, to which someone or something is assigned: *people identified me with a homely farmer's wife and I could never escape that pigeonhole*.
▶ verb [with obj.] **1** assign to a particular category, typically an overly restrictive one: *I was **pigeonholed as** a 'youth writer'*.
2 put (a document) in a pigeonhole. ■ put aside for future consideration: *she pigeonholed her worry about him*.

pigeonite ▶ noun [mass noun] a calcium-poor pyroxene mineral occurring chiefly in basalt.
– ORIGIN early 20th cent.: named after *Pigeon Point*, Minnesota, + **-ITE¹**.

pigeon pair ▶ noun dialect a boy and girl as twins, or as the only children in a family.

pigeon pea ▶ noun **1** a dark red tropical pealike seed.
2 the woody Old World plant which yields pigeon peas, with pods and foliage that are used as fodder. ● *Cajanus cajan*, family Leguminosae.

pigeon's milk ▶ noun [mass noun] a curd-like secretion from a pigeon's crop, which it regurgitates and feeds to its young.

pigeon-toed ▶ adjective (of a person or horse) having the toes or feet turned inwards.

pigface ▶ noun Austral./NZ a succulent creeping plant with bright flowers, related to Hottentot fig. ● Genera *Carpobrotus* and *Disphyma* (both formerly *Mesembryanthemum*), family Aizoaceae.
– ORIGIN early 19th cent.: named with reference to the large pink flowers.

pigfish ▶ noun (pl. **same** or **pigfishes**) **1** a deep-bodied scaleless fish with a protuberant snout, which lives in the cooler seas of the southern hemisphere. ● Family Congiopodidae: several genera and species.
2 [usu. with modifier] any of a number of other marine fishes, especially one that grunts: ● a western Atlantic grunt (*Orthopristis chrysoptera*, family Pomadasyidae). ● Austral./NZ a wrasse or groper (genera *Bodianus* and *Achoerodus*, family Labridae). Compare with **HOGFISH**.

pig-footed bandicoot ▶ noun an Australian bandicoot with toes that form a paired foot pad on the forelimbs, and a single foot pad on the hindlimbs. It is believed to be extinct. ● *Chaeropus ecaudatus*, family Peramelidae.

piggery ▶ noun (pl. **piggeries**) **1** a farm where pigs are bred or kept. ■ a pigsty.
2 [mass noun] behaviour regarded as characteristic of pigs in greed or unpleasantness.

piggish ▶ adjective resembling a pig, especially in being unpleasant.
– DERIVATIVES **piggishly** adverb, **piggishness** noun.

Piggott /ˈpɪgət/, Lester (Keith) (b.1935), English jockey. He was champion jockey nine times between 1960 and 1971 and again in 1981 and 1982; he won the Derby a record nine times.

piggy ▶ noun (pl. **piggies**) a child's word for a pig or piglet.
▶ adjective resembling a pig, especially in features or appetite: *three pairs of little piggy eyes*.
– PHRASES **piggy** (also **pig**) **in the middle** chiefly Brit. a game in which two people attempt to throw a ball to each other without a third person in the middle catching it. ■ a person who is placed in an awkward situation between two others.

piggyback ▶ noun a ride on someone's back and shoulders.
▶ adjective on the back and shoulders of another person: *a piggyback ride*. ■ attached to or riding on a larger object: *a telescope with fittings for piggyback cameras*.
▶ adverb on the back and shoulders of another person: *I had to carry him piggyback*.
▶ verb [with obj.] carry by or as if by means of a piggyback. ■ link to or take advantage of (an existing system or body of work): *they have **piggybacked** their own networks **on to** the system*. ■ [no obj.] use existing work or an existing product as a basis or support: *yesterday's experiment **piggybacks on** previous trials*.
– ORIGIN mid 16th cent. (as an adverb): the word's origins are uncertain.

piggy bank ▶ noun a money box, typically one shaped like a pig.

pig-headed ▶ adjective stupidly obstinate.
– DERIVATIVES **pig-headedly** adverb, **pig-headedness** noun.

pightle /ˈpʌɪt(ə)l/ ▶ noun dialect a small field or enclosure.
– ORIGIN Middle English: origin obscure, apparently diminutive.

pig-ignorant ▶ adjective informal extremely stupid or crude.

pig iron ▶ noun [mass noun] crude iron as first obtained from a smelting furnace, in the form of oblong blocks. Compare with **PIG** (sense 4 of the noun).

Pig Island (also **Pig Islands**) Austral./NZ informal a nickname for New Zealand.
– ORIGIN said to be so named because of the pigs left there by Captain Cook.

pig Latin ▶ noun [mass noun] a secret language formed from English by transferring the initial consonant or consonant cluster of each word to the end of the word and adding a vocalic syllable (usually /eɪ/): so *igpay atinlay*.

piglet ▶ noun a young pig.

pigman ▶ noun (pl. **pigmen**) a person who looks after pigs on a farm.

pigment ▶ noun the natural colouring matter of animal or plant tissue. ■ a substance used for colouring or painting, especially a dry powder, which when mixed with oil, water, or another medium constitutes a paint or ink.
▶ verb [with obj.] (usu. as adj. **pigmented**) colour (something) with or as if with pigment: *precast pigmented concrete panels*.
– DERIVATIVES **pigmentary** adjective.
– ORIGIN Middle English, from Latin *pigmentum*, from *pingere* 'to paint'. The verb dates from the early 20th cent.

P

pigmentation ▸ noun [mass noun] the natural colouring of animal or plant tissue. ■ abnormal colouring of a person's skin, typically resulting from disease.

pigmy ▸ noun variant spelling of PYGMY.

pignut ▸ noun another term for EARTHNUT (sense 1).

pigpen ▸ noun N. Amer. a pigsty.

pig-root Austral./NZ informal ▸ verb [no obj.] (of a horse or other animal) kick upwards with the hind legs, keeping the head down and the forelegs firmly planted.
▸ noun the act of pig-rooting.

Pigs, Bay of a bay on the SW coast of Cuba, scene of an unsuccessful attempt in 1961 by US-backed Cuban exiles to invade the country and overthrow the regime of Fidel Castro.

pigskin ▸ noun **1** the hide of a domestic pig. ■ [mass noun] leather made from this.
2 N. Amer. informal a football.

pig-sticking ▸ noun [mass noun] the activity of hunting wild boar with a spear, carried out on horseback.
– DERIVATIVES **pig-sticker** noun.

pigsty ▸ noun (pl. **pigsties**) a pen or enclosure for a pig or pigs. ■ a very dirty or untidy house or room.

pigswill ▸ noun [mass noun] kitchen refuse and scraps fed to pigs.

pigtail ▸ noun **1** a plaited lock of hair worn singly at the back or on each side of the head.
2 a short length of braided wire connecting a stationary part to a moving part in an electrical device.
3 a thin twist of tobacco.
– DERIVATIVES **pigtailed** adjective.

pigweed ▸ noun [mass noun] **1** an amaranth that grows as a weed or is used for fodder. ● Genus *Amaranthus*, family Amaranthaceae: several species, in particular *A. retroflexus* and *A. albus*.
2 North American term for FAT HEN.

pi-jaw ▸ noun [mass noun] informal, dated tedious moralizing talk.

pika /ˈpʌɪkə, ˈpiːkə/ ▸ noun a small mammal related to the rabbits, having rounded ears, short limbs, and a very small tail, found mainly in the mountains and deserts of Asia. Also called MOUSE HARE. ● Family Ochotonidae and genus *Ochotona*: many species, including the **collared pika** (*O. collaris*), of western North America.
– ORIGIN early 19th cent.: from Tungus *piika*.

pike[1] ▸ noun (pl. **same**) a long-bodied predatory freshwater fish with a pointed snout and large teeth, of both Eurasia and North America. ● Family Esocidae and genus *Esox*: five species, including the widespread **northern pike** (*E. lucius*).
■ used in names of predatory fish with large teeth other than the true pike, e.g. **garpike**.
– ORIGIN Middle English: from PIKE[2] (because of the fish's pointed jaw).

P

pike[2] ▸ noun **1** historical an infantry weapon with a pointed steel or iron head on a long wooden shaft.
2 N. English (in names of hills in the Lake District) a hill with a peaked top: *Scafell Pike*.
▸ verb [with obj.] historical kill or thrust (someone) through with a pike.
– ORIGIN early 16th cent.: from French *pique*, back-formation from *piquer* 'pierce', from *pic* 'pick, pike'; compare with Old English *pīc* 'point, prick' (of unknown origin). Sense 2 of the noun is apparently of Scandinavian origin; compare with West Norwegian dialect *pīk* 'pointed mountain'.

pike[3] ▸ noun N. Amer. short for TURNPIKE.
– PHRASES **come down the pike** informal appear on the scene; come to notice.

pike[4] ▸ noun [often as modifier] a jackknife position in diving or gymnastics.
– ORIGIN 1920s: of unknown origin.

pike[5] ▸ verb [no obj.] Austral./NZ informal **1** (**pike out**) withdraw from or go back on (a plan or agreement).
2 (**pike on**) let (someone) down.
– ORIGIN late Middle English (as *pike oneself* 'take up a pilgrim's staff'): compare with Danish *pigge af* 'hasten off'. The current senses date from the mid 20th cent.

pikelet ▸ noun a thin kind of crumpet.
– ORIGIN late 18th cent.: from Welsh (*bara*) *pyglyd* 'pitchy (bread)'.

pikeman ▸ noun (pl. **pikemen**) historical **1** the keeper of a turnpike.
2 a soldier armed with a pike.

pikeperch ▸ noun (pl. **same**) a predatory pike-like freshwater fish of the perch family, especially the zander. ● Genus *Stizostedion*, family Percidae: five species, including the sauger and the walleye.

piker ▸ noun informal **1** N. Amer. a gambler who makes only small bets. ■ a mean or cautious person.
2 Austral./NZ a person who withdraws from a plan, commitment, etc.
– ORIGIN late 19th cent.: from PIKE[5].

pikestaff ▸ noun historical the wooden shaft of a pike.
– PHRASES **(as) plain as a pikestaff 1** very obvious. **2** ordinary or unattractive in appearance. [alteration of *as plain as a packstaff*, the staff being that of a pedlar, on which he rested his pack of wares.]
– ORIGIN late 16th cent.: from PIKE[2] + STAFF[1].

pikey ▸ noun Brit. informal, offensive a Gypsy.
– ORIGIN mid 19th cent.: from an old sense of *pike*, 'a road on which a toll is collected'.

piki /ˈpiːki/ ▸ noun [mass noun] maize-meal bread in the form of very thin sheets, made by the Hopi Indians of the south-western US.
– ORIGIN Hopi.

pikkie /ˈpəki, ˈpɪki/ ▸ noun (pl. **pikkies**) S. African informal a child.
– ORIGIN Afrikaans, literally 'bantam', from Dutch dialect *piek* 'chicken', later also 'small child'.

Pik Pobedy /ˌpiːk pəˈbjɛdi/ a mountain in eastern Kyrgyzstan, situated close to the border with China. Rising to a height of 7,439 m (24,406 ft), it is the highest peak in the Tien Shan range.
– ORIGIN from Russian, literally 'Victory Peak'.

pilaf /pɪˈlaf/ (also **pilaff, pilau, pulao**) ▸ noun a Middle Eastern or Indian dish of rice or wheat, vegetables, and spices, typically having added meat or fish.
– ORIGIN from Turkish *pilâv*.

pilaster /pɪˈlastə/ ▸ noun a rectangular column, especially one projecting from a wall.
– DERIVATIVES **pilastered** adjective.
– ORIGIN late 16th cent.: from French *pilastre*, from Italian *pilastro* or medieval Latin *pilastrum*, from Latin *pila* 'pillar'.

Pilate /ˈpʌɪlət/, Pontius (died *c.*36 AD), Roman procurator of Judaea *c.*26–*c.*36. He is remembered for presiding at the trial of Jesus Christ and authorizing his crucifixion.

Pilates /pɪˈlɑːtiːz/ ▸ noun a system of exercises using special apparatus, designed to improve physical strength, flexibility, and posture, and enhance mental awareness: *this quest for better training has led many dancers to Pilates* | [as modifier] *the Pilates method*.
– ORIGIN 1960s: named after the German physical fitness specialist Joseph *Pilates* (1880–1967), who devised the system.

pilau rice /pɪˈlaʊ, ˈpiːlaʊ/ ▸ noun [mass noun] (in Indian cookery) rice seasoned with spices and cooked with vegetables or meat.

pilchard ▸ noun a small, edible, commercially valuable marine fish of the herring family. ● *Sardinops* and other genera, family Clupeidae: several species, including the European *Sardina pilchardus*. See also SARDINE[1].
– ORIGIN mid 16th cent.: of unknown origin.

pile[1] ▸ noun **1** a heap of things laid or lying one on top of another: *he placed the books in a neat pile* | *tottering piles of dirty dishes*. ■ informal a large amount of something: *he's making piles of money*. ■ archaic a funeral pyre.
2 a large imposing building or group of buildings: *a Victorian Gothic pile*.
3 a series of plates of dissimilar metals laid one on another alternately to produce an electric current.
4 (also **atomic pile**) dated a nuclear reactor.
▸ verb **1** [with obj. and adverbial] place (things) one on top of the other: *she piled all the groceries on the counter*. ■ (**be piled with**) be stacked or loaded with: *his in tray was piled high with papers*. ■ (**pile up/pile something up**) increase or cause to increase in quantity: [no obj.] *the work is piling up*. ■ (**pile something on**) informal intensify or exaggerate something for effect: *you can pile on the guilt but my heart has turned to stone*.
2 [no obj.] (**pile into/out of**) (of a group of people) get into or out of (a vehicle) in a disorganized manner: *ten of us piled into the minibus*. ■ (**pile into**) (of a vehicle) crash into: *60 cars piled into each other on the M62*.
– PHRASES **make a** (or **one's**) **pile** informal make a lot of money. **pile arms** place a number of rifles (usually four) with their butts on the ground and the muzzles together. **pile it on** informal exaggerate the seriousness of a situation for effect.
– ORIGIN late Middle English: from Old French, from Latin *pila* 'pillar, pier'.

pile[2] ▸ noun **1** a heavy stake or post driven vertically into the bed of a river, soft ground, etc., to support the foundations of a superstructure.
2 Heraldry a triangular charge or ordinary formed by two lines meeting at an acute angle, usually pointing down from the top of the shield.
▸ verb [with obj.] strengthen or support (a structure) with piles.
– DERIVATIVES **piling** noun.
– ORIGIN Old English *pīl* 'dart, arrow', also 'pointed stake', of Germanic origin; related to Dutch *pijl* and German *Pfeil*, from Latin *pilum* '(heavy) javelin'.

pile[3] ▸ noun [mass noun] the soft projecting surface of a carpet or a fabric such as velvet or flannel, consisting of many small threads.
– ORIGIN Middle English (in the sense 'downy feather'): from Latin *pilus* 'hair'. The current sense dates from the mid 16th cent.

pilea /ˈpʌɪlɪə/ ▸ noun a plant of the nettle family which lacks stinging hairs, native to warm regions and widely grown as an indoor plant. ● Genus *Pilea*, family Urticaceae.
– ORIGIN modern Latin, from Latin *pileus* 'felt cap'.

pileated woodpecker /ˈpʌɪlɪeɪtɪd/ ▸ noun a large North American woodpecker with mainly black plumage and a red cap and crest. ● *Dryocopus pileatus*, family Picidae.
– ORIGIN late 18th cent.: *pileated* from Latin *pileatus* 'capped', from *pileus* 'felt cap'.

piledriver ▸ noun a machine for driving piles into the ground. ■ Brit. informal a forceful act, blow, or shot: *Varney's last-minute winning piledriver*.
– DERIVATIVES **piledriving** noun & adjective.

pile dwelling ▸ noun (in prehistoric times) a dwelling built on piles over a lake.

piles ▸ plural noun haemorrhoids.
– ORIGIN late Middle English: probably from Latin *pila* 'ball' (because of the globular form of external haemorrhoids).

pile-up ▸ noun **1** a crash involving several vehicles.
2 an accumulation of a specified thing: *a massive pile-up of data*.

pileus /ˈpʌɪlɪəs/ ▸ noun (pl. **pilei** /-lɪʌɪ/) Botany the cap of a mushroom or toadstool.
– ORIGIN mid 18th cent.: from Latin, literally 'felt cap'.

pilewort ▸ noun the lesser celandine.
– ORIGIN late Middle English: from PILES (because of its reputed efficacy against piles) + WORT.

pilfer ▸ verb [with obj.] steal (things of little value).
– DERIVATIVES **pilferage** noun, **pilferer** noun.
– ORIGIN late Middle English (as a noun in the sense 'action of pilfering, something pilfered'): from Old French *pelfrer* 'to pillage', of unknown origin. Compare with PELF.

pilgrim ▸ noun **1** a person who journeys to a sacred place for religious reasons. ■ chiefly literary a person regarded as journeying through life.
2 (usu. **Pilgrim**) a member of the Pilgrim Fathers.
▸ verb (**pilgrims, pilgriming, pilgrimed**) [no obj., with adverbial of direction] archaic travel or wander like a pilgrim.
– ORIGIN Middle English: from Provençal *pelegrin*, from Latin *peregrinus* 'foreign' (see PEREGRINE).

pilgrimage ▸ noun a pilgrim's journey. ■ a journey to a place of particular interest or significance: *his passion was opera and he made annual pilgrimages to Bayreuth*. ■ chiefly literary life viewed as a journey.
▸ verb [no obj., with adverbial of direction] go on a pilgrimage.
– ORIGIN Middle English: from Provençal *pelegrinage*, from *pelegrin* (see PILGRIM).

Pilgrim Fathers the pioneers of British colonization of North America. A group of 102 people led by English Puritans fleeing religious persecution sailed in the *Mayflower* and founded the colony of Plymouth, Massachusetts, in 1620.

Pilipino /ˌpɪlɪˈpiːnəʊ/ ▸ noun & adjective variant of FILIPINO.

pill[1] ▸ noun **1** a small round mass of solid medicine for swallowing whole. ■ (**the pill**) an oral contraceptive in pill form: *is she on the pill?*
2 informal, dated a tedious or unpleasant person.
3 informal, dated (in some sports) a humorous term for a ball.
– PHRASES **a bitter pill (to swallow)** an unpleasant or painful necessity (to accept). **sugar** (or **sweeten**) **the pill** make an unpleasant or painful necessity more palatable.
– ORIGIN late Middle English: ultimately from Latin *pilula* 'little ball', diminutive of *pila*; compare with Middle Dutch, Middle Low German *pille*.

pill² ▶ verb [no obj.] (of knitted fabric) form small balls of fluff on its surface.
– ORIGIN 1960s: from the noun *pill* denoting a small ball of fluff, extended sense of PILL¹.

pillage ▶ verb [with obj.] rob a (place) using violence, especially in wartime: *the abbey was plundered and pillaged.* ■ steal (something) using violence, especially in wartime: *artworks pillaged from churches and museums.*
▶ noun [mass noun] the action of pillaging a place or property, especially in war.
– DERIVATIVES **pillager** noun.
– ORIGIN late Middle English (as a noun): from Old French, from *piller* 'to plunder'.

pillar ▶ noun a tall vertical structure of stone, wood, or metal, used as a support for a building, or as an ornament or monument. ■ something shaped like a pillar: *a pillar of rock.* ■ a solid mass of coal left to support the roof of a mine. ■ a person or thing regarded as reliably providing essential support for something: *he was a pillar of his local community.*
– PHRASES **from pillar to post** from one place to another in an unceremonious or fruitless manner: *they were pushed from pillar to post from the moment they left their homes.*
– DERIVATIVES **pillared** adjective.
– ORIGIN Middle English: from Anglo-Norman French *piler*, based on Latin *pila* 'pillar'.

pillar box ▶ noun (in the UK) a large red cylindrical public postbox.

pillar-box red ▶ noun [mass noun] Brit. a bright red colour, like that in which pillar boxes are painted.

pillar rose ▶ noun a climbing rose suitable for training on an upright.

Pillars of Hercules an ancient name for two promontories on either side of the Strait of Gibraltar (the Rock of Gibraltar and Mount Acho in Ceuta), held by legend to have been parted by the arm of Hercules.

pill beetle ▶ noun a small convex beetle which is able to feign death by retracting its legs and contracting into a ball. ● Family Byrrhidae: several genera.

pillbox ▶ noun **1** a small shallow cylindrical box for holding pills.
2 a woman's hat with straight sides, a flat top, and no brim.
3 a small enclosed, partly underground, concrete fort used as an outpost.

pill bug ▶ noun another term for PILL WOODLOUSE.

pillion ▶ noun a seat for a passenger behind a motorcyclist. ■ historical a woman's light saddle. ■ historical a cushion attached to the back of a saddle, on which a second person may ride.
– PHRASES **ride pillion** travel seated behind a motorcyclist.
– ORIGIN late 15th cent. (denoting a light saddle): from Scottish Gaelic *pillean*, Irish *pillín* 'small cushion', diminutive of *pell*, from Latin *pellis* 'skin'.

pilliwinks /ˈpɪlɪwɪŋks/ ▶ plural noun historical an instrument of torture used for squeezing the fingers.
– ORIGIN late Middle English *pyrwykes*, *pyrewinkes*, of unknown origin.

pillock ▶ noun Brit. informal a stupid person.
– ORIGIN mid 16th cent.: variant of archaic *pillicock* 'penis', the early sense of *pillock* in northern English.

pillory ▶ noun (pl. **pillories**) a wooden framework with holes for the head and hands, in which offenders were formerly imprisoned and exposed to public abuse.
▶ verb (**pillories**, **pillorying**, **pilloried**) [with obj.]
1 historical put (someone) in a pillory.
2 attack or ridicule publicly: *he found himself pilloried by members of his own party.*
– ORIGIN Middle English: from Old French *pilori*, probably from Provençal *espilori* (associated by some with a Catalan word meaning 'peephole', of uncertain origin).

pillow ▶ noun a rectangular cloth bag stuffed with feathers or other soft materials, used to support the head when lying or sleeping. ■ short for LACE PILLOW.
▶ verb [with obj.] rest (one's head) as if on a pillow: *his head was pillowed on his arm.* ■ literary serve as a pillow for.
– DERIVATIVES **pillowy** adjective.
– ORIGIN Old English *pyle*, *pylu*, of West Germanic origin; related to Dutch *peluw* and German *Pfühl*, based on Latin *pulvinus* 'cushion'.

pillow book ▶ noun (in Japanese classical literature) a type of private journal or diary.

pillowcase ▶ noun a removable cloth cover for a pillow.

pillow fight ▶ noun a mock fight using pillows.

pillow lace ▶ noun [mass noun] lace made by hand using a lace pillow.

pillow lava ▶ noun [mass noun] lava which has solidified as rounded masses, characteristic of eruption under water.

pillow sham ▶ noun N. Amer. a decorative pillowcase for covering a pillow when it is not in use.

pillowslip ▶ noun a pillowcase.

pillow talk ▶ noun [mass noun] intimate conversation in bed.

pill popper ▶ noun informal a person who takes pills freely.
– DERIVATIVES **pill-popping** noun.

pillule ▶ noun variant spelling of PILULE.

pill woodlouse ▶ noun a woodlouse with a thick cuticle, which is able to roll up into a ball when threatened. Also called PILL BUG. ● Genus *Armadillidium*, order Isopoda.

pillwort ▶ noun a creeping grass-like aquatic fern which has slender stem-like shoots with small globular spore-producing bodies at their bases, growing on the muddy margins of ponds and lakes in western Europe. ● *Pilularia globulifera*, family Marsileaceae.

pilocarpine /ˌpʌɪlə(ʊ)ˈkɑːpiːn/ ▶ noun [mass noun] Chemistry a volatile alkaloid obtained from jaborandi leaves, used to contract the pupils and to relieve pressure in the eye in glaucoma patients.
– ORIGIN late 19th cent.: from modern Latin *Pilocarpus* (genus name of the jaborandi) + -INE⁴.

pilose /ˈpʌɪləʊz/ (also **pilous**) ▶ adjective Botany & Zoology covered with long soft hairs.
– DERIVATIVES **pilosity** noun.
– ORIGIN mid 18th cent.: from Latin *pilosus*, from *pilus* 'hair'.

pilot ▶ noun **1** a person who operates the flying controls of an aircraft. ■ a person with expert local knowledge qualified to take charge of a ship entering or leaving a harbour. ■ a navigational handbook for use at sea. ■ informal a jockey. ■ archaic a guide or leader.
2 a television or radio programme made to test audience reaction with a view to the production of a series. ■ [as modifier] done as an experiment or test before being introduced more widely: *a pilot scheme for training workers.* ■ [often as modifier] Telecommunications an unmodulated reference signal transmitted with another signal for the purposes of control or synchronization.
3 another term for COWCATCHER.
▶ verb (**pilots**, **piloting**, **piloted**) [with obj.] **1** be the pilot of (an aircraft or ship): *he piloted the helicopter from Paris to Deauville.* ■ [with obj. and adverbial of direction] guide or steer: *Melissa piloted her through the booking hall.*
2 test (a scheme, project, etc.) before introducing it more widely: *one-day workshops for part-time staff were piloted in June.*
– DERIVATIVES **pilotage** noun, **pilotless** adjective.
– ORIGIN early 16th cent. (denoting a person who steers a ship): from French *pilote*, from medieval Latin *pilotus*, an alteration of *pedota*, based on Greek *pēdon* 'oar', (plural) 'rudder'.

pilot balloon ▶ noun a small meteorological balloon used to track air currents.

pilot bird ▶ noun a brown ground-dwelling Australian songbird, noted for its habit of accompanying superb lyrebirds to feed on disturbed insects. ● *Pycnoptilus floccosus*, family Acanthizidae.

pilot biscuit ▶ noun North American term for SHIP'S BISCUIT.

pilot chute ▶ noun a small parachute used to bring the main one into operation.

pilot cloth ▶ noun [mass noun] thick blue woollen cloth, used to make seamen's coats.

pilotfish ▶ noun (pl. **same** or **pilotfishes**) a fish of warm seas that is often seen swimming close to large fish such as sharks and sometimes turtles and boats. ● *Naucrates ductor*, family Carangidae.

pilot hole ▶ noun a small hole drilled ahead of a full-sized hole as a guide.

pilot house ▶ noun another term for WHEELHOUSE (sense 1).

pilot jacket ▶ noun another term for PEA JACKET.

pilot light ▶ noun **1** a small gas burner kept alight permanently to light a larger burner when needed, especially on a gas cooker or boiler.
2 an electric indicator light or control light.

pilot officer ▶ noun the lowest rank of officer in the RAF, above warrant officer and below flying officer.

pilot whale ▶ noun a toothed whale that has black skin with a grey anchor-shaped marking on the chin, a low dorsal fin, and a square bulbous head. Also called BLACKFISH. ● Genus *Globicephala*, family Delphinidae: the short-finned *G. macrorhyncus* of subtropical waters, and the long-finned *G. melas* of temperate waters.

pilous /ˈpʌɪləs/ ▶ adjective another term for PILOSE.

Pils /pɪlz, -s/ ▶ noun [mass noun] a type of lager beer similar to Pilsner.
– ORIGIN 1960s: abbreviation of PILSNER.

Pilsen /ˈpɪls(ə)n/ an industrial city in the western part of the Czech Republic; pop. 164,230 (2007). Czech name PLZEŇ.

Pilsner /ˈpɪlznə, ˈpɪls-/ (also **Pilsener**) ▶ noun [mass noun] a lager beer with a strong hop flavour, originally brewed at Pilsen (Plzeň) in the Czech Republic.

Piltdown man /ˈpɪltdaʊn/ ▶ noun a fraudulent fossil composed of a human cranium and an ape jaw, allegedly discovered near Lewes in East Sussex and presented in 1912 as a genuine hominid of the early Pleistocene, but shown to be a hoax in 1953.
– ORIGIN *Piltdown*, the name of a village in Sussex.

pilule /ˈpɪljuːl/ (also **pillule**) ▶ noun a small pill.
– ORIGIN late Middle English: from French, from Latin *pilula* 'small ball', diminutive of *pila*.

PIM ▶ abbreviation personal information manager.

Pima /ˈpiːmə/ ▶ noun (pl. **same** or **Pimas**) **1** a member of an American Indian people living chiefly along the Gila and Salt Rivers in Arizona and in northern Mexico.
2 [mass noun] the Uto-Aztecan language of the Pima and the Papago.
▶ adjective relating to the Pima or their language.
– ORIGIN Spanish, shortening of *Pimahito*, from Pima *pimahaitu* 'nothing'.

pimento /pɪˈmɛntəʊ/ ▶ noun (pl. **pimentos**) **1** variant spelling of PIMIENTO.
2 chiefly W. Indian another term for ALLSPICE (sense 2).
– ORIGIN late 17th cent.: from Spanish *pimiento* (see PIMIENTO).

pi-meson ▶ noun another term for PION.

pimiento /ˌpɪmɪˈɛntəʊ, pɪmˈjɛn-/ (also **pimento**) ▶ noun (pl. **pimientos**) a red sweet pepper.
– ORIGIN mid 17th cent.: from Spanish, from medieval Latin *pigmentum* 'spice', from Latin, 'pigment'.

Pimm's ▶ noun trademark a gin-based alcoholic drink, served typically with lemonade or soda water and fresh mint.
– ORIGIN early 20th cent.: from the name of the proprietor of the restaurant where the drink was created.

P

pimp ▶ noun **1** a man who controls prostitutes and arranges clients for them, taking a percentage of their earnings in return.
2 Austral. informal a telltale or informer.
▶ verb **1** [no obj.] (often as noun **pimping**) act as a pimp. ■ [with obj.] provide (someone) as a prostitute. ■ [with obj.] informal sell or promote (something) in an extravagant or persistent way: *he pimped their debut album to all the staff writers at NME.*
2 [with obj.] informal make (something) more showy or impressive: *he pimped up the car with spoilers and twin-spoke 18-inch alloys.*
3 [no obj.] (**pimp on**) Austral. informal inform on.
– ORIGIN late 16th cent.: of unknown origin.

> **WORD TRENDS** How do completely negative words gain a positive meaning? **Pimp** is a telling example of this process in action. Even the modern extended sense of 'sell or promote in an extravagant or persistent way' carries a strong dose of moral disapproval: *they need to release quality music instead of pimping boy bands.* However, the popularity of hip-hop culture has made the **pimp** a figure of social aspiration for some people, with the word increasingly associated with a glamorous world of champagne, fast cars, and flashy jewellery. This image has spawned a positive sense of the verb, inspired in part by the MTV show *Pimp my Ride*, in which worn-out cars were transformed and customized: *we've got to get that minivan pimped out | I could have hired PR people to pimp up my material.*

pimpernel /ˈpɪmpənɛl/ ▶ noun a small European plant of the primrose family, with creeping stems

and flat five-petalled flowers. ● Genera *Anagallis* and *Lysimachia*, family Primulaceae: several species, in particular the **scarlet pimpernel**.
– ORIGIN late Middle English (denoting the great burnet and the salad burnet): from Old French *pimpernelle*, based on Latin *piper* 'pepper' (because of the resemblance of the burnet's fruit to a peppercorn).

pimping ▶ **adjective** archaic small or insignificant.
– ORIGIN late 17th cent.: of unknown origin.

pimple ▶ **noun** a small hard inflamed spot on the skin.
– DERIVATIVES **pimpled adjective, pimply adjective (pimplier, pimpliest).**
– ORIGIN Middle English: related to Old English *piplian* 'break out in pustules'.

pimpmobile ▶ **noun** US informal a large ostentatious car, of a style associated with pimps.

PIN (also **PIN number**) ▶ **abbreviation** personal identification number.

pin ▶ **noun 1** a thin piece of metal with a sharp point at one end and a round head at the other, used for fastening pieces of cloth, paper, etc. ■ a small brooch or badge. ■ Medicine a steel rod used to join the ends of fractured bones while they heal. ■ a metal peg that holds down the activating lever of a hand grenade, preventing its explosion. ■ a hairpin. ■ Music a peg round which one string of a musical instrument is fastened.
2 a metal projection from a plug or an integrated circuit which makes an electrical connection with a socket or another part of a circuit.
3 Golf a stick with a flag placed in a hole to mark its position. ■ a skittle in bowling.
4 (**pins**) informal a person's legs: *she was very nimble on her pins.*
5 Chess an attack on a piece or pawn which is thereby pinned.
6 Brit. historical a half-firkin cask for beer.
▶ **verb** (**pins, pinning, pinned**) [with obj. and adverbial]
1 attach or fasten with a pin or pins: *he pinned the badge on to his lapel | her hair was pinned back.*
2 hold (someone) firmly in a specified position so they are unable to move: *she was standing **pinned against** the door | Richards **pinned** him **down** until the police arrived.*
3 [with obj.] Chess hinder or prevent (a piece or pawn) from moving because of the danger to a more valuable piece standing behind it along the line of an attack.
– PHRASES **(as) clean** (or **neat**) **as a new pin** extremely clean or neat. **for two pins I'd** (or **he'd, she'd**, etc.) —— Brit. used to convey strong temptation to do something, typically from annoyance or irritation: *for two pins I'd have tipped that bowl and all its contents over her.* **be able to hear a pin drop** used to describe absolute silence or stillness. **pin one's colours to the mast** see MAST[1]. **pin one's ears back** listen carefully. **pin one's hopes** (or **faith**) **on** rely heavily on: *ministers were pinning their hopes on a big-spending Christmas.*
– PHRASAL VERBS **pin someone down** force someone to be specific or make a commitment: *he's very hard to pin down.* **pin something down** define or identify something precisely: *the government's ideology is bafflingly difficult to pin down.* **pin something on** attribute the blame or responsibility for something to (someone): *they pinned the blame for the loss of jobs on the trade unions.*
– ORIGIN late Old English *pinn*, of West Germanic origin; related to Dutch *pin* 'pin, peg', from Latin *pinna* 'point, tip, edge'.

pina colada /ˌpiːnə kəˈlɑːdə/ ▶ **noun** a cocktail made with rum, pineapple juice, and coconut.
– ORIGIN from Spanish *piña colada*, literally 'strained pineapple'.

pinafore ▶ **noun** (also Brit. **pinafore dress**) a collarless sleeveless dress worn over a blouse or jumper. ■ a woman's loose sleeveless garment, typically full length and worn over clothes to keep them clean. ■ a sleeveless apron-like garment worn over a young girl's dress, typically having ties or buttons at the back.
– ORIGIN late 18th cent.: from PIN + AFORE (because the term originally denoted an apron with a bib pinned on the front of a dress).

Pinang variant spelling of PENANG.

pinaster /pʌɪˈnastə/ ▶ **noun** another term for MARITIME PINE.

piñata /piːnˈjɑːtə/ ▶ **noun** chiefly N. Amer. a decorated figure of an animal containing toys and sweets that is suspended from a height and broken open by blindfolded children as part of a celebration.
– ORIGIN mid 19th cent.: Spanish, literally 'pot'.

Pinatubo, Mount /ˌpɪnəˈtuːbəʊ/ a volcano on the island of Luzon, in the Philippines. It erupted in 1991, killing more than 300 people and destroying the homes of more than 200,000.

pinball ▶ **noun** [mass noun] a game in which small metal balls are shot across a sloping board and score points by striking various targets.

pinboard ▶ **noun** a board covered with cork and fixed to a wall so that messages and pictures can be pinned on to it for display.

pince-nez /pãsˈneɪ/ ▶ **noun** [treated as sing. or pl.] a pair of eyeglasses with a nose clip instead of earpieces.
– ORIGIN late 19th cent.: from French, literally '(that) pinches (the) nose'.

pincer ▶ **noun 1** (**pincers** or **a pair of pincers**) a tool made of two pieces of metal with blunt concave jaws that are arranged like the blades of scissors, used for gripping and pulling things.
2 a front claw of a lobster, crab, or similar crustacean.
– ORIGIN Middle English: from Anglo-Norman French, from Old French *pincier* 'to pinch'.

pincer movement ▶ **noun** a movement by two separate bodies of troops converging on the enemy.

pincette /pɪnˈsɛt, pãˈsɛt/ ▶ **noun** a small pair of pincers; tweezers.
– ORIGIN mid 16th cent.: from French, diminutive of *pince* 'pair of pincers'.

pinch ▶ **verb** [with obj.] **1** grip (something, typically a person's flesh) tightly and sharply between finger and thumb: *she pinched his cheek.* ■ (of a shoe) hurt (a foot) by being too tight. ■ compress (one's lips), especially from worry or tension.
2 [no obj.] live in a frugal way: *if I **scraped and pinched** a bit, I might manage.*
3 informal steal or take without permission: *he pinched a handful of sweets.* ■ Brit. arrest (someone): *I was pinched for dangerous driving last month.*
4 remove (buds or leaves) from a plant to encourage bushy growth.
5 Sailing sail (a boat) so close to the wind that the sails begin to lose power.
▶ **noun 1** an act of pinching someone: *he gave her a gentle pinch.* ■ an amount of an ingredient that can be held between fingers and thumb: *add **a pinch of** salt.*
2 Baseball a critical point in the game.
– PHRASES **at** (or N. Amer. **in**) **a pinch** if absolutely necessary. **feel the pinch** experience hardship, especially financial. **have to pinch oneself** used to convey that a good situation is so surprising that the person involved has to make sure they are not imagining it: *sometimes I have to pinch myself to realize it isn't all a dream.*
– ORIGIN Middle English (as a verb): from an Old Northern French variant of Old French *pincier* 'to pinch'.

pinchbeck ▶ **noun** [mass noun] an alloy of copper and zinc resembling gold, used in watchmaking and cheap jewellery.
▶ **adjective** appearing valuable, but actually cheap or tawdry.
– ORIGIN mid 18th cent.: named after Christopher *Pinchbeck* (died 1732), English watchmaker.

pinched ▶ **adjective 1** tense and pale from cold, worry, or hunger: *her pinched, sallow face.*
2 suffering from financial hardship.

pinch effect ▶ **noun** Physics the constriction of a plasma through which a large electric current is flowing, caused by the attractive force of the current's own magnetic field.

pinch-hit ▶ **verb** [no obj.] Baseball bat instead of another player, typically at a critical point in the game. ■ N. Amer. informal act as a substitute for someone, especially in an emergency.
– DERIVATIVES **pinch-hitter noun.**

pinchpenny ▶ **noun** (pl. **pinchpennies**) [usu. as modifier] a miserly person.

pinch point ▶ **noun** a place or point where congestion occurs or is likely to occur, especially on a road: *the transport secretary has set out plans to ease traffic jams at ninety-two pinch points.*

pinch-run ▶ **verb** [no obj.] Baseball substitute for another as a base runner, typically at a critical point in the game.
– DERIVATIVES **pinch-runner noun.**

pin curl ▶ **noun** a curl which has been held by a hairpin while setting.

pincushion ▶ **noun 1** a small pad for holding pins.
2 (also **pincushion distortion**) [mass noun] a form of optical distortion in which straight lines along the edge of a screen or a lens bulge towards the centre.
3 (also **pincushion protea**) S. African an African shrub or tree related to the proteas, with rounded flower heads that resemble pincushions. ● Genus *Leucospermum*, family Proteaceae.

Pindar /ˈpɪndə/ (*c.*518–*c.*438 BC), Greek lyric poet. He is famous for his odes (the *Epinikia*), which celebrate victories in athletic contests at Olympia and elsewhere and relate them to religious and moral themes.
– DERIVATIVES **Pindaric** /pɪnˈdarɪk/ **adjective.**

Pindus Mountains /ˈpɪndəs/ a range of mountains in west central Greece, stretching from the border with Albania southwards to the Gulf of Corinth. The highest peak is Mount Smolikas, which rises to 2,637 m (8,136 ft). Greek name **Píndhos** /ˈpinðɔs/.

pine[1] ▶ **noun 1** (also **pine tree**) an evergreen coniferous tree which has clusters of long needle-shaped leaves. Many kinds are grown for the soft timber, which is widely used for furniture and pulp, or for tar and turpentine. Compare with FIR. ● Genus *Pinus*, family Pinaceae: many species, including the **Scots pine** and **stone pine**.
■ used in names of coniferous trees of families other than that of the pine, e.g. **Chile pine**. ■ used in names of unrelated plants that resemble the pines in some way, e.g. **ground pine**, **screw pine**. ■ [as modifier] having the scent of pine needles: *pine potpourri.*
2 informal, chiefly W. Indian a pineapple.
– DERIVATIVES **pinery noun.**
– ORIGIN Old English, from Latin *pinus*, reinforced in Middle English by Old French *pin*.

pine[2] ▶ **verb** [no obj.] suffer a mental and physical decline, especially because of a broken heart: *she thinks I am **pining away** from love.* ■ (**pine for**) miss or long for: *she's still **pining for** him.*
– ORIGIN Old English *pīnian* '(cause to) suffer', of Germanic origin; related to Dutch *pijnen*, German *peinen* 'experience pain', also to obsolete *pine* 'punishment'; ultimately based on Latin *poena* 'punishment'.

pineal /ˈpɪnɪəl, ˈpʌɪ-/ (also **pineal gland, pineal body**) ▶ **noun** a pea-sized conical mass of tissue behind the third ventricle of the brain, secreting a hormone-like substance in some mammals.
– ORIGIN late 17th cent.: from French *pinéal*, from Latin *pinea* 'pine cone'. The anatomical term refers to the shape of the gland.

pineal eye ▶ **noun** Zoology (in some reptiles and lower vertebrates) an eye-like structure on the top of the head, covered by almost transparent skin and derived from or linked to the pineal.

pineapple ▶ **noun 1** a large juicy tropical fruit consisting of aromatic edible yellow flesh surrounded by a tough segmented skin and topped with a tuft of stiff leaves.
2 the widely cultivated tropical American plant that bears the pineapple. It is low-growing, with a spiral of spiny sword-shaped leaves on a thick stem. ● *Ananas comosus*, family Bromeliaceae.
3 informal a hand grenade.
– PHRASES **the rough end of the pineapple** Austral. informal a situation in which someone receives unfair or harsh treatment.
– ORIGIN late Middle English (denoting a pine cone): from PINE[1] + APPLE. The word was applied to the fruit in the mid 17th cent., because of its resemblance to a pine cone.

pineapple weed ▶ **noun** [mass noun] a small mayweed with a smell resembling that of pineapple, having flowers that lack ray florets. ● Genus *Matricaria*, family Compositae: the European *M. matricarioides* and the North American *M. discoidea*.

pine beauty ▶ **noun** a brown European moth whose caterpillars feed on pine needles and are a serious pest of plantations. ● *Panolis flammea*, family Noctuidae.

pine cone ▶ **noun** the conical or rounded woody fruit of a pine tree, with scales which open to release the seeds.

pine marten ▶ **noun** an arboreal weasel-like mammal that has a dark brown coat with a yellowish throat and a bushy tail, native to northern Eurasia. ● *Martes martes*, family Mustelidae.

pinene /ˈpʌɪniːn/ ▶ **noun** [mass noun] Chemistry a colourless flammable liquid present in turpentine, juniper oil, and other natural extracts. ● A bicyclic terpene; chem. formula: $C_{10}H_{16}$; four isomers, especially **α-pinene**, the main constituent of turpentine.
– ORIGIN late 19th cent.: from Latin *pinus* 'pine' + -ENE.

P

pine nut ▸ noun the edible seed of various pine trees.

pinesap ▸ noun N. Amer. a woodland plant related to wintergreen, lacking chlorophyll and bearing one or more waxy bell-shaped flowers. ● Two species in the family Monotropaceae: the violet-scented **sweet pinesap** (*Monotropsis odorata*), and the yellow bird's-nest.

Pine Tree State informal name for MAINE.

pinetum /pʌɪˈniːtəm/ ▸ noun (pl. **pineta** /-tə/) a plantation of pine trees or other conifers planted for scientific or ornamental purposes.
– ORIGIN mid 19th cent.: from Latin, from *pinus* 'pine'.

pinewood ▸ noun **1** [mass noun] the timber from pine trees.
2 (usu. **pinewoods**) a forest of pine trees.

piney ▸ adjective variant spelling of PINY.

pin feather ▸ noun Ornithology an immature feather, before the veins have expanded and while the shaft is full of fluid.

pinfold historical ▸ noun a pound for stray animals.
▸ verb [with obj.] confine (a stray animal) in a pinfold.
– ORIGIN late Old English *pundfald*, from a base shared by POND and POUND[3] + FOLD[2].

ping ▸ noun an abrupt high-pitched ringing sound.
▸ verb **1** make or cause to make a ping: [no obj.] *the doorbell pinged* | [with obj.] *Victoria pinged the bell.*
2 [with obj.] Computing query (another computer on a network) to determine whether there is a connection to it. ■ send an email or other electronic message to (someone): *at least a dozen people have pinged me or called to tell me this.*
3 US another term for PINK[4].
– DERIVATIVES **pinger** noun.
– ORIGIN mid 19th cent.: imitative.

pingo /ˈpɪŋɡəʊ/ ▸ noun (pl. **pingos**) Geology a dome-shaped mound consisting of a layer of soil over a large core of ice, occurring in permafrost areas.
– ORIGIN 1920s: from Inuit *pinguq* 'nunatak'.

ping-pong (also US trademark **Ping-Pong**) ▸ noun informal table tennis.
– ORIGIN early 20th cent.: imitative of the sound of a bat striking a ball.

pinguid /ˈpɪŋɡwɪd/ ▸ adjective formal of the nature of or resembling fat; oily or greasy.
– ORIGIN mid 17th cent.: from Latin *pinguis* 'fat' + -ID[1].

pinguin /ˈpɪŋɡwɪn/ (also **pingwing** /ˈpɪŋwɪŋ/) ▸ noun a large prickly plant related to the pineapple, native to tropical America and the Caribbean. Its fruit is edible but contains enzymes that can irritate the throat. ● *Bromelia pinguin*, family Bromeliaceae.
– ORIGIN late 17th cent.: of unknown origin.

pinhead ▸ noun **1** the round head of a pin. ■ a very small round object or mark: [as modifier] *pinhead dots.*
2 informal a stupid or foolish person.

pinheaded ▸ adjective informal stupid; foolish.

pin-high ▸ adjective Golf (of a ball) at the same distance from the tee as the hole, but off to one side.

pinhole ▸ noun a very small hole.

pinhole borer ▸ noun the larva of an ambrosia beetle, which makes minute round holes in timber.

pinhole camera ▸ noun a camera with a pinhole aperture and no lens.

pinion[1] /ˈpɪnjən/ ▸ noun the outer part of a bird's wing including the flight feathers. ■ literary a bird's wing as used in flight.
▸ verb [with obj.] **1** restrain or immobilize (someone) by tying up or holding their arms or legs: *he was pinioned to the ground.* ■ tie up or hold (the arms or legs) of a person: *I struggled to rise but my arms were pinioned.*
2 cut off the pinion of (a wing or bird) to prevent flight.
– ORIGIN late Middle English: from Old French *pignon*, based on Latin *pinna*, *penna* 'feather'.

pinion[2] /ˈpɪnjən/ ▸ noun a small cogwheel or spindle engaging with a large cogwheel.
– ORIGIN mid 17th cent.: from French *pignon*, alteration of obsolete *pignol*, from Latin *pinea* 'pine cone', from *pinus* 'pine'.

pink[1] ▸ adjective **1** of a colour intermediate between red and white, as of coral or salmon: *bright pink lipstick* | *her face was pink with embarrassment.* ■ (of wine) rosé.
2 informal, often derogatory having or showing left-wing tendencies: *pink politicians.*
3 of or associated with homosexuals: *a boom in the pink economy* | *the pink pound.*
▸ noun **1** [mass noun] pink colour, pigment, or material: *soft pastel shades of pink and blue.* ■ (also **hunting pink**) the scarlet jacket worn by fox-hunters or the material from which this is made. ■ [count noun] the pink ball in snooker. ■ informal rosé wine.
2 (**the pink of**) the best condition or degree: *the economy is not in the pink of health.*
▸ verb **1** [no obj.] become pink: *Cheryl's cheeks pinked with sudden excitement.*
2 [with obj.] Austral./NZ shear (a sheep) so closely that the colour of the skin is visible.
– PHRASES **in the pink** informal in extremely good health and spirits. **turn** (or **go**) **pink** blush: *I felt myself go pink.*
– DERIVATIVES **pinkish** adjective, **pinkly** adverb, **pinkness** noun, **pinky** adjective (**pinkier**, **pinkiest**).
– ORIGIN mid 17th cent.: from PINK[2], the early use of the adjective being to describe the colour of the flowers of this plant.

pink[2] ▸ noun a herbaceous Eurasian plant with sweet-smelling pink or white flowers and slender, typically grey-green leaves. ● Genus *Dianthus*, family Caryophyllaceae (the **pink family**). This family includes the campions, chickweeds, stitchworts, and the cultivated carnations. See also CLOVE[1] (sense 3).
– ORIGIN late 16th cent.: perhaps short for *pink eye*, literally 'small or half-shut eye'; compare with the synonymous French word *oeillet*, literally 'little eye'.

pink[3] ▸ verb [with obj.] **1** cut a scalloped or zigzag edge on: (as adj. **pinked**) *a bonnet with pinked edging.* ■ wound or nick (someone) slightly with a weapon or missile.
2 archaic decorate: *April pinked the earth with flowers.*
– ORIGIN early 16th cent. (in the sense 'pierce or nick slightly'): compare with Low German *pinken* 'strike, peck'.

pink[4] ▸ verb [no obj.] Brit. (of a vehicle engine) make a series of rattling sounds as a result of over-rapid combustion of the fuel–air mixture in the cylinders.
– ORIGIN early 20th cent.: imitative.

pink[5] ▸ noun historical a small square-rigged sailing ship, typically with a narrow, overhanging stern.
– ORIGIN late 15th cent.: from Middle Dutch *pin(c)ke*, of unknown ultimate origin; compare with Spanish *pinque* and Italian *pinco*.

pink[6] ▸ noun [mass noun] dated a yellowish lake pigment made by combining vegetable colouring matter with a white base.
– ORIGIN mid 17th cent.: of unknown origin.

pink-collar ▸ adjective relating to work traditionally associated with women.

pink elephants ▸ plural noun informal hallucinations supposedly typical of those experienced by a person who is drunk.

Pinkerton, Allan (1819–84), Scottish-born American detective. In 1850 he established the first American private detective agency.

pink-eye ▸ noun [mass noun] **1** a viral disease of horses, symptoms of which include fever, abortion, and redness of the eyes. ● The virus belongs to the genus *Arterivirus*.
2 conjunctivitis in humans and some livestock.

pink fir apple ▸ noun a potato of a pink-skinned knobbly variety.

pink gin ▸ noun Brit. gin flavoured with angostura bitters.

pinkie[1] ▸ noun informal the little finger.
– ORIGIN early 19th cent.: partly from Dutch *pink* 'the little finger', reinforced by PINK[1].

pinkie[2] ▸ noun (pl. **pinkies**) informal **1** a derogatory term used by black people for a white person.
2 (usu. **pinkies**) the maggot of the greenbottle fly, used as fishing bait.
– ORIGIN late 19th cent.: from PINK[2], of obscure origin.

pinking shears (also **pinking scissors**) ▸ plural noun shears with a serrated blade, used to cut a zigzag edge in fabric to prevent it fraying.

pink noise ▸ noun [mass noun] Physics random noise having equal energy per octave, and so having more low-frequency components than white noise.

pinko ▸ noun (pl. **pinkos** or **pinkoes**) informal, derogatory, chiefly N. Amer. a person with left-wing or liberal views.

pink salmon ▸ noun another term for HUMPBACK (sense 2). ■ [mass noun] the pale pink flesh of the humpback salmon used as food.

pink slip N. Amer. informal ▸ noun a notice of dismissal from employment.
▸ verb (**pink-slip**) [with obj.] dismiss (someone) from employment.

Pinkster /ˈpɪŋ(k)stə/ ▸ noun US dialect Whitsuntide.
– ORIGIN mid 18th cent.: from Dutch, 'Pentecost', from celebrations in areas of former Dutch influence, such as New York.

pin money ▸ noun [mass noun] a small sum of money for spending on inessentials.
ORIGIN late 17th cent.: from PIN in the sense 'decorative clasp for the hair or a garment' + MONEY. The term originally denoted an allowance made to a woman for dress and other personal expenses by her husband.

pinna /ˈpɪnə/ ▸ noun (pl. **pinnae** /-niː/) **1** Anatomy & Zoology the external part of the ear in humans and other mammals; the auricle.
2 Botany a primary division of a pinnate leaf, especially of a fern.
3 Zoology any of a number of animal structures resembling fins or wings.
– ORIGIN late 18th cent.: modern Latin, from a variant of Latin *penna* 'feather, wing, fin'.

pinnace /ˈpɪnɪs/ ▸ noun chiefly historical a small boat, typically with sails and/or several oars, forming part of the equipment of a warship or other large vessel.
– ORIGIN mid 16th cent.: from French *pinace*, probably based on Latin *pinus* 'pine' (see PINE[1]); compare with Italian *pinaccia* and Spanish *pinaza*.

pinnacle ▸ noun **1** the most successful point; the culmination: *he had reached **the pinnacle of** his career.*
2 a high, pointed piece of rock. ■ a small pointed turret built as an ornament on a roof.
▸ verb [with obj.] literary **1** form the culminating point or example of.
2 set on or as if on a pinnacle.
– DERIVATIVES **pinnacled** adjective.
– ORIGIN Middle English: from Old French, from late Latin *pinnaculum*, diminutive of *pinna* 'wing, point'.

pinnae plural form of PINNA.

pinnate ▸ adjective Botany (of a compound leaf) having leaflets arranged on either side of the stem, typically in pairs opposite each other. ■ Zoology (especially of an invertebrate animal) having branches, tentacles, etc., on each side of an axis, like the vanes of a feather.
– DERIVATIVES **pinnated** adjective, **pinnately** adverb, **pinnation** /-ˈneɪʃ(ə)n/ noun.
– ORIGIN early 18th cent.: from Latin *pinnatus* 'feathered', from *pinna*, *penna* (see PINNA).

pinnatifid /pɪˈneɪtɪfɪd, -ˈnatɪ-/ ▸ adjective Botany (of a leaf) pinnately divided, but not all the way down to the central axis.
– ORIGIN mid 18th cent.: from modern Latin *pinnatifidus*, from Latin *pinnatus* 'feathered' + *fid-* 'cleft' (from the verb *findere*).

pinni- /ˈpɪni/ ▸ combining form relating to wings or fins: *pinniped.*
– ORIGIN from Latin *pinna*, *penna* 'wing, fin'.

pinniped Zoology ▸ noun a carnivorous aquatic mammal of the order Pinnipedia, such as a seal or walrus.
▸ adjective relating to or denoting pinnipeds.

Pinnipedia /ˌpɪnɪˈpiːdɪə/ ▸ plural noun Zoology an order of carnivorous aquatic mammals which comprises the seals, sea lions, and walrus. They are distinguished by their flipper-like limbs. ● Order Pinnipedia: three families.
– ORIGIN modern Latin (plural), from Latin *pinna* 'wing, fin' + *pes*, *ped-* foot.

pinnule /ˈpɪnjuːl/ ▸ noun Botany a secondary division of a pinnate leaf, especially of a fern. ■ Zoology a part or organ like a small wing or fin, especially a side branch on the arm of a crinoid.
– ORIGIN late 16th cent. (denoting one of the sights of an astrolabe): from Latin *pinnula* 'small wing', diminutive of *pinna*.

PIN number ▸ noun see PIN.

pinny ▸ noun (pl. **pinnies**) Brit. informal a pinafore.
– ORIGIN mid 19th cent.: abbreviation.

Pinochet /ˈpɪnəʃeɪ/, Augusto (b.1915), Chilean general and statesman, President 1974–90; full name *Augusto Pinochet Ugarte*. Having masterminded the military coup which overthrew President Allende in 1973, he imposed a military dictatorship until forced to call elections in 1989. He was replaced by a democratically elected president in 1990.

pinochle /ˈpiːnɒk(ə)l/ ▸ noun [mass noun] a North American card game for two or more players using a 48-card pack consisting of two of each card from nine to ace, the object being to score points for various combinations and to win tricks. ■ the combination of queen of spades and jack of diamonds in the game of pinochle.
– ORIGIN mid 19th cent.: of unknown origin.

P

pinocytosis /ˌpiːnəʊsʌɪˈtəʊsɪs, ˌpɪnəʊ-, ˌpʌɪnəʊ-/ ▸ **noun** [mass noun] Biology the ingestion of liquid into a cell by the budding of small vesicles from the cell membrane.
– ORIGIN late 19th cent.: from Greek *pino* 'drink' + *-cytosis* on the pattern of *phagocytosis*.

pinole /piːˈnəʊleɪ, -li/ ▸ **noun** [mass noun] US flour made from parched cornflour mixed with sweet flour made of mesquite beans, sugar, and spice.
– ORIGIN mid 19th cent.: from Latin American Spanish, from Nahuatl *pinolli*.

piñon /pɪˈnjɒn, ˈpɪnjəʊn/ (also **pinyon** or **piñon pine**) ▸ **noun** a small pine tree with edible seeds, native to Mexico and the south-western US. ● *Pinus cemebroides*, family Pinaceae.
■ (also **piñon nut**) a pine nut obtained from the piñon.
– ORIGIN mid 19th cent.: from Spanish, from Latin *pinea* 'pine cone'.

Pinot /ˈpiːnəʊ/ ▸ **noun** [mass noun] any of several varieties of wine grape, especially the chief varieties **Pinot Noir**, a black grape, and **Pinot Blanc**, a white grape.
■ a wine made from Pinot grapes.
– ORIGIN variant of earlier *Pineau*, diminutive of *pin* 'pine' (because of the shape of the grape cluster).

pinotage /ˈpɪnə(ʊ)tɑːʒ/ ▸ **noun** [mass noun] a variety of red wine grape grown in South Africa, produced by crossing Pinot Noir and other varieties. ■ red wine made from the pinotage grape.
– ORIGIN blend of *Pinot* (*Noir*) and *Hermitage*, names of types of grape.

pinout ▸ **noun** Electronics a diagram showing the arrangement of pins on an integrated circuit and their functions.

pinpoint ▸ **noun** a tiny dot or point: *a pinpoint of light*.
▸ **adjective** [attrib.] **1** absolutely precise; to the finest degree: *this weapon fired shells with pinpoint accuracy*.
2 tiny: *a pinpoint hole*.
▸ **verb** [with obj.] find or identify with great accuracy or precision: *one flare had pinpointed the target | it is difficult to pinpoint the source of his life's inspiration*.

pinprick ▸ **noun 1** a prick caused by a pin. ■ a minor annoyance or irritation.
2 a very small dot or amount: *the stars were pinpricks of light*.

pins and needles ▸ **plural noun** [treated as sing.] a tingling sensation in a limb recovering from numbness.
– PHRASES **on pins and needles** in an agitated state of suspense.

P

Pinsent, Sir Matthew (b.1970), English rower. He won four consecutive Olympic gold medals between 1992 and 2004.

pinspot ▸ **noun** a small powerful spotlight for sharp illumination of a very small area.

pinstripe ▸ **noun** a very narrow stripe in cloth, especially of the type used for formal suits. ■ a suit made of pinstripe cloth: *a double-breasted navy pinstripe*.
– DERIVATIVES **pinstriped** **adjective**.

pint (abbrev.: **pt**) ▸ **noun** a unit of liquid or dry capacity equal to one eighth of a gallon, in Britain equal to 0.568 litre and in the US equal to 0.473 litre (for liquid measure) or 0.551 litre (for dry measure).
■ Brit. informal a pint of beer: *we'll probably go for a pint on the way home*. ■ Brit. a pint of milk. ■ Brit. a measure of shellfish, the amount containable in a pint mug.
– ORIGIN late Middle English: from Old French *pinte*, of unknown origin.

pinta ▸ **noun** Brit. informal a pint of milk.
– ORIGIN 1950s: representing a pronunciation of *pint of*.

pintado petrel /pɪnˈtɑːdəʊ/ ▸ **noun** a common petrel of southern oceans, having black plumage with white markings. ● *Daption capense*, family Procellariidae.
– ORIGIN early 17th cent.: from Portuguese and Spanish *pintado* 'guinea fowl' + PETREL.

pintail ▸ **noun** a mainly migratory duck with a pointed tail. ● Genus *Anas*, family Anatidae: three species, in particular the **northern pintail** (*A. acuta*) of Eurasia and North America, the male of which has boldly marked plumage and two long tail streamers.
■ informal any of a number of other birds with long pointed tails, especially (US) a grouse.

Pinter /ˈpɪntə/, Harold (1930–2008), English dramatist, actor, and director. His plays are associated with the Theatre of the Absurd and are typically marked by a sense of menace. Notable plays: *The Birthday Party* (1958), *The Caretaker* (1960), and *Party Time* (1991). Nobel Prize for Literature (2005).

pintle /ˈpɪnt(ə)l/ ▸ **noun** a pin or bolt on which a rudder or other part turns.
– ORIGIN Old English *pintel* 'penis', perhaps a diminutive; compare with Dutch *pint* and German *Pint* 'penis', of unknown ultimate origin.

pinto /ˈpɪntəʊ/ N. Amer. ▸ **adjective** piebald.
▸ **noun** (pl. **pintos**) a piebald horse.
– ORIGIN mid 19th cent.: from Spanish, literally 'mottled', based on Latin *pictus*, past participle of *pingere* 'to paint'.

pinto bean ▸ **noun** a medium-sized speckled variety of kidney bean.
– ORIGIN early 20th cent.: *pinto* from PINTO, because of the mottled seed of this variety of bean.

pint pot ▸ **noun** a beer glass or mug that holds a pint, especially one made of pewter.

pint-sized (also **pint-size**) ▸ **adjective** informal (especially of a person) very small.

pintuck ▸ **noun** a very narrow ornamental tuck in a garment.

pin-up ▸ **noun** a poster showing a famous or attractive person. ■ a person featured in a pin-up.

pinwheel chiefly N. Amer. ▸ **noun** a small firework resembling a Catherine wheel. ■ something shaped or rotating like a pinwheel.
▸ **verb** [no obj.] spin or rotate like a pinwheel.

pinworm ▸ **noun** a small nematode worm which is an internal parasite of vertebrates. ● Family Oxyuridae, class Phasmida, including *Enterobius vermicularis* (in humans) and *Oxyuris equi* (in horses).

piny (also **piney**) ▸ **adjective** relating to or covered with pines.

Pinyin /pɪnˈjɪn/ ▸ **noun** [mass noun] the standard system of romanized spelling for transliterating Chinese.
– ORIGIN 1960s: from Chinese *pīn-yīn*, literally 'spell-sound'.

pinyon ▸ **noun** variant spelling of PIÑON.

piolet /pjəʊˈleɪ/ ▸ **noun** Climbing an ice pick.
– ORIGIN mid 19th cent.: from French dialect, literally 'little pick', diminutive of *piolo*; related to *pioche* 'pickaxe'.

pion /ˈpʌɪɒn/ ▸ **noun** Physics a meson having a mass approximately 270 times that of an electron. Also called PI-MESON.
– ORIGIN 1950s: from PI[1] (the letter used as a symbol for the particle) + -ON.

Pioneer a series of American space probes launched between 1958 and 1973, two of which provided the first clear pictures of Jupiter and Saturn (1973–9).

pioneer ▸ **noun** a person who is among the first to explore or settle a new country or area. ■ a person who is among the first to research and develop a new area of knowledge or activity: *a famous pioneer of birth control*. ■ (in the former Soviet Union and other communist countries) a member of a children's movement that aimed to foster communist ideals.
■ a member of an infantry group preparing roads or terrain for the main body of troops. ■ (in Ireland) a member of the Pioneer Total Abstinence Association, a Catholic temperance society.
▸ **verb** [with obj.] develop or be the first to use or apply (a new method, area of knowledge, or activity): *the technique was pioneered by a Swiss doctor in the 1930s*. ■ open up (a road or terrain) as a pioneer.
– ORIGIN early 16th cent. (as a military term denoting a member of the infantry): from French *pionnier* 'foot soldier, pioneer', Old French *paonier*, from *paon*, from Latin *pedo*, *pedon-* (see PAWN[1]).

pioneering ▸ **adjective** involving new ideas or methods: *his pioneering work on consciousness*.

pious ▸ **adjective 1** devoutly religious: *a deeply pious woman*. ■ making or constituting a hypocritical display of virtue: *his pious platitudes*. ■ archaic dutiful or loyal, especially towards one's parents.
2 [attrib.] (of a hope) sincere but unlikely to be fulfilled.
– DERIVATIVES **piously** **adverb**, **piousness** **noun**.
– ORIGIN late Middle English: from Latin *pius* 'dutiful, pious' + -OUS.

pious fraud ▸ **noun** a deception intended to benefit those deceived, especially to strengthen religious belief.

pip[1] ▸ **noun** a small hard seed in a fruit. ■ S. African the stone of soft fruits such as peaches and plums.
– PHRASES **squeeze someone until the pips squeak** Brit. informal extract the maximum amount of money from someone.
– ORIGIN late 18th cent.: abbreviation of PIPPIN.

pip[2] ▸ **noun** (usu. **the pips**) Brit. a short high-pitched sound used especially to indicate the time on the radio or to instruct a caller using a public telephone to insert more money.
– ORIGIN early 20th cent.: imitative.

pip[3] ▸ **noun 1** Brit. a star (one to three according to rank) on the shoulder of an army officer's uniform.
2 any of the spots on a playing card, dice, or domino.
3 an image of an object on a radar screen.
– ORIGIN late 16th cent. (originally *peep*, denoting each of the dots on playing cards, dice, and dominoes): of unknown origin.

pip[4] ▸ **noun** [mass noun] a disease of poultry or other birds causing thick mucus in the throat and white scale on the tongue.
– PHRASES **give someone the pip** informal, dated make someone angry or depressed.
– ORIGIN late Middle English: from Middle Dutch *pippe*, probably from an alteration of Latin *pituita* 'slime'. In the late 15th cent. the word came to be applied humorously to unspecified human diseases, and later to ill humour.

pip[5] ▸ **verb** (**pips**, **pipping**, **pipped**) [with obj.] Brit. informal defeat by a small margin or at the last moment: *you were just pipped for the prize*. ■ dated hit or wound (someone) with a gun.
– PHRASES **pip someone at** (or **to**) **the post** defeat someone at the last moment.
– ORIGIN late 19th cent.: from PIP[1] or PIP[3].

pip[6] ▸ **verb** (**pips**, **pipping**, **pipped**) [with obj.] (of a young bird) crack (the shell of the egg) when hatching.
– ORIGIN late 19th cent.: perhaps of imitative origin.

pipa[1] /pɪˈpɑː, ˈpʌɪpə, ˈpɪpə/ ▸ **noun** another term for SURINAME TOAD.
– ORIGIN early 18th cent.: probably from Galibi.

pipa[2] /ˈpiːpə/ ▸ **noun** a shallow-bodied, four-stringed Chinese instrument resembling a lute.
– ORIGIN Chinese.

pipal /ˈpiːp(ə)l/ ▸ **noun** variant spelling of PEEPUL.

pipe ▸ **noun 1** a tube used to convey water, gas, oil, or other fluid substances. ■ a cylindrical vein of ore or rock, especially one in which diamonds are found.
■ a cavity in cast metal. ■ informal a duct, vessel, or tubular structure in the body, or in an animal or plant. ■ Computing a connection to the Internet or to a website.
2 a device for smoking tobacco, consisting of a narrow tube made from wood, clay, etc. with a bowl at one end in which the tobacco is burned, the smoke from which is drawn into the mouth. ■ a quantity of tobacco held by a pipe. ■ a device for smoking illegal drugs: *a crack pipe*.
3 a wind instrument consisting of a single tube with holes along its length that are covered by the fingers to produce different notes. ■ (usu. **pipes**) bagpipes.
■ (**pipes**) a set of musical pipes joined together, as in pan pipes. ■ any of the cylindrical tubes by which notes are produced in an organ. ■ a boatswain's whistle. ■ [in sing.] a high-pitched cry or song, especially of a bird.
4 Computing a command which causes the output from one routine to be the input for another. [short for PIPELINE.] ■ the symbol |.
5 a cask for wine, especially as a measure equal to two hogsheads, usually equivalent to 105 gallons (about 477 litres).
▸ **verb 1** [with obj. and adverbial of direction] convey (water, gas, oil, or other fluid substances) through a pipe or pipes: *water from the lakes is piped to Manchester*.
■ transmit (music, a radio or television programme, signal, etc.) by wire or cable.
2 [with obj.] play (a tune) on a pipe or pipes. ■ [with obj. and adverbial of direction] play a pipe or pipes as a ceremonial accompaniment to the arrival or departure of (someone): *the Duke was piped on board*. ■ [with obj. and adverbial] use a boatswain's whistle to summon (the crew) to work or a meal: *the hands were piped to breakfast*.
3 [no obj.] (of a bird) sing in a high or shrill voice.
■ [with direct speech] say something in a high, shrill voice: *'No, miss,' piped Lucy*.
4 [with obj.] decorate (clothing or soft furnishings) with thin cord covered in fabric and inserted into a seam.
5 arrange (food, particularly icing or cream) in decorative lines or patterns.

6 [with obj.] propagate (a pink [redacted] ing a cutting at the joint of a [redacted]
– PHRASES **put that in your pi**[redacted] informal used to indicate that the [redacted] will have to accept a particular situa[redacted] even if it is unwelcome.
– PHRASAL VERBS **pipe someone away** (or **down**) Nautical dismiss someone from duty. **pipe something away** Nautical give a signal for a boat to start. **pipe down** [often in imperative] informal stop talking; be less noisy. **pipe up** say something suddenly.
– DERIVATIVES **pipeful** noun (pl. **pipefuls**), **pipeless** adjective, **pipy** adjective.
– ORIGIN Old English *pīpe* 'musical tube', *pīpian* 'play a pipe', of Germanic origin; related to Dutch *pijp* and German *Pfeife*, based on Latin *pipare* 'to peep, chirp', reinforced in Middle English by Old French *piper* 'to chirp, squeak'.

pipe band ▸ noun a band, especially a military one, consisting of bagpipe players, drummers, and a pipe major.

pipe berth (Brit. also **pipe cot**) ▸ noun a collapsible bed with a frame of metal pipes, used on a boat.

pipe bomb ▸ noun a home-made bomb, the components of which are contained in a pipe.

pipeclay ▸ noun [mass noun] a fine white clay, used especially for making tobacco pipes or for whitening leather.
▸ verb [with obj.] whiten (leather) with pipeclay.

pipe cleaner ▸ noun a piece of wire covered with fibre, used to clean a tobacco pipe.

piped music ▸ noun [mass noun] pre-recorded background music played through loudspeakers in a public place.

pipe dream ▸ noun an unattainable or fanciful hope or scheme.
– ORIGIN late 19th cent.: referring to a dream experienced when smoking an opium pipe.

pipefish ▸ noun (pl. **same** or **pipefishes**) a narrow elongated chiefly marine fish with segmented bony armour beneath the skin and a long tubular snout. The male typically has a brood pouch in which the eggs develop. ● *Syngnathus* and other genera, family Syngnathidae: numerous species.

pipe jacking ▸ noun [mass noun] a method of laying underground pipes without digging a trench, in which the pipes are assembled in an access shaft and then pushed into position by a hydraulic jack.

pipeline ▸ noun **1** a long pipe, typically underground, for conveying oil, gas, etc. over long distances. ■ a channel or system supplying goods or information: *the biggest heroin pipeline in history*.
2 Computing a linear sequence of specialized modules used for pipelining.
3 (in surfing) the hollow formed by the breaking of a very large wave.
▸ verb **1** [with obj. and adverbial of direction] convey (a substance) by a pipeline.
2 [with obj.] (often as adj. **pipelined**) Computing design or execute (a computer or instruction) using the technique of pipelining.
– PHRASES **in the pipeline** in the process of being planned or developed.

pipelining ▸ noun [mass noun] **1** the laying of pipelines. ■ transportation by means of pipelines.
2 Computing a form of computer organization in which successive steps of an instruction sequence are executed in turn by a sequence of modules able to operate concurrently, so that another instruction can be begun before the previous one is finished.

pipe major ▸ noun an NCO commanding regimental pipes and drums.

pip emma ▸ adverb & noun Brit. dated informal term for **P.M.**
– ORIGIN First World War: signallers' name for the letters P and M.

pipe-opener ▸ noun Brit. informal a period of exercise taken as a warm-up. ■ an introductory or preliminary event, typically in a sports contest.

pipe organ ▸ noun Music an organ using pipes instead of or as well as reeds.

Piper, John (1903–92), English painter and decorative designer. He is best known for his watercolours and aquatints of buildings and for his stained glass in Coventry and Llandaff cathedrals.

piper ▸ noun **1** a bagpipe player.
2 a person who plays a pipe, especially an itinerant musician.
– ORIGIN Old English *pipere*.

[redacted] of holding tobacco pipes.

[redacted]perəziːn, pʌɪ-/ ▸ noun [mass noun] [redacted]nthetic crystalline compound with basic p[redacted]ties, sometimes used as an anthelmintic and insecticide. ● A heterocyclic compound; chem. formula: $C_4H_{10}N_2$.
– ORIGIN late 19th cent.: from **PIPERIDINE** + **AZINE**.

piperidine /pɪˈpɛrɪdiːn, pʌɪ-/ ▸ noun [mass noun] Chemistry a peppery-smelling liquid formed by the reduction of pyridine. ● Chem. formula: $C_5H_{11}N$.
– ORIGIN mid 19th cent.: from Latin *piper* 'pepper' + **-IDE** + **-INE**[4].

pipe roll ▸ noun the annual records of the British Exchequer from the 12th to the 19th century.
– ORIGIN probably so named because subsidiary documents were rolled in pipe form.

pipe snake ▸ noun any of a number of slender tropical burrowing snakes, in particular: ● a South American snake marked with bold red and black stripes (*Anilius scytale*, the only member of the family Aniliidae). ● an Asian snake which displays its bright under-tail coloration when alarmed (genus *Cylindrophis*, family Uropeltidae).

pipestone ▸ noun [mass noun] hard red clay used by North American Indians for tobacco pipes.

pipette /pɪˈpɛt/ ▸ noun a slender tube attached to or incorporating a bulb, for transferring or measuring out small quantities of liquid, especially in a laboratory.
▸ verb [with obj. and adverbial of direction] pour, convey, or draw off using a pipette.
– ORIGIN mid 19th cent.: from French, literally 'little pipe', diminutive of *pipe*.

pipework ▸ noun [mass noun] pipes that make up a network in a house, heating system, etc.

pipewort ▸ noun an aquatic or marsh plant with leafless stems bearing heads of inconspicuous flowers, native to western Ireland, the Hebrides, and North America. ● *Eriocaulon aquaticum*, family Eriocaulaceae.

pipi[1] /ˈpɪpi/ ▸ noun (pl. **same** or **pipis**) either of two edible marine bivalve molluscs native to New Zealand. ● *Amphidesma australe* (family Amphidesmatidae) and *Chione stutchburyi* (family Veneridae).
– ORIGIN mid 19th cent.: from Maori.

pipi[2] /ˈpiːpiː/ ▸ noun variant spelling of **PEE-PEE**.

piping ▸ noun [mass noun] **1** lengths of pipe made of metal, plastic, or other materials.
2 thin lines of icing or cream, used to decorate cakes and desserts.
3 thin cord covered in fabric, used to decorate clothing or soft furnishings and reinforce seams.
4 the action or art of playing a pipe or pipes.
5 [count noun] a cutting of a pink or similar plant taken at a joint.
▸ adjective [attrib.] high-pitched: *the piping voice of a little girl*.

piping hot ▸ adjective (of food or water) very hot.
– ORIGIN *piping*, because of the whistling sound made by very hot liquid or food.

pipistrelle /ˌpɪpɪˈstrɛl, ˈpɪp-/ (also **pipistrelle bat**) ▸ noun a small insectivorous Old World bat with jerky, erratic flight. ● Genus *Pipistrellus*, family Vespertilionidae: numerous species, including *P. pipistrellus*, which is the commonest bat in Eurasia.
– ORIGIN late 18th cent.: from French, from Italian *pipistrello*, from Latin *vespertilio(n-)* 'bat', from *vesper* 'evening'.

pipit /ˈpɪpɪt/ ▸ noun a mainly ground-dwelling songbird of open country, typically having brown streaky plumage. ● Family Motacillidae: three genera, in particular *Anthus*, and many species, e.g. the meadow pipit.
– ORIGIN mid 18th cent.: probably imitative.

pipkin ▸ noun a small earthenware pot or pan.
– ORIGIN mid 16th cent.: of unknown origin.

pippin ▸ noun **1** a red and yellow dessert apple. ■ an apple grown from seed.
2 informal, chiefly N. Amer. an excellent person or thing.
– ORIGIN Middle English: from Old French *pepin*, of unknown ultimate origin.

pip pip ▸ exclamation informal, dated goodbye.
– ORIGIN early 20th cent.: imitative, probably of the repeated short blasts on the horn of a motor car or bicycle.

pipsissewa /pɪpˈsɪsɪwə/ ▸ noun a North American plant of the wintergreen family, with whorled evergreen leaves. ● *Chimaphila umbellata*, family Pyrolaceae. ■ [mass noun] a preparation of the leaves of the pipsissewa, used as a diuretic and tonic.
– ORIGIN late 18th cent.: from Abnaki, literally 'flower of the woods'.

pipsqueak ▸ noun informal a person considered to be insignificant, especially because they are small or young.
– ORIGIN early 20th cent.: symbolic and imitative.

piquancy /ˈpiːk(ə)nsi/ ▸ noun [mass noun] a pleasantly sharp and appetizing flavour; spiciness: *the tangy soy dip gave them a slightly Asian piquancy*. ■ the quality of being pleasantly stimulating or exciting; interest: *the tragedy only adds piquancy to the tale*.

piquant /ˈpiːk(ə)nt, -kɒnt/ ▸ adjective having a pleasantly sharp taste or appetizing flavour: *a piquant tartare sauce*. ■ pleasantly stimulating or exciting to the mind.
– DERIVATIVES **piquantly** adverb.
– ORIGIN early 16th cent. (in the sense 'severe, bitter'): from French, literally 'stinging, pricking', present participle of *piquer*.

pique[1] /piːk/ ▸ noun [mass noun] a feeling of irritation or resentment resulting from a slight, especially to one's pride: *he left in a fit of pique*.
▸ verb (**piques, piquing, piqued**) **1** [with obj.] arouse (interest or curiosity).
2 (**be piqued**) feel irritated or resentful: *she was piqued by his curtness*.
3 (**pique oneself**) archaic pride oneself.
– ORIGIN mid 16th cent. (denoting animosity between two or more people): from French *piquer* 'prick, irritate'.

pique[2] /piːk/ ▸ noun (in piquet) the scoring of 30 points on declarations and play before one's opponent scores anything. Compare with **REPIQUE**.
▸ verb (**piques, piquing, piqued**) [with obj.] score a pique against (one's opponent).
– ORIGIN mid 17th cent.: from French *pic*, from the Old French sense 'stabbing blow', of unknown ultimate origin.

piqué /ˈpiːkeɪ/ ▸ noun [mass noun] stiff fabric, typically cotton, woven in a strongly ribbed or raised pattern.
– ORIGIN mid 19th cent.: from French, literally 'backstitched', past participle of *piquer*.

piquet[1] /ˈpiːkeɪ, pɪˈkɛt/ ▸ noun [mass noun] a trick-taking card game for two players, using a 32-card pack consisting of the seven to the ace only.
– ORIGIN mid 17th cent.: from French, of unknown origin.

piquet[2] ▸ noun variant spelling of **PICKET** (sense 2 of the noun).

piquillo /pɪˈkiːjəʊ/ ▸ noun (pl. **piquillos**) a sweet pepper of a variety grown in Spain, often sold roasted and preserved in oil.
– ORIGIN Spanish, literally 'little beak'.

PIR ▸ abbreviation passive infrared (denoting a type of sensor).

pir /pɪə/ ▸ noun a Muslim saint or holy man.
– ORIGIN from Persian *pīr* 'old man'.

piracy ▸ noun **1** [mass noun] the practice of attacking and robbing ships at sea. ■ a practice similar to piracy but in other contexts, especially hijacking: *air piracy*.
2 the unauthorized use or reproduction of another's work: *software piracy*.
– ORIGIN mid 16th cent.: via medieval Latin from Greek *pirateia*, from *peiratēs* (see **PIRATE**).

Piraeus /pʌɪˈriːəs, pɪˈreɪəs/ the chief port of Athens, situated on the Saronic Gulf 8 km (5 miles) SW of the city; pop. 178,400 (est. 2009). Greek name **Piraiévs** or **Piraiéus** /ˌpireˈefs/.

piragua /pɪˈragwə/ ▸ noun another term for **PIROGUE**.
– ORIGIN Spanish from Carib, literally 'dugout'.

Pirandello /ˌpɪrənˈdɛləʊ/, Luigi (1867–1936), Italian dramatist and novelist. His plays, including *Six Characters in Search of an Author* (1921) and *Henry IV* (1922), challenged the conventions of naturalism. Notable novels: *The Outcast* (1901) and *The Late Mattia Pascal* (1904). Nobel Prize for Literature (1934).

Piranesi /ˌpɪrəˈneɪzi/, Giovanni Battista (1720–78), Italian engraver. He is known for his dramatically conceived etchings of the buildings of Rome, in which the altered scale adds to their grandeur; he also produced an influential series of etchings of imagined and fantastical prisons, *Carceri d'Invenzioni* (1745–61).

piranha /pɪˈrɑːnə, -njə/ ▸ noun a deep-bodied South American freshwater fish that typically lives in shoals and has very sharp teeth that are used to tear flesh from prey. It has a reputation as a fearsome

P

predator. ● *Serrosalmus* and other genera, family Characidae: several species.
– ORIGIN mid 18th cent.: via Portuguese from Tupi *pirá* 'fish' + *sainha* 'tooth'.

pirate ▶ **noun** a person who attacks and robs ships at sea. ■ a person who appropriates or reproduces the work of another for profit without permission, usually in contravention of patent or copyright: [as modifier] *pirate recordings*. ■ a person or organization that broadcasts radio or television programmes without official authorization: [as modifier] *a pirate radio station*.
▶ **verb** [with obj.] **1** (often as adj. **pirated**) use or reproduce (another's work) for profit without permission, usually in contravention of patent or copyright: *pirated tapes of Hollywood blockbusters*.
2 dated rob or plunder (a ship).
– DERIVATIVES **piratic** adjective, **piratical** adjective, **piratically** adverb.
– ORIGIN Middle English: from Latin *pirata*, from Greek *peiratēs*, from *peirein* 'to attempt, attack' (from *peira* 'an attempt').

WORD TRENDS Though they no longer come with parrots and peg legs, modern **pirates** are as big a threat as the swashbuckling figures of history. And their numbers are rising, with the Oxford English Corpus showing a more than fourfold explosion in use since 2007. The Corpus also shows that *Somali* is the most common modifier of **pirate**, reflecting a recent surge in piracy around the Horn of Africa. But the high seas are not the only place where **pirates** lurk—online piracy is also on the increase. The use of **pirate** to refer to someone who steals the work of another has been around since the 17th century, but the ease of copying and sharing files via the Internet has led to a massive increase. While those who download films and music over the Web may not consider themselves to be criminals, production companies have a different view: *Internet pirates cost US industry hundreds of billions of dollars in lost revenue every year*.

piriform ▶ **adjective** variant spelling of PYRIFORM.

piripiri /ˈpɪrɪˌpɪri/ (also **pirri-pirri burr**) ▶ **noun** (pl. **piripiris**) a New Zealand plant of the rose family, with prickly burrs. ● Genus *Acaena*, family Rosaceae: several species, in particular *A. anserinifolia*.
– ORIGIN mid 19th cent.: from Maori.

piri-piri /ˈpɪrɪˌpɪri/ ▶ **noun** [mass noun] a very hot sauce made with red chilli peppers.
– ORIGIN Ronga (a Bantu language of southern Mozambique), literally 'pepper'.

pirk /pəːk/ ▶ **noun** a metal weight fitted with a hook, used as a lure for sea fishing.
– ORIGIN perhaps a variant of PERCH¹, PERCH³.

P

pirog /pɪˈrɒg/ ▶ **noun** (pl. **pirogi** /-gi/ or **pirogen** /-g(ə)n/) (in Russian cookery) a large pie.
– ORIGIN Russian.

pirogi /pəˈrəʊgi/ ▶ **noun** variant spelling of PIEROGI.

pirogue /pɪˈrəʊg/ ▶ **noun** a long, narrow canoe made from a single tree trunk, especially in Central America and the Caribbean.
– ORIGIN early 17th cent.: from French, probably from Carib.

piroplasmosis /ˌpʌɪrə(ʊ)plazˈməʊsɪs/ ▶ **noun** another term for BABESIOSIS.

piroshki /pɪˈrɒʃki/ (also **pirozhki** /-ʒki/) ▶ **plural noun** small Russian savoury pastries or patties, filled with meat or fish and rice.
– ORIGIN from Russian *pirozhki*, plural of *pirozhok*, diminutive of *pirog* (see PIROG).

pirouette /ˌpɪrʊˈɛt/ ▶ **noun** chiefly Ballet an act of spinning on one foot, typically with the raised foot touching the knee of the supporting leg. ■ a movement performed in advanced dressage and classical riding, in which the horse makes a circle by pivoting on a hind leg, while cantering.
▶ **verb** [no obj.] perform a pirouette.
– ORIGIN mid 17th cent.: from French, literally 'spinning top', of unknown ultimate origin.

pirri-pirri burr ▶ **noun** see PIRIPIRI.

Pisa /ˈpiːzə/ a city in west central Italy, in Tuscany, on the River Arno; pop. 87,398 (2008). It is noted for the 'Leaning Tower of Pisa', a circular bell tower which leans about 5 m (17 ft) from the perpendicular over its height of 55 m (181 ft).

pis aller /piːz ˈaleɪ/, French /piz ale/ ▶ **noun** a course of action followed as a last resort.
– ORIGIN French, from *pis* 'worse' + *aller* 'go'.

Pisan, Christine de, see DE PISAN.

Pisano¹ /pɪˈsɑːnəʊ/, Andrea [redacted] Nino, his son (died *c.*1368), Italia[redacted] created the earliest pair of bronze doors [redacted] baptistery at Florence (completed 1336). [redacted] one of the earliest to specialize in free-standing life-size figures.

Pisano² /pɪˈsɑːnəʊ/ two Italian sculptors, **Nicola** (*c.*1220–*c.*1278) and his son **Giovanni** (*c.*1250–*c.*1314). Nicola's work departed from medieval conventions and signalled a revival of interest in classical sculpture. His most famous works are the pulpits in the baptistery at Pisa and in Siena cathedral. Giovanni's works include the richly decorated facade of Siena cathedral.

piscary /ˈpɪskəri/ ▶ **noun** (in phrase **common of piscary**) Brit., chiefly historical the right of fishing in another's water.
– ORIGIN late 15th cent.: from medieval Latin *piscaria* 'fishing rights', neuter plural of Latin *piscarius* 'relating to fishing', from *piscis* 'fish'.

piscatorial /ˌpɪskəˈtɔːrɪəl/ ▶ **adjective** formal of or concerning fishermen or fishing.
– ORIGIN early 19th cent.: from Latin *piscatorius* 'relating to fishing' (from *piscator* 'fisherman', from *piscis* 'fish') + -AL.

piscatory /ˈpɪskət(ə)ri/ ▶ **adjective** another term for PISCATORIAL.

Pisces /ˈpʌɪsiːz, ˈpɪskiːz/ **1** Astronomy a large constellation (the Fish or Fishes), said to represent a pair of fish tied together by their tails.
2 Astrology the twelfth sign of the zodiac, which the sun enters about 20 February. ■ (**a Pisces**) (pl. **same**) a person born when the sun is in the sign of Pisces.
– DERIVATIVES **Piscean** /ˈpʌɪsɪən/ noun & adjective (sense 2).
– ORIGIN Latin, plural of *piscis* 'fish'.

pisciculture /ˈpɪsɪˌkʌltʃə/ ▶ **noun** [mass noun] the controlled breeding and rearing of fish.
– ORIGIN mid 19th cent.: from Latin *piscis* 'fish' + CULTURE, on the pattern of words such as *agriculture*.

piscina /pɪˈsiːnə, pɪˈsʌɪnə/ ▶ **noun** (pl. **piscinas** or **piscinae** /-niː/) **1** a stone basin near the altar in Catholic and pre-Reformation churches for draining water used in the Mass.
2 (in ancient Roman architecture) a pool or pond for bathing or swimming.
– ORIGIN late 16th cent. (in sense 2): from Latin, literally 'fish pond', from *piscis* 'fish'; sense 1 was found in medieval Latin.

piscine /ˈpɪsʌɪn/ ▶ **adjective** of or concerning fish.
– ORIGIN late 18th cent.: from Latin *piscis* 'fish' + -INE¹.

Piscis Austrinus /ˌpʌɪsɪs ɒˈstrʌɪnəs/ (also **Piscis Australis** /ɒˈstreɪlɪs/) Astronomy a southern constellation (the Southern Fish), south of Aquarius and Capricornus. It contains the bright star Fomalhaut.
– ORIGIN Latin.

piscivorous /pɪˈsɪv(ə)rəs/ ▶ **adjective** Zoology (of an animal) feeding on fish.
– DERIVATIVES **piscivore** noun.
– ORIGIN mid 17th cent.: from Latin *piscis* 'fish' + -VOROUS.

pisco /ˈpɪskəʊ/ ▶ **noun** (pl. **piscos**) [mass noun] a white brandy made in Peru from muscat grapes.
– ORIGIN named after a port in Peru.

pisé /ˈpiːzeɪ/ ▶ **noun** [mass noun] building material of stiff clay or earth, forced between boards which are removed as it hardens.
– ORIGIN late 18th cent.: French, literally 'pounded', past participle of *piser*.

pish ▶ **exclamation** dated used to express annoyance, impatience, or disgust.
– ORIGIN natural utterance: first recorded in English in the late 16th cent.

pisher ▶ **noun** N. Amer. informal an insignificant or contemptible person.
– ORIGIN 1940s: Yiddish, literally 'pisser', from the verb *pissen*.

pishogue /pɪˈʃəʊg/ (also **pishrogue** /pɪˈʃrəʊg/) ▶ **noun** Irish a superstitious belief. ■ a spell or charm.
– ORIGIN early 19th cent.: from Irish *piseog* 'witchcraft'.

Pishpek /pɪʃˈpɛk/ former name (until 1926) for BISHKEK.

Pisidia /pʌɪˈsɪdɪə/ an ancient region of Asia Minor, between Pamphylia and Phrygia. It was incorporated into the Roman province of Galatia in 25 BC.
– DERIVATIVES **Pisidian** adjective & noun.

pisiform /ˈpʌɪsɪfɔːm, ˈpɪzɪ-/ (also **pisiform bone**) ▶ **noun** a small rounded carpal bone situated where [redacted] meets the outer edge of the [redacted] with the triquetral. [redacted] t.: from modern Latin *pisi-* [redacted], from *pisum* 'pea' + *forma* 'shape'.

Pisistratus [redacted] /pʌɪˈsɪstrətəs/ (also **Peisistratus**) (*c.*600–*c.*527 BC), tyrant of Athens. He reduced aristocratic power in rural Attica and promoted the financial prosperity and cultural pre-eminence of Athens.

pisky (also **piskey**) ▶ **noun** (pl. **piskies** or **piskeys**) Brit. (especially in Cornwall) a pixie.
– ORIGIN late 19th cent.: dialect variant of PIXIE.

pismire /ˈpɪsmʌɪə/ ▶ **noun** archaic an ant.
– ORIGIN Middle English: from PISS (alluding to the smell of an anthill) + obsolete *mire* 'ant'.

pisolite /ˈpɪzəlʌɪt, ˈpʌɪsə-/ ▶ **noun** [mass noun] Geology a sedimentary rock, especially limestone, made up of small pea-shaped pieces.
– DERIVATIVES **pisolitic** adjective.
– ORIGIN early 19th cent.: from modern Latin *pisolithus* (see PISOLITH) + -LITE.

pisolith /ˈpɪzəlɪθ, ˈpʌɪsə-/ ▶ **noun** Geology any of the component pieces of which pisolite consists.
– ORIGIN late 18th cent.: from modern Latin *pisolithus*, from Greek *pisos* 'pea'.

piss vulgar slang ▶ **verb** [no obj.] urinate. ■ [with obj.] discharge (something, especially blood) when urinating. ■ (**piss oneself/one's pants**) urinate involuntarily (often used to indicate a loss of self-control through fear or hilarity). ■ (**piss down**) rain heavily.
▶ **noun** [mass noun] urine. ■ [in sing.] an act of urinating.
– PHRASES **be** (or **go**) **on the piss** Brit. be engaged in (or go on) a heavy drinking session. **not have a pot to piss in** N. Amer. be very poor. **a piece of piss** Brit. a very easy thing to do. **piss in the wind** do something that is ineffective or a waste of time. **take the piss** (**out of someone/thing**) Brit. mock someone or something.
– PHRASAL VERBS **piss about/around** Brit. spend time doing stupid or unimportant things. **piss off** [usu. in imperative] go away. **piss someone off** annoy someone. **piss on/over** show complete contempt for. **piss something up** spoil or ruin something.
– ORIGIN Middle English: from Old French *pisser*, probably of imitative origin.

pissabed ▶ **noun** the dandelion.
– ORIGIN late 16th cent.: from the verb PISS (because of its diuretic properties) + ABED, suggested by the French name for the dandelion, *pissenlit*.

pissaladière /ˌpɪsaləˈdjɛː/ ▶ **noun** a Provençal open tart resembling pizza, typically made with onions, anchovies, and black olives.
– ORIGIN French, from Provençal *pissaladiero*, from *pissala* 'salt fish'.

piss and vinegar ▶ **noun** [mass noun] vulgar slang aggressive energy.

pissant /ˈpɪsant/ US vulgar slang ▶ **noun** an insignificant or contemptible person or thing.
▶ **adjective** worthless or contemptible.
– ORIGIN mid 17th cent.: from the noun PISS + -ANT.

Pissarro /pɪˈsɑːrəʊ/, Camille (1830–1903), French painter and graphic artist. He was a leading figure of the Impressionist movement, typically painting landscapes and cityscapes. He also experimented with pointillism in the 1880s.

piss artist ▶ **noun** Brit. vulgar slang a drunkard. ■ a person who wastes time or behaves stupidly.

pissed ▶ **adjective** vulgar slang **1** (also **pissed up**) Brit. drunk.
2 (**pissed off**) (N. Amer. also **pissed**) very annoyed.
– PHRASES **as pissed as a newt** (or **fart**) Brit. very drunk.

pisser ▶ **noun** vulgar slang a person who urinates. ■ a toilet. ■ [in sing.] an annoying or disappointing event or circumstance.

pisshead ▶ **noun** Brit. vulgar slang a drunkard.

piss-hole ▶ **noun** vulgar slang a squalid place.

pissing ▶ **adjective** [attrib.] vulgar slang **1** (of rain) heavy.
2 used for emphasis or to express annoyance or contempt.

pissoir /piːˈswɑː, ˈpɪswɑː/, French /piswaʀ/ ▶ **noun** a public urinal.
– ORIGIN French.

piss-poor ▶ **adjective** vulgar slang of a very low standard.

pisspot ▶ **noun** vulgar slang a chamber pot.

piss-take ▶ **noun** Brit. vulgar slang an act of mockery.
– DERIVATIVES **piss-taker** noun, **piss-taking** noun.

piss-up ▶ **noun** Brit. vulgar slang a heavy drinking session.

pissy ▸ adjective vulgar slang **1** relating to or suggestive of urine. ▪ inferior or contemptible.
2 chiefly US arrogantly argumentative.

pistachio /pɪˈstɑːʃɪəʊ, pɪˈstatʃəʊ/ ▸ noun (pl. **pistachios**) **1** (also **pistachio nut**) the edible pale green seed of an Asian tree. ▪ [mass noun] a pale green colour.
2 the evergreen tree which produces the pistachio, with small brownish-green flowers and oval reddish fruit. It is widely cultivated, especially around the Mediterranean and in the US. ● *Pistacia vera*, family Anacardiaceae.
– ORIGIN late Middle English *pistace*, from Old French, superseded in the 16th cent. by forms from Italian *pistaccio*, via Latin from Greek *pistakion*, from Old Persian.

piste /piːst/ ▸ noun a ski run of compacted snow.
– ORIGIN French, literally 'racetrack'.

pisteur /piːˈstəː/ ▸ noun a person employed to prepare the snow on a piste.
– ORIGIN French.

pistil /ˈpɪstɪl/ ▸ noun Botany the female organs of a flower, comprising the stigma, style, and ovary.
– ORIGIN early 18th cent.: from French *pistile* or Latin *pistillum* 'pestle'.

pistillate /ˈpɪstɪlət/ ▸ adjective Botany (of a plant or flower) having pistils but no stamens. Compare with STAMINATE.

pistol ▸ noun a small firearm designed to be held in one hand.
▸ verb (**pistols, pistolling, pistolled**; US **pistols, pistoling, pistoled**) [with obj.] dated shoot (someone) with a pistol.
– ORIGIN mid 16th cent.: from obsolete French *pistole*, from German *Pistole*, from Czech *pišťala*, of which the original meaning was 'whistle', hence 'a firearm' by the resemblance in shape.

pistole /pɪˈstəʊl/ ▸ noun any of various gold coins used in Europe or Scotland in the 17th and 18th centuries.
– ORIGIN late 16th cent.: from French, abbreviation of *pistolet*, in the same sense, of uncertain ultimate origin.

pistoleer /ˌpɪstəˈlɪə/ ▸ noun archaic a soldier armed with a pistol.

pistolero /ˌpɪstəˈlɛːrəʊ/ ▸ noun (pl. **pistoleros** /-ɒs, -əʊz/) (in Spain and Spanish-speaking areas) a gunman or gangster.
– ORIGIN Spanish.

pistol grip ▸ noun a handle shaped like the butt of a pistol.

pistol shot ▸ noun a shot fired from a pistol. ▪ [mass noun] the range of a pistol.

pistol-whip ▸ verb [with obj.] hit or beat (someone) with the butt of a pistol.

piston /ˈpɪst(ə)n/ ▸ noun a disc or short cylinder fitting closely within a tube in which it moves up and down against a liquid or gas, used in an internal-combustion engine to derive motion, or in a pump to impart motion. ▪ a valve in a brass musical instrument in the form of a piston, depressed to alter the pitch of a note.
– ORIGIN early 18th cent.: from French, from Italian *pistone*, variant of *pestone* 'large pestle', augmentative of *pestello* 'pestle'.

piston corer ▸ noun Geology a piston-driven cylindrical device for taking samples of material from the seabed.

piston engine ▸ noun an engine, especially in an aircraft, in which power is derived from cylinders and pistons rather than a turbine.
– DERIVATIVES **piston-engined** adjective.

piston ring ▸ noun a ring on a piston sealing the gap between the piston and the cylinder wall.

piston rod ▸ noun a rod or crankshaft attached to a piston to drive a wheel or to impart motion.

pistou /ˈpiːstuː/ ▸ noun [mass noun] sauce or paste made from crushed basil, garlic, and cheese, used especially in Provençal dishes. ▪ a thick vegetable soup made with pistou.
– ORIGIN Provençal; compare with PESTO.

pit[1] ▸ noun **1** a large hole in the ground. ▪ a large deep hole from which stones or minerals are quarried. ▪ a coal mine: [as modifier] *the recent protests over planned pit closures.* ▪ a low or wretched psychological state: *a black pit of depression.* ▪ (**the pit**) literary hell.
2 an area reserved or enclosed for a specific purpose, in particular: ▪ (usu. **the pits**) an area at the side of a track where racing cars are serviced and refuelled. ▪ a sunken area in a workshop floor allowing access to a car's underside. ▪ an orchestra pit. ▪ a part of the floor of a stock exchange in which a particular stock or commodity is traded. ▪ (**the pit**) Brit. dated the seating at the back of the stalls of a theatre. ▪ chiefly historical an enclosure in which animals are made to fight: *a bear pit.*
3 a hollow or indentation in a surface. ▪ a small indentation left on the skin by a pustule or spot; a pockmark.
4 Brit. informal a person's bed.
5 informal a person's armpit.
▸ verb (**pits, pitting, pitted**) [with obj.] **1** (**pit someone/thing against**) set someone or something in conflict or competition with: *you'll get the chance to pit your wits against the world champions.* ▪ historical set an animal to fight against (another animal) for sport. [because formerly set against each other in a 'pit' or enclosure.]
2 make a hollow or indentation in the surface of: *rain poured down, pitting the bare earth.* ▪ [no obj.] sink in or contract so as to form a pit or hollow.
3 [no obj.] drive a racing car into the pits for fuel or maintenance.
– PHRASES **be the pits** informal be extremely bad or the worst of its kind. **dig a pit for** try to trap. **the pit of one's** (or **the**) **stomach** the lower abdomen regarded as the seat of strong feelings, especially anxiety.
– ORIGIN Old English *pytt*, of West Germanic origin; related to Dutch *put* and German *Pfütze*, based on Latin *puteus* 'well, shaft'.

pit[2] chiefly N. Amer. ▸ noun the stone of a fruit.
▸ verb (**pits, pitting, pitted**) [with obj.] remove the pit from (fruit).
– ORIGIN mid 19th cent.: apparently from Dutch; related to PITH.

pita ▸ noun N. Amer. variant spelling of PITTA[1].

pitahaya /ˌpɪtəˈhʌɪə/ ▸ noun any tall cactus of Mexico and the south-western US, in particular the saguaro. ▪ the edible fruit of a pitahaya cactus.
– ORIGIN late 18th cent.: from Spanish, from Haitian Creole.

pit-a-pat (also **pitapat**) ▸ adverb with a sound like quick light steps or taps: *her heart went pit-a-pat.*
▸ noun [in sing.] a sound like quick light steps or taps.
– ORIGIN early 16th cent.: imitative of alternating sounds.

pit boss ▸ noun informal, chiefly US an employee in a casino in charge of gaming tables.

pit bull (in full **pit bull terrier**) ▸ noun a dog of an American variety of bull terrier, noted for its ferocity.

Pitcairn Islands /ˈpɪtkɛːn/ a British overseas territory comprising a group of volcanic islands in the South Pacific, east of French Polynesia. The colony's only settlement is Adamstown, on Pitcairn Island, the chief island of the group; pop. 50 (est. 2009). Pitcairn Island was discovered in 1767, and remained uninhabited until settled in 1790 by mutineers from HMS *Bounty*.
– ORIGIN named after the midshipman who first sighted the islands.

pitch[1] ▸ noun **1** [mass noun] the quality of a sound governed by the rate of vibrations producing it; the degree of highness or lowness of a tone: *her voice rose steadily in pitch.* ▪ a standard degree of highness or lowness used in performance: *the guitars were strung and tuned to pitch.* See also CONCERT PITCH.
2 [mass noun] the steepness of a slope, especially of a roof. ▪ [count noun] Climbing a section of a climb, especially a steep one. ▪ the height to which a hawk soars before swooping on its prey.
3 [in sing.] a level of the intensity of something, especially a high level: *the media furore reached such a pitch that the company withdrew the product.*
4 Brit. an area of ground marked out or used for play in an outdoor team game: *a football pitch.* ▪ Cricket the strip of ground between the two sets of stumps.
5 Baseball a delivery of the ball by the pitcher. ▪ (also **pitch of the ball**) Cricket the spot where the ball bounces when bowled. ▪ (also **pitch shot**) Golf a high approach shot on to the green.
6 a form of words used when trying to persuade someone to buy or accept something: *he put over a very strong sales pitch.*
7 Brit. a place where a street vendor or performer stations themselves or sets up a stall.
8 [mass noun] a swaying or oscillation of a ship, aircraft, or vehicle around a horizontal axis perpendicular to the direction of motion.
9 [mass noun] technical the distance between successive corresponding points or lines, for example between the teeth of a cogwheel. ▪ a measure of the angle of the blades of a screw propeller, equal to the distance forward a blade would move in one revolution if it exerted no thrust on the medium. ▪ the density of typed or printed characters on a line, typically expressed as numbers of characters per inch.
▸ verb **1** [with obj. and adverbial] set (one's voice or a piece of music) at a particular pitch: *you've pitched the melody very high.* ▪ set or aim at a particular level, target, or audience: *he should pitch his talk at a suitable level for the age group.*
2 [with obj. and adverbial of direction] throw roughly or casually: *he crumpled the page up and pitched it into the fireplace.* ▪ [no obj., with adverbial of direction] fall heavily, especially headlong: *she pitched forward into blackness.*
3 [with obj.] Baseball throw (the ball) for the batter to try to hit. ▪ Cricket (of a bowler) cause (the ball) to strike the ground at a particular point: *all too often you pitch the ball short.* ▪ Golf hit (the ball) on to the green with a pitch shot. ▪ [no obj.] Cricket & Golf (of the ball) strike the ground in a particular spot.
4 [no obj.] make a bid to obtain a contract or other business: *I've been pitching for this account for over a month.* ▪ [with obj.] try to persuade someone to buy or accept (something): *they pitched the story to various magazines and newspapers.*
5 [with obj.] set up and fix in position: *we pitched camp for the night.* ▪ Cricket fix (the stumps) in the ground and place the bails in preparation for play.
6 [no obj.] (of a moving ship, aircraft, or vehicle) rock or oscillate around a lateral axis, so that the front moves up and down: *the little steamer pressed on, pitching gently.* ▪ (of a vehicle) move with a vigorous jolting motion: *a Land Rover came pitching round the hillside.*
7 [with obj.] cause (a roof) to slope downwards from the ridge: *the roof was pitched at an angle of 75 degrees.* ▪ [no obj.] slope downwards: *the ravine pitches down to the creek.*
8 [with obj.] pave (a road) with stones.
9 [with obj.] (in brewing) add yeast to (wort) to induce fermentation.
– PHRASES **make a pitch** make a bid to obtain a contract or other business.
– PHRASAL VERBS **pitch someone/thing against** informal pit someone or something against. **pitch in** informal vigorously join in to help with a task or activity. ▪ join in a fight or dispute. **pitch into** informal vigorously tackle or begin to deal with. ▪ forcefully assault. **pitch up** informal turn up; arrive. **pitch something up** (or **pitch up**) Cricket bowl a ball so that it bounces near the batsman.
– ORIGIN Middle English (as a verb in the senses 'thrust (something pointed) into the ground' and 'fall headlong'): perhaps related to Old English *picung* 'stigmata', of unknown ultimate origin. The sense development is obscure.

pitch[2] ▸ noun [mass noun] a sticky resinous black or dark brown substance that is semi-liquid when hot and hardens when cold, obtained by distilling tar or turpentine and used for waterproofing. ▪ any of various substances similar to pitch, such as asphalt or bitumen.
▸ verb [with obj.] chiefly archaic cover, coat, or smear with pitch.
– ORIGIN Old English *pic* (noun), *pician* (verb), of Germanic origin; related to Dutch *pek* and German *Pech*; based on Latin *pix, pic-*.

pitch and putt ▸ noun [mass noun] a form of golf played on a miniature course in which the green can be reached in one stroke from the tee.

pitch and run ▸ noun Golf a pitch shot with a lower trajectory and no backspin, so that the ball runs forward on landing.

pitch-and-toss ▸ noun [mass noun] a gambling game in which the player who manages to throw a coin closest to a mark gets to toss all the coins, winning those that land with the head up.

pitch bend ▸ noun [mass noun] a facility in a synthesizer that enables the player to change the pitch of the note played by a small amount.

pitch-black (also **pitch-dark**) ▸ adjective completely dark.
– DERIVATIVES **pitch-blackness** noun.

pitchblende /ˈpɪtʃblɛnd/ ▸ noun [mass noun] a form of the mineral uraninite occurring in brown or black pitch-like masses and containing radium.
– ORIGIN late 18th cent.: from German *Pechblende*, from *Pech* 'pitch' + *Blende* (see BLENDE).

P

pitch circle ▶ noun Mechanics an imaginary circle concentric to a toothed wheel, along which the pitch of the teeth is measured.

pitch control ▶ noun [mass noun] **1** control of the pitch of a helicopter's rotors or an aircraft's propellers. **2** control of the pitching motion of an aircraft.

pitched battle ▶ noun a battle in which the time and place are determined beforehand, rather than a casual or chance skirmish. ■ a violent confrontation involving large numbers of people.

pitcher[1] ▶ noun **1** a large jug. ■ the contents of a pitcher: *a pitcher of water*.
2 (**pitchers**) broken pottery crushed and reused.
3 the modified leaf of a pitcher plant.
– DERIVATIVES **pitcherful** noun (pl. **pitcherfuls**).
– ORIGIN Middle English: from Old French *pichier* 'pot', based on late Latin *picarium*.

pitcher[2] /ˈpɪtʃə/ ▶ noun **1** Baseball the player who delivers the ball to the batter.
2 a stone used for paving.

pitcher plant ▶ noun a plant with a deep pitcher-shaped pouch that contains fluid into which insects are attracted and drowned. Nutrients are then absorbed from their bodies by the plant. ● Three families, in particular Sarraceniaceae (New World) and Nepenthaceae (Old World): many species, including the purple-flowered *Sarracenia purpurea*, naturalized in Ireland.

pitchfork ▶ noun a farm tool with a long handle and two sharp metal prongs, used for lifting hay.
▶ verb [with obj. and adverbial of direction] lift with a pitchfork. ■ thrust (someone) suddenly into an unexpected and difficult situation: *he was* **pitchforked into** *the job for six months*.
– ORIGIN late Middle English: from earlier *pickfork*, influenced by the verb PITCH[1] (because the tool is used for 'pitching' or throwing sheaves on to a stack).

pitchman ▶ noun (pl. **pitchmen** /-mɛn/) N. Amer. informal a person delivering a sales pitch.

pitchout ▶ noun **1** Baseball a pitch thrown intentionally beyond the reach of the batter to allow the catcher a clear throw at an advancing base runner.
2 American Football a lateral pass, especially from the quarterback to a running back.

pitch pine ▶ noun a pine tree with hard, heavy, resinous timber that is used in building, especially the longleaf pine of North America.

pitch pipe ▶ noun Music a small pipe blown to set the pitch for singing or tuning an instrument.

pitchpole ▶ verb [no obj.] dialect somersault. ■ Nautical (of a boat) be overturned so that its stern pitches forward over its bows.
▶ noun dialect a somersault.
– ORIGIN mid 17th cent. (as a noun): from the verb PITCH[1] + POLL.

pitchside ▶ noun the area adjacent to the side of a football or other sports pitch.
▶ adjective & adverb at, on, or towards the side of a football or other sports pitch: [as adj.] *a pitchside briefing* | [as adv.] *reporters will be pitchside with the fans*.

pitchstone ▶ noun [mass noun] Geology a dull vitreous rock resembling hardened pitch, formed by weathering of obsidian.

pitchy ▶ adjective (**pitchier**, **pitchiest**) like or as dark as pitch.

piteous ▶ adjective deserving or arousing pity: *a piteous cry*.
– DERIVATIVES **piteously** adverb, **piteousness** noun.
– ORIGIN Middle English: from Old French *piteus*, from Latin *pietas* 'piety, pity' (see PIETY).

pitfall ▶ noun **1** a hidden or unsuspected danger or difficulty: *the pitfalls of buying goods at public auctions*.
2 a covered pit for use as a trap.

pith ▶ noun [mass noun] **1** the spongy white tissue lining the rind of oranges, lemons, and other citrus fruits. ■ Botany the spongy cellular tissue in the stems and branches of many higher plants. ■ archaic spinal marrow.
2 the essence of something: *the pith and core of socialism*.
3 vigour and conciseness of expression: *he writes with a combination of pith and exactitude*.
▶ verb [with obj.] **1** remove the pith from.
2 pierce or sever the spinal cord of (an animal) so as to kill or immobilize it.
– DERIVATIVES **pithless** adjective.
– ORIGIN Old English *pitha*, of West Germanic origin.

pithead ▶ noun the top of a mineshaft. ■ the area surrounding a pithead.

Pithecanthropus /ˌpɪθɪˈkanθrəpəs/ ▶ noun a former genus name applied to some fossil hominids found in Java in 1891. See JAVA MAN.
– ORIGIN late 19th cent.: modern Latin, from Greek *pithēkos* 'ape' + *anthrōpos* 'man'.

pith helmet ▶ noun a lightweight sun helmet made from the dried pith of the sola or a similar tropical plant.

pithivier /ˌpɪtɪˈvjeɪ/ ▶ noun a tart with a rich almond filling.
– ORIGIN from French *Pithiviers*, the name of a small town in the department of the Loiret.

pithos /ˈpɪθɒs/ ▶ noun (pl. **pithoi** /-θɔɪ/) Archaeology a large earthenware storage jar.
– ORIGIN Greek.

pithy ▶ adjective (**pithier**, **pithiest**) **1** (of a fruit or plant) containing much pith.
2 (of language or style) terse and vigorously expressive: *his characteristically pithy comments*.
– DERIVATIVES **pithily** adverb, **pithiness** noun.

pitiable ▶ adjective **1** deserving or arousing pity: *the men were in a pitiable condition*.
2 contemptibly poor or small: *a pitiable imitation of the real thing*.
– DERIVATIVES **pitiableness** noun, **pitiably** adverb.
– ORIGIN late Middle English: from Old French *piteable*, from *piteer* 'to pity'.

pitiful ▶ adjective **1** deserving or arousing pity: *two children in a very pitiful state*. ■ archaic compassionate.
2 very small or poor; inadequate: *a pitiful attempt to impress her*.
– DERIVATIVES **pitifully** adverb, **pitifulness** noun.

pitiless ▶ adjective showing no pity; cruel: *a pitiless executioner*. ■ (especially of weather) unrelentingly harsh or severe.
– DERIVATIVES **pitilessly** adverb, **pitilessness** noun.

Pitman, Sir Isaac (1813–97), English inventor of a shorthand system, published as *Stenographic Sound Hand* (1837). Pitman shorthand is still widely used in the UK and elsewhere.

pitman ▶ noun **1** (pl. **pitmen**) a coal miner.
2 (pl. **pitmans**) N. Amer. a connecting rod.

piton /ˈpiːtɒn/ ▶ noun a peg or spike driven into a rock or crack to support a climber or a rope. ■ (**the Pitons**) two conical mountains in St Lucia in the Caribbean. Reaching a height of 798 m (2,618 ft) and 750 m (2,461 ft), they rise up out of the sea just off the SW coast of the island.
– ORIGIN late 19th cent.: from French, literally 'eye bolt'.

pitot tube /ˈpiːtəʊ/ (also **pitot**) ▶ noun an open-ended right-angled tube pointing in opposition to the flow of a fluid and used to measure pressure. ■ (also **pitot-static tube**, **pitot head**) a device consisting of a pitot tube inside or adjacent to a parallel tube closed at the end but with holes along its length, the pressure difference between them being a measure of the relative velocity of the fluid, or the airspeed of an aircraft.
– ORIGIN late 19th cent.: named after Henri *Pitot* (1695–1771), French physicist.

pitpan ▶ noun a flat-bottomed boat made from a hollowed tree trunk, used in Central America.
– ORIGIN late 18th cent.: from Miskito *pitban* 'boat'.

pit pony ▶ noun Brit. historical a pony that hauled loads in a coal mine.

pit prop ▶ noun a large wooden beam used to support the roof of a coal mine.

pit saw ▶ noun historical a large saw with handles at the top and bottom, used in a vertical position by two men, one standing above the timber to be cut, the other in a pit below it.

pit stop ▶ noun Motor Racing a stop at a pit for servicing and refuelling, especially during a race. ■ informal a brief rest, especially during a journey.

Pitt the name of two British Tory statesmen: ■ **William**, 1st Earl of Chatham (1708–78); known as **Pitt the Elder**. As Secretary of State (effectively Prime Minister), he headed coalition governments 1756–61 and 1766–8. He brought the Seven Years War to an end in 1763 and also masterminded the conquest of French possessions overseas, particularly in Canada and India. ■ **William** (1759–1806), Prime Minister 1783–1801 and 1804–6, the son of Pitt the Elder; known as **Pitt the Younger**. The youngest-ever Prime Minister, he introduced reforms to reduce the national debt.

pitta[1] /ˈpɪtə/ (also **pitta bread**, N. Amer. **pita**) ▶ noun [mass noun] flat, hollow, slightly leavened bread which can be split open to hold a filling.
– ORIGIN modern Greek, literally 'cake or pie'; compare with Turkish *pide*, in a similar sense.

pitta[2] /ˈpɪtə/ ▶ noun a small ground-dwelling thrush-like bird with brightly coloured plumage and a very short tail, found in the Old World tropics. ● Family Pittidae and genus *Pitta*: many species.
– ORIGIN mid 19th cent.: from Telugu *piṭṭa* '(young) bird'.

pittance ▶ noun **1** [usu. in sing.] a very small or inadequate amount of money: *he paid his workers a pittance*.
2 historical a pious bequest to a religious house or order to provide extra food and wine at particular festivals, or on the anniversary of the benefactor's death.
– ORIGIN Middle English: from Old French *pitance*, from medieval Latin *pitantia*, from Latin *pietas* 'pity'.

pitted ▶ adjective **1** having a hollow or indentation on the surface: *his jowled and pitted face*.
2 (of a fruit) having had the stone removed: *pitted black olives*.

pitter-patter ▶ noun a sound like that of quick light steps or taps: *the soft pitter-patter of the rain on the leaves*.
▶ adverb with a sound like that of quick light steps or taps: *footsteps that go pitter-patter*.
▶ verb [no obj.] move with or make such a sound: *the rain pitter-pattered on my windows*.
– ORIGIN late Middle English: reduplication (expressing rhythmic repetition) of the verb PATTER[1].

Pitti /ˈpɪti/ an art gallery and museum in Florence, housed in the Pitti Palace (built 1440–*c*.1549). Its contents include masterpieces from the Medici collections and Gobelin tapestries.

Pitt Island see CHATHAM ISLANDS.

pittosporum /ˌpɪtəˈspɔːrəm/ ▶ noun an evergreen shrub or small tree that typically has small fragrant flowers and is chiefly native to Australasia. ● Genus *Pittosporum*, family Pittosporaceae.
– ORIGIN modern Latin, from Greek *pitta* 'pitch' (because of the resinous pulp around the seeds) + *sporos* 'seed'.

Pitt-Rivers, Augustus Henry Lane Fox (1827–1900), English archaeologist and anthropologist. He developed a new scientific approach to archaeology. His collection of weapons and artefacts from different cultures formed the basis of the ethnological museum in Oxford which bears his name.

Pittsburgh /ˈpɪtsbəːg/ an industrial city in SW Pennsylvania, at the junction of the Allegheny and Monongahela Rivers; pop. 310,037 (est. 2008).

pituitary /pɪˈtjuːɪt(ə)ri/ ▶ noun (pl. **pituitaries**) (in full **pituitary gland** or **pituitary body**) the major endocrine gland, a pea-sized body attached to the base of the brain that is important in controlling growth and development and the functioning of the other endocrine glands. Also called HYPOPHYSIS.
▶ adjective relating to the pituitary gland.
– ORIGIN early 17th cent.: from Latin *pituitarius* 'secreting phlegm', from *pituita* 'phlegm'.

pit viper ▶ noun a venomous snake of a group distinguished by visible sensory pits on the head which can detect prey by heat. They are found in both America and Asia. ● Subfamily Crotalinae, family Viperidae: numerous genera and species, including the rattlesnakes.

pity ▶ noun (pl. **pities**) **1** [mass noun] the feeling of sorrow and compassion caused by the sufferings and misfortunes of others: *her voice was full of pity*.
2 [in sing.] a cause for regret or disappointment: *it's a pity you didn't contact us first* | *what a pity we can't be friends*.
▶ verb (**pities**, **pitying**, **pitied**) [with obj.] feel sorrow for the misfortunes of: *I could see from their faces that they pitied me* | (as adj. **pitying**) *he gave her a pitying look*.
– PHRASES **for pity's sake** informal used to express impatience or make an urgent appeal: *for pity's sake, get a move on!* **more's the pity** informal used to express regret about a fact that has just been stated: *you're not the one who has to pay the bills, more's the pity*. **take** (or **have**) **pity** show compassion: *the old couple took pity on him and gave him food*.
– DERIVATIVES **pityingly** adverb.
– ORIGIN Middle English (also in the sense 'clemency, mildness'): from Old French *pite* 'compassion', from Latin *pietas* 'piety'; compare with PIETY.

pity party ▶ **noun** informal, chiefly US an instance of indulging in self-pity or eliciting pity from other people: *I'm not going to throw a pity party—I don't think many people would show up.*

pityriasis /ˌpɪtɪˈrʌɪəsɪs/ ▶ **noun** [mass noun] [with modifier] Medicine a skin disease characterized by the shedding of fine flaky scales.
– ORIGIN late 17th cent.: modern Latin, from Greek *pituriasis* 'scurf', from *pituron* 'bran'.

più mosso /pjuː ˈmɒsəʊ/ ▶ **adverb & adjective** Music (especially as a direction) more quickly.
– ORIGIN Italian.

Pius XII /ˈpʌɪəs/ (1876–1958), pope 1939–58; born *Eugenio Pacelli*. He upheld the neutrality of the Roman Catholic Church during the Second World War, and was criticized after the war for failing to condemn Nazi atrocities.

pivot ▶ **noun** the central point, pin, or shaft on which a mechanism turns or oscillates. ■ [usu. in sing.] a person or thing that plays a central part in a situation or enterprise: *the* ***pivot of*** *community life was the chapel.* ■ the person or position from which a body of troops takes its reference point when moving or changing course. ■ (also **pivotman**) chiefly N. Amer. a player in a central position in a team sport. ■ Basketball a movement in which the player holding the ball may move in any direction with one foot, while keeping the other (the pivot foot) in contact with the floor.
▶ **verb** (**pivots, pivoting, pivoted**) [no obj.] turn on or as if on a pivot: *he swung round,* ***pivoting on*** *his heel.* ■ [with obj.] provide (a mechanism) with a pivot; fix (a mechanism) on a pivot: (as adj. **pivoted**) *a pivoted bracket.* ■ (**pivot on**) depend on: *the government's reaction pivoted on the response of the Prime Minister.*
– DERIVATIVES **pivotable** adjective.
– ORIGIN late Middle English: from French, probably from the root of dialect *pue* 'tooth of a comb' and Spanish *pu(y)a* 'point'. The verb dates from the mid 19th cent.

pivotal ▶ **adjective** 1 of crucial importance in relation to the development or success of something else: *Japan's pivotal role in the world economy.*
2 fixed on or as if on a pivot: *a sliding or pivotal motion.*

pix ▶ **plural noun** informal pictures, especially photographs.
– ORIGIN 1930s: pluralized abbreviation.

pixel /ˈpɪks(ə)l, -sɛl/ ▶ **noun** Electronics a minute area of illumination on a display screen, one of many from which an image is composed.
– ORIGIN 1960s: abbreviation of *picture element* (compare with PIX).

pixelate /ˈpɪksəleɪt/ (also **pixellate** or **pixilate**) ▶ **verb** [with obj.] divide (an image) into pixels, typically for display or storage in a digital format. ■ display an image of (someone or something) on television as a small number of large pixels, typically in order to disguise someone's identity.
– DERIVATIVES **pixelation** noun.

pixie (also **pixy**) ▶ **noun** (pl. **pixies**) a supernatural being in folklore and children's stories, typically portrayed as small and human-like in form, with pointed ears and a pointed hat.
– DERIVATIVES **pixieish** adjective.
– ORIGIN mid 17th cent.: of unknown origin.

pixie hat (also **pixie hood**) ▶ **noun** a child's hat with a pointed crown.

pixilate ▶ **verb** variant spelling of PIXELATE.

pixilated (also **pixillated**) ▶ **adjective** bewildered; confused. ■ informal, dated drunk.
– ORIGIN mid 19th cent.: variant of *pixie-led*, literally 'led astray by pixies', figuratively 'confused', or from PIXIE, on the pattern of words such as *elated* and *emulated*.

pixilation (also **pixillation**) ▶ **noun** [mass noun] 1 a technique used in film whereby the movements of real people are filmed or edited in such a way that they appear to move like artificial animations.
2 the state of being pixilated.
3 variant spelling of PIXELATION (see PIXELATE).

Pizan, Christine de, see DE PISAN.

Pizarro /pɪˈzɑːrəʊ/, Francisco (*c.*1478–1541), Spanish conquistador. He defeated the Inca empire and in 1533 set up a puppet monarchy at Cuzco, building his own capital at Lima (1535), where he was assassinated.

pizza /ˈpiːtsə, ˈpɪtsə/ ▶ **noun** a dish of Italian origin, consisting of a flat round base of dough baked with a topping of tomatoes and cheese, typically with added meat, fish, or vegetables.
– ORIGIN Italian, literally 'pie'.

pizza box ▶ **noun** a computer casing which is not very tall and has a square cross section.

pizzazz (also **pizazz, pazazz,** or **pzazz**) ▶ **noun** [mass noun] informal an attractive combination of vitality and glamour: *a summer collection with pizzazz.*
– ORIGIN said to have been invented by Diana Vreeland, fashion editor of *Harper's Bazaar* in the 1930s.

pizzeria /ˌpiːtsəˈriːə, ˈpɪtsə-/ ▶ **noun** a place where pizzas are made or sold; a pizza restaurant.
– ORIGIN Italian.

pizzicato /ˌpɪtsɪˈkɑːtəʊ/ Music ▶ **adverb** (often as a direction) plucking the strings of a violin or other stringed instrument with one's finger.
▶ **adjective** performed pizzicato.
▶ **noun** (pl. **pizzicatos** or **pizzicati** /-ti/) [mass noun] the technique of playing pizzicato. ■ [count noun] a note or passage played pizzicato.
– ORIGIN Italian, literally 'pinched, twitched', past participle of *pizzicare*, based on *pizza* 'point, edge'.

pizzle ▶ **noun** chiefly Austral. or archaic the penis of an animal, especially a bull, formerly used for flogging people.
– ORIGIN late 15th cent.: from Low German *pēsel* or Flemish *pezel* (diminutives of Middle Low German *pēse* and Middle Dutch *pēze*).

PJs ▶ **plural noun** informal pyjamas.

PK ▶ **abbreviation** ■ Pakistan (international vehicle registration). ■ psychokinesis.

pK ▶ **noun** Chemistry a figure expressing the acidity or alkalinity of a solution of a weak electrolyte in a similar way to pH, equal to $-\log_{10} K$, where *K* is the dissociation (or ionization) constant of the electrolyte.
– ORIGIN from *p* as in *pH*, and *K* representing a constant.

pk ▶ **abbreviation** ■ (also **Pk**) park. ■ peak. ■ peck(s). ■ pack.

PKU ▶ **abbreviation** phenylketonuria.

PL ▶ **abbreviation** ■ Poland (international vehicle registration). ■ Computing programming language.

pl. ▶ **abbreviation** ■ (also **Pl.**) place: *3 Palmerston Pl., Edinburgh.* ■ plate (referring to illustrations in a book). ■ chiefly Military platoon. ■ Grammar plural.

PLA ▶ **abbreviation** ■ People's Liberation Army. ■ (in the UK) Port of London Authority.

placable /ˈplakəb(ə)l/ ▶ **adjective** archaic easily calmed; gentle and forgiving.
– DERIVATIVES **placability** noun.
– ORIGIN late Middle English (in the sense 'pleasing, agreeable'): from Old French, or from Latin *placabilis*, from *placare* 'appease'.

placard /ˈplakɑːd/ ▶ **noun** a printed or handwritten notice or sign for public display, either fixed to a wall or carried during a demonstration.
▶ **verb** also /plaˈkɑːd/ [with obj.] cover with notices: *they were placarding the town with posters.*
– ORIGIN late 15th cent. (denoting a warrant or licence): from Old French *placquart*, from *plaquier* 'to plaster, lay flat', from Middle Dutch *placken*. The current sense of the verb dates from the early 19th cent.

placate /pləˈkeɪt, ˈplakeɪt, ˈpleɪ-/ ▶ **verb** [with obj.] make (someone) less angry or hostile: *they attempted to placate the students with promises.*
– DERIVATIVES **placating** adjective, **placatingly** adverb, **placation** noun.
– ORIGIN late 17th cent.: from Latin *placat-* 'appeased', from the verb *placare*.

placatory /pləˈkeɪt(ə)ri/ ▶ **adjective** intended to make someone less angry or hostile; conciliatory: *his hands held in a placatory gesture.*

place ▶ **noun** 1 a particular position, point, or area in space; a location: *I can't be in two places at once | the monastery was a peaceful place | that street was* ***no place for*** *a lady* | figurative *he would always have a special place in her heart.* ■ a particular area on a larger surface: *he lashed out and cut the policeman's hand in three places.* ■ a building or area used for a specified purpose or activity: *the town has many excellent eating places | a place of worship.* ■ informal a person's home: *what about dinner at my place?* ■ a point in a book or other text reached by a reader at a particular time: *I must have lost my place in the script.*
2 a portion of space designated or available for or being used by someone: *they hurried to their places at the table | Jackie had saved her a place.* ■ a vacancy or available position: *he was offered a place at Liverpool University.* ■ the regular or proper position of something: *she put the book back in its place.* ■ a person's rank or status: *occupation structures a person's place in society.* ■ [usu. with negative] a right or privilege resulting from someone's role or position: *I'm sure she has a story to tell, but it's* ***not my place*** *to ask.* ■ the role played by or importance attached to someone or something in a particular context: *the place of computers in improving office efficiency.*
3 a position in a sequence or series, typically one ordered on the basis of merit: *his score left him in ninth place.* ■ Brit. any of the first three or sometimes four positions in a race (used especially of the second, third, or fourth positions). ■ N. Amer. the second position, especially in a horse race. ■ the degree of priority given to something: *accurate reportage* ***takes second place to*** *lurid detail.* ■ the position of a figure in a series indicated in decimal or similar notation, especially one after the decimal point: *calculate the ratios to one* ***decimal place.***
4 [in place names] a square or short street: *the lecture theatre is in New Burlington Place.* ■ a country house with its grounds.
▶ **verb** [with obj.] 1 [with obj. and adverbial] put in a particular position: *a newspaper had been placed beside my plate.* ■ cause to be in a particular situation: *enemy officers were placed under arrest | you are not placing yourself under any obligation.* ■ allocate or assign (an abstract quality) to something: *they place a great deal of emphasis on positive thought.* ■ (**be placed**) have a specified degree of advantage or convenience as a result of one's position or circumstances: [with infinitive] *the company is well placed to seize the opportunity.*
2 find a home or employment for: *the children were placed with foster-parents.* ■ dispose of (something, especially shares) by selling to a customer. ■ arrange for the recognition and implementation of (an order, bet, etc.): *they placed a contract for three boats.* ■ order or obtain a connection for (a telephone call) through an operator.
3 [with obj. and adverbial] identify or classify as being of a specified type or as holding a specified position in a sequence or hierarchy: *a survey placed the company 13th for achievement.* ■ [with obj.] [usu. with negative] be able to remember or identify (someone or something): *she eventually said she couldn't place him.* ■ (**be placed**) Brit. achieve a specified position in a race: *he was placed eleventh in the long individual race.* ■ [no obj.] be among the first three or four in a race (or the first three in the US).
4 Rugby & American Football score (a goal) by a place kick.
– PHRASES **give place to** be succeeded or replaced by. **go places** informal travel. ■ be increasingly successful: *a pop star who's definitely going places.* **in place 1** working or ready to work; established: *contingency plans should be in place | the rules which we shall* ***put in place*** *in the months ahead meet these criteria.* **2** N. Amer. on the spot; not travelling any distance. **in place of** instead of. **keep someone in his** (or **her**) **place** keep someone from becoming presumptuous. **out of place** not in the proper position; disarranged. ■ in a setting where one is or feels inappropriate or incongruous. **a place in the sun** a position of favour or advantage. **put oneself in another's place** consider a situation from another's point of view. **put someone in his** (or **her**) **place** deflate or humiliate someone regarded as being presumptuous. **take place** occur: *people laid flowers at the spot where the crash took place.* **take one's place** take up one's usual or recognized position. **take the place of** replace.
– DERIVATIVES **placeless** adjective.
– ORIGIN Middle English: from Old French, from an alteration of Latin *platea* 'open space', from Greek *plateia (hodos)* 'broad (way)'.

place bet ▶ **noun** (in the UK) a bet on a horse to win a place in a race, usually first, second, or third. ■ (in the US) a bet on a horse to come first or second.
– DERIVATIVES **place betting** noun.

placebo /pləˈsiːbəʊ/ ▶ **noun** (pl. **placebos**) a medicine or procedure prescribed for the psychological benefit to the patient rather than for any physiological effect. ■ a substance that has no therapeutic effect, used as a control in testing new drugs. ■ a measure designed merely to humour or placate someone.
– ORIGIN late 18th cent.: from Latin, literally 'I shall be acceptable or pleasing', from *placere* 'to please'.

placebo effect ▶ **noun** a beneficial effect produced by a placebo drug or treatment, which cannot be attributed to the properties of the placebo itself, and must therefore be due to the patient's belief in that treatment.

P

place brick ▶ noun a brick which has been imperfectly fired due to being on the outward side of the kiln.

place card ▶ noun a card bearing a person's name, placed on a table to indicate where they should sit.

placeholder ▶ noun **1** Mathematics a significant zero in the decimal representation of a number. ■ a symbol or piece of text used in a mathematical expression or in an instruction in a computer program to denote a missing quantity or operator.
2 Linguistics an element of a sentence that is required by syntactic constraints but carries little or no semantic information, for example the word *it* as a subject in *it is a pity that she left*, where the true subject is *that she left*.

place kick American Football, Rugby, & Soccer ▶ noun a kick made after the ball is first placed on the ground.
▶ verb (**place-kick**) [no obj.] (often as noun **place-kicking**) take a place kick.
– DERIVATIVES **place-kicker** noun.

placeman ▶ noun (pl. **placemen**) Brit. derogatory a person appointed to a position, especially in government service, for personal profit and as a reward for political support.

place mat ▶ noun a small mat underneath a person's dining plate, used to protect the table from the heat of the plate and food.

placement ▶ noun [mass noun] the action of placing someone or something somewhere: *the proper placement of microphones*. ■ the action of finding a home, job, or school for someone: *a baby put up for adoption may wait up to three years or more for placement* | [count noun] *a placement in a special school*. ■ Brit. the temporary posting of someone in a workplace to enable them to gain work experience: *students spend one year on industrial placement*.

place name ▶ noun the name of a geographical location, such as a town, lake, or a range of hills.

placenta /plə'sɛntə/ ▶ noun (pl. **placentae** /-tiː/ or **placentas**) **1** a flattened circular organ in the uterus of pregnant eutherian mammals, nourishing and maintaining the fetus through the umbilical cord.

> The placenta consists of vascular tissue in which oxygen and nutrients can pass from the mother's blood into that of the fetus, and waste products can pass in the reverse direction. The placenta is expelled from the uterus at the birth of the fetus, when it is often called the afterbirth. Marsupials and monotremes do not develop placentas.

2 Botany (in flowers) part of the ovary wall to which the ovules are attached.
– ORIGIN late 17th cent.: from Latin, from Greek *plakous, plakount-* 'flat cake', based on *plax, plak-* 'flat plate'.

P

placental ▶ adjective relating to a placenta. ■ Zoology relating to or denoting mammals that possess a placenta; eutherian.
▶ noun Zoology a placental mammal. See **EUTHERIA**.

placental abruption ▶ noun see **ABRUPTION**.

placenta praevia /'priːvɪə/ (US **placenta previa**) ▶ noun [mass noun] Medicine a condition in which the placenta partially or wholly blocks the neck of the uterus, so interfering with normal delivery of a baby.
– ORIGIN early 19th cent.: from **PLACENTA** and Latin *praevia* 'going before', feminine of *praevius*.

placentation /ˌplas(ə)n'teɪʃ(ə)n/ ▶ noun [mass noun] Anatomy & Zoology the formation or arrangement of a placenta or placentae in a woman's or female animal's uterus. ■ Botany the arrangement of the placenta or placentae in the ovary of a flower.

placer¹ ▶ noun [often as modifier] a deposit of sand or gravel in the bed of a river or lake, containing particles of valuable minerals: *placer gold deposits*.
– ORIGIN early 19th cent.: from Latin American Spanish, literally 'deposit, shoal'; related to *placel* 'sandbank', from *plaza* 'a place'.

placer² ▶ noun **1** [with modifier] a person or animal gaining a specified position in a competition or race: *last year's fifth placer had a good run*.
2 a person who positions, sets, or arranges something: *he was a shrewd placer of the ball*. ■ a person who puts the material ready for firing in a pottery kiln.
3 Brit. informal a dealer in stolen goods.

place setting ▶ noun a complete set of crockery and cutlery provided for one person at a meal.

placet /'pleɪsɛt/ ▶ noun Brit. an affirmative vote in a Church or university assembly.
– ORIGIN Latin, literally 'it pleases'.

place value ▶ noun the numerical value that a digit has by virtue of its position in a number.

placid ▶ adjective not easily upset or excited: *a placid, contented man*. ■ calm and peaceful, with little movement or activity: *the placid waters of a small lake*.
– DERIVATIVES **placidity** noun, **placidly** adverb, **placidness** noun.
– ORIGIN early 17th cent.: from French *placide*, from Latin *placidus*, from *placere* 'to please'.

placing ▶ noun **1** [mass noun] the action of putting something in position or the fact of being positioned: *the placing of the lights*. ■ the action of making an order.
2 (usu. **placings**) a ranking one is given during or after a sports race or other competition.
3 a post that is found for a job-seeker.
4 a sale or new issue of a large quantity of shares.

placket ▶ noun an opening or slit in a garment, covering fastenings or for access to a pocket, or the flap of fabric under such an opening.
– ORIGIN early 17th cent.: variant of **PLACARD** in an obsolete sense 'garment worn under an open coat or gown'.

placoderm /'plakə(ʊ)dəːm/ ▶ noun a fossil fish of the Devonian period, having the front part of the body encased in broad flat bony plates. ● Class Placodermi: several orders.
– ORIGIN mid 19th cent.: from Greek *plax, plak-* 'flat plate' + *derma* 'skin'.

placodont /'plakə(ʊ)dɒnt/ ▶ noun a fossil marine shellfish-eating reptile of the Triassic period, having short flat grinding palatal teeth and sometimes a turtle-like shell. ● Suborder Placodontia, superorder Sauropterygia: several families and genera, including *Placodus*.
– ORIGIN late 19th cent.: from Greek *plax, plak-* 'flat plate' + *odous, odont-* 'tooth'.

placoid /'plakɔɪd/ ▶ adjective Zoology (of fish scales) tooth-like, being made of dentine with a pointed backward projection of enamel, as in sharks and rays. Compare with **CTENOID** and **GANOID**.
– ORIGIN mid 19th cent.: from Greek *plax, plak-* 'flat plate' + **-OID**.

Placozoa /ˌplakə'zəʊə/ ▶ plural noun Zoology a minor phylum that contains a single minute marine invertebrate (*Trichoplax adhaerens*), which has a flattened body with two cell layers and is the simplest known metazoan.
– ORIGIN modern Latin (plural), from Greek *plakos* 'flat' + *zōia* 'animals'.

plafond /pla'fɔ̃(d)/ ▶ noun an ornately decorated ceiling.
– ORIGIN French, from *plat* 'flat' + *fond* 'bottom, base'.

plagal /'pleɪg(ə)l/ ▶ adjective Music (of a church mode) containing notes between the dominant and the note an octave higher. Compare with **AUTHENTIC**.
– ORIGIN late 16th cent.: from medieval Latin *plagalis*, from *plaga* 'plagal mode', from Latin *plagius*, from medieval Greek *plagios* (*hēkhos*) 'plagal (mode)', from Greek *plagos* 'side'.

plagal cadence ▶ noun Music a cadence in which the chord of the subdominant immediately precedes that of the tonic.

plage ▶ noun **1** /plɑːʒ/ dated a beach by the sea, especially at a fashionable resort.
2 /pleɪdʒ/ Astronomy an unusually bright region on the sun.
– ORIGIN French.

plagiarism ▶ noun [mass noun] the practice of taking someone else's work or ideas and passing them off as one's own.
– DERIVATIVES **plagiarist** noun, **plagiaristic** adjective.
– ORIGIN early 17th cent.: from Latin *plagiarius* 'kidnapper' (from *plagium* 'a kidnapping', from Greek *plagion*) + **-ISM**.

plagiarize /'pleɪdʒərʌɪz/ (also **plagiarise**) ▶ verb [with obj.] take (the work or an idea of someone else) and pass it off as one's own. ■ take the work or an idea of (someone) and pass it off as one's own.
– DERIVATIVES **plagiarizer** noun.

plagio- /'pleɪdʒɪəʊ, 'plagɪəʊ/ ▶ combining form oblique: *plagioclase*.
– ORIGIN from Greek *plagios* 'slanting', from *plagos* 'side'.

plagioclase /'pleɪdʒɪə(ʊ)kleɪz, 'plagɪəʊ-/ (also **plagioclase feldspar**) ▶ noun [mass noun] a form of feldspar consisting of aluminosilicates of sodium and/or calcium, common in igneous rocks and typically white.
– ORIGIN mid 19th cent.: from **PLAGIO-** 'oblique' + Greek *klasis* 'cleavage' (because originally characterized as having two cleavages at an oblique angle).

plague ▶ noun **1** (usu. **the plague**) a contagious bacterial disease characterized by fever and delirium, typically with the formation of buboes (see **BUBONIC PLAGUE**) and sometimes infection of the lungs (**pneumonic plague**). ■ any contagious disease that spreads rapidly and kills many people.
2 an unusually large number of insects or animals infesting a place and causing damage: *a plague of locusts*.
3 [in sing.] a thing causing trouble or irritation: *staff theft is usually **the plague of** restaurants*. ■ (**a plague on**) archaic used as a curse: *a plague on all their houses!* [echoing Shakespeare's *Romeo and Juliet* (III. i. 94).]
▶ verb (**plagues, plaguing, plagued**) [with obj.] cause continual trouble or distress to: *he has been plagued by ill health*. ■ pester or harass (someone) continually: *he was plaguing her with questions*.
– ORIGIN late Middle English: Latin *plaga* 'stroke, wound', probably from Greek (Doric dialect) *plaga*, from a base meaning 'strike'.

plaguy /'pleɪgi/ (also **plaguey**) ▶ adjective informal troublesome or annoying.

plaice ▶ noun (pl. **same**) a North Atlantic flatfish which is a commercially important food fish. ● Two species in the family Pleuronectidae: the European *Pleuronectes platessa*, often found in very shallow water, and the American *Hippoglossoides platessoides*, found in deeper waters.
– ORIGIN Middle English: from Old French *plaiz*, from late Latin *platessa*, from Greek *platus* 'broad'.

plaid /plad/ ▶ noun [mass noun] chequered or tartan twilled cloth, typically made of wool. ■ [count noun] a long piece of tartan worn over the shoulder as part of Scottish Highland dress.
– DERIVATIVES **plaided** adjective.
– ORIGIN early 16th cent.: from Scottish Gaelic *plaide* 'blanket', of unknown ultimate origin.

Plaid Cymru /plʌɪd 'kʌmri/ the Welsh Nationalist party, founded in 1925 and dedicated to seeking autonomy for Wales. It won its first parliamentary seat in 1966, and since 1974 has maintained a small number of representatives in Parliament.
– ORIGIN Welsh, 'party of Wales'.

plain¹ ▶ adjective **1** not decorated or elaborate; simple or basic in character: *good plain food* | *everyone dined at a plain wooden table*. ■ without a pattern; in only one colour: *a plain fabric*. ■ bearing no indication as to contents or affiliation: *donations can be put in a plain envelope*. ■ (of paper) without lines.
2 easy to perceive or understand; clear: *the advantages were plain to see* | *it was plain that something was wrong*. ■ [attrib.] (of written or spoken usage) clearly expressed, without the use of technical or abstruse terms: *an insurance policy written in plain English*. ■ not using concealment or deception; frank: *there were indrawn breaths at such plain speaking*.
3 not distinguished by any particular beauty; ordinary looking: *a plain, round-faced woman*. ■ having no pretensions; not remarkable or special: *a plain, honest man with no nonsense about him*.
4 [attrib.] sheer; simple (used for emphasis): *the main problem is just plain exhaustion*.
5 (of a knitting stitch) made by putting the needle through the front of the stitch from left to right. Compare with **PURL¹**.
▶ adverb informal **1** [as submodifier] used for emphasis: *perhaps the youth was just plain stupid*.
2 clearly or unequivocally: *I'm finished with you, I'll tell you plain*.
▶ noun a large area of flat land with few trees.
– PHRASES **as plain as the nose on someone's face** informal very obvious. **plain and simple** informal used to emphasize the statement preceding or following: *she was a nuisance, plain and simple*. **plain as day** informal very clearly.
– DERIVATIVES **plainly** adverb [as sentence adverb] *her mother was plainly anxious to leave*, **plainness** noun.
– ORIGIN Middle English: from Old French *plain*, from Latin *planus*, from a base meaning 'flat'.

plain² ▶ verb [no obj.] archaic mourn or lament. ■ complain. ■ emit a mournful or plaintive sound.
– ORIGIN Middle English: from Old French *plaindre*, from Latin *plangere* 'to lament'.

plain card ▶ noun a playing card that is neither a trump nor a court card.

plainchant ▶ noun another term for **PLAINSONG**.

plain chocolate ▶ noun [mass noun] Brit. dark, slightly bitter, chocolate without added milk.

plain clothes ▶ plural noun ordinary clothes rather than uniform, especially when worn by police officers.
– DERIVATIVES **plain-clothed** adjective.

plain dealing ▶ noun [mass noun] honest and straightforward behaviour towards others.

plain flour ▶ noun [mass noun] Brit. flour that does not contain a raising agent.

plain hunting ▶ noun another term for **HUNTING** (sense 3).

Plain People ▶ plural noun US the Amish, the Mennonites, and the Dunkers, three strict Christian sects emphasizing a simple way of life.

plain sailing ▶ noun [mass noun] [often with negative] smooth and easy progress in a process or activity: *team-building was not all plain sailing.*
– ORIGIN mid 18th cent.: probably a popular use of *plane sailing*, denoting the practice of determining a ship's position on the theory that it is moving on a plane.

plain sawing ▶ noun [mass noun] the method or action of sawing timber tangential to the growth rings, so that the rings make angles of less than 45° with the faces of the boards produced.

plain service ▶ noun a church service without music.

Plains Indian ▶ noun a member of any of various North American Indian peoples who formerly inhabited the Great Plains area.

> Although a few of the Plains Indian peoples were sedentary farmers, most, including the Blackfoot, Cheyenne, and Comanche, were nomadic buffalo hunters, who gathered in tribes during the summer and dispersed into family groups in the winter.

plainsman ▶ noun (pl. **plainsmen**) a person who lives on a plain, especially a frontiersman who lived on the Great Plains of North America.

Plains of Abraham a plateau beside the city of Quebec, overlooking the St Lawrence River. It was the scene in 1759 of a battle in which the British army under General Wolfe, having scaled the heights above the city under cover of darkness, surprised and defeated the French. The battle led to British control over Canada.

plainsong ▶ noun [mass noun] unaccompanied church music sung in unison in medieval modes and in free rhythm corresponding to the accentuation of the words, which are taken from the liturgy. Compare with **GREGORIAN CHANT**.
– ORIGIN late Middle English: translating Latin *cantus planus*.

plain-spoken ▶ adjective outspoken or blunt.

plain suit ▶ noun (in bridge and whist) a suit that is not trumps.

plains-wanderer ▶ noun a short-tailed quail-like bird found in the sparse grasslands of SE Australia. ● *Pedionomus torquatus*, the only member of the family Pedionomidae.

plaint ▶ noun **1** Law, Brit. an accusation or charge.
2 chiefly literary a complaint or lamentation.
– ORIGIN Middle English: from Old French *plainte*, feminine past participle of *plaindre* 'complain', or from Old French *plaint*, from Latin *planctus* 'beating of the breast'.

plain text ▶ noun [mass noun] text that is not written in code.

plaintiff ▶ noun Law a person who brings a case against another in a court of law. Compare with **DEFENDANT**.
– ORIGIN late Middle English: from Old French *plaintif* 'plaintive' (used as a noun). The *-f* ending has come down through Law French; the word was originally the same as *plaintive*.

> **USAGE** In England and Wales the term **plaintiff** was officially replaced by **claimant** in 1999.

plain tiger ▶ noun a migratory African butterfly related to the monarch, with orange, white, and black wing markings. ● *Danaus chrysippus*, subfamily Danainae, family Nymphalidae.

plain tile ▶ noun a kind of flat tile used in roofing.

plaintive ▶ adjective sounding sad and mournful: *a plaintive cry.*
– DERIVATIVES **plaintively** adverb, **plaintiveness** noun.
– ORIGIN late Middle English: from Old French *plaintif, -ive*, from *plainte* 'lamentation' (see **PLAINT**).

plain weave ▶ noun [mass noun] a style of weave in which the weft alternates over and under the warp.

plait /plat/ ▶ noun **1** Brit. a single length of hair, straw, rope, or other material made up of three or more interlaced strands.
2 archaic term for **PLEAT**.
▶ verb [with obj.] form (hair, straw, rope, or other material) into a plait or plaits. ■ make (something) by forming material into a plait or plaits: *a basket plaited from strips of flax.*
– ORIGIN late Middle English: from Old French *pleit* 'a fold', based on Latin *plicare* 'to fold'. The word was formerly often pronounced like 'plate'; since late Middle English there has been an alternative spelling *plat*, to which the current pronunciation corresponds.

plan ▶ noun **1** a detailed proposal for doing or achieving something: *the UN peace plan.* ■ [with modifier] a scheme for the regular payment of contributions towards a pension, savings account, or insurance policy: *a personal pension plan.*
2 an intention or decision about what one is going to do: *I have no plans to retire.*
3 a detailed map or diagram: *a street plan.* ■ a drawing or diagram made by projection on a horizontal plane, especially one showing the layout of a building or one floor of a building. Compare with **ELEVATION** (sense 3). ■ a diagram showing how something will be arranged: *look at the seating plan.* ■ (in the Methodist Church) a document listing the preachers for all the services in a circuit during a given period.
▶ verb (**plans, planning, planned**) [with obj.] **1** decide on and make arrangements for in advance: *they were planning a trip to Egypt* | [with infinitive] *he plans to fly on Wednesday* | [no obj.] *we* ***plan on*** *getting married in the near future.*
2 design or make a plan of (something to be made or built): *she had planned the garden from scratch.*
– PHRASES **someone's** (or **the**) **best plan** a person's (or the) most sensible course of action: *William's best plan would be to get a job.* **go according to plan** happen as one arranged or intended. **make a plan** S. African devise a way of overcoming difficulties. **plan of action** (or **campaign** or **attack**) an organized programme of measures to be taken in order to achieve a goal.
– ORIGIN late 17th cent.: from French, from earlier *plant* 'ground plan, plane surface', influenced in sense by Italian *pianta* 'plan of building'. Compare with **PLANT**.

planar /ˈpleɪnə/ ▶ adjective Mathematics relating to or in the form of a plane: *planar surfaces.*

planarian /pləˈnɛːrɪən/ ▶ noun a free-living flatworm which has a three-branched intestine and a tubular pharynx, typically located halfway down the body. ● Order Tricladida, class Turbellaria: *Planaria* and other genera.
– ORIGIN mid 19th cent.: from modern Latin *Planaria* (feminine of Latin *planarius* 'lying flat') + **-IAN**.

planation /pləˈneɪʃ(ə)n/ ▶ noun [mass noun] the levelling of a landscape by erosion.
– ORIGIN late 19th cent.: from **PLANE[1]** + **-ATION**.

planche /plɑːntʃ, plɑːnʃ/ ▶ noun (in gymnastics) a position in which the body is held parallel with the ground by the arms, performed on the parallel bars, rings, or floor.
– ORIGIN early 20th cent.: French, literally 'plank'.

planchet /ˈplɑːn(t)ʃɪt/ ▶ noun a plain metal disc from which a coin is made.
– ORIGIN early 17th cent.: diminutive of earlier *planch* 'slab of metal', from Old French *planche* 'plank, slab'.

planchette /plɑːnˈʃɛt/ ▶ noun a small board supported on castors, typically heart-shaped and fitted with a vertical pencil, used for automatic writing and in seances.
– ORIGIN mid 19th cent.: from French, literally 'small plank', diminutive of *planche*.

Planck /plaŋk/, Max (Karl Ernst Ludwig) (1858–1947), German theoretical physicist who founded quantum theory, announcing the radiation law named after him in 1900. Nobel Prize for Physics (1918).

Planck's constant (also **Planck constant**) ▶ noun Physics a fundamental constant, equal to the energy of a quantum of electromagnetic radiation divided by its frequency, with a value of 6.626×10^{-34} joules.

Planck's law ▶ noun Physics a law, forming the basis of quantum theory, which states that electromagnetic radiation from heated bodies is not emitted as a continuous flow but is made up of discrete units or quanta of energy, the size of which involve a fundamental physical constant (Planck's constant).

plane[1] ▶ noun **1** a flat surface on which a straight line joining any two points on it would wholly lie: *the horizontal plane.* ■ an imaginary flat surface through or joining material objects: *the planets orbit the sun in roughly the same plane.* ■ a flat or level surface of a material object: *the* ***plane of*** *his forehead.* ■ a flat surface producing lift by the action of air or water over and under it.
2 a level of existence, thought, or development: *everything is connected on the spiritual plane.*
▶ adjective [attrib.] completely level or flat: *a plane surface.* ■ relating to only two-dimensional surfaces or magnitudes: *plane and solid geometry.*
▶ verb [no obj., with adverbial] (of a bird or an airborne object) soar without moving the wings; glide: *seagulls swooped and planed overhead.* ■ [no obj.] (of a boat, surfboard, etc.) skim over the surface of water as a result of lift produced by hydrodynamic means.
– ORIGIN early 17th cent.: from Latin *planum* 'flat surface', neuter of the adjective *planus* 'plain'. The adjective was suggested by French *plan(e)* 'flat'. The word was introduced to differentiate the geometrical senses, previously expressed by **PLAIN[1]**, from the latter's other meanings.

plane[2] ▶ noun an aeroplane.
▶ verb [no obj., with adverbial of direction] travel in an aeroplane.
– ORIGIN early 20th cent.: shortened form.

plane[3] ▶ noun a tool consisting of a block with a projecting steel blade, used to smooth a wooden or other surface by paring shavings from it.
▶ verb [with obj.] smooth (wood or other material) with a plane: *plane the edges of the wood to a smooth finish.* ■ [with obj. and adverbial] reduce or remove (unwanted material) with a plane: *plane off any swollen wood before repainting.*
– ORIGIN Middle English: from a variant of obsolete French *plaine* 'planing instrument', from late Latin *plana* (in the same sense), from Latin *planare* 'make level', from *planus* 'plain, level'.

plane[4] (also **plane tree**) ▶ noun a tall spreading tree of the northern hemisphere, with maple-like leaves and bark which peels in uneven patches. ● Genus *Platanus*, family Platanaceae. See also **LONDON PLANE, CHINAR**.
– ORIGIN late Middle English: from Old French, from Latin *platanus*, from Greek *platanos*, from *platus* 'broad'.

planeload ▶ noun an amount of cargo or number of passengers that will fill an aircraft: ***a planeload of*** *holidaymakers.*

plane polarization ▶ noun [mass noun] a process restricting the vibrations of electromagnetic radiation, especially light, to one direction.
– DERIVATIVES **plane-polarized** adjective.

planer ▶ noun another term for **PLANE[3]**.

planet ▶ noun a celestial body moving in an elliptical orbit round a star. ■ (**the planet**) the earth: *no generation has the right to pollute the planet.* ■ chiefly Astrology & historical a celestial body distinguished from the fixed stars by having an apparent motion of its own (including the moon and sun), especially with reference to its supposed influence on people and events.

> The planets of the solar system are either gas giants—Jupiter, Saturn, Uranus, and Neptune—or smaller rocky bodies—Mercury, Venus, Earth, and Mars. Pluto, formerly regarded as the ninth planet, was in 2006 reclassified as a dwarf planet. The minor planets, or asteroids, orbit mainly between the orbits of Mars and Jupiter. Only Earth and Venus have substantial atmospheres.

– PHRASES **what planet are you on?** Brit. informal used to indicate that someone is out of touch with reality.
– DERIVATIVES **planetologist** noun, **planetology** noun.
– ORIGIN Middle English: from Old French *planete*, from late Latin *planeta, planetes*, from Greek *planētēs* 'wanderer, planet', from *planan* 'wander'.

plane table ▶ noun a surveying instrument used for direct plotting in the field, with a circular drawing board and pivoted alidade.

planetarium /ˌplanɪˈtɛːrɪəm/ ▶ noun (pl. **planetariums** or **planetaria** /-rɪə/) **1** a domed building in which images of stars, planets, and constellations are projected for public entertainment or education. ■ a device used to project images of stars, planets, and constellations.
2 another term for **ORRERY**.
– ORIGIN mid 18th cent.: modern Latin, from Latin *planetarius* 'relating to the planets'.

planetary ▶ **adjective** relating or belonging to a planet or planets. ■ relating to the earth as a planet.
– ORIGIN late 16th cent.: from late Latin *planetarius* 'relating to the planets' (recorded only as a noun meaning 'astrologer'), from *planeta* 'planet'.

planetary gear (also **planetary wheel**) ▶ **noun** another term for **PLANET GEAR**.

planetary nebula ▶ **noun** Astronomy a ring-shaped nebula formed by an expanding shell of gas round an ageing star.

planetesimal /ˌplanɪˈtɛsɪm(ə)l/ Astronomy ▶ **noun** a minute planet; a body which could come together with many others under gravitation to form a planet.
▶ **adjective** denoting or relating to planetesimals.
– ORIGIN early 20th cent.: from **PLANET**, on the pattern of *infinitesimal*.

planetfall ▶ **noun** [mass noun] (chiefly in science fiction) a landing or arrival on a planet after a journey through space.

planet gear (also **planet wheel**) ▶ **noun** see **SUN-AND-PLANET GEAR**.

planetoid ▶ **noun** another term for **ASTEROID**.

planform ▶ **noun** the shape or outline of an aircraft wing as projected upon a horizontal plane.

plangent /ˈplan(d)ʒ(ə)nt/ ▶ **adjective** chiefly literary (of a sound) loud and resonant, with a mournful tone.
– DERIVATIVES **plangency** noun, **plangently** adverb.
– ORIGIN early 19th cent.: from Latin *plangent-* 'lamenting', from the verb *plangere*.

planification /ˌplanɪfɪˈkeɪʃ(ə)n/ ▶ **noun** [mass noun] the management of resources according to a plan of economic or political development.
– ORIGIN 1950s: from French *planifier* 'to plan' (see **-FICATION**).

planigale /ˈplanɪgeɪl, ˌplanɪˈgeɪli/ ▶ **noun** a very small mouse-like carnivorous marsupial with a long tail, native to Australia and New Guinea. ● Genus *Planigale*, family Dasyuridae: several species.
– ORIGIN 1940s: modern Latin, from Latin *planus* 'flat' (referring to the flat skull of the marsupial), on the pattern of *phascogale*.

planigraphy /pləˈnɪgrəfi/ ▶ **noun** [mass noun] Medicine the process of obtaining a visual representation of a plane section through living tissue, by such techniques as tomography, ultrasonography, etc.
– ORIGIN 1930s: from Dutch *planigraphie*, from Latin *planus* 'flat, level' + Greek *-graphia* (see **-GRAPHY**).

planimeter /pləˈnɪmɪtə/ ▶ **noun** an instrument for mechanically measuring the area of a plane figure.
– DERIVATIVES **planimetric** adjective, **planimetry** noun.
– ORIGIN mid 19th cent.: from French *planimètre*, from Latin *planus* 'level' + *-mètre* '(instrument) measuring'.

planish /ˈplanɪʃ/ ▶ **verb** [with obj.] flatten (sheet metal) with a smooth-faced hammer or between rollers.
– ORIGIN late Middle English (in the sense 'make level'): from obsolete French *planiss-*, lengthened stem of *planir* 'to smooth', from *plain* 'smooth, level'.

planisphere /ˈplanɪsfɪə/ ▶ **noun** a map formed by the projection of a sphere or part of a sphere on a plane, especially an adjustable circular star map that shows the appearance of the heavens at a specific time and place.
– DERIVATIVES **planispheric** /-ˈsfɛrɪk/ adjective.
– ORIGIN late Middle English *planisperie*, from medieval Latin *planisphaerium*, from Latin *planus* 'level' + *sphaera* 'sphere'; later influenced by French *planisphère*.

plank ▶ **noun 1** a long, thin, flat piece of timber, used especially in building and flooring.
2 a fundamental point of a political or other programme: *the central plank of the bill is the curb on industrial polluters*.
3 Brit. informal a stupid person.
▶ **verb** [with obj.] **1** make, provide, or cover with planks: (as adj. **planked**) *the planked wooden steps*.
2 informal, chiefly N. Amer. & Irish put or set (something) down forcefully or abruptly: *Ned planked the glasses in front of him*.
3 Scottish hide (something): *he had planked £1,000 under the mattress*. [alteration of the verb **PLANT**.]
– PHRASES **walk the plank** (in former times) be forced by pirates to walk blindfold along a plank over the side of a ship to one's death in the sea.
– ORIGIN Middle English: from Old Northern French *planke*, from late Latin *planca* 'board', feminine (used as a noun) of *plancus* 'flat-footed'.

planking ▶ **noun** [mass noun] planks collectively, especially when used for flooring or as part of a boat.

planktivorous /ˌplaŋkˈtɪv(ə)rəs/ ▶ **adjective** feeding on plankton.

plankton /ˈplaŋ(k)t(ə)n, -tɒn/ ▶ **noun** [mass noun] the small and microscopic organisms drifting or floating in the sea or fresh water, consisting chiefly of diatoms, protozoans, small crustaceans, and the eggs and larval stages of larger animals. Many animals are adapted to feed on plankton, especially by filtering the water. Compare with **NEKTON**.
– DERIVATIVES **planktic** adjective, **planktonic** adjective.
– ORIGIN late 19th cent.: from German, from Greek *planktos* 'wandering', from the base of *plazein* 'wander'.

planned economy ▶ **noun** an economy in which production, investment, prices, and incomes are determined centrally by the government.

planned obsolescence ▶ **noun** [mass noun] a policy of producing consumer goods that rapidly become obsolete and so require replacing, achieved by frequent changes in design, termination of the supply of spare parts, and the use of non-durable materials.

planner ▶ **noun 1** a person who makes plans. ■ a person who controls or plans urban development: *city planners*.
2 a list or chart with information that is an aid to planning: *my day planner*.

planning ▶ **noun** [mass noun] the process of making plans for something. ■ the control of urban development by a local government authority, from which a licence must be obtained to build a new property or change an existing one: *planning applications*.

planning blight ▶ **noun** [mass noun] the reduction of economic activity or property values in a particular area resulting from expected or possible future development or restriction of development.

planning gain ▶ **noun** [mass noun] provision by a developer to include in a proposal projects beneficial to a community in exchange for permission for a commercially promising but potentially unacceptable development.

planning permission ▶ **noun** [mass noun] Brit. formal permission from a local authority for the erection or alteration of buildings or similar development.

plano- /ˈpleɪnəʊ/ ▶ **combining form** level; flat: *planoconvex* | *planometer*.
– ORIGIN from Latin *planus* 'flat'.

planoconcave ▶ **adjective** (of a lens) with one surface plane and the opposite one concave.

planoconvex ▶ **adjective** (of a lens) with one surface plane and the opposite one convex.

planographic ▶ **adjective** Printing relating to or denoting a printing process in which the printing surface is flat, as in lithography.
– DERIVATIVES **planography** noun.

planometer /pləˈnɒmɪtə/ ▶ **noun** a flat plate, typically of cast iron, used in metalwork as a standard gauge for plane surfaces.

plant ▶ **noun 1** a living organism of the kind exemplified by trees, shrubs, herbs, grasses, ferns, and mosses, typically growing in a permanent site, absorbing water and inorganic substances through its roots, and synthesizing nutrients in its leaves by photosynthesis using the green pigment chlorophyll. ■ a small plant, as distinct from a shrub or tree: *garden plants*.

> Plants differ from animals in lacking specialized sense organs, having no capacity for voluntary movement, having cell walls, and growing to suit their surroundings rather than having a fixed body plan.

2 a place where an industrial or manufacturing process takes place: *a giant car plant*. ■ [mass noun] machinery used in an industrial or manufacturing process: *inadequate investment in new plant*.
3 a person placed in a group as a spy or informer: *we thought he was a CIA plant spreading disinformation*. ■ a thing put among someone's belongings to incriminate or compromise them.
4 Snooker a shot in which the cue ball is made to strike one of two touching or nearly touching balls with the result that the second is potted.
▶ **verb** [with obj.] **1** put (a seed, bulb, or plant) in the ground so that it can grow: *we planted a lot of fruit trees*. ■ cover or supply (an area of land) with plants: *the garden is planted with herbs*. ■ (**plant something out**) place a plant in the ground out of doors so it can grow, especially after growing it from seed in an indoor environment. ■ informal bury (someone).
2 [with obj. and adverbial of place] set or place in a particular position: *he planted himself squarely in front of her* | *she planted a kiss on his cheek*. ■ establish (an idea) in someone's mind: *the seed of doubt is planted in his mind*. ■ secretly place (a bomb that is set to go off at a later time). ■ put or hide (something) among someone's belongings to compromise or incriminate the owner: *they claimed that the drugs had been planted on them by police*. ■ send (someone) to join a group or organization to act as a spy or informer. ■ found or establish (a colony, city, or community). ■ deposit (young fish, spawn, oysters, etc.) in a river or lake.
– PHRASES **have** (or **keep**) **one's feet firmly planted on the ground** be (or remain) level-headed and sensible.
– DERIVATIVES **plantable** adjective, **plantlet** noun, **plant-like** adjective.
– ORIGIN Old English *plante* 'seedling', *plantian* (verb), from Latin *planta* 'sprout, cutting' (later influenced by French *plante*) and *plantare* 'plant, fix in a place'.

Plantagenet /planˈtadʒɪnɪt/ ▶ **adjective** relating to the English royal dynasty which held the throne from the accession of Henry II in 1154 until the death of Richard III in 1485.
▶ **noun** a member of the Plantagenet dynasty.
– ORIGIN from Latin *planta genista* 'sprig of broom', said to be worn as a crest by and given as a nickname to Geoffrey, count of Anjou, the father of Henry II.

plantain[1] /ˈplantɪn, -teɪn/ ▶ **noun** a low-growing plant which typically has a rosette of leaves and a slender green flower spike, occurring widely as a weed of lawns. ● Genus *Plantago*, family Plantaginaceae: many species.
– ORIGIN late Middle English: from Old French, from Latin *plantago*, *plantagin-*, from *planta* 'sole of the foot' (because of its broad prostrate leaves).

plantain[2] /ˈplantɪn, -teɪn/ ▶ **noun 1** a banana containing high levels of starch and little sugar, which is harvested green and widely used as a cooked vegetable in the tropics.
2 the plant which bears the plantain. ● *Musa* × *paradisiaca*, family Musaceae.
– ORIGIN mid 16th cent.: from Spanish *plá(n)tano*, probably by assimilation of a South American word to the Spanish *plá(n)tano* 'plane tree'.

plantain-eater ▶ **noun** an African bird of the turaco family, especially a grey one with a long tail. ● Family Musophagidae, in particular two species in the genus *Crinifer*.

plantain lily ▶ **noun** another term for **HOSTA**.

plantar /ˈplantə/ ▶ **adjective** Anatomy relating to the sole of the foot.
– ORIGIN early 18th cent.: from Latin *plantaris*, from *planta* 'sole'.

plantation ▶ **noun 1** an estate on which crops such as coffee, sugar, and tobacco are grown. ■ an area in which trees have been planted, especially for commercial purposes.
2 [mass noun] colonization or settlement of emigrants, especially of English and then Scottish families in Ireland in the 16th–17th centuries under government sponsorship. ■ historical a colony.
– ORIGIN late Middle English (denoting the action of planting seeds): from Latin *plantatio(n-)*, from the verb *plantare* 'to plant'.

plantation song ▶ **noun** a song of the kind formerly sung by black slaves on American plantations.

planter ▶ **noun 1** [often with modifier] a manager or owner of a plantation: *wealthy coffee planters*.
2 a machine or person that plants seeds, bulbs, etc. ■ a decorative container in which plants are grown.
3 (in Irish history) an English or Scottish settler on confiscated land during the 17th century.

planter's punch ▶ **noun** a cocktail containing rum, lemon or lime juice, and sugar.
– ORIGIN 1920s: probably so called because drunk by plantation owners.

plant geography ▶ **noun** another term for **PHYTOGEOGRAPHY**.

plant hopper ▶ **noun** a small widely distributed plant-sucking bug that leaps when disturbed. Some kinds are pests of rice and sugar cane. ● Delphacidae and other families, suborder Homoptera.

plantigrade /ˈplantɪgreɪd/ ▶ **adjective** (of a mammal) walking on the soles of the feet, like a human or a bear. Compare with **DIGITIGRADE**.

– ORIGIN mid 19th cent.: from French, from modern Latin *plantigradus*, from Latin *planta* 'sole' + *-gradus* '-walking'.

plant louse ▶ noun a small bug that infests plants and feeds on the sap or tender shoots, especially an aphid. ● Several families in the series Sternorrhyncha, suborder Homoptera. See also JUMPING PLANT LOUSE.

plantocracy /plɑːn'tɒkrəsi/ ▶ noun (pl. **plantocracies**) a population of planters regarded as the dominant class, especially in the West Indies.

plantsman (or **plantswoman**) ▶ noun (pl. **plantsmen** or **plantswomen**) an expert in garden plants and gardening.

planula /'planjʊlə/ ▶ noun (pl. **planulae** /-liː/) Zoology a free-swimming coelenterate larva with a flattened, ciliated, solid body.
– ORIGIN late 19th cent.: modern Latin, diminutive of Latin *planus* 'plane, flat'.

plan view ▶ noun a view of an object as projected on a horizontal plane.

plaque /plak, plɑːk/ ▶ noun **1** an ornamental tablet, typically of metal, porcelain, or wood, that is fixed to a wall or other surface in commemoration of a person or event.
2 [mass noun] a sticky deposit on teeth in which bacteria proliferate.
3 Medicine a small, distinct, typically raised patch or region on or within the body resulting from local damage or deposition of material, such as a fatty deposit on an artery wall in atherosclerosis or a site of localized damage of brain tissue in Alzheimer's disease. ■ Microbiology a clear area in a cell culture caused by the inhibition of growth or destruction of cells by an agent such as a virus.
4 a flat counter used in gambling.
– DERIVATIVES **plaquette** /pla'kɛt/ noun.
– ORIGIN mid 19th cent.: from French, from Dutch *plak* 'tablet', from *plakken* 'to stick'.

plash[1] literary ▶ noun **1** a splashing sound: *the plash of the fountain.*
2 a pool or puddle.
▶ verb [no obj.] make a splashing sound: *the oars plashed in the silence.* ■ [with obj.] strike the surface of (water) with a splashing sound.
– DERIVATIVES **plashy** adjective.
– ORIGIN early 16th cent.: probably imitative.

plash[2] ▶ verb [with obj.] archaic bend down and interweave (branches and twigs) to form a hedge. ■ make or renew (a hedge) by bending and interweaving branches and twigs.
– ORIGIN late 15th cent.: from Old French *plaissier*, based on Latin *plectere* 'to plait'. Compare with PLEACH.

plasma /'plazmə/ (also **plasm** /'plaz(ə)m/) ▶ noun [mass noun] **1** the colourless fluid part of blood, lymph, or milk, in which corpuscles or fat globules are suspended.
2 an ionized gas consisting of positive ions and free electrons in proportions resulting in more or less no overall electric charge, typically at low pressures (as in the upper atmosphere and in fluorescent lamps) or at very high temperatures (as in stars and nuclear fusion reactors). ■ a substance analogous to ionized-gas plasma, consisting of mobile charged particles (such as a molten salt or the electrons within a metal).
3 a bright green, translucent variety of quartz used in mosaic and for other decorative purposes.
4 another term for CYTOPLASM or PROTOPLASM.
– DERIVATIVES **plasmatic** adjective, **plasmic** adjective.
– ORIGIN early 18th cent. (in the sense 'mould, shape'): from late Latin, literally 'mould', from Greek *plasma*, from *plassein* 'to shape'.

plasma cell ▶ noun Physiology a fully differentiated B-lymphocyte (white blood cell) which produces a single type of antibody.

plasmalemma /'plazmə,lɛmə/ ▶ noun Biology a plasma membrane which bounds a cell, especially one immediately within the wall of a plant cell.
– DERIVATIVES **plasmalemmal** adjective.
– ORIGIN 1920s: from PLASMA + Greek *lemma* 'rind'.

plasma membrane ▶ noun Biology a microscopic membrane of lipids and proteins which forms the external boundary of the cytoplasm of a cell or encloses a vacuole, and regulates the passage of molecules in and out of the cytoplasm.

plasmapause ▶ noun Astronomy the outer limit of a plasmasphere, marked by a sudden change in plasma density.

plasmapheresis /,plazmə'fɛrɪsɪs, -fə'riːsɪs/ ▶ noun [mass noun] Medicine a method of removing blood plasma from the body by withdrawing blood, separating it into plasma and cells, and transfusing the cells back into the bloodstream. It is performed especially to remove antibodies in treating autoimmune conditions.
– ORIGIN 1920s: from PLASMA + Greek *aphairesis* 'taking away' (from *apo-* 'from' + *hairein* 'take').

plasma screen ▶ noun a flat display screen using an array of cells containing a gas plasma to produce different colours in each cell.

plasma sheet ▶ noun Astronomy a layer of plasma in the magnetotail of the earth (or another planet), lying in the equatorial plane beyond the plasmapause, with two divergent branches that reach the earth at polar latitudes.

plasmasphere ▶ noun Astronomy the roughly toroidal region surrounding and thought to rotate with the earth (or another planet) at latitudes away from the poles, containing a relatively dense plasma of low-energy electrons and protons.

plasmid /'plazmɪd/ ▶ noun Biology a genetic structure in a cell that can replicate independently of the chromosomes, typically a small circular DNA strand in the cytoplasm of a bacterium or protozoan. Plasmids are much used in the laboratory manipulation of genes. Compare with EPISOME.
– ORIGIN 1950s: from PLASMA + -ID[2].

plasmin /'plazmɪn/ ▶ noun [mass noun] Biochemistry an enzyme, formed in the blood in some circumstances, which destroys blood clots by attacking fibrin.
– ORIGIN mid 19th cent.: from French *plasmine*, from late Latin *plasma* 'mould, image'.

plasminogen /plaz'mɪnədʒ(ə)n/ ▶ noun [mass noun] Biochemistry the inactive precursor of the enzyme plasmin, present in blood.

plasmodesma /,plazmə(ʊ)'dɛzmə/ ▶ noun (pl. **plasmodesmata** /-mətə/) Botany a narrow thread of cytoplasm that passes through the cell walls of adjacent plant cells and allows communication between them.
– ORIGIN early 20th cent.: from German *Plasmodesma*, from late Latin *plasma* 'mould, formation' + Greek *desma* 'bond, fetter'.

plasmodium /plaz'məʊdɪəm/ ▶ noun (pl. **plasmodia** /-dɪə/) **1** a parasitic protozoan of a genus which includes those causing malaria. ● Genus *Plasmodium*, phylum Sporozoa.
2 Biology a form within the life cycle of some simple organisms such as slime moulds, typically consisting of a mass of protoplasm containing many nuclei.
– DERIVATIVES **plasmodial** adjective.
– ORIGIN late 19th cent.: modern Latin, based on late Latin *plasma* 'mould, formation'.

plasmolyse /'plazməlʌɪz/ (US **plasmolyze**) ▶ verb [with obj.] Botany subject to plasmolysis.

plasmolysis /plaz'mɒlɪsɪs/ ▶ noun [mass noun] Botany contraction of the protoplast of a plant cell as a result of loss of water from the cell.
– ORIGIN late 19th cent.: modern Latin, from *plasmo-* from late Latin *plasma* 'mould' + Greek *lusis* 'loosening' (because of the separation of the plasma membrane from the cell wall).

plasmon /'plazmɒn/ ▶ noun Physics a quantum or quasi-particle associated with a local collective oscillation of charge density.
– ORIGIN 1950s: from PLASMA + -ON.

Plassey /'plasi/ a village in NE India, in West Bengal, north-west of Kolkata (Calcutta). It was the scene in 1757 of a battle in which a small British army under Robert Clive defeated the forces of the nawab of Bengal, establishing British supremacy in Bengal. Modern name PALASHI.

plasteel /'plastiːl/ ▶ noun [mass noun] (in science fiction) an ultra-strong non-metallic material.
– ORIGIN 1970s: blend of PLASTIC and STEEL.

plaster ▶ noun **1** [mass noun] a soft mixture of sand and cement and sometimes lime with water, for spreading on walls, ceilings, or other structures, to form a smooth hard surface when dried. ■ (also **plaster of Paris**) a hard white substance made by the addition of water to powdered and partly dehydrated gypsum, used for holding broken bones in place and making sculptures and casts. ■ the powder from which plaster of Paris is made.
2 (also **sticking plaster**) Brit. an adhesive strip of material for covering cuts and wounds. ■ dated a bandage on which a poultice or liniment is spread for application. See MUSTARD PLASTER.
▶ verb [with obj.] **1** cover (a wall, ceiling, or other structure) with plaster. ■ (**plaster something with/in**) coat or cover something with (a substance), especially to an extent considered excessive: *a face plastered in heavy make-up.* ■ [with obj. and adverbial] make (hair) lie flat by applying a liquid to it: *his hair was plastered down with water.* ■ [with obj. and adverbial] display widely and conspicuously: *her story was plastered all over the December issue.*
2 apply a plaster cast or medical plaster to (a part of the body).
3 informal, dated bomb or shell (a target) heavily.
– DERIVATIVES **plastery** adjective.
– ORIGIN Old English, denoting a bandage spread with a curative substance, from medieval Latin *plastrum* (shortening of Latin *emplastrum*, from Greek *emplastron* 'daub, salve'), later reinforced by the Old French noun *plastre*. Sense 1 dates from late Middle English.

plasterboard ▶ noun [mass noun] board made of plaster set between two sheets of paper, used especially to form or line the inner walls of houses.

plaster cast ▶ noun see CAST[1] (sense 1 of the noun).

plastered ▶ adjective **1** informal very drunk.
2 covered with or made of plaster.

plasterer ▶ noun a person whose job it is to apply plaster to walls, ceilings, or other structures.

plaster of Paris ▶ noun see PLASTER (sense 1 of the noun).

plaster saint ▶ noun a person who makes a show of being without moral faults or human weakness, especially in a hypocritical way.

plasterwork ▶ noun [mass noun] plaster as part of the interior of a building, especially covering the surface of a wall or formed into decorative shapes and patterns.

plastic ▶ noun [mass noun] a synthetic material made from a wide range of organic polymers such as polyethylene, PVC, nylon, etc., that can be moulded into shape while soft, and then set into a rigid or slightly elastic form. ■ informal credit cards or other types of plastic card that can be used as money: *he pays with cash instead of with plastic.*
▶ adjective **1** made of plastic: *plastic bags.* ■ artificial or unnatural: *a holiday rep with huge white teeth and a plastic smile.*
2 (of substances or materials) easily shaped or moulded: *rendering the material more plastic.* ■ relating to moulding or modelling in three dimensions, or to produce three-dimensional effects: *the plastic arts.* ■ (in science and technology) of or relating to the permanent deformation of a solid without fracture by the temporary application of force.
3 Biology exhibiting adaptability to change or variety in the environment.
– DERIVATIVES **plastically** adverb.
– ORIGIN mid 17th cent. (in the sense 'characteristic of moulding'): from French *plastique* or Latin *plasticus*, from Greek *plastikos*, from *plassein* 'to mould'.

plastic bomb ▶ noun a bomb containing plastic explosive.

plastic bullet ▶ noun a bullet made of PVC or another plastic material, typically used by security and police forces for riot control.

plastic explosive ▶ noun [mass noun] a putty-like explosive capable of being moulded by hand.

plasticine ▶ noun [mass noun] trademark a soft modelling material, used especially by children.
– ORIGIN late 19th cent.: from the adjective PLASTIC + -INE[4].

plasticity ▶ noun [mass noun] **1** the quality of being easily shaped or moulded.
2 Biology the adaptability of an organism to changes in its environment or differences between its various habitats.

plasticize (also **plasticise**) ▶ verb [with obj.] (often as adj. **plasticized**) make plastic or mouldable, especially by the addition of a plasticizer. ■ treat or make with plastic: *plasticized cotton.*
– DERIVATIVES **plasticization** noun.

plasticizer (also **plasticiser**) ▶ noun a substance (typically a solvent) added to a synthetic resin to produce or promote plasticity and flexibility and to reduce brittleness.

plasticky ▶ adjective looking or feeling like plastic: *the tables were covered with plasticky tablecloths.*

plastic surgery ▶ noun [mass noun] the process of reconstructing or repairing parts of the body by the

P

transfer of tissue, either in the treatment of injury or for cosmetic reasons.
– DERIVATIVES **plastic surgeon** noun.

plastic wood ▶ noun [mass noun] a mouldable material which hardens to resemble wood and is used for filling cracks in wood.

plastic wrap ▶ noun North American term for CLING FILM.

plastid /ˈplastɪd/ ▶ noun Botany any of a class of small organelles in the cytoplasm of plant cells, containing pigment or food.
– ORIGIN late 19th cent.: from German, based on Greek *plastos* 'shaped'.

plastique /plaˈstiːk/ ▶ noun [mass noun] plastic explosive.
– ORIGIN mid 20th cent.: French, literally 'plastic' (adjective used as a noun).

plastisol /ˈplastɪsɒl/ ▶ noun a liquid substance which can be converted into a solid plastic simply by heating, consisting of particles of synthetic resin dispersed in a non-volatile liquid.
– ORIGIN 1940s: from the noun PLASTIC + SOL[2].

plastron /ˈplastrən/ ▶ noun **1** a large pad worn by a fencer to protect the chest. ■ historical a steel breastplate worn beneath a hauberk.
2 an ornamental front of a woman's bodice or shirt consisting of colourful material with lace or embroidery, fashionable in the late 19th century. ■ a man's starched shirt front without pleats.
3 Zoology the underside part of a tortoise's or turtle's shell. ■ a similar ventral plate in some invertebrate animals. ■ Entomology (in an aquatic insect) a patch of cuticle covered with hairs which retain a thin layer of air that acts like a gill for breathing under water.
– DERIVATIVES **plastral** adjective.
– ORIGIN early 16th cent.: from French, from Italian *piastrone*, augmentative of *piastra* 'breastplate', from Latin *emplastrum* 'a plaster' (see PLASTER).

-plasty ▶ combining form moulding, grafting, or formation of a specified part, especially a part of the body: *rhinoplasty*.
– ORIGIN based on Greek *plastos* 'formed, moulded'.

plat[1] N. Amer. ▶ noun a plot of land. ■ a map or plan of an area of land showing actual or proposed features.
▶ verb [with obj.] plan out or make a map of (an area of land, especially a proposed site for construction).
– ORIGIN late Middle English: variant of the noun PLOT in the sense 'piece of ground'. The current verb sense dates from the early 18th cent.

plat[2] ▶ noun & verb variant spelling of PLAIT.

Plataea, Battle of /pləˈtiːə/ a battle in 479 BC, during the Persian Wars, in which the Persian forces were defeated by the Greeks near the city of Plataea in Boeotia.

P

platan /ˈplat(ə)n/ ▶ noun literary a plane tree.
– ORIGIN late Middle English: via Latin from Greek *platanos* 'plane tree'.

platanna /plaˈtanə/ ▶ noun South African term for CLAWED FROG.
– ORIGIN mid 19th cent.: from Afrikaans, apparently from Dutch *plat* 'flat' + *-hander*, literally 'handed one'.

plat du jour /ˌplɑː d(j)uː ˈʒʊə/, French /pla dy ʒuʀ/ ▶ noun (pl. **plats du jour** pronunc. **same**) a dish specially prepared by a restaurant on a particular day, in addition to the usual menu.
– ORIGIN French, literally 'dish of the day'.

plate ▶ noun **1** a flat dish, typically circular and made of china, from which food is eaten or served. ■ an amount of food on a plate: ***a plate of spaghetti***. ■ N. Amer. a main course of a meal, served on one plate: *he recommended the roast beef plate*. ■ Austral./NZ a plate of food contributed by a guest to a social gathering. ■ a dish, typically made of metal or wood, passed round a church congregation in order to collect donations of money. ■ Biology a shallow glass dish on which a culture of cells or microorganisms may be grown.
2 [mass noun] dishes, bowls, cups, and other utensils made of gold, silver, or other metal. [from Old French *vaisselle en plate* 'dishes and plates made of a single piece of metal'.] ■ [count noun] a silver or gold dish or trophy awarded as a prize in a race or competition. ■ [in names] a race or competition in which a silver or gold dish or trophy is awarded: *the final of the Ladies' Plate at Henley*.
3 a thin, flat sheet or strip of metal or other material, typically one used to join or strengthen things or forming part of a machine: *he underwent surgery to have a steel plate put into his leg*. ■ a small, flat piece of metal or other material bearing a name or inscription and attached to a door or other object: *a discreet brass plate announced William Marsden, RA*. ■ short for NUMBER PLATE. ■ Baseball short for HOME PLATE. ■ a horizontal timber laid along the top of a wall to support the ends of joists or rafters. ■ a light horseshoe for a racehorse.
4 Botany & Zoology a thin, flat organic structure or formation: *the fused bony plates protect the tortoise's soft parts*.
5 Geology each of the several rigid pieces of the earth's lithosphere which together make up the earth's surface. (See also PLATE TECTONICS.)
6 a sheet of metal, plastic, or other material bearing an image of type or illustrations from which multiple copies are printed. ■ a printed photograph, picture, or illustration, especially one on superior-quality paper in a book. ■ a thin sheet of metal, glass, or other substance coated with a light-sensitive film on which an image is formed, used in larger or older types of camera.
7 a thin piece of plastic moulded to the shape of a person's mouth and gums, to which artificial teeth or another orthodontic appliance are attached. ■ informal a complete denture or orthodontic appliance.
8 a thin piece of metal that acts as an electrode in a capacitor, battery, or cell. ■ N. Amer. the anode of a thermionic valve.
▶ verb [with obj.] **1** cover (a metal object) with a thin coating of a different metal. ■ cover (an object) with plates of metal for decoration, protection, or strength.
2 serve or arrange (food) on a plate or plates: *overcooked vegetables won't look appetizing, no matter how they are plated*.
3 Baseball score or cause to score (a run or runs).
4 Biology inoculate (cells or infective material) on to a culture plate, especially with the object of isolating a particular strain of micro-organisms or estimating viable cell numbers.
– PHRASES **on a plate** informal used to indicate that something has been achieved with little or no effort. **on one's plate** chiefly Brit. occupying one's time or energy: *you've got a lot on your plate at the moment*. **plates of meat** rhyming slang a person's feet.
– DERIVATIVES **plateful** noun (pl. **platefuls**), **plateless** adjective, **plater** noun.
– ORIGIN Middle English (denoting a flat, thin sheet, usually of metal): from Old French, from medieval Latin *plata* 'plate armour', based on Greek *platus* 'flat'. Sense 1 of the noun represents Old French *plat* 'platter, large dish', also 'dish of meat', noun use of Old French *plat* 'flat'.

Plate, River /pleɪt/ a wide estuary on the Atlantic coast of South America at the border between Argentina and Uruguay, formed by the confluence of the Rivers Paraná and Uruguay. The cities of Buenos Aires and Montevideo lie on its shores. In 1939 it was the scene of a naval battle in which the British defeated the Germans. Spanish name **Río de la Plata**.
– ORIGIN *Plate* from Spanish *plata* 'silver', exported from the region in the Spanish colonial period.

plate armour ▶ noun [mass noun] protective armour of metal plates, especially as worn in medieval times by knights.

plateau /ˈplatəʊ/ ▶ noun (pl. **plateaux** /-təʊz/ or **plateaus**) **1** an area of fairly level high ground. ■ [as modifier] denoting a group of American Indian peoples of the high plains of western Canada and the US, including the Nez Percé.
2 a state of little or no change following a period of activity or progress: *the peace process had reached a plateau*.
▶ verb (**plateaus**, **plateauing**, **plateaued**) [no obj.] reach a state of little or no change after a period of activity or progress: *the industry's problems have plateaued out*.
– ORIGIN late 18th cent.: from French, from Old French *platel*, diminutive of *plat* 'level'.

plate glass ▶ noun [mass noun] [often as modifier] thick fine-quality glass, typically used for shop windows and doors and originally cast in plates.

platelayer ▶ noun Brit. a person employed in laying and maintaining railway track.

platelet ▶ noun Physiology a small colourless disc-shaped cell fragment without a nucleus, found in large numbers in blood and involved in clotting. Also called THROMBOCYTE.

platemaker ▶ noun a person or machine that makes printing plates.

platen /ˈplat(ə)n/ ▶ noun **1** the plate in a small letterpress printing press which presses the paper against the type.
2 the cylindrical roller in a typewriter against which the paper is held.
– ORIGIN late 16th cent.: from French *platine* 'flat piece' from *plat* 'flat'.

plate number ▶ noun a serial number in the margin of a plate from which postage stamps are printed.

plate rack ▶ noun Brit. a rack in which plates are stored or placed to drain after being washed.

plateresque /ˌplatəˈrɛsk/ ▶ adjective (especially of Spanish architecture) richly ornamented in a style suggesting silverware.
– ORIGIN late 19th cent.: from Spanish *plateresco*, from *platero* 'silversmith', from *plata* 'silver'.

plate tectonics ▶ plural noun [treated as sing.] a theory explaining the structure of the earth's crust and many associated phenomena as resulting from the interaction of rigid lithospheric plates which move slowly over the underlying mantle.

plate tracery ▶ noun [mass noun] Architecture tracery with perforations in otherwise continuous stone.

platform ▶ noun **1** a raised level surface on which people or things can stand: *there are viewing platforms where visitors may gape at the chasm*. ■ a raised floor or stage used by public speakers or performers so that they can be seen by their audience. ■ a raised structure along the side of a railway track where passengers get on and off trains at a station. ■ Brit. the floor area at the entrance to a bus. ■ a raised structure standing in the sea from which oil or gas wells can be drilled or regulated. ■ [usu. with modifier] a raised structure or orbiting satellite from which rockets or missiles may be launched. ■ a standard for the hardware of a computer system, which determines what kinds of software it can run.
2 [usu. in sing.] the declared policy of a political party or group: *seeking election on a platform of low taxes*. ■ an opportunity to voice one's views or initiate action: *the forum will provide a platform for discussion of communication issues*.
3 (**platforms**) shoes with very thick soles: [as modifier] *yellow platform shoes*.
– ORIGIN mid 16th cent.: from French *plateforme* 'ground plan', literally 'flat shape'.

platformer ▶ noun informal term for PLATFORM GAME.

platform game ▶ noun a type of video game featuring two-dimensional graphics where the player controls a character jumping or climbing between solid platforms at different positions on the screen.

platform ticket ▶ noun Brit. historical a ticket allowing a non-traveller access to a railway station platform.

Plath /plaθ/, Sylvia (1932–63), American poet, wife of Ted Hughes. Her work is notable for its treatment of extreme and painful states of mind. In 1963 she committed suicide. Notable works: *Ariel* (poems, 1965) and *The Bell Jar* (novel, 1963).

plating ▶ noun [mass noun] **1** a thin coating of gold, silver, or other metal. ■ the process of applying plating.
2 an outer covering of flat metal sections: *the tractors carried steel plating for protection*.
3 the process of knitting two yarns together so that each yarn appears mainly on one side of the finished piece.
4 the racing of horses in which the prize for the winner is a plate.

platinic /pləˈtɪnɪk/ ▶ adjective of or containing platinum, especially in its tetravalent state.
– ORIGIN mid 19th cent.: from PLATINUM, on the pattern of words such as *ferric*.

platinize /ˈplatɪnʌɪz/ (also **platinise**) ▶ verb [with obj.] (usu. as adj. **platinized**) coat (something) with platinum.
– DERIVATIVES **platinization** noun.

platinoid /ˈplatɪnɔɪd/ ▶ noun [mass noun] an alloy of copper with zinc, nickel, and sometimes tungsten, used for its high electrical resistance.

platinum /ˈplatɪnəm/ ▶ noun [mass noun] a precious silvery-white metal, the chemical element of atomic number 78. It was first encountered by the Spanish in South America in the 16th century, and is used in jewellery, electrical contacts, laboratory equipment, and industrial catalysts. (Symbol: **Pt**) ■ [often as modifier] greyish white or silvery like platinum: *a platinum wig*.
– PHRASES **go platinum** (of a recording) achieve sales meriting a platinum disc.
– ORIGIN early 19th cent.: alteration of earlier *platina*, from Spanish, diminutive of *plata* 'silver'.

platinum black ▶ **noun** [mass noun] platinum in the form of a finely divided black powder, used as a catalyst and absorbent for gases.

platinum blonde (also **platinum blond**) ▶ **adjective** (of hair) silvery-blonde.
▶ **noun** a person with silvery-blonde hair.

platinum disc ▶ **noun** a framed platinum disc awarded to a recording artist or group for sales of a record exceeding a specified high figure.

platinum metals ▶ **plural noun** Chemistry the six metals platinum, palladium, ruthenium, osmium, rhodium, and iridium, which have similar properties and tend to occur together in nature.

platitude /ˈplatɪtjuːd/ ▶ **noun** a remark or statement, especially one with a moral content, that has been used too often to be interesting or thoughtful: *she began uttering liberal platitudes*.
– DERIVATIVES **platitudinize** (also **platitudinise**) **verb**.
– ORIGIN early 19th cent.: from French, from *plat* 'flat'.

platitudinous /ˌplatɪˈtjuːdɪnəs/ ▶ **adjective** (of a remark or statement) used too often to be interesting or thoughtful; hackneyed: *this may sound platitudinous*.

Plato /ˈpleɪtəʊ/ (*c.*429–*c.*347 BC), Greek philosopher.

> A disciple of Socrates and the teacher of Aristotle, Plato founded the Academy in Athens. An integral part of his thought is the theory of 'ideas' or 'forms', in which abstract entities or **universals** are contrasted with their objects or **particulars** in the material world. His philosophical writings are presented in the form of dialogues, with Socrates as the principal speaker; they include the *Symposium* and the *Timaeus*. Plato's political theories appear in the *Republic*, in which he explored the nature and structure of a just society.

Platonic /pləˈtɒnɪk/ ▶ **adjective 1** of or associated with the Greek philosopher Plato or his ideas.
2 (**platonic**) (of love or friendship) intimate and affectionate but not sexual: *their relationship is purely platonic*.
3 (**platonic**) confined to words, theories, or ideals, and not leading to practical action.
– DERIVATIVES **platonically** adverb.
– ORIGIN mid 16th cent.: via Latin from Greek *Platōnikos*, from *Platōn* 'Plato'.

Platonic solid (also **Platonic body**) ▶ **noun** one of five regular solids (a tetrahedron, cube, octahedron, dodecahedron, or icosahedron).

Platonism /ˈpleɪt(ə)nɪz(ə)m/ ▶ **noun** [mass noun] the philosophy of Plato or his followers. See **PLATO**. ■ any of various revivals of Platonic doctrines or related ideas, especially Neoplatonism and Cambridge Platonism (a 17th century attempt to reconcile Christianity with humanism and science). ■ the theory that numbers or other abstract objects are objective, timeless entities, independent of the physical world and of the symbols used to represent them.
– DERIVATIVES **Platonist** noun.

platoon ▶ **noun** a subdivision of a company of soldiers, usually forming a tactical unit that is commanded by a subaltern or lieutenant and divided into three sections. ■ a group of people acting together: *platoons of sharp lawyers*. ■ [as modifier] (in South Africa) denoting a school or schooling system in which two separate sets of teachers and pupils use the same buildings, one in the morning and one in the afternoon. ■ [as modifier] Baseball engaged in platooning: *a platoon player*.
▶ **verb 1** [with obj.] (in South Africa) apply the platoon system to (a school).
2 [with obj.] Baseball use the strategy of alternating (a pair of players or one player with another) in a specified field position in successive games.
– ORIGIN mid 17th cent.: from French *peloton* 'platoon', literally 'small ball', diminutive of *pelote*.

Plattdeutsch /ˈplatdɔɪtʃ/ ▶ **noun & adjective** another term for **LOW GERMAN**.
– ORIGIN German, from Dutch *Platduits*, from *plat* 'flat, low' + *Duits* 'German'.

platteland /ˈplataland/ S. African ▶ **noun** [mass noun] remote country districts.
▶ **adjective** belonging to or characteristic of remote country districts; rustic.
– ORIGIN Afrikaans, literally 'flat land'.

platter ▶ **noun 1** a large flat dish or plate for serving food. ■ a quantity of food served on a platter: *huge platters of cooked meat*. ■ a meal or selection of food placed on a platter, especially one served in a restaurant: *dinner was a bowl of soup and a cold platter*.
2 something shaped like a platter, in particular: ■ informal, dated a record: *dig out some old platters*. ■ the rotating metal disc forming the turntable of a record player. ■ Computing a rigid rotating disk on which data is stored in a disk drive; a hard disk (considered as a physical object).
– PHRASES **on a (silver) platter** informal used to indicate that someone receives or achieves something with little or no effort.
– ORIGIN Middle English: from Anglo-Norman French *plater*, from *plat* 'large dish' (see **PLATE**).

platy /ˈplati/ ▶ **noun** (pl. **platies**) a small live-bearing freshwater fish of Central America, which is popular in aquaria. ● Genus *Xiphophorus*, family Poeciliidae: several species, in particular *X. maculatus*, which has been bred in a wide variety of colours.
– ORIGIN early 20th cent.: colloquial abbreviation of modern Latin *Platypoecilus* (former genus name), from Greek *platus* 'broad' + *poikilos* 'variegated'.

platy- ▶ **combining form** broad; flat: *platypus*.
– ORIGIN from Greek *platus* 'broad, flat'.

platyhelminth /ˌplatɪˈhɛlmɪnθ/ ▶ **noun** Zoology an invertebrate of the phylum Platyhelminthes; a flatworm.

Platyhelminthes /ˌplatɪhɛlˈmɪnθiːz/ ▶ **plural noun** Zoology a phylum of invertebrates that comprises the flatworms.
– ORIGIN modern Latin (plural), from **PLATY-** 'flat' + Greek *helminth* 'worm'.

platypus /ˈplatɪpəs/ ▶ **noun** (pl. **platypuses**) a semi-aquatic egg-laying mammal which frequents lakes and streams in eastern Australia. It has a sensitive pliable bill shaped like that of a duck, webbed feet with venomous spurs, and dense fur. Also called **DUCKBILL** or **DUCK-BILLED PLATYPUS**. ● *Ornithorhynchus anatinus*, the only member of the family Ornithorhynchidae, order Monotremata.
– ORIGIN late 18th cent.: modern Latin, from Greek *platupous* 'flat-footed', from *platus* 'flat' + *pous* 'foot'.

platyrrhine /ˈplatɪrʌɪn/ Zoology ▶ **adjective** relating to primates of a group that comprises the New World monkeys, marmosets, and tamarins. They are distinguished by having nostrils that are far apart and directed forwards or sideways, and typically have a prehensile tail. Compare with **CATARRHINE**.
▶ **noun** a platyrrhine primate. ● Infraorder Platyrrhini, order Primates: families Cebidae and Callitrichidae.
– ORIGIN mid 19th cent.: from **PLATY-** 'flat' + Greek *rhis, rhin-* 'nose' + **-INE**[1].

platysma /pləˈtɪzmə/ ▶ **noun** (pl. **platysmas** or **platysmata** /-mətə/) Anatomy a broad sheet of muscle fibres extending from the collar bone to the angle of the jaw.
– ORIGIN late 17th cent.: modern Latin, from Greek *platusma* 'flat piece, plate'.

plaudits /ˈplɔːdɪts/ ▶ **plural noun** praise: *the network has received plaudits for its sports coverage*. ■ the applause of an audience: *the plaudits for the winner died down*.
– ORIGIN early 17th cent.: *plaudit* shortened from Latin *plaudite* 'applaud!' (said by Roman actors at the end of a play), imperative plural of *plaudere*.

plausible ▶ **adjective** (of an argument or statement) seeming reasonable or probable: *a plausible explanation* | *it seems plausible that one of two things may happen*. ■ (of a person) skilled at producing persuasive arguments, especially ones intended to deceive: *a plausible liar*.
– DERIVATIVES **plausibility** noun, **plausibly** adverb.
– ORIGIN mid 16th cent. (also in the sense 'deserving applause or approval'): from Latin *plausibilis*, from *plaus-* 'applauded', from the verb *plaudere*.

Plautus /ˈplɔːtəs/, Titus Maccius (*c.*250–184 BC), Roman comic dramatist. His plays, such as *Rudens*, are modelled on Greek New Comedy.

play ▶ **verb 1** [no obj.] engage in activity for enjoyment and recreation rather than a serious or practical purpose: *the children were playing by a pool* | *her friends were playing with their dolls*. ■ [with obj.] engage in (a game or activity) for enjoyment: *I want to play Snakes and Ladders*. ■ amuse oneself by engaging in imaginative pretence: *the boys were playing at soldiers*. ■ (**play at**) engage in without proper seriousness or understanding: *it would be wrong to assume that he is simply playing at right-wing politics*. ■ (**play with**) treat inconsiderately for one's own amusement: *she likes to play with people's emotions*. ■ (**play with**) fiddle or tamper with: *has somebody been playing with these taps?* ■ [with negative or in questions] (**be playing at**) used to convey one's irritation at someone's actions or one's failure to understand their motives: *what on earth do you think you're playing at?*
2 [with obj.] take part in (a sport): *I play squash and badminton*. ■ participate in (a sporting match or contest): *the squad will have played 14 games in six weeks*. ■ compete against (another player or team) in a sporting match: *the team will play France on Wednesday*. ■ [no obj.] be part of a team, especially in a specified position, in a sporting contest: *he played in goal*. ■ strike (a ball) or execute (a stroke) in a game. ■ [no obj., with adverbial] (of a cricket ground) be in such condition as to have a specified effect on play. ■ assign to take part in a match, especially in a specified position: *the manager played his strongest side of the season*. ■ move (a piece) or display (a playing card) in one's turn in a game: *he played his queen*. ■ bet or gamble at or on: *he didn't gamble or play the ponies*.
3 [no obj.] [usu. with negative] be cooperative: *he needs financial backing, but the building societies won't play*.
4 [with obj.] represent (a character) in a theatrical performance or a film: *early in her career she played Ophelia*. ■ [no obj.] perform in a film or theatrical production: *he was proud to be playing opposite a famous actor*. ■ put on or take part in (a theatrical performance, film, or concert): *the show was one of the best we ever played*. ■ give a dramatic performance at (a particular theatre or place). ■ behave as though one were (a specified type of person): *the skipper played the innocent, but smuggled goods were found on his vessel*. ■ (**play someone for**) treat someone as being of (a specified type): *don't imagine you can play me for a fool*.
5 [with obj.] perform on (a musical instrument): *a man was playing a guitar*. ■ possess the skill of performing on (a musical instrument): *he taught himself to play the violin*. ■ produce (notes) from a musical instrument; perform (a piece of music): *they played a violin sonata*. ■ make (a record, record player, radio, etc.) produce sounds. ■ [no obj.] (of a musical instrument, record, record player, etc.) produce sounds: *somewhere within, a harp was playing*. ■ [with obj. and adverbial of direction] accompany (someone) with music as they are moving in a specified direction: *the bagpipes played them out of the dining room*.
6 [no obj.] move lightly and quickly, so as to appear and disappear; flicker: *little beams of light played over the sea*. ■ (of a fountain or similar source of water) emit a stream of gently moving water.
7 [with obj.] allow (a fish) to exhaust itself pulling against a line before reeling it in.
▶ **noun** [mass noun] **1** activity engaged in for enjoyment and recreation, especially by children: *a child at play may use a stick as an aeroplane*. ■ behaviour or speech that is not intended seriously: *I flinched, but only in play*. ■ [as modifier] designed to be used in games of pretence; not real: *play families are arranged in play houses*.
2 the conducting of a sporting match: *rain wrecked the second day's play*. ■ the action or manner of engaging in a sport or game: *he maintained the same rhythm of play throughout the game*. ■ the status of the ball in a game as being available to be played according to the rules: *the ball was put in play*. ■ the state of being active, operative, or effective. ■ [count noun] a move or manoeuvre in a sport or game: *the best play is to lead the 3 of clubs*. ■ archaic the activity of gambling.
3 [count noun] a dramatic work for the stage or to be broadcast: *the actors put on a new play*.
4 the space in or through which a mechanism can or does move: *the steering rack was loose, and there was a little play*. ■ scope or freedom to act or operate: *our policy allows the market to have freer play*.
5 light and constantly changing movement: *the artist exploits the play of light across the surface*.
– PHRASES **bring** (or **call**) **into play** cause something to start working so that one can make use of it: *he cannot afford to bring into play the kind of leadership veto that operated all those years ago*. **come into play** become active, operational, or effective: *luck comes into play*. **make a play for** informal attempt to attract or attain. **make (great) play of** (or **with**) draw attention to in an ostentatious manner, typically to gain prestige or advantage: *the company made great play of their recent growth in profits*. **make play with** treat frivolously. **not playing with a full deck** see **DECK**. **play ball** see **BALL**[1]. **play both ends against the middle** keep one's options open by supporting or favouring opposing sides. **play something by ear** perform music without having to

P

read from a score. ■ **(play it by ear)** informal proceed instinctively according to results and circumstances rather than according to rules or a plan. **play by the rules** follow what is generally held to be the correct line of behaviour. **play one's cards close to one's chest** see CHEST. **play one's cards right** (or **well**) see CARD[1]. **play ducks and drakes with** see DUCKS AND DRAKES. **play fair** observe principles of justice; avoid cheating. **play someone false** prove treacherous or deceitful towards someone. **play fast and loose** behave irresponsibly or immorally. **play favourites** N. Amer. show favouritism towards someone or something. **play the field** see FIELD. **play for time** use specious excuses or unnecessary manoeuvres to gain time. **play the game** see GAME[1]. **play God** see GOD. **play havoc with** see HAVOC. **play hell** see HELL. **play hookey** see HOOKEY. **play a** (or **one's**) **hunch** make an instinctive choice. **play oneself in** Brit. become accustomed to the circumstances and conditions of a game or activity. **play into someone's hands** act in such a way as unintentionally to give someone an advantage. **play it cool** informal make an effort to be or appear to be calm and unemotional. **play the market** speculate in stocks. **a play on words** a pun. **play a part** make a contribution to a situation: *social and economic factors may have also played a part* | *he personally wanted to thank those nurses and staff who had* ***played a part in*** *his recovery*. **play** (or **play it**) **safe** (or **for safety**) take precautions; avoid risks. **play to the gallery** see GALLERY. **play a trick** (or **joke**) **on** behave in a deceptive or teasing way towards. **play truant** see TRUANT. **play with oneself** informal masturbate. **play with fire** take foolish risks. **played out** informal used or seen too many times before so no longer interesting: *the melodrama is a little played out to be entirely satisfying*.

– PHRASAL VERBS **play about** (or **around**) behave in a casual, foolish, or irresponsible way: *you shouldn't* ***play around with*** *a child's future*. ■ informal (of a married person) have a love affair. **play along** perform a piece of music at the same time as it is playing on a tape or record. ■ pretend to cooperate: *she had to play along and be polite*. **play someone along** informal deceive or mislead someone over a period of time. **play away** Brit. play a sports fixture on an opponent's ground. ■ informal (of a married person) have a love affair. **play something back** play sounds that one has recently recorded, especially to monitor recording quality. **play something down** represent something as being less important than it in fact is: *he tried to play down the seriousness of his illness*. **play someone off** bring people into conflict or competition for one's own advantage: *top footballers were able to* ***play*** *clubs* ***off against*** *each other to gain higher pay*. **play off** (of two teams or competitors) play an extra match to decide a draw or tie. **play on** exploit (a weak or vulnerable point in someone): *he played on his opponent's nerves*. **play out 1** develop in a particular way: *the position of the sub-tropical jet stream across North America will determine how winter plays out*. **2** happen; take place: *this scenario plays out all across the country*. **play someone out** drain someone of strength or life. **play something out** act the whole of a drama; enact a scene or role. **play up** Brit. **1** informal (of a child) misbehave: *I hadn't had much sleep – the kids had been playing up*. ■ fail to function properly: *his phone line was constantly playing up*. **2** put all one's energy into a game. **play someone up** (of a part of the body or an illness) cause pain or discomfort to someone. **play something up** emphasize the extent or importance of something: *the mystery surrounding his death was played up by the media*. **play up to** exploit, trade on, or make the most of.

– DERIVATIVES **playability** noun, **playable** adjective.

– ORIGIN Old English *pleg(i)an* 'to exercise', *plega* 'brisk movement', related to Middle Dutch *pleien* 'leap for joy, dance'.

playa[1] /ˈplʌɪə/ ▶ noun an area of flat, dried-up land, especially a desert basin from which water evaporates quickly.

– ORIGIN mid 19th cent.: from Spanish, literally 'beach', from late Latin *plagia*.

playa[2] /ˈpleɪə/ ▶ noun see PLAYER (sense 1).

play-act ▶ verb [no obj.] act in a play. ■ [with obj.] act (a scene, role, etc.). ■ (usu. as noun **play-acting**) engage in histrionic pretence: *the defender indulged in some play-acting after tumbling to the ground*.

– DERIVATIVES **play-actor** noun.

playback ▶ noun [mass noun] the reproduction of previously recorded sounds or moving images. ■ [count noun] a pre-recorded musical soundtrack mimed to by an actor.

P

playback singer ▶ noun (especially in Indian cinema) a singer who records songs to be mimed in films by actors.

playbill ▶ noun a poster announcing a theatrical performance. ■ N. Amer. a theatre programme.

playbook ▶ noun N. Amer. a book containing a sports team's strategies and plays, especially in American football.

playboy ▶ noun a wealthy man who spends his time enjoying himself, especially one who behaves irresponsibly or is sexually promiscuous.

play-by-play ▶ noun N. Amer. a detailed running commentary on a sporting contest.

play centre ▶ noun a place separate from school where children can play under supervision. ■ chiefly NZ a preschool playgroup.

play date ▶ noun a social occasion arranged for children to play together.

playdown ▶ noun chiefly Canadian & Scottish a game or match forming part of a play-off.

Player, Gary (b.1935), South African golfer. He has won numerous championships including the British Open (1959; 1968; 1974), the Masters (1961; 1974; 1978), and the PGA (1962; 1972).

player ▶ noun **1** a person taking part in a sport or game: *a tennis player*. ■ a person or body that is involved and influential in an area or activity: *the country's isolationism made it a secondary player in world political events*. ■ (also **playa**) informal a confident, successful man with many sexual partners: *she's so wary of playas, she's declared herself celibate*. **2** [usu. with modifier] a person who plays a musical instrument: *a guitar player*. ■ a device for playing CDs, records, etc.

3 an actor: *there are moments of tenderness beautifully expressed by the players*.

player-manager ▶ noun a person who both plays in a sports team and manages it.

player-piano ▶ noun a piano fitted with a pneumatic apparatus enabling it to be played automatically by means of a rotating perforated roll signalling the notes to be played.

playfellow ▶ noun a playmate.

playful ▶ adjective fond of games and amusement; light-hearted. ■ intended for one's own or others' amusement rather than seriously: *he gave me a playful punch on the arm*. ■ giving or expressing pleasure and amusement: *the ballet accents the playful use of movement*.

– DERIVATIVES **playfully** adverb, **playfulness** noun.

playgoer ▶ noun a person who goes to the theatre regularly: *the actor was a great favourite with the London playgoers*.

playground ▶ noun an outdoor area provided for children to play in, especially at a school or public park. ■ a place where a particular group of people choose to enjoy themselves: *the mountains are a* ***playground for*** *hang-gliders*.

playgroup ▶ noun Brit. a regular meeting of a group of preschool children at a particular place, organized by parents for their children to take part in supervised creative and social play.

playhouse ▶ noun **1** (also **Playhouse**) a theatre. **2** a toy house for children to play in.

playing card ▶ noun each of a set of rectangular pieces of card having a sequence of numbers and symbols on one side, used to play various games, some involving gambling. A standard pack contains 52 cards divided into four suits.

playing field ▶ noun a field used for outdoor team games.

– PHRASES **a level playing field** see LEVEL.

playlet ▶ noun a short play or dramatic piece.

playlist ▶ noun a list of recorded songs or pieces of music chosen to be broadcast on a radio show or by a particular radio station.

▶ verb [with obj.] place (a song or piece of music) on a playlist.

playmaker ▶ noun a player in a team game who leads attacks or brings other players on the same side into a position from which they could score.

– DERIVATIVES **playmaking** noun.

playmate ▶ noun **1** a friend with whom a child plays. **2** used euphemistically to refer to a person's lover.

play-off ▶ noun an additional match played to decide the outcome of a contest.

playpen ▶ noun a small portable enclosure in which a baby or small child can play safely.

play-play S. African informal ▶ adjective [attrib.] not genuine; make-believe: *they're at the age when they want more than a play-play watch*.

▶ verb [no obj.] engage in make-believe: [with clause] *I could play-play I was a beach boy*.

playroom ▶ noun a room in a house that is set aside for children to play in.

playscheme ▶ noun a local project or scheme providing recreational facilities and activities for children for a certain period of time, typically during the school holidays.

playschool ▶ noun Brit. a playgroup.

playsuit ▶ noun an all-in-one stretchy garment for a baby or very young child, covering the body, arms, and legs. ■ a women's all-in-one garment, or matching set of garments.

plaything ▶ noun a toy. ■ a person treated as amusing but unimportant by someone else: *she was the mistress and plaything of a wealthy businessman*.

playtime ▶ noun a period in the school day when children are allowed to go outside and play: *they chant their tables before playtime*.

playwright ▶ noun a person who writes plays.

playwriting ▶ noun [mass noun] the activity or process of writing plays.

plaza ▶ noun chiefly N. Amer. **1** a public square, marketplace, or similar open space in a built-up area. **2** a shopping centre.

– ORIGIN late 17th cent.: from Spanish, literally 'place'.

plc (also **PLC**) ▶ abbreviation Brit. public limited company.

plea ▶ noun **1** a request made in an urgent and emotional manner: *he made a dramatic plea for disarmament*. ■ a claim that a circumstance means that one should not be blamed for or should not be forced to do something: *her plea of a headache was not entirely false*.

2 Law a formal statement by or on behalf of a defendant or prisoner, stating guilt or innocence in response to a charge, offering an allegation of fact, or claiming that a point of law should apply: *he changed his plea to not guilty*.

– PHRASES **plea of tender** Law a plea that the defendant has always been ready to satisfy the plaintiff's claim and now brings the sum into court.

– ORIGIN Middle English (in the sense 'lawsuit'): from Old French *plait, plaid* 'agreement, discussion', from Latin *placitum* 'a decree', neuter past participle of *placere* 'to please'.

plea bargaining ▶ noun [mass noun] Law an arrangement between prosecutor and defendant whereby the defendant pleads guilty to a lesser charge in exchange for a more lenient sentence or an agreement to drop other charges.

– DERIVATIVES **plea-bargain** verb, **plea bargain** noun.

pleach /pliːtʃ/ ▶ verb [with obj.] (usu. as adj. **pleached**) entwine or interlace (tree branches) to form a hedge or provide cover for an outdoor walkway: *an avenue of pleached limes*.

– ORIGIN late Middle English: from an Old French variant of *plaissier* (see PLASH[2]).

plead ▶ verb (past and past participle **pleaded** or N. Amer., Scottish, or dialect **pled**) **1** [reporting verb] make an emotional appeal: [no obj.] *she* ***pleaded with*** *them not to gag the boy* | [with direct speech] *'Don't go,' she pleaded* | [with infinitive] *Anne pleaded to go with her* | (as adj. **pleading**) *he gave her a pleading look*.

2 [with obj.] present and argue for (a position), especially in court or in another public context. ■ [no obj.] Law address a court as an advocate on behalf of a party. ■ [no obj., with complement] Law state formally in court whether one is guilty or not guilty of the offence with which one is charged: *the youth pleaded guilty to murdering the girl*. ■ Law invoke (a reason or a point of law) as an accusation or defence: *on trial for attempted murder, she pleaded self-defence*. ■ offer or present as an excuse for doing or not doing something: *he pleaded family commitments as a reason for not attending*.

– DERIVATIVES **pleader** noun, **pleadingly** adverb.

– ORIGIN Middle English (in the sense 'to wrangle'): from Old French *plaidier* 'go to law', from *plaid* 'discussion' (see PLEA).

USAGE In a law court a person can **plead guilty** or **plead not guilty**. The phrase **plead innocent** is not a technical legal term, although it is commonly found in general use.

pleadable ▸ adjective Law able to be offered as a formal plea in court.

pleading ▸ noun **1** [mass noun] the action of making an emotional or earnest appeal to someone: *he ignored her pleading.*
2 (usu. **pleadings**) Law a formal statement of the cause of an action or defence.

pleasance ▸ noun a secluded enclosure or part of a garden, especially one attached to a large house.
– ORIGIN Middle English (in the sense 'pleasure'): from Old French *plaisance*, from *plaisant* 'pleasing' (see PLEASANT).

pleasant ▸ adjective (**pleasanter**, **pleasantest**) giving a sense of happy satisfaction or enjoyment: *a very pleasant evening.* ■ (of a person or their manner) friendly and considerate; likeable: *they found him pleasant and cooperative.*
– DERIVATIVES **pleasantly** adverb, **pleasantness** noun.
– ORIGIN Middle English (in the sense 'pleasing'): from Old French *plaisant* 'pleasing', from the verb *plaisir* (see PLEASE).

pleasantry ▸ noun (pl. **pleasantries**) (usu. **pleasantries**) an inconsequential remark made as part of a polite conversation: *after an exchange of pleasantries, I proceeded to outline a plan.* ■ a mild joke: *he laughed at his own pleasantry.*
– ORIGIN late 16th cent.: from French *plaisanterie*, from Old French *plaisant* 'pleasing' (see PLEASANT).

please ▸ verb [with obj.] **1** cause to feel happy and satisfied: *he arranged a fishing trip to please his son* | [with obj. and infinitive] ***it pleased** him to be seen with someone in the news.* ■ [no obj.] give satisfaction: *she was quiet and eager to please.* ■ satisfy aesthetically.
2 (**please oneself**) take only one's own wishes into consideration in deciding how to act or proceed: *this is the first time in ages that I can just please myself.* ■ [no obj.] wish or desire to do something: *feel free to wander around **as you please**.* ■ (**it pleases**, **pleased**, etc., **someone to do something**) dated it is someone's choice to do something: *instead of attending the meeting, it pleased him to go off hunting.*
▸ adverb used in polite requests or questions: *please address letters to the Editor* | *what type of fish is this, please?* ■ used to add urgency and emotion to a request: *please, please come home!* ■ used to agree politely to a request: *'May I ring you at home?' 'Please do.'* ■ used in polite or emphatic acceptance of an offer: *'Would you like a drink?' 'Yes, please.'* ■ used to ask someone to stop doing something of which the speaker disapproves: *Rita, please—people are looking.* ■ used to express incredulity or irritation: *Oh please, is that meant to be a serious argument?*
– PHRASES **as —— as you please** informal used to emphasize the manner in which someone does something, especially when this is seen as surprising: *she walked forward as calm as you please.* **if you please 1** used in polite requests: *follow me, if you please.* **2** used to express indignation at something perceived as unreasonable: *she wants me to make fifty cakes in time for the festival, if you please!* **please yourself** used to express indifference, especially when someone does not cooperate or behave as expected: *'I can manage on my own.' 'Please yourself.'*
– ORIGIN Middle English: from Old French *plaisir* 'to please', from Latin *placere*.

pleased ▸ adjective feeling or showing pleasure and satisfaction, especially at an event or a situation: *both girls were **pleased with** their new hairstyles* | *he seemed really **pleased that** she was there* | *a pleased smile.* ■ [with infinitive] willing or glad to do something: *we will be pleased to provide an independent appraisal.* ■ (**pleased with oneself**) proud of one's achievements, especially excessively so; self-satisfied.
– PHRASES **(as) pleased as Punch** see PUNCH[4]. **not best pleased** Brit. informal annoyed or irritated: *the government-backed organizations were not best pleased by the criticism.* **pleased to meet you** said on being introduced to someone: *'This is my wife.' 'Pleased to meet you.'*
– DERIVATIVES **pleasedly** adverb.

pleasing ▸ adjective satisfying or appealing: *the pleasing austerity of the surroundings.*
– DERIVATIVES **pleasingly** adverb [as submodifier] *a pleasingly unpretentious late night lounge bar.*

pleasurable ▸ adjective pleasing; enjoyable.
– DERIVATIVES **pleasurableness** noun, **pleasurably** adverb.
– ORIGIN late 16th cent.: from PLEASURE, on the pattern of *comfortable*.

pleasure ▸ noun [mass noun] a feeling of happy satisfaction and enjoyment: *she smiled with pleasure at being praised.* ■ enjoyment and entertainment, as opposed to necessity: *she had not travelled for pleasure for a long time.* ■ [count noun] an event or activity from which one derives enjoyment: *the car makes driving in the city a pleasure.* ■ sensual gratification: *the touch of his fingers gave her such pleasure.*
▸ adjective [attrib.] used or intended for entertainment rather than business: *pleasure boats.*
▸ verb [with obj.] give sexual enjoyment or satisfaction to: *tell me what will pleasure you.* ■ [no obj.] (**pleasure in**) derive enjoyment from: *risky verbal exchanges that the pair might pleasure in.*
– PHRASES **at Her** (or **His**) **Majesty's pleasure** detained in a British prison: *his sharp practice cost him a term at Her Majesty's pleasure.* **at someone's pleasure** as and when someone wishes: *the landlord could terminate the agreement at his pleasure.* **have the pleasure of something** (or **of doing something**) used in formal requests and descriptions: *he asked if he might have the pleasure of taking her to lunch.* **my pleasure** used as a polite reply to thanks. **take pleasure in** derive happiness or enjoyment from: *they take a perverse pleasure in causing trouble.* **what's your pleasure?** what would you like? (used especially when offering someone a choice): *'What's your pleasure?' 'A cappuccino, please.'* **with pleasure** gladly (used to express polite agreement or acceptance).
– ORIGIN late Middle English: from Old French *plaisir* 'to please' (used as a noun). The second syllable was altered under the influence of abstract nouns ending in *-ure*, such as *measure*.

pleasure principle ▸ noun Psychoanalysis the instinctive drive to seek pleasure and avoid pain, expressed by the id as a basic motivating force which reduces psychic tension.

pleat ▸ noun a double or multiple fold in a garment or other item made of cloth, held by stitching the top or side.
▸ verb [with obj.] fold into pleats: (as adj. **pleated**) *a short pleated skirt.*
– ORIGIN late Middle English: a variant of PLAIT. The written form of the word became obsolete between *c.*1700 and the end of the 19th cent.

pleather ▸ noun [mass noun] imitation leather made from polyurethane.
– ORIGIN 1980s: blend of POLYURETHANE and LEATHER.

pleb ▸ noun (usu. **plebs**) informal, derogatory an ordinary person, especially one from the lower social classes.
– DERIVATIVES **plebby** adjective.

plebe /pliːb/ ▸ noun US informal a newly entered cadet or freshman, especially at a military or naval academy.
– ORIGIN early 17th cent.: perhaps an abbreviation of PLEBEIAN.

plebeian /plɪˈbiːən/ ▸ noun (in ancient Rome) a commoner. ■ a member of the lower social classes.
▸ adjective of or belonging to the commoners of ancient Rome. ■ of or belonging to the lower social classes. ■ lacking in refinement: *he is a man of plebeian tastes.*
– ORIGIN mid 16th cent.: from Latin *plebeius* (from *plebs, pleb-* 'the common people') + -AN.

plebiscite /ˈplɛbɪsʌɪt, -sɪt/ ▸ noun the direct vote of all the members of an electorate on an important public question such as a change in the constitution. ■ Roman History a law enacted by the plebeians' assembly.
– DERIVATIVES **plebiscitary** /-ˈbɪsɪt(ə)ri/ adjective.
– ORIGIN mid 16th cent. (referring to Roman history): from French *plébiscite*, from Latin *plebiscitum*, from *plebs, pleb-* 'the common people' + *scitum* 'decree' (from *sciscere* 'vote for'). The sense 'direct vote of the whole electorate' dates from the mid 19th cent.

Plecoptera /plɪˈkɒptərə/ ▸ plural noun Entomology an order of insects that comprises the stoneflies. ■ (**plecoptera**) insects of the Plecoptera order; stoneflies.
– DERIVATIVES **plecopteran** noun & adjective.
– ORIGIN modern Latin (plural), from Greek *plekos* 'wickerwork' (from *plekein* 'to plait') + *pteron* 'wing'.

plectrum /ˈplɛktrəm/ ▸ noun (pl. **plectrums** or **plectra** /-trə/) a thin flat piece of plastic, tortoiseshell, or other slightly flexible material held by or worn on the fingers and used to pluck the strings of a musical instrument such as a guitar. ■ the mechanical part corresponding to a plectrum which plucks the strings of an instrument such as a harpsichord.
– ORIGIN late Middle English: via Latin from Greek *plēktron* 'something with which to strike', from *plēssein* 'to strike'.

pled North American, Scottish, or dialect past participle of PLEAD.

pledge ▸ noun **1** a solemn promise or undertaking: [with infinitive] *the conference ended with a joint pledge to limit pollution.* ■ a promise of a donation to charity: *appeals for emergency relief met with pledges totalling £250,000,000.* ■ (**the pledge**) a solemn undertaking to abstain from alcohol: *she persuaded Arthur to take the pledge.*
2 Law a thing that is given as security for the fulfilment of a contract or the payment of a debt and is liable to forfeiture in the event of failure. ■ a thing given as a token of love, favour, or loyalty.
3 archaic the drinking of a person's health; a toast.
▸ verb **1** [with obj. and infinitive] commit (a person or organization) by a solemn promise: *the government pledged itself to deal with environmental problems.* ■ [with clause] formally declare or promise that something is or will be the case: *the Prime Minister pledged that there would be no increase in VAT.* ■ [no obj., with infinitive] solemnly undertake to do something: *they pledged to continue the campaign for funding.* ■ [with obj.] undertake formally to give: *Japan pledged $100 million in humanitarian aid.*
2 [with obj.] Law give as security on a loan: *the creditor to whom the land is pledged.*
3 [with obj.] archaic drink to the health of.
– PHRASES **pledge one's troth** see TROTH.
– DERIVATIVES **pledger** noun, **pledgor** noun (Law).
– ORIGIN Middle English (denoting a person acting as surety for another): from Old French *plege*, from medieval Latin *plebium*, perhaps related to the Germanic base of PLIGHT[2].

pledgee ▸ noun a person to whom a pledge is given.

Pledge of Allegiance (in the US) a solemn oath of loyalty to the United States, declaimed as part of flag-saluting ceremonies.

pledget /ˈplɛdʒɪt/ ▸ noun a small wad of lint or other soft material used to stop up a wound or an opening in the body.
– ORIGIN mid 16th cent.: of unknown origin.

-plegia /pliːdʒə/ ▸ suffix Medicine forming nouns denoting a kind of paralysis, as *hemiplegia*, *paraplegia*.
– DERIVATIVES **-plegic** suffix forming corresponding adjectives.
– ORIGIN from Greek *plēgē* 'blow, stroke' (from *plēssein* 'to strike') + -IA[1].

pleiad /ˈplʌɪəd/ ▸ noun literary an outstanding group of seven people or things.
– ORIGIN early 17th cent.: from PLEIADES.

Pleiades /ˈplʌɪədiːz/ **1** Greek Mythology the seven daughters of the Titan Atlas and the Oceanid Pleione, who were pursued by the hunter Orion until Zeus changed them into a cluster of stars.
2 Astronomy a well-known open cluster of stars in the constellation Taurus. Six (or more) stars are visible to the naked eye but there are actually some five hundred present, formed very recently in stellar terms. Also called SEVEN SISTERS.
– ORIGIN via Latin from Greek.

plein-air /plɛn ˈɛː/, French /plɛn ɛʀ/ ▸ adjective denoting or in the manner of a 19th-century style of painting outdoors, which became a central feature of French Impressionism.
– ORIGIN from French *en plein air* 'in the open air'.

pleiotropy /plʌɪˈɒtrəpi/ ▸ noun [mass noun] Genetics the production by a single gene of two or more apparently unrelated effects.
– DERIVATIVES **pleiotropic** /-ˈtrəʊpɪk, -ˈtrɒpɪk/ adjective, **pleiotropism** noun.
– ORIGIN 1930s: from Greek *pleiōn* 'more' + *tropē* 'turning'.

Pleistocene /ˈplʌɪstəsiːn/ ▸ adjective Geology relating to or denoting the first epoch of the Quaternary period, between the Pliocene and Holocene epochs. ■ (as noun **the Pleistocene**) the Pleistocene epoch or the system of deposits laid down during it.

> The Pleistocene epoch lasted from 1,640,000 to about 10,000 years ago. It was marked by great fluctuations in temperature that caused the ice ages, with glacial periods followed by warmer interglacial periods. Several forms of fossil human, leading up to modern humans, appeared during this epoch.

– ORIGIN mid 19th cent.: from Greek *pleistos* 'most' + *kainos* 'new'.

P

plenary /ˈpliːnəri/ ▶ **adjective 1** unqualified; absolute: *crusaders were offered a plenary indulgence by the Pope.*
2 (of a meeting) to be attended by all participants at a conference or assembly, who otherwise meet in smaller groups: *a plenary session of the European Parliament.*
▶ **noun** a meeting or session attended by all participants at a conference or assembly.
– ORIGIN late Middle English: from late Latin *plenarius* 'complete', from *plenus* 'full'.

plenipotentiary /ˌplɛnɪpəˈtɛnʃ(ə)ri/ ▶ **noun** (pl. **plenipotentiaries**) a person, especially a diplomat, invested with the full power of independent action on behalf of their government, typically in a foreign country.
▶ **adjective** having full power to take independent action: [postpositive] ***a minister plenipotentiary.*** ■ (of power) absolute.
– ORIGIN mid 17th cent.: from medieval Latin *plenipotentiarius*, from *plenus* 'full' + *potentia* 'power'.

plenitude ▶ **noun** an abundance: *an ancient Celtic god thought to bring **a plenitude of** wealth or food.* ■ [mass noun] the condition of being full or complete: *the plenitude of the Pope's powers.*
– ORIGIN late Middle English: from Old French, from late Latin *plenitudo*, from *plenus* 'full'.

plenteous ▶ **adjective** literary plentiful.
– DERIVATIVES **plenteously** adverb, **plenteousness** noun.
– ORIGIN Middle English: from Old French *plentivous*, from *plentif*, *-ive*, from *plente* 'plenty'. Compare with **BOUNTEOUS**.

plentiful ▶ **adjective** existing in or yielding great quantities; abundant: *coal is cheap and plentiful.*
– DERIVATIVES **plentifully** adverb, **plentifulness** noun.

plentitude ▶ **noun** rare term for **PLENITUDE**.

plenty ▶ **pronoun** a large or sufficient amount or quantity; more than enough: *I would have **plenty of** time to get home before my parents arrived | you'll have plenty to keep you busy | there are shops **in plenty*** | [as determiner] informal or dialect *there was plenty room.*
▶ **noun** [mass noun] a situation in which food and other necessities are available in sufficiently large quantities: *such natural phenomena as famine and plenty.*
▶ **adverb** [usu. as submodifier] informal used to emphasize the degree of something: *she has **plenty more** ideas.*
– ORIGIN Middle English (in the sense 'fullness, perfection'): from Old French *plente*, from Latin *plenitas*, from *plenus* 'full'.

Plenty, Bay of a region of the North Island, New Zealand, extending around the bay of the same name. The port of Tauranga is situated on it.

plenum /ˈpliːnəm/ ▶ **noun 1** an assembly of all the members of a group or committee. [influenced by Russian *plenum* 'plenary session'.]
2 Physics a space completely filled with matter, or the whole of space so regarded.
– ORIGIN late 17th cent.: from Latin, literally 'full space', neuter of *plenus* 'full'.

pleo- ▶ **combining form** having more than the usual or expected number: *pleocytosis*.
– ORIGIN from Greek *pleōn* 'more'.

pleochroic /ˌpliːə(ʊ)ˈkrəʊɪk/ ▶ **adjective** (of a crystal) absorbing different wavelengths of light differently depending on the direction of incidence of the rays or their plane of polarization, often resulting in the appearance of different colours according to the direction of view.
– DERIVATIVES **pleochroism** noun.
– ORIGIN mid 19th cent.: from **PLEO-** 'more' + *khrōs* 'colour' + **-IC**.

pleocytosis /ˌpliːə(ʊ)sʌɪˈtəʊsɪs/ ▶ **noun** [mass noun] Medicine the presence of an abnormally large number of lymphocytes in the cerebrospinal fluid.

pleomorphism /ˌpliːə(ʊ)ˈmɔːfɪz(ə)m/ ▶ **noun** [mass noun] the occurrence of more than one distinct form of a natural object, such as a crystalline substance, a virus, the cells in a tumour, or an organism at different stages of the life cycle.
– DERIVATIVES **pleomorphic** adjective.
– ORIGIN mid 19th cent.: from Greek *pleiōn* 'more' + *morphē* 'form' + **-ISM**.

pleonasm /ˈpliːə(ʊ)ˌnaz(ə)m/ ▶ **noun** [mass noun] the use of more words than are necessary to convey meaning (e.g. *see with one's eyes*), either as a fault of style or for emphasis.
– DERIVATIVES **pleonastic** adjective, **pleonastically** adverb.
– ORIGIN mid 16th cent.: via late Latin from Greek *pleonasmos*, from *pleonazein* 'be superfluous'.

pleopod /ˈpliːə(ʊ)pɒd/ ▶ **noun** Zoology a forked swimming limb of a crustacean, five pairs of which are typically attached to the abdomen. Also called **SWIMMERET**.
– ORIGIN mid 19th cent.: from Greek *plein* 'swim, sail' + *pous*, *pod-* 'foot'.

pleroma /pləˈrəʊmə/ ▶ **noun** [in sing.] **1** (in Gnosticism) the spiritual universe as the abode of God and of the totality of the divine powers and emanations.
2 (in Christian theology) the totality or fullness of the Godhead which dwells in Christ.
– DERIVATIVES **pleromatic** adjective.
– ORIGIN mid 18th cent.: from Greek *plērōma* 'that which fills', from *plēroun* 'make full', from *plērēs* 'full'.

plesiosaur /ˈpliːsɪəsɔː, ˈpliːz-/ ▶ **noun** a large fossil marine reptile of the Mesozoic era, with a broad flat body, large paddle-like limbs, and typically a long flexible neck and small head. ● Infraorder Plesiosauria, superorder Sauropterygia: several families, including Plesiosauridae.
– ORIGIN mid 19th cent.: from modern Latin *Plesiosaurus*, from Greek *plēsios* 'near' + *sauros* 'lizard'.

plessor /ˈplɛsə/ ▶ **noun** variant spelling of **PLEXOR**.

plethora /ˈplɛθ(ə)rə/ ▶ **noun 1** a large or excessive amount of something: ***a plethora of** committees and subcommittees | Allen won a plethora of medals during his illustrious career.*
2 Medicine an excess of a bodily fluid, particularly blood.
– DERIVATIVES **plethoric** /ˈplɛθ(ə)rɪk, plɪˈθɒrɪk/ adjective (archaic or Medicine).
– ORIGIN mid 16th cent. (in the medical sense): via late Latin from Greek *plēthōrē*, from *plēthein* 'be full'.

> **USAGE** Strictly, a **plethora** is not just an abundance of something, it is an excessive amount. However, the new, looser sense is now so dominant that it must be regarded as part of standard English.

plethysmograph /plɪˈθɪzməgrɑːf/ ▶ **noun** Medicine an instrument for recording and measuring variation in the volume of a part of the body, especially as caused by changes in blood pressure.
– DERIVATIVES **plethysmographic** adjective.
– ORIGIN late 19th cent.: from Greek *plēthusmos* 'enlargement' (based on *plēthus* 'fullness') + **-GRAPH**.

pleura[1] /ˈplʊərə/ ▶ **noun** (pl. **pleurae** /-riː/) **1** each of a pair of serous membranes lining the thorax and enveloping the lungs in humans and other mammals.
2 Zoology a lateral part in an animal body or structure. Compare with **PLEURON**.
– DERIVATIVES **pleural** adjective.
– ORIGIN late Middle English: via medieval Latin from Greek, literally 'side of the body, rib'.

pleura[2] plural form of **PLEURON**.

pleurisy /ˈplʊərɪsi/ ▶ **noun** [mass noun] Medicine inflammation of the pleurae, which impairs their lubricating function and causes pain when breathing. It is caused by pneumonia and other diseases of the chest or abdomen.
– DERIVATIVES **pleuritic** adjective.
– ORIGIN late Middle English: from Old French *pleurisie*, from late Latin *pleurisis*, alteration of earlier Latin *pleuritis*, from Greek *pleura* 'side of the body, rib'.

pleuro- ▶ **combining form** relating to the pleura or pleurae: *pleuropneumonia*.
– ORIGIN from Greek *pleura* 'side', *pleuron* 'rib'.

pleurodynia /ˌplʊərə(ʊ)ˈdɪnɪə/ ▶ **noun** [mass noun] Medicine severe pain in the muscles between the ribs or in the diaphragm.
– ORIGIN early 19th cent.: from **PLEURO-** 'of the pleura' + Greek *odunē* 'pain'.

pleuron /ˈplʊərɒn/ ▶ **noun** (pl. **pleura** /-rə/) Zoology the side wall of each segment of the body of an arthropod.
– ORIGIN early 18th cent.: from Greek, literally 'side of the body, rib'.

pleuropneumonia ▶ **noun** [mass noun] pneumonia complicated with pleurisy.

Pleven /ˈplɛv(ə)n/ an industrial town in northern Bulgaria, north-east of Sofia; pop. 112,372 (2008). An important fortress town and trading centre of the Ottoman Empire, it was taken from the Turks by the Russians in the Russo-Turkish War of 1877, after a siege of 143 days.

plew /pluː/ ▶ **noun** Canadian historical a beaver skin, used as a standard unit of value in the fur trade.
– ORIGIN mid 19th cent.: from Canadian French *pélu* 'hairy', from French *poil* 'hair, bristle'.

plexiglas /ˈplɛksɪglɑːs/ ▶ **noun** [mass noun] trademark, chiefly N. Amer. a solid transparent plastic made of polymethyl methacrylate (the same material as perspex or lucite).
– ORIGIN 1930s: from Greek *plēxis* 'percussion' + **GLASS**.

plexor /ˈplɛksə/ (also **plessor**) ▶ **noun** a small hammer with a rubber head used to test reflexes and in medical percussion.
– ORIGIN mid 19th cent.: formed irregularly from Greek *plēxis* 'percussion' (from *plēssein* 'to strike') + **-OR**[1].

plexus ▶ **noun** (pl. **same** or **plexuses**) Anatomy a network of nerves or vessels in the body. ■ an intricate network or web-like formation.
– DERIVATIVES **plexiform** adjective.
– ORIGIN late 17th cent.: from Latin, literally 'plaited formation', past participle of *plectere* 'to plait'.

pliability ▶ **noun** [mass noun] the quality of being easily bent; flexibility: *an excellent combination of strength, pliability, and elasticity.*

pliable ▶ **adjective 1** easily bent; flexible: *quality leather is pliable and will not crack.*
2 easily influenced: *pliable teenage minds.*
– DERIVATIVES **pliably** adverb.
– ORIGIN late Middle English: from French, from *plier* 'to bend' (see **PLY**[1]).

pliant ▶ **adjective 1** easily bent: *pliant willow stems.*
2 easily influenced or directed; yielding: *a more pliant prime minister.*
– DERIVATIVES **pliancy** noun, **pliantly** adverb.
– ORIGIN Middle English: from French, literally 'bending', present participle of *plier*.

plica /ˈplɪkə, ˈplʌɪkə/ ▶ **noun 1** (pl. **plicae** /-kiː/ or **plicas**) Anatomy a fold or ridge of tissue. ■ Botany a small lobe between the petals of a flower.
2 [mass noun] Medicine a densely matted condition of the hair.
– ORIGIN mid 17th cent.: modern Latin, from medieval Latin, 'fold', from *plicare* 'to fold'.

plicate /ˈplʌɪkət, ˈplʌɪkeɪt/ ▶ **adjective** Biology & Geology folded, crumpled, or corrugated.
– DERIVATIVES **plicated** /plɪˈkeɪtɪd/ adjective.
– ORIGIN mid 18th cent.: from Latin *plicatus* 'folded', past participle of *plicare*.

plication ▶ **noun** a fold or corrugation. ■ [mass noun] the manner of folding or condition of being folded.
– ORIGIN late Middle English: via Old French from medieval Latin *plicatio(n-)*, from Latin *plicare* 'to fold'.

plié /ˈpliːeɪ/ Ballet ▶ **noun** a movement in which a dancer bends the knees and straightens them again, usually with the feet turned right out and heels firmly on the ground.
▶ **verb** [no obj.] perform a plié.
– ORIGIN French, literally 'bent', past participle of *plier* (see also **PLY**[1]).

pliers (also **a pair of pliers**) ▶ **plural noun** pincers with parallel, flat, and typically serrated surfaces, used chiefly for gripping small objects or bending wire.
– ORIGIN mid 16th cent.: from dialect *ply* 'bend', from French *plier* 'to bend', from Latin *plicare* 'to fold'.

plight[1] ▶ **noun** a dangerous, difficult, or otherwise unfortunate situation: *we must direct our efforts towards relieving the plight of children living in poverty.*
– ORIGIN Middle English: from Anglo-Norman French *plit* 'fold'. The *-gh-* spelling is by association with **PLIGHT**[2].

plight[2] ▶ **verb** [with obj.] archaic pledge or solemnly promise (one's faith or loyalty). ■ (**be plighted to**) be engaged to be married to.
– PHRASES **plight one's troth** see **TROTH**.
– ORIGIN Old English *plihtan* 'endanger', of Germanic origin; related to Dutch *plicht* and German *Pflicht* 'duty'. The current sense is recorded only from Middle English, but is probably original, in view of the related Germanic words.

plimsoll (also **plimsole**) ▶ **noun** Brit. a light rubber-soled canvas shoe, worn especially for sports.
– ORIGIN late 19th cent.: probably from the resemblance of the side of the sole to a **PLIMSOLL LINE**.

Plimsoll line (also **Plimsoll mark**) ▶ **noun** a marking on a ship's side showing the limit of legal submersion when loaded with cargo under various sea conditions.

– ORIGIN named after Samuel *Plimsoll* (1824–98), the English politician whose agitation in the 1870s resulted in the Merchant Shipping Act of 1876, ending the practice of sending to sea overloaded and heavily insured old ships, from which the owners profited if they sank.

Plinian /ˈplɪnɪən/ ▸ **adjective** Geology relating to or denoting a type of volcanic eruption in which a narrow stream of gas and ash is violently ejected from a vent to a height of several miles.
– ORIGIN mid 17th cent.: from Italian *pliniano*, with reference to the eruption of Vesuvius in AD 79, in which Pliny the Elder died.

plink ▸ **verb** [no obj.] emit a short, sharp, metallic or ringing sound. ■ play a musical instrument in such a way as to produce short, sharp, ringing sounds. ■ [with obj.] chiefly N. Amer. shoot at (a target) casually.
▸ **noun** a short, sharp, metallic or ringing sound.
– DERIVATIVES **plinky** adjective.
– ORIGIN 1940s: imitative.

plinth ▸ **noun** a heavy base supporting a statue or vase. ■ Architecture the lower square slab at the base of a column. ■ Architecture the base course of a building, or projecting base of a wall.
– ORIGIN late 16th cent.: from Latin *plinthus*, from Greek *plinthos* 'tile, brick, squared stone'. The Latin form was in early use in English.

Pliny[1] /ˈplɪni/ (23–79), Roman statesman and scholar; Latin name *Gaius Plinius Secundus*; known as **Pliny the Elder**. His *Natural History* (77) is a vast encyclopedia of the natural and human worlds. He died while observing the eruption of Vesuvius.

Pliny[2] /ˈplɪni/ (*c.*61–*c.*112), Roman senator and writer, nephew of Pliny the Elder; Latin name *Gaius Plinius Caecilius Secundus*; known as **Pliny the Younger**. He is noted for his books of letters which deal with both public and private affairs and which include a description of the eruption of Vesuvius in 79.

Pliocene /ˈplʌɪə(ʊ)siːn/ ▸ **adjective** Geology relating to or denoting the last epoch of the Tertiary period, between the Miocene and Pleistocene epochs. ■ (as noun **the Pliocene**) the Pliocene epoch or the system of rocks deposited during it.

> The Pliocene epoch lasted from 5.2 to 1.64 million years ago. Temperatures were falling at this time and many mammals were becoming extinct. The first hominids, including *Australopithecus* and *Homo habilis*, appeared.

– ORIGIN mid 19th cent.: from Greek *pleiōn* 'more' + *kainos* 'new'.

Plio-Pleistocene ▸ **adjective** Geology relating to or linking the Pliocene and Pleistocene epochs or rock systems together. ■ (as noun **the Plio-Pleistocene**) the Pliocene and Pleistocene epochs together or the system of rocks deposited during them.

pliosaur /ˈplʌɪəsɔː/ ▸ **noun** a plesiosaur with a short neck, large head, and massive toothed jaws. ● Family Pliosauridae, infraorder Plesiosauria: several genera, including *Pliosaurus*.
– ORIGIN mid 19th cent.: from modern Latin *Pliosaurus* (genus name), from Greek *pleiōn* 'more' + *sauros* 'lizard' (because of its greater similarity to a lizard than the ichthyosaur).

plissé /ˈpliːseɪ/ ▸ **adjective** (of fabric) treated to give a permanent puckered or crinkled effect.
▸ **noun** [mass noun] material treated so as to be permanently puckered or crinkled.
– ORIGIN late 19th cent.: French, literally 'pleated', past participle of *plisser*.

PLO ▸ **abbreviation** Palestine Liberation Organization.

plock ▸ **verb** [no obj.] make a short, low clicking sound.
▸ **noun** a short, low clicking sound.
– ORIGIN 1930s: imitative.

plod ▸ **verb** (**plods**, **plodding**, **plodded**) [no obj., with adverbial of direction] walk doggedly and slowly with heavy steps: *we plodded back up the hill*. ■ work slowly and perseveringly at a dull task: *we were plodding through a textbook*.
▸ **noun 1** a slow, heavy walk: *he settled down to a steady plod*.
2 (also **PC Plod**) Brit. informal a police officer. [with allusion to Mr *Plod* the Policeman in Enid Blyton's *Noddy* stories for children.]
– DERIVATIVES **plodder** noun.
– ORIGIN mid 16th cent.: probably symbolic of a heavy gait.

plodding ▸ **adjective** slow-moving and unexciting: *a plodding comedy drama*. ■ (of a person) thorough and hard-working but lacking in imagination or intelligence.
– DERIVATIVES **ploddingly** adverb.

-ploid ▸ **combining form** Biology denoting the number of sets of chromosomes in a cell: *triploid*.
– ORIGIN based on *(ha)ploid* and *(di)ploid*.

ploidy /ˈplɔɪdi/ ▸ **noun** [mass noun] Genetics the number of sets of chromosomes in a cell, or in the cells of an organism.
– ORIGIN 1940s: from words such as *(di)ploidy* and *(poly)ploidy*.

Ploieşti /plɔɪˈɛʃti/ an oil-refining city in central Romania, north of Bucharest; pop. 231,620 (2006).

plongeur /plɔ̃ˈʒəː/ ▸ **noun** a person employed to wash dishes and carry out other menial tasks in a restaurant or hotel.
– ORIGIN French, literally 'person who plunges'.

plonk[1] informal, chiefly Brit. ▸ **verb 1** [with obj. and adverbial of place] set down heavily or carelessly: *she plonked her glass on the table*. ■ (**plonk oneself**) sit down heavily and without ceremony: *he plonked himself down on the sofa*.
2 [no obj.] play unskilfully on a musical instrument: *people plonking around on expensive instruments*.
▸ **noun** a sound as of something being set down heavily: *he sat down with a plonk*.
– ORIGIN late 19th cent. (originally dialect): imitative; compare with **PLUNK**.

plonk[2] ▸ **noun** [mass noun] Brit. informal cheap wine of inferior quality.
– ORIGIN 1930s (originally Australian): probably an alteration of *blanc* in French *vin blanc* 'white wine'.

plonker ▸ **noun** Brit. **1** informal a foolish or inept person.
2 vulgar slang a man's penis.
– ORIGIN mid 19th cent. (as a dialect word meaning 'something large of its kind'): from the verb **PLONK**[1] + **-ER**[1].

plook /pluːk/ ▸ **noun** Scottish a spot or pimple.
– ORIGIN Middle English: of unknown origin.

plop ▸ **noun** a short sound as of a small, solid object dropping into water without a splash.
▸ **verb** (**plops**, **plopping**, **plopped**) fall or cause to fall with a plop: [no obj.] *the stone plopped into the pond* | [with obj.] *she plopped a sugar cube into the cup*. ■ (**plop oneself down**) sit or lie down gently but clumsily: *he plopped himself down on the nearest chair*.
– ORIGIN early 19th cent.: imitative.

plosion /ˈpləʊʒ(ə)n/ ▸ **noun** [mass noun] Phonetics the sudden release of air in the pronunciation of a plosive consonant.
– ORIGIN early 20th cent.: shortening of **EXPLOSION**.

plosive /ˈpləʊsɪv, -z-/ Phonetics ▸ **adjective** denoting a consonant that is produced by stopping the airflow using the lips, teeth, or palate, followed by a sudden release of air.
▸ **noun** a plosive speech sound. The basic plosives in English are *t*, *k*, and *p* (voiceless) and *d*, *g*, and *b* (voiced).
– ORIGIN late 19th cent.: shortening of **EXPLOSIVE**.

plot ▸ **noun 1** a plan made in secret by a group of people to do something illegal or harmful: [with infinitive] *there's a plot to overthrow the government*.
2 the main events of a play, novel, film, or similar work, devised and presented by the writer as an interrelated sequence.
3 a small piece of ground marked out for a purpose such as building or gardening: *a vegetable plot*.
4 a graph showing the relation between two variables. ■ chiefly US a diagram, chart, or map.
▸ **verb** (**plots**, **plotting**, **plotted**) [with obj.] **1** secretly make plans to carry out (an illegal or harmful action): *the two men are serving sentences for plotting a bomb campaign* | [no obj.] *brother plots against brother*.
2 devise the sequence of events in (a play, novel, film, or similar work).
3 mark (a route or position) on a chart: *he started to plot lines of ancient sites*. ■ mark out or allocate (points) on a graph. ■ make (a curve) by marking out a number of points on a graph. ■ illustrate by use of a graph: *it is possible to plot fairly closely the rate at which recruitment of girls increased*.
– PHRASES **lose the plot** Brit. informal lose one's ability to understand or cope with what is happening: *many people believe that he is feeling the strain or has lost the plot*. **the plot thickens** see **THICKEN**.
– DERIVATIVES **plotless** adjective.
– ORIGIN late Old English (in sense 3 of the noun), of unknown origin. The sense 'secret plan', dating from the late 16th cent., is associated with Old French *complot* 'dense crowd, secret project', the same term being used occasionally in English from the mid 16th cent. Compare with **PLAT**[1].

Plotinus /plәˈtʌɪnəs/ (*c.*205–70), philosopher, probably of Roman descent. He was the founder and leading exponent of Neoplatonism; his writings were published after his death by his pupil Porphyry.

plot line ▸ **noun** the course or main features of the plot of a play, novel, or film.

plot ratio ▸ **noun** a ratio representing the density of building in a specified area of land.

Plott (also **Plott hound**) ▸ **noun** a hunting dog of a breed developed from German stock by the Plott family of North Carolina. It has a smooth dark brown coat and large drooping ears.

plotter ▸ **noun 1** someone who secretly makes plans to do something illegal or harmful; a conspirator: *the trial of alleged coup plotters*.
2 a piece of equipment that marks out points on a chart: *a GPS chart plotter*.

plotty ▸ **adjective** informal (of a novel, play, or film) having an excessively elaborate or complicated plot.

plotz ▸ **verb** [no obj.] N. Amer. informal collapse or be beside oneself with frustration, annoyance, or other strong emotion: *lots of directors plotz while making their films*.
– ORIGIN 1960s: from Yiddish *platsen*, literally 'to burst', from Middle High German *platzen*.

plough (US **plow**) ▸ **noun 1** a large farming implement with one or more blades fixed in a frame, drawn over soil to turn it over and cut furrows in preparation for the planting of seeds. ■ [mass noun] land that has been ploughed: *she saw a brown strip of plough*. ■ chiefly N. Amer. a snowplough.
2 (**the Plough**) Brit. a prominent formation of seven stars in the constellation Ursa Major (the Great Bear), containing the Pointers that indicate the direction to the Pole Star. Also called **THE BIG DIPPER** (N. Amer.), **CHARLES'S WAIN** (formerly, in Britain).
▸ **verb** [with obj.] **1** turn up the earth of (an area of land) with a plough, especially before sowing: *the fields had all been ploughed up* | (as adj. **ploughed**) *a ploughed field*. ■ cut (a furrow or line) with or as if with a plough: *icebergs have ploughed furrows on the seabed*. ■ (of a ship or boat) travel through (an area of water): *cruise liners plough the long-sailed routes*. ■ (**plough something up**) unearth something while using a plough: *some day someone will plough up the bomb and lose a leg*.
2 [no obj., with adverbial of direction] (especially of a vehicle) move in a fast and uncontrolled manner: *the car ploughed into the side of a van*. ■ advance or progress laboriously or forcibly: *they ploughed their way through deep snow* | *the students are ploughing through a set of grammar exercises*. ■ (**plough on**) continue steadily despite difficulties or warnings to stop: *he ploughed on, trying to outline his plans*.
3 chiefly N. Amer. clear snow from (a road) using a snowplough.
4 Brit. informal, dated fail (an examination).
– PHRASES **plough a lonely** (or **one's own**) **furrow** follow a course of action in which one is isolated or in which one can act independently. **put** (or **set**) **one's hand to the plough** embark on a task. [with biblical allusion to Luke 9:62.]
– PHRASAL VERBS **plough something in/back** plough grass or other material into the soil to enrich it. ■ invest money in a business or reinvest profits in the enterprise producing them.
– DERIVATIVES **ploughable** adjective, **plougher** noun.
– ORIGIN late Old English *plōh*, of Germanic origin; related to Dutch *ploeg* and German *Pflug*. The spelling *plough* became common in England in the 18th cent.; earlier (16th–17th cents) the noun was normally spelled *plough*, the verb *plow*.

ploughland (US **plowland**) ▸ **noun** [mass noun] land that is ploughed for growing crops; arable land. ■ [count noun] a measure of land used in the northern and eastern counties of England after the Norman conquest, based on the area able to be ploughed in a year by a team of eight oxen.

ploughman (US **plowman**) ▸ **noun** (pl. **ploughmen**) a person who uses a plough.

ploughman's lunch ▸ **noun** Brit. a meal of bread and cheese, typically with pickle and salad.

ploughman's spikenard ▸ **noun** a European plant of the daisy family, with purple and yellow flower heads. ● *Inula conyzae*, family Compositae.

Plough Monday ▸ **noun** the first Monday after Epiphany, formerly marked by popular festivals or observances in some regions.
– ORIGIN from the custom of dragging a plough through the streets to mark the beginning of the ploughing season.

P

plough pan ▶ **noun** a compacted layer in cultivated soil resulting from repeated ploughing.

ploughshare (US **plowshare**) ▶ **noun** the main cutting blade of a plough, behind the coulter.
– ORIGIN late Middle English: from PLOUGH + Old English *scær*, *scear* 'ploughshare' (related to SHEAR).

Plovdiv /ˈplɒvdɪf/ an industrial and commercial city in southern Bulgaria; pop. 347,600 (2008). Known to the ancient Greeks as Philippopolis and to the Romans as Trimontium, it assumed its present name after the First World War.

plover /ˈplʌvə/ ▶ **noun** a short-billed gregarious wading bird, typically found by water but sometimes frequenting grassland, tundra, and mountains. ● Family Charadriidae (the **plover family**): several genera and numerous species, especially the **ringed plovers** (*Charadrius*), **grey** and **golden plovers** (*Pluvialis*), and lapwings (*Vanellus*).
■ used in names of birds similar to the plover in other families, e.g. **Egyptian plover**.
– ORIGIN Middle English: from Anglo-Norman French, based on Latin *pluvia* 'rain'.

plow ▶ **noun & verb** US spelling of PLOUGH.

ploy ▶ **noun** a cunning plan or action designed to turn a situation to one's own advantage: *the president has dismissed the referendum as a ploy to buy time*. ■ an activity done for amusement: *the eternal cross-stitch I was set to do before I could indulge my own ploys*.
– ORIGIN late 17th cent. (originally Scots and northern English in the sense 'pastime'): of unknown origin. The notion of 'a calculated plan' dates from the 1950s.

PLP ▶ **abbreviation** (in the UK) Parliamentary Labour Party.

PLR ▶ **abbreviation** (in the UK) Public Lending Right.

pls ▶ **abbreviation** informal please: *if you have any suggestions, pls email me*.

pluck ▶ **verb** [with obj.] **1** take hold of (something) and quickly remove it from its place: *she plucked a blade of grass* | *he plucked a tape from the shelf*. ■ catch hold of and pull quickly: *she plucked his sleeve* | [no obj.] *brambles* ***plucked at*** *her jeans*. ■ pull the feathers from (a bird's carcass) to prepare it for cooking.
■ pull some of the hairs from (one's eyebrows) to make them look neater. ■ Geology (of glacier ice) break off (pieces of rock) by mechanical force.
2 quickly or suddenly remove someone from a dangerous or unpleasant situation: *the baby was plucked from a grim orphanage*.
3 sound (a musical instrument or its strings) with one's finger or a plectrum.
▶ **noun** [mass noun] **1** spirited and determined courage.
2 the heart, liver, and lungs of an animal as food.
– PHRASES **pluck up courage** see COURAGE.
– DERIVATIVES **plucker noun** [usu. in combination] *a goose-plucker*.
– ORIGIN late Old English *ploccian*, *pluccian*, of Germanic origin; related to Flemish *plokken*; probably from the base of Old French *(es)peluchier* 'to pluck'. Sense 1 of the noun is originally boxers' slang.

P

plucky ▶ **adjective** (**pluckier**, **pluckiest**) having or showing determined courage in the face of difficulties.
– DERIVATIVES **pluckily adverb**, **pluckiness noun**.

plug ▶ **noun 1** a piece of solid material fitting tightly into a hole and blocking it up: *somewhere in the pipes there is a plug of ice blocking the flow*. ■ a circular piece of metal, rubber, or plastic used to stop the plughole of a bath or basin and keep the water in it.
■ N. Amer. informal a baby's dummy. ■ a mass of solidified lava filling the neck of a volcano. ■ (in gardening) a young plant or clump of grass with a small mass of soil protecting its roots, for planting out.
2 a device for making an electrical connection between an appliance and the mains, consisting of an insulated casing with metal pins that fit into holes in a socket. ■ a socket into which an electric plug can be fitted. ■ short for SPARK PLUG.
3 informal a piece of publicity promoting a product, event, or establishment: *he threw in a plug, boasting that the restaurant offered many entrées for under £5*.
4 a piece of tobacco cut from a larger cake for chewing. ■ [mass noun] (also **plug tobacco**) tobacco in large cakes designed to be cut for chewing.
5 Fishing a lure with one or more hooks attached.
6 short for FIREPLUG.
7 N. Amer. informal a tired or old horse.
▶ **verb** (**plugs**, **plugging**, **plugged**) [with obj.] **1** block or fill in (a hole or cavity): *trucks arrived loaded with gravel to plug the hole and clear the road*. ■ fill: *the new sanctions are meant to plug the gaps in the trade embargo*. ■ insert (something) into an opening so as to fill it: *the baby plugged his thumb into his mouth*.
2 informal mention (a product, event, or establishment) publicly in order to promote it: *during the show he plugged his new record*.
3 N. Amer. informal shoot or hit (someone or something).
4 [no obj., with adverbial] informal proceed steadily and laboriously with a journey or task: *during the years of poverty, he* ***plugged away at*** *his writing*.
– PHRASES **plug the gap** (or **gaps**) provide something that is lacking in a particular situation: *the government is to borrow £29 billion to plug the gap in public spending*.
– PHRASAL VERBS **plug something in** connect an electrical appliance to the mains by inserting a plug in a socket. **plug into** (of an electrical appliance) be connected to another appliance by a lead inserted in a socket. ■ gain or have access to a system of computerized information: *we plug into the research facilities available at the institute*. ■ become knowledgeable about and involved with: *the workshops are a great way to plug into radical ideas and radical groups*.
– DERIVATIVES **plugger noun**.
– ORIGIN early 17th cent.: from Middle Dutch and Middle Low German *plugge*, of unknown ultimate origin.

Plug and Play ▶ **noun** a standard for the connection of peripherals to personal computers, whereby a device only needs to be connected to a computer in order to be configured to work perfectly, without any action by the user.

plugboard ▶ **noun** a board containing several sockets into which plugs may be inserted to interconnect electric circuits, telephone lines, or computer components, by means of short lengths of wire.

plug-compatible ▶ **adjective** relating to or denoting computing equipment which is compatible with devices or systems produced by different manufacturers, to the extent that it can be plugged in and operated successfully.
▶ **noun** a piece of plug-compatible computing equipment.

plug flow ▶ **noun** [mass noun] Geology & Physics the flow of a body of ice or viscous fluid with no shearing between adjacent layers; idealized flow without any mixing of particles of fluid.

plug fuse ▶ **noun** a fuse designed to be pushed into a socket in a panel or board.

plug gauge ▶ **noun** a gauge in the form of a plug, used for measuring the diameter of a hole.

plugged-in ▶ **adjective** informal up to date; aware of the latest developments or trends.

plughole ▶ **noun** Brit. a hole at the lowest point of a bath, basin, or sink, down which waste water drains away and which can be stopped with a plug.
– PHRASES **go down the plughole** informal be unsuccessful, lost, or wasted: *the company went down the plughole*.

plug-in ▶ **adjective** able to be connected by means of a plug: *a plug-in kettle*. ■ Computing (of a module or software) able to be added to a system to give extra features or functions: *a plug-in graphics card*.
▶ **noun 1** Computing a plug-in module or plug-in software.
2 Canadian an electric socket in a car park or garage for plugging in the block heater of a vehicle to prevent the engine from freezing.

plug-ugly informal, chiefly N. Amer. ▶ **noun** (pl. **plug-uglies**) a thug or villain.
▶ **adjective** (of a person) very ugly.
– ORIGIN by association with the verb PLUG in the informal sense 'hit with the fist'.

plum ▶ **noun 1** an oval fleshy fruit which is purple, reddish, or yellow when ripe and contains a flattish pointed stone. ■ [usu. with modifier] W. Indian a small edible fruit from any of a number of trees.
2 (also **plum tree**) the deciduous tree which bears plums. ● Several species in the genus *Prunus*, family Rosaceae, in particular *P. domestica*.
3 [mass noun] a reddish-purple colour.
4 [usu. as modifier] informal a thing, typically a job, considered to be highly desirable: *he landed a plum assistant producer's job*.
▶ **adverb** chiefly US variant spelling of PLUMB¹: *the helicopter crashed plum on the cabins*.
– PHRASES **have a plum in one's mouth** Brit. have an accent thought typical of the English upper classes. **like a ripe plum** (or **ripe plums**) used to convey that something can be obtained with little or no effort: *the country is likely to fall into the enemy's hands like a ripe plum*.
– ORIGIN Old English *plūme*, from medieval Latin *pruna*, from Latin *prunum* (see PRUNE¹).

plumage /ˈpluːmɪdʒ/ ▶ **noun** [mass noun] a bird's feathers collectively.
– DERIVATIVES **plumaged adjective** [usu. in combination] *a grey-plumaged bird*.
– ORIGIN late Middle English: from Old French, from *plume* 'feather'.

plumb¹ ▶ **verb** [with obj.] **1** measure (the depth of a body of water). ■ [no obj., with adverbial] (of water) be of a specified depth: *at its deepest the lake scarcely plumbed seven feet*. ■ explore or experience fully or to extremes: *she had* ***plumbed the depths of*** *depravity*.
2 test (an upright surface) to determine the vertical.
▶ **noun** a ball of lead or other heavy object attached to the end of a line for finding the depth of water or determining the vertical on an upright surface.
▶ **adverb 1** informal exactly: *trading opportunities plumb in the centre of central Europe*. ■ [as submodifier] N. Amer. extremely or completely: *they must both be plumb crazy*.
2 archaic vertically: *drapery fell from their human forms plumb down*.
▶ **adjective** vertical: *ensure that the skirting is straight and plumb*. ■ Cricket (of the wicket) level; true.
– PHRASES **out of plumb** not exactly vertical: *the towers are inclined, from four to ten feet out of plumb*.
– ORIGIN Middle English (originally in the sense 'sounding lead'): via Old French from Latin *plumbum* 'lead'.

plumb² ▶ **verb** [with obj.] (**plumb something in**) Brit. install an appliance such as a bath, toilet, or washing machine and connect to water and drainage pipes.
■ install and connect water and drainage pipes in (a building or room): *the kitchen is* ***plumbed for*** *a washing machine*.
– ORIGIN late 19th cent. (in the sense 'work as a plumber'): back-formation from PLUMBER.

plumbago /plʌmˈbeɪɡəʊ/ ▶ **noun** (pl. **plumbagos**)
1 old-fashioned term for GRAPHITE. [early 17th cent. (denoting an ore such as galena containing lead): from Latin, from *plumbum* 'lead'. The sense 'graphite' arose through its use for pencil leads.]
2 an evergreen flowering shrub or climber which is widely distributed in warm regions and grown elsewhere as a greenhouse or indoor plant. Also called LEADWORT. [named from the colour of the flowers.]
● Genus *Plumbago*, family Plumbaginaceae.

plumbate /ˈplʌmbeɪt/ ▶ **noun** Chemistry a salt in which the anion contains both lead and oxygen, especially one of the anion PbO_3^{2-}.
– ORIGIN mid 19th cent.: from Latin *plumbum* 'lead' + -ATE¹.

plumb bob ▶ **noun** a bob of lead or other heavy material forming the weight of a plumb line.

plumbeous /ˈplʌmbɪəs/ ▶ **adjective** of or like lead.
■ Ornithology of the dull grey colour of lead.
– ORIGIN late 16th cent.: from Latin *plumbeus* 'leaden' (from *plumbum* 'lead') + -OUS.

plumber ▶ **noun** a person who fits and repairs the pipes, fittings, and other apparatus of water supply, sanitation, or heating systems.
– ORIGIN late Middle English (originally denoting a person dealing in and working with lead): from Old French *plommier*, from Latin *plumbarius*, from *plumbum* 'lead'.

plumber's snake ▶ **noun** see SNAKE.

plumbic /ˈplʌmbɪk/ ▶ **adjective** Chemistry of lead with a valency of four; of lead(IV). Compare with PLUMBOUS.
■ Medicine caused by the presence of lead.
– ORIGIN late 18th cent.: from Latin *plumbum* 'lead' + -IC.

plumbing ▶ **noun** [mass noun] the system of pipes, tanks, fittings, and other apparatus required for the water supply, heating, and sanitation in a building.
■ the work of installing and maintaining a plumbing system. ■ informal used as a humorous euphemism for the excretory tracts and urinary system: *I'd never discuss my plumbing with ladies*.

plumbism /ˈplʌmbɪz(ə)m/ ▶ **noun** technical term for LEAD POISONING.

plumbless /ˈplʌmlɪs/ ▶ **adjective** literary (of a body of water) extremely deep.

plumb line ▶ **noun** a line with a plumb attached to it, used for finding the depth of water or determining the vertical on an upright surface.

plumbous /ˈplʌmbəs/ ▶ **adjective** Chemistry of lead with a valency of two; of lead(II). Compare with PLUMBIC.

– ORIGIN late 17th cent.: from Latin *plumbosus* 'full of lead'.

plumb rule ▶ noun a plumb line attached to a board, used by builders and surveyors.

plum duff ▶ noun a rich, spiced suet pudding made with raisins or currants.

plume ▶ noun **1** a long, soft feather or arrangement of feathers used by a bird for display or worn by a person for ornament: *a hat with a jaunty ostrich plume.* ■ Zoology a part of an animal's body that resembles a feather: *the antennae are divided into large feathery plumes.*
2 a long cloud of smoke or vapour resembling a feather as it spreads from its point of origin: *as he spoke, the word was accompanied by a white plume of breath.* ■ a mass of material, typically a pollutant, spreading from a source: *a radioactive plume.*
3 (also **mantle plume**) Geology a localized column of hotter magma rising by convection in the mantle, believed to cause volcanic activity in locations away from plate margins.
▶ verb **1** [no obj.] spread out in a shape resembling a feather: *smoke plumed from the chimneys.* ■ [with obj.] decorate with or as if with feathers: (as adj. **plumed**) *rain began to beat down on my plumed cap.*
2 (**plume oneself**) chiefly archaic (of a bird) preen itself. ■ feel a great sense of self-satisfaction about something: *she **plumed herself on** being cosmopolitan.*
– DERIVATIVES **plumeless** adjective, **plume-like** adjective.
– ORIGIN late Middle English: from Old French, from Latin *pluma* 'down'.

plumed serpent ▶ noun a mythical creature depicted as part bird, part snake, in particular Quetzalcóatl, a god of the Toltec and Aztec civilizations having this form.

plume moth ▶ noun a small, slender long-legged moth with narrow wings divided into feathery plumes. At rest the wings are rolled and held out sideways, giving the moth the shape of a letter T.
● Family Pterophoridae: several genera.

plumeria /pluːˈmɪərɪə/ ▶ noun a fragrant flowering tropical tree of a genus which includes frangipani.
● Genus *Plumeria*, family Apocynaceae.
– ORIGIN modern Latin, named after Charles *Plumier* (1646–1704), French botanist.

plummet ▶ verb (**plummets, plummeting, plummeted**) [no obj.] fall or drop straight down at high speed: *a climber was killed when he plummeted 300 feet down an icy gully.* ■ decrease rapidly in value or amount: *hardware sales plummeted.*
▶ noun **1** a steep and rapid fall or drop.
2 a plumb or plumb line.
– ORIGIN late Middle English (as a noun): from Old French *plommet* 'small sounding lead', diminutive of *plomb* 'lead'. The current verb sense dates from the 1930s.

plummy ▶ adjective (**plummier, plummiest**)
1 resembling a plum: *cosy reds and plummy blues.*
2 Brit. informal (of a person's voice) having an accent thought typical of the English upper classes.
3 Brit. informal choice; highly desirable: *there are some plummy roles for the taking here.*

plumose /ˈpluːməʊs, ˈpluːməʊs, -z/ ▶ adjective chiefly Biology having many fine filaments or branches which give a feathery appearance.
– ORIGIN mid 18th cent.: from Latin *plumosus* 'full of down or feathers', from *pluma* 'down'.

plump¹ ▶ adjective having a full rounded shape: *the berries were plump and sweet.* ■ (of a person) rather fat.
▶ verb [with obj.] shake or pat (a cushion or pillow) to adjust its stuffing and make it rounded and soft: *she **plumped up** her pillows.* ■ [no obj.] (**plump up**) become rounder and fatter: *stew the dried fruits gently until they plump up.*
– DERIVATIVES **plumpish** adjective, **plumply** adverb, **plumpy** adjective.
– ORIGIN late 15th cent. (in the sense 'blunt, forthright'): related to Middle Dutch *plomp*, Middle Low German *plump*, *plomp* 'blunt, obtuse, blockish'. The sense has become appreciative, perhaps by association with PLUM.

plump² ▶ verb **1** [with obj. and adverbial of place] set down heavily or unceremoniously: *she plumped her bag on the table.* ■ (**plump oneself**) sit down heavily and unceremoniously: *she plumped herself down in the nearest seat* | [no obj.] *he plumped down on the bench beside me.*
2 [no obj.] (**plump for**) decide definitely in favour of (one of two or more possibilities): *offered a choice of drinks, he plumped for brandy.*
▶ noun archaic an abrupt plunge; a heavy fall.
▶ adverb informal **1** with a sudden or heavy fall: *she sat down plump on the bed.*
2 dated directly and bluntly: *he must tell her plump and plain that he was on the dole.*
– ORIGIN late Middle English: related to Middle Low German *plumpen*, Middle Dutch *plompen* 'fall into water', probably of imitative origin.

plumpness ▶ noun [mass noun] the quality of having a full rounded shape: *the plumpness of the peaches.* ■ a person's quality of being rather fat; chubbiness: *she grew up being teased for her plumpness.*

plum pox ▶ noun [mass noun] an aphid-borne virus disease of plum trees characterized by yellow blotches on the leaves and pockets of dead tissue in the fruit.

plum pudding ▶ noun a rich boiled suet pudding containing raisins, currants, and spices.
– ORIGIN early 18th cent.: so named because the pudding was originally made with plums, the word *plum* being retained later to denote 'raisin', which became a substituted ingredient.

plum tomato ▶ noun a tomato of an Italian variety which is large and shaped like a plum.

plumule /ˈpluːmjuːl/ ▶ noun **1** Botany the rudimentary shoot or stem of an embryo plant.
2 Ornithology a bird's down feather, numbers of which form an insulating layer under the contour feathers.
– ORIGIN early 18th cent.: from French *plumule* or Latin *plumula* 'small feather', diminutive of *pluma* 'down'.

plumy ▶ adjective (**plumier, plumiest**) resembling or decorated with feathers.

plunder ▶ verb [with obj.] steal goods from (a place or person), typically using force and in a time of war or civil disorder: *looters moved into the disaster area to plunder shops.* ■ steal (goods), typically using force and in a time of disorder. ■ take material from (artistic or academic work) for one's own purposes: *we shall plunder related sciences to assist our research.*
▶ noun [mass noun] the violent and dishonest acquisition of property: *the commander refused to maintain his troops through pillage and plunder.* ■ property acquired illegally and violently: *the army sacked the city and carried off huge quantities of plunder.*
– DERIVATIVES **plunderer** noun.
– ORIGIN mid 17th cent.: from German *plündern*, literally 'rob of household goods', from Middle High German *plunder* 'household effects'. Early use of the verb was with reference to the Thirty Years War (reflecting German usage); on the outbreak of the Civil War in 1642, the word and activity were associated with the forces under Prince Rupert.

plunge ▶ verb **1** [no obj., with adverbial] jump or dive quickly and energetically: *our little daughters whooped as they **plunged into** the sea.* ■ fall suddenly and uncontrollably: *a car swerved to avoid a bus and plunged into a ravine.* ■ (as adj. **plunging**) denoting a very low-cut neckline on a woman's garment. ■ embark impetuously on a speech or course of action: *he came to a decision, and plunged on before he had time to reconsider it.* ■ suffer a rapid decrease in value: *shares in the company plunged 18p on news that profits had fallen.* ■ (of a ship) pitch: *the ship plunged through the 20-foot seas.* ■ [no obj.] (of a horse) rear violently.
2 [with obj. and adverbial] push or thrust quickly: *he plunged his hands into his pockets.* ■ quickly immerse in liquid: *to peel fruit, cover with boiling water and then plunge them into iced water.* ■ suddenly bring into a specified condition or state: *for a moment the scene was illuminated, then it was plunged back into darkness.* ■ [with obj.] sink (a pot containing a plant) in the ground: *pot up and plunge spring-flowering bulbs.*
▶ noun an act of jumping or diving into water: *fanatics went straight from the hot room to take a cold plunge.* ■ a swift and drastic fall in value or amount: *the central bank declared a 76% plunge in its profits.*
– PHRASES **take the plunge** informal commit oneself to a course of action about which one is nervous.
– ORIGIN late Middle English: from Old French *plungier* 'thrust down', based on Latin *plumbum* 'lead, plummet'.

plunge pool ▶ noun **1** a deep basin excavated at the foot of a waterfall by the action of the falling water.
2 a small, deep swimming pool, typically one filled with cold water and used to refresh or invigorate the body after a sauna.

plunger ▶ noun **1** a part of a device or mechanism that works with a plunging or thrusting movement. ■ a device consisting of a rubber cup on a long handle, used to clear blocked pipes by means of suction.
2 informal a person who gambles or spends money recklessly.

plunk informal ▶ verb **1** [no obj.] play a keyboard or plucked stringed instrument in an inexpressive way.
2 [with obj.] US hit (someone) abruptly.
3 [with obj. and adverbial] chiefly N. Amer. set down heavily or abruptly: *she plunked her pack on top of the bar.* ■ (**plunk something down**) pay a sum of money: *I plunked down £14.95 for the new paperback edition.*
▶ noun **1** the sound made by abruptly plucking a string of a stringed instrument.
2 US a heavy blow.
– ORIGIN early 19th cent.: probably imitative.

pluperfect ▶ adjective Grammar (of a tense) denoting an action completed prior to some past point of time specified or implied, formed in English by *had* and the past participle, as in *he had gone by then.*
▶ noun the pluperfect tense.
– ORIGIN late 15th cent.: from modern Latin *plusperfectum*, from Latin (*tempus praeteritum*) *plus quam perfectum* '(past tense) more than perfect'.

plural ▶ adjective **1** Grammar (of a word or form) denoting more than one, or (in languages with dual number) more than two: [postpositive] *the first person plural.* ■ more than one in number: *the meanings of the text are plural.*
2 containing several diverse elements: *a plural society.*
▶ noun Grammar a plural word or form. ■ (**the plural**) the plural number: *the verb is in the plural.*
– DERIVATIVES **plurally** adverb.
– ORIGIN late Middle English: from Old French *plurel* or Latin *pluralis*, from *plus*, *plur-* 'more'.

pluralism ▶ noun [mass noun] **1** a condition or system in which two or more states, groups, principles, sources of authority, etc., coexist. ■ a political theory or system of power-sharing among a number of political parties. ■ a theory or system of devolution and autonomy for individual bodies in preference to monolithic state control. ■ a form of society in which the members of minority groups maintain their independent cultural traditions. ■ Philosophy a theory or system that recognizes more than one ultimate principle. Compare with MONISM.
2 the practice of holding more than one ecclesiastical office at a time.
– DERIVATIVES **pluralist** noun & adjective, **pluralistic** adjective, **pluralistically** adverb.

plurality ▶ noun (pl. **pluralities**) **1** [mass noun] the fact or state of being plural: *some languages add an extra syllable to mark plurality.* ■ [in sing.] a large number of people or things: *a plurality of critical approaches.*
2 US the number of votes cast for a candidate who receives more than any other but does not receive an absolute majority. ■ the number by which plurality exceeds the number of votes cast for the candidate placed second.
3 chiefly historical another term for PLURALISM (sense 2).
– ORIGIN late Middle English: from Old French *pluralite*, from late Latin *pluralitas*, from Latin *pluralis* 'relating to more than one' (see PLURAL).

pluralize (also **pluralise**) ▶ verb [with obj.] **1** cause to become more numerous. ■ cause to be made up of several different elements.
2 give a plural form to (a word).
– DERIVATIVES **pluralization** noun.

plural society ▶ noun a society composed of different ethnic groups or cultural traditions, or in the political structure of which ethnic or cultural differences are reflected.

plural voting ▶ noun [mass noun] the system or practice of casting more than one vote, or of voting in more than one constituency.

pluri- ▶ combining form several: *pluripotent.*
– ORIGIN from Latin *plus*, *plur-* 'more', *plures* 'several'.

pluripotent /ˌplʊərɪˈpəʊt(ə)nt/ ▶ adjective Biology (of an immature cell or stem cell) capable of giving rise to several different cell types.
– ORIGIN 1940s: from PLURI- 'several' + Latin *potent-* 'being able' (see POTENT¹).

plus ▶ preposition **1** with the addition of: *two plus four is six* | *he was awarded the full amount plus interest.* ■ informal together with: *all apartments have a small kitchen plus private bathroom.*
2 (of temperature) above zero: *the temperature is frequently plus 35 degrees at midday.*

P

▸ **adjective 1** [postpositive] (after a number or amount) at least: *companies put losses at $500,000 plus.* ▪ (after a grade) rather better than: *B plus.*
2 (before a number) above zero; positive: *plus 60 degrees centigrade.*
3 having a positive electric charge.
▸ **noun 1** short for **plus sign**. ▪ a mathematical operation of addition.
2 an advantage: *knowing the language is a decided plus* | [as modifier] *on the plus side, the staff are enthusiastic and good-natured.*
▸ **conjunction** informal furthermore; also: *it's packed full of medical advice, plus it keeps you informed about the latest research.*
– ORIGIN mid 16th cent.: from Latin, literally 'more'.

plus ça change /ˌpluː sa ˈʃɒ̃ʒ/, French /ply sa ʃɑ̃ʒ/ ▸ **exclamation** used to express resigned acknowledgement of the fundamental immutability of human nature and institutions.
– ORIGIN French, from *plus ça change, plus c'est la même chose* 'the more it changes, the more it stays the same'.

plus fours ▸ **plural noun** baggy knickerbockers reaching below the knee, formerly worn by men for hunting and golf.
– ORIGIN 1920s: so named because the overhang at the knee required an extra four inches of material.

plush ▸ **noun** [mass noun] a rich fabric of silk, cotton, wool, or a combination of these, with a long, soft nap: [as modifier] *plush upholstery.*
▸ **adjective** richly luxurious and expensive: *a plush Mayfair flat.*
– DERIVATIVES **plushly** adverb, **plushness** noun.
– ORIGIN late 16th cent.: from obsolete French *pluche*, contraction of *peluche*, from Old French *peluchier* 'to pluck', based on Latin *pilus* 'hair'. The sense 'luxurious' dates from the 1920s.

plush velvet ▸ **noun** [mass noun] a kind of plush with a short, soft, dense nap, resembling velvet.

plushy US ▸ **adjective** (**plushier**, **plushiest**) made of or resembling plush; soft to the touch: *her heels sank into the plushy carpet.*
▸ **noun** (also **plushie**) (pl. **plushies**) a soft toy.

plus-minus ▸ **noun** [often as modifier] Ice Hockey a running total used as an indication of a player's effectiveness, calculated by adding one for each goal scored by the player's team in even-strength play while the player is on the ice, and subtracting one for each goal conceded.
▸ **adverb** S. African more or less; roughly: *it was plus-minus 8.30 a.m.*

plus-one ▸ **noun** informal a person's guest at a social function.

P

plus sign ▸ **noun** the symbol +, indicating addition or a positive value.

plus-size ▸ **adjective** N. Amer. (of a woman or women's clothing) of a larger size than normal; outsize.

plus twos ▸ **plural noun** a shorter version of plus fours.

Plutarch /ˈpluːtɑːk/ (*c.*46–*c.*120), Greek biographer and philosopher; Latin name *Lucius Mestrius Plutarchus*. He is chiefly known for *Parallel Lives*, a collection of biographies of prominent Greeks and Romans.

pluteus /ˈpluːtɪəs/ ▸ **noun** (pl. **plutei** /ˈpluːtɪʌɪ/) Zoology the planktonic larva of some echinoderms, being somewhat triangular with lateral projections.
– ORIGIN late 19th cent.: from Latin, literally 'barrier' (with reference to its shape).

Plutino /pluːˈtiːnəʊ/ ▸ **noun** a small planet-like body orbiting the sun in the region of the Kuiper belt and in resonance with Neptune.
– ORIGIN 1990s: from the name of **Pluto** (because they have a similar orbit) + the Italian diminutive suffix *-ino*.

Pluto 1 Greek Mythology the god of the underworld. Also called **Hades**.
2 Astronomy a small planetary body orbiting the sun, discovered in 1930 by Clyde Tombaugh.

> Pluto usually orbits beyond Neptune at an average distance of 5,900 million km from the sun, though its orbit is so eccentric that at perihelion it is closer to the sun than Neptune (as in 1979–99). Pluto is smaller than earth's moon (diameter about 2,250 km), but it was discovered in 1978 to have its own large satellite (Charon). From the time of its discovery it was regarded as the ninth (outermost) planet of the solar system, but in the 1990s its unusual characteristics led astronomers to question its planetary nature. In August 2006 the International Astronomical Union formally declared Pluto to be a dwarf planet rather than a planet proper.

– ORIGIN via Latin from *Ploutōn*, the Greek name of the god of the underworld.

plutocracy /pluːˈtɒkrəsi/ ▸ **noun** (pl. **plutocracies**) [mass noun] government by the wealthy. ▪ [count noun] a state or society governed by the wealthy. ▪ [count noun] an elite or ruling class whose power derives from their wealth.
– DERIVATIVES **plutocratic** adjective, **plutocratically** adverb.
– ORIGIN mid 17th cent.: from Greek *ploutokratia*, from *ploutos* 'wealth' + *kratos* 'strength, authority'.

plutocrat ▸ **noun** often derogatory a person whose power derives from their wealth.

pluton /ˈpluːt(ə)n/ ▸ **noun** Geology a body of intrusive igneous rock.
– ORIGIN 1930s: back-formation from **plutonic**.

Plutonian ▸ **adjective 1** of or associated with the underworld.
2 relating to the dwarf planet Pluto.

plutonic ▸ **adjective 1** Geology relating to or denoting igneous rock formed by solidification at considerable depth beneath the earth's surface.
2 (**Plutonic**) relating to the underworld or the god Pluto.

plutonism ▸ **noun** [mass noun] Geology the formation of intrusive igneous rocks by solidification of magma beneath the earth's surface. ▪ (**Plutonism**) historical the theory (now accepted) that rocks such as granite were formed by solidification from the molten state, as proposed by James Hutton and others, rather than by precipitation from the sea. Compare with **Neptunism**.
– DERIVATIVES **Plutonist** noun & adjective (historical).

plutonium ▸ **noun** [mass noun] the chemical element of atomic number 94, a dense silvery radioactive metal of the actinide series, used as a fuel in nuclear reactors and as an explosive in nuclear fission weapons. Plutonium only occurs in trace amounts in nature but is manufactured in nuclear reactors from uranium-238. (Symbol: **Pu**)
– ORIGIN 1940s: from Greek 'Pluto', on the pattern of *neptunium*, being the next planet beyond Neptune.

pluvial chiefly Geology ▸ **adjective** relating to or characterized by rainfall.
▸ **noun** a period marked by increased rainfall.
– ORIGIN mid 17th cent.: from Latin *pluvialis*, from *pluvia* 'rain'.

Pluviose /ˈpluːvɪəʊs/ (also **Pluviôse** French /plyvjəʊz/) ▸ **noun** the fifth month of the French Republican calendar (1793–1805), originally running from 20 January to 18 February.
– ORIGIN French *Pluviôse*, from Latin *pluviosus* 'relating to rain'.

ply[1] ▸ **noun** (pl. **plies**) **1** a thickness or layer of a folded or laminated material. ▪ [usu. in combination] a strand of yarn or rope. ▪ the number of multiple layers or strands of which something is made: *the yarn can be any ply from two to eight.*
2 short for **plywood**.
3 [mass noun] (in game theory) the number of levels at which branching occurs in a tree of possible outcomes, typically corresponding to the number of moves ahead (in chess strictly half-moves ahead) considered by a computer program. ▪ [count noun] a half-move (i.e. one player's move) in computer chess.
– ORIGIN late Middle English (in the sense 'fold'): from French *pli* 'fold', from the verb *plier*, from Latin *plicare* 'to fold'.

ply[2] ▸ **verb** (**plies**, **plying**, **plied**) [with obj.] **1** work steadily with (a tool): *a tailor delicately plying his needle.* ▪ work steadily at (one's business or trade).
2 [no obj., with adverbial of direction] (of a vessel or vehicle) travel regularly over a route, typically for commercial purposes: *ferries ply across a strait to the island.* ▪ [with obj.] regularly travel over (a route): *the fleet has plied the Bristol Channel since Victorian times.*
3 (**ply someone with**) provide someone with (food or drink) in a continuous or insistent way: *she plied me with tea and scones.* ▪ direct (numerous questions) at someone: *she plied him with questions about his visit.*
– PHRASES **ply for hire** Brit. search for or be available for customers to hire.
– ORIGIN late Middle English: shortening of **apply**.

Plymouth /ˈplɪməθ/ **1** a port and naval base in Devon, SW England; pop. 251,900 (est. 2009). In 1620 it was the scene of the Pilgrim Fathers' departure to North America in the *Mayflower*. ▪ a shipping forecast area covering the English Channel roughly between the meridians of the Scilly Isles in the west and Start Point in the east.
2 a town in SE Massachusetts, on the Atlantic coast; pop. 55,705 (est. 2008). The site in 1620 of the landing of the Pilgrim Fathers, it was the earliest permanent European settlement in New England.
3 the capital of the island of Montserrat in the Caribbean. It was abandoned following the eruption of the Soufrière Hills volcano from 1995.

Plymouth Brethren a strict Calvinistic religious body formed at Plymouth in Devon *c.*1830, having no formal creed and no official order of ministers. Its teaching emphasizes an expected millennium and members renounce many secular occupations, allowing only those compatible with New Testament standards.

Plymouth Rock[1] a granite boulder at Plymouth, Massachusetts, on to which the Pilgrim Fathers are said to have stepped from the *Mayflower*.

Plymouth Rock[2] ▸ **noun** a chicken of a large domestic breed of American origin, having grey plumage with blackish stripes, and a yellow beak, legs, and feet.

plyometrics ▸ **plural noun** [treated as sing.] a form of exercise that involves rapid and repeated stretching and contracting of the muscles, designed to increase strength.
– DERIVATIVES **plyometric** adjective.
– ORIGIN 1970s: from Greek *plio* 'more' + **metric**[1].

ply rating ▸ **noun** a number indicating the strength of a tyre casing.
– ORIGIN 1950s: formerly referring to the number of cord plies in a casing.

plywood ▸ **noun** [mass noun] a type of strong thin wooden board consisting of two or more layers glued and pressed together with the direction of the grain alternating.

Plzeň /ˈplʼzɛɲ/ Czech name for **Pilsen**.

PM informal ▸ **abbreviation** ▪ post-mortem. ▪ Provost Marshal.
▸ **noun** (pl. **PMs**) **1** chiefly Brit. the Prime Minister: *a private meeting with the PM.*
2 (in the context of Internet message boards) a private message, sent directly from one user to another: *drop me a PM if you want more details.*
▸ **verb** [with obj.] (**PMs**, **PMing**, **PMd**) send (another user of an Internet message board) a private message: *I'll PM you when I'm back online.*

Pm ▸ **symbol** the chemical element promethium.

p.m. ▸ **abbreviation** after noon, used after times of day between noon and midnight not expressed using the 24-hour clock: *at 3.30 p.m.*
– ORIGIN from Latin *post meridiem*.

PMG ▸ **abbreviation** ▪ Paymaster General. ▪ Postmaster General.

PMS ▸ **abbreviation** premenstrual syndrome.

PMT ▸ **abbreviation** chiefly Brit. premenstrual tension.

PNdB ▸ **abbreviation** perceived noise decibel(s).

pneuma /ˈnjuːmə/ ▸ **noun** Philosophy (in Stoic thought) the vital spirit, soul, or creative force of a person.
– ORIGIN Greek, literally 'that which is breathed or blown'.

pneumatic ▸ **adjective** containing or operated by air or gas under pressure. ▪ Zoology (chiefly of cavities in the bones of birds) containing air.
– DERIVATIVES **pneumatically** adverb, **pneumaticity** noun.
– ORIGIN mid 17th cent.: from French *pneumatique* or Latin *pneumaticus*, from Greek *pneumatikos*, from *pneuma* 'wind', from *pnein* 'breathe'.

pneumatic drill ▸ **noun** Brit. a large, heavy mechanical drill driven by compressed air, used for breaking up a hard surface such as a road.

pneumatics ▸ **plural noun** [treated as sing.] the branch of physics or technology concerned with the mechanical properties of gases.

pneumatic tyre ▸ **noun** a tyre inflated with air.

pneumatique /ˌnjuːməˈtiːk/, French /pnømatik/ ▸ **noun** (pl. pronunc. **same**) (in Paris) a system of conveying mail along tubes by air pressure. ▪ a message conveyed by pneumatique.
– ORIGIN French.

pneumato- /ˈnjuːmətəʊ/ ▸ **combining form 1** of or containing air: *pneumatophore.*
2 relating to the spirit: *pneumatology.*
– ORIGIN from Greek *pneuma*, *pneumat-* 'wind, breath, spirit'.

pneumatology ▶ noun [mass noun] the branch of Christian theology concerned with the Holy Ghost and other spiritual concepts.
– DERIVATIVES **pneumatological** adjective.

pneumatolysis /ˌnjuːməˈtɒlɪsɪs/ ▶ noun [mass noun] Geology the chemical alteration of rocks and the formation of minerals by the action of hot magmatic gases and vapours.
– DERIVATIVES **pneumatolytic** adjective.

pneumatophore /ˈnjuːmətəfɔː/ ▶ noun **1** Zoology the gas-filled float of some colonial coelenterates, such as the Portuguese man-of-war.
2 Botany (in mangroves and other swamp plants) an aerial root specialized for gaseous exchange.

pneumo- ▶ combining form **1** relating to the lungs: *pneumogastric*.
2 relating to the presence of air or gas: *pneumothorax*.
– ORIGIN Sense 1 from Greek *pneumōn* 'lung'; sense 2 from Greek *pneuma* 'air'.

pneumococcus /ˌnjuːmə(ʊ)ˈkɒkəs/ ▶ noun (pl. **pneumococci** /-ˈkɒk(s)ʌɪ, -ˈkɒk(s)iː/) a bacterium associated with pneumonia and some forms of meningitis. ● *Streptococcus pneumoniae*, a Gram-positive diplococcus.
– DERIVATIVES **pneumococcal** adjective.

pneumoconiosis /ˌnjuːmə(ʊ)kəʊnɪˈəʊsɪs/ ▶ noun [mass noun] Medicine a disease of the lungs due to inhalation of dust, characterized by inflammation, coughing, and fibrosis.
– ORIGIN late 19th cent.: from PNEUMO- 'relating to the lungs' + Greek *konis* 'dust' + -OSIS.

pneumocystis /ˌnjuːmə(ʊ)ˈsɪstɪs/ ▶ noun [mass noun] Medicine a parasitic protozoan that can cause fatal pneumonia in people affected with immunodeficiency disease. ● *Pneumocystis carinii*, phylum Sporozoa.

pneumogastric ▶ adjective relating to the lungs and stomach.

pneumonectomy /ˌnjuːmə(ʊ)ˈnɛktəmi/ ▶ noun (pl. **pneumonectomies**) [mass noun] surgical removal of a lung or part of a lung.

pneumonia /njuːˈməʊnɪə/ ▶ noun [mass noun] lung inflammation caused by bacterial or viral infection, in which the air sacs fill with pus and may become solid. Inflammation may affect both lungs (**double pneumonia**) or only one (**single pneumonia**).
– DERIVATIVES **pneumonic** adjective.
– ORIGIN early 17th cent.: via Latin from Greek, from *pneumōn* 'lung'.

pneumonic plague ▶ noun see PLAGUE.

pneumonitis /ˌnjuːmə(ʊ)ˈnʌɪtɪs/ ▶ noun [mass noun] Medicine inflammation of the walls of the alveoli (air sacs) in the lungs.

pneumonoultramicroscopicsilicovolcanoconiosis ▶ noun [mass noun] an artificial long word said to mean a lung disease caused by inhaling very fine ash and sand dust.

pneumotachograph ▶ noun an apparatus for recording the rate of airflow during breathing.

pneumothorax ▶ noun [mass noun] Medicine the presence of air or gas in the cavity between the lungs and the chest wall, causing collapse of the lung.

PNG ▶ abbreviation Papua New Guinea.

p–n junction ▶ noun Electronics a boundary between p-type and n-type material in a semiconductor device, functioning as a rectifier.

PNP ▶ adjective Electronics denoting a semiconductor device in which an n-type region is sandwiched between two p-type regions.
▶ abbreviation (in computing) Plug and Play.

Pnyx /pnɪks/ the public place of assembly in ancient Athens, a semicircular level cut out of the side of a small hill west of the Acropolis.
– ORIGIN from Greek *pnux*.

PO ▶ abbreviation ■ Petty Officer. ■ Pilot Officer. ■ postal order. ■ Post Office.

Po¹ /pəʊ/ a river in northern Italy. Italy's longest river, it rises in the Alps near the border with France and flows 652 km (405 miles) eastwards to the Adriatic.

Po² ▶ symbol the chemical element polonium.

po /pəʊ/ ▶ noun (pl. **pos**) Brit. informal a chamber pot.
– ORIGIN late 19th cent.: from French *pot de chambre* 'chamber pot'.

po' /pɔː/ ▶ adjective US short for POOR, used to represent dialectal speech.

poach¹ ▶ verb [with obj.] cook (an egg) without its shell in or over boiling water. ■ cook by simmering in a small amount of liquid.
– ORIGIN late Middle English: from Old French *pochier*, earlier in the sense 'enclose in a bag', from *poche* 'bag, pocket'.

poach² ▶ verb [with obj.] **1** illegally hunt or catch (game or fish) on land that is not one's own or in contravention of official protection. ■ take or acquire in an unfair or clandestine way: *employers risk having their newly trained workers poached by other firms.* ■ [no obj.] (in ball games) take a shot that a partner or teammate would have expected to take.
2 (of an animal) trample or cut up (turf) with its hoofs. ■ [no obj.] (of land) become sodden by being trampled.
– PHRASES **poach on someone's territory** encroach on someone else's rights.
– ORIGIN early 16th cent. (in the sense 'push roughly together'): apparently related to POKE¹; sense 1 is perhaps partly from French *pocher* 'enclose in a bag' (see POACH¹).

poached egg fungus ▶ noun another term for PORCELAIN FUNGUS.

poacher¹ ▶ noun [usu. with modifier] a pan for cooking eggs or other food by poaching: *an egg poacher*.

poacher² ▶ noun **1** a person who hunts or catches game or fish illegally.
2 a small spiny fish which has an armour of overlapping plates and lives chiefly in cooler coastal waters. ● Family Agonidae: several genera and species.
– PHRASES **poacher turned gamekeeper** chiefly Brit. someone who now protects the interests they previously attacked.

poblano /pɒˈblɑːnəʊ/ ▶ noun (pl. **poblanos**) a large dark green chilli pepper of a mild-flavoured variety.
– ORIGIN Spanish.

po'boy ▶ noun another term for POOR BOY.

Pocahontas /ˌpɒkəˈhɒntəs/ (*c.*1595–1617), American Indian princess, daughter of an Algonquian chief in Virginia. According to an English colonist, Pocahontas rescued him from death at the hands of her father. In 1613 she was seized as a hostage by the English and she later married another colonist, John Rolfe.

pochard /ˈpɒtʃəd, ˈpəʊtʃəd/ ▶ noun (pl. **same** or **pochards**) a diving duck, the male of which typically has a reddish-brown head and a black breast. ● Genera *Aythya* and *Netta*, family Anatidae: five species, in particular the common *A. ferina* of Eurasia.
– ORIGIN mid 16th cent.: of unknown origin.

pochette /pɒˈʃɛt/ ▶ noun a woman's small handbag shaped like an envelope.
– ORIGIN late 19th cent.: from French, literally 'small pocket', diminutive of *poche*.

pocho /ˈpɒtʃəʊ/ informal, often derogatory ▶ noun (pl. **pochos**) a US citizen of Mexican origin; a culturally Americanized Mexican.
▶ adjective relating to US citizens of Mexican origin.
– ORIGIN via Mexican Spanish from Spanish, literally 'discoloured, pale'.

pock ▶ noun a pockmark.
– DERIVATIVES **pocked** adjective, **pocky** adjective (archaic).
– ORIGIN Old English *poc* 'pustule', of Germanic origin; related to Dutch *pok* and German *Pocke*. Compare with POX.

pocket ▶ noun **1** a small bag sewn into or on clothing so as to form part of it, used for carrying small articles. ■ a pouch-like compartment providing separate storage space, for example in a suitcase or car door. ■ S. African a narrow sack in which agricultural produce is sold, used as a measure for trading. ■ Billiards & Snooker an opening at the corner or on the side of the table into which balls are struck. ■ informal a person's financial resources: *the food was all priced to suit the hard-up airman's pocket.*
2 a small patch of something: *some of the gardens still had pockets of dirty snow in them.* ■ a small, isolated group or area: *there were pockets of disaffection in parts of the country.* ■ a cavity in a rock or stratum filled with ore or other material.
▶ adjective [attrib.] of a suitable size for carrying in a pocket: *a pocket German dictionary.* ■ on a small scale: *a 6,000 acre pocket paradise.*
▶ verb (**pockets**, **pocketing**, **pocketed**) [with obj.] put into one's pocket: *she watched him lock up and pocket the key.* ■ take or receive (money or other valuables) for oneself, especially dishonestly: *local politicians were found to have been pocketing the proceeds of fund-raisers.* ■ Billiards & Snooker drive (a ball) into a pocket. ■ enclose as though in a pocket: *the fillings can be pocketed in a pitta bread.* ■ suppress (one's feelings) and proceed despite them: *they were prepared to pocket their pride.*
– PHRASES **in pocket** Brit. having enough money or money to spare; having gained in a transaction. ■ (of money) gained by someone from a transaction. **in someone's pocket 1** dependent on someone financially and therefore under their influence. **2** very close to and closely involved with someone: *I'm tired of villages where everyone lives in everyone else's pocket.* **out of pocket** having lost money in a transaction. ■ (**out-of-pocket**) [as modifier] (of an expense or cost) paid for directly rather than being put on account or charged to some other person or organization. **pay out of pocket** US pay for something with one's own money, rather than from a particular fund or account. **put one's hand in one's pocket** spend or provide one's own money.
– DERIVATIVES **pocketable** adjective, **pocketful** noun (pl. **pocketfuls**), **pocketless** adjective.
– ORIGIN Middle English (in the sense 'bag, sack', also used as a measure of quantity): from Anglo-Norman French *poket(e)*, diminutive of *poke* 'pouch'. The verb dates from the late 16th cent. Compare with POKE².

pocket battleship ▶ noun any of a class of cruisers with large-calibre guns, operated by the German navy in the Second World War.

pocketbook ▶ noun **1** Brit. a notebook.
2 US a wallet, purse, or handbag. ■ N. Amer. one's financial resources: *they provide packages for every taste and every pocketbook.*
3 (**pocket book**) N. Amer. a paperback or other small or cheap edition of a book.

pocket borough ▶ noun (in the UK) a borough in which the election of political representatives was controlled by one person or family. Such boroughs were abolished by the Reform Acts of 1832 and 1867.

pocket gopher ▶ noun see GOPHER (sense 1).

pocketknife ▶ noun chiefly N. Amer. a penknife.

pocket money ▶ noun [mass noun] Brit. a small amount of money given to a child by its parents, typically on a regular basis. ■ a small amount of money suitable for minor expenses.

pocket mouse ▶ noun a small nocturnal rodent with large cheek pouches for carrying food, native to the deserts of North and Central America. ● Genus *Perognathus*, family Heteromyidae: several species.

pocket veto ▶ noun an indirect veto of a legislative bill by the US President or a state governor by retaining the bill unsigned until it is too late for it to be dealt with during the legislative session.

pocket watch ▶ noun a watch on a chain, intended to be carried in the pocket of a jacket or waistcoat.

pockmark ▶ noun a pitted scar or mark on the skin left by a pustule or spot. ■ a scar, mark, or pitted area disfiguring a surface.
▶ verb [with obj.] cover or disfigure with pockmarks: *the area is pockmarked by gravel pits* | (as adj. **pockmarked**) *a pockmarked face.*

poco /ˈpəʊkəʊ/ ▶ adverb Music (in directions) a little; rather: *poco adagio*.
– ORIGIN Italian.

Pocomania /ˌpəʊkə(ʊ)ˈmeɪnɪə/ ▶ noun [mass noun] a Jamaican folk religion combining revivalism with ancestor worship and spirit possession.
– ORIGIN 1930s: probably a Hispanicized form of a local word, the second element being interpreted as -MANIA.

pod¹ ▶ noun **1** an elongated seed vessel of a leguminous plant such as the pea, splitting open on both sides when ripe. ■ the egg case of a locust. ■ Geology a body of rock or sediment whose length greatly exceeds its other dimensions. ■ a narrow-necked purse net for catching eels.
2 [often with modifier] a detachable or self-contained unit on an aircraft, spacecraft, vehicle, or vessel, having a particular function: *the torpedo's sensor pod.*
▶ verb (**pods**, **podding**, **podded**) **1** [no obj.] (of a plant) bear or form pods: *the peas have failed to pod.*
2 [with obj.] remove (peas or beans) from their pods prior to cooking.
– PHRASES **in pod** informal, dated pregnant.
– ORIGIN late 17th cent.: back-formation from dialect *podware*, *podder* 'field crops', of unknown origin.

pod² ▶ noun a small herd or school of marine animals, especially whales.
– ORIGIN mid 19th cent. (originally US): of unknown origin.

podagra /pɒˈdagrə, ˈpɒdəgrə/ ▶ noun [mass noun] Medicine gout of the foot, especially the big toe.

P

– ORIGIN Middle English: from Latin, from Greek *pous, pod-* 'foot' + *agra* 'seizure'.

podcast ▶ noun a multimedia digital file made available on the Internet for downloading to a portable media player, computer, etc.
▶ verb (past and past participle **podcast**) [with obj.] make (a multimedia digital file) available as a podcast.
– DERIVATIVES **podcastable** adjective, **podcaster** noun, **podcasting** noun.
– ORIGIN early 21st cent.: from **IPOD**.

podge ▶ noun informal a short, fat person. ■ [mass noun] excess weight; fat: *pregnancy podge*.
– ORIGIN mid 19th cent.: of unknown origin.

podger ▶ noun a short bar of iron or steel used as a lever, especially for tightening a box spanner.

Podgorica /ˈpɒdˌɡɔːrɪtsə/ the capital of Montenegro; pop. 142,500 (est. 2007). It was under Turkish rule from 1474 until 1878. Between 1946 and 1993 it was named Titograd in honour of Marshal Tito.

podgy ▶ adjective (**podgier**, **podgiest**) Brit. informal (of a person or part of their body) rather fat; chubby: *he put a podgy arm round Alan's shoulders*.
– DERIVATIVES **podginess** noun.

podiatry /pə(ʊ)ˈdʌɪətri/ ▶ noun another term for **CHIROPODY**.
– DERIVATIVES **podiatrist** noun.
– ORIGIN early 20th cent.: from Greek *pous, pod-* 'foot' + *iatros* 'physician'.

podium /ˈpəʊdɪəm/ ▶ noun (pl. **podiums** or **podia** /ˈpəʊdɪə/) a small platform on which a person may stand to be seen by an audience, as when making a speech or conducting an orchestra. ■ N. Amer. a lectern. ■ a continuous projecting base or pedestal under a building. ■ a projecting lower structure around the base of a tower block. ■ a raised platform surrounding the arena in an ancient amphitheatre.
– ORIGIN mid 18th cent.: via Latin from Greek *podion*, diminutive of *pous, pod-* 'foot'.

podocarp /ˈpəʊdə(ʊ)kɑːp/ ▶ noun a coniferous tree or shrub chiefly native to the southern hemisphere, widely grown as an ornamental or timber tree.
● Genus *Podocarpus*, family Podocarpaceae.
– ORIGIN mid 19th cent.: from modern Latin *Podocarpus*, from Greek *pous, pod-* 'foot' + *karpos* 'fruit'.

Podolsk /pəˈdɒlsk/ an industrial city in Russia, south of Moscow; pop. 180,000 (est. 2008).

Podunk /ˈpəʊdʌŋk/ ▶ noun [usu. as modifier] US informal a hypothetical small town regarded as typically dull or insignificant.
– ORIGIN mid 19th cent.: a place name of southern New England, of Algonquian origin.

P

podzol /ˈpɒdzɒl/ (also **podsol** /ˈpɒdsɒl/) ▶ noun Soil Science an infertile acidic soil having an ash-like subsurface layer (from which minerals have been leached) and a lower dark stratum, occurring typically under temperate coniferous woodland.
– DERIVATIVES **podzolic** adjective, **podzolization** noun.
– ORIGIN early 20th cent.: from Russian, from *pod* 'under' + *zola* 'ashes'.

Poe /pəʊ/, Edgar Allan (1809–49), American short-story writer, poet, and critic. His fiction and poetry are Gothic in style and characterized by their exploration of the macabre and the grotesque. Notable works: 'The Fall of the House of Usher' (short story, 1840); 'The Murders in the Rue Morgue' (detective story, 1841); 'The Raven' (poem, 1845).

poem ▶ noun a piece of writing in which the expression of feelings and ideas is given intensity by particular attention to diction (sometimes involving rhyme), rhythm, and imagery.
– ORIGIN late 15th cent.: from French *poème* or Latin *poema*, from Greek *poēma*, early variant of *poiēma* 'fiction, poem', from *poiein* 'create'.

poenskop /ˈpʊnzkɒp, ˈpʊnskɒp/ ▶ noun (pl. **same** or **poenskops**) S. African a large South African sea bream of shallow waters, which typically has a fleshy bump on the snout. ● *Cymatoceps* and other genera, family Sparidae.
– ORIGIN Afrikaans, from South African Dutch, probably from Dutch *pots* 'bump' + *kop* 'head'.

poesy /ˈpəʊɪzi, -si/ ▶ noun [mass noun] archaic or literary poetry. ■ the art or composition of poetry.
– ORIGIN late Middle English: from Old French *poesie*, via Latin from Greek *poēsis*, variant of *poiēsis* 'making, poetry', from *poiein* 'create'.

poet ▶ noun a person who writes poems. ■ a person possessing special powers of imagination or expression.
– ORIGIN Middle English: from Old French *poete*, via Latin from Greek *poētēs*, variant of *poiētēs* 'maker, poet', from *poiein* 'create'.

poetaster /ˌpəʊɪˈtastə/ ▶ noun a person who writes inferior poetry.
– ORIGIN late 16th cent.: modern Latin, from Latin *poeta* 'poet' + **-ASTER**.

poète maudit /pəʊˌɛt məʊˈdi/ ▶ noun (pl. **poètes maudits**) a poet who is insufficiently appreciated by their contemporaries.
– ORIGIN French, literally 'cursed poet'.

poetess ▶ noun a female poet.

poetic ▶ adjective relating to or used in poetry: *the muse is a poetic convention*. ■ written in verse rather than prose: *a poetic drama*. ■ having an imaginative or sensitively emotional style of expression: *the orchestral playing was colourful and poetic*.
– DERIVATIVES **poetical** adjective, **poetically** adverb.
– ORIGIN mid 16th cent.: from French *poétique*, from Latin *poeticus* 'poetic, relating to poets', from Greek *po(i)ētikos*, from *po(i)ētēs* (see **POET**).

poeticize (also **poeticise**) ▶ verb [with obj.] make poetic in character. ■ [no obj.] write or speak poetically.
– DERIVATIVES **poeticism** noun.

poetic justice ▶ noun [mass noun] the fact of experiencing a fitting or deserved retribution for one's actions.

poetic licence ▶ noun [mass noun] the freedom to depart from the facts of a matter or from the conventional rules of language when speaking or writing in order to create an effect.

poetics ▶ plural noun [treated as sing.] the art of writing poetry. ■ the study of linguistic techniques in poetry and literature.

poetize (also **poetise**) ▶ verb [no obj.] dated write or speak in verse or in a poetic style. ■ [with obj.] represent in poetic form.

Poet Laureate ▶ noun (pl. **Poets Laureate** or **Poet Laureates**) an eminent poet appointed as a member of the British royal household.

> The first Poet Laureate in the modern sense was Ben Jonson, but the title became established with the appointment of John Dryden in 1668. The Poet Laureate was formerly expected to write poems for state occasions, but since Victorian times the post has carried no specific duties. Since 2009 the post has been held by Carol Ann Duffy.

poetry ▶ noun [mass noun] literary work in which the expression of feelings and ideas is given intensity by the use of distinctive style and rhythm; poems collectively or as a genre of literature. ■ a quality of beauty and intensity of emotion regarded as characteristic of poems: *poetry and fire are nicely balanced in the music*. ■ something regarded as comparable to poetry in its beauty: *the music department is housed in a building which is pure poetry*.
– ORIGIN late Middle English: from medieval Latin *poetria*, from Latin *poeta* 'poet'. In early use the word sometimes referred to creative literature in general.

Poets' Corner part of Westminster Abbey where several poets are buried or commemorated.

po-faced ▶ adjective Brit. humourless and disapproving: *don't be so po-faced about everything*.
– ORIGIN 1930s: perhaps from **PO**, influenced by *poker-faced*.

pogey /ˈpəʊɡi/ ▶ noun [mass noun] Canadian informal unemployment or welfare benefit: *so you want me to end up on pogey?*
– ORIGIN late 19th cent.: of unknown origin.

pogo ▶ noun (also **pogo stick**) (pl. **pogos**) a toy for jumping about on, consisting of a long, spring-loaded pole with a handle at the top and rests for a person's feet near the bottom.
▶ verb (**pogoes**, **pogoing**, **pogoed**) [no obj.] informal jump up and down as if on a pogo stick as a form of dancing to rock music, especially punk.
– ORIGIN 1920s: of unknown origin.

pogonia /pəˈɡəʊnɪə/, /pɒˈɡəʊnɪə/ ▶ noun an orchid of the northern hemisphere whose purple or yellowish-green flowers have a fringed lip. ● Genus *Pogonia*, family Orchidaceae.
– ORIGIN modern Latin, from Greek *pōgōn* beard + **-IA**[1].

Pogonophora /ˌpəʊɡəˈnɒfərə/ ▶ plural noun Zoology a small phylum of long deep-sea worms which live in upright tubes of protein and chitin. They lack mouths and guts, subsisting mainly on the products of symbiotic bacteria.
– DERIVATIVES **pogonophoran** noun & adjective.
– ORIGIN modern Latin (plural), from Greek *pōgōn* 'beard' + *pherein* 'to bear'.

pogrom /ˈpɒɡrəm, ˈpɒɡrɒm/ ▶ noun an organized massacre of a particular ethnic group, in particular that of Jews in Russia or eastern Europe.
– ORIGIN early 20th cent.: from Russian, literally 'devastation', from *gromit* 'destroy by the use of violence'.

Po Hai /pəʊ ˈhʌɪ/ variant of **BO HAI**.

pohutukawa /pə(ʊ)ˌhuːtəˈkɑːwə/ ▶ noun an evergreen New Zealand tree of the myrtle family, which bears crimson flowers in December and January.
● *Metrosideros excelsa*, family Myrtaceae.
– ORIGIN mid 19th cent.: from Maori.

poi[1] /pɔɪ/ ▶ noun [mass noun] a Hawaiian dish made from the fermented root of the taro which has been baked and pounded to a paste.
– ORIGIN Polynesian.

poi[2] /pɔɪ/ ▶ noun (pl. **same** or **pois**) a small light ball of woven flax, swung rhythmically on the end of a string in Maori action songs and dances.
– ORIGIN Maori.

poignancy /ˈpɔɪnjənsi/ ▶ noun [mass noun] the quality of evoking a keen sense of sadness or regret; pathos: *the pregnancy has a special poignancy for her family*.
– DERIVATIVES **poignance** noun.

poignant /ˈpɔɪnjənt/ ▶ adjective evoking a keen sense of sadness or regret: *a poignant reminder of the passing of time*. ■ archaic sharp or pungent in taste or smell.
– DERIVATIVES **poignantly** adverb.
– ORIGIN late Middle English: from Old French, literally 'pricking', present participle of *poindre*, from Latin *pungere* 'to prick'.

poikilitic /ˌpɔɪkɪˈlɪtɪk/ ▶ adjective Geology relating to or denoting the texture of an igneous rock in which small crystals of one mineral occur within crystals of another.
– ORIGIN mid 19th cent.: from Greek *poikilos* 'variegated' + **-ITE**[1] + **-IC**.

poikilo- ▶ combining form variegated: *poikiloblastic*. ■ variable: *poikilotherm*.
– ORIGIN from Greek *poikilos* 'variegated, varied'.

poikiloblastic /ˌpɔɪkɪlə(ʊ)ˈblastɪk/ ▶ adjective Geology relating to or denoting the texture of a metamorphic rock in which small crystals of an original mineral occur within crystals of its metamorphic product.

poikilotherm /ˈpɔɪkɪlə(ʊ)ˌθəːm/ ▶ noun Zoology an organism that cannot regulate its body temperature except by behavioural means such as basking or burrowing. Often contrasted with **HOMEOTHERM**.
– DERIVATIVES **poikilothermal** adjective, **poikilothermic** adjective, **poikilothermy** noun.

poilu /pwʌˈluː/, French /pwaly/ ▶ noun historical, informal an infantry soldier in the French army, especially one who fought in the First World War.
– ORIGIN French, literally 'hairy', by extension 'brave', whiskers being associated with virility.

Poincaré /ˈpwãkareɪ/, French /pwɛ̃kaʀe/, Jules-Henri (1854–1912), French mathematician and philosopher of science, who transformed celestial mechanics and was one of the pioneers of algebraic topology. He proposed a relativistic philosophy which implied the absolute velocity of light, which nothing could exceed.

Poincaré map ▶ noun Mathematics & Physics a representation of the phase space of a dynamic system, indicating all possible trajectories. ■ (also **Poincaré section**) the intersection of this representation with a given line, plane, etc.

poinciana /ˌpɔɪnsɪˈɑːnə/ ▶ noun a tropical tree of the pea family, with showy red or red and yellow flowers. ● Genera *Caesalpinia* and *Delonix* (formerly *Poinciana*), family Leguminosae: several species, including the flamboyant.
– ORIGIN mid 18th cent.: modern Latin, named after M. de *Poinci*, a 17th-cent. governor of the Antilles.

poind /pɔɪnd, pɪnd/ ▶ verb [with obj.] Scots Law distrain or impound (a person's property). ■ subject (someone) to the distraint or impounding of their property.
– ORIGIN late Middle English: variant of dialect *pind* 'impound'.

Poindexter /ˈpɔɪndɛkstə/ ▶ noun US informal a boringly studious or socially inept person.
– ORIGIN 1980s: apparently from the name of one of the main characters in the comedy film *Revenge of the Nerds* (1984).

poinsettia /ˌpɔɪnˈsɛtɪə/ ▶ noun a small Mexican shrub with large showy scarlet bracts surrounding the small yellow flowers, popular as a houseplant at

Christmas. ● *Euphorbia* (formerly *Poinsettia*) *pulcherrima*, family Euphorbiaceae.
– ORIGIN mid 19th cent.: modern Latin, named after Joel R. *Poinsett* (1779–1851), American diplomat and amateur botanist.

point /pɔɪnt/ ▶ noun **1** the tapered, sharp end of a tool, weapon, or other object: *the point of his dagger* | *a pencil point*. ■ Archaeology a pointed flake or blade, especially one that has been worked. ■ Ballet another term for POINTE. ■ Boxing the tip of a person's chin as a spot for a blow. ■ the prong of a deer's antler.
2 a dot or other punctuation mark, in particular a full stop. ■ a decimal point: *fifty-five point nine*. ■ a dot or small stroke used in Semitic languages to indicate vowels or distinguish particular consonants. ■ a very small dot or mark: *the sky was studded with points of light*.
3 a particular spot, place, or position in an area or on a map, object, or surface: *turn left at the point where you see a sign to Appleford* | *the furthermost point of the gallery* | *the check-in point*. ■ a particular moment in time or stage in a process: *from this point onwards the teacher was completely won over*. ■ (usu. **the point**) the critical or decisive moment: *when it came to the point he would probably do what was expected of him*. ■ (**the point of**) the verge or brink of (doing or being something): *she was **on the point of** leaving*. ■ [usu. with modifier] a stage or level at which a change of state occurs: *local kennels are full to bursting point*. ■ [with modifier] Brit. a socket in a wall for connecting a device to an electrical supply or communications network: *a power point*. ■ (in geometry) something having position but not spatial extent, magnitude, dimension, or direction, for example the intersection of two lines.
4 a single item or detail in an extended discussion, list, or text: *the main points of the Edinburgh agreement*. ■ an argument or idea: *he **made the point that** economic regulation involves controls on pricing*. ■ (usu. **the point**) the significant or essential element of something being planned or discussed: *it took her a long time to **come to the point***. ■ [in sing.] [usu. with negative or in questions] advantage or purpose that can be gained from doing something: *there was **no point in** denying the truth* | ***what's the point of** having things I don't need?* ■ [mass noun] relevance or effectiveness. ■ a distinctive feature or characteristic, typically a good one, of a person or thing: *he has his good points*.
5 (in sports and games) a mark or unit of scoring awarded for success or performance: *he kicked a penalty goal to put Bangor eight points ahead*. ■ a unit used in measuring value, achievement, or extent: *the shares index was down seven points*. ■ an advantage or success in an argument or discussion: *she smiled, assuming she had **won her point***. ■ a unit of credit towards an award or benefit: *points were allocated according to the inadequacy of the existing accommodation*. ■ a percentage of the profits from a film or recording offered to certain people involved in its production. ■ (**point of**) (in piquet) the longest suit in a player's hand, containing a specified number of up to eight cards. ■ a unit of weight (2 mg) for diamonds. ■ a unit of varying value, used in quoting the price of stocks, bonds, or futures. ■ Bridge a value assigned to certain cards (4 points for an ace, 3 for a king, 2 for a queen, and 1 for a jack, sometimes with extra points for long or short suits) by a player in assessing the strength of their hand.
6 each of thirty-two directions marked at equal distances round a compass. ■ a direction towards the horizon corresponding to the direction marked on a compass. ■ the angular interval between two successive points of a compass, i.e. one eighth of a right angle (11° 15′). ■ (**points ——**) unspecified places considered in terms of their direction from a specified place: *they headed down Highway 401 to Ontario and points west*.
7 a narrow piece of land jutting out into the sea: *the boat came round the point* | [in names] *Blakeney Point*.
8 (usu. **points**) Brit. a junction of two railway lines, with a pair of linked tapering rails that can be moved laterally to allow a train to pass from one line to the other.
9 Printing a unit of measurement for type sizes and spacing (in the UK and US 0.351 mm, in Europe 0.376 mm).
10 Cricket a fielding position on the off side near the batsman. ■ a fielder at the point position. ■ Ice Hockey either of two areas to the left and right of the net, just inside the blue line where it meets the boards.
11 (usu. **points**) (in a motor vehicle) each of a set of electrical contacts in the distributor.
12 a small leading party of an advanced guard of troops. ■ [mass noun] chiefly N. Amer. the position at the head of a column or wedge of troops: *he **walked point** and I took the tail*. ■ chiefly N. Amer. short for POINT MAN.
13 (usu. **points**) the extremities of an animal, typically a horse or cat, such as the face, paws, and tail of a Siamese cat.
14 Hunting a spot to which a straight run is made. ■ a straight run: *our fox **made his point** to Moorhill*.
15 (usu. **points**) historical a tagged piece of ribbon or cord used for lacing a garment or attaching a hose to a doublet.
16 a short piece of cord at the lower edge of a sail for tying up a reef.
17 [mass noun] the action or position of a dog in pointing: *a bird dog **on point***.
18 Music an important phrase or subject, especially in a contrapuntal composition.
▶ verb **1** [no obj.] direct someone's attention towards something by extending one's finger or something held in one's hand: *the lads were nudging each other and pointing at me*. ■ [with adverbial] indicate a particular time, direction, or reading: *a sign pointing left*. ■ [with obj.] direct or aim (something) at someone or something: *he **pointed** the torch beam **at** the floor*. ■ [with adverbial of direction] face or be turned in a particular direction: *two of its toes point forward and two point back*.
2 [no obj., with adverbial] cite a fact or situation as evidence of something: *he **points to** several factors supporting this conclusion*. ■ (**point to**) (of a fact or situation) indicate that (something) is likely to happen or be the case: *everything pointed to an Eastern attack*. ■ [with obj.] give force or emphasis to (words or actions): *he wouldn't miss the opportunity to point a moral*.
3 [with obj.] chiefly Ballet extend (the toes) by tensing the foot and ankle so as to form a point.
4 [with obj.] fill the joints of (brickwork or masonry) with smoothly finished mortar.
5 [with obj.] give a sharp, tapered point to: *he twisted and pointed his moustache*.
6 [with obj.] insert points in (written text of Semitic languages). ■ mark (Psalms) with signs for chanting.
7 [with obj.] (of a dog) indicate the presence of (game) by standing rigid while looking towards it.
– PHRASES **beside** (or **off**) **the point** irrelevant. **case in point** an instance or example that illustrates what is being discussed: *the 'green revolution' in agriculture is a good case in point*. **in point of fact** see FACT. **make one's point** put across a proposition clearly and convincingly. **make a point of** make a special and noticeable effort to do (a specified thing): *she made a point of taking a walk each day*. **on point** chiefly US apposite; relevant. **point the finger** openly accuse someone or apportion blame. **the point of no return** the point in a journey or enterprise at which it becomes essential or more practical to continue to the end rather than turn back. **point of sailing** a sailing boat's heading in relation to the wind. **score points** deliberately make oneself appear superior to someone else by making clever remarks: *she was constantly trying to think of ways to **score points off** him*. **take someone's point** chiefly Brit. accept the validity of someone's idea or argument. **to the point** relevant: *his evidence was brief and to the point*. **up to a point** to some extent but not completely. **win on points** Boxing win by scoring more points than one's opponent (as awarded by the judges and/or the referee) rather than by a knockout.
– PHRASAL VERBS **point something out** direct someone's gaze or attention towards, especially by extending one's finger: *I pointed out a conical heap of stones*. ■ [reporting verb] say something to make someone aware of a fact or circumstance: [with clause] *she pointed out that his van had been in the car park all day* | [with direct speech] *'Most of the people round here are very poor,' I pointed out*. **point something up** reveal the true nature or importance of something: *he did so much to point up their plight in the 1960s*.
– ORIGIN Middle English: the noun partly from Old French *point*, from Latin *punctum* 'something that is pricked', giving rise to the senses 'unit, mark, point in space or time'; partly from Old French *pointe*, from Latin *puncta* 'pricking', giving rise to the senses 'sharp tip, promontory'. The verb is from Old French *pointer*, and in some senses from the English noun.

point bar ▶ noun Geology an alluvial deposit that forms by accretion inside an expanding loop of a river.

point-blank ▶ adjective & adverb (of a shot) fired from very close to its target: [as adj.] *the bullet, fired at point-blank range, hit him in the middle of the back* | [as adv.] *Waxman fired the pistol point-blank at Clyde*. ■ (of a statement or question) direct and without explanation or qualification: [as adv.] *he refuses point-blank to be photographed or give interviews*.
– ORIGIN late 16th cent.: probably from POINT + BLANK in the contemporaneous sense 'white spot in the centre of a target'.

point blanket ▶ noun Canadian a type of Hudson's Bay blanket with distinctive markings or points woven in to indicate weight.

point break ▶ noun (in surfing) a type of wave characteristic of a coast with a headland.

point charge ▶ noun chiefly Physics an electric charge regarded as concentrated in a mathematical point, without spatial extent.

point contact ▶ noun Electronics the contact of a metal point with the surface of a semiconductor so as to form a rectifying junction.

point d'appui /ˌpwã daˈpwiː/, French /pwɛ̃ dapɥi/ ▶ noun (pl. **points d'appui**) a support or prop.
– ORIGIN French, literally 'point of support'.

point duty ▶ noun [mass noun] Brit. the duties of a police officer or other official stationed at a junction to control traffic.

pointe /pwãt/ ▶ noun (pl. pronunc. **same**) Ballet the tips of the toes. ■ (also **pointe work**) [mass noun] dance performed on the tips of the toes.
– PHRASES **on** (or **en**) **pointe** on the tips of the toes.
– ORIGIN French, literally 'tip'.

Pointe-à-Pitre /ˌpwãtaˈpiːtr(ə)/ the chief port and commercial capital of the French island of Guadeloupe in the Caribbean; pop. 19,000 (est. 2007).

pointed ▶ adjective **1** having a sharpened or tapered tip or end: *his face tapers to a pointed chin*.
2 (of a remark or look) expressing criticism in a direct and unambiguous way.
– DERIVATIVES **pointedly** adverb (sense 2), **pointedness** noun.

pointelle /ˌpɔɪnˈtɛl/ (also trademark **Pointelle**) ▶ noun [mass noun] a type of knitwear or woollen fabric with small eyelet holes that create a lacy effect.
– ORIGIN 1950s: probably from *point* in the sense 'lace made entirely with a needle' + the French diminutive suffix *-elle*.

Pointe-Noire /pwãtˈnwɑː/ the chief seaport of Congo, an oil terminal on the Atlantic coast; pop. 792,382 (2009).

pointer ▶ noun **1** a long, thin piece of metal on a scale or dial which moves to indicate a figure or position. ■ a rod used for pointing to features on a map or chart. ■ a hint as to what might happen in the future: *the figures were a **pointer to** gradual economic recovery*. ■ a small piece of advice; a tip: *here are some **pointers on** how to go about the task*. ■ Computing another term for CURSOR. ■ Computing a variable whose value is the address of another variable; a link.
2 a dog of a breed that on scenting game stands rigid looking towards it.

Pointers Astronomy (in the northern hemisphere) two stars of the Plough or Big Dipper in Ursa Major, through which a line points nearly to the Pole Star. ■ (in the southern hemisphere) two stars in the constellation Crux, through which a line points nearly to the south celestial pole.

point estimate ▶ noun Statistics a single value given as an estimate of a parameter of a population. Compare with INTERVAL ESTIMATE.

point group ▶ noun Crystallography any of the 32 sets of symmetry operations which can be used to characterize three-dimensional lattices and are the basis of the system of crystal classes.

point guard ▶ noun Basketball the player who directs the team's offence.

pointillism /ˈpwantɪlɪz(ə)m/ ▶ noun [mass noun] a technique of neo-Impressionist painting using tiny dots of various pure colours, which become blended in the viewer's eye. It was developed by Seurat with the aim of producing a greater degree of luminosity and brilliance of colour.
– DERIVATIVES **pointillist** noun & adjective, **pointillistic** adjective.
– ORIGIN early 20th cent.: from French *pointillisme*, from *pointiller* 'mark with dots'.

pointing ▶ noun [mass noun] the action of filling the joints of brickwork or masonry with mortar.

pointing device ▶ noun Computing a generic term for any device (e.g. a graphics tablet, mouse, stylus, or trackball) used to control the movement of a cursor on a computer screen.

P

point lace ▸ noun [mass noun] lace made with a needle on a parchment pattern.

pointless ▸ adjective having little or no sense, use, or purpose: *speculating like this is a pointless exercise* | [with infinitive] *it's pointless to plan too far ahead.*
– DERIVATIVES **pointlessly** adverb, **pointlessness** noun.

point man ▸ noun the soldier at the head of a patrol; the leader of an armed force. ■ N. Amer. (especially in a political context) a person at the forefront of an activity or endeavour.

point mutation ▸ noun Genetics a mutation affecting only one or very few nucleotides in a gene sequence.

point of departure ▸ noun the starting point of a line of thought or course of action; an initial assumption: *Keynes took these current events as his point of departure.*

point of honour ▸ noun an action or circumstance that affects one's reputation or conscience: *he languished in jail refusing, as a point of honour, to talk.*

point of inflection ▸ noun another term for **INFLECTION POINT** (sense 1).

point of order ▸ noun a query in a formal debate or meeting as to whether correct procedure is being followed.

point of sale (abbrev.: **POS**) ▸ noun the place at which a retail transaction is carried out: *refunds will be provided at the point of sale.*

point of view ▸ noun a particular attitude or way of considering a matter: *I'm trying to get Matthew to change his point of view.* ■ (in fictional writing) the narrator's position in relation to a story being told: *this story is told from a child's point of view.* ■ the position from which something or someone is observed.

pointsman ▸ noun (pl. **pointsmen**) Brit. a person in charge of railway points.

point source ▸ noun **1** Physics a source of energy, such as light or sound, which can be regarded as having negligible dimensions.
2 a localized and stationary source of pollution. Compare with **NON-POINT SOURCE**.

point spread ▸ noun **1** N. Amer. a forecast of the number of points constituting the margin by which a stronger team is expected to defeat a weaker one, used for betting purposes.
2 Physics & Physiology the spread of energy from a point source, especially with respect to light coming into an optical instrument or eye.

points system (also **point system**) ▸ noun a system for distributing or allocating resources or for ranking or evaluating candidates or claimants on the basis of points allocated or accumulated.

point-to-point ▸ noun (pl. **point-to-points**) Brit. an amateur steeplechase for horses used in hunting, over a set cross-country course.
▸ adjective (of a route or journey) from one place to the next without stopping or changing; direct. ■ (of a telecommunication or computer link) directly from the sender to the receiver.
– DERIVATIVES **point-to-pointer** noun, **point-to-pointing** noun.

pointy ▸ adjective (**pointier**, **pointiest**) informal having a pointed tip or end: *pointy ears.*

pointy-headed ▸ adjective N. Amer. informal, chiefly derogatory expert; intellectual: *some pointy-headed college professor.*
– DERIVATIVES **pointy-head** noun.
– ORIGIN by association with **EGGHEAD**.

poise[1] ▸ noun [mass noun] **1** graceful and elegant bearing in a person: *poise and good deportment can be cultivated.* ■ composure and dignity of manner: *at least he had a moment to think, to recover his poise.*
2 archaic balance; equilibrium.
▸ verb be or cause to be balanced or suspended: [no obj.] *he poised motionless on his toes* | [with obj.] figurative *the world was poised between peace and war.* ■ (**be poised**) be ready and prepared to do something: [with infinitive] *teachers are poised to resume their attack on government school tests.*
– ORIGIN late Middle English (in the sense 'weight'): from Old French *pois, peis* (noun), *peser* (verb), from an alteration of Latin *pensum* 'weight', from the verb *pendere* 'weigh'. From the early senses of 'weight' and 'measure of weight' arose the notion of 'equal weight, balance', leading to the extended senses 'composure' and 'elegant bearing'.

poise[2] ▸ noun Physics a unit of dynamic viscosity, such that a tangential force of one dyne per square centimetre causes a velocity change one centimetre per second between two parallel planes separated by one centimetre in a liquid.
– ORIGIN early 20th cent.: from the name of Jean L. M. *Poiseuille* (1799–1869), French physician.

poised ▸ adjective having a composed and self-assured manner. ■ having a graceful and elegant bearing.

Poiseuille flow /pwaˈzəːi/ ▸ noun [mass noun] Physics laminar or streamline flow of an incompressible viscous fluid, especially through a long, narrow cylinder.
– ORIGIN 1940s: named after Jean L. M. *Poiseuille* (1799–1869), French physician.

poisha /ˈpɔɪʃə/ ▸ noun (pl. **same**) a monetary unit of Bangladesh, equal to one hundredth of a taka.
– ORIGIN Bengali, alteration of **PAISA**.

poison ▸ noun [mass noun] a substance that when introduced into or absorbed by a living organism causes illness or death: *he killed himself with poison* | [count noun] *strong chemical poisons.* ■ Chemistry a substance that reduces the activity of a catalyst. ■ Physics an additive or impurity in a nuclear reactor that slows a reaction by absorbing neutrons. ■ something that has a destructive or corrupting influence: *the late 1930s, when Nazism was spreading its poison.*
▸ verb [with obj.] administer poison to (a person or animal), either deliberately or accidentally: *he tried to poison his wife* | (as noun **poisoning**) *symptoms of poisoning may include nausea, diarrhoea, and vomiting.* ■ adulterate or contaminate with poison: *the Amazon basin is being poisoned by the mercury used by gold prospectors.* ■ (usu. as adj. **poisoned**) treat (a weapon or missile) with poison in order to augment its lethal effect: *poisoned arrows.* ■ prove harmful or destructive to: *his disgust had poisoned his attitude toward everyone.* ■ Chemistry (of a substance) reduce the activity of (a catalyst).
– PHRASES **what's your poison?** informal used to ask someone what they would like to drink.
– DERIVATIVES **poisoner** noun.
– ORIGIN Middle English (denoting a harmful medicinal draught): from Old French *poison* 'magic potion', from Latin *potio(n-)* 'potion', related to *potare* 'to drink'.

poison arrow frog ▸ noun a small, slender tropical American frog which is typically brightly coloured. The skin of these frogs secretes a virulent poison, formerly used by American Indians to coat their arrows. ● Family Dendrobatidae: several genera and numerous species.

poisoned chalice ▸ noun chiefly Brit. an assignment, award, or honour which is likely to prove a disadvantage or source of problems to the recipient: *many thought the new minister had been handed a poisoned chalice.*

poison gas ▸ noun [mass noun] poisonous gas or vapour, used especially to disable an enemy in warfare.

poison ivy ▸ noun a North American climbing plant which secretes an irritant oil from its leaves that can cause dermatitis. ● *Rhus radicans*, family Anacardiaceae.

poison oak ▸ noun a North American climbing shrub related to poison ivy and having similar properties. ● *Rhus toxicodendron*, family Anacardiaceae.

poisonous ▸ adjective (of an animal or insect) producing poison as a means of attacking enemies or prey: *a poisonous snake.* ■ (of a plant or substance) causing or capable of causing death or illness if taken into the body: *poisonous chemicals.* ■ extremely unpleasant or malicious: *there was a poisonous atmosphere at the office.*
– DERIVATIVES **poisonously** adverb.

poison pen letter ▸ noun an anonymous letter that is libellous, abusive, or malicious.

poison pill ▸ noun Finance a tactic used by a company threatened with an unwelcome takeover bid to make itself unattractive to the bidder.

Poisson /ˈpwʌsɒ̃/, Siméon-Denis (1781–1840), French mathematical physicist. His major contributions were in probability theory, in which he greatly improved Laplace's work and developed several concepts that are now named after him.

Poisson distribution /ˈpwʌsɒ̃/ ▸ noun Statistics a discrete frequency distribution which gives the probability of a number of independent events occurring in a fixed time.

Poisson's ratio ▸ noun Physics the ratio of the proportional decrease in a lateral measurement to the proportional increase in length in a sample of material that is elastically stretched.

Poitiers /ˈpwʌtɪeɪ/ a city in west central France, the chief town of Poitou-Charentes region and capital of the former province of Poitou; pop. 91,395 (2006).

Poitou /ˈpwʌtuː/ a former province of west central France, now united with Charente to form the region of Poitou-Charentes. Formerly part of Aquitaine, it was held by the French and English in succession until it was finally united with France at the end of the Hundred Years War.

Poitou-Charentes /ˌpwʌtuːʃaˈrɒ̃t/, French /pwatuʃaʀɑ̃t/ a region of western France, on the Bay of Biscay, centred on Poitiers.

poke[1] ▸ verb **1** [with obj.] jab or prod (someone or something) with one's finger or a sharp object: *he poked Benny in the ribs and pointed* | [no obj.] *they sniffed, felt, and poked at everything they bought.* ■ (on the social networking site Facebook) attract the attention of (another member of the site) by using the 'poke' facility. ■ prod and stir (a fire) with a poker to make it burn more fiercely. ■ make (a hole) in something by prodding or jabbing at it. ■ vulgar slang (of a man) have sexual intercourse with (a woman).
2 [with obj. and adverbial of direction] thrust (something, such as one's head) in a particular direction: *I poked my head around the door to see what was going on.* ■ [no obj., with adverbial] protrude and be visible: *she had wisps of grey hair poking out from under her bonnet.*
▸ noun **1** an act of poking someone or something: *she gave the fire a poke.* ■ vulgar slang an act of sexual intercourse.
2 (**a poke round/around**) informal a look or search around a place.
3 [mass noun] Brit. informal power or acceleration in a car: *I expect you'd prefer something with a bit more poke.*
4 (also **poke bonnet**) a woman's bonnet with a projecting brim or front, popular especially in the early 19th century.
– PHRASES **be better than a poke in the eye with a sharp** (or Austral. **burnt**) **stick** humorous be welcome or pleasing: *I got a tax rebate—not a huge amount but better than a poke in the eye with a sharp stick.* **poke fun at** tease or make fun of. **poke one's nose into** informal take an intrusive interest in. **take a poke at someone** informal hit or punch someone. ■ criticize someone.
– PHRASAL VERBS **poke about/around** informal look around a place, typically in search of something: *she poked about in the cupboard for a minute or two.*
– ORIGIN Middle English: origin uncertain; compare with Middle Dutch and Middle Low German *poken*, of unknown ultimate origin. The noun dates from the late 18th cent.

poke[2] ▸ noun chiefly Scottish a bag or small sack: *he fished out a poke of crisps from under the counter.* ■ N. Amer. informal a purse or wallet.
– PHRASES **a pig in a poke** see **PIG**.
– ORIGIN Middle English: from Old Northern French *poke*, variant of Old French *poche* 'pocket'. Compare with **POUCH**.

poke[3] ▸ noun **1** another term for **POKEWEED**.
2 (**Indian poke**) a North American plant of the lily family with a poisonous black rhizome and tall sprays of yellow-green flowers. ● *Veratrum viride*, family Liliaceae.
– ORIGIN early 18th cent.: from Algonquian *poughkone* (see **PUCCOON**).

poke-check ▸ verb [with obj.] Ice Hockey poke the puck off the stick of (an opposing player).

poker[1] ▸ noun a metal rod with a handle, used for prodding and stirring an open fire.

poker[2] ▸ noun [mass noun] a card game played by two or more people who bet on the value of the hands dealt to them. A player wins the pool either by having the highest combination at the showdown or by forcing all opponents to concede without a showing of the hand, sometimes by means of bluff.
– ORIGIN mid 19th cent.: of US origin; perhaps related to German *pochen* 'to brag', *Pochspiel* 'bragging game'.

poker dice ▸ plural noun dice with card designs (from nine to ace) on the faces instead of spots. ■ [mass noun] a dice game in which the thrower aims for combinations of several dice similar to winning hands in poker.

poker face ▸ noun an impassive expression that hides one's true feelings. ■ a person with a poker face.
– DERIVATIVES **poker-faced** adjective.

pokerwork ▸ noun British term for **PYROGRAPHY**.

pokeweed ▸ noun [mass noun] a North American plant with red stems, spikes of cream flowers, and purple

berries. Also called **POKE³**. ● *Phytolacca americana*, family Phytolaccaceae.
– ORIGIN early 18th cent.: *poke* from Algonquian *poughkone*.

pokey ▸ noun (usu. **the pokey**) informal, chiefly N. Amer. prison.
– ORIGIN early 20th cent.: alteration of **POGEY** (an early sense being 'hostel for the needy'), perhaps influenced by **POKY**.

pokey hat (also **poky hat**) ▸ noun Scottish an ice-cream cone.

pokie ▸ noun (pl. **pokies**) Austral. a fruit machine.
– ORIGIN 1960s: from *poker machine*, a type of fruit machine on which playing-card symbols appear.

poky (also **pokey**) ▸ adjective (**pokier**, **pokiest**)
1 (of a room or building) uncomfortably small and cramped: *five of us shared the poky little room*.
2 informal (especially of a car) having considerable power or acceleration.
3 N. Amer. annoyingly slow: *his speech was poky, like he was a little simple*.
– DERIVATIVES **pokily** adverb, **pokiness** noun.
– ORIGIN mid 19th cent. (in the sense 'concerned with petty matters'): from **POKE¹** (in a contemporaneous sense 'confine') + **-Y¹**.

pol ▸ noun N. Amer. informal a politician.

Polack /ˈpəʊlak/ (also **polack**) derogatory, chiefly N. Amer. ▸ noun a person from Poland or of Polish descent.
▸ adjective of Polish origin or descent.
– ORIGIN late 16th cent.: from Polish *Polak*.

Poland a country in central Europe with a coastline on the Baltic Sea; pop. 38,482,900 (est. 2009); official language, Polish; capital, Warsaw. Polish name **POLSKA**.

> First united as a nation in the 11th century, Poland became a dominant power in the region in the 16th century but thereafter suffered severely from the rise of Russian, Swedish, Prussian, and Austrian power, being partitioned in the late 18th century. Poland regained full independence (as a republic) after the First World War. Its invasion by German forces in 1939 precipitated the Second World War, from which it eventually emerged as a communist state under Soviet domination. In the 1980s the rise of the independent trade union movement Solidarity eventually led to the end of communist rule (1989).

Polanski /pəˈlanski/, Roman (b.1933), French film director, of Polish descent. His second wife, the actress **Sharon Tate** (1943–69), was one of the victims of a multiple murder by followers of the cult leader Charles Manson. Notable films: *Rosemary's Baby* (1968), *Chinatown* (1974) and *The Pianist* (2002), for which he won an Oscar.

polar ▸ adjective 1 relating to the North or South Pole: *the polar regions*. ■ (of an animal or plant) living in the north or south polar region. ■ Astronomy relating to the poles of a celestial body. ■ Astronomy relating to a celestial pole. ■ Geometry relating to the poles of a sphere. See **POLE²**. ■ Biology relating to the poles of a cell, organ, or part.
2 Physics & Chemistry having electrical or magnetic polarity. ■ (of a liquid, especially a solvent) consisting of molecules with a dipole moment. ■ (of a solid) ionic.
3 directly opposite in character or tendency: *depression and its polar opposite, mania*.
▸ noun 1 Geometry the straight line joining the two points at which tangents from a fixed point touch a conic section.
2 Astronomy a variable binary star which emits strongly polarized light, one component being a strongly magnetic white dwarf.
– ORIGIN mid 16th cent.: from medieval Latin *polaris* 'heavenly', from Latin *polus* 'end of an axis' (see **POLE²**).

polar axis ▸ noun Astronomy the axis of an equatorially mounted telescope which is at right angles to the declination axis and parallel to the earth's axis of rotation, about which the telescope is turned to follow the apparent movement of celestial objects resulting from the earth's rotation.

polar bear ▸ noun a large white arctic bear which lives mainly on the pack ice. It is a powerful swimmer and feeds chiefly on seals. ● *Thalarctos maritimus*, family Ursidae.

polar body ▸ noun Biology each of the small cells which bud off from an oocyte at the two meiotic divisions and do not develop into ova.

polar cap ▸ noun Astronomy a region of ice or other frozen matter surrounding a pole of a planet.

polar coordinates ▸ plural noun Geometry a pair of coordinates locating the position of a point in a plane, the first being the length of the straight line (*r*) connecting the point to the origin, and the second the angle (θ) made by this line with a fixed line. ■ the coordinates in a three-dimensional extension of polar coordinates.

polar curve ▸ noun Geometry a curve drawn on polar coordinates around a fixed point, as in a polar diagram.

polar diagram ▸ noun chiefly Physics & Electronics a diagram in which a point of origin is surrounded by a curve whose radius at any given point is proportional to the magnitude of some property measured in the direction of that point. Polar diagrams are often used to depict the directional sensitivity of aerials and microphones.

polar distance ▸ noun Geometry the angular distance of a point on a sphere from the nearest pole.

Polari /pəˈlɑːri/ (also **Palari** or **Palare**) ▸ noun [mass noun] a form of theatrical slang incorporating Italianate words, rhyming slang, and Romany, used especially by homosexuals.
– ORIGIN mid 19th cent.: from Italian *parlare* 'to speak'.

polarimeter /ˌpəʊləˈrɪmɪtə/ ▸ noun an instrument for measuring the polarization of light, and especially for determining the effect of a substance in rotating the plane of polarization of light.
– DERIVATIVES **polarimetric** adjective, **polarimetry** noun.
– ORIGIN mid 19th cent.: from medieval Latin *polaris* 'polar' + **-METER**.

Polaris /pəˈlɑːrɪs/ 1 Astronomy the Pole Star.
2 a type of submarine-launched ballistic missile designed to carry nuclear warheads, formerly in service with the US and British navies.
– ORIGIN mid 19th cent.: from medieval Latin *polaris* 'heavenly', from Latin *polus* 'end of an axis'.

polariscope /pəˈlarɪskəʊp/ ▸ noun another term for **POLARIMETER**.
– DERIVATIVES **polariscopic** adjective.
– ORIGIN early 19th cent.: from medieval Latin *polaris* 'polar' + **-SCOPE**.

polarity ▸ noun (pl. **polarities**) [mass noun] the property of having poles or being polar: *it exhibits polarity when presented to a magnetic needle*. ■ the relative orientation of poles; the direction of a magnetic or electric field. ■ the state of having two opposite or contradictory tendencies, opinions, or aspects: *the polarity between male and female* | [count noun] *the Cold War's neat polarities can hardly be carried on*. ■ Biology the tendency of living organisms or parts to develop with distinct anterior and posterior (or uppermost and lowermost) ends, or to grow or orientate in a particular direction.

polarity therapy ▸ noun [mass noun] a system of treatment used in alternative medicine, intended to restore a balanced distribution of the body's energy, and incorporating manipulation, exercise, and dietary restrictions.

polarize (also **polarise**) ▸ verb 1 [with obj.] Physics restrict the vibrations of (a transverse wave, especially light) wholly or partially to one direction.
2 [with obj.] Physics cause (something) to acquire polarity.
3 divide or cause to divide into two sharply contrasting groups or sets of opinions or beliefs: [no obj.] *the cultural sphere has **polarized into** two competing ideological positions*.
– DERIVATIVES **polarizable** adjective, **polarization** noun, **polarizer** noun.

polarizing filter ▸ noun a photographic or optical filter that polarizes the light passing through it, used chiefly for reducing reflections and improving contrast.

polarography /ˌpəʊləˈrɒgrəfi/ ▸ noun [mass noun] Chemistry a method of analysis in which a sample is subjected to electrolysis using a special electrode and a range of applied voltages, a plot of current against voltage showing steps corresponding to particular chemical species and proportional to their concentration.
– DERIVATIVES **polarographic** adjective.
– ORIGIN 1930s: from *polarization* (see **POLARIZE**) + **-GRAPHY**.

Polaroid ▸ noun trademark 1 [mass noun] material in thin plastic sheets that produces a high degree of plane polarization in light passing through it. ■ (**Polaroids**) sunglasses with lenses made from Polaroid plastic.
2 a photograph taken with a Polaroid camera.
▸ adjective Photography relating to or denoting a type of camera with internal processing that produces a finished print rapidly after each exposure.
– ORIGIN 1930s: from **POLARIZE** + **-OID**.

polar orbit ▸ noun a satellite orbit that passes over polar regions, especially one whose plane contains the polar axis.

polar star ▸ noun Astronomy a star at or close to a celestial pole, especially the Pole Star.

polar wandering ▸ noun [mass noun] the slow erratic movement of the earth's poles relative to the continents throughout geological time, due largely to continental drift.

polder /ˈpəʊldə/ ▸ noun a piece of low-lying land reclaimed from the sea or a river and protected by dykes, especially in the Netherlands.
– ORIGIN early 17th cent.: from Dutch, from Middle Dutch *polre*.

Pole ▸ noun a native or inhabitant of Poland, or a person of Polish descent.
– ORIGIN via German from Polish *Polanie*, literally 'field-dwellers', from *pole* 'field'.

pole¹ ▸ noun 1 a long, slender, rounded piece of wood or metal, typically used with one end placed in the ground as a support for something: *a tent pole*. ■ a young tree with a straight slender trunk and no lower branches. ■ short for **SKI POLE**. ■ a wooden shaft fitted to the front of a cart or carriage drawn by animals and attached to their yokes or collars. ■ a simple fishing rod.
2 historical, chiefly Brit. another term for **PERCH³** (sense 1). ■ (also **square pole**) another term for **PERCH³** (sense 2).
▸ verb [with obj.] propel (a boat) by pushing a pole against the bottom of a river, canal, or lake.
– PHRASES **under bare poles** Sailing with no sail set. **up the pole** informal 1 Brit. mad: ***taxes can be enough to drive you up the pole***. 2 chiefly Irish pregnant.
– ORIGIN late Old English *pāl* (in early use without reference to thickness or length), of Germanic origin; related to Dutch *paal* and German *Pfahl*, based on Latin *palus* 'stake'.

pole² ▸ noun either of the two locations (**North Pole** or **South Pole**) on the surface of the earth (or of a celestial object) which are the northern and southern ends of the axis of rotation. See also **MAGNETIC POLE**. ■ Geometry either of the two points at which the axis of a circle cuts the surface of a sphere. ■ Geometry a fixed point to which other points or lines are referred, e.g. the origin of polar coordinates or the point of which a line or curve is a polar. ■ Biology an extremity of the main axis of a cell, organ, or part. ■ each of the two opposite points on the surface of a magnet at which magnetic forces are strongest. ■ each of two terminals (positive and negative) of an electric cell, battery, or machine. ■ one of two opposed or contradictory principles or ideas.
– PHRASES **be poles apart** have nothing in common.
– DERIVATIVES **poleward** adjective, **polewards** adjective & adverb.
– ORIGIN late Middle English: from Latin *polus* 'end of an axis', from Greek *polos* 'pivot, axis, sky'.

pole³ ▸ noun short for **POLE POSITION**.

poleaxe (US also **poleax**) ▸ noun another term for **BATTLEAXE** (sense 1). ■ a short-handled axe with a spike at the back, formerly used in naval warfare for boarding, resisting boarders, and cutting ropes. ■ a butcher's axe with a hammer head at the back, used to slaughter animals.
▸ verb [with obj.] hit, kill, or knock down with or as if with a poleaxe. ■ cause great shock to: *I was poleaxed by this revelation*.
– ORIGIN Middle English: related to Middle Dutch *pol(l)aex*, Middle Low German *pol(l)exe* (see **POLL**, **AXE**). The change in the first syllable was due to association with **POLE¹**; the first element *poll-* may have referred to a special head of the axe or to the head of an enemy.

pole barn ▸ noun a farm building which has sides consisting of poles covered with wire mesh.

pole bean ▸ noun N. Amer. a climbing bean.

polecat ▸ noun a weasel-like Eurasian mammal with mainly dark brown fur and a darker mask across the eyes, noted for its fetid smell. ● Genus *Mustela*, family Mustelidae: three species, in particular the **European polecat** (*M. putorius*), which is the probable ancestor of the domestic ferret. ■ North American term for **SKUNK**.

P

– ORIGIN Middle English: perhaps from Old French *pole* 'chicken' + CAT[1].

polecat-ferret ▸ noun a domestic ferret of a variety that has the darker colouring of the wild polecat.

pole dancing ▸ noun [mass noun] erotic dancing which involves swinging around a fixed pole.
– DERIVATIVES **pole dancer** noun.

pole lathe ▸ noun an ancient form of lathe operated by a treadle, in which the work is turned by a cord passing round it and rotated back by the action of a springy pole or sapling attached to the top end.

polemic /pəˈlɛmɪk/ ▸ noun a strong verbal or written attack on someone or something: *his polemic against the cultural relativism of the Sixties* | [mass noun] *a writer of feminist polemic.* ■ (usu. **polemics**) the practice of engaging in controversial debate or dispute: *the history of science has become embroiled in religious polemics.*
▸ adjective another term for POLEMICAL.
– DERIVATIVES **polemicist** noun, **polemicize** (also **polemicise**) verb.
– ORIGIN mid 17th cent.: via medieval Latin from Greek *polemikos*, from *polemos* 'war'.

polemical ▸ adjective of or involving strongly critical or disputatious writing or speech: *a polemical essay.*
– DERIVATIVES **polemically** adverb.

polenta /pəˈlɛntə/ ▸ noun [mass noun] maize flour as used in Italian cookery; cornmeal. ■ a paste or dough made from polenta, which is boiled and typically then fried or baked.
– ORIGIN late 16th cent.: Italian, from Latin, 'pearl barley' (a sense of *polenta* in Old English).

pole piece ▸ noun Physics a mass of iron forming the end of an electromagnet, through which the lines of magnetic force are concentrated and directed.

pole position ▸ noun the most favourable position at the start of a motor race. ■ a leading or dominant position: *a company boasting the pole position in the communications business.*
– ORIGIN 1950s: from a 19th-cent. use of *pole* in horse racing, denoting the starting position next to the inside boundary fence.

Pole Star Astronomy a fairly bright star located within one degree of the celestial north pole, in the constellation Ursa Minor. It is a triple star, the bright component of which is a cepheid variable. Also called NORTH STAR, POLARIS.

pole vault ▸ noun [mass noun] (**the pole vault**) an athletic event in which competitors attempt to vault over a high bar with the aid of an extremely long flexible pole. ■ [count noun] a vault performed in the pole vault athletic event.
▸ verb (**pole-vault**) [no obj.] perform a pole vault.
– DERIVATIVES **pole-vaulter** noun.

police ▸ noun [treated as pl.] (usu. **the police**) the civil force of a state, responsible for the prevention and detection of crime and the maintenance of public order. ■ members of a police force: *there are fewer women police than men.* ■ [with adj. or noun modifier] an organization engaged in the enforcement of official regulations in a specified domain: *transport police.*
▸ verb [with obj.] (of a police force) have the duty of maintaining law and order in or at (an area or event): (as noun **policing**) *a ten-point plan to improve policing.* ■ enforce regulations or an agreement in (a particular area or domain): *a UN resolution to use military force to police the no-fly zone.* ■ enforce the provisions of (a law, agreement, or treaty): *the regulations will be policed by factory inspectors.*
– ORIGIN late 15th cent. (in the sense 'public order'): from French, from medieval Latin *politia* 'citizenship, government' (see POLICY[1]). Current senses date from the early 19th cent.

police constable ▸ noun see CONSTABLE.

police dog ▸ noun a dog, especially an Alsatian, trained for use in police work.

police force ▸ noun an organized body of police officers responsible for a country, district, or town.

policeman ▸ noun (pl. **policemen**) a male member of a police force.

Police Motu ▸ noun see MOTU.

police officer ▸ noun a policeman or policewoman.

police procedural ▸ noun chiefly N. Amer. a crime novel in which the emphasis is on the procedures used by the police in solving the crime.

police record ▸ noun (usu. **police records**) a dossier kept by the police on all people convicted of crime. ■ (**a police record**) a personal history which includes some conviction for crime: *a well-known character with a police record.*

police state ▸ noun a totalitarian state controlled by a political police force that secretly supervises the citizens' activities.

police station ▸ noun the office or headquarters of a local police force.

policewoman ▸ noun (pl. **policewomen**) a female member of a police force.

policier /ˌpɒlɪˈsjeɪ/, French /pɔlisje/ ▸ noun a film based on a police novel, portraying crime and its detection by police.
– ORIGIN French, from *roman policier* 'detective novel'.

policy[1] ▸ noun (pl. **policies**) a course or principle of action adopted or proposed by an organization or individual: *the government's controversial economic policies* | [mass noun] *it is not company policy to dispense with our older workers.* ■ [mass noun] archaic prudent or expedient conduct or action.
– ORIGIN late Middle English: from Old French *policie* 'civil administration', via Latin from Greek *politeia* 'citizenship', from *politēs* 'citizen', from *polis* 'city'.

policy[2] ▸ noun (pl. **policies**) a contract of insurance: *they took out a joint policy.*
– ORIGIN mid 16th cent.: from French *police* 'bill of lading, contract of insurance', from Provençal *poliss(i)a*, probably from medieval Latin *apodissa*, *apodixa*, based on Greek *apodeixis* 'evidence, proof', from *apodeiknunai* 'demonstrate, show'.

policyholder ▸ noun a person or group in whose name an insurance policy is held.

policymaker ▸ noun a person responsible for or involved in formulating policies, especially in politics.
– DERIVATIVES **policymaking** noun.

polio ▸ noun short for POLIOMYELITIS.

poliomyelitis /ˌpəʊlɪəʊmʌɪəˈlʌɪtɪs, ˌpɒlɪəʊ-/ ▸ noun [mass noun] Medicine an infectious viral disease that affects the central nervous system and can cause temporary or permanent paralysis.
– ORIGIN late 19th cent.: modern Latin, from Greek *polios* 'grey' + *muelos* 'marrow'.

poliovirus ▸ noun Medicine any of a group of enteroviruses including those that cause poliomyelitis.

polis[1] /ˈpəʊlɪs, ˈpɒlɪs/ ▸ noun Scottish and Irish form of POLICE.

polis[2] /ˈpɒlɪs/ ▸ noun (pl. **poleis**) a city-state in ancient Greece, especially as considered in its ideal form for philosophical purposes.
– ORIGIN Greek.

Polisario /ˌpɒlɪˈsɑːrɪəʊ/ (also **Polisario Front**) an independence movement in Western (formerly Spanish) Sahara, formed in 1973.
– ORIGIN Spanish acronym, from *Frente Popular para la Liberación de Sagnia el-Hamra y Río de Oro* 'Popular Front for the Liberation of Sagnia el-Hamra and Rio de Oro'.

Polish /ˈpəʊlɪʃ/ ▸ adjective relating to Poland, its inhabitants, or their language.
▸ noun [mass noun] the Western Slavic language of Poland, spoken by some 38 million people.

polish /ˈpɒlɪʃ/ ▸ verb [with obj.] make the surface of (something) smooth and shiny by rubbing it: *behind the bar the steward polished glasses busily.* ■ improve, refine, or add the finishing touches to: *he's got to polish up his French for his job.*
▸ noun [mass noun] a substance used to give something a smooth and shiny surface when rubbed in: *a tin of shoe polish.* ■ [in sing.] an act of rubbing something to give it a shiny surface: *I could give the wardrobe a polish.* ■ smoothness or glossiness produced by rubbing or friction: *the machine refines the shape of the stone and gives it polish.* ■ refinement or elegance in a person or thing: *his poetry has clarity and polish.*
– PHRASAL VERBS **polish something off** quickly finish or consume something: *they polished off most of the sausages.*
– DERIVATIVES **polishable** adjective, **polisher** noun.
– ORIGIN Middle English: from Old French *poliss-*, lengthened stem of *polir* 'to polish', from Latin *polire*.

Polish Corridor a former region of Poland which extended northwards to the Baltic coast and separated East Prussia from the rest of Germany, granted to Poland after the First World War to ensure Polish access to the coast. Its annexation by Germany in 1939, with the German occupation of the rest of Poland, precipitated the Second World War. After the war the area was restored to Poland.

polished ▸ adjective shiny as a result of being rubbed: *a polished mahogany table.* ■ accomplished and skilful: *his polished performance in the film.* ■ refined, sophisticated, or elegant: *he was polished and charming.* ■ (of rice) having had the outer husk removed during milling.

Polish notation ▸ noun [mass noun] Logic & Computing a system of formula notation without brackets or special punctuation, frequently used to represent the order in which arithmetical operations are performed in many computers and calculators. In the usual form (**reverse Polish notation**), operators follow rather than precede their operands.

politburo /ˈpɒlɪtˌbjʊərəʊ/ ▸ noun (pl. **politburos**) the principal policymaking committee of a communist party. ■ (**Politburo**) the principal policymaking committee in the former Soviet Union, founded in 1917. Also called (1952–66) the PRESIDIUM.
– ORIGIN from Russian *politbyuro*, from *polit(icheskoe) byuro* 'political bureau'.

polite ▸ adjective (**politer**, **politest**) having or showing behaviour that is respectful and considerate of other people: *they thought she was wrong but were too polite to say so.* ■ [attrib.] relating to people who regard themselves as more cultured and refined than others: *the picture outraged polite society.*
– DERIVATIVES **politely** adverb, **politeness** noun.
– ORIGIN late Middle English (in the Latin sense): from Latin *politus* 'polished, made smooth', past participle of *polire*.

politesse /ˌpɒlɪˈtɛs/ ▸ noun [mass noun] formal politeness or etiquette.
– ORIGIN early 18th cent.: French, from Italian *politezza*, *pulitezza*, from *pulito* 'polite'.

politic ▸ adjective (of an action) seeming sensible and judicious in the circumstances: [with infinitive] *I did not think it politic to express my reservations.* ■ (also **politick**) archaic (of a person) prudent and sagacious.
▸ verb (**politics**, **politicking**, **politicked**) [no obj.] (often as noun **politicking**) often derogatory engage in political activity: *the cumbersome bureaucracy and politicking of the European Community.*
– DERIVATIVES **politicly** adverb (rare).
– ORIGIN late Middle English: from Old French *politique* 'political', via Latin from Greek *politikos*, from *politēs* 'citizen', from *polis* 'city'.

political ▸ adjective **1** of or relating to the government or public affairs of a country: *a period of political and economic stability.* ■ relating to the ideas or strategies of a particular party or group in politics: *a decision taken for purely political reasons.* ■ interested in or active in politics: *I'm not very political.* ■ motivated by a person's beliefs or actions concerning politics: *a political crime.*
2 chiefly derogatory done or acting in the interests of status or power within an organization rather than as a matter of principle.
– DERIVATIVES **politically** adverb [sentence adverb] *politically, it was safer to sit on the fence.*

political animal ▸ noun chiefly informal a person who is interested in social and political issues, especially one who actively participates in politics.

political asylum ▸ noun see ASYLUM.

political commissar ▸ noun a person responsible for political education and organization in a military unit in China.

political correctness (also **political correctitude**) ▸ noun [mass noun] the avoidance of forms of expression or action that are perceived to exclude, marginalize, or insult groups of people who are socially disadvantaged or discriminated against.

political economy ▸ noun [mass noun] dated economics as a branch of knowledge or academic discipline.
– DERIVATIVES **political economist** noun.

political geography ▸ noun [mass noun] the branch of geography that deals with the boundaries, divisions, and possessions of states.

politically correct (or **incorrect**) ▸ adjective exhibiting (or failing to exhibit) political correctness: *it is not politically correct to laugh at speech impediments.*

political offence ▸ noun Law an offence regarded as justifiable or deserving of special consideration because of its political motivation.

political prisoner ▸ noun a person imprisoned for their political beliefs or actions.

political refugee ▸ noun a refugee from an oppressive government.

political science ▶ noun [mass noun] the branch of knowledge that deals with the state and systems of government; the scientific analysis of political activity and behaviour.
– DERIVATIVES **political scientist** noun.

politician ▶ noun a person who is professionally involved in politics, especially as a holder of an elected office. ■ chiefly US a person who acts in a manipulative and devious way, typically to gain advancement within an organization.

politicize (also **politicise**) ▶ verb [with obj.] (often as adj. **politicized**) cause (an activity or event) to become political in character: *wage bargaining in the public sector became more politicized.* ■ make (someone) politically aware: *we successfully politicized a generation of women.* ■ [no obj.] engage in or talk about politics.
– DERIVATIVES **politicization** noun.

politick ▶ adjective archaic spelling of POLITIC.

politico ▶ noun (pl. **politicos**) informal, chiefly derogatory a politician or person with strong political views.
– ORIGIN Spanish and Italian, 'politic' or 'political person'.

politico- ▶ combining form politically: *politico-ethical.* ■ political and ...: *politico-economic.*
– ORIGIN from Greek *politikos* 'civic, political'.

politics ▶ plural noun **1** [usu. treated as sing.] the activities associated with the governance of a country or area, especially the debate between parties having power: *the party quickly gained influence in French politics | thereafter he dropped out of active politics.* ■ the activities of governments concerning the political relations between states: *in the conduct of global politics, economic status must be backed by military capacity.* ■ the academic study of government and the state: [as modifier] *a politics lecturer.* ■ a particular set of political beliefs or principles: *people do not buy their paper purely for its politics.* ■ (often **the politics of**) the principles relating to or inherent in a sphere or activity, especially when concerned with power and status: *the politics of gender.*
2 activities aimed at improving someone's status or increasing power within an organization: *yet another discussion of office politics and personalities.*
– PHRASES **play politics** act for political or personal gain rather than from principle.

polity /ˈpɒlɪti/ ▶ noun (pl. **polities**) a form or process of civil government or constitution. ■ an organized society; a state as a political entity.
– ORIGIN mid 16th cent.: from obsolete French *politie*, via Latin from Greek *politeia* 'citizenship, government', from *politēs* 'citizen', from *polis* 'city'.

polje /ˈpɒljə/ ▶ noun Geology a flat-floored depression in a karstic region, especially in Slovenia, with steep enclosing walls and a covering of alluvium.
– ORIGIN late 19th cent.: from Serbian and Croatian.

Polk /pəʊk/, James Knox (1795–1849), American Democratic statesman, 11th President of the US 1845–9. His term of office resulted in major territorial additions to the US: Texas was admitted to the Union in 1845 and conflict with Mexico resulted in the annexation of California and the south-west two years later.

polka /ˈpɒlkə, ˈpəʊlkə/ ▶ noun a lively dance of Bohemian origin in duple time. ■ a piece of music for the polka.
▶ verb (**polkas, polkaing, polkaed** or **polka'd**) [no obj.] dance the polka.
ORIGIN mid 19th cent.: via French and German from Czech *půlka* 'half-step', from *půl* 'half'.

polka dot ▶ noun one of a number of round dots repeated to form a regular pattern on fabric: [as modifier] *a red and white polka-dot shirt.*
– DERIVATIVES **polka-dotted** adjective.

poll /pəʊl/ ▶ noun **1** (often **the polls**) the process of voting in an election: *the country went to the polls on March 10.* ■ the number of votes cast in an election: *the ruling party won 24 seats, narrowly topping the poll.* ■ (**the polls**) the places where votes are cast in an election: *the polls have only just closed.* ■ short for OPINION POLL.
2 dialect a person's head. ■ the part of the head on which hair grows; the scalp.
3 a hornless animal, especially one of a breed of hornless cattle. See also RED POLL.
▶ verb [with obj.] **1** record the opinion or vote of: *over half of those polled do not believe the prime minister usually tells the truth.* ■ [no obj., with adverbial] (of a candidate in an election) receive a specified number of votes: *the Green candidate polled 3.6 per cent.*
2 Telecommunications & Computing check the status of (a device), especially as part of a repeated cycle.
3 cut the horns off (an animal, especially a young cow). ■ archaic cut off the top of (a tree or plant), typically to encourage further growth; pollard.
– ORIGIN Middle English (in the sense 'head'): perhaps of Low German origin. The original sense was 'head', and hence 'an individual person among a number', from which developed the sense 'number of people ascertained by counting of heads' and then 'counting of heads or of votes' (17th cent.).

pollack /ˈpɒlək/ (also **pollock**) ▶ noun (pl. **same** or **pollacks**) an edible greenish-brown fish of the cod family, with a protruding lower jaw. Found in the NE Atlantic, it is popular with anglers. ● *Pollachius pollachius*, family Gadidae.
– ORIGIN late Middle English: perhaps of Celtic origin.

Pollaiuolo /ˌpɒlʌɪˈwəʊləʊ/, Antonio (*c.*1432–98) and Piero (1443–96), Italian sculptors, painters, and engravers. Both brothers worked on the monuments to Popes Sixtus IV and Innocent VIII in St Peter's, and Antonio is particularly known for his realistic depiction of the human form.

pollan /ˈpɒlən/ ▶ noun an Arctic cisco (fish) of a variety which occurs in Irish lakes.
– ORIGIN early 18th cent.: from Irish *pollán*, perhaps based on *poll* 'pool'.

pollard /ˈpɒləd/ ▶ verb [with obj.] (often as adj. **pollarded**) cut off the top and branches of (a tree) to encourage new growth at the top.
▶ noun **1** a tree whose top and branches have been pollarded.
2 archaic an animal that has lost its horns or cast its antlers.
– ORIGIN early 17th cent.: from the verb POLL + -ARD.

polled /pəʊld/ ▶ adjective (of cattle, sheep, or goats) lacking horns, either naturally or because they have been removed.

pollen ▶ noun [mass noun] a fine powdery substance, typically yellow, consisting of microscopic grains discharged from the male part of a flower or from a male cone. Each grain contains a male gamete that can fertilize the female ovule, to which pollen is transported by the wind, insects, or other animals.
– ORIGIN mid 18th cent.: from Latin, literally 'fine powder'.

pollen basket ▶ noun Entomology a flattened area fringed with hairs on the hind leg of a social bee, used for carrying pollen. Also called CORBICULA.

pollen count ▶ noun an index of the amount of pollen in the air, published chiefly for the benefit of those allergic to it.

pollen tube ▶ noun Botany a hollow tube which develops from a pollen grain when deposited on the stigma of a flower. It penetrates the style and conveys the male gametes to the ovule.

pollen zone ▶ noun a characteristic assemblage of pollen obtained by pollen analysis. Each zone (denoted by a Roman numeral) corresponds to one of the climatic stages of the late-glacial and postglacial periods.

pollex /ˈpɒlɛks/ ▶ noun (pl. **pollices** /-lɪsiːz/) Anatomy & Zoology the innermost digit of a forelimb, especially the thumb in primates.
– ORIGIN mid 19th cent.: from Latin, literally 'thumb or big toe'.

pollie ▶ noun variant spelling of POLLY.

pollinate ▶ verb [with obj.] convey pollen to or deposit pollen on (a stigma, ovule, flower, or plant) and so allow fertilization.
– DERIVATIVES **pollination** noun, **pollinator** noun.
– ORIGIN late 19th cent.: from Latin *pollen, pollin-* 'pollen' + -ATE³.

polling booth ▶ noun Brit. a compartment with one open side in which one voter at a time stands to mark their ballot paper.

polling day ▶ noun Brit. the day of a local or general election.

polling station (N. Amer. also **polling place**) ▶ noun a building, such as a school or community centre, where voting takes place during an election.

pollinium /pəˈlɪnɪəm/ ▶ noun (pl. **pollinia** /pəˈlɪnɪə/) Botany a coherent mass of pollen grains that is the product of each anther lobe of some flowers, especially orchids. Single or paired pollinia are often attached to, and carried by, pollinating insects.
– ORIGIN mid 19th cent.: modern Latin, from Latin *pollen, pollin-* 'pollen'.

polliwog (also **pollywog**) ▶ noun **1** N. Amer. & dialect a tadpole.
2 N. Amer. informal a new sailor, especially one crossing the equator for the first time.
– ORIGIN late Middle English (earlier as *pollywiggle*): from POLL in the sense 'head' + the verb WIGGLE.

pollo /ˈpɒləʊ/ ▶ noun [mass noun] chicken (as used in the names of Italian, Spanish, or Mexican dishes).
– ORIGIN Spanish and Italian.

Pollock, (Paul) Jackson (1912–56), American painter. He was a leading figure in the abstract expressionist movement and from 1947 became the chief exponent of the style known as action painting, whereby he poured, splashed, or dripped paint on to the canvas.

pollock ▶ noun **1** North American term for SAITHE.
2 variant spelling of POLLACK.

pollster /ˈpəʊlstə/ ▶ noun a person who conducts or analyses opinion polls.

poll tax ▶ noun [mass noun] a tax levied on every adult, without reference to their income or resources. ■ informal term for COMMUNITY CHARGE.

pollutant ▶ noun a substance that pollutes something, especially water or the atmosphere: *chemical pollutants* | [as modifier] *pollutant gases.*

pollute ▶ verb [with obj.] contaminate (water, the air, etc.) with harmful or poisonous substances: *the explosion polluted the town with dioxin* | (as adj. **polluted**) *the Mersey is one of Europe's most polluted rivers.* ■ defile or corrupt: *a society polluted by racism.*
– DERIVATIVES **polluter** noun.
– ORIGIN late Middle English: from Latin *pollut-* 'soiled, defiled', from the verb *polluere*, based on the root of *lutum* 'mud'.

pollution ▶ noun [mass noun] the presence in or introduction into the environment of a substance which has harmful or poisonous effects: *the level of pollution in the air is rising.*
– ORIGIN late Middle English: from Latin *pollutio(n-)*, from the verb *polluere* (see POLLUTE).

Pollux /ˈpɒləks/ **1** Greek Mythology the twin brother of Castor. Also called POLYDEUCES. See DIOSCURI.
2 Astronomy the brightest star in the constellation Gemini, close to Castor.

polly (also **pollie**) ▶ noun (pl. **pollies**) Austral./NZ informal a politician.
– ORIGIN 1960s: abbreviation.

Pollyanna ▶ noun an excessively cheerful or optimistic person.
– DERIVATIVES **Pollyannaish** adjective, **Pollyannaism** noun.
– ORIGIN early 20th cent.: the name of the optimistic heroine created by Eleanor Hodgman Porter (1868–1920), American author of children's stories.

pollywog ▶ noun variant spelling of POLLIWOG.

Polo, Marco, see MARCO POLO.

polo ▶ noun [mass noun] a game of Eastern origin resembling hockey, played on horseback with a long-handled mallet.
– ORIGIN late 19th cent.: from Balti, 'ball'.

poloidal /pəˈlɔɪd(ə)l/ ▶ adjective Physics relating to or denoting a magnetic field associated with a toroidal electric field, in which each line of force is confined to a radial or meridian plane.
– ORIGIN 1940s: from POLAR, on the pattern of *toroidal*.

Polokwane /ˌpɒlə(ʊ)ˈkwɑːni/ a town in northern South Africa, capital of the Limpopo province; pop. 136,100 (est. 2009). Former name (until 2002) PIETERSBURG.

polonaise /ˌpɒləˈneɪz/ ▶ noun **1** a slow dance of Polish origin in triple time, consisting chiefly of an intricate march or procession. ■ a piece of music for the polonaise.
2 historical a woman's dress with a tight bodice and a skirt open from the waist downwards, looped up to show a decorative underskirt.
▶ adjective (of a dish) garnished with chopped hard-boiled egg yolk, breadcrumbs, and parsley.
– ORIGIN mid 18th cent.: from French, feminine of *polonais* 'Polish', from medieval Latin *Polonia* 'Poland'.

polo neck ▶ noun Brit. a high, close-fitting, turned-over collar on a sweater. ■ a sweater with a polo neck.
– DERIVATIVES **polo-necked** adjective.

polonium /pəˈləʊnɪəm/ ▶ noun [mass noun] the chemical element of atomic number 84, a radioactive metal occurring in nature only as a product of radioactive decay of uranium. (Symbol: Po)

– ORIGIN late 19th cent.: modern Latin, from medieval Latin *Polonia* 'Poland' (the native country of Marie Curie, the element's co-discoverer).

Polonnaruwa /ˌpɒləˈnɑːruwə/ a town in NE Sri Lanka; pop. 13,900 (est. 2009). Succeeding Anuradhapura in the 8th century as the capital of Ceylon, it became an important Buddhist centre in the 12th century. It was subsequently deserted until a modern town was built there in the 20th century.

polony /pəˈləʊni/ ▸ noun (pl. **polonies**) Brit. another term for **BOLOGNA**.
– ORIGIN mid 18th cent.: apparently an alteration of **BOLOGNA**.

polo pony ▸ noun a horse used in playing polo, typically bred for speed and agility.

polo shirt ▸ noun a casual short-sleeved cotton shirt with a collar and several buttons at the neck.

polo stick ▸ noun a long-handled mallet used for playing polo.

Pol Pot /pɒl ˈpɒt/ (*c.*1925–98), Cambodian communist leader of the Khmer Rouge, Prime Minister 1976–9; born *Saloth Sar*. During his regime the Khmer Rouge embarked on a brutal reconstruction programme in which many millions of Cambodians were killed. Overthrown in 1979, Pol Pot led the Khmer Rouge in a guerrilla war against the new Vietnamese-backed government until his official retirement in 1985.

Polska /ˈpɒlska/ Polish name for **POLAND**.

Poltava /pɒlˈtɑːvə/ a city in east central Ukraine; pop. 301,600 (est. 2009).

poltergeist /ˈpɒltəgʌɪst/ ▸ noun a ghost or other supernatural being supposedly responsible for physical disturbances such as making loud noises and throwing objects about.
– ORIGIN mid 19th cent.: from German *Poltergeist*, from *poltern* 'create a disturbance' + *Geist* 'ghost'.

Poltoratsk /ˌpɒltəˈrɑːtsk/ former name (1919–27) for **ASHGABAT**.

poltroon /pɒlˈtruːn/ ▸ noun archaic or literary an utter coward.
– DERIVATIVES **poltroonery** noun.
– ORIGIN early 16th cent.: from French *poltron*, from Italian *poltrone*, perhaps from *poltro* 'sluggard'.

poly ▸ noun (pl. **polys**) informal **1** polyester.
2 Brit. historical a polytechnic.
3 polythene.

poly- ▸ combining form many; much: *polyandry* | *polychrome*. ■ Chemistry denoting the presence of many atoms or groups of a particular kind in a molecule: *polycarbonate*.
– ORIGIN from Greek *polus* 'much', *polloi* 'many'.

polyacetylene /ˌpɒlɪəˈsɛtɪliːn/ ▸ noun [mass noun] Chemistry a black electrically conducting solid which is a hydrocarbon polymer containing chains of carbon atoms joined by alternate double and single bonds.

polyacrylamide /ˌpɒlɪəˈkrɪləmʌɪd/ ▸ noun [mass noun] a synthetic resin made by polymerizing acrylamide, especially a water-soluble polymer used to form or stabilize gels and as a thickening or clarifying agent.

polyadic /ˌpɒlɪˈadɪk/ ▸ adjective involving three or more quantities, elements, or individuals.
– ORIGIN early 20th cent.: from **POLY-** 'many', on the pattern of words such as *dyadic*, *monadic*.

polyamide /ˌpɒlɪˈeɪmʌɪd, -ˈam-/ ▸ noun [mass noun] a synthetic polymer of a type made by the linkage of an amino group of one molecule and a carboxylic acid group of another, including many synthetic fibres such as nylon.

polyamory /ˌpɒlɪˈam(ə)ri/ ▸ noun [mass noun] the practice of engaging in multiple sexual relationships with the consent of all the people involved.
– DERIVATIVES **polyamorist** noun, **polyamorous** adjective.
– ORIGIN 1990s: from **POLY-** 'many' + Latin *amor* 'love'.

polyandry /ˈpɒlɪandri/ ▸ noun [mass noun] polygamy in which a woman has more than one husband. Compare with **POLYGYNY**. ■ Zoology a pattern of mating in which a female animal has more than one male mate.
– DERIVATIVES **polyandrous** adjective.
– ORIGIN late 17th cent.: from **POLY-** 'many' + Greek *anēr*, *andr-* 'male'.

polyanthus /ˌpɒlɪˈanθəs/ ▸ noun (pl. **same**) a herbaceous flowering plant which is a complex hybrid between the wild primrose and primulas, cultivated in Europe since the 17th century. ● *Primula × polyantha*, family Primulaceae.
– ORIGIN early 18th cent.: modern Latin, from **POLY-** 'many' + Greek *anthos* 'flower'.

polyatomic ▸ adjective consisting of many atoms.

polybag ▸ noun informal a bag made of polythene film.

Polybius /pəˈlɪbɪəs/ (*c.*200–*c.*118 BC), Greek historian. His forty books of *Histories* (only partially extant) chronicled the rise of the Roman Empire from 220 to 146 BC.

polycarbonate ▸ noun [mass noun] a synthetic resin in which the polymer units are linked through carbonate groups, including many moulding materials and films.

Polycarp, St /ˈpɒlɪkɑːp/ (*c.*69–*c.*155), Greek bishop of Smyrna in Asia Minor. The leading Christian figure in Smyrna, he was arrested during a pagan festival, refused to recant his faith, and was burnt to death. Feast day, 23 February.

Polychaeta /ˌpɒlɪˈkiːtə/ ▸ plural noun Zoology a class of marine annelid worms which comprises the bristle worms.
– ORIGIN modern Latin (plural), from Greek *polu-* 'many' + *khaitē* 'mane' (taken to mean 'bristle').

polychaete /ˈpɒlɪkiːt/ ▸ noun Zoology a marine annelid worm of the class Polychaeta; a bristle worm.

polychlorinated biphenyl (abbrev.: **PCB**) ▸ noun Chemistry any of a class of toxic aromatic compounds, often formed as waste in industrial processes, whose molecules contain two benzene rings in which hydrogen atoms have been replaced by chlorine atoms.

polychromatic ▸ adjective of two or more or of varying colours; multicoloured: *patterned polychromatic brickwork*. ■ Physics (of light or other radiation) of a number of wavelengths or frequencies.

polychrome ▸ adjective painted or printed in several colours.
▸ noun [mass noun] varied colouring. ■ [count noun] a work of art in several colours, especially a statue.
▸ verb [with obj.] (usu. as adj. **polychromed**) execute (a work of art) in several colours.
– ORIGIN early 19th cent.: from French, from Greek *polukhrōmos*, from *polu-* 'many' + *khrōma* 'colour'.

polychromy /ˈpɒlɪkrəʊmi/ ▸ noun [mass noun] the art of painting in several colours, especially as applied to ancient pottery, sculpture, and architecture.

polyclinic ▸ noun a clinic (typically one independent of a hospital) where both general and specialist examinations and treatments are available to outpatients.

Polyclitus /ˌpɒlɪˈklʌɪtəs/ (5th century BC), Greek sculptor, known for his statues of idealized male athletes. Two Roman copies of his works survive, the *Doryphoros* (spear-bearer) and the *Diadumenos* (youth fastening a band round his head).

polyclonal /ˌpɒlɪˈkləʊn(ə)l/ ▸ adjective Medicine & Biology consisting of or derived from many clones.

polycotton ▸ noun [mass noun] fabric made from a mixture of cotton and polyester fibre.

polycrystalline ▸ adjective (of a metal or other solid) consisting of many crystalline parts that are randomly oriented with respect to each other.

polyculture ▸ noun [mass noun] the simultaneous cultivation or exploitation of several crops or kinds of animals.

polycyclic /ˌpɒlɪˈsʌɪklɪk, -ˈsɪk-/ ▸ adjective relating to or resulting from many cycles. ■ Chemistry (of an organic compound) having several rings of atoms in the molecule. ■ Geology (of a landform or deposit) having undergone two or more cycles of erosion and deposition.

polycystic ▸ adjective Medicine characterized by multiple cysts.

polycythaemia /ˌpɒlɪsʌɪˈθiːmɪə/ (US **polycythemia**) ▸ noun [mass noun] Medicine an abnormally increased concentration of haemoglobin in the blood, either through reduction of plasma volume or increase in red cell numbers. It may be a primary disease of unknown cause, or a secondary condition linked to respiratory or circulatory disorder or cancer.
– ORIGIN mid 19th cent.: modern Latin, from **POLY-** 'many' + **-CYTE** 'cell' + **HAEMO-** 'blood' + **-IA**[1].

polydactyly /ˌpɒlɪˈdaktɪli/ ▸ noun [mass noun] a condition in which a person or animal has more than five fingers or toes on one, or on each, hand or foot.
– DERIVATIVES **polydactyl** adjective & noun.
– ORIGIN late 19th cent.: from Greek *poludaktulos* (from *polu-* 'many' + *daktulos* 'finger') + **-Y**[3].

Polydeuces /ˌpɒlɪˈdjuːsiːz/ another name for **POLLUX** (sense 1).

polydipsia /ˌpɒlɪˈdɪpsɪə/ ▸ noun [mass noun] Medicine abnormally great thirst as a symptom of disease (such as diabetes) or psychological disturbance.
– ORIGIN mid 17th cent.: from Greek *poludipsios* 'very thirsty', *poludipsos* 'causing great thirst', based on *dipsa* 'thirst'.

polydrug ▸ adjective relating to or denoting the use of several, typically illegal, drugs together: *prolonged polydrug abuse*.

polyelectrolyte /ˌpɒlɪɪˈlɛktrəlʌɪt/ ▸ noun Chemistry a polymer which has several ionizable groups along the molecule, especially any of those used for coagulating and flocculating particles during water treatment or for making electrophoretic gels.

polyembryony /ˌpɒlɪˈɛmbrɪəni/ ▸ noun [mass noun] Biology the formation of more than one embryo from a single fertilized ovum or in a single seed.
– DERIVATIVES **polyembryonic** adjective.

polyene /ˈpɒlijiːn/ ▸ noun Chemistry a hydrocarbon with several carbon–carbon double bonds, especially one having a chain of conjugated single and double bonds.

polyester ▸ noun [mass noun] a synthetic resin in which the polymer units are linked by ester groups, used chiefly to make synthetic textile fibres. ■ a fabric made from polyester fibre.

polyethnic ▸ adjective belonging to, comprising, or containing many ethnic groups.
– DERIVATIVES **polyethnicity** noun.

polyethylene /ˌpɒlɪˈɛθɪliːn/ ▸ noun another term for **POLYTHENE**.

polyethylene glycol ▸ noun [mass noun] a synthetic resin made by polymerizing ethylene glycol, in particular any of a series of water-soluble oligomers and polymers used chiefly as solvents or waxes.

polyethylene terephthalate /ˌtɛrəfˈθaleɪt/ (abbrev.: **PET**) ▸ noun [mass noun] a synthetic resin made by copolymerizing ethylene glycol and terephthalic acid, widely used to make polyester fibres.

Polyfilla ▸ noun [mass noun] trademark a type of plaster used to make minor building repairs, such as filling small holes.

polygamous ▸ adjective relating to or involving polygamy: *polygamous societies*. ■ Zoology (of an animal) typically having more than one mate. ■ Botany (of a plant) bearing some flowers with stamens only, some with pistils only, and some with both, on the same or different plants.
– DERIVATIVES **polygamously** adverb.
– ORIGIN early 17th cent.: from Greek *polugamos* (from *polu-* 'much, often' + *-gamos* 'marrying') + **-OUS**.

polygamy ▸ noun [mass noun] the practice or custom of having more than one wife or husband at the same time. ■ Zoology a pattern of mating in which an animal has more than one mate. ■ Botany the condition of bearing some flowers with stamens only, some with pistils only, and some with both, on the same or different plants.
– DERIVATIVES **polygamist** noun.
– ORIGIN late 16th cent.: from French *polygamie*, via late Latin from Greek *polugamia*, from *polugamos* 'often marrying'.

polygene ▸ noun Genetics a gene whose individual effect on a phenotype is too small to be observed, but which can act together with others to produce observable variation.
– ORIGIN 1940s: back-formation from **POLYGENIC**.

polygenesis /ˌpɒlɪˈdʒɛnɪsɪs/ ▸ noun [mass noun] **1** Biology the hypothetical origination of a race or species from a number of independent stocks. Compare with **POLYGENY**.
2 the hypothetical origination of language or of a surname from a number of independent sources in different places at different times.

polygenetic ▸ adjective relating to polygenesis; having more than one origin or source. ■ Geology denoting or originating from a volcano that has erupted several times.

polygenic /ˌpɒlɪˈdʒɛnɪk/ ▸ adjective Genetics relating to or determined by polygenes.
– DERIVATIVES **polygenically** adverb.
– ORIGIN 1940s: from Greek *polugenēs* 'of many kinds' + **-IC**.

polygenism /pəˈlɪdʒɪnɪz(ə)m/ ▸ noun [mass noun] the doctrine of polygeny.
– DERIVATIVES **polygenist** noun & adjective.

polygeny /pəˈlɪdʒ(ə)ni/ ▸ noun [mass noun] the theory (not now generally held) that humans evolved from several independent pairs of ancestors. Compare with **POLYGENESIS**.

polyglot /ˈpɒlɪglɒt/ ▶ **adjective** knowing or using several languages: *a polyglot career woman.* ■ (of a book) having the text translated into several languages.
▶ **noun** a person who knows and is able to use several languages.
– DERIVATIVES **polyglottal** /ˈglɒt(ə)l/ **adjective**.
– ORIGIN mid 17th cent.: from French *polyglotte*, from Greek *poluglōttos*, from *polu-* 'many' + *glōtta* 'tongue'.

polygon /ˈpɒlɪg(ə)n/ ▶ **noun** Geometry a plane figure with at least three straight sides and angles, and typically five or more.
– DERIVATIVES **polygonal** **adjective**.
– ORIGIN late 16th cent.: via late Latin from Greek *polugōnon*, neuter (used as a noun) of *polugōnos* 'many-angled'.

polygon of forces ▶ **noun** Physics a polygon that represents by the length and direction of its sides all the forces acting on a body or point.

polygonum /pəˈlɪg(ə)nəm/ ▶ **noun** a plant of a genus that includes knotgrass and knotweed, some of which are weeds and some are garden ornamentals.
● Genus *Polygonum*, family Polygonaceae.
– ORIGIN modern Latin, from Greek *polu-* 'many' + *gonu* 'knee, joint' (because of the swollen joints sheathed by stipules).

polygraph ▶ **noun** a machine designed to detect and record changes in physiological characteristics, such as a person's pulse and breathing rates, used especially as a lie detector. ■ a lie-detector test carried out with a polygraph.
– DERIVATIVES **polygraphic** **adjective**.

polygyne ▶ **adjective** Entomology (of a social insect) having more than one egg-laying queen in each colony.

polygyny /pəˈlɪdʒɪni/ ▶ **noun** [mass noun] polygamy in which a man has more than one wife. Compare with **POLYANDRY**. ■ Zoology a pattern of mating in which a male animal has more than one female mate.
– DERIVATIVES **polygynous** /pəˈlɪdʒɪnəs/ **adjective**.
– ORIGIN late 18th cent.: from **POLY-** 'many' + Greek *gunē* 'woman'.

polyhedron /ˌpɒlɪˈhiːdrən, -ˈhɛd-/ ▶ **noun** (pl. **polyhedra** /-drə/ or **polyhedrons**) Geometry a solid figure with many plane faces, typically more than six.
– DERIVATIVES **polyhedral** **adjective**.
– ORIGIN late 16th cent.: from Greek *poluedron*, neuter (used as a noun) of *poluedros* 'many-sided'.

polyhistor /ˌpɒlɪˈhɪstə/ ▶ **noun** another term for **POLYMATH**.
– ORIGIN late 16th cent.: from Greek *poluistōr* 'very learned', from *polu-* 'much, very' + *histōr* 'wise man'.

Polyhymnia /ˌpɒlɪˈhɪmnɪə/ Greek & Roman Mythology the Muse of the art of mime.
– ORIGIN via Latin from Greek, literally 'she of the many hymns'.

polyimide /ˌpɒlɪˈɪmʌɪd/ ▶ **noun** [mass noun] a synthetic resin in which the polymer units are linked by imide groups, used chiefly for heat-resistant films and coatings.

polymath /ˈpɒlɪmaθ/ ▶ **noun** a person of wide knowledge or learning.
– DERIVATIVES **polymathic** **adjective**, **polymathy** /pəˈlɪməθi/ **noun**.
– ORIGIN early 17th cent.: from Greek *polumathēs* 'having learned much', from *polu-* 'much' + the stem of *manthanein* 'learn'.

polymer /ˈpɒlɪmə/ ▶ **noun** Chemistry a substance which has a molecular structure built up chiefly or completely from a large number of similar units bonded together, e.g. many synthetic organic materials used as plastics and resins.
– DERIVATIVES **polymeric** **adjective**.
– ORIGIN mid 19th cent.: from German, from Greek *polumeros* 'having many parts', from *polu-* 'many' + *meros* 'a share'.

polymerase /ˈpɒlɪməreɪz, pəˈlɪməreɪz/ ▶ **noun** Biochemistry an enzyme which brings about the formation of a particular polymer, especially DNA or RNA.

polymerase chain reaction ▶ **noun** Biochemistry a method of making multiple copies of a DNA sequence, involving repeated reactions with a polymerase.

polymerize (also **polymerise**) ▶ **verb** Chemistry combine or cause to combine to form a polymer.
– DERIVATIVES **polymerizable** **adjective**, **polymerization** **noun**.

polymerous /pəˈlɪm(ə)rəs/ ▶ **adjective** Biology having or consisting of many parts.

polymetallic ▶ **adjective** chiefly Geology containing or involving several metals or their ores.

polymethyl methacrylate /pɒlɪˌmiːθʌɪl mɪˈθakrɪlət, -ˌmɛθ-, -θɪl/ ▶ **noun** [mass noun] a glassy synthetic resin obtained by polymerizing methyl methacrylate.

polymict /ˈpɒlɪmɪkt/ ▶ **adjective** Geology (of a conglomerate) consisting of fragments of several different rock types.
– ORIGIN 1950s: from **POLY-** 'much' + Greek *miktos* 'mixed'.

polymorph ▶ **noun** an organism or inorganic object or material which takes various forms. ■ Physiology a polymorphonuclear leucocyte.
– ORIGIN early 19th cent.: from Greek *polumorphos*, from *polu-* 'many' + *morphē* 'form'.

polymorphism ▶ **noun** [mass noun] the occurrence of something in several different forms, in particular: ■ Biology the occurrence of different forms among the members of a population or colony, or in the life cycle of an individual organism. ■ Genetics the presence of genetic variation within a population, upon which natural selection can operate. ■ Computing a feature of a programming language that allows routines to use variables of different types at different times.
– DERIVATIVES **polymorphic** **adjective**, **polymorphous** **adjective**.

polymorphonuclear /ˌpɒlɪˌmɔːfə(ʊ)ˈnjuːklɪə/ ▶ **adjective** Physiology (of a leucocyte) having a nucleus with several lobes and a cytoplasm that contains granules, as in an eosinophil or basophil.

polymorphous perversity ▶ **noun** [mass noun] Psychology a generalized sexual desire that can be excited and gratified in many ways, normal in young children but unusual in adults.
– DERIVATIVES **polymorphously perverse** **adjective**.

polymyositis /ˌpɒlɪmʌɪə(ʊ)ˈsʌɪtɪs/ ▶ **noun** [mass noun] Medicine a condition marked by inflammation and degeneration of skeletal muscle throughout the body.

polymyxin /ˌpɒlɪˈmɪksɪn/ ▶ **noun** Medicine any of a group of polypeptide antibiotics that are active chiefly against Gram-negative bacteria. ● Polymyxins are obtained from soil bacteria of the genus *Bacillus*, in particular *B. polymyxa*.
– ORIGIN 1940s: from modern Latin *polymyxa*, from Greek *polu-* 'much' + *muxa* 'slime' + **-IN**[1].

Polynesia /ˌpɒlɪˈniːʒə, -ˈniːzɪə/ a region of the central Pacific, lying to the east of Micronesia and Melanesia and containing the easternmost of the three great groups of Pacific islands, including Hawaii, the Marquesas Islands, Samoa, the Cook Islands, and French Polynesia.
– ORIGIN from **POLY-** 'many' + Greek *nēsos* 'island'.

Polynesian ▶ **adjective** relating to Polynesia, its people, or their languages.
▶ **noun 1** a native or inhabitant of Polynesia, or a person of Polynesian descent.
2 [mass noun] a group of Austronesian languages spoken in Polynesia, including Maori, Hawaiian, and Samoan.

polyneuritis /ˌpɒlɪnjʊəˈrʌɪtɪs/ ▶ **noun** [mass noun] Medicine any disorder that affects the peripheral nerves collectively.

polyneuropathy /ˌpɒlɪnjʊəˈrɒpəθi/ ▶ **noun** [mass noun] Medicine a general degeneration of peripheral nerves that spreads towards the centre of the body.

polynomial /ˌpɒlɪˈnəʊmɪəl/ ▶ **adjective** consisting of several terms.
▶ **noun** Mathematics an expression of more than two algebraic terms, especially the sum of several terms that contain different powers of the same variable(s). ■ Biology a Latin name with more than two parts.
– ORIGIN late 17th cent.: from **POLY-** 'many', on the pattern of *multinomial*.

polynomial time ▶ **noun** [mass noun] Computing the time required for a computer to solve a problem, where this time is a simple polynomial function of the size of the input.

polynuclear ▶ **adjective** Chemistry (of a complex) containing more than one metal atom. ■ (of a compound) polycyclic.

polynucleotide ▶ **noun** Biochemistry a linear polymer whose molecule is composed of many nucleotide units, constituting a section of a nucleic acid molecule.

polynya /pə(ʊ)ˈlɪnjə/ ▶ **noun** a stretch of open water surrounded by ice, especially in Arctic seas.
– ORIGIN mid 19th cent.: from Russian, from the base of *pole* 'field'.

polyoma virus /ˌpɒlɪˈəʊmə/ ▶ **noun** Medicine any of a group of papovaviruses that are usually endemic in their host species without causing disease but which can cause tumours when injected into other species.

polyp /ˈpɒlɪp/ ▶ **noun 1** Zoology a solitary or colonial sedentary form of a coelenterate such as a sea anemone, typically having a columnar body with the mouth uppermost surrounded by a ring of tentacles. In some species, polyps are a phase in the life cycle which alternates with a medusoid phase. Compare with **MEDUSA**.
2 Medicine a small growth, usually benign and with a stalk, protruding from a mucous membrane.
– DERIVATIVES **polypous** **adjective** (sense 2).
– ORIGIN late Middle English (in sense 2): from Old French *polipe*, from Latin *polypus* (see **POLYPUS**). Sense 1 dates from the mid 18th cent.

polypary /ˈpɒlɪp(ə)ri/ ▶ **noun** (pl. **polyparies**) Zoology the common stem or skeletal support of a colony of polyps, to which the individual zooids are attached.
– ORIGIN mid 18th cent.: from modern Latin *polyparium*, from Latin *polypus* (see **POLYPUS**).

polypeptide ▶ **noun** Biochemistry a linear organic polymer consisting of a large number of amino-acid residues bonded together in a chain, forming part of (or the whole of) a protein molecule.
– ORIGIN early 20th cent.: from **POLY-** 'many' + **PEPTONE** + **-IDE**.

polyphagous /pəˈlɪfəgəs/ ▶ **adjective** Zoology (of an animal) able to feed on various kinds of food.
– ORIGIN early 19th cent.: from Greek *poluphagos* 'eating to excess' + **-OUS**.

polyphase ▶ **adjective** consisting of or occurring in a number of separate stages. ■ (of an electrical device) simultaneously using several alternating currents of the same voltage and frequency but with different phases.
– DERIVATIVES **polyphasic** **adjective**.

Polyphemus /ˌpɒlɪˈfiːməs/ Greek Mythology a Cyclops who trapped Odysseus and some of his companions in a cave, from which they escaped by putting out his one eye while he slept. In another story Polyphemus loved the sea nymph Galatea, and in jealousy killed his rival Acis.

polyphenol /ˌpɒlɪˈfiːnɒl/ ▶ **noun** Chemistry a compound containing more than one phenolic hydroxyl group.
– DERIVATIVES **polyphenolic** **adjective**.

polyphonic ▶ **adjective** producing or involving many sounds or voices. ■ Music (especially of vocal music) in two or more parts each having a melody of its own; contrapuntal. Compare with **HOMOPHONIC**. ■ Music (of an instrument) capable of producing more than one note at a time.
– DERIVATIVES **polyphonically** **adverb**.
– ORIGIN late 18th cent.: from Greek *poluphōnos* (from *polu-* 'many' + *phōnē* 'voice, sound') + **-IC**.

polyphony /pəˈlɪf(ə)ni/ ▶ **noun** (pl. **polyphonies**) [mass noun] Music the style of simultaneously combining a number of parts, each forming an individual melody and harmonizing with each other. ■ [count noun] a composition written, played, or sung in polyphony ■ the ability of an electronic keyboard or synthesizer to play a number of notes simultaneously.
– DERIVATIVES **polyphonist** **noun**, **polyphonous** **adjective**.
– ORIGIN early 19th cent.: from Greek *poluphōnia*, from *polu-* 'many' + *phōnē* 'sound'.

polyphosphate /ˌpɒlɪˈfɒsfeɪt/ ▶ **noun** Chemistry a salt or ester of an oxyacid with two or more phosphorus atoms in its anion, especially any of a number used chiefly as detergents or food additives.

polyphyletic /ˌpɒlɪfʌɪˈlɛtɪk/ ▶ **adjective** Biology (of a group of organisms) derived from more than one common evolutionary ancestor or ancestral group and therefore not suitable for placing in the same taxon.

polypi plural form of **POLYPUS**.

polyploid /ˈpɒlɪplɔɪd/ Biology ▶ **adjective** of or denoting cells or nuclei containing more than two homologous sets of chromosomes.
▶ **noun** a polyploid organism, variety, or species.
– DERIVATIVES **polyploidy** **noun**.

polypod ▶ **adjective** Zoology having many feet or foot-like appendages, especially denoting a phase of insect larval development characterized by a

segmented abdomen with rudimentary or functional appendages.
– ORIGIN mid 18th cent. (as a noun denoting an animal having many feet): from French *polypode* 'many-footed', from Greek *polupous, polupod-*, from *polu-* 'many' + *pous, pod-* 'foot'.

polypody /ˈpɒlɪpəʊdi/ ▶ **noun** (pl. **polypodies**) a widely distributed fern which has stout scaly creeping rhizomes and remains green during the winter, growing on trees, walls, and stones, especially in limestone areas. ● Genus *Polypodium*, family Polypodiaceae: several species, in particular the **common polypody** (*P. vulgare*).
– ORIGIN late Middle English: via Latin from Greek *polupodion*, denoting a kind of fern, from *polu-* 'many' + *pous, pod-* 'foot'.

polypoid /ˈpɒlɪpɔɪd/ ▶ **adjective 1** Zoology relating to or resembling a polyp or hydra. ■ relating to or denoting the polyp stage in the life cycle of a coelenterate. Also called HYDROID. Compare with MEDUSOID.
2 Medicine (of a growth) resembling or in the form of a polyp.

polypore /ˈpɒlɪpɔː/ ▶ **noun** a bracket fungus in which the spores are expelled through fine pores on the underside. ● Several families in the order Aphyllophorales, class Hymenomycetes, in particular Polyporaceae, which includes the **beech polypore** (*Piptoporus* (formerly *Polyporus*) *betulinus*).

polyposis /ˌpɒlɪˈpəʊsɪs/ ▶ **noun** [mass noun] Medicine a condition characterized by the presence of numerous internal polyps, especially a hereditary disease (**familial adenomatous polyposis**) which affects the colon and in which the polyps may become malignant.

polypropylene /ˌpɒlɪˈprəʊpɪliːn/ ▶ **noun** [mass noun] a synthetic resin which is a polymer of propylene, used chiefly for films, fibres, or moulding materials.

polyptych /ˈpɒlɪptɪk/ ▶ **noun** a painting, typically an altarpiece, consisting of more than three leaves or panels joined by hinges or folds.
– ORIGIN mid 19th cent.: from late Latin *polyptycha* (neuter plural) 'registers', from Greek *poluptukhos* 'having many folds', from *polu-* 'many' + *ptukhē* 'fold'.

polypus /ˈpɒlɪpəs/ ▶ **noun** (pl. **polypi** /-pʌɪ/) archaic or technical term for POLYP.
– ORIGIN late Middle English: via Latin from a variant of Greek *polupous* 'cuttlefish, polyp', from *polu-* 'many' + *pous, pod-* 'foot'.

polyrhythm ▶ **noun** Music a rhythm which makes use of two or more different rhythms simultaneously.
– DERIVATIVES **polyrhythmic** adjective.

polyribosome /ˌpɒlɪˈrʌɪbəsəʊm/ ▶ **noun** another term for POLYSOME.

P

polysaccharide ▶ **noun** Biochemistry a carbohydrate (e.g. starch, cellulose, or glycogen) whose molecules consist of a number of sugar molecules bonded together.

polysemy /ˈpɒlɪsiːmi, pəˈlɪsɪmi/ ▶ **noun** [mass noun] Linguistics the coexistence of many possible meanings for a word or phrase.
– DERIVATIVES **polysemic** adjective, **polysemous** adjective.
– ORIGIN early 20th cent.: from POLY- 'many' + Greek *sēma* 'sign'.

polysexual ▶ **adjective** incorporating many different kinds of sexuality; pansexual.

polysome /ˈpɒlɪsəʊm/ ▶ **noun** Biology a cluster of ribosomes held together by a strand of messenger RNA which each is translating.

polystyrene /ˌpɒlɪˈstʌɪriːn/ ▶ **noun** [mass noun] a synthetic resin which is a polymer of styrene, used chiefly as lightweight rigid foams and films.

polysulphide (US **polysulfide**) ▶ **noun** Chemistry a compound containing two or more sulphur atoms bonded together as an anion or group. ■ a synthetic rubber or other polymer in which the units are linked through such groups.

polysyllabic ▶ **adjective** (of a word) having more than one syllable. ■ using or characterized by words of many syllables: *polysyllabic jargon*.
– DERIVATIVES **polysyllabically** adverb.

polysyllable ▶ **noun** a polysyllabic word.

polysymptomatic ▶ **adjective** (of a disease condition or a person or animal) involving or exhibiting many symptoms.

polysynthetic ▶ **adjective** denoting or relating to a language characterized by complex words consisting of several morphemes, in which a single word may function as a whole sentence. Many American Indian languages are polysynthetic.

polytechnic ▶ **noun** an institution of higher education offering courses at degree level or below, especially in vocational subjects.
– ORIGIN early 19th cent.: from French *polytechnique*, from Greek *polutekhnos*, from *polu-* 'many' + *tekhnē* 'art'.

USAGE In Britain the term **polytechnic** has largely dropped out of use. In 1989 British polytechnics gained autonomy from local education authorities and in 1992 were able to call themselves **universities**.

polytene /ˈpɒlɪtiːn/ ▶ **adjective** Genetics relating to or denoting a giant chromosome which is composed of many parallel copies of the genetic material, as found in *Drosophila* fruit flies where they are much used in genetic research.
– ORIGIN 1930s: from POLY- 'many' + *-tene* (from Greek *tainia* 'band, ribbon') denoting stages of the first meiotic division.

polytetrafluoroethylene /ˌpɒlɪˌtɛtrəˌflʊərəʊˈɛθɪliːn, -ˌflɔː-/ ▶ **noun** [mass noun] another term for TEFLON.

polytheism /ˈpɒlɪˌθiːɪz(ə)m/ ▶ **noun** [mass noun] the belief in or worship of more than one god.
– DERIVATIVES **polytheist** noun, **polytheistic** adjective.
– ORIGIN early 17th cent.: from French *polythéisme*, from Greek *polutheos* 'of many gods', from *polu-* 'many' + *theos* 'god'.

polythene ▶ **noun** [mass noun] Brit. a tough, light flexible synthetic resin made by polymerizing ethylene, chiefly used for plastic bags, food containers, and other packaging.
– ORIGIN 1930s: contraction of POLYETHYLENE.

polythetic /ˌpɒlɪˈθɛtɪk/ ▶ **adjective** relating to or sharing a number of characteristics which occur commonly in members of a group or class, but none of which is essential for membership of that group or class.
– ORIGIN 1960s: from POLY- 'many' + Greek *thetos* 'placed, arranged' + -IC.

polytonality ▶ **noun** [mass noun] the simultaneous use of two or more keys in a musical composition.
– DERIVATIVES **polytonal** adjective.

polytunnel ▶ **noun** an elongated polythene-covered frame under which seedlings or other plants are grown outdoors.

polytype ▶ **noun** Crystallography any of a number of forms of a crystalline substance which differ only in one of the dimensions of the unit cell.
– DERIVATIVES **polytypic** adjective, **polytypism** noun.

polyunsaturated ▶ **adjective** Chemistry (of an organic compound, especially a fat or oil molecule) containing several double or triple bonds between carbon atoms.

polyunsaturates ▶ **plural noun** polyunsaturated fats or fatty acids.

polyurethane /ˌpɒlɪˈjʊərɪθeɪn/ ▶ **noun** [mass noun] a synthetic resin in which the polymer units are linked by urethane groups, used chiefly as constituents of paints, varnishes, adhesives, and foams.
▶ **verb** [with obj.] (usu. as adj. **polyurethaned**) coat with polyurethane paint or varnish.

polyuria /ˌpɒlɪˈjʊərɪə/ ▶ **noun** [mass noun] Medicine production of abnormally large volumes of dilute urine. Compare with DIURESIS.
– DERIVATIVES **polyuric** adjective.

polyvalent /ˌpɒlɪˈveɪl(ə)nt/ ▶ **adjective 1** Chemistry having a valency of three or more.
2 Medicine active against several toxins or strains of pathogen.
3 having many different functions, forms, or facets: *the polyvalent character of his thought*.
– DERIVATIVES **polyvalence** noun.

polyvinyl /ˌpɒlɪˈvʌɪn(ə)l/ ▶ **adjective** denoting materials or objects made from polymers of vinyl compounds.

polyvinyl acetate (abbrev.: **PVA**) ▶ **noun** [mass noun] a synthetic resin made by polymerizing vinyl acetate, used chiefly in paints and adhesives.

polyvinyl chloride (abbrev.: **PVC**) ▶ **noun** [mass noun] a tough chemically resistant synthetic resin made by polymerizing vinyl chloride and used for a wide variety of products including pipes, flooring, and sheeting.

polyvinylpyrrolidone /ˌpɒlɪˌvʌɪn(ə)lpɪˈrɒlɪdəʊn/ ▶ **noun** [mass noun] Chemistry a water-soluble polymer of vinyl pyrrolidone, used as a synthetic blood plasma substitute and in the cosmetic, drug, and food-processing industries.

Polyzoa /ˌpɒlɪˈzəʊə/ ▶ **plural noun** Zoology another term for BRYOZOA.
– DERIVATIVES **polyzoan** noun & adjective.
– ORIGIN modern Latin (plural), from POLY- 'many' + *zōion* 'animal'.

Pom[1] ▶ **noun** Austral./NZ informal, often derogatory a British person.
– ORIGIN early 20th cent.: short for POMMY.

Pom[2] ▶ **noun** short for POMERANIAN.

poma /ˈpəʊmə/ ▶ **noun** trademark a ski lift in which a pole attached to a moving cable pulls each skier uphill on their skis.
– ORIGIN 1950s: named after Jan *Pomagalski* (died 1969), its Polish inventor.

pomace /ˈpʌmɪs/ ▶ **noun** [mass noun] (especially in cider-making) the pulpy residue remaining after fruit has been crushed in order to extract its juice. ■ the pulpy matter remaining after a substance such as fish or castor oil seeds has been pressed to extract the oil or juice.
– ORIGIN late 16th cent.: apparently from medieval Latin *pomacium* 'cider', from Latin *pomum* 'apple'.

pomade /pəˈmeɪd, -ˈmɑːd/ ▶ **noun** [mass noun] a scented ointment or oil for dressing the hair.
▶ **verb** [with obj.] (often as adj. **pomaded**) apply pomade to.
– ORIGIN mid 16th cent.: from French *pommade*, based on Latin *pomum* 'apple' (from which it was originally made).

Pomak /ˈpəʊmak/ ▶ **noun** a Muslim Bulgarian.
– ORIGIN Bulgarian.

pomander /pəˈmandə, ˈpɒməndə/ ▶ **noun** a ball or perforated container of aromatic substances, placed in a cupboard or room to perfume the air or (formerly) carried as a supposed protection against infection. ■ a piece of fruit, typically an orange, studded with cloves and hung in a wardrobe to perfume it.
– ORIGIN late 15th cent.: from Old French *pome d'embre*, from medieval Latin *pomum de ambra* 'apple of ambergris'.

pomarine skua /ˈpɒmərʌɪn/ ▶ **noun** a large Arctic-breeding skua, having dark brown plumage with (in some birds) pale underparts. ● *Stercorarius pomarinus*, family Stercorariidae. North American name: **pomarine jaeger**.
– ORIGIN mid 19th cent.: *pomarine* from French *pomarin*, from Greek *pōma* 'cover, lid' + *rhis, rhin-* 'nose' (because the bird's nostrils are partly covered by a cere).

pomatum /pə(ʊ)ˈmeɪtəm/ ▶ **noun & verb** old-fashioned term for POMADE.
– ORIGIN mid 16th cent.: modern Latin, from Latin *pomum* 'apple'.

pombe /ˈpɒmbeɪ/ ▶ **noun** [mass noun] (in Central and East Africa) a fermented drink made from various kinds of grain and fruit.
– ORIGIN Kiswahili.

pome /pəʊm/ ▶ **noun** Botany a fruit consisting of a fleshy enlarged receptacle and a tough central core containing the seeds, e.g. an apple, pear, or quince.
– ORIGIN late Middle English: from Old French, based on Latin *poma*, plural of *pomum* 'apple'.

pomegranate /ˈpɒmɪɡranɪt/ ▶ **noun 1** a spherical fruit with a tough golden-orange outer skin and sweet red gelatinous flesh containing many seeds.
2 the tree that bears the pomegranate, native to North Africa and western Asia. ● *Punica granatum*, family Punicaceae.
– ORIGIN Middle English: from Old French *pome grenate*, from *pome* 'apple' + *grenate* 'pomegranate' (from Latin (*malum*) *granatum* '(apple) having many seeds', from *granum* 'seed').

pomelo /ˈpɒmələʊ, ˈpʌm-/ (also **pummelo**) ▶ **noun** (pl. **pomelos**) **1** the largest of the citrus fruits, with a thick yellow skin and bitter pulp which resembles grapefruit in flavour. Also called SHADDOCK.
2 the tree which bears the pomelo. ● *Citrus maxima*, family Rutaceae.
– ORIGIN mid 19th cent.: of unknown origin.

Pomerania /ˌpɒməˈreɪnɪə/ a region of north central Europe, extending along the south shore of the Baltic Sea between Stralsund in NE Germany and the Vistula in Poland. The region was controlled variously by Germany, Poland, the Holy Roman Empire, Prussia, and Sweden, until the larger part was restored to Poland in 1945, the western portion becoming a part of the German state of Mecklenburg-West Pomerania.

Pomeranian ▸ **noun** a small dog of a breed with long silky hair, a pointed muzzle, and pricked ears.

Pomerol /ˈpɒmərɒl/ ▸ **noun** [mass noun] a red Bordeaux wine produced in Pomerol, a region in the Gironde, France.

pomfret /ˈpɒmfrɪt/ ▸ **noun** a deep-bodied fish of open seas, which typically has scales on the dorsal and anal fins. ● Family Bramidae: several genera and species, including the edible *Brama brama* of the North Atlantic (also called **RAY'S BREAM**).
– ORIGIN early 18th cent.: apparently from Portuguese *pampo*.

pomfret cake /ˈpɒmfrɪt, ˈpʌm-/ ▸ **noun** archaic variant of **PONTEFRACT CAKE**.

pomiculture /ˈpəʊmɪˌkʌltʃə/ ▸ **noun** [mass noun] fruit-growing.
– ORIGIN late 19th cent.: from Latin *pomum* 'fruit' + **CULTURE**, on the pattern of words such as *agriculture*.

pommel /ˈpʌm(ə)l/ ▸ **noun 1** a rounded knob on the end of the handle of a sword, dagger, or old-fashioned gun.
2 the upward curving or projecting part of a saddle in front of the rider.
▸ **verb** (**pommels, pommelling, pommelled**; US **pommels, pommeling, pommeled**) another term for **PUMMEL**.
– ORIGIN Middle English (denoting a finial at the top of a tower): from Old French *pomel*, from a diminutive of Latin *pomum* 'fruit, apple'.

pommel horse ▸ **noun** a vaulting horse fitted with a pair of curved handgrips, used for a gymnastic exercise consisting of swings of the legs and body.

pommes frites /pɒm ˈfriːt/ ▸ **plural noun** (especially in recipes or on menus) fried potato chips.
– ORIGIN French, from *pommes de terre frites*, literally 'fried potatoes'.

Pommy (also **Pommie**) Austral./NZ informal, often derogatory ▸ **adjective** British: *a Pommy accent*.
▸ **noun** (pl. **Pommies**) a British person.
– ORIGIN early 20th cent.: of unknown origin; said by some to be short for *pomegranate*, as a near rhyme to *immigrant*, but evidence is lacking.

po-mo ▸ **abbreviation** informal postmodern.

pomology /pə(ʊ)ˈmɒlədʒi/ ▸ **noun** [mass noun] the science of fruit-growing.
– DERIVATIVES **pomological** adjective, **pomologist** noun.
– ORIGIN early 19th cent.: from Latin *pomum* 'fruit' + **-LOGY**.

pomp ▸ **noun** [mass noun] ceremony and splendid display: *entertaining overseas visitors with the right degree of pomp*. ■ (also **pomps**) archaic vain and ostentatious display: *I perceived Captain Delmar, in all the pomp and pride of full uniform*.
– ORIGIN Middle English: from Old French *pompe*, via Latin from Greek *pompē* 'procession, pomp', from *pempein* 'send'.

Pompadour /ˈpɒmpədʊə/, Jeanne Antoinette Poisson, Marquise de (1721–64), French noblewoman; known as **Madame de Pompadour**. In 1744 she became the mistress of Louis XV, gaining considerable influence at court, but she later became unpopular as a result of her interference in political affairs.

pompadour /ˈpɒmpədɔː, -dʊə/ ▸ **noun** a woman's hairstyle in which the hair is turned back off the forehead in a roll. ■ N. Amer. a man's hairstyle in which the hair is combed back from the forehead without a parting.
▸ **verb** [with obj.] (usu. as adj. **pompadoured**) N. Amer. arrange (hair) in a pompadour.
– ORIGIN late 19th cent.: named after Madame de **POMPADOUR**.

pompano /ˈpɒmpənəʊ/ ▸ **noun** (pl. **pompanos**) **1** an edible butterfish that lives in shoals along the west coast of North America. ● *Peprillus simillimus*, family Stromateidae.
2 another term for **JACK**[1] (sense 11).
– ORIGIN late 18th cent.: from Spanish *pámpano*, perhaps from *pámpana* 'vine leaf', because of its shape.

Pompeii /pɒmˈpeɪi/ an ancient city in western Italy, south-east of Naples. The city was buried by an eruption of Mount Vesuvius in AD 79; excavations of the site began in 1748, revealing well-preserved remains of buildings, mosaics, furniture, and the personal possessions of the city's inhabitants.

Pompey /ˈpɒmpi/ (106–48 BC), Roman general and statesman; Latin name *Gnaeus Pompeius Magnus*; known as **Pompey the Great**. He founded the First Triumvirate, but later quarrelled with Caesar, who defeated him at the battle of Pharsalus. He then fled to Egypt, where he was murdered.

Pompidou /ˈpɒmpɪduː/, Georges (Jean Raymond) (1911–74), French statesman, Prime Minister 1962–8 and President 1969–74. He was instrumental in ending the conflict in Algeria between French forces and nationalist guerrillas.

Pompidou Centre a modern art gallery, exhibition centre, and concert hall in Paris, designed by Sir Richard Rogers and the Italian architect Renzo Piano (b.1937) and opened in 1977. Also called **BEAUBOURG CENTRE**.

pompier /ˈpɒmpɪə/ ▸ **noun** (pl. pronunc. **same**) an artist regarded as painting in an academic, imitative, and vulgarly neoclassical style.
– ORIGIN mid 19th cent.: from French, literally 'fireman', said to derive from the similarity between firemen's helmets and those worn by the Greek gods and heroes depicted by late Classical artists.

pom-pom[1] (also **pompon**) ▸ **noun** a small woollen ball attached to a garment, especially a hat, for decoration. ■ a large round cluster of brightly coloured streamers waved in pairs by cheerleaders. ■ a dahlia, chrysanthemum, or aster with small tightly clustered petals.
– ORIGIN mid 18th cent. (originally denoting a bunch of ribbons, feathers, etc. worn by women in the hair or on a dress): French *pompon*, of unknown origin.

pom-pom[2] ▸ **noun** Brit. an automatic quick-firing two-pounder cannon of the Second World War period, typically mounted on a ship and used against aircraft.
– ORIGIN late 19th cent.: imitative of the sound of the discharge.

pomposity ▸ **noun** [mass noun] the quality of being pompous; self-importance: *his reputation for arrogance and pomposity*.

pompous ▸ **adjective 1** affectedly grand, solemn, or self-important: *a pompous ass who pretends he knows everything*.
2 archaic characterized by pomp or splendour: *processions and other pompous shows*.
– DERIVATIVES **pompously** adverb, **pompousness** noun.
– ORIGIN late Middle English: from Old French *pompeux* 'full of grandeur', from late Latin *pomposus*, from *pompa* 'pomp'.

'pon ▸ **preposition** literary or dialect form of **UPON**.

ponce Brit. informal ▸ **noun 1** derogatory an effeminate man.
2 a man who lives off a prostitute's earnings.
▸ **verb** [no obj.] live off a prostitute's earnings. ■ [with obj.] seek to obtain (something) without paying for it or doing anything in return: *I ponced a ciggie off her*.
– PHRASAL VERBS **ponce about/around** behave in an affected or ineffectual way: *I ponced around in front of the mirror*. **ponce something up** make overly elaborate and unnecessary changes to something in an attempt to improve it: *they would not let the food alone, they had to ponce it up in some way or other*.
– ORIGIN late 19th cent.: perhaps from the verb **POUNCE**[1].

Ponce de León /ˌpɒnseɪ də leɪˈɒn/, Spanish /ˌpəɔnθe de leˈəɔn, ˌpəɔnse/, Juan (*c*.1460–1521), Spanish explorer. He accompanied Columbus on his second voyage to the New World in 1493, became governor of Puerto Rico (1510–12), and landed on the coast of Florida in 1513, claiming the area for Spain.

poncey (also **poncy**) ▸ **adjective** (**poncier, ponciest**) Brit. informal pretentious or affected: *a poncey wine bar*.

poncho ▸ **noun** (pl. **ponchos**) a garment of a type originally worn in South America, made of a thick piece of woollen cloth with a slit in the middle for the head. ■ a waterproof garment in this style worn as a raincoat.
– ORIGIN early 18th cent.: from South American Spanish, from Araucanian.

pond ▸ **noun** a small body of still water formed naturally or by artificial means. ■ (**the pond**) humorous the Atlantic Ocean: *he's relatively unknown on this side of the pond*.
▸ **verb** [with obj.] hold back or dam up (flowing water or another liquid) to form a pond. ■ [no obj.] (of flowing water or other liquids) form a pond.
– ORIGIN Middle English: alteration of **POUND**[3], commonly used in dialect in the same sense.

ponder ▸ **verb** [with obj.] think about (something) carefully, especially before making a decision or reaching a conclusion: *I pondered the question of what clothes to wear for the occasion* | [no obj.] *she sat pondering over her problem*.
– DERIVATIVES **ponderation** noun (rare).
– ORIGIN Middle English (in the sense 'appraise, judge the worth of'): from Old French *ponderer* 'consider', from Latin *ponderare* 'weigh, reflect on', from *pondus, ponder-* 'weight'.

ponderable ▸ **adjective** literary having appreciable weight or significance.
– DERIVATIVES **ponderability** noun.
– ORIGIN mid 17th cent.: from late Latin *ponderabilis*, from *ponderare* 'weigh, reflect on' (see **PONDER**).

ponderal index /ˈpɒnd(ə)r(ə)l/ ▸ **noun** Medicine an index of weight in relation to height or length.
– ORIGIN early 17th cent.: *ponderal* from Latin *pondus, ponder-* 'weight' + **-AL**.

ponderosa /ˌpɒndəˈrəʊzə, -sə/ (also **ponderosa pine**) ▸ **noun** a tall, slender North American pine tree, planted for timber and as an ornamental. ● *Pinus ponderosa*, family Pinaceae.
– ORIGIN late 19th cent.: feminine of Latin *ponderosus* 'massive', used as a specific epithet in *Pinus ponderosa*.

ponderous ▸ **adjective** slow and clumsy because of great weight: *a swarthy, ponderous giant of a man*. ■ (especially of speech or writing) dull or laborious: *the show is loaded down with ponderous one-liners*.
– DERIVATIVES **ponderosity** noun, **ponderously** adverb, **ponderousness** noun.
– ORIGIN late Middle English: via French from Latin *ponderosus*, from *pondus, ponder-* 'weight'.

Pondicherry /ˌpɒndɪˈtʃɛri/ former name (until 2006) for **PUDUCHERRY**.

pond life ▸ **noun** [mass noun] **1** the animals, especially the invertebrates, that live in ponds or stagnant water.
2 Brit. informal a contemptible or worthless person or group of people: *gangs of foul-mouthed pond life*.

pondok /ˈpɒndɒk/ (also **pondokkie**) ▸ **noun** (pl. **pondoks** or **pondokkies**) S. African a rough shelter made of scraps of wood, cardboard, or corrugated iron.
– ORIGIN Afrikaans, from Malay.

pond scum ▸ **noun** [mass noun] N. Amer. a mass of algae forming a green film on the surface of stagnant water. ■ informal a worthless or contemptible person or group of people.

pond skater ▸ **noun** a slender predatory bug which moves quickly across the surface film of water, using its front legs for catching prey. ● Family Gerridae, suborder Heteroptera: *Gerris* and other genera, and many species, in particular the common European *G. lacustris*.

pond snail ▸ **noun** an aquatic European snail with a brown conical shell, living typically in fresh water. ● Genus *Limnaea*, family Limnaeidae.

pond terrapin (also **European pond terrapin**) ▸ **noun** a terrapin with a dark shell that is typically patterned with yellow, native to Europe, western Asia, and NW Africa. ● *Emys orbicularis*, family Emydidae.

pondweed ▸ **noun** [mass noun] a submerged aquatic plant that grows in still or running water and sometimes has floating leaves. ● Genus *Potamogeton*, family Potamogetonaceae.

pone /pəʊn/ (also **corn pone** or **pone bread**) ▸ **noun** [mass noun] US unleavened maize bread in the form of flat oval cakes or loaves, originally as prepared with water by North American Indians and cooked in hot ashes.
– ORIGIN Algonquian, 'bread'.

pong Brit. informal ▸ **noun** a strong, unpleasant smell.
▸ **verb** [no obj.] smell strongly and unpleasantly.
– DERIVATIVES **pongy** adjective (**pongier, pongiest**).
– ORIGIN early 20th cent.: of unknown origin.

ponga /ˈpʌŋə/ (also **punga**) ▸ **noun** NZ a tree fern found in forests throughout New Zealand. Also called **SILVER FERN**. ● *Cyathea dealbata*, family Cyatheaceae.
– ORIGIN mid 19th cent.: from Maori.

pongal /ˈpɒŋg(ə)l/ ▸ **noun** the Tamil New Year festival, celebrated by the cooking of new rice. ■ [mass noun] a southern Indian dish of rice cooked with various herbs and spices.
– ORIGIN from Tamil *poṅkal*, literally 'boiling, swelling' (with reference to the cooking process of rice).

pongee /pʌnˈdʒiː, pɒn-/ ▸ **noun** [mass noun] a soft, unbleached type of Chinese fabric, originally made from threads of raw silk and now also other fibres such as cotton which are usually mercerized.
– ORIGIN early 18th cent.: from Chinese (Mandarin dialect) *běnjī* literally 'own loom' or *běnzhī* literally 'home-woven'.

P

pongid /ˈpɒn(d)ʒɪd/ ▶ **noun** Zoology a primate of a family (Pongidae) which comprises the great apes. See also **HOMINID**.
– ORIGIN 1950s: from modern Latin *Pongidae* (plural), from the genus name *Pongo* (see **PONGO**).

pongo ▶ **noun** (pl. **pongos**) Brit. military slang a soldier (used especially by members of the Royal Navy or RAF).
– ORIGIN early 17th cent. (denoting a large African ape): from Congolese *mpongo*. The slang sense dates from the early 20th cent.

poniard /ˈpɒnjəd/ ▶ **noun** historical a small, slim dagger.
– ORIGIN mid 16th cent.: from French *poignard*, based on Latin *pugnus* 'fist'.

pons /pɒnz/ (in full **pons Varolii** /vəˈrəʊlɪʌɪ/) ▶ **noun** (pl. **pontes** /ˈpɒntiːz/) Anatomy the part of the brainstem that links the medulla oblongata and the thalamus.
– ORIGIN late 17th cent.: from Latin, literally 'bridge', (in full) 'bridge of Varolius', named after C. Varoli (1543–75), Italian anatomist.

pons asinorum /ˌasɪˈnɔːrəm/ ▶ **noun** the point at which many learners fail, especially a theory or formula that is difficult to grasp.
– ORIGIN mid 18th cent.: Latin, literally 'bridge of asses', term taken from the fifth proposition of the first book of Euclid.

pont /pɒnt/ ▶ **noun** S. African a flat-bottomed ferry worked on cables or ropes.
– ORIGIN Dutch.

Ponte, Lorenzo Da, see **DA PONTE**.

Pontefract cake /ˈpɒntɪfrakt/ ▶ **noun** Brit. a flat round liquorice sweet.
– ORIGIN mid 19th cent.: named after *Pontefract* (earlier *Pomfret*), a town in northern England where the sweets were first made.

pontes plural form of **PONS**.

Pontiac fever /ˈpɒntɪak/ ▶ **noun** [mass noun] Medicine a mild systemic disease with symptoms resembling influenza, probably caused by a legionella infection.
– ORIGIN 1960s: named after *Pontiac*, Michigan, US, where the first major outbreak was recorded.

Pontianak /ˌpɒntɪˈɑːnak/ a seaport in Indonesia, on the west coast of Borneo at the delta of the Kapuas River; pop. 469,400 (est. 2009).

Pontic ▶ **adjective** relating to ancient Pontus.

pontifex /ˈpɒntɪfɛks/ ▶ **noun** (pl. **pontifices** /-ˈtɪfɪsiːz/) (in ancient Rome) a member of the principal college of priests.
– ORIGIN Latin, from *pons, pont-* 'bridge' + *-fex* from *facere* 'make'.

Pontifex Maximus /ˈmaksɪməs/ ▶ **noun** (in ancient Rome) the head of the principal college of priests. ■ (in the Roman Catholic Church) a title of the Pope.
– ORIGIN *Maximus*, superlative of Latin *magnus* 'great'.

pontiff (also **sovereign** or **supreme pontiff**) ▶ **noun** the Pope.
– ORIGIN late 17th cent. (denoting an early Christian bishop): from French *pontife*, from Latin *pontifex* (see **PONTIFEX**).

pontifical /pɒnˈtɪfɪk(ə)l/ ▶ **adjective 1** (in the Roman Catholic Church) relating to the pontiff or pope: *a pontifical commission*.
2 characterized by a pompous air of infallibility: *such explanations were greeted with pontifical disdain*.
▶ **noun** (in the Roman Catholic Church) an office book of the Western Church containing rites to be performed by the Pope or bishops. ■ (**pontificals**) the vestments and insignia of a bishop, cardinal, or abbot: *a bishop in full pontificals*.
– DERIVATIVES **pontifically** adverb.
– ORIGIN late Middle English: from Latin *pontificalis*, from *pontifex* (see **PONTIFEX**).

pontifical Mass ▶ **noun** (in the Roman Catholic Church) a High Mass celebrated by a cardinal or bishop.

pontificate ▶ **verb** /pɒnˈtɪfɪkeɪt/ [no obj.] **1** express one's opinions in a pompous and dogmatic way: *he was pontificating about art and history*.
2 (in the Roman Catholic Church) officiate as bishop, especially at Mass.
▶ **noun** /pɒnˈtɪfɪkət/ (in the Roman Catholic Church) the office or period of office of a pope or bishop: *Pope Gregory VIII enjoyed only a ten-week pontificate*.
– DERIVATIVES **pontification** /-ˈkeɪʃ(ə)n/ noun.
– ORIGIN late Middle English (as a noun): from Latin *pontificatus*, from *pontifex* (see **PONTIFEX**). The verb dates from the early 19th cent.

pontifices plural form of **PONTIFEX**.

pontil /ˈpɒntɪl/ (also **punty** /ˈpʌnti/) ▶ **noun** (in glass-making) an iron rod used to hold or shape soft glass.
– ORIGIN mid 19th cent.: from French, apparently from Italian *pontello* 'small point', diminutive of *punto*.

pontine /ˈpɒntʌɪn/ ▶ **adjective** Anatomy relating to or affecting the pons of the brain.
– ORIGIN late 19th cent.: from Latin *pons, pont-* 'bridge' + **-INE¹**.

Pontine Marshes /ˈpɒntʌɪn/ an area of marshland in western Italy, on the Tyrrhenian coast south of Rome. It became infested with malaria in ancient Roman times, and it was not until 1928 that an extensive scheme to drain the marshes was begun. Several new towns have since been built in the region, which is now a productive agricultural area. Italian name **AGRO PONTINO**.

Pont l'Évêque /ˌpɔ̃ ləˈvɛk/ ▶ **noun** [mass noun] a kind of creamy soft cheese made originally at Pont l'Évêque in Normandy, France.

pontoon¹ /pɒnˈtuːn/ ▶ **noun** [mass noun] Brit. the card game blackjack or vingt-et-un. ■ [count noun] a hand of two cards totalling 21 in pontoon.
– ORIGIN early 20th cent.: probably an alteration of *vingt-et-un* 'twenty-one'.

pontoon² /pɒnˈtuːn/ ▶ **noun 1** a flat-bottomed boat or hollow metal cylinder used with others to support a temporary bridge or floating landing stage. ■ a bridge or landing stage supported by pontoons. ■ each of a pair of floats fitted to an aircraft to enable it to land on water.
2 a large flat-bottomed barge or lighter equipped with cranes and tackle for careening ships and salvage work.
– ORIGIN late 17th cent.: from French *ponton*, from Latin *ponto, ponton-*, from *pons, pont-* 'bridge'.

Pontormo /pɒnˈtɔːməʊ/, Jacopo da (1494–1557), Italian painter, whose use of dynamic composition, anatomical exaggeration, and bright colours placed him at the forefront of early Mannerism.

Pontus /ˈpɒntəs/ an ancient region of northern Asia Minor, on the Black Sea coast north of Cappadocia. Between 120 and 63 BC, under Mithridates VI, it dominated the whole of Asia Minor; by the end of the 1st century BC it had been defeated by Rome and absorbed into the Roman Empire.

pony ▶ **noun** (pl. **ponies**) **1** a horse of a small breed, especially one below 15 hands (or 14 hands 2 inches). ■ (**the ponies**) informal, chiefly N. Amer. racehorses: *he had been playing the ponies on the side*.
2 informal a small glass or measure of alcohol: *a pony of vodka*.
3 Brit. informal a sum of £25.
▶ **verb** (**ponies, ponying, ponied**) [with obj.] (**pony something up**) N. Amer. informal pay a sum of money, especially as a contribution or unavoidable expense: *he ponied up $450 for the project*.
– ORIGIN mid 17th cent.: probably from French *poulenet* 'small foal', diminutive of *poulain*, from late Latin *pullanus*, from Latin *pullus* 'young animal'.

Pony Express (in the US) a system of mail delivery operating from 1860–1 between St Joseph in Missouri and Sacramento in California, using continuous relays of horse riders.

ponytail ▶ **noun** a hairstyle in which the hair is drawn back and tied at the back of the head so as to hang down.
– DERIVATIVES **ponytailed** adjective.

pony-trekking ▶ **noun** [mass noun] Brit. the activity of riding across country on a pony or horse for pleasure, typically as a holiday activity.
– DERIVATIVES **pony-trekker** noun.

Ponzi scheme /ˈpɒnzi/ ▶ **noun** a form of fraud in which belief in the success of a non-existent enterprise is fostered by the payment of quick returns to the first investors from money invested by later investors.
– ORIGIN named after Charles *Ponzi* (died 1949), who carried out such a fraud (1919–20).

ponzu /ˈpɒnzuː/ ▶ **noun** [mass noun] (in Japanese cookery) a sauce or dip made with soy sauce and citrus juice.
– ORIGIN Japanese, from *pon* 'smack, pop' + *zu*, from *su* 'vinegar'.

poo ▶ **exclamation, noun, & verb** see **POOH**.

pooch¹ ▶ **noun** informal a dog.
– ORIGIN 1920s: of unknown origin.

pooch² ▶ **verb** US informal protrude or cause to protrude: [no obj.] *a dress that made her stomach pooch out even more than usual*.
– ORIGIN mid 17th cent.: from the noun **POUCH**.

poodle ▶ **noun** a dog of a breed with a curly coat that is usually clipped. ■ Brit. a person or organization who is overly willing to obey another: *the council is being made a poodle of central government*.
▶ **verb** [no obj., with adverbial of direction] Brit. informal move or travel in a leisurely manner: *the chap who just wants to poodle along the road at 50 mph*.
– ORIGIN early 19th cent.: from German *Pudel(hund)*, from Low German *pud(d)eln* 'splash in water' (the poodle being a water-dog).

poodlefaker ▶ **noun** Brit. informal, dated a man who habitually chooses to socialize with women.

poof¹ /pʊf, puːf/ (also **pouf** or **poove**) ▶ **noun** Brit. informal, derogatory an effeminate or homosexual man.
– DERIVATIVES **poofy** adjective (**poofier, poofiest**).
– ORIGIN mid 19th cent.: perhaps an alteration of the archaic noun *puff* in the sense 'braggart'.

poof² /pʊf/ (also **pouf**) ▶ **exclamation 1** used to describe a sudden disappearance: *once you've used it, poof—it's gone*.
2 used to express contemptuous dismissal: *'Oh, poof!' said Will. 'You say that every year.'*
– ORIGIN early 19th cent.: symbolic.

poofter /ˈpʊftə, ˈpuː-/ ▶ **noun** another term for **POOF¹**.
– ORIGIN early 20th cent.: extended form.

pooh (also **poo**) informal ▶ **exclamation 1** used to express disgust at an unpleasant smell.
2 used to express impatience or contempt: *Oh pooh! Don't be such a spoilsport*.
▶ **noun** [mass noun] (usu. **poo**) excrement. ■ [in sing.] an act of defecating.
▶ **verb** [no obj.] (usu. **poo**) defecate.
– ORIGIN natural exclamation: first recorded in English in the late 16th cent.

pooh-bah /puːˈbɑː/ ▶ **noun** a person having much influence or holding many offices at the same time, especially one who is perceived as pompously self-important.
– ORIGIN from the name of a character in W. S. Gilbert's *The Mikado* (1885).

pooh-pooh ▶ **verb** [with obj.] informal dismiss (an idea or suggestion) as being foolish or impractical.
– ORIGIN late 18th cent.: reduplication of **POOH**.

Poohsticks ▶ **noun** [mass noun] a game in which each player throws a stick over the upstream side of a bridge into a stream or river, the winner being the person whose stick emerges first from under the bridge.
– ORIGIN 1920s: from Winnie-the-*Pooh*, the name of a toy bear in the children's books of A. A. Milne.

pooja ▶ **noun** variant spelling of **PUJA**.

pooka¹ /ˈpuːkə/ ▶ **noun** (in Irish mythology) a hobgoblin or sprite able to take on the form of various animals.
– ORIGIN from Irish *púca*.

pooka² ▶ **noun** variant spelling of **PUKA**.

pool¹ ▶ **noun** a small area of still water, typically one formed naturally. ■ a shallow patch of liquid lying on a surface: *a pool of blood* | figurative *the lamps cast pools of light on the wet streets*. ■ a swimming pool. ■ a deep place in a river.
▶ **verb** [no obj.] (of liquid) form a pool on the ground or another surface: *sweat pooled in the hollow of my back*. ■ (of blood) accumulate in parts of the venous system.
– ORIGIN Old English *pōl*, of West Germanic origin; related to Dutch *poel* and German *Pfuhl*.

pool² ▶ **noun 1** a shared supply of vehicles or resources to be drawn on when needed: *a car pool*. ■ a group of people available for work when required or considered as a resource: *the typing pool*. ■ a common fund into which all contributors pay and from which financial backing is provided: *big public investment pools*. ■ the collective amount of players' stakes in gambling or sweepstakes; a kitty. ■ (usu. **the pools**) another term for **FOOTBALL POOL**.
2 [mass noun] a game played on a small billiard table using two sets of seven coloured and numbered balls together with one black ball and a white cue ball, with the aim of pocketing all one's own balls and then the black.
3 a group of contestants who compete against each other in a tournament for the right to advance to the next round.

4 an arrangement, illegal in many countries, between competing parties to fix prices or rates and share business in order to eliminate competition.
▶ **verb** [with obj.] (of two or more people or organizations) put (money or other assets) into a common fund: *they entered a contract to pool any gains and invest them profitably*. ■ share (resources or information) for the benefit of all involved: *the skills of teachers can be pooled and shared*.
– ORIGIN late 17th cent. (originally denoting a game of cards having a pool): from French *poule* in the sense 'stake, kitty', associated with POOL[1].

Poole a port and resort town in Dorset on the south coast of England, just west of Bournemouth; pop. 135,800 (est. 2009).

pool hall ▶ **noun** a place where pool is played.

poolroom ▶ **noun** N. Amer. **1** a place for playing pool. **2** a betting shop.

poolside ▶ **noun** the area adjoining a swimming pool.
▶ **adjective & adverb** towards or beside a swimming pool: [as adj.] *a poolside bar* | [as adv.] *she and her parents lounged poolside*.

poon[1] ▶ **noun** Austral. informal a simple or foolish person.
– ORIGIN 1940s: origin unknown.

poon[2] ▶ **verb** [no obj.] (**poon up**) Austral. informal dress in such a way as to attract attention, typically with sexual success in view.
– ORIGIN 1940s: of unknown origin.

poon[3] ▶ **noun** short for POONTANG.

Poona former name for PUNE.

poontang /ˈpuːntaŋ/ ▶ **noun** [mass noun] N. Amer. vulgar slang sexual activity. ■ a woman or women regarded solely in terms of potential sexual gratification.
– ORIGIN 1920s: alteration of French *putain* 'prostitute'.

poop[1] ▶ **noun** (also **poop deck**) the aftermost and highest deck of a ship, especially in a sailing ship where it typically forms the roof of a cabin in the stern.
▶ **verb** [with obj.] (of a wave) break over the stern of (a ship), sometimes causing it to capsize.
– ORIGIN late Middle English: from Old French *pupe*, from a variant of Latin *puppis* 'stern'.

poop[2] ▶ **verb** N. Amer. informal [with obj.] (often as adj. **pooped**) exhaust: *I was pooped and just flopped into bed*.
– PHRASAL VERBS **poop out** stop functioning: *the analogue tape fluttered slightly in pitch but didn't poop out*.
– ORIGIN 1930s: of unknown origin.

poop[3] informal, chiefly N. Amer. ▶ **noun** [mass noun] excrement.
▶ **verb** [no obj.] defecate.
– ORIGIN early 18th cent.: imitative.

poop[4] ▶ **noun** [mass noun] informal, chiefly N. Amer. up-to-date or inside information.
– ORIGIN 1940s: of unknown origin.

poop[5] ▶ **noun** informal, chiefly N. Amer. a stupid or ineffectual person.
– DERIVATIVES **poopy** adjective (**poopier**, **poopiest**).
– ORIGIN early 20th cent.: perhaps a shortening of NINCOMPOOP.

pooper scooper (also **poop scoop**) ▶ **noun** an implement for clearing up dog excrement.

poor ▶ **adjective 1** lacking sufficient money to live at a standard considered comfortable or normal in a society: *they were too poor to afford a telephone* | (as plural noun **the poor**) *the gap between the rich and the poor has widened*. ■ (of a place) inhabited by people with little money: *the world's poorest countries*.
2 of a low or inferior standard or quality: *many people are eating a very poor diet* | *her work was poor*. ■ (**poor in**) deficient or lacking in: *the water is poor in nutrients*. ■ dated used ironically to deprecate something belonging to or offered by oneself: *he is, in my poor opinion, a more handsome young man*.
3 [attrib.] (of a person) deserving of pity or sympathy: *they enquired after poor Dorothy's broken hip*.
– PHRASES **(as) poor as a church mouse** extremely poor. **poor little rich boy** (or **girl**) a wealthy young person whose money brings them no contentment. **the poor man's ——** an inferior or cheaper substitute for the thing specified: *corduroy has always been the poor man's velvet*. **poor relation** a person or thing that is considered inferior or subordinate to others of the same type or group: *for many years radio has been **the poor relation of** the media*. **take a poor view of** regard with disapproval.
– ORIGIN Middle English: from Old French *poure*, from Latin *pauper*.

poor box ▶ **noun** historical a collection box, especially one in a church, for gifts of money or other articles towards the relief of the poor.

poor boy (also **poor-boy sandwich**) ▶ **noun** US a large oval sandwich filled with a range of simple but substantial ingredients.

Poor Clare ▶ **noun** a member of an order of Franciscan nuns founded by St Clare of Assisi in *c.*1212.

poorhouse ▶ **noun** Brit. another term for WORKHOUSE.

Poor Law ▶ **noun** Brit. historical a law relating to the support of the poor. Originally the responsibility of the parish, the relief and employment of the poor passed over to the workhouses in 1834. In the early 20th century the Poor Law was replaced by schemes of social security.

poorly ▶ **adverb 1** in a way that is unsatisfactory or inadequate: *schools that were performing poorly* | [as submodifier] *a poorly attended church*.
2 with insufficient money: *he lived as poorly as his peasant parishioners*.
▶ **adjective** chiefly Brit. unwell: *she looked poorly*.

poor man's orchid ▶ **noun** another term for SCHIZANTHUS.

poor man's weather glass ▶ **noun** the scarlet pimpernel.
– ORIGIN mid 19th cent.: so named because its flowers close before rain.

poor-me-one ▶ **noun** W. Indian the common potoo (bird), which has a nocturnal call consisting of a number of descending notes.
– ORIGIN imitative of its call.

poor mouth N. Amer. & Irish informal ▶ **noun** a person who claims to be poor in order to benefit from others.
▶ **verb** (**poor-mouth**) **1** [no obj.] claim to be poor.
2 [with obj.] talk disparagingly about: *don't let those girls poor-mouth you*.

poorness ▶ **noun** [mass noun] the state of lacking or being deficient in some desirable quality or constituent: *the poorness of the food*.

poor rate ▶ **noun** historical a local tax levied by a parish to finance the relief or support of the poor.

poor relief ▶ **noun** [mass noun] historical financial assistance given to the poor from state or local community funds.

poor-spirited ▶ **adjective** archaic timid; cowardly.

poort /ˈpʊət/ ▶ **noun** [often in place names] S. African a narrow pass through mountains.
– ORIGIN South African Dutch, 'passage', from Dutch *poort* 'gate'.

poor white ▶ **noun** derogatory a member of an impoverished white underclass, especially one living in the southern US.

poorwill ▶ **noun** a small nightjar found mainly in central and western North America. ● Three genera in the family Caprimulgidae: four species, in particular the **common poorwill** (*Phalaenoptilus nuttallii*), which hibernates in cold weather.
– ORIGIN late 19th cent.: imitative of its call.

Pooterish /ˈpuːtərɪʃ/ ▶ **adjective** self-important and mundane or narrow-minded: *a Pooterish, inhibited man*.
– ORIGIN 1960s: from the name of Charles *Pooter*, the central character of *Diary of a Nobody* (1892) by George and Weedon Grossmith.

pootle ▶ **verb** [no obj., with adverbial of direction] Brit. informal move or travel in a leisurely manner: *they were pootling down a canal in their new boat*.
– ORIGIN 1970s: blend of the verbs POODLE and TOOTLE.

poove /puːv/ ▶ **noun** variant spelling of POOF[1].

POP ▶ **abbreviation** ■ persistent organic pollutant. ■ (also **PoP**) Computing point of presence, denoting equipment that provides access to the Internet. ■ (in the UK) Post Office Preferred, used to specify the size of envelopes and other items. ■ Computing Post Office Protocol.

pop[1] ▶ **verb** (**pops, popping, popped**) **1** make or cause to make a light explosive sound: [no obj.] *corks popped and glasses tinkled* | [with obj.] *teenagers were popping balloons with darts*. ■ [no obj.] (of a person's ears) make a small popping sound within the head as pressure is equalized, typically because of a change of altitude. ■ [with obj.] heat (popcorn or another foodstuff) until it bursts open.
2 [no obj., with adverbial of direction] go somewhere for a short time, often without notice: *she popped in to see if she could help*. ■ [with obj. and adverbial of direction] put or move (something) somewhere quickly: *she popped a pen into her pocket*. ■ [with obj.] N. Amer. release, open, or engage (something) quickly or suddenly: *he pulled a can of beer from the refrigerator and popped its tab*.
3 [no obj.] (of a person's eyes) open wide and appear to bulge, especially with surprise.
4 [with obj.] informal take or inject (a drug).
5 [with obj.] Brit. informal pawn (something).
▶ **noun 1** a light explosive sound: *there were a few pops, perhaps from pistols*.
2 [mass noun] informal, dated a sweet fizzy drink such as lemonade. ■ [count noun] N. Amer. a can of sweet fizzy drink: *fruit-flavoured pops*.
3 a patch of bright colour: *I like wearing a neutral outfit with one pop of yellow*.
4 (also **pop fly** or **pop-up**) Baseball a ball hit high in the air but not far from the home plate, providing an easy catch.
▶ **adverb** with a light explosive sound: *the champagne went pop*.
– PHRASES **—— a pop** N. Amer. informal costing a specified amount per item: *those swimsuits she wears are £50 a pop*. **have** (or **take**) **a pop at** informal attack physically or verbally. **make someone's eyes pop** (or US **pop out**) informal cause great astonishment to someone. **pop one's clogs** Brit. informal die. **pop the question** informal propose marriage.
– PHRASAL VERBS **pop off** informal die. **pop up 1** appear or occur suddenly: *these memories can pop up from time to time*. ■ Computing (of a browser window) appear without having been requested, especially for the purpose of advertising. **2** Cricket (of a cricket ball) rise sharply off the pitch.
– ORIGIN late Middle English (in the senses 'a blow, knock' and 'to strike'): imitative.

pop[2] ▶ **noun** (also **pop music**) [mass noun] commercial popular music, in particular accessible, tuneful music of a kind popular since the 1950s and sometimes contrasted with rock, soul, or other forms of popular music.
▶ **adjective** [attrib.] **1** relating to commercial popular music: *a pop star* | *a pop group*.
2 often derogatory (especially of a scientific or academic subject) made accessible to the general public; popularized: *pop psychology*.
– ORIGIN late 19th cent.: abbreviation of POPULAR.

pop[3] ▶ **noun** chiefly US informal term for FATHER.
– ORIGIN mid 19th cent.: abbreviation of POPPA.

pop. ▶ **abbreviation** population.

popadom (also **popadum**) ▶ **noun** variant spellings of POPPADOM.

pop art ▶ **noun** [mass noun] art based on modern popular culture and the mass media, especially as a critical or ironic comment on traditional fine art values.

> The term is applied specifically to the works, largely from the mid 1950s and 1960s, of a group of artists including Andy Warhol, Roy Lichtenstein, Jasper Johns, and Peter Blake, who used images from comic books, advertisements, consumer products, television, and cinema.

P

popcorn ▶ **noun** [mass noun] maize of a variety with hard kernels that swell up and burst open when heated. ■ maize kernels when popped, typically eaten as a snack.

pop culture ▶ **noun** [mass noun] commercial culture based on popular taste.

Pope, Alexander (1688–1744), English poet. A major figure of the Augustan age, he is famous for his caustic wit and metrical skill, in particular his use of the heroic couplet. Notable works: *The Rape of the Lock* (1712; enlarged 1714); *An Essay on Man* (1733–4).

pope[1] ▶ **noun 1** (usu. **the Pope**) the Bishop of Rome as head of the Roman Catholic Church. ■ the head of the Coptic Church, the Bishop or Patriarch of Alexandria.
2 another term for RUFFE.
– PHRASES **is the Pope (a) Catholic?** informal used to indicate that something is blatantly obvious: *Did he bet that day? Is the Pope Catholic?*
– DERIVATIVES **popedom** noun.
– ORIGIN Old English, via ecclesiastical Latin from ecclesiastical Greek *papas* 'bishop, patriarch', variant of Greek *pappas* 'father'.

pope[2] ▶ **noun** a parish priest of the Orthodox Church in Russia and the Balkans.
– ORIGIN mid 17th cent.: from Russian *pop*, from Old Church Slavonic *popŭ*.

Pope Joan (according to a legend widely believed in the Middle Ages) a woman in male disguise who (*c.*1100) became a distinguished scholar and then pope, reigned for more than two years, and died after giving birth to a child during a procession.

Popemobile ▸ noun informal a bulletproof vehicle with a raised viewing area, used by the Pope on official visits.

popery ▸ noun [mass noun] derogatory, chiefly archaic the doctrines, practices, and ceremonies associated with the Pope or the papal system; Roman Catholicism.

pope's eye ▸ noun Scottish an edible lymph gland surrounded with fat in a sheep's leg.

pope's nose ▸ noun US term for PARSON'S NOSE.

pop-eyed ▸ adjective (of a person) having bulging or staring eyes, typically through surprise or fear.

pop festival ▸ noun a large outdoor event, typically lasting several days, at which popular music is performed.

pop fly ▸ noun Baseball see POP[1].

popgun ▸ noun a child's toy gun which shoots a harmless pellet or cork. ■ a small, inefficient, or antiquated gun.

pop-hole ▸ noun a hole in a fence or divider through which animals can pass, especially one allowing poultry access to the outside or allowing piglets access to the sow.

popinjay /ˈpɒpɪndʒeɪ/ ▸ noun **1** dated a vain or conceited person, especially one who dresses or behaves extravagantly.
2 archaic a parrot.
– ORIGIN Middle English: from Old French *papingay*, via Spanish from Arabic *babbaġā*. The change in the ending was due to association with JAY.

popish ▸ adjective derogatory Roman Catholic.
– DERIVATIVES **popishly** adverb.

Popish Plot a fictitious Jesuit plot concocted by Titus Oates in 1678, involving a plan to kill Charles II, massacre Protestants, and put the Catholic Duke of York on the English throne. The 'discovery' of the plot led to widespread panic and the execution of about thirty-five Catholics.

poplar ▸ noun **1** a tall, fast-growing tree of north temperate regions, widely grown in shelter belts and for timber and pulp. ● Genus *Populus*, family Salicaceae: many species, including the North American cottonwoods and the balm of Gilead poplars.
2 (**yellow poplar**) North American term for TULIP TREE.
– ORIGIN Middle English: from Old French *poplier*, from Latin *populus* 'poplar'.

poplin ▸ noun [mass noun] a plain-woven fabric, typically a very lightweight cotton, with a corded surface.
– ORIGIN early 18th cent.: from obsolete French *papeline*, perhaps from Italian *papalina* (feminine) 'papal', referring to the town of Avignon (residence of popes in exile (1309–77), and site of papal property), where it was first made.

P

popliteal /pɒˈplɪtɪəl, ˌpɒplɪˈtiːəl/ ▸ adjective Anatomy relating to or situated in the hollow at the back of the knee.
– ORIGIN early 18th cent.: from modern Latin *popliteus* (from Latin *poples*, *poplit-* 'ham, hough') + -AL.

pop music ▸ noun fuller form of POP[2].

Popocatépetl /ˌpɒpəˈkatəˌpɛt(ə)l, -ˌkatəˈpɛt(ə)l/ an active volcano in Mexico, south-east of Mexico City, which rises to 5,452 m (17,887 ft).

pop-out ▸ noun Baseball an act of being put out by a caught fly ball.
▸ adjective N. Amer. denoting something designed to be easily removable for use: *a pop-out panel*.

popover ▸ noun N. Amer. a very light cake made from a thin batter, which rises to form a hollow shell when baked.

poppa ▸ noun N. Amer. informal term for FATHER.
– ORIGIN late 19th cent.: alteration of PAPA.

poppadom /ˈpɒpədəm/ (also **poppadum** or **popadom**) ▸ noun (in Indian cookery) a large circular piece of thin, spiced bread made from ground lentils and fried in oil.
– ORIGIN from Tamil *pappaḍam*.

Popper, Sir Karl Raimund (1902–94), Austrian-born British philosopher. In *The Logic of Scientific Discovery* (1934) he argued that scientific hypotheses can never be finally confirmed as true, but are tested by attempts to falsify them. In *The Open Society and its Enemies* (1945) he criticized the historicist social theories of Plato, Hegel, and Marx.

popper ▸ noun **1** Brit. informal a press stud.
2 informal a small vial of amyl nitrite used for inhalation, which makes a popping sound when opened.
3 (in fishing) an artificial lure which makes a popping sound when moved over the surface of the water.
4 N. Amer. a utensil for popping corn.

poppet ▸ noun **1** Brit. informal an endearingly sweet or pretty child (often used as an affectionate form of address): *'Here you are, poppet,' the nurse said.*
2 chiefly historical a small figure of a human being used in sorcery and witchcraft.
3 (also **poppet valve**) Engineering a mushroom-shaped valve with a flat end piece that is lifted in and out of an opening by an axial rod.
– ORIGIN late Middle English: based on Latin *pup(p)a* 'girl, doll'. Compare with PUPPET.

poppet-head ▸ noun Brit. the frame at the top of a mineshaft, supporting pulleys for the ropes used in hoisting.

popping crease ▸ noun Cricket a line four feet (1.22 metres) in front of and parallel to the line of the stumps, within which the batsman must keep the bat or one foot grounded to avoid the risk of being stumped or run out.
– ORIGIN late 18th cent.: from the verb POP[1], perhaps in the obsolete sense 'strike'.

popple ▸ verb [no obj.] (of water) flow in a tumbling or rippling way.
▸ noun [in sing.] a rolling or rippling of water.
– ORIGIN late Middle English: probably from Middle Dutch *popelen* 'to murmur', of imitative origin.

poppy[1] ▸ noun a herbaceous plant with showy flowers, milky sap, and rounded seed capsules. Many poppies contain alkaloids and are a source of drugs such as morphine and codeine. ● *Papaver* and other genera, family Papaveraceae (the **poppy family**): many species, including the wild red-flowered **corn poppy** (*P. rhoeas*). The poppy family also includes the corydalis, greater celandine, and bloodroot.
– DERIVATIVES **poppied** adjective.
– ORIGIN Old English *popig*, *papæg*, from a medieval Latin alteration of Latin *papaver*.

poppy[2] ▸ adjective (**poppier**, **poppiest**) (of popular music) tuneful and immediately appealing: *catchy, poppy tunes*.

poppycock ▸ noun [mass noun] informal nonsense.
– ORIGIN mid 19th cent.: from Dutch dialect *pappekak*, from *pap* 'soft' + *kak* 'dung'.

Poppy Day ▸ noun Brit. another name for REMEMBRANCE SUNDAY.

poppy head ▸ noun **1** the seed capsule of a poppy.
2 an ornamental top on the end of a church pew.

pop quiz ▸ noun N. Amer. a short test given to students without any prior warning.

pop rivet ▸ noun a tubular rivet that is inserted into a hole and clinched by the withdrawing of a central rod, used where only one side of the work is accessible.
▸ verb (**pop-rivet**) (**pop-rivets**, **pop-riveting**, **pop-riveted**) [with obj.] secure or fasten with pop rivets.

pop shop ▸ noun Brit. informal, dated a pawnbroker's shop.

Popsicle ▸ noun N. Amer. trademark an ice lolly.
– ORIGIN 1920s: fanciful formation.

popsock ▸ noun a type of nylon stocking with an elasticated top, reaching to the wearer's knee.

popster ▸ noun informal a pop musician.

popstrel ▸ noun informal, chiefly Brit. a young female pop singer: *a teenage popstrel*.
– ORIGIN 1990s: from POP[2] and MINSTREL.

popsy (also **popsie**) ▸ noun (pl. **popsies**) informal, chiefly Brit. an attractive young woman.
– ORIGIN mid 19th cent.: alteration of POPPET.

pop-top ▸ noun North American term for RING PULL: [as modifier] *a pop-top beer can*.

populace /ˈpɒpjʊləs/ ▸ noun [treated as sing. or pl.] the people living in a particular country or area: *the party misjudged the mood of the populace*.
– ORIGIN late 16th cent.: from French, from Italian *popolaccio* 'common people', from *popolo* 'people' + the pejorative suffix *-accio*.

popular ▸ adjective **1** liked or admired by many people or by a particular person or group: *she was one of the most popular girls in the school | these cheeses are very popular in Europe*.
2 [attrib.] (of cultural activities or products) intended for or suited to the taste, understanding, or means of the general public rather than specialists or intellectuals: *editorials accusing the government of wanting to gag the popular press*. ■ (of a belief or attitude) held by the majority of the general public: *many adult cats, contrary to popular opinion, dislike milk*.
3 [attrib.] (of political activity) carried on by the people as a whole rather than restricted to politicians or political parties: *a popular revolt against colonial rule*.
– DERIVATIVES **popularism** noun.
– ORIGIN late Middle English (in the sense 'prevalent among the general public'): from Latin *popularis*, from *populus* 'people'. Sense 1 dates from the early 17th cent.

popular etymology ▸ noun another term for FOLK ETYMOLOGY.

popular front ▸ noun a party or coalition representing left-wing elements, in particular (**the Popular Front**) an alliance of communist, radical, and socialist elements formed and gaining some power in countries such as France and Spain in the 1930s.

popularity ▸ noun [mass noun] the state or condition of being liked, admired, or supported by many people: *he was at the height of his popularity*.

popularize (also **popularise**) ▸ verb [with obj.] cause (something) to become generally liked: *his books have done much to popularize the sport*. ■ make (a scientific or academic subject) accessible to the general public by presenting it in an understandable form: *they are skilled at popularizing the technical aspects of genetics*.
– DERIVATIVES **popularization** noun, **popularizer** noun.

popularly ▸ adverb by many or most people; generally: *advancing age is popularly associated with a declining capacity to work*. ■ (of a term, name, or title) in informal, common, or non-specialist use: *the community charge (popularly known as the poll tax)*. ■ (of a politician or government) chosen by the majority of the voters; democratically: *a popularly elected Parliament*.

popular music ▸ noun [mass noun] music appealing to the popular taste, including rock and pop and also soul, reggae, rap, and dance music.

populate ▸ verb [with obj.] form the population of (a place): *the island is populated by scarcely 40,000 people | a cosy rural town populated with friendly folk*. ■ cause people to settle in (a place). ■ fill or be present in (a place or sphere): *the film is an epic fantasy populated by grotesque weirdos*. ■ Computing fill in (data).
– ORIGIN late 16th cent.: from medieval Latin *populat-* 'supplied with people', from the verb *populare*, from *populus* 'people'.

populated ▸ adjective **1** [often with submodifier] inhabited: *a densely populated area | populated countries*.
2 Electronics (of a printed circuit board) having components fitted.

population ▸ noun **1** all the inhabitants of a particular place: *the island has a population of about 78,000*. ■ [with adj. or noun modifier] a particular group or type of people living in a place: *measures to speed up integration of the country's immigrant population*. ■ [mass noun] [with adj.] the extent to which an area is or has been populated: *areas of sparse population*. ■ [mass noun] the action of populating a place.
2 Biology a community of animals, plants, or humans among whose members interbreeding occurs.
3 Statistics a finite or infinite collection of items under consideration.
4 Astronomy each of three groups (designated I, II, and III) into which stars can be approximately divided on the basis of their manner of formation.
– ORIGIN late 16th cent. (denoting an inhabited place): from late Latin *populatio(n-)*, from the verb *populare*, from *populus* 'people'.

population explosion ▸ noun a sudden, large increase in the size of a population.

population group ▸ noun (in South Africa during the apartheid era) the official term for an ethnic group.

population inversion ▸ noun see INVERSION (sense 1).

populist ▸ noun a member or adherent of a political party seeking to represent the interests of ordinary people. ■ a person who supports or seeks to appeal to the concerns of ordinary people.
▸ adjective relating to or characteristic of a populist or populists: *populist tabloid newspapers*.
– DERIVATIVES **populism** noun, **populistic** adjective.
– ORIGIN late 19th cent. (originally referring to a US political party): from Latin *populus* 'people' + -IST.

populous ▸ adjective having a large population; densely populated: *the populous city of Shanghai*.
– DERIVATIVES **populousness** noun.
– ORIGIN late Middle English: from late Latin *populosus*, from *populus* 'people'.

pop-up ▸ adjective [attrib.] (of a book or greetings card) containing folded cut-out pictures that rise up to form a three-dimensional scene or figure when the page is turned. ■ (of an electric toaster) operating so as to push up a piece of toast quickly when it is ready. ■ Computing (of a menu or other utility) able to be superimposed on the screen being worked on and suppressed rapidly.
▸ noun **1** a pop-up picture in a book. ■ a book containing pop-up pictures.
2 Baseball see POP[1] (sense 4 of the noun).
3 Computing a pop-up menu or other utility. ■ an unrequested browser window, especially one generated for the purpose of advertising.

porangi /ˈpɔːraŋi/ ▸ adjective NZ informal mad; crazy.
– ORIGIN Maori.

porbeagle /ˈpɔːbiːg(ə)l/ ▸ noun a large, active shark which is found chiefly in the open seas of the North Atlantic and in the Mediterranean. Also called MACKEREL SHARK. ● *Lamna nasus*, family Lamnidae.
– ORIGIN mid 18th cent.: perhaps from Cornish *porth* 'harbour, cove' + *bugel* 'shepherd'.

porcelain /ˈpɔːs(ə)lɪn/ ▸ noun [mass noun] a white vitrified translucent ceramic; china. See also HARD-PASTE, SOFT-PASTE. ■ [count noun] (usu. **porcelains**) an article made of porcelain. ■ porcelain articles collectively: *a collection of Chinese porcelain*.
– DERIVATIVES **porcellaneous** /ˌpɔːsɪˈleɪnɪəs/ adjective.
– ORIGIN mid 16th cent.: from French *porcelaine*, from Italian *porcellana* 'cowrie shell', hence 'chinaware' (from its resemblance to the dense polished shells).

porcelain clay ▸ noun another term for KAOLIN.

porcelain crab ▸ noun a marine crablike crustacean with long antennae, related to the hermit crabs. ● *Porcellana* and other genera, superfamily Galatheoidea.
– ORIGIN mid 19th cent.: so named because of its smooth and polished shell.

porcelain fungus ▸ noun a common edible Eurasian mushroom which is white and covered with a slimy fluid, growing on beech trees. Also called POACHED EGG FUNGUS. ● *Oudemansiella mucida*, family Tricholomataceae, class Hymenomycetes.

porch ▸ noun a covered shelter projecting in front of the entrance of a building. ■ N. Amer. a veranda.
– DERIVATIVES **porched** adjective.
– ORIGIN Middle English: from Old French *porche*, from Latin *porticus* 'colonnade', from *porta* 'passage'.

porcine /ˈpɔːsʌɪn/ ▸ adjective of, affecting, or resembling a pig or pigs: *his flushed, porcine features*.
– ORIGIN mid 17th cent.: from French *porcin* or Latin *porcinus*, from *porcus* 'pig'.

porcini /pɔːˈtʃiːni/ ▸ plural noun chiefly N. Amer. ceps (wild mushrooms), especially as an item on a menu.
– ORIGIN Italian, literally 'little pigs'.

porcupine ▸ noun a large rodent with defensive spines or quills on the body and tail. ● Suborder Hystricomorpha: families Hystricidae (three Old World genera) and Erethizontidae (four New World genera).
– ORIGIN late Middle English: from Old French *porc espin*, from Provençal *porc espi(n)*, from Latin *porcus* 'pig' + *spina* 'thorn'.

porcupine fish ▸ noun a tropical marine fish which has a parrot-like beak and is covered with sharp spines. It inflates itself like a balloon when threatened. ● Family Diodontidae: three genera and several species, including the widely distributed *Diodon hystrix*. See also BURRFISH.

pore[1] ▸ noun a minute opening in a surface, especially the skin or integument of an organism, through which gases, liquids, or microscopic particles may pass.
– ORIGIN late Middle English: from Old French, via Latin from Greek *poros* 'passage, pore'.

pore[2] ▸ verb [no obj.] (**pore over/through**) be absorbed in reading or studying (something): *I spent hours poring over cookery books*. ■ archaic think intently; ponder: *he has thought and pored on it*.
– ORIGIN Middle English: perhaps related to PEER[1].

> **USAGE** People frequently confuse the verbs **pore** and **pour**. **Pore** is used with **over** or **through** and means 'be absorbed in reading something' (*I spent hours poring over cookery books*), while **pour** means 'flow or cause to flow in a steady stream' (*water poured off the stones | pour the marinade over the pork | pour the tea*). As **pore** is a much less common word, people often choose the more familiar **pour**, producing sentences such as *she was pouring over books and studying till midnight*. Although increasingly common, this use is incorrect in standard English.

porgy /ˈpɔːgi/ ▸ noun (pl. **porgies**) a deep-bodied fish related to the sea breams, which is typically silvery but sometimes changes to a blotched pattern. It usually lives in warm coastal waters. ● *Calamus* and other genera, family Sparidae: many species.
– ORIGIN mid 17th cent.: alteration of Spanish and Portuguese *pargo*.

Pori /ˈpɔːri/ an industrial port in SW Finland, on the Gulf of Bothnia; pop. 76,525 (2009).

Porifera /pəˈrɪf(ə)rə/ ▸ plural noun Zoology a phylum of aquatic invertebrate animals that comprises the sponges.
– ORIGIN modern Latin (plural), from Latin *porus* 'pore' + *-fer* 'bearing'.

poriferan Zoology ▸ noun an aquatic invertebrate animal of the phylum Porifera; a sponge.
▸ adjective relating to or denoting poriferans.

porin /ˈpɔːrɪn/ ▸ noun Biochemistry any of a class of proteins whose molecules can form channels (large enough to allow the passage of small ions and molecules) through cellular membranes.
– ORIGIN 1970s: from Greek *poros* 'pore' + -IN[1].

pork ▸ noun [mass noun] **1** the flesh of a pig used as food, especially when uncured.
2 short for PORK BARREL.
▸ verb **1** [with obj.] vulgar slang, chiefly US (of a man) have sexual intercourse with.
2 [no obj.] (**pork out**) informal gorge oneself with food.
– ORIGIN Middle English: from Old French *porc*, from Latin *porcus* 'pig'.

pork barrel ▸ noun N. Amer. informal used in reference to the utilization of government funds for projects designed to please voters or legislators and win votes: *the lesson that power is based on the pork barrel and purchased with patronage*.
– DERIVATIVES **pork-barrelling** noun.
– ORIGIN early 20th cent.: from the use of a barrel to keep a reserve supply of meat.

porker ▸ noun a young pig raised and fattened for food. ■ informal, derogatory a fat person.

porkling ▸ noun a young or small pig; a piglet.

pork pie ▸ noun Brit. a raised pie made with minced, cooked pork, typically eaten cold.

pork-pie hat ▸ noun a hat with a flat crown and a brim turned up all round.

pork scratchings ▸ plural noun see SCRATCHINGS.

porky[1] ▸ adjective (**porkier, porkiest**) **1** informal (of a person or part of their body) fleshy or fat.
2 of or resembling pork.
▸ noun (pl. **porkies**) (also **porky-pie**) Brit. rhyming slang a lie: *you've been telling porkies*.

porky[2] ▸ noun (pl. **porkies**) US informal a porcupine.

porn (also **porno**) informal ▸ noun [mass noun] pornography: *hardcore porn*. ■ television programmes, books, etc., regarded as catering for a voyeuristic or obsessive interest in a specified subject: *gastro-porn*.
▸ adjective pornographic: *a porn film*.
– ORIGIN 1950s: abbreviation.

pornographic ▸ adjective constituting or resembling pornography; obscene: *pornographic images*.
– DERIVATIVES **pornographically** adverb.

pornography ▸ noun [mass noun] printed or visual material containing the explicit description or display of sexual organs or activity, intended to stimulate sexual excitement.
– DERIVATIVES **pornographer** noun.
– ORIGIN mid 19th cent.: from Greek *pornographos* 'writing about prostitutes', from *pornē* 'prostitute' + *graphein* 'write'.

porous ▸ adjective (of a rock or other material) having minute interstices through which liquid or air may pass. ■ not retentive or secure: *he ran through a porous home defence to score easily*.
– DERIVATIVES **porosity** noun, **porousness** noun.
– ORIGIN late Middle English: from Old French *poreux*, based on Latin *porus* 'pore'.

porphyria /pɔːˈfɪrɪə/ ▸ noun [mass noun] Medicine a rare hereditary disease in which there is abnormal metabolism of the blood pigment haemoglobin. Porphyrins are excreted in the urine, which becomes dark; other symptoms include mental disturbances and extreme sensitivity of the skin to light.
– ORIGIN 1920s: modern Latin, from PORPHYRIN.

porphyrin /ˈpɔːfɪrɪn/ ▸ noun Biochemistry any of a class of pigments (including haem and chlorophyll) whose molecules contain a flat ring of four linked heterocyclic groups, sometimes with a central metal atom.
– ORIGIN early 20th cent.: from Greek *porphura* 'purple' + -IN[1].

porphyritic /ˌpɔːfɪˈrɪtɪk/ ▸ adjective Geology relating to or denoting a rock texture containing distinct crystals or crystalline particles embedded in a compact groundmass.

porphyroblast /ˈpɔːfɪrə(ʊ)blast/ ▸ noun Geology a larger recrystallized grain occurring in a finer groundmass in a metamorphic rock.
– DERIVATIVES **porphyroblastic** adjective.

Porphyry /ˈpɔːfɪri/ (*c*.232–303), Neoplatonist philosopher; born *Malchus*. He was a pupil of Plotinus, whose works he edited after the latter's death.

porphyry /ˈpɔːfɪri/ ▸ noun (pl. **porphyries**) [mass noun] a hard igneous rock containing crystals of feldspar in a fine-grained groundmass.
– ORIGIN late Middle English: via medieval Latin from Greek *porphuritēs*, from *porphura* 'purple'.

porpoise /ˈpɔːpəs, ˈpɔpɔɪs/ ▸ noun a small toothed whale with a low triangular dorsal fin and a blunt rounded snout. ● Family Phocoenidae: three genera and several species, in particular the **common** (or **harbour**) **porpoise** (*Phocoena phocoena*), of the North Atlantic and North Pacific.
▸ verb [no obj.] move through the water like a porpoise, alternately rising above it and submerging: *the boat began to porpoise badly*.
– ORIGIN Middle English: from Old French *porpois*, based on Latin *porcus* 'pig' + *piscis* 'fish', rendering earlier *porcus marinus* 'sea hog'.

porridge ▸ noun [mass noun] **1** chiefly Brit. a dish consisting of oatmeal or another meal or cereal boiled in water or milk.
2 Brit. informal time spent in prison: *I'm sweating it out doing porridge*.
– DERIVATIVES **porridgy** adjective.
– ORIGIN mid 16th cent. (denoting soup thickened with barley): alteration of POTTAGE. Sense 2 dates from the 1950s.

porringer /ˈpɒrɪn(d)ʒə/ ▸ noun historical a small bowl, typically with a handle, used for soup, stew, or similar dishes.
– ORIGIN late Middle English (earlier as *potager* and *pottinger*): from Old French *potager*, from *potage* 'contents of a pot'.

Porro prism /ˈpɒrəʊ/ ▸ noun a reflecting prism in which the light is reflected on two 45° surfaces and returned parallel to the incoming beam. Compare with ROOF PRISM. ■ (**porro prisms** or **porro-prism binoculars**) a pair of binoculars using two Porro prisms at right angles, resulting in a conventional instrument with objective lenses that are further apart than the eyepieces.
– ORIGIN named after the Italian scientist Ignazio *Porro* (1801–75).

Porsche /pɔːʃ/, German /ˈpɔrʃə/, Ferdinand (1875–1952), Austrian car designer. In 1934 he designed the Volkswagen ('people's car'). His name has since become famous for the high-performance sports and racing cars produced by his company, originally to his designs.

Porsenna /pɔːˈsɛnə/ (also **Porsena** /ˈpɔːsɪnə/), Lars (6th century BC), a legendary Etruscan chieftain, king of the town of Clusium. Summoned by Tarquinius Superbus after the latter's overthrow and exile from Rome, Porsenna subsequently laid siege to the city, but did not succeed in capturing it.

port[1] ▸ noun a town or city with a harbour or access to navigable water where ships load or unload. ■ a harbour: [as modifier] *Belfast's port facilities*.
– PHRASES **any port in a storm** proverb in adverse circumstances one welcomes any source of relief or escape. **port of call** a place where a ship stops on a voyage. ■ a point, typically one of a series, at which one stops briefly or to which one has recourse during a journey or procedure: *his last port of call that day was the bank*. **port of entry** a harbour or airport where customs officers are stationed to oversee people and goods entering or leaving a country.
– ORIGIN Old English, from Latin *portus* 'haven, harbour', reinforced in Middle English by Old French.

port[2] (also **port wine**) ▸ noun [mass noun] a strong, sweet dark red (occasionally brown or white) fortified wine, originally from Portugal, typically drunk as a dessert wine.

– ORIGIN shortened form of OPORTO, a major port from which the wine is shipped.

port³ ▶ **noun** the side of a ship or aircraft that is on the left when one is facing forward. The opposite of STARBOARD.
▶ **verb** [with obj.] turn (a ship or its helm) to port.
– ORIGIN mid 16th cent.: probably originally the side containing an entry port or facing the port (quayside) for loading.

port⁴ ▶ **noun 1** an opening in the side of a ship for boarding or loading. ■ a porthole. ■ (also **gun port**) an opening in the body of an aircraft or in a wall or armoured vehicle through which a gun may be fired. ■ an opening for the passage of steam, liquid, or gas: *loss of fuel from the exhaust port.*
2 Electronics a socket in a computer network into which a device can be plugged.
3 chiefly Scottish a gate or gateway, especially into a walled city.
– ORIGIN Old English (in the sense 'gateway'), from Latin *porta* 'gate'; reinforced in Middle English by Old French *porte*. The later sense 'opening in the side of a ship' led to the general sense 'aperture'.

port⁵ ▶ **verb** [with obj. and adverbial of direction] **1** Computing transfer (software) from one system or machine to another: *the software can be ported to practically any platform*
2 carry or convey. ■ [with obj.] [often in imperative] Military carry (a rifle or other weapon) diagonally across and close to the body with the barrel or blade near the left shoulder: *Detail! For inspection—port arms!*
▶ **noun 1** Military the position required by an order to port a weapon: *Parker had his rifle at the port.*
2 literary a person's carriage or bearing: *she has the proud port of a princess.*
3 Computing a transfer of software from one system or machine to another.
– PHRASES **at port arms** Military in the position adopted when given a command to port one's weapon.
– ORIGIN Middle English (in sense 2 of the noun): from Old French *port* 'bearing, gait', from the verb *porter*, from Latin *portare* 'carry'. The verb (from French *porter*) dates from the mid 16th cent.

port⁶ ▶ **noun** Austral. informal a suitcase or travelling bag: *she packed her ports and walked out.*
– ORIGIN early 20th cent.: abbreviation of PORTMANTEAU.

porta- ▶ **combining form** denoting something that is movable or portable, often used as part of a proprietary name: *Portaloo | Portakabin.*
– ORIGIN from PORTABLE.

portable ▶ **adjective** able to be easily carried or moved, especially because being of a lighter and smaller version than usual: *a portable television.* ■ Computing (of software) able to be transferred from one machine or system to another. ■ Brit. (of a loan or pension) capable of being transferred or adapted in altered circumstances.
▶ **noun** a small version of something, such as a television, that can be easily carried. ■ N. Amer. a small transportable building used as a classroom.
– DERIVATIVES **portability** noun, **portably** adverb.
– ORIGIN late Middle English: from Old French *portable*, from late Latin *portabilis*, from Latin *portare* 'carry'.

portage /ˈpɔːtɪdʒ, pɔːˈtɑːʒ/ ▶ **noun** [mass noun] the carrying of a boat or its cargo between two navigable waters: *the return journey was made much simpler by portage.* ■ [count noun] a place at which portage is necessary: *a portage over the weir.* ■ archaic the action of carrying or transporting something.
▶ **verb** [with obj.] carry (a boat or its cargo) between navigable waters: *we portaged everything here.* ■ [no obj., with adverbial] (of a boat) be carried between or across unnavigable waters.
– ORIGIN late Middle English: from French, from *porter* 'carry'. The sense relating to carrying between navigable waters dates from the late 17th cent.

Portakabin ▶ **noun** Brit. trademark a portable building, used as a temporary office, classroom, etc.
– ORIGIN 1960s: from PORTA- and an alteration of CABIN.

portal¹ ▶ **noun** a doorway, gate, or other entrance, especially a large and imposing one. ■ an Internet site providing access or links to other sites.
– ORIGIN late Middle English: from Old French, from medieval Latin *portale*, neuter (used as a noun) of *portalis* 'like a gate', from Latin *porta* 'door, gate'.

portal² ▶ **adjective** Anatomy relating to an opening in an organ through which major blood vessels pass, especially the transverse fissure of the liver.
– ORIGIN mid 19th cent.: from modern Latin *portalis*, from Latin *porta* 'gate'.

portal frame ▶ **noun** Engineering a rigid structural frame consisting essentially of two uprights connected at the top by a third member.

Portaloo ▶ **noun** Brit. trademark a portable building containing a toilet.

portal system ▶ **noun** Anatomy the system of blood vessels consisting of the hepatic portal vein with its tributaries and branches. ■ any system of blood vessels which has a capillary network at each end.

portal vein (in full **hepatic portal vein**) ▶ **noun** Anatomy a vein conveying blood to the liver from the spleen, stomach, pancreas, and intestines.

portamento /ˌpɔːtəˈmɛntəʊ/ ▶ **noun** (pl. **portamentos** or **portamenti** /-ti/) Music **1** a slide from one note to another, especially in singing or playing the violin.
2 [mass noun] piano playing in a manner intermediate between legato and staccato.
– ORIGIN Italian, literally 'carrying'.

Port Arthur former name (1898–1905) for LUSHUN.

Portastudio ▶ **noun** (pl. **Portastudios**) trademark a portable multitrack recording and mixing desk.

portative organ ▶ **noun** chiefly historical a small portable pipe organ.
– ORIGIN early 16th cent. (as a compound): *portative* from Old French *portatif, -ive*, apparently an alteration of *portatil*, based on Latin *portare* 'carry'.

Port-au-Prince /ˌpɔːtəʊˈprɪns/, French /pɔʀtəpʀɛ̃s/ the capital of Haiti, a port on the west coast; pop. 1,998,000 (est. 2007). Founded by the French in 1749, it became capital of the new republic in 1806.

Port Blair a port on the southern tip of South Andaman Island in the Bay of Bengal; pop. 127,100 (est. 2009). It is the capital of the Andaman and Nicobar Islands.

portcullis ▶ **noun** a strong, heavy grating that can be lowered down grooves on each side of a gateway to block it.
– DERIVATIVES **portcullised** adjective.
– ORIGIN Middle English: from Old French *porte coleice* 'sliding door', from *porte* 'door' (from Latin *porta*) + *coleice* 'sliding' (feminine of *couleis*, from Latin *colare* 'to filter').

port de bras /ˌpɔː də ˈbrɑː/ ▶ **noun** (pl. **ports de bras** pronunc. **same**) chiefly Ballet an act or manner of moving and posing the arms. ■ an exercise designed to develop graceful movement and disposition of the arms, typically involving a bend accompanied by arm movement.
– ORIGIN French, literally 'bearing of (the) arms'.

Port de France former name for NOUMÉA.

Porte /pɔːt/ (in full **the Sublime** or **Ottoman Porte**) historical the Ottoman court at Constantinople.
– ORIGIN early 17th cent.: from French *la Sublime Porte* 'the exalted gate', translation of the Turkish title of the central office of the Ottoman government.

porte cochère /ˌpɔːt kɒˈʃɛː/ ▶ **noun** a covered entrance large enough for vehicles to pass through, typically opening into a courtyard. ■ N. Amer. a porch where vehicles stop to set down passengers.
– ORIGIN late 17th cent.: French, literally 'coach gateway'.

Port Elizabeth a port in South Africa, on the coast of the province of Eastern Cape; pop. 1,146,400 (est. 2009).

portend ▶ **verb** [with obj.] be a sign or warning that (something, especially something momentous or calamitous) is likely to happen: *the eclipses portend some major events.*
– ORIGIN late Middle English: from Latin *portendere*, based on *pro-* 'forth' + *tendere* 'stretch'.

portent /ˈpɔːtɛnt, -t(ə)nt/ ▶ **noun 1** a sign or warning that a momentous or calamitous event is likely to happen: *many birds are regarded as being portents of death.* ■ [mass noun] future significance: *an omen of grave portent for the tribe.*
2 literary an exceptional or wonderful person or thing: *what portent can be greater than a pious notary?*
– ORIGIN late 16th cent.: from Latin *portentum* 'omen, token', from the verb *portendere* (see PORTEND).

portentous ▶ **adjective** of or like a portent; of momentous significance: *this portentous year in Canadian history.* ■ done in a pompously or overly solemn manner so as to impress: *the author's portentous moralizings.*
– DERIVATIVES **portentously** adverb, **portentousness** noun.

Porter, Cole (1892–1964), American songwriter. He is known for songs such as 'Let's Do It', 'Night and Day', and 'Begin the Beguine' and the musicals *Anything Goes* (1934) and *Kiss me, Kate* (1948).

porter¹ ▶ **noun 1** a person employed to carry luggage and other loads, especially in a railway station, airport, hotel, or market. ■ (also **hospital porter**) a hospital employee who moves equipment or patients. ■ a person employed to carry supplies on a mountaineering expedition. ■ N. Amer. a sleeping-car attendant.
2 [mass noun] dark brown bitter beer brewed from malt partly charred or browned by drying at a high temperature. [originally made as a drink for porters.]
– ORIGIN Middle English: from Old French *porteour*, from medieval Latin *portator*, from Latin *portare* 'carry'.

porter² ▶ **noun** Brit. an employee in charge of the entrance of a hotel, block of flats, college, or other large building.
– ORIGIN Middle English: from Old French *portier*, from late Latin *portarius*, from *porta* 'gate, door'.

porterage ▶ **noun** [mass noun] the work of carrying luggage or other loads, done by porters or labourers.

porterhouse ▶ **noun** historical, chiefly N. Amer. an establishment at which porter and sometimes steaks were served.
– ORIGIN mid 18th cent.: from PORTER¹ (sense 2) + HOUSE.

porterhouse steak ▶ **noun** a thick steak cut from the thick end of a sirloin.

porter's knot ▶ **noun** historical a double shoulder pad and forehead loop used for carrying loads.

Port Étienne /eɪˈtjɛn/ former name for NOUADHIBOU.

portfire ▶ **noun** historical a handheld fuse used for firing cannons, igniting explosives in mining, etc.
– ORIGIN mid 17th cent.: partial Anglicization of French *porte-feu*, from *porter* 'carry' + *feu* 'fire'.

portfolio ▶ **noun** (pl. **portfolios**) **1** a large, thin, flat case for loose sheets of paper such as drawings or maps. ■ a set of pieces of creative work intended to demonstrate a person's ability to a potential employer. ■ a varied set of photographs of a model or actor intended to be shown to a potential employer.
2 a range of investments held by a person or organization: *a portfolio of insured municipal securities.* ■ a range of products or services offered by an organization: *an unrivalled portfolio of quality brands.*
3 [as modifier] denoting or engaged in an employment pattern which involves a succession of short-term contracts and part-time work, rather than the more traditional model of a single job for life: *portfolio careers allow women to balance work with family.*
4 the position and duties of a Minister or Secretary of State: *he took on the Foreign Affairs portfolio.*
– ORIGIN early 18th cent.: from Italian *portafogli*, from *portare* 'carry' + *foglio* 'leaf' (from Latin *folium*).

Port-Gentil /ˌpɔːʒɒnˈtiː/ the principal port of Gabon, on the Atlantic coast south of Libreville; pop. 150,000 (est. 2009).

Port Harcourt /ˈhɑːkɔːt/ a port in SE Nigeria, on the Gulf of Guinea at the eastern edge of the Niger delta; pop. 1,020,000 (est. 2007).

Port Hedland a seaport on the NW coast of Western Australia; pop. 13,357 (2009).

porthole ▶ **noun 1** a small window on the outside of a ship or aircraft.
2 historical an opening for firing a cannon through.

portico /ˈpɔːtɪkəʊ/ ▶ **noun** (pl. **porticoes** or **porticos**) a structure consisting of a roof supported by columns at regular intervals, typically attached as a porch to a building.
– ORIGIN early 17th cent.: from Italian, from Latin *porticus* 'porch'.

portière /ˌpɔːtɪˈɛː/ ▶ **noun** a curtain hung over a door or doorway.
– ORIGIN mid 19th cent.: French, from *porte* 'door', from Latin *porta* 'gate, door'.

Porţile de Fier /pɔrˌtsiːlɛ dɛ ˈfjɛr/ Romanian name for IRON GATE.

portion ▶ **noun 1** a part of a whole: *a portion of the jetty still stands | he could repeat large portions of Shakespeare.* ■ a part of something divided between people; a share: *she wanted the right to decide how her portion of the allowance should be spent.* ■ an amount of food suitable for or served to one person: *a portion of ice cream | burger joints offering huge portions.* ■ Law the part or share of an estate given or descending by law to an heir. ■ (also **marriage portion**) archaic a dowry given to a bride at her marriage.

P

2 archaic a person's destiny or lot: *what will be my portion?*
▶ verb [with obj.] divide (something) into parts and share out: *for centuries meadowland with common hay rights was **portioned out**.* ■ (usu. as adj., with submodifier **portioned**) serve (food) in an amount suitable for one person: *generously portioned lunches.* ■ archaic give a dowry to (a bride).
– ORIGIN Middle English: from Old French *porcion*, from Latin *portio(n-)*, from the phrase *pro portione* 'in proportion'.

portionless ▶ adjective archaic (of a woman) without a dowry.

Port Jackson willow ▶ noun either of two Australian acacias which were introduced into South Africa where they have become naturalized. ● Genus *Acacia*, family Leguminosae: *A. longifolia* and *A. cyanophylla*, which is a useful sand-binding tree.
– ORIGIN mid 19th cent.: named after the harbour of Sydney, Australia.

Portland 1 an industrial port in NW Oregon, on the Willamette River near its confluence with the Columbia River; pop. 557,706 (est. 2008).
2 a shipping forecast area covering the English Channel roughly between the meridians of Start Point in the west and Poole in the east, taking its name from the Isle of Portland.

Portland, Isle of a rocky limestone peninsula on the south coast of England, in Dorset. Its southernmost tip is known as the Bill of Portland or Portland Bill. The peninsula is quarried for its fine building stone.

Portland cement ▶ noun [mass noun] cement manufactured from chalk and clay which hardens under water and when hard resembles Portland stone in colour.

Portland stone ▶ noun [mass noun] limestone from the Isle of Portland in Dorset, highly prized as a building material.

Portland vase a dark blue Roman glass vase with white decoration, dating from around the 1st century AD. Acquired in the 18th century by the Duchess of Portland, it is now in the British Museum.

Portlaoise /pɔːtˈliːʃ/ (also **Portlaoighise**) the county town of Laois in the Republic of Ireland; pop. 3,281 (2006). It is the site of a top-security prison.

portlet /ˈpɔːtlɪt/ ▶ noun Computing an application used by a portal website to receive requests from clients and return information.
– ORIGIN blend of PORTAL[1] and -LET, after APPLET, SERVLET.

Port Louis /ˈluːɪs, ˈluːi/ the capital of Mauritius, a port on the NW coast; pop. 150,000 (est. 2007).

portly ▶ adjective (**portlier**, **portliest**) 1 (especially of a man) rather fat.
2 archaic of a stately or dignified appearance and manner: *he was a man of portly presence.*
– DERIVATIVES **portliness** noun.
– ORIGIN late 15th cent.: from PORT[5] in the sense 'bearing' + -LY[1].

Port Mahon another name for MAHON.

portmanteau /pɔːtˈmantəʊ/ ▶ noun (pl. **portmanteaus** or **portmanteaux** /-əʊz/) a large travelling bag, typically made of stiff leather and opening into two equal parts. ■ [as modifier] consisting of or combining two or more aspects or qualities: *a portmanteau movie composed of excerpts from his most famous films.*
– ORIGIN mid 16th cent.: from French *portemanteau*, from *porter* 'carry' + *manteau* 'mantle'.

portmanteau word ▶ noun a word blending the sounds and combining the meanings of two others, for example *motel* or *brunch*.

Port Moresby /ˈmɔːzbi/ the capital of Papua New Guinea, situated on the south coast of the island of New Guinea, on the Coral Sea; pop. 307,600 (est. 2009).

Port Natal former name (until 1835) for DURBAN.

Porto /ˈpɔərtu/ Portuguese name for OPORTO.

Pôrto Alegre /ˌpɔːtuː əˈlɛɡreɪ/ a major port and commercial city in SE Brazil, capital of the state of Rio Grande do Sul; pop. 1,420,667 (2007). It is situated on the Lagoa dos Patos, a lagoon separated from the Atlantic by a sandy peninsula.

portobello /ˌpɔːtəˈbɛləʊ/ (also **portobello mushroom**) ▶ noun (pl. **portobellos**) a large mature mushroom with an open flat cap.
– ORIGIN 1990s: perhaps alteration of Italian *pratarolo* 'meadow mushroom'.

Port of London Authority the corporate body controlling the London harbour and docks.

Port-of-Spain the capital of Trinidad and Tobago, a port on the NW coast of the island of Trinidad; pop. 54,000 (est. 2007).

portolan /ˈpɔːtəlan/ (also **portolano** /ˌpɔːtəˈlɑːnəʊ/) ▶ noun (pl. **portolans** or **portolanos**) historical a book of sailing directions with charts and descriptions of harbours and coasts.
– ORIGIN mid 19th cent.: from Italian *portolano*, from *porto* 'harbour'.

Porto Novo /ˌpɔːtəʊ ˈnəʊvəʊ/ the capital of Benin, a port on the Gulf of Guinea close to the border with Nigeria; pop. 255,878 (2006). It was a centre of the Portuguese slave trade.

Pôrto Velho /ˌpɔːtuː ˈvɛljuː/ a town in western Brazil, capital of the state of Rondônia; pop. 369,345 (2007).

Port Petrovsk /pɪˈtrɒfsk/ former name (until 1922) for MAKHACHKALA.

Port Pirie /ˈpɪri/ a port on the coast of South Australia, on the Spencer Gulf north of Adelaide; pop. 17,950 (2008).

portrait ▶ noun **1** a painting, drawing, photograph, or engraving of a person, especially one depicting only the face or head and shoulders. ■ a representation or impression of someone or something in language or on film or television: *the writer builds up a fascinating portrait of a community.*
2 [as modifier] denoting a format of printed matter which is higher than it is wide. Compare with LANDSCAPE (sense 2 of the noun).
– DERIVATIVES **portraitist** noun (sense 1).
– ORIGIN mid 16th cent.: from French, past participle (used as a noun) of Old French *portraire* 'portray'.

portraiture ▶ noun [mass noun] the art of painting or taking portraits. ■ vivid and detailed description: *his strength as a novelist lay in his portraiture of upper-class families.* ■ [count noun] formal a portrait.
– ORIGIN late Middle English: from Old French, from *portrait* (see PORTRAIT).

portray ▶ verb [with obj.] depict (someone or something) in a work of art or literature: *the ineffectual Oxbridge dons portrayed by Evelyn Waugh.* ■ describe (someone or something) in a particular way: *the book **portrayed him as** a self-serving careerist.* ■ (of an actor) play the part of (someone) in a film or play: *he chose Trevor Howard to portray Captain Bligh.*
– DERIVATIVES **portrayable** adjective, **portrayer** noun.
– ORIGIN Middle English: from Old French *portraire*, based on *traire* 'to draw', from an alteration of Latin *trahere*.

portrayal ▶ noun a depiction of someone or something in a work of art or literature; a picture: *a realistic portrayal of war.* ■ a description of someone or something in a particular way; a representation: *the media portrayal of immigration.* ■ an instance of an actor playing a part in a film or play; a performance: *his portrayal of the title character.*

Port Said /sʌɪd/ a port in Egypt, on the Mediterranean coast at the north end of the Suez Canal; pop. 570,600 (est. 2006). It was founded in 1859 at the start of the construction of the Suez Canal.

Port Salut /ˌpɔː saˈluː/ ▶ noun [mass noun] a pale, mild type of cheese.
– ORIGIN named after the Trappist monastery in France, where it was first produced.

Portsmouth a port and naval base on the south coast of England, in Hampshire; pop. 201,800 (est. 2009). The naval dockyard was established there in 1496.

Port Stanley another name for STANLEY[1].

Port Sudan the chief port of Sudan, on the Red Sea; pop. 284,000 (est. 2008).

Port Sunlight a village on the south bank of the Mersey. Founded and built in the 1880s by Viscount Leverhulme, it provided model housing for the employees of his 'Sunlight' soap factory.

Portugal /ˈpɔːtjʊɡ(ə)l, ˈpɔːtʃʊ-/ a country occupying the western part of the Iberian peninsula in SW Europe; pop. 10,707,900 (est. 2009); official language, Portuguese; capital, Lisbon.

> The country was linked with Spain until it became an independent kingdom in the 12th century. In the 15th and 16th centuries it emerged as one of the leading European colonial powers. Portugal became a republic in 1911, after the expulsion of the monarchy. A long period of dictatorship by Antonio Salazar (Prime Minister 1932–68) and his successor Marcello Caetano (1906–80) was ended in 1974 by a military coup, which led to Portugal's rapid withdrawal from its African colonies and eventually to democratic reform. Portugal became a member of the EC in 1986.

Portuguese /ˌpɔːtjʊˈɡiːz, -tʃʊ-/ ▶ adjective relating to Portugal or its people or language.
▶ noun (pl. **same**) **1** a native or inhabitant of Portugal, or a person of Portuguese descent.
2 [mass noun] the language of Portugal and Brazil, a Romance language spoken by about 160 million people.
– ORIGIN from Portuguese *português*, from medieval Latin *portugalensis*.

Portuguese man-of-war ▶ noun a floating colonial coelenterate with a number of polyps and a conspicuous float. It bears long tentacles which are able to inflict painful stings and occurs chiefly in warm seas. ● *Physalia physalis*, order Siphonophora, class Hydrozoa.

Port Vila another name for VILA.

port watch ▶ noun see WATCH (sense 2 of the noun).

port wine ▶ noun see PORT[2].

port wine stain ▶ noun a kind of large, deep red birthmark, a persistent haemangioma or naevus, typically on the face.

POS ▶ abbreviation point of sale.

posada /pəˈsɑːdə/ ▶ noun (in Spanish-speaking countries) a hotel or inn.
– ORIGIN Spanish, from *posar* 'to lodge'.

pose[1] ▶ verb **1** [with obj.] present or constitute (a problem or danger): *the sheer number of visitors is posing a threat to the area.* ■ raise (a question or matter for consideration): *the statement posed more questions than it answered.*
2 [no obj.] assume a particular position in order to be photographed, painted, or drawn: *the prime minister posed for photographers.* ■ [with obj.] place (someone) in a particular position in order to be photographed, painted, or drawn.
3 [no obj.] (**pose as**) pretend to be (someone or something): *an armed gang posed as policemen to ambush a postman* | figurative *a literary novel posing as a spy thriller.*
4 [no obj.] behave affectedly in order to impress others: *some people like to drive kit cars, but most just like to pose in them.*
▶ noun **1** a way of standing or sitting, especially in order to be photographed, painted, or drawn: *photographs of boxers in ferocious poses.*
2 a particular way of behaving adopted in order to impress or to give a false impression: *the man dropped his pose of amiability.*
– DERIVATIVES **posable** adjective.
– ORIGIN Middle English: from Old French *poser* (verb), from late Latin *pausare* 'to pause', which replaced Latin *ponere* 'to place'. The noun dates from the early 19th cent.

P

pose[2] ▶ verb [with obj.] archaic puzzle or perplex (someone) with a question or problem: *we have thus posed the mathematician and the historian.*
– ORIGIN early 16th cent.: shortening of obsolete *appose*, from Old French *aposer*, variant of *oposer* 'oppose'.

Poseidon /pəˈsʌɪd(ə)n/ Greek Mythology the god of the sea, water, earthquakes, and horses, son of Cronus and Rhea and brother of Zeus. He is often depicted with a trident in his hand. Roman equivalent NEPTUNE.

Posen /ˈpəʊːzn/ German name for POZNAŃ.

poser[1] ▶ noun a person who poses; a poseur.

poser[2] ▶ noun a difficult or perplexing question or problem.

poseur /pəʊˈzəː/ ▶ noun a person who behaves affectedly in order to impress others.
– ORIGIN French, from *poser* 'to place'.

poseuse /pəʊˈzəːz/ ▶ noun humorous a female poser.
– ORIGIN French, feminine of *poseur* (see POSEUR).

posey (also **posy**) ▶ adjective (**posier**, **posiest**) informal (of a person or their behaviour) affected and attempting to impress others; pretentious.

posh informal ▶ adjective elegant or stylishly luxurious: *a posh hotel* | *I'll have to look posh.* ■ Brit. typical of or belonging to the upper class: *she had a posh accent.*
▶ adverb Brit. in an upper-class way: *trying to talk posh.*
▶ noun [mass noun] Brit. the quality of being elegant, stylish, or upper class: *we finally bought a colour TV, which seemed the height of posh.*
▶ verb [with obj.] (**posh someone/thing up**) Brit. smarten someone or something up: *we will be getting all poshed up for the company summer ball.*

– DERIVATIVES **poshly** adverb, **poshness** noun.
– ORIGIN early 20th cent.: perhaps from slang *posh*, denoting a dandy. There is no evidence to support the folk etymology that *posh* is formed from the initials of *port out starboard home* (referring to the more comfortable accommodation, out of the heat of the sun, on ships between England and India).

posho¹ ▶ noun (pl. **poshos**) Brit. informal an upper-class person.

posho² ▶ noun [mass noun] (in East Africa) daily rations consisting typically of maize or rice, given to soldiers or in payment for menial work.
– ORIGIN Kiswahili, literally 'daily rations'.

posing pouch ▶ noun a man's garment covering only the genitals.

posit /ˈpɒzɪt/ ▶ verb (**posits, positing, posited**) **1** [with obj.] put forward as fact or as a basis for argument: *the Confucian view posits a perfectible human nature.* ■ (**posit something on**) base something on the truth of (a particular assumption): *these plots are posited on a false premise about women's nature as inferior.*
2 [with obj. and adverbial] put in position; place: *the Professor posits Cohen in his second category of poets.*
▶ noun Philosophy a statement which is made on the assumption that it will prove to be true.
– ORIGIN mid 17th cent.: from Latin *posit-* 'placed', from the verb *ponere*.

positif /ˈpɒzɪtɪf/ ▶ noun Music (in some organs) a separate division of stops with its own manual, similar to a choir organ.
– ORIGIN French.

position ▶ noun **1** a place where someone or something is located or has been put: *the distress call had given the ship's position* | *Mrs Snell took up her position on the bottom step of the stairs.* ■ [mass noun] the correct location of someone or something: *sew the band into position* | *make sure that no slates have slipped* ***out of position.*** ■ (often **positions**) a place where part of a military force is posted for strategic purposes: *the guns were shelling the German positions.*
2 a particular way in which someone or something is placed or arranged: *he moved himself into a reclining position* | [mass noun] *cramp forced her to change position.* ■ the configuration of the pieces and pawns on the board at any point in a game of chess. ■ Music a particular location of the hand on the fingerboard of a stringed instrument: *be familiar with the first six positions across the four strings.* ■ Music the arrangement of the constituent notes of a chord.
3 a situation, especially as it affects one's power to act: *the company's financial position is grim* | [with infinitive] *we were not in a position to judge the merits of the case.* ■ [mass noun] the state of being placed where one has an advantage over one's rivals or competitors: *sleek motor launches jostled for position.* ■ a person's place or level of importance in relation to others: *he made up ground to finish in second position.* ■ [mass noun] high rank or social standing: *a woman of supposed wealth and position.* ■ a job: *she retired from her position as marketing director.* ■ (in team games) a role assigned to a particular player based on the location in which they play.
4 a person's point of view or attitude towards something: *the party's* ***position on*** *abortion.*
5 the extent to which an investor, dealer, or speculator has made a commitment in the market by buying or selling securities: *traders were covering short positions.*
6 Logic a proposition laid down or asserted; a tenet or assertion.
▶ verb [with obj. and adverbial] put or arrange (someone or something) in a particular place or way: *he pulled out a chair and positioned it between them* | *she positioned herself on a bench.* ■ promote (a product, service, or business) within a particular sector of a market, or as the fulfilment of that sector's specific requirements: *a development plan which will* ***position*** *the city* ***as*** *a major economic force in the region.*
– ORIGIN late Middle English: from Old French, from Latin *positio(n-)*, from *ponere* 'to place'. The current sense of the verb dates from the early 19th cent.

positional ▶ adjective relating to or determined by position: *United will be forced to make several positional changes.*
– DERIVATIVES **positionally** adverb.

positional goods ▶ plural noun Economics goods which are in limited supply and which become more sought after and relatively more expensive as material prosperity increases.

positioner ▶ noun a device for moving an object into position and automatically keeping it there.

position paper ▶ noun (in business and politics) a written report outlining someone's attitude or intentions regarding a particular matter.

positive ▶ adjective **1** consisting in or characterized by the presence rather than the absence of distinguishing features. ■ expressing or implying affirmation, agreement, or permission: *the company received a positive response from investors.* ■ (of the results of a test or experiment) indicating that a certain substance or condition is present or exists: *a player had tested positive for cocaine use.* ■ [in combination] (of a person or their blood) having a specified substance or condition: *HIV-positive.*
2 constructive, optimistic, or confident: *there needs to be a positive approach to young offenders* | *adopt a positive outlook on life.* ■ showing progress or improvement: *the prospects for positive growth in the economy do not look good.*
3 with no possibility of doubt; definite: *he made a positive identification of a glossy ibis.* ■ convinced in one's opinion; certain: *'You are sure it was the same man?' 'Positive!' said George.* ■ [attrib.] informal downright; complete (used for emphasis): *it's a positive delight to see you.*
4 (of a quantity) greater than zero.
5 containing, producing, or denoting an electric charge opposite to that carried by electrons.
6 (of a photographic image) showing lights and shades or colours true to the original.
7 Grammar denoting the primary degree of an adjective or adverb, which expresses simple quality without qualification. Contrasted with **COMPARATIVE** and **SUPERLATIVE**.
8 chiefly Philosophy dealing only with matters of fact and experience; not speculative or theoretical. Compare with **POSITIVISM** (sense 1).
9 Astrology relating to or denoting any of the air or fire signs, considered active in nature.
▶ noun **1** a desirable or constructive quality or attribute: *take your weaknesses and translate them into positives* | *to manage your way out of recession, accentuate* ***the positive.***
2 a positive photographic image, especially one printed from a negative.
3 a result of a test or experiment indicating that a certain substance or condition is present or exists.
4 [mass noun] the part of an electric circuit that is at a higher electrical potential than another point designated as having zero electrical potential.
5 a number greater than zero.
6 Grammar an adjective or adverb in the positive degree.
– DERIVATIVES **positiveness** noun, **positivity** noun.
– ORIGIN late Middle English: from Old French *positif, -ive* or Latin *positivus*, from *posit-* 'placed', from the verb *ponere*. The original sense referred to laws as being formally 'laid down', which gave rise to the sense 'explicitly laid down and admitting no question', hence 'certain'.

positive discrimination ▶ noun [mass noun] Brit. (in the context of the allocation of resources or employment) the practice or policy of favouring individuals belonging to groups which suffer discrimination.

positive feedback ▶ noun [mass noun] chiefly Biology the enhancing or amplification of an effect by its own influence on the process which gives rise to it.
■ Electronics the return of part of an output signal to the input, which is in phase with it, so that the amplifier gain is increased and often the output is distorted.

positive geotropism ▶ noun [mass noun] Botany the tendency of roots to grow downwards.

positive law ▶ noun [mass noun] statutes which have been laid down by a legislature, court, or other human institution and can take whatever form the authors want. Compare with **NATURAL LAW**.

positive logic ▶ noun [mass noun] a method using electrical signals to represent binary digits, in which the positive signal is taken to represent 1 and the negative signal 0.

positively ▶ adverb in a positive way, in particular: ■ with certainty: *experts could not positively identify the voices.* ■ [as submodifier] used to emphasize that something is the case, even though it may seem surprising: *some of the diets may be positively dangerous.*

positive organ ▶ noun chiefly historical a large but movable pipe organ. Compare with **PORTATIVE ORGAN**.
– ORIGIN early 18th cent.: *positive* in the sense 'adapted to be placed in position'.

positive pole ▶ noun Physics a north-seeking pole of a magnet.

positive prescription ▶ noun see **PRESCRIPTION** (sense 3).

positive pressure ▶ noun [mass noun] air or gas pressure greater than that of the atmosphere, as used e.g. in the artificial ventilation of the lungs.

positive sign ▶ noun Mathematics another term for **PLUS SIGN**.

positive vetting ▶ noun [mass noun] Brit. a process of exhaustive inquiry into the background and character of a candidate for a civil service post that involves access to secret material.

positivism ▶ noun [mass noun] Philosophy **1** a philosophical system recognizing only that which can be scientifically verified or which is capable of logical or mathematical proof, and therefore rejecting metaphysics and theism. [from French *positivisme*, coined by the French philosopher Auguste Comte.] ■ another term for **LOGICAL POSITIVISM**.
2 the theory that laws and their operation derive validity from the fact of having been enacted by authority or of deriving logically from existing decisions, rather than from any moral considerations (e.g. that a rule is unjust).
– DERIVATIVES **positivist** noun & adjective, **positivistic** adjective, **positivistically** adverb.

positron /ˈpɒzɪtrɒn/ ▶ noun Physics a subatomic particle with the same mass as an electron and a numerically equal but positive charge.
– ORIGIN 1930s: from **POSITIVE** + **-TRON**.

Posix /ˈpɒsɪks/ ▶ noun [mass noun] Computing a set of formal descriptions that provide a standard for the design of operating systems, especially ones which are compatible with Unix.
– ORIGIN 1980s: from the initial letters of *portable operating system* + *-ix* suggested by **UNIX**.

posology /pəˈsɒlədʒi/ ▶ noun [mass noun] rare the part of medicine concerned with dosage.
– ORIGIN early 19th cent.: from French *posologie*, from Greek *posos* 'how much' + *-logia* (see **-LOGY**).

poss ▶ abbreviation possible: *if poss* | *as soon as poss.*

posse /ˈpɒsi/ ▶ noun **1** US historical a body of men summoned by a sheriff to enforce the law. ■ (also **posse comitatus** /ˌkɒmɪˈteɪtəs/) Brit. historical the body of men above the age of fifteen in a county (excluding peers, the clergy, or the infirm), whom the sheriff could summon to repress a riot or for other purposes. [*comitatus* from medieval Latin, 'of the county'.]
2 informal a group of people who have a common characteristic or occupation: *tea was handed round by a posse of mothers.* ■ a group of young people who socialize together, especially to go to clubs or raves.
– ORIGIN mid 17th cent.: from medieval Latin, literally 'power', from Latin *posse* 'be able'.

possess ▶ verb [with obj.] **1** have as belonging to one; own: *I do not possess a television set.* ■ Law have possession of as distinct from ownership: *a two-year suspended sentence for possessing cocaine.* ■ have as an ability, quality, or characteristic: *he did not possess a sense of humour* | (**be possessed of**) *a fading blonde possessed of a powerful soprano voice.* ■ (**possess oneself of**) archaic take for one's own.
2 (of a demon or spirit, especially an evil one) have complete power over (someone) and be manifested through their speech or actions: *she was possessed by the Devil.* ■ (of an emotion, idea, etc.) dominate the mind of: *I was possessed by a desire to tell her everything.*
3 literary (of a man) have sexual intercourse with.
4 archaic maintain (oneself or one's mind or soul) in a state of patience or quiet: *I tried to* ***possess*** *my soul in patience.* [often with biblical allusion to Luke 21:19, the proper sense ('gain your souls') being misunderstood.]
– PHRASES **what possessed you?** used to express surprise at an action regarded as extremely unwise: *what possessed you to come here?*
– ORIGIN late Middle English: from Old French *possesser*, from Latin *possess-* 'occupied, held', from the verb *possidere*, from *potis* 'able, capable' + *sedere* 'sit'.

possessed ▶ adjective (of a person) completely controlled by an evil spirit: *she ran like a possessed person.*
– PHRASES **like a man** (or **woman**) **possessed** in a frenzy; madly: *the striker charged down on goal like a man possessed.*

possession ▶ noun **1** [mass noun] the state of having, owning, or controlling something: *she had taken possession of the sofa* | *the book came into my*

possession | *he remains* ***in full possession of*** *his sanity.* ■ Law visible power or control over something, as distinct from lawful ownership; holding or occupancy as distinct from ownership: *the landlord wishes to* ***gain possession of*** *the accommodation.* ■ informal the state of possessing an illegal drug: *they're charged with possession.* ■ (in soccer, rugby, and other ball games) temporary control of the ball by a player or team: *the ball hit a defender and Brown's quick reaction put him* ***in possession****.*
2 (usu. **possessions**) something that is owned or possessed: *I had no money or possessions* | *that photograph was Bert's most precious possession.* ■ a territory or country controlled or governed by another: *France's former colonial possessions.*
3 [mass noun] the state of being controlled by a demon or spirit: *they said prayers to protect the people inside the hall from demonic possession.* ■ the state of being completely dominated by an idea or emotion: *fear* ***took possession of*** *my soul.*
– DERIVATIVES **possessionless** adjective.
– ORIGIN Middle English: from Old French, from Latin *possessio(n-)*, from the verb *possidere* (see **POSSESS**).

possession order ▸ noun chiefly Brit. an order made by a court directing that possession of a property be given to the owner or other claimant.

possessive ▸ adjective **1** demanding someone's total attention and love: *has he become jealous or possessive?* | *he placed a firm, possessive hand on her elbow.* ■ showing an unwillingness to share one's possessions: *young children are proud and possessive of their own property.*
2 Grammar relating to or denoting the case of nouns and pronouns expressing possession.
▸ noun Grammar a possessive word or form. ■ (**the possessive**) the possessive case.
– DERIVATIVES **possessively** adverb, **possessiveness** noun.

possessive determiner ▸ noun Grammar a determiner indicating possession, for example *my, your, her, their.*

possessive pronoun ▸ noun Grammar a pronoun indicating possession, for example *mine, yours, hers, theirs.*

possessor ▸ noun a person who owns something or has a particular quality: *his father was the possessor of a considerable fortune.* ■ Law a person who takes, occupies, or holds something without necessarily having ownership, or as distinguished from the owner.
– DERIVATIVES **possessory** adjective.

posset /ˈpɒsɪt/ ▸ noun historical a drink made of hot milk curdled with ale, wine, or other alcohol and typically flavoured with spices.
▸ verb (**possets, possetting, possetted**) [no obj.] (of a baby) regurgitate curdled milk.
– ORIGIN late Middle English: of unknown origin. The verb is first recorded in English dialect in the late 19th cent.

possibility ▸ noun (pl. **possibilities**) a thing that may happen or be the case: *relegation remains a distinct possibility* | [with clause] *there was the possibility that he might be turned down.* ■ [mass noun] the state or fact of being possible; likelihood: *there is* ***no possibility of*** *any government achieving this level of expenditure.* ■ a thing that may be chosen or done out of several possible alternatives: *one possibility is to allow all firms to participate.* ■ (**possibilities**) unspecified qualities of a promising nature; potential: *the house was old but it had possibilities.*
– ORIGIN late Middle English: from Old French *possibilite*, from late Latin *possibilitas*, from *possibilis* 'able to be done' (see **POSSIBLE**).

possible ▸ adjective **1** able to be done or achieved: *surely it's not* ***possible for*** *a man to live so long?* | *contact me* ***as soon as possible*** | *I'd like the report this afternoon,* ***if possible****.* ■ [attrib.] able to be or become; potential: *he was a possible future customer.* ■ [with superlative] having as much or as little of a specified quality as can be achieved: *children need the best education possible* | *the shortest possible route.* ■ [attrib.] (of a number or score) as high as is achievable in a test, competition, or game: *the team have taken just three points from a possible twelve.*
2 that may exist or happen, but that is not certain or probable: *the possible effects of global warming* | [with clause] *it is possible that he will have to return to hospital.*
▸ noun a potential candidate for a job or team: *I have marked five possibles with an asterisk.* ■ (**the possible**) that which is likely or achievable: *they were living right at the edge of the possible.* ■ the highest possible score, especially in a shooting competition: *Mickey scored the possible.*
– ORIGIN late Middle English: from Old French, or from Latin *possibilis*, from *posse* 'be able'.

possibly ▸ adverb **1** [sentence adverb] perhaps (used to indicate doubt or hesitancy): *he found himself alone, possibly the only survivor.* ■ [with modal] used in polite requests: *could you possibly pour me another cup of tea?*
2 [usu. with modal] in accordance with what is likely or achievable, in particular: ■ used to emphasize that one feels that something is surprising, or bewildering: *what can you possibly mean?* ■ used to emphasize that someone has or will put all their effort into something: *be as noisy as you possibly can.*

possie /ˈpɒzi/ (also **pozzy**) ▸ noun Austral./NZ informal a place or position: *the bridge will provide a good fishing possie.* ■ a job.
– ORIGIN early 20th cent.: from **POSITION** + **-IE**.

POSSLQ /ˈpɒs(ə)l,kjuː/ ▸ abbreviation US person of the opposite sex sharing living quarters (used to refer to a live-in sexual partner).

possum ▸ noun a tree-dwelling Australasian marsupial that typically has a prehensile tail. ● Four families, especially Petauridae: many species, including the ringtails. ■ N. Amer. informal an opossum.
– PHRASES **play possum 1** pretend to be asleep or unconscious (as an opossum does when threatened). **2** feign ignorance.
– ORIGIN early 17th cent.: shortening of **OPOSSUM**.

post[1] ▸ noun **1** a long, sturdy piece of timber or metal set upright in the ground and used as a support or marker: *follow the blue posts until the track meets a road.* ■ a goalpost: *Robertson, at the near post, headed wide.* ■ (**the post**) a starting post or winning post.
2 an Internet posting.
▸ verb [with obj.] **1** display (a notice) in a public place: *a curt notice had been posted on the door.* ■ put notices on or in: *we have posted all the bars.*
2 announce or publish (something, especially a financial result): *the company posted a £460,000 loss.* ■ [with obj. and complement] publish the name of (a member of the armed forces) as missing or dead: *a whole troop had been posted missing.* ■ make (information) available on the Internet. ■ submit (a message) to an Internet message board or blog.
3 (of a player or team) achieve or record (a particular score or result): *Smith and Lamb posted a century partnership.*
– PHRASES **go** (or **come**) **to post** (of a racehorse) start a race.
– PHRASAL VERBS **post up** Basketball play in a position near the basket, along the side of the key.
– ORIGIN Old English, from Latin *postis* 'doorpost', later 'rod, beam', probably reinforced in Middle English by Old French *post* 'pillar, beam' and Middle Dutch, Middle Low German *post* 'doorpost'.

post[2] ▸ noun **1** [mass noun] chiefly Brit. the official service or system that delivers letters and parcels: *winners will be notified by post* | *the tickets are in the post.* ■ letters and parcels delivered: *she was opening her post.* ■ [in sing.] a single collection or delivery of mail: *entries must be received no later than first post on 14 June.* ■ used in names of newspapers: *the Washington Post.*
2 historical each of a series of couriers who carried mail on horseback between fixed stages. ■ archaic a person or vehicle that carries mail.
▸ verb **1** [with obj.] chiefly Brit. send (a letter or parcel) via the postal system: *I've just been to post a letter* | ***post off*** *your order form today.*
2 [with obj.] (in bookkeeping) enter (an item) in a ledger. ■ complete (a ledger) by entering items.
3 [no obj., with adverbial] historical travel with relays of horses: *we posted in an open carriage.* ■ [with adverbial of direction] archaic travel with haste; hurry: *he comes posting up the street.*
▸ adverb archaic with haste: *come now, come post.*
– PHRASES **keep someone posted** keep someone informed of the latest developments or news.
– ORIGIN early 16th cent. (in sense 2 of the noun): from French *poste*, from Italian *posta*, from a contraction of Latin *posita*, feminine past participle of *ponere* 'to place'.

post[3] ▸ noun **1** a position of paid employment; a job: *he resigned from the post of Foreign Minister* | *a teaching post.*
2 a place where someone is on duty or where a particular activity is carried out: *a shift worker asleep at his post* | *a customs post.* ■ a place where a soldier or police officer is stationed or which they patrol: *he gave the men orders not to leave their posts.* ■ N. Amer. a force stationed at a permanent position or camp; a garrison. ■ US a local group in an organization of military veterans.
3 historical the status or rank of full-grade captain in the Royal Navy: *Captain Miller was* ***made post*** *in 1796.*
▸ verb [with obj. and adverbial] send (someone) to a place to take up an appointment: *he was posted to Washington as military attaché.* ■ station (someone, especially a soldier or police officer) in a particular place: *a guard was posted at the entrance.*
– ORIGIN mid 16th cent.: from French *poste*, from Italian *posto*, from a contraction of popular Latin *positum*, neuter past participle of *ponere* 'to place'.

post[4] ▸ preposition subsequent to; after: *American poetry post the 1950s hasn't had the same impact.*
– ORIGIN 1960s: independent usage of **POST-**.

post- ▸ prefix after in time or order: *post-date* | *post-operative.*
– ORIGIN from Latin *post* 'after, behind'.

postage ▸ noun [mass noun] the sending of letters and parcels by post: *proof of postage is required.* ■ the amount required to send a letter or parcel by post: *the prices include postage and packing.*

postage meter ▸ noun N. Amer. a franking machine.

postage stamp ▸ noun a small adhesive piece of paper of specified value issued by a national Post Office to be affixed to a letter or parcel to indicate the amount of postage paid.

postal ▸ adjective relating to the post: *postal services.* ■ chiefly Brit. done by post: *a postal ballot.*
▸ noun US informal a postcard.
– PHRASES **go postal** US informal go mad, especially from stress. [with reference to cases in which postal employees ran amok and shot colleagues.]
– DERIVATIVES **postally** adverb.
– ORIGIN mid 19th cent.: from French, from *poste* 'postal service'.

postal card ▸ noun US term for **POSTCARD**.

postal code ▸ noun another term for **POSTCODE**.

postal note ▸ noun Australian and NZ term for **POSTAL ORDER**.

postal order ▸ noun Brit. an order for payment of a specified sum to a named payee, issued by the Post Office.

Postal Service ▸ noun US term for **POST OFFICE** (sense 1).

postal vote ▸ noun Brit. a vote sent in by post rather than cast in person.

post-and-beam ▸ adjective (of a building or a method of construction) having or using a framework of upright and horizontal beams.

postbag ▸ noun British term for **MAILBAG**.

post-bellum /ˈbɛləm/ ▸ adjective occurring or existing after a war, in particular the American Civil War.
– ORIGIN late 19th cent.: from Latin *post* 'after' + *bellum* 'war'.

postbox ▸ noun a large public box with a slot into which post is placed for collection by the post office. ■ British term for **MAILBOX**.

post captain ▸ noun historical a Royal Navy officer holding the full rank of captain, as opposed to a commander with the courtesy title of captain.

postcard ▸ noun a card for sending a message by post without an envelope, typically having a photograph or other illustration on one side.

post-chaise /ˈpəʊs(t)ʃeɪz/ ▸ noun (pl. **post-chaises** pronunc. **same**) historical a horse-drawn carriage used for transporting passengers or mail, especially in the 18th and early 19th centuries.
– ORIGIN late 17th cent.: from **POST**[2] + **CHAISE** in the sense 'horse-drawn carriage'.

post-classical ▸ adjective relating to or denoting a time after the classical period of any language, art, or culture, in particular in ancient Greek and Latin culture.

postcode ▸ noun Brit. a group of numbers or letters and numbers which are added to a postal address to assist the sorting of mail.
– DERIVATIVES **postcoded** adjective.

postcode lottery ▸ noun Brit. a situation in which someone's access to health services or medical treatment is determined by the area of the country in which they live.

post-coital ▸ adjective occurring or done after sexual intercourse: *post-coital contraception.*
– DERIVATIVES **post-coitally** adverb.

P

postcolonial ▶ **adjective** occurring or existing after the end of colonial rule: *the postcolonial government* | *postcolonial literature*.

post-date ▶ **verb** [with obj.] **1** (usu. as adj. **post-dated**) affix or assign a date later than the actual one to (a document or event): *a post-dated cheque*.
2 occur or come at a later date than: *Stonehenge was presumed to post-date these structures*.

postdoc ▶ **noun** informal a person engaged in postdoctoral research. ■ [mass noun] postdoctoral research.

postdoctoral ▶ **adjective** relating to or denoting research undertaken after the completion of doctoral research: *a postdoctoral fellowship*.

poster ▶ **noun 1** a large printed picture used for decoration. ■ a large printed picture, notice, or advertisement displayed in a public place: [as modifier] *a poster campaign*.
2 a person who posts a message on an Internet message board or blog.
▶ **verb** [no obj.] (usu. as noun **postering**) put up posters in an area: *illegal postering in downtown Montreal*.

poster boy (or **poster girl** or **poster child**) ▶ **noun** N. Amer. a person or thing that epitomizes or represents a specified quality, cause, etc.: *the ever-grinning* ***poster boy for*** *the coastal good life*.
– ORIGIN from the use in print advertisements of good-looking young people and appealing children.

poste restante /pəʊst ˈrɛst(ə)nt/ ▶ **noun** [mass noun] Brit. a service offered by a post office whereby mail is kept for an agreed period until collected by the addressee.
– ORIGIN mid 18th cent.: from French, literally 'mail remaining'.

posterior ▶ **adjective 1** chiefly Anatomy further back in position; of or nearer the rear or hind end: *the posterior part of the gut* | *a basal body situated just* ***posterior to*** *the nucleus*. The opposite of **ANTERIOR**. ■ Medicine relating to or denoting presentation of a fetus in which the rear or caudal end is nearest the cervix and emerges first at birth: *a posterior labour*.
2 formal coming after in time or order; later: *a date* ***posterior to*** *the first Reform Bill*.
▶ **noun** humorous a person's buttocks.
– DERIVATIVES **posteriority** noun, **posteriorly** adverb.
– ORIGIN early 16th cent. (as a plural noun denoting descendants): from Latin, comparative of *posterus* 'following', from *post* 'after'.

posterior probability ▶ **noun** the statistical probability that a hypothesis is true calculated in the light of relevant observations.

posterity ▶ **noun** [mass noun] all future generations of people: *the victims' names are recorded for posterity*. ■ [in sing.] archaic the descendants of a person: *God offered Abraham a posterity like the stars of heaven*.
– ORIGIN late Middle English: from Old French *posterite*, from Latin *posteritas*, from *posterus* 'following'.

P

posterize /ˈpəʊstərʌɪz/ (also **posterise**) ▶ **verb** [with obj.] print or display (a photograph or other image) using only a small number of different tones.
– DERIVATIVES **posterization** noun.

postern /ˈpɒst(ə)n, ˈpəʊst-/ ▶ **noun** a back or side entrance: [as modifier] *a small postern door*.
– ORIGIN Middle English: from Old French *posterne*, alteration of *posterle*, from late Latin *posterula*, diminutive of *posterus* 'following'.

poster paint ▶ **noun** [mass noun] an opaque paint with a water-soluble binder, used for posters and children's paintings.

post exchange ▶ **noun** a shop at a US military camp, selling food, clothing, and other items.

postface ▶ **noun** a brief explanatory comment or note at the end of a book or other piece of writing.

post-feminist ▶ **adjective** coming after the feminism of the 1960s and subsequent decades, in particular moving beyond or rejecting some of the ideas of feminism as out of date.
▶ **noun** a person holding post-feminist views.
– DERIVATIVES **post-feminism** noun.

postfix ▶ **verb** [with obj.] Biology treat (a biological substance or specimen) with a second fixative.

post-Fordism ▶ **noun** [mass noun] the theory that modern industrial production should change from the large-scale mass-production methods pioneered by Henry Ford towards the use of small flexible manufacturing units.
– DERIVATIVES **post-Fordist** noun & adjective.

post-free ▶ **adjective & adverb** Brit. carried by post free of charge to the customer.

postfrontal ▶ **noun** Zoology a bone behind the orbit of the eye in some vertebrates.

postgenomic ▶ **adjective** Genetics relating to or denoting the study of the expression of the set of genes in an organism.

postglacial ▶ **adjective** Geology relating to the period since the last (Weichsel or Devensian) glaciation, from the sudden rise in temperature that marks the beginning of the Flandrian about 10,000 years ago. Compare with **LATE-GLACIAL**.

postgrad ▶ **adjective & noun** informal short for **POSTGRADUATE**.

postgraduate ▶ **adjective** relating to or denoting a course of study undertaken after completing a first degree: *a postgraduate degree*.
▶ **noun** a student engaged in a postgraduate course.

post-haste ▶ **adverb** with great speed or immediacy: *she would go post-haste to England*.
– ORIGIN mid 16th cent.: from the direction 'haste, post, haste', formerly given on letters.

post hoc /ˈhɒk/ ▶ **adjective** occurring or done after the event, especially with reference to the fallacious assumption that the occurrence in question has a logical relationship with the event it follows: *this rhetoric offers a post hoc justification for the changes*.
▶ **adverb** after the event.
– ORIGIN Latin, literally 'after this'.

post horn ▶ **noun** historical a valveless horn used to signal the arrival or departure of a mounted courier or mail coach.

posthumous /ˈpɒstjʊməs/ ▶ **adjective** occurring, awarded, or appearing after the death of the originator: *he was awarded a posthumous Military Cross* | *a posthumous collection of his articles*. ■ (of a child) born after the death of its father.
– DERIVATIVES **posthumously** adverb.
– ORIGIN early 17th cent.: from Latin *postumus* 'last' (superlative from *post* 'after'), in late Latin spelled *posth-* by association with *humus* 'ground'.

post-hypnotic ▶ **adjective** relating to or denoting the giving of ideas or instructions to a subject under hypnosis that are intended to affect behaviour after the hypnotic trance ends: *post-hypnotic suggestion*.

postiche /pɒˈstiːʃ/ ▶ **noun** rare a hairpiece.
– ORIGIN early 18th cent.: from French, literally 'false', from Italian *posticcio* 'counterfeit, feigned'.

postie ▶ **noun** Brit. informal a postman or postwoman.
– ORIGIN late 19th cent.: abbreviation.

postil /ˈpɒstɪl/ ▶ **noun** archaic a marginal note or comment, especially on a biblical text. ■ a homily or book of homilies.
– ORIGIN late Middle English: from Old French *postille*, from medieval Latin *postilla*, perhaps from Latin *post illa (verba)* 'after those words', written as a direction to a scribe.

postilion /pɒˈstɪlɪən/ (also **postillion**) ▶ **noun** a person who rides the leading nearside (left-hand side) horse of a team or pair drawing a coach or carriage, especially when there is no coachman.
– ORIGIN mid 16th cent. (in the sense 'forerunner acting as guide to the post-horse rider'): from French *postillon*, from Italian *postiglione* 'post-boy', from *posta* (see **POST**[2]).

post-Impressionism ▶ **noun** [mass noun] the work or style of a varied group of late 19th-century and early 20th-century artists including Van Gogh, Gauguin, and Cézanne. They reacted against the naturalism of the Impressionists to explore colour, line, and form, and the emotional response of the artist, a concern which led to the development of expressionism.
– DERIVATIVES **post-Impressionist** noun & adjective, **post-Impressionistic** adjective.

post-industrial ▶ **adjective** relating to or denoting an economy which no longer relies on heavy industry: *a post-industrial society*.
– DERIVATIVES **post-industrialism** noun.

posting[1] ▶ **noun** chiefly Brit. an appointment to a job, especially one abroad or in the armed forces: *he requested a posting to Japan*. ■ the location of an appointment abroad: *Norway was an attractive posting because of its quality of life*.

posting[2] ▶ **noun** a message submitted to an Internet message board or blog.

Post-it (also **Post-it note**) ▶ **noun** trademark a piece of paper with an adhesive strip on one side, designed to be stuck prominently to an object or surface and easily removed when necessary.

postlapsarian /ˌpəʊstlapˈsɛːrɪən/ ▶ **adjective** Theology or literary occurring or existing after the Fall of Man.
– ORIGIN mid 18th cent.: from **POST-** 'occurring after'.

postlude ▶ **noun** a concluding piece of music. ■ an epilogue or afterword.
– ORIGIN mid 19th cent.: from **POST-** 'later, after', on the pattern of *prelude*.

postman ▶ **noun** (pl. **postmen**) Brit. a person who is employed to deliver or collect letters and parcels.

postman's knock ▶ **noun** Brit. a game, played especially by children, in which imaginary letters are delivered in exchange for kisses.

postmark ▶ **noun** an official mark stamped on a letter or other postal package, giving the place, date, and time of posting, and serving to cancel the postage stamp: *the package had a York postmark*.
▶ **verb** [with obj.] stamp (a postal package) with a postmark: [with obj. and complement] *the letter was postmarked New York*.

postmaster ▶ **noun** a man in charge of a post office.

postmaster general ▶ **noun** the head of a country's postal service (abolished in the UK as an office in 1969).

post mill ▶ **noun** chiefly historical a windmill supported by a post on which it pivots to catch the wind.

postmillennial /ˌpəʊs(t)mɪˈlɛnɪəl/ ▶ **adjective** (especially in Christian doctrine) following the millennium.

postmillennialism ▶ **noun** [mass noun] (among fundamentalist Christians) the doctrine that the Second Coming of Christ will be the culmination of the prophesied millennium of blessedness.
– DERIVATIVES **postmillennialist** noun.

postmistress ▶ **noun** a woman in charge of a post office.

postmodern ▶ **adjective** subsequent to or coming later than that which is modern. ■ relating to or characterized by postmodernism, especially in being self-referential: *postmodern deconstructionist theories*.

postmodernism ▶ **noun** [mass noun] a late 20th-century style and concept in the arts, architecture, and criticism, which represents a departure from modernism and is characterized by the self-conscious use of earlier styles and conventions, a mixing of different artistic styles and media, and a general distrust of theories.
– DERIVATIVES **postmodernist** noun & adjective, **postmodernity** noun.

postmodify ▶ **verb** (**postmodifies**, **postmodifying**, **postmodified**) [with obj.] Grammar modify the sense of (a noun or other word) by being placed after it.
– DERIVATIVES **postmodification** noun, **postmodifier** noun.

post-mortem ▶ **noun** (also **post-mortem examination**) an examination of a dead body to determine the cause of death. ■ an analysis or discussion of an event held soon after it has occurred, especially in order to determine why it was a failure: *an election post-mortem on why the party lost*.
▶ **adjective** [attrib.] relating to a post-mortem. ■ happening after death: *post-mortem changes in his body* | [as adv.] *assessment of morphology in nerves taken post-mortem*.
– ORIGIN mid 18th cent.: from Latin, literally 'after death'.

postmultiply ▶ **verb** (**postmultiplies**, **postmultiplying**, **postmultiplied**) [with obj.] Mathematics multiply (a vector, matrix, or element of a group) non-commutatively by a following factor.

postnatal ▶ **adjective** relating to or denoting the period after childbirth: *postnatal care*.
– DERIVATIVES **postnatally** adverb.

postnatal depression ▶ **noun** [mass noun] depression suffered by a mother following childbirth, typically arising from the combination of hormonal changes, psychological adjustment to motherhood, and fatigue.

postnuptial ▶ **adjective** occurring in or relating to the period after marriage. ■ Zoology occurring in or relating to the period after the mating season of an animal.

post-obit ▶ **adjective** archaic taking effect after death.
– ORIGIN mid 18th cent.: from Latin *post obitum*, from *post* 'after' + *obitus* 'decease' (from *obire* 'to die').

post office ▶ **noun 1** the public department or corporation responsible for postal services and (in some

countries) telecommunications. ▪ a building where postal business is transacted.
2 US term for **POSTMAN'S KNOCK**.

post office box (also **PO box**) ▶ **noun** a numbered box in a post office assigned to a person or organization, where letters for them are kept until called for.

post-op ▶ **abbreviation** post-operative.

post-operative ▶ **adjective** during, relating to, or denoting the period following a surgical operation: *post-operative care.*

postorbital chiefly Zoology ▶ **adjective** situated at the back of the orbit or eye socket, in particular denoting a process of the frontal bone which in some reptiles forms a separate bone.
▶ **noun** a postorbital bone.

post-paid ▶ **adjective & adverb** (with reference to a letter or parcel) on which postage has already been paid: [as adj.] *use the post-paid envelope provided.*

post-partum /ˈpɑːtəm/ ▶ **adjective** Medicine & Veterinary Medicine following childbirth or the birth of young.
– ORIGIN mid 19th cent.: from Latin *post partum* 'after childbirth'.

postpone ▶ **verb** [with obj.] cause or arrange for (something) to take place at a time later than that first scheduled: *the visit had to be postponed for some time* | [with present participle] *he postponed implementing the scheme until industry and business were consulted.*
– DERIVATIVES **postponable** adjective, **postponer** noun.
– ORIGIN late 15th cent.: from Latin *postponere*, from *post* 'after' + *ponere* 'to place'.

postponement ▶ **noun** [mass noun] the action of postponing something; deferral: *the postponement of the elections* | [count noun] *after repeated postponements, Berlin's new Jewish Museum is officially open.*

postpose ▶ **verb** [with obj.] Grammar place (a modifying word or morpheme) after the word that it modifies.
– ORIGIN late 16th cent. (in the sense 'place later or lower'): from French *postposer*, from *post-* 'after' + *poser* 'to place'. The current sense dates from the 1920s.

postposition ▶ **noun** Grammar a word or morpheme placed after the word it governs, for example *-ward* in *homeward*.
– DERIVATIVES **postpositional** adjective.
– ORIGIN mid 19th cent.: from **PREPOSITION**, by substitution of the prefix **POST-** for *pre-*.

postpositive ▶ **adjective** (of a word) placed after or as a suffix on the word that it relates to.
▶ **noun** a postpositive word.
– DERIVATIVES **postpositively** adverb.

postprandial ▶ **adjective** formal or humorous during or relating to the period after dinner or lunch: *we were jolted from our postprandial torpor.* ▪ Medicine occurring or done after a meal.
– ORIGIN early 19th cent.: from **POST-** 'after' + Latin *prandium* 'a meal' + **-AL**.

post-production ▶ **noun** [mass noun] [often as modifier] work done on a film or recording after filming or recording has taken place: *post-production editing.*

post-punk ▶ **adjective** denoting a style of rock music inspired by punk but less aggressive in performance and musically more experimental.
▶ **noun** [mass noun] post-punk music.

post room ▶ **noun** Brit. the department of a company that deals with incoming and outgoing mail.

PostScript ▶ **noun** Computing, trademark a language used as a standard for describing pages of text.

postscript ▶ **noun** an additional remark at the end of a letter, after the signature and introduced by 'PS'. ▪ an extra piece of information about an event that is added after it has happened: *as a postscript to this, Paul did finally marry.*
– ORIGIN mid 16th cent.: from Latin *postscriptum*, neuter past participle (used as a noun) of *postscribere* 'write under, add', from *post* 'after, later' + *scribere* 'write'.

postseason ▶ **adjective** chiefly N. Amer. (of a sporting fixture or other event) taking place after the end of the regular season.
▶ **noun** the period following the regular season. ▪ a game or competition held during the postseason.

post-structuralism ▶ **noun** [mass noun] an extension and critique of structuralism, especially as used in critical textual analysis.

> Emerging in French intellectual life in the late 1960s and early 1970s, post-structuralism embraced Jacques Derrida's deconstructionism and the later work of Roland Barthes, the psychoanalytic theories of Jacques Lacan and Julia Kristeva (b.1941), the historical critiques of Michel Foucault, and the writings of Jean-François Lyotard and Jean Baudrillard. It departed from the claims to objectivity and comprehensiveness made by structuralism and emphasized instead plurality and deferral of meaning, rejecting the fixed binary oppositions of structuralism and the validity of authorial authority.

– DERIVATIVES **post-structural** adjective, **post-structuralist** noun & adjective.

post-synch ▶ **verb** [with obj.] add a sound recording to (film or video footage) at a later time.

post-tax ▶ **adjective** (of income or profits) remaining after the deduction of taxes.

post-tension ▶ **verb** [with obj.] strengthen (reinforced concrete) by applying tension to the reinforcing rods after the concrete has set.

post town ▶ **noun** Brit. a town having a main branch of the Post Office or its own postcode.

post-traumatic stress disorder ▶ **noun** [mass noun] Medicine a condition of persistent mental and emotional stress occurring as a result of injury or severe psychological shock, typically involving disturbance of sleep and constant vivid recall of the experience, with dulled responses to others and to the outside world.

postulant /ˈpɒstjʊl(ə)nt/ ▶ **noun** a candidate, especially one seeking admission into a religious order.
– ORIGIN mid 18th cent.: from French *postulant* or Latin *postulant-* 'asking', from the verb *postulare* (see **POSTULATE**).

postulate ▶ **verb** /ˈpɒstjʊleɪt/ [with obj.] **1** suggest or assume the existence, fact, or truth of (something) as a basis for reasoning, discussion, or belief: *his theory postulated a rotatory movement for hurricanes* | [with clause] *she postulated that the environmentalists might have a case.*
2 (in ecclesiastical law) nominate or elect (someone) to an ecclesiastical office subject to the sanction of a higher authority.
▶ **noun** /ˈpɒstjʊlət/ formal a thing suggested or assumed as true as the basis for reasoning, discussion, or belief: *perhaps the postulate of Babylonian influence on Greek astronomy is incorrect.* ▪ Mathematics an assumption used as a basis for mathematical reasoning.
– DERIVATIVES **postulation** noun.
– ORIGIN late Middle English (in sense 2 of the verb): from Latin *postulat-* 'asked', from the verb *postulare*.

postulator ▶ **noun 1** a person who postulates something.
2 a person who presents a case for the canonization or beatification of someone in the Roman Catholic Church.

posture ▶ **noun 1** a particular position of the body: *I got out of the car in an alert posture.* ▪ the characteristic way in which someone holds their body when standing or sitting: *he took ballet lessons to improve his posture.* ▪ Zoology a particular pose adopted by a bird or other animal, interpreted as a signal of a specific pattern of behaviour.
2 a particular approach or attitude: *trade unions adopted a more militant posture in wage negotiations.* ▪ a way of behaving that is intended to convey a false impression; a pose.
▶ **verb 1** [no obj.] (often as noun **posturing**) behave in a way that is intended to impress or mislead: *a masking of fear with macho posturing.* ▪ [with obj.] adopt (a particular attitude) so as to impress or mislead: *the companies may posture regret, but they have a vested interest in increasing Third World sales.*
2 [with obj. and adverbial] archaic place (someone) in a particular attitude or pose.
– DERIVATIVES **postural** adjective, **posturer** noun.
– ORIGIN late 16th cent. (denoting the relative position of one thing to another): from French, from Italian *postura*, from Latin *positura* 'position', from *posit-* 'placed', from the verb *ponere*.

postviral syndrome (also **postviral fatigue syndrome**) ▶ **noun** [mass noun] myalgic encephalomyelitis following a viral infection.

postvocalic ▶ **adjective** (of a speech sound) occurring immediately after a vowel.

post-war ▶ **adjective** occurring or existing after a war (especially the Second World War): *post-war Britain* | *post-war reconstruction.*

postwoman ▶ **noun** (pl. **postwomen**) a woman who is employed to deliver or collect letters and parcels.

posy¹ ▶ **noun** (pl. **posies**) **1** a small bunch of flowers.
2 archaic a short motto or line of verse inscribed inside a ring.
– ORIGIN late Middle English (in sense 2): contraction of **POESY**.

posy² ▶ **adjective** variant spelling of **POSEY**.

pot¹ ▶ **noun 1** a rounded or cylindrical container, typically of metal, used for cooking: *pots and pans hung from a rack.* ▪ [usu. with modifier or in combination] any of various containers made for a particular purpose, especially one used for storage: *a yogurt pot* | *a coffee pot.* ▪ a container for holding drink, especially beer. ▪ the contents of a pot: ***a pot of** coffee.*
2 (**the pot**) the total sum of the bets made on a round in poker, brag, etc.: *Jim raked in half the pot.* ▪ all the money contributed by a group of people for a particular purpose: *in insurance, everybody puts money into the pot used to pay claims.*
3 informal a prize in a sporting contest, especially a silver cup.
4 informal a pot belly.
5 informal an engine cylinder.
6 Billiards & Snooker a shot in which a player strikes a ball into a pocket.
▶ **verb** (**pots, potting, potted**) [with obj.] **1** plant in a flowerpot. ▪ (**pot something on**) transplant a plant from a small flowerpot to a larger one. ▪ (**pot something up**) transplant a seedling into a flowerpot.
2 preserve (food, especially meat or fish) in a sealed pot or jar: *venison can be potted in the same way as tongue.*
3 Billiards & Snooker strike (a ball) into a pocket: *he failed to pot a red at close range.*
4 informal hit or kill by shooting: *he was shot in the eye as neighbours potted clay pigeons.* ▪ succeed in obtaining (something desirable); win: *do you fancy potting a fine trophy?*
5 [no obj.] make articles from earthenware or baked clay: *why not paint or pot in the sun this winter?*
6 Brit. sit (a young child) on a potty.
7 encapsulate (an electrical component or circuit) in a synthetic resin or similar insulating material which sets solid.
– PHRASES **for the pot** for food or cooking: *he shot a pigeon for the pot.* **go to pot** informal deteriorate through neglect: *the foundry was allowed to go to pot in the seventies.* **the pot calling the kettle black** used to convey that the criticisms a person is aiming at someone else could equally well apply to themselves. **pot of gold** see **GOLD**. **pots of money** informal a very large amount of money. **shit** (or **piss**) **or get off the pot** vulgar slang used to convey that someone should stop wasting time and get on with something. **a watched pot never boils** proverb time seems to drag endlessly when you're waiting for something to happen.
– DERIVATIVES **potful** noun (pl. **potfuls**).
– ORIGIN late Old English *pott*, probably reinforced in Middle English by Old French *pot*; of unknown ultimate origin (compare with late Latin *potus* 'drinking cup'). Current senses of the verb date from the early 17th cent.

pot² ▶ **noun** [mass noun] informal cannabis.
– ORIGIN 1930s: probably from Mexican Spanish *potiguaya* 'cannabis leaves'.

pot³ ▶ **noun 1** a shot aimed at someone or something; a potshot.
2 (chiefly in rugby) an attempt to score a goal with a kick.
▶ **verb** (**pots, potting, potted**) [with obj.] score (a goal).

pot⁴ ▶ **noun** short for **POTENTIOMETER** (sense 2).

potable /ˈpəʊtəb(ə)l/ ▶ **adjective** formal safe to drink; drinkable: *there is no supply of potable water available.*
– DERIVATIVES **potability** noun.
– ORIGIN late Middle English: from French *potable*, from late Latin *potabilis*, from Latin *potare* 'to drink'.

potage /pɒˈtɑːʒ/ ▶ **noun** [mass noun] thick soup.
– ORIGIN mid 16th cent.: from French. Compare with **POTTAGE**.

potager /ˈpɒtədʒə/ ▶ **noun** a kitchen garden.
– ORIGIN mid 17th cent.: from French *jardin potager* 'garden providing vegetables for the pot'.

potamology /ˌpɒtəˈmɒlədʒi/ ▶ **noun** [mass noun] Geography the study of rivers.
– ORIGIN early 19th cent.: from Greek *potamos* 'river' + **-LOGY**.

potash ▶ **noun** [mass noun] an alkaline potassium compound, especially potassium carbonate or hydroxide.
– ORIGIN early 17th cent.: from *pot-ashes*, from obsolete Dutch *potasschen*, originally obtained by

P

leaching vegetable ashes and evaporating the solution in iron pots.

potash alum ▶ noun see ALUM.

potassium /pəˈtasɪəm/ ▶ noun [mass noun] the chemical element of atomic number 19, a soft silvery-white reactive metal of the alkali-metal group. (Symbol: **K**)
– DERIVATIVES **potassic** adjective (Mineralogy).
– ORIGIN early 19th cent.: from POTASH (earlier *potass*, from French *potasse*) + -IUM.

potassium–argon dating ▶ noun [mass noun] Geology a method of dating rocks from the relative proportions of radioactive potassium-40 and its decay product, argon-40.

potassium hydroxide ▶ noun [mass noun] a strongly alkaline white deliquescent compound used in many industrial processes, e.g. soap manufacture. ● Chem. formula: KOH.

potassium nitrate ▶ noun [mass noun] a white crystalline salt which occurs naturally in nitre and is used in preserving meat and as a constituent of gunpowder. ● Chem. formula: KNO_3.

potation /pə(ʊ)ˈteɪʃ(ə)n/ ▶ noun archaic or humorous an alcoholic drink. ■ [mass noun] the action of drinking alcohol: *you did rather abstain from potation.* ■ (often **potations**) a drinking bout.
– ORIGIN late Middle English: from Old French, from Latin *potatio(n-)*, from *potare* 'to drink'.

potato ▶ noun (pl. **potatoes**) **1** a starchy plant tuber which is one of the most important food crops, cooked and eaten as a vegetable: *roast potatoes* | [mass noun] *mashed potato.*
2 the plant of the nightshade family which produces potatoes on underground runners. ● *Solanum tuberosum*, family Solanaceae. It was first cultivated in the Andes about 1,800 years ago and was introduced to Europe in c.1570.
3 Brit. informal a large hole in a sock or stocking, especially one in the heel.
– ORIGIN mid 16th cent.: from Spanish *patata*, variant of Taino *batata* 'sweet potato'. The English word originally denoted the sweet potato and gained its current sense in the late 16th cent.

potato blight ▶ noun [mass noun] a destructive fungal disease of potatoes resulting in dry brown rot of the tubers. ● **Early blight** is caused by *Alternaria solani* (subdivision Deuteromycotina), and **late blight** is caused by *Phytophthora infestans* (subdivision Mastigomycotina).

potato chip ▶ noun see CHIP (sense 2 of the noun).

potato crisp ▶ noun see CRISP.

potato pancake ▶ noun a small flat cake of grated potatoes mixed with flour and egg and fried.

potato salad ▶ noun [mass noun] a side dish consisting of cold cooked potato chopped and mixed with mayonnaise and seasonings.

P

potato vine ▶ noun a semi-evergreen climbing plant with pale blue or white flowers, related to the potato and native to South and Central America. ● *Solanum jasminoides*, family Solanaceae.

pot-au-feu /ˌpɒtəʊˈfəː/ ▶ noun (pl. **same**) [mass noun] a French soup of meat, typically boiled beef, and vegetables cooked in a large pot.
– ORIGIN French, literally 'pot on the fire'.

Potawatomi /ˌpɒtəˈwɒtəmi/ ▶ noun (pl. **same** or **Potawatomis**) **1** a member of an American Indian people inhabiting the Great Lakes region, principally in Michigan and Wisconsin.
2 [mass noun] the Algonquian language of the Potawatomi, now with few speakers.
▶ adjective relating to the Potawatomi or their language.
– ORIGIN the name in Ojibwa.

pot-bellied pig (in full **Vietnamese pot-bellied pig**) ▶ noun a pig of a small dark breed with short legs and a large stomach, sometimes kept as a pet.

pot-bellied stove ▶ noun a small bulbous-sided wood-burning stove.

pot belly ▶ noun a large, protruding, rotund stomach.
– DERIVATIVES **pot-bellied** adjective.

potboiler ▶ noun informal a book, film, or other creative work produced solely to make the originator a living by catering to popular taste.

pot-bound ▶ adjective (of a plant) having roots which fill the flowerpot, leaving no room for them to expand.

potch (also **potch opal**) ▶ noun [mass noun] opal which has no play of colour and is of no value.
– ORIGIN late 19th cent.: of unknown origin.

pot cheese ▶ noun [mass noun] US a coarse type of cottage cheese.

poteen /pɒˈtiːn/ (also **potheen**) ▶ noun [mass noun] chiefly Irish alcohol made illicitly, typically from potatoes.
– ORIGIN early 19th cent.: from Irish (*fuisce*) *poitín* 'little pot (of whiskey)', diminutive of *pota* 'pot'.

Potemkin[1] /pəˈtɛmkɪn/ a battleship whose crew mutinied in the Russian Revolution of 1905 when in the Black Sea, bombarding Odessa before seeking asylum in Romania. The incident persuaded the tsar to agree to a measure of reform.

Potemkin[2] /pəˈtɛmkɪn/ ▶ adjective informal having a false or deceptive appearance, especially one presented for the purpose of propaganda: *it is a Potemkin party; there is little behind the impressive parliamentary group seen on television.*
– ORIGIN 1930s: from Grigori Aleksandrovich *Potyomkin* (often transliterated *Potemkin*), a favourite of Empress Catherine II of Russia, who reputedly gave the order for sham villages to be built for the empress's tour of the Crimea in 1787.

potency ▶ noun (pl. **potencies**) [mass noun] **1** the power of something to affect the mind or body: *a myth of enormous potency* | *the unexpected potency of the rum punch.* ■ [count noun] (in homeopathy) the number of times a remedy has been diluted and succussed, taken as a measure of the strength of the effect it will produce: *she was given a low potency twice daily.* ■ Genetics the extent of the contribution of an allele towards the production of a phenotypic characteristic. ■ Biology a capacity in embryonic tissue for developing into a particular specialized tissue or organ.
2 a male's ability to achieve an erection or to reach orgasm: *the myth of declining sexual potency with increasing age.*

potent[1] ▶ adjective **1** having great power, influence, or effect: *thrones were potent symbols of authority* | *a potent drug.*
2 (of a male) able to achieve an erection or to reach an orgasm.
– DERIVATIVES **potence** noun, **potently** adverb.
– ORIGIN late Middle English: from Latin *potent-* 'being powerful, being able', from the verb *posse*.

potent[2] Heraldry ▶ adjective [postpositive] **1** formed of crutch-shaped pieces; (especially of a cross) having a straight bar across the end of each extremity.
2 of the fur called potent (as a tincture).
▶ noun [mass noun] fur resembling vair, but with the alternating pieces T-shaped.
– ORIGIN late Middle English (denoting a crutch): alteration of Old French *potence* 'crutch', from Latin *potentia* 'power' (in medieval Latin 'crutch'), from *potent-* (see POTENT[1]).

potentate ▶ noun a monarch or ruler, especially an autocratic one.
– ORIGIN late Middle English: from Latin *potentatus* 'dominion', from *potent-* 'being able or powerful' (see POTENT[1]).

potential ▶ adjective [attrib.] having or showing the capacity to develop into something in the future: *a campaign to woo potential customers.*
▶ noun **1** [mass noun] latent qualities or abilities that may be developed and lead to future success or usefulness: *a young broadcaster with great potential* | [count noun] *the potentials of the technology were never wholly controllable.* ■ (often **potential for/to do something**) the possibility of something happening or of someone doing something in the future: *pesticides with the potential to cause cancer.*
2 Physics the quantity determining the energy of mass in a gravitational field or of charge in an electric field.
– DERIVATIVES **potentiality** noun, **potentialize** (also **potentialise**) verb, **potentially** adverb [as submodifier] *potentially dangerous products.*
– ORIGIN late Middle English: from late Latin *potentialis*, from *potentia* 'power', from *potent-* 'being able' (see POTENT[1]). The noun dates from the early 19th cent.

potential barrier ▶ noun Physics a region within a force field in which the potential is significantly higher than at points either side of it, so that a particle requires energy to pass through it.

potential difference ▶ noun Physics the difference of electrical potential between two points.

potential divider ▶ noun another term for VOLTAGE DIVIDER.

potential energy ▶ noun [mass noun] Physics the energy possessed by a body by virtue of its position relative to others, stresses within itself, electric charge, and other factors. Compare with KINETIC ENERGY.

potential well ▶ noun Physics a region in a field of force, in particular the region in which an atomic nucleus is situated, in which the potential is significantly lower than at points immediately outside it, so that a particle in it is likely to remain there unless it gains a relatively large amount of energy.

potentiate /pə(ʊ)ˈtɛnʃɪeɪt/ ▶ verb [with obj.] technical increase the power, effect, or likelihood of (something, especially a drug or physiological reaction): *the glucose will potentiate intestinal absorption of sodium.*
– ORIGIN early 19th cent.: from POTENT[1], on the pattern of *substantiate*.

potentiation ▶ noun [mass noun] Physiology the increase in strength of nerve impulses along pathways which have been used previously, either short-term or long-term.

potentilla /ˌpəʊt(ə)nˈtɪlə/ ▶ noun a plant of a genus that includes the cinquefoils, especially (in gardening) a small shrub with yellow or red flowers. ● Genus *Potentilla*, family Rosaceae: many species.
– ORIGIN modern Latin, based on Latin *potent-* 'being powerful' (with reference to its herbal qualities) + the diminutive suffix *-illa*.

potentiometer /pə(ʊ)ˌtɛnʃɪˈɒmɪtə/ ▶ noun **1** an instrument for measuring an electromotive force by balancing it against the potential difference produced by passing a known current through a known variable resistance.
2 a variable resistor with a third adjustable terminal. The potential at the third terminal can be adjusted to give any fraction of the potential across the ends of the resistor.

potentiometry ▶ noun [mass noun] Chemistry the measurement of electrical potential as a technique in chemical analysis.
– DERIVATIVES **potentiometric** adjective.

potentize (also **potentise**) ▶ verb [with obj.] rare make stronger or more potent. ■ make (a homeopathic medicine) more powerful by diluting and shaking it.
– DERIVATIVES **potentization** noun.

Potenza /pəˈtɛnzə/ a market town in southern Italy, capital of Basilicata region; pop. 68,594 (2008).

pothead ▶ noun informal a person who smokes cannabis.

potheen /pɒˈtʃiːn/ ▶ noun chiefly Irish variant spelling of POTEEN.

pother /ˈpɒðə/ ▶ noun [in sing.] a commotion or fuss: *what a pother you make!*
– ORIGIN late 16th cent.: of unknown origin.

pot-herb ▶ noun any herb grown for culinary use.

pot holder ▶ noun N. Amer. a piece of quilted or thick fabric for handling hot dishes and pans.

pothole ▶ noun **1** a deep natural underground cave formed by the erosion of rock, especially by the action of water. ■ a deep circular hole in a riverbed formed by the erosion of the rock by the rotation of stones in an eddy. ■ (also **pothole lake**) N. Amer. a pond formed by a natural hollow in the ground in which water has collected.
2 a depression or hollow in a road surface caused by wear or subsidence.
▶ verb [no obj.] (often as noun **potholing**) Brit. explore underground potholes as a pastime: *they went potholing in the Pennines.*
– DERIVATIVES **potholed** adjective, **potholer** noun.
– ORIGIN early 19th cent.: from Middle English *pot* 'pit' (perhaps of Scandinavian origin) + HOLE.

pot-hook ▶ noun **1** chiefly historical a hook used for hanging a pot over a hearth or for lifting a hot pot.
2 dated a curved stroke in handwriting, especially as made by children learning to write.

pot-house ▶ noun dated a small tavern.

pothunter ▶ noun a person who hunts solely to achieve a kill, rather than as a sport. ■ informal a person who takes part in a contest merely for the sake of the prize.

potion ▶ noun a liquid with healing, magical, or poisonous properties: *a love potion.*
– ORIGIN Middle English: from Old French, from Latin *potio(n-)* 'drink, poisonous draught', related to *potare* 'to drink'.

Potiphar /ˈpɒtɪfə/ (in the Bible) an Egyptian officer whose wife tried to seduce Joseph and then falsely accused him of attempting to rape her (Gen. 39).

potjie /ˈpɔiki, ˈpʊiki/ ▶ noun (pl. **potjies**) S. African a lidded, usually three-legged cast-iron pot for use over an open fire. ■ (also **potjiekos**) [mass noun] a stew cooked in such a pot.
– ORIGIN Afrikaans, literally 'little pot'.

potlatch ▸ noun (among North American Indian peoples of the north-west coast) an opulent ceremonial feast at which possessions are given away or destroyed to display wealth or enhance prestige.
▸ verb [no obj.] hold such a feast or ceremony.
– ORIGIN Chinook Jargon, from Nootka *p'ačiƛ* 'make a gift at a potlatch'.

pot liquor ▸ noun [mass noun] chiefly US liquor in which meat, fish, or vegetables have been boiled; stock.

pot luck ▸ noun a situation in which one must take a chance that whatever is available will prove to be good or acceptable: *he could take pot luck in a town not noted for its restaurants.* ■ (usu. **potluck**) N. Amer. a meal or party to which each of the guests contributes a dish: [as modifier] *a potluck supper.*

potman ▸ noun (pl. **potmen** /ˈpɒtmɛn/) dated a man who serves drinks in a pub or bar.

Potomac /pəˈtəʊmək/ a river of the eastern US, which rises in the Appalachian Mountains in West Virginia and flows about 459 km (285 miles) through Washington DC into Chesapeake Bay on the Atlantic coast.

potoo /pəˈtuː/ ▸ noun a nocturnal insectivorous bird resembling a large nightjar, found in tropical America. ● Genus *Nyctibius* and family Nyctibiidae: five species, in particular the **common potoo** (*N. griseus*).
– ORIGIN mid 19th cent.: from Jamaican creole, from Akan, of imitative origin.

potoroo /ˌpɒtəˈruː/ ▸ noun a small nocturnal rat-kangaroo with long hindlimbs and typically a hopping gait, native to Australia. ● Genus *Potorous*, family Potoroidae: three species.
– ORIGIN late 18th cent.: probably from Dharuk *badaru*.

Potosí /ˌpɒtəʊˈsiː/ a city in southern Bolivia; pop. 153,328 (2009). Situated at an altitude of about 4,205 m (13,780 ft), it is one of the highest cities in the world.

pot pie ▸ noun chiefly N. Amer. **1** a savoury pie baked in a deep dish, typically with a top crust only.
2 a stew with dumplings.

pot plant ▸ noun Brit. a plant grown or suitable for growing in a flowerpot, especially indoors.

potpourri /pəʊˈpʊəri, -ˈriː, pɒtˈpʊəri/ ▸ noun (pl. **potpourris**) [mass noun] a mixture of dried petals and spices placed in a bowl to perfume a room. ■ a mixture or medley of things: *he played a potpourri of tunes from Gilbert and Sullivan.*
– ORIGIN early 17th cent. (denoting a stew made of different kinds of meat): from French, literally 'rotten pot'.

potrero /pɒˈtrɛːrəʊ/ ▸ noun (pl. **potreros**) (in the south-western US and South America) a paddock or pasture for horses or cattle.
– ORIGIN mid 19th cent.: from Spanish, from *potro* 'colt, pony'.

pot roast ▸ noun a piece of meat cooked slowly in a covered dish.
▸ verb (**pot-roast**) [with obj.] cook (a piece of meat) slowly in a covered dish.

Potsdam /ˈpɒtsdam/ a city in eastern Germany, the capital of Brandenburg, situated just south-west of Berlin on the Havel River; pop. 148,800 (est. 2006). It is the site of the rococo Sans Souci palace built for Frederick II between 1745 and 1747.

Potsdam Conference a meeting held in Potsdam in the summer of 1945 between US, Soviet, and British leaders, which established principles for the Allied occupation of Germany following the end of the Second World War.

potsherd /ˈpɒtʃəːd/ ▸ noun a broken piece of ceramic material, especially one found on an archaeological site.

potshot ▸ noun a shot aimed at a person or thing that happens to be within easy reach: *a sniper took a potshot at him.* ■ a criticism, especially a random or unfounded one: *the show takes wickedly funny potshots at as many movies as it can muster.*
– ORIGIN mid 19th cent.: originally a *shot* at an animal intended for the *pot*, i.e. purely for food, rather than for display (which would require skilled shooting according to hunting rules).

potsticker ▸ noun a Chinese wonton dumpling which is fried until brown on one side, then turned and simmered in a small amount of broth.

pot still ▸ noun a still to which heat is applied directly and not by means of a steam jacket.

pottage ▸ noun [mass noun] archaic soup or stew.
– PHRASES **sell something for a mess of pottage** sell something for a ridiculously small amount. [with biblical allusion to the story of Esau, who sold his birthright (Gen. 25:31).]
– ORIGIN Middle English (as *potage*): from Old French *potage* 'that which is put into a pot'. Compare with POTAGE and PORRIDGE.

potted ▸ adjective **1** (of a plant) planted or grown in a flowerpot and usually kept indoors: *an array of exotic potted palms.*
2 chiefly Brit. (of meat or fish) preserved in a sealed pot or jar: *potted shrimps.* ■ (of a biographical or historical account) put into a short and easily assimilable form: *a potted history of the band's career.*
3 N. Amer. informal intoxicated by drink or drugs, especially cannabis: *everybody was pretty potted.*
4 (of an electrical component or circuit) encapsulated in insulating material.

Potter, (Helen) Beatrix (1866–1943), English writer for children. She is known for her series of animal stories, illustrated with her own delicate watercolours, which began with *The Tale of Peter Rabbit* (first published privately in 1900).

potter¹ (N. Amer. **putter**) ▸ verb [no obj.] occupy oneself in a desultory but pleasant way: *I'm quite happy just to potter about by myself here.* ■ [with adverbial of direction] move or go in a casual, unhurried way: *I might potter into Nice for the day.*
▸ noun [in sing.] an act or period of occupying oneself in a desultory but pleasant way: *an afternoon's potter through the rooms and possessions of the rich.*
– DERIVATIVES **potterer** noun.
– ORIGIN mid 16th cent. (in the sense 'poke repeatedly'): frequentative of dialect *pote* 'to push, kick, or poke' of unknown origin.

potter² ▸ noun a person who makes ceramic ware.
– ORIGIN late Old English *pottere* (see POT¹, -ER¹).

potter's field ▸ noun historical a burial place for paupers and strangers.
– ORIGIN the name of an area of land near Jerusalem bought for this purpose with the money given to Judas Iscariot for betraying Jesus (Matt. 27:7).

potter's wheel ▸ noun a horizontal revolving disc on which wet clay is shaped into pots or other round ceramic objects.

potter wasp ▸ noun a solitary wasp which builds a flask-shaped nest of mud into which it seals an egg and a supply of food for the larva. ● Genus *Eumenes*, family Eumenidae: many species, including *E. coarctatus* of European heathland.

pottery ▸ noun (pl. **potteries**) **1** [mass noun] pots, dishes, and other articles made of fired clay. Pottery can be broadly divided into earthenware, porcelain, and stoneware. ■ the craft or profession of making pottery: *courses include drawing, painting, and pottery.*
2 a factory or workshop where pottery is made. ■ (**the Potteries**) the area around Stoke-on-Trent, Staffordshire, where the English pottery industry is based.
– ORIGIN Middle English: from Old French *poterie*, from *potier* 'a potter'.

potting compost ▸ noun [mass noun] a mixture of loam, peat, sand, and nutrients, used as a growing medium for plants in containers.

potting shed ▸ noun chiefly Brit. a shed which is used for potting plants and in which plants and garden tools and supplies are stored.

pottle ▸ noun **1** archaic a measure for liquids equal to a half gallon.
2 archaic a small conical punnet for strawberries or other fruit. ■ NZ a small plastic or cardboard food container: *a pottle of apricot yogurt.*
– ORIGIN Middle English (in sense 1): from Old French *potel* 'little pot', diminutive of *pot*.

potto /ˈpɒtəʊ/ ▸ noun (pl. **pottos**) a small, slow-moving nocturnal primate with a short tail, living in the tropical forests of Africa. ● *Perodicticus potto*, family Lorisidae, suborder Prosimii.
– ORIGIN early 18th cent.: perhaps from Guinea dialect.

Pott's fracture ▸ noun a fracture of the lower end of the fibula, usually involving a dislocation of the ankle.
– ORIGIN mid 19th cent.: named after Sir Percivall Pott (1713–88), English surgeon.

potty¹ ▸ adjective (**pottier**, **pottiest**) informal, chiefly Brit. **1** mad; crazy: *he's driving me potty.* ■ [predic.] extremely enthusiastic about or fond of someone or something: *she's potty about you.*
2 [attrib.] insignificant or feeble: *a potty little place.*
– DERIVATIVES **pottiness** noun.
– ORIGIN mid 19th cent.: of unknown origin.

potty² ▸ noun (pl. **potties**) a bowl used by small children as a toilet.

potty-mouthed ▸ adjective informal using or characterized by bad language: *a potty-mouthed rapper.*
– DERIVATIVES **potty mouth** noun.

potty-train ▸ verb [with obj.] train (a small child) to use a potty.

POTUS /ˈpəʊtəs/ ▸ noun US informal President of the United States.
– ORIGIN early 20th cent.: acronym.

pot-valiant ▸ adjective archaic courageous as a result of drinking alcohol.
– DERIVATIVES **pot-valour** noun.

pouch ▸ noun **1** a small flexible bag, typically carried in a pocket or attached to a belt: *a tobacco pouch | webbing with pouches for stun grenades.* ■ a lockable bag for mail or dispatches.
2 a pocket-like abdominal receptacle in which marsupials carry their young during lactation. ■ any of a number of similar animal structures, such as those in the cheeks of rodents.
3 (often **pouches**) a baggy area of skin underneath a person's eyes.
▸ verb [with obj.] **1** put into a pouch: *he stopped, pouched his tickets, and plodded on.* ■ informal succeed in securing: *he pouched his fifth first prize by beating Higginson in the final.* ■ Cricket catch (the ball): *Hick pouched his fourth catch with ease.*
2 make (part of a garment) hang like a pouch: *the muslin is lightly pouched over the belt.*
– DERIVATIVES **pouched** adjective, **pouchy** adjective.
– ORIGIN Middle English (as a noun): from Old Northern French *pouche*, variant of Old French *poche* 'bag'. Compare with POKE².

pouchong /puːˈ(t)ʃɒŋ/ ▸ noun [mass noun] a kind of China tea made by fermenting the withered leaves only briefly, typically scented with rose petals.
– ORIGIN Chinese.

pouf¹ ▸ noun variant spelling of POOF¹, POUFFE.
▸ exclamation variant spelling of POOF².

pouf² /puːf/ ▸ noun a part of a dress in which a large mass of material has been gathered so that it stands away from the body. ■ a bouffant hairstyle.
– ORIGIN early 19th cent.: from French, of imitative origin.

pouffe /puːf/ (also **pouf**) ▸ noun a cushioned footstool or low seat with no back.
– ORIGIN late 19th cent.: from French *pouf* (see POUF²).

poui /ˈpuːi/ ▸ noun (pl. **same** or **pouis**) a Caribbean and tropical American tree with trumpet-shaped flowers, grown as an ornamental and valued for its timber. ● Genus *Tabebuia*, family Bignoniaceae.
– ORIGIN mid 19th cent.: a local word in Trinidad.

Pouilly /puːlji/ ▸ noun [mass noun] any of various dry white wines produced in central France.
– ORIGIN the name, or part of the name, of several French villages where such wines are produced.

Poulenc /ˈpuːlãk/, French /pulɛ̃k/, Francis (Jean Marcel) (1899–1963), French composer. He was a member of Les Six. His work is characterized by lyricism as well as the use of idioms of popular music such as jazz, and includes songs and the ballet *Les Biches* (1923).

poult¹ /pəʊlt/ ▸ noun Farming a young domestic chicken, turkey, pheasant, or other fowl being raised for food.
– ORIGIN late Middle English: contraction of PULLET.

poult² /puːlt, pʊlt/ (also **poult-de-soie** /ˌpuːdəˈswɑː/) ▸ noun [mass noun] a fine corded silk or taffeta, typically coloured and used as a dress fabric.
– ORIGIN 1930s: from French *poult-de-soie*, from *poult* (of unknown origin) + *de soie* 'of silk'.

poulterer ▸ noun Brit. a dealer in poultry and, typically, game.
– ORIGIN late 16th cent.: from archaic *poulter*, in the same sense, from Old French *pouletier*.

poultice /ˈpəʊltɪs/ ▸ noun a soft, moist mass of material, typically consisting of bran, flour, herbs, etc., applied to the body to relieve soreness and inflammation and kept in place with a cloth.
▸ verb [with obj.] apply a poultice to: *he poulticed the wound.*
– ORIGIN late Middle English: from Latin *pultes* (plural), from *puls*, *pult-* 'pottage, pap'.

poultry /ˈpəʊltri/ ▸ noun [mass noun] domestic fowl, such as chickens, turkeys, ducks, and geese.

P

– ORIGIN Middle English: from Old French *pouletrie*, from *poulet* 'pullet'.

poultryman ▶ noun (pl. **poultrymen**) a person who rears or sells poultry for a living.

pounamu /paʊˈnɑːmuː/ ▶ noun [mass noun] NZ a variety of jade; greenstone.
– ORIGIN mid 19th cent.: from Maori.

pounce[1] ▶ verb [no obj.] (of an animal or bird of prey) spring or swoop suddenly so as to catch prey: *as he watched, a mink* ***pounced on*** *the vole.* ■ (of a person) spring forward suddenly so as to attack or seize someone or something: *the gang* ***pounced on*** *him and knocked him to the ground.* ■ notice and take swift advantage of a mistake or sign of weakness: *the paper* ***pounced on*** *her admission that she is still a member of CND.*
▶ noun **1** a sudden swoop or spring.
2 archaic a bird's claw.
– ORIGIN late Middle English (as a noun denoting a tool for stamping or punching): origin obscure, perhaps from PUNCHEON[1]. The noun sense 'a bird's claw' arose in the late 15th cent. and gave rise to the verb (late 17th cent.).

pounce[2] ▶ noun [mass noun] **1** a fine resinous powder formerly used to prevent ink from spreading on unglazed paper or to prepare parchment to receive writing.
2 powdered charcoal or other fine powder dusted over a perforated pattern to transfer the design to the object beneath.
▶ verb [with obj.] **1** smooth down by rubbing with pounce or pumice.
2 transfer (a design) by the use of pounce.
– ORIGIN late 16th cent. (as a verb): from French *poncer*, based on Latin *pumex* 'pumice'.

pouncet box /ˈpaʊnsɪt/ ▶ noun archaic a small box with a perforated lid used for holding a substance impregnated with perfume.
– ORIGIN late 16th cent.: perhaps originally erroneously from *pounced* (= perforated) *box*.

Pound, Ezra (Weston Loomis) (1885–1972), American poet and critic, resident in Europe 1908–45. Initially associated with imagism, he later developed a highly eclectic poetic voice, drawing on a vast range of classical and other references and establishing a reputation as a modernist poet. Notable works: *Hugh Selwyn Mauberley* (1920) and *Cantos* (series, 1917–70).

pound[1] ▶ noun **1** (abbrev.: **lb**) a unit of weight equal to 16 oz. avoirdupois (0.4536 kg), or 12 oz. troy (0.3732 kg).
2 (also **pound sterling**) (pl. **pounds sterling**) the basic monetary unit of the UK, equal to 100 pence. ■ another term for PUNT[4]. ■ the basic monetary unit of several Middle Eastern countries, equal to 100 piastres. ■ the former basic monetary unit of Cyprus, equal to 100 cents. ■ the basic monetary unit of the Sudan.
– PHRASES **one's pound of flesh** something one is strictly or legally entitled to, but which it is ruthless or inhuman to demand. [with allusion to Shakespeare's *Merchant of Venice*.]
– ORIGIN Old English *pund*, of Germanic origin; related to Dutch *pond* and German *Pfund*, from Latin (*libra*) *pondo*, denoting a Roman 'pound weight' of 12 ounces.

P

pound[2] ▶ verb [with obj.] **1** strike or hit heavily and repeatedly: *Patrick pounded the couch with his fists* | [no obj.] *pounding on the door, she shouted at the top of her voice.* ■ [no obj.] beat or throb with a strong regular rhythm: *her heart was pounding.* ■ [no obj., with adverbial of direction] walk or run with heavy steps: *I heard him pounding along the gangway.*
2 crush or grind (something) into a powder or paste: *pound the cloves with salt and pepper until smooth.* ■ informal defeat (an opponent) in a resounding way: [with obj. and complement] *he pounded the unseeded American 6–2 7–5 7–5.*
– PHRASES **pound the beat** (of a police officer) patrol an allocated route or area.
– PHRASAL VERBS **pound something out** produce a text or piece of music with heavy strokes on a keyboard or instrument: *an old typewriter on which she pounded out her poems.*
– ORIGIN Old English *pūnian*; related to Dutch *puin*, Low German *pün* '(building) rubbish'.

pound[3] ▶ noun a place where stray animals, especially dogs, may be officially taken and kept until claimed by their owners. ■ a place where illegally parked motor vehicles removed by the police are kept until their owners pay a fine in order to reclaim them. ■ archaic a place of confinement; a trap or prison.
▶ verb [with obj.] archaic shut (an animal) in a pound.
– ORIGIN late Middle English (earlier in compounds): of uncertain origin. Early use referred to an enclosure for the detention of stray or trespassing cattle.

poundage ▶ noun **1** Brit. a payment of a particular amount per pound sterling of the sum involved in a transaction. ■ a percentage of the total earnings of a business, paid as wages.
2 [mass noun] weight, especially when regarded as excessive: *reduce excess poundage without risking overexertion.*

poundal /ˈpaʊnd(ə)l/ ▶ noun Physics a unit of force equal to that required to give a mass of one pound an acceleration of one foot per second per second.
– ORIGIN late 19th cent.: from POUND[1] + the suffix *-al*, perhaps suggested by QUINTAL.

pound cake ▶ noun N. Amer. a rich cake containing a pound, or equal weights, of each chief ingredient, typically flour, butter, and sugar.

pounder ▶ noun [usu. in combination] **1** a person or thing weighing a specified number of pounds: *Sloan set a blue-shark record with a 184-pounder.* ■ a gun designed to fire a shell weighing a specified number of pounds.
2 a person or thing that pounds something: *he's direct, but not abrasive, not a desk-pounder.*

pounding ▶ noun [mass noun] repeated and heavy striking or hitting of someone or something: *the pounding of the surf on a sandy beach.* ■ rhythmical beating or throbbing: *all she could hear was the pounding of her heart.*
– PHRASES **take** (or **get**) **a pounding** be repeatedly hit or attacked: *the town took a hell of a pounding from the Luftwaffe* | figurative *shares took a pounding this month.*

pound lock ▶ noun fuller term for LOCK[1] (sense 2 of the noun).
– ORIGIN late 18th cent.: *pound* from POUND[3], in the sense 'body of still water, pond'.

pound sign ▶ noun **1** the sign '£', representing a pound sterling.
2 North American term for HASH[3].

pound sterling ▶ noun see POUND[1] (sense 2).

pour ▶ verb [no obj., with adverbial of direction] **1** flow rapidly in a steady stream: *water poured off the roof* | figurative *words poured from his mouth.* ■ [with obj. and adverbial of direction] cause (a liquid) to flow from a container in a steady stream: *she poured a little whisky into a glass* | *the remaining liquid is* ***poured out***. ■ [with obj.] prepare and serve (a drink): *he poured a cup of coffee* | [with two objs] *Harry poured her a drink.* ■ [with obj.] (**pour something into**) contribute money to (an enterprise or project) in copious amounts: *Belgium has been pouring money into the company.* ■ [with obj.] (**pour something out**) express one's feelings in an unrestrained way: *in his letters, Edward poured out his hopes.* ■ [with obj.] (**pour oneself into**) humorous (of a woman) put on (a tight-fitting garment): *I poured myself into a short Lycra skirt.*
2 [no obj.] (of rain) fall heavily: *the storm clouds gathered and the rain* ***poured down*** | *it's pouring with rain.*
3 come or go in a steady stream and in large numbers: *people poured out of the train.*
– PHRASES **it never rains but it pours** proverb misfortunes or difficult situations tend to follow each other in rapid succession or to arrive all at the same time. **pour cold water on** see COLD. **pour it on** N. Amer. informal progress or work quickly or with all one's energy. **pour oil on troubled waters** try to settle a disagreement or dispute with words intended to placate or pacify those involved. **pour scorn on** see SCORN.
– DERIVATIVES **pourable** adjective, **pourer** noun.
– ORIGIN Middle English: of unknown origin.

> **USAGE** On the confusion of **pour** and **pore**, see USAGE at PORE[2].

pourboire /pʊəˈbwɑː/ ▶ noun a gratuity; a tip.
– ORIGIN French, from *pour boire*, literally '(money) for drinking'.

pousada /pəʊˈsɑːdə/ ▶ noun a hotel in Portugal owned and administered by the government.
– ORIGIN Portuguese, literally 'resting place'.

pousse-café /ˌpuːskaˈfeɪ/ ▶ noun (pl. pronunc. **same**) a glass of various liqueurs or cordials poured in successive layers, taken immediately after coffee.
– ORIGIN French, literally 'push coffee'.

Poussin /ˈpuːsã/, French /pusɛ̃/, Nicolas (1594–1665), French painter. He is regarded as the chief representative of French classicism and a master of the grand manner. His subject matter included biblical scenes (*The Adoration of the Golden Calf*, c.1635), classical mythology (*Et in Arcadia Ego*, c.1655), and historical landscapes.

poussin /ˈpuːsã/ ▶ noun a chicken killed young for eating.
– ORIGIN French.

pout[1] ▶ verb [no obj.] push one's lips or one's bottom lip forward as an expression of petulant annoyance or in order to make oneself look sexually attractive: *she lounged on the steps, pouting* | (as adj. **pouting**) *pouting actresses* | [with obj.] *he shrugged and pouted his lips.*
▶ noun a pouting expression: *his lower lip protruded in a sulky pout.*
– DERIVATIVES **poutingly** adverb, **pouty** adjective (**poutier**, **poutiest**).
– ORIGIN Middle English (as a verb): perhaps from the base of Swedish dialect *puta* 'be inflated'. Compare with POUT[2].

pout[2] ▶ noun **1** (also **pouting**) another term for BIB[1] (sense 2).
2 North American term for EELPOUT.
– ORIGIN Old English *pūta* (only in *ǣlepūta* 'eelpout'); related to Dutch *puit* 'frog, chub', *puitaal* 'eelpout', and perhaps to POUT[1].

pouter ▶ noun a kind of pigeon able to inflate its crop considerably.

poutine /puːˈtiːn/ ▶ noun Canadian a dish of potato chips topped with cheese curds and gravy.
– ORIGIN 1980s: Canadian French, either from French *pouding* 'pudding' or directly from PUDDING.

POV ▶ abbreviation point of view.

poverty ▶ noun [mass noun] **1** the state of being extremely poor: *thousands of families are living in abject poverty.* ■ the renunciation of the right to individual ownership of property as part of a religious vow.
2 the state of being inferior in quality or insufficient in amount: *the poverty of her imagination.*
– ORIGIN Middle English: from Old French *poverte*, from Latin *paupertas*, from *pauper* 'poor'.

poverty line ▶ noun the estimated minimum level of income needed to secure the necessities of life.

poverty-stricken ▶ adjective extremely poor.

poverty trap ▶ noun Brit. a situation in which an increase in someone's income is offset by a consequent loss of state benefits, leaving them no better off.

povidone iodine /ˈpɒvɪdəʊn/ ▶ noun [mass noun] Medicine a brown powder used as an antiseptic for external application, consisting of a complex of polyvinylpyrrolidone and iodine.
– ORIGIN 1950s: *povidone*, contraction of POLYVINYLPYRROLIDONE.

POW ▶ abbreviation prisoner of war.

pow ▶ exclamation expressing the sound of a blow or explosion: *Pow! Bombs went off on six beaches at once.*
– ORIGIN late 19th cent. (originally US): imitative.

powan /ˈpəʊwən/ ▶ noun a widely distributed freshwater whitefish of lakes and rivers in northern Eurasia, especially one of a variety occurring only in two Scottish lochs. ● *Coregonus lavaretus*, family Salmonidae. See also GWYNIAD, SCHELLY.
– ORIGIN mid 17th cent.: Scots variant of POLLAN.

powder ▶ noun [mass noun] fine, dry particles produced by the grinding, crushing, or disintegration of a solid substance: *add four tablespoons of cocoa powder* | [count noun] *crush the poppy seeds to a powder.* ■ (also **face powder**) a cosmetic in the form of powder, applied to a person's face with a brush or soft pad. ■ [count noun] dated a medicine or drug in the form of powder, usually designed to be dissolved in a liquid. ■ (also **powder snow**) loose, dry newly fallen snow. ■ gunpowder.
▶ verb [with obj.] **1** apply cosmetic powder to (the face or body): *she powdered her face and put on a dab of perfume.* ■ sprinkle or cover (a surface) with powder or a powdery substance: *broken glass powdered the floor.*
2 reduce (a substance) to a powder by drying or crushing it: *then the rose petals are dried and powdered.*
– PHRASES **keep one's powder dry** remain cautious and ready for a possible emergency. **powder one's nose** euphemistic (of a woman) go to the toilet. **take a powder** N. Amer. informal depart quickly, especially in order to avoid a difficult situation.

– ORIGIN Middle English: from Old French *poudre*, from Latin *pulvis, pulver-* 'dust'.

powder blue ▶ noun [mass noun] a soft, pale blue: [as modifier] *a powder-blue jumpsuit.*

powder-coat ▶ verb [with obj.] cover (an object) with a polyester or epoxy powder, which is then heated to fuse into a protective layer.

powdered ▶ adjective in the form of powder: *powdered milk.*

powdered sugar ▶ noun North American term for ICING SUGAR.

powder flask ▶ noun historical a small container with a nozzle for carrying and dispersing gunpowder.

powder horn ▶ noun historical the horn of an ox, cow, or similar animal used to hold gunpowder, with the wide end filled in and a nozzle at the pointed end.

powder keg ▶ noun a barrel of gunpowder. ■ a dangerous or volatile situation: *the place had been a powder keg since the uprising.*

powder metallurgy ▶ noun [mass noun] the production and working of metals as fine powders which can be pressed and sintered to form objects.

powder monkey ▶ noun historical a boy employed on a sailing warship to carry powder to the guns. ■ N. Amer. a person who works with explosives.

powder-post beetle ▶ noun a small brown beetle whose wood-boring larvae reduce wood to a very fine powder. ● Family Lyctidae: several genera.

powder puff ▶ noun a soft pad for applying powder to the skin, especially the face. ■ informal an ineffectual person or thing: [as modifier] *a powder-puff bowler.*

powder room ▶ noun euphemistic a women's toilet in a public building. ■ N. Amer. a toilet in a domestic house.

powder snow ▶ noun see POWDER.

powdery ▶ adjective resembling or characteristic of powder in texture: *when the package was opened, a powdery white substance fell out.*

powdery mildew ▶ noun [mass noun] mildew on a plant which is marked by a white floury covering consisting of conidia. Compare with DOWNY MILDEW. ● Family Erysiphaceae, subdivision Ascomycotina.

Powell[1] /ˈpəʊəl/, Anthony (Dymoke) (1905–2000), English novelist. He is best known for his sequence of twelve novels *A Dance to the Music of Time* (1951–75), a satirical portrayal of the English upper middle classes between the two World Wars.

Powell[2] /ˈpaʊəl/, (John) Enoch (1912–98), British Conservative and Ulster Unionist politician, noted for his condemnation of multiracial immigration into Britain and his opposition to British entry into the Common Market.

Powell[3] /ˈpaʊəl/, Michael (Latham) (1905–90), English film director, producer, and scriptwriter. He founded The Archers Company with the Hungarian scriptwriter **Emeric Pressburger** (1902–88); their films included *A Matter of Life and Death* (1946) and *The Red Shoes* (1948).

power ▶ noun [mass noun] **1** the ability or capacity to do something or act in a particular way: ***the power of speech*** | *I will* ***do everything in my power*** *to help you* | (**powers**) *his* ***powers of concentration.*** **2** the capacity or ability to direct or influence the behaviour of others or the course of events: *a political process that offers people power over their own lives* | *she had me in her power.* ■ political or social authority or control, especially that exercised by a government: *the party had been in power for eight years.* ■ authority that is given or delegated to a person or body: *police do not have the power to stop and search.* ■ the military strength of a state: *the sea power of Venice.* ■ [count noun] a state or country, especially one viewed in terms of its international influence and military strength: *a great colonial power.* ■ [count noun] a person or organization that is strong or influential within a particular context: *he was a power in the university.* ■ [count noun] a supernatural being, deity, or force: *the powers of darkness.* ■ (**powers**) (in traditional Christian angelology) the sixth-highest order of the ninefold celestial hierarchy. ■ [with modifier] used in the names of movements aiming to enhance the status of a specified group: *gay power.* **3** physical strength and force exerted by something or someone: *the power of the storm* | figurative *the lyrical power of his prose.* ■ capacity or performance of an engine or other device: *a surge of power from the engine.* ■ [as modifier] denoting a sports player, team, or style of play that makes use of power rather than finesse: *a power pitcher.* ■ the magnifying capacity of a lens. **4** energy that is produced by mechanical, electrical, or other means and used to operate a device: *generating power from waste* | [as modifier] *power cables.* ■ electrical energy supplied to an area, building, etc.: *30,000 homes were left without power.* ■ [as modifier] driven by electrical energy: *a power drill.* **5** Physics the rate of doing work, measured in watts or less frequently horse power. **6** Mathematics the product obtained when a number is multiplied by itself a certain number of times: *2* ***to the power of*** *4 equals 16.* **7** (**a power of**) chiefly dialect a large number or amount of something: *there's a power of difference between farming now and when I was a lad.*

▶ verb **1** [with obj.] supply (a device) with mechanical or electrical energy: *the car is powered by a fuel-injected 3.0-litre engine* | (as adj., in combination **-powered**) *a nuclear-powered submarine.* ■ (**power something up/down**) switch a device on or off: *the officer powered up the fighter's radar.* **2** [no obj., with adverbial of direction] move or travel with great speed or force: *he powered round a bend.* ■ [with obj.] direct (something, especially a ball) with great force: *Nicholas powered a header into the net* | *Nicholas powered a header into the net.*

– PHRASES **do someone/thing a power of good** informal be very beneficial to someone or something. **in the power of** under the control of: *what happens to them is in the power of the management.* **more power to your elbow!** (or **to you** etc.) Brit. used to encourage someone or express approval of their actions. **power behind the throne** a person who exerts authority or influence without having formal status. **the powers that be** the authorities. [with biblical allusion to Rom. 13:1.]

– ORIGIN Middle English: from Anglo-Norman French *poeir*, from an alteration of Latin *posse* 'be able'.

power-assisted ▶ adjective (especially of steering or brakes in a motor vehicle) using an inanimate source of power to assist manual operation.

power base ▶ noun a source of authority, influence, or support, especially in politics or negotiations: *the party's power base was confined to one province.*

powerboat ▶ noun a fast motor boat designed for racing or recreation.
– DERIVATIVES **powerboating** noun.

power breakfast ▶ noun a meeting between powerful politicians, executives, etc., held early in the morning while they eat breakfast.

power broker ▶ noun a person who deliberately affects the distribution of political or economic power by exerting influence or by intrigue.
– DERIVATIVES **power-broking** noun & adjective.

power cut ▶ noun Brit. a temporary withdrawal or failure of an electrical power supply.

power dive ▶ noun a steep dive of an aircraft with the engines providing thrust.
▶ verb (**power-dive**) [no obj.] perform a power dive.

power dressing ▶ noun [mass noun] the practice of dressing in a style intended to show that one holds an important position in business, politics, etc.

power factor ▶ noun the ratio of the actual electrical power dissipated by an AC circuit to the product of the r.m.s. values of current and voltage. The difference between the two is caused by reactance in the circuit and represents power that does no useful work.

power forward ▶ noun Basketball a large forward who plays in the area near the opposing team's basket.

powerful ▶ adjective having great power or strength: *a fast, powerful car* | *computers are now more compact and powerful.* ■ having control and influence over people and events: *the world's most powerful nation.* ■ having a strong effect on people's feelings or thoughts: *his photomontages are powerful anti-war images.*
▶ adverb [as submodifier] chiefly dialect very: *walking is powerful hot work.*
– DERIVATIVES **powerfully** adverb, **powerfulness** noun.

powerhead ▶ noun a part of an engine or other device that supplies power.

powerhouse ▶ noun **1** a person or thing of great energy, strength, or power. **2** dated or US another term for POWER STATION.

power law ▶ noun Mathematics a relationship between two quantities such that one is proportional to a fixed power of the other.

powerless ▶ adjective [often with infinitive] without ability, influence, or power: *troops were powerless to stop last night's shooting.*
– DERIVATIVES **powerlessly** adverb, **powerlessness** noun.

powerlifting ▶ noun [mass noun] a form of competitive weightlifting in which contestants attempt three types of lift in a set sequence.
– DERIVATIVES **powerlifter** noun.

power line ▶ noun a cable carrying electrical power, especially one supported by pylons or poles.

power lunch ▶ noun a working lunch, especially one at which powerful politicians, executives, etc. hold important discussions.

power nap ▶ noun a short sleep taken during the working day in order to restore one's mental alertness.

power of attorney ▶ noun [mass noun] Law the authority to act for another person in specified or all legal or financial matters.

power pack ▶ noun a self-contained and typically transportable unit which stores and supplies electrical power. ■ a transformer for converting an alternating current (from the mains) to a direct current at a different (usually lower) voltage.

power plant ▶ noun another term for POWER STATION. ■ an engine or other apparatus which provides power for a machine, building, etc.

power play ▶ noun [mass noun] **1** tactics exhibiting or intended to increase a person's power or influence: *the sexual power play of their relationship.* **2** offensive tactics in a team sport involving the concentration of players at a particular point. **3** [count noun] Ice Hockey a temporary situation in which a team has a numerical advantage over its opponents because one or more players is serving a penalty.

PowerPoint ▶ noun trademark a software package designed to create electronic presentations consisting of a series of separate pages or slides.

power politics ▶ plural noun [treated as sing. or pl.] political action by a person or group which makes use of or is intended to increase their power or influence.

power pop ▶ noun [mass noun] a style of pop music characterized by a strong melody line, heavy use of guitars, and simple rhythm.

power series ▶ noun Mathematics an infinite series of the form $\Sigma a_n x^n$ (where *n* is a positive integer). ■ a generalization of this for more than one variable.

power-sharing ▶ noun [mass noun] a policy agreed between political parties or within a coalition to share responsibility for decision-making and political action.

power shovel ▶ noun a mechanical excavator.

power shower ▶ noun a shower using an electric pump to produce a high-pressure spray.

power slide ▶ noun a deliberate controlled skid in a vehicle, performed in order to turn corners at high speed.

power spectrum ▶ noun Physics the distribution of the energy of a waveform among its different frequency components.

power station ▶ noun an installation where electrical power is generated for distribution.

power steering ▶ noun [mass noun] power-assisted steering on a motor vehicle.

power stroke ▶ noun the stage of the cycle of an internal-combustion engine in which the piston is driven outward by the expansion of gases.

power take-off ▶ noun a device which transfers mechanical power from an engine to another piece of equipment, especially on a tractor or similar vehicle.

power train ▶ noun the mechanism that transmits the drive from the engine of a vehicle to its axle. ■ this mechanism, the engine, and the axle considered collectively.

power-up ▶ noun **1** [mass noun] the action of switching on an electrical device, especially a computer. **2** (in a computer game) a bonus which a player can collect and which gives their character an advantage such as more strength or firepower.

power user ▶ noun Computing a knowledgeable and sophisticated user of computers.

power walking ▶ noun [mass noun] brisk walking as a form of aerobic exercise.
– DERIVATIVES **power-walk** noun & verb, **power-walker** noun.

P

Powhatan /ˈpaʊətan/ ▶ **noun** (pl. **same** or **Powhatans**) **1** a member of an American Indian people of eastern Virginia.
2 [mass noun] the extinct Algonquian language of the Powhatan.
▶ **adjective** relating to the Powhatan or their language.
– ORIGIN Virginia Algonquian.

powwow ▶ **noun 1** a North American Indian ceremony involving feasting and dancing.
2 a conference or meeting for discussion, especially among friends or colleagues.
▶ **verb** [no obj.] informal hold a powwow; confer: *news squads powwowed nervously*.
– ORIGIN early 17th cent.: from Narragansett *powah, powwaw* 'magician' (literally 'he dreams').

Powys /ˈpaʊɪs, ˈpaʊ-/ a county of east central Wales, on the border with England, formed in 1974 from the former counties of Montgomeryshire, Radnorshire, and most of Breconshire; administrative centre, Llandrindod Wells. ■ a former Welsh kingdom. At its most powerful in the early 12th century, Powys was conquered by the English in 1284.

pox ▶ **noun** any of several viral diseases producing a rash of pimples that become pus-filled and leave pockmarks on healing. ■ **(the pox)** informal syphilis. ■ **(the pox)** historical smallpox.
– PHRASES **a pox on** archaic used as a curse: *a pox on both their houses!*
– ORIGIN late Middle English: alteration of *pocks*, plural of POCK.

poxvirus ▶ **noun** Medicine any of a group of large DNA viruses that cause smallpox and similar infectious diseases in vertebrates.

poxy ▶ **adjective (poxier, poxiest)** informal, chiefly Brit. of poor quality; worthless: *they've won one poxy trophy*.

Pozidriv /ˈpɒzɪdrʌɪv/ (US **Poz-i-Driv**) ▶ **noun** trademark a type of cross-head screwdriver with a smaller ridge bisecting each quarter of the cross.

Poznań /ˈpɒznaɲ/ a city in NW Poland; pop. 564,035 (2007). An area of German colonization since the 13th century, it was the centre of Polish power in the 15th–17th centuries, but passed to Prussia in 1793. It was under German control almost continuously until the First World War, and was overrun by the Germans again in 1939. German name POSEN.

Pozsony Hungarian /ˈpoʒoɲ/ Hungarian name for BRATISLAVA.

pozzolana /ˌpɒtsəˈlɑːnə/ ▶ **noun** [mass noun] a type of volcanic ash used for mortar or for cement that sets under water.
– ORIGIN early 18th cent.: from Italian, from *pozz(u)olana* '(earth) of Pozzuoli', a town near Naples.

P

pp ▶ **abbreviation** ■ **(pp.)** pages: *pp. 71–73*. ■ (also **p.p.**) per procurationem (used when signing a letter on someone else's behalf). [Latin.] ■ Music pianissimo.

> **USAGE** The traditional way to use **pp** when signing a letter on someone else's behalf is to place **pp** before one's own name rather than before the name of the other person. This is because the original Latin phrase **per procurationem** means 'through the agency of'. However, **pp** is now often taken to mean 'on behalf of' and is placed before the name of the person who has not signed, and this has become standard practice in many offices.

PPARC ▶ **abbreviation** (in the UK) Particle Physics and Astronomy Research Council.

PPE ▶ **abbreviation** philosophy, politics, and economics (a degree course at Oxford University).

ppi ▶ **abbreviation** Computing pixels per inch, a measure of the resolution of display screens, scanners, and printers.

ppl ▶ **abbreviation** informal people.

ppm ▶ **abbreviation** ■ part(s) per million: *water containing 1 ppm fluoride*. ■ Computing page(s) per minute, a measure of the speed of printers.

PPP ▶ **abbreviation** ■ Pakistan People's Party. ■ Computing point to point protocol, which allows data conforming to the Internet protocol IP to be handled on a serial line. ■ purchasing power parity (a way of measuring what an amount of money will buy in different countries). ■ Brit. public-private partnership, an arrangement whereby a public project or service is partially financed or run by a private company.

PPS ▶ **abbreviation** ■ additional postscript: *PS Those photos are ghastly! PPS Can I have your other address?* ■ Brit. Parliamentary Private Secretary.

PPU ▶ **abbreviation** Peace Pledge Union.

PPV ▶ **abbreviation** pay-per-view.

PQ ▶ **abbreviation** ■ Parti Québécois. ■ Province of Quebec.

PR ▶ **abbreviation** ■ proportional representation. ■ public relations. ■ N. Amer. Puerto Rico.

Pr ▶ **symbol** the chemical element praseodymium.

pr ▶ **abbreviation** ■ pair: *patterned gloves, £7.99/pr*. ■ archaic per: *$6 pr day*.

PRA ▶ **abbreviation** progressive retinal atrophy (a disease afflicting dogs).

practicability ▶ **noun** [mass noun] the quality of being practicable; viability: *the practicability of his ideas has nothing to do with their truth*.

practicable ▶ **adjective** able to be done or put into practice successfully: *the measures will be put into effect as soon as is reasonably practicable*. ■ able to be used; useful: *signal processing can let you transform a signal into a practicable form*.
– DERIVATIVES **practicably** adverb.
– ORIGIN mid 17th cent.: from French *praticable*, from *pratiquer* 'put into practice'.

practical ▶ **adjective 1** of or concerned with the actual doing or use of something rather than with theory and ideas: *there are two obvious practical applications of the research*.
2 (of an idea, plan, or method) likely to succeed or be effective in real circumstances; feasible: *neither of these strategies are practical for smaller businesses*. ■ suitable for a particular purpose: *a practical, stylish kitchen*. ■ (of a person) sensible and realistic in their approach to a situation or problem: *I'm merely being practical—we must find a ground-floor flat*. ■ (of a person) skilled at manual tasks: *Steve'll fix it—he's quite practical*.
3 so nearly the case that it can be regarded as so; virtual: ***for all practical purposes**, she's his girlfriend*.
▶ **noun** Brit. an examination or lesson in which theories and procedures learned are applied to the actual making or doing of something.
– ORIGIN late 16th cent.: from archaic *practic* 'practical' (from Old French *practique*, via late Latin from Greek *praktikos* 'concerned with action', from *prattein* 'do, act') + -AL.

practicality ▶ **noun** (pl. **practicalities**) **1** [mass noun] the quality or state of being practical: *there are still major doubts about the practicality of the proposal*.
2 (practicalities) the aspects of a situation that involve the actual doing or experience of something rather than theories or ideas: *the practicalities of living at sea*.

practical joke ▶ **noun** a trick played on someone in order to make them look foolish and to amuse others.
– DERIVATIVES **practical joker** noun.

practically ▶ **adverb 1** virtually; almost: *the strike lasted practically a fortnight | the place was practically empty*.
2 in a practical manner.

practical nurse ▶ **noun** (in North America) a nurse who has completed a training course of a lower standard than a registered nurse.

practice ▶ **noun** [mass noun] **1** the actual application or use of an idea, belief, or method, as opposed to theories relating to it: *the principles and practice of teaching | the recommendations proved too expensive to **put into practice***. ■ the carrying out or exercise of a profession, especially that of a doctor or lawyer: *he abandoned medical practice for the Church*. ■ [count noun] the business or premises of a doctor or lawyer: *Dr Apps has a practice in Neasham Road*.
2 the customary, habitual, or expected procedure or way of doing of something: *product placement is common practice in American movies* | [count noun] *modern child-rearing practices*. ■ an established method of legal procedure.
3 repeated exercise in or performance of an activity or skill so as to acquire or maintain proficiency in it: *it must have taken a lot of practice to become so fluent*. ■ [count noun] a period of time spent doing this: *daily choir practices*.
▶ **verb** US spelling of PRACTISE.
– PHRASES **in practice 1** in reality (used to refer to what actually happens as opposed to what is meant or believed to happen): *in theory this method is ideal—in practice it is unrealistic*. **2** currently proficient in a particular activity or skill as a result of repeated exercise or performance of it. **out of practice** not currently proficient in a particular activity or skill through not having exercised or performed it for some time: *he was out of practice at interrogation*. **practice makes perfect** regular exercise of an activity or skill is the way to become proficient in it.
– ORIGIN late Middle English: from PRACTISE, on the pattern of pairs such as *advise, advice*.

> **USAGE** Care should be taken with the use of the words **practice** and **practise** as there are differences in British and US usage. **Practice** is the correct spelling for the noun in both British and US English and it is also the spelling of the verb in US English. However, in British English the verb should be spelled **practise**.

practician ▶ **noun** archaic a person who practises a profession or occupation, especially a practical one; a practitioner.
– ORIGIN late 15th cent.: from Old French *practicien*, from *practique* 'practical' (see PRACTICAL).

practicum /ˈpraktɪkəm/ ▶ **noun** (pl. **practicums**) chiefly N. Amer. a practical section of a course of study.
– ORIGIN early 20th cent.: from late Latin, neuter of *practicus* 'practical'.

practise (US **practice**) ▶ **verb** [with obj.] **1** perform (an activity) or exercise (a skill) repeatedly or regularly in order to acquire, improve or maintain proficiency in it: *I need to practise my French* | [no obj.] *they were practising for the Olympics*.
2 carry out or perform (a particular activity, method, or custom) habitually or regularly: *we still practise some of these rituals today*. ■ actively pursue or be engaged in (a particular profession or occupation): *he began to practise law* | [no obj.] *he practised as a barrister* | (as adj. **practising**) *a practising architect*. ■ observe the teaching and rules of (a particular religion): (as adj. **practising**) *a practising Roman Catholic*.
3 [no obj.] archaic scheme or plot for an evil purpose: *what a tangled web we weave when we first practise to deceive*.
– PHRASES **practise what one preaches** do what one advises others to do.
– DERIVATIVES **practiser** noun.
– ORIGIN late Middle English: from Old French *practiser* or medieval Latin *practizare*, alteration of *practicare* 'perform, carry out', from *practica* 'practice', from Greek *praktikē*, feminine (used as a noun), of *praktikos* (see PRACTICAL).

> **USAGE** On the difference between **practise** and **practice**, see USAGE at PRACTICE.

practised (US **practiced**) ▶ **adjective** expert, typically as the result of much experience: *admiring the dress with a practised eye | the waiter was practised at disrupting moments of intimacy*.

practitioner ▶ **noun** a person actively engaged in an art, discipline, or profession, especially medicine: *patients are treated by skilled practitioners*.
– ORIGIN mid 16th cent.: extension of obsolete *practitian*, variant of PRACTICIAN.

prad ▶ **noun** informal, chiefly Austral./NZ a horse.
– ORIGIN late 18th cent.: altered form of Dutch *paard* 'horse'.

Prader–Willi syndrome /ˌprɑːdəˈvɪli/ ▶ **noun** [mass noun] a rare congenital disorder characterized by learning difficulties, growth abnormalities, and obsessive eating, caused especially by the absence of certain genes normally present on the copy of chromosome 15 inherited from the father.
– ORIGIN 1960s: named after Andrea *Prader* (born 1919) and Heinrich *Willi* (1900–71), Swiss paediatricians.

Prado /ˈprɑːdəʊ/ the Spanish national art gallery in Madrid, established in 1818.

prae- ▶ **prefix** (used especially in words regarded as Latin or relating to Roman antiquity) equivalent to PRE-.
– ORIGIN from Latin.

praecipe /ˈpriːsɪpi/ ▶ **noun** Law an order requesting a writ or other legal document. ■ historical a writ demanding action or an explanation of non-action.
– ORIGIN Latin (the first word of the writ), imperative of *praecipere* 'enjoin, command'. See also PRECEPT.

praemunire /ˌpriːmjuːˈnʌɪri/ ▶ **noun** [mass noun] historical the offence of asserting or maintaining papal jurisdiction in England. ■ [count noun] a writ charging a sheriff to summon a person accused of this offence.
– ORIGIN late Middle English: from medieval Latin, 'forewarn', from Latin *praemonere*, from *prae* 'beforehand' + *monere* 'warn'. The term comes from *praemunire facias* 'that you warn (a person to appear)', part of the wording in the writ.

praenomen /priːˈnəʊmɛn/ ▶ **noun** an ancient Roman's first or personal name, for example *Marcus* Tullius Cicero.
– ORIGIN Latin, from *prae* 'before' + *nomen* 'name'.

praepostor /prɪˈpɒstə/ ▶ **noun** Brit. (at some public schools) a prefect or monitor.
– ORIGIN mid 18th cent.: from *praepositor*, alteration of Latin *praepositus* 'head, chief', past participle of *praeponere* 'set over', from *prae* 'ahead' + *ponere* 'to place'.

Praesepe /prʌɪˈsiːpi/ Astronomy a large open cluster of stars in the constellation Cancer, the Beehive.
– ORIGIN Latin, literally 'manger, hive'.

praesidium ▶ **noun** variant spelling of PRESIDIUM.

praetor /ˈpriːtə, ˈpriːtɔː/ (US also **pretor**) ▶ **noun** Roman History each of two ancient Roman magistrates ranking below consul.
– DERIVATIVES **praetorship** noun.
– ORIGIN Latin, perhaps from *prae* 'before' + *it-* 'gone' (from the verb *ire*).

praetorian (US also **pretorian**) ▶ **adjective** Roman History of or having the powers of a praetor.
▶ **noun** a man of praetorian rank.

praetorian guard ▶ **noun** Roman History the bodyguard of the Roman emperor.

pragmatic ▶ **adjective** dealing with things sensibly and realistically in a way that is based on practical rather than theoretical considerations: *a pragmatic approach to politics*. ■ relating to philosophical or political pragmatism. ■ Linguistics relating to pragmatics.
– DERIVATIVES **pragmatically** adverb.
– ORIGIN late 16th cent. (in the senses 'busy, interfering, conceited'): via Latin from Greek *pragmatikos* 'relating to fact', from *pragma* 'deed' (from the stem of *prattein* 'do'). The current senses date from the mid 19th cent.

pragmatics ▶ **plural noun** [usu. treated as sing.] the branch of linguistics dealing with language in use and the contexts in which it is used, including such matters as deixis, the taking of turns in conversation, text organization, presupposition, and implicature.

pragmatic sanction ▶ **noun** historical an imperial or royal decree that has the force of law. ■ (**Pragmatic Sanction**) a document drafted in 1717 by the Emperor Charles VI providing for his daughter Maria Theresa to succeed to all his territories should he die without a son. Opposition to it led to the War of the Austrian Succession on Charles's death in 1740.
– ORIGIN translating Law Latin *pragmatica sanctio*.

pragmatism ▶ **noun** [mass noun] **1** a pragmatic attitude or policy: *ideology had been tempered with pragmatism*.
2 Philosophy an approach that evaluates theories or beliefs in terms of the success of their practical application.
– DERIVATIVES **pragmatist** noun, **pragmatistic** adjective.
– ORIGIN mid 19th cent.: from Greek *pragma*, *pragmat-* 'deed' (see PRAGMATIC) + -ISM.

Prague /prɑːg/ the capital of the Czech Republic, in the north east on the River Vltava; pop. 1,196,454 (2007). Czech name **Praha**.

> Prague was the capital of Czechoslovakia from 1918 until the partition of 1993. The capital of Bohemia from the 14th century, it was the scene of much religious conflict. In 1618 Protestant citizens threw Catholic officials from the windows of Hradčany Castle, an event, known as the **Defenestration of Prague**, which contributed to the outbreak of the Thirty Years War.

Prague School a group of linguists established in Prague in 1926 who developed distinctive feature theory in phonology and communicative dynamism in language teaching. Leading members were Nikolai Trubetzkoy (1890–1938) and Roman Jakobson.

Prague Spring a brief period of liberalization in Czechoslovakia, ending in August 1968, during which a programme of political, economic, and cultural reform was initiated.

Praha /ˈprɑːhɑː/ Czech name for PRAGUE.

prahu /ˈprɑːuː/ ▶ **noun** variant spelling of PROA.

Praia /ˈprʌɪə/ the capital of the Cape Verde Islands, a port on the island of São Tiago; pop. 126,000 (est. 2007).

Prairial /ˈprɛːrɪəl/, French /prɛrjal/ ▶ **noun** the ninth month of the French Republican calendar (1793–1805), originally running from 20 May to 18 June.
– ORIGIN French, from *prairie* 'meadow'.

prairie ▶ **noun 1** a large open area of grassland, especially in North America.
2 (**Prairie**) [often as modifier] a steam locomotive of 2-6-2 wheel arrangement.
– ORIGIN late 18th cent.: from French, from Old French *praerie*, from Latin *pratum* 'meadow'.

prairie chicken (also **prairie hen**) ▶ **noun** a large North American grouse found on the prairies, the male being noted for the display dance in which it inflates two orange neck pouches and makes a booming sound. ● Genus *Tympanuchus*, family Tetraonidae: two species.

prairie dog ▶ **noun** a gregarious ground squirrel that lives in interconnected burrows which may cover many hectares, native to the grasslands of North America. ● Genus *Cynomys*, family Sciuridae: several species.

prairie-dogging ▶ **noun** [mass noun] humorous the practice of workers in an open-plan office raising their heads above the partitions surrounding their desks when they hear a loud voice or other noise.
– ORIGIN 1990s: prairie dogs are known for frequently standing on their hind legs to look around for danger.

prairie oyster ▶ **noun 1** a drink made with a raw egg and seasoning, drunk as a cure for a hangover.
2 (**prairie oysters**) chiefly N. Amer. the testicles of a calf cooked and served as food.

prairie schooner ▶ **noun** N. Amer. a covered wagon used by the 19th-century pioneers in crossing the North American prairies.

Prairie State informal name for ILLINOIS.

prairie wolf ▶ **noun** North American term for COYOTE.

prairie wool ▶ **noun** [mass noun] Canadian the natural grassy plant cover of prairie land.

praise ▶ **verb** [with obj.] **1** express warm approval or admiration of: *we can't praise Chris enough—he did a brilliant job*.
2 express one's respect and gratitude towards (a deity), especially in song: *we praise God for past blessings*.
▶ **noun** [mass noun] (also **praises**) **1** the expression of approval or admiration for someone or something: *the audience was full of praise for the whole production*.
2 the expression of respect and gratitude as an act of worship: *give praise to God*.
– PHRASES **praise be** archaic used as an expression of relief, joy, or gratitude. **sing the praises of** express enthusiastic approval or admiration of: *Uncle Felix never stopped singing her praises*.
– DERIVATIVES **praiseful** adjective, **praiser** noun.
– ORIGIN Middle English (also in the sense 'set a price on, attach value to'): from Old French *preisier* 'to prize, praise', from late Latin *pretiare*, from Latin *pretium* 'price'. Compare with PRIZE¹.

praise singer (also **praise poet**) ▶ **noun** S. African another term for IMBONGI.

praiseworthy ▶ **adjective** deserving approval and admiration: *the government's praiseworthy efforts*.
– DERIVATIVES **praiseworthily** adverb, **praiseworthiness** noun.

prajna /ˈpraʒnə/ ▶ **noun** [mass noun] Buddhism direct insight into the truth taught by the Buddha, as a faculty required to attain enlightenment.
– ORIGIN from Sanskrit *prajñā*.

Prakrit /ˈprɑːkrɪt/ ▶ **noun** any of the ancient or medieval vernacular dialects of north and central India which existed alongside or were derived from Sanskrit.
– ORIGIN from Sanskrit *prākṛta* 'unrefined, natural'. Compare with SANSKRIT.

praline /ˈprɑːliːn, ˈpreɪliːn/ ▶ **noun** [mass noun] a smooth, sweet substance made by boiling nuts in sugar and grinding the mixture, used especially as a filling for chocolates. ■ [count noun] a chocolate filled with praline.
– ORIGIN early 18th cent.: from French, named after Marshal de Plessis-*Praslin* (1598–1675), the French soldier whose cook invented it.

pralltriller /ˈprɑːl,trɪlə/ ▶ **noun** Music an ornament consisting of one rapid alternation of the written note with the note immediately above it.
– ORIGIN mid 19th cent.: from German, from *prallen* 'rebound' + *Triller* 'a trill'.

pram¹ /pram/ ▶ **noun** Brit. a four-wheeled carriage for a baby, pushed by a person on foot.
– ORIGIN late 19th cent.: contracted abbreviation of PERAMBULATOR.

pram² /prɑːm, pram/ ▶ **noun** a flat-bottomed sailing boat. ■ US a small flat-bottomed rowing boat for fishing.
– ORIGIN late Middle English: from Middle Dutch *prame*, Middle Low German *prāme*, perhaps from Czech *prám* 'raft'.

prana /ˈprɑːnə/ ▶ **noun** [mass noun] Hinduism breath, considered as a life-giving force.
– ORIGIN Sanskrit.

pranam /prəˈnɑːm/ ▶ **noun** [mass noun] (in South Asia) a respectful greeting made by putting one's palms together and often touching the feet of the person greeted: *she joined her palms in pranam*.
– ORIGIN from Hindi *praṇām*.

pranayama /,prɑːnʌˈjɑːmə/ ▶ **noun** [mass noun] (in yoga) the regulation of the breath through certain techniques and exercises.
– ORIGIN Sanskrit, from *prāṇa* 'breath' + *āyāma* 'restraint'.

prance ▶ **verb** [no obj., with adverbial of direction] (of a horse) move with high springy steps: *the pony was prancing around the paddock*. ■ (of a person) walk or move around with ostentatious, exaggerated movements: *she pranced around the lounge impersonating her favourite pop stars*.
▶ **noun** an act or instance of prancing.
– DERIVATIVES **prancer** noun.
– ORIGIN late Middle English (as a verb): of unknown origin.

prandial /ˈprandɪəl/ ▶ **adjective** formal or humorous during or relating to dinner or lunch. ■ Medicine during or relating to the eating of food.
– ORIGIN early 19th cent.: from Latin *prandium* 'meal' + -AL.

Prandtl /ˈprant(ə)l/, Ludwig (1875–1953), German physicist. He established the existence of the boundary layer and made important studies on streamlining.

Prandtl number ▶ **noun** Physics a dimensionless parameter used in calculations of heat transfer between a moving fluid and a solid body, equal to $c_p v/k$, where c_p is the heat capacity per unit volume of the fluid, v its kinematic viscosity, and k its thermal conductivity.

prang Brit. informal ▶ **verb** [with obj.] crash (a motor vehicle or aircraft). ■ dated bomb (a target) successfully from the air.
▶ **noun** a crash involving a motor vehicle or aircraft. ■ dated a bombing raid.
– ORIGIN 1940s: imitative.

prank ▶ **noun** a practical joke or mischievous act.
– DERIVATIVES **prankish** adjective, **prankishness** noun.
– ORIGIN early 16th cent. (denoting a wicked deed): of unknown origin.

prankster ▶ **noun** a person fond of playing pranks.

P

prasad /prʌˈsɑːd/ ▶ **noun** Hinduism a devotional offering made to a god, typically consisting of food that is later shared among devotees.
– ORIGIN from Sanskrit *prasāda* 'clearness, kindness, grace'.

prase /preɪz/ ▶ **noun** [mass noun] a translucent leek-green variety of quartz.
– ORIGIN late 18th cent.: from French, via Latin from Greek *prasios* 'leek-green', from *prason* 'leek'.

praseodymium /,preɪzɪə(ʊ)ˈdɪmɪəm/ ▶ **noun** [mass noun] the chemical element of atomic number 59, a soft silvery-white metal of the lanthanide series. (Symbol: **Pr**)
– ORIGIN late 19th cent.: modern Latin, from German *Praseodym*, from Greek *prasios* 'leek-green' (because of its green salts) + German *Didym* 'didymium'.

prat ▶ **noun** informal **1** Brit. an incompetent or stupid person; an idiot.
2 a person's buttocks.
– ORIGIN mid 16th cent. (in sense 2): of unknown origin. Sense 1 dates from the 1960s.

prate ▶ **verb** [no obj.] talk foolishly or at tedious length about something: *I sat in my pew and heard him prate on for at least an hour and a half*.
– DERIVATIVES **prater** noun (rare).
– ORIGIN late Middle English: from Middle Dutch, Middle Low German *praten*, probably of imitative origin.

pratfall ▶ **noun** informal a fall on to one's buttocks: *he took a pratfall into the sand*. ■ an embarrassing failure or mistake: *the first political pratfalls of the new administration*.

pratie /ˈpreɪti/ ▶ **noun** chiefly Irish a potato.
– ORIGIN late 18th cent.: from Irish *prátaí*, plural of *práta*.

pratincole /ˈpratɪŋkəʊl/ ▶ noun a long-winged fork-tailed insectivorous bird related to the plovers, resembling a swallow in flight and typically living near water. ● Genus *Glareola* (and *Stiltia*), family Glareolidae: several species, in particular *G. pratincola* of Africa and the Mediterranean.
– ORIGIN late 18th cent.: from modern Latin *pratincola*, from Latin *pratum* 'meadow' + *incola* 'inhabitant'.

pratique /ˈpratɪk/ ▶ noun [mass noun] historical permission granted to a ship to have dealings with a port, given after quarantine or on showing a clean bill of health.
– ORIGIN early 17th cent.: from French, literally 'practice', via Italian from medieval Latin *practica*, feminine (used as a noun) of *practicus* 'practical'.

Prato /ˈprɑːtəʊ/ a city in west central Italy, north-west of Florence; pop. 185,091 (2008).

prattle ▶ verb [no obj.] talk at length in a foolish or inconsequential way: *she began to* ***prattle on*** *about her visit to the dentist.*
▶ noun [mass noun] foolish or inconsequential talk: *do you intend to keep up this childish prattle?*
– DERIVATIVES **prattler** noun.
– ORIGIN mid 16th cent.: from Middle Low German *pratelen*, from *praten* (see PRATE).

prau ▶ noun variant spelling of PROA.

Pravda /ˈprɑːvdə/ a Russian daily newspaper, founded in 1912 and from 1918 to 1991 the official organ of the Soviet Communist Party.
– ORIGIN Russian, literally 'truth'.

prawn ▶ noun a marine crustacean which resembles a large shrimp. ● *Leander* and other genera, class Malacostraca. See also DUBLIN BAY PRAWN, KING PRAWN.
– PHRASES **don't come the raw prawn with me** see RAW.
– ORIGIN late Middle English: of unknown origin.

prawn cracker ▶ noun (in Chinese cooking) a light crisp made from rice or tapioca flour with prawn flavouring, which puffs up when deep-fried.

prawner ▶ noun a boat used for fishing for prawns.
– DERIVATIVES **prawning** noun.

praxis /ˈpraksɪs/ ▶ noun [mass noun] formal **1** practice, as distinguished from theory: *modern political praxis is now thoroughly permeated with a productivist ethos.* **2** accepted practice or custom: *patterns of Christian praxis in Church and society.*
– ORIGIN late 16th cent.: via medieval Latin from Greek, literally 'doing', from *prattein* 'do'.

Praxiteles /prakˈsɪtəliːz/ (mid 4th century BC), Athenian sculptor. Only one of his works, *Hermes Carrying the Infant Dionysus*, survives. He is also noted for a statue of Aphrodite, of which there are only Roman copies.

P

pray ▶ verb [no obj.] address a prayer to God or another deity: *the whole family are* ***praying for*** *Michael.* ■ wish or hope strongly for a particular outcome or situation: *after several days of rain, we were* ***praying for*** *sun* | [with clause] *I prayed that James wouldn't notice.*
▶ adverb formal or archaic used as a preface to polite requests or instructions: *ladies and gentlemen, pray be seated.* ■ used as a way of adding ironic or sarcastic emphasis to a question: *and what, pray, was the purpose of that?*
– ORIGIN Middle English (in the sense 'ask earnestly'): from Old French *preier*, from late Latin *precare*, alteration of Latin *precari* 'entreat'.

prayer /prɛː/ ▶ noun a solemn request for help or expression of thanks addressed to God or another deity: *I'll say a prayer for him* | [mass noun] *the peace of God is ours through prayer.* ■ (**prayers**) a religious service, especially a regular one, at which people gather in order to pray together: *500 people were detained as they attended Friday prayers.* ■ an earnest hope or wish: *it is our prayer that the current progress on human rights will be sustained.*
– PHRASES **not have a prayer** informal have no chance at all of succeeding at something.
– ORIGIN Middle English: from Old French *preiere*, based on Latin *precarius* 'obtained by entreaty', from *prex, prec-* 'prayer'.

prayer beads ▶ plural noun a string of beads used to keep count while uttering prayers.

prayer book ▶ noun a book containing the forms of prayer regularly used in Christian worship, especially a Book of Common Prayer.

prayer flag ▶ noun (especially in Tibetan Buddhism) a flag on which prayers are inscribed.

prayerful ▶ adjective characterized by or expressive of prayer: *the church has a prayerful atmosphere.* ■ (of a person) given to praying; devout.
– DERIVATIVES **prayerfully** adverb, **prayerfulness** noun.

prayer mat (also **prayer rug**) ▶ noun a small carpet used by Muslims for kneeling on when praying.

prayer meeting ▶ noun (especially among Nonconformists) a religious gathering or service during which prayers are offered.

Prayer of Manasses /məˈnasiːz/ a book of the Apocrypha consisting of a penitential prayer put into the mouth of Manasseh, king of Judah.

prayer plant ▶ noun a Brazilian plant with variegated leaves which are erect at night but lie flat during the day, grown as a houseplant. ● *Maranta leuconeura*, family Marantaceae.

prayer shawl ▶ noun Judaism another term for TALLITH.

prayer stick ▶ noun a stick decorated with feathers, used by various American Indian peoples in their religious ceremonies.

prayer wheel ▶ noun a small revolving cylinder inscribed with or containing prayers, a revolution of which symbolizes the repetition of a prayer, used by Tibetan Buddhists.

praying mantis ▶ noun see MANTIS.

praziquantel /ˌprazɪˈkwantəl, ˌpreɪzɪˈkwɒntəl/ ▶ noun [mass noun] Medicine a synthetic anthelmintic drug used in the treatment of schistosomiasis and other infestations of humans and animals with parasitic trematodes or cestodes.
– ORIGIN 1970s: from *p(y)razi(ne)* + *-quantel* (perhaps from elements of QUINOLINE and ANTHELMINTIC).

PRC ▶ abbreviation People's Republic of China.

pre ▶ preposition previous to; before: *the tree was almost certainly planted pre 1700.*
– ORIGIN 1960s: independent usage of PRE-.

pre- ▶ prefix before (in time, place, order, degree, or importance): *pre-adolescent* | *precaution* | *precede.*
– ORIGIN from Latin *prae-*.

preach ▶ verb [no obj.] deliver a sermon or religious address to an assembled group of people, typically in church: *he preached to a large congregation* | [with obj.] *our pastor will preach the sermon* | (as noun **preaching**) *large numbers of people would come to hear his preaching.* ■ [with obj.] publicly proclaim or teach (a religious message or belief): *he preached the word of God.* ■ [with obj.] earnestly advocate (a belief or course of action): *my parents have always preached toleration and moderation.* ■ give moral advice to someone in a pompously self-righteous way: *viewers want to be entertained, not* ***preached at.***
– PHRASES **preach to the converted** advocate something to people who already share one's convictions about its merits or importance.
– ORIGIN Middle English: from Old French *prechier*, from Latin *praedicare* 'proclaim', in ecclesiastical Latin 'preach', from *prae* 'before' + *dicare* 'declare'.

preacher ▶ noun a person who preaches, especially a minister of religion.
– ORIGIN Middle English: from Old French *precheor*, from ecclesiastical Latin *praedicator*, from the verb *praedicare* (see PREACH).

preacher bench ▶ noun an apparatus on which weightlifting exercises are performed, having a seat and a padded bar at chest height to support the arms.

preachify ▶ verb (**preachifies, preachifying, preachified**) [no obj.] informal preach or moralize tediously: *he's a fund-raiser as well as a minister, but he's a preacher who doesn't preachify.*

preachment ▶ noun [mass noun] dogmatic instruction and exhortation: *successful leadership is a process of persuasion rather than preachment.*
– ORIGIN Middle English: from Old French *prechement*, from late Latin *praedicamentum*.

preachy ▶ adjective (**preachier, preachiest**) informal having or showing a tendency to give moral advice in a tedious or self-righteous way: *his patriotic pictures had a preachy tone.*
– DERIVATIVES **preachiness** noun.

preadaptation ▶ noun Biology an adaptation which serves a different purpose from the one for which it evolved. ■ [mass noun] the process by which a preadaptation arises.
– DERIVATIVES **preadapt** verb.

preadolescent ▶ adjective (of a child) having nearly reached adolescence. ■ relating to the two or three years preceding adolescence: *Mozart's preadolescent sonatas.*
▶ noun a preadolescent child.
– DERIVATIVES **preadolescence** noun.

preagricultural ▶ adjective denoting a people, tribe, or culture that has not developed agriculture as a means of subsistence.

pre-AIDS ▶ adjective following infection with HIV but before the full development of AIDS: *pre-AIDS patients.*

preamble /priːˈamb(ə)l, ˈpriː-/ ▶ noun a preliminary or preparatory statement; an introduction: *he could tell that what she said was by way of a preamble* | [mass noun] *I gave him the bad news without preamble.* ■ Law the introductory part of a statute or deed, stating its purpose, aims, and justification.
– DERIVATIVES **preambular** adjective (formal).
– ORIGIN late Middle English: from Old French *preambule*, from medieval Latin *praeambulum*, from late Latin *praeambulus* 'going before'.

preamp ▶ noun short for PREAMPLIFIER.

preamplifier ▶ noun an electronic device that amplifies a very weak signal, for example from a microphone or pickup, and transmits it to a main amplifier.
– DERIVATIVES **preamplify** verb (**preamplifies, preamplifying, preamplified**).

prearrange ▶ verb [with obj.] (usu. as adj. **prearranged**) arrange or agree upon (something) in advance: *did she have a prearranged meeting?*
– DERIVATIVES **prearrangement** noun.

Preb. ▶ abbreviation Prebendary.

prebaiting ▶ noun [mass noun] the practice of accustoming vermin or fish to harmless bait, so that they will take poisoned or hooked bait more readily.

prebend /ˈprɛb(ə)nd/ ▶ noun **1** historical the portion of the revenues of a cathedral or collegiate church formerly granted to a canon or member of the chapter as his stipend. ■ the property from which such a stipend was derived.
2 another term for PREBENDARY.
– ORIGIN late Middle English: from Old French *prebende*, from late Latin *praebenda* 'things to be supplied, pension', neuter plural gerundive of Latin *praebere* 'to grant', from *prae* 'before' + *habere* 'hold, have'.

prebendal /prɪˈbɛnd(ə)l/ ▶ adjective relating to a prebend or prebendary: *the prebendal manor.*

prebendary /ˈprɛb(ə)nd(ə)ri/ ▶ noun (pl. **prebendaries**) an honorary canon. ■ historical a canon of a cathedral or collegiate church whose income originally came from a prebend.
– ORIGIN late Middle English: from medieval Latin *praebendarius*, from late Latin *praebenda* 'pension' (see PREBEND).

prebiotic ▶ adjective **1** existing or occurring before the emergence of life.
2 promoting the growth of beneficial intestinal microorganisms.
▶ noun a non-digestible food ingredient that promotes the growth of beneficial microorganisms in the intestines.

preboard ▶ verb [with obj.] allow (a particular passenger or group of passengers) to board an aircraft before the rest of the passengers.

pre-book ▶ verb [with obj.] (usu. as adj. **pre-booked**) book (something) in advance: *a pre-booked hotel reservation.*
– DERIVATIVES **pre-bookable** adjective.

Preboreal /priːˈbɔːrɪəl/ ▶ adjective Geology relating to or denoting the first climatic stage of the postglacial period in northern Europe, between the Younger Dryas and Boreal stages (about 10,000 to 9,000 years ago). The stage was marked by a rapid spread of birch and pine forests. ■ (as noun **the Preboreal**) the Preboreal climatic stage.

prebuttal /priːˈbʌt(ə)l/ ▶ noun (in politics) a response formulated in anticipation of a criticism; a pre-emptive rebuttal.
– ORIGIN 1990s: blend of PRE- and REBUTTAL.

Precambrian /priːˈkambrɪən/ ▶ adjective Geology relating to or denoting the earliest aeon of the earth's history, preceding the Cambrian period and the Phanerozoic aeon. Compare with CRYPTOZOIC. ■ (as noun **the Precambrian**) the Precambrian aeon or the system of rocks deposited during it.

The Precambrian extended from the origin of the earth (believed to have been about 4,600 million years ago) to about 570 million years ago, representing nearly ninety per cent of geological time. The oldest known Precambrian rocks have been dated to about 3,800 million years old, and the earliest living organisms date from the latter part of the aeon. The Precambrian is now replaced in formal stratigraphic schemes by the Archaean, Proterozoic, and (in some schemes) Priscoan aeons.

precancerous ▶ **adjective** Medicine (of a cell or medical condition) likely to develop into cancer if untreated: *precancerous skin lesions.*

precarious ▶ **adjective** not securely held or in position; dangerously likely to fall or collapse: *a precarious ladder.* ■ dependent on chance; uncertain: *he made a precarious living as a painter.*
– DERIVATIVES **precariously** adverb, **precariousness** noun.
– ORIGIN mid 17th cent.: from Latin *precarius* 'obtained by entreaty' (from *prex, prec-* 'prayer') + **-OUS**.

precast ▶ **verb** (**precasts, precasting**; past and past participle **precast**) [with obj.] (usu. as adj. **precast**) cast (an object or material, typically concrete) in its final shape before positioning: *precast concrete beams.*

precatory /ˈprɛkət(ə)ri/ ▶ **adjective** formal relating to or expressing a wish or request. ■ Law (in a will) expressing a wish or request of the testator but not necessarily binding.
– ORIGIN mid 17th cent.: from late Latin *precatorius*, from *precat-* 'prayed', from the verb *precari*.

precaution ▶ **noun** a measure taken in advance to prevent something dangerous, unpleasant, or inconvenient from happening: *he had **taken the precaution of** seeking legal advice.* ■ (**precautions**) informal contraception: *we never **took precautions**.*
– ORIGIN late 16th cent. (in the sense 'prudent foresight'): from French *précaution*, from late Latin *praecautio(n-)*, from Latin *praecavere*, from *prae* 'before' + *cavere* 'take heed, beware of'.

precautionary ▶ **adjective** carried out as a precaution; preventive: *she was taken to hospital as a precautionary measure.*

precede ▶ **verb** [with obj.] come before (something) in time: *a gun battle had preceded the explosions.* ■ come before in order or position: *take time to read the chapters that precede the recipes* | (as adj. **preceding**) *the preceding pages.* ■ go in front or ahead of: *he let her precede him through the gate.* ■ (**precede something with**) preface or introduce something with: *he preceded the book with a collection of poems.*
– ORIGIN late Middle English: from Old French *preceder*, from Latin *praecedere*, from *prae* 'before' + *cedere* 'go'.

precedence /ˈprɛsɪd(ə)ns, prɪˈsiːd(ə)ns/ ▶ **noun** [mass noun] the condition of being considered more important than someone or something else; priority in importance, order, or rank: *his desire for power soon **took precedence over** any other consideration.* ■ the order to be ceremonially observed by people of different rank, according to an acknowledged or legally determined system: *quarrels over precedence among the Bonaparte family marred the coronation.*

precedent ▶ **noun** /ˈprɛsɪd(ə)nt/ an earlier event or action that is regarded as an example or guide to be considered in subsequent similar circumstances: *there are substantial precedents for using interactive media in training.* ■ Law a previous case or legal decision that may be or (**binding precedent**) must be followed in subsequent similar cases: *we hope to **set a legal precedent** to protect hundreds of miles of green lanes.*
▶ **adjective** /prɪˈsiːd(ə)nt, ˈprɛsɪ-/ preceding in time, order, or importance: *a precedent case.*
– ORIGIN late Middle English: from Old French, literally 'preceding'.

precentor /prɪˈsɛntə/ ▶ **noun** a person who leads a congregation in its singing or (in a synagogue) prayers. ■ a minor canon who administers the musical life of a cathedral.
– DERIVATIVES **precent** verb, **precentorship** noun.
– ORIGIN early 17th cent.: from French *précenteur* or Latin *praecentor*, from *praecent-* 'sung before', from the verb *praecinere*, from *prae* 'before' + *canere* 'sing'.

precept /ˈpriːsɛpt/ ▶ **noun 1** a general rule intended to regulate behaviour or thought: *the legal precept of being innocent until proven guilty* | [mass noun] *children learn far more by example than by precept.*
2 a writ or warrant: *the Commissioner issued precepts requiring the companies to provide information.*
3 Brit. an order issued by one local authority to another specifying the rate of tax to be charged on its behalf. ■ a rate or tax set by a precept.
– DERIVATIVES **preceptive** adjective.
– ORIGIN late Middle English: from Latin *praeceptum*, neuter past participle of *praecipere* 'warn, instruct', from *prae* 'before' + *capere* 'take'.

preceptor /prɪˈsɛptə/ ▶ **noun** (fem. **preceptress**) a teacher or instructor.
– DERIVATIVES **preceptorial** /ˌpriːsɛpˈtɔːrɪəl/ adjective, **preceptorship** noun.
– ORIGIN late Middle English: from Latin *praeceptor*, from *praecept-* 'warned, instructed', from the verb *praecipere* (see **PRECEPT**).

precession ▶ **noun** [mass noun] Physics the slow movement of the axis of a spinning body around another axis due to a torque (such as gravitational influence) acting to change the direction of the first axis. It is seen in the circle slowly traced out by the pole of a spinning gyroscope.
– DERIVATIVES **precess** verb, **precessional** adjective.
– ORIGIN late 16th cent. (as a term in astronomy, referring to the **PRECESSION OF THE EQUINOXES**): from late Latin *praecessio(n-)*, from *praecedere* 'go before' (see **PRECEDE**).

precession of the equinoxes ▶ **noun** [mass noun] Astronomy the slow retrograde motion of equinoctial points along the ecliptic. ■ the resulting earlier occurrence of equinoxes in each successive sidereal year.

As the earth rotates about its axis it responds to the gravitational attraction of the sun upon its equatorial bulge, so that its axis of rotation describes a circle in the sky, with a period of about 26,000 years. The precession of the equinoxes was discovered by Hipparchus in c.125 BC, when the vernal equinox was in Aries.

pre-Christian ▶ **adjective** relating to a time before Christ or the advent of Christianity: *the pre-Christian world.*

precinct /ˈpriːsɪŋ(k)t/ ▶ **noun 1** (usu. **precincts**) the area within the walls or perceived boundaries of a particular building or place: *a former MP who still works in the precincts of the House.* ■ an enclosed or clearly defined area of ground around a cathedral, church, or college.
2 Brit. an area in a town designated for specific or restricted use, especially one which is closed to traffic: *a pedestrian precinct.*
3 N. Amer. a district of a city or town as defined for policing purposes. ■ the police station situated in such a subdivision. ■ an electoral district of a city or town served by a single polling station.
– ORIGIN late Middle English (denoting an administrative district): from medieval Latin *praecinctum*, neuter past participle (used as a noun) of *praecingere* 'encircle', from *prae* 'before' + *cingere* 'gird'.

preciosity /ˌprɛʃɪˈɒsɪti/ ▶ **noun** [mass noun] excessive refinement in art, music, or language.
– ORIGIN mid 19th cent.: suggested by French *préciosité*, a sense derived from Molière's *Les Précieuses Ridicules* (1659), a comedy in which ladies frequenting the literary salons of Paris were satirized.

precious ▶ **adjective 1** of great value; not to be wasted or treated carelessly: *precious works of art* | *my time's precious.* ■ greatly loved or treasured by someone: *look after my daughter—she's very **precious to** me.* ■ [attrib.] informal used for emphasis, often in an ironic context: *you and your precious schedule—you've got to lighten up!* | *a precious lot you know about dogs!*
2 derogatory affectedly concerned with elegant or refined behaviour, language, or manners: *his exaggerated, precious manner.*
▶ **noun** used as a term of address for a beloved person: *don't be frightened, my precious.*
– PHRASES **precious little** (or **few**) extremely little or few (used for emphasis): *police still know precious little about the dead man.*
– DERIVATIVES **preciously** adverb, **preciousness** noun.
– ORIGIN Middle English: from Old French *precios*, from Latin *pretiosus* 'of great value', from *pretium* 'price'.

precious coral ▶ **noun** another term for **RED CORAL**.

precious metals ▶ **plural noun** gold, silver, and platinum.

precious stone ▶ **noun** a highly attractive and valuable piece of mineral, used especially in jewellery; a gemstone.

precipice ▶ **noun** a very steep rock face or cliff, especially a tall one: *we swerved toward the edge of the precipice.*
– ORIGIN late 16th cent. (denoting a headlong fall): from French *précipice* or Latin *praecipitium* 'abrupt descent', from *praeceps, praecip(it)-* 'steep, headlong'.

precipitancy ▶ **noun** [mass noun] rashness or suddenness of action: *matters were taken out of his control by the precipitancy of his commander.*

precipitant ▶ **noun 1** a cause of a particular action or event: *the immediate precipitants of the conflict.* ■ chiefly Psychology a cause or stimulus which precipitates a particular condition: *depression may be a precipitant in many cases.*
2 Chemistry a substance that causes the precipitation of a specified substance: *a protein precipitant.*
– DERIVATIVES **precipitance** noun.
– ORIGIN early 17th cent.: from obsolete French *précipitant* 'precipitating', present participle of *précipiter*.

precipitate ▶ **verb** /prɪˈsɪpɪteɪt/ [with obj.] **1** cause (an event or situation, typically one that is undesirable) to happen suddenly, unexpectedly, or prematurely: *the incident precipitated a political crisis.* ■ [with obj. and adverbial of direction] cause to move suddenly and with force: *suddenly the ladder broke, precipitating them down into a heap.* ■ (**precipitate someone/thing into**) send someone or something suddenly into a particular state or condition: *they were precipitated into a conflict for which they were quite unprepared.*
2 Chemistry cause (a substance) to be deposited in solid form from a solution. ■ cause (drops of moisture or particles of dust) to be deposited from the atmosphere or from a vapour or suspension.
▶ **adjective** /prɪˈsɪpɪtət/ done, made, or acting suddenly or without careful consideration: *I must apologize for my staff—their actions were precipitate.* ■ occurring suddenly or abruptly: *a precipitate decline in Labour fortunes.*
▶ **noun** /prɪˈsɪpɪtət, -teɪt/ Chemistry a substance precipitated from a solution.
– DERIVATIVES **precipitable** adjective, **precipitately** adverb, **precipitateness** noun.
– ORIGIN early 16th cent.: from Latin *praecipitat-* 'thrown headlong', from the verb *praecipitare*, from *praeceps, praecip(it)-* 'headlong', from *prae* 'before' + *caput* 'head'. The original sense of the verb was 'hurl down, send violently'; hence 'cause to move rapidly', which gave rise to sense 1 (early 17th cent.).

precipitation ▶ **noun** [mass noun] **1** Chemistry the action or process of precipitating a substance from a solution.
2 rain, snow, sleet, or hail that falls to or condenses on the ground.
3 archaic the fact or quality of acting suddenly and rashly: *Cora was already regretting her precipitation.*
– ORIGIN late Middle English (denoting the action of falling or throwing down): from Latin *praecipitatio(n-)*, from *praecipitare* 'throw down or headlong' (see **PRECIPITATE**).

precipitator ▶ **noun** an apparatus for causing precipitation, especially a device for removing dust from a gas.

precipitin /prɪˈsɪpɪtɪn/ ▶ **noun** Biochemistry an antibody that produces a visible precipitate when it reacts with its antigen.
– ORIGIN early 20th cent.: from the verb **PRECIPITATE** + **-IN**[1].

precipitous /prɪˈsɪpɪtəs/ ▶ **adjective 1** dangerously high or steep: *the track skirted a precipitous drop.* ■ (of a change to a worse situation or condition) sudden and dramatic: *a precipitous slide in the government's popularity.*
2 (of an action) done suddenly and without careful consideration: *precipitous intervention.*
– DERIVATIVES **precipitously** adverb, **precipitousness** noun.
– ORIGIN mid 17th cent.: from obsolete French *précipiteux*, from Latin *praeceps, praecip(it)-* 'steep, headlong' (see **PRECIPITATE**).

precis /ˈpreɪsi/ ▶ **noun** (pl. **same** /-siːz/) a summary or abstract of a text or speech.
▶ **verb** (**precises** /-siːz/, **precising** /-siːɪŋ/, **precised** /-siːd/) [with obj.] make a precis of (a text or speech).
– ORIGIN mid 18th cent.: from French *précis*, literally 'precise' (adjective used as a noun).

precise ▶ **adjective** marked by exactness and accuracy of expression or detail: *precise directions* | *I want as precise a time of death as I can get.* ■ (of a person) exact, accurate, and careful about details: *the director was precise with his camera positions.* ■ [attrib.] used to emphasize that one is referring to an exact and particular thing: *at that precise moment the car stopped.*
– DERIVATIVES **preciseness** noun.

P

– ORIGIN late Middle English: from Old French *prescis*, from Latin *praecis-* 'cut short', from the verb *praecidere*, from *prae* 'in advance' + *caedere* 'to cut'.

precisely ▶ **adverb** in exact terms; without vagueness: *the guidelines are precisely defined.* ■ exactly (used to emphasize the complete accuracy or truth of a statement): *at 2.00 precisely, the phone rang | kids will love it precisely because it will irritate their parents.* ■ used as a reply to confirm or agree with a previous statement: *'You mean it was a conspiracy?' 'Precisely.'*

precisian /prɪˈsɪʒ(ə)n/ ▶ **noun** chiefly archaic a person who is rigidly precise or punctilious, especially as regards religious rules.

precision ▶ **noun** [mass noun] the quality, condition, or fact of being exact and accurate: *the deal was planned and executed with military precision.* ■ [as modifier] marked by or adapted for accuracy and exactness: *a precision instrument.* ■ technical refinement in a measurement, calculation, or specification, especially as represented by the number of digits given: *a technique which examines and identifies each character with the highest level of precision* | [count noun] *a precision of six decimal figures.* Compare with **ACCURACY**.

– ORIGIN mid 18th cent.: from French *précision* or Latin *praecisio(n-)*, from *praecidere* 'cut off' (see **PRECISE**).

pre-classical ▶ **adjective** relating to a time before a period regarded as classical, especially in music, literature, or ancient history.

preclinical ▶ **adjective** Medicine **1** relating to or denoting the first, chiefly theoretical, stage of a medical education: *preclinical students.*
2 relating to or denoting the stage in a disease prior to the appearance of symptoms that make a diagnosis possible.
3 relating to or denoting the stage of drug testing that precedes the clinical stage.

preclude ▶ **verb** [with obj.] prevent from happening; make impossible: *the secret nature of his work precluded official recognition.* ■ (**preclude someone from**) (of a situation or condition) prevent someone from doing something: *his difficulties preclude him from leading a normal life.*

– DERIVATIVES **preclusion** noun, **preclusive** adjective.

– ORIGIN late 15th cent. (in the sense 'bar a route or passage'): from Latin *praecludere*, from *prae* 'before' + *claudere* 'to shut'.

precocial /prɪˈkəʊʃ(ə)l/ Zoology ▶ **adjective** (of a young bird or other animal) hatched or born in an advanced state and able to feed itself almost immediately. Also called **NIDIFUGOUS**. Often contrasted with **ALTRICIAL**. ■ (of a particular species) having precocial young.

– ORIGIN late 19th cent.: from modern Latin *Praecoces* (the name of a former division of birds, plural of Latin *praecox* 'mature before its time') + **-IAL**.

precocious ▶ **adjective** (of a child) having developed certain abilities or inclinations at an earlier age than usual: *a precocious, solitary boy.* ■ (of behaviour or ability) indicative of such development: *a precocious talent for computing.* ■ (of a plant) flowering or fruiting earlier than usual.

– DERIVATIVES **precociously** adverb, **precociousness** noun, **precocity** noun.

– ORIGIN mid 17th cent.: from Latin *praecox*, *praecoc-* (from *praecoquere* 'ripen fully', from *prae* 'before' + *coquere* 'to cook') + **-IOUS**.

precognition ▶ **noun 1** [mass noun] foreknowledge of an event, especially as a form of extrasensory perception.
2 Law, chiefly Scottish the preliminary examination of witnesses, especially to decide whether there is ground for a trial.

– DERIVATIVES **precognitive** adjective (sense 1).

– ORIGIN late Middle English: from late Latin *praecognitio(n-)*, based on Latin *cognoscere* 'know'.

precoital ▶ **adjective** occurring before or as a preliminary to sexual intercourse.

precolonial ▶ **adjective** occurring or existing before the beginning of colonial rule: *the two main kingdoms that flourished in precolonial times.*

pre-Columbian ▶ **adjective** relating to the history and cultures of the Americas before the arrival of Columbus in 1492.

preconceived ▶ **adjective** (of an idea or opinion) formed before having the evidence for its truth or usefulness: *the same set of facts can be tailored to fit any preconceived belief.*

preconception ▶ **noun** a preconceived idea or prejudice.

preconcert /ˌpriːkənˈsəːt/ ▶ **verb** [with obj.] archaic arrange or organize (something) in advance: (as adj. **preconcerted**) *a preconcerted signal.*

precondition ▶ **noun** a condition that must be fulfilled before other things can happen or be done: *a precondition for peace.*
▶ **verb** [with obj.] **1** condition (an action) to happen in a certain way: *enquiries are always preconditioned by cultural assumptions.* ■ condition or influence (a person or animal) by exposing them to stimuli or information prior to the relevant behavioural situation: [with obj. and infinitive] *the anthropologist is not preconditioned to interact with those he studies* | (as noun **preconditioning**) *the protective effect of preconditioning.*
2 bring (something) into the desired state for use: (as adj. **preconditioned**) *preconditioned paper.*

preconfigure ▶ **verb** [with obj.] Computing configure in advance: *an application preconfigured for the insurance industry.*

preconize /ˈpriːkənʌɪz/ (also **preconise**) ▶ **verb** [with obj.] rare proclaim or commend publicly. ■ (of the Pope) publicly approve the appointment of (a bishop).

– ORIGIN late Middle English: from medieval Latin *praeconizare*, from Latin *praeco(n-)* 'herald'.

pre-Conquest ▶ **adjective** occurring or existing before the Norman conquest of England.

preconscious ▶ **adjective** Psychoanalysis of or associated with a part of the mind below the level of immediate conscious awareness, from which memories and emotions that have not been repressed can be recalled: *beliefs and values which are on a preconscious level.*
▶ **noun** (**one's/the preconscious**) Psychology the part of the mind in which preconscious thoughts or memories reside.

– DERIVATIVES **preconsciousness** noun.

pre-cook ▶ **verb** [with obj.] cook in advance: (as adj. **pre-cooked**) *a pre-cooked pastry case.*

pre-cool ▶ **verb** [with obj.] cool in advance.

precordium /priːˈkɔːdɪəm/ ▶ **noun** Anatomy the region of the thorax immediately in front of or over the heart.

– DERIVATIVES **precordial** adjective.

– ORIGIN late 19th cent.: singular of Latin *praecordia* 'diaphragm, entrails'.

precursor ▶ **noun** a person or thing that comes before another of the same kind; a forerunner: *a three-stringed precursor of the violin.* ■ a substance from which another is formed, especially by metabolic reaction: *pepsinogen is the inactive precursor of pepsin.*

– ORIGIN late Middle English: from Latin *praecursor*, from *praecurs-* 'preceded', from *praecurrere*, from *prae* 'beforehand' + *currere* 'to run'.

precursory (also **precursive**) ▶ **adjective** preceding something in time, development, or position; preliminary: *precursory seismic activity.*

– ORIGIN late 16th cent.: from Latin *praecursorius*, from *praecurs-* 'preceded' (see **PRECURSOR**).

pre-cut ▶ **verb** [with obj.] (usu. as adj. **pre-cut**) cut into the desired shape or sections in advance: *pre-cut pieces of cloth.*

predacious /prɪˈdeɪʃəs/ (also **predaceous**) ▶ **adjective** (of an animal) predatory: *predacious insects.*

– DERIVATIVES **predacity** noun.

– ORIGIN early 18th cent.: from Latin *praeda* 'booty' + **-ACIOUS**.

predate[1] /priːˈdeɪt/ ▶ **verb** [with obj.] exist or occur at a date earlier than (something): *here parish boundaries seem clearly to predate Roman roads.*

predate[2] /prɪˈdeɪt/ ▶ **verb** [with obj.] (of an animal) act as a predator of; catch and eat (prey).

– ORIGIN 1940s: back-formation from **PREDATION**.

predation /prɪˈdeɪʃ(ə)n/ ▶ **noun** [mass noun] **1** the preying of one animal on others: *an effective defence against predation.*
2 the action of attacking or plundering: *the old story of male predation and female vulnerability* | [count noun] *the predations of would-be pirates.*

– ORIGIN late 15th cent. (in the Latin sense): from Latin *praedatio(n-)* 'taking of booty', from the verb *praedari* 'seize as plunder', from *praeda* 'booty'. The zoological sense dates from the 1930s.

predator ▶ **noun 1** an animal that naturally preys on others: *wolves are major predators of small mammals.*
2 a person who ruthlessly exploits others: *a sexual predator.* ■ a company that tries to take over another.

– ORIGIN 1920s: from Latin *praedator* 'plunderer', from *praedat-* 'seized as plunder', from the verb *praedari* (see **PREDATION**).

predatory ▶ **adjective 1** (of an animal) preying naturally on others: *predatory species of shark.*
2 seeking to exploit others: *she always felt at the mercy of predatory men.*

– DERIVATIVES **predatorily** adverb, **predatoriness** noun.

– ORIGIN late 16th cent. (in the sense 'relating to plundering'): from Latin *praedatorius*, from *praedator* 'plunderer' (see **PREDATOR**).

predatory pricing ▶ **noun** [mass noun] the pricing of goods or services at such a low level that other firms cannot compete and are forced to leave the market.

predawn ▶ **adjective** relating to or taking place before dawn: *in a predawn raid, troops stormed the university campus.*

predecease formal ▶ **verb** [with obj.] die before (another person, typically a relative): *his second wife predeceased him.*
▶ **noun** a death preceding that of another person.

predecessor ▶ **noun** a person who held a job or office before the current holder: *the new President's foreign policy is very similar to that of his predecessor.* ■ a thing that has been followed or replaced by another: *the chapel was built in 1864 on the site of its predecessor.*

– ORIGIN late Middle English: from late Latin *praedecessor*, from Latin *prae* 'beforehand' + *decessor* 'retiring officer' (from *decedere* 'depart').

predefined ▶ **adjective** defined, limited, or established in advance: *the terms are keyed in as predefined codes.*

predella /prɪˈdɛlə/ ▶ **noun** a step or platform on which an altar is placed. ■ a raised shelf above an altar. ■ a painting or sculpture on this, typically forming an appendage to an altarpiece.

– ORIGIN mid 19th cent.: from Italian, literally 'stool'.

predestinarian /prɪˌdɛstɪˈnɛːrɪən/ ▶ **noun** a person who believes in the doctrine of predestination.
▶ **adjective** upholding, affirming, or relating to the doctrine of predestination.

predestinate ▶ **verb** /priːˈdɛstɪneɪt/ [with obj.] predestine.
▶ **adjective** /priːˈdɛstɪnət/ predestined.

– ORIGIN late Middle English: from ecclesiastical Latin *praedestinat-* 'made firm beforehand', from the verb *praedestinare*, from *prae* 'in advance' + *destinare* 'establish'.

predestination ▶ **noun** [mass noun] (in Christian theology) the doctrine that God has ordained all that will happen, especially with regard to the salvation of some and not others. It has been particularly associated with the teachings of St Augustine of Hippo and of Calvin.

– ORIGIN Middle English: from ecclesiastical Latin *praedestinatio(n-)*, from *praedestinare* 'make firm beforehand' (see **PREDESTINATE**).

predestine ▶ **verb** [with obj.] (of God) destine (someone) for a particular fate or purpose: *Calvinists believed that every person was predestined by God to go to heaven or to hell.* ■ determine (an outcome or course of events) in advance by divine will or fate: (as adj. **predestined**) *our predestined end.*

– ORIGIN late Middle English: from Old French *predestiner* or ecclesiastical Latin *praedestinare* (see **PREDESTINATE**).

predetermine ▶ **verb** [with obj.] establish or decide in advance: *closed questions almost predetermine the response given* | (as adj. **predetermined**) *a predetermined level of spending.* ■ predestine (an outcome or course of events): *a strong sense that life had been predetermined.*

– DERIVATIVES **predeterminable** adjective, **predeterminate** adjective, **predetermination** noun.

– ORIGIN early 17th cent.: from late Latin *praedeterminare*, from *prae* 'beforehand' + *determinare* 'limit, settle'.

predeterminer ▶ **noun** Grammar a word or phrase that occurs before a determiner, typically quantifying the noun phrase, for example *both* or *a lot of*.

predial /ˈpriːdɪəl/ ▶ **adjective** archaic relating to land or the cultivation of land. ■ historical (of a tithe) consisting of agricultural produce. ■ historical relating to or denoting a slave or tenant attached to farms or the land.
▶ **noun** historical a predial slave.

– ORIGIN late Middle English: from medieval Latin *praedialis*, from Latin *praedium* 'farm'.

predicable /ˈprɛdɪkəb(ə)l/ ▶ adjective that may be predicated or affirmed.
▶ noun a thing that is predicable. ■ (usu. **predicables**) (in Aristotelian logic) each of the classes to which predicates belong, usually listed as genus, species, difference, property, and accident.
– DERIVATIVES **predicability** noun.
– ORIGIN mid 16th cent.: from medieval Latin *praedicabilis* 'able to be affirmed', from Latin *praedicare* 'declare' (see PREDICATE).

predicament /prɪˈdɪkəm(ə)nt/ ▶ noun **1** a difficult, unpleasant, or embarrassing situation: *the club's financial predicament*.
2 (in Aristotelian logic) each of the ten 'categories', often listed as: substance or being, quantity, quality, relation, place, time, posture, having or possession, action, and passion.
– ORIGIN late Middle English (in sense 2): from late Latin *praedicamentum* 'something predicated' (rendering Greek *katēgoria* 'category'), from Latin *praedicare* (see PREDICATE). From the sense 'category' arose the sense 'state of being, condition'; hence 'unpleasant situation'.

predicant /ˈprɛdɪk(ə)nt/ ▶ adjective archaic (especially of the religious order of the Dominicans) characterized by preaching.
▶ noun archaic a preacher, especially a Dominican friar.
– ORIGIN late 16th cent.: from Latin *praedicant* 'declaring', from the verb *praedicare*, in ecclesiastical Latin meaning 'preach'.

predicate ▶ noun /ˈprɛdɪkət/ **1** Grammar the part of a sentence or clause containing a verb and stating something about the subject (e.g. *went home* in *John went home*).
2 Logic something which is affirmed or denied concerning an argument of a proposition.
▶ verb /ˈprɛdɪkeɪt/ [with obj.] **1** Grammar & Logic state, affirm, or assert (something) about the subject of a sentence or an argument of a proposition: *a word which predicates something about its subject* | *aggression is* ***predicated of*** *those who act aggressively*. ■ declare or affirm (something) as true or existing; postulate or assert.
2 (**predicate something on/upon**) found or base something on: *the theory of structure on which later chemistry was predicated*.
– DERIVATIVES **predication** noun.
– ORIGIN late Middle English (as a noun): from Latin *praedicatum* 'something declared', neuter of *praedicatus* 'declared, proclaimed', past participle of the verb *praedicare*, from *prae* 'beforehand' + *dicare* 'make known'.

predicate calculus ▶ noun [mass noun] the branch of symbolic logic that deals with propositions containing predicates, names, and quantifiers.

predicative /prɪˈdɪkətɪv/ ▶ adjective **1** Grammar (of an adjective or noun) forming or contained in the predicate, as *old* in *the dog is old* (but not in *the old dog*) and *house* in *there is a large house*. Contrasted with ATTRIBUTIVE. ■ denoting a use of the verb *to be* to assert something about the subject.
2 Logic acting as a predicate.
– DERIVATIVES **predicatively** adverb.
– ORIGIN mid 19th cent.: from Latin *praedicativus*, from *praedicat-* 'declared' (in medieval Latin 'predicated'), from the verb *praedicare* (see PREDICATE).

predicator /ˈprɛdɪkeɪtə/ ▶ noun (in systemic grammar) a verb phrase considered as a constituent of clause structure, along with subject, object, and adjunct.

predict ▶ verb [with obj.] say or estimate that (a specified thing) will happen in the future or will be a consequence of something: *it is too early to predict a result* | [with clause] *he predicts that the trend will continue* | (as adj. **predicted**) *the predicted growth in road traffic*.
– DERIVATIVES **predictor** noun.
– ORIGIN early 17th cent.: from Latin *praedict-* 'made known beforehand, declared', from the verb *praedicere*, from *prae-* 'beforehand' + *dicere* 'say'.

predictable ▶ adjective able to be predicted: *the market is volatile and never predictable*. ■ derogatory always behaving or occurring in the way expected: *the characters are stereotyped and extremely predictable*.
– DERIVATIVES **predictability** noun, **predictably** adverb [sentence adverb] *predictably, Margaret found an excuse to interrupt him*.

prediction ▶ noun a thing predicted; a forecast: *a prediction that economic growth would resume*. ■ [mass noun] the action of predicting something: *the prediction of future behaviour*.
– ORIGIN mid 16th cent.: from Latin *praedictio(n-)*, from *praedicere* 'make known beforehand' (see PREDICT).

predictive ▶ adjective relating to or having the effect of predicting an event or result: *predictive accuracy* | *rules are not* ***predictive of*** *behaviour*.
– DERIVATIVES **predictively** adverb.

predigest ▶ verb (of an animal) treat (food) by a process similar to digestion in order to make it more digestible when subsequently eaten. ■ simplify (information) so as to make it easier to understand or absorb.
– DERIVATIVES **predigestion** noun.

predigital ▶ adjective belonging to or characteristic of the period preceding the widespread adoption of digital technologies: *the predigital age*.

predikant /ˌprɛdɪˈkant, ˌprɪədə-/ ▶ noun S. African a minister of the Dutch Reformed Church.
– ORIGIN Dutch, from ecclesiastical Latin *praedicare* 'preach'.

predilection /ˌpriːdɪˈlɛkʃ(ə)n/ ▶ noun a preference or special liking for something; a bias in favour of something: *your* ***predilection for*** *pretty girls*.
– ORIGIN mid 18th cent.: from French *prédilection*, from Latin *praedilect-* 'preferred', from the verb *praediligere*, from *prae* 'in advance' + *diligere* 'to select'.

predispose ▶ verb [with obj.] (**predispose someone to/to do something**) make someone liable or inclined to a specified attitude, action, or condition: *lack of exercise may predispose an individual to high blood pressure* | *I'm kind of* ***predisposed towards*** *disliking them*.

predisposition ▶ noun a liability or tendency to suffer from a particular condition, hold a particular attitude, or act in a particular way: *a child may inherit a* ***predisposition to*** *schizophrenia* | [mass noun] *factors including genetic predisposition*.

prednisolone /prɛdˈnɪsələʊn/ ▶ noun [mass noun] Medicine a synthetic steroid with similar properties and uses to those of prednisone, of which it is a reduced derivative.
– ORIGIN 1950s: from PREDNISONE, with the insertion of -OL.

prednisone /ˈprɛdnɪzəʊn/ ▶ noun [mass noun] Medicine a synthetic drug similar to cortisone, used to relieve rheumatic and allergic conditions and to treat leukaemia.
– ORIGIN 1950s: perhaps from *pre(gnane)* (a synthetic hydrocarbon) + *d(ie)n(e)* + *(cort)isone*.

predominance ▶ noun [mass noun] the state or condition of being greater in number or amount: *the predominance of women in such professions as social work and nursing* | [in sing.] *churches with a predominance of African-American members*. ■ the possession or exertion of control or power: *Hollywood's continued predominance in the international film market*.

predominant ▶ adjective present as the strongest or main element: *the predominant colour was white*. ■ having or exerting control or power: *the predominant political forces*.
– ORIGIN mid 16th cent.: from Old French, from medieval Latin *predominant-* 'predominating', from the verb *predominari* (see PREDOMINATE).

predominantly ▶ adverb mainly; for the most part: [sentence adverb] *it is predominantly a coastal bird* | *predominantly Russian areas*.

predominate ▶ verb [no obj.] be the strongest or main element; be greater in number or amount: *small-scale producers predominate in the south*. ■ have or exert control or power: *private interest was not allowed to* ***predominate over*** *the public good*.
– ORIGIN late 16th cent.: from medieval Latin *predominat-* 'predominated', from the verb *predominari* (see PRE-, DOMINATE).

predominately ▶ adverb another term for PREDOMINANTLY.

predoom ▶ verb [with obj.] literary condemn or determine the fate of (someone or something) in advance: *he was predoomed by the decrees of heaven*.

predorsal /priːˈdɔːs(ə)l/ ▶ adjective in front of the dorsal region.

predynastic /ˌpriːdɪˈnastɪk, -dʌɪ-/ ▶ adjective relating to a period before the normally recognized dynasties, especially in ancient Egypt before about 3000 BC.

pre-echo ▶ noun (pl. **pre-echoes**) **1** a faint copy heard just before an actual sound in a recording, caused by the accidental transfer of signals.
2 a foreshadowing: *one can detect pre-echoes of both the later works*.
▶ verb [with obj.] foreshadow: *these three sonatas all pre-echo things to come*.

pre-eclampsia ▶ noun [mass noun] a condition in pregnancy characterized by high blood pressure, sometimes with fluid retention and proteinuria.
– DERIVATIVES **pre-eclamptic** adjective & noun.

pre-elect ▶ verb [with obj.] (at Oxford and Cambridge Universities) elect (someone) to a post before the time they take up the appointment: *she was pre-elected to a junior research fellowship*.

pre-embryo ▶ noun technical a human embryo or fertilized ovum in the first fourteen days after fertilization, before implantation in the womb has occurred.
– DERIVATIVES **pre-embryonic** adjective.

preemie /ˈpriːmi/ ▶ noun (pl. **preemies**) N. Amer. informal a baby born prematurely.
– ORIGIN 1920s (as *premy*): from PREMATURE + -IE.

pre-eminence ▶ noun [mass noun] the fact of surpassing all others; superiority: *the Edinburgh Festival maintains its pre-eminence because of the quality of its programming*.

pre-eminent ▶ adjective surpassing all others; very distinguished in some way: *the world's pre-eminent expert on asbestos*.
– ORIGIN late Middle English: from Latin *praeeminent-* 'towering above, excelling', from the verb *praeeminere*, from *prae* 'before' + *eminere* 'stand out'.

pre-eminently ▶ adverb [sentence adverb] above all; in particular: *the novel is pre-eminently a realistic genre*.

pre-empt ▶ verb [with obj.] **1** take action in order to prevent (an anticipated event) happening; forestall: *the government pre-empted a coup attempt*. ■ act in advance of (someone) in order to prevent them doing something: *it looked as if she'd ask him more, but Parr pre-empted her*.
2 acquire or appropriate (something) in advance: *many tables were already pre-empted by family parties*. ■ N. Amer. occupy (public land) so as to have a pre-emptive right to buy it before others.
3 [no obj.] Bridge make a pre-emptive bid.
▶ noun Bridge a pre-emptive bid.
– DERIVATIVES **pre-emptor** noun.
– ORIGIN mid 19th cent.: back-formation from PRE-EMPTION.

pre-emption ▶ noun [mass noun] **1** the purchase of goods or shares by one person or party before the opportunity is offered to others: *the commission had the right of pre-emption*. ■ historical, chiefly N. Amer. & Austral./NZ the right to purchase public land in this way.
2 the action of pre-empting or forestalling, especially of making a pre-emptive attack: *damaging retaliation for any attempt at pre-emption*.
– ORIGIN early 17th cent.: from medieval Latin *praeemptio(n-)*, from the verb *praeemere*, from *prae* 'in advance' + *emere* 'buy'.

P

pre-emptive ▶ adjective serving or intended to pre-empt or forestall something, especially to prevent attack by disabling the enemy: *a pre-emptive strike*. ■ relating to the purchase of goods or shares by one person or party before the opportunity is offered to others: *pre-emptive rights*. ■ Bridge denoting a bid, typically an opening bid, intended to be so high that it prevents or interferes with effective bidding by the opponents.
– DERIVATIVES **pre-emptively** adverb.

preen ▶ verb [no obj.] (of a bird) tidy and clean its feathers with its beak: *reed buntings preened at the pool's edge* | [with obj.] *the pigeon preened her feathers*. ■ (also **preen oneself**) (of a person) devote effort to making oneself look attractive and then admire one's appearance: *adolescents preening in their bedroom mirrors*. ■ (**preen oneself**) congratulate or pride oneself: *he's busy* ***preening himself on*** *acquiring such a pretty girlfriend*.
– ORIGIN late Middle English: apparently a variant of obsolete *prune* (based on Latin *ungere* 'anoint'), in the same sense, associated with Scots and northern English dialect *preen* 'pierce, pin' (because of the 'pricking' action of the bird's beak).

preen gland ▶ noun Ornithology a gland at the base of a bird's tail, which produces the oil used in preening.

pre-establish ▶ verb [with obj.] (usu. as adj. **pre-established**) establish (something) in advance: *he had no pre-established plan*.

pre-exist ▸ **verb** [no obj.] (usu. as adj. **pre-existing**) exist at or from an earlier time: *a pre-existing contractual obligation.* ■ [with obj.] exist at or from an earlier time than (something): *demons who pre-existed the Great Flood.*
– DERIVATIVES **pre-existence** noun, **pre-existent** adjective.

pre-exposure ▸ **noun** previous or premature exposure to something, especially to a disease or infection: [as modifier] *pre-exposure vaccination.*

pref. ▸ **abbreviation** ■ preface. ■ preference (with reference to preference shares). ■ preferred (with reference to a preferred share).

prefab ▸ **noun** informal a prefabricated building.
– ORIGIN 1930s: abbreviation.

prefabricate ▸ **verb** [with obj.] (usu. as adj. **prefabricated**) manufacture sections of (a building or piece of furniture) to enable quick assembly on site: *prefabricated homes.*
– DERIVATIVES **prefabrication** noun.

preface /ˈprɛfəs/ ▸ **noun** an introduction to a book, typically stating its subject, scope, or aims. ■ a preliminary explanation. ■ Christian Church the introduction to the central part of the Eucharist, historically forming the first part of the canon or prayer of consecration. In the Western Church it comes between the Sursum Corda and the Sanctus and varies with the season.
▸ **verb** [with obj.] provide (a book) with a preface: *the book is prefaced by a quotation from William Faulkner.* ■ (**preface something with/by**) introduce or begin (a speech or event) with or by doing something: *it is important to preface the debate with a general comment.*
– ORIGIN late Middle English: via Old French from medieval Latin *praefatia*, alteration of Latin *praefatio(n-)* 'words spoken beforehand', from the verb *praefari*, from *prae* 'before' + *fari* 'speak'.

prefatory /ˈprɛfət(ə)ri/ ▸ **adjective** serving as an introduction; introductory: *in his prefatory remarks the author claims that ...*

prefect ▸ **noun 1** chiefly Brit. (in some schools) a senior pupil who is authorized to enforce discipline.
2 a chief officer, magistrate, or regional governor in certain countries. ■ a senior magistrate or governor in the ancient Roman world.
– DERIVATIVES **prefectoral** adjective, **prefectorial** adjective.
– ORIGIN late Middle English (in sense 2): from Old French, from Latin *praefectus*, past participle of *praeficere* 'set in authority over', from *prae* 'before' + *facere* 'make'. Sense 1 dates from the early 19th cent.

prefecture ▸ **noun** (in certain countries) a district under the authority of a prefect or governor. ■ a prefect's office or tenure. ■ the official residence or headquarters of a prefect.
– DERIVATIVES **prefectural** adjective.
– ORIGIN late Middle English: from Latin *praefectura*, from *praefectus* '(person) set in authority over' (see PREFECT).

P

prefer ▸ **verb** (**prefers, preferring, preferred**) [with obj.] **1** like (one thing or person) better than another or others; tend to choose: *I prefer Venice to Rome* | [with infinitive] *I would prefer to discuss the matter in private* | [with clause] *Val would presumably prefer that you didn't get arrested.*
2 formal submit (a charge or a piece of information) for consideration: *the police will prefer charges.*
3 archaic promote or advance (someone) to a prestigious position: *he was eventually **preferred to** the bishopric of Durham.*
– ORIGIN late Middle English: from Old French *preferer*, from Latin *praeferre*, from *prae* 'before' + *ferre* 'to bear, carry'.

preferable ▸ **adjective** more desirable or suitable: *lower interest rates were **preferable to** higher ones.*
– DERIVATIVES **preferability** noun.

preferably ▸ **adverb** [sentence adverb] ideally; if possible: *he would like a place of his own, preferably outside the town.*

preference ▸ **noun 1** a greater liking for one alternative over another or others: *her **preference for** white wine* | *he chose a clock **in preference to** a watch.* ■ a thing preferred: *nearly 40 per cent named acid house as their musical preference.* ■ [mass noun] favour shown to one person or thing over another or others: *preference is given to those who make a donation.*
2 Law a prior right or precedence, especially in connection with the payment of debts.
– ORIGIN late Middle English (in the sense 'promotion'): from Old French, from medieval Latin *praeferentia*, from Latin *praeferre* 'carry in front' (see PREFER).

preference share (or **stock**) (N. Amer. **preferred share** or **stock**) ▸ **noun** a share which entitles the holder to a fixed dividend, whose payment takes priority over that of ordinary share dividends.

preferential ▸ **adjective** of or involving preference or partiality; constituting a favour or privilege: *preferential interest rates may be offered to employees* | *preferential trade terms.* ■ (of voting or an election) in which the voter puts candidates in order of preference. ■ (of a creditor) having a claim on the receipt of payment from a debtor which will be met before those of other creditors.
– DERIVATIVES **preferentially** adverb.
– ORIGIN mid 19th cent.: from PREFERENCE, on the pattern of *differential.*

preferment ▸ **noun** [mass noun] promotion or appointment to a position or office: *after ordination, preferment was fast* | [count noun] *most of her ministers owed their first preferment to her.*

prefetch Computing ▸ **verb** /priːˈfɛtʃ/ [with obj.] transfer (data) from main memory to temporary storage in readiness for later use.
▸ **noun** /priːˈfɛtʃ/ a process involving such a transfer.

prefigure ▸ **verb** [with obj.] **1** be an early indication or version of (something): *the Hussite movement prefigured the Reformation.*
2 archaic imagine beforehand: *I lay awake, prefiguring the future.*
– DERIVATIVES **prefiguration** noun, **prefigurative** adjective, **prefigurement** noun.
– ORIGIN late Middle English: from ecclesiastical Latin *praefigurare* 'represent beforehand', from *prae* 'before' + *figurare* 'to form, fashion'.

prefix ▸ **noun** a word, letter, or number placed before another: *the Institute was granted the prefix 'Royal' in 1961.* ■ an element placed at the beginning of a word to adjust or qualify its meaning (e.g. *ex-*, *non-*, *re-*) or (in some languages) as an inflection. ■ a title placed before a name (e.g. *Mr*).
▸ **verb** [with obj.] add (something) at the beginning as a prefix or introduction: *a preface is **prefixed to** the book.* ■ add a prefix or introduction to (something): *all three-digit numbers will now be prefixed by 580.*
– DERIVATIVES **prefixation** noun.
– ORIGIN mid 16th cent. (as a verb): from Old French *prefixer*, from Latin *praefixus* 'fixed in front', from the verb *praefigere*, from *prae* 'before' + *figere* 'to fix'. The noun is from modern Latin *praefixum*, neuter (used as a noun) of *praefixus*, and dates from the mid 17th cent.

preflight ▸ **adjective** occurring before a flight in an aircraft: *our detailed preflight briefing.*
▸ **verb** [with obj.] prepare (an aircraft) for a flight by carrying out systematic checks.

prefocus ▸ **adjective** relating to or denoting a light bulb which is designed so that its beam is focused automatically when it is fitted inside a lamp, especially a vehicle headlamp.

preform ▸ **verb** [with obj.] (usu. as adj. **preformed**) form (something) beforehand: *a preformed pool.*

preformation ▸ **noun** [mass noun] the action or process of preforming something. ■ Biology, historical the theory, now discarded, that an embryo develops from a complete miniature version of the organism. Often contrasted with EPIGENESIS.
– DERIVATIVES **preformationist** noun & adjective.

prefrontal ▸ **adjective 1** Anatomy in or relating to the foremost part of the frontal lobe of the brain: *the prefrontal cortex.*
2 Zoology relating to or denoting a bone in front of the eye socket in some lower vertebrates (equivalent to part of the human ethmoid bone).
▸ **noun** Zoology a prefrontal bone.

pregenital ▸ **adjective 1** Psychoanalysis relating to psychosexual development before the genital phase.
2 Zoology situated in front of the genital region.

preggers ▸ **adjective** [predic.] informal, chiefly Brit. pregnant.

preglacial ▸ **adjective** relating to or denoting a time before a glacial period.

pregnable ▸ **adjective** vulnerable to attack; not impregnable: *the fort's pregnable approaches.*
– ORIGIN late Middle English: from Old French *prenable*, literally 'takable', from Latin *prehendere* 'seize'. The *g* was sometimes written in French, perhaps indicating palatal *n*, but has come to be pronounced as a separate sound in English.

pregnancy ▸ **noun** (pl. **pregnancies**) [mass noun] the condition or period of being pregnant: *the first weeks of pregnancy* | [count noun] *a straightforward pregnancy.*

pregnant ▸ **adjective 1** (of a woman or female animal) having a child or young developing in the uterus: *she was heavily **pregnant with** her second child* | *she was six months pregnant.*
2 full of meaning; significant or suggestive: *a pregnant pause* | *a development **pregnant with** implications.*
– DERIVATIVES **pregnantly** adverb.
– ORIGIN late Middle English: from Latin *praegnant-*, probably from *prae* 'before' + the base of *gnasci* 'be born'.

preheat ▸ **verb** [with obj.] heat (something, especially an oven or grill) beforehand: *preheat the oven to 200°C.*

prehensile /prɪˈhɛnsʌɪl/ ▸ **adjective** (chiefly of an animal's limb or tail) capable of grasping.
– DERIVATIVES **prehensility** noun.
– ORIGIN late 18th cent.: from French *préhensile*, from Latin *prehens-* 'grasped', from the verb *prehendere*, from *prae* 'before' + *hendere* 'to grasp'.

prehension ▸ **noun** [mass noun] **1** Zoology & Psychology the action of grasping or seizing.
2 Philosophy an interaction of a subject with an event or entity which involves perception but not necessarily cognition.
– ORIGIN early 19th cent.: from Latin *prehensio(n-)*, from *prehendere* 'to grasp'.

prehistoric ▸ **adjective** relating to or denoting the period before written records: *prehistoric man.* ■ informal very old, primitive, or out of date: *my dad's electric typewriter was a prehistoric machine.*
– DERIVATIVES **prehistorically** adverb.
– ORIGIN mid 19th cent.: from French *préhistorique* (see PRE-, HISTORIC).

prehistory ▸ **noun** [mass noun] the period of time before written records: *myths that stretch back into prehistory.* ■ the events or conditions leading up to a particular occurrence or phenomenon: *the prehistory of capitalism.*
– DERIVATIVES **prehistorian** noun.

prehuman ▸ **adjective** relating to or denoting the time before the appearance of human beings, especially the evolutionary stage immediately preceding the development of modern humans.
▸ **noun** a precursor of the human species.

pre-ignition ▸ **noun** [mass noun] the premature combustion of the fuel–air mixture in an internal-combustion engine.

pre-industrial ▸ **adjective** relating to a time before industrialization: *a pre-industrial society.*

pre-install (also **pre-instal**) ▸ **verb** another term for PRELOAD.

prejudge ▸ **verb** [with obj.] form a judgement on (an issue or person) prematurely and without having adequate information: *it is wrong to prejudge an issue on the basis of speculation.*
– DERIVATIVES **prejudgement** (also **prejudgment**) noun.

prejudice ▸ **noun** [mass noun] **1** preconceived opinion that is not based on reason or actual experience: *English **prejudice against** foreigners* | [count noun] *deep-rooted class prejudices.* ■ dislike, hostility, or unjust behaviour formed on such a basis: *accusations of racial prejudice.*
2 chiefly Law harm or injury that results or may result from some action or judgement: *prejudice resulting from delay in the institution of the proceedings.*
▸ **verb** [with obj.] **1** give rise to prejudice in (someone); make biased: *the statement might prejudice the jury.*
2 chiefly Law cause harm to (a state of affairs): *delay is likely to prejudice the child's welfare.*
– PHRASES **with prejudice** Law extinguishing any right to pursue a claim in another suit. **without prejudice** Law without detriment to any existing right or claim: *the payment was made **without** any **prejudice to** her rights.*
– ORIGIN Middle English (in sense 2 of the noun): from Old French, from Latin *praejudicium*, from *prae* 'in advance' + *judicium* 'judgement'.

prejudiced ▸ **adjective** having or showing a dislike or distrust that is derived from prejudice; bigoted: *people are **prejudiced against** us* | *prejudiced views.*

prejudicial ▸ **adjective** harmful to someone or something; detrimental: *the proposals were considered **prejudicial to** the city centre.*
– DERIVATIVES **prejudicially** adverb.

– ORIGIN late Middle English: from Old French *prejudiciel*, from *prejudice* (see PREJUDICE).

prelacy /ˈprɛləsi/ ▶ **noun** (pl. **prelacies**) [mass noun] chiefly archaic the government of the Christian Church by clerics of high social rank and power. ■ [count noun] the office or rank of a prelate. ■ (**the prelacy**) prelates collectively.
– ORIGIN Middle English: from Anglo-Norman French *prelacie*, from medieval Latin *prelatia*, from *praelatus* (see PRELATE).

prelapsarian /ˌpriːlapˈsɛːrɪən/ ▶ **adjective** Theology or literary characteristic of the time before the Fall of Man; innocent and unspoilt: *a prelapsarian Eden of astonishing plenitude*.
– ORIGIN late 19th cent.: from PRE- 'before' + Latin *lapsus*, from *labi* 'to fall'.

prelate /ˈprɛlət/ ▶ **noun** formal or historical a bishop or other high ecclesiastical dignitary.
– DERIVATIVES **prelatic** /prɪˈlatɪk/ adjective, **prelatical** /prɪˈlatɪk(ə)l/ adjective.
– ORIGIN Middle English: from Old French *prelat*, from medieval Latin *praelatus* 'civil dignitary', past participle (used as a noun) of Latin *praeferre* 'carry before', also 'place before in esteem'.

prelature ▶ **noun** the office, rank, or sphere of authority of a prelate. ■ (**the prelature**) prelates collectively.
– ORIGIN early 17th cent.: from French *prélature*, from medieval Latin *praelatura*, from *praelatus* 'civil dignitary' (see PRELATE).

prelim /ˈpriːlɪm, prɪˈlɪm/ ▶ **noun** informal **1** an event which precedes or prepares for another, in particular: ■ a preliminary examination, especially at a university. ■ a preliminary round in a sporting competition: *the prelims of the 400-meter free relay*.
2 (**prelims**) the pages preceding the main text of a book, including the title, contents, and preface.
– ORIGIN late 19th cent.: abbreviation of PRELIMINARY.

preliminary ▶ **adjective** preceding or done in preparation for something fuller or more important: *a preliminary draft* | *the discussions were seen as* ***preliminary to*** *the policy paper*.
▶ **noun** (pl. **preliminaries**) a preliminary action or event: *the bombardment was resumed as* ***a preliminary to*** *an infantry attack*. ■ (**preliminaries**) business or talk, especially of a formulaic or polite nature, taking place before an action or event: *she began speaking, without preliminaries*. ■ a preliminary round in a sporting competition. ■ (**preliminaries**) the prelims of a text.
– PHRASES **preliminary to** preparatory to; in advance of.
– DERIVATIVES **preliminarily** adverb.
– ORIGIN mid 17th cent.: from modern Latin *praeliminaris* or French *préliminaire*, from Latin *prae* 'before' + *limen, limin-* 'threshold'.

prelingually deaf ▶ **adjective** deaf from birth or from a time in infancy before the development of the ability to speak.

prelinguistic ▶ **adjective** of or at a stage before the development of language (by the human species) or the acquisition of speech (by a child).

preliterate ▶ **adjective** relating to or denoting a society or culture that has not developed the use of writing.

preload ▶ **verb** [with obj.] load beforehand: *the camera comes preloaded with a 24-exposure film*. ■ give (a mechanical component) an internal load independent of any working load, typically in order to reduce distortion or noise in operation.
▶ **noun** a thing loaded or applied as a load beforehand.

pre-loved ▶ **adjective** informal second-hand.

prelude /ˈprɛljuːd/ ▶ **noun 1** an action or event serving as an introduction to something more important: *a ceasefire had been agreed as* ***a prelude to*** *full peace negotiations*.
2 an introductory piece of music, most commonly an orchestral opening to an act of an opera, the first movement of a suite, or a piece preceding a fugue. ■ a short piece of music of a similar style, especially for the piano. ■ the introductory part of a poem or other literary work.
▶ **verb** [with obj.] serve as a prelude or introduction to: *the bombardment preluded an all-out final attack*.
– DERIVATIVES **preludial** adjective.
– ORIGIN mid 16th cent.: from French *prélude*, from medieval Latin *praeludium*, from Latin *praeludere* 'play beforehand', from *prae* 'before' + *ludere* 'to play'.

premarital ▶ **adjective** occurring or existing before marriage: *premarital sex*.
– DERIVATIVES **premaritally** adverb.

premaster ▶ **verb** [with obj.] Computing make a master copy of (data) on a hard disk before writing it to a CD-ROM.

prematch ▶ **adjective** in or relating to the period before a sports match: *his prematch press conference*.

premature ▶ **adjective** occurring or done before the usual or proper time; too early: *the sun can cause premature ageing* | [with infinitive] *it would be premature to draw any firm conclusions at this stage*. ■ (of a baby) born before the end of the full term of gestation, especially three or more weeks before.
– DERIVATIVES **prematurity** noun.
– ORIGIN late Middle English (in the sense 'ripe, mature'): from Latin *praematurus* 'very early', from *prae* 'before' + *maturus* 'ripe'.

premature ejaculation ▶ **noun** [mass noun] ejaculation of semen during sexual intercourse before or immediately after penetration.

prematurely ▶ **adverb** before the due time; ahead of time: *his son died prematurely* | *prematurely grey hair*.

premaxillary ▶ **adjective** Anatomy situated in front of the maxilla.

pre-med ▶ **noun 1** chiefly N. Amer. a premedical course. ■ a student on a pre-med course.
2 short for PREMEDICATION.
▶ **adjective** short for PREMEDICAL.

premedical ▶ **adjective** relating to or engaged in study in preparation for medical school.

premedication ▶ **noun** [mass noun] medication which is given in preparation for an operation or other treatment.

premeditate ▶ **verb** [with obj.] (usu. as adj. **premeditated**) think out or plan (an action, especially a crime) beforehand: *premeditated murder*.
– ORIGIN mid 16th cent. (earlier (late Middle English) as *premeditation*): from Latin *praemeditat-* 'thought out before', from the verb *praemeditari*, from *prae* 'before' + *meditari* 'meditate'.

premeditation ▶ **noun** [mass noun] the action of planning something (especially a crime) beforehand; intent: *the defendant said there was no planning or premeditation*.

premenopausal /priːˌmɛnəˈpɔːz(ə)l/ ▶ **adjective** of or in the period of a woman's life immediately preceding the menopause.

premenstrual /priːˈmɛnstrʊəl/ ▶ **adjective** of, occurring, or experienced before menstruation: *premenstrual tension*.
– DERIVATIVES **premenstrually** adverb.

premenstrual syndrome (abbrev.: **PMS**) ▶ **noun** [mass noun] any of a complex of symptoms (including emotional tension and fluid retention) experienced by some women in the days immediately before menstruation.

premier /ˈprɛmɪə, ˈpriː-/ ▶ **adjective** [attrib.] first in importance, order, or position; leading: *Germany's premier rock band* | *the premier league*. ■ of earliest creation: *he holds the premier barony in the UK—created in 1269*.
▶ **noun** a Prime Minister or other head of government. ■ (in Australia and Canada) the chief minister of a government of a state or province.
– ORIGIN late 15th cent.: from Old French, 'first', from Latin *primarius* 'principal'.

premier cru /ˌprɛmɪə ˈkruː/, French /pʀəmje kʀy/ ▶ **noun** (pl. **premiers crus** pronunc. **same**) (chiefly in French official classifications) a wine of a superior grade, or the vineyard that produces it. Compare with GRAND CRU.
– ORIGIN French, literally 'first growth'.

premiere /ˈprɛmɪɛː/ ▶ **noun** the first performance of a musical or theatrical work or the first showing of a film.
▶ **verb** [with obj.] give the first performance of: *his first stage play was premiered at the Birmingham Repertory Theatre*. ■ [no obj.] (of a musical or theatrical work or a film) have its first performance: *the show premiered in New York this week*.
– ORIGIN late 19th cent.: French *première*, feminine of *premier* 'first' (see PREMIER).

premiership ▶ **noun** [mass noun] **1** the office or position of a Prime Minister or other head of government.
2 (**the Premiership**) the top division of professional soccer in England.

premillennial ▶ **adjective 1** existing or occurring before a new millennium.
2 Christian Theology relating to or believing in premillennialism.

premillennialism ▶ **noun** [mass noun] (among Christian fundamentalists) the doctrine that the prophesied millennium of blessedness will begin with the imminent Second Coming of Christ.
– DERIVATIVES **premillennialist** noun.

Preminger /ˈprɛmɪndʒə/, Otto (Ludwig) (1906–86), Austrian-born American film director, noted for films such as *The Moon is Blue* (1953), *The Man with the Golden Arm* (1955), and *Bonjour Tristesse* (1959).

premise ▶ **noun** /ˈprɛmɪs/ (Brit. also **premiss**) Logic a previous statement or proposition from which another is inferred or follows as a conclusion: *if the premise is true, then the conclusion must be true*. ■ an assertion or proposition which forms the basis for a work or theory: *the fundamental premise of the report*.
▶ **verb** /prɪˈmʌɪz/ [with obj.] (**premise something on/upon**) base an argument, theory, or undertaking on: *the reforms were premised on our findings*. ■ state or presuppose (something) as a premise: [with clause] *one school of thought premised that the cosmos is indestructible*. ■ archaic state by way of introduction.
– ORIGIN late Middle English: from Old French *premisse*, from medieval Latin *praemissa* (*propositio*) '(proposition) set in front', from Latin *praemittere*, from *prae* 'before' + *mittere* 'send'.

premises ▶ **plural noun** a house or building, together with its land and outbuildings, occupied by a business or considered in an official context: *the company has moved to new premises* | *alcohol is not allowed on the premises* | [treated as sing.] *the three had negotiated a lease for a premises in Boothstown, Manchester*.

premium ▶ **noun** (pl. **premiums**) **1** an amount to be paid for a contract of insurance.
2 a sum added to an ordinary price or charge: *customers are reluctant to pay a premium for organic fruit*. ■ a sum added to interest or wages; a bonus. ■ [as modifier] relating to or denoting a commodity of superior quality and therefore a higher price: *premium lagers*. ■ Stock Exchange the amount by which the price of a share or other security exceeds its issue price, its nominal value, or the value of the assets it represents: *the shares jumped to a 70 per cent premium on the first day*.
3 something given as a reward, prize, or incentive: *the Society of Arts awarded him a premium*.
– PHRASES **at a premium 1** scarce and in demand: *space was at a premium*. **2** above the usual or nominal price: *touts sell the tickets at a premium*. **put** (or **place**) **a premium on** regard or treat as particularly valuable or important: *he put a premium on peace and stability*.
– ORIGIN early 17th cent. (in the sense 'reward, prize'): from Latin *praemium* 'booty, reward', from *prae* 'before' + *emere* 'buy, take'.

Premium Bond (also **Premium Savings Bond**) ▶ **noun** (in the UK) a government security that offers no interest or capital gain but is entered in regular draws for cash prizes.

premix ▶ **verb** [with obj.] mix in advance.
▶ **noun** a substance or product consisting of ready-mixed elements or materials.

premodify ▶ **verb** (**premodifies, premodifying, premodified**) [with obj.] Grammar modify the sense of (a noun or other word) by being placed before it.
– DERIVATIVES **premodification** noun, **premodifier** noun.

premolar ▶ **noun** a tooth situated between the canine and the molar teeth. An adult human normally has eight, two in each jaw on each side.

premonition /ˌprɛməˈnɪʃ(ə)n, ˌpriː-/ ▶ **noun** a strong feeling that something is about to happen, especially something unpleasant: *he had* ***a premonition of*** *imminent disaster*.
– DERIVATIVES **premonitory** adjective.
– ORIGIN mid 16th cent. (in the sense 'advance warning'): from French *prémonition*, from late Latin *praemonitio(n-)*, from Latin *praemonere*, from *prae* 'before' + *monere* 'warn'.

Premonstratensian /ˌpriːmɒnstrəˈtɛnsɪən/ ▶ **noun** a member of an order of regular canons founded at Prémontré in France in 1120, or of the corresponding order of nuns. Also called NORBERTINE.
▶ **adjective** relating to the Premonstratensians.
– ORIGIN from medieval Latin *Praemonstratensis*, from *Praemonstratus* (literally 'foreshown'), the Latin name of the abbey of Prémontré, so named

P

because the site was prophetically pointed out by the order's founder, St Norbert.

premorbid ▸ adjective Medicine & Psychiatry preceding the occurrence of symptoms of disease or disorder.

premotor ▸ adjective Anatomy relating to or denoting the anterior part of the motor cortex in the frontal lobe of the brain, which is concerned with coordinating voluntary movement.

premultiply ▸ verb (**premultiplies**, **premultiplying**, **premultiplied**) [with obj.] Mathematics multiply (a vector, matrix, or element of a group) non-commutatively by a preceding factor.

prenatal ▸ adjective before birth; during or relating to pregnancy: *prenatal development*.
– DERIVATIVES **prenatally** adverb.

prenominal ▸ adjective Grammar (of a word or part of speech) preceding a noun.
– ORIGIN mid 17th cent.: from Latin *praenomen*, *praenomin-* 'first name' + **-AL**.

prentice ▸ noun & verb archaic term for **APPRENTICE**.
– DERIVATIVES **prenticeship** noun.

prenup ▸ noun N. Amer. informal a prenuptial agreement.

prenuptial ▸ adjective existing or occurring before marriage: *prenuptial pregnancy*. ■ Zoology existing or occurring before mating.

prenuptial agreement ▸ noun chiefly N. Amer. an agreement made by a couple before they marry concerning the ownership of their respective assets should the marriage fail.

preoccupation ▸ noun [mass noun] the state or condition of being preoccupied or engrossed with something: *his* ***preoccupation with*** *politics*. ■ [count noun] a subject or matter that engrosses someone: *their main preoccupation was how to feed their families*.
– ORIGIN late 16th cent. (first used in rhetoric in the sense 'anticipating and meeting objections beforehand'): from Latin *praeoccupatio(n-)*, from *praeoccupare* 'seize beforehand' (see **PREOCCUPY**).

preoccupy ▸ verb (**preoccupies**, **preoccupying**, **preoccupied**) [with obj.] (of a matter or subject) dominate or engross the mind of (someone) to the exclusion of other thoughts: *his mother was* ***preoccupied with*** *paying the bills* | (as adj. **preoccupied**) *she seemed a bit preoccupied*.
– ORIGIN mid 16th cent.: from **PRE-** + **OCCUPY**, suggested by Latin *praeoccupare* 'seize beforehand'.

preocular ▸ adjective in front of the eye.

pre-op informal ▸ adjective short for **PREOPERATIVE**.
▸ noun a tranquillizing injection or other treatment administered in preparation for a surgical operation.

preoperative ▸ adjective denoting, administered in, or occurring in the period before a surgical operation.
– DERIVATIVES **preoperatively** adverb.

preorbital ▸ adjective chiefly Zoology situated in front of the orbit or eye socket.

preordain ▸ verb [with obj.] decide or determine (an outcome or course of action) beforehand: *you might think the company's success was preordained* | (as adj. **preordained**) *a divinely preordained plan of creation*.

pre-order ▸ verb [with obj.] place an order for (an item) before it is available for purchase: *click on the link below to pre-order the DVD*.
▸ noun an order for a product placed before it is available for purchase.

pre-owned ▸ adjective chiefly N. Amer. second-hand.

prep[1] ▸ noun informal **1** [mass noun] Brit. (especially in an independent school) schoolwork that is set to be done outside lessons. ■ a period set aside for this.
2 [as modifier] relating to education in a preparatory school: *sixth-formers and prep pupils*.
3 N. Amer. a student in a preparatory school.
– ORIGIN mid 19th cent.: abbreviation of **PREPARATION**.

prep[2] informal, chiefly N. Amer. ▸ verb (**preps**, **prepping**, **prepped**) [with obj.] prepare (something); make ready: *scores of volunteers help prep the food*. ■ [no obj.] prepare oneself for an event: *to prep for his role he trimmed his unruly locks*.
▸ noun [mass noun] preparation: *I do the prep*.
– ORIGIN 1920s: abbreviation of **PREPARE** or **PREPARATION**.

prep. ▸ abbreviation preposition.

pre-pack (also **pre-package**) ▸ verb [with obj.] (usu. as adj. **pre-packed**) pack or wrap (goods, especially food) on the site of production or before sale: *pre-packed salmon steaks*.

prepaid past and past participle of **PREPAY**.

preparation ▸ noun **1** [mass noun] the action or process of preparing or being prepared for use or consideration: *the preparation of a draft contract* | *the project is* ***in preparation***. ■ [count noun] (usu. **preparations**) something done to get ready for an event or undertaking: *she continued her* ***preparations for*** *the party*.
2 a substance that is specially made up, especially a medicine or food. ■ a specimen that has been prepared for scientific or medical examination: *a microscope preparation*.
3 Music (in conventional harmony) the sounding of the discordant note in a chord in the preceding chord where it is not discordant, lessening the effect of the discord.
4 Brit. dated fuller form of **PREP**[1] (sense 1).
– ORIGIN late Middle English: via Old French from Latin *praeparatio(n-)*, from *praeparare* 'make ready before' (see **PREPARE**).

preparative ▸ adjective preparatory.
▸ noun a preparatory act, procedure, or circumstance.
– DERIVATIVES **preparatively** adverb.

preparatory ▸ adjective serving as or carrying out preparation for a task or undertaking: *more preparatory work is needed*. ■ Brit. relating to education in a preparatory school: *preparatory schooling*.
– PHRASES **preparatory to** as a preparation for: *she applied her make-up preparatory to leaving*.
– ORIGIN late Middle English: from late Latin *praeparatorius*, from *praeparat-* 'made ready beforehand', from the verb *praeparare* (see **PREPARE**).

preparatory school ▸ noun **1** Brit. a private school for pupils between the ages of seven and thirteen.
2 N. Amer. a private school that prepares pupils for college or university.

prepare ▸ verb [with obj.] **1** make (something) ready for use or consideration: *prepare a brief summary of the article*. ■ (as adj. **prepared**) created in advance; pre-planned: *the spokesman was reading a prepared statement*. ■ make (food or a meal) ready for cooking or eating: *she was busy preparing lunch*. ■ make (a substance) by a chemical reaction or series of reactions.
2 make (someone) ready or able to do or deal with something: *schools should* ***prepare*** *children* ***for*** *life* | [no obj.] *she took time off to* ***prepare for*** *her exams*. ■ (**be prepared to do something**) be willing to do something: *I wasn't prepared to go along with that*.
3 Music (in conventional harmony) lead up to (a discord) by means of preparation.
– DERIVATIVES **preparer** noun.
– ORIGIN late Middle English: from French *préparer* or Latin *praeparare*, from *prae* 'before' + *parare* 'make ready'.

preparedness ▸ noun [mass noun] a state of readiness, especially for war: *the country maintained a high level of military preparedness*.

prepared piano ▸ noun a piano with objects placed on or between the strings, or some strings retuned, to produce an unusual tonal effect.

prepay ▸ verb (**prepays**, **prepaying**; past and past participle **prepaid**) [with obj.] (usu. as adj. **prepaid**) pay for in advance: *prepaid licence fees*. ■ (as adj. **prepaid**) (of an envelope or address label) supplied with the postage already paid for contents up to a certain weight.
– DERIVATIVES **prepayable** adjective, **prepayment** noun.

prepense /prɪˈpɛns/ ▸ adjective [usu. postpositive] chiefly Law, dated deliberate; intentional: *malice prepense*.
– DERIVATIVES **prepensely** adverb.
– ORIGIN early 18th cent.: alteration of *prepensed*, past participle of obsolete *prepense*, from Old French *purpenser*, from *por-* 'beforehand' + *penser* 'think'. The prefix *pre-* was substituted to emphasize the notion of 'beforehand'.

pre-plan ▸ verb [with obj.] (usu. as adj. **pre-planned**) plan in advance: *a pre-planned route*.

prepolymer ▸ noun Chemistry a substance which represents an intermediate stage in polymerization, and can be usefully manipulated before polymerization is completed.

preponderance ▸ noun [mass noun] the quality or fact of being greater in number, quantity, or importance: *the preponderance of women among older people* | [count noun] *a preponderance of lower-paid jobs*.

preponderant ▸ adjective predominant in influence, number, or importance: *the preponderant influence of the US within the alliance*.
– DERIVATIVES **preponderantly** adverb.
– ORIGIN late Middle English: from Latin *preponderant-* 'weighing more', from the verb *praeponderare* (see **PREPONDERATE**).

preponderate ▸ verb [no obj.] be greater in number, influence, or importance: *the advantages* ***preponderate over*** *this apparent disadvantage*.
– ORIGIN early 17th cent. (in the sense 'weigh more, have greater intellectual weight'): from Latin *praeponderat-* 'of greater weight', from the verb *praeponderare*, from *prae* 'before' + *ponderare* 'weigh, consider'.

prepone /priːˈpəʊn/ ▸ verb [with obj.] Indian bring (something) forward to an earlier date or time: *the publication date has been preponed from July to June*.
– ORIGIN 1970s: from **PRE-** + **POSTPONE**.

prepose ▸ verb [with obj.] Linguistics place (an element or word) in front of another.
– ORIGIN late 15th cent. (in the sense 'place in authority'): from French *préposer*, suggested by Latin *praeponere* 'put before'.

preposition /ˌprɛpəˈzɪʃ(ə)n/ ▸ noun Grammar a word governing, and usually preceding, a noun or pronoun and expressing a relation to another word or element in the clause, as in 'the man *on* the platform', 'she arrived *after* dinner', 'what did you do it *for*?'.
– DERIVATIVES **prepositional** adjective, **prepositionally** adverb.
– ORIGIN late Middle English: from Latin *praepositio(n-)*, from the verb *praeponere*, from *prae* 'before' + *ponere* 'to place'.

> **USAGE** There is a traditional view, first set forth by the 17th-century poet and dramatist John Dryden, that it is incorrect to put a preposition at the end of a sentence, as in *where do you come* ***from***? or *she's not a writer I've ever come* ***across***. The rule was formulated on the basis that, since in Latin a preposition cannot come after the word it governs or is linked with, the same should be true of English. The problem is that English is not like Latin in this respect, and in many cases (particularly in questions and with phrasal verbs) the attempt to move the preposition produces awkward, unnatural-sounding results. Winston Churchill famously objected to the rule, saying, *'This is the sort of English* ***up with*** *which I will not* ***put***.*'* In standard English the placing of a preposition at the end of a sentence is widely accepted, provided the use sounds natural and the meaning is clear.

prepositional object ▸ noun Grammar a noun phrase governed by a preposition.

prepositive /priːˈpɒzɪtɪv/ ▸ adjective Grammar (of a word, particle, etc.) placed in front of the word that it governs or modifies.
– ORIGIN late 16th cent.: from late Latin *praepositivus* (see **PRE-**, **POSITIVE**).

prepossessing ▸ adjective [often with negative] attractive or appealing in appearance: *he was not a prepossessing sight*.
– DERIVATIVES **prepossession** noun.

preposterous ▸ adjective contrary to reason or common sense; utterly absurd or ridiculous: *a preposterous suggestion*.
– DERIVATIVES **preposterously** adverb, **preposterousness** noun.
– ORIGIN mid 16th cent.: from Latin *praeposterus* 'reversed, absurd' (from *prae* 'before' + *posterus* 'coming after') + **-OUS**.

prepotent ▸ adjective greater than others in power or influence. ■ (of a breeding animal) showing great effectiveness in transmitting hereditary characteristics to its offspring.
– DERIVATIVES **prepotency** noun.
– ORIGIN late Middle English: from Latin *praepotent-* 'having greater power', from *prae* 'before, ahead' + *posse* 'be able'.

preppy (also **preppie**) informal, chiefly US ▸ noun (pl. **preppies**) a pupil or graduate of an expensive preparatory school, or a person resembling such a pupil in dress or appearance.
▸ adjective (**preppier**, **preppiest**) of or typical of such a person, especially with reference to their neat style of dress: *the preppy look*.
– ORIGIN early 20th cent.: from **PREP SCHOOL** + **-Y**[2].

preprandial ▸ adjective formal or humorous done or taken before dinner or lunch: *a preprandial glass of sherry*. ■ Medicine occurring or done before a meal.
– ORIGIN early 19th cent.: from **PRE-** 'before' + Latin *prandium* 'a meal' + **-AL**.

prepreg ▸ noun [mass noun] a fibrous material pre-impregnated with a particular synthetic resin, used in making reinforced plastics.
– ORIGIN 1950s: from **PRE-** 'before' + *(im)preg(nated)*.

pre-prepare ▸ verb [with obj.] (usu as adj. **pre-prepared**) prepare or produce (something, especially food) in advance: *a takeaway or pre-prepared meal.*

pre-press ▸ adjective relating to composition, page layout, and other work done on a publication before it is actually printed.

preprint ▸ verb [with obj.] (usu. as adj. **preprinted**) print (something) in advance: *a preprinted form.*
▸ noun something which is printed in advance, especially a part of a work printed and issued before general publication of that work.

preprocess ▸ verb [with obj.] subject (data) to preliminary processing.

preprocessor ▸ noun a computer program that modifies data to conform with the input requirements of another program.

pre-production ▸ noun [mass noun] work done on a product, especially a film or broadcast programme, before full-scale production begins: [as modifier] *the pre-production script.*

preprogram ▸ verb (**preprogrammes, preprogramming, preprogrammed**) [with obj.] (usu. as adj. **preprogrammed**) program (a computer or other electronic device) in advance: *a preprogrammed function key.* ▪ program (something) into a computer or other electronic device before use: *preprogrammed messages.*

prep school ▸ noun another term for **PREPARATORY SCHOOL**.

prepubertal ▸ adjective another term for **PREPUBESCENT**.
– DERIVATIVES **prepuberty** noun.

prepubescent ▸ adjective relating to or in the period preceding puberty: *a prepubescent girl.*
▸ noun a prepubescent boy or girl.
– DERIVATIVES **prepubescence** noun.

prepublication ▸ adjective issued or occurring before publication: *prepublication censorship.*
▸ noun [mass noun] publication in advance.

prepuce /ˈpriːpjuːs/ ▸ noun Anatomy **1** technical term for **FORESKIN**.
2 the fold of skin surrounding the clitoris.
– DERIVATIVES **preputial** adjective.
– ORIGIN late Middle English: from French *prépuce*, from Latin *praeputium*.

pre-qualify ▸ verb [no obj.] qualify in advance to take part in a sporting event: (as adj. **pre-qualifying**) *players who fail at the pre-qualifying stage.*

prequel /ˈpriːkw(ə)l/ ▸ noun a story or film containing events which precede those of an existing work: *the film is a prequel to the cult TV series.*
– ORIGIN 1970s: from **PRE-** 'before' + **SEQUEL**.

Pre-Raphaelite /priːˈrafəlʌɪt/ ▸ noun a member of a group of English 19th-century artists, including Holman Hunt, Millais, and D. G. Rossetti, who consciously sought to emulate the simplicity and sincerity of the work of Italian artists from before the time of Raphael.

> Seven young English artists and writers founded the **Pre-Raphaelite Brotherhood** in 1848 as a reaction against the slick sentimentality and academic convention of much Victorian art. Their work is characterized by strong line and colour, naturalistic detail, and often biblical or literary subjects. The group began to disperse in the 1850s, and the term became applied to the rather different later work of Rossetti, and that of Burne-Jones and William Morris, in which a romantic and decorative depiction of classical and medieval themes had come to predominate.

▸ adjective relating to the Pre-Raphaelites. ▪ (especially of a woman) reminiscent of a Pre-Raphaelite painting, typically in having long, thick, wavy auburn hair, pale skin, and a fey demeanour.
– DERIVATIVES **Pre-Raphaelitism** noun.

pre-record ▸ verb [with obj.] (often as adj. **pre-recorded**) record (sound or film) in advance: *a pre-recorded talk.* ▪ record sound on (a tape) beforehand: *pre-recorded digital audiotapes.*

preregistration ▸ noun [mass noun] **1** the action of registering or being registered in advance: *members are entitled to free preregistration.*
2 [as modifier] relating to or denoting the period of a doctor's training between qualification and registration: *the preregistration year.*
– DERIVATIVES **preregister** verb.

pre-release ▸ adjective **1** relating to or denoting a record, film, or other product that has not yet been generally released: *a pre-release version of the software.*
2 relating to the period before the release of a suspect or prisoner.
▸ noun a film, record, or other product given restricted availability before being generally released.

prerequisite /priːˈrɛkwɪzɪt/ ▸ noun a thing that is required as a prior condition for something else to happen or exist: *sponsorship is not a* **prerequisite for** *any of our courses.*
▸ adjective required as a prior condition: *the student must have the prerequisite skills.*

prerogative /prɪˈrɒgətɪv/ ▸ noun a right or privilege exclusive to a particular individual or class: *in some countries, higher education is predominantly the prerogative of the rich.* ▪ (also **royal prerogative**) [mass noun] the right of the sovereign, which in British law is theoretically subject to no restriction. ▪ a faculty or property distinguishing a person or class: *it's not a female prerogative to feel insecure.*
▸ adjective Law, Brit. arising from the prerogative of the Crown (usually delegated to the government or the judiciary) and based in common law rather than statutory law: *the monarch retained the formal prerogative power to appoint the Prime Minister.*
– ORIGIN late Middle English: via Old French from Latin *praerogativa* '(the verdict of) the political division which was chosen to vote first in the assembly', feminine (used as noun) of *praerogativus* 'asked first', from *prae* 'before' + *rogare* 'ask'.

prerogative court ▸ noun historical (in the UK) either of two ecclesiastical courts at Canterbury and York formerly responsible for the probate of wills involving property in more than one diocese.

prerogative of mercy ▸ noun [mass noun] the right and power of a sovereign, state president, or other supreme authority to commute a death sentence, to change the mode of execution, or to pardon an offender.

pre-Roman ▸ adjective relating to a period before the rise or dominance of ancient Rome, or before the conquest of a particular region by the ancient Romans: *the Celtic kingdoms of pre-Roman Britain.*

Pres. ▸ abbreviation President.

presage /ˈprɛsɪdʒ/ ▸ verb also /prɪˈseɪdʒ/ [with obj.] be a sign or warning of (an imminent event, typically an unwelcome one): *the heavy clouds above the moorland presaged snow.* ▪ archaic (of a person) predict: *lands he could measure, terms and tides presage.*
▸ noun an omen or portent: *the fever was a sombre presage of his final illness.* ▪ archaic a feeling of presentiment or foreboding: *he had a strong presage that he had only a very short time to live.*
– DERIVATIVES **presager** noun (archaic).
– ORIGIN late Middle English (as a noun): via French from Latin *praesagium*, from *praesagire* 'forebode', from *prae* 'before' + *sagire* 'perceive keenly'.

presbyopia /ˌprɛzbɪˈəʊpɪə/ ▸ noun [mass noun] long-sightedness caused by loss of elasticity of the lens of the eye, occurring typically in middle and old age.
– DERIVATIVES **presbyopic** adjective.
– ORIGIN late 18th cent.: modern Latin, from Greek *presbus* 'old man' + *ōps, ōp-* 'eye'.

presbyter /ˈprɛzbɪtə/ ▸ noun historical an elder or minister of the Christian Church. ▪ formal (in Presbyterian Churches) an elder. ▪ formal (in episcopal Churches) a minister of the second order, under the authority of a bishop.
– DERIVATIVES **presbyteral** /-ˈbɪt(ə)r(ə)l/ adjective, **presbyterate** noun, **presbyterial** adjective.
– ORIGIN late 16th cent.: via ecclesiastical Latin from Greek *presbuteros* 'elder' (used in the New Testament to denote an elder of the early church), comparative of *presbus* 'old (man)'.

Presbyterian /ˌprɛzbɪˈtɪərɪən/ ▸ adjective relating to or denoting a Christian Church or denomination governed by elders according to the principles of Presbyterianism.
▸ noun a member of a Presbyterian Church. ▪ an advocate of the Presbyterian system.
– ORIGIN mid 17th cent.: from ecclesiastical Latin *presbyterium* (see **PRESBYTERY**) + **-AN**.

Presbyterianism ▸ noun [mass noun] a form of Protestant Church government in which the Church is administered locally by the minister with a group of elected elders of equal rank, and regionally and nationally by representative courts of ministers and elders.

> Presbyterianism was first introduced in Geneva in 1541 under John Calvin, in the belief that it best represented the pattern of the early church. There are now many Presbyterian Churches (often called Reformed Churches) worldwide, notably in the Netherlands and Scotland and in countries with which they have historic links (including the United States and Northern Ireland). They typically subscribe (more or less strictly) to the Westminster Confession.

presbytery /ˈprɛzbɪt(ə)ri/ ▸ noun (pl. **presbyteries**)
1 [treated as sing. or pl.] a body of Church elders and ministers, especially (in Presbyterian Churches) an administrative body (court) representing all the local congregations of a district. ▪ a district represented by such a body of elders and ministers.
2 the house of a Roman Catholic parish priest.
3 chiefly Architecture the eastern part of a church chancel beyond the choir; the sanctuary.
– ORIGIN late Middle English (in sense 3): from Old French *presbiterie*, via ecclesiastical Latin from Greek *presbuterion*, from *presbuteros* (see **PRESBYTER**).

preschool ▸ adjective relating to the time before a child is old enough to go to school: *a preschool playgroup.*
▸ noun a nursery school.
– DERIVATIVES **preschooler** noun.

prescience ▸ noun [mass noun] the fact of knowing something in advance; foreknowledge: *with extraordinary prescience, Jung actually predicted the Nazi eruption.*

prescient /ˈprɛsɪənt/ ▸ adjective having or showing knowledge of events before they take place: *a prescient warning.*
– DERIVATIVES **presciently** adverb.
– ORIGIN early 17th cent.: from Latin *praescient-* 'knowing beforehand', from the verb *praescire*, from *prae* 'before' + *scire* 'know'.

pre-scientific ▸ adjective relating to the time before the development of modern science or the application of scientific method.

prescind /prɪˈsɪnd/ ▸ verb [no obj.] (**prescind from**) formal leave out of consideration: *such traditionalists have prescinded from novel practices and attitudes.* ▪ [with obj.] detach or separate from something: *his is an idea entirely prescinded from all of the others.*
– ORIGIN mid 17th cent. (in the sense 'cut off abruptly or prematurely'): from Latin *praescindere*, from *prae* 'before' + *scindere* 'to cut'.

prescribe ▸ verb [with obj.] **1** (of a medical practitioner) advise and authorize the use of (a medicine or treatment) for someone, especially in writing: *her doctor prescribed sleeping tablets* | [with two objs] *he was prescribed a course of antibiotics.* ▪ recommend (a substance or action) as something beneficial: *marriage is often prescribed as a universal remedy.*
2 state authoritatively or as a rule that (an action or procedure) should be carried out: *rules prescribing five acts for a play are purely arbitrary.*
– DERIVATIVES **prescribable** adjective, **prescriber** noun.
– ORIGIN late Middle English (in the sense 'confine within bounds', also as a legal term meaning 'claim by prescription'): from Latin *praescribere* 'direct in writing', from *prae* 'before' + *scribere* 'write'.

> **USAGE** The verbs **prescribe** and **proscribe** do not have the same meaning. **Prescribe** is a much commoner word and means either 'issue a medical prescription' or 'recommend with authority', as in *the doctor* ***prescribed*** *antibiotics*. **Proscribe**, on the other hand, is a formal word meaning 'condemn or forbid', as in *gambling was strictly* ***proscribed*** *by the authorities*.

prescript /ˈpriːskrɪpt/ ▸ noun formal or dated an ordinance, law, or command.
– ORIGIN mid 16th cent.: from Latin *praescriptum* 'something directed in writing', neuter past participle of *praescribere* (see **PRESCRIBE**).

prescription ▸ noun **1** an instruction written by a medical practitioner that authorizes a patient to be issued with a medicine or treatment: *he scribbled a prescription for tranquillizers* | [mass noun] *the lotion is available* **on prescription**. ▪ [mass noun] the action of prescribing a medicine or treatment: *the unnecessary prescription of antibiotics.* ▪ a medicine or remedy that is prescribed: *I've got to pick up my prescription from the chemist's.*
2 a recommendation that is authoritatively put forward: *effective prescriptions for sustaining rural communities.*
3 (also **positive prescription**) [mass noun] Law the establishment of a claim founded on the basis of a long or indefinite period of uninterrupted use or of long-standing custom.
– ORIGIN late Middle English (as a legal term): via Old French from Latin *praescriptio(n-)*, from the verb

P

praescribere (see **PRESCRIBE**). Sense 1 dates from the late 16th cent.

prescriptive ▸ **adjective 1** relating to the imposition or enforcement of a rule or method: *these guidelines are not intended to be prescriptive.* ■ Linguistics attempting to impose rules of correct usage on the users of a language: *a prescriptive grammar book.* Often contrasted with **DESCRIPTIVE**.
2 (of a right, title, or institution) having become legally established or accepted by long usage or the passage of time: *a prescriptive right of way.* ■ archaic arising from long-standing custom or usage: *for her own mother she felt no more than a prescriptive affection.*
– DERIVATIVES **prescriptively** adverb, **prescriptiveness** noun, **prescriptivism** noun, **prescriptivist** noun & adjective.
– ORIGIN mid 18th cent.: from late Latin *praescriptivus* 'relating to a legal exception', from *praescript-* 'directed in writing', from the verb *praescribere* (see **PRESCRIBE**).

preseason ▸ **adjective** (of a sporting fixture) taking place before the regular season.
▸ **noun** the period of time before the regular season.

preselect ▸ **verb** [with obj.] select or set in advance: *four British swimmers were preselected for the Olympics.*
– DERIVATIVES **preselection** noun, **preselective** adjective.

preselector ▸ **noun** a device for selecting a mechanical or electrical operation in advance of its execution.

pre-sell ▸ **verb** [with obj.] promote or market (a product) before it is officially launched: *producers can pre-sell a film on the basis of the script.*

presence ▸ **noun** [mass noun] the state or fact of existing, occurring, or being present: *my presence in the flat made her happy | the presence of chlorine in the atmosphere | the memorial was unveiled **in the presence of** 24 veterans.* ■ [count noun] a person or thing that exists or is present in a place but is not seen: *the monks became aware of a strange presence.* ■ [in sing.] a group of people, especially soldiers or police, stationed in a particular place: *the USA would maintain a presence in the Indian Ocean region.* ■ the impressive manner or appearance of a person: *Richard was not a big man but his presence was overwhelming.*
– PHRASES **make one's presence felt** have a strong and obvious effect or influence on others or on a situation. **presence of mind** the ability to remain calm and take quick, sensible action: *he had the presence of mind to record the scene on video.*
– ORIGIN Middle English: via Old French from Latin *praesentia* 'being at hand', from the verb *praeesse* (see **PRESENT[1]**).

presence chamber ▸ **noun** a room, especially one in a palace, in which a monarch or other distinguished person receives visitors.

presenile /priːˈsiːnʌɪl/ ▸ **adjective** occurring in or characteristic of the period of life preceding old age: *Alzheimer's disease is a form of presenile dementia.*

present[1] /ˈprɛz(ə)nt/ ▸ **adjective 1** [predic.] in a particular place: *a doctor must be present at the ringside | the speech caused embarrassment to all those present.* ■ existing or occurring in a place or thing: *gases present in the atmosphere.*
2 [attrib.] existing or occurring now: *she did not expect to find herself in her present situation.* ■ now being considered or discussed: *the present article cannot answer every question.* ■ Grammar (of a tense or participle) expressing an action now going on or habitually performed, or a condition now existing.
▸ **noun 1** (usu. **the present**) the period of time now occurring: *they are happy and at peace, refusing to think beyond the present.*
2 Grammar a present tense: *the verbs are all in the present.* See also **HISTORIC PRESENT**.
– PHRASES **all present and correct** used to indicate that not a single thing or person is missing. **at present** now: *membership at present stands at about 5,000.* **for the present** for now; temporarily. (**there is**) **no time like the present** an action should be done now rather than later. **present company excepted** excluding those who are here now. **these presents** Law, formal this document: *the premises outlined in red on the Plan annexed to these presents.*
– ORIGIN Middle English: via Old French from Latin *praesent-* 'being at hand', present participle of *praeesse*, from *prae* 'before' + *esse* 'be'.

present[2] /prɪˈzɛnt/ ▸ **verb** [with obj.] **1** give or award formally or ceremonially: *the duke **presented** certificates **to** the men | a local celebrity will present the prizes.* ■ (**present someone with**) give someone (a gift or award) in such a way: *my pupils presented me with some flowers.* ■ show or offer (something) for others to scrutinize or consider: *he stopped and presented his passport.* ■ formally deliver (a cheque or bill) for acceptance or payment: *a cheque presented by Mr Jackson was returned by the bank.* ■ Law bring (a complaint, petition, or evidence) formally to the notice of a court.
2 formally introduce (someone) to someone else: *may I present my wife?* ■ (**present oneself**) appear formally before others: *he failed to present himself in court.* ■ (**present someone to**) (in church use) recommend an ordained minister to a bishop for institution to (a benefice). ■ [no obj.] (often **present with**) Medicine (of a patient) come forward for initial medical examination for a particular condition or symptom: *the patient presented with mild clinical encephalopathy.*
3 introduce or announce the various items of (a television or radio show) as a participant: *the Late Show was presented by Cynthia Rose.* ■ (of a company or producer) put (a show or exhibition) before the public.
4 be the cause of (a problem or difficulty): *the suspect may present a danger to himself or others.* ■ exhibit (a particular state or appearance) to others: *the EC presented a united front over the crisis.* ■ represent (someone or something) to others in a particular way: *the prime minister **presented himself as** a radical figure.* ■ (**present itself**) (of an opportunity or idea) occur and be available for use or exploitation: *when a favourable opportunity presented itself he would submit his proposition.* ■ [no obj.] Medicine (of an illness) manifest itself.
5 [no obj.] Medicine (of a part of a fetus) be directed towards the cervix during labour.
6 hold out or aim (a firearm) at something so as to be ready to fire: *they were to present their rifles, take aim, and fire.*
▸ **noun** (**the present**) the position of a firearm when aimed or held ready to be aimed, especially the position from which a rifle is fired.
– PHRASES **present arms** hold a rifle vertically in front of the body as a salute.
– ORIGIN Middle English: from Old French *presenter*, from Latin *praesentare* 'place before' (in medieval Latin 'present as a gift'), from *praesent-* 'being at hand' (see **PRESENT[1]**).

present[3] /ˈprɛz(ə)nt/ ▸ **noun** a thing given to someone as a gift: *a Christmas present.*
– PHRASES **make a present of** give as a gift: *he had made a present of a hacienda to the president.*
– ORIGIN Middle English: from Old French, originally in the phrase *mettre une chose en present à quelqu'un* 'put a thing into the presence of a person'.

presentable ▸ **adjective** clean, smart, or decent enough to be seen in public: *I did my best to make myself look presentable.*
– DERIVATIVES **presentability** noun, **presentably** adverb.

presentation ▸ **noun 1** [mass noun] the giving of something to someone, especially as part of a formal ceremony: *the presentation of certificates to new members | [count noun] the Lord Lieutenant made the presentations.* ■ the manner or style in which something is given, offered, or displayed: *the presentation of foods is designed to stimulate your appetite.* ■ a formal introduction of someone, especially at court. ■ chiefly historical the action or right of formally proposing a candidate for a Church benefice or other position: *the Earl of Pembroke offered Herbert the presentation of the living of Bremerton.*
2 a speech or talk in which a new product, idea, or piece of work is shown and explained to an audience: *a sales presentation.*
3 Medicine the position of a fetus in relation to the cervix at the time of delivery: *breech presentation.*
4 (**Presentation of Christ**) another term for **CANDLEMAS**.
– DERIVATIVES **presentational** adjective, **presentationally** adverb.
– ORIGIN late Middle English: via Old French from late Latin *praesentatio(n-)*, from Latin *praesentare* 'place before' (see **PRESENT[2]**).

presentative ▸ **adjective** historical (of a benefice) to which a patron has the right of presentation.
– ORIGIN mid 16th cent.: probably from medieval Latin, based on Latin *praesentare* (see **PRESENT[2]**).

present-day ▸ **adjective** relating to the current period of time: *present-day technological developments.*

presentee ▸ **noun** a person nominated or recommended for an office or position, especially a Church living.
– ORIGIN late 15th cent.: from Anglo-Norman French, literally 'presented', from the verb *presenter* (see **PRESENT[2]**).

presenteeism ▸ **noun** [mass noun] the practice of being present at one's place of work for more hours than is required, especially as a manifestation of insecurity about one's job.

presenter ▸ **noun** Brit. a person who introduces and appears in a television or radio programme.

presentient /prɪˈsɛnʃ(ə)nt, -ˈzɛn-/ ▸ **adjective** rare having a presentiment.
– ORIGIN early 19th cent.: from Latin *praesentient-* 'perceiving beforehand', from the verb *praesentire*, from *prae* 'before' + *sentire* 'to feel'.

presentiment /prɪˈzɛntɪm(ə)nt, -ˈsɛn-/ ▸ **noun** an intuitive feeling about the future, especially one of foreboding: *a presentiment of disaster.*
– ORIGIN early 18th cent.: from obsolete French *présentiment*.

presentism ▸ **noun** [mass noun] uncritical adherence to present-day attitudes, especially the tendency to interpret past events in terms of modern values and concepts.
– DERIVATIVES **presentist** adjective.

presently ▸ **adverb 1** at the present time; now: *there are presently 1,128 people on the waiting list.*
2 after a short time; soon: *this will be examined in more detail presently.*

> **USAGE** Presently can mean both 'now, at this moment' and 'soon'. Both senses go back to the Middle Ages. The former sense fell into disfavour between the 17th and 20th centuries and some traditionalists still object to it, but it is widely used and generally regarded as acceptable standard English.

presentment /prɪˈzɛntm(ə)nt/ ▸ **noun** Law a formal presentation of information to a court, especially by a sworn jury regarding an offence or other matter.
– ORIGIN Middle English: from Old French *presentement*, from *presenter* 'place before' (see **PRESENT[2]**).

present participle ▸ **noun** Grammar the form of a verb, ending in *-ing* in English, which is used in forming continuous tenses, e.g. in *I'm thinking*, alone in non-finite clauses, e.g. in *sitting here, I haven't a care in the world*, as a noun, e.g. in *good thinking*, and as an adjective, e.g. in *running water*.

present value (also **net present value**) ▸ **noun** Finance the value in the present of a sum of money, in contrast to some future value it will have when it has been invested at compound interest.

preservation ▸ **noun** [mass noun] the action of preserving something: *the preservation of the city's green spaces | food preservation.* ■ the state of being preserved, especially to a specified degree: *the chapel is in a poor state of preservation.*
– ORIGIN late Middle English: via Old French from medieval Latin *praeservatio(n-)*, from late Latin *praeservare* 'to keep' (see **PRESERVE**).

preservationist ▸ **noun** a supporter or advocate of the preservation of something, especially of historic buildings and artefacts.

preservation order ▸ **noun** chiefly Brit. a legal obligation laid on an owner to preserve a building of historic interest, or to conserve trees and natural habitat regarded as contributing amenity value to the environment.

preservative ▸ **noun** a substance used to preserve foodstuffs, wood, or other materials against decay.
▸ **adjective** acting to preserve something: *the preservative effects of freezing.*
– ORIGIN late Middle English: via Old French from medieval Latin *praeservativus*, from late Latin *praeservat-* 'kept', from the verb *praeservare* (see **PRESERVE**).

preserve ▸ **verb** [with obj.] **1** maintain (something) in its original or existing state: *all records of the past were zealously preserved* | (as adj. **preserved**) *a magnificently preserved monastery.* ■ retain (a condition or state of affairs): *a fight to preserve local democracy.* ■ maintain or keep alive (a memory or quality): *the film has preserved all the qualities of the novel.* ■ keep safe from harm or injury: *a place for preserving endangered species.* ■ keep (game or an area where game is found) undisturbed to allow private hunting or shooting.

2 treat (food) to prevent its decomposition. ■ prepare (fruit) for long-term storage by boiling it with sugar.
▶ **noun 1** [mass noun] a foodstuff made with fruit preserved in sugar, such as jam or marmalade: *a jar of cherry preserve* | [count noun] *home-made preserves.*
2 a sphere of activity regarded as being reserved for a particular person or group: *the civil service became the preserve of the educated middle class.*
3 chiefly N. Amer. a place where game is protected and kept for private hunting or shooting.
– DERIVATIVES **preservable** adjective, **preserver** noun.
– ORIGIN late Middle English (in the sense 'keep safe from harm'): from Old French *preserver*, from late Latin *praeservare*, from *prae-* 'before, in advance' + *servare* 'to keep'.

pre-service ▶ **adjective** relating to the period before a person takes a job that requires training: *pre-service courses for graduates.*

preset ▶ **verb** (**presets**, **presetting**; past and past participle **preset**) [with obj.] (usu. as adj. **preset**) set or adjust (a value that controls the operation of a device) in advance of its use: *the water is heated quickly to a preset temperature.*
▶ **noun** a control on electronic equipment that is set or adjusted beforehand to facilitate use.

pre-shrunk ▶ **adjective** (of a fabric or garment) having undergone a shrinking process during manufacture to prevent further shrinking in use.
– DERIVATIVES **pre-shrink** verb.

preside ▶ **verb** [no obj.] **1** be in the position of authority in a meeting or other gathering: *the prime minister will preside at an emergency cabinet meeting* | (as adj. **presiding**) *the sentence imposed by the presiding judge.* ■ (**preside over**) be in charge of (a place or situation): *Johnson has presided over eight matches since Beck's dismissal.*
2 (**preside at**) play (a musical instrument, especially a keyboard instrument) at a public gathering.
– ORIGIN early 17th cent.: from French *présider*, from Latin *praesidere*, from *prae* 'before' + *sedere* 'sit'.

presidency ▶ **noun** (pl. **presidencies**) **1** the office of president: *the presidency of the United States.* ■ the period of a president's office: *the liberal climate that existed during Carter's presidency.*
2 Christian Church the role of the priest or minister who conducts a Eucharist.
– ORIGIN late 16th cent.: from medieval Latin *praesidentia*, from *praesidere* 'sit before' (see **PRESIDE**).

president ▶ **noun 1** the elected head of a republican state: *the Irish president* | [as title] *President Kennedy.* ■ the head of a society, council, or other organization: *the president of the European Union.* ■ the head of certain colleges. ■ N. Amer. the head of a university. ■ N. Amer. the head of a company.
2 Christian Church the celebrant at a Eucharist.
– DERIVATIVES **presidential** adjective, **presidentially** adverb, **presidentship** noun (archaic).
– ORIGIN late Middle English: via Old French from Latin *praesident-* 'sitting before' (see **PRESIDE**).

president-elect ▶ **noun** (pl. **presidents-elect**) a person who has been elected president but has not yet taken up office.

Presidential Medal of Freedom ▶ **noun** (in the US) a medal constituting the highest award that can be given to a civilian in peacetime.

presiding officer ▶ **noun** an official in charge of a polling station at an election.

presidio /prɛˈsɪdɪəʊ/ ▶ **noun** (pl. **presidios**) (in Spain and Spanish America) a fortified military settlement.
– ORIGIN Spanish, from Latin *praesidium* 'garrison'.

presidium /prɪˈsɪdɪʌm, -ˈzɪ-/ (also **praesidium**) ▶ **noun** a standing executive committee in a communist country. ■ (**Presidium**) (in the former Soviet Union) the committee which functioned as the legislative authority when the Supreme Soviet was not sitting.
– ORIGIN 1920s: from Russian *prezidium*, from Latin *praesidium* 'protection, garrison' (see **PRESIDE**).

Presley, Elvis (Aaron) (1935–77), American rock-and-roll and pop singer. He was the dominant personality of early rock and roll with songs such as 'Heartbreak Hotel' and 'Blue Suede Shoes' (both 1956). He also made a number of films, including *King Creole* (1958).

presoak ▶ **verb** [with obj.] soak (something) as a preliminary process or treatment.

Presocratic /ˌpriːsəˈkratɪk/ ▶ **adjective** relating to or denoting the speculative philosophers active in the ancient Greek world in the 6th and 5th centuries BC (before the time of Socrates), who attempted to find rational explanations for natural phenomena. They included Parmenides, Anaxagoras, Empedocles, and Heraclitus.
▶ **noun** a Presocratic philosopher.

press[1] ▶ **verb 1** move or cause to move into a position of contact with something by exerting continuous physical force: [with obj. and adverbial of direction] *he pressed his face to the glass* | [no obj., with adverbial of direction] *her body pressed against his.* ■ [with obj.] exert continuous physical force on (something), typically in order to operate a device: *he pressed a button and the doors slid open.* ■ [with obj.] squeeze (someone's arm or hand) as a sign of affection. ■ [no obj., with adverbial of direction] move in a specified direction by pushing: *the mob was still pressing forward.* ■ (of an enemy or opponent) attack persistently and fiercely: [no obj.] *their enemies pressed in on all sides.* ■ [no obj.] (**press on/ahead**) continue in one's action: *he stubbornly **pressed on with** his work.*
2 [with obj.] apply pressure to (something) to flatten, shape, or smooth it, typically by ironing: *she pressed her nicest blouse* | (as adj. **pressed**) *immaculately pressed trousers.* ■ apply pressure to (a flower or leaf) between sheets of paper in order to dry and preserve it. ■ extract (juice or oil) by crushing or squeezing fruit, vegetables, etc.: (as adj. **pressed**) *freshly pressed orange juice.* ■ squeeze or crush (fruit, vegetables, etc.) to extract the juice or oil. ■ manufacture (something, especially a record) by moulding under pressure.
3 [with obj.] forcefully put forward (an opinion, claim, or course of action): *Rose did not press the point.* ■ make strong efforts to persuade or force (someone) to do something: *when I **pressed** him **for** precise figures he evaded the subject* | [with infinitive] *the marketing directors were pressed to justify their expenditure* | [no obj.] *they continued to **press for** changes in legislation.* ■ (**press something on/upon**) insist that (someone) accepts an offer or gift: *he pressed dinner invitations on her.* ■ [no obj.] (of time) be in short supply, necessitating immediate action: *she was almost 45 years old and time was pressing.* ■ (**be pressed**) have barely enough of something, especially time: *I'm terribly **pressed for** time.* ■ (**be pressed to do something**) have difficulty doing or achieving something: *they may be **hard pressed** to keep their promise.*
4 [with obj.] Weightlifting raise (a specified weight) by lifting it to shoulder height and then gradually pushing it upwards above the head.
5 [no obj.] Golf try too hard to achieve distance with a shot, at the risk of inaccuracy.
▶ **noun 1** a device for applying pressure to something in order to flatten or shape it or to extract juice or oil: *a flower press* | *a wine press.* ■ a machine that applies pressure to a workpiece by means of a tool, in order to punch shapes.
2 a printing press. ■ [often in names] a business that prints or publishes books: *the Clarendon Press.*
3 (**the press**) [treated as sing. or pl.] newspapers or journalists viewed collectively: *the incident was not reported in the press* | [as modifier] *press coverage of the trial.* ■ [mass noun] coverage in newspapers and magazines: *there's no point in demonstrating if you don't get any press* | [in sing.] *the government has had a bad press for years.*
4 an act of pressing something: *the system summons medical help at the press of a button* | *these clothes could do with a press.* ■ [in sing.] a closely packed crowd or mass of people or things: *among the press of cars he saw a taxi.* ■ dated pressure of business. ■ Basketball any of various forms of close guarding by the defending team.
5 Weightlifting an act of raising a weight to shoulder height and then gradually pushing it upwards above the head.
6 chiefly Irish & Scottish a large cupboard.
– PHRASES **go to press** go to be printed. **press charges** see **CHARGE**. **press something home** see **HOME**. **press (the) flesh** informal (of a celebrity or politician) greet people by shaking hands.
– DERIVATIVES **presser** noun.
– ORIGIN Middle English: from Old French *presse* (noun), *presser* (verb), from Latin *pressare* 'keep pressing', frequentative of *premere*.

press[2] ▶ **verb** [with obj.] **1** (**press someone/thing into**) put someone or something to a specified use, especially as a temporary or makeshift measure: *she was **pressed into service** as an interpreter.*
2 historical force (a man) to enlist in the army or navy.
▶ **noun** historical a forcible enlistment of men, especially for the navy.
– ORIGIN late 16th cent.: alteration (by association with **PRESS**[1]) of obsolete *prest* 'pay given on enlistment, enlistment by such payment', from Old French *prest* 'loan, advance pay', based on Latin *praestare* 'provide'.

press agent ▶ **noun** a person employed to organize advertising and publicity in the press on behalf of an organization or celebrity.

pressboard ▶ **noun** [mass noun] chiefly N. Amer. a smooth, hard, dense board typically made from wood or textile pulp or laminated waste paper, used as an electrical insulator and for making light furniture.

pressbook ▶ **noun 1** a book of press cuttings.
2 a booklet or leaflet put together by a film producer to publicize a new film.

press box ▶ **noun** an area or room reserved for journalists at a sports event.

Pressburg /ˈprɛsbʊrk/ German name for **BRATISLAVA**.

press card ▶ **noun** an official authorization carried by a journalist, especially one that gives admission to an event.

press conference ▶ **noun** an interview given to journalists by a prominent person in order to make an announcement or answer questions.

Press Council ▶ **noun** a body established in the UK in 1953 to raise and maintain professional standards among journalists.

press cutting ▶ **noun** Brit. a paragraph or short article cut out of a newspaper or magazine.

pressé /ˈpreseɪ/ ▶ **noun** a drink made from freshly squeezed fruit juice, sugar, and ice: *an orange pressé.*
– ORIGIN French, 'pressed, squeezed'.

presser foot ▶ **noun** the footplate of a sewing machine which holds the material down on to the part which feeds it under the needle.

press fit ▶ **noun** technical an interference fit between two parts in which one part is forced under pressure into a slightly smaller hole in the other.
– DERIVATIVES **press-fitted** adjective.

press gallery ▶ **noun** a place reserved for journalists observing the proceedings in a parliament or law court.

press gang ▶ **noun** historical a body of men employed to enlist men forcibly into service in the army or navy.
▶ **verb** [with obj.] (**press-gang**) chiefly historical forcibly enlist (someone) into service in the army or navy. ■ (**press-gang someone into**) force someone to do something: *we press-ganged Simon into playing.*

pressie ▶ **noun** variant spelling of **PREZZIE**.

pressing ▶ **adjective** requiring quick or immediate action or attention: *inflation was the most pressing problem* | *he had pressing business in Scotland.* ■ expressing something strongly or persistently: *a pressing invitation.*
▶ **noun 1** an act or instance of applying force or weight to something: *pure-grade olive oil is the product of the second or third pressings.*
2 a record or other object made by the application of force or weight. ■ a series of objects pressed at one time: *the EP sold out its first pressing in one day.*
– DERIVATIVES **pressingly** adverb.

pressman ▶ **noun** (pl. **pressmen**) **1** chiefly Brit. a journalist.
2 a person who operates a printing press.

pressmark ▶ **noun** Brit. (especially in older libraries) a mark on a library book indicating its location.

pressor ▶ **adjective** Physiology producing an increase in blood pressure by stimulating constriction of the blood vessels: *a pressor response.*

press release ▶ **noun** an official statement issued to newspapers giving information on a particular matter.

press stud ▶ **noun** Brit. a small fastener on clothing, engaged by pressing its two halves together.

press-up ▶ **noun** Brit. an exercise in which a person lies facing the floor and, keeping their back straight, raises their body by pressing down on their hands.

pressure ▶ **noun** [mass noun] **1** continuous physical force exerted on or against an object by something in contact with it: *the gate was buckling under the pressure of the crowd outside.* ■ [count noun] the force per unit area exerted by a fluid against a surface with which it is in contact: *gas can be fed to the turbines at a pressure of around 250 psi.*
2 the use of persuasion or intimidation to make someone do something: *backbenchers put pressure on the government to provide safeguards* | [count noun] *the many pressures on girls to worry about their looks.*

P

■ the influence or effect of someone or something: *oil prices came under some downwards pressure.* ■ a sense of stressful urgency caused by having too many demands on one's time or resources: *he resigned due to pressure of work* | [count noun] *the pressures of city life.*
▸ **verb** [with obj.] attempt to persuade or coerce (someone) into doing something: *it might be possible to* ***pressure him into resigning*** | [with obj. and infinitive] *she pressured her son to accept a job offer from the bank.*
– ORIGIN late Middle English: from Old French, from Latin *pressura*, from *press-* 'pressed', from the verb *premere* (see PRESS[1]).

pressure cooker ▸ **noun** an airtight pot in which food can be cooked quickly under steam pressure. ■ a highly stressful situation or assignment: *an academic pressure cooker which turns teenagers into depressives.*
– DERIVATIVES **pressure-cook** verb.

pressure group ▸ **noun** a group that tries to influence public policy in the interest of a particular cause: *an environmental pressure group.*

pressure hull ▸ **noun** the inner hull of a submarine, in which approximately normal pressure is maintained when the vessel is submerged.

pressure lamp ▸ **noun** a portable oil or paraffin lamp in which the fuel is forced up into the mantle or burner by air pressure in the reservoir, which can be increased by pumping with a plunger.

pressure point ▸ **noun** a point on the surface of the body sensitive to pressure. ■ a point where an artery can be pressed against a bone to inhibit bleeding.

pressure suit ▸ **noun** an inflatable suit that protects the wearer against low pressure, for example when flying at a high altitude.

pressure vessel ▸ **noun** a container designed to hold material at high pressures. ■ an enclosed structure containing a nuclear reactor core immersed in pressurized coolant.

pressurize (also **pressurise**) ▸ **verb** [with obj.] **1** produce or maintain raised pressure artificially in (a gas or its container): *the mixture was pressurized to 1,900 atmospheres* | (as adj. **pressurized**) *a pressurized can.* ■ maintain a tolerable atmospheric pressure in (an aircraft cabin) at a high altitude: (as adj. **pressurized**) *a pressurized cabin.*
2 [with obj.] attempt to persuade or coerce (someone) into doing something: *don't let anyone* ***pressurize you into*** *snap decisions* | [with obj. and infinitive] *people had been pressurized to vote.*
– DERIVATIVES **pressurization** noun.

pressurized-water reactor (abbrev.: **PWR**) ▸ **noun** a nuclear reactor in which the fuel is uranium oxide clad in zircaloy and the coolant and moderator is water at high pressure so that it does not boil at the operating temperature of the reactor.

P

presswork ▸ **noun** [mass noun] **1** the shaping of metal by pressing or drawing it into a shaped hollow die. **2** the process of using a printing press. ■ printed matter, especially with regard to its quality.

Prester John /ˈprɛstə/ a legendary medieval Christian king of Asia, said to have defeated the Muslims and to be destined to bring help to the Holy Land.
– ORIGIN Middle English: from Old French *prestre Jehan*, from medieval Latin *presbyter Johannes* 'priest John'.

prestidigitation /ˌprɛstɪˌdɪdʒɪˈteɪʃ(ə)n/ ▸ **noun** [mass noun] formal conjuring tricks performed as entertainment.
– DERIVATIVES **prestidigitator** noun.
– ORIGIN mid 19th cent.: from French, from *preste* 'nimble' + Latin *digitus* 'finger' + -ATION.

prestige ▸ **noun** [mass noun] widespread respect and admiration felt for someone or something on the basis of a perception of their achievements or quality: *the firm has recently gained considerable prestige.* ■ [as modifier] denoting something that arouses widespread respect or admiration: *prestige diplomatic posts* | *a prestige car.*
– DERIVATIVES **prestigeful** adjective.
– ORIGIN mid 17th cent. (in the sense 'illusion, conjuring trick'): from French, literally 'illusion, glamour', from late Latin *praestigium* 'illusion', from Latin *praestigiae* (plural) 'conjuring tricks'. The transference of meaning occurred by way of the sense 'dazzling influence, glamour', at first depreciatory.

prestige pricing ▸ **noun** [mass noun] the practice of pricing goods at a high level in order to give the appearance of quality.

prestigious ▸ **adjective** inspiring respect and admiration; having high status: *a prestigious academic post.*
– DERIVATIVES **prestigiously** adverb, **prestigiousness** noun.
– ORIGIN mid 16th cent. (in the sense 'practising conjuring tricks'): from late Latin *praestigiosus*, from *praestigiae* 'conjuring tricks'. The current sense dates from the early 20th cent.

prestissimo /prɛˈstɪsɪməʊ/ Music ▸ **adverb & adjective** (especially as a direction) in a very quick tempo.
▸ **noun** (pl. **prestissimos**) a movement or passage marked to be performed in a very quick tempo.
– ORIGIN Italian, superlative of *presto* 'quick, quickly' (see PRESTO).

presto ▸ **adverb & adjective** Music (especially as a direction) in a quick tempo.
▸ **noun** (pl. **prestos**) Music a movement or passage marked to be performed in a quick tempo.
▸ **exclamation** another way of saying HEY PRESTO.
– ORIGIN Italian, 'quick, quickly', from late Latin *praestus* 'ready', from Latin *praesto* 'at hand'.

Preston a city in NW England, the administrative centre of Lancashire, on the River Ribble; pop. 165,600 (est. 2009). It was the site in the 18th century of the first English cotton mills.

Prestonpans, Battle of /ˌprɛstənˈpanz/ a battle in 1745 near the town of Prestonpans just east of Edinburgh, the first major engagement of the Jacobite uprising of 1745–6. The Jacobites routed the Hanoverians, leaving the way clear for Charles Edward Stuart's subsequent invasion of England.

prestressed ▸ **adjective** strengthened by the application of stress during manufacture, especially (of concrete) by means of rods or wires inserted under tension before the material is set.
– DERIVATIVES **prestressing** noun.

Prestwick a town to the south of Glasgow in South Ayrshire, SW Scotland, the site of an international airport; pop. 14,800 (est. 2009).

presumably ▸ **adverb** [sentence adverb] used to convey that what is stated is very likely though not known for certain: *it was not yet ten o'clock, so presumably the boys were still at the pub.*

presume ▸ **verb 1** [with clause] suppose that something is the case on the basis of probability: *I presumed that the man had been escorted from the building* | [with obj. and complement] *two of the journalists went missing and are presumed dead.* ■ take for granted that something exists or is the case: *the argument presumes that only one person can do the work.*
2 [no obj., with infinitive] be arrogant or impertinent enough to do something: *kindly don't presume to issue me orders in my own house.* ■ [no obj.] make unjustified demands; take liberties: *forgive me if I have presumed.* ■ [no obj.] (**presume on/upon**) unjustifiably regard (something) as entitling one to privileges: *he was wary of presuming on the close friendship between them.*
– DERIVATIVES **presumable** adjective.
– ORIGIN late Middle English: from Old French *presumer*, from Latin *praesumere* 'anticipate' (in late Latin 'take for granted'), from *prae* 'before' + *sumere* 'take'.

presuming ▸ **adjective** archaic presumptuous.

presumption ▸ **noun 1** an idea that is taken to be true on the basis of probability: *underlying presumptions about human nature.* ■ [mass noun] the acceptance of something as true although it is not known for certain: *the presumption of innocence.* ■ chiefly Law an attitude adopted in law or as a matter of policy towards an action or proposal in the absence of acceptable reasons to the contrary: *the planning policy shows a general* ***presumption in favour of*** *development.*
2 [mass noun] behaviour perceived as arrogant, disrespectful, and transgressing the limits of what is permitted or appropriate: *he lifted her off the ground, and she was enraged at his presumption.*
– ORIGIN Middle English: from Old French *presumpcion*, from Latin *praesumptio(n-)* 'anticipation', from the verb *praesumere* (see PRESUME).

presumptive ▸ **adjective 1** of the nature of a presumption; presumed in the absence of further information: *a presumptive diagnosis.* ■ Law giving grounds for the inference of a fact or of the appropriate interpretation of the law.
2 another term for PRESUMPTUOUS.
– DERIVATIVES **presumptively** adverb.
– ORIGIN late Middle English: from French *présomptif, -ive*, from late Latin *praesumptivus*, from *praesumpt-* 'taken before', from the verb *praesumere* (see PRESUME).

presumptuous ▸ **adjective** (of a person or their behaviour) failing to observe the limits of what is permitted or appropriate: *I hope I won't be considered presumptuous if I offer some advice.*
– DERIVATIVES **presumptuously** adverb, **presumptuousness** noun.
– ORIGIN Middle English: from Old French *presumptueux*, from late Latin *praesumptuosus*, variant of *praesumptiosus* 'full of boldness', from *praesumptio* (see PRESUMPTION).

presuppose ▸ **verb** [with obj.] require as a precondition of possibility or coherence: *their original prediction presupposed a universe only three billion years old.* ■ [with clause] tacitly assume at the beginning of a line of argument or course of action that something is the case: *your argument presupposes that it does not matter who is in power.*
– ORIGIN late Middle English: from Old French *presupposer*, suggested by medieval Latin *praesupponere*, from *prae* 'before' + *supponere* 'place under' (see SUPPOSE).

presupposition ▸ **noun** a thing tacitly assumed beforehand at the beginning of a line of argument or course of action: *both men shared certain ethical presuppositions about the universe.* ■ [mass noun] the action or state of presupposing or being presupposed.
– ORIGIN mid 16th cent.: from medieval Latin *praesuppositio(n-)*, from the verb *praesupponere* (see PRESUPPOSE).

presynaptic /ˌpriːsɪˈnaptɪk/ ▸ **adjective** Physiology relating to or denoting a nerve cell that releases a transmitter substance into a synapse during transmission of an impulse.
– DERIVATIVES **presynaptically** adverb.

prêt-à-porter /ˌprɛtəˈpɔːteɪ/ ▸ **noun** [mass noun] designer clothes sold ready to wear rather than made to measure.
– ORIGIN French, literally 'ready to wear'.

pre-tax ▸ **adjective** (of income or profits) considered or calculated before the deduction of taxes: *pre-tax profits rose 23 per cent.*

pre-teen ▸ **adjective** relating to a child of about eleven or twelve years of age.
▸ **noun** a pre-teen child.

pretence (US **pretense**) ▸ **noun 1** an attempt to make something that is not the case appear true: *his anger is masked by a pretence that all is well* | [mass noun] *they have finally abandoned their secrecy and pretence.* ■ [mass noun] the practice of inventing imaginary situations in play: *before the age of two, children start to engage in pretence.* ■ [mass noun] affected and ostentatious speech and behaviour.
2 (**pretence to**) a claim to have a particular skill or quality: *he was quick to disclaim any pretence to superiority.*
– ORIGIN late Middle English: from Anglo-Norman French *pretense*, based on medieval Latin *pretensus* 'pretended', alteration of Latin *praetentus*, from the verb *praetendere* (see PRETEND).

pretend ▸ **verb 1** [with clause or infinitive] behave so as to make it appear that something is the case when in fact it is not: *I closed my eyes and pretended I was asleep* | *she turned the pages and pretended to read.* ■ engage in an imaginative game or fantasy: *children pretending to be grown-ups.* ■ [with obj.] give the appearance of feeling or possessing (an emotion or quality); simulate: *she pretended a greater surprise than she felt.*
2 [no obj.] (**pretend to**) lay claim to (a quality or title): *he cannot pretend to sophistication.*
▸ **adjective** [attrib.] informal not really what it is represented as being; imaginary: *the children poured out pretend tea for the dolls.*
– ORIGIN late Middle English: from Latin *praetendere* 'stretch forth, claim', from *prae* 'before' + *tendere* 'stretch'. The adjective dates from the early 20th cent.

pretended ▸ **adjective** not genuine; assumed: *eating ice cream with pretended unconcern.*

pretender ▸ **noun** a person who claims or aspires to a title or position: *the* ***pretender to*** *the throne.*

pretense ▸ **noun** US spelling of PRETENCE.

pretension ▸ **noun 1** (**pretension to**) a claim or assertion of a claim to something: *his pretensions to the imperial inheritance* | [mass noun] *all that we cannot tolerate is pretension to infallibility.* ■ (often **pretensions**) a claim or aspiration to a particular quality: *another ageing rocker with literary pretensions.*

2 [mass noun] the use of affectation to impress; pretentiousness: *he spoke simply, without pretension.*
– ORIGIN late Middle English: from medieval Latin *praetensio(n-)*, from *praetens-* 'alleged', from the verb *praetendere* (see **PRETEND**).

pre-tension ▸ verb [with obj.] apply tension to (an object) before manufacture or use. ▪ strengthen (reinforced concrete) by applying tension to the reinforcing rods before the concrete has set.
– DERIVATIVES **pre-tensioner** noun.

pretentious ▸ adjective attempting to impress by affecting greater importance or merit than is actually possessed: *pretentious art films | the pretentious jargon of wine experts.*
– DERIVATIVES **pretentiously** adverb, **pretentiousness** noun.
– ORIGIN mid 19th cent.: from French *prétentieux*, from *prétention* (see **PRETENSION**).

preter- /ˈpriːtə/ ▸ combining form more than: *preternatural.*
– ORIGIN from Latin *praeter* 'past, beyond'.

preterite /ˈprɛt(ə)rɪt/ (US also **preterit**) Grammar ▸ adjective expressing a past action or state.
▸ noun a simple past tense or form.
– ORIGIN Middle English (in the sense 'bygone, former'): from Latin *praeteritus* 'gone by', past participle of *praeterire*, from *praeter* 'past, beyond' + *ire* 'go'.

preterition /ˌpriːtəˈrɪʃ(ə)n/ ▸ noun [mass noun] the action of passing over or disregarding a matter, especially the rhetorical technique of making summary mention of something by professing to omit it.
– ORIGIN late 16th cent.: from late Latin *praeteritio(n-)*, from *praeterire* 'pass, go by'.

preterm Medicine ▸ adjective born or occurring after a pregnancy significantly shorter than normal, especially after no more than 37 weeks of pregnancy.
▸ adverb after a short pregnancy; prematurely: *babies born preterm are likely to lack surfactant in the lungs.*

pretermit /ˌpriːtəˈmɪt/ ▸ verb (**pretermits**, **pretermitting**, **pretermitted**) [with obj.] archaic **1** omit to do or mention: *some points of conduct we advisedly pretermit.*
2 abandon (a custom or continuous action) for a time: *the pleasant musical evenings were now entirely pretermitted.*
– DERIVATIVES **pretermission** /-ˈmɪʃ(ə)n/ noun.
– ORIGIN late 15th cent.: from Latin *praetermittere*, from *praeter* 'past, beyond' + *mittere* 'let go'.

preternatural /ˌpriːtəˈnatʃ(ə)r(ə)l/ (also **praeternatural**) ▸ adjective beyond what is normal or natural: *autumn had arrived with preternatural speed.*
– DERIVATIVES **preternaturally** adverb.

pretest ▸ noun a preliminary test or trial.
▸ verb [with obj.] carry out a preliminary test or trial of: *prior to its use, the questionnaire was pretested on two groups of trainees.*

pretext ▸ noun a reason given in justification of a course of action that is not the real reason: *the rebels had the perfect pretext for making their move | he called round **on the pretext of** asking after her mother.*
– ORIGIN early 16th cent.: from Latin *praetextus* 'outward display', from the verb *praetexere* 'to disguise', from *prae* 'before' + *texere* 'weave'.

pretor ▸ noun US spelling of **PRAETOR**.

Pretoria /prɪˈtɔːrɪə/ the administrative capital of South Africa; pop. 1,679,200 (est. 2009). It was founded in 1855 by Marthinus Wessel Pretorius (1819–1901), the first President of the South African Republic, and named after his father Andries.

pretorian ▸ adjective & noun US spelling of **PRAETORIAN**.

Pretoria-Witwatersrand-Vereeniging /fəˈriːnɪkɪŋ/ former name (until 1995) for **GAUTENG**.

pretreat ▸ verb [with obj.] treat (something) with a chemical before use.
– DERIVATIVES **pretreatment** noun.

pretrial ▸ adjective in or relating to the period before a judicial trial: *a pretrial hearing.*

prettify ▸ verb (**prettifies**, **prettifying**, **prettified**) [with obj.] make (someone or something) appear superficially pretty or attractive: *nothing has been done to prettify the site.*
– DERIVATIVES **prettification** noun, **prettifier** noun.

pretty ▸ adjective (**prettier**, **prettiest**) **1** (of a person, especially a woman or child) attractive in a delicate way without being truly beautiful: *a pretty little girl with an engaging grin.* ▪ (of a thing) pleasing to the eye or the ear: *a pretty summer dress.*
2 [attrib.] informal used ironically to express annoyance or displeasure: *he led me a pretty dance.*
▸ adverb [as submodifier] informal to a moderately high degree; fairly: *he looked pretty fit for his age.*
▸ noun (pl. **pretties**) informal an attractive thing, especially a trinket: *he buys her lots of pretties—bangles and rings.* ▪ used to refer in a condescending way to an attractive person: *six pretties in sequined leotards.*
▸ verb (**pretties**, **prettying**, **prettied**) [with obj.] make pretty or attractive: *she'll be all **prettied up** and ready to go in an hour.*
– PHRASES **pretty much** (or **nearly** or **well**) informal very nearly: *the case is pretty well over.* **a pretty penny** informal a large sum of money. **pretty please** used as a wheedling form of request. **be sitting pretty** informal be in an advantageous situation: *if she could get sponsors, she would be sitting pretty.*
– DERIVATIVES **prettily** adverb, **prettiness** noun, **prettyish** adjective.
– ORIGIN Old English *prættig*; related to Middle Dutch *pertich* 'brisk, clever', obsolete Dutch *prettig* 'humorous, sporty', from a West Germanic base meaning 'trick'. The sense development 'deceitful, cunning, clever, skilful, admirable, pleasing, nice' has parallels in adjectives such as *canny, fine, nice*, etc.

pretty boy ▸ noun informal, often derogatory a foppish or effeminate man.

pretty-face wallaby ▸ noun another term for **WHIPTAIL WALLABY**.

pretzel /ˈprɛts(ə)l/ ▸ noun a crisp biscuit baked in the form of a knot or stick and flavoured with salt.
▸ verb (**pretzels**, **pretzeling**, **pretzeled**) [with obj.] N. Amer. twist, bend, or contort: *he found the snake pretzeled into a tangle of knots.*
– ORIGIN mid 19th cent. (originally US): from German *Pretzel*.

prevail ▸ verb [no obj.] **1** prove more powerful or superior: *it is hard for logic to **prevail over** emotion.* ▪ be widespread or current in a particular area or at a particular time: *a friendly atmosphere prevailed among the crowds.*
2 (**prevail on/upon**) persuade (someone) to do something: *she was prevailed upon to give an account of her work.*
– ORIGIN late Middle English: from Latin *praevalere* 'have greater power', from *prae* 'before' + *valere* 'have power'.

prevailing ▸ noun existing at a particular time; current: *the unfavourable prevailing economic conditions.* ▪ having most appeal or influence; prevalent: *the prevailing mood within Whitehall circles.*
– DERIVATIVES **prevailingly** adverb.

prevailing wind ▸ noun a wind from the direction that is predominant or most usual at a particular place or season.

prevalence ▸ noun [mass noun] the fact or condition of being prevalent; commonness: *the prevalence of obesity in adults.*

prevalent /ˈprɛv(ə)l(ə)nt/ ▸ adjective [attrib.] widespread in a particular area or at a particular time: *the social ills prevalent in society today.* ▪ archaic predominant; powerful.
– DERIVATIVES **prevalently** adverb.
– ORIGIN late 16th cent.: from Latin *praevalent-* 'having greater power', from the verb *praevalere* (see **PREVAIL**).

prevaricate /prɪˈvarɪkeɪt/ ▸ verb [no obj.] speak or act in an evasive way: *he seemed to prevaricate when journalists asked pointed questions.*
– DERIVATIVES **prevarication** noun, **prevaricator** noun.
– ORIGIN mid 16th cent. (earlier (Middle English) as *prevarication* and *prevaricator*), in the sense 'go astray, transgress': from Latin *praevaricat-* 'walked crookedly, deviated', from the verb *praevaricari*, from *prae* 'before' + *varicari* 'straddle'.

prevenient /prɪˈviːnɪənt/ ▸ adjective formal preceding in time or order; antecedent.
– ORIGIN early 17th cent.: from Latin *praevenient-* 'coming before', from the verb *praevenire*, from *prae* 'before' + *venire* 'come'.

prevent ▸ verb [with obj.] **1** keep (something) from happening: *action must be taken to prevent further accidents.* ▪ stop (someone) from doing something: *locks won't **prevent** a determined burglar **from** getting in.*
2 archaic (of God) go before (someone) with spiritual guidance and help.
– DERIVATIVES **preventability** noun, **preventable** (also **preventible**) adjective.
– ORIGIN late Middle English (in the sense 'act in anticipation of'): from Latin *praevent-* 'preceded, hindered', from the verb *praevenire*, from *prae* 'before' + *venire* 'come'.

preventative ▸ adjective & noun another term for **PREVENTIVE**.
– DERIVATIVES **preventatively** adverb.

preventer ▸ noun a person or thing that prevents something: *a power-surge preventer.* ▪ Sailing an extra line or wire rigged to support a piece of rigging under strain, or to hold the boom and prevent it from gybing.

prevention ▸ noun [mass noun] the action of stopping something from happening or arising: *crime prevention | the treatment and prevention of AIDS.*
– PHRASES **prevention is better than cure** (or US **an ounce of prevention is worth a pound of cure**) proverb it's easier to stop something happening in the first place than to repair the damage after it has happened.

preventive ▸ adjective designed to keep something undesirable such as illness or harm from occurring: *preventive medicine.*
▸ noun a medicine or other treatment designed to prevent disease or ill health.
– DERIVATIVES **preventively** adverb.

preventive detention ▸ noun [mass noun] Law the imprisonment of a person with the aim of preventing them from committing further offences or of maintaining public order.

preverbal ▸ adjective **1** existing or occurring before the development of speech: *preverbal communication.*
2 Grammar occurring before a verb: *preverbal particles.*

preview ▸ noun an opportunity to view something before it is acquired or becomes generally available: *I have photos of the goods if anyone would like a preview.* ▪ a showing of a film, exhibition, etc. before its official opening. ▪ a trailer for a film. ▪ a publicity article or review of a forthcoming film, book, etc., based on an advance viewing. ▪ Computing a facility for inspecting the appearance of a document before it is printed.
▸ verb [with obj.] display (a product, film, etc.) before it is made generally available: *the company will preview an enhanced version of its database.* ▪ see or inspect (something) before it is used or becomes generally available: *the teacher should preview teaching aids to ensure that they are at the right level.* ▪ comment on (a forthcoming event): *next week we'll be previewing the new season.*
– DERIVATIVES **previewer** noun.

Previn /ˈprɛvɪn/, André (George) (b.1929), German-born American conductor, pianist, and composer. He is most famous as a conductor, notably with the London Symphony Orchestra (1968–79), the Pittsburgh Symphony Orchestra (1976–86), and the Royal Philharmonic Orchestra (1987–91).

P

previous ▸ adjective **1** [attrib.] existing or occurring before in time or order: *she looked tired after her exertions of the previous evening | the boat's previous owner.*
2 informal overhasty in acting: *I admit I may have been a bit previous.*
▸ noun [mass noun] Brit. informal previous convictions; a criminal record: *he's got previous—theft and wounding.*
– PHRASES **previous to** before: *the month previous to publication.*
– ORIGIN early 17th cent.: from Latin *praevius* 'going before' (from *prae* 'before' + *via* 'way') + **-OUS**.

previously ▸ adverb at a previous or earlier time; before: *museums and art galleries which had previously been open to the public | they discovered a previously unknown gene.*

previous question ▸ noun (in parliamentary procedure) a motion to decide whether to vote on a main question, moved before the main question itself is put.

previse /prɪˈvʌɪz/ ▸ verb [with obj.] literary foresee or predict (an event): *he had intelligence to previse the possible future.*
– DERIVATIVES **prevision** noun, **previsional** adjective.
– ORIGIN late 16th cent.: from Latin *praevis-* 'foreseen, anticipated', from the verb *praevidere*, from *prae* 'before' + *videre* 'to see'.

prevocalic /ˌpriːvəˈkalɪk/ ▸ adjective occurring immediately before a vowel.

pre-vocational ▸ adjective given or performed as preparation for vocational training.

Prévost d'Exiles /ˌpreɪvəʊ dɛgˈziːl/, French /pʀevo dɛkzil/, Antoine-François (1696–1763), French novelist; known as **Abbé Prévost**. A Benedictine monk and priest, he is remembered for his novel *Manon Lescaut* (1731), which inspired operas by Jules Massenet and Puccini.

pre-war ▶ **adjective** existing, occurring, or built before a war: *the pre-war years*.

pre-wash ▶ **noun** a preliminary wash, especially one performed as part of a cycle in an automatic washing machine. ■ a substance applied as a treatment before washing.
▶ **verb** [with obj.] give a preliminary wash to.

prewire ▶ **verb** [with obj.] wire (something requiring electrical circuitry) in advance of usual installation.

prexy (also **prex**) ▶ **noun** (pl. **prexies**) US informal a president, especially the president of a college or society.
– ORIGIN early 19th cent. (as *prex*): college slang.

prey ▶ **noun** [mass noun] **1** an animal that is hunted and killed by another for food: *the kestrel pounced on its prey*. ■ a person who is easily deceived or harmed: *he was easy prey for the two con men*.
2 archaic plunder or (in biblical use) a prize.
▶ **verb** [no obj.] (**prey on/upon**) hunt and kill for food: *small birds that prey on insect pests*. ■ take advantage of or harm: *this is a mean type of theft by ruthless people preying on the elderly*. ■ cause constant distress to: *the problem had begun to prey on my mind*.
– PHRASES **fall prey to** (also **be** or **become prey to**) be hunted and killed by (an animal): *small rodents fell prey to domestic cats*. ■ be vulnerable to or overcome by: *he would often fall prey to melancholy | the settlers become prey to nameless fears*.
– DERIVATIVES **preyer** noun.
– ORIGIN Middle English (also denoting plunder taken in war): the noun from Old French *preie*, from Latin *praeda* 'booty', the verb from Old French *preier*, based on Latin *praedari* 'seize as plunder', from *praeda*.

Prez, Josquin des, see **DES PREZ**.

prez ▶ **noun** informal term for **PRESIDENT**.

prezzie (also **pressie**) ▶ **noun** Brit. informal a present.
– ORIGIN 1930s (as *presee*): abbreviation.

prial /ˈprʌɪəl/ ▶ **noun** (in card games) a set of three cards of the same denomination.
– ORIGIN early 19th cent.: alteration of *pair royal*.

Priam /ˈprʌɪam/ Greek Mythology the king of Troy at the time of its destruction by the Greeks under Agamemnon. The father of Paris and Hector and husband of Hecuba, he was slain by Neoptolemus, son of Achilles.

P

priapic /prʌɪˈapɪk/ ▶ **adjective** relating to or resembling a phallus: *priapic carvings*. ■ relating to male sexuality and sexual activity: *the spirit of these pages is downright priapic*. ■ Medicine (of a man) having a persistently erect penis.
– ORIGIN late 18th cent.: from *Priapos* (Greek form of **PRIAPUS**) + **-IC**.

priapism /ˈprʌɪəpɪz(ə)m/ ▶ **noun** [mass noun] Medicine persistent and painful erection of the penis.
– ORIGIN late Middle English: via late Latin from Greek *priapismos*, from *priapizein* 'be lewd', from *Priapos* (Greek form of **PRIAPUS**).

Priapulida /ˌprʌɪəˈpjʊlɪdə/ ▶ **plural noun** Zoology a small phylum of burrowing worm-like marine invertebrates which have a thick body, a large eversible proboscis, and a terminal tail.
– DERIVATIVES **priapulid** /prʌɪˈapjʊlɪd/ **noun & adjective**.
– ORIGIN modern Latin (plural), from *Priapulus* (genus name), diminutive of **PRIAPUS**.

Priapus /prʌɪˈeɪpəs/ Greek Mythology a god of fertility, whose cult spread to Greece (and, later, Italy) from Turkey after Alexander's conquests. He was also a god of gardens and the patron of seafarers and shepherds.

Pribilof Islands /ˈprɪbɪlɒf/ a group of four islands in the Bering Sea, off the coast of SW Alaska. First visited in 1786 by the Russian explorer Gavriil Loginovich Pribylov (d.1796), they came into US possession after the purchase of Alaska in 1867.

Price, Vincent (1911–93), American actor, best known for his performances in a series of films based on stories by Edgar Allan Poe, such as *The Pit and the Pendulum* (1961).

price ▶ **noun 1** the amount of money expected, required, or given in payment for something: *land could be sold for a high price | house prices have fallen | [mass noun] large cars are dropping in price*. ■ the odds in betting. ■ [mass noun] archaic value; worth: *the parable of the pearl of great price*.
2 an unwelcome experience or action undergone or done as a condition of achieving an objective: *the price of their success was an entire day spent in discussion*.
▶ **verb** [with obj.] **1** decide the amount required as payment for (something offered for sale): *the watches are priced at £55*. ■ attach price labels or tickets to (an item for sale).
2 discover or establish the price of (something for sale).
– PHRASES **at any price** no matter what expense or difficulty is involved: *they wanted peace at any price*. **at a price** requiring great expense or involving unwelcome consequences: *his generosity comes at a price*. **beyond** (or **without**) **price** so valuable that no price can be stated. **a price on someone's head** a reward offered for someone's capture or death. **price oneself out of the market** become unable to compete commercially. **put a price on** determine the value of: *you can't put a price on what she has to offer*. **what price ——? 1** used to ask what has become of something or to suggest that something has or would become worthless: *what price justice if he were allowed to go free?* **2** used to state that something seems unlikely: *what price cricket at the Olympics?*
– DERIVATIVES **pricer** noun.
– ORIGIN Middle English: the noun from Old French *pris*, from Latin *pretium* 'value, reward'; the verb, a variant (by assimilation to the noun) of earlier *prise* 'estimate the value of' (see **PRIZE**[1]). Compare with **PRAISE**.

price discrimination ▶ **noun** [mass noun] the action of selling the same product at different prices to different buyers, in order to maximize sales and profits.

price–earnings ratio (also **price–earnings multiple**) ▶ **noun** Finance the current market price of a company share divided by the earnings per share of the company.

price elasticity ▶ **noun** [mass noun] Economics a measure of the effect of a price change or a change in the quantity supplied on the demand for a product or service.

price-fixing ▶ **noun** [mass noun] a practice whereby rival companies come to an illicit agreement not to sell goods or services below a certain price.

price leadership ▶ **noun** [mass noun] Economics the setting of prices in a market by a dominant company, which is followed by others in the same market.

priceless ▶ **adjective 1** so precious that its value cannot be determined: *priceless works of art*.
2 informal very amusing: *darling, you're priceless!*
– DERIVATIVES **pricelessly** adverb, **pricelessness** noun.

price lining ▶ **noun** [mass noun] the sale of a related range of products at different prices, each representing a distinct level of quality.

price list ▶ **noun** a list of the current prices of items on sale.

price point ▶ **noun** a point on a scale of possible prices at which something might be marketed.

price relative ▶ **noun** the ratio of the price of something at one time to its price at another.

price ring ▶ **noun** a group of traders or companies acting illegally to fix a minimum retail price for their competing products, thus forming a cartel.

price-sensitive ▶ **adjective** denoting a product whose sales are greatly influenced by its price. ■ (of information) likely to affect share prices if it were made public.

price support ▶ **noun** [mass noun] Economics government assistance in maintaining the levels of market prices regardless of supply or demand.

price system ▶ **noun** an economic system in which prices are determined by market forces.

price tag ▶ **noun** a label showing the price of an item for sale. ■ the cost of something: *a $400 billion price tag was put on the venture*.

price-taker ▶ **noun** Economics a company that must accept the prevailing prices in the market of its products, its own transactions being unable to affect the market price.

price war ▶ **noun** a period of fierce competition in which traders cut prices in an attempt to increase their share of the market.

pricey (also **pricy**) ▶ **adjective** (**pricier**, **priciest**) informal expensive: *boutiques selling pricey clothes*.
– DERIVATIVES **priciness** noun.

prick ▶ **verb** [with obj.] **1** make a small hole in (something) with a sharp point; pierce slightly: *prick the potatoes all over with a fork*. ■ [no obj.] feel a sensation as though a sharp point were sticking into one: *she felt her scalp prick and her palms were damp*. ■ (of tears) cause the sensation of imminent weeping in (a person's eyes): *tears of disappointment were pricking her eyelids*. ■ cause mental or emotional discomfort to: *her conscience pricked her as she told the lie*. ■ provoke to action: *the police were pricked into action by the horrifying sight*.
2 (especially of a horse or dog) make (the ears) stand erect when on the alert.
▶ **noun 1** an act of piercing something with a sharp point: *the pin prick had produced a drop of blood*. ■ a small hole or mark made by pricking something. ■ a sharp pain caused by being pierced with a sharp point. ■ a sudden feeling of an unpleasant emotion: *she felt a prick of resentment*.
2 vulgar slang a man's penis. ■ a stupid or contemptible man.
3 archaic a goad for oxen.
– PHRASES **kick against the pricks** hurt oneself by persisting in useless resistance or protest. [with biblical allusion to Acts 9:5.] **one's ears prick up** one becomes suddenly attentive: *my ears pricked up when I overheard two guys discussing the actress*. **prick up one's ears** (especially of a horse or dog) make the ears stand erect when on the alert. ■ (of a person) become suddenly attentive.
– PHRASAL VERBS **prick something out 1** draw a pattern by making small holes in a surface: *he pricked out a rough design with his dagger*. ■ decorate a surface by pricking out a pattern. **2** plant seedlings in small holes made in the earth.
– DERIVATIVES **pricker** noun.
– ORIGIN Old English *pricca* (noun), *prician* (verb), probably of West Germanic origin and related to Low German and Dutch *prik* (noun), *prikken* (verb).

pricket ▶ **noun 1** a male fallow deer in its second year, having straight, unbranched horns.
2 historical a spike for holding a candle.
– ORIGIN late Middle English: from **PRICK** + **-ET**[1].

prickle ▶ **noun** a short pointed outgrowth on the bark or epidermis of a plant; a small thorn: *the prickles of the gorse bushes*. ■ a small spine or pointed outgrowth on the skin of certain animals. ■ a tingling sensation on a person's skin, typically caused by strong emotion: *Kathleen felt a prickle of excitement*.
▶ **verb** [no obj.] (of a part of the body) experience a tingling sensation, especially as a result of strong emotion: *the sound made her skin prickle with horror*. ■ [with obj.] cause a tingling sensation in: *I hate the way the fibres prickle your skin*. ■ (of a person) react defensively or angrily to something: *she prickled at the implication that she had led a protected life*.
– ORIGIN Old English *pricel* 'instrument for pricking, sensation of being pricked'; related to Middle Dutch *prickel*, from the Germanic base of **PRICK**. The verb is partly a diminutive of the verb **PRICK**.

prickleback ▶ **noun** a long, slender fish with a spiny dorsal fin running the length of the body. It lives in cooler seas of the northern hemisphere, typically in shallow inshore waters. ● Family Stichaeidae: many genera and species.

prickly ▶ **adjective** (**pricklier**, **prickliest**) **1** covered in prickles: *masses of prickly brambles*. ■ resembling prickles: *his hair was prickly and short*. ■ having or causing a tingling or itching sensation: *prickly velvet seats | my skin feels prickly*.
2 (of a person) ready to take offence. ■ (of a subject, issue, etc.) likely to cause offence or controversy: *this is a prickly subject*.
– DERIVATIVES **prickliness** noun.

prickly ash ▶ **noun** a spiny North American shrub or tree with prickly branches and bark that can be used medicinally. ● Genus *Zanthoxylum*, family Rutaceae: the northern *Z. americanum* and the southern *Z. clava-herculis* (also called **HERCULES' CLUB**).
■ [mass noun] a medicinal preparation made from the bark of the prickly ash.

prickly heat ▶ **noun** [mass noun] an itchy inflammation of the skin, typically with a rash of small vesicles, common in hot, humid weather. Also called **MILIARIA**.

prickly pear ▶ **noun** a cactus with jointed stems and oval flattened segments, having barbed bristles and large pear-shaped prickly fruits. ● Genus *Opuntia*, family Cactaceae: several species, in particular *O. ficus-indica*, which has become naturalized in the Mediterranean.
■ the edible orange or red fruit of the prickly pear.

prickly poppy ▶ noun a Central American plant with prickly leaves and large scented yellow flowers. It has become a weed in many tropical regions, but is cultivated in cooler regions as an ornamental.
● *Argemone mexicana*, family Papaveraceae.

prick-teaser (also **prick-tease**) ▶ noun vulgar slang another term for COCK-TEASER.

pricy ▶ adjective variant spelling of PRICEY.

pride ▶ noun [mass noun] **1** a feeling of deep pleasure or satisfaction derived from one's own achievements, the achievements of one's close associates, or from qualities or possessions that are widely admired: *the faces of the children's parents glowed with pride* | *he takes **great pride in** his appearance.* ■ a person or thing which arouses a feeling of deep pleasure or satisfaction: *the pride of the village is the swimming pool.* ■ literary the best state of something; the prime: *in the pride of youth.*
2 consciousness of one's own dignity: *he swallowed his pride and asked for help.* ■ the quality of having an excessively high opinion of oneself or one's importance: *the worst sin in a ruler was pride.*
3 [count noun] a group of lions forming a social unit.
▶ verb (**pride oneself on/upon**) be especially proud of (a particular quality or skill): *he prided himself on his honesty.*
– PHRASES **one's pride and joy** a person or thing of which one is very proud: *the car was his pride and joy.* **pride goes** (or **comes**) **before a fall** proverb if you're too conceited or self-important, something will happen to make you look foolish. **pride of place** the most prominent position among a group of things: *the certificate has pride of place on my wall.*
– DERIVATIVES **prideful** adjective, **pridefully** adverb.
– ORIGIN late Old English *prȳde* 'excessive self-esteem', variant of *prȳtu*, *prȳte*, from *prūd* (see PROUD).

pride of India ▶ noun any of a number of Asian trees which are cultivated as ornamentals, in particular:
● the chinaberry. ● a yellow-flowered tree which has become naturalized in parts of southern Europe (*Koelreuteria paniculata*, family Sapindaceae).

Pride's Purge the exclusion or arrest of about 140 members of parliament likely to vote against a trial of the captive Charles I by soldiers under the command of Colonel Thomas Pride (d.1658) in December 1648. Following the purge, the remaining members, known as the Rump Parliament, voted for the trial which resulted in Charles's execution.

prie-dieu /priː'djəː/ ▶ noun (pl. **prie-dieux** pronunc. **same**) a piece of furniture for use during prayer, consisting of a kneeling surface and a narrow upright front with a rest for the elbows or for books.
– ORIGIN mid 18th cent.: French, literally 'pray God'.

priest ▶ noun **1** an ordained minister of the Catholic, Orthodox, or Anglican Church, authorized to perform certain rites and administer certain sacraments. ■ a person who performs religious ceremonies and duties in a non-Christian religion.
2 a mallet used to kill fish caught when angling. [with allusion to the priest's function in performing the last rites.]
▶ verb [with obj.] formal ordain to the priesthood.
– DERIVATIVES **priestlike** adjective.
– ORIGIN Old English *prēost*, of Germanic origin; related to Dutch *priester*, German *Priester*, based on ecclesiastical Latin *presbyter* 'elder' (see PRESBYTER).

priestcraft ▶ noun [mass noun] often derogatory the knowledge and work of a priest.

priestess ▶ noun a female priest of a non-Christian religion.

priesthood ▶ noun [mass noun] (often **the priesthood**) the office or position of a priest. ■ priests in general.

priest-in-charge ▶ noun (pl. **priests-in-charge**) (in the Anglican Church) an ordained minister who has charge of a parish but has not been formally appointed as its incumbent.

Priestley[1], J. B. (1894–1984), English novelist, dramatist, and critic; full name *John Boynton Priestley*. He is noted for works such as *The Good Companions* (1929), a picaresque novel, and the mystery drama *An Inspector Calls* (1947).

Priestley[2], Joseph (1733–1804), English scientist and theologian. Priestley was the author of about 150 books, mostly theological or educational. His chief work was on the chemistry of gases, in which his most significant discovery was of 'dephlogisticated air' (oxygen) in 1774; he demonstrated that it was important to animal life, and that plants give it off in sunlight.

priestly ▶ adjective relating to or befitting a priest or priests: *performing priestly duties.*
– DERIVATIVES **priestliness** noun.
– ORIGIN Old English *prēostlic* (see PRIEST, -LY[1]).

priest's hole ▶ noun historical a hiding place for a Roman Catholic priest during times of religious persecution.

prig ▶ noun a self-righteously moralistic person who behaves as if they are superior to others.
– DERIVATIVES **priggery** noun.
– ORIGIN mid 16th cent.: of unknown origin. The earliest sense was 'tinker' or 'petty thief', whence 'disliked person', especially 'someone who is affectedly and self-consciously precise' (late 17th cent.).

priggish ▶ adjective self-righteously moralistic and superior: *a priggish little pedant* | *she was priggish about sex.*
– DERIVATIVES **priggishly** adverb, **priggishness** noun.

prill ▶ noun a pellet or solid globule of a substance formed by the congealing of a liquid during an industrial process.
– DERIVATIVES **prilled** adjective.
– ORIGIN late 18th cent. (as a term in copper mining, denoting rich copper ore remaining after removal of low-grade material): of unknown origin.

prim ▶ adjective (**primmer**, **primmest**) feeling or showing disapproval of anything regarded as improper; stiffly correct: *a very prim and proper lady.*
▶ verb (**prims**, **primming**, **primmed**) [with obj.] purse (the mouth or lips) into a prim expression: *Laurie primmed up his mouth.*
– DERIVATIVES **primly** adverb, **primness** noun.
– ORIGIN late 17th cent. (as a verb): probably ultimately from Old French *prin*, Provençal *prim* 'excellent, delicate', from Latin *primus* 'first'.

prima ballerina /'priːmə/ ▶ noun the chief female dancer in a ballet or ballet company.
– ORIGIN late 19th cent.: Italian, literally 'first ballerina'.

primacy /'prʌɪməsi/ ▶ noun [mass noun] **1** the fact of being pre-eminent or most important: *London's primacy as a financial centre.*
2 the office, period of office, or authority of a primate of the Church.
3 [usu. as modifier] Psychology the fact of an item having been presented earlier to the subject (especially as increasing its likelihood of being remembered): *the **primacy effect** is thought to reflect recall from a long-term memory store.*
– ORIGIN late Middle English: from Old French *primatie*, from medieval Latin *primatia*, from Latin *primas*, *primat-* 'of the first rank' (see PRIMATE[1]).

prima donna /ˌpriːmə 'dɒnə/ ▶ noun the chief female singer in an opera or opera company. ■ a very temperamental person with an inflated view of their own talent or importance.
– DERIVATIVES **prima donna-ish** adjective.
– ORIGIN late 18th cent.: Italian, literally 'first lady'.

primaeval ▶ adjective variant spelling of PRIMEVAL.

prima facie /ˌprʌɪmə 'feɪʃi/ ▶ adjective & adverb Law based on the first impression; accepted as correct until proved otherwise: [as adj.] *a prima facie case of professional misconduct* | [as adv.] *the original lessee prima facie remains liable for the payment of the rent.*
– ORIGIN Latin, from *primus* 'first' + *facies* 'face'.

primal /'prʌɪm(ə)l/ ▶ adjective **1** relating to an early stage in evolutionary development; primeval: *primal hunting societies.* ■ Psychology relating to or denoting the needs, fears, or behaviour that are postulated (especially in Freudian theory) to form the origins of emotional life: *he preys on people's primal fears.*
2 most important; primary or fundamental: *rivers were the primal highways of life.*
– DERIVATIVES **primally** adverb.
– ORIGIN early 17th cent.: from medieval Latin *primalis*, from Latin *primus* 'first'.

primal horde ▶ noun Anthropology (in Freudian theory) a hypothetical patriarchal unit of prehistoric human social organization.

primal scene ▶ noun Psychology (in Freudian theory) the occasion on which a child becomes aware of its parents' sexual intercourse, the timing of which is thought to be crucial in determining predisposition to future neuroses.

primal scream ▶ noun a release of intense basic frustration, anger, and aggression, especially that rediscovered by means of primal therapy.

primal therapy ▶ noun [mass noun] a form of psychotherapy which focuses on a patient's earliest emotional experiences and encourages verbal expression of childhood suffering, typically using an empty chair or other prop to represent a parent towards whom anger is directed.

primaquine /'prʌɪməkwiːn, 'priːmə-/ ▶ noun [mass noun] Medicine a synthetic compound derived from quinoline, used in the treatment of malaria.
– ORIGIN 1940s: apparently from Latin *prima* (feminine of *primus* 'first') + *quin(olin)e*.

primarily /'prʌɪm(ə)rɪli, prʌɪ'mɛr-/ ▶ adverb for the most part; mainly: *around 80 per cent of personal computers are used primarily for word processing.*

primary ▶ adjective **1** of chief importance; principal: *the government's primary aim is to see significant reductions in unemployment.*
2 earliest in time or order: *the primary stage of their political education.* ■ Biology & Medicine belonging to or directly derived from the first stage of development or growth: *a primary bone tumour.* ■ (**Primary**) Geology former term for PALAEOZOIC.
3 not derived from, caused by, or based on anything else: *the research involved the use of primary source materials.*
4 chiefly Brit. relating to or denoting education for children between the ages of about five and eleven: *a primary teacher.*
5 relating to or denoting the input side of a transformer or other inductive device.
6 Chemistry (of an organic compound) having its functional group located on a carbon atom which is bonded to no more than one other carbon atom. ■ (chiefly of amines) derived from ammonia by replacement of one hydrogen atom by an organic group.
▶ noun (pl. **primaries**) **1** (also **primary election**) (in the US) a preliminary election to appoint delegates to a party conference or to select the candidates for a principal, especially presidential, election.
2 a primary colour. ■ Ornithology a primary feather. ■ Astronomy the body orbited by a smaller satellite or companion. ■ a primary coil or winding in an electrical transformer.
3 (**the Primary**) Geology, dated the Palaeozoic era.
– ORIGIN late Middle English (in the sense 'original, not derivative'): from Latin *primarius*, from *primus* 'first'. The noun uses date from the 18th cent.

primary care (also **primary health care**) ▶ noun [mass noun] health care provided in the community for people making an initial approach to a medical practitioner or clinic for advice or treatment.

primary cell ▶ noun an electric cell that produces current by an irreversible chemical reaction.

primary colour ▶ noun any of a group of colours from which all other colours can be obtained by mixing.

> The primary colours for pigments are red, blue, and yellow. The primary additive colours for light are red, green, and blue; the primary subtractive colours (which give the primary additive colours when subtracted from white light) are magenta, cyan, and yellow.

primary evidence ▶ noun [mass noun] Law evidence, such as the original of a document, that by its nature does not suggest that better evidence is available.

primary feather ▶ noun any of the largest flight feathers in a bird's wing, growing from the manus.

primary group ▶ noun Sociology a group held together by relationships formed by family and environmental associations, regarded as basic to social life and culture.

primary industry ▶ noun [mass noun] Economics industry, such as mining, agriculture, or forestry, that is concerned with obtaining or providing natural raw materials for conversion into commodities and products for the consumer.

primary planet ▶ noun a planet that directly orbits the sun.

primary poverty ▶ noun [mass noun] Economics effective poverty due to insufficiency of means rather than waste, inefficiency, or some other drain on resources.

primary process ▶ noun Psychoanalysis an unconscious thought process arising from the pleasure principle, such as condensation or displacement, which is irrational and not subject to compulsion.

primary production ▶ noun [mass noun] the production of raw materials for industry.

primary qualities ▶ plural noun Philosophy properties or qualities, such as size, motion, shape, number, etc., belonging to physical matter independently of an observer. ■ the four original qualities of matter (hot, cold, wet, and dry) recognized by Aristotle, from which other qualities were held to derive.

P

primary school ▶ **noun** Brit. a school for children between the ages of about five and eleven.

primary sector ▶ **noun** Economics the sector of the economy concerned with or relating to primary industry.

primary structure ▶ **noun 1** Biochemistry the characteristic sequence of amino acids forming a protein or polypeptide chain, considered as the most basic element of its structure.
2 Aeronautics the parts of an aircraft whose failure would seriously endanger safety.

primary treatment ▶ **noun** [mass noun] the sedimentation and removal of most suspended matter from sewage effluent.

primate[1] /ˈprʌɪmeɪt, -mət/ ▶ **noun** Christian Church the chief bishop or archbishop of a province: *Cardinal Glemp, the primate of Poland.*
– DERIVATIVES **primatial** /-ˈmeɪʃ(ə)l/ **adjective**.
– ORIGIN Middle English: from Old French *primat*, from Latin *primas, primat-* 'of the first rank', from *primus* 'first'.

primate[2] /ˈprʌɪmeɪt/ ▶ **noun** Zoology a mammal of an order that includes the lemurs, bushbabies, tarsiers, marmosets, monkeys, apes, and humans. They are distinguished by having hands, hand-like feet, and forward-facing eyes, and are typically agile tree-dwellers. ● Order Primates: several families.
– ORIGIN late 19th cent.: from Latin *primas, primat-* 'of the first rank' (see PRIMATE[1]).

Primate of All England ▶ **noun** a title of the Archbishop of Canterbury.

Primate of All Ireland ▶ **noun** a title of both the Catholic and Anglican Archbishops of Armagh.

Primate of England ▶ **noun** a title of the Archbishop of York.

primatology /ˌprʌɪməˈtɒlədʒi/ ▶ **noun** [mass noun] the branch of zoology that deals with primates.
– DERIVATIVES **primatological adjective**, **primatologist noun**.

primavera /ˌpriːməˈvɛːrə/ ▶ **noun** [mass noun] the hard, light-coloured timber of a Central American tree.
● The tree is *Cybistax donnellsmithii*, family Bignoniaceae.
▶ **adjective** [postpositive] (of a pasta dish) made with lightly sautéed spring vegetables: *linguine primavera.*
– ORIGIN late 19th cent.: from Spanish, denoting the season of spring, from Latin *primus* 'first, earliest' + *ver* 'spring' (alluding to the tree's early flowering).

prime[1] ▶ **adjective 1** of first importance; main: *a nurse's prime concern is the well-being of the patient.* ■ from which another thing may derive or proceed: *Diogenes' conclusion that air is the prime matter.*
2 [attrib.] of the best possible quality; excellent: *prime cuts of meat.* ■ having all the typical characteristics of something: *the novel is a prime example of the genre.* ■ most suitable or likely: *any hospital with high costs is a prime candidate for closure.*
3 Mathematics (of a number) divisible only by itself and unity (e.g. 2, 3, 5, 7, 11). ■ [predic.] (of two or more numbers in relation to each other) having no common factor but unity.
▶ **noun 1** [in sing.] the state or time of greatest vigour or success in a person's life: *you're in the prime of life | he wasn't elderly, but clearly past his prime.* ■ archaic the beginning of something: *the prime of the world.*
2 Christian Church a service forming part of the Divine Office of the Western Church, traditionally said at the first hour of the day (i.e. 6 a.m.), but now little used.
3 a prime number.
4 Printing a symbol (′) written after a letter or symbol as a distinguishing mark or after a figure as a symbol for minutes or feet.
5 Fencing the first of eight parrying positions, used to protect the upper inside of the body, with the sword hand at head height in pronation and the tip of the blade pointing downwards. [French.]
6 a special section in a cycle race, attracting a special prize.
– DERIVATIVES **primeness noun**.
– ORIGIN Old English *prīm* (in sense 2 of the noun), from Latin *prima (hora)* 'first (hour)', reinforced in Middle English by Old French *prime*; the adjective dates from late Middle English, via Old French from Latin *primus* 'first'.

P

prime[2] ▶ **verb** [with obj.] **1** make (something) ready for use or action, in particular: ■ prepare (a firearm or explosive device) for firing or detonation. ■ cover (a surface) with a primer. ■ pour or spray liquid into (a pump) before starting in order to seal the moving parts and facilitate its operation. ■ inject extra fuel into (the cylinder or carburettor of an internal-combustion engine) in order to facilitate starting. ■ [no obj.] (of a steam engine or its boiler) mix water with the steam being passed into the cylinder. ■ Biology & Medicine induce a susceptibility or proclivity in (an animal, person, or tissue): *artificial milk can prime the baby's body for future allergic reactions.* ■ Biochemistry serve as a starting material for (a polymerization process).
2 prepare (someone) for a situation, typically by supplying them with relevant information: [with obj. and infinitive] *the sentries had been primed to admit him without challenge.*
– PHRASES **prime the pump** stimulate the growth or success of something by supplying it with money: *the money was intended to prime the community care pump.*
– ORIGIN early 16th cent. (in the sense 'fill, load'): origin uncertain; probably based on Latin *primus* 'first', since the sense expressed is a 'first' operation prior to something else.

prime cost ▶ **noun** the direct cost of a commodity in terms of the materials and labour involved in its production, excluding fixed costs.

prime lens ▶ **noun** Photography a lens of fixed focal length.

prime meridian ▶ **noun** a planet's meridian adopted as the zero of longitude.

prime minister ▶ **noun** the head of an elected government; the principal minister of a sovereign or state.

> In current use, the terms *Premier* and *Prime Minister* refer to the same office in Britain, but in Canada and Australia the government of a province or state is headed by a Premier, that of the federal government by a Prime Minister. In countries such as France, where the President has an executive function, the Prime Minister is in a subordinate position.

prime mover ▶ **noun 1** a person who is chiefly responsible for the creation or execution of a plan.
2 an initial source of motive power.

primer[1] ▶ **noun 1** [mass noun] a substance used as a preparatory coat on wood, metal, or canvas, especially to prevent the absorption of subsequent layers of paint or the development of rust.
2 a cap or cylinder containing a compound which responds to friction or an electrical impulse and ignites the charge in a cartridge or explosive.
3 a small pump for pumping fuel to prime an internal-combustion engine, especially in an aircraft.
4 Biochemistry a molecule that serves as a starting material for a polymerization process.

primer[2] ▶ **noun** an elementary textbook that serves as an introduction to a subject of study or is used for teaching children to read.
– ORIGIN late Middle English: from medieval Latin *primarius (liber)* 'primary (book)' and *primarium (manuale)* 'primary (manual)'.

prime rate ▶ **noun** chiefly N. Amer. the lowest rate of interest at which money may be borrowed commercially.

prime rib ▶ **noun** N. Amer. a roast or steak cut from the seven ribs immediately before the loin.

prime time ▶ **noun** the time at which a radio or television audience is expected to be at its highest: *the show is networked at prime time* | [as modifier] *prime-time television.*

primeur /priːˈməː/ ▶ **noun 1** (**primeurs**) fruit or vegetables grown to be available very early in the season.
2 [mass noun] newly produced wines which have recently been made available.
– ORIGIN French, literally 'newness'.

primeval /prʌɪˈmiːv(ə)l/ (also **primaeval**) ▶ **adjective** of the earliest time in history: *mile after mile of primeval forest.* ■ (of emotion or behaviour) strongly instinctive and unreasoning: *a primeval desire.*
– DERIVATIVES **primevally adverb**.
– ORIGIN mid 17th cent.: from Latin *primaevus* (from *primus* 'first' + *aevum* 'age') + -AL.

primeval soup ▶ **noun** another term for PRIMORDIAL SOUP.

prime vertical ▶ **noun** Astronomy a great circle in the celestial sphere passing through the zenith and the east and west points of the horizon.

primigravida /ˌpriːmɪˈgravɪdə, ˌprʌɪm-/ ▶ **noun** (pl. **primigravidae** /-diː/) Medicine a woman who is pregnant for the first time.
– ORIGIN late 19th cent.: modern Latin (feminine), from Latin *primus* 'first' + *gravidus* 'pregnant' (see GRAVID).

priming ▶ **noun** [mass noun] a substance which primes something for use or action, in particular: ■ another term for PRIMER[1]. ■ gunpowder placed in the pan of a firearm to ignite a charge.

primipara /prʌɪˈmɪp(ə)rə/ ▶ **noun** (pl. **primiparae** /-riː/) Medicine a woman who is giving birth for the first time.
– DERIVATIVES **primiparous adjective**.
– ORIGIN mid 19th cent.: modern Latin (feminine), from *primus* 'first' + *-parus* 'bringing forth' (from the verb *parere*).

primitive ▶ **adjective 1** relating to, denoting, or preserving the character of an early stage in the evolutionary or historical development of something: *primitive mammals | Primitive Germanic.* ■ relating to or denoting a preliterate, non-industrial society or culture characterized by simple social and economic organization: *primitive people.* ■ (of behaviour or emotion) apparently originating in unconscious needs or desires and unaffected by objective reasoning: *the primitive responses we share with many animals.* ■ of or denoting a simple, naive style of art that deliberately rejects sophisticated artistic techniques.
2 very basic or unsophisticated in terms of comfort, convenience, or efficiency: *the accommodation at the camp was a bit primitive.*
3 not developed or derived from anything else: *primitive material of the universe.* ■ Linguistics denoting a word, base, or root from which another is historically derived. ■ Mathematics (of an algebraic or geometric expression) from which another is derived, or which is not itself derived from another.
4 Biology (of a part or structure) in the first or early stage of formation or growth; rudimentary. See also PRIMITIVE STREAK.
▶ **noun 1** a person belonging to a preliterate, non-industrial society.
2 a pre-Renaissance painter, or one who imitates the pre-Renaissance style. ■ an artist deliberately employing a simple, naive style. ■ a painting by a primitive artist, or an object in a primitive style.
3 Linguistics a word, base, or root from which another is historically derived. ■ Mathematics an algebraic or geometric expression from which another is derived; a curve of which another is the polar or reciprocal. ■ Computing any of a set of basic geometric shapes which may be generated in computer graphics.
– DERIVATIVES **primitively adverb**, **primitiveness noun**.
– ORIGIN late Middle English (in the sense 'original, not derivative'): from Old French *primitif, -ive*, from Latin *primitivus* 'first of its kind', from *primus* 'first'.

primitive cell ▶ **noun** Crystallography the smallest possible unit cell of a lattice, having lattice points at each of its eight vertices only.

Primitive Methodist ▶ **noun** historical a member of a society of Methodists which was formed in 1811 and joined the united Methodist Church in 1932.

primitive streak ▶ **noun** Embryology the faint streak which is the earliest trace of the embryo in the fertilized ovum of a higher vertebrate.

primitivism ▶ **noun** [mass noun] **1** a belief in the value of what is simple and unsophisticated, expressed as a philosophy of life or through art or literature.
2 instinctive and unreasoning behaviour.
– DERIVATIVES **primitivist noun & adjective**.

primo /ˈpriːməʊ/ ▶ **noun** (pl. **primos**) Music the leading or upper part in a duet.
▶ **adjective** N. Amer. informal of top quality or importance: *the primo team in the land.*
– ORIGIN mid 18th cent.: Italian, literally 'first'.

Primo de Rivera /ˌpriːməʊ deɪ rɪˈvɛːrə/, Spanish /ˌprimɑo ðe riˈβera/, Miguel (1870–1930), Spanish general and statesman, head of state 1923–30. He assumed dictatorial powers after leading a military coup. His son, **José Antonio Primo de Rivera** (1903–36), founded the Falange in 1933 and was executed by Republicans in the Spanish Civil War.

primogenitor /ˌprʌɪmə(ʊ)ˈdʒɛnɪtə/ ▶ **noun** an ancestor, especially the earliest ancestor of a people; a progenitor.
– ORIGIN mid 17th cent.: variant of PROGENITOR, on the pattern of *primogeniture*.

primogeniture /ˌprʌɪmə(ʊ)ˈdʒɛnɪtʃə/ ▶ **noun** [mass noun] the state of being the firstborn child. ■ (also **right of primogeniture**) the right of succession belonging to the firstborn child, especially the feudal

rule by which the whole real estate of an intestate passed to the eldest son.
– ORIGIN early 17th cent.: from medieval Latin *primogenitura*, from Latin *primo* 'first' + *genitura* 'geniture'.

primordial /prʌɪˈmɔːdɪəl/ ▶ **adjective** existing at or from the beginning of time; primeval: *the primordial oceans.* ■ (especially of a feeling or state) basic and fundamental: *the primordial needs of the masses.* ■ Biology (of a cell, part, or tissue) in the earliest stage of development.
– DERIVATIVES **primordiality** noun, **primordially** adverb.
– ORIGIN late Middle English: from late Latin *primordialis* 'first of all', from *primordius* 'original' (see PRIMORDIUM).

primordial soup ▶ **noun** [mass noun] a solution rich in organic compounds in the primitive oceans of the earth, from which life is thought to have originated.

primordium /prʌɪˈmɔːdɪəm/ ▶ **noun** (pl. **primordia** /-dɪə/) Biology an organ, structure, or tissue in the earliest stage of development.
– ORIGIN late 19th cent.: from Latin, neuter of *primordius* 'original', from *primus* 'first' + *ordiri* 'begin'.

Primorsky /priːˈmɔːski/ a krai (administrative territory) in the far south-east of Siberian Russia, between the Sea of Japan and the Chinese border; capital, Vladivostok.

primo uomo /ˌpriːməʊ ˈwəʊməʊ/, Italian /ˌpriːmo ˈwɔːmo/ ▶ **noun** (pl. **primi uomini** or **primo uomos**) the principal male singer in an opera or opera company.
– ORIGIN Italian, literally 'first man'.

primp ▶ **verb** [no obj.] spend time making minor adjustments to one's hair, make-up, or clothes: *girls were primping in front of the mirror* | [with obj.] *she was primping her stiff hair.*
– ORIGIN late 16th cent.: related to PRIM.

primrose ▶ **noun** a European plant of woodland and hedgerows, which produces pale yellow flowers in the early spring. ● *Primula vulgaris*, family Primulaceae (the **primrose family**). This family also includes the cowslip, pimpernels, and cyclamens.
■ (also **primrose yellow**) [mass noun] a pale yellow colour.
– PHRASES **primrose path** the pursuit of pleasure, especially when it is seen to bring disastrous consequences: *blithely unaware of his doom, he continued down his primrose path.* [with allusion to Shakespeare's *Hamlet* I. iii. 50.]
– ORIGIN late Middle English: compare with Old French *primerose* and medieval Latin *prima rosa*, literally 'first rose'.

Primrose League a political association, formed in memory of Benjamin Disraeli (whose favourite flower was reputedly the primrose) in 1883, to promote and sustain the principles of Conservatism as represented by him.

primula /ˈprɪmjʊlə/ ▶ **noun** a plant of a genus that includes primroses, cowslips, and polyanthuses. Many kinds are cultivated as ornamentals, bearing flowers in a wide variety of colours in the spring. ● Genus *Primula*, family Primulaceae.
– ORIGIN modern Latin, from medieval Latin, feminine of *primulus*, diminutive of *primus* 'first'.

primulaceous ▶ **adjective** Botany relating to or denoting plants of the primrose family (Primulaceae).
– ORIGIN mid 19th cent.: from modern Latin *Primulaceae* (plural), based on medieval Latin *primula* (see PRIMULA), + -OUS.

primum mobile /ˌprʌɪməm ˈməʊbɪleɪ, ˌpriːməm ˈməʊbɪli/ ▶ **noun 1** the most important source of motion or action.
2 (in the medieval version of the Ptolemaic system) an outer sphere supposed to move round the earth in twenty-four hours carrying the inner spheres with it.
– ORIGIN from medieval Latin, literally 'first moving thing'.

Primus /ˈprʌɪməs/ ▶ **noun** trademark a brand of portable cooking stove that burns vaporized oil.

primus /ˈprʌɪməs/ ▶ **noun** the presiding bishop of the Scottish Episcopal Church, elected by the bishops from among their number.
– ORIGIN late 16th cent.: from Latin, literally 'first'.

primus inter pares /ˌpriːməs ɪntə ˈpɑːriːz, ˌprʌɪməs/ ▶ **noun** a first among equals; the senior or representative member of a group.
– ORIGIN Latin.

prince ▶ **noun** the son of a monarch. ■ a close male relative of a monarch, especially a grandson. ■ a male monarch of a small state, actually, nominally, or originally subject to a king or emperor. ■ (in France, Germany, and other European countries) a nobleman, usually ranking next below a duke. ■ (**prince of/among**) a man or thing regarded as pre-eminent in a particular sphere or group: *arctic char is a prince among fishes.*
– PHRASES **prince of the blood** a man who is a prince by right of his royal descent.
– DERIVATIVES **princedom** noun, **princelike** adjective.
– ORIGIN Middle English: via Old French from Latin *princeps, princip-* 'first, chief, sovereign', from *primus* 'first' + *capere* 'take'.

Prince Albert, Prince Charles, etc. see ALBERT, PRINCE; CHARLES, PRINCE, etc.

Prince Charming a fairy-tale hero in *King Charming* or *Prince Charming* by James Robinson Planché (1796–1880). The name was later adopted for the hero of various fairy-tale pantomimes. ■ (as noun also **a Prince Charming**) an ideal male lover who is both handsome and of admirable character.
– ORIGIN partial translation of French *Roi Charmant*, literally 'King Charming'.

Prince Consort ▶ **noun** the husband of a reigning female sovereign who is himself a prince.

Prince Edward Island an island in the Gulf of St Lawrence, in eastern Canada, the country's smallest province; pop. 135,851 (2006); capital, Charlottetown. Explored by Jacques Cartier in 1534 and colonized by the French, it was ceded to the British in 1763. It became a province of Canada in 1873.

princeling ▶ **noun** chiefly derogatory the ruler of a small principality or domain. ■ a young prince.

princely ▶ **adjective** (**princelier**, **princeliest**) of or relating to a prince: *the princely states of India.* ■ suitable for a prince; very grand: *princely accommodation.* ■ (of a sum of money) large or generous (often used ironically): *he provided a first-class funeral for the princely sum of £2.*
– DERIVATIVES **princeliness** noun.

Prince of Darkness ▶ **noun** a name for the Devil.

Prince of Peace ▶ **noun** a title given to Jesus Christ (in allusion to Isa. 9:6).

prince of the blood ▶ **noun** see PRINCE.

Prince of the Church ▶ **noun** historical a dignitary in the Church, especially a wealthy or influential cardinal or bishop.

Prince of Wales ▶ **noun** a title traditionally granted to the heir apparent to the British throne (usually the eldest son of the sovereign) since Edward I of England gave the title to his son in 1301 after the conquest of Wales.

Prince of Wales check ▶ **noun** [usu. as modifier] a large check pattern: *a Prince of Wales check suit.*

Prince of Wales' feathers ▶ **plural noun** a plume of three ostrich feathers, first adopted as a crest by the eldest son of Edward III, Edward Plantagenet, the Black Prince.

Prince of Wales Island 1 an island in the Canadian Arctic, in the Northwest Territories to the east of Victoria Island.
2 former name for PENANG.

Prince Regent ▶ **noun** a prince who acts as regent, in particular the title of the future George IV, who was regent from 1811 until he became king in 1820.

Prince Royal ▶ **noun** the eldest son of a reigning monarch.

Prince Rupert's Land another name for RUPERT'S LAND.

prince's feather ▶ **noun** a tall South American plant with upright brush-like spikes of small red flowers. ● *Amaranthus hypochondriacus*, family Amaranthaceae.

Princes in the Tower the young sons of Edward IV, namely **Edward, Prince of Wales** (b.1470) and **Richard, Duke of York** (b.1472), supposedly murdered in the Tower of London in or shortly after 1483. They were taken to the Tower of London by their uncle (the future Richard III) and are generally assumed to have been murdered, but whether at the instigation of Richard III or of another is not known; two skeletons discovered in 1674 are thought to have been those of the princes.

princess ▶ **noun** the daughter of a monarch. ■ a close female relative of a monarch, especially a granddaughter. ■ the wife or widow of a prince. ■ the female monarch of a small state, actually, nominally, or originally subject to a king or emperor. ■ (**princess of/among**) a woman or thing regarded as pre-eminent in a particular sphere or group: *the princess of American politics.* ■ a spoilt or arrogant young woman: *support your husband and stop being such a princess.* ■ Brit. informal a form of address used by a man to a girl or woman: *is something the matter, princess?*
– PHRASES **princess of the blood** a woman who is a princess by right of her royal descent.
– ORIGIN late Middle English: from Old French *princesse*, from *prince* (see PRINCE).

Princess Anne, Princess Margaret, etc. see ANNE, PRINCESS, MARGARET, PRINCESS, etc.

princesse lointaine /prɛ̃ˌsɛs lwɛ̃ˈtɛn/ ▶ **noun** (pl. **princesses lointaines**) literary an ideal but unattainable woman.
– ORIGIN French, literally 'distant princess', from the title of a play by E. ROSTAND, based on a theme in troubadour poetry.

Princess Regent ▶ **noun** a princess who acts as regent. ■ the wife of a Prince Regent.

Princess Royal ▶ **noun** the eldest daughter of a reigning monarch (especially as a title conferred by the British monarch).

Princeton University /ˈprɪnstən/ a university at Princeton in New Jersey, one of the most prestigious in the US. It was founded in 1746.

principal ▶ **adjective** [attrib.] **1** first in order of importance; main: *the country's principal cities.*
2 denoting an original sum invested or lent: *the principal amount of your investment.*
▶ **noun 1** the most important or senior person in an organization or group: *a design consultancy whose principal is based in San Francisco.* ■ the head of a school, college, or other educational institution. ■ the leading performer in a concert, play, ballet, or opera. ■ Music the leading player in each section of an orchestra. ■ (in certain professions) a fully qualified practitioner. ■ (in the UK) a senior civil servant in charge of a particular section.
2 [in sing.] a sum of money lent or invested, on which interest is paid: *the winners are paid from the interest without even touching the principal.*
3 a person for whom another acts as an agent or representative: *stockbrokers in Tokyo act as agents rather than as principals.*
4 Law the person directly responsible for a crime. ■ historical each of the combatants in a duel.
5 a main rafter supporting purlins.
6 an organ stop sounding a main register of open flue pipes typically an octave above the diapason.
– PHRASES **principal in the first degree** Law a person who directly perpetrates a crime. **principal in the second degree** Law a person who directly aids the perpetration of a crime.
– DERIVATIVES **principalship** noun.
– ORIGIN Middle English: via Old French from Latin *principalis* 'first, original', from *princeps, princip-* 'first, chief'.

P

> **USAGE** On the confusion of **principal** and **principle**, see **USAGE** at **PRINCIPLE**.

principal axis ▶ **noun** Physics each of three mutually perpendicular axes in a body about which the moment of inertia is at a maximum. ■ another term for OPTICAL AXIS.

principal boy ▶ **noun** Brit. the leading male role in a pantomime, usually played by a woman.

principal component analysis ▶ **noun** [mass noun] Statistics a method of analysis which involves finding the linear combination of a set of variables that has maximum variance and removing its effect, repeating this successively.

principal diagonal ▶ **noun** Mathematics the set of elements of a matrix that lie on the line joining the top left corner to the bottom right corner.

principality ▶ **noun** (pl. **principalities**) **1** a state ruled by a prince. ■ (**the Principality**) Brit. Wales.
2 (**principalities**) (in traditional Christian angelology) the fifth-highest order of the ninefold celestial hierarchy.
– ORIGIN Middle English (denoting the rank of a prince): from Old French *principalite*, from late Latin *principalitas*, from Latin *principalis* 'first, original' (see PRINCIPAL).

principally ▶ **adverb** [sentence adverb] for the most part; chiefly: *he was principally a landscape painter.*

principal parts ▶ **plural noun** Grammar the forms of a verb from which all other inflected forms can be deduced, for example *swim, swam, swum.*

principate /ˈprɪnsɪpət/ ▶ **noun** the rule of the early Roman emperors, during which some features of republican government were retained.
– ORIGIN late Middle English (denoting a principality): from Latin *principatus* 'first place', from *princeps, princip-* 'first, chief' (see **PRINCE**). The current sense dates from the mid 19th cent.

principe /ˈprɪntʃɪpeɪ/ ▶ **noun** (pl. **principi** /ˈprɪntʃɪpi/) (in Italy) a prince.
– ORIGIN Italian, from Latin *princeps, princip-* 'first, chief' (see **PRINCE**).

principessa /ˌprɪntʃɪˈpɛsə/ ▶ **noun** (pl. **principesse** /ˌprɪntʃɪˈpɛseɪ/) (in Italy) a princess.
– ORIGIN Italian, from medieval Latin *principissa*, from Latin *princeps, princip-* (see **PRINCE**).

principle ▶ **noun 1** a fundamental truth or proposition that serves as the foundation for a system of belief or behaviour or for a chain of reasoning: *the basic principles of justice*. ■ (usu. **principles**) a rule or belief governing one's behaviour: *struggling to be true to their own principles* | [mass noun] *she resigned over a matter of principle*. ■ [mass noun] morally correct behaviour and attitudes: *a man of principle*.
2 a general scientific theorem or law that has numerous special applications across a wide field. ■ a natural law forming the basis for the construction or working of a machine: *these machines all operate on the same general principle*.
3 a fundamental source or basis of something: *the first principle of all things was water*. ■ a fundamental quality determining the nature of something: *the combination of male and female principles*. ■ [with adj.] Chemistry an active or characteristic constituent of a substance, obtained by simple analysis or separation: *the active principle of Spanish fly*.
– PHRASES **in principle** as a general idea or plan, although the details are not yet established: *the government agreed in principle to a peace plan that included a ceasefire*. ■ used to indicate that although something is theoretically possible, in reality it may not actually happen: *in principle, the banks are entitled to withdraw these loans when necessary*. **on principle** because of or in order to demonstrate one's adherence to a particular belief: *he refused, on principle, to pay the fine*.
– ORIGIN late Middle English: from Old French, from Latin *principium* 'source', *principia* (plural) 'foundations', from *princeps, princip-* 'first, chief'.

> **USAGE** The words **principle** and **principal** are pronounced in the same way but they do not have the same meaning. **Principle** is normally used as a noun meaning 'a fundamental basis of a system of thought or belief', as in *this is one of the basic* ***principles*** *of democracy*. **Principal**, on the other hand, is normally an adjective meaning 'main or most important', as in *one of the country's* ***principal*** *cities*. **Principal** can also be a noun, where it is used to refer to the most senior or most important person in an organization or other group: *the deputy* ***principal***.

P

principled ▶ **adjective 1** (of a person or their behaviour) acting in accordance with morality and showing recognition of right and wrong: *a principled politician*.
2 (of a system or method) based on a given set of rules: *a coherent and principled approach*.

principle of parsimony ▶ **noun** see **PARSIMONY**.

prink ▶ **verb** (**prink oneself**) spend time making minor adjustments to one's appearance: *women were prinking themselves in front of the looking glass*.
– ORIGIN late 16th cent.: probably related to archaic *prank* 'dress or adorn in a showy manner'; related to Middle Low German *prank* 'pomp', Dutch *pronk* 'finery'.

print ▶ **verb** [with obj.] **1** produce (books, newspapers, etc.), especially in large quantities, by a mechanical process involving the transfer of text or designs to paper: *a thousand copies of the book were printed*. ■ produce (text or a picture) by a printing process: *the words had been printed in dark type*. ■ (of a newspaper or magazine) publish (a piece of writing) within its pages: *the article was printed in the first edition*. ■ (of a publisher or printer) arrange for (a book, manuscript, etc.) to be reproduced in large quantities. ■ produce a paper copy of (information stored on a computer): *the results of a search can be* ***printed out***. ■ produce (a photographic print) from a negative.
2 write (text) clearly without joining the letters together: *print your name and address on the back of the cheque*.
3 mark (a surface, typically a fabric or garment) with a coloured design or pattern: *a delicate fabric printed with roses*. ■ transfer (a design or pattern) to a surface: *patterns of birds and trees were printed on the cotton*. ■ make (a mark or indentation) by pressing something on a surface or in a soft substance. ■ mark (the surface of a soft substance): *we printed the butter with carved wooden butter moulds*. ■ fix (something) firmly or indelibly in someone's mind: *his face was* ***printed on*** *her memory*.
▶ **noun 1** [mass noun] the text appearing in a book, newspaper, or other printed publication, especially with reference to its size, form, or style: *she forced herself to concentrate on the tiny print* | *bold print*. ■ the state of being available in published form: *the news will never* ***get into print***. ■ (usu. **the prints**) informal a newspaper: *the report's contents were widely summarized in the public prints*. ■ [as modifier] relating to the printing industry or the printed media: *the print unions*.
2 an indentation or mark made on a surface or soft substance: *there were paw prints everywhere*. ■ (**prints**) fingerprints: *the FBI matched the prints to those of the robbery suspect*.
3 a picture or design printed from a block or plate or copied from a painting by photography: *the walls were hung with sporting prints*. ■ a photograph printed on paper from a negative or transparency. ■ a copy of a motion picture on film, especially a particular version of it.
4 a piece of fabric or clothing with a coloured pattern or design printed on it: *light summer prints* | [as modifier] *a floral print dress*. ■ a pattern or design printed on a garment or fabric.
– PHRASES **appear in print** (of an author) have one's work published. **in print 1** (of a book) available from the publisher. **2** in printed or published form: *she did not live to see her work in print*. **out of print** (of a book) no longer available from the publisher. **the printed word** language or ideas as expressed in books, newspapers, or other publications, especially when contrasted with their expression in speech: *he understood the power of the printed word*.
– ORIGIN Middle English (denoting the impression made by a stamp or seal): from Old French *preinte* 'pressed', feminine past participle of *preindre*, from Latin *premere* 'to press'.

printability ▶ **noun** [mass noun] the ability of paper to take print: *the paper's printability and porosity*.

printable ▶ **adjective** suitable or fit to be printed or published: *break photographs up into printable form* | *he was called a drunk and a racist, among printable epithets*. ■ Computing (of text) able to be printed.

printed circuit ▶ **noun** an electronic circuit consisting of thin strips of a conducting material such as copper, which have been etched from a layer fixed to a flat insulating sheet called a **printed circuit board**, and to which integrated circuits and other components are attached.

printer ▶ **noun** a person whose job or business is commercial printing. ■ a machine for printing text or pictures, especially one linked to a computer.

printer's devil ▶ **noun** historical a person, typically a young boy serving as an apprentice, who ran errands in a printing office.

printer's mark ▶ **noun** a logo serving as a printer's trademark.

printery ▶ **noun** (pl. **printeries**) a printing works.

printhead ▶ **noun** Computing a component in a printer that assembles and holds the characters and from which the images of the characters are transferred to the printing medium.

printing ▶ **noun** [mass noun] the production of books, newspapers, or other printed material. ■ [count noun] a single impression of a book: *the second printing was ready just after Christmas*. ■ handwriting in which the letters are written separately rather than being joined together.

printing press ▶ **noun** a machine for printing text or pictures from type or plates.

printmaker ▶ **noun** a person who makes pictures or designs by printing them from specially prepared plates or blocks.
– DERIVATIVES **printmaking** noun.

printout ▶ **noun** Computing a page or set of pages of printed material obtained from a computer's printer.

print run ▶ **noun** the number of copies of a book, magazine, etc. printed at one time.

print-through ▶ **noun** [mass noun] the accidental transfer of recorded signals to adjacent layers in a reel of magnetic tape.

printworks ▶ **noun** [treated as sing. or pl.] a factory where the printing of textiles takes place.

prion[1] /ˈprʌɪən/ ▶ **noun** a small petrel of southern seas, having a wide bill fringed with comb-like plates for feeding on planktonic crustaceans. ● Genus *Pachyptila*, family Procellariidae: six species.
– ORIGIN mid 19th cent.: modern Latin (former genus name), from Greek *priōn* 'a saw' (referring to its saw-like bill).

prion[2] /ˈpriːɒn/ ▶ **noun** Microbiology a protein particle that is believed to be the cause of brain diseases such as BSE, scrapie, and CJD. Prions are not visible microscopically, contain no nucleic acid, and are highly resistant to destruction. Compare with **VIRINO**.
– ORIGIN 1980s: by rearrangement of elements from *pro(teinaceous) in(fectious particle)*.

prior[1] ▶ **adjective** [attrib.] existing or coming before in time, order, or importance: *he has a prior engagement this evening*.
▶ **noun** N. Amer. informal a previous criminal conviction: *he had no juvenile record, no priors*.
– PHRASES **prior to** before: *she visited me on the day prior to her death*.
– ORIGIN early 18th cent.: from Latin, literally 'former, elder', related to *prae* 'before'.

prior[2] ▶ **noun** the male head of a house or group of houses of certain religious orders, in particular: ■ the man next in rank below an abbot. ■ the head of a house of friars.
– DERIVATIVES **priorate** noun, **priorship** noun.
– ORIGIN late Old English, from a medieval Latin noun use of Latin *prior* 'elder, former' (see **PRIOR**[1]).

prior charge ▶ **noun** Finance a class of stock or capital on which claims for payment take precedence over the claims of ordinary stock or capital.

prioress ▶ **noun** a woman who is head of a house of certain orders of nuns. ■ the woman who is next in rank below an abbess.

prioritize (also **prioritise**) ▶ **verb** [with obj.] designate or treat (something) as being very or most important: *the department has failed to prioritize safety within the oil industry*. ■ determine the order for dealing with (a series of items or tasks) according to their relative importance: *age affects the way people prioritize their goals*.
– DERIVATIVES **prioritization** noun.

priority ▶ **noun** (pl. **priorities**) [mass noun] the fact or condition of being regarded or treated as more important than others: *the safety of the country* ***takes priority over*** *any other matter*. ■ [count noun] a thing that is regarded as more important than others: *housework didn't figure high on her list of priorities*. ■ Brit. the right to proceed before other traffic: *priority is given to traffic already on the roundabout*.
– ORIGIN late Middle English (denoting precedence in time or rank): from Old French *priorite*, from medieval Latin *prioritas*, from Latin *prior* 'former' (see **PRIOR**[1]).

prior probability ▶ **noun** Statistics a probability as assessed before making reference to certain relevant observations, especially subjectively or on the assumption that all possible outcomes be given the same probability.

priory ▶ **noun** (pl. **priories**) a small monastery or nunnery that is governed by a prior or prioress.
– ORIGIN Middle English: from Anglo-Norman French *priorie*, medieval Latin *prioria*, from Latin *prior* 'elder, superior' (see **PRIOR**[2]).

Pripyat /ˈpriːpjət/ (also **Pripet** /-pət/) a river of NW Ukraine and southern Belarus, which rises in Ukraine near the border with Poland and flows some 710 km (440 miles) eastwards through the Pripyat Marshes to join the River Dnieper north of Kiev.

Priscian /ˈprɪʃɪən/ (6th century AD), Byzantine grammarian; full name *Priscianus Caesariensis*. His *Grammatical Institutions* became one of the standard Latin grammatical works in the Middle Ages.

Priscoan /prɪˈskəʊən, ˈprɪ-/ ▶ **adjective** Geology relating to or denoting the aeon that (in some schemes) constitutes the earliest part of the Precambrian, preceding the Archaean aeon. It extended from the origin of the earth to about 4,000 million years ago, and has left no identifiable rocks. ■ (as noun **the Priscoan**) the Priscoan aeon.
– ORIGIN formed irregularly from Latin *priscus* 'ancient' + **-AN**.

prise (US **prize**) ▶ **verb** [with obj. and adverbial of direction] use force in order to move, apart, or open (something): *I tried to prise Joe's fingers away from the stick*. ■ (**prise something out of/from**) obtain

something from (someone) with effort or difficulty: *I got the loan, though I had to prise it out of him.*
– ORIGIN late 17th cent.: from dialect *prise* 'lever', from Old French *prise* 'grasp, taking hold'. Compare with PRY².

prism /ˈprɪz(ə)m/ ▸ noun Geometry a solid geometric figure whose two ends are similar, equal, and parallel rectilinear figures, and whose sides are parallelograms. ■ Optics a glass or other transparent object in the form of a prism, especially one that is triangular with refracting surfaces at an acute angle with each other and that separates white light into a spectrum of colours.
– ORIGIN late 16th cent.: via late Latin from Greek *prisma* 'thing sawn', from *prizein* 'to saw'.

prismatic /prɪzˈmatɪk/ ▸ adjective relating to or having the form of a prism or prisms: *a prismatic structure.* ■ (of an instrument) incorporating a prism or prisms: *a prismatic compass.* ■ (of colours) formed, separated, or distributed by or as if by an optical prism: *a flash of prismatic light on the edge of the glass.*
– DERIVATIVES **prismatically** adverb.
– ORIGIN early 18th cent.: from French *prismatique*, from Greek *prisma* 'thing sawn' (see PRISM).

prismatic layer ▸ noun Zoology the middle layer of the shell of a mollusc, consisting of crystalline calcite or aragonite.

prismoid /ˈprɪzmɔɪd/ ▸ noun Geometry a body like a prism, in which the end faces have the same number of sides but are not equal.

prison ▸ noun a building to which people are legally committed as a punishment for a crime or while awaiting trial: *he died **in prison** | both men were **sent to prison**.*
▸ verb (**prisons, prisoning, prisoned**) [with obj.] literary imprison: *the young man was prisoned behind the doors.*
– ORIGIN late Old English, from Old French *prisun*, from Latin *prensio(n-)*, variant of *prehensio(n-)* 'laying hold of', from the verb *prehendere*.

prison camp ▸ noun a camp where prisoners of war or political prisoners are kept under guard.

prisoner ▸ noun a person legally committed to prison as a punishment for a crime or while awaiting trial. ■ a person captured and kept confined by an enemy or criminal: *she may have been **held prisoner** before being killed | 200 rebels were **taken prisoner**.* ■ a person who is or feels confined or trapped by a situation: *he's become a prisoner of the publicity he's generated.*
– PHRASES **take no prisoners** be ruthlessly aggressive or uncompromising in the pursuit of one's objectives.
– ORIGIN late Middle English: from Old French *prisonier*, from *prison* (see PRISON).

prisoner of conscience ▸ noun a person who has been put in prison for holding political or religious views that are not tolerated in the state in which they live.

prisoner of state (also **state prisoner**) ▸ noun a person confined on the authority of the state for political reasons.

prisoner of war (abbrev.: **POW**) ▸ noun a person who has been captured and imprisoned by the enemy in war.

prisoner's base ▸ noun [mass noun] a chasing game played by two groups of children each occupying a distinct base or home.

prisoner's dilemma ▸ noun (in game theory) a situation in which two players each have two options whose outcome depends crucially on the simultaneous choice made by the other, often formulated in terms of two prisoners separately deciding whether to confess to a crime.

prison officer ▸ noun Brit. a guard in a prison.

prissy ▸ adjective (**prissier, prissiest**) fussily and excessively respectable: *a middle-class family with two prissy children.*
– DERIVATIVES **prissily** adverb, **prissiness** noun.
– ORIGIN late 19th cent.: perhaps a blend of PRIM and SISSY.

Priština /ˈpriːʃtɪnə/ a city in the Balkans, the capital of Kosovo; pop. 210,800 (est. 2009). The capital of medieval Serbia, it was under Ottoman control from 1389 until 1912.

pristine /ˈprɪstiːn, -stʌɪn/ ▸ adjective in its original condition; unspoilt: *pristine copies of an early magazine.* ■ clean and fresh as if new; spotless: *a pristine white shirt.*
– DERIVATIVES **pristinely** adverb.
– ORIGIN mid 16th cent. (in the sense 'original, former, primitive and undeveloped'): from Latin *pristinus* 'former'. The senses 'unspoilt' and 'spotless' date from the 1920s.

Pritchett /ˈprɪtʃɪt/, Sir V. S. (1900–97), English writer and critic; full name *Victor Sawdon Pritchett*. He is chiefly remembered for his short stories.

prithee /ˈprɪðiː/ ▸ exclamation archaic please (used to convey a polite request): *prithee, Jack, answer me honestly.*
– ORIGIN late 16th cent.: abbreviation of *I pray thee*.

privacy /ˈprɪvəsi, ˈprʌɪ-/ ▸ noun [mass noun] a state in which one is not observed or disturbed by other people: *she returned to the privacy of her own home.* ■ the state of being free from public attention: *a law to restrict newspapers' freedom to invade people's privacy.*

private ▸ adjective **1** belonging to or for the use of one particular person or group of people only: *all bedrooms have private facilities | his private plane.* ■ (of a conversation, activity, or gathering) involving only a particular person or group, and often dealing with matters that are not to be disclosed to others: *this is a private conversation | a small private service in the chapel.* ■ (of thoughts and feelings) not to be revealed to others: *she felt awkward at intruding on private grief.* ■ (of a person) choosing not to reveal their thoughts and feelings to others: *he was a very private man.* ■ (of a place) quiet and free from people who may interrupt: *can we go somewhere a little more private?* ■ [predic.] (especially of two people) alone and undisturbed by others: *we can phone from the library—we'll be private in there.*
2 (of a person) having no official or public role or position: *the paintings were sold to a private collector.* ■ not connected with one's work or official position: *the ambassador visited the school in a private capacity.*
3 (of a service or industry) provided or owned by an individual or an independent, commercial company rather than the state. ■ (of education or medical treatment) conducted outside the state system and charging fees to those who make use of it: *private education | if I could afford it I'd **go private**.* ■ relating to or denoting a transaction between individuals and not involving commercial organizations: *it was a private sale—no estate agent's commission.*
▸ noun **1** the lowest rank in the army, below lance corporal or private first class.
2 (**privates**) informal short for PRIVATE PARTS.
– PHRASES **in private** with no one else present: *I've got to talk to you in private.*
– ORIGIN late Middle English (originally denoting a person not acting in an official capacity): from Latin *privatus* 'withdrawn from public life', a use of the past participle of *privare* 'bereave, deprive', from *privus* 'single, individual'.

private bill ▸ noun a legislative bill affecting the interests only of a particular body or individual.

private company ▸ noun Brit. a company whose shares may not be offered to the public for sale and which operates under legal requirements less strict than those for a public company.

private detective (also **private investigator**) ▸ noun a freelance detective who carries out covert investigations on behalf of private clients.

private enterprise ▸ noun [mass noun] business or industry that is managed by independent companies or private individuals rather than being controlled by the state.

privateer /ˌprʌɪvəˈtɪə/ ▸ noun **1** historical an armed ship owned and crewed by private individuals holding a government commission and authorized for use in war, especially in the capture of merchant shipping. ■ a commander or crew member of a privateer, often regarded as a pirate.
2 an advocate or exponent of private enterprise.
3 Motor Racing a competitor who races as a private individual rather than as a member of a team.
– DERIVATIVES **privateering** noun.
– ORIGIN mid 17th cent.: from PRIVATE, on the pattern of *volunteer*.

privateersman ▸ noun (pl. **privateersmen**) historical a commander or crew member of a privateer.

private eye ▸ noun informal a private detective.

private first class ▸ noun a rank in the US army, above private and below corporal.

private income ▸ noun another term for UNEARNED INCOME.

private investigator ▸ noun another term for PRIVATE DETECTIVE.

private key ▸ noun see PUBLIC KEY.

private law ▸ noun [mass noun] a branch of the law that deals with the relations between individuals or institutions, rather than relations between these and the state.

private life ▸ noun a person's personal relationships, interests, etc., as distinct from their public or professional life.

privately ▸ adverb in a private way, manner, or capacity: *I must insist we speak privately | their children were privately educated.* ■ [often sentence adverb] used to refer to a situation in which someone's thoughts and feelings are not revealed: *privately, Robert considered that she was overreacting.*

private means ▸ plural noun Brit. income from investments, property, or inheritance, as opposed to earned income or state benefit.

private member ▸ noun (in the UK, Canada, Australia, and New Zealand) a member of a parliament who is not a minister or does not hold government office.

private member's bill ▸ noun (in the UK, Canada, Australia, and New Zealand) a legislative bill that is introduced by a private Member of Parliament and is not part of a government's planned legislation. Such bills rarely become law.

private nuisance ▸ noun Law an unlawful interference with the use and enjoyment of land.

private parts ▸ plural noun euphemistic a person's genitals.

private practice ▸ noun [mass noun] the work of a professional practitioner such as a doctor or lawyer who is self-employed. ■ Brit. medical practice that is not part of the National Health Service.

private press ▸ noun a printing establishment operated on a small scale by a private person or group, in which the emphasis is on quality and individuality rather than profit.

private school ▸ noun **1** Brit. an independent school supported wholly by the payment of fees.
2 N. Amer. a school supported by a private organization or private individuals rather than by the state.

private secretary ▸ noun **1** a secretary who deals with the personal and confidential concerns of a business person or public figure.
2 a civil servant acting as an aide to a senior government official.

private sector ▸ noun the part of the national economy that is not under direct state control.

private soldier ▸ noun a soldier of the lowest rank. ■ US a soldier of the lowest rank who is not a recruit.

private treaty ▸ noun [mass noun] the agreement for the sale of a property at a price negotiated directly between the vendor and purchaser or their agents.

private view ▸ noun an event attended by invited guests at which an art exhibition may be seen before it is opened to the public.

private war ▸ noun **1** a feud between people or families that is conducted without regard to the law.
2 hostilities against members of another state that take place without government sanction.

privation /prʌɪˈveɪʃ(ə)n/ ▸ noun [mass noun] **1** a state in which food and other essentials for well being are lacking: *years of rationing and privation* | [count noun] ***the privations of life at the front.***
2 formal the loss or absence of a quality or attribute that is normally present: *cold is the privation of heat.*
– ORIGIN Middle English: from Latin *privatio(n-)*, from *privat-* 'deprived', from the verb *privare* (see PRIVATE).

privatism /ˈprʌɪvətɪz(ə)m/ ▸ noun [mass noun] a tendency to be concerned with ideas or issues only in so far as they affect one as an individual.

privative /ˈprɪvətɪv/ ▸ adjective (of an action or state) marked by the absence or loss of some quality or attribute that is normally present. ■ (of a statement or term) denoting the absence or loss of an attribute or quality: *parliament may insert a privative clause to achieve this result.* ■ Grammar (of a particle or affix) expressing absence or negation, for example the Greek *a-*, meaning 'not', in *atypical*.
– ORIGIN late 16th cent.: from Latin *privativus* 'denoting privation', from *privat-* 'deprived' (see PRIVATION).

P

privatize (also **privatise**) ▶ **verb** [with obj.] transfer (a business, industry, or service) from public to private ownership and control: *they were opposed to plans to privatize electricity and water.*
– DERIVATIVES **privatization** noun, **privatizer** noun.

privet /ˈprɪvɪt/ ▶ **noun** a shrub of the olive family, with small white heavily scented flowers and poisonous black berries. ● Genus *Ligustrum*, family Oleaceae: several species, in particular the evergreen *L. ovalifolium*, often used as hedging in towns.
– ORIGIN mid 16th cent.: of unknown origin.

privilege ▶ **noun** a special right, advantage, or immunity granted or available only to a particular person or group: *education is a right, not a privilege* | [mass noun] *he has been accustomed all his life to wealth and privilege.* ■ something regarded as a special honour: *I had the privilege of giving the Sir George Brown memorial lecture.* ■ (also **absolute privilege**) (especially in a parliamentary context) the right to say or write something without the risk of incurring punishment or legal action for defamation. ■ the right of a lawyer or official to refuse to divulge confidential information. ■ chiefly historical a grant to an individual, corporation, or place of special rights or immunities, especially in the form of a franchise or monopoly.
▶ **verb** [with obj.] formal grant a privilege or privileges to: *English inheritance law privileged the eldest son.* ■ exempt (someone) from a liability or obligation to which others are subject: *barristers **are privileged** from arrest going to, coming from, and abiding in court.*
– ORIGIN Middle English: via Old French from Latin *privilegium* 'bill or law affecting an individual', from *privus* 'private' + *lex, leg-* 'law'.

privileged ▶ **adjective 1** having special rights, advantages, or immunities: *in the nineteenth century only a privileged few had the vote.* ■ [with infinitive] having been granted a special honour: *I felt I had been privileged to compete in such a race.*
2 (of information) legally protected from being made public.

privity /ˈprɪvɪti/ ▶ **noun** (pl. **privities**) Law a relation between two parties that is recognized by law, such as that of blood, lease, or service: *the parties no longer have privity with each other.*
– ORIGIN Middle English (in the sense 'secrecy, intimacy'): from Old French *privete*, from medieval Latin *privitas*, from Latin *privus* 'private'.

privity of contract ▶ **noun** [mass noun] Law the relation between the parties in a contract which entitles them to sue each other but prevents a third party from doing so.

P

privy ▶ **adjective 1** (**privy to**) sharing in the knowledge of (something secret or private): *he was no longer privy to her innermost thoughts.*
2 archaic hidden; secret: *a privy place.*
▶ **noun** (pl. **privies**) **1** a toilet located in a small shed outside a house or other building.
2 Law a person having a part or interest in any action, matter, or thing.
– DERIVATIVES **privily** adverb.
– ORIGIN Middle English (originally in the sense 'belonging to one's own private circle'): from Old French *prive* 'private' (also used as a noun meaning 'private place' and 'familiar friend'), from Latin *privatus* 'withdrawn from public life' (see **PRIVATE**).

privy chamber ▶ **noun** a private apartment in a royal residence.

Privy Council ▶ **noun** a body of advisers appointed by a sovereign or a Governor General (now chiefly on an honorary basis and including present and former government ministers). ■ chiefly historical a sovereign's or Governor General's private counsellors.

privy counsellor (also **privy councillor**) ▶ **noun** a member of a Privy Council.

privy purse ▶ **noun** (in the UK) taxed funds provided by the Duchy of Lancaster to meet some official expenditure incurred by the monarch, plus his or her private expenses.

privy seal ▶ **noun** (in the UK) a seal affixed to state documents.

Prix de Rome /ˌpriː də ˈrəʊm/, French /pʀi də ʀɔm/ ▶ **noun** historical a prize awarded annually by the French government in a competition for artists, sculptors, architects, and musicians.
– ORIGIN French, literally 'prize of Rome', because the winner of the first prize in each category was funded for a period of study in Rome.

prix fixe /ˌpriː ˈfɪks/, French /pʀi fiks/ ▶ **noun** a meal consisting of several courses served at a total fixed price: [as modifier] *the prix fixe menu of the day.*
– ORIGIN French, literally 'fixed price'.

Prix Goncourt /ˌpriː ɡɒ̃ˈkʊə/, French /pʀi ɡɔ̃kuʀ/ ▶ **noun** an award given annually for a work of French literature. See **GONCOURT**.

prize[1] ▶ **noun 1** a thing given as a reward to the winner of a competition or in recognition of an outstanding achievement: *her invention won first prize in a national contest.* ■ a thing, especially an amount of money or a valuable object, that can be won in a game of chance: *the star prize in the charity raffle* | [as modifier] *prize money.* ■ something of great value that is worth struggling to achieve: *the prize will be victory in the general election.*
2 chiefly historical an enemy ship captured during the course of naval warfare. [late Middle English: from Old French *prise* 'taking, booty', from *prendre* 'take'.]
▶ **adjective** [attrib.] having been or likely to be awarded a prize in a competition: *a prize bull.* ■ denoting something for which a prize is awarded: *a prize crossword.* ■ excellent of its kind; outstanding: *a prize example of how well organic farming can function.* ■ complete; utter: *you must think I'm a prize idiot.*
▶ **verb** [with obj.] value extremely highly: *the berries were prized for their healing properties* | (as adj. **prized**) *the bicycle was her most prized possession.*
– PHRASES (**there are**) **no prizes for guessing** used to convey that something is obvious: *there's no prizes for guessing what you two have been up to!*
– ORIGIN Middle English: the noun, a variant of **PRICE**; the verb (originally in the sense 'estimate the value of') from Old French *pris-*, stem of *preisier* 'to praise, appraise' (see **PRAISE**).

prize[2] ▶ **verb** US spelling of **PRISE**.

prize court ▶ **noun** a naval court that adjudicates on the distribution of ships and property captured in the course of naval warfare.

prizefight ▶ **noun** a boxing match, typically an unlicensed one, fought for prize money.
– DERIVATIVES **prizefighter** noun, **prizefighting** noun.

prize-giving ▶ **noun** Brit. a ceremonial event at which prizes are awarded, especially one held at a school.

prizeman ▶ **noun** (pl. **prizemen**) a winner of a prize, especially an academic one.

prize money ▶ **noun** [mass noun] money offered or received as a prize.

prize ring ▶ **noun** a ring used for prizefighting. ■ (**the prize ring**) the practice of prizefighting; boxing.

prizewinner ▶ **noun** a winner of a prize.
– DERIVATIVES **prizewinning** adjective.

PRO ▶ **abbreviation** ■ Public Record Office. ■ public relations officer.

pro[1] ▶ **noun** (pl. **pros**) informal **1** a professional, especially in sport: *a tennis pro.*
2 a prostitute.
▶ **adjective** (of a person or an event) professional: *a pro golfer.*
– ORIGIN mid 19th cent.: abbreviation.

pro[2] ▶ **noun** (pl. **pros**) (usu. **pros**) an advantage or argument in favour of something: ***the pros and cons** of share ownership.*
▶ **preposition & adverb** in favour of: [as prep.] *they were pro the virtues of individualism.*
– ORIGIN late Middle English (as a noun): from Latin, literally 'for, on behalf of'.

pro-[1] ▶ **prefix 1** favouring; supporting: *pro-choice.*
2 acting as a substitute or deputy for: *proconsul.*
3 denoting motion forwards, out, or away: *proceed* | *propel* | *prostrate.*
– ORIGIN from Latin *pro* 'in front of, on behalf of, instead of, on account of'.

pro-[2] ▶ **prefix** before in time, place, order, etc.: *proactive* | *prothalamium.*
– ORIGIN from Greek *pro* 'before'.

proa /ˈprəʊə/ (also **prau** or **prahu**) ▶ **noun** a type of sailing boat originating in Malaysia and Indonesia that may be sailed with either end at the front, typically having a large triangular sail and an outrigger.
– ORIGIN late 16th cent.: from Malay *perahu*.

pro-abortion ▶ **adjective** in favour of the availability of medically induced abortion.
– DERIVATIVES **pro-abortionist** noun & adjective.

proactive ▶ **adjective** (of a person or action) creating or controlling a situation rather than just responding to it after it has happened: ***employers must take a proactive approach to equal pay.***
– DERIVATIVES **proaction** noun, **proactively** adverb, **proactivity** noun.
– ORIGIN 1930s: from **PRO-**[2] (denoting earlier occurrence), on the pattern of *reactive*.

proactive interference (also **proactive inhibition**) ▶ **noun** [mass noun] Psychology the tendency of previously learned material to hinder subsequent learning.

pro-am ▶ **adjective** (of a sports event) involving both professionals and amateurs: *a pro-am golf tournament.*
▶ **noun** a pro-am event.

prob ▶ **noun** informal a problem: *there's no prob.*
– ORIGIN 1930s: abbreviation.

probabilistic ▶ **adjective** based on or adapted to a theory of probability; subject to or involving chance variation: *the main approaches are either rule-based or probabilistic.*
– DERIVATIVES **probabilistically** adverb.

probability ▶ **noun** (pl. **probabilities**) [mass noun] the quality or state of being probable; the extent to which something is likely to happen or be the case: *the rain will make the probability of a postponement even greater.* ■ [count noun] a probable or the most probable event: *for a time revolution was a strong probability.* ■ Mathematics the extent to which an event is likely to occur, measured by the ratio of the favourable cases to the whole number of cases possible: *the area under the curve represents probability* | [count noun] *a probability of 0.5.*
– PHRASES **in all probability** used to convey that something is very likely: *he would in all probability make himself known.*
– ORIGIN late Middle English: from Latin *probabilitas*, from *probabilis* 'provable, credible' (see **PROBABLE**).

probability density function ▶ **noun** Statistics a function of a continuous random variable, whose integral across an interval gives the probability that the value of the variable lies within the same interval.

probability distribution ▶ **noun** Statistics a function of a discrete variable whose integral over any interval is the probability that the variate specified by it will lie within that interval.

probability theory ▶ **noun** [mass noun] the branch of mathematics that deals with quantities having random distributions.

probable ▶ **adjective** [often with clause] likely to happen or be the case: *it is **probable that** the economic situation will deteriorate further* | *the probable consequences of his action.*
▶ **noun** Brit. a person who is likely to become or do something, especially one who is likely to be chosen for a team: *Merson and Wright are probables.*
– ORIGIN late Middle English (in the sense 'worthy of belief'): via Old French from Latin *probabilis*, from *probare* 'to test, demonstrate'.

probable cause ▶ **noun** [mass noun] Law, chiefly N. Amer. reasonable grounds to believe that a particular person has committed a crime, especially to justify making a search or preferring a charge.

probably ▶ **adverb** [sentence adverb] almost certainly; as far as one knows or can tell: ***she would probably never see him again*** | *'A bomb, do you think?' 'Probably.'*

proband /ˈprəʊbənd/ ▶ **noun** Medicine & Genetics a person serving as the starting point for the genetic study of a family.
– ORIGIN 1920s: from Latin *probandus* 'to be proved', gerundive of *probare* 'to test'.

probang /ˈprəʊbaŋ/ ▶ **noun** Medicine a strip of flexible material with a sponge or tuft at the end, used to remove an object from the throat or apply medication to it.
– ORIGIN mid 17th cent. (named *provang* by its inventor): perhaps an alteration suggested by **PROBE**.

probate ▶ **noun** [mass noun] the official proving of a will: *the house has been valued for probate.* ■ [count noun] a verified copy of a will with a certificate as handed to the executors.
▶ **verb** [with obj.] N. Amer. establish the validity of (a will).
– ORIGIN late Middle English: from Latin *probatum* 'something proved', neuter past participle of *probare* 'to test, prove'.

probation ▶ **noun** [mass noun] Law the release of an offender from detention, subject to a period of good behaviour under supervision: *I went to court and was **put on probation**.* ■ a process of testing or observing the character or abilities of a person who is new to a role or job: *for an initial period of probation your manager will closely monitor your progress.*

– DERIVATIVES **probational** adjective, **probationary** adjective.
– ORIGIN late Middle English (denoting testing or investigation): from Old French *probacion*, from Latin *probatio(n-)*, from *probare* 'to test, prove' (see PROVE). The legal use dates from the late 19th cent.

probationer ▸ noun 1 a person who is serving a probationary or trial period in a job or position to which they are newly appointed.
2 an offender on probation.

probation officer ▸ noun a person appointed to supervise offenders who are on probation.

probative /ˈprəʊbətɪv/ ▸ adjective chiefly Law having the quality or function of proving or demonstrating something; affording proof or evidence: *it places the probative burden on the defendant.*
– ORIGIN late Middle English (describing something that serves as a test): from Latin *probativus*, from *probat-* 'proved', from the verb *probare* (see PROVE).

probe ▸ noun 1 a blunt-ended surgical instrument used for exploring a wound or part of the body. ■ a small device, especially an electrode, used for measuring, testing, or obtaining information.
2 a thorough investigation into a crime or other matter: *a probe into city hall corruption.*
3 (also **space probe**) an unmanned exploratory spacecraft designed to transmit information about its environment.
4 a projecting device for engaging in a drogue, either on an aircraft for use in in-flight refuelling or on a spacecraft for use in docking with another craft.
▸ verb [with obj.] explore or examine (something), especially with the hands or an instrument: *hands probed his body from top to bottom.* ■ [no obj.] enquire into someone or something closely: *what right had he to **probe into** her personal life?* | (as adj. **probing**) *his dark probing eyes* | [with obj.] *police are probing a nightwatchman's murder.*
– DERIVATIVES **prober** noun, **probingly** adverb.
– ORIGIN late Middle English (as a noun): from late Latin *proba* 'proof' (in medieval Latin 'examination'), from Latin *probare* 'to test'. The verb dates from the mid 17th cent.

probenecid /prəʊˈbɛnɪsɪd/ ▸ noun [mass noun] Medicine a synthetic sulphur-containing compound which promotes increased excretion of uric acid and is used to treat gout.
– ORIGIN 1950s: from *pro(pyl)* + *ben(zoic)* + *-e-* + *(a)cid.*

probiotic /ˌprəʊbʌɪˈɒtɪk/ ▸ adjective denoting a substance which stimulates the growth of microorganisms, especially those with beneficial properties (such as those of the intestinal flora).
▸ noun a probiotic substance or preparation. ■ a microorganism introduced into the body for its beneficial qualities.

probit /ˈprɒbɪt/ ▸ noun Statistics a unit of probability based on deviation from the mean of a standard distribution.
– ORIGIN 1930s: from *prob(ability un)it.*

probity /ˈprəʊbɪti, ˈprɒb-/ ▸ noun [mass noun] formal the quality of having strong moral principles; honesty and decency: *financial probity.*
– ORIGIN late Middle English: from Latin *probitas*, from *probus* 'good'.

problem ▸ noun 1 a matter or situation regarded as unwelcome or harmful and needing to be dealt with and overcome: *they have financial problems* | *the problem of ageism in Hollywood.* ■ a thing that is difficult to achieve: *motivation of staff can also be a problem.*
2 Physics & Mathematics an inquiry starting from given conditions to investigate or demonstrate a fact, result, or law. ■ Geometry a proposition in which something has to be constructed. Compare with THEOREM. ■ (in chess) an arrangement of pieces in which the solver has to achieve a specified result.
– PHRASES **have a problem with** disagree with or have an objection to: *I have no problem with shopping on Sundays.* **no problem** used to express one's agreement or acquiescence: *'Can you come over here right away?' 'No problem.'* **that's your** (or **his**, **her**, etc.) **problem** used to express one's lack of interest in or sympathy with another person's problems: *he'd made a mistake but that was his problem.*
– ORIGIN late Middle English (originally denoting a riddle or a question for academic discussion): from Old French *probleme*, via Latin from Greek *problēma*, from *proballein* 'put forth', from *pro* 'before' + *ballein* 'to throw'.

problematic ▸ adjective constituting or presenting a problem: *the situation was problematic for teachers.*
▸ noun a thing that constitutes a problem: *the problematics of artificial intelligence.*
– DERIVATIVES **problematical** adjective, **problematically** adverb.
– ORIGIN early 17th cent.: via French from late Latin *problematicus*, from Greek *problēmatikos*, from *problēma* (see PROBLEM).

problematize (also **problematise**) ▸ verb [with obj.] make into or regard as a problem requiring a solution: *he problematized the concept of history.*
– DERIVATIVES **problematization** noun.

problem child ▸ noun a child with behavioural or other difficulties.

pro bono publico /prəʊ ˌbɒnəʊ ˈpʊblɪkəʊ, ˌbəʊnəʊ ˈpʌblɪkəʊ/ ▸ adverb & adjective for the public good: [as adv.] *the burden they carried pro bono publico.* ■ (usu. **pro bono**) chiefly N. Amer. denoting legal work undertaken without charge, especially for a client on low income: [as adv.] *the attorneys are representing him pro bono* | [as adj.] *pro bono legal services.*
– ORIGIN Latin.

Proboscidea /ˌprɒbəˈsɪdɪə/ ▸ plural noun Zoology an order of large mammals that comprises the elephants and their extinct relatives. They are distinguished by the possession of a trunk and tusks.
– ORIGIN modern Latin (plural), from PROBOSCIS.

proboscidean (also **proboscidian**) Zoology ▸ noun a mammal of the order Proboscidea, which comprises the elephants and their extinct relatives.
▸ adjective relating to or denoting proboscideans.

proboscis /prəˈbɒsɪs/ ▸ noun (pl. **probosces** /-siːz/, **proboscides** /-sɪdiːz/, or **proboscises**) the nose of a mammal, especially when it is long and mobile such as the trunk of an elephant or the snout of a tapir. ■ Entomology (in many insects) an elongated sucking mouthpart that is typically tubular and flexible. ■ Zoology (in some worms) an extensible tubular sucking organ.
– ORIGIN early 17th cent.: via Latin from Greek *proboskis* 'means of obtaining food', from *pro* 'before' + *boskein* '(cause to) feed'.

proboscis monkey ▸ noun a leaf-eating monkey native to the forests of Borneo, the male of which is twice the weight of the female and has a large pendulous nose. ● *Nasalis larvatus*, family Cercopithecidae.

proboscis worm ▸ noun another term for RIBBON WORM.

procaine /ˈprəʊkeɪn/ ▸ noun [mass noun] a synthetic compound derived from benzoic acid, used as a local anaesthetic, especially in dentistry.
– ORIGIN early 20th cent.: from PRO-[1] (denoting substitution) + *-caine* (from COCAINE).

procaine penicillin ▸ noun [mass noun] Medicine a slow-acting antibiotic made from a salt of procaine and a form of penicillin.

procaryote ▸ noun variant spelling of PROKARYOTE.

procedure ▸ noun an established or official way of doing something: *the police are now reviewing procedures* | [mass noun] *parliamentary procedure.* ■ a series of actions conducted in a certain order or manner: *the standard procedure for informing new employees about conditions of work.* ■ a surgical operation: *the procedure is carried out under general anaesthetic.* ■ Computing another term for SUBROUTINE.
– DERIVATIVES **procedural** adjective, **procedurally** adverb.
– ORIGIN late 16th cent.: from French *procédure*, from *procéder* (see PROCEED).

proceed ▸ verb [no obj.] 1 begin a course of action: *the consortium could **proceed with** the plan.* ■ [with infinitive] do something after something else: *opposite the front door was a staircase which I proceeded to climb.* ■ (of an action) carry on or continue: *my studies are proceeding well.* ■ Law start a lawsuit against someone: *he may still be able to **proceed against** the contractor under negligence rules.*
2 [no obj., with adverbial of direction] move forward: *from the High Street, proceed over Magdalen Bridge.* ■ Brit. dated advance to a higher rank, status, or education: *he did not **proceed to** university in his seventeenth year.*
3 originate from: *his claim that all power **proceeded from** God.*
– ORIGIN late Middle English: from Old French *proceder*, from Latin *procedere*, from *pro-* 'forward' + *cedere* 'go'.

proceedings ▸ plural noun an event or a series of activities involving a set procedure: *you complete a form to start proceedings.* ■ Law action taken in a court to settle a dispute: *criminal proceedings were brought against him.* ■ a published report of a set of meetings or a conference.

proceeds ▸ plural noun money obtained from an event or activity: *proceeds from the event will go to aid the work of the charity.*
– ORIGIN early 17th cent.: plural of the obsolete noun *proceed*, in the same sense, earlier meaning 'procedure'.

process[1] /ˈprəʊsɛs/ ▸ noun 1 a series of actions or steps taken in order to achieve a particular end: *military operations could jeopardize the peace process.* ■ a natural series of changes: *the ageing process.* ■ a systematic series of mechanized or chemical operations that are performed in order to produce something: *the manufacturing process is relatively simple.* ■ a series of interdependent operations carried out by computer. ■ [as modifier] Printing relating to or denoting printing using ink in three colours (cyan, magenta, and yellow) and black to produce a complete range of colour: *process inks.*
2 Law a summons or writ requiring a person to appear in court.
3 Biology & Anatomy a natural appendage or outgrowth on or in an organism, such as a protuberance on a bone.
▸ verb [with obj.] perform a series of mechanical or chemical operations on (something) in order to change or preserve it: *the salmon is quickly processed after harvest to preserve the flavour.* ■ deal with (someone or something) using an official procedure: *the immigration authorities who processed him.* ■ Computing operate on (data) by means of a program.
– PHRASES **be in the process of doing something** be continuing with an action already started: *I was in the process of buying a house.* **in the process** as an unintended part of a course of action: *she would make him pay for this, even if she killed herself in the process.* **in process of time** as time goes on.
– DERIVATIVES **processable** adjective.
– ORIGIN Middle English: from Old French *proces*, from Latin *processus* 'progression, course', from the verb *procedere* (see PROCEED). Current senses of the verb date from the late 19th cent.

process[2] /prəˈsɛs/ ▸ verb [no obj., with adverbial of direction] walk or march in procession: *they processed down the aisle.*
– ORIGIN early 19th cent.: back-formation from PROCESSION.

process engineering ▸ noun [mass noun] the branch of engineering that is concerned with industrial processes, especially continuous ones such as the production of petrochemicals.
– DERIVATIVES **process engineer** noun.

procession ▸ noun 1 a number of people or vehicles moving forward in an orderly fashion, especially as part of a ceremony: *a funeral procession.* ■ [mass noun] the action of moving forward in an orderly way: *the fully robed civic dignitaries walk **in procession**.* ■ a relentless succession of people or things: *magistrates complain that they see **a procession of** recidivist minor offenders.*
2 [mass noun] Theology the emanation of the Holy Spirit.
– DERIVATIVES **processionist** noun.
– ORIGIN late Old English, via Old French from Latin *processio(n-)*, from *procedere* 'move forward' (see PROCEED).

P

processional ▸ adjective relating to or used in a religious or ceremonial procession: *a processional cross.*
▸ noun a book containing litanies and hymns for use in religious processions. ■ a hymn or other piece of music sung or played during a religious procession.

processionary ▸ noun (also **processionary moth**) (pl. **processionaries**) a greyish moth whose caterpillars live communally in silken tents in trees, marching out at night in procession to feed, causing substantial damage. ● Family Thaumetopoeidae: several species, in particular the European **pine processionary** (*Thaumetopoea pityocampa*). ■ (also **processionary caterpillar**) the larva of the processionary moth.

processor ▸ noun a machine that processes something: *the processor overexposed the film.* ■ Computing another term for CENTRAL PROCESSING UNIT.

process server ▸ noun a sheriff's officer (or, in the US, anyone) who serves writs; a bailiff.

processual /prəˈsɛsjʊəl/ ▸ adjective relating to or involving the study of processes rather than discrete events.

procès-verbal /ˌprɒseɪvəːˈbɑːl/ ▸ noun (pl. **procès-verbaux** /-ˈbəʊ/) a written report of proceedings.
– ORIGIN mid 17th cent.: French.

prochlorperazine /ˌprəʊklɔːˈpɛrəziːn/ ▸ **noun** [mass noun] Medicine a synthetic compound derived from phenothiazine, used as a tranquillizer.
– ORIGIN 1950s: from *pro(pyl)* + *chlor(ine)* + *(pi)perazine*.

pro-choice ▸ **adjective** advocating the legal right of a woman to choose whether or not she will have an abortion: *a pro-choice demonstration.*
– DERIVATIVES **pro-choicer** noun.

proclaim ▸ **verb 1** [with clause] announce officially or publicly: *the government's chief scientific adviser proclaimed that the epidemic was under control* | [with obj.] *army commanders proclaimed a state of emergency.* ■ [with obj. and complement] declare officially or publicly to be: *he* ***proclaimed*** *King James II* ***as*** *King of England.* ■ say something emphatically; declare: *she proclaimed that what I had said was untrue* | [with obj. and infinitive] *he proclaimed the car to be in sound condition.*
2 [with obj.] indicate clearly: *his high, intelligent forehead proclaimed a strength of mind that was almost tangible* | [with obj. and complement] *he had a rolling gait that proclaimed him a man of the sea.*
– DERIVATIVES **proclaimer** noun, **proclamatory** adjective.
– ORIGIN late Middle English *proclame*, from Latin *proclamare* 'cry out', from *pro-* 'forth' + *clamare* 'to shout'. The change in the second syllable was due to association with the verb CLAIM.

proclamation ▸ **noun** a public or official announcement dealing with a matter of great importance: *the issuing by the monarch of a proclamation dissolving Parliament.* ■ [mass noun] the public or official announcement of an important matter: *the government restricted the use of water by proclamation.* ■ a clear declaration of something: *they often make proclamations about their heterosexuality.*
– ORIGIN late Middle English: via Old French from Latin *proclamatio(n-)*, from *proclamare* 'shout out' (see PROCLAIM).

proclitic /prə(ʊ)ˈklɪtɪk/ Linguistics ▸ **noun** a word pronounced with so little emphasis that it is shortened and forms part of the following word, e.g. *at* in *at home*. Compare with ENCLITIC.
▸ **adjective** denoting or relating to a proclitic.
– ORIGIN mid 19th cent.: from modern Latin *procliticus* (from Greek *proklinein* 'lean forward'), on the pattern of late Latin *encliticus* (see ENCLITIC).

proclivity /prəˈklɪvɪti/ ▸ **noun** (pl. **proclivities**) a tendency to choose or do something regularly; an inclination or predisposition towards a particular thing: *a* ***proclivity for*** *hard work.*
– ORIGIN late 16th cent.: from Latin *proclivitas*, from *proclivis* 'inclined', from *pro-* 'forward, down' + *clivus* 'slope'.

P

Procne /ˈprɒkni/ Greek Mythology the sister of Philomel.

procoagulant /ˌprəʊkəʊˈagjʊl(ə)nt/ Biochemistry ▸ **adjective** relating to or denoting substances that promote the conversion in the blood of the inactive protein prothrombin to the clotting enzyme thrombin.
▸ **noun** a procoagulant substance.

Proconsul /prəʊˈkɒns(ə)l/ ▸ **noun** a fossil hominoid primate found in Lower Miocene deposits in East Africa, one of the last common ancestors of both humans and the great apes. ● Genus *Proconsul*, family Pongidae.

proconsul /prəʊˈkɒns(ə)l/ ▸ **noun 1** a governor of a province in ancient Rome, having much of the authority of a consul.
2 a governor or deputy consul of a modern colony.
– DERIVATIVES **proconsular** adjective, **proconsulate** noun, **proconsulship** noun.
– ORIGIN from Latin *pro consule* '(one acting) for the consul'.

Procopius /prəˈkəʊpɪəs/ (*c.*500–*c.*562), Byzantine historian, born in Caesarea in Palestine. He accompanied Justinian's general Belisarius on his campaigns between 527 and 540. His principal works are the *History of the Wars of Justinian* and *On Justinian's Buildings*.

procrastinate /prə(ʊ)ˈkrastɪneɪt/ ▸ **verb** [no obj.] delay or postpone action; put off doing something: *the temptation will be to procrastinate until the power struggle plays itself out.*
– DERIVATIVES **procrastinator** noun, **procrastinatory** adjective.
– ORIGIN late 16th cent.: from Latin *procrastinat-* 'deferred till the morning', from the verb *procrastinare*, from *pro-* 'forward' + *crastinus* 'belonging to tomorrow' (from *cras* 'tomorrow').

procrastination /prə(ʊ)ˌkrastɪˈneɪʃ(ə)n/ ▸ **noun** [mass noun] the action of delaying or postponing something: *your first tip is to avoid procrastination.*

procreate ▸ **verb** [no obj.] (of people or animals) produce young; reproduce: *species that procreate by copulation.*
– DERIVATIVES **procreant** adjective (archaic), **procreation** noun, **procreative** adjective, **procreator** noun.
– ORIGIN late Middle English: from Latin *procreat-* 'generated, brought forth', from the verb *procreare*, from *pro-* 'forth' + *creare* 'create'.

Procrustean /prə(ʊ)ˈkrʌstɪən/ ▸ **adjective** (especially of a framework or system) enforcing uniformity or conformity without regard to natural variation or individuality: *a fixed Procrustean rule.*
– ORIGIN mid 19th cent.: from the name PROCRUSTES + -AN.

Procrustes /prəʊˈkrʌstiːz/ Greek Mythology a robber who forced travellers to lie on a bed and made them fit it by stretching their limbs or cutting off the appropriate length of leg. Theseus killed him in like manner.
– ORIGIN from Greek *prokroustēs*, literally 'stretcher', from *prokrouein* 'beat out'.

proctitis /prɒkˈtʌɪtɪs/ ▸ **noun** [mass noun] Medicine inflammation of the rectum and anus.
– ORIGIN early 19th cent.: from Greek *prōktos* 'anus' + -ITIS.

proctology /prɒkˈtɒlədʒi/ ▸ **noun** [mass noun] the branch of medicine concerned with the anus and rectum.
– DERIVATIVES **proctological** adjective, **proctologist** noun.
– ORIGIN late 19th cent.: from Greek *prōktos* 'anus' + -LOGY.

proctor ▸ **noun 1** Brit. an officer (usually one of two) at certain universities, appointed annually and having mainly disciplinary functions.
2 N. Amer. an invigilator at a university or college examination.
3 (in the Church of England) an elected representative of the clergy in the convocation of Canterbury or York. ■ historical a qualified practitioner of law in ecclesiastical and certain other courts. See also QUEEN'S PROCTOR.
▸ **verb** [with obj.] N. Amer. invigilate (an examination).
– DERIVATIVES **proctorial** adjective, **proctorship** noun.
– ORIGIN late Middle English: contraction of PROCURATOR.

proctoscope /ˈprɒktəskəʊp/ ▸ **noun** a medical instrument with an integral lamp for examining the anus and lower part of the rectum or carrying out minor medical procedures.
– DERIVATIVES **proctoscopy** noun.
– ORIGIN late 19th cent.: from Greek *prōktos* 'anus' + -SCOPE.

procumbent /prə(ʊ)ˈkʌmb(ə)nt/ ▸ **adjective** Botany (of a plant or stem) growing along the ground without throwing out roots.
– ORIGIN mid 17th cent.: from Latin *procumbent-* 'falling forwards', from the verb *procumbere*, from *pro-* 'forwards, down' + a verb related to *cubare* 'to lie'.

procuracy /prəˈkjʊərəsi/ ▸ **noun** (pl. **procuracies**) the position or office of a procurator.

procuration ▸ **noun** [mass noun] Law, dated the appointment, authority, or action of an attorney. ■ archaic the action of procuring or obtaining something.
– ORIGIN late Middle English: via Old French from Latin *procuratio(n-)*, from *procurare* 'attend to, take care of' (see PROCURE).

procurator /ˈprɒkjʊreɪtə/ ▸ **noun 1** Law an agent representing others in a court of law in countries retaining Roman civil law. ■ (in Scotland) a lawyer practising before the lower courts.
2 historical a treasury officer in a province of the Roman Empire.
– DERIVATIVES **procuratorial** adjective, **procuratorship** noun.
– ORIGIN Middle English (denoting a steward): from Old French *procuratour* or Latin *procurator* 'administrator, finance agent', from *procurat-* 'taken care of', from the verb *procurare* (see PROCURE).

procurator fiscal ▸ **noun** (in Scotland) a local coroner and public prosecutor.

procure ▸ **verb** [with obj.] **1** obtain (something), especially with care or effort: *food procured for the rebels* | [with two objs] *he persuaded a friend to procure him a ticket.* ■ obtain (someone) as a prostitute for another person.
2 [with obj. and infinitive] Law persuade or cause (someone) to do something: *he procured his wife to sign the mandate for the joint account.* ■ archaic or Law cause (something) to happen: *he was charged with procuring the death of the Earl of Lancaster.*
– DERIVATIVES **procurable** adjective.
– ORIGIN Middle English: from Old French *procurer*, from Latin *procurare* 'take care of, manage', from *pro-* 'on behalf of' + *curare* 'see to'.

procurement ▸ **noun** [mass noun] the action of obtaining or procuring something: *financial assistance for the procurement of legal advice* | [count noun] *the company's procurements from foreign firms.* ■ the action or occupation of acquiring military equipment and supplies: *defence procurement.*

procurer ▸ **noun 1** a person who obtains a prostitute for another person.
2 Law a person who causes someone to do something or something to happen.
– ORIGIN late Middle English (denoting a steward): from Anglo-Norman French *procurour*, from Latin *procurator* (see PROCURATOR). Sense 1 dates from the mid 17th cent.

procuress ▸ **noun** a female procurer.

Procyon /ˈprəʊsɪən/ Astronomy the eighth-brightest star in the sky, and the brightest in the constellation Canis Minor.
– ORIGIN Greek, literally 'before the dog' (because it rises before Sirius, the Dog Star).

procyonid /ˌprəʊsɪˈɒnɪd, -sʌɪ-/ ▸ **noun** Zoology a mammal of the raccoon family (Procyonidae).
– ORIGIN early 20th cent.: from modern Latin *Procyonidae* (plural), from the genus name *Procyon* (see PROCYON).

Prod ▸ **noun** informal, offensive (especially in Ireland) a Protestant.
– ORIGIN 1940s: abbreviation representing a pronunciation.

prod ▸ **verb** (**prods**, **prodding**, **prodded**) [with obj.] poke with a finger, foot, or pointed object: *he prodded her in the ribs* | [no obj.] *she took up a fork and* ***prodded at*** *the food.* ■ stimulate or persuade (someone who is reluctant or slow) to do something: *they attempted to* ***prod*** *the central bank* ***into*** *cutting interest rates.*
▸ **noun 1** a poke with a finger, foot, or pointed object: *he gave the wire netting an experimental prod.* ■ an act of stimulating or reminding someone to do something: *you need a gentle prod to remind you that life is only what you make it.*
2 a pointed implement, typically one discharging an electric current and used as a goad: *a cattle prod.*
– PHRASES **on the prod** N. Amer. informal looking for trouble: *a gangster on the prod.*
– DERIVATIVES **prodder** noun.
– ORIGIN mid 16th cent. (as a verb): perhaps symbolic of a short poking movement, or a blend of POKE[1] and dialect *brod* 'to goad, prod'. The noun dates from the mid 18th cent.

Proddie (also **Proddy**) ▸ **noun** (pl. **Proddies**) informal, offensive (especially in Ireland) a Protestant.

pro-democracy ▸ **noun** denoting or relating to political activism directed towards the establishment of democratic government in a country: *the pro-democracy movement.*

pro Deo /prəʊ ˈdeɪəʊ/ ▸ **adjective & adverb** Law, S. African with legal costs paid by the state at the instruction of the court: [as adv.] *the counsel defended him pro Deo.* ■ free of charge: [as adv.] *who'd work pro Deo in this day and age?*
– ORIGIN Latin, literally 'for God'.

prodigal ▸ **adjective 1** spending money or using resources freely and recklessly; wastefully extravagant: *prodigal habits die hard.*
2 having or giving something on a lavish scale: *the dessert was prodigal with whipped cream.*
▸ **noun** a person who spends money in a recklessly extravagant way. ■ (also **prodigal son** or **daughter**) a person who leaves home to lead a prodigal life but later makes a repentant return. [with biblical allusion to the parable in Luke 15:11–32.]
– DERIVATIVES **prodigality** noun, **prodigally** adverb.
– ORIGIN late Middle English: from late Latin *prodigalis*, from Latin *prodigus* 'lavish'.

prodigious /prəˈdɪdʒəs/ ▸ **adjective 1** remarkably or impressively great in extent, size, or degree: *the stove consumed a prodigious amount of fuel* | *her memory was prodigious.*
2 archaic unnatural or abnormal: *rumours of prodigious happenings, such as monstrous births.*
– DERIVATIVES **prodigiously** adverb [as submodifier] *a prodigiously gifted artist*, **prodigiousness** noun.

– ORIGIN late 15th cent. (in the sense 'portentous'): from Latin *prodigiosus*, from *prodigium* 'portent' (see PRODIGY).

prodigy ▶ noun (pl. **prodigies**) [often with modifier] a young person with exceptional qualities or abilities: *a Russian pianist who was a child prodigy in his day.* ■ an outstanding example of a particular quality: *Germany seemed **a prodigy of** industrial discipline.* ■ an amazing or unusual thing, especially one out of the ordinary course of nature: *omens and prodigies abound in Livy's work.*
– ORIGIN late 15th cent. (denoting something extraordinary considered to be an omen): from Latin *prodigium* 'portent'.

prodromal /prəʊˈdrəʊm(ə)l/ ▶ adjective Medicine relating to or denoting the period between the appearance of initial symptoms and the full development of a rash or fever.

prodrome /ˈprəʊdrəʊm, ˈprɒdrəʊm/ ▶ noun Medicine an early symptom indicating the onset of a disease or illness.
– ORIGIN early 17th cent.: from French, from modern Latin *prodromus*, from Greek *prodromos* 'precursor', from *pro* 'before' + *dromos* 'running'.

prodrug ▶ noun a biologically inactive compound which can be metabolized in the body to produce a drug.

produce ▶ verb /prəˈdjuːs/ [with obj.] **1** make or manufacture from components or raw materials: *the company have just produced a luxury version of the aircraft.* ■ (of a place or process) yield, grow, or supply: *the vineyards in the Val d'Or produce excellent wines.* ■ create or form (something) as part of a physical, biological, or chemical process: *the plant produces blue flowers in late autumn.* ■ make (something) using creative skills: *the garden where the artist produced many of his flower paintings.*
2 cause (a particular result or situation) to happen or exist: *no conventional drugs had produced any significant change.*
3 show or provide (something) for consideration, inspection, or use: *he produced a sheet of paper from his pocket.*
4 administer the financial and managerial aspects of (a film or broadcast) or the staging of (a play, opera, etc.). ■ supervise the making of (a musical recording), especially by determining the overall sound.
5 Geometry, dated extend or continue (a line).
▶ noun /ˈprɒdjuːs/ [mass noun] agricultural and other natural products collectively: *dairy produce.* ■ the result of a person's or efforts: *the work was in some degree the produce of their joint efforts.*
– DERIVATIVES **producibility** noun, **producible** adjective.
– ORIGIN late Middle English (in sense 3 of the verb): from Latin *producere*, from *pro-* 'forward' + *ducere* 'to lead'. Current noun senses date from the late 17th cent.

producer ▶ noun **1** a person, company, or country that makes, grows, or supplies goods or commodities for sale: *an oil producer.* ■ a person or thing that makes or causes something: *the mould is the producer of the toxin aflatoxin.*
2 a person responsible for the financial and managerial aspects of the making of a film or broadcast or for staging a play, opera, etc. ■ a person who supervises the making of a musical recording.

producer gas ▶ noun [mass noun] a low-grade fuel gas consisting largely of nitrogen and carbon monoxide, formed by passing air, or air and steam, through red-hot carbon.

product ▶ noun **1** an article or substance that is manufactured or refined for sale: *dairy products.* ■ a substance produced during a natural, chemical, or manufacturing process: *waste products.* ■ [mass noun] commercially manufactured articles, especially recordings, viewed collectively: *too much product of too little quality.*
2 a thing or person that is the result of an action or process: *her perpetual suntan was the product of a solarium.* ■ a person whose character and identity have been formed by a particular period or situation: *an ageing academic who is a product of the 1960s.*
3 Mathematics a quantity obtained by multiplying quantities together, or from an analogous algebraic operation.
– ORIGIN late Middle English (as a mathematical term): from Latin *productum* 'something produced', neuter past participle (used as a noun) of *producere* 'bring forth' (see PRODUCE).

product differentiation ▶ noun [mass noun] Economics the marketing of generally similar products with minor variations that are used by consumers when making a choice.

production ▶ noun [mass noun] **1** the action of making or manufacturing from components or raw materials, or the process of being so manufactured: *banning the production of chemical weapons | the car is no longer **in production**.* ■ the harvesting or refinement of something natural: *non-intensive methods of food production.* ■ the total amount of something that is produced: *steel production had peaked in 1974.* ■ the creation of something as part of a physical, biological, or chemical process: *excess production of collagen by the liver.* ■ [as modifier] denoting a car or other vehicle which has been manufactured in large numbers, as opposed to a prototype or other special version: *a production model.*
2 the provision of something for consideration, inspection, or use: *members are entitled to a discount **on production of** their membership card.*
3 the process of or management involved in making a film, play, or record: *the film was still **in production**.* ■ [count noun] a film, record, play, etc., viewed in terms of its making or staging: *an exciting new production of La Traviata.* ■ [in sing.] the overall sound of a musical recording, as determined by the way in which it is produced: *the record's production is gloriously relaxed.*
– PHRASES **make a production of** informal do (something) in an unnecessarily complicated way.
– DERIVATIVES **productional** adjective.
– ORIGIN late Middle English: via Old French from Latin *productio(n-)*, from *producere* 'bring forth' (see PRODUCE).

production line ▶ noun an arrangement in a factory in which a thing being manufactured is passed through a set linear sequence of mechanical or manual operations.

production number ▶ noun a spectacular musical item, typically including song and dance and involving all or most of the cast, in a theatrical show or film.

production platform ▶ noun a platform which houses equipment necessary to keep an oil or gas field in production, with facilities for temporarily storing the output of several wells.

productive ▶ adjective **1** producing or able to produce large amounts of goods, crops, or other commodities: *the most productive employees.* ■ relating to or engaged in the production of goods, crops, or other commodities: *the country's productive capacity.* ■ achieving a significant amount or result: *a long and productive career | the therapy sessions became more productive.* ■ [predic.] (**productive of**) producing or giving rise to: *the hotel was not productive of amusing company.* ■ Linguistics (of a prefix, suffix, or other linguistic unit) currently used in forming new words or expressions.
2 Medicine (of a cough) that raises mucus from the respiratory tract.
– DERIVATIVES **productively** adverb, **productiveness** noun.
– ORIGIN early 17th cent.: from French *productif, -ive* or late Latin *productivus*, from *product-* 'brought forth', from the verb *producere* (see PRODUCE).

productivity ▶ noun [mass noun] the state or quality of being productive: *the long-term productivity of land.* ■ the effectiveness of productive effort, especially in industry, as measured in terms of the rate of output per unit of input: *workers have boosted productivity by 30 per cent.* ■ Ecology the rate of production of new biomass by an individual, population, or community; the fertility or capacity of a given habitat or area: *nutrient-rich waters with high primary productivity.*

productize (also **productise**) ▶ verb [with obj.] make or develop (a service, concept, etc.) into a product: *additional development will be required to productize the technology.*
– DERIVATIVES **productization** noun.

product liability ▶ noun [mass noun] the legal liability a manufacturer or trader incurs for producing or selling a faulty product.

product placement ▶ noun [mass noun] a practice in which manufacturers of goods or providers of a service gain exposure for their products by paying for them to be featured in films and television programmes.

proem /ˈprəʊɪm/ ▶ noun formal a preface or preamble to a book or speech.
– ORIGIN late Middle English: from Old French *proeme*, via Latin from Greek *prooimion* 'prelude', from *pro* 'before' + *oimē* 'song'.

proenzyme ▶ noun Biochemistry a biologically inactive substance which is metabolized into an enzyme.

pro-European ▶ adjective favouring or supporting closer links with the European Union.
▶ noun a pro-European person.

prof ▶ noun informal a professor.
– ORIGIN mid 19th cent.: abbreviation.

Prof. ▶ abbreviation professor: [as title] *Prof. Smith.*

pro-family ▶ adjective chiefly US promoting family life and traditional moral values.

profane /prəˈfeɪn/ ▶ adjective **1** not relating to that which is sacred or religious; secular: *a talk that tackled topics both sacred and profane.* ■ (of a person) not initiated into religious rites or any esoteric knowledge: *he was an agnostic, a profane man.*
2 (of a person or their behaviour) not respectful of religious practice; irreverent: *a profane person might be tempted to violate the tomb.* ■ (of language) blasphemous or obscene.
▶ verb [with obj.] treat (something sacred) with irreverence or disrespect: *it was a serious matter to profane a tomb.*
– DERIVATIVES **profanation** noun, **profanely** adverb, **profaneness** noun, **profaner** noun.
– ORIGIN late Middle English (in the sense 'heathen'): from Old French *prophane*, from Latin *profanus* 'outside the temple, not sacred', from *pro-* (from Latin *pro* 'before') + *fanum* 'temple'.

profanity /prəˈfanɪti/ ▶ noun (pl. **profanities**) [mass noun] blasphemous or obscene language: *an outburst of profanity.* ■ [count noun] a swear word; an oath. ■ irreligious or irreverent behaviour.
– ORIGIN mid 16th cent.: from late Latin *profanitas*, from Latin *profanus* 'not sacred' (see PROFANE).

proferens /prəˈfɛrɛnz/ ▶ noun (pl. **proferentes** /ˌprɒfəˈrɛntiːz/) Law the party which proposes or adduces a contract or a condition in a contract.
– ORIGIN Latin, literally 'uttering'.

profess ▶ verb [with obj.] **1** claim, often falsely, that one has (a quality or feeling): *he had professed his love for her only to walk away | [with infinitive] I don't profess to be an expert | [with complement] (**profess oneself**) he professed himself amazed at the boy's ability.* ■ archaic have or claim knowledge or skill in (a subject or accomplishment): *though knowing little of the arts I professed, he proved a natural adept.*
2 affirm one's faith in or allegiance to (a religion or set of beliefs): *a people professing Christianity.* ■ (**be professed**) be received into a religious order under vows: *she entered St Margaret's Convent, and was professed in 1943.*
3 archaic or humorous teach (a subject) as a professor: *a professor—what does he profess?*
– ORIGIN Middle English (as *be professed* 'be received into a religious order'): from Latin *profess-* 'declared publicly', from the verb *profiteri*, from *pro-* 'before' + *fateri* 'confess'.

professed ▶ adjective **1** (of a quality, feeling, or belief) claimed openly but often falsely: *for all her professed populism, she was seen as remote from ordinary people.*
2 (of a person) openly declared to be: *a professed and conforming Anglican.* ■ (of a monk or nun) having taken the vows of a religious order. ■ archaic claiming to be qualified as a particular specialist; professional.

professedly ▶ adverb [sentence adverb] ostensibly; apparently (used in reference to something claimed or asserted, possibly falsely): *restrictions professedly designed to stop the use of political propaganda.*

profession ▶ noun **1** a paid occupation, especially one that involves prolonged training and a formal qualification: *his chosen profession of teaching | a barrister **by profession**.* ■ [treated as sing. or pl.] a body of people engaged in a particular profession: *the legal profession has become increasingly business-conscious.*
2 an open but often false claim: *his profession of delight rang hollow.*
3 a declaration of belief in a religion. ■ the declaration or vows made on entering a religious order. ■ [mass noun] the ceremony or fact of being professed in a religious order: *after profession she taught in Maidenhead.*
– PHRASES **the oldest profession** humorous the practice of working as a prostitute.
– ORIGIN Middle English (denoting the vow made on entering a religious order): via Old French from Latin *professio(n-)*, from *profiteri* 'declare publicly'

P

(see PROFESS). Sense 1 derives from the notion of an occupation that one 'professes' to be skilled in.

professional ▶ adjective **1** relating to or belonging to a profession: *young professional people*. ■ worthy of or appropriate to a professional person; competent, skilful, or assured: *his professional expertise* | *their music is both memorable and professional*.
2 engaged in a specified activity as one's main paid occupation rather than as an amateur: *a professional boxer*. ■ informal, derogatory habitually making a feature of a particular activity or attribute: *a professional gloom-monger*.
▶ noun a person engaged or qualified in a profession: *professionals such as lawyers and surveyors*. ■ a person engaged in a specified activity, especially a sport, as a main paid occupation rather than as a pastime. ■ a person competent or skilled in a particular activity: *she was a real professional on stage*.
– DERIVATIVES **professionally** adverb.

professional foul ▶ noun Brit. (especially in soccer) a deliberate foul to deny an opponent an advantageous position.

professionalism ▶ noun **1** [mass noun] the competence or skill expected of a professional: *the key to quality and efficiency is professionalism*.
2 the practising of an activity, especially a sport, by professional rather than amateur players: *the trend towards professionalism*.

professionalize (also **professionalise**) ▶ verb [with obj.] give (an occupation, activity, or group) professional qualities, typically by increasing training or raising required qualifications: *attempts to professionalize the police are resisted by many*.
– DERIVATIVES **professionalization** noun.

professor ▶ noun **1** (N. Amer. also **full professor**) a university academic of the highest rank; the holder of a university chair.
2 N. Amer. a university teacher.
3 a person who affirms a faith in or allegiance to something: *the professors of true religion*.
– DERIVATIVES **professorate** noun, **professorial** adjective, **professorially** adverb, **professoriate** noun, **professorship** noun.
– ORIGIN late Middle English: from Latin *professor*, from *profess-* 'declared publicly', from the verb *profiteri* (see PROFESS).

proffer ▶ verb [with obj.] hold out or put forward (something) to someone for acceptance: *she proffered a glass of wine* | *he proffered his resignation*.
▶ noun literary an offer or proposal.
– ORIGIN Middle English: from Anglo-Norman French *proffrir*, from Latin *pro-* 'before' + *offerre* 'to offer'.

proficiency ▶ noun [mass noun] a high degree of skill; expertise: *he demonstrated his* ***proficiency in*** *Chinese*.

proficient ▶ adjective competent or skilled in doing or using something: *I was* ***proficient at*** *my job* | *she felt reasonably* ***proficient in*** *Italian*.
– DERIVATIVES **proficiently** adverb.
– ORIGIN late 16th cent.: from Latin *proficient-* 'advancing', from the verb *proficere*, from *pro-* 'on behalf of' + *facere* 'do, make'.

profile ▶ noun **1** an outline of something, especially a person's face, as seen from one side: *the man turned and she caught his profile*. ■ a drawing or other representation of the outline of something. ■ a vertical cross section of a structure: *skilfully made vessels with an S-shaped profile*. ■ Geography an outline of part of the earth's surface, e.g. the course of a river, as seen in a vertical section. ■ a flat outline piece of scenery on stage.
2 a short article giving a description of a person or organization: *a profile of a Texas tycoon*.
3 [in sing.] the extent to which a person or organization attracts public notice: *raising the profile of women in industry*.
4 a graphical or other representation of information relating to particular characteristics of something, recorded in quantified form: *a sleep profile for someone on a shift system*. ■ a record of a person's psychological or behavioural characteristics, preferences, etc.: *they had been using personal details to build customer profiles*.
▶ verb [with obj.] **1** describe (a person or organization) in a short article: *he was to profile a backbench MP*.
2 represent in outline from one side: *he was standing motionless, profiled on the far side of the swimming pool*. ■ (**be profiled**) have a specified shape in outline: *a proud bird profiled like a phoenix*. ■ shape (something), especially by means of a tool guided by a template: (as adj. **profiled**) *profiled and plain tiles*.
– PHRASES **in profile** (in reference to someone's face) as seen from one side: *a photograph of Leon in profile*.
– DERIVATIVES **profiler** noun.
– ORIGIN mid 17th cent.: from obsolete Italian *profilo*, from the verb *profilare*, from *pro-* 'forth' + *filare* 'to spin', formerly 'draw a line' (from Latin *filare*, from *filum* 'thread').

profile component ▶ noun an attainment target in a particular subject, forming part of a general assessment of a pupil.

profiling ▶ noun [mass noun] the recording and analysis of a person's psychological and behavioural characteristics, so as to assess or predict their capabilities in a certain sphere or to assist in identifying categories of people.

profit ▶ noun **1** a financial gain, especially the difference between the amount earned and the amount spent in buying, operating, or producing something: *record pre-tax profits* | [mass noun] *his eyes brightened at the prospect of profit*.
2 [mass noun] advantage; benefit: *there's no profit in screaming at referees from the bench*.
▶ verb (**profits, profiting, profited**) [no obj.] obtain a financial advantage or benefit: *the only people to* ***profit from*** *the episode were the lawyers*. ■ obtain an advantage or benefit: *not all children would* ***profit from*** *this kind of schooling*. ■ [with obj.] be beneficial to: *it would profit us to change our plans*.
– PHRASES **at a profit** making more money than is spent in buying, operating, or producing something: *doing up houses and selling them at a profit*.
– ORIGIN Middle English (in the sense 'advantage, benefit'): from Old French, from Latin *profectus* 'progress, profit', from *proficere* 'to advance', from *pro-* 'on behalf of' + *facere* 'do'. The verb is from Old French *profiter*.

profitable ▶ adjective **1** (of a business or activity) yielding profit or financial gain.
2 beneficial; useful: *he'd had a profitable day*.
– DERIVATIVES **profitability** noun, **profitably** adverb.
– ORIGIN Middle English: from Old French, from the verb *profiter* (see PROFIT).

profit and loss account ▶ noun an account in the books of an organization to which incomes and gains are credited and expenses and losses debited, so as to show the net profit or loss over a given period. ■ a financial statement showing a company's net profit or loss in a given period.

profit centre ▶ noun a part of an organization with assignable revenues and costs and hence ascertainable profitability.

profiteer ▶ verb [no obj.] (often as noun **profiteering**) make or seek to make an excessive or unfair profit, especially illegally: *seven food merchants were charged with profiteering*.
▶ noun a person who profiteers.

profiterole /prəˈfɪtərəʊl/ ▶ noun a small ball of soft, sweet choux pastry filled with cream and covered with chocolate sauce, served as a dessert.
– ORIGIN French, diminutive of *profit* 'profit'.

profitless ▶ adjective without benefit or advantage; pointless: *a long and profitless public row*.

profit margin ▶ noun the amount by which revenue from sales exceeds costs in a business.

profit-sharing ▶ noun [mass noun] a system in which the people who work for a company receive a direct share of the profits.

profit-taking ▶ noun [mass noun] the sale of securities that have risen in price.

profit warning ▶ noun a statement issued by a company advising the stock market that profits will be lower than expected.

profligate /ˈprɒflɪgət/ ▶ adjective **1** recklessly extravagant or wasteful in the use of resources: *profligate consumers of energy*.
2 licentious; dissolute: *he succumbed to drink and a profligate lifestyle*.
▶ noun a licentious, dissolute person.
– DERIVATIVES **profligacy** noun, **profligately** adverb.
– ORIGIN mid 16th cent. (in the sense 'overthrown, routed'): from Latin *profligatus* 'dissolute', past participle of *profligare* 'overthrow, ruin', from *pro-* 'forward, down' + *fligere* 'strike down'.

pro-form ▶ noun Linguistics a word or lexical unit which is dependent for its meaning on reference to some other part of the context, for example a pronoun or the verb *do* in *she likes chocolate and so do I*.

pro forma /prəʊ ˈfɔːmə/ ▶ adjective done or produced as a matter of form: *pro forma reports*. ■ denoting a standard document or form, especially an invoice sent in advance of or with goods supplied. ■ (of a financial statement) showing potential or expected income, costs, assets, or liabilities, especially in relation to some planned act or situation.
▶ adverb as a matter of form or politeness: *he nodded to him pro forma*.
▶ noun a pro forma document or form.
– ORIGIN early 16th cent.: from Latin.

profound ▶ adjective (**profounder, profoundest**)
1 (of a state, quality, or emotion) very great or intense: *profound feelings of disquiet* | *the implications of this discovery are profound*. ■ (of a disease or disability) very severe: *a case of profound liver failure*.
2 (of a person or statement) having or showing great knowledge or insight: *a profound philosopher*. ■ (of a subject or idea) demanding deep study or thought: *expressing profound truths in simple language*.
3 archaic very deep: *profound crevasses*.
▶ noun (**the profound**) literary the deepest part of something, especially the ocean. ■ profound quality.
– DERIVATIVES **profoundness** noun.
– ORIGIN Middle English: from Old French *profund*, from Latin *profundus* 'deep', from Latin *pro* 'before' + *fundus* 'bottom'. The word was used earliest in the sense 'showing deep insight'.

profoundly ▶ adverb ■ [as submodifier] to a profound extent; extremely: *a profoundly disturbing experience*. in a profound way; greatly: *he profoundly altered the whole course of my life*.

Profumo /prəˈfjuːməʊ/, John (Dennis) (1915–2006), British Conservative politician. In 1960 he was appointed Secretary of State for War under Harold Macmillan. Three years later news broke of his relationship with the mistress of a Soviet diplomat, Christine Keeler, raising fears of a security breach and precipitating his resignation.

profundity ▶ noun (pl. **profundities**) [mass noun] great depth of insight or knowledge: *the simplicity and profundity of the message*. ■ great depth or intensity of a state, quality, or emotion: *the profundity of her misery*. ■ [count noun] a statement or idea that shows great knowledge or insight.

profuse ▶ adjective (especially of something offered or discharged) very plentiful; abundant: *I offered my profuse apologies*. ■ archaic (of a person) extravagant: *they are* ***profuse in*** *hospitality*.
– DERIVATIVES **profusely** adverb, **profuseness** noun.
– ORIGIN late Middle English (in the sense 'extravagant'): from Latin *profusus* 'lavish, spread out', past participle of *profundere*, from *pro-* 'forth' + *fundere* 'pour'.

profusion ▶ noun [in sing.] an abundance or large quantity of something: *a rich* ***profusion of*** *flowers* | [mass noun] *the beautiful pink foxgloves growing* ***in profusion*** *among the ferns*.
– ORIGIN mid 16th cent.: via French from Latin *profusio(n-)*, from *profundere* 'pour out'. Early use expressed the senses 'extravagance', 'squandering', and 'waste'.

prog informal ▶ noun a television or radio programme: *Britain's best-loved pop prog*.
▶ adjective (of rock music) progressive: *prog rock bands*.

progenitive ▶ adjective formal having the power to produce offspring.

progenitor /prə(ʊ)ˈdʒɛnɪtə/ ▶ noun a person or thing from which a person, animal, or plant is descended or originates; an ancestor or parent: *his children were the progenitors of many of Scotland's noble families*. ■ a person who originates a cultural or intellectual movement: *the progenitor of modern jazz*.
– ORIGIN late Middle English: from Old French *progeniteur*, from Latin *progenitor*, from *progenit-* 'begotten', from the verb *progignere*, from *pro-* 'forward' + *gignere* 'beget'.

progeniture /prə(ʊ)ˈdʒɛnɪtʃə/ ▶ noun [mass noun] formal the production of offspring; procreation. ■ progeny; offspring.
– ORIGIN late 15th cent.: from *progenit-* 'begotten' (from the verb *progignere*) + -URE.

progeny /ˈprɒdʒəni/ ▶ noun [treated as sing. or pl.] a descendant or the descendants of a person, animal, or plant; offspring: *shorthorn cattle are highly effective in bestowing their characteristics on their progeny*.
– ORIGIN Middle English: from Old French *progenie*, from Latin *progenies*, from *progignere* 'beget' (see PROGENITOR).

progeria /prə(ʊ)ˈdʒɪərɪə/ ▶ **noun** [mass noun] Medicine a rare syndrome in children characterized by physical symptoms suggestive of premature old age.
– ORIGIN early 20th cent.: modern Latin, from Greek *progērōs* 'prematurely old'.

progesterone /prəˈdʒɛstərəʊn/ ▶ **noun** [mass noun] Biochemistry a steroid hormone released by the corpus luteum that stimulates the uterus to prepare for pregnancy.
– ORIGIN 1930s: blend of **PROGESTIN** and the German synonym *Luteosteron* (from **CORPUS LUTEUM** + **STEROL**).

progestin /prə(ʊ)ˈdʒɛstɪn/ ▶ **noun** Biochemistry another term for **PROGESTOGEN**.
– ORIGIN 1930s: from **PRO-**[1] + **GESTATION** + **-IN**[1].

progestogen /prə(ʊ)ˈdʒɛstədʒ(ə)n/ ▶ **noun** Biochemistry a natural or synthetic steroid hormone, such as progesterone, that maintains pregnancy and prevents further ovulation during pregnancy.
– ORIGIN 1940s: from **PROGESTIN** + **-GEN**.

proglottid /prəʊˈglɒtɪd/ ▶ **noun** Zoology each segment in the strobila of a tapeworm, containing a complete sexually mature reproductive system.
– ORIGIN late 19th cent.: from Greek *proglōssis*, *proglōssid-* 'point of the tongue', based on *glōssa*, *glōtta* 'tongue' (because of its shape).

prognathous /prɒgˈneɪθəs, ˈprɒgnəθəs/ ▶ **adjective** having a projecting lower jaw or chin. ■ (of a lower jaw or chin) projecting.
– DERIVATIVES **prognathic** /prɒgˈnaθɪk/ adjective, **prognathism** noun.
– ORIGIN mid 19th cent.: from **PRO-**[2] 'before' + Greek *gnathos* 'jaw' + **-OUS**.

prognosis /prɒgˈnəʊsɪs/ ▶ **noun** (pl. **prognoses** /-siːz/) the likely course of a medical condition: *the disease has a poor prognosis.* ■ an opinion, based on medical experience, of the likely course of a medical condition: *it is very difficult to make an accurate prognosis.* ■ a forecast of the likely outcome of a situation: *gloomy prognoses about overpopulation.*
– ORIGIN mid 17th cent.: via late Latin from Greek *prognōsis*, from *pro-* 'before' + *gignōskein* 'know'.

prognostic /prɒgˈnɒstɪk/ ▶ **adjective** relating to or serving to predict the likely course of a medical condition.
▶ **noun** archaic an advance indication of a future event; an omen: *a pale moon and watery sun are known as prognostics of rain.*
– DERIVATIVES **prognostically** adverb.
– ORIGIN late Middle English: from Latin *prognosticus* from Greek *prognōstikos*, from *prognōsis* (see **PROGNOSIS**).

prognosticate ▶ **verb** [with obj.] foretell or prophesy (a future event): *the economists were prognosticating financial Armageddon.*
– DERIVATIVES **prognosticator** noun, **prognosticatory** adjective.
– ORIGIN late Middle English: from medieval Latin *prognosticat-*, from the verb *prognosticare* 'make a prediction' (see **PROGNOSTIC**).

prognostication ▶ **noun** [mass noun] the action of prophesying future events. ■ [count noun] a prophecy: *these gloomy prognostications proved to be unfounded.*
– ORIGIN late Middle English: from Old French *prognosticacion*, from medieval Latin *prognosticatio(n-)*, from the verb *prognosticare* (see **PROGNOSTICATE**).

prograde /ˈprəʊgreɪd/ ▶ **adjective 1** Astronomy (of planetary motion) proceeding from west to east; direct. The opposite of **RETROGRADE**.
2 Geology (of a metamorphic change) resulting from an increase in temperature or pressure.
▶ **verb** [no obj.] Geology (of a coastline) advance towards the sea as a result of the accumulation of waterborne sediment.
– DERIVATIVES **progradation** noun.
– ORIGIN early 20th cent. (as a verb): from **PRO-**[1] 'forwards' + **RETROGRADE**.

program ▶ **noun & verb** US spelling of **PROGRAMME** (also widely used in computing contexts).

programmatic ▶ **adjective 1** of the nature of or according to a programme, schedule, or method: *a programmatic approach to change.*
2 of the nature of programme music.
– DERIVATIVES **programmatically** adverb.

programme (US **program**) ▶ **noun 1** a planned series of future events or performances: *a weekly programme of films | the programme includes Dvořák's New World symphony.* ■ a set of related measures or activities with a particular long-term aim: *the British nuclear power programme.*
2 a sheet or booklet giving details of items or performers at an event or performance: *a theatre programme.*
3 an item broadcast between stated times on radio or television: *a nature programme.* ■ dated a radio or television channel.
4 (**program**) a series of coded software instructions to control the operation of a computer or other machine.
▶ **verb** (**programmes, programming, programmed**; US **programs, programing, programed**) [with obj.]
1 (**program**) provide (a computer or other machine) with coded instructions for the automatic performance of a task: *it is a simple matter to program the computer to recognize such symbols.* ■ input (instructions for the automatic performance of a task) into a computer or other machine: *simply* ***program in*** *your desired volume level.* ■ cause (a person or animal) to behave in a predetermined way: *all members of a species are* ***programmed to*** *build nests in the same way.*
2 arrange according to a plan or schedule: *we learn how to programme our own lives.* ■ schedule (an item) within a plan: *the next stage of the treaty is programmed for next year.*
3 US broadcast (an item): *the station does not program enough contemporary works.*
– PHRASES **get with the program** [often in imperative] N. Amer. informal do what is expected of one; adopt the prevailing viewpoint.
– DERIVATIVES **programmability** noun, **programmable** adjective.
– ORIGIN early 17th cent. (in the sense 'written notice'): via late Latin from Greek *programma*, from *prographein* 'write publicly', from *pro* 'before' + *graphein* 'write'.

programmed cell death ▶ **noun** less technical term for **APOPTOSIS**.

programmed learning ▶ **noun** [mass noun] a teaching method in which information is broken into simple sections on which pupils are able to test themselves.

programme evaluation and review technique (abbrev.: **PERT**) ▶ **noun** a network analysis technique which is used to determine the time it will take to complete a complex process.

programme music ▶ **noun** [mass noun] music that is intended to evoke images or convey the impression of events. Compare with **ABSOLUTE MUSIC**.

programmer (US also **programer**) ▶ **noun** a person who writes computer programs. ■ a device that automatically controls the operation of something in accordance with a prescribed program.

programme trading ▶ **noun** [mass noun] the simultaneous purchase and sale of many different stocks, or of stocks and related futures contracts, with the use of a computer program to exploit price differences in different markets.

programming ▶ **noun** [mass noun] **1** the process of writing computer programs.
2 the process of scheduling something, especially radio or television programmes. ■ radio or television programmes that are scheduled or broadcast: *the station is to expand its late-night programming.*

progress ▶ **noun** /ˈprəʊgrɛs/ [mass noun] **1** forward or onward movement towards a destination: *the darkness did not stop my progress | they failed to* ***make*** *any* ***progress*** *up the estuary.* ■ [count noun] archaic a state journey or official tour, especially by royalty.
2 development towards an improved or more advanced condition: *we are* ***making progress*** *towards equal rights.*
▶ **verb** /prəˈgrɛs/ [no obj.] **1** move forward or onward in space or time: *as the century progressed the quality of telescopes improved.* ■ [with obj.] (usu. as adj. **progressed**) Astrology calculate the position of (a planet) or of all the planets and coordinates of (a chart) according to the technique of progression.
2 develop towards an improved or more advanced condition: *work on the pond is progressing.* ■ [with obj.] cause (a task or undertaking) to make progress: *I cannot predict how quickly we can progress the matter.*
– PHRASES **in progress** in the course of being done or carried out: *a meeting was in progress.*
– ORIGIN late Middle English (as a noun): from Latin *progressus* 'an advance', from the verb *progredi*, from *pro-* 'forward' + *gradi* 'to walk'. The verb became obsolete in British English use at the end of the 17th cent. and was readopted from American English in the early 19th cent.

progress chaser ▶ **noun** a person in an organization who is responsible for checking that work is done efficiently and to schedule.

progression ▶ **noun 1** [mass noun] the process of developing gradually towards a more advanced state: *good opportunities for career progression* | [count noun] *a steady progression towards your goals.* ■ movement towards a destination: *their mode of progression through the forest.* ■ [count noun] Music a passage or movement from one note or chord to another: *a blues progression.* ■ [count noun] Astrology a predictive technique in which the daily movement of the planets, starting from the day of birth, represents a year in the subject's life.
2 a number of things in a series: *the vista unfolds in a progression of castles and vineyards as seemingly endless as the Rhine itself.*
– DERIVATIVES **progressional** adjective.
– ORIGIN late Middle English: from Old French, from Latin *progressio(n-)*, from the verb *progredi* (see **PROGRESS**).

progressionist chiefly historical ▶ **noun 1** Biology a supporter of the theory that all life forms gradually evolve to a higher form.
2 an advocate of or believer in political or social progress.
▶ **adjective** Biology supporting or relating to the theory that all life forms evolve to a higher form: *progressionist evolutionists.*

progressive ▶ **adjective 1** happening or developing gradually or in stages: *a progressive decline in popularity.* ■ (of a medical condition) increasing in severity: *progressive liver failure.* ■ (of taxation or a tax) increasing as a proportion of the sum taxed as that sum increases: *steeply progressive income taxes.*
2 (of a person or idea) favouring social reform: *a relatively progressive Minister of Education.* ■ favouring change or innovation: *the most progressive art school in Britain.* ■ relating to or denoting a style of rock music popular especially in the 1970s and characterized by classical influences, the use of keyboard instruments, and lengthy compositions.
3 Grammar denoting an aspect or tense of a verb that expresses an action in progress, e.g. *am writing, was writing.* Also called **CONTINUOUS**.
4 (of a card game or dance) involving a series of sections for which participants successively change place or relative position.
5 archaic engaging in or constituting forward motion.
▶ **noun 1** an advocate of social reform.
2 Grammar a progressive tense or aspect: *the present progressive.*
3 (also **progressive proof**) (usu. **progressives**) Printing each of a set of proofs of colour work, showing all the colours separately and the cumulative effect of overprinting them.
– DERIVATIVES **progressively** adverb, **progressiveness** noun, **progressivism** noun, **progressivist** noun & adjective.
– ORIGIN early 17th cent.: from French *progressif, -ive* or medieval Latin *progressivus*, from *progress-* 'gone forward', from the verb *progredi* (see **PROGRESS**).

Progressive Conservative Party a Canadian political party advocating free trade and holding moderate views on social policies. Founded in the mid 19th century but operating under its present name since 1942, the party was in power 1984–93 under Brian Mulroney.

proguanil /prəʊˈgwɑːnɪl/ ▶ **noun** [mass noun] Medicine a bitter-tasting synthetic compound derived from biguanide, used in the prevention and treatment of malaria.
– ORIGIN 1940s: from *pro(pyl)* + *(bi)guan(ide)* (a crystalline base) + **-IL**.

pro hac vice /ˌprəʊ hɑːk ˈvʌɪsi/ ▶ **adverb** for or on this occasion only.
– ORIGIN Latin.

prohibit ▶ **verb** (**prohibits, prohibiting, prohibited**) [with obj.] formally forbid (something) by law, rule, or other authority: *all ivory trafficking between nations is prohibited.* ■ formally forbid someone from doing something: *he is* ***prohibited from*** *becoming a director.* ■ (of a fact or situation) make (something) impossible; prevent: *the budget agreement had prohibited any tax cuts.*
– DERIVATIVES **prohibitor** noun, **prohibitory** adjective.
– ORIGIN late Middle English: from Latin *prohibit-* 'kept in check', from the verb *prohibere*, from *pro-* 'in front' + *habere* 'to hold'.

P

prohibited ▸ adjective that has been forbidden; banned: *they had deliberately fed prohibited material to their herd.*

prohibited degrees ▸ plural noun another term for **THE FORBIDDEN DEGREES** (see **FORBIDDEN**).

prohibition /ˌprəʊhɪˈbɪʃ(ə)n, prəʊɪ-/ ▸ noun [mass noun] **1** the action of forbidding something, especially by law: *they argue that prohibition of drugs will always fail.* ▪ [count noun] a law or regulation forbidding something: *prohibitions on insider dealing.* ▪ [count noun] English Law a writ from a superior court forbidding an inferior court from proceeding in a suit deemed to be beyond its cognizance.
2 (**Prohibition**) the prevention by law of the manufacture and sale of alcohol, especially in the US between 1920 and 1933.
– DERIVATIVES **prohibitionary** adjective, **Prohibitionist** noun.
– ORIGIN late Middle English: from Old French, from Latin *prohibitio(n-)*, from *prohibere* 'keep in check' (see **PROHIBIT**).

prohibitive ▸ adjective **1** (of a law or rule) forbidding or restricting something: *prohibitive legislation.* ▪ preventing someone from doing something: *books made browser-proof with prohibitive cellophane wrapping.*
2 (of a price or charge) so high as to prevent something being done or bought: *the cost of converting existing power stations is likely to be prohibitive.*
– DERIVATIVES **prohibitively** adverb, **prohibitiveness** noun.
– ORIGIN late Middle English (in sense 1): from French *prohibitif, -ive* or Latin *prohibitivus*, from *prohibit-* 'kept in check', from the verb *prohibere* (see **PROHIBIT**).

proinsulin ▸ noun [mass noun] Biochemistry a substance produced by the pancreas which is converted to insulin.

project ▸ noun **1** an individual or collaborative enterprise that is carefully planned to achieve a particular aim: *a research project | a project to build a new power station.* ▪ a piece of research work undertaken by a school or college student: *a history project.* ▪ a proposed or planned undertaking: *the novel undermines its own stated project of telling a story.*
2 (also **housing project**) N. Amer. a government-subsidized housing development with relatively low rents: *her family still lives in the projects.*
▸ verb [with obj.] **1** estimate or forecast (something) on the basis of present trends: *spending was **projected** at £72,900 million.* ▪ (often as adj. **projected**) plan (a scheme or undertaking): *a projected exhibition of contemporary art.*
2 [no obj.] extend outwards beyond something else; protrude: *I noticed a slip of paper **projecting from** the book* | (as adj. **projecting**) *a projecting bay window.*
3 [with obj. and adverbial of direction] throw or cause to move forward or outward: *seeds are projected from the tree.* ▪ cause (light, shadow, or an image) to fall on a surface: *the one light projected shadows on the wall.* ▪ cause (a sound) to be heard at a distance: *being audible depends on your ability to project your voice.* ▪ imagine (oneself, a situation, etc.) as having moved to a different place or time: *people may be **projecting** the present **into** the past.*
4 present or promote (a particular view or image): *he strives to project an image of youth.* ▪ present (someone or something) in a particular way: *she liked to project herself more as a friend than a doctor.* ▪ display (an emotion or quality) in one's behaviour: *everyone would be amazed that a young girl could project such depths of emotion.* ▪ (**project something on to**) attribute or transfer an emotion or desire to (another person), especially unconsciously: *men may sometimes project their own fears on to women.*
5 Geometry draw straight lines through (a given figure) to produce a corresponding figure on a surface or a line.
6 make a projection of (the earth, sky, etc.) on a plane surface.
– ORIGIN late Middle English (in the sense 'preliminary design, tabulated statement'): from Latin *projectum* 'something prominent', neuter past participle of *proicere* 'throw forth', from *pro-* 'forth' + *jacere* 'to throw'. Early senses of the verb were 'plan' and 'cause to move forward'.

projectile ▸ noun a missile designed to be fired from a gun. ▪ an object propelled through the air, especially one thrown as a weapon: *they tried to shield Johnson from the projectiles that were being thrown.*
▸ adjective denoting or relating to a projectile: *a projectile weapon.* ▪ propelled with great force.
– ORIGIN mid 17th cent.: modern Latin, from *project-* 'thrown forth', from the verb *proicere* (see **PROJECT**).

projection ▸ noun **1** an estimate or forecast of a future situation based on a study of present trends: *plans based on projections of slow but positive growth* | [mass noun] *population projection is essential for planning.*
2 [mass noun] the presentation of an image on a surface, especially a cinema screen: *quality illustrations for overhead projection.* ▪ [count noun] an image projected on a surface: *the band use stage projections featuring moon shots.* ▪ the ability to make a sound heard at a distance: *I taught him voice projection.*
3 [mass noun] the presentation or promotion of someone or something in a particular way: *the legal profession's projection of an image of altruism.* ▪ [count noun] a mental image viewed as reality: *monsters can be understood as mental projections of mankind's fears.* ▪ the unconscious transfer of one's desires or emotions to another person: *we protect the self by a number of defence mechanisms, including repression and projection.*
4 a thing that extends outwards from something else: *the chipboard covered all the sharp projections.*
5 [mass noun] Geometry the action of projecting a figure.
6 [mass noun] the representation on a plane surface of part of the surface of the earth or a celestial sphere. ▪ (also **map projection**) [count noun] a method for representing part of the surface of the earth or a celestial sphere on a plane surface.
– DERIVATIVES **projectionist** noun (sense 2).
– ORIGIN mid 16th cent. (in sense 6): from Latin *projectio(n-)*, from *proicere* 'throw forth' (see **PROJECT**).

projection television ▸ noun a large television receiver in which the image is projected optically on to a large viewing screen.

projective ▸ adjective **1** Geometry relating to or derived by projection: *projective transformations.* ▪ (of a property of a figure) unchanged by projection.
2 Psychology relating to the unconscious transfer of one's desires or emotions to another person: *the projective contents of wish fantasies.* ▪ relating to the unconscious expression or introduction of one's impressions or feelings.
– DERIVATIVES **projectively** adverb.

projective geometry ▸ noun [mass noun] the study of the projective properties of geometric figures.

projective test ▸ noun a psychological test in which words, images, or situations are presented to a person and the responses analysed for unconscious expression of elements of personality that they reveal.

project manager ▸ noun the person in overall charge of the planning and execution of a particular project.
– DERIVATIVES **project-manage** verb.

projector ▸ noun **1** a device that is used to project rays of light, especially an apparatus with a system of lenses for projecting slides or film on to a screen.
2 archaic a person who plans and sets up a project.

prokaryote /prəʊˈkarɪəʊt, -ɒt/ (also **procaryote**) ▸ noun Biology a microscopic single-celled organism which has neither a distinct nucleus with a membrane nor other specialized organelles, including the bacteria and cyanobacteria. Compare with **EUKARYOTE**.
– DERIVATIVES **prokaryotic** adjective.
– ORIGIN 1960s: from **PRO-**[2] 'before' + Greek *karuon* 'nut, kernel' + *-ote* as in **ZYGOTE**.

Prokofiev /prəˈkɒfɪɛf/, Sergei (Sergeevich) (1891–1953), Russian composer. Notable works include seven symphonies, the opera *The Love for Three Oranges* (1919), the ballet music for *Romeo and Juliet* (1935–6), and *Peter and the Wolf* (1936), a young person's guide to the orchestra in the form of a fairy tale.

Prokopyevsk /prəˈkɒpjɛfsk/ a coal-mining city in southern Russia, in the Kuznets Basin industrial region to the south of Kemerovo; pop. 213,200 (est. 2008).

prolactin /prəʊˈlaktɪn/ ▸ noun [mass noun] Biochemistry a hormone released from the anterior pituitary gland that stimulates milk production after childbirth.
– ORIGIN 1930s: from **PRO-**[2] 'before' + **LACTATION**.

prolapse ▸ noun /ˈprəʊlaps, prəˈlaps/ a slipping forward or down of a part or organ of the body: *a rectal prolapse.* ▪ a prolapsed part or organ, especially a uterus or rectum.
▸ verb /prəʊˈlaps/ [no obj.] (usu. as adj. **prolapsed**) (of a part or organ of the body) slip forward or down: *a prolapsed uterus.*
– ORIGIN mid 18th cent.: from Latin *prolaps-* 'slipped forward', from the verb *prolabi*, from *pro-* 'forward, down' + *labi* 'to slip'.

prolapsed disc (also **prolapsed intervertebral disc**) ▸ noun another term for **SLIPPED DISC**.

prolapsus /prəʊˈlapsəs/ ▸ noun [mass noun] technical term for **PROLAPSE**.
– ORIGIN late 18th cent.: modern Latin, from late Latin, literally 'fall'.

prolate /ˈprəʊleɪt/ ▸ adjective Geometry (of a spheroid) lengthened in the direction of a polar diameter. Often contrasted with **OBLATE**[2].
– ORIGIN late 17th cent.: from Latin *prolatus* 'carried forward', past participle of *proferre* 'prolong', from *pro-* 'forward' + *ferre* 'carry'.

prole informal, derogatory ▸ noun a member of the working class.
▸ adjective working class.
– ORIGIN late 19th cent.: abbreviation of **PROLETARIAT**.

proleg ▸ noun Entomology a fleshy abdominal limb of a caterpillar or similar insect larva.

prolegomenon /ˌprəʊlɪˈɡɒmɪnən/ ▸ noun (pl. **prolegomena**) a critical or discursive introduction to a book.
– ORIGIN mid 17th cent.: via Latin from Greek, passive present participle (neuter) of *prolegein* 'say beforehand', from *pro* 'before' + *legein* 'say'.

prolepsis /prəʊˈlɛpsɪs, -ˈliːpsɪs/ ▸ noun (pl. **prolepses** /-siːz/) [mass noun] **1** Rhetoric the anticipation and answering of possible objections in rhetorical speech.
2 the representation of a thing as existing before it actually does or did so, as in *he was a dead man when he entered.* ▪ literary a figurative device in narrative, in which a future event is prefigured.
– DERIVATIVES **proleptic** adjective.
– ORIGIN late Middle English (as a term in rhetoric): via late Latin from Greek *prolēpsis*, from *prolambanein* 'anticipate', from *pro* 'before' + *lambanein* 'take'.

proletarian /ˌprəʊlɪˈtɛːrɪən/ ▸ adjective relating to the proletariat: *a proletarian ideology.*
▸ noun a member of the proletariat.
– DERIVATIVES **proletarianism** noun, **proletarianization** (also **proletarianisation**) noun, **proletarianize** (also **proletarianise**) verb.
– ORIGIN mid 17th cent.: from Latin *proletarius* (from *proles* 'offspring'), denoting a person having no wealth in property, who only served the state by producing offspring, + **-AN**.

proletariat (also archaic **proletariate**) ▸ noun [treated as sing. or pl.] working-class people regarded collectively (often used with reference to Marxism): *the growth of the industrial proletariat.* ▪ the lowest class of citizens in ancient Rome.
– ORIGIN mid 19th cent.: from French *prolétariat*, from Latin *proletarius* (see **PROLETARIAN**).

pro-life ▸ adjective opposing abortion and euthanasia: *she is a pro-life activist.*
– DERIVATIVES **pro-lifer** noun.

proliferate /prəˈlɪfəreɪt/ ▸ verb [no obj.] increase rapidly in number; multiply: *the science-fiction magazines which proliferated in the 1920s.* ▪ (of a cell, structure, or organism) reproduce rapidly: *cultured cells often proliferate indefinitely.* ▪ [with obj.] cause (cells, tissue, structures, etc.) to reproduce rapidly.
– DERIVATIVES **proliferative** adjective, **proliferator** noun.
– ORIGIN late 19th cent.: back-formation from **PROLIFERATION**.

proliferation ▸ noun [mass noun] rapid increase in the number or amount of something: *a continuing threat of nuclear proliferation.* ▪ rapid reproduction of a cell, part, or organism: *we attempted to measure cell proliferation.* ▪ [in sing.] a large number of something: *stress levels are high, forcing upon them **a proliferation of** ailments.*
– ORIGIN mid 19th cent.: from French *prolifération*, from *prolifère* 'proliferous'.

proliferous ▸ adjective Biology (of a plant) producing buds or side shoots from a flower or other terminal part. ▪ (of a plant or invertebrate) propagating or multiplying by means of buds or offsets.
– ORIGIN mid 17th cent.: from Latin *proles* 'offspring' + **-FEROUS**.

prolific ▸ adjective **1** (of a plant, animal, or person) producing much fruit or foliage or many offspring: *in captivity tigers are prolific breeders.* ▪ (of an artist,

author, or composer) producing many works: *he was a prolific composer of operas.* ■ (of a sports player) high-scoring: *a prolific goalscorer.*
2 present in large numbers or quantities; plentiful: *mahogany was once prolific in the tropical forests.* ■ characterized by plentiful wildlife or produce: *the prolific rivers around Galway.*
– DERIVATIVES **prolificacy** noun, **prolifically** adverb, **prolificness** noun.
– ORIGIN mid 17th cent.: from medieval Latin *prolificus*, from Latin *proles* 'offspring' (see PROLIFEROUS).

proline /ˈprəʊliːn/ ▸ **noun** [mass noun] Biochemistry an amino acid which is a constituent of most proteins, especially collagen. ● A heterocyclic compound; chem. formula: $C_5H_9NO_2$.
– ORIGIN early 20th cent.: contraction of the chemical name *p(yr)rol(id)ine-2-*carboxylic acid.

prolix /ˈprəʊlɪks, prəˈlɪks/ ▸ **adjective** (of speech or writing) using or containing too many words; tediously lengthy: *he found the narrative too prolix and discursive.*
– DERIVATIVES **prolixity** noun, **prolixly** adverb.
– ORIGIN late Middle English: from Old French *prolixe* or Latin *prolixus* 'poured forth, extended', from *pro-* 'outward' + *liquere* 'be liquid'.

prolocutor /ˈprəʊləˌkjuːtə, ˈprɒl-, prə(ʊ)ˈlɒkjʊtə/ ▸ **noun 1** a chairperson of the lower house of convocation in a province of the Church of England.
2 archaic or formal a spokesman.
– ORIGIN late Middle English (in sense 2): from Latin, from *prolocut-* 'spoken out', from the verb *proloqui*, from *pro* 'before' + *loqui* 'speak'.

Prolog /ˈprəʊlɒg/ ▸ **noun** [mass noun] Computing a high-level computer programming language first devised for artificial intelligence applications.
– ORIGIN 1970s: from the first elements of PROGRAMMING and LOGIC.

prologue (US **prolog**) ▸ **noun 1** a separate introductory section of a literary, dramatic, or musical work. ■ archaic the actor who delivers the prologue in a play.
2 an event or act that leads to another: *the events from 1945 to 1956 provided the* **prologue to** *the post-imperial era.* ■ (in professional cycling) a short preliminary time trial held before a race to establish a leader.
– ORIGIN Middle English: from Old French, via Latin from Greek *prologos*, from *pro-* 'before' + *logos* 'saying'.

prolong ▸ **verb** [with obj.] extend the duration of: *an idea which prolonged the life of the engine by many years.* ■ technical extend in spatial length: *the line of his lips was prolonged in a short red scar.*
– DERIVATIVES **prolongation** noun, **prolonger** noun.
– ORIGIN late Middle English: from Old French *prolonguer*, from late Latin *prolongare*, from *pro-* 'forward, onward' + *longus* 'long'.

prolonged ▸ **adjective** continuing for a long time or longer than usual; lengthy: *the region suffered a prolonged drought.*
– DERIVATIVES **prolongedly** adverb.

prolusion /prəˈl(j)uːʒ(ə)n/ ▸ **noun** archaic or formal a preliminary action or event; a prelude. ■ a preliminary essay or article.
– ORIGIN early 17th cent.: from Latin *prolusio(n-)*, from *prolus-* 'practised beforehand', from the verb *proludere*, from *pro* 'before' + *ludere* 'to play'.

prom ▸ **noun** informal **1** Brit. short for PROMENADE (sense 1 of the noun): *she took a short cut along the prom.*
2 (also **Prom**) Brit. short for PROMENADE CONCERT: *the last night of the Proms.*
3 N. Amer. a formal dance, especially one held by a class in high school or college at the end of a year.

promenade /ˌprɒməˈnɑːd, -ˈneɪd, ˈprɒm-/ ▸ **noun 1** a paved public walk, typically one along the seafront at a resort. ■ a leisurely walk, or sometimes a ride or drive, taken in a public place so as to meet or be seen by others: *an evening promenade.* ■ (in country dancing) a movement in which couples follow one another in a given direction, each couple having both hands joined.
2 N. Amer. archaic term for PROM (sense 3).
▸ **verb** [no obj.] take a leisurely public walk, ride, or drive so as to meet or be seen by others: *they promenaded along the waterfront.* ■ [with obj.] take a promenade through (a place): *people began to promenade the streets.* ■ [with obj.] dated escort (someone) about a place, especially so as to be seen by others: *the governor of Utah promenades the daughter of the Maryland governor.*
– ORIGIN mid 16th cent. (denoting a leisurely walk in public): from French, from *se promener* 'to walk', reflexive of *promener* 'take for a walk'.

promenade concert ▸ **noun** Brit. a concert of classical music at which a part of the audience stands in an area without seating, for which tickets are sold at a reduced price. The most famous series of such concerts is the annual BBC Promenade Concerts (known as **the Proms**), instituted by Sir Henry Wood in 1895.

promenade deck ▸ **noun** an open-air upper deck on a passenger ship on which passengers may walk.

promenader ▸ **noun 1** a person who takes a leisurely walk, ride, or drive in public.
2 Brit. a person attending a promenade concert and choosing to stand in the area without seating.

promethazine /prə(ʊ)ˈmɛθəziːn/ ▸ **noun** [mass noun] Medicine a synthetic antihistamine drug derived from phenothiazine, used chiefly to treat the symptoms of allergies and motion sickness.
– ORIGIN 1950s: from *pro(pyl)* + *(di)meth(ylamine)*, a colourless gas + *(phenothi)azine*.

Prometheus /prəˈmiːθɪəs/ Greek Mythology a demigod, one of the Titans, who was worshipped by craftsmen. When Zeus hid fire away from man Prometheus stole it by trickery and returned it to earth. As punishment Zeus chained him to a rock where an eagle fed each day on his liver, which grew again each night; he was rescued by Hercules.
– DERIVATIVES **Promethean** adjective.

promethium /prəˈmiːθɪəm/ ▸ **noun** [mass noun] the chemical element of atomic number 61, a radioactive metal of the lanthanide series. It was first produced artificially in a nuclear reactor and occurs in nature in traces as a product of uranium fission. (Symbol: **Pm**)
– ORIGIN 1940s: modern Latin, from the name of the Titan PROMETHEUS.

prominence ▸ **noun** [mass noun] **1** the state of being important, famous, or noticeable: *she* **came to prominence** *as an artist in the 1960s* | [in sing.] *the commission gave the case a prominence which it might otherwise have escaped.*
2 the fact or state of projecting from something: *radiographs showed enlargement of the right heart with prominence of the pulmonary outflow tract.* ■ [count noun] a thing that projects from something, such as a projecting feature of the landscape or a protuberance on a part of the body: *the steep, rocky prominence resembled a snow-capped mountain.* ■ [count noun] Astronomy a stream of incandescent gas projecting above the sun's chromosphere.
– DERIVATIVES **prominency** noun.
– ORIGIN late 16th cent. (denoting something that juts out): from obsolete French, from Latin *prominentia* 'jutting out', from the verb *prominere* (see PROMINENT).

prominent ▸ **adjective 1** important; famous: *she was a prominent member of the city council.*
2 projecting from something; protuberant: *a man with big, prominent eyes like a lobster's.*
3 situated so as to catch the attention; noticeable: *the new housing estates are prominent landmarks.*
▸ **noun** (also **prominent moth**) a stout drab-coloured moth with tufts on the forewings which stick up while at rest, the caterpillars of which typically have fleshy growths on the back. ● Family Notodontidae: many species.
– DERIVATIVES **prominently** adverb.
– ORIGIN late Middle English (in the sense 'projecting'): from Latin *prominent-* 'jutting out', from the verb *prominere*. Compare with EMINENT.

prominenti /ˌprɒmɪˈnɛnti/ ▸ **plural noun** distinguished or eminent people: *a restaurant which attracted the prominenti.*
– ORIGIN Italian, from *prominente* 'prominent'.

promiscuity ▸ **noun** [mass noun] the fact or state of being promiscuous; immorality: *some fear this will lead to greater sexual promiscuity amongst teens.*

promiscuous /prəˈmɪskjʊəs/ ▸ **adjective 1** having or characterized by many transient sexual relationships: *she's a wild, promiscuous, good-time girl* | *promiscuous behaviour.*
2 demonstrating or implying an unselective approach; indiscriminate or casual: *the city fathers were promiscuous with their honours.* ■ consisting of a wide range of different things: *Americans are free to choose from a promiscuous array of values.*
– DERIVATIVES **promiscuously** adverb, **promiscuousness** noun.
– ORIGIN early 17th cent.: from Latin *promiscuus* 'indiscriminate', (based on *miscere* 'to mix') + **-ous**. The early sense was 'consisting of elements mixed together', giving rise to 'indiscriminate' and 'undiscriminating', whence the notion of 'casual'.

promise ▸ **noun 1** a declaration or assurance that one will do something or that a particular thing will happen: *what happened to all those firm promises of support?* | [with infinitive] *I did not keep my promise to go home early.* ■ [in sing.] an indication that something is likely to occur: *dawn came with the promise of fine weather.*
2 [mass noun] the quality of potential excellence: *he showed great promise even as a junior officer.*
▸ **verb 1** [reporting verb] assure someone that one will definitely do something or that something will happen: [with infinitive] *he promised to forward my mail* | [with clause] *she made him promise that he wouldn't do it again* | [with direct speech] *'I'll bring it straight back,' she promised* | [with two objs] *he promised her the job.* ■ [with obj.] archaic pledge (someone, especially a woman) to marry someone else; betroth: *I've been promised to him for years.*
2 [with obj.] give good grounds for expecting (a particular occurrence): *forthcoming concerts promise a feast of music* | [with infinitive] *it promised to be a night that all would remember.* ■ announce (something) as being expected to happen: *forecasters were promising a record snowfall in Boston* | [with two objs] *we're promised more winter weather tonight.* ■ (**promise oneself**) contemplate the pleasant expectation of: *he tidied up the sitting room, promising himself an early night.*
– PHRASES **I promise** (or **I promise you**) informal used for emphasis, especially so as to reassure, encourage, or threaten someone: *oh, I'm not joking, I promise you.* **on a promise** informal confidently assured of something, especially of having sexual intercourse: *a shop where Tom and I are on a promise with the girls serving there.* **promise (someone) the earth** (or **moon**) make extravagant promises to someone that are unlikely to be fulfilled: *interactive technology titillates, promises the earth but delivers nothing.* **promises, promises** informal used to indicate that the speaker is sceptical about someone's stated intention to do something.
– DERIVATIVES **promiser** noun.
– ORIGIN late Middle English: from Latin *promissum* 'something promised', neuter past participle of *promittere* 'put forth, promise', from *pro-* 'forward' + *mittere* 'send'.

Promised Land ▸ **noun** (in the Bible) the land of Canaan, that was promised to Abraham and his descendants (Gen. 12:7). ■ (**the promised land**) a place or situation in which someone expects to find great happiness: *Italy is the promised land for any musician.*

promisee ▸ **noun** Law a person to whom a promise is made.

promising ▸ **adjective** showing signs of future success: *a promising film actor* | *a promising start to the season.*
– DERIVATIVES **promisingly** adverb.

promisor ▸ **noun** Law a person who makes a promise.

promissory /ˈprɒmɪs(ə)ri/ ▸ **adjective 1** chiefly Law conveying or implying a promise: *statements that are promissory in nature* | *promissory words.*
2 archaic indicative of something to come; full of promise: *the glow of evening is* **promissory of** *the splendid days to come.*
– ORIGIN late Middle English: from medieval Latin *promissorius*, from *promiss-* 'promised', from the verb *promittere* (see PROMISE).

promissory note ▸ **noun** a signed document containing a written promise to pay a stated sum to a specified person or the bearer at a specified date or on demand.

prommer ▸ **noun** Brit. informal a person attending a promenade concert and choosing to stand in the area without seating; a promenader.

promo /ˈprəʊməʊ/ informal ▸ **noun** (pl. **promos**) a piece of publicity or advertising, especially in the form of a short film or video.
– ORIGIN 1960s: abbreviation of PROMOTION.

promontory /ˈprɒm(ə)nt(ə)ri/ ▸ **noun** (pl. **promontories**) **1** a point of high land that juts out into the sea or a large lake; a headland: *a rocky promontory.*
2 Anatomy a protuberance on an organ or other bodily structure.
– ORIGIN mid 16th cent.: from Latin *promontorium*, variant (influenced by *mons, mont-* 'mountain') of *promunturium*.

promote ▸ **verb** [with obj.] **1** support or actively encourage (a cause, venture, etc.); further the progress of:

P

some regulation is still required to promote competition. ■ give publicity to (a product, organization, or venture) so as to increase sales or public awareness: *they are using famous personalities to promote the library nationally.* ■ attempt to ensure the passing of (a private Act of Parliament).
2 raise (someone) to a higher position or rank: *she was* **promoted to** *General Manager.* ■ transfer (a sports team) to a higher division of a league: *they were promoted from the Third Division last season.*
■ Chess exchange (a pawn) for a more powerful piece of the same colour, typically a queen, when it reaches the opponent's end of the board. ■ Bridge enable (a relatively low card) to win a trick by playing off the higher ones first.
3 Chemistry (of an additive) act as a promoter of (a catalyst).
– DERIVATIVES **promotability** noun, **promotable** adjective, **promotive** adjective.
– ORIGIN late Middle English: from Latin *promot-* 'moved forward', from the verb *promovere*, from *pro-* 'forward, onward' + *movere* 'to move'.

promoter ▶ noun **1** a person or company that finances or organizes a sporting event, concert, or theatrical production: *a boxing promoter.*
2 a supporter of a cause or aim: *Mitterrand was a fierce promoter of European integration.*
3 (also **promotor**) Chemistry an additive that increases the activity of a catalyst. ■ Biology a region of a DNA molecule which forms the site at which transcription of a gene starts.
– ORIGIN late Middle English: from Anglo-Norman French *promotour*, from medieval Latin *promotor* (see **PROMOTE**).

promotion ▶ noun [mass noun] **1** activity that supports or encourages a cause, venture, or aim: *the promotion of cultural and racial diversity.*
2 the publicizing of a product, organization, or venture so as to increase sales or public awareness: [as modifier] *a sales promotion company.* ■ [count noun] a publicity campaign: *the paper is reaping the rewards of a series of promotions.* ■ (often as modifier **promotions**) the activity of organizing publicity campaigns: *she's the promotions manager for EMI.* ■ [count noun] a sporting event, especially a series of boxing matches, staged for profit: *a boxing promotion.*
3 the action of promoting someone or something to a higher position or rank or the fact of being so promoted: *majors designated for* **promotion to** *lieutenant colonel | United won promotion last season |* [count noun] *a promotion to Sales Director.*
4 Chemistry the action of promoting a catalyst.
– ORIGIN late Middle English (in sense 3): via Old French from Latin *promotio(n-)*, from *promovere* 'move forward' (see **PROMOTE**).

promotional ▶ adjective relating to the publicizing of a product, organization, or venture so as to increase sales or public awareness: *she was on a promotional tour for her books.*

prompt ▶ verb [with obj.] **1** (of an event or fact) cause or bring about (an action or feeling): *the violence prompted a wave of refugees to flee the country.* ■ (**prompt someone to/to do something**) cause someone to take a course of action: *curiosity prompted him to look inside.*
2 encourage (a hesitating speaker) to say something: [with direct speech] *'And the picture?' he prompted.* ■ supply a forgotten word or line to (an actor) during the performance of a play. ■ Computing (of a computer) request input from (a user).
▶ noun **1** an act of encouraging a hesitating speaker: *with barely a prompt, Barbara talked on.* ■ a word or phrase spoken as a reminder to an actor of a forgotten word or line. ■ another term for **PROMPTER**. ■ Computing a word or symbol on a screen to show that the system is waiting for input.
2 the time limit for the payment of an account, stated on a prompt note.
▶ adjective done without delay; immediate: *she would have died but for the prompt action of two ambulancemen.* ■ (of a person) acting without delay: *the fans were prompt in complying with police requests.* ■ (of goods) for immediate delivery and payment.
▶ adverb Brit. exactly (with reference to a specified time): *I set off at three-thirty prompt.*
– DERIVATIVES **promptitude** noun, **promptness** noun.
– ORIGIN Middle English (as a verb): based on Old French *prompt* or Latin *promptus* 'brought to light', also 'prepared, ready', past participle of *promere* 'to produce', from *pro-* 'out, forth' + *emere* 'take'.

prompt book ▶ noun an annotated copy of a play for the use of a prompter during a performance.

prompt box ▶ noun an area in a theatre in which a prompter sits, located in front of the footlights beneath the stage.

prompter ▶ noun a person seated out of sight of the audience who supplies a forgotten word or line to an actor during the performance of a play.

prompting ▶ noun [mass noun] the action of saying something to persuade, encourage, or remind someone to do or say something: *after some prompting, the defendant gave the police his name.*

promptly ▶ adverb **1** with little or no delay; immediately: *he paid the fine promptly.* ■ used to express surprise, and slight disapproval, when someone does something shortly after something else: *every time she managed to pay her credit card off, she promptly went shopping again.*
2 at exactly a specified time; punctually: *Jamie arrived promptly at 8:30.*

prompt note ▶ noun a note sent to a customer as a reminder of payment due.

prompt side ▶ noun the side of the stage where the prompter sits, usually to the actor's left in the UK and to the actor's right in the US.

promulgate /ˈprɒm(ə)lgeɪt/ ▶ verb [with obj.] promote or make widely known (an idea or cause): *these objectives have to be promulgated within the organization.* ■ put (a law or decree) into effect by official proclamation: *in January 1852 the new Constitution was promulgated.*
– DERIVATIVES **promulgation** noun, **promulgator** noun.
– ORIGIN mid 16th cent. (earlier (late 15th cent.) as *promulgation*): from Latin *promulgat-* 'exposed to public view', from the verb *promulgare*, from *pro-* 'out, publicly' + *mulgere* 'cause to come forth' (literally 'to milk').

promulge /prəˈmʌldʒ/ ▶ verb archaic variant of **PROMULGATE**.
– ORIGIN late 15th cent.: from Latin *promulgare*.

pronaos /prəʊˈneɪɒs/ ▶ noun (pl. **pronaoi** /-ˈneɪɔɪ/) a vestibule at the front of a classical temple, enclosed by a portico and projecting side walls.
– ORIGIN via Latin from Greek *pronaos* 'hall of a temple', from *pro* 'before' + *naos* 'temple'.

pronate /ˈprəʊneɪt/ ▶ verb [with obj.] Anatomy turn or hold (a hand, foot, or limb) so that the palm or sole is facing downwards or inwards: (as adj. **pronated**) *a pronated foot.* Compare with **SUPINATE**. ■ [no obj.] walk or run with most of the weight on the inside edge of the feet.
– DERIVATIVES **pronation** noun.
– ORIGIN mid 19th cent.: back-formation from *pronation*, based on Latin *pronus* 'leaning forward'.

pronator ▶ noun Anatomy **1** a muscle whose contraction produces or assists in the pronation of a limb or part of a limb.
2 a person who pronates when walking or running.

prone ▶ adjective **1** (**prone to/to do something**) likely or liable to suffer from, do, or experience something unpleasant or regrettable: *farmed fish are prone to disease |* [in combination] *he was written off by many as too injury-prone.*
2 lying flat, especially face downwards: *I was lying prone on a foam mattress | a prone position.* ■ technical denoting the position of the forearm with the palm of the hand facing downwards. ■ archaic with a downward slope or direction.
– ORIGIN late Middle English: from Latin *pronus* 'leaning forward', from *pro* 'forwards'.

proneness ▶ noun [mass noun] liability to suffer from or experience something disagreeable; susceptibility: *his proneness to injury will seriously mar a promising career.*

prong ▶ noun **1** each of two or more projecting pointed parts at the end of a fork. ■ a projecting part on various other devices. ■ vulgar slang a man's penis.
2 each of the separate parts of an attack or operation, typically approaching a place or subject from different positions: *the three main prongs of the government's programme.*
▶ verb [with obj.] pierce or stab with a fork: *he passed his fork to the right hand to prong the meat.*
– DERIVATIVES **pronged** adjective [in combination] *a three-pronged attack.*
– ORIGIN late 15th cent. (denoting a forked implement): perhaps related to Middle Low German *prange* 'pinching instrument'. The verb dates from the mid 19th cent.

pronghorn (also **pronghorn antelope**) ▶ noun a deer-like North American mammal with a stocky body, long slim legs, and black horns that are shed and regrown annually. ● *Antilocapra americana*, the only member of the family Antilocapridae.

pronk ▶ verb [no obj.] (of a springbok or other antelope) leap in the air with an arched back and stiff legs, typically as a form of display or when threatened.
– ORIGIN late 19th cent.: from Afrikaans, literally 'show off', from Dutch *pronken* 'to strut'.

pronominal /prəʊˈnɒmɪn(ə)l/ ▶ adjective relating to or serving as a pronoun: *a pronominal form.*
– DERIVATIVES **pronominalization** (also **pronominalisation**) noun, **pronominally** adverb.
– ORIGIN mid 17th cent.: from late Latin *pronominalis* 'belonging to a pronoun', from Latin *pronomen* (see **PRONOUN**).

pronoun ▶ noun a word that can function as a noun phrase used by itself and that refers either to the participants in the discourse (e.g. *I*, *you*) or to someone or something mentioned elsewhere in the discourse (e.g. *she*, *it*, *this*).
– ORIGIN late Middle English: from **PRO-**[1] 'on behalf of', + **NOUN**, suggested by French *pronom*, Latin *pronomen* (from *pro-* 'for, in place of' + *nomen* 'name').

pronounce ▶ verb [with obj.] **1** make the sound of (a word or part of a word) in the correct or a particular way: *Gerry pronounced the hero's name 'Cahoolin'.*
2 declare or announce in a formal or solemn way: *allow history to pronounce the verdict |* [with complement] *she was pronounced dead at the scene |* [with clause] *Asquith pronounced that this was the right course.* ■ [no obj.] (**pronounce on**) pass judgement or make a decision on: *the Secretary of State will shortly pronounce on alternative measures.*
– DERIVATIVES **pronounceability** noun, **pronounceable** adjective, **pronouncer** noun.
– ORIGIN late Middle English: from Old French *pronuncier*, from Latin *pronuntiare*, from *pro-* 'out, forth' + *nuntiare* 'announce' (from *nuntius* 'messenger').

pronounced ▶ adjective very noticeable or marked; conspicuous: *he had a pronounced squint.*
– DERIVATIVES **pronouncedly** adverb.

pronouncement ▶ noun a formal or authoritative announcement or declaration: *distrust of the pronouncements of politicians was endemic.*

pronto ▶ adverb informal promptly; quickly: *put it in the refrigerator, pronto.*
– ORIGIN early 20th cent.: from Spanish, from Latin *promptus* (see **PROMPT**).

Prontosil /ˈprɒntəsɪl/ ▶ noun [mass noun] Medicine, historical the first sulphonamide antibiotic, a reddish-brown crystalline pigment formerly used to treat a range of infections.
– ORIGIN 1930s: from German, an invented proprietary name.

pronucleus /prəʊˈnjuːklɪəs/ ▶ noun (pl. **pronuclei**) Biology either of a pair of gametic nuclei, in the stage following meiosis but before their fusion leads to the formation of the nucleus of the zygote.
– DERIVATIVES **pronuclear** adjective.

pronunciamento /prəˌnʌnsɪəˈmɛntəʊ/ ▶ noun (pl. **pronunciamentos**) (especially in Spain and Spanish-speaking countries) a political manifesto or proclamation.
– ORIGIN Spanish *pronunciamiento*, from *pronunciar* 'pronounce'.

pronunciation /prənʌnsɪˈeɪʃ(ə)n/ ▶ noun [mass noun] the way in which a word is pronounced: *spelling does not determine pronunciation |* [count noun] *similar pronunciations are heard in Ulster.*
– ORIGIN late Middle English: from Latin *pronuntiatio(n-)*, from the verb *pronuntiare* (see **PRONOUNCE**).

> **USAGE** The word **pronunciation** is often pronounced, by analogy with **pronounce**, as if the second syllable rhymed with **bounce**. This is not correct in standard English: the standard pronunciation has the second syllable rhyming with **dunce**. The correct spelling is **pronunciation**, never **pronounciation**.

pro-nuncio /prəʊˈnʌnsɪəʊ, -ʃɪəʊ/ ▶ noun (pl. **pro-nuncios**) a papal ambassador to a country that does not accord the Pope's ambassador automatic precedence over other ambassadors.
– ORIGIN 1960s: from Italian *pro-nunzio*, from *pro-* 'before' + *nunzio* 'nuncio'.

proof ▶ noun **1** [mass noun] evidence or argument establishing a fact or the truth of a statement: *you will be asked to give proof of your identity |* [count noun] *this is not a proof for the existence of God.* ■ Law the

spoken or written evidence in a trial. ■ the action of establishing the truth of a statement: *spatial dimensions whose very existence is beyond all hope of proof.* ■ [count noun] a series of stages in the resolution of a mathematical or philosophical problem.
2 Printing a trial impression of a page, taken from type or film and used for making corrections before final printing. ■ a trial photographic print made for initial selection. ■ each of a number of impressions from an engraved plate, especially (in commercial printing) of a limited number before the ordinary issue is printed and before an inscription or signature is added. ■ a specially struck specimen coin with a polished or frosted finish.
3 [mass noun] the strength of distilled alcoholic spirits, relative to proof spirit taken as a standard of 100: [in combination] *powerful 132-proof rum.*
4 a test or trial of something.
5 Scots Law a trial or a civil case before a judge without a jury.
▸ **adjective 1** able to withstand something damaging; resistant: *the marine battle armour was* ***proof against*** *most weapons* | [in combination] *the system comes with idiot-proof instructions.*
2 denoting a trial impression of a page or printed work: *a proof copy is sent up for checking.*
▸ **verb** [with obj.] **1** make (fabric) waterproof: (as adj. **proofed**) *the flysheet is made from proofed nylon.*
2 make a proof of (a printed work, engraving, etc.): (as noun **proofing**) *proofing could be done on a low-cost printer.* ■ proofread (a text): *William proofed much of her work.*
3 N. Amer. activate (yeast) by the addition of liquid. ■ knead (dough) until light and smooth. ■ [no obj.] (of dough) prove: *shape into a baguette and let proof for a few minutes.*
– PHRASES **the proof of the pudding is in the eating** proverb the real value of something can be judged only from practical experience or results and not from appearance or theory.
– ORIGIN Middle English *preve*, from Old French *proeve*, from late Latin *proba*, from Latin *probare* 'to test, prove'. The change of vowel in late Middle English was due to the influence of **PROVE**. Current senses of the verb date from the late 19th cent.

proof positive ▸ **noun** [mass noun] evidence taken to be final or absolute proof of the existence of something: *he still needs proof positive of her love.*

proofread ▸ **verb** (past and past participle **proofread**) [with obj.] read (printer's proofs or other written or printed material) and mark any errors.
– DERIVATIVES **proofreader** noun.

proof sheet ▸ **noun** Printing a page of proofed text; a proof.

proof spirit ▸ **noun** [mass noun] a mixture of alcohol and water containing (in the UK) 57.1 per cent alcohol by volume or (in the US) 50 per cent alcohol by volume, used as a standard of strength of distilled alcoholic spirits.

proof text ▸ **noun** a passage of the Bible to which appeal is made in support of an argument or position in theology.

prop[1] ▸ **noun 1** a pole or beam used as a temporary support or to keep something in position: *he looked around for a prop to pin the door open.* ■ a person or thing that is a major source of support or assistance: *he found himself becoming the emotional prop of the marriage.* ■ Grammar a word used to fill a syntactic role without any specific meaning of its own, for example *it* in *it is raining.*
2 (also **prop forward**) Rugby a forward at either end of the front row of a scrum.
3 chiefly Austral. a sudden stop made by a horse moving at speed.
▸ **verb** (**props, propping, propped**) **1** [with obj. and adverbial of place] support or keep in position: *she propped her chin in the palm of her right hand.* ■ lean (something) against something else: *a jug of milk with a note propped against it* | *she propped the picture up on the mantlepiece.* ■ use an object to keep (something) in position: *he found that the door was* ***propped open.***
2 [no obj.] chiefly Austral. (of a horse) come to a dead stop with the forelegs rigid.
– PHRASES **prop up the bar** informal spend a considerable time drinking in a pub.
– PHRASAL VERBS **prop someone/thing up** support or assist someone or something that would otherwise fail or decline: *the government spent £3 billion in an attempt to prop up the pound.*
– ORIGIN late Middle English: probably from Middle Dutch *proppe* 'support (for vines)'.

prop[2] ▸ **noun** (usu. **props**) a portable object other than furniture or costumes used on the set of a play or film. ■ (**props**) [treated as sing.] informal, dated a property man or mistress.
– ORIGIN mid 19th cent.: abbreviation of **PROPERTY**.

prop[3] ▸ **noun** informal an aircraft propeller.
– ORIGIN early 20th cent.: abbreviation.

prop. ▸ **abbreviation** ■ proposition. ■ proprietor.

propaedeutic /ˌprəʊpiːˈdjuːtɪk/ formal ▸ **adjective** (of an area of study) serving as a preliminary instruction or as an introduction to further study.
▸ **noun** an introduction to a subject or area of study.
– DERIVATIVES **propaedeutical** adjective.
– ORIGIN late 18th cent.: from **PRO-[2]** 'before' + Greek *paideutikos* 'of or for teaching', suggested by Greek *propaideuein* 'teach beforehand'.

propaganda ▸ **noun 1** [mass noun] information, especially of a biased or misleading nature, used to promote a political cause or point of view: *he was charged with distributing enemy propaganda.* ■ the dissemination of such information as a political strategy: *the party's leaders believed that a long period of education and propaganda would be necessary.*
2 (**Propaganda**) a committee of cardinals of the Roman Catholic Church responsible for foreign missions, founded in 1622 by Pope Gregory XV.
– ORIGIN Italian, from modern Latin *congregatio de propaganda fide* 'congregation for propagation of the faith' (see sense 2). Sense 1 dates from the early 20th cent.

propagandist chiefly derogatory ▸ **noun** a person who disseminates propaganda: *a highly persuasive political propagandist.*
▸ **adjective** consisting of or spreading propaganda: *propagandist films.*
– DERIVATIVES **propagandism** noun, **propagandistic** adjective, **propagandistically** adverb.

propagandize (also **propagandise**) ▸ **verb** [no obj.] chiefly derogatory promote a particular cause or view by using propaganda: *abolitionist leaders had not specifically* ***propagandized for*** *emancipation.* ■ [with obj.] attempt to influence (someone) by using propaganda.

propagate ▸ **verb** [with obj.] **1** breed specimens of (a plant or animal) by natural processes from the parent stock: *try propagating your own houseplants from cuttings.* ■ [no obj.] (of a plant or animal) reproduce in such a way: *the plant propagates freely from stem cuttings.*
2 spread and promote (an idea, theory, etc.) widely: *the French propagated the idea that the English were drunkards.*
3 [with adverbial of direction] (with reference to motion, light, sound, etc.) transmit or be transmitted in a particular direction or through a medium: [with obj.] *electromagnetic effects can be propagated at a finite velocity only through material substances.*
– DERIVATIVES **propagation** noun, **propagative** adjective.
– ORIGIN late Middle English: from Latin *propagat-* 'multiplied from layers or shoots', from the verb *propagare*; related to *propago* 'young shoot' (from a base meaning 'fix').

propagator ▸ **noun 1** a covered, typically heated container filled with earth or compost, used for germinating or raising seedlings.
2 a person who spreads and promotes an idea, theory, etc.

propagule /ˈprɒpəgjuːl/ ▸ **noun** Botany a vegetative structure that can become detached from a plant and give rise to a new plant, e.g. a bud, sucker, or spore.
– ORIGIN mid 19th cent.: from modern Latin *propagulum* 'small shoot', diminutive of *propago* 'shoot, runner'.

propane /ˈprəʊpeɪn/ ▸ **noun** [mass noun] Chemistry a flammable hydrocarbon gas of the alkane series, present in natural gas and used as bottled fuel. ● Chem. formula: C_3H_8.
– ORIGIN mid 19th cent.: from **PROPIONIC ACID** + **-ANE[2]**.

propanoic acid /ˌprəʊpəˈnəʊɪk/ ▸ **noun** Chemistry another term for **PROPIONIC ACID**.

propanol /ˈprəʊpənɒl/ ▸ **noun** [mass noun] Chemistry each of two isomeric liquid alcohols used as solvents; propyl alcohol. ● Chem. formula: $CH_3CH_2CH_2OH$ (**1-propanol, propan-1-ol**) and $CH_3CH(OH)CH_3$ (**2-propanol, propan-2-ol**).
– ORIGIN late 19th cent.: from **PROPANE** + **-OL**.

propanone /ˈprəʊpənəʊn/ ▸ **noun** Chemistry another term for **ACETONE**.

propel ▸ **verb** (**propels, propelling, propelled**) [with obj.] drive or push something forwards: *the boat is propelled by using a very long paddle* | (as adj., in combination **-propelled**) *a rocket-propelled grenade launcher.* ■ [with obj. and adverbial of direction] spur or drive into a particular situation: *fear propelled her out of her stillness.*
– ORIGIN late Middle English (in the sense 'expel, drive out'): from Latin *propellere*, from *pro-* 'forward' + *pellere* 'to drive'.

propellant ▸ **noun** a substance that propels something, in particular: ■ an inert fluid, liquefied under pressure, in which the active contents of an aerosol are dispersed. ■ an explosive that fires bullets from a firearm. ■ a substance used as a reagent in a rocket engine to provide thrust.
▸ **adjective** capable of propelling something: *propellant gases.*
– ORIGIN mid 17th cent.: originally from Latin *propellent-* 'driving ahead (of oneself)', from the verb *propellere*, later from **PROPEL**.

propeller (also **propellor**) ▸ **noun** a mechanical device for propelling a boat or aircraft, consisting of a revolving shaft with two or more broad, angled blades attached to it.

propeller-head ▸ **noun** informal a person who has an obsessive interest in computers or technology.
– ORIGIN 1980s: probably with reference to a beanie hat with a propeller on top, popularized by science-fiction enthusiasts.

propeller shaft ▸ **noun** a shaft transmitting power from an engine to a propeller or to the wheels of a motor vehicle.

propeller turbine ▸ **noun** another term for **TURBOPROP**.

propelling pencil ▸ **noun** Brit. a pencil with a plastic or metal case and a thin replaceable lead that may be extended as the point is worn away by twisting the outer casing.

propene /ˈprəʊpiːn/ ▸ **noun** Chemistry another term for **PROPYLENE**.
– ORIGIN mid 19th cent.: blend of **PROPANE** and **ALKENE**.

propenoic acid /ˌprəʊpəˈnəʊɪk/ ▸ **noun** systematic chemical name for **ACRYLIC ACID**.

propensity ▸ **noun** (pl. **propensities**) an inclination or natural tendency to behave in a particular way: *his* ***propensity for*** *violence* | [with infinitive] *their innate propensity to attack one another.*
– ORIGIN late 16th cent.: from archaic *propense* (from Latin *propensus* 'inclined', past participle of *propendere*, from *pro-* 'forward, down' + *pendere* 'hang') + **-ITY**.

proper ▸ **adjective 1** [attrib.] chiefly Brit. denoting something that is truly what it is said or regarded to be; genuine: *she's never had a proper job* | *a proper meal.* ■ [postpositive] strictly so called; in its true form: *after this event, three countries will progress to the World Cup proper.* ■ informal used as an intensifier, especially in derogatory contexts: *a* ***proper little*** *do-gooder, aren't I?*
2 [attrib.] of the required or correct type or form; suitable or appropriate: *an artist needs the proper tools* | *they had not followed the proper procedures.* ■ according to or respecting social standards or conventions; respectable, especially excessively so: *her parents' view of what was* ***proper for*** *a well-bred girl* | *a very prim and proper Swiss lady.*
3 (**proper to**) belonging or relating exclusively or distinctively to; particular to: *the two elephant types proper to Africa and to southern Asia.* ■ (of a psalm, lesson, prayer, etc.) appointed for a particular day, occasion, or season. ■ archaic belonging to oneself or itself; own: *to judge with my proper eyes.*
4 [usu. postpositive] Heraldry in the natural colours.
5 archaic or dialect (of a person) good-looking: *he is a proper youth!*
6 Mathematics denoting a subset or subgroup that does not constitute the entire set or group, especially one that has more than one element.
▸ **adverb** Brit. informal or dialect satisfactorily or correctly: *my eyes were all blurry and I couldn't see proper.* ■ thoroughly: *he blotted his copybook* ***good and proper.***
▸ **noun** the part of a church service that varies with the season or feast.
– DERIVATIVES **properness** noun.
– ORIGIN Middle English: from Old French *propre*, from Latin *proprius* 'one's own, special'.

properdin /prəʊˈpəːdɪn/ ▸ **noun** [mass noun] Biochemistry a protein present in the blood, involved in the body's response to certain kinds of infection.
– ORIGIN 1950s: from **PRO-[2]** 'before' + Latin *perdere* 'destroy' + **-IN[1]**.

P

proper fraction ▸ noun a fraction that is less than one, with the numerator less than the denominator.

properly ▸ adverb **1** correctly or satisfactorily: *ensuring the work is carried out properly | a properly drafted agreement.* ▪ appropriately for the circumstances; suitably or respectably: *I'm trying to get my mother to behave properly.*
2 [sentence adverb] in the strict sense; exactly: *algebra is, properly speaking, the analysis of equations.*
3 [usu. as submodifier] informal, chiefly Brit. thoroughly; completely: *on the first day she felt properly well, Millie sat out on the front steps.*

proper motion ▸ noun [mass noun] Astronomy the part of the apparent motion of a fixed star that is due to its actual movement in space relative to the sun.

proper noun (also **proper name**) ▸ noun a name used for an individual person, place, or organization, spelled with an initial capital letter, e.g. *Jane, London,* and *Oxfam.* Often contrasted with **COMMON NOUN**.

propertied ▸ adjective (of a person or group) owning property and land, especially in large amounts: *a propertied country gentleman.*

Propertius /prəˈpəːʃəs/, Sextus (*c.*50–*c.*16 BC), Roman poet. His four books of elegies are largely concerned with his love affair with a woman whom he called Cynthia.

property ▸ noun (pl. **properties**) **1** [mass noun] a thing or things belonging to someone; possessions collectively: *she wanted Oliver and his property out of her flat | the stolen property was not recovered.* ▪ a building or buildings and the land belonging to it or them: *he's expanding now, buying property* | [count noun] *the renovation of council properties.* ▪ (**properties**) shares or investments in property. ▪ Law the right to the possession, use, or disposal of something; ownership: *rights of property.* ▪ old-fashioned term for **PROP**[2].
2 an attribute, quality, or characteristic of something: *the property of heat to expand metal at uniform rates.*
– ORIGIN Middle English: from an Anglo-Norman French variant of Old French *propriete,* from Latin *proprietas,* from *proprius* 'one's own, particular' (see **PROPER**).

property mistress (or **property man**) ▸ noun dated a person in charge of theatrical props.

property qualification ▸ noun chiefly historical a qualification for office or for the exercise of a right, especially the right to vote, based on the ownership of property.

prop forward ▸ noun see **PROP**[1] (sense 2 of the noun).

prophage /ˈprəʊfeɪdʒ/ ▸ noun Microbiology the genetic material of a bacteriophage, incorporated into the genome of a bacterium and able to produce phages if specifically activated.
– ORIGIN 1950s: from **PRO-**[2] 'before' + **PHAGE**.

prophase ▸ noun [mass noun] Biology the first stage of cell division, before metaphase, during which the chromosomes become visible as paired chromatids and the nuclear envelope disappears. The first prophase of meiosis includes the reduction division.
– ORIGIN late 19th cent.: from **PRO-**[2] 'before' + **PHASE**.

prophecy /ˈprɒfɪsi/ ▸ noun (pl. **prophecies**) a prediction of what will happen in the future: *a bleak prophecy of war and ruin.* ▪ [mass noun] the faculty or practice of prophesying: *the gift of prophecy.*
– ORIGIN Middle English: from Old French *profecie,* via late Latin from Greek *prophēteia,* from *prophētēs* (see **PROPHET**).

prophesy /ˈprɒfɪsʌɪ/ ▸ verb (**prophesies, prophesying, prophesied**) [with obj.] say that (a specified thing) will happen in the future: *Jacques was prophesying a bumper harvest* | [with clause] *the papers prophesied that he would resign after the weekend.*
– DERIVATIVES **prophesier** noun.
– ORIGIN Middle English: from Old French *profecier,* from *profecie* (see **PROPHECY**).

> **USAGE** The words **prophesy** and **prophecy** are often confused. **Prophesy** is the spelling that should be used for the verb (*he was prophesying a bumper harvest*), whereas **prophecy** is the correct spelling for the noun (*a bleak prophecy of war and ruin*). The differentiation between the spellings of the noun and verb was not established until after 1700 and has no etymological basis, *prophesy* being at first a spelling variant of both the noun and the verb.

prophet ▸ noun **1** a person regarded as an inspired teacher or proclaimer of the will of God: *the Old Testament prophet, Jeremiah.* ▪ (**the Prophet**) (among Muslims) Muhammad. ▪ a person who advocates or speaks in a visionary way about a new cause or theory: *he is repeatedly hailed as a prophet of modernism.* ▪ a person who predicts what will happen in the future: *the prime minister ignored **the prophets of doom**.*
2 (**the Prophets**) (in Christian use) the books of Isaiah, Jeremiah, Ezekiel, Daniel, and the twelve minor prophets. ▪ (in Jewish use) one of the three canonical divisions of the Hebrew Bible, distinguished from the Law and the Hagiographa, and comprising the books of Joshua, Judges, Samuel, Kings, Jeremiah, Ezekiel, Isaiah, and the twelve minor prophets.
– PHRASES **a prophet is not without honour save in his own country** proverb a person's gifts and talents are rarely appreciated by those close to them. [with biblical allusion to Matt. 13:57.]
– DERIVATIVES **prophethood** noun, **prophetism** noun.
– ORIGIN Middle English: from Old French *prophete,* via Latin from Greek *prophētēs* 'spokesman', from *pro* 'before' + *phētēs* 'speaker' (from *phēnai* 'speak').

prophetess ▸ noun a female prophet.

prophetic /prəˈfɛtɪk/ ▸ adjective **1** accurately predicting what will happen in the future: *his warnings proved prophetic.*
2 relating to or characteristic of a prophet or prophecy: *the prophetic books of the Old Testament.*
– DERIVATIVES **prophetical** adjective, **prophetically** adverb.
– ORIGIN late 15th cent.: from French *prophétique* or late Latin *propheticus,* from Greek *prophētikos* 'predicting' (see **PROPHET**).

prophylactic /ˌprɒfɪˈlaktɪk/ ▸ adjective intended to prevent disease: *prophylactic measures.*
▸ noun **1** a medicine or course of action used to prevent disease: *I took malaria prophylactics.*
2 N. Amer. a condom.
– DERIVATIVES **prophylactically** adverb.
– ORIGIN late 16th cent.: from French *prophylactique,* from Greek *prophulaktikos,* from *pro* 'before' + *phulassein* 'to guard'.

prophylaxis /ˌprɒfɪˈlaksɪs/ ▸ noun [mass noun] treatment given or action taken to prevent disease.
– ORIGIN mid 19th cent.: modern Latin, from **PRO-**[2] 'before' + Greek *phulaxis* 'act of guarding'.

propinquity /prəˈpɪŋkwɪti/ ▸ noun [mass noun] **1** formal the state of being close to someone or something; proximity: *he kept his distance as though afraid propinquity might lead him into temptation.*
2 technical close kinship.
– ORIGIN late Middle English: from Old French *propinquité,* from Latin *propinquitas,* from *propinquus* 'near', from *prope* 'near to'.

propionate /ˈprəʊpɪəneɪt/ ▸ noun Chemistry a salt or ester of propionic acid.

propionibacterium /ˌprəʊpɪˌɒnɪbakˈtɪərɪəm/ ▸ noun (pl. **propionibacteria** /-rɪə/) a bacterium which metabolizes carbohydrate, some kinds being involved in the fermentation of dairy products and the aetiology of acne. ● Genus *Propionibacterium*; Gram-positive rods.
– ORIGIN modern Latin, from *propionic* (see **PROPIONIC ACID**) + **BACTERIUM**.

propionic acid /ˌprəʊpɪˈɒnɪk/ ▸ noun [mass noun] Chemistry a colourless pungent liquid organic acid produced in some forms of fermentation and used for inhibiting the growth of mould in bread. ● Alternative name: **propanoic acid**; chem. formula: C_2H_5COOH.
– ORIGIN mid 19th cent.: *propionic* from French *propionique,* from Greek *pro* 'before' + *piōn* 'fat', it being the first member of the fatty acid series to form fats.

propitiate /prəˈpɪʃɪeɪt/ ▸ verb [with obj.] win or regain the favour of (a god, spirit, or person) by doing something that pleases them: *the pagans thought it was important to propitiate the gods with sacrifices.*
– DERIVATIVES **propitiation** noun, **propitiator** noun, **propitiatory** adjective.
– ORIGIN late Middle English (as *propitiation*): from Latin *propitiat-* 'made favourable', from the verb *propitiare,* from *propitius* 'favourable, gracious' (see **PROPITIOUS**).

propitious /prəˈpɪʃəs/ ▸ adjective giving or indicating a good chance of success; favourable: *the timing for such a meeting seemed propitious.* ▪ archaic favourably disposed towards someone.
– DERIVATIVES **propitiously** adverb, **propitiousness** noun.
– ORIGIN late Middle English: from Old French *propicieus* or Latin *propitius* 'favourable, gracious'.

prop jet ▸ noun a turboprop aircraft or engine.

propolis /ˈprɒp(ə)lɪs/ ▸ noun [mass noun] a red or brown resinous substance collected by honeybees from tree buds, used by them to fill crevices and to fix and varnish honeycombs.
– ORIGIN early 17th cent.: via Latin from Greek *propolis* 'suburb', also 'bee glue', from *pro* 'before' + *polis* 'city'.

proponent /prəˈpəʊnənt/ ▸ noun a person who advocates a theory, proposal, or course of action: *a strong proponent of the free market and liberal trade policies.*
– ORIGIN late 16th cent.: from Latin *proponent-* 'putting forth', from the verb *proponere* (see **PROPOUND**).

Propontis /prəˈpɒntɪs/ ancient name for the Sea of Marmara (see **MARMARA, SEA OF**).

proportion ▸ noun a part, share, or number considered in comparative relation to a whole: *the proportion of greenhouse gases in the atmosphere is rising.* ▪ the relationship of one thing to another in terms of quantity, size, or number; ratio: *the proportion of examination to coursework | the bleach can be diluted with water in the proportion one part bleach to ten parts water.* ▪ (**proportions**) the comparative measurements or size of different parts of a whole: *the view of what constitutes perfect bodily proportions changes from one generation to the next.* ▪ (**proportions**) dimensions; size: *the room, despite its ample proportions, seemed too small for him.* ▪ [mass noun] the correct, attractive, or ideal relationship between one thing and another or between the parts of a whole: *perceptions of colour, form, harmony, and proportion.*
▸ verb [with obj.] formal adjust or regulate (something) so that it has a particular or suitable relationship to something else: *a life after death in which happiness can be **proportioned to** virtue.*
– PHRASES **in proportion 1** according to a particular relationship in size, amount, or degree: *the pension was docked **in proportion to** earnings.* ▪ in comparison with; in relation to: *the cuckoo's eggs are unusually small **in proportion to** its size.* **2** in the correct or appropriate relation to the size, shape, or position of other things: *her figure was completely in proportion.* ▪ correctly or realistically regarded in terms of relative importance or seriousness: *the problem of hooliganism has to be **kept in proportion**.* **out of proportion** in the wrong relation to the size, shape, or position of other things: *the sculpture seemed out **of proportion to** its surroundings.* ▪ wrongly or unrealistically regarded in terms of relative importance or seriousness. **sense of proportion** the ability to judge the relative importance or seriousness of things.
– ORIGIN late Middle English: from Old French, from Latin *proportio(n-),* from *pro portione* 'in respect of (its or a person's) share'.

proportionable ▸ adjective archaic term for **PROPORTIONAL**.
– DERIVATIVES **proportionably** adverb.

proportional ▸ adjective corresponding in size or amount to something else: *the punishment should be **proportional to** the crime.* ▪ Mathematics (of a variable quantity) having a constant ratio to another quantity.
– DERIVATIVES **proportionality** noun, **proportionally** adverb.
– ORIGIN late Middle English: from late Latin *proportionalis,* from *proportio(n-)* (see **PROPORTION**).

proportional counter ▸ noun Physics an ionization chamber in which the operating voltage is large enough to produce amplification but not so large that the output pulse ceases to be proportional to the initial ionization.

proportional representation (abbrev.: **PR**) ▸ noun [mass noun] an electoral system in which parties gain seats in proportion to the number of votes cast for them.

proportionate ▸ adjective another term for **PROPORTIONAL**.
– DERIVATIVES **proportionately** adverb.

proportioned ▸ adjective [with submodifier] having dimensions or a comparative relationship of parts of a specified type: *she was tall and perfectly proportioned.*

proposal ▸ noun **1** a plan or suggestion, especially a formal or written one, put forward for consideration by others: *a set of **proposals for** a major new high-speed rail link.* ▪ [mass noun] the action of proposing a

plan or suggestion: *the proposal of a flexible school-leaving age*.
2 an offer of marriage.

propose ▶ **verb 1** [with obj.] put forward (a plan or suggestion) for consideration by others: *he proposed a new nine-point peace plan* | [with clause] *I proposed that the government should retain a 51 per cent stake in the company*. ■ nominate (someone) for an elected office or as a member of a society: *Roy Thomson was proposed as chairman*. ■ put forward (a motion) to a legislature or committee: *the government put its slim majority to the test by proposing a vote of confidence*. ■ [with infinitive] intend to do something: *he proposed to attend the meeting*.
2 [no obj.] make an offer of marriage to someone: *I have already* ***proposed to*** *Sarah* | [with obj.] *one girl* ***proposed marriage to*** *him on the spot*.
– PHRASES **propose a toast** (or **propose someone's health**) ask a group of people at a social occasion to drink to the health and happiness of a specified person: *the Lord Mayor* ***proposed a toast to*** *the Queen*.
– DERIVATIVES **proposer** noun.
– ORIGIN Middle English: from Old French *proposer*, from Latin *proponere* (see PROPONENT), but influenced by Latin *propositus* 'put or set forth' and Old French *poser* 'to place'.

proposition ▶ **noun 1** a statement or assertion that expresses a judgement or opinion: *the proposition that high taxation is undesirable*. ■ Logic a statement that expresses a concept that can be true or false. ■ Mathematics a formal statement of a theorem or problem, typically including the demonstration.
2 a suggested scheme or plan of action, especially in a business context: *a detailed investment proposition*. ■ US a constitutional proposal; a bill. ■ informal an offer of sexual intercourse made to a person with whom one is not involved, especially one that is made in an unsubtle way.
3 [with adj.] a project, task, idea, etc. considered in terms of its likely success or difficulty: *setting up your own business can seem an attractive proposition*.
▶ **verb** [with obj.] informal make a suggestion of sexual intercourse to (someone), especially in an unsubtle way: *she had been propositioned at the party by a sub-editor with bad breath*. ■ make an offer or suggestion to: *I was propositioned by the editor about becoming film critic of the paper*.
– DERIVATIVES **propositional** adjective (chiefly Logic).
– ORIGIN Middle English: from Old French, from Latin *propositio(n-)*, from the verb *proponere* (see PROPOUND).

propositional attitude ▶ **noun** Philosophy the relation that a person has with a proposition, such as having an opinion concerning it or responding emotionally to it.

propositional calculus ▶ **noun** [mass noun] the branch of symbolic logic that deals with propositions and the relations between them, without examination of their content.

propound /prəˈpaʊnd/ ▶ **verb** [with obj.] put forward (an idea or theory) for consideration by others: *he began to propound the idea of a 'social monarchy' as an alternative to Franco*.
– DERIVATIVES **propounder** noun.
– ORIGIN mid 16th cent.: alteration of archaic *propone*, from Latin *proponere* 'set forth', from *pro-* 'forward' + *ponere* 'put'. The addition of the final *-d* can be compared with that in *expound* and *compound*.

propoxyphene /prəʊˈpɒksɪfiːn/ ▶ **noun** [mass noun] Medicine a synthetic compound chemically related to methadone, used as a mild narcotic analgesic.
– ORIGIN 1950s: from PROPYL + OXY-[1] + *-phene* (from PHENYL).

propranolol /prəʊˈpranəlɒl/ ▶ **noun** [mass noun] Medicine a synthetic compound which acts as a beta blocker and is used mainly in the treatment of cardiac arrhythmia. ● Chemical formula: $C_{16}H_{21}NO_2$.
– ORIGIN 1960s: from *pro(pyl)* + *pr(op)anol*, with the reduplication of *-ol*.

proprietary ▶ **adjective 1** relating to an owner or ownership: *the company has a proprietary right to the property*. ■ behaving as if one owned something or someone: *he looked about him with a proprietary air*.
2 (of a product) marketed under and protected by a registered trade name: *proprietary brands of insecticide*.
– ORIGIN late Middle English (as a noun denoting a member of a religious order who held property): from late Latin *proprietarius* 'proprietor', from *proprietas* (see PROPERTY).

proprietary name (also **proprietary term**) ▶ **noun** a name of a product or service registered by its owner as a trademark and not usable by others without permission.

proprietor ▶ **noun** the owner of a business, or a holder of property.
– DERIVATIVES **proprietorship** noun.

proprietorial /prəˌprʌɪəˈtɔːrɪəl/ ▶ **adjective** behaving as if one owned a particular thing or person; possessive: *Louis draped his arm across her shoulders in a proprietorial way*.
– DERIVATIVES **proprietorially** adverb.

proprietress ▶ **noun** a female proprietor.

propriety ▶ **noun** (pl. **proprieties**) [mass noun] conformity to conventionally accepted standards of behaviour or morals: *he always behaved with the utmost propriety*. ■ (**proprieties**) the details or rules of behaviour conventionally considered to be correct: *she's a great one for the proprieties*. ■ the condition of being right, appropriate, or fitting: *they questioned the propriety of certain investments made by the council*.
– ORIGIN late Middle English (in the sense 'peculiarity, essential quality'): from Old French *propriete*, from Latin *proprietas* (see PROPERTY).

proprioceptive /ˌprəʊprɪə(ʊ)ˈsɛptɪv/ ▶ **adjective** Physiology relating to stimuli that are produced and perceived within an organism, especially those connected with the position and movement of the body. Compare with EXTEROCEPTIVE and INTEROCEPTIVE.
– ORIGIN early 20th cent.: from Latin *proprius* 'own' + RECEPTIVE.

proprioceptor /ˈprəʊprɪə(ʊ)sɛptə/ ▶ **noun** Physiology a sensory receptor which receives stimuli from within the body, especially one that responds to position and movement.
– ORIGIN early 20th cent.: from Latin *proprius* 'own' + RECEPTOR.

props ▶ **noun** [mass noun] black slang due respect: *certain sectors of the music fraternity still refuse to give him props*.
– ORIGIN 1990s: from *proper respect*.

propshaft ▶ **noun** a propeller shaft, especially of a motor vehicle.

proptosis /prɒpˈtəʊsɪs/ ▶ **noun** [mass noun] Medicine abnormal protrusion or displacement of an eye or other body part.
– ORIGIN late 17th cent.: via late Latin from Greek *proptōsis*, from *pro* 'before' + *piptein* 'to fall'.

propulsion ▶ **noun** [mass noun] the action of driving or pushing forwards: *they dive and use their wings for propulsion under water*.
– DERIVATIVES **propulsive** adjective, **propulsively** adverb.
– ORIGIN early 17th cent. (in the sense 'expulsion'): from medieval Latin *propulsio(n-)*, from Latin *propellere* 'drive before (oneself)'.

propulsor ▶ **noun** a ducted propeller which can be swivelled to give forward, upward, or downward flight to an airship.

propyl /ˈprəʊpʌɪl, -pɪl/ ▶ **noun** [as modifier] Chemistry of or denoting the alkyl radical $-C_3H_7$, derived from propane. Compare with ISOPROPYL.

propyla plural form of PROPYLON.

propylaeum /ˌprɒpɪˈliːəm/ ▶ **noun** (pl. **propylaea** /-ˈliːə/) Architecture the structure forming the entrance to a temple. ■ (**the Propylaeum**) the entrance to the Acropolis at Athens.
– ORIGIN via Latin from Greek *propulaion*, neuter (used as a noun) of *propulaios* 'before the gate', from *pro* 'before' + *pulē* 'gate'.

propylene /ˈprəʊpɪliːn/ ▶ **noun** [mass noun] Chemistry a gaseous hydrocarbon of the alkene series, made by cracking alkanes. ● Alternative name: **propene**; chem. formula: C_3H_6.

propylene glycol ▶ **noun** [mass noun] Chemistry a liquid alcohol which is used as a solvent, in antifreeze, and in the food, plastics, and perfume industries. ● Chem. formula: $C_3H_6(OH)_2$; two isomers.

propylon /ˈprɒpɪlɒn/ ▶ **noun** (pl. **propylons** or **propyla** /-lə/) another term for PROPYLAEUM.
– ORIGIN mid 19th cent.: via Latin from Greek *propulon*, from *pro* 'before' + *pulē* 'gate'.

pro rata /prəʊ ˈrɑːtə, ˈreɪtə/ ▶ **adjective** proportional: *as the pound has fallen costs have risen on a pro rata basis*.
▶ **adverb** proportionally: *their fees will rise pro rata with salaries*.
– ORIGIN late 16th cent.: Latin, literally 'according to the rate'.

prorate /prəʊˈreɪt, ˈprəʊ-/ ▶ **verb** [with obj.] chiefly N. Amer. allocate, distribute, or assess pro rata: *bonuses are prorated over the life of a player's contract*.
– DERIVATIVES **proration** noun.

prorogue /prəˈrəʊg/ ▶ **verb** (**prorogues, proroguing, prorogued**) [with obj.] discontinue a session of (a parliament or other legislative assembly) without dissolving it.
– DERIVATIVES **prorogation** /-rəˈgeɪʃ(ə)n/ noun.
– ORIGIN late Middle English: from Old French *proroger*, from Latin *prorogare* 'prolong, extend', from *pro-* 'in front of, publicly' + *rogare* 'ask'.

prosaic /prə(ʊ)ˈzeɪɪk/ ▶ **adjective** having or using the style or diction of prose as opposed to poetry; lacking imaginativeness or originality: *prosaic language can't convey the experience*. ■ commonplace; unromantic: *the masses were too preoccupied by prosaic day-to-day concerns*.
– DERIVATIVES **prosaically** adverb, **prosaicness** noun.
– ORIGIN late 16th cent. (as a noun denoting a prose writer): from late Latin *prosaicus*, from Latin *prosa* 'straightforward (discourse)' (see PROSE). Current senses of the adjective date from the mid 18th cent.

prosaist /ˈprəʊzeɪɪst/ ▶ **noun 1** a person who writes in prose.
2 a prosaic person.
– DERIVATIVES **prosaism** noun.
– ORIGIN early 19th cent.: from French *prosaïste*, from Latin *prosa* 'straightforward (discourse)' (see PROSE).

prosauropod /prəʊˈsɔːrəpɒd, -ˈsaʊr-/ ▶ **noun** an elongated partly bipedal herbivorous dinosaur of the late Triassic and early Jurassic periods, related to the ancestors of sauropods. ● Infraorder Prosauropoda, suborder Sauropodomorpha, order Saurischia.
– ORIGIN 1950s: from PRO-[2] 'before in time' + SAUROPOD.

proscenium /prə(ʊ)ˈsiːnɪəm/ ▶ **noun** (pl. **prosceniums** or **proscenia** /-nɪə/) the part of a theatre stage in front of the curtain. ■ the stage of an ancient theatre. ■ short for PROSCENIUM ARCH.
– ORIGIN early 17th cent.: via Latin from Greek *proskēnion*, from *pro* 'before' + *skēnē* 'stage'.

proscenium arch ▶ **noun** an arch framing the opening between the stage and the auditorium in some theatres.

prosciutto /prəˈʃuːtəʊ/ ▶ **noun** [mass noun] raw cured Italian ham, eaten especially in thin slices as an hors d'oeuvre.
– ORIGIN Italian.

proscribe ▶ **verb** [with obj.] forbid, especially by law: *strikes remained proscribed in the armed forces*. ■ denounce or condemn: *certain customary practices which the Catholic Church proscribed, such as polygyny*. ■ historical outlaw (someone).
– DERIVATIVES **proscriptive** adjective.
– ORIGIN late Middle English (in the sense 'to outlaw'): from Latin *proscribere*, from *pro-* 'in front of' + *scribere* 'write'.

> **USAGE** **Proscribe** does not have the same meaning as **prescribe**: see **USAGE** at **PRESCRIBE**.

proscription ▶ **noun** [mass noun] the action of forbidding something; banning: *the proscription of the party after the 1715 Rebellion*. ■ condemnation or denunciation of something.

prose ▶ **noun** [mass noun] **1** written or spoken language in its ordinary form, without metrical structure: *a short story in prose* | [as modifier] *a prose passage*. ■ [count noun] a passage of prose for translation into a foreign language. ■ plain or dull writing, discourse, or expression: *closely typed in best office prose*.
2 another term for SEQUENCE (sense 4 of the noun).
▶ **verb 1** [no obj.] talk tediously: *he was still prosing away about the advantages of a warm climate*.
2 [with obj.] dated compose in or convert into prose.
– DERIVATIVES **proser** noun.
– ORIGIN Middle English: via Old French from Latin *prosa (oratio)* 'straightforward (discourse)', feminine of *prosus*, earlier *prorsus* 'direct'.

Prosecco /prə(ʊ)ˈsɛkəʊ/ ▶ **noun** [mass noun] (trademark in the UK) a sparkling white wine from the Veneto region of NE Italy.
– ORIGIN Italian, probably from *Prosecco*, a town near Trieste.

prosector /prə(ʊ)ˈsɛktə/ ▶ **noun** chiefly N. Amer. a person who dissects dead bodies for examination or anatomical demonstration.

P

– ORIGIN mid 19th cent.: from late Latin, literally 'anatomist', based on Latin *secare* 'to cut', perhaps via French *prosecteur*.

prosecute ▶ **verb** [with obj.] **1** institute or conduct legal proceedings against (a person or organization): *they were prosecuted for obstructing the highway* | [no obj.] *the company didn't prosecute because of his age.* ■ institute legal proceedings in respect of (a claim or offence): *the state's attorney's office seemed to decide that this was a case worth prosecuting.*
2 continue with (a course of action) with a view to its completion: *a serious threat to the government's ability to prosecute the war.* ■ archaic carry on (a trade or pursuit).
– DERIVATIVES **prosecutable** adjective.
– ORIGIN late Middle English (in sense 2): from Latin *prosecut-* 'pursued, accompanied', from the verb *prosequi*, from *pro-* 'onward' + *sequi* 'follow'.

prosecution ▶ **noun** [mass noun] **1** the institution and conducting of legal proceedings against someone in respect of a criminal charge: *the organizers are facing prosecution for noise nuisance* | [count noun] *they lacked the funds to embark on private prosecutions.* ■ (**the prosecution**) [treated as sing. or pl.] the party instituting or conducting legal proceedings against someone in a lawsuit: *the main witness for the prosecution.*
2 the continuation of a course of action with a view to its completion: *the BBC's prosecution of its commercial ends.*
– ORIGIN mid 16th cent. (in sense 2): from Old French, or from late Latin *prosecutio(n-)*, from *prosequi* 'pursue, accompany' (see PROSECUTE).

prosecutor ▶ **noun** a person, especially a public official, who institutes legal proceedings against someone. ■ a barrister or other lawyer who conducts the case against a defendant in a criminal court.
– DERIVATIVES **prosecutorial** adjective.

proselyte /ˈprɒsɪlʌɪt/ ▶ **noun** a person who has converted from one opinion, religion, or party to another. ■ a Gentile who has converted to Judaism.
▶ **verb** US term for PROSELYTIZE.
– DERIVATIVES **proselytism** /-lɪtɪz(ə)m/ noun.
– ORIGIN late Middle English: via late Latin from Greek *prosēluthos* 'stranger, convert', from *prosēluth-*, past stem of *proserkhesthai* 'approach'.

proselytize /ˈprɒsɪlɪtʌɪz/ (also **proselytise**) ▶ **verb** [with obj.] convert or attempt to convert (someone) from one religion, belief, or opinion to another: *the programme did have a tremendous evangelical effect, proselytizing many* | [no obj.] *proselytizing for converts* | (as noun **proselytizing**) *no amount of proselytizing was going to change their minds.* ■ advocate or promote (a belief or course of action): *Davis wanted to share his concept and proselytize his ideas.*
– DERIVATIVES **proselytization** noun, **proselytizer** noun.

P

prosencephalon /ˌprɒsɛnˈsɛfəlɒn, -ˈkɛf-/ ▶ **noun** another term for FOREBRAIN.
– ORIGIN mid 19th cent.: from Greek *prosō* 'forwards' + *enkephalos* 'brain'.

prosenchyma /prɒˈsɛŋkɪmə/ ▶ **noun** [mass noun] Biology a plant tissue consisting of elongated cells with interpenetrating tapering ends, occurring especially in vascular tissue.
– ORIGIN mid 19th cent.: from Greek *pros* 'towards' + *enkhuma* 'infusion', on the pattern of *parenchyma*.

prose poem ▶ **noun** a piece of imaginative poetic writing in prose.
– DERIVATIVES **prose poetry** noun.

Proserpina /prəˈsəːpɪnə/ (also **Proserpine** /-pɪni/) Roman Mythology Roman name for PERSEPHONE.

pro shop ▶ **noun** a retail outlet at a golf club, typically run by the resident professional, where golfing equipment can be purchased or repaired.

prosimian /prəʊˈsɪmɪən/ Zoology ▶ **noun** a primitive primate of a group that includes the lemurs, lorises, bushbabies, and tarsiers. ● Suborder Prosimii, order Primates: several families.
▶ **adjective** relating to the prosimians. Compare with SIMIAN.
– ORIGIN late 19th cent.: from PRO-² 'before' + SIMIAN.

prosit /ˈprəʊzɪt/ ▶ **exclamation** an expression used in drinking a person's health.
– ORIGIN German, from Latin, literally 'may it benefit'.

Prosobranchia /ˌprɒsə(ʊ)ˈbraŋkɪə/ ▶ **plural noun** Zoology a group of molluscs which includes the limpets, abalones, and many terrestrial and aquatic snails. They all have a shell, and many have an operculum. ● Subclass Prosobranchia, class Gastropoda.
– DERIVATIVES **prosobranch** /ˈprɒsəbraŋk/ noun.
– ORIGIN modern Latin (plural), from Greek *prosō* 'forwards' + *brankhia* 'gills'.

prosocial ▶ **adjective** Psychology relating to or denoting behaviour which is positive, helpful, and intended to promote social acceptance and friendship.

prosodic analysis /prəˈsɒdɪk/ ▶ **noun** [mass noun] Linguistics analysis of a language based on its patterns of stress and intonation in different contexts. In systemic grammar, prosodic analysis is regarded as an essential foundation for the analysis of syntax and meaning.

prosody /ˈprɒsədi/ ▶ **noun** [mass noun] **1** the patterns of rhythm and sound used in poetry: *the translator is not obliged to reproduce the prosody of the original.* ■ the theory or study of prosody.
2 the patterns of stress and intonation in a language.
– DERIVATIVES **prosodic** adjective, **prosodist** noun.
– ORIGIN late 15th cent.: from Latin *prosodia* 'accent of a syllable', from Greek *prosōidia* 'song sung to music, tone of a syllable', from *pros* 'towards' + *ōidē* 'song'.

prosoma /prə(ʊ)ˈsəʊmə/ ▶ **noun** another term for CEPHALOTHORAX.
– ORIGIN late 19th cent.: from PRO-² 'before' + Greek *sōma* 'body'.

prosopagnosia /ˌprɒsə(ʊ)pagˈnəʊsɪə, -ˈnəʊzɪə/ ▶ **noun** [mass noun] Psychiatry the inability to recognize the faces of familiar people, typically as a result of damage to the brain.
– ORIGIN 1950s: modern Latin, from Greek *prosōpon* 'face' + *agnōsia* 'ignorance'.

prosopography /ˌprɒsə(ʊ)ˈpɒgrəfi/ ▶ **noun** (pl. **prosopographies**) a description of a person's appearance, personality, career, etc., or a collection of such descriptions. ■ [mass noun] the study of such descriptions, especially as an aspect of the study of Roman history.
– DERIVATIVES **prosopographical** /-pəˈgrafɪk(ə)l/ adjective.
– ORIGIN 1920s: from modern Latin *prosopographia*, from Greek *prosōpon* 'face, person' + *-graphia* 'writing'.

prosopopoeia /ˌprɒsəpəˈpiːə/ ▶ **noun** [mass noun]
1 a figure of speech in which an abstract thing is personified.
2 a figure of speech in which an imagined, absent, or dead person or thing is represented as speaking.
– ORIGIN mid 16th cent.: via Latin from Greek *prosōpopoiia*, from *prosōpon* 'person' + *poiein* 'to make'.

prospect ▶ **noun 1** [mass noun] the possibility or likelihood of some future event occurring: *there was no prospect of a reconciliation* | [count noun] *some training which offered a prospect of continuous employment.* ■ [in sing.] a mental picture of a future or anticipated event: *this presents a disturbing prospect of one-party government.* ■ (**prospects**) chances or opportunities for success or wealth: *the poor prospects for the steel industry.*
2 a person regarded as likely to succeed or as a potential customer, client, etc.: *Norwich's unbeaten heavyweight prospect* | *clients deemed likely prospects for active party membership.*
3 a place likely to yield mineral deposits.
4 an extensive view of landscape: *a viewpoint commanding a magnificent prospect of the estuary.*
▶ **verb** [no obj.] search for mineral deposits, especially by drilling and excavation: *the company is also prospecting for gold.* ■ (**prospect for**) search for; seek: *many charities are prospecting for new donors.*
– DERIVATIVES **prospectless** adjective, **prospector** noun.
– ORIGIN late Middle English (as a noun denoting the action of looking towards a distant object): from Latin *prospectus* 'view', from *prospicere* 'look forward', from *pro-* 'forward' + *specere* 'to look'. Early use, referring to a view of landscape, gave rise to the meaning 'mental picture' (mid 16th cent.), whence 'anticipated event'.

prospective ▶ **adjective** [attrib.] expected or expecting to be the specified thing in the future: *she showed a prospective buyer around the house.* ■ likely to happen at a future date: *a meeting to discuss prospective changes in government legislation.*
– DERIVATIVES **prospectively** adverb.
– ORIGIN late 16th cent. (in the sense 'looking forward, having foresight'): from obsolete French *prospectif, -ive* or late Latin *prospectivus*, from Latin *prospectus* 'view' (see PROSPECT).

prospectus ▶ **noun** (pl. **prospectuses**) a printed booklet advertising a school or university to potential parents or students or giving details of a share offer for the benefit of investors.
– ORIGIN mid 18th cent.: from Latin, literally 'view, prospect', from the verb *prospicere*, from *pro-* 'forward' + *specere* 'to look'.

prosper ▶ **verb** [no obj.] succeed in material terms; be financially successful: *his business prospered* | *the state hopes to prosper from free trade with the United States.* ■ flourish physically; grow strong and healthy: *areas where grey squirrels cannot prosper.* ■ [with obj.] archaic make successful: *God has wonderfully prospered this nation.*
– ORIGIN late Middle English: from Old French *prosperer*, from Latin *prosperare*, from *prosperus* 'doing well'.

prosperity ▶ **noun** [mass noun] the state of being prosperous: *a long period of peace and prosperity.*
– ORIGIN Middle English: from Old French *prosperite*, from Latin *prosperitas*, from *prosperus* 'doing well'.

prosperous ▶ **adjective** successful in material terms; flourishing financially: *prosperous middle-class professionals.* ■ bringing wealth and success: *we wish you a Merry Christmas and a prosperous New Year.*
– DERIVATIVES **prosperously** adverb, **prosperousness** noun.
– ORIGIN late Middle English: from Old French *prospereus*, from Latin *prosperus* 'doing well'.

prostacyclin /ˌprɒstəˈsʌɪklɪn/ ▶ **noun** [mass noun] Biochemistry a compound of the prostaglandin type produced in arterial walls, which functions as an anticoagulant and vasodilator.
– ORIGIN 1970s: from PROSTAGLANDIN + CYCLIC + -IN¹.

prostaglandin /ˌprɒstəˈglandɪn/ ▶ **noun** Biochemistry any of a group of compounds with varying hormone-like effects, notably the promotion of uterine contractions. They are cyclic fatty acids.
– ORIGIN 1930s: from PROSTATE + GLAND¹ + -IN¹.

prostate (also **prostate gland**) ▶ **noun** a gland surrounding the neck of the bladder in male mammals and releasing a fluid component of semen.
– DERIVATIVES **prostatic** adjective.
– ORIGIN mid 17th cent.: via French from modern Latin *prostata*, from Greek *prostatēs* 'one that stands before', from *pro* 'before' + *statos* 'standing'.

prostatectomy /ˌprɒstəˈtɛktəmi/ ▶ **noun** (pl. **prostatectomies**) a surgical operation to remove all or part of the prostate gland.

prostate-specific antigen (abbrev.: **PSA**) ▶ **noun** [mass noun] Medicine an antigenic enzyme released in the prostate and found in abnormally high concentrations in the blood of men with prostate cancer.

prostatitis /ˌprɒsteɪˈtʌɪtɪs/ ▶ **noun** [mass noun] Medicine inflammation of the prostate gland.

prosthesis /prɒsˈθiːsɪs, ˈprɒsθɪsɪs/ ▶ **noun** (pl. **prostheses** /-siːz/) **1** an artificial body part, such as a limb, a heart, or a breast implant.
2 Linguistics the addition of a letter or syllable at the beginning of a word, as in Spanish *escuela* derived from Latin *scola*.
– DERIVATIVES **prosthetic** /-ˈθɛtɪk/ adjective, **prosthetically** adverb.
– ORIGIN mid 16th cent. (in sense 2): via late Latin from Greek *prosthesis*, from *prostithenai*, from *pros* 'in addition' + *tithenai* 'to place'.

prosthetic group ▶ **noun** Biochemistry a non-protein group forming part of or combined with a protein.

prosthetics /prɒsˈθɛtɪks/ ▶ **plural noun** artificial body parts; prostheses. ■ [treated as sing.] the branch of surgery concerned with the making and fitting of artificial body parts. ■ pieces of flexible material applied to actors' faces to transform their appearance.

prosthetist /ˈprɒsθɪtɪst/ ▶ **noun** a specialist in prosthetics.

prosthodontics /ˌprɒsθəˈdɒntɪks/ ▶ **plural noun** [treated as sing.] the branch of dentistry concerned with the design, manufacture, and fitting of artificial replacements for teeth and other parts of the mouth.
– DERIVATIVES **prosthodontist** noun.
– ORIGIN 1940s: from PROSTHESIS, on the pattern of *orthodontics*.

prostitute ▶ **noun** a person, typically a woman, who engages in sexual activity for payment.
▶ **verb** [with obj.] offer (someone, typically a woman) for sexual activity in exchange for payment: *although she was paid £15 to join a man at his table, she never prostituted herself.* ■ put (oneself or one's talents) to an unworthy or corrupt use for personal or financial gain: *his willingness to prostitute himself to the worst instincts of the electorate.*

– ORIGIN mid 16th cent. (as a verb): from Latin *prostitut-* 'exposed publicly, offered for sale', from the verb *prostituere*, from *pro-* 'before' + *statuere* 'set up, place'.

prostitution ▶ noun [mass noun] the practice or occupation of engaging in sexual activity with someone for payment. ■ the unworthy or corrupt use of one's talents for personal or financial gain.

prostrate ▶ adjective /ˈprɒstreɪt/ **1** lying stretched out on the ground with one's face downwards. ■ [predic.] completely overcome or helpless, especially with distress or exhaustion: *his wife was* **prostrate with** *shock*.
2 Botany growing along the ground.
▶ verb /prɒˈstreɪt/ [with obj.] **1** (**prostrate oneself**) throw oneself flat on the ground so as to be lying face downwards, especially in reverence or submission: *she prostrated herself on the bare floor of the church*.
2 reduce (someone) to extreme physical weakness: *she was so prostrated by migraine that she could scarcely totter up the stairs to bed*.
– ORIGIN Middle English: from Latin *prostratus* 'thrown down', past participle of *prosternere*, from *pro-* 'before' + *sternere* 'lay flat'.

prostration /prɒˈstreɪʃ(ə)n/ ▶ noun [mass noun] the action of lying stretched out on the ground. ■ the state of being extremely weak or subservient: *the refusal to call a strike reflects the union leadership's* **prostration before** *the company*. ■ extreme physical weakness or emotional exhaustion.

prostyle /ˈprəʊstʌɪl/ ▶ noun Architecture a portico with a maximum of four columns.
– ORIGIN late 17th cent.: from Latin *prostylos* '(building) having pillars in front', from Greek *pro* 'before' + *stulos* 'column'.

prosumer /prəʊˈsuːmə/ ▶ noun **1** a person who buys electronic goods that are of a standard between those aimed at consumers and professionals.
2 a consumer who becomes involved with designing or customizing products for their own needs.
– ORIGIN 1980s: from **PROFESSIONAL** or **PRODUCER** + **CONSUMER**.

prosy /ˈprəʊzi/ ▶ adjective (**prosier**, **prosiest**) (especially of speech or writing) showing no imagination; commonplace or dull.
– DERIVATIVES **prosily** adverb, **prosiness** noun.

prot- ▶ combining form variant spelling of **PROTO-** before a vowel (as in *protamine*).

protactinium /ˌprəʊtakˈtɪnɪəm/ ▶ noun [mass noun] the chemical element of atomic number 91, a radioactive metal of the actinide series, occurring in small amounts as a product of the natural decay of uranium. (Symbol: **Pa**)
– ORIGIN early 20th cent.: from **PROTO-** 'original, earlier' + **ACTINIUM**, so named because one of its isotopes decays to form actinium.

protagonist ▶ noun **1** the leading character or one of the major characters in a play, film, novel, etc. ■ the main figure or one of the most prominent figures in a situation: *in this colonial struggle the main protagonists were Great Britain and France*.
2 an advocate or champion of a particular cause or idea: *he's a strenuous protagonist of the new agricultural policy*.
– ORIGIN late 17th cent.: from Greek *prōtagōnistēs*, from *prōtos* 'first in importance' + *agōnistēs* 'actor'.

> **USAGE** The basic sense of **protagonist**, as originally used in connection with ancient Greek drama, is 'the main character in a play'. Some traditionalists object to the looser use to refer to a number of characters (rather than just the main one) in a play, film, etc., as for example *the play's half-dozen protagonists were well cast*, although this is both common and well established. Traditionalists also dislike the meaning 'a supporter of a cause', as in *he's a strenuous* ***protagonist*** *of the new agricultural policy*. This sense, recorded from the 19th century, probably arose by analogy with **antagonist**, the **pro-** in **protagonist** being interpreted as meaning 'in favour of'. In fact, **prot-** here derives from the Greek root meaning 'first'.

protamine /ˈprəʊtəmiːn/ ▶ noun Biochemistry any of a group of simple proteins found combined with nucleic acids, especially in fish sperm.
– ORIGIN late 19th cent.: from **PROTO-** 'original' + **AMINE**.

protandrous /prəʊˈtandrəs/ ▶ adjective Botany & Zoology (of a hermaphrodite flower or animal) having the male reproductive organs come to maturity before the female. The opposite of **PROTOGYNOUS**.
– DERIVATIVES **protandry** noun.

protanope /ˈprəʊt(ə)nəʊp/ ▶ noun a person suffering from protanopia.

protanopia /ˌprəʊtəˈnəʊpɪə/ ▶ noun [mass noun] colour blindness resulting from insensitivity to red light, causing confusion of greens, reds, and yellows. It is hereditary, and is the commonest form of colour blindness. Also called **DALTONISM**. Compare with **DEUTERANOPIA**, **TRITANOPIA**.
– ORIGIN early 20th cent.: from **PROTO-** 'original' (red being regarded as the first component of colour vision) + **AN-**[1] 'lacking' + **-OPIA**.

pro tanto /prəʊ ˈtantəʊ/ ▶ adjective & adverb to such an extent; to that extent.
– ORIGIN Latin, literally 'for so much'.

protasis /ˈprɒtəsɪs/ ▶ noun (pl. **protases** /-siːz/) Grammar the clause expressing the condition in a conditional sentence (e.g. *if you asked me* in *if you asked me I would agree*). Often contrasted with **APODOSIS**.
– ORIGIN late 16th cent.: via Latin from Greek *protasis* 'proposition', from *pro* 'before' + *teinein* 'to stretch'.

protea /ˈprəʊtɪə/ ▶ noun an evergreen shrub or small tree with large nectar-rich cone-like flower heads surrounded by brightly coloured bracts, chiefly native to South Africa. ● Genus *Protea*, family Proteaceae: many species, including *P. repens*, which was formerly used as a source of sweet syrup.
– ORIGIN modern Latin, from **PROTEUS**, with reference to the many species of the genus.

protean /ˈprəʊtɪən, prəʊˈtiːən/ ▶ adjective tending or able to change frequently or easily: *it is difficult to comprehend the whole of this protean subject*. ■ able to do many different things; versatile: *protean thinkers who scan the horizons of work and society*.
– ORIGIN late 16th cent.: from **PROTEUS** + **-AN**.

protease /ˈprəʊtɪeɪz/ ▶ noun Biochemistry an enzyme which breaks down proteins and peptides.
– ORIGIN early 20th cent.: from **PROTEIN** + **-ASE**.

proteasome /ˈprəʊtɪəˌsəʊm/ ▶ noun Biochemistry a complex of proteinases involved in breaking down selected intracellular proteins.
– ORIGIN 1980s: from **PROTEIN** + **-SOME**[3].

protect ▶ verb [with obj.] keep safe from harm or injury: *he tried to* **protect** *Kelly* **from** *the attack* | [no obj.] *use a sunscreen that* **protects against** *both UVA and UVB*. ■ (often as adj. **protected**) aim to preserve (a threatened species or area) by legislating against collecting, hunting, or development: *the natterjack toad is a protected species* | *logging is continuing in protected areas in violation of an international agreement*. ■ Economics shield (a domestic industry) from competition by imposing import duties on foreign goods. ■ Computing restrict access to or use of (data or a memory location).
– DERIVATIVES **protectable** adjective.
– ORIGIN late Middle English: from Latin *protect-* 'covered in front', from the verb *protegere*, from *pro-* 'in front' + *tegere* 'to cover'.

protectant ▶ noun a substance that provides protection, e.g. against disease or ultraviolet radiation.

protection ▶ noun [mass noun] the action of protecting, or the state of being protected: *the B vitamins give* **protection against** *infection* | *his son was put under police protection*. ■ a person or thing that protects someone or something: *the castle was built as protection against the Saxons* | [in sing.] *a protection against the evil eye*. ■ [count noun] (usu. **protections**) a legal or other formal measure intended to preserve civil liberties and rights. ■ [count noun] a document guaranteeing immunity from harm to the person specified in it. ■ the practice of paying money to criminals so as to prevent them from attacking oneself or one's property: [as modifier] *a protection racket* | *protection money*. ■ money paid to criminals on this basis, especially on a regular basis. ■ Climbing the number and quality of running belays or other equipment employed to safeguard a pitch.
– ORIGIN Middle English: from Old French, from late Latin *protectio(n-)*, from *protegere* 'cover in front' (see **PROTECT**).

protectionism ▶ noun [mass noun] Economics the theory or practice of shielding a country's domestic industries from foreign competition by taxing imports.
– DERIVATIVES **protectionist** noun & adjective.

protective ▶ adjective intended to protect someone or something: *protective gloves are worn to minimize injury*. ■ having or showing a strong wish to protect someone or something: *I felt protective towards her* | *as adults we are naturally protective of children*. ■ Economics relating to the protection of domestic industries from foreign competition: *protective tariffs*.
▶ noun Brit. a thing that protects someone or something: *an effectual protective against the midge*. ■ dated a condom.
– DERIVATIVES **protectively** adverb, **protectiveness** noun.

protective colouring (also **protective coloration**) ▶ noun [mass noun] colouring that disguises or camouflages a plant or animal.

protective custody ▶ noun [mass noun] the detention of a person for their own protection.

protector ▶ noun **1** a person or thing that protects someone or something: *a man who became her protector, adviser, and friend* | *ear protectors*.
2 (usu. **Protector**) historical a regent in charge of a kingdom during the minority, absence, or incapacity of the sovereign. ■ (also **Lord Protector of the Commonwealth**) the title of the head of state in England during the later period of the Commonwealth between 1653 and 1659, first Oliver Cromwell (1653–8), then his son Richard (1658–9).
– DERIVATIVES **protectoral** adjective, **protectorship** noun.

protectorate ▶ noun **1** a state that is controlled and protected by another. ■ the relationship between a protectorate and the state that controls it: *a French protectorate had been established over Tunis*.
2 (usu. **Protectorate**) historical the position or period of office of a Protector, especially that in England of Oliver and Richard Cromwell.

protectress ▶ noun a female protector.

protégé /ˈprɒtɪʒeɪ, -tɛʒeɪ, ˈprəʊ-/ ▶ noun (fem. **protégée** pronunc. **same**) a person who is guided and supported by an older and more experienced or influential person: *Ruskin submitted his protégé's name for election*.
– ORIGIN late 18th cent.: French, literally 'protected', past participle of *protéger*, from Latin *protegere* 'cover in front' (see **PROTECT**).

protein ▶ noun any of a class of nitrogenous organic compounds which have large molecules composed of one or more long chains of amino acids and are an essential part of all living organisms, especially as structural components of body tissues such as muscle, hair, etc., and as enzymes and antibodies. ■ [mass noun] proteins collectively, especially as a dietary component: *a diet high in protein*.
– DERIVATIVES **proteinaceous** adjective, **proteinic** /-ˈtiːnɪk/ adjective, **proteinous** /-ˈtiːnəs, -ˈtiːɪnəs/ adjective.
– ORIGIN mid 19th cent.: from French *protéine*, German *Protein*, from Greek *prōteios* 'primary', from *prōtos* 'first'.

proteinase /ˈprəʊtiːneɪz/ ▶ noun another term for **ENDOPEPTIDASE**.

P

protein engineering ▶ noun [mass noun] the manipulation of the structures of proteins so as to produce desired properties, or the synthesis of proteins with particular structures.

proteinuria /ˌprəʊtiːˈnjʊərɪə/ ▶ noun [mass noun] Medicine the presence of abnormal quantities of protein in the urine, which may indicate damage to the kidneys.

pro tem /prəʊ ˈtɛm/ ▶ adverb & adjective for the time being: [as adv.] *a printer which Marisa could use pro tem* | [as adj.] *a pro tem committee*.
– ORIGIN abbreviation of Latin *pro tempore*.

proteoglycan /ˌprəʊtɪəʊˈɡlʌɪkan/ ▶ noun Biochemistry a compound consisting of a protein bonded to mucopolysaccharide groups, present especially in connective tissue.

proteolysis /ˌprəʊtɪˈɒlɪsɪs/ ▶ noun [mass noun] Biochemistry the breakdown of proteins or peptides into amino acids by the action of enzymes.
– DERIVATIVES **proteolytic** adjective, **proteolytically** adverb.
– ORIGIN late 19th cent.: modern Latin, from **PROTEIN** + **-LYSIS**.

proteome /ˈprəʊtɪəʊm/ ▶ noun Genetics the entire complement of proteins that is or can be expressed by a cell, tissue, or organism.
– ORIGIN 1990s: a blend of **PROTEIN** and **GENOME**.

proteomics /ˌprəʊtɪˈɒmɪks/ ▶ plural noun [treated as sing.] the branch of molecular biology concerned with determining the proteome.
– DERIVATIVES **proteomic** adjective.

Proterozoic /ˌprəʊt(ə)rəˈzəʊɪk/ ▶ adjective Geology relating to or denoting the aeon that constitutes the later part of the Precambrian, between the Archaean aeon and the Cambrian period, in which the earliest forms of life evolved. ■ (as noun **the Proterozoic**) the

Proterozoic aeon or the system of rocks deposited during it.

> The Proterozoic lasted from about 2,500 to 570 million years ago. For millions of years only bacteria and single-celled organisms existed, and the early invertebrates that followed were soft-bodied and rarely left any trace in the form of fossils.

– ORIGIN late 19th cent.: from Greek *proteros* 'former' + *zōē* 'life', *zōos* 'living' + **-IC**.

protest ▶ **noun** /'prəʊtɛst/ **1** a statement or action expressing disapproval of or objection to something: *the British team lodged an official protest* | [mass noun] *two senior scientists resigned **in protest**.* ■ an organized public demonstration expressing strong objection to an official policy or course of action: *a protest over planned pit closures* | [as modifier] *a protest march.*
2 Law a written declaration, typically by a notary public, that a bill has been presented and payment or acceptance refused.
▶ **verb** /prə'tɛst/ **1** [no obj.] express an objection to what someone has said or done: *before Muriel could protest, he had filled both glasses.* ■ publicly demonstrate strong objection to an official policy or course of action: *doctors and patients **protested against** plans to cut services at the hospital* | [with obj.] N. Amer. *the workers were protesting economic measures enacted a week earlier.*
2 [reporting verb] declare (something) firmly and emphatically in response to doubt or accusation: [with direct speech] *'I'm not being coy!' Lucy protested* | [with obj.] *she has always protested her innocence.*
3 [with obj.] Law write or obtain a protest in regard to (a bill).
– PHRASES **under protest** after expressing one's objection or reluctance; unwillingly: *'I'm only here under protest,' Jenna said shortly.*
– DERIVATIVES **protestingly** adverb.
– ORIGIN late Middle English (as a verb in the sense 'make a solemn declaration'): from Old French *protester*, from Latin *protestari*, from *pro-* 'forth, publicly' + *testari* 'assert' (from *testis* 'witness').

Protestant /'prɒtɪst(ə)nt/ ▶ **noun** a member or follower of any of the Western Christian Churches that are separate from the Roman Catholic Church in accordance with the principles of the Reformation, including the Baptist, Presbyterian, and Lutheran Churches.

> Protestants are so called after the declaration (*protestatio*) of Martin Luther and his supporters dissenting from the decision of the Diet of Spires (1529), which reaffirmed the edict of the Diet of Worms against the Reformation. All Protestants reject the authority of the papacy, both religious and political, and find authority in the text of the Bible, made available to all in vernacular translation.

▶ **adjective** relating to or belonging to any of the Protestant Churches.
– DERIVATIVES **Protestantization** (also **Protestantisation**) noun, **Protestantize** (also **Protestantise**) verb.
– ORIGIN mid 16th cent.: via German or French from Latin *protestant-* 'protesting', from Latin *protestari* (see **PROTEST**).

Protestant ascendancy ▶ **noun** historical the domination of the Anglo-Irish Protestant minority in Ireland, especially in the 18th and 19th centuries. ■ the members of the landed aristocracy comprising this minority.

Protestant ethic (also **Protestant work ethic**) ▶ **noun** the view that a person's duty and responsibility is to achieve success through hard work and thrift.
– ORIGIN translating German *die protestantische Ethik*, coined (1904) by the economist Max Weber in his thesis on the relationship between the teachings of Calvin and the rise of capitalism.

Protestantism ▶ **noun** [mass noun] the faith, practice, and Church order of the Protestant Churches. ■ adherence to the forms of Christian doctrine which are generally regarded as Protestant rather than Catholic or Eastern Orthodox.

protestation /ˌprɒtɪ'steɪʃ(ə)n/ ▶ **noun 1** an emphatic declaration in response to doubt or accusation: *her protestations of innocence were in vain* | [mass noun] *no amount of protestation made any difference.*
2 an objection or protest: *he was warned by the referee for his loud protestations.*
– ORIGIN Middle English: from Old French, from late Latin *protestatio(n-)*, from *protestari* 'to protest' (see **PROTEST**).

protester (also **protestor**) ▶ **noun** a person who publicly demonstrates opposition to something; a demonstrator: *the decision was hailed by **protesters against** the closure as a triumph.*

Proteus /'prəʊtɪəs/ **1** Greek Mythology a minor sea god who had the power of prophecy but would assume different shapes to avoid answering questions.
2 Astronomy a satellite of Neptune, the sixth closest to the planet, discovered by the Voyager 2 space probe in 1989 (diameter 400 km).

proteus /'prəʊtɪəs/ ▶ **noun 1** a bacterium found in the intestines of animals and in the soil. ● Genus *Proteus*; motile Gram-negative rods.
2 another term for **OLM**.
– ORIGIN early 19th cent.: from **PROTEUS**.

prothalamium /ˌprəʊθə'leɪmɪəm/ ▶ **noun** (pl. **prothalamia** /-mɪə/) literary a song or poem celebrating a forthcoming wedding.
– ORIGIN late 16th cent.: from *Prothalamion*, the title of a poem by Spenser, on the pattern of *epithalamium*.

prothallus /prəʊ'θaləs/ ▶ **noun** (pl. **prothalli** /-lʌɪ, -liː/) Botany the gametophyte of ferns and related plants.
– DERIVATIVES **prothallial** adjective.
– ORIGIN mid 19th cent.: modern Latin, from **PRO-**[2] 'before, earlier' + Greek *thallos* 'green shoot'.

prothesis /'prɒθɪsɪs/ ▶ **noun** (pl. **protheses** /-siːz/)
1 [mass noun] Christian Church (especially in the Orthodox Church) the action of placing the Eucharistic elements on the credence table. ■ [count noun] a credence table. ■ [count noun] the part of a church where the credence table stands.
2 Linguistics another term for **PROSTHESIS** (sense 2).
– DERIVATIVES **prothetic** adjective.
– ORIGIN late 16th cent. (in sense 2): from Greek, 'placing before or in public view', from *pro* 'before' + *thesis* 'placing'.

prothonotary /ˌprəʊθə'nəʊt(ə)ri, prə'θɒnə-/ ▶ **noun** variant spelling of **PROTONOTARY**.

prothonotary warbler ▶ **noun** a North American warbler, the male of which has a golden-yellow head, breast, and underparts. ● *Protonotaria citrea*, family Parulidae.
– ORIGIN late 18th cent.: named with reference to the saffron colour of the robes worn by clerks to the Pope (see **PROTONOTARY APOSTOLIC**).

prothorax ▶ **noun** Entomology the anterior segment of the thorax of an insect, not bearing any wings.
– DERIVATIVES **prothoracic** adjective.

prothrombin /prəʊ'θrɒmbɪn/ ▶ **noun** [mass noun] Biochemistry a protein present in blood plasma which is converted into active thrombin during coagulation.

Protista /prəʊ'tɪstə/ ▶ **plural noun** Biology a kingdom or large grouping that comprises mostly single-celled organisms such as the protozoa, simple algae and fungi, slime moulds, and (formerly) the bacteria. They are now divided among up to thirty phyla, and some have both plant and animal characteristics.
– DERIVATIVES **protist** /'prəʊtɪst/ noun, **protistan** adjective & noun, **protistology** noun.
– ORIGIN modern Latin (plural), from Greek *prōtista*, neuter plural of *prōtistos* 'very first', superlative of *prōtos* 'first'.

protium /'prəʊtɪəm/ ▶ **noun** [mass noun] Chemistry the common, stable isotope of hydrogen, as distinct from deuterium and tritium.
– ORIGIN 1930s: modern Latin, from Greek *prōtos* 'first'.

proto- (usu. **prot-** before a vowel) ▶ **combining form** original or primitive: *prototherian* | *prototype.* ■ first or earliest: *protomartyr* | *protozoon.*
– ORIGIN from Greek *prōtos* 'first'.

protoceratops /ˌprəʊtə(ʊ)'sɛrətɒps/ ▶ **noun** a small quadrupedal dinosaur of the late Cretaceous period, having a bony frill above the neck and probably ancestral to triceratops. ● Genus *Protoceratops*, infraorder Ceratopsia, order Ornithischia.

protocol ▶ **noun 1** [mass noun] the official procedure or system of rules governing affairs of state or diplomatic occasions: *protocol forbids the prince from making any public statement in his defence.* ■ the accepted or established code of procedure or behaviour in any group, organization, or situation: *what is the protocol at a smart lunch if one's neighbour dozes off during the speeches?*
2 the original draft of a diplomatic document, especially of the terms of a treaty agreed to in conference and signed by the parties. ■ an amendment or addition to a treaty or convention: *a protocol to the treaty allowed for this Danish referendum.*
3 a formal or official record of scientific experimental observations. ■ a procedure for carrying out a scientific experiment or a course of medical treatment.
4 Computing a set of rules governing the exchange or transmission of data between devices.
– ORIGIN late Middle English (denoting the original minute of an agreement, forming the legal authority for future dealings relating to it): from Old French *prothocole*, via medieval Latin from Greek *prōtokollon* 'first page, flyleaf', from *prōtos* 'first' + *kolla* 'glue'. Sense 1 derives from French *protocole*, the collection of set forms of etiquette to be observed by the French head of state, and the name of the government department responsible for this (in the 19th cent.).

Protoctista /ˌprəʊtɒk'tɪstə/ ▶ **plural noun** Biology a kingdom or large grouping that is either synonymous with the Protista or equivalent to the Protista together with their multicellular descendants.
– DERIVATIVES **protoctist** noun.
– ORIGIN modern Latin (plural), based on Greek *prōtos* 'first'.

protogalaxy ▶ **noun** (pl. **protogalaxies**) Astronomy a vast mass of gas from which a galaxy is thought to develop.
– DERIVATIVES **protogalactic** adjective.

Proto-Germanic ▶ **noun** see **GERMANIC**.

protogynous /prəʊ'tɒdʒɪnəs/ ▶ **adjective** Botany & Zoology (of a hermaphrodite flower or animal) having the female reproductive organs come to maturity before the male. The opposite of **PROTANDROUS**.
– DERIVATIVES **protogyny** noun.

protohuman Anthropology ▶ **noun** a hypothetical prehistoric primate, resembling humans and thought to be their ancestor, whose profile has been compiled mainly from fossil evidence.
▶ **adjective** relating to or denoting a protohuman.

Proto-Indo-European ▶ **noun** [mass noun] the lost language from which all Indo-European languages derive. See **INDO-EUROPEAN**.
▶ **adjective** relating to Proto-Indo-European.

protolanguage ▶ **noun** a hypothetical lost parent language from which actual languages are derived.

protomartyr ▶ **noun** the first martyr for a cause, especially the first Christian martyr, St Stephen.

proton /'prəʊtɒn/ ▶ **noun** Physics a stable subatomic particle occurring in all atomic nuclei, with a positive electric charge equal in magnitude to that of an electron.

> The mass of the proton is 1,836 times greater than that of the electron. The atoms of each chemical element have a characteristic number of protons in the nucleus; this is known as the atomic number. The common isotope of hydrogen has a nucleus consisting of a single proton.

– DERIVATIVES **protonic** adjective.
– ORIGIN 1920s: from Greek, neuter of *prōtos* 'first'.

protonate /'prəʊt(ə)neɪt/ ▶ **verb** [with obj.] Chemistry transfer a proton to (a molecule, group, or atom) which forms a coordinate bond to the proton.
– DERIVATIVES **protonation** noun.

protonotary /ˌprəʊtə'nəʊt(ə)ri, prə'tɒnət(ə)ri/ (also **prothonotary**) ▶ **noun** (pl. **protonotaries**) chiefly historical a chief clerk in some law courts, originally in the Byzantine court.
– ORIGIN late Middle English: via medieval Latin from late Greek *prōtonotarios*, from *prōtos* 'first' + *notarios* 'notary'.

Protonotary Apostolic (also **Protonotary Apostolical**) ▶ **noun** a member of the Roman Catholic college of prelates who register papal acts and direct the canonization of saints.

protopathic /ˌprəʊtə(ʊ)'paθɪk/ ▶ **adjective** Physiology relating to or denoting those sensory nerve fibres of the skin which are capable of discriminating only between relatively coarse stimuli, chiefly heat, cold, and pain. Often contrasted with **EPICRITIC**.
– ORIGIN mid 19th cent.: from **PROTO-** 'primitive' + Greek *pathos* 'suffering, feeling' + **-IC**.

protoplasm /'prəʊtə(ʊ)ˌplaz(ə)m/ ▶ **noun** [mass noun] Biology the colourless material comprising the living part of a cell, including the cytoplasm, nucleus, and other organelles.
– DERIVATIVES **protoplasmic** adjective.
– ORIGIN mid 19th cent.: from Greek *prōtoplasma* (see **PROTO-**, **PLASMA**).

protoplast /'prəʊtə(ʊ)plast, -plɑːst/ ▶ **noun** chiefly Botany the protoplasm of a living plant or bacterial cell whose cell wall has been removed.
– ORIGIN late 19th cent.: from Greek *prōtoplastos* 'first formed', from *prōtos* 'first' + *plassein* 'to mould'.

protopodite /prəʊˈtɒpədʌɪt/ (also **protopod** /ˈprəʊtə(ʊ)pɒd/) ▸ **noun** Zoology the basal segments of the biramous limb or appendage of a crustacean. Compare with **ENDOPODITE**, **EXOPODITE**.
– ORIGIN late 19th cent.: from **PROTO-** 'early, original' + Greek *pous*, *pod-* 'foot' + **-ITE**[1].

protostar ▸ **noun** Astronomy a contracting mass of gas which represents an early stage in the formation of a star, before nucleosynthesis has begun.

protostome /ˈprəʊtə(ʊ)stəʊm/ ▸ **noun** Zoology a multicellular organism whose mouth develops from a primary embryonic opening, such as an annelid, mollusc, or arthropod.
– ORIGIN 1950s: from **PROTO-** 'primitive' + Greek *stoma* 'mouth'.

Prototheria /ˌprəʊtə(ʊ)ˈθɪərɪə/ ▸ **plural noun** Zoology a group of mammals that comprises the monotremes and their extinct relatives. Compare with **THERIA**.
● Subclass Prototheria, class Mammalia.
– ORIGIN modern Latin (plural), from **PROTO-** 'first, original' + Greek *thēr* 'wild beast'.

prototherian Zoology ▸ **noun** a mammal of the group Prototheria, which comprises the monotremes and their extinct relatives.
▸ **adjective** relating to or denoting prototherians.

prototype ▸ **noun 1** a first or preliminary version of a device or vehicle from which other forms are developed: *the firm is testing a prototype of the weapon.* ■ the first, original, or typical form of something; an archetype: *these objects are the prototypes of a category of rapidly spinning neutron stars.*
2 Electronics a basic filter network with specified cut-off frequencies, from which other networks may be derived to obtain sharper cut-offs, constancy of characteristic impedance with frequency, etc.
▸ **verb** [with obj.] make a prototype of (a product).
– DERIVATIVES **prototypal** adjective, **prototypic** adjective, **prototypical** adjective, **prototypically** adverb.
– ORIGIN late 16th cent. (denoting the original of which something else is a copy or derivative): via French or late Latin from Greek *prōtotupos* (see **PROTO-**, **TYPE**).

Protozoa /ˌprəʊtəˈzəʊə/ ▸ **plural noun** Zoology a phylum or grouping of phyla which comprises the single-celled microscopic animals, which include amoebas, flagellates, ciliates, sporozoans, and many other forms. They are now usually treated as a number of phyla belonging to the kingdom Protista. ■ (**protozoa**) organisms of this group.
– ORIGIN modern Latin (plural), from **PROTO-** 'first' + Greek *zōion* 'animal'.

protozoan Zoology ▸ **noun** a single-celled microscopic animal of a group of phyla of the kingdom Protista, such as an amoeba, flagellate, ciliate, or sporozoan.
▸ **adjective** relating to or denoting protozoans.
– DERIVATIVES **protozoal** adjective, **protozoic** adjective, **protozoon** noun.

protract ▸ **verb** [with obj.] prolong: *he had certainly taken his time, even protracting the process.*
– ORIGIN mid 16th cent.: from Latin *protract-* 'prolonged', from the verb *protrahere*, from *pro-* 'out' + *trahere* 'to draw'.

protracted ▸ **adjective** lasting for a long time or longer than expected or usual: *a protracted and bitter dispute.*
– DERIVATIVES **protractedly** adverb.

protractile /prəˈtraktʌɪl, -tɪl/ ▸ **adjective** another term for **PROTRUSIBLE**.

protraction ▸ **noun** [mass noun] **1** the action of prolonging something or the state of being prolonged: *the protraction of the war.*
2 the action of extending a part of the body.
– ORIGIN mid 16th cent.: from French, or from late Latin *protractio(n-)*, from *protrahere* 'prolong' (see **PROTRACT**).

protractor ▸ **noun 1** an instrument for measuring angles, typically in the form of a flat semicircle marked with degrees along the curved edge.
2 (also **protractor muscle**) chiefly Zoology a muscle serving to extend a part of the body. Compare with **RETRACTOR**.

protrude ▸ **verb** [no obj.] extend beyond or above a surface: *something like a fin protruded from the water.* ■ [with obj.] (of an animal) cause (a body part) to protrude.
– DERIVATIVES **protrusive** adjective.
– ORIGIN early 17th cent. (in the sense 'thrust something forward or onward'): from Latin *protrudere*, from *pro-* 'forward, out' + *trudere* 'to thrust'.

protruding ▸ **adjective** sticking out; projecting: *a stocky guy with a furrowed brow and a protruding bottom lip.*

protrusible (also **protrusile**) ▸ **adjective** Zoology (of a body part, such as the jaws of a fish) capable of being protruded or extended.
– ORIGIN mid 19th cent.: from Latin *protrus-* 'extended or thrust forward' (from the verb *protrudere*) + **-IBLE**.

protrusion ▸ **noun** something that protrudes; a protuberance: *a protrusion of rock jutted from the mountainside.*

protuberance /prəˈtjuːb(ə)r(ə)ns/ ▸ **noun** a thing that protrudes from something else: *some dinosaurs evolved protuberances on top of their heads.* ■ [mass noun] the fact or state of protruding: *the large size and protuberance of the incisors.*

protuberant ▸ **adjective** protruding; bulging: *his protuberant eyes fluttered open.*
– ORIGIN mid 17th cent.: from late Latin *protuberant-* 'swelling out', from the verb *protuberare*, from *pro-* 'forward, out' + *tuber* 'bump'.

Protura /prə(ʊ)ˈtjʊərə/ ▸ **plural noun** Entomology an order of minute white wingless insects with slender bodies. They lack eyes and antennae, using the first pair of legs as sensory organs. ● Order Protura, subclass Apterygota, class Insecta (or Hexapoda).
– DERIVATIVES **proturan** noun & adjective.
– ORIGIN modern Latin (plural), from Greek *prōtos* 'first, primitive'.

proud ▸ **adjective 1** feeling deep pleasure or satisfaction as a result of one's own achievements, qualities, or possessions or those of someone with whom one is closely associated: *a proud grandma of three boys* | *she got nine passes and he was so* **proud of** *her.* ■ (of an event, achievement, etc.) causing someone to feel proud: *we have a proud history of innovation.*
2 having or showing a high or excessively high opinion of oneself or one's importance: *he was a proud, arrogant man.* ■ conscious of one's own dignity: *I was too proud to go home.* ■ imposing; splendid: *bulrushes emerge tall and proud from the middle of the pond.*
3 [predic.] Brit. slightly projecting from a surface: *balls standing* **proud of** *the fabric.* ■ denoting flesh that has grown round a healing wound with excessive granulation of the tissues.
– PHRASES **do someone proud** informal act in a way that gives someone cause to feel pleased or satisfied: *they did themselves proud in a game which sent the fans home happy.* ■ treat someone very well, typically by lavishly feeding or entertaining them.
– DERIVATIVES **proudly** adverb, **proudness** noun.
– ORIGIN late Old English *prūt*, *prūd* 'having a high opinion of one's own worth', from Old French *prud* 'valiant', based on Latin *prodesse* 'be of value'. The phrase *proud flesh* dates back to late Middle English, but the sense 'slightly projecting' is first recorded in English dialect of the 19th cent.

Proudhon /ˈpruːdɒ̃/, French /pʀydɔ̃/, Pierre Joseph (1809–65), French social philosopher and journalist. His pamphlet *What is Property?* (1840) argues that property, in the sense of the exploitation of one person's labour by another, is theft.

Proust[1] /pruːst/, Joseph Louis (1754–1826), French analytical chemist. He proposed the law of constant proportions, demonstrating that any pure sample of a chemical compound (such as an oxide of a metal) always contains the same elements in fixed proportions.

Proust[2] /pruːst/, Marcel (1871–1922), French novelist, essayist, and critic. He devoted much of his life to writing his novel *À la recherche du temps perdu* (published in seven sections between 1913 and 1927). Its central theme is the recovery of the lost past and the releasing of its creative energies through the stimulation of unconscious memory.
– DERIVATIVES **Proustian** adjective.

Prov. ▸ **abbreviation** ■ Proverbs (in biblical references). ■ chiefly Canadian Province or Provincial.

prove /pruːv/ ▸ **verb** (past participle **proved** or **proven** /ˈpruːv(ə)n, ˈprəʊ-/) **1** [with obj.] demonstrate the truth or existence of (something) by evidence or argument: *the concept is difficult to prove* | (as adj. **proven**) *a proven ability to work hard.* ■ (US **prove something up**) Law establish the genuineness and validity of (a will).
2 [with obj. and complement] demonstrate to be the specified thing by evidence or argument: *if they are proved guilty we won't trade with them.* ■ [no obj., with complement] be seen or found to be: *the scheme has proved a great success.* ■ (**prove oneself**) demonstrate one's abilities or courage. ■ [with obj.] rare test the accuracy of (a mathematical calculation). ■ [with obj.] subject (a gun) to a testing process.
3 [no obj.] (of bread dough) become aerated by the action of yeast; rise.
– PHRASES **not proven** Scots Law a verdict that there is insufficient evidence to establish guilt or innocence. **prove someone wrong** show that what someone says is wrong or incorrect: *if you can prove me wrong let me know and I'll update the review.*
– DERIVATIVES **provability** noun, **provable** adjective, **provably** adverb, **prover** noun.
– ORIGIN Middle English: from Old French *prover*, from Latin *probare* 'test, approve, demonstrate', from *probus* 'good'.

> **USAGE** For complex historical reasons, **prove** developed two past participles: **proved** and **proven**. Both are correct and can be used more or less interchangeably (*this hasn't been* **proved** *yet*; *this hasn't been* **proven** *yet*). In British English **proved** is more common, with the exception that **proven** is always used when the word is an adjective coming before the noun: *a* **proven** *talent*, not *a* **proved** *talent*.

provenance /ˈprɒv(ə)nəns/ ▸ **noun** [mass noun] the place of origin or earliest known history of something: *an orange rug of Iranian provenance.* ■ [count noun] a record of ownership of a work of art or an antique, used as a guide to authenticity or quality: *the manuscript has a distinguished provenance.*
– ORIGIN late 18th cent.: from French, from the verb *provenir* 'come or stem from', from Latin *provenire*, from *pro-* 'forth' + *venire* 'come'.

Provençal /ˌprɒvɒ̃ˈsɑːl/, French /pʀɔvɑ̃sal/ ▸ **adjective** relating to or denoting Provence or its people or language.
▸ **noun 1** a native or inhabitant of Provence.
2 [mass noun] the language of Provence.

> Provençal is a Romance language closely related to French, Italian, and Catalan; it is sometimes called *langue d'oc* (or Occitan), though strictly speaking it is one dialect of this. In the 12th–14th centuries it was the language of the troubadours and cultured speakers of southern France, but the spread of the northern dialects of French led to its decline.

– ORIGIN French, from Latin *provincialis* 'provincial'.

provençale /ˌprɒvɒ̃ˈsɑːl/ ▸ **adjective** [postpositive] denoting a dish cooked in a sauce made with tomatoes, garlic, and olive oil: *chicken provençale.*
– ORIGIN from French *à la provençale* 'in the Provençal style'.

Provence /prɒˈvɒ̃s/, French /pʀɔvɑ̃s/ a former province of SE France, on the Mediterranean coast east of the Rhône. Settled by the Greeks in the 6th century BC, the area around Marseilles became, in the 1st century BC, part of the Roman colony of Gaul. It was united with France in 1481 and is now part of the region of Provence–Alpes–Côte d'Azur.
– ORIGIN from Latin *provincia* 'province', a colloquial name for southern Gaul, the first Roman province to be established outside Italy.

provender /ˈprɒvɪndə/ ▸ **noun** [mass noun] dated animal fodder. ■ chiefly humorous food.
– ORIGIN Middle English: from Old French *provendre*, based on an alteration of Latin *praebenda* 'things to be supplied' (see **PREBEND**).

provenience /prəˈviːnɪəns/ ▸ **noun** US term for **PROVENANCE**.

proventriculus /ˌprəʊvɛnˈtrɪkjʊləs/ ▸ **noun** (pl. **proventriculi**) Zoology the narrow glandular first region of a bird's stomach between the crop and the gizzard. ■ the thick-walled muscular expansion of the oesophagus above the stomach of crustaceans and insects.
– ORIGIN mid 19th cent.: from **PRO-**[2] 'before' + Latin *ventriculus* 'small belly', diminutive of *venter*, *ventr-* 'belly'.

proverb ▸ **noun** a short, well-known pithy saying, stating a general truth or piece of advice.
– ORIGIN Middle English: from Old French *proverbe*, from Latin *proverbium*, from *pro-* '(put) forth' + *verbum* 'word'.

proverbial ▸ **adjective** (of a word or phrase) referred to in a proverb or idiom: *I'm going to stick out like the proverbial sore thumb.* ■ well known, especially so as to be stereotypical: *the Welsh people, whose hospitality is proverbial.*
▸ **noun** used to stand for a word or phrase that is normally part of a proverb or idiom but is not actually uttered: *one word out of line, and the proverbial hits the fan.*

– DERIVATIVES **proverbiality** noun, **proverbially** adverb.
– ORIGIN late Middle English: from Latin *proverbialis*, from *proverbium* (see PROVERB).

Proverbs (also **Book of Proverbs**) a book of the Bible containing maxims attributed mainly to Solomon.

pro-vice-chancellor ▸ noun an assistant or deputy vice chancellor of a university.

provide ▸ verb **1** [with obj.] make available for use; supply: *these clubs provide a much appreciated service for this area.* ■ (**provide someone with**) equip or supply someone with (something useful or necessary): *we were provided with a map of the area.* ■ present or yield (something useful): *neither will provide answers to these problems.*
2 [no obj.] (**provide for**) make adequate preparation for (a possible event): *new qualifications must provide for changes in technology.* ■ supply sufficient money to ensure the maintenance of (someone): *Emma was handsomely provided for in Frannie's will.* ■ (of a law) enable or allow (something to be done).
3 [with clause] stipulate in a will or other legal document: *the order should be varied to provide that there would be no contact with the father.*
4 [with obj.] (**provide someone to**) Christian Church, historical appoint an incumbent to (a benefice).
– ORIGIN late Middle English (also in the sense 'prepare to do, get ready'): from Latin *providere* 'foresee, attend to', from *pro-* 'before' + *videre* 'to see'.

provided ▸ conjunction on the condition or understanding that: *cutting corners was acceptable, provided that you could get away with it.*

Providence the state capital of Rhode Island, a port on the Atlantic coast; pop. 171,557 (est. 2008). It was founded in 1636 as a haven for religious dissenters.

providence ▸ noun [mass noun] **1** the protective care of God or of nature as a spiritual power: *they found their trust in divine providence to be a source of comfort.* ■ (**Providence**) God or nature as providing protective care: *I live out my life as Providence decrees.*
2 timely preparation for future eventualities: *it was considered a duty to encourage providence.*
– ORIGIN late Middle English: from Old French, from Latin *providentia*, from *providere* 'foresee, attend to' (see PROVIDE).

provident ▸ adjective making or indicative of timely preparation for the future: *she had learned to be provident.*
– DERIVATIVES **providently** adverb.
– ORIGIN late Middle English: from Latin *provident-* 'foreseeing, attending to', from the verb *providere* (see PROVIDE).

P

provident fund ▸ noun (especially in South East Asia) an investment fund contributed to by employees, employers, and (sometimes) the state, out of which a lump sum is provided to each employee on retirement.

providential ▸ adjective **1** occurring at a favourable time; opportune: *his appearance had seemed more than just providential.*
2 involving divine foresight or providence.
– DERIVATIVES **providentially** adverb.
– ORIGIN mid 17th cent.: from PROVIDENCE, on the pattern of *evidential*.

Provident Society ▸ noun Brit. another term for FRIENDLY SOCIETY.

provider ▸ noun a person or thing that provides something: *a leading provider of personal financial services.* ■ a person who earns money to support their family.

providing ▸ conjunction on the condition or understanding that: *we have the team which can win the league, providing we avoid bad injuries.*

Provie /'prəʊvi, 'prɒvi/ ▸ noun informal another term for **Provo**.

province ▸ noun **1** a principal administrative division of a country or empire: *Chengdu, capital of Sichuan province.* ■ (**the Province**) Brit. Northern Ireland. ■ Christian Church a district under an archbishop or a metropolitan. ■ Roman History a territory outside Italy under a Roman governor.
2 (**the provinces**) Brit. the whole of a country outside the capital, especially when regarded as lacking in sophistication or culture: *I made my way home to the dreary provinces by train.*
3 (**one's province**) an area of special knowledge, interest, or responsibility: *she knew little about wine—that had been her father's province.*
– ORIGIN late Middle English: from Old French, from Latin *provincia* 'charge, province', of uncertain ultimate origin.

provincial ▸ adjective **1** of or concerning a province of a country or empire: *provincial elections.*
2 of or concerning the regions outside the capital city of a country, especially when regarded as unsophisticated or narrow-minded: *provincial towns | the whole exhibition struck one as being very provincial.*
▸ noun **1** an inhabitant of a province of a country or empire.
2 an inhabitant of the regions outside the capital city of a country, especially when regarded as unsophisticated or narrow-minded. ■ (**provincials**) Brit. local newspapers, as contrasted with national ones.
3 Christian Church the head or chief of a province or of a religious order in a province.
– DERIVATIVES **provinciality** noun, **provincially** adverb.
– ORIGIN late Middle English: from Old French, from Latin *provincialis* 'belonging to a province' (see PROVINCE).

provincialism ▸ noun [mass noun] **1** the way of life characteristic of the regions outside the capital city of a country, especially when regarded as unsophisticated or narrow-minded. ■ narrow-mindedness, insularity, or lack of sophistication.
2 concern for one's own area or region at the expense of national or supranational unity.
3 [count noun] a word or phrase peculiar to a local area.
4 Ecology the degree to which plant or animal communities are restricted to particular areas.
– DERIVATIVES **provincialist** noun & adjective.

proving ground ▸ noun an area or situation in which a person or thing is tested or proved.

provirus /prəʊ'vʌɪrəs/ ▸ noun Microbiology the genetic material of a virus as incorporated into, and able to replicate with, the genome of a host cell.
– DERIVATIVES **proviral** adjective.

provision ▸ noun [mass noun] **1** the action of providing or supplying something for use: *new contracts for the provision of services.* ■ (**provision for/against**) financial or other arrangements for future eventualities or requirements: *farmers have been slow to **make provision for** their retirement.* ■ [count noun] an amount set aside out of profits in the accounts of an organization for a known liability, especially a bad debt or the diminution in value of an asset.
2 an amount or thing supplied or provided: *changing levels of transport provision.* ■ (**provisions**) supplies of food, drink, or equipment, especially for a journey.
3 [count noun] a condition or requirement in a legal document: *the first private prosecution **under the provisions of** the 1989 Water Act.*
4 [count noun] Christian Church, historical an appointment to a benefice, especially directly by the Pope rather than by the patron, and originally before it became vacant.
▸ verb **1** [with obj.] supply with food, drink, or equipment, especially for a journey.
2 [no obj.] set aside an amount in an organization's accounts for a known liability: *financial institutions have to **provision against** loan losses.*
– DERIVATIVES **provisioner** noun.
– ORIGIN late Middle English (also in the sense 'foresight'): via Old French from Latin *provisio(n-)*, from *providere* 'foresee, attend to' (see PROVIDE). The verb dates from the early 19th cent.

provisional ▸ adjective **1** arranged or existing for the present, possibly to be changed later: *a provisional government | provisional bookings.* ■ Brit. (of a driving licence) to be obtained before starting to learn to drive and upgraded to a full licence on passing a driving test. ■ (of a postage stamp) put into circulation temporarily, usually owing to the unavailability of the definitive issue.
2 (**Provisional**) denoting the unofficial wings of the IRA and Sinn Fein established in 1969 and advocating terrorism.
▸ noun **1** a provisional stamp.
2 (**Provisional**) a member of the Provisional wings of the IRA or Sinn Fein.
– DERIVATIVES **provisionality** noun.

provisionally ▸ adverb subject to further confirmation; for the time being: *the film, provisionally entitled Skin, is due to be released next year.*

proviso /prə'vʌɪzəʊ/ ▸ noun (pl. **provisos**) a condition or qualification attached to an agreement or statement: *he let his house **with the proviso that** his own staff should remain to run it.*
– ORIGIN late Middle English: from the medieval Latin phrase *proviso (quod)* 'it being provided (that)', from Latin *providere* 'foresee, provide'.

provisor ▸ noun **1** (in the Roman Catholic Church) a deputy of a bishop or archbishop.
2 Christian Church, historical the holder of a provision.
– ORIGIN late Middle English: from Anglo-Norman French *provisour*, from Latin *provisor*, from *provis-* 'provided' (see PROVISION).

provisory ▸ adjective rare **1** subject to a proviso; conditional.
2 provisional.
– ORIGIN early 17th cent.: from French *provisoire* or medieval Latin *provisorius*, from *provis-* 'foreseen, attended to', from the verb *providere* (see PROVIDE).

provitamin ▸ noun Biochemistry a substance which is converted into a vitamin within an organism.

Provo /'prəʊvəʊ/ ▸ noun (pl. **Provos**) informal term for PROVISIONAL (sense 2 of the noun).

provocation ▸ noun [mass noun] **1** action or speech that makes someone angry, especially deliberately: *you should remain calm and not respond to provocation | he burst into tears **at the slightest provocation**.* ■ Law action or speech held to be likely to prompt physical retaliation: *the assault had taken place **under provocation**.*
2 the action of arousing sexual desire or interest, especially deliberately: *walking with deliberate provocation, she struck a pose, then giggled.*
3 Medicine testing to elicit a particular response or reflex.
– ORIGIN late Middle English: from Old French, from Latin *provocatio(n-)*, from the verb *provocare* (see PROVOKE).

provocative ▸ adjective causing anger or another strong reaction, especially deliberately: *a provocative article | his provocative remarks on race.* ■ intended or intending to arouse sexual desire or interest: *a provocative sidelong glance.*
– DERIVATIVES **provocatively** adverb, **provocativeness** noun.
– ORIGIN late Middle English: from Old French *provocatif, -ive*, from late Latin *provocativus*, from *provocat-* 'called forth, challenged', from the verb *provocare* (see PROVOKE).

provoke ▸ verb [with obj.] stimulate or give rise to (a reaction or emotion, typically a strong or unwelcome one) in someone: *the decision provoked a storm of protest from civil rights organizations.* ■ stimulate or incite (someone) to do or feel something, especially by arousing anger in them: *a teacher can **provoke** you **into** working harder.* ■ deliberately make (someone) annoyed or angry: *Rachel refused to be provoked.*
– DERIVATIVES **provokable** adjective, **provoker** noun.
– ORIGIN late Middle English (also in the sense 'invoke, summon'): from Old French *provoquer*, from Latin *provocare* 'challenge', from *pro-* 'forth' + *vocare* 'to call'.

provoking ▸ adjective **1** causing annoyance; irritating: *there is evidence of provoking conduct and loss of self-control.*
2 [in combination] giving rise to the specified reaction or emotion: *fear-provoking | laughter-provoking.*
– DERIVATIVES **provokingly** adverb.

provolone /ˌprɒvə'ləʊneɪ, -'ləʊni/ ▸ noun [mass noun] an Italian soft smoked cheese made from cow's milk and having a mellow flavour.
– ORIGIN Italian, from *provola* 'buffalo's milk cheese'.

provost /'prɒvəst/ ▸ noun **1** Brit. the head of certain university colleges, especially at Oxford or Cambridge, and public schools. ■ N. Amer. a senior administrative officer in certain universities.
2 Scottish term for MAYOR. See also LORD PROVOST.
3 the head of a chapter in a cathedral. ■ the Protestant minister of the principal church of a town or district in Germany and certain other European countries. ■ historical the head of a Christian community.
4 short for PROVOST MARSHAL.
5 historical the chief magistrate of a French or other European town.
– DERIVATIVES **provostship** noun.
– ORIGIN late Old English *profost* 'head of a chapter, prior', reinforced in Middle English by Anglo-Norman French *provost*, from medieval Latin *propositus*, synonym of Latin *praepositus* 'head, chief' (see PRAEPOSTOR).

provost guard ▸ noun US a detachment of soldiers acting as military police under the command of a provost marshal.

provost marshal ▶ noun the head of military police in camp or on active service. ■ (in the Royal Navy) a senior commissioned officer in the Regulatory Branch or Naval Dockyard Port.

prow /praʊ/ ▶ noun the pointed front part of a ship; the bow. ■ the pointed or projecting front part of something such as a car or building.
– ORIGIN mid 16th cent.: from Old French *proue*, from Provençal *proa*, probably via Latin from Greek *prōira*, from a base represented by Latin *pro* 'in front'.

prowess ▶ noun [mass noun] **1** skill or expertise in a particular activity or field: *his prowess as a fisherman* | *her culinary prowess.*
2 bravery in battle.
– ORIGIN Middle English (in sense 2): from Old French *proesce*, from *prou* 'valiant'. Sense 1 dates from the early 20th cent.

prowfish /ˈpraʊfɪʃ/ ▶ noun (pl. **same** or **prowfishes**) any of a number of marine fishes that typically have dark spots and a dorsal fin extending the length of the body: ● a scaleless Australian fish that has a deep head and tapers towards the tail (family Pataecidae: several genera). ● a fish of the North Pacific (*Zaprora silenus*, the only member of the family Zaproridae).

prowl ▶ verb [no obj.] (of a person or animal) move about restlessly and stealthily, especially in search of prey: *lions prowling in the bush* | [with obj.] *youngsters were prowling the streets in droves.*
▶ noun an act of prowling.
– PHRASES **on the prowl** prowling around in search of prey.
– ORIGIN late Middle English: of unknown origin.

prowl car ▶ noun US a police squad car.

prowler ▶ noun a person who moves stealthily about or loiters near a place with a view to committing a crime.

prox. ▶ abbreviation proximo.

prox. acc. ▶ abbreviation proxime accessit.

proxemics /prɒkˈsiːmɪks/ ▶ plural noun [treated as sing.] the branch of knowledge that deals with the amount of space that people feel it necessary to set between themselves and others.
– ORIGIN 1960s: from PROXIMITY, on the pattern of words such as *phonemics*.

Proxima Centauri /ˌprɒksɪmə sɛnˈtɔːrʌɪ/ Astronomy a faint red dwarf star associated with the bright binary star Alpha Centauri. It is the closest known star to the solar system (distance 4.24 light years).
– ORIGIN Latin, 'nearest (star) of Centaurus'.

proximal ▶ adjective Anatomy situated nearer to the centre of the body or the point of attachment: *the proximal end of the forearm.* The opposite of DISTAL. ■ Geology relating to or denoting an area close to a centre of a geological process such as sedimentation or volcanism.
– DERIVATIVES **proximally** adverb.
– ORIGIN early 19th cent. (as a term in anatomy and zoology): from Latin *proximus* 'nearest' + -AL. In geology, usage dates from the 1940s.

proximate ▶ adjective **1** (especially of the cause of something) closest in relationship; immediate. ■ closest in space or time: *the failure of the proximate military power to lend assistance.*
2 nearly accurate; approximate.
– DERIVATIVES **proximately** adverb, **proximation** noun.
– ORIGIN late 16th cent.: from Latin *proximatus* 'drawn near', past participle of *proximare*, from *proximus* 'nearest'.

proxime accessit /ˌprɒksɪmeɪ akˈsɛsɪt, -mɪ/ ▶ noun used to name the person who comes second in an examination or is runner-up for an award: *winner: J. W. Wright; proxime accessit: T. G. Broadbent.*
– ORIGIN Latin, literally 'came very near'.

proximity ▶ noun [mass noun] nearness in space, time, or relationship: *do not operate microphones in close proximity to television sets.*
– ORIGIN late 15th cent.: from French *proximité*, from Latin *proximitas*, from *proximus* 'nearest'.

proximity fuse ▶ noun an electronic detonator that causes a projectile to explode when it comes within a preset distance of its target.

proximo /ˈprɒksɪməʊ/ ▶ adjective [postpositive] dated of next month: *he must be in Edinburgh on 1st proximo.*
– ORIGIN from Latin *proximo mense* 'in the next month'.

proxy ▶ noun (pl. **proxies**) **1** [mass noun] the authority to represent someone else, especially in voting: *Britons overseas may register to vote **by proxy**.* ■ [count noun] a person authorized to act on behalf of another. ■ [count noun] a document authorizing a person to vote on another's behalf.
2 a figure that can be used to represent the value of something in a calculation: *the use of a US wealth measure as **a proxy for** the true worldwide measure.*
– ORIGIN late Middle English: contraction of PROCURACY.

proxy war ▶ noun a war instigated by a major power which does not itself become involved.

Prozac /ˈprəʊzak/ ▶ noun trademark for FLUOXETINE.
– ORIGIN 1980s: an invented name.

prozone /ˈprəʊzəʊn/ ▶ noun [mass noun] Medicine (in testing for antigens) the range of relative quantities of precipitin (or agglutinin) and antigen within which any precipitation (or agglutination) is inhibited by the predominance of one component.
– ORIGIN early 20th cent.: from PRO-² 'before' + (*agglutination*) *zone*.

PRS ▶ abbreviation ■ Performing Rights Society. ■ (in the UK) President of the Royal Society.

prude ▶ noun a person who is or claims to be easily shocked by matters relating to sex or nudity.
– DERIVATIVES **prudery** noun.
– ORIGIN early 18th cent.: from French, back-formation from *prudefemme*, feminine of *prud'homme* 'good man and true', from *prou* 'worthy'.

prudence ▶ noun [mass noun] the quality of being prudent; cautiousness: *we need to **exercise prudence** in such important matters.*

prudent ▶ adjective acting with or showing care and thought for the future: *no prudent money manager would authorize a loan without first knowing its purpose.*
– DERIVATIVES **prudently** adverb.
– ORIGIN late Middle English: from Old French, or from Latin *prudent-*, contraction of *provident-* 'foreseeing, attending to' (see PROVIDENT).

prudential ▶ adjective involving or showing care and forethought, especially in business.
– DERIVATIVES **prudentially** adverb.
– ORIGIN late Middle English: from PRUDENT, on the pattern of words such as *evidential*.

Prudhoe Bay /ˈpruːdəʊ/ an inlet of the Arctic Ocean on the north coast of Alaska. It is a major centre of Alaskan oil production.

prudish ▶ adjective having or revealing a tendency to be easily shocked by matters relating to sex or nudity; excessively concerned with sexual propriety: *the prudish moral climate of the late 19th century.*
– DERIVATIVES **prudishly** adverb, **prudishness** noun.

pruinose /ˈpruːɪnəʊs, -z/ ▶ adjective chiefly Botany covered with white powdery granules; frosted in appearance.
ORIGIN early 19th cent.: from Latin *pruinosus*, from *pruina* 'hoar frost'.

prune¹ ▶ noun **1** a plum preserved by drying and having a black, wrinkled appearance.
2 informal an unpleasant or disagreeable person: *he was a good leader, but a right miserable old prune.*
– ORIGIN Middle English: from Old French, via Latin from Greek *prou(m)non* 'plum'.

prune² ▶ verb [with obj.] trim (a tree, shrub, or bush) by cutting away dead or overgrown branches or stems, especially to increase fruitfulness and growth. ■ cut away (a branch or stem) in this way: ***prune back** the branches.* ■ reduce the extent of (something) by removing superfluous or unwanted parts: *the workforce was pruned.* ■ remove (superfluous or unwanted parts) from something: *Eliot deliberately **pruned away** details.*
▶ noun [in sing.] an instance of trimming a tree, shrub, or bush.
– DERIVATIVES **pruner** noun.
– ORIGIN late 15th cent. (in the sense 'abbreviate'): from Old French *pro(o)ignier*, possibly based on Latin *rotundus* 'round'.

prunella¹ /prʊˈnɛlə/ ▶ noun a plant of a genus that includes self-heal. Several kinds are cultivated as ground cover and rockery plants. ● Genus *Prunella*, family Labiatae.
– ORIGIN modern Latin, literally 'quinsy', in medieval Latin *brunella*, diminutive of *brunus* 'brown', denoting a disease causing a brown coating on the tongue. Self-heal was a reputed cure for the disease.

prunella² /prʊˈnɛlə/ ▶ noun [mass noun] a strong silk or worsted fabric used formerly for barristers' gowns and the uppers of women's shoes.
– ORIGIN mid 17th cent.: perhaps from French *prunelle* 'sloe' (because of its dark colour).

pruning hook ▶ noun a cutting tool used for pruning, consisting of a hooked blade on a long handle.

prunus /ˈpruːnəs/ ▶ noun a tree or shrub of a large genus that includes many varieties grown for their spring blossom (cherry and almond) or for their fruit (plum, peach, and apricot). ● Genus *Prunus*, family Rosaceae.
– ORIGIN modern Latin, from Latin, literally 'plum tree'.

prurient /ˈprʊərɪənt/ ▶ adjective having or encouraging an excessive interest in sexual matters, especially the sexual activity of others: *she'd been the subject of much prurient curiosity.*
– DERIVATIVES **prurience** noun, **pruriency** noun, **pruriently** adverb.
– ORIGIN late 16th cent. (in the sense 'having a mental itching'): from Latin *prurient-* 'itching, longing' and 'being wanton', from the verb *prurire*.

prurigo /prʊəˈrʌɪgəʊ/ ▶ noun [mass noun] Medicine a chronic skin disease causing severe itching.
– ORIGIN mid 17th cent.: from Latin, from *prurire* 'to itch'.

pruritus /prʊˈrʌɪtəs/ ▶ noun [mass noun] Medicine severe itching of the skin, as a symptom of various ailments.
– DERIVATIVES **pruritic** adjective.
– ORIGIN mid 17th cent.: from Latin, 'itching' (see PRURIGO).

prusik /ˈprʌsɪk/ Climbing ▶ noun [mass noun] a method of ascending or descending a rope by means of two loops, each attached to it by a special knot tightening when weight is applied and slackening when it is removed, enabling the loop to be moved along the rope. ■ (also **prusik knot**) [count noun] a sliding knot that locks under pressure enabling a person to climb in this way.
▶ verb (**prusiks**, **prusiking**, **prusiked**) [no obj.] (usu. as noun **prusiking**) climb using the prusik method.
– ORIGIN 1930s: from the name of Karl *Prusik*, the Austrian mountaineer who devised this method of climbing.

Prussia a former kingdom of Germany. Originally a small country on the SE shores of the Baltic, under Frederick the Great it became a major European power covering much of modern NE Germany and Poland. After the Franco-Prussian War of 1870–1 it became the centre of Bismarck's new German Empire, but following Germany's defeat in the First World War the Prussian monarchy was abolished.
– DERIVATIVES **Prussian** adjective & noun.

Prussian blue ▶ noun [mass noun] a deep blue pigment used in painting and dyeing, made from or in imitation of ferric ferrocyanide. ■ the deep blue colour of this pigment.

prussic acid /ˈprʌsɪk/ ▶ noun old-fashioned term for HYDROCYANIC ACID.
– DERIVATIVES **prussiate** noun.
– ORIGIN late 18th cent.: *prussic* from French *prussique* 'relating to Prussian blue'.

Prut /pruːt/ (also **Pruth**) a river of SE Europe, which rises in the Carpathian Mountains in southern Ukraine and flows south east for 850 km (530 miles), joining the Danube near Galaţi in Romania. For much of its course it forms the border between Romania and Moldova.

pry¹ ▶ verb (**pries**, **prying**, **pried**) [no obj.] enquire too inquisitively into a person's private affairs: *I'm sick of you **prying into** my personal life.*
– ORIGIN Middle English (in the sense 'peer inquisitively'): of unknown origin.

pry² ▶ verb (**pries**, **prying**, **pried**) chiefly N. Amer. another term for PRISE: *prying open the door* | *he pried his left leg free.*
– ORIGIN early 19th cent.: from the verb PRISE, interpreted as *pries*, third person singular of the present tense.

pry bar ▶ noun N. Amer. a small, flattish iron bar used in the same way as a crowbar.

prying ▶ adjective excessively interested in a person's private affairs; too inquisitive: *she felt there was no place where she could escape from the prying eyes.*
– DERIVATIVES **pryingly** adverb.

prytany /ˈprɪtəni/ ▶ noun (pl. **prytanies**) (in ancient Greece) each of the ten divisions of the Athenian Council of Five Hundred. ■ a period of five weeks for which each of these ten divisions presided in turn.

P

– ORIGIN from Greek *prutaneia*, from *prutanis* 'prince, ruler'.

Przewalski's horse /ˌpəːʒəˈvalski/ ▸ **noun** a stocky wild Mongolian horse with a dun-coloured coat and a dark brown erect mane, now extinct in the wild. It is the only true wild horse, and is the ancestor of the domestic horse. ● *Equus ferus*, family Equidae.
– ORIGIN late 19th cent.: named after Nikolai M. *Przheval'sky* (1839–88), Russian explorer.

PS ▸ **abbreviation** ■ Police Sergeant. ■ postscript. ■ private secretary. ■ (in the theatre) prompt side.

Ps. ▸ **abbreviation** (pl. **Pss.**) Psalm or Psalms.

PSA ▸ **abbreviation** prostate-specific antigen.

psalm /sɑːm/ ▸ **noun** a sacred song or hymn, in particular any of those contained in the biblical Book of Psalms and used in Christian and Jewish worship. ■ (**the Psalms** or **the Book of Psalms**) a book of the Bible comprising a collection of religious verses, sung or recited in both Jewish and Christian worship.
– DERIVATIVES **psalmic** adjective.
– ORIGIN Old English (*p*)*sealm*, via ecclesiastical Latin from Greek *psalmos* 'song sung to harp music', from *psallein* 'to pluck'.

psalmist ▸ **noun** the author or composer of a psalm, especially of any of the biblical Psalms.
– ORIGIN late 15th cent.: from late Latin *psalmista*, from *psalmus* 'song sung to harp music' (see **PSALM**).

psalmody /ˈsɑːmədi, ˈsalm-/ ▸ **noun** [mass noun] the singing of psalms or similar sacred canticles, especially in public worship. ■ psalms arranged for singing: *these books offer a useful collection of psalmody.*
– DERIVATIVES **psalmodic** adjective.
– ORIGIN Middle English: via late Latin from Greek *psalmōidia* 'singing to a harp', from *psalmos* (see **PSALM**) + *ōidē* 'song'.

psalter /ˈsɔːltə, ˈsɒl-/ ▸ **noun** (**the psalter**) the Book of Psalms. ■ a copy of the biblical Psalms, especially for liturgical use.
– ORIGIN Old English (*p*)*saltere*, via Latin *psalterium* from Greek *psaltērion* 'stringed instrument'.

psalterium /sɔːlˈtɪərɪəm, sɒl-/ ▸ **noun** another term for **OMASUM**.
– ORIGIN mid 19th cent.: from Latin, literally 'psalter' (see **PSALTER**), because of its many folds of tissue, resembling pages of a book.

psaltery /ˈsɔːlt(ə)ri, ˈsɒl-/ ▸ **noun** (pl. **psalteries**) an ancient and medieval musical instrument like a dulcimer but played by plucking the strings with the fingers or a plectrum.
– ORIGIN Middle English *sautrie*, from Old French *sauterie*, from Latin *psalterium* (see **PSALTER**).

P

PSBR ▸ **abbreviation** Brit. public-sector borrowing requirement.

psephology /sɛˈfɒlədʒi, sɪ-/ ▸ **noun** [mass noun] the statistical study of elections and trends in voting.
– DERIVATIVES **psephological** adjective, **psephologically** adverb, **psephologist** noun.
– ORIGIN 1950s: from Greek *psēphos* 'pebble, vote' (from the ancient Greeks' practice of using pebbles to cast votes) + **-LOGY**.

pseud /sjuːd/ ▸ **noun** Brit. informal a pretentious person, especially one who claims to know a great deal about art, literature, etc.
– ORIGIN 1960s: abbreviation of **PSEUDO**.

pseud- ▸ **combining form** variant spelling of **PSEUDO-** reduced before a vowel (as in *pseudepigrapha*).

pseudepigrapha /ˌsjuːdɪˈpɪɡrəfə/ ▸ **plural noun** spurious or pseudonymous writings, especially Jewish writings ascribed to various biblical patriarchs and prophets but composed within approximately 200 years of the birth of Christ.
– DERIVATIVES **pseudepigraphal** adjective, **pseudepigraphic** adjective.
– ORIGIN late 17th cent.: neuter plural of Greek *pseudepigraphos* 'with false title' (see **PSEUDO-**, **EPIGRAPH**).

pseudo /ˈsjuːdəʊ/ ▸ **adjective 1** not genuine; sham: *a pseudo Georgian facade.*
2 informal pretentious or insincere: *his lyrics sound like pseudo intellectual rubbish.*
▸ **noun** (pl. **pseudos**) informal a pretentious or insincere person.
– ORIGIN late Middle English: independent use of **PSEUDO-**.

pseudo- (also **pseud-** before a vowel) ▸ **combining form 1** supposed or purporting to be but not really so; false; not genuine: *pseudonym* | *pseudoscience.*
2 resembling or imitating: *pseudo-hallucination.*
– ORIGIN from Greek *pseudes* 'false', *pseudos* 'falsehood'.

pseudobulb ▸ **noun** Botany a bulb-like enlargement of the stem in many orchids, especially tropical and epiphytic ones.

pseudocarp ▸ **noun** technical term for **FALSE FRUIT**.
– ORIGIN mid 19th cent.: from **PSEUDO-** 'false' + Greek *karpos* 'fruit'.

pseudocholinesterase /ˌsjuːdəʊˌkəʊlɪˈnɛstəreɪz/ ▸ **noun** [mass noun] Biochemistry an enzyme present in the blood and certain organs which hydrolyses acetylcholine more slowly than acetylcholinesterase.

pseudo-classical ▸ **adjective** having a false or spurious classical style.

pseudo-cleft (also **pseudo-cleft sentence**) ▸ **noun** Grammar a sentence which resembles a cleft sentence by conveying emphasis or politeness through the use of a relative clause, such as *what we want is money* representing *we want money.*

pseudocode ▸ **noun** [mass noun] Computing a notation resembling a simplified programming language, used in program design.

pseudocopulation /ˌsjuːdəʊˌkɒpjʊˈleɪʃ(ə)n/ ▸ **noun** [mass noun] Biology attempted copulation by a male insect with a flower (especially an orchid) that resembles the female, carrying pollen to it in the process.

pseudocyesis /ˌsjuːdəʊsʌɪˈiːsɪs/ ▸ **noun** technical term for **PHANTOM PREGNANCY**.
– ORIGIN mid 19th cent.: from **PSEUDO-** 'false' + Greek *kuēsis* 'conception'.

pseudocyst ▸ **noun** Medicine a fluid-filled cavity resembling a cyst but lacking a wall or lining.

Pseudo-Dionysius (6th century AD), the unidentified author of important theological works formerly attributed to Dionysius the Areopagite.

pseudoephedrine /sjuːdəʊˈɛfədriːn/ ▸ **noun** [mass noun] a drug obtained from plants of the genus *Ephedra* (or prepared synthetically) and used as a nasal decongestant.

pseudoextinction ▸ **noun** [mass noun] Palaeontology the apparent extinction of a group of organisms of which modified descendant forms survive.

pseudogene ▸ **noun** Genetics a section of a chromosome that is an imperfect copy of a functional gene.

pseudohermaphroditism /ˌsjuːdəʊhəːˈmafrədʌɪtɪz(ə)m/ ▸ **noun** [mass noun] Medicine the condition in which an individual of one sex has external genitalia superficially resembling those of the other sex.

pseudomembrane ▸ **noun** Medicine a layer of exudate resembling a membrane, formed on the surface of the skin or of a mucous membrane, especially the conjunctiva.
– DERIVATIVES **pseudomembranous** adjective.

pseudomonas /ˌsjuːdə(ʊ)ˈməʊnəs, sjuːˈdɒmənas/ ▸ **noun** Microbiology a bacterium which occurs in soil and detritus, including a number that are pathogens of plants or animals. ● Genus *Pseudomonas*; aerobic Gram-negative bacteria.
– ORIGIN modern Latin, from **PSEUDO-** 'false' + *monas* 'monad'.

pseudomorph /ˈsjuːdə(ʊ)mɔːf/ Crystallography ▸ **noun** a crystal consisting of one mineral but having the form of another.
▸ **verb** [with obj.] replace (another substance) to form a pseudomorph.
– DERIVATIVES **pseudomorphic** adjective, **pseudomorphism** noun, **pseudomorphous** adjective.
– ORIGIN mid 19th cent.: from **PSEUDO-** 'false' + Greek *morphē* 'form'.

pseudonym /ˈsjuːdənɪm/ ▸ **noun** a fictitious name, especially one used by an author.
– ORIGIN mid 19th cent.: from French *pseudonyme*, from Greek *pseudōnymos*, from *pseudēs* 'false' + *onoma* 'name'.

pseudonymous /sjuːˈdɒnɪməs/ ▸ **adjective** writing or written under a false name.
– DERIVATIVES **pseudonymity** /-ˈnɪmɪti/ noun, **pseudonymously** adverb.

pseudopod /ˈsjuːdə(ʊ)pɒd/ ▸ **noun** another term for **PSEUDOPODIUM**.

pseudopodium /ˌsjuːdə(ʊ)ˈpəʊdɪəm/ ▸ **noun** (pl. **pseudopodia** /-dɪə/) Biology a temporary protrusion of the surface of an amoeboid cell for movement and feeding.
– ORIGIN mid 19th cent.: modern Latin, from **PSEUDO-** + **PODIUM**.

pseudopregnancy ▸ **noun** (pl. **pseudopregnancies**) another term for **PHANTOM PREGNANCY**.

pseudorabies /ˌsjuːdəʊˈreɪbiːz/ ▸ **noun** [mass noun] Veterinary Medicine an infectious herpesvirus disease of the central nervous system in domestic animals that causes convulsions and intense itching and is usually fatal.

pseudorandom ▸ **adjective** (of a number, a sequence of numbers, or any digital data) satisfying one or more statistical tests for randomness but produced by a definite mathematical procedure.
– DERIVATIVES **pseudorandomly** adverb.

pseudoscience ▸ **noun** a collection of beliefs or practices mistakenly regarded as being based on scientific method.
– DERIVATIVES **pseudoscientific** adjective, **pseudoscientist** noun.

pseudoscorpion ▸ **noun** another term for **FALSE SCORPION**.

pseudouridine /ˌsjuːdəʊˈjʊərɪdiːn/ ▸ **noun** [mass noun] Biochemistry a nucleoside present in transfer RNA and differing from uridine in having the sugar residue attached at a carbon atom instead of nitrogen.

pshaw /pʃɔː, ʃɔː/ dated or humorous ▸ **exclamation** an expression of contempt or impatience: *'Poison? Pshaw! The very idea!'*
▸ **verb** [no obj.] say 'pshaw': *when I suggested that free trade might dilute Canadian culture, he pshawed.*
– ORIGIN natural exclamation: first recorded in English in the late 17th cent.

PSHE ▸ **abbreviation** (in the UK) personal, social, and health education (as a school subject).

psi /psʌɪ, sʌɪ/ ▸ **noun 1** the twenty-third letter of the Greek alphabet (Ψ, ψ), transliterated as 'ps'. ■ (**Psi**) [followed by Latin genitive] Astronomy the twenty-third star in a constellation: *Psi Aquarii.*
2 [mass noun] supposed parapsychological or psychic faculties or phenomena: [as modifier] *psi powers.*
– ORIGIN Greek.

p.s.i. ▸ **abbreviation** pounds per square inch.

psilocybin /ˌsʌɪlə(ʊ)ˈsʌɪbɪn/ ▸ **noun** [mass noun] Chemistry a hallucinogenic compound of the alkaloid class, found in the liberty cap and related toadstools.
– ORIGIN 1950s: from modern Latin *Psilocybe* (genus name), from Greek *psilos* 'bald' + *kubē* 'head'.

psionic /sʌɪˈɒnɪk/ ▸ **adjective** relating to or denoting the practical use of psychic powers or paranormal phenomena: *psionic communication.*
– DERIVATIVES **psionically** adverb.
– ORIGIN 1950s: from **PSI**, on the pattern of *electronic*.

psittacine /ˈsɪtəkʌɪn, -sʌɪn/ Ornithology ▸ **adjective** relating to or denoting birds of the parrot family: *psittacine beak and feather disease.*
▸ **noun** a bird of the parrot family.
– ORIGIN late 19th cent.: from Latin *psittacinus* 'of a parrot', from *psittacus*, from Greek *psittakos* 'parrot'.

psittacosis /ˌsɪtəˈkəʊsɪs/ ▸ **noun** [mass noun] a contagious disease of birds, caused by chlamydiae and transmissible (especially from parrots) to human beings as a form of pneumonia.
– ORIGIN late 19th cent.: from Latin *psittacus* 'parrot' + **-OSIS**.

PSNI ▸ **abbreviation** Police Service of Northern Ireland, the police force which replaced the RUC in 2001.

psoas /ˈsəʊas/ (also **psoas major**) ▸ **noun** Anatomy each of a pair of large muscles which run from the lumbar spine through the groin on either side and, with the iliacus, flex the hip. A second muscle, the **psoas minor**, has a similar action but is often absent.
– ORIGIN late 17th cent.: from Greek, accusative plural of *psoa*, interpreted as singular.

psocid /ˈsəʊkɪd, -sɪd/ ▸ **noun** Entomology a small or minute insect of an order that includes the booklice. Many psocids are wingless and somewhat resemble lice or aphids, and most live on bark and among foliage. ● Order Psocoptera: many families, including the large family Psocidae.
– ORIGIN late 19th cent.: from modern Latin *Psocidae* (plural), from *Psocus* (genus name), from Greek *psōkhein* 'to grind'.

Psocoptera /sə(ʊ)ˈkɒptərə/ ▸ **plural noun** Entomology an order of insects that comprises the booklice and other psocids.
– DERIVATIVES **psocopteran** noun & adjective.
– ORIGIN modern Latin (plural), from *Psocus* (genus name) + *pteron* 'wing'.

psoralen /ˈsɔːrəlɛn/ ▸ **noun** [mass noun] Chemistry a compound present in certain plants which is used in perfumery and (in combination with ultraviolet

light) to treat psoriasis and other skin disorders.
● A tricyclic lactone; chem. formula: $C_{11}H_6O_3$.
– ORIGIN 1930s: from modern Latin *Psoralea* (former genus name), from Greek *psōraleos* 'itchy' (from *psōra* 'itch') + the suffix *-en* (compare with **-ENE**).

psoriasis /sɒˈrʌɪəsɪs/ ▶ **noun** [mass noun] Medicine a skin disease marked by red, itchy, scaly patches.
– DERIVATIVES **psoriatic** /ˌsɔːrɪˈatɪk/ **adjective**.
– ORIGIN late 17th cent.: modern Latin, from Greek *psōriasis*, from *psōrian* 'have an itch', from *psōra* 'itch'.

psst ▶ **exclamation** used to attract someone's attention surreptitiously: *Psst! Want to know a secret?*
– ORIGIN 1920s: imitative.

PST ▶ **abbreviation** Pacific Standard Time (see **PACIFIC TIME**).

PSV ▶ **abbreviation** Brit. public service vehicle.

psych /sʌɪk/ (also **psyche**) ▶ **verb** [with obj.] **1** (usu. **psych someone up**) informal mentally prepare (someone) for a testing task or occasion: *we had to psych ourselves up for the race.* ■ (as adj. **psyched**) excited and full of anticipation: *we've told him you were coming—he's really psyched.*
2 analyse (something) in psychological terms. ■ subject (someone) to psychological investigation or psychotherapy.
3 (usu. **psyche**) [no obj.] Bridge make a psychic bid.
▶ **noun 1** informal short for **PSYCHIATRIST** or **PSYCHOLOGIST**. ■ [mass noun] short for **PSYCHIATRY** or **PSYCHOLOGY**.
2 (usu. **psyche**) Bridge a psychic bid.
▶ **adjective** informal **1** short for **PSYCHIATRIC**.
2 short for **PSYCHEDELIC**: *a rare old psych album.*
– PHRASAL VERBS **psych someone out** intimidate an opponent or rival by appearing very confident or aggressive: *we won't be* **psyched out of** *beating them.*

Psyche /ˈsʌɪki/ Greek Mythology a Hellenistic personification of the soul as female, or sometimes as a butterfly. The allegory of Psyche's love for Cupid is told in *The Golden Ass* by Apuleius.

psyche¹ /ˈsʌɪki/ ▶ **noun** the human soul, mind, or spirit: *I will never really fathom the female psyche.*
– ORIGIN mid 17th cent.: via Latin from Greek *psukhē* 'breath, life, soul'.

psyche² /sʌɪk/ ▶ **verb, noun, & adjective** variant spelling of **PSYCH**.

psychedelia /ˌsʌɪkəˈdiːlɪə/ ▶ **noun** [mass noun] music, culture, or art based on the experiences produced by psychedelic drugs.
– ORIGIN 1960s: back-formation from **PSYCHEDELIC**.

psychedelic /ˌsʌɪkəˈdɛlɪk, -ˈdiːlɪk/ ▶ **adjective** relating to or denoting drugs (especially LSD) that produce hallucinations and apparent expansion of consciousness. ■ (of music, especially rock) characterized by musical experimentation and drug-related lyrics. ■ having intense, vivid colours or a swirling abstract pattern: *a psychedelic T-shirt.*
▶ **noun** a psychedelic drug.
– DERIVATIVES **psychedelically** **adverb**.
– ORIGIN 1950s: formed irregularly from **PSYCHE¹** + Greek *dēlos* 'clear, manifest' + **-IC**.

psychiatric /ˌsʌɪkɪˈatrɪk/ ▶ **adjective** relating to mental illness or its treatment: *a psychiatric disorder.*
– DERIVATIVES **psychiatrically** **adverb**.

psychiatrist ▶ **noun** a medical practitioner specializing in the diagnosis and treatment of mental illness.

psychiatry /sʌɪˈkʌɪətri/ ▶ **noun** [mass noun] the study and treatment of mental illness, emotional disturbance, and abnormal behaviour.
– ORIGIN mid 19th cent.: from Greek *psukhē* 'soul, mind' + *iatreia* 'healing' (from *iatros* 'healer').

psychic /ˈsʌɪkɪk/ ▶ **adjective 1** relating to or denoting faculties or phenomena that are apparently inexplicable by natural laws, especially involving telepathy or clairvoyance: *psychic powers.* ■ appearing or considered to have powers of telepathy or clairvoyance: *I could sense it—I must be psychic.*
2 relating to the soul or mind: *he dulled his psychic pain with gin.*
3 Bridge denoting a bid that deliberately misrepresents the bidder's hand, in order to mislead the opponents.
▶ **noun** a person considered or claiming to have psychic powers; a medium. ■ (**psychics**) [treated as sing. or pl.] the study of psychic phenomena.
– DERIVATIVES **psychical** **adjective** (sense 1 of the adjective), **psychically** **adverb**, **psychism** **noun** (sense 1 of the adjective).
– ORIGIN early 19th cent.: from Greek *psukhikos* (see **PSYCHE¹**).

psychic income ▶ **noun** [mass noun] Economics the non-monetary or non-material satisfactions that accompany an occupation or economic activity.

psycho informal ▶ **noun** (pl. **psychos**) a psychopath.
▶ **adjective** psychopathic.
– ORIGIN 1930s: abbreviation.

psycho- ▶ **combining form** relating to the mind or psychology: *psychobabble* | *psychometrics.*
– ORIGIN from Greek *psukhē* 'breath, soul, mind'.

psychoacoustics ▶ **plural noun** [treated as sing.] the branch of psychology concerned with the perception of sound and its physiological effects.
– DERIVATIVES **psychoacoustic** **adjective**.

psychoactive ▶ **adjective** (chiefly of a drug) affecting the mind.

psychoanalysis ▶ **noun** [mass noun] a system of psychological theory and therapy which aims to treat mental disorders by investigating the interaction of conscious and unconscious elements in the mind and bringing repressed fears and conflicts into the conscious mind by techniques such as dream interpretation and free association.
– DERIVATIVES **psychoanalyse** (US **psychoanalyze**) **verb**, **psychoanalytic** **adjective**, **psychoanalytical** **adjective**, **psychoanalytically** **adverb**.

psychoanalyst ▶ **noun** a person who practises psychoanalysis.

psychobabble ▶ **noun** [mass noun] informal, derogatory jargon used in popular psychology.

psychobiology ▶ **noun** [mass noun] the branch of science that deals with the biological basis of behaviour and mental phenomena.
– DERIVATIVES **psychobiological** **adjective**, **psychobiologist** **noun**.

psychodrama ▶ **noun 1** [mass noun] a form of psychotherapy in which patients act out events from their past.
2 a play, film, or novel in which psychological elements are the main interest.

psychodynamics ▶ **plural noun** [treated as sing.] the interrelation of the unconscious and conscious mental and emotional forces that determine personality and motivation. ■ the branch of psychology that deals with psychodynamics.
– DERIVATIVES **psychodynamic** **adjective**, **psychodynamically** **adverb**.

psychogenesis /ˌsʌɪkə(ʊ)ˈdʒɛnɪsɪs/ ▶ **noun** the psychological cause to which a mental illness or behavioural disturbance may be attributed (as distinct from a physical cause).

psychogenic /ˌsʌɪkə(ʊ)ˈdʒɛnɪk/ ▶ **adjective** having a psychological origin or cause rather than a physical one: *psychogenic ill health.*

psychogeriatrics ▶ **plural noun** [treated as sing.] the branch of health care concerned with mental illness in elderly people.
– DERIVATIVES **psychogeriatric** **adjective**, **psychogeriatrician** **noun**.

psychographics ▶ **plural noun** [treated as sing.] the study and classification of people according to their attitudes, aspirations, and other psychological criteria, especially in market research.
– DERIVATIVES **psychographic** **adjective**.

psychohistory ▶ **noun** (pl. **psychohistories**) [mass noun] the interpretation of historical events with the aid of psychological theory. ■ [count noun] a psychological history of an individual.
– DERIVATIVES **psychohistorian** **noun**, **psychohistorical** **adjective**.

psychokinesis /ˌsʌɪkəʊkɪˈniːsɪs, -kʌɪ-/ ▶ **noun** [mass noun] the supposed ability to move objects by mental effort alone.
– DERIVATIVES **psychokinetic** **adjective**.

psycholinguistics ▶ **plural noun** [treated as sing.] the study of the relationships between linguistic behaviour and psychological processes, including the process of language acquisition.
– DERIVATIVES **psycholinguist** **noun**, **psycholinguistic** **adjective**.

psychological ▶ **adjective** of, affecting, or arising in the mind; related to the mental and emotional state of a person: *the victim had sustained physical and psychological damage.* ■ relating to psychology: *psychological research.* ■ (of an ailment or problem) having a mental rather than a physical cause: *it was concluded that her pain was psychological.*
– DERIVATIVES **psychologically** **adverb**.

psychological block ▶ **noun** another term for **MENTAL BLOCK**.

psychological moment ▶ **noun** the moment at which something will or would have the greatest psychological effect: *there was a psychological moment when they might have accepted the report.*

psychological warfare ▶ **noun** [mass noun] actions intended to reduce an opponent's morale.

psychologism ▶ **noun** [mass noun] Philosophy a tendency to interpret events or arguments in subjective terms, or to exaggerate the relevance of psychological factors.

psychologist ▶ **noun** an expert or specialist in psychology.

psychologize (also **psychologise**) ▶ **verb** [with obj.] analyse or regard in psychological terms. ■ [no obj.] theorize or speculate concerning psychology.

psychology ▶ **noun 1** [mass noun] the scientific study of the human mind and its functions, especially those affecting behaviour in a given context.
2 [in sing.] the mental characteristics or attitude of a person or group: *the psychology of child-killers.* ■ the mental factors governing a situation or activity: *the psychology of interpersonal relationships.*
– ORIGIN late 17th cent.: from modern Latin *psychologia* (see **PSYCHO-**, **-LOGY**).

psychometric /ˌsʌɪkə(ʊ)ˈmɛtrɪk/ ▶ **adjective** relating to psychometry or psychometrics.
– DERIVATIVES **psychometrically** **adverb**.

psychometrics ▶ **plural noun** [treated as sing.] the science of measuring mental capacities and processes.

psychometry /sʌɪˈkɒmɪtri/ ▶ **noun** [mass noun] **1** the supposed ability to discover facts about an event or person by touching inanimate objects associated with them.
2 another term for **PSYCHOMETRICS**.
– DERIVATIVES **psychometrician** **noun**, **psychometrist** **noun**.

psychomotor ▶ **adjective** relating to the origination of movement in conscious mental activity.

psychoneuroimmunology /ˌsʌɪkə(ʊ)ˌnjʊərəʊˌɪmjʊˈnɒlədʒi/ ▶ **noun** [mass noun] Medicine the study of the effect of the mind on health and resistance to disease.

psychoneurosis ▶ **noun** another term for **NEUROSIS**.

psychopath ▶ **noun** a person suffering from chronic mental disorder with abnormal or violent social behaviour. ■ informal an unstable and aggressive person.

psychopathic ▶ **adjective** suffering from or constituting a chronic mental disorder with abnormal or violent social behaviour: *a psychopathic disorder.* ■ informal abnormal and obsessive; manic: *an obsessive attention to detail that looked almost psychopathic.*
– DERIVATIVES **psychopathically** **adverb**.

psychopathology ▶ **noun 1** [mass noun] the scientific study of mental disorders.
2 features of people's mental health considered collectively. ■ mental or behavioural disorder.
– DERIVATIVES **psychopathological** **adjective**, **psychopathologist** **noun**.

psychopathy /sʌɪˈkɒpəθi/ ▶ **noun** [mass noun] mental illness or disorder.

psychopharmacology ▶ **noun** [mass noun] the branch of psychology concerned with the effects of drugs on the mind and behaviour.
– DERIVATIVES **psychopharmacological** **adjective**, **psychopharmacologist** **noun**.

psychophysics ▶ **plural noun** [treated as sing.] the branch of psychology that deals with the relations between physical stimuli and mental phenomena.
– DERIVATIVES **psychophysical** **adjective**.

psychophysiology ▶ **noun** [mass noun] Psychology the study of the relationship between physiological and psychological phenomena. ■ the way in which the mind and body interact.
– DERIVATIVES **psychophysiological** **adjective**, **psychophysiologist** **noun**.

psychopomp /ˈsʌɪkə(ʊ)pɒmp/ (also **psychopompos**) ▶ **noun** (in Greek mythology) a guide of souls to the place of the dead. ■ the spiritual guide of a living person's soul.
– ORIGIN from Greek *psukhopompos*, from *psukhē* 'soul' + *pompos* 'conductor'.

psychosexual ▶ **adjective** of or involving the psychological aspects of the sexual impulse.
– DERIVATIVES **psychosexually** **adverb**.

psychosis /sʌɪˈkəʊsɪs/ ▸ **noun** (pl. **psychoses** /-siːz/) a severe mental disorder in which thought and emotions are so impaired that contact is lost with external reality.
– ORIGIN mid 19th cent.: from Greek *psukhōsis* 'animation', from *psukhoō* 'I give life to', from *psukhē* 'soul, mind'.

psychosocial ▸ **adjective** relating to the interrelation of social factors and individual thought and behaviour.
– DERIVATIVES **psychosocially** adverb.

psychosomatic /ˌsʌɪkə(ʊ)səˈmatɪk/ ▸ **adjective 1** (of a physical illness or other condition) caused or aggravated by a mental factor such as internal conflict or stress: *her doctor was convinced that most of Edith's problems were psychosomatic.*
2 relating to the interaction of mind and body.
– DERIVATIVES **psychosomatically** adverb.

psychosurgery ▸ **noun** [mass noun] brain surgery, such as leucotomy, used to treat mental disorder.
– DERIVATIVES **psychosurgical** adjective.

psychosynthesis ▸ **noun** [mass noun] Psychoanalysis the integration of separated elements of the psyche or personality.

psychotherapy ▸ **noun** [mass noun] the treatment of mental disorder by psychological rather than medical means.
– DERIVATIVES **psychotherapeutic** adjective, **psychotherapist** noun.

psychotic /sʌɪˈkɒtɪk/ ▸ **adjective** relating to, denoting, or suffering from a psychosis: *a psychotic disturbance.*
▸ **noun** a person suffering from a psychosis.
– DERIVATIVES **psychotically** adverb.

psychotomimetic /sʌɪˌkɒtə(ʊ)mɪˈmɛtɪk/ ▸ **adjective** relating to or denoting drugs which are capable of producing an effect on the mind similar to a psychotic state.
▸ **noun** a psychotomimetic drug.

psychotronic /ˌsʌɪkə(ʊ)ˈtrɒnɪk/ ▸ **adjective 1** denoting or relating to a genre of films that typically have a science fiction, horror, or fantasy theme and were made on a low budget.
2 relating to psychotronics.

psychotronics ▸ **plural noun** [treated as sing.] a particular branch of parapsychology which supposes an energy or force to emanate from living organisms and affect matter.
– ORIGIN 1970s: from **PSYCHO-**, on the pattern of *electronics.*

psychotropic /ˌsʌɪkə(ʊ)ˈtrəʊpɪk, ˌsʌɪkə(ʊ)ˈtrɒpɪk/ ▸ **adjective** relating to or denoting drugs that affect a person's mental state.
▸ **noun** a psychotropic drug.

psychrometer /sʌɪˈkrɒmɪtə/ ▸ **noun** a hygrometer consisting of wet-bulb and dry-bulb thermometers, the difference in the two thermometer readings being used to determine atmospheric humidity.
– ORIGIN early 18th cent.: from Greek *psukhros* 'cold' + **-METER.**

psychrophile /ˈsʌɪkrə(ʊ)fʌɪl/ ▸ **noun** Biology an organism that grows best at temperatures close to freezing.
– DERIVATIVES **psychrophilic** adjective.
– ORIGIN 1920s: from Greek *psukhros* 'cold' + **-PHILE.**

psyllid /ˈsɪlɪd/ ▸ **noun** Entomology a minute insect of a family (Psyllidae) that comprises the jumping plant lice.
– ORIGIN late 19th cent.: from modern Latin *Psyllidae* (plural), from Greek *psulla* 'flea'.

psyllium /ˈsɪlɪəm/ ▸ **noun** a leafy-stemmed Eurasian plantain, the seeds of which are used as a laxative and as a bulking agent in the treatment of obesity. ● *Plantago psafra*, family Plantaginaceae.
– ORIGIN mid 16th cent.: via Latin from Greek *psullion*, from *psulla* 'flea' (because the seeds resemble fleas).

psy-ops /ˈsʌɪɒps/ ▸ **plural noun** tactics intended to manipulate one's opponents or enemies, such as the dissemination of propaganda or the use of psychological warfare.
– ORIGIN 1960s: contraction of *psychological operations.*

psy-war /ˈsʌɪwɔː/ ▸ **noun** [mass noun] psychological warfare.

PT ▸ **abbreviation** Brit. physical training.

Pt ▸ **abbreviation** ■ Part: *Pt 1 of the Consumer Protection Act 1987.* ■ (**pt**) pint. ■ (in scoring) point. ■ Printing point (as a unit of measurement): *12 pt type.* ■ (**Pt.**) Point (on maps): *Pt. Cloates.* ■ (**pt**) (denoting a side of a ship or aircraft) port.
▸ **symbol** the chemical element platinum.

PTA ▸ **abbreviation** ■ parent–teacher association. ■ (in the UK) Passenger Transport Authority, a local body responsible for operating public transport in a particular region.

Ptah /tɑː/ Egyptian Mythology an ancient deity of Memphis, creator of the universe, god of artisans, and husband of Sekhmet. He became one of the chief deities of Egypt, and was identified by the Greeks with Hephaestus.

ptarmigan /ˈtɑːmɪɡ(ə)n/ ▸ **noun** a northern grouse of mountainous and Arctic regions, with feathered legs and feet and plumage that typically changes to white in winter. ● Genus *Lagopus*, family Tetraonidae: two species, in particular the (**rock**) **ptarmigan** (*L. mutus*) of Eurasia and North America.
– ORIGIN late 16th cent.: from Scottish Gaelic *tàrmachan*. The spelling with *p-* was introduced later, suggested by Greek words starting with *pt-*.

PT boat ▸ **noun** US a motor torpedo boat used by the military.
– ORIGIN 1940s: from *P(atrol) T(orpedo) boat.*

PTE ▸ **abbreviation** (in the UK) Passenger Transport Executive, a local body responsible for implementing public transport policy in a particular region.

Pte ▸ **abbreviation** Brit. Private (in the army).

pteranodon /tɛˈranədɒn/ ▸ **noun** a large tailless pterosaur of the Cretaceous period, with a long toothless beak, a long bony crest, and a wingspan of up to 7 m. ● Genus *Pteranodon*, family Pteranodontidae, order Pterosauria.
– ORIGIN modern Latin, from Greek *pteron* 'wing' + *an-* 'without' + *odous, odont-* 'tooth'.

pteridology /ˌtɛrɪˈdɒlədʒi/ ▸ **noun** [mass noun] the study of ferns and related plants.
– DERIVATIVES **pteridologist** noun.
– ORIGIN mid 19th cent.: from Greek *pteris, pterid-* 'fern' + **-LOGY.**

Pteridophyta /ˌtɛrɪdə(ʊ)ˈfʌɪtə/ ▸ **plural noun** Botany a division of flowerless green plants that comprises the ferns and their relatives. ● Division Pteridophyta: classes Filicopsida (ferns), Sphenopsida (horsetails), and Lycopsida (clubmosses).
– ORIGIN modern Latin (plural), from Greek *pteris, pterid-* 'fern' + *phuton* 'plant'.

pteridophyte /ˈtɛrɪdə(ʊ)fʌɪt/ ▸ **noun** Botany a flowerless green plant of the division Pteridophyte, which comprises the ferns and their relatives.

pteridosperm /ˈtɛrɪdəʊspəːm/ ▸ **noun** a fossil plant which is intermediate between the ferns and seed-bearing plants, dying out in the Triassic period. Also called **SEED FERN.** ● Formerly placed in their own taxon (class Pteridospermeae), but now included with the gymnosperms.
– ORIGIN early 20th cent.: from modern Latin *pteridospermeae*, from Greek *pteris, pterid-* 'fern'.

ptero- /ˈtɛrəʊ/ ▸ **combining form** relating to wings; having wings: *pterosaur.*
– ORIGIN from Greek *pteron* 'feather, wing'.

pterobranch /ˈtɛrə(ʊ)braŋk/ ▸ **noun** Zoology a minute tube-dwelling colonial acorn worm found chiefly in deep water. ● Class Pterobranchia, phylum Hemichordata.

pterodactyl /ˌtɛrəˈdaktɪl/ ▸ **noun** a pterosaur of the late Jurassic period, with a long slender head and neck and a very short tail. ● Family Pterodactylidae, order Pterosauria: several genera, including *Pterodactylus.*
■ (in general use) any pterosaur.
– ORIGIN early 19th cent.: from modern Latin *Pterodactylus* (genus name), from Greek *pteron* 'wing' + *daktulos* 'finger'.

pteropod /ˈtɛrəpɒd/ ▸ **noun** Zoology a sea butterfly.
– ORIGIN mid 19th cent.: from modern Latin *Pteropoda* (plural), from Greek *pteron* 'wing' + *pous, pod-* 'foot'.

pterosaur /ˈtɛrəsɔː/ ▸ **noun** a fossil warm-blooded flying reptile of the Jurassic and Cretaceous periods, with membranous wings supported by a greatly lengthened fourth finger, and probably covered with fur. ● Order Pterosauria, subdivision Archosauria: several families, including pterodactyls, pteranodons, etc.
– ORIGIN mid 19th cent.: from modern Latin *Pterosauria* (plural), from Greek *pteron* 'wing' + *sauros* 'lizard'.

pteroylglutamic acid /ˌtɛrəʊʌɪlɡluˈtamɪk, -rəʊɪl-/ ▸ **noun** another term for **FOLIC ACID.**
– ORIGIN 1940s: the initial element of *pteroylglutamic* is from Greek *pteron* 'wing', with reference to insect pigments.

pterygoid process /ˈtɛrɪɡɔɪd/ ▸ **noun** Anatomy each of a pair of projections from the sphenoid bone in the skull.
– ORIGIN early 18th cent.: from modern Latin *pterygoides* (plural), from Greek *pterux, pterug-* 'wing'.

Pterygota /ˈtɛrɪɡəʊtə/ ▸ **plural noun** Entomology a large group of insects that comprises those that have wings or winged ancestors, including the majority of modern species. Compare with **APTERYGOTA.** ● Subclass Pterygota, class Insecta (or Hexapoda): many orders.
– DERIVATIVES **pterygote** noun.
– ORIGIN modern Latin (plural), from Greek *pterugōtos* 'winged', from *pteron, pterug-* 'wing'.

PTFE ▸ **abbreviation** polytetrafluoroethylene.

PTO ▸ **abbreviation** ■ Brit. please turn over (written at the foot of a page to indicate that the text continues on the reverse). ■ (also **pto**) (in a tractor or other vehicle) power take-off.

Ptolemaic /ˌtɒləˈmeɪɪk/ ▸ **adjective 1** relating to the Greek astronomer Ptolemy or his theories.
2 relating to the Ptolemies of Egypt (see **PTOLEMY[1]**).

Ptolemaic system (also **Ptolemaic theory**) ▸ **noun** Astronomy, historical the theory that the earth is the stationary centre of the universe, with the planets moving in epicyclic orbits within surrounding concentric spheres. Compare with **COPERNICAN SYSTEM.**

Ptolemy[1] /ˈtɒlɪmi/ the name of all the Macedonian rulers of Egypt, a dynasty founded by Ptolemy, the close friend and general of Alexander the Great, who took charge of Egypt after the latter's death and declared himself king (Ptolemy I) in 304 BC. The dynasty ended with the death of Cleopatra in 30 BC.

Ptolemy[2] /ˈtɒlɪmi/ (2nd century) Greek astronomer and geographer. His teachings had enormous influence on medieval thought, the geocentric view of the cosmos being adopted as Christian doctrine until the late Renaissance. Ptolemy's *Geography*, giving lists of places with their longitudes and latitudes, was also a standard work for centuries, despite its inaccuracies.

ptomaine /ˈtəʊmeɪn/ ▸ **noun** Chemistry, dated any of a group of amine compounds of unpleasant taste and odour formed in putrefying animal and vegetable matter and formerly thought to cause food poisoning.
– ORIGIN late 19th cent.: from French *ptomaïne*, from Italian *ptomaina*, formed irregularly from Greek *ptōma* 'corpse'.

P2P ▸ **abbreviation** Computing peer-to-peer.

ptosis /ˈtəʊsɪs/ ▸ **noun** [mass noun] Medicine drooping of the upper eyelid due to paralysis or disease, or as a congenital condition.
– DERIVATIVES **ptotic** /ˈtəʊtɪk/ adjective.
– ORIGIN mid 18th cent.: from Greek *ptōsis*, from *piptein* 'to fall'.

P-trap ▸ **noun** a trap consisting of a U-bend with the upper part of its outlet arm bent horizontally.
– ORIGIN late 19th cent.: so named because of its shape.

PTSD ▸ **abbreviation** post-traumatic stress disorder.

Pty ▸ **abbreviation** Austral. & S. African proprietary (used in the names of companies): *Apex Engineering Pty Ltd.*

ptyalin /ˈtʌɪəlɪn/ ▸ **noun** [mass noun] Biochemistry a form of amylase found in the saliva of humans and some other animals.
– ORIGIN mid 19th cent.: from Greek *ptualon* 'spittle' + **-IN[1].**

p-type ▸ **adjective** Electronics denoting a region in a semiconductor in which electrical conduction is due chiefly to the movement of positive holes. Compare with **N-TYPE.**

Pu ▸ **symbol** the chemical element plutonium.

pub Brit. ▸ **noun** an establishment for the sale of beer and other drinks, and sometimes also food, to be consumed on the premises: *let's go to the pub | a country pub.* ■ Austral. a hotel.
▸ **verb** (**pubs, pubbing, pubbed**) [no obj.] (usu. as noun **pubbing**) informal frequent pubs.
– ORIGIN mid 19th cent.: abbreviation of **PUBLIC HOUSE.**

pub. ▸ **abbreviation** ■ publication(s). ■ published. ■ publisher.

pub crawl Brit. informal ▸ **noun** a tour taking in several pubs or drinking places, with one or more drinks at each.
▸ **verb** (**pub-crawl**) [no obj.] go on a pub crawl.

pube /pjuːb/ ▸ **noun** informal a pubic hair.

puberty ▸ **noun** [mass noun] the period during which adolescents reach sexual maturity and become capable of reproduction.

– DERIVATIVES **pubertal** adjective.
– ORIGIN late Middle English: from Latin *pubertas*, from *puber* 'adult', related to *pubes* (see PUBES).

pubes ▶ noun **1** /'pju:bi:z/ (pl. **same**) the lower part of the abdomen at the front of the pelvis, covered with hair from puberty.
2 /'pju:bi:z/ plural form of PUBIS.
3 /pju:bz/ informal plural form of PUBE.
– ORIGIN late 16th cent.: from Latin, 'pubic hair, groin, genitals'.

pubescence /pjʊ'bɛs(ə)ns/ ▶ noun [mass noun] **1** the time when puberty begins.
2 Botany & Zoology soft down on the leaves and stems of plants or on various parts of animals, especially insects.
– ORIGIN late Middle English: from French, or from medieval Latin *pubescentia*, from Latin *pubescent-* 'reaching puberty' (see PUBESCENT).

pubescent ▶ adjective **1** relating to or denoting a person at or approaching the age of puberty.
2 Botany & Zoology covered with short soft hair; downy.
▶ noun a person at or approaching the age of puberty.
– ORIGIN mid 17th cent.: from French, or from Latin *pubescent-* 'reaching puberty', from the verb *pubescere*.

pubic ▶ adjective relating to the pubes or pubis: *pubic hair*.

pubis /'pju:bɪs/ ▶ noun (pl. **pubes** /-bi:z/) either of a pair of bones forming the two sides of the pelvis.
– ORIGIN late 16th cent.: from Latin *os pubis* 'bone of the pubes'.

public ▶ adjective **1** of or concerning the people as a whole: *public concern | public affairs*. ■ open to or shared by all the people of an area or country: *a public library*. ■ of or involved in the affairs of the community, especially in government or entertainment: *he was forced to withdraw from public life | a public figure*.
2 done, perceived, or existing in open view: *he wanted a public apology in the Wall Street Journal | we should talk somewhere less public*.
3 of or provided by the state rather than an independent, commercial company: *public spending | public services*.
4 Brit. of, for, or acting for a university: *public examination results*.
▶ noun **1** (**the public**) [treated as sing. or pl.] ordinary people in general; the community: *the library is open to the public | **the general public** have a right to know*. ■ [with adj. or noun modifier] a section of the community having a particular interest or connection: *the reading public*. ■ (**one's public**) informal the people who watch or are interested in an artist, writer, or performer: *some famous last words to give my public*.
2 Brit. short for PUBLIC BAR or PUBLIC HOUSE.
– PHRASES **go public 1** become a public company. **2** reveal details about a previously private concern: *Bates **went public with** the news at a press conference*. **in public** in view of other people; when others are present: *men don't cry in public*. **the public eye** the state of being known or of interest to people in general, especially through the media: *the pressures of being constantly **in the public eye***.
– ORIGIN late Middle English: from Old French, from Latin *publicus*, blend of *poplicus* 'of the people' (from *populus* 'people') and *pubes* 'adult'.

public act ▶ noun a law that affects the public as a whole.

public address system ▶ noun a system of microphones, amplifiers, and loudspeakers used to amplify speech or music in a large building or at an outdoor gathering.

publican ▶ noun **1** Brit. a person who owns or manages a pub. ■ Austral. a person who owns or manages a hotel.
2 (in ancient Roman and biblical times) a collector or farmer of taxes: *publicans and sinners*.
– ORIGIN Middle English (in sense 2): from Old French *publicain*, from Latin *publicanus*, from *publicum* 'public revenue', neuter (used as a noun) of *publicus* 'of the people'. Sense 1 dates from the early 18th cent.

public analyst ▶ noun Brit. a health official who analyses food.

publication ▶ noun [mass noun] the preparation and issuing of a book, journal, or piece of music for public sale: *the publication of her first novel*. ■ the action of making something generally known: *the publication of April trade figures*. ■ [count noun] a book or journal issued for public sale: *scientific publications*.
– ORIGIN late Middle English (in the sense 'public announcement or declaration'): via Old French from Latin *publicatio(n-)*, from *publicare* 'make public' (see PUBLISH).

public bar ▶ noun Brit. the more plainly furnished bar in a pub. Compare with LOUNGE BAR.

public bill ▶ noun a proposed law that affects the public as a whole.

public company (N. Amer. **public corporation**) ▶ noun a company whose shares are traded freely on a stock exchange.

public defender ▶ noun US Law a lawyer employed by the state in a criminal trial to represent a defendant who is unable to afford legal assistance.

public domain ▶ noun the state of belonging or being available to the public as a whole, especially through not being subject to copyright or other legal restrictions.

public enemy ▶ noun a notorious wanted criminal. ■ a person or thing regarded as the greatest threat to a group or community: *he identified inflation as **public enemy number one***.

public good ▶ noun **1** Economics a commodity or service that is provided without profit to all members of a society, either by the government or by a private individual or organization.
2 the benefit or well-being of the public: *the frequent conflict between the public good and private interests*.

public house ▶ noun Brit. formal term for PUB.

public housing ▶ noun [mass noun] housing provided for people on low incomes, subsidized by public funds.

public interest immunity ▶ noun [mass noun] (in the UK and some Commonwealth countries) a principle by which the government can request that sensitive documents are not used as evidence in a trial, on the grounds that to do so would be against the public or national interest.

publicist ▶ noun **1** a person responsible for publicizing a product, person, or company.
2 dated a journalist, especially one concerned with current affairs.
3 archaic a writer or other person skilled in international law.
– DERIVATIVES **publicistic** adjective.
– ORIGIN late 18th cent.: from French *publiciste*, from Latin *(jus) publicum* 'public (law)'.

publicity ▶ noun [mass noun] notice or attention given to someone or something by the media: *the case attracted wide publicity in the press*. ■ the giving out of information about a product, person, or company for advertising or promotional purposes: [as modifier] *a publicity campaign*. ■ material or information used for such a purpose: *we distributed publicity from a stall in the marketplace*.
– ORIGIN late 18th cent.: from French *publicité*, from *public* 'public' (see PUBLIC).

publicity agent ▶ noun another term for PUBLICIST (sense 1).

publicize (also **publicise**) ▶ verb [with obj.] make (something) widely known: *use the magazine to publicize human rights abuses*. ■ give out information about (a product, person, or company) for advertising or promotional purposes: *Judy had started to publicize books and celebrities*.
– DERIVATIVES **publicization** noun.

public key ▶ noun Computing a cryptographic key that can be obtained and used by anyone to encrypt messages intended for a particular recipient, such that the encrypted messages can be deciphered only by using a second key that is known only to the recipient (the **private key**).

public law ▶ noun [mass noun] the law of relations between individuals and the state.

public lending right ▶ noun [mass noun] (in the UK) the right of authors to receive payment when their books or other works are lent out by public libraries.

public limited company ▶ noun (in the UK) a company registered under the Companies Act (1980), with statutory minimum capital requirements and shares offered to the public subject to conditions of limited liability.

publicly ▶ adverb **1** so as to be seen by other people; in public: *some weep publicly*. ■ [often sentence adverb] used in reference to views expressed to others and not necessarily genuinely felt: *publicly, officials criticized the resolution, but privately they thought it tolerable*.
2 by the state rather than an independent, commercial company: *a publicly owned company*.

USAGE Note that the spelling is **publicly**, not **-ally**.

public nuisance ▶ noun Brit. an act that is illegal because it interferes with the rights of the public generally. ■ informal an obnoxious or dangerous person or group of people.

public opinion ▶ noun [mass noun] views prevalent among the public.

public orator ▶ noun see ORATOR.

public policy ▶ noun [mass noun] **1** the principles, often unwritten, on which social laws are based.
2 Law the principle that injury to the public good is a basis for denying the legality of a contract or other transaction.

public prosecutor ▶ noun Brit. a law officer who conducts criminal proceedings on behalf of the state or in the public interest. Compare with CROWN PROSECUTOR.

public purse ▶ noun the funds raised by a government by taxation or other means.

Public Record Office ▶ noun (in the UK) an institution where official archives are kept for public inspection.

public relations ▶ plural noun [also treated as sing.] the professional maintenance of a favourable public image by a company or other organization or a famous person. ■ the state of the relationship between a company or other organization or a famous person and the public: *companies justify the cost in terms of improved public relations*.

public school ▶ noun **1** (in the UK) a private fee-paying secondary school, especially one for boarders.
2 (chiefly in North America) a school supported by public funds.
– ORIGIN late 16th cent.: from Latin *publica schola*, denoting a school maintained at the public expense; in England *public school* (a term recorded from 1580) originally denoted a grammar school under public management, founded for the benefit of the public (contrasting with *private school*, run for the profit of the proprietor); since the 19th cent. the term has been applied to the old endowed English grammar schools, and newer schools modelled on them, which have developed into fee-paying boarding schools.

public sector ▶ noun the part of an economy that is controlled by the state.

public servant ▶ noun a person who works for the state or for local government, such as a judge or teacher. ■ Australian and NZ term for CIVIL SERVANT.

public service ▶ noun Australian and NZ term for CIVIL SERVICE.

public spirit ▶ noun [mass noun] willingness to do things that help the public.

public-spirited ▶ adjective willing to help the wider community; socially concerned: *those public-spirited people who call attention to low standards in high places*.
– DERIVATIVES **public-spiritedly** adverb, **public-spiritedness** noun.

public transport (N. Amer. **public transportation**) ▶ noun [mass noun] buses, trains, and other forms of transport that are available to the public, charge set fares, and run on fixed routes.

public utility ▶ noun an organization supplying the community with electricity, gas, water, or sewerage.

public works ▶ plural noun the work of building such things as roads, schools, and hospitals, carried out by the state for the community.

publish ▶ verb [with obj.] **1** prepare and issue (a book, journal, or piece of music) for public sale: *we publish practical reference books* | [no obj.] *the pressures on researchers to publish*. ■ print (something) in a book or journal so as to make it generally known: *we pay £5 for every letter we publish*. ■ (usu. as adj. **published**) prepare and issue the works of (a particular writer): *a published author*. ■ formally announce or read (an edict or marriage banns).
2 Law communicate (a libel) to a third party.
– DERIVATIVES **publishable** adjective.
– ORIGIN Middle English (in the sense 'make generally known'): from the stem of Old French *puplier*, from Latin *publicare* 'make public', from *publicus* (see PUBLIC).

publisher ▶ noun (also **publishers**) a company or person that prepares and issues books, journals, or music for sale: *the publishers of Vogue | a commercial*

P

music publisher. ■ chiefly N. Amer. a newspaper proprietor.

publishing ▸ **noun** [mass noun] the occupation or activity of preparing and issuing books, journals, and other material for sale: *she worked in publishing.*

Puccini /pʊˈtʃiːni/, Giacomo (1858–1924), Italian composer. Puccini's sense of the dramatic, gift for melody, and skilful use of the orchestra have contributed to his enduring popularity. Notable operas: *La Bohème* (1896), *Tosca* (1900), and *Madama Butterfly* (1904).

puccoon /pʌˈkuːn/ ▸ **noun** a North American plant which yields a pigment from which dye or medicinal products were formerly obtained. ● a yellow-flowered plant with slender leaves (genus *Lithospermum*, family Boraginaceae). ● (**red puccoon**) another term for **BLOODROOT** (sense 1).
– ORIGIN early 17th cent.: from Algonquian *poughkone*.

puce /pjuːs/ ▸ **adjective** of a dark red or purple-brown colour: *his face was puce with rage and frustration.*
▸ **noun** [mass noun] a dark red or purple-brown colour.
– ORIGIN late 18th cent.: from French, literally 'flea(-colour)', from Latin *pulex, pulic-*.

Puck ▸ **noun** another name for **ROBIN GOODFELLOW**. ■ (**puck**) a mischievous or evil sprite.
– ORIGIN Old English *pūca*; it is unclear whether the word is of Celtic or Germanic origin.

puck ▸ **noun 1** a black disc made of hard rubber, used in ice hockey.
2 Computing an input device resembling a mouse, dragged across a mat which senses its position to move the cursor on the screen.
– ORIGIN late 19th cent.: of unknown origin.

pucker ▸ **verb** (especially with reference to a person's face) tightly gather or contract into wrinkles or small folds: [no obj.] *the child's face puckered, ready to cry* | [with obj.] *the baby stirred,* ***puckering up*** *its face* | *she puckered her lips.*
▸ **noun** a tightly gathered wrinkle or small fold: *a pucker between his eyebrows.*
– DERIVATIVES **puckery** adjective.
– ORIGIN late 16th cent. (as a verb): probably frequentative, from the base of **POKE**[2] and **POCKET** (suggesting the formation of small purse-like gatherings).

puckeroo /ˌpʌkəˈruː/ NZ ▸ **adjective** broken; useless.
▸ **verb** [with obj.] [often as adj] (**puckerooed**) ruin or break.
– ORIGIN late 19th cent. (as a verb): from Maori *pakaru* 'broken'.

puckish ▸ **adjective** playful, especially in a mischievous way: *a puckish sense of humour.*
– DERIVATIVES **puckishly** adverb, **puckishness** noun.

pud ▸ **noun** Brit. informal short for **PUDDING**.

P

pudding ▸ **noun** chiefly Brit. **1** a cooked sweet dish served after the main course of a meal: *a rice pudding* | [mass noun] *a good helping of pudding.* ■ [mass noun] the dessert course of a meal: *what's for pudding?* ■ N. Amer. a dessert with a soft or creamy consistency.
2 a sweet or savoury steamed dish made with suet and flour: *a steak and kidney pudding.* ■ the intestines of a pig or sheep stuffed with oatmeal, spices, and meat and boiled. ■ informal a fat or stupid person: *away with you, you big pudding!*
– PHRASES **in the pudding club** Brit. informal pregnant.
– DERIVATIVES **puddingy** adjective.
– ORIGIN Middle English (denoting a sausage such as *black pudding*): apparently from Old French *boudin* 'black pudding', from Latin *botellus* 'sausage, small intestine'.

pudding basin ▸ **noun** Brit. a deep round bowl used for mixing and cooking steamed puddings. ■ [as modifier] denoting a hairstyle produced or seemingly produced by inverting a pudding basin on a person's head and cutting away all the hair that sticks out under it: *a pudding-basin haircut.*

pudding cloth ▸ **noun** a cloth used for tying up some puddings for boiling.

pudding face ▸ **noun** informal a large fat face.
– DERIVATIVES **pudding-faced** adjective.

pudding-head ▸ **noun** informal a stupid person.

puddingstone ▸ **noun** [mass noun] a conglomerate rock in which dark-coloured round pebbles contrast with a paler fine-grained matrix.

puddle ▸ **noun 1** a small pool of liquid, especially of rainwater on the ground: *splashing through deep puddles* | figurative *a little puddle of light.*
2 [mass noun] clay and sand mixed with water and used as a watertight covering for embankments.
3 Rowing a circular patch of disturbed water made by the blade of an oar at each stroke.
▸ **verb** [with obj.] **1** wet or cover (a surface) with water, especially rainwater: *the cobbles under our feet were wet and puddled.* ■ [no obj.] (of liquid) form a small pool: *rivulets of water coursed down the panes, puddling on the sill.* ■ [no obj.] archaic dabble or wallow in mud or shallow water: *children are playing and puddling about in the dirt.* ■ [no obj.] (**puddle about/around**) informal occupy oneself in a disorganized or unproductive way: *the Internet is just the latest excuse for puddling around at work.*
2 line (a hole) with puddle. ■ knead (clay and sand) into puddle. ■ work (mixed water and clay) to separate gold or opal. ■ (usu. as noun **puddling**) chiefly historical stir (molten iron) with iron oxide in a furnace, to produce wrought iron by oxidizing carbon.
– DERIVATIVES **puddler** noun, **puddly** adjective.
– ORIGIN Middle English: diminutive of Old English *pudd* 'ditch, furrow'; compare with German dialect *Pfudel* 'pool'.

puddle jumper ▸ **noun** informal, chiefly N. Amer. a small light aeroplane which is fast and manoeuvrable and used for short trips.

pudency /ˈpjuːd(ə)nsi/ ▸ **noun** literary modesty or embarrassment.
– ORIGIN early 17th cent.: from late Latin *pudentia*.

pudendum /pjʊˈdɛndəm/ ▸ **noun** (pl. **pudenda** /-də/) a person's external genitals, especially a woman's.
– DERIVATIVES **pudendal** adjective, **pudic** /ˈpjuːdɪk/ adjective.
– ORIGIN mid 17th cent.: from Latin *pudenda* (*membra*) '(parts) to be ashamed of', neuter plural of the gerundive of *pudere* 'be ashamed'.

pudeur /pjuːˈdəː/, French /pydœʀ/ ▸ **noun** [mass noun] a sense of shame or embarrassment, especially with regard to matters of a sexual or personal nature.
– ORIGIN 1930s: French, literally 'modesty'.

pudge ▸ **noun** [mass noun] N. Amer. informal fat on a person's body.
– ORIGIN early 19th cent. (denoting a fat person): of unknown origin; compare with **PODGE**.

pudgy ▸ **adjective** (**pudgier**, **pudgiest**) informal (of a person or part of their body) rather fat: *his pudgy fingers.*
– DERIVATIVES **pudgily** adverb, **pudginess** noun.

pudu /ˈpuːduː/ ▸ **noun** a very small and rare deer found in the lower Andes of South America. ● Genus *Pudu*, family Cervidae: two species.
– ORIGIN late 19th cent.: from Araucanian.

Puducherry /ˌpʊdʊˈtʃɛri/ a Union Territory of SE India, on the Coromandel Coast, formed from several former French territories and incorporated into India in 1954. Former name (until 2006) **PONDICHERRY**. ■ the capital city of Puducherry; pop. 232,300 (est. 2009).

Puebla /ˈpwɛblə/ a state of south central Mexico. ■ its capital city; pop. 1,399,519 (2005). It lies at the edge of the central Mexican plateau at an altitude of 2,150 m (7,055 ft). Full name **Puebla de Zaragoza** /deɪ ˌsarəˈgɒsə/.

pueblo /ˈpwɛbləʊ/ ▸ **noun** (pl. **pueblos**) **1** a town or village in Spain, Latin America, or the south-western US, especially an American Indian settlement.
2 (**Pueblo**) (pl. **same** or **Pueblos**) a member of any of various American Indian peoples, including the Hopi, occupying pueblo settlements chiefly in New Mexico and Arizona.
▸ **adjective** (**Pueblo**) relating to or denoting the Pueblo or their culture.
– ORIGIN Spanish, literally 'people', from Latin *populus*.

puerile /ˈpjʊərʌɪl/ ▸ **adjective** childishly silly and immature: *a puerile argument.*
– DERIVATIVES **puerilely** adverb, **puerility** noun (pl. **puerilities**).
– ORIGIN late 16th cent. (in the sense 'like a boy'): from French *puéril* or Latin *puerilis*, from *puer* 'boy'.

puerperal fever ▸ **noun** [mass noun] fever caused by uterine infection following childbirth.

puerperium /ˌpjuːəˈpɛrɪəm, ˌpjuːəˈpiːrɪəm/ ▸ **noun** [mass noun] Medicine the period of about six weeks after childbirth during which the mother's reproductive organs return to their original non-pregnant condition.
– DERIVATIVES **puerperal** adjective.
– ORIGIN early 17th cent.: from Latin, from *puerperus* 'parturient' (from *puer* 'child' + *-parus* 'bearing').

Puerto Cortés /ˌpwɛːtəʊ kɔːˈtɛz/ a port in NW Honduras, on the Caribbean coast at the mouth of the Ulua River; pop. 66,000 (est. 2008).

Puerto Limón another name for **LIMÓN**.

Puerto Plata /ˈplɑːtə/ a resort town in the Dominican Republic, on the north coast; pop. 134,200 (est. 2009).

Puerto Rico /ˈriːkəʊ/ an island of the Greater Antilles in the Caribbean; pop. 3,966,200 (est. 2009); official languages, Spanish and English; capital, San Juan. One of the earliest Spanish settlements in the New World, it was ceded to the US in 1898 after the Spanish-American War, and in 1952 it became a commonwealth in voluntary association with the US, with full powers of local government.
– DERIVATIVES **Puerto Rican** adjective & noun.

Puerto Rico Trench an ocean trench extending in an east–west direction to the north of Puerto Rico and the Leeward Islands. It reaches a depth of 9,220 m (28,397 ft).

puff ▸ **noun 1** a short, explosive burst of breath or wind: *a puff of wind swung the weathercock round.* ■ the sound of air or vapour escaping suddenly: *the whistle and puff of steam.* ■ a small quantity of vapour or smoke, emitted in one blast: *the fire breathed out* ***a puff of*** *blue smoke.* ■ an act of drawing quickly on a pipe, cigarette, or cigar: *he took a puff of his cigar.* ■ [mass noun] Brit. informal breath: *after a chase of over three miles he had finally run out of puff.*
2 [usu. with modifier or in combination] a light pastry case, typically one made of puff pastry, containing a sweet or savoury filling: *a jam puff.*
3 informal a review of a work of art, book, or theatrical production, especially an excessively complimentary one: *the publishers sent him a copy of the book hoping for a puff.* ■ Brit. an advertisement, especially one exaggerating the value of the goods advertised.
4 a gathered mass of material in a dress or other garment. ■ a rolled protuberant mass of hair. ■ N. Amer. an eiderdown.
5 a powder puff.
▸ **verb 1** [no obj.] breathe in repeated short gasps: *exercises that make you puff.* ■ [with adverbial] move with short, noisy breaths or bursts of air or steam: *the train came puffing in.* ■ smoke a pipe, cigarette, or cigar: *he* ***puffed on*** *his pipe contentedly.* ■ [with obj.] blow (dust, smoke, or a light object) with a quick breath or blast of air: *he puffed out smoke through his long cigarette holder.* ■ move through the air in short bursts: *his breath puffed out like white smoke.*
2 (**puff something out/up** or **puff out/up**) swell or become swollen: [with obj.] *he suddenly sucked his stomach in and puffed his chest out* | [no obj.] *when he was in a temper, his cheeks puffed up and his eyes shrank.* ■ (**be puffed up**) be conceited: *he was never puffed up about his writing.*
3 [with obj.] advertise with exaggerated or false praise: *publishers have puffed the book on the grounds that it contains new discoveries.*
– PHRASES **in all one's puff** Brit. informal in one's whole life. **puff and blow** breathe in gasps during or after exertion.
– ORIGIN Middle English: imitative of the sound of a breath, perhaps from Old English *pyf* (noun), *pyffan* (verb).

Puffa (also **Puffa jacket**) ▸ **noun** Brit. trademark a type of thick padded jacket.
– ORIGIN 1990s: origin uncertain; perhaps respelling of **PUFFER**.

puff adder ▸ **noun** a large, sluggish, mainly nocturnal African viper which inflates the upper part of its body and hisses loudly when under threat. ● *Bitis arietans*, family Viperidae.
■ North American term for **HOGNOSE SNAKE**.

puffback (also **puff-back shrike**) ▸ **noun** a small black-and-white African shrike, the male of which displays by puffing up the feathers of the lower back. ● Genus *Dryoscopus*, family Laniidae: several species.

puffball ▸ **noun 1** a fungus that produces a spherical or pear-shaped fruiting body which ruptures when ripe to release a cloud of spores. ● Families Lycoperdaceae, class Gasteromycetes, in particular genus *Lycoperdon*.
2 a short full skirt gathered around the hemline to produce a soft puffy shape.

puffbird ▸ **noun** a stocky large-headed bird somewhat resembling a kingfisher, found in tropical American forests. ● Family Bucconidae: several genera and many species.

puffed ▸ **adjective 1** (also **puffed out**) Brit. out of breath: *he felt puffed after climbing to the top of the apartment block.*
2 (also **puffed up**) swollen: *symptoms include puffed eyelids.* ■ (of a sleeve or other part of a garment) gathered so as to have a rounded shape.

puffer ▶ noun **1** a person or thing that puffs. ■ chiefly Scottish a steamboat, especially a small coastal freighter. ■ informal a steam train. ■ informal an aerosol inhaler used for administering a drug for a condition such as asthma.
2 short for **PUFFERFISH**.

pufferfish ▶ noun (pl. **same** or **pufferfishes**) a stout-bodied marine or freshwater fish which typically has spiny skin and inflates itself like a balloon when threatened. It is sometimes used as food, but some parts are highly toxic. ● Family Tetraodontidae: several genera and many species, including the **common pufferfish** (*Tetraodon cutcutia*).

puffery ▶ noun [mass noun] chiefly N. Amer. exaggerated or false praise.

puffin ▶ noun an auk (seabird) of northern and Arctic waters which nests in holes, with a large head and a massive brightly coloured triangular bill. ● Genera *Fratercula* and *Lunda*, family Alcidae: three species, in particular the (**Atlantic**) **puffin** (*F. arctica*).
– ORIGIN Middle English (denoting the Manx shearwater): apparently from **PUFF** + **-ING³**, with reference to the Manx shearwater's fat nestlings. The later use is a confusion, by association of nesting habits and habitat.

puffin crossing ▶ noun (in the UK) a pedestrian crossing with traffic lights which go green again only when no more pedestrians are detected on the crossing by infrared detectors and mats.
– ORIGIN 1990s: *puffin* from *p(edestrian) u(ser) f(riendly) in(telligent)*, respelled after the bird's name by analogy with *pelican crossing*.

puff pastry ▶ noun [mass noun] light flaky pastry, used for pie crusts, canapés, and sweet pastries.

puff sleeve ▶ noun a short sleeve gathered at the top and cuff and full in the middle.

puffy ▶ adjective (**puffier**, **puffiest**) **1** (especially of part of the body) unusually swollen: *her eyes were puffy and full of tears.*
2 soft, rounded, and light: *small puffy clouds.* ■ (of a garment) padded or gathered to give a rounded shape: *a puffy blue ski-jacket.*
3 (of wind or breath) coming in short bursts: *his breath was puffy and fast.*
– DERIVATIVES **puffily** adverb, **puffiness** noun.

puftaloon /ˈpʌftəluːn/ ▶ noun Austral. a small fried cake, spread with jam, sugar, or honey, and usually eaten hot.
– ORIGIN late 19th cent.: origin uncertain; perhaps related to **PUFF**.

pug¹ ▶ noun **1** (also **pug dog**) a dog of a dwarf breed like a bulldog with a broad flat nose and deeply wrinkled face.
2 a small, slender moth which rests with its wings stretched out to the sides. ● *Eupithecia* and other genera, family Geometridae.
– DERIVATIVES **puggish** adjective, **puggy** adjective.
– ORIGIN mid 18th cent.: perhaps of Low German origin.

pug² ▶ noun [mass noun] loam or clay mixed and worked into a soft, plastic condition without air pockets for making bricks or pottery.
▶ verb (**pugs**, **pugging**, **pugged**) [with obj.] **1** (usu. as adj. **pugged**) prepare (clay) in this way.
2 (usu. as noun **pugging**) pack (a space) with pug, sawdust, or other material in order to deaden sound.
– ORIGIN early 19th cent.: of unknown origin.

pug³ ▶ noun informal a boxer.
– ORIGIN mid 19th cent.: abbreviation of **PUGILIST**.

pug⁴ ▶ noun the footprint of an animal: [as modifier] *I saw the pug marks of the tigress in the soft earth.*
▶ verb (**pugs**, **pugging**, **pugged**) [with obj.] track (an animal) by its footprints.
– ORIGIN mid 19th cent.: from Hindi *pag* 'footprint'.

pug dog ▶ noun another term for **PUG¹** (sense 1).

Puget Sound /ˈpjuːdʒɪt/ an inlet of the Pacific on the coast of Washington State in the US. It is linked to the ocean by the Strait of Juan de Fuca.
– ORIGIN named after Peter *Puget*, the aide of George Vancouver who explored it in 1792.

puggaree /ˈpʌg(ə)riː/ ▶ noun **1** another term for **PAGRI**.
2 a thin muslin scarf tied round a sun helmet so as to hang down over the wearer's neck and shield it from the sun.
– ORIGIN from Hindi *pagṛī* 'turban'.

pugilism ▶ noun [mass noun] dated or humorous the profession or hobby of boxing: *I do not go to displays of pugilism.*

pugilist /ˈpjuːdʒɪlɪst/ ▶ noun dated or humorous a boxer, especially a professional one.
– DERIVATIVES **pugilistic** adjective.
– ORIGIN mid 18th cent.: from Latin *pugil* 'boxer' + **-IST**.

Pugin /ˈpjuːdʒɪn/, Augustus Welby Northmore (1812–52), English architect, theorist, and designer. He believed that the Gothic style was the only proper architectural style because of its origins in medieval Christian society. He is known particularly for his work on the external detail and internal fittings for the Houses of Parliament, designed by Sir Charles Barry.

Puglia /ˈpulja/ Italian name for **APULIA**.

pug mill ▶ noun a machine for mixing and working clay and other materials into pug (see **PUG²**).

pugnacious /pʌgˈneɪʃəs/ ▶ adjective eager or quick to argue, quarrel, or fight: *the increasingly pugnacious demeanour of right-wing politicians.*
– DERIVATIVES **pugnaciously** adverb, **pugnacity** noun.
– ORIGIN mid 17th cent.: from Latin *pugnax*, *pugnac-* (from *pugnare* 'to fight', from *pugnus* 'fist') + **-IOUS**.

pug nose ▶ noun a short nose with an upturned tip.
– DERIVATIVES **pug-nosed** adjective.

Pugwash conferences /ˈpʌgwɒʃ/ a series of international conferences first held in Pugwash (a village in Nova Scotia) in 1957 by scientists to promote the peaceful application of scientific discoveries.

puha /ˈpuːhɑː/ ▶ noun [mass noun] NZ the leaves of the sowthistle used as a vegetable.
– ORIGIN mid 19th cent.: from Maori.

puisne /ˈpjuːni/ ▶ adjective Law (in the UK and some other countries) denoting a judge of a superior court inferior in rank to chief justices.
– ORIGIN late 16th cent. (as a noun, denoting a junior or inferior person): from Old French, from *puis* (from Latin *postea* 'afterwards') + *ne* 'born' (from Latin *natus*). Compare with **PUNY**.

puisne mortgage ▶ noun Law, chiefly Brit. a second or subsequent mortgage of unregistered land of which the title deeds are retained by a first mortgagee.

puissance /ˈpjuːɪs(ə)ns, ˈpwiː-, ˈpwɪ-/ ▶ noun [mass noun] **1** also /ˈpwiːsɒ̃s/ (**Puissance**) a competitive test of a horse's ability to jump large obstacles in showjumping.
2 archaic or literary great power, influence, or prowess.
– ORIGIN late Middle English (in sense 2): from Old French, 'power', from *puissant* 'having power' (see **PUISSANT**). Sense 1 dates from the 1950s.

puissant /ˈpjuːɪs(ə)nt, ˈpwiː-, ˈpwɪ-/ ▶ adjective archaic or literary having great power or influence.
– DERIVATIVES **puissantly** adverb.
– ORIGIN late Middle English: via Old French from Latin *posse* 'be able'.

puja /ˈpuːdʒɑː/ (also **pooja**) ▶ noun [mass noun] Hinduism & Buddhism the act of worship: *I perform puja every day* | [count noun] *the entire family gets together for a puja.*
– ORIGIN Sanskrit *pūjā* 'worship'.

pujari /pʊˈdʒɑːri/ ▶ noun (pl. **pujaris**) a Hindu priest.
– ORIGIN via Hindi from Sanskrit *pūjā* 'worship'.

puka /ˈpuːkə/ (also **puka shell**, **pooka**) ▶ noun a small spiral shell typically strung with others to make necklaces or bracelets.
– ORIGIN Hawaiian, literally 'hole'.

puke informal ▶ verb vomit: [no obj.] *wild with shame at **puking up** like a baby* | [with obj.] *he **puked up** his pizza.*
▶ noun [mass noun] vomit.
– DERIVATIVES **pukey** (also **puky**) adjective (**pukier**, **pukiest**).
– ORIGIN late 16th cent.: probably imitative; first recorded as a verb in: 'At first the infant, mewling, and puking in the nurse's arms', in Shakespeare's *As you like it* (II. vii. 144).

pukeko /ˈpuːkɛkəʊ/ ▶ noun (pl. **pukekos**) NZ another term for **SWAMPHEN**.
– ORIGIN mid 19th cent.: from Maori.

pukka /ˈpʌkə/ (also **pukkah**) ▶ adjective informal
1 genuine: *the more expensive brands are pukka natural mineral waters.* ■ of or appropriate to high or respectable society: *it wouldn't be considered the pukka thing to do.*
2 Brit. excellent: *hey, man, that shirt's pukka.*
– ORIGIN late 17th cent.: from Hindi *pakkā* 'cooked, ripe, substantial'.

puku¹ /ˈpuːkuː/ ▶ noun (pl. **pukus**) an antelope with a shaggy golden-yellow coat and short thick horns, native to wetland areas of southern Africa. ● *Kobus vardonii*, family Bovidae.
– ORIGIN late 19th cent.: from Zulu *mpuku*.

puku² /ˈpʊkuː/ ▶ noun NZ a person's stomach or belly.
– ORIGIN early 20th cent.: from Maori.

pul /puːl/ ▶ noun (pl. **puls** or **puli**) a monetary unit of Afghanistan, equal to one hundredth of an afghani.
– ORIGIN Pashto, from Persian *pūl* 'copper coin'.

pula /ˈpʊlə/ ▶ noun (pl. **same**) the basic monetary unit of Botswana, equal to 100 thebe.
– ORIGIN Setswana, literally 'rain'.

pulao /pəˈlaʊ/ ▶ noun variant spelling of **PILAF**.

pulaski /pʊˈlaski/ ▶ noun (pl. **pulaskis**) chiefly US a hatchet with a head that forms an axe blade on one side and an adze on the other.
– ORIGIN 1920s: named after Edward C. *Pulaski* (1866–1931), the American forest ranger who designed it.

Pulau Seribu /ˌpuːlaʊ ˈsɛrɪbuː/ Indonesian name for **THOUSAND ISLANDS** (sense 2).

pulchritude /ˈpʌlkrɪtjuːd/ ▶ noun [mass noun] literary beauty.
– DERIVATIVES **pulchritudinous** adjective.
– ORIGIN late Middle English: from Latin *pulchritudo*, from *pulcher*, *pulchr-* 'beautiful'.

pule /pjuːl/ ▶ verb [no obj.] (often as adj. **puling**) literary cry querulously or weakly: *she's no puling infant.*
– ORIGIN late Middle English (originally referring to a bird's cry): probably imitative; compare with French *piauler*, in the same sense.

puli /ˈpuːli/ ▶ noun (pl. **pulik** /ˈpuːlɪk/) a sheepdog of a black, grey, or white breed with a long thick coat.
– ORIGIN 1930s: from Hungarian.

Pulitzer /ˈpʊlɪtsə/, Joseph (1847–1911), Hungarian-born American newspaper proprietor and editor. A pioneer of campaigning popular journalism, he owned a number of newspapers. He made provisions in his will for the establishment of the annual Pulitzer Prizes.

Pulitzer Prize ▶ noun an award for an achievement in American journalism, literature, or music. There are thirteen made each year.

pull ▶ verb [with obj.] **1** [usu. with adverbial] exert force on (someone or something) so as to cause movement towards oneself: *he pulled her down on to the couch* | [with obj. and complement] *I pulled the door shut behind me* | figurative *they are pulled in incompatible directions by external factors and their own beliefs* | [no obj.] *the little boy **pulled at** her skirt.* ■ (of an animal or vehicle) be attached to the front and be the source of forward movement of (a vehicle): *the carriage was pulled by four horses.* ■ [no obj.] (of an engine) exert propulsive force; deliver power: *the engine warmed up quickly and pulled well.* ■ [with obj. and adverbial] remove or extract (something) by grasping and exerting force on it: *she pulled a handkerchief out of her pocket* | *he pulled on his boots* | *I pulled up some onions.* ■ [with adverbial of direction] (**pull oneself**) move in a specified direction with effort, especially by taking hold of something and exerting force: *he pulled himself into the saddle.* ■ damage (a muscle, ligament, etc.) by abnormal strain. ■ informal bring out (a weapon) for use against someone: *it's not every day a young woman **pulls a gun on** a burglar.* ■ Brit. draw (beer) from a barrel to serve. ■ [no obj.] (**pull at/on**) inhale deeply while smoking (a pipe, cigarette, or cigar).
2 [no obj., with adverbial] move steadily in a specified direction or manner: *the bus was about to pull away* | *the boy pulled ahead and disappeared round the corner.* ■ [no obj., with adverbial of direction] move one's body in a specified direction, especially against resistance: *she tried to **pull away from** him.*
3 attract (someone) as a customer; cause to show interest in something: *anyone can enter the show if they have a good act and the ability to pull a crowd* | *tourist attractions which **pull in** millions of foreign visitors.* ■ Brit. informal succeed in attracting sexually: *I used my sense of humour to pull girls.* ■ informal carry out or achieve (something clever or duplicitous): *the magazine pulled its trick of producing the right issue at the right time.*
4 informal cancel or withdraw (an entertainment or advertisement): *the gig was pulled at the first sign of difficulty.* ■ N. Amer. withdraw or disqualify (a player) from a game. ■ arrest: *I am never likely to get pulled for speeding.* ■ check the speed of (a horse), especially so as to make it lose a race.
5 Cricket play (the ball) round to the leg side from the off. ■ Golf & Baseball strike (the ball) in the direction of one's follow-through so that it travels to the left (or, with a left-handed player, the right).

6 [no obj.] American Football (of a lineman) withdraw from and cross behind the line of scrimmage to block opposing players and clear the way for a runner.
7 print (a proof).
8 Computing retrieve (an item of data) from the top of a stack.
▶ **noun 1** an act of pulling something: *give the hair a quick pull and it comes out by the roots.* ■ a handle to hold while pulling. ■ a deep draught of a drink. ■ an act of inhaling while smoking a pipe, cigarette, or cigar: *he took a pull on his cheroot.* ■ [in sing.] Brit. an act of moving steadily or with effort: *a pull for ten minutes brought me to the summit.* ■ an injury to a muscle or ligament caused by abnormal strain: *he was ruled out of the game with a hamstring pull.*
2 [in sing.] a force drawing someone or something in a particular direction: *the pull of the water tore her away* | figurative *the pull of her home town was a strong one.* ■ [count noun] something exerting an influence or attraction: *one of the pulls of urban life is the opportunity of finding employment.* ■ [mass noun] ability to exercise influence: *the team might be seeded because of their pull within soccer's international body.* ■ Brit. informal an attempt to attract someone sexually: *an eligible bachelor* ***on the pull.***
3 Sport a pulling stroke.
4 a printer's proof.
– PHRASES **like pulling teeth** informal used to convey that something is extremely difficult to do: *it had been like pulling teeth to extract these two small items from Moore.* **pull a boner** see BONER. **pull a face** (or **faces**) see FACE. **pull a fast one** see FAST[1]. **pull one's head in** Austral./NZ informal mind one's own business. **pull someone's leg** deceive someone playfully; tease someone. **pull the other one** (**it's got bells on**) Brit. informal used to express a suspicion that one is being deceived or teased: *Your boat was sunk by a swordfish? Pull the other one!* **pull out all the stops** see STOP. **pull the plug** informal prevent something from happening or continuing: *the company* ***pulled the plug on the deal.*** **pull** (**one's**) **punches** [usu. with negative] be less forceful, severe, or violent than one could be: *a smooth-tongued critic who doesn't pull his punches.* **pull rank** see RANK[1]. **pull one's socks up** see SOCK. **pull strings** make use of one's influence and contacts to gain an advantage unofficially or unfairly. **pull the strings** be in control of events or of other people's actions. **pull together** cooperate in a task or undertaking. **pull oneself together** recover control of one's emotions. **pull someone/thing to pieces** see PIECE. **pull one's weight** do one's fair share of work. **pull wires** US another way of saying PULL STRINGS above. **pull the wool over someone's eyes** see WOOL.
– PHRASAL VERBS **pull back** (or **pull someone/thing back**) **1** retreat or cause troops to retreat from an area: *the pact called on the rival forces to pull back and allow a neutral force to take control.* ■ (**pull back**) withdraw from an undertaking: *the party pulled back from its only positive policy.* **2** Sport improve or restore a team's position by scoring a goal: *he pulled back a goal three minutes before half time* | *Rovers pulled back to 4–3 with a goal two minutes from time.* **pull something down 1** demolish a building. **2** informal earn a sum of money: *he was pulling down sixty grand a year.* **pull in** Brit. **1** (of a vehicle) move to the side of or off the road: *he pulled in at the kerb.* **2** (of a bus or train) arrive to take passengers. **pull someone/thing in 1** succeed in securing or obtaining something: *the party pulled in 10 per cent of the vote.* ■ informal earn a sum of money: *you could pull in £100,000.* **2** informal arrest someone: *I'd pull him in for questioning.* **3** use reins to check a horse. **pull something off** informal succeed in achieving or winning something difficult: *he pulled off a brilliant first round win.* **pull out 1** withdraw from an undertaking: *he was forced to* ***pull out of*** *the championship because of an injury.* ■ retreat or cause to retreat from an area: *the army pulled out, leaving the city in ruins* | (**pull someone out**) *the CIA had pulled its operatives out of Tripoli.* **2** (of a bus or train) leave with its passengers. **3** (of a vehicle) move out from the side of the road, or from its normal position in order to overtake: *as he turned the corner a police car pulled out in front of him.* **pull over** (of a vehicle) move to the side of or off the road. **pull someone over** (of the police) cause a driver to pull off the road: *he was pulled over for speeding.* **pull round** chiefly Brit. recover from an illness. **pull through** (or **pull someone/thing through**) get through an illness or other dangerous or difficult situation: *the illness is difficult to overcome, but we hope she'll pull through.* **pull up 1** (of a vehicle) come to a halt: *he pulled up outside the cottage.* **2** increase the altitude of an aircraft. **pull someone up** cause someone to stop or pause; check: *the shock of his words* ***pulled her up short.*** ■ Brit. reprimand someone.
– DERIVATIVES **puller** noun.
– ORIGIN Old English *pullian* 'pluck, snatch'; origin uncertain; the sense has developed from expressing a short sharp action to one of sustained force.

pullback ▶ **noun 1** an act of withdrawing troops.
2 a reduction in price or demand: *wait for pullbacks to buy international stocks.*

pull-down ▶ **adjective** Computing (of a menu) appearing below a menu title only while selected. Compare with DROP-DOWN.

pullet ▶ **noun** a young hen, especially one less than one year old.
– ORIGIN late Middle English: from Old French *poulet*, diminutive of *poule*, from the feminine of Latin *pullus* 'chicken, young animal'.

pulley ▶ **noun** (pl. **pulleys**) a wheel with a grooved rim around which a cord passes, which acts to change the direction of a force applied to the cord and is used to raise heavy weights. ■ a wheel or drum fixed on a shaft and turned by a belt, used for the application or transmission of power.
▶ **verb** (**pulleys**, **pulleying**, **pulleyed**) [with obj.] hoist with a pulley.
– ORIGIN Middle English: from Old French *polie*, probably from a medieval Greek diminutive of *polos* 'pivot, axis'.

pull hitter ▶ **noun** Baseball a hitter who normally strikes the ball in the direction in which they follow through.

pull-in ▶ **noun** Brit. dated a roadside cafe.

pulling guard ▶ **noun** American Football an offensive guard who pulls back from the line of scrimmage and runs toward the sideline to block for a runner.

Pullman ▶ **noun** (pl. **Pullmans**) [usu. as modifier] a railway carriage giving special comfort: *a train of Pullman cars.* ■ a train consisting of Pullman carriages. ■ (also **Pullman case**) N. Amer. a large suitcase designed to fit under the seat in a Pullman carriage.
– ORIGIN mid 19th cent.: named after George M. *Pullman* (1831–97), its American designer.

pull-out ▶ **adjective** (of a section of a magazine, newspaper, or other publication) designed to be detached and kept.
▶ **noun 1** a pull-out section of a magazine or newspaper: *don't miss Monday's 8-page Games pull-out.*
2 a withdrawal, especially from military involvement or participation in a commercial venture.

pullover ▶ **noun** a knitted garment put on over the head and covering the top half of the body.

pull-quote ▶ **noun** US a brief, attention-catching quotation taken from the main text of an article and used as a subheading or graphic feature.

pull tab ▶ **noun 1** North American term for RING PULL.
2 US a gambling card with a tab that can be pulled back to reveal a row or rows of symbols, with prizes for matching symbols.

pullulate /ˈpʌljʊleɪt/ ▶ **verb** [no obj.] (often as adj. **pullulating**) breed or spread prolifically or rapidly: *a pullulating little swarm of fish.* ■ be very crowded and lively: *our pullulating megalopolis.*
– DERIVATIVES **pullulation** noun.
– ORIGIN early 17th cent.: from Latin *pullulat-* 'sprouted', from the verb *pullulare*, from *pullulus*, diminutive of *pullus* 'young animal'.

pull-up ▶ **noun 1** an exercise involving raising oneself with one's arms by pulling up against a horizontal bar fixed above one's head.
2 Brit. dated a roadside cafe.

pulmonaria /ˌpʌlməˈnɛːrɪə/ ▶ **noun** a plant of a genus that includes lungwort. ● Genus *Pulmonaria*, family Boraginaceae.
– ORIGIN modern Latin, from medieval Latin *pulmonaria* (*herba*), feminine (used as a noun) of Latin *pulmonarius* 'relating to the lungs' (from the belief in its efficacy in curing lung diseases).

pulmonary /ˈpʌlmən(ə)ri/ ▶ **adjective** relating to the lungs: *pulmonary blood flow.*
– ORIGIN mid 17th cent.: from Latin *pulmonarius*, from *pulmo*, *pulmon-* 'lung'.

pulmonary artery ▶ **noun** the artery carrying blood from the right ventricle of the heart to the lungs for oxygenation.

pulmonary tuberculosis ▶ **noun** see TUBERCULOSIS.

pulmonary vein ▶ **noun** a vein carrying oxygenated blood from the lungs to the left atrium of the heart.

Pulmonata /ˌpʌlməˈneɪtə/ ▶ **plural noun** Zoology a group of molluscs which includes the land snails and slugs and many freshwater snails. They have a modified mantle cavity which acts as a lung for breathing air. ● Subclass Pulmonata, class Gastropoda.
– ORIGIN modern Latin (plural), from Latin *pulmo*, *pulmon-* 'lung'.

pulmonate Zoology ▶ **noun** a mollusc of the group Pulmonata, which includes the land snails and slugs and many freshwater snails.
▶ **adjective** relating to or denoting pulmonates.

pulmonic /pʌlˈmɒnɪk/ ▶ **adjective** another term for PULMONARY.

pulmonic airstream ▶ **noun** Phonetics the flow of air from the lungs under comparatively constant pressure, used in forming speech sounds. Contrasted with VELARIC AIRSTREAM.

pulp ▶ **noun** [mass noun] **1** a soft, wet, shapeless mass of material: *boiling with soda will reduce your peas to pulp.* ■ the soft fleshy part of a fruit. ■ a soft wet mass of fibres derived from rags or wood, used in papermaking. ■ vascular tissue filling the interior cavity and root canals of a tooth. ■ Mining pulverized ore mixed with water.
2 [usu. as modifier] popular or sensational writing that is regarded as being of poor quality: *the story is a mix of pulp fiction and Greek tragedy.* [because formerly printed on cheap paper.]
▶ **verb** [with obj.] crush into a soft, wet, shapeless mass. ■ withdraw (a publication) from the market and recycle the paper.
– PHRASES **beat** (or **smash**) **someone to a pulp** beat someone severely.
– DERIVATIVES **pulper** noun.
– ORIGIN late Middle English (denoting the soft fleshy part of fruit): from Latin *pulpa*. The verb dates from the mid 17th cent.

pulpit ▶ **noun 1** a raised enclosed platform in a church or chapel from which the preacher delivers a sermon. ■ (**the pulpit**) religious teaching as expressed in sermons: *the movies could rival the pulpit as an agency moulding the ideas of the mass public.*
2 a raised platform in the bows of a fishing boat or whaler. ■ a guard rail enclosing a small area at the bow of a yacht.
– ORIGIN Middle English: from Latin *pulpitum* 'scaffold, platform', in medieval Latin 'pulpit'.

pulpwood ▶ **noun** [mass noun] timber suitable for making into pulp.

pulpy ▶ **adjective** (**pulpier**, **pulpiest**) **1** resembling or consisting of pulp; mushy: *simmer gently until the fruit is very soft and pulpy.*
2 (of writing) sensationalist and of poor quality; trashy: *pulpy detective novels.*
– DERIVATIVES **pulpiness** noun.

pulque /ˈpʊlkeɪ, ˈpʊlki/ ▶ **noun** [mass noun] a Mexican alcoholic drink made by fermenting sap from the maguey plant.
– ORIGIN via American Spanish from Nahuatl *puliúhki* 'decomposed'.

pulsar /ˈpʌlsɑː/ ▶ **noun** Astronomy a celestial object, thought to be a rapidly rotating neutron star, that emits regular pulses of radio waves and other electromagnetic radiation at rates of up to one thousand pulses per second.
– ORIGIN from *puls(ating st)ar*, on the pattern of *quasar*.

pulsate /pʌlˈseɪt, ˈpʌlseɪt/ ▶ **verb** [no obj.] expand and contract with strong regular movements: *blood vessels throb and pulsate.* ■ (often as adj. **pulsating**) produce a regular throbbing sensation or sound: *dance the night away in one of the pulsating discos.* ■ (usu. as adj. **pulsating**) be very exciting: *victory in a pulsating semi-final.*
– DERIVATIVES **pulsation** noun, **pulsator** noun, **pulsatory** /ˈpʌlsət(ə)ri/ adjective.
– ORIGIN late 18th cent. (earlier (Middle English) as *pulsation*): from Latin *pulsat-* 'throbbed, pulsed', from the verb *pulsare*, frequentative of *pellere* 'to drive, beat'.

pulsatile /ˈpʌlsətʌɪl/ ▶ **adjective** chiefly Physiology pulsating; relating to pulsation: *pulsatile tinnitus.*
– ORIGIN late Middle English: from medieval Latin *pulsatilis* (in *vena pulsatilis* 'artery'), from the verb *pulsare* (see PULSATE).

pulsatilla /ˌpʌlsəˈtɪlə/ ▶ **noun** a plant of a genus that includes the pasque flower. ● Genus *Pulsatilla*, family Ranunculaceae.
– ORIGIN modern Latin, diminutive of *pulsatus* 'beaten about', expressing the notion 'small flower beaten by the wind'.

pulse¹ ▶ noun **1** a rhythmical throbbing of the arteries as blood is propelled through them, typically as felt in the wrists or neck: *the doctor found a faint pulse* | *the idea was enough to set my pulse racing.* ■ each successive throb of the arteries or heart.
2 a single vibration or short burst of sound, electric current, light, or other wave: *a pulse of gamma rays* | [as modifier] *a pulse generator.* ■ a musical beat or other regular rhythm.
3 the central point of energy and organization in an area or activity: *those close to the financial and economic pulse maintain that there have been fundamental changes.*
4 Biochemistry a measured amount of an isotopic label given to a culture of cells.
▶ verb **1** [no obj.] throb rhythmically; pulsate: *a knot of muscles at the side of his jaw pulsed.*
2 [with obj.] modulate (a wave or beam) so that it becomes a series of pulses. ■ apply a pulsed signal to (a device). ■ Biochemistry short for PULSE-LABEL.
– PHRASES **feel** (or **take**) **the pulse of** determine the heart rate of (someone) by feeling and timing the pulsation of an artery. ■ ascertain the general mood or opinion of: *the conference will be an opportunity to feel the pulse of those working in the field.*
– DERIVATIVES **pulseless** adjective.
– ORIGIN late Middle English: from Latin *pulsus* 'beating', from *pellere* 'to drive, beat'.

pulse² ▶ noun the edible seed of a leguminous plant, for example a chickpea, lentil, or bean. ■ a plant producing pulses.
– ORIGIN Middle English: from Old French *pols*, from Latin *puls* 'porridge of meal or pulse'; related to POLLEN.

pulse code modulation ▶ noun [mass noun] Electronics a pulse modulation technique in which the amplitude of an analogue signal is converted to a binary value represented as a series of pulses.

pulse dialling ▶ noun [mass noun] a method of telephone dialling in which each digit is transmitted as a corresponding number of electronic pulses, now being superseded by tone dialling.

pulse jet ▶ noun a type of jet engine in which combustion is intermittent, the ignition and expulsion of each charge of mixture causing the intake of a fresh charge.

pulse-label ▶ verb [with obj.] Biochemistry subject (cells in a culture) to a pulse of an isotopic label.

pulse modulation ▶ noun [mass noun] Electronics a type of modulation in which pulses are varied in some respect, such as width or amplitude, to represent the amplitude of a signal.

pulse oximeter ▶ noun an oximeter that measures the proportion of oxygenated haemoglobin in the blood in pulsating vessels, especially the capillaries of the finger or ear.

pultrude /pʊlˈtruːd, pʌl-/ ▶ verb [with obj.] (usu. as adj. **pultruded**) make (a reinforced plastic article) by drawing resin-coated glass fibres through a heated die.
– DERIVATIVES **pultrusion** noun.
– ORIGIN 1960s: from *pul(ling)* + EXTRUDE.

pulverize (also **pulverise**) ▶ verb [with obj.] reduce to fine particles: *the brick of the villages was pulverized by the bombardment.* ■ informal, chiefly Brit. defeat utterly: *he had a winning car and pulverized the opposition.*
– DERIVATIVES **pulverization** noun, **pulverizer** noun.
– ORIGIN late Middle English: from late Latin *pulverizare*, from *pulvis, pulver-* 'dust'.

pulverulent /pʌlˈvɛrʊl(ə)nt/ ▶ adjective archaic consisting of fine particles; powdery or crumbly.
– ORIGIN mid 17th cent.: from Latin *pulverulentus*, from *pulvis, pulver-* 'dust'.

pulvinus /pʌlˈvʌɪnəs/ ▶ noun (pl. **pulvini** /-nʌɪ/) Botany an enlarged section at the base of a leaf stalk in some plants, which is subject to changes of rigidity leading to movements of the leaf or leaflet.
– ORIGIN mid 19th cent.: from Latin, literally 'cushion'.

puma ▶ noun a large American wild cat with a plain tawny to greyish coat, found from Canada to Patagonia. Also called COUGAR, PANTHER, and MOUNTAIN LION in North America. ● *Felis concolor*, family Felidae.
– ORIGIN late 18th cent.: via Spanish from Quechua.

pumice /ˈpʌmɪs/ ▶ noun [mass noun] a very light and porous volcanic rock formed when a gas-rich froth of glassy lava solidifies rapidly. ■ (also **pumice stone**) [count noun] a piece of pumice used as an abrasive, especially for removing hard skin.
▶ verb [with obj.] rub with pumice to smooth or clean.
– DERIVATIVES **pumiceous** /pjuːˈmɪʃəs/ adjective.
– ORIGIN late Middle English: from Old French *pomis*, from a Latin dialect variant of *pumex, pumic-*. Compare with POUNCE².

pummel ▶ verb (**pummels, pummelling, pummelled**; US **pummels, pummeling, pummeled**) [with obj.] strike repeatedly with the fists: *he felt like a boxer who had been pummelled mercilessly against the ropes.* ■ N. Amer. informal criticize severely: *he has been pummelled by the reviewers.*
– ORIGIN mid 16th cent.: variant of POMMEL.

pummelo ▶ noun variant spelling of POMELO.

pump¹ ▶ noun **1** a mechanical device using suction or pressure to raise or move liquids, compress gases, or force air into inflatable objects such as tyres: *a petrol pump.* ■ [in sing.] an instance of moving something by or as if by a pump: *the pump of blood to her heart.*
2 [with modifier] Physiology an active transport mechanism in living cells by which specific ions are moved through the cell membrane against a concentration gradient: *the bacterium's sodium pump.*
▶ verb [with obj.] **1** [with adverbial of direction] force (liquid, gas, etc.) to move by or as if by means of a pump: *the blood is pumped around the body.* ■ [no obj., with adverbial of direction] move in spurts as though driven by a pump: *blood was pumping from a wound in his shoulder.*
2 fill (something such as a tyre or balloon) with liquid or gas using a pump: *I fetched the bike and **pumped up** the back tyre* | *my veins had been **pumped full of** glucose.* ■ informal shoot (bullets) into (a target). ■ (as adj. **pumped** or **pumped up**) informal very enthusiastic or excited: *the team came out really pumped up.*
3 move vigorously up and down: [with obj.] *we had to pump the handle like mad* | [no obj.] *that's superb running—look at his legs pumping.* ■ apply and release (a brake pedal or lever) several times in quick succession, typically to prevent skidding.
4 informal try to elicit information from (someone) by persistent questioning: *she began to **pump** her friend **for** details.*
– PHRASES **pump someone's hand** shake a person's hand vigorously. **pump iron** informal exercise with weights.
– PHRASAL VERBS **pump something in/into** informal invest a large sum of money in (something): *he pumped all his savings into building the boat.* **pump something out** produce or emit something in large quantities or amounts: *carnival bands pumping out music.* **pump something up** informal turn up the volume of music.
– DERIVATIVES **pumper** noun.
– ORIGIN late Middle English (originally in nautical use): related to Dutch *pomp* 'ship's pump' (earlier in the sense 'wooden or metal conduit'), probably partly of imitative origin.

pump² ▶ noun a light shoe, in particular: ■ chiefly N. English a sports shoe; a plimsoll. ■ Brit. a light shoe for dancing. ■ N. Amer. a court shoe.
– ORIGIN mid 16th cent.: of unknown origin.

pump-action ▶ adjective **1** denoting a repeating firearm in which a new round is brought from the magazine into the breech by a slide action in line with the barrel: *a pump-action shotgun.*
2 denoting an unpressurized spray dispenser for liquid that is worked by finger action rather than by internal pressure (as in an aerosol).

pump-and-dump ▶ adjective informal denoting the fraudulent practice of encouraging investors to buy shares in a company in order to inflate the price artificially, and then selling one's own shares while the price is high.

pumpernickel /ˈpʊmpəˌnɪk(ə)l, ˈpʌm-/ ▶ noun [mass noun] dark, dense German bread made from coarsely ground wholemeal rye.
– ORIGIN mid 18th cent.: transferred use of German *Pumpernickel* 'lout, bumpkin', of unknown ultimate origin.

pump gun ▶ noun a pump-action rifle with a tubular magazine.

pumpkin ▶ noun **1** a large rounded orange-yellow fruit with a thick rind, the flesh of which can be used in sweet or savoury dishes.
2 the plant of the gourd family which produces pumpkins, having tendrils and large lobed leaves and native to warm regions of America. ● Genus *Cucurbita*, family Cucurbitaceae: several species, in particular *C. pepo*. ■ Brit. another term for SQUASH².
– ORIGIN late 17th cent.: alteration of earlier *pumpion*, from obsolete French *pompon*, via Latin from Greek *pepōn* 'large melon' (see PEPO).

pumpkinseed ▶ noun (pl. **same** or **pumpkinseeds**) a small, edible brightly coloured freshwater fish of the sunfish family, native to North America. It is popular in aquaria and has been introduced into many European waters. ● *Lepomis gibbosus*, family Centrarchidae.

pump-priming ▶ noun [mass noun] **1** the introduction of fluid into a pump to prepare it for working.
2 the stimulation of economic activity by investment: [as modifier] *a pump-priming fund.*
– DERIVATIVES **pump-prime** verb, **pump-primer** noun.

pump room ▶ noun a room, building, or compartment in which pumps are housed or from which they are controlled. ■ a room at a spa where medicinal water is dispensed.

pum-pum /ˈpʊmpʊm/ ▶ noun W. Indian vulgar slang the female genitals.
– ORIGIN from a West African language.

pun¹ ▶ noun a joke exploiting the different possible meanings of a word or the fact that there are words which sound alike but have different meanings.
▶ verb (**puns, punning, punned**) [no obj.] (often as adj. **punning**) make a pun.
– DERIVATIVES **punningly** adverb, **punster** noun.
– ORIGIN mid 17th cent.: perhaps an abbreviation of obsolete *pundigrion*, as a fanciful alteration of PUNCTILIO.

pun² ▶ verb (**puns, punning, punned**) [with obj.] Brit. consolidate (earth or rubble) by pounding it.
– DERIVATIVES **punner** noun.
– ORIGIN mid 16th cent.: dialect variant of POUND².

puna /ˈpuːnə/ ▶ noun **1** a high treeless plateau in the Peruvian Andes.
2 another term for ALTITUDE SICKNESS.
– ORIGIN via American Spanish from Quechua.

Punan /puːˈnɑːn/ ▶ noun (pl. **same** or **Punans**) **1** a member of any of various groups of Dayak peoples inhabiting parts of Borneo.
2 [mass noun] any of the related languages of the Punan, now with fewer than 4,000 speakers.
▶ adjective relating to the Punan or their languages.
– ORIGIN the name in Dayak.

punani /pʊˈnɑːni/ (also **punany**) ▶ noun black slang the female genitals. ■ [mass noun] women regarded sexually.
– ORIGIN 1980s: origin uncertain.

punch¹ ▶ verb [with obj.] **1** strike with the fist: *he punched her in the face and ran off.*
2 press (a button or key on a machine): *I punched the button to summon the lift.* ■ (**punch something in/into**) enter information by punching a button or key on a machine.
3 N. Amer. drive (cattle) by prodding them with a stick.
▶ noun a blow with the fist. ■ [mass noun] informal the strength needed to deliver a blow: *he has the punch to knock out anyone in his division.* ■ [in sing.] informal the power to impress or attract attention; impact: *photos give their arguments an extra visual punch.*
– PHRASES **beat someone to the punch** informal anticipate or forestall someone's actions. **punch above one's weight** informal engage in an activity or contest perceived as being beyond one's abilities. **punch the (time) clock** N. Amer. (of an employee) clock in or out. ■ be employed in a conventional job with regular hours. **punch someone's lights out** see LIGHTS.
– PHRASAL VERBS **punch in** (or **out**) N. Amer. (of an employee) clock in (or out).
– DERIVATIVES **puncher** noun.
– ORIGIN late Middle English (as a verb in the sense 'puncture, prod'): variant of POUNCE¹.

punch² ▶ noun **1** a device or machine for making holes in materials such as paper, leather, or metal.
2 a tool or machine for impressing a design or stamping a die on a material.
▶ verb [with obj.] pierce a hole in (paper, leather, metal, etc.) with or as though with a punch. ■ pierce (a hole) with or as though with a punch.
– ORIGIN early 16th cent.: perhaps an abbreviation of PUNCHEON¹, or from the verb PUNCH¹.

punch³ ▶ noun [mass noun] a drink made from wine or spirits mixed with water, fruit juices, spices, etc., and typically served hot.
– ORIGIN mid 17th cent.: apparently from Sanskrit *pañca* 'five, five kinds of' (because the drink had five ingredients).

punch⁴ ▶ noun **1** (**Punch**) a grotesque, hook-nosed humpbacked buffoon, the chief male character of the Punch and Judy puppet show. Punch is the English variant of a stock character derived ultimately from Italian commedia dell'arte. Also called PUNCHINELLO.

P

2 (in full **Suffolk punch**) a draught horse of a short-legged thickset breed.
– PHRASES **as pleased** (or **proud**) **as Punch** feeling great delight or pride.
– ORIGIN mid 17th cent. (as a dialect term denoting a short, fat person): abbreviation of PUNCHINELLO.

Punch and Judy an English puppet show presented on the miniature stage of a tall collapsible booth traditionally covered with striped canvas. The show was probably introduced from the Continent in the 17th century. Punch is on the manipulator's right hand, remaining on stage all the time, while the left hand provides a series of characters—baby, wife (Judy), priest, doctor, policeman, hangman—for him to nag, beat, and finally kill.

punchbag ▸ **noun** Brit. a stuffed cylindrical bag suspended so it can be punched for exercise or training, especially by boxers. ■ a person on whom another person vents their anger.

punchball ▸ **noun 1** Brit. a stuffed or inflated ball suspended or mounted on a stand, used for punching as exercise or training, especially by boxers.
2 [mass noun] US a team ball game in which a rubber ball is punched or headed.

punchboard ▸ **noun** N. Amer. a board with holes containing slips of paper which are punched out as a form of gambling, with the object of locating a winning slip.

punchbowl ▸ **noun** a bowl used for mixing and serving punch. ■ chiefly Brit. a deep round hollow in a hilly area.

punch-drunk ▸ **adjective** stupefied by or as if by a series of heavy blows to the head.

punched card (also **punchcard**) ▸ **noun** a card perforated according to a code, formerly used to program computers.

punched tape ▸ **noun** a paper tape perforated according to a code, formerly used for conveying instructions or data to a data processor.

puncheon[1] /ˈpʌn(t)ʃ(ə)n/ ▸ **noun 1** a short post, especially one used for supporting the roof in a coal mine. ■ US a rough board or other length of wood, used for flooring or building.
2 another term for PUNCH[2].
– ORIGIN Middle English: from Old French *poinchon*, probably based on Latin *punct-* 'punctured', from the verb *pungere*. Compare with the noun POUNCE[1].

puncheon[2] /ˈpʌn(t)ʃ(ə)n/ ▸ **noun** historical a large cask for liquids or other commodities, holding from 72 to 120 gallons.
– ORIGIN late Middle English: from Old French *poinchon*, of uncertain origin although forms in Old French and English correspond to those of PUNCHEON[1].

P

Punchinello /ˌpʌn(t)ʃɪˈnɛləʊ/ ▸ **noun** (pl. **Punchinellos**) another name for PUNCH[4] (sense 1). ■ archaic a short, stout, comical-looking person.
– ORIGIN mid 17th cent.: alteration of Neapolitan dialect *Polecenella*, perhaps a diminutive of *pollecena* 'young turkey cock with a hooked beak', from *pulcino* 'chicken', from Latin *pullus*.

punching bag ▸ **noun** North American term for PUNCHBAG.

punchline ▸ **noun** the final phrase or sentence of a joke or story, providing the humour or some other crucial element.

punch press ▸ **noun** a press that is designed to drive a punch for shaping metal.

punch-up ▸ **noun** Brit. informal a disorderly bout of fighting with the fists; a brawl.

punchy ▸ **adjective** (**punchier**, **punchiest**) **1** having an immediate impact; forceful: *his style is journalistic, with short punchy sentences*.
2 informal, chiefly N. Amer. another term for PUNCH-DRUNK.
– DERIVATIVES **punchily** adverb, **punchiness** noun.

puncta plural form of PUNCTUM.

punctae /ˈpʌŋ(k)tiː/ ▸ **plural noun** Biology minute rounded dots or spots of colour, or small elevations or depressions on a surface.
– ORIGIN modern Latin (plural).

punctate /ˈpʌŋ(k)teɪt/ ▸ **adjective** Biology studded with or denoting dots or tiny holes.
– DERIVATIVES **punctation** noun.
– ORIGIN mid 18th cent.: from Latin *punctum* 'point' + -ATE[2].

punctilio /pʌŋ(k)ˈtɪlɪəʊ/ ▸ **noun** (pl. **punctilios**) a fine or petty point of conduct or procedure.
– ORIGIN late 16th cent.: from Italian *puntiglio(n-)* and Spanish *puntillo*, diminutive of *punto* 'a point'.

punctilious /pʌŋ(k)ˈtɪlɪəs/ ▸ **adjective** showing great attention to detail or correct behaviour: *he was punctilious in providing every amenity for his guests*.
– DERIVATIVES **punctiliously** adverb, **punctiliousness** noun.
– ORIGIN mid 17th cent.: from French *pointilleux*, from *pointille*, from Italian *puntiglio* (see PUNCTILIO).

punctual /ˈpʌŋ(k)tʃʊəl, -tjʊəl/ ▸ **adjective 1** happening or doing something at the agreed or proper time: *he's the sort of man who's always punctual*.
2 Grammar denoting or relating to an action that takes place at a particular point in time. Contrasted with DURATIVE.
– DERIVATIVES **punctuality** noun.
– ORIGIN late 17th cent.: from medieval Latin *punctualis*, from Latin *punctum* 'a point'.

punctually ▸ **adverb** at the agreed or proper time; promptly: *four out of five trains were arriving punctually*.

punctuate /ˈpʌŋ(k)tʃʊeɪt, -tjʊ-/ ▸ **verb** [with obj.]
1 insert punctuation marks in (text).
2 occur at intervals throughout (an area or period): *the country's history has been punctuated by coups*. ■ (**punctuate something with**) interrupt or intersperse something with: *she punctuates her conversation with snatches of song*.
– ORIGIN mid 17th cent. (in the sense 'point out'): from medieval Latin *punctuat-* 'brought to a point', from the verb *punctuare*, from *punctum* 'a point'.

punctuated equilibrium ▸ **noun** [mass noun] Biology the hypothesis that evolutionary development is marked by isolated episodes of rapid speciation between long periods of little or no change.

punctuation ▸ **noun** [mass noun] **1** the marks, such as full stop, comma, and brackets, used in writing to separate sentences and their elements and to clarify meaning.
2 Biology rapid or sudden speciation, as suggested by the theory of punctuated equilibrium.
– DERIVATIVES **punctuational** adjective.
– ORIGIN mid 17th cent.: from medieval Latin *punctuatio(n-)*, from the verb *punctuare* (see PUNCTUATE).

punctuationist ▸ **noun** Biology a person who believes in or advocates the hypothesis of punctuated equilibrium.
– DERIVATIVES **punctuationalism** noun.

punctuation mark ▸ **noun** a mark, such as a full stop, comma, or question mark, used in writing to separate sentences and their elements and to clarify meaning.

punctum /ˈpʌŋ(k)təm/ ▸ **noun** (pl. **puncta** /-tə/) technical a small, distinct point. ■ Anatomy the opening of a tear duct.
– ORIGIN late 16th cent. (figuratively, denoting a point): from Latin, literally 'a point'.

puncture ▸ **noun** a small hole in a tyre resulting in an escape of air: *she was on her way home when she had a puncture*. ■ a small hole in something such as the skin, caused by a sharp object: [as modifier] *a puncture wound*.
▸ **verb** [with obj.] **1** make a puncture in (something): *one of the knife blows had punctured a lung*. ■ [no obj.] sustain a puncture: *the tyre had punctured and it would have to be replaced*.
2 cause a sudden collapse of (mood or feeling): *the earlier mood of optimism was punctured*.
– ORIGIN late Middle English: from Latin *punctura*, from *punct-* 'pricked', from the verb *pungere*. The verb dates from the late 17th cent.

pundit /ˈpʌndɪt/ ▸ **noun 1** an expert in a particular subject or field who is frequently called upon to give their opinions to the public: *political pundits were tipping him for promotion*.
2 variant spelling of PANDIT.
– DERIVATIVES **punditry** noun (sense 1).
– ORIGIN from Sanskrit *paṇḍita* 'learned'.

punditocracy /pʌndɪˈtɒkrəsi/ ▸ **noun** [mass noun] an elite or influential class of experts or political commentators.

Pune /ˈpuːnə/ an industrial city in Maharashtra, western India, in the hills south-east of Mumbai (Bombay); pop. 3,337,500 (est. 2009). It was a military and administrative centre under British rule. Formerly called POONA.

punga /ˈpʌŋə/ ▸ **noun** variant spelling of PONGA.

pungent ▸ **adjective** having a sharply strong taste or smell: *the pungent smell of frying onions*. ■ (of comment, criticism, or humour) having a sharp and caustic quality.
– DERIVATIVES **pungency** noun, **pungently** adverb.
– ORIGIN late 16th cent. (in the sense 'very painful or distressing'): from Latin *pungent-* 'pricking', from the verb *pungere*.

Punic /ˈpjuːnɪk/ ▸ **adjective** relating to ancient Carthage.
▸ **noun** [mass noun] the language of Carthage, related to Phoenician.
– ORIGIN from Latin *Punicus* (earlier *Poenicus*), from *Poenus*, from Greek *Phoinix* 'Phoenician'.

Punic Wars three wars between Rome and Carthage, which led to the unquestioned dominance of Rome in the western Mediterranean.

> In the first Punic War (264–241 BC), Rome secured Sicily from Carthage and established herself as a naval power; in the second (218–201 BC), the defeat of Hannibal (largely through the generalship of Fabius Cunctator and Scipio Africanus) put an end to Carthage's position as a Mediterranean power; the third (149–146 BC) ended in the total destruction of the city of Carthage.

punish ▸ **verb** [with obj.] inflict a penalty or sanction on (someone) as retribution for an offence, especially a transgression of a legal or moral code: *I have done wrong and I'm being* ***punished for*** *it*. ■ inflict a penalty or sanction on someone for (such an offence): *fraudulent acts would be punished by up to two years in prison*. ■ informal capitalize on (an opponent's mistake), especially in sport: *Australia punished Ireland's handling blunders and scored three tries*. ■ treat (someone) in an unfairly harsh way: *a rise in prescription charges would punish the poor*. ■ subject to severe and debilitating treatment.
– DERIVATIVES **punisher** noun.
– ORIGIN Middle English: from Old French *puniss-*, lengthened stem of *punir* 'punish', from Latin *punire*, from *poena* 'penalty'.

punishable ▸ **adjective** (of an act) subject to a judicial punishment: *a criminal offence* ***punishable by*** *up to three years in jail* | *a punishable offence*.

punishing ▸ **adjective** physically and mentally demanding; arduous: *the band's punishing tour schedule*. ■ severe and debilitating: *the recession was having a punishing effect on our business*.
– DERIVATIVES **punishingly** adverb.

punishment ▸ **noun** [mass noun] the infliction or imposition of a penalty as retribution for an offence: *crime demands just punishment*. ■ the penalty inflicted: *she assisted her husband to escape punishment for the crime* | [count noun] *he approved of stiff punishments for criminals*. ■ informal rough treatment or handling: *your machine can take a fair amount of punishment before falling to bits*.
– ORIGIN late Middle English: from Old French *punissement*, from the verb *punir* (see PUNISH).

punitive /ˈpjuːnɪtɪv/ (also **punitory** /-t(ə)ri/) ▸ **adjective** inflicting or intended as punishment: *he called for punitive measures against the Eastern bloc*. ■ (of a tax or other charge) extremely high: *a current punitive interest rate of 31.3 per cent*.
– DERIVATIVES **punitively** adverb, **punitiveness** noun.
– ORIGIN early 17th cent.: from French *punitif*, *-ive* or medieval Latin *punitivus*, from Latin *punit-* 'punished', from the verb *punire* (see PUNISH).

punitive damages ▸ **plural noun** Law damages exceeding simple compensation and awarded to punish the defendant.

Punjab /pʌnˈdʒɑːb, ˈpʌndʒɑːb, pʊn-/ (also **the Punjab**) a region of NW India and Pakistan, a wide, fertile plain traversed by the Indus and the five tributaries which gave the region its name. ■ a province of Pakistan; capital, Lahore. ■ a state of India; capital, Chandigarh. Until 1966 the Punjab also encompassed what is now the state of Haryana.

> The region became a centre of Sikhism in the 15th century and, after the capture of Lahore in 1799 by Ranjit Singh, a powerful Sikh kingdom. It was annexed by the British in 1849 and became a part of British India. In the partition of 1947 it was divided between Pakistan and India.

– ORIGIN Hindi *Panjāb*, from Persian *panj* 'five' + *āb* 'water'.

Punjabi /pʌnˈdʒɑːbi, pʊn-/ (also **Panjabi**) ▸ **noun** (pl. **Punjabis**) **1** a native or inhabitant of Punjab.
2 [mass noun] the Indic language of Punjab, spoken by over 92 million people.
3 (**punjabi**) a long kurta (loose collarless shirt).
▸ **adjective** relating to Punjab or its people or language.

punji stick /ˈpʌndʒi/ (also **punji stake**) ▸ **noun** a sharpened bamboo stake, typically one tipped with

poison, set in a camouflaged hole in the ground as a means of defence, especially in SE Asia.
– ORIGIN late 19th cent.: *punji* probably of Tibeto-Burman origin.

punk ▶ noun **1** N. Amer. informal a worthless person (often used as a general term of abuse). ■ a criminal or thug. ■ US (in prison slang) a passive male homosexual. ■ an inexperienced young person.
2 (also **punk rock**) [mass noun] a loud, fast-moving, and aggressive form of rock music, popular in the late 1970s. ■ (also **punk rocker**) [count noun] an admirer or player of punk rock, typically characterized by coloured spiked hair and clothing decorated with safety pins or zips.
3 [mass noun] chiefly N. Amer. soft, crumbly wood that has been attacked by fungus, used as tinder.
▶ adjective **1** N. Amer. informal in poor condition: *I felt too punk to eat.*
2 relating to punk rock and its associated subculture: *a punk band* | *a punk haircut.*
– DERIVATIVES **punkish** adjective, **punky** adjective (**punkier**, **punkiest**).
– ORIGIN late 17th cent. (in sense 3 of the noun): perhaps, in some senses, related to archaic *punk* 'prostitute', also to SPUNK.

punkah /ˈpʌŋkə, -kɑː/ ▶ noun chiefly historical (in India) a large cloth fan on a frame suspended from the ceiling, moved backwards and forwards by pulling on a cord. ■ Indian an electric fan.
– ORIGIN via Hindi from Sanskrit *pakṣaka*, from *pakṣa* 'wing'.

punker ▶ noun chiefly N. Amer. a punk rocker.

punkette ▶ noun a female punk rocker.
– ORIGIN 1980s: from PUNK + the feminine suffix -ETTE.

punnet ▶ noun Brit. a small light basket or other container for fruit or vegetables: ***a punnet of** strawberries.*
– ORIGIN early 19th cent.: perhaps a diminutive of dialect *pun* 'a pound'.

punt1 /pʌnt/ ▶ noun a long, narrow flat-bottomed boat, square at both ends and propelled with a long pole, used on inland waters chiefly for recreation.
▶ verb travel or convey in a punt: [no obj.] *in summer you can enjoy punting along the river.*
– ORIGIN Old English, from Latin *ponto*, denoting a flat-bottomed ferry boat; readopted in the early 16th cent. from Middle Low German *punte* or Middle Dutch *ponte* 'ferry boat', of the same origin.

punt2 /pʌnt/ ▶ verb [with obj.] **1** [with adverbial of direction] Soccer kick (the ball) a long distance upfield.
2 American Football & Rugby kick the ball after it has dropped from the hands and before it reaches the ground.
▶ noun an act of punting a ball.
– ORIGIN mid 19th cent.: probably from dialect *punt* 'push forcibly'. Compare with BUNT1.

punt3 /pʌnt/ ▶ verb [no obj.] (in some gambling card games) lay a stake against the bank. ■ Brit. informal bet or speculate on something: *investors are **punting on** a takeover.*
▶ noun Brit. informal a bet: *those **taking a punt on** the company's success.*
– PHRASES **take** (or **have**) **a punt at** Austral./NZ informal attempt to do (something).
– ORIGIN early 18th cent.: from French *ponte* 'player against the bank', from Spanish *punto* 'a point'.

punt4 /pʊnt/ ▶ noun (until the introduction of the euro in 2002) the basic monetary unit of the Republic of Ireland, equal to 100 pence.
– ORIGIN Irish, literally 'pound'.

Punta Arenas /ˌpʊntə əˈreɪnəs/ a port in southern Chile, on the Strait of Magellan; pop. 120,000 (est. 2006).

punter ▶ noun **1** informal, chiefly Brit. a person who gambles, places a bet, or makes a risky investment. ■ a customer or client, especially a member of an audience. ■ a prostitute's client.
2 American Football & Rugby a player who punts.
3 a person who propels or travels in a punt.

punty /ˈpʌnti/ ▶ noun (pl. **punties**) variant spelling of PONTIL.

puny /ˈpjuːni/ ▶ adjective (**punier**, **puniest**) small and weak: *white-faced, puny children.* ■ poor in quality, amount, or size: *the army was reduced to a puny 100,000 men.*
– DERIVATIVES **punily** adverb, **puniness** noun.
– ORIGIN mid 16th cent. (as a noun denoting a younger or more junior person): phonetic spelling of PUISNE.

pup ▶ noun a young dog. ■ a young wolf, seal, rat, or other mammal. ■ dated a cheeky or arrogant boy or young man: *you saucy young pup!*
▶ verb (**pups**, **pupping**, **pupped**) [no obj.] (of bitches and certain other female animals) give birth to young.
– PHRASES **in pup** (of a bitch) pregnant. **sell someone a pup** Brit. informal swindle someone by selling them something worthless.
– ORIGIN late 16th cent. (in the sense 'arrogant young man'): back-formation from PUPPY, interpreted as a diminutive.

pupa /ˈpjuːpə/ ▶ noun (pl. **pupae** /-piː/) an insect in its inactive immature form between larva and adult, e.g. a chrysalis.
– DERIVATIVES **pupal** adjective.
– ORIGIN late 18th cent.: modern Latin, from Latin *pupa* 'girl, doll'.

puparium /pjuːˈpɛːrɪəm/ ▶ noun (pl. **puparia** /-rɪə/) Entomology the hardened last larval skin which encloses the pupa in some insects, especially higher diptera. ■ a pupa enclosed in a puparium.
– ORIGIN early 19th cent.: modern Latin, from PUPA, on the pattern of words such as *herbarium*.

pupate ▶ verb [no obj.] (of a larva) become a pupa.
– DERIVATIVES **pupation** noun.

pupfish ▶ noun (pl. **same** or **pupfishes**) a small fish found in fresh or brackish water in the deserts of the south-western US and northern Mexico. ● Genus *Cyprinodon*, family Cyprinodontidae: several species.

pupil1 ▶ noun a person who is taught by another, especially a schoolchild or student in relation to a teacher. ■ Brit. a trainee barrister.
– ORIGIN late Middle English (in the sense 'orphan, ward'): from Old French *pupille*, from Latin *pupillus* (diminutive of *pupus* 'boy') and *pupilla* (diminutive of *pupa* 'girl').

pupil2 ▶ noun the dark circular opening in the centre of the iris of the eye, which varies in size to regulate the amount of light reaching the retina.
– DERIVATIVES **pupillary** adjective.
– ORIGIN late Middle English: from Old French *pupille* or Latin *pupilla*, diminutive of *pupa* 'doll' (so named from the tiny reflected images visible in the eye).

pupillage (also **pupilage**) ▶ noun [mass noun] the state of being a pupil or student. ■ Law (in the UK) apprenticeship to a member of the Bar, which qualifies a barrister to practise independently.

pupil-master ▶ noun Brit. a barrister in charge of a trainee barrister.

pupiparous /pjuːˈpɪp(ə)rəs/ ▶ adjective Entomology (of certain flies, e.g. the tsetse) producing young which are already ready to pupate.
– ORIGIN early 19th cent.: from modern Latin *pupipara* (neuter plural of *pupiparus* 'bringing forth young') + -OUS.

puppet ▶ noun a movable model of a person or animal that is typically moved either by strings controlled from above or by a hand inside it. ■ a person, group, or country under the control of another: *a former revolutionary hero who is now a puppet of the state.*
– DERIVATIVES **puppetry** noun.
– ORIGIN mid 16th cent. (denoting a doll): later form of POPPET, generally having a more unfavourable connotation.

puppeteer ▶ noun a person who operates puppets.
– DERIVATIVES **puppeteering** noun.

puppetmaster ▶ noun a person, group, or country that covertly controls another: *the puppetmaster behind the current administration.*

Puppis /ˈpʌpɪs/ Astronomy a southern constellation (the Poop or Stern), lying partly in the Milky Way south of Canis Major and originally part of Argo.
– ORIGIN Latin.

puppy ▶ noun (pl. **puppies**) a young dog. ■ dated a cheeky or arrogant boy or young man: *you ungrateful puppy!* ■ informal, chiefly N. Amer. a person or thing of a specified kind: *these puppies were way over my budget.*
– DERIVATIVES **puppyhood** noun, **puppyish** adjective.
– ORIGIN late 15th cent. (denoting a lapdog): perhaps from Old French *poupee* 'doll, plaything'; compare with PUPPET, synonymous with dialect *puppy* (as in *puppy-show* 'puppet show').

puppy dog ▶ noun a child's word for a puppy.

puppy fat ▶ noun [mass noun] Brit. fat on the body of a baby or child which disappears around adolescence.

puppy love ▶ noun [mass noun] intense but relatively shallow romantic attachment, associated with adolescents.

pup tent ▶ noun N. Amer. a small triangular tent, especially one for two people and without side walls.

pur- ▶ prefix equivalent to PRO-1 (as in *purloin*, *pursue*).
– ORIGIN from Anglo Norman French, from Latin *por-*, *pro-*.

Purana /pʊˈrɑːnə/ ▶ noun (usu. **Puranas**) any of a class of Sanskrit sacred writings on Hindu mythology and folklore of varying date and origin, the most ancient of which dates from the 4th century AD.
– DERIVATIVES **Puranic** adjective.
– ORIGIN from Sanskrit *purāṇa* 'ancient (legend)', from *purā* 'formerly'.

Purbeck marble /ˈpəːbɛk/ (also **Purbeck stone**) ▶ noun [mass noun] a hard limestone from Purbeck in Dorset, which is polished and used for decorative parts of buildings, fonts, and effigies.

purblind /ˈpəːblʌɪnd/ ▶ adjective literary having impaired or defective vision; partially blind. ■ slow or unable to understand; dim-witted.
– DERIVATIVES **purblindness** noun.
– ORIGIN Middle English (as two words in the sense 'completely blind'): from the adverb PURE 'utterly' (later assimilated to PUR-) + BLIND.

Purcell /pəːˈsɛl, ˈpəːs(ə)l/, Henry (1659–95), English composer. Organist for Westminster Abbey (1679–95), he composed choral odes and songs for royal occasions. His main interest was music for the theatre; he composed the first English opera *Dido and Aeneas* (1689) and incidental music for many plays.

purchase ▶ verb [with obj.] **1** acquire (something) by paying for it; buy: *Mr Gill spotted the manuscript at a local auction and purchased it for £1,500.* ■ archaic obtain or achieve with effort or suffering: *the victory was purchased by the death of Rhiwallon.*
2 Nautical haul up (a rope, cable, or anchor) by means of a pulley or lever.
▶ noun **1** [mass noun] the action of buying something: *the large number of videos currently available for purchase* | [count noun] *she **made her purchases** carefully.* ■ [count noun] a thing that has been bought: *she stowed her purchases in the car.* ■ Law the acquisition of property by one's personal action rather than by inheritance. ■ archaic the annual rent or return from land.
2 [mass noun] firm contact or grip: *the horse's hooves fought for purchase on the slippery pavement* | [in sing.] *an attempt to gain a purchase on the soft earth.* ■ [count noun] a pulley or similar device for moving heavy objects.
– DERIVATIVES **purchasable** adjective.
– ORIGIN Middle English: from Old French *pourchacier* 'seek to obtain or bring about', the earliest sense also in English, which soon gave rise to the senses 'gain' (hence, in nautical use, the notion of 'gaining' one portion of rope after another) and 'buy'.

purchaser ▶ noun a person who buys something; a buyer: *one of the club's prospective purchasers.*

purchase tax ▶ noun a tax added to the price of goods sold to consumers.

purchasing power ▶ noun [mass noun] the financial ability to buy products and services. ■ the value of a sum of money.

purdah /ˈpəːdə/ ▶ noun [mass noun] the practice in certain Muslim and Hindu societies of screening women from men or strangers, especially by means of a curtain: *he never required them to observe purdah* | *she was supposed to be **in purdah** upstairs.* ■ [count noun] a curtain used for screening off women in this way.
– ORIGIN early 19th cent.: from Urdu and Persian *parda* 'veil, curtain'.

pure ▶ adjective **1** not mixed or adulterated with any other substance or material: *cars can run on pure alcohol* | *the jacket was pure wool.* ■ without any extraneous and unnecessary elements: *the romantic notion of pure art devoid of social responsibility.* ■ free of any contamination: *the pure, clear waters of Scotland.* ■ (also **pure-bred**) (of an animal or plant) of unmixed origin or descent; pedigree: *the pure Charolais is white or light wheat in the coat* | *80 pure-bred stallions were on parade.*
2 (of a sound) perfectly in tune and with a clear tone.
3 wholesome and untainted by immorality, especially that of a sexual nature: *our fondness for each other is pure and innocent.*

P

4 (of a subject of study) dealing with abstract concepts and not practical application: *a theoretical discipline such as pure physics*. Compare with APPLIED.
5 [attrib.] involving or containing nothing else but; sheer (used for emphasis): *a shout of pure anger | an outcome which may be a matter of pure chance | it was revenge, **pure and simple**.*
6 Phonetics (of a vowel) not joined with another to form a diphthong.
– DERIVATIVES **pureness** noun.
– ORIGIN Middle English: from Old French *pur* 'pure', from Latin *purus*.

pure culture ▶ noun Microbiology a culture in which only one strain or clone is present.

purée /ˈpjʊəreɪ/ ▶ noun [mass noun] a smooth cream of liquidized or crushed fruit or vegetables: *tomato purée*.
▶ verb (**purées**, **puréeing**, **puréed**) [with obj.] make a purée of (fruit or vegetables).
– ORIGIN early 18th cent.: French, literally 'purified', feminine past participle of *purer*.

pure line ▶ noun Biology an inbred line of genetic descent.

purely ▶ adverb 1 in a pure manner: *act nobly, speak purely, and think charitably*.
2 entirely; exclusively: *the purpose of the meeting was purely to give information*.

pure mathematics ▶ plural noun see MATHEMATICS.

pure play (also **pure player**) ▶ noun [usu. as modifier] a company that focuses exclusively on a particular product or service in order to obtain a large market share. ■ a company that operates only on the Internet.

pure science ▶ noun a science depending on deductions from demonstrated truths, such as mathematics or logic, or studied without regard to practical applications.

purfle /ˈpəːf(ə)l/ ▶ noun an ornamental border, typically one inlaid on the back or belly of a violin. ■ archaic an embroidered edge of a garment.
▶ verb [with obj.] (often as noun **purfling**) decorate (something) with an ornamental border.
– ORIGIN Middle English (as a verb): from Old French *porfil* (noun), *porfiler* (verb), based on Latin *pro* 'forward' + *filum* 'thread'.

purgation /pəːˈɡeɪʃ(ə)n/ ▶ noun [mass noun] 1 purification or cleansing. ■ (in Catholic doctrine) the spiritual cleansing of a soul in purgatory. ■ historical the action of clearing oneself of accusation or suspicion by taking an oath or undergoing an ordeal.
2 evacuation of the bowels brought about by taking laxatives.
– ORIGIN late Middle English: from Old French *purgacion*, from Latin *purgatio(n-)*, from *purgare* 'purify' (see PURGE).

P

purgative /ˈpəːɡətɪv/ ▶ adjective strongly laxative in effect. ■ having the effect of ridding one of unwanted feelings or memories: *the purgative action of language*.
▶ noun a laxative. ■ a thing that rids one of unwanted feelings or memories: *confrontation would be a purgative*.
– ORIGIN late Middle English: from Old French *purgatif, -ive*, from late Latin *purgativus*, from *purgat-* 'purified', from the verb *purgare* (see PURGE).

purgatory /ˈpəːɡət(ə)ri/ ▶ noun (pl. **purgatories**) (often **Purgatory**) (in Catholic doctrine) a place or state of suffering inhabited by the souls of sinners who are expiating their sins before going to heaven. ■ [mass noun] mental anguish or suffering: *this was purgatory, worse than anything she'd faced in her life*.
▶ adjective archaic having the quality of cleansing or purifying: *infernal punishments are purgatory and medicinal*.
– DERIVATIVES **purgatorial** adjective.
– ORIGIN Middle English: from Anglo-Norman French *purgatorie* or medieval Latin *purgatorium*, neuter (used as a noun) of late Latin *purgatorius* 'purifying', from the verb *purgare* (see PURGE).

purge ▶ verb [with obj.] 1 rid (someone) of an unwanted feeling, memory, or condition: *Bob had helped **purge** Martha **of** the terrible guilt that had haunted her*. ■ remove (an unwanted feeling, memory, etc.) in such a way: *his hatred was purged*. ■ remove (a group of people considered undesirable) from an organization or place in an abrupt or violent manner: *he purged all but 26 of the central committee members*. ■ remove someone from (an organization or place) in such a way: *an opportunity to **purge** the party **of** unsatisfactory members*. ■ Law atone for or wipe out (contempt of court).
2 physically remove (something) completely: *a substance designed to purge impurities from the body*. ■ [no obj.] evacuate one's bowels, especially as a result of taking a laxative.
▶ noun 1 an abrupt or violent removal of a group of people: *the savagery of government's political purges*.
2 dated a laxative.
– DERIVATIVES **purger** noun.
– ORIGIN Middle English (in the legal sense 'clear oneself of a charge'): from Old French *purgier*, from Latin *purgare* 'purify', from *purus* 'pure'.

puri /ˈpuːri/ ▶ noun (pl. **puris**) (in Indian cookery) a small, round piece of bread made of unleavened wheat flour, deep-fried and served with meat or vegetables.
– ORIGIN via Hindi from Sanskrit *pūrikā*.

purify ▶ verb (**purifies**, **purifying**, **purified**) [with obj.] remove contaminants from: *the filtration plant is able to purify 70 tons of water a day* | (as adj. **purified**) *purified linseed oil* | figurative *they set out to purify art by reviving the spirit and style of early religious painting*. ■ (**purify something from**) extract something from: *genomic DNA was purified from whole blood*. ■ make ceremonially clean: *a ritual bath to purify the soul*.
– DERIVATIVES **purification** noun, **purificatory** adjective, **purifier** noun.
– ORIGIN Middle English: from Old French *purifier*, from Latin *purificare*, from *purus* 'pure'.

Purim /ˈpʊərɪm, pʊˈriːm/ ▶ noun a lesser Jewish festival held in spring (on the 14th or 15th day of Adar) to commemorate the defeat of Haman's plot to massacre the Jews as recorded in the book of Esther.
– ORIGIN Hebrew, plural of *pūr*, explained in the book of Esther (3:7, 9:24) as meaning 'lot', with allusion to the casting of lots by Haman.

purine /ˈpjʊəriːn/ ▶ noun [mass noun] Chemistry a colourless crystalline compound with basic properties, forming uric acid on oxidation. ● A bicyclic compound; chem. formula: $C_5H_4N_4$.
■ (also **purine base**) [count noun] a substituted derivative of purine, especially the bases adenine and guanine present in DNA.
– ORIGIN late 19th cent.: from German *Purin*, from Latin *purus* 'pure' + *uricum* 'uric acid' + -INE[4].

purism ▶ noun [mass noun] 1 scrupulous or exaggerated observance of or insistence on traditional rules or structures, especially in language or style.
2 (**Purism**) an early 20th-century artistic style and movement founded by Le Corbusier and the French painter Amédée Ozenfant (1886–1966) and emphasizing purity of geometric form. It arose out of a rejection of cubism and was characterized by a return to the representation of recognizable objects.

purist ▶ noun 1 a person who insists on absolute adherence to traditional rules or structures, especially in language or style.
2 (**Purist**) an adherent of Purism.
– DERIVATIVES **puristic** adjective.
– ORIGIN early 18th cent.: from French *puriste*, from *pur* 'pure'.

puritan ▶ noun (**Puritan**) a member of a group of English Protestants of the late 16th and 17th centuries who regarded the Reformation of the Church under Elizabeth I as incomplete and sought to simplify and regulate forms of worship. ■ a person with censorious moral beliefs, especially about self-indulgence and sex.
▶ adjective (usu. **Puritan**) relating to the Puritans. ■ having or displaying censorious moral beliefs, especially about self-indulgence and sex.
– DERIVATIVES **puritanism** noun.
– ORIGIN late 16th cent.: from late Latin *puritas* 'purity' + -AN.

puritanical ▶ adjective having or displaying a very strict or censorious moral attitude towards self-indulgence or sex: *his puritanical parents saw any kind of pleasure as the road to damnation*.
– DERIVATIVES **puritanically** adverb.

purity ▶ noun [mass noun] 1 freedom from adulteration or contamination: *the purity of our drinking water*.
2 freedom from immorality, especially of a sexual nature: *white is meant to represent purity and innocence*.
– ORIGIN Middle English: from Old French *purete*, later assimilated to late Latin *puritas*, from Latin *purus* 'pure'.

Purkinje cell /pəːˈkɪndʒi/ ▶ noun Anatomy a nerve cell of a large, branched type found in the cortex of the cerebellum.
– ORIGIN mid 19th cent.: named after Jan E. *Purkinje* (1787–1869), Bohemian physiologist.

purl[1] ▶ noun [mass noun] 1 a knitting stitch made by putting the needle through the front of the stitch from right to left. Compare with PLAIN[1] (sense 5 of the adjective).
2 a cord of twisted gold or silver wire used for bordering or edging something. ■ an ornamental edging of lace or ribbon.
▶ verb [with obj.] knit with a purl stitch: *knit one, purl one*.
– ORIGIN mid 17th cent.: of uncertain origin.

purl[2] literary ▶ verb [no obj.] (of a stream or river) flow with a swirling motion and babbling sound.
▶ noun [in sing.] a purling motion or sound.
– ORIGIN early 16th cent. (denoting a small swirling stream): probably imitative; compare with Norwegian *purla* 'bubble up'.

purler ▶ noun Brit. informal a headlong fall: *the horse went a purler at the last fence*.
– ORIGIN mid 19th cent.: from dialect *purl* 'upset, overturn'.

purlieu /ˈpəːljuː/ ▶ noun (pl. **purlieus** or **purlieux**) 1 (**purlieus**) the area near or surrounding a place: *the photogenic purlieus of Cambridge*. ■ a person's usual haunts.
2 Brit. historical a tract on the border of a forest, especially one earlier included in it and still partly subject to forest laws.
– ORIGIN late 15th cent. (denoting a tract on the border of a forest): probably an alteration (suggested by French *lieu* 'place') of Anglo-Norman French *puralee* 'a going round to settle the boundaries'.

purlin /ˈpəːlɪn/ ▶ noun a horizontal beam along the length of a roof, resting on principals and supporting the common rafters or boards.
– ORIGIN late Middle English: perhaps of French origin.

purloin /pəːˈlɔɪn/ ▶ verb [with obj.] formal or humorous steal (something): *he must have managed to purloin a copy of the key*.
– DERIVATIVES **purloiner** noun.
– ORIGIN Middle English (in the sense 'put at a distance'): from Anglo-Norman French *purloigner* 'put away', from *pur-* 'forth' + *loign* 'far'.

puro /ˈpʊərəʊ/ ▶ noun (pl. **puros**) (in Spain and Spanish-speaking countries) a cigar.
– ORIGIN Spanish, literally 'pure'.

puromycin /ˌpjʊərə(ʊ)ˈmʌɪsɪn/ ▶ noun [mass noun] Medicine an antibiotic used to treat sleeping sickness and amoebic dysentery. ● This antibiotic is produced by the bacterium *Streptomyces alboniger*.
– ORIGIN 1950s: from PURINE + -MYCIN.

purple ▶ noun [mass noun] 1 a colour intermediate between red and blue: *the painting was mostly in shades of blue and purple*. ■ purple clothing or material.
2 (also **Tyrian purple**) a crimson dye obtained from some molluscs, formerly used for fabric worn by an emperor or senior magistrate in ancient Rome or Byzantium. ■ (**the purple**) (in ancient Rome or Byzantium) clothing of this colour. ■ (**the purple**) (in ancient Rome) a position of rank, authority, or privilege: *he was too young to assume the purple*. ■ (**the purple**) the scarlet official dress of a cardinal.
▶ adjective of a colour intermediate between red and blue: *a faded purple T-shirt*.
▶ verb make or become purple in colour: [no obj.] *Edmund's cheeks purpled* | [with obj.] *the neon was purpling the horizon above the highway*.
– PHRASES **born in** (or **to**) **the purple** born into a reigning family or privileged class.
– DERIVATIVES **purpleness** noun, **purplish** adjective, **purply** adjective.
– ORIGIN Old English (describing the clothing of an emperor), alteration of *purpre*, from Latin *purpura* 'purple', from Greek *porphura*, denoting molluscs that yielded a crimson dye, also cloth dyed with this.

purple emperor ▶ noun a large European woodland butterfly that has iridescent purplish-black wings with white markings. ● *Apatura iris*, subfamily Apaturinae, family Nymphalidae.

purple gallinule ▶ noun another term for SWAMPHEN.

purple heart ▶ noun 1 (**Purple Heart**) (in the US) a decoration for members of the armed forces wounded or killed in action, established in 1782 and re-established in 1932.
2 a large tree of the rainforests of Central and South America, with dark purplish-brown timber which blackens on contact with water. ● Genus *Peltogyne*, family Leguminosae: several species.

3 Brit. informal a purple heart-shaped amphetamine tablet.

purple passage ▸ noun an elaborate or excessively ornate passage in a literary composition.

purple patch ▸ noun 1 Brit. informal a run of success or good luck: *people expect me to score in every game now I've hit a purple patch.*
2 another term for **PURPLE PASSAGE**.

purple prose ▸ noun [mass noun] prose that is too elaborate or ornate.

purple swamphen ▸ noun see **SWAMPHEN**.

purport ▸ verb /pəˈpɔːt/ [with infinitive] appear to be or do something, especially falsely: *she is not the person she purports to be* | (as adj. **purported**) *the purported marriage was void.*
▸ noun /ˈpəːpɔːt/ [mass noun] the meaning or sense of something, typically a document or speech: *I do not understand the purport of your remarks.* ■ the purpose or intention of something: *the purport of existence.*
– DERIVATIVES **purportedly** adverb.
– ORIGIN late Middle English (in the sense 'express, signify'): from Old French *purporter*, from medieval Latin *proportare*, from Latin *pro-* 'forth' + *portare* 'carry, bear'. The sense 'appear to be' dates from the late 18th cent.

purpose ▸ noun 1 the reason for which something is done or created or for which something exists: *the purpose of the meeting is to appoint a trustee* | *the building is no longer needed for its original purpose.* ■ (usu. **purposes**) a particular requirement or consideration, typically one that is temporary or restricted in scope or extent: *state pensions are considered as earned income for tax purposes.*
2 [mass noun] a person's sense of resolve or determination: *there was a new* ***sense of purpose*** *in her step as she set off.*
▸ verb [with obj.] formal have as one's intention or objective: *God has allowed suffering, even purposed it.*
– PHRASES **accidentally on purpose** informal apparently by accident but in fact intentionally. **on purpose** intentionally: *he was being annoying on purpose.* **to no purpose** with no result or effect; pointlessly. **to the purpose** relevant or useful: *you may have heard something from them which is to the purpose.*
– ORIGIN Middle English: from Old French *porpos*, from the verb *porposer*, variant of *proposer* (see **PROPOSE**).

purpose-built (also **purpose-made**) ▸ adjective Brit. built or made for a particular purpose: *purpose-built accommodation for the elderly.*

purposeful ▸ adjective 1 having or showing determination or resolve: *the purposeful stride of a great barrister.*
2 having a useful purpose: *purposeful activities.*
3 intentional: *if his sudden death was not accidental, it must have been purposeful.*
– DERIVATIVES **purposefully** adverb, **purposefulness** noun.

purposeless ▸ adjective done or made with no discernible point or purpose: *purposeless vandalism.* ■ having no aim or plan: *his purposeless life.*
– DERIVATIVES **purposelessly** adverb, **purposelessness** noun.

purposely ▸ adverb on purpose; intentionally: *she had purposely made it difficult.*

purposive ▸ adjective having or done with a purpose: *teaching is a purposive activity.*
– DERIVATIVES **purposively** adverb, **purposiveness** noun.

purpura /ˈpəːpjʊrə/ ▸ noun [mass noun] Medicine a rash of purple spots on the skin caused by internal bleeding from small blood vessels. ■ [with modifier] any of a number of diseases characterized by such a rash: *psychogenic purpura.*
– DERIVATIVES **purpuric** /-ˈpjʊərɪk/ adjective.
– ORIGIN mid 18th cent.: from Latin, from Greek *porphura* 'purple'.

purpure /ˈpəːpjʊə/ ▸ noun [mass noun] purple, as a heraldic tincture.
– ORIGIN Old English (in the sense 'purple garment'), from Latin *purpura* (see **PURPURA**), reinforced by Old French *purpre* and influenced by words ending in *-ure*.

purpurin /ˈpəːpjʊrɪn/ ▸ noun [mass noun] Chemistry a red dye originally extracted from madder and also prepared artificially by the oxidation of alizarin. ● An anthraquinone derivative; chem. formula: $C_{14}H_8O_5$.
– ORIGIN mid 19th cent.: from Latin *purpura* 'purple' + **-IN**[1].

purr ▸ verb [no obj.] (of a cat) make a low continuous vibratory sound expressing contentment. ■ [no obj., with adverbial of direction] (of a vehicle or engine) move smoothly while making a similar sound: *a sleek blue BMW purred past him.* ■ speak in a low, soft voice, especially when expressing contentment or acting seductively: [with direct speech] *'Would you like a coffee?' she purred.*
▸ noun a purring sound.
– ORIGIN early 17th cent.: imitative.

purse ▸ noun 1 chiefly Brit. a small pouch of leather or plastic used for carrying money, typically by a woman. ■ the money possessed by or available to a person or country: *institutions are funded from the same general purse.* ■ a sum of money given as a prize in a sporting contest, especially a boxing match.
2 N. Amer. a handbag.
▸ verb (with reference to the lips) pucker or contract, typically to express disapproval or irritation: [with obj.] *Marianne took a glance at her reflection and pursed her lips disgustedly* | [no obj.] *under stress his lips would purse slightly.*
– PHRASES **hold the purse strings** have control of expenditure. **tighten** (or **loosen**) **the purse strings** restrict (or increase) the amount of money available to be spent.
– ORIGIN late Old English, alteration of late Latin *bursa* 'purse', from Greek *bursa* 'hide, leather'. The current verb sense (from the notion of drawing purse strings) dates from the early 17th cent.

purse net ▸ noun a bag-shaped net with a mouth that can be drawn together with cords, for catching fish or rabbits.

purser ▸ noun an officer on a ship who keeps the accounts, especially the head steward on a passenger vessel.

purse seine /seɪn/ ▸ noun a large seine (fishing net) which may be drawn into the shape of a bag, used for catching shoal fish.
– DERIVATIVES **purse-seiner** noun.

purslane /ˈpəːslən/ ▸ noun any of a number of small, typically fleshy-leaved plants which grow in damp or marshy habitats, in particular: ● (also **sea purslane**) an edible plant which grows in salt marshes (*Atriplex portulacoides*, family Chenopodiaceae). ● (also **pink purslane**) a small pink-flowered North American plant of damp places (genus *Claytonia*, family Portulacaceae).
– ORIGIN late Middle English: from Old French *porcelaine*, probably from Latin *porcil(l)aca*, variant of *portulaca*, influenced by French *porcelaine* 'porcelain'.

pursuance ▸ noun [mass noun] formal engagement in an activity or course of action: *you have a right to use public areas* ***in the pursuance of*** *your lawful hobby.* ■ the action of trying to achieve something: *staff took industrial action* ***in pursuance of*** *a better deal.*

pursuant /pəˈsjuːənt/ ▸ adverb (**pursuant to**) formal in accordance with (a law or a legal document or resolution): *the local authority applied for care orders pursuant to section 31 of the Children Act 1989.*
▸ adjective archaic following; going in pursuit.
– ORIGIN late Middle English *poursuiant* (as a noun in the sense 'prosecutor'): from Old French, 'pursuing', from the verb *poursuir*; later influenced in spelling by **PURSUE**.

pursue ▸ verb (**pursues, pursuing, pursued**) [with obj.] 1 follow or chase (someone or something): *the officer pursued the van* | figurative *a heavily indebted businessman was being pursued by creditors.* ■ persistently seek to form a sexual relationship with (someone): *Sophie was being pursued by a number of men.* ■ seek to attain or accomplish (a goal) over a long period: *should people pursue their own happiness at the expense of others?* ■ archaic or literary (of something unpleasant) persistently afflict (someone): *mercy lasts as long as sin pursues man.*
2 continue or proceed along (a path or route): *the road pursued a straight course over the scrubland.* ■ engage in (an activity or course of action): *Andrew was determined to pursue a computer career* | *the council decided not to pursue an appeal.* ■ continue to investigate or explore (an idea or argument): *we shall not pursue the matter any further.*
– DERIVATIVES **pursuable** adjective.
– ORIGIN Middle English (originally in the sense 'follow with enmity'): from Anglo-Norman French *pursuer*, from an alteration of Latin *prosequi* 'prosecute'.

pursuer ▸ noun a person or thing that pursues another. ■ Scots Law a person who brings a case against another into court; a plaintiff.

pursuit ▸ noun 1 [mass noun] the action of pursuing someone or something: *the cat crouched in the grass* ***in pursuit of*** *a bird* | *those whose business is the pursuit of knowledge.* ■ [count noun] a cycling race in which competitors set off from different parts of a track and attempt to overtake one another. ■ Physiology the action of the eye in following a moving object.
2 an activity of a specified kind, especially a recreational or sporting one: *a whole range of leisure pursuits.*
– PHRASES **give pursuit** (of a person, animal, or vehicle) start to chase another.
– ORIGIN late Middle English: from Anglo-Norman French *purseute* 'following after', from *pursuer* (see **PURSUE**). Early senses included 'persecution, annoyance' and in legal contexts 'petition, prosecution'.

pursuivant /ˈpəːsɪv(ə)nt/ ▸ noun 1 Brit. an officer of the College of Arms ranking below a herald. The four ordinary pursuivants are Rouge Croix, Bluemantle, Rouge Dragon, and Portcullis.
2 archaic a follower or attendant.
– ORIGIN late Middle English (denoting a junior heraldic officer): from Old French *pursivant*, present participle (used as a noun) of *pursivre* 'follow after'.

pursy ▸ adjective archaic 1 (especially of a horse) short of breath; asthmatic.
2 (of a person) fat.
– ORIGIN late Middle English: reduction of Anglo-Norman French *porsif*, alteration of Old French *polsif*, from *polser* 'breathe with difficulty', from Latin *pulsare* 'set in violent motion'.

purulent /ˈpjʊərʊl(ə)nt/ ▸ adjective Medicine consisting of, containing, or discharging pus.
– ORIGIN late Middle English: from Latin *purulentus* 'festering', from *pus, pur-* (see **PUS**).

purvey ▸ verb [with obj.] formal provide or supply (food, drink, or other goods) as one's business: *shops purveying cooked food.* ■ spread or promote (an idea, view, etc.): *the majority of newspapers purvey a range of right-wing attitudes.*
– ORIGIN Middle English: from Anglo-Norman French *purveier*, from Latin *providere* 'foresee, attend to' (see **PROVIDE**). Early senses included 'foresee', 'attend to in advance', and 'equip'.

purveyance ▸ noun [mass noun] formal the action of purveying something. ■ Brit. historical the right of the sovereign to buy provisions and use horses and vehicles for a fixed price lower than the market value.
– ORIGIN Middle English (in the senses 'foresight' and 'prearrangement'): from Old French *porveance*, from Latin *providentia* 'foresight' (see **PROVIDENCE**).

purveyor ▸ noun a person who sells or deals in particular goods: *a purveyor of large luxury vehicles.* ■ a person or group who spreads or promotes an idea, view, etc.: *a purveyor of traditional Christian values.*

P

purview ▸ noun [in sing.] formal the scope of the influence or concerns of something: *such a case might be within the purview of the legislation.* ■ range of experience or thought: *social taboos meant that little information was likely to come within the purview of women generally.*
– ORIGIN late Middle English: from Anglo-Norman French *purveu* 'foreseen', past participle of *purveier* (see **PURVEY**). Early use was as a legal term specifying the body of a statute following the words 'be it enacted ...'.

pus ▸ noun [mass noun] a thick yellowish or greenish opaque liquid produced in infected tissue, consisting of dead white blood cells and bacteria with tissue debris and serum.
– ORIGIN late Middle English: from Latin.

Pusan /puːˈsan/ an industrial city and seaport on the SE coast of South Korea; pop. 3,596,100 (est. 2008).

Pusey /ˈpjuːzi/, Edward Bouverie (1800–82), English theologian. In 1833, while professor of Hebrew at Oxford, he founded the Oxford Movement, and became its leader after the withdrawal of John Henry Newman (1841). His many writings include a series of *Tracts for the Times*.
– DERIVATIVES **Puseyism** noun, **Puseyite** noun.

push ▸ verb 1 [with obj., usu. with adverbial] exert force on (someone or something) in order to move them away from oneself: *she pushed her glass towards him* | [with obj. and complement] *Lydia pushed the door shut* | [no obj.] ***he pushed at*** *the skylight, but it wouldn't budge.* ■ hold and exert force on (something) so as to cause it to move in front of one: *a woman was pushing a pram.* ■ [with adverbial] move one's body or a part of it into a specified position with effort: *she pushed her hands into her pockets.* ■ press (a part of a machine or other device): *the lift boy pushed the button for*

the twentieth floor. ■ [with adverbial] cause to reach a particular level or state: *competition in the retail sector will push down prices | the political chaos could push the country into recession.*
2 [no obj., with adverbial] move forward by using force to pass people or cause them to move aside: *she **pushed her way** through the crowded streets | he pushed past an old woman in his haste.* ■ (of an army) advance over territory: *the guerrillas have pushed south to within 100 miles of the capital.* ■ exert oneself to attain something or surpass others: *I was pushing hard until about 10 laps from the finish.* ■ (**be pushing**) informal be nearly (a particular age or amount): *she must be pushing forty, but she's still a good looker.*
3 [with obj.] compel or urge (someone) to do something, especially to work hard: *she believed he was pushing their daughter too hard.* ■ [no obj.] (**push for**) demand persistently: *the council continued to push for the better management of water resources.* ■ (**be pushed**) informal have very little of something, especially time: *I'm a bit **pushed for** time at the moment.* ■ (**be pushed to do something**) informal find it difficult to achieve something: *he will be pushed to retain the title as his form this season has been below par.*
4 [with obj.] informal promote the use, sale, or acceptance of: *the company has been pushing a document management system.* ■ sell (a narcotic drug) illegally.
5 [with obj.] Computing prepare (a stack) to receive a piece of data on the top. ■ transfer (data) to the top of a stack.
6 [with obj.] Photography develop (a film) so as to compensate for deliberate underexposure.
▸ **noun 1** an act of pushing someone or something in order to move them away from oneself: *he closed the door with a push.* ■ an act of pressing a part of a machine or device: *the door locks at the push of a button.*
2 a vigorous effort to do or obtain something: *many clubs are joining in the fund-raising push | he determined to make one last push for success.* ■ a military attack in force: *the army was engaged in a push against guerrilla strongholds.* ■ [mass noun] forcefulness and enterprise: *an investor with the necessary money and push.* ■ (**a push**) informal something that is hard to achieve: *we're managing on our own but it's a push.*
– PHRASES **at a push** Brit. informal if absolutely necessary; only with a certain degree of difficulty: *there's room for four people, or five at a push.* **get** (or **give someone**) **the push** (or **shove**) Brit. informal be dismissed (or dismiss someone) from a job. ■ be rejected in (or end) a relationship. **push at** (or **against**) **an open door** have no difficulty in accomplishing a task. **push the boat out** see BOAT. **push someone's buttons** see BUTTON. **be pushing up the daisies** see DAISY. **push one's luck** informal take a risk on the assumption that one will continue to be successful or in favour. **when push comes to shove** informal when one must commit oneself to an action or decision: *when push came to shove, I always stood up for him.*
– PHRASAL VERBS **push ahead** proceed with or continue a course of action: *he promised to **push ahead** with economic reform.* **push someone around** (or **about**) informal treat someone roughly or inconsiderately. **push in** Brit. go in front of people who are already queuing. **push off 1** use an oar, boathook, etc. to exert pressure so as to move a boat out from a bank. **2** Brit. informal go away. **push on** continue on a journey: *the light was already fading, but she pushed on.* **push something through** get a proposed measure completed or accepted quickly.
– ORIGIN Middle English (as a verb): from Old French *pousser*, from Latin *pulsare* 'to push, beat, pulse' (see PULSE[1]). The early sense was 'exert force on', giving rise later to 'make a strenuous effort, endeavour'.

pushback ▸ **noun** [mass noun] chiefly US a negative or unfavourable reaction or response: *we got some pushback on the new pricing.*

pushbike ▸ **noun** Brit. informal a bicycle.

push-button ▸ **noun** [usu. as modifier] a button that is pushed to operate an electrical device: *a push-button telephone.*

pushcart ▸ **noun** a small handcart or barrow.

pushchair ▸ **noun** Brit. a folding chair on wheels, in which a baby or young child can be pushed along.

pusher ▸ **noun 1** informal a person who sells illegal drugs.
2 a person or thing that pushes something: [in combination] *the checkout trolley-pushers.*

pushful ▸ **adjective** arrogantly self-assertive; pushy.

Pushkin /ˈpʊʃkɪn/, Aleksandr (Sergeevich) (1799–1837), Russian poet, novelist, and dramatist. He wrote prolifically in many genres; his first success was the romantic narrative poem *Ruslan and Ludmilla* (1820). Other notable works include the verse novel *Eugene Onegin* (1833) and the blank-verse historical drama *Boris Godunov* (1831).

pushover ▸ **noun 1** informal a person who is easy to overcome or influence: *Colonel Moore was benevolent but no pushover.* ■ a thing that is very easily done: *this is going to be a pushover.*
2 (also **pushover try**) Rugby a try in which one side in a scrum pushes the ball over the opponents' goal line.

pushpin ▸ **noun** N. Amer. a drawing pin with a spherical or cylindrical head of coloured plastic.

pushpit ▸ **noun** a raised safety rail in the stern of a yacht.
– ORIGIN 1960s: humorous formation, suggested by PULPIT.

push poll ▸ **noun** an ostensible opinion poll in which the true objective is to sway voters by using loaded questions.
– DERIVATIVES **push-polling** noun.

push processing ▸ **noun** [mass noun] Photography the development of film so as to compensate for deliberate underexposure, thereby increasing the effective film speed.

push-pull ▸ **adjective** operated by pushing and pulling. ■ Electronics having or involving two matched valves or transistors that operate 180 degrees out of phase, conducting alternately for increased output.

pushrod ▸ **noun** a rod operated by cams that opens and closes the valves in an internal-combustion engine.

push-start ▸ **verb** [with obj.] start (a motor vehicle) by pushing it in order to make the engine turn.
▸ **noun** an act of push-starting a motor vehicle.

push technology ▸ **noun** [mass noun] Computing a service in which the user downloads software from a provider which then continually supplies information from the Internet in categories selected by the user.

Pushtu /ˈpʌʃtuː/ ▸ **noun** variant of PASHTO.

push-up ▸ **adjective** (of a bra) designed to give uplift to the breasts.
▸ **noun** chiefly N. Amer. another term for PRESS-UP.

pushy ▸ **adjective** (**pushier**, **pushiest**) excessively or unpleasantly self-assertive or ambitious.
– DERIVATIVES **pushily** adverb, **pushiness** noun.

pusillanimous /ˌpjuːsɪˈlanɪməs/ ▸ **adjective** showing a lack of courage or determination; timid.
– DERIVATIVES **pusillanimity** /-ləˈnɪmɪti/ noun, **pusillanimously** adverb.
– ORIGIN late Middle English: from ecclesiastical Latin *pusillanimis* (translating Greek *olugopsukhos*), from *pusillus* 'very small' + *animus* 'mind', + -OUS.

Puskas /ˈpʊʃkəs/, Ferenc (1927–2006), Hungarian footballer. A striker, he came to prominence in the Hungarian national team of the early 1950s. In 1956 he went to play for Real Madrid, scoring four goals in their 1960 European Cup Final victory.

puss[1] ▸ **noun** informal, chiefly Brit. a cat. ■ [usu. with modifier] a playful or coquettish girl or young woman.
– ORIGIN early 16th cent.: probably from Middle Low German *pūs* (also *pūskatte*) or Dutch *poes*, of unknown origin.

puss[2] ▸ **noun** Irish & Scottish a person's face, mouth, or expression.
– ORIGIN late 19th cent.: from Irish *pus* 'lip, mouth'.

puss moth ▸ **noun** a large furry greyish-white moth with darker markings. The boldly marked caterpillar rears up when threatened, waving whip-like appendages and spitting formic acid. ● *Cerura vinula*, family Notodontidae.

pussy ▸ **noun** (pl. **pussies**) **1** informal a cat.
2 vulgar slang a woman's genitals. ■ [mass noun] women in general, considered sexually. ■ N. Amer. informal a weak, cowardly, or effeminate man.

pussycat ▸ **noun** informal **1** a cat.
2 a gentle, mild-mannered, or easy-going person: *he may look scary, but people assure us he's really a pussycat.*

pussycat bow ▸ **noun** a large, soft, floppy bow at the neck of a woman's blouse.

pussyfoot ▸ **verb** [no obj., with adverbial] act in a cautious or non-committal way: *I realized I could no longer pussyfoot around.* ■ move stealthily or warily: *they make a great show of pussyfooting through the greenery.*

pussy-whip ▸ **verb** [with obj.] (usu. as adj. **pussy-whipped**) vulgar slang (of a woman) continually criticize or nag (a man).

pussy willow ▸ **noun** a willow with soft fluffy yellow or silvery catkins that appear before the leaves. Also called SALLOW[2]. ● Genus *Salix*, family Salicaceae: several species, in particular (in the US) the glaucous willow (*S. discolor*), and (in Britain) the goat willow (*S. caprea*) and grey willow (*S. cinerea*).
– ORIGIN mid 19th cent.: originally a child's word, because of the resemblance of the soft fluffy catkins to a cat's fur.

pustulate ▸ **verb** /ˈpʌstjʊleɪt/ [no obj.] form into pustules: (as adj. **pustulating**) *pustulating epidermal ulcers.*
▸ **adjective** /ˈpʌstjʊlət/ chiefly Biology having or covered with pustules: *the surface is coarsely pustulate.*
– DERIVATIVES **pustulation** noun.
– ORIGIN late Middle English (as an adjective): from late Latin *pustulatus*, past participle of *pustulare* 'to blister', from *pustula* 'pustule'.

pustule /ˈpʌstjuːl/ ▸ **noun** a small blister or pimple on the skin containing pus. ■ Biology a small raised spot or rounded swelling, especially one on a plant resulting from fungal infection.
– DERIVATIVES **pustular** adjective.
– ORIGIN late Middle English: from Latin *pustula*.

put ▸ **verb** (**puts**, **putting**; past and past participle **put**) [with obj. and adverbial] **1** move to or place in a particular position: *Harry put down his cup | I put my hand out towards her | watch where you're putting your feet!* ■ cause (someone or something) to go to a particular place and remain there for a time: *India has put three experimental satellites into space.* ■ [no obj., with adverbial of direction] (of a ship) proceed in a particular direction: *she stepped into the boat and **put out to sea** | they **put in** at Cuba to refit.* ■ [no obj., with adverbial of direction] US archaic (of a river) flow in a particular direction.
2 bring into a particular state or condition: *they tried to put me at ease | a large aid programme was put into practice | he **is putting himself** at risk.* ■ (**put oneself in**) imagine oneself in (a particular situation): *it was no use trying to put herself in his place.* ■ write or print (something) in a particular place: *they put my name on the cover page.* ■ express (a thought or comment) in a particular way: *to put it bluntly, he was not really divorced.*
3 (**put something on/on to**) cause (someone or something) to be subject to something: *commentators put some of the blame on Congress | he defended his decision to put VAT on domestic fuel.* ■ assign a particular value, figure, or limit to: *it is very difficult to put a figure on the size of the budget.* ■ (**put something at**) estimate something to be (a particular amount): *estimates put the war's cost at £1 million a day.*
4 throw (a shot or weight) as an athletic sport: *she set a women's record by putting the shot 56′ 7″.*
▸ **noun 1** a throw of a shot or weight.
2 Stock Exchange short for PUT OPTION.
– PHRASES **not know where to put oneself** informal feel deeply embarrassed. **put something behind one** get over a bad experience by distancing oneself from it: *they have tried to put their grief behind them and rebuild their lives.* **put the clocks back** (or **forward**) adjust clocks or watches backwards (or forwards) to take account of official changes in time. **put someone's eyes out** blind someone in a violent way. **put one's hands together** applaud; clap: *I want you all to put your hands together for Barry.* **put one's hands up** raise one's hands in surrender. **put it** (or **oneself**) **about** Brit. informal be sexually promiscuous. **put it there** [in imperative] informal used to indicate that the speaker wishes to shake hands with someone in agreement or congratulation. **put one over on** informal deceive (someone) into accepting something false. **put up or shut up** informal justify oneself or remain silent: *they called for the minister to either put up or shut up.*
– PHRASAL VERBS **put about** Nautical (of a ship) turn on the opposite tack. **put someone about** chiefly Scottish & N. English upset or trouble someone. **put something about** Brit. spread information or rumours. **put something across** (or **over**) communicate something effectively. **put something aside 1** save money for future use. **2** forget or disregard something, typically a feeling or a past difference of opinion. **put someone away** informal confine someone in a prison or psychiatric hospital: *he deserves to be put away forever.* **put something away 1** save money for future use. **2** informal consume food or drink in

large quantities. **3** informal (in sport) dispatch or score a goal or shot. **put something back** reschedule a planned event to a later time or date. ■ delay something: *greater public control may put back the modernization of the industry.* **put something by** chiefly Brit. another way of saying PUT SOMETHING ASIDE (sense 1) above). **put someone down 1** informal criticize someone. **2** Brit. lay a baby down to sleep. **put something down 1** record something in writing: *he's putting a few thoughts down on paper.* ■ make a recording of a piece of music. **2** suppress a rebellion, coup, or riot by force. **3** kill an animal because it is sick, injured, or old. **4** pay a specified sum as a deposit: *he put a thousand down and paid the rest over six months.* **5** preserve or store food or wine for future use. **6** (also **put down**) land an aircraft. **put someone down as** consider or judge someone or something to be: *I'd have put you down as a Vivaldi man.* **put someone down for** enter someone's name on a list as wishing to do, join, or subscribe to (something): *he put his son down for Eton.* **put something down to** attribute something to: *if I forget anything, put it down to old age.* **put someone forward** recommend someone as a suitable candidate for a job or position: *he put me forward as head of publicity.* **put something forward** submit a plan, proposal, or theory for consideration. **put in** [with direct speech] interrupt in a conversation or discussion: *'But you're a sybarite, Roger,' put in Isobel.* **put something in/into 1** present or submit something formally: *the airport had put in a claim for damages.* ■ (**put in for**) chiefly Brit. apply formally for: *Adam put in for six months' leave.* **2** devote time or effort to (something): *employed mothers put in the longest hours of all women.* **3** invest money or resources in. **put someone off 1** cancel or postpone an appointment with someone: *he'd put off Martin until nine o'clock.* **2** cause someone to lose interest or enthusiasm: *she wanted to be a nurse, but the thought of night shifts put her off.* ■ cause someone to feel dislike or distrust: *she had a coldness that just put me off.* **3** distract someone: *don't put me off—I'm trying to concentrate.* **put something off** postpone something: *they can't put off a decision much longer.* **put someone on** informal tease or playfully deceive someone. **put something on 1** place a garment, jewellery, etc. on part of one's body: *Juliet had put on a cotton dress | she put on fresh make-up.* **2** cause a device to operate: *shall I put the light on?* ■ start to play recorded music or a video. **3** organize or present a play, exhibition, or event. ■ provide a public transport service: *so many people wanted to visit this spot that an extra train had to be put on.* **4** increase in body weight; become heavier by a specified amount: *she's given up her diet and put on 20 lb.* ■ add a specified amount to (the cost of something): *the news put 12 pence on the share price.* ■ Cricket (of batsmen) score a particular number of runs in a partnership: *Gooch and Broad put on 125 for the first wicket.* **5** assume a particular expression, accent, etc.: *he put on a lugubrious look.* ■ behave deceptively: *she doesn't feel she has to put on an act.* **6** bet a specified amount of money on: *he put £1,000 on the horse to win.* **put someone on to** draw someone's attention to (someone or something useful, notable, or interesting): *Pike put me on to the Department's Legal Section.* **put out** N. Amer. informal agree to have sexual intercourse with someone. **put someone out 1** cause someone trouble or inconvenience: *would it put you out too much to let her visit you for a couple of hours?* ■ upset or annoy someone: *he was not put out by the rebuff.* **2** (in sport) defeat a player or side and so eliminate them from a competition. **3** make someone unconscious by means of drugs or an anaesthetic. **put something out 1** extinguish something that is burning: *fire crews from Grangetown put out the blaze.* ■ turn off a light. **2** lay something out ready for use: *she put out glasses and paper napkins.* **3** issue or broadcast something: *a limited-edition single was put out to promote the album.* **4** dislocate a joint: *she fell off her horse and put her shoulder out.* **5** (of a company) allocate work to a contractor or freelancer to be done off the premises. **6** (of an engine or motor) produce a particular amount of power: *the non-turbo is expected to put out about 250 bhp.* **put something over 1** another way of saying PUT SOMETHING ACROSS above. **2** N. Amer. postpone something. **put someone through 1** connect someone by telephone to another person or place: *put me through to the police office, please.* **2** subject someone to an unpleasant or demanding experience: *I hate Brian for what he put me through.* **3** pay for one's child to attend school or college. **put something through** initiate something and see it through to a successful conclusion: *he put through a reform programme to try to save the regime.* **put someone to** cause (inconvenience or difficulty) to someone: *I don't want to put you to any trouble.* **put something to 1** submit something to (someone) for consideration or attention: *we are making a takeover bid and putting an offer to the shareholders.* ■ (**put it to**) [with clause] make a statement or allegation to (someone) and challenge them to deny it: *I put it to him that he was just a political groupie.* **2** devote something to (a particular use or purpose): *they put the land to productive use.* **3** couple an animal with (another of the opposite sex) for breeding. **put something together** make something by assembling different parts or people: *he can take a clock apart and put it back together again | they decided to put a new band together.* **put someone under** another way of saying PUT SOMEONE OUT (sense 3) above. **put up** stay temporarily in accommodation other than one's own home: *we put up at a hotel in the city centre.* **put someone up 1** accommodate someone temporarily. **2** propose someone for election or adoption: *the party had put up a candidate in each constituency.* **put something up 1** construct or erect something: *I put up the tent and cooked a meal.* **2** raise one's hand to signal that one wishes to answer or ask a question. **3** display a notice, sign, or poster. ■ present a proposal, theory, or argument for discussion or consideration. **4** chiefly Brit. increase the cost of something: *I'm afraid I've got to put your rent up.* **5** provide money as backing for an enterprise: *the sponsors are putting up £5,000 for the event.* **6** offer or show a particular degree of resistance, effort, or skill in a fight or competitive situation: *he put up a brave fight.* **7** offer something for sale or auction. **8** cause game to rise from cover. **9** archaic return a sword to its sheath. **be put upon** informal (often as adj. **put-upon**) be taken advantage of through having one's good nature exploited: *a put-upon drudge who slaved for her employer.* **put someone up to 1** informal encourage someone to do (something wrong or unwise): *Who else would play a trick like that on me? I expect Rose put him up to it.* **2** archaic inform someone about (something). **put up with** tolerate; endure: *I'm too tired to put up with any nonsense.*

– ORIGIN Old English (recorded only in the verbal noun *putung*), of unknown origin; compare with dialect *pote* 'to push, thrust' (an early sense of the verb *put*).

puta /ˈputa/ ▸ **noun** informal (in Spanish-speaking countries or parts of America) a prostitute or promiscuous woman.
– ORIGIN Spanish.

putamen /pjʊˈteɪmɛn/ ▸ **noun** (pl. **putamina** /-ˈteɪmɪnə/ or **putamens**) Anatomy the outer part of the lentiform nucleus of the brain.
– ORIGIN late 19th cent.: from Latin, literally 'shell remaining after pruning'.

putative /ˈpjuːtətɪv/ ▸ **adjective** [attrib.] generally considered or reputed to be: *the putative father of her children.*
– DERIVATIVES **putatively** adverb.
– ORIGIN late Middle English: from Old French *putatif, -ive* or late Latin *putativus*, from Latin *putat-* 'thought', from the verb *putare*.

put-down ▸ **noun** informal a remark intended to humiliate or criticize someone.

puter ▸ **noun** informal a computer.
– ORIGIN 1990s: abbreviation.

Putin /ˈpuːtɪn/, Vladimir (b.1952), Russian statesman, President 2000–8 and Prime Minister since 2008.

put-in ▸ **noun** Rugby an act or the right of putting the ball into a scrum.

putlog /ˈpʌtlɒg/ (also **putlock** /-lɒk/) ▸ **noun** a short horizontal pole projecting from a wall, on which scaffold floorboards rest.
– ORIGIN mid 17th cent.: of unknown origin.

put-on ▸ **noun** N. Amer. informal a deception; a hoax.

putonghua /puːtʊŋˈhwɑː/ ▸ **noun** [mass noun] the standard spoken form of modern Chinese, based on the dialect of Beijing.
– ORIGIN Chinese, literally 'common spoken language'.

put option ▸ **noun** Stock Exchange an option to sell assets at an agreed price on or before a particular date.

put-put /ˈpʌtpʌt/ ▸ **noun & verb** another term for PUTTER².
– ORIGIN early 20th cent.: imitative.

putrefaction ▸ **noun** [mass noun] the process of decay or rotting in a body or other organic matter.
– ORIGIN late Middle English: from Old French, or from late Latin *putrefactio(n-)*, from *putrefacere* 'make rotten' (see PUTREFY).

putrefactive ▸ **adjective** relating to or causing decay: *they were killed by the putrefactive bacteria.*

putrefy /ˈpjuːtrɪfʌɪ/ ▸ **verb** (**putrefies, putrefying, putrefied**) [no obj.] (of a body or other organic matter) decay or rot and produce a fetid smell.
– ORIGIN late Middle English: via French from Latin *putrefacere*, from *puter, putr-* 'rotten'.

putrescent /pjuːˈtrɛs(ə)nt/ ▸ **adjective** undergoing the process of decay; rotting: *the odour of putrescent flesh.*
– DERIVATIVES **putrescence** noun.
– ORIGIN mid 18th cent.: from Latin *putrescent-* 'beginning to go rotten', inceptive of *putrere* 'to rot' (see PUTRID).

putrescible ▸ **adjective** liable to decay; subject to putrefaction: *putrescible domestic waste.*

putrid ▸ **adjective 1** (of organic matter) decaying or rotting and emitting a fetid smell. ■ of or characteristic of rotting matter: *the putrid smells from the slaughterhouses.*
2 informal very unpleasant; repulsive: *the cocktail is a putrid pink colour.*
– DERIVATIVES **putridity** noun, **putridly** adverb, **putridness** noun.
– ORIGIN late Middle English: from Latin *putridus*, from *putrere* 'to rot', from *puter, putr-* 'rotten'.

putsch /pʊtʃ/ ▸ **noun** a violent attempt to overthrow a government; a coup.
– DERIVATIVES **putschist** noun.
– ORIGIN 1920s: from Swiss German, literally 'thrust, blow'.

putt /pʌt/ ▸ **verb** (**putts, putting, putted**) [no obj.] try to hit a golf ball into the hole by striking it gently so that it rolls across the green.
▸ **noun** a stroke of this kind made in an attempt to hole the ball.
– ORIGIN mid 17th cent. (originally Scots): differentiated from PUT.

puttanesca /pʊtəˈnɛskə/ ▸ **adjective** [usu. postpositive] denoting a pasta sauce including tomatoes, garlic, black olives, and anchovies: *pasta puttanesca.*
– ORIGIN Italian, from *puttana* 'prostitute' (the sauce is said to have been devised by prostitutes as one which could be cooked quickly between clients' visits).

puttee /ˈpʌti/ ▸ **noun** a long strip of cloth wound spirally round the leg from ankle to knee for protection and support. ■ N. Amer. a leather legging.
– ORIGIN late 19th cent.: from Hindi *paṭṭī* 'band, bandage'.

putter¹ /ˈpʌtə/ ▸ **noun 1** a golf club designed for use in putting, typically with a flat-faced mallet-like head.
2 [with adj.] a golfer considered in terms of their skill at putting: *you'll need to be a good putter to break par.*

putter² /ˈpʌtə/ ▸ **noun** the rapid intermittent sound of a small petrol engine: *the putter of an old aeroplane.*
▸ **verb** [no obj.] move with or make a puttering sound: *barges puttered slowly through the water.*
– ORIGIN 1940s: imitative.

putter³ /ˈpʌtə/ ▸ **verb** North American term for POTTER¹.
– ORIGIN late 19th cent.: alteration.

putting green ▸ **noun** a smooth area of short grass surrounding a hole, either as part of a golf course or as a separate area for putting.

Puttnam /ˈpʌtnəm/, Sir David (Terence) (b.1941), English film producer. Puttnam produced *Chariots of Fire* (1981), which won four Oscars, *The Killing Fields* (1984), and *The Mission* (1986).

putto /ˈpʊtəʊ/ ▸ **noun** (pl. **putti** /-ti/) a representation of a naked child, especially a cherub or a cupid in Renaissance art.
– ORIGIN Italian, literally 'boy', from Latin *putus*.

putty ▸ **noun** [mass noun] **1** a soft, malleable greyish-yellow paste, made from ground chalk and raw linseed oil, that hardens after a few hours and is used for sealing glass in window frames and filling holes in wood. ■ [usu. with modifier] any of a number of similar malleable substances used inside and outside buildings, e.g. **plumber's putty, lime putty**, or used for modelling or casting, e.g. **epoxy putty**.
2 a polishing powder, usually made from tin oxide, used in jewellery work.
▸ **verb** (**putties, puttying, puttied**) [with obj.] seal or cover (something) with putty.
– PHRASES **be (like) putty in someone's hands** be easily manipulated or dominated by someone.

P

– ORIGIN mid 17th cent.: from French *potée*, literally 'potful', from *pot* 'pot'.

put-up ▸ adjective [attrib.] arranged beforehand in order to deceive someone: *the whole thing could be a put-up job to get his wife over to Ireland.*

put-you-up ▸ noun Brit. a sofa or settee that can be converted into a bed.

putz /pʊts, pʌts/ N. Amer. informal ▸ noun **1** a stupid or worthless person.
2 vulgar slang a man's penis.
▸ verb [no obj.] engage in inconsequential or unproductive activity: *too much **putzing around** up there would ruin them.*
– ORIGIN 1960s: Yiddish, literally 'penis'.

puy /pwiː/ ▸ noun a small extinct volcanic cone in the Auvergne, France.
– ORIGIN mid 19th cent.: French, literally 'hill', from Latin *podium* (see **PODIUM**).

puy lentil /pwiː/ ▸ noun a small variety of green lentil with blue marbling, highly regarded for its flavour.
– ORIGIN named after the French town of Le *Puy* in the Auvergne.

puzzle ▸ verb [with obj.] cause (someone) to feel confused because they cannot understand something: *she was puzzled by the doctor's manner.* ■ [no obj.] think hard about something because one cannot understand it: *she was still **puzzling over** this problem when she reached the office.* ■ (**puzzle something out**) solve or understand something by thinking hard.
▸ noun **1** a game, toy, or problem designed to test ingenuity or knowledge. ■ a jigsaw puzzle.
2 a person or thing that is difficult to understand or explain; an enigma: *the meaning of the poem has always been a puzzle.*
– DERIVATIVES **puzzlement** noun.
– ORIGIN late 16th cent. (as a verb): of unknown origin.

puzzled ▸ adjective unable to understand; perplexed: *the questioners were met with puzzled looks | she looked puzzled and angry with him.*

puzzler ▸ noun **1** a difficult question or problem.
2 a person who solves puzzles as a pastime.

puzzling ▸ adjective causing one to be puzzled; perplexing: *only one very puzzling question remains unanswered.*
– DERIVATIVES **puzzlingly** adverb [sentence adverb] *puzzlingly, he was never able to attend gatherings of contributors in Oxford.*

PVA ▸ abbreviation polyvinyl acetate.

PVC ▸ abbreviation polyvinyl chloride.

PVR ▸ abbreviation personal video recorder.

PVS ▸ abbreviation Medicine ■ persistent vegetative state. ■ postviral (fatigue) syndrome (another term for **ME**).

Pvt. ▸ abbreviation ■ (in the US army) private. ■ private (in company names).

PW ▸ abbreviation policewoman.

p.w. ▸ abbreviation per week.

PWA ▸ abbreviation person with AIDS.

PWR ▸ abbreviation pressurized-water reactor.

PWV ▸ abbreviation Pretoria-Witwatersrand-Vereeniging.

PX ▸ abbreviation post exchange.

PY ▸ abbreviation Paraguay (international vehicle registration).

pya /pjɑː/ ▸ noun a monetary unit of Burma (Myanmar), equal to one hundredth of a kyat.
– ORIGIN Burmese.

pyaemia /pʌɪˈiːmɪə/ (US **pyemia**) ▸ noun [mass noun] blood poisoning (septicaemia) caused by the spread in the bloodstream of pus-forming bacteria released from an abscess.
– ORIGIN mid 19th cent.: modern Latin, from Greek *puon* 'pus' + *haima* 'blood'.

pycnocline /ˈpɪknə(ʊ)klʌɪn/ ▸ noun Geography a layer in an ocean or other body of water in which water density increases rapidly with depth.
– ORIGIN 1950s: from Greek *puknos* 'thick' + **CLINE**.

pye-dog /ˈpʌɪdɒg/ (also **pie-dog** or **pi-dog**) ▸ noun a stray mongrel, especially in Asia.
– ORIGIN mid 19th cent.: from Anglo-Indian *pye*, Hindi *pāhī* 'outsider' + **DOG**.

pyelitis /ˌpʌɪəˈlʌɪtɪs/ ▸ noun [mass noun] Medicine inflammation of the renal pelvis.
– ORIGIN mid 19th cent.: from Greek *puelos* 'trough, basin' + **-ITIS**.

pyelography /ˌpʌɪəˈlɒgrəfi/ ▸ noun [mass noun] Medicine an X-ray technique for producing an image of the renal pelvis and urinary tract by the introduction of a radiopaque fluid. Also called **UROGRAPHY**.
– DERIVATIVES **pyelogram** /ˈpʌɪələ(ʊ)gram/ noun.
– ORIGIN early 20th cent.: from Greek *puelos* 'trough, basin' + **-GRAPHY**.

pyelonephritis /ˌpʌɪələʊnɪˈfrʌɪtɪs/ ▸ noun [mass noun] Medicine inflammation of the kidney as a result of bacterial infection.
– DERIVATIVES **pyelonephritic** adjective.
– ORIGIN mid 19th cent.: from Greek *puelos* 'trough, basin' + **NEPHRITIS**.

pyemia ▸ noun US spelling of **PYAEMIA**.

pygidium /pʌɪˈdʒɪdɪəm, pʌɪˈgɪdɪəm/ ▸ noun (pl. **pygidia** /pʌɪˈdʒɪdɪə, pʌɪˈgɪdɪə/) Zoology the terminal part or hind segment of the body in certain invertebrates.
– ORIGIN mid 19th cent.: modern Latin, from Greek *pugē* 'rump'.

Pygmalion[1] /pɪgˈmeɪlɪən/ Greek Mythology a king of Cyprus who fashioned an ivory statue of a beautiful woman and loved it so deeply that in answer to his prayer Aphrodite gave it life. The woman (at some point named Galatea) bore him a daughter, Paphos.

Pygmalion[2] /pɪgˈmeɪlɪən/ a legendary king of Tyre, brother of Elissa (Dido), whose husband he killed in the hope of obtaining his fortune.

pygmy (also **pigmy**) ▸ noun (pl. **pygmies**) **1** (**Pygmy**) a member of certain peoples of very short stature in equatorial Africa and parts of SE Asia. Pygmies (e.g. the Mbuti and Twa peoples) are typically nomadic hunter-gatherers with an average male height not above 150 cm (4 ft 11 in.).
2 chiefly derogatory a very small person, animal, or thing. ■ a person who is insignificant or is deficient in a particular respect: *he regarded them as intellectual pygmies.*
▸ adjective very small or insignificant. ■ used in names of animals and plants that are much smaller than more typical kinds, e.g. **pygmy shrew**, **pygmy water lily**.
– ORIGIN late Middle English (originally in the plural, denoting a mythological race of small people): via Latin from Greek *pugmaios* 'dwarf', from *pugmē* 'the length measured from elbow to knuckles'.

pygmy chimpanzee ▸ noun another term for **BONOBO**.

pygmy owl ▸ noun a very small owl found in America and northern Eurasia. ● Genus *Glaucidium*, family Strigidae: several species.

pygmy shrew ▸ noun a shrew which is one of the smallest known mammals. ● Genus *Sorex*, family Soricidae: several species.

pygostyle /ˈpʌɪgə(ʊ)stʌɪl/ ▸ noun Ornithology (in a bird) a triangular plate formed of the fused caudal vertebrae, typically supporting the tail feathers.
– ORIGIN late 19th cent.: from Greek *pugē* 'rump' + *stulos* 'column'.

pyinkado /pjɪŋkədəʊ/ ▸ noun (pl. **pyinkados**) a southern Asian tree of the pea family, yielding hard durable timber which is used in heavy construction work. ● *Xylia dolabriformis*, family Leguminosae.
– ORIGIN mid 19th cent.: from Burmese.

pyjamas (US **pajamas**) ▸ plural noun a loose-fitting jacket and trousers for sleeping in: *a pair of pyjamas |* (as modifier **pyjama**) *pyjama trousers.* ■ a pair of loose trousers tied by a drawstring around the waist, worn by both sexes in some Asian countries.
– ORIGIN early 19th cent.: from Urdu and Persian, from *pāy* 'leg' + *jāma* 'clothing'.

pyknic /ˈpɪknɪk/ ▸ adjective Anthropology relating to or denoting a stocky physique with a rounded body and head, thickset trunk, and a tendency to fat.
– ORIGIN 1920s: from Greek *puknos* 'thick' + **-IC**. The word was first used by the German psychiatrist, Ernst Kretschmer (1888–1964), in his tripartite classification of human types (the other two being *asthenic* and *athletic*).

pylon ▸ noun **1** a tall tower-like structure used for carrying electricity cables high above the ground. ■ a tower or post marking a path for light aircraft, cars, or other vehicles, especially in racing.
2 a pillar-like structure on the wing of an aircraft used for carrying an engine, weapon, fuel tank, or other load.
3 a monumental gateway to an ancient Egyptian temple formed by two truncated pyramidal towers.
4 N. Amer. a plastic cone used to mark areas of roads.
– ORIGIN mid 19th cent.: from Greek *pulōn*, from *pulē* 'gate'.

pyloric /pʌɪˈlɒrɪk/ ▸ adjective Anatomy & Medicine relating to or affecting the region where the stomach opens into the duodenum: *pyloric stenosis.*

pylorus /pʌɪˈlɔːrəs/ ▸ noun (pl. **pylori** /pʌɪˈlɔːrʌɪ/) Anatomy the opening from the stomach into the duodenum.
– ORIGIN early 17th cent.: via late Latin from Greek *pulouros* 'gatekeeper', from *pulē* 'gate' + *ouros* 'warder'.

Pynchon /ˈpɪntʃən/, Thomas (Ruggles) (b.1937), American novelist. He is an elusive author who shuns public attention, while his works abandon the normal conventions of the novel. Notable works: *V* (1963), *The Crying of Lot 49* (1966), and *Gravity's Rainbow* (1972).

pyoderma /ˌpʌɪə(ʊ)ˈdəːmə/ ▸ noun [mass noun] Medicine a skin infection with formation of pus.
– ORIGIN 1930s: from Greek *puo-* (from *puon* 'pus') + *derma* 'skin'.

pyogenic /ˌpʌɪə(ʊ)ˈdʒɛnɪk/ ▸ adjective Medicine involving or relating to the production of pus.
– ORIGIN mid 19th cent.: from Greek *puo-* (from *puon* 'pus') + **-GENIC**.

Pyongyang /pjɒŋˈjaŋ/ the capital of North Korea; pop. 3,255,400 (est. 2008). The oldest city on the Korean peninsula, it was first mentioned in records of 108 BC. It developed as an industrial city during the years of Japanese occupation, from 1910 to 1945.

pyorrhoea /ˌpʌɪəˈriːə/ (US **pyorrhea**) ▸ noun another term for **PERIODONTITIS**.
– ORIGIN early 19th cent.: from Greek *puo-* (from *puon* 'pus') + *rhoia* 'flux' (from *rhein* 'to flow').

pyracantha /ˌpʌɪrəˈkanθə/ ▸ noun a thorny evergreen Eurasian shrub with white flowers and bright red or yellow berries, which is a popular ornamental. Also called **FIRETHORN**. ● Genus *Pyracantha*, family Rosaceae.
– ORIGIN modern Latin, via Latin from Greek *purakantha*, the name of an unidentified plant, from *pur* 'fire' + *akantha* 'thorn'.

pyralid /pʌɪˈralɪd, -ˈreɪl-/ ▸ noun Entomology an insect of a family (Pyralidae) of small delicate moths with narrow forewings. The larvae of many species are pests of stored foodstuffs.
– ORIGIN late 19th cent.: from modern Latin *Pyralidae* (plural), based on Greek *puralis*, denoting a mythical fly said to live in fire.

pyramid /ˈpɪrəmɪd/ ▸ noun **1** a monumental structure with a square or triangular base and sloping sides that meet in a point at the top, especially one built of stone as a royal tomb in ancient Egypt.

> Pyramids were built as tombs for Egyptian pharaohs from the 3rd dynasty (c.2649 BC) until c.1640 BC. The early step pyramid, with several levels and a flat top, developed into the true pyramid, such as the three largest at Giza near Cairo (**the Pyramids**, including the Great Pyramid of Cheops) which were one of the Seven Wonders of the World. Monuments of similar shape are associated with the Aztec and Maya civilizations of around 1200 BC–AD 750, and, like those in Egypt, were part of large ritual complexes.

2 an object, shape, or arrangement with such a form: *a pyramid of logs |* [as modifier] *a pyramid roof.* ■ Geometry a polyhedron of which one face is a polygon of any number of sides, and the other faces are triangles with a common vertex: *a three-sided pyramid.* ■ Anatomy a structure of more or less pyramidal form, especially in the brain or the renal medulla. ■ an organization or system that is structured with fewer people or things at each level as one approaches the top: *the lowest strata of the social pyramid.* ■ (**pyramids**) a game played on a billiard table with fifteen coloured balls arranged in a triangle and a cue ball.
3 a system of financial growth achieved by a small initial investment, with subsequent investments being funded by using unrealized profits as collateral. ■ a form of investment in which each paying participant recruits two further participants, with returns being given to early participants using money contributed by later ones.
▸ verb [with obj.] chiefly N. Amer. **1** stack or arrange in the shape of a pyramid.
2 achieve a substantial return on (money or property) after making a small initial investment.
– DERIVATIVES **pyramidic** adjective, **pyramidical** /-ˈmɪdɪk(ə)l/ adjective.

– ORIGIN late Middle English (in the geometrical sense): via Latin from Greek *puramis, puramid-*, of unknown ultimate origin.

pyramidal /pɪˈramɪd(ə)l/ ▸ **adjective 1** resembling a pyramid in shape.
2 Anatomy & Medicine relating to or denoting a tract of motor nerves within the pyramid of the medulla oblongata.

pyramidal orchid ▸ **noun** a small orchid of calcareous grassland, with a conical spike of pinkish-purple flowers. ● *Anacamptis pyramidalis*, family Orchidaceae.

pyramid selling ▸ **noun** [mass noun] a system of selling goods in which agency rights are sold to an increasing number of distributors at successively lower levels.

Pyramus /ˈpɪrəməs/ Roman Mythology a Babylonian youth, lover of Thisbe.

> Forbidden to marry by their parents, who were neighbours, the lovers conversed through a chink in a wall and agreed to meet at a tomb outside the city. There, Thisbe was frightened away by a lioness coming from its kill, and Pyramus, seeing her bloodstained cloak and supposing her dead, stabbed himself. Thisbe, finding his body when she returned, threw herself upon his sword.

pyrargyrite /pʌɪˈrɑːdʒɪrʌɪt/ ▸ **noun** [mass noun] a dark reddish-grey mineral consisting of a sulphide of silver and antimony.
– ORIGIN mid 19th cent.: from Greek *puro-* (from *pur* 'fire') + *arguros* 'silver' + -ITE[1].

pyre ▸ **noun** a heap of combustible material, especially one for burning a corpse as part of a funeral ceremony.
– ORIGIN mid 17th cent.: via Latin from Greek *pura*, from *pur* 'fire'.

pyrene /ˈpʌɪriːn/ ▸ **noun** [mass noun] Chemistry a crystalline aromatic hydrocarbon present in coal tar.
● A tetracyclic compound; chemical formula: $C_{16}H_{10}$.
– ORIGIN mid 19th cent.: from Greek *pur* 'fire' + -ENE.

Pyrenean mountain dog ▸ **noun** a large heavily built dog of a white breed, with a thick shaggy double coat.

Pyrenean sheepdog ▸ **noun** a sheepdog of a small fawn or grey long-coated breed, often with white markings.

Pyrenees /ˌpɪrəˈniːz/ a range of mountains extending along the border between France and Spain from the Atlantic coast to the Mediterranean. Its highest peak is the Pico de Aneto in northern Spain, which rises to a height of 3,404 m (11,168 ft).
– DERIVATIVES **Pyrenean** adjective.

pyrethrin /pʌɪˈriːθrɪn/ ▸ **noun** Chemistry any of a group of insecticidal compounds present in pyrethrum flowers.
– ORIGIN 1920s: from PYRETHRUM + -IN[1].

pyrethroid /pʌɪˈriːθrɔɪd/ ▸ **noun** Chemistry a pyrethrin or related insecticidal compound.

pyrethrum /pʌɪˈriːθrəm/ ▸ **noun** an aromatic plant of the daisy family, typically having feathery foliage and brightly coloured flowers. ● Genus *Tanacetum* (formerly *Chrysanthemum* or *Pyrethrum*), family Compositae: several species, in particular *T. coccineum*, grown as an ornamental, and *T. cinerariifolium*, grown as a source of the insecticide pyrethrum.
■ [mass noun] an insecticide made from the dried flowers of pyrethrum plants.
– ORIGIN Middle English (denoting pellitory): from Latin, from Greek *purethron* 'feverfew'. The current senses (based on the former genus name) date from the late 19th cent.

pyretic /pʌɪˈrɛtɪk, pɪ-/ ▸ **adjective** feverish or inducing fever.
– ORIGIN early 18th cent. (as a noun, denoting an antipyretic drug): from modern Latin *pyreticus*, from Greek *puretos* 'fever'.

Pyrex ▸ **noun** [mass noun] [usu. as modifier] trademark a hard heat-resistant type of glass, typically used for ovenware: *a set of Pyrex dishes*.
– ORIGIN early 20th cent.: an invented word.

pyrexia /pʌɪˈrɛksɪə, pɪ-/ ▸ **noun** [mass noun] Medicine raised body temperature; fever.
– DERIVATIVES **pyrexial** adjective, **pyrexic** adjective.
– ORIGIN mid 18th cent.: modern Latin, from Greek *purexis*, from *puressein* 'be feverish', from *pur* 'fire'.

pyridine /ˈpɪrɪdiːn/ ▸ **noun** [mass noun] Chemistry a colourless volatile liquid with an unpleasant odour, present in coal tar and used chiefly as a solvent. ● A heteroaromatic compound; chem. formula: C_5H_5N.
– ORIGIN mid 19th cent.: from Greek *pur* 'fire' + -IDE + -INE[4].

pyridostigmine /ˌpɪrɪdə(ʊ)ˈstɪɡmiːn/ ▸ **noun** [mass noun] Medicine a synthetic compound related to neostigmine, with similar but weaker and longer-acting effects.
– ORIGIN 1950s: blend of PYRIDINE and NEOSTIGMINE.

pyridoxal /ˌpɪrɪˈdɒksəl/ ▸ **noun** [mass noun] Biochemistry an oxidized derivative of pyridoxine which acts as a coenzyme in transamination and other processes.
– ORIGIN 1940s: from PYRIDOXINE + -AL.

pyridoxine /ˌpɪrɪˈdɒksɪn, -iːn/ ▸ **noun** [mass noun] Biochemistry a colourless weakly basic solid present chiefly in cereals, liver oils, and yeast, and important in the metabolism of unsaturated fatty acids. Also called VITAMIN B_6. ● An alcohol derived from pyridine; chem. formula: $C_8H_{11}NO_3$.
– ORIGIN 1930s: from *pyrid(ine)* + OX- 'oxygen' + -INE[4].

pyriform /ˈpɪrɪfɔːm/ (also **piriform**) ▸ **adjective** Anatomy & Biology pear-shaped: *the pyriform fossa*.
– ORIGIN mid 18th cent.: from modern Latin *pyriformis*, from *pyrum* (misspelling of *pirum* 'pear') + -IFORM.

pyrimethamine /ˌpɪrɪˈmɛθəmiːn/ ▸ **noun** [mass noun] Medicine a synthetic compound derived from pyrimidine, used to treat malaria.

pyrimidine /pɪˈrɪmɪdiːn/ ▸ **noun** [mass noun] Chemistry a colourless crystalline compound with basic properties. ● A heteroaromatic compound; chem. formula: $C_4H_4N_2$.
■ (also **pyrimidine base**) [count noun] a substituted derivative of pyrimidine, especially the bases thymine and cytosine present in DNA.
– ORIGIN late 19th cent.: from German *Pyrimidin*, from PYRIDINE, with the insertion of *-im-* from IMIDE.

pyrites /pʌɪˈrʌɪtiːz/ (also **iron pyrites**; Mineralogy **pyrite**) ▸ **noun** [mass noun] a shiny yellow mineral consisting of iron disulphide and typically occurring as intersecting cubic crystals. See also COPPER PYRITES.
– DERIVATIVES **pyritic** adjective, **pyritize** (also **pyritise**) verb.
– ORIGIN late Middle English (denoting a mineral used for kindling fire): via Latin from Greek *puritēs* 'of fire', from *pur* 'fire'.

pyro ▸ **noun** (pl. **pyros**) informal a pyromaniac.

pyro- ▸ **combining form 1** relating to fire: *pyromania*.
2 Chemistry & Mineralogy denoting a compound or mineral that is formed or affected by heat or has a fiery colour: *pyrophosphate | pyroxene*.
– ORIGIN from Greek *pur* 'fire'.

pyroclastic /ˌpʌɪrə(ʊ)ˈklastɪk/ Geology ▸ **adjective** relating to, consisting of, or denoting fragments of rock erupted by a volcano.
▸ **plural noun (pyroclastics)** pyroclastic fragments.
– DERIVATIVES **pyroclast** noun.

pyroclastic flow ▸ **noun** Geology a dense, destructive mass of very hot ash, lava fragments, and gases ejected explosively from a volcano and typically flowing at great speed.

pyroelectric ▸ **adjective** having or using the property of becoming electrically charged when heated: *a pyroelectric sensor*.
– DERIVATIVES **pyroelectricity** noun.

pyrogallol /ˌpʌɪrə(ʊ)ˈɡalɒl/ ▸ **noun** [mass noun] Chemistry a weakly acid crystalline compound chiefly used as a developer in photography. Also called **pyrogallic acid**. ● Alternative name: **1,3,5-trihydroxybenzene**; chem. formula: $C_6H_3(OH)_3$.

pyrogen /ˈpʌɪrədʒ(ə)n/ ▸ **noun** Medicine a substance, typically produced by a bacterium, which produces fever when introduced or released into the blood.

pyrogenic ▸ **adjective 1** Medicine inducing fever.
2 caused or produced by combustion or the application of heat.
– DERIVATIVES **pyrogenicity** noun.

pyrography /pʌɪˈrɒɡrəfi/ ▸ **noun** [mass noun] the art or technique of decorating wood or leather by burning a design on the surface with a heated metallic point. Also called POKERWORK in Britain.

pyrolusite /ˌpʌɪrə(ʊ)ˈluːsʌɪt/ ▸ **noun** [mass noun] a black or dark grey mineral with a metallic lustre, consisting of manganese dioxide.
– ORIGIN early 19th cent.: from PYRO- 'fire, heat' + Greek *lousis* 'washing' (because of the mineral's use in decolorizing glass).

pyrolyse /ˈpʌɪrəlʌɪz/ (US **pyrolyze**) ▸ **verb** Chemistry make or become decomposed through heating to a high temperature.
– ORIGIN 1920s: from PYROLYSIS, on the pattern of *analyse*.

pyrolysis /pʌɪˈrɒlɪsɪs/ ▸ **noun** [mass noun] Chemistry decomposition brought about by high temperatures.
– DERIVATIVES **pyrolytic** adjective.

pyromania ▸ **noun** [mass noun] an obsessive desire to set fire to things.
– DERIVATIVES **pyromanic** adjective.

pyromaniac ▸ **noun** a person suffering from pyromania: *a ten-year-old pyromaniac*.
– DERIVATIVES **pyromaniacal** adjective.

pyrometallurgy ▸ **noun** [mass noun] the branch of science and technology concerned with the use of high temperatures to extract and purify metals.

pyrometer /pʌɪˈrɒmɪtə/ ▸ **noun** an instrument for measuring high temperatures, especially in furnaces and kilns.
– DERIVATIVES **pyrometric** adjective, **pyrometry** noun.

pyrometric cone ▸ **noun** see CONE (sense 1 of the noun).

pyromorphite /ˌpʌɪrə(ʊ)ˈmɔːfʌɪt/ ▸ **noun** [mass noun] a mineral consisting of a chloride and phosphate of lead, typically occurring as green, yellow, or brown crystals in the oxidized zones of lead deposits.
– ORIGIN early 19th cent.: from PYRO- 'fire, heat' + Greek *morphē* 'form' + -ITE[1].

pyrope /ˈpʌɪrəʊp/ (also **pyrope garnet**) ▸ **noun** [mass noun] a deep red variety of garnet.
– ORIGIN early 19th cent.: from German *Pyrop*, via Latin from Greek *purōpos* 'gold-bronze', literally 'fiery eyed', from *pur* 'fire' + *ōps* 'eye'.

pyrophoric /ˌpʌɪrə(ʊ)ˈfɒrɪk/ ▸ **adjective** liable to ignite spontaneously on exposure to air. ■ (of an alloy) emitting sparks when scratched or struck.
– ORIGIN mid 19th cent.: from modern Latin *pyrophorus*, from Greek *purophoros* 'fire-bearing', from *pur* 'fire' + *pherein* 'to bear'.

pyrophosphate ▸ **noun** Chemistry a salt or ester of pyrophosphoric acid.

pyrophosphoric acid /ˌpʌɪrə(ʊ)fɒsˈfɒrɪk/ ▸ **noun** [mass noun] Chemistry a glassy solid obtained by heating phosphoric acid. ● A tetrabasic acid; chem. formula: $H_4P_2O_7$.

pyrosis /pʌɪˈrəʊsɪs/ ▸ **noun** another term for HEARTBURN.
– ORIGIN late 18th cent.: modern Latin, from Greek *purōsis*, from *puroun* 'set on fire', from *pur* 'fire'.

pyrotechnic /ˌpʌɪrə(ʊ)ˈtɛknɪk/ ▸ **adjective 1** relating to fireworks: *a pyrotechnic display*.
2 brilliant or sensational: *his writing contains more pyrotechnic energy, more colour and action*.
– DERIVATIVES **pyrotechnician** noun, **pyrotechnical** adjective, **pyrotechnist** noun.
– ORIGIN early 19th cent.: from PYRO- 'fire' + Greek *tekhnē* 'art' + -IC.

pyrotechnics ▸ **plural noun 1** a firework display.
■ [treated as sing.] the art of making or displaying fireworks.
2 a brilliant performance or display of a specified skill: *he thrilled his audience with vocal pyrotechnics*.

pyrotechny ▸ **noun** [mass noun] **1** historical the use of fire in alchemy.
2 another term for PYROTECHNICS.
– ORIGIN late 16th cent.: from French *pyrotechnie* or modern Latin *pyrotechnia*, from Greek *pur* + *tekhnē* 'art'.

pyroxene /pʌɪˈrɒksiːn/ ▸ **noun** any of a large class of rock-forming silicate minerals, generally containing calcium, magnesium, and iron and typically occurring as prismatic crystals.
– ORIGIN early 19th cent.: from PYRO- 'fire' + Greek *xenos* 'stranger' (because the mineral group was supposed alien to igneous rocks).

pyroxenite /pʌɪˈrɒksɪnʌɪt/ ▸ **noun** [mass noun] Geology a dark, greenish, granular intrusive igneous rock consisting chiefly of pyroxenes and olivine.
– ORIGIN mid 19th cent.: from PYROXENE + -ITE[1].

pyroxylin /pʌɪˈrɒksɪlɪn/ ▸ **noun** [mass noun] Chemistry a form of nitrocellulose which is less highly nitrated and is soluble in ether and alcohol.
– ORIGIN mid 19th cent.: from French *pyroxyline*, from Greek *pur* 'fire' + *xulon* 'wood'.

Pyrrha /ˈpɪrə/ Greek Mythology the wife of Deucalion.

pyrrhic[1] /ˈpɪrɪk/ ▸ **adjective** (of a victory) won at too great a cost to have been worthwhile for the victor.
– ORIGIN late 19th cent.: from the name PYRRHUS + -IC.

pyrrhic[2] /ˈpɪrɪk/ ▸ **noun** a metrical foot of two short or unaccented syllables.
▸ **adjective** written in or based on such a measure.

– ORIGIN early 17th cent.: via Latin from Greek *purrhikhios (pous)* 'pyrrhic (foot)', the metre of a song accompanying a war dance, named after *Purrhikhos*, inventor of the dance.

Pyrrho /ˈpɪrəʊ/ (*c.*365–*c.*270 BC), Greek philosopher, regarded as the founder of scepticism. He is credited with arguing that happiness comes from suspending judgement because certainty of knowledge is impossible.

Pyrrhonism /ˈpɪrənɪz(ə)m/ ▶ **noun** [mass noun] the philosophy of Pyrrho. ■ philosophic doubt; scepticism.
– DERIVATIVES **Pyrrhonist noun & adjective.**

pyrrhotite /ˈpɪrətʌɪt/ ▶ **noun** [mass noun] a reddish-bronze mineral consisting of iron sulphide, typically forming massive or granular deposits.
– ORIGIN mid 19th cent.: from Greek *purrhotēs* 'redness' + **-ITE**[1].

Pyrrhus /ˈpɪrəs/ (*c.*318–272 BC), king of Epirus *c.*307–272. After invading Italy in 280, he defeated the Romans at Asculum in 279, but sustained heavy losses; the term *pyrrhic victory* is named in allusion to this.

pyrrole /ˈpɪrəʊl/ ▶ **noun** [mass noun] Chemistry a weakly basic sweet-smelling liquid compound present in coal tar. ● A heteroaromatic compound; chem. formula: C_4H_4NH.
– ORIGIN mid 19th cent.: from Greek *purrhos* 'reddish' + Latin *oleum* 'oil'.

pyrrolidine /pɪˈrɒlɪdiːn/ ▶ **noun** [mass noun] Chemistry a pungent liquid made by the reduction of pyrrole. ● Chem. formula: C_4H_8NH.

pyrrolidone /pɪˈrɒlɪdəʊn/ ▶ **noun** [mass noun] Chemistry a colourless weakly basic solid which is a keto derivative of pyrrolidine. ● Chem. formula: C_4H_7NO.

pyruvate /pʌɪˈruːveɪt/ ▶ **noun** Biochemistry a salt or ester of pyruvic acid.

pyruvic acid /pʌɪˈruːvɪk/ ▶ **noun** [mass noun] Biochemistry a yellowish organic acid which occurs as an intermediate in many metabolic processes, especially glycolysis. ● A keto acid; chem. formula: $CH_3COCOOH$.
– ORIGIN mid 19th cent.: from modern Latin *acidum pyruvicum*, from *acidum* 'acid' + *pyruvicum* based on **PYRO-** (denoting an acid) + Latin *uva* 'grape'.

Pythagoras /pʌɪˈθagərəs/ (*c.*580–500 BC), Greek philosopher; known as **Pythagoras of Samos**. Pythagoras sought to interpret the entire physical world in terms of numbers, and founded their systematic and mystical study; he is best known for the theorem of the right-angled triangle. His analysis of the courses of the sun, moon, and stars into circular motions was not set aside until the 17th century.
– DERIVATIVES **Pythagorean** /-ˌθagəˈriːən/ **adjective & noun.**

Pythagoras' theorem ▶ **noun** a theorem attributed to Pythagoras that the square on the hypotenuse of a right-angled triangle is equal in area to the sum of the squares on the other two sides.

Pythia /ˈpɪθɪə/ the priestess of Apollo at Delphi in ancient Greece. See **DELPHI**.
– DERIVATIVES **Pythian adjective.**
– ORIGIN from *Puthō*, a former name of Delphi.

Pythias /ˈpɪθɪas/ see **DAMON**.

python ▶ **noun 1** a large heavy-bodied non-venomous snake occurring throughout the Old World tropics, killing prey by constriction and asphyxiation. ● Family Pythonidae: genera *Python* (of Asia and Africa), and *Morelia* and *Aspidites* (of Australasia).
2 (**Python**) [mass noun] Computing a high-level general-purpose programming language.
– DERIVATIVES **pythonic adjective.**
– ORIGIN late 16th cent. (in the Greek sense): via Latin from Greek *Puthōn*, the name of a huge serpent killed by Apollo. The current sense dates from the mid 19th cent.

Pythonesque ▶ **adjective** denoting or resembling the absurdist or surrealist humour or style of *Monty Python's Flying Circus*, a British television comedy series (1969–74).

pythoness ▶ **noun** archaic a woman believed to be possessed by a familiar spirit and to be able to foresee the future.
– ORIGIN late Middle English: from Old French *phitonise*, from an alteration of late Latin *pythonissa*, based on Greek *puthōn* 'soothsaying demon'. Compare with **PYTHIA**.

pyuria /pʌɪˈjʊərɪə/ ▶ **noun** [mass noun] Medicine the presence of pus in the urine, typically from bacterial infection.
– ORIGIN early 19th cent.: from Greek *puon* 'pus' + **-URIA**.

pyx /pɪks/ ▶ **noun 1** Christian Church the container in which the consecrated bread of the Eucharist is kept. **2** (in the UK) a box at the Royal Mint in which specimen gold and silver coins are deposited to be tested annually at the **trial of the pyx** by members of the Goldsmiths' Company.
– ORIGIN late Middle English: from Latin *pyxis*, from Greek *puxis* 'box'.

pyxidium /pɪkˈsɪdɪəm/ ▶ **noun** (pl. **pyxidia** /-dɪə/) Botany a seed capsule that splits open so that the top comes off like the lid of a box.
– ORIGIN mid 19th cent.: modern Latin, from Greek *puxidion*, diminutive of *puxis* 'box'.

Pyxis /ˈpɪksɪs/ Astronomy a small and inconspicuous southern constellation (the Compass Box or Mariner's Compass), lying in the Milky Way between Vela and Puppis.
– ORIGIN Latin.

pzazz ▶ **noun** variant spelling of **PIZZAZZ**.

P

Qq

Q[1] (also **q**) ▸ **noun** (pl. **Qs** or **Q's**) the seventeenth letter of the alphabet. ▪ denoting the next after P in a set of items, categories, etc.

Q[2] ▸ **abbreviation** ▪ quarter (used to refer to a specified quarter of the financial year): *we expect to have an exceptional Q4.* ▪ queen (used especially in describing card games and recording moves in chess): *17 Qb4.* ▪ question: *Q: What's the problem? A: I don't feel well.* ▪ Theology denoting the hypothetical source of the passages shared by the gospels of Matthew and Luke, but not found in Mark. [probably from German *Quelle* 'source'.]

q ▸ **symbol** Physics electric charge.
– ORIGIN mid 19th cent.: initial letter of *quantity*.

QA ▸ **abbreviation** quality assurance.

Qabalah ▸ **noun** variant spelling of **Kabbalah**.

Qabis variant spelling of **Gabès**.

Qaddafi variant spelling of **Gaddafi**.

qanat /kəˈnɑːt/ (also **kanat**) ▸ **noun** (in the Middle East) a gently sloping underground channel or tunnel constructed to lead water from the interior of a hill to a village below.
– ORIGIN Persian, from Arabic *qanāt* 'reed, pipe, channel'.

Qantas /ˈkwɒntəs/ the international airline of Australia.
– ORIGIN acronym from *Queensland and Northern Territory Aerial Services*.

Qaraghandy /ˈkarəˌgandi/ an industrial city in eastern Kazakhstan, at the centre of a major coal-mining region; pop. 446,100 (est. 2006). Russian name **Karaganda**.

qat ▸ **noun** variant spelling of **khat**.

Qatar /kaˈtɑː, ˈkʌtə/ a sheikhdom occupying a peninsula on the west coast of the Persian Gulf; pop. 833,300 (est. 2009); official language, Arabic; capital, Doha. The country was a British protectorate from 1916 until 1971, when it became a sovereign independent state. Oil is the chief source of revenue.
– DERIVATIVES **Qatari adjective & noun**.

Qattara Depression /kəˈtɑːrə/ an extensive, low-lying, and largely impassable area of desert in NE Africa, to the west of Cairo, that falls to 133 m (436 ft) below sea level.

qawwal /kaˈwɑːl/ ▸ **noun** a performer of qawwali.
– ORIGIN Urdu and Persian *qawwāl*, from Arabic, 'reciter, chanter' (see **qawwali**).

qawwali /kaˈwɑːli/ ▸ **noun** [mass noun] a style of Muslim devotional music now associated particularly with Sufis.
– ORIGIN from Arabic *qawwāli*, from *qawwāl* 'loquacious', also 'singer'.

QB ▸ **abbreviation** ▪ American Football quarterback. ▪ Law Queen's Bench.

QC ▸ **abbreviation** ▪ quality control. ▪ Quebec (in official postal use). ▪ Law Queen's Counsel.

QCD ▸ **abbreviation** quantum chromodynamics.

Q-Celtic ▸ **noun & adjective** another term for **Goidelic**.
– ORIGIN Q, from the retention of the Indo-European *kw* sound as *q* or *c* in this group of languages.

QED ▸ **abbreviation** ▪ quantum electrodynamics. ▪ quod erat demonstrandum.

Q fever ▸ **noun** [mass noun] an infectious fever caused by rickettsiae and transmitted to humans from cattle, sheep, and goats by unpasteurized milk.
– ORIGIN 1930s: from Q for *query* + **fever**.

qi /kiː/ ▸ **noun** variant spelling of **chi**[2].

qiblah /ˈkɪblə/ (also **qibla, kibla**) ▸ **noun** the direction of the Kaaba (the sacred building at Mecca), to which Muslims turn at prayer.
– ORIGIN mid 17th cent.: Arabic, 'that which is opposite'.

qigong /tʃiːˈgɒŋ/ ▸ **noun** [mass noun] a Chinese system of physical exercises and breathing control related to tai chi.
– ORIGIN Chinese.

Qin /tʃɪn/ (also **Ch'in**) a dynasty that ruled China 221–206 BC and was the first to establish rule over a united China. The construction of the Great Wall of China was begun during this period.

Qing /tʃɪŋ/ (also **Ch'ing**) a dynasty established by the Manchus that ruled China 1644–1912. Its overthrow in 1912 by Sun Yat-sen and his supporters ended imperial rule in China.

Qingdao /tʃɪŋˈdaʊ/ a port in eastern China, in Shandong province on the Yellow Sea coast; pop. 2,654,300 (est. 2006).

Qinghai /tʃɪŋˈhʌɪ/ (also **Tsinghai**) a mountainous province in north central China; capital, Xining.

qintar /ˈkɪntɑː/ ▸ **noun** (pl. **same, qintars**, or **qindarka**) a monetary unit of Albania, equal to one hundredth of a lek.
– ORIGIN from Albanian *qindar*, from *qind* 'hundred'.

Qiqihar /ˌtʃɪtʃɪˈhɑː/ a port on the River Nen, in Heilongjiang province, NE China; pop. 1,115,100 (est. 2006).

Qld ▸ **abbreviation** Queensland.

QM ▸ **abbreviation** Quartermaster.

QMG ▸ **abbreviation** Quartermaster General.

QMS ▸ **abbreviation** Quartermaster Sergeant.

Qom /kʊm/ (also **Qum** or **Kum**) a city in central Iran; pop. 964,706 (2006). It is a holy city and centre of learning among Shiite Muslims.

Qomolungma /ˌtsəʊmə(ʊ)ˈlʊŋmə/ (also **Chomolungma**) Tibetan name for **Everest, Mount**.

QPM ▸ **abbreviation** (in the UK) Queen's Police Medal.

qr ▸ **abbreviation** quarter(s).

Q-ship ▸ **noun** historical a merchant ship with concealed weapons, used by the British in the First and Second World Wars in an attempt to destroy submarines.
– ORIGIN First World War: from Q as a non-explicit symbol of the type of vessel + **ship**.

QSO ▸ **abbreviation** quasi-stellar object, a quasar.

qt ▸ **abbreviation** quart(s).

q.t. ▸ **noun** (in phrase **on the q.t.**) informal secretly; secret.
– ORIGIN late 19th cent.: abbreviation of *quiet*.

qua /kweɪ, kwɑː/ ▸ **conjunction** formal in the capacity of; as being: ***shareholders qua members may be under obligations to the company.***
– ORIGIN Latin, ablative feminine singular of *qui* 'who'.

Quaalude /ˈkweɪl(j)uːd/ ▸ **noun** trademark for **methaqualone**.
– ORIGIN 1960s: an invented name.

quack[1] ▸ **noun** the characteristic harsh sound made by a duck.
▸ **verb** [no obj.] (of a duck) make a quack. ▪ informal (of a person) talk loudly and foolishly.
– ORIGIN mid 16th cent. (as a verb): imitative.

quack[2] ▸ **noun** a person who dishonestly claims to have special knowledge and skill in some field, typically medicine. ▪ Brit. informal a doctor.
– DERIVATIVES **quackery noun, quackish adjective**.
– ORIGIN mid 17th cent.: abbreviation of earlier *quacksalver*, from Dutch, probably from obsolete *quacken* 'prattle' + *salf, zalf* (see **salve**[1]).

quack grass ▸ **noun** North American term for **couch**[2].
– ORIGIN early 19th cent.: *quack*, variant of *quick*, northern form of **quitch**.

quad ▸ **noun 1** informal short for: ▪ a quadrangle. ▪ a quadruplet (child). ▪ a quadriceps. ▪ a quad bike. ▪ quadraphony.
2 (in telephony) a group of four insulated conductors twisted together, usually forming two circuits. [abbreviation of *quadruplex*, a telegraphic device invented by Thomas Edison, by means of which four messages could be sent simultaneously over one wire.]
3 a radio aerial in the form of a square or rectangle broken in the middle of one side. [abbreviation of **quadrilateral**.]
4 informal a traditional four-wheeled roller skate.
5 Printing a small metal block in various sizes, lower than type height, used in letterpress printing for filling up short lines. [abbreviation of the late 17th-cent. printing term *quadrat*.]
▸ **adjective** informal quadruple or quadraphonic.

quad bike ▸ **noun** a motorcycle with four large tyres, for off-road use.

quadragenarian /ˌkwɒdrədʒɪˈnɛːrɪən/ ▸ **noun** a person who is between 40 and 49 years old.
– ORIGIN mid 19th cent.: from late Latin *quadragenarius* (based on Latin *quadraginta* 'forty') + **-an**.

Quadragesima /ˌkwɒdrəˈdʒɛsɪmə/ (also **Quadragesima Sunday**) ▸ **noun** the first Sunday in Lent.
– ORIGIN from ecclesiastical Latin, feminine of Latin *quadragesimus* 'fortieth', from *quadraginta* 'forty' (Lent lasting forty days).

quadragesimal ▸ **adjective** archaic (of a fast, especially one in Lent) lasting forty days. ▪ belonging or appropriate to the period of Lent.

quadrangle ▸ **noun 1** Geometry a four-sided plane figure, especially a square or rectangle.
2 a square or rectangular space or courtyard enclosed by buildings.
– ORIGIN late Middle English: from Old French, or from late Latin *quadrangulum* 'square', neuter of *quadrangulus*, from Latin *quadri-* 'four' + *angulus* 'corner, angle'.

quadrangular ▸ **adjective** (of an object or architectural structure) having four sides. ▪ Brit. (of a sporting contest) involving four teams competing against each other.

quadrant ▸ **noun** technical **1** each of four quarters of a circle. ▪ each of four parts of a plane, sphere, space, or body divided by two lines or planes at right angles: *the right upper quadrant of the kidney.*
2 historical an instrument used for taking angular measurements of altitude in astronomy and navigation, typically consisting of a graduated quarter circle and a sighting mechanism.

Q

3 a frame fixed to the head of a ship's rudder, to which the steering mechanism is attached. ▪ a panel with slots through which a lever is moved to orient or otherwise control a mechanism.
– DERIVATIVES **quadrantal** adjective.
– ORIGIN late Middle English (denoting the astronomical instrument): from Latin *quadrans, quadrant-* 'quarter', from *quattuor* 'four'.

Quadrantids /kwɒˈdrantɪdz/ Astronomy an annual meteor shower with a radiant in the constellation Boötes, reaching a peak about 3 January.
– ORIGIN from Latin *Quadrans Muralis* 'the Mural Quadrant', the name of a former constellation.

quadraphonic (also **quadrophonic**) ▶ **adjective** (of sound reproduction) transmitted through four channels.
– DERIVATIVES **quadraphonically** adverb, **quadraphonics** plural noun, **quadraphony** /-ˈdrɒf(ə)ni/ noun.
– ORIGIN 1960s: from QUADRI- 'four' + a shortened form of STEREOPHONIC.

quadrat /ˈkwɒdrət/ ▶ **noun** Ecology each of a number of small areas of habitat, typically of one square metre, selected at random to act as samples for assessing the local distribution of plants or animals. ▪ a portable frame, typically with an internal grid, used to mark out a quadrat.
– ORIGIN early 20th cent.: variant of QUADRATE.

quadrate ▶ **noun** /ˈkwɒdrət/ **1** (also **quadrate bone**) Zoology (in the skull of a bird or reptile) a squarish bone with which the jaw articulates, thought to be homologous with the incus of the middle ear in mammals.
2 Anatomy another term for QUADRATUS.
▶ **adjective** /ˈkwɒdrət/ roughly square or rectangular.
▶ **verb** /kwɒˈdreɪt, ˈkwɒdreɪt/ archaic **1** [with obj.] make square.
2 [no obj.] conform with or correspond to something.
– ORIGIN late Middle English (as an adjective): from Latin *quadrat-* 'made square', from the verb *quadrare*, from *quattuor* 'four'.

quadratic /kwɒˈdratɪk/ ▶ **adjective** Mathematics involving the second and no higher power of an unknown quantity or variable: *a quadratic equation*.
▶ **noun** a quadratic equation.
– ORIGIN mid 17th cent.: from French *quadratique* or modern Latin *quadraticus*, from *quadratus* 'made square', past participle of *quadrare* (see QUADRATE).

quadrature /ˈkwɒdrətʃə/ ▶ **noun** [mass noun] **1** Mathematics the process of constructing a square with an area equal to that of a circle, or of another figure bounded by a curve.
2 Astronomy the position of the moon or a planet when it is 90° from the sun as viewed from the earth.
3 Electronics a phase difference of 90 degrees between two waves of the same frequency, as in the colour difference signals of a television screen.
– ORIGIN mid 16th cent. (as a mathematical term): from Latin *quadratura* 'a square, squaring', from *quadrare* (see QUADRATE).

Q

quadrature amplitude modulation ▶ **noun** [mass noun] Telecommunications a modulation system used in microwave and satellite communication, involving phase and amplitude modulation of a carrier wave.

quadratus /kwɒˈdreɪtəs/ ▶ **noun** (pl. **quadrati** /-tʌɪ/) Anatomy any of several roughly square or rectangular muscles, e.g. in the abdomen, thigh, and eye socket.
– ORIGIN mid 18th cent.: from Latin, literally 'made square'.

quadrennial /kwɒˈdrɛnɪəl/ ▶ **adjective** recurring every four years. ▪ lasting for or relating to a period of four years.
– DERIVATIVES **quadrennially** adverb.
– ORIGIN mid 17th cent.: from QUADRENNIUM + -AL.

quadrennium /kwɒˈdrɛnɪəm/ ▶ **noun** (pl. **quadrennia** /-nɪə/ or **quadrenniums**) a specified period of four years.
– ORIGIN early 19th cent.: from Latin *quadriennium*, from *quadri-* 'four' + *annus* 'year'.

quadri- ▶ **combining form** four; having four: *quadriceps | quadriplegia*.
– ORIGIN from Latin, from *quattuor* 'four'.

quadric /ˈkwɒdrɪk/ Geometry ▶ **adjective** (of a surface or curve) described by an equation of the second degree.
▶ **noun** a quadric surface or curve.
– ORIGIN mid 19th cent.: from Latin *quadra* 'square' + -IC.

quadriceps /ˈkwɒdrɪsɛps/ ▶ **noun** (pl. **same**) Anatomy the large muscle at the front of the thigh, which is divided into four distinct portions and acts to extend the leg.
– ORIGIN mid 16th cent.: from Latin, literally 'four-headed'.

quadrilateral ▶ **noun** a four-sided figure.
▶ **adjective** having four straight sides.
– ORIGIN mid 17th cent.: from late Latin *quadrilaterus* (from Latin *quadri-* 'four' + *latus, later-* 'side') + -AL.

quadrille[1] /kwɒˈdrɪl/ ▶ **noun** a square dance performed typically by four couples and containing five figures, each of which is a complete dance in itself. ▪ a piece of music for a quadrille.
– ORIGIN mid 18th cent.: from French from Spanish *cuadrilla* or Italian *quadriglia* 'troop, company', from *cuadra, quadra* 'square', based on Latin *quadrare* 'make square'.

quadrille[2] /kwɒˈdrɪl/ ▶ **noun** [mass noun] a trick-taking card game for four players using a pack of forty cards (i.e. one lacking eights, nines, and tens), fashionable in the 18th century.
– ORIGIN early 18th cent.: from French, perhaps from Spanish *cuartillo* (from *cuarto* 'fourth'). The change in the first syllable was due to association with QUADRILLE[1].

quadrille[3] /kwɒˈdrɪl/ ▶ **noun** [mass noun] a ruled grid of small squares, especially on paper.
– ORIGIN late 19th cent.: from French *quadrillé*, from *quadrille* 'small square', from Spanish *cuadrillo* 'small block'.

quadrillion /kwɒˈdrɪljən/ ▶ **cardinal number** (pl. **quadrillions** or (with numeral) **same**) a thousand raised to the power of five (10^{15}). ▪ dated, chiefly Brit. a thousand raised to the power of eight (10^{24}).
– DERIVATIVES **quadrillionth** ordinal number.
– ORIGIN late 17th cent.: from French, from *million*, by substitution of the prefix *quadri-* 'four' for the initial letters.

quadripartite /ˌkwɒdrɪˈpɑːtʌɪt/ ▶ **adjective** consisting of four parts. ▪ shared by or involving four parties.
– ORIGIN late Middle English: from Latin *quadripartitus*, from *quadri-* 'four' + *partitus* 'divided'.

quadriplegia /ˌkwɒdrɪˈpliːdʒə/ ▶ **noun** [mass noun] Medicine paralysis of all four limbs; tetraplegia.
– DERIVATIVES **quadriplegic** adjective & noun.
– ORIGIN 1920s: from QUADRI- 'four' + a shortened form of PARAPLEGIA.

quadrivalent /ˌkwɒdrɪˈveɪl(ə)nt/ ▶ **adjective** Chemistry another term for TETRAVALENT.

quadrivium /kwɒˈdrɪvɪəm/ ▶ **noun** a medieval university course involving the 'mathematical arts' of arithmetic, geometry, astronomy, and music. Compare with TRIVIUM.
– ORIGIN Latin, literally 'the place where four roads meet' (in late Latin 'the four branches of mathematics'), from *quadri-* 'four' + *via* 'road'.

quadroon /kwɒˈdruːn/ ▶ **noun** dated a person who is one-quarter black by descent.
– ORIGIN early 18th cent. (earlier as *quarteron*): via French from Spanish *cuarterón*, from *cuarto* 'quarter', from Latin *quartus*; later assimilated to words beginning with QUADRI-.

quadrophonic ▶ **adjective** variant spelling of QUADRAPHONIC.

quadrumanous /kwɒˈdruːmənəs, ˌkwɒdrʊˈmɑːnəs/ ▶ **adjective** Zoology, dated (of primates other than humans) having all four feet modified as hands, i.e. having opposable digits.
– ORIGIN late 17th cent.: from modern Latin *Quadrumana* (former order name, neuter plural of *quadrumanus*, from *quadru-* 'four' + Latin *manus* 'hand') + -OUS.

quadruped /ˈkwɒdrʊpɛd/ ▶ **noun** an animal which has four feet, especially an ungulate mammal.
– DERIVATIVES **quadrupedal** /-ˈpiːd(ə)l, -ˈruːpɪd(ə)l/ adjective, **quadrupedalism** noun.
– ORIGIN mid 17th cent.: from French *quadrupède* or Latin *quadrupes, quadruped-*, from *quadru-* 'four' + *pes, ped-* 'foot'.

quadruple /ˈkwɒdrʊp(ə)l, kwɒˈdruːp(ə)l/ ▶ **adjective** [attrib.] consisting of four parts or elements: *a quadruple murder*. ▪ consisting of four times as much or as many as usual: *a quadruple vodka*. ▪ (of time in music) having four beats in a bar.
▶ **verb** increase or be increased fourfold: [no obj.] *oil prices quadrupled in the 1970s*.
▶ **noun** a quadruple number or amount.
– DERIVATIVES **quadruply** adverb.
– ORIGIN late Middle English (as a verb): via French from Latin *quadruplus*, from *quadru-* 'four' + *-plus* as in *duplus* (see DUPLE).

Quadruple Alliance a union or association between four powers or states, notably that formed in 1813 between Britain, Russia, Austria, and Prussia in order to defeat Napoleon and to maintain the international order established in Europe at the end of the Napoleonic Wars.

quadruplet /ˈkwɒdrʊplɪt, kwɒˈdruːplɪt/ ▶ **noun** **1** (usu. **quadruplets**) each of four children born at one birth.
2 Music a group of four notes to be performed in the time of three.
– ORIGIN late 18th cent.: from QUADRUPLE, on the pattern of *triplet*.

quadruplicate ▶ **adjective** /kwɒˈdruːplɪkət/ consisting of four parts or elements. ▪ of which four copies are made.
▶ **verb** /kwɒˈdruːplɪkeɪt/ [with obj.] multiply (something) by four. ▪ (usu. as adj. **quadruplicated**) make or provide in quadruplicate.
– PHRASES **in quadruplicate** in four identical copies.
– DERIVATIVES **quadruplication** noun.
– ORIGIN mid 17th cent.: from Latin *quadruplicat-* 'quadrupled', from the verb *quadruplicare*, from *quadruplex, quadruplic-* 'fourfold', from *quadru-* 'four' + *plicare* 'to fold'.

quadrupole /ˈkwɒdrʊpəʊl/ ▶ **noun** Physics a distribution of electric charge or magnetization consisting of four equal monopoles, or two equal dipoles, arranged close together with alternating polarity and operating as a unit. ▪ a device using a quadrupole arrangement directed at one point to focus beams of subatomic particles.

quaestor /ˈkwiːstə/ ▶ **noun** (in ancient Rome) any of a number of officials who had charge of public revenue and expenditure.
– DERIVATIVES **quaestorship** noun.
– ORIGIN Latin, from an old form of *quaesit-* 'sought', from the verb *quaerere*.

quaff /kwɒf, kwɑːf/ ▶ **verb** [with obj.] drink (something, especially an alcoholic drink) heartily.
▶ **noun** informal, dated an alcoholic drink.
– DERIVATIVES **quaffable** adjective, **quaffer** noun.
– ORIGIN early 16th cent.: probably imitative of the sound of drinking.

quag /kwag, kwɒg/ ▶ **noun** archaic a marshy or boggy place.
– DERIVATIVES **quaggy** adjective.
– ORIGIN late 16th cent.: related to dialect *quag* 'shake, quiver'; probably symbolic, the *qu-* suggesting movement (as in *quake* and *quick*).

quagga /ˈkwagə/ ▶ **noun** a South African zebra, extinct since 1883, that had a yellowish-brown coat with darker stripes. ● *Equus quagga*, family Equidae; recent studies have shown that it was probably a variety of the common zebra.
– ORIGIN South African Dutch, probably from Khoikhoi, imitative of its braying.

quagmire /ˈkwagmʌɪə, ˈkwɒg-/ ▶ **noun** a soft boggy area of land that gives way underfoot: *torrential rain turned the building site into a quagmire*. ▪ an awkward, complex, or hazardous situation: *a legal quagmire*.
– ORIGIN late 16th cent.: from QUAG + MIRE.

quahog /ˈkwɔːhɒg, ˈkwɑː-/ (also **quahaug** /-hɔːg/) ▶ **noun** N. Amer. a large, rounded edible clam of the Atlantic coast of North America. Also called HARD CLAM, HARDSHELL CLAM. ● *Venus mercenaria*, family Veneridae.
– ORIGIN mid 18th cent.: from Narragansett *poquaûhock*.

quaich /kweɪk, -x/ (also **quaigh**) ▶ **noun** Scottish a shallow drinking cup, typically made of wood and having two handles.
– ORIGIN mid 16th cent.: from Scottish Gaelic *cuach* 'cup'.

Quai d'Orsay /ˌkeɪ dɔːˈseɪ/, French /kɛ dɔʀsɛ/ a riverside street on the left bank of the Seine in Paris. ▪ the French ministry of foreign affairs, which has its headquarters in this street.

quail[1] ▶ **noun** (pl. **same** or **quails**) **1** a small short-tailed Old World game bird resembling a tiny partridge, typically having brown camouflaged plumage. ● Family Phasianidae: three genera, in particular *Coturnix*, and several species, e.g. the widespread migratory **common quail** (*C. coturnix*).
2 a small or medium-sized New World game bird, the male of which has distinctive facial markings. ● Family Phasianidae (or Odontophoridae): several genera and many species, including the bobwhite.
– ORIGIN Middle English: from Old French *quaille*, from medieval Latin *coacula* (probably imitative of its call).

quail[2] ▶ verb [no obj.] feel or show fear or apprehension: *she quailed at his heartless words.*
– ORIGIN late Middle English (in the sense 'waste away, come to nothing'): of unknown origin.

quaint ▶ adjective attractively unusual or old-fashioned: *quaint country cottages | a quaint old custom.*
– DERIVATIVES **quaintly** adverb, **quaintness** noun.
– ORIGIN Middle English: from Old French *cointe*, from Latin *cognitus* 'ascertained', past participle of *cognoscere*. The original sense was 'wise, clever', also 'ingenious, cunningly devised', hence 'out of the ordinary' and the current sense (late 18th cent.).

quake ▶ verb [no obj.] (especially of the earth) shake or tremble: *the rumbling vibrations set the whole valley quaking.* ■ (of a person) shake or shudder with fear: *those words should have them* ***quaking in their boots.***
▶ noun informal an earthquake.
– DERIVATIVES **quaky** adjective (**quakier**, **quakiest**).
– ORIGIN Old English *cwacian*.

Quaker ▶ noun a member of the Religious Society of Friends, a Christian movement founded by George Fox *c.*1650 and devoted to peaceful principles. Central to the Quakers' belief is the doctrine of the 'Inner Light', or sense of Christ's direct working in the soul. This has led them to reject both formal ministry and all set forms of worship.
– DERIVATIVES **Quakerish** adjective, **Quakerism** noun.
– ORIGIN from **QUAKE** + **-ER**[1], perhaps alluding to George Fox's direction to his followers to 'tremble at the name of the Lord', or from fits supposedly experienced by worshippers when moved by the Spirit. Compare with **SHAKER** (sense 2).

quaking bog ▶ noun a bog formed over water or soft mud, which shakes underfoot.

quaking grass ▶ noun [mass noun] a slender-stalked grass with oval or heart-shaped flower heads which tremble in the wind. ● Genus *Briza*, family Gramineae: several species, including *B. media*, which is sometimes cultivated as an ornamental.

quale /ˈkweɪli/ ▶ noun (pl. **qualia** /ˈkweɪlɪə/) (usu. **qualia**) Philosophy a quality or property as perceived or experienced by a person.
– ORIGIN late 17th cent.: from Latin, neuter of *qualis* 'of what kind'.

qualification ▶ noun **1** a pass of an examination or an official completion of a course, especially one conferring status as a recognized practitioner of a profession or activity: *I left school at 15 with no qualifications.* ■ [mass noun] the action or fact of becoming qualified as a recognized practitioner of a profession or activity: *her qualification as a barrister.* ■ a quality or accomplishment that makes someone suitable for a particular job or activity: *only one qualification required—fabulous sense of humour.*
2 a condition that must be fulfilled before a right can be acquired; an official requirement: *the five-year residency qualification for presidential candidates.*
3 [mass noun] the action or fact of qualifying or being eligible for something: *they need to beat Poland to ensure qualification for the World Cup finals.*
4 a statement or assertion that makes another less absolute: *this important qualification needs to be remembered when interpreting the results* | [mass noun] *I welcome without qualification the Minister's statement.*
5 [mass noun] Grammar the attribution of a quality to a word, especially a noun.
– DERIVATIVES **qualificatory** adjective.
– ORIGIN mid 16th cent.: from medieval Latin *qualificatio(n-)*, from the verb *qualificare* (see **QUALIFY**).

qualified ▶ adjective **1** officially recognized as being trained to perform a particular job; certified: *newly qualified nurses.* ■ [with infinitive] competent or knowledgeable to do something; capable: *I was less well qualified than almost anyone present to recollect the olden days.*
2 not complete or absolute; limited: *I could only judge this CD a qualified success.*

qualifier ▶ noun **1** a person or team that qualifies for a competition or its final rounds. ■ a match or contest to decide which individuals or teams qualify for a competition or its final rounds.
2 Grammar a word or phrase, especially an adjective, used to attribute a quality to another word, especially a noun. ■ (in systemic grammar) a word or phrase added after a noun to qualify its meaning.

qualify ▶ verb (**qualifies**, **qualifying**, **qualified**) **1** [no obj.] be entitled to a particular benefit or privilege by fulfilling a necessary condition: *a pensioner who does not qualify for income support.* ■ become eligible for a competition or its final rounds, by reaching a certain standard or defeating a competitor: *England are in danger of failing to qualify.* ■ be or make properly entitled to be classed in a particular way: [no obj.] *he qualifies as a genuine political refugee.*
2 [no obj.] become officially recognized as a practitioner of a particular profession or activity, typically by undertaking a course and passing examinations: *the training necessary to* ***qualify as*** *a solicitor | I've only just qualified.* ■ [with obj.] officially recognize or establish (someone) as a practitioner of a particular profession or activity: *the courses qualify you as an instructor of the sport.* ■ [with obj. and infinitive] make (someone) competent or knowledgeable enough to do something: *I'm not qualified to write on the subject.*
3 [with obj.] make (a statement or assertion) less absolute; add reservations to: *she felt obliged to qualify her first short answer.* ■ archaic make (something) less severe or extreme: *his sincere piety, his large heart always qualify his errors.* ■ archaic alter the strength or flavour of (something, especially a liquid): *he qualified his mug of water with a plentiful infusion of the liquor.*
4 [with obj.] Grammar (of a word or phrase) attribute a quality to (another word, especially a preceding noun). ■ (**qualify something as**) archaic attribute a specified quality to something; describe something as: *the propositions have been qualified as heretical.*
– DERIVATIVES **qualifiable** adjective.
– ORIGIN late Middle English (in the sense 'describe in a particular way'): from French *qualifier*, from medieval Latin *qualificare*, from Latin *qualis* 'of what kind, of such a kind' (see **QUALITY**).

qualitative /ˈkwɒlɪtətɪv/ ▶ adjective relating to, measuring, or measured by the quality of something rather than its quantity: *a qualitative change in the undergraduate curriculum.* Often contrasted with **QUANTITATIVE.** ■ Grammar (of an adjective) describing the quality of something in size, appearance, value, etc. Such adjectives can be submodified by words such as *very* and have comparative and superlative forms. Contrasted with **CLASSIFYING.**
– DERIVATIVES **qualitatively** adverb.
– ORIGIN late Middle English: from late Latin *qualitativus*, from Latin *qualitas* (see **QUALITY**).

qualitative analysis ▶ noun [mass noun] Chemistry identification of the constituents, e.g. elements or functional groups, present in a substance.

quality ▶ noun (pl. **qualities**) **1** [mass noun] the standard of something as measured against other things of a similar kind; the degree of excellence of something: *an improvement in product quality* | [count noun] *people today enjoy a better quality of life.* ■ general excellence of standard or level: *a masterpiece for connoisseurs of quality.* ■ (usu. **qualities**) Brit. short for **QUALITY PAPER.** ■ archaic high social standing: *commanding the admiration of people of quality.* ■ [treated as pl.] archaic people of high social standing: *he's dazed at being called on to speak before quality.*
2 a distinctive attribute or characteristic possessed by someone or something: *he shows strong leadership qualities | the plant's aphrodisiac qualities.* ■ Phonetics the distinguishing characteristic or characteristics of a speech sound. ■ Astrology any of three properties (cardinal, fixed, or mutable), representing types of movement, that a zodiacal sign can possess.
▶ adjective informal of good quality; excellent: *he's a quality player.*
– ORIGIN Middle English (in the senses 'character, disposition' and 'particular property or feature'): from Old French *qualite*, from Latin *qualitas* (translating Greek *poiotēs*), from *qualis* 'of what kind, of such a kind'.

quality assurance ▶ noun [mass noun] the maintenance of a desired level of quality in a service or product, especially by means of attention to every stage of the process of delivery or production.

quality circle ▶ noun a group of employees who meet regularly to consider ways of resolving problems and improving production in their organization.

quality control ▶ noun [mass noun] a system of maintaining standards in manufactured products by testing a sample of the output against the specification.
– DERIVATIVES **quality controller** noun.

quality factor ▶ noun Physics a parameter of an oscillatory system or device, such as a laser, expressing the relationship between stored energy and energy dissipation. ■ a figure expressing the ability of ionizing radiation to cause biological damage, relative to a standard dose of X-rays.

quality paper (also **quality newspaper**) ▶ noun Brit. a newspaper, typically a broadsheet, that is considered to deal seriously with issues and to have high editorial standards.

quality time ▶ noun [mass noun] time in which one's child, partner, or other loved person receives one's undivided attention, in such a way as to strengthen the relationship.

qualm /kwɑːm, kwɔːm/ ▶ noun an uneasy feeling of doubt, worry, or fear, especially about one's own conduct; a misgiving: *military regimes generally* ***have no qualms about*** *controlling the press.* ■ archaic a momentary faint or sick feeling.
– DERIVATIVES **qualmish** adjective.
– ORIGIN early 16th cent. (in the sense 'momentary sick feeling'): perhaps related to Old English *cw(e)alm* 'pain', of Germanic origin.

quamash /kwəˈmaʃ, ˈkwɒmaʃ/ ▶ noun variant spelling of **CAMAS.**

quandary /ˈkwɒnd(ə)ri/ ▶ noun (pl. **quandaries**) a state of perplexity or uncertainty over what to do in a difficult situation: *Kate was* ***in a quandary.*** ■ a difficult situation; a practical dilemma: *a legal quandary.*
– ORIGIN late 16th cent.: perhaps partly from Latin *quando* 'when'.

quandong /ˈkwɒndɒŋ, ˈkwan-/ ▶ noun either of two Australian trees: ● a small tree of the sandalwood family, which has round red fruit with an edible pulp and kernel (*Eucarya acuminata*, family Santalaceae). ● (also **blue quandong**) a large tree of the subtropical rainforest, which has blue berries (*Elaeocarpus grandis*, family Elaeocarpaceae).
– ORIGIN mid 19th cent.: from Wiradhuri.

quango /ˈkwaŋgəʊ/ ▶ noun (pl. **quangos**) Brit., chiefly derogatory a semi-public administrative body outside the civil service but receiving financial support from the government, which makes senior appointments to it.
– ORIGIN 1970s (originally US): acronym from *quasi* (or *quasi-autonomous*) *non-government(al) organization.*

Quant /kwɒnt/, Mary (b.1934), English fashion designer. She was a principal creator of the '1960s look', launching the miniskirt in 1966 and promoting bold colours and geometric designs. She was also one of the first to design for the ready-to-wear market.

quant[1] /kwɒnt/ ▶ noun informal a quantity analyst.
– ORIGIN late 20th cent.: abbreviation.

quant[2] /kwɒnt, kwant/ ▶ noun Brit. a pole for propelling a barge or punt, especially one with a prong at the bottom to prevent it sinking into the mud.
– ORIGIN late Middle English: perhaps from Latin *contus*, from Greek *kontos* 'boat pole'.

quanta plural form of **QUANTUM.**

quantal /ˈkwɒnt(ə)l/ ▶ adjective technical composed of discrete units; varying in steps rather than continuously: *a quantal release of neurotransmitter.* ■ Physics relating to a quantum or quanta, or to quantum theory. ■ chiefly Physiology relating to or denoting an all-or-none response or state.
– ORIGIN early 20th cent.: from **QUANTUM** + **-AL.**

quantic ▶ noun Mathematics a homogeneous function of two or more variables having rational or integral coefficients.
– ORIGIN mid 19th cent.: from Latin *quantus* 'how great, how much' + **-IC.**

quantifier ▶ noun Logic an expression (e.g. *all, some*) that indicates the scope of a term to which it is attached. ■ Grammar a determiner or pronoun indicative of quantity (e.g. *all, both*).

quantify ▶ verb (**quantifies**, **quantifying**, **quantified**) [with obj.] **1** express or measure the quantity of: *it is impossible to quantify the extent of the black economy.*
2 Logic define the application of (a term or proposition) by the use of *all, some*, etc., e.g. 'for all *x* if *x* is A then *x* is B'.
– DERIVATIVES **quantifiability** noun, **quantifiable** adjective, **quantification** noun.
– ORIGIN mid 16th cent.: from medieval Latin *quantificare*, from Latin *quantus* 'how much'.

quantile /ˈkwɒntʌɪl/ ▶ noun Statistics each of any set of values of a variate which divide a frequency distribution into equal groups, each containing the same fraction of the total population. ■ any of the groups so produced, e.g. a quartile or percentile.
– ORIGIN 1940s: from Latin *quantus* 'how great, how much' + **-ILE.**

Q

quantitate /ˈkwɒntɪteɪt/ ▸ **verb** [with obj.] Medicine & Biology determine the quantity or extent of (something in numerical terms); quantify.
– DERIVATIVES **quantitation** noun.
– ORIGIN 1960s: from QUANTITY + -ATE[3].

quantitative /ˈkwɒntɪˌtətɪv, -ˌteɪtɪv/ ▸ **adjective** relating to, measuring, or measured by the quantity of something rather than its quality: *quantitative analysis*. Often contrasted with QUALITATIVE. ■ denoting or relating to verse whose metre is based on the length of syllables, as in Latin, as opposed to the stress, as in English.
– DERIVATIVES **quantitatively** adverb.
– ORIGIN late 16th cent. (in the sense 'having magnitude or spatial extent'): from medieval Latin *quantitativus*, from Latin *quantitas* (see QUANTITY).

quantitative analysis ▸ **noun** [mass noun] Chemistry measurement of the quantities of particular constituents present in a substance.

quantitative easing ▸ **noun** [mass noun] Finance the introduction of new money into the money supply by a central bank.

quantitative linguistics ▸ **plural noun** [treated as sing.] the comparative study of the frequency and distribution of words and syntactic structures in different texts.

quantitive ▸ **adjective** another term for QUANTITATIVE.
– DERIVATIVES **quantitively** adverb.

quantity ▸ **noun** (pl. **quantities**) [mass noun] **1** the amount or number of a material or abstract thing not usually estimated by spatial measurement: *the quantity and quality of the fruit can be controlled*. ■ [count noun] a certain, usually specified, amount or number of something: ***a small quantity of** food* | *if taken in large quantities, the drug can result in liver failure*. ■ (often **quantities**) a considerable number or amount of something: *she was able to drink **quantities of** beer without degenerating into giggles* | [mass noun] *many people like to buy in quantity*.
2 Phonetics the perceived length of a vowel sound or syllable.
3 Mathematics & Physics a value or component that may be expressed in numbers. ■ [count noun] the figure or symbol representing this.
– ORIGIN Middle English: from Old French *quantite*, from Latin *quantitas* (translating Greek *posotēs*), from *quantus* 'how great, how much'.

quantity surveyor ▸ **noun** Brit. a person who calculates the amount of materials needed for building work, and how much they will cost.

quantity theory (also **the quantity theory of money**) ▸ **noun** [mass noun] Economics the hypothesis that changes in prices correspond to changes in the monetary supply.

Q

quantize (also **quantise**) ▸ **verb** [with obj.] **1** Physics form into quanta, in particular restrict the number of possible values of (a quantity) or states of (a system) so that certain variables can assume only certain discrete magnitudes.
2 Electronics approximate (a continuously varying signal) by one whose amplitude is restricted to a prescribed set of values.
– DERIVATIVES **quantization** noun, **quantizer** noun (sense 2).

quantum /ˈkwɒntəm/ ▸ **noun** (pl. **quanta** /-tə/) **1** Physics a discrete quantity of energy proportional in magnitude to the frequency of the radiation it represents. ■ an analogous discrete amount of any other physical quantity, such as momentum or electric charge. ■ Physiology the unit quantity of acetylcholine released at a neuromuscular junction by a single synaptic vesicle, contributing a discrete small voltage to the measured end-plate potential.
2 a required or allowed amount, especially an amount of money legally payable in damages. ■ a share or portion: *each man has only a quantum of compassion*.
– ORIGIN mid 16th cent. (in the general sense 'quantity'): from Latin, neuter of *quantus* (see QUANTITY). Sense 1 dates from the early 20th cent.

quantum bit ▸ **noun** Computing the basic unit of information in a quantum computer.

quantum chromodynamics (abbrev.: **QCD**) ▸ **plural noun** [treated as sing.] Physics a quantum field theory in which the strong interaction is described in terms of an interaction between quarks mediated by gluons, both quarks and gluons being assigned a quantum number called 'colour'.

quantum computer ▸ **noun** a computer which makes use of the quantum states of subatomic particles to store information.
– DERIVATIVES **quantum computing** noun.

quantum dot ▸ **noun** Physics a semiconductor crystal of nanometre dimensions with distinctive conductive properties determined by its size.

quantum electrodynamics ▸ **plural noun** [treated as sing.] a quantum field theory that deals with the electromagnetic field and its interaction with electrically charged particles.

quantum field theory ▸ **noun** Physics a field theory that incorporates quantum mechanics and the principles of the theory of relativity.

quantum gravity ▸ **noun** [mass noun] Physics a theory that attempts to explain gravitational physics in terms of quantum mechanics.

quantum jump ▸ **noun 1** Physics an abrupt transition of an electron, atom, or molecule from one quantum state to another, with the absorption or emission of a quantum.
2 another term for QUANTUM LEAP.

quantum leap ▸ **noun** a sudden large increase or advance: *there has been a quantum leap in the quality of wines marketed in the UK*.

quantum mechanics ▸ **plural noun** [treated as sing.] Physics the branch of mechanics that deals with the mathematical description of the motion and interaction of subatomic particles, incorporating the concepts of quantization of energy, wave–particle duality, the uncertainty principle, and the correspondence principle.
– DERIVATIVES **quantum-mechanical** adjective.

quantum meruit /ˌkwɒntəm ˈmɛrʊɪt/ ▸ **noun** [mass noun] [usu. as modifier] Law a reasonable sum of money to be paid for services rendered or work done when the amount due is not stipulated in a legally enforceable contract.
– ORIGIN Latin, literally 'as much as he has deserved'.

quantum number ▸ **noun** Physics a number which occurs in the theoretical expression for the value of some quantized property of a subatomic particle, atom, or molecule and can only have certain integral or half-integral values.

quantum state ▸ **noun** Physics a state of a quantized system which is described by a set of quantum numbers.

quantum theory ▸ **noun** [mass noun] Physics a theory of matter and energy based on the concept of quanta, especially quantum mechanics.

Quapaw /ˈkwɔːpɔː/ ▸ **noun** (pl. **same** or **Quapaws**) **1** a member of an American Indian people of the Arkansas River region, now living mainly in NE Oklahoma.
2 [mass noun] the extinct Siouan language of the Quapaw.
▸ **adjective** relating to the Quapaw or their language.
– ORIGIN from Quapaw *okáxpa*, originally the name of a village.

quarantine /ˈkwɒrəntiːn/ ▸ **noun** [mass noun] a state, period, or place of isolation in which people or animals that have arrived from elsewhere or been exposed to infectious or contagious disease are placed: *many animals die **in quarantine***.
▸ **verb** [with obj.] put (a person or animal) in quarantine.
– ORIGIN mid 17th cent.: from Italian *quarantina* 'forty days', from *quaranta* 'forty'.

quark[1] /kwɑːk, kwɔːk/ ▸ **noun** Physics any of a number of subatomic particles carrying a fractional electric charge, postulated as building blocks of the hadrons. Quarks have not been directly observed but theoretical predictions based on their existence have been confirmed experimentally.
– ORIGIN 1960s: a word invented by Murray GELL-MANN. Originally *quork*, the term was changed by association with the line 'Three quarks for Muster Mark' in Joyce's *Finnegans Wake* (1939).

quark[2] /kwɑːk/ ▸ **noun** [mass noun] a type of low-fat curd cheese.
– ORIGIN 1930s: from German *Quark* 'curd, curds'.

quarrel[1] ▸ **noun** an angry argument or disagreement: *he made the mistake of **picking a quarrel** with John*. ■ [usu. with negative] a reason for disagreement with a person, group, or principle: *we **have no quarrel with** the people of the country, only with the dictator*.
▸ **verb** (**quarrels**, **quarrelling**, **quarrelled**; US **quarrels**, **quarreling**, **quarreled**) [no obj.] have an angry argument or disagreement: *stop **quarrelling with** your sister*. ■ (**quarrel with**) take exception to or disagree with (something): *some people quarrel with this approach*. ■ W. Indian complain or scold someone: *he will quarrel like hell if he see black pods on the trees*.
– DERIVATIVES **quarreller** noun.
– ORIGIN Middle English (in the sense 'reason for disagreement with a person'): from Old French *querele*, from Latin *querel(l)a* 'complaint', from *queri* 'complain'.

quarrel[2] ▸ **noun** historical a short, heavy square-headed arrow or bolt used in a crossbow or arbalest.
– ORIGIN Middle English: from Old French, based on late Latin *quadrus* 'square'. Compare with QUARRY[3].

quarrelsome ▸ **adjective** given to or characterized by quarrelling: *a moody, quarrelsome man*.
– DERIVATIVES **quarrelsomeness** noun.

quarrion /ˈkwɒrɪən/ (also **quarrien**) ▸ **noun** Austral. another term for COCKATIEL.
– ORIGIN early 20th cent.: from Wiradhuri *guwarraying*.

quarry[1] ▸ **noun** (pl. **quarries**) a place, typically a large, deep pit, from which stone or other materials are or have been extracted.
▸ **verb** (**quarries**, **quarrying**, **quarried**) [with obj.] extract (stone or other materials) from a quarry. ■ cut into (rock or ground) to obtain stone or other materials.
– DERIVATIVES **quarrier** noun.
– ORIGIN Middle English: from a variant of medieval Latin *quareria*, from Old French *quarriere*, based on Latin *quadrum* 'a square'. The verb dates from the late 18th cent.

quarry[2] ▸ **noun** (pl. **quarries**) an animal pursued by a hunter, hound, predatory mammal, or bird of prey. ■ a thing or person that is chased or sought: *the security police crossed the border in pursuit of their quarry*.
– ORIGIN Middle English: from Old French *cuiree*, alteration, influenced by *cuir* 'leather' and *curer* 'clean, disembowel', of *couree*, based on Latin *cor* 'heart'. Originally the term denoted the parts of a deer that were placed on the hide and given as a reward to the hounds.

quarry[3] ▸ **noun** (pl. **quarries**) **1** a diamond-shaped pane of glass as used in lattice windows.
2 (also **quarry tile**) an unglazed floor tile.
– ORIGIN mid 16th cent. (in sense 2): alteration of QUARREL[2], which in late Middle English denoted a lattice windowpane.

quarryman ▸ **noun** (pl. **quarrymen**) a worker in a quarry.

quart ▸ **noun 1** a unit of liquid capacity equal to a quarter of a gallon or two pints, equivalent in Britain to approximately 1.13 litres and in the US to approximately 0.94 litre. ■ N. Amer. a unit of dry capacity equivalent to approximately 1.10 litres.
2 /kɑːt/ (also **quarte** or **carte**) Fencing the fourth of eight parrying positions.
3 (in piquet) a sequence of four cards of the same suit.
– PHRASES **you can't get a quart into a pint pot** Brit. proverb you cannot achieve the impossible.
– ORIGIN Middle English: from Old French *quarte*, from Latin *quarta* (*pars*) 'fourth (part)', from *quartus* 'fourth', from *quattuor* 'four'.

quartan /ˈkwɔːt(ə)n/ ▸ **adjective** Medicine denoting a mild form of malaria causing a fever that recurs every third day: *quartan fever*. ● Quartan malaria (or quartan ague) is caused by infection with *Plasmodium malariae*. Compare with TERTIAN.
– ORIGIN late Middle English: from Latin (*febris*) *quartana*, based on Latin *quartus* 'fourth' (because, by inclusive reckoning, the fever recurs every fourth day).

quarter ▸ **noun 1** each of four equal or corresponding parts into which something is or can be divided: *she cut each apple into quarters* | *a page and a quarter* | *a quarter of a mile*. ■ a period of three months regarded as one fourth of a year, used especially in reference to financial transactions such as the payment of bills or a company's earnings: *the first quarter of the fiscal year*. ■ a period of fifteen minutes or a point of time marking the transition from one fifteen-minute period to the next: *he sat with his pint until a quarter past nine*. ■ a coin representing 25 cents, a quarter of a US or Canadian dollar. ■ each of the four parts into which an animal's or bird's carcass may be divided, each including a leg or wing. ■ one fourth of a lunar month. ■ (in basketball, American football, and Australian Rules) each of four equal periods into which a game is divided. ■ chiefly US one of four terms into which a school or university year may be divided.
2 one fourth of a pound weight (avoirdupois, equal to 4 ounces). ■ one fourth of a hundredweight (Brit.

28 lb or US 25 lb). ■ Brit. a grain measure equivalent to 8 bushels.
3 (**quarters**) the haunches or hindquarters of a horse.
4 a part of a town or city having a particular character or use: *a beautiful port city with a fascinating medieval quarter.*
5 the direction of one of the points of the compass, especially as a direction from which the wind blows. ■ a particular but unspecified person, group of people, or area: *we have just had help from an unexpected quarter.* ■ either side of a ship aft of the beam: *he trained his glasses over the starboard quarter.*
6 (**quarters**) rooms or lodgings, especially those allocated to servicemen or to staff in domestic service: *they lived in RAF married quarters.*
7 [mass noun] pity or mercy shown towards an enemy or opponent who is in one's power: *the riot squad gave no quarter.*
8 Heraldry each of four or more roughly equal divisions of a shield separated by vertical and horizontal lines. ■ a square charge which covers the top left (dexter chief) quarter of the field.
▶ **verb** [with obj.] **1** divide into four equal or corresponding parts: *peel and quarter the bananas.* ■ historical cut (the body of an executed person) into four parts: *the plotters were hanged, drawn, and quartered.* ■ cut (a log) into quarters, and these into planks so as to show the grain well.
2 (**be quartered**) [with adverbial of place] be stationed or lodged in a specified place: *many were quartered in tents.* ■ (**quarter someone on**) impose someone on (another person) as a lodger: *you would have had her quartered on you forever.*
3 range over or traverse (an area) in every direction: *we watched a pair of kingfishers quartering the river looking for minnows.* ■ [no obj., with adverbial of direction] move at an angle; go in a diagonal or zigzag direction: *his young dog quartered back and forth in quick turns.*
4 Heraldry display (different coats of arms) in quarters of a shield, especially to show arms inherited from heiresses who have married into the bearer's family: *Edward III* ***quartered*** *the French royal arms* ***with*** *his own.* ■ divide (a shield) into four or more parts by vertical and horizontal lines.
– ORIGIN Middle English: from Old French *quartier*, from Latin *quartarius* 'fourth part of a measure', from *quartus* 'fourth', from *quattuor* 'four'.

quarterage ▶ **noun** archaic a sum paid or received quarterly.

quarterback ▶ **noun** American Football a player stationed behind the centre who directs a team's offensive play. ■ N. Amer. a person who directs or coordinates an operation or project.
▶ **verb** [with obj.] American Football play as a quarterback for (a particular team). ■ N. Amer. direct or coordinate (an operation or project).

quarter binding ▶ **noun** [mass noun] a type of bookbinding in which the spine is bound in one material (usually leather) and the rest of the cover in another.
– DERIVATIVES **quarter-bound** adjective.

quarter day ▶ **noun** Brit. each of four days fixed by custom as marking off the quarters of the year, on which some tenancies begin and end and quarterly payments of rent and other charges fall due.

quarterdeck ▶ **noun** the part of a ship's upper deck near the stern, traditionally reserved for officers. ■ the officers of a ship or the navy.

quarter-final ▶ **noun** a match or round of a knockout competition that precedes the semi-final.
– DERIVATIVES **quarter-finalist** noun.

Quarter Horse ▶ **noun** a horse of a small stocky breed noted for agility and speed over short distances. It is reputed to be the fastest breed of horse over distances of a quarter of a mile.

quarter-hour (also **quarter of an hour**) ▶ **noun** a period of fifteen minutes. ■ a point of time fifteen minutes before or after any hour.

quartering ▶ **noun 1** (**quarterings**) Heraldry the coats of arms marshalled on a shield to denote the marriages into a family of the heiresses of others.
2 [mass noun] the provision of accommodation or lodgings, especially for troops.
3 [mass noun] the action of dividing something into four parts.

quarter-light ▶ **noun** Brit. a window in the side of a motor vehicle other than the main door window.

quarterly ▶ **adjective 1** done, produced, or occurring once every quarter of a year: *a quarterly newsletter is distributed to members.*
2 Heraldry (of a shield or charge) divided into four (or occasionally more) subdivisions by vertical and horizontal lines.
▶ **adverb 1** once every quarter of a year: *interest is paid quarterly.*
2 Heraldry in the four, or in two diagonally opposite, quarters of a shield. [on the pattern of Old French *quartile*.]
▶ **noun** (pl. **quarterlies**) a magazine or journal that is published four times a year.

quartermaster ▶ **noun 1** a regimental officer, usually commissioned from the ranks, responsible for administering barracks, laying out the camp, and looking after supplies.
2 a naval petty officer with particular responsibility for steering and signals.

Quartermaster General ▶ **noun** the head of the army department in charge of the quartering and equipment of troops.

quartermaster sergeant ▶ **noun** a senior rank of non-commissioned officer in the army, above sergeant, employed on administrative duties.

quartern /'kwɔːt(ə)n/ ▶ **noun** archaic a quarter of a pint.
– ORIGIN Middle English (in the general sense 'a quarter'): from Old French *quart(e)ron*, from *quart(e)* (see QUART).

quartern loaf ▶ **noun** archaic a loaf of bread weighing four pounds.

quarter note ▶ **noun** Music, chiefly N. Amer. a crotchet.

quarter pipe ▶ **noun** a ramp with a slightly convex surface, used by skateboarders, rollerbladers, or snowboarders to perform jumps and other manoeuvres.

quarter plate ▶ **noun** Brit. a photographic plate measuring $3^1/_4 \times 4^1/_4$ inches (*c.*8.3×10.8 cm). ■ a photograph reproduced from a quarter plate.

quarter-pounder ▶ **noun** a hamburger that weighs a quarter of a pound.

quarter-saw ▶ **verb** [with obj.] (usu. as adj. **quarter-sawn**) saw (a log) radially into quarters and then into boards. ■ produce (a board or a piece of furniture) using this technique.

quarter section ▶ **noun** N. Amer. a quarter of a square mile of land; 160 acres (approximately 64.7 hectares).

quarter sessions ▶ **plural noun** historical (in England, Wales, and Northern Ireland) a court of limited criminal and civil jurisdiction and of appeal, usually held quarterly in counties or boroughs, and replaced in 1972 by crown courts.

quarterstaff ▶ **noun** historical a stout pole 6–8 feet long, formerly used as a weapon.

quarter-tone ▶ **noun** Music half a semitone.

quartet (also **quartette**) ▶ **noun** a group of four people playing music or singing together. ■ a composition for a quartet. ■ a set of four people or things.
– ORIGIN early 17th cent. (in the general sense 'set of four'): from French *quartette*, from Italian *quartetto*, from *quarto* 'fourth', from Latin *quartus*.

quartic /'kwɔːtɪk/ Mathematics ▶ **adjective** involving the fourth and no higher power of an unknown quantity or variable.
▶ **noun** a quartic equation, function, curve, or surface.
– ORIGIN mid 19th cent.: from Latin *quartus* 'fourth' + -IC.

quartier /'kɑːtɪeɪ/, French /kartje/ ▶ **noun** (pl. pronunc. same) a district of a French city.
– ORIGIN French.

quartile /'kwɔːtʌɪl/ ▶ **noun** Statistics each of four equal groups into which a population can be divided according to the distribution of values of a particular variable. ■ each of the three values of the random variable which divide a population into quartiles.
– ORIGIN late 19th cent.: from medieval Latin *quartilis*, from Latin *quartus* 'fourth'.

quarto /'kwɔːtəʊ/ (abbrev.: **4to**) ▶ **noun** (pl. **quartos**) [mass noun] Printing a size of book page resulting from folding each printed sheet into four leaves (eight pages). ■ [count noun] a book of quarto size. ■ a size of writing paper, 10 in. × 8 in. (254 × 203 mm).
– ORIGIN late 16th cent.: from Latin *(in) quarto* ('in) the fourth (of a sheet'), ablative of *quartus* 'fourth'.

quartz ▶ **noun** [mass noun] a hard mineral consisting of silica, found widely in igneous and metamorphic rocks and typically occurring as colourless or white hexagonal prisms. It is often coloured by impurities (as in amethyst, citrine, and cairngorm).
– ORIGIN mid 18th cent.: from German *Quarz*, from Polish dialect *kwardy*, corresponding to Czech *tvrdý* 'hard'.

quartz clock ▶ **noun** an electric clock in which the current is regulated and accuracy maintained by the regular vibrations of a quartz crystal.

quartz-halogen ▶ **adjective** (of a high-intensity electric lamp) using a quartz bulb containing the vapour of a halogen, usually iodine.

quartzite ▶ **noun** [mass noun] Geology an extremely compact, hard, granular rock consisting essentially of quartz. It often occurs as silicified sandstone, as in sarsen stones.

quartz lamp ▶ **noun** an electric lamp in which the envelope is made of quartz, which allows ultraviolet light to pass through it. It may be a bulb containing a halogen or a tube containing mercury vapour.

quartz watch ▶ **noun** a watch operated by vibrations of an electrically driven quartz crystal.

quasar /'kweɪzɑː, -sɑː/ ▶ **noun** Astronomy a massive and extremely remote celestial object, emitting exceptionally large amounts of energy, which typically has a starlike image in a telescope. It has been suggested that quasars contain massive black holes and may represent a stage in the evolution of some galaxies.
– ORIGIN 1960s: contraction of *quasi-stellar*.

quash ▶ **verb** [with obj.] reject as invalid, especially by legal procedure: *his conviction was quashed on appeal.* ■ put an end to; suppress: *a hospital executive quashed rumours that nursing staff will lose jobs.*
– ORIGIN Middle English: from Old French *quasser* 'annul', from late Latin *cassare* (medieval Latin also *quassare*), from *cassus* 'null, void'. Compare with SQUASH[1].

quasi- /'kweɪzʌɪ, -sʌɪ, 'kwɑːzi/ ▶ **combining form** apparently but not really; seemingly: *quasi-American | quasi-scientific.* ■ being partly or almost: *quasi-crystalline.*
– ORIGIN from Latin *quasi* 'as if, almost'.

quasi-contract ▶ **noun** an obligation of one party to another imposed by law independently of an agreement between the parties.
– DERIVATIVES **quasi-contractual** adjective.

quasicrystal ▶ **noun** Physics a locally regular aggregation of molecules resembling a crystal in certain properties (such as that of diffraction) but not having a consistent spatial periodicity.
– DERIVATIVES **quasicrystalline** adjective.

Quasimodo /ˌkwɒzɪ'məʊdəʊ/ the name of the hunchback in Victor Hugo's novel *Notre-Dame de Paris* (1831).

quasiparticle ▶ **noun** Physics a quantum of energy in a crystal lattice or other system of bodies which has momentum and position and can in some respects be regarded as a particle.

quassia /'kwɒʃə, 'kwɒʃɪə, 'kwasɪə/ ▶ **noun** a South American shrub or small tree related to ailanthus.
● Genera *Quassia* and *Picrasma*, family Simaroubaceae: several species, in particular *Q. amara*.
■ [mass noun] the wood, bark, or root of the quassia, yielding a bitter medicinal tonic, insecticide, and vermifuge.
– ORIGIN named after Graman *Quassi*, an 18th-cent. Surinamese slave who discovered its medicinal properties in 1730.

Q

quatercentenary /ˌkwatəsɛn'tiːn(ə)ri, -'tɛn-, ˌkweɪtə-/ ▶ **noun** (pl. **quatercentenaries**) the four-hundredth anniversary of a significant event.
▶ **adjective** relating to a four-hundredth anniversary.
– ORIGIN late 19th cent.: from Latin *quater* 'four times' + CENTENARY.

quaternary /kwə'təːn(ə)ri/ ▶ **adjective 1** fourth in order or rank; belonging to the fourth order.
2 (**Quaternary**) Geology relating to or denoting the most recent period in the Cenozoic era, following the Tertiary period and comprising the Pleistocene and Holocene epochs.
3 Chemistry denoting an ammonium compound containing a cation of the form NR_4^+, where R represents organic groups or atoms other than hydrogen. ■ (of a carbon atom) bonded to four other carbon atoms.
▶ **noun** (**the Quaternary**) Geology the Quaternary period or the system of deposits laid down during it.

> The Quaternary began about 1,640,000 years ago and is still current. Humans and other mammals evolved into their present forms, and were strongly affected by the ice ages of the Pleistocene.

– ORIGIN late Middle English (as a noun denoting a set of four): from Latin *quaternarius*, from *quaterni* 'four at once', from *quater* 'four times', from *quattuor* 'four'.

quaternion /kwəˈtəːnɪən/ ▸ noun **1** Mathematics a complex number of the form *w* + *xi* + *yj* + *zk*, where *w*, *x*, *y*, *z* are real numbers and *i*, *j*, *k* are imaginary units that satisfy certain conditions.
2 rare a set of four people or things.
– ORIGIN mid 19th cent.: from late Latin *quaternio(n-)*, from Latin *quaterni* (see QUATERNARY).

quatorze /kəˈtɔːz/ ▸ noun (in piquet) a set of four aces, kings, queens, jacks, or tens held in one hand.
– ORIGIN early 18th cent.: French, literally 'fourteen', from Latin *quattuordecim*.

quatrain /ˈkwɒtreɪn/ ▸ noun a stanza of four lines, especially one having alternate rhymes.
– ORIGIN late 16th cent.: from French, from *quatre* 'four'.

quatrefoil /ˈkatrəfɔɪl/ ▸ noun an ornamental design of four lobes or leaves as used in architectural tracery, resembling a flower or clover leaf.
– ORIGIN late 15th cent.: from Anglo-Norman French, from Old French *quatre* 'four' + *foil* 'leaf'.

quattrocento /ˌkwatrə(ʊ)ˈtʃɛntəʊ/ ▸ noun (**the quattrocentro**) the 15th century as a period of Italian art or architecture.
– ORIGIN Italian, literally '400' (shortened from *milquattrocento* '1400'), used with reference to the years 1400–99.

quaver ▸ verb [no obj.] (of a person's voice) shake or tremble in speaking, typically through nervousness or emotion.
▸ noun **1** a shake or tremble in a person's voice.
2 Music, chiefly Brit. a note having the time value of an eighth of a semibreve or half a crotchet, represented by a large dot with a hooked stem. Also called EIGHTH NOTE.
– DERIVATIVES **quaveringly** adverb, **quavery** adjective.
– ORIGIN late Middle English (as a verb in the general sense 'tremble'): from dialect *quave* 'quake, tremble', probably from an Old English word related to QUAKE. The noun is first recorded (mid 16th cent.) as a musical term.

quay ▸ noun a stone or metal platform lying alongside or projecting into water for loading and unloading ships.
– DERIVATIVES **quayage** noun.
– ORIGIN late Middle English *key*, from Old French *kay*, of Celtic origin. The change of spelling in the late 17th cent. was influenced by the modern French spelling *quai*.

quayside ▸ noun a quay and the area around it.

qubit ▸ noun Computing another term for QUANTUM BIT.
– ORIGIN 1990s: from *quantum bit*, with punning allusion to *cubit*.

Que. ▸ abbreviation Quebec.

quean /kwiːn/ ▸ noun archaic an impudent or badly behaved girl or woman. ■ a prostitute.
– ORIGIN Old English *cwene* 'woman', of Germanic origin; related to Dutch *kween* 'barren cow', from an Indo-European root shared by Greek *gunē*.

Q

queasy ▸ adjective (**queasier**, **queasiest**) nauseous; feeling sick: *in the morning he was still pale and queasy*. ■ inducing a feeling of nausea: *the queasy swell of the boat*. ■ slightly nervous or worried about something.
– DERIVATIVES **queasily** adverb, **queasiness** noun.
– ORIGIN late Middle English *queisy*, *coisy* 'causing nausea', of uncertain origin; perhaps related to Old French *coisier* 'to hurt'.

Quebec /kwɪˈbɛk/ **1** a heavily forested province in eastern Canada; pop. 7,546,131 (2006). It was settled by the French in 1608, ceded to the British in 1763, and became one of the original four provinces in the Dominion of Canada in 1867. The majority of its residents are French-speaking and it is a focal point of the French-Canadian nationalist movement, which advocates independence for Quebec. French name **Québec** /kebɛk/. ■ (also **Quebec City**) the capital city of Quebec, a port on the St Lawrence River; pop. 491,142 (2006). Founded in 1608, it is Canada's oldest city. It was captured from the French by a British force in 1759 after the battle of the Plains of Abraham, and became capital of Lower Canada (later Quebec) in 1791.
2 a code word representing the letter Q, used in radio communication.
– DERIVATIVES **Quebecker** (also **Quebecer**) noun.

quebracho /kɪˈbrɑːtʃəʊ/ ▸ noun (pl. **quebrachos**) a South American tree whose timber and bark are a rich source of tannin. ● Genera *Aspidosperma* (family Apocynaceae) and *Schinopsis* (family Anacardiaceae).
– ORIGIN late 19th cent.: from Spanish, from *quebrar* 'to break' + *hacha* 'axe'.

Quechua /ˈkɛtʃwə/ (also **Quecha** /ˈkɛtʃə/, **Quichua**) ▸ noun (pl. **same** or **Quechuas**) **1** a member of an American Indian people of Peru and parts of Bolivia, Chile, Colombia, and Ecuador.
2 [mass noun] the language or group of languages of the Quechua, spoken by some 11 million people.
▸ adjective relating to the Quechua or their language.
– DERIVATIVES **Quechuan** (also **Quechan**) adjective & noun.
– ORIGIN Spanish, from Quechua *ghechwa* 'temperate valleys'.

queen ▸ noun **1** the female ruler of an independent state, especially one who inherits the position by right of birth. ■ (also **Queen Consort**) a king's wife. ■ a woman or thing regarded as the finest or most outstanding in a particular sphere or group: *the queen of the social columns*. ■ a woman or girl chosen to hold the most important position in a festival or event: *she's the official carnival queen*. ■ (**the Queen**) dated (in the UK) the national anthem when there is a female sovereign. ■ informal a man's wife or girlfriend.
2 the most powerful chess piece that each player has, able to move in any direction along a rank, file, or diagonal on which it stands.
3 a playing card bearing a representation of a queen, normally ranking next below a king and above a jack.
4 Entomology a reproductive female in a colony of social ants, bees, wasps, or termites, frequently the only one present in a colony.
5 an adult female cat that has not been spayed.
6 informal a male homosexual, typically one regarded as ostentatiously effeminate.
▸ verb [with obj.] **1** (**queen it over**) (of a woman) behave in an unpleasantly superior way towards (someone).
2 Chess convert (a pawn) into a queen when it reaches the opponent's back rank on the board.
– DERIVATIVES **queendom** noun, **queenless** adjective, **queen-like** adjective, **queenship** noun.
– ORIGIN Old English *cwēn*, of Germanic origin; related to QUEAN.

Queen Anne ▸ adjective denoting a style of English furniture or architecture characteristic of the early 18th century. The furniture is noted for its simple, proportioned style and for its cabriole legs and walnut veneer; the architecture is characterized by the use of red brick in simple, basically rectangular designs.

Queen Anne's Bounty ▸ noun [mass noun] historical duties called 'first fruits and tenths', payable originally to the Pope but made payable to the Crown by Henry VIII, and directed by Queen Anne in 1704 to be used to augment the livings of the poorer clergy.

Queen Anne's lace ▸ noun another term for COW PARSLEY.

queen bee ▸ noun the single reproductive female in a hive or colony of honeybees. ■ informal a woman who has a dominant or controlling position in a particular group or sphere.

queen cake ▸ noun a small, soft, typically heart-shaped currant cake.

Queen Charlotte Islands a group of more than 150 islands off the west coast of Canada, in British Columbia.

Queen City ▸ noun N. Amer. the pre-eminent city of a region.

Queen Consort ▸ noun see QUEEN (sense 1 of the noun).

Queen Dowager ▸ noun the widow of a king.

queenfish ▸ noun (pl. **same** or **queenfishes**) an edible marine fish, in particular: ● a popular sporting fish of the Indo-Pacific (*Chorinemus lysan*, family Carangidae). ● a drumfish of the Pacific coast of North America (*Seriphus politus*, family Sciaenidae).

queenie ▸ noun old-fashioned term for QUEEN (sense 6 of the noun).

Queen in Council ▸ noun (in the UK) the Privy Council as issuing Orders in Council or receiving petitions when the reigning monarch is a queen.

queenly ▸ adjective (**queenlier**, **queenliest**) resembling, fit for, or appropriate to a queen.
– DERIVATIVES **queenliness** noun.

Queen Maud Land /mɔːd/ a part of Antarctica bordering the Atlantic Ocean, claimed since 1939 by Norway.
– ORIGIN named after *Queen Maud* of Norway (1869–1938).

Queen Mother ▸ noun the widow of a king and mother of the sovereign.

queen of puddings ▸ noun a pudding made with bread, jam, and meringue.

Queen of the May ▸ noun another term for MAY QUEEN.

queen post ▸ noun either of two upright timbers between the tie beam and principal rafters of a roof truss.

Queens a borough of New York City, at the western end of Long Island; pop. 2,225,200 (2006).

Queen's Award ▸ noun (in the UK) any of a number of annual awards given to firms for achievements in exporting goods or services or in advancing technology.

Queen's Bench (in full **Queen's Bench Division**) ▸ noun (in the UK) a division of the High Court of Justice.

Queensberry Rules /ˈkwiːnzb(ə)ri/ ▸ plural noun the standard rules of boxing, originally drawn up in 1867 to govern the sport in Britain. ■ standard rules of polite or acceptable behaviour.
– ORIGIN late 19th cent.: named after John Sholto Douglas (1844–1900), 9th Marquess of *Queensberry*, who supervised the preparation of the rules.

queen's bishop ▸ noun Chess each player's bishop on the queen's side of the board at the start of a game.

Queen's bounty ▸ noun in the reign of a queen, the term for KING'S BOUNTY.

queen scallop ▸ noun a small edible European scallop. ● *Chlamys opercularis*, family Pectinidae.

Queen's Champion ▸ noun another term for CHAMPION OF ENGLAND.

Queen's colour ▸ noun (in the UK) a silk union flag carried by a particular regiment along with its regimental colour.

Queen's Counsel (abbrev.: **QC**) ▸ noun a senior barrister appointed on the recommendation of the Lord Chancellor.

Queen's County former name for LAOIS.

Queen's English ▸ noun [mass noun] (**the Queen's English**) the English language as written and spoken correctly by educated people in Britain.

Queen's evidence ▸ noun [mass noun] English Law evidence for the prosecution given by a participant in or accomplice to the crime being tried: *what happens if they turn Queen's evidence?*

Queen's Guide ▸ noun (in the UK) a Guide who has reached the highest rank of proficiency.

Queen's highway ▸ noun [mass noun] Brit. formal the public road network, regarded as being under royal protection.

queenside ▸ noun Chess the half of the board on which both queens stand at the start of a game (the left-hand side for White, right for Black).

queen-sized (also **queen-size**) ▸ adjective (especially of a commercial product) of a larger size than the standard but smaller than something that is king-sized: *queen-sized fitted sheets*.

queen's knight ▸ noun Chess each player's knight on the queen's side of the board at the start of a game.

Queensland a state comprising the NE part of Australia; pop. 4,293,915 (2008); capital, Brisbane. Originally established in 1824 as a penal settlement, Queensland was constituted a separate colony in 1859, having previously formed part of New South Wales, and was federated with the other states of Australia in 1901.
– DERIVATIVES **Queenslander** noun.

Queensland blue ▸ noun Austral. **1** (also **Queensland blue heeler**) a cattle dog with a dark speckled body.
2 a pumpkin of a slaty-grey variety.

Queen's Messenger ▸ noun (in the UK) a courier in the diplomatic service, employed by the government to carry important official papers within Britain and abroad.

queen's pawn ▸ noun Chess the pawn occupying the square immediately in front of each player's queen at the start of a game.

Queen's Proctor ▸ noun Law (in the UK) an official who has the right to intervene in probate, divorce, and nullity cases when collusion or the suppression of facts is alleged.

queen's rook ▸ noun Chess each player's rook on the queen's side of the board at the start of a game.

Queen's Scout ▸ noun (in the UK) a Scout who has reached the highest standard of proficiency.

Queen's Speech ▸ noun (in the UK) a statement read by the sovereign at the opening of a new session of parliament, detailing the government's proposed legislative programme.

queensware ▸ noun [mass noun] a type of fine, cream-coloured Wedgwood pottery.
– ORIGIN mid 18th cent. (as *Queen's ware*): named in honour of Queen Charlotte (wife of George III), who had been presented with a set in 1765.

queeny ▸ adjective (**queenier**, **queeniest**) informal (of a homosexual man) flamboyantly effeminate.

queer ▸ adjective **1** strange; odd: *she had a queer feeling that they were being watched.* ■ [predic.] Brit. informal, dated slightly ill.
2 informal, derogatory (of a man) homosexual.
▸ noun informal, derogatory a homosexual man.
▸ verb [with obj.] informal spoil or ruin (an agreement, event, or situation): *Reg didn't want someone meddling and queering the deal at the last minute.*
– PHRASES **in Queer Street** Brit. informal, dated in difficulty, typically by being in debt. **queer fish** Brit. informal a person whose behaviour seems strange or unusual. **queer someone's pitch** Brit. spoil someone's plans or chances of doing something, especially secretly or maliciously.
– DERIVATIVES **queerish** adjective, **queerly** adverb, **queerness** noun.
– ORIGIN early 16th cent.: considered to be from German *quer* 'oblique, perverse', but the origin is doubtful.

> **USAGE** The word **queer** was first used to mean 'homosexual' in the early 20th century: it was originally, and usually still is, a deliberately offensive and aggressive term when used by heterosexual people. In recent years, however, gay people have taken the word **queer** and deliberately used it in place of **gay** or **homosexual**, in an attempt, by using the word positively, to deprive it of its negative power. This use of **queer** is now well established and widely used among gay people (especially as an adjective or noun modifier, as in *queer rights*; *queer-bashing*) and at present exists alongside the other use.

quelea /ˈkwiːlɪə/ ▸ noun a brownish weaver bird found in Africa, the male of which has either a black face or a red head. Also called DIOCH. ● Genus *Quelea*, family Ploceidae: three species, in particular the **red-billed quelea** (*Q. quelea*), which occurs in huge numbers and is an important pest of crops.
– ORIGIN modern Latin, perhaps from medieval Latin *qualea* 'quail'.

quell ▸ verb [with obj.] put an end to (a rebellion or other disorder), typically by the use of force: *extra police were called to quell the disturbance.* ■ subdue or silence (someone): *Connor quelled him with a look.* ■ suppress (a feeling): *she quelled an urge to race up the stairs.*
– DERIVATIVES **queller** noun.
– ORIGIN Old English *cwellan* 'kill', of Germanic origin; related to Dutch *kwellen* and German *quälen*.

quench ▸ verb [with obj.] **1** satisfy (one's thirst) by drinking. ■ satisfy (a desire): *he only pursued her to quench an aching need.*
2 extinguish (a fire): *firemen hauled on hoses in a desperate bid to quench the flames.* ■ stifle or suppress (a feeling): *fury rose in him, but he quenched it.* ■ dated reduce (someone) to silence: *she quenched Anne by a curt command to hold her tongue.*
3 rapidly cool (red-hot metal or other material), especially in cold water or oil. ■ Physics & Electronics suppress or damp (an effect such as luminescence, or an oscillation or discharge).
▸ noun an act of quenching a very hot substance.
– DERIVATIVES **quenchable** adjective, **quencher** noun (chiefly Physics & Metallurgy), **quenchless** adjective (literary).
– ORIGIN Old English *-cwencan* (in *acwencan* 'put out, extinguish'), of Germanic origin.

quenelle /kəˈnɛl/ ▸ noun (usu. **quenelles**) a small seasoned ball of pounded fish or meat.
– ORIGIN French, probably from Alsatian German *Knödel*.

quercetin /ˈkwəːsɪtɪn/ ▸ noun [mass noun] Chemistry a yellow crystalline pigment present in plants, used as a food supplement to reduce allergic responses or boost immunity. ● A flavone derivative; chem. formula: $C_{15}H_{10}O_7$.
– ORIGIN mid 19th cent.: probably from Latin *quercetum* 'oak grove' (from *quercus* 'oak') + -IN[1].

Quercia, Jacopo della, see DELLA QUERCIA.

querencia /kɛˈrɛnθɪə/, Spanish /keˈrenθja, -sja/ ▸ noun the part of a bullring where the bull takes its stand.
– ORIGIN Spanish, literally 'lair, home ground', from *querer* 'desire, love', from Latin *quaerere* 'seek'.

Querétaro /kɛˈrɛtərəʊ/ a state of central Mexico.
■ the capital city of Querétaro; pop. 596,450 (2005). In 1847 it was the scene of the signing of the treaty ending the US–Mexican war.

querist /ˈkwɪərɪst/ ▸ noun chiefly archaic a person who asks questions; a questioner.
– ORIGIN mid 17th cent.: from Latin *quaerere* 'ask' + -IST.

quern /kwəːn/ ▸ noun a simple hand mill for grinding corn, typically consisting of two circular stones, the upper of which is rotated or rubbed to and fro on the lower one.
– ORIGIN Old English *cweorn(e)*, of Germanic origin; related to Old Norse *kvern* and Dutch *kweern*.

quernstone ▸ noun chiefly Archaeology either of the two circular stones forming a quern, found at prehistoric sites from the Neolithic onwards.

querulous /ˈkwɛrʊləs, ˈkwɛrjʊləs/ ▸ adjective complaining in a rather petulant or whining manner: *she became querulous and demanding.*
– DERIVATIVES **querulously** adverb, **querulousness** noun.
– ORIGIN late 15th cent.: from late Latin *querulosus*, from Latin *querulus*, from *queri* 'complain'.

query ▸ noun (pl. **queries**) a question, especially one expressing doubt or requesting information: *if you have any queries please telephone our office.* ■ chiefly Printing a question mark.
▸ verb (**queries**, **querying**, **queried**) [reporting verb] ask a question about something, especially in order to express one's doubts about it or to check its validity or accuracy: [with clause] *many people queried whether any harm had been done* | [with obj.] *I rang the water company to query my bill* | [with direct speech] *'Why not?' he queried.* ■ [with obj.] chiefly N. Amer. put a question or questions to (someone): *when these officers were queried, they felt unhappy.*
– ORIGIN mid 17th cent.: anglicized form of the Latin imperative *quaere!*, used in the 16th cent. in English as a verb in the sense 'inquire' and as a noun meaning 'query', from Latin *quaerere* 'ask, seek'.

query language ▸ noun [mass noun] Computing a language for the specification of procedures for the retrieval (and sometimes also modification) of information from a database.

quesadilla /ˌkeɪsəˈdiːljə, -ˈdiːjə/ ▸ noun a tortilla filled with cheese and heated.
– ORIGIN Spanish.

que sera sera /ˈkeɪ sərɑː sərɑː/ ▸ exclamation used to convey a fatalistic recognition that future events are out of the speaker's control.
– ORIGIN Spanish *qué será será* 'what will be, will be', popularized by the 1956 song 'Que Sera, Sera'.

quest ▸ noun a long or arduous search for something: *the quest for a reliable vaccine has intensified.* ■ (in medieval romance) an expedition made by a knight to accomplish a prescribed task.
▸ verb [no obj.] search for something: *he was a real scientist, questing after truth.* ■ [with obj.] literary search for; seek out.
– DERIVATIVES **quester** (also **questor**) noun, **questingly** adverb.
– ORIGIN late Middle English: from Old French *queste* (noun), *quester* (verb), based on Latin *quaerere* 'ask, seek'. See also INQUEST.

question ▸ noun **1** a sentence worded or expressed so as to elicit information: *we hope this leaflet has been helpful in answering your questions.* ■ a doubt about the truth or validity of something: *there's no question that the company's true financial situation is different.* ■ [mass noun] the raising of a doubt about or objection to something: *Edward was the only one she obeyed **without question** | her loyalty is really **beyond question**.*
2 a matter requiring resolution or discussion: *the question of local government funding worried ministers.* ■ a matter or concern depending on or involving a specified condition or thing: *it was not simply a **question of** age and hierarchy.*
▸ verb [with obj.] ask (someone) questions, especially in an official context: *four men were being questioned about the killings* | (as noun **questioning**) *the young lieutenant escorted us to the barracks for questioning.* ■ feel or express doubt about; raise objections to: *members had questioned the cost of the scheme.*
– PHRASES **be a question of time** be certain to happen sooner or later: *it is only a question of time before somebody is killed.* **bring something into question** raise an issue for further consideration or discussion: *technology had brought into question the whole future of work.* **come into question** become an issue for further consideration or discussion: *our Sunday Trading laws have come into question.* **in question 1** being considered or discussed: *on the day in question, there were several serious emergencies.* **2** in doubt: *all of the old certainties are in question.* **no question of** no possibility of. **out of the question** too impracticable or unlikely to merit discussion. **put the question** (in a formal debate or meeting) require supporters and opponents of a proposal to record their votes.
– DERIVATIVES **questioner** noun, **questioningly** adverb.
– ORIGIN late Middle English: from Old French *question* (noun), *questionner* (verb), from Latin *quaestio(n-)*, from *quaerere* 'ask, seek'.

questionable ▸ adjective doubtful as regards truth or validity: [with clause] *it is **questionable whether** any of these exceptions is genuine.* ■ likely to be dishonourable or morally suspect: *his questionable financial deals.*
– DERIVATIVES **questionability** noun, **questionableness** noun, **questionably** adverb.

questionary ▸ noun (pl. **questionaries**) chiefly Medicine a questionnaire.
– ORIGIN late 19th cent.: from French *questionnaire* (see QUESTIONNAIRE).

question mark ▸ noun a punctuation mark (?) indicating a question. ■ used to express doubt or uncertainty about something: *there's **a question mark over** his future.*

question master ▸ noun Brit. a person who presides over a quiz or panel game.

questionnaire /ˌkwɛstʃəˈnɛː, ˌkɛstjə-/ ▸ noun a set of printed or written questions with a choice of answers, devised for the purposes of a survey or statistical study.
– ORIGIN late 19th cent.: from French, from *questionner* 'to question'.

question time ▸ noun (in the UK) a period during parliamentary proceedings in the House of Commons when MPs may question ministers.

Quetta /ˈkwɛtə/ a city in western Pakistan, the capital of Baluchistan province; pop. 860,000 (est. 2009).

quetzal /ˈkɛts(ə)l, ˈkwɛt-/ ▸ noun **1** a bird of the trogon family, with iridescent green plumage and typically red underparts, found in the forests of tropical America. ● Genus *Pharomachrus*, family Trogonidae: five species, especially the **resplendent quetzal** (*P. mocinno*), the male of which has very long tail coverts and was venerated by the Aztecs.
2 the basic monetary unit of Guatemala, equal to 100 centavos.
– ORIGIN early 19th cent. (in sense 1): from Spanish, from Aztec *quetzalli* 'brightly coloured tail feather'.

Q

Quetzalcóatl /ˌkɛts(ə)lkəʊˈat(ə)l/ the plumed serpent god of the Toltec and Aztec civilizations.

quetzalcoatlus /ˌkwɛts(ə)lkəʊˈatləs/ ▸ noun a giant pterosaur of the late Cretaceous period, which was the largest ever flying animal with a wingspan of up to 15 m. ● Genus *Quetzalcoatlus*, family Azhdarchidae, order Pterosauria.
– ORIGIN modern Latin, from the name of the Aztec god QUETZALCÓATL.

queue ▸ noun **1** chiefly Brit. a line or sequence of people or vehicles awaiting their turn to be attended to or to proceed.
2 Computing a list of data items, commands, etc., stored so as to be retrievable in a definite order, usually the order of insertion.
3 archaic a plait of hair worn at the back.
▸ verb (**queues**, **queuing** or **queueing**, **queued**)
1 [no obj.] chiefly Brit. take one's place in a queue: *in the war they had **queued for** food.* ■ (**queue up**) be extremely keen to do or have something: *companies are queuing up to move to the bay.*
2 [with obj.] Computing arrange in a queue.
– ORIGIN late 16th cent. (as a heraldic term denoting the tail of an animal): from French, based on Latin *cauda* 'tail'. Compare with CUE[2]. Sense 1 of the noun dates from the mid 19th cent.

queue-jump ▸ verb [no obj.] Brit. push into a queue in order to be served or dealt with before one's turn. ■ take unfair precedence over others: (as noun **queue-jumping**) *the initiative has facilitated queue-jumping, with private patients transferred to NHS hospitals.*
– DERIVATIVES **queue-jumper** noun.

Quezon City /ˈkeɪzɒn/ a city on the island of Luzon in the northern Philippines; pop. 2,679,500 (est. 2007). It was established in 1940 and from 1948 to 1976 it was the capital of the Philippines.
– ORIGIN named after Manuel Luis *Quezon* (1878–1944), the first President of the republic.

Qufu /tʃuːˈfuː/ a small town in Shandong province in eastern China, where Confucius was born in 551 BC and lived for much of his life.

quibble ▶ noun **1** a slight objection or criticism: *the only quibble about this book is the price.*
2 archaic a play on words; a pun.
▶ verb [no obj.] argue or raise objections about a trivial matter: *they are always quibbling about the amount they are prepared to pay.*
– DERIVATIVES **quibbler** noun, **quibblingly** adverb.
– ORIGIN early 17th cent. (in the sense 'play on words, pun'): diminutive of obsolete *quib* 'a petty objection', probably from Latin *quibus*, dative and ablative plural of *qui, quae, quod* 'who, what, which', frequently used in legal documents and so associated with subtle distinctions or verbal niceties.

quiche /kiːʃ/ ▶ noun a baked flan or tart with a savoury filling thickened with eggs, usually eaten cold.
– ORIGIN French, from Alsatian dialect *Küchen*; related to German *Kuchen* 'cake'.

Quiché /kiːˈtʃeɪ/ ▶ noun (pl. **same** or **Quichés**) **1** a member of a people inhabiting the western highlands of Guatemala.
2 [mass noun] the Mayan language of the Quiché, with around 800,000 speakers.
▶ adjective relating to the Quiché or their language.
– ORIGIN the name in Quiché.

Quichua /ˈkɪtʃwə/ ▶ noun & adjective variant spelling of **Quechua**.

quick ▶ adjective **1** moving fast or doing something in a short time: *in the qualifying session he was two seconds quicker than his teammate* | [with infinitive] *he was always quick to point out her faults.* ■ lasting or taking a short time: *Brian gave her a quick look* | *we went to the pub for a quick drink.* ■ happening with little or no delay; prompt: *children like to see quick results from their efforts.*
2 prompt to understand, think, or learn; intelligent: *it was quick of him to spot the mistake.* ■ (of a person's eye or ear) keenly perceptive; alert. ■ (of a person's temper) easily roused.
▶ adverb informal at a fast rate; quickly: *he'll find some place where he can make money quicker* | [as exclamation] *Get out, quick!*
▶ noun **1** (**the quick**) the soft tender flesh below the growing part of a fingernail or toenail. ■ the central or most sensitive part of someone or something.
2 (as plural noun **the quick**) archaic those who are living: *the quick and the dead.*
3 Cricket, informal a fast bowler.
– PHRASES **be quick off the mark** see **mark**¹. **cut someone to the quick** cause someone deep distress by a hurtful remark or action. **(as) quick as a flash** see **flash**¹. **quick and dirty** informal, chiefly US makeshift; done or produced hastily: *a quick and dirty synopsis of their work.* **quick on the draw** see **draw**. **a quick one** informal a rapidly consumed alcoholic drink. **quick with child** archaic at a stage of pregnancy when movements of the fetus have been felt.
– DERIVATIVES **quickness** noun.
– ORIGIN Old English *cwic, cwicu* 'alive, animated, alert', of Germanic origin; related to Dutch *kwiek* 'sprightly' and German *keck* 'saucy', from an Indo-European root shared by Latin *vivus* 'alive' and Greek *bios, zōē* 'life'.

Q

quickbeam ▶ noun another term for **mountain ash** (sense 1).
– ORIGIN Old English, apparently from **quick** (although the sense of the adjective is unclear) + **beam**.

quicken ▶ verb **1** make or become faster or quicker: [with obj.] *she quickened her pace, desperate to escape* | [no obj.] *I felt my pulse quicken.*
2 stimulate or become stimulated: [no obj.] *her interest quickened* | (as adj. **quickening**) *he looked with quickening curiosity through the smoke.* ■ [with obj.] give or restore life to: *on the third day after his death the human body of Jesus was quickened by the Spirit.* ■ [with obj.] archaic make (a fire) burn brighter.
3 [no obj.] archaic (of a woman) reach a stage in pregnancy when movements of the fetus can be felt. ■ (of a fetus) begin to show signs of life.

quick-fire ▶ adjective **1** unhesitating and rapid; in quick succession: *quick-fire repartee.*
2 (of a gun) able to fire shots in rapid succession.

quick-freeze ▶ verb [with obj.] freeze (food) rapidly so as to preserve its nutritional value.

quickie informal ▶ noun **1** a rapidly consumed alcoholic drink.
2 a brief act of sexual intercourse.
3 Cricket a fast bowler.
▶ adjective done or made quickly: *a quickie divorce.*

quicklime ▶ noun see **lime**¹.

quickly ▶ adverb at a fast speed; rapidly: *Reg's illness progressed frighteningly quickly.* ■ with little or no delay; promptly: *we moved quickly to deal with our auditor's questions.*

quick march ▶ noun a brisk military march.
▶ exclamation a command to begin marching quickly.

quick-release ▶ adjective (of a device) designed for rapid release: *a quick-release button.*

quicksand ▶ noun [mass noun] (also **quicksands**) loose wet sand that yields easily to pressure and sucks in anything resting on or falling into it. ■ a bad or dangerous situation from which it is hard to escape: *John found himself sinking fast in financial quicksand.*

quickset ▶ noun [mass noun] Brit. hedging, especially of hawthorn, grown from slips or cuttings.

quicksilver ▶ noun [mass noun] the liquid metal mercury. ■ [as modifier] moving or changing rapidly and unpredictably: *his quicksilver wit.*

quickstep ▶ noun **1** a dance similar to a fast foxtrot. ■ a piece of music written for a quickstep.
2 a step used when marching in quick time.
▶ verb (**quicksteps**, **quickstepping**, **quickstepped**) [no obj.] dance the quickstep.

quick-tempered ▶ adjective easily made angry.

quickthorn ▶ noun another term for **hawthorn**.

quick time ▶ noun [mass noun] Military marching that is conducted at about 120 paces per minute.

quick trick ▶ noun (usu. **quick tricks**) Bridge a card such as an ace (or a king in a suit where the ace is also held) that can normally be relied on to win a trick.

quick-witted ▶ adjective showing or characterized by an ability to think or respond quickly and effectively.
– DERIVATIVES **quick-wittedness** noun.

Quicunque vult /kwiːˈkʊŋkweɪ ˌvʊlt/ ▶ noun another term for **Athanasian Creed**.
– ORIGIN from Latin *quicunque vult (salvus esse)* 'whosoever wishes (to be saved)', the opening words of the creed.

quid¹ ▶ noun (pl. **same**) Brit. informal one pound sterling: *we paid him four hundred quid.*
– PHRASES **not the full quid** Austral./NZ informal not very intelligent. **quids in** Brit. informal in a position where one has profited or is likely to profit from something.
– ORIGIN late 17th cent. (denoting a sovereign): of obscure origin.

quid² ▶ noun a lump of tobacco for chewing.
– ORIGIN early 18th cent.: variant of **cud**.

quiddity /ˈkwɪdɪti/ ▶ noun (pl. **quiddities**) **1** [mass noun] chiefly Philosophy the inherent nature or essence of someone or something.
2 a distinctive feature; a peculiarity: *his quirks and quiddities.*
– ORIGIN late Middle English: from medieval Latin *quidditas*, from Latin *quid* 'what'.

quidnunc /ˈkwɪdnʌŋk/ ▶ noun archaic an inquisitive and gossipy person.
– ORIGIN early 18th cent.: from Latin *quid nunc?* 'what now?'

quid pro quo /ˌkwɪd prəʊ ˈkwəʊ/ ▶ noun (pl. **quid pro quos**) a favour or advantage granted in return for something: *the pardon was a quid pro quo for their help in releasing hostages.*
– ORIGIN mid 16th cent. (denoting a medicine substituted for another): Latin, 'something for something'.

quiescent /kwɪˈɛs(ə)nt, kwʌɪ-/ ▶ adjective in a state or period of inactivity or dormancy: *strikes were headed by groups of workers who had previously been quiescent.*
– DERIVATIVES **quiescence** noun, **quiescently** adverb.
– ORIGIN mid 17th cent.: from Latin *quiescent-* 'being still', from the verb *quiescere*, from *quies* 'quiet'.

quiet ▶ adjective (**quieter**, **quietest**) **1** making little or no noise: *the car has a quiet, economical engine* | *I was as quiet as I could be, but he knew I was there.* ■ (of a place, period of time, or situation) without much activity, disturbance, or excitement: *the street below was quiet, little traffic braving the snow.* ■ without being disturbed or interrupted: *all he wanted was a quiet drink.*
2 carried out discreetly, secretly, or with moderation: *we wanted a quiet wedding* | *I'll have a quiet word with him.* ■ (of a person) mild and reserved by nature: *his quiet, middle-aged parents.* ■ expressed in a restrained or understated way: *Molly spoke with quiet confidence.* ■ (of a colour or garment) unobtrusive; not bright or showy.
▶ noun [mass noun] absence of noise or bustle; silence; calm: *the ringing of the telephone shattered the early morning quiet.* ■ freedom from disturbance or interruption by others: *he understood her wish for peace and quiet.* ■ a peaceful or settled state of affairs in social or political life: *after several months of comparative quiet, the scandal re-erupted in August.*
▶ verb chiefly N. Amer. make or become silent, calm, or still: [with obj.] *there are ways of **quieting kids down*** | [no obj.] *the journalists **quieted down** as Judy stepped on to the dais.*
– PHRASES **do anything for a quiet life** see **life**. **keep quiet** (or **keep someone quiet**) refrain or prevent someone from speaking or from disclosing something secret. **keep something quiet** (or **keep quiet about something**) refrain from disclosing information about something; keep something secret. **on the quiet** informal without anyone knowing or noticing; secretly or unobtrusively. **(as) quiet as the grave** see **grave**¹. **(as) quiet as a mouse** (or **lamb**) (of a person or animal) extremely quiet or docile.
– DERIVATIVES **quietness** noun.
– ORIGIN Middle English (originally as a noun denoting peace as opposed to war): via Old French, based on Latin *quies, quiet-* 'repose, quiet'.

quieten ▶ verb chiefly Brit. make or become quiet and calm: [with obj.] *her mother was trying to quieten her* | *things seemed to have quietened down.*

quietism ▶ noun [mass noun] **1** (in the Christian faith) devotional contemplation and abandonment of the will as a form of religious mysticism.
2 calm acceptance of things as they are without attempts to resist or change them: *political quietism.*
– DERIVATIVES **quietist** noun & adjective, **quietistic** adjective.
– ORIGIN late 17th cent. (denoting the religious mysticism based on the teachings of the Spanish priest Miguel de Molinos (*c.*1640–97)): from Italian *quietismo*, based on Latin *quies, quiet-* 'quiet'.

quietly ▶ adverb in a quiet manner: *he worked quietly and diligently* | [as submodifier] *she was quietly confident that they'd win.*
– PHRASES **just quietly** Austral./NZ informal confidentially.

quietude ▶ noun [mass noun] a state of stillness, calmness, and quiet in a person or place.
– ORIGIN late 16th cent.: from French *quiétude* or medieval Latin *quietudo*, from Latin *quietus* 'quiet'.

quietus /kwʌɪˈiːtəs/ ▶ noun (pl. **quietuses**) literary death or something that causes death, regarded as a release from life. ■ archaic something that has a calming or soothing effect.
– ORIGIN late Middle English: abbreviation of medieval Latin *quietus est* 'he is quit' (see **quit**¹), originally used as a form of receipt or discharge on payment of a debt.

quiff ▶ noun chiefly Brit. a piece of hair brushed upwards and backwards from a man's forehead.
– ORIGIN late 19th cent. (originally denoting a lock of hair plastered down on the forehead, especially as worn by soldiers): of unknown origin.

quila /ˈkɪlʌ/ ▶ noun Indian a fort or fortress.
– ORIGIN from Urdu *qila*.

quill ▶ noun **1** (also **quill feather**) any of the main wing or tail feathers of a bird. ■ the hollow shaft of a feather, especially the lower part or calamus that lacks barbs. ■ (also **quill pen**) a pen made from a main wing or tail feather of a large bird by pointing and slitting the end of the shaft.
2 the hollow sharp spines of a porcupine, hedgehog, or other spiny mammal.
3 (**quills**) another term for **penne**.
4 (**quills**) US informal, dated pan pipes.
▶ verb [with obj.] form (fabric) into small cylindrical folds.
– ORIGIN late Middle English (in the senses 'hollow stem' and 'shaft of a feather'): probably from Middle Low German *quiele*.

quilling ▶ noun a piece of quilled lace or other fabric used as a trim. ■ [mass noun] N. Amer. a type of ornamental craftwork involving the shaping of paper, fabric, or glass into delicate pleats or folds.

quillwork ▶ noun [mass noun] a type of decoration for clothing and possessions characteristic of certain North American Indian peoples, using softened and dyed porcupine quills to make elaborate applied designs.

quillwort ▶ noun a plant related to the clubmosses, with a dense rosette of long slender leaves, the bases of which contain the spore-producing organs, occurring typically as a submerged aquatic. ● Genus *Isoetes*, family Isoetaceae, class Lycopsida.

quilt[1] ▶ noun a warm bed covering made of padding enclosed between layers of fabric and kept in place by lines of stitching, typically applied in a decorative design. ■ a knitted or fabric bedspread with decorative stitching. ■ a duvet. ■ a layer of padding used for insulation.
▶ verb [with obj.] (often as adj. **quilted**) join together (layers of fabric or padding) with lines of stitching to form a bed covering, a warm garment, or for decorative effect.
– DERIVATIVES **quilter** noun.
– ORIGIN Middle English: from Old French *cuilte*, from Latin *culcita* 'mattress, cushion'.

quilt[2] ▶ verb [with obj.] Austral. informal, dated punch (someone).
– ORIGIN mid 19th cent.: perhaps a transferred use of the verb QUILT[1] (with the association of quilting for protection).

quilting ▶ noun [mass noun] the making of quilts as a craft or leisure activity. ■ the work produced in quilting; quilted material. ■ the pattern of stitching used for quilting.

quim ▶ noun Brit. vulgar slang a woman's genitals.
– ORIGIN mid 18th cent.: of unknown origin.

quin ▶ noun Brit. informal short for QUINTUPLET.

quinacridone /kwɪˈnakrɪdəʊn/ ▶ noun Chemistry any of a group of synthetic organic compounds whose molecules contain three benzene and two pyridine rings arranged alternately. They include a number of red to violet pigments.
– ORIGIN early 20th cent.: from *quin(oline)* + *acrid(ine)* + -ONE.

quinacrine /ˈkwɪnəkriːn, -krɪn/ ▶ noun [mass noun] Medicine a synthetic compound derived from acridine, used as an anthelmintic and antimalarial drug. ■ (in full **quinacrine mustard**) Biochemistry a nitrogen mustard derived from quinacrine, used as a fluorescent stain for chromosomes.
– ORIGIN 1930s: blend of QUININE and ACRIDINE.

quinary /ˈkwʌɪnəri/ ▶ adjective relating to the number five, in particular: ■ of the fifth order or rank. ■ Zoology, historical relating to or denoting a former system of classification in which the animal kingdom is divided into five subkingdoms, and each subkingdom into five classes.
– ORIGIN early 17th cent.: from Latin *quinarius*, from *quini* 'five at once, a set of five', from *quinque* 'five'.

quinate /ˈkwʌɪneɪt/ ▶ noun Chemistry a salt or ester of quinic acid.

quince ▶ noun 1 a hard, acid pear-shaped fruit used in preserves or as flavouring.
2 the shrub or small tree which bears quinces, native to western Asia. ● *Cydonia oblonga*, family Rosaceae.
■ (**Japanese quince**) another term for JAPONICA.
– ORIGIN Middle English (originally a collective plural): from Old French *cooin*, from Latin *(malum) cotoneum*, variant of *(malum) cydonium* 'apple of Cydonia (= Chania, in Crete)'.

quincentenary /ˌkwɪnsɛnˈtiːn(ə)ri, -ˈtɛn-/ ▶ noun (pl. **quincentenaries**) the five-hundredth anniversary of a significant event.
▶ adjective relating to a five-hundredth anniversary.
– ORIGIN late 19th cent.: from Latin *quinque* 'five' + CENTENARY.

quincentennial ▶ noun & adjective another term for QUINCENTENARY.

Quincey, Thomas De, see **De Quincey**.

quincunx /ˈkwɪnkʌŋks/ ▶ noun (pl. **quincunxes**) 1 an arrangement of five objects with four at the corners of a square or rectangle and the fifth at its centre, used for the five on a dice or playing card, and in planting trees.
2 [mass noun] Astrology an aspect of 150°, equivalent to five zodiacal signs.
– DERIVATIVES **quincuncial** adjective, **quincuncially** adverb.
– ORIGIN mid 17th cent.: from Latin, literally 'five twelfths', from *quinque* 'five' + *uncia* 'twelfth'.

Quine /kwʌɪn/, Willard Van Orman (1908–2000), American philosopher and logician. A radical critic of modern empiricism, Quine took issue with the philosophy of language proposed by Rudolf Carnap, arguing that 'no statement is immune from revision' and that even the principles of logic themselves can be questioned and replaced.

quinella /kwɪˈnɛlə/ ▶ noun a bet in which the first two places in a race must be predicted, but not necessarily in the correct order. Compare with PERFECTA.
– ORIGIN 1940s (originally US): from Latin American Spanish *quiniela*.

quinic acid /ˈkwɪnɪk/ ▶ noun [mass noun] Chemistry an acid present in cinchona bark and other plant products, used in the synthesis of pharmaceuticals. ● A cyclic carboxylic acid; chem. formula $C_6H_7(OH)_4COOH$.
– ORIGIN early 19th cent.: from modern Latin *quinatus*, from Latin *quini* (see QUINARY).

quinidine /ˈkwɪnɪdiːn/ ▶ noun [mass noun] Medicine a compound obtained from cinchona bark and used to treat irregularities of heart rhythm. It is an isomer of quinine.
– ORIGIN mid 19th cent.: from Spanish *quina* 'cinchona bark' (from Quechua *kina* 'bark') + -IDE + -INE[4].

quinine /ˈkwɪniːn, kwɪˈniːn/ ▶ noun [mass noun] a bitter crystalline compound present in cinchona bark, used as a tonic and formerly as an antimalarial drug. ● An alkaloid; chem. formula: $C_{20}H_{24}N_2O_2$.
– ORIGIN early 19th cent.: from Spanish *quina* 'cinchona bark' (from Quechua *kina* 'bark') + -INE[4].

quinoa /ˈkiːnəʊə, kwɪˈnəʊə/ ▶ noun [mass noun] a plant of the goosefoot family found in the Andes, where it was widely cultivated for its edible starchy seeds prior to the introduction of Old World grains.
● *Chenopodium quinoa*, family Chenopodiaceae.
■ the grain-like seeds of the quinoa, used as food and in the production of alcoholic drinks.
– ORIGIN early 17th cent.: Spanish spelling of Quechua *kinua, kinoa*.

quinol /ˈkwɪnɒl/ ▶ noun another term for HYDROQUINONE.
– ORIGIN late 19th cent.: from Spanish *quina* (see QUININE) + -OL.

quinoline /ˈkwɪnəliːn/ ▶ noun [mass noun] Chemistry a pungent oily liquid present in coal tar. ● A heteroaromatic compound with fused benzene and pyridine rings; chem. formula: C_9H_7N.
– ORIGIN mid 19th cent.: from Spanish *quina* (see QUININE) + -OL + -INE[4].

quinolone /ˈkwɪnələʊn/ ▶ noun [mass noun] an antibiotic derived from quinoline and used chiefly against Gram-negative organisms.
– ORIGIN 1930s: from *quin-* (in QUINOLINE) + -ONE.

quinone /ˈkwɪnəʊn, kwɪˈnəʊn/ ▶ noun [mass noun] Chemistry another term for 1,4-benzoquinone (see BENZOQUINONE). ■ [count noun] any compound with the same ring structure as 1,4-benzoquinone.
– ORIGIN mid 19th cent.: from Spanish *quina* (see QUININE) + -ONE.

quinquagenarian /ˌkwɪŋkwədʒɪˈnɛːrɪən/ ▶ noun a person who is between 50 and 59 years old.
– ORIGIN early 19th cent.: from Latin *quinquagenarius* (based on *quinquaginti* 'fifty') + -AN.

Quinquagesima /ˌkwɪŋkwəˈdʒɛsɪmə/ (also **Quinquagesima Sunday**) ▶ noun the Sunday before the beginning of Lent.
– ORIGIN medieval Latin, feminine of Latin *quinquagesimus* 'fiftieth', on the pattern of *Quadragesima* (because it is fifty days before Easter).

quinque- ▶ combining form five; having five: *quinquevalent*.
– ORIGIN from Latin *quinque* 'five'.

quinquennial /kwɪŋˈkwɛnɪəl/ ▶ adjective recurring every five years. ■ lasting for or relating to a period of five years.
– DERIVATIVES **quinquennially** adverb.
– ORIGIN late 15th cent. (in the sense 'lasting five years'): from Latin *quinquennis* (from *quinque* 'five' + *annus* 'year') + -AL.

quinquennium /kwɪŋˈkwɛnɪəm/ ▶ noun (pl. **quinquennia** /-nɪə/ or **quinquenniums**) a specified period of five years.
– ORIGIN early 17th cent.: from Latin, from *quinque* 'five' + *annus* 'year'.

quinquereme /ˈkwɪŋkwɪˌriːm/ ▶ noun an ancient Roman or Greek galley of a kind believed to have had three banks of oars, the oars in the top two banks being rowed by pairs of oarsmen and the oars in the bottom bank being rowed by single oarsmen.
– ORIGIN mid 16th cent.: from Latin *quinqueremis*, from *quinque* 'five' + *remus* 'oar'.

quinquevalent /ˌkwɪnkwɪˈveɪl(ə)nt/ ▶ adjective Chemistry another term for PENTAVALENT.

quinsy /ˈkwɪnzi/ ▶ noun [mass noun] inflammation of the throat, especially an abscess in the region of the tonsils.
– ORIGIN Middle English: from Old French *quinencie*, from medieval Latin *quinancia*, from Greek *kunankhē* 'canine quinsy', from *kun-* 'dog' + *ankhein* 'throttle'.

quint /kɪnt, kwɪnt/ ▶ noun 1 (in piquet) a sequence of five cards of the same suit. A run of ace, king, queen, jack, and ten is a **quint major** and one of jack, ten, nine, eight, and seven a **quint minor**. [late 17th cent.: from French, from Latin *quintus* 'fifth', from *quinque* 'five'.]
2 N. Amer. short for QUINTUPLET.

quinta /ˈkwɪntə, ˈkɪntə/ ▶ noun (in Spain, Portugal, and Latin America) a large house in the country or on the outskirts of a town. ■ a country estate, in particular a wine-growing estate in Portugal.
– ORIGIN Spanish and Portuguese, from *quinta parte* 'fifth part' (originally referring to the amount of a farm's produce paid in rent).

quintain /ˈkwɪntɪn/ ▶ noun historical a post set up as a mark in tilting with a lance, typically with a sandbag attached that would swing round and strike an unsuccessful tilter. ■ (**the quintain**) the medieval military exercise of tilting at a quintain.
– ORIGIN late Middle English: from Old French *quintaine*, perhaps based on Latin *quintana*, a street in a Roman camp separating the fifth and sixth maniples, where military exercises were performed (from *quintus* 'fifth').

quintal /ˈkwɪnt(ə)l/ ▶ noun a unit of weight equal to a hundredweight (112 lb) or, formerly, 100 lb. ■ a unit of weight equal to 100 kg.
– ORIGIN late Middle English: via Old French from medieval Latin *quintale*, from Arabic *qinṭār*, based on Latin *centenarius* 'containing a hundred'.

Quintana Roo /kiːn,tɑːnə ˈrəʊ/ a state of SE Mexico, on the Yucatán Peninsula; capital, Chetumal.

quinte /kãt/ ▶ noun Fencing the fifth of eight parrying positions.
– ORIGIN early 18th cent.: French, from Latin *quintus* 'fifth', from *quinque* 'five'.

quintessence /kwɪnˈtɛs(ə)ns/ ▶ noun 1 the most perfect or typical example of a quality or class: *he was the quintessence of political professionalism*.
■ the aspect of something regarded as the intrinsic and central constituent of its character: *we were all brought up to believe that advertising is the quintessence of marketing*.
2 a refined essence or extract of a substance.
3 (in classical and medieval philosophy) a fifth substance in addition to the four elements, thought to compose the heavenly bodies and to be latent in all things.
– ORIGIN late Middle English (as a term in philosophy): via French from medieval Latin *quinta essentia* 'fifth essence'.

quintessential /ˌkwɪntɪˈsɛnʃ(ə)l/ ▶ adjective representing the most perfect or typical example of a quality or class: *he was the quintessential tough guy—strong, silent, and self-contained*.
– DERIVATIVES **quintessentially** adverb.

quintet ▶ noun a group of five people playing music or singing together. ■ a musical composition for a quintet. ■ any group of five people or things: *a novel about a quintet of interrelated lovers*.
– ORIGIN late 18th cent.: from French *quintette* or Italian *quintetto*, from *quinto* 'fifth', from Latin *quintus*.

quintile /ˈkwɪntɪl, -ʌɪl/ ▶ noun 1 Statistics any of five equal groups into which a population can be divided according to the distribution of values of a particular variable. ■ each of the four values of the random variable which divide a population into quintiles.
2 [mass noun] Astrology an aspect of 72° (one fifth of a circle).
– ORIGIN early 17th cent.: from Latin *quintilis (mensis)* 'fifth month, July', from *quintus* 'fifth'.

Quintilian /kwɪnˈtɪlɪən/ (c.35–c.96 AD), Roman rhetorician; Latin name *Marcus Fabius Quintilianus*. He is best known for his *Education of an Orator*, a comprehensive treatment of the art of rhetoric and the training of an orator.

quintillion /kwɪnˈtɪljən/ ▶ cardinal number (pl. **quintillions** or (with numeral) **same**) a thousand raised to the power of six (10^{18}). ■ dated, chiefly Brit. a million raised to the power of five (10^{30}).
– DERIVATIVES **quintillionth** ordinal number.

Q

– ORIGIN late 17th cent.: from French, from *million*, by substitution of the prefix *quinti-* 'five' (from Latin *quintus* 'fifth') for the initial letters.

quintuple /ˈkwɪntjʊp(ə)l, kwɪnˈtjuːp(ə)l/ ▶ **adjective** [attrib.] consisting of five parts or things. ■ five times as much or as many. ■ (of time in music) having five beats in a bar.
▶ **verb** increase or cause to increase fivefold.
▶ **noun** a fivefold number or amount; a set of five.
– DERIVATIVES **quintuply** adverb.
– ORIGIN late 16th cent.: via French from medieval Latin *quintuplus*, from Latin *quintus* 'fifth' + *-plus* as in *duplus* (see DUPLE).

quintuplet /ˈkwɪntjʊˌplɪt, kwɪnˈtjuːplɪt/ ▶ **noun** **1** (usu. **quintuplets**) each of five children born at one birth.
2 Music a group of five notes to be performed in the time of three or four.
– ORIGIN late 19th cent.: from QUINTUPLE, on the pattern of words such as *triplet*.

quintuplicate ▶ **adjective** fivefold. ■ of which five copies are made.
▶ **verb** [with obj.] multiply by five.
– PHRASES **in quintuplicate** in five identical copies. ■ in groups of five.
– ORIGIN mid 17th cent.: from QUINTUPLE, on the pattern of words such as *quadruplicate*.

quip ▶ **noun** a witty remark. ■ archaic a play on words.
▶ **verb** (**quips, quipping, quipped**) [no obj.] make a witty remark: [with direct speech] *'Flattery will get you nowhere,' she quipped.*
– DERIVATIVES **quipster** noun.
– ORIGIN mid 16th cent.: perhaps from Latin *quippe* 'indeed, forsooth'.

quipu /ˈkiːpuː, ˈkwɪ-/ ▶ **noun** an ancient Inca device for recording information, consisting of variously coloured threads knotted in different ways.
– ORIGIN from Quechua *khipu* 'knot'.

quire /kwʌɪə/ ▶ **noun** four sheets of paper or parchment folded to form eight leaves, as in medieval manuscripts. ■ any collection of leaves one within another in a manuscript or book. ■ 25 (formerly 24) sheets of paper; one twentieth of a ream.
– ORIGIN Middle English: from Old French *quaier*, from Latin *quaterni* 'set of four'.

quirk ▶ **noun** **1** a peculiar aspect of a person's character or behaviour: *they accepted her attitude as one of her little quirks.* ■ a strange chance occurrence: *a strange quirk of fate had led her to working for Nathan.* ■ a sudden twist, turn, or curve: *wry humour put a slight quirk in his mouth.*
2 Architecture an acute hollow between convex or other mouldings.
▶ **verb** (with reference to a person's mouth or eyebrow) move or twist suddenly, especially to express surprise or amusement: [no obj.] *his lips quirked disbelievingly.*
– DERIVATIVES **quirkish** adjective.
– ORIGIN early 16th cent. (as a verb): of unknown origin. The early sense of the noun was 'subtle verbal twist, quibble', later 'unexpected twist'.

Q

quirky ▶ **adjective** (**quirkier, quirkiest**) having or characterized by peculiar or unexpected traits or aspects: *her sense of humour was decidedly quirky.*
– DERIVATIVES **quirkily** adverb, **quirkiness** noun.

quirt /kwəːt/ ▶ **noun** a short-handled riding whip with a braided leather lash.
▶ **verb** [with obj.] hit with a quirt.
– ORIGIN mid 19th cent. (originally US): from Spanish *cuerda* 'cord' (from Latin *chorda* 'cord') or from Mexican Spanish *cuarta* 'whip'.

quisling /ˈkwɪzlɪŋ/ ▶ **noun** a traitor who collaborates with an enemy force occupying their country.
– ORIGIN Second World War: from the name of Major Vidkun *Quisling* (1887–1945), the Norwegian army officer and diplomat who ruled Norway on behalf of the German occupying forces (1940–45).

quit[1] ▶ **verb** (**quits, quitting**; past and past participle **quitted** or **quit**) **1** [with obj.] leave (a place), usually permanently: *hippies finally quit two sites in Hampshire last night.* ■ [no obj.] (of a tenant) leave rented accommodation: *the landlord issued a notice to quit.* ■ informal resign from (a job): *she quit her job in a pizza restaurant* | [no obj.] *he quit as manager of the struggling Third Division team.* ■ informal, chiefly N. Amer. stop or discontinue (an action or activity): *quit moaning!* | *I want to quit smoking.*
2 (**quit oneself**) [with adverbial] archaic behave in a specified way: *quit yourselves like men, and fight.*
▶ **adjective** (**quit of**) rid of: *I want to be quit of him.*
– PHRASES **quit hold of** archaic let go of.
– ORIGIN Middle English (in the sense 'set free'): from Old French *quiter* (verb), *quite* (adjective), from Latin *quietus*, past participle of *quiescere* 'be still', from *quies* 'quiet'.

quit[2] ▶ **noun** [in combination] used in names of various small songbirds found in the Caribbean area, e.g. **bananaquit, grassquit**.
– ORIGIN mid 19th cent.: probably imitative.

quitch (also **quitch grass**) ▶ **noun** another term for COUCH[2].
– ORIGIN Old English *cwice*, of uncertain origin; perhaps related to QUICK (with reference to its vigorous growth).

quitclaim ▶ **noun** Law, historical & US a formal renunciation or relinquishing of a claim.

quite ▶ **adverb** [usu. as submodifier] **1** to the utmost or most absolute extent or degree; absolutely; completely: *it's quite out of the question* | *are you quite certain about this?* | *this is quite a different problem* | *I quite agree* | *quite frankly, I don't blame you.* ■ US very; really (used as an intensifier): *'You've no intention of coming back?' 'I'm quite sorry, but no, I have not.'* ■ W. Indian all the way: *dresses quite from Port of Spain.*
2 to a certain or fairly significant extent or degree; fairly: *it's quite warm outside* | *he's quite an attractive man.*
▶ **exclamation** (also **quite so**) expressing agreement with or understanding of a remark or statement: *'I don't want to talk about that now.' 'Quite.'*
– PHRASES **not quite** not completely or entirely: *my hair's not quite dry* | *she hasn't quite got the hang of it yet.* **not quite the thing** dated not well, healthy, or normal: *I'm afraid Oliver isn't feeling quite the thing this morning.* ■ socially unacceptable: *it wouldn't be quite the thing to turn up in a raincoat and wellies.* **quite a ——** (also often ironic **quite the ——**) used to indicate that the specified person or thing is perceived as particularly notable, remarkable, or impressive: *quite a party, isn't it?* | *quite the little horsewoman, aren't you?* **quite a few** see FEW. **quite a lot** (or **a bit**) a considerable number or amount of something: *my job involves quite a lot of travel* | *he's quite a bit older than she is.* **quite some 1** a considerable amount of: *she hasn't been seen for quite some time.* **2** informal way of saying QUITE A ——. **quite something** see SOMETHING.
– ORIGIN Middle English: from the obsolete adjective *quite*, variant of QUIT[1].

Quito /ˈkiːtəʊ/ the capital of Ecuador; pop. 1,579,200 (est. 2008). It is situated in the Andes just south of the equator, at an altitude of 2,850 m (9,350 ft).

quit-rent ▶ **noun** historical a rent, typically a small one, paid by a freeholder or copyholder in lieu of services which might be required of them.

quits ▶ **adjective** [predic.] (of two people) on even terms, especially because a debt or score has been settled: *I think we're just about quits now, don't you?*
– PHRASES **call it quits** agree or acknowledge that terms are now equal, especially on the settlement of a debt: *take this cheque and we'll call it quits.* ■ decide to abandon an activity or venture: *surely, after covering eleven wars, he could be forgiven for calling it quits?*
– ORIGIN late 15th cent. (in the sense 'freed from a liability or debt'): perhaps a colloquial abbreviation of medieval Latin *quittus*, from Latin *quietus*, used as a receipt (see QUIETUS).

quittance ▶ **noun** archaic or literary a release or discharge from a debt or obligation. ■ a document certifying this; a receipt.
– ORIGIN Middle English: from Old French *quitance*, from *quiter* 'to release' (see QUIT[1]).

quitter ▶ **noun** [usu. with negative] informal a person who gives up easily or does not have the courage or determination to finish a task.

quiver[1] ▶ **verb** [no obj.] tremble or shake with a slight rapid motion: *the tree's branches stopped quivering* | *Juliet's lower lip quivered.* ■ [with obj.] cause (something) to make a slight rapid motion: *the bird runs along in a zigzag path, quivering its wings.*
▶ **noun** a slight trembling movement or sound, especially one caused by a sudden strong emotion: *she couldn't help the quiver in her voice.*
– DERIVATIVES **quiveringly** adverb, **quivery** adjective.
– ORIGIN Middle English: from Old English *cwifer* 'nimble, quick'. The initial *qu-* is probably symbolic of quick movement (as in *quaver* and *quick*).

quiver[2] ▶ **noun** an archer's portable case for holding arrows. ■ a set of surfboards of different lengths and shapes for use with different types of waves.
– PHRASES **an arrow in the quiver** one of a number of resources or strategies that can be drawn on or followed.
– ORIGIN Middle English: from Anglo-Norman French *quiveir*, of West Germanic origin; related to Dutch *koker* and German *Köcher*.

quiverful ▶ **noun** (pl. **quiverfuls**) the amount of arrows a quiver can hold. ■ Brit. humorous a large number of offspring. [with biblical allusion to Ps. 127:5.]
– ORIGIN mid 19th cent.: from QUIVER[2] + -FUL.

quiver tree ▶ **noun** a tropical aloe which forms a tree, the hollow branches of which were formerly used by the San (Bushmen) as quivers. ● *Aloe dichotoma*, family Liliaceae (or Aloeaceae).

qui vive /kiː ˈviːv/ ▶ **noun** (in phrase **on the qui vive**) on the alert or lookout: *duty requires the earnest liberal to spend most of his time on the qui vive for fascism.*
– ORIGIN late 16th cent.: from French, literally '(long) live who?', i.e. 'on whose side are you?', used as a sentry's challenge.

Quixote see DON QUIXOTE.

quixotic /kwɪkˈsɒtɪk/ ▶ **adjective** extremely idealistic; unrealistic and impractical: *a vast and perhaps quixotic project.*
– DERIVATIVES **quixotically** adverb, **quixotism** /ˈkwɪksətɪz(ə)m/ noun, **quixotry** /ˈkwɪksətri/ noun.
– ORIGIN late 18th cent.: from DON QUIXOTE + -IC.

quiz[1] ▶ **noun** (pl. **quizzes**) a test of knowledge, especially as a competition between individuals or teams as a form of entertainment. ■ informal, chiefly Brit. an act of questioning someone. ■ N. Amer. an informal written test or examination given to students.
▶ **verb** (**quizzes, quizzing, quizzed**) [with obj.] ask (someone) questions: *four men have been quizzed about the murder.* ■ N. Amer. give (a student or class) an informal written test or examination.
– ORIGIN mid 19th cent. (as a verb; originally US): possibly from QUIZ[2], influenced by INQUISITIVE.

quiz[2] archaic ▶ **verb** (**quizzes, quizzing, quizzed**) [with obj.] **1** look curiously or intently at (someone) through or as if through an eyeglass: *deep-set eyes quizzed her in the candlelight.*
2 make fun of: *is it possible he has heard of my foible and is quizzing me?*
▶ **noun** (pl. **quizzes**) **1** a practical joke or hoax. ■ a person who ridicules or hoaxes another.
2 an odd or eccentric person.
– DERIVATIVES **quizzer** noun.
– ORIGIN late 18th cent.: sometimes said to have been invented by a Dublin theatre proprietor who, having made a bet that a nonsense word could be made known within 48 hours throughout the city, and that the public would give it a meaning, had the word written up on walls all over the city. There is no evidence to support this theory.

quizmaster ▶ **noun** Brit. a person who asks the questions and enforces the rules in a television or radio quiz programme.

quiz show ▶ **noun** a broadcast entertainment programme in which people compete in a quiz, typically for prizes.

quizzical ▶ **adjective** (of a person's expression or behaviour) indicating mild or amused puzzlement: *she gave me a quizzical look.* ■ rare amusingly odd or strange.
– DERIVATIVES **quizzicality** noun, **quizzically** adverb, **quizzicalness** noun.

Qum variant spelling of QOM.

Qumran /kʊmˈrɑːn/ a region on the western shore of the Dead Sea. The Dead Sea scrolls were found (1947–56) in caves at nearby Khirbet Qumran, the site of an ancient Jewish settlement.

quod /kwɒd/ ▶ **noun** Brit. informal, dated prison: *ten years in quod.*
– ORIGIN late 17th cent.: of unknown origin.

quod erat demonstrandum /kwɒd ˌɛrat dɛmənˈstrandʊm/ (abbrev.: **QED**) ▶ **exclamation** used to convey that a fact or situation demonstrates the truth of one's theory or claim, especially to mark the conclusion of a formal proof.
– ORIGIN Latin, literally 'which was to be demonstrated'.

quodlibet /ˈkwɒdlɪbɛt/ ▶ **noun** **1** archaic a topic for or exercise in philosophical or theological discussion.
2 literary a light-hearted medley of well-known tunes.
– DERIVATIVES **quodlibetarian** /-bɪˈtɛːrɪən/ noun.
– ORIGIN late Middle English: from Latin, from *quod* 'what' + *libet* 'it pleases'.

quoin /kɔɪn, kwɔɪn/ ▶ **noun 1** an external angle of a wall or building. ■ (also **quoin stone**) any of the stones or bricks forming a quoin; a cornerstone.
2 Printing a wedge or expanding mechanical device used for locking a letterpress forme into a chase.
3 a wedge for raising the level of a gun barrel or for keeping it from rolling.
▶ **verb** [with obj.] **1** provide (a wall) with quoins or corners.
2 Printing lock up (a forme) with a quoin.
– ORIGIN Middle English: variant of COIN, used earlier in the sense 'cornerstone' and 'wedge'.

quoining ▶ **noun** [mass noun] the stone or brick used to form a quoin of a wall or building.

quoit /kɔɪt, kwɔɪt/ ▶ **noun 1** a ring of iron, rope, or rubber thrown in a game to encircle or land as near as possible to an upright peg. ■ (**quoits**) [treated as sing.] a game consisting of aiming and throwing quoits.
2 the flat covering stone of a dolmen. ■ [often in place names] the dolmen itself.
3 Austral. informal a person's buttocks.
▶ **verb** [with obj. and adverbial of direction] archaic throw or propel like a quoit.
– ORIGIN late Middle English: probably of French origin.

quokka /ˈkwɒkə/ ▶ **noun** a small short-tailed wallaby with a short face, round ears, and some tree-climbing ability, native to Western Australia. ● *Setonix brachyurus*, family Macropodidae.
– ORIGIN mid 19th cent.: from Nyungar *kwaka*.

quoll /kwɒl/ ▶ **noun** a catlike carnivorous marsupial with short legs and a white-spotted coat, native to the forests of Australia and New Guinea. Also called DASYURE, NATIVE CAT, TIGER CAT. ● Genus *Dasyurus*, family Dasyuridae: several species.
– ORIGIN late 18th cent.: from Guugu Yimidhirr (an Aboriginal language) *dhigul*.

quondam /ˈkwɒndəm, -dam/ ▶ **adjective** [attrib.] formal that once was; former: *quondam dissidents joined the establishment*.
– ORIGIN late 16th cent.: from Latin, 'formerly'.

Quonset /ˈkwɒnsɪt/ (also **Quonset hut**) ▶ **noun** N. Amer. trademark a building made of corrugated metal and having a semicircular cross section.
– ORIGIN Second World War: named after *Quonset* Point, Rhode Island, where such huts were first made.

quorate /ˈkwɔːrət, -reɪt/ ▶ **adjective** Brit. (of a meeting) attended by a quorum and so having valid proceedings.

Quorn /kwɔːn/ ▶ **noun** [mass noun] Brit. trademark a type of textured vegetable protein made from an edible fungus and used as a meat substitute.
– ORIGIN 1980s: the name of a former company in the Leicestershire village of Quorndon.

quorum /ˈkwɔːrəm/ ▶ **noun** (pl. **quorums**) the minimum number of members of an assembly or society that must be present at any of its meetings to make the proceedings of that meeting valid.
– ORIGIN late Middle English (referring to justices of the peace): used in commissions for committee members designated by the Latin *quorum vos ... unum (duos*, etc.) *esse volumus* 'of whom we wish that you ... be one (two, etc.)'.

quota ▶ **noun** a limited or fixed number or amount of people or things, in particular: ■ a limited quantity of a particular product which under official controls can be produced, exported, or imported: *the country may be exceeding its OPEC quota of 1,100,000 barrels of oil per day*. ■ a fixed share of something that a person or group is entitled to receive or is bound to contribute: *they were arrested to help fill the quota of arrests the security police had to make during the crackdown*. ■ a fixed minimum or maximum number of a particular group of people allowed to do something, e.g. immigrants to enter a country, workers to undertake a job, or students to enrol for a course: *the removal of entry quotas encouraged young people to enter universities*. ■ (in a system of proportional representation) the minimum number of votes required to elect a candidate. ■ (also **diocesan quota**) (in the Anglican Church) the proportion of the funds of a parish contributed to the finances of the diocese.
– ORIGIN early 17th cent.: from medieval Latin *quota* (*pars*) 'how great (a part)', feminine of *quotus*, from *quot* 'how many'.

quotable ▶ **adjective** suitable for or worth quoting: *a script peppered with quotable one-liners*.
– DERIVATIVES **quotability** noun.

quota sample ▶ **noun** Statistics a sample taken from a stratified population by sampling until a pre-assigned quota in each stratum is represented.
– DERIVATIVES **quota sampling** noun.

quotation ▶ **noun 1** a group of words taken from a text or speech and repeated by someone other than the original author or speaker: *a quotation from Mark Twain*. ■ a short musical passage or visual image taken from one piece of music or work of art and used in another. ■ [mass noun] the action of quoting from a text, speech, piece of music, or work of art: *a great argument with much quotation of Darwin*.
2 a formal statement setting out the estimated cost for a particular job or service: *ensure you receive a written quotation covering all aspects of the job*. ■ Stock Exchange a price offered by a market-maker for the sale or purchase of a stock or other security.
3 Stock Exchange a registration granted to a company enabling their shares to be officially listed and traded.
– ORIGIN mid 16th cent. (denoting a marginal reference to a passage of text): from medieval Latin *quotatio(n-)*, from the verb *quotare* (see QUOTE).

quotation mark ▶ **noun** each of a set of punctuation marks, single (' ') or double (" "), used either to mark the beginning and end of a title or quoted passage, or to indicate that a word or phrase is regarded as slang or jargon or is being discussed rather than used within the sentence.

quote ▶ **verb** [with obj.] **1** repeat or copy out (words from a text or speech written or spoken by another person): *I realized she was quoting passages from Shakespeare* | [no obj.] *he quoted from the scriptures*. ■ repeat a statement by (someone): *a military spokesman was* **quoted as saying** *that the border was now quiet*. ■ mention or refer to (someone or something) to provide evidence or authority for a statement or opinion: *the examples quoted above could be multiplied from case studies from all over England*. ■ (**quote someone/thing as**) put forward or describe someone or something as being: *heavy teaching loads are often quoted as a bad influence on research*.
2 give someone (the estimated price of a job or service): [with two objs] *a garage quoted him £30*. ■ (**quote someone/thing at/as**) name at (specified odds): *he is quoted as 9–2 favourite to score the first goal of the match*.
3 Stock Exchange give (a company) a quotation or listing on a stock exchange: *a British conglomerate* **quoted** *on the London Stock Exchange*.
▶ **noun 1** a quotation from a text or speech: *a quote from Wordsworth*.
2 a quotation giving the estimated cost for a particular job or service: *quotes from different insurance companies*. ■ Stock Exchange a price offered by a market-maker for the sale or purchase of a stock or other security.
3 Stock Exchange a quotation or listing of a company on a stock exchange.
4 (**quotes**) quotation marks: *use double quotes around precise phrases you wish to search for*.
– PHRASES **quote —— unquote** (also **quote, unquote**) informal used parenthetically when speaking to indicate the beginning and end of a statement or passage that one is repeating: *the second sentence says, quote, There has never been a better time to invest in the commodities market, unquote* | *the brochure describes the view as, quote, unquote, unforgettably breathtaking*.
– ORIGIN late Middle English: from medieval Latin *quotare*, from *quot* 'how many', or from medieval Latin *quota* (see QUOTA). The original sense was 'mark a book with numbers, or with marginal references', later 'give a reference by page or chapter', hence 'cite a text or person' (late 16th cent.).

quoth /kwəʊθ/ ▶ **verb** [with direct speech] archaic or humorous said (used only in first and third person singular before the subject): *'Ah,' quoth he, as soon as the bike started, 'a blown cylinder head gasket.'*
– ORIGIN Middle English: past tense of obsolete *quethe* 'say, declare', of Germanic origin.

quotidian /kwɒˈtɪdɪən, kwəʊ-/ ▶ **adjective 1** of or occurring every day; daily: *the car sped noisily off through the quotidian traffic*. ■ ordinary or everyday; mundane: *his story is an achingly human one, mired in quotidian details*.
2 Medicine denoting the malignant form of malaria.
– ORIGIN Middle English: via Old French from Latin *quotidianus*, earlier *cotidianus*, from *cotidie* 'daily'.

quotient /ˈkwəʊʃ(ə)nt/ ▶ **noun 1** Mathematics a result obtained by dividing one quantity by another.
2 a degree or amount of a specified quality or characteristic: *the increase in Washington's cynicism quotient*.
– ORIGIN late Middle English: from Latin *quotiens* 'how many times' (from *quot* 'how many'), by confusion with participial forms ending in *-ens*, *-ent-*.

quo warranto /ˌkwəʊ wəˈrantəʊ/ ▶ **noun** [usu. as modifier] Law, historical & US a writ or legal action requiring a person to show by what warrant an office or franchise is held, claimed, or exercised.
– ORIGIN Law Latin, literally 'by what warrant'.

Qur'an /kəˈrɑːn/ (also **Quran**) ▶ **noun** Arabic spelling of KORAN.

qursh /kʊəʃ/ ▶ **noun** (pl. **same**) a monetary unit of Saudi Arabia, equal to one twentieth of a rial.
– ORIGIN from Arabic *qirsh*, from Slavic *groš*, via Old High German *grosch* from medieval Latin (*denarius*) *grossus* 'thick (penny)'. Compare with GROSCHEN.

q.v. ▶ **abbreviation** used to direct a reader to another part of a book or article for further information.
– ORIGIN from Latin *quod vide*, literally 'which see'.

QwaQwa /ˈkwakwə/ a former homeland established in South Africa for the South Sotho people, situated in the Drakensberg Mountains in Free State province.

QWERTY /ˈkwəːti/ ▶ **adjective** denoting the standard layout on English-language typewriters and keyboards, having *q*, *w*, *e*, *r*, *t*, and *y* as the first keys from the left on the top row of letters.

Rr

R[1] (also **r**) ▸ **noun** (pl. **Rs** or **R's**) the eighteenth letter of the alphabet. ▪ denoting the next after Q in a set of items, categories, etc.
– PHRASES **the R months** the months with R in their names (September to April), considered to be the season for eating oysters. **the three Rs** reading, writing, and arithmetic, regarded as the fundamentals of learning.

R[2] ▸ **abbreviation** ▪ rand: *a farm worth nearly R1,3 million.* ▪ (in names of sports clubs) Rangers or Rovers. ▪ Réaumur (a temperature scale, now obsolete). ▪ Regina or Rex: *Elizabeth R.* ▪ (also ®) registered as a trademark. ▪ (in the US) Republican. ▪ N. Amer. (in film classification) restricted (denoting films restricted to viewers over a certain age). ▪ (on a gear shift) reverse. ▪ (**R.**) River (chiefly on maps). ▪ roentgen(s). ▪ Romania (international vehicle registration). ▪ rook (in recording moves in chess): *21.Rh4.* ▪ Cricket (on scorecards) run(s).
▸ **symbol** ▪ Chemistry an unspecified alkyl or other organic radical or group. [abbreviation of RADICAL.] ▪ electrical resistance. ▪ Chemistry the gas constant.

r ▸ **abbreviation** ▪ recto. ▪ (giving position or direction) right: *l to r: Evan, Nic, and David.* ▪ Law rule.
▸ **symbol** ▪ radius. ▪ Statistics correlation coefficient.

RA ▸ **abbreviation** ▪ Argentina (international vehicle registration). [from Spanish *República Argentina* 'Argentine Republic'.] ▪ Astronomy right ascension. ▪ (in the UK) Royal Academician. ▪ (in the UK) Royal Academy. ▪ (in the UK) Royal Artillery. ▪ (in the UK) Rugby Association (in the names of rugby clubs).

Ra[1] /rɑː/ (also **Re**) Egyptian Mythology the sun god, the supreme Egyptian deity, worshipped as the creator of all life and typically portrayed with a falcon's head bearing the solar disc. From earliest times he was associated with the pharaoh.

R

Ra[2] ▸ **symbol** the chemical element radium.

RAAF ▸ **abbreviation** Royal Australian Air Force.

Rabat /rəˈbat/ the capital of Morocco, an industrial port on the Atlantic Coast; pop. 1,787,300 (est. 2009). It was founded as a military fort in the 12th century by the Almohads.

Rabaul /rəˈbaʊl/ the chief town and port of the island of New Britain, Papua New Guinea; pop. 7,000 (est. 2009).

rabbet /ˈrabɪt/ ▸ **noun & verb** archaic or North American term for REBATE[2].
– ORIGIN late Middle English: from Old French *rabbat* 'abatement, recess'.

rabbi /ˈrabʌɪ/ ▸ **noun** (pl. **rabbis**) a Jewish scholar or teacher, especially one who studies or teaches Jewish law. ▪ a person appointed as a Jewish religious leader.
– DERIVATIVES **rabbinate** /ˈrabɪnət/ **noun**.
– ORIGIN late Old English, via ecclesiastical Latin and Greek from Hebrew *rabbī* 'my master', from *raḇ* 'master'.

rabbinic /rəˈbɪnɪk/ ▸ **adjective** relating to rabbis or to Jewish law or teachings.
– DERIVATIVES **rabbinical** adjective, **rabbinically** adverb.

rabbit ▸ **noun 1** a gregarious burrowing plant-eating mammal, with long ears, long hind legs, and a short tail. ● Family Leporidae: several genera and species, in particular the **European rabbit** (*Oryctolagus cuniculus*), which is often kept as a pet or raised for food.
▪ [mass noun] the flesh of the rabbit as food. ▪ [mass noun] the fur of the rabbit. ▪ North American term for HARE. ▪ informal a poor performer in a sport or game, in particular (in cricket) a poor batsman. ▪ US a runner who acts as pacesetter in the first laps of a race.
2 Brit. informal a conversation: *we had quite a heated rabbit about it.* [from *rabbit and pork*, rhyming slang for 'talk'.]
▸ **verb** (**rabbits**, **rabbiting**, **rabbited**) [no obj.] **1** (usu. as noun **rabbiting**) hunt rabbits: *locate the area where you can go* ***rabbiting***.
2 Brit. informal talk at length, especially about trivial matters: *stop* ***rabbiting on***, *will you, and go to bed!*
– PHRASES **breed like rabbits** informal reproduce prolifically. **pull** (or **bring**) **a rabbit out of the** (or **a**) **hat** do something unexpected but ingeniously effective in response to a problem: *everyone is waiting to see if the king can pull a rabbit out of the hat and announce a ceasefire.*
– DERIVATIVES **rabbity** adjective.
– ORIGIN late Middle English: apparently from Old French (compare with French dialect *rabotte* 'young rabbit'), perhaps of Dutch origin (compare with Flemish *robbe*).

rabbitbrush (also **rabbitbush**) ▸ **noun** a North American shrub of the daisy family, which bears clusters of small yellow flowers. ● *Chrysothamnus nauseosus*, family Compositae.

rabbit-eared bandicoot (also **rabbit bandicoot**) ▸ **noun** a burrowing Australian bandicoot with long ears, long limbs, and a long furry tail. Also called BILBY. ● Family Thylacomyidae and genus *Macrotis*: two species, one of which is possibly extinct.

rabbit fever ▸ **noun** informal term for TULARAEMIA.

rabbitfish ▸ **noun** (pl. **same** or **rabbitfishes**) **1** a ratfish found in the NE Atlantic and around South Africa. Also called RAT-TAIL. ● *Chimaera monstrosa*, family Chimaeridae.
2 a fish with a blunt snout and rabbit-like jaws, found in inshore waters of the tropical Indo-Pacific, especially around reefs. ● Family Siganidae: several genera and species, in particular *Siganus oramin*.

rabbit food ▸ **noun** [mass noun] humorous salad, seen as insubstantial or tasteless.

rabbit punch ▸ **noun** a sharp chop with the edge of the hand to the back of the neck.

rabbit's foot ▸ **noun** the foot of a rabbit carried as a good luck charm.

rabbit warren ▸ **noun** see WARREN.

rabble ▸ **noun** a disorderly crowd; a mob: *he was met by a rabble of noisy, angry youths.* ▪ (**the rabble**) ordinary people, especially when regarded as socially inferior or uncouth.
– ORIGIN late Middle English (in the senses 'string of meaningless words' and 'pack of animals'): perhaps related to dialect *rabble* 'to gabble'.

rabble-rouser ▸ **noun** a person who speaks with the intention of inflaming the emotions of a crowd of people, typically for political reasons.
– DERIVATIVES **rabble-rousing** adjective & noun.

Rabelais /ˈrabəleɪ, French ʀablɛ/, François (c.1494–1553), French satirist. His writings are noted for their earthy humour, their parody of medieval learning and literature, and their affirmation of humanist values. Notable works: *Pantagruel* (1532) and *Gargantua* (1534).

Rabelaisian /ˌrabəˈleɪzɪən/ ▸ **adjective** displaying earthy humour; bawdy: *the conversation was often highly Rabelaisian.*

rabi /ˈrʌbiː/ ▸ **noun** [mass noun] (in South Asia) the grain crop sown in September and reaped in the spring.
– ORIGIN Hindi *rabī'*.

rabid /ˈrabɪd, ˈreɪ-/ ▸ **adjective 1** having or proceeding from an extreme or fanatical support of or belief in something: *a rabid feminist.*
2 (of an animal) affected with rabies. ▪ of or connected with rabies.
– DERIVATIVES **rabidity** /rəˈbɪdɪti/ **noun**, **rabidly** adverb, **rabidness** noun.
– ORIGIN early 17th cent. (in the sense 'furious, madly violent'): from Latin *rabidus*, from *rabere* 'to rave'.

rabies /ˈreɪbiːz, -ɪz/ ▸ **noun** [mass noun] a contagious and fatal viral disease of dogs and other mammals, transmissible through the saliva to humans and causing madness and convulsions. Also called HYDROPHOBIA.
– ORIGIN late 16th cent.: from Latin, from *rabere* 'rave'.

Rabin /rəˈbiːn/, Yitzhak (1922–95), Israeli statesman and military leader, Prime Minister 1974–7 and 1992–5. In 1993 he negotiated a PLO–Israeli peace accord with Yasser Arafat, for which he shared the 1994 Nobel Peace Prize with Arafat and Shimon Peres. He was assassinated by a Jewish extremist.

RAC ▸ **abbreviation** ▪ (in the UK) Royal Armoured Corps. ▪ (in the UK) Royal Automobile Club.

raccoon /rəˈkuːn/ (also **racoon**) ▸ **noun** a greyish-brown American mammal which has a foxlike face with a black mask, a ringed tail, and the habit of washing its food in water. ● Genus *Procyon*, family Procyonidae (the **raccoon family**): two species, in particular the **common raccoon** (*P. lotor*), which often occurs in urban areas in North America. The raccoon family also includes the coati, kinkajou, cacomistle, and olingo.
▪ [mass noun] the fur of the raccoon.
– ORIGIN early 17th cent.: from Virginia Algonquian *aroughcun*.

raccoon dog ▸ **noun** a small wild dog with a black facial mask and long brindled fur, native to the forests of southern and eastern Asia. ● *Nyctereutes procyonoides*, family Canidae.

race[1] ▸ **noun 1** a competition between runners, horses, vehicles, etc. to see which is the fastest in covering a set course: *Hill started from pole position and won the race.* ▪ (**the races**) a series of such competitions for horses or dogs, held at a fixed time on a set course. ▪ [in sing.] a situation in which individuals or groups compete to be first to achieve a particular objective: ***the race for*** *nuclear power.* ▪ archaic the course of the sun or moon through the heavens.
2 a strong or rapid current flowing through a narrow channel in the sea or a river: *angling for tuna in turbulent tidal races.*
3 a groove, channel, or passage, in particular: ▪ a water channel, especially one built to lead water to or from a point where its energy is utilized, as in a mill or mine. ▪ a smooth ring-shaped groove or guide in which a ball bearing or roller bearing runs. ▪ a fenced passageway in a stockyard through which animals pass singly for branding, loading, washing, etc. ▪ (in weaving) the channel along which the shuttle moves.

▸ **verb 1** [no obj.] compete with another or others to see who is fastest at covering a set course or achieving an objective: *the vet took blood samples from the horses before they raced* | [with obj.] *two drivers **raced** each other through a housing estate.* ■ compete regularly in races as a sport or leisure activity: *next year, he raced again for the team.* ■ [with obj.] prepare and enter (an animal or vehicle) for races: *he raced his three horses simply for the fun of it.*
2 [no obj., with adverbial] move or progress swiftly or at full speed: *I raced into the house* | figurative *she spoke automatically, while her mind raced ahead.* ■ operate or cause to operate at excessive speed: [no obj.] *the truck came to rest against a tree with its engine racing.* ■ [no obj.] (of a person's heart or pulse) beat faster than usual because of fear or excitement.
– PHRASES **be at the races** (or Austral./NZ **in the race**) [usu. with negative] Brit. informal competing with a chance of success: *they were never quite at the races against Rangers.* **a race against time** a situation in which something must be done before a particular point in time: *it was a race against time to reach shore before the dinghy sank.*
– ORIGIN late Old English, from Old Norse *rás* 'current'. It was originally a northern English word with the sense 'rapid forward movement', which gave rise to the senses 'contest of speed' (early 16th cent.) and 'channel, path' (i.e. the space traversed). The verb dates from the late 15th cent.

race² ▸ **noun** each of the major divisions of humankind, having distinct physical characteristics: *people of all races, colours, and creeds.* ■ [mass noun] the fact or condition of belonging to a racial division or group; the qualities or characteristics associated with this. ■ a group of people sharing the same culture, history, language, etc.; an ethnic group: *we Scots were a bloodthirsty race then.* ■ a group or set of people or things with a common feature or features: *some male firefighters still regarded women as **a race apart**.* ■ Biology a population within a species that is distinct in some way, especially a subspecies: *people have killed so many tigers that two races are probably extinct.* ■ (in non-technical use) each of the major divisions of living creatures: *a member of the human race* | *the race of birds.* ■ literary a group of people descended from a common ancestor: *a prince of the race of Solomon.* ■ [mass noun] archaic ancestry: *two coursers of ethereal race.*

> Although ideas of race are centuries old, it was not until the 19th century that attempts to systematize racial divisions were made. Ideas of supposed racial superiority and social Darwinism reached their culmination in Nazi ideology of the 1930s and gave pseudoscientific justification to policies and attitudes of discrimination, exploitation, slavery, and extermination. Theories of race asserting a link between racial type and intelligence are now discredited. Scientifically it is accepted as obvious that there are subdivisions of the human species, but it is also clear that genetic variation between individuals of the same race can be as great as that between members of different races.

– ORIGIN early 16th cent. (denoting a group with common features): via French from Italian *razza*, of unknown ultimate origin.

> **USAGE** In recent years, the associations of **race** with the ideologies and theories that grew out of the work of 19th-century anthropologists and physiologists has led to the use of the word **race** itself becoming problematic. Although still used in general contexts, it is now often replaced by other words which are less emotionally charged, such as **people(s)** or **community**.

race³ ▸ **noun** dated a ginger root.
– ORIGIN late Middle English: from Old French *rais*, from Latin *radix, radic-* 'root'.

racecard ▸ **noun** a programme giving information about the races scheduled for a particular race meeting.

racecourse ▸ **noun** a ground or track for horse or dog racing.

racegoer ▸ **noun** a person attending a race meeting, especially one who does so frequently.

racehorse ▸ **noun** a horse bred, trained, and kept for racing.

racemate /ˈrasɪmeɪt/ ▸ **noun** Chemistry a racemic mixture.

raceme /ˈrasiːm, rəˈsiːm/ ▸ **noun** Botany a flower cluster with the separate flowers attached by short equal stalks at equal distances along a central stem. The flowers at the base of the central stem develop first. Compare with CYME and SPIKE².
– ORIGIN late 18th cent.: from Latin *racemus* 'bunch of grapes'.

race meeting ▸ **noun** Brit. a sporting event consisting of a series of races, typically horse races, held at a particular course over one or more days.

race memory ▸ **noun** a supposedly inherited subconscious memory of events in human history or prehistory.

racemic /rəˈsiːmɪk, rəˈsɛmɪk/ ▸ **adjective** Chemistry composed of dextrorotatory and laevorotatory forms of a compound in equal proportion.
– DERIVATIVES **racemize** /ˈrasɪmʌɪz/ (also **racemise**) **verb**.
– ORIGIN early 19th cent. (in *racemic acid*): from French *racémique* 'derived from grape juice' (originally referring to tartaric acid in this) + -IC.

racemose /ˈrasɪməʊs, -z/ ▸ **adjective** Botany (of a flower cluster) taking the form of a raceme. ■ Anatomy (especially of compound glands) having the form of a cluster.
– ORIGIN late 17th cent.: from Latin *racemosus*, from *racemus* (see RACEME).

race music ▸ **noun** [mass noun] US dated music popular among or played by black people, especially jazz and blues.

racer ▸ **noun 1** an animal or means of transport bred or designed for racing: *tall-masted ocean racers.* ■ a person who competes in races. ■ [as modifier] denoting an article of clothing that has a T-shaped back behind the shoulder blades to allow ease of movement in sporting activities: *a racer bra.*
2 a fast-moving, harmless, and typically slender-bodied snake. ● Several genera in the family Colubridae: genus *Coluber*, including the American *C. constrictor* and the European *C. gemonensis* (see also WHIP SNAKE), and the Asian genera *Ptyas* and *Argyrogena* (also called RAT SNAKE).
3 a circular horizontal rail along which the carriage or traversing platform of a heavy gun moves.

racerback ▸ **adjective** denoting an article of clothing, typically a singlet, swimsuit, or bra, in which the shoulder straps are joined between the shoulder blades.

race relations ▸ **plural noun** relations between members or communities of different races within one country.

race riot ▸ **noun** a public outbreak of violence due to racial antagonism.

racerunner ▸ **noun** any of a number of fast-moving active lizards with longitudinal markings and a pointed snout, in particular: ● an American lizard (genus *Cnemidophorus*, family Teiidae). ● (**desert racerunner**) an East European lizard (*Eremias arguta*, family Lacertidae).

racetrack ▸ **noun** a racecourse. ■ a track for motor racing.

raceway ▸ **noun** chiefly N. Amer. **1** a water channel, especially an artificial one of running water in which fish are reared. ■ a groove or race in which bearings run. ■ a pipe or tubing enclosing electric wires.
2 a track for trotting, pacing, or harness racing. ■ a track for motor racing.

rachis /ˈreɪkɪs/ (also **rhachis**) ▸ **noun** (pl. **rachides** /-kɪdiːz/) **1** Botany a stem of a plant, especially a grass, bearing flower stalks at short intervals. ■ the midrib of a compound leaf or frond.
2 Anatomy the vertebral column or the cord from which it develops.
3 Ornithology the shaft of a feather, especially the part bearing the barbs.
– ORIGIN late 18th cent.: modern Latin, from Greek *rhakhis* 'spine'. The English plural *-ides* is by false analogy.

rachitis /rəˈkʌɪtɪs/ ▸ **noun** old-fashioned medical term for RICKETS.
– DERIVATIVES **rachitic** /-ˈkɪtɪk/ **adjective**.
– ORIGIN early 18th cent.: modern Latin, from Greek *rhakhitis*, from *rhakhis* 'spine'.

Rachmaninov /rakˈmanɪnɒf/, Sergei (Vasilevich) (1873–1943), Russian composer and pianist, resident in the US from 1917. Part of the Russian romantic tradition, he is primarily known for his compositions for piano, including concertos and the Prelude in C sharp minor (1892).

Rachmanism /ˈrakmənɪz(ə)m/ ▸ **noun** [mass noun] Brit. the exploitation and intimidation of tenants by unscrupulous landlords.
– ORIGIN named after Peter *Rachman* (1919–62), a London landlord whose practices became notorious in the early 1960s.

racial ▸ **adjective** relating to race: *a racial minority.* ■ on the grounds of or connected with difference in race: *racial abuse.*
– DERIVATIVES **racially** adverb.

racialism ▸ **noun** another term for RACISM.
– DERIVATIVES **racialist** noun & adjective, **racialize** (also **racialise**) verb.

racial profiling ▸ **noun** [mass noun] US the use of race or ethnicity as grounds for suspecting someone of having committed an offence.

Racine /raˈsiːn, French rasin/, Jean (1639–99), French dramatist, the principal tragedian of the French classical period. Central to most of his tragedies is a perception of the blind folly of human passion, continually enslaved and unsatisfied. Notable works: *Andromaque* (1667) and *Phèdre* (1677).

racing ▸ **noun** [mass noun] short for HORSE RACING. ■ any sport that involves competing in races: *cycle racing* | *yacht racing.*
▸ **adjective 1** moving swiftly: *he controlled his racing thoughts.*
2 (of a person) following horse racing: *Kevin was not a racing man.*

racing car ▸ **noun** a car built for racing on a prepared track.

racing demon ▸ **noun** [mass noun] a competitive version of the card game patience played simultaneously by a number of players.

racing driver ▸ **noun** a person who drives racing cars as a profession.

racism ▸ **noun** [mass noun] the belief that all members of each race possess characteristics, abilities, or qualities specific to that race, especially so as to distinguish it as inferior or superior to another race or races. ■ prejudice, discrimination, or antagonism directed against someone of a different race based on such a belief: *a programme to combat racism.*

racist ▸ **noun** a person who believes that a particular race is superior to another.
▸ **adjective** having or showing the belief that a particular race is superior to another: *we are investigating complaints about racist abuse at a newsagents.*

rack¹ ▸ **noun 1** a framework, typically with rails, bars, hooks, or pegs, for holding or storing things: *a spice rack* | *a letter rack.* ■ an overhead shelf on a coach, train, or aircraft for stowing luggage. ■ a vertically barred frame for holding animal fodder: *a hay rack.* ■ N. Amer. informal a bed.
2 a cogged or toothed bar or rail engaging with a wheel or pinion, or using pegs to adjust the position of something: *a steering rack.*
3 (**the rack**) historical an instrument of torture consisting of a frame on which the victim was stretched by turning rollers to which the wrists and ankles were tied.
4 a triangular structure for positioning the balls in pool. ■ a single game of pool.
5 N. Amer. a set of antlers.
6 a digital effects unit for a guitar or other instrument, typically giving many different sounds.
7 N. Amer. informal a woman's breasts: *that chick's got a nice rack.*
▸ **verb** [with obj.] **1** (also **wrack**) cause extreme pain, anguish, or distress to: *he was racked with guilt.* ■ historical torture (someone) on the rack.
2 [with obj. and adverbial of place] place in or on a rack: *the shoes were racked neatly beneath the dresses.*
3 move by a rack and pinion.
4 chiefly archaic raise (rent) above a fair or normal amount. See also RACK RENT. ■ oppress (a tenant) by exacting excessive rent.
– PHRASES **go to rack** (or **wrack**) **and ruin** gradually deteriorate in condition because of neglect; fall into disrepair. [*rack* from Old English *wræc* 'vengeance'; related to WREAK.] **off the rack** North American term for OFF THE PEG (see PEG). **on the rack** suffering intense distress or strain. **rack** (or **wrack**) **one's brains** (or **brain**) make a great effort to think of or remember something.
– PHRASAL VERBS **rack something up** accumulate or achieve something, typically a score or amount: *Japan is racking up record trade surpluses with the United States.*
– ORIGIN Middle English: from Middle Dutch *rec*, Middle Low German *rek* 'horizontal bar or shelf', probably from *recken* 'to stretch, reach' (possibly the source of sense 1 of the verb).

> **USAGE** The relationship between the forms **rack** and **wrack** is complicated. The most common noun sense of **rack**, 'a framework for holding and storing things',

R

is always spelled **rack**, never **wrack**. In the phrase **rack something up** the word is also always spelled **rack**. Figurative senses of the verb, deriving from the type of torture in which someone is stretched on a **rack**, can, however, be spelled either **rack** or **wrack**: thus ***racked*** *with guilt* or ***wracked*** *with guilt*; ***rack*** *your brains* or ***wrack*** *your brains*. In addition, the phrase **rack and ruin** can also be spelled **wrack and ruin**.

rack² ▸ **noun** a horse's gait in which both hoofs on either side in turn are lifted almost simultaneously, and all four hoofs are off the ground together at certain moments.
▸ **verb 1** [no obj., with adverbial of direction] (of a horse) move with such a gait.
2 [no obj., in imperative] (**rack off**) Austral. informal go away.
– ORIGIN mid 16th cent.: of unknown origin.

rack³ ▸ **noun** a joint of meat, typically lamb, that includes the front ribs.
– ORIGIN late 16th cent.: of unknown origin.

rack⁴ ▸ **verb** [with obj.] draw off (wine, beer, etc.) from the sediment in the barrel: *the wine is* ***racked off*** *into large oak casks*.
– ORIGIN late 15th cent.: from Provençal *arracar*, from *raca* 'stems and husks of grapes, dregs'.

rack⁵ ▸ **noun** variant spelling of **WRACK³**.
▸ **verb** [no obj., with adverbial of direction] archaic (of a cloud) be driven before the wind.
– ORIGIN Middle English (denoting a rush or collision): probably of Scandinavian origin; compare with Norwegian and Swedish dialect *rak* 'wreckage', from *reka* 'to drive'.

rack-and-pinion ▸ **adjective** denoting a mechanism (e.g. for a car steering system) using a fixed cogged or toothed bar or rail engaging with a smaller cog.

racket¹ (also **racquet**) ▸ **noun** a bat with a round or oval frame strung with catgut, nylon, etc., used especially in tennis, badminton, and squash: *a squash racket*. ■ chiefly N. Amer. a snowshoe resembling a racket.
– ORIGIN early 16th cent.: from French *raquette* (see **RACKETS**).

racket² ▸ **noun 1** [in sing.] a loud unpleasant noise; a din: *the kids were making a racket*. ■ archaic the noise and liveliness of fashionable society.
2 informal an illegal or dishonest scheme for obtaining money: *a protection racket*. ■ a person's line of business or way of life: *I'm in the insurance racket*.
▸ **verb** (**rackets, racketing, racketed**) [no obj., with adverbial] **1** make or move with a loud unpleasant noise: *trains racketed by*.
2 (**racket about/around**) enjoy oneself socially; go in pursuit of pleasure or entertainment.
– DERIVATIVES **rackety** adjective.
– ORIGIN mid 16th cent.: perhaps imitative of clattering.

racketball ▸ **noun** variant spelling of **RACQUETBALL**.

racketeer ▸ **noun** a person who engages in dishonest and fraudulent business dealings.
– DERIVATIVES **racketeering** noun.

R

rackets ▸ **plural noun** [treated as sing.] a ball game for two or four people played with rackets in a plain four-walled court, distinguished from squash in particular by the use of a solid, harder ball.
– ORIGIN late Middle English (also in the singular): from French *raquette*, via Italian from Arabic *rāḥa*, *rāḥat-* 'palm of the hand'.

racket-tail (also **racquet-tail**) ▸ **noun** a South American hummingbird with long racket-shaped tail feathers. • Genera *Ocreatus* and *Loddigesia*, family Trochilidae: two species.
■ any of a number of other birds, in particular certain parrots, drongos, and motmots, with racket-shaped tails.

Rackham /ˈrakəm/, Arthur (1867–1939), English illustrator, noted for his illustrations of books such as the Grimm brothers' *Fairy Tales* (1900) and *Peter Pan* (1906).

rack mounting ▸ **noun** [mass noun] [usu. as modifier] the use of standardized racks for supporting electrical or electronic equipment.
– DERIVATIVES **rack-mounted** adjective.

rack railway ▸ **noun** a railway with a toothed rail between the bearing rails which engages with a cogwheel under the locomotive, for very steep slopes.

rack rate ▸ **noun** the official or advertised price of a hotel room, on which a discount is usually negotiable.

rack rent ▸ **noun** an extortionate or very high rent.
▸ **verb** (**rack-rent**) [with obj.] dated exact an excessive or extortionate rent from (a tenant) or for (a property).
– DERIVATIVES **rack-renter** noun.
– ORIGIN late 16th cent. (as *rack-rented*): from the verb **RACK¹** (in the sense 'cause stress') + the noun **RENT¹**.

raclette /raˈklɛt/ ▸ **noun** [mass noun] a Swiss dish of melted cheese, typically eaten with potatoes.
– ORIGIN French, literally 'small scraper', referring to the practice of holding the cheese over the heat and scraping it on to a plate as it melts.

racon /ˈreɪkɒn/ ▸ **noun** chiefly US a radar beacon that can be identified and located by its response to a specific radar signal.
– ORIGIN 1940s: blend of **RADAR** and **BEACON**.

raconteur /ˌrakɒnˈtəː/ ▸ **noun** a person who tells anecdotes in a skilful and amusing way.
– ORIGIN early 19th cent.: French, from *raconter* 'relate, recount'.

raconteuse /ˌrakɒnˈtəːz/ ▸ **noun** a female raconteur.
– ORIGIN mid 19th cent.: French, feminine of *raconteur* (see **RACONTEUR**).

racoon ▸ **noun** variant spelling of **RACCOON**.

racquet ▸ **noun** variant spelling of **RACKET¹**.

racquetball (also **racketball**) ▸ **noun** chiefly N. Amer. a game played with a small hard ball and a short-handled racket in a four-walled handball court.

racy ▸ **adjective** (**racier, raciest**) **1** lively, entertaining, and typically sexually titillating: *the novel was considered rather racy at the time*. ■ showing vigour or spirit. ■ (of a wine, flavour, etc.) having a characteristic quality in a high degree.
2 (of a vehicle or animal) designed or bred to be suitable for racing: *the yacht is fast and racy*.
– DERIVATIVES **racily** adverb, **raciness** noun.

RAD ▸ **abbreviation** (in the UK) Royal Academy of Dance.

rad¹ ▸ **abbreviation** radian(s).

rad² ▸ **noun** informal a political radical.
– ORIGIN early 19th cent.: abbreviation.

rad³ ▸ **noun** Physics a unit of absorbed dose of ionizing radiation, corresponding to the absorption of 0.01 joule per kilogram of absorbing material.
– ORIGIN early 20th cent.: acronym from *radiation absorbed dose*.

rad⁴ ▸ **adjective** informal, chiefly N. Amer. excellent; impressive: *his style is so rad | a really rad game*.
– ORIGIN 1980s: probably an abbreviation of **RADICAL**.

rad⁵ ▸ **noun** short for **RADIATOR**.

RADA /ˈrɑːdə/ ▸ **abbreviation** (in the UK) Royal Academy of Dramatic Art.

radar ▸ **noun** [mass noun] a system for detecting the presence, direction, distance, and speed of aircraft, ships, and other objects, by sending out pulses of radio waves which are reflected off the object back to the source. ■ [count noun] an apparatus used for this. ■ a person's capacity for intuitive perception; a special sensitivity for factors, trends, etc.: *keep your radar tuned to changes at work*. ■ used to indicate that someone or something has or has not come to the attention of a person or group: *he's* ***off the radar*** *in the UK but in his country of birth he's a well-known figure*.
– ORIGIN 1940s: from *ra(dio) d(etection) a(nd) r(anging)*.

radar gun ▸ **noun** a handheld device used by traffic police to estimate the speed of a passing vehicle.

radar trap ▸ **noun** an area of road in which radar is used by the police to detect vehicles exceeding a speed limit.

RADC ▸ **abbreviation** (in the UK) Royal Army Dental Corps.

Radcliffe, Mrs Ann (1764–1823), English novelist, a leading exponent of the Gothic novel. Notable works: *The Mysteries of Udolpho* (1794) and *The Italian* (1797).

raddle ▸ **noun** another term for **REDDLE**. ■ [count noun] a block or stick of reddle.
▸ **verb** [with obj.] colour with reddle.
– ORIGIN early 16th cent.: related to **RED**; compare with **RUDDLE**.

raddled ▸ **adjective 1** showing signs of age or fatigue: *she's beginning to look quite raddled*.
2 coloured with or as if with raddle: *raddled sheep*.
– ORIGIN Sense 1 from **RADDLE** in the sense 'rouge', by association with its exaggerated use in make-up.

radge Scottish informal ▸ **noun** a wild, crazy, or violent person.
▸ **adjective** wild, crazy, or violent.
– ORIGIN 1920s: apparently an alteration of **RAGE**.

Radha /ˈrɑːdɑː, ˈrɑːðɑː/ Hinduism the favourite mistress of the god Krishna, and an incarnation of Lakshmi.
– ORIGIN from Sanskrit, literally 'prosperity'.

Radhakrishnan /ˌrɑːdəˈkrɪʃnən/, Sir Sarvepalli (1888–1975), Indian philosopher and statesman, President 1962–7. He introduced classical Indian philosophy to the West through works such as *Indian Philosophy* (1923–7).

radial ▸ **adjective 1** of or arranged like rays or the radii of a circle; diverging in lines from a common centre. ■ (of a road or route) running directly from a town or city centre to an outlying district. ■ (also **radial-ply**) denoting a tyre in which the layers of fabric have their cords running at right angles to the circumference of the tyre and the tread is strengthened by further layers round the circumference.
2 Anatomy & Zoology relating to the radius.
▸ **noun 1** a radial tyre.
2 a radial road.
3 Zoology a supporting ray in a fish's fin.
4 a radial engine.
– DERIVATIVES **radially** adverb.
– ORIGIN late 16th cent.: from medieval Latin *radialis*, from Latin *radius* (see **RADIUS**).

radial engine ▸ **noun** a type of internal-combustion engine used chiefly in aircraft, having its cylinders fixed radially around a rotating crankshaft.

radial keratotomy ▸ **noun** see **KERATOTOMY**.

radial symmetry ▸ **noun** [mass noun] chiefly Biology symmetry about a central axis, as in a starfish or a tulip flower.

radial velocity ▸ **noun** chiefly Astronomy the velocity of a star or other body along the line of sight of an observer.

radian /ˈreɪdɪən/ ▸ **noun** Geometry a unit of measurement of angles equal to about 57.3°, equivalent to the angle subtended at the centre of a circle by an arc equal in length to the radius.

radiance ▸ **noun** [mass noun] **1** light or heat as emitted or reflected by something: *the radiance of the sunset dwindled and died*. ■ great joy or love, apparent in someone's expression or bearing: *the radiance of the bride's smile*. ■ a glowing quality of the skin, especially as indicative of good health or youth.
2 Physics the flux of radiation emitted per unit solid angle in a given direction by a unit area of a source.

radiant ▸ **adjective 1** sending out light; shining or glowing brightly: *a bird with radiant green and red plumage*. ■ (of a person or their expression) clearly emanating great joy, love, or health: *she gave him a radiant smile*. ■ (of an emotion or quality) emanating powerfully from someone or something; very conspicuous: *he praised her radiant self-confidence*.
2 [attrib.] (of electromagnetic energy, especially heat) transmitted by radiation, rather than conduction or convection. ■ (of an appliance) designed to emit radiant energy, especially for cooking or heating.
▸ **noun** a point or object from which light or heat radiates, especially a heating element in an electric or gas heater. ■ Astronomy a radiant point.
– DERIVATIVES **radiancy** noun, **radiantly** adverb.
– ORIGIN late Middle English: from Latin *radiant-* 'emitting rays', from the verb *radiare* (see **RADIATE**).

radiant point ▸ **noun** a centre point from which rays or radii proceed. ■ Astronomy the apparent focal point of a meteor shower.

radiate ▸ **verb 1** [with obj.] emit (energy, especially light or heat) in the form of rays or waves: *the hot stars radiate energy*. ■ [no obj., with adverbial of direction] (of light, heat, or other energy) be emitted in the form of rays or waves: *the continual stream of energy which radiates from the sun*. ■ (of a person) clearly emanate (a strong feeling or quality) through their expression or bearing: *she lifted her chin, radiating defiance*. ■ (**radiate from**) (of a feeling or quality) emanate clearly from: *leadership and confidence radiate from her*.
2 [no obj., with adverbial of direction] diverge or spread from or as if from a central point: *he ran down one of the passages that radiated from the room*. ■ (as adj. **radiated**) used in names of animals with markings arranged like rays, e.g. **radiated tortoise**. ■ Biology (of an animal or plant group) evolve into a variety of forms adapted to new ways of life.
▸ **adjective** rare arranged in or having a radial pattern: *the radiate crown*.
– DERIVATIVES **radiative** adjective (sense 1 of the verb).

– ORIGIN early 17th cent.: from Latin *radiat-* 'emitted in rays', from the verb *radiare*, from *radius* 'ray, spoke'.

radiation ▸ noun [mass noun] **1** Physics the emission of energy as electromagnetic waves or as moving subatomic particles, especially high-energy particles which cause ionization. ■ the energy transmitted in this way.
2 chiefly Biology divergence out from a central point, in particular evolution from an ancestral animal or plant group into a variety of new forms.
– DERIVATIVES **radiational** adjective.
– ORIGIN late Middle English (denoting the action of sending out rays of light): from Latin *radiatio(n-)*, from *radiare* 'emit rays' (see RADIATE).

radiation belt ▸ noun Astronomy a region surrounding a planet where charged particles accumulate under the influence of the planet's magnetic field.

radiation chemistry ▸ noun [mass noun] the branch of chemistry concerned with the effects of radiation on matter.

radiation pattern ▸ noun Physics the directional variation in intensity of the radiation from an aerial or other source.

radiation sickness ▸ noun [mass noun] illness caused by exposure of the body to ionizing radiation, characterized by nausea, hair loss, diarrhoea, bleeding, and damage to the bone marrow and central nervous system.

radiation therapy (also **radiation treatment**) ▸ noun another term for RADIOTHERAPY.

radiator ▸ noun **1** a thing that radiates or emits light, heat, or sound. ■ a device for heating a room consisting of a metal tank connected by pipes through which hot water is pumped by a central heating system. ■ a portable oil or electric heater resembling such a device.
2 an engine-cooling device in a motor vehicle or aircraft consisting of a bank of thin tubes in which circulating water is cooled by the surrounding air.

radical ▸ adjective **1** (especially of change or action) relating to or affecting the fundamental nature of something; far-reaching or thorough: *a radical overhaul of the existing regulatory framework*. ■ forming an inherent or fundamental part of the nature of someone or something: *the assumption of radical differences between the mental attributes of literate and non-literate peoples*. ■ (of surgery or medical treatment) thorough and intended to be completely curative.
2 characterized by departure from tradition; innovative or progressive: *the city is known for its radical approach to transport policy*. ■ advocating or based on thorough or complete political or social reform; representing or supporting an extreme or progressive section of a political party: *a radical American activist*. ■ Brit. historical belonging to an extreme section of the Liberal party during the 19th century.
3 relating to the root of something, in particular: ■ Mathematics of the root of a number or quantity. ■ denoting or relating to the roots of a word. ■ Music belonging to the root of a chord. ■ Botany of, or springing direct from, the root or stem base of a plant.
4 [usu. as exclamation] N. Amer. informal very good; excellent: *Okay, then. Seven o'clock. Radical!*
▸ noun **1** a person who advocates thorough or complete political or social reform; a member of a political party or part of a party pursuing such aims.
2 Chemistry a group of atoms behaving as a unit in a number of compounds. See also FREE RADICAL.
3 the root or base form of a word. ■ any of the basic set of approximately 214 Chinese characters constituting semantically or functionally significant elements in the composition of other characters and used as a means of classifying characters in dictionaries.
4 Mathematics a quantity forming or expressed as the root of another. ■ a radical sign.
– DERIVATIVES **radicalism** noun, **radically** adverb [as submodifier] *a radically different approach*, **radicalness** noun.
– ORIGIN late Middle English (in the senses 'forming the root' and 'inherent'): from late Latin *radicalis*, from Latin *radix*, *radic-* 'root'.

radical chic ▸ noun [mass noun] the fashionable affectation of radical left-wing views. ■ the dress, lifestyle, or people associated with this.
– ORIGIN 1970: coined by the US writer Tom Wolfe.

radicalize (also **radicalise**) ▸ verb [with obj.] **1** cause (someone) to become an advocate of radical political or social reform: *some of those involved had been radicalized by the Vietnam War*.
2 introduce fundamental or far-reaching changes in: *the push to radicalize 16–19 science education*.
– DERIVATIVES **radicalization** noun.

radical sign ▸ noun Mathematics the sign √ which indicates the square root of the number following (or a higher root indicated by a preceding superscript numeral).

radicchio /raˈdiːkɪəʊ/ ▸ noun (pl. **radicchios**) chicory of a variety which has dark red leaves.
– ORIGIN Italian.

radices plural form of RADIX.

radicle /ˈradɪk(ə)l/ ▸ noun Botany the part of a plant embryo that develops into the primary root. ■ Anatomy a root-like subdivision of a nerve or vein.
– DERIVATIVES **radicular** adjective (Anatomy).
– ORIGIN late 17th cent.: from Latin *radicula*, diminutive of *radix*, *radic-* 'root'.

radii plural form of RADIUS.

radio ▸ noun (pl. **radios**) **1** [mass noun] the transmission and reception of electromagnetic waves of radio frequency, especially those carrying sound messages: *cellular phones are linked by radio rather than wires*.
2 [mass noun] the activity or industry of broadcasting sound programmes to the public: *she has written much material for radio* | [as modifier] *a radio station*. ■ radio programmes: *we used to listen to a lot of radio*. ■ [in names] a broadcasting station or channel: *Radio One*.
3 an apparatus for receiving radio programmes: *he switched the radio on*. ■ an apparatus capable of both receiving and transmitting radio messages between individuals, ships, planes, etc.: *a ship-to-shore radio*.
▸ verb (**radioes**, **radioing**, **radioed**) [no obj.] communicate or send a message by radio: *we radioed for help*. ■ [with obj.] communicate with (a person or place) by radio: *we'll radio Athens right away*.
– ORIGIN early 20th cent.: abbreviation of RADIO-TELEPHONY.

radio- ▸ combining form **1** denoting radio waves or broadcasting: *radio-controlled* | *radiogram*.
2 Physics connected with rays, radiation, or radioactivity: *radiogenic* | *radiograph*. ■ denoting artificially prepared radioisotopes of elements: *radio-cobalt*.
3 Anatomy belonging to the radius in conjunction with some other part: *radio-carpal*.
– ORIGIN from RADIO or RADIUS.

radioactive ▸ adjective emitting or relating to the emission of ionizing radiation or particles: *radioactive decay* | *the water was radioactive*.
– DERIVATIVES **radioactively** adverb.

radioactivity ▸ noun [mass noun] the emission of ionizing radiation or particles caused by the spontaneous disintegration of atomic nuclei. ■ radioactive substances, or the radiation emitted by these.

radio astronomy ▸ noun [mass noun] the branch of astronomy concerned with radio emissions from celestial objects.

radiobiology ▸ noun [mass noun] the branch of biology concerned with the effects of ionizing radiation on organisms and the application in biology of radiological techniques.
– DERIVATIVES **radiobiological** adjective, **radiobiologically** adverb, **radiobiologist** noun.

radio button ▸ noun Computing (in a graphical display) an icon representing one of a set of options, only one of which can be selected at any time.

radio car ▸ noun a car, especially a police car, equipped with a two-way radio.

radiocarbon ▸ noun [mass noun] Chemistry a radioactive isotope of carbon.

radiocarbon dating ▸ noun another term for CARBON DATING.

radiochemistry ▸ noun [mass noun] the branch of chemistry concerned with radioactive substances.
– DERIVATIVES **radiochemical** adjective, **radiochemist** noun.

radio-controlled ▸ adjective (of an device) controllable from a distance by radio.

radio-element ▸ noun a radioactive element or isotope.

radio frequency ▸ noun a frequency or band of frequencies in the range 10^4 to 10^{11} or 10^{12} Hz, suitable for use in telecommunications.

radio galaxy ▸ noun a galaxy emitting radiation in the radio-frequency range of the electromagnetic spectrum.

radiogenic /ˌreɪdɪə(ʊ)ˈdʒɛnɪk, -ˈdʒiːn-/ ▸ adjective **1** produced by radioactivity: *a radiogenic isotope*.
2 well suited in style or subject for broadcasting by radio: *a radiogenic series*.
– DERIVATIVES **radiogenically** adverb.

radiogram ▸ noun **1** Brit. a combined radio and record player built into a cabinet with a speaker. [from RADIO- + GRAMOPHONE.]
2 another term for RADIOGRAPH.
3 a telegram sent by radio.

radiograph ▸ noun an image produced on a sensitive plate or film by X-rays, gamma rays, or similar radiation, and typically used in medical examination.
▸ verb [with obj.] produce an image of (something) on a sensitive plate or film by X-rays, gamma rays, or similar radiation.
– DERIVATIVES **radiographic** adjective, **radiographically** adverb.

radiography ▸ noun [mass noun] the process or occupation of taking radiographs to assist in medical examinations.
– DERIVATIVES **radiographer** noun.

radio ham ▸ noun see HAM[2] (sense 2 of the noun).

radioimmunoassay ▸ noun Medicine a technique for determining antibody levels by introducing an antigen labelled with a radioisotope and measuring the subsequent radioactivity of the antibody component.

radioimmunology ▸ noun [mass noun] the use of radioactively labelled antigens and antibodies in medical and biological research.

radioisotope ▸ noun Chemistry a radioactive isotope.
– DERIVATIVES **radioisotopic** adjective.

radio jockey ▸ noun chiefly Indian a radio presenter or disc jockey.

radiolaria /ˌreɪdɪə(ʊ)ˈlɛːrɪə/ ▸ plural noun Zoology radiolarians collectively.
– ORIGIN late 19th cent.: modern Latin (former order name), from late Latin *radiolus* 'faint ray', diminutive of *radius* 'ray'.

radiolarian Zoology ▸ noun a single-celled aquatic animal which has a spherical amoeba-like body with a spiny skeleton of silica. Their skeletons can accumulate as a slimy deposit on the seabed. ● Three classes of the phylum Actinopoda, kingdom Protista (formerly subclass or order Radiolaria).
▸ adjective relating to or formed from radiolarians.

radiology ▸ noun [mass noun] the science dealing with X-rays and other high-energy radiation, especially the use of such radiation for the diagnosis and treatment of disease.
– DERIVATIVES **radiologic** adjective, **radiological** adjective, **radiologically** adverb, **radiologist** noun.

radiolucent /ˌreɪdɪəʊˈluːsənt/ ▸ adjective transparent to X-rays.
– DERIVATIVES **radiolucency** noun.

radiometer /ˌreɪdɪˈɒmɪtə/ ▸ noun an instrument for detecting or measuring the intensity or force of radiation.
– DERIVATIVES **radiometry** noun.

radiometric ▸ adjective Physics relating to the measurement of radioactivity.
– DERIVATIVES **radiometrically** adverb.

radiometric dating ▸ noun [mass noun] a method of dating geological specimens by determining the relative proportions of particular radioactive isotopes present in a sample.

radionics /ˌreɪdɪˈɒnɪks/ ▸ plural noun [treated as sing.] a system of alternative medicine based on the supposition that detectable electromagnetic radiation emitted by living matter can be interpreted diagnostically and transmitted to treat illness at a distance by complex electrical instruments.
– ORIGIN 1940s: from RADIO- 'radiation', on the pattern of *electronics*.

radionuclide ▸ noun a radioactive nuclide.

radiopaque /ˌreɪdɪəʊˈpeɪk/ (also **radio-opaque**) ▸ adjective (of a substance) opaque to X-rays or similar radiation.
– DERIVATIVES **radiopacity** noun.

radiophonic ▸ adjective relating to or denoting sound, especially music, produced electronically.

radioscopy /ˌreɪdɪˈɒskəpi/ ▸ noun [mass noun] Physics the examination by X-rays or similar radiation of objects opaque to light.
– DERIVATIVES **radioscopic** adjective.

radiosonde /ˈreɪdɪəʊˌsɒnd/ ▸ noun an instrument carried by balloon or other means to various levels

R

of the atmosphere and transmitting measurements by radio.
– ORIGIN 1930s: from **RADIO-** (relating to broadcasting) + German *Sonde* 'probe'.

radio-telephony ▶ **noun** [mass noun] telephony using radio transmission.
– DERIVATIVES **radio-telephone** noun, **radio-telephonic** adjective.

radio telescope ▶ **noun** Astronomy an instrument used to detect radio emissions from the sky, whether from natural celestial objects or from artificial satellites.

radiotherapy ▶ **noun** [mass noun] the treatment of disease, especially cancer, using X-rays or similar forms of radiation.
– DERIVATIVES **radiotherapeutic** adjective, **radiotherapist** noun.

radio wave ▶ **noun** an electromagnetic wave of a frequency between about 10^4 and 10^{11} or 10^{12} Hz, as used for long-distance communication.

radish ▶ **noun 1** a swollen pungent-tasting edible root, especially a variety which is small, spherical, and red, and eaten raw with salad.
2 the plant of the cabbage family which yields the radish. ● *Raphanus sativus*, family Cruciferae.
– ORIGIN Old English *rædic*, from Latin *radix*, *radic-* 'root'.

radium /ˈreɪdɪəm/ ▶ **noun** [mass noun] the chemical element of atomic number 88, a rare radioactive metal of the alkaline earth series. It was formerly used as a source of radiation for radiotherapy. (Symbol: **Ra**)
– ORIGIN late 19th cent.: from Latin *radius* 'ray' + **-IUM**.

radium emanation ▶ **noun** archaic term for **RADON**.

radius /ˈreɪdɪəs/ ▶ **noun** (pl. **radii** /-dɪʌɪ/ or **radiuses**)
1 a straight line from the centre to the circumference of a circle or sphere. ■ a radial line from the focus to any point of a curve. ■ a specified distance from a centre in all directions: *there are plenty of local pubs within a two-mile radius*.
2 Anatomy the thicker and shorter of the two bones in the human forearm. Compare with **ULNA**. ■ Zoology the corresponding bone in a vertebrate's foreleg or a bird's wing. ■ Entomology any of the main veins in an insect's wing.
3 Zoology a radially symmetric feature in an echinoderm or coelenterate, e.g. an arm of a starfish.
▶ **verb** (**radiuses**, **radiusing**, **radiused**) [with obj.] (often as adj. **radiused**) give a rounded form to (a corner or edge).
– ORIGIN late 16th cent. (in sense 2 of the noun): from Latin, literally 'staff, spoke, ray'.

radius of curvature ▶ **noun** Mathematics the radius of a circle which touches a curve at a given point and has the same tangent and curvature at that point.

radius vector ▶ **noun** Mathematics a line of variable length drawn from a fixed origin to a curve. ■ Astronomy such a line joining a satellite or other celestial object to its primary.

radix /ˈradɪks, ˈreɪ-/ ▶ **noun** (pl. **radices** /-dɪsiːz/)
1 Mathematics the base of a system of numeration.
2 rare a source or origin of something.
– ORIGIN early 17th cent. (in sense 2): from Latin, literally 'root'. Sense 1 dates from the late 18th cent.

R

Radnorshire /ˈradnəʃɪə, -ʃə/ a former county of eastern Wales. It became part of Powys in 1974.

Radom /ˈrɑːdɒm/ an industrial city in central Poland; pop. 225,292 (2007).

radome /ˈreɪdəʊm/ ▶ **noun** a dome or other structure protecting radar equipment and made from material transparent to radio waves, especially one on the outer surface of an aircraft.
– ORIGIN 1940s: blend of **RADAR** and **DOME**.

radon /ˈreɪdɒn/ ▶ **noun** [mass noun] the chemical element of atomic number 86, a rare radioactive gas belonging to the noble gas series. (Symbol: **Rn**)
– ORIGIN early 20th cent.: from **RADIUM**, on the pattern of *argon*.

radula /ˈradjʊlə/ ▶ **noun** (pl. **radulae** /-liː/) Zoology (in a mollusc) a rasp-like structure of tiny teeth used for scraping food particles off a surface and drawing them into the mouth.
– DERIVATIVES **radular** adjective.
– ORIGIN late 19th cent.: from Latin, literally 'scraper', from *radere* 'to scrape'.

radwaste /ˈradweɪst/ ▶ **noun** [mass noun] informal radioactive waste.

Raeburn /ˈreɪbəːn/, Sir Henry (1756–1823), Scottish portrait painter. The leading Scottish portraitist of his day, he depicted the local intelligentsia and Highland chieftains in a bold and distinctive style.

Raelian /rʌɪˈiːlɪən/ ▶ **noun** a member of an atheistic cult based on the belief that humans originated from alien scientists who came to earth in UFOs.
▶ **adjective** relating to the Raelians or their beliefs.
– ORIGIN 1990s: from *Rael*, assumed name of Claude Vorilhon, French singer and journalist, author of *The Message Given to me by Extraterrestrials* (1974).

RAF ▶ **abbreviation** (in the UK) Royal Air Force.

Rafferty's rules /ˈrafətɪz/ ▶ **plural noun** Austral./NZ informal no rules at all: *the campaign was fought according to Rafferty's rules*.
– ORIGIN 1920s: *Rafferty*, probably an English dialect alteration of **REFRACTORY**.

raffia ▶ **noun** a palm tree native to tropical Africa and Madagascar, with a short trunk and leaves which may be up to 18 m (60 feet) long. ● *Raphia ruffia*, family Palmae.
■ [mass noun] the fibre from the leaves of the raffia tree, used for making items such as hats and baskets.
– ORIGIN early 18th cent.: from Malagasy.

raffinate /ˈrafɪneɪt/ ▶ **noun** Chemistry a liquid from which impurities have been removed by solvent extraction.
– ORIGIN 1920s: from French *raffiner* or German *raffinieren* 'refine' + **-ATE**[1].

raffinose /ˈrafɪnəʊz, -s/ ▶ **noun** [mass noun] Chemistry a sugar present in sugar beet, cotton seed, and many cereals. It is a trisaccharide containing glucose, galactose, and fructose units.
– ORIGIN late 19th cent.: from French *raffiner* 'refine' + **-OSE**[2].

raffish ▶ **adjective** unconventional and slightly disreputable, especially in an attractive way: *his raffish air*.
– DERIVATIVES **raffishly** adverb, **raffishness** noun.
– ORIGIN early 19th cent.: from **RIFF-RAFF** + **-ISH**[1].

raffle[1] ▶ **noun** a means of raising money by selling numbered tickets, one or some of which are subsequently drawn at random, the holder or holders of such tickets winning a prize.
▶ **verb** [with obj.] offer as a prize in a raffle.
– ORIGIN late Middle English (denoting a kind of dice game): from Old French, of unknown origin. The current sense dates from the mid 18th cent.

raffle[2] ▶ **noun** [mass noun] dialect rubbish; refuse: *the raffle of the yard below*.
– ORIGIN late Middle English (in the sense 'rabble, riff-raff'): perhaps from Old French *ne rifle ne rafle* 'nothing at all'.

Raffles, Sir (Thomas) Stamford (1781–1826), British colonial administrator. As Lieutenant General of Sumatra he persuaded the East India Company to purchase the undeveloped island of Singapore (1819), undertaking much of the preliminary work for transforming it into an international port and centre of commerce.

rafflesia /rəˈfliːʒɪə, -ˈzɪə/ ▶ **noun** a parasitic plant which lacks chlorophyll and bears a single very large flower which smells of carrion, native to Malaysia and Indonesia. ● Genus *Rafflesia*, family Rafflesiaceae: several species, including *R. arnoldii*, with flowers over 60 cm (2 ft) across.
– ORIGIN modern Latin, named after Sir T. Stamford **RAFFLES**.

raft[1] ▶ **noun 1** a flat buoyant structure of timber or other materials fastened together, used as a boat or floating platform. ■ a small inflatable rubber or plastic boat, especially one for use in emergencies. ■ a floating mass of fallen trees, vegetation, ice, or other material. ■ a dense flock of swimming birds or mammals: *great* ***rafts of*** *cormorants, often 5,000 strong*.
2 a layer of reinforced concrete forming the foundation of a building.
▶ **verb 1** [no obj., with adverbial of direction] travel on or as if on a raft: *I have rafted along the Rio Grande*. ■ [with obj. and adverbial of direction] transport on or as if on a raft: *the stores were rafted ashore*. ■ (of an ice floe) be driven on top of or underneath another floe.
2 [with obj.] bring or fasten together (a number of boats or other objects) side by side.
– ORIGIN late Middle English (in the sense 'beam, rafter'): from Old Norse *raptr* 'rafter'. The verb dates from the late 17th cent.

raft[2] ▶ **noun** a large amount of something: ***a raft of*** *government initiatives*.
– ORIGIN mid 19th cent.: alteration of dialect *raff* 'abundance' (perhaps of Scandinavian origin), by association with **RAFT**[1] in the sense 'floating mass'.

rafter[1] ▶ **noun** a beam forming part of the internal framework of a roof.
– ORIGIN Old English *ræfter*, of Germanic origin; related to **RAFT**[1].

rafter[2] ▶ **noun** a person who travels on a raft. ■ a lumberjack who fastens logs into a raft to transport them by water.

raftered ▶ **adjective** (of a room or ceiling) having exposed rafters.

rafting ▶ **noun** [mass noun] the sport or pastime of travelling down a river on a raft.

raftsman ▶ **noun** (pl. **raftsmen**) a man who works on a raft.

raft spider ▶ **noun** a large European spider which frequents pools and swamps, reaching through the surface to capture insects, tadpoles, and sometimes small fish. ● Genus *Dolomedes*, family Pisauridae.

rag[1] /rag/ ▶ **noun 1** a piece of old cloth, especially one torn from a larger piece, used typically for cleaning things: *he wiped his hands on an oily rag* | [mass noun] *a piece of rag*. ■ (**rags**) old or tattered clothes: *street urchins dressed* ***in rags***. ■ [with negative] archaic the smallest scrap of cloth or clothing: *not a rag of clothing has arrived to us this winter*.
2 informal a newspaper, typically one regarded as being of low quality: *the local rag*.
▶ **verb** (**rags**, **ragging**, **ragged**) [with obj.] give a decorative effect to (a painted surface) by applying paint, typically of a different colour, with a rag. ■ apply (paint) to a surface with a rag.
– PHRASES **be on the rag** informal, chiefly N. Amer. be menstruating. [from *rag* in the sense 'sanitary towel'.] **lose one's rag** Brit. informal lose one's temper. (**from**) **rags to riches** used to describe a person's rise from a state of extreme poverty to one of great wealth: *it was the old rags-to-riches fantasy*.
– ORIGIN Middle English: probably a back-formation from **RAGGED** or **RAGGY**.

rag[2] /rag/ ▶ **noun** [mass noun] [usu. as modifier] Brit. a programme of stunts, parades, and other entertainments organized by students to raise money for charity: *rag week*. ■ [count noun] informal, dated a boisterous prank or practical joke.
▶ **verb** (**rags**, **ragging**, **ragged**) [with obj.] **1** make fun of (someone) in a boisterous manner.
2 rebuke severely.
3 Ice Hockey keep possession of (the puck) by skilful stick-handling and avoidance of opponents, so as to waste time.
– PHRASAL VERBS **rag on** N. Amer. informal complain about or criticize continually.
– ORIGIN mid 18th cent.: of unknown origin.

rag[3] /rag/ ▶ **noun 1** a large coarse roofing slate.
2 (also **ragstone**) [mass noun] Brit. a hard, coarse sedimentary rock that can be broken into thick slabs.
– ORIGIN late Middle English (in sense 2): of unknown origin; later associated with **RAG**[1].

rag[4] /rag/ ▶ **noun** a ragtime composition or tune.
– ORIGIN late 19th cent.: perhaps from **RAGGED**; compare with **RAGTIME**.

rag[5] /rɑːg/ ▶ **noun** variant of **RAGA**.

raga /ˈrɑːgə, ˈrɑːgɑː/ (also **rag**) ▶ **noun** (in Indian classical music) each of the six basic musical modes which express different moods in certain characteristic progressions, with more emphasis placed on some notes than others. ■ a piece using a particular raga.
– ORIGIN late 18th cent.: from Sanskrit, literally 'colour, musical tone'.

ragamuffin (also **raggamuffin**) ▶ **noun 1** a person, typically a child, in ragged, dirty clothes.
2 an exponent or follower of ragga, typically one dressing in scruffy clothes. ■ another term for **RAGGA**.
– ORIGIN Middle English: probably based on **RAG**[1], with a fanciful suffix.

rag-and-bone man ▶ **noun** Brit. an itinerant dealer in old clothes, furniture, and second-hand items.

ragbag ▶ **noun** a bag in which scraps of fabric and old clothes are kept for use. ■ a miscellaneous collection of things: ***a ragbag of*** *reforms is now being discussed*. ■ Brit. informal a woman dressed in an untidy way.

rag bolt ▶ **noun** a bolt with barbs to keep it tight when it has been driven in.

rag book ▶ **noun** Brit. a book for very small children made of strong cloth that cannot be torn.

rag doll ▶ **noun** a soft doll made from pieces of cloth.

rage ▶ **noun 1** [mass noun] violent uncontrollable anger: *her face was distorted with rage* | [count noun] *he flew into a rage*. ■ [with modifier] anger or aggression associated with conflict arising from a particular situation: *office rage is on the increase*. ■ the violent action of a natural agency: *the rising rage of the sea*.

2 [in sing.] a vehement desire or passion: ***a rage for absolute honesty informs much western art.*** ■ **(the rage)** a widespread temporary enthusiasm or fashion: *computer games are **all the rage**.* ■ literary prophetic, poetic, or martial enthusiasm or ardour.
3 Austral./NZ informal a lively party.
▸ **verb** [no obj.] **1** feel or express violent uncontrollable anger: *he **raged at** the futility of it all* | [with direct speech] *'That's unfair!' Maggie raged.* ■ [with adverbial] (of a natural agency or a conflict) continue violently or with great force: *the argument raged for days.* ■ [with adverbial of direction] (of an illness or fire) spread very rapidly or uncontrollably: *the great cholera epidemic which raged across Europe in 1831.* ■ (of an emotion) have or reach a high degree of intensity: *she couldn't hide the fear that raged within her.*
2 Austral./NZ informal go out and enjoy oneself socially: *get ready to rage!*
– DERIVATIVES **rager** noun.
– ORIGIN Middle English (also in the sense 'madness'): from Old French *rage* (noun), *rager* (verb), from a variant of Latin *rabies* (see **RABIES**).

ragfish ▸ **noun** (pl. **same** or **ragfishes**) a large fish of the North Pacific, the bones of which are mostly cartilaginous, causing the body to feel limp when held. ● *Icosteus aenigmaticus*, the only member of the family Icosteidae.

ragga /ˈraɡə/ ▸ **noun** [mass noun] a style of dance music originating in Jamaica and derived from reggae, in which a DJ improvises lyrics over a sampled or electronic backing track.
– ORIGIN 1990s: from **RAGAMUFFIN**, because of the style of clothing worn by its followers.

raggamuffin ▸ **noun** variant spelling of **RAGAMUFFIN**.

ragged /ˈraɡɪd/ ▸ **adjective** **1** (of cloth or clothes) old and torn. ■ wearing old and torn clothes: *a ragged child.*
2 having a rough or irregular surface or edge: *a ragged coastline.* ■ (of an animal) having a rough, shaggy coat. ■ Printing (especially of a right margin) uneven because the lines are unjustified.
3 lacking finish, smoothness, or uniformity: *the ragged discipline of the players.* ■ (of a sound) not controlled; uneven: *his breathing became ragged.*
4 suffering from exhaustion or stress: *he looked a little ragged, a little shadowy beneath the eyes.*
– PHRASES **run someone ragged** exhaust someone by making them undertake a lot of physical activity.
– DERIVATIVES **raggedly** adverb, **raggedness** noun.
– ORIGIN Middle English: of Scandinavian origin; compare with Old Norse *rǫgvathr* 'tufted' and Norwegian *ragget* 'shaggy'.

ragged robin ▸ **noun** a pink-flowered European campion of damp grassland, with divided petals that give it a tattered appearance. ● *Lychnis flos-cuculi*, family Caryophyllaceae.

raggedy ▸ **adjective** informal, chiefly N. Amer. scruffy; shabby.

raggedy-ass (also **raggedy-assed**) ▸ **adjective** N. Amer. informal in poor condition; shabby: *she finally sold that raggedy-ass house.* ■ (of a person) new and inexperienced.

raggle-taggle ▸ **adjective** untidy and scruffy.
– ORIGIN early 20th cent.: apparently a fanciful variant of **RAGTAG**.

raggy ▸ **adjective** (**raggier**, **raggiest**) informal ragged: *his raggy clothes.*
– ORIGIN late Old English, of Scandinavian origin.

raghead ▸ **noun** N. Amer. informal, offensive a person who wears a turban or keffiyeh (often used as a term of abuse for an Arab or Muslim).

ragi /ˈrɑːɡiː/ ▸ **noun** [mass noun] chiefly Indian another term for **FINGER MILLET** (see **MILLET**).
– ORIGIN from Sanskrit and Hindi *rāgī*, from Telugu.

raging ▸ **adjective** showing rage: *a raging bull.* ■ continuing with overpowering force; very powerful: *the stream could become a raging torrent in wet weather.* ■ informal tremendous: *he had been a raging success in Spain.*

ragini /ˈrɑːɡəni, ˈrʌɡəni/ ▸ **noun** (pl. **raginis** /ˈrɑːɡəniz, ˈrʌɡəniz/) (in Indian classical music) a derivative melody related to a raga.
– ORIGIN Sanskrit *rāgiṇī*, literally 'coloured, impassioned'; compare with **RAGA**.

raglan ▸ **adjective** having or denoting sleeves that continue in one piece up to the neck of a garment, without a shoulder seam.
▸ **noun** an overcoat with raglan sleeves.
– ORIGIN mid 19th cent.: named after Lord *Raglan* (1788–1855), a British commander in the Crimean War.

ragman ▸ **noun** (pl. **ragmen**) a person who collects or deals in rags, old clothes, and other items.

Ragnarök /ˈraɡnərɒk/ Scandinavian Mythology the final battle between the gods and the powers of evil, the Scandinavian equivalent of the *Götterdämmerung*.
– ORIGIN from Old Norse *ragnarǫkr* 'twilight of the gods'.

ragout /raˈɡuː/ ▸ **noun** a highly seasoned dish of small pieces of meat stewed with vegetables.
– ORIGIN from French *ragoût*, from *ragoûter* 'revive the taste of'.

rag paper ▸ **noun** [mass noun] paper made from cotton, originally from cotton rags, but now from cotton linters.

ragpicker ▸ **noun** a person who collects and sells rags.

rag-roll ▸ **verb** [with obj.] create a striped or marbled effect on (a surface) by painting it with a rag crumpled up into a roll.
– DERIVATIVES **rag-rolled** adjective, **rag-rolling** noun.

rag rug ▸ **noun** a rug made from small strips of fabric hooked into or pushed through a base material such as hessian.

ragstone ▸ **noun** see **RAG**[3] (sense 2).

ragtag ▸ **adjective** [attrib.] untidy, disorganized, or incongruously varied in character: *a ragtag group of idealists.*
▸ **noun** (also **ragtag and bobtail**) [in sing.] a disreputable or disorganized group of people.
– ORIGIN early 19th cent.: superseding earlier *tag-rag* and *tag and rag* (see **RAG**[1], **TAG**[1]).

ragtime ▸ **noun** [mass noun] a kind of music evolved by black American musicians in the 1890s and played especially on the piano, characterized by a syncopated melodic line and regularly accented accompaniment.
▸ **adjective** informal, dated disorderly; disreputable: *a ragtime army.*
– ORIGIN probably from **RAG**[4] (from the syncopation) + **TIME**.

ragtop ▸ **noun** informal a car with a convertible roof.

rag trade ▸ **noun** (**the rag trade**) informal the clothing or fashion industry.

raguly /ˈraɡjʊli/ ▸ **adjective** [usu. postpositive] Heraldry having an edge with oblique notches like a row of sawn-off branches.
– ORIGIN mid 17th cent.: perhaps from **RAGGED**, on the pattern of *nebuly*.

Ragusa /raˈɡuːzə/ Italian name (until 1918) for **DUBROVNIK**.

ragweed ▸ **noun** [mass noun] a North American plant of the daisy family. Its tiny green flowers produce copious amounts of pollen, making it a major causative agent of hay fever in some areas. ● *Ambrosia artemisia*, family Compositae.

ragworm ▸ **noun** a predatory marine bristle worm which is frequently used as bait by fishermen. ● Family Nereidae: several genera and species, especially *Nereis diversicolor*.

ragwort ▸ **noun** a yellow-flowered ragged-leaved European plant of the daisy family, which is a common weed of grazing land and is toxic to livestock. ● Genus *Senecio*, family Compositae: several species, in particular *S. jacobaea*.

rah informal ▸ **exclamation** chiefly N. Amer. a cheer of encouragement or approval.
▸ **noun** Brit. an upper-class person.
– ORIGIN late 19th cent.: shortening of **HURRAH**.

Rahman see **ABDUL RAHMAN**, **MUJIBUR RAHMAN**.

rah-rah N. Amer. informal ▸ **adjective** marked by great or uncritical enthusiasm or excitement: *many players were turned off by his rah-rah style.*
▸ **noun** [mass noun] great or uncritical enthusiasm and excitement.
– ORIGIN early 20th cent.: reduplication of **RAH**.

rah-rah skirt ▸ **noun** a short skirt with layered flounces, of a kind typically worn by cheerleaders.

rai /rʌɪ/ ▸ **noun** [mass noun] a style of music fusing Arabic and Algerian folk elements with Western rock.
– ORIGIN 1980s: perhaps from Arabic *ha er-ray*, literally 'that's the thinking, here is the view', a phrase frequently found in the songs.

RAID ▸ **abbreviation** Computing redundant array of independent (or inexpensive) disks, a system for providing greater capacity, faster access, and security against data corruption by spreading data across several disk drives.

raid ▸ **noun** a rapid surprise attack on an enemy by troops, aircraft, or other armed forces: *a bombing raid.* ■ a rapid surprise attack to commit a crime, especially to steal from business premises: *an early morning **raid on** a bank.* ■ a surprise visit by police to arrest suspects or seize illicit goods. ■ Stock Exchange a hostile attempt to buy a major or controlling interest in the shares of a company.
▸ **verb** [with obj.] conduct a raid on: *officers raided thirty homes yesterday.* ■ quickly and illicitly take something from (a place): *she crept downstairs to raid the larder.*
– ORIGIN late Middle English (as a noun): Scots variant of **ROAD** in the early senses 'journey on horseback', 'foray'. The noun became rare from the end of the 16th cent. but was revived by Sir Walter Scott; the verb dates from the mid 19th cent.

raider ▸ **noun** a person who attacks an enemy in their territory; a marauder: *Scandinavian raiders put down their roots in Cumbria.* ■ a person who attacks business premises in order to steal: *masked raiders burst into the 100-seater restaurant.*

rail[1] /reɪl/ ▸ **noun** **1** a bar or series of bars fixed on upright supports or attached to a wall or ceiling, serving as part of a barrier or used to hang things on: *a curtain rail.* ■ (**the rails**) the inside boundary fence of a racecourse.
2 a steel bar or continuous line of bars laid on the ground as one of a pair forming a railway track: *the goods train left the rails.* ■ [mass noun] [often as modifier] railways as a means of transport: *rail fares* | *travelling by rail.*
3 a horizontal piece in the frame of a panelled door or sash window. Compare with **STILE**[2].
4 the edge of a surfboard or sailboard.
5 Electronics a conductor which is maintained at a fixed potential and to which other parts of a circuit are connected.
▸ **verb** **1** [with obj.] provide or enclose (a space or place) with a rail or rails: *the altar is **railed off from** the nave.*
2 [with obj. and adverbial of direction] convey (goods) by rail: *perishables were railed into Manhattan.*
3 [no obj.] (in windsurfing) sail the board on its edge.
– PHRASES **go off the rails** informal begin behaving in an uncontrolled or unacceptable way. **on the rails** **1** informal behaving or functioning in a normal or regulated way: *he is determined to get the club back **on the rails**.* **2** (of a racehorse or jockey) in a position on the racetrack nearest the inside fence.
– DERIVATIVES **railage** noun, **railless** adjective.
– ORIGIN Middle English: from Old French *reille* 'iron rod', from Latin *regula* 'straight stick, rule'.

rail[2] ▸ **verb** [no obj.] (**rail against/at/about**) complain or protest strongly and persistently about: *he railed at human fickleness.*
– DERIVATIVES **railer** noun.
– ORIGIN late Middle English: from French *railler*, from Provençal *ralhar* 'to jest', based on an alteration of Latin *rugire* 'to bellow'.

rail[3] ▸ **noun** a secretive bird with drab grey and brown plumage, typically having a long bill and found in dense waterside vegetation. ● Family Rallidae (the **rail family**): several genera, especially *Rallus*, and numerous species. The rail family also includes the crakes, gallinules, moorhens, and coots.
– ORIGIN late Middle English: from Old Northern French *raille*, perhaps of imitative origin.

rail-babbler ▸ **noun** a long-tailed songbird of the logrunner family, with bold blue, red-brown, and white plumage, found mainly in the forests of New Guinea. ● Genus *Ptilorrhoa* (and *Eupetes*), family Orthonychidae: four species.

railbird ▸ **noun** N. Amer. a spectator at a horse race, especially one who watches from the railings along the track.

railbus ▸ **noun** a lightweight diesel or petrol-driven railway passenger vehicle, typically with four wheels.

railcar ▸ **noun** Brit. a powered railway passenger vehicle designed to operate singly or as part of a multiple unit. ■ (**rail car**) N. Amer. any railway carriage or wagon.

railcard ▸ **noun** Brit. a pass entitling the holder to reduced rail fares on off-peak trains.

rail fence ▸ **noun** chiefly N. Amer. a fence, typically a wooden one, made of posts and rails.

R

railhead ▸ noun a point on a railway from which roads and other transport routes begin. ■ the furthest point reached in constructing a railway.

railing ▸ noun (usu. **railings**) a fence or barrier made of rails.

raillery /ˈreɪləri/ ▸ noun [mass noun] good-humoured teasing.
– ORIGIN mid 17th cent.: from French *raillerie*, from *railler* 'to rail' (see RAIL[2]).

railman ▸ noun (pl. **railmen**) another term for RAILWAYMAN.

railroad ▸ noun North American term for RAILWAY.
▸ verb **1** [with obj.] informal rush or coerce (someone) into doing something: *she hesitated, unwilling to be* ***railroaded into*** *a decision.* ■ cause (a measure) to be passed or approved quickly by applying pressure: *the Bill had been* ***railroaded through*** *the House.* ■ N. Amer. send (someone) to prison without a fair trial.
2 [no obj.] (usu. as noun **railroading**) N. Amer. travel or work on the railways.

railway ▸ noun Brit. **1** a track made of steel rails along which trains run: [as modifier] *a railway line* | *a railway station.* ■ a set of tracks for other vehicles.
2 a network of tracks with the trains, organization, and personnel required for its working: *the carriage of freight on the railways.*

railwayman ▸ noun (pl. **railwaymen**) Brit. a man who works on a railway.

raiment /ˈreɪm(ə)nt/ ▸ noun [mass noun] (also **raiments**) archaic or literary clothing: *ladies clothed in raiment bedecked with jewels.*
– ORIGIN late Middle English: shortening of obsolete *arrayment* 'dress, outfit'.

rain ▸ noun [mass noun] the condensed moisture of the atmosphere falling visibly in separate drops: *the rain had not stopped for days* | *it's pouring with rain.* ■ (**rains**) falls of rain: *the plants were washed away by unusually heavy rains.* ■ [in sing.] a large or overwhelming quantity of things that fall or descend: *he fell under the* ***rain of*** *blows.*
▸ verb [no obj.] (**it rains, it is raining**, etc.) rain falls: *it was beginning to rain.* ■ literary (of the sky, the clouds, etc.) send down rain. ■ [with adverbial of direction] fall or cause to fall in large or overwhelming quantities: [no obj.] *bombs rained down* | [with obj.] *she rained blows on to him.* ■ [with obj.] (**it rains ——, it is raining ——**, etc.) used to convey that a specified thing is falling in large quantities: *it was just raining glass.*
– PHRASES **be as right as rain** be perfectly fit and well. **it never rains but it pours** see POUR. **rain cats and dogs** rain very hard. [origin uncertain; first recorded in 1738, used by Jonathan Swift, but the phrase *rain dogs and polecats* was used a century earlier in Richard Brome's *The City Witt.*] **rain on someone's parade** informal prevent someone from enjoying an event; spoil someone's plans. **(come) rain or shine** whether it rains or not; whatever the weather: *he runs six miles every morning, rain or shine.*
– PHRASAL VERBS **be rained off** (or N. Amer. **out**) (of an event) be cancelled or terminated because of rain: *the match was rained off.*
– DERIVATIVES **rainless** adjective.
– ORIGIN Old English *regn* (noun), *regnian* (verb), of Germanic origin; related to Dutch *regen* and German *Regen*.

rainbird ▸ noun a bird that is said to foretell rain by its call, especially (in Britain) the green woodpecker or (in South Africa) a kind of coucal.

rainbow ▸ noun an arch of colours visible in the sky, caused by the refraction and dispersion of the sun's light by rain or other water droplets in the atmosphere. The colours of the rainbow are generally said to be red, orange, yellow, green, blue, indigo, and violet. ■ a display of the colours of the spectrum produced by dispersion of light. ■ a wide range of related and typically colourful things: ***a rainbow of*** *medals decorated his chest.* ■ [as modifier] many-coloured: *a big rainbow packet of felt pens.*
– PHRASES **at the end of the rainbow** used to refer to something much sought after but impossible to attain. [with allusion to the story of a crock of gold supposedly to be found by anyone reaching the end of a rainbow.] **chase rainbows** (or **a rainbow**) pursue an illusory goal.
– ORIGIN Old English *regnboga* (see RAIN, BOW[1]).

Rainbow Bridge a bridge of natural rock, the world's largest natural bridge, situated in southern Utah, just north of the border with Arizona. Its span is 86 m (278 ft).

rainbow coalition ▸ noun (especially in the US) a political alliance of several different groups, representing social, ethnic, and other minorities.

rainbowfish ▸ noun (pl. **same** or **rainbowfishes**) any of a number of small brightly coloured fish of warm waters, in particular: ● an Australian freshwater fish (genus *Melanotaenia*, family Melanotaenidae). ● (**Celebes rainbowfish**) a freshwater fish native to Sulawesi and popular in aquaria (*Telmatherina ladigesi*, family Atherinidae).

rainbow lorikeet (also **rainbow lory**) ▸ noun a small vividly coloured Australasian parrot, found in many different races on SW Pacific islands. ● *Trichoglossus haematodus*, family Loridae (or Psittacidae).

rainbow runner ▸ noun a colourfully striped fish of the jack family, of warm seas worldwide. ● *Elagatis bipinnulata*, family Carangidae.

rainbow trout ▸ noun a large, partly migratory trout native to the Pacific seaboard of North America. It has been widely introduced elsewhere, both as a farmed food fish and as a sporting fish. ● *Onchorhynchus mykiss*, family Salmonidae.

rain check ▸ noun N. Amer. **1** a ticket given for later use when a sporting fixture or other outdoor event is interrupted or postponed by rain.
2 a coupon issued to a customer by a shop, guaranteeing that a sale item which is out of stock may be purchased by that customer at a later date at the same reduced price.
– PHRASES **take a rain check** used to refuse an offer politely, with the implication that one may take it up at a later date.

raincoat ▸ noun a long coat, typically having a belt, made from waterproofed or water-resistant fabric.

rain dance ▸ noun a ritual dance to summon rain, as practised by some Pueblo Indians and other peoples.

raindrop ▸ noun a single drop of rain.
– ORIGIN Old English *regndropa* (see RAIN, DROP).

rainfall ▸ noun [mass noun] the fall of rain. ■ the quantity of rain falling within a given area in a given time: *low rainfall.*

rainfast ▸ adjective (of a chemical spray or other substance) not able to be washed away by rain.

rainfly ▸ noun (pl. **rainflies**) **1** N. Amer. the flysheet of a tent.
2 W. Indian a winged ant or termite, seen in numbers after rain.

rainforest ▸ noun a luxuriant, dense forest rich in biodiversity, found typically in tropical areas with consistently heavy rainfall.

rain gauge ▸ noun a device for collecting and measuring the amount of rain which falls.

Rainier, Mount /rəˈnɪə, ˈreɪnɪə/ a volcanic peak in the south-west of Washington State in the US. Rising to a height of 4,395 m (14,410 ft), it is the highest peak in the Cascade Range.

rainmaker ▸ noun **1** a person who attempts to cause rain to fall, either by rituals or by a scientific technique such as seeding clouds with crystals.
2 N. Amer. informal a person who generates income for a business or organization by brokering deals or attracting clients or funds.
– DERIVATIVES **rainmaking** noun.

rainout ▸ noun N. Amer. a cancellation or premature ending of an event because of rain.

rainproof ▸ adjective (especially of a building or garment) impervious to rain: *a rainproof coat.*

rain scald ▸ noun [mass noun] a skin disease of horses caused by infection with actinomycete bacteria, typically contracted in persistently rainy conditions.

rain shadow ▸ noun a region having little rainfall because it is sheltered from prevailing rain-bearing winds by a range of hills.

rain stick ▸ noun a ceremonial instrument originating in the Andes, consisting of a hollow branch sealed at both ends and containing small hard objects such as seeds or pebbles, which make a noise like falling rain when the branch is tilted.

rainstorm ▸ noun a storm with heavy rain.

rainswept ▸ adjective exposed to or frequently experiencing rain and wind: *the rainswept quayside.*

rain tree ▸ noun a large tropical American tree which is widely planted as a street tree. It has grooved bark which typically supports epiphytic plants, and 'rain' is excreted by cicadas that live in the tree. ● *Albizia saman*, family Leguminosae.

rainwash ▸ noun [mass noun] the washing away of soil or other loose material by rain.

rainwater ▸ noun [mass noun] water that has fallen as or been obtained from rain.

rainwear ▸ noun [mass noun] waterproof or water-resistant clothes suitable for wearing in the rain.

rainworm ▸ noun **1** the earthworm, which often comes to the surface after rain.
2 a soil-dwelling nematode worm, the juveniles of which parasitize grasshoppers. ● *Mermis nigrescens*, class Aphasmida (or Adenophorea).

rainy ▸ adjective (**rainier, rainiest**) (of weather, a period, or an area) having or characterized by considerable rainfall: *a rainy afternoon.*
– PHRASES **a rainy day** used in reference to a possible time in the future when money will be needed: *putting money by for a rainy day.*
– DERIVATIVES **raininess** noun.
– ORIGIN Old English *rēnig* (see RAIN, -Y[1]).

Raipur /rʌɪˈpʊə/ a city in central India, capital of the state of Chhattisgarh; pop. 759,600 (est. 2009).

raise ▸ verb [with obj.] **1** lift or move to a higher position or level: *she raised both arms above her head* | *his flag was raised over the city.* ■ lift or move to a vertical position; set upright: *Melody managed to raise him to his feet.* ■ construct or build (a structure): *a fence was being raised around the property.* ■ cause to rise or form: *the galloping horse raised a cloud of dust.* ■ bring to the surface (a ship that has sunk). ■ cause (bread) to rise, especially by the action of yeast.
2 increase the amount, level, or strength of: *the bank raised interest rates* | *the need to raise the quality of education* | *he had to raise his voice to make himself heard.* ■ promote (someone) to a higher rank: *the king* ***raised*** *him* ***to*** *the title of Count Torre Bella.* ■ (**raise something to**) Mathematics multiply a quantity to (a specified power): *3 raised to the 7th power is 2,187.* ■ [with two objs] (in poker or brag) bet (a specified amount) more than (another player): *I'll raise you another hundred dollars.* ■ Bridge make a higher bid in the same suit as that bid by (one's partner).
3 cause to occur or to be considered: *the alarm was raised when he failed to return home* | *universities are meant to raise doubts about every axiom.*
4 collect, levy, or bring together (money or resources): *it is hoped that the event will raise £50,000.* ■ generate (an invoice or other document).
5 bring up (a child): *he was born and raised in San Francisco.* ■ breed or grow (animals or plants): *they raised pigs and kept a pony.*
6 bring (someone) back from death: *God* ***raised*** *Jesus* ***from the dead.*** ■ cause (a ghost or spirit) to appear.
7 abandon or force an enemy to abandon (a siege, blockade, or embargo). ■ drive (an animal) from its lair: *the rabbit was only 250 yards from where he first raised it.*
8 (of someone at sea) come in sight of (land or another ship): *they raised the low coast by evening.* ■ Brit. informal establish contact with (someone) by telephone or radio: *I raised him on the open line.*
9 Medicine stimulate production of (an antiserum, antibody, or other biologically active substance) against the appropriate target cell or substance.
▸ noun **1** N. Amer. an increase in salary: *he wants a raise and some perks.*
2 (in poker or brag) an increase in a stake. ■ Bridge a higher bid in the suit that one's partner has bid.
3 [usu. with adj. or noun modifier] Weightlifting an act of lifting or raising a part of the body while holding a weight: *bent-over raises.*
– PHRASES **raise Cain** see CAIN. **raise the devil** informal make a noisy disturbance. **raise one's eyebrows** see EYEBROW. **raise one's glass** drink a toast: *I* ***raised my glass*** *to Susan.* **raise one's hand** strike or seem to be about to strike someone: *she* ***raised her hand to*** *me.* **raise one's hat** briefly remove one's hat as a gesture of courtesy or respect to someone. **raise hell** informal make a noisy disturbance. ■ complain vociferously: *he raised hell with polluters.* **raise hob** see HOB[2]. **raise a laugh** make people laugh. **raise the roof** make a great deal of noise, especially through cheering: *when I finally scored the fans raised the roof.*
– DERIVATIVES **raisable** adjective, **raiser** noun.
– ORIGIN Middle English: from Old Norse *reisa*; related to the verb REAR[2].

raised ▸ adjective **1** elevated to a higher position or level; lifted: *the lord and his family ate on a raised platform at one end of the hall.* ■ embossed; in relief: *the building features raised lettering.* ■ (of pastry) standing without support.

2 more intense or strong than usual; higher: *a neighbour heard raised voices from the other's flat | as we age we are more likely to have raised blood pressure.*

raised beach ▶ noun Geology a former beach now lying above water level owing to geological changes since its formation.

raised bog ▶ noun a peat bog in which growth is most rapid at the centre, giving it a domed shape.

raisin ▶ noun a partially dried grape.
– DERIVATIVES **raisiny** adjective.
– ORIGIN Middle English: from Old French, 'grape', from an alteration of Latin *racemus* 'grape bunch'.

raison d'état /ˌreɪzɒ̃ deɪˈtɑː/, French /ʀɛzɔ̃ deta/ ▶ noun (pl. **raisons d'état** pronunc. **same**) a purely political reason for action on the part of a ruler or government, especially where a departure from openness, justice, or honesty is involved.
– ORIGIN French, literally 'reason of state'.

raison d'être /ˌreɪzɒ̃ ˈdɛtrə/, French /ʀɛzɔ̃ dɛtʀ/ ▶ noun (pl. **raisons d'être** pronunc. **same**) the most important reason or purpose for someone or something's existence: *seeking to shock is the catwalk's raison d'être.*
– ORIGIN French, literally 'reason for being'.

raita /ˈrʌɪtə/ ▶ noun [mass noun] an Indian side dish of yogurt containing chopped cucumber or other vegetables, and spices.
– ORIGIN from Hindi *rāytā*.

Raj /rɑː(d)ʒ/ ▶ noun (**the Raj**) historical British sovereignty in India: *the last days of the Raj.* ■ (**raj**) [mass noun] Indian rule; government
– ORIGIN from Hindi *rāj* 'reign'.

raja /ˈrɑːdʒɑː/ (also **rajah**) ▶ noun historical an Indian king or prince. ■ a title extended to minor dignitaries and nobles in India during the British Raj. ■ a title extended by the British to a Malay or Javanese ruler or chief.
– ORIGIN from Hindi *rājā*, Sanskrit *rājan* 'king'.

Rajasthan /ˌrɑːdʒəˈstɑːn/ a state in western India, on the Pakistani border; capital, Jaipur. The western part of the state consists largely of the Thar Desert.
– DERIVATIVES **Rajasthani** noun & adjective.

Rajasthan Canal former name for **INDIRA GANDHI CANAL**.

raja yoga ▶ noun [mass noun] a form of yoga intended to achieve control over the mind and emotions.
– ORIGIN from Sanskrit, from *rājan* 'king' + **YOGA**.

Rajkot /rɑːdʒˈkəʊt/ a city in Gujarat, western India; pop. 1,395,000 (est. 2009).

Rajput /ˈrɑːdʒpʊt/ ▶ noun a member of a Hindu military caste claiming Kshatriya descent.
– ORIGIN from Hindi *rājpūt*, from Sanskrit *rājan* 'king' + *putra* 'son'.

Rajputana /ˌrɑːdʒpʊˈtɑːnə/ an ancient region of India consisting of a collection of princely states ruled by dynasties. Following independence from Britain in 1947, they united to form the state of Rajasthan, parts also being incorporated into Gujarat and Madhya Pradesh.

Rajshahi /rɑːdʒˈʃɑːhi/ a port on the Ganges River in western Bangladesh; pop. 472,775 (2008).

Rajya Sabha /ˌrɑːdʒjə sʌˈbɑː/ the upper house of the Indian parliament. Compare with **LOK SABHA**.
– ORIGIN from Sanskrit *rājya* 'State' + *sabhā* 'council'.

rake[1] ▶ noun an implement consisting of a pole with a toothed crossbar or fine tines at the end, used especially for drawing together cut grass or smoothing loose soil or gravel. ■ an implement similar to a rake used for other purposes, e.g. by a croupier drawing in money at a gaming table. ■ [in sing.] an act of raking: *giving the lawn a rake.*
▶ verb [with obj.] **1** gather together with a rake or similar implement: *they started* **raking up** *hay.* ■ make (ground) smooth with a rake: *I sometimes* **rake over** *the allotment.*
2 scratch or scrape (something, especially a person's flesh) with a long sweeping movement: *her fingers raked Bill's face.* ■ [with obj. and adverbial of direction] draw or drag (something) through something with a sweeping movement: *she raked a comb through her hair.* ■ sweep (something) from end to end with gunfire, a look, or a beam of light: *the road was raked with machine-gun fire.* ■ [no obj., with adverbial of direction] move across something with a long sweeping movement: *his icy gaze raked mercilessly over Lissa's slender figure.* ■ [no obj., with adverbial] search or rummage through something: *he raked through his pockets and brought out a five-pound note.*
– PHRASES **rake and scrape** black English be extremely thrifty; scrimp and save. **rake over (old) coals** (or **rake over the ashes**) chiefly Brit. revive the memory of an incident which is best forgotten. **(as) thin as a rake** (of a person) very thin.
– PHRASAL VERBS **rake something in** informal make a lot of money: *the shop's raking it in now.* **rake something up/over** revive the memory of an incident or period that is best forgotten: *I have no desire to rake over the past.*
– DERIVATIVES **raker** noun.
– ORIGIN Old English *raca, racu*, of Germanic origin; related to Dutch *raak* and German *Rechen*, from a base meaning 'heap up'; the verb is partly from Old Norse *raka* 'to scrape, shave'.

rake[2] ▶ noun a fashionable or wealthy man of dissolute or promiscuous habits.
– PHRASES **a rake's progress** a progressive deterioration, especially through self-indulgence. [from the title of a series of engravings by Hogarth (1735).]
– ORIGIN mid 17th cent.: abbreviation of archaic *rakehell* in the same sense.

rake[3] ▶ verb [with obj.] set (something) at a sloping angle: *the floor is steeply raked.* ■ [no obj.] (of a ship's mast or funnel) incline from the perpendicular towards the stern. ■ [no obj.] (of a ship's bow or stern) project at its upper part beyond the keel.
▶ noun **1** [in sing.] the angle at which a thing slopes.
2 the angle of the edge or face of a cutting tool.
– ORIGIN early 17th cent.: probably related to German *ragen* 'to project', of unknown ultimate origin; compare with Swedish *raka*.

rake[4] ▶ noun Brit. a number of railway carriages or wagons coupled together.
– ORIGIN early 20th cent. (originally Scots and northern English): from Old Norse *rák* 'stripe, streak', from an alteration of *rek-* 'to drive'. The word was in earlier use in the senses 'path, groove' and 'vein of ore'.

rake-off ▶ noun informal a commission or share of the profits from a deal, especially one that is disreputable.

rakhi /ˈrɑːki/ ▶ noun (pl. **rakhis**) a cotton bracelet, typically bearing elaborate ornamentation, given at Raksha Bandhan by a girl or woman to a brother or someone she considers as one, who must then treat her as a sister.
– ORIGIN from Hindi *rākhī*.

raki /rəˈkiː, ˈraki/ ▶ noun [mass noun] a strong alcoholic spirit made in eastern Europe or the Middle East.
– ORIGIN from Turkish *rakı*.

raking light ▶ noun [mass noun] (in art or photography) bright light, usually beamed obliquely, used to reveal such features as texture and detail.

rakish[1] ▶ adjective having or displaying a dashing, jaunty, or slightly disreputable quality or appearance: *he had a rakish, debonair look.*
– DERIVATIVES **rakishly** adverb, **rakishness** noun.
– ORIGIN early 18th cent.: from **RAKE[2]** + **-ISH[1]**.

rakish[2] ▶ adjective (especially of a boat or car) smart and fast-looking, with streamlined angles and curves.
– ORIGIN early 19th cent.: from **RAKE[3]** + **-ISH[1]**.

Rákosi /ˈrɑːkɒʃi/, Mátyás (1892–1971), Hungarian Communist statesman, First Secretary of the Hungarian Socialist Workers' Party 1945–56 and Prime Minister 1952–3 and 1955–6. After the Communist seizure of power in 1945 he did much to establish a firmly Stalinist regime. He was ousted as Premier by the more liberal Imre Nagy in 1953.

Raksha Bandhan /ˌrʌkʃɑː ˈbʌnd(ə)n/ ▶ noun (in South Asia) a popular annual festival, usually in August, during which a girl or woman gives a cotton bracelet (rakhi) to a brother or someone she considers as one, who in turn treats her as a sister.

raku /ˈrɑːkuː/ ▶ noun [mass noun] [usu. as modifier] a kind of lead-glazed Japanese earthenware, used especially for the tea ceremony.
– ORIGIN Japanese, literally 'enjoyment'.

rakyat /ˈrɑːkjɑːt/ ▶ noun (in South East Asia) the ordinary people, especially when considered in relation to the government.
– ORIGIN Malay, from Arabic *raʿiyya* 'herd at pasture, subjects of a shepherd or king'.

rale /rɑːl/ ▶ noun (usu. **rales**) Medicine an abnormal rattling sound heard when examining unhealthy lungs with a stethoscope.
– ORIGIN early 19th cent.: from French *râle*, from *râler* 'to rattle'.

Raleigh[1] /ˈrɑːli/ the state capital of North Carolina; pop. 392,552 (est. 2008).

Raleigh[2] /ˈrɑːli, ˈrɔːli/ (also **Ralegh**), Sir Walter (*c.*1552–1618), English explorer, courtier, and writer. A favourite of Elizabeth I, he organized several voyages of exploration and colonization to the Americas, and introduced potato and tobacco plants to England. Imprisoned in 1603 by James I on a charge of conspiracy, he was released in 1616 to lead an expedition in search of El Dorado, but was executed on the original charge when he returned empty-handed.

rall. ▶ abbreviation Music rallentando.

rallentando /ˌralənˈtandəʊ/ Music ▶ adverb & adjective (especially as a direction) with a gradual decrease of speed.
▶ noun (pl. **rallentandos** or **rallentandi** /-di/) a gradual decrease in speed.
– ORIGIN Italian, literally 'slowing down', from the verb *rallentare*.

ralli car (also **ralli cart**) ▶ noun Brit. historical a light two-wheeled horse-drawn vehicle for four people.
– ORIGIN late 19th cent.: from *Ralli*, the name of the first purchaser of such a vehicle.

rally[1] ▶ verb (**rallies, rallying, rallied**) [no obj.] **1** (of troops) come together again in order to continue fighting after a defeat or dispersion: *De Montfort's troops rallied and drove back the king's infantry.* ■ [with obj.] bring together (forces) again in order to continue fighting. ■ assemble in a mass meeting: *up to 50,000 people rallied in the city centre.* ■ bring or come together in order to support a person or cause: [no obj., with infinitive] *colleagues* **rallied round** *to help Ann* | [with obj.] *a series of meetings to rally support for the union.*
2 recover or cause to recover in health, spirits, or poise: [no obj.] *he floundered for a moment, then rallied again* | [with obj.] *they rallied her with a drink.* ■ (of share, currency, or commodity prices) increase after a fall: *prices of metals have rallied.*
3 drive in a rally.
▶ noun (pl. **rallies**) **1** a mass meeting of people making a political protest or showing support for a cause: *a banned nationalist rally.* ■ an open-air event for people who own a particular kind of vehicle: *a traction engine rally.*
2 a long-distance race for motor vehicles over public roads or rough terrain, typically in several stages: [as modifier] *a rally driver.*
3 a quick or marked recovery after a decline: *the market staged a late rally.*
4 (in tennis and other racket sports) an extended exchange of strokes between players.
– DERIVATIVES **rallier** noun, **rallyist** noun (sense 2 of the noun).
– ORIGIN early 17th cent. (in the sense 'bring together again'): from French *rallier*, from *re-* 'again' + *allier* 'to ally'.

rally[2] ▶ verb (**rallies, rallying, rallied**) [with obj.] archaic subject (someone) to good-humoured ridicule; tease: *he rallied her on the length of her pigtail.*
– ORIGIN mid 17th cent.: from French *railler* 'to rib, tease' (see **RAIL[2]**).

rallycross ▶ noun [mass noun] Brit. a form of motor racing in which cars are driven in heats over a course including rough terrain and made roads, but not public roads. Compare with **AUTOCROSS**.

R

rallying ▶ noun [mass noun] **1** the action or process of coming together to support a person or cause.
2 the sport or action of participating in a motor rally: *established names in international rallying.*
▶ adjective having the effect of calling people to action: *a rallying cry.*

ralph /ralf/ ▶ verb [no obj.] informal, chiefly N. Amer. vomit.
– ORIGIN 1960s: origin uncertain; apparently a use of the male given name *Ralph*, but perhaps imitative.

RAM ▶ abbreviation ■ Computing random-access memory. ■ (in the UK) Royal Academy of Music.

ram ▶ noun **1** an uncastrated male sheep. ■ (**the Ram**) the zodiacal sign or constellation Aries.
2 a battering ram. ■ historical a beak or other projecting part of the bow of a warship, for piercing the sides of other ships.
3 the falling weight of a piledriving machine.
4 a hydraulic water-raising or lifting machine. ■ the piston of a hydrostatic press.
▶ verb (**rams, ramming, rammed**) [with obj. and adverbial of direction] **1** roughly force (something) into place: *he rammed his stick into the ground.* ■ [with obj.] (of a vehicle or vessel) be driven violently into (another vehicle or vessel) in an attempt to stop or damage it: *their boat was rammed by a Japanese warship.* ■ [no obj., with adverbial] crash violently against something: *the stolen car rammed into the front of the house.* ■ [with obj.] (often as adj. **rammed**) beat (earth) with a heavy implement to make it hard and firm.

2 (**be rammed**) Brit. informal (of a place) be very crowded: *the club is rammed to the rafters every week.*
– PHRASES **ram something down someone's throat** see THROAT. **ram something home** see HOME.
– DERIVATIVES **rammer** noun.
– ORIGIN Old English *ram(m)*, of Germanic origin; related to Dutch *ram*.

Rama /ˈrɑːmə/ the hero of the Ramayana, husband of Sita. He is the Hindu model of the ideal man, the seventh incarnation of Vishnu, and is widely venerated, by some sects as the supreme god.

ramada /rəˈmɑːdə/ ▶ **noun** US an arbour or porch.
– ORIGIN mid 19th cent.: from Spanish.

Ramadan /ˈramədan, ˌraməˈdan/ (also **Ramadhan** /-zan/) ▶ **noun** the ninth month of the Muslim year, during which strict fasting is observed from dawn to sunset.
– ORIGIN from Arabic *ramaḍān*, from *ramaḍa* 'be hot'. The lunar reckoning of the Muslim calendar brings the fast eleven days earlier each year, eventually causing Ramadan to occur in any season; originally it was supposed to be in one of the hot months.

ram air ▶ **noun** [mass noun] technical air which is forced to enter a moving aperture, such as the air intake of an aircraft.

Ramakrishna /ˌrɑːməˈkrɪʃnə/ (1836–86), Indian yogi and mystic; born *Gadadhar Chatterjee*. He condemned lust, money, and the caste system, preaching that all religions leading to the attainment of mystical experience are equally good and true.

Raman /ˈrɑːmən/, Sir Chandrasekhara Venkata (1888–1970), Indian physicist. He discovered the Raman effect, one of the most important proofs of the quantum theory of light. Nobel Prize for Physics (1930).

Raman effect ▶ **noun** [mass noun] Physics a change of wavelength exhibited by some of the radiation scattered in a medium. The effect is specific to the molecules which cause it, and so can be used in spectroscopic analysis. Compare with RAYLEIGH SCATTERING.

Ramapithecus /ˌrɑːməˈpɪθɪkəs/ ▶ **noun** a fossil anthropoid ape of the Miocene epoch, known from remains found in SW Asia and East Africa, and probably ancestral to the orang-utan. ● Genus *Ramapithecus*, family Pongidae.
– ORIGIN modern Latin, from RAMA + Greek *pithēkos* 'ape'.

Ramayana /rɑːˈmɑːjʌnə/ one of the two great Sanskrit epics of the Hindus, composed *c.*300 BC. It describes how Rama, aided by his brother and the monkey Hanuman, rescued his wife Sita from Ravana, the ten-headed demon king of Lanka.
– ORIGIN Sanskrit, literally 'exploits of Rama'.

Rambert /ˈrɒmbɛː/, Dame Marie (1888–1982), British ballet dancer, teacher, and director, born in Poland; born *Cyvia Rambam*. After moving to London in 1917 she formed and directed the Ballet Club, which became known as the Ballet Rambert in 1935.

R

ramble ▶ **verb** [no obj.] **1** walk for pleasure in the countryside.
2 talk or write at length in a confused or inconsequential way: *Willy* ***rambled on*** *about Norman archways.*
3 (of a plant) put out long shoots and grow over walls or other plants.
▶ **noun** a walk taken for pleasure in the countryside.
– ORIGIN late Middle English (in sense 2 of the verb): probably related to Middle Dutch *rammelen*, used of animals in the sense 'wander about on heat', also to the noun RAM.

rambler ▶ **noun 1** a person who walks in the countryside for pleasure.
2 a straggling or climbing rose.

rambling ▶ **adjective 1** (of writing or speech) lengthy and confused or inconsequential.
2 (of a plant) putting out long shoots and growing over walls or other plants: *rambling roses.* ■ (of a building or path) spreading or winding irregularly in various directions: *a big old rambling house.*
▶ **noun** [mass noun] the activity of walking in the countryside for pleasure: [as modifier] *a rambling club.*
– DERIVATIVES **ramblingly** adverb.

Rambo /ˈrambəʊ/ ▶ **noun** (pl. **Rambos**) an exceptionally tough, aggressive man.
– ORIGIN the name of the hero of David Morrell's novel *First Blood* (1972), popularized in the films *First Blood* (1982) and *Rambo: First Blood Part II* (1985).

rambunctious /ramˈbʌŋ(k)ʃəs/ ▶ **adjective** informal, chiefly N. Amer. uncontrollably exuberant; boisterous.
– DERIVATIVES **rambunctiously** adverb, **rambunctiousness** noun.
– ORIGIN mid 19th cent.: of unknown origin.

rambutan /ramˈb(j)uːt(ə)n/ ▶ **noun 1** a red, plum-sized tropical fruit with soft spines and a slightly acidic taste.
2 the Malaysian tree that bears the rambutan. ● *Nephelium lappaceum*, family Sapindaceae.
– ORIGIN early 18th cent.: from Malay *rambūtan*, from *rambut* 'hair', with allusion to the fruit's spines.

RAMC ▶ **abbreviation** (in the UK) Royal Army Medical Corps.

Rameau /ˈrɑːməʊ/, French /ʀamo/, Jean-Philippe (1683–1764), French composer, musical theorist, and organist. He is best known for his four volumes of harpsichord pieces (1706–41), which are noted for their bold harmonies and textural diversity.

ramekin /ˈramɪkɪn, ˈramkɪn/ (also **ramekin dish**) ▶ **noun** a small dish for baking and serving an individual portion of food. ■ a quantity of food served in a ramekin, in particular a small quantity of cheese baked with breadcrumbs, eggs, and seasoning.
– ORIGIN mid 17th cent.: from French *ramequin*, of Low German or Dutch origin; compare with obsolete Flemish *rameken* 'toasted bread'.

ramen /ˈrɑːmɛn/ ▶ **plural noun** (in oriental cuisine) quick-cooking noodles, typically served in a broth with meat and vegetables.
– ORIGIN Japanese, from Chinese *lā* 'to pull' + *miàn* 'noodles'.

Rameses /ˈramɪsiːz/ variant spelling of RAMSES.

ramie /ˈrami/ ▶ **noun** [mass noun] **1** a vegetable fibre noted for its length and toughness. ■ cloth woven from ramie.
2 the plant of the nettle family which yields ramie, native to tropical Asia. ● *Boehmeria nivea*, family Urticaceae.
– ORIGIN mid 19th cent.: from Malay *rami*.

ramification ▶ **noun** (usu. **ramifications**) a complex or unwelcome consequence of an action or event: *any change is bound to have legal ramifications.* ■ a subdivision of a complex structure or process: *an extended family with its ramifications of neighbouring in-laws.* ■ [mass noun] formal or technical the action of ramifying or the state of being ramified.
– ORIGIN mid 17th cent.: from French, from *ramifier* 'form branches' (see RAMIFY).

ramify /ˈramɪfʌɪ/ ▶ **verb** (**ramifies, ramifying, ramified**) [no obj.] formal or technical form branches or offshoots; branch out: *an elaborate system of canals was built, ramifying throughout the UK.* ■ [with obj.] (often as adj. **ramified**) cause to branch out: *a ramified genealogical network.*
– ORIGIN late Middle English: from Old French *ramifier*, from medieval Latin *ramificare*, from Latin *ramus* 'branch'.

Ramillies, Battle of /ˈramɪlɪz/, French /ʀamiji/ a battle in the War of the Spanish Succession which took place in 1706 near the village of Ramillies, north of Namur, in Belgium. The British army under General Marlborough defeated the French.

ramin /raˈmiːn/ ▶ **noun** a hardwood tree of Malaysian swamp forests, which yields pale lightweight timber. ● *Gonystylus bancanus*, family Thymelaeaceae.
– ORIGIN 1950s: from Malay.

ramjet ▶ **noun** a type of jet engine in which the air drawn in for combustion is compressed solely by the forward motion of the aircraft.

ramkie /ˈramki/ ▶ **noun** a stringed instrument resembling a guitar, formerly played by the Khoikhoi people of southern Africa.
– ORIGIN early 19th cent.: from Afrikaans, from Nama *rangi-b*, perhaps from Portuguese *rabequinha*, diminutive of *rabeca* 'fiddle'.

rammies /ˈramɪz/ ▶ **plural noun** Austral. & S. African informal, dated trousers.
– ORIGIN early 20th cent.: perhaps related to RAMIE, or representing a reduced form of *round me (or the) houses*, rhyming slang for *trousers*.

rammy ▶ **noun** (pl. **rammies**) Scottish a quarrel or brawl.
– ORIGIN 1930s: perhaps from Scots *rammle* 'row, uproar', variant of RAMBLE.

ramose /ˈraməʊs, ˈreɪ-/ ▶ **adjective** technical having branches; branched.
– ORIGIN late 17th cent.: from Latin *ramosus*, from *ramus* 'branch'.

ramp ▶ **noun 1** a sloping surface joining two different levels, as at the entrance or between floors of a building: *a wheelchair ramp.* ■ a movable set of steps for entering or leaving an aircraft. ■ Brit. a transverse ridge in a road to control the speed of vehicles. ■ N. Amer. an inclined slip road leading on to or off a main road or motorway: *an exit ramp.* ■ North American term for CATWALK (sense 1).
2 an upward bend in a stair rail.
3 an electrical waveform in which the voltage increases or decreases linearly with time.
4 Brit. informal a swindle, especially one involving a fraudulent increase of the price of a share.
▶ **verb 1** [with obj.] provide with a ramp.
2 [no obj.] archaic (of an animal) rear up on its hind legs in a threatening posture. ■ [with adverbial of direction] rush about uncontrollably. ■ [with adverbial of direction] (of a plant) grow or climb luxuriantly: *ivy ramped over the flower beds.*
3 [no obj.] (of an electrical waveform) increase or decrease voltage linearly with time.
4 [with obj.] Brit. drive up the price of (a company's shares) in order to gain a financial advantage. [late 20th cent.: of unknown origin; a 19th-cent. slang use of the term was 'rob, swindle'.] ■ increase the level or amount of (something) sharply: *the company has moved into new quarters in order to* ***ramp up*** *production.*
– ORIGIN Middle English (as a verb in the sense 'rear up', also used as a heraldic term): from Old French *ramper* 'creep, crawl', of unknown origin. Sense 1 of the noun dates from the late 18th cent.

rampage ▶ **verb** /ramˈpeɪdʒ/ [no obj., with adverbial of direction] (especially of a large group of people) move through a place in a violent and uncontrollable manner: *several thousand demonstrators rampaged through the city.*
▶ **noun** /ramˈpeɪdʒ, ˈrampeɪdʒ/ [usu. in sing.] a period of violent and uncontrollable behaviour by a group of people: *thugs* ***went on the rampage*** *and wrecked a classroom.*
– DERIVATIVES **rampager** noun.
– ORIGIN late 17th cent.: perhaps based on the verb RAMP and the noun RAGE.

rampageous ▶ **adjective** archaic boisterously or violently uncontrollable.

rampant ▶ **adjective 1** (especially of something unwelcome) flourishing or spreading unchecked: *political violence was rampant | rampant inflation.* ■ unrestrained in action or performance: *rampant sex.* ■ (of a plant) lush in growth; luxuriant: *a rich soil soon becomes home to rampant weeds.*
2 [usu. postpositive] Heraldry (of an animal) represented standing on one hind foot with its forefeet in the air (typically in profile, facing the dexter side, with right hind foot and tail raised): *two gold lions rampant.*
– DERIVATIVES **rampancy** noun, **rampantly** adverb.
– ORIGIN Middle English (as a heraldic term): from Old French, literally 'crawling', present participle of *ramper* (see RAMP). From the original use describing a wild animal arose the sense 'fierce', whence the current notion of 'unrestrained'.

rampart ▶ **noun** (usu. **ramparts**) a defensive wall of a castle or walled city, having a broad top with a walkway and typically a stone parapet. ■ a defensive or protective barrier: *the open Pacific broke on the far-off ramparts of the reef.*
▶ **verb** [with obj.] fortify or surround with or as if with a rampart: *the town's streets were ramparted with tall mounds of rubble.*
– ORIGIN late 16th cent.: from French *rempart*, from *remparer* 'fortify, take possession of again', based on Latin *ante* 'before' + *parare* 'prepare'.

rampion /ˈrampɪən/ ▶ **noun** a Eurasian plant of the bellflower family, some kinds of which have a root that can be eaten in salads: ● a Mediterranean plant with a long, narrow spike of bluish flowers and a thick taproot (*Campanula rapunculus*, family Campanulaceae). ● (**horned rampion**) a grassland plant with dense rounded flower heads of inward curving, typically blue, tubular flowers (genus *Phyteuma*, family Campanulaceae).
– ORIGIN late 16th cent.: from a variant of medieval Latin *rapuncium*; compare with German *Rapunzel* 'lamb's lettuce'.

ram raid ▶ **noun** Brit. a robbery in which a shop window is rammed with a vehicle and looted.
– DERIVATIVES **ram-raider** noun, **ram-raiding** noun.

ramrod ▶ **noun 1** a rod for ramming down the charge of a muzzle-loading firearm. ■ used in similes and metaphors to describe an erect or rigid posture: *he held himself ramrod straight.*
2 N. Amer. a foreman or manager, especially one who is a strict disciplinarian.

▸ **verb** (**ramrods**, **ramrodding**, **ramrodded**) [with obj.] (**ramrod something through**) chiefly N. Amer. force a proposed measure to be accepted or completed quickly: *they ramrodded through legislation voiding the court injunctions*.

Ramsay[1] /ˈramzi/, Allan (1713–84), Scottish portrait painter. His style is noted for its French rococo grace and sensitivity, particularly in his portraits of women.

Ramsay[2] /ˈramzi/, Sir William (1852–1916), Scottish chemist, discoverer of the noble gases. He first discovered argon, helium, and (with the help of **M. W. Travers**, 1872–1961) neon, krypton, and xenon, determining their atomic weights and places in the periodic table. In 1910, with Frederick Soddy and **Sir Robert Whytlaw-Gray** (1877–1958), Ramsay identified the last noble gas, radon. Nobel Prize for Chemistry (1904).

Ramses /ˈramsiːz/ (also **Rameses**) the name of eleven Egyptian pharaohs, notably: ■ **Ramses II** (died *c.*1225 BC), reigned *c.*1292–*c.*1225 BC; known as **Ramses the Great**. The third pharaoh of the 19th dynasty, he built vast monuments and statues, including the two rock temples at Abu Simbel. ■ **Ramses III** (died *c.*1167 BC), reigned *c.*1198–*c.*1167 BC. The second pharaoh of the 20th dynasty, he fought decisive battles against the Libyans and the Sea Peoples. After his death the power of Egypt declined.

Ramsey /ˈramzi/, Sir Alf (1920–99), English footballer and manager; full name *Alfred Ernest Ramsey*. He played as a defender for Southampton, Tottenham Hotspur, and England, and managed England from 1963 to 1974, winning the World Cup in 1966.

ramshackle ▸ **adjective** (especially of a house or vehicle) in a state of severe disrepair: *a ramshackle cottage*.
– ORIGIN early 19th cent. (originally dialect in the sense 'irregular, disorderly'): alteration of earlier *ramshackled*, altered form of obsolete *ransackled* 'ransacked'.

ramshorn snail /ˈramzhɔːn/ ▸ **noun** a European freshwater snail which has a flat spiral shell. ● Family Planorbidae: several genera.

ramsons /ˈrams(ə)nz/ ▸ **plural noun** [usu. treated as sing.] a Eurasian woodland plant with broad shiny leaves and round heads of white flowers, producing a strong aroma of garlic. Also called **WILD GARLIC**. ● *Allium ursinum*, family Liliaceae (or Alliaceae).
– ORIGIN Old English *hramsan*, plural of *hramsa* 'wild garlic', later interpreted as singular.

ramus /ˈreɪməs/ ▸ **noun** (pl. **rami** /ˈreɪmʌɪ, ˈreɪmiː/)
1 Anatomy an arm or branch of a bone, in particular those of the ischium and pubes or of the jawbone. ■ a major branch of a nerve.
2 Zoology a structure in an invertebrate that has the form of a projecting arm, typically one of two or more that are conjoined or adjacent. ■ a barb of a feather.
– DERIVATIVES **ramal** adjective.
– ORIGIN mid 17th cent.: from Latin, literally 'branch'.

RAN ▸ **abbreviation** Royal Australian Navy.

ran past of **RUN**.

ranch ▸ **noun 1** a large farm, especially in North America or Australia, where cattle or other animals are bred. ■ (also **ranch house**) N. Amer. a single-storey house.
2 (also **ranch dressing**) [mass noun] N. Amer. a type of thick white salad dressing made with sour cream.
▸ **verb** [no obj.] (often as noun **ranching**) run a ranch: *cattle ranching*. ■ [with obj.] (often as adj. **ranched**) breed (animals) on a ranch. ■ [with obj.] use (land) as a ranch.
– ORIGIN early 19th cent.: from Spanish *rancho* 'group of persons eating together'.

rancher ▸ **noun 1** a person who owns or runs a ranch.
2 N. Amer. a ranch house.

ranchera /rɑːnˈtʃɛːrə/ ▸ **noun** [mass noun] a type of Mexican country music typically played with guitars and horns. ■ [count noun] a ranchera tune or song.
– ORIGIN 1980s: from Spanish *canción ranchera* 'farmers' song'.

rancheria /ˌrɑːn(t)ʃəˈriːə/ ▸ **noun** (in Spanish America and the western US) a small Indian settlement.
– ORIGIN Spanish, from *rancho* (see **RANCH**).

ranchero /rɑːnˈtʃɛːrəʊ/ ▸ **noun** (pl. **rancheros**) N. Amer. a person who farms or works on a ranch, especially in the south-western US and Mexico.
– ORIGIN Spanish, from *rancho* (see **RANCH**).

Ranchi /ˈrɑːntʃi/ a city in NE India, capital of the state of Jharkhand; pop. 1,047,500 (est. 2009).

rancid ▸ **adjective** (of foods containing fat or oil) smelling or tasting unpleasant as a result of being old and stale. ■ highly unpleasant; repugnant: *his columns are just rationales for every kind of rancid prejudice*.
– DERIVATIVES **rancidity** noun, **rancidly** adverb, **rancidness** noun.
– ORIGIN early 17th cent.: from Latin *rancidus* 'stinking'.

rancorous ▸ **adjective** characterized by bitterness or resentment: *sixteen miserable months of rancorous disputes* | *a rancorous debate*.
– DERIVATIVES **rancorously** adverb.

rancour (US **rancor**) ▸ **noun** [mass noun] bitterness or resentfulness, especially when long standing: *he spoke without rancour*.
– ORIGIN Middle English: via Old French from late Latin *rancor* 'rankness' (in the Vulgate 'bitter grudge'), related to Latin *rancidus* 'stinking'.

Rand[1] /rand, rɑːnt/ (**the Rand**) another name for **WITWATERSRAND**.

Rand[2] /rand/, Ayn (1905–82), Russian-born American writer and philosopher; born *Alissa Rozenbaum*. She developed a philosophy of 'objectivism', arguing for 'rational self-interest', individualism, and laissez-faire capitalism, which she presented in both non-fiction works and novels. Notable novels: *The Fountainhead* (1943) and *Atlas Shrugged* (1957).

rand[1] /rand, rɑːnt/ ▸ **noun 1** the basic monetary unit of South Africa, equal to 100 cents.
2 S. African a long rocky ridge.
– ORIGIN sense 1 is from *the Rand*, the name of a goldfield district near Johannesburg; sense 2 is from Afrikaans, literally 'edge' (related to **RAND**[2]).

rand[2] /rand/ ▸ **noun** a strip of leather placed under the back part of a shoe or boot to make it level before the lifts of the heel are attached.
– ORIGIN Old English (denoting a border): of Germanic origin; related to Dutch *rand* and German *Rand* 'edge'. The current sense dates from the 16th cent.

randan ▸ **noun** (in phrase **on the randan**) Scottish out celebrating or enjoying oneself: *I went out on the randan with some of my old pals*.
– ORIGIN mid 17th cent.: perhaps an alteration of **RANDOM**.

R & B (also **R 'n' B**) ▸ **noun** [mass noun] **1** rhythm and blues.
2 a kind of pop music of black origin with a soulful vocal style featuring much improvisation.

R & D ▸ **abbreviation** research and development.

Randers /ˈrɑːnəz/ a port of Denmark, on the Randers Fjord on the east coast of the Jutland peninsula; pop. 59,842 (2009).

random ▸ **adjective 1** made, done, or happening without method or conscious decision: *apparently random violence*. ■ Statistics governed by or involving equal chances for each item: *a random sample of 100 households*. ■ (of masonry) with stones of irregular size and shape.
2 informal odd, unusual, or unexpected: *the class was hard but he was so random that it was always fun*.
– PHRASES **at random** without method or conscious decision: *he opened the book at random*.
– DERIVATIVES **randomly** adverb, **randomness** noun.
– ORIGIN Middle English (in the sense 'impetuous headlong rush'): from Old French *randon* 'great speed', from *randir* 'gallop', from a Germanic root shared by **RAND**[2].

> **WORD TRENDS** In the 1990s teenagers called everything and everyone **sad**; in the early 2000s they used **random**. Although the slang sense of **random** arose in the 1970s in US computing circles, it didn't take off in British English until the 21st century. As with **sad**, the change in meaning is quite small, with the biggest difference being the context and way that the word is used. **Random** can be rather disparaging (*Mum, you are so random*), but it is often used in a positive way, or at least with the implication that the subject, though undeniably odd, is also amusing and entertaining: *I find it impossible to not laugh at such a random guy* | *the park was so random that I'm rather glad I stuck around.*

random access ▸ **noun** [mass noun] Computing the process of transferring information to or from memory in which every memory location can be accessed directly rather than being accessed in a fixed sequence: [as modifier] *random-access programming*.

random error ▸ **noun** Statistics an error in measurement caused by factors which vary from one measurement to another.

randomize (also **randomise**) ▸ **verb** [with obj.] (usu. as adj. **randomized**) technical make random in order or arrangement; employ random selection or sampling in (an experiment or procedure).
– DERIVATIVES **randomization** noun.

random walk ▸ **noun** Physics the movements of an object or changes in a variable that follow no discernible pattern or trend.

R & R ▸ **abbreviation** ■ informal rest and recreation. ■ Medicine rescue and resuscitation. ■ (also **R 'n' R**) rock and roll.

Randstad /ˈrandstat/ a conurbation in the north-west of the Netherlands that stretches in a horseshoe shape from Dordrecht and Rotterdam round to Utrecht and Amersfoort via The Hague, Leiden, Haarlem, and Amsterdam. The majority of the people of the Netherlands live in this area.

randy ▸ **adjective** (**randier**, **randiest**) **1** informal sexually aroused or excited.
2 Scottish archaic having a rude, aggressive manner.
– DERIVATIVES **randily** adverb, **randiness** noun.
– ORIGIN mid 17th cent.: perhaps from obsolete *rand* 'rant, rave', from obsolete Dutch *randen* 'to rant'.

ranee /ˈrɑːniː/ ▸ **noun** archaic spelling of **RANI**.

rang past of **RING**[2].

rangatira /ˌraŋəˈtɪərə/ ▸ **noun** NZ a Maori chief or noble.
– ORIGIN Maori.

range ▸ **noun 1** the area of variation between upper and lower limits on a particular scale: *the cost will be in the range of $1–5 million a day* | *grand hotels were outside my price range*. ■ the scope of a person's knowledge or abilities: *in this film he gave some indication of his range*. ■ the compass of a person's voice or a musical instrument: *she was gifted with an incredible vocal range*. ■ the period of time covered by something such as a forecast. ■ the area covered by or included in something: *a guide to the range of debate this issue has generated*. ■ Mathematics the set of values that a given function can take as its argument varies.
2 a set of different things of the same general type: *the area offers a wide range of activities for the tourist*.
3 [mass noun] the distance within which a person can see or hear: *something lurked just beyond her range of vision*. ■ the maximum distance at which a radio transmission can be effectively received: *planets within radio range of Earth*. ■ [count noun] the distance that can be covered by a vehicle or aircraft without refuelling: *the vans have a range of 125 miles*. ■ the maximum distance to which a gun will shoot or over which a missile will travel: *a duck came within range* | [count noun] *these rockets have a range of 30 to 40 miles*. ■ [count noun] the distance between a camera and the subject to be photographed.
4 a line or series of mountains or hills: *a mountain range*. ■ (**ranges**) Austral./NZ mountainous or hilly country.
5 a large area of open land for grazing or hunting. ■ an area of land or sea used as a testing ground for military equipment. ■ an open or enclosed area with targets for shooting practice. ■ the area over which a plant or animal is distributed.
6 a large cooking stove with burners or hotplates and one or more ovens, all of which are kept continually hot. ■ N. Amer. an electric or gas cooker.
7 a row of buildings. ■ a continuous stretch of a building.
8 [mass noun] archaic the direction or position in which something lies: *the range of the hills and valleys is nearly from north to south*.
▸ **verb 1** [no obj., with adverbial] vary or extend between specified limits: *prices range from £30 to £100*.
2 [with obj. and adverbial] place or arrange in a row or rows or in a specified manner: *a table with half a dozen chairs ranged around it*. ■ [no obj., with adverbial of direction] run or extend in a line in a particular direction: *he regularly came to the benches that ranged along the path*. ■ Printing, Brit. (with reference to type) align or be aligned, especially at the ends of successive lines.
3 (**range someone against** or **be ranged against**) place oneself or be placed in opposition to (a person or group): *Japan ranged herself against the European nations*.
4 [no obj., with adverbial of direction] (of a person or animal) travel or wander over a wide area: *patrols ranged deep into enemy territory* | [with obj.] *tribes who ranged the windswept lands of the steppe* | (as adj., in combination **-ranging**) *free-ranging groups of baboons*. ■ (of a person's eyes) pass from one person or thing to

R

another: *his eyes* ***ranged over*** *them.* ■ (of something written or spoken) cover a wide number of different topics: *tutorials* ***ranged over*** *a variety of subjects.*
5 [no obj.] obtain the range of a target by adjustment after firing past it or short of it, or by the use of radar or laser equipment: *radar-type transmissions which appeared to be* ***ranging on*** *our convoys.* ■ [with adverbial] (of a projectile) cover a specified distance. ■ [with adverbial] (of a gun) send a projectile over a specified distance.
– PHRASES **at a range of** with a specified distance between one person or thing and another: *she fired at a range of a few inches.*
– ORIGIN Middle English (in the sense 'line of people or animals'): from Old French *range* 'row, rank', from *rangier* 'put in order', from *rang* 'rank'. Early usage also included the notion of 'movement over an area'.

rangé /ˈrɒ̃ʒeɪ, rɒ̃ˈʒeɪ/ ▸ **adjective** literary (of a person or their lifestyle) orderly; settled.
– ORIGIN French, literally 'in order', past participle of *ranger*.

rangefinder ▸ **noun** an instrument for estimating the distance of an object, especially for use with a camera or gun.

rangeland ▸ **noun** [mass noun] (also **rangelands**) open country used for grazing or hunting animals.

Ranger a series of nine American moon probes launched between 1961 and 1965, the last three of which took many photographs before crashing into the moon.

ranger ▸ **noun 1** a keeper of a park, forest, or area of countryside.
2 a member of a body of armed men, in particular: ■ a mounted soldier. ■ US a commando.
3 (**Ranger** or **Ranger Guide**) Brit. a member of the senior branch of the Guides.
4 a person or thing that wanders over a particular area: *rangers of the mountains.*

ranging pole (also **ranging rod**) ▸ **noun** Surveying a pole or rod used for setting a straight line.

rangoli /rʌŋˈgəʊli/ ▸ **noun** [mass noun] traditional Indian decoration and patterns made with ground rice, particularly during festivals.
– ORIGIN from Marathi *rāgoḷī*.

Rangoon /raŋˈguːn/ the former capital of Burma (Myanmar), a port in the Irrawaddy delta; pop. 4,088,000 (est. 2007). For centuries a Buddhist religious centre, it is the site of the Shwe Dagon Pagoda, built over 2,500 years ago. The modern city was established by the British in the mid 19th century and was the capital from 1886 until it was replaced by Naypyidaw in 2005. Burmese name **YANGON**.

rangy /ˈreɪn(d)ʒi/ ▸ **adjective** (**rangier**, **rangiest**) (of a person) tall and slim with long, slender limbs: *the rangy, untidy figure of the young magician.*
– DERIVATIVES **ranginess** noun.

rani /ˈrɑːniː/ (also **ranee**) ▸ **noun** (pl. **ranis**) historical a Hindu queen.
– ORIGIN from Hindi *rānī*, Sanskrit *rājñī*, feminine of *rājan* 'king'.

R

ranitidine /raˈnɪtɪdiːn, -ˈnʌɪt-/ ▸ **noun** [mass noun] Medicine a synthetic compound with antihistamine properties, used to treat ulcers and related conditions.
– ORIGIN 1970s: blend of **FURAN** and **NITRO-**, + **-IDE** + **-INE**[4].

Ranjit Singh /ˌrʌndʒɪt ˈsɪŋ/ (1780–1839), Indian maharaja, founder of the Sikh state of Punjab; known as the **Lion of the Punjab**. He proclaimed himself maharaja of Punjab in 1801, and went on to make it the most powerful state in India. Most of his territory was annexed by Britain after the Sikh Wars which followed his death.

Rank, J. Arthur, 1st Baron (1888–1972), English industrialist and film executive; full name *Joseph Arthur Rank*. In 1941 he founded the Rank Organization, a film production and distribution company that acquired control of the leading British studios and cinema chains in the 1940s and 1950s.

rank[1] ▸ **noun 1** a position in the hierarchy of the armed forces: *an army officer of high rank | he was promoted to the rank of Captain.* ■ a position within the hierarchy of an organization or society: *only two cabinet members had held ministerial rank before.* ■ [mass noun] high social position: *persons of rank and breeding.* ■ Statistics a number specifying position in a numerically ordered series. ■ (in systemic grammar) the level of a linguistic unit or set of linguistic units in relation to other sets in the hierarchy.
2 a single line of soldiers or police officers drawn up abreast. ■ a regular row or line of things or people: *conifer plantations growing in serried ranks.* ■ Chess each of the eight rows of eight squares running from side to side across a chessboard. Compare with **FILE**[2]. ■ Brit. short for **TAXI RANK**.
3 (**ranks**) the people belonging to or constituting a group or class: *the ranks of Britain's unemployed.* ■ (**the ranks**) (in the armed forces) those who are not commissioned officers: *he was fined and* ***reduced to the ranks.***
4 Mathematics the value or the order of the largest non-zero determinant of a given matrix.
▸ **verb** [with obj. and adverbial] **1** give (someone or something) a rank or place within a grading system: *students ranked the samples in order of preference |* [with obj. and complement] *she is ranked number four in the world.* ■ [no obj., with adverbial] have a specified rank or place within a grading system: *he now ranks third in America.* ■ [with obj.] US take precedence over (someone) in respect of rank; outrank: *the Secretary of State ranks all the other members of the cabinet.*
2 arrange in a row or rows: *the tents were ranked in orderly rows.*
– PHRASES **break rank** (or **ranks**) (of soldiers or police officers) fail to remain in line. ■ fail to maintain solidarity: *the government is prepared to* ***break ranks with*** *the Allied states.* **close ranks** (of soldiers or police officers) come closer together in a line. ■ unite in order to defend common interests: *the family had always closed ranks in times of crisis.* **keep rank** (of soldiers or police officers) remain in line. **pull rank** take unfair advantage of one's seniority. **rise through** (or **from**) **the ranks** (of a private or a non-commissioned officer) receive a commission. ■ advance in an organization by one's own efforts: *he rose through the ranks to become managing director.*
– ORIGIN Middle English (in the sense 'row of things'): from Old French *ranc*, of Germanic origin; related to **RING**[1].

rank[2] ▸ **adjective 1** (of vegetation) growing too thickly and coarsely.
2 having a foul or offensive smell: *breathing rank air.* ■ informal very unpleasant: *the tea at work is nice but the coffee's pretty rank.*
3 [attrib.] (especially of something bad or deficient) complete and utter (used for emphasis): *rank stupidity | a rank outsider.*
– DERIVATIVES **rankly** adverb, **rankness** noun.
– ORIGIN Old English *ranc* 'proud, rebellious, sturdy', also 'fully grown', of Germanic origin. An early sense 'luxuriant' gave rise to 'too luxuriant', whence the negative connotation of modern usage.

rank and file ▸ **noun** [treated as pl.] (**the rank and file**) the ordinary members of an organization as opposed to its leaders: *the rank and file of the Labour Party |* [as modifier] *rank-and-file members.*
– ORIGIN referring to the 'ranks' and 'files' into which privates and non-commissioned officers form on parade.

rank correlation ▸ **noun** Statistics an assessment of the degree of correlation between two ways of assigning ranks to the members of a set.

ranker[1] ▸ **noun 1** chiefly Brit. a soldier in the ranks; a private. ■ a commissioned officer who has been in the ranks.
2 [in combination] a person or animal of a specified rank: *of the 26 top-rankers in humanities, 18 are girls.*

ranker[2] ▸ **noun** Soil Science a simple soil consisting of a layer of humus lying directly on an unaltered substrate such as bedrock, glacial drift, or volcanic ash.
– ORIGIN based on Austrian German *Rank* 'steep slope'.

ranking ▸ **noun** a position in a hierarchy or scale: *his world number-one ranking.* ■ [mass noun] the action or process of giving a specified rank to someone or something: *the ranking of students.*
▸ **adjective** [in combination] having a specified rank in a hierarchy: *high-ranking army officers.* ■ [attrib.] N. Amer. having a high rank: *I'm the ranking officer here.*

rankle ▸ **verb** [no obj.] **1** (of a comment or fact) cause continuing annoyance or resentment: *the casual manner of his dismissal still rankles.* ■ [with obj.] annoy or irritate (someone): *Lisa was rankled by his assertion.*
2 archaic (of a wound or sore) continue to be painful; fester.
– ORIGIN Middle English: from Old French *rancler*, from *rancle, draoncle* 'festering sore', from an alteration of medieval Latin *dracunculus*, diminutive of *draco* 'serpent'.

rankshift ▸ **noun** (in systemic grammar) a use of a linguistic unit at a lower rank than the one to which it ordinarily belongs.
▸ **verb** (**be rankshifted**) (of a linguistic unit) be used at a lower rank.

Rann of Kutch see **KUTCH, RANN OF**.

ransack ▸ **verb** [with obj.] go through (a place) stealing things and causing damage: *burglars ransacked her home.* ■ search (a place or receptacle) thoroughly, especially in such a way as to cause harm: *man has ransacked the planet for fuel.*
– DERIVATIVES **ransacker** noun.
– ORIGIN Middle English: from Old Norse *rannsaka*, from *rann* 'house' + a second element related to *sœkja* 'seek'.

Ransom, John Crowe (1888–1974), American poet and critic. With *The New Criticism* (1941) he started a school of criticism which rejected the Victorian emphasis on literature as a moral force and advocated a close analysis of textual structure in isolation from the social background of the text.

ransom ▸ **noun** a sum of money demanded or paid for the release of a captive. ■ [mass noun] the holding or freeing of a captive in return for payment of a ransom: *the capture and ransom of the king.*
▸ **verb** [with obj.] obtain the release of (a captive) by paying a ransom: *the lord was captured in war and had to be ransomed.* ■ hold (a captive) and demand a ransom for their release. ■ release (a captive) after receiving a ransom.
– PHRASES **hold someone to ransom** hold someone captive and demand payment for their release. ■ demand concessions from a person or organization by threatening damaging action. **a king's ransom** a huge amount of money.
– ORIGIN Middle English: from Old French *ransoun* (noun), *ransouner* (verb), from Latin *redemptio(n-)* 'ransoming, releasing' (see **REDEMPTION**). Early use also occurred in theological contexts expressing 'deliverance' and 'atonement'.

Ransome, Arthur (Michell) (1884–1967), English novelist and journalist, best known for the children's classic *Swallows and Amazons* (1930).

rant ▸ **verb** [no obj.] speak or shout at length in an angry, impassioned way: *she was still* ***ranting on about*** *the unfairness of it all.*
▸ **noun** a spell of ranting; a tirade: *his rants against organized religion.*
– PHRASES **rant and rave** shout and complain angrily and at length.
– ORIGIN late 16th cent. (in the sense 'behave boisterously'): from Dutch *ranten* 'talk nonsense, rave'.

ranter ▸ **noun 1** a person who rants.
2 (**Ranter**) a member of an antinomian Christian sect in England during the mid 17th century which denied the authority of scripture and clergy. ■ (in the 19th century) a member of certain Nonconformist, in particular Methodist, groups.

ranting ▸ **noun** (usu. **rantings**) a long, angry, and impassioned speech: *the reactionary rantings of an embittered old man.*
– DERIVATIVES **rantingly** adverb.

ranunculaceous /rəˌnʌŋkjʊˈleɪʃəs/ ▸ **adjective** Botany relating to or denoting plants of the buttercup family (Ranunculaceae).
– ORIGIN mid 19th cent.: from modern Latin *Ranunculaceae* (plural), based on Latin *ranunculus* 'little frog', + **-OUS**.

ranunculus /rəˈnʌŋkjʊləs/ ▸ **noun** (pl. **ranunculuses** or **ranunculi** /-lʌɪ, -liː/) a temperate plant of a genus that includes the buttercups and water crowfoots, typically having yellow or white bowl-shaped flowers and lobed or toothed leaves. ● Genus *Ranunculus*, family Ranunculaceae: many species, including several garden ornamentals.
– ORIGIN modern Latin, from Latin, literally 'little frog', diminutive of *rana*.

Ranvier's node ▸ **noun** see **NODE OF RANVIER**.

RAOC ▸ **abbreviation** (in the UK) Royal Army Ordnance Corps.

rap[1] ▸ **verb** (**raps**, **rapping**, **rapped**) **1** [with obj.] strike (a hard surface) with a series of rapid audible blows, especially in order to attract attention: *he stood up and rapped the table |* [no obj.] *she* ***rapped on*** *the window.* ■ strike (something) several times against a hard surface: *she rapped her stick on the floor.* ■ strike sharply with a stick or similar implement: *she rapped my fingers with a ruler.* ■ informal criticize severely: *certain banks are to be rapped for delaying interest rate cuts.* ■ say sharply or suddenly: *the ambassador* ***rapped out*** *an order.*
2 [no obj.] informal, chiefly N. Amer. talk or chat in an easy and familiar manner: *we could be here all night rapping about spiritualism.*

3 [no obj.] perform rap music.
▶ noun 1 a quick, sharp knock or blow: *there was a confident rap at the door.* ■ informal a sharp criticism: *social services were smarting from an Ombudsman's rap.*
2 [mass noun] a type of popular music of US black origin in which words are recited rapidly and rhythmically over an instrumental backing. ■ [count noun] a piece of rap, or the words themselves.
3 informal, chiefly N. Amer. a lengthy or impromptu conversation: *dropping in after work for a rap over a beer.*
4 [usu. with adj. or noun modifier] N. Amer. informal a criminal charge, especially of a specified kind: *he's just been acquitted on a murder rap.*
5 N. Amer. informal a person's reputation, typically a bad one: *why should drag queens get a bad rap?*
– PHRASES **beat the rap** N. Amer. informal escape punishment for or be acquitted of a crime. **a rap on** (or **over**) **the knuckles** a reprimand. **rap someone on** (or **over**) **the knuckles** reprimand or criticize someone. **take the rap** informal be punished or blamed, especially for something that is not one's fault.
– ORIGIN Middle English (originally in the senses 'severe blow with a weapon' and 'deliver a heavy blow'): probably imitative and of Scandinavian origin; compare with Swedish *rappa* 'beat, drub', also with CLAP[1] and FLAP.

rap[2] ▶ noun [in sing., with negative] the smallest amount (used for emphasis): *he doesn't care a rap whether it's true or not.*
– ORIGIN early 19th cent.: from Irish *ropaire* 'robber'; used as the name of a counterfeit coin in 18th-cent Ireland.

rapacious /rəˈpeɪʃəs/ ▶ adjective aggressively greedy or grasping: *rapacious landlords.*
– DERIVATIVES **rapaciously** adverb, **rapaciousness** noun.
– ORIGIN mid 17th cent.: from Latin *rapax*, *rapac-* (from *rapere* 'to snatch') + -IOUS.

rapacity /rəˈpasɪti/ ▶ noun [mass noun] aggressive greed: *the rapacity of landowners seeking greater profit from their property.*

RAPC ▶ abbreviation (in the UK) Royal Army Pay Corps.

rape[1] ▶ noun [mass noun] 1 the crime, typically committed by a man, of forcing another person to have sexual intercourse with the offender against their will: *he denied two charges of rape* | [count noun] *he had committed at least two rapes.* ■ archaic the abduction of a woman, especially for the purpose of having sexual intercourse with her: *the Rape of the Sabine Women.*
2 the wanton destruction or spoiling of a place: *the rape of the countryside.*
▶ verb [with obj.] 1 (especially of a man) force (another person) to have sexual intercourse with the offender against their will.
2 spoil or destroy (a place): *timber men doubt the government's ability to ensure the forests are not raped.*
– DERIVATIVES **raper** noun (chiefly US).
– ORIGIN late Middle English (originally denoting violent seizure of property, later carrying off a woman by force): from Anglo-Norman French *rap* (noun), *raper* (verb), from Latin *rapere* 'seize'.

rape[2] ▶ noun [mass noun] a plant of the cabbage family with bright yellow heavily scented flowers, especially a variety (**oilseed rape**) grown for its oil-rich seed and as stockfeed. Also called COLZA. ● Genus *Brassica*, family Cruciferae, in particular *B. napus* subsp. oleifera.
– ORIGIN late Middle English (originally denoting the turnip plant): from Latin *rapum*, *rapa* 'turnip'.

rape[3] ▶ noun historical (in the UK) any of the six ancient divisions of Sussex.
– ORIGIN Old English, variant of ROPE, with reference to the fencing-off of land.

rape[4] ▶ noun [mass noun] (also **rapes**) the stalks and skins of grapes left after winemaking, used in making vinegar.
– ORIGIN early 17th cent. (as *rape wine*): from French *râpe*, medieval Latin *raspa* 'bunch of grapes'.

rape crisis centre ▶ noun an agency offering advice and support to victims of violent sexual crime.

rape oil ▶ noun [mass noun] an oil obtained from rapeseed, used as a lubricant, in alternative fuels, and in foodstuffs.

rapeseed ▶ noun [mass noun] seeds of the rape plant, used chiefly for oil. See RAPE[2].

Raphael[1] /ˈrafeɪəl/ (in the Bible) one of the seven archangels in the apocryphal Book of Enoch. He is said to have 'healed' the earth when it was defiled by the sins of the fallen angels.

Raphael[2] /ˈrafeɪəl/ (1483–1520), Italian painter and architect; Italian name *Raffaello Sanzio*. Regarded as one of the greatest artists of the Renaissance, he is particularly noted for his madonnas, including his altarpiece the *Sistine Madonna* (*c.*1513).

raphe /ˈreɪfi/ ▶ noun (pl. **raphae** /ˈreɪfiː/) Anatomy & Biology a groove, ridge, or seam in an organ or tissue, typically marking the line where two halves fused in the embryo, in particular: ■ the connecting ridge between the two halves of the medulla oblongata or the tegmentum of the midbrain. ■ Botany a longitudinal ridge on the side of certain ovules or seeds. ■ Botany a longitudinal groove in the valve of many diatoms.
– ORIGIN mid 18th cent.: modern Latin, from Greek *rhaphē* 'seam'.

raphide /ˈreɪfʌɪd/ ▶ noun Botany a needle-shaped crystal of calcium oxalate occurring in clusters within the tissues of certain plants.
– ORIGIN mid 19th cent.: via French from Greek *rhaphis*, *rhaphid-* 'needle'.

rapid ▶ adjective happening in a short time or at a great rate: *the country's rapid economic decline* | *they lost three wickets in rapid succession.* ■ (of an action) characterized by great speed: *they made a rapid exit.*
▶ noun (usu. **rapids**) a fast-flowing and turbulent part of the course of a river.
– DERIVATIVES **rapidness** noun.
– ORIGIN mid 17th cent.: from Latin *rapidus*, from *rapere* 'take by force'.

rapid eye movement ▶ noun a jerky motion of a person's eyes occurring in REM sleep.

rapid-fire ▶ adjective another term for QUICK-FIRE.

rapidity ▶ noun [mass noun] the quality of moving or reacting with great speed: *the fish sank into the sand with such rapidity that it must be seen to be believed.* ■ the fact of happening at a great rate; swiftness: *technology spreads with extraordinary rapidity.*

rapidly ▶ adverb very quickly; at a great rate: *the business is expanding rapidly* | *the problem is rapidly worsening.*

rapid transit ▶ noun [mass noun] [usu. as modifier] a form of high-speed urban passenger transport such as an elevated railway system.

rapier ▶ noun a thin, light sharp-pointed sword used for thrusting. ■ [as modifier] (especially of speech or intelligence) quick and incisive: *rapier wit.*
– ORIGIN early 16th cent.: from French *rapière*, from *râpe* 'rasp, grater' (because the perforated hilt resembles a rasp or grater).

rapine /ˈrapʌɪn, -pɪn/ ▶ noun [mass noun] literary the violent seizure of someone's property.
– ORIGIN late Middle English: from Old French, or from Latin *rapina*, from *rapere* 'seize'.

rapini /rəˈpiːni/ ▶ noun a Mediterranean variety of turnip widely grown for its broccoli-like shoots and florets. ● *Brassica rapa* var. *rapa*, family Cruciferae.
– ORIGIN Italian, diminutive of *rapa* 'turnip'.

rapist ▶ noun a man who commits rape.

rapparee /ˌrapəˈriː/ ▶ noun a bandit or irregular soldier in Ireland in the 17th century.
– ORIGIN from Irish *rapaire* 'short pike'.

rappee /raˈpiː/ ▶ noun [mass noun] a type of coarse snuff.
– ORIGIN mid 18th cent.: from French (*tabac*) *râpé* 'rasped (tobacco)'.

rappel /raˈpɛl/ ▶ noun & verb (**rappels**, **rappelling**, **rappelled**) another term for ABSEIL.
– ORIGIN 1930s: from French, literally 'a recalling', from *rappeler* in the sense 'bring back to oneself' (with reference to the rope manoeuvre).

rappen /ˈrap(ə)n/ ▶ noun (pl. **same**) a monetary unit in the German-speaking cantons of Switzerland and in Liechtenstein, equal to one hundredth of the Swiss franc.
– ORIGIN from German *Rappe* 'raven', with reference to the depiction of the head of a raven on a medieval coin.

rapper ▶ noun a person who performs rap music.

rapport /raˈpɔː/ ▶ noun a close and harmonious relationship in which the people or groups concerned understand each other's feelings or ideas and communicate well: *she was able to establish a good rapport with the children* | *she **had an instant rapport with** animals* | [mass noun] *there was little rapport between them.*
– ORIGIN mid 17th cent.: French, from *rapporter* 'bring back'.

rapporteur /ˌrapɔːˈtəː/ ▶ noun a person who is appointed by an organization to report on the proceedings of its meetings: *the UN rapporteur.*
– ORIGIN late 18th cent.: French, from *rapporter* 'bring back'.

rapprochement /raˈprɒʃmɒ̃/ ▶ noun (especially in international affairs) an establishment or resumption of harmonious relations: *there were signs of a growing rapprochement between the two countries.*
– ORIGIN French, from *rapprocher*, from *re-* (expressing intensive force) + *approcher* 'to approach'.

rapscallion /rapˈskalɪən/ ▶ noun archaic or humorous a mischievous person.
– ORIGIN late 17th cent.: alteration of earlier *rascallion*, perhaps from RASCAL.

rap sheet ▶ noun N. Amer. informal a criminal record.

rapt ▶ adjective 1 completely fascinated or absorbed by what one is seeing or hearing: *a rapt teenage audience.* ■ characterized by a state of fascination: *they listened with rapt attention.* ■ filled with an intense and pleasurable emotion; enraptured: *she shut her eyes and seemed rapt with desire.* ■ Austral./NZ informal another term for WRAPPED.
2 archaic having been carried away bodily or transported to heaven: *he was rapt on high.*
– DERIVATIVES **raptly** adverb, **raptness** noun.
– ORIGIN late Middle English (in the sense 'transported by religious feeling'): from Latin *raptus* 'seized', past participle of *rapere*.

raptor ▶ noun 1 a bird of prey, e.g. an eagle or hawk.
2 informal a dromaeosaurid dinosaur, especially a velociraptor or utahraptor. [from VELOCIRAPTOR, a shortened form used originally by palaeontologists, popularized by the film *Jurassic Park* (1993).]
– ORIGIN late Middle English: from Latin, literally 'plunderer', from *rapt-* 'seized', from the verb *rapere*.

raptorial ▶ adjective chiefly Zoology (of a bird or other animal) predatory. ■ (of a limb or other organ) adapted for seizing prey.
– ORIGIN early 19th cent.: from Latin *raptor* 'plunderer' + -IAL.

rapture ▶ noun 1 [mass noun] a feeling of intense pleasure or joy: *Leonora listened with rapture.* ■ (**raptures**) expressions of intense pleasure or enthusiasm about something: *the tabloids **went into raptures about** her.*
2 (**the Rapture**) N. Amer. (according to some millenarian teaching) the transporting of believers to heaven at the Second Coming of Christ.
▶ verb [with obj.] N. Amer. (according to some millenarian teaching) transport (a believer) from earth to heaven at the Second Coming of Christ.
– PHRASES **rapture of the deep** informal nitrogen narcosis.
– ORIGIN late 16th cent. (in the sense 'seizing and carrying off'): from obsolete French, or from medieval Latin *raptura* 'seizing', partly influenced by RAPT.

rapturous ▶ adjective characterized by, feeling, or expressing great pleasure or enthusiasm: *he was greeted with rapturous applause.*
– DERIVATIVES **rapturously** adverb.

rara avis /ˌrɛːrə ˈeɪvɪs, ˌrɑːrə ˈavɪs/ ▶ noun (pl. **rarae aves** /-riː, -viːz/) another term for RARE BIRD.
– ORIGIN Latin.

rare[1] ▶ adjective (**rarer**, **rarest**) (of an event, situation, or condition) not occurring very often: *a rare genetic disorder* | [with infinitive] *it's rare to see a house so little altered.* ■ (of a thing) not found in large numbers and so of interest or value: *one of Britain's rarest birds, the honey buzzard.* ■ unusually good or remarkable: *he plays with rare sensitivity.*
– DERIVATIVES **rareness** noun.
– ORIGIN late Middle English (in the sense 'widely spaced, infrequent'): from Latin *rarus*.

rare[2] ▶ adjective (**rarer**, **rarest**) (of meat, especially beef) lightly cooked, so that the inside is still red.
– ORIGIN late 18th cent.: variant of obsolete *rear* 'half-cooked' (used to refer to soft-boiled eggs, from the mid 17th to mid 19th centuries).

rare bird ▶ noun an exceptional person or thing; a rarity: *the style is a rare bird in Brazilian music.*
– ORIGIN translating Latin *rara avis* (Juvenal's *Satires*, vi.165).

rarebit (also **Welsh rarebit**) ▶ noun [mass noun] a dish of melted and seasoned cheese on toast, sometimes with other ingredients.
– ORIGIN late 18th cent.: alteration of *rabbit* in WELSH RABBIT; the reason for the use of the term *rabbit* is unknown.

R

rare earth (also **rare earth element** or **rare earth metal**) ▶ **noun** Chemistry any of a group of chemically similar metallic elements comprising the lanthanide series and (usually) scandium and yttrium. They are not especially rare, but they tend to occur together in nature and are difficult to separate from one another.

raree-show /ˈrɛːriːʃəʊ/ ▶ **noun** archaic a form of entertainment, especially one carried in a box, such as a peep show.
– ORIGIN late 17th cent.: apparently representing *rare show*, as pronounced by Savoyard showmen.

rarefaction /ˌrɛːrɪˈfakʃ(ə)n/ ▶ **noun** [mass noun] reduction in the density of something, especially air or a gas. ■ Medicine the lessening of density of tissue, especially of nervous tissue or bone.
– ORIGIN early 17th cent.: from medieval Latin *rarefactio(n-)*, from the verb *rarefacere* 'grow thin, become rare'.

rarefied /ˈrɛːrɪfʌɪd/ ▶ **adjective 1** (of air, especially that at high altitudes) of lower pressure than usual; thin.
2 distant from the lives and concerns of ordinary people; esoteric: *rarefied scholarly pursuits*.

rarefy /ˈrɛːrɪfʌɪ/ (also **rarify**) ▶ **verb** (**rarefies, rarefying, rarefied**) make or become less dense or solid.
– DERIVATIVES **rarefication** noun, **rarefactive** adjective.
– ORIGIN late Middle English: from Old French *rarefier*, or medieval Latin *rareficare*, based on Latin *rarus* 'rare' + *facere* 'make'.

rare gas ▶ **noun** another term for NOBLE GAS.

rarely ▶ **adverb 1** not often; seldom: *I rarely drive above 50 mph*.
2 archaic remarkably well: *you can write rarely now, after all your schooling*. ■ to an unusual degree; exceptionally: [as submodifier] *the rarely fine Sheraton bookcase*.

raring ▶ **adjective** [with infinitive] informal very enthusiastic and eager to do something: *she was raring to get back to her work* | *I'll be ready and* ***raring to go***.
– ORIGIN 1920s: present participle of *rare*, dialect variant of ROAR or REAR[2].

rarity ▶ **noun** (pl. **rarities**) [mass noun] the state or quality of being rare: *the rarity of the condition*. ■ [count noun] a rare thing, especially one having particular value: *to take the morning off was a rarity*.
– ORIGIN late Middle English: from Latin *raritas*, from *rarus* 'far apart, infrequently found' (see RARE[1]).

Rarotonga /ˌrarəˈtɒŋgə/ a mountainous island in the South Pacific, the chief island of the Cook Islands. Its chief town, Avarua, is the capital of the Cook Islands.
– DERIVATIVES **Rarotongan** noun & adjective.

rasa /ˈrʌsəː/ ▶ **noun** [mass noun] Hinduism the agreeable quality of something, especially the emotional or aesthetic impression of a work of art.
– ORIGIN Sanskrit, literally 'flavour, juice (of food)'.

Ras al-Khaimah /ˌrɑːs alˈkʌɪmə/ one of the seven member states of the United Arab Emirates; pop. 171,900 (est. 2009). It joined the United Arab Emirates in 1972, after the British withdrawal from the Persian Gulf. ■ the capital of Ras al-Khaimah, a port on the Gulf; pop. 107,900 (est. 2009).

R

rasam /ˈrʌsəm/ ▶ **noun** [mass noun] a thin, very spicy southern Indian soup served with other dishes, typically as a drink.
– ORIGIN Tamil.

rascal ▶ **noun** a mischievous or cheeky person, especially a child or man (typically used in an affectionate way).
– DERIVATIVES **rascality** noun (pl. **rascalities**), **rascally** adjective.
– ORIGIN Middle English (in the senses 'a mob' and 'member of the rabble'): from Old French *rascaille* 'rabble', of uncertain origin.

rascasse /rasˈkas/ ▶ **noun** a small scorpionfish with brick-red skin and spiny fins, found chiefly in the Mediterranean and used as an ingredient of bouillabaisse. ● *Scorpaena scrofa*, family Scorpaenidae.
– ORIGIN 1920s: from French.

rase ▶ **verb** variant spelling of RAZE.

rasgulla /rʌsˈgʊlə/ ▶ **noun** an Indian sweet consisting of a ball of paneer (curd cheese) cooked in syrup.
– ORIGIN from Hindi *rasgullā*, from *ras* 'juice' + *gullā* 'ball'.

rash[1] ▶ **adjective** acting or done without careful consideration of the possible consequences; impetuous: *it would be extremely rash to make such an assumption* | *a rash decision*.
– DERIVATIVES **rashly** adverb, **rashness** noun.
– ORIGIN late Middle English (also in Scots and northern English in the sense 'nimble, eager'): of Germanic origin; related to German *rasch*.

rash[2] ▶ **noun 1** an area of redness and spots on a person's skin, appearing especially as a result of illness.
2 a series of things of the same type, especially when unwelcome, happening within a short space of time: *a rash of strikes by health-service workers*.
– ORIGIN early 18th cent.: probably related to Old French *rasche* 'eruptive sores, scurf'; compare with Italian *raschia* 'itch'.

rasher ▶ **noun** a thin slice of bacon.
– ORIGIN late 16th cent.: of unknown origin.

ras malai /ˈrʌs mʌˌlʌɪ/ ▶ **noun** [mass noun] an Indian sweet dish consisting of small, flat cakes of paneer (curd cheese) in sweetened, thickened milk.
– ORIGIN from Hindi *ras* 'juice' and *malāi* 'cream'.

rasp ▶ **noun 1** [in sing.] a harsh, grating noise: *the rasp of the engine*.
2 a coarse file or similar metal tool for scraping, filing, or rubbing down objects of metal, wood, or other hard material.
▶ **verb 1** [no obj.] make a harsh, grating noise: *my breath rasped in my throat*. ■ [with direct speech] say in a harsh, grating voice: *'Stay where you are!' he rasped*.
2 [with obj.] scrape or file (something) with a rasp. ■ (of a rough surface or object) scrape in a painful or unpleasant way.
– DERIVATIVES **raspy** adjective (**raspier, raspiest**).
– ORIGIN Middle English (as a verb): from Old French *rasper*, perhaps of Germanic origin.

raspberry ▶ **noun** (pl. **raspberries**) **1** an edible soft fruit related to the blackberry, consisting of a cluster of reddish-pink drupelets.
2 the plant which yields the raspberry, forming tall stiff prickly stems or 'canes'. ● *Rubus idaeus*, family Rosaceae; cultivars include the loganberry, tayberry, and veitchberry.
3 [mass noun] a deep reddish-pink colour: [as modifier] *a raspberry tweed jacket*.
4 informal a sound made with the tongue and lips, expressing derision or contempt: *Clare* ***blew a raspberry***. [from *raspberry tart*, rhyming slang for 'fart'.]
– ORIGIN early 17th cent.: from dialect *rasp*, abbreviation of obsolete *raspis* 'raspberry' (also used as a collective), of unknown origin, + BERRY.

raspberry cane ▶ **noun** a cultivated raspberry plant.

rasper ▶ **noun** a person or thing that scrapes something with or as if with a rasp. ■ Hunting a high fence that is difficult to jump.

rasp fern ▶ **noun** a small robust fern with prickly toothed edges to the lobes, growing in woodland and rainforests in Australasia and Polynesia, typically in rocky crevices. ● Genus *Doodia*, family Blechnaceae.

rasping ▶ **adjective** harsh-sounding and unpleasant; grating: *his cracked, rasping voice narrates the story*.
– DERIVATIVES **raspingly** adverb.

Rasputin /raˈspjuːtɪn/, Grigori (Efimovich) (1871–1916), Russian monk. He came to exert great influence over Tsar Nicholas II and his family during the First World War; this influence, combined with his reputation for debauchery, steadily discredited the imperial family, and he was assassinated by a group loyal to the tsar.

rass /rɑːs/ ▶ **noun** black slang a person's buttocks. ■ a contemptible person.
– ORIGIN late 18th cent.: alteration of ARSE, perhaps partly from *your arse*.

rassle ▶ **verb** N. Amer. non-standard spelling of WRESTLE, representing a regional pronunciation.
– DERIVATIVES **rassler** noun.

Rasta /ˈrastə/ ▶ **noun & adjective** informal short for RASTAFARIAN.

Rastafari /ˌrastəˈfɑːri/ ▶ **noun** [mass noun] [usu. as modifier] the Rastafarian movement.
– ORIGIN from *Ras Tafari*, the name by which Haile Selassie was known (1916–30).

Rastafarian /ˌrastəˈfɑːrɪən, -ˈfɛːrɪən/ ▶ **adjective** relating to a religious movement of Jamaican origin holding that Emperor Haile Selassie of Ethiopia was the Messiah and that blacks are the chosen people and will eventually return to their African homeland.
▶ **noun** a member of the Rastafarian religious movement. Rastafarians have distinctive codes of behaviour and dress, including the wearing of dreadlocks and the smoking of cannabis, and they follow a diet that excludes pork, shellfish, and milk.
– DERIVATIVES **Rastafarianism** noun.

Rastaman /ˈrastəman/ ▶ **noun** (pl. **Rastamen**) informal a male Rastafarian.

raster /ˈrastə/ ▶ **noun** a rectangular pattern of parallel scanning lines followed by the electron beam on a television screen or computer monitor.
– ORIGIN 1930s: from German *Raster*, literally 'screen', from Latin *rastrum* 'rake', from *ras-* 'scraped', from the verb *radere*.

raster image processor (abbrev.: **RIP**) ▶ **noun** Computing a device that rasterizes an image.

rasterize (also **rasterise**) ▶ **verb** [with obj.] Computing convert (an image stored as an outline) into pixels that can be displayed on a screen or printed.
– DERIVATIVES **rasterization** noun, **rasterizer** noun.

Rastyapino /raˈstjɑːpɪnəʊ/ former name (1919–29) for DZERZHINSK.

rat ▶ **noun 1** a rodent that resembles a large mouse, typically having a pointed snout and a long tail. Some kinds have become cosmopolitan and are sometimes responsible for transmitting diseases. ● Family Muridae: many genera, including *Rattus* (the Old World rats), and several hundred species.
2 informal a despicable person, especially a man who has been deceitful or disloyal. ■ an informer.
3 [with modifier] N. Amer. informal a person who is associated with or frequents a specified place: *LA mall rats*.
4 US a pad used to give shape and fullness to a woman's hair.
▶ **exclamation** (**rats**) informal used to express mild annoyance or irritation.
▶ **verb** (**rats, ratting, ratted**) [no obj.] **1** (usu. as noun **ratting**) hunt or kill rats.
2 informal desert one's party, side, or cause.
3 [with obj.] US shape (hair) with a rat.
– PHRASAL VERBS **rat on** (also N. Amer. **rat someone out**) informal inform on (someone): *he refused to rat on his buddies*. ■ break (an agreement or promise): *he accused the government of ratting on an earlier pledge*.
– ORIGIN Old English *ræt*, probably of Romance origin; reinforced in Middle English by Old French *rat*. The verb dates from the early 19th cent.

rata /ˈrɑːtə/ ▶ **noun** a large New Zealand tree of the myrtle family, with crimson flowers and hard red timber. ● Genus *Metrosideros*, family Myrtaceae: several species, in particular *M. robusta*.
– ORIGIN late 18th cent.: from Maori.

ratable ▶ **adjective** variant spelling of RATEABLE.

ratafia /ˌratəˈfɪə/ ▶ **noun** [mass noun] a liqueur flavoured with almonds or the kernels of peaches, apricots, or cherries. ■ (also **ratafia biscuit**) [count noun] an almond-flavoured biscuit resembling a small macaroon.
– ORIGIN late 17th cent.: from French; perhaps related to TAFIA.

ratamacue /ˈratəməˌkjuː/ ▶ **noun** Music one of the basic patterns (rudiments) of drumming, consisting of a two-beat figure, the first beat of which is played as a triplet and preceded by two grace notes.
– ORIGIN 1940s: imitative.

Ratana /ˈrɑːtənə/, Tahupotiki Wiremu (1873–1939), Maori political and religious leader. He founded the Ratana Church (1920), a religious revival movement which aimed to unite all Maori people.

rataplan /ˌratəˈplan/ ▶ **noun** [in sing.] a drumming or beating sound.
– ORIGIN mid 19th cent.: from French, of imitative origin.

rat-arsed ▶ **adjective** Brit. vulgar slang very drunk.

ratatat ▶ **noun** variant of RAT-TAT.

ratatouille /ˌratəˈtuːi, -ˈtwiː/ ▶ **noun** [mass noun] a vegetable dish consisting of onions, courgettes, tomatoes, aubergines, and peppers, fried and stewed in oil and sometimes served cold.
– ORIGIN a French dialect word.

ratbag ▶ **noun** Brit. informal an unpleasant or disliked person.

rat-bite fever ▶ **noun** Medicine a disease contracted from the bite of a rat which causes inflammation of the skin and fever or vomiting. ● This disease can be caused by either the bacterium *Spirillum minus* or the fungus *Streptobacillus moniliformis*.

rat-catcher ▶ **noun** a person whose job is to catch or destroy rats.

ratchet ▶ **noun 1** a device consisting of a bar or wheel with a set of angled teeth in which a pawl, cog, or tooth engages, allowing motion in one direction only. ■ a bar or wheel that forms part of a ratchet.

2 a situation or process that is perceived to be changing in a series of irreversible steps: *the upward ratchet of property taxes.*
▶ **verb** (**ratchets, ratcheting, ratcheted**) [with obj.]
1 operate by means of a ratchet.
2 (**ratchet something up/down**) cause something to rise (or fall) as a step in what is perceived as an irreversible process: *the Bank of Japan ratcheted up interest rates again.*
– ORIGIN mid 17th cent.: from French *rochet*, originally denoting a blunt lance head, later in the sense 'bobbin, ratchet'; related to the base of archaic *rock* 'quantity of wool on a distaff for spinning'.

rate¹ ▶ **noun 1** a measure, quantity, or frequency, typically one measured against another quantity or measure: *the island has the lowest crime rate in the world | buying up sites at a rate of one a month.* ■ the speed with which something moves or happens: *the band is shedding vocalists at an alarming rate | your heart rate.*
2 a fixed price paid or charged for something: *a £3.40 minimum hourly rate of pay | advertising rates.* ■ the amount of a charge or payment expressed as a percentage of another amount, or as a basis of calculation: *you'll find our current interest rate very competitive.* ■ (**rates**) (in the UK) a tax on commercial land and buildings paid to a local authority; (in Northern Ireland and formerly in the UK) a tax levied on private property.
▶ **verb 1** [with obj.] assign a standard or value to (something) according to a particular scale: *they were asked to rate their ability at different driving manoeuvres* | [with obj. and complement] *the hotel, rated four star, had no hot water.* ■ [with obj. and adverbial] assign a standard, optimal, or limiting rating to (a piece of equipment): *the average life of the new bulb is **rated at** approximately 500 hours.* ■ (in the UK) assess the value of (a property) for the purpose of levying a local tax.
2 [with obj. and adverbial] consider to be of a certain quality or standard: *Atkinson rates him as Europe's top defender* | [with obj. and complement] *the program has been rated a great success.* ■ [no obj., with adverbial] be regarded in a specified way: *Jeff still rates as one of the nicest people I have ever met.* ■ [with obj.] informal have a high opinion of: *Mike certainly rated her, goodness knows why.* ■ [with obj.] be worthy of; merit: *the ambassador rated a bulletproof car and a police escort.*
– PHRASES **at any rate** whatever happens or may have happened: *for the moment, at any rate, he was safe.* ■ used to clarify or emphasize a statement: *the story, or at any rate, a public version of it, was known and remembered.* **at this** (or **that**) **rate** if matters continue in this or that way: *at this rate, I won't have a job to go back to.* **rate of return** the annual income from an investment expressed as a proportion (usually a percentage) of the original investment.
– ORIGIN late Middle English (expressing a notion of 'estimated value'): from Old French, from medieval Latin *rata* (from Latin *pro rata parte* (or *portione*) 'according to the proportional share'), from *ratus* 'reckoned', past participle of *reri*.

rate² ▶ **verb** [with obj.] archaic scold (someone) angrily: *he rated the young man soundly for his want of respect.*
– ORIGIN late Middle English: of unknown origin.

rate³ ▶ **verb** variant spelling of RET.

rateable (also **ratable**) ▶ **adjective** able to be rated or estimated.
– DERIVATIVES **rateability** noun, **rateably** adverb.

rateable value ▶ **noun** (in the UK) a value ascribed to a domestic or commercial building based on its size, location, and other factors, used to determine the rates payable by its owner.

rate-capping ▶ **noun** [mass noun] (formerly in the UK) the imposition of an upper limit on the rates leviable by a local authority.
– DERIVATIVES **rate-cap** verb.

rate constant ▶ **noun** Chemistry a coefficient of proportionality relating the rate of a chemical reaction at a given temperature to the concentration of reactant (in a unimolecular reaction) or to the product of the concentrations of reactants.

ratel /ˈreɪt(ə)l, ˈrɑː-/ ▶ **noun** a badger-like mammal with a white or grey back and black underparts, native to Africa and Asia. In Africa it is attracted by the honeyguide bird to bee nests, which it breaks open to gain access to the grubs and honey. Also called HONEY BADGER. ● *Mellivora capensis*, family Mustelidae.
– ORIGIN late 18th cent.: from Afrikaans, of unknown ultimate origin.

rate of exchange ▶ **noun** another term for EXCHANGE RATE.

ratepayer ▶ **noun 1** (in the UK) a person liable to pay rates.
2 N. Amer. a customer of a public utility.

rate tart ▶ **noun** Brit. informal a person who switches from one credit card or mortgage provider to another in order to take advantage of special introductory offers.

ratfish ▶ **noun** (pl. **same** or **ratfishes**) **1** a blunt-nosed chimaera with rodent-like front teeth and a long, thin tail, found chiefly in cooler waters. See also RABBITFISH. ● Genera *Chimaera* and *Hydrolagus*, family Chimaeridae: several species, including *H. colliei* of the eastern North Pacific.
2 a long, thin purplish edible fish which lives in shallow temperate waters of the Indo-Pacific where it burrows in the sand. ● *Gonorhynchus gonorhynchus*, the only member of the family Gonorhynchidae.

rath¹ /rɑːθ/ ▶ **noun** Archaeology (in Ireland) a strong circular earthen wall forming an enclosure and serving as a fort and residence for a tribal chief.
– ORIGIN Irish.

rath² /rʌθ/ ▶ **noun** Indian a chariot, especially one used to carry an idol in a ceremonial procession. See also RATH YATRA.
– ORIGIN Hindi.

Rathaus /ˈrathaʊs/ ▶ **noun** (pl. **Rathäuser** /ˈrathɔɪzə/) a town hall in a German-speaking country.
– ORIGIN German, from *Rat* 'council' + *Haus* 'house'.

rathe /reɪð/ ▶ **adjective** archaic or literary (of a person or their actions) prompt and eager. ■ (of flowers or fruit) blooming or ripening early in the year.
– ORIGIN Old English *hræth, hræd*, of Germanic origin; perhaps related to the base of RASH¹.

rather ▶ **adverb 1** (**would rather**) used to indicate one's preference in a particular matter: *would you like some wine or would you rather stick to sherry?* | *she'd **rather** die **than** cause a scene* | [with clause] *I'd rather you didn't tell him.*
2 [as submodifier] to a certain or significant extent or degree: *she's been behaving rather strangely | he's rather an unpleasant man.* ■ used before verbs so as to make the expression of a feeling or opinion less assertive: *I rather think he wants me to marry him | we were rather hoping you might do that for us.*
3 used to suggest that the opposite of a previous statement is the case; on the contrary: [sentence adverb] *There is no shortage of basic skills in the workplace. Rather, the problem is poor management.* ■ more precisely: *I walked, **or rather** limped, the two miles home.* ■ instead of; as opposed to: *she seemed indifferent **rather than** angry.*
▶ **exclamation** Brit. dated used to express emphatic affirmation, agreement, or acceptance: *'You are glad to be home, aren't you?' 'Rather!'*
– PHRASES **had rather** literary or archaic would rather: *I had rather not see him.* **rather you** (or **him** or **her** etc.) **than me** used to convey that one would be reluctant oneself to undertake a particular task undertaken by someone else.
– ORIGIN Old English *hrathor* 'earlier, sooner', comparative of *hræthe* 'without delay', from *hræth* 'prompt' (see RATHE).

rathe-ripe ▶ **adjective** archaic or literary (of fruits or grain) ripening early in the year. ■ (of a person) maturing early.

Rathlin Island /ˈraθlɪn/ an island in the North Channel, off the north coast of Ireland.

rathole ▶ **noun 1** informal a cramped or squalid room or building.
2 N. Amer. informal used to refer to the waste of money or resources: *pouring our assets **down the rathole** of military expenditure.*
3 (in the oil industry) a shallow hole drilled near a well to accommodate the drill string joint when not in use. ■ a small hole drilled at the bottom of a larger hole.
▶ **verb** [with obj.] N. Amer. informal hide (money or goods), typically as part of a deception.

rathskeller /ˈrɑːtsˌkɛlə/ ▶ **noun** US a beer hall or restaurant in a basement.
– ORIGIN early 20th cent.: from obsolete German (now *Ratskeller*), from *Rathaus* 'town hall' + *Keller* 'cellar', denoting the place where beer and wine were sold.

rath yatra /rʌθ jɑːtrɑː/ ▶ **noun** Hinduism a ceremonial procession centred around a chariot carrying an idol, specifically the procession of the Juggernaut. ■ (in India) a political demonstration consisting of a convoy of motor vehicles travelling over a long distance.
– ORIGIN via Hindi from Sanskrit *ratha* 'chariot' + *yātrā* from *yā* 'to travel'.

ratify ▶ **verb** (**ratifies, ratifying, ratified**) [with obj.] sign or give formal consent to (a treaty, contract, or agreement), making it officially valid.
– DERIVATIVES **ratifiable** adjective, **ratification** noun, **ratifier** noun.
– ORIGIN late Middle English: from Old French *ratifier*, from medieval Latin *ratificare*, from Latin *ratus* 'fixed' (see RATE¹).

rating¹ ▶ **noun 1** a classification or ranking of someone or something based on a comparative assessment of their quality, standard, or performance: *the hotel regained its five-star rating.* ■ (**ratings**) the estimated audience size of a particular television or radio programme: *the soap's ratings have recently picked up.* ■ the value of a property or condition which is claimed to be standard, optimal, or limiting for a substance, material, or device: *fuel with a low octane rating.* ■ any of the classes into which racing yachts are assigned according to dimensions.
2 Brit. a non-commissioned sailor in the navy. [so named from the position or rating held by a sailor, recorded on a ship's books.]

rating² ▶ **noun** dated an angry reprimand.

ratio ▶ **noun** (pl. **ratios**) the quantitative relation between two amounts showing the number of times one value contains or is contained within the other: *the ratio of men's jobs to women's is 8 to 1.*
– ORIGIN mid 17th cent.: from Latin, literally 'reckoning', from *rat-* 'reckoned', from the verb *reri*.

ratiocinate /ˌratɪˈɒsɪneɪt, ˌraʃɪ-/ ▶ **verb** [no obj.] formal form judgements by a process of logic; reason.
– DERIVATIVES **ratiocination** noun, **ratiocinative** adjective, **ratiocinator** noun.
– ORIGIN mid 17th cent.: from Latin *ratiocinat-* 'deliberated, calculated', from the verb *ratiocinari*, from *ratio* (see RATIO).

ratio decidendi /ˌdɛsɪˈdɛndiː/ ▶ **noun** (pl. **rationes decidendi** /ˌratɪˈəʊniːz/) Law the rule of law on which a judicial decision is based.
– ORIGIN Latin, literally 'reason for deciding'.

ration ▶ **noun** a fixed amount of a commodity officially allowed to each person during a time of shortage, as in wartime: *1947 saw the bread ration reduced.* ■ (**rations**) an amount of food supplied on a regular basis, especially to members of the armed forces during a war. ■ (**rations**) food; provisions: *their emergency rations ran out.* ■ a fixed amount of a particular thing: *holidaymakers who like **a** generous **ration of** activity.*
▶ **verb** [with obj.] allow each person to have only a fixed amount of (a commodity): *petrol was so strictly rationed that bikes were always in demand.* ■ (**ration someone to**) allow someone to have only (a fixed amount of a commodity): *the population was rationed to four litres of water per person per day.*
– PHRASES **come up** (or **be given**) **with the rations** military slang (of a medal) be awarded automatically and without regard to merit.
– ORIGIN early 18th cent.: from French, from Latin *ratio(n-)* 'reckoning, ratio'.

rational ▶ **adjective 1** based on or in accordance with reason or logic: *I'm sure there's a perfectly rational explanation.* ■ able to think sensibly or logically: *Ursula's upset—she's not being very rational.* ■ endowed with the capacity to reason: *man is a rational being.*
2 Mathematics (of a number, quantity, or expression) expressible, or containing quantities which are expressible, as a ratio of whole numbers.
– DERIVATIVES **rationality** noun, **rationally** adverb.
– ORIGIN late Middle English (in the sense 'having the ability to reason'): from Latin *rationalis*, from *ratio(n-)* 'reckoning, reason' (see RATIO).

rational dress ▶ **noun** [mass noun] a style of women's dress introduced in the late 19th century, characterized by the wearing of knickerbockers or bloomers in place of a skirt.

rationale /ˌraʃəˈnɑːl/ ▶ **noun** a set of reasons or a logical basis for a course of action or belief: *he explained the rationale behind the change.*
– ORIGIN mid 17th cent.: modern Latin, neuter (used as a noun) of Latin *rationalis* 'endowed with reason' (see RATIONAL).

rationalism ▶ **noun** [mass noun] the practice or principle of basing opinions and actions on reason and knowledge rather than on religious belief or emotional response: *scientific rationalism.* ■ Philosophy the theory that reason rather than experience is the foundation of certainty in knowledge. ■ Theology the practice of treating reason as the ultimate authority in religion.

R

– DERIVATIVES **rationalist** noun, **rationalistic** adjective, **rationalistically** adverb.

rationalize (also **rationalise**) ▶ **verb** [with obj.] **1** attempt to explain or justify (behaviour or an attitude) with logical reasons, even if these are not appropriate: *she couldn't rationalize her urge to return to the cottage.* **2** Brit. make (a company, process, or industry) more efficient, especially by dispensing with superfluous personnel or equipment: *if we rationalize production, will that mean redundancies?* ■ reorganize (a process or system) so as to make it more logical and consistent: *Parliament should seek to rationalize the country's court structure.* **3** Mathematics convert (a function or expression) to a rational form.
– DERIVATIVES **rationalization** noun, **rationalizer** noun.

ration book (also **ration card**) ▶ **noun** an official document entitling the holder to a ration of food, clothes, or other goods.

ratite /ˈratʌɪt/ Ornithology ▶ **adjective** (of a bird) having a flat breastbone without a keel, and so unable to fly. Contrasted with CARINATE.
▶ **noun** any of the mostly large, flightless birds with a ratite breastbone, i.e. the ostrich, rhea, emu, cassowary, and kiwi, together with the extinct moa and elephant bird.
– ORIGIN late 19th cent.: from Latin *ratis* 'raft' + -ITE[1].

rat-kangaroo ▶ **noun** a small rat-like Australian marsupial with long hindlimbs used for hopping. ● Family Potoroidae: several genera and species.

ratlines /ˈratlɪnz/ ▶ **plural noun** a series of small rope lines fastened across a sailing ship's shrouds like the rungs of a ladder, used for climbing the rigging.
– ORIGIN late Middle English: of unknown origin.

ratoon /rəˈtuːn/ ▶ **noun** a new shoot or sprout springing from the base of a crop plant, especially sugar cane, after cropping.
▶ **verb** [no obj.] (of sugar cane) produce ratoons. ■ [with obj.] cut down (a plant) to cause it to produce ratoons.
– ORIGIN mid 17th cent.: from Spanish *retoño* 'a sprout'.

rat pack[1] ▶ **noun** informal **1** a group of journalists and photographers who pursue celebrities in a relentless or aggressive way. **2** (**the Rat Pack**) the name given to the group of 1960s actors that included Dean Martin, Frank Sinatra, and Sammy Davis Jr. ■ N. Amer. a group of friends or associates.

rat pack[2] ▶ **noun** Brit. informal a ration pack issued by the army to men on duty away from base camp.

rat race ▶ **noun** informal a way of life in which people are caught up in a fiercely competitive struggle for wealth or power.

rat run ▶ **noun** Brit. informal a minor, typically residential street used by drivers during peak periods to avoid congestion on main roads.

ratsbane ▶ **noun** [mass noun] archaic rat poison.

R

rat snake ▶ **noun** a harmless constricting snake that feeds on rats and other small mammals. ● Several genera and species in the family Colubridae: genus *Elaphe* of America, in particular *E. obsoleta*, and genera *Ptyas* and *Argyrogena* of Asia (also called RACER), in particular *P. mucosus*.

rat-tail ▶ **noun 1** (also **rat's tail**) a narrow hairless tail like that of a rat, or something that resembles one. ■ (**rat's tails**) Brit. informal hair hanging in lank, damp or greasy strands. **2** a fish with a long, thin tail, in particular: ■ another term for GRENADIER (sense 2). ■ another term for RABBITFISH (sense 1).

rat-tailed maggot ▶ **noun** the aquatic larva of the drone fly, with a tail-like telescopic breathing tube that enables it to breathe air while submerged.

rattan /rəˈtan/ ▶ **noun 1** [mass noun] the thin jointed stems of a palm, used to make furniture. ■ [count noun] a length of rattan used as a walking stick. **2** the tropical Old World climbing palm which yields rattan, with long, spiny, jointed stems. ● Genus *Calamus*, family Palmae.
– ORIGIN mid 17th cent.: from Malay *rotan*, probably from *raut* 'pare, trim'.

rat-tat (also **rat-tat-tat** or **rat-a-tat**) ▶ **noun** a rapping sound (used especially in reference to a sequence of knocks on a door or the sound of gunfire).
– ORIGIN late 17th cent.: imitative.

ratted ▶ **adjective** Brit. informal very drunk.

ratter ▶ **noun** a dog or other animal that is used for hunting rats.

Rattle, Sir Simon (Denis) (b.1955), English conductor. Principal conductor with the City of Birmingham Symphony Orchestra 1980–91, he became chief conductor of the Berlin Philharmonic Orchestra in 2000 and its artistic director in 2002.

rattle ▶ **verb 1** make or cause to make a rapid succession of short, sharp knocking sounds: [no obj.] *the roof rattled with little gusts of wind* | [with obj.] *he rattled some change in his pocket.* ■ [no obj., with adverbial of direction] (of a vehicle or its occupants) move or travel with a knocking sound: *trains rattled past at frequent intervals.* ■ [no obj.] (**rattle about/around in**) be in or occupy (an unnecessarily spacious room or building): *the house was too big—we just rattled around in it.* **2** [with obj.] informal make (someone) nervous, worried, or irritated: *she turned quickly, rattled by his presence.*
▶ **noun 1** a rapid succession of short, sharp, sounds: *the rattle of teacups on the tray.* ■ a gurgling sound in the throat of a dying person. **2** a thing used to make a rattling sound, in particular: ■ a baby's toy consisting of a container filled with small pellets, which makes a noise when shaken. ■ Brit. a wooden device that makes a loud noise when whirled around, formerly used by spectators at football matches. ■ the set of horny rings at the end of a rattlesnake's tail, shaken as a warning. **3** archaic a person who talks incessantly in a lively or inane way.
– PHRASES **rattle someone's cage** (or **chain**) informal anger or irritate someone. **rattle sabres** threaten to take aggressive action. See also SABRE-RATTLING.
– PHRASAL VERBS **rattle something off** say, perform, or produce something quickly and effortlessly: *he rattled off some instructions.* **rattle on/away** talk rapidly and at length, especially in an inane way: *she found herself rattling on about unhappiness and happiness.*
– DERIVATIVES **rattly** adjective (**rattlier**, **rattliest**).
– ORIGIN Middle English: related to Middle Dutch and Low German *ratelen*, of imitative origin.

rattlebox ▶ **noun** used in reference to something that rattles, such as an old or rickety vehicle.

rattler ▶ **noun 1** a thing that rattles, especially an old or rickety vehicle. **2** N. Amer. informal a rattlesnake.

rattlesnake ▶ **noun** a heavy-bodied American pit viper with a series of horny rings on the tail that produce a characteristic rattling sound when vibrated as a warning. ● Genera *Crotalus* and *Sistrurus*, family Viperidae: several species.

rattletrap ▶ **noun** informal an old or rickety vehicle.

rattling ▶ **adjective 1** making a series of knocking sounds: *a rattling old lift.* **2** informal, dated very good of its kind (used for emphasis): *a rattling good story.*

rat trap ▶ **noun** informal **1** an unpleasant situation that offers no prospect of improvement. **2** a squalid or ramshackle building.

ratty ▶ **adjective** (**rattier**, **rattiest**) **1** resembling or characteristic of a rat: *his ratty eyes glittered.* ■ (of a place) infested with rats. ■ informal in bad condition; shabby or ramshackle: *a ratty old armchair.* **2** [predic.] Brit. informal bad-tempered and irritable: *I was a bit ratty with the children.*
– DERIVATIVES **rattily** adverb, **rattiness** noun.

raucous /ˈrɔːkəs/ ▶ **adjective** making or constituting a disturbingly harsh and loud noise: *raucous youths.*
– DERIVATIVES **raucously** adverb, **raucousness** noun.
– ORIGIN mid 18th cent.: from Latin *raucus* 'hoarse' + -OUS.

rauli /ˈraʊli/ ▶ **noun** a southern beech tree with showy autumn foliage, native to Chile and cultivated as an ornamental. ● *Nothofagus procera*, family Fagaceae.
– ORIGIN early 20th cent.: via American Spanish from Mapuche *ruili*.

raunch ▶ **noun** [mass noun] informal energetic earthiness; vulgarity: *the raunch of his first album.*
– ORIGIN 1960s: back-formation from RAUNCHY.

raunchy ▶ **adjective** (**raunchier**, **raunchiest**) informal **1** energetically earthy and sexually explicit: *his raunchy new novel.* **2** US shabby or grubby: *the restaurant's style is raunchy and the sanitation chancy.*
– DERIVATIVES **raunchily** adverb, **raunchiness** noun.
– ORIGIN 1930s: of unknown origin.

Rauschenberg /ˈraʊʃ(ə)nbəːg/, Robert (1925–2008), American artist. His series of 'combine' paintings, such as *Charlene* (1954) and *Rebus* (1955), incorporate three-dimensional objects such as nails, rags, and bottles.

rauwolfia /raʊˈwʊlfɪə, raʊˈvɒlfɪə/ (also **rauvolfia**) ▶ **noun** a tropical shrub or small tree, some kinds of which are cultivated for medicinal drugs. ● Genus *Rauwolfia* (or *Rauvolfia*), family Apocynaceae: many species, in particular the Indian snakeroot (*R. serpentina*), from which the drug reserpine is obtained.
– ORIGIN modern Latin, named after Leonhard *Rauwolf* (died 1596), German botanist.

rav /rɒv/ ▶ **noun** Judaism a rabbi, especially one who holds a position of authority or who acts as a personal mentor. [partly via Yiddish.] ■ (**Rav**) (in orthodox Judaism) a title of respect and form of address preceding a personal name.
– ORIGIN from Hebrew and Aramaic *raḇ* 'master'.

ravage ▶ **verb** [with obj.] cause severe and extensive damage to: *the hurricane ravaged southern Florida.*
▶ **noun** (**ravages**) the destructive effects of something: *his face had withstood* ***the ravages of time.*** ■ acts of destruction: *the ravages committed by man.*
– DERIVATIVES **ravager** noun.
– ORIGIN early 17th cent.: from French *ravager*, from earlier *ravage*, alteration of *ravine* 'rush of water'.

ravaged ▶ **adjective** severely damaged; devastated: *he hopes to visit his ravaged homeland.* ■ disfigured by age or illness: *the ravaged faces of the elderly cancer victims.*

rave[1] ▶ **verb** [no obj.] **1** talk incoherently, as if one were delirious or mad: *Nancy's having hysterics and raving about a black ghost.* ■ address someone in an angry, uncontrolled way: [with direct speech] *'Never mind how he feels!' Melissa raved.* **2** speak or write about someone or something with great enthusiasm or admiration: *New York's critics raved about the acting.* **3** informal attend a rave party.
▶ **noun 1** [usu. as modifier] informal an extremely enthusiastic recommendation or appraisal: *their tour received* ***rave reviews.*** ■ a person or thing that inspires intense and widely shared enthusiasm: *last year's fave raves are back for a live performance.* ■ Brit. informal, dated a passionate and usually transitory infatuation. **2** informal a lively party involving dancing and drinking: *their annual fancy-dress rave.* ■ a very large party or similar event with dancing to loud, fast electronic music. ■ [mass noun] electronic dance music of the kind played at a rave.
– DERIVATIVES **ravey** adjective (informal).
– ORIGIN Middle English (in the sense 'show signs of madness'): probably from Old Northern French *raver*; related obscurely to (Middle) Low German *reven* 'be senseless, rave'.

rave[2] ▶ **noun** a rail of a cart. ■ (**raves**) a permanent or removable framework added to the sides of a cart to increase its capacity.
– ORIGIN mid 16th cent.: variant of the synonymous dialect word *rathe*, of unknown origin.

Ravel /raˈvɛl/, French /ʀavɛl/, Maurice (Joseph) (1875–1937), French composer. His works are somewhat impressionistic in style, employing colourful orchestration and unresolved dissonances. Notable works: the ballets *Daphnis and Chloë* (1912) and *Boléro* (1928) and the orchestral work *La Valse* (1920).

ravel ▶ **verb** (**ravels**, **ravelling**, **ravelled**; US **ravels**, **raveling**, **raveled**) **1** [with obj.] (**ravel something out**) untangle something: *Davy had finished ravelling out his herring net.* **2** [no obj.] unravel; fray. **3** [with obj.] confuse or complicate (a question or situation).
▶ **noun** a tangle, cluster, or knot: *a ravel of knitting.*
– ORIGIN late Middle English (in the sense 'entangle, confuse'): probably from Dutch *ravelen* 'fray out, tangle'.

ravelin /ˈravlɪn/ ▶ **noun** historical an outwork of fortifications, with two faces forming a salient angle, constructed beyond the main ditch and in front of the curtain.
– ORIGIN late 16th cent.: from French, from obsolete Italian *ravellino*, of unknown origin.

ravelling ▶ **noun** a thread from a woven or knitted fabric that has frayed or started to unravel.

raven[1] /ˈreɪv(ə)n/ ▶ **noun** a large heavily built crow with mainly black plumage, feeding chiefly on carrion. ● Genus *Corvus*, family Corvidae: several species, in particular the widespread all-black **common raven** (*C. corax*).
▶ **adjective** (especially of hair) of a glossy black colour.
– ORIGIN Old English *hræfn*, of Germanic origin; related to Dutch *raaf* and German *Rabe*.

raven² /ˈrav(ə)n/ ▶ **verb** [no obj.] archaic (of a wild animal) hunt voraciously for prey. ■ [with obj.] devour voraciously.
– ORIGIN late 15th cent. (in the sense 'take as spoil'): from Old French *raviner*, originally 'to ravage', based on Latin *rapina* 'pillage'.

ravening ▶ **adjective** (of a ferocious wild animal) extremely hungry and hunting for prey: *they turned on each other like ravening wolves.*

Ravenna /rəˈvɛnə/ a city near the Adriatic coast in NE central Italy; pop. 155,997 (2008). Ravenna became the capital of the Western Roman Empire in 402 and then of the Ostrogothic kingdom of Italy, afterwards serving as capital of Byzantine Italy. It is noted for its ancient mosaics dating from the early Christian period.

ravenous ▶ **adjective** extremely hungry: *I'd been out all day and was ravenous.* ■ (of hunger or need) very great; voracious: *a ravenous appetite.*
– DERIVATIVES **ravenously** adverb, **ravenousness** noun.
– ORIGIN late Middle English: from Old French *ravineus*, from *raviner* 'to ravage' (see RAVEN²).

raver ▶ **noun** informal **1** Brit. a person who has an exciting and uninhibited social life.
2 a person who regularly goes to raves.
3 a person who talks incoherently.

rave-up ▶ **noun** Brit. informal a lively, noisy party involving dancing and drinking. ■ N. Amer. a fast, loud, or danceable piece of pop music.

Ravi /ˈrʌvi/ a river in southern Asia, one of the headwaters of the Indus, which rises in the Himalayas in Himachel Pradesh, NW India, and flows generally south-westwards into Pakistan, where it empties into the Chenab River just north of Multan. It is one of the five rivers that gave Punjab its name.

ravigote /ˈravɪgɒt/ (also **ravigotte**) ▶ **noun** [mass noun] a mixture of chopped chervil, chives, tarragon, and shallots, used in cookery to give piquancy to a sauce or as a base for a herb butter.
– ORIGIN French, from *ravigoter* 'invigorate'.

ravin /ˈravɪn/ ▶ **noun** [mass noun] archaic violent seizure of prey or property; plunder.
– ORIGIN Middle English: from Old French *ravine*, from Latin *rapina* 'pillage' (see RAPINE).

ravine /rəˈviːn/ ▶ **noun** a deep, narrow gorge with steep sides.
– DERIVATIVES **ravined** adjective.
– ORIGIN late 18th cent.: from French, 'violent rush (of water)' (see RAVIN).

raving ▶ **noun** (usu. **ravings**) irrational or incoherent talk: *the ravings of a madwoman.*
▶ **adjective** informal used to emphasize a particular quality: *she'd never been a raving beauty* | [as submodifier] *have you gone **raving mad**?*

ravioli /ˌravɪˈəʊli/ ▶ **plural noun** small pasta envelopes containing minced meat, fish, cheese, or vegetables, usually served with a sauce.
– ORIGIN Italian.

ravish ▶ **verb** [with obj.] **1** archaic seize and carry off (someone) by force. ■ dated (of a man) rape (a woman).
2 literary fill (someone) with intense delight; enrapture: *ravished by a sunny afternoon, she had agreed without even thinking.*
– DERIVATIVES **ravisher** noun, **ravishment** noun.
– ORIGIN Middle English: from Old French *raviss-*, lengthened stem of *ravir*, from an alteration of Latin *rapere* 'seize'.

ravishing ▶ **adjective** delightful; entrancing: *she looked ravishing.*
– DERIVATIVES **ravishingly** adverb.

raw ▶ **adjective** **1** (of food) not cooked: *raw eggs* | *salsify can be eaten raw in salads.* ■ (of a material or substance) in its natural state; unprocessed: *raw silk* | *raw sewage.* ■ (of data) not analysed, evaluated, or processed for use.
2 (of a part of the body) red and painful, especially as the result of skin abrasion: *he scrubbed his hands until they were raw.* ■ (of a person's nerves) very sensitive.
3 (of an emotion or quality) strong and undisguised: *he exuded an air of raw, vibrant masculinity.* ■ frank and realistic in the depiction of unpleasant situations: *a raw, uncompromising portrait.* ■ US informal (of language) coarse or crude, typically in relation to sexual matters.
4 (of the weather) cold and damp; bleak: *a raw February night.*
5 new to an activity or job and therefore lacking experience or skill: *they were replaced by raw recruits.*
6 (of the edge of a piece of cloth) not having a hem or selvedge.
7 S. African derogatory from a traditional tribal or rural culture.
– PHRASES **don't come the raw prawn with me** Austral. informal don't treat me like a foolish or gullible person. **in the raw 1** in its true state; in a starkly realistic way: *he didn't much care for nature in the raw.* **2** informal naked: *I slept in the raw.* **a raw deal** informal a situation in which someone receives unfair or harsh treatment. **touch someone on the raw** Brit. upset someone by referring to a subject about which they are extremely sensitive.
– DERIVATIVES **rawly** adverb, **rawness** noun.
– ORIGIN Old English *hrēaw*, of Germanic origin; related to Dutch *rauw* and German *roh*, from an Indo-European root shared by Greek *kreas* 'raw flesh'.

Rawalpindi /rɔːlˈpɪndi, ˌrɑːwəl-/ a city in Punjab province, northern Pakistan, in the foothills of the Himalayas; pop. 1,933,900 (est. 2009). A former military station, it was the interim capital of Pakistan, 1959–67, during the construction of Islamabad.

raw bar ▶ **noun** US a bar or counter which sells raw oysters and other seafood.

raw-boned ▶ **adjective** having a bony or gaunt physique: *raw-boned farmhands.*

rawhide ▶ **noun** [mass noun] stiff untanned leather. ■ [count noun] N. Amer. a whip or rope made of rawhide.

Rawlplug /ˈrɔːlplʌg/ ▶ **noun** Brit. trademark a thin plastic or fibre sheath that is inserted into a hole in masonry in order to hold a screw.
– ORIGIN early 20th cent.: from *Rawlings* (the name of the engineers who introduced it) + PLUG.

Rawls /rɔːlz/, John (1921–2002), American philosopher. His books *A Theory of Justice* (1971) and *Political Liberalism* (1993) consider the basic institutions of a just society as those chosen by rational people under conditions which ensure impartiality.

raw material ▶ **noun** the basic material from which a product is made.

raw sienna ▶ **noun** see SIENNA.

raw umber ▶ **noun** see UMBER.

Ray¹ /reɪ/, John (1627–1705), English naturalist. Ray was the first to classify flowering plants into monocotyledons and dicotyledons, and he established the species as the basic taxonomic unit. His systematic scheme was not improved upon until that of Linnaeus.

Ray² /reɪ/, Man (1890–1976), American photographer, painter, and film-maker; born *Emmanuel Rudnitsky*. A leading figure in the Dada and surrealist movements, he is known for his photographs in which images were manipulated and superimposed on one another.

Ray³ /rʌɪ/, Satyajit (1921–92), Indian film director, the first to bring Indian films to the attention of Western audiences. Notable films: *Pather Panchali* (1955).

ray¹ ▶ **noun** **1** each of the lines in which light (and heat) may seem to stream from the sun or any luminous body, or pass through a small opening: *a ray of sunlight came through the window.* ■ the straight line in which light or other electromagnetic radiation travels to a given point. ■ (with adj. or noun modifier **rays**) a specified form of non-luminous radiation: *ultraviolet rays.* ■ (**rays**) informal, chiefly N. Amer. sunlight considered in the context of sunbathing: ***catch some rays** on a sandy beach.* ■ an initial or slight indication of a positive or welcome quality: *if only I could see some **ray of hope**.*
2 Mathematics any of a set of straight lines passing through one point.
3 a thing that is arranged radially, in particular: ■ Botany any of the individual strap-shaped florets around the edge of the flower of a daisy or related plant. ■ (also **fin ray**) Zoology each of the long slender bony supports in the fins of most bony fishes. ■ Zoology each radial arm of a starfish.
▶ **verb** [no obj., with adverbial of direction] spread from or as if from a central point: *delicate lines rayed out at each corner of her eyes.* ■ [with obj. and adverbial of direction] literary radiate (light): *the sun rays forth its natural light into the air.*
– PHRASES **ray of sunshine** informal a person who brings happiness into the lives of others.
– DERIVATIVES **rayless** adjective (chiefly Botany).
– ORIGIN Middle English: from Old French *rai*, based on Latin *radius* 'spoke, ray'. The verb dates from the late 16th cent.

ray² ▶ **noun** a broad flat marine or freshwater fish with a cartilaginous skeleton, wing-like pectoral fins, and a long slender tail. Many rays have venomous spines or electric organs. ● Order Batiformes: several families, including Rajidae (the skates).
– ORIGIN Middle English: from Old French *raie*, from Latin *raia*.

ray³ (also **re**) ▶ **noun** Music (in tonic sol-fa) the second note of a major scale. ■ the note D in the fixed-doh system.
– ORIGIN Middle English *re*, representing (as an arbitrary name for the note) the first syllable of *resonare*, taken from a Latin hymn (see SOLMIZATION).

rayed ▶ **adjective** [in combination] chiefly Biology having rays of a specified number or kind: *white-rayed daisies.*

ray-finned fish ▶ **noun** a fish of a large group having thin fins strengthened by slender rays, including all bony fishes apart from the coelacanth and lungfishes. Compare with LOBE-FINNED FISH, TELEOST. ● Subclass (or class) Actinopterygii: numerous orders.

ray floret ▶ **noun** Botany (in a composite flower head of the daisy family) any of a number of strap-shaped and typically sterile florets that form the ray. In plants such as dandelions the flower head is composed entirely of ray florets. Compare with DISC FLORET.

ray gun ▶ **noun** (in science fiction) a gun causing injury or damage by the emission of rays.

Rayleigh /ˈreɪli/, John William Strutt, 3rd Baron (1842–1919), English physicist. He established the electrical units of resistance, current, and electromotive force. With William Ramsay he discovered argon and other inert gases. Nobel Prize for Physics (1904).

Rayleigh number ▶ **noun** Physics a dimensionless parameter that is a measure of the instability of a layer of fluid due to differences of temperature and density at the top and bottom.

Rayleigh scattering ▶ **noun** [mass noun] Physics the scattering of light by particles in a medium, without change in wavelength. It accounts, for example, for the blue colour of the sky, since blue light is scattered slightly more efficiently than red. Compare with RAMAN EFFECT.

Rayleigh wave ▶ **noun** Physics an undulating wave that travels over the surface of a solid, especially of the ground in an earthquake, with a speed independent of wavelength, the motion of the particles being in ellipses.

Raynaud's disease /ˈreɪnəʊ/ (also **Raynaud's syndrome**) ▶ **noun** [mass noun] a disease characterized by spasm of the arteries in the extremities, especially the fingers (**Raynaud's phenomenon**). It is typically brought on by constant cold or vibration, and leads to pallor, pain, numbness, and in severe cases, gangrene.
– ORIGIN late 19th cent.: named after Maurice *Raynaud* (1834–81), French physician.

rayon ▶ **noun** [mass noun] a textile fibre or fabric made from regenerated cellulose (viscose).
– ORIGIN 1920s: an arbitrary formation.

rayonnant /ˌreɪjɒˈnɒ̃/, French /rɛjɔnɑ̃/ ▶ **adjective** relating to or denoting a French style of Gothic architecture prevalent from *c.*1230 to *c.*1350, characterized by distinctive rose windows.
– ORIGIN French, literally 'radiating', from the pattern of radiating lights in the windows.

Ray's bream ▶ **noun** see POMFRET.
– ORIGIN mid 19th cent.: named after John Ray (see RAY¹).

raze (also **rase**) ▶ **verb** [with obj.] completely destroy (a building, town, or other settlement): *villages were **razed to the ground**.*
– ORIGIN Middle English (in the sense 'scratch, incise'): from Old French *raser* 'shave closely', from Latin *ras-* 'scraped', from the verb *radere*.

razoo /rɑːˈzuː/ ▶ **noun** [with negative] Austral./NZ informal used to denote an imaginary coin of little value or a very small sum of money: *the lousy government never gave them a **brass razoo**.*
– ORIGIN 1930s: of unknown origin.

razor ▶ **noun** an instrument with a sharp blade or set of blades, used to remove unwanted hair from the face or body.
▶ **verb** [with obj.] cut with a razor.

R

– ORIGIN Middle English: from Old French *rasor*, from *raser* 'shave closely' (see RAZE).

razorback ▶ noun **1** (also **razorback hog**) a pig of a half-wild breed common in the southern US, with the back formed into a high narrow ridge.
2 (also **razorback ridge**) a steep-sided narrow ridge of land.

razorbill ▶ noun a black-and-white auk (seabird) with a deep bill that is said to resemble a cut-throat razor, found in the North Atlantic and Baltic Sea. ● *Alca torda*, family Alcidae.

razor blade ▶ noun a blade used in a razor, typically a flat piece of metal with a sharp edge or edges used in a safety razor.

razor clam ▶ noun North American term for RAZOR SHELL.

razor cut ▶ noun a short or tapered haircut effected with a razor.
▶ verb (**razor-cut**) [with obj.] cut (hair) with a razor.

razor edge (also **razor's edge**) ▶ noun a sharp edge of a knife or similar implement. ■ a critical or precarious situation: *politically we are on a razor edge.* ■ (**the razor edge**) the most advanced stage in the development of something; the cutting edge: *in 1960 jet planes were* ***the razor edge of*** *chic.*
– DERIVATIVES **razor-edged** adjective.

razorfish ▶ noun (pl. **same** or **razorfishes**) **1** a small fish of the Indo-Pacific, with a long flattened snout and a laterally compressed body encased in thin bony shields that meet to form a sharp ridge on the belly. ● Family Centriscidae: several genera and species, including *Aeoliscus strigatus*, which swims in a head-down vertical posture.
2 a small brightly coloured wrasse with a steeply sloping forehead, living chiefly in coastal waters of the western Atlantic. ● Genus *Hemipteronotus*, family Labridae: several species.
3 another term for RAZOR SHELL.

razor grass ▶ noun [mass noun] W. Indian a tall sedge or grass with leaf blades that have sharp cutting edges. ● Genera *Scleria* (family Cyperaceae) and *Paspalum* (family Gramineae): several species.

razor-sharp ▶ adjective extremely sharp: *razor-sharp teeth* | figurative *his razor-sharp mind.*

razor shell ▶ noun a burrowing bivalve mollusc with a long slender shell which resembles the handle of a cut-throat razor. Also called JACKKNIFE CLAM or RAZOR CLAM in North America. ● Family Solenidae: *Ensis* and other genera.

razor-thin ▶ adjective extremely thin: *razor-thin slices of salmon.* ■ (especially of a margin of victory) very slim; barely achieved: *a razor-thin margin of eight votes.*

razor wire ▶ noun [mass noun] a metal wire or ribbon with sharp edges or studded with small sharp blades, used as a barrier to deter intruders.

razz informal, chiefly N. Amer. ▶ verb [with obj.] tease (someone) playfully.
▶ noun another term for RASPBERRY (sense 4).
– ORIGIN early 20th cent.: from informal *razzberry*, alteration of RASPBERRY.

R

razzia /ˈrazɪə/ ▶ noun historical a hostile raid for purposes of conquest, plunder, and capture of slaves, especially one carried out by Moors in North Africa.
– ORIGIN mid 19th cent.: via French from Algerian Arabic *ġāziya* 'raid'.

razzle ▶ noun (in phrase **on the razzle**) Brit. informal out celebrating or enjoying oneself: *he's gone out on the razzle again.*
– ORIGIN early 20th cent.: abbreviation of RAZZLE-DAZZLE.

razzle-dazzle ▶ noun another term for RAZZMATAZZ.
– ORIGIN late 19th cent.: reduplication of DAZZLE.

razzmatazz (also **razzamatazz**) ▶ noun [mass noun] informal noisy, showy, and exciting activity and display designed to attract and impress: *the razzmatazz of a political campaign.*
– ORIGIN late 19th cent.: probably an alteration of RAZZLE-DAZZLE.

RB ▶ abbreviation Botswana (international vehicle registration).
– ORIGIN from *Republic of Botswana.*

Rb ▶ symbol the chemical element rubidium.

RBI ▶ abbreviation Baseball run batted in (a run credited to the batter for enabling a runner to score during his play).

RC ▶ abbreviation ■ (in cycling) racing club. ■ Red Cross. ■ reinforced concrete. ■ Electronics resistance/capacitance (or resistor/capacitor). ■ Roman Catholic.

RCA ▶ abbreviation ■ Central African Republic (international vehicle registration). [from French *République Centrafricaine.*] ■ (in the US) Radio Corporation of America. ■ (in the UK) Royal College of Art.

RCAF ▶ abbreviation Royal Canadian Air Force.

RCH ▶ abbreviation Chile (international vehicle registration).
– ORIGIN from Spanish *República de Chile.*

RCM ▶ abbreviation (in the UK) Royal College of Music.

RCMP ▶ abbreviation Royal Canadian Mounted Police.

RCN ▶ abbreviation (in the UK) Royal College of Nursing.

RCP ▶ abbreviation (in the UK) Royal College of Physicians.

RCS ▶ abbreviation ■ (in the UK) Royal College of Scientists. ■ (in the UK) Royal College of Surgeons. ■ (in the UK) Royal Corps of Signals.

RCVS ▶ abbreviation (in the UK) Royal College of Veterinary Surgeons.

RD ▶ abbreviation ■ Brit. refer to drawer (used by banks when suspending payment of a cheque). ■ (in the UK) Royal Naval Reserve Decoration.

Rd ▶ abbreviation Road (used in street names).

RDA ▶ abbreviation ■ recommended daily (or dietary) allowance, the quantity of a particular nutrient which should be consumed daily in order to maintain good health. ■ (in the UK) Regional Development Agency.

RDBMS ▶ abbreviation Computing relational database management system.

RDC ▶ abbreviation historical (in the UK) Rural District Council.

RDF ▶ abbreviation ■ radio direction finder (or finding). ■ (in the US) rapid deployment force.

RDI ▶ abbreviation recommended (or reference) daily intake, another term for **RDA**.

RDS ▶ abbreviation ■ radio data system, in which a digital signal is transmitted with a normal radio signal to provide further data or control the receiver. ■ respiratory distress syndrome.

RDX ▶ noun [mass noun] a type of high explosive.
– ORIGIN 1940s: from *R(esearch) D(epartment) (E)x(plosive).*

RE ▶ abbreviation ■ religious education (as a school subject). ■ (in the UK) Royal Engineers.

Re¹ /reɪ/ variant spelling of RA¹.

Re² ▶ symbol the chemical element rhenium.

re¹ /riː, reɪ/ ▶ preposition in the matter of (used typically as the first word in the heading of an official document or to introduce a reference in a formal letter): *re: invoice 87.* ■ about; concerning: *I saw the deputy head re the incident.*
– ORIGIN Latin, ablative of *res* 'thing'.

> **USAGE** The traditional view is that **re** should be used in headings and references, as in **Re:** *Ainsworth versus Chambers*, but not as a normal word meaning 'about', as in *I saw the deputy head re the incident.* However, the evidence suggests that **re** is now widely used in the second context in official and semi-official contexts, and is now generally accepted. It is hard to see any compelling logical argument against using it as an ordinary English word in this way.

re² ▶ noun variant spelling of RAY³.

're ▶ abbreviation informal are (usually after the pronouns you, we, and they): *we're a bit worried.*

re- ▶ prefix **1** once more; afresh; anew: *reaccustom* | *reactivate.* ■ with return to a previous state: *revert.*
2 (also **red-**) in return; mutually: *react* | *resemble.* ■ in opposition: *repel* | *resistance.*
3 behind or after: *relic* | *remain.* ■ in a withdrawn state: *recluse* | *reticent.* ■ back and away; down: *recede* | *relegation.*
4 with frequentative or intensive force: *refine* | *resound.*
5 with negative force: *recant.*
– ORIGIN from Latin *re-*, *red-* 'again, back'.

> **USAGE** In modern English the tendency is for words formed with prefixes such as **re-** to be unhyphenated: **restore, remain, reacquaint.** One general exception to this is when the word to which **re-** attaches begins with **e**: in this case a hyphen is often inserted for clarity: **re-examine, re-enter, re-enact.** A hyphen is sometimes also used where the word formed with the prefix would be identical to an already existing word: **re-cover** (meaning 'cover again', as in *we decided to re-cover the dining-room chairs*) not **recover** (meaning 'get better in health'). Similar guidelines apply to other prefixes, such as **pre-**.

reabsorb ▶ verb [with obj.] absorb (something) again.
– DERIVATIVES **reabsorption** noun.

reaccept ▶ verb [with obj.] accept (someone or something) again.
– DERIVATIVES **reacceptance** noun.

reaccustom ▶ verb [with obj.] accustom (someone) to something again.

reach ▶ verb **1** [no obj., with adverbial of direction] stretch out an arm in a specified direction in order to touch or grasp something: *he reached over and turned off his bedside light.* ■ (**reach for**) extend one's hand or arm in an attempt to touch or grasp (something): *Leith reached for the nearest folder.* ■ [with obj.] (**reach something out**) stretch out one's hand or arm: *he reached out a hand and touched her hair.* ■ [with obj.] (**reach something down**) stretch upwards to pick something up and bring it to a lower level: *she reached down a plate from the cupboard.* ■ [with two objs] hand (something) to (someone): *reach me those glasses.* ■ [no obj.] be able to touch something with an outstretched arm or leg: *I had to stand on tiptoe and even then I could hardly reach.*
2 [with obj.] arrive at; get as far as: *'Goodbye,' she said as they reached the door* | *the show is due to reach our screens early next year.* ■ [no obj.] W. Indian arrive: *just round that corner, by them mango trees, and we reach.*
3 [with obj.] attain or extend to (a specified point, level, or condition): *unemployment reached a peak in 1933* | [no obj.] *denim shorts that reach to his knees.* ■ succeed in achieving: *the conference reached agreement on the draft treaty.* ■ succeed in influencing or having an effect on: *he seeks opportunities to reach viewers without journalistic interference.*
4 [with obj.] make contact with (someone) by telephone or other means: *I've been trying to reach you all morning.* ■ (of a broadcast or other communication) be received by: *television reached those parts of the electorate that other news sources could not.*
5 [no obj.] Sailing sail with the wind blowing from the side of the ship.
▶ noun **1** an act of reaching out with one's arm: *she made a reach for him.* ■ [in sing.] the distance to which someone, especially a boxer, can stretch out their hand: *a giant, over six feet seven with a reach of over 81 inches.*
2 the extent or range of something's application, effect, or influence: *he told a story to illustrate the reach of his fame.* ■ the number of people who watch or listen to a particular broadcast or channel during a specified period: *the programme's daily reach is 400,000.*
3 (often **reaches**) a continuous extent of water, especially a stretch of river between two bends, or the part of a canal between locks: *the upper reaches of the Nile.*
4 Sailing a distance traversed in reaching.
– PHRASES **out of** (or **beyond**) **reach** outside the distance to which someone can stretch out their hand. ■ beyond the capacity of someone to attain something: *she thought university was out of her reach.* **within** (or **in**) **reach** inside the distance to which someone can stretch out their hand. ■ inside a distance that can be travelled: *a 1930s semi* ***within easy reach of*** *the town centre.* ■ within the capacity of someone to attain something.
– DERIVATIVES **reachable** adjective.
– ORIGIN Old English *rǣcan*, of West Germanic origin; related to Dutch *reiken* and German *reichen*.

reacher ▶ noun **1** a thing which reaches, especially a device that enables a disabled or elderly person to pick up objects that are difficult to reach.
2 a kind of jib on a sailing ship.

reach-me-down Brit. informal, dated ▶ adjective [attrib.] (of a garment) ready-made or second-hand.
▶ noun a second-hand or ready-made garment. ■ (**reach-me-downs**) trousers.

reacquaint ▶ verb [with obj.] make (someone) acquainted or familiar with someone or something again: *he was able to* ***reacquaint himself with*** *an old school chum.*
– DERIVATIVES **reacquaintance** noun.

reacquire ▶ verb [with obj.] acquire (something) again.
– DERIVATIVES **reacquisition** noun.

react ▶ verb [no obj.] **1** act in response to something; respond in a particular way: *he reacted angrily to the news of his dismissal* | *the market reacted by falling a*

further 3.1%. ■ (**react against**) respond with hostility or a contrary course of action to: *they reacted against the elite art music of their time.* ■ suffer from adverse physiological effects after ingesting, breathing, or touching a substance: *many babies react to soy-based formulas.* ■ Stock Exchange (of share prices) fall after rising.
2 Chemistry & Physics interact and undergo a chemical or physical change: *the sulphur in the coal* ***reacts with*** *the limestone during combustion.* ■ [with obj.] cause (a substance) to undergo a chemical or physical change by interacting with another substance.
– ORIGIN mid 17th cent.: from **RE-** (expressing intensive force or reversal) + **ACT**, originally suggested by medieval Latin *react-* 'done again', from the verb *reagere.*

reactance ▸ **noun** [mass noun] Physics the non-resistive component of impedance in an AC circuit, arising from the effect of inductance or capacitance or both and causing the current to be out of phase with the electromotive force causing it.

reactant ▸ **noun** Chemistry a substance that takes part in and undergoes change during a reaction.

reaction ▸ **noun 1** something done, felt, or thought in response to a situation or event: *my immediate reaction was one of relief* | [mass noun] *prices fell* ***in reaction to*** *intense competition.* ■ (**reactions**) a person's ability to respond physically and mentally to external stimuli: *a skilled driver with quick reactions.* ■ an adverse physiological response to a substance that has been breathed in, ingested, or touched: *such allergic reactions as hay fever and asthma.* ■ a mode of thinking or behaving that is deliberately different from previous modes of thought and behaviour: *the work of these painters was a* ***reaction against*** *Fauvism.* ■ [mass noun] opposition to political or social progress or reform: *the institution is under threat from the forces of reaction.*
2 a chemical process in which substances act mutually on each other and are changed into different substances, or one substance changes into other substances. ■ Physics an analogous transformation of atomic nuclei or other particles.
3 [mass noun] Physics a force exerted in opposition to an applied force.
– DERIVATIVES **reactionist** noun & adjective.
– ORIGIN mid 17th cent.: from **REACT** + **-ION**, originally suggested by medieval Latin *reactio(n-)*, from *react-* 'done again' (see **REACT**).

reactionary ▸ **adjective** opposing political or social progress or reform: *reactionary attitudes toward women's rights.*
▸ **noun** (pl. **reactionaries**) a reactionary person.

reaction formation ▸ **noun** [mass noun] Psychoanalysis the tendency of a repressed wish or feeling to be expressed at a conscious level in a contrasting form.

reactivate ▸ **verb** [with obj.] restore (something) to a state of activity; bring back into action.
– DERIVATIVES **reactivation** noun.

reactive ▸ **adjective 1** showing a response to a stimulus: *pupils are reactive to light.* ■ Physiology showing an immune response to a specific antigen. ■ (of a disease or illness) caused by a reaction to something: *reactive arthritis* | *reactive depression.* ■ having a tendency to react chemically: *nitrogen dioxide is a highly reactive gas.*
2 acting in response to a situation rather than creating or controlling it: *a proactive rather than a reactive approach.*
3 Physics relating to reactance: *a reactive load.*

reactive inhibition ▸ **noun** [mass noun] Psychology the inhibiting effect of fatigue or boredom on the response to a stimulus and ability to learn.

reactivity ▸ **noun** [mass noun] the quality of being reactive or the degree to which something is reactive. ■ the extent to which a nuclear reactor deviates from a steady state.

reactor ▸ **noun 1** (also **nuclear reactor**) an apparatus or structure in which fissile material can be made to undergo a controlled, self-sustaining nuclear reaction with the consequent release of energy. ■ a container or apparatus in which substances are made to react chemically, especially one in an industrial plant.
2 Medicine a person who shows an immune response to a specific antigen or an adverse reaction to a drug or other substance.
3 Physics a coil or other component which provides reactance in a circuit.

read /riːd/ ▸ **verb** (past and past participle **read** /rɛd/) [with obj.] **1** look at and comprehend the meaning of (written or printed matter) by interpreting the characters or symbols of which it is composed: *it's the best novel I've ever read* | *I never learned to read music* | *Emily* ***read over*** *her notes* | [no obj.] *I'll go to bed and read for a while.* ■ [no obj.] have the ability to look at and comprehend the meaning of written or printed matter: *only three of the girls could read and none could write.* ■ speak (the written or printed matter that one is reading) aloud: *I read the letter to her* | *the charges against him were* ***read out*** | [no obj.] *I'll read to you if you like.* ■ habitually read (a particular newspaper or periodical). ■ [no obj., with complement] (of a passage, text, or sign) have a certain wording: *the placard read 'We want justice'.* ■ used to indicate that a particular word in a text or passage is incorrect and that another should be substituted for it: *for madam read madman.* ■ [no obj.] (**read for**) (of an actor) audition for (a role).
2 discover (information) by reading it in a written or printed source: *he was arrested yesterday—I read it in the paper* | [no obj.] *I read about the course in a magazine.* ■ (as adj., with submodifier **read**) having a specified level of knowledge as a result of reading: *Ada was* ***well read in*** *French literature.* ■ discern (a fact, emotion, or quality) in someone's eyes or expression: *she looked down, terrified that he would read fear on her face.*
3 understand or interpret the nature or significance of: *he didn't dare look away, in case this was read as a sign of weakness.* ■ [no obj., with adverbial] (of a piece of writing) convey a specified impression to the reader: *the brief note read like a cry for help.*
4 inspect and record the figure indicated on (a measuring instrument): *I've come to read the gas meter.* ■ [no obj., with complement] (of a measuring instrument) indicate a specified measurement or figure: *the thermometer read 0° C.*
5 chiefly Brit. study (an academic subject) at a university: *I'm reading English at Cambridge* | [no obj.] *he went to Manchester to* ***read for*** *a BA in Economics.*
6 (of a computer) copy, transfer, or interpret (data). ■ [with obj. and adverbial] enter or extract (data) in an electronic storage device. ■ (of a device) obtain data from (light or other input).
7 present (a bill or other measure) before a legislative assembly.
8 hear and understand the words of (someone speaking on a radio transmitter): *'Do you read me? Over.'*
▸ **noun** [usu. in sing.] chiefly Brit. a period or act of reading something: *I was having a quiet read of the newspaper.* ■ [with adj.] informal a book considered in terms of its readability: *the book is a thoroughly entertaining read.* ■ US a person's interpretation of something: *their* ***read on*** *the national situation may be correct.*
– PHRASES **read between the lines** look for or discover a meaning that is implied rather than explicitly stated. **read someone like a book** understand someone's thoughts and motives easily. **read someone's mind** (or **thoughts**) discern what someone is thinking. **read my lips** N. Amer. informal listen carefully (used to emphasize the importance of the speaker's words). **take something as read** Brit. assume something without the need for further discussion. **you wouldn't read about it** Austral./NZ informal used to express incredulity, disgust, or ruefulness.
– PHRASAL VERBS **read something into** attribute a meaning or significance to (something) that it may not in fact possess: *was I reading too much into his behaviour?* **read someone out of** chiefly US formally expel someone from (an organization). [with reference to the reading of the formal sentence of expulsion.] **read up on something** (or **read something up**) acquire information about a particular subject by studying it intensively: *she spent the time reading up on antenatal care.*
– ORIGIN Old English *rǣdan*, of Germanic origin; related to Dutch *raden* and German *raten* 'advise, guess'. Early senses included 'advise' and 'interpret (a riddle or dream)' (see **REDE**).

readable ▸ **adjective 1** able to be read or deciphered; legible. ■ easy or enjoyable to read: *a marvellously readable book.*
2 (of data or a storage medium or device) capable of being processed or interpreted by a computer or other electronic device.
– DERIVATIVES **readability** noun, **readably** adverb.

readapt ▸ **verb** [no obj.] become adjusted to changed conditions again: *the limpets readapted to submerged life.* ■ [with obj.] change (something) as a result of new or different conditions: *she'll be the one readapting her life.*
– DERIVATIVES **readaptation** noun.

readdress ▸ **verb** [with obj.] **1** change the address written or printed on (a letter or parcel).
2 look at or attend to (an issue or problem) once again.

reader ▸ **noun 1** a person who reads or who is fond of reading: *she's an avid reader.* ■ a person who reads a particular newspaper, magazine, or text: *Guardian readers.* ■ a person entitled to use a particular library. ■ a person who reads and reports to a publisher or producer on the merits of manuscripts submitted for publication or production, or who provides critical comments on the text. ■ a proofreader. ■ short for **LAY READER**.
2 a person who inspects and records the figure indicated on a measuring instrument: *a meter reader.*
3 a book containing extracts of a text or texts, designed to give learners of a language practice in reading.
4 (**Reader**) Brit. a university lecturer of the highest grade below professor.
5 a device that produces on a screen a magnified, readable image of a microfiche or microfilm. ■ Computing a device or piece of software used for reading or obtaining data stored on tape, cards, or other media.
– ORIGIN Old English *rǣdere* 'interpreter of dreams, reader'.

readerly ▸ **adjective** relating to a reader: *he tries one's readerly patience to breaking point.*

readership ▸ **noun 1** [treated as sing. or pl.] the readers of a newspaper, magazine, or book regarded collectively: *the magazine has a readership of just 65,000.*
2 (**Readership**) Brit. the position of Reader at a university.

readily ▸ **adverb** without hesitation or reluctance; willingly: *he readily admits that the new car surpasses its predecessors.* ■ without delay or difficulty; easily: [as submodifier] *transport is readily available.*

read-in ▸ **noun** [mass noun] Computing the input or entry of data to a computer or storage device.

readiness ▸ **noun** [mass noun] **1** the state of being fully prepared for something: *your muscles tense* ***in readiness for*** *action.*
2 [in sing.] [with infinitive] willingness to do something: *Spain had indicated a readiness to accept his terms.*
3 the quality of being immediate, quick, or prompt: *quickness of hearing and readiness of speech were essential.*

Reading /ˈrɛdɪŋ/ a town in Berkshire, southern England, on the River Kennet near its junction with the Thames; pop. 142,300 (est. 2009).

reading ▸ **noun 1** [mass noun] the action or skill of reading: *the reading of a will* | *suggestions for further reading* | [as modifier] *reading skills.* ■ written or printed matter that can be read: *his main reading was detective stories* | [with adj.] *I found the article fascinating reading.* ■ [usu. with adj.] knowledge of literature: *a man of wide reading.*
2 an occasion at which pieces of literature are read to an audience. ■ a piece of literature or passage of scripture that is read aloud: *readings from the Bible.*
3 a particular interpretation of a text or situation: *feminist readings of Goethe.*
4 a figure or amount shown by a meter or other measuring instrument: *radiation readings were taken every hour.*
5 a stage of debate in parliament through which a Bill must pass before it can become law: *the Bill returns to the House for its final reading next week.*

reading age ▸ **noun** a child's reading ability expressed with reference to an average age at which a comparable ability is found.

reading frame ▸ **noun** Genetics the grouping of three successive bases in a sequence of DNA that constitutes the codons for the amino acids encoded by the DNA.

readjust ▸ **verb** [with obj.] set or adjust (something) again: *I readjusted the rear-view mirror.* ■ [no obj.] adjust or adapt to a changed situation: *it can take years to* ***readjust to*** *this situation.*
– DERIVATIVES **readjustment** noun.

readmit ▸ **verb** (**readmits**, **readmitting**, **readmitted**) [with obj.] admit (someone) to a place or organization again: *they were readmitted to hospital.*
– DERIVATIVES **readmission** noun, **readmittance** noun.

read-only memory (abbrev.: **ROM**) ▸ **noun** Computing memory read at high speed but not capable of being changed by program instructions.

R

readopt ▶ **verb** [with obj.] adopt (a physical position) again. ■ start to follow (a principle or course of action) again.
– DERIVATIVES **readoption** noun.

read-out ▶ **noun** a visual record or display of the output from a computer or scientific instrument.

read-through ▶ **noun** an initial rehearsal of a play at which actors read their parts from scripts.

re-advertise ▶ **verb** [with obj.] advertise (something, especially a job vacancy) again.
– DERIVATIVES **re-advertisement** noun.

read-write ▶ **adjective** Computing capable of reading existing data and accepting alterations or further input.

ready ▶ **adjective** (**readier**, **readiest**) **1** [predic.] in a suitable state for an action or situation; fully prepared: *are you ready, Carrie?* | *I* ***got ready for*** *bed* | [with infinitive] *she was about ready to leave.* ■ (of a thing) made suitable and available for immediate use: *dinner's ready!* | *could you have the list ready by this afternoon?* ■ (**ready with**) keen or quick to give: *every time I rang up, she was ready with some excuse.* ■ (**ready for**) in need of or having a desire for: *I expect you're ready for a drink.*
2 [with infinitive] willing or eager to do something: *she is ready to die for her political convictions.* ■ in such a condition as to be likely to do something: *by the time he arrived he was ready to drop.*
3 easily available or obtained; within reach: *there was a ready supply of drink* | *the murderer knew that the mallet would be* ***ready to hand.*** ■ [attrib.] immediate, quick, or prompt: *those who have ready access to the arts* | *a girl with a ready smile.*
▶ **adverb** [usu. in combination] done in advance of being needed: *ready-cooked meals.*
▶ **noun** (pl. **readies**) (**readies** or **the ready**) Brit. informal available money; cash.
▶ **verb** (**readies**, **readying**, **readied**) [with obj.] prepare for an action or purpose: *the spare transformer was readied for shipment* | [with obj. and infinitive] *she readied herself to speak first.*
– PHRASES **at the ready** prepared or available for immediate use: *the men walk with their guns at the ready.* **make ready** prepare: *they were told to* ***make ready*** *for the journey home.* **ready, steady, go** (also N. Amer. **ready, set, go**) used to announce the beginning of a race.
– ORIGIN Middle English: from Old English *rǣde* (from a Germanic base meaning 'arrange, prepare'; related to Dutch *gereed*) + -Y[1].

-ready ▶ **combining form** denoting something that is available, suitable, or prepared for a particular use or purpose: *an oven-ready chicken* | *camera-ready artwork.*

ready-made ▶ **adjective** made to a standard size or specification rather than to order: *a range of ready-made curtains.* ■ available immediately; not needing to be specially created or devised: *we have no ready-made answers.* ■ (of food) sold ready or almost ready to be served: *a ready-made Christmas cake.*
▶ **noun** (usu. **ready-mades**) a ready-made article: *he smokes ready-mades now.* ■ (especially in Dadaism) a mass-produced article selected by an artist and displayed as a work of art.

R

ready meal ▶ **noun** Brit. a meal sold in a pre-cooked form that only requires reheating.

ready-mix ▶ **noun** [mass noun] ready-mixed concrete.

ready-mixed ▶ **adjective** (of concrete, paint, food, etc.) having some or all of the constituents already mixed together.

ready money (also **ready cash**) ▶ **noun** [mass noun] money in the form of cash that is immediately available.

ready reckoner ▶ **noun** a book or table listing standard numerical calculations or other kinds of information presented formulaically.

ready-to-wear ▶ **adjective** (of clothes) made for the general market and sold through shops rather than made to order for an individual customer.

reaffirm ▶ **verb** [reporting verb] state again strongly: *the prime minister reaffirmed his commitment to the agreement* | [with clause] *he reaffirmed that it was essential to strengthen the rule of law.* ■ [with obj.] confirm the validity of (something previously established): *the election reaffirmed his position as leader.*
– DERIVATIVES **reaffirmation** noun.

reafforest ▶ **verb** Brit. another term for REFOREST.
– DERIVATIVES **reafforestation** noun.

Reagan /ˈreɪɡ(ə)n/, Ronald (Wilson) (1911–2004), American Republican statesman, 40th President of the US 1981–9. He was a Hollywood actor before entering politics. His presidency saw the launch of the Strategic Defense Initiative and cuts in taxes and social services budgets, as well as the Irangate scandal and the signing of an intermediate nuclear forces non-proliferation treaty, both in 1987.
– DERIVATIVES **Reaganism** noun, **Reaganite** adjective & noun.

reagency /rɪˈeɪdʒ(ə)nsi/ ▶ **noun** [mass noun] Chemistry reactive power or operation.

reagent /rɪˈeɪdʒ(ə)nt/ ▶ **noun** a substance or mixture for use in chemical analysis or other reactions: *this compound is a very sensitive reagent for copper.*

reagent grade ▶ **noun** [mass noun] Chemistry a grade of commercial chemicals of a high standard of purity suitable for use in chemical analysis.

reagin /rɪˈeɪdʒɪn/ ▶ **noun** [mass noun] Medicine the antibody which is involved in allergic reactions, causing the release of histamine when it combines with antigen in tissue, and capable of producing sensitivity to the antigen when introduced into the skin of a normal individual. ■ the substance in the blood which is responsible for a positive response to the Wassermann test.
– DERIVATIVES **reaginic** adjective.
– ORIGIN early 20th cent.: coined in German from *reagieren* 'react'.

real[1] /riːl/ ▶ **adjective 1** actually existing as a thing or occurring in fact; not imagined or supposed: *Julius Caesar was a real person* | *her many illnesses, real and imaginary.* ■ used to emphasize the significance or seriousness of a situation: *there is a real danger of civil war* | *the competitive threat from overseas is very real.* ■ Philosophy relating to something as it is, not merely as it may be described or distinguished.
2 (of a thing) not imitation or artificial; genuine: *the earring was presumably real gold.* ■ true or actual: *his real name is James* | *this isn't my real reason for coming.* ■ [attrib.] rightly so called; proper: *he's my idea of a real man.*
3 [attrib.] informal complete; utter (used for emphasis): *the tour turned out to be a real disaster.*
4 [attrib.] adjusted for changes in the value of money; assessed by purchasing power: *real incomes had fallen by 30 per cent* | *an increase* ***in real terms*** *of 11.6 per cent.*
5 Mathematics (of a number or quantity) having no imaginary part. See IMAGINARY.
6 Optics (of an image) of a kind in which the light that forms it actually passes through it; not virtual.
▶ **adverb** [as submodifier] informal, chiefly N. Amer. really; very: *my head hurts real bad.*
– PHRASES **for real** informal used to assert that something is genuine or is actually the case: *I'm not playing games—this is for real!* ■ N. Amer. used in questions to express surprise or to question the truth or seriousness of what one has seen or heard: *are these guys for real?* **get real!** informal, chiefly N. Amer. used to convey that an idea or statement is foolish or overly idealistic: *You want teens to have committed sexual relationships? Get real!* **a real live ——** humorous used to emphasize the existence or presence of something surprising or unusual: *a real live detective had been at the factory.* **real money** informal a significant amount of money. **the real thing** informal a thing that is absolutely genuine or authentic: *you've never been in love before, so how can you be sure this is the real thing?*
– DERIVATIVES **realness** noun.
– ORIGIN late Middle English (as a legal term meaning 'relating to things, especially real property'): from Anglo-Norman French, from late Latin *realis*, from Latin *res* 'thing'.

real[2] /reɪˈɑːl/ ▶ **noun** the basic monetary unit of Brazil since 1994, equal to 100 centavos. ■ a former coin and monetary unit of various Spanish-speaking countries.
– ORIGIN Spanish, literally 'royal' (adjective used as a noun).

real account ▶ **noun** Finance an account dealing with the material assets of a business, such as its property.

real ale ▶ **noun** [mass noun] Brit. cask-conditioned beer that is served traditionally, without additional gas pressure.

real estate ▶ **noun** [mass noun] chiefly N. Amer. property consisting of land or buildings: *most of her real estate is in New Mexico.*

real estate agent ▶ **noun** N. Amer. an estate agent.
– DERIVATIVES **real estate agency** noun.

realgar /rɪˈalɡə/ ▶ **noun** [mass noun] a soft reddish mineral consisting of arsenic sulphide, formerly used as a pigment and in fireworks.
– ORIGIN late Middle English: via medieval Latin from Arabic *rahj al-ġār* 'arsenic', literally 'dust of the cave'.

realia /reɪˈɑːlɪə, rɪˈeɪlɪə/ ▶ **noun** [mass noun] objects and material from everyday life used as teaching aids.
– ORIGIN 1950s: from late Latin, neuter plural (used as a noun) of *realis* 'relating to things' (see REAL[1]).

realign ▶ **verb** [with obj.] change or restore to a different or former position or state: *they worked to relieve his shoulder pain and realign the joint* | *the president realigned his government to reflect the balance of parties.* ■ (**realign oneself with**) change one's opinion with regard to: *he wished to realign himself with Bagehot's more pessimistic position.*
– DERIVATIVES **realignment** noun.

realism ▶ **noun** [mass noun] **1** the attitude or practice of accepting a situation as it is and being prepared to deal with it accordingly: *the summit was marked by a new mood of realism.* ■ the view that the subject matter of politics is political power, not matters of principle. ■ the doctrine that the law is better understood by analysis of judges rather than the judgements given.
2 the quality or fact of representing a person or thing in a way that is accurate and true to life: *British soaps will stay because of their gritty realism.* ■ an artistic or literary movement or style characterized by the representation of people or things as they actually are. Often contrasted with IDEALISM (sense 1).
3 Philosophy the doctrine that universals or abstract concepts have an objective or absolute existence. The theory that universals have their own reality is sometimes called **Platonic realism** because it was first outlined by Plato's doctrine of 'forms' or ideas. Often contrasted with NOMINALISM. ■ the doctrine that matter as the object of perception has real existence and is neither reducible to universal mind or spirit nor dependent on a perceiving agent. Often contrasted with IDEALISM (sense 2).
– DERIVATIVES **realist** noun & adjective.

realistic ▶ **adjective 1** having or showing a sensible and practical idea of what can be achieved or expected: *I thought we had a realistic chance of winning.*
2 representing things in a way that is accurate and true to life: *a realistic human drama.*
– DERIVATIVES **realistically** adverb [sentence adverb] *realistically, there was little prospect of any improvement.*

reality ▶ **noun** (pl. **realities**) [mass noun] **1** the state of things as they actually exist, as opposed to an idealistic or notional idea of them: *he refuses to face reality* | *Laura was losing touch with reality.* ■ [count noun] a thing that is actually experienced or seen, especially when this is unpleasant: *the harsh* ***realities of*** *life in a farming community.* ■ [count noun] a thing that exists in fact, having previously only existed in one's mind: *we want to make the dream a reality.* ■ the quality of being lifelike: *the reality of Marryat's detail.* ■ [as modifier] relating to reality TV: *a reality show.*
2 the state or quality of having existence or substance: *youth, when death has no reality.* ■ Philosophy existence that is absolute, self-sufficient, or objective, and not subject to human decisions or conventions.
– PHRASES **in reality** in actual fact (used to contrast a false idea of what is true or possible with one that is more accurate): *she had believed she could control these feelings, but in reality that was not so easy.* **the reality is ——** used to assert that the truth of a matter is not what one would think or expect.
– ORIGIN late 15th cent.: via French from medieval Latin *realitas*, from late Latin *realis* 'relating to things' (see REAL[1]).

WORD TRENDS When did **reality** become quite so artificial? The word that supposedly describes life and experience exactly as we know it is increasingly used to refer to deeply unrealistic concepts and situations. *Reality TV* is intended to be unscripted and spontaneous, but events in such shows are often manipulated and the footage extensively edited before it reaches the viewing public. The sense 'relating to reality TV' now provides many of the word's commonest collocates, such as *show*, *series*, *star*, *game*, and *programme*.

reality check ▶ **noun** [usu. in sing.] informal an occasion on which one is reminded of the state of things in the real world.

reality principle ▶ **noun** Psychoanalysis the control by the ego of the pleasure-seeking activity of the id in order to meet the demands of the external world.

reality testing ▶ **noun** [mass noun] Psychology the objective evaluation of an emotion or thought against real life, as a faculty present in normal individuals but defective in psychotics.

reality TV (also **reality television**) ▶ **noun** [mass noun] television programmes in which real people are continuously filmed, designed to be entertaining rather than informative.

realizable (also **realisable**) ▶ **adjective 1** able to be achieved or made to happen: *the need to define realizable targets.*
2 in or able to be converted into cash: *10 per cent of realizable assets.*
– DERIVATIVES **realizability** noun.

realization (also **realisation**) ▶ **noun 1** [in sing.] an act of becoming fully aware of something as a fact: *a growing realization of the need to create common economic structures* | [mass noun] *realization dawned suddenly.*
2 [mass noun] the achievement of something desired or anticipated: *he did not live to see the realization of his dream.* ■ [count noun] an actual form given to a concept or work: *a perfect realization of Bartók's Second Violin Concerto on disc.* ■ Linguistics the way in which a particular linguistic feature is used in speech or writing on a particular occasion. ■ [count noun] Mathematics an instance or embodiment of an abstract group as the set of symmetry operations of some object or set. ■ [count noun] Statistics a particular series which might be generated by a specified random process.
3 [mass noun] the conversion of an asset into cash. ■ [count noun] a sale of goods: *auction realizations.*

realize (also **realise**) ▶ **verb** [with obj.] **1** become fully aware of (something) as a fact; understand clearly: *he realized his mistake at once* | [with clause] *they realized that something was wrong.*
2 cause to happen: *his worst fears have been realized.* ■ achieve (something desired or anticipated); fulfil: *it is only now that she is beginning to realize her potential.*
3 give actual or physical form to: *the stage designs have been beautifully realized.* ■ use (a linguistic feature) in a particular spoken or written form. ■ Music add to or complete (a piece of music left sparsely notated by the composer).
4 make (a profit) from a transaction: *she realized a profit of $100,000.* ■ be sold for: *the drawings are expected to realize £500,000.* ■ convert (an asset) into cash: *he realized all the assets in her trust fund.*
– DERIVATIVES **realizer** noun.
– ORIGIN early 17th cent.: from **REAL**[1], on the pattern of French *réaliser*.

real life ▶ **noun** [mass noun] life as it is lived in reality, involving unwelcome as well as welcome experiences, as distinct from a fictional or idealized world: [as modifier] *real-life situations.*

real line ▶ **noun** Mathematics a notional line in which every real number is conceived of as represented by a point.

reallocate ▶ **verb** [with obj.] allocate again or in a different way.
– DERIVATIVES **reallocation** noun.

reallot ▶ **verb** (**reallots**, **reallotting**, **reallotted**) [with obj.] allot again or differently.
– DERIVATIVES **reallotment** noun.

really ▶ **adverb 1** in actual fact, as opposed to what is said or imagined to be true or possible: *so what really happened?* | *they're not really my aunt and uncle* | [sentence adverb] *really, there are only three options.* ■ used to emphasize a statement or opinion: *I really want to go* | *I'm sorry, Ruth, I really am.* ■ seriously (used in questions and exclamations with an implied negative answer): *do you really expect me to believe that?*
2 [as submodifier] very; thoroughly: *I think she's really great* | *a really cold day.*
▶ **exclamation** used to express interest, surprise, or doubt: *'I've been working hard.' 'Really?'* ■ used to express mild protest: *really, Marjorie, you do jump to conclusions!* ■ chiefly US used to express agreement: *'It's a nightmare finding somewhere to live in this town.' 'Yeah, really.'*
– PHRASES **really and truly** used to emphasize the sincerity of a statement or opinion: *I sometimes wonder whether you really and truly love me.*

realm ▶ **noun** archaic, literary, or Law a kingdom: *the defence of the realm.* ■ a field or domain of activity or interest: *the realm of applied chemistry* | *an overall Labour majority is not beyond the realms of possibility.* ■ Zoology a primary biogeographical division of the earth's surface.
– ORIGIN Middle English *rewme*, from Old French *reaume*, from Latin *regimen* 'government' (see **REGIMEN**). The spelling with *-l-* (standard from *c.*1600) was influenced by Old French *reiel* 'royal'.

realo /ˈriːələʊ, reɪˈaləʊ/ ▶ **noun** (pl. **realos**) informal a member of the pragmatic, as opposed to the radical, wing of the Green movement. Often contrasted with **FUNDIE**.
– ORIGIN 1980s: from German, from *Realist* 'realist'.

realpolitik /reɪˈɑːlpɒlɪˌtiːk/ ▶ **noun** [mass noun] a system of politics or principles based on practical rather than moral or ideological considerations.
– ORIGIN early 20th cent.: from German *Realpolitik* 'practical politics'.

real presence ▶ **noun** Christian Theology the actual presence of Christ's body and blood in the Eucharistic elements.

real property ▶ **noun** [mass noun] Law property consisting of land or buildings. Compare with **PERSONAL PROPERTY**.

real tennis ▶ **noun** [mass noun] the original form of tennis, played with a solid ball on an enclosed court divided into equal but dissimilar halves, the service side (from which service is always delivered) and the hazard side (on which service is received). A similar game was played in monastery cloisters in the 11th century.

real time ▶ **noun** the actual time during which a process or event occurs. ■ [as modifier] Computing relating to a system in which input data is processed within milliseconds so that it is available virtually immediately as feedback to the process from which it is coming, e.g. in a missile guidance system.

realtor /ˈrɪəltə/ ▶ **noun** N. Amer. trademark an estate agent.
– ORIGIN early 20th cent.: from **REALTY** + **-OR**[1].

realty /ˈrɪəlti/ ▶ **noun** [mass noun] Law a person's real property. The opposite of **PERSONALTY**.

real wages ▶ **plural noun** income expressed in terms of purchasing power as opposed to actual money received.

ream[1] ▶ **noun** 500 (formerly 480) sheets of paper. ■ (usu. **reams**) a large quantity of something, especially paper or writing: ***reams of*** *paper have been used to debate these questions.*
– ORIGIN late Middle English: from Old French *raime*, based on Arabic *rizma* 'bundle'.

ream[2] ▶ **verb** [with obj.] **1** widen (a hole) with a special tool. ■ widen a bore or hole in (a gun or other metal object) with a special tool. ■ N. Amer. clear out or remove (material) from something.
2 N. Amer. informal rebuke (someone) fiercely: *the agent* ***reamed*** *him* ***out*** *for walking away from the deal.*
3 N. Amer. vulgar slang have anal intercourse with.
– ORIGIN early 19th cent.: of unknown origin.

reamer ▶ **noun 1** a tool for widening or finishing drilled holes.
2 North American term for **LEMON-SQUEEZER**.

reanalyse (US **reanalyze**) ▶ **verb** [with obj.] conduct a further analysis of; analyse again.
– DERIVATIVES **reanalysis** noun.

reanimate ▶ **verb** [with obj.] restore to life or consciousness; revive. ■ give fresh vigour or impetus to: *his personal dislike of the man was reanimated.*
– DERIVATIVES **reanimation** noun.

reap ▶ **verb** [with obj.] cut or gather (a crop or harvest). ■ harvest the crop from (a piece of land). ■ receive (something, especially something beneficial) as a consequence of one's own or another's actions: *the company is poised to reap the benefits of this investment.*
– PHRASES **reap the harvest** (or **fruits**) **of** suffer the results or consequences of: *we are now reaping the harvest of our permissive ways.* **you reap what you sow** proverb you eventually have to face up to the consequences of your actions.
– ORIGIN Old English *ripan*, *reopan*, of unknown origin.

reaper ▶ **noun** a person or machine that harvests a crop. ■ (**the Reaper**) short for **THE GRIM REAPER** at **GRIM**.

reappear ▶ **verb** [no obj.] appear again: *her symptoms reappeared.*
– DERIVATIVES **reappearance** noun.

reapply ▶ **verb** (**reapplies**, **reapplying**, **reapplied**)
1 [no obj.] make another application or request: *he intended to reapply for his old post.*
2 [with obj.] apply (an existing rule or principle) in a different context.
3 [with obj.] spread (a substance) on a surface again: *reapply the sunscreen hourly.*
– DERIVATIVES **reapplication** noun.

reappoint ▶ **verb** [with obj.] appoint (someone) once again to a position they have previously held.
– DERIVATIVES **reappointment** noun.

reapportion ▶ **verb** [with obj.] assign or distribute (something) again or in a different way.
– DERIVATIVES **reapportionment** noun.

reappraise ▶ **verb** [with obj.] appraise or assess again or in a different way: *the Tory party has reappraised its strategy.*
– DERIVATIVES **reappraisal** noun.

rear[1] ▶ **noun** [in sing.] the back part of something, especially a building or vehicle: *the kitchen door at the rear of the house.* ■ the space or position at the back of something or someone: *the field at the rear of the church.* ■ the hindmost part of an army, fleet, or line of people: *two policemen at the rear fell out of the formation.* ■ (also **rear end**) informal a person's buttocks.
▶ **adjective** [attrib.] at the back: *the car's rear window.*
– PHRASES **bring up the rear** be at the very end of a line of people. ■ come last in a race or other contest. **take someone in rear** attack an army from behind.
– ORIGIN Middle English (first used as a military term): from Old French *rere*, based on Latin *retro* 'back'.

rear[2] ▶ **verb 1** [with obj.] bring up and care for (a child) until they are fully grown: *Nigel was born and reared in Bath* | *I was reared on stories of collieries.* ■ (of an animal) care for (its young) until they are fully grown. ■ breed and raise (animals): *the calves are reared for beef.* ■ grow or cultivate (plants): (as adj., in combination **-reared**) *laboratory-reared plantlets.*
2 [no obj.] (of a horse or other animal) raise itself upright on its hind legs: *the horse reared in terror* | *a rattlesnake* ***reared up*** *at his elbow.* ■ [with adverbial of place] (of a building, mountain, etc.) extend or appear to extend to a great height: *houses reared up on either side.* ■ (**rear up**) (of a person) show anger or irritation: *if anyone said the wrong thing, I used to rear up.* ■ [with obj.] archaic set upright.
– PHRASES **rear one's head** raise one's head. ■ (**rear its head**) (of an unpleasant matter) present itself: *elitism is* ***rearing its ugly head*** *again.*
– DERIVATIVES **rearer** noun.
– ORIGIN Old English *rǣran* 'set upright, construct, elevate', of Germanic origin; related to **RAISE** (which has supplanted *rear* in many applications), also to **RISE**.

rear admiral ▶ **noun** a rank of naval officer, above commodore and below vice admiral.

rear commodore ▶ **noun** an officer in a yacht club ranking below vice commodore.

rear echelon ▶ **noun** the section of an army concerned with administrative and supply duties.

rearguard ▶ **noun** the soldiers at the rear of a body of troops, especially those protecting a retreating army. ■ a reactionary or conservative element in an organization or community: *the academies acted as powerful guardians of the rearguard.* ■ (in team sports) a defending player or players.
– ORIGIN late Middle English (denoting the rear part of an army): from Old French *rereguarde*.

R

rearguard action ▶ **noun** a defensive action carried out by a retreating army.

rear light (also **rear lamp**) ▶ **noun** chiefly Brit. a red light at the rear of a vehicle; a tail light.

rearm ▶ **verb** [with obj.] provide with a new supply of weapons: *his plan to rearm Germany.* ■ [no obj.] acquire or build up a new supply of weapons.
– DERIVATIVES **rearmament** noun.

rearmost ▶ **adjective** furthest back: *the rearmost door.*

rearrange ▶ **verb** [with obj.] change the position of: *she rearranged her skirt as she sat back in her chair.* ■ change (the position, time, or order of something): *he had rearranged his schedule.*
– DERIVATIVES **rearrangement** noun.

rearrest ▶ **verb** [with obj.] arrest (someone) again.
▶ **noun** an act of rearresting someone.

rear sight ▶ **noun** the sight nearest to the stock on a firearm.

rear-view mirror ▶ **noun** a small angled mirror fixed inside the windscreen of a motor vehicle enabling the driver to see the vehicle or road behind.

rearward ▶ **adjective** directed towards the back: *a slight rearward movement.*
▶ **adverb** (also **rearwards**) towards the back: *the engine nozzles point rearward.*
▶ **noun** (usu. **in/at/on the rearward**) archaic the part or position at the back of something.

– ORIGIN Middle English (as a noun denoting the rear part of an army): from Anglo-Norman French *rerewarde* 'rearguard'; the adjective dates from the early 17th cent. and is from **REAR**[1] + **-WARD**.

rear-wheel drive ▶ noun [mass noun] a transmission system that provides power to the rear wheels of a motor vehicle: [as modifier] *a rear-wheel drive coupé*.

reascend ▶ verb [no obj.] ascend again or to a former position: *the fallen angel reascends to the upper air*.
– DERIVATIVES **reascension** noun.

reason ▶ noun **1** a cause, explanation, or justification for an action or event: *she asked him to return, but didn't give a reason* | *I resigned for personal reasons* | [with clause] *Giles is the reason that I am here*. ■ [mass noun] good or obvious cause to do something: *we have reason to celebrate*. ■ Logic a premise of an argument in support of a belief, especially a minor premise when given after the conclusion.
2 [mass noun] the power of the mind to think, understand, and form judgements logically: *there is a close connection between reason and emotion*. ■ what is right, practical, or possible; common sense: *people are willing, **within reason**, to pay for schooling*.
■ (**one's reason**) one's sanity: *she is in danger of losing her reason*.
▶ verb [no obj.] think, understand, and form judgements logically: *humans do not reason entirely from facts*. ■ [with obj.] (**reason something out**) find an answer to a problem by considering possible options. ■ (**reason with**) persuade (someone) with rational argument: *I tried to reason with her, but without success*.
– PHRASES **beyond** (**all**) **reason** to a foolishly excessive degree: *he indulged Andrew beyond all reason*. **by reason of** formal because of: *persons who, by reason of age, are in need of care*. **for some reason** used to convey that one does not know the reason for a particular situation, often with the implication that one finds it strange or surprising: *for some reason he likes you*. **listen to reason** be persuaded to act sensibly. **theirs** (or **ours**) **not to reason why** used to suggest that it is not someone's (or one's) place to question a situation. [with allusion to Tennyson's 'Charge of the Light Brigade' (1854).] **reason of state** another term for **RAISON D'ÉTAT**. (**it**) **stands to reason** it is obvious or logical: *it stands to reason that if you can eradicate the fear the nervousness will subside*.
– DERIVATIVES **reasoner** noun, **reasonless** adjective (archaic).
– ORIGIN Middle English: from Old French *reisun* (noun), *raisoner* (verb), from a variant of Latin *ratio(n-)*, from the verb *reri* 'consider'.

> **USAGE** **1** Many people object to the construction **the reason why ...**, on the grounds that the subordinate clause should express a statement, using a *that*-clause, not imply a question with a *why*-clause: ***the reason (that)*** *I decided not to phone* rather than ***the reason why*** *I decided not to phone*.
> **2** The construction **the reason ... is because**, as in ***the reason*** *I didn't phone* ***is because*** *my mother has been ill*, is also disliked, on the grounds that either 'because' or 'the reason' is redundant; it is better to use the word **that** instead (***the reason*** *I didn't phone* ***is that***...) or rephrase altogether (*I didn't phone because ...*).
> Nevertheless, both the above usages are well established and, although they may be inelegant, they are generally accepted in standard English.

R

reasonable ▶ adjective **1** having sound judgement; fair and sensible: *no reasonable person could have objected*. ■ based on good sense: *it seems a reasonable enough request* | *the guilt of a person on trial must be proved beyond reasonable doubt*. ■ archaic able to reason logically: *man is by nature reasonable*.
2 as much as is appropriate or fair; moderate: *a police officer may use reasonable force to gain entry*. ■ fairly good; average: *the carpet is in reasonable condition*.
■ (of a price or product) not too expensive: *a restaurant serving excellent food at reasonable prices* | *they are lovely shoes and very reasonable*.
– DERIVATIVES **reasonableness** noun.
– ORIGIN Middle English: from Old French *raisonable*, suggested by Latin *rationabilis* 'rational', from *ratio* (see **REASON**).

reasonably ▶ adverb **1** in a sensible way: *he began to talk calmly and reasonably about his future*. ■ by sensible standards of judgement; justifiably: *a constable who reasonably believes a breach of the peace is about to take place* | [sentence adverb] *it was assumed, **reasonably enough**, that the murder had taken place by the pond*.
2 to a moderate or acceptable degree; fairly: [as submodifier] *she played the piano reasonably well*.
■ inexpensively: *ski wear which looks good and is reasonably priced*.

reasoned ▶ adjective based on logic or good sense: *a reasoned judgement*.

reasoned amendment ▶ noun (in the UK) an amendment to a parliamentary bill that seeks to prevent a further reading by proposing reasons for its alteration or rejection.

reasoning ▶ noun [mass noun] the action of thinking about something in a logical, sensible way: *he explained the **reasoning behind** his decision at a media conference*.

reassemble ▶ verb [no obj.] (of a group) gather together again: *after lunch the class reassembled*.
■ [with obj.] put (something) together again: *the trucks had to be reassembled on arrival*.
– DERIVATIVES **reassembly** noun.

reassert ▶ verb [with obj.] assert again: *he moved quickly to reassert his control*.
– DERIVATIVES **reassertion** noun.

reassess ▶ verb [with obj.] consider or assess again, in the light of new or different factors: *we have decided to reassess our timetable*.
– DERIVATIVES **reassessment** noun.

reassign ▶ verb [with obj.] appoint (someone) to a different post or role. ■ allocate or distribute (work or resources) differently: *he ordered the ministries to reassign the vehicles*.
– DERIVATIVES **reassignment** noun.

reassume ▶ verb [with obj.] take on or gain (something) again: *he reassumed the title of Governor General*.
– DERIVATIVES **reassumption** noun.

reassurance ▶ noun [mass noun] the action of removing someone's doubts or fears: *children need reassurance and praise*. ■ [count noun] a statement that removes someone's doubts or fears: *we have been given reassurances that the water is safe to drink*.

reassure ▶ verb [with obj.] say or do something to remove the doubts and fears of (someone): *he understood her feelings and tried to reassure her* | [with obj. and clause] *Joachim reassured him that he was needed* | (as adj. **reassuring**) *Gina gave her a reassuring smile*.
– DERIVATIVES **reassuringly** adverb.

reattach ▶ verb [with obj.] attach (something that has fallen or been taken off) in its former position.
– DERIVATIVES **reattachment** noun.

reattain ▶ verb [with obj.] attain (an objective or position) again.
– DERIVATIVES **reattainment** noun.

reattempt ▶ verb [with obj.] attempt to achieve (something) again: *I reattempted entry*.

Réaumur scale /ˈreɪə(ʊ),mjʊə/ ▶ noun an obsolete scale of temperature at which water freezes at 0° and boils at 80° under standard conditions.
– ORIGIN late 18th cent.: named after René A. F. de *Réaumur* (1683–1757), French naturalist.

reave /riːv/ ▶ verb (past and past participle **reft** /rɛft/) [no obj.] archaic carry out raids in order to plunder. ■ [with obj.] rob (a person or place) of something by force: *reft of a crown, he yet may share the feast*. ■ [with obj.] steal (something).
– DERIVATIVES **reaver** noun.
– ORIGIN Old English *rēafian*, of Germanic origin; related to Dutch *roven*, German *rauben*, also to **ROB**.

reawaken ▶ verb (with reference to a feeling or state) emerge or cause to emerge again; awaken again: [no obj.] *a sense of community started to reawaken in the 1970s* | [with obj.] *his departure reawakened deep divisions within the party*.

Reb[1] /rɛb/ ▶ noun a traditional Jewish title or form of address, corresponding to *Sir*, for a man who is not a rabbi (used preceding the forename or surname).
– ORIGIN Yiddish.

Reb[2] /rɛb/ (also **Johnny Reb**) ▶ noun US informal a Confederate soldier in the American Civil War.
– ORIGIN abbreviation of **REBEL**.

rebab /rɪˈbab/ ▶ noun a bowed or plucked stringed instrument of Arab origin, used especially in North Africa, the Middle East, and South Asia.
– ORIGIN mid 18th cent.: from Arabic *rabāb*.

rebadge ▶ verb [with obj.] relaunch (a product) under a new name or logo.

rebalance ▶ verb [with obj.] restore the correct balance to; balance again or differently: *the Pilates method aims to rebalance and restore correct posture*.

rebar ▶ noun [mass noun] reinforcing steel used as rods in concrete: *a piece of rebar*.

rebarbative /rɪˈbɑːbətɪv/ ▶ adjective formal unattractive and objectionable: *rebarbative modern buildings*.
– ORIGIN late 19th cent.: from French *rébarbatif, -ive*, from Old French *se rebarber* 'face each other 'beard to beard' aggressively', from *barbe* 'beard'.

rebase ▶ verb [with obj.] establish a new base level for (a tax level, price index, etc.).

rebate[1] /ˈriːbeɪt/ ▶ noun a partial refund to someone who has paid too much for tax, rent, or a utility. ■ a deduction or discount on a sum of money due.
▶ verb [with obj.] pay back (a sum of money) as a rebate.
– DERIVATIVES **rebatable** adjective.
– ORIGIN late Middle English (as a verb in the sense 'diminish (a sum or amount)'): from Anglo-Norman French *rebatre* 'beat back', also 'deduct'.

rebate[2] /ˈriːbeɪt/ ▶ noun a step-shaped recess cut along the edge or in the face of a piece of wood, typically forming a match to the edge or tongue of another piece.
▶ verb (**rebates**, **rebating**, **rebated**) [with obj.] make a rebate in (a piece of wood). ■ [with obj. and adverbial] join or fix (a piece of wood) to another with a rebate: *the oak boarding was rebated in*.
– ORIGIN late 17th cent.: alteration of **RABBET**.

rebbe /ˈrɛbə/ ▶ noun Judaism a rabbi, especially a religious leader of the Hasidic sect.
– ORIGIN Yiddish, from Hebrew *rabbī* 'rabbi'.

rebbetzin /ˈrɛbɪtsɪn/ (also **rebbitzin**) ▶ noun Judaism
1 the wife of a rabbi.
2 a female religious teacher.
– ORIGIN Yiddish, feminine of *rebbe* (see **REBBE**).

rebec /ˈriːbɛk/ (also **rebeck**) ▶ noun a medieval stringed instrument played with a bow, typically having three strings.
– ORIGIN late Middle English: from French, based on Arabic *rabāb*.

rebel ▶ noun /ˈrɛb(ə)l/ a person who rises in opposition or armed resistance against an established government or leader: *Tory rebels* | [as modifier] *rebel forces*. ■ a person who resists authority, control, or convention.
▶ verb /rɪˈbɛl/ (**rebels**, **rebelling**, **rebelled**) [no obj.] rise in opposition or armed resistance to an established government or leader: *the Earl of Pembroke subsequently rebelled against Henry III*. ■ resist authority, control, or convention: *respect did not prevent children from rebelling against their parents*. ■ show or feel repugnance for or resistance to something: *as I came over the hill my legs rebelled—I could walk no further*.
– ORIGIN Middle English: from Old French *rebelle* (noun), *rebeller* (verb), from Latin *rebellis* (used originally with reference to a fresh declaration of war by the defeated), based on *bellum* 'war'.

rebellion ▶ noun an act of armed resistance to an established government or leader: *the authorities put down a rebellion by landless colonials* | [mass noun] *the Bretons rose in rebellion against the King*. ■ [mass noun] the action or process of resisting authority, control, or convention: *an act of teenage rebellion*.
– ORIGIN Middle English: from Old French, from Latin *rebellio(n-)*, from *rebellis* (see **REBEL**).

rebellious ▶ adjective showing a desire to resist authority, control, or convention: *I became very rebellious and opted out*. ■ engaged in opposition or armed resistance to an established government or leader: *the rebellious republics*. ■ (of a thing) not easily controlled or kept in place: *he smoothed back a rebellious lock of hair*.
– DERIVATIVES **rebelliously** adverb, **rebelliousness** noun.

rebetika /rɪˈbɛtɪkə/ (also **rembetika**) ▶ noun [mass noun] a type of Greek popular song accompanied by instruments such as violins and bouzoukis.
– ORIGIN modern Greek *rempetika* (pl.), used as noun of *rempetikos* 'of vagrants or rebels', probably from *rempetēs* 'vagrant'.

rebid ▶ verb (**rebids**, **rebidding**; past and past participle **rebid**) [no obj.] bid again: *the group can rebid after June 18*.
▶ noun a further bid.

rebind ▶ verb (past and past participle **rebound**) [with obj.] give a new binding to (a book).

rebirth ▶ noun [mass noun] the process of being reincarnated or born again: *the endless cycle of birth, death, and rebirth*. ■ [count noun] a period of new life, growth, or activity; a revival: *the rebirth of a defeated nation*.

rebirthing ▶ noun [mass noun] a form of therapy involving controlled breathing intended to simulate the trauma of being born.
– DERIVATIVES **rebirther** noun.

reblochon /ˈrəblɒʃɒ̃/ ▶ **noun** [mass noun] a kind of soft French cheese, made originally and chiefly in Savoy.
– ORIGIN French.

reboard ▶ **verb** [with obj.] (of a passenger) board (a ship or vehicle) again.

rebook ▶ **verb** [with obj.] book (accommodation or a ticket) again: *passengers whose plans were disrupted must rebook their flights.*

reboot ▶ **verb** (with reference to a computer system) boot or be booted again.
▶ **noun** an act of booting a computer system again.

rebore ▶ **verb** [with obj.] make a new or wider boring in (the cylinders of an internal-combustion engine).
▶ **noun** an act of reboring an engine's cylinders. ■ an engine with rebored cylinders.

reborn ▶ **adjective** brought back to life or activity: *a reborn version of social democracy.* ■ having experienced a complete spiritual change: *a reborn Catholic.*

rebound[1] ▶ **verb** /rɪˈbaʊnd/ [no obj.] **1** bounce back through the air after hitting something hard: *his shot hammered into the post and rebounded across the goal.* ■ Basketball gain possession of a missed shot after it bounces off the backboard or basket rim.
2 recover in value, amount, or strength after a decrease or decline: *the Share Index rebounded to show a twenty-point gain.*
3 (**rebound on/upon**) (of an event or action) have an unexpected adverse consequence for (someone, especially the person responsible for it): *Nicholas's tricks are rebounding on him.*
▶ **noun** /ˈriːbaʊnd/ **1** (in sporting contexts) a ball or shot that bounces back after striking a hard surface: *he blasted the rebound into the net.* ■ Basketball a recovery of possession of a missed shot.
2 an increase in value, amount, or strength after a previous decline: *they revealed a big rebound in profits for last year.* ■ [usu. as modifier] the recurrence of a medical condition, especially after withdrawal of medication: *rebound hypertension.*
– PHRASES **on the rebound** while still distressed by the ending of a romantic relationship: *I was on the rebound when I met Jack.*
– ORIGIN late Middle English: from Old French *rebondir*, from *re-* 'back' + *bondir* 'bounce up'.

rebound[2] past and past participle of **REBIND**.

rebounder ▶ **noun 1** a small circular trampoline used for exercising.
2 Basketball a player who rebounds the ball.

rebozo /rɪˈbəʊzəʊ/ ▶ **noun** (pl. **rebozos**) a long scarf covering the head and shoulders, traditionally worn by Spanish-American women.
– ORIGIN Spanish.

rebrand ▶ **verb** [with obj.] (usu. as noun **rebranding**) change the corporate image of (a company or organization).

rebreathe ▶ **verb** [with obj.] breathe in (exhaled air).

rebreather ▶ **noun** an aqualung in which the diver's exhaled breath is partially purified of carbon dioxide, mixed with more oxygen, and then breathed again by the diver.

rebroadcast ▶ **verb** (past and past participle **rebroadcast**) [with obj.] broadcast or relay (a programme or signal) again.
▶ **noun** a repeated or relayed broadcast.

rebuff ▶ **verb** [with obj.] reject (someone or something) in an abrupt or ungracious manner: *I asked her to be my wife, and was rebuffed in no uncertain terms.*
▶ **noun** an abrupt or ungracious rejection of an offer, request, or friendly gesture: *his reserve was not intended as a rebuff* | [mass noun] *callers phoning a chatline need have no fear of rebuff.*
– ORIGIN late 16th cent.: from obsolete French *rebuffer* (verb), *rebuffe* (noun), from Italian *ri-* (expressing opposition) + *buffo* 'a gust, puff', of imitative origin.

rebuild ▶ **verb** (past and past participle **rebuilt**) [with obj.] build (something) again after it has been damaged or destroyed: *after the earthquake people set about rebuilding their homes* | figurative *we try to help them rebuild their lives.*
▶ **noun** an instance of rebuilding. ■ a thing that has been rebuilt, especially a vehicle or other machine.
– DERIVATIVES **rebuildable** adjective, **rebuilder** noun.

rebuke ▶ **verb** [with obj.] express sharp disapproval or criticism of (someone) because of their behaviour or actions: *she had **rebuked** him **for** drinking too much* | *the judge publicly rebuked the jury.*
▶ **noun** an expression of sharp disapproval or criticism: *he hadn't meant it as a rebuke, but Neil flinched.*
– DERIVATIVES **rebuker** noun.
– ORIGIN Middle English (originally in the sense 'force back, repress'): from Anglo-Norman French and Old Northern French *rebuker*, from *re-* 'back, down' + *bukier* 'to beat' (originally 'cut down wood', from Old French *busche* 'log').

rebury ▶ **verb** (**reburies**, **reburying**, **reburied**) [with obj.] bury again.
– DERIVATIVES **reburial** noun.

rebus /ˈriːbəs/ ▶ **noun** (pl. **rebuses**) a puzzle in which words are represented by combinations of pictures and individual letters; for instance, *apex* might be represented by a picture of an ape followed by a letter *X*. ■ historical an ornamental device associated with a person to whose name it punningly alludes.
– ORIGIN early 17th cent.: from French *rébus*, from Latin *rebus*, ablative plural of *res* 'thing'.

rebut /rɪˈbʌt/ ▶ **verb** (**rebuts**, **rebutting**, **rebutted**) [with obj.] **1** claim or prove that (evidence or an accusation) is false: *he had to rebut charges of acting for the convenience of his political friends.*
2 archaic drive back or repel (a person or attack).
– DERIVATIVES **rebuttable** adjective.
– ORIGIN Middle English (in the senses 'rebuke' and 'repulse'): from Anglo-Norman French *rebuter*, from Old French *re-* (expressing opposition) + *boter* 'to butt'. Sense 1 (originally a legal use) dates from the early 19th cent.

rebuttal ▶ **noun** an instance of rebutting evidence or an accusation. ■ another term for **REBUTTER**.

rebutter ▶ **noun** Law, archaic a defendant's reply to the plaintiff's surrejoinder.
– ORIGIN mid 16th cent.: from Anglo-Norman French *rebuter* (from Old French *rebut* 'a reproach or rebuke').

rec ▶ **noun** informal **1** Brit. a recreation ground.
2 N. Amer. recreation: [as modifier] *the rec centre.*

recalcitrant /rɪˈkalsɪtr(ə)nt/ ▶ **adjective** having an obstinately uncooperative attitude towards authority or discipline: *a class of recalcitrant fifteen-year-olds.*
▶ **noun** a person with a recalcitrant attitude.
– DERIVATIVES **recalcitrance** noun, **recalcitrantly** adverb.
– ORIGIN mid 19th cent.: from Latin *recalcitrant-* 'kicking out with the heels', from the verb *recalcitrare*, based on *calx*, *calc-* 'heel'.

recalculate ▶ **verb** [with obj.] calculate again, typically using different data.
– DERIVATIVES **recalculation** noun.

recalescence /ˌriːkəˈlɛs(ə)ns/ ▶ **noun** [mass noun] Metallurgy a temporary rise in temperature during cooling of a metal, caused by a change in crystal structure.
– ORIGIN late 19th cent.: from **RE-** 'again' + Latin *calescere* 'grow hot' + **-ENCE**.

recalibrate ▶ **verb** [with obj.] calibrate (something) again or differently: *the sensors had to be recalibrated.*

recall /rɪˈkɔːl/ ▶ **verb** [with obj.] **1** bring (a fact, event, or situation) back into one's mind; remember: *I can still vaguely recall being taken to the hospital* | [with clause] *he recalled how he felt at the time.* ■ cause one to remember or think of: *the film's analysis of contemporary concerns recalls The Big Chill.* ■ (**recall someone/thing to**) bring the memory or thought of someone or something to (a person or their mind): *the smell of a blackcurrant bush has ever since recalled to me that evening.* ■ call up (stored computer data) for processing or display.
2 officially order (someone) to return to a place: *the Panamanian ambassador was recalled from Peru.* ■ select (a sports player) as a member of a team from which they have previously been dropped: *the Fulham defender has been **recalled to** the Welsh squad for the World Cup.* ■ (of a manufacturer) request all the purchasers of (a certain product) to return it, as the result of the discovery of a fault. ■ bring (someone) out of a state of inattention or reverie: *her action **recalled** him **to** the present.* ■ archaic revoke or annul (an action or decision).
▶ **noun** also /ˈriːkɔːl/ **1** [mass noun] the action or faculty of remembering something learned or experienced: *people's understanding and subsequent recall of stories or events.*
2 an act or instance of officially recalling someone or something: *a recall of Parliament.* ■ N. Amer. the removal of an elected government official from office by a petition followed by voting.
3 Computing the proportion of the number of relevant documents retrieved from a database in response to an enquiry.
– PHRASES **beyond recall** in such a way that restoration is impossible: *shopping developments have already blighted other parts of the city beyond recall.*
– DERIVATIVES **recallable** adjective.
– ORIGIN late 16th cent. (as a verb): from **RE-** 'again' + **CALL**, suggested by Latin *revocare* or French *rappeler* 'call back'.

recant /rɪˈkant/ ▶ **verb** [no obj.] say that one no longer holds an opinion or belief, especially one considered heretical: *heretics were burned if they would not recant* | [with obj.] *Galileo was forced to recant his assertion that the earth orbited the sun.*
– DERIVATIVES **recanter** noun.
– ORIGIN mid 16th cent.: from Latin *recantare* 'revoke', from *re-* (expressing reversal) + *cantare* 'sing, chant'.

recantation /ˌriːkanˈteɪʃ(ə)n/ ▶ **noun** a statement that one no longer holds a particular opinion or belief; a retraction: *every writer interprets Galileo's recantation in a different way.*

recap ▶ **verb** (**recaps**, **recapping**, **recapped**) [with obj.] state again as a summary; recapitulate: *a way of recapping the story so far* | [no obj.] *to recap, the committee has decided to ask Farris, Cullen, and Jurgens to go.*
▶ **noun** a summary of what has been said; a recapitulation: *a quick recap of the idea and its main advantages.*
– ORIGIN 1950s. abbreviation.

recapitalize (also **recapitalise**) ▶ **verb** [with obj.] provide (a business) with more capital, especially by replacing debt with stock.
– DERIVATIVES **recapitalization** noun.

recapitulate /ˌriːkəˈpɪtjʊleɪt/ ▶ **verb** [with obj.] summarize and state again the main points of: *he began to recapitulate his argument with care.* ■ Biology repeat (an evolutionary or other process) during development and growth.
– DERIVATIVES **recapitulatory** adjective.
– ORIGIN late 16th cent.: from late Latin *recapitulat-* 'gone through heading by heading', from *re-* 'again' + *capitulum* 'chapter' (diminutive of *caput* 'head').

recapitulation /ˌriːkəpɪtjʊˈleɪʃ(ə)n/ ▶ **noun** an act or instance of summarizing and restating the main points of something: *his recapitulation of the argument.* ■ [mass noun] Biology the repetition of an evolutionary or other process during development or growth. ■ Music a part of a movement (especially one in sonata form) in which themes from the exposition are restated.

recaption ▶ **noun** [mass noun] Law the action of taking back, without legal process, property of one's own that has been wrongfully taken or withheld.
– ORIGIN mid 18th cent.: from Anglo-Latin *recaptio(n-)*, from *re-* 'back' + Latin *captio(n-)* 'taking'.

recapture ▶ **verb** [with obj.] capture (a person or animal that has escaped): *armed police have recaptured a prisoner who's been on the run for five days.* ■ recover (something taken or lost): *Edward I recaptured the castle* | *Leeds failed to recapture the form which had swept them to the title.* ■ recreate or experience again (a past time, event, or feeling): *the programmes give viewers a chance to recapture their own childhoods.*
▶ **noun** [in sing.] an act of recapturing someone or something.

recast ▶ **verb** (past and past participle **recast**) [with obj.] **1** give (a metal object) a different form by melting it down and reshaping it. ■ present or organize in a different form or style: *his doctoral thesis has been recast for the general reader.*
2 allocate the parts in (a play or film) to different actors: *there were moves to recast the play.*

recce /ˈrɛki/ Brit. ▶ **noun** informal term for **RECONNAISSANCE**.
▶ **verb** (**recces**, **recceing**, **recced**) informal term for **RECONNOITRE**.
– ORIGIN 1940s: abbreviation.

recd ▶ **abbreviation** received.

recede ▶ **verb** [no obj.] **1** go or move back or further away from a previous position: *the floodwaters had receded* | *his footsteps receded down the corridor.* ■ (usu. as adj. **receding**) (of a facial feature) slope backwards: *a slightly receding chin.* ■ (**recede from**) archaic withdraw from (a promise or agreement).
2 (of a quality, feeling, or possibility) gradually diminish: *the prospects of an early end to the war receded.*
3 (of a man's hair) cease to grow at the temples and above the forehead: *his dark hair was receding a little* | (as adj. **receding**) *a receding hairline.*

R

– ORIGIN late 15th cent. (in the sense 'depart from a usual state or standard'): from Latin *recedere*, from *re-* 'back' + *cedere* 'go'.

receipt ▶ **noun 1** [mass noun] the action of receiving something or the fact of its being received: *I would be grateful if you would acknowledge receipt of this letter* | *families* ***in receipt of*** *supplementary benefit.* ■ [count noun] a written or printed statement acknowledging that something has been paid for or that goods have been received. ■ (**receipts**) an amount of money received during a particular period by an organization or business: *box office receipts.*
2 archaic a recipe.
▶ **verb** [with obj.] (usu. as adj. **receipted**) mark (a bill) as paid: *the receipted hotel bill.*
– ORIGIN late Middle English: from Anglo-Norman French *receite*, from medieval Latin *recepta* 'received', feminine past participle of Latin *recipere*. The *-p-* was inserted in imitation of the Latin spelling.

receivable ▶ **adjective** able to be received.
▶ **plural noun** (**receivables**) amounts owed to a business, regarded as assets.

receive ▶ **verb** [with obj.] **1** be given, presented with, or paid (something): *the band will receive a £100,000 advance* | *she received her prize from the manager.* ■ take delivery of (something sent or communicated): *he received fifty enquiries after advertising the job.* ■ consent to hear (an oath or confession): *he failed to find a magistrate to receive his oath.* ■ buy or accept goods known to be stolen: *he was deprived of his licence for receiving a stolen load of whisky.*
2 suffer, experience, or be subject to (specified treatment): *the event received wide press coverage* | *she received only cuts and bruises.* ■ [with obj. and adverbial] respond to (something) in a specified way: *her first poem was not well received.* ■ meet and have to withstand: *the landward slopes receive the full force of the wind.* ■ meet with (a specified reaction): *the rulings have received widespread acceptance.* ■ (as adj. **received**) widely accepted as authoritative or true: *the myths and received wisdom about the country's past.*
3 greet or welcome (a visitor) formally: *representatives of the club will be received by the Mayor.* ■ be visited by: *she was not allowed to receive visitors.* ■ admit as a member: *hundreds of converts were* ***received into*** *the Church.*
4 form (an idea or impression) as a result of perception or experience: *the impression she received was one of unhurried leisure.*
5 detect or pick up (broadcast signals): *the systems work by comparing time signals received from different satellites.*
6 serve as a receptacle for: *the basin that receives your blood.* ■ provide space or accommodation for: *the remaining lines receive the general rolling stock.*
7 (in tennis and similar games) be the player to whom the server serves (the ball).
8 eat or drink (the Eucharistic bread or wine): *he received Communion and left.*
– PHRASES **be at** (or **on**) **the receiving end** informal be subjected to something: *she found herself on the receiving end of a good deal of teasing.*
– ORIGIN Middle English: from Anglo-Norman French *receivre*, based on Latin *recipere*, from *re-* 'back' + *capere* 'take'.

R

received pronunciation (also **received standard**) ▶ **noun** [mass noun] the standard form of British English pronunciation, based on educated speech in southern England, widely accepted as a standard elsewhere.

receiver ▶ **noun 1** the part of a telephone apparatus contained in the earpiece, in which electrical signals are converted into sounds. ■ a complete telephone handset: *he picked up the receiver.* ■ a piece of radio or television apparatus that detects broadcast signals and converts them into visible or audible form: *a satellite receiver.*
2 a person who gets or accepts something that has been sent or given to them: *the receiver of a gift.* ■ a person who buys or accepts goods known to be stolen. ■ (in tennis and similar games) the player to whom the ball is served to begin play. ■ American Football a player who specializes in catching passes.
3 (Brit. also **official receiver**) a person or company appointed by a court to manage the financial affairs of a business or person that has gone bankrupt: *the company is in the hands of the receivers.*
4 Chemistry a container for collecting the products of distillation, chromatography, or other process.
5 the part of a firearm which houses the action and to which the barrel and other parts are attached.

receivership ▶ **noun** [mass noun] the state of being dealt with by an official receiver: *the company went* ***into receivership*** *last week.*

receiving line ▶ **noun** a collection of people who gather in a row to greet guests as they arrive at a formal social event.

receiving order ▶ **noun** Brit. a court order authorizing an official receiver to act in a case of bankruptcy (since 1986 superseded by a bankruptcy order).

recension /rɪˈsɛnʃ(ə)n/ ▶ **noun** a revised edition of a text. ■ [mass noun] the revision of a text.
– ORIGIN mid 17th cent. (in the sense 'survey, review'): from Latin *recensio(n-)*, from *recensere* 'revise', from *re-* 'again' + *censere* 'to review'.

recent ▶ **adjective 1** having happened, begun, or been done not long ago; belonging to a past period comparatively close to the present: *his recent visit to Britain* | *a recent edition of the newspaper.*
2 (**Recent**) Geology another term for **HOLOCENE**.
▶ **noun** (**the Recent**) Geology the Holocene epoch.
– DERIVATIVES **recency** noun, **recentness** noun.
– ORIGIN late Middle English (in the sense 'fresh'): from Latin *recens, recent-* or French *récent*.

recently ▶ **adverb** at a recent time; not long ago: *I recently bought a CD player* | *until recently we had a female doctor.*

receptacle /rɪˈsɛptək(ə)l/ ▶ **noun 1** a hollow object used to contain something: *fast-food receptacles.*
2 N. Amer. an electrical socket.
3 chiefly Zoology an organ or structure which receives a secretion, eggs, sperm, etc.
4 Botany an enlarged area at the apex of a stem on which the parts of a flower or the florets of a flower head are inserted. ■ a structure supporting the sexual organs in some algae, mosses, and liverworts.
– ORIGIN late Middle English: from Latin *receptaculum*, from *receptare* 'receive back', frequentative of *recipere* (see **RECEIVE**).

reception ▶ **noun 1** [mass noun] the action or process of receiving something sent, given, or inflicted: *sensation is not the passive reception of stimuli.* ■ [count noun] the way in which a person or group of people reacts to someone or something: *the election budget got a stony reception in the City.* ■ the process of receiving broadcast signals: *a microchip that will allow parents to block reception of violent programmes.* ■ the quality of broadcast signals received: *I had to put up with poor radio reception.* ■ American Football an act of catching a pass.
2 [mass noun] the action of admitting someone to a place, group, or institution or the process of being admitted: *their reception into the Church.* ■ the formal or ceremonious welcoming of a guest: *his reception by the Prime Minister.* ■ [count noun] a formal social occasion held to welcome someone or to celebrate an event: *a wedding reception.*
3 chiefly Brit. the area in a hotel or organization where guests and visitors are greeted and dealt with: *wait for me downstairs* ***in reception*** | [as modifier] *the reception desk.*
4 [usu. as modifier] Brit. the first class in an infant school: *the reception class.*
– ORIGIN late Middle English: from Old French, or from Latin *receptio(n-)*, from the verb *recipere* (see **RECEIVE**).

reception centre ▶ **noun** Brit. a hostel providing temporary accommodation for distressed people such as refugees, the homeless, and those with psychiatric difficulties.

receptionist ▶ **noun** a person who greets and deals with clients and visitors to a surgery, office, etc. ■ Brit. a person employed in a hotel to receive guests and deal with their bookings.

reception order ▶ **noun** Brit. an order authorizing the admission and detention of a patient in a psychiatric hospital.

reception room ▶ **noun** a room in a hotel or other building used for functions such as parties and meetings. ■ Brit. a room in a private house suitable for entertaining visitors.

receptive ▶ **adjective** willing to consider or accept new suggestions and ideas: *a receptive audience* | *the institution was* ***receptive to*** *new ideas.* ■ able to receive signals or stimuli. ■ (of a female animal) ready to mate.
– DERIVATIVES **receptively** adverb, **receptiveness** noun, **receptivity** noun.

receptor /rɪˈsɛptə/ ▶ **noun** Physiology an organ or cell able to respond to light, heat, or other external stimulus and transmit a signal to a sensory nerve. ■ a region of tissue, or a molecule in a cell membrane, which responds specifically to a particular neurotransmitter, hormone, antigen, or other substance.
– ORIGIN early 20th cent.: coined in German from Latin *receptor*, from *recept-* 'taken back', from the verb *recipere* (see **RECEIVE**).

recess /rɪˈsɛs, ˈriːsɛs/ ▶ **noun 1** a small space created by building part of a wall further back from the rest: *a table set into a recess.* ■ a hollow space inside something: *the concrete block has a recess in its base.* ■ (usu. **recesses**) a remote, secluded, or secret place: *the recesses of the silent pine forest* | figurative *the dark recesses of his soul.*
2 a period of time when the proceedings of a parliament, committee, court of law, or other official body are temporarily suspended: *talks resumed after a month's recess* | *Parliament was* ***in recess.*** ■ chiefly N. Amer. a break between school classes: *the mid-morning recess.*
▶ **verb 1** [with obj.] (often as adj. **recessed**) attach (a fitment) by setting it back into the wall or surface to which it is fixed: *recessed ceiling lights.*
2 [no obj.] chiefly N. Amer. (of formal proceedings) be temporarily suspended: *the talks recessed at 2.15.* ■ [with obj.] suspend (formal proceedings) temporarily. ■ (of an official body) suspend its proceedings for a period of time.
– ORIGIN mid 16th cent. (in the sense 'withdrawal, departure'): from Latin *recessus*, from *recedere* 'go back' (see **RECEDE**). The verb dates from the early 19th cent.

recession ▶ **noun 1** a period of temporary economic decline during which trade and industrial activity are reduced, generally identified by a fall in GDP in two successive quarters: *the country is in the depths of a recession* | [mass noun] *measures to pull the economy out of recession.*
2 [mass noun] chiefly Astronomy the action of receding; motion away from an observer.
– DERIVATIVES **recessionary** adjective.
– ORIGIN mid 17th cent.: from Latin *recessio(n-)*, from *recess-* 'gone back', from the verb *recedere* (see **RECEDE**).

recessional ▶ **adjective 1** relating to an economic recession: *recessional times.*
2 chiefly Astronomy relating to or denoting motion away from the observer.
3 Geology (of a moraine or other deposit) left during a pause in the retreat of a glacier or ice sheet.
▶ **noun** a hymn sung while the clergy and choir process out of church at the end of a service.

recessive ▶ **adjective 1** Genetics relating to or denoting heritable characteristics controlled by genes which are expressed in offspring only when inherited from both parents. Often contrasted with **DOMINANT**.
2 undergoing an economic recession: *the recessive housing market.*
3 Phonetics (of the stress on a word or phrase) tending to fall on the first syllable.
4 Linguistics tending to fall into disuse.
▶ **noun** Genetics a recessive trait or gene.
– DERIVATIVES **recessively** adverb, **recessiveness** noun, **recessivity** noun.
– ORIGIN late 17th cent.: from **RECESS**, on the pattern of *excessive*.

Rechabite /ˈrɛkəbʌɪt/ ▶ **noun** (in the Bible) a member of an Israelite family, descended from Rechab, who refused to drink wine or live in houses (Jer. 35). ■ a member of the Independent Order of Rechabites, a benefit society of teetotallers, founded in 1835.

recharge ▶ **verb** [with obj.] restore electrical energy in (a battery or a battery-operated device) by connecting it to a power supply: *he plugged his razor in to recharge it.* ■ [no obj.] (of a battery or battery-operated device) be refilled with electrical energy: *the drill takes about three hours to recharge.* ■ refill (a cup, glass, or other container) with liquid: *we recharged our glasses.* ■ [no obj.] (of a person) return to a normal state of mind or strength after a period of exertion: *she needs a bit of time to recharge after giving so much of herself.*
▶ **noun** [mass noun] the replenishment of an aquifer by the absorption of water.
– PHRASES **recharge one's batteries** regain one's strength and energy by resting for a time.
– DERIVATIVES **rechargeable** adjective, **recharger** noun.

réchauffé /reɪˈʃəʊfeɪ/ ▶ **noun** a dish of warmed-up food left over from a previous meal.
– ORIGIN French, literally 'reheated', past participle of *réchauffer*.

recheck ▶ **verb** [with obj.] check or verify again: *switch off at once and recheck all the wiring.*
▶ **noun** an act of checking or verifying something again.

recherché /rəˈʃɛːʃeɪ/ ▶ **adjective** rare, exotic, or obscure: *a few linguistic terms are perhaps a bit recherché for the average readership.*
– ORIGIN French, literally 'carefully sought out', past participle of *rechercher*.

rechipping ▶ **noun** [mass noun] Brit. the practice of changing the electronic identification numbers of a stolen mobile phone so as to enable it to be reused.

rechristen ▶ **verb** [with obj. and complement] give a new name to: *the brewery rechristened the pub The Brown Trout.*

recidivist /rɪˈsɪdɪvɪst/ ▶ **noun** a convicted criminal who reoffends, especially repeatedly.
▶ **adjective** relating to recidivists: *the third lowest recidivist rate in the country.* ■ tending to reoffend: *women are rarely recidivist.*
– DERIVATIVES **recidivism** noun, **recidivistic** adjective.
– ORIGIN late 19th cent.: from French *récidiviste*, from *récidiver* 'fall back', based on Latin *recidivus* 'falling back', from the verb *recidere*, from *re-* 'back' + *cadere* 'to fall'.

Recife /rəˈsiːfi/ a port on the Atlantic coast of NE Brazil, capital of the state of Pernambuco; pop. 1,533,580 (2007). Former name **PERNAMBUCO**.

recipe /ˈrɛsɪpi/ ▶ **noun** a set of instructions for preparing a particular dish, including a list of the ingredients required: *a traditional Yorkshire recipe.* ■ something which is likely to lead to a particular outcome: *sky-high interest rates are **a recipe for** disaster.* ■ archaic a medical prescription.
– ORIGIN late Middle English: from Latin, literally 'receive!' (first used as an instruction in medical prescriptions), imperative of *recipere*.

recipient ▶ **noun** a person or thing that receives or is awarded something: *the recipient of the Nobel Peace Prize.*
▶ **adjective** [attrib.] receiving or capable of receiving something: *a recipient country.*
– DERIVATIVES **recipiency** noun.
– ORIGIN mid 16th cent.: from Latin *recipient-* 'receiving', from the verb *recipere*.

reciprocal /rɪˈsɪprək(ə)l/ ▶ **adjective 1** given, felt, or done in return: *she was hoping for some reciprocal comment or gesture.*
2 (of an agreement or obligation) bearing on or binding each of two parties equally: *the treaty is a bilateral commitment with reciprocal rights and duties.* ■ Grammar (of a pronoun or verb) expressing mutual action or relationship.
3 (of a course or bearing) differing from a given course or bearing by 180 degrees.
4 Mathematics (of a quantity or function) related to another so that their product is unity.
▶ **noun 1** Mathematics an expression or function so related to another that their product is unity; the quantity obtained by dividing the number one by a given quantity.
2 Grammar a pronoun or verb expressing mutual action or relationship, e.g. *each other*, *fight*.
– DERIVATIVES **reciprocality** noun, **reciprocally** adverb.
– ORIGIN late 16th cent.: from Latin *reciprocus* (based on *re-* 'back' + *pro-* 'forward') + **-AL**.

reciprocal cross ▶ **noun** Genetics a pair of crosses between a male of one strain and a female of another, and vice versa.

reciprocate /rɪˈsɪprəkeɪt/ ▶ **verb 1** [with obj.] respond to (a gesture or action) by making a corresponding one: *the favour was reciprocated* | [no obj.] *perhaps I was expected to reciprocate with some remark of my own.* ■ feel (affection or love) for someone in the same way that they feel it for oneself: *her passion for him was not reciprocated.*
2 [no obj.] (usu. as adj. **reciprocating**) (of a part of a machine) move backwards and forwards in a straight line: *a reciprocating blade.*
– DERIVATIVES **reciprocation** noun, **reciprocator** noun.
– ORIGIN late 16th cent.: from Latin *reciprocat-* 'moved backwards and forwards', from the verb *reciprocare*, from *reciprocus* (see **RECIPROCAL**).

reciprocating engine ▶ **noun** an engine in which one or more pistons move up and down in cylinders; a piston engine.

reciprocity /ˌrɛsɪˈprɒsɪti/ ▶ **noun** [mass noun] the practice of exchanging things with others for mutual benefit, especially privileges granted by one country or organization to another.
– ORIGIN mid 18th cent.: from French *réciprocité*, from *réciproque*, from Latin *reciprocus* 'moving backwards and forwards' (see **RECIPROCATE**).

recirculate ▶ **verb** [with obj.] circulate again.
– DERIVATIVES **recirculation** noun.

recital ▶ **noun 1** a performance of a programme of music by a soloist or small group: *I gave my first recital at the Royal College.*
2 an enumeration or listing of connected names, facts, or events: *they launched into a recital of their misadventures.*
3 (usu. **recitals**) Law the part of a legal document that explains its purpose and gives other factual information.
– DERIVATIVES **recitalist** noun.

recitation ▶ **noun** the action of repeating something aloud from memory: *the recitation of traditional poems.* ■ the repetition of a list of facts.

recitative /ˌrɛsɪtəˈtiːv/ ▶ **noun** [mass noun] musical declamation of the kind usual in the narrative and dialogue parts of opera and oratorio, sung in the rhythm of ordinary speech with many words on the same note: *singing in recitative.*
– ORIGIN mid 17th cent.: from Italian *recitativo*, from Latin *recitare* 'to read out' (see **RECITE**).

recitativo /ˌrɛsɪtəˈtiːvəʊ/ ▶ **noun** (pl. **recitativos**) another term for **RECITATIVE**.
– ORIGIN Italian.

recite ▶ **verb** [with obj.] repeat aloud or declaim (a poem or passage) from memory before an audience: *he recited passages of Dante.* ■ say aloud (a series of names, facts, etc.): *she recited the dates and names of kings and queens.*
– DERIVATIVES **reciter** noun.
– ORIGIN late Middle English (as a legal term in the sense 'state (a fact) in a document'): from Old French *reciter* or Latin *recitare* 'read out', from *re-* (expressing intensive force) + *citare* 'cite'.

reck ▶ **verb** [no obj.] [with negative or in questions] archaic pay heed to something: *ye reck not of lands or goods.* ■ (**it recks**) it is of importance: *what recks it?*
– ORIGIN Old English, of Germanic origin; compare with **RECKLESS**. The word became common in rhetorical and poetic language in the 19th cent.

reckless ▶ **adjective** heedless of danger or the consequences of one's actions; rash or impetuous: *you mustn't be so reckless* | *reckless driving.*
– DERIVATIVES **recklessly** adverb, **recklessness** noun.
– ORIGIN Old English *recceléas*, from the Germanic base (meaning 'care') of **RECK**.

reckon ▶ **verb 1** [with obj.] establish by calculation: *his debts were **reckoned at** £300,000* | *the Byzantine year was reckoned from 1 September.* ■ (**reckon someone/thing among**) include someone or something in (a class or group): *the society can reckon among its members males of the royal blood.*
2 [with clause] informal be of the opinion: *he reckons that the army should pull out entirely* | *I reckon I can manage that.* ■ [with obj. and complement] consider or regard in a specified way: *the event was reckoned a failure.* ■ [no obj.] (**reckon on/to**) informal have a specified view or opinion of: *'What do you reckon on this place?' she asked.* ■ [with obj.] Brit. informal rate highly: *I don't reckon his chances.*
3 [no obj.] (**reckon on**) rely on or be sure of: *they had reckoned on a day or two more of privacy.* ■ [with infinitive] informal expect to do a particular thing: *I reckon to get away by two-thirty.*
– PHRASES **a —— to be reckoned with** (or **to reckon with**) a thing or person that is not to be ignored or underestimated: *the trade unions were a political force to be reckoned with.*
– PHRASAL VERBS **reckon with** (or **without**) take (or fail to take) into account: *they hadn't reckoned with a visit from Eunice.* **reckon with** archaic settle accounts with.
– ORIGIN Old English *(ge)recenian* 'recount, relate', of West Germanic origin; related to Dutch *rekenen* and German *rechnen* 'to count (up)'. Early senses included 'give an account of items received' and 'mention things in order', which gave rise to the notion of 'calculation' and hence of 'being of an opinion'.

reckoner ▶ **noun** a table or device designed to assist with calculation.

reckoning ▶ **noun** [mass noun] **1** the action or process of calculating or estimating something: *the sixth, or by another reckoning eleventh, Earl of Mar.* ■ a person's opinion or judgement: *by ancient reckoning, bacteria are plants.* ■ [count noun] archaic a bill or account, or its settlement.
2 the avenging or punishing of past mistakes or misdeeds: *the fear of being brought to reckoning* | [count noun] *there will be a terrible reckoning.*
3 (**the reckoning**) contention for a place in a team or among the winners of a contest: *he has hit the sort of form which could thrust him **into the reckoning**.*

reclaim ▶ **verb** [with obj.] **1** retrieve or recover (something previously lost, given, or paid); obtain the return of: *you can reclaim £25 of the £435 deducted* | *when Dennis emerged I reclaimed my room.* ■ dated redeem (someone) from a state of vice; reform: *societies for reclaiming beggars and prostitutes.* ■ archaic tame or civilize (an animal or person).
2 bring (waste land or land formerly under water) under cultivation: *much of the Camargue has now been reclaimed* | (as adj. **reclaimed**) *reclaimed land.* ■ recover (material) for reuse; recycle: *a sufficient weight of plastic could easily be reclaimed.*
▶ **noun** [mass noun] the action or process of reclaiming or being reclaimed: *VAT reclaim.*
– DERIVATIVES **reclaimable** adjective, **reclaimer** noun, **reclamation** noun.
– ORIGIN Middle English (used in falconry in the sense 'recall'): from Old French *reclamer*, from Latin *reclamare* 'cry out against', from *re-* 'back' + *clamare* 'to shout'.

reclassify ▶ **verb** (**reclassifies, reclassifying, reclassified**) [with obj.] assign to a different class or category: *what was previously tax relief may be reclassified as government expenditure.* ■ (in South Africa during the apartheid era) officially assign (someone) to a different legally defined ethnic group.
– DERIVATIVES **reclassification** noun.

recline ▶ **verb** [no obj.] lean or lie back in a relaxed position with the back supported: *she was reclining in a deckchair* | (as adj. **reclining**) *a reclining figure.* ■ (of a seat) be able to have the back moved into a sloping position: *all the seats recline.*
– DERIVATIVES **reclinable** adjective.
– ORIGIN late Middle English (in the sense 'cause to lean back'): from Old French *recliner* or Latin *reclinare* 'bend back, recline', from *re-* 'back' + *clinare* 'to bend'.

recliner ▶ **noun** a chair with a reclining back, especially one with an integral footrest.

reclothe ▶ **verb** [with obj.] dress again, especially in different clothes: *she was ceremonially reclothed in a new robe.*

recluse /rɪˈkluːs/ ▶ **noun** a person who lives a solitary life and tends to avoid other people.
▶ **adjective** archaic favouring a solitary life.
– DERIVATIVES **reclusion** noun.
– ORIGIN Middle English: from Old French *reclus*, past participle of *reclure*, from Latin *recludere* 'enclose', from *re-* 'again' + *claudere* 'to shut'.

reclusive ▶ **adjective** avoiding the company of other people; solitary: *he led a reclusive life.*
– DERIVATIVES **reclusively** adverb, **reclusiveness** noun.

recoat ▶ **verb** [with obj.] apply another coat of paint, varnish, etc. to.

recode ▶ **verb** [with obj.] put (something, especially a computer program) into a different code. ■ assign a different code to.

recognition ▶ **noun** [mass noun] the action or process of recognizing or being recognized, in particular: ■ identification of a thing or person from previous encounters or knowledge: *she saw him pass by without a sign of recognition* | *methods of production have improved **out of all recognition**.* ■ acknowledgement of the existence, validity, or legality of something: *the unions must receive proper recognition.* ■ appreciation or acclaim for an achievement, service, or ability: *his work was slow to gain recognition* | *she received the award **in recognition of** her human rights work.* ■ (also **diplomatic recognition**) formal acknowledgement by a country that another political entity fulfils the conditions of statehood and is eligible to be dealt with as a member of the international community.
– PHRASES **beyond recognition** so as to be no longer recognizable: *within a few years, the Soviet Union changed almost beyond recognition* | *methods of production have improved **beyond all recognition**.*
– ORIGIN late 15th cent. (denoting the acknowledgement of a service): from Latin *recognitio(n-)*, from the verb *recognoscere* 'know again, recall to mind' (see **RECOGNIZE**).

recognizable (also **recognisable**) ▶ **adjective** able to be recognized or identified from previous

R

encounters or knowledge: *there was no recognizable photograph of him* | *his car was instantly recognizable.*
– DERIVATIVES **recognizability** noun, **recognizably** adverb.

recognizance /rɪˈkɒ(g)nɪz(ə)ns/ (also **recognisance**) ▶ **noun** Law a bond by which a person undertakes before a court or magistrate to observe some condition, especially to appear when summoned.
– ORIGIN Middle English: from Old French *reconnissance*, from *reconnaistre* 'recognize'.

recognizant /rɪˈkɒgnɪz(ə)nt/ (also **recognisant**) ▶ **adjective** (**recognizant of**) formal conscious or aware of (something, especially a favour).

recognize (also **recognise**) ▶ **verb** [with obj.] **1** identify (someone or something) from having encountered them before; know again: *I recognized her when her wig fell off* | *Julia hardly recognized Jill when they met.* ■ identify from knowledge of appearance or character: *Pat is very good at recognizing wild flowers.* ■ (of a computer or other machine) automatically identify and respond correctly to (a sound, printed character, etc.).
2 acknowledge the existence, validity, or legality of: *the defence is recognized in British law* | *he was recognized as an international authority.* ■ show official appreciation of; reward formally: *his work was recognized by an honorary degree from Glasgow University.* ■ officially regard (a qualification) as valid or proper: *these qualifications are recognized by the Department of Education.* ■ grant diplomatic recognition to (a country or government). ■ (of a person presiding at a meeting or debate) call on (someone) to speak.
– DERIVATIVES **recognizer** noun.
– ORIGIN late Middle English (earliest attested as a term in Scots law): from Old French *reconniss-*, stem of *reconnaistre*, from Latin *recognoscere* 'know again, recall to mind', from *re-* 'again' + *cognoscere* 'learn'.

recoil ▶ **verb** [no obj.] **1** suddenly spring or flinch back in fear, horror, or disgust: *he recoiled in horror.* ■ feel fear, horror, or disgust at the thought of something: *Ronni felt herself recoil at the very thought.*
2 rebound or spring back through force of impact or elasticity: *the muscle has the ability to recoil.* ■ (of a gun) move abruptly backwards as a reaction on firing a bullet, shell, or other missile. ■ (**recoil on/upon**) (of an action) have an adverse reactive effect on (the originator).
▶ **noun** [mass noun] the action of recoiling: *his body jerked with the recoil of the rifle.*
– DERIVATIVES **recoilless** adjective.
– ORIGIN Middle English (denoting the act of retreating): from Old French *reculer* 'move back', based on Latin *culus* 'buttocks'.

recollect[1] /ˌrɛkəˈlɛkt/ ▶ **verb** [with obj.] remember (something); call to mind: *he could not quite recollect the reason* | *'Can you recollect how he reacted?'*
– ORIGIN early 16th cent. (in the sense 'gather'): from Latin *recollect-* 'gathered back', from the verb *recolligere*, from *re-* 'back' + *colligere* 'collect'.

recollect[2] /ˌriːkəˈlɛkt/ ▶ **verb** [with obj.] **1** (**recollect oneself**) bring oneself back to a state of composure: *he had a look round, recollected himself, and prepared for the day.*
2 rare collect or gather together again.
– ORIGIN early 17th cent.: later form of RECOLLECT[1], from RE- 'once more' + the verb COLLECT[1].

R

recollection /ˌrɛkəˈlɛkʃ(ə)n/ ▶ **noun** [mass noun] the action or faculty of remembering or recollecting something: ***to the best of my recollection** no one ever had a bad word to say about him.* ■ [count noun] a thing recollected; a memory: *a biography based on his wife's recollections.*
– DERIVATIVES **recollective** adjective.
– ORIGIN late 16th cent. (denoting the action of gathering things together again): from French or medieval Latin *recollectio(n-)*, from the verb *recolligere* 'gather again' (see RECOLLECT[1]).

Recollet /ˈrɛkəleɪ/ (also **Recollect** /ˈrɛkəlɛkt/) ▶ **noun** historical a member of a reformed branch of the Franciscan order, founded in France in the late 16th century.
– ORIGIN from French *récollet*, from medieval Latin *recollectus* 'gathered together', expressing a notion of concentration, and absorption in thought.

recolonize (also **recolonise**) ▶ **verb** [with obj.] (chiefly of a plant or animal species) colonize (a region or habitat) again.
– DERIVATIVES **recolonization** noun.

recolour (US **recolor**) ▶ **verb** [with obj.] colour again or differently.

recombinant /rɪˈkɒmbɪnənt/ Genetics ▶ **adjective** [attrib.] relating to or denoting an organism, cell, or genetic material formed by recombination.
▶ **noun** a recombinant organism, cell, or piece of genetic material.

recombinant DNA ▶ **noun** [mass noun] DNA that has been formed artificially by combining constituents from different organisms.

recombinase /rɪˈkɒmbɪneɪz/ ▶ **noun** Biochemistry an enzyme which promotes genetic recombination.

recombination ▶ **noun** [mass noun] the process of recombining things. ■ Genetics the rearrangement of genetic material, especially by crossing over in chromosomes or by the artificial joining of segments of DNA from different organisms.

recombine ▶ **verb** combine or cause to combine again or differently: [no obj.] *carbohydrates can recombine with oxygen* | [with obj.] *decompose the calculation into components and recombine them to find the solution.*

recommence ▶ **verb** begin or cause to begin again: [no obj.] *the war recommenced* | [with obj.] *it was agreed to recommence talks.*
– DERIVATIVES **recommencement** noun.

recommend ▶ **verb** [with obj.] **1** put forward (someone or something) with approval as being suitable for a particular purpose or role: *George had recommended some local architects* | *a book I **recommended to** a friend of mine.* ■ advise or suggest (something) as a course of action: *some doctors recommend putting a board under the mattress* | [with clause] *the report recommended that criminal charges be brought* | (as adj. **recommended**) *the recommended daily intake of vitamins.* ■ [with obj. and infinitive] advise (someone) to do something: *you are strongly recommended to seek professional advice.* ■ make (someone or something) appealing or desirable: *the house had much to recommend it.*
2 (**recommend someone/thing to**) archaic commend or entrust someone or something to (someone).
– DERIVATIVES **recommendable** adjective, **recommendatory** adjective, **recommender** noun.
– ORIGIN late Middle English (in sense 2): from medieval Latin *recommendare*, from Latin *re-* (expressing intensive force) + *commendare* 'commit to the care of'.

recommendation ▶ **noun** a suggestion or proposal as to the best course of action, especially one put forward by an authoritative body: *the committee put forward forty recommendations for change.* ■ [mass noun] the action of recommending something or someone: *he selected his staff by personal recommendation.*

recommission ▶ **verb** [with obj.] commission again.

recommit ▶ **verb** (**recommits, recommitting, recommitted**) [with obj.] commit again. ■ return (a motion, proposal, or parliamentary bill) to a committee for further consideration.
– DERIVATIVES **recommitment** noun, **recommittal** noun.

recompense /ˈrɛkəmpɛns/ ▶ **verb** [with obj.] make amends to (someone) for loss or harm suffered; compensate: *offenders should recompense their victims* | *he was recompensed for the wasted time.* ■ pay or reward (someone) for effort or work: *he was handsomely recompensed.* ■ make amends to or reward someone for (loss, harm, or effort): *losses up to £20,000 are recompensed.* ■ archaic punish or reward (someone) for an action.
▶ **noun** [mass noun] compensation or reward given for loss or harm suffered or effort made: *adequate recompense for workers who lose their jobs* | *substantial damages were paid **in recompense**.* ■ archaic restitution made or punishment inflicted for a wrong or injury.
– ORIGIN late Middle English: from Old French, from the verb *recompenser* 'do a favour to requite a loss', from late Latin *recompensare*, from Latin *re-* 'again' (also expressing intensive force) + *compensare* 'weigh one thing against another'.

recompile ▶ **verb** [with obj.] compile (a computer program) again or differently.
▶ **noun** an act of recompiling a computer program.
– DERIVATIVES **recompilation** noun.

recompose ▶ **verb** [with obj.] compose again or differently: *a marble panel recomposed from fragments.*
– DERIVATIVES **recomposition** noun.

recon /rɪˈkɒn/ N. Amer. informal ▶ **noun** short for RECONNAISSANCE.
▶ **verb** (**recons, reconning, reconned**) short for RECONNOITRE.

reconcilable ▶ **adjective** capable of being reconciled; compatible: *the two propositions are hardly reconcilable* | *the theory was quite **reconcilable with** industrialization.*
– DERIVATIVES **reconcilability** noun.

reconcile /ˈrɛk(ə)nsʌɪl/ ▶ **verb** [with obj.] **1** restore friendly relations between: *the king and the archbishop were publicly reconciled* | *she wanted to be **reconciled with** her father.* ■ settle (a quarrel): *advice on how to reconcile the conflict.* ■ make or show to be compatible: *the agreement had to be reconciled with the city's new international relations policy.* ■ (**reconcile someone to**) make someone accept (a disagreeable or unwelcome thing): *he was reconciled to leaving.*
2 make (one account) consistent with another, especially by allowing for transactions begun but not yet completed: *it is not necessary to reconcile the cost accounts to the financial accounts.*
– DERIVATIVES **reconcilement** noun, **reconciler** noun, **reconciliatory** adjective.
– ORIGIN late Middle English: from Old French *reconcilier* or Latin *reconciliare*, from Latin *re-* 'back' (also expressing intensive force) + *conciliare* 'bring together'.

reconciliation /ˌrɛk(ə)nsɪlɪˈeɪʃ(ə)n/ ▶ **noun 1** the restoration of friendly relations: *his **reconciliation with** your uncle* | [count noun] *the earl was seeking **a reconciliation with** his wife.*
2 the action of making one view or belief compatible with another: *any possibility of **reconciliation between** such clearly opposed positions.*
3 the action of making financial accounts consistent; harmonization: *the reconciliation process should be consistent with the business strategy.*

recondite /ˈrɛk(ə)ndʌɪt, rɪˈkɒn-/ ▶ **adjective** (of a subject or knowledge) little known; abstruse: *the book is full of recondite information.*
– ORIGIN mid 17th cent.: from Latin *reconditus* 'hidden, put away', past participle of *recondere*, from *re-* 'back' + *condere* 'put together, secrete'.

recondition ▶ **verb** [with obj.] condition again. ■ Brit. overhaul or renovate (a vehicle engine or piece of equipment): *a ship was being reconditioned* | (as adj. **reconditioned**) *a reconditioned engine.*

reconfigure ▶ **verb** [with obj.] configure (something) differently: *you don't have to reconfigure the modem each time you make a connection.*
– DERIVATIVES **reconfigurable** adjective, **reconfiguration** noun.

reconfirm ▶ **verb** [with obj.] confirm again.
– DERIVATIVES **reconfirmation** noun.

reconnaissance /rɪˈkɒnɪs(ə)ns/ ▶ **noun** [mass noun] military observation of a region to locate an enemy or ascertain strategic features: *an excellent aircraft for low-level reconnaissance* | [count noun] *after a reconnaissance British forces took the island.* ■ preliminary surveying or research: *conducting client reconnaissance.*
– ORIGIN early 19th cent.: from French, from *reconnaître* 'recognize' (see RECONNOITRE).

reconnect ▶ **verb** [with obj.] connect back together: *surgeons had to reconnect tendons, nerves, and veins.* ■ [no obj.] re-establish a bond of communication or emotion: *in order to keep your marriage healthy, it is important to reconnect as mature individuals.*
– DERIVATIVES **reconnection** noun.

reconnoitre /ˌrɛkəˈnɔɪtə/ (US **reconnoiter**) ▶ **verb** [with obj.] make a military observation of (a region): *they reconnoitred the beach some weeks before the landing* | [no obj.] *the raiders were reconnoitring for further attacks.*
▶ **noun** an act of reconnoitring: *a nocturnal reconnoitre of the camp.*
– ORIGIN early 18th cent.: from obsolete French *reconnoître*, from Latin *recognoscere* 'know again' (see RECOGNIZE).

reconquer ▶ **verb** [with obj.] conquer again.
– DERIVATIVES **reconquest** noun.

reconsecrate ▶ **verb** [with obj.] consecrate (someone or something) again.
– DERIVATIVES **reconsecration** noun.

reconsider ▶ **verb** [with obj.] consider (something) again, especially for a possible change of decision regarding it: *they called on the US government to reconsider its policy* | [no obj.] *I beg you to reconsider.*

reconsideration ▶ **noun** the act of considering something again; review.

reconsign ▶ **verb** [with obj.] consign again or differently.
– DERIVATIVES **reconsignment** noun.

reconsolidate ▶ **verb** [with obj.] consolidate (something) again or anew.
– DERIVATIVES **reconsolidation** noun.

reconstitute ▸ verb [with obj.] **1** build up again from parts; reconstruct. ■ change the form and organization of (an institution): *he reconstituted his cabinet.* **2** restore (something dried) to its original state by adding water to it: (as adj. **reconstituted**) *reconstituted milk.*
– DERIVATIVES **reconstitution** noun.

reconstruct ▸ verb [with obj.] build or form (something) again after it has been damaged or destroyed: *a small area of painted Roman plaster has been reconstructed.* ■ reorganize (something): *later emperors reconstructed the army.* ■ form an impression, model, or re-enactment of (a past event or thing) from the available evidence: *from copies of correspondence it is possible to reconstruct the broad sequence of events.*
– DERIVATIVES **reconstructable** (also **reconstructible**) adjective, **reconstructive** adjective, **reconstructor** noun.

reconstruction ▸ noun **1** [mass noun] the action or process of reconstructing or being reconstructed: *the economic reconstruction of Russia.* ■ [count noun] a thing that has been rebuilt after being damaged or destroyed: *comparison between the original and the reconstruction.* ■ [count noun] an impression, model, or re-enactment of a past event formed from the available evidence: *a reconstruction of the accident would be staged to try to discover the cause of the tragedy* **2** (**the Reconstruction**) the period 1865–77 following the American Civil War, during which the Southern states of the Confederacy were controlled by federal government and social legislation, including the granting of new rights to black people, was introduced.

reconvene ▸ verb convene or cause to convene again, especially after a pause in proceedings: [no obj.] *parliament reconvenes on 1st June* | [with obj.] *it was agreed to reconvene the permanent commission.*

reconvert ▸ verb [with obj.] convert back to a former state.
– DERIVATIVES **reconversion** noun.

reconvict ▸ verb [with obj.] convict (someone) of a further criminal offence: *many prisoners are reconvicted within two years of release.*
– DERIVATIVES **reconviction** noun.

record ▸ noun **1** a thing constituting a piece of evidence about the past, especially an account kept in writing or some other permanent form: *identification was made through dental records* | *a record of meter readings.* ■ (also **court record**) Law an official report of the proceedings and judgement in a court. ■ Computing a number of related items of information which are handled as a unit. **2** the sum of the past achievements or performance of a person, organization, or thing: *the safety record at the airport is first class* | *the team preserved their unbeaten home record.* ■ short for CRIMINAL RECORD. **3** the best performance or most remarkable event of its kind: *he held the world record for over a decade* | [as modifier] *record profits.* **4** a thin plastic disc carrying recorded sound in grooves on each surface, for reproduction by a record player. ■ a piece or collection of music reproduced on a record or on another medium: *my favourite record.*
▸ verb [with obj.] **1** set down in writing or some other permanent form for later reference: *they were asked to keep a diary and record everything they ate or drank* | (as adj. **recorded**) *levels of recorded crime.* ■ state or set down publicly or officially: *the coroner recorded a verdict of accidental death.* ■ (of an instrument or observer) show or register (a measurement or result): *the temperature was the lowest recorded since 1926.* ■ achieve (a certain score or result): *they recorded their first win of the season.* **2** convert (sound or a performance) into a permanent form on tape, disc, etc. for subsequent reproduction or broadcast: *they were recording a guitar recital.* ■ produce (a programme, or a piece or collection of music) by such means: *they go into the studio next week to record their debut album* | *they recorded an episode of the show.*
– PHRASES **for the record** so that the true facts are recorded or known: *for the record, I have never been to the flat.* **a matter of record** a thing that is established as a fact through being officially recorded. **off the record** not made as an official or attributable statement. **on record 1** (also **on the record**) used in reference to the making of an official or public statement: *I would like to* ***place on record*** *my sincere thanks.* **2** officially measured and noted: *it proved to be one of the warmest Decembers on record.* **put** (or **set**) **the record straight** give the true version of events that have been reported incorrectly.
– DERIVATIVES **recordable** adjective.
– ORIGIN Middle English: from Old French *record* 'remembrance', from *recorder* 'bring to remembrance', from Latin *recordari* 'remember', based on *cor, cord-* 'heart'. The noun was earliest used in law to denote the fact of being written down as evidence. The verb originally meant 'narrate orally or in writing', also 'repeat so as to commit to memory'.

record-breaking ▸ adjective surpassing a record or best-ever achievement: *the fair attracted a record-breaking 10,678 visitors.*
– DERIVATIVES **record-breaker** noun.

recorded delivery ▸ noun Brit. a Post Office service in which the sender receives a certificate that a letter or parcel has been posted and the Post Office obtains a signature from the recipient as a record that it has been delivered.

recorder ▸ noun **1** an apparatus for recording sound, pictures, or data. **2** a person who keeps records: *a recorder of rural life.* **3** (**Recorder**) (in England and Wales) a barrister appointed to serve as a part-time judge. ■ Brit. historical a judge in certain courts. **4** a simple wind instrument without keys, held vertically and played by blowing air through a shaped mouthpiece against a sharp edge.
– DERIVATIVES **recordership** noun (sense 3).
– ORIGIN late Middle English (denoting a kind of judge): from Anglo-Norman French *recordour*, from Old French *recorder* 'bring to remembrance'; partly reinforced by the verb RECORD (also used in the obsolete sense 'practise a tune': see sense 4).

record holder ▸ noun a person who has achieved the best-ever performance, especially in a particular sport: *the Commonwealth 800 metres record holder.*
– DERIVATIVES **record-holding** adjective.

recording ▸ noun [mass noun] the action or process of recording sound or a performance for subsequent reproduction or broadcast: [as modifier] *a recording studio.* ■ [count noun] a recorded broadcast or performance: *a bootleg live recording.* ■ a disc or tape on which sounds or visual images have been recorded.

recording angel ▸ noun an angel that is believed to register each person's good and bad actions.

recordist ▸ noun a person who makes recordings, especially of sound: *a sound recordist.*

record player ▸ noun an apparatus for reproducing sound from records, comprising a turntable that spins the record at a constant speed and a stylus that slides along in the groove and picks up the sound, together with an amplifier and a loudspeaker.

recork ▸ verb [with obj.] put back or replace the cork in (a bottle of wine).

recount[1] /rɪˈkaʊnt/ ▸ verb [reporting verb] tell someone about something; give an account of an event or experience: [with obj.] *I recounted the tale to Steve* | [with clause] *he recounts how they often talked of politics.*
▸ noun an act or instance of giving an account of an event or experience.
– ORIGIN late Middle English: from Old Northern French *reconter* 'tell again', based on Old French *counter* (see COUNT[1]).

recount[2] ▸ verb /riːˈkaʊnt/ [with obj.] count again.
▸ noun /ˈriːkaʊnt/ an act of counting something again, especially votes in an election.

recoup ▸ verb [with obj.] regain (something lost or expended): *rains have helped recoup water levels* | *sleep was what she needed to recoup her strength* | [no obj.] *he's just resting, recouping from the trial.* ■ regain (money spent) through subsequent profits: *oil companies are keen to recoup their investment.* ■ reimburse or compensate (someone) for money spent or lost. ■ Law deduct or keep back (part of a sum due).
– DERIVATIVES **recoupable** adjective, **recoupment** noun.
– ORIGIN early 17th cent. (as a legal term): from French *recouper* 'retrench, cut back', from *re-* 'back' + *couper* 'to cut'.

recourse ▸ noun [in sing.] a source of help in a difficult situation: *surgery may be the only recourse.* ■ [mass noun] (**recourse to**) the use of (someone or something) as a source of help in a difficult situation: *a means of solving disputes without recourse to courts of law* | *all three countries had recourse to the IMF for standby loans.* ■ [mass noun] the legal right to demand compensation or payment: *the bank* ***has recourse against*** *the exporter for losses incurred.*
– PHRASES **without recourse** Finance a formula used to disclaim responsibility for future non-payment, especially of a negotiable financial instrument.
– ORIGIN late Middle English (also in the sense 'running or flowing back'): from Old French *recours*, from Latin *recursus*, from *re-* 'back, again' + *cursus* 'course, running'.

recover ▸ verb **1** [no obj.] return to a normal state of health, mind, or strength: ***Neil is still recovering from*** *shock* | *the economy has begun to recover.* ■ (**be recovered**) (of a person) be well again: *you'll be fully recovered before you know it.* **2** [with obj.] find or regain possession of (something stolen or lost): *police recovered a stolen video.* ■ regain control of (oneself or of a physical or mental state): *he recovered his balance and sped on.* ■ regain or secure (money spent or lost or compensation) by legal process or the making of profits: *many companies recovered their costs within six months.* ■ make up for (a loss in position or time): *the French recovered the lead.* **3** remove or extract (an energy source or industrial chemical) for use, reuse, or waste treatment.
▸ noun (**the recover**) a defined position of a firearm forming part of a military drill: *bring the firelock* ***to the recover.***
– DERIVATIVES **recoverer** noun.
– ORIGIN Middle English (originally with reference to health): from Anglo-Norman French *recoverer*, from Latin *recuperare* 'get again'.

re-cover ▸ verb [with obj.] put a new cover or covering on: *the cost of re-covering the armchair.*

recoverable ▸ adjective **1** (of something lost) able to be regained or retrieved: *even unreadable disks may contain information that is recoverable.* ■ (of compensation or money spent or lost) able to be regained or secured by means of a legal process or subsequent profits. **2** (of an energy source) able to be economically extracted from the ground or sea.
– DERIVATIVES **recoverability** noun.

recovery ▸ noun (pl. **recoveries**) [mass noun] **1** a return to a normal state of health, mind, or strength: *signs of recovery in the housing market* | [count noun] *it is hoped that Lawrence can* ***make a full recovery.*** **2** the action or process of regaining possession or control of something stolen or lost: *a team of salvage experts to ensure the recovery of family possessions.* ■ the action of regaining or securing compensation or money lost or spent by means of a legal process or subsequent profits: *debt recovery.* ■ [count noun] an object or amount of money recovered: *the recoveries included gold jewellery.* ■ the action of taking a vehicle or aircraft that has broken down or crashed to a place for repair: [as modifier] *a recovery vehicle.* ■ (also **recovery shot**) [count noun] Golf a stroke bringing the ball from the rough or from a hazard back on to the fairway or the green. ■ [count noun] American Football an act of regaining a dropped ball. ■ (in rowing, cycling, or swimming) the action of returning the paddle, leg, or arm to its initial position ready to make a new stroke. **3** the process of removing or extracting an energy source or industrial chemical for use, reuse, or waste treatment.
– PHRASES **in recovery** recovering from mental illness or drug addiction.
– ORIGIN late Middle English (denoting a means of restoration): from Anglo-Norman French *recoverie*, from *recovrer* 'get back'.

recovery position ▸ noun Brit. a position used in first aid to prevent choking in unconscious patients, in which the body is placed facing downwards and slightly to the side, supported by the bent limbs. Also called SEMI-PRONE POSITION.

recovery stock ▸ noun Finance a share that has fallen in price but is thought to have the potential of climbing back to its original level.

recovery time ▸ noun the time required for a material or piece of equipment to resume its former or usual condition following an action, such as the passage of a current through electrical equipment.

recreant /ˈrɛkrɪənt/ archaic ▸ adjective **1** cowardly. **2** unfaithful to a belief; apostate.
▸ noun **1** a coward. **2** a person who is unfaithful to a belief; an apostate.
– DERIVATIVES **recreancy** noun.
– ORIGIN Middle English: from Old French, literally 'surrendering', present participle of *recroire*, from medieval Latin *(se) recredere* 'surrender (oneself)', from *re-* (expressing reversal) + *credere* 'entrust'.

R

recreate ▶ verb [with obj.] create again: *the door was now open to recreate a single German state.* ■ reproduce; re-enact: *he recreated Mallory's 1942 climb for TV.*

recreation[1] /ˌrɛkrɪˈeɪʃ(ə)n/ ▶ noun [mass noun] activity done for enjoyment when one is not working: *she rides for recreation* | [as modifier] *sport and recreation facilities* | [count noun] *his recreations included golf and rugby.*
– ORIGIN late Middle English (also in the sense 'mental or spiritual consolation'): via Old French from Latin *recreatio(n-)*, from *recreare* 'create again, renew'.

recreation[2] /ˌriːkrɪˈeɪʃ(ə)n/ ▶ noun [mass noun] the action or process of creating something again: *the periodic destruction and recreation of the universe.* ■ [count noun] a re-enactment or simulation of something.
– ORIGIN early 16th cent.: from RE- 'again' + CREATION.

recreational ▶ adjective relating to or denoting activity done for enjoyment when one is not working: *money to provide recreational facilities.* ■ relating to or denoting drugs taken on an occasional basis for enjoyment.
– DERIVATIVES **recreationally** adverb.

recreation ground ▶ noun Brit. a piece of public land used for sports and games.

recreative /ˈrɛkrɪˌeɪtɪv, ˌriːkrɪˈeɪtɪv/ ▶ adjective another term for RECREATIONAL.

recriminate /rɪˈkrɪmɪneɪt/ ▶ verb [no obj.] archaic make counter accusations: *his party would never recriminate, never return evil for evil.*
– ORIGIN early 17th cent.: from medieval Latin *recriminat-* 'accused in return', from the verb *recriminari*, from *re-* (expressing opposition) + *criminare* 'accuse' (from *crimen* 'crime').

recrimination ▶ noun (usu. **recriminations**) an accusation in response to one from someone else: *there are no tears, no recriminations* | [mass noun] *there was a period of bitter recrimination.*

recriminative ▶ adjective archaic term for RECRIMINATORY.

recriminatory ▶ adjective involving or of the nature of mutual or counter accusations: *his habit of rendering love in terms of recriminatory bickering.*

rec room ▶ noun N. Amer. a room in a private house, especially in the basement, used for recreation and entertainment.

recross ▶ verb [with obj.] cross or pass over again.

recrudesce /ˌriːkruːˈdɛs, ˌrɛk-/ ▶ verb [no obj.] formal break out again; recur.
– DERIVATIVES **recrudescence** noun, **recrudescent** adjective.
– ORIGIN late 19th cent.: back-formation from *recrudescence* 'recurrence', from Latin *recrudescere* 'become raw again', from *re-* 'again' + *crudus* 'raw'.

recruit ▶ verb [with obj.] **1** enlist (someone) in the armed forces: *we recruit our toughest soldiers from the desert tribes* | [no obj.] *the regiment was still actively recruiting.* ■ form (an army or other force) by enlisting new people. ■ enrol (someone) as a member or worker in an organization or as a supporter of a cause: *there are plans to recruit more staff later this year.* ■ [with obj. and infinitive] informal persuade to do or help with something: *she recruited her children to help run the racket.*
2 dated replenish or reinvigorate (numbers, strength, etc.): *travelling was said to recruit the constitution.*
▶ noun a person newly enlisted in the armed forces and not yet fully trained. ■ a new member of an organization or supporter of a cause.
– DERIVATIVES **recruitable** adjective, **recruiter** noun.
– ORIGIN mid 17th cent. (in the senses 'fresh body of troops' and 'supplement the numbers in a group'): from obsolete French dialect *recrute*, based on Latin *recrescere* 'grow again', from *re-* 'again' + *crescere* 'grow'.

recruitment ▶ noun **1** [mass noun] the action of enlisting new people in the armed forces. ■ the action of finding new people to join an organization or support a cause: *this was a deterrent to the recruitment of nurses.*
2 Ecology the increase in a natural population as progeny grow and new members arrive.
3 Physiology the incorporation of cells from elsewhere in the body into a tissue or region.

recrystallize (also **recrystallise**) ▶ verb form or cause to form crystals again.
– DERIVATIVES **recrystallization** noun.

recta plural form of RECTUM.

rectal ▶ adjective relating to or affecting the rectum: *rectal cancer.*
– DERIVATIVES **rectally** adverb.

rectangle ▶ noun a plane figure with four straight sides and four right angles, especially one with unequal adjacent sides, in contrast to a square.
– ORIGIN late 16th cent.: from medieval Latin *rectangulum*, from late Latin *rectiangulum*, based on Latin *rectus* 'straight' + *angulus* 'an angle'.

rectangular ▶ adjective **1** denoting or shaped like a rectangle: *a neat rectangular area.* ■ (of a solid) having a base, section, or side shaped like a rectangle: *a rectangular prism.*
2 placed or having parts placed at right angles.
– DERIVATIVES **rectangularity** noun, **rectangularly** adverb.

rectangular coordinates ▶ plural noun a pair of coordinates measured along axes at right angles to one another.

rectangular hyperbola ▶ noun a hyperbola with rectangular asymptotes.

recti plural form of RECTUS.

rectified spirit ▶ noun [mass noun] (also **rectified spirits**) a mixture of ethanol (95.6 per cent) and water produced as an azeotrope by distillation.

rectifier ▶ noun an electrical device which converts an alternating current into a direct one by allowing a current to flow through it in one direction only.

rectify ▶ verb (**rectifies, rectifying, rectified**) [with obj.] **1** put right; correct: *mistakes made now cannot be rectified later* | *efforts to rectify the situation.*
2 convert (alternating current) to direct current.
3 find a straight line equal in length to (a curve).
– DERIVATIVES **rectifiable** adjective, **rectification** noun.
– ORIGIN late Middle English: from Old French *rectifier*, from medieval Latin *rectificare*, from Latin *rectus* 'right'.

rectilinear /ˌrɛktɪˈlɪnɪə/ (also **rectilineal** /-nɪəl/) ▶ adjective contained by, consisting of, or moving in a straight line or lines: *a rectilinear waveform.* ■ Photography relating to a straight line or lines: *rectilinear distortion.* ■ Photography (of a wide-angle lens) corrected as much as possible, so that straight lines in the subject appear straight in the image.
– DERIVATIVES **rectilinearity** noun, **rectilinearly** adverb.
– ORIGIN mid 17th cent.: from late Latin *rectilineus* (from Latin *rectus* 'straight' + *linea* 'line') + -AR[1].

rectitude ▶ noun [mass noun] formal morally correct behaviour or thinking; righteousness: *Mattie is a model of rectitude.*
– ORIGIN late Middle English (denoting straightness): from Old French, from late Latin *rectitudo*, from Latin *rectus* 'right, straight'.

recto ▶ noun (pl. **rectos**) a right-hand page of an open book, or the front of a loose document. Contrasted with VERSO.
– ORIGIN early 19th cent.: from Latin *recto (folio)* 'on the right (leaf)'.

rectocele /ˈrɛktə(ʊ)siːl/ ▶ noun Medicine a prolapse of the wall between the rectum and the vagina.
– ORIGIN mid 19th cent.: from RECTUM + -CELE.

rector ▶ noun **1** (in the Church of England) the incumbent of a parish where all tithes formerly passed to the incumbent. Compare with VICAR. ■ (in other Anglican Churches) a member of the clergy who has charge of a parish. ■ (in the Roman Catholic Church) a priest in charge of a church or of a religious institution.
2 the head of certain universities, colleges, and schools. ■ (in Scotland) an elected representative of students on a university's governing body.
– DERIVATIVES **rectorate** noun, **rectorial** adjective, **rectorship** noun.
– ORIGIN late Middle English: from Latin *rector* 'ruler', from *rect-* 'ruled', from the verb *regere*.

rectory ▶ noun (pl. **rectories**) a rector's house. ■ a Church of England benefice held by a rector.
– ORIGIN mid 16th cent.: from Old French *rectorie* or medieval Latin *rectoria*, from Latin *rector* (see RECTOR).

rectrices /ˈrɛktrɪsiːz/ ▶ plural noun (sing. **rectrix** /-trɪks/) Ornithology the larger feathers in a bird's tail, used for steering in flight. Compare with REMIGES.
– ORIGIN mid 18th cent.: from Latin, feminine plural of *rector* 'ruler' (see RECTOR).

rectum ▶ noun (pl. **rectums** or **recta** /-tə/) the final section of the large intestine, terminating at the anus.
– ORIGIN mid 16th cent.: from Latin *rectum (intestinum)* 'straight (intestine)'.

rectus /ˈrɛktəs/ ▶ noun (pl. **recti** /-tʌɪ/) Anatomy any of several straight muscles, in particular: ■ (also **rectus abdominis** /abˈdɒmɪnɪs/) each of a pair of long flat muscles at the front of the abdomen, joining the sternum to the pubis and acting to bend the whole body forwards or sideways. ■ any of a number of muscles controlling the movement of the eyeball.
– ORIGIN early 18th cent.: from Latin, literally 'straight'.

recumbent /rɪˈkʌmb(ə)nt/ ▶ adjective (especially of a person or effigy) lying down: *recumbent statues.* ■ (of a plant) growing close to the ground.
▶ noun a type of bicycle designed to be ridden lying almost flat on one's back.
– DERIVATIVES **recumbency** noun.
– ORIGIN mid 17th cent.: from Latin *recumbent-* 'reclining', from the verb *recumbere*, from *re-* 'back' + a verb related to *cubare* 'to lie'.

recuperate /rɪˈkuːpəreɪt/ ▶ verb **1** [no obj.] recover from illness or exertion: *she has been recuperating from a knee injury* | *Christmas is a time to recuperate.*
2 [with obj.] recover or regain (something lost or taken): *they will seek to recuperate the returns that go with investment.*
– DERIVATIVES **recuperable** adjective.
– ORIGIN mid 16th cent.: from Latin *recuperat-* 'regained', from the verb *recuperare*, from *re-* 'back' + *capere* 'take'.

recuperation ▶ noun [mass noun] **1** recovery from illness or exertion: *the human body has amazing powers of recuperation.*
2 the recovery or regaining of something: *the recuperation of the avant-garde for art.* ■ the action of a recuperator in imparting heat to incoming air or gaseous fuel from hot waste gases.

recuperative ▶ adjective **1** having the effect of restoring health or strength: *the body's recuperative powers.*
2 relating to the action of a recuperator or a similar heat exchanger.

recuperator ▶ noun a form of heat exchanger in which hot waste gases from a furnace are conducted continuously along a system of flues where they impart heat to incoming air or gaseous fuel.

recur ▶ verb (**recurs, recurring, recurred**) [no obj.] occur again periodically or repeatedly: *when the symptoms recurred, the doctor diagnosed something different* | (as adj. **recurring**) *a recurring theme.* ■ (of a thought, image, or memory) come back to one's mind: *Oglethorpe's words kept recurring to him.* ■ (**recur to**) go back to (something) in thought or speech: *the book remained a favourite and she constantly recurred to it.*
– DERIVATIVES **recurrence** noun, **recurringly** adverb.
– ORIGIN Middle English (in the sense 'return to'): from Latin *recurrere*, from *re-* 'again, back' + *currere* 'run'.

recurrent ▶ adjective **1** occurring often or repeatedly: *she had a recurrent dream about falling.*
2 Anatomy (of a nerve or blood vessel) turning back so as to reverse direction.
– DERIVATIVES **recurrently** adverb.
– ORIGIN late 16th cent. (in sense 2): from Latin *recurrent-* 'running back', from the verb *recurrere* (see RECUR).

recurring decimal ▶ noun a decimal fraction in which a figure or group of figures is repeated indefinitely, as in *0.666 ...* or as in *1.851851851 ....*

recursion /rɪˈkəːʃ(ə)n/ ▶ noun [mass noun] Mathematics & Linguistics the repeated application of a recursive procedure or definition. ■ [count noun] a recursive definition.
– ORIGIN 1930s: from late Latin *recursio(n-)*, from *recurrere* 'run back' (see RECUR).

recursion formula ▶ noun Mathematics an equation relating the value of a function for a given value of its argument (or arguments) to its values for other values of the argument(s).

recursive ▶ adjective characterized by recurrence or repetition, in particular: ■ Mathematics & Linguistics relating to or involving the repeated application of a rule, definition, or procedure to successive results. ■ Computing relating to or involving a program or routine of which a part requires the application of the whole, so that its explicit interpretation requires in general many successive executions.

R

– DERIVATIVES **recursively** adverb.
– ORIGIN late 18th cent. (in the general sense): from late Latin *recurs-* 'returned' (from the verb *recurrere* 'run back') + **-IVE**. Specific uses have arisen in the 20th cent.

recurve ▸ verb [no obj.] chiefly Biology bend backwards: (as adj. **recurved**) *large recurved tusks*.
▸ noun Archery a bow that curves forward at the ends, which straighten out under tension when the bow is drawn.
– DERIVATIVES **recurvature** noun.
– ORIGIN late 16th cent.: from Latin *recurvare* 'bend something back', from *re-* 'back' + *curvare* 'to bend'.

recusant /'rɛkjʊz(ə)nt/ ▸ noun a person who refuses to submit to an authority or to comply with a regulation. ■ historical a person who refused to attend services of the Church of England.
▸ adjective of or denoting a recusant.
– DERIVATIVES **recusancy** noun.
– ORIGIN mid 16th cent.: from Latin *recusant-* 'refusing', from the verb *recusare* (see **RECUSE**).

recuse /rɪ'kjuːz/ ▸ verb [with obj.] chiefly N. Amer. challenge (a judge or juror) as unqualified to perform legal duties because of a potential conflict of interest or lack of impartiality: *he was recused when he referred to the corporation as 'a bunch of villains'*. ■ (**recuse oneself**) (of a judge) excuse oneself from a case because of a potential conflict of interest or lack of impartiality.
– DERIVATIVES **recusal** noun.
– ORIGIN late Middle English (in the sense 'reject', specifically 'object to a judge as prejudiced'): from Latin *recusare* 'to refuse', from *re-* (expressing opposition) + *causa* 'a cause'. The current sense dates from the early 19th cent.

recut ▸ verb (**recuts**, **recutting**; past and past participle **recut**) [with obj.] remove further or different material from (a film or screenplay): *director Tony Scott is recutting several key scenes*.

recyclable ▸ adjective able to be recycled.
▸ noun (usu. **recyclables**) a substance or object that can be recycled.
– DERIVATIVES **recyclability** noun.

recycle ▸ verb [with obj.] convert (waste) into reusable material: *car hulks were recycled into new steel* | (as noun **recycling**) *a call for the recycling of all paper*. ■ return (material) to a previous stage in a cyclic process. ■ use again: *he reserves the right to recycle his own text*.
– DERIVATIVES **recycler** noun.

red ▸ adjective (**redder**, **reddest**) **1** of a colour at the end of the spectrum next to orange and opposite violet, as of blood, fire, or rubies: *her red lips* | *the sky was turning red outside*. ■ (of a person or their face) flushed or rosy, especially with embarrassment, anger, or heat: *there were some red faces in headquarters* | *he went bright red*. ■ (of a person's eyes) bloodshot or having pink rims, especially with tiredness or crying: *her eyes were red and swollen*. ■ (of hair or fur) of a reddish-brown colour. ■ dated, offensive (of a people) having reddish skin. ■ of or denoting the suits hearts and diamonds in a pack of cards: *a red queen*. ■ (of wine) made from dark grapes and coloured by their skins. ■ denoting a red light or flag used as a signal to stop. ■ used to denote something forbidden, dangerous, or urgent: *the force went on red alert*. ■ (of a ski run) of the second-highest level of difficulty, as indicated by coloured markers on the run. ■ Physics denoting one of three colours of quark.
2 (**Red**) informal, chiefly derogatory communist or socialist (used especially during the Cold War with reference to the Soviet Union).
3 archaic or literary involving bloodshed or violence: *red battle stamps his foot and nations feel the shock*.
4 (also **red-blanket**) S. African (of a Xhosa) coming from a traditional tribal culture. Contrasted with **SCHOOL**[1]. [with reference to the blankets traditionally worn by the Xhosa people.]
▸ noun **1** [mass noun] red colour or pigment: *their work is marked in red by the teacher*. ■ red clothes or material: *she could not wear red*.
2 a red thing, in particular: ■ a red wine. ■ a red ball in snooker or billiards. ■ a red light.
3 (also **Red**) informal, chiefly derogatory a communist or socialist.
4 (**the red**) the situation of owing money to a bank because one has spent more than is in one's account: *the company was £4 million in the red*. [from the conventional use of red ink to indicate debt items.]
– PHRASES **better dead than red** (or **better red than dead**) a cold-war slogan claiming that the prospect of nuclear war is preferable to that of a communist society (or vice versa). (**as**) **red as a beetroot** (N. Amer. **beet**) (of a person) red-faced, typically through embarrassment. **red in tooth and claw** involving savage or merciless conflict or competition: *nature, red in tooth and claw*. [from Tennyson's *In Memoriam*.] **the red planet** a name for Mars. **a red rag to a bull** an object, utterance, or act which is certain to provoke someone: *the refusal to discuss the central issue was like a red rag to a bull*. **reds under the bed** used during the cold war with reference to the feared presence and influence of communist sympathizers. **see red** informal become very angry suddenly: *the mere thought of Piers with Nicole made her see red*.
– DERIVATIVES **reddish** adjective, **reddy** adjective, **redly** adverb, **redness** noun.
– ORIGIN Old English *rēad*, of Germanic origin; related to Dutch *rood* and German *rot*, from an Indo-European root shared by Latin *rufus*, *ruber*, Greek *eruthros*, and Sanskrit *rudhira* 'red'.

red- ▸ prefix variant spelling of **RE-** before a vowel (as in *redolent*).

redact /rɪ'dakt/ ▸ verb [with obj.] edit (text) for publication. ■ censor or obscure (part of a text) for legal or security purposes.
– DERIVATIVES **redactor** noun.
– ORIGIN mid 19th cent.: back-formation from **REDACTION**.

redaction ▸ noun [mass noun] the process of editing text for publication. ■ the censoring or obscuring of part of a text for legal or security purposes. ■ [count noun] a version of a text, such as a new edition or an abridged version.
– DERIVATIVES **redactional** adjective.
– ORIGIN late 18th cent.: from French *rédaction*, from late Latin *redactio(n-)*, from *redigere* 'bring back'.

red admiral ▸ noun a migratory butterfly which has dark wings marked with red bands and white spots. ● Genus *Vanessa*, subfamily Nymphalinae, family Nymphalidae: several species, in particular *V. atalanta*.

red algae ▸ noun a large group of algae that includes many seaweeds that are mainly red in colour. Some kinds yield useful products (agar, alginates) or are used as food (laver, dulse, carrageen). ● Division Rhodophyta (or phylum Rhodophyta, kingdom Protista).

redan /rɪ'dan/ ▸ noun an arrow-shaped embankment forming part of a fortification.
– ORIGIN late 17th cent.: from French, from *redent* 'notching (of a saw)', from *re-* 'again' (expressing repetition) + *dent* 'tooth'.

Red Army the army of the Soviet Union, formed after the Revolution of 1917. The name was officially dropped in 1946. ■ the army of China or some other Communist countries.

Red Army Faction a left-wing terrorist group in former West Germany, active from 1968 onwards. It was originally led by Andreas Baader (1943–77) and Ulrike Meinhof (1934–76). Also called **BAADER–MEINHOF GROUP**.

red arsenic ▸ noun another term for **REALGAR**.

redback (also **redback spider**) ▸ noun a highly venomous Australasian spider which is black with a bright red stripe down the back, closely related to the American black widow. ● *Latrodectus mactans hasseltii*, family Theridiidae.

red-bait ▸ verb [with obj.] (often as noun **red-baiting**) N. Amer. informal harass or persecute (someone) on account of known or suspected communist sympathies.
▸ noun S. African a large sea squirt which is a popular bait with sea anglers. ● *Pyura stolonifera*, class Ascidiaceae.
– DERIVATIVES **red-baiter** noun.

red beds ▸ plural noun Geology sandstones or other sedimentary strata coloured red by haematite coating the grains.

red biddy ▸ noun [mass noun] Brit. informal, dated a mixture of cheap wine and methylated spirits.

red blood cell ▸ noun less technical term for **ERYTHROCYTE**.

red-blooded ▸ adjective (of a man) vigorous or virile, especially in having strong heterosexual appetites: *he was attracted to her, as any red-blooded male would be*.
– DERIVATIVES **red-bloodedness** noun.

redbone ▸ noun a dog with a red or red and tan coat of an American breed formerly used to hunt raccoons.

red book ▸ noun the title given to any of various official books of economic or political significance.
– ORIGIN *red* being the conventional colour of the binding of official books.

red box ▸ noun Brit. a box, typically covered with red leather, used by a Minister of State to hold official documents.

redbreast ▸ noun informal, chiefly Brit. a robin.

red-brick ▸ adjective built with red bricks. ■ (of a British university) founded in the late 19th or early 20th century and with buildings of brick, as distinct from the older universities built of stone.

Red Brigades an extreme left-wing terrorist organization based in Italy, which from the early 1970s was responsible for carrying out kidnappings, murders, and acts of sabotage.

redbud ▸ noun a North American tree of the pea family, with pink flowers that grow from the trunk, branches, and twigs. ● Genus *Cercis*, family Leguminosae.

redbush ▸ noun another term for **ROOIBOS**.
– ORIGIN translation of Afrikaans *rooibos*.

redcap ▸ noun **1** Brit. informal a member of the military police.
2 N. Amer. a railway porter.

red card ▸ noun (in soccer and some other games) a red card shown by the referee to a player who is being sent off the field. Compare with **YELLOW CARD**.
▸ verb (**red-card**) [with obj.] (of a referee) send (a player) off the field by showing a red card.

red carpet ▸ noun a long, narrow red carpet laid on the ground for a distinguished visitor to walk along when arriving. ■ (**the red carpet**) used in reference to privileged treatment of a distinguished visitor: [as modifier] *the group gets red-carpet treatment in most places*.

red cedar ▸ noun either of two North American coniferous trees with reddish-brown bark: ● Two species in the family Cupressaceae: the **western red cedar** (*Thuja plicata*), which yields strong, lightweight timber and is cultivated in Europe, and the **eastern red cedar** (*Juniperus virginiana*), found chiefly in the eastern US.

red cell ▸ noun less technical term for **ERYTHROCYTE**.

red cent ▸ noun N. Amer. a one-cent coin. ■ [usu. with negative] the smallest amount of money: *some of the people don't deserve a single red cent*.
– ORIGIN early 19th cent.: so named because it was formerly made of copper.

red channel ▸ noun (at a customs area in an airport or port) the passage which should be taken by arriving passengers who have goods to declare.

redcoat ▸ noun **1** historical a British soldier.
2 (in the UK) an organizer and entertainer at a Butlin's holiday camp.
– ORIGIN early 16th cent. (in sense 1): so named because of the colour of the uniform. Sense 2 dates from the 1950s.

red coral (also **precious coral**) ▸ noun a branching pinkish-red horny coral which is used in jewellery. ● Genus *Corallium*, order Gorgonacea, class Anthozoa.

Red Crescent a national branch in Muslim countries of the International Movement of the Red Cross and the Red Crescent.

Red Cross the International Movement of the Red Cross and the Red Crescent, an international humanitarian organization bringing relief to victims of war or natural disaster. The Red Cross was set up in 1864 at the instigation of the Swiss philanthropist Henri Dunant (1828–1910) according to the Geneva Convention, and its headquarters are at Geneva.

redcurrant ▸ noun **1** a small, sweet red berry, chiefly used to make a jelly eaten as an accompaniment to cold meats.
2 the shrub which produces the redcurrant, related to the blackcurrant. ● *Ribes rubrum*, family Grossulariaceae.

redd[1] ▸ verb (past and past participle **redd**) [with obj.] (**redd something up**) Scottish & Irish put something in order; tidy: *you take this baby while I redd the room up*.
– ORIGIN late Middle English (in the sense 'clear space'): perhaps related to **RID**.

redd[2] ▸ noun a hollow in a riverbed made by a trout or salmon to spawn in.
– ORIGIN mid 17th cent. (originally Scots and northern English in the sense 'spawn'): of unknown origin.

red deer ▸ noun a deer with a rich red-brown summer coat that turns dull brownish-grey in winter, the male having large branched antlers. It is native to North America, Eurasia, and North Africa. ● *Cervus elaphus*, family Cervidae. Compare with **WAPITI**.

Red Delicious ▸ noun a widely grown dessert apple of a soft-fleshed red-skinned variety.

R

redden ▸ **verb** make or become red: [with obj.] *bare arms reddened by sun and wind* | [no obj.] *the sky is reddening.* ▪ [no obj.] (of a person) blush: *Lyn reddened at the description of herself.* ▪ [no obj.] (of the eyes) become pink at the rims as a result of crying.

Redding, Otis (1941–67), American soul singer. 'Dock of the Bay', released after Redding's death in an air crash, became a number-one US hit in 1968.

Redditch an industrial town in west central England, in Worcestershire; pop. 75,300 (est. 2009).

reddle ▸ **noun** [mass noun] a red pigment consisting of ochre.
– ORIGIN early 18th cent.: variant of **RUDDLE**.

red dog ▸ **noun** another term for **DHOLE**.

red duster ▸ **noun** Brit. informal term for **RED ENSIGN**.

red dwarf ▸ **noun** Astronomy a small, old, relatively cool star.

rede /riːd/ archaic ▸ **noun** [mass noun] advice or counsel given by one person to another.
▸ **verb** [with obj.] **1** advise (someone): [with obj. and infinitive] *therefore, my son, I rede thee stay at home.*
2 interpret (a riddle or dream).
– ORIGIN Old English *rǣd*, of Germanic origin; related to Dutch *raad*, German *Rat*. The verb is a variant of **READ**, of the same origin.

redecorate ▸ **verb** [with obj.] apply paint or wallpaper in (a room or building) again, typically differently.
– DERIVATIVES **redecoration** noun.

rededicate ▸ **verb** [with obj.] dedicate again: *the cathedral was eventually rededicated in June 1997.*
– DERIVATIVES **rededication** noun.

redeem ▸ **verb** [with obj.] **1** compensate for the faults or bad aspects of: *a disappointing debate redeemed only by an outstanding speech.* ▪ (**redeem oneself**) do something that compensates for poor past performance or behaviour: *Australia redeemed themselves by dismissing India for 153.* ▪ atone or make amends for (sin, error, or evil): *the thief on the cross who by a single act redeemed a life of evil.* ▪ save (someone) from sin, error, or evil: *he was a sinner, redeemed by the grace of God.*
2 gain or regain possession of (something) in exchange for payment: *statutes enabled state peasants to redeem their land.* ▪ Finance repay (a stock, bond, or other instrument) at the maturity date. ▪ exchange (a coupon, voucher, or trading stamp) for goods, a discount, or money. ▪ pay the necessary money to clear (a debt): *owners were unable to redeem their mortgages.* ▪ archaic free (oneself or another) from slavery or captivity by paying a ransom.
3 fulfil or carry out (a pledge or promise): *the party prepared to redeem the pledges of the past three years.*
– DERIVATIVES **redeemable** adjective.
– ORIGIN late Middle English (in the sense 'buy back'): from Old French *redimer* or Latin *redimere*, from *re-* 'back' + *emere* 'buy'.

R

redeemer ▸ **noun** a person who redeems someone or something. ▪ (often **the Redeemer**) Christ.

redeeming ▸ **adjective 1** compensating for someone's or something's faults; compensatory: *tuneless dirges with few redeeming features.*
2 able to save people from sin, error, or evil: *the transforming power of God's redeeming grace.*

redefine ▸ **verb** [with obj.] define again or differently: *the role of the Emperor was redefined.*
– DERIVATIVES **redefinition** noun.

redemption ▸ **noun** [mass noun] **1** the action of saving or being saved from sin, error, or evil: *God's plans for the redemption of his world.* ▪ [in sing.] a thing that saves someone from error or evil: *his marginalization from the Hollywood jungle proved to be his redemption.*
2 the action of regaining or gaining possession of something in exchange for payment, or clearing a debt. ▪ archaic the action of buying one's freedom.
– PHRASES **beyond** (or **past**) **redemption** too bad to be improved or saved.
– ORIGIN late Middle English: from Old French, from Latin *redemptio(n-)*, from *redimere* 'buy back' (see **REDEEM**).

redemption yield ▸ **noun** Finance the yield of a stock calculated as a percentage of the redemption price with an adjustment made for any capital gain or loss which that price represents relative to the current price.

redemptive ▸ **adjective** acting to save someone from error or evil: *the healing power of redemptive love.*

red ensign ▸ **noun** a red flag with the Union Jack in the top corner next to the flagstaff, flown by British-registered ships.

redeploy ▸ **verb** [with obj.] assign (troops, employees, or resources) to a new place or task: *units concentrated in Buenos Aires would be redeployed to the provinces.*
– DERIVATIVES **redeployment** noun.

redeposit ▸ **verb** [with obj.] deposit (something) again.
– DERIVATIVES **redeposition** noun.

redesign ▸ **verb** [with obj.] design (something) again or in a different way: *the front seats have been redesigned.*
▸ **noun** [mass noun] the action or process of redesigning something.

redesignate ▸ **verb** [with obj.] give (someone or something) a different official name, description, or title: *the territories have been **redesignated as** national parks.*
– DERIVATIVES **redesignation** noun.

redetermine ▸ **verb** [with obj.] determine (something) again or differently.
– DERIVATIVES **redetermination** noun.

redevelop ▸ **verb** [with obj.] develop (something) again or differently. ▪ construct new buildings in (an urban area), typically after demolishing the existing buildings: *plans to redevelop London's docklands.*
– DERIVATIVES **redeveloper** noun, **redevelopment** noun.

red-eye ▸ **noun 1** [mass noun] the undesirable effect in flash photography of people appearing to have red eyes, caused by a reflection from the retina when the flashgun is too near the camera lens. ▪ (also **red-eye flight**) [in sing.] informal, chiefly N. Amer. a flight on which a passenger cannot expect to get much sleep on account of the time of departure or arrival: *she caught the red-eye back to New York.*
2 a freshwater fish with red eyes, in particular: ▪ Brit. a rudd. ▪ N. Amer. a rock bass.
3 [mass noun] US informal cheap whisky. ▪ Canadian a drink made from tomato juice and beer.

red-eye gravy ▸ **noun** [mass noun] US gravy made by adding liquid to the fat from cooked ham.

red-faced ▸ **adjective** having a red face, especially as a result of embarrassment or shame: *Steve was left red-faced when a fan tried to rip his trousers off.*

red-figure ▸ **noun** [usu. as modifier] a type of ancient Greek pottery, originating in Athens in the late 6th century BC, in which figures are outlined and details added in black, and the background is then filled in with black to leave the figures in the red colour of the clay: *a red-figure vase.* Compare with **BLACK-FIGURE**.

redfish ▸ **noun** (pl. **same** or **redfishes**) **1** a bright red edible marine fish, in particular: ● a North Atlantic rockfish (genus Sebastes, family Scorpaenidae, in particular the commercially important *S. marinus*). ● the red drum of the western Atlantic, popular as a game fish (*Sciaenops ocellatus*, family Sciaenidae). ● a bottom-dwelling Australian fish (*Centroberyx affinis*, family Berycidae). Also called **NANNYGAI**.
2 Brit. a male salmon in the spawning season.

red fish ▸ **noun** [mass noun] fish with dark flesh, such as herring, mackerel, sardine, and pilchard. Compare with **WHITE FISH**.

red flag ▸ **noun** a red flag as the symbol of socialist revolution or a warning of danger. ▪ (**the Red Flag**) the anthem of Britain's Labour Party, a socialist song with words written in 1889 by James Connell (1852–1929) and sung to the tune of the German song 'O Tannenbaum'.

Redford, (Charles) Robert (b.1936), American film actor and director. He made his name playing opposite Paul Newman in *Butch Cassidy and the Sundance Kid* (1969), co-starring again with him in *The Sting* (1973). Other notable films include *Ordinary People* (1980), for which he won an Oscar as director.

red fox ▸ **noun** a common fox with a reddish coat, native to both Eurasia and North America and living from the Arctic tundra to the centres of cities. ● *Vulpes vulpes*, family Canidae.

red giant ▸ **noun** Astronomy a very large star of high luminosity and low surface temperature. Red giants are thought to be in a late stage of evolution when no hydrogen remains in the core to fuel nuclear fusion.

red gold ▸ **noun** [mass noun] an alloy of gold and copper.

Redgrave[1] the name of a family of English actors, notably: ▪ **Sir Michael (Scudamore)** (1908–85). A well-known stage actor, he played numerous Shakespearean roles and also starred in films such as *The Browning Version* (1951) and *The Importance of Being Earnest* (1952). ▪ **Vanessa** (b.1937), Sir Michael's eldest daughter. Her career in the theatre and cinema includes the films *Mary Queen of Scots* (1972), *Julia* (1976), for which she won an Oscar, and *Howard's End* (1992).

Redgrave[2], Sir Steve (b.1962), English rower; full name *Steven Geoffrey Redgrave*. He won five consecutive Olympic gold medals between 1984 and 2000.

red–green ▸ **adjective** denoting colour blindness in which reds and greens are confused, either protanopia (daltonism) or deuteranopia.

red grouse ▸ **noun** a bird of a race of the willow grouse having entirely reddish-brown plumage, native only to the British Isles and familiar as a moorland game bird. ● *Lagopus lagopus scoticus*, family Phasianidae (or Tetraonidae).

Red Guard ▸ **noun** any of various radical or socialist groups, in particular an organized detachment of workers during the Russian Revolution of 1917 and a militant youth movement in China (1966–76) which carried out attacks on intellectuals and other disfavoured groups as part of Mao Zedong's Cultural Revolution. ▪ a member of one of these groups.

red gum ▸ **noun** an Australian gum tree with smooth bark and hard dark red timber. ● Genera *Eucalyptus* (and *Angophora*), family Myrtaceae: many species, in particular the widespread **river red gum** (*E. camaldulensis*).
▪ [mass noun] astringent reddish kino gum obtained from some red gum trees, used for medicinal purposes and for tanning.

red hand ▸ **noun** the arms or badge of Ulster, a red left hand cut off squarely at the wrist. Also called **BLOODY HAND**.

red-handed ▸ **adjective** used to indicate that a person has been discovered in or just after the act of doing something wrong or illegal: *I **caught him red-handed**, stealing a wallet.*

red hat ▸ **noun** a cardinal's hat, especially as the symbol of a cardinal's office.

redhead ▸ **noun 1** a person with reddish hair.
2 a North American diving duck with a reddish-brown head, related to and resembling the pochard. ● *Aythya americana*, family Anatidae.

red-headed ▸ **adjective** [attrib.] (of a person) having reddish-brown hair. ▪ used in names of birds, insects, and other animals with red heads, e.g. **red-headed woodpecker**.

red heat ▸ **noun** [mass noun] the temperature or state of something so hot that it emits red light.

red herring ▸ **noun 1** a dried smoked herring, which is turned red by the smoke.
2 a clue or piece of information which is or is intended to be misleading or distracting: *the argument about women's choices is largely a red herring.* [so named from the practice of using the scent of red herring in training hounds.]

red-hot ▸ **adjective 1** so hot as to glow red: *red-hot coals* | *the red-hot handle burnt his hand.*
2 very exciting, interesting, or good: *our red-hot creativity department.* ▪ very passionate: *a red-hot lover.* ▪ (of a favourite in a race or other contest) most strongly expected to win: *Ipswich Town are red-hot favourites for the championship.*

red-hot poker ▸ **noun** a South African plant with tall erect spikes of tubular flowers, the upper ones of which are typically red and the lower ones yellow. ● *Kniphofia uvaria*, family Liliaceae: many cultivars.

redial ▸ **verb** (**redials, redialling, redialled**; US **redials, redialing, redialed**) [with obj.] dial (a telephone number) again.
▸ **noun** (also **last number redial**) the facility on a telephone by which the number just dialled may be automatically redialled by pressing a single button.

redid past of **REDO**.

rediffusion ▸ **noun** [mass noun] Brit. the relaying of broadcast programmes, especially by cable from a central receiver.

Red Indian ▸ **noun** old-fashioned term for **AMERICAN INDIAN**.

> **USAGE** The term **Red Indian**, first recorded in the early 19th century, has largely fallen out of use, associated as it is with stereotypes of cowboys and Indians and the Wild West, and today may cause offence. The normal terms in modern use are **American Indian** and **Native American** or, if appropriate, the name of the specific people (**Cherokee, Iroquois**, and so on).

redingote /ˈrɛdɪŋɡəʊt/ ▸ **noun** a woman's long coat with a cutaway or contrasting front. ■ a man's double-breasted topcoat with a full skirt.
– ORIGIN late 18th cent.: French, from English *riding coat*.

red ink ▸ **noun** [mass noun] chiefly N. Amer. used in reference to financial deficit or debt: *he voted for many of the projects that have left the state awash in red ink*.

redintegrate /rɛˈdɪntɪɡreɪt/ ▸ **verb** [with obj.] archaic restore (something) to a state of wholeness, unity, or perfection.
– DERIVATIVES **redintegration** noun, **redintegrative** adjective.
– ORIGIN late Middle English: from Latin *redintegrat-* 'made whole', from the verb *redintegrare*, from *re(d)-* 'again' + *integrare* 'restore'.

redirect ▸ **verb** [with obj.] direct (something) to a new or different place or purpose: *get the post office to redirect your mail* | *resources were redirected to a major project*.
– DERIVATIVES **redirection** noun.

rediscount Finance ▸ **verb** [with obj.] (of a central bank) discount (a bill of exchange or similar instrument) that has already been discounted by a commercial bank.
▸ **noun** [mass noun] the action of rediscounting something.

rediscover ▸ **verb** [with obj.] discover (something forgotten or ignored) again: *he was trying to rediscover his Gaelic roots*.
– DERIVATIVES **rediscovery** noun (pl. **rediscoveries**).

redisplay ▸ **verb** [with obj.] display (something) again or differently.

redissolve ▸ **verb** dissolve or cause to dissolve again.
– DERIVATIVES **redissolution** noun.

redistribute ▸ **verb** [with obj.] distribute (something) differently or again, typically to achieve greater social equality: *their primary concern was to redistribute income from rich to poor*.
– DERIVATIVES **redistribution** noun, **redistributive** adjective.

redistributionist ▸ **noun** a person who advocates the redistribution of wealth.
▸ **adjective** relating to the belief that wealth should be redistributed: *redistributionist measures*.
– DERIVATIVES **redistributionism** noun.

redivide ▸ **verb** [with obj.] divide (something) again or differently: *the Balkans were redivided among Slovene, Croat, and Serb*.
– DERIVATIVES **redivision** noun.

redivivus /ˌrɛdɪˈviːvəs/ ▸ **adjective** [postpositive] literary come back to life; reborn: *one is tempted to think of Poussin as a sort of Titian redivivus*.
– ORIGIN late 16th cent.: from Latin, from *re(d)-* 'again' + *vivus* 'living'.

red kangaroo ▸ **noun** a large kangaroo of Australian grasslands, the male of which has a russet-red coat and the female (also called **BLUE FLYER**) typically a blue-grey coat. ● *Macropus rufus*, family Macropodidae.

red kite ▸ **noun** a bird of prey with reddish-brown plumage and a forked tail, found chiefly in Europe. ● *Milvus milvus*, family Accipitridae.

red lead ▸ **noun** [mass noun] a red form of lead oxide used as a pigment.

Red Leicester ▸ **noun** see **LEICESTER**[3].

red-letter day ▸ **noun** a day that is pleasantly noteworthy or memorable.
– ORIGIN early 18th cent.: from the practice of highlighting a festival in red on a calendar.

red light ▸ **noun** a red traffic light or similar signal that instructs moving vehicles to stop. ■ a refusal or an order to stop an action: *some subsidies would get a red light and be prohibited*.

red-light district ▸ **noun** an area of a town or city containing many brothels, strip clubs, and other sex businesses.
– ORIGIN late 19th cent.: from the use of a red light as the sign of a brothel.

redline N. Amer. informal ▸ **verb** [with obj.] **1** drive with (a car engine) at or above its rated maximum revolutions per minute: *both his engines were redlined now*.
2 refuse (a loan or insurance) to someone because they live in an area deemed to be a poor financial risk. ■ cancel (a project).
▸ **noun 1** the maximum number of revolutions per minute for a car engine.
2 a boundary or limit which should not be crossed.
– ORIGIN from the use of *red* as a limit marker, in sense 2 of the verb a limit marked out by ringing a section of a map.

red man ▸ **noun** dated, offensive an American Indian.

red meat ▸ **noun** [mass noun] meat that is red when raw, for example beef or lamb. Often contrasted with **WHITE MEAT**.

Redmond, John (Edward) (1856–1918), Irish politician, leader of the Irish Nationalist Party in the House of Commons 1891–1918. The Home Rule Bill of 1912 was introduced with his support, although it was never implemented because of the First World War.

red mullet ▸ **noun** an elongated fish with long barbels on the chin, living in warmer seas and widely valued as a food fish. ● Family Mullidae: several genera and many species, in particular *Muletus surmuletus* of the Mediterranean and East Atlantic.

redneck ▸ **noun** N. Amer. informal, derogatory a working-class white person from the southern US, especially a politically reactionary one: [as modifier] *redneck towns*.
– DERIVATIVES **rednecked** adjective.

redo ▸ **verb** (**redoes**, **redoing**; past **redid**; past participle **redone**) [with obj.] do (something) again or differently: *a whole day's work has to be redone*. ■ redecorate (a room or building): *the house is being redone exactly to suit his taste*.

redolent /ˈrɛdəl(ə)nt/ ▸ **adjective 1** (**redolent of/with**) strongly reminiscent or suggestive of: *names redolent of history and tradition*. ■ literary strongly smelling of: *the church was old, dark, and redolent of incense*.
2 archaic or literary fragrant or sweet-smelling: *a rich, inky, redolent wine*.
– DERIVATIVES **redolence** noun, **redolently** adverb.
– ORIGIN late Middle English (in the sense 'fragrant'): from Old French, or from Latin *redolent-* 'giving out a strong smell', from *re(d)-* 'back, again' + *olere* 'to smell'.

Redon /rəˈdɒ̃/, French /ʀədɔ̃/, Odilon (1840–1916), French painter and graphic artist. He was a leading exponent of symbolism and forerunner of surrealism, especially in his early charcoal drawings of fantastic or nightmarish subjects.

redouble ▸ **verb** make or become much greater, more intense, or more numerous: [with obj.] *we will redouble our efforts to reform agricultural policy* | [no obj.] *pressure to solve the problem has redoubled*. ■ [no obj.] Bridge double a bid already doubled by an opponent.
▸ **noun** Bridge a call that doubles a bid already doubled by an opponent.
– ORIGIN late Middle English: from French *redoubler*, from *re-* 'again' + *doubler* 'to double'. The noun dates from the early 20th cent.

redoubt ▸ **noun** Military a temporary or supplementary fortification, typically square or polygonal and without flanking defences: *the British stormed the rebel redoubt* | figurative *branch 200 was a redoubt of left-wing trade unionism*.
– ORIGIN early 17th cent.: from French *redoute*, from obsolete Italian *ridotta* and medieval Latin *reductus* 'refuge', from Latin *reducere* 'withdraw'. The *-b-* was added by association with **DOUBT**.

redoubtable ▸ **adjective** often humorous (of a person) formidable, especially as an opponent: *he was a redoubtable debater* | *the redoubtable ladies*.
– DERIVATIVES **redoubtably** adverb.
– ORIGIN late Middle English: from Old French *redoutable*, from *redouter* 'to fear', from *re-* (expressing intensive force) + *douter* 'to doubt'.

redound /rɪˈdaʊnd/ ▸ **verb** [no obj.] **1** (**redound to**) formal contribute greatly to (a person's credit or honour): *his latest diplomatic effort will redound to his credit*.
2 (**redound upon**) archaic come back upon; rebound on: *may his sin redound upon his head!* [probably by association with **REBOUND**[1].]
– ORIGIN late Middle English (in the sense 'surge up, overflow'): from Old French *redonder*, from Latin *redundare* 'surge', from *re(d)-* 'again' + *unda* 'a wave'.

redox /ˈriːdɒks, ˈrɛdɒks/ ▸ **noun** [mass noun] [usu. as modifier] Chemistry oxidation and reduction considered together as complementary processes: *redox reactions involve electron transfer*.
– ORIGIN 1920s: blend of **REDUCTION** and **OXIDATION**.

red panda ▸ **noun** a raccoon-like mammal with thick reddish-brown fur and a bushy tail, native to high bamboo forests from the Himalayas to southern China. Also called **LESSER PANDA, CAT-BEAR**. ● *Ailurus fulgens*; it is variously placed with the raccoons or bears, or in its own family (Ailurudae).

red pepper ▸ **noun** the ripe red fruit of a sweet pepper.

red phosphorus ▸ **noun** see **PHOSPHORUS**.

red pine ▸ **noun** any of a number of coniferous trees which yield reddish timber, in particular: ● a North American pine (*Pinus resinosa*, family Pinaceae). ● NZ another term for **RIMU**.

redpoll /ˈrɛdpəʊl/ ▸ **noun 1** a mainly brown finch with a red forehead, related to the linnet and widespread in Eurasia and North America. ● *Acanthis flammea*, family Fringillidae; occurs in a number of races that were formerly regarded as separate species.
2 (**red poll**) an animal of a breed of red-haired polled cattle.

redraft ▸ **verb** [with obj.] draft (a document, text, or map) again in a different way: *it is important to redraft your will in the event of family breakdown*.
▸ **noun** a document, text, or map which has been redrafted.

red rattle ▸ **noun** a pink-flowered lousewort of marshy places, the seeds of which produce a rattling sound inside their capsule when ripe. ● *Pedicularis palustris*, family Scrophulariaceae.

redraw ▸ **verb** (past **redrew**; past participle **redrawn**) [with obj.] draw or draw up again or differently: *the rota was redrawn*.

redress ▸ **verb** [with obj.] **1** remedy or set right (an undesirable or unfair situation): *the question is how to redress the consequences of racist land policies*.
2 archaic set upright again.
▸ **noun** [mass noun] remedy or compensation for a wrong or grievance: *those seeking redress for an infringement of public law rights*.
– PHRASES **redress the balance** restore equality in a situation.
– DERIVATIVES **redressable** adjective, **redressal** noun, **redresser** noun.
– ORIGIN Middle English: the verb from Old French *redresser*; the noun via Anglo-Norman French *redresse*.

re-dress ▸ **verb** [with obj.] dress (someone or something) again: *he re-dressed the wound*.

red ribbon ▸ **noun 1** US an award given for coming second in a competition.
2 Canadian an award for coming first in a competition.

Red River 1 a river in SE Asia, which rises in southern China and flows 1,175 km (730 miles) generally south-eastwards through northern Vietnam to the Gulf of Tonkin. Chinese name **YUAN JIANG**, Vietnamese name **SONG HONG**.
2 a river in the southern US, a tributary of the Mississippi, which rises in northern Texas and flows 1,966 km (1,222 miles) generally south-eastwards, forming part of the border between Texas and Oklahoma, and enters the Mississippi in Louisiana. Also called **Red River of the South**.
3 a river in the northern US and Canada, which rises in North Dakota and flows 877 km (545 miles) northwards, forming for most of its length the border between North Dakota and Minnesota, before entering Canada and emptying into Lake Winnipeg. Also called **Red River of the North**.

R

red river hog ▸ **noun** another term for **BUSH PIG**.

red roan ▸ **adjective** denoting an animal's coat consisting of bay or chestnut mixed with white or grey.
▸ **noun** a red roan animal.

red rose ▸ **noun 1** the emblem of Lancashire or the Lancastrians.
2 the symbol of the British Labour Party.

red salmon ▸ **noun** another term for **SOCKEYE**. ■ [mass noun] the reddish-pink flesh of the sockeye salmon used as food.

red sandalwood ▸ **noun** either of two SE Asian trees of the pea family which yield red timber. ● Two species in the family Leguminosae: *Pterocarpus santalinus*, from which a red dye is obtained, and *Adenanthera pavonina*, whose seeds were formerly used as weights by goldsmiths.

Red Sea a long, narrow nearly landlocked sea separating Africa from the Arabian peninsula. It is linked to the Indian Ocean in the south by the Gulf of Aden and to the Mediterranean in the north by the Suez Canal.

red setter ▸ **noun** less formal term for **IRISH SETTER**.

redshank ▸ **noun** a large Eurasian sandpiper with long red legs and brown, grey, or blackish plumage. ● Genus *Tringa*, family Scolopacidae: two species, in particular *T. totanus*.

red shift ▸ **noun** Astronomy the displacement of spectral lines towards longer wavelengths (the red end of the spectrum) in radiation from distant galaxies and celestial objects. This is interpreted as a Doppler shift which is proportional to the velocity of recession and thus to distance. Compare with BLUE SHIFT.

redshirt ▸ **noun 1** US informal a college athlete who is withdrawn from university sporting events for a year to develop their skills and extend their period of playing eligibility by a further year at this level of competition.
2 a supporter of Garibaldi, in particular one of the thousand who sailed with him in 1860 to conquer Sicily.
▸ **verb** [with obj.] US informal keep (an athlete) out of university competition for a year: *he was less developed at the outset, so he was redshirted.* ■ [no obj.] (of a college athlete) be barred from university competition for a year: *he redshirted last season.*
– ORIGIN from the red shirts worn by such athletes in practices with regular team members.

redskin ▸ **noun** dated or offensive an American Indian.

red snapper ▸ **noun** a reddish marine fish which is of commercial value as a food fish, in particular: ● a tropical fish of the snapper family (genus *Lutjanus*, family Lutjanidae). ● a North Pacific rockfish (*Sebastes ruberrimus*, family Scorpaenidae).

red sorrel ▸ **noun** see SORREL[1] (sense 2).

Red Square a large square in Moscow next to the Kremlin. In existence since the late 15th century, under Communism the square was the scene of great parades celebrating May Day and the October Revolution.

red squirrel ▸ **noun** a small tree squirrel with a reddish coat: ● a Eurasian squirrel with distinctive ear tufts during the winter months and (in Britain) a whitish tail (*Sciurus vulgaris*, family Sciuridae). ● a North American squirrel with a pale belly and a black line along the sides during the summer (*Tamiasciurus hudsonicus*, family Sciuridae).

red star ▸ **noun** chiefly historical the emblem of some communist countries.

redstart ▸ **noun 1** a Eurasian and North African songbird related to the chats, having a reddish tail and underparts. ● *Phoenicurus* and other genera, family Turdidae: several species.
2 an American warbler, the male of which is black with either a red belly or orange markings. ● Genera *Setophaga* and *Myioborus*, family Parulidae: several species.

red state ▸ **noun** a US state that predominantly votes for or supports the Republican Party. Compare with BLUE STATE.
– ORIGIN from the typical colour used to represent the Republican Party on maps during elections.

red tabby ▸ **noun** a cat with a reddish-orange coat striped or dappled in a deeper red. This is a technical term for the colouring commonly called ginger or marmalade.

red-tailed hawk ▸ **noun** the commonest and most widespread buzzard of North and Central America, with a reddish tail. ● *Buteo jamaicensis*, family Accipitridae.

R

red tape ▸ **noun** [mass noun] excessive bureaucracy or adherence to official rules and formalities: *this law will just create more red tape.*
– ORIGIN early 18th cent.: so named because of the red or pink tape used to bind official documents.

red tide ▸ **noun** a discoloration of seawater caused by a bloom of toxic red dinoflagellates.

red top ▸ **noun** Brit. a tabloid newspaper.
– ORIGIN 1990s: from the red background on which the titles of certain British newspapers are printed.

reduce ▸ **verb** [with obj.] **1** make smaller or less in amount, degree, or size: *the need for businesses to reduce costs | the workforce has been reduced to some 6,100.* ■ [no obj.] become smaller or less in size, amount, or degree: *the number of priority homeless cases has reduced slightly.* ■ boil (a sauce or other liquid) in cooking so that it becomes thicker and more concentrated. ■ [no obj.] chiefly N. Amer. (of a person) lose weight, typically by dieting: *by May she had reduced to 9 stone.* ■ Photography make (a negative or print) less dense. ■ Phonetics articulate (a speech sound) in a way requiring less muscular effort, giving rise in vowels to a more central articulatory position.
2 (**reduce someone/thing to**) bring someone or something to (a worse or less desirable state or condition): *she has been reduced to near poverty | the church was reduced to rubble.* ■ (**be reduced to doing something**) be forced by difficult circumstances into doing something desperate: *ordinary soldiers are reduced to begging.* ■ make someone helpless with (shock, anguish, or amusement): *Olga was reduced to stunned silence.* ■ force someone into (obedience or submission): *he reduced his grandees to due obedience.*
3 (**reduce something to**) change a substance to (a different or more basic form): *it is difficult to understand how lava could have been reduced to dust.* ■ present a problem or subject in (a simplified form): *he reduces unimaginable statistics to manageable proportions.* ■ convert a fraction to (the form with the lowest terms).
4 Chemistry cause to combine chemically with hydrogen. ■ undergo or cause to undergo a reaction in which electrons are gained from another substance or molecule. The opposite of OXIDIZE.
5 restore (a dislocated part of the body) to its proper position by manipulation or surgery.
6 archaic besiege and capture (a town or fortress).
– PHRASES **reduced circumstances** used euphemistically to refer to the state of being poor after being relatively wealthy: *a divorcee living in reduced circumstances.* **reduce someone to the ranks** demote a non-commissioned officer to an ordinary soldier.
– DERIVATIVES **reducer** noun.
– ORIGIN late Middle English: from Latin *reducere*, from *re-* 'back, again' + *ducere* 'bring, lead'. The original sense was 'bring back' (hence 'restore', now surviving in sense 5); this led to 'bring to a different state', then 'bring to a simpler or lower state' (hence sense 3); and finally 'diminish in size or amount' (sense 1, dating from the late 18th cent.).

reducible ▸ **adjective 1** [predic.] (of a subject or problem) capable of being simplified in presentation or analysis: *Shakespeare's major soliloquies are not **reducible to** categories.*
2 Mathematics (of a polynomial) able to be factorized into two or more polynomials of lower degree. ■ (of a group) expressible as the direct product of two of its subgroups.
– DERIVATIVES **reducibility** noun.

reducing agent ▸ **noun** Chemistry a substance that tends to bring about reduction by being oxidized and losing electrons.

reductant ▸ **noun** Chemistry a reducing agent.

reductase /rɪˈdʌkteɪz/ ▸ **noun** [usu. with modifier] Biochemistry an enzyme which promotes the chemical reduction of a specified substance.

reductio ad absurdum /rɪˌdʌktɪəʊ ad abˈsəːdəm/ ▸ **noun** Philosophy a method of proving the falsity of a premise by showing that its logical consequence is absurd or contradictory.
– ORIGIN Latin, literally 'reduction to the absurd'.

reduction ▸ **noun** [mass noun] **1** the action or fact of making something smaller or less in amount, degree, or size: *talks on arms reduction* | [count noun] *there had been **a reduction in** the number of casualties.* ■ [count noun] the amount by which something is made smaller, less, or lower in price: *special reductions on knitwear.* ■ the simplification of a subject or problem to a particular form in presentation or analysis: *the **reduction of** classical genetics **to** molecular biology.* ■ Mathematics the process of converting an amount from one denomination to a smaller one, or of bringing down a fraction to its lowest terms. ■ Biology the halving of the number of chromosomes per cell that occurs at one of the two anaphases of meiosis.
2 [count noun] a thing that is made smaller or less in size or amount, in particular: ■ an arrangement of an orchestral score for piano or for a smaller group of performers. ■ a thick and concentrated liquid or sauce made by boiling. ■ a copy of a picture or photograph made on a smaller scale than the original.
3 the action of remedying a dislocation or fracture by returning the affected part of the body to its normal position.
4 Chemistry the process or result of reducing or being reduced.
5 Phonetics substitution of a sound which requires less muscular effort to articulate: *the process of vowel reduction.*
– ORIGIN late Middle English (denoting the action of bringing back): from Old French, or from Latin *reductio(n-)*, from *reducere* 'bring back, restore' (see REDUCE). The sense development was broadly similar to that of REDUCE; sense 1 dates from the late 17th cent.

reduction gear ▸ **noun** a system of gearwheels in which the driven shaft rotates more slowly than the driving shaft.

reductionism ▸ **noun** [mass noun] often derogatory the practice of analysing and describing a complex phenomenon in terms of its simple or fundamental constituents, especially when this is said to provide a sufficient explanation.
– DERIVATIVES **reductionist** noun & adjective, **reductionistic** adjective.

reductive ▸ **adjective 1** tending to present a subject or problem in a simplified form, especially one viewed as crude: *such a conclusion by itself would be reductive.* ■ (with reference to art) minimal: *he combines his reductive abstract shapes with a rippled surface.*
2 relating to chemical reduction.
– DERIVATIVES **reductively** adverb, **reductiveness** noun.

reductivism ▸ **noun 1** another term for MINIMALISM.
2 another term for REDUCTIONISM.

redundancy ▸ **noun** (pl. **redundancies**) [mass noun] the state of being no longer needed or useful: *the redundancy of 19th-century heavy plant machinery.* ■ Brit. the state of being no longer in employment because there is no more work available: *the factory's workers face redundancy* | [count noun] *the car giant is expected to announce around 5,000 redundancies.* ■ Engineering the inclusion of extra components which are not strictly necessary to functioning, in case of failure in other components.

redundant ▸ **adjective** no longer needed or useful; superfluous: *an appropriate use for a redundant church | many of the old skills had become redundant.* ■ Brit. no longer in employment because there is no more work available: *eight permanent staff were **made redundant**.* ■ Engineering (of a component) not strictly necessary to functioning but included in case of failure in another component.
– DERIVATIVES **redundantly** adverb.
– ORIGIN late 16th cent. (in the sense 'abundant'): from Latin *redundant-* 'surging up', from the verb *redundare* (see REDOUND).

reduplicate ▸ **verb** [with obj.] repeat or copy so as to form another of the same kind: *the upper parts of the harmony may be reduplicated at the octave above.* ■ repeat (a syllable or other linguistic element) exactly or with a slight change (e.g. *hurly-burly*, *see-saw*).
– DERIVATIVES **reduplication** noun, **reduplicative** adjective.
– ORIGIN late 16th cent.: from late Latin *reduplicat-* 'doubled again', from the verb *reduplicare*, from *re-* 'again' + *duplicare* (see DUPLICATE).

redux /ˈriːdʌks/ ▸ **adjective** [postpositive] brought back; revived: *Damian has the veneer of the angry young man redux.*
– ORIGIN late 19th cent.: from Latin, from *reducere* 'bring back'.

redwater (also **redwater fever**) ▸ **noun** [mass noun] the disease babesiosis in cattle.

red wiggler ▸ **noun** N. Amer. another term for REDWORM (sense 1).

redwing ▸ **noun 1** a small migratory thrush that breeds mainly in northern Europe, with red underwings showing in flight. ● *Turdus iliacus*, family Turdidae.
2 any of a number of red-winged birds, especially the American red-winged blackbird. ● Several species, in particular *Agelaius phoeniceus*, family Icteridae.

red wolf ▸ **noun** a fairly small wolf with a cinnamon or tawny coloured coat, native to the south-eastern US but possibly extinct in the wild. ● *Canis rufus*, family Canidae.

redwood ▸ **noun** either of two giant conifers with thick fibrous bark, native to California and Oregon. They are the tallest known trees and are among the largest living organisms. ● Two species in the family Taxodiaceae: the **California** (or **coast**) **redwood** (*Sequoia sempervirens*), which can grow to a height of c.110 m (328 ft), and the **giant redwood**, giant sequoia, wellingtonia, or big tree (*Sequoiadendron giganteum*), which can reach a trunk diameter of 11 m (36 ft).
■ used in names of a number of chiefly tropical trees with reddish timber, e.g. **Andaman redwood**.

redworm ▸ **noun 1** a red earthworm used in composting kitchen waste and as fishing bait. ● *Lumbricus rubellus*, family Lumbricidae.
2 a parasitic nematode worm occurring in the intestines of horses. ● Genus *Strongylus*, class Phasmida.

red zone ▸ **noun** a red sector on a gauge or dial corresponding to conditions that exceed safety limits: *ozone readings edged into the red zone.* ■ a region that is dangerous or forbidden, or in which a particular activity is prohibited. ■ American Football the region between the opposing team's 20-yard line and goal line, which is a major focus of their attack strategy.

reebok ▸ noun variant spelling of RHEBOK.

re-echo ▸ verb (**re-echoes, re-echoing, re-echoed**) echo again or repeatedly: [no obj.] *Dawn's words re-echoed in her mind.*

Reed, Sir Carol (1906–76), English film director. His films include *Odd Man Out* (1947), *The Third Man* (1949), and the musical *Oliver!* (1968), for which he won an Oscar.

reed ▸ noun **1** a tall, slender-leaved plant of the grass family, which grows in water or on marshy ground. ● Genera *Phragmites* and *Arundo*, family Gramineae: several species, in particular the **common** (or **Norfolk**) **reed** (*P. australis*), which is used for thatching.
■ used in names of plants similar to the reed and growing in wet habitats, e.g. **bur-reed**. ■ a tall straight stalk of a reed plant, used especially as a material in making thatch or household items. ■ [mass noun] Brit. straw used for thatching. ■ literary a rustic musical pipe made from a reed or from straw.
2 a thing or person resembling or likened to a reed, in particular: ■ a weak or impressionable person: *the jurors were mere* **reeds in the wind**. ■ literary an arrow. ■ (**reeds**) a set of semi-cylindrical adjacent mouldings like reeds laid together.
3 a piece of thin cane or metal, sometimes doubled, which vibrates in a current of air to produce the sound of various musical instruments, as in the mouthpiece of a clarinet or oboe or at the base of some organ pipes. ■ a wind instrument played with a reed. ■ an organ stop with reed pipes.
4 an electrical contact used in a magnetically operated switch or relay.
5 a weaver's comb-like implement (originally made from reed or cane) for separating the threads of the warp and correctly positioning the weft.
– PHRASES **a broken reed** a weak or ineffectual person.
– ORIGIN Old English *hrēod*, of West Germanic origin; related to Dutch *riet* and German *Ried*.

reed bed ▸ noun an area of water or marshland dominated by reeds.

reedbuck (S. African also **rietbok**) ▸ noun an African antelope with a distinctive whistling call and high bouncing jumps. ● Genus *Redunca*, family Bovidae: three species.

reed bunting ▸ noun a Eurasian bunting that frequents reed beds and hedgerows, the male having a black head and white collar. ● *Emberiza schoeniclus*, family Emberizidae (subfamily Emberizinae).

reeded ▸ adjective **1** shaped into or decorated with semi-cylindrical adjacent mouldings: *a front door with a reeded glass panel.*
2 (of a wind instrument) having a reed or reeds: [in combination] *a double-reeded oboe.*

reeding ▸ noun a small semi-cylindrical moulding or ornamentation. ■ [mass noun] the making of reeded mouldings.

re-edit ▸ verb (**re-edits, re-editing, re-edited**) [with obj.] edit (a text or film) again.
– DERIVATIVES **re-edition** noun.

reedling (also **bearded reedling**) ▸ noun another term for BEARDED TIT.

reed mace ▸ noun another term for BULRUSH (sense 1).

reed organ ▸ noun a keyboard instrument similar to a harmonium, in which air is drawn upwards past metal reeds.

reed pipe ▸ noun a simple wind instrument having or made from a reed. ■ an organ pipe with a reed.

reed stop ▸ noun an organ stop controlling reed pipes.

re-educate ▸ verb [with obj.] educate or train (someone) in order to change their beliefs or behaviour: *criminals are to be re-educated.*
– DERIVATIVES **re-education** noun.

reed warbler ▸ noun a Eurasian and African songbird with plain plumage, frequenting reed beds. ● Genus *Acrocephalus*, family Sylviidae: several species, in particular the common *A. scirpaceus*.

reedy ▸ adjective (**reedier, reediest**) **1** (of a sound or voice) high and thin in tone: *Franco's reedy voice.*
2 (of water or land) full of or edged with reeds: *low reedy islands.*
3 (of a person) tall and thin: *a reedy twelve-year-old.*
– DERIVATIVES **reediness** noun.

reef¹ ▸ noun a ridge of jagged rock, coral, or sand just above or below the surface of the sea. ■ a vein of ore in the earth, especially one containing gold.
– ORIGIN late 16th cent. (earlier as *riff*): from Middle Low German and Middle Dutch *rif*, *ref*, from Old Norse *rif*, literally 'rib', used in the same sense; compare with REEF².

reef² Sailing ▸ noun each of the several strips across a sail which can be taken in or rolled up to reduce the area exposed to the wind.
▸ verb [with obj.] take in one or more reefs of (a sail): *reef the mainsail in strong winds.* ■ shorten (a topmast or a bowsprit).
– ORIGIN Middle English: from Middle Dutch *reef*, *rif*, from Old Norse *rif*, literally 'rib', used in the same sense; compare with REEF¹.

reef-builder ▸ noun a marine organism, especially a coral, which builds reefs.
– DERIVATIVES **reef-building** noun.

reefer¹ ▸ noun informal a cannabis cigarette. ■ [mass noun] cannabis.
– ORIGIN 1930s: perhaps related to Mexican Spanish *grifo* '(smoker of) cannabis'.

reefer² ▸ noun **1** short for REEFER JACKET.
2 Sailing a person who reefs a sail. ■ Nautical slang, archaic a midshipman.

reefer³ ▸ noun informal a refrigerated lorry, railway wagon, or ship.
– ORIGIN early 20th cent.: abbreviation.

reefer jacket ▸ noun a thick close-fitting double-breasted jacket.

reef flat ▸ noun the horizontal upper surface of a coral reef.

reef knot ▸ noun chiefly Brit. a type of double knot which is made symmetrically to hold securely and cast off easily.

reefpoint ▸ noun Sailing each of several short pieces of rope attached to a sail to secure it when reefed.

reek ▸ verb [no obj.] smell strongly and unpleasantly; stink: *the yard* **reeked of** *wet straw and horse manure.* ■ be suggestive of something unpleasant or undesirable: *the speeches* **reeked of** *anti-Semitism.* ■ archaic give off smoke, steam, or fumes: *while temples crash, and towers in ashes reek.*
▸ noun **1** [in sing.] a foul smell: *the reek of cattle dung.*
2 [mass noun] chiefly Scottish smoke.
– DERIVATIVES **reeky** adjective.
– ORIGIN Old English *rēocan* 'give out smoke or vapour', *rēc* (noun) 'smoke', of Germanic origin; related to Dutch *rieken* 'to smell', *rook* 'smoke', German *riechen* 'to smell', *Rauch* 'smoke'.

reel ▸ noun **1** a cylinder on which film, wire, thread, or other flexible materials can be wound: *a cotton reel.* ■ a length of something wound on to a reel: *a reel of copper wire.* ■ a part of a film: *in the final reel he is transformed from unhinged sociopath into local hero.*
2 a lively Scottish or Irish folk dance. ■ a piece of music for a reel, typically in simple or duple time.
▸ verb **1** [with obj.] (**reel something in**) wind something on to a reel by turning the reel. ■ bring in a fish attached to a line by turning a reel and winding in the line: *he reeled in a good perch.*
2 [no obj.] lose one's balance and stagger or lurch violently: *he punched Connolly in the ear, sending him reeling | she reeled back against the van.* ■ [with adverbial of direction] walk in a staggering or lurching manner, especially while drunk: *the two reeled out of the bar arm in arm.* ■ feel shocked, bewildered, or giddy: *the Prime Minister was reeling from a savaging inflicted in the Commons | the alcohol made my head reel.*
3 [no obj.] dance a reel.
– PHRASAL VERBS **reel something off** say or recite something very rapidly and without apparent effort: *she proceeded to reel off the various dishes of the day.*
– DERIVATIVES **reeler** noun.
– ORIGIN Old English *hrēol*, denoting a rotatory device on which spun thread is wound; of unknown origin.

re-elect ▸ verb [with obj.] elect (someone) to a further term of office: *Wilson was re-elected in September 1974.*
– DERIVATIVES **re-election** noun.

re-eligible ▸ adjective eligible for re-election to a further term of office.

reel-to-reel ▸ adjective denoting a tape recorder in which the tape passes between two reels mounted separately rather than within a cassette, now generally superseded by cassette players except for professional use.

re-embark ▸ verb [no obj.] go on board ship again.
– DERIVATIVES **re-embarkation** noun.

re-emerge ▸ verb [no obj.] emerge again; come into sight or prominence once more: *nationalism has re-emerged in western Europe.*
– DERIVATIVES **re-emergence** noun, **re-emergent** adjective.

re-emphasize (also **re-emphasise**) ▸ verb [with obj.] place emphasis on (something) again: *the latter document re-emphasized the need for a national curriculum.*
– DERIVATIVES **re-emphasis** noun.

re-employ ▸ verb [with obj.] employ (a former employee) again.
– DERIVATIVES **re-employment** noun.

re-enact ▸ verb [with obj.] **1** act out (a past event): *bombers were gathered together to re-enact the historic first air attack.*
2 bring (a law) into effect again when the original statute has been repealed or has expired.
– DERIVATIVES **re-enactment** noun, **re-enactor** noun.

re-energize (also **re-energise**) ▸ verb [with obj.] give fresh vitality, enthusiasm, or impetus to: *new reconstruction projects will re-energize the flagging economy.*

re-engineer ▸ verb [with obj.] redesign (a device or machine). ■ (often as noun **re-engineering**) restructure (a company or part of its operations), especially by exploiting information technology.

re-enlist ▸ verb [no obj.] enlist again in the armed forces.

re-enter ▸ verb [with obj.] enter (something) again: *women who wish to re-enter the labour market.*
– DERIVATIVES **re-entrance** noun.

re-entrant ▸ adjective (of an angle) pointing inwards. The opposite of SALIENT. ■ having an inward-pointing angle or angles.
▸ noun **1** a re-entrant angle. ■ an indentation or depression in terrain.
2 a person who has re-entered something, especially the labour force.

re-entry ▸ noun (pl. **re-entries**) [mass noun] **1** the action or process of re-entering something: *programmes designed to prepare you for re-entry to the profession.* ■ the return of a spacecraft or missile into the earth's atmosphere.
2 Law the action of retaking or repossession.
3 [count noun] a visible duplication of part of the design for a postage stamp due to an inaccurate first impression. ■ a stamp displaying such a duplication.

re-equip ▸ verb (**re-equips, re-equipping, re-equipped**) [with obj.] provide with new equipment: *the mill was re-equipped with modern machinery.*
– DERIVATIVES **re-equipment** noun.

re-erect ▸ verb [with obj.] erect (something, especially a building) again.
– DERIVATIVES **re-erection** noun.

re-establish /ˌriːɪˈstablɪʃ, ˌriːɛ-/ ▸ verb [with obj.] establish (something) again or anew: *this project will re-establish contact with students.*
– DERIVATIVES **re-establishment** noun.

re-evaluate ▸ verb [with obj.] evaluate again or differently: *fifteen patients were re-evaluated after six months | I began to re-evaluate my life.*
– DERIVATIVES **re-evaluation** noun.

reeve¹ ▸ noun chiefly historical a local official, in particular the chief magistrate of a town or district in Anglo-Saxon England. ■ historical an official supervising a landowner's estate. ■ Canadian the president of a village or town council.
– ORIGIN Old English *rēfa*.

reeve² ▸ verb (past and past participle **rove** or **reeved**) [with obj.] Nautical thread (a rope or rod) through a ring or other aperture: *one end of the new rope was* **reeved through** *the chain.*
ORIGIN early 17th cent.: probably from Dutch *reven* 'reef (a sail)' (see REEF²).

reeve³ ▸ noun a female ruff. See RUFF¹ (sense 4).
– ORIGIN early 17th cent.: variant of dialect *ree*, of unknown origin.

re-examine ▸ verb [with obj.] examine again or further: *I will have the body re-examined.* ■ Law examine (one's own witness) again, after cross-examination by the opposing counsel.
– DERIVATIVES **re-examination** noun.

re-export ▸ verb /ˌriːɪkˈspɔːt, -ɛk-/ [with obj.] export (imported goods), typically after they have undergone further processing or manufacture.
▸ noun /riːˈɛkspɔːt/ [mass noun] the action of re-exporting something. ■ [count noun] a thing that has been or will be re-exported.
– DERIVATIVES **re-exportation** noun, **re-exporter** /ˌriːɪkˈspɔːtə, -ɛk-/ noun.

ref informal ▸ noun (in sports) a referee.

R

▸ **verb** (**refs, reffing, reffed**) [with obj.] act as referee in (a game or match).
– ORIGIN late 19th cent.: abbreviation.

ref. ▸ **abbreviation** ■ reference. ■ refer to.

reface ▸ **verb** [with obj.] put a new facing on (a building): *part of the tower was refaced with brick.*

refashion ▸ **verb** [with obj.] fashion (something) again or differently.

refasten ▸ **verb** [with obj.] fasten again: *Norman stooped to refasten the padlock.*

refection ▸ **noun** [mass noun] literary refreshment by food or drink. ■ [count noun] a light meal. ■ Zoology the eating of partly digested faecal pellets, as practised by rabbits.
– ORIGIN Middle English: from Old French, from Latin *refectio(n-)*, from *reficere* 'renew' (see REFECTORY).

refectory ▸ **noun** (pl. **refectories**) a room used for communal meals in an educational or religious institution.
– ORIGIN late Middle English: from late Latin *refectorium*, from Latin *reficere* 'refresh, renew', from *re-* 'back' + *facere* 'make'.

refectory table ▸ **noun** a long, narrow table.

refer /rɪˈfəː/ ▸ **verb** (**refers, referring, referred**) **1** [no obj.] (**refer to**) mention or allude to: *her mother never referred to him again | the Royal Navy is referred to as the Senior Service.* ■ [with obj.] (**refer someone to**) direct the attention of someone to: *I refer my honourable friend to the reply that I gave some moments ago.* ■ (**refer to**) (of a word, phrase, or symbol) describe or denote; have as a referent: *the star refers to items which are intended for the advanced learner.*
2 [with obj.] (**refer something to**) pass a matter to (a higher body) for a decision: *the prisoner may require the Secretary of State to refer his case to the Parole Board.* ■ (**refer someone to**) send or direct someone to a medical specialist: *she was referred to a clinical psychologist for counselling.* ■ [no obj.] (**refer to**) read or otherwise use (a source of information) in order to ascertain something; consult: *I always refer to a dictionary when I come upon a new word.*
3 [with obj.] (**refer something to**) archaic trace or attribute something to (someone or something) as a cause or source: *the God to whom he habitually referred his highest inspirations.* ■ regard something as belonging to (a certain period, place, or class).
4 [with obj.] fail (a candidate in an examination).
– PHRASES **refer to drawer** Brit. a phrase used by banks when suspending payment of a cheque.
– DERIVATIVES **referable** /rɪˈfəːrəb(ə)l, ˈrɛf(ə)r-/ **adjective**, **referrer noun**.
– ORIGIN late Middle English: from Old French *referer* or Latin *referre* 'carry back', from *re-* 'back' + *ferre* 'bring'.

referee ▸ **noun 1** an official who watches a game or match closely to ensure that the rules are adhered to and (in some sports) to arbitrate on matters arising from the play.
2 Brit. a person willing to testify in writing about the character or ability of someone, especially an applicant for a job. ■ a person appointed to examine and assess for publication a scientific or other academic work.
▸ **verb** (**referees, refereeing, refereed**) [with obj.] act as the referee of: *he had refereed two of the first-round group matches.*

reference ▸ **noun** [mass noun] **1** the action of mentioning or alluding to something: ***he made reference to** the enormous power of the mass media* | [count noun] *references to Darwinism and evolution.* ■ [count noun] a mention or citation of a source of information in a book or article. ■ [count noun] a source of information cited in a book or article.
2 the use of a source of information in order to ascertain something: *popular works of reference* | [as modifier] *a reference work.* ■ the sending of a matter to an authority for decision or consideration: *the publishers reprinted and sold the work **without reference** to the author.*
3 [count noun] a letter from a previous employer testifying to someone's ability or reliability, used when applying for a new job.
▸ **verb** [with obj.] **1** provide (a book or article) with citations of sources of information: *each chapter is referenced, citing literature up to 1990.*
2 mention or refer to: *the media referenced our association in almost 40 articles.*
– PHRASES **for future reference** for use at a later date. **terms of reference** the scope and limitations of an activity or area of knowledge: *the minister will present a plan outlining the inquiry's terms of reference.* **with** (or **in**) **reference to** in relation to; as regards: *war can only be explained with reference to complex social factors.*

reference book ▸ **noun 1** a book intended to be consulted for information on specific matters.
2 S. African historical another term for PASS[1] (sense 3 of the noun).

reference electrode ▸ **noun** Electronics an electrode having an accurately maintained potential, used as a reference for measurement by other electrodes.

reference frame ▸ **noun** see FRAME OF REFERENCE.

reference library ▸ **noun** a library, typically one holding many reference books, in which the books are not for loan but may be read on site.

reference point ▸ **noun** a basis or standard for evaluation, assessment, or comparison; a criterion.

referendum /ˌrɛfəˈrɛndəm/ ▸ **noun** (pl. **referendums** or **referenda** /-də/) a general vote by the electorate on a single political question which has been referred to them for a direct decision.
– ORIGIN mid 19th cent.: from Latin, gerund ('referring') or neuter gerundive ('something to be brought back or referred') of *referre* (see REFER).

referent ▸ **noun** Linguistics the thing in the world that a word or phrase denotes or stands for.
– ORIGIN mid 19th cent.: from Latin *referent-* 'bringing back', from the verb *referre* (see REFER).

referential ▸ **adjective 1** containing or of the nature of references or allusions.
2 Linguistics relating to a referent, in particular having the external world rather than a text or language as a referent.
– DERIVATIVES **referentiality noun**, **referentially adverb**.

referral ▸ **noun** an act of referring someone or something for consultation, review, or further action. ■ [mass noun] the directing of a patient to a medical specialist by a GP. ■ a person whose case has been referred to a specialist doctor or a professional body.

referred pain ▸ **noun** [mass noun] Medicine pain felt in a part of the body other than its actual source.

reffo ▸ **noun** (pl. **reffos**) Austral. informal, offensive a refugee from Europe, in particular one who left Germany or German-occupied Europe before the Second World War.

refill ▸ **verb** /riːˈfɪl/ [with obj.] fill (a container) again: *she paused and refilled her glass with wine before going on.* ■ [no obj.] (of a container) become full again: *the empty pool will rapidly refill from rain and snow.*
▸ **noun** /ˈriːfɪl/ an act of refilling or a glass that is refilled: *he proffered his glass for a refill | the waitress appeared with refills.*
– DERIVATIVES **refillable adjective**.

refinance ▸ **verb** [with obj.] finance (something) again, typically with new loans at a lower rate of interest.

refine ▸ **verb** [with obj.] remove impurities or unwanted elements from (a substance), typically as part of an industrial process: *sugar was refined by boiling it in huge iron vats.* ■ make minor changes so as to improve or clarify (a theory or method): *ease of access to computers has refined analysis and presentation of data.*
– DERIVATIVES **refiner noun**.
– ORIGIN late 16th cent.: from RE- 'again' + the verb FINE[1], influenced by French *raffiner*.

refined ▸ **adjective** with impurities or unwanted elements having been removed by processing: *refined sugar.* ■ elegant and cultured in appearance, manner, or taste: *her voice was very low and refined.* ■ developed or improved so as to be precise or subtle: *building up a more refined profile of the customer's needs.*

refinement ▸ **noun** [mass noun] the process of removing impurities or unwanted elements from a substance: *the refinement of uranium.* ■ the improvement or clarification of something by the making of small changes: *this gross figure needs considerable refinement* | [count noun] *recent **refinements to** production techniques.* ■ cultured elegance in behaviour or manner: *her carefully cultivated veneer of refinement.* ■ sophisticated and superior good taste: *the refinement of Hellenistic art.*

refinery ▸ **noun** (pl. **refineries**) an industrial installation where a substance is refined: *an oil refinery.*

refinish ▸ **verb** [with obj.] apply a new finish to (a surface or object).
▸ **noun** an act of refinishing a surface or object.

refit ▸ **verb** (**refits, refitting, refitted**) [with obj.] replace or repair machinery, equipment, and fittings in (a ship, building, etc.): *a lucrative contract to refit a submarine fleet.*
▸ **noun** a restoration or repair of machinery, equipment, or fittings.

refix ▸ **verb** [with obj.] fix in position again or differently.

reflag ▸ **verb** (**reflags, reflagging, reflagged**) [with obj.] change the national registration of (a ship).

reflate ▸ **verb** [with obj.] expand the level of output of (an economy) by government stimulus, using either fiscal or monetary policy.
– DERIVATIVES **reflation noun**, **reflationary adjective**.
– ORIGIN 1930s: from RE- 'again', on the pattern of *inflate, deflate*.

reflect ▸ **verb 1** [with obj.] (of a surface or body) throw back (heat, light, or sound) without absorbing it: *when the sun's rays hit the Earth a lot of the heat is reflected back into space.* ■ (of a mirror or shiny surface) show an image of: *he could see himself reflected in Keith's mirrored glasses.* ■ embody or represent (something) in a faithful or appropriate way: *schools should reflect cultural differences.* ■ (of an action or situation) bring (credit or discredit) to the relevant parties: *the main contract is progressing well, which reflects great credit on those involved.* ■ [no obj.] (**reflect well/badly on**) bring about a good or bad impression of: *the incident reflects badly on the operating practices of the airlines.*
2 [no obj.] (usu. **reflect on/upon**) think deeply or carefully about: *he reflected with sadness on the unhappiness of his marriage* | [with clause] *Charles reflected that maybe there was hope for the family after all.* ■ archaic make disparaging remarks about: *the clergy were strictly charged not to reflect on the Catholic religion in their discourses.*
– ORIGIN late Middle English: from Old French *reflecter* or Latin *reflectere*, from *re-* 'back' + *flectere* 'to bend'.

reflectance ▸ **noun** Physics the measure of the proportion of light or other radiation striking a surface which is reflected off it.

reflected glory ▸ **noun** [mass noun] fame or approval achieved through association with someone else rather than through one's own efforts.

reflecting telescope ▸ **noun** a telescope in which a mirror is used to collect and focus light.

reflection ▸ **noun 1** [mass noun] the throwing back by a body or surface of light, heat, or sound without absorbing it: *the reflection of light.* ■ [count noun] an amount of light, heat, or sound that is reflected by a body or surface: *the reflections from the street lamps gave them just enough light.* ■ [count noun] an image seen in a mirror or shiny surface: *Marianne surveyed her reflection in the mirror.* ■ [count noun] a thing that is a consequence of or arises from something else: *a healthy skin is a reflection of good health in general.* ■ [in sing.] a thing bringing discredit to someone or something: *it was a sad **reflection on** society that because of his affliction he was picked on.*
2 [mass noun] serious thought or consideration: *he doesn't get much time for reflection.* ■ [count noun] an idea about something, especially one that is written down or expressed: *reflections on human destiny and art.*
3 [count noun] Mathematics the conceptual operation of inverting a system or event with respect to a plane, each element being transferred perpendicularly through the plane to a point the same distance the other side of it.
– ORIGIN late Middle English: from Old French *reflexion* or late Latin *reflexio(n-)*, from Latin *reflex-* 'bent back', from the verb *reflectere*.

reflection coefficient ▸ **noun** another term for REFLECTANCE.

reflective ▸ **adjective 1** providing a reflection; capable of reflecting light or other radiation: *reflective glass | reflective clothing.* ■ produced by reflection: *a colourful reflective glow.*
2 relating to or characterized by deep thought; thoughtful: *a quiet, reflective, astute man.*
– DERIVATIVES **reflectively adverb**, **reflectiveness noun**.

reflectivity ▸ **noun** Physics the property of reflecting light or radiation, especially reflectance as measured independently of the thickness of a material.

reflectometer /ˌriːflɛkˈtɒmɪtə/ ▸ **noun** an instrument for measuring quantities associated with reflection, in particular (also **time domain reflectometer**) an instrument for locating discontinuities (e.g. faults in electric cables) by detecting and measuring reflected pulses of energy.
– DERIVATIVES **reflectometry noun**.

R

reflector ▶ noun a piece of glass or metal for reflecting light in a required direction, e.g. a red one on the back of a motor vehicle or bicycle. ■ an object or device which reflects radio waves, seismic vibrations, sound, or other waves. ■ a reflecting telescope.

reflet /rəˈfleɪ/ ▶ noun [mass noun] lustre or iridescence, especially on ceramics.
– ORIGIN French, literally 'reflection'.

reflex ▶ noun **1** an action that is performed without conscious thought as a response to a stimulus: *a newborn baby is equipped with basic reflexes.* ■ (in reflexology) a response in a part of the body to stimulation of a corresponding point on the feet, hands, or head.
2 a thing which is determined by and reproduces the essential features or qualities of something else: *politics was no more than a reflex of economics.* ■ a word formed by development from an earlier stage of a language.
3 archaic a reflected source of light.
▶ adjective **1** (of an action) performed without conscious thought as an automatic response to a stimulus: *sneezing is a reflex action.*
2 (of an angle) exceeding 180°.
3 archaic (of light) reflected. ■ bent or turned backwards.
– DERIVATIVES **reflexly** adverb.
– ORIGIN early 16th cent. (as a noun denoting reflection): from Latin *reflexus* 'a bending back', from *reflectere* 'bend back' (see REFLECT).

reflex arc ▶ noun Physiology the nerve pathway involved in a reflex action, including at its simplest a sensory nerve and a motor nerve with a synapse between.

reflex camera ▶ noun a camera with a ground-glass focusing screen on which the image is formed by a combination of lens and mirror, enabling the scene to be correctly composed and focused.

reflexible ▶ adjective chiefly technical capable of being reflected.
– DERIVATIVES **reflexibility** noun.

reflexion ▶ noun archaic spelling of REFLECTION.

reflexive ▶ adjective **1** Grammar denoting a pronoun that refers back to the subject of the clause in which it is used, e.g. *myself, themselves.* ■ (of a verb or clause) having a reflexive pronoun as its object (e.g. *wash oneself*).
2 Logic (of a relation) always holding between a term and itself.
3 (of a method or theory in the social sciences) taking account of itself or of the effect of the personality or presence of the researcher on what is being investigated.
4 (of an action) performed as a reflex, without conscious thought: *at concerts like this one standing ovations have become reflexive.*
▶ noun a reflexive word or form, especially a pronoun.
– DERIVATIVES **reflexively** adverb, **reflexiveness** noun, **reflexivity** noun.

reflexology ▶ noun [mass noun] **1** a system of massage used to relieve tension and treat illness, based on the theory that there are reflex points on the feet, hands, and head linked to every part of the body.
2 Psychology the scientific study of reflex action as it affects behaviour.
– DERIVATIVES **reflexologist** noun (sense 1).

refloat ▶ verb [with obj.] set afloat again.

reflow ▶ noun [mass noun] **1** (in word processing) the action of rearranging text on a page having varied such features as type size, line length, and spacing.
2 Electronics a soldering technique in which surface-mount components are held in position on a circuit board using a paste containing solder which melts to form soldered joints when the circuit board is heated.
▶ verb [with obj.] **1** (in word processing) rearrange (text) on a page having varied such features as type size, line length, and spacing.
2 Electronics attach (a surface-mount component) using the reflow technique.

refluent /ˈrɛflʊənt/ ▶ adjective literary flowing back; ebbing: *the refluent waters of the Mississippi.*
– ORIGIN late Middle English: from Latin *refluent-* 'flowing back', from the verb *refluere*, from *re-* 'back' + *fluere* 'to flow'.

reflux /ˈriːflʌks/ ▶ noun [mass noun] **1** Chemistry the process of boiling a liquid so that any vapour is liquefied and returned to the stock.
2 technical the flowing back of a liquid, especially that of a fluid in the body.
▶ verb **1** [no obj.] Chemistry boil or cause to boil in circumstances such that the vapour returns to the stock of liquid after condensing.
2 [no obj., with adverbial of direction] technical (of a liquid, especially a bodily fluid) flow back.
– ORIGIN Middle English: from RE- and FLUX.

refocus ▶ verb (**refocuses, refocusing, refocused** or **refocusses, refocussing, refocussed**) [with obj.] adjust the focus of (a lens or one's eyes). ■ focus (attention or resources) on something new or different: *refocus attention on yourself through repeating your main points.*

refold ▶ verb [with obj.] fold (something) up again: *she refolded the newspaper and placed it back on the counter.*

reforest ▶ verb [with obj.] replant with trees; cover again with forest: *a project to reforest the country's coastal areas.*
– DERIVATIVES **reforestation** noun.

reforge ▶ verb [with obj.] forge or create again or differently: *they wanted to reforge the identity of the nation.*

reform ▶ verb [with obj.] **1** make changes in (something, especially an institution or practice) in order to improve it: *the Bill will reform the tax system.* ■ cause (someone) to relinquish an immoral, criminal, or self-destructive lifestyle: *the state has a duty to reform criminals* | (as adj. **reformed**) *I'm considered a reformed character these days.* ■ [no obj.] relinquish an immoral, criminal, or self-destructive lifestyle.
2 Chemistry subject (hydrocarbons) to a catalytic process in which straight-chain molecules are converted to branched forms for use as petrol.
▶ noun [mass noun] the action or process of reforming an institution or practice: *the reform of the divorce laws* | [count noun] *economic reforms.*
– DERIVATIVES **reformable** adjective, **reformative** adjective, **reformer** noun.
– ORIGIN Middle English (as a verb in the senses 'restore (peace)' and 'bring back to the original condition'): from Old French *reformer* or Latin *reformare*, from *re-* 'back' + *formare* 'to form, shape'. The noun dates from the mid 17th cent.

re-form ▶ verb form or cause to form again: [no obj.] *the clouds re-formed over the sun.*

Reform Act ▶ noun an act framed to amend the system of parliamentary representation, especially any of those introduced in Britain during the 19th century.

> The first Reform Act (1832) disenfranchised various rotten boroughs and lowered the property qualification, widening the electorate by about 50 per cent to include most of the male members of the upper middle class. The second (1867) doubled the electorate to about 2 million men by again lowering the property qualification, and the third (1884) increased it to about 5 million.

reformat ▶ verb (**reformats, reformatting, reformatted**) [with obj.] chiefly Computing give a new format to; revise or represent in another format.

reformation ▶ noun **1** [mass noun] the action or process of reforming an institution or practice: *the reformation of the Senate.*
2 (**the Reformation**) a 16th-century movement for the reform of abuses in the Roman Church ending in the establishment of the Reformed and Protestant Churches.

> The roots of the Reformation go back to the 14th-century attacks on the wealth and hierarchy of the Church made by groups such as the Lollards and the Hussites. But the Reformation is usually thought of as beginning in 1517 when Martin Luther issued ninety-five theses criticizing Church doctrine and practice. In Denmark, Norway, Sweden, Saxony, Hesse, and Brandenburg, supporters broke away and established Protestant Churches, while in Switzerland a separate movement was led by Zwingli and later Calvin.

– DERIVATIVES **reformational** adjective.
– ORIGIN late Middle English: from Latin *reformatio(n-)*, from *reformare* 'shape again' (see REFORM).

re-formation ▶ noun [mass noun] the action or process of forming again.

reformatory /rɪˈfɔːmət(ə)ri/ ▶ noun (pl. **reformatories**) archaic or N. Amer. dated an institution to which young offenders are sent as an alternative to prison.
▶ adjective tending or intended to produce reform.

Reformed Church ▶ noun a Church that has accepted the principles of the Reformation, especially a Calvinist Church (as distinct from Lutheran).

reformist ▶ adjective supporting or advancing gradual reform rather than abolition or revolution.
▶ noun a person who advocates gradual reform rather than abolition or revolution.
– DERIVATIVES **reformism** noun.

Reform Judaism ▶ noun [mass noun] a form of Judaism, initiated in Germany by the philosopher Moses Mendelssohn (1729–86), which has reformed or abandoned aspects of Orthodox Jewish worship and ritual in an attempt to adapt to modern changes in social, political, and cultural life.
– DERIVATIVES **Reform Jew** noun.

reform school ▶ noun historical an institution to which young offenders were sent as an alternative to prison.

reformulate ▶ verb [with obj.] formulate again or differently: *pupils benefit from the opportunity to reformulate their thinking in a helpful atmosphere.*
– DERIVATIVES **reformulation** noun.

refound ▶ verb [with obj.] found (a city or institution) again; re-establish: *Westminster was refounded as a Benedictine monastery under Mary Tudor.*
– DERIVATIVES **refoundation** noun.

refract ▶ verb [with obj.] (of water, air, or glass) make (a ray of light) change direction when it enters at an angle: *the rays of light are refracted by the material of the lens.* ■ measure the focusing characteristics of (an eye) or of the eyes of (someone).
– ORIGIN early 17th cent.: from Latin *refract-* 'broken up', from the verb *refringere*, from *re-* 'back' + *frangere* 'to break'.

refracting telescope ▶ noun a telescope which uses a converging lens to collect the light.

refraction ▶ noun [mass noun] Physics the fact or phenomenon of light, radio waves, etc. being deflected in passing obliquely through the interface between one medium and another or through a medium of varying density. ■ change in direction of propagation of any wave as a result of its travelling at different speeds at different points along the wave front. ■ measurement of the focusing characteristics of an eye or eyes.
– ORIGIN mid 17th cent.: from late Latin *refractio(n-)*, from *refringere* 'break up' (see REFRACT).

refractive ▶ adjective of or involving refraction.
– DERIVATIVES **refractively** adverb.

refractive index ▶ noun the ratio of the velocity of light in a vacuum to its velocity in a specified medium.

refractometer /ˌriːfrakˈtɒmɪtə/ ▶ noun an instrument for measuring a refractive index.
– DERIVATIVES **refractometric** adjective, **refractometry** noun.

refractor ▶ noun a lens or other object which causes refraction. ■ a refracting telescope.

refractory ▶ adjective formal **1** stubborn or unmanageable: *his refractory pony.*
2 resistant to a process or stimulus. ■ Medicine (of a person, illness, or diseased tissue) not yielding to treatment: *healing of previously refractory ulcers.* ■ Medicine, rare (of a person or animal) resistant to infection. ■ technical (of a substance) resistant to heat; hard to melt or fuse.
▶ noun (pl. **refractories**) technical a substance that is resistant to heat.
– DERIVATIVES **refractoriness** noun.
– ORIGIN early 17th cent.: alteration of obsolete *refractary*, from Latin *refractarius* 'stubborn' (see also REFRACT).

refractory period ▶ noun Physiology a period immediately following stimulation during which a nerve or muscle is unresponsive to further stimulation.

refrain¹ ▶ verb [no obj.] stop oneself from doing something: *she refrained from comment.*
– ORIGIN Middle English (in the sense 'restrain a thought or feeling'): from Old French *refrener*, from Latin *refrenare*, from *re-* (expressing intensive force) + *frenum* 'bridle'.

refrain² ▶ noun a repeated line or number of lines in a poem or song, typically at the end of each verse. ■ the musical accompaniment for a refrain. ■ a comment or complaint that is often repeated: *'Poor Tom' had become the constant refrain of his friends.*
– ORIGIN late Middle English: from Old French, from *refraindre* 'break', based on Latin *refringere* 'break up' (because the refrain 'broke' the sequence).

reframe ▶ verb [with obj.] **1** place (a picture or photograph) in a new frame.
2 frame or express (words or a concept or plan) differently: *I reframed my question.*

R

refrangible ▶ adjective able to be refracted.
– DERIVATIVES **refrangibility** noun.
– ORIGIN late 17th cent.: from modern Latin *refrangibilis*, from *refrangere* 'break up' (see REFRACT).

refreeze ▶ verb (past **refroze**; past participle **refrozen**) make or become frozen again.

refresh ▶ verb **1** [with obj.] give new strength or energy to; reinvigorate: *the shower had refreshed her* | (as adj. **refreshed**) *I awoke feeling calm and refreshed.* ▪ stimulate or jog (someone's memory) by checking or going over previous information: *he was able to refresh her memory on many points.* ▪ revise or update (skills or knowledge): *short-term courses give nurses an opportunity to refresh their skills.* ▪ Computing update the display on (a screen). ▪ place or keep (food) in cold water so as to cool it or maintain its freshness.
2 chiefly N. Amer. pour more (drink) for someone or refill (a container) with drink: *the tea is cold and the pot needs refreshing.*
▶ noun Computing an act or function of updating the display on a screen.
– ORIGIN late Middle English: from Old French *refreschier*, from *re-* 'back' + *fres(che)* 'fresh'.

refresher ▶ noun **1** [usu. as modifier] an activity that refreshes one's skills or knowledge: *candidates take some refresher training before coming back.*
2 Law, Brit. an extra fee payable to counsel in a prolonged case.

refresher course ▶ noun a short course reviewing or updating previous studies or training connected with one's profession.

refreshing ▶ adjective serving to refresh or reinvigorate someone: *a refreshing drink.* ▪ welcome or stimulating because new or different: *it makes a* ***refreshing change*** *to be able to write about something nice* | *her directness is refreshing.*
– DERIVATIVES **refreshingly** adverb.

refreshment ▶ noun **1** (usu. **refreshments**) a light snack or drink: *light refreshments are available* | [mass noun] *an ample supply of liquid refreshment.*
2 [mass noun] the giving of fresh strength or energy: *holidays are for refreshment and recreation.*
– ORIGIN late Middle English (in sense 2): from Old French *refreschement*, from the verb *refreschier* (see REFRESH).

refried beans ▶ plural noun pinto beans boiled and fried in advance and reheated when required, used especially in Mexican cooking.

refrigerant ▶ noun a substance used for refrigeration.
▶ adjective causing cooling or refrigeration.
– ORIGIN late 16th cent. (denoting a substance that cools or allays fever): from French *réfrigérant* or Latin *refrigerant-* 'making cool', from the verb *refrigerare* (see REFRIGERATE).

refrigerate ▶ verb [with obj.] subject (food or drink) to cold in order to chill or preserve it, typically by placing it in a refrigerator: *refrigerate the dough for one hour.*
– DERIVATIVES **refrigeration** noun, **refrigeratory** adjective.
– ORIGIN late Middle English: from Latin *refrigerat-* 'made cool', from the verb *refrigerare*, from *re-* 'back' + *frigus, frigor-* 'cold'.

refrigerated ▶ adjective (of food or drink) chilled in a refrigerator: *sandwiches must be kept refrigerated in shops* | *refrigerated meat.* ▪ (of a vehicle or container) used to keep or transport food or drink in a chilled condition.

refrigerator ▶ noun an appliance or compartment which is artificially kept cool and used to store food and drink. Modern refrigerators generally make use of the cooling effect produced when a volatile liquid is forced to evaporate in a sealed system in which it can be condensed back to liquid outside the refrigerator.

refringent /rɪˈfrɪn(d)ʒ(ə)nt/ ▶ adjective Physics refractive.
– ORIGIN late 18th cent.: from Latin *refringent-*, literally 'breaking again', from the verb *refringere*.

refroze past of REFREEZE.

refrozen past participle of REFREEZE.

reft past and past participle of REAVE.

refuel ▶ verb (**refuels**, **refuelling**, **refuelled**; US **refuels**, **refueling**, **refueled**) [with obj.] supply (a vehicle) with more fuel: *the authorities agreed to refuel the plane.* ▪ [no obj.] (of a vehicle) be supplied with more fuel.

refuge ▶ noun [mass noun] the state of being safe or sheltered from pursuit, danger, or difficulty: *he was forced to take refuge in the French embassy* | *I sought refuge in drink.* ▪ [count noun] a place or situation providing safety or shelter: *the family came to be seen as a refuge from a harsh world.* ▪ [count noun] an institution providing safe accommodation for women who have suffered violence from a husband or partner. ▪ [count noun] Brit. a traffic island.
– ORIGIN late Middle English: from Old French, from Latin *refugium*, from Latin *re-* 'back' + *fugere* 'flee'.

refugee ▶ noun a person who has been forced to leave their country in order to escape war, persecution, or natural disaster: *tens of thousands of refugees fled their homes* | [as modifier] *a refugee camp.*
– ORIGIN late 17th cent.: from French *réfugié* 'gone in search of refuge', past participle of *(se) réfugier*, from *refuge* (see REFUGE).

refugium /rɪˈfjuːdʒɪəm/ ▶ noun (pl. **refugia** /-dʒɪə/) Biology an area in which a population of organisms can survive through a period of unfavourable conditions, especially glaciation.
– ORIGIN 1950s: from Latin, literally 'place of refuge'.

refulgent /rɪˈfʌldʒ(ə)nt/ ▶ adjective literary shining very brightly: *refulgent blue eyes.*
– DERIVATIVES **refulgence** noun, **refulgently** adverb.
– ORIGIN late 15th cent.: from Latin *refulgent-* 'shining out', from the verb *refulgere*, from *re-* (expressing intensive force) + *fulgere* 'to shine'.

refund ▶ verb /rɪˈfʌnd/ [with obj.] pay back (money), typically to a customer who is not satisfied with goods or services bought. ▪ pay back money to: *I'll refund you for the apples and any other damage.*
▶ noun /ˈriːfʌnd/ a repayment of a sum of money: *you may be allowed to claim a refund of the tax.*
– DERIVATIVES **refundable** adjective.
– ORIGIN late Middle English (in the senses 'pour back' and 'restore'): from Old French *refonder* or Latin *refundere*, from *re-* 'back' + *fundere* 'pour', later associated with the verb FUND. The noun dates from the mid 19th cent.

refurb ▶ noun informal an act or instance of refurbishing a building: *the theatre closes next year for its £100m refurb.*

refurbish ▶ verb [with obj.] renovate and redecorate (something, especially a building): *the premises have been completely refurbished in our corporate style.*
– DERIVATIVES **refurbishment** noun.

refurnish ▶ verb [with obj.] furnish (a room or building) again or differently.

refusal ▶ noun [usu. with infinitive] an act of refusing to do something: *he became tired of his friend's refusal to see him.* ▪ an expression of unwillingness to accept or grant an offer or request: *an appeal against the refusal of a licence.* ▪ an instance of a horse stopping short or running aside at a jump.

refuse[1] /rɪˈfjuːz/ ▶ verb [no obj., with infinitive] indicate or show that one is not willing to do something: *I refused to answer* | [no obj.] *he was severely beaten when he refused.* ▪ [with obj.] indicate that one is not willing to accept or grant (something offered or requested): *she refused a cigarette* | [with two objs] *the old lady was refused admission to four hospitals.* ▪ informal (of a thing) fail to perform a required action: *the car refused to start.* ▪ [with obj.] dated decline to accept an offer of marriage from (someone): *he's so conceited he'd never believe anyone would refuse him.* ▪ [with obj.] (of a horse) stop short or run aside at (a fence or other obstacle) instead of jumping it.
– DERIVATIVES **refuser** noun.
– ORIGIN Middle English: from Old French *refuser*, probably an alteration of Latin *recusare* 'to refuse', influenced by *refutare* 'refute'.

refuse[2] /ˈrɛfjuːs/ ▶ noun [mass noun] matter thrown away or rejected as worthless; rubbish: *heaps of refuse* | [as modifier] *refuse collection.*
– ORIGIN late Middle English: perhaps from Old French *refusé* 'refused', past participle of *refuser* (see REFUSE[1]).

refusenik /rɪˈfjuːznɪk/ ▶ noun **1** a Jew in the former Soviet Union who was refused permission to emigrate to Israel.
2 a person who refuses to follow orders or obey the law, especially as a protest.
– ORIGIN 1970s: from REFUSE[1] + -NIK.

refute /rɪˈfjuːt/ ▶ verb [with obj.] prove (a statement or theory) to be wrong or false; disprove: *these claims have not been convincingly refuted.* ▪ prove that (someone) is wrong. ▪ deny or contradict (a statement or accusation): *a spokesman totally refuted the allegation of bias.*
– DERIVATIVES **refutable** adjective, **refutation** noun, **refuter** noun.
– ORIGIN mid 16th cent.: from Latin *refutare* 'repel, rebut'.

> **USAGE** The core meaning of **refute** is 'prove a statement or theory to be wrong', as in *attempts to* ***refute*** *Einstein's theory.* In the second half of the 20th century a more general sense developed, meaning simply 'deny', as in *I absolutely* ***refute*** *the charges made against me.* Traditionalists object to this newer use as an unacceptable degradation of the language, but it is widely encountered.

reg ▶ noun [usu. in combination] Brit. informal a vehicle's registration mark, especially the letter denoting the year of manufacture: *a B-reg lorry.*
– ORIGIN 1960s: abbreviation.

regain ▶ verb [with obj.] obtain possession or use of (something, typically a quality or ability) again after losing it: *he soon regained his composure.* ▪ reach (a place, position, or thing) again; get back to: *they were unable to regain their boats.*
– ORIGIN mid 16th cent.: from French *regagner* (see RE-, GAIN).

regal ▶ adjective of, resembling, or fit for a monarch, especially in being magnificent or dignified: *her regal bearing.*
▶ noun Music a small portable reed organ of the 16th and 17th centuries, with a pair of horizontal bellows on top.
– DERIVATIVES **regally** adverb.
– ORIGIN late Middle English: from Old French, or from Latin *regalis*, from *rex, reg-* 'king'.

regale ▶ verb [with obj.] entertain or amuse (someone) with talk: *he* ***regaled*** *her* ***with*** *a colourful account of that afternoon's meeting.* ▪ lavishly supply (someone) with food or drink: *he was regaled with excellent home cooking.*
– DERIVATIVES **regalement** noun (rare).
– ORIGIN mid 17th cent.: from French *régaler*, from *re-* (expressing intensive force) + Old French *gale* 'pleasure'.

regalia /rɪˈɡeɪlɪə/ ▶ plural noun [treated as sing. or pl.] the emblems or insignia of royalty, especially the crown, sceptre, and other ornaments used at a coronation. ▪ the distinctive clothing worn and ornaments carried at formal occasions as an indication of status: *the Bishop of Florence* ***in full regalia.***
– ORIGIN mid 16th cent. (in the sense 'royal powers'): from medieval Latin, literally 'royal privileges', from Latin, neuter plural of *regalis* 'regal'.

> **USAGE** The word **regalia** comes from Latin and is, technically speaking, the plural of *regalis*. However, in the way the word is used in English today it behaves as a collective noun, similar to words like **staff** or **government**. This means that it can be used with either a singular or plural verb (*the* ***regalia*** *of Russian tsardom* ***is*** *now displayed in the Kremlin* or *the* ***regalia*** *of Russian tsardom* ***are*** *now displayed in the Kremlin*), but it has no other singular form.

regalian ▶ adjective formal belonging or relating to a monarch; regal: *regalian rights.*
– ORIGIN early 19th cent.: from French *régalien*, from Latin *regalis* 'regal'.

regalism ▶ noun [mass noun] the doctrine of a sovereign's supremacy in ecclesiastical matters.
– DERIVATIVES **regalist** noun & adjective.

regality ▶ noun (pl. **regalities**) [mass noun] **1** the state of being a king or queen. ▪ the demeanour or dignity appropriate to a king or queen: *Enid awaited her guests, radiating regality.*
2 historical (in Scotland) territorial jurisdiction granted by the king to a powerful subject. ▪ [count noun] a territory subject to regality jurisdiction
3 [count noun] archaic a royal privilege.
– ORIGIN late Middle English: from Anglo-Norman French *regalite* or medieval Latin *regalitas*, from *regalis* 'royal' (see REGAL).

regard ▶ verb **1** [with obj. and adverbial] consider or think of in a specified way: *she regarded London as her base* | *he was highly regarded by senators of both parties.* ▪ gaze at steadily in a particular way: *Professor Ryker regarded him with a faint smile* | *Nuala regarded him unflinchingly.* ▪ [with obj.] archaic pay attention to; heed: *he talk'd very wisely, but I regarded him not.*
2 [with obj.] archaic (of a thing) relate to; concern.
▶ noun **1** [mass noun] attention to or concern for something: *the court must have* ***regard to*** *the principle of welfare* | *she rescued him* ***without regard for*** *herself.* ▪ liking and respect; esteem: *they hold dolphins in high regard* | [count noun] *she had a particular regard for*

Eliot. ■ [in sing.] a steady or significant look: *he shifted uneasily before their clear regard.*
2 (**regards**) best wishes (used to express friendliness in greetings): *give her my regards.*
– PHRASES **as regards** concerning; in respect of: *as regards content, the programme will cover important current issues.* **in this** (or **that**) **regard** in connection with the point previously mentioned: *there was little incentive for them to be active in this regard.* **with** (or **in** or **having**) **regard to** as concerns; in respect of: *he made enquiries with regard to Beth.*
– DERIVATIVES **regardable** adjective.
– ORIGIN Middle English: from Old French *regarder* 'to watch', from *re-* 'back' (also expressing intensive force) + *garder* 'to guard'.

regardant /rɪˈɡɑːd(ə)nt/ ▶ adjective [usu. postpositive] Heraldry looking backwards.
– ORIGIN late Middle English: from Anglo-Norman French and Old French, present participle of *regarder* 'look (again)'.

regardful ▶ adjective (**regardful of**) formal paying attention to; mindful of: *Parker was not overly regardful of public opinion.*
– DERIVATIVES **regardfully** adverb.

regarding ▶ preposition in respect of; concerning: *your recent letter regarding the above proposal.*

regardless ▶ adverb despite the prevailing circumstances: *they were determined to carry on regardless.* ■ (**regardless of**) without regard or consideration for: *the allowance is paid regardless of age or income.*
– DERIVATIVES **regardlessly** adverb, **regardlessness** noun.

regather ▶ verb **1** [with obj.] collect or gather again: *after 1910 the workers' movement regathered momentum.*
2 [no obj.] meet or come together again.

regatta ▶ noun a sporting event consisting of a series of boat or yacht races.
– ORIGIN early 17th cent.: from Italian (Venetian dialect), literally 'a fight, contest'.

regd ▶ abbreviation registered.

regelate /ˌriːdʒɪˈleɪt/ ▶ verb [no obj.] technical (chiefly of pieces of ice thawed apart) freeze together again.
– DERIVATIVES **regelation** noun.
– ORIGIN mid 19th cent.: from **RE-** 'again' + Latin *gelat-* 'frozen' (from the verb *gelare*).

regency /ˈriːdʒ(ə)nsi/ ▶ noun (pl. **regencies**) the office of or period of government by a regent. ■ a commission acting as regent. ■ (**the Regency**) the particular period of a regency, especially (in Britain) from 1811 to 1820 and (in France) from 1715 to 1723.
▶ adjective (**Regency**) relating to or denoting British architecture, clothing, and furniture of the Regency or, more widely, of the late 18th and early 19th centuries. Regency style was contemporary with the Empire style and shares many of its features: elaborate and ornate, it is generally neoclassical, with a generous borrowing of Greek and Egyptian motifs.
– ORIGIN late Middle English: from medieval Latin *regentia*, from Latin *regent-* 'ruling' (see **REGENT**).

regenerate ▶ verb /rɪˈdʒɛnəreɪt/ [with obj.] **1** (of a living organism) grow (new tissue) after loss or damage: *the lizard has to find the wherewithal to regenerate its tail.* ■ [no obj.] (of an organ or tissue) grow again: *once destroyed, brain cells do not regenerate.*
2 bring new and more vigorous life to (an area, industry, institution, etc.); revive, especially in economic terms: *the money will be used to regenerate the heart of the town.* ■ (especially in Christian use) give a new and higher spiritual nature to.
3 (usu. as adj. **regenerated**) Chemistry precipitate (a natural polymer, especially cellulose or a protein) as fibres following chemical processing.
▶ adjective /rɪˈdʒɛn(ə)rət/ reformed or reborn, especially in a spiritual or moral sense: *he was not truly regenerate.*
– DERIVATIVES **regenerator** noun.
– ORIGIN late Middle English (as an adjective): from Latin *regeneratus* 'created again', past participle of *regenerare*, from *re-* 'again' + *generare* 'create'. The verb dates from the mid 16th cent.

regeneration ▶ noun [mass noun] the action or process of regenerating or being regenerated: *the regeneration of inner cities.* ■ the formation of new animal or plant tissue. ■ Electronics positive feedback. ■ Chemistry the action or process of regenerating polymer fibres.
– ORIGIN Middle English: from Latin *regeneratio(n-)*, from *regenerare* 'create again' (see **REGENERATE**).

regenerative ▶ adjective tending to or characterized by regeneration: *natural regenerative processes.*
– DERIVATIVES **regeneratively** adverb.

regenerative braking ▶ noun [mass noun] a method of braking in which energy is extracted from the parts braked, to be stored and reused.

regent ▶ noun **1** a person appointed to administer a state because the monarch is a minor or is absent or incapacitated.
2 N. Amer. a member of the governing body of a university or other academic institution.
▶ adjective [postpositive] acting as regent for a monarch: *the queen regent of Portugal.* See also **PRINCE REGENT**.
– ORIGIN late Middle English: from Old French, or from Latin *regent-* 'ruling', from the verb *regere*.

regex (also **regexp**) ▶ noun Computing a regular expression.

reggae /ˈrɛɡeɪ/ ▶ noun [mass noun] a style of popular music with a strongly accented subsidiary beat, originating in Jamaica. Reggae evolved in the late 1960s from ska and other local variations on calypso and rhythm and blues, and became widely known in the 1970s through the work of Bob Marley; its lyrics are much influenced by Rastafarian ideas.
– ORIGIN 1960s: perhaps related to Jamaican English *rege-rege* 'quarrel, row'.

reggaeton /ˈrɛɡeɪtəʊn/ ▶ noun [mass noun] a form of dance music of Puerto Rican origin, characterized by a fusion of Latin rhythms, dancehall, and hip hop or rap.
– ORIGIN early 21st cent.: from **REGGAE** and Spanish *ton* after *-thon* as in **-ATHON**.

Reggio di Calabria /ˌrɛdʒɪəʊ diː kəˈlabrɪə/ a port at the southern tip of the 'toe' of Italy, on the Strait of Messina; pop. 185,621 (2008). The original settlement was founded about 720 BC by Greek colonists as Rhegion (Latin Rhegium).

reggo ▶ noun variant spelling of **REGO**.

regicide /ˈrɛdʒɪsʌɪd/ ▶ noun [mass noun] the action of killing a king. ■ [count noun] a person who kills or takes part in killing a king.
– DERIVATIVES **regicidal** adjective.
– ORIGIN mid 16th cent.: from Latin *rex*, *reg-* 'king' + **-CIDE**, probably suggested by French *régicide*.

regild ▶ verb [with obj.] gild (something) again.

regime /reɪˈʒiːm/ ▶ noun **1** a government, especially an authoritarian one: *ideological opponents of the regime.*
2 a system or ordered way of doing things: *detention centres with a very tough physical regime | a tax regime.* ■ a coordinated programme for the promotion or restoration of health; a regimen: *a low-calorie, low-fat regime.* ■ the conditions under which a scientific or industrial process occurs.
– ORIGIN late 15th cent. (in the sense 'regimen'): French *régime*, from Latin *regimen* 'rule' (see **REGIMEN**). Sense 1 dates from the late 18th cent. (with original reference to the Ancien Régime).

regime change ▶ noun the replacement of one administration or government by another, especially by means of military force.

regimen /ˈrɛdʒɪmən/ ▶ noun **1** a prescribed course of medical treatment, diet, or exercise for the promotion or restoration of health: *a regimen of one or two injections per day.*
2 archaic a system of government.
– ORIGIN late Middle English (denoting the action of governing): from Latin, from *regere* 'to rule'.

regiment ▶ noun /ˈrɛdʒɪm(ə)nt/ **1** a permanent unit of an army typically commanded by a lieutenant colonel and divided into several companies, squadrons, or batteries and often into two battalions: [in names] *the Royal Highland Regiment.* ■ an operational unit of artillery. ■ a large array or number of people or things: *the whole regiment of women MPs.*
2 [mass noun] archaic rule or government.
▶ verb /ˈrɛdʒɪmɛnt/ [with obj.] organize according to a strict system or pattern: *every aspect of their life is strictly regimented.*
– DERIVATIVES **regimentation** noun.
– ORIGIN late Middle English (in the sense 'rule or government'): via Old French from late Latin *regimentum* 'rule', from *regere* 'to rule'.

regimental ▶ adjective relating to a regiment: *a regimental badge | regimental traditions.*
– DERIVATIVES **regimentally** adverb.

regimental colour ▶ noun (in the UK) a regimental standard in the form of a silk flag, carried by a particular regiment along with its Queen's colour.

regimentals ▶ plural noun military uniform, especially that of a particular regiment.

regimental sergeant major ▶ noun see **SERGEANT MAJOR** (sense 1).

regimented /ˈrɛdʒɪmɛntɪd/ ▶ adjective very strictly organized or controlled: *the regimented life of a long-term prisoner.*

Regina¹ /rɪˈdʒʌɪnə/ the capital of Saskatchewan, situated in the centre of the wheat-growing plains of south central Canada; pop. 179,246 (2006).

Regina² /rɪˈdʒʌɪnə/ ▶ noun the reigning queen (used following a name or in the titles of lawsuits, e.g. *Regina v. Jones*, the Crown versus Jones).
– ORIGIN Latin, literally 'queen'.

Regiomontanus /ˌrɛdʒɪəʊmɒnˈtɑːnəs/, Johannes (1436–76), German astronomer and mathematician; born *Johannes Müller*. He translated Ptolemy's *Mathematical Syntaxis* and wrote four monumental works on mathematics and astronomy.

region ▶ noun **1** an area, especially part of a country or the world having definable characteristics but not always fixed boundaries: *the equatorial regions | a major wine-producing region.* ■ an administrative district of a city or country. ■ (**the regions**) Brit. the parts of a country outside the capital or chief seat of government: *the promotion of investment in the regions.* ■ an area of activity or thought: *his work takes needlework into the region of folk art.*
2 a part of the body, especially around or near an organ: *the lumbar region.*
– PHRASES **in the region of** approximately: *annual sales in the region of 30 million.*
– ORIGIN Middle English: from Old French, from Latin *regio(n-)* 'direction, district', from *regere* 'to rule, direct'.

regional ▶ adjective relating to or characteristic of a region: *regional and local needs | regional variations.* ■ Brit. relating to the regions of a country rather than the capital: *a regional accent.*
▶ noun (usu. **regionals**) a stamp, newspaper, or other thing produced or used in a particular region. ■ (**regionals**) N. Amer. a sporting contest involving competitors from a particular region.
– DERIVATIVES **regionally** adverb.

regionalism ▶ noun **1** [mass noun] the theory or practice of regional rather than central systems of administration or economic, cultural, or political affiliation: *a strong expression of regionalism.*
2 a linguistic feature peculiar to a particular region and not part of the standard language of a country.
– DERIVATIVES **regionalist** noun & adjective.

regionalize (also **regionalise**) ▶ verb [with obj.] (usu. as adj. **regionalized**) organize (a country, area, or enterprise) on a regional basis: *a regionalized system.*
– DERIVATIVES **regionalization** noun.

regisseur /ˌreʒɪˈsəː/ ▶ noun a person who stages a theatrical production, especially a ballet.
– ORIGIN from French *régisseur*.

register ▶ noun **1** an official list or record of names or items: *a membership register.* ■ a book or record of attendance, for example of pupils in a class or guests in a hotel.
2 a particular part of the range of a voice or instrument: *boy trebles singing in a high register.* ■ a sliding device controlling a set of organ pipes which share a tonal quality. ■ a set of organ pipes controlled by a sliding device.
3 Linguistics a variety of a language or a level of usage, as determined by degree of formality and choice of vocabulary, pronunciation, and syntax, according to the communicative purpose, social context, and standing of the user.
4 [mass noun] Printing & Photography the exact correspondence of the position of colour components in a printed positive. ■ Printing the exact correspondence of the position of printed matter on the two sides of a leaf.
5 (in electronic devices) a location in a store of data, used for a specific purpose and with quick access time.
6 an adjustable plate for widening or narrowing an opening and regulating a draught, especially in a fire grate.
7 Art one of a number of bands or sections into which a design is divided.
▶ verb [with obj.] **1** enter or record on an official list or directory: *the vessel is registered as British | his father was late in registering his birth* | (as adj. **registered**) *a registered charity.* ■ [no obj.] enter one's name and other details on an official list or directory: *you register at the site with a user ID and a password* | [with infinitive] *34,500 registered to vote.* ■ [no obj.] put one's name in a register as a guest in a hotel. ■ [no obj.] N. Amer. (of a couple to be married) have a list of wedding gifts compiled and kept at a shop for consultation by gift buyers. ■ entrust (a letter or parcel) to a post office

R

for transmission by registered post: (as adj. **registered**) *a registered letter*.
2 (of an instrument) detect and show (a reading) automatically: *the electroscope was too insensitive to register the tiny changes*. ■ [no obj., with complement] (of an event) give rise to a specified reading on an instrument: *the blast registered 5.4 on the Richter scale*.
3 express or convey (an opinion or emotion): *I wish to register an objection* | *his features registered amusement*. ■ [no obj.] (of an emotion) show in a person's face or gestures: *nothing registered on their faces*. ■ [usu. with negative] notice or become aware of: *he hadn't even registered her presence*. ■ [no obj.] [usu. with negative] make an impression on a person's mind: *the content of her statement did not register*.
4 achieve (a certain score or result) in a game or match: *they registered their third consecutive draw*.
5 Printing & Photography correspond or cause to correspond exactly in position.
– DERIVATIVES **registrable** adjective.
– ORIGIN late Middle English: from Old French *regestre* or medieval Latin *regestrum*, *registrum*, alteration of *regestum*, singular of late Latin *regesta* 'things recorded', from *regerere* 'enter, record'.

registered nurse (abbrev.: **RN**) ▸ **noun** N. Amer. a fully trained nurse with an official state certificate of competence. ■ Brit. short for **State Registered Nurse**.

registered post (N. Amer. **registered mail**) ▸ **noun** a postal procedure with special precautions for safety and for compensation in case of loss.

register office ▸ **noun** (in the UK) a local government building where civil marriages are conducted and births, marriages, and deaths are recorded with the issue of certificates.

> **USAGE** The form **register office** is the official term, but **registry office** is the form which dominates in informal and non-official use.

register ton ▸ **noun** see **TON[1]** (sense 2 of the noun).

registrant ▸ **noun** a person who registers something.

registrar /ˈrɛdʒɪstrɑː, ˌrɛdʒɪˈstrɑː/ ▸ **noun 1** an official responsible for keeping a register or official records: *the registrar of births and deaths*. ■ the chief administrative officer in a university. ■ (in the UK) the judicial and administrative officer of the High Court.
2 Brit. a middle-ranking hospital doctor undergoing training as a specialist.
– DERIVATIVES **registrarship** noun.
– ORIGIN late 17th cent.: from medieval Latin *registrarius*, from *registrum* (see **REGISTER**).

registrar general ▸ **noun** a government official responsible for holding a population census.

registrary /ˈrɛdʒɪstr(ə)ri/ ▸ **noun** (pl. **registraries**) the chief administrative officer of Cambridge University.

registration ▸ **noun 1** [mass noun] the action or process of registering or of being registered: *the registration of births, marriages, and deaths* | [count noun] *the number of new private car registrations has increased*. ■ [count noun] a certificate that attests to the registering of a person, car, etc. ■ the action or process of acquiring full British citizenship by a Commonwealth resident or a person of British descent.
2 (also **registration mark** or **registration number**) Brit. the series of letters and figures identifying a motor vehicle, assigned on registration and displayed on a number plate: *her car registration is H53 UVO*.
3 [mass noun] Music a combination of stops used when playing the organ.
– ORIGIN mid 16th cent.: from medieval Latin *registratio(n-)*, based on Latin *regerere* 'enter, record' (see **REGISTER**).

registration document (also **vehicle registration document**) ▸ **noun** (in the UK) a document giving registered information about a vehicle, such as the owner's name, the date of its manufacture, and the engine and chassis numbers.

registration plate ▸ **noun** Brit. another term for **NUMBER PLATE**.

registry ▸ **noun** (pl. **registries**) **1** a place where registers or records are kept. ■ an official list or register.
2 [mass noun] registration. ■ the nationality of a merchant ship: *converted trawlers of local registry*.

registry office ▸ **noun** another term for **REGISTER OFFICE** (in informal and non-official use).

Regius professor /ˈriːdʒɪəs/ ▸ **noun** (in the UK) the holder of a university chair founded by a sovereign (especially one at Oxford or Cambridge instituted by Henry VIII) or filled by Crown appointment.
– ORIGIN Latin *regius* 'royal', from *rex*, *reg-* 'king'.

reglaze ▸ **verb** [with obj.] glaze (a window) again.

reglet /ˈrɛglɪt/ ▸ **noun 1** Printing a thin strip of wood or metal used to separate type.
2 Architecture a narrow strip used to separate mouldings or panels from one another.
– ORIGIN mid 17th cent.: from French *réglet*, diminutive of *règle* 'rule'.

regnal /ˈrɛgn(ə)l/ ▸ **adjective** [attrib.] of a reign or monarch.
– ORIGIN early 17th cent.: from Anglo-Latin *regnalis*, from Latin *regnum* 'kingdom'.

regnal year ▸ **noun** a year reckoned from the date or anniversary of a sovereign's accession.

regnant /ˈrɛgnənt/ ▸ **adjective 1** [often postpositive] reigning; ruling: *a queen regnant*.
2 formal currently having the greatest influence; dominant: *the regnant belief*.
– ORIGIN early 17th cent.: from Latin *regnant-* 'reigning', from the verb *regnare*.

rego /ˈrɛdʒəʊ/ (also **reggo**) ▸ **noun** (pl. **regos**) Austral./NZ informal **1** a motor-vehicle registration: *no rego, one headlamp, baldy tyres*.
2 [mass noun] the action of registering, especially for an activity; registration: *footy rego day*.
– ORIGIN 1960s: abbreviation of **REGISTRATION** + the colloquial suffix **-o**.

regolith /ˈrɛgəlɪθ/ ▸ **noun** [mass noun] Geology the layer of unconsolidated solid material covering the bedrock of a planet.
– ORIGIN late 19th cent.: from Greek *rhēgos* 'rug, blanket' + **-LITH**.

regorge ▸ **verb** [with obj.] archaic bring up again; disgorge. ■ [no obj.] flow back again.
– ORIGIN early 17th cent.: from French *regorger*, or from **RE-** 'again' + the verb **GORGE**.

regrade ▸ **verb** [with obj.] (often as noun **regrading**) grade again or differently: *a demand for a regrading of pay levels*.

regress ▸ **verb** /rɪˈgrɛs/ **1** [no obj.] return to a former or less developed state: *they would not regress to pre-technological tribalism*. ■ return mentally to a former stage of life or a supposed previous life, especially through hypnosis: [no obj.] *she claims to be able to regress to the Roman era* | [with obj.] *I regressed Sylvia to early childhood*.
2 [with obj.] Statistics calculate the coefficient or coefficients of regression of (a variable) against or on another variable.
▸ **noun** /ˈriːgrɛs/ [mass noun] **1** the action of returning to a former or less developed state.
2 Philosophy a series of statements in which a logical procedure is continually reapplied to its own result without approaching a useful conclusion (e.g. defining something in terms of itself).
– ORIGIN late Middle English (as a noun): from Latin *regressus*, from *regredi* 'go back, return', from *re-* 'back' + *gradi* 'to walk'.

regression ▸ **noun** [mass noun] **1** a return to a former or less developed state: *it is easy to blame unrest on economic regression*. ■ a return to an earlier stage of life or a supposed previous life, especially through hypnosis. ■ a lessening of the severity of a disease or its symptoms: *there was 46.7 per cent complete regression in the placebo group*.
2 Statistics a measure of the relation between the mean value of one variable (e.g. output) and corresponding values of other variables (e.g. time and cost).

regressive ▸ **adjective 1** returning to a former or less developed state; characterized by regression: *regressive aspects of recent local government reform*. ■ relating to or marked by psychological regression.
2 (of a tax) taking a proportionally greater amount from those on lower incomes.
3 Philosophy proceeding from effect to cause or from particular to universal.
– DERIVATIVES **regressively** adverb, **regressiveness** noun.

regret ▸ **verb** (**regrets**, **regretting**, **regretted**) [with obj.] feel sad, repentant, or disappointed over (something that one has done or failed to do): *she immediately regretted her words* | [with clause] *I always regretted that I never trained*. ■ used in polite formulas to express apology for or sadness over something undesirable: *any inconvenience to readers is regretted* | [with clause] *we regret that no tickets may be exchanged*. ■ archaic feel sorrow for the loss or absence of (something pleasant): *my home, when shall I cease to regret you!*
▸ **noun** [mass noun] a feeling of sadness, repentance, or disappointment over an occurrence or something that one has done or failed to do: *she expressed her regret at Virginia's death* | *he had to decline, to his regret*. ■ (often **one's regrets**) used in polite formulas to express apology for or sadness at an occurrence or an inability to accept an invitation: *please give your grandmother my regrets*.
– ORIGIN late Middle English: from Old French *regreter* 'bewail (the dead)', perhaps from the Germanic base of **GREET[2]**.

regretful ▸ **adjective** feeling or showing regret: *he sounded regretful but pointed out that he had committed himself*.
– DERIVATIVES **regretfulness** noun.

regretfully ▸ **adverb** in a regretful manner. ■ [sentence adverb] it is regrettable that: *regretfully, mounting costs forced the branch to close*.

> **USAGE** The adjectives **regretful** and **regrettable** are distinct in meaning: **regretful** means 'feeling or showing regret', as in *she shook her head with a* ***regretful*** *smile*, while **regrettable** means 'giving rise to regret; undesirable', as in *the loss of jobs is* ***regrettable***. The adverbs **regretfully** and **regrettably** have not, however, preserved the same distinction. **Regretfully** is used as a normal adverb to mean 'in a regretful manner' (*he sighed* ***regretfully***), but it is also used as a sentence adverb meaning 'it is regrettable that' (***regretfully****, mounting costs forced the branch to close*). In this latter use it is synonymous with **regrettably**. Despite objections from traditionalists, this use is now well established and is included in most modern dictionaries without comment.

regrettable ▸ **adjective** (of conduct or an event) giving rise to regret; undesirable; unwelcome: *the loss of this number of jobs is regrettable* | *irresponsible and regrettable actions*.

regrettably ▸ **adverb** [sentence adverb] unfortunately (used to express apology for or sadness at something): *regrettably, last night's audience was a meagre one*.

> **USAGE** On the use of **regrettably** and **regretfully**, see **USAGE** at **REGRETFULLY**.

regroup ▸ **verb** reassemble or cause to reassemble into organized groups, typically after being attacked or defeated: [no obj.] *by November 1971 the opposition was regrouping* | [with obj.] *he regrouped his fighters in the hills*.
– DERIVATIVES **regroupment** noun.

regrow ▸ **verb** (past **regrew**; past participle **regrown**) grow or cause to grow again.
– DERIVATIVES **regrowth** noun.

regs ▸ **abbreviation** informal regulations.

Regt ▸ **abbreviation** Regiment.

regulable ▸ **adjective** able to be regulated.

regular ▸ **adjective 1** arranged in or constituting a constant or definite pattern, especially with the same space between individual instances: *plant the flags at regular intervals* | *a regular arrangement*. ■ (of a structure or arrangement) arranged in or constituting a symmetrical or harmonious pattern: *beautifully regular, heart-shaped leaves*. ■ Botany (of a flower) having radial symmetry.
2 recurring at short uniform intervals: *a regular monthly check* | *her breathing became more regular*. ■ done or happening frequently: *regular border clashes* | *parties were a fairly regular occurrence*. ■ doing the same thing often or at uniform intervals: *regular worshippers*. ■ defecating or menstruating at predictable times or intervals.
3 conforming to or governed by an accepted standard of procedure or convention: *policies carried on by his ministers through regular channels* | *a regular job*. ■ [attrib.] of or belonging to the permanent professional armed forces of a country: *a regular soldier*. ■ properly trained or qualified and pursuing a full-time occupation: *a strong distrust of regular doctors*. ■ Christian Church subject to or bound by religious rule; belonging to a religious or monastic order: *the regular clergy*. Contrasted with **SECULAR** (sense 2 of the adjective). ■ informal, dated rightly so called; complete; absolute (used for emphasis): *this place is a regular fisherman's paradise*.
4 used, done, or happening on a habitual basis; usual: *I couldn't get an appointment with my regular barber* | *the bar became one of his regular haunts*. ■ chiefly N. Amer. of a normal or ordinary kind: *egg pasta is richer than regular pasta*. ■ N. Amer. not pretentious or arrogant; ordinary and friendly: *he's a regular guy, not a glamour puss*. ■ denoting merchandise, especially food or clothing, of average or standard size: *a shake and regular fries*. ■ (in surfing and other board sports) with the left leg in front of the right on the board.

R

5 Grammar (of a word) following the normal pattern of inflection: *a regular verb*.
6 Geometry (of a figure) having all sides and all angles equal: *a regular polygon*. ■ (of a solid) bounded by a number of equal figures.
▸ **noun** a regular customer, member of a team, etc.: *pub regulars | the absence of four first-team regulars*. ■ a regular member of the armed forces. ■ Christian Church one of the regular clergy.
– PHRASES **keep regular hours** go to bed and get up at the same time each day.
– DERIVATIVES **regularly** adverb.
– ORIGIN late Middle English: from Old French *reguler*, from Latin *regularis*, from *regula* 'rule'.

regular canon ▸ **noun** see CANON².

regular expression ▸ **noun** Computing a sequence of symbols and characters expressing a string or pattern to be searched for within a longer piece of text.

regularity ▸ **noun** (pl. **regularities**) [mass noun] the state or quality of being regular: *he came to see her with increasing regularity* | [count noun] *the patterns and regularities of social life*.

regularize (also **regularise**) ▸ **verb** [with obj.] make (something) regular: *an electrical implant to regularize the heartbeat*. ■ establish (a hitherto temporary or provisional arrangement) on an official basis: *immigrants applying to regularize their status as residents*.
– DERIVATIVES **regularization** noun.

regulate ▸ **verb** [with obj.] control or maintain the rate or speed of (a machine or process) so that it operates properly: *a hormone which regulates metabolism*. ■ control (something, especially a business activity) by means of rules and regulations: *the Code regulates the takeovers of all public companies*. ■ set (a clock or other apparatus) according to an external standard.
– DERIVATIVES **regulative** adjective.
– ORIGIN late Middle English (in the sense 'control by rules'): from late Latin *regulat-* 'directed, regulated', from the verb *regulare*, from Latin *regula* 'rule'.

regulation ▸ **noun 1** a rule or directive made and maintained by an authority: *planning regulations*. ■ [as modifier] in accordance with regulations; of the correct type: *regulation army footwear*. ■ [as modifier] informal of a familiar or predictable type; formulaic: *a regulation Western parody*.
2 [mass noun] the action or process of regulating or being regulated: *the regulation of financial markets*.

regulator ▸ **noun** a person or thing that regulates something, in particular: ■ a person or body that supervises a particular industry or business activity. ■ a device for controlling the rate of working of machinery or for controlling fluid flow, in particular a handle controlling the supply of steam to the cylinders of a steam engine. ■ a device for adjusting the balance of a clock or watch in order to regulate its speed.

regulatory /ˈrɛgjʊlət(ə)ri, ˌrɛgjʊˈleɪt(ə)ri/ ▸ **adjective** serving or intended to regulate something: *the existing legal and regulatory framework*.

regulo /ˈrɛgjʊləʊ/ ▸ **noun** Brit. trademark used before a numeral to denote a setting on a temperature scale in a gas oven: *preheat the oven to 420° (regulo 7)*.

Regulus /ˈrɛgjʊləs/ Astronomy the brightest star in the constellation Leo. It is a triple system of which the primary is a hot dwarf star.
– ORIGIN Latin, literally 'little king'.

regulus /ˈrɛgjʊləs/ ▸ **noun** (pl. **reguluses** or **reguli** /-lʌɪ, -liː/) **1** Chemistry, archaic a metallic form of a substance, obtained by smelting or reduction.
2 a petty king or ruler.
– ORIGIN late 16th cent.: from Latin, diminutive of *rex, reg-* 'king'; originally in the phrase *regulus of antimony* (denoting metallic antimony), apparently so named because of its readiness to combine with gold.

regurgitate /rɪˈgəːdʒɪteɪt/ ▸ **verb** [with obj.] bring (swallowed food) up again to the mouth: *gulls regurgitate food for the chicks*. ■ repeat (information) without analysing or comprehending it: *facts which can then be regurgitated at examinations*.
– DERIVATIVES **regurgitation** noun.
– ORIGIN late 16th cent.: from medieval Latin *regurgitat-*, from the verb *regurgitare*, from Latin *re-* 'again, back' + *gurges, gurgit-* 'whirlpool'.

rehab /ˈriːhab/ informal ▸ **noun 1** [mass noun] a course of treatment for drug or alcohol dependence, typically at a residential facility: *the star has been in rehab for a week*.
2 US a building that has been rehabilitated or restored.
▸ **verb** (**rehabs, rehabbing, rehabbed**) [with obj.] N. Amer. rehabilitate or restore: *they don't rehab you at all in jail* | (as adj. **rehabbed**) *newly rehabbed apartments for rent*.
– ORIGIN 1940s: abbreviation of REHABILITATE and REHABILITATION.

rehabilitate ▸ **verb** [with obj.] restore (someone) to health or normal life by training and therapy after imprisonment, addiction, or illness: *helping to rehabilitate former criminals*. ■ restore (someone) to former privileges or reputation after a period of disfavour: *with the fall of the government many former dissidents were rehabilitated*. ■ return (something, especially a building or environmental feature) to its former condition.
– DERIVATIVES **rehabilitation** noun, **rehabilitative** adjective.
– ORIGIN late 16th cent. (earlier (late 15th cent.) as *rehabilitation*) (in the sense 'restore to former privileges'): from medieval Latin *rehabilitat-*, from the verb *rehabilitare* (see RE-, HABILITATE).

rehang ▸ **verb** /riːˈhaŋ/ (past and past participle **rehung**) [with obj.] hang (something) again or differently.
▸ **noun** /ˈriːhaŋ/ an act of rehanging works of art in a gallery.

rehash ▸ **verb** [with obj.] reuse (old ideas or material) without significant change or improvement: *he endlessly rehashes songs from his American era*. ■ chiefly N. Amer. consider or discuss (something) at length after it has happened: *is it really necessary to rehash that trauma all over again?*
▸ **noun** a reuse of old ideas or material without significant change or improvement.

rehear ▸ **verb** (past and past participle **reheard**) hear or listen to again. ■ Law hear (a case or plaintiff) in a court again: (as noun **rehearing**) *the parents produced fresh evidence and won a rehearing*.

rehearsal ▸ **noun** a practice or trial performance of a play or other work for later public performance: ***rehearsals for*** *the opera season*. ■ [mass noun] the action or process of rehearsing: *I've had a fortnight* ***in rehearsal***.

rehearse ▸ **verb** [with obj.] **1** practise (a play, piece of music, or other work) for later public performance: *we were rehearsing a radio play* | [no obj.] *she was* ***rehearsing for*** *her world tour*. ■ supervise (a performer or group) during a rehearsal: *he listened to Charlie rehearsing the band*. ■ mentally prepare or recite (words one intends to say): *he had rehearsed a thousand fine phrases*.
2 state (a list of points that have been made many times before): *criticisms of factory farming have been rehearsed often enough*.
– DERIVATIVES **rehearser** noun.
– ORIGIN Middle English (in the sense 'repeat aloud'): from Old French *rehercier*, perhaps from *re-* 'again' + *hercer* 'to harrow', from *herse* 'harrow' (see HEARSE).

reheat ▸ **verb** [with obj.] heat (something, especially cooked food) again.
▸ **noun** [mass noun] the process of using the hot exhaust to burn extra fuel in a jet engine and produce extra power. ■ [count noun] an afterburner.

reheel ▸ **verb** [with obj.] fit (a shoe) with a new heel.

rehire ▸ **verb** [with obj.] hire (a former employee) again: *the company dismissed its workers and rehired them on a lower rate*.

Rehoboam /ˌriːəˈbəʊəm/, son of Solomon, king of ancient Israel *c.*930–*c.*915 BC. His reign witnessed the secession of the northern tribes and their establishment of a new kingdom under Jeroboam, leaving Rehoboam as the first king of Judah (1 Kings 11–14).

rehoboam ▸ **noun** a wine bottle of about six times the standard size.
– ORIGIN late 19th cent.: from the name REHOBOAM.

rehome ▸ **verb** [with obj.] find a new home for (a pet).

rehouse ▸ **verb** [with obj.] provide (someone) with new housing: *tenants will be rehoused in hotels until their homes are habitable*.

rehung past and past participle of REHANG.

rehydrate ▸ **verb** absorb or cause to absorb moisture after dehydration: [no obj.] *cubes of dried food which rehydrated in the mouth*.
– DERIVATIVES **rehydratable** adjective, **rehydration** noun.

Reich¹ /rʌɪk, -x/, German /raɪç/ the former German state, most often used to refer to the Third Reich, the Nazi regime from 1933 to 1945. The **First Reich** was considered to be the Holy Roman Empire, 962–1806, and the **Second Reich** the German Empire, 1871–1918, but neither of these terms is part of normal historical terminology.
– ORIGIN German, literally 'empire'.

Reich² /rʌɪx/, Steve (b.1936), American composer; full name *Stephen Michael Reich*. A leading minimalist, he uses the repetition of short phrases within a simple harmonic field. Influences include Balinese and West African music.

Reichstag /ˈrʌɪxsˌtɑːg, ˈrʌɪks-/ the main legislature of the German state under the Second and Third Reichs. ■ the building in which the main German legislature met, badly damaged by fire on the Nazi accession to power in 1933.
– ORIGIN German, from *Reichs* 'of the empire' + *Tag* 'diet' (see DIET²).

reify /ˈriːɪfʌɪ, ˈreɪɪ-/ ▸ **verb** (**reifies, reifying, reified**) [with obj.] formal make (something abstract) more concrete or real: *these instincts are, in man, reified as verbal constructs*.
– DERIVATIVES **reification** noun, **reificatory** adjective.
– ORIGIN mid 19th cent.: from Latin *res, re-* 'thing' + -FY.

reign ▸ **verb** [no obj.] hold royal office; rule as monarch: *Queen Elizabeth* ***reigns over*** *the UK*. ■ be the best or most important in a particular area or domain: *in America, baseball* ***reigns supreme***. ■ (of a quality or condition) be the dominant feature of a situation or place: *confusion reigned*.
▸ **noun** the period of rule of a monarch: *the original chapel was built in the reign of Charles I*. ■ the period during which someone or something is predominant or pre-eminent: *she was hoping for a long reign as world champion*.
– ORIGIN Middle English: from Old French *reignier* 'to reign', *reigne* 'kingdom', from Latin *regnum*, related to *rex, reg-* 'king'.

USAGE The correct idiomatic phrase is a **free rein**, not a **free reign**; see USAGE at REIN.

reigning ▸ **adjective** occupying the throne; ruling: *the official residence of the reigning monarch*. ■ currently holding a particular sporting title: *the reigning European champions*.

reignite ▸ **verb** ignite or cause to ignite again: [no obj.] *oven burners automatically reignite if blown out*.

reign of terror ▸ **noun** a period of remorseless repression or bloodshed, in particular (**Reign of Terror**) the period of the Terror during the French Revolution.

reiki /ˈreɪki/ ▸ **noun** [mass noun] a healing technique based on the principle that the therapist can channel energy into the patient by means of touch, to activate the natural healing processes of the patient's body and restore physical and emotional well-being.
– ORIGIN Japanese, literally 'universal life energy'.

reimagine ▸ **verb** [with obj.] reinterpret (an event, work of art, etc.) imaginatively.

reimburse /ˌriːɪmˈbəːs/ ▸ **verb** [with obj.] repay (a person who has spent or lost money): *the investors should be reimbursed for their losses*. ■ repay (a sum of money that has been spent or lost): *your expenses will be reimbursed*.
– DERIVATIVES **reimbursable** adjective, **reimbursement** noun.
– ORIGIN early 17th cent.: from RE- 'back, again' + obsolete *imburse* 'put in a purse', from medieval Latin *imbursare*, from *in-* 'into' + late Latin *bursa* 'purse'.

reimport ▸ **verb** [with obj.] import (goods processed or made from exported materials).
▸ **noun** [mass noun] the action of reimporting something. ■ [count noun] a reimported item.
– DERIVATIVES **reimportation** noun.

reimpose ▸ **verb** [with obj.] impose (something, especially a law or regulation) again after a lapse.
– DERIVATIVES **reimposition** noun.

Reims /riːmz/, French /rɛ̃s/ (also **Rheims**) a city of northern France, chief town of Champagne-Ardenne region; pop. 188,078 (2006). It was the traditional coronation place of most French kings and is noted for its fine 13th-century Gothic cathedral.

rein ▸ **noun** (usu. **reins**) a long, narrow strap attached at one end to a horse's bit, typically used in pairs to guide or check a horse in riding or driving. ■ Brit. a pair of straps used to restrain a young child. ■ the power to direct and control: *a new chairperson will soon take over the reins*.
▸ **verb** [with obj. and adverbial] check or guide (a horse) by pulling on its reins: *he reined in his horse and waited*. ■ keep under control; restrain: *with an effort, she*

R

reined back her impatience | the government had failed to rein in public spending.

– PHRASES **draw rein** Brit. stop one's horse. **(a) free rein** freedom of action or expression: *he was given free rein to work out his designs.* **keep a tight rein on** exercise strict control over: *her only chance of survival was to keep a tight rein on her feelings.*

– ORIGIN Middle English: from Old French *rene*, based on Latin *retinere* 'retain'.

> **USAGE** The idiomatic phrase **a free rein**, which derives from the literal meaning of using reins to control a horse, is sometimes misinterpreted and written as **a free reign**. More than a third of the citations for the phrase in the Oxford English Corpus use **reign** instead of **rein**.

reincarnate ▶ verb /ˌriːɪnˈkɑːneɪt/ [with obj.] cause (someone) to undergo rebirth in another body: *a man may be reincarnated in animal form* | (as adj. **reincarnated**) *a reincarnated soul.* ■ [no obj.] be reborn in another body: *they were afraid she would reincarnate as a vampire.*

▶ adjective /ˌriːɪnˈkɑːnət/ [usu. postpositive] reborn in another body: *he claims that the girl is his dead daughter reincarnate.*

reincarnation ▶ noun [mass noun] the rebirth of a soul in another body. ■ [count noun] a person or animal in whom a particular soul is believed to have been reborn: *he believed he was the* ***reincarnation of*** *Louis XVI.* ■ [count noun] a new version of something from the past: *the latest reincarnation of the hippie look.*

reincorporate ▶ verb [with obj.] make (something) a part of something else once more: *a campaign to reincorporate the visual arts into religious devotion.*

– DERIVATIVES **reincorporation** noun.

reindeer ▶ noun (pl. **same** or **reindeers**) a deer of the tundra and subarctic regions of Eurasia and North America, both sexes of which have large branching antlers. Most Eurasian reindeer are domesticated and used for drawing sledges and as a source of milk, flesh, and hide. Called **CARIBOU** in North America.

● *Rangifer tarandus*, family Cervidae.

– ORIGIN late Middle English: from Old Norse *hreindýri*, from *hreinn* 'reindeer' + *dýr* 'deer'.

reindeer moss ▶ noun a large branching bluish-grey lichen which grows in arctic and subarctic regions, sometimes providing the chief winter food of reindeer. ● *Cladonia rangiferina*, order Cladoniales.

reindustrialize (also **reindustrialise**) ▶ verb [with obj.] revitalize or modernize the industry of (a country or area).

– DERIVATIVES **reindustrialization** noun.

reinfect ▶ verb [with obj.] cause to become infected again.

– DERIVATIVES **reinfection** noun.

reinflate ▶ verb [with obj.] **1** fill (something, especially a tyre) with air or gas again.

2 cause inflation of (a currency) or in (an economy) again.

– DERIVATIVES **reinflation** noun.

R

reinforce ▶ verb [with obj.] strengthen or support (an object or substance), especially with additional material: *the helmet has been reinforced with a double layer of cork.* ■ strengthen (an existing feeling, idea, or habit): *the next few months reinforced my opinion of Vince as a man of his word.* ■ strengthen (a military force) with additional personnel or equipment.

– DERIVATIVES **reinforcer** noun.

– ORIGIN late Middle English: from French *renforcer*, influenced by *inforce*, an obsolete spelling of **ENFORCE**; the sense of providing military support is probably from Italian *rinforzare*.

reinforced concrete ▶ noun [mass noun] concrete in which metal bars or wire is embedded to increase its tensile strength.

reinforcement ▶ noun [mass noun] the action or process of reinforcing or strengthening. ■ the process of encouraging or establishing a belief or pattern of behaviour. ■ (**reinforcements**) extra personnel sent to increase the strength of an army or similar force: *a small force would hold the position until reinforcements could be sent.* ■ the strengthening structure or material employed in reinforced concrete or plastic.

reinhabit ▶ verb [with obj.] inhabit (a place) again.

Reinhardt[1] /ˈrʌɪnhɑːt/, Django (1910–53), Belgian jazz guitarist; born *Jean Baptiste Reinhardt*. He became famous in Paris in the 1930s for his improvisational style, blending swing with influences from his Gypsy background. In 1934, together with violinist Stephane Grappelli, he formed the Quintette du Hot Club de France.

Reinhardt[2] /ˈrʌɪnhɑːt/, Max (1873–1943), Austrian director and impresario; born *Max Goldmann*. He produced large-scale versions of such works as Sophocles' *Oedipus Rex* (1910), and helped establish the Salzburg Festival, with Richard Strauss and Hugo von Hofmannsthal.

reinsert ▶ verb [with obj.] place (something) back into its previous position.

– DERIVATIVES **reinsertion** noun.

reinstall (also **reinstal**) ▶ verb (**reinstalls** or **reinstals**, **reinstalling**, **reinstalled**) [with obj.] **1** place or fix (equipment or machinery) in position again. ■ install (computer software) again: *I reinstalled the program.*

2 place (someone) in a position of authority again; reinstate.

▶ noun an act of reinstalling something, especially software.

– DERIVATIVES **reinstallation** noun.

reinstate ▶ verb [with obj.] restore (someone or something) to their former position or state: *the union threatened strike action if Owen was not reinstated.*

reinstatement ▶ noun [mass noun] the action of giving someone back a position they have lost: *the student body gave its support to the two expelled students and demanded their reinstatement.* ■ the restoration of something such as a law or custom: *others have demanded the reinstatement of the death penalty.*

reinstitute ▶ verb [with obj.] institute or introduce again: *by reinstituting conscription they could alienate a new generation of American youth.*

– DERIVATIVES **reinstitution** noun.

reinsure ▶ verb [with obj.] (of an insurer) transfer (all or part of a risk) to another insurer to provide protection against the risk of the first insurance.

– DERIVATIVES **reinsurance** noun, **reinsurer** noun.

reintegrate ▶ verb [with obj.] restore (elements regarded as disparate) to unity. ■ integrate (someone) back into society: *it can be difficult for an offender to be reintegrated into the community.*

– DERIVATIVES **reintegration** noun.

reinter ▶ verb [with obj.] bury (a corpse) again, often in a different place to that of the first burial.

– DERIVATIVES **reinterment** noun.

reinterpret ▶ verb (**reinterprets**, **reinterpreting**, **reinterpreted**) [with obj.] interpret (something) in a new or different light.

– DERIVATIVES **reinterpretation** noun.

reintroduce ▶ verb [with obj.] bring (something, especially a law or system) into existence or effect again: *thirty-six states have reintroduced the death penalty.* ■ put (a species of animal or plant) back into a former habitat: *a scheme to reintroduce wolves to Yellowstone National Park.*

– DERIVATIVES **reintroduction** noun.

reinvade ▶ verb [with obj.] invade (something, especially a country or region) again.

– DERIVATIVES **reinvasion** noun.

reinvent ▶ verb [with obj.] change (something) so much that it appears to be entirely new: *he brought opera to the masses and reinvented the waltz.* ■ (**reinvent oneself**) take up a radically new job or way of life: *the actor wants to reinvent himself as an independent movie mogul.*

– PHRASES **reinvent the wheel** waste a great deal of time or effort in creating something that already exists.

– DERIVATIVES **reinvention** noun.

reinvest ▶ verb [with obj.] put (the profit on a previous investment) back into the same scheme.

– DERIVATIVES **reinvestment** noun.

reinvestigate ▶ verb [with obj.] investigate (a matter) again: *detectives made the decision to reinvestigate the case.*

– DERIVATIVES **reinvestigation** noun.

reinvigorate ▶ verb [with obj.] give new energy or strength to: *we are fully committed to reinvigorating the economy of the area.*

– DERIVATIVES **reinvigoration** noun.

reishi /ˈreɪʃi/ ▶ noun a mushroom with a shiny cap which typically grows on dead or dying timber, found in Asia and North America. Preparations made from it are credited with various stimulant and health-giving properties. ● *Ganoderma lucidum*, family Ganodermaceae, class Hymenomycetes.

– ORIGIN Japanese.

reissue ▶ verb (**reissues**, **reissuing**, **reissued**) [with obj.] make a new supply or different form of (a product, especially a book or record) available for sale: *the book was reissued with a new epilogue.*

▶ noun a new issue of a product.

reiterate ▶ verb [reporting verb] say something again or a number of times, typically for emphasis or clarity: [with clause] *she reiterated that the government would remain steadfast in its support* | [with direct speech] *'I just want to forget it all,' he reiterated* | [with obj.] *he reiterated the points made in his earlier speech.*

– DERIVATIVES **reiteration** noun, **reiterative** adjective.

– ORIGIN late Middle English (in the sense 'do an action repeatedly'): from Latin *reiterat-* 'gone over again', from the verb *reiterare*, from *re-* 'again' + *iterare* 'do a second time'.

Reiter's syndrome /ˈrʌɪtəz/ (also **Reiter's disease**) ▶ noun [mass noun] a medical condition typically affecting young men, characterized by arthritis, conjunctivitis, and urethritis, and caused by an unknown pathogen, possibly a chlamydia.

– ORIGIN 1920s: named after Hans *Reiter* (1881–1969), German bacteriologist.

Reith /riːθ/, John (Charles Walsham), 1st Baron (1889–1971), Scottish administrator and politician, first general manager (1922–7) and first director general (1927–38) of the BBC. He played a major part in the growth of the BBC and championed the moral and intellectual role of broadcasting in the community.

reive /riːv/ ▶ verb [no obj.] (usu. as noun **reiving**) chiefly Scottish another term for **REAVE**.

– DERIVATIVES **reiver** noun.

– ORIGIN Middle English: variant of **REAVE**; the usual spelling when referring to the historical practice of cattle-raiding on the Scottish Borders.

reject ▶ verb /rɪˈdʒɛkt/ [with obj.] dismiss as inadequate, unacceptable, or faulty: *union negotiators rejected a 1.5 per cent pay award | these explanations of criminal behaviour have been rejected by sociologists.* ■ refuse to agree to (a request): *an application to hold a pop concert at the club was rejected.* ■ fail to show due affection or concern for (someone); rebuff: *she didn't want him to feel he had been rejected after his sister was born.* ■ Medicine show an immune response to (a transplanted organ or tissue) so that it fails to survive.

▶ noun /ˈriːdʒɛkt/ a person or thing dismissed as inadequate or unacceptable: *some of the team's rejects have gone on to prove themselves in championships.* ■ an item sold cheaply because of minor flaws: [as modifier] *reject china plates.*

– DERIVATIVES **rejectable** adjective, **rejective** adjective (rare), **rejector** noun.

– ORIGIN late Middle English: from Latin *reject-* 'thrown back', from the verb *reicere*, from *re-* 'back' + *jacere* 'to throw'.

rejection ▶ noun [mass noun] the dismissing or refusing of a proposal, idea, etc.: *the Union decided last night to recommend rejection of the offer.* ■ the action of spurning a person's affections: *some people are reluctant to try it, because they fear rejection.*

rejectionist ▶ noun [often as modifier] a person who rejects a proposed policy, especially an Arab who refuses to accept a negotiated peace with Israel.

rejection slip ▶ noun a formal notice sent by an editor or publisher to an author with a rejected manuscript or typescript.

rejig Brit. ▶ verb (**rejigs**, **rejigging**, **rejigged**) [with obj.] **1** organize (something) differently; rearrange: *the organizers scrambled frantically to rejig schedules.*

2 dated re-equip with machinery; refit.

▶ noun a reorganization: *a cabinet rejig.*

rejigger ▶ verb US term for **REJIG** (sense 1 of the verb).

rejoice ▶ verb [no obj.] feel or show great joy or delight: *we spent the evening* ***rejoicing at*** *our victory | he* ***rejoiced in*** *her spontaneity.* ■ (**rejoice in**) Brit. used ironically to draw attention to a strange characteristic, especially a name: *the guard rejoiced in the name of Blossom.* ■ [with obj.] archaic cause joy to: *I love to rejoice their poor Hearts at this season.*

– ORIGIN Middle English (in the sense 'cause joy to'): from Old French *rejoiss-*, lengthened stem of *rejoir*, from *re-* (expressing intensive force) + *joir* 'experience joy'.

rejoicing ▶ noun [mass noun] great joy; jubilation: *the ban was lifted in 1990 amid general rejoicing.*

– DERIVATIVES **rejoicingly** adverb.

rejoin[1] ▸ verb [with obj.] join together again; reunite: *the stone had been cracked and crudely rejoined.* ▪ return to (a companion, organization, or route that one has left): *the soldiers were returning from leave to rejoin their unit.*

rejoin[2] ▸ verb [reporting verb] say something in reply, typically in a quick or critical manner: [with direct speech] *'It's nice to talk under the stars.' 'No stars tonight,' he rejoined.*
– ORIGIN late Middle English (in the sense 'reply to a charge in a lawsuit'): from Old French *rejoindre*, from *re-* 'again' + *joindre* 'to join'.

rejoinder ▸ noun a reply, especially a sharp or witty one: *she would have made some cutting rejoinder but none came to mind.* ▪ Law, dated a defendant's answer to the plaintiff's reply or replication.
– ORIGIN late Middle English: from Anglo-Norman French *rejoindre* (infinitive used as a noun) (see REJOIN[2]).

rejuvenate /rɪˈdʒuːvəneɪt/ ▸ verb [with obj.] make (someone or something) look or feel better, younger, or more vital: *a bid to rejuvenate the town centre* | (as adj. **rejuvenating**) *the rejuvenating effects of therapeutic clay.* ▪ (often as adj. **rejuvenated**) restore (a river or stream) to a condition characteristic of a younger landscape.
– DERIVATIVES **rejuvenation** noun, **rejuvenator** noun.
– ORIGIN early 19th cent.: from RE- 'again' + Latin *juvenis* 'young' + -ATE[3], suggested by French *rajeunir*.

rejuvenescence /rɪˌdʒuːvəˈnɛsəns/ ▸ noun [mass noun] the renewal of youth or vitality. ▪ Biology the reactivation of vegetative cells, resulting in regrowth from old or injured parts.
– ORIGIN mid 17th cent.: from late Latin *rejuvenescere* (from Latin *re-* 'again' + *juvenis* 'young') + -ENCE.

rekey ▸ verb (**rekeys, rekeying, rekeyed**) [with obj.] chiefly Computing enter (text or other data) again using a keyboard.

rekindle ▸ verb [with obj.] relight (a fire). ▪ revive (something lost or lapsed): *he tried to rekindle their friendship.*

-rel ▸ suffix forming nouns with diminutive or derogatory force such as *cockerel, scoundrel.*
– ORIGIN from Old French *-erel(le)*.

relabel ▸ verb (**relabels, relabelling, relabelled**; US **relabels, relabeling, relabeled**) [with obj.] label (something) again or differently.

relaid past and past participle of RELAY[2].

relapse /rɪˈlaps/ ▸ verb [no obj.] (of a sick or injured person) deteriorate after a period of improvement. ▪ (**relapse into**) return to (a less active or a worse state): *he relapsed into silence.*
▸ noun also /ˈriːlaps/ a deterioration in someone's state of health after a temporary improvement: *he responded well to treatment, but then suffered a relapse.*
– DERIVATIVES **relapser** noun.
– ORIGIN late Middle English: from Latin *relaps-* 'slipped back', from the verb *relabi*, from *re-* 'back' + *labi* 'to slip'. Early senses referred to a return to heresy or wrongdoing.

relapsing fever ▸ noun [mass noun] an infectious bacterial disease marked by recurrent fever. • The disease is caused by spirochaetes of the genus *Borrelia*.

relatable ▸ adjective **1** able to be related to something else: *the growth of the welfare state will be clearly relatable to the growth of democracy.*
2 enabling a person to feel that they can relate to someone or something: *Mary-Kate's problems make her more relatable.*
DERIVATIVES **relatability** noun.

relate ▸ verb [with obj.] **1** make or show a connection between: *the study examines social change within the city and **relates** it **to** developments in the country as a whole* | *a supercomputer could relate all those factors.* ▪ (**be related**) be causally connected: *high unemployment is **related to** high crime rates.* ▪ (**be related**) be connected by blood or marriage: *he was **related to** my mother* | *people who are distantly related.* ▪ [no obj.] (**relate to**) have reference to; concern: *the new legislation related to corporate activities.*
2 [no obj.] (**relate to**) feel sympathy for or identify with: *kids related to him because he was so rebellious.*
3 give an account of; narrate: *various versions of the story have been related by the locals.*
– ORIGIN mid 16th cent.: from Latin *relat-* 'brought back', from the verb *referre* (see REFER).

related ▸ adjective belonging to the same family, group, or type; connected: *sleeping sickness and related diseases.* ▪ [in combination] associated with the specified item or process, especially causally: *income-related benefits.*
– DERIVATIVES **relatedness** noun.

relater (also **relator**) ▸ noun a person who tells a story; a narrator.

relation ▸ noun **1** the way in which two or more people or things are connected; a thing's effect on or relevance to another: *questions about the **relation between** writing and reality* | *the size of the targets **bore no relation to** their importance.* ▪ (**relations**) the way in which two or more people or groups feel about and behave towards each other: *the improvement in relations between the two countries* | *the meetings helped cement Anglo-American relations.* ▪ (**relations**) formal sexual intercourse: *did you always have good, healthy relations with your wife?*
2 a person who is connected by blood or marriage; a relative: *he has no close relations.*
3 [mass noun] the action of telling a story.
– PHRASES **in relation to** in the context of; in connection with: *there is an ambiguity in the provisions in relation to children's hearings.*
– ORIGIN Middle English: from Old French, or from Latin *relatio(n-)*, from *referre* 'bring back' (see RELATE).

relational ▸ adjective concerning the way in which two or more people or things are connected: *there was no relational link between the killer and his victim.*
– DERIVATIVES **relationally** adverb.

relational database ▸ noun Computing a database structured to recognize relations between stored items of information.

relationship ▸ noun the way in which two or more people or things are connected, or the state of being connected: *the study will assess the **relationship between** unemployment and political attitudes.* ▪ the state of being connected by blood or marriage: *they can trace their relationship to a common ancestor.* ▪ the way in which two or more people or groups regard and behave towards each other: *the landlord–tenant relationship* | *she was proud of her good relationship with the staff.* ▪ an emotional and sexual association between two people: *she has a daughter from a previous relationship.*

relative /ˈrɛlətɪv/ ▸ adjective **1** considered in relation or in proportion to something else: *the relative effectiveness of the various mechanisms is not known.* ▪ existing or possessing a specified characteristic only in comparison to something else; not absolute: *she went down the steps into the relative darkness of the dining room* | *the firms are relative newcomers to computers.*
2 Grammar denoting a pronoun, determiner, or adverb that refers to an expressed or implied antecedent and attaches a subordinate clause to it, e.g. *which, who.* ▪ (of a clause) attached to an antecedent by a relative word.
3 Music (of major and minor keys) having the same key signature.
4 (of a service rank) corresponding in grade to another in a different service.
▸ noun **1** a person connected by blood or marriage: *much of my time is spent visiting relatives.* ▪ a species related to another by common origin: *the plant is a relative of ivy.*
2 Grammar a relative pronoun, determiner, or adverb.
3 Philosophy a term or concept which is dependent on something else.
– PHRASES **relative to 1** in comparison with: *the figures suggest that girls are underachieving relative to boys.* ▪ in terms of a connection to: *we must consider the location of the hospital relative to its catchment area.* **2** about; concerning.
– ORIGIN late Middle English: from Old French *relatif, -ive*, from late Latin *relativus* 'having reference or relation' (see RELATE).

relative atomic mass ▸ noun Chemistry the ratio of the average mass of one atom of an element to one twelfth of the mass of an atom of carbon-12.

relative density ▸ noun Chemistry the ratio of the density of a substance to the density of a standard, usually water for a liquid or solid, and air for a gas.

relative humidity ▸ noun the amount of water vapour present in air expressed as a percentage of the amount needed for saturation at the same temperature.

relatively ▸ adverb [sentence adverb] in relation, comparison, or proportion to something else: *they were very poor, but, **relatively speaking**, they had been lucky.* ▪ [as submodifier] regarded in comparison with something else rather than absolutely; quite: *the site was cheap and relatively clean.*

relative molecular mass ▸ noun Chemistry the ratio of the average mass of one molecule of an element or compound to one twelfth of the mass of an atom of carbon-12.

relativism /ˈrɛlətɪvɪz(ə)m/ ▸ noun [mass noun] the doctrine that knowledge, truth, and morality exist in relation to culture, society, or historical context, and are not absolute.
– DERIVATIVES **relativist** noun.

relativistic ▸ adjective Physics accurately described only by the theory of relativity.
– DERIVATIVES **relativistically** adverb.

relativity ▸ noun [mass noun] **1** the absence of standards of absolute and universal application: *moral relativity.*
2 Physics the dependence of various physical phenomena on relative motion of the observer and the observed objects, especially regarding the nature and behaviour of light, space, time, and gravity.

> The concept of relativity was set out in Einstein's **special theory of relativity**, published in 1905. This states that all motion is relative and that the velocity of light in a vacuum has a constant value which nothing can exceed. Among its consequences are the following: the mass of a body increases and its length (in the direction of motion) shortens as its speed increases; the time interval between two events occurring in a moving body appears greater to a stationary observer; and mass and energy are equivalent and interconvertible. Einstein's **general theory of relativity**, published in 1915, extended the theory to accelerated motion and gravitation, which was treated as a curvature of the space–time continuum. It predicted that light rays would be deflected, and shifted in wavelength, when passing through a substantial gravitational field, effects which have been experimentally confirmed.

relativize (also **relativise**) ▸ verb [with obj.] chiefly Linguistics & Philosophy make or treat as relative to or dependent on something else. ▪ Physics treat (a phenomenon or concept) according to the principles of the theory of relativity.
– DERIVATIVES **relativization** noun.

relator ▸ noun **1** Law a person who brings a public lawsuit, typically in the name of the Attorney General, regarding the abuse of an office or franchise.
2 variant spelling of RELATER.

relaunch ▸ verb [with obj.] launch (something, especially a product) again or in a different form: *he relaunched the paper as a tabloid.*
▸ noun an instance of relaunching a product.

relax ▸ verb **1** make or become less tense or anxious: [no obj.] *he relaxed and smiled confidently* | (as adj. **relaxing**) *a relaxing holiday.* ▪ [no obj.] rest from work or engage in an enjoyable activity so as to become less tired or anxious: *the team relax with a lot of skiing.* ▪ [with obj.] cause (a limb or muscle) to become less rigid: *relax the leg by bringing the knee towards the chest.* ▪ [with obj.] make (something) less firm or tight: *Cicely relaxed her hold.* ▪ [with obj.] straighten or partially uncurl (hair) using a chemical product.
2 [with obj.] make (a rule or restriction) less strict: *the ministry relaxed some of the restrictions.*
– DERIVATIVES **relaxer** noun.
– ORIGIN late Middle English: from Latin *relaxare*, from *re-* (expressing intensive force) + *laxus* 'lax, loose'.

relaxant ▸ noun a drug used to promote relaxation or reduce tension: *a muscle relaxant.* ▪ a thing having a relaxing effect: *sex can be a great relaxant.*
▸ adjective causing relaxation.

relaxation ▸ noun [mass noun] **1** the state of being free from tension and anxiety. ▪ recreation or rest, especially after a period of work: *his favourite form of relaxation was reading detective novels.* ▪ the loss of tension in a part of the body, especially in a muscle when it ceases to contract.
2 the action of making a rule or restriction less strict: *relaxation of censorship rules.*
3 Physics the restoration of equilibrium following disturbance.

relaxation oscillator ▸ noun Electronics an oscillator in which sharp, sometimes aperiodic oscillations result from the rapid discharge of a capacitor or inductance.

relaxed ▸ adjective free from tension and anxiety: *we were having a great time and feeling very relaxed* | *the relaxed atmosphere of the hotel.* ▪ (of a muscle or other body part) not tense.
– DERIVATIVES **relaxedly** adverb, **relaxedness** noun.

R

relaxin /rɪˈlaksɪn/ ▶ **noun** [mass noun] Biochemistry a hormone secreted by the placenta that causes the cervix to dilate and prepares the uterus for the action of oxytocin during labour.

relay¹ /ˈriːleɪ/ ▶ **noun 1** a group of people or animals engaged in a task or activity for a period of time and then replaced by a similar group: *the wagons were pulled by relays of horses | gangs of workers were sent **in relays**.* ■ [usu. as modifier] a race between teams of runners, each team member in turn covering part of the total distance: *a 550-metre relay race.*
2 an electrical device, typically incorporating an electromagnet, which is activated by a current or signal in one circuit to open or close another circuit.
3 a device to receive, reinforce, and retransmit a radio or television signal. ■ a signal or broadcast transmitted by a relay: *a relay of a performance live from the concert hall.*
▶ **verb** also /rɪˈleɪ/ [with obj.] receive and pass on (information or a message): *she intended to relay everything she had learned.* ■ broadcast (something) by passing signals received from elsewhere through a transmitting station: *the speech was relayed live from the palace.*
– ORIGIN late Middle English (referring to the provision of fresh hounds on the track of a deer): from Old French *relai* (noun), *relayer* (verb), based on Latin *laxare* 'slacken'.

relay² /riːˈleɪ/ ▶ **verb** (past and past participle **relaid**) [with obj.] lay again or differently: *they plan to relay about half a mile of the track.*

relearn ▶ **verb** (past and past participle **relearned** or chiefly Brit. **relearnt**) [with obj.] learn (something) again: *I've been relearning my Latin and Greek.*

release ▶ **verb** [with obj.] **1** allow or enable to escape from confinement; set free: *the government announced that the prisoners would be released.*
2 allow (something) to move, act, or flow freely: *she released his arm and pushed him aside | growth hormone is released into the blood during sleep.* ■ remove restrictions or obligations from (someone or something) so that they become available for other activity: *the strategy would release forces for service in other areas.* ■ remove (part of a machine or appliance) from a fixed position, allowing something else to move or function: *he released the handbrake.* ■ allow (something) to return to its resting position by ceasing to put pressure on it: *press the cap down and release.*
3 allow (information) to be generally available: *no details about the talks were released.* ■ make (a film, recording, or other product) available to the public: *they released a flurry of great singles.*
4 Law remit or discharge (a debt). ■ surrender (a right). ■ make over (property or money) to another.
▶ **noun** [mass noun] **1** the action or process of releasing or being released: *a campaign by the prisoner's mother resulted in his release.* ■ [count noun] a handle or catch that releases part of a mechanism.
2 the action of making a film, recording, or other product available to the public: *the movie will be **on release** from Christmas.* ■ [count noun] a film or other product made available to the public: *his current album release has topped the charts for six months.*
3 Law the action of releasing property, money, or a right to another. ■ [count noun] a document effecting a release of property, money, etc.
– DERIVATIVES **releasable** adjective, **releasee** noun (Law), **releaser** noun, **releasor** noun (Law).
– ORIGIN Middle English: from Old French *reles* (noun), *relesser* (verb), from Latin *relaxare* 'stretch out again, slacken' (see RELAX).

release agent ▶ **noun** a substance applied to a surface, typically the surface of a mould or container, to prevent other substances from sticking to it.

releasing factor ▶ **noun** Biochemistry a substance which, when secreted by the hypothalamus, promotes the release of a specified hormone from the anterior lobe of the pituitary gland.

relegate ▶ **verb** [with obj.] assign an inferior rank or position to: *they aim to prevent women from being **relegated to** a secondary role.* ■ Brit. transfer (a sports team) to a lower division of a league: *United were relegated to division two.*
– DERIVATIVES **relegation** noun.
– ORIGIN late Middle English (in the sense 'send into exile'): from Latin *relegat-* 'sent away, referred', from the verb *relegare*, from *re-* 'again' + *legare* 'send'.

relent ▶ **verb** [no obj.] abandon or mitigate a severe or harsh attitude, especially by finally yielding to a request: *she was going to refuse his request, but relented.* ■ become less severe or intense: *the rain relented.*
– ORIGIN late Middle English (in the sense 'dissolve, melt'): based on Latin *re-* 'back' + *lentare* 'to bend' (from *lentus* 'flexible').

relentless ▶ **adjective** unceasingly intense: *the relentless heat of the desert.* ■ harsh or inflexible: *a patient but relentless taskmaster.*
– DERIVATIVES **relentlessly** adverb, **relentlessness** noun.

relet chiefly Brit. ▶ **verb** (**relets**, **reletting**; past and past participle **relet**) [with obj.] let (a property) for a further period or to a new tenant.
▶ **noun** an act of letting a property again.

relevant ▶ **adjective** closely connected or appropriate to the matter in hand: *what small companies need is relevant advice | the candidate's experience is **relevant to** the job.*
– DERIVATIVES **relevance** noun, **relevancy** noun, **relevantly** adverb.
– ORIGIN early 16th cent. (as a Scots legal term meaning 'legally pertinent'): from medieval Latin *relevant-* 'raising up', from Latin *relevare*.

relevé /ˌrələˈveɪ/ ▶ **noun 1** Ballet a movement in which the dancer rises on the tips of the toes.
2 Ecology each of a number of small plots of vegetation, analysed as a sample of a wider area.
– ORIGIN French, literally 'raised up'.

reliable ▶ **adjective** consistently good in quality or performance; able to be trusted: *a reliable source of information.*
▶ **noun** (usu. **reliables**) a reliable person or thing: *the supporting cast includes old reliables like Mitchell.*
– DERIVATIVES **reliability** noun, **reliableness** noun, **reliably** adverb.

reliance ▶ **noun** [mass noun] dependence on or trust in someone or something: *the farmer's **reliance on** pesticides.* ■ [count noun] archaic a person or thing on which someone depends.
– DERIVATIVES **reliant** adjective.

relic ▶ **noun** an object surviving from an earlier time, especially one of historical interest: *a museum of railway relics.* ■ a part of a deceased holy person's body or belongings kept as an object of reverence. ■ a person or thing that has survived from an earlier time but is now outmoded: *the supermodel has become an embarrassing relic from the early 1990s.*
– ORIGIN Middle English: from Old French *relique* (originally plural), from Latin *reliquiae* (see RELIQUIAE).

relicense ▶ **verb** [with obj.] license or authorize again.

relict /ˈrɛlɪkt/ ▶ **noun 1** a thing which has survived from an earlier period or in a primitive form. ■ an animal or plant that has survived while others of its group have become extinct, e.g. the coelacanth. ■ a population that now survives in only a few localities.
2 archaic a widow.
– ORIGIN late Middle English (in sense 2): from Old French *relicte* '(woman) left behind', from late Latin *relicta*, from the verb *relinquere* 'leave behind'. Sense 1 arose in the early 20th cent. and is from Latin *relictus*, past participle of *relinquere*.

relief ▶ **noun** [mass noun] **1** a feeling of reassurance and relaxation following release from anxiety or distress: *much to her relief, she saw the door open.* ■ [count noun] a cause of or occasion for relief: *it was a relief to find somewhere to stay.* ■ the alleviation of pain, discomfort, or distress: *tablets for the relief of pain.* ■ (usu. **light relief**) something interesting or enjoyable that provides a short respite from a tense or tedious situation: *the kiss-and-tell tale gave the nation some light relief from page after page of war coverage.*
2 financial or practical assistance given to those in special need or difficulty: *raising money for famine relief* | [as modifier] *relief workers.* ■ a remission of tax normally due: *employees who donate to charity will receive tax relief.* ■ chiefly Law the redress of a hardship or grievance. ■ the action of raising the siege of a besieged town: *the relief of Mafeking.*
3 [usu. as modifier] a person or group of people replacing others who have been on duty: *the relief nurse was late.* ■ Brit. an extra vehicle providing supplementary public transport at peak times or in emergencies.
4 the state of being clearly visible or obvious due to being accentuated: *the setting sun threw the snow-covered peaks **into relief**.* ■ a method of moulding, carving, or stamping in which the design stands out from the surface, to a greater (**high relief**) or lesser (**low relief**) extent. ■ [count noun] a piece of sculpture in relief. ■ a representation of relief given by an arrangement of line or colour or shading. ■ Geography difference in height from the surrounding terrain: *the sharp relief of many mountains.* [via French from Italian *rilievo*, from *rilevare* 'raise', from Latin *relevare*.]
– PHRASES **in relief** Baseball acting as a substitute pitcher. **on relief** chiefly N. Amer. receiving state assistance because of need.
– ORIGIN late Middle English: from Old French, from *relever* 'raise up, relieve', from Latin *relevare* 'raise again, alleviate'.

relief map ▶ **noun** a map indicating hills and valleys by shading rather than by contour lines alone. ■ a map model with elevations and depressions representing hills and valleys, typically on an exaggerated relative scale.

relief printing ▶ **noun** [mass noun] printing from raised images, as in letterpress and flexography.

relief road ▶ **noun** Brit. a road taking traffic around, rather than through, a congested urban area.

relieve ▶ **verb** [with obj.] **1** cause (pain, distress, or difficulty) to become less severe or serious: *the drug was used to promote sleep and to relieve pain.* ■ cause (someone) to stop feeling distressed or anxious: *he was relieved by her change of tone.*
2 release (someone) from duty by taking their place: *another signalman relieved him at 5.30.* ■ bring military support for (a besieged place): *he dispatched an expedition to relieve the city.*
3 (**relieve someone of**) take (a burden) from someone: *he relieved her of her baggage.* ■ free someone from (a tiresome responsibility): *she relieved me of the household chores.* ■ used ironically to indicate that someone has been deprived of something: *he was relieved of his world title.*
4 make less tedious or monotonous by the introduction of variety: *the bird's body is black, relieved only by white under the tail.*
5 (**relieve oneself**) used as a formal or euphemistic expression for urination or defecation.
6 archaic make (something) stand out: *the twilight relieving in purple masses the foliage of the island.*
– DERIVATIVES **relievable** adjective, **reliever** noun.
– ORIGIN Middle English: from Old French *relever*, from Latin *relevare*, from *re-* (expressing intensive force) + *levare* 'raise' (from *levis* 'light').

relieved ▶ **adjective** no longer feeling distressed or anxious; reassured: *relieved parents who had waited anxiously for news.*
– DERIVATIVES **relievedly** adverb.

relieving officer ▶ **noun** historical an official appointed by a parish or union to administer relief to the poor.

relievo /rɪˈliːvəʊ/ (also **rilievo**) ▶ **noun** (pl. **relievos**) chiefly Art another term for RELIEF (sense 4).
– ORIGIN Italian *rilievo*.

relight ▶ **verb** (past and past participle **relighted** or **relit**) [with obj.] light (something) again: *he reached for the matches to relight his pipe.*

religio- /rɪˈlɪdʒɪəʊ/ ▶ **combining form** religious and ...: *religio-political | religio-national.*
– ORIGIN from RELIGION or RELIGIOUS.

religion ▶ **noun** [mass noun] the belief in and worship of a superhuman controlling power, especially a personal God or gods: *ideas about the relationship between science and religion.* ■ [count noun] a particular system of faith and worship: *the world's great religions.* ■ [count noun] a pursuit or interest followed with great devotion: *consumerism is the new religion.*
– PHRASES **get religion** informal be converted to religious belief and practices.
– DERIVATIVES **religionless** adjective.
– ORIGIN Middle English (originally in the sense 'life under monastic vows'): from Old French, or from Latin *religio(n-)* 'obligation, bond, reverence', perhaps based on Latin *religare* 'to bind'.

religionism ▶ **noun** [mass noun] excessive religious zeal.
– DERIVATIVES **religionist** noun.

religiose /rɪˈlɪdʒɪəʊs/ ▶ **adjective** excessively religious.
– DERIVATIVES **religiosity** noun.
– ORIGIN mid 19th cent.: from Latin *religiosus*, from *religio* 'reverence, obligation'.

religious ▶ **adjective** relating to or believing in a religion: *both men were deeply religious and moralistic | religious music.* ■ (of a belief or practice) forming part of someone's faith in a divine being: *she has strong religious convictions.* ■ belonging or relating to a monastic order or other group of people who are united by their practice of religion: *religious houses were built on ancient pagan sites.* ■ treated or regarded with a devotion and scrupulousness

R

appropriate to worship: *I have a religious aversion to reading manuals.*
▶ **noun** (pl. **same**) a person bound by monastic vows.
– DERIVATIVES **religiously** adverb, **religiousness** noun.
– ORIGIN Middle English: from Old French, from Latin *religiosus*, from *religio* 'reverence, obligation' (see RELIGION).

Religious Society of Friends official name for the Quakers (see QUAKER).

reline ▶ **verb** [with obj.] replace the lining of: *the heavily brocaded drapes that she had relined.* ■ attach a new backing canvas to (a painting).

relinquish ▶ **verb** [with obj.] voluntarily cease to keep or claim; give up: *he relinquished his managerial role to become chief executive.*
– DERIVATIVES **relinquishment** noun.
– ORIGIN late Middle English: from Old French *relinquiss-*, lengthened stem of *relinquir*, from Latin *relinquere*, from *re-* (expressing intensive force) + *linquere* 'to leave'.

reliquary /ˈrɛlɪkwəri/ ▶ **noun** (pl. **reliquaries**) a container for holy relics.
– ORIGIN mid 16th cent.: from French *reliquaire*, from Old French *relique* (see RELIC).

reliquiae /rɪˈlɪkwɪiː/ ▶ **plural noun** formal remains.
– ORIGIN mid 17th cent.: Latin, feminine plural (used as a noun) of *reliquus* 'remaining', based on *linquere* 'to leave'.

relish ▶ **noun 1** [mass noun] great enjoyment: *she swigged a mouthful of wine with relish.* ■ liking for or pleasurable anticipation of something: *I was appointed to a post for which I had little relish.*
2 a piquant sauce or pickle eaten with plain food to add flavour.
3 archaic an appetizing flavour: *the tired glutton finds no relish in the sweetest meat.* ■ a distinctive taste or tinge: *the relish of wine.*
▶ **verb** [with obj.] **1** enjoy greatly: *he was relishing his moment of glory.* ■ anticipate with pleasure: *we did not relish the idea of a strike.*
2 archaic make pleasant to the taste; add relish to: *I have also a novel to relish my wine.*
– DERIVATIVES **relishable** adjective.
– ORIGIN Middle English: alteration of obsolete *reles*, from Old French *reles* 'remainder', from *relaisser* 'to release'. The early noun sense was 'odour, taste' giving rise to 'appetizing flavour, piquant taste' (mid 17th cent.), and hence sense 2 of the noun (late 18th cent.).

relist ▶ **verb** [with obj.] place (something, especially shares) on a list again.

relive ▶ **verb** [with obj.] live through (an experience or feeling, especially an unpleasant one) again in one's imagination or memory: *he broke down sobbing as he relived the attack.*

relleno /rɛˈljeɪnəʊ/ ▶ **noun** (pl. **rellenos**) short for CHILE RELLENO.

rellie (Austral. also **rello**) ▶ **noun** (pl. **rellies** or **rellos**) informal, chiefly Austral./NZ a relative.

reload ▶ **verb** [with obj.] load (something, especially a gun that has been fired) again: *he reloaded the chamber of the shotgun with fresh cartridges* | [no obj.] *Charlie reloaded and took aim.*

relocate ▶ **verb** [no obj.] move to a new place and establish one's home or business there: *sixty workers could face redundancy because the firm is relocating* | [with obj.] *distribution staff will be relocated to Holland.*
– DERIVATIVES **relocation** noun.

relock ▶ **verb** [with obj.] lock (a door, container, vehicle, etc.) again.

reluctance ▶ **noun** [mass noun] **1** unwillingness or disinclination to do something: *she sensed his reluctance to continue.*
2 Physics the property of a magnetic circuit of opposing the passage of magnetic flux lines, equal to the ratio of the magnetomotive force to the magnetic flux.

reluctant ▶ **adjective** unwilling and hesitant; disinclined: [with infinitive] *she seemed reluctant to answer.*
– DERIVATIVES **reluctantly** adverb.
– ORIGIN mid 17th cent. (in the sense 'writhing, offering opposition'): from Latin *reluctant-* 'struggling against', from the verb *reluctari*, from *re-* (expressing intensive force) + *luctari* 'to struggle'.

rely ▶ **verb** (**relies, relying, relied**) [no obj.] (**rely on/upon**) depend on with full trust or confidence: *I know I can rely on your discretion.* ■ be dependent on: *the charity has to rely entirely on public donations.*
– ORIGIN Middle English: from Old French *relier* 'bind together', from Latin *religare*, from *re-* (expressing intensive force) + *ligare* 'bind'. The original sense was 'gather together', later 'turn to, associate with', whence 'depend upon with confidence'.

rem ▶ **noun** (pl. **same**) a unit of effective absorbed dose of ionizing radiation in human tissue, loosely equivalent to one roentgen of X-rays.
– ORIGIN 1940s: acronym from *roentgen equivalent man*.

remade past and past participle of REMAKE.

remain ▶ **verb** [no obj.] **1** continue to exist, especially after other similar people or things have ceased to do so: *a cloister is all that remains of the monastery.* ■ stay in the place that one has been occupying: *her husband remained at the flat in Regent's Park.* ■ [with complement] continue to possess a particular quality or fulfil a particular role: *he had remained alert the whole time.*
2 be left over or outstanding after others or other parts have been completed, used, or dealt with: *a more intractable problem remains.*
– PHRASES **remain to be seen** used to express the notion that something is not yet known: *she has broken her leg, but it remains to be seen how badly.*
– ORIGIN late Middle English: from Old French *remain-*, stressed stem of *remanoir*, from Latin *remanere*, from *re-* (expressing intensive force) + *manere* 'to stay'.

remainder ▶ **noun 1** a part, number, or quantity that is left over: *leave a few mushrooms for garnish and slice the remainder.* ■ Mathematics the number which is left over in a division in which one quantity does not exactly divide another. ■ a copy of a book left unsold when demand has fallen.
2 a part that is still to come: *the remainder of the year.*
3 Law a property interest that becomes effective in possession only when a prior interest (created at the same time) ends.
▶ **verb** [with obj.] dispose of (a book left unsold) at a reduced price: *titles are being remaindered increasingly quickly to save on overheads.*
– ORIGIN late Middle English (in sense 3 of the noun): from Anglo-Norman French, from Latin *remanere* (see REMAIN).

remaining ▶ **adjective 1** still existing, present, or in use; surviving: *Lilly was my last remaining close relative* | *the few* ***remaining*** *employees are working part-time.*
2 not yet used, dealt with, or resolved; outstanding: *they advertised for any remaining creditors to come forward.*
3 still to happen; future: *England have forbidden him to play in the remaining fixtures.*

remains ▶ **plural noun** the parts left over after other parts have been removed, used, or destroyed: *the remains of a sandwich lunch were on the table.* ■ historical or archaeological relics: *Roman remains.* ■ a person's body after death.
– ORIGIN late Middle English (occasionally treated as singular): from Old French *remain*, from *remaindre*, from an informal form of Latin *remanere* (see REMAIN).

remake ▶ **verb** (past and past participle **remade**) [with obj.] make (something) again or differently: *the bed would be more comfortable if it were remade.*
▶ **noun** a film or piece of music that has been filmed or recorded again and re-released.

reman ▶ **verb** (**remans, remanning, remanned**) [with obj.] **1** equip with new personnel.
2 literary make (someone) manly or courageous again.

remand Law ▶ **verb** [with obj.] place (a defendant) on bail or in custody, especially when a trial is adjourned: *he was remanded in custody for a week.* ■ return (a case) to a lower court for reconsideration.
▶ **noun** a committal to custody.
– PHRASES **on remand** in custody pending trial.
– ORIGIN late Middle English (as a verb in the sense 'send back again'): from late Latin *remandare*, from *re-* 'back' + *mandare* 'commit'. The noun dates from the late 18th cent.

remand centre ▶ **noun** (in the UK and Canada) an institution in which people accused of a crime are held in custody while awaiting trial.

remanent /ˈrɛmənənt/ ▶ **adjective** (of magnetism) remaining after the magnetizing field has been removed.
– DERIVATIVES **remanence** noun.
– ORIGIN late Middle English: from Latin *remanent-* 'remaining', from the verb *remanere*.

remap ▶ **verb** (**remaps, remapping, remapped**) [with obj.] Computing assign (a function) to a different key.

remark ▶ **verb 1** [reporting verb] say something as a comment; mention: [with direct speech] *'Tom's looking peaky,' she remarked* | [with clause] *he remarked that he had some work to finish* | [no obj.] *the judges* ***remarked on*** *the high standard of the entries.*
2 [with obj.] regard with attention; notice: *he remarked the man's inflamed eyelids.*
▶ **noun** a written or spoken comment: *I decided to ignore his rude remarks.* ■ [mass noun] notice or comment: *the landscape, familiar since childhood, was not worthy of remark.*
– ORIGIN late 16th cent. (in sense 2 of the verb): from French *remarquer* 'note again', from *re-* (expressing intensive force) + *marquer* 'to mark, note'.

re-mark ▶ **verb** [with obj.] mark (an examination paper or piece of academic work) again.
▶ **noun** [in sing.] an act of marking an examination or piece of academic work again.

remarkable ▶ **adjective** worthy of attention; striking: *a remarkable coincidence.*
– DERIVATIVES **remarkableness** noun, **remarkably** adverb [sentence adverb] *remarkably, I finished ahead of schedule* | [as submodifier] *they got on remarkably well.*
– ORIGIN early 17th cent.: from French *remarquable*, from *remarquer* 'take note of' (see REMARK).

Remarque /rɪˈmɑːk/, Erich Maria (1898–1970), German-born American novelist. His first novel, *All Quiet on the Western Front* (1929), was a huge international success. All of his ten novels deal with the horror of war and its aftermath.

remarry ▶ **verb** (**remarries, remarrying, remarried**) [no obj.] marry again.
– DERIVATIVES **remarriage** noun.

remaster ▶ **verb** [with obj.] make a new master of (a recording), typically in order to improve the sound quality.

rematch ▶ **noun** a second match or game between two sports teams or players.

rembetika ▶ **noun** variant spelling of REBETIKA.

Rembrandt /ˈrɛmbrant/ (1606–69), Dutch painter; full name *Rembrandt Harmensz van Rijn*.

> He made his name as a portrait painter with the *Anatomy Lesson of Dr Tulp* (1632). With his most celebrated painting, *The Night Watch* (1642), he used chiaroscuro to give his subjects a more spiritual and introspective quality, a departure which was to transform the Dutch portrait tradition. Rembrandt is especially identified with the series of more than sixty self-portraits painted from 1629 to 1669.

REME ▶ **abbreviation** (in the British army) Royal Electrical and Mechanical Engineers.

remeasure ▶ **verb** [with obj.] measure again.
– DERIVATIVES **remeasurement** noun.

remediable ▶ **adjective** capable of being cured; treatable: *a remediable condition that may have serious consequences if not recognised.* ■ capable of being remedied; rectifiable: *these grievances are remediable.*

remedial ▶ **adjective** giving or intended as a remedy or cure: *remedial surgery.* ■ provided or intended for children with learning difficulties: *remedial education.*
– DERIVATIVES **remedially** adverb.
– ORIGIN mid 17th cent.: from late Latin *remedialis*, from Latin *remedium* 'cure, medicine' (see REMEDY).

remediation /rɪˌmiːdɪˈeɪʃ(ə)n/ ▶ **noun** [mass noun] the action of remedying something, in particular of reversing or stopping environmental damage. ■ the giving of remedial teaching or therapy.
– DERIVATIVES **remediate** verb.
– ORIGIN early 19th cent.: from Latin *remediatio(n-)*, from *remediare* 'heal, cure' (see REMEDY).

remedy ▶ **noun** (pl. **remedies**) **1** a medicine or treatment for a disease or injury: *herbal remedies for aches and pains.* ■ a means of counteracting or eliminating something undesirable: *shopping became* ***a remedy for*** *personal problems.* ■ a means of legal reparation: *compensation is available* ***as a remedy against*** *governmental institutions.*
2 the margin within which coins as minted may differ from the standard fineness and weight.
▶ **verb** (**remedies, remedying, remedied**) [with obj.] set right (an undesirable situation): *money will be given to remedy the poor funding of nurseries.*
– ORIGIN Middle English: from Anglo-Norman French *remedie*, from Latin *remedium*, from *re-* 'back' (also expressing intensive force) + *mederi* 'heal'.

remember ▸ **verb 1** [with obj.] have in or be able to bring to one's mind an awareness of (someone or something from the past): *I remember the screech of the horn as the car came towards me* | *no one remembered his name.* ■ bear (someone) in mind by making them a gift or making provision for them: *he has remembered the boy in his will.* ■ pray for the well-being of: *the congress should be remembered in our prayers.* ■ (**remember someone to**) convey greetings from one person to (another): *remember me to Charlie.* ■ (**remember oneself**) recover one's manners after a lapse.
2 [with infinitive] do something that one has undertaken to do or that is necessary or advisable: *did you remember to post the letters?* ■ [with clause] used to emphasize the importance of what is asserted: *you must remember that this is a secret.*
– DERIVATIVES **rememberer** noun.
– ORIGIN Middle English: from Old French *remembrer*, from late Latin *rememorari* 'call to mind', from *re-* (expressing intensive force) + Latin *memor* 'mindful'.

remembrance ▸ **noun** [mass noun] the action of remembering something: *a flash of remembrance passed between them.* ■ the action of remembering the dead: *a chapel of remembrance.* ■ [count noun] a memory or recollection: *they exchanged fond remembrances of his gentle ways.* ■ [count noun] a thing kept or given as a reminder or in commemoration of someone.
– ORIGIN Middle English: from Old French, from *remembrer* (see REMEMBER).

Remembrance Day ▸ **noun 1** another term for **REMEMBRANCE SUNDAY**.
2 historical another term for **ARMISTICE DAY**.

remembrancer ▸ **noun 1** a chronicler.
2 Brit. an official of the Court of Exchequer.

Remembrance Sunday ▸ **noun** (in the UK) the Sunday nearest 11 November, when those who were killed in the First and Second World Wars and later conflicts are commemorated. Also called **POPPY DAY**.

remex ▸ **noun** singular form of **REMIGES**.

remiges /ˈrɛmɪdʒiːz/ ▸ **plural noun** (sing. **remex** /ˈriːmɛks/) Ornithology flight feathers. Compare with **RECTRICES**.
– ORIGIN mid 18th cent.: from Latin, literally 'rowers', based on *remus* 'oar'.

remilitarize (also **remilitarise**) ▸ **verb** [with obj.] supply (a place that has previously been demilitarized) with new military resources: *the Rhineland was remilitarized in 1936.*
– DERIVATIVES **remilitarization** noun.

remind ▸ **verb** [with obj.] **1** cause (someone) to remember someone or something: *he would have forgotten my birthday if you hadn't reminded him* | [with obj. and direct speech] *'You had an accident,' he reminded her.* ■ (**remind someone of**) cause someone to think of (something) because of a resemblance: *his impassive, fierce stare reminded her of an owl.*
2 cause (someone) to fulfil an obligation or to take note of something: [with obj. and clause] *the barman reminded them that singing was not permitted* | [with obj. and infinitive] *she reminded me to be respectful.*
– ORIGIN mid 17th cent.: from **RE-** 'again' + the verb **MIND**, probably suggested by obsolete *rememorate*, in the same sense.

reminder ▸ **noun** a thing that causes someone to remember something: *her mushroom omelette is a blissful reminder of Sunday suppers.* ■ a letter sent to remind someone of an obligation, especially to pay a bill.

remindful ▸ **adjective** acting as a reminder: *his humour is remindful of that of Max.*

remineralize (also **remineralise**) ▸ **verb** [with obj.] restore the depleted mineral content of (a part of the body, especially the bones or teeth).
– DERIVATIVES **remineralization** noun.

reminisce /ˌrɛmɪˈnɪs/ ▸ **verb** [no obj.] indulge in enjoyable recollection of past events: *they reminisced about their summers abroad.*
– DERIVATIVES **reminiscer** noun.
– ORIGIN early 19th cent.: back-formation from **REMINISCENCE**.

reminiscence ▸ **noun 1** a story told about a past event remembered by the narrator: *his reminiscences of his early days in Parliament.* ■ [mass noun] the enjoyable recollection of past events: *his story made me smile in reminiscence.* ■ (**reminiscences**) a collection in literary form of incidents that someone remembers.
2 a characteristic of one thing that is suggestive of another: *his first works are too full of reminiscences of earlier poetry.*
– ORIGIN late 16th cent. (denoting the action of remembering): from late Latin *reminiscentia*, from Latin *reminisci* 'remember'.

reminiscent ▸ **adjective 1** tending to remind one of something: *the sights were* ***reminiscent of*** *my childhood.* ■ absorbed in or suggesting absorption in memories: *her expression was wistful and reminiscent.*
2 suggesting something by resemblance: *her robes were vaguely* ***reminiscent of*** *military dress.*
– DERIVATIVES **reminiscently** adverb.
– ORIGIN mid 18th cent.: from Latin *reminiscent-* 'remembering', from the verb *reminisci*.

remise /rɪˈmiːz/ Fencing ▸ **verb** [no obj.] make a second thrust after the first has failed.
▸ **noun** a second thrust made after the first has failed.
– ORIGIN French, past participle of *remettre* 'put back'.

remiss /rɪˈmɪs/ ▸ **adjective** [predic.] lacking care or attention to duty; negligent: *it would be very remiss of me not to pass on that information.*
– DERIVATIVES **remissly** adverb, **remissness** noun.
– ORIGIN late Middle English: from Latin *remissus* 'slackened', past participle of *remittere*. The early senses were 'weakened in colour or consistency' and (in describing sound) 'faint, soft'.

remissible ▸ **adjective** (especially of sins) able to be pardoned.
– ORIGIN late 16th cent.: from French *rémissible* or late Latin *remissibilis*, from *remiss-* 'slackened', from the verb *remittere* (see **REMISS**).

remission ▸ **noun** [mass noun] **1** the cancellation of a debt, charge, or penalty: *the scheme allows for the partial remission of tuition fees.* ■ Brit. the reduction of a prison sentence, especially as a reward for good behaviour. ■ formal forgiveness of sins.
2 a temporary diminution of the severity of disease or pain: *ten patients remained* ***in remission***.
– ORIGIN Middle English: from Old French, or from Latin *remissio(n-)*, from *remittere* 'send back, restore' (see **REMIT**).

remit ▸ **verb** /rɪˈmɪt/ (**remits, remitting, remitted**) [with obj.] **1** cancel or refrain from exacting or inflicting (a debt or punishment): *the excess of the sentence over 12 months was remitted.* ■ Theology forgive (a sin).
2 send (money) in payment or as a gift: *the income they remitted to their families.*
3 refer (a matter for decision) to an authority: *the request for an investigation was remitted to a special committee.* ■ Law send back (a case) to a lower court. ■ Law send (someone) from one tribunal to another for a trial or hearing. ■ archaic postpone. ■ archaic consign again to a previous state: *thus his indiscretion remitted him to the nature of an ordinary person.*
4 [no obj.] archaic diminish: *phobias may remit spontaneously without any treatment.*
▸ **noun** /ˈriːmɪt, rɪˈmɪt/ **1** chiefly Brit. the task or area of activity officially assigned to an individual or organization: *the committee was becoming caught up in issues that did not fall within its remit.*
2 an item referred to someone for consideration.
– DERIVATIVES **remittal** noun, **remitter** noun.
– ORIGIN late Middle English: from Latin *remittere* 'send back, restore', from *re-* 'back' + *mittere* 'send'. The noun dates from the early 20th cent.

remittance ▸ **noun** a sum of money sent in payment or as a gift. ■ [mass noun] the action of sending money in payment or as a gift.

remittance man ▸ **noun** chiefly historical an emigrant supported or assisted by payments of money from home.

remittent ▸ **adjective** (of a fever) characterized by fluctuating body temperatures.
– ORIGIN late 17th cent.: from Latin *remittent-* 'sending back', from the verb *remittere* (see **REMIT**).

remix ▸ **verb** [with obj.] mix (something) again. ■ produce a different version of (a musical recording) by altering the balance of the separate tracks.
▸ **noun** a version of a musical recording produced by remixing.
– DERIVATIVES **remixer** noun.

remnant ▸ **noun 1** a part or quantity that is left after the greater part has been used, removed, or destroyed: *the bogs are an endangered* ***remnant of*** *a primeval landscape.* ■ a piece of cloth left when the greater part has been used or sold. ■ a surviving trace: ***a remnant of the past.***
2 Christian Theology a small minority of people who will remain faithful to God and so be saved (in allusion to biblical prophecies concerning Israel).
▸ **adjective** [attrib.] remaining: *remnant strands of hair.*
– ORIGIN Middle English: contraction of obsolete *remenant* from Old French *remenant*, from *remenoir*, *remanoir* 'remain'.

remodel ▸ **verb** (**remodels, remodelling, remodelled**; US **remodels, remodeling, remodeled**) [with obj.] change the structure or form of (something, especially a building): *the station was remodelled and enlarged in 1927.* ■ shape (a figure or object) again or differently: *she remodelled the head with careful fingers.*

remodeler ▸ **noun** N. Amer. a person who carries out structural alterations to an existing building, such as adding a new bathroom.

remodify ▸ **verb** (**remodifies, remodifying, remodified**) [with obj.] modify again.
– DERIVATIVES **remodification** noun.

remold ▸ **verb** US spelling of **REMOULD**.

remonetize (also **remonetise**) ▸ **verb** [with obj.] rare restore (a metal) to its former position as legal tender.
– DERIVATIVES **remonetization** noun.

remonstrance /rɪˈmɒnstr(ə)ns/ ▸ **noun** a forcefully reproachful protest: *angry remonstrances in the Commons* | [mass noun] *he shut his ears to any remonstrance.* ■ (**the Remonstrance**) a document drawn up in 1610 by the Arminians of the Dutch Reformed Church, presenting the differences between their doctrines and those of the strict Calvinists.
– ORIGIN late 16th cent. (in the sense 'evidence'): from Old French, or from medieval Latin *remonstrantia*, from *remonstrare* 'demonstrate, show' (see **REMONSTRATE**).

Remonstrant /rɪˈmɒnstrənt/ ▸ **noun** a member of the Arminian party in the Dutch Reformed Church.
– ORIGIN early 17th cent.: from medieval Latin *remonstrant-* 'demonstrating' (see also **REMONSTRANCE**).

remonstrate /ˈrɛmənstreɪt/ ▸ **verb** [no obj.] make a forcefully reproachful protest: *he turned angrily to* ***remonstrate with*** *Tommy* | [with direct speech] *'You don't mean that,' she remonstrated.*
– DERIVATIVES **remonstration** noun, **remonstrative** adjective.
– ORIGIN late 16th cent. (in the sense 'make plain'): from medieval Latin *remonstrat-* 'demonstrated', from the verb *remonstrare*, from *re-* (expressing intensive force) + *monstrare* 'to show'.

remontant /rɪˈmɒnt(ə)nt/ ▸ **adjective** (of a plant) blooming or producing a crop more than once a season.
▸ **noun** a remontant plant.
– ORIGIN late 19th cent.: from French, literally 'coming up again', from the verb *remonter*.

remora /ˈrɛmərə/ ▸ **noun** a slender marine fish which attaches itself to large fish by means of a sucker on top of the head. It generally feeds on the host's external parasites. Also called **SHARK-SUCKER**, **SUCKERFISH**. ● Family Echeneidae: several genera and species, in particular the widespread *Remora remora*.
– ORIGIN mid 16th cent.: from Latin, literally 'hindrance', from *re-* 'back' + *mora* 'delay' (because of the former belief that the fish slowed down ships).

remorse ▸ **noun** [mass noun] deep regret or guilt for a wrong committed: *they were filled with remorse and shame.*
– ORIGIN late Middle English: from Old French *remors*, from medieval Latin *remorsus*, from Latin *remordere* 'vex', from *re-* (expressing intensive force) + *mordere* 'to bite'.

remorseful ▸ **adjective** filled with remorse; sorry: *the defendant was* ***remorseful for*** *what he had done.*
– DERIVATIVES **remorsefully** adverb.

remorseless ▸ **adjective 1** without regret or guilt: *a remorseless killer.*
2 (of something unpleasant) never ending or improving; relentless: *remorseless poverty.*
– DERIVATIVES **remorselessly** adverb, **remorselessness** noun.

remortgage ▸ **verb** [with obj.] take out another or a different kind of mortgage on (a property).
▸ **noun** a different or additional mortgage.

remote ▸ **adjective** (**remoter, remotest**) **1** (of a place) situated far from the main centres of population; distant: *the valley is* ***remote from*** *the usual tourist routes* | *a remote Welsh valley.* ■ (of an electronic device) operating or operated at a distance by means of radio or infrared signals. ■ distant in time: *a golden age in the remote past.*
2 having very little connection with or relationship to: *the theory seems rather intellectual and remote*

from everyday experience. ■ distantly related: *a remote cousin.*
3 (of a chance or possibility) unlikely to occur: *chances of a lasting peace became even more remote.*
4 aloof and unfriendly in manner: *Maud seemed remote and patronizing.*
5 Computing denoting a device which can only be accessed by means of a network. Compare with LOCAL.
▸ **noun** a remote control device.
– DERIVATIVES **remoteness** noun.
– ORIGIN late Middle English (in the sense 'far apart'): from Latin *remotus* 'removed', past participle of *removere* (see REMOVE).

remote control ▸ **noun** [mass noun] control of a machine or apparatus from a distance by means of radio or infrared signals transmitted from a device. ■ (also **remote controller**) [count noun] a device that controls an apparatus by means of radio or infrared signals.
– DERIVATIVES **remote-controlled** adjective.

remotely ▸ **adverb 1** from a distance; without physical contact: *new electronic meters that can be read remotely.*
2 [as submodifier] [usu. with negative] in the slightest degree: *he had never been remotely jealous.*

remote sensing ▸ **noun** [mass noun] the scanning of the earth by satellite or high-flying aircraft in order to obtain information about it.

remoulade /ˈrɛmʊlɑːd/ ▸ **noun** [mass noun] salad or seafood dressing made with hard-boiled egg yolks, oil, and vinegar, and flavoured with mustard, capers, and herbs.
– ORIGIN French *rémoulade*, from Italian *remolata*.

remould (US **remold**) ▸ **verb** /riːˈməʊld/ [with obj.] change the appearance, structure, or character of: *did the welfare state remould capitalism to give it a more human face?* ■ Brit. put a new tread on (a worn tyre).
▸ **noun** /ˈriːməʊld/ Brit. a tyre that has been given a new tread.

remount ▸ **verb** /riːˈmaʊnt/ [with obj.] **1** get on (a horse or vehicle) in order to ride it again: *she went to remount her horse* | [no obj.] *I remounted and rode on.*
2 attach to a new frame or setting: *remount the best photos in glass-fronted mounts.*
3 organize and embark on (a course of action) again: *the raid was remounted in August.* ■ produce (a play or exhibition) again.
▸ **noun** /ˈriːmaʊnt/ a fresh horse for a rider. ■ historical a supply of fresh horses for a regiment.

removal ▸ **noun** [mass noun] the action of removing someone or something, in particular: ■ the action of taking away or abolishing something unwanted: *the removal of the brain tumour* | *the removal of all legal barriers to the free movement of goods* | [count noun] *the forced removals of the Acadians began in late 1755.* ■ [usu. as modifier] Brit. the transfer of furniture and other contents when moving house: *removal men.* ■ the dismissal of someone from a job. ■ S. African historical the forcing of individuals or communities to leave their place of residence, especially to move to ethnically homogeneous rural settlements. ■ (also **removal of remains**) Irish the formal procedure of taking a body from the house to the church for the funeral service.

removalist ▸ **noun** Austral. a person or firm engaged in household or business removals.

remove ▸ **verb** [with obj.] **1** take (something) away or off from the position occupied: *Customs officials* ***removed*** *documents* ***from*** *the premises* | *she sat down to remove her make-up.* ■ take off (clothing): *he sat down and quickly removed his shoes and socks.* ■ [no obj.] (**remove to**) dated change one's home or place of residence by moving to (another place): *he removed to Wales and began afresh.* ■ S. African historical compel (someone) by law to move to another area: *a man is removed to the tribal district of his forbears.*
2 abolish or get rid of: *exchange controls have finally been removed* | *they* ***removed*** *thousands of needy youngsters* ***from*** *the benefit system.* ■ dismiss from a job: *he was* ***removed from*** *his position as teacher.*
3 (**be removed**) be distant from: *it is an isolated place,* ***far removed from*** *the London art world.* ■ be very different from: *an explanation which is* ***far removed from*** *the truth.*
4 (as adj. **removed**) separated by a particular number of steps of descent: *his second cousin once removed.*
▸ **noun 1** a degree of remoteness or separation: *at this remove, the whole incident seems insane.*
2 (also **Remove**) chiefly historical a form or division in some British schools: *a member of the Fifth Remove.*
– DERIVATIVES **removability** noun, **removable** adjective, **remover** noun.
– ORIGIN Middle English (as a verb): from the Old French stem *remov-*, from Latin *removere*, from *re-* 'back' + *movere* 'to move'.

REM sleep ▸ **noun** [mass noun] a kind of sleep that occurs at intervals during the night and is characterized by rapid eye movements, more dreaming and bodily movement, and faster pulse and breathing.

remuage /ˌrɛmjʊˈɑːʒ/, French /ʀəmɥaʒ/ ▸ **noun** [mass noun] the periodic turning or shaking of bottled wine, especially champagne, to move sediment towards the cork.
– ORIGIN French, literally 'moving about'.

remuda /rəˈmuːdə/ ▸ **noun** N. Amer. a herd of horses that have been saddle-broken, from which ranch hands choose their mounts for the day.
– ORIGIN late 19th cent.: via American Spanish, from Spanish, literally 'exchange, replacement'.

remunerate /rɪˈmjuːnəreɪt/ ▸ **verb** [with obj.] pay (someone) for services rendered or work done: *they should be remunerated fairly for their work.*
– ORIGIN early 16th cent.: from Latin *remunerat-* 'rewarded, recompensed', from the verb *remunerari*, from *re-* (expressing intensive force) + *munus, muner-* 'gift'.

remuneration /rɪˌmjuːnəˈreɪʃ(ə)n/ ▸ **noun** [mass noun] money paid for work or a service.

remunerative /rɪˈmjuːn(ə)rətɪv/ ▸ **adjective** financially rewarding; lucrative: *highly remunerative activities.* ■ earning a salary; paid: *since June 2003 he has not had any remunerative employment.*

Remus /ˈriːməs/ Roman Mythology the twin brother of Romulus.

REN ▸ **abbreviation** ringer equivalent number, a measure of the load a device will place on a telephone line. The maximum REN allowed on a single line is usually limited by telephone companies.

Renaissance /rɪˈneɪs(ə)ns, -ɒ̃s/ the revival of European art and literature under the influence of classical models in the 14th–16th centuries. ■ the culture and style of art and architecture developed during this era. ■ (as noun **a renaissance**) a revival of or renewed interest in something: *cinema-going is enjoying something of a renaissance.*

> The Renaissance is generally regarded as beginning in Florence, where there was a revival of interest in classical antiquity. Important early figures are the writers Petrarch, Dante, and Boccaccio and the painter Giotto. Music flourished, from madrigals to the polyphonic masses of Palestrina, with a wide variety of instruments such as viols and lutes. The period from the end of the 15th century has become known as the High Renaissance, when Venice and Rome began to share Florence's importance and Raphael, Leonardo da Vinci, and Michelangelo were active. Renaissance thinking spread to the rest of Europe from the early 16th century, and was influential for the next hundred years.

– ORIGIN from French *renaissance*, from *re-* 'back, again' + *naissance* 'birth' (from Latin *nascentia*, from *nasci* 'be born').

Renaissance man ▸ **noun** a man with many talents or areas of knowledge.

renal /ˈriːn(ə)l/ ▸ **adjective** technical relating to the kidneys: *renal failure.*
– ORIGIN mid 17th cent.: from French *rénal*, from late Latin *renalis*, from Latin *renes* 'kidneys'.

renal calculus ▸ **noun** another term for KIDNEY STONE.

renal pelvis ▸ **noun** see PELVIS (sense 2).

renal tubule ▸ **noun** another term for KIDNEY TUBULE.

rename ▸ **verb** [with obj. and complement] give a new name to: *after independence Celebes was renamed Sulawesi.*

Renan /rəˈnɒ̃/, French /ʀənɑ̃/, (Joseph) Ernest (1823–92), French historian, theologian, and philosopher. He provoked a controversy with the publication of his *Life of Jesus* (1863), which rejected the supernatural element in Jesus's life.

renascence /rɪˈnas(ə)ns, -ˈneɪ-/ ▸ **noun** formal the revival of something that has been dormant: *the renascence of poetry as an oral art.* ■ another term for RENAISSANCE.

renascent ▸ **adjective** becoming active or popular again: *renascent fascism.*
– ORIGIN early 18th cent.: from Latin *renascent-* 'being born again', from the verb *renasci*, from *re-* 'back, again' + *nasci* 'be born'.

renationalize (also **renationalise**) ▸ **verb** [with obj.] transfer (a privatized industry) back into state ownership or control.
– DERIVATIVES **renationalization** noun.

Renault /ˈrɛnəʊ/, French /ʀənɔ/, Louis (1877–1944), French engineer and motor manufacturer. He and his brothers established the Renault company in 1898, manufacturing racing cars, and later industrial and agricultural machinery and military technology.

rencontre /rɛnˈkɒntə/ ▸ **noun** archaic variant spelling of RENCOUNTER.
– ORIGIN early 17th cent.: French.

rencounter /rɛnˈkaʊntə/ archaic ▸ **noun** a chance meeting with someone. ■ a battle, skirmish, or duel.
▸ **verb** [with obj.] meet by chance: *I wonder who those fellows were we rencountered last night.*
– ORIGIN early 16th cent.: from French *rencontre* (noun), *rencontrer* 'meet face to face'.

rend ▸ **verb** (past and past participle **rent**) [with obj.] tear (something) into pieces: *snapping teeth that would rend human flesh to shreds* | figurative *the speculation and confusion which was rending the civilized world.* ■ [with obj. and adverbial of direction] archaic wrench (something) violently: *he rent the branch out of the tree.* ■ literary cause great emotional pain to: *you tell me this in order to make me able to betray you without rending my heart.*
– PHRASES **rend the air** literary sound piercingly: *a shrill scream rent the air.* **rend one's garments** (or **hair**) tear one's clothes (or pull one's hair out) as a sign of extreme grief or distress.
– ORIGIN Old English *rendan*; related to Middle Low German *rende*.

render ▸ **verb** [with obj.] **1** provide or give (a service, help, etc.): *money serves as a reward for* ***services rendered*** | *Mrs Evans would* ***render*** *assistance* ***to*** *those she thought were in need.* ■ submit or present for inspection or consideration: *he would render income tax returns at the end of the year.* ■ deliver (a verdict or judgement): *the jury's finding amounted to the clearest verdict yet rendered upon the scandal.* ■ literary give up; surrender: *he will* ***render up*** *his immortal soul.*
2 [with obj. and complement] cause to be or become; make: *the rains rendered his escape impossible.*
3 represent or depict artistically: *the eyes and the cheeks are exceptionally well rendered.* ■ perform (a piece of music): *a soprano solo reverently rendered by Linda Howie.* ■ translate: *the phrase was* ***rendered into*** *English.* ■ Computing process (an outline image) using colour and shading in order to make it appear solid and three-dimensional.
4 covertly send (a foreign criminal or terrorist suspect) for interrogation abroad; subject to extraordinary rendition.
5 melt down (fat) in order to clarify it. ■ process (the carcass of an animal) in order to extract proteins, fats, and other usable parts: (as adj. **rendered**) *the* ***rendered down*** *remains of sheep.*
6 cover (stone or brick) with a coat of plaster: *external walls will be rendered and tiled.*
▸ **noun** [mass noun] a first coat of plaster applied to a brick or stone surface.
– DERIVATIVES **renderer** noun.
– ORIGIN late Middle English: from Old French *rendre*, from an alteration of Latin *reddere* 'give back', from *re-* 'back' + *dare* 'give'. The earliest senses were 'recite', 'translate', and 'give back' (hence 'represent' and 'perform'); 'hand over' (hence 'give help' and 'submit for consideration'); 'cause to be'; and 'melt down'.

WORD TRENDS See RENDITION.

rendering ▸ **noun 1** a performance of a piece of music or drama: *a lively rendering of 'Ilkley Moor'.* ■ a translation: *a literal rendering of an idiom.* ■ an artistic depiction of something: *a trompe l'oeil rendering of Mount Rushmore.* ■ [mass noun] Computing the processing of an outline image using colour and shading to make it appear solid and three-dimensional.
2 [mass noun] the action of applying plaster to a wall. ■ [count noun] a coating of plaster applied to a wall.
3 [mass noun] formal the action of giving or surrendering something: *the rendering of Church dues.*

render-set ▸ **verb** [with obj.] plaster (a wall) with two coats.
▸ **noun** [mass noun] plastering consisting of two coats.

rendezvous /ˈrɒndɪvuː, -deɪvuː/ ▸ **noun** (pl. **same** /-vuːz/) a meeting at an agreed time and place: *Edward turned up late for their rendezvous.* ■ a meeting place. ■ a bar, restaurant, or similar establishment that is used as a popular meeting place.
▸ **verb** (**rendezvouses** /-vuːz/, **rendezvousing** /-vuːɪŋ/, **rendezvoused** /-vuːd/) [no obj.] meet at an agreed time and place: *I rendezvoused with Bea as planned.*

R

– ORIGIN late 16th cent.: from French *rendez-vous!* 'present yourselves!', imperative of *se rendre*.

rendition ▸ **noun 1** a performance or interpretation, especially of a dramatic role or piece of music: *a wonderful rendition of 'Nessun Dorma'*. ■ a visual representation or reproduction: *a pen-and-ink rendition of Mars with his sword drawn*. ■ a translation or transliteration.
2 (also **extraordinary rendition**) [mass noun] (especially in the US) the practice of sending a foreign criminal or terrorist suspect covertly to be interrogated in a country with less rigorous regulations for the humane treatment of prisoners.
– ORIGIN early 17th cent.: from obsolete French, from *rendre* 'give back, render'.

> **WORD TRENDS** Although recorded as far back as 1980, the new sense of **rendition** is generally regarded as a product of the 'War on Terror'. It refers to the morally and legally ambiguous practice of sending suspects to be questioned in countries known to use harsh interrogation techniques and even torture. The Oxford English Corpus has shown a steady increase in examples throughout the last decade, with a particular rise in the phrase *extraordinary rendition*, which is now the most common collocate of **rendition** by far. The practice has also spawned a new sense of the verb **render**, meaning 'send someone abroad for interrogation'. Like *extraordinary rendition*, this has seen a surge in use in the last two years: *he was seized in Pakistan and later secretly rendered to Morocco*.

rendzina /rɛn(d)ˈziːnə/ ▸ **noun** Soil Science a fertile lime-rich soil with dark humus above a pale soft calcareous layer, typical of grassland on chalk or limestone.
– ORIGIN 1920s: via Russian from Polish *rędzina*.

renegade /ˈrɛnɪɡeɪd/ ▸ **noun** a person who deserts and betrays an organization, country, or set of principles. ■ archaic a person who abandons religion; an apostate. ■ a person who behaves in a rebelliously unconventional manner: *he was a renegade and social malcontent*.
▸ **adjective** having treacherously changed allegiance: *a renegade bodyguard*. ■ archaic having abandoned one's religious beliefs: *a renegade monk*.
▸ **verb** [no obj.] archaic become a renegade: *Johnson had renegaded from the Confederacy*.
– ORIGIN late 15th cent.: from Spanish *renegado*, from medieval Latin *renegatus* 'renounced', past participle (used as a noun) of *renegare*, from *re-* (expressing intensive force) + Latin *negare* 'deny'.

renegado /ˌrɛnɪˈɡeɪdəʊ/ ▸ **noun** (pl. **renegadoes**) archaic term for **RENEGADE**.
– ORIGIN Spanish.

renege /rɪˈneɪɡ, rɪˈniːɡ/ (also **renegue**) ▸ **verb** [no obj.] go back on a promise, undertaking, or contract: *the government had **reneged on** its election promises*. ■ another term for **REVOKE** (sense 2). ■ [with obj.] archaic renounce or abandon: *there's one of them, anyhow, that didn't renege him*.
– DERIVATIVES **reneger** noun.
– ORIGIN mid 16th cent. (in the sense 'desert'): from medieval Latin *renegare*, from Latin *re-* (expressing intensive force) + *negare* 'deny'.

R

renegotiate ▸ **verb** [with obj.] negotiate (something) again in order to change the original agreed terms: *the parties will renegotiate the price*.
– DERIVATIVES **renegotiable** adjective, **renegotiation** noun.

renew ▸ **verb** [with obj.] **1** resume (an activity) after an interruption: *the parents renewed their campaign to save the school*. ■ re-establish (a relationship): *he had renewed an acquaintance with MacAlister*. ■ repeat (a statement): *detectives renewed their appeal for witnesses to contact them*.
2 (usu. as adj. **renewed**) give fresh life or strength to: *she would face the future with renewed determination*. ■ extend the period of validity of (a licence, subscription, or contract): *her contract had not been renewed*.
3 replace (something that is broken or worn out): *a generator was replaced and filters were renewed*.
– DERIVATIVES **renewer** noun.

renewable ▸ **adjective** capable of being renewed: *we are on renewable annual contracts*. ■ (of energy or its source) not depleted when used: *a shift away from fossil fuels to renewable energy*.
▸ **noun** (usu. **renewables**) a source of energy that is not depleted by use, such as water, wind, or solar power.
– DERIVATIVES **renewability** noun.

renewal ▸ **noun 1** an instance of resuming something after an interruption: *a renewal of hostilities*.
2 [mass noun] the action of extending the period of validity of a licence, subscription, or contract: *the contracts came up for renewal* | [count noun] *a renewal of his passport*.
3 [mass noun] the replacement or repair of something: *the need for urban renewal*. ■ (among charismatic Christians) the state or process of being made spiritually new in the Holy Spirit.

Renfrewshire /ˈrɛnfruːʃɪə, -ʃə/ a council area and former county of west central Scotland, on the Firth of Clyde, divided into **Renfrewshire** and **East Renfrewshire**.

renga /ˈrɛŋɡə/ ▸ **noun** (pl. **same** or **rengas**) a Japanese poem in the form of a tanka (or series of tanka), with the first three lines composed by one person and the second two by another.
– ORIGIN Japanese, from *ren* 'linking' + *ga* (from *ka* 'poetry').

reniform /ˈriːnɪfɔːm/ ▸ **adjective** chiefly Mineralogy & Botany kidney-shaped.
– ORIGIN mid 18th cent.: from Latin *ren* 'kidney' + **-IFORM**.

renin /ˈriːnɪn/ ▸ **noun** [mass noun] Biochemistry an enzyme secreted by and stored in the kidneys which promotes the production of the protein angiotensin.
– ORIGIN late 19th cent.: from Latin *ren* 'kidney' + **-IN**[1].

renminbi /ˈrɛnmɪnbi/ ▸ **noun** [mass noun] the system of currency of the People's Republic of China, introduced in 1948. ■ another term for **YUAN**.
– ORIGIN from Chinese *rénmínbì*, from *rénmín* 'people' + *bì* 'currency'.

Rennes /rɛn/, French /ʀɛn/ an industrial city in NW France; pop. 214,813 (2006). It was established as the capital of a Celtic tribe, the Redones, from whom it derives its name, later becoming the capital of the ancient kingdom of Brittany.

rennet /ˈrɛnɪt/ ▸ **noun** [mass noun] curdled milk from the stomach of an unweaned calf, containing rennin and used in curdling milk for cheese. ■ a preparation containing rennin.
– ORIGIN late 15th cent.: probably related to **RUN**.

Rennie, John (1761–1821), Scottish civil engineer. He is best known as the designer of the London and East India Docks (built *c.*1800), and Waterloo Bridge, Southwark Bridge, and London Bridge (1811–31).

rennin /ˈrɛnɪn/ ▸ **noun** [mass noun] an enzyme secreted into the stomach of unweaned mammals causing the curdling of milk.
– ORIGIN late 19th cent.: from **RENNET** + **-IN**[1].

Reno /ˈriːnəʊ/ a city in western Nevada; pop. 217,016 (est. 2008). It is noted as a gambling resort and for its liberal laws enabling quick marriages and divorces.

Renoir[1] /rəˈnwɑː, ˈrɛnwɑː/, French /ʀənwaʀ/, Jean (1894–1979), French film director, son of Auguste Renoir. Notable films: *La Grande illusion* (1937) and *La Règle du jeu* (1939).

Renoir[2] /rəˈnwɑː, ˈrɛnwɑː/, French /ʀənwaʀ/, (Pierre) Auguste (1841–1919), French painter. An early Impressionist, he developed a style characterized by light, fresh colours and indistinct, subtle outlines. Notable works: *Les Grandes baigneuses* (1884–7).

renominate ▸ **verb** [with obj.] nominate (someone) for a further term of office.
– DERIVATIVES **renomination** noun.

renormalization (also **renormalisation**) ▸ **noun** [mass noun] Physics a method used in quantum mechanics in which unwanted infinities are removed from the solutions of equations by redefining parameters such as the mass and charge of subatomic particles.
– DERIVATIVES **renormalize** verb.

renosterbos /rɛˈnɒstəbɒs/ ▸ **noun** a grey-leaved, evergreen southern African shrub of the daisy family. ● *Elytropappus rhinocerotis*, family Compositae.
– ORIGIN early 19th cent.: from Afrikaans, from *renoster* 'rhinoceros' + *bos* 'bush'.

renosterveld /rɛˈnɒstəvɛlt/ ▸ **noun** [mass noun] S. African land on which the dominant vegetation is renosterbos.
– ORIGIN 1950s: blend of **RENOSTERBOS** and **VELD**.

renounce ▸ **verb** [with obj.] formally declare one's abandonment of (a claim, right, or possession): *Isabella offered to renounce her son's claim to the French Crown*. ■ [no obj.] Law refuse or resign a right or position, especially one as an heir or trustee: *there will be forms enabling the allottee to renounce*. ■ refuse to continue to recognize or abide by: *these agreements were renounced after the fall of the Tsarist regime*. ■ reject or abandon (a cause, bad habit, or way of life): *they renounced the armed struggle* | *he renounced alcohol completely*.
– PHRASES **renounce the world** completely withdraw from society in order to lead a more spiritually fulfilling life.
– DERIVATIVES **renounceable** adjective, **renouncement** noun, **renouncer** noun.
– ORIGIN late Middle English: from Old French *renoncer*, from Latin *renuntiare* 'protest against', from *re-* (expressing reversal) + *nuntiare* 'announce'.

renovate /ˈrɛnəveɪt/ ▸ **verb** [with obj.] restore (something old, especially a building) to a good state of repair: *the old school has been tastefully renovated as a private house*. ■ archaic refresh; reinvigorate: *a little warm nourishment renovated him for a short time*.
– DERIVATIVES **renovator** noun.
– ORIGIN early 16th cent.: from Latin *renovat-* 'made new again', from the verb *renovare*, from *re-* 'back, again' + *novus* 'new'.

renovation ▸ **noun** [mass noun] the action of renovating a building: *this property is in need of complete renovation* | [count noun] *older churches underwent major renovations*.

renown ▸ **noun** [mass noun] the condition of being known or talked about by many people; fame: *authors of great renown*.
– ORIGIN Middle English: from Anglo-Norman French *renoun*, from Old French *renomer* 'make famous', from *re-* (expressing intensive force) + *nomer* 'to name', from Latin *nominare*.

renowned ▸ **adjective** known or talked about by many people; famous: *Britain is **renowned for** its love of animals* | *a renowned author*.

rent[1] ▸ **noun** [mass noun] a tenant's regular payment to a landlord for the use of property or land. ■ a sum paid for the hire of equipment.
▸ **verb** [with obj.] pay someone for the use of (something, typically property, land, or a car): *they rented a house together in Sussex* | (as adj. **rented**) *a rented apartment*. ■ (of an owner) allow someone to use (something) in return for payment: *he purchased a large tract of land and **rented it out** to local farmers*. ■ [no obj.] N. Amer. be let or hired out at a specified rate: *skis or snowboards **rent for** $60–80 for six days*.
– PHRASES **for rent** available to be rented.
– ORIGIN Middle English: from Old French *rente*, from a root shared by **RENDER**.

rent[2] ▸ **noun** a large tear in a piece of fabric: *Eddie was dismayed by the rent in the roof of the tent* | figurative *they stared at the rents in the clouds*.
– ORIGIN mid 16th cent.: from obsolete *rent* 'pull to pieces, lacerate', variant of **REND**.

rent[3] past and past participle of **REND**.

rent-a- ▸ **combining form** often humorous denoting availability for hire of a specified thing: *rent-a-car* | *rent-a-crowd*.

rentable ▸ **adjective** available or suitable for renting: *rentable office space*.
– DERIVATIVES **rentability** noun.

rental ▸ **noun** an amount paid or received as rent. ■ [mass noun] the action of renting something: *the office was **on** weekly **rental***. ■ N. Amer. a rented house or car.
▸ **adjective** relating to or available for rent: *rental accommodation*.
– ORIGIN late Middle English: from Anglo-Norman French, or from Anglo-Latin *rentale*, from Old French *rente* (see **RENT**[1]).

rental library ▸ **noun** US a library which rents books and other material for a fee.

rent boy ▸ **noun** Brit. informal a young male prostitute.

renter ▸ **noun 1** a person who rents a flat, car, or other object.
2 US a rented car or video cassette.
3 Brit. informal a male prostitute.

rent-free ▸ **adjective & adverb** with exemption from rent: [as adj.] *rent-free periods* | [as adv.] *you could live in the cottage rent-free*.

rentier /ˈrɒntɪeɪ/, French /ʀɑ̃tje/ ▸ **noun** a person living on income from property or investments.
– ORIGIN French, from *rente* 'dividend'.

rent party ▸ **noun** US a party held to raise money to pay rent by charging guests for attendance.

rent roll ▸ **noun** a register of a landlord's lands and buildings with the rents due from them. ■ a landlord's total income from rent.

rent table ▸ **noun** a circular or octagonal office table of a kind made in the 18th century.

renumber ▸ **verb** [with obj.] change the number or numbers assigned to (something).

renunciation ▸ **noun** [mass noun] the formal rejection of something, typically a belief, claim, or course of action: *the life of the Spirit required renunciation of marriage* | [count noun] *a renunciation of violence.* ■ Law express or tacit abandonment of a right or position, usually without assignment to another person.
– DERIVATIVES **renunciant** noun & adjective, **renunciative** /rɪˈnʌnsɪətɪv/ adjective, **renunciatory** /rɪˈnʌnʃət(ə)ri/ adjective.
– ORIGIN late Middle English: from late Latin *renuntiatio(n-)*, from Latin *renuntiare* 'protest against' (see RENOUNCE).

renvers /ˈrɛnvəs/ (also **renverse**) ▸ **noun** a movement performed in dressage, in which the horse moves parallel to the side of the arena, with its hindquarters carried closer to the wall than its shoulders and its body curved away from the centre.
– ORIGIN French.

renvoi /ˈrɒ̃vwʌ/ ▸ **noun** [mass noun] Law the action or process of referring a case or dispute to the jurisdiction of another country.
– ORIGIN late 19th cent.: French, from *renvoyer* 'send back'.

reoccupy ▸ **verb** (**reoccupies, reoccupying, reoccupied**) [with obj.] occupy (a place or position) again: *the English reoccupied the border counties.*
– DERIVATIVES **reoccupation** noun.

reoccur ▸ **verb** (**reoccurs, reoccurring, reoccurred**) [no obj.] occur again or repeatedly: *ulcers tend to reoccur after treatment has stopped.*
– DERIVATIVES **reoccurrence** noun.

reoffend ▸ **verb** [no obj.] commit a further offence: *people who reoffend while on bail.*
– DERIVATIVES **reoffender** noun.

reopen ▸ **verb** [with obj.] open again: *after being renovated the house was reopened to the public* | [no obj.] *the trial reopens on 6 March.*

reorder ▸ **verb** [with obj.] **1** request (something) to be made, supplied, or served again: *reps reorder any titles which fall below the agreed number.*
2 arrange (something) again or differently: *he fixed his bed and reordered his books.*
▸ **noun** a renewed or repeated order for goods.

reorg ▸ **noun** informal a reorganization.

reorganize (also **reorganise**) ▸ **verb** [with obj.] change the way in which (something) is organized: *we have to reorganize the entire workload* | [no obj.] *the company reorganized into fewer key areas.*
– DERIVATIVES **reorganization** noun, **reorganizer** noun.

reorient /riːˈɔːrɪɛnt, -ˈɒr-/ ▸ **verb** [with obj.] change the focus or direction of: *the country began reorienting its economic and social policies in 1988.* ■ (**reorient oneself**) find one's position again in relation to one's surroundings: *slowly they advanced, stopping every so often and then reorienting themselves.*
– DERIVATIVES **reorientate** verb, **reorientation** noun.

reovirus /ˈriːə(ʊ),vʌɪrəs/ ▸ **noun** any of a group of RNA viruses that are sometimes associated with respiratory and enteric infection.
– ORIGIN 1950s: from the initial letters of *respiratory, enteric,* and *orphan* (referring to a virus not identified with a particular disease) + VIRUS.

rep[1] informal ▸ **noun** a representative: *a union rep.* ■ a sales representative.
▸ **verb** (**reps, repping, repped**) [no obj.] act as a sales representative: *at eighteen she was working for her dad, repping on the road.*
– ORIGIN late 19th cent.: abbreviation.

rep[2] ▸ **noun** [mass noun] informal repertory: *once, when I was in rep, I learned Iago in three days.* ■ [count noun] a repertory theatre or company.
– ORIGIN 1920s: abbreviation.

rep[3] (also **repp**) ▸ **noun** [mass noun] a fabric with a ribbed surface, used in curtains and upholstery.
– ORIGIN mid 19th cent.: from French *reps*, of unknown ultimate origin.

rep[4] ▸ **noun** N. Amer. informal short for REPUTATION: *I don't know why caffeine's suddenly got such a bad rep.*

rep[5] ▸ **noun** (in bodybuilding) a repetition of a set of exercises.
▸ **verb** (**reps, repping, repped**) [with obj.] (in knitting patterns) repeat (stitches or part of a design).
– ORIGIN 1950s: abbreviation.

Rep. ▸ **abbreviation** ■ (in the US Congress) Representative. ■ Republic. ■ US a Republican.

repack ▸ **verb** [with obj.] pack (a suitcase or bag) again.

repackage ▸ **verb** [with obj.] package again or differently: *excess stock may be given to charities or repackaged.* ■ present in a new way: *the commission has repackaged its ideas.*
– DERIVATIVES **repackaging** noun.

repaginate ▸ **verb** [with obj.] renumber the pages of (a book, magazine, or other printed item).
– DERIVATIVES **repagination** noun.

repaid past and past participle of REPAY.

repaint ▸ **verb** [with obj.] cover with a new coat of paint.
▸ **noun** [in sing.] an act of painting something again.

repair[1] ▸ **verb** [with obj.] restore (something damaged, faulty, or worn) to a good condition: *faulty electrical appliances should be repaired by an electrician.* ■ make good (damage). ■ put right (an unwelcome situation): *the new government moved quickly to repair relations with the USA.*
▸ **noun** [mass noun] the action of repairing something: *the truck was* ***beyond repair*** | [count noun] *the abandoned house they bought needs repairs.* ■ [count noun] a result of repairing something: *a coat of French polish was brushed over the repair.* ■ the relative physical condition of an object: *the hospital is* ***in a bad state of repair.***
– DERIVATIVES **repairable** adjective, **repairer** noun.
– ORIGIN late Middle English: from Old French *reparer*, from Latin *reparare*, from *re-* 'back' + *parare* 'make ready'.

repair[2] ▸ **verb** [no obj.] (**repair to**) formal or humorous go to (a place), especially in company: *we repaired to the tranquillity of a nearby cafe.*
▸ **noun** [mass noun] archaic frequent or habitual visiting of a place: *she exhorted repair to the church.* ■ [count noun] a place which is frequently visited or occupied: *the repairs of wild beasts.*
– ORIGIN Middle English: from Old French *repairer*, from late Latin *repatriare* 'return to one's country' (see REPATRIATE).

repairman ▸ **noun** (pl. **repairmen**) a person who repairs vehicles, machinery, or appliances.

repaper ▸ **verb** [with obj.] apply new wallpaper to (a wall or room).

reparable /ˈrɛp(ə)rəb(ə)l/ ▸ **adjective** (especially of an injury or loss) possible to rectify or repair.
– ORIGIN late 16th cent.: from French *réparable*, from Latin *reparabilis*, from *reparare* 'make ready again' (see REPAIR[1]).

reparation /,rɛpəˈreɪʃ(ə)n/ ▸ **noun** [mass noun] **1** the action of making amends for a wrong one has done, by providing payment or other assistance to those who have been wronged: *the courts required a convicted offender to* ***make financial reparation to*** *his victim.* ■ (**reparations**) the compensation for war damage paid by a defeated state.
2 archaic the action of repairing something: *the old hall was pulled down to avoid the cost of reparation.*
– DERIVATIVES **reparative** /ˈrɛp(ə)rətɪv, rɪˈparətɪv/ adjective.
– ORIGIN late Middle English: from Old French, from late Latin *reparatio(n-)*, from *reparare* 'make ready again' (see REPAIR[1]).

repartee /,rɛpɑːˈtiː/ ▸ **noun** [mass noun] conversation or speech characterized by quick, witty comments or replies.
– ORIGIN mid 17th cent.: from French *repartie* 'replied promptly', feminine past participle of *repartir*, from *re-* 'again' + *partir* 'set off'.

repartition ▸ **verb** [with obj.] partition or divide (something) again.

repass ▸ **verb** [no obj.] pass again, especially on the way back.
– ORIGIN late Middle English: from Old French *repasser*.

repast /rɪˈpɑːst/ ▸ **noun** formal a meal: *a sumptuous repast.*
– ORIGIN late Middle English: from Old French, based on late Latin *repascere*, from *re-* (expressing intensive force) + *pascere* 'to feed'.

repat /ˈriːpat, riːˈpat/ ▸ **noun** Brit. informal, dated a person who has been repatriated.
– ORIGIN 1940s: abbreviation.

repatriate /riːˈpatrɪeɪt, -ˈpeɪ-/ ▸ **verb** [with obj.] send (someone) back to their own country: *the last German POWs were repatriated in November 1948.* ■ send or bring (money) back to one's own country: *foreign firms would be permitted to repatriate all profits.*
▸ **noun** a person who has been repatriated.
– DERIVATIVES **repatriation** noun.
– ORIGIN early 17th cent. (earlier (late 16th cent.) as *repatriation*): from late Latin *repatriat-* 'returned to one's country', from the verb *repatriare*, from *re-* 'back' + Latin *patria* 'native land'.

repay ▸ **verb** (past and past participle **repaid**) [with obj.] pay back (a loan): *the loans were to be repaid over a 20-year period.* ■ pay back money borrowed from (someone): *most of his fortune had been spent repaying creditors.* ■ do or give something as recompense for (a favour or kindness received): *the manager has given me another chance and I'm desperate to repay that faith.* ■ Brit. be worth devoting time to (a specified action): *these sites would repay more detailed investigation.*
– DERIVATIVES **repayable** adjective.
– ORIGIN late Middle English: from Old French *repaier*.

repayment ▸ **noun** [mass noun] the action of paying back a loan. ■ [count noun] an amount of money paid back: *minimum monthly repayments.*

repayment mortgage ▸ **noun** Brit. a mortgage in which the borrower repays the capital and interest together in fixed instalments over a fixed period.

repeal ▸ **verb** [with obj.] revoke or annul (a law or act of parliament): *the legislation was repealed five months later.*
▸ **noun** [mass noun] the action of revoking or annulling a law or act of parliament: *the House voted in favour of repeal.*
– DERIVATIVES **repealable** adjective.
– ORIGIN late Middle English: from Anglo-Norman French *repeler*, from Old French *re-* (expressing reversal) + *apeler* 'to call, appeal'.

repeat ▸ **verb 1** [reporting verb] say again something one has already said: [with direct speech] *'Are you hurt?' he repeated* | [with obj.] *Billy repeated his question* | [with clause] *Ann repeated that she was very comfortable.* ■ say again (something said or written by someone else): *he repeated the words after me* | [with clause] *she repeated what I'd said.* ■ (**repeat oneself**) say or do the same thing again.
2 [with obj.] do (something) again or more than once: *earlier experiments were repeated on a larger scale.* ■ broadcast (a television or radio programme) again. ■ undertake (a course or period of instruction) again: *Mark had to repeat first and second grades.* ■ (**repeat itself**) occur again in the same way or form: *I don't intend to let history repeat itself.* ■ [no obj.] US illegally vote more than once in an election. ■ [no obj.] N. Amer. attain an achievement again, especially by winning a championship for the second consecutive time: *the first team in nineteen years to repeat as NBA champions.*
3 [no obj.] chiefly Brit. (of food) be tasted intermittently for some time after being swallowed as a result of belching or indigestion: *that cucumber* ***repeated on me*** *for hours.*
▸ **noun** something that occurs or is done again: *the final will be a repeat of last year.* ■ a repeated broadcast of a television or radio programme. ■ [as modifier] occurring, done, or used more than once: *a repeat prescription* | *a repeat offender.* ■ a consignment of goods similar to one already received. ■ a decorative pattern which is repeated uniformly over a surface. ■ Music a passage intended to be repeated. ■ Music a mark indicating a passage to be repeated.
– DERIVATIVES **repeatability** noun, **repeatable** adjective.
– ORIGIN late Middle English: from Old French *repeter*, from Latin *repetere*, from *re-* 'back' + *petere* 'seek'.

repeated ▸ **adjective** done or occurring again several times in the same way: *there were repeated attempts to negotiate* | *despite repeated requests, neither company gave a satisfactory answer.*

repeatedly ▸ **adverb** over and over again; constantly: *they have been warned repeatedly with no effect.*

repeater ▸ **noun** a person or thing that repeats something, in particular: ■ a firearm which fires several shots without reloading. ■ a watch or clock which repeats its last strike when required. ■ a device for the automatic retransmission or amplification of an electrically transmitted message. ■ a railway signal indicating the state of another that is out of sight.

repeat fee ▸ **noun** a fee paid to a radio or television artist each time their performance is rebroadcast.

repeating ▸ **adjective 1** (of a firearm) capable of firing several shots in succession without reloading.
2 (of a pattern) recurring uniformly over a surface.

repeating decimal ▸ **noun** a recurring decimal.

R

repêchage /ˈrɛpəʃɑːʒ/ ▶ **noun** (in rowing and other sports) a contest in which the runners-up in the eliminating heats compete for a place in the final.
– ORIGIN early 20th cent.: French, from *repêcher* 'fish out, rescue'.

repel ▶ **verb** (**repels**, **repelling**, **repelled**) [with obj.] **1** drive or force (an attack or attacker) back or away: *government units sought to repel the rebels.* ■ (of a magnetic pole or electric field) force (something similarly magnetized or charged) away from itself: *electrically charged objects attract or repel one another* | [no obj.] *like poles repel and unlike poles attract.* ■ (of a substance) resist mixing with or be impervious to (another substance): *boots with good-quality leather uppers to repel moisture.*
2 be repulsive or distasteful to: *she was repelled by the permanent smell of drink on his breath.*
3 formal refuse to accept (something, especially an argument or theory): *the alleged right of lien led by the bankrupt's solicitor was repelled.*
– DERIVATIVES **repeller** noun.
– ORIGIN late Middle English: from Latin *repellere*, from *re-* 'back' + *pellere* 'to drive'.

repellent (also **repellant**) ▶ **adjective 1** [often in combination] able to repel a particular thing; impervious to a particular substance: *water-repellent nylon.*
2 causing disgust or distaste: *the idea was slightly repellent to her.*
▶ **noun 1** a substance that dissuades particular insects or other pests from approaching or settling: *a flea repellent.*
2 a substance used to treat something, especially fabric or stone, so as to make it impervious to water: *treat brick with a silicone water repellent.*
– DERIVATIVES **repellence** noun, **repellency** noun, **repellently** adverb.
– ORIGIN mid 17th cent.: from Latin *repellent-* 'driving back', from the verb *repellere* (see REPEL).

repent ▶ **verb** [no obj.] feel or express sincere regret or remorse about one's wrongdoing or sin: *the Padre urged his listeners to repent* | *he repented of his action.* ■ [with obj.] view or think of (an action or omission) with deep regret or remorse: *Marian came to repent her hasty judgement.* ■ (**repent oneself**) archaic feel regret or penitence about: *I repent me of all I did.*
– DERIVATIVES **repenter** noun.
– ORIGIN Middle English: from Old French *repentir*, from *re-* (expressing intensive force) + *pentir* (based on Latin *paenitere* 'cause to repent').

repentance ▶ **noun** [mass noun] the action of repenting; sincere regret or remorse: *each person who turns to God in genuine repentance and faith will be saved.*

repentant ▶ **adjective** expressing or feeling sincere regret and remorse; remorseful: *he is truly repentant for his incredible naivety and stupidity.*

repeople ▶ **verb** [with obj.] repopulate (a place).

repercussion ▶ **noun 1** (usu. **repercussions**) an unintended consequence of an event or action, especially an unwelcome one: *the move would have grave repercussions for the entire region.*
2 archaic the recoil of something after impact.
3 archaic an echo or reverberation.
– DERIVATIVES **repercussive** adjective.
– ORIGIN late Middle English (as a medical term meaning 'repressing of infection'): from Old French, or from Latin *repercussio(n-)*, from *repercutere* 'cause to rebound, push back', from *re-* 'back, again' + *percutere* 'to strike'. The early sense 'driving back, rebounding' (mid 16th cent.) gave rise later to 'blow given in return', hence sense 1 (early 20th cent.).

R

reperfusion /riːpəˈfjuːʒ(ə)n/ ▶ **noun** [mass noun] Medicine the action of restoring the flow of blood to an organ or tissue, typically after a heart attack or stroke.

repertoire /ˈrɛpətwɑː/ ▶ **noun** a stock of plays, dances, or items that a company or a performer knows or is prepared to perform. ■ the whole body of items which are regularly performed: *the mainstream concert repertoire.* ■ a stock of skills or types of behaviour that a person habitually uses: *his repertoire of denigratory gestures.*
– ORIGIN mid 19th cent.: from French *répertoire*, from late Latin *repertorium* (see REPERTORY).

repertory /ˈrɛpət(ə)ri/ ▶ **noun** (pl. **repertories**) **1** [mass noun] the performance of various plays, operas, or ballets by a company at regular short intervals: [as modifier] *a repertory actor.* ■ repertory theatres regarded collectively. ■ [count noun] a repertory company.
2 another term for REPERTOIRE. ■ a repository or collection, especially of information.
– ORIGIN mid 16th cent. (denoting an index or catalogue): from late Latin *repertorium*, from Latin *repert-* 'found, discovered', from the verb *reperire*. Sense 1 (arising from the fact that a company has a 'repertory' of pieces for performance) dates from the late 19th cent.

repertory company ▶ **noun** a theatrical company that performs plays from its repertoire for regular, short periods of time, moving on from one play to another.

repetend /ˈrɛpɪtɛnd, ˌrɛpɪˈtɛnd/ ▶ **noun** Mathematics the repeating figure or figures of a recurring decimal fraction. ■ formal a recurring word or phrase; a refrain.
– ORIGIN early 18th cent.: from Latin *repetendum* 'something to be repeated', neuter gerundive of *repetere* (see REPEAT).

répétiteur /rɛˌpɛtɪˈtəː/ ▶ **noun** a tutor or coach of ballet dancers or musicians, especially opera singers.
– ORIGIN French.

repetition ▶ **noun** [mass noun] **1** the action of repeating something that has already been said or written: *her comments are worthy of repetition* | [count noun] *a repetition of his reply to the delegation.* ■ [count noun] archaic a piece set by a teacher to be learned by heart and recited.
2 [often with negative] the recurrence of an action or event: *there was to be no repetition of the interwar years* | [count noun] *I didn't want a repetition of the scene in my office that morning.* ■ [count noun] a thing repeated: *the geometric repetitions of Islamic art.* ■ [count noun] a training exercise which is repeated, especially a series of repeated raisings and lowerings of the weight in weight training. ■ Music the repeating of a passage or note.
– DERIVATIVES **repetitional** adjective.
– ORIGIN late Middle English: from Old French *repeticion* or Latin *repetitio(n-)*, from *repetere* (see REPEAT).

repetitious ▶ **adjective** another term for REPETITIVE: *many hours of repetitious labour.*
– DERIVATIVES **repetitiously** adverb, **repetitiousness** noun.

repetitive ▶ **adjective** containing or characterized by repetition, especially when unnecessary or tiresome: *a repetitive task.*
– DERIVATIVES **repetitively** adverb, **repetitiveness** noun.

repetitive strain injury (abbrev.: **RSI**) ▶ **noun** [mass noun] a condition in which the prolonged performance of repetitive actions, typically with the hands, causes pain or impairment of function in the tendons and muscles involved.

rephrase ▶ **verb** [with obj.] express (an idea or question) in an alternative way, especially for the purpose of clarification: *rephrase the statement so that it is clear.*

repine ▶ **verb** [no obj.] literary feel or express discontent; fret: *you mustn't let yourself repine.*
– ORIGIN early 16th cent.: from RE- 'again' + the verb PINE², on the pattern of *repent*.

repique /rɪˈpiːk/ ▶ **noun** (in piquet) the scoring of 30 points on declarations alone before beginning to play. Compare with PIQUE².
▶ **verb** (**repiques**, **repiquing**, **repiqued**) [with obj.] score a repique against (one's opponent).
– ORIGIN mid 17th cent.: from French *repic*; compare with Italian *ripicco*.

replace ▶ **verb** [with obj.] **1** take the place of: *Ian's smile was replaced by a frown.* ■ provide a substitute for (something that is broken, old, or inoperative): *the glass had not long been replaced after a fight.* ■ fill the role of (someone or something) with a substitute: *the government dismissed 3,000 of its customs inspectors, replacing them with new recruits.*
2 put (something) back in a previous place or position: *he drained his glass and replaced it on the bar.*
– DERIVATIVES **replacer** noun.

replaceable ▶ **adjective** able to be replaced: *a knife with a replaceable blade.* ■ Chemistry denoting those hydrogen atoms in an acid which can be displaced by metal atoms when forming salts.

replacement ▶ **noun** [mass noun] the action or process of replacing someone or something: *the replacement of religion by poetry* | [count noun] *a hip replacement.* ■ a person or thing that takes the place of another.

replacement therapy ▶ **noun** [mass noun] Medicine treatment aimed at making up a deficit of a substance normally present in the body.

replan ▶ **verb** (**replans**, **replanning**, **replanned**) [with obj.] plan (something, especially the layout of buildings or cities) differently or again.

replant ▶ **verb** [with obj.] plant (a tree or plant which has been dug up) again, especially in a larger pot or new site. ■ provide (an area) with new plants or trees: *38 per cent of ancient woodland has been replanted with conifers.* ■ surgically reattach to the body (a part that has been removed or severed).

replaster ▶ **verb** [with obj.] plaster (a surface) again.

replay ▶ **verb** [with obj.] **1** play back (a recording on tape, video, or film): *he could stop the tape and replay it whenever he wished.*
2 repeat (something, especially an event): *she replayed in her mind every detail of the night before.* ■ play (a match) again to decide a winner after the original encounter ended in a draw or contentious result.
▶ **noun 1** [mass noun] the playing again of part of a recording, especially so as to be able to watch an incident more closely: *clouds can be studied in speeded-up replay* | [count noun] *the umpire studied TV replays.*
2 an occurrence which closely follows the pattern of a previous event: *the second goal was a replay of the first.* ■ a replayed match.

replenish ▶ **verb** [with obj.] fill (something) up again: *he replenished Justin's glass with mineral water.* ■ restore (a stock or supply) to a former level or condition: *all creatures need sleep to replenish their energies.*
– DERIVATIVES **replenisher** noun, **replenishment** noun.
– ORIGIN late Middle English (in the sense 'supply abundantly'): from Old French *repleniss-*, lengthened stem of *replenir*, from *re-* 'again' (also expressing intensive force) + *plenir* 'fill' (from Latin *plenus* 'full').

replete /rɪˈpliːt/ ▶ **adjective** [predic.] filled or well-supplied with something: *sensational popular fiction, replete with adultery and sudden death.* ■ very full of or sated by food: *I went out into the sun-drenched streets again, replete and relaxed.*
– DERIVATIVES **repletion** noun.
– ORIGIN late Middle English: from Old French *replet(e)* or Latin *repletus* 'filled up', past participle of *replere*, from *re-* 'back, again' + *plere* 'fill'.

replevin /rɪˈplɛvɪn/ ▶ **noun** [mass noun] Law a procedure whereby seized goods may be provisionally restored to their owner pending the outcome of an action to determine the rights of the parties concerned. ■ [count noun] an action arising from the process of replevin.
– ORIGIN late Middle English: from Anglo-Norman French, from Old French *replevir* 'recover' (see REPLEVY).

replevy /rɪˈplɛvi/ ▶ **verb** (**replevies**, **replevying**, **replevied**) [with obj.] Law recover (seized goods) by replevin.
– ORIGIN mid 16th cent.: from Old French *replevir* 'recover'; apparently related to PLEDGE.

replica ▶ **noun** an exact copy or model of something, especially one on a smaller scale: *a replica of the Empire State Building.*
– ORIGIN mid 18th cent. (as a musical term in the sense 'a repeat'): from Italian, from *replicare* 'to reply'.

replicant ▶ **noun** (in science fiction) a genetically engineered or artificial being created as an exact replica of a particular human being.
– ORIGIN from REPLICA + -ANT: first used in the film *Blade Runner* (1982).

replicase /ˈrɛplɪkeɪz/ ▶ **noun** [mass noun] Biochemistry an enzyme which catalyses the synthesis of a complementary RNA molecule using an RNA template.
– ORIGIN 1960s: from the verb REPLICATE + -ASE.

replicate ▶ **verb** /ˈrɛplɪkeɪt/ [with obj.] make an exact copy of; reproduce: *it might be impractical to replicate Eastern culture in the west.* ■ (**replicate itself**) (of genetic material or a living organism) reproduce or give rise to a copy of itself: *interleukin-16 prevents the virus from replicating itself.* ■ repeat (a scientific experiment or trial) to obtain a consistent result: *these findings have been replicated by Metzger and Antes.*
▶ **adjective** /ˈrɛplɪkət/ [attrib.] of the nature of a copy: *a replicate Earth.* ■ of the nature of a repetition of a scientific experiment or trial: *the variation of replicate measurements.*
▶ **noun** /ˈrɛplɪkət/ **1** a close or exact copy; a replica. ■ a repeated experiment or trial.
2 Music a tone one or more octaves above or below the given tone.
– DERIVATIVES **replicability** /ˌrɛplɪkəˈbɪlɪti/ noun, **replicable** /ˈrɛplɪkəb(ə)l/ adjective.
– ORIGIN late Middle English (in the sense 'repeat'): from Latin *replicat-*, from the verb *replicare*, from

re- 'back, again' + *plicare* 'to fold'. The current senses date from the late 19th cent.

replication ▶ **noun 1** [mass noun] the action of copying or reproducing something. ■ [count noun] a copy: *a twentieth-century building would be cheaper than a replication of what was there before.* ■ the repetition of a scientific experiment or trial to obtain a consistent result. ■ the process by which genetic material or a living organism gives rise to a copy of itself. **2** Law, dated a plaintiff's reply to the defendant's plea.
– ORIGIN late Middle English: from Old French *replicacion*, from Latin *replicatio(n-)*, from *replicare* 'fold back, repeat', later 'make a reply' (see REPLICATE).

replicative /ˈrɛplɪkətɪv/ ▶ **adjective** Biology relating to or involving the replication of genetic material or living organisms.

replicator ▶ **noun** a thing which replicates or copies something. ■ Biology a structural gene at which replication of a specific replicon is believed to be initiated.

replicon /ˈrɛplɪkɒn/ ▶ **noun** Biology a nucleic acid molecule, or part of one, which replicates as a unit, beginning at a specific site within it.
– ORIGIN 1960s: from REPLICATION + -ON.

reply ▶ **verb** (**replies, replying, replied**) [reporting verb] say something in response to something someone has said: [no obj.] *he was gone before we could* ***reply to*** *his last remark* | [with clause] *she replied that she had been sound asleep* | [with direct speech] *'I'm OK—just leave me alone,' he replied.* ■ [no obj.] write back in answer to someone: *she replied with a long letter the next day.* ■ [no obj.] respond by a similar action or gesture: *they* ***replied to*** *the shelling with a heavy mortar attack.*
▶ **noun** (pl. **replies**) a verbal or written answer: *I received a reply from the managing director* | *'No,' was the curt reply.* ■ [mass noun] the action of answering someone or something: *I am writing* ***in reply to*** *your letter.* ■ a response in the form of a gesture, action, or expression: *Clough scored the first goal and Speed hit a late reply.* ■ Law a plaintiff's response to the defendant's plea.
– DERIVATIVES **replier** noun.
– ORIGIN late Middle English (as a verb): from Old French *replier*, from Latin *replicare* 'repeat', later 'make a reply' (see REPLICATE).

reply coupon ▶ **noun** a coupon used for prepaying the postage for the reply to a letter sent to another country.

reply-paid ▶ **adjective** Brit. (of an envelope or card) having the postage for a reply prepaid.

repo /ˈriːpəʊ/ N. Amer. informal ▶ **noun** (pl. **repos**) **1** another term for REPURCHASE AGREEMENT.
2 a car or other item which has been repossessed.
▶ **verb** (**repo's, repo'ing, repo'd**) [with obj.] repossess (a car or other item) when a buyer defaults on payments.
– ORIGIN 1960s: abbreviation.

repoint ▶ **verb** [with obj.] fill in or repair the joints of (brickwork).

repolish ▶ **verb** [with obj.] polish (something) again.

repo man ▶ **noun** N. Amer. informal a person employed to repossess goods for which a purchaser has defaulted on payment.

repopulate ▶ **verb** [with obj.] introduce a population into (a previously occupied area or country): *the area was repopulated largely by Russians.* ■ populate or fill again: *probiotics help repopulate your gut with the healthy bacteria.*
– DERIVATIVES **repopulation** noun.

report ▶ **verb 1** [reporting verb] give a spoken or written account of something that one has observed, heard, done, or investigated: [with obj.] *the minister reported a decline in milk production* | [with clause] *police reported that the floods were abating* | [no obj.] *the teacher should* ***report on*** *the child's progress.* ■ [no obj.] cover an event or subject as a journalist or a reporter: *the press* ***reported on*** *Republican sex scandals* | [with clause] *the Egyptian news agency reported that a coup attempt had taken place.* ■ (**be reported**) used to indicate that something has been stated, although one cannot confirm its accuracy: [with infinitive] *hoaxers are reported to be hacking into airline frequencies to impersonate air traffic controllers* | (as adj. **reported**) *he's now a reported £50,000 in debt.* ■ [with obj.] make a formal statement or complaint about (someone or something) to the necessary authority: *undisclosed illegalities are* ***reported to*** *the company's directors* | [with obj. and complement] *eight Yorkshire terriers have been reported missing in the last month.* ■ [with obj.] Brit. (of a parliamentary committee chairman) formally announce that the committee has dealt with (a bill). ■ (**report something out**) US (of a committee of Congress) return a bill to the legislative body for action.
2 [no obj.] present oneself formally as having arrived at a particular place or as ready to do something: *he had to* ***report to*** *the headmaster at 4 p.m.* ■ (**report back**) return to work or duty after a period of absence.
3 [no obj.] (**report to**) be responsible to (a superior or supervisor): *he reports to the chairman of the committee.*
▶ **noun 1** an account given of a particular matter, especially in the form of an official document, after thorough investigation or consideration by an appointed person or body: *the chairman's annual report.* ■ a spoken or written description of an event or situation, especially one intended for publication or broadcasting in the media: *press reports suggested that the secret police were helping to maintain public order.* ■ Brit. a teacher's written assessment of a pupil's work, progress, and conduct, issued at the end of a term or school year. ■ Law a detailed formal account of a case heard in a court, giving the main points in the judgement, especially as prepared for publication.
2 a piece of information that is unsupported by firm evidence: *reports were circulating that the chairman was about to resign.* ■ [mass noun] dated rumour: ***report has it*** *that the beetles have now virtually disappeared.*
3 a sudden loud noise of or like an explosion or gunfire.
4 an employee who reports to another employee.
5 [mass noun] archaic the reputation of someone or something: *whatsoever things are lovely and of* ***good report.***
– PHRASES **on report 1** Brit. during the report stage of a bill in the House of Commons or House of Lords. **2** (especially of a prisoner or member of the armed forces) on a disciplinary charge.
– DERIVATIVES **reportable** adjective.
– ORIGIN late Middle English: from Old French *reporter* (verb), *report* (noun), from Latin *reportare* 'bring back', from *re-* 'back' + *portare* 'carry'. The sense 'give an account' gave rise to 'submit a formal report', hence 'inform an authority of one's presence' (sense 2 of the verb, mid 19th cent.) and 'be accountable to a superior' (sense 3 of the verb, late 19th cent.).

reportage /ˌrɛpɔːˈtɑːʒ, rɪˈpɔːtɪdʒ/ ▶ **noun** [mass noun] the reporting of news by the press and the broadcasting media: *extensive reportage of elections.* ■ the factual, journalistic presentation of an account in a book or other text.
– ORIGIN early 17th cent.: French, from Old French *reporter* 'carry back' (see REPORT).

report card ▶ **noun** chiefly N. Amer. a teacher's written assessment of a pupil's work, progress, and conduct, sent home to a parent or guardian. ■ an evaluation of performance: *Democrat legislators fared poorly in a recent report card.*

reportedly ▶ **adverb** [sentence adverb] according to what some say (used to express the speaker's belief that the information given is not necessarily true): *he was in El Salvador, reportedly on his way to Texas.*

reported speech ▶ **noun** [mass noun] a speaker's words reported in subordinate clauses governed by a reporting verb, with the required changes of person and tense (e.g. *he said that he would go,* based on *I will go*). Also called INDIRECT SPEECH. Contrasted with DIRECT SPEECH.

reporter ▶ **noun** a person who reports, especially one employed to report news or conduct interviews for the press or broadcasting media.

reporting verb ▶ **noun** a verb belonging to a class of verbs conveying the action of speaking and used with both direct and reported speech. Reporting verbs may also be used with a direct object and with an infinitive construction.

reportorial /ˌrɛpɒˈtɔːrɪəl/ ▶ **adjective** N. Amer. of or characteristic of newspaper reporters: *reportorial ambition and curiosity.*
– DERIVATIVES **reportorially** adverb.
– ORIGIN mid 19th cent.: from REPORTER, on the pattern of *editorial.*

report stage ▶ **noun** (in the UK and Canada) the stage in the process of a bill becoming law at which it is debated in the House of Commons or House of Lords after it is reported.

reposado /ˌrɛpɒˈsɑːdəʊ/ ▶ **noun** [mass noun] (pl. **reposados**) a type of tequila which has been aged in oak for between two months and a year.
– ORIGIN Spanish, literally 'rested'.

repose[1] /rɪˈpəʊz/ ▶ **noun** [mass noun] a state of rest, sleep, or tranquillity: ***in repose*** *her face looked relaxed.* ■ the state of being calm and composed: *he had lost none of his grace or his repose.* ■ Art harmonious arrangement of colours and forms, providing a restful visual effect.
▶ **verb** [no obj., with adverbial of place] be situated or kept in a particular place: *the diamond now reposes in the Louvre.* ■ lie down in rest: *how sweetly he would repose in the four-poster bed.* ■ [with obj.] literary (**repose something on/in**) lay something to rest in or on: *I'll go to him, and repose our distresses on his friendly bosom.* ■ [with obj.] archaic give rest to: *he halted to repose his way-worn soldiers.*
– DERIVATIVES **reposeful** adjective, **reposefully** adverb.
– ORIGIN late Middle English: from Old French *repos* (noun), *reposer* (verb), from late Latin *repausare*, from *re-* (expressing intensive force) + *pausare* 'to pause'.

repose[2] /rɪˈpəʊz/ ▶ **verb** [with obj.] (**repose something in**) place something, especially one's confidence or trust, in: *we have never betrayed the trust that you have reposed in us.*
– DERIVATIVES **reposal** noun (rare).
– ORIGIN late Middle English (in the sense 'put back in the same position'): from RE- 'again' + the verb POSE[1], suggested by Latin *reponere* 'replace', from *re-* (expressing intensive force) + *ponere* 'to place'.

reposition ▶ **verb** [with obj.] place in a different position; adjust or alter the position of: *try repositioning the thermostat in another room.* ■ change the image of (a company, product, etc.) to target a new or wider market: *we are trying to reposition the brand with a premium image.*

repository /rɪˈpɒzɪt(ə)ri/ ▶ **noun** (pl. **repositories**) a place where or receptacle in which things are or may be stored: *a deep repository for nuclear waste.* ■ a place where something, especially a natural resource, is found in significant quantities: *accessible repositories of water.* ■ a person or thing regarded as a store of information or in which a particular quality may be found: *his mind was a rich repository of the past.*
– ORIGIN late 15th cent.: from Old French *repositoire* or Latin *repositorium*, from *reposit-* 'placed back', from the verb *reponere* (see REPOSE[2]).

repossess ▶ **verb** [with obj.] retake possession of (something) when a buyer defaults on payments: *565 homes were repossessed for non-payment of mortgages.*
– DERIVATIVES **repossession** noun.

repossessor ▶ **noun** chiefly N. Amer. a person hired by a credit company to repossess an item when the buyer defaults on payments.

repost ▶ **verb** [with obj.] make (information) available on the Internet again. ■ send (a message) to an Internet message board or newsgroup again.
▶ **noun** a message reposted on the Internet.

repot ▶ **verb** (**repots, repotting, repotted**) [with obj.] put (a plant) in another pot, especially a larger one.

repoussé /rəˈpuːseɪ/ ▶ **adjective** (of metalwork) hammered into relief from the reverse side.
▶ **noun** [mass noun] repoussé metalwork.
– ORIGIN mid 19th cent.: French, literally 'pushed back', past participle of *repousser*, from *re-* (expressing intensive force) + *pousser* 'to push'.

repp ▶ **noun** variant spelling of REP[3].

repr. ▶ **abbreviation** reprint or reprinted.

reprehend /ˌrɛprɪˈhɛnd/ ▶ **verb** [with obj.] reprimand: *a recklessness which cannot be too severely reprehended.*
– DERIVATIVES **reprehension** noun.
– ORIGIN Middle English: from Latin *reprehendere* 'seize, check, rebuke', from *re-* (expressing intensive force) + *prehendere* 'seize'.

reprehensible ▶ **adjective** deserving censure or condemnation: *his complacency and reprehensible laxity.*
– DERIVATIVES **reprehensibility** noun, **reprehensibly** adverb.
– ORIGIN late Middle English: from late Latin *reprehensibilis*, from *reprehens-* 'rebuked', from the verb *reprehendere* (see REPREHEND).

represent ▶ **verb** [with obj.] **1** be entitled or appointed to act or speak for (someone), especially in an official capacity: *for purposes of litigation, an infant can and must be represented by an adult.* ■ (of a competitor) participate in a sporting event on behalf of (one's club, town, region, or country): *Wade represented Great Britain.* ■ be an elected Member of Parliament or member of a legislature for (a particular

R

constituency or party): *she became the first woman to represent a South Wales mining valley.* ■ act as a substitute for (someone), especially on an official occasion: *the Duke of Edinburgh was represented by the Countess Mountbatten.*
2 constitute; amount to: *this figure represents eleven per cent of the company's total sales.* ■ be a specimen or example of; typify: *twenty parents, picked to represent a cross section of Scottish life.* ■ (**be represented**) be present in something to a particular degree: *abstraction is well represented in this exhibition.*
3 depict (a particular subject) in a work of art: *santos are small wooden figures representing saints.* ■ [with obj. and adverbial or infinitive] describe or portray in a particular way: *the young were consistently represented as being in need of protection.* ■ (of a sign or symbol) have a particular signification; stand for: *numbers 1–15 represent the red balls.* ■ be a symbol or embodiment of: *the three heads of Cerberus represent the past, present, and future.* ■ play (a role) in a theatrical production.
4 formal state or point out clearly: *it was represented to him that she would be an unsuitable wife.* ■ [with clause] allege; claim: *the vendors have represented that such information is accurate.*
– DERIVATIVES **representability** noun, **representable** adjective.
– ORIGIN late Middle English: from Old French *representer* or Latin *repraesentare*, from *re-* (expressing intensive force) + *praesentare* 'to present'.

re-present ▸ verb [with obj.] present (something) again, especially for further consideration or in an altered form: *I will re-present Eikmeyer's model here.* ■ present (a cheque or bill) again for payment.
– DERIVATIVES **re-presentation** noun.

representation ▸ noun [mass noun] **1** the action of speaking or acting on behalf of someone or the state of being so represented: *you may qualify for free legal representation.*
2 the description or portrayal of someone or something in a particular way: *the representation of women in newspapers.* ■ the depiction of someone or something in a work of art: *Picasso is striving for some absolute representation of reality.* ■ [count noun] a picture, model, or other depiction of someone or something: *a striking representation of a vase of flowers.* ■ (in some theories of perception) a mental state or concept regarded as corresponding to a thing perceived.
3 (**representations**) formal statements made to an authority, especially so as to communicate an opinion or register a protest: *the Law Society will make representations to the Lord Chancellor.* ■ [count noun] a statement or allegation: *any buyer was relying on a representation that the tapes were genuine.*
– ORIGIN late Middle English (in the sense 'image, likeness'): from Old French *representation* or Latin *repraesentatio(n-)*, from *repraesentare* 'bring before, exhibit' (see REPRESENT).

representational ▸ adjective relating to or characterized by representation: *representational democracy.* ■ relating to or denoting art which aims to depict the physical appearance of things. Contrasted with ABSTRACT.
– DERIVATIVES **representationally** adverb.

representationalism ▸ noun [mass noun] **1** the practice or advocacy of representational art.
2 Philosophy another term for REPRESENTATIONISM.
– DERIVATIVES **representationalist** adjective & noun.

representationism ▸ noun [mass noun] Philosophy the doctrine that thought is the manipulation of mental representations which correspond to external states or objects.
– DERIVATIVES **representationist** noun.

representative ▸ adjective **1** typical of a class, group, or body of opinion: *Churchill was not properly representative of influential opinion in Britain.* ■ containing typical examples of many or all types: *a representative sample of young people in Scotland.*
2 (of a legislative assembly or deliberative body) consisting of people chosen to act and speak on behalf of a wider group. ■ (of a government or political system) based on elected or chosen representatives: *free elections and representative democracy.*
3 serving as a portrayal or symbol of something: *the show would be more* ***representative of*** *how women really are.* ■ (of art) representational: *the bust involves a high degree of representative abstraction.*
4 Philosophy relating to mental representation.
▸ noun **1** a person chosen or appointed to act or speak for another or others, in particular: ■ an agent of a firm who travels to potential clients to sell its products. ■ an employee of a travel company who lives in a resort and looks after the needs of its holidaymakers. ■ a person chosen or elected to speak and act on behalf of others in a legislative assembly or deliberative body. ■ a delegate who attends a conference, negotiations, etc., so as to represent the interests of another person or group. ■ a person who takes the place of another on an official occasion.
2 an example of a class or group: *fossil representatives of lampreys and hagfishes.*
– DERIVATIVES **representatively** adverb, **representativeness** noun.

repress ▸ verb [with obj.] subdue (someone or something) by force: *the uprisings were repressed.* ■ restrain, prevent, or inhibit (the expression or development of something): *Isabel couldn't repress a sharp cry of fear.* ■ suppress (a thought or desire) so that it becomes or remains unconscious: *the thought that he had killed his brother was so terrible that he repressed it.* ■ Biology prevent the transcription of (a gene).
– DERIVATIVES **represser** noun, **repressible** adjective.
– ORIGIN Middle English (in the sense 'keep back something objectionable'): from Latin *repress-* 'pressed back, checked', from the verb *reprimere*, from *re-* 'back' + *premere* 'to press'.

repressed ▸ adjective restrained or oppressed: *repressed indigenous groups.* ■ (of a thought or desire) kept suppressed and unconscious in one's mind: *repressed homosexuality.* ■ characterized by the repression of thoughts or desires, especially sexual ones: *a very repressed, almost Victorian, household.*

repression ▸ noun [mass noun] the action of subduing someone or something by force. ■ the restraint, prevention, or inhibition of a feeling, quality, etc.: *the repression of anger can be positively harmful.* ■ the action or process of suppressing a thought or desire in oneself so that it remains unconscious.

repressive ▸ adjective (especially of a social or political system) inhibiting or restraining personal freedom: *a repressive regime.* ■ inhibiting or preventing the expression or awareness of thoughts or desires: *a repressive moral code.*
– DERIVATIVES **repressively** adverb, **repressiveness** noun.

repressor ▸ noun Biochemistry a substance which acts on an operon to inhibit enzyme synthesis.

reprice ▸ verb [with obj.] put a different price on (a product or commodity).

reprieve ▸ verb [with obj.] cancel or postpone the punishment of (someone, especially someone condemned to death): *under the new regime, prisoners under sentence of death were reprieved.* ■ abandon or postpone plans to close or abolish (something): *the threatened pits could be reprieved.*
▸ noun a cancellation or postponement of a punishment. ■ a cancellation or postponement of an undesirable event: *a mother who faced eviction has been given a reprieve.*
– ORIGIN late 15th cent. (as the past participle *repryed*): from Anglo-Norman French *repris*, past participle of *reprendre*, from Latin *re-* 'back' + *prehendere* 'seize'. The insertion of *-v-* (16th cent.) remains unexplained. Sense development has undergone a reversal, from the early meaning 'send back to prison', via 'postpone a legal process', to the current sense 'rescue from impending punishment'.

reprimand /ˈrɛprɪmɑːnd/ ▸ noun a formal expression of disapproval.
▸ verb [with obj.] address a reprimand to: *officials were reprimanded for poor work.*
– ORIGIN mid 17th cent.: from French *réprimande*, via Spanish from Latin *reprimenda*, 'things to be held in check', neuter plural gerundive of *reprimere* (see REPRESS).

reprint ▸ verb [with obj.] print again or in a different form: *his book was reprinted several times after his death.*
▸ noun an act of printing more copies of a work. ■ a copy of a book or other material that has been reprinted. ■ an offprint.
– DERIVATIVES **reprinter** noun.

reprisal ▸ noun an act of retaliation: *three youths died in the reprisals which followed* | [mass noun] *the threat of reprisal.* ■ [mass noun] historical the forcible seizure of a foreign subject or their goods as an act of retaliation.
– ORIGIN late Middle English: from Anglo-Norman French *reprisaille*, from medieval Latin *reprisalia* (neuter plural), based on Latin *repraehens-* 'seized', from the verb *repraehendere* (see REPREHEND). The current sense dates from the early 18th cent.

reprise /rɪˈpriːz/ ▸ noun a repeated passage in music. ■ a repetition or further performance of something: *a stale reprise of past polemic.*
▸ verb [with obj.] repeat (a piece of music or a performance).
– ORIGIN early 18th cent.: French, literally 'taken up again', feminine past participle of *reprendre* (see REPRIEVE).

repro ▸ noun (pl. **repros**) [usu. as modifier] informal **1** a reproduction or copy, particularly of a piece of furniture: *a Georgian repro cabinet.*
2 [mass noun] the reproduction of a document or image: *in-house repro and some finishing.*

reproach ▸ verb [with obj.] express to (someone) one's disapproval of or disappointment in their actions: *her friends* ***reproached*** *her* ***for*** *not thinking enough about her family* | [with direct speech] *'You know that isn't true,' he reproached her.* ■ (**reproach someone with**) accuse someone of: *his wife reproached him with cowardice.* ■ archaic censure or rebuke (an offence).
▸ noun [mass noun] the expression of disapproval or disappointment: *he gave her a look of reproach* | [count noun] *a farrago of warnings and pained reproaches.* ■ (**a reproach to**) a thing that makes the failings of (someone or something else) more apparent: *his elegance is a living reproach to our slovenly habits.* ■ (**Reproaches**) (in the Roman Catholic Church) a set of antiphons and responses for Good Friday representing the reproaches of Christ to his people.
– PHRASES **above** (or **beyond**) **reproach** such that no criticism can be made; perfect.
– DERIVATIVES **reproachable** adjective, **reproaching** adjective, **reproachingly** adverb.
– ORIGIN Middle English: from Old French *reprochier* (verb), from a base meaning 'bring back close', based on Latin *prope* 'near'.

reproachful ▸ adjective expressing disapproval or disappointment: *she gave him a reproachful look.*
– DERIVATIVES **reproachfully** adverb, **reproachfulness** noun.

reprobate /ˈrɛprəbeɪt/ ▸ noun **1** an unprincipled person.
2 archaic (in Calvinism) a sinner who is not of the elect and is predestined to damnation.
▸ adjective **1** unprincipled: *reprobate behaviour.*
2 archaic (in Calvinism) predestined to damnation.
▸ verb [with obj.] archaic express or feel disapproval of: *his neighbours reprobated his method of proceeding.*
– DERIVATIVES **reprobation** noun.
– ORIGIN late Middle English (as a verb): from Latin *reprobat-* 'disapproved', from the verb *reprobare*, from *re-* (expressing reversal) + *probare* 'approve'.

reprocess ▸ verb [with obj.] process (something, especially spent nuclear fuel) again or differently, typically in order to reuse it.

reproduce ▸ verb [with obj.] **1** produce a copy of: *his works are reproduced on postcards and posters.* ■ [no obj., with adverbial] be copied with a specified degree of success: *you'll be amazed to see how well half-tones reproduce.* ■ produce something very similar to (something else) in a different medium or context: *the problems are difficult to reproduce in the laboratory.*
2 (of an organism) produce offspring by a sexual or asexual process: *bacteria normally divide and* ***reproduce themselves*** *every twenty minutes* | [no obj.] *an individual needs to avoid being eaten until it has reproduced.*
– DERIVATIVES **reproducer** noun, **reproducibility** noun, **reproducible** adjective, **reproducibly** adverb.

reproduction ▸ noun [mass noun] **1** the action or process of copying something: *the cost of colour reproduction in publication is high.* ■ [count noun] a copy of a work of art, especially a print or photograph of a painting. ■ [as modifier] made to imitate the style of an earlier period or of a particular craftsman: *reproduction French classical beds.* ■ the quality of reproduced sound: *the design was changed to allow louder reproduction.*
2 the production of offspring by a sexual or asexual process.

reproductive ▸ adjective relating to or effecting reproduction: *the female reproductive system.*
– DERIVATIVES **reproductively** adverb, **reproductiveness** noun, **reproductivity** noun.

reprogram (also **reprogramme**) ▸ verb (**reprograms, reprogramming, reprogrammed**; US also **reprograms, reprograming, reprogramed**) [with obj.]

program (a computer or something likened to one) again or differently.
– DERIVATIVES **reprogrammable** adjective.

reprographics ▶ plural noun [treated as sing.] another term for REPROGRAPHY.

reprography /rɪˈprɒɡrəfi/ ▶ noun [mass noun] the science and practice of copying and reproducing documents and graphic material.
– DERIVATIVES **reprographer** noun, **reprographic** adjective.
– ORIGIN 1960s: from REPRODUCE + -GRAPHY.

reproof[1] /rɪˈpruːf/ ▶ noun an expression of blame or disapproval: *she welcomed him with a mild reproof for leaving her alone* | [mass noun] *a look of reproof.*
– ORIGIN Middle English: from Old French *reprove*, from *reprover* 'reprove'. Early senses included 'ignominy, personal shame' and 'scorn'.

reproof[2] /riːˈpruːf/ ▶ verb [with obj.] **1** Brit. make (a garment) waterproof again.
2 make a fresh proof of (printed matter).

reprove ▶ verb [with obj.] reprimand (someone): *he was reproved for obscenity* | [with direct speech] *'Don't be childish, Hilary,' he reproved mildly* | (as adj. **reproving**) *a reproving glance.*
– DERIVATIVES **reprovable** adjective, **reprover** noun, **reprovingly** adverb.
– ORIGIN Middle English (also in the senses 'reject' and 'censure'): from Old French *reprover*, from late Latin *reprobare* 'disapprove' (see REPROBATE).

reptile ▶ noun **1** a cold-blooded vertebrate animal of a class that includes snakes, lizards, crocodiles, turtles, and tortoises. They are distinguished by having a dry scaly skin, and typically laying soft-shelled eggs on land. ● Class Reptilia: orders Chelonia (turtles and tortoises), Squamata (snakes and lizards), Rhynchocephalia (the tuatara), and Crocodylia (crocodilians). Among several extinct groups are the dinosaurs, pterosaurs, and ichthyosaurs.
2 informal a person regarded with loathing and contempt.
▶ adjective [attrib.] belonging to a reptile or to the class of reptiles: *reptile eggs.*
– ORIGIN late Middle English: from late Latin, neuter of *reptilis*, from Latin *rept-* 'crawled', from the verb *repere.*

reptilian /rɛpˈtɪlɪən/ ▶ adjective **1** relating to or characteristic of reptiles: *the reptilian ancestors of mammals.*
2 (of a person) deeply disliked and despised; repulsive: *a reptilian villain with no redeeming features.*
▶ noun an animal belonging to the class Reptilia; a reptile.

Repton /ˈrɛpt(ə)n/, Humphry (1752–1818), English landscape gardener. His parks were carefully informal after the model of Capability Brown. Important designs include the park at Cobham in Kent (*c.*1789–*c.*1793).

republic ▶ noun a state in which supreme power is held by the people and their elected representatives, and which has an elected or nominated president rather than a monarch. ■ archaic a group with a certain equality between its members.
– ORIGIN late 16th cent.: from French *république*, from Latin *respublica*, from *res* 'concern' + *publicus* 'of the people, public'.

republican ▶ adjective **1** (of a form of government, constitution, etc.) belonging to or characteristic of a republic. ■ advocating republican government: *the republican movement.*
2 (**Republican**) (in the US) supporting the Republican Party.
▶ noun **1** an advocate of republican government.
2 (**Republican**) (in the US) a member or supporter of the Republican Party.
3 an advocate of a united Ireland.
– DERIVATIVES **republicanism** noun.

Republican Party one of the two main US political parties (the other being the Democratic Party), favouring a right-wing stance, limited central government, and tough, interventionist foreign policy. It was formed in 1854 in support of the anti-slavery movement preceding the Civil War.

Republic Day ▶ noun the day on which the foundation of a republic is commemorated, in particular (in India) 26 January.

republish ▶ verb [with obj.] publish (a text) again, especially in a new edition.
– DERIVATIVES **republication** noun.

repudiate /rɪˈpjuːdɪeɪt/ ▶ verb [with obj.] **1** refuse to accept; reject: *she has repudiated policies associated with previous party leaders.* ■ chiefly Law refuse to fulfil or discharge (an agreement, obligation, or debt): *breach of a condition gives the other party the right to repudiate a contract.* ■ (in the past or in non-Christian religions) disown or divorce (one's wife).
2 deny the truth or validity of: *the minister repudiated allegations of human rights abuses.*
– DERIVATIVES **repudiator** noun.
– ORIGIN late Middle English (originally an adjective in the sense 'divorced'): from Latin *repudiatus* 'divorced, cast off', from *repudium* 'divorce'.

repudiation ▶ noun [mass noun] **1** rejection of a proposal or idea: *the repudiation of reformist policies* | [count noun] *a repudiation of left-wing political ideas.* ■ refusal to fulfil or discharge an agreement, obligation, or debt.
2 denial of the truth or validity of something.

repudiatory /rɪˈpjuːdɪə,t(ə)ri/ ▶ adjective Law relating to or constituting repudiation of a contract: *a repudiatory breach of the partnership agreement.*

repugnance /rɪˈpʌɡnəns/ ▶ noun [mass noun] intense disgust: *our repugnance at the bleeding carcasses.*
– ORIGIN late Middle English (in the sense 'opposition'): from Old French *repugnance* or Latin *repugnantia*, from *repugnare* 'oppose', from *re-* (expressing opposition) + *pugnare* 'to fight'.

repugnancy ▶ noun [mass noun] formal inconsistency or incompatibility of ideas or statements.

repugnant ▶ adjective **1** extremely distasteful, unacceptable: *cannibalism seems **repugnant to** us.*
2 (**repugnant to**) in conflict or incompatible with: *a by-law must not be repugnant to the general law of the country.* ■ archaic given to stubborn resistance.
– DERIVATIVES **repugnantly** adverb.
– ORIGIN late Middle English (in the sense 'offering resistance'): from Old French *repugnant* or Latin *repugnant-* 'opposing', from the verb *repugnare* (see REPUGNANCE).

repulse ▶ verb [with obj.] **1** drive back (an attack or attacker) by force: *rioters tried to storm the Ministry but were repulsed by police.* ■ reject or rebuff (an approach or offer or the person making it): *she left, feeling hurt because she had been repulsed.*
2 cause to feel intense distaste and aversion: *audiences were repulsed by the film's brutality.*
▶ noun [mass noun] the action of driving back an attack or of being driven back: *the repulse of the invaders.* ■ [count noun] a discouraging response to an offer or approach: *his evasion of her scheme had been another repulse.*
– ORIGIN late Middle English: from Latin *repuls-* 'driven back', from the verb *repellere* (see REPEL).

repulsion ▶ noun [mass noun] **1** a feeling of intense distaste or disgust: *people talk about the case with a mixture of fascination and repulsion.*
2 Physics a force under the influence of which objects tend to move away from each other, e.g. through having the same magnetic polarity or electric charge.

repulsive ▶ adjective **1** arousing intense distaste or disgust: *a repulsive smell.*
2 relating to repulsion between physical objects.
3 archaic lacking friendliness or sympathy.
– DERIVATIVES **repulsively** adverb, **repulsiveness** noun.

repurchase ▶ verb [with obj.] buy (something) back.
▶ noun [mass noun] the action of buying something back.

repurchase agreement ▶ noun Finance a contract in which the vendor of a security agrees to repurchase it from the buyer at an agreed price.

repurify ▶ verb (**repurifies, repurifying, repurified**) [with obj.] purify (something) again.
– DERIVATIVES **repurification** noun.

repurpose ▶ verb [with obj.] adapt for use in a different purpose.

reputable ▶ adjective having a good reputation: *a reputable company.*
– DERIVATIVES **reputably** adverb.
– ORIGIN early 17th cent.: from obsolete French, or from medieval Latin *reputabilis*, from Latin *reputare* 'reflect upon' (see REPUTE).

reputation ▶ noun the beliefs or opinions that are generally held about someone or something: *his reputation was tarnished by allegations of bribery.* ■ a widespread belief that someone or something has a particular characteristic: *his knowledge of his subject earned him a reputation as an expert.*
– DERIVATIVES **reputational** adjective.
– ORIGIN Middle English: from Latin *reputatio(n-)*, from *reputare* 'think over' (see REPUTE).

repute ▶ noun [mass noun] the opinion generally held of someone or something; the state of being regarded in a particular way: *pollution could bring the authority's name into bad repute.* ■ the state of being highly regarded; fame: *chefs of international repute.*
▶ verb (**be reputed**) be generally regarded as having done something or as having particular characteristics: *he was reputed to have a fabulous house.* ■ (usu. as adj. **reputed**) be generally believed to exist or be the case, despite not being so: *this area gave the lie to the reputed flatness of the country.* ■ (usu. as adj. **reputed**) be widely known and well thought of: *intensive training with reputed coaches.*
– ORIGIN late Middle English: from Old French *reputer* or Latin *reputare* 'think over', from *re-* (expressing intensive force) + *putare* 'think'.

reputedly ▶ adverb according to what people say or believe; supposedly: *he reputedly gained a £1.2-million settlement at the end of their marriage.*

requalify ▶ verb (**requalifies, requalifying, requalified**) [no obj.] qualify or become eligible for something again.
– DERIVATIVES **requalification** noun.

request ▶ noun an act of asking politely or formally for something: *a **request for** information* | *the club's excursion was postponed **at the request of** some of the members.* ■ a thing that is asked for: *to have our ideas taken seriously is surely a reasonable request.* ■ an instruction to a computer to provide information or perform another function. ■ a tune or song played on a radio programme, typically accompanied by a personal message, in response to a listener's request. ■ [mass noun] archaic the state of being sought after: *human intelligence, which is in constant request in a family.*
▶ verb [with obj.] politely or formally ask for: *he received the information he had requested* | [with clause] *the chairman requested that the reports be considered.* ■ [with infinitive] politely or formally ask (someone) to do something: *the letter requested him to report to London.*
– PHRASES **by** (or **on**) **request** in response to an expressed wish.
– DERIVATIVES **requester** noun.
– ORIGIN Middle English: from Old French *requeste* (noun), based on Latin *requirere* (see REQUIRE).

request stop ▶ noun Brit. a bus stop at which the bus halts only if requested by a passenger or if hailed.

requiem /ˈrɛkwɪəm, -ɪɛm/ ▶ noun (especially in the Roman Catholic Church) a Mass for the repose of the souls of the dead. ■ a musical composition setting parts of a requiem Mass, or of a similar character. ■ an act or token of remembrance: *he designed the epic as a requiem for his wife.*
– ORIGIN Middle English: from Latin (first word of the Mass), accusative of *requies* 'rest'.

requiem shark ▶ noun a migratory, live-bearing shark of warm seas, sometimes also found in brackish or fresh water. ● Family Carcharhinidae: many species, including the tiger shark, blue shark, and tope.
– ORIGIN mid 17th cent.: from obsolete French *requiem*, variant of *requin* 'shark', influenced by REQUIEM.

R

requiescat /ˌrɛkwɪˈɛskat/ ▶ noun a wish or prayer for the repose of a dead person.
– ORIGIN Latin, from *requiescat in pace* (see RIP[1]).

requinto /rɛˈkɪntəʊ/ ▶ noun (pl. **requintos**) (in Spanish-speaking countries) a small guitar, typically tuned a fifth higher than a standard guitar.
– ORIGIN Spanish, literally 'second fifth subtracted from a quantity'.

require ▶ verb [with obj.] need for a particular purpose: *three patients required operations* | *please indicate how many tickets you require.* ■ make necessary: *it would have required much research to produce a comprehensive list.* ■ specify as compulsory: *the minimum car insurance required by law.* ■ [with obj. and infinitive] (of someone in authority) instruct or expect (someone) to do something: *you will be required to attend for cross-examination.* ■ (**require something of**) regard an action, ability, or quality as due from (someone) by virtue of their position: *the care and diligence required of him as a trustee.*
– ORIGIN late Middle English: from Old French *requere*, from Latin *requirere*, from *re-* (expressing intensive force) + *quaerere* 'seek'.

required ▶ adjective officially compulsory, or otherwise considered essential; indispensable: *eight editions were published, each **required reading** for trainees.* ■ in keeping with one's wishes; desired: *the corset, the garment that ensured the required female shape.*

requirement ▸ **noun** a thing that is needed or wanted: *choose the type of window that suits your requirements best.* ■ a thing that is compulsory; a necessary condition: *applicants must satisfy the normal entry requirements.*

requisite /ˈrɛkwɪzɪt/ ▸ **adjective** made necessary by particular circumstances or regulations: *the application will not be processed until the requisite fee is paid.*
▸ **noun** a thing that is necessary for the achievement of a specified end: *she believed privacy to be* ***a requisite for*** *a peaceful life.*
– DERIVATIVES **requisitely** adverb.
– ORIGIN late Middle English: from Latin *requisitus* 'searched for, deemed necessary', past participle of *requirere* (see REQUIRE).

requisition /ˌrɛkwɪˈzɪʃ(ə)n/ ▸ **noun** an official order laying claim to the use of property or materials: *I had to make various requisitions for staff and accommodation.* ■ a formal written demand that something should be performed or put into operation. ■ (also **requisition on title**) Law a demand to the vendor of a property for the official search relating to the title. ■ [mass noun] the appropriation of goods for military or public use.
▸ **verb** [with obj.] demand the use or supply of (something) by official order: *the government had assumed powers to requisition cereal products at fixed prices.* ■ demand the performance or occurrence of: *a stakeholder has requisitioned an extraordinary general meeting.*
– DERIVATIVES **requisitioner** noun.
– ORIGIN late Middle English (as a noun in the sense 'request, demand'): from Old French, or from Latin *requisitio(n-)*, from *requirere* 'search for' (see REQUIRE). The verb dates from the mid 19th cent.

requite /rɪˈkwʌɪt/ ▸ **verb** [with obj.] formal make appropriate return for (a favour, service, or wrongdoing): *they are quick to requite a kindness.* ■ avenge or retaliate for (an injury or wrong). ■ return a favour to (someone): *to win enough to requite my friends.* ■ respond to (love or affection): *she did not requite his love.*
– DERIVATIVES **requital** noun.
– ORIGIN early 16th cent.: from RE- 'back' + obsolete *quite*, variant of the verb QUIT[1].

reran past of RERUN.

rerate ▸ **verb** [with obj.] (often as noun **rerating**) rate or assess (something, especially shares or a company) again.

reread ▸ **verb** (past and past participle **reread**) [with obj.] read (a text) again: *I reread the poem.*
▸ **noun** [in sing.] an act of reading something again.
– DERIVATIVES **rereadable** adjective.

re-record ▸ **verb** [with obj.] record (sound, especially music) again.

reredos /ˈrɪədɒs/ ▸ **noun** (pl. **same**) Christian Church an ornamental screen covering the wall at the back of an altar.
– ORIGIN late Middle English: from Anglo-Norman French, from Old French *areredos*, from *arere* 'behind' + *dos* 'back'.

re-release ▸ **verb** [with obj.] release (a recording or film) again: *he is re-releasing his 1983 hit single.*
▸ **noun** [mass noun] the action of releasing a recording or film again: *the long awaited re-release of my favourite film.* ■ [count noun] a re-released recording or film.

re-roof ▸ **verb** [with obj.] provide (a building) with a new or substantially repaired roof.

re-route ▸ **verb** [with obj.] send by or along a different route: *the police had re-routed the march.*

rerun ▸ **verb** (**reruns, rerunning**; past **reran**; past participle **rerun**) [with obj.] show, stage, or perform again: *she can stop the video and rerun a short sequence.*
▸ **noun** an event or programme which is run again.

res ▸ **abbreviation** informal resolution: *high-res images.*

resale ▸ **noun** [mass noun] the sale of a thing previously bought.
– DERIVATIVES **resaleable** (also **resalable**) adjective.

resale price maintenance ▸ **noun** [mass noun] Brit. an agreement between a manufacturer and a wholesaler or retailer not to sell a product below a specified price.

resat past and past participle of RESIT.

rescale ▸ **verb** [with obj.] change the scale of (something).

reschedule ▸ **verb** [with obj.] change the time of (a planned event): *the concert has been rescheduled for September.* ■ arrange a new scheme of repayments of (a debt).

rescind /rɪˈsɪnd/ ▸ **verb** [with obj.] revoke, cancel, or repeal (a law, order, or agreement): *the government eventually rescinded the directive.*
– DERIVATIVES **rescindable** adjective.
– ORIGIN mid 16th cent.: from Latin *rescindere*, from *re-* (expressing intensive force) + *scindere* 'to divide, split'.

rescission /rɪˈsɪʒ(ə)n/ ▸ **noun** [mass noun] formal the revocation, cancellation, or repeal of a law, order, or agreement.
– ORIGIN mid 17th cent.: from late Latin *rescissio(n-)*, from *resciss-*, 'split again', from the verb *rescindere* (see RESCIND).

rescore ▸ **verb** [with obj.] revise the score of (a piece of music).

rescript /ˈriːskrɪpt/ ▸ **noun** an official edict or announcement. ■ historical a Roman emperor's written reply to an appeal for guidance, especially on a legal point. ■ the Pope's decision on a question of Roman Catholic doctrine or papal law.
– ORIGIN late Middle English (denoting a papal decision): from Latin *rescriptum*, neuter past participle of *rescribere* 'write back', from *re-* 'back' + *scribere* 'write'.

rescue ▸ **verb** (**rescues, rescuing, rescued**) [with obj.] save (someone) from a dangerous or difficult situation: *firemen rescued a man trapped in the river.* ■ informal keep from being lost or abandoned; retrieve: *he got out of his chair to rescue his cup of coffee.*
▸ **noun** an act of saving or being saved from danger or difficulty: *he* ***came to our rescue*** *with a loan of £100.*
– DERIVATIVES **rescuable** adjective, **rescuer** noun.
– ORIGIN Middle English: from Old French *rescoure* from Latin *re-* (expressing intensive force) + *excutere* 'shake out, discard'.

reseal ▸ **verb** [with obj.] seal (something) again.
– DERIVATIVES **resealable** adjective.

research /rɪˈsəːtʃ, ˈriːsəːtʃ/ ▸ **noun** [mass noun] (also **researches**) the systematic investigation into and study of materials and sources in order to establish facts and reach new conclusions: *the group carries out research in geochemistry | medical research | he prefaces his study with a useful summary of his own researches.* ■ [as modifier] engaged in or intended for research: *a research student | a research paper.*
▸ **verb** [with obj.] investigate systematically: *she has spent the last five years researching her people's history* | [no obj.] *the team have been* ***researching into*** *flora and fauna.* ■ discover or verify information for use in (a book, programme, etc.): *I was in New York researching my novel* | (as adj., with submodifier **researched**) *a well-researched and readable account.*
– DERIVATIVES **researchable** adjective, **researcher** noun.
– ORIGIN late 16th cent.: from obsolete French *recerche* (noun), *recercher* (verb), from Old French *re-* (expressing intensive force) + *cerchier* 'to search'.

> **USAGE** The traditional pronunciation in British English puts the stress on the second syllable, -search. In US English the stress is reversed and comes on the re-. The US pronunciation is becoming more common in British English and, while some traditionalists view it as incorrect, it is now generally accepted as a standard variant of British English.

research and development ▸ **noun** [mass noun] (in industry) work directed towards the innovation, introduction, and improvement of products and processes.

reseat ▸ **verb** [with obj.] **1** cause (someone) to sit down again after they have risen: *he reseated himself in his armchair.* ■ sit (someone) in a new position: *we reseated the orchestra for each variation.* ■ realign or repair (a tap, valve, or other object) in order to fit it into its correct position.
2 equip with new seats: *the coaches were reseated last year to increase capacity.*

réseau /ˈreɪzəʊ/ ▸ **noun** (pl. **réseaux** pronunc. **same**) a network or grid. ■ a plain net ground used in lacemaking. ■ a reference marking pattern on a photograph, used in astronomy and surveying. ■ a spy or intelligence network, especially in the French resistance movement during the German occupation.
– ORIGIN late 16th cent. (as a term in lacemaking): French, literally 'net, web'.

resect /rɪˈsɛkt/ ▸ **verb** [with obj.] (often as adj. **resected**) Surgery cut out (tissue or part of an organ): *a small piece of resected colon.*
– DERIVATIVES **resectable** adjective, **resection** noun, **resectional** adjective.
– ORIGIN mid 17th cent. (in the sense 'remove, cut away'): from Latin *resect-* 'cut off', from the verb *resecare*, from *re-* 'back' + *secare* 'to cut'.

reseda /ˈrɛsɪdə, rɪˈsiːdə/ ▸ **noun** a plant of the genus *Reseda* (family Resedaceae), especially (in gardening) a mignonette.
– ORIGIN mid 18th cent.: from Latin, interpreted in the sense 'assuage!', imperative of *resedare*, with reference to its supposed curative powers.

reseed ▸ **verb** [with obj.] sow (an area of land) with seed, especially grass seed, again.

reselect ▸ **verb** [with obj.] select (someone or something) again or differently: *he was reselected as candidate for Sunderland South.*
– DERIVATIVES **reselection** noun.

resell ▸ **verb** (past and past participle **resold**) [with obj.] sell (something one has bought) to someone else: *products can be resold on the black market for huge profits.*
– DERIVATIVES **reseller** noun.

resemblance ▸ **noun** [mass noun] the state of resembling or being alike: *they* ***bear some resemblance to*** *Italian figurines* | [count noun] *there was a close* ***resemblance between*** *herself* ***and*** *Anne.* ■ [count noun] a way in which two or more things are alike: *the physical resemblances between humans and apes.*
– DERIVATIVES **resemblant** adjective.
– ORIGIN Middle English: from Anglo-Norman French, from the verb *resembler* (see RESEMBLE).

resemble ▸ **verb** [with obj.] have a similar appearance to or qualities in common with (someone or something); look or seem like: *some people resemble their dogs | they* ***resembled each other*** *closely.*
– ORIGIN Middle English: from Old French *resembler*, based on Latin *similare* (from *similis* 'like').

resent ▸ **verb** [with obj.] feel bitterness or indignation at (a circumstance, action, or person): *she resented the fact that I had children.*
– ORIGIN late 16th cent.: from obsolete French *resentir*, from *re-* (expressing intensive force) + *sentir* 'feel' (from Latin *sentire*). The early sense was 'experience an emotion or sensation', later 'feel deeply', giving rise to 'feel aggrieved by'.

resentful ▸ **adjective** feeling or expressing bitterness or indignation at having been treated unfairly: *he was angry and* ***resentful of*** *their intrusion.*
– DERIVATIVES **resentfully** adverb, **resentfulness** noun.

resentment ▸ **noun** [mass noun] bitter indignation at having been treated unfairly: *his* ***resentment at*** *being demoted* | [count noun] *some people harbour resentments going back many years.*
– ORIGIN early 17th cent.: from Italian *risentimento* or French *ressentiment*, from obsolete French *resentir* (see RESENT).

reserpine /rɪˈsəːpiːn/ ▸ **noun** [mass noun] Medicine a compound of the alkaloid class obtained from Indian snakeroot and other plants and used in the treatment of hypertension.
– ORIGIN 1950s: from the modern Latin species name *R(auwolfia) serp(entina)*, named after Leonhard *Rauwolf* (see RAUWOLFIA), + -INE[4].

reservation ▸ **noun 1** [mass noun] the action of reserving something: *the reservation of positions for non-Americans.* ■ [count noun] an arrangement whereby something, especially a seat or room, is reserved for a particular person: *do you have a reservation?* ■ (in church use) the practice of retaining a portion of the consecrated elements after Mass for communion of the sick or as a focus for devotion.
2 an expression of doubt qualifying overall approval of a plan or statement: *some generals voiced reservations about making air strikes.*
3 an area of land set aside for occupation by North American Indians or Australian Aborigines.
4 Law a right or interest retained in an estate being conveyed.
5 [mass noun] (in the Roman Catholic Church) the action of a superior of reserving to himself the power of absolution. ■ [count noun] a right reserved to the Pope of nomination to a vacant benefice.
– ORIGIN late Middle English (denoting the Pope's right of nomination to a benefice): from Old French, or from late Latin *reservatio(n-)*, from *reservare* 'keep back' (see RESERVE).

reservation policy ▸ **noun** Indian the policy of reserving a certain percentage of jobs or school or college places for members of scheduled castes, scheduled tribes, or other groups.

reserve ▸ verb [with obj.] **1** retain for future use: *roll out half the dough and reserve the other half.* ▪ **(reserve something for)** use or engage in something only in or at (a particular circumstance or time): *Japanese food has been presented as expensive and reserved for special occasions.* ▪ (in church use) retain (a portion of the consecrated elements) after Mass for communion of the sick or as a focus for devotion. ▪ retain or hold (a right or entitlement), especially by formal or legal stipulation: [with obj. and infinitive] *the editor reserves the right to edit letters.*
2 arrange for (a room, seat, ticket, etc.) to be kept for the use of a particular person: *a place was reserved for her in the front row.*
3 refrain from delivering (a judgement or decision) without due consideration or evidence: *I'll reserve my views on his ability until he's played again.*
▸ noun **1** (often **reserves**) a supply of a commodity not needed for immediate use but available if required: *Australia has major coal, gas, and uranium reserves.* ▪ funds kept available by a bank, company, or government: *foreign exchange reserves.* ▪ a part of a company's profits added to capital rather than paid as a dividend.
2 a body of troops withheld from action to reinforce or protect others, or additional to the regular forces and available in an emergency. ▪ a member of the military reserve.
3 an extra player in a team, serving as a possible substitute. ▪ **(the reserves)** the second-choice team.
4 a place set aside for special use, in particular: ▪ a reservation for an indigenous people. ▪ a protected area for wildlife.
5 [mass noun] a lack of warmth or openness in manner or expression: *she smiled and some of her natural reserve melted.* ▪ a feeling of doubt qualifying acceptance of a person, statement, or plan: *she trusted him without reserve.*
6 short for RESERVE PRICE.
7 (in the decoration of ceramics or textiles) an area in which the original material or background colour remains visible.
– PHRASES **in reserve** unused and available if required: *the platoon had been kept in reserve.*
– DERIVATIVES **reservable** adjective, **reserver** noun.
– ORIGIN Middle English: from Old French *reserver*, from Latin *reservare* 'keep back', from *re-* 'back' + *servare* 'to keep'.

re-serve ▸ verb [no obj.] (in various sports) serve again.

reserve bank ▸ noun **1** (in the US) a regional bank operating under and implementing the policies of the Federal Reserve.
2 Austral./NZ & S. African a central bank.

reserve currency ▸ noun a strong currency widely used in international trade that a central bank is prepared to hold as part of its foreign exchange reserves.

reserved ▸ adjective **1** slow to reveal emotion or opinions: *he is a reserved, almost taciturn man.*
2 kept specially for a particular person: *a reserved seat.*
– DERIVATIVES **reservedly** adverb, **reservedness** noun.

reserved occupation ▸ noun Brit. an occupation from which a person will not be taken for military service.

reserved word ▸ noun Computing a word in a programming language which has a fixed meaning and cannot be redefined by the programmer.

reserve grade ▸ noun Austral./NZ (in sport) a second division.

reserve price ▸ noun the price stipulated as the lowest acceptable by the seller for an item sold at auction.

reservist ▸ noun a member of the military reserve forces.

reservoir ▸ noun **1** a large natural or artificial lake used as a source of water supply. ▪ a supply or source of something: *Scotland has always had a fine reservoir of comic talent.* ▪ [usu. with modifier] a place where fluid collects, especially in rock strata or in the body. ▪ a receptacle or part of a machine designed to hold fluid.
2 Medicine a population, tissue, etc. which is chronically infested with the causative agent of a disease and can act as a source of further infection.
– ORIGIN mid 17th cent.: from French *réservoir*, from *réserver* 'to reserve, keep'.

reset ▸ verb (**resets, resetting**; past and past participle **reset**) [with obj.] set again or differently: *I must reset the alarm.* ▪ Electronics cause (a binary device) to enter the state representing the numeral 0.
– DERIVATIVES **resettable** adjective.

resettle ▸ verb settle or cause to settle in a different place: [with obj.] *they offered to resettle 300,000 refugees* | [no obj.] *144,000 East Germans had resettled in West Germany.*
– DERIVATIVES **resettlement** noun.

res gestae /reɪz ˈɡɛstʌɪ, riːz ˈdʒɛstiː/ ▸ plural noun Law the events, circumstances, remarks, etc. which relate to a particular case, especially as constituting admissible evidence in a court of law.
– ORIGIN Latin, literally 'things done'.

reshape ▸ verb [with obj.] shape or form (something) differently or again: *the decrees will thoroughly reshape Poland's economy.*

resharpen ▸ verb [with obj.] sharpen (a blade or implement) again.

reshoot ▸ verb (past and past participle **reshot**) [with obj.] shoot (a scene of a film) again or differently: *they had to reshoot the whole thing with another actor.*
▸ noun an act of reshooting a scene of a film.

reshow ▸ verb (past participle **reshown** or **reshowed**) [with obj.] show for a second or subsequent time: *the programme will be reshown on August 11.*

reshuffle ▸ verb [with obj.] **1** interchange the positions of (members of a team, especially government ministers): *the president was forced to reshuffle his cabinet.* ▪ put in a new order; rearrange: *genetic constituents are constantly reshuffled into individual organisms.*
2 shuffle (playing cards) again.
▸ noun an act of reorganizing or rearranging something: *he was brought into the government in the last reshuffle.*

reside ▸ verb [no obj., with adverbial of place] **1** have one's permanent home in a particular place: *people who work in the city actually reside in neighbouring towns.* ▪ be situated: *the paintings now reside on the walls of a restaurant.*
2 (of power or a right) belong to a person or body: *legislative powers reside with the Federal Assembly.* ▪ (of a quality) be present or inherent in something: *the meaning of an utterance does not wholly reside in the semantic meaning.*
– ORIGIN late Middle English (in the sense 'be in residence as an official'): probably a back-formation from RESIDENT, influenced by French *résider* or Latin *residere* 'remain', from *re-* 'back' + *sedere* 'sit'.

residence ▸ noun a person's home, especially a large and impressive one. ▪ the official home of a government minister or other public or official figure. ▪ [mass noun] the fact of living in a particular place: *Rome was his main place of residence* | *she **took up residence** in Paris.*
– PHRASES **in residence** living in a particular place: *the guests currently in residence at the hotel.* ▪ **(— in residence)** a person with a particular occupation (especially an artist or writer) paid to work in a college or other institution.
– ORIGIN late Middle English (denoting the fact of living in a place): from Old French, or from medieval Latin *residentia*, from Latin *residere* 'remain' (see RESIDE).

residence time ▸ noun technical the average length of time during which a substance, a portion of material, or an object is in a given location or condition, such as adsorption or suspension.

residency ▸ noun (pl. **residencies**) **1** [mass noun] the fact of living in a place: *a government ruling confirmed the returning refugees' right to residency.* ▪ [count noun] a residential post held by a writer, musician, or artist, typically for teaching purposes.
2 historical the official residence of the Governor General's representative or other government agent, especially at the court of an Indian state.
3 an organization of intelligence agents in a foreign country.
4 Brit. a musician's regular engagement at a club or other venue.
5 N. Amer. a period of specialized medical training in a hospital; the position of a resident.

resident ▸ noun **1** a person who lives somewhere permanently or on a long-term basis. ▪ a bird, butterfly, or other animal of a species that does not migrate. ▪ Brit. a guest in a hotel who stays for one or more nights. ▪ US a pupil who boards at a boarding school. ▪ historical a British government agent in any semi-independent state, especially the Governor General's agent at the court of an Indian state. ▪ an intelligence agent in a foreign country.
2 N. Amer. a medical graduate engaged in specialized practice under supervision in a hospital.
▸ adjective **1** living somewhere on a long-term basis: *he has been resident in Brazil for a long time.* ▪ having quarters on the premises of one's work: *resident farm workers.* ▪ attached to and working regularly for a particular institution: *the film studio needed a resident historian.* ▪ (of a bird, butterfly or other animal) remaining in an area throughout the year; non-migratory.
2 (of a computer program, file, etc.) immediately available in computer memory, rather than having to be loaded from elsewhere.
– DERIVATIVES **residentship** noun (historical).
– ORIGIN Middle English: from Latin *resident-* 'remaining', from the verb *residere* (see RESIDE).

resident commissioner ▸ noun a delegate elected to represent Puerto Rico in the US House of Representatives. They are able to speak in the House and serve on committees, but may not vote.

residential ▸ adjective designed for people to live in: *private residential and nursing homes.* ▪ providing accommodation in addition to other services: *a residential sixth-form college.* ▪ occupied by private houses: *quieter traffic in residential areas.* ▪ concerning or relating to residence: *land has been diverted from residential use.*
– DERIVATIVES **residentially** adverb.

residential school ▸ noun a boarding school. ▪ (in Canada) a government-supported boarding school for children from American Indian and Inuit communities.

residentiary ▸ adjective relating to or involving residence in a place. ▪ (of a canon) required to live officially in a cathedral or collegiate church.
▸ noun (pl. **residentiaries**) a residentiary canon.
– ORIGIN early 16th cent. (as a noun): from medieval Latin *residentiarius*, from Latin *resident-* 'remaining' (see RESIDENT).

residua plural form of RESIDUUM.

residual ▸ adjective remaining after the greater part or quantity has gone: *the withdrawal of residual occupying forces.* ▪ (of a quantity) left after other items have been subtracted: *residual income after tax and mortgage payments.* ▪ (of a physical state or property) remaining after the removal of or present in the absence of a causative agent: *residual stenosis.* ▪ (of an experimental or arithmetical error) not accounted for or eliminated. ▪ (of a soil or other deposit) formed in situ by weathering.
▸ noun **1** a quantity remaining after other things have been subtracted or allowed for. ▪ a difference between a value measured in a scientific experiment and the theoretical or true value. ▪ Geology a portion of rocky or high ground remaining after erosion.
2 a royalty paid to a performer, writer, etc. for a repeat of a play, television show, etc.
3 the resale value of a new car or other item at a specified time after purchase, expressed as a percentage of its purchase price.
– DERIVATIVES **residually** adverb.

residual current ▸ noun an electric current which flows briefly in a circuit after the voltage is reduced to zero, due to the momentum of the charge carriers.

residual current device ▸ noun a current-activated circuit-breaker used as a safety device for mains-operated electrical tools and appliances.

residual stress ▸ noun [mass noun] Physics the stress present in an object in the absence of any external load or force.

residuary ▸ adjective technical residual. ▪ Law relating to the residue of an estate: *a residuary legatee.*
– ORIGIN early 18th cent.: from RESIDUUM + -ARY[1].

residue /ˈrɛzɪdjuː/ ▸ noun a small amount of something that remains after the main part has gone or been taken or used: *the fine residue left after the sorting of tea* | figurative *the residue of the country's colonial past.* ▪ a substance that remains after a process such as combustion or evaporation. ▪ Law the part of an estate that is left after the payment of charges, debts, and bequests.
– ORIGIN late Middle English: from Old French *residu*, from Latin *residuum* 'something remaining' (see RESIDUUM).

residuum /rɪˈzɪdjʊəm/ ▸ noun (pl. **residua** /-djʊə/)
1 technical a chemical residue.
2 Sociology a class of society that is unemployed and without privileges or opportunities.
– ORIGIN late 17th cent.: from Latin, neuter of *residuus* 'remaining', from the verb *residere*.

R

resign ▶ verb **1** [no obj.] voluntarily leave a job or office: *he **resigned from** the government in protest at the policy.* ■ [with obj.] give up (an office, privilege, etc.): *four deputies resigned their seats.* ■ Chess end a game by conceding defeat without being checkmated: *he lost his Queen and resigned in 45 moves.*
2 (**resign oneself to**) accept that something undesirable cannot be avoided: *she resigned herself to a lengthy session | he seems resigned to a shortened career.* ■ archaic surrender oneself to another's guidance.
– DERIVATIVES **resigner** noun.
– ORIGIN late Middle English: from Old French *resigner*, from Latin *resignare* 'unseal, cancel', from *re-* 'back' + *signare* 'sign, seal'.

re-sign ▶ verb [with obj.] sign (a document) again. ■ engage (a sports player) to play for a team for a further period.

resignal ▶ verb (**resignals, resignalling, resignalled**; US **resignals, resignaling, resignaled**) [with obj.] (often as noun **resignalling**) equip (a railway line) with new signal equipment.

resignation ▶ noun **1** an act of resigning from a job or office: *he announced his resignation.* ■ a document conveying someone's intention of resigning: *I've handed in my resignation.* ■ Chess an act of ending a game by conceding defeat without being checkmated.
2 [mass noun] the acceptance of something undesirable but inevitable: *a shrug of resignation.*
– ORIGIN late Middle English: via Old French from medieval Latin *resignatio(n-)*, from *resignare* 'unseal, cancel' (see **RESIGN**).

resigned ▶ adjective having accepted something unpleasant that one cannot do anything about: *my response is a resigned shrug of the shoulders.*
– DERIVATIVES **resignedly** adverb.

resile /rɪˈzʌɪl/ ▶ verb [no obj.] formal abandon a position or a course of action: *can he **resile from** the agreement?*
– ORIGIN early 16th cent.: from obsolete French *resilir* or Latin *resilire* 'to recoil', from *re-* 'back' + *salire* 'to jump'.

resilience ▶ noun [mass noun] **1** the ability of a substance or object to spring back into shape; elasticity: *nylon is excellent in wearability, abrasion resistance and resilience.*
2 the capacity to recover quickly from difficulties; toughness: *the often remarkable resilience of so many British institutions.*
– DERIVATIVES **resiliency** noun.

resilient ▶ adjective **1** (of a substance or object) able to recoil or spring back into shape after bending, stretching, or being compressed.
2 (of a person or animal) able to withstand or recover quickly from difficult conditions: *babies are generally far more resilient than new parents realize | the fish are **resilient to** most infections.*
– DERIVATIVES **resiliently** adverb.
– ORIGIN mid 17th cent.: from Latin *resilient-* 'leaping back', from the verb *resilire* (see **RESILE**).

R

resilin /ˈrɛzɪlɪn/ ▶ noun [mass noun] Biochemistry an elastic material formed of cross-linked protein chains, found in insect cuticles, especially in the hinges and ligaments of wings.
– ORIGIN 1960s: from Latin *resilire* 'leap back, recoil' + **-IN**[1].

resin /ˈrɛzɪn/ ▶ noun **1** [mass noun] a sticky flammable organic substance, insoluble in water, exuded by some trees and other plants (notably fir and pine). Compare with **GUM**[1] (sense 1 of the noun).
2 (also **synthetic resin**) a solid or liquid synthetic organic polymer used as the basis of plastics, adhesives, varnishes, or other products.
▶ verb (**resins, resining, resined**) [with obj.] (usu. as adj. **resined**) rub or treat with resin: *resined canvas.*
– DERIVATIVES **resinoid** adjective & noun, **resinous** adjective.
– ORIGIN late Middle English: from Latin *resina*; related to Greek *rhētinē* 'pine resin'. Compare with **ROSIN**.

resinate ▶ verb /ˈrɛzɪneɪt/ [with obj.] (usu. as adj. **resinated**) impregnate or flavour with resin: *resinated white wine.*
▶ noun /ˈrɛzɪnət/ Chemistry a salt of an acid derived from resin.

res ipsa loquitur /ˌreɪz ˌɪpsə ˈlɒkwɪtə/ ▶ noun Law the principle that the mere occurrence of some types of accident is sufficient to imply negligence.
– ORIGIN Latin, literally 'the matter speaks for itself'.

resist ▶ verb [with obj.] withstand the action or effect of: *antibodies help us to resist infection.* ■ try to prevent by action or argument: *we will resist changes to the treaty.* ■ refrain from doing (something tempting or unwise): *I couldn't resist buying the blouse.* ■ [no obj.] struggle or fight back when attacked: *without giving her time to resist, he dragged her off her feet.*
▶ noun a resistant substance applied as a coating to protect a surface during a process, for example to prevent dye or glaze adhering.
– DERIVATIVES **resister** noun, **resistibility** noun, **resistible** adjective.
– ORIGIN late Middle English: from Old French *resister* or Latin *resistere*, from *re-* (expressing opposition) + *sistere* 'stop' (reduplication of *stare* 'to stand'). The current sense of the noun dates from the mid 19th cent.

resistance ▶ noun **1** [mass noun] the refusal to accept or comply with something: *they displayed a narrow-minded **resistance to** change.* ■ the use of force or violence to oppose someone or something: *government forces were unable to crush guerrilla-style resistance | she **put up** no **resistance to** being led away.* ■ (also **resistance movement**) a secret organization resisting authority, especially in an occupied country. ■ (**the Resistance**) the underground movement formed in France during the Second World War to fight the German occupying forces and the Vichy government. Also called **MAQUIS**.
2 the ability not to be affected by something, especially adversely: *some of us have a lower **resistance to** cold than others.* ■ [mass noun] Medicine & Biology lack of sensitivity to a drug, insecticide, etc., especially as a result of continued exposure or genetic change.
3 the impeding or stopping effect exerted by one material thing on another: *air resistance was reduced by streamlining.*
4 the degree to which a substance or device opposes the passage of an electric current, causing energy dissipation. By Ohm's law resistance (measured in ohms) is equal to the voltage divided by the current. ■ [count noun] a resistor or other circuit component which opposes the passage of an electric current.
– PHRASES **the line** (or **path**) **of least resistance** the easiest course of action.
– ORIGIN late Middle English: from French *résistance*, from late Latin *resistentia*, from the verb *resistere* 'hold back' (see **RESIST**).

resistance thermometer ▶ noun Physics an instrument used to measure a change in temperature by its effect on the electrical resistance of a platinum or other metal wire.

resistance training ▶ noun another term for **WEIGHT TRAINING**.

resistant ▶ adjective offering resistance to something or someone: *some of the old Churches are **resistant to** change* | [in combination] *a water-resistant adhesive.*

resistive /rɪˈzɪstɪv/ ▶ adjective technical able to withstand the action or effect of something. ■ Physics of or concerning electrical resistance.

resistivity /ˌrɪzɪˈstɪvɪti/ ▶ noun [mass noun] Physics a measure of the resisting power of a specified material to the flow of an electric current.

resistless ▶ adjective archaic powerful and irresistible: *a resistless impulse.* ■ powerless to resist the effect of someone or something; unresisting.
– DERIVATIVES **resistlessly** adverb.

resistor ▶ noun Physics a device having resistance to the passage of an electric current.

resit Brit. ▶ verb (**resits, resitting**; past and past participle **resat**) [with obj.] take (an examination) again after failing it: *she is resitting her maths GCSE.*
▶ noun an examination that is resat.

resite ▶ verb [with obj.] place or situate in a different place: *they want the statue to be resited in the national headquarters.*

resize ▶ verb [with obj.] alter the size of (something, especially a computer window or image).

res judicata /reɪz ˌdʒuːdɪˈkɑːtə/ ▶ noun (pl. **res judicatae** /ˌdʒuːdɪˈkɑːtʌɪ, ˌdʒuːdɪˈkɑːtiː/) Law a matter that has been adjudicated by a competent court and therefore may not be pursued further by the same parties.
– ORIGIN Latin, literally 'judged matter'.

reskill ▶ verb [with obj.] teach (a person, especially an unemployed person) new skills.

reskin ▶ verb (**reskins, reskinning, reskinned**) [with obj.] replace or repair the skin of (an aircraft or motor vehicle).

Resnais /rəˈneɪ/, French /ʀɛnɛ/, Alain (b.1922), French film director. One of the foremost directors of the *nouvelle vague*, he used experimental techniques to explore memory and time. Notable films: *Hiroshima mon amour* (1959) and *L'Année dernière à Marienbad* (1961).

resold past and past participle of **RESELL**.

resole ▶ verb [with obj.] provide (a boot, shoe, etc.) with a new sole.

resoluble /rɪˈzɒljʊb(ə)l/ ▶ adjective archaic able to be resolved.
– ORIGIN early 17th cent.: from French *résoluble* or late Latin *resolubilis*, based on Latin *solvere* 'release, loosen'.

re-soluble ▶ adjective able to dissolve or be dissolved again: *the re-soluble nature of the paint.*

resolute /ˈrɛzəluːt/ ▶ adjective admirably purposeful, determined, and unwavering: *he was resolute in his fight to uphold liberal values.*
– DERIVATIVES **resolutely** adverb, **resoluteness** noun.
– ORIGIN late Middle English (in the sense 'paid', describing a rent): from Latin *resolutus* 'loosened, released, paid', past participle of *resolvere* (see **RESOLVE**).

resolution ▶ noun **1** a firm decision to do or not to do something: *she kept her resolution not to see Anne any more | a New Year's resolution.* ■ a formal expression of opinion or intention agreed on by a legislative body or other formal meeting, typically after taking a vote: *the conference passed two resolutions.*
2 [mass noun] the quality of being determined or resolute: *he handled the last British actions of the war with resolution.*
3 [mass noun] the action of solving a problem or contentious matter: *the peaceful resolution of all disputes* | [count noun] *a successful resolution to the problem.* ■ Music the passing of a discord into a concord during the course of changing harmony. ■ Medicine the disappearance of a symptom or condition.
4 [mass noun] chiefly Chemistry the process of reducing or separating something into constituent parts or components. ■ Physics the replacing of a single force or other vector quantity by two or more jointly equivalent to it.
5 the smallest interval measurable by a telescope or other scientific instrument; the resolving power. ■ [mass noun] the degree of detail visible in a photographic or television image: *a high-resolution monitor.*
– ORIGIN late Middle English: from Latin *resolutio(n-)*, from *resolvere* 'loosen, release' (see **RESOLVE**).

resolutive /ˈrɛzəluːtɪv/ ▶ adjective formal or archaic having the power or ability to dissolve or dispel something.
– ORIGIN late Middle English: from medieval Latin *resolutivus*, from *resolut-* 'released', from the verb *resolvere* (see **RESOLVE**).

resolve ▶ verb **1** [with obj.] settle or find a solution to (a problem or contentious matter): *the firm aims to resolve problems within 30 days.* ■ [with obj.] Medicine cause (a symptom or condition) to heal or subside: *endoscopic biliary drainage can rapidly resolve jaundice.* ■ [no obj.] (of a symptom or condition) heal or subside. ■ Music (with reference to a discord) pass or cause to pass into a concord during the course of harmonic change.
2 [no obj.] decide firmly on a course of action: [with infinitive] *she resolved to ring Dana as soon as she got home.* ■ [with clause] (of a legislative body or other formal meeting) make a decision by a formal vote: *the executive resolved that a strike would be detrimental to all concerned* | [with infinitive] *the conference resolved to support an alliance.*
3 chiefly Chemistry separate or cause to be separated into constituent parts or components. ■ [with obj.] (**resolve something into**) reduce a subject, statement, etc. by mental analysis into (separate elements or a more elementary form): *the ability to resolve facts into their legal categories.* ■ [with obj.] Physics analyse (a force or velocity) into components acting in particular directions.
4 [no obj.] (of something seen at a distance) turn into a different form when seen more clearly: *the orange light **resolved itself** into four roadwork lanterns.* ■ [with obj.] (of optical or photographic equipment) separate or distinguish between (closely adjacent objects): *Hubble was able to resolve six variable stars in M31.* ■ [with obj.] separately distinguish (peaks in a graph or spectrum).
▶ noun **1** [mass noun] firm determination to do something: *she received information that strengthened her resolve.*
2 US a formal resolution by a legislative body or public meeting.

– DERIVATIVES **resolvability** noun, **resolvable** adjective, **resolver** noun.
– ORIGIN late Middle English (in the senses 'dissolve, disintegrate' and 'solve (a problem)'): from Latin *resolvere*, from *re-* (expressing intensive force) + *solvere* 'loosen'.

resolved ▶ adjective [predic., with infinitive] firmly determined to do something: *Constance was resolved not to cry.*
– DERIVATIVES **resolvedly** adverb.

resolvent Mathematics ▶ adjective denoting an equation, function, or expression that is introduced in order to reach or complete a solution.
▶ noun a resolvent equation, function, or expression.

resolving power ▶ noun [mass noun] the ability of an optical instrument or type of film to separate or distinguish small or closely adjacent images.

resonance ▶ noun [mass noun] **1** the quality in a sound of being deep, full, and reverberating: *the resonance of his voice.* ■ the power to evoke enduring images, memories, and emotions: *the concepts lose their emotional resonance.*
2 Physics the reinforcement or prolongation of sound by reflection from a surface or by the synchronous vibration of a neighbouring object.
3 the condition in which an electric circuit or device produces the largest possible response to an applied oscillating signal. ■ Mechanics the condition in which an object or system is subjected to an oscillating force having a frequency close to its own natural frequency.
4 Astronomy the occurrence of a simple ratio between the periods of revolution of two bodies about a single primary.
5 Chemistry the state of having a molecular structure which cannot adequately be represented by a single structural formula but is a composite of two or more structures of higher energy.
6 [count noun] Physics a short-lived subatomic particle that is an excited state of a more stable particle.
– ORIGIN late Middle English: from Old French, from Latin *resonantia* 'echo', from *resonare* 'resound' (see RESONANT).

resonant ▶ adjective **1** (of sound) deep, clear, and continuing to sound or reverberate: *a full-throated and resonant guffaw.* ■ (**resonant with**) (of a place) filled or resounding with (a sound): *alpine valleys resonant with the sound of church bells.* ■ having the ability to evoke enduring images, memories, or emotions: *the prints are* ***resonant with*** *traditions of Russian folk art and story.*
2 (of a room, musical instrument, or hollow body) tending to reinforce or prolong sounds, especially by synchronous vibration.
3 technical relating to or bringing about resonance in a circuit, atom, or other object.
4 (of a colour) enhancing or enriching another colour or colours by contrast.
– DERIVATIVES **resonantly** adverb.
– ORIGIN late 16th cent.: from French *résonnant* or Latin *resonant-* 'resounding', from the verb *resonare*, from *re-* (expressing intensive force) + *sonare* 'to sound'.

resonate ▶ verb [no obj.] **1** produce or be filled with a deep, full, reverberating sound: *the sound of the siren resonated across the harbour.* ■ evoke images, memories, and emotions: *the words* ***resonate with*** *so many different meanings.* ■ chiefly US (of an idea or action) meet with agreement: *the judge's ruling resonated among many of the women.*
2 technical produce electrical or mechanical resonance: *the crystal resonates at 16 MHz.*
– DERIVATIVES **resonation** noun.
– ORIGIN late 19th cent.: from Latin *resonat-* 'resounded', from the verb *resonare* (see RESOUND).

resonator ▶ noun an apparatus that increases the resonance of a sound, especially a hollow part of a musical instrument. ■ a musical or scientific instrument responding to a single sound or note, used for detecting it when it occurs in combination with other sounds. ■ Physics a device that displays electrical resonance, especially one used for the detection of radio waves. ■ Physics a hollow enclosure with conducting walls capable of containing electromagnetic fields having particular frequencies of oscillation and exchanging electrical energy with them, used to detect or amplify microwaves.

resorb /rɪˈsɔːb/ ▶ verb [with obj.] technical absorb (something) again: *the ability to resorb valuable solutes from the urine.* ■ Physiology remove (cells, or a tissue or structure) by gradual breakdown into component materials and dispersal in the circulation: *bone tissue will be resorbed.*
– ORIGIN mid 17th cent.: from Latin *resorbere*, from *re-* (expressing intensive force) + *sorbere* 'absorb'.

resorcinol /rɪˈzɔːsɪnɒl/ ▶ noun [mass noun] Chemistry a crystalline compound originally obtained from galbanum resin, used in the production of dyes, resins, and cosmetics. ● Alternative name: **1,3-dihydroxybenzene**; chem. formula: $C_6H_4(OH)_2$.
– ORIGIN late 19th cent.: from the earlier term *resorcin* + -OL.

resorption /rɪˈzɔːpʃ(ə)n, -ˈsɔːp-/ ▶ noun [mass noun] the process or action by which something is reabsorbed: *the resorption of water.* ■ Physiology the absorption into the circulation of cells or tissue.
– DERIVATIVES **resorptive** adjective.
– ORIGIN early 19th cent.: from RESORB, on the pattern of the pair *absorb, absorption.*

resort ▶ noun **1** a place that is frequented for holidays or recreation or for a particular purpose: *a seaside resort | a health resort.* ■ [mass noun] archaic the tendency of a place to be frequented by many people: *places of public resort.*
2 [mass noun] the action of resorting to a course of action in a difficult situation: *Germany and Italy tried to resolve their economic and social failures by* ***resort to*** *fascism.* ■ [in sing.] a course of action that is resorted to: *her only resort is a private operation.*
▶ verb [no obj.] (**resort to**) **1** turn to and adopt (a course of action, especially an extreme or undesirable one) so as to resolve a difficult situation: *the duke was prepared to resort to force if negotiation failed.*
2 formal go often or in large numbers to.
– PHRASES **as a first** (or **last** or **final**) **resort** before anything else is attempted (or when all else has failed). **in the last resort** ultimately: *in the last resort what really moves us is our personal convictions.* [suggested by French *en dernier ressort.*]
– ORIGIN late Middle English (denoting something one can turn to for assistance): from Old French *resortir*, from *re-* 'again' + *sortir* 'come or go out'. The sense 'place frequently visited' dates from the mid 18th cent.

re-sort ▶ verb [with obj.] sort (something) again or differently.

resound /rɪˈzaʊnd/ ▶ verb **1** [no obj., with adverbial] (of a sound, voice, etc.) fill or echo throughout a place: *another scream resounded through the school.* ■ (of a place) be filled or echo with a sound or sounds: *the office* ***resounds with*** *the metronomic clicking of keyboards.* ■ (of fame, an achievement, etc.) be much talked of: *whatever they do in the Nineties will not resound in the way that their earlier achievements did.*
2 [with obj.] literary sing (the praises) of: *Horace resounds the praises of Italy.*
– ORIGIN late Middle English: from RE- 'again' + the verb SOUND[1], suggested by Old French *resoner* or Latin *resonare* 'sound again'.

resounding ▶ adjective **1** (of a sound) loud enough to reverberate: *a resounding smack across the face.*
2 [attrib.] unmistakable; total: *the evening was a resounding success.*
– DERIVATIVES **resoundingly** adverb.

resource /rɪˈsɔːs, rɪˈzɔːs/ ▶ noun **1** (usu. **resources**) a stock or supply of money, materials, staff, and other assets that can be drawn on by a person or organization in order to function effectively: *local authorities complained that they lacked resources.* ■ (**resources**) a country's collective means of supporting itself or becoming wealthier, as represented by its reserves of minerals, land, and other natural assets. ■ a source of help or information: *census records are an invaluable resource for the historian | the database could be used as a reference and teaching resource.* ■ (**resources**) N. Amer. available assets.
2 an action or strategy which may be adopted in adverse circumstances: *sometimes anger is the only resource left in a situation like this.* ■ (**resources**) personal attributes and capabilities regarded as able to help or sustain one in adverse circumstances: *we had been left very much to our own resources.* ■ [mass noun] dated the ability to find clever ways to overcome difficulties; resourcefulness: *a man of resource.*
3 dated a leisure occupation.
▶ verb [with obj.] provide with resources: *a strategy which ensures that primary health care workers are adequately resourced.*
– DERIVATIVES **resourceless** adjective, **resourcelessness** noun.
– ORIGIN early 17th cent.: from obsolete French *ressourse*, feminine past participle (used as a noun) of Old French dialect *resourdre* 'rise again, recover' (based on Latin *surgere* 'to rise').

resourceful ▶ adjective having the ability to find quick and clever ways to overcome difficulties.
– DERIVATIVES **resourcefully** adverb, **resourcefulness** noun.

respecify ▶ verb (**respecifies, respecifying, respecified**) [with obj.] specify again or differently.

respect ▶ noun **1** [mass noun] a feeling of deep admiration for someone or something elicited by their abilities, qualities, or achievements: *the director had a lot of* ***respect for*** *Douglas as an actor.* ■ the state of being admired or respected: *his first chance in over fifteen years to regain respect in the business.* ■ (**respects**) a person's polite greetings: *give my respects to their Excellencies.* ■ informal used to express the speaker's approval of someone or something: ***respect to*** *Hill for a truly non-superficial piece on the techno scene.*
2 due regard for the feelings, wishes, or rights of others: *young people's lack of* ***respect for*** *their parents.*
3 a particular aspect, point, or detail: *the government's record* ***in this respect*** *is a mixed one.*
▶ verb [with obj.] **1** admire (someone or something) deeply, as a result of their abilities, qualities, or achievements: *she was respected by everyone she worked with* | (as adj. **respected**) *a respected academic.*
2 have due regard for (someone's feelings, wishes, or rights): *I respected his views.* ■ avoid harming or interfering with: *it is incumbent upon all hill users to respect the environment.* ■ agree to recognize and abide by (a legal requirement): *the crown and its ministers ought to respect the ordinary law.*
– PHRASES **in respect of** (or **with respect to**) as regards; with reference to: *the two groups were similar with respect to age, sex, and diagnoses.* **in respect that** because. **pay one's** (**last**) **respects** see PAY[1]. **with** (or **with all due**) **respect** used as a polite formula preceding, and intended to mitigate the effect of, an expression of disagreement: *with all due respect, Father, I think you've got to be more broadminded these days.*
– ORIGIN late Middle English: from Latin *respectus*, from the verb *respicere* 'look back at, regard', from *re-* 'back' + *specere* 'look at'.

respectability ▶ noun [mass noun] the quality of being socially acceptable: *provincial notions of respectability.* ■ the quality of being accepted as valid or important within a particular field: *scientific respectability.*

respectable ▶ adjective **1** regarded by society to be good, proper, or correct: *they thought the stage no life for a respectable lady.* ■ (of a person's appearance, clothes, or behaviour) decent or presentable: *a perfectly respectable pair of pyjamas.*
2 of some merit or importance: *a respectable botanical text.* ■ adequate or acceptable in number, size, or amount: *America's GDP grew by a respectable 2.6 per cent.*
– DERIVATIVES **respectably** adverb.

respecter ▶ noun [usu. with negative] a person who has a high regard for someone or something: *he was no respecter of the female sex.*
– PHRASES **be no respecter of persons** treat everyone in the same way, without being influenced by their status or wealth.

respectful ▶ adjective feeling or showing deference and respect: *they sit in respectful silence.*
– DERIVATIVES **respectfully** adverb, **respectfulness** noun.

respecting ▶ preposition dated or formal with reference or regard to: *he began to have serious worries respecting his car.*

respective ▶ adjective [attrib.] belonging or relating separately to each of two or more people or things: *they chatted about their respective childhoods.*
– ORIGIN late Middle English (in the sense 'relative, comparative'): from medieval Latin *respectivus*, from *respect-* 'regarded, considered', from the verb *respicere* (see RESPECT), reinforced by French *respectif, -ive.*

respectively ▶ adverb separately or individually and in the order already mentioned (used when enumerating two or more items or facts that refer back to a previous statement): *they received sentences of one year and eight months respectively.*

respell ▶ verb (past and past participle **respelled** or chiefly Brit. **respelt**) [with obj.] spell (a word) again or differently, especially phonetically in order to indicate its pronunciation.

R

Respighi /rɛˈspiːgi/, Ottorino (1879–1936), Italian composer. He is best known for his suites the *Fountains of Rome* (1917) and the *Pines of Rome* (1924), based on the poems of Gabriele d'Annunzio.

respirable /ˈrɛsp(ə)rəb(ə)l, rɪˈspʌɪ-/ ▸ **adjective** (of the air or a gas) able or fit to be breathed. ■ (of particles in the air) able to be breathed in: *woodworking can create quantities of fine respirable dust.*
– ORIGIN late 18th cent.: from French *respirable* or late Latin *respirabilis*, from *respirare* 'breathe out' (see RESPIRE).

respirate /ˈrɛspɪreɪt/ ▸ **verb** [with obj.] Medicine & Biology assist (a person or animal) to breathe by means of artificial respiration.
– ORIGIN mid 17th cent.: back-formation from RESPIRATION.

respiration ▸ **noun** [mass noun] the action of breathing: *opiates affect respiration.* ■ [count noun] chiefly Medicine a single breath. ■ Biology a process in living organisms involving the production of energy, typically with the intake of oxygen and the release of carbon dioxide from the oxidation of complex organic substances.
– ORIGIN late Middle English: from Latin *respiratio(n-)*, from *respirare* 'breathe out' (see RESPIRE).

respirator ▸ **noun** an apparatus worn over the mouth and nose or the entire face to prevent the inhalation of dust, smoke, or other noxious substances. ■ an apparatus used to induce artificial respiration.

respiratory /rɪˈspɪrət(ə)ri, ˈrɛsp(ə)rət(ə)ri, rɪˈspʌɪ-/ ▸ **adjective** relating to or affecting respiration or the organs of respiration: *respiratory disease.*

respiratory distress syndrome ▸ **noun** another term for HYALINE MEMBRANE DISEASE.

respiratory pigment ▸ **noun** Biochemistry a substance (such as haemoglobin or haemocyanin) with a molecule consisting of protein with a pigmented prosthetic group, involved in the physiological transport of oxygen or electrons.

respiratory quotient ▸ **noun** Physiology the ratio of the volume of carbon dioxide evolved to that of oxygen consumed by an organism, tissue, or cell in a given time.

respiratory syncytial virus ▸ **noun** Medicine a paramyxovirus which causes disease of the respiratory tract. It is a major cause of bronchiolitis and pneumonia in young children, and may be a contributing factor in cot death.

respiratory tract ▸ **noun** the passage formed by the mouth, nose, throat, and lungs, through which air passes during breathing.

respire ▸ **verb** [no obj.] **1** breathe: *he lay back, respiring deeply* | [with obj.] *a country where fresh air seems impossible to respire.* ■ (of a plant) carry out respiration, especially at night when photosynthesis has ceased.
2 archaic recover hope, courage, or strength after a time of difficulty: *the archduke, newly respiring from so long a war.*
– ORIGIN late Middle English: from Old French *respirer* or Latin *respirare* 'breathe out', from *re-* 'again' + *spirare* 'breathe'.

R

respirometer ▸ **noun** Biology a device which measures the rate of consumption of oxygen by a living organism. ■ Medicine an instrument for measuring the air capacity of the lungs.

respite /ˈrɛspʌɪt, -spɪt/ ▸ **noun** [mass noun] a short period of rest or relief from something difficult or unpleasant: *the refugee encampments will provide some* ***respite from*** *the suffering* | [in sing.] *a brief* ***respite from*** *the heat.* ■ a short delay permitted before an unpleasant obligation is met or a punishment is carried out.
▸ **verb** [with obj.] rare postpone (a sentence, obligation, etc.): *the execution was only respited a few months.* ■ archaic grant a respite to (someone, especially a person condemned to death).
– ORIGIN Middle English: from Old French *respit*, from Latin *respectus* 'refuge, consideration'.

respite care ▸ **noun** [mass noun] temporary institutional care of a sick, elderly, or disabled person, providing relief for their usual carer.

resplendent /rɪˈsplɛnd(ə)nt/ ▸ **adjective** attractive and impressive through being richly colourful or sumptuous: *she was resplendent in a sea-green dress.*
– DERIVATIVES **resplendence** noun, **resplendency** noun, **resplendently** adverb.
– ORIGIN late Middle English: from Latin *resplendent-* 'shining out', from the verb *resplendere*, from *re-* (expressing intensive force) + *splendere* 'to glitter'.

respond ▸ **verb 1** [reporting verb] say something in reply: [no obj.] *she could not get Robert to* ***respond to*** *her words* | [with clause] *he responded that it would not be feasible* | [with direct speech] *'It's not part of my job,' Belinda responded.* ■ (of a congregation) say or sing the response in reply to a priest.
2 [no obj.] (of a person) do something as a reaction to someone or something: *she* ***responded to*** *his grin with a smile.* ■ react quickly or positively to a stimulus or treatment: *his back injury has failed to respond to treatment.* ■ [with obj.] Bridge make (a bid) in answer to one's partner's preceding bid.
▸ **noun 1** Architecture a half-pillar or half-pier attached to a wall to support an arch, especially at the end of an arcade.
2 (in church use) a response to a versicle; a responsory.
– DERIVATIVES **respondence** noun (archaic) **responder** noun.
– ORIGIN late Middle English (as a noun): from Old French, from *respondre* 'to answer', from Latin *respondere*, from *re-* 'again' + *spondere* 'to pledge'. The verb dates from the mid 16th cent.

respondent ▸ **noun 1** Law a party against whom a petition is filed, especially one in an appeal or a divorce case.
2 a person who replies to something, especially one supplying information for a questionnaire or responding to an advertisement.
▸ **adjective** [attrib.] **1** Law in the position of a party defending against a petition: *the respondent defendant.*
2 replying to something: *the respondent firms in the survey.*
3 Psychology involving or denoting a response, especially a conditioned reflex, to a specific stimulus.
– ORIGIN early 16th cent. (in sense 2 of the noun): from Latin *respondent-* 'answering, offering in return', from the verb *respondere* (see RESPOND).

responsa plural form of RESPONSUM.

response ▸ **noun 1** a verbal or written answer: *there was laughter at his response to the question* | [mass noun] *we received 400 applications* ***in response to*** *one job ad.* ■ an answer to a question in a test, questionnaire, etc. ■ (usu. **responses**) a part of a religious liturgy said or sung by a congregation in answer to a minister or cantor.
2 a reaction to something: *an extended, jazzy piano solo drew the biggest* ***response from*** *the crowd* | [mass noun] *an Honours degree course in Japanese has been established* ***in response to*** *an increasing demand.* ■ Psychology & Physiology an excitation of a nerve impulse caused by a change or event; a physical reaction to a specific stimulus or situation. ■ the way in which a mechanical or electrical device responds to a stimulus or stimuli. ■ Bridge a bid made in answer to one's partner's preceding bid.
– ORIGIN Middle English: from Old French *respons* or Latin *responsum* 'something offered in return', neuter past participle of *respondere* (see RESPOND).

response time ▸ **noun** the length of time taken for a person or system to react to a given stimulus or event. ■ Electronics the time taken for a circuit or measuring device, when subjected to a change in input signal, to change its state by a specified fraction of its total response to that change.

response variable ▸ **noun** another term for DEPENDENT VARIABLE.

responsibility ▸ **noun** (pl. **responsibilities**) [mass noun]
1 the state or fact of having a duty to deal with something or of having control over someone: *women bear children and* ***take responsibility for*** *childcare.*
2 the state or fact of being accountable or to blame for something: *the group has claimed responsibility for a string of murders.* ■ [in sing.] (**responsibility to/towards**) a moral obligation to behave correctly towards or in respect of: *individuals have a responsibility to control their behaviour.*
3 the opportunity or ability to act independently and take decisions without authorization: *we expect individuals to take on more responsibility.* ■ [count noun] (often **responsibilities**) a thing which one is required to do as part of a job, role, or legal obligation: *he will take over the responsibilities of Overseas Director.*
– PHRASES **on one's own responsibility** without authorization.

responsible ▸ **adjective 1** [predic.] having an obligation to do something, or having control over or care for someone, as part of one's job or role: *the cabinet minister* ***responsible for*** *Education.* ■ (**responsible to**) having to report to (a superior) and be answerable to them for one's actions: *the Prime Minister and cabinet are responsible to Parliament.*
2 being the primary cause of something and so able to be blamed or credited for it: *Gooch was* ***responsible for*** *198 of his side's 542 runs.* ■ morally accountable for one's behaviour: *the progressive emergence of the child as a responsible being.*
3 (of a job or position) involving important duties, independent decision-making, or control over others. ■ capable of being trusted: *a responsible adult.*
– DERIVATIVES **responsibleness** noun, **responsibly** adverb.
– ORIGIN late 16th cent. (in the sense 'answering to, corresponding'): from obsolete French *responsible*, from Latin *respons-* 'answered, offered in return', from the verb *respondere* (see RESPOND).

responsive ▸ **adjective 1** reacting quickly and positively: *a flexible service that is* ***responsive to*** *changing social patterns.* ■ responding readily and with interest: *our most enthusiastic and responsive students.*
2 in response; answering: *I'm distracted by a nibble on my line: I jig it several times, but there is no responsive tug.* ■ (of a section of liturgy) using responses.
– DERIVATIVES **responsively** adverb, **responsiveness** noun.

responsorial /ˌrɪspɒnˈsɔːrɪəl/ ▸ **adjective** (of a psalm or liturgical chant) recited in parts with a congregational response between each part.

responsory /rɪˈspɒns(ə)ri/ ▸ **noun** (pl. **responsories**) (in the Christian Church) an anthem said or sung by a soloist and choir after a lesson.
– ORIGIN late Middle English: from late Latin *responsorium*, from Latin *respons-* 'answered' from the verb *respondere* (see RESPOND).

responsum /rɪˈspɒnsəm/ ▸ **noun** (pl. **responsa** /rɪˈspɒnsə/) a written reply by a rabbi or Talmudic scholar to an inquiry on some matter of Jewish law.
– ORIGIN Latin, literally 'reply'.

respray ▸ **verb** /riːˈspreɪ/ [with obj.] spray (something, especially a vehicle) with a new coat of paint.
▸ **noun** /ˈriːspreɪ/ an instance of respraying something.

res publica /reɪz ˈpʊblɪkə, ˈpʌblɪkə/ ▸ **noun** the state, republic, or commonwealth.
– ORIGIN Latin, literally 'public matter'.

ressentiment /rəˈsɒ̃tɪmɒ̃/ ▸ **noun** [mass noun] a psychological state resulting from suppressed feelings of envy and hatred which cannot be satisfied.
– ORIGIN via German (used by Nietzsche in this sense) from French *ressentiment* 'feeling'.

rest[1] ▸ **verb** [no obj.] **1** cease work or movement in order to relax, sleep, or recover strength: *he needed to rest after the feverish activity* | *I'm going to* ***rest up*** *before travelling to England.* ■ [with obj.] allow to be inactive in order to regain strength or health: *her friend read to her while she rested her eyes.* ■ (**be resting**) Brit. used euphemistically by actors to indicate that they are out of work. ■ [with obj.] leave (a player) out of a team temporarily: *both men were rested for the cup final.* ■ (of a problem or subject) be left without further investigation or discussion: *the council has urged the planning committee not to allow the matter to rest.* ■ [with obj.] allow (land) to lie fallow.
2 [no obj., with adverbial of place] be placed or supported so as to stay in a specified position: *her elbow was resting on the arm of the sofa.* ■ (of a body) lie buried: *the king's body rested in his tomb.* ■ [with obj. and adverbial of place] place (something) so that it is supported in a specified position: *he rested a hand on her shoulder.* ■ (**rest on/upon**) (of a look) alight or be steadily directed on: *his eyes rested briefly on the boy.*
3 (**rest on/upon**) be based on; depend on: *the country's security rested on its alliances.* ■ [with obj.] (**rest something in/on**) place hope, trust, or confidence on or in: *she rested her hopes in her attorney.* ■ be the responsibility of or belong to a specified person: *the final say* ***rests with*** *the regional assemblies.*
4 Law, N. Amer. conclude presentation of either party's case in a suit or prosecution: *the prosecution rests.* See also REST ONE'S CASE below.
▸ **noun 1** an instance or period of resting: *you look as though you need a rest* | [mass noun] *a couple of days of complete rest.* ■ [mass noun] a motionless state: *the car accelerates rapidly from rest.*
2 Music an interval of silence of a specified duration. ■ the sign denoting a musical rest. ■ a pause in speech or verse.
3 [in combination] an object that is used to support something: *a shoulder rest.* ■ a support or hook for a telephone receiver when not in use. ■ a support for a cue in billiards or snooker.

– PHRASES **at rest** not moving or exerting oneself. ■ not agitated or troubled: *if you think something's wrong, consult the doctor to set your mind at rest.* ■ dead and buried. **come to rest** stop moving; settle: *the lift came to rest at the first floor*. **give it a rest** Brit. informal used to ask someone to stop talking about something that the speaker finds irritating. **no rest for the wicked** see WICKED. **rest one's case** conclude one's presentation of evidence and arguments in a lawsuit. ■ humorous said to show that one believes one has presented sufficient evidence for one's views. **rest on one's laurels** see LAUREL. **rest** (or **God rest**) **his** (or **her**) **soul** used to express a wish that God should grant someone's soul peace.
– ORIGIN Old English *ræst, rest* (noun), *ræstan, restan* (verb), of Germanic origin, from a root meaning 'league' or 'mile' (referring to a distance after which one rests).

rest² ▶ noun **1** [in sing.] the remaining part of something: *what do you want to do for the rest of your life? | I'll tell you the rest tomorrow night.* ■ [treated as pl.] the remaining people or things; the others: *the rest of us were experienced skiers.*
2 Anatomy a small, detached portion of an organ or tissue.
3 a rally in real tennis.
▶ verb [no obj., with complement] remain or be left in a specified condition: *you can rest assured she will do everything she can.*
– PHRASES **and the rest** informal used to assert that something is an understatement: *'You mean it took three hours?' 'And the rest.'* **and (all) the rest (of it)** and everything else of a similar type that might be mentioned: *it's all very well to talk about natural affection and love and the rest of it.* **for the rest** Brit. as far as other matters are concerned. **the rest is history** see HISTORY.
– ORIGIN late Middle English: from Old French *reste* (noun), *rester* (verb), from Latin *restare* 'remain', from *re-* 'back' + *stare* 'to stand'.

restage ▶ verb [with obj.] present (a performance or public event) again or differently.

rest area ▶ noun North American term for LAY-BY.

restart ▶ verb start again: [no obj.] *the talks will restart in September* | [with obj.] *he tried to restart his stalled car.*
▶ noun [in sing.] a new start or beginning.

restate ▶ verb [with obj.] state (something) again or differently, especially more clearly or convincingly: *he restated his opposition to abortion.*
– DERIVATIVES **restatement** noun.

restaurant /ˈrɛst(ə)rɒnt, -r(ə)nt, -rɒ̃/ ▶ noun a place where people pay to sit and eat meals that are cooked and served on the premises.
– ORIGIN early 19th cent.: from French, from *restaurer* 'provide food for' (literally 'restore to a former state').

restaurant car ▶ noun Brit. a dining car.

restaurateur /ˌrɛst(ə)rəˈtəː, ˌrɛstɒr-/ ▶ noun a person who owns and manages a restaurant.
– ORIGIN late 18th cent.: French, from the verb *restaurer* (see RESTAURANT).

> **USAGE** The word **restaurateur** is taken directly from the French form. Although common, **restauranteur** with an *n* is a misspelling.

rest cure ▶ noun a period spent in inactivity or leisure with the intention of improving one's physical or mental health.

restenosis /ˌriːstɛˈnəʊsɪs/ ▶ noun [mass noun] Medicine the recurrence of abnormal narrowing of an artery or valve after corrective surgery.
– ORIGIN 1950s: from RE- 'again' + STENOSIS.

rest frame ▶ noun Physics a frame of reference relative to which a given body is at rest.

restful ▶ adjective having a quiet and soothing quality: *the rooms were cool and restful.*
– DERIVATIVES **restfully** adverb, **restfulness** noun.

restharrow ▶ noun a sticky Old World plant of the pea family, which has pink flowers and creeping woody stems with spines. ● Genus *Ononis*, family Leguminosae.
– ORIGIN mid 16th cent.: from obsolete *rest* 'stop, arrest' + HARROW (because the tough stems impeded the progress of a harrow).

rest home ▶ noun a residential institution where old or frail people are cared for.

rest house ▶ noun (in parts of Asia and Africa) a house or small hotel offering accommodation for travellers.

resting place ▶ noun used in reference to the grave or death: *he would share her final resting place in the cemetery.*

resting potential ▶ noun Physiology the electrical potential of a neuron or other excitable cell relative to its surroundings when not stimulated or involved in passage of an impulse.

restio /ˈrɛstɪəʊ/ ▶ noun (pl. **restios**) a wiry rush- or reed-like plant of southern Africa, used for thatching and brooms. ● Genus *Restio*, family Restionaceae: many species.
– ORIGIN modern Latin (genus name), from Latin *restis* 'a rope'.

restitutio in integrum /rɛstɪˌtjuːtɪəʊ ɪn ɪnˈtɛɡrəm/ ▶ noun [mass noun] Law restoration of an injured party to the situation which would have prevailed had no injury been sustained; restoration to the original or pre-contractual position.
– ORIGIN Latin, literally 'restoration to the whole (i.e. uninjured) state'.

restitution ▶ noun [mass noun] **1** the restoration of something lost or stolen to its proper owner: *the ANC had demanded the restitution of land seized from blacks.*
2 recompense for injury or loss: *he was ordered to pay £6,000 in restitution.*
3 the restoration of something to its original state: *restitution of the damaged mucosa.* ■ Physics the resumption of an object's original shape or position through elastic recoil.
– DERIVATIVES **restitutionary** adjective, **restitutive** adjective.
– ORIGIN Middle English: from Old French, or from Latin *restitutio(n-)*, from *restituere* 'restore', from *re-* 'again' + *statuere* 'establish'.

restive ▶ adjective (of a person) unable to remain still, silent, or submissive, especially because of boredom or dissatisfaction. ■ (of a horse) stubbornly standing still or moving backwards or sideways; refusing to advance.
– DERIVATIVES **restively** adverb, **restiveness** noun.
– ORIGIN late 16th cent.: from Old French *restif, -ive*, from Latin *restare* 'remain'. The original sense, 'inclined to remain still', has undergone a reversal; the association with the refractory movements of a horse gave rise to the current sense 'restless'.

restless ▶ adjective unable to rest or relax as a result of anxiety or boredom: *the audience grew restless and inattentive.* ■ offering no physical or emotional rest; involving constant activity: *a restless night.*
– DERIVATIVES **restlessly** adverb, **restlessness** noun.
– ORIGIN Old English *restlēas* (see REST¹, -LESS).

restless legs syndrome ▶ noun [mass noun] a disorder characterized by an unpleasant tickling or twitching sensation in the leg muscles when sitting or lying down, relieved only by moving the legs.

rest mass ▶ noun Physics the mass of a body when at rest.

resto ▶ noun (pl. **restos**) N. Amer. informal a restaurant.
– ORIGIN 1980s: abbreviation.

restock ▶ verb [with obj.] replenish (a store) with fresh stock or supplies: *work began at once to restock the fishery.*

restoration ▶ noun [mass noun] **1** the action of returning something to a former owner, place, or condition: *the restoration of Andrew's sight.* ■ the process of restoring a building, work of art, etc. to its original condition: *the altar paintings seem in need of restoration.* ■ the reinstatement of a previous practice, right, or situation: *the restoration of capital punishment.* ■ [count noun] Dentistry a structure provided to replace or repair dental tissue so as to restore its form and function, such as a filling, crown, or bridge. ■ [count noun] a model or drawing representing the supposed original form of an extinct animal, ruined building, etc.
2 the return of a monarch to a throne, a head of state to government, or a regime to power. ■ (**the Restoration**) the re-establishment of Charles II as King of England in 1660. After the death of Oliver Cromwell in 1658, his son Richard (1626–1712) proved incapable of maintaining the Protectorate, and General Monck organized the king's return from exile. ■ (**Restoration**) [usu. as modifier] the period following the Restoration of Charles II: *Restoration drama.* ■ (**the Restoration**) the restoration of the Bourbon monarchy in France in 1814, following the fall of Napoleon. Louis XVIII was recalled from exile by Talleyrand.
– ORIGIN late 15th cent. (denoting the action of restoring to a former state): partly from Old French, partly an alteration of obsolete *restauration* (from late Latin *restauratio(n-)*, from the verb *restaurare*), suggested by RESTORE.

Restoration comedy ▶ noun [mass noun] a style of drama which flourished in London after the Restoration in 1660, typically having a complicated plot marked by wit, cynicism, and licentiousness. Principal exponents include William Congreve, William Wycherley, George Farquhar, and Sir John Vanbrugh.

restorationism ▶ noun [mass noun] a charismatic Christian movement seeking to restore the beliefs and practices of the early Church.
– DERIVATIVES **restorationist** noun & adjective.

restorative ▶ adjective **1** having the ability to restore health, strength, or well-being: *the restorative power of long walks.*
2 Surgery & Dentistry relating to the restoration of form or function to a damaged tooth or other part of the body.
▶ noun a thing that restores health, strength, or well-being, especially a medicine or drink.
– DERIVATIVES **restoratively** adverb.
– ORIGIN late Middle English: from an Old French variant of *restauratif, -ive*, from *restorer* (see RESTORE).

restore ▶ verb [with obj.] bring back or re-establish (a previous right, practice, or situation): *the government restored confidence in the housing market | order was eventually restored by riot police.* ■ return (someone or something) to a former condition, place, or position: *the effort to restore him to office isn't working.* ■ repair or renovate (a building, work of art, etc.) so as to return it to its original condition: *the building has been lovingly restored.* ■ give (something stolen, taken away, or lost) back to the original owner or recipient: *the government will restore land to those who lost it through confiscation.*
– DERIVATIVES **restorable** adjective, **restorer** noun.
– ORIGIN Middle English: from Old French *restorer*, from Latin *restaurare* 'rebuild, restore'.

restrain ▶ verb [with obj.] prevent (someone or something) from doing something; keep under control or within limits: *the need to restrain public expenditure | he had to be restrained from walking out* | (as adj. **restraining**) *Cara put a restraining hand on his arm.* ■ control (a strong urge or emotion): *Amiss had to restrain his impatience.* ■ deprive (someone) of freedom of movement or personal liberty: *leg cuffs are used for restraining and transporting violent criminals.* ■ (of a seat belt) hold (a person or part of their body) down and back while in a vehicle seat.
– DERIVATIVES **restrainable** adjective, **restrainer** noun.
– ORIGIN Middle English: from Old French *restreign-*, stem of *restreindre*, from Latin *restringere*, from *re-* 'back' + *stringere* 'to tie, pull tight'.

restrained ▶ adjective characterized by reserve or moderation; unemotional or dispassionate: *his restrained, gentlemanly voice.* ■ (of colour, decoration, etc.) not excessively showy or ornate; understated.
– DERIVATIVES **restrainedly** adverb.

restraining order ▶ noun a temporary court order issued to prohibit an individual from carrying out a particular action, especially approaching or contacting a specified person.

restraint ▶ noun **1** (often **restraints**) a measure or condition that keeps someone or something under control: *decisions are made within the financial restraints of the budget.* ■ [mass noun] the action of keeping someone or something under control. ■ [mass noun] deprivation or restriction of personal liberty or freedom of movement: *he remained aggressive and required physical restraint.* ■ a device which limits or prevents freedom of movement: *car safety restraints.*
2 [mass noun] unemotional, dispassionate, or moderate behaviour; self-control: *he urged the protestors to exercise restraint.* ■ understatement, especially of artistic expression: *with strings and piano, all restraint vanished.*
– ORIGIN late Middle English: from Old French *restreinte*, feminine past participle of *restreindre* 'hold back' (see RESTRAIN).

restraint of trade ▶ noun [mass noun] Law action that interferes with free competition in a market. ■ [count noun] a clause in a contract that restricts a person's right to carry on their trade or profession.

restrict ▶ verb [with obj.] put a limit on; keep under control: *some roads may have to be closed at peak times to restrict the number of visitors.* ■ deprive (someone or something) of freedom of movement or action:

R

cities can restrict groups of protesters from gathering on a residential street. ■ (**restrict someone to**) limit someone to only doing or having (a particular thing) or staying in (a particular place): *I shall restrict myself to a single example.* ■ (**restrict something to**) limit something to (a particular place, time, or group): *the Zoological Gardens were at first restricted to members and their guests.* ■ withhold (information) from general disclosure: *at first the Americans tried to restrict news of their involvement in Vietnam.*
– ORIGIN mid 16th cent.: from Latin *restrict-* 'confined, bound fast', from the verb *restringere* (see **RESTRAIN**).

restricted ▶ adjective limited in extent, number, scope, or action: *Western scientists had only restricted access to the site.* ■ Brit. (of a document or information) not to be disclosed to the public for reasons of national security. ■ Biology (of a virus) unable to reproduce at its normal rate in certain hosts. ■ Biochemistry (of DNA) subject to degradation by a restriction enzyme.
– DERIVATIVES **restrictedly** adverb, **restrictedness** noun.

restriction ▶ noun (often **restrictions**) a limiting condition or measure, especially a legal one: *planning restrictions on commercial development.* ■ [mass noun] the limitation or control of someone or something, or the state of being restricted: *the restriction of local government power.*
– DERIVATIVES **restrictionism** noun, **restrictionist** adjective & noun.
– ORIGIN late Middle English: from Old French, or from Latin *restrictio(n-)*, from *restringere* 'bind fast, confine' (see **RESTRICT**).

restriction enzyme (also **restriction endonuclease**) ▶ noun Biochemistry an enzyme produced chiefly by certain bacteria, that has the property of cleaving DNA molecules at or near a specific sequence of bases.

restriction fragment ▶ noun Biochemistry a fragment of a DNA molecule that has been cleaved by a restriction enzyme.

restriction fragment length polymorphism ▶ noun Genetics a variation in the length of restriction fragments produced by a given restriction enzyme in a sample of DNA. Such variation is used in forensic investigations and to map hereditary disease.

restrictive ▶ adjective **1** imposing restrictions on someone's activities or freedom: *a web of restrictive regulations.*
2 Grammar (of a relative clause or descriptive phrase) serving to specify the particular instance or instances being mentioned.
– DERIVATIVES **restrictively** adverb, **restrictiveness** noun.

USAGE What is the difference between *the books which were on the table once belonged to my aunt* and *the books, which were on the table, once belonged to my aunt?* In the first sentence the speaker uses the relative clause to pick out a subset of books (the ones on the table) and imply a contrast with some other set of books. In the second sentence the size of the set of books referred to is unaffected by the relative clause; the speaker merely offers the additional information that they happen to be on the table.
This distinction is between **restrictive** and **non-restrictive** relative clauses. In writing, a non-restrictive relative clause is set off within commas, while in speech the difference is expressed by a difference in intonation. Ignorance of the distinction can lead to unintentionally comic effects: for example, strictly speaking, the relative clause in *if you are in need of assistance, please ask any member of staff who will be pleased to help* implies contrast with another set of staff who will not be pleased to help. A comma is needed before **who**.

restrictive covenant ▶ noun Law a covenant imposing a restriction on the use of land so that the value and enjoyment of adjoining land will be preserved.

restrictive practice ▶ noun Brit. an arrangement by a group of workers to limit output or restrict the entry of new workers in order to protect their own interests. ■ an arrangement in industry or trade that restricts competition between firms.

restring ▶ verb (past and past participle **restrung**) [with obj.] **1** fit new or different strings to (a musical instrument or sports racket).
2 thread (objects such as beads) on a new string.

restroom ▶ noun **1** Brit. a room in a public building for people to relax or recover in.
2 N. Amer. a toilet in a public building.

restructure ▶ verb [with obj.] organize differently: *a plan to strengthen and restructure the EC.* ■ Finance convert (the debt of a business in difficulty) into another kind of debt, typically one that is repayable at a later time.

restudy ▶ verb (**restudies, restudying, restudied**) [with obj.] study (something) again.
▶ noun an instance of studying something again.

restyle ▶ verb [with obj.] **1** rearrange or remake in a new shape or layout: *Nick restyled Rebecca's hair.*
2 give a new designation to: *the Association decided to restyle his job as performance director.*
▶ noun an instance of restyling something. ■ a new shape or arrangement.

resubmit ▶ verb [with obj.] submit (something, such as a plan, application, or resignation) again.
– DERIVATIVES **resubmission** noun.

result ▶ noun **1** a thing that is caused or produced by something else; a consequence or outcome: *the tower collapsed **as a result of** safety violations | different approaches have been tried with somewhat mixed results.* ■ a favourable outcome of an undertaking or contest: *determination and persistence guarantee results | if we can get a result in that game we might qualify.* ■ (usu. **results**) the outcome of a business's trading over a given period, expressed as a statement of profit or loss: *oil companies have reported better results.* ■ a final score, mark, or placing in a sporting event or examination.
2 an item of information obtained by experiment or some other scientific method; a quantity or formula obtained by calculation.
▶ verb [no obj.] occur or follow as the consequence of something: *anger may **result from** an argument* | (as adj. **resulting**) *talk of a general election and the resulting political uncertainty.* ■ (**result in**) have (a specified outcome): *talks in July had resulted in stalemate.*
– PHRASES **without result** in vain: *Denny had inquired about getting work, without result.*
– ORIGIN late Middle English (as a verb): from medieval Latin *resultare* 'to result', earlier in the sense 'spring back', from *re-* (expressing intensive force) + *saltare* (frequentative of *salire* 'to jump'). The noun dates from the early 17th cent.

resultant ▶ adjective [attrib.] occurring or produced as a result of something: *restructuring and the resultant cost savings.*
▶ noun technical a force, velocity, or other vector quantity which is equivalent to the combined effect of two or more component vectors acting at the same point.
– ORIGIN mid 17th cent. (in the adjectival sense): from Latin *resultant-* 'springing back', from the verb *resultare* (see **RESULT**). The noun sense dates from the early 19th cent.

resultative Grammar ▶ adjective expressing, indicating, or relating to the outcome of an action.
▶ noun a resultative verb, conjunction, or clause.

resume ▶ verb begin again or continue after a pause or interruption: [with obj.] *a day later normal service was resumed* | [no obj.] *the talks resumed in April.* ■ [no obj.] begin speaking again after a pause or interruption: *he sipped at the glass of water and then resumed.* ■ take or put on again: *the judge resumed his seat.*
▶ noun N. Amer. variant spelling of **RÉSUMÉ** (sense 2).
– DERIVATIVES **resumable** adjective.
– ORIGIN late Middle English: from Old French *resumer* or Latin *resumere*, from *re-* 'back' + *sumere* 'take'.

résumé /ˈrezjʊmeɪ/ ▶ noun **1** a summary: *I gave him a quick résumé of events.*
2 N. Amer. a curriculum vitae.
– ORIGIN early 19th cent.: French, literally 'resumed', past participle (used as a noun) of *résumer*.

resumption ▶ noun [mass noun] **1** the action of beginning something again after a pause or interruption.
2 Law, chiefly Austral. the action, on the part of the Crown or other authority, of reassuming possession of lands, rights, etc., previously granted to another.
– ORIGIN late Middle English (in the sense 'the action of reassuming possession of lands etc.'): from Old French *resumption* or late Latin *resumptio(n-)*, from Latin *resumpt-*, past participle of *resumere* (see **RESUME**).

resumptive ▶ adjective Grammar indicating resumption of a topic that has previously been referred to.

resupinate /rɪˈsuːpɪneɪt, -ˈsjuː-/ ▶ adjective Botany (of a leaf, flower, fruiting body, etc.) upside down.
– DERIVATIVES **resupination** noun.
– ORIGIN late 18th cent.: from Latin *resupinatus* 'bent back', past participle of *resupinare*, based on *supinus* 'lying on the back'.

resupply ▶ verb (**resupplies, resupplying, resupplied**) [with obj.] provide with a fresh supply: *he planned to use 216 Squadron to resupply his force.* ■ [no obj.] acquire a fresh supply: *phase two envisaged a period to regroup and resupply.*
▶ noun an act or instance of resupplying something or being resupplied.

resurface ▶ verb **1** [with obj.] put a new coating on or re-form (a surface, especially a road).
2 [no obj.] come back up to the surface of water: *he resurfaced beside the boat.* ■ arise or become evident again: *serious concerns about the welfare of animals eventually resurfaced.* ■ (of a person) come out of hiding or obscurity: *he resurfaced under a false identity in Australia.*

resurgence ▶ noun [in sing.] an increase or revival after a period of little activity, popularity, or occurrence: *a resurgence of interest in religion.*

resurgent ▶ adjective increasing or reviving after a period of little activity, popularity, or occurrence: *resurgent nationalism.*
– ORIGIN early 19th cent. (earlier as a noun): from Latin *resurgent-* 'rising again', from the verb *resurgere*, from *re-* 'again' + *surgere* 'to rise'.

resurrect ▶ verb [with obj.] restore (a dead person) to life: *he queried whether Jesus was indeed resurrected.* ■ revive or revitalize (something that is inactive, disused, or forgotten): *the deal collapsed and has yet to be resurrected.*
– ORIGIN late 18th cent.: back-formation from **RESURRECTION**.

resurrection ▶ noun [mass noun] the action or fact of resurrecting or being resurrected: *the story of the resurrection of Osiris.* ■ (**the Resurrection**) (in Christian belief) the rising of Christ from the dead. ■ (**the Resurrection**) (in Christian belief) the rising of the dead at the Last Judgement. ■ the revitalization or revival of something: *the resurrection of the country under a charismatic leader.*
– ORIGIN Middle English: from Old French, from late Latin *resurrectio(n-)*, from the verb *resurgere* 'rise again' (see **RESURGENT**).

resurrection man ▶ noun historical a person who illicitly retrieved corpses for dissection from rivers, scenes of disaster, or burial grounds.

resurrection plant ▶ noun any of a number of plants which are able to survive drought, typically folding up when dry and unfolding when moistened, in particular: ● a fern of tropical and warm-temperate America (*Polypodium polypodioides*, family Polypodiaceae). ● a Californian clubmoss (*Selaginella lepidophylla*, family Selaginellaceae). ● the rose of Jericho.

resurvey ▶ verb [with obj.] survey (a district) again. ■ study or investigate again: *the same people surveyed in 1992 will be resurveyed periodically.*
▶ noun an act of surveying a district or studying something again.

resuscitate /rɪˈsʌsɪteɪt/ ▶ verb [with obj.] revive (someone) from unconsciousness or apparent death. ■ make (something) active or vigorous again: *measures to resuscitate the ailing economy.*
– DERIVATIVES **resuscitation** noun, **resuscitative** adjective, **resuscitator** noun.
– ORIGIN early 16th cent.: from Latin *resuscitat-* 'raised again', from the verb *resuscitare*, from *re-* 'back' + *suscitare* 'raise'.

resuspend ▶ verb [with obj.] place (cells or particles) in suspension in a fluid again.
– DERIVATIVES **resuspension** noun.

resveratrol /rezˈvɛrətrɒl/ ▶ noun [mass noun] Chemistry a polyphenol compound found in certain plants and in red wine, which has antioxidant properties and has been investigated for possible anti-carcinogenic effects.
– ORIGIN 1930s: blend of **RESIN** and **VERATRUM** (the plant from which the compound was first obtained) + **-OL**.

ret /rɛt/ (also **rate**) ▶ verb (**rets, retting, retted**) [with obj.] soak (flax or hemp) in water to soften it.
– ORIGIN late Middle English: related to Dutch *reten*, also to **ROT**.

ret. ▶ abbreviation retired.

retable /rɪˈteɪb(ə)l/ (also **retablo** /rɪˈtɑːbləʊ/) ▶ noun (pl. **retables** or **retablos**) a frame or shelf enclosing decorated panels or revered objects above and behind an altar. ■ a painting or other image above and behind an altar.

– ORIGIN early 19th cent.: from French *rétable*, from Spanish *retablo*, from medieval Latin *retrotabulum* 'rear table', from Latin *retro* 'backwards' + *tabula* 'table'.

retail /ˈriːteɪl/ ▶ **noun** [mass noun] the sale of goods to the public in relatively small quantities for use or consumption rather than for resale: [as modifier] *the retail trade.*
▶ **verb** also /rɪˈteɪl/ [with obj.] **1** sell (goods) to the public by retail. ■ [no obj.] **(retail at/for)** (of goods) be sold by retail for (a specified price): *the product retails for around £20.*
2 relate the details of (a story or incident) to others: *his inimitable way of retailing a diverting anecdote.*
– DERIVATIVES **retailer** noun.
– ORIGIN late Middle English: from an Anglo-Norman French use of Old French *retaille* 'a piece cut off', from *retaillier*, from *re-* (expressing intensive force) + *tailler* 'to cut'.

retail park ▶ **noun** a shopping development situated outside a town or city, typically containing a number of large chain stores.

retail politics ▶ **plural noun** [also treated as sing.] US a style of political campaigning in which the candidate attends local events in order to target voters on a small-scale or individual basis.
– ORIGIN early 20th cent.: first referring to the practice of paying for votes.

retail price index ▶ **noun** (in the UK) an index of the variation in the prices of retail goods and other items.

retail price maintenance ▶ **noun** another term for **RESALE PRICE MAINTENANCE.**

retail therapy ▶ **noun** [mass noun] humorous the practice of shopping in order to make oneself feel more cheerful.

retain ▶ **verb** [with obj] **1** continue to have (something); keep possession of: *Labour retained the seat | built in 1830, the house retains many of its original features.* ■ not abolish or alter; maintain: *the rights of defendants must be retained.* ■ keep in one's memory: *I retained a few French words and phrases.*
2 absorb and continue to hold (a substance): *limestone is known to retain water.*
3 (often as adj. **retaining**) keep (something) in place; hold fixed: *remove the retaining bar.*
4 keep (someone) engaged in one's service: *he has been retained as a freelance.* ■ secure the services of (a barrister) with a preliminary payment.
– DERIVATIVES **retainability** noun, **retainable** adjective, **retainment** noun.
– ORIGIN late Middle English: via Anglo-Norman French from Old French *retenir*, from Latin *retinere*, from *re-* 'back' + *tenere* 'hold'.

retainer ▶ **noun 1** a thing that holds something in place: *a guitar string retainer.*
2 (also **retaining fee**) a fee paid in advance to someone, especially a barrister, in order to secure their services for use when required. ■ Brit. a reduced rent paid to retain accommodation during a period of non-occupancy.
3 a servant, especially one who has worked for a person or family for a long time.

retaining wall ▶ **noun** a wall that holds back earth or water.

retake ▶ **verb** (past **retook**; past participle **retaken**) [with obj.] take again, in particular: ■ take (a test or examination) again after failing: *Dawn had to retake her driving test.* ■ regain possession or control of: *in 799 the Moors retook Barcelona.* ■ reshoot (a film sequence or photograph) or re-record (a piece of music).
▶ **noun 1** a test or examination that is retaken.
2 an instance of filming a scene or recording a piece of music again.

retaliate /rɪˈtalɪeɪt/ ▶ **verb** [no obj.] make an attack in return for a similar attack: *the blow stung and she retaliated immediately.* ■ [with obj.] archaic repay (an injury or insult) in kind: *they used their abilities to retaliate the injury.*
– DERIVATIVES **retaliative** adjective, **retaliator** noun, **retaliatory** adjective.
– ORIGIN early 17th cent.: from Latin *retaliat-* 'returned in kind', from the verb *retaliare*, from *re-* 'back' + *talis* 'such'.

retaliation ▶ **noun** [mass noun] the action of returning a military attack; counter-attack: *the bombings are believed to be in retaliation for the trial of 15 suspects.* ■ the action of harming someone because they have harmed oneself; revenge: *she rejected as preposterous any suggestion that she had acted in retaliation.*

retard ▶ **verb** /rɪˈtɑːd/ [with obj.] delay or hold back in terms of progress or development: *his progress was retarded by his limp.*
▶ **noun** /ˈriːtɑːd/ offensive a person who has a mental disability (often used as a general term of abuse).
– PHRASES **in retard** Brit. formal behind in terms of development or progress: *I was in retard of them in real knowledge.*
– DERIVATIVES **retardation** noun **retarder** noun, **retardment** noun (rare).
– ORIGIN late 15th cent.: from French *retarder*, from Latin *retardare*, from *re-* 'back' + *tardus* 'slow'.

retardant ▶ **adjective** [in combination] (chiefly of a synthetic or treated fabric or substance) not readily susceptible to fire: *fire-retardant polymers.*
▶ **noun** a fabric or substance that prevents or inhibits something, especially the outbreak of fire.
– DERIVATIVES **retardancy** noun.

retardataire /rɪˌtɑːdəˈtɛː/ ▶ **adjective** (of a work of art or architecture) executed in an earlier or outdated style.
– ORIGIN French.

retardate /rɪˈtɑːdeɪt/ ▶ **noun** N. Amer., dated or offensive a person who has a mental disability.
– ORIGIN 1950s: from Latin *retardat-* 'slowed down', from the verb *retardare* (see **RETARD**).

retarded ▶ **adjective** less advanced in mental, physical, or social development than is usual for one's age.

retch ▶ **verb** [no obj.] make the sound and movement of vomiting. ■ [with obj.] vomit.
▶ **noun** a movement or sound of vomiting.
– ORIGIN mid 19th cent.: variant of dialect *reach*, from a Germanic base meaning 'spittle'.

retd (also **ret.**) ▶ **abbreviation** retired (used after the name of a retired armed forces officer or in recording that a sports player retired from a game).

rete /ˈriːti/ ▶ **noun** (pl. **retia** /-tɪə, -ʃɪə/) Anatomy an elaborate network of blood vessels or nerve cells.
– ORIGIN mid 16th cent.: from Latin *rete* 'net'.

reteach ▶ **verb** (past and past participle **retaught**) [with obj.] teach (someone or something) again.

retell ▶ **verb** (past and past participle **retold**) [with obj.] tell (a story) again or differently: *Walker retells the history of the world from the black perspective.*

retention ▶ **noun** [mass noun] **1** the continued possession, use, or control of something: *the retention of direct control by central government.* ■ the fact of keeping something in one's memory: *the children's retention of facts.*
2 the action of absorbing and continuing to hold a substance: *the soil's retention of moisture.* ■ failure to eliminate a substance from the body: *eating too much salt can lead to fluid retention.*
– ORIGIN late Middle English (denoting the power to retain something): from Old French, from Latin *retentio(n-)*, from *retinere* 'hold back' (see **RETAIN**).

retentive ▶ **adjective 1** (of a person's memory) effective in retaining facts and impressions.
2 (of a substance) able to absorb and hold moisture. ■ chiefly Medicine serving to keep something in place.
– DERIVATIVES **retentively** adverb, **retentiveness** noun.
– ORIGIN late Middle English: from Old French *retentif, -ive* or medieval Latin *retentivus*, from *retent-* 'held back', from the verb *retinere* (see **RETAIN**).

retentivity ▶ **noun** (pl. **retentivities**) Physics the ability of a substance to retain or resist magnetization, frequently measured as the strength of the magnetic field that remains in a sample after removal of an inducing field.

retest ▶ **verb** /riːˈtɛst/ [with obj.] test (someone or something) again.
▶ **noun** /ˈriːtɛst/ an act of retesting someone or something.

retexture ▶ **verb** [with obj.] treat (material or a garment) so as to restore firmness to its texture.

rethatch ▶ **verb** [with obj.] thatch (a roof or building) again.

rethink ▶ **verb** (past and past participle **rethought**) [with obj.] consider or assess (something, especially a course of action) again, especially in order to change it: *the government were forced to rethink their plans.*
▶ **noun** [in sing.] a reassessment, especially one that results in changes being made: *a last-minute rethink of their tactics.*

Rethymnon /ˈrɛθɪmnɒn/ a port on the north coast of Crete; pop. 27,900 (est. 2009). Greek name **Réthimnon** /ˈrɛθɪmnɒn/.

retia plural form of **RETE.**

retiarius /ˌrɛtɪˈɑːrɪəs, -ˈɛːrɪəs/ ▶ **noun** (pl. **retiarii** /-rɪʌɪ, -rɪiː/) an ancient Roman gladiator who used a net to trap his opponent.
– ORIGIN Latin, from *rete* 'net'.

reticence ▶ **noun** [mass noun] the quality of being reticent; reserve: *the traditional emotional reticence of the British.*

reticent /ˈrɛtɪs(ə)nt/ ▶ **adjective** not revealing one's thoughts or feelings readily: *she was extremely reticent about her personal affairs.*
– DERIVATIVES **reticently** adverb.
– ORIGIN mid 19th cent.: from Latin *reticent-* 'remaining silent', from the verb *reticere*, from *re-* (expressing intensive force) + *tacere* 'be silent'.

reticle /ˈrɛtɪk(ə)l/ ▶ **noun** North American term for **GRATICULE.**
– ORIGIN mid 18th cent.: from Latin *reticulum* 'net'.

reticula plural form of **RETICULUM.**

reticular formation (also **reticular activating system**) ▶ **noun** Anatomy a diffuse network of nerve pathways in the brainstem connecting the spinal cord, cerebrum, and cerebellum, and mediating the overall level of consciousness.

reticulate ▶ **verb** /rɪˈtɪkjʊleɪt/ [with obj.] rare divide or mark (something) in such a way as to resemble a net or network: *the numerous canals and branches of the river reticulate the flat alluvial plain.*
▶ **adjective** /rɪˈtɪkjʊlət/ chiefly Botany & Zoology reticulated.
– ORIGIN mid 17th cent.: from Latin *reticulatus* 'reticulated', from *reticulum* (see **RETICULUM**).

reticulated ▶ **adjective** constructed, arranged, or marked like a net or network: *a pinafore of a finely reticulated pattern.* ■ (of porcelain) having a pattern of interlacing lines forming a net or web. ■ Architecture relating to or denoting a style of decorated tracery characterized by circular shapes drawn at top and bottom into ogees, resulting in a net-like framework.

reticulated python ▶ **noun** a very large Asian python patterned with dark patches outlined in black. It is the longest snake at up to 11 m. ● *Python reticulatus*, family Pythonidae.

reticulation ▶ **noun 1** [mass noun] a pattern or arrangement of interlacing lines resembling a net: *the fish should have a blue back with white reticulation.* ■ Photography the formation of a network of wrinkles or cracks in a photographic emulsion.
2 chiefly Austral./NZ a network of pipes used in irrigation and water supply.

reticule /ˈrɛtɪkjuːl/ ▶ **noun 1** chiefly historical a woman's small handbag, typically having a drawstring and decorated with embroidery or beading.
2 variant spelling of **RETICLE.**
– ORIGIN early 18th cent.: from French *réticule*, from Latin *reticulum* (see **RETICULUM**).

reticulin /rɪˈtɪkjʊlɪn/ ▶ **noun** [mass noun] Biochemistry a structural protein resembling collagen, present in connective tissue as a network of fine fibres, especially around muscle and nerve fibres.
– ORIGIN late 19th cent.: from *reticular* (see **RETICULUM**) + **-IN**[1].

reticulocyte /rɪˈtɪkjʊlə(ʊ)sʌɪt/ ▶ **noun** Physiology an immature red blood cell without a nucleus, having a granular or reticulated appearance when suitably stained.
– ORIGIN 1920s: from **RETICULATED** + **-CYTE.**

reticuloendothelial /rɪˌtɪkjʊləʊɛndə(ʊ)ˈθiːlɪəl/ ▶ **adjective** Physiology relating to or denoting a diverse system of fixed and circulating phagocytic cells (macrophages and monocytes) involved in the immune response. They are spread throughout the body, and are especially common in the liver, spleen, and lymphatic system. Also called **LYMPHORETICULAR.**
– ORIGIN 1920s: from **RETICULUM** + *endothelial* (see **ENDOTHELIUM**).

reticuloendotheliosis /rɪˌtɪkjʊləʊɛndə(ʊ)ˈθiːlɪəʊsɪs/ ▶ **noun** [mass noun] Medicine overgrowth of some part of the reticuloendothelial system, causing isolated swelling of the bone marrow and in severe cases the destruction of the bones of the skull.

Reticulum /rɪˈtɪkjʊləm/ Astronomy a small southern constellation (the Net), between Dorado and Hydrus.
– ORIGIN Latin, diminutive of *rete* 'net'.

reticulum /rɪˈtɪkjʊləm/ ▶ **noun** (pl. **reticula** /-lə/) **1** a fine network or net-like structure.
2 Zoology the second stomach of a ruminant, having a honeycomb-like structure, receiving food from the rumen and passing it to the omasum.
– DERIVATIVES **reticular** adjective.

R

– ORIGIN mid 17th cent.: from Latin, diminutive of *rete* 'net'.

retie ▶ verb (**reties, retying, retied**) [with obj.] tie (something) again.

retiform /ˈriːtɪfɔːm, ˈrɛtɪ-/ ▶ adjective rare net-like.
– ORIGIN late 17th cent.: from Latin *rete* 'net' + **-IFORM**.

retighten ▶ verb [with obj.] tighten again; make tighter: *loosen the tourniquet every hour or so and then retighten it*.

retile ▶ verb [with obj.] tile (a room or surface) again.

retime ▶ verb [with obj.] set a different time for: *management would have retimed jobs and cut the piece rates*.

retina /ˈrɛtɪnə/ ▶ noun (pl. **retinas** or **retinae** /-niː/) a layer at the back of the eyeball that contains cells sensitive to light, which trigger nerve impulses that pass via the optic nerve to the brain, where a visual image is formed.
– DERIVATIVES **retinal** adjective.
– ORIGIN late Middle English: from medieval Latin, from Latin *rete* 'net'.

retinitis /ˌrɛtɪˈnʌɪtɪs/ ▶ noun [mass noun] Medicine inflammation of the retina of the eye.

retinitis pigmentosa /ˌpɪgmɛnˈtəʊsə/ ▶ noun [mass noun] Medicine a chronic hereditary eye disease characterized by black pigmentation and gradual degeneration of the retina.
– ORIGIN mid 19th cent.: *pigmentosa*, feminine of Latin *pigmentosus*, from *pigmentum* 'pigment'.

retinoblastoma /ˌrɛtɪnəʊblaˈstəʊmə/ ▶ noun [mass noun] Medicine a rare malignant tumour of the retina, affecting young children.

retinoic acid /rɛtɪˈnəʊɪk/ ▶ noun [mass noun] a carboxylic acid, obtained from retinol by oxidation and used in ointments to treat acne. ● Chem. formula: $C_{19}H_{27}COOH$.

retinoid /ˈrɛtɪnɔɪd/ ▶ noun Biochemistry any of a group of compounds having effects in the body like those of vitamin A.

retinol /ˈrɛtɪnɒl/ ▶ noun [mass noun] Biochemistry a yellow compound found in green and yellow vegetables, egg yolk, and fish-liver oil. It is essential for growth and for vision in dim light. Also called **VITAMIN A**.
● A carotenoid alcohol; chem. formula: $C_{20}H_{29}OH$.
– ORIGIN 1960s: from **RETINA** + **-OL**.

retinopathy /ˌrɛtɪˈnɒpəθi/ ▶ noun [mass noun] Medicine disease of the retina which results in impairment or loss of vision.

retinotopic /ˌrɛtɪnə(ʊ)ˈtɒpɪk/ ▶ adjective Physiology relating to or preserving the spatial relations of the sensory receptors of the retina.

retinue /ˈrɛtɪnjuː/ ▶ noun a group of advisers, assistants, or others accompanying an important person.
– ORIGIN late Middle English: from Old French *retenue*, feminine past participle (used as a noun) of *retenir* 'keep back, retain'.

retiral /rɪˈtʌɪr(ə)l/ ▶ noun (in Scotland) a person's retirement from a job or office.

R

retire ▶ verb **1** [no obj.] leave one's job and cease to work, typically on reaching the normal age for leaving service: *he* **retired from** *the Navy in 1986*. ■ [with obj.] compel (an employee) to leave their job, especially before they have reached retirement age. ■ (of a player) cease to participate in competitive sport: *he retired from football several years ago*. ■ (of a sports player) withdraw from a race or match as a result of accident or injury: *he was forced to retire with a damaged oil tank* | [with complement] *Stewart retired hurt*. ■ [with obj.] Baseball put out (a batter); cause (a side) to end a turn at bat: *Dopson retired twelve batters in a row*.
2 [no obj.] withdraw to or from a particular place: *she retired into the bathroom*. ■ go to bed: *everyone retired early that night*. ■ (of a jury) leave the courtroom to decide the verdict of a trial. ■ (of a military force) retreat from an enemy or an attacking position: *lack of numbers compelled the British force to retire*. ■ [with obj.] order (a military force) to retreat.
3 [with obj.] Economics withdraw (a bill or note) from circulation or currency.
4 [with obj.] Finance pay off or cancel (a debt).
– DERIVATIVES **retiree** noun, **retirer** noun.
– ORIGIN mid 16th cent. (in the sense 'withdraw to a place of safety or seclusion'): from French *retirer*, from *re-* 'back' + *tirer* 'draw'.

retiré /rəˈtɪəreɪ/ ▶ noun (pl. pronunc. **same**) Ballet a movement in which one leg is raised at right angles to the body until the toe is in line with the knee of the supporting leg.
– ORIGIN French, literally 'drawn back'.

retired ▶ adjective **1** having left one's job and ceased to work: *a retired headmaster*.
2 archaic (of a place) quiet and secluded: *this retired corner of the world*. ■ (of a person's way of life) quiet and involving little contact with other people. ■ (of a person) reserved; uncommunicative.
– DERIVATIVES **retiredness** noun (archaic).

retirement ▶ noun [mass noun] **1** the action or fact of leaving one's job and ceasing to work: *a man nearing retirement* | [count noun] *the library has seen a large number of retirements this year*. ■ the period of one's life after retiring from work: *he spent much of his retirement travelling in Europe*. ■ the action or fact of ceasing to play a sport competitively.
2 the withdrawal of a jury from the courtroom to decide their verdict. ■ [count noun] the period of time during which a jury decides their verdict: *a three-hour retirement*.
3 seclusion: *he lived in retirement in Kent*. ■ [count noun] archaic a secluded or private place: *Exmouth, where he has a sweet country retirement*.

retirement age (also Brit. **retiring age**) ▶ noun the age at which most people normally retire from work.

retirement home ▶ noun a house or flat in a group or block designed for the needs of old and retired people. ■ an institution for elderly people needing care.

retirement pension ▶ noun Brit. a pension paid by the state to retired people above a certain age.

retiring ▶ adjective shy and fond of being on one's own: *a retiring, acquiescent woman*.
– DERIVATIVES **retiringly** adverb.

retitle ▶ verb [with obj.] give a different title to.

retold past and past participle of **RETELL**.

retook past of **RETAKE**.

retool ▶ verb [with obj.] equip (a factory) with new or adapted tools. ■ N. Amer. alter the form or character of; reshape: *he has a little time to retool his candidacy*.

retort[1] ▶ verb **1** [reporting verb] say something in answer to a remark, typically in a sharp, angry, or witty manner: [with direct speech] *'No need to be rude,' retorted Isabel* | [with clause] *he retorted that this was nonsense*.
2 [with obj.] archaic repay (an insult or injury): *it was now his time to retort the humiliation*. ■ turn (an insult or accusation) back on the person who has issued it: *he was resolute to retort the charge of treason on his foes*. ■ use (an opponent's argument) against them.
▶ noun a sharp, angry, or witty reply: *she opened her mouth to make a suitably cutting retort*.
– ORIGIN late 15th cent. (in the sense 'hurl back an accusation or insult'): from Latin *retort-* 'twisted back, cast back', from the verb *retorquere*, from *re-* 'in return' + *torquere* 'to twist'.

retort[2] ▶ noun a container or furnace for carrying out a chemical process on a large or industrial scale. ■ historical a glass container with a long neck, used in distilling liquids and other chemical operations.
▶ verb [with obj.] heat in a retort in order to separate or purify: *the raw shale is retorted at four crude oil works*.
– ORIGIN early 17th cent.: from French *retorte*, from medieval Latin *retorta*, feminine past participle of *retorquere* 'twist back' (with reference to the long recurved neck of the laboratory container).

retortion ▶ noun [mass noun] (in international law) retaliation by a state on another's subjects.
– ORIGIN late 16th cent. (in the sense 'bending or turning backwards'): from **RETORT**[1], perhaps on the pattern of *contortion*.

retouch ▶ verb [with obj.] improve or repair (a painting, photograph, or other image) by making slight additions or alterations.
– DERIVATIVES **retoucher** noun.
– ORIGIN late 17th cent.: probably from French *retoucher*.

retrace ▶ verb [with obj.] go back over (the same route that one has just taken): *he began to* **retrace his steps** *to the station car park*. ■ discover and follow (a route taken by someone else): *I've tried to retrace some of her movements*. ■ trace (something) back to its source or beginning: *I wanted to retrace a particular evolutionary pathway*.
– ORIGIN late 17th cent.: from French *retracer*.

retract ▶ verb **1** draw or be drawn back or back in: [with obj.] *she retracted her hand as if she'd been burnt* | [no obj.] *the tentacle retracted quickly*.
2 [with obj.] withdraw (a statement or accusation) as untrue or unjustified: *he retracted his allegations*. ■ withdraw or go back on (an undertaking): *the parish council was forced to retract a previous resolution*.
– DERIVATIVES **retractable** adjective, **retraction** noun, **retractive** adjective.
– ORIGIN late Middle English: from Latin *retract-* 'drawn back', from the verb *retrahere* (from *re-* 'back' + *trahere* 'drag'); the senses 'withdraw (a statement)' and 'go back on' via Old French from *retractare* 'reconsider' (based on *trahere* 'drag').

retractile /rɪˈtraktʌɪl/ ▶ adjective Zoology capable of being retracted: *a long retractile proboscis*.
– ORIGIN late 18th cent.: from **RETRACT**, on the pattern of *contractile*.

retractor ▶ noun a device for retracting something: *seat belts with automatic retractors*. ■ (also **retractor muscle**) chiefly Zoology a muscle serving to retract a part of the body. Compare with **PROTRACTOR**.

retrain ▶ verb [with obj.] teach (someone) new skills to enable them to do a different job. ■ [no obj.] learn new skills so as to be able to do a different job: *a workforce which is willing to retrain*.

retranslate /ˌriːtransˈleɪt, -trɑːns-, -nz-/ ▶ verb [with obj.] translate again.
– DERIVATIVES **retranslation** noun.

retransmit /ˌriːtranzˈmɪt, -trɑːnz-, -ns-/ ▶ verb (**retransmits, retransmitting, retransmitted**) [with obj.] transmit (data, a radio signal, or a broadcast programme) again or on to another receiver.
– DERIVATIVES **retransmission** /-ˈmɪʃ(ə)n/ noun.

retread ▶ verb **1** (past **retrod**; past participle **retrodden**) [with obj.] go back over (a path or one's steps): *they never retread the same ground*.
2 (past and past participle **retreaded**) [with obj.] put a new tread on (a worn tyre).
▶ noun **1** a tyre that has been given a new tread; a remould.
2 N. Amer. informal a superficially altered version of a film, book, etc.: *a retread of the 30s romantic comedy*.
3 informal a person retrained for new work or recalled for service.

retreat ▶ verb [no obj.] **1** (of an army) withdraw from enemy forces as a result of their superior power or after a defeat: *the French retreated in disarray*. ■ move back or withdraw: *it becomes so hot that the lizards retreat into the shade* | *the ice retreated during warmer periods called interglacials* | (as adj. **retreating**) *the sound of retreating footsteps*. ■ withdraw to a quiet or secluded place: *after the funeral he retreated to Scotland*. ■ [with obj.] Chess move (a piece) back from a forward or threatened position on the board.
2 change one's mind or plans as a result of criticism or difficulty: *his proposals were clearly unreasonable and he was forced to retreat*.
3 (of shares) decline in value.
▶ noun **1** an act of moving back or withdrawing: *a speedy retreat* | [mass noun] *the army was* **in retreat**. ■ an act of changing one's mind or plans as a result of criticism or difficulty: *the trade unions made a retreat from their earlier position*.
2 a signal for a military force to withdraw: *the bugle sounded a retreat*. ■ [mass noun] a military musical ceremony carried out at sunset, originating in the playing of drums and bugles to tell soldiers to return to camp for the night.
3 a quiet or secluded place in which one can rest and relax: *their country retreat in Ireland*. ■ a period or place of seclusion for the purposes of prayer and meditation: *the bishop is away on his annual retreat* | [mass noun] *before his ordination he* **went into retreat**.
4 a decline in the value of shares.
– PHRASES **beat a retreat** see **BEAT**.
– ORIGIN late Middle English: from Old French *retret* (noun), *retraiter* (verb), from Latin *retrahere* 'pull back' (see **RETRACT**).

retrench ▶ verb [no obj.] (of an organization or individual) reduce costs or spending in response to economic difficulty: *as a result of the recession the company retrenched* | [with obj.] *if people are forced to retrench their expenditure trade will suffer*. ■ [with obj.] Austral. & S. African make (an employee) redundant: *if there are excess staff they should be retrenched*. ■ [with obj.] formal reduce (something) in extent or quantity: *right-wing parties which seek to retrench the welfare state*.
– DERIVATIVES **retrenchment** noun.
– ORIGIN late 16th cent. (in the now formal usage): from obsolete French *retrencher*, variant of *retrancher*, from *re-* (expressing reversal) + *trancher* 'to cut, slice'.

retrial ▶ noun Law a second or further trial on the same issues and with the same parties.

retribution ▸ **noun** [mass noun] punishment inflicted on someone as vengeance for a wrong or criminal act: *settlers drove the Navajo out of Arizona **in retribution for** their raids.*
– DERIVATIVES **retributive** /rɪˈtrɪbjʊtɪv/ **adjective**, **retributory** /rɪˈtrɪbjʊt(ə)ri/ **adjective**.
– ORIGIN late Middle English (also in the sense 'recompense for merit or a service'): from late Latin *retributio(n-)*, from *retribut-* 'assigned again', from the verb *retribuere*, from *re-* 'back' + *tribuere* 'assign'.

retrieval ▸ **noun 1** [mass noun] the process of getting something back from somewhere: *the investigation was completed after the retrieval of plane wreckage.*
2 the action of obtaining or consulting material stored in a computer system.

retrieve ▸ **verb** [with obj.] **1** get or bring (something) back from somewhere: *I was sent to retrieve the balls from his garden | Steven stooped and retrieved his hat.* ■ (of a dog) find and bring back (game that has been shot). ■ [no obj.] reel or bring in a fishing line.
2 find or extract (information stored in a computer). ■ recall (something): *the police hope to encourage him to retrieve forgotten memories.*
3 put right or improve (an unwelcome situation): *he made one last desperate attempt to retrieve the situation.*
▸ **noun 1** an act of retrieving something, especially game that has been shot. ■ an act of reeling or drawing in a fishing line.
2 [mass noun] archaic the possibility of recovery: *he ruined himself **beyond retrieve**.*
– DERIVATIVES **retrievability** noun, **retrievable** adjective.
– ORIGIN late Middle English (in the sense 'find lost game'): from Old French *retroeve-*, stressed stem of *retrover* 'find again'.

retriever ▸ **noun 1** a dog of a breed used for retrieving game.
2 a person who retrieves something.

retro[1] ▸ **adjective** imitative of a style or fashion from the recent past: *retro 60s fashions.*
▸ **noun** [mass noun] retro clothes, music, or style: *a look which mixes Italian casual wear and American retro.*
– ORIGIN 1960s: from French *rétro*, abbreviation of *rétrograde* 'retrograde'.

retro[2] ▸ **noun** (pl. **retros**) short for RETROROCKET.

retro- ▸ **combining form 1** denoting action that is directed backwards or is reciprocal: *retrocede | retroject.*
2 denoting location behind: *retrosternal | retrochoir.*
– ORIGIN from Latin *retro* 'backwards'.

retroactive /rɛtrəʊˈaktɪv/ ▸ **adjective** (especially of legislation) taking effect from a date in the past: *a big retroactive tax increase.*
– DERIVATIVES **retroaction** noun, **retroactively** adverb, **retroactivity** noun.

retroactive interference (also **retroactive inhibition**) ▸ **noun** [mass noun] Psychology the tendency of later learning to hinder the memory of previously learned material.

retrobulbar /ˌrɛtrəʊˈbʌlbə/ ▸ **adjective** Anatomy & Medicine situated or occurring behind the eyeball: *a retrobulbar abscess.*

retrocede /ˌrɛtrə(ʊ)ˈsiːd/ ▸ **verb** [with obj.] rare cede (territory) back again: *Spain retroceded the colony to France.*
– DERIVATIVES **retrocession** noun.
– ORIGIN early 19th cent.: from French *rétrocéder*.

retrochoir /ˈrɛtrəʊˌkwʌɪə/ ▸ **noun** the interior of a cathedral or large church behind the high altar.
– ORIGIN mid 19th cent.: from medieval Latin *retrochorus* (see RETRO-, CHOIR).

retrod past of RETREAD (sense 1 of the verb).

retrodden past participle of RETREAD (sense 1 of the verb).

retrodiction /ˌrɛtrə(ʊ)ˈdɪkʃ(ə)n/ ▸ **noun** [mass noun] the explanation or interpretation of past actions or events inferred from the laws that are assumed to have governed them.
– DERIVATIVES **retrodict** verb.

retroelement ▸ **noun** Biochemistry a sequence of DNA in a chromosome that arose by the copying of an RNA virus into DNA by reverse transcriptase and integration of the DNA copy into the chromosome.

retrofit /ˈrɛtrəʊfɪt/ ▸ **verb** (**retrofits, retrofitting, retrofitted**) [with obj.] add (a component or accessory) to something that did not have it when manufactured: *motorists who retrofit catalysts to older cars.* ■ provide (something) with a component or accessory not fitted during manufacture: *buses have been retrofitted with easy-access features.*
▸ **noun** an act of retrofitting a component or accessory. ■ a component or accessory added to something after manufacture.
– ORIGIN 1950s: blend of RETROACTIVE and REFIT.

retroflex /ˈrɛtrə(ʊ)flɛks/ (also **retroflexed**) ▸ **adjective** Anatomy & Medicine turned backwards: *a retroflexed endoscope.* ■ Phonetics pronounced with the tip of the tongue curled up towards the hard palate: *the retroflex /r/.*
– DERIVATIVES **retroflexion** noun.
– ORIGIN late 18th cent.: from Latin *retroflex-* 'bent backwards', from the verb *retroflectere*, from *retro* 'backwards' + *flectere* 'to bend'.

retrofuturism ▸ **noun** [mass noun] the use of a style or aesthetic considered futuristic in an earlier era.
– DERIVATIVES **retro-futuristic** adjective.

retrogradation /ˌrɛtrəʊgrəˈdeɪʃ(ə)n/ ▸ **noun** [mass noun] Astronomy & Astrology the apparent temporary reverse motion of a planet (from east to west), resulting from the relative orbital progress of the earth and the planet. ■ the orbiting or rotation of a planet or planetary satellite in a reverse direction from that normal in the solar system.
– ORIGIN mid 16th cent.: from late Latin *retrogradation-* (see RETRO-, GRADATION).

retrograde ▸ **adjective 1** directed or moving backwards: *a retrograde flow.* ■ Astronomy & Astrology (of the apparent motion of a planet) in a reverse direction from normal (from east to west), resulting from the relative orbital progress of the earth and the planet. The opposite of PROGRADE. ■ Astronomy (of the orbit or rotation of a planet or planetary satellite) in a reverse direction from that normal in the solar system.
2 reverting to an earlier and inferior condition: *to go back on the progress that has been made would be a retrograde step.*
3 (of the order of something) reversed; inverse: *the retrograde form of these inscriptions.*
4 Geology (of a metamorphic change) resulting from a decrease in temperature or pressure.
▸ **noun** rare a degenerate person.
▸ **verb** [no obj.] **1** archaic go back in position or time: *our history must retrograde for the space of a few pages.* ■ revert to an earlier and inferior condition.
2 Astronomy show retrograde motion.
– DERIVATIVES **retrogradely** adverb.
– ORIGIN late Middle English (as a term in astronomy): from Latin *retrogradus*, from *retro* 'backwards' + *gradus* 'step' (from *gradi* 'to walk').

retrogress /ˌrɛtrə(ʊ)ˈgrɛs/ ▸ **verb** [no obj.] go back to an earlier state, typically a worse one: *she retrogressed to the starting point of her rehabilitation.*
– ORIGIN early 19th cent.: from RETRO- 'back', on the pattern of the verb *progress*.

retrogression ▸ **noun** [mass noun] **1** the process of returning to an earlier state, typically a worse one: *a retrogression to 19th-century attitudes.*
2 Astronomy another term for RETROGRADATION.
– DERIVATIVES **retrogressive** adjective.
– ORIGIN mid 17th cent.: from RETRO- 'backwards', on the pattern of *progression*.

retroject /ˌrɛtrə(ʊ)ˈdʒɛkt/ ▸ **verb** [with obj.] rare project backwards: *the rabbinic interpretation is retrojected into the biblical text.*
– ORIGIN mid 19th cent.: from RETRO- 'backwards', on the pattern of the verb *project*.

retronym /ˈrɛtrə(ʊ)nɪm/ ▸ **noun** a new term created from an existing word in order to distinguish the original referent of the existing word from a later one that is the product of progress or technological development (e.g. *acoustic guitar* for *guitar*).
– ORIGIN 1980s: blend of RETRO- and -ONYM.

retroperitoneal /ˌrɛtrəʊˌpɛrɪtəˈniːəl/ ▸ **adjective** Anatomy & Medicine situated or occurring behind the peritoneum.

retroreflector ▸ **noun** a device which reflects light back along the incident path, irrespective of the angle of incidence.
– DERIVATIVES **retroreflective** adjective.

retrorocket ▸ **noun** a small auxiliary rocket on a spacecraft or missile, fired in the direction of travel to slow the craft down, for example when landing on the surface of a planet.

retrorse /rɪˈtrɔːs/ ▸ **adjective** Biology turned or pointing backwards: *retrorse spines.*
– ORIGIN early 19th cent.: from Latin *retrorsus*, contraction of *retroversus*, from *retro* 'backwards' + *versus* 'turned' (past participle of *vertere*).

retrospect ▸ **noun** a survey or review of a past course of events or period of time.
– PHRASES **in retrospect** when looking back on a past event or situation; with hindsight: *perhaps, in retrospect, I shouldn't have gone.*
– ORIGIN early 17th cent.: from RETRO- 'back', on the pattern of the noun *prospect*.

retrospection ▸ **noun** [mass noun] the action of looking back on or reviewing past events or situations, especially those in one's own life: *he was disinclined to indulge in retrospection.*
– ORIGIN mid 17th cent.: probably from RETROSPECT (used as a verb).

retrospective ▸ **adjective** looking back on or dealing with past events or situations: *our survey was retrospective.* ■ (of an exhibition or compilation) showing the development of an artist's work over a period of time. ■ (of a statute or legal decision) taking effect from a date in the past: *retrospective pay awards.*
▸ **noun** an exhibition or compilation showing the development of an artist's work over a period of time: *a Georgia O'Keeffe retrospective.*
– DERIVATIVES **retrospectively** adverb.

retrosternal /ˌrɛtrə(ʊ)ˈstəːn(ə)l/ ▸ **adjective** Anatomy & Medicine behind the breastbone.

retrotransposon /ˌrɛtrəʊtransˈpəʊzɒn, -trɑːns-, -tranz-/ ▸ **noun** Genetics a transposon whose sequence shows homology with that of a retrovirus.

retroussé /rəˈtruːseɪ/ ▸ **adjective** (of a person's nose) turned up at the tip in an attractive way.
– ORIGIN early 19th cent.: French, literally 'tucked up', past participle of *retrousser*.

retroverted /ˈrɛtrəʊvəːtɪd/ ▸ **adjective** Anatomy (of the uterus) tilted abnormally backwards.
– DERIVATIVES **retroversion** noun.
– ORIGIN late 18th cent.: from Latin *retrovertere* 'turn backwards' + -ED[2].

Retrovir /ˈrɛtrə(ʊ)vɪə/ ▸ **noun** trademark for ZIDOVUDINE.
– ORIGIN 1980s: abbreviation of RETROVIRUS.

retrovirus /ˈrɛtrəʊˌvʌɪrəs/ ▸ **noun** Biology any of a group of RNA viruses which insert a DNA copy of their genome into the host cell in order to replicate, e.g. HIV.
– DERIVATIVES **retroviral** adjective.
– ORIGIN 1970s: modern Latin, from the initial letters of *reverse transcriptase* + VIRUS.

retry ▸ **verb** (**retries, retrying, retried**) **1** [with obj.] Law try (a defendant or case) again.
2 [no obj.] Computing re-enter a command, especially because an error was made the first time. ■ (of a system) transmit data again because the first attempt was unsuccessful.
▸ **noun** an instance of re-entering a command or retransmitting data.

retsina /rɛtˈsiːnə/ ▸ **noun** [mass noun] a Greek white or rosé wine flavoured with resin.
– ORIGIN modern Greek.

retune ▸ **verb** [with obj.] tune (something) again or differently, in particular: ■ put (a musical instrument) back in tune or alter its pitch. ■ tune (a radio, television, or other piece of electronic equipment) to a different frequency.

returf ▸ **verb** [with obj.] Brit. cover (ground) or replace (a lawn or sports field) with new turf.

return ▸ **verb 1** [no obj.] come or go back to a place or person: *he **returned to** America in the late autumn.* ■ (**return to**) go back to (a particular situation): *I'll be glad when things return to normal.* ■ (**return to**) divert one's attention back to: *he returned to his newspaper.* ■ (especially of a feeling) reoccur after a period of absence: *her appetite had returned.* ■ Golf play the last nine holes in a round of eighteen holes: *McAllister went out in 43 and returned in 32.*
2 [with obj.] give, put, or send (something) back to a place or person: *complete the application form and **return** it **to** this address.* ■ feel, say, or do (the same feeling, action, etc.) in response: *she returned his kiss.* ■ (in tennis and other sports) hit or send (the ball) back to an opponent. ■ American Football intercept (a pass, kick, or fumble by the opposing team) and run upfield with the ball. ■ (of a judge or jury) state or present (a decision or verdict) in response to a formal request. ■ Bridge lead (a card, especially one of a suit led earlier by one's partner) after taking a trick.
3 [with obj.] yield or make (a profit): *the company returned a profit of £4.3 million.*
4 [with obj.] (of an electorate) elect (a person or party) to office: *the city of Glasgow returned eleven Labour MPs.*

R

5 Architecture continue (a wall) in a changed direction, especially at right angles.
▶ **noun 1** an act of coming or going back to a place or activity: *he celebrated his safe return from the war* | [as modifier] *a return flight.* ■ [in sing.] an act of going back to an earlier state or situation: *the designer advocated a return to elegance.* ■ [mass noun] the action of returning something: *the tape is ready to despatch to you on return of the documents.* ■ (in tennis and other sports) a stroke played in response to a serve or other stroke by one's opponent. ■ a thing which has been given or sent back, especially an unwanted ticket for a sporting event or play. ■ (also **return ticket**) Brit. a ticket which allows someone to travel to a place and back again. ■ an electrical conductor bringing a current back to its source. ■ (also **return match** or **game**) a second contest between the same opponents.
2 (also **returns**) a profit from an investment: *product areas are being developed to produce maximum returns.* ■ [mass noun] a good rate of return.
3 an official report or statement submitted in response to a formal demand: *census returns.* ■ a returning officer's announcement of an election result. ■ Law an endorsement or report by a court officer or sheriff on a writ.
4 [mass noun] election to office: *I campaigned for the return of forty-four MPs.*
5 (also **carriage return**) a mechanism or key on a typewriter that returns the carriage to a fixed position at the start of a new line. ■ (also **return key**) a key pressed on a computer keyboard to simulate a carriage return in a word-processing program, or to indicate the end of a command or data string.
6 Architecture a part receding from the line of the front, for example the side of a house or of a window opening.
– PHRASES **by return (of post)** Brit. in the next available mail delivery to the sender. **in return** as a response, exchange, or reward for something: *he left the house to his sister in return for her kindness.* **many happy returns (of the day)** used as a greeting to someone on their birthday.
– DERIVATIVES **returnable** adjective, **returner** noun.
– ORIGIN Middle English: the verb from Old French *returner*, from Latin *re-* 'back' + *tornare* 'to turn'; the noun via Anglo-Norman French.

return crease ▶ noun Cricket each of two lines on either side of the wicket, at right angles to the bowling and popping creases, between which the bowler must deliver the ball.

returnee ▶ noun a person who returns, in particular: ■ a refugee returning from abroad. ■ a member of the armed forces returning from overseas duty. ■ a person returning to work, especially after bringing up a family.

returning officer ▶ noun (in the UK, Canada, Australia, and New Zealand) the official in each constituency or electorate who conducts an election and announces the result.

retying present participle of RETIE.

R

retype ▶ verb [with obj.] type (text) again on a typewriter or computer, especially to correct errors.

Reuben /ˈruːbɪn/ (in the Bible) a Hebrew patriarch, eldest son of Jacob and Leah (Gen. 29:32). ■ the tribe of Israel traditionally descended from Reuben.

reunify ▶ verb (**reunifies, reunifying, reunified**) [with obj.] restore political unity to (a place or group, especially a divided territory): *on 20 June 1991, Germany was reunified.*
– DERIVATIVES **reunification** noun.

reunion ▶ noun an instance of two or more people coming together again after a period of separation: *she had a tearful reunion with her parents.* ■ a social gathering attended by members of a group of people who have not seen each other for some time: *a school reunion.* ■ [mass noun] the action of being brought together again as a unified whole: *the reunion of East and West Germany.*
– ORIGIN early 17th cent.: from French *réunion* or Anglo-Latin *reunio(n-)*, from Latin *reunire* 'unite'.

Réunion /riːˈjuːnjən, -nɪən/, French /ʀeynjɔ̃/ a volcanically active, subtropical island in the Indian Ocean east of Madagascar, one of the Mascarene Islands; pop. 807,000 (est. 2007); capital, Saint-Denis. A French possession since 1638, the island became an administrative region of France in 1974.

reunite ▶ verb come together or cause to come together again after a period of separation or disunity: [no obj.] *the three friends reunited in 1959* | [with obj.] *Stephanie was reunited with her parents.*

reupholster ▶ verb [with obj.] upholster with new materials, especially with a different covering fabric: *the bed was reupholstered in chintz.*
– DERIVATIVES **reupholstery** noun.

reuptake ▶ noun [mass noun] Physiology the absorption by a presynaptic nerve ending of a neurotransmitter that it has secreted.

reuse ▶ verb /riːˈjuːz/ [with obj.] use again or more than once: *the tape could be magnetically erased and reused.*
▶ noun /riːˈjuːs/ [mass noun] the action of using something again: *the ballast was cleaned ready for reuse.*
– DERIVATIVES **reusable** adjective.

Reuters /ˈrɔɪtəz/ an international news agency founded in London in 1851 by Paul Julius Reuter (1816–99). The agency pioneered the use of telegraphy, building up a service used today by newspapers and radio and television stations in most countries.

reutilize (also **reutilise**) ▶ verb [with obj.] utilize again or for a different purpose.
– DERIVATIVES **reutilization** noun.

rev informal ▶ noun (usu. **revs**) a revolution of an engine per minute: *an engine speed of 1,750 revs.* ■ an act of increasing the speed of revolution of a vehicle's engine by pressing the accelerator.
▶ verb (**revs, revving, revved**) [with obj.] increase the running speed of (an engine) or the engine speed of (a vehicle) by pressing the accelerator, especially while the clutch is disengaged: *he revved up the engine and drove off.* ■ [no obj.] (of an engine) operate with increasing speed when the accelerator is pressed, especially while the clutch is disengaged: *he could hear the sound of an engine revving nearby.* ■ make or become more active or energetic: [no obj.] *he's revving up for next week's World Cup game* | [with obj.] *we need to rev up the economy.*
– ORIGIN early 20th cent.: abbreviation of REVOLUTION.

Rev. ▶ abbreviation ■ the book of Revelation (in biblical references). ■ (as the title of a priest) Reverend.

revaccinate ▶ verb [with obj.] vaccinate again for the same disease.
– DERIVATIVES **revaccination** noun.

revalue ▶ verb (**revalues, revaluing, revalued**) [with obj.] assess the value of (something) again. ■ Economics adjust the value of (a currency) in relation to other currencies.
– DERIVATIVES **revaluation** noun.

revamp ▶ verb [with obj.] give new and improved form, structure, or appearance to: *an attempt to revamp the museum's image* | (as adj. **revamped**) *a revamped magazine.*
▶ noun [usu. in sing.] an act of improving the form, structure, or appearance of something: *the brand was given a $1 million revamp.* ■ a new and improved version: *the show was a revamp of an old idea.*

revanchism /rɪˈvan(t)ʃɪz(ə)m/ ▶ noun [mass noun] a policy of seeking to retaliate, especially to recover lost territory.
– DERIVATIVES **revanchist** adjective & noun.
– ORIGIN 1950s: from French *revanche*, 'revenge' + -ISM.

revarnish ▶ verb [with obj.] varnish (something) again.

rev counter ▶ noun an instrument that measures and displays the rate of revolutions of an engine.

Revd ▶ abbreviation Brit. (as the title of a priest) Reverend.

reveal[1] ▶ verb [with obj.] make (previously unknown or secret information) known to others: *Brenda was forced to reveal Robbie's whereabouts* | [with clause] *he revealed that he had received death threats.* ■ cause or allow (something) to be seen: *the clouds were breaking up to reveal a clear blue sky.* ■ make (something) known to humans by divine or supernatural means: *the truth revealed at the Incarnation.*
– DERIVATIVES **revealable** adjective, **revealer** noun.
– ORIGIN late Middle English: from Old French *reveler* or Latin *revelare*, from *re-* 'again' (expressing reversal) + *velum* 'veil'.

reveal[2] ▶ noun either side surface of an aperture in a wall for a door or window.
– ORIGIN late 17th cent.: from obsolete *revale* 'to lower', from Old French *revaler*, from *re-* 'back' + *avaler* 'go down, sink'.

revealed religion ▶ noun [mass noun] religion based on divine revelation rather than reason.

revealing ▶ adjective making interesting or significant information known, especially of a personal nature: *a revealing radio interview.* ■ (of an item of clothing) allowing more of the wearer's body to be seen than is usual: *a very revealing dress.*
– DERIVATIVES **revealingly** adverb.

revegetate ▶ verb [with obj.] chiefly N. Amer. produce a new growth of vegetation on (disturbed or barren ground).
– DERIVATIVES **revegetation** noun.

reveille /rɪˈvali/ ▶ noun [in sing.] a signal sounded especially on a bugle or drum to wake personnel in the armed forces.
– ORIGIN mid 17th cent.: from French *réveillez!* 'wake up!', imperative plural of *réveiller*, based on Latin *vigilare* 'keep watch'.

réveillon /ˌrɛveɪˈjɒ̃/, French /ʀevɛjɔ̃/ ▶ noun (usu. **Le Réveillon**) (in France and French-speaking countries) a night-time celebration, especially a feast traditionally held after midnight on Christmas morning.
– ORIGIN French, from *réveiller* 'awaken'.

revel ▶ verb (**revels, revelling, revelled**; US **revels, reveling, reveled**) [no obj.] enjoy oneself in a lively and noisy way, especially with drinking and dancing: (as noun **revelling**) *a night of drunken revelling.* ■ (**revel in**) gain great pleasure from (a situation): *Bill said he was secretly revelling in his new-found fame.*
▶ noun (**revels**) lively and noisy enjoyment, especially with drinking and dancing.
– ORIGIN late Middle English: from Old French *reveler* 'rise up in rebellion', from Latin *rebellare* 'to rebel'.

revelation ▶ noun **1** a surprising and previously unknown fact that has been disclosed to others: *revelations about his personal life.* ■ [mass noun] the making known of something that was previously secret or unknown: *the revelation of a plot to assassinate the king.* ■ used to emphasize the remarkable quality of someone or something: *seeing them play at international level was a revelation.*
2 [mass noun] the divine or supernatural disclosure to humans of something relating to human existence: *an attempt to reconcile Darwinian theories with biblical revelation* | [count noun] *a divine revelation.* ■ (**Revelation** or **Revelations**; in full **the Revelation of St John the Divine**) the last book of the New Testament, recounting a divine revelation of the future to St John.
– DERIVATIVES **revelational** adjective.
– ORIGIN Middle English (in the theological sense): from Old French, or from late Latin *revelatio(n-)*, from *revelare* 'lay bare' (see REVEAL[1]). Sense 1 dates from the mid 19th cent.

revelationist ▶ noun a believer in divine revelation.

revelatory /ˌrɛvəˈleɪt(ə)ri, ˈrɛv(ə)lət(ə)ri/ ▶ adjective revealing something hitherto unknown: *a revelatory experience.*

reveller (US **reveler**) ▶ noun a person who is enjoying themselves in a lively and noisy way: *drunken revellers brawled in the town centre in the early hours.*

revelry ▶ noun (pl. **revelries**) [mass noun] (also **revelries**) lively and noisy festivities, especially when these involve drinking a large amount of alcohol: *sounds of revelry issued into the night* | *New Year revelries.*

revenant /ˈrɛv(ə)nənt/ ▶ noun a person who has returned, especially supposedly from the dead.
– ORIGIN early 19th cent.: French, literally 'coming back', present participle (used as a noun) of *revenir*.

revenge ▶ noun [mass noun] the action of hurting or harming someone in return for an injury or wrong suffered at their hands: *other spurned wives have taken public revenge on their husbands.* ■ the desire to repay an injury or wrong: *it was difficult not to be overwhelmed with feelings of hate and revenge.* ■ (in sporting contexts) the defeat of a person or team by whom one was beaten in a previous encounter: *Zimbabwe snatched the game 18–16, but the Spanish had their revenge later.*
▶ verb (**revenge oneself** or **be revenged**) chiefly literary inflict hurt or harm on someone for an injury or wrong done to oneself: *I'll be revenged on the whole pack of you.* ■ [with obj.] inflict revenge on behalf of (someone else): *it's a pity he chose that way to revenge his sister.* ■ inflict retribution for (a wrong or injury done to oneself or another): *her brother was slain, and she revenged his death.*
– PHRASES **revenge is a dish best served (or eaten) cold** proverb vengeance is often more satisfying if it is not exacted immediately.
– DERIVATIVES **revenger** noun (literary).
– ORIGIN late Middle English: from Old French *revencher*, from late Latin *revindicare*, from *re-* (expressing intensive force) + *vindicare* 'claim, avenge'.

revengeful ▶ adjective eager for revenge.
– DERIVATIVES **revengefully** adverb, **revengefulness** noun.

revenge tragedy ▶ noun [mass noun] a style of drama, popular in England during the late 16th and 17th centuries, in which the basic plot was a quest for vengeance and which typically featured scenes of carnage and mutilation. Examples of the genre include Thomas Kyd's *The Spanish Tragedy* (1592) and John Webster's *The Duchess Of Malfi* (1623).

revenue ▶ noun [mass noun] (also **revenues**) income, especially when of an organization and of a substantial nature: *traders have lost £10,000 in revenue since the traffic scheme was implemented.* ■ a state's annual income from which public expenses are met. ■ (often **the revenue**) the department of the civil service collecting state revenue. See also INLAND REVENUE.
– ORIGIN late Middle English: from Old French *revenu(e)* 'returned', past participle (used as a noun) of *revenir*, from Latin *revenire* 'return', from *re-* 'back' + *venire* 'come'.

revenue tariff ▶ noun a tariff imposed principally to raise government revenue rather than to protect domestic industries.

reverb /ˈriːvəːb, rɪˈvəːb/ ▶ noun [mass noun] an effect whereby the sound produced by an amplifier or an amplified musical instrument is made to reverberate slightly.
– ORIGIN 1960s: abbreviation.

reverberate ▶ verb [no obj., usu. with adverbial] **1** (of a loud noise) be repeated several times as an echo: *her deep booming laugh reverberated around the room.* ■ (of a place) appear to vibrate because of a loud noise: *the hall **reverberated with** laughter.* ■ [with obj.] archaic return or re-echo (a sound): *oft did the cliffs reverberate the sound.*
2 have continuing and serious effects: *the statements by the professor reverberated through the Capitol.*
– DERIVATIVES **reverberant** adjective, **reverberantly** adverb, **reverberative** adjective, **reverberator** noun, **reverberatory** adjective.
– ORIGIN late 15th cent. (in the sense 'drive or beat back'): from Latin *reverberat-* 'struck again', from the verb *reverberare*, from *re-* 'back' + *verberare* 'to lash' (from *verbera* (plural) 'scourge').

reverberation ▶ noun **1** [mass noun] prolongation of a sound; resonance: *electronic effects have been added, such as echo and reverberation.*
2 (usu. **reverberations**) a continuing effect; a repercussion: *the attack has had reverberations around the world.*

reverberatory furnace ▶ noun a furnace in which the roof and walls are heated by flames and radiate heat on to material in the centre of the furnace.

Revere /rɪˈvɪə/, Paul (1735–1818), American patriot. In 1775 he rode from Boston to Lexington to warn fellow American revolutionaries of the approach of British troops.

revere /rɪˈvɪə/ ▶ verb [with obj.] feel deep respect or admiration for (something): *Cézanne's still lifes were revered by his contemporaries.*
– ORIGIN mid 17th cent.: from French *révérer* or Latin *revereri*, from *re-* (expressing intensive force) + *vereri* 'to fear'.

reverence ▶ noun [mass noun] deep respect for someone or something: *rituals showed honour and reverence for the dead.* ■ [count noun] archaic a gesture indicative of deep respect; a bow or curtsy: *the messenger **made his reverence**.* ■ (**His/Your Reverence**) a title or form of address to a member of the clergy, especially a priest in Ireland.
▶ verb [with obj.] regard or treat with deep respect: *the many divine beings reverenced by Hindu tradition.*
– ORIGIN Middle English: from Old French, from Latin *reverentia*, from *revereri* 'stand in awe of' (see REVERE).

reverend ▶ adjective used as a title or form of address to members of the clergy: *the Reverend Pat Tilly.*
▶ noun informal a clergyman.
– ORIGIN late Middle English: from Old French, or from Latin *reverendus* 'person to be revered', gerundive of *revereri* (see REVERE).

> **USAGE** As a title **Reverend** is used for members of the clergy; the traditionally correct form of address is *the Reverend James Smith* or *the Reverend J. Smith*, rather than *Reverend Smith* or simply *Reverend*. Other words are prefixed in titles of more senior clergy: bishops are **Right Reverend**, archbishops are **Most Reverend**, and deans are **Very Reverend**.

Reverend Mother ▶ noun the title of the Mother Superior of a convent.

reverent ▶ adjective feeling or showing deep and solemn respect: *a reverent silence.*
– DERIVATIVES **reverently** adverb.
– ORIGIN late Middle English: from Latin *reverent-* 'revering', from the verb *revereri* (see REVERE).

reverential ▶ adjective of the nature of, due to, or characterized by reverence: *their names are always mentioned in reverential tones.*
– DERIVATIVES **reverentially** adverb.

reverie /ˈrɛv(ə)ri/ ▶ noun a state of being pleasantly lost in one's thoughts; a daydream: *a knock on the door broke her reverie* | [mass noun] *I slipped into reverie.* ■ Music an instrumental piece suggesting a dreamy or musing state. ■ archaic a fanciful or impractical idea or theory.
– ORIGIN early 17th cent.: from obsolete French *resverie*, from Old French *reverie* 'rejoicing, revelry', from *rever* 'be delirious', of unknown ultimate origin.

revers /rɪˈvɪə/ ▶ noun (pl. **same** /-ˈvɪəz/) the turned-back edge of a garment revealing the undersurface, especially at the lapel.
– ORIGIN mid 19th cent.: from French, literally 'reverse'.

reversal ▶ noun **1** a change to an opposite direction, position, or course of action: *a dramatic reversal in population decline in the Alps* | [mass noun] *the reversal of tidal currents.* ■ Law an annulment of a judgement, sentence, or decree made by a lower court or authority: *a reversal by the House of Lords of the Court of Appeal's decision.* ■ an adverse change of fortune: *the champions suffered a League reversal at Gloucester last month.*
2 [mass noun] Photography direct production of a positive image from an exposed film or plate; direct reproduction of a positive or negative image.
– ORIGIN late 15th cent. (as a legal term): from REVERSE + -AL.

reversal film ▶ noun [mass noun] Photography film that gives a positive image directly when processed, used chiefly for making transparencies.

reverse /rɪˈvəːs/ ▶ verb **1** [no obj.] move backwards: *the lorry reversed into the back of a bus.* ■ [with obj.] cause (a vehicle) to move backwards: *she reversed the car into a side turn.* ■ (of an engine) work in a contrary direction: *the ship's engines reversed and cut out altogether.*
2 [with obj.] make (something) the opposite of what it was: *the damage done to the ozone layer may be reversed.* ■ exchange (the position or function) of two people or things: *the experimenter and the subject reversed roles and the experiment was repeated.* ■ Law revoke or annul (a judgement, sentence, or decree made by a lower court or authority): *the court reversed his conviction.*
3 [with obj.] turn (something) the other way round or up or inside out: (as adj. **reversed**) *a reversed S-shape.*
4 [with obj.] Printing make (type or a design) appear as white in a block of solid colour or a half-tone: *their press ads had a headline **reversed out of** the illustration.*
▶ adjective [attrib.] going in or turned towards the direction opposite to that previously stated: *the trend appears to be going in the reverse direction.* ■ operating, behaving, or ordered in a way opposite to that which is usual or expected: *indiscriminate bombing had a reverse effect on popular morale.* ■ Electronics (of a voltage applied to a semiconductor junction) in the direction which does not allow significant current to flow. ■ Geology denoting a fault in which a relative downward movement occurred in the strata on the underside of the fault plane.
▶ noun **1** a complete change of direction or action: *the gall actuates a reverse of photosynthesis.* ■ [mass noun] reverse gear on a motor vehicle; the position of a gear lever or selector corresponding to this. ■ American Football a play in which a player reverses the direction of attack by passing the ball to a teammate moving in the opposite direction.
2 (**the reverse**) the opposite to that previously stated: *he didn't feel homesick—quite the reverse.*
3 an adverse change of fortune; a setback or defeat: *United suffered their heaviest reverse of the season.*
4 the opposite side or face to the observer: *the address is given on the reverse of this leaflet.* ■ a left-hand page of an open book, or the back of a loose document. ■ the side of a coin or medal bearing the value or secondary design. ■ the design or inscription on the reverse of a coin or medal.
– PHRASES **in** (or **into**) **reverse** (of a motor vehicle) in reverse gear so as to travel backwards. ■ in the opposite direction or manner from usual: *a similar ride next year will do the route in reverse.* **reverse arms** hold a rifle with the butt upwards, typically as a drill movement at a military or state funeral. **reverse the charges** make the recipient of a telephone call responsible for payment.
– DERIVATIVES **reversely** adverb, **reverser** noun.
– ORIGIN Middle English: from Old French *revers*, *reverse* (nouns), *reverser* (verb), from Latin *reversus* 'turned back', past participle of *revertere*, from *re-* 'back' + *vertere* 'to turn'.

reverse-charge ▶ adjective chiefly Brit. denoting a telephone call paid for by the recipient.

reverse discrimination ▶ noun another term for POSITIVE DISCRIMINATION.

reverse engineering ▶ noun [mass noun] the reproduction of another manufacturer's product following detailed examination of its construction or composition.
– DERIVATIVES **reverse-engineer** verb.

reverse gear ▶ noun a gear used to make a vehicle or piece of machinery move or work backwards.

reverse osmosis ▶ noun [mass noun] Chemistry a process by which a solvent passes through a porous membrane in the direction opposite to that for natural osmosis when subjected to a hydrostatic pressure greater than the osmotic pressure.

reverse Polish notation ▶ noun see POLISH NOTATION.

reverse takeover ▶ noun a takeover of a public company by a smaller company.

reverse transcriptase ▶ noun see TRANSCRIPTASE.

reverse transcription ▶ noun [mass noun] Biochemistry the reverse of normal transcription, occurring in some RNA viruses, in which a sequence of nucleotides is copied from an RNA template during the synthesis of a molecule of DNA.

reversible ▶ adjective **1** able to be turned the other way round: *a reversible pushchair seat.* ■ (of a garment or fabric) faced on both sides so as to be worn or used with either outside.
2 (of the effects of a process or condition) capable of being reversed so that the previous state is restored: *potentially reversible forms of renal failure.* ■ Chemistry (of a reaction) occurring together with its converse, and so yielding an equilibrium mixture of reactants and products. ■ Physics (of a change or process) capable of complete and detailed reversal, especially denoting or undergoing an ideal change in which a system is in thermodynamic equilibrium at all times. ■ Chemistry (of a colloid) capable of being changed from a gel into a sol by a reversal of the treatment which turns the sol into a gel.
– DERIVATIVES **reversibility** noun, **reversibly** adverb.

reversing light ▶ noun Brit. a white light at the rear of a vehicle that comes on when the vehicle is reversing.

reversion /rɪˈvəːʃ(ə)n/ ▶ noun **1** [mass noun] a return to a previous state, practice, or belief: *there was some reversion to polytheism* | [in sing.] ***a reversion to** the two-party system.* ■ Biology the action of reverting to a former or ancestral type.
2 [mass noun] Law the right, especially of the original owner or their heirs, to possess or succeed to property on the death of the present possessor or at the end of a lease. ■ [count noun] a property to which someone has the right of reversion. ■ the right of succession to an office or post after the death or retirement of the holder: *he was given a promise of **the reversion of** Boraston's job.*
3 a sum payable on a person's death, especially by way of life insurance.
4 (also **reversion disease**) [mass noun] an incurable disease of the blackcurrant transmitted by the blackcurrant gall mite.
– DERIVATIVES **reversionary** adjective.
– ORIGIN late Middle English (denoting the action of returning to or from a place): from Old French, or from Latin *reversio(n-)*, from *revertere* 'turn back' (see REVERSE).

reversionary bonus ▶ noun a sum added to the amount of an insurance policy payable at the maturation of the policy or the death of the person insured.

reversioner ▶ noun Law a person who possesses the reversion to a property or privilege.

revert ▶ verb **1** [no obj.] (**revert to**) return to (a previous state, practice, topic, etc.): *he reverted to his native language* | *he ignored her words by reverting to*

R

the former subject. ■ convert to (the Islamic faith). ■ Biology return to (a former or ancestral type): *it is impossible that a fishlike mammal will actually revert to being a true fish.* ■ Law (of property) return to (the original owner) by reversion.
2 [with obj.] archaic turn (one's eyes or steps) back: *on reverting our eyes, every step presented some new and admirable scene.*
▸ **noun** a person who has converted to the Islamic faith.
– DERIVATIVES **reverter** noun (Law), **revertible** adjective (Law).
– ORIGIN Middle English: from Old French *revertir* or Latin *revertere* 'turn back'. Early senses included 'recover consciousness' and 'return to a position'.

revertant Biology ▸ **adjective** (of a cell, organism, or strain) having reverted to the normal type from a mutant or abnormal form.
▸ **noun** a revertant cell, organism, or strain.

revet /rɪˈvɛt/ ▸ **verb** (**revets, revetting, revetted**) [with obj.] (usu. as adj. **revetted**) face (a rampart, wall, etc.) with masonry, especially in fortification: *sandbagged and revetted trenches.*
– ORIGIN early 19th cent.: from French *revêtir*, from late Latin *revestire*, from *re-* 'again' + *vestire* 'clothe' (from *vestis* 'clothing').

revetment /rɪˈvɛtm(ə)nt/ ▸ **noun** (especially in fortification) a retaining wall or facing of masonry or other material, supporting or protecting a rampart, wall, etc. ■ a barricade of earth or sandbags set up to provide protection from blast or to prevent aircraft from overrunning when landing.
– ORIGIN late 18th cent.: from French *revêtement*, from the verb *revêtir* (see REVET).

review ▸ **noun 1** a formal assessment of something with the intention of instituting change if necessary: *a comprehensive review of UK defence policy* | [mass noun] *all areas of the company will come under review.* ■ Law a reconsideration of a judgement, sentence, etc. by a higher court or authority: *a review of her sentence* | [mass noun] *his case comes up for review in January.* Compare with JUDICIAL REVIEW. ■ a report on or evaluation of a subject or past events: *the Director General's end-of-year review.*
2 a critical appraisal of a book, play, film, etc. published in a newspaper or magazine. ■ [often in names] a periodical publication with critical articles on culture and current events.
3 a ceremonial display and formal inspection of military or naval forces, typically by a sovereign or commander-in-chief.
4 a facility for playing a tape recording during a fast wind or rewind, so that it can be stopped at a particular point.
▸ **verb** [with obj.] **1** assess (something) formally with the intention of instituting change if necessary: *the Home Secretary was called on to review Britain's gun laws.* ■ Law submit (a sentence, case, etc.) for reconsideration by a higher court or authority: *the Attorney General asked the court to review the sentence.* ■ survey or evaluate (a subject or past events): *in the next chapter we review a number of recent empirical studies.*
2 write a critical appraisal of (a book, play, film, etc.) for publication in a newspaper or magazine: *I reviewed his first novel.*
3 (of a sovereign, commander-in-chief, etc.) make a ceremonial and formal inspection of (military or naval forces).
4 view or inspect again: *all slides were then reviewed by one pathologist.*
– DERIVATIVES **reviewable** adjective, **reviewal** noun.
– ORIGIN late Middle English (as a noun denoting a formal inspection of military or naval forces): from obsolete French *reveue*, from *revoir* 'see again'.

reviewer ▸ **noun 1** a person who writes critical appraisals of books, plays, films, etc. for publication.
2 a person who formally assesses something with a view to changing it if necessary: *a rent reviewer.*

revile ▸ **verb** [with obj.] criticize in an abusive or angrily insulting manner: *he was now reviled by the party that he had helped to lead.*
– DERIVATIVES **revilement** noun, **reviler** noun.
– ORIGIN Middle English: from Old French *reviler*, based on *vil* 'vile'.

revise ▸ **verb 1** [with obj.] reconsider and alter (something) in the light of further evidence: *he had cause to revise his opinion a moment after expressing it.* ■ examine and improve or amend (written or printed matter): *the book was published in 1960 and revised in 1968* | (as adj. **revised**) *a revised edition.* ■ alter so as to make more efficient: (as adj. **revised**) *the revised finance and administrative groups.*
2 [no obj.] Brit. reread work done previously to improve one's knowledge of a subject, typically to prepare for an examination: *students frantically revising for exams* | [with obj.] *revise your lecture notes on the topic.*
▸ **noun** Printing a proof including corrections made in an earlier proof.
– DERIVATIVES **revisable** adjective, **revisal** noun, **reviser** noun, **revisory** adjective.
– ORIGIN mid 16th cent. (in the sense 'look again or repeatedly (at)'): from French *réviser* 'look at', or Latin *revisere* 'look at again', from *re-* 'again' + *visere* (intensive form of *videre* 'to see').

Revised Standard Version (abbrev.: **RSV**) ▸ **noun** a modern English translation of the Bible, published 1946–57 and based on the American Standard Version of 1901.

Revised Version (abbrev.: **RV**) ▸ **noun** an English translation of the Bible published in 1881–95 and based on the Authorized Version.

revision ▸ **noun** [mass noun] the action of revising: *the scheme needs drastic revision.* ■ [count noun] a revised edition or form of something.
– DERIVATIVES **revisionary** adjective.

revisionism ▸ **noun** [mass noun] often derogatory a policy of revision or modification, especially of Marxism on evolutionary socialist (rather than revolutionary) or pluralist principles. ■ the theory or practice of revising one's attitude to a previously accepted situation or point of view.
– DERIVATIVES **revisionist** noun & adjective.

revisit ▸ **verb** (**revisits, revisiting, revisited**) [with obj.] come back to or visit again: *she was anxious to revisit some of her old haunts in Paris.* ■ consider (a situation or problem) again or from a different perspective: *the council will have to revisit the issue at a general meeting this summer.*

revitalize (also **revitalise**) ▸ **verb** [with obj.] imbue (something) with new life and vitality: *a package of spending cuts to revitalize the economy.*
– DERIVATIVES **revitalization** noun.

revival ▸ **noun 1** an improvement in the condition, strength, or fortunes of someone or something: *a revival in the fortunes of the party* | *an economic revival.* ■ a restoration to life or consciousness.
2 an instance of something becoming popular, active, or important again: *cross-country skiing is enjoying a revival.* ■ a new production of an old play or similar work. ■ a reawakening of religious fervour, especially by means of evangelistic meetings: *the revivals of the nineteenth century* | [mass noun] *a wave of religious revival.*

revivalism ▸ **noun** [mass noun] belief in or the promotion of a revival of religious fervour. ■ a tendency or desire to revive a former custom or practice: *Seventies revivalism.*
– DERIVATIVES **revivalist** noun & adjective, **revivalistic** adjective.

revive ▸ **verb** [with obj.] restore to life or consciousness: *both men collapsed, but were revived.* ■ [no obj.] regain life, consciousness, or strength: *she was beginning to revive from her faint.* ■ give new strength or energy to: *the cool, refreshing water revived us all.* ■ restore interest in or the popularity of: *many pagan traditions are being revived.* ■ improve the position or condition of: *the paper made panicky attempts to revive falling sales.*
– DERIVATIVES **revivable** adjective, **reviver** noun.
– ORIGIN late Middle English: from Old French *revivre* or late Latin *revivere*, from Latin *re-* 'back' + *vivere* 'live'.

revivify /rɪˈvɪvɪfʌɪ/ ▸ **verb** (**revivifies, revivifying, revivified**) [with obj.] give new life or vigour to: *they revivified a wine industry that had all but vanished.*
– DERIVATIVES **revivification** noun.
– ORIGIN late 17th cent.: from French *revivifier* or late Latin *revivificare* (see RE-, VIVIFY).

revocable /ˈrɛvəkəb(ə)l/ ▸ **adjective** capable of being revoked or cancelled: *a revocable settlement.*
– DERIVATIVES **revocability** noun.

revoke ▸ **verb 1** [with obj.] officially cancel (a decree, decision, or promise): *the men appealed and the sentence was revoked.*
2 [no obj.] (in bridge, whist, and other card games) fail to follow suit despite being able to do so.
– DERIVATIVES **revocation** noun, **revoker** noun.
– ORIGIN late Middle English: from Old French *revoquer* or Latin *revocare*, from *re-* 'back' + *vocare* 'to call'.

revolt ▸ **verb 1** [no obj.] take violent action against an established government or ruler; rebel: *the Iceni revolted and had to be suppressed.* ■ refuse to acknowledge someone or something as having authority: *voters may revolt when they realize the cost of the measures.* ■ (as adj. **revolted**) archaic having rebelled: *the emperor was leading an expedition against the revolted Bretons.*
2 [with obj.] cause to feel disgust: *he was revolted by the stench that greeted him.* ■ [no obj.] archaic feel disgust: *'tis just the main assumption reason most revolts at.*
▸ **noun** an attempt to end the authority of a person or body by rebelling: *a country-wide* ***revolt against*** *the government* | [mass noun] *the peasants rose in revolt.* ■ a refusal to continue to obey or conform: *a revolt over tax increases.*
– ORIGIN mid 16th cent.: from French *révolte* (noun), *révolter* (verb), from Italian *rivoltare*, based on Latin *revolvere* 'roll back' (see REVOLVE).

revolting ▸ **adjective** causing intense disgust; disgusting: *there was a revolting smell that lingered in the air.*
– DERIVATIVES **revoltingly** adverb [as submodifier] *when I was a kid I was revoltingly precocious.*

revolute /ˈrɛvəl(j)uːt/ ▸ **adjective** Botany (especially of the edge of a leaf) curved or curled back.
– ORIGIN mid 18th cent.: from Latin *revolutus* 'unrolled', past participle of *revolvere* (see REVOLVE).

revolution ▸ **noun 1** a forcible overthrow of a government or social order, in favour of a new system. ■ (often **the Revolution**) (in Marxism) the class struggle which is expected to lead to political change and the triumph of communism. ■ a dramatic and wide-reaching change in conditions, attitudes, or operation: *marketing underwent a revolution.*
2 an instance of revolving: *one revolution a second.* ■ [mass noun] the movement of an object in a circular or elliptical course around another or about an axis or centre: *revolution about the axis of rotation.* ■ a single orbit or course of this kind.
– DERIVATIVES **revolutionism** noun, **revolutionist** noun.
– ORIGIN late Middle English: from Old French, or from late Latin *revolutio(n-)*, from *revolvere* 'roll back' (see REVOLVE).

revolutionary ▸ **adjective 1** involving or causing a complete or dramatic change: *a revolutionary new drug.*
2 engaged in or promoting political revolution: *the revolutionary army.* ■ (**Revolutionary**) relating to a particular revolution, especially the War of American Independence.
▸ **noun** (pl. **revolutionaries**) a person who advocates or engages in political revolution.

Revolutionary Tribunal a court established in Paris in October 1793 to try political opponents of the French Revolution. There was no right of appeal and from June 1794 the only penalty was death.

revolutionize (also **revolutionise**) ▸ **verb** [with obj.] change (something) radically or fundamentally: *this fabulous new theory will revolutionize the whole of science.*

Revolutions of 1848 a series of revolts against monarchical rule in Europe during 1848.

> They sprang from a shared background of autocratic government, lack of representation for the middle classes, economic grievances, and growing nationalism. Revolution occurred first in France, and in the German and Italian states there were uprisings and demonstrations; in Austria rioting caused the flight of the emperor. All of the revolutions ended in failure and repression, but some of the liberal reforms gained as a result survived.

revolve ▸ **verb** [no obj.] move in a circle on a central axis: *overhead, the fan revolved slowly.* ■ (**revolve about/around**) move in a circular orbit around: *the earth revolves around the sun.* ■ (**revolve around**) treat as the most important element: *her life revolved around her husband.* ■ [with obj.] consider (something) repeatedly and from different angles: *her mind revolved the possibilities.*
– ORIGIN late Middle English (in the senses 'turn (the eyes) back', 'restore', 'consider'): from Latin *revolvere*, from *re-* 'back' (also expressing intensive force) + *volvere* 'roll'.

revolver ▸ **noun 1** a pistol with revolving chambers enabling several shots to be fired without reloading.
2 an agreement to provide revolving credit.

revolving credit ▸ **noun** [mass noun] credit that is automatically renewed as debts are paid off.

revolving door ▸ **noun** an entrance to a large building in which four partitions turn about a central axis. ■ used to refer to a situation in which the same events recur in a continuous cycle: *many patients are*

R

trapped in a revolving door of admission, discharge, and readmission. ■ [usu. as modifier] an organization that people tend to enter and leave very quickly: *the newsroom became a revolving-door workplace.*

revolving fund ▶ noun a fund that is continually replenished as withdrawals are made.

revote ▶ noun a second or repeated vote.

revue /rɪˈvjuː/ ▶ noun a light theatrical entertainment consisting of a series of short sketches, songs, and dances, typically dealing satirically with topical issues.
– ORIGIN French, literally 'review'.

revulsion ▶ noun [mass noun] **1** a sense of disgust and loathing: *news of the attack will be met with sorrow and revulsion.*
2 Medicine, chiefly historical the drawing of disease or blood congestion from one part of the body to another, e.g. by counterirritation.
– DERIVATIVES **revulsive** adjective & noun.
– ORIGIN mid 16th cent. (in sense 2): from French, or from Latin *revulsio(n-)*, from *revuls-* 'torn out', from the verb *revellere* (from *re-* 'back' + *vellere* 'pull'). Sense 1 dates from the early 19th cent.

reward ▶ noun a thing given in recognition of service, effort, or achievement: *the holiday was a reward for 40 years' service with the company | he's **reaping the rewards** of his hard work and perseverance* | figurative *the emotional rewards of being a carer.* ■ a fair return for good or bad behaviour: *a slap on the face was his reward for his cheek.* ■ a sum offered for information leading to the solving of a crime, the detection of a criminal, etc.
▶ verb [with obj.] give something to (someone) in recognition of their services, efforts, or achievements: *the engineer who supervised the work was **rewarded with** the MBE.* ■ show one's appreciation of (an action or quality): *an effective organization rewards creativity and initiative.* ■ (**be rewarded**) receive what one deserves: *their hard work was rewarded by the winning of a five-year contract.*
– PHRASES **go to one's reward** euphemistic die.
– DERIVATIVES **rewardless** adjective.
– ORIGIN Middle English: from Anglo-Norman French, variant of Old French *reguard* 'regard, heed', also an early sense of the English word.

rewarding ▶ adjective providing satisfaction; gratifying: *skiing can be hugely rewarding.*
– DERIVATIVES **rewardingly** adverb.

rewarewa /ˈreɪwəˌreɪwə/ ▶ noun a tall red-flowered tree native to New Zealand, which yields decorative timber used for cabinetmaking. ● *Knightia excelsa*, family Proteaceae.
– ORIGIN mid 19th cent.: from Maori.

reweigh ▶ verb [with obj.] weigh (something) again.

rewind ▶ verb (past and past participle **rewound**) (with reference to a film or tape) wind or be wound back to the beginning: [with obj.] *I rewound the film and stopped it.*
▶ noun a mechanism for rewinding a film or tape.
– DERIVATIVES **rewinder** noun.

rewire ▶ verb [with obj.] provide (an appliance, building, or vehicle) with new electric wiring.
▶ noun [in sing.] an instance of rewiring something.

reword ▶ verb [with obj.] put (something) into different words: *there is a sound reason for rewording that clause.*

rework ▶ verb [with obj.] make changes to (something), especially in order to make it more up to date: *he reworked the orchestral score for two pianos* | (as noun **reworking**) *a reworking of the Sherwood Forest legend.*

rewound past and past participle of **REWIND**.

rewrap ▶ verb (**rewraps, rewrapping, rewrapped**) [with obj.] wrap (something) again or differently.

rewritable ▶ adjective Computing (of a storage device) supporting overwriting of previously recorded data.

rewrite ▶ verb (past **rewrote**; past participle **rewritten**) [with obj.] write (something) again so as to alter or improve it: *I cobbled together a rough draft and then rewrote it.*
▶ noun an instance of rewriting something. ■ a piece of text that has been rewritten.
– PHRASES **rewrite history** select or present past events in a way that suits one's particular purposes. **rewrite the record books** (of a sports player or team) break a record or records.

Rex¹ ▶ noun the reigning king (used following a name or in the titles of lawsuits, e.g. *Rex v. Jones*: the Crown versus Jones).
– ORIGIN Latin, literally 'king'.

Rex² ▶ noun a cat of a breed with curly fur, which lacks guard hairs.
– ORIGIN 1960s: from Latin, literally 'king'.

Rexine /ˈrɛksiːn/ ▶ noun [mass noun] Brit. trademark an artificial leather, used in upholstery and bookbinding.
– ORIGIN early 20th cent.: of unknown origin.

Reye's syndrome /ˈreɪz, ˈrʌɪz/ ▶ noun [mass noun] a life-threatening metabolic disorder in young children, of uncertain cause but sometimes precipitated by aspirin and involving encephalitis and liver failure.
– ORIGIN 1960s: named after Ralph D. K. *Reye* (1912–78), Australian paediatrician.

Reykjavik /ˈreɪkjəvɪk, -viːk/ the capital of Iceland, a port on the west coast; pop. 119,357 (2009).
– ORIGIN from Icelandic *rejkja* 'smoky', referring to the steam from its many hot springs.

Reynard /ˈrɛnɑːd, ˈreɪ-/ ▶ noun literary a name for a fox.
– ORIGIN from Old French *renart*; the spelling was influenced by Middle Dutch *Reynaerd*.

Reynolds¹ /ˈrɛn(ə)ldz/, Albert (b.1933), Irish Fianna Fáil statesman, Taoiseach (Prime Minister) 1992–4. He was involved with John Major in drafting the 'Downing Street Declaration' (1993), intended as the basis of a peace initiative in Northern Ireland.

Reynolds² /ˈrɛn(ə)ldz/, Sir Joshua (1723–92), English painter. The first president of the Royal Academy (1768), he sought to raise portraiture to the status of historical painting by adapting poses and settings from classical statues and Renaissance paintings.

Reynolds number ▶ noun Physics a dimensionless number used in fluid mechanics to indicate whether fluid flow past a body or in a duct is steady or turbulent. ● This is evaluated as $\rho \upsilon d/\mu$, where d is a diameter or other characteristic length of the system, υ is a typical speed, ρ is the fluid density, and μ is the viscosity of the fluid. The **magnetic Reynolds number** is an analogous number used in the description of the dynamic behaviour of a magnetized plasma.
– ORIGIN early 20th cent.: named after Osborne *Reynolds* (1842–1912), English physicist.

Reynolds stress ▶ noun Physics the net rate of transfer of momentum across a surface in a fluid resulting from turbulence in the fluid.
– ORIGIN 1940s: named after Osborne *Reynolds* (see **REYNOLDS NUMBER**).

Reza Shah /ˌreɪzə ˈʃɑː/ see **PAHLAVI¹**.

rezone ▶ verb [with obj.] chiefly N. Amer. assign (land or property) to a different planning zone: *they submitted a proposal to rezone part of the Brooklyn waterfront.*

RF ▶ abbreviation radio frequency.

Rf ▶ symbol the chemical element rutherfordium.

RFA ▶ abbreviation (in the UK) Royal Fleet Auxiliary.

RFC ▶ abbreviation ■ (in computing) request for comment, a document circulated on the Internet which forms the basis of a technical standard. ■ historical Royal Flying Corps. ■ Rugby Football Club.

RFID ▶ abbreviation radio frequency identification, a method for tracking goods by means of tags which transmit a radio signal.

RFLP ▶ abbreviation restriction fragment length polymorphism.

RFP ▶ abbreviation chiefly N. Amer. request for proposal.

Rg ▶ symbol the chemical element roentgenium.

RGN ▶ abbreviation Registered General Nurse.

RGS ▶ abbreviation Royal Geographical Society.

Rh ▶ abbreviation rhesus (factor).
▶ symbol the chemical element rhodium.

r.h. ▶ abbreviation right hand.

RHA ▶ abbreviation ■ (in the UK) regional health authority. ■ (in the UK) Royal Horse Artillery.

rhabdom /ˈrabdəʊm/ (also **rhabdome**) ▶ noun Zoology a translucent cylinder forming part of the light-sensitive receptor in the eye of an arthropod.
– ORIGIN late 19th cent.: from late Greek *rhabdōma*, from *rhabdos* 'rod'.

rhabdomancy /ˈrabdəˌmansi/ ▶ noun [mass noun] formal dowsing with a rod or stick.
– ORIGIN mid 17th cent.: from Greek *rhabdomanteia*, from *rhabdos* 'rod'.

rhabdomyolysis /ˌrabdə(ʊ)mʌɪˈɒlɪsɪs/ ▶ noun [mass noun] Medicine the destruction of striated muscle cells; (especially in horses) azoturia.
– ORIGIN 1950s: from Greek *rhabdos* 'rod' + **MYO-** + **-LYSIS**.

rhabdomyosarcoma /ˌrabdə(ʊ)ˌmʌɪə(ʊ)sɑːˈkəʊmə/ ▶ noun (pl. **rhabdomyosarcomas** or **rhabdomyosarcomata** /-mətə/) Medicine a rare malignant tumour involving striated muscle tissue.
– ORIGIN late 19th cent.: from Greek *rhabdos* 'rod' + **MYO-** + **SARCOMA**.

rhachis ▶ noun variant spelling of **RACHIS**.

Rhadamanthine /ˌradəˈmanθʌɪn/ ▶ adjective literary showing stern and inflexible judgement.
– ORIGIN mid 17th cent.: from **RHADAMANTHUS** + **-INE¹**.

Rhadamanthus /ˌradəˈmanθəs/ Greek Mythology the son of Zeus and Europa, and brother of Minos, who, as a ruler and judge in the underworld, was renowned for his justice.

Rhaeto-Romance /ˌriːtə(ʊ)rəʊˈmans/ (also **Rhaeto-Romanic** /-ˈmanɪk/) ▶ adjective relating to or denoting the Romance dialects spoken in parts of SE Switzerland, NE Italy, and Tyrol, especially Romansh and Ladin.
▶ noun [mass noun] the Rhaeto-Romance dialects.
– ORIGIN from Latin *Rhaetus* 'of *Rhaetia*' (the name of a Roman province in the Alps) + **ROMANCE**.

rhamnose /ˈramnəʊz, -s/ ▶ noun [mass noun] Chemistry a sugar of the hexose class which occurs widely in plants, especially in berries of the common buckthorn.
– ORIGIN late 19th cent.: from modern Latin *Rhamnus* (genus name) + **-OSE²**.

rhapsode /ˈrapsəʊd/ ▶ noun a person who recites epic poems, especially one of a group in ancient Greece whose profession it was to recite the Homeric poems.
– ORIGIN from Greek *rhapsōidos*, from *rhapsōidia* (see **RHAPSODY**).

rhapsodist ▶ noun **1** a person who rhapsodizes.
2 another term for **RHAPSODE**.

rhapsodize (also **rhapsodise**) ▶ verb [no obj.] speak or write about someone or something with great enthusiasm and delight: *he began to rhapsodize about Gaby's beauty and charm.*

rhapsody ▶ noun (pl. **rhapsodies**) **1** an effusively enthusiastic or ecstatic expression of feeling: *rhapsodies of praise.* ■ Music a free instrumental composition in one extended movement, typically one that is emotional in character.
2 (in ancient Greece) an epic poem, or part of a poem, of a suitable length for recitation at one time.
– DERIVATIVES **rhapsodic** /rapˈsɒdɪk/ adjective, **rhapsodical** adjective, **rhapsodically** adverb.
– ORIGIN mid 16th cent. (in sense 2): via Latin from Greek *rhapsōidia*, from *rhaptein* 'to stitch' + *ōidē* 'song, ode'.

rhatany /ˈratəni/ ▶ noun **1** [mass noun] an astringent extract of the root of a South American shrub, used in medicine.
2 the partially parasitic South American shrub which yields rhatany, which is also used as a source of dye. ● Genus *Krameria*, family Krameriaceae.
– ORIGIN early 19th cent.: from modern Latin *rhatania*, via Portuguese and Spanish from Quechua *ratánya*.

RHD ▶ abbreviation right-hand drive.

Rhea /ˈriːə/ **1** Greek Mythology one of the Titans, wife of Cronus and mother of Zeus, Demeter, Poseidon, Hera, and Hades. Frightened of betrayal by their children, Cronus ate them; Rhea rescued Zeus from this fate by hiding him and giving Cronus a stone wrapped in blankets instead.
2 Astronomy a satellite of Saturn, the fourteenth closest to the planet, discovered by Cassini in 1672 (diameter 1,530 km).

rhea /ˈriːə/ ▶ noun a large flightless bird of South American grasslands, resembling a small ostrich with greyish-brown plumage. ● Family Rheidae: two species, *Rhea americana* and *Pterocnemia pennata*.
– ORIGIN early 19th cent.: modern Latin (genus name), from the name of the Titan **RHEA**.

rhebok /ˈriːbɒk/ (also **reebok**, **grey rhebok**, or **rhebuck**) ▶ noun a small South African antelope with a woolly brownish-grey coat, a long slender neck, and short straight horns. ● *Pelea capreolus*, family Bovidae.
– ORIGIN late 18th cent.: from Dutch *reebok* 'roebuck'.

Rheims variant spelling of **REIMS**.

Rhein /rʌɪn/ German name for **RHINE**.

Rheinland /ˈrʌɪnlant/ German name for **RHINELAND**.

Rheinland-Pfalz /ˌrʌɪnlantˈpfalts/ German name for **RHINELAND-PALATINATE**.

rheme /riːm/ ▶ noun Linguistics the part of a clause that gives information about the theme.

R

– ORIGIN late 19th cent.: from Greek *rhēma* 'that which is said'.

Rhenish /ˈrɛnɪʃ/ ▶ adjective of the Rhine and the regions adjoining it.
▶ noun [mass noun] wine from the Rhine region.
– ORIGIN late Middle English: from Anglo-Norman French *reneis*, from a medieval Latin alteration of Latin *Rhenanus*, from *Rhenus* 'Rhine'.

rhenium /ˈriːnɪəm/ ▶ noun [mass noun] the chemical element of atomic number 75, a rare silvery-white metal which occurs in trace amounts in ores of molybdenum and other metals. (Symbol: **Re**)
– ORIGIN 1920s: modern Latin, from *Rhenus*, the Latin name of the River **RHINE**.

rheology /rɪˈɒlədʒi/ ▶ noun [mass noun] the branch of physics that deals with the deformation and flow of matter, especially the non-Newtonian flow of liquids and the plastic flow of solids.
– DERIVATIVES **rheological** adjective, **rheologist** noun.
– ORIGIN 1920s: from Greek *rheos* 'stream' + **-LOGY**.

rheometer /rɪˈɒmɪtə/ ▶ noun an instrument for measuring the rheological properties of a substance.

rheostat /ˈriːəstat/ ▶ noun an electrical instrument used to control a current by varying the resistance.
– DERIVATIVES **rheostatic** adjective.
– ORIGIN mid 19th cent.: from Greek *rheos* 'stream' + **-STAT**.

rhesus baby /ˈriːsəs/ ▶ noun an infant suffering from haemolytic disease of the newborn.
– ORIGIN 1960s: see **RHESUS FACTOR**.

rhesus factor ▶ noun [in sing.] an antigen occurring on the red blood cells of many humans (around 85 per cent) and some other primates. It is particularly important as a cause of haemolytic disease of the newborn and of incompatibility in blood transfusions.
– ORIGIN 1940s: *rhesus* from **RHESUS MONKEY**, in which the antigen was first observed.

rhesus monkey (also **rhesus macaque**) ▶ noun a small brown macaque with red skin on the face and rump, native to southern Asia. It is often kept in captivity and is widely used in medical research. ● *Macaca mulatta*, family Cercopithecidae.
– ORIGIN early 19th cent.: modern Latin *rhesus*, arbitrary use of Latin *Rhesus* (from Greek *Rhēsos*, the name of a mythical king of Thrace).

rhesus negative ▶ adjective lacking the rhesus factor.

rhesus positive ▶ adjective having the rhesus factor.

rhetor /ˈriːtə/ ▶ noun (in ancient Greece and Rome) a teacher of rhetoric. ■ an orator.
– ORIGIN via Latin from Greek *rhētōr*.

rhetoric /ˈrɛtərɪk/ ▶ noun [mass noun] the art of effective or persuasive speaking or writing, especially the exploitation of figures of speech and other compositional techniques. ■ language designed to have a persuasive or impressive effect, but which is often regarded as lacking in sincerity or meaningful content: *all we have from the Opposition is empty rhetoric.*
– ORIGIN Middle English: from Old French *rethorique*, via Latin from Greek *rhētorikē* (*tekhnē*) '(art) of rhetoric', from *rhētōr* 'rhetor'.

rhetorical /rɪˈtɒrɪk(ə)l/ ▶ adjective **1** relating to or concerned with the art of rhetoric: *repetition is a common rhetorical device.* ■ expressed in terms intended to persuade or impress: *the rhetorical commitment of the government to give priority to primary education.*
2 (of a question) asked in order to produce an effect or to make a statement rather than to elicit information.
– DERIVATIVES **rhetorically** adverb.
– ORIGIN late Middle English (first used in the sense 'eloquently expressed'): via Latin from Greek *rhētorikos* (from *rhētor* 'rhetor') + **-AL**.

rhetorician ▶ noun an expert in formal rhetoric. ■ a speaker whose words are primarily intended to impress or persuade.
– ORIGIN late Middle English: from Old French *rethoricien*, from *rhetorique* (see **RHETORIC**).

rheum /ruːm/ ▶ noun [mass noun] chiefly literary a watery fluid that collects in or drips from the nose or eyes.
– ORIGIN late Middle English: from Old French *reume*, via Latin from Greek *rheuma* 'stream' (from *rhein* 'to flow').

rheumatic /rʊˈmatɪk/ ▶ adjective relating to or caused by rheumatism: *rheumatic pains.* ■ (of a person or part of the body) affected by rheumatism.
▶ noun a person affected by rheumatism.
– DERIVATIVES **rheumaticky** adjective (informal).
– ORIGIN late Middle English (originally referring to infection characterized by rheum): from Old French *reumatique*, or via Latin from Greek *rheumatikos*, from *rheuma* 'bodily humour, flow' (see **RHEUM**).

rheumatic fever ▶ noun [mass noun] a non-contagious acute fever marked by inflammation and pain in the joints. It chiefly affects young people and is caused by a streptococcal infection.

rheumatics ▶ plural noun [usu. treated as sing.] informal rheumatism; rheumatic pains.

rheumatism ▶ noun [mass noun] any disease marked by inflammation and pain in the joints, muscles, or fibrous tissue, especially rheumatoid arthritis.
– ORIGIN late 17th cent.: from French *rhumatisme*, or via Latin from Greek *rheumatismos*, from *rheumatizein* 'to snuffle', from *rheuma* 'stream': the disease was originally supposed to be caused by the internal flow of 'watery' humours.

rheumatoid /ˈruːmətɔɪd/ ▶ adjective Medicine relating to, affected by, or resembling rheumatism.

rheumatoid arthritis ▶ noun [mass noun] a chronic progressive disease causing inflammation in the joints and resulting in painful deformity and immobility, especially in the fingers, wrists, feet, and ankles. Compare with **OSTEOARTHRITIS**.

rheumatoid factor ▶ noun Medicine any of a group of autoantibodies which are present in the blood of many people with rheumatoid arthritis.

rheumatology /ˌruːməˈtɒlədʒi/ ▶ noun [mass noun] Medicine the study of rheumatism, arthritis, and other disorders of the joints, muscles, and ligaments.
– DERIVATIVES **rheumatological** adjective, **rheumatologist** noun.

rheumy ▶ adjective (**rheumier**, **rheumiest**) (especially of the eyes) full of rheum; watery.

rhinal /ˈrʌɪn(ə)l/ ▶ adjective Anatomy relating to the nose or the olfactory part of the brain.
– ORIGIN mid 19th cent.: from Greek *rhis, rhin-* 'nose' + **-AL**.

Rhine /rʌɪn/ a river in western Europe which rises in the Swiss Alps and flows for 1,320 km (820 miles) to the North Sea. It forms the border between Germany and Switzerland in the south, then Germany and France, before flowing north through Germany and westwards through the Netherlands to empty into the North Sea near Rotterdam. French name **Rhin** /rɛ̃/; German name **Rhein**.

Rhineland the region of western Germany through which the Rhine flows, especially the part to the west of the river. German name **RHEINLAND** /ˈraɪnlant/.

Rhineland-Palatinate a state of western Germany; capital, Mainz. German name **RHEINLAND-PFALZ**.

rhinestone ▶ noun an imitation diamond, used in cheap jewellery and to decorate clothes.
– ORIGIN late 19th cent.: translating French *caillou du Rhin*, literally 'pebble of the Rhine'.

rhinitis /rʌɪˈnʌɪtɪs, rɪ-/ ▶ noun [mass noun] Medicine inflammation of the mucous membrane of the nose, caused by a virus infection (e.g. the common cold) or by an allergic reaction (e.g. hay fever).

rhino ▶ noun (pl. **same** or **rhinos**) informal a rhinoceros.
– ORIGIN late 19th cent.: abbreviation.

rhino- ▶ combining form relating to the nose: *rhinoplasty.*
– ORIGIN from Greek *rhis, rhin-* 'nose'.

rhinoceros /rʌɪˈnɒs(ə)rəs/ ▶ noun (pl. **same** or **rhinoceroses**) a large, heavily built plant-eating mammal with one or two horns on the nose and thick folded skin, native to Africa and southern Asia. All kinds have become endangered through hunting. ● Family Rhinocerotidae: four genera and five species.
– ORIGIN Middle English: via Latin from Greek *rhinokerōs*, from *rhis, rhin-* 'nose' + *keras* 'horn'.

rhinoceros beetle ▶ noun a very large mainly tropical beetle, the male of which has a curved horn extending from the head and typically another from the thorax. In some parts of Asia males are put to fight as a spectator sport. ● Several genera and species in the family Scarabaeidae, including *Oryctes rhinoceros*, which is a serious pest of cocoa palms.

rhinoceros bird ▶ noun another term for **OXPECKER**.

rhinoceros horn ▶ noun [mass noun] a mass of keratinized fibres that comprises the horn of a rhinoceros, reputed in Eastern medicine to have medicinal or aphrodisiac powers.

rhinoplasty /ˈrʌɪnə(ʊ)ˌplasti/ ▶ noun (pl. **rhinoplasties**) [mass noun] Medicine plastic surgery performed on the nose.
– DERIVATIVES **rhinoplastic** adjective.

rhinovirus /ˈrʌɪnəʊˌvʌɪrəs/ ▶ noun Medicine any of a group of picornaviruses including those which cause some forms of the common cold.

rhizo- ▶ combining form Botany relating to a root or roots: *rhizomorph.*
– ORIGIN from Greek *rhiza* 'root'.

rhizobium /rʌɪˈzəʊbɪəm/ ▶ noun a nitrogen-fixing bacterium that is common in the soil, especially in the root nodules of leguminous plants. ● Genus *Rhizobium*; Gram-negative rods.
– ORIGIN 1920s: modern Latin, from **RHIZO-** 'root' + Greek *bios* 'life'.

rhizoctonia /ˌrʌɪzɒkˈtəʊnɪə/ ▶ noun [mass noun] a common soil fungus that sometimes causes plant diseases such as damping off, foot rot, and eyespot. ● Genus *Rhizoctonia*, subdivision Deuteromycotina, in particular *R. solani*.
– ORIGIN late 19th cent.: modern Latin (genus name), from Greek *rhiza* 'root' + *ktonos* 'murder'.

rhizoid /ˈrʌɪzɔɪd/ ▶ noun Botany a filamentous outgrowth or root hair on the underside of the thallus in some lower plants, especially mosses and liverworts, serving both to anchor the plant and (in terrestrial forms) to conduct water.
– DERIVATIVES **rhizoidal** adjective.

rhizome /ˈrʌɪzəʊm/ ▶ noun Botany a continuously growing horizontal underground stem which puts out lateral shoots and adventitious roots at intervals. Compare with **BULB** (sense 1).
– ORIGIN mid 19th cent.: from Greek *rhizōma*, from *rhizousthai* 'take root', based on *rhiza* 'root'.

rhizomorph /ˈrʌɪzə(ʊ)mɔːf/ ▶ noun Botany a root-like aggregation of hyphae in certain fungi.

Rhizopoda /ˌrʌɪzəˈpəʊdə, rʌɪˈzɒpədə/ ▶ plural noun Zoology a phylum of single-celled animals which includes the amoebas and their relatives, which have extensible pseudopodia.
– DERIVATIVES **rhizopod** noun.
– ORIGIN modern Latin (plural), from **RHIZO-** 'root' + Greek *pous, pod-* 'foot'.

rhizosphere /ˈrʌɪzə(ʊ)ˌsfɪə/ ▶ noun Ecology the region of soil in the vicinity of plant roots in which the chemistry and microbiology is influenced by their growth, respiration, and nutrient exchange.

rho /rəʊ/ ▶ noun (pl. **rhos**) the seventeenth letter of the Greek alphabet (Ρ, ρ), transliterated as 'r' or (when written with a rough breathing) 'rh'. ■ (**Rho**) [followed by Latin genitive] Astronomy the seventeenth star in a constellation: *Rho Cassiopeiae.*
▶ symbol ■ (ρ) density. ■ (ρ) Spearman's correlation coefficient.
– ORIGIN Greek.

rhodamine /ˈrəʊdəmiːn/ ▶ noun Chemistry any of a number of synthetic dyes derived from xanthene, used to colour textiles.
– ORIGIN late 19th cent.: from **RHODO-** 'rose-coloured' + **AMINE**.

Rhode Island /rəʊd/ a state in the north-eastern US, on the Atlantic coast; pop. 1,050,788 (est. 2008); capital, Providence. Settled from England in the 17th century, it was one of the original thirteen states of the Union (1776) and is the smallest and most densely populated.
– DERIVATIVES **Rhode Islander** noun.

Rhode Island Red ▶ noun a bird of a breed of reddish-black domestic chicken, originally from America.

Rhodes[1] /rəʊdz/ a Greek island in the SE Aegean, off the Turkish coast, the largest of the Dodecanese and the most easterly island in the Aegean; pop. 130,000 (est. 2004). Greek name **RÓDHOS**. ■ its capital, a port on the northernmost tip; pop. 55,900 (est. 2009). It was founded *c.*408 BC and was the site of the Colossus of Rhodes.

Rhodes[2] /rəʊdz/, Cecil (John) (1853–1902), British-born South African statesman, Prime Minister of Cape Colony 1890–6. He expanded British territory in southern Africa, annexing Bechuanaland (now Botswana) in 1884 and developing Rhodesia from 1889. By 1890 he had acquired 90 per cent of the world's production of diamonds.

Rhodesia /rəʊˈdiːʃə, -ˈdiːʒə/ the former name of a large territory in central southern Africa which was divided into Northern Rhodesia (now Zambia) and Southern Rhodesia (now Zimbabwe).

The region was developed by Cecil Rhodes through the British South Africa Company, which administered it until Southern Rhodesia became a self-governing British colony in 1923 and Northern Rhodesia a British protectorate in 1924. From 1953 to 1963 Northern and Southern Rhodesia were united with Nyasaland (now Malawi) to form the Federation of Rhodesia and Nyasaland. The name Rhodesia was adopted by Southern Rhodesia when Northern Rhodesia left the Federation in 1963 to become the independent republic of Zambia; Rhodesia became independent Zimbabwe in 1979.

– DERIVATIVES **Rhodesian** adjective & noun.

Rhodesian ridgeback ▸ noun a dog of a breed having a short light brown coat and a ridge of hair along the middle of the back, growing in the opposite direction to the rest of the coat.

Rhodes Scholarship ▸ noun any of several scholarships awarded annually and tenable at Oxford University by students from certain Commonwealth countries, the United States, and Germany.
– DERIVATIVES **Rhodes Scholar** noun.
– ORIGIN named after Cecil *Rhodes* (see **RHODES²**), who founded the scholarships in 1902.

rhodium /ˈrəʊdɪəm/ ▸ noun [mass noun] the chemical element of atomic number 45, a hard silvery-white metal of the transition series, typically occurring in association with platinum. (Symbol: **Rh**)
– ORIGIN early 19th cent.: modern Latin, from Greek *rhodon* 'rose' (from the colour of the solution of its salts).

rhodo- ▸ combining form chiefly Mineralogy & Chemistry rose-coloured: *rhodochrosite*.
– ORIGIN from Greek *rhodon* 'rose'.

rhodochrosite /ˌrəʊdə(ʊ)ˈkrəʊsʌɪt/ ▸ noun [mass noun] a mineral consisting of manganese carbonate, typically occurring as pink, brown, or grey rhombohedral crystals.
– ORIGIN mid 19th cent.: from Greek *rhodokhrōs* 'rose-coloured' + **-ITE¹**.

rhododendron /ˌrəʊdəˈdɛndr(ə)n/ ▸ noun a shrub or small tree of the heather family, with large clusters of bell-shaped flowers and typically with large evergreen leaves, widely grown as an ornamental. ● Genus *Rhododendron*, family Ericaceae: many cultivars.
– ORIGIN via Latin from Greek, from *rhodon* 'rose' + *dendron* 'tree'.

rhodonite /ˈrəʊd(ə)nʌɪt/ ▸ noun [mass noun] a brownish or rose-pink mineral consisting of a silicate of manganese and other elements.
– ORIGIN early 19th cent.: from Greek *rhodon* 'rose' + **-ITE¹**.

Rhodope Mountains /ˈrɒdəpi/ a mountain system in the Balkans, SE Europe, on the frontier between Bulgaria and Greece, rising to a height of over 2,000 m (6,600 ft) and including the Rila Mountains in the north-west.

Rhodophyta /ˌrəʊdə(ʊ)ˈfʌɪtə/ ▸ plural noun Botany a division of lower plants that comprises the red algae.
– ORIGIN modern Latin (plural), from **RHODO-** 'rose-coloured' + Greek *phuta* 'plants'.

rhodophyte ▸ noun Botany a lower plant of the division Rhodophyta, which comprises the red algae.

rhodopsin /rə(ʊ)ˈdɒpsɪn/ ▸ noun another term for **VISUAL PURPLE**.
– ORIGIN late 19th cent.: from Greek *rhodon* 'rose' + *opsis* 'sight' + **-IN¹**.

rhodora /rə(ʊ)ˈdɔːrə/ ▸ noun a pink-flowered North American shrub of the heather family. ● *Rhododendron canadense*, family Ericaceae.
– ORIGIN late 18th cent.: modern Latin (former genus name), based on Greek *rhodon* 'rose'.

rhomb /rɒm(b)/ ▸ noun a rhombohedral crystal.
■ a rhombus.
– DERIVATIVES **rhombic** adjective.
– ORIGIN early 19th cent.: from Latin *rhombus* (see **RHOMBUS**).

rhombencephalon /ˌrɒmbɛnˈsɛf(ə)lɒn, -ˈkɛf-/ ▸ noun Anatomy another term for **HINDBRAIN**.
– ORIGIN late 19th cent.: from **RHOMB** + **ENCEPHALON**.

rhombi plural form of **RHOMBUS**.

rhombohedral /ˌrɒmbə(ʊ)ˈhiːdr(ə)l/ ▸ adjective (chiefly of a crystal) shaped like a rhombohedron.

rhombohedron /ˌrɒmbə(ʊ)ˈhiːdr(ə)n, -ˈhɛd-/ ▸ noun (pl. **rhombohedra** /-drə/ or **rhombohedrons**) a solid figure whose faces are six equal rhombuses. ■ a rhombohedral crystal or other solid object.
– ORIGIN mid 19th cent.: from **RHOMBUS** + **-HEDRON**, on the pattern of words such as *polyhedron*.

rhomboid /ˈrɒmbɔɪd/ ▸ adjective having or resembling the shape of a rhombus.
▸ noun **1** a parallelogram in which adjacent sides are unequal.
2 (also **rhomboid muscle**) another term for **RHOMBOIDEUS**.
– DERIVATIVES **rhomboidal** adjective.
– ORIGIN late 16th cent. (as a noun): from French *rhomboïde*, or via late Latin from Greek *rhomboeidēs*, from *rhombos* (see **RHOMBUS**).

rhomboideus /rɒmˈbɔɪdɪəs/ ▸ noun (pl. **rhomboidei** /-dɪʌɪ/) Anatomy a muscle connecting the shoulder blade to the vertebrae.
– ORIGIN mid 19th cent.: modern Latin, from *rhomboideus (musculus)* (see **RHOMBOID**).

Rhombozoa /ˌrɒmbə(ʊ)ˈzəʊə/ ▸ plural noun Zoology a minor phylum of mesozoan worms which are parasites in the kidneys of cephalopod molluscs.
– DERIVATIVES **rhombozoan** noun & adjective.
– ORIGIN modern Latin (plural), from Greek *rhombos* 'rhombus' + *zōia* 'animals'.

rhombus /ˈrɒmbəs/ ▸ noun (pl. **rhombuses** or **rhombi** /-bʌɪ/) Geometry a quadrilateral all of whose sides have the same length.
– ORIGIN mid 16th cent.: via Latin from Greek *rhombos*.

Rhondda /ˈrɒndə/ an urbanized district of South Wales, which extends along the valleys of the Rivers Rhondda Fawr and Rhondda Fach. It was formerly noted as a coal-mining area.

Rhône /rəʊn/ a river in SW Europe which rises in the Swiss Alps and flows 812 km (505 miles), through Lake Geneva into France, then to Lyons, Avignon, and the Mediterranean west of Marseilles, where it forms a wide delta that includes the Camargue.

Rhône-Alpes /rəʊnˈalp/ a region of SE France, extending from the Rhône valley to the borders with Switzerland and Italy and including much of the former duchy of Savoy.

rhotacization /ˌrəʊtəsʌɪˈzeɪʃ(ə)n/ (also **rhotacisation**) ▸ noun [mass noun] Phonetics pronunciation of a vowel to reflect a following *r* in the orthography, as for example in American English *farm, bird*.
– ORIGIN 1970s: from *rhotacize* (from Greek *rhōtakizein*) + **-ATION**.

rhotic /ˈrəʊtɪk/ ▸ adjective Phonetics relating to or denoting a dialect or variety of English (e.g. in America and SW England) in which *r* is pronounced before a consonant (as in *hard*) and at the ends of words (as in *far*).
– DERIVATIVES **rhoticity** /rəʊˈtɪsɪti/ noun.
– ORIGIN 1960s: from Greek *rhot-*, stem of *rho* (see **RHO**) + **-IC**.

RHS ▸ abbreviation ■ Royal Historical Society. ■ Royal Horticultural Society. ■ Royal Humane Society.

rhubarb ▸ noun [mass noun] **1** the thick reddish or green leaf stalks of a cultivated plant of the dock family, which are eaten as a fruit after cooking.
2 the large-leaved Eurasian plant which produces rhubarb. ● *Rheum rhaponticum* (or *rhabarbarum*), family Polygonaceae.
■ used in names of other plants of this genus, several of which are used medicinally, e.g. **Chinese rhubarb**.
3 Brit. informal the noise made by a group of actors to give the impression of indistinct background conversation, especially by the random repetition of the word 'rhubarb'. ■ nonsense: *it was all rhubarb, about me, about her daughter, about art*.
4 [count noun] N. Amer. informal a heated dispute.
– ORIGIN late Middle English (denoting the rootstock of other plants of this genus used medicinally): from Old French *reubarbe*, from a shortening of medieval Latin *rheubarbarum*, alteration (by association with *rheum* 'rhubarb') of *rhabarbarum* 'foreign rhubarb', from Greek *rha* (also meaning 'rhubarb') + *barbaros* 'foreign'.

Rhum /rʌm/ (also **Rum**) an island in the Inner Hebrides, to the south of Skye. In 1957 it was designated a nature reserve.

rhumb /rʌm/ ▸ noun Nautical **1** (also **rhumb line**) an imaginary line on the earth's surface cutting all meridians at the same angle, used as the standard method of plotting a ship's course on a chart.
2 any of the 32 points of the compass.
– ORIGIN late 16th cent.: from French *rumb* (earlier *ryn (de vent)* 'point of the compass'), probably from Dutch *ruim* 'space, room'. The spelling change was due to association with Latin *rhombus* (see **RHOMBUS**).

rhumba ▸ noun variant spelling of **RUMBA**.

rhyme ▸ noun [mass noun] correspondence of sound between words or the endings of words, especially when these are used at the ends of lines of poetry. ■ [count noun] a short poem in which the sound of the word or syllable at the end of each line corresponds with that at the end of another. ■ rhyming poetry or verse: *the clues were written in rhyme*. ■ [count noun] a word that has the same sound as another.
▸ verb [no obj.] (of a word, syllable, or line) have or end with a sound that corresponds to another: *balloon rhymes with moon* | (as adj. **rhyming**) *rhyming couplets*. ■ (of a poem or song) be composed in rhyme: *the poem would have been better if it rhymed*. ■ [with obj.] (**rhyme something with**) put a word together with (another word that has a corresponding sound), as when writing poetry: *I'm not sure about rhyming perestroika with balalaika*. ■ literary compose verse or poetry: *Musa rhymed and sang*.
– PHRASES **rhyme or reason** [with negative] logical explanation or reason: *without rhyme or reason his mood changed*.
– DERIVATIVES **rhymer** noun.
– ORIGIN Middle English *rime*, from Old French, from medieval Latin *rithmus*, via Latin from Greek *rhuthmos* (see **RHYTHM**). The current spelling was introduced in the early 17th cent. under the influence of *rhythm*.

rhyme scheme ▸ noun the ordered pattern of rhymes at the ends of the lines of a poem or verse.

rhymester ▸ noun a person who composes rhymes, especially simple ones.

rhyming slang ▸ noun [mass noun] a type of slang that replaces words with rhyming words or phrases, typically with the rhyming element omitted. For example *butcher's*, short for *butcher's hook*, means 'look' in Cockney rhyming slang.

rhynchosaur /ˈrɪŋkə(ʊ)sɔː/ ▸ noun a tusked herbivorous reptile of the Triassic period. ● Order Rhynchosauria, subclass Diapsida.
– ORIGIN mid 19th cent.: from modern Latin *Rhynchosaurus* (genus name), from Greek *rhunkos* 'snout' + *sauros* 'lizard'.

rhynchosporium /ˌrɪŋkə(ʊ)ˈspɔːrɪəm/ ▸ noun a fungus which causes foliage discoloration in barley and rye. ● Genus *Rhynchosporium*, subdivision Deuteromycotina.
■ [mass noun] a disease caused by rhynchosporium.
– ORIGIN modern Latin, from Greek *rhunkos* 'snout, beak' (because of the shape of the fungus) + **SPORE**.

rhyolite /ˈrʌɪəlʌɪt/ ▸ noun [mass noun] Geology a pale fine-grained volcanic rock of granitic composition, typically porphyritic in texture.
– ORIGIN mid 19th cent.: from German *Rhyolit*, from Greek *rhuax* 'lava stream' + *lithos* 'stone'.

rhythm /ˈrɪð(ə)m/ ▸ noun **1** a strong, regular repeated pattern of movement or sound: *Ruth listened to the rhythm of his breathing*. ■ [mass noun] the systematic arrangement of musical sounds, principally according to duration and periodical stress. ■ a particular pattern formed by musical rhythm: *melodies with deep African rhythms*. ■ [mass noun] a person's natural feeling for musical rhythm: *they've got no rhythm*.
2 [mass noun] the measured flow of words and phrases in verse or prose as determined by the relation of long and short or stressed and unstressed syllables.
3 a regularly recurring sequence of events or processes: *the twice daily rhythms of the tides*. ■ Art a harmonious sequence or correlation of colours or elements.
– DERIVATIVES **rhythmless** adjective.
– ORIGIN mid 16th cent. (also originally in the sense 'rhyme'): from French *rhythme*, or via Latin from Greek *rhuthmos* (related to *rhein* 'to flow').

rhythm and blues (abbrev.: **R & B**) ▸ noun [mass noun] a form of popular music of US black origin which arose during the 1940s from blues, with the addition of driving rhythms taken from jazz. It was an immediate precursor of rock and roll.

rhythmic ▸ adjective **1** having or relating to rhythm: *a rhythmic dance*.
2 occurring regularly: *there are rhythmic changes in our bodies*.
– DERIVATIVES **rhythmical** adjective, **rhythmically** adverb.
– ORIGIN early 17th cent.: from French *rhythmique* or via Latin from Greek *rhuthmikos*, from *rhuthmos* (see **RHYTHM**).

rhythmic gymnastics ▸ plural noun [usu. treated as sing.] a form of gymnastics emphasizing dance-like rhythmic routines, typically accentuated by the use of ribbons or hoops.

R

rhythmicity ▶ noun [mass noun] rhythmical quality or character: *the nursery rhymes' rhythmicity makes them easy to learn.*

rhythm method ▶ noun a method of avoiding conception favoured by the Roman Catholic Church, by which sexual intercourse is restricted to the times of a woman's menstrual cycle when ovulation is least likely to occur.

rhythm section ▶ noun the part of a pop or jazz group supplying the rhythm, generally regarded as consisting of bass and drums and sometimes piano or guitar.

rhyton /ˈrʌɪtɒn, ˈrɪtɒn/ ▶ noun (pl. **rhytons** or **rhyta** /ˈrʌɪtə, ˈrɪtə/) a type of drinking container used in ancient Greece, typically having the form of an animal's head or a horn, with the hole for drinking from located at the lower or pointed end.
– ORIGIN from Greek *rhuton*, neuter of *rhutos* 'flowing'; related to *rhein* 'to flow'.

RI ▶ abbreviation ■ Indonesia (international vehicle registration). [from Bahasa Indonesia *Républik Indonésia*.] ■ Rex et Imperator (King and Emperor) or Regina et Imperatrix (Queen and Empress). [Latin.] ■ Rhode Island (in official postal use). ■ Royal Institute or Institution.

RIA ▶ abbreviation ■ radioimmunoassay. ■ Royal Irish Academy.

ria /ˈriːə/ ▶ noun Geography a long, narrow inlet formed by the partial submergence of a river valley.
– ORIGIN late 19th cent.: from Spanish *ría* 'estuary'.

riad /ˈriːad/ ▶ noun (in Morocco) a large traditional house built around a central courtyard, often converted into a hotel.
– ORIGIN Arabic *riyāḍ*, *riad*, literally 'gardens', plural of *rawḍa* 'garden'.

rial /ˈriːɑːl/ (also **riyal**) ▶ noun **1** the basic monetary unit of Iran and Oman, equal to 100 dinars in Iran and 1,000 baiza in Oman.
2 (usu. **riyal**) the basic monetary unit of Saudi Arabia, Qatar, and Yemen, equal to 100 halala in Saudi Arabia, 100 dirhams in Qatar, and 100 fils in Yemen.
– ORIGIN via Persian from Arabic *riyāl*, from Spanish *real* 'royal'.

Rialto /rɪˈaltəʊ/ an island in Venice, containing the old mercantile quarter of medieval Venice. The Rialto Bridge, completed in 1591, crosses the Grand Canal between Rialto and San Marco islands.

RIB ▶ noun a small open boat with a fibreglass hull and inflatable rubber sides.
– ORIGIN acronym from *rigid inflatable boat*.

rib ▶ noun **1** each of a series of slender curved bones articulated in pairs to the spine (twelve pairs in humans), protecting the thoracic cavity and its organs. ■ a rib of an animal with meat adhering to it used as food; a joint consisting of animal ribs.
2 a long raised piece of strengthening or supporting material, in particular: ■ Architecture a curved member supporting a vault or defining its form. ■ a curved transverse strut of metal or timber in a ship, extending up from the keel and forming part of the framework of the hull. ■ each of the curved pieces of wood forming the body of a lute or the sides of a violin. ■ each of the hinged rods supporting the fabric of an umbrella. ■ Aeronautics a structural member in an aerofoil, extending back from the leading edge and serving to define the contour of the aerofoil.
3 a vein of a leaf or an insect's wing. ■ a ridge of rock or land.
4 [mass noun] Knitting a combination of alternate plain and purl stitches producing a ridged, slightly elastic fabric.
▶ verb (**ribs**, **ribbing**, **ribbed**) [with obj.] **1** mark with or form into ridges: *the road was ribbed with furrows of slush.* ■ provide with ribs.
2 informal tease good-naturedly: *the first time I appeared in the outfit I was ribbed mercilessly.*
– ORIGIN Old English *rib*, *ribb* (noun), of Germanic origin; related to Dutch *rib(be)* and German *Rippe*. Sense 1 of the verb dates from the mid 16th cent.; the sense 'tease' was originally a US slang usage meaning 'to fool, dupe' (1930s).

RIBA ▶ abbreviation Royal Institute of British Architects.

ribald /ˈrɪb(ə)ld, ˈrʌɪbɔːld/ ▶ adjective referring to sexual matters in an amusingly rude or irreverent way: *a ribald comment.*
– ORIGIN Middle English (as a noun denoting a lowly retainer or a licentious or irreverent person): from Old French *ribauld*, from *riber* 'indulge in licentious pleasures', from a Germanic base meaning 'prostitute'.

ribaldry ▶ noun [mass noun] ribald talk or behaviour.

riband /ˈrɪb(ə)nd/ ▶ noun archaic a ribbon.
– ORIGIN Middle English: from Old French *riban*, probably from a Germanic compound of the noun BAND[1].

ribbed ▶ adjective **1** (especially of a fabric or garment) having a pattern of raised bands: *a ribbed cashmere sweater.*
2 Architecture (of a vault or other structure) strengthened with ribs.

Ribbentrop /ˈrɪb(ə)ntrɒp/, Joachim von (1893–1946), German Nazi politician. As Foreign Minister (1938–45) he signed the non-aggression pact with the Soviet Union (1939). He was convicted as a war criminal in the Nuremberg trials and hanged.

ribber ▶ noun an attachment on a knitting machine for producing rib stitch.

ribbing ▶ noun [mass noun] **1** a rib-like structure or pattern.
2 informal good-natured teasing.

ribbon ▶ noun **1** a long, narrow strip of fabric, used for tying something or for decoration: *the tiny pink ribbons in her hair* | [mass noun] *four lengths of ribbon.* ■ a ribbon of a special colour or design awarded as a prize or worn to indicate the holding of an honour, especially a small multicoloured piece of ribbon worn in place of the medal it represents. ■ (**ribbons**) prizes; honours: *in the Silk Cup trophy class Mullins stayed **in the ribbons**.*
2 a long, narrow strip: *slice the peppers into ribbons lengthways.* ■ a narrow band of impregnated material wound on a spool and forming the inking agent in some typewriters and computer printers.
▶ verb [no obj., with adverbial of direction] extend or move in a long, narrow strip like a ribbon: *miles of concrete ribboned behind the bus.*
– PHRASES **cut a** (or **the**) **ribbon** ceremonially open a building or road, typically by cutting a ribbon across the entrance. **cut** (or **tear**) **something to ribbons** cut (or tear) something so badly that only ragged strips remain. ■ damage something severely: *the country has seen its economy torn to ribbons by recession.*
– DERIVATIVES **ribboned** adjective.
– ORIGIN early 16th cent.: variant of RIBAND. The French spelling *ruban* was also frequent in the 16th–18th cents.

ribbon cable ▶ noun a cable for transmitting electronic signals consisting of several insulated wires connected together to form a flat ribbon.

ribbon development ▶ noun [mass noun] Brit. the building of houses along a main road, especially one leading out of a town or village.

ribbonfish ▶ noun (pl. **same** or **ribbonfishes**) any of a number of long slender fishes which typically have a dorsal fin running the length of the body, in particular: ● a fish of the dealfish family (Trachipteridae). ● a fish of the cutlassfish family (Trichiuridae). ● another term for OARFISH.

ribbon-grass ▶ noun another term for TAPE-GRASS.

ribbon worm ▶ noun a chiefly aquatic worm with an elongated, unsegmented, flattened body that is typically brightly coloured and tangled in knots, and a long proboscis for catching food. ● Phylum Nemertea: two classes.

ribby ▶ adjective having prominent ribs: *ribby, bony-rumped cattle.*

ribcage ▶ noun the bony frame formed by the ribs round the chest.

Ribera /rɪˈbɛːrə/, José (or Jusepe) de (*c.*1591–1652), Spanish painter and etcher, resident in Italy from 1616; known as **Lo Spagnoletto** ('the little Spaniard'). He is best known for his religious and genre paintings, for example the *Martyrdom of St Bartholomew* (*c.*1630).

rib-eye ▶ noun [usu. as modifier] a cut of beef from the outer side of the ribs: *a rib-eye steak.*

ribitol /ˈrʌɪbɪtɒl, ˈrɪb-/ ▶ noun [mass noun] Chemistry a colourless crystalline compound which is formed by reduction of ribose and occurs in certain plants. ● An alcohol; chem. formula: $HOCH_2(CHOH)_3CH_2OH$.
– ORIGIN 1940s: from RIBOSE + -ITE[1] + -OL.

riboflavin /ˌrʌɪbə(ʊ)ˈfleɪvɪn/ ▶ noun [mass noun] Biochemistry a yellow vitamin of the B complex which is essential for metabolic energy production. It is present in many foods, especially milk, liver, eggs, and green vegetables, and is also synthesized by the intestinal flora. Also called VITAMIN B_2.
– ORIGIN 1930s: from RIBOSE + Latin *flavus* 'yellow' + -IN[1].

ribonuclease /ˌrʌɪbə(ʊ)ˈnjuːklɪeɪz/ ▶ noun another term for RNASE.

ribonucleic acid /ˌrʌɪbə(ʊ)njuːˈkleɪɪk, -ˈkliːɪk/ ▶ noun see RNA.
– ORIGIN 1930s: *ribonucleic* from RIBOSE + NUCLEIC ACID.

ribose /ˈrʌɪbəʊz, -s/ ▶ noun [mass noun] Chemistry a sugar of the pentose class which occurs widely in nature as a constituent of nucleosides and several vitamins and enzymes.
– ORIGIN late 19th cent.: arbitrary alteration of ARABINOSE, a related sugar.

ribosome /ˈrʌɪbə(ʊ)səʊm/ ▶ noun Biochemistry a minute particle consisting of RNA and associated proteins found in large numbers in the cytoplasm of living cells. They bind messenger RNA and transfer RNA to synthesize polypeptides and proteins.
– DERIVATIVES **ribosomal** adjective.
– ORIGIN 1950s: from RIBONUCLEIC ACID + -SOME[3].

ribozyme /ˈrʌɪbə(ʊ)zʌɪm/ ▶ noun Biochemistry an RNA molecule capable of acting as an enzyme.
– ORIGIN 1980s: blend of RIBONUCLEIC ACID and ENZYME.

rib-tickler ▶ noun informal a very amusing joke or story.
– DERIVATIVES **rib-tickling** adjective, **rib-ticklingly** adverb.

ribulose /ˈrʌɪbjʊləʊz, -s/ ▶ noun [mass noun] Chemistry a sugar of the pentose class which is an important intermediate in carbohydrate metabolism and photosynthesis.
– ORIGIN 1930s: from RIBOSE + *-ulose*.

ribwort (also **ribwort plantain**) ▶ noun a Eurasian plantain with erect ribbed leaves and a rounded flower spike. ● *Plantago lanceolata*, family Plantaginaceae.

Ricardian /rɪˈkɑːdiən/ ▶ adjective **1** relating to the time of any of three kings of England, Richard I, II, and III. ■ of or holding the view that Richard III was a just king who was misrepresented by Shakespeare and other writers.
2 relating to the political economist David Ricardo.
▶ noun **1** a contemporary or supporter of Richard III.
2 an adherent of the theories of David Ricardo.
– DERIVATIVES **Ricardianism** noun.
– ORIGIN from medieval Latin *Ricardus* 'Richard' + -IAN.

Ricardo /rɪˈkɑːdəʊ/, David (1772–1823), English political economist, of Dutch parentage. He is best known for *On the Principles of Political Economy and Taxation* (1817), in which he set out his views on prices, wages, and profits. A supporter of free trade and the repeal of the Corn Laws, he was elected to Parliament in 1819.

Ricci tensor /ˈriːtʃi/ ▶ noun Mathematics a set of components that describes part of the curvature of space–time. It is a symmetric second-order tensor.
– ORIGIN 1920s: named after Curbastro G. *Ricci* (1853–1925), Italian mathematician.

Rice, Sir Tim (b.1944), English lyricist and entertainer; full name *Timothy Miles Bindon Rice*. Together with Andrew Lloyd Webber he co-wrote a number of hit musicals, including *Joseph and the Amazing Technicolor Dreamcoat* (1968), *Jesus Christ Superstar* (1971), and *Evita* (1978). He has won three Oscars for best original film song (1992, 1994, and 1996).

rice ▶ noun [mass noun] a swamp grass which is widely cultivated as a source of food, especially in Asia. ● *Oryza sativa*, family Gramineae. **African rice** belongs to the related species *O. glaberrima*, whereas the so-called **wild rice** is not a true rice at all.
■ the grains of rice used as food.

> Rice provides the staple diet of half the world's population and is second only to wheat in terms of total output. Rice seedlings are usually planted in flooded fields or paddies, so that terraces are necessary on hillsides and a reliable source of water is essential.

▶ verb [with obj.] N. Amer. force (cooked potatoes or other vegetables) through a sieve or ricer.
– ORIGIN Middle English: from Old French *ris*, from Italian *riso*, from Greek *oruza*.

rice bowl ▶ noun **1** an area in which abundant quantities of rice are grown.
2 [in sing.] one's livelihood (used especially with reference to Asia): *vested interests will fight to the death to protect their rice bowl.*

rice paper ▶ noun [mass noun] thin translucent edible paper made from the flattened and dried pith of a shrub, used in oriental painting and in baking biscuits and cakes. ● This paper is obtained from the Chinese plant *Tetrapanax papyriferus* (family Araliaceae) or from the Indo-Pacific plant *Scaevola sericea* (family Goodeniaceae).

ricer ▶ noun N. Amer. a utensil with small holes through which boiled potatoes or other soft food can be pushed to form particles of a similar size to grains of rice.

rice rat ▶ **noun** a nocturnal rat that typically lives in marshy or damp areas, native to America, the Caribbean, and the Galapagos Islands. ● *Oryzomys* and other genera, family Muridae: numerous species.

ricercar /ˌriːtʃəˈkɑː, ˈriːtʃəˌkɑː/ (also **ricercare** /ˌriːtʃəˈkɑːreɪ, -ri/) ▶ **noun** (pl. **ricercars** or **ricercari**) Music an elaborate contrapuntal instrumental composition in fugal or canonic style, typically of the 16th to 18th centuries.
– ORIGIN from Italian *ricercare* 'search out'.

rich ▶ **adjective 1** having a great deal of money or assets; wealthy: *a rich and famous family* | (as plural noun **the rich**) *every day the split between the rich and the poor widens.* ■ (of a country or region) having valuable natural resources or a successful economy. ■ of expensive materials or workmanship; demonstrating wealth: *rich mahogany furniture.* ■ generating wealth; valuable: *not all footballers enjoy rich rewards from the game.*
2 existing in plentiful quantities; abundant: *the rich flora and fauna of the forest.* ■ having (a particular thing) in large amounts: *many vegetables and fruits are rich in vitamins* | [in combination] *a protein-rich diet.* ■ (of food) containing a large amount of fat, spices, sugar, etc.: *dishes with wonderfully rich sauces.* ■ (of drink) full-bodied: *a rich and hoppy best bitter.* ■ (of the fuel and air mixture in an internal-combustion engine) containing a high proportion of fuel.
3 producing a large quantity of something: *novels have always been a rich source of material for the film industry.* ■ (of land) having the properties necessary to produce fertile growth. ■ (of a mine or mineral deposit) yielding a large quantity of precious metal.
4 (of a colour, sound, smell, etc.) pleasantly deep or strong: *his rich bass voice* | *basmati rice has a rich aroma.*
5 interesting because full of variety: *what a full, rich life you lead!*
6 informal (of a remark) causing ironic amusement or indignation: *these comments are* ***a bit rich*** *coming from a woman with no money worries.*
– DERIVATIVES **richen** verb, **richness** noun.
– ORIGIN Old English *rīce* 'powerful, wealthy', of Germanic origin, related to Dutch *rijk* and German *reich*; ultimately from Celtic; reinforced in Middle English by Old French *riche* 'rich, powerful'.

Richard[1] the name of three kings of England:
■ **Richard I** (1157–99), son of Henry II, reigned 1189–99; known as **Richard Coeur de Lion** or **Richard the Lionheart**. He led the Third Crusade, defeating Saladin at Arsuf (1191) but failing to capture Jerusalem. Returning home, he was held hostage by the Holy Roman emperor Henry VI until being released in 1194 on payment of a huge ransom. ■ **Richard II** (1367–1400), son of the Black Prince, reigned 1377–99. Following his minority, he executed or banished most of his former opponents. His confiscation of his uncle John of Gaunt's estate on the latter's death provoked Henry Bolingbroke's return from exile to overthrow him. ■ **Richard III** (1452–85), brother of Edward IV, reigned 1483–5. He served as Protector to his nephew Edward V, who, after two months, was declared illegitimate and subsequently disappeared. Richard's brief rule ended at Bosworth Field, where he was defeated by Henry Tudor and killed.

Richard[2], Sir Cliff (b.1940), British pop singer, born in India; born *Harry Roger Webb*. With his group the Drifters (later called the Shadows), he recorded such songs as 'Living Doll' (1959). Since the 1970s he has combined a successful solo pop career with evangelism.

Richards, Viv (b.1952), West Indian cricketer; full name *Isaac Vivian Alexander Richards*. He captained the West Indian team from 1985 until 1991, and scored over 6,000 runs during his test career.

Richardson[1], Sir Ralph (David) (1902–83), English actor. He played many Shakespearean roles as well as leading parts in plays including Harold Pinter's *No Man's Land* (1975) and films including *Oh! What a Lovely War* (1969).

Richardson[2], Samuel (1689–1761), English novelist. His first novel *Pamela* (1740–1), entirely in the form of letters and journals, popularized the epistolary novel. He experimented further with the genre in *Clarissa Harlowe* (1747–8).

Richard the Lionheart /ˈlʌɪənhɑːt/, Richard I of England (see **RICHARD[1]**).

Richelieu /ˈriːʃ(ə)ljəː/, French /ʀiʃəljø/, Armand Jean du Plessis, duc de (1585–1642), French cardinal and statesman. As chief minister of Louis XIII (1624–42) he dominated French government. In 1635 he established the Académie française.

riches ▶ **plural noun** material wealth: *riches beyond their wildest dreams.* ■ valuable or abundant resources: *the riches of the world's waters* | *the riches of the Serbian oral tradition.*
– ORIGIN Middle English: variant (later interpreted as a plural form) of archaic *richesse*, from Old French *richeise* (from *riche* 'rich').

Richler /ˈrɪtʃlə/, Mordecai (1931–2001), Canadian writer. His best-known novel is probably *The Apprenticeship of Duddy Kravitz* (1959).

richly ▶ **adverb** in an elaborate, generous, or plentiful way: *she was richly dressed in the height of fashion* | *Levkas and its neighbouring islands reward explorers richly.* ■ [as submodifier] fully (used to emphasize that something is merited and just): *give your family a richly deserved holiday.*

Richmond /ˈrɪtʃmənd/ **1** a town in northern England, on the River Swale in North Yorkshire; pop. 9,000 (est. 2009).
2 a residential borough of Greater London, situated on the Thames. It contains Hampton Court Palace and the Royal Botanic Gardens at Kew. Full name **Richmond-upon-Thames.**
3 the state capital of Virginia, a port on the James River; pop. 202,002 (est. 2008). During the American Civil War it was the Confederate capital from July 1861 until its capture in 1865.

Richter scale /ˈrɪktə/ ▶ **noun** Geology a numerical scale for expressing the magnitude of an earthquake on the basis of seismograph oscillations. The more destructive earthquakes typically have magnitudes between about 5.5 and 8.9; it is a logarithmic scale and a difference of one represents an approximate thirtyfold difference in magnitude.
– ORIGIN 1930s: named after Charles F. *Richter* (1900–85), American geologist.

Richthofen /ˈrɪxtˌhəʊv(ə)n/, German /ˈrɪçtˌhoːfn/, Manfred, Freiherr von (1882–1918), German fighter pilot; known as **the Red Baron**. He joined a fighter squadron in 1915, flying a distinctive bright red aircraft. He was eventually shot down after destroying eighty enemy planes.

ricin /ˈrʌɪsɪn, ˈrɪsɪn/ ▶ **noun** [mass noun] Chemistry a highly toxic protein obtained from the pressed seeds of the castor oil plant.
– ORIGIN late 19th cent.: from modern Latin *Ricinus communis* (denoting the castor oil plant) + **-IN[1]**.

rick[1] ▶ **noun** a stack of hay, corn, straw, or similar material, especially one formerly built into a regular shape and thatched. ■ N. Amer. a pile of firewood somewhat smaller than a cord. ■ N. Amer. a set of shelving for storing barrels.
▶ **verb** [with obj.] form into a rick or ricks; stack.
– ORIGIN Old English *hrēac*, of Germanic origin; related to Dutch *rook*.

rick[2] ▶ **noun** a slight sprain or strain, especially in a person's neck or back.
▶ **verb** [with obj.] Brit. strain (one's neck or back) slightly.
– ORIGIN late 18th cent. (as a verb): of dialect origin

rickets /ˈrɪkɪts/ ▶ **noun** [mass noun treated as sing. or pl.] Medicine a disease of children caused by vitamin D deficiency, characterized by imperfect calcification, softening, and distortion of the bones typically resulting in bow legs.
– ORIGIN mid 17th cent.: perhaps an alteration of Greek *rhakhitis* (see **RACHITIS**).

rickettsia /rɪˈkɛtsɪə/ ▶ **noun** (pl. **rickettsiae** /-iːː/ or **rickettsias**) any of a group of very small bacteria that include the causative agents of typhus and various other febrile diseases in humans. Like viruses, many of them can only grow inside living cells, and they are frequently transmitted by mites, ticks, or lice. ● Genus *Rickettsia*, order Rickettsiales; Gram-negative rods.
– DERIVATIVES **rickettsial** adjective.
– ORIGIN modern Latin, named after Howard Taylor *Ricketts* (1871–1910), American pathologist.

rickety ▶ **adjective 1** (of a structure or piece of equipment) poorly made and likely to collapse: *we went carefully up the rickety stairs* | figurative *a rickety banking system.*
2 affected by rickets.
– DERIVATIVES **ricketiness** noun.
– ORIGIN late 17th cent.: from **RICKETS** + **-Y[1]**.

rickey ▶ **noun** (pl. **rickeys**) N. Amer. a drink consisting of a spirit, typically gin, mixed with lime or lemon juice, carbonated water, and ice.
– ORIGIN late 19th cent.: probably from the surname *Rickey*.

rickle ▶ **noun** Scottish, Irish, & N. English a loosely piled heap: *a rickle of bones.*
– ORIGIN late 15th cent.: perhaps from Norwegian dialect *rikl*, or from **RICK[1]**.

rickrack (also **ricrac**) ▶ **noun** [mass noun] braided trimming in a zigzag pattern, used as decoration on clothes.
– ORIGIN late 19th cent.: of unknown origin.

rickshaw (also **ricksha** /-ʃə/) ▶ **noun** a light two-wheeled passenger vehicle drawn by one or more people, chiefly used in Asian countries. ■ short for **CYCLE RICKSHAW**.
– ORIGIN late 19th cent.: abbreviation of **JINRICKSHA**.

RICO ▶ **abbreviation** (in the US) Racketeer Influenced and Corrupt Organizations Act.

ricochet /ˈrɪkəʃeɪ, -ʃɛt/ ▶ **verb** (**ricochets, ricocheting** /-ʃeɪɪŋ/, **ricocheted** /-ʃeɪd/ or **ricochets, ricochetting** /-ʃɛtɪŋ/, **ricochetted** /-ʃɛtɪd/) [no obj., with adverbial of direction] (of a bullet or other projectile) rebound off a surface: *a bullet ricocheted off a nearby wall.* ■ [with obj. and adverbial of direction] cause to rebound off a surface: *they fired off a couple of rounds, ricocheting the bullets against a wall.* ■ appear to move with a series of ricochets: *the sound ricocheted around the hall.*
▶ **noun** a shot or hit that rebounds off a surface. ■ [mass noun] the action or movement of a bullet or other projectile when ricocheting.
– ORIGIN mid 18th cent.: from French, of unknown origin.

ricotta /rɪˈkɒtə/ ▶ **noun** [mass noun] a soft white unsalted Italian cheese.
– ORIGIN Italian, literally 'recooked, cooked twice'.

ricrac ▶ **noun** variant spelling of **RICKRACK**.

RICS ▶ **abbreviation** (in the UK) Royal Institution of Chartered Surveyors.

rictus /ˈrɪktəs/ ▶ **noun** a fixed grimace or grin: *their faces were each frozen in a terrified rictus.*
– DERIVATIVES **rictal** adjective.
– ORIGIN early 19th cent.: from Latin, literally 'open mouth', from *rict-* 'gaped', from the verb *ringi*.

rid ▶ **verb** (**rids, ridding**; past and past participle **rid** or archaic **ridded**) [with obj.] (**rid someone/thing of**) make someone or something free of (an unwanted person or thing): *boil the peel to rid it of bitterness.* ■ (**be rid of**) be freed or relieved of: *she couldn't wait to be rid of us.*
– PHRASES **be well rid of** be in a better state for having removed (a troublesome or unwanted person or thing). **get rid of** take action so as to be free of (a troublesome or unwanted person or thing).
– ORIGIN Middle English: from Old Norse *rythja*. The original sense 'to clear' described clearing land of trees and undergrowth; this gave rise to 'free from rubbish or encumbrances', later becoming generalized.

riddance ▶ **noun** [mass noun] the action of getting rid of a troublesome or unwanted person or thing.
– PHRASES **good riddance** said to express relief at being free of an unwanted person or thing.

ridden past participle of **RIDE**.

riddim /ˈrɪdɪm/ ▶ **noun** non-standard spelling of **RHYTHM**: *dancehall riddims.*
– ORIGIN representing a Jamaican pronunciation.

riddle[1] ▶ **noun** a question or statement intentionally phrased so as to require ingenuity in ascertaining its answer or meaning. ■ a person or thing that is difficult to understand or explain: *the riddle of her death.*
▶ **verb** [no obj.] archaic speak in or pose riddles. ■ [with two objs] solve or explain (a riddle) to (someone): *riddle me this then.*
– PHRASES **talk** (or **speak**) **in riddles** express oneself in an ambiguous or puzzling manner.
– DERIVATIVES **riddler** noun.
– ORIGIN Old English *rǣdels, rǣdelse* 'opinion, conjecture, riddle'; related to Dutch *raadsel*, German *Rätsel*, also to **READ**.

riddle[2] ▶ **verb** [with obj.] **1** make many holes in (someone or something), especially with gunshot: *his car was riddled by sniper fire.* ■ fill or permeate (someone or something), especially with something undesirable: *the existing law is riddled with loopholes* | *her body was riddled with arthritis.*
2 pass (a substance) through a large coarse sieve: *for final potting, the soil mixture is not riddled.* ■ remove

ashes or other unwanted material from (something, especially a fire or stove) with a sieve.
▸ **noun** a large coarse sieve, especially one used for separating ashes from cinders or sand from gravel.
– ORIGIN late Old English *hriddel*, of Germanic origin; from an Indo-European root shared by Latin *cribrum* 'sieve', *cernere* 'separate', and Greek *krinein* 'decide'.

riddling ▸ **adjective** speaking or expressed in riddles; enigmatic: *the riddling sphinx.*
– DERIVATIVES **riddlingly** adverb.

ride ▸ **verb** (past **rode**; past participle **ridden**) [with obj.] **1** sit on and control the movement of (an animal, typically a horse): *Jane and Rory were riding their ponies* | [no obj.] *I haven't ridden much since the accident.* ■ [no obj., with adverbial] travel on a horse or other animal: *we rode on horseback* | *some of the officers were riding back.* ■ sit on and control (a bicycle or motorcycle): *he rode a Harley Davidson across the United States.* ■ [no obj.] (**ride in/on**) travel in or on (a vehicle) as a passenger: *I started riding on the buses.* ■ chiefly N. Amer. travel in (a vehicle or lift): *she rides the bus across 42nd Street.* ■ go through or over (an area) on a horse, bicycle, etc.: *ride the full length of the Ridgeway.* ■ compete in (a race) on a horse, bicycle, or motorcycle: *I rode a good race.* ■ [no obj., with adverbial or complement] (of a vehicle, animal, racetrack, etc.) be of a particular character for riding on or in: *the Metro rode as well as some cars of twice the price.* ■ informal transport (someone) in a vehicle. ■ S. African transport (goods): *neighbours rode loads of prickly pear to feed their animals.*
2 be carried or supported by (something moving with great momentum): *a stream of young surfers fighting the elements to ride the waves* | figurative *the fund rode the growth boom in the 1980s.* ■ [no obj.] move so as to project or overlap: *when two lithospheric plates collide, one tends to **ride over** the other.* ■ [no obj.] (of a vessel) sail or float: *a large cedar barque **rode at anchor*** | figurative *the moon was riding high in the sky.*
3 (**be ridden**) be full of or dominated by: *you must not think him ridden with angst* | (as adj., in combination **-ridden**) *the crime-ridden streets.*
4 yield to (a blow) so as to reduce its impact: *Harrison drew back his jaw as if riding the blow.*
5 vulgar slang have sexual intercourse with.
6 N. Amer. annoy, pester, or tease: *if you don't give all the kids a chance to play, the parents ride you.*
▸ **noun 1** a journey made on a horse, bicycle, or motorcycle, or in a vehicle: *I took them for a ride in the van* | figurative *investors have had a bumpy ride.* ■ N. Amer. a person giving someone a lift in a vehicle: *their ride into town had dropped them off near the bridge.* ■ US informal a motor vehicle. ■ the quality of comfort or smoothness offered by a vehicle while it is being driven: *the ride is comfortable, though there is a slight roll when cornering.* ■ a path, typically one through woods, for horse riding. ■ Canadian a demonstration of horse riding as an entertainment.
2 a roller coaster, roundabout, or other amusement ridden at a fair or amusement park.
3 vulgar slang an act of sexual intercourse. ■ a sexual partner of a specified ability.
4 (also **ride cymbal**) a cymbal used for keeping up a continuous rhythm.
– PHRASES **be riding for a fall** see FALL. **for the ride** used to convey that someone is participating in activity for pleasure or as an observer only: *she's obviously just **along for the ride**.* **let something ride** take no immediate action over something. **ride the clutch** partially depress the clutch pedal of a vehicle while driving. **ride herd on** N. Amer. keep watch over: *a man to ride herd on this frenetically paced enterprise.* **ride high** be successful: *the economy will be riding high on the top of the next boom.* **ride the pine** (or **bench**) N. Amer. informal (of an athlete) sit on the sidelines rather than participate in a game or event. **ride the rods** (or **rails**) Canadian informal ride on a freight train surreptitiously without paying. **ride roughshod over** carry out one's own plans or wishes with arrogant disregard for (someone or something): *he rode roughshod over everyone else's opinions.* —— **rides again** used to indicate that someone or something has reappeared unexpectedly and with new vigour. **ride shotgun** chiefly N. Amer. travel as a guard next to the driver of a vehicle. ■ ride in the passenger seat of a vehicle. ■ act as a protector: *we are to have armed guards riding shotgun on domestic aeroplanes.* **ride to hounds** chiefly Brit. go fox-hunting on horseback. **a rough** (or **easy**) **ride** a difficult (or easy) time doing something: *the prime minister was given a rough ride by left-wing MPs yesterday.* **take someone for a ride** informal deceive or cheat someone.
– PHRASAL VERBS **ride someone down** trample or overtake someone while on horseback. **ride on** depend on: *there is a great deal of money riding on the results of these studies.* **ride something out** come safely through a dangerous or difficult situation: *the fleet had **ridden out the storm**.* **ride up** (of a garment) gradually work or move upwards out of its proper position.
– DERIVATIVES **rideable** (also **ridable**) adjective.
– ORIGIN Old English *rīdan*, of Germanic origin; related to Dutch *rijden* and German *reiten*.

ride-off ▸ **noun** N. Amer. (in a riding competition) a round held to resolve a tie or determine qualifiers for a later stage; a jump-off.

ride-on ▸ **adjective** denoting a power-driven machine, especially a lawnmower, on which the operator rides.
▸ **noun 1** a ride-on lawnmower.
2 chiefly N. Amer. a toy car that a child can sit in and move.

rider ▸ **noun 1** a person who is riding or who can ride a horse, bicycle, motorcycle, etc.
2 a condition or proviso added to something already agreed: *one **rider to the deal**—if the hurricane heads north, we run for shelter.* ■ Brit. an addition or amendment to a bill at its third reading. ■ Brit. a recommendation or comment added by the jury to a judicial verdict. ■ a supplementary clause in a performer's contract specifying food, drink, etc., to be provided.
3 a small weight positioned on the beam of a balance for fine adjustment.
– DERIVATIVES **riderless** adjective.
– ORIGIN late Old English *rīdere* 'mounted warrior, knight' (see RIDE, -ER[1]).

ridership ▸ **noun** [mass noun] chiefly N. Amer. the number of passengers using a particular form of public transport.

ridge ▸ **noun 1** a long, narrow hilltop, mountain range, or watershed: *the North-East ridge of Everest.* ■ the line or edge formed where the two sloping sides of a roof meet at the top. ■ a narrow raised band on a surface: *buff your nails in order to smooth ridges.* ■ a raised strip of arable land, especially (in medieval fields) one of a set separated by furrows.
2 Meteorology an elongated region of high barometric pressure.
▸ **verb** [with obj.] (often as adj. **ridged**) mark with or form into ridges: *the ridged sand of the beach* | *a field ploughed in narrow stretches that are **ridged up** slightly.* ■ [no obj.] (of a surface) form into or rise up as a ridge.
– DERIVATIVES **ridgy** adjective.
– ORIGIN Old English *hrycg* 'spine, crest', of Germanic origin; related to Dutch *rug* and German *Rücken* 'back'.

ridgeback ▸ **noun** short for RHODESIAN RIDGEBACK.

ridge piece (also **ridge tree**) ▸ **noun** a horizontal beam along the ridge of a roof, into which the rafters are fastened.

ridge pole ▸ **noun 1** the horizontal pole of a long tent.
2 another term for RIDGE PIECE.

ridge runner ▸ **noun** US informal a mountain farmer of the Southern states of the US.

ridge tent ▸ **noun** a tent having a central ridge supported by a pole or frame at each end.

ridge tile ▸ **noun** a semicircular or curved tile used in making a roof ridge.

ridgeway ▸ **noun** a road or track along a ridge, especially (**the Ridgeway**) a prehistoric trackway following the ridge of the downs in Wiltshire and Berkshire, in southern England.

ridgy-didge ▸ **adjective** Austral. informal genuine, original, or good: *a true-blue ridgy-didge Aussie.*
– ORIGIN 1950s: from *ridge*, an old slang term meaning 'gold, gold coin'.

ridicule ▸ **noun** [mass noun] the subjection of someone or something to mockery and derision: *he is held up **as an object of ridicule**.*
▸ **verb** [with obj.] subject to mockery and derision: *his theory was ridiculed and dismissed.*
– ORIGIN late 17th cent.: from French, or from Latin *ridiculum*, neuter (used as a noun) of *ridiculus* 'laughable', from *ridere* 'to laugh'.

ridiculous ▸ **adjective** deserving or inviting derision or mockery; absurd: *that ridiculous tartan cap.*
– DERIVATIVES **ridiculousness** noun.
– ORIGIN mid 16th cent.: from Latin *ridiculosus*, from *ridiculus* 'laughable' (see RIDICULE).

ridiculously ▸ **adverb** so as to invite mockery or derision; absurdly: [sentence adverb] *ridiculously, I felt like crying.* ■ [as submodifier] so as to cause surprise or disbelief: *it had been ridiculously easy to track him down.*

riding[1] ▸ **noun** [mass noun] the sport or activity of riding horses. ■ [count noun] a path for horse riding, typically one through woods.

riding[2] ▸ **noun 1** (usu. **the East/North/West Riding**) one of three former administrative divisions of Yorkshire.
2 an electoral district of Canada.
– ORIGIN Old English *trithing*, from Old Norse *thrithjungr* 'third part', from *thrithi* 'third'. The initial *th-* was lost due to assimilation with the preceding *-t* of *East*, *West*, or with the *-th* of *North*.

riding crop ▸ **noun** a short flexible whip with a loop for the hand, used in riding horses.

riding habit ▸ **noun** a woman's riding dress, consisting of a skirt worn with a double-breasted jacket.

riding light ▸ **noun** a light shown by a ship at anchor.

riding school ▸ **noun** an establishment where horse riding is taught.

Ridley, Nicholas (*c.*1500–55), English Protestant bishop and martyr. He was appointed bishop of Rochester (1547) and then of London (1550). He opposed the Catholic policies of Mary I, for which he was burnt at the stake in Oxford.

ridley (also **ridley turtle**) ▸ **noun** (pl. **ridleys**) a small turtle of tropical seas. ● Genus *Lepidochelys*, family Cheloniidae: **Kemp's ridley** (*L. kempi*) of the Atlantic, and the larger **olive ridley** (*L. olivacea*) of the Pacific.
– ORIGIN late 19th cent.: of unknown origin.

Rie /riː/, Lucie (1902–95), Austrian-born British potter. Her pottery and stoneware were admired for their precise simple shapes and varied subtle glazes.

riebeckite /ˈriːbɛkʌɪt/ ▸ **noun** [mass noun] a dark blue or black mineral of the amphibole group, occurring chiefly in alkaline igneous rocks or as blue asbestos (crocidolite).
– ORIGIN late 19th cent.: from the name of Emil *Riebeck* (died 1885), German explorer, + -ITE[1].

Riefenstahl /ˈriːf(ə)n,ʃtɑːl/, Leni (1902–2003), German film-maker and photographer; full name *Bertha Helene Amalie Riefenstahl*. She was chiefly known for *Triumph of the Will* (1934), a depiction of the 1934 Nuremberg Nazi Party rallies. Though she was not working for the Nazi Party, outside Germany her work was regarded as Nazi propaganda.

Riel /riːˈɛl/, Louis (1844–85), Canadian political leader. He led the rebellion of the Metis at Red River Settlement in 1869, later forming a provisional government and negotiating terms for the union of Manitoba with Canada. He was executed for treason after leading a further rebellion.

riel /ˈriːəl/ ▸ **noun** the basic monetary unit of Cambodia, equal to 100 sen.
– ORIGIN Khmer.

riem /rɪm, riːm/ (also **riempie** /ˈrɪmpi, ˈriːmpi/) ▸ **noun** (pl. **riems** or **riempies**) S. African a strip of rawhide or worked leather, used as a rope or in making chairs and other furniture.
– ORIGIN Dutch.

Riemann /ˈriːmən/, German /ˈriːman/, (Georg Friedrich) Bernhard (1826–66), German mathematician. He founded Riemannian geometry, which is of fundamental importance to both mathematics and physics. The **Riemann hypothesis**, about the complex numbers which are roots of a certain transcendental equation, remains an unsolved problem.

Riemannian geometry /riːˈmanɪən/ ▸ **noun** [mass noun] a form of differential non-Euclidean geometry developed by Bernhard Riemann, used to describe curved space. It provided Einstein with a mathematical basis for his general theory of relativity.

Riesling /ˈriːzlɪŋ, ˈriːs-/ ▸ **noun** [mass noun] a variety of wine grape grown in Germany, Austria, and elsewhere. ■ a dry white wine made from the Riesling grape.
– ORIGIN German.

rietbok /ˈriːtbɒk/ ▸ **noun** S. African another term for REEDBUCK.
– ORIGIN South African Dutch.

rifampicin /rɪˈfampɪsɪn/ (also **rifampin**) ▸ **noun** [mass noun] Medicine a reddish-brown antibiotic used chiefly to treat tuberculosis and leprosy. ● The antibiotic is obtained from the bacterium *Nocardia mediterranei*.
– ORIGIN 1960s: from *rifamycin* (an antibiotic first isolated from the bacterium *Streptomyces mediterranei*) + the insertion of *pi-* from PIPERAZINE.

rife ▸ **adjective** [predic.] (especially of something undesirable) of common occurrence; widespread: *male*

chauvinism was rife in medicine. ■ (**rife with**) full of: *the streets were rife with rumour and fear.*
▶ **adverb** in an unchecked or widespread manner: *speculation **ran rife** that he was an arms dealer.*
– ORIGIN late Old English *rȳfe*, probably from Old Norse *rífr* 'acceptable'.

riff ▶ **noun** a short repeated phrase in popular music and jazz, frequently played over changing chords or harmonies or used as a background to a solo improvisation: *a brilliant guitar riff.* ■ a monologue or spoken improvisation, especially a humorous one, on a particular subject: *extended **riffs on** the pitfalls of contemporary romance.*
▶ **verb** [no obj.] play riffs: *the other horns would be riffing behind him.* ■ perform a monologue or spoken improvisation on a particular subject: *he also **riffs on** racism and the economy.*
– ORIGIN 1930s: perhaps an abbreviation of **REFRAIN**.

riffage /ˈrɪfɪdʒ/ ▶ **noun** [mass noun] informal guitar riffs, especially in rock music.

riffle ▶ **verb 1** [no obj.] turn over something, especially the pages of a book, quickly and casually: *he **riffled through** the pages* | [with obj.] *she opened a book and riffled the pages.* ■ (**riffle through**) search quickly through (something): *she riffled through her leather handbag.* ■ [with obj.] disturb the surface of; ruffle: *there was a slight breeze that riffled her hair.*
2 [with obj.] shuffle (playing cards) by flicking up and releasing the corners or sides of two piles of cards so that they intermingle and may be slid together to form a single pile.
▶ **noun 1** [usu. in sing.] an act or sound of riffling through something.
2 chiefly N. Amer. a rocky or shallow part of a stream or river where the water flows brokenly. ■ a patch of waves or ripples.
– ORIGIN late 18th cent. (in sense 2 of the noun): perhaps from a variant of the verb **RUFFLE**, influenced by **RIPPLE**.

riffler ▶ **noun** a narrow elongated tool with a curved file surface at each end, used in filing concave surfaces.
– ORIGIN late 18th cent.: from French *rifloir*, from Old French *rifler* 'to scrape'.

riff-raff ▶ **noun** [mass noun] disreputable or undesirable people.
– ORIGIN late 15th cent. (as *riff and raff*): from Old French *rif et raf* 'one and all, every bit', of Germanic origin.

rifle¹ ▶ **noun** a gun, especially one fired from shoulder level, having a long spirally grooved barrel intended to make a bullet spin and thereby have greater accuracy over a long distance: *a hunting rifle.* ■ (**rifles**) troops armed with rifles: [in names] *the Burma Rifles.*
▶ **verb 1** [with obj.] (usu. as adj. **rifled**) make spiral grooves in (a gun or its barrel or bore) to make a bullet spin and thereby have greater accuracy over a long distance: *a line of replacement rifled barrels.*
2 [with obj. and adverbial of direction] hit or kick (a ball) hard and straight: *Ferguson rifled home his fourth goal of the season.*
– ORIGIN mid 17th cent.: from French *rifler* 'graze, scratch', of Germanic origin. The earliest noun usage was in *rifle gun*, which had 'rifles' or spiral grooves cut into the inside of the barrel.

rifle² ▶ **verb** [no obj.] search through something in a hurried way in order to find or steal something: *she **rifled through** the cassette tapes* | [with obj.] *she rifled the house for money.* ■ [with obj.] steal: *he rifled the dead man's possessions.*
– ORIGIN Middle English: from Old French *rifler* 'graze, plunder', of Germanic origin.

rifle bird ▶ **noun** a bird of paradise, the male of which has mainly velvety-black plumage and a display call that sounds like a whistling bullet. ● Genus *Ptiloris*, family Paradisaeidae: three species.

rifleman ▶ **noun** (pl. **riflemen**) **1** a soldier armed with a rifle, especially a private in a rifle regiment. ■ a person skilled at using a rifle.
2 a very small, short-tailed, greenish-yellow songbird which feeds on insects on tree bark, native to New Zealand. [perhaps so named from a comparison between its plumage and an early military uniform.] ● *Acanthisitta chloris*, family Xenicidae.

rifle microphone ▶ **noun** a type of gun microphone with several tubes of different lengths in front of the diaphragm to enhance its directional focus.

rifle range ▶ **noun** a place for practising shooting with rifles. ■ an attraction at a fairground in which people fire rifles at targets in order to win prizes.

riflescope ▶ **noun** informal a telescopic sight on a rifle.

rifle shot ▶ **noun** a shot fired from a rifle. ■ [mass noun] the range of a rifle: *the schooner had escaped out of rifle shot.*

rifling /ˈrʌɪflɪŋ/ ▶ **noun** [mass noun] the arrangement of spiral grooves on the inside of a rifle barrel.

Rif Mountains /rɪf/ (also **Er Rif**) a mountain range of northern Morocco, running parallel to the Mediterranean for about 290 km (180 miles) eastwards from Tangier. Rising to over 2,250 m (7,000 ft), it forms a westward extension of the Atlas Mountains.

rift ▶ **noun 1** a crack, split, or break in something: *the wind had torn open a rift in the clouds.* ■ Geology a major fault separating blocks of the earth's surface; a rift valley.
2 a serious break in friendly relations: *the **rift between** the two branches of the legal profession.*
▶ **verb** [no obj.] chiefly Geology form fissures or breaks, especially through large-scale faulting; move apart: *a fragment of continental crust which rifted away from eastern Australia.* ■ [with obj.] (usu. as adj. **rifted**) tear or force (something) apart: *the nascent rifted margins of the Red Sea.*
– ORIGIN Middle English: of Scandinavian origin; compare with Norwegian and Danish *rift* 'cleft, chink'.

rift valley ▶ **noun** a steep-sided valley formed by the downward displacement of a block of the earth's surface between nearly parallel faults or fault systems.

rig¹ ▶ **verb** (**rigs, rigging, rigged**) **1** [with obj.] provide (a sailing boat) with sails and rigging: *the catamaran will be rigged as a ketch* | (as adj., in combination **-rigged**) *a gaff-rigged cutter.* ■ assemble and adjust (the equipment of a sailing boat, aircraft, etc.) in readiness for operation: *most sails are kept ready rigged.*
2 set up (equipment or a device or structure), typically in a makeshift or hasty way: *he had **rigged up** a sort of tent* | [with obj. and infinitive] *the power plant of the lifeboat had been rigged to explode.*
3 provide (someone) with clothes of a particular type: *a cavalry regiment **rigged out** in green and gold.*
▶ **noun 1** the particular way in which a sailing boat's masts, sails, and rigging are arranged: *a ketch rig.* ■ the sail, mast, and boom of a windsurfer.
2 a device or piece of equipment designed for a particular purpose: *a lighting rig.* ■ an oil rig or drilling rig. ■ (in CB and short-wave radio) a transmitter and receiver. ■ a set of amplifiers and speakers used by a live band or a DJ in a club. ■ a particular type of construction for fishing tackle that bears the bait and hook.
3 a person's costume, outfit, or style of dress: *the rig of the American Army Air Corps.*
4 chiefly N. Amer. & Austral./NZ a truck.
– PHRASES (**in**) **full rig** informal (wearing) smart or ceremonial clothes.
– ORIGIN late 15th cent. (in nautical use): perhaps of Scandinavian origin: compare with Norwegian *rigga* 'bind or wrap up'. The noun dates from the early 19th cent.

rig² ▶ **verb** (**rigs, rigging, rigged**) [with obj.] manage or conduct (something) fraudulently so as to gain an advantage: *the results of the elections had been rigged* | (as noun, in combination **-rigging**) *charges of vote-rigging.* ■ cause an artificial rise or fall in prices in (the stock market) with a view to personal profit: *he accused games firms of rigging the market.*
▶ **noun** archaic a trick or swindle.
– ORIGIN late 18th cent. (in the noun sense): of unknown origin.

Riga /ˈriːɡə/ a port on the Baltic Sea, capital of Latvia; pop. 722,000 (est. 2007).

rigadoon /ˌrɪɡəˈduːn/ ▶ **noun** a lively dance for couples, in duple or quadruple time, of Provençal origin.
– ORIGIN late 17th cent.: from French *rigaudon*, perhaps named after its inventor, said to be a dance teacher called *Rigaud*.

rigatoni /ˌrɪɡəˈtəʊni/ ▶ **plural noun** pasta in the form of short hollow fluted tubes.
– ORIGIN Italian.

Rigel /ˈrʌɪdʒəl, ˈrʌɪɡ(ə)l/ Astronomy the seventh-brightest star in the sky, and the brightest in the constellation Orion. It is a blue supergiant nearly sixty thousand times as luminous as our sun.
– ORIGIN from Arabic *rijl* 'foot (of Orion)'.

rigger¹ ▶ **noun 1** [in combination] a ship rigged in a particular way: *a square-rigger.*
2 a person who rigs or attends to the rigging of a sailing ship, aircraft, or parachute. ■ a person who erects and maintains scaffolding, cranes, etc. ■ a person who works on or helps construct an oil rig.
3 (also **rigger brush**) an artist's long-haired sable brush.
4 an outrigger carrying a rowlock on a racing rowing boat.

rigger² ▶ **noun** a person who fraudulently manipulates something so as to produce a result or situation to their advantage.

rigging ▶ **noun** [mass noun] **1** the system of ropes or chains employed to support a ship's masts (**standing rigging**) and to control or set the yards and sails (**running rigging**).
2 the ropes and wires supporting the structure of an airship, biplane, hang-glider, or parachute. ■ the system of cables and fittings controlling the flight surfaces and engines of an aircraft.

right ▶ **adjective 1** morally good, justified, or acceptable: *I hope we're doing the right thing* | [with infinitive] *you were quite right to criticize him.*
2 true or correct as a fact: *I'm not sure I know the right answer* | *her theories were proved right.* ■ [predic.] correct in one's opinion or judgement: *she was right about Tom having no money.* ■ according to what is correct for a particular situation: *is this the right way to the cottage?* | *you're not holding it the right way up.* ■ best or most appropriate for a particular situation: *he was clearly the right man for the job* | *I was waiting for the right moment to ask him.* ■ socially fashionable or important: *he was seen at all the right places.*
3 [predic.] in a satisfactory, sound, or normal state or condition: *that sausage doesn't smell right* | *if only I could have helped **put** matters **right**.*
4 on, towards, or relating to the side of a human body or of a thing which is to the east when the person or thing is facing north: *my right elbow* | *the right edge of the field.*
5 [attrib.] Brit. informal complete; absolute (used for emphasis): *I felt a right idiot.*
6 relating to a person or group favouring conservative views: *are you politically right, left, or centre?*
▶ **adverb 1** to the furthest or most complete extent or degree (used for emphasis): *the car spun right off the track* | *I'm right out of ideas.* ■ exactly; directly (used to emphasize the precise location or time of something): *Harriet was standing right behind her.* ■ informal without delaying or hesitating; immediately: *I'll be right back.* ■ [as submodifier] dialect or archaic very: *it's right spooky in there!*
2 correctly: *he had guessed right.* ■ in the required or necessary way; satisfactorily: *nothing's going right for me this season.*
3 on or to the right side: *turn right off the B1269.*
▶ **noun 1** [mass noun] that which is morally correct, just, or honourable: *she doesn't understand the difference between right and wrong* | [count noun] *the rights and wrongs of the matter.*
2 a moral or legal entitlement to have or do something: [with infinitive] *she had every right to be angry* | *you're quite **within your rights** to ask for your money back* | [mass noun] *there is no **right of** appeal against the decision.* ■ (**rights**) the authority to perform, publish, film, or televise a particular work, event, etc.: *they sold the paperback rights.*
3 (**the right**) the right-hand part, side, or direction: *take the first turning on the right* | (**one's right**) *she seated me on her right.* ■ (in football or a similar sport) the right-hand half of the field when facing the opponent's goal. ■ the right wing of an army. ■ a right turn: *he made a right in Dorchester Avenue.* ■ a road or entrance on the right: *take the first right over the stream.* ■ a person's right fist, especially a boxer's. ■ a blow given with the right fist: *the young copper swung a terrific right.*
4 (often **the Right**) [treated as sing. or pl.] a group or party favouring conservative views and supporting capitalist principles: *the Right got in at the election* | *his proposal was viewed with alarm by the right of the party.*
▶ **verb 1** [with obj.] restore to a normal or upright position: *we righted the capsized dinghy.*
2 restore to a normal or correct state: *righting the economy demanded major cuts in defence spending.* ■ redress or rectify (a wrong or mistaken action): *she was determined to right the wrongs done to her father.* ■ archaic make reparation to (someone) for a wrong done to them: *we'll see you righted.*
▶ **exclamation** informal used to indicate agreement or to acknowledge a statement or order: *'Barry's here.' 'Oh, right'* | ***right you are**, sir.* ■ used as an interrogative at the end of a statement as a way of inviting confirmation or approval: *you went to see Angie on Monday, right?* ■ used as a filler in speech or to introduce an utterance or exhortation: *right, let's have a drink* | *and I didn't think any more of it, right, but Mum said I should take him to a doctor.*

R

– PHRASES **bang** (or N. Amer. **dead**) **to rights** informal (of a criminal) with positive proof of guilt: *we've got you bang to rights handling stolen property.* **be in the right** be morally or legally justified in one's views or actions. **by rights** if things had happened or been done fairly or correctly: *by rights, he should not be playing next week.* **do right by** treat (someone) fairly. **in one's own right** as a result of one's own claims, qualifications, or efforts, rather than an association with someone else: *he was already established as a poet in his own right.* (**not**) **in one's right mind** (not) sane. **not right in the head** informal (of a person) not completely sane. (**as**) **of right** (or **by right**) as a result of having a moral or legal claim or entitlement: *the state will be obliged to provide health care as of right.* **on the right side of** on the safe, appropriate, or desirable side of: *her portrayal of his neurotic wife falls just on the right side of caricature.* ■ in a position to be viewed with favour by: *he hasn't always remained on the right side of the law.* ■ somewhat less than (a specified age): *she's on the right side of forty.* **the right stuff** the necessary qualities for a given task or job: *he had the right stuff to enter this business.* **put** (or **set**) **someone right 1** restore someone to health. **2** make someone understand the true facts of a situation. **put** (or **set**) **something to rights** restore something to its correct or normal state. (**as**) **right as rain** informal (of a person) feeling completely well or healthy. **right** (or **straight**) **away** (or informal **off**) immediately. **right enough** informal certainly; undeniably: *your record's bad right enough.* **right on** informal used as an expression of strong support, approval, or encouragement. See also **RIGHT-ON**. **a right one** Brit. informal a silly or foolish person. **she's** (or **she'll be**) **right** Austral./NZ informal that will be all right; don't worry. **too right** Brit. informal used to express one's enthusiastic agreement with a statement.

– DERIVATIVES **righter** noun, **rightish** adjective, **rightless** adjective, **rightness** noun, **rightward** adjective, **rightwards** adjective & adverb.

– ORIGIN Old English *riht* (adjective and noun), *rihtan* (verb), *rihte* (adverb), of Germanic origin; related to Latin *rectus* 'ruled', from an Indo-European root denoting movement in a straight line.

right about (also **right about-face**) ▸ **noun** Military a right turn continued through 180° so as to face in the opposite direction: [as exclamation] *By twos—right about—march!*

right angle ▸ **noun** an angle of 90°, as in a corner of a square, or formed by dividing a circle into quarters.

– PHRASES **at right angles** (or **a right angle**) **to** forming an angle of 90° with (something): *hold the brush at right angles to the surface.*

right-angled ▸ **adjective** containing or being a right angle: *a right-angled triangle.*

right ascension ▸ **noun** Astronomy the distance of a point east of the First Point of Aries, measured along the celestial equator and expressed in hours, minutes, and seconds. Compare with **DECLINATION** and **CELESTIAL LONGITUDE**.

right back ▸ **noun** a defender in soccer or field hockey who plays primarily in a position on the right of the field.

Right Bank a district of the city of Paris, situated on the right bank of the River Seine, to the north of the river. The area contains the Champs-Élysées and the Louvre.

right bank ▸ **noun** the bank of a river, on the right as one faces downstream.

right brain ▸ **noun** the right-hand side of the human brain, which is believed to be associated with creative thought and the emotions.

right-click ▸ **verb** [no obj.] Computing click on a link or other screen object by depressing the right-hand button on the mouse: *right-click on My Network Places and select Properties.*

righten ▸ **verb** [with obj.] archaic make (something) right, correct, or straight: *thy stubborn mind will not be rightened.*

righteous /ˈrʌɪtʃəs/ ▸ **adjective 1** morally right or justifiable: *feelings of righteous indignation about pay and conditions.* ■ (of a person) morally good; virtuous: *he stood up for what he knew was right and died a righteous person.*

2 US informal, chiefly black English very good; excellent: *righteous eggs, man!* ■ correctly so called; genuine: *he is righteous trash.*

– DERIVATIVES **righteously** adverb.

– ORIGIN Old English *rihtwīs*, from *riht* 'right' + *wīs* 'manner, state, condition'. The change in the ending in the 16th cent. was due to association with words such as *bounteous*.

righteousness ▸ **noun** [mass noun] the quality of being morally right or justifiable: *we had little doubt about the righteousness of our cause.*

right field ▸ **noun** Baseball the part of the outfield to the right of the batter when facing the pitcher: *a ball hit to right field.*

right-footed ▸ **adjective** (of a person) using the right foot more naturally than the left. ■ (of a kick) done with the right foot.

rightful ▸ **adjective** [attrib.] having a legitimate right to property, position, or status: *the rightful owner of the jewels.* ■ legitimately claimed; fitting: *they are determined to take their rightful place in a new South Africa.*

– DERIVATIVES **rightfully** adverb, **rightfulness** noun.

– ORIGIN Old English *rihtful* 'upright, righteous' (see **RIGHT**, **-FUL**). The notion of 'legitimacy' dates from Middle English.

right hand ▸ **noun** the hand of a person's right side. ■ the region or direction on the right side of a person or thing: *a great wall loomed above the street on the right hand.* ■ the most important position next to someone: *the place of honour at his host's right hand.* ■ (also **right arm**) an efficient or indispensable assistant: *she could have helped him, been her father's right hand.*

▸ **adjective** [attrib.] on or towards the right side of a person or thing: *the top right-hand corner.* ■ done with or using the right hand: *wild right-hand punches.*

right-hand drive ▸ **noun** [mass noun] a motor-vehicle steering system with the steering wheel and other controls fitted on the right side, designed for use in countries where vehicles drive on the left side of the road. ■ [count noun] a vehicle with right-hand drive steering.

right-handed ▸ **adjective 1** (of a person) using the right hand more naturally than the left: *a right-handed golfer.* ■ (of a tool or item of equipment) made to be used with the right hand: *a right-handed guitar.* ■ made or done with the right hand: *right-handed batting.*

2 (of a screw) advanced by turning clockwise. ■ Biology (of a spiral shell or helix) dextral. ■ (of a racecourse) turning clockwise.

▸ **adverb** with the right hand: *Jackson bats right-handed.*

– DERIVATIVES **right-handedly** adverb, **right-handedness** noun.

right-hander ▸ **noun 1** a right-handed person. ■ a blow struck with the right hand.

2 a corner on a road or racing track that bends to the right.

right-hand man ▸ **noun** an indispensable helper or chief assistant.

Right Honourable ▸ **noun** Brit. a title given to certain high officials such as Privy Counsellors and government ministers.

rightism ▸ **noun** [mass noun] the political views or policies of the right.

– DERIVATIVES **rightist** noun & adjective.

rightly ▸ **adverb 1** correctly: *if I remember rightly, she never gives interviews.* ■ with good reason: *the delicious cuisine for which her country was rightly famous.*

2 in accordance with justice or what is morally right: *the key rightly belonged to Craig.*

right-minded ▸ **adjective** having sound views and principles.

– DERIVATIVES **right-mindedness** noun.

rightmost ▸ **adjective** [attrib.] situated furthest to the right.

righto (also **righty-ho**) ▸ **exclamation** Brit. informal expressing agreement or assent: *'Coming to pick up the kids?' 'Righto.'*

right of abode ▸ **noun** [mass noun] chiefly Brit. a person's right to take up residence or remain resident in a country.

right of common ▸ **noun** see **COMMON** (sense 4 of the noun).

right of primogeniture ▸ **noun** see **PRIMOGENITURE**.

right of search ▸ **noun** [mass noun] the right of a ship of a belligerent state to stop and search a neutral merchant vessel for prohibited goods.

right of way ▸ **noun** [mass noun] **1** the legal right, established by usage or grant, to pass along a specific route through grounds or property belonging to another. ■ [count noun] a path or thoroughfare subject to such a right.

2 the legal right of a pedestrian, vehicle, or ship to proceed with precedence over others in a particular situation or place.

3 N. Amer. the right to build and operate a railway line, road, or utility on land belonging to another. ■ [count noun] the land on which a railway line, road, or utility is built.

right-on ▸ **adjective** informal, often derogatory in keeping with fashionable liberal or left-wing opinions and values: *the right-on music press.*

Right Reverend ▸ **noun** a title given to a bishop, especially in the Anglican Church.

rights issue ▸ **noun** an issue of shares offered at a special price by a company to its existing shareholders in proportion to their holding of old shares.

rightsize ▸ **verb** [with obj.] chiefly US convert (something) to an appropriate or optimum size. ■ reduce the size of (a company or organization) by shedding staff.

rights of man ▸ **plural noun** rights held to be justifiably belonging to any person; human rights. The phrase is associated with the Declaration of the Rights of Man and of the Citizen, adopted by the French National Assembly in 1789 and used as a preface to the French Constitution of 1791.

right-thinking ▸ **adjective** right-minded.

right-to-life ▸ **adjective** another term for **PRO-LIFE**.

– DERIVATIVES **right-to-lifer** noun.

right-to-work ▸ **adjective** chiefly US relating to or promoting a worker's right not to be required to join a trade union: *Kansas is a right-to-work state.*

right triangle ▸ **noun** N. Amer. a right-angled triangle.

right turn ▸ **noun** a turn that brings a person's front to face the way their right side did before: *take a right turn into Barracks Lane.*

right whale ▸ **noun** a baleen whale with a large head and a deeply curved jaw, of Arctic and temperate waters. ● Family Balaenidae: two genera and three species, in particular *Balaena glacialis*, which has distinctive patches of callosities on the snout. See also **BOWHEAD**.

right wing ▸ **noun** (**the right wing**) **1** the conservative or reactionary section of a political party or system. [with reference to the National Assembly in France (1789–91), where the nobles sat to the president's right and the commons to the left.]

2 the right side of a team on the field in soccer, rugby, and field hockey: *he reverted to his normal position on the right wing.* ■ the right side of an army.

▸ **adjective** conservative or reactionary: *a right-wing Republican senator.*

– DERIVATIVES **right-winger** noun.

righty ▸ **noun** (pl. **righties**) N. Amer. informal **1** a right-handed person.

2 a person who supports or is involved in right-wing politics.

righty-ho ▸ **exclamation** variant spelling of **RIGHTO**.

rigid ▸ **adjective 1** unable to bend or be forced out of shape; not flexible: *a seat of rigid orange plastic.* ■ (of a person or part of their body) stiff and unmoving, especially as a result of shock or fear: *Beatrice was rigid with terror.*

2 not able to be changed or adapted: *rigid bureaucratic controls.* ■ not adaptable in outlook, belief, or response: *the College had not wanted to be too rigid in imposing teaching methods.*

▸ **noun** a lorry which is not articulated.

– DERIVATIVES **rigidify** verb (**rigidifies**, **rigidifying**, **rigidified**), **rigidity** noun, **rigidly** adverb, **rigidness** noun.

– ORIGIN late Middle English: from Latin *rigidus*, from *rigere* 'be stiff'.

rigid designator ▸ **noun** Philosophy a term that identifies the same object or individual in every possible world.

Rigil Kentaurus /ˌrʌɪdʒɪl kɛnˈtɔːrəs/ (also **Rigil Kent**) Astronomy the star Alpha Centauri.

– ORIGIN Arabic, literally 'the foot of the Centaur'.

rigmarole /ˈrɪɡmərəʊl/ ▸ **noun** a lengthy and complicated procedure: *he went through the rigmarole of securing the front door.* ■ a long, rambling story or statement.

– ORIGIN mid 18th cent.: apparently an alteration of *ragman roll*, originally denoting a legal document recording a list of offences.

rigor[1] /ˈrɪɡɔː, ˈrʌɪɡɔː, -ɡə/ ▸ **noun** Medicine a sudden feeling of cold with shivering accompanied by a rise in temperature, often with copious sweating, especially at the onset or height of a fever. ■ short for **RIGOR MORTIS**.

– ORIGIN late Middle English: from Latin, literally 'stiffness', from *rigere* 'be stiff'.

rigor[2] ▶ **noun** US spelling of RIGOUR.

rigorism ▶ **noun** [mass noun] extreme strictness in interpreting or enforcing a law or principle. ■ the Roman Catholic doctrine that in doubtful cases of conscience the strict course is always to be followed.
– DERIVATIVES **rigorist noun & adjective.**

rigor mortis /ˈmɔːtɪs/ ▶ **noun** [mass noun] Medicine stiffening of the joints and muscles of a body a few hours after death, usually lasting from one to four days.
– ORIGIN mid 19th cent.: from Latin, literally 'stiffness of death'.

rigorous ▶ **adjective** extremely thorough and careful: *the rigorous testing of consumer products.* ■ (of a rule, system, etc.) strictly applied or adhered to: *rigorous controls on mergers.* ■ (of a person) adhering strictly to a belief or system: *a rigorous teetotaller.* ■ harsh and demanding: *many of the expedition had passed rigorous SAS courses.*
– DERIVATIVES **rigorously adverb, rigorousness noun.**
– ORIGIN late Middle English: from Old French *rigorous* or late Latin *rigorosus*, from *rigor* 'stiffness' (see RIGOR[1]).

rigour (US **rigor**) ▶ **noun** [mass noun] the quality of being extremely thorough and careful: *his analysis is lacking in rigour.* ■ severity or strictness: *the full rigour of the law.* ■ (**rigours**) harsh and demanding conditions: *the rigours of a harsh winter.*
– ORIGIN late Middle English: from Old French *rigour* from Latin *rigor* 'stiffness'.

rig-out ▶ **noun** informal, chiefly Brit. an outfit of clothes.

Rig Veda /rɪɡ ˈveɪdə, ˈviːdə/ Hinduism the oldest and principal of the Vedas, composed in the 2nd millennium BC and containing a collection of hymns in early Sanskrit. See VEDA.
– ORIGIN from Sanskrit *ṛgveda*, from *ṛc* '(sacred) stanza' + *veda* '(sacred) knowledge'.

Rijeka /riːˈɛkə/ a port on the Adriatic coast of Croatia; pop. 138,600 (est. 2009). Italian name FIUME.

Rijksmuseum /ˈrʌɪksmuːˌzeɪəm/ the national art gallery of the Netherlands, in Amsterdam. It contains the most representative collection of Dutch art in the world.

rijsttafel /ˈrʌɪstˌtɑːf(ə)l/ ▶ **noun** [mass noun] a meal of SE Asian food consisting of a selection of spiced rice dishes.
– ORIGIN Dutch, from *rijst* 'rice' + *tafel* 'table'.

rikishi /ˈrɪkɪʃi/ ▶ **noun** (pl. **same**) a sumo wrestler.
– ORIGIN Japanese, from *riki* 'strength' + *shi* 'warrior'.

Riksmål /ˈriːksmɔːl/ ▶ **noun** another term for BOKMÅL.
– ORIGIN Norwegian, from *rike* 'state, nation' + *mål* 'language'.

Rila Mountains /ˈriːlə/ a range of mountains in western Bulgaria, forming the westernmost extent of the Rhodope Mountains. It is the highest range in Bulgaria, rising to a height of 2,925 m (9,596 ft) at Mount Musala.

rile ▶ **verb** [with obj.] **1** informal make (someone) annoyed or irritated: *he has been riled by suggestions that his Arsenal future is in doubt.*
2 N. Amer. make (water) turbulent or muddy.
– ORIGIN early 19th cent.: variant of ROIL.

Riley[1] ▶ **noun** (in phrase **the life of Riley**) informal a luxurious or carefree existence.
– ORIGIN early 20th cent.: of unknown origin.

Riley[2], Bridget (Louise) (b.1931), English painter. A leading exponent of op art, she worked with flat patterns to create optical illusions of light and movement. Notable paintings: *Fall* (1963).

rilievo /rɪˈljeɪvəʊ/ ▶ **noun** variant spelling of RELIEVO.

Rilke /ˈrɪlkə/, Rainer Maria (1875–1926), Austrian poet, born in Bohemia; pseudonym of *René Karl Wilhelm Josef Maria Rilke.* His conception of art as a quasi-religious vocation culminated in his best-known works, the *Duino Elegies* and *Sonnets to Orpheus* (both 1923).

rill /rɪl/ ▶ **noun** a small stream. ■ a shallow channel cut in the surface of soil or rocks by running water. ■ variant spelling of RILLE.
– ORIGIN mid 16th cent.: probably of Low German origin.

rille /rɪl/ (also **rill**) ▶ **noun** Astronomy a fissure or narrow channel on the moon's surface.
– ORIGIN mid 19th cent.: from German (see RILL).

rillettes /ˈriːjɛt/ ▶ **plural noun** pâté made of minced pork or other light meat, seasoned and combined with fat.
– ORIGIN French, diminutive (plural) of Old French *rille* 'strip of pork'.

RIM ▶ **abbreviation** Mauritania (international vehicle registration).
– ORIGIN from French *République Islamique de Mauritanie.*

rim[1] ▶ **noun** the upper or outer edge of an object, typically something circular or approximately circular: *a china egg cup with a gold rim.* ■ the outer edge of a wheel, on which the tyre is fitted. ■ the part of a spectacle frame surrounding the lenses. ■ a limit or boundary: *the outer rim of the solar system.* ■ an encircling stain or deposit: *a thick rim of suds.*
▶ **verb** (**rims, rimming, rimmed**) [with obj.] form or act as an outer edge or rim for: *a huge lake rimmed by glaciers* | (as adj., in combination **-rimmed**) *steel-rimmed glasses.* ■ mark with an encircling stain or deposit: *his collar was rimmed with dirt.*
– DERIVATIVES **rimless adjective.**
– ORIGIN Old English *rima* 'a border, coast'; compare with Old Norse *rimi* 'ridge, strip of land' (the only known cognate).

rim[2] ▶ **verb** (**rims, rimming, rimmed**) [with obj.] vulgar slang lick or suck the anus of (someone) as a means of sexual stimulation.
– ORIGIN perhaps a variant of REAM[2].

Rimbaud /ˈrambəʊ/, French /rɛ̃bo/, (Jean Nicholas) Arthur (1854–91), French poet. Known for poems such as 'Le Bateau ivre' (1871) and the collection of symbolist prose poems *Une Saison en enfer* (1873), and for his stormy relationship with Paul Verlaine, he stopped writing at about the age of 20 and spent the rest of his life travelling.

rim brake ▶ **noun** a brake acting on the rim of a wheel.

rime[1] /rʌɪm/ ▶ **noun** (also **rime ice**) [mass noun] frost formed on cold objects by the rapid freezing of water vapour in cloud or fog. ■ literary hoar frost.
▶ **verb** [with obj.] literary cover (an object) with hoar frost: *he does not brush away the frost that rimes his beard.*
– ORIGIN Old English *hrīm*, of Germanic origin; related to Dutch *rijm*. The word became rare in Middle English but was revived in literary use at the end of the 18th cent.

rime[2] ▶ **noun & verb** archaic spelling of RHYME.

rimfire ▶ **adjective** relating to or denoting guns whose cartridges have the primer around the edge of the base.

Rimini /ˈrɪmɪni/ a port and resort on the Adriatic coast of NE Italy; pop. 140,137 (2008).

rimland ▶ **noun** [mass noun] (also **rimlands**) a peripheral region, especially one with political or strategic significance.

rim lock ▶ **noun** a lock that is fitted to the surface of a door, as opposed to a mortise lock.

Rimmon /ˈrɪmən/ (in the Bible) a deity worshipped in ancient Damascus (2 Kings 5: 18).

rimrock ▶ **noun** [mass noun] chiefly N. Amer. an outcrop of resistant rock forming a margin to a gravel deposit, especially one forming a cliff at the edge of a plateau.

rim-shot ▶ **noun** a drum stroke in which the stick strikes the rim and the head of the drum simultaneously.

Rimsky-Korsakov /ˌrɪmskɪˈkɔːsəkɒf/, Nikolai (Andreevich) (1844–1908), Russian composer. He achieved fame with his orchestral suite *Scheherazade* (1888) and his many operas drawing on Russian and Slavic folk tales.

rimu /ˈriːmuː/ ▶ **noun** a tall coniferous tree with dark brown flaking bark, which is the chief native softwood tree of New Zealand. The timber is used for furniture and interior fittings. Also called RED PINE.
● *Dacrydium cupressinum*, family Podocarpaceae.
– ORIGIN mid 19th cent.: from Maori.

rimy /ˈrʌɪmi/ ▶ **adjective** (**rimier, rimiest**) literary covered with frost.

rind ▶ **noun** [mass noun] the tough outer skin of certain fruit, especially citrus fruit. ■ the hard outer edge of cheese or bacon. ■ the bark of a tree or plant. ■ the hard outer layer of a rhizomorph or other part of a fungus. ■ the skin or blubber of a whale.
▶ **verb** [with obj.] strip the bark from (a tree).
– DERIVATIVES **rinded adjective** [in combination] *yellow-rinded lemons*, **rindless adjective.**
– ORIGIN Old English *rind(e)* 'bark of a tree'; related to Dutch *run* and German *Rinde*, of unknown origin.

rinderpest /ˈrɪndəpɛst/ ▶ **noun** [mass noun] Veterinary Medicine an infectious disease of ruminants, especially cattle, caused by a paramyxovirus. It is characterized by fever, dysentery, and inflammation of the mucous membranes. Also called CATTLE PLAGUE.
– PHRASES **before** (or **since**) **the rinderpest** S. African a long time ago (or for a very long time). [referring to the 1896 epidemic, treated as a landmark.]
– ORIGIN mid 19th cent.: from German, from *Rinder* 'cattle' + *Pest* 'plague'.

ring[1] ▶ **noun 1** a small circular band, typically of precious metal and often set with one or more gemstones, worn on a finger as an ornament or a token of marriage, engagement, or authority. ■ Ornithology, Brit. an aluminium strip secured round a bird's leg to identify it.
2 a ring-shaped or circular object: *an inflatable rubber ring* | *fried onion rings.* ■ a circular marking or pattern: *she had black rings round her eyes.* ■ a group of people or things arranged in a circle: *a ring of trees* | *everyone sat in a ring, holding hands.* ■ a circular or spiral course: *they were dancing energetically in a ring.* ■ chiefly Brit. a flat circular device forming part of a gas or electric hob, providing heat from below: *a gas ring.* ■ Astronomy a thin band or disc of rock and ice particles round a planet. ■ short for TREE RING. ■ short for RING ROAD. ■ [usu. as modifier] Archaeology a circular prehistoric earthwork, typically consisting of a bank and ditch: *a ring ditch.* ■ vulgar slang a person's anus.
3 an enclosed space, surrounded by seating for spectators, in which a sport, performance, or show takes place: *a circus ring.* ■ a roped enclosure for boxing or wrestling. ■ (**the ring**) the profession, sport, or institution of boxing.
4 a group of people engaged in a shared enterprise, especially one involving illegal or unscrupulous activity: *the police had been investigating the drug ring.*
5 Chemistry a number of atoms bonded together to form a closed loop in a molecule.
6 Mathematics a set of elements with two binary operations, addition and multiplication, the second being distributive over the first and associative.
▶ **verb** [with obj.] **1** surround (someone or something), especially for protection or containment: *the courthouse was ringed with police.* ■ form a line around the edge of (something circular): *dark shadows ringed his eyes.* ■ chiefly Brit. draw a circle round (something), especially to focus attention on it: *an area of Soho had been ringed in red.*
2 Ornithology, Brit. put an aluminium strip around the leg of (a bird) for subsequent identification. ■ put a circular band through the nose of (a bull, pig, or other farm animal) to lead or otherwise control it.
3 [with obj.] informal fraudulently change the identity of (a motor vehicle), typically by changing its registration plate. [1960s: from an earlier slang use in the general sense 'exchange' (compare with RINGER).]
4 short for RINGBARK.
– PHRASES **hold the ring** monitor a dispute or conflict without becoming involved in it. **run** (or **make**) **rings round** (or **around**) **someone** informal outclass or outwit someone very easily. **throw one's hat in the ring** see HAT.
– DERIVATIVES **ringed adjective** [in combination] *the five-ringed Olympic emblem*, **ringless adjective.**
– ORIGIN Old English *hring*, of Germanic origin; related to Dutch *ring*, German *Ring*, also to the noun RANK[1].

ring[2] ▶ **verb** (past **rang**; past participle **rung**) **1** [no obj.] make a clear resonant or vibrating sound: *a shot rang out* | *a bell rang loudly.* ■ [with obj.] cause (a bell or alarm) to ring: *he walked up to the door and rang the bell.* ■ (of a telephone) produce a series of resonant or vibrating sounds to signal an incoming call: *the phone rang again as I replaced it.* ■ call for service or attention by sounding a bell: *Ruth, will you ring for some tea?* ■ [with obj.] sound (the hour, a peal, etc.) on a bell or bells: *a bell ringing the hour.*
2 [with obj.] Brit. call by telephone: *I rang her this morning* | *Harriet rang Dorothy up next day* | [no obj.] *she rang to tell him the good news.*
3 [no obj.] (**ring with/to**) (of a place) resound or reverberate with (a sound or sounds): *the room rang with laughter.* ■ (of a person's ears) be filled with a continuous buzzing or humming sound, especially as the after-effect of a blow or loud noise: *he yelled so loudly that my eardrums rang.* ■ (**ring with**) be filled or permeated with (a particular quality): *a clever retort which rang with contempt.* ■ [no obj., with complement] convey a specified impression or quality: *the author's honesty rings true.*
▶ **noun 1** an act of ringing a bell, or the resonant sound caused by this: *there was a ring at the door.* ■ each of a series of resonant or vibrating sounds signalling an incoming telephone call. ■ Brit. informal a telephone

R

call: *I'd better give her a ring tomorrow.* ■ [in sing.] a loud, clear sound or tone: *the ring of sledgehammers on metal.* ■ a set of bells, especially church bells.
2 [in sing.] a particular quality conveyed by something heard or expressed: *the song had a curious ring of nostalgia to it.*
– PHRASES **ring a bell** see BELL[1]. **ring the changes** see CHANGE. **ring down** (or **up**) **the curtain** cause a theatre curtain to be lowered (or raised). ■ mark the end (or the beginning) of an enterprise or event: *the sendoff **rings down the curtain on** a major chapter in television history.* **ring in one's ears** (or **head**) linger in the memory: *he left Washington with the president's praises ringing in his ears.* **ring off the hook** N. Amer. (of a telephone) be constantly ringing due to a large number of incoming calls.
– PHRASAL VERBS **ring someone/thing in** (or **out**) usher someone or something in (or out) by ringing a bell: *the bells were beginning to ring out the old year.* **ring off** end a telephone call by replacing the receiver: *before I ring off can I have a quick word with Colin?* **ring something up** record an amount on a cash register: *he took the money for the drinks and rang it up.*
– ORIGIN Old English *hringan*, of Germanic origin, perhaps imitative.

ring-a-ring o' roses ▶ noun [mass noun] a singing game played by children, in which the players hold hands and dance in a circle, falling down at the end of the song.
– ORIGIN said to refer to the inflamed ('rose-coloured') ring of buboes, symptomatic of the plague; the final part of the game is symbolic of death.

ringbark ▶ verb [with obj.] remove a ring of bark from (a tree) in order to kill it or to check rapid growth and thereby improve fruit production.

ring binder ▶ noun Brit. a loose-leaf binder with ring-shaped clasps that can be opened to pass through holes in the paper.

ringbolt ▶ noun a bolt with a ring attached for fitting a rope to.

ringbone ▶ noun [mass noun] osteoarthritis of the pastern joint of a horse, causing swelling and lameness.

ring-bound ▶ adjective bound in a ring binder.

ring circuit ▶ noun an electric circuit serving a number of power points, with one circuit-breaker in the supply.

ringdove ▶ noun a dove or pigeon with a ring-like mark on the neck, in particular: ● Brit. the wood pigeon. ● N. Amer. a captive or feral African collared dove (*Streptopelia roseogrisea*, family Columbidae).

ring dyke ▶ noun Geology a dyke that is roughly circular in plan, formed by upwelling of magma in a conical or cylindrical fracture system.

ringed plover ▶ noun a small plover found chiefly in Eurasia, with white underparts and a black collar, breeding on sand or shingle beaches. ● Genus *Charadrius*, family Charadriidae : three species, in particular *Charadrius hiaticula*.

R

ringed seal ▶ noun a seal of arctic and subarctic waters, which has pale ring-shaped markings on the back and sides and a short muzzle. ● *Phoca hispida*, family Phocidae.

ringer ▶ noun 1 informal an athlete or horse fraudulently substituted for another in a competition or event. ■ a motor vehicle whose identity has been fraudulently changed by the substitution of a different registration plate. ■ a highly proficient person brought in supplement a team or group.
2 (also **dead ringer**) informal a person or thing that looks very like another: *he is **a dead ringer for** his late papa.*
3 a person or device that rings something.
4 Austral./NZ a shearer with the highest tally of sheep shorn in a given period. [late 19th cent.: special use of dialect *ringer* 'something exceptionally good'.]
5 Austral. a stockman, especially one employed in droving. [early 20th cent.: from *ring* 'turn (a group of cattle) back on itself, work as a drover'.]

Ringer's solution ▶ noun [mass noun] Biology a physiological saline solution that typically contains, in addition to sodium chloride, salts of potassium and calcium.
– ORIGIN late 19th cent.: named after Sydney *Ringer* (1834–1910), English physician.

ringette ▶ noun [mass noun] Canadian a game resembling ice hockey, played (especially by women and girls) with a straight stick and a rubber ring, and in which no intentional body contact is allowed.

ring fence ▶ noun a fence completely enclosing a farm or piece of land. ■ an effective or comprehensive barrier.
▶ verb (**ring-fence**) [with obj.] 1 enclose (a piece of land) with a ring fence.
2 Brit. guarantee that (funds allocated for a particular purpose) will not be spent on anything else: *the government failed to ring-fence the money provided to schools.*

ring finger ▶ noun the finger next to the little finger, especially of the left hand, on which the wedding ring is worn.

ring fort ▶ noun Archaeology a prehistoric earthwork, especially an Iron Age hill fort, defended by circular ramparts and ditches.

ringgit /'rɪŋgɪt/ ▶ noun (pl. **same** or **ringgits**) the basic monetary unit of Malaysia, equivalent to 100 sen.
– ORIGIN Malay.

ringhals /'rɪŋhals/ ▶ noun variant spelling of RINKHALS.

ring-in ▶ noun Austral./NZ a horse or an athlete fraudulently substituted for another in a competition or event. ■ a person or thing that is not a genuine member of a group or set: *are you a fair dinkum pom or a ring-in?*

ringing ▶ adjective having or emitting a clear resonant sound: *a ringing voice.* ■ (of a statement) forceful and unequivocal: *the Russian leader received a ringing declaration of support.*
▶ noun an act or sound of ringing: *the ringing of fire alarms.*
– DERIVATIVES **ringingly** adverb.

ringing tone ▶ noun a sound heard by a telephone caller when the number dialled is being rung.

ringleader ▶ noun a person who initiates or leads an illicit or illegal activity.

ringlet ▶ noun 1 a lock of hair hanging in a corkscrew-shaped curl.
2 a brown butterfly with wings bearing eyespots. ● *Aphantopus*, *Erebia*, and other genera in the subfamily Satyrinae, family Nymphalidae: several species.
– DERIVATIVES **ringletted** (also **ringleted**) adjective.

ring main ▶ noun Brit. 1 an electrical supply serving a series of consumers and returning to the original source, so that each consumer has an alternative path in the event of a failure. ■ another term for RING CIRCUIT.
2 an arrangement of pipes forming a closed loop into which steam, water, or sewage may be fed and whose points of draw-off are supplied by flow from two directions.

ringmaster ▶ noun the person directing a circus performance.

ring modulator ▶ noun an electronic circuit, especially in a musical instrument, that incorporates a closed loop of four diodes and can be used for the balanced mixing and modulation of signals.

ringneck ▶ noun any of a number of ring-necked birds, in particular: ● a common pheasant of a variety having a white neck ring. ● Austral. a green parrot with a yellow collar (genus *Barnardius*, family Psittacidae: two species). ● N. Amer. a ring-necked duck (*Aythya collaris*, family Anatidae).

ring-necked ▶ adjective used in names of birds and reptiles with a band or bands of colour round the neck, e.g. **ring-necked parakeet**.

ring ouzel (also **ring ousel**) ▶ noun a European thrush that resembles a blackbird with a white crescent across the breast, inhabiting upland moors and mountainous country. ● *Turdus torquatus*, family Turdidae.

ring pull ▶ noun Brit. a ring on a can that is pulled to break the seal in order to open it.

ring road ▶ noun Brit. a road encircling a town.

ringside ▶ noun the area immediately beside a boxing ring or circus ring.
▶ adjective & adverb beside a boxing ring or circus ring: [as adj.] *a ringside judge* | [as adv.] *Ed and I were seated ringside.*
– DERIVATIVES **ringsider** noun.

ringside seat ▶ noun a seat immediately adjacent to a boxing ring. ■ an advantageous position from which to observe or monitor something.

ring spanner ▶ noun a spanner in which the jaws form a ring with internal serrations which fit completely around a nut, usable in confined spaces.

ringster ▶ noun N. Amer. dated 1 a member of a political or price-fixing ring.
2 a boxer.

ringtail ▶ noun 1 a ring-tailed cat or lemur. ■ a female hen harrier or related harrier. ■ a golden eagle up to its third year.
2 (also **ringtail** or **ring-tailed possum**) a nocturnal tree-dwelling Australian possum that habitually curls its prehensile tail into a ring or spiral. ● Genus *Pseudocheirus* and other genera, family Petauridae: several species.

ring-tailed ▶ adjective used in names of mammals and birds that have the tail banded in contrasting colours, e.g. **ring-tailed lemur**, or curled at the end, e.g. **ring-tailed possum** (see RINGTAIL (sense 2)).

ring-tailed cat ▶ noun a nocturnal raccoon-like mammal with a dark-ringed tail, found in North America. Also called RINGTAIL, CACOMISTLE. ● *Bassariscus astutus*, family Procyonidae.

ring-tailed lemur ▶ noun a gregarious lemur with a grey coat, black rings around the eyes, and distinctive black-and-white banding on the tail. ● *Lemur catta*, family Lemuridae.

ringtone ▶ noun a sound made by a mobile phone when an incoming call is received.

ringwork ▶ noun Archaeology the circular entrenchment of a minor medieval castle, especially a fortified Norman manor.

ringworm ▶ noun [mass noun] a contagious itching skin disease occurring in small circular patches, caused by any of a number of fungi and affecting chiefly the scalp or the feet. The commonest form is athlete's foot. Also called TINEA.

rink ▶ noun 1 (also **ice rink**) an enclosed area of ice for skating, ice hockey, or curling. ■ (also **roller rink**) a smooth enclosed floor of wood or asphalt for roller skating. ■ a building containing an ice rink or roller rink. ■ (also **bowling rink**) the strip of a bowling green used for playing a match.
2 a team in curling or bowls.
– ORIGIN late Middle English (originally Scots in the sense 'jousting ground'): perhaps originally from Old French *renc* 'rank'.

rinkhals /'rɪŋkhals/ (also **ringhals**) ▶ noun a large nocturnal spitting cobra of southern Africa, with one or two white rings across the throat. ● *Hemachatus haemachatus*, family Elapidae.
– ORIGIN late 18th cent.: from Afrikaans *rinkhals*, from *ring* 'ring' + *hals* 'neck'.

rinky-dink ▶ adjective informal, chiefly N. Amer. old-fashioned, amateurish, or shoddy: *the fifty-third issue of the quarterly looked just as rinky-dink as the first.*
– ORIGIN late 19th cent.: of unknown origin.

Rinpoche /'rɪnpɒtʃeɪ/ ▶ noun a religious teacher held in high regard among Tibetan Buddhists (often used as an honorific title).
– ORIGIN Tibetan, literally 'precious jewel'.

rinse ▶ verb [with obj.] wash (something) with clean water to remove soap, detergent, dirt, or impurities: *always rinse your hair thoroughly* | [no obj.] *drain the beans and rinse well.* ■ wash (something) quickly, especially without soap: *Rose **rinsed out** a tumbler* | *Karen **rinsed** her mouth **out**.* ■ (**rinse something off/out**) remove (soap, detergent, dirt, or impurities) by washing with clean water: *the conditioning mousse doesn't have to be rinsed out.*
▶ noun 1 an act of rinsing something: *I gave my hands a quick rinse.*
2 an antiseptic solution for cleansing the mouth.
3 a preparation for conditioning or temporarily tinting the hair.
– DERIVATIVES **rinser** noun.
– ORIGIN Middle English (as a verb): from Old French *rincer*, of unknown ultimate origin.

Rio Branco /ˌriːuː 'braŋkuː/ a city in western Brazil, capital of the state of Acre; pop. 290,639 (2007).

Rio de Janeiro /ˌriːəʊ də dʒə'nɪərəʊ/ a state of eastern Brazil, on the Atlantic coast. ■ (also **Rio**) its capital; pop. 6,093,472 (2007). The chief port of Brazil, it was the country's capital from 1763 until 1960, when it was replaced by Brasilia.

Río de la Plata /ˌrriəʊ ðe la 'plata/ Spanish name for the River Plate (see PLATE, RIVER).

Río de Oro /ˌriːəʊ deɪ 'ɔːrəʊ/ an arid region on the Atlantic coast of NW Africa, forming the southern part of Western Sahara. It was united with Saguia el-Hamra in 1958 to form the province of Spanish Sahara (now Western Sahara).

Rio Grande /ˌriːəʊ 'grand, 'grandi/ a river of North America which rises in the Rocky Mountains of SW Colorado and flows 3,030 km (1,880 miles) generally south-eastwards to the Gulf of Mexico, forming the US–Mexico frontier from El Paso to the sea.

Rio Grande do Norte /ˌriːuː ˌɡrandi duː ˈnɔːti/ a state of NE Brazil, on the Atlantic coast; capital, Natal.

Rio Grande do Sul /ˌriːuː ˌɡrandi duː ˈsʊl/ a state of Brazil, situated on the Atlantic coast at the southern tip of the country, on the border with Uruguay; capital, Pôrto Alegre.

Rioja /rɪˈɒhə, rɪˈɒkə/ ▶ **noun** [mass noun] a wine produced in La Rioja, Spain.

Rio Muni /ˌriːəʊ ˈmuːni/ the part of Equatorial Guinea that lies on the mainland of West Africa. Its chief town is Bata.

Rio Negro /ˌriːəʊ ˈneɪɡrəʊ, ˈnɛɡ-/ a river of South America, which rises as the Guainia in eastern Colombia and flows for about 2,255 km (1,400 miles) through NW Brazil before joining the Amazon near Manaus.

riot ▶ **noun 1** a violent disturbance of the peace by a crowd: *riots broke out in the capital* | [mass noun] *he was convicted on charges of riot and assault* | [as modifier] *riot police.* ■ an uproar: *the film's sex scenes caused a riot in Cannes.* ■ an outburst of uncontrolled feelings: ***a riot of** emotions raged through Fabia.* ■ [mass noun] archaic uncontrolled revelry; rowdy behaviour.
2 [in sing.] an impressively large or varied display of something: *the garden was **a riot of** colour.*
3 [in sing.] informal a highly amusing or entertaining person or thing: *everyone thought she was a riot.*
▶ **verb** [no obj.] take part in a violent public disturbance: *students rioted in Paris* | (as noun **rioting**) *another night of rioting.* ■ behave in an unrestrained way: *another set of emotions rioted through him.* ■ archaic act in a dissipated way: *an unrepentant prodigal son, rioting off to far countries.*
– PHRASES **run riot** behave in a violent and unrestrained way. ■ (of a mental faculty or emotion) function or be expressed without restraint: *her imagination ran riot.* ■ proliferate or spread uncontrollably: *traditional prejudices were allowed to run riot.*
– DERIVATIVES **rioter** noun.
– ORIGIN Middle English (originally in the sense 'dissolute living'): from Old French *riote* 'debate', from *rioter* 'to quarrel', of unknown ultimate origin.

Riot Act an Act passed by the British government in 1715 and repealed in 1967, designed to prevent civil disorder. The Act made it a felony for an assembly of more than twelve people to refuse to disperse after being ordered to do so and having been read a specified section of the Act by lawful authority.
– PHRASES **read someone the Riot Act** Brit. give someone a severe warning or reprimand.

riot gear ▶ **noun** [mass noun] protective clothing and equipment worn by police or prison officers in situations of crowd violence.

riot girl (also **riot grrrl**) ▶ **noun** a member of a movement of young feminists associated with aggressive punk-style rock music.

riotous ▶ **adjective** marked by or involving public disorder: *a riotous crowd.* ■ characterized by wild and uncontrolled behaviour: *a riotous party.* ■ having a vivid, varied appearance: *a riotous display of bright red, green, and yellow vegetables.* ■ hilariously funny: *a riotous account of the making of the movie.*
– DERIVATIVES **riotously** adverb, **riotousness** noun.
– ORIGIN Middle English (in the sense 'troublesome'): from Old French, from *riote* (see **RIOT**).

RIP¹ ▶ **abbreviation** rest in peace (used on graves).
– ORIGIN from Latin *requiescat* (or, in the plural, *requiescant*) *in pace.*

RIP² /rɪp/ ▶ **noun** a raster image processor.
▶ **verb** (usu. **rip**) (**rips, ripping, ripped**) [with obj.] rasterize (an image): *once you are happy with the image, you can rip it out.*
– ORIGIN 1970s: abbreviation.

rip¹ ▶ **verb** (**rips, ripping, ripped**) **1** [with obj. and adverbial of direction] tear or pull (something) quickly or forcibly away from something or someone: *a fan tried to rip his trousers off during a show* | figurative *countries ripped apart by fighting.* ■ [with obj.] make a long tear or cut in: *you've ripped my jacket* | (as adj. **ripped**) *ripped jeans.* ■ [with obj.] make (a hole) by force: *the truck was struck by lightning and had a hole ripped out of its roof.* ■ [no obj.] come violently apart; tear: *the skirt of her frock ripped.*
2 [no obj., with adverbial of direction] move forcefully and rapidly: *fire **ripped through** her bungalow.*
3 [with obj.] Computing use a program to copy (material from a CD or DVD) on to a computer's hard drive.
▶ **noun 1** a long tear or cut. ■ [in sing.] an act of tearing something forcibly.
2 N. Amer. informal a fraud or swindle; a rip-off.
– PHRASES **let rip** informal do something vigorously or without restraint: *the brass sections let rip with sheer gusto.* ■ express oneself vehemently or angrily. **let something rip** informal allow something, especially a vehicle, to go at full speed. ■ allow something to happen forcefully or without interference: *once she started a tirade, it was best to let it rip.* ■ utter or express something forcefully and noisily: *when I passed the exam I let rip a 'yippee'.*
– PHRASAL VERBS **rip into** informal make a vehement verbal attack on: *he ripped into me just for going into the caravan.* **rip someone off** informal cheat someone, especially financially: *she thought he was ripping her off over her royalties.* **rip something off** steal or plagiarize something: *they have ripped off £6.7 billion* | *the film is a shameless collection of ideas ripped off from other movies.* **rip something up** tear something violently into small pieces so as to destroy it: *he ripped up her pile of old letters.*
– ORIGIN late Middle English (as a verb): of unknown origin; compare with the verb **REAP**. The noun dates from the early 18th cent.

rip² ▶ **noun** a stretch of fast-flowing and rough water in the sea or in a river, caused by the meeting of currents. ■ short for **RIP CURRENT**.
– ORIGIN late 18th cent.: perhaps related to **RIP¹**.

rip³ ▶ **noun** informal, dated **1** an immoral or unpleasant person. ■ a mischievous person, especially a child.
2 a worthless horse.
– ORIGIN late 18th cent.: perhaps from *rep*, abbreviation of **REPROBATE**.

riparian /rʌɪˈpɛːrɪən/ ▶ **adjective** chiefly Law relating to or situated on the banks of a river: *all the riparian states must sign an agreement.* ■ Ecology relating to wetlands adjacent to rivers and streams.
– ORIGIN mid 19th cent.: from Latin *riparius* (from *ripa* 'bank') + **-AN**.

ripcord ▶ **noun** a cord that is pulled to open a parachute.

rip current ▶ **noun** an intermittent strong surface current flowing seaward from the shore.

ripe ▶ **adjective 1** (of fruit or grain) developed to the point of readiness for harvesting and eating: *a ripe tomato.* ■ (of a cheese or wine) fully matured. ■ (of a smell or flavour) rich, intense, or pungent: *rich, ripe flavours emanate from this wine.*
2 having arrived at the fitting stage or time for a particular action or purpose): *land **ripe for** development* | *they felt that **the time was ripe for** a new approach.* ■ (**ripe with**) full of: *a population ripe with discontent.*
3 [attrib.] (of a person's age) advanced: *she lived to a ripe old age.*
4 (of a female fish or insect) ready to lay eggs or spawn.
5 informal (of a person's language) beyond the bounds of propriety; coarse.
– DERIVATIVES **ripely** adverb, **ripeness** noun.
– ORIGIN Old English *ripe*, of West Germanic origin; related to Dutch *rijp* and German *reif*.

ripen ▶ **verb** become or make ripe: [no obj.] *honeydew melons ripen slowly* | [with obj.] *for ease of harvesting, the fruit is ripened to order.*

ripieno /ˌrɪpɪˈeɪnəʊ/ ▶ **noun** (pl. **ripienos** or **ripieni** /-ni/) [usu. as modifier] Music the body of instruments accompanying the concertino in baroque concerto music: *the concertino is accompanied by ripieno strings.*
– ORIGIN early 18th cent. (in the sense 'supplementary'): from Italian, from *ri-* 'again' + *pieno* 'full'.

rip-off ▶ **noun** informal a fraud or swindle, especially something that is grossly overpriced: *designer label clothes are just expensive rip-offs.* ■ an inferior imitation of something: *rip-offs of all the latest styles.*

riposte /rɪˈpɒst/ ▶ **noun 1** a quick, clever reply to an insult or criticism.
2 a quick return thrust in fencing.
▶ **verb 1** [with direct speech] make a quick, clever reply to an insult or criticism: *'You've got a strange sense of honour,' Grant riposted.*
2 [no obj.] make a quick return thrust in fencing.
– ORIGIN early 18th cent.: from French *risposte* (noun), *risposter* (verb), from Italian *risposta* 'response'.

ripper ▶ **noun 1** a tool that is used to tear or break something. ■ a murderer who mutilates victims' bodies.
2 informal, chiefly Austral. a thing that is particularly good: *a ripper of a gig.* ■ a good snowboarder.
▶ **adjective** informal, chiefly Austral. particularly good; excellent: *everyone had a ripper time* | *this record still sounds ripper.*

ripping ▶ **adjective** Brit. informal, dated splendid; excellent: *she's going to have a ripping time.*
– DERIVATIVES **rippingly** adverb.

ripple ▶ **noun 1** a small wave or series of waves on the surface of water, especially as caused by a slight breeze or an object dropping into it. ■ a thing resembling a ripple or ripples in appearance or movement: *the sand undulated and was ridged with ripples.* ■ a gentle rising and falling sound that spreads through a group of people: *a ripple of laughter ran around the room.* ■ a particular feeling or effect that spreads through someone or something: *his words set off a ripple of excitement within her.* ■ Physics a wave on a fluid surface, the restoring force for which is provided by surface tension rather than gravity, and which consequently has a wavelength shorter than that corresponding to the minimum speed of propagation. ■ [mass noun] small periodic, usually undesirable, variations in electrical voltage superposed on a direct voltage or on an alternating voltage of lower frequency.
2 [mass noun] a type of ice cream with wavy lines of coloured flavoured syrup running through it: *a family block of raspberry ripple.*
▶ **verb** [no obj.] (of water) form or flow with small waves on the surface: *the Mediterranean rippled and sparkled* | (as adj. **rippling**) *the rippling waters.* ■ [with obj.] cause (the surface of water) to form small waves: *a cool wind rippled the surface of the estuary.* ■ move in a way resembling small waves: [no obj.] *fields of grain rippling in the wind.* ■ [no obj., with adverbial of direction] (of a sound or feeling) spread through a person, group, or place: *applause **rippled around** the tables.*
– DERIVATIVES **ripplet** noun, **ripply** adjective.
– ORIGIN late 17th cent. (as a verb): of unknown origin.

ripple effect ▶ **noun** the continuing and spreading results of an event or action.

ripple marks ▶ **plural noun** a system of parallel wavy ridges and furrows left on sand, mud, or rock by the action of water or wind.

riprap N. Amer. ▶ **noun** [mass noun] loose stone used to form a foundation for a breakwater or other structure.
▶ **verb** (**ripraps, riprapping, riprapped**) [with obj.] strengthen with riprap.
– ORIGIN mid 19th cent.: reduplication of **RAP¹**.

rip-roaring ▶ **adjective** full of energy and vigour: *a rip-roaring derby match.*
– DERIVATIVES **rip-roaringly** adverb.

ripsaw ▶ **noun** a coarse saw for cutting wood along the grain.

ripsnorting ▶ **adjective** N. Amer. informal showing great vigour or intensity: *a ripsnorting editorial.*
– DERIVATIVES **ripsnorter** noun, **ripsnortingly** adverb.

ripstop ▶ **noun** [mass noun] nylon fabric that is woven so that a tear will not spread.

R

rip tide ▶ **noun** another term for **RIP²**.

Rip Van Winkle the hero of a story in Washington Irving's *Sketch Book* (1819–20), who fell asleep in the Catskill Mountains and awoke after twenty years to find the world completely changed.

RISC ▶ **noun** [usu. as modifier] Computing computers or computing based on a form of microprocessor designed to perform a limited set of operations extremely quickly.
– ORIGIN 1980s: acronym from *reduced instruction set computer* (or *computing*).

rise ▶ **verb** (past **rose**; past participle **risen**) [no obj.] **1** move from a lower position to a higher one; come or go up: *the tiny aircraft rose from the ground.* ■ (of the sun, moon, or another celestial body) appear above the horizon: *the sun had just risen.* ■ (of a fish) come to the surface of water: *a fish rose and was hooked and landed.* ■ reach a higher position in society or one's profession: *the officer was a man of great courage who **had risen from the ranks.*** ■ (**rise above**) succeed in not being limited or constrained by (a restrictive environment or situation): *he struggled to rise above his humble background.* ■ (**rise above**) be superior to: *I try to rise above prejudice.*
2 get up from lying, sitting, or kneeling: *she pushed back her chair and rose.* ■ get out of bed, especially in the morning: *I rose and got dressed.* ■ chiefly Brit. (of a meeting or a session of a court) adjourn: *the judge's*

remark heralded the signal for the court to rise. ■ be restored to life: *three days later he rose from the dead.*
3 cease to be submissive, obedient, or peaceful: *the activists urged militant factions to **rise up**.* ■ (**rise to**) find the strength or ability to respond adequately to (a challenging situation): *many participants in the race had never sailed before, but they **rose to the challenge**.* ■ (**rise to**) (of a person) react with annoyance or argument to (provocation): *he didn't rise to my teasing.*
4 (of a river) have its source: *the Euphrates rises in Turkey.* ■ (of a wind) start to blow or to blow more strongly: *the wind continued to rise.*
5 (of land or a natural feature) incline upwards; become higher: *the moorlands rise and fall in gentle folds.* ■ (of a structure or natural feature) be much taller than the surrounding landscape: *the cliff rose more than a hundred feet above us.* ■ (of someone's hair) stand on end: *he felt the hairs rise on the back of his neck.* ■ (of a building) undergo construction from the foundations: *rows of two-storey houses are slowly rising.* ■ (of dough) swell by the action of yeast: *leave the dough in a warm place to rise.* ■ (of a bump, blister, or weal) appear as a swelling on the skin: *blisters rose on his burned hand.* ■ (of a person's stomach) become nauseated: *Fabio's stomach **rose** at the foul bedding.*
6 increase in number, size, amount, or degree: *land prices had risen.* ■ (of the sea, a river, or other body of water) increase in level, typically through tidal action or flooding: *the river level rose so high the work had to be abandoned.* ■ (of a barometer or other measuring instrument) give a higher reading. ■ (of a sound) become louder or higher in pitch: *my voice rose an octave or two as I screamed.* ■ (of an emotion) develop and become more intense: *he felt a tide of resentment rising in him.* ■ (of a person's mood) become more cheerful: *her spirits rose as they left the ugly city behind.* ■ (of the colour in a person's face) become deeper, especially as a result of embarrassment: *he was teasing her, and she could feel her colour rising.*
7 (**rising**) approaching (a specified age): *she was thirty-nine rising forty.*
▸ **noun 1** an upward movement; an instance of rising: *the bird has a display flight of steep flapping rises.* ■ an instance of social, commercial, or political advancement: *few models have had such a meteoric rise.* ■ an upward slope or hill. ■ the vertical height of a step, arch, or incline. ■ another term for **RISER** (sense 2).
2 an increase in number, size, amount, or degree: *local people are worried by the rise in crime.* ■ Brit. an increase in salary or wages.
3 an increase in sound or pitch: *the rise and fall of his voice.*
4 [in sing.] a source or origin: *it was here that the brook had its rise.*
– PHRASES **get** (or **take**) **a rise out of** informal provoke an angry or irritated response from (someone), especially by teasing. **on the rise** becoming greater or more numerous; increasing: *prices were on the rise.* ■ becoming more successful: *young stars on the rise.* **rise and shine** [usu. in imperative] informal wake up and get out of bed promptly. **rise to the bait** see **BAIT**. **rise with the sun** (or **lark**) get up early in the morning. **one's star is rising** one is becoming more successful or popular.
– ORIGIN Old English *rīsan* 'make an attack', 'wake, get out of bed', of Germanic origin; related to Dutch *rijzen* and German *reisen*.

riser ▸ **noun 1** [with adj.] a person who habitually gets out of bed at a particular time of the morning: *late risers always exasperate early risers.*
2 a vertical section between the treads of a staircase.
3 a vertical pipe for the upward flow of liquid or gas.
4 a low platform on a stage or in an auditorium, used to give greater prominence to a speaker or performer.
5 a strip of webbing joining the harness and the rigging lines of a parachute or paraglider.

rise time ▸ **noun** Electronics the time required for a pulse to rise from 10 per cent to 90 per cent of its steady value.

rishi /ˈrɪʃi/ ▸ **noun** (pl. **rishis**) a Hindu sage or saint.
– ORIGIN from Sanskrit *ṛṣi*.

risible /ˈrɪzɪb(ə)l/ ▸ **adjective** provoking laughter through being ludicrous: *a risible scene of lovemaking in a tent.*
– DERIVATIVES **risibility noun**, **risibly adverb**.
– ORIGIN mid 16th cent. (in the sense 'inclined to laughter'): from late Latin *risibilis*, from Latin *ris-* 'laughed', from the verb *ridere*.

rising ▸ **noun** an armed protest against authority; a revolt.
▸ **adjective 1** going up, increasing, or sloping upward: *the rising temperature | rising ground.* ■ advancing to maturity or high standing: *the rising generation of American writers.* ■ approaching (a specified age): *the rising fives on the verge of school.* ■ Astrology (of a sign) ascendant.
2 [postpositive] Heraldry (of a bird) depicted with the wings open but not fully displayed, as if preparing for flight.

rising damp ▸ **noun** [mass noun] Brit. moisture absorbed from the ground into a wall.

rising main ▸ **noun** Brit. a vertical pipe that rises from the ground to supply mains water to a building. ■ the vertical pipe of a water pump.

rising sign ▸ **noun** Astrology an ascendant sign.

rising trot ▸ **noun** Riding a style of riding in which a rider rises from the saddle on every second stride of a horse's trotting pace.

risk ▸ **noun** a situation involving exposure to danger: *flouting the law was too much of a risk* | [mass noun] *all outdoor activities carry an element of risk.* ■ [in sing.] the possibility that something unpleasant or unwelcome will happen: *reduce the risk of heart disease.* ■ [with modifier] a person or thing regarded as a threat or likely source of danger: *she's a security risk | gloss paint can burn strongly and pose a fire risk.* ■ (usu. **risks**) a possibility of harm or damage against which something is insured. ■ [with adj.] a person or thing regarded as likely to turn out well or badly in a particular context or respect: *Western banks regarded Romania as a good risk.* ■ [mass noun] the possibility of financial loss: *the Bank is rigorous when it comes to analysing and evaluating risk.*
▸ **verb** [with obj.] expose (someone or something valued) to danger, harm, or loss: *he risked his life to save his dog.* ■ act in such a way as to bring about the possibility of (an unpleasant or unwelcome event): *coal producers must sharpen up or risk losing half their business.* ■ incur the chance of unfortunate consequences by engaging in (an action): *Shelley was far too intelligent to risk attempting to deceive him.*
– PHRASES **at risk** exposed to harm or danger: *23 million people in Africa are **at risk from** starvation.* **at one's (own) risk** taking responsibility for one's own safety or possessions: *they undertook the adventure at their own risk.* **at the risk of doing something** although there is the possibility of something unpleasant resulting: *at the risk of boring people to tears, I repeat the most important rule in painting.* **at risk to** with the possibility of endangering: *he visited prisons at considerable risk to his health.* **risk one's neck** put one's life in danger. **run** (or **take**) **the risk** (or **risks**) expose oneself to the possibility of something unpleasant occurring: *she preferred not to **run the risk of** encountering his sister.*
– ORIGIN mid 17th cent.: from French *risque* (noun), *risquer* (verb), from Italian *risco* 'danger' and *rischiare* 'run into danger'.

risk assessment ▸ **noun** a systematic process of evaluating the potential risks that may be involved in a projected activity or undertaking.

risk capital ▸ **noun** another term for **VENTURE CAPITAL**.

risk management ▸ **noun** [mass noun] (in business) the forecasting and evaluation of financial risks together with the identification of procedures to avoid or minimize their impact.

risky ▸ **adjective** (**riskier**, **riskiest**) **1** full of the possibility of danger, failure, or loss: *it was much too risky to try to disarm him.*
2 risqué: *their risky patter made the guests laugh.*
– DERIVATIVES **riskily adverb**, **riskiness noun**.

Risorgimento /rɪˌsɔːdʒɪˈmɛntəʊ/ a movement for the unification and independence of Italy, which was achieved in 1870.

> The restoration of repressive regimes after the Napoleonic Wars led to revolts in Naples and Piedmont (1821) and Bologna (1831). With French aid, the Austrians were driven out of northern Italy by 1859, and the south was won over by Garibaldi. Voting resulted in the acceptance of Victor Emmanuel II as the first king of a united Italy in 1861.

– ORIGIN Italian, literally 'resurrection'.

risotto /rɪˈzɒtəʊ/ ▸ **noun** (pl. **risottos**) an Italian dish of rice cooked in stock with ingredients such as vegetables and meat or seafood.
– ORIGIN Italian, from *riso* 'rice'.

risqué /rɪˈskeɪ, ˈrɪskeɪ, ˈriːskeɪ/ ▸ **adjective** slightly indecent and liable to shock, especially by being sexually suggestive: *his risqué humour.*
– ORIGIN mid 19th cent.: French, past participle of *risquer* 'to risk'.

Riss /rɪs/ ▸ **noun** [usu. as modifier] Geology the penultimate Pleistocene glaciation in the Alps, possibly corresponding to the Saale of northern Europe. ■ the system of deposits laid down at this time.
– ORIGIN early 20th cent.: from the name of a tributary of the River Danube in Germany.

rissole ▸ **noun** Brit. a compressed mixture of meat and spices, coated in breadcrumbs and fried.
– ORIGIN early 18th cent.: from French, from Old French dialect *ruissole*, from a feminine form of late Latin *russeolus* 'reddish', from Latin *russus* 'red'.

Risso's dolphin /ˈrɪsəʊz/ ▸ **noun** a grey dolphin which has a rounded snout with no beak, and long black flippers, living mainly in temperate seas. Also called **GRAMPUS**. ● *Grampus griseus*, family Delphinidae.
– ORIGIN late 19th cent.: named after Giovanni A. *Risso* (1777–1845), Italian naturalist.

ristorante /ˌrɪstɒˈranteɪ, -ti/ ▸ **noun** (pl. **ristoranti** /-ti/) an Italian restaurant.
– ORIGIN Italian.

ristretto /rɪˈstrɛtəʊ/ ▸ **noun** (pl. **ristrettos**) a drink of very strong, concentrated espresso coffee.
– ORIGIN Italian, literally 'restricted', from *restringere* 'restrict'.

rit. ▸ **abbreviation** Music ■ ritardando. ■ ritenuto.

Ritalin /ˈrɪtəlɪn/ ▸ **noun** trademark for **METHYLPHENIDATE**.

ritardando /ˌrɪtɑːˈdandəʊ/ ▸ **adverb, adjective, & noun** (pl. **ritardandos** or **ritardandi** /-di/) Music another term for **RALLENTANDO**.
– ORIGIN Italian.

rite ▸ **noun** a religious or other solemn ceremony or act. ■ a body of customary observances characteristic of a Church or a part of it: *the Byzantine rite.* ■ a social custom, practice, or conventional act: *the British family Christmas rite.*
– PHRASES **rite of passage** a ceremony or event marking an important stage in someone's life, especially birth, the transition from childhood to adulthood, marriage, and death.
– ORIGIN Middle English: from Latin *ritus* '(religious) usage'.

rite de passage /ˌriːt də paˈsɑːʒ/ ▸ **noun** (pl. **rites de passage** pronunc. **same**) another term for **RITE OF PASSAGE** (see **RITE**).
– ORIGIN French.

ritenuto /ˌrɪtɛˈn(j)uːtəʊ/ Music ▸ **adverb & adjective** (especially as a direction) with an immediate reduction of speed.
▸ **noun** (pl. **ritenutos** or **ritenuti** /-ti/) an immediate reduction of speed.
– ORIGIN Italian, literally 'retained, restrained'.

ritornello /ˌrɪtɔːˈnɛləʊ/ ▸ **noun** (pl. **ritornellos** or **ritornelli** /-li/) Music a short instrumental refrain or interlude in a vocal work.
– ORIGIN Italian, diminutive of *ritorno* 'return'.

ritual ▸ **noun** a religious or solemn ceremony consisting of a series of actions performed according to a prescribed order: *ancient fertility rituals* | [mass noun] *the role of ritual in religion.* ■ a prescribed order of performing such a ceremony, especially one characteristic of a particular religion or Church. ■ a series of actions or type of behaviour regularly and invariably followed by someone: *her visits to Joy became a ritual.*
▸ **adjective** [attrib.] relating to or done as a religious or solemn rite: *ritual burial | a ritual murder.* ■ (of an action) arising from convention or habit: *the players gathered for the ritual pre-match huddle.*
– DERIVATIVES **ritually adverb**.
– ORIGIN late 16th cent. (as an adjective): from Latin *ritualis*, from *ritus* (see **RITE**).

ritual abuse (also **satanic abuse**) ▸ **noun** [mass noun] the alleged sexual abuse or murder of people, especially children, supposedly committed as part of satanic rituals.

ritualistic ▸ **adjective** relating to or characteristic of rituals followed as part of a religious or solemn ceremony: *a ritualistic act of worship.* ■ invariably performed in the same way: *the party's ritualistic display of support for their leader.*
– DERIVATIVES **ritualism noun**, **ritualist noun**, **ritualistically adverb**.

ritualization (also **ritualisation**) ▸ **noun** [mass noun] the action or process of ritualizing something. ■ Zoology the evolutionary process by which an action or behaviour pattern in an animal loses its original function but is retained for its role in display or other social interaction.

R

ritualize (also **ritualise**) ▶ **verb** [with obj.] (usu. as adj. **ritualized**) make (something) into a ritual by following a pattern of actions or behaviour: *interpreting football hooliganism as a ritualized expression of aggression.* ■ Zoology cause (an action or behaviour pattern) to undergo ritualization.

ritz ▶ **noun** [mass noun] informal **1** chiefly N. Amer. ostentatious luxury and glamour.
2 (**the Ritz**) [usu. with negative] used in reference to luxurious accommodation: *it's not the Ritz, but it's convenient, clean, and good value for money.*
– PHRASES **put on the ritz** chiefly N. Amer. make a show of luxury or extravagance.
– ORIGIN early 20th cent.: from *Ritz*, a proprietary name of luxury hotels, from César *Ritz* (1850–1918), a Swiss hotel owner.

ritzy ▶ **adjective** (**ritzier**, **ritziest**) informal expensively stylish: *the ritzy Plaza Hotel.*
– DERIVATIVES **ritzily** adverb, **ritziness** noun.

rival ▶ **noun** a person or thing competing with another for the same objective or for superiority in the same field of activity: *he has no serious rival for the job* | [as modifier] *gun battles between rival gangs.* ■ [with negative] a person or thing that equals another in quality: *she has no rivals as a female rock singer.*
▶ **verb** (**rivals**, **rivalling**, **rivalled**; US **rivals**, **rivaling**, **rivaled**) [with obj.] be or seem to be equal or comparable to: *the efficiency of the Bavarians* ***rivals that of*** *the Viennese.*
– ORIGIN late 16th cent.: from Latin *rivalis*, originally in the sense 'person using the same stream as another', from *rivus* 'stream'.

rivalrous ▶ **adjective** prone to or subject to rivalry: *rivalrous presidential aspirants.*

rivalry ▶ **noun** (pl. **rivalries**) [mass noun] competition for the same objective or for superiority in the same field: *there always has been intense rivalry between the clubs* | [count noun] *personal and political rivalries.*

rive /rʌɪv/ ▶ **verb** (past **rived**; past participle **riven** /ˈrɪv(ə)n/) literary split or tear apart violently: *the party was riven by disagreements over Europe* | figurative *he was riven with guilt.* ■ archaic split or crack (wood or stone): *the wood was riven with deep cracks.*
– ORIGIN Middle English: from Old Norse *rífa*, of unknown ultimate origin.

river ▶ **noun** a large natural stream of water flowing in a channel to the sea, a lake, or another river: *the River Danube* | *the Mekong River* | [as modifier] *river pollution.* ■ a large quantity of a flowing substance: *great* ***rivers of*** *molten lava.* ■ used in names of animals and plants living in or associated with rivers, e.g. **river dolphin**.
– PHRASES **sell someone down the river** informal betray someone, especially so as to benefit oneself. [earlier referring to the sale of a troublesome slave to the owner of a sugar-cane plantation on the lower Mississippi, where conditions were relatively harsher.] **up the river** N. Amer. informal to or in prison. [with allusion to Sing Sing prison, situated up the Hudson River from the city of New York.]
– DERIVATIVES **rivered** adjective.
– ORIGIN Middle English: from Anglo-Norman French, based on Latin *riparius*, from *ripa* 'bank of a river'.

Rivera /rɪˈvɛːrə/, Spanish /riˈβera/, Diego (1886–1957), Mexican painter. He inspired a revival of fresco painting in Latin America and the US. His largest mural is a history of Mexico for the National Palace in Mexico City (unfinished, 1929–57). He was married to Frida Kahlo.

riverbank ▶ **noun** the bank of a river.

riverbed ▶ **noun** the bed or channel in which a river flows.

river blindness ▶ **noun** [mass noun] a tropical skin disease caused by a parasitic filarial worm, transmitted by the bite of blackflies (*Simulium damnosum*) which breed in fast-flowing rivers. The larvae of the parasite can migrate into the eye and cause blindness. Also called ONCHOCERCIASIS. ● The worm is *Onchocerca volvulus*, class Phasmida.

riverboat ▶ **noun** a boat designed for use on rivers.

river capture ▶ **noun** [mass noun] Geology the natural diversion of the headwaters of one stream into the channel of another, typically resulting from rapid headward erosion by the latter stream.

river dolphin ▶ **noun** a solitary dolphin with a long slender beak, a small dorsal fin, and very poor eyesight. It lives in rivers and coastal waters of South America, India, and China, using echolocation to find its prey. ● Family Platanistidae: four genera and species.

riverfront ▶ **noun** the land or property alongside a river: *warehouses line the riverfront* | [as modifier] *a riverfront restaurant.*

riverine /ˈrɪvərʌɪn/ ▶ **adjective** technical or literary relating to or situated on a river or riverbank; riparian: *a riverine village.*

riverscape ▶ **noun** a view or prospect of a river. ■ a painting of a river or riverside scene.

Riverside a city in southern California, situated in the centre of an orange-growing region; pop. 295,357 (est. 2008).

riverside ▶ **noun** [often as modifier] the ground along a riverbank: *a riverside car park.*

rivet /ˈrɪvɪt/ ▶ **noun** a short metal pin or bolt for holding together two plates of metal, its headless end being beaten out or pressed down when in place. ■ a similar device for holding seams of clothing together.
▶ **verb** (**rivets**, **riveting**, **riveted**) [with obj.] **1** join or fasten (plates of metal) with a rivet or rivets.
2 fix (someone or something) so as to make them incapable of movement: *the grip on her arm was firm enough to* ***rivet her to the spot.*** ■ attract and completely engross (someone): *he was riveted by the newsreels shown on television.* ■ direct (one's eyes or attention) intently: *all eyes* ***were riveted on*** *him.*
– DERIVATIVES **riveter** noun.
– ORIGIN Middle English: from Old French, from *river* 'fix, clinch', of unknown ultimate origin.

riveting ▶ **adjective** completely engrossing; compelling: *the book is a riveting account of the legendary freedom fighter.*
– DERIVATIVES **rivetingly** adverb.

riviera /ˌrɪvɪˈɛːrə/ ▶ **noun** a coastal region with a subtropical climate and vegetation. ■ (**the Riviera**) part of the Mediterranean coastal region of southern France and northern Italy, extending from Cannes to La Spezia, famous for its beauty, mild climate, and fashionable resorts.
– ORIGIN mid 18th cent.: from Italian, literally 'seashore'.

rivière /ˌrɪvɪˈɛː/ ▶ **noun** a necklace of gems that increase in size towards a large central stone, typically consisting of more than one string.
– ORIGIN late 19th cent.: French, literally 'river'.

Rivne /ˈrɪvnə/ an industrial city in western Ukraine north-east of Lviv; pop. 249,000 (est. 2009). Russian name ROVNO.

rivulet /ˈrɪvjʊlɪt/ ▶ **noun 1** a small stream of water or another liquid: *sweat ran in rivulets down his back.* ■ literary a very small river or stream.
2 a brownish European moth with white markings, occurring in rough grassland. ● *Perizoma affinitatum*, family Geometridae.
– ORIGIN late 16th cent.: alteration of obsolete *riveret* (from French, literally 'small river'), perhaps suggested by Italian *rivoletto*, diminutive of *rivolo*, based on Latin *rivus* 'stream'.

rivulus /ˈrɪvjʊləs/ ▶ **noun** a small tropical American killifish of fresh and brackish water. ● Genus *Rivulus*, family Cyprinodontidae: several species, many of which are spotted.
– ORIGIN modern Latin, from Latin, literally 'small stream'.

Riyadh /riːˈjɑːd/ the capital of Saudi Arabia; pop. 4,465,000 (est. 2007). It is situated on a high plateau in the centre of the country.

riyal ▶ **noun** variant spelling of RIAL.

RKO a US film production and distribution company founded in 1928, which produced classic films such as *King Kong* (1933) and *Citizen Kane* (1941).
– ORIGIN abbreviation of *Radio-Keith-Orpheum*, from a merger of Radio Corporation of America (RCA) with the *Keith* and *Orpheum* cinema chains.

RL ▶ **abbreviation** ■ rugby league. ■ Lebanon (international vehicle registration). [from *Republic of Lebanon*.]

RLS ▶ **abbreviation** restless legs syndrome.

rly ▶ **abbreviation** railway.

RM ▶ **abbreviation** ■ Madagascar (international vehicle registration). [from French *République de Madagascar*.] ■ (in the UK) Royal Mail. ■ (in the UK) Royal Marines.

rm ▶ **abbreviation** room.

RMA ▶ **abbreviation** Royal Military Academy.

RMM ▶ **abbreviation** Mali (international vehicle registration).

RMP ▶ **abbreviation** Royal Military Police.

RMS ▶ **abbreviation** Royal Mail Ship.

r.m.s. ▶ **abbreviation** Mathematics root mean square.

RMT ▶ **abbreviation** (in the UK) National Union of Rail, Maritime, and Transport Workers.

RN ▶ **abbreviation** ■ Niger (international vehicle registration). [from French *République du Niger*.] ■ (chiefly in North America) Registered Nurse. ■ (in the UK) Royal Navy.

Rn ▶ **symbol** the chemical element radon.

RNA ▶ **noun** [mass noun] Biochemistry ribonucleic acid, a nucleic acid present in all living cells. Its principal role is to act as a messenger carrying instructions from DNA for controlling the synthesis of proteins, although in some viruses RNA rather than DNA carries the genetic information.

RNAS ▶ **abbreviation** (in the UK) Royal Naval Air Station.

RNase ▶ **noun** [mass noun] Biochemistry an enzyme which promotes the breakdown of RNA into oligonucleotides and smaller molecules.
– ORIGIN 1950s: from **RNA** + **-ASE**.

RNA virus ▶ **noun** a virus in which the genetic information is stored in the form of RNA (as opposed to DNA).

RNLI ▶ **abbreviation** (in the UK) Royal National Lifeboat Institution.

RNZAF ▶ **abbreviation** Royal New Zealand Air Force.

RNZN ▶ **abbreviation** Royal New Zealand Navy.

roach[1] ▶ **noun** (pl. **same**) an edible Eurasian freshwater fish of the carp family, popular with anglers. It can hybridize with related fishes, notably rudd and bream. ● *Rutilus rutilus*, family Cyprinidae.
– ORIGIN Middle English: from Old French *roche*, of unknown ultimate origin.

roach[2] ▶ **noun** informal **1** N. Amer. a cockroach.
2 a roll of card or paper that forms the butt of a cannabis cigarette.

roach[3] ▶ **noun** Sailing a curved part of a fore-and-aft sail extending beyond a straight line between any two of its three corners, especially on the leech side.
– ORIGIN late 18th cent.: of unknown origin.

roached ▶ **adjective** US **1** (of an animal's back) having an upward curve.
2 (of a person's hair) brushed upwards or forwards into a roll. ■ (of a horse's mane) clipped or trimmed short so that the hair stands on end.

road ▶ **noun 1** a wide way leading from one place to another, especially one with a specially prepared surface which vehicles can use: *a country road* | [as modifier] *a road accident* | [in names] *they live at 15 Park Road* | [mass noun] *the shipment of freight* ***by road.*** ■ the part of a road intended for vehicles, especially in contrast to a verge or pavement. ■ [with modifier] historical a regular trade route for a particular commodity: *the Silk Road across Asia to the West.* ■ Mining an underground passage or gallery in a mine. ■ N. Amer. a railroad. ■ Brit. a railway track, especially as clear (or otherwise) for a train to proceed: *they waited for a clear road at Hellifield Junction.*
2 a series of events or a course of action that will lead to a particular outcome: *he's well* ***on the road to*** *recovery.* ■ a particular course or direction taken or followed: *the low road of apathy and alienation*
3 [often in place names] (usu. **roads**) a partly sheltered stretch of water near the shore in which ships can ride at anchor: *Boston Roads.*
– PHRASES **down the road** informal, chiefly N. Amer. in the future. **the end of the road** see END. **hit the road** see HIT. **in** (or **out of**) **the** (or **one's**) **road** [often in imperative] informal in (or out of) someone's way. **one for the road** informal a final drink before leaving a place. **on the road 1** on a long journey or series of journeys, especially as part of one's job as a sales representative or a performer. ■ (of a person) without a permanent home and moving from place to place. **2** (of a car) in use; able to be driven. **a road to nowhere** see NOWHERE. **take to the road** (or **take the road**) set out on a journey or series of journeys.
– DERIVATIVES **roadless** adjective.
– ORIGIN Old English *rād* 'journey on horseback', 'foray'; of Germanic origin; related to the verb RIDE.

roadbed ▶ **noun** the material laid down to form a road. ■ N. Amer. the part of a road on which vehicles travel. ■ another term for TRACKBED.

road bike ▶ **noun 1** a motorcycle that meets the legal requirements for use on ordinary roads.
2 a bicycle suitable for use only on ordinary roads.

roadblock ▶ **noun** a barrier or barricade on a road, especially one set up by the authorities to stop and

R

examine traffic. ■ US a hindrance or obstruction: *the biggest roadblock to solar power is its price tag.*

road car ▶ noun a car that meets the legal requirements for use on ordinary roads, especially a racing car adapted for road use.

road fund ▶ noun Brit. historical a fund for the construction and maintenance of roads and bridges.

road fund licence ▶ noun Brit. a disc displayed on a vehicle certifying payment of road tax.

road-going ▶ adjective (of a car) meeting legal requirements for use on ordinary roads.

road hog ▶ noun informal a motorist who drives recklessly or inconsiderately, making it difficult for others to pass.

roadholding ▶ noun [mass noun] the ability of a vehicle to remain stable when moving, especially when cornering at high speeds.

roadhouse ▶ noun an inn or club on a country road.

road hump ▶ noun another term for **SLEEPING POLICEMAN**.

roadie informal ▶ noun a person employed by a touring band of musicians to set up and maintain equipment.
▶ verb [no obj.] work as a roadie.

roadkill ▶ noun a killing of an animal on the road by a vehicle. ■ [mass noun] animals killed on the road by vehicles.

roadman ▶ noun (pl. **roadmen**) archaic a man employed to repair or maintain roads.

road manager ▶ noun the organizer and supervisor of a musicians' tour.

road map ▶ noun **1** a map, especially one designed for motorists, showing the roads of a country or area.
2 a plan or strategy intended to achieve a particular goal: *a road map for peace in the region.*

road metal ▶ noun see **METAL** (sense 2 of the noun).

road movie ▶ noun a film of a genre in which the main character is travelling, either in flight or on a journey of self-discovery.

road noise ▶ noun [mass noun] noise resulting from the movement of a vehicle's tyres over the road surface.

road pricing ▶ noun [mass noun] the practice of charging motorists to use busy roads at certain times, especially to relieve congestion in urban areas.

road rage ▶ noun [mass noun] sudden violent anger provoked in a motorist by the actions of another driver.

roadroller ▶ noun a motor vehicle with a heavy roller, used in road-making.

roadrunner ▶ noun a slender fast-running bird of the cuckoo family, found chiefly in arid country from the southern US to Central America. ● Genus *Geococcyx*, family Cuculidae: two species, in particular the **(greater) roadrunner** (*G. californianus*).

road sense ▶ noun [mass noun] Brit. a person's capacity for safe behaviour on the road, especially in traffic.

roadshow ▶ noun a touring show of performers, especially pop musicians. ■ a touring political or promotional campaign. ■ each of a series of radio or television programmes broadcast on location from different venues.

R

roadside ▶ noun [often as modifier] the strip of land beside a road: *roadside cafes.*

road sign ▶ noun a sign giving information or instructions to road users.

roadstead ▶ noun another term for **ROAD** (sense 3).
– ORIGIN mid 16th cent.: from **ROAD** + obsolete *stead* 'a place'.

roadster ▶ noun an open-top car with two seats. ■ a bicycle designed for use on the road. ■ a horse for riding on the road.

road tax ▶ noun [mass noun] Brit. a periodic tax payable on motor vehicles using public roads.

road test ▶ noun a test of the performance of a vehicle or engine on the road. ■ a test of equipment carried out under actual operating conditions.
▶ verb (**road-test**) [with obj.] test (a vehicle or engine) on the road. ■ try out (something) under actual operating conditions for review or prior to purchase or release: *we road-tested a new laptop computer.*

Road Town the capital of the British Virgin Islands, situated on the island of Tortola; pop. 9,300 (est. 2009).

road train ▶ noun chiefly Austral. a large lorry pulling one or more trailers.

road trip ▶ noun **1** a journey made by car, bus, etc.
2 N. Amer. a series of sporting fixtures played away from home.
▶ verb (**road-trip**) [no obj.] N. Amer. make a journey by car, bus, etc.: *they road-tripped from New Jersey to Hollywood.*
– DERIVATIVES **road-tripper** noun.

road warrior ▶ noun US informal a person who travels frequently as part of their job and does much work while travelling.

roadway ▶ noun a road. ■ the part of a road intended for vehicles, in contrast to the pavement or verge. ■ the part of a bridge or railway used by traffic.

roadwork ▶ noun [mass noun] **1** (**roadworks**) Brit. work done in building or repairing roads.
2 athletic exercise or training involving running on roads.

roadworthy ▶ adjective (of a motor vehicle or bicycle) fit to be used on the road.
– DERIVATIVES **roadworthiness** noun.

roam ▶ verb [no obj., with adverbial of direction] move about or travel aimlessly or unsystematically, especially over a wide area: *tigers once **roamed over** most of Asia* | (as adj. **roaming**) *roaming elephants.* ■ [with obj.] travel unsystematically over, through, or about (a place): *gangs of youths roamed the streets unopposed.* ■ (of a person's eyes or hands) pass lightly over something without stopping: *her eyes roamed over the chattering women* | [with obj.] *he let his eyes roam her face.* ■ [no obj.] (of a person's mind or thoughts) drift along without dwelling on anything in particular: *he let his mind roam as he walked.* ■ (often as noun **roaming**) use a mobile phone on another operator's network, typically while abroad: *packages in which you pay a slightly higher fee when roaming on other networks.*
▶ noun [in sing.] an aimless walk.
– DERIVATIVES **roamer** noun.
– ORIGIN Middle English: of unknown origin.

roan[1] ▶ adjective denoting an animal, especially a horse or cow, having a coat of a main colour thickly interspersed with hairs of another colour, typically bay, chestnut, or black mixed with white.
▶ noun [usu. with modifier] a roan animal: *a blue roan.*
– ORIGIN mid 16th cent.: from Old French, of unknown origin.

roan[2] ▶ noun [mass noun] soft flexible leather made from sheepskin, used in bookbinding as a substitute for morocco.
– ORIGIN early 19th cent.: perhaps from *Roan*, the old name of the French town of **ROUEN**.

roan antelope ▶ noun an African antelope with black-and-white facial markings, a mane of stiff hair, and large backwardly curving horns. ● *Hippotragus equinus*, family Bovidae.

ROAR ▶ abbreviation right of admission reserved.

roar ▶ noun a full, deep, prolonged cry uttered by a lion or other large wild animal. ■ a loud, deep sound uttered by a person or crowd, generally as an expression of pain, anger, or approval: *he gave a roar of rage.* ■ a loud outburst of laughter. ■ a very loud, deep, prolonged sound made by something inanimate: *the roar of the sea.*
▶ verb **1** [no obj.] (of a lion or other large wild animal) utter a full, deep, prolonged cry. ■ (of a person or crowd) utter a loud, deep, prolonged sound, typically from anger, pain, or excitement: *Manfred roared with rage.* ■ (of something inanimate) make a very loud, deep, prolonged sound: *a huge fire roared in the grate.* ■ [with obj.] utter or express in a loud tone: *the crowd roared its approval* | [with direct speech] *'Get out of my way!' he roared.* ■ [with obj. and adverbial] (of a crowd) encourage (someone) to do something by loud shouts or cheering: *Damon Hill will be **roared on** this weekend by a huge home crowd.* ■ laugh loudly: *Shirley roared in amusement.* ■ (of a horse) make a loud noise in breathing as a symptom of disease of the larynx.
2 [no obj., with adverbial] (especially of a vehicle) move at high speed making a loud prolonged sound: *a car roared past.* ■ act or happen fast and decisively or conspicuously: *Swindon roared back with two goals.*
– DERIVATIVES **roarer** noun.
– ORIGIN Old English *rārian* (verb), imitative of a deep prolonged cry, of West Germanic origin; related to German *röhren*. The noun dates from late Middle English.

roaring ▶ adjective [attrib.] **1** making or uttering a roar: *he was greeted everywhere with roaring crowds* | *a swollen, roaring river.* ■ (of a fire) burning fiercely and noisily. ■ chiefly archaic behaving or living in a noisy riotous manner: *a roaring boy.* ■ (of a period of time) characterized by prosperity, optimism, and excitement: *the Roaring Twenties.*
2 informal very obviously or unequivocally the thing mentioned (used for emphasis): *last week's 70s night was a **roaring success*** | [as submodifier] *two roaring drunk firemen.*
– PHRASES **do a roaring trade** (or **business**) informal do very good business. **the roaring forties** stormy ocean tracts between latitudes 40° and 50° south.
– DERIVATIVES **roaringly** adverb.

roast ▶ verb [with obj.] **1** cook (food, especially meat) by prolonged exposure to heat in an oven or over a fire: *she was going to roast a leg of mutton for Sunday dinner* | (as adj. **roasted**) *roasted chestnuts.* ■ [no obj.] (of food) be cooked in such a way: *she checked the meat roasting in the oven for lunch.* ■ process (a foodstuff, metal ore, etc.) by subjecting it to intense heat: *decaffeinated coffee beans are roasted and ground.* ■ make or become very warm, especially through exposure to the heat of the sun or a fire: [with obj.] *the fire was hot enough to roast anyone who stood close to it* | [no obj.] *Jessica could feel her face begin to roast.*
2 informal criticize or reprimand severely: *if you waste his time he'll roast you.*
3 N. Amer. informal tease in a good-natured way.
▶ adjective [attrib.] (of food) having been roasted: *a plate of cold roast beef.*
▶ noun a joint of meat that has been roasted or that is intended for roasting: *carving the Sunday roast.* ■ [mass noun] the process of roasting something, especially coffee, or the result of this. ■ [with adj.] a particular type of roasted coffee: *continental roasts.* ■ an outdoor party at which meat is roasted: *Harold put on a terrific pig roast.*
– ORIGIN Middle English: from Old French *rostir*, of West Germanic origin.

roaster ▶ noun a container, oven, furnace, or apparatus for roasting something. ■ a foodstuff that is particularly suitable for roasting, especially a chicken.

roasting ▶ noun **1** [mass noun] the action of cooking something in an oven or over an open fire.
2 [in sing.] informal a severe criticism or reprimand: *banks are to get a roasting from the Treasury.*
▶ adjective informal very hot and dry: *a roasting day in London.*

rob ▶ verb (**robs, robbing, robbed**) [with obj.] take property unlawfully from (a person or place) by force or threat of force: *he tried, with three others, to rob a bank* | *she was **robbed of** her handbag.* ■ informal overcharge (someone) for something: *Bob thinks my suit cost £70, and even then he thinks I was robbed.* ■ informal or dialect steal: *someone had robbed my jacket.* ■ (**rob someone of**) deprive someone of (something needed or deserved): *poor health has robbed her of a normal social life.* ■ Soccer deprive (an opposing player) of the ball: *Hughes robbed Vonk yards inside the City half.*
– PHRASES **rob Peter to pay Paul** take something away from one person to pay another; discharge one debt only to incur another. [probably with reference to the saints and apostles *Peter* and *Paul*; the allusion is uncertain, the phrase often showing variations such as 'unclothe Peter and clothe Paul', 'borrow from Peter ...', etc.]
– ORIGIN Middle English: from Old French *rober*, of Germanic origin; related to the verb **REAVE**.

robata /rɒˈbɑːtə/ ▶ noun a type of charcoal grill used in Japanese cooking.
– ORIGIN Japanese, literally 'open fireplace'.

Robbe-Grillet /rɒbˈɡriːeɪ/, French /ʀɔbɡʀijɛ/, Alain (1922–2008), French novelist. His first novel, *The Erasers* (1953), was an early example of the *nouveau roman*. He also wrote essays and screenplays.

Robben Island /ˈrɒb(ə)n/ a small island off the coast of South Africa, near Cape Town. It is the site of the former prison used for the detention of political prisoners, including Nelson Mandela.

robber ▶ noun a person who commits robbery.
– ORIGIN Middle English: from Anglo-Norman French and Old French *robere*, from the verb *rober* (see **ROB**).

robber baron ▶ noun a ruthless and unscrupulous plutocrat.
– ORIGIN originally denoting a feudal lord who engaged in plundering.

robber crab ▶ noun a large terrestrial crablike crustacean which climbs coconut palms to feed on the nuts, found on islands in the Indo-Pacific area. Also called **COCONUT CRAB**. ● *Birgus latro*, family Paguridae.

robber fly ▶ noun a large, powerful predatory fly which darts out and grabs insect prey on the wing. ● Family Asilidae: many genera.

robbery ▶ noun (pl. **robberies**) [mass noun] the action of robbing a person or place: *he was involved in drugs, extortion, and robbery* | [count noun] *an armed robbery.* ■ informal unashamed swindling or overcharging.
– ORIGIN Middle English: from Anglo-Norman French and Old French *roberie*, from the verb *rober* (see **ROB**).

Robbia see **DELLA ROBBIA**.

Robbins, Jerome (1918–98), American ballet dancer and choreographer. He choreographed a number of successful musicals, including *The King and I* (1951), *West Side Story* (1957), and *Fiddler on the Roof* (1964).

robe ▶ noun **1** a long, loose outer garment reaching to the ankles. ■ (often **robes**) a robe worn, especially on formal or ceremonial occasions, as an indication of the wearer's rank, office, or profession. ■ a dressing gown or bathrobe.
2 N. Amer. a lap robe.
▶ verb [with obj.] (usu. as adj. **robed**) clothe in a robe: *a circle of robed figures* | [in combination] *a white-robed Bedouin.* ■ [no obj.] put on robes, especially for a formal or ceremonial occasion: *I went into the vestry and robed for the Mass.*
– ORIGIN Middle English: from Old French, from the Germanic base (in the sense 'booty') of **ROB** (because clothing was an important component of booty).

Robert the name of three kings of Scotland:
■ **Robert I** (1274–1329), reigned 1306–29; known as **Robert the Bruce**. He campaigned against Edward I, and defeated Edward II at Bannockburn (1314). He re-established Scotland as a separate kingdom, negotiating the Treaty of Northampton (1328).
■ **Robert II** (1316–90), grandson of Robert the Bruce, reigned 1371–90. He was steward of Scotland from 1326 to 1371, and the first of the Stuart line.
■ **Robert III** (*c.*1337–1406), son of Robert II, reigned 1390–1406; born *John*. An accident made him physically disabled, resulting in a power struggle among members of his family.

Roberts, Frederick Sleigh, 1st Earl Roberts of Kandahar (1832–1914), British Field Marshal. He helped suppress the Indian Mutiny of 1857–8, secured victory at Kandahar (1880), ending the Second Afghan War, and planned the successful march on the Boer capital of Pretoria (1900) during the Second Boer War.

Robert the Bruce see **ROBERT**.

Robeson /ˈrəʊbs(ə)n/, Paul (Bustill) (1898–1976), American singer and actor. His singing of 'Ol' Man River' in the musical *Showboat* (1927) established his international reputation. His black activism and Communist sympathies led to ostracism in the 1950s.

Robespierre /ˈrəʊbzpjɛː/, French /ʀɔbɛspjɛʀ/, Maximilien François Marie Isidore de (1758–94), French revolutionary. As leader of the radical Jacobins in the National Assembly he backed the execution of Louis XVI, implemented a purge of the Girondists, and initiated the Terror, but the following year he fell from favour and was guillotined.

Robey, Sir George (1869–1954), English comedian and actor; born *George Edward Wade*. He performed in music halls and films.

robin ▶ noun **1** a small Old World thrush related to the chats, typically having a brown back with red on the breast or other colourful markings. ● *Erithacus* and other genera, family Turdidae: numerous species, e.g. the familiar **European robin** or redbreast (*E. rubecula*), which has an orange-red face and breast.
2 [usu. with adj. or noun modifier] any of a number of other birds that resemble the European robin, especially in having a red breast: ● a large New World thrush (genus *Turdus*, family Turdidae), in particular the **American robin** (*T. migratorius*). ● Austral./NZ a small songbird related to the flycatchers (family Eopsaltridae, in particular genus *Petroica*).
– ORIGIN mid 16th cent.: from Old French, pet form of the given name *Robert*.

robin-chat ▶ noun an African chat with a mainly dark back and orange underparts. ● Genus *Cossypha* (and *Pseudocossyphus*), family Turdidae: several species.

Robin Goodfellow a mischievous sprite or goblin believed, especially in the 16th and 17th centuries, to haunt the English countryside. Also called **PUCK**.

robing room ▶ noun a room where holders of ceremonial office put on official robes.

Robin Hood a semi-legendary English medieval outlaw, reputed to have robbed the rich and helped the poor. Although he is generally associated with Sherwood Forest in Nottinghamshire, it seems likely that the real Robin Hood operated in Yorkshire in the early 13th century. ■ (as noun **a Robin Hood**) a person considered to be taking from the wealthy and giving to the poor.

robinia /rəˈbɪnɪə/ ▶ noun a North American tree or shrub of a genus that includes the false acacia. ● Genus *Robinia*, family Leguminosae.
– ORIGIN modern Latin, named after Jean and Vespasien *Robin*, 17th-cent. French gardeners to the royal family in Paris.

robin's-egg (also **robin's-egg blue** or **robin-egg**) ▶ noun [mass noun] N. Amer. a greenish-blue colour.

Robinson[1], Edward G. (1893–1972), Romanian-born American actor; born *Emanuel Goldenberg*. He appeared in a number of gangster films in the 1930s, starting with *Little Caesar* (1930).

Robinson[2], (William) Heath (1872–1944), English cartoonist and illustrator. He lampooned the machine age by inventing absurdly complicated 'Heath Robinson contraptions' to perform elementary or ridiculous actions.

Robinson[3], Smokey (b.1940), American soul singer and songwriter; born *William Robinson*. He is known for a series of successes with his group the Miracles, such as 'Tracks of my Tears' (1965).

Robinson[4], Sugar Ray (1920–89), American boxer; born *Walker Smith*. He was world welterweight champion and seven times middleweight champion.

Robinson Crusoe /ˈkruːsəʊ/ the hero of Daniel Defoe's novel *Robinson Crusoe* (1719), who survives a shipwreck and lives for years on a desert island.

robin's pincushion ▶ noun another term for **BEDEGUAR**.

robocall ▶ noun US an automated telephone call which delivers a recorded message, typically on behalf of a political party or telemarketing company.
– ORIGIN 1990s: blend of **ROBOT** and **CALL**.

robot /ˈrəʊbɒt/ ▶ noun **1** a machine capable of carrying out a complex series of actions automatically, especially one programmable by a computer. ■ (especially in science fiction) a machine resembling a human being and able to replicate certain human movements and functions automatically. ■ a person who behaves in a mechanical or unemotional manner: *public servants are not expected to be mindless robots.*
2 another term for **CRAWLER** (in the computing sense).
3 S. African a set of automatic traffic lights.
– ORIGIN from Czech, from *robota* 'forced labour'. The term was coined in K. Čapek's play *R.U.R.* 'Rossum's Universal Robots' (1920).

robotic /rə(ʊ)ˈbɒtɪk/ ▶ adjective relating to robots: *a robotic device for performing surgery.* ■ resembling or characteristic of a robot, especially in being stiff or unemotional: *his robotic voice.*
– DERIVATIVES **robotically** adverb.

robotics ▶ plural noun [treated as sing.] the branch of technology that deals with the design, construction, operation, and application of robots.

robotize (also **robotise**) ▶ verb [with obj.] (usu. as adj. **robotized**) convert (a production system, factory, etc.) to operation by robots.
– DERIVATIVES **robotization** noun.

Rob Roy[1] (1671–1734), Scottish outlaw; born *Robert Macgregor*. His reputation as a Scottish Robin Hood was exaggerated in Sir Walter Scott's novel of the same name (1817).

Rob Roy[2] ▶ noun a cocktail made of Scotch whisky and vermouth.

Robsart /ˈrɒbsɑːt/, Amy (1532–60), English noblewoman, wife of Robert Dudley, Earl of Leicester. Her mysterious death aroused suspicions that her husband had had her killed so that he could be free to marry Queen Elizabeth I.

robust ▶ adjective (**robuster**, **robustest**) **1** (of an object) sturdy in construction: *a robust metal cabinet.* ■ strong and healthy; vigorous: *the Caplan family are a robust lot.* ■ (of a system, organization, etc.) able to withstand or overcome adverse conditions: *the country's political system has continued to be robust in spite of its economic problems.* ■ uncompromising and forceful: *he took quite a robust view of my case.*
2 (of wine or food) strong and rich in flavour or smell: *a robust mixture of fish, onions, capers and tomatoes.*
– DERIVATIVES **robustly** adverb, **robustness** noun.
– ORIGIN mid 16th cent.: from Latin *robustus* 'firm and hard', from *robus*, earlier form of *robur* 'oak, strength'.

robusta ▶ noun **1** [mass noun] coffee or coffee beans from a widely grown kind of coffee plant. Beans of this variety are often used in the manufacture of instant coffee.
2 the tropical West African bush that produces robusta coffee beans. ● *Coffea canephora* (formerly *robusta*), family Rubiaceae. See also **ARABICA**.
– ORIGIN early 20th cent.: modern Latin, feminine of Latin *robustus* 'robust'.

ROC ▶ abbreviation historical (in the UK) Royal Observer Corps.

roc ▶ noun a gigantic mythological bird described in the Arabian Nights.
– ORIGIN late 16th cent.: ultimately from Persian *ruḵ*.

rocaille /rə(ʊ)ˈkʌɪ/ ▶ noun **1** [mass noun] an 18th-century artistic or architectural style of decoration characterized by elaborate ornamentation with pebbles and shells, typical of grottos and fountains.
2 a tiny ornamental bead.
– ORIGIN French, from *roc* 'rock'.

rocambole /ˈrɒk(ə)mbəʊl/ ▶ noun a Eurasian plant that is closely related to garlic and is sometimes used as a flavouring. ● *Allium scorodoprasum*, family Liliaceae (or Alliaceae).
– ORIGIN late 17th cent.: from French, from German *Rockenbolle*.

ROCE ▶ abbreviation Finance return on capital employed.

Roche limit /rəʊʃ/ (also **Roche's limit**) ▶ noun Astronomy the distance within which the gravitational field of a large body is strong enough to prevent any smaller body from being held together by gravity.
– ORIGIN late 19th cent.: named after Edouard Albert *Roche* (1820–83), French mathematician.

roche moutonnée /ˌrɒʃ muːˈtɒneɪ/ ▶ noun (pl. **roches moutonnées** pronunc. **same**) Geology a small bare outcrop of rock shaped by glacial erosion, with one side smooth and gently sloping and the other steep, rough, and irregular.
– ORIGIN mid 19th cent.: French, literally 'fleecy rock'.

Rochester[1] /ˈrɒtʃɪstə/ **1** a town on the Medway estuary in Kent, SE England; pop. 31,000 (est. 2009).
2 a city in NW New York State, on Lake Ontario; pop. 206,886 (est. 2008).

Rochester[2] /ˈrɒtʃɪstə/, John Wilmot, 2nd Earl of (1647–80), English poet and courtier. Infamous for his dissolute life at the court of Charles II, he wrote sexually explicit love poems and verse satires.

rochet /ˈrɒtʃɪt/ ▶ noun Christian Church a vestment resembling a surplice, used chiefly by bishops and abbots.
– ORIGIN Middle English: from Old French, a diminutive from a Germanic base shared by German *Rock* 'coat'.

rock[1] ▶ noun **1** [mass noun] the solid mineral material forming part of the surface of the earth and other similar planets, exposed on the surface or underlying the soil. ■ [count noun] a mass of rock projecting above the earth's surface or out of the sea: *there are dangerous rocks around the island.* ■ [count noun] Geology any natural material, hard or soft (e.g. clay), having a distinctive mineral composition. ■ (**the Rock**) informal name for Gibraltar or (Canadian) Newfoundland.
2 a large piece of rock which has become detached from a cliff or mountain; a boulder: *the stream flowed through a jumble of rocks.* ■ N. Amer. a stone of any size. ■ [mass noun] Brit. a kind of hard confectionery in the form of cylindrical peppermint-flavoured sticks. ■ informal a precious stone, especially a diamond. ■ informal a small piece of crack cocaine. ■ (**rocks**) vulgar slang a man's testicles.
3 used to refer to someone or something that is extremely strong, reliable, or hard: *the Irish scrum has been as solid as a rock.*
4 (usu. **rocks**) (especially with allusion to shipwrecks) a source of danger or destruction: *the new system is **heading for the rocks**.*
5 (**rocks**) US informal, dated money.
– PHRASES **between a rock and a hard place** informal faced with two equally undesirable alternatives. **get one's rocks off** vulgar slang have an orgasm. ■ obtain pleasure or satisfaction. **on the rocks** informal **1** (of a relationship or enterprise) experiencing difficulties and likely to fail. **2** (of a drink) served undiluted and with ice cubes.
– DERIVATIVES **rock-like** adjective.
– ORIGIN Middle English: from Old French *rocque*, from medieval Latin *rocca*, of unknown ultimate origin.

rock[2] ▶ verb **1** move gently to and fro or from side to side: [with obj.] *she rocked the baby in her arms* | [no obj.] *the vase rocked back and forth on its base* | (as adj. **rocking**) *the rocking movement of the boat.* ■ (with

reference to a building or region) shake or cause to shake or vibrate, especially because of an impact, earthquake, or explosion: [with obj.] *minutes later a second blast rocked the city* | [no obj.] *the building began to rock on its foundations.* ■ [with obj.] cause great shock or distress to (someone or something), especially so as to weaken or destabilize: *diplomatic upheavals that rocked the British Empire.*
2 [no obj.] informal dance to or play rock music. ■ (of a place) be exciting or full of social activity: *the new town really rocks* | (as adj. **rocking**) *a rocking resort.* ■ be very good or pleasing: *this is when the job really rocks.*
3 [with obj.] informal wear (a garment) or affect (an attitude or style), especially in a confident or flamboyant way: *she was rocking a clingy little leopard-skin number.*
▶ **noun 1** [mass noun] rock music: [as modifier] *a rock star.* ■ rock and roll.
2 a gentle movement to and fro or from side to side: *she placed the baby in the cot and gave it a rock.*
– PHRASES **rock the boat** see BOAT.
– PHRASAL VERBS **rock out** perform rock music loudly and vigorously. **rock up** Brit. informal arrive; turn up: *they rocked up at about 2.00 p.m.*
– ORIGIN late Old English *roccian*, probably from a Germanic base meaning 'remove, move'; related to Dutch *rukken* 'jerk, tug' and German *rücken* 'move'.

rockabilly ▶ **noun** [mass noun] a type of popular music, originating in the south-eastern US in the 1950s, combining elements of rock and roll and country music.
– ORIGIN 1950s: blend of ROCK AND ROLL and HILLBILLY.

Rockall a rocky islet in the North Atlantic, about 400 km (250 miles) north-west of Ireland. It was formally annexed by Britain in 1955 but has since become the subject of territorial dispute between Britain, Denmark, Iceland, and Ireland. ■ a shipping forecast area in the NE Atlantic, containing the islet of Rockall near its northern boundary.

rock and roll (also **rock 'n' roll**) ▶ **noun** [mass noun] a type of popular dance music originating in the 1950s, characterized by a heavy beat and simple melodies. Rock and roll was an amalgam of black rhythm and blues and white country music, usually based around a twelve-bar structure and an instrumentation of guitar, double bass, and drums.
– DERIVATIVES **rock and roller** noun.

rock bass ▶ **noun** a red-eyed North American freshwater fish of the sunfish family, found chiefly in rocky streams. Also called RED-EYE. ● *Ambloplites rupestris*, family Centrarchidae.

rock borer ▶ **noun** any of a number of burrowing bivalve molluscs which bore into rock and other hard materials, in particular: ● a mussel with a cigar shaped shell, occurring in warm seas (genus *Lithophaga*, family Mytilidae). ● a clam with an oval to oblong shell (genus *Hiatella*, family Hiatellidae).

rock-bottom ▶ **adjective** at the lowest possible level: *rock-bottom prices.* ■ fundamental: *a pure, rock-bottom kind of realism.*
▶ **noun** (**rock bottom**) the lowest possible level: *the morale of Britain's family doctors was* **at rock bottom**.

R

rock-bound ▶ **adjective** (of a coast or shore) rocky and inaccessible.

rockburst ▶ **noun** Mining a sudden, violent rupture or collapse of highly stressed rock in a mine.

rock cake ▶ **noun** chiefly Brit. a small currant cake with a hard rough surface.

rock candy ▶ **noun** [mass noun] N. Amer. a kind of hard confectionery typically made of masses of crystallized sugar.

rock climbing ▶ **noun** [mass noun] the sport or pastime of climbing rock faces, especially with the aid of ropes and special equipment.
– DERIVATIVES **rock-climb** verb, **rock climber** noun.

rock cod ▶ **noun** any of a number of marine fishes that frequent rocky habitats, especially in Australian waters. ● Several species, chiefly in the families Scorpaenidae and Serranidae.

Rock Cornish (also **Rock Cornish hen** or **Rock Cornish game hen**) ▶ **noun** a stocky chicken of a breed which is kept for its meat.

rock cress ▶ **noun** another term for ARABIS.

rock crystal ▶ **noun** [mass noun] transparent quartz, typically in the form of colourless hexagonal crystals.

rock cycle ▶ **noun** Geology an idealized cycle of processes undergone by rocks in the earth's crust, involving igneous intrusion, uplift, erosion, transportation, deposition as sedimentary rock, metamorphism, and further melting and igneous intrusion.

rock dove ▶ **noun** a mainly grey Old World pigeon that frequents coastal and inland cliffs. It is the ancestor of domestic and feral pigeons. ● *Columba livia*, family Columbidae.

Rockefeller /ˈrɒkəfɛlə/, John D. (1839–1937), American industrialist and philanthropist; full name *John Davison Rockefeller*. By 1880 he exercised a virtual monopoly over oil refining in the US. Both he and his son, **John D. Rockefeller Jr** (1874–1960), established many philanthropic institutions.

rocker ▶ **noun 1** a person who performs, dances to, or enjoys rock music: *a punk rocker.* ■ a rock song. ■ Brit. a young person, especially in the 1960s, belonging to a subculture characterized by leather clothing, riding motorcycles, and a liking for rock music.
2 a rocking device forming part of a mechanism, especially one for controlling the positions of brushes in a dynamo.
3 a curved bar or similar support on which something such as a chair or cradle can rock. ■ a rocking chair.
4 [mass noun] the amount of curvature in the longitudinal contour of a boat or surfboard.
– PHRASES **off one's rocker** informal mad.

rocker arm ▶ **noun** a rocking lever in an engine, especially one in an internal-combustion engine which serves to work a valve and is operated by a pushrod from the camshaft.

rocker panel ▶ **noun** (in a motor vehicle) a panel forming part of the bodywork below the level of the passenger door.

rocker switch ▶ **noun** an electrical on/off switch incorporating a spring-loaded rocker.

rockery ▶ **noun** (pl. **rockeries**) a heaped arrangement of rough stones with soil between them, planted with rock plants, especially alpines.

rocket[1] ▶ **noun 1** a cylindrical projectile that can be propelled to a great height or distance by the combustion of its contents, used typically as a firework or signal. ■ (also **rocket engine** or **rocket motor**) an engine operating on the same principle, providing thrust as in a jet engine but without depending on the intake of air for combustion. ■ an elongated rocket-propelled missile or spacecraft. ■ used to refer to a person or thing that moves very fast or to an action that is done with great force: *she shot out of her chair like a rocket.*
2 [in sing.] Brit. informal a severe reprimand.
▶ **verb** (**rockets**, **rocketing**, **rocketed**) **1** [no obj.] (of an amount, price, etc.) increase very rapidly and suddenly: *sales of milk in supermarkets are rocketing* | (as adj. **rocketing**) *rocketing prices.* ■ [with adverbial of direction] move very rapidly: [no obj.] *he rocketed to national stardom* | [with obj.] *she showed the kind of form that rocketed her to the semi-finals last year.*
2 [with obj.] attack with rocket-propelled missiles: *the city was rocketed and bombed from the air.*
– PHRASES **rise like a rocket** (**and fall like a stick**) rise suddenly and dramatically (and subsequently fall in a similar manner).
– ORIGIN early 17th cent.: from French *roquette*, from Italian *rocchetto*, diminutive of *rocca* 'distaff (for spinning)', with reference to its cylindrical shape.

rocket[2] ▶ **noun** (also **garden rocket** or **salad rocket**) [mass noun] Brit. an edible Mediterranean plant of the cabbage family, whose leaves are eaten in salads. ● *Eruca vesicaria sativa*, family Cruciferae.
■ used in names of other fast-growing plants of this family, e.g. **London rocket**, **sweet rocket**.
– ORIGIN late 15th cent.: from French *roquette*, from Italian *ruchetta*, diminutive of *ruca*, from Latin *cruca* 'downy-stemmed plant'.

rocketeer ▶ **noun** a person who works with space rockets; a rocket enthusiast.

rocketry ▶ **noun** [mass noun] the branch of science that deals with rockets and rocket propulsion. ■ the use of rockets.

rocket science ▶ **noun** [mass noun] [usu. with negative] humorous something very difficult to understand: *we want you to get out and vote—it's not exactly rocket science.*
– DERIVATIVES **rocket scientist** noun.

rock face ▶ **noun** a bare vertical surface of natural rock.

rockfall ▶ **noun** an avalanche of loose rocks. ■ a mass of fallen rock.

rockfish ▶ **noun** (pl. **same** or **rockfishes**) a marine fish of the scorpionfish family with a laterally compressed body. It is generally a bottom-dweller in rocky areas and is frequently of sporting or commercial value. ● Genus *Sebastes*, family Scorpaenidae: numerous species.

rock flour ▶ **noun** [mass noun] finely powdered rock formed by glacial or other erosion.

rockfowl ▶ **noun** a long-necked crow-sized bird with a brightly coloured bare head, found in the forests of West Africa and nesting in caves. Also called BALD CROW. ● Genus *Picathartes*, family Picathartidae (or Timaliidae): two species.

rock garden ▶ **noun** a mound or bank built of earth and stones, and planted with rock plants; a rockery. ■ a garden in which rockeries are the chief feature.

Rockhampton a port on the Fitzroy River, in Queensland, NE Australia; pop. 58,749 (2006). It is the centre of Australia's largest beef-producing area.

rockhopper (also **rockhopper penguin**) ▶ **noun** a small penguin with a yellowish crest, breeding on subantarctic coastal cliffs which it ascends by hopping from rock to rock. ● *Eudyptes chrysocome*, family Spheniscidae.

rockhound ▶ **noun** informal, chiefly N. Amer. a geologist or amateur collector of mineral specimens.
– DERIVATIVES **rockhounding** noun.

rock hyrax ▶ **noun** an African hyrax (mammal) that lives on rocky outcrops and cliffs and feeds mainly on grass. Also called DASSIE. ● Genus *Procavia* (and *Heterohyrax*), family Procaviidae: several species.

Rockies another name for the ROCKY MOUNTAINS.

rocking chair ▶ **noun** a chair mounted on rockers or springs, which can rock back and forth.

rocking horse ▶ **noun** a model of a horse mounted on rockers or springs for a child to sit on and rock to and fro.

rocking stone ▶ **noun** a boulder poised in such a way that it can be easily rocked.

rockling ▶ **noun** a slender marine fish of the cod family, typically occurring in shallow water or tidal pools. ● Genera *Ciliata* and *Rhinomenus*, family Gadidae: several species.

rock lobster ▶ **noun** another term for SPINY LOBSTER.

rock maple ▶ **noun** North American term for SUGAR MAPLE.

rock melon ▶ **noun** another term for CANTALOUPE.

rock music ▶ **noun** [mass noun] a form of popular music which evolved from rock and roll and pop music during the mid and late 1960s. Harsher and often self-consciously more serious than its predecessors, it was initially characterized by musical experimentation and drug-related or anti-establishment lyrics. ■ another term for ROCK AND ROLL.

rock 'n' roll ▶ **noun** variant spelling of ROCK AND ROLL.

Rock of Gibraltar see GIBRALTAR.

rock pigeon ▶ **noun** another term for ROCK DOVE.

rock pipit ▶ **noun** a dark-coloured pipit frequenting rocky shores in NW Europe. ● *Anthus petrosus*, family Motacillidae; formerly thought to be conspecific with the water pipit.

rock plant ▶ **noun** a plant that grows on or among rocks.

rock pool ▶ **noun** a pool of water among rocks, typically along a shoreline.

rock python ▶ **noun** a large dark-skinned constricting snake with paler markings and a distinctive pale mark on the crown. ● Genera *Python* and *Morelia*, family Pythonidae: several species, including *P. sebae* of Africa, *P. molurus* of Asia, and *M. amethistina* of Australia.

rock rabbit ▶ **noun 1** South African term for ROCK HYRAX.
2 another term for PIKA.

rock-ribbed ▶ **adjective** N. Amer. resolute or uncompromising, especially with respect to political allegiance: *a rock-ribbed Republican.*

rock rose ▶ **noun** a herbaceous or shrubby plant with rose-like flowers, native to temperate and warm regions. Also called SUN ROSE. ● Genera *Cistus* and *Helianthemum*, family Cistaceae.

rock salmon ▶ **noun 1** a tropical snapper which occurs both in the sea and in rivers, valued for food and sport. ● *Lutjanus argentimaculatus*, family Lutjanidae.
2 [mass noun] Brit. dogfish or wolf fish as food.

rock salt ▶ **noun** [mass noun] common salt occurring naturally as a mineral; halite.

rock samphire ▶ **noun** see SAMPHIRE.

rockslide ▶ **noun** an avalanche of rock or other stony material. ■ a mass of stony material deposited by a rockslide.

rock snake ▶ noun the Asian rock python.

rock solid ▶ adjective unlikely to change, fail, or collapse: *her love was rock solid.*

rocksteady ▶ noun [mass noun] an early form of reggae music originating in Jamaica in the 1960s, characterized by a slow tempo.

rock thrush ▶ noun an Old World thrush found in mountains and rocky habitats, with a grey or blue head and typically orange underparts. ● Genus *Monticola*, family Turdidae: several species, including the **blue rock thrush** (*M. solitarius*), the male of which is entirely slate-blue.

rockumentary ▶ noun informal a documentary about rock music and musicians.
– ORIGIN 1970s: from ROCK² + DOCUMENTARY.

rock wallaby ▶ noun an agile Australian wallaby that lives among cliffs and rocks, having feet with thick pads and fringes of stiff hair. ● Genus *Petrogale*, family Macropodidae: several species.

Rockwell, Norman (Percevel) (1894–1978), American illustrator. Known for his sentimental portraits of small-town American life, he was an illustrator for *Life* and the *Saturday Evening Post*.

rock wool ▶ noun [mass noun] inorganic material made into matted fibre used especially for insulation or soundproofing.

rocky ▶ adjective (**rockier, rockiest**) **1** consisting or full of rock or rocks: *a rocky crag above the village* | *hillsides of dry, rocky soil.*
2 tending to rock or shake; unsteady.
3 difficult and full of problems: *the marriage seemingly got off to a rocky start* | *the rocky road to success.*
4 relating to or characteristic of rock music: *rocky and acoustic folk bands.*
– DERIVATIVES **rockily** adverb, **rockiness** noun.

Rocky Mountain goat ▶ noun see MOUNTAIN GOAT (sense 1).

Rocky Mountains (also **the Rockies**) the chief mountain system of North America, which extends from the US–Mexico border to the Yukon Territory of northern Canada. It forms the Continental Divide. Several peaks rise to over 4,300 m (14,000 ft), the highest being Mount Elbert at 4,399 m (14,431 ft).

Rocky Mountain spotted fever ▶ noun see SPOTTED FEVER.

rococo /rəˈkəʊkəʊ/ ▶ adjective denoting furniture or architecture characterized by an elaborately ornamental late baroque style of decoration prevalent in 18th-century continental Europe, with asymmetrical patterns involving motifs and scrollwork. ■ (especially of music or literature) extravagantly or excessively ornate.
▶ noun [mass noun] the rococo style of art, decoration, or architecture.
– ORIGIN mid 19th cent.: from French, humorous alteration of ROCAILLE.

rod ▶ noun **1** a thin straight bar, especially of wood or metal. ■ a wand or staff as a symbol of office, authority, or power. ■ a slender straight stick or shoot growing on or cut from a tree or bush. ■ a stick used for caning or flogging. ■ (**the rod**) the use of such a stick as punishment: *if you'd been my daughter, you'd have felt the rod.* ■ vulgar slang a man's penis.
2 a fishing rod. ■ an angler.
3 historical, chiefly Brit. another term for PERCH³ (sense 1). ■ (also **square rod**) another term for PERCH³ (sense 2).
4 US informal a pistol or revolver.
5 Anatomy a light-sensitive cell of one of the two types present in large numbers in the retina of the eye, responsible mainly for monochrome vision in poor light. Compare with CONE (sense 3 of the noun).
– PHRASES **kiss the rod** see KISS. **make a rod for one's own back** do something likely to cause difficulties for oneself later. **rule with a rod of iron** control or govern very strictly or harshly. **spare the rod and spoil the child** proverb if children are not physically punished when they do wrong their personal development will suffer.
– DERIVATIVES **rodless** adjective, **rodlet** noun, **rod-like** adjective.
– ORIGIN late Old English *rodd* 'slender shoot growing on or cut from a tree', also 'straight stick or bundle of twigs used to inflict punishment'; probably related to Old Norse *rudda* 'club'.

rode¹ past of RIDE.

rode² ▶ verb [no obj.] (of a woodcock) fly on a regular circuit in the evening as a territorial display, making sharp calls and grunts.
– ORIGIN mid 18th cent. (in the sense 'fly landwards in the evening'): of unknown origin.

rode³ ▶ noun Nautical, N. Amer. a rope, especially one securing an anchor or trawl.
– ORIGIN early 17th cent.: of unknown origin.

rodent ▶ noun a gnawing mammal of an order that includes rats, mice, squirrels, hamsters, porcupines, and their relatives, distinguished by strong constantly growing incisors and no canine teeth. They constitute the largest order of mammals. ● Order Rodentia: three suborders. See SCIUROMORPHA, MYOMORPHA, and HYSTRICOMORPHA.
– ORIGIN mid 19th cent.: from Latin *rodent-* 'gnawing', from the verb *rodere*.

rodenticide /rəˈdɛntɪsʌɪd/ ▶ noun a poison used to kill rodents.

rodent ulcer ▶ noun Medicine a slow-growing malignant tumour of the face (basal cell carcinoma).

rodeo /ˈrəʊdɪəʊ, rə(ʊ)ˈdeɪəʊ/ ▶ noun (pl. **rodeos**) **1** an exhibition or contest in which cowboys show their skill at riding broncos, roping calves, wrestling steers, etc. ■ an exhibition or contest demonstrating other skills, such as motorcycle riding or canoeing.
2 a round-up of cattle on a ranch for branding, counting, etc. ■ an enclosure for such a round-up.
▶ verb (**rodeos, rodeoing, rodeoed**) [no obj.] compete in a rodeo.
– ORIGIN mid 19th cent.: from Spanish, from *rodear* 'go round', based on Latin *rotare* 'rotate'.

Rodgers, Richard (Charles) (1902–79), American composer. He worked with librettist **Lorenz Hart** (1895–1943) before collaborating with Oscar Hammerstein II on a succession of popular musicals, including *The Sound of Music* (1959).

rodgersia /rɒˈdʒəːzɪə/ ▶ noun an Asian plant which is sometimes cultivated for its attractive foliage. ● Genus *Rodgersia*, family Saxifragaceae.
– ORIGIN modern Latin, named after John *Rodgers* (1812–82), American admiral.

rodham /ˈrɒdəm/ ▶ noun (in the Fen district of East Anglia) a raised bank formed from silt deposits on the bed of a dry river course.
– ORIGIN mid 19th cent.: of unknown origin; other spellings are recorded but *rodham* is preferred in local use.

Ródhos /ˈrɔðɔs/ Greek name for RHODES¹.

Rodin /ˈrəʊdã/, French /ʀɔdɛ̃/, Auguste (1840–1917), French sculptor. He was chiefly concerned with the human form. Notable works: *The Thinker* (1880) and *The Kiss* (1886).

rodomontade /ˌrɒdə(ʊ)mɒnˈteɪd/ ▶ noun [mass noun] boastful or inflated talk or behaviour.
▶ verb [no obj.] archaic talk boastfully.
– ORIGIN early 17th cent.: from French, from obsolete Italian *rodomontada*, from Italian *rodomonte*, from the name of a boastful character in the medieval *Orlando* epics.

Rodrigo /rɒˈdriːgəʊ/, Spanish /rəˈðriγəo/, Joaquín (1901–99), Spanish composer; known in particular for his *Concierto de Aranjuez* for guitar and orchestra (1939). Rodrigo was blind from the age of three.

ROE ▶ abbreviation ■ Finance return on equity. ■ rules of engagement (in combat).

Roe, Sir (Edwin) Alliott Verdon (1877–1958), English engineer and aircraft designer. With his brother H. V. Roe he founded the Avro Company and built a number of planes, including the Avro 504 biplane of the First World War; in 1928 he formed the Saunders-Roe Company to design and manufacture flying boats.

roe¹ ▶ noun (also **hard roe**) [mass noun] the mass of eggs contained in the ovaries of a female fish or shellfish, especially when ripe and used as food; the full ovaries themselves. ■ (**soft roe**) the ripe testes of a male fish, especially when used as food.
– ORIGIN late Middle English: related to Middle Low German, Middle Dutch *roge*.

roe² (also **roe deer**) ▶ noun (pl. **same** or **roes**) a small Eurasian deer which lacks a visible tail and has a reddish summer coat that turns greyish in winter. ● Genus *Capreolus*, family Cervidae: two species, in particular the **European roe deer** (*C. capreolus*).
– ORIGIN Old English *rā(ha)*, of Germanic origin; related to Dutch *ree* and German *Reh*.

roebuck ▶ noun a male roe deer.

Roedean an independent boarding school for girls, on the south coast of England east of Brighton. It was founded in 1885.

Roeg /rəʊg/, Nicolas (Jack) (b.1928), English film director. His work is often impressionistic, and uses cutting techniques to create disjointed narratives. Notable works: *Performance* (1970) and *The Man Who Fell to Earth* (1975).

roentgen /ˈrʌntdʒən, ˈrəːnt-, ˈrɒntgən, -gən/ (abbrev.: **R**) ▶ noun a unit of ionizing radiation, the amount producing one electrostatic unit of positive or negative ionic charge in one cubic centimetre of air under standard conditions.
– ORIGIN 1920s: named after Wilhelm Conrad *Röntgen* (1845–1923), German physicist, discoverer of X-rays.

roentgenium /rʌntˈdʒɛnɪəm, rəːnt-, rɒnt-, -ˈgɛn-/ ▶ noun the chemical element of atomic number 111, a radioactive element produced artificially. (Symbol: **Rg**)
– ORIGIN early 21st cent.: named after Wilhelm Conrad *Röntgen* (see ROENTGEN).

roentgenogram /ˈrʌntdʒənə(ʊ)gram, ˈrəːnt-, ˈrɒnt-, -gənəʊ-/ ▶ noun chiefly Medicine an X-ray photograph.

roentgenography /ˌrʌntdʒəˈnɒgrəfi, ˌrəːnt-, ˌrɒnt-/ ▶ noun [mass noun] chiefly Medicine X-ray photography.
– DERIVATIVES **roentgenographic** adjective, **roentgenographically** adverb.

roentgenology /ˌrʌntdʒəˈnɒlədʒi, ˌrəːnt-, ˌrɒnt-/ ▶ noun chiefly Medicine another term for RADIOLOGY.

roentgen rays ▶ plural noun dated X-rays.

Roeselare /ˈruːsəˌlaːrə/ a town in NW Belgium, in the province of West Flanders; pop. 56,547 (2008). French name ROULERS.

ROFL (also **ROTFL**) ▶ abbreviation informal rolling on the floor laughing (used to convey great amusement): *just read this, it's absolutely hysterical—am still ROFL.*

rogan josh /ˌrəʊg(ə)n ˈdʒəʊʃ/ ▶ noun [mass noun] an Indian dish of curried meat, typically lamb, in a rich tomato-based sauce.
– ORIGIN from Urdu *roġan još*.

rogation /rə(ʊ)ˈgeɪʃ(ə)n/ ▶ noun [usu. as modifier] (in the Christian Church) a solemn supplication consisting of the litany of the saints chanted on the three days before Ascension Day: *Rogation Week.*
– ORIGIN late Middle English: from Latin *rogatio(n-)*, from *rogare* 'ask'.

Rogation Days (in the Western Christian Church) the three days before Ascension Day, traditionally marked by fasting and prayer, particularly for the blessing of the harvest (after the pattern of pre-Christian rituals).

Rogation Sunday ▶ noun the Sunday preceding the Rogation Days.

Rogationtide ▶ noun the period of the Rogation Days.

roger ▶ exclamation your message has been received (used in radio communication): *'Roger; we'll be with you in about ten minutes.'* ■ informal used to express assent or understanding: *'Go light the stove.' 'Roger, Mister Bossman,' Frank replied.*
▶ verb [with obj.] Brit. vulgar slang (of a man) have sexual intercourse with.
– ORIGIN mid 16th cent.: from the given name *Roger*. The verb (dating from the early 18th cent.) is from an obsolete noun sense 'penis'.

R

Rogers¹, Ginger (1911–95), American actress and dancer; born *Virginia Katherine McMath*. She is known for her dancing partnership with Fred Astaire, during which she appeared in musicals including *Top Hat* (1935). Her solo acting career included the film *Kitty Foyle* (1940), for which she won an Oscar.

Rogers², Richard (George), Baron Rogers of Riverside (b.1933), British architect, born in Italy. A leading exponent of high-tech architecture, his major works include the Pompidou Centre in Paris (1971–7), designed with the Italian architect Renzo Piano (b.1937), and the Lloyd's Building in London (1986).

Roget /ˈrɒʒeɪ/, Peter Mark (1779–1869), English scholar. He worked as a physician but is remembered as the compiler of *Roget's Thesaurus of English Words and Phrases*, first published in 1852.

rogue ▶ noun **1** a dishonest or unprincipled man: *you are a rogue and an embezzler.* ■ a person whose behaviour one disapproves of but who is nonetheless likeable or attractive: *Cenzo, you old rogue!*
2 [usu. as modifier] an elephant or other large wild animal living apart from the herd and having savage or destructive tendencies: *a rogue elephant.* ■ a person or thing that behaves in an aberrant or unpredictable

way, typically with damaging or dangerous effects: *he hacked into data and ran rogue programs* | *a rogue cop who took the law into his own hands.* ■ a seedling or plant deviating from the standard variety.

▶ verb [with obj.] remove inferior or defective plants or seedlings from (a crop).

– ORIGIN mid 16th cent. (denoting an idle vagrant): probably from Latin *rogare* 'beg, ask', and related to obsolete slang *roger* 'vagrant beggar' (many such cant terms were introduced towards the middle of the 16th cent.).

roguery ▶ noun (pl. **rogueries**) [mass noun] conduct characteristic of a rogue, especially acts of dishonesty or playful mischief: *there has always been roguery associated with horse dealing.*

rogues' gallery ▶ noun informal a collection of photographs of known criminals, used by police to identify suspects. ■ a collection of people or creatures notable for a certain shared quality or characteristic, typically a disreputable one: *a rogues' gallery of bureaucrats and cold-hearted advocates of 'progress'.*

rogue state ▶ noun a nation or state regarded as breaking international law and posing a threat to the security of other nations.

rogue trader ▶ noun a securities trader who engages in speculative trading without authorization.

roguish ▶ adjective **1** characteristic of a dishonest or unprincipled person: *he led a roguish and uncertain existence.*
2 playfully mischievous: *he gave her a roguish smile.*
– DERIVATIVES **roguishly** adverb, **roguishness** noun.

Rohmer /ˈrəʊmə/, French /ʀɔmɛʀ/, Eric (1920–2010), born *Jean-Marie Maurice Scherer*, French film director and critic, member of the *nouvelle vague*. His films, many of which deal with issues of conscience, include *My Night at Maud's* (1968), *Claire's Knee* (1970), and the costume drama *The Lady and the Duke* (2002).

Rohypnol /rəʊˈhɪpnɒl/ ▶ noun [mass noun] trademark a powerful sedative drug of the benzodiazepine class.
– ORIGIN 1970s: invented name.

ROI ▶ abbreviation Finance return on investment.

roil /rɔɪl/ ▶ verb **1** [with obj.] literary make (a liquid) turbid or muddy by disturbing the sediment: *winds roil these waters.* ■ [no obj.] (of a liquid) move in a turbulent, swirling manner: *the sea roiled below her.*
2 US term for RILE (sense 1).
– ORIGIN late 16th cent.: perhaps from Old French *ruiler* 'mix mortar', from late Latin *regulare* 'regulate'.

roily ▶ adjective N. Amer. muddy; turbulent: *those waters were roily, high and muddy.*

roister /ˈrɔɪstə/ ▶ verb [no obj.] enjoy oneself or celebrate in a noisy or boisterous way: *workers from the refinery roistered in the bars.*
– DERIVATIVES **roisterer** noun, **roisterous** adjective.
– ORIGIN late 16th cent.: from obsolete *roister* 'roisterer', from French *rustre* 'ruffian', variant of *ruste*, from Latin *rusticus* 'rustic'.

ROK ▶ abbreviation South Korea (international vehicle registration).
– ORIGIN from *Republic of Korea*.

R

roko /ˈrəʊkəʊ/ ▶ noun (pl. **rokos**) Indian a protest or demonstration: *services to and from Bangalore were affected today due to the rail roko.*
– ORIGIN Hindi, from *roknaa* 'prevent, hinder'.

Roland /ˈrəʊlənd/ the most famous of Charlemagne's paladins, hero of the *Chanson de Roland* (12th century). He is said to have become a friend of Oliver, another paladin, after engaging him in single combat in which neither won. Roland was killed at the Battle of Roncesvalles.
– PHRASES **a Roland for an Oliver** archaic an effective or adequate retort or response: *he had given Mrs Carr a Roland for her Oliver.*

role (also **rôle**) ▶ noun an actor's part in a play, film, etc.: *Dietrich's role as a wife in war-torn Paris.* ■ the function assumed or part played by a person or thing in a particular situation: *the equipment will play a vital role in the fight against cancer.*
– ORIGIN early 17th cent.: from obsolete French *roule* 'roll', referring originally to the roll of paper on which the actor's part was written.

role model ▶ noun a person looked to by others as an example to be imitated.

role playing (also **role play**) ▶ noun [mass noun] **1** chiefly Psychology the acting out or performance of a particular role, either consciously (as a technique in psychotherapy or training) or unconsciously, in accordance with the perceived expectations of society as regards a person's behaviour in a particular context.
2 participation in a role-playing game.
– DERIVATIVES **role-play** verb, **role player** noun.

role-playing game ▶ noun a game in which players take on the roles of imaginary characters who engage in adventures, typically in a particular fantasy setting overseen by a referee.

role reversal ▶ noun a situation in which someone adopts a role the reverse of that which they normally assume in relation to someone else, who typically assumes their role in exchange.

Rolfing ▶ noun [mass noun] a massage technique aimed at the vertical realignment of the body, and therefore deep enough to release muscular tension at skeletal level, which can contribute to the relief of long-standing tension and neuroses.
– DERIVATIVES **Rolf** verb.
– ORIGIN 1970s: from the name of Ida P. *Rolf* (1897–1979), American physiotherapist, + -ING[1].

roll ▶ verb **1** move in a particular direction by turning over and over on an axis: [no obj., with adverbial of direction] *the car rolled down into a ditch* | [with obj. and adverbial of direction] *she rolled the ball across the floor.* ■ turn over to face a different direction: [no obj., with adverbial] *she rolled on to her side* | [with obj. and adverbial] *they rolled him over on to his back.* ■ [with obj.] turn (one's eyes) upwards, typically to show surprise or disapproval: *Sarah rolled her eyes to the ceiling.* ■ [no obj., with adverbial] lie down and turn over and over while remaining in the same place: *the buffalo rolled in the dust.* ■ [no obj.] (of a moving ship, aircraft, or vehicle) rock or oscillate around an axis parallel to the direction of motion: *the ship pitched and rolled.* ■ [no obj., with adverbial] move along or from side to side unsteadily or uncontrollably: *they were rolling about with laughter.* ■ [with obj.] N. Amer. informal overturn (a vehicle): *he rolled his Mercedes in a 100 mph crash.* ■ [with obj.] throw (a die or dice). ■ [with obj.] obtain (a particular score) by doing this: *roll a 2, 3, or 12.*
2 [no obj., with adverbial of direction] (of a vehicle) move or run on wheels: *the van was rolling along the lane.* ■ [with obj. and adverbial of direction] move or push (a wheeled object): *Pat rolled the trolley to and fro.* ■ (**roll something up/down**) make a car window or a window blind move up or down by turning a handle: *do not roll down the window to give a stranger directions.* ■ (of a drop of liquid) flow: *huge tears rolled down her cheeks.* ■ (of time) elapse steadily: *the years rolled by.* ■ (**roll off**) (of a product) issue from (an assembly line or machine): *the first copies of the newspaper rolled off the presses.* ■ (of waves, smoke, cloud, or fog) move or flow forward with an undulating motion: *the fog rolled across the fields.* ■ [no obj.] (of land) extend in gentle undulations. ■ [no obj.] (of credits for a film or television programme) be displayed as if moving on a roller up the screen. ■ (with reference to a machine, device, or system) operate or begin operating: [no obj.] *the cameras started to roll* | [with obj.] *roll the camera.*
3 [with obj. and adverbial] turn (something flexible) over and over on itself to form a cylinder, tube, or ball: *she started to* **roll up** *her sleeping bag.* ■ [with obj.] (**roll something up** (or **back**)) fold the edge of a garment over on itself a number of times to shorten it: *she rolled up her sleeves to wash her hands.* ■ [with obj.] make (something) by forming material into a cylinder or ball: [with two objs] *Harry rolled himself a joint.* ■ [no obj., with adverbial] curl up tightly: *the shock made the hedgehog roll into a ball.*
4 [with obj. and adverbial] flatten (something) by passing a roller over it or by passing it between rollers: *roll out the dough on a floured surface.*
5 [no obj., with adverbial of direction] (of a loud, deep sound) reverberate: *the first peals of thunder rolled across the sky.* ■ [with obj.] pronounce (a consonant, typically an *r*) with a trill: *when he wanted to emphasize a point he rolled his rrrs.* ■ [with obj.] utter (a word or words) with a reverberating or vibratory effect: *he rolled the word around his mouth.* ■ (of words) flow effortlessly or mellifluously: *the names of his colleagues rolled off his lips.*
6 informal rob (someone, typically when they are intoxicated or asleep): *if you don't get drunk, you don't get rolled.*

▶ noun **1** a cylinder formed by winding flexible material around a tube or by turning it over and over on itself without folding: *a roll of carpet.* ■ a cylindrical mass of something or a number of items arranged in a cylindrical shape: *a roll of mints.* ■ [with modifier] an item of food that is made by wrapping a flat sheet of pastry, cake, meat, or fish round a sweet or savoury filling: *salmon and rice rolls.* ■ N. Amer. & Austral. a quantity of banknotes rolled together.
2 a movement in which someone or something turns or is turned over on itself: *a roll of the dice.* ■ a gymnastic exercise in which the body is rolled into a tucked position and turned in a forward or backward circle: *a forward roll.* ■ a complete rotation by a flying aircraft about its longitudinal axis. ■ [mass noun] a swaying or oscillation of a ship, aircraft, or vehicle around an axis parallel to the direction of motion: *the car corners capably with a minimum of roll.*
3 a prolonged, deep, reverberating sound: *thunder exploded, roll after roll.* ■ Music one of the basic patterns (rudiments) of drumming, consisting of a sustained, rapid alternation of single or double strokes of each stick.
4 a very small loaf of bread: *a bacon roll.*
5 an official list or register of names. ■ the total numbers on such a list: *a review of secondary schools to assess the effects of falling rolls.* ■ a document, typically an official record, historically kept in scroll form.
6 [mass noun] undulation of the landscape: *hidden by the roll of the land was a refinery.*
7 a roller for flattening something, especially one used to shape metal in a rolling mill.
– PHRASES **a roll in the hay** (or **the sack**) informal an act of sexual intercourse. **be rolling in it** (or **in money**) informal be very rich. **on a roll** informal experiencing a prolonged spell of success or good luck: *the organization is on a roll.* **rolled into one** (of characteristics drawn from different people or things) combined in one person or thing: *banks are several businesses rolled into one.* **rolling drunk** so drunk as to be swaying or staggering. **rolling in the aisles** informal (of an audience) laughing uncontrollably. **roll of honour** Brit. a list of people whose deeds or achievements are honoured, or who have died in battle. **roll one's own** informal make one's own cigarettes from loose tobacco. **roll up one's sleeves** prepare to fight or work. **roll with the punches** (of a boxer) move one's body away from an opponent's blows so as to lessen the impact. ■ adapt oneself to adverse circumstances. **strike someone off the roll** Brit. debar a solicitor from practising as a penalty for dishonesty or other misconduct.
– PHRASAL VERBS **roll something back** reverse the progress or reduce the power or importance of something: *the public sector of the economy has been rolled back.* **roll in** informal **1** be received in large amounts: *the money was rolling in.* **2** casually arrive at a place late: *Steve rolled in about lunchtime.* **roll on** [in imperative] Brit. informal used to indicate that one wants a particular time or event to come quickly: *roll on January!* **roll something out** officially launch or introduce a new product or service: *the firm rolled out its newest generation of supercomputers.* **roll something over** Finance contrive or extend a particular financial arrangement. ■ Brit. carry over prize money in a lottery from one draw to the next, typically because the jackpot has not been won. **roll up** informal arrive: *we rolled up at the same time.* ■ [in imperative] used to encourage passers-by to look at or participate in something, typically at a fairground: *roll up, roll up, for all the fun of the fair.* **roll something up** Military drive the flank of an enemy line back and round so that the line is shortened or surrounded.
– DERIVATIVES **rollable** adjective.
– ORIGIN Middle English: from Old French *rolle* (noun), *roller* (verb), from Latin *rotulus* 'a roll', variant of *rotula* 'little wheel', diminutive of *rota*.

rollaway ▶ noun N. Amer. a bed fitted with wheels or castors, allowing it to be moved easily.

rollback ▶ noun **1** chiefly N. Amer. a reduction or decrease: *a 5 per cent rollback of personal income taxes.*
2 Computing the process of restoring a database or program to a previously defined state, typically to recover from an error.
▶ verb [with obj.] Computing restore (a database) to a previously defined state.

roll bar ▶ noun a metal bar running up the sides and across the top of a vehicle, especially one used in motor sport, strengthening its frame and protecting the occupants if the vehicle overturns.

roll cage ▶ noun a framework of reinforcements protecting a car's passenger cabin in the event that it should roll on to its roof.

roll call ▶ noun the process of calling out a list of names to establish who is present. ■ a list or group of people or things that are notable in some specified way: *a roll call of young hopefuls.*

roll cast ▸ noun Fishing a cast in which the angler does not throw the line backwards.

rolled gold ▸ noun [mass noun] gold in the form of a thin coating applied to a baser metal by rolling.

rolled oats ▸ plural noun oats that have been husked and crushed.

roller[1] ▸ noun **1** a cylinder that rotates about a central axis and is used in various machines and devices to move, flatten, or spread something. ▪ an absorbent revolving cylinder attached to a handle, used to apply paint. ▪ a small cylinder around which hair is rolled in order to produce curls. ▪ (also **roller bandage**) a long surgical bandage rolled up for convenient application.
2 a long swelling wave that appears to roll steadily towards the shore.
3 [as modifier] relating to or involving roller skates: *roller hockey*.
4 a brightly coloured crow-sized bird with predominantly blue plumage, having a characteristic tumbling display flight. ● Genera *Coracias* and *Eurystomus*, family Coraciidae: several species, especially the widespread **European roller** (*C. garrulus*).
5 a bird of a breed of tumbler pigeon.
6 a breed of canary with a trilling song.

roller[2] ▸ noun Brit. informal a car made by Rolls-Royce.

rollerball ▸ noun **1** a ballpoint pen using thinner ink than other ballpoints.
2 Computing an input device containing a ball which is moved with the fingers to control the cursor.

roller bearing ▸ noun a bearing similar to a ball bearing but using small cylindrical rollers instead of balls. ▪ a roller used in such a bearing.

Rollerblade ▸ noun trademark an in-line skate.
▸ verb [no obj.] skate using Rollerblades.
– DERIVATIVES **rollerblader** noun.

roller blind ▸ noun a window blind fitted on a roller.

roller coaster ▸ noun a fairground attraction that consists of a light railway track which has many tight turns and steep slopes on which people ride in small, fast open carriages: [as modifier] *a roller-coaster ride*. ▪ something characterized by wild and unpredictable changes: *a terrific roller coaster of a book*.
▸ verb (**roller-coaster**) (also **roller-coast**) [no obj.] move, change, or occur in a dramatically changeable manner: *the twentieth century fades behind us and history roller-coasters on*.

roller derby ▸ noun a type of speed-skating competition on roller skates.

roller rink ▸ noun see **RINK**.

roller skate ▸ noun each of a pair of boots or metal frames fitted to shoes with four or more small wheels, for gliding across a hard surface.

roller skating ▸ noun [mass noun] skating on a hard surface other than ice, as a sport or a pastime.
– DERIVATIVES **roller-skate** verb, **roller skater** noun.

roller towel ▸ noun a long towel with the ends joined and hung on a roller or one fed through a device from one roller holding the clean part to another holding the used part.

roll feed ▸ noun a feed mechanism supplying material in sheet form, e.g. paper, by means of rollers.

roll film ▸ noun [mass noun] photographic film with a protective lightproof backing paper wound on to a spool.

rollick ▸ verb [no obj.] act or behave in a jovial and exuberant fashion.
– ORIGIN early 19th cent.: probably dialect, perhaps a blend of **ROMP** and **FROLIC**.

rollicking[1] ▸ adjective [attrib.] exuberantly lively and amusing: *this is all good rollicking fun*.

rollicking[2] (also **rollocking**) ▸ noun Brit. informal a severe reprimand: *I've had a bit of a rollicking for not riding with more restraint*.
– ORIGIN 1930s: euphemistic alteration of **BOLLOCKING**.

rolling ▸ adjective **1** moving by turning over and over on an axis: *a rolling ball*.
2 (of land) extending in gentle undulations: *the rolling countryside*.
3 done or happening in a steady and continuous way: *a rolling programme of reforms* | *a rolling news service*.

rolling hitch ▸ noun a kind of hitch used to attach a rope to a spar or larger rope.

rolling mill ▸ noun a factory or machine for rolling steel or other metal into sheets.

rolling pin ▸ noun a cylinder rolled over pastry or dough to flatten or shape it.

rolling stock ▸ noun [mass noun] locomotives, carriages, wagons, or other vehicles used on a railway. ▪ US the road vehicles of a trucking company.

rolling stone ▸ noun a person who is unwilling to settle for long in one place.
– PHRASES **a rolling stone gathers no moss** proverb a person who does not settle in one place will not accumulate wealth or status, or responsibilities or commitments.

Rolling Stones an English rock group featuring singer Mick Jagger and guitarist Keith Richards. Originally a rhythm-and-blues band, they became successful with a much-imitated rebel image, and are known for songs such as 'Satisfaction' (1965) and 'Jumping Jack Flash' (1968).

rolling strike ▸ noun a strike consisting of a coordinated series of consecutive limited strikes by small groups of workers.

roll-in roll-out ▸ noun [mass noun] Computing a method or the process of switching data or code between main and auxiliary memories in order to process several tasks simultaneously.

rollmop ▸ noun a rolled uncooked pickled herring fillet.
– ORIGIN early 20th cent.: from German *Rollmops*.

roll-neck ▸ noun a high loosely turned over collar: [as modifier] *a black roll-neck sweater*. ▪ a garment with a roll-neck collar.

rollocking ▸ noun variant spelling of **ROLLICKING[2]**.

roll-off ▸ noun the smooth fall of response to zero at either end of the frequency range of a piece of audio equipment.

roll-on ▸ adjective denoting a deodorant or cosmetic applied by means of a rotating ball in the neck of the container.
▸ noun **1** a roll-on deodorant or cosmetic.
2 Brit. a light elastic corset.

roll-on roll-off ▸ adjective Brit. denoting a passenger ferry in which vehicles are driven directly on at the start of the voyage and driven off at the end of it.

roll-out ▸ noun **1** the unveiling of a new aircraft or spacecraft. ▪ the official launch or introduction of a new product or service.
2 Aeronautics the stage of an aircraft's landing during which it travels along the runway while losing speed.
3 American Football a play in which a quarterback moves out toward the sideline before attempting to pass.

rollover ▸ noun **1** Finance the extension or transfer of a debt or other financial arrangement. ▪ Brit. (in a lottery) the accumulative carry-over of prize money to the following draw.
2 informal the overturning of a vehicle.
3 a facility on an electronic keyboard enabling one or several keystrokes to be registered correctly while another key is depressed.

Rolls, Charles Stewart (1877–1910), English motoring and aviation pioneer. He and Henry Royce formed the company Rolls-Royce Ltd in 1906. Rolls was the first Englishman to fly across the English Channel, and made the first double crossing in 1910 shortly before he was killed in an air crash. The Rolls-Royce company established its reputation with luxury cars and produced aircraft engines used in both world wars.

Rolls-Royce /ˈrəʊlzˈrɔɪs/ noun **1** trademark a luxury car produced by the British Rolls-Royce company.
2 a product that is the most luxurious or highly specified of its kind: *the one I have at the moment is the Rolls Royce of accordions*.

roll-top desk ▸ noun a writing desk with a semicircular flexible cover sliding in curved grooves.

roll-up ▸ noun **1** (chiefly N. Amer. also **roll-your-own**) Brit. informal a hand-rolled cigarette.
2 Austral. informal an assembly or its turnout: *we should get a big roll-up*.
▸ adjective [attrib.] **1** denoting something which can be rolled up: *roll-up panels*.
2 Finance denoting an investment fund in which returns are reinvested and tax liabilities can be reduced.

Rolodex /ˈrəʊlə(ʊ)dɛks/ ▸ noun N. Amer. trademark a type of desktop card index.

roly-poly ▸ adjective informal (of a person) having a round, plump appearance: *a roly-poly young boy*.
▸ noun **1** (also **roly-poly pudding**) [mass noun] Brit. a pudding made of a sheet of suet pastry covered with jam or fruit, formed into a roll, and steamed or baked.
2 Austral. a bushy tumbleweed. ● Several species, in particular a saltwort (*Salsola kali*, family Chenopodiaceae) which is able to grow away from saline habitats.
– ORIGIN early 17th cent.: fanciful formation from the verb **ROLL**.

ROM ▸ abbreviation Computing read-only memory.

Rom ▸ noun (pl. **Roma** /ˈrɒmə/) **1** a Gypsy, especially a man or boy.
2 (as plural noun **Roma**) Gypsy people collectively.
– ORIGIN mid 19th cent.: Romany, 'man, husband'.

Rom. ▸ abbreviation Epistle to the Romans (in biblical references).

rom. ▸ abbreviation roman (used as an instruction for a typesetter).

Roma /ˈrəʊmə/ Italian name for **ROME**.

Romaic /rə(ʊ)ˈmeɪɪk/ dated ▸ noun [mass noun] the vernacular language of modern Greece.
▸ adjective relating to Romaic.
– ORIGIN from modern Greek *romaiikos* 'Roman', used specifically of the eastern Roman Empire.

romaine /rə(ʊ)ˈmeɪn/ ▸ noun a cos lettuce.
– ORIGIN early 20th cent.: from French, feminine of *romain* 'Roman'.

romaji /ˈrəʊmədʒi/ ▸ noun [mass noun] a system of romanized spelling used to transliterate Japanese.
– ORIGIN early 20th cent.: from Japanese, from *rōma* 'Roman' + *ji* 'letter(s)'.

Roman ▸ adjective **1** relating to ancient Rome or its empire or people: *an old Roman road*. ▪ relating to medieval or modern Rome: *the Roman and Pisan lines of popes*.
2 dated short for **ROMAN CATHOLIC**: *the Roman Church's instructions to its clergy*.
3 denoting the alphabet (or any of the letters in it) used for writing Latin, English, and most European languages, developed in ancient Rome.
4 (**roman**) (of type) of a plain upright kind used in ordinary print, especially as distinguished from italic and Gothic.
▸ noun **1** a citizen or soldier of the ancient Roman Republic or Empire. ▪ a citizen of modern Rome.
2 dated a Roman Catholic.
3 (**roman**) [mass noun] roman type.
– ORIGIN Middle English: from Old French *Romain*, from Latin *Romanus*, from *Roma* 'Rome'.

roman (also **roman fish**) ▸ noun (pl. **same** or **romans**) S. African a red or pink South African sea bream. ● *Chrysoblephus* and other genera, family Sparidae: several species, in particular *C. laticeps*.
– ORIGIN late 18th cent.: from Afrikaans *rooi* 'red' + *man* 'man'.

roman-à-clef /ˌrəʊmɒ̃ɑːˈkleɪ/, French /ʀɔmɑ̃akle/ ▸ noun (pl. **romans-à-clef** pronunc. **same**) a novel in which real people or events appear with invented names.
– ORIGIN French, literally 'novel with a key'.

R

Roman baths ▸ plural noun a building containing a complex of rooms designed for bathing, relaxing, and socializing, as used in ancient Rome.

Roman blind ▸ noun a window blind made of fabric that draws up into pleats.

Roman Britain Britain during the period AD 43–410, when most of Britain was part of the Roman Empire.

> The frontier of the Roman province of Britain was eventually established at Hadrian's Wall; the more northerly Antonine Wall was breached and abandoned (c.181). Roman settlers and traders built villas, and Roman towns including London (Londinium), York (Eboracum), Lincoln (Lindum Colonia), St Albans (Verulamium), and Colchester (Camulodunum) were established or developed.

Roman candle ▸ noun a firework giving off a series of flaming coloured balls and sparks.

Roman Catholic ▸ adjective relating to the Roman Catholic Church: *a Roman Catholic bishop*.
▸ noun a member of the Roman Catholic Church.
– DERIVATIVES **Roman Catholicism** noun.
– ORIGIN late 16th cent.: translation of Latin (*Ecclesia*) *Romana Catholica* (*et Apostolica*) 'Roman Catholic (and Apostolic Church)'. It was apparently first used as a conciliatory term in place of the earlier *Roman*, *Romanist*, or *Romish*, considered derogatory.

Roman Catholic Church the part of the Christian Church which acknowledges the Pope as its head, especially as it has developed since the Reformation.

> It is the largest Christian Church, dominant particularly in South America and southern Europe. Roman Catholicism differs from Protestantism in the importance it grants to tradition, ritual, and the authority of the Pope as successor to the Apostle St Peter, and especially in its doctrines of papal infallibility (formally defined in 1870) and of the Eucharist (transubstantiation), its celibate male priesthood, its emphasis on confession, and the veneration of the Virgin Mary and other saints. Much modern Roman Catholic thought and practice arises from scholastic theology and from the response to the Reformation made by the Council of Trent (1545–63). It became less rigid after the Second Vatican Council (1962–5), but its continuing opposition to divorce, abortion, and artificial contraception remains controversial.

Romance /rə(ʊ)ˈmans, ˈrəʊmans/ ▶ **noun** [mass noun] the group of Indo-European languages descended from Latin, principally French, Spanish, Portuguese, Italian, Catalan, Occitan, and Romanian.
▶ **adjective** relating to or denoting this group of languages: *the Romance languages*.
– ORIGIN Middle English (originally denoting the vernacular language of France as opposed to Latin): from Old French *romanz*, based on Latin *Romanicus* 'Roman'.

romance /rə(ʊ)ˈmans, ˈrəʊmans/ ▶ **noun 1** [mass noun] a feeling of excitement and mystery associated with love: *I had a thirst for romance*. ■ love, especially when sentimental or idealized: *he asked her for a date and romance blossomed*. ■ [count noun] a love affair, especially one that is not very serious or long-lasting: *a holiday romance*. ■ [count noun] a book or film dealing with love in a sentimental or idealized way: *light historical romances*. ■ a genre of fiction dealing with love in such a way: *wartime passion from the master of romance*.
2 [mass noun] a quality or feeling of mystery, excitement, and remoteness from everyday life: *the romance of the sea*.
3 a medieval tale dealing with a hero of chivalry, of the kind common in the Romance languages: *the Arthurian romances*.
4 a work of fiction depicting a setting and events remote from everyday life, especially one of a kind popular in the 16th and 17th centuries: *Elizabethan pastoral romances*.
5 Music a short informal piece.
▶ **verb** [with obj.] **1** dated try to gain the love of; court: *the wealthy estate owner romanced her*. ■ informal seek the attention or custom of (someone), especially by the use of flattery: *he is being romanced by the big boys in New York*. ■ [no obj.] engage in a love affair: *we started romancing*.
2 another term for ROMANTICIZE: *to a certain degree I am romancing the past*.
– DERIVATIVES **romancer** noun.
– ORIGIN Middle English: from ROMANCE, originally denoting a composition in the vernacular as opposed to works in Latin. Early use denoted vernacular verse on the theme of chivalry; the sense 'genre centred on romantic love' dates from the mid 17th cent.

Roman de la rose /ˌrəʊmɒ̃ də la ˈrəʊz/, French /ʀɔmɑ̃ də la ʀoz/ an extremely influential French poem of the 13th century, an allegorical romance embodying the aristocratic ethic of courtly love. It was composed by two different authors some forty years apart.
– ORIGIN French, literally 'romance of the rose'.

Roman Empire the empire established by Augustus in 27 BC and divided by Theodosius in AD 395 into the Western or Latin and Eastern or Greek Empire.

> At its greatest extent Roman rule or influence extended from Armenia and Mesopotamia in the east to the Iberian peninsula in the west, and from the Rhine and Danube in the north to Egypt and provinces on the Mediterranean coast of North Africa. The empire was divided after the death of Theodosius I (AD 395) into the Western Empire and the Eastern or Byzantine Empire (centred on Constantinople). Peace was maintained largely by the substantial presence of the Roman army, and a degree of unity was achieved by an extensive network of roads, a single legal system, and a common language (Latin in the West, Greek in the East). Rome was sacked by the Visigoths under Alaric in 410, and the last emperor of the West, Romulus Augustulus, was deposed in 476. The Eastern Empire, which was stronger, lasted until 1453.

Romanesque /ˌrəʊməˈnɛsk/ ▶ **adjective** relating to a style of architecture which prevailed in Europe *c.*900–1200, although sometimes dated back to the end of the Roman Empire (5th century).
▶ **noun** [mass noun] Romanesque architecture.

> Romanesque architecture is characterized by round arches and massive vaulting, and by heavy piers, columns, and walls with small windows. Although disseminated throughout western Europe, the style reached its fullest development in central and northern France; the equivalent style in England is usually called Norman.

– ORIGIN French, from *roman* 'romance'.

roman-fleuve /ˌrəʊmɒ̃ˈfləːv/, French /ʀɔmɑ̃flœv/ ▶ **noun** (pl. **romans-fleuves** pronunc. **same**) a novel featuring the leisurely description of the lives of closely related people. ■ a sequence of related, self-contained novels.
– ORIGIN French, literally 'river novel'.

Roman holiday ▶ **noun** an occasion on which enjoyment or profit is derived from others' suffering or discomfort.
– ORIGIN early 19th cent.: from Byron's *Childe Harold*, originally with reference to a holiday given for a gladiatorial combat.

Romania /rəʊˈmeɪnɪə/ (also **Rumania**) a country in SE Europe with a coastline on the Black Sea; pop. 22,215,400 (est. 2009); official language, Romanian; capital, Bucharest.

> In the Middle Ages the area consisted of the principalities of Wallachia and Moldavia, which were swallowed up by the Ottoman Empire in the 15th–16th centuries. The two principalities gained independence in 1878. After the Second World War, in which it supported Germany, Romania became a Communist state under Soviet domination. After 1974 the country pursued an increasingly independent course under the virtual dictatorship of Nicolae Ceaușescu. His regime collapsed in violent popular unrest in 1989 and a new democratic constitution was introduced. Romania joined the EU in 2007.

Romanian (also **Rumanian**) ▶ **adjective** relating to Romania or its people or language.
▶ **noun 1** a native or inhabitant of Romania, or a person of Romanian descent.
2 [mass noun] the language of Romania, a Romance language influenced by the neighbouring Slavic languages. It is spoken by over 23 million people in Romania itself and by the majority of the population of Moldova.

Romanic /rə(ʊ)ˈmanɪk/ ▶ **noun & adjective** less common term for ROMANCE.
– ORIGIN early 18th cent.: from Latin *Romanicus*, from *Romanus* 'Roman'.

Romanism ▶ **noun** [mass noun] dated Roman Catholicism.

Romanist ▶ **noun 1** an expert in or student of Roman antiquities or law, or of the Romance languages.
2 chiefly derogatory a member or supporter of the Roman Catholic Church.
▶ **adjective** chiefly derogatory belonging or adhering to the Roman Catholic Church.

Romanize /ˈrəʊmənʌɪz/ (also **Romanise**) ▶ **verb** [with obj.] **1** historical bring (a region, people, etc.) under Roman influence or authority.
2 make Roman Catholic in character: *he has Romanized the services of his church*.
3 (**romanize**) put (text) into the Roman alphabet or into roman type: *Atatürk's decision to romanize the written language*.
– DERIVATIVES **Romanization** noun.

Roman law ▶ **noun** [mass noun] the law code of the ancient Romans forming the basis of civil law in many countries today.

Roman nose ▶ **noun** a nose with a high bridge.

Roman numeral ▶ **noun** any of the letters representing numbers in the Roman numerical system: I = 1, V = 5, X = 10, L = 50, C = 100, D = 500, M = 1,000. In this system a letter placed after another of greater value adds (thus XVI or xvi is 16), whereas a letter placed before another of greater value subtracts (thus XC is 90).

Romano /rə(ʊ)ˈmɑːnəʊ/ ▶ **noun** [mass noun] a strong-tasting hard cheese, originally made in Italy.
– ORIGIN Italian, literally 'Roman'.

Romano- /rə(ʊ)ˈmɑːnəʊ/ ▶ **combining form** Roman; Roman and ...: *Romano-British*.

Romanov /rəʊˈmɑːnɒf/ a dynasty that ruled in Russia from the accession of Michael Romanov (1596–1645) in 1613 until the overthrow of the last tsar, Nicholas II, in 1917.

Roman Republic the ancient Roman state from the expulsion of the Etruscan monarchs in 509 BC (see TARQUINIUS) until the assumption of power by Augustus (Octavian) in 27 BC.

> The republic was dominated by a landed aristocracy, the patricians, who ruled through the advisory Senate and two annually elected chief magistrates or consuls; the plebeians or common people had their own representatives, the tribunes, who in time gained the power of veto over the other magistrates. During the life of the republic Rome came to dominate the rest of Italy and, following the Punic and Macedonian Wars, began to acquire extensive dominions in the Mediterranean and Asia Minor. Dissatisfaction with the Senate's control of government led to civil wars, which culminated in Julius Caesar's brief dictatorship. This established the principle of personal autocracy, and after Caesar's assassination another round of civil war ended with Octavian's assumption of authority.

Romans, Epistle to the a book of the New Testament, an epistle of St Paul to the Church at Rome.

Romansh /rə(ʊ)ˈmanʃ, -ˈmɑːnʃ/ (also **Rumansh**) ▶ **noun** [mass noun] the Rhaeto-Romance language spoken in the Swiss canton of Grisons by fewer than 30,000 people. It has several dialects, and is an official language of Switzerland.
▶ **adjective** relating to the Romansh language.
– ORIGIN from Romansh *Roman(t)sch*, from medieval Latin *romanice* 'in the Romanic manner'.

Roman snail ▶ **noun** another term for EDIBLE SNAIL.

romantic ▶ **adjective 1** conducive to or characterized by the expression of love: *a romantic candlelit dinner*. ■ (of a person) readily demonstrating feelings of love: *he's very handsome, and so romantic*. ■ relating to love, especially in a sentimental or idealized way: *a romantic comedy*.
2 of, characterized by, or suggestive of an idealized view of reality: *a romantic attitude to the past* | *some romantic dream of country peace*.
3 (usu. **Romantic**) relating to or denoting the movement of romanticism: *the Romantic tradition*.
▶ **noun 1** a person with romantic beliefs or attitudes: *I am an incurable romantic*.
2 (usu. **Romantic**) a writer or artist of the Romantic movement.
– DERIVATIVES **romantically** adverb.
– ORIGIN mid 17th cent. (referring to the characteristics of romance in a narrative): from archaic *romaunt* 'tale of chivalry', from an Old French variant of *romanz* (see ROMANCE).

romanticism ▶ **noun** [mass noun] a movement in the arts and literature which originated in the late 18th century, emphasizing inspiration, subjectivity, and the primacy of the individual. Often contrasted with CLASSICISM.

> Romanticism was a reaction against the order and restraint of classicism and neoclassicism, and a rejection of the rationalism which characterized the Enlightenment. In music, the period embraces much of the 19th century, with composers including Schubert, Schumann, Liszt, and Wagner. Writers exemplifying the movement include Wordsworth, Coleridge, Byron, Shelley, and Keats; among romantic painters are such stylistically diverse artists as William Blake, J. M. W. Turner, Delacroix, and Goya.

– DERIVATIVES **romanticist** noun.

romanticize (also **romanticise**) ▶ **verb** [with obj.] deal with or describe in an idealized or unrealistic fashion; make (something) seem better or more appealing than it really is: *the tendency to romanticize non-industrial societies* | [no obj.] *she was romanticizing about the past*.
– DERIVATIVES **romanticization** noun.

Romany /ˈrəʊməni, ˈrɒm-/ (also **Romani**) ▶ **noun** (pl. **Romanies**) **1** [mass noun] the language of the Gypsies, which is an Indo-European language related to Hindi. It is spoken by a dispersed group of about 1 million people, and has many dialects.
2 a Gypsy.
▶ **adjective** relating to Gypsies or their language.
– ORIGIN early 19th cent.: from Romany *Romani*, feminine and plural of the adjective *Romano*, from *Rom* 'man, husband' (see ROM).

Romberg /ˈrɒmbəːg/, Sigmund (1887–1951), Hungarian-born American composer. He wrote a succession of popular operettas, including *The Student Prince* (1924), *The Desert Song* (1926), and *New Moon* (1928).

romcom /ˈrɒmkɒm/ ▶ **noun** informal (in film or television) a romantic comedy.

Rome the capital of Italy and of the Lazio region, situated on the River Tiber about 25 km (16 miles) inland; pop. 2,724,347 (2008). Italian name **Roma**. ■ used allusively to refer to the Roman Catholic Church.

> According to tradition the ancient city was founded by Romulus (after whom it is named) in 753 BC on the Palatine Hill; as it grew it spread to the other six hills of Rome (Aventine, Caelian, Capitoline, Esquiline, Quirinal, and Viminal). Rome was ruled by kings until the expulsion of Tarquinius Superbus in 510 BC led to the establishment of the Roman Republic. By the mid 2nd century BC Rome had subdued the whole of Italy and had come to dominate the western Mediterranean and the Hellenistic world in the east, acquiring the first of the overseas possessions that became the Roman Empire. By the time of the empire's fall the city was overshadowed politically by Constantinople, but emerged as the seat of the papacy and as the spiritual capital of Western Christianity. In the 14th and 15th centuries Rome became a centre of the Renaissance. It remained under papal control, forming part of the Papal States, until 1871, when it was made the capital of a unified Italy.

– PHRASES **all roads lead to Rome** proverb there are many different ways of reaching the same goal or conclusion. **Rome was not built in a day** proverb a complex task is bound to take a long time and should not be rushed. **when in Rome (do as the Romans do)** proverb when abroad or in an unfamiliar environment you should adopt the customs or behaviour of those around you.

Rome, Treaty of a treaty setting up and defining the aims of the European Economic Community. It was signed at Rome on 25 March 1957 by France, West Germany, Italy, Belgium, the Netherlands, and Luxembourg.

Romeo /ˈrəʊmɪəʊ/ ▸ **noun 1** (pl. **Romeos**) an attractive, passionate male seducer or lover.
2 a code word representing the letter R, used in radio communication.
– ORIGIN from the name of the hero of Shakespeare's romantic tragedy *Romeo and Juliet*.

romer /ˈrəʊmə/ ▸ **noun** a small piece of plastic or card bearing perpendicularly aligned scales or (if transparent) a grid, used to determine the precise reference of a point within the grid printed on a map.
– ORIGIN 1930s: named after Carrol *Romer* (1883–1951), its British inventor.

Romish /ˈrəʊmɪʃ/ ▸ **adjective** chiefly derogatory Roman Catholic: *Romish ideas*.

Rommel /ˈrɒm(ə)l/, Erwin (1891–1944), German Field Marshal; known as **the Desert Fox**. As commander of the Afrika Korps he deployed a series of surprise manoeuvres and succeeded in capturing Tobruk (1942), but was defeated by Montgomery at El Alamein later that year. He was forced to commit suicide after being implicated in the officers' conspiracy against Hitler in 1944.

Romney /ˈrɒmni, ˈrʌmni/, George (1734–1802), English portrait painter. From the early 1780s he produced over fifty portraits of Lady Hamilton in historical costumes and poses.

romp ▸ **verb** [no obj.] (especially of a child or animal) play roughly and energetically: *the noisy pack of children romped around the gardens*. ■ [with adverbial] informal proceed without effort to achieve something: *Newcastle romped to victory* | *a 33–1 'no-hoper' romped home*. ■ informal engage in sexual activity, especially illicitly: *a colleague stumbled on the couple romping in an office*.
▸ **noun** a spell of rough, energetic play: *a romp in the snow*. ■ a light-hearted film or other work: *an enjoyably gross sci-fi romp*. ■ informal an easy victory: *their UEFA Cup romp against the Luxembourg part-timers*. ■ informal a spell of sexual activity, especially an illicit one: *three-in-a-bed sex romps*.
– ORIGIN early 18th cent.: perhaps an alteration of **ramp**.

rompers (also **romper suit**) ▸ **plural noun** a young child's one-piece outer garment.

Romulus /ˈrɒmjʊləs/ Roman Mythology one of the traditional founders of Rome, with his brother Remus. The twin sons of Mars by a Vestal Virgin, Romulus and Remus were abandoned at birth but were found and suckled by a she-wolf and brought up by a shepherd family. Remus is said to have been killed by Romulus during an argument about the new city.

Roncesvalles, Battle of /ˈrɒnsəval/ a battle which took place in 778 at a mountain pass in the Pyrenees, near the village of Roncesvalles in northern Spain. The rearguard of Charlemagne's army was attacked by the Basques and massacred. French name **Roncevaux** /rɔ̃svəʊ/.

rondavel /rɒnˈdɑːv(ə)l/ ▸ **noun** S. African a traditional circular African dwelling with a conical thatched roof.
– ORIGIN from Afrikaans *rondawel*.

rond de jambe /ˌrɔ̃ də ˈʒɒmb/ ▸ **noun** (pl. **ronds de jambes** or **ronds de jambe**) Ballet a circular movement of the leg which can be performed on the ground or during a jump.
– ORIGIN French.

ronde /rɒnd/ ▸ **noun** a dance in which the dancers move in a circle.
– ORIGIN 1930s: French, feminine of *rond* 'round'.

rondeau /ˈrɒndəʊ/ ▸ **noun** (pl. **rondeaux** pronunc. **same** or /-əʊz/) a poem of ten or thirteen lines with only two rhymes throughout and with the opening words used twice as a refrain.
– ORIGIN early 16th cent.: French, later form of *rondel* (see **rondel**).

rondel /ˈrɒnd(ə)l/ ▸ **noun** a rondeau, especially one of three stanzas of thirteen or fourteen lines with a two line refrain.
– ORIGIN Middle English: from Old French, from *rond* 'round'; compare with **roundel**.

rondo /ˈrɒndəʊ/ ▸ **noun** (pl. **rondos**) a musical form with a recurring leading theme, often found in the final movement of a sonata or concerto.
– ORIGIN late 18th cent.: Italian, from French *rondeau* (see **rondeau**).

Rondônia /rɒnˈdɒnjə/ a state of NW Brazil, on the border with Bolivia; capital, Pôrto Velho.

rone /rəʊn/ ▸ **noun** Scottish a gutter for carrying off rain from a roof.
– ORIGIN mid 18th cent.: of unknown origin.

rongo-rongo /ˌrɒŋgəʊˈrɒŋgəʊ/ ▸ **noun** [mass noun] Archaeology an ancient script of hieroglyphic signs found on wooden tablets on Easter Island. The symbols have not yet been deciphered.
– ORIGIN early 20th cent.: a local word.

ronin /ˈrəʊnɪn/ ▸ **noun** (pl. **same** or **ronins**) historical (in feudal Japan) a wandering samurai who had no lord or master.
– ORIGIN Japanese.

ronquil /ˈrɒŋkɪl/ ▸ **noun** a slender bottom-dwelling fish that lives in cold coastal waters of the North Pacific. ● Family Bathymasteridae: several genera and species.
– ORIGIN late 19th cent.: from Spanish *ronquillo* 'slightly hoarse'.

Röntgen /ˈrʌntjən, ˈrɒntg(ə)n/, German /ˈrœntgn/, Wilhelm Conrad (1845–1923), German physicist, the discoverer of X-rays. He was a skilful experimenter and worked in a variety of areas as well as radiation. He was awarded the first Nobel Prize for Physics in 1901.

röntgen etc. ▸ **noun** variant spelling of **roentgen** etc.

roo ▸ **noun** Austral. informal a kangaroo.
– ORIGIN early 20th cent.: shortened form.

roo bar ▸ **noun** Australian term for **bull bar**.

rood /ruːd/ ▸ **noun 1** a crucifix, especially one positioned above the rood screen of a church or on a beam over the entrance to the chancel.
2 historical, chiefly Brit. a measure of land area equal to a quarter of an acre (40 square perches, approximately 0.1012 hectare).
– ORIGIN Old English *rōd*; related to Dutch *roede* and German *Rute* 'rod'.

rood loft ▸ **noun** a gallery on top of the rood screen of a church.

rood screen ▸ **noun** a screen, typically of richly carved wood or stone, separating the nave from the chancel of a church. Rood screens are found throughout western Europe and date chiefly from the 14th–16th centuries.

roof ▸ **noun** (pl. **roofs** or **rooves** /ruːvz/) **1** the structure forming the upper covering of a building or vehicle. ■ the top inner surface of a covered area or space; the ceiling: *the roof of the cave fell in*. ■ used to signify a house or other building, especially in the context of hospitality or shelter: *helping those without a roof over their heads* | *they slept under the same roof*.
2 the upper limit or level of prices or wages: *starting salary £12,185, rising to a roof of £16,835*.
▸ **verb** [with obj.] cover with a roof: *the yard had been roughly roofed over with corrugated iron*. ■ function as the roof of: *fan vaults roof these magnificent buildings*.
– PHRASES **go through the roof** informal **1** (of prices or figures) reach extreme or unexpected heights. **2** (also **hit the roof**) suddenly become very angry. **raise the roof** see **raise**. **the roof of the world** the Himalayas.
– DERIVATIVES **roofless** adjective.
– ORIGIN Old English *hrōf*, of Germanic origin; related to Old Norse *hróf* 'boat shed', Dutch *roef* 'deckhouse'. English alone has the general sense 'covering of a house'; other Germanic languages use forms related to *thatch*.

roof bolt ▸ **noun** Mining a tensioned rod anchoring the roof of a working to the strata above.
– DERIVATIVES **roof-bolting** noun.

roofer ▸ **noun** a person who constructs or repairs roofs.

roof garden ▸ **noun** a garden on the flat roof of a building.

roofie ▸ **noun** informal a tablet of the drug Rohypnol.

roofing ▸ **noun** [mass noun] material for constructing a building's roof: *a house with corrugated iron roofing*. ■ the process of constructing a roof or roofs: *jobs such as roofing*.

roofline ▸ **noun** the design or proportions of a vehicle's roof.

roof of the mouth ▸ **noun** the palate.

roof prism ▸ **noun** a reflecting prism in which the reflecting surface is in two parts that are angled like the two sides of a pitched roof. Compare with **Porro prism**. ■ (**roof prisms**) (also **roof-prism binoculars**) a pair of binoculars using two such prisms, resulting in an instrument with parallel sides and objective lenses that are the same distance apart as the eyepieces.

roof rack ▸ **noun** a framework for carrying luggage on the roof of a vehicle.

roof rat ▸ **noun** another term for **black rat**.

roofscape ▸ **noun** a scene or view of roofs, especially when considered in terms of its aesthetic appeal.

rooftop ▸ **noun** the outer surface of a building's roof.
– PHRASES **shout something from the rooftops** see **shout**.

roof-tree ▸ **noun** the ridge piece of a roof.

rooibos /ˈrɔɪbɒs/ ▸ **noun** S. African an evergreen South African shrub of the pea family. ● Genus *Aspalathus*, family Leguminosae.
■ (**rooibos tea**) [mass noun] an infusion of the leaves of the rooibos plant drunk as tea.
– ORIGIN early 20th cent.: from Afrikaans, literally 'red bush'.

rooigras /ˈrɔɪxras/ ▸ **noun** [mass noun] S. African a valuable southern African pasture grass which has a reddish tint in winter. ● *Themeda triandra*, family Poaceae.
– ORIGIN late 19th cent.: from Afrikaans, literally 'red grass'.

rooikat /ˈrɔɪkat/ ▸ **noun** South African term for **caracal**.
– ORIGIN late 18th cent.: from Afrikaans, literally 'red cat'.

rooinek /ˈrɔɪnɛk/ ▸ **noun** S. African informal, offensive an English person or an English-speaking South African (used chiefly by Afrikaners).
– ORIGIN Afrikaans, literally 'red-neck'.

rook[1] ▸ **noun** a gregarious Eurasian crow with black plumage and a bare face, nesting in colonies in treetops. ● *Corvus frugilegus*, family Corvidae.
▸ **verb** [with obj.] informal defraud, overcharge, or swindle (someone).
– ORIGIN Old English *hrōc*, probably imitative and of Germanic origin; related to Dutch *roek*.

rook[2] ▸ **noun** a chess piece, typically with its top in the shape of a battlement, that can move in any direction along a rank or file on which it stands. Each player starts the game with two rooks at opposite ends of the first rank. See also **castle**.
– ORIGIN Middle English: from Old French *rock*, based on Arabic *rukk* (of which the sense remains uncertain).

rookery ▸ **noun** (pl. **rookeries**) **1** a breeding colony of rooks, typically seen as a collection of nests high in a clump of trees. ■ a breeding colony of seabirds, seals, or turtles. ■ North American term for **heronry**.
2 a dense collection of housing, especially in a slum area.

rookie ▸ **noun** informal a new recruit, especially in the army or police: [as modifier] *a rookie cop*. ■ a member of a sports team in their first full season.

R

– ORIGIN late 19th cent.: perhaps an alteration of RECRUIT, influenced by ROOK[1].

rookoo /ˈruːkuː/ ▶ noun variant spelling of ROUCOU.

room /ruːm, rʊm/ ▶ noun **1** [mass noun] space that can be occupied or where something can be done: *there's only room for a single bed in there* | *she* ***made room*** *for Josh on the sofa* | [with infinitive] *he was trapped without room to move.* ■ opportunity or scope for something to happen or be done: *there's* ***room for*** *improvement in the way the programme is managed* | [with infinitive] *a policy which left the government with very little room to manoeuvre.*
2 a part or division of a building enclosed by walls, floor, and ceiling: *he wandered from room to room.* ■ the people present in a room: *the whole room burst into an uproar of approval.* ■ (**rooms**) Brit. a set of rooms, typically rented, in which a person, couple, or family live: *my rooms at Mrs Jenks's house.*
▶ verb [no obj.] N. Amer. share a room, house, or flat, especially a rented one at a college or similar institution: *I was rooming with my cousin.* ■ [with obj.] provide with a shared room or lodging: *they roomed us together.*
– PHRASES **no** (or **not**) **room to swing a cat** humorous used in reference to a very confined space: *there's not even room to swing a cat!* [*cat* in the sense 'cat-o'-nine-tails'.] **smoke-filled rooms** used in reference to political decision-making conducted privately by a small group of influential people rather than more openly or democratically.
– DERIVATIVES **roomed** adjective [in combination] *a four-roomed house*, **roomful** noun (pl. **roomfuls**).
– ORIGIN Old English *rūm*, of Germanic origin; related to Dutch *ruim*, German *Raum*.

roomer ▶ noun N. Amer. a lodger occupying a room without board.

roomette ▶ noun N. Amer. **1** a private single compartment in a railway sleeping car.
2 a small bedroom for letting.

roomie ▶ noun N. Amer. informal a room-mate.

rooming house ▶ noun chiefly N. Amer. a lodging house.

room-mate ▶ noun a person occupying the same room as another. ■ N. Amer. a person occupying the same room, flat, or house as another.

room service ▶ noun [mass noun] a service provided in a hotel allowing guests to order food and drink to be brought to their rooms.

room temperature ▶ noun [mass noun] a comfortable ambient temperature, generally taken as about 20°C.

roomy ▶ adjective (**roomier**, **roomiest**) (especially of accommodation) having plenty of room; spacious.
– DERIVATIVES **roominess** noun.

Rooney, Mickey (b.1920), American actor; born *Joseph Yule Jr.* He received Oscar nominations for his roles in *Babes in Arms* (1939) and *The Human Comedy* (1943).

Roosevelt[1] /ˈrəʊzəvɛlt/, (Anna) Eleanor (1884–1962), American humanitarian and diplomat. She was the niece of Theodore Roosevelt, and married Franklin D. Roosevelt in 1905. She was involved in a wide range of liberal causes; as chair of the UN Commission on Human Rights she helped draft the Declaration of Human Rights (1948).

R

Roosevelt[2] /ˈrəʊzəvɛlt/, Franklin D. (1882–1945), American Democratic statesman, 32nd President of the US 1933–45; full name *Franklin Delano Roosevelt*; known as **FDR**. His New Deal of 1933 helped to lift the US out of the Great Depression, and he played an important part in Allied policy during the Second World War. In 1940 he became the first American President to be elected for a third term in office and he subsequently secured a fourth term.

Roosevelt[3] /ˈrəʊzəvɛlt/, Theodore (1858–1919), American Republican statesman, 26th President of the US 1901–9; known as **Teddy Roosevelt**. He was noted for his antitrust laws and successfully engineered the American bid to build the Panama Canal (1904–14). He won the Nobel Peace Prize in 1906 for negotiating the end of the Russo-Japanese War.

roost[1] ▶ noun a place where birds regularly settle or congregate to rest at night, or where bats congregate to rest in the day.
▶ verb [no obj.] (of a bird or bat) settle or congregate for rest or sleep: *migrating martins and swallows were settling to roost.*
– PHRASES **come home to roost** (of an action in the past) have an unexpected adverse consequence for the person responsible: *for the overextended borrowers,* ***the chickens have come home to roost.*** [from the proverb 'curses, like chickens, come home to roost']
– ORIGIN Old English *hrōst*, related to Dutch *roest*; of unknown ultimate origin.

roost[2] ▶ noun (in the Orkneys and Shetlands) a tidal race.
– ORIGIN mid 17th cent.: from Old Norse *rǫst*.

rooster ▶ noun chiefly N. Amer. a male domestic fowl; a cock.

rooster tail ▶ noun N. Amer. informal the spray of water thrown up behind a speedboat or surfboard. ■ a spray of dust, gravel, etc. thrown up behind a motor vehicle.

root[1] ▶ noun **1** the part of a plant which attaches it to the ground or to a support, typically underground, conveying water and nourishment to the rest of the plant via numerous branches and fibres. ■ the persistent underground part of a plant, especially when fleshy and enlarged and used as a vegetable, e.g. a turnip or carrot. ■ any plant grown for such a root. ■ the embedded part of a bodily organ or structure such as a hair, tooth, or nail: *her hair was fairer at the roots.* ■ the part of a thing attaching it to a greater or more fundamental whole; the end or base.
2 the basic cause, source, or origin of something: *money is the root of all evil* | *jealousy was at the root of it* | [as modifier] *the root cause of the problem.* ■ (**roots**) family, ethnic, or cultural origins: *it's always nice to return to my roots.* ■ (as modifier **roots**) denoting or relating to something from a particular ethnic or cultural origin, especially a non-Western one: *roots music.* ■ (in biblical use) a scion; a descendant: *the root of David.* ■ Linguistics a morpheme, not necessarily surviving as a word in itself, from which words have been made by the addition of prefixes or suffixes or by other modification. ■ (also **root note**) Music the fundamental note of a chord.
3 Mathematics a number or quantity that when multiplied by itself, typically a specified number of times, gives a specified number or quantity. ■ short for SQUARE ROOT. ■ a value of an unknown quantity satisfying a given equation.
4 Austral./NZ & Irish vulgar slang an act of sexual intercourse. ■ [with adj.] a sexual partner of a specified ability.
▶ verb [with obj.] **1** cause (a plant or cutting) to grow roots: *root your own cuttings from stock plants.* ■ [no obj.] (of a plant or cutting) establish roots: *large trees had rooted in the canal bank.*
2 establish deeply and firmly: *vegetarianism is* ***rooted in*** *Indian culture.* ■ (**be rooted in**) have as an origin or cause: *the Latin verb is rooted in an Indo-European word.*
3 [with obj. and adverbial] (often as adj. **rooted**) cause (someone) to stand immobile through fear or amazement: *she found herself* ***rooted to the spot*** *in disbelief.*
4 [with obj.] Austral./NZ & Irish vulgar slang have sexual intercourse with. ■ exhaust (someone) or frustrate their efforts.
– PHRASES **at root** basically; fundamentally: *it is a moral question at root.* **put down roots** (of a plant) begin to draw nourishment from the soil through its roots. ■ (of a person) begin to have a settled life in a particular place. **root and branch** used to express the thorough or radical nature of a process or operation: *root-and-branch reform of personal taxation.* **strike at the root** (or **roots**) **of** affect in a vital area with potentially destructive results: *the proposals struck at the roots of community life.* **take root** (of a plant) begin to grow and draw nourishment from the soil through its roots. ■ become fixed or established: *the idea had taken root in my mind.*
– PHRASAL VERBS **root something out** (also **root something up**) dig or pull up a plant by the roots. ■ find and get rid of someone or something pernicious or dangerous: *a campaign to root out corruption.*
– DERIVATIVES **rootedness** noun, **rootlet** noun, **root-like** adjective, **rooty** adjective (**rootier**, **rootiest**).
– ORIGIN late Old English *rōt*, from Old Norse *rót*; related to Latin *radix*, also to WORT.

root[2] ▶ verb [no obj., with adverbial] (of an animal) turn up the ground with its snout in search of food: *stray dogs rooting around for bones and scraps.* ■ search unsystematically through an untidy mass or area; rummage: *she was rooting through a pile of papers.* ■ [with obj.] (**root something out**) find or extract something by rummaging: *he managed to root out the cleaning kit.*
▶ noun [in sing.] an act of rooting: *I had a root through the open drawers.*
– PHRASAL VERBS **root for** informal support or hope for the success of (a person or group entering a contest or undertaking a challenge): *the whole of this club is rooting for him.* **root someone on** N. Amer. informal cheer or spur someone on: *his mother rooted him on enthusiastically from ringside.*
– ORIGIN Old English *wrōtan*, of Germanic origin; related to Old English *wrōt* 'snout', German *Rüssel* 'snout', and perhaps ultimately to Latin *rodere* 'gnaw'.

root ball ▶ noun the mass formed by the roots of a plant and the soil surrounding them.

root beer ▶ noun [mass noun] N. Amer. an effervescent drink made from an extract of the roots and bark of certain plants.

root-bound ▶ adjective another term for POT-BOUND.

root canal ▶ noun the pulp-filled cavity in the root of a tooth. ■ N. Amer. a procedure to replace infected pulp in a root canal with an inert material.

root cellar ▶ noun N. Amer. a domestic cellar used for storing root vegetables.

root crop ▶ noun a crop that is a root vegetable or other root, e.g. sugar beet.

root directory ▶ noun Computing the directory at the highest level of a hierarchy.

rooter ▶ noun N. Amer. informal a supporter or fan of a sports team or player.

root fly ▶ noun a dark slender fly whose larvae may cause serious damage to the roots of crops. ● Family Anthomyiidae: many genera and species, including the **cabbage root fly** (*Delia radicum*).

root hair ▶ noun Botany each of a large number of elongated microscopic outgrowths from the outer layer of cells in a root, absorbing moisture and nutrients from the soil.

rootin'-tootin' ▶ adjective informal, chiefly N. Amer. brashly or boisterously enthusiastic: *a rootin'-tootin' Wild West show.*
– ORIGIN late 19th cent.: reduplication of *rooting* in the sense 'inquisitive', an early dialect sense of the compound.

rootkit ▶ noun Computing a set of software tools that enable an unauthorized user to gain control of a computer system without being detected.

root-knot ▶ noun [mass noun] a disease of cultivated flowers and vegetables caused by eelworm infestation, resulting in galls on the roots. ● The eelworms belong to the genus *Meloidogyne*, class Nematoda.

rootle ▶ verb Brit. informal term for ROOT[2].
– ORIGIN early 19th cent.: frequentative of ROOT[2].

rootless ▶ adjective **1** (of a plant) not having roots.
2 having no settled home or social or family ties: *a rootless nomad.*
– DERIVATIVES **rootlessness** noun.

root mean square ▶ noun Mathematics the square root of the arithmetic mean of the squares of a set of values.

root nodule ▶ noun see NODULE (sense 1).

root note ▶ noun see ROOT[1] (sense 2 of the noun).

root run ▶ noun the space over which the roots of a plant extend.

root sign ▶ noun Mathematics another term for RADICAL SIGN.

rootstock ▶ noun **1** a rhizome.
2 a plant on to which another variety is grafted. ■ a primary form or source from which offshoots have arisen: *the rootstock of all post-Triassic ammonites.*

rootsy ▶ adjective (**rootsier**, **rootsiest**) informal (of music) uncommercialized and full-blooded, typically showing traditional or ethnic origins.

root vegetable ▶ noun the fleshy enlarged root of a plant used as a vegetable, e.g. a carrot, swede, or beetroot.

rootworm ▶ noun an insect larva that feeds on the roots of plants.

rooves plural form of ROOF.

rope ▶ noun **1** a length of thick strong cord made by twisting together strands of hemp, sisal, nylon, or similar material. ■ N. Amer. a lasso. ■ (**the rope**) used in reference to execution by hanging: *executions by the rope continued well into the twentieth century.* ■ (**the ropes**) the ropes enclosing a boxing or wrestling ring.
2 a quantity of roughly spherical objects such as onions or beads strung together: *a rope of pearls.*
3 (**the ropes**) informal the established procedures in an organization or area of activity: *I want you to* ***show her the ropes.*** [mid 19th cent.: with reference to ropes used in sailing.]
▶ verb [with obj.] **1** catch, fasten, or secure with rope: *the calves must be roped and led out of the stockade* | *the*

climbers were all roped together. ■ **(rope something off)** enclose or separate an area with a rope or tape: *police roped off the area.* ■ [no obj.] Climbing (of a party of climbers) connect each other together with a rope: *we stopped at the foot of the ridge and* ***roped up.*** ■ [no obj.] **(rope down/up)** Climbing climb down or up using a rope: *the party had been roping down a hanging glacier.*
2 (rope someone in/into) persuade someone, despite reluctance, to take part in (an activity): *anyone who could sing in tune was roped in.*
– PHRASES **give a man enough rope (**or **plenty of rope) and he will hang himself** proverb given enough freedom of action a person will bring about their own downfall. **money for old rope** see MONEY. **on the rope** Climbing roped together. **on the ropes** Boxing forced against the ropes by the opponent's attack. ■ in state of near collapse or defeat: *behind the apparent success the company was on the ropes.* **a rope of sand** literary used in allusion to something providing only illusory security or coherence: *our union will become a mere rope of sand.*
– ORIGIN Old English *rāp*, of Germanic origin; related to Dutch *reep* and German *Reif*.

ropeable /ˈrəʊpəb(ə)l/ (also **ropable**) ▶ **adjective** Austral./NZ informal angry; furious: *the idea of it gets him absolutely ropeable.*
– ORIGIN late 19th cent.: from the notion that the person requires to be restrained.

rope-a-dope ▶ **noun** [mass noun] US informal a boxing tactic of pretending to be trapped against the ropes, goading an opponent to throw tiring ineffective punches.
– ORIGIN 1970s: coined by Muhammad Ali, referring to a tactic in a boxing match with George Foreman.

rope ladder ▶ **noun** two long ropes connected by short crosspieces, typically made of wood or metal, used as a ladder.

ropemanship ▶ **noun** [mass noun] skill in climbing with ropes.

rope-moulding ▶ **noun** a moulding cut in an interweaving spiral in imitation of rope strands.

rope's end historical ▶ **noun** a short piece of rope used for flogging, especially on ships.
▶ **verb (rope's-end)** [with obj.] flog with a rope's end.

rope-walk ▶ **noun** historical a long piece of ground where ropes are made.

rope-walker ▶ **noun** dated a performer on a tightrope.
– DERIVATIVES **rope-walking** noun.

ropeway ▶ **noun** a transport system for materials or people, used especially in mines or mountainous areas, in which carriers are suspended from moving cables powered by a motor.

ropey ▶ **adjective** variant spelling of ROPY.

roping ▶ **noun** [mass noun] **1** the action of catching or securing something with ropes: *calf roping.*
2 ropes collectively.

ropy (also **ropey**) ▶ **adjective (ropier, ropiest)**
1 resembling a rope, especially in being long, strong, and fibrous: *the ropy roots of the old tree.*
2 Brit. informal of poor quality: *a portrait by a pretty ropy artist.* ■ slightly ill: *I did feel a bit ropy earlier.*
– DERIVATIVES **ropily** adverb, **ropiness** noun.

roque /rəʊk/ ▶ **noun** [mass noun] US a form of croquet played on a hard court surrounded by a bank.
– ORIGIN late 19th cent.: alteration of ROQUET.

Roquefort /ˈrɒkfɔː/ ▶ **noun** [mass noun] trademark a soft blue cheese made from ewes' milk. It is ripened in limestone caves and has a strong flavour.
– ORIGIN from the name of a village in southern France.

roquet /ˈrəʊkeɪ, -ki/ Croquet ▶ **verb (roquets, roqueting, roqueted)** [with obj.] strike (another ball) with one's own.
▶ **noun** an act of roqueting.
– ORIGIN mid 19th cent.: apparently an arbitrary alteration of the verb CROQUET, originally used in the same sense.

roquette /rɒˈkɛt/ ▶ **noun** another term for ROCKET[2].
– ORIGIN French.

Roraima /rɔːˈrʌɪmə/ **1** a mountain in the Guiana Highlands of South America, situated at the junction of the borders of Venezuela, Brazil, and Guyana. Rising to 2,774 m (9,094 ft), it is the highest peak in the range.
2 a state of northern Brazil, on the borders with Venezuela and Guyana; capital, Boa Vista.

ro-ro ▶ **abbreviation** Brit. roll-on roll-off.
– ORIGIN 1960s: abbreviation.

rorqual /ˈrɔːkw(ə)l/ ▶ **noun** a baleen whale of streamlined appearance with pleated skin on the underside.
● Family Balaenopteridae: two genera and six species, including the **common rorqual** (or fin whale).
– ORIGIN early 19th cent.: via French from Norwegian *røyrkval*, from Old Norse *reythr*, the specific name, + *hvalr* 'whale'.

Rorschach test /ˈrɔːʃɑːk/ ▶ **noun** Psychology a type of projective test used in psychoanalysis, in which a standard set of symmetrical ink blots of different shapes and colours is presented one by one to the subject, who is asked to describe what they suggest or resemble.
– ORIGIN 1920s: named after Hermann *Rorschach* (1884–1922), Swiss psychiatrist.

rort /rɔːt/ ▶ **noun** informal **1** Austral./NZ a fraudulent or dishonest act or practice: *a tax rort.*
2 Austral. dated a wild party.
▶ **verb** [no obj.] Austral./NZ engage in sharp practice. ■ [with obj.] manipulate (a ballot or records) fraudulently; rig. ■ [with obj.] work (a system) to obtain the greatest benefit while remaining within the letter of the law.
– ORIGIN 1930s: back-formation from RORTY.

rorty ▶ **adjective (rortier, rortiest)** Brit. informal boisterous and high-spirited.
– ORIGIN mid 19th cent.: of unknown origin.

Rosa /ˈrəʊzə/, Salvator (1615–73), Italian painter and etcher. His landscapes, often peopled with bandits and containing scenes of violence in wild natural settings, were an important influence on the romantic art of the 18th and 19th centuries.

rosace /ˈrəʊzeɪs/ ▶ **noun** an ornamentation resembling a rose, in particular a rose window.
– ORIGIN mid 19th cent.: from French, from Latin *rosaceus* 'rose-like' (see ROSACEOUS).

rosacea /rəʊˈzeɪʃɪə/ (also **acne rosacea**) ▶ **noun** [mass noun] Medicine a condition in which certain facial blood vessels enlarge, giving the cheeks and nose a flushed appearance.
– ORIGIN late 19th cent.: from Latin, feminine of *rosaceus* in the sense 'rose-coloured'.

rosaceous /rəʊˈzeɪʃəs/ ▶ **adjective** Botany relating to or denoting plants of the rose family (Rosaceae).
– ORIGIN mid 18th cent.: from modern Latin *Rosaceae* (based on Latin *rosa* 'rose') + -OUS.

rosaline /ˈrəʊzəliːn/ ▶ **noun** [mass noun] a variety of fine needlepoint or pillow lace.
– ORIGIN early 20th cent. (as *rosaline point*): probably from French.

rosaniline /rə(ʊ)ˈzanɪliːn, -lɪn, -lʌɪn/ ▶ **noun** [mass noun] Chemistry a reddish-brown synthetic compound which is a base used in making a number of red dyes, notably fuchsin. ● A triphenylmethane derivative; chem. formula: $C_{20}H_{19}N_3$.
– ORIGIN mid 19th cent.: from ROSE[1] + ANILINE.

rosarian /rəʊˈzɛːrɪən/ ▶ **noun** a person who cultivates roses, especially as an occupation.
– ORIGIN mid 19th cent.: from Latin *rosarium* 'rose garden, rosary' + -AN.

Rosario /rəʊˈsɑːrɪəʊ/ an inland port on the Paraná River in east central Argentina; pop. 923,800 (est. 2005).

rosarium /rəʊˈzɛːrɪəm/ ▶ **noun** (pl. **rosariums** or **rosaria**) formal a rose garden.
– ORIGIN mid 19th cent.: from Latin (see ROSARY).

rosary /ˈrəʊz(ə)ri/ ▶ **noun** (pl. **rosaries**) (in the Roman Catholic Church) a form of devotion in which five (or fifteen) decades of Hail Marys are repeated, each decade preceded by an Our Father and followed by a Glory Be. ■ a string of beads for keeping count in a rosary or in the devotions of some other religions, in Roman Catholic use 55 or 165 in number. ■ a book containing a rosary.
– ORIGIN late Middle English (in the sense 'rose garden'): from Latin *rosarium* 'rose garden', based on *rosa* 'rose'.

Roscius /ˈrɒsɪəs, ˈrɒʃɪ-/ (d.62 BC), Roman actor; full name *Quintus Roscius Gallus*. Many notable English actors from the 16th century onwards were nicknamed in reference to his great skill.

roscoe /ˈrɒskəʊ/ ▶ **noun** US informal, dated a gun, especially a pistol or revolver.
– ORIGIN early 20th cent.: from the surname *Roscoe*.

Roscommon /rɒsˈkɒmən/ a county in the north central part of the Republic of Ireland, in the province of Connacht; pop. 58,768 (2006). ■ the county town of Roscommon; pop. 5,017 (2006).

rose[1] ▶ **noun 1** a prickly bush or shrub that typically bears red, pink, yellow, or white fragrant flowers, native to north temperate regions and widely grown as an ornamental. ● Genus *Rosa*, family Rosaceae (the **rose family**); many species, hybrids, and cultivars. This large family includes most temperate fruits (apple, plum, peach, cherry, blackberry, strawberry) as well as the hawthorns, rowans, and potentillas.
■ the flower of a rose bush: *he sent her a dozen red roses.* ■ used in names of other plants whose flowers resemble roses, e.g. **Christmas rose, rose of Sharon**.
2 a stylized representation of a rose in heraldry or decoration, typically with five petals (especially as a national emblem of England): *the Tudor rose.*
3 [mass noun] a warm pink or light crimson colour: *the rose and gold of dawn* | [as modifier] *the 100% cotton range is available in rose pink and ocean blue* | [in combination] *leaves with rose-red margins.* ■ **(usu. roses)** used in reference to a rosy complexion: *the fresh air will soon put the roses back in her cheeks.*
4 (roses) used to refer to favourable circumstances or ease of success: *all is not roses in the firm today.*
5 a perforated cap attached to a shower, the spout of a watering can, or the end of a hose to produce a spray.
6 short for COMPASS ROSE.
▶ **verb** [with obj.] literary make rosy: *a warm flush now rosed her hitherto blue cheeks.*
– PHRASES **a bed of roses** see BED. **come up roses** (of a situation) develop in a very favourable way: *new boyfriend, successful career — everything was coming up roses.* **come up (**or **out) smelling of roses** emerge from a difficult situation with one's reputation intact. **under the rose** archaic in secret; sub rosa.
– DERIVATIVES **rose-like** adjective.
– ORIGIN Old English *rōse*, of Germanic origin, from Latin *rosa*; reinforced in Middle English by Old French *rose*.

rose[2] past of RISE.

rosé /ˈrəʊzeɪ/ ▶ **noun** [mass noun] any light pink wine, coloured by only brief contact with red grape skins.
– ORIGIN French, literally 'pink'.

roseapple ▶ **noun** a tropical evergreen tree cultivated for its foliage and fruit. ● Genus *Syzygium*, family Myrtaceae: several species, in particular the SE Asian *S. jambos*.
■ the spherical white rose-scented fruit of the roseapple.

roseate /ˈrəʊzɪət/ ▶ **adjective** rose-coloured: *the early, roseate light.* ■ used in names of birds with partly pink plumage, e.g. **roseate tern**.
– ORIGIN late Middle English: from Latin *roseus* 'rosy' (from *rosa* 'rose') + -ATE[2].

Roseau /rəʊˈzəʊ/ the capital of Dominica in the Caribbean; pop. 14,000 (est. 2007).

rosebay ▶ **noun 1** (also **rosebay willowherb**) a tall willowherb with pink flowers, native to north temperate regions and often spreading on burnt ground. ● *Epilobium* (or *Chamaenerion*) *angustifolium*, family Onagraceae.
2 N. Amer. a rhododendron. ● Genus *Rhododendron*, family Ericaceae: several species, in particular **Lapland rosebay** (*R. lapponicum*), a dwarf shrub of northern latitudes.

Rosebery /ˈrəʊzbəri/, Archibald Philip Primrose, 5th Earl of (1847–1929), British Liberal statesman, Prime Minister 1894–5.

R

rose bowl ▶ **noun** a bowl for displaying cut roses.

rose-breasted grosbeak ▶ **noun** a North American grosbeak, the male of which is black and white with a pinkish-red breast patch. ● *Pheucticus ludovicianus*, family Emberizidae (subfamily Cardinalinae).

rosebud ▶ **noun** an unopened flower of a rose. ■ archaic a pretty young woman.

rose campion ▶ **noun** an ornamental garden campion with woolly leaves and magenta flowers.
● *Lychnis coronaria*, family Caryophyllaceae.

rose chafer ▶ **noun** a brilliant green or copper-coloured day-flying chafer (beetle) which feeds on roses and other flowers. The larvae typically live in rotting timber. ● Genus *Cetonia*, family Scarabaeidae: several species, in particular the European *C. aurata*.

rose-coloured ▶ **adjective** of a warm pink colour: *rose-coloured silks.* ■ used in reference to a naively optimistic or idealistic viewpoint: *you are still seeing the profession* ***through rose-coloured spectacles.***

rose-coloured starling ▶ **noun** a starling with a pink back and underparts, found from eastern Europe to central Asia and fond of feeding on locusts. ● *Sturnus roseus*, family Sturnidae.

rose comb ▶ **noun** a fleshy comb which lies flat on the head of certain breeds of domestic fowl.

rose-cut ▶ **adjective** (of a gem) cut in tiny triangular facets.

rose diamond ▸ noun a hemispherical diamond with the curved part cut in triangular facets.

rose engine (also **rose-engine lathe**) ▸ noun a lathe for engraving curved or intricate patterns.

rosefinch ▸ noun an Asian finch found chiefly in mountainous areas, the male of which has predominantly pinkish-red plumage. ● *Carpodacus* and other genera, family Fringillidae: many species.

rosefish ▸ noun (pl. **same** or **rosefishes**) N. Amer. the redfish of the North Atlantic (*Sebastes marinus*).

rose geranium ▸ noun a pink-flowered pelargonium with fragrant leaves. ● *Pelargonium graveolens*, family Geraniaceae.

rose hip ▸ noun see HIP².

rosella /rə(ʊ)ˈzɛlə/ ▸ noun an Australian parakeet with vivid green, red, yellow, or blue plumage. ● Genus *Platycercus*, family Psittacidae: several species.
– ORIGIN mid 19th cent.: alteration of *Rosehill*, New South Wales, where the bird was first found.

rose madder ▸ noun [mass noun] a pale shade of pink.

rosemaling /ˈrəʊsəˌmɑːlɪŋ, -ˌmɔːlɪŋ, -zə-/ ▸ noun [mass noun] chiefly N. Amer. the art, originating in Norway, of painting wooden furniture and objects with flower motifs. ■ painted flower motifs as used in rosemaling.
– DERIVATIVES **rosemaled** adjective.
– ORIGIN 1940s: from Norwegian, literally 'rose painting'.

rose mallow ▸ noun an ornamental hibiscus. ● Genus *Hibiscus*, family Malvaceae, in particular *H. rosa-sinensis*.

rosemary ▸ noun [mass noun] an evergreen aromatic shrub of the mint family, native to southern Europe. The narrow leaves are used as a culinary herb, in perfumery, and as an emblem of remembrance. ● *Rosmarinus officinalis*, family Labiatae.
– ORIGIN Middle English *rosmarine*, based on Latin *ros marinus*, from *ros* 'dew' + *marinus* 'of the sea'. The spelling change was due to association with ROSE¹ and MARY¹.

rose of Jericho ▸ noun an annual desert plant whose dead branches fold inwards around the mature seeds forming a ball which is blown about, native to North Africa and the Middle East. ● *Anastatica hierochuntica*, family Cruciferae.

rose of Sharon ▸ noun a low shrub with dense foliage and large golden-yellow flowers, native to SE Europe and Asia Minor and widely cultivated for ground cover. ● *Hypericum calycinum*, family Guttiferae. ■ (in biblical use) a flowering plant of unknown identity.

roseola /rə(ʊ)ˈziːələ, ˌrəʊzɪˈəʊlə/ ▸ noun [mass noun] Medicine a rose-coloured rash occurring in measles, typhoid fever, syphilis, and some other diseases. ■ (in full **roseola infantum** /ɪnˈfantəm/) a disease of young children in which a fever is followed by a rash, caused by a herpesvirus.
– ORIGIN early 19th cent.: modern variant of RUBEOLA, from Latin *roseus* 'rose-coloured'.

R

rose-point ▸ noun [mass noun] point lace with a design of roses.

rose quartz ▸ noun [mass noun] a translucent pink variety of quartz.

roseroot ▸ noun a yellow-flowered stonecrop whose roots smell of roses when dried or bruised, native to north temperate regions. ● *Rhodiola rosea*, family Crassulaceae.

Roses, Wars of the see WARS OF THE ROSES.

Rose Theatre a theatre in Southwark, London, built in 1587. Many of Shakespeare's plays were performed there, some for the first time. Remains of the theatre, which was demolished *c.*1605, were uncovered in 1989.

rose-tinted ▸ adjective another term for ROSE-COLOURED.

Rosetta Stone /rə(ʊ)ˈzɛtə/ an inscribed stone found near Rosetta on the western mouth of the Nile in 1799. Its text is written in three scripts: hieroglyphic, demotic, and Greek. The deciphering of the hieroglyphs by Jean-François Champollion in 1822 led to the interpretation of many other early records of Egyptian civilization. ■ (as noun **a Rosetta stone**) a key to some previously undecipherable mystery or unattainable knowledge: *zero point energy could be the Rosetta stone of physics.*

rosette ▸ noun **1** a rose-shaped decoration, typically made of ribbon, worn by supporters of a sports team or political party or awarded as a prize.
2 an object or arrangement resembling a rose, in particular: ■ Architecture a carved or moulded ornament resembling or representing a rose. ■ Biology a marking or group of markings resembling a rose. ■ a radial arrangement of horizontally spreading leaves at the base of a low-growing plant. ■ a rose diamond.
– DERIVATIVES **rosetted** adjective.
– ORIGIN mid 18th cent.: from French, diminutive of *rose* (see ROSE¹).

rose water ▸ noun [mass noun] scented water made with rose petals, used as a perfume and formerly for medicinal and culinary purposes.

rose window ▸ noun a circular window with mullions or tracery radiating in a form suggestive of a rose.

rosewood ▸ noun **1** [mass noun] close-grained tropical timber with a distinctive fragrance, used particularly for making furniture and musical instruments.
2 the tree which produces rosewood. ● Genus *Dalbergia*, family Leguminosae: several species, in particular *D. nigra* of Brazil.
■ used in names of other trees which yield similar timber, e.g. **African rosewood**.

Rosh Hashana /ˌrɒʃ həˈʃɑːnə/ (also **Rosh Hashanah**) ▸ noun the Jewish New Year festival, held on the first (and sometimes the second) day of Tishri (in September). It is marked by the blowing of the shofar, and begins the ten days of penitence culminating in Yom Kippur.
– ORIGIN Hebrew, literally 'head (i.e. beginning) of the year'.

Roshi /ˈrəʊʃi/ ▸ noun (pl. **Roshis**) the spiritual leader of a community of Zen Buddhist monks.
– ORIGIN Japanese.

Rosicrucian /ˌrəʊzɪˈkruːʃ(ə)n/ ▸ noun a member of a secretive 17th- and 18th-century society devoted to the study of metaphysical, mystical, and alchemical lore. An anonymous pamphlet of 1614 about a mythical 15th-century knight called Christian Rosenkreuz is said to have launched the movement. ■ a member of any of a number of later organizations deriving from the Rosicrucian society.
▸ adjective relating to the Rosicrucians.
– DERIVATIVES **Rosicrucianism** noun.
– ORIGIN from modern Latin *rosa crucis* (or *crux*), Latinization of German *Rosenkreuz*, + -IAN.

Rosie Lee ▸ noun [mass noun] Brit. rhyming slang tea.

rosin /ˈrɒzɪn/ ▸ noun [mass noun] resin, especially the solid amber residue obtained after the distillation of crude turpentine oleoresin, or of naphtha extract from pine stumps. It is used in adhesives, varnishes, and inks and for treating the bows of stringed instruments.
▸ verb (**rosins**, **rosining**, **rosined**) [with obj.] rub (something, especially a violin bow or string) with rosin.
– DERIVATIVES **rosiny** adjective.
– ORIGIN Middle English: from medieval Latin *rosina*, from Latin *resina* (see RESIN).

Roskilde /ˈrɒskɪlə/ a port in Denmark, on the island of Zealand; pop. 46,292 (2009). It was the seat of Danish kings from *c.*1020 and the capital of Denmark until 1443.

rosolio /rə(ʊ)ˈzəʊlɪəʊ/ ▸ noun (pl. **rosolios**) [mass noun] a sweet cordial made in Italy from alcohol, raisins, sugar, rose petals, cloves, and cinnamon.
– ORIGIN Italian, from modern Latin *ros solis* 'dew of the sun'.

RoSPA /ˈrɒspə/ ▸ abbreviation (in the UK) Royal Society for the Prevention of Accidents.

Ross¹, Diana (b.1944), American pop and soul singer. Originally the lead singer of the Supremes, she went on to become a successful solo artist. She received an Oscar for her role as Billie Holiday in the film *Lady Sings the Blues* (1973).

Ross², Sir James Clark (1800–62), British explorer. He discovered the north magnetic pole in 1831, and headed an expedition to the Antarctic from 1839 to 1843, in the course of which he discovered Ross Island, Ross Dependency, and the Ross Sea. He was the nephew of Sir John Ross.

Ross³, Sir John (1777–1856), British explorer. He led an expedition to Baffin Bay in 1818 and another in search of the North-West Passage between 1829 and 1833.

Ross and Cromarty a former county of northern Scotland, stretching from the Moray Firth to the North Minch. In 1975 it became part of Highland region.

Ross Dependency part of Antarctica administered by New Zealand, consisting of everything lying to the south of latitude 60° south between longitudes 160° east and 150° west.
– ORIGIN named after J. C. *Ross* (see ROSS²).

Rossellini /ˌrɒsəˈliːni/, Roberto (1906–77), Italian film director. He is known for his neo-realist films, particularly his quasi-documentary trilogy about the Second World War: *Rome, Open City* (1945), *Paisà* (1946), and *Germany, Year Zero* (1948).

Rossetti¹ /rəˈzɛti/, Christina (Georgina) (1830–94), English poet. She wrote much religious poetry (reflecting her High Anglican faith), love poetry, and children's verse. Notable works: *Goblin Market and Other Poems* (1862). She was the sister of Dante Gabriel Rossetti.

Rossetti² /rəˈzɛti/, Dante Gabriel (1828–82), English painter and poet; full name *Gabriel Charles Dante Rossetti*. A founder member of the Pre-Raphaelite brotherhood (1848), he is best known for his idealized images of women, including *Beata Beatrix* (*c.*1863) and *The Blessed Damozel* (1871–9). He was the brother of Christina Rossetti.

Rossini /rɒˈsiːni/, Gioacchino Antonio (1792–1868), Italian composer, one of the creators of Italian bel canto. He wrote over thirty operas, including *The Barber of Seville* (1816) and *William Tell* (1829).

Rosslare /rɒsˈlɛː/ a ferry port on the SE coast of the Republic of Ireland, in County Wexford.

Ross Sea a large arm of the Pacific forming a deep indentation in the coast of Antarctica.
– ORIGIN named after J. C. *Ross* (see ROSS²).

Ross seal ▸ noun a small Antarctic seal with a short muzzle and large eyes, breeding on the pack ice. ● *Ommatophoca rossi*, family Phocidae.

Rostand /ˈrɒstɒ̃/, French /ʀɔstɑ̃/, Edmond (1868–1918), French dramatist and poet. He romanticized the life of the 17th-century soldier, duellist, and writer Cyrano de Bergerac in his poetic drama of that name (1897).

roster /ˈrɒstə/ ▸ noun a list or plan showing turns of duty or leave for individuals or groups in an organization: *next week's duty roster.* ■ a list of members of a team or organization, in particular of sports players available for team selection.
▸ verb [with obj.] chiefly Brit. place on or assign according to a duty roster: *the locomotive is rostered for service on Sunday.*
– ORIGIN early 18th cent. (originally denoting a list of duties and leave for military personnel): from Dutch *rooster* 'list', earlier 'gridiron', from *roosten* 'to roast', with reference to its parallel lines.

rösti /ˈrəːsti/ ▸ noun (pl. **same**) [mass noun] a Swiss dish of grated potatoes formed into a small flat cake and fried. ■ [count noun] a flat cake of grated potato.
– ORIGIN 1950s: from Swiss German.

Rostock /ˈrɒstɒk/ an industrial port on the Baltic coast of Germany; pop. 199,900 (est. 2006).

Rostov /ˈrɒstɒv/ a port and industrial city in SW Russia, on the River Don near its point of entry into the Sea of Azov; pop. 1,048,700 (est. 2008). The city is built around a fortress erected by the Turks in the 18th century. Full name **Rostov-on-Don**.

rostra plural form of ROSTRUM.

rostral /ˈrɒstr(ə)l/ ▸ adjective **1** Anatomy situated or occurring near the front end of the body, especially in the region of the nose and mouth or (in an embryo) near the hypophyseal region: *the rostral portion of the brain.*
2 Zoology of or on the rostrum: *in these snakes the rostral shield is enlarged and flattened.*
– DERIVATIVES **rostrally** adverb.
– ORIGIN early 19th cent.: from ROSTRUM + -AL.

rostrum /ˈrɒstrəm/ ▸ noun (pl. **rostra** /-trə/ or **rostrums**) **1** a raised platform on which a person stands to make a public speech, receive an award or medal, play music, or conduct an orchestra. ■ a similar platform for supporting a film or television camera.
2 chiefly Zoology a beak-like projection, especially a stiff snout or anterior prolongation of the head in an insect, crustacean, or cetacean.
– DERIVATIVES **rostrate** /-strət/ (also **rostrated**) adjective (sense 2).
– ORIGIN mid 16th cent.: from Latin, literally 'beak' (from *rodere* 'gnaw'). The word was originally used (at first in the plural *rostra*) to denote part of the Forum in Rome, which was decorated with the beaks of captured galleys, and was used as a platform for public speakers.

Roswell /ˈrɒswɛl/ a town in New Mexico, the scene of a mysterious crash in July 1947. Controversy has surrounded claims by some investigators that the crashed object was a UFO.

rosy ▶ adjective (**rosier, rosiest**) **1** (especially of a person's skin) coloured like a pink or red rose, typically as an indication of health, youth, or embarrassment: *the memory had the power to make her cheeks turn rosy* | [in combination] *a rosy-cheeked schoolgirl.*
2 promising or suggesting good fortune or happiness; hopeful: *the strategy has produced results beyond the most rosy forecasts.* ■ easy and pleasant: *life could never be rosy for them.*
– DERIVATIVES **rosily** adverb, **rosiness** noun.

rosy cross ▶ noun an equal-armed cross with a rose at its centre, the emblem of the Rosicrucians.

rosy finch ▶ noun a finch found in Asia and western North America, the male of which has pinkish underparts and rump. ● Genus *Leucosticte*, family Fringillictae: three species, in particular *L. arctoa*.

rot ▶ verb (**rots, rotting, rotted**) **1** (chiefly of animal or vegetable matter) decay or cause to decay by the action of bacteria and fungi; decompose: [no obj.] *the chalets were neglected and their woodwork was **rotting away*** | [with obj.] *caries sets in at a weak point and spreads to rot the whole tooth.* ■ [no obj.] gradually deteriorate, especially through neglect: *the education system has been allowed to rot.*
2 [with obj.] Brit. informal, dated make fun of; tease: *has anybody been rotting you?*
▶ noun [mass noun] **1** the process of decaying: *the leaves were turning black with rot.* ■ rotten or decayed matter. ■ [usu. with modifier] any of a number of fungal or bacterial diseases that cause tissue deterioration, especially in plants. ■ (often **the rot**) liver rot in sheep.
2 (**the rot**) Brit. a process of deterioration; a decline in standards: *there is enough talent in the team to **stop the rot**.* ■ US corruption on the part of officials.
3 informal, chiefly Brit. nonsense; rubbish: *don't talk rot* | [as exclamation] *'Rot!' she said with vehemence.*
– ORIGIN Old English *rotian* (verb), of Germanic origin; related to Dutch *rotten*; the noun (Middle English) may have come via Scandinavian.

rota ▶ noun **1** Brit. a list showing when each of a number of people has to do a particular job: *a cleaning rota*. Compare with **ROSTER**.
2 (**the Rota**) the supreme ecclesiastical and secular court of the Roman Catholic Church.
– ORIGIN early 17th cent.: from Latin, literally 'wheel'.

rotamer /ˈrəʊtəmə/ ▶ noun Chemistry any of a number of isomers of a molecule which can be interconverted by rotation of part of the molecule about a particular bond.
– ORIGIN 1960s: from *rotational* (see **ROTATION**) + **-MER**.

Rotary (in full **Rotary International**) a worldwide charitable society of business and professional people, formed in 1905.
– DERIVATIVES **Rotarian** noun & adjective
– ORIGIN so named because members hosted events in rotation.

rotary ▶ adjective (of motion) revolving around a centre or axis; rotational. ■ (of a thing) acting by means of rotation, especially (of a machine) operating through the rotation of some part: *a rotary mower.*
▶ noun (pl. **rotaries**) **1** a rotary machine, engine, or device.
2 N. Amer. a traffic roundabout.
– ORIGIN mid 18th cent.: from medieval Latin *rotarius*, from *rota* 'wheel'.

Rotary club ▶ noun a local branch of Rotary.

rotary cutter ▶ noun a machine which produces material for use in veneering by rotating a log longitudinally against a blade.
– DERIVATIVES **rotary cutting** noun.

rotary engine ▶ noun an engine which produces rotary motion or which has a rotating part or parts, in particular: ■ an aircraft engine with a fixed crankshaft around which cylinders and propeller rotate. ■ a Wankel engine.

rotary press ▶ noun a printing press that prints from a rotating cylindrical surface on to paper forced against it by another cylinder.

rotary wing ▶ noun [usu. as modifier] an aerofoil that rotates in an approximately horizontal plane, providing all or most of the lift in a helicopter or autogiro.

rotate /rə(ʊ)ˈteɪt/ ▶ verb **1** move or cause to move in a circle round an axis or centre: [no obj.] *the wheel continued to rotate* | (as adj. **rotating**) *a rotating drum* | [with obj.] *the small directional side rockets rotated the craft.*
2 [no obj.] pass to each member of a group in a regularly recurring order: *the job of chairing the meeting rotates.* ■ [with obj.] grow (different crops) in succession on a particular piece of land to avoid exhausting the soil: *these crops were sometimes rotated with grass.* ■ [with obj.] change the position of (tyres) on a motor vehicle to distribute wear.
– DERIVATIVES **rotatable** adjective, **rotative** /ˈrəʊtətɪv/ adjective, **rotatory** /ˈrəʊtət(ə)ri, -ˈteɪt(ə)ri/ adjective.
– ORIGIN late 17th cent.: from Latin *rotat-* 'turned in a circle', from the verb *rotare*, from *rota* 'wheel'.

rotation ▶ noun [mass noun] **1** the action of rotating about an axis or centre: *the moon moves in the same direction as the earth's rotation* | [count noun] *several solar rotations.* ■ Mathematics the conceptual operation of turning a system about an axis. ■ Mathematics another term for **CURL** (sense 3 of the noun).
2 the passing of a privilege or responsibility to each member of a group in a regularly recurring order: *it has become common for senior academics to act as heads of department **in rotation**.* ■ (also **crop rotation**) the action or system of rotating crops. ■ Forestry the cycle of planting, felling, and replanting. ■ [count noun] US a tour of duty, especially by a medical practitioner in training.
– DERIVATIVES **rotational** adjective, **rotationally** adverb.
– ORIGIN mid 16th cent.: from Latin *rotatio(n-)*, from the verb *rotare* (see **ROTATE**).

rotator ▶ noun a thing which rotates or which causes something to rotate. ■ Anatomy a muscle whose contraction causes or assists in the rotation of a part of the body.

rotator cuff ▶ noun Anatomy, chiefly N. Amer. a tough sheath of tendons and ligaments that supports the arm at the shoulder joint.

rotavator /ˈrəʊtəveɪtə/ (also **rotovator**) ▶ noun trademark a machine with rotating blades for breaking up or tilling the soil.
– DERIVATIVES **rotavate** verb.
– ORIGIN 1930s: a blend of **ROTARY** + **CULTIVATOR**.

rotavirus /ˈrəʊtə,vʌɪrəs/ ▶ noun Medicine any of a group of RNA viruses, some of which cause acute enteritis in humans.
– ORIGIN 1970s: modern Latin, from Latin *rota* 'wheel' + **VIRUS**.

ROTC ▶ abbreviation (in the US) Reserve Officers' Training Corps.

rote ▶ noun [mass noun] mechanical or habitual repetition of something to be learned: *a poem learnt **by rote** in childhood* | [as modifier] *rote learning.*
– ORIGIN Middle English (also in the sense 'habit, custom'): of unknown origin.

rotenone /ˈrəʊtənəʊn/ ▶ noun [mass noun] Chemistry a toxic crystalline substance obtained from the roots of derris and related plants, widely used as an insecticide. ● A polycyclic ketone; chem. formula: $C_{23}H_{22}O_6$.
– ORIGIN 1920s: from Japanese *rotenon* (from *roten* 'derris') + **-ONE**.

rotgut ▶ noun [mass noun] informal poor-quality and potentially harmful alcoholic drink.

Roth /rɒθ/, Philip (Milton) (b.1933), American novelist and short-story writer. He often writes about the complexity and diversity of contemporary American Jewish life. Notable works: *Portnoy's Complaint* (1969).

Rotherham /ˈrɒðərəm/ an industrial town in South Yorkshire, northern England; pop. 112,800 (est. 2009).

Rothko /ˈrɒθkəʊ/, Mark (1903–70), American painter, born in Latvia; born *Marcus Rothkovich*. A leading figure in colour-field painting, he painted hazy and apparently floating rectangles of colour.

Rothschild /ˈrɒθs,tʃʌɪld, ˈrɒθ,tʃʌɪld/, Meyer Amschel (1743–1812), German financier. He founded the Rothschild banking house in Frankfurt at the end of the 18th century.

roti /ˈrəʊti/ ▶ noun (pl. **rotis**) [mass noun] Indian bread, especially a flat round bread cooked on a griddle.
– ORIGIN from Hindi *roṭī*.

rotifer /ˈrəʊtɪfə/ ▶ noun Zoology a minute multicellular aquatic animal of the phylum Rotifera.

Rotifera /rəʊˈtɪf(ə)rə/ ▶ plural noun Zoology a small phylum of minute multicellular aquatic animals which have a characteristic wheel-like ciliated organ used in swimming and feeding.
– ORIGIN modern Latin (plural), from Latin *rota* 'wheel' + *ferre* 'to bear'.

rotisserie /rə(ʊ)ˈtɪs(ə)ri/ ▶ noun **1** a restaurant specializing in roasted or barbecued meat.
2 a cooking appliance with a rotating spit for roasting and barbecuing meat.
– ORIGIN mid 19th cent.: from French *rôtisserie*, from *rôtir* 'to roast'.

rotogravure /,rəʊtə(ʊ)grəˈvjʊə/ ▶ noun [mass noun] a printing system using a rotary press with intaglio cylinders, typically running at high speed and used for long print runs of magazines and stamps. ■ [count noun] chiefly N. Amer. a sheet or magazine printed with the rotogravure system, especially the colour magazine of a Sunday newspaper.
– ORIGIN early 20th cent.: from German *Rotogravur*, part of the name of a printing company.

rotor ▶ noun **1** a rotary part of a machine, in particular: ■ a hub with a number of radiating aerofoils that is rotated in an approximately horizontal plane to provide the lift for a rotary wing aircraft. ■ the rotating assembly in a turbine. ■ the armature of an electric motor. ■ (also **rotor arm**) the rotating part of the distributor of an internal-combustion engine which successively makes and breaks electrical contacts so that each spark plug fires in turn. ■ the rotating container in a centrifuge.
2 Meteorology a large eddy in which the air circulates about a horizontal axis, especially in the lee of a mountain.
– ORIGIN early 20th cent.: formed irregularly from **ROTATOR**.

rotorcraft ▶ noun (pl. **same**) a rotary wing aircraft, such as a helicopter or autogiro.

Rotorua /,rəʊtəˈruːə/ a city and major tourist destination in the North Island, New Zealand, on the southwest shore of Lake Rotorua; pop. 53,800 (est. 2006). It lies at the centre of a region of thermal springs and geysers.

rotoscope ▶ noun a device which projects and enlarges individual frames of filmed live action to permit them to be used to create cartoon animation and composite film sequences. ■ a computer application which combines live action and other images in a film.
▶ verb [with obj.] transfer (an image from live action film) into another film sequence using a rotoscope.
– ORIGIN 1950s: origin obscure; perhaps the same word as 19th-cent. *rotascope*, denoting a kind of gyroscope.

rototiller /ˈrəʊtə(ʊ),tɪlə/ ▶ noun trademark North American term for **ROTAVATOR**.
– DERIVATIVES **rototill** verb.

rotovator (also **Rotovator**) ▶ noun variant spelling of **ROTAVATOR**.

rotten ▶ adjective (**rottener, rottenest**) **1** suffering from decay: *rotten eggs* | *the supporting beams were rotten.* ■ morally, socially, or politically corrupt: *he believed that the whole art business was rotten.*
2 informal very bad: *she was a rotten cook.* ■ extremely unpleasant: *it's rotten for you having to cope on your own.* ■ unwell: *she tried to tell me she felt rotten.*
▶ adverb informal to an extreme degree; very much: *your mother said that I **spoiled you rotten*** | *we used to send him up **something rotten**.*
– DERIVATIVES **rottenly** adverb, **rottenness** noun.
– ORIGIN Middle English: from Old Norse *rotinn*.

rotten apple ▶ noun informal used to refer to a morally corrupt person in a group, regarded as capable of having an adverse effect on others: *chartered accountants have no time for rotten apples in their professional barrel.*

rotten borough ▶ noun Brit. historical a borough that was able to elect an MP despite having very few voters, the choice of MP typically being in the hands of one person or family.
– ORIGIN so named because the borough was found to have 'decayed' to the point of no longer having a constituency.

rottenstone ▶ noun [mass noun] decomposed siliceous limestone used as a powder or paste for polishing metals.

rotter ▶ noun informal, dated, chiefly Brit. a cruel, mean, or unkind person: *Rosemary had decided that all men were rotters.*

Rotterdam /ˈrɒtədam/ a city in the Netherlands, at the mouth of the River Meuse, 25 km (15 miles) inland from the North Sea; pop. 582,951 (2008). It is one of the world's largest ports and a major oil refinery, with extensive shipbuilding and petrochemical industries.

Rottweiler /ˈrɒtvʌɪlə, -wʌɪlə/ ▶ **noun** a large powerful dog of a tall black-and-tan breed.
– ORIGIN early 20th cent.: German, from *Rottweil*, the name of a town in SW Germany.

rotund /rə(ʊ)ˈtʌnd/ ▶ **adjective 1** (of a person) large and plump. ■ round or spherical: *huge stoves held great rotund cauldrons.*
2 (of speech or literary style) sonorous; grandiloquent.
– DERIVATIVES **rotundity** noun, **rotundly** adverb.
– ORIGIN late 15th cent.: from Latin *rotundus*, from *rotare* 'rotate'.

rotunda ▶ **noun** a round building or room, especially one with a dome.
– ORIGIN early 17th cent.: alteration of Italian *rotonda* (*camera*) 'round (chamber)', feminine of *rotondo* 'round' (see ROTUND).

rouble /ˈruːb(ə)l/ (also chiefly N. Amer. **ruble**) ▶ **noun** the basic monetary unit of Russia and some other former republics of the USSR, equal to 100 kopeks.
– ORIGIN via French from Russian *rubl'*.

roucou /ruːˈkuː/ (also **rookoo**) ▶ **noun** West Indian term for ANNATTO.
– ORIGIN from Carib.

roué /ˈruːeɪ/ ▶ **noun** a debauched man, especially an elderly one.
– ORIGIN early 19th cent.: French, literally 'broken on a wheel', referring to the instrument of torture thought to be deserved by such a person.

Rouen /ˈruːɒn/, French /ʀwɑ̃/ a port on the River Seine in NW France, chief town of Haute-Normandie; pop. 110,276 (2006). Rouen was in English possession from the time of the Norman Conquest until captured by the French in 1204, and again 1419–49; in 1431 Joan of Arc was tried and burnt at the stake there.

Rouen duck ▶ **noun** a bird of a breed of large duck resembling the wild mallard in colouring.

rouge[1] /ruːʒ/ ▶ **noun 1** [mass noun] a red powder or cream used as a cosmetic for colouring the cheeks or lips.
2 short for JEWELLER'S ROUGE.
▶ **verb** [with obj.] (often as adj. **rouged**) colour with rouge: *her brightly rouged cheeks.* ■ [no obj.] archaic apply rouge to one's cheeks.
▶ **adjective** (of wine) red.
– ORIGIN late Middle English (denoting the colour red): from French, 'red', from Latin *rubeus*. The cosmetic term dates from the mid 18th cent.

rouge[2] /ruː(d)ʒ/ ▶ **noun** (in Canadian football) a single point awarded when the receiving team fails to run a kick out of its own end zone.
– ORIGIN late 19th cent.: of unknown origin.

rouge et noir /ˌruːʒ eɪ ˈnwɑː/ ▶ **noun** [mass noun] a gambling card game in which cards are turned up on a table marked with red and black diamonds.
– ORIGIN late 18th cent.: French, literally 'red and black'.

rouget /ʀuʒɛ/ ▶ **noun** French term for RED MULLET, used especially in cookery.
– ORIGIN French.

R

rough ▶ **adjective 1** having an uneven or irregular surface; not smooth or level: *they had to carry the victim across the rough, stony ground* | *her skin felt dry and rough.* ■ denoting the face of a tennis or squash racket on which the loops formed from the stringing process project (used as a call when the racket is spun to decide the right to serve first or to choose ends).
2 (of a person or their behaviour) not gentle; violent or boisterous: *pushchairs should be capable of withstanding rough treatment.* ■ (of an area or occasion) characterized by violent behaviour: *the workmen hate going to the rough estates.* ■ (of weather or the sea) wild and stormy: *the lifeboat crew braved rough seas to rescue a couple.*
3 not finished tidily or decoratively; plain and basic: *the customers sat at rough wooden tables.* ■ put together as a temporary measure; makeshift: *he had one arm in a rough sling.* ■ lacking sophistication or refinement: *she took care of him in her rough, kindly way.* ■ not fully worked out or including every detail: *he had a rough draft of his new novel.* ■ (of stationery) used for making preliminary notes: *rough paper.*
4 (of a voice) harsh and rasping: *his voice was rough with barely suppressed fury.* ■ (of wine or another alcoholic drink) sharp or harsh in taste.
5 not exact or precise; approximate: *they had a rough idea of when the murder took place* | *it'll cost about £50, at a rough guess.*
6 informal difficult and unpleasant: *the teachers gave me* ***a rough time*** *because my image didn't fit.* ■ Brit. hard; severe: *the first day of a job is* ***rough on*** *everyone.* ■ unwell: *the altitude had hit her and she was feeling rough.*
▶ **adverb** informal in a manner that lacks gentleness; harshly or violently: *treat 'em rough but treat 'em fair.*
▶ **noun 1** chiefly Brit. a disreputable and violent person.
2 [mass noun] (on a golf course) longer grass around the fairway and the green: *his second shot lay* ***in the rough.***
3 a preliminary sketch: *I did a rough to work out the scale of the lettering.*
4 an uncut precious stone.
▶ **verb** [with obj.] **1** work or shape (something) in a rough, preliminary fashion: *flat surfaces of wood are* ***roughed down.*** ■ (**rough something out**) produce a preliminary and unfinished version of something: *the engineer roughed out a diagram on his notepad.*
2 make uneven: ***rough up*** *the icing with a palette knife.*
3 (**rough it**) informal live in discomfort with only basic necessities: *she'd had to rough it alone in digs.*
– PHRASES **bit of rough** informal a male sexual partner whose toughness or lack of sophistication is a source of attraction. **in the rough 1** without decoration or other treatment; in a natural state: *a diamond in the rough.* **2** in difficulties: *even before the recession hit, the project was in the rough.* **rough and ready** crude but effective: *a rough-and-ready estimating method.* ■ (of a person or place) unsophisticated or unrefined. **rough around the edges** having a few imperfections. **rough as bags** Austral./NZ informal lacking refinement; coarse. **the rough edge** (or **side**) **of someone's tongue** a scolding: *you two stop quarrelling or you'll get the rough edge of my tongue.* **rough edges** small imperfections. **rough justice** treatment that is not scrupulously fair or in accordance with the law. **rough passage** a journey over rough sea. ■ a difficult time or experience: *the rough passage faced by the legislation.* **a rough ride** see RIDE. **sleep rough** Brit. sleep in uncomfortable conditions, typically out of doors. **take the rough with the smooth** accept the unpleasant aspects of life as well as the good.
– PHRASAL VERBS **rough someone up** informal beat someone up: *he was roughed up in jail while awaiting trial.*
– DERIVATIVES **roughish** adjective, **roughness** noun.
– ORIGIN Old English *rūh*, of West Germanic origin; related to Dutch *ruw* and German *rauh*.

roughage ▶ **noun** [mass noun] fibrous indigestible material in vegetable foodstuffs which aids the passage of food and waste products through the gut. ■ Farming coarse, fibrous fodder.

rough and tumble ▶ **noun** a situation without rules or organization; a free-for-all: *the rough and tumble of political life* | [as modifier] *the rough-and-tumble atmosphere of the dealing room.*
– ORIGIN early 19th cent.: originally boxing slang.

rough breathing ▶ **noun** see BREATHING (sense 2).

roughcast ▶ **noun** [mass noun] plaster of lime, cement, and gravel, used on outside walls.
▶ **adjective 1** (of a building or part of a building) coated with roughcast.
2 (of a person) lacking refinement: *she thought of the roughcast yeomen she would meet.*
▶ **verb** (past and past participle **roughcast**) [with obj.] coat (a wall) with roughcast.

rough-coated ▶ **adjective** (of a dog or other animal) having relatively coarse fur which does not lie flat: *a rough-coated Jack Russell.*

rough collie ▶ **noun** a dog of a rough-coated breed of collie, typically black and white or black, white, and tan.

rough copy ▶ **noun 1** a first draft of a piece of writing.
2 a copy of a picture showing only the essential features.

rough cut ▶ **noun** the first version of a film after preliminary editing.
▶ **verb** (**rough-cut**) [with obj.] cut (something) rapidly and without particular attention to quality or accuracy.

rough diamond ▶ **noun** an uncut diamond. ■ Brit. a person who is generally of good character but lacks manners, education, or style.

rough-dry ▶ **verb** [with obj.] dry (something) roughly or imperfectly: *she continued to rough-dry her hair.*

roughen ▶ **verb** make or become rough: [with obj.] *the wind was roughening the surface of the river* | [no obj.] *his voice roughened.*

rough grazing ▶ **noun** [mass noun] uncultivated land used for grazing livestock. ■ [count noun] a piece of such land.

rough-hewn ▶ **adjective** denoting wood or stone that has been cut with a tool such as an axe, so that its surface is not smooth: *rough-hewn logs.* ■ not sophisticated, polished, or elegant: *a rough-hewn cinematic style.* ■ denoting or possessing attractively strong or bony facial features: *his angular, rough-hewn face.*
– DERIVATIVES **rough-hew** verb.

rough hound ▶ **noun** another term for DOGFISH (sense 1).

rough house informal, chiefly N. Amer. ▶ **noun** a violent disturbance.
▶ **verb** (**rough-house**) [no obj.] act in a boisterous, violent manner: *they rough-house on street corners.* ■ [with obj.] handle (someone) roughly or violently: *he had them rough-housed by his servants.*

roughie ▶ **noun 1** dialect & Austral., dated a hooligan. ■ Austral./NZ an unfair or unreasonable act.
2 Austral./NZ an outsider in a horse race.
3 variant spelling of ROUGHY.

roughing ▶ **noun** [mass noun] Ice Hockey unnecessary or excessive use of force, for which a minor penalty may be given.

roughly ▶ **adverb 1** in a manner lacking gentleness; harshly or violently: *the man picked me up roughly.*
2 in a manner lacking refinement and precision: *people were crouching over roughly built brick fireplaces.*
3 approximately: *this is a walk of roughly 13 miles* | [sentence adverb] *the narrative is,* ***roughly speaking,*** *contemporary with the earliest of the gospels.*

roughneck informal ▶ **noun 1** a rough and uncouth person.
2 an oil rig worker.
▶ **verb** [no obj.] (usu. as noun **roughnecking**) work on an oil rig.

rough-rider ▶ **noun** N. Amer. a person who rides horses frequently. ■ a person who breaks in or can ride unbroken horses. ■ (**Rough Rider**) a member of a volunteer cavalry force during the Spanish-American War.

roughshod ▶ **adjective** archaic (of a horse) having shoes with nail heads projecting to prevent slipping.
– PHRASES **ride roughshod over** see RIDE.

rough timber ▶ **noun** [mass noun] partly dressed timber, having only the branches removed.

rough tongue ▶ **noun** the habit of speaking rudely: *he was known as a jovial fellow but was not without a vicious temper and a rough tongue.*
– DERIVATIVES **rough-tongued** adjective.

rough trade ▶ **noun** [mass noun] informal male homosexual prostitution, especially when involving brutality or sadism. ■ people involved in prostitution of this type.

roughy /ˈrʌfi/ (also **roughie**) ▶ **noun** (pl. **roughies**) Austral./NZ **1** a marine fish with a deeply laterally compressed body and large rough-edged scales which become spiny on the belly. ● Family Trachichthyidae: several genera and species, including the small Australian *Trachichthys australis*, which occurs on rocky reefs.
2 another term for RUFF[2] (sense 1).

rouille /ˈruːi/ ▶ **noun** [mass noun] a Provençal sauce made from pounded red chillies, garlic, breadcrumbs, and other ingredients blended with stock, typically added to bouillabaisse.
– ORIGIN French, literally 'rust', with reference to the colour.

roulade /ruːˈlɑːd/ ▶ **noun 1** a dish cooked or served in the form of a roll, typically made from a flat piece of meat, fish, or sponge, spread with a soft filling and rolled up into a spiral.
2 a florid passage of runs in classical music for a solo virtuoso, especially one sung to one syllable.
– ORIGIN French, from *rouler* 'to roll'.

rouleau /ˈruːləʊ, ruːˈləʊ/ ▶ **noun** (pl. **rouleaux** or **rouleaus** /-əʊz/) **1** a cylindrical packet of coins.
2 a coil or roll of ribbon, knitted wool, or other material, especially used as trimming.
– ORIGIN late 17th cent.: French, from obsolete French *roule* 'a roll'.

roulement /ˈruːlmɒ̃/ ▶ **noun** [mass noun] Military movement of troops or equipment, especially for a short period of duty to relieve another force.
– ORIGIN early 20th cent.: French, literally 'rolling'.

Roulers /ruːˈlɛː/ French name for **ROESELARE**.

roulette ▶ **noun 1** [mass noun] a gambling game in which a ball is dropped on to a revolving wheel with numbered compartments, the players betting on the number at which the ball comes to rest.
2 a tool or machine with a revolving toothed wheel, used in engraving or for making slit-shaped perforations between postage stamps.
▶ **verb** [with obj.] make slit-shaped perforations in (paper, especially sheets of postage stamps).
– ORIGIN mid 18th cent.: from French, diminutive of *rouelle* 'wheel', from late Latin *rotella*, diminutive of Latin *rota* 'wheel'.

Roumania /ruːˈmeɪnɪə/ old-fashioned variant of **ROMANIA**.

Roumanian /ruːˈmeɪnɪən/ ▶ **adjective & noun** old-fashioned variant of **ROMANIAN**.

Roumelia variant spelling of **RUMELIA**.

round ▶ **adjective 1** shaped like a circle or cylinder: *she was seated at a small, round table.* ■ having a curved shape like part of the circumference of a circle: *round brackets.* ■ (of a person's shoulders) bent forward from the line of the back.
2 shaped like a sphere: *a round glass ball | the grapes are small and round.* ■ (of a person's body) plump. ■ having a curved surface with no sharp projections: *the boulders look round and smooth.*
3 (of a voice) rich and mellow; not harsh.
4 [attrib.] (of a number) expressed in convenient units rather than exactly, for example to the nearest whole number or multiple of ten: *the size of the fleet is given in round numbers.* ■ used to show that a figure has been completely and exactly reached: *the batsman made a round 100 | a round dozen.* ■ archaic (of a sum of money) considerable: *his business is worth a round sum to me.*
5 not omitting or disguising anything; frank: *she berated him in good round terms.*
▶ **noun 1** a circular piece of something: *cut the pastry into rounds.* ■ a thick disc of beef cut from the haunch as a joint.
2 an act of visiting a number of people or places in turn: *she* ***did the rounds of*** *her family to say goodbye.* ■ a regular tour of inspection in which the well-being of those visited is checked: *the doctor is just* ***making his rounds*** *in the wards.* ■ chiefly Brit. a journey along a fixed route delivering goods as part of one's job or a job involving such journeys: *I did a newspaper round.*
3 each of a sequence of sessions in a process, typically characterized by development between one session and another: *the two sides held three rounds of talks.* ■ a division of a contest such as a boxing or wrestling match. ■ each of a succession of stages in a competition, in each of which more candidates are eliminated: *the FA Cup first round.* ■ an act of playing all the holes in a golf course once: *Eileen enjoys the occasional* ***round of golf***.
4 a regularly recurring sequence of activities: *their lives were a* ***daily round*** *of housework and laundry.* ■ a set of drinks bought for all the members of a group, typically as part of a sequence in which each member in turn buys such a set: *it's my round.*
5 Music a song for three or more unaccompanied voices or parts, each singing the same theme but starting one after another, at the same pitch or in octaves; a simple canon.
6 Brit. a slice of bread: *two rounds of toast.* ■ the quantity of sandwiches made from two slices of bread.
7 the amount of ammunition needed to fire one shot. ■ Archery a fixed number of arrows shot from a fixed distance.
▶ **adverb** chiefly Brit. **1** so as to rotate or cause rotation; with circular motion: *a plane circled round overhead | she turned her glass* ***round and round***. ■ so as to cover or take in the whole area surrounding a particular centre: *she paused to glance round admiringly at the décor.* ■ so as to reach everyone in a particular group or area: *he passed round a newspaper cutting.*
2 so as to rotate and face in the opposite direction: *he swung round to face her.* ■ so as to lead in another direction: *it was the last house before the road curved round.* ■ used in describing the position of something, typically with regard to the direction in which it is facing or its relation to other items: *the picture shows the pieces the wrong way round.* ■ used to describe a situation in terms of the relation between people, actions, or events: *it was he who was attacking her, not the other way round.*
3 so as to surround someone or something: *everyone crowded round | a pool with banks all the way round.* ■ used in stating the girth of something: *the trunk is nine feet round.*
4 so as to reach a new place or position, typically by moving to the other side of something: *he made his way round to the back of the building | they went the* ***long way round*** *by the main road.* ■ used to convey an ability to navigate or orientate oneself: *I like pupils to* ***find their own way round***. ■ informal used to convey the idea of visiting someone else: *why don't you come round to my flat?*
5 used to suggest idle and purposeless motion or activity: *he was driving round aimlessly.*
6 so as to give support and companionship: *if one girl is distraught the others will rally round.*
▶ **preposition** chiefly Brit. **1** on every side of (a focal point): *the area round the school | with shifting sands all round me.* ■ (of something abstract) having (the thing mentioned) as a focus: *the text is built round real practical examples.*
2 so as to encircle (someone or something): *he wrapped the blanket round him | she drew a red circle round his name.* ■ (of a person's arm or arms) partially encircling (another person) as a gesture of affection: *Angus put an arm round Flora and kissed her.*
3 following an approximately circular route past (a corner or obstacle): *a bus appeared round the corner.* ■ on the other side of (a corner or obstacle): *Steven parked the car round the corner.* ■ so as to hit (something) in passing: *if he didn't shut up he might get a clip round the ear.*
4 so as to cover or take in the whole area of (a place): *she went round the house and saw that all the windows were barred.*
▶ **verb** [with obj.] **1** pass and go round (something) so as to move on in a changed direction: *the ship rounded the cape and sailed north.*
2 alter (a number) to one less exact but more convenient for calculations: *we'll* ***round*** *the weight* ***up*** *to the nearest kilo | the committee* ***rounded down*** *the figure.*
3 give a round shape to: *a lathe that rounded chair legs.* ■ [no obj.] become circular in shape: *her eyes rounded in dismay.* ■ Phonetics pronounce (a vowel) with the lips narrowed and protruded.
– PHRASES **go the round** (or **rounds**) (of a story or joke) be passed on from person to person. **in the round 1** (of sculpture) standing free with all sides shown, rather than carved in relief against a ground. ■ fully and thoroughly; with all aspects shown: *to understand social phenomena one must see them in the round.* **2** (of a theatrical performance) with the audience placed on at least three sides of the stage. **round about 1** on all sides or in all directions: *everything round about was covered with snow.* **2** at a point or time approximately equal to: *they arrived round about nine.* **round the bend** see **BEND**[1]. **round the twist** see **TWIST**.
– PHRASAL VERBS **round something off** make the edges or corners of something smooth. ■ complete something in a satisfying or suitable way: *a pint at the pub will round off the day nicely.* **round on** make a sudden verbal attack on: *she rounded on me angrily.* **round something out** make something more complete: *his father insisted he went to university to round out his education.* **round someone/thing up** drive or collect a number of people or animals together for a particular purpose: *in the afternoon the cows are rounded up for milking.* ■ arrest a number of people.
– DERIVATIVES **roundish** adjective, **roundness** noun.
– ORIGIN Middle English: from the Old French stem *round-*, from a variant of Latin *rotundus* 'rotund'.

USAGE Are round and around (as preposition and adverbial particle) interchangeable in all contexts? In many contexts in British English they are, as in *she put her arm* ***round*** *him*; *she put her arm* ***around*** *him*. There is, however, a general preference for **round** to be used for definite, specific movement (*she turned* ***round***; *a bus came* ***round*** *the corner*), while **around** tends to be used in contexts which are less definite (*she wandered* ***around*** *for ages*; *costing* ***around*** *£3,000*) or for abstract uses (*a rumour circulating* ***around*** *the cocktail bars*).
In US English the situation is different. The normal form in most contexts is **around**; **round** is generally regarded as informal or non-standard and is only standard in certain fixed expressions, as in *all year* ***round*** and *they went* ***round and round*** *in circles*.

roundabout ▶ **noun 1** Brit. a road junction at which traffic moves in one direction round a central island to reach one of the roads converging on it.
2 Brit. a large revolving device in a playground, for children to ride on. ■ a merry-go-round.
▶ **adjective** not following a short direct route; circuitous: *we need to take a roundabout route to throw off any pursuit.* ■ not saying what is meant clearly and directly; circumlocutory: *in a roundabout way, he was fishing for information.*

round-arm ▶ **adjective** Cricket (of bowling) performed with an outward horizontal swing of the arm.

roundball ▶ **noun** US informal term for **BASKETBALL**.
– DERIVATIVES **roundballer** noun.

round brackets ▶ **plural noun** Brit. brackets of the form ( ).

round dance ▶ **noun** a folk dance in which the dancers form one large circle. ■ a ballroom dance such as a waltz or polka in which couples move in circles round the ballroom.

rounded ▶ **adjective 1** having a smooth, curved surface: *rounded grey hills.* ■ having a spherical shape: *his large, rounded stomach.* ■ forming circular or elliptical shapes: *his writing was firm and rounded.* ■ Phonetics (of a vowel) pronounced with the lips narrowed and protruded.
2 well developed in all aspects; complete and balanced: *we should educate children to become rounded human beings.*

roundel /ˈraʊnd(ə)l/ ▶ **noun 1** a small disc, especially a decorative medallion. ■ a picture or pattern contained in a circle. ■ Heraldry a plain filled circle as a charge (often with a special name according to colour). ■ a circular identifying mark painted on military aircraft, as, for example, the red, white, and blue of the RAF.
2 a short poem consisting of three stanzas of three lines each, rhyming alternately, with the opening words repeated as a refrain after the first and third stanzas. The form, a variant of the rondeau, was developed by Swinburne.
– ORIGIN Middle English: from Old French *rondel*, from *ro(u)nd-* (see **ROUND**).

roundelay /ˈraʊndəleɪ/ ▶ **noun** literary a short, simple song with a refrain. ■ a circle dance.
– ORIGIN late Middle English: from Old French *rondelet*, from *rondel* (see **RONDEL**). The change in the ending was due to association with the final syllable of **VIRELAY**.

rounder ▶ **noun 1** (in rounders) a complete run of a player through all the bases as a unit of scoring.
2 N. Amer. informal a habitual criminal or disreputable person.

rounders ▶ **plural noun** [treated as sing.] a ball game played (chiefly in British schools) with a cylindrical wooden bat, in which players run round a circuit of bases after hitting the ball.

round game ▶ **noun** a game, typically a card game, for more than two players in which each player plays as an individual, not as part of a team.

round hand ▶ **noun** a style of handwriting in which the letters have clear rounded shapes.

Roundhead ▶ **noun** historical a member or supporter of the Parliamentary party in the English Civil War.
– ORIGIN so named because of the short-cropped hairstyle of the Puritans, who formed an important element in the party.

roundheel ▶ **noun** N. Amer. informal a promiscuous woman.
– DERIVATIVES **roundheeled** adjective.
– ORIGIN 1950s: with reference to worn-down heels, allowing the wearer to lean backwards.

roundhouse ▶ **noun 1** a railway locomotive maintenance shed built around a turntable.
2 informal a blow given with a wide sweep of the arm. ■ Baseball a slow, widely curving pitch. ■ a wide turn on a surfboard.
3 chiefly historical a cabin or set of cabins on the after part of the quarterdeck of a sailing ship.

roundhouse kick ▶ **noun** (chiefly in karate) a kick made with a wide sweep of the leg and rotation of the body.

roundly ▶ **adverb 1** in a vehement or emphatic manner: *the latest attacks have been roundly condemned by campaigners for peace.* ■ so thoroughly as to leave no doubt: *the army was roundly beaten.* ■ too plainly for politeness; bluntly: *she told him roundly to get to the point.*
2 so as to form a circular or roughly circular shape: *he was a middle-aged, roundly built man.*

round-nose ▶ **adjective 1** (of a tool) having the end rounded, so as to produce a rounded cut or surface or to prevent accidents or damage.
2 (of a bullet) having a rounded front end.
▶ **noun** a bullet with a rounded front end.
– DERIVATIVES **round-nosed** adjective.

R

round robin ▶ **noun 1** [often as modifier] a tournament in which each competitor plays in turn against every other: *a round-robin competition.* ■ a series or sequence: *an inconclusive round robin of talks in Cairo, Washington, and New York.*
2 a petition, especially one with signatures written in a circle to conceal the order of writing.

round shot ▶ **noun** [mass noun] historical ammunition in the form of cast-iron or steel spherical balls for firing from cannon.

round-shouldered ▶ **adjective** having the shoulders bent forward so that the back is rounded: *a thin, round-shouldered man.*

roundsman ▶ **noun** (pl. **roundsmen**) **1** Brit. a trader's employee who goes round delivering and taking orders: *a milk roundsman.*
2 US a police officer in charge of a patrol.
3 Austral. a journalist covering a specified subject.

Round Table ▶ **noun 1** the table at which King Arthur and his knights sat so that none should have precedence.
2 an international charitable association which holds discussions and undertakes community service, open to men between the ages of 18 and 45, typically from business and professional groups.
3 (usu. as modifier **round table**) an assembly for discussion, especially at a conference: *round-table talks.*

round trip ▶ **noun** a journey to one or more places and back again, especially by a route that does not cover the same ground twice. ■ [often as modifier] chiefly N. Amer. a journey to a place and back again, along the same route: *a round-trip air fare.*

round turn ▶ **noun** a complete turn of a rope around another rope or an anchoring point.

round-up ▶ **noun** a systematic gathering together of people or things: *mass police round-ups and detentions.* ■ a summary of facts or events: *a news round-up every fifteen minutes.*

round window ▶ **noun** informal term for **FENESTRA ROTUNDA** (see **FENESTRA**).

roundwood ▶ **noun** [mass noun] timber which is left as small logs, not sawn into planks or chopped for fuel, typically taken from near the tops of trees and used for furniture.

roundworm ▶ **noun** a nematode worm, especially a parasitic one found in the intestines of mammals.
● Many species in the class Phasmida, including the large *Ascaris lumbricoides* in humans.

roup[1] /raʊp/ chiefly Scottish & N. English ▶ **noun** an auction.
▶ **verb** [with obj.] sell (something) by auction: *his effects were rouped.*
– ORIGIN Middle English (in the sense 'roar, croak'): of Scandinavian origin; compare with Old Norse *raupa* 'boast, brag'.

roup[2] /ruːp/ ▶ **noun** [mass noun] an infectious disease of poultry affecting the respiratory tract.
– ORIGIN mid 16th cent.: of unknown origin.

rouse /raʊz/ ▶ **verb** [with obj.] **1** cause to stop sleeping: *she was roused from a deep sleep by a hand on her shoulder.* ■ [no obj.] cease to sleep or to be inactive; wake up: *she roused, took off her eyepads, and looked around.* ■ bring out of inactivity: *once the enemy camp was roused, they would move on the castle | she'd just stay a few more minutes, then* ***rouse herself*** *and go back.* ■ startle (game) from a lair or cover.
2 make angry or excited: *the crowds were* ***roused to*** *fever pitch by the drama of the race.* ■ give rise to (an emotion or feeling): *his evasiveness roused my curiosity.*
3 stir (a liquid, especially beer while brewing): *rouse the beer as the hops are introduced.*
– DERIVATIVES **rousable** adjective, **rouser** noun.
– ORIGIN late Middle English (originally as a hawking and hunting term): probably from Anglo-Norman French, of unknown ultimate origin.

R

rouseabout ▶ **noun** Austral./NZ an unskilled labourer or odd jobber on a farm, especially in a shearing shed.
– ORIGIN mid 19th cent.: originally dialect in the sense 'rough bustling person', from the verb **ROUSE**.

rousette /ruˈzɛt/ (also **rousette fruit bat**) ▶ **noun** a fruit bat that feeds mainly on nectar and pollen, forming very large colonies in caves from Africa to the Solomon Islands. ● Genus *Rousettus*, family Pteropodidae: several species.
– ORIGIN late 18th cent.: from French *roussette*, feminine of Old French *rousset* 'reddish', from *roux* 'red'.

rousing ▶ **adjective 1** exciting; stirring: *a rousing speech.*
2 archaic (of a fire) blazing strongly.
– DERIVATIVES **rousingly** adverb.

Rous sarcoma /raʊs/ ▶ **noun** a form of tumour, caused by an RNA virus, which affects birds, particularly poultry.
– ORIGIN early 20th cent.: named after Francis P. *Rous* (1879–1970), American physician.

Rousse variant spelling of **RUSE**.

Rousseau[1] /ˈruːsəʊ/, French /ʀuso/, Henri (Julien) (1844–1910), French painter; known as **le Douanier** ('customs officer'). After retiring as a customs official in 1893, he created bold and colourful paintings of fantastic dreams and exotic jungle landscapes, such as *Sleeping Gypsy* (1897) and *Tropical Storm with Tiger* (1891).

Rousseau[2] /ˈruːsəʊ/, French /ʀuso/, Jean-Jacques (1712–78), French philosopher and writer, born in Switzerland. He believed that civilization warps the fundamental goodness of human nature, but that the ill effects can be moderated by active participation in democratic consensual politics. Notable works: *Émile* (1762) and *The Social Contract* (1762).

Rousseau[3] /ˈruːsəʊ/, French /ʀuso/, (Pierre Étienne) Théodore (1812–67), French painter. A leading landscapist of the Barbizon School, his works typically depict the scenery and changing light effects of the forest of Fontainebleau, for example *Under the Birches, Evening* (1842–4).

Roussillon /ˈruːsɪjɒn/, French /ʀusijɔ̃/ a former province of southern France, on the border with Spain in the eastern Pyrenees, now part of Languedoc-Roussillon. Part of Spain until 1659, Roussillon retains many of its Spanish characteristics and traditions and Catalan is widely spoken.

roust /raʊst/ ▶ **verb** [with obj.] **1** N. Amer. cause to get up or start moving; rouse: *I rousted him out of his bed with a cup of tea.*
2 informal treat roughly; harass: *the detectives who had rousted him the night of the murder.*
– ORIGIN mid 17th cent.: perhaps an alteration of **ROUSE**.

roustabout /ˈraʊstəbaʊt/ ▶ **noun** an unskilled or casual labourer. ■ a labourer on an oil rig. ■ N. Amer. a dock labourer or deckhand. ■ N. Amer. a circus labourer. ■ Austral./NZ variant spelling of **ROUSEABOUT**.
– ORIGIN mid 19th cent.: from the verb **ROUST**.

rout[1] /raʊt/ ▶ **noun 1** a disorderly retreat of defeated troops: *the retreat degenerated into a rout.* ■ a decisive defeat: *the party lost more than half their seats in the rout.*
2 Law, dated an assembly of people who have made a move towards committing an illegal act which would constitute an offence of riot. ■ archaic a disorderly or tumultuous crowd of people: *a rout of strangers ought not to be admitted.*
3 archaic a large evening party or reception.
▶ **verb** [with obj.] defeat and cause to retreat in disorder: *in a matter of minutes the attackers were routed.*
– PHRASES **put to rout** put to flight; defeat utterly.
– ORIGIN Middle English: ultimately based on Latin *ruptus* 'broken', from the verb *rumpere*; sense 1 and the verb (late 16th cent.) are from obsolete French *route*, probably from Italian *rotta* 'break-up of an army'; the other senses are via Anglo-Norman French *rute*.

rout[2] /raʊt/ ▶ **verb 1** [with obj.] cut a groove, or any pattern not extending to the edges, in (a wooden or metal surface).
2 [no obj.] dialect (of an animal) turn up ground with its snout in search of food. ■ rummage about.
3 [with obj.] find (someone or something), or force them from a place: *Simon routed him from the stable.*
– ORIGIN mid 16th cent. (in sense 2): alteration of the verb **ROOT**[2]. Sense 1 dates from the early 19th cent.

route /ruːt/ ▶ **noun** a way or course taken in getting from a starting point to a destination: *the scenic route from Florence to Siena.* ■ the line of a road, path, railway, etc. ■ N. Amer. a round travelled in delivering, selling, or collecting goods. ■ a method or process leading to a specified result: *the many routes to a healthier diet will be described.*
▶ **verb** (**routes**, **routeing** or **routing**, **routed**) [with obj. and adverbial of direction] send or direct along a specified course: *all lines of communication were routed through London.*
– ORIGIN Middle English: from Old French *rute* 'road', from Latin *rupta (via)* 'broken (way)', feminine past participle of *rumpere*.

route man ▶ **noun** North American term for **ROUNDSMAN** (sense 1).

route march ▶ **noun** a march for troops over a designated route, typically via roads or tracks.

route one ▶ **noun** [mass noun] Soccer, Brit. the use of a long kick upfield as an attacking tactic.
– ORIGIN from a phrase used in the 1960s television quiz show *Quizball*, in which questions (graded in difficulty) led to scoring a goal, *Route One* being the direct path.

router[1] /ˈraʊtə/ ▶ **noun** a power tool with a shaped cutter, used in carpentry for making grooves for joints, decorative mouldings, etc.

router[2] /ˈruːtə/ ▶ **noun** a device which forwards data packets to the appropriate parts of a computer network.

routier /ˈruːtɪeɪ/, French /ʀutje/ ▶ **noun** (pl. **routiers** pronunc. **same**) **1** a member of a band of mercenaries in France in the late medieval period.
2 (in France) a long-distance lorry driver.
– ORIGIN French, from *route* 'road'.

routine ▶ **noun** a sequence of actions regularly followed: *I settled down into a routine of work and sleep |* [mass noun] *as a matter of routine a report will be sent to the director.* ■ a set sequence in a performance such as a dance or comedy act: *he was trying to persuade her to have a tap routine in the play.* ■ Computing a sequence of instructions for performing a task that forms a program or a distinct part of one.
▶ **adjective** performed as part of a regular procedure rather than for a special reason: *the Ministry insisted that this was just a routine annual drill.*
▶ **verb** [with obj.] rare organize according to a routine: *all had been routined with smoothness.*
– DERIVATIVES **routinely** adverb.
– ORIGIN late 17th cent. (denoting a regular course or procedure): from French, from *route* 'road' (see **ROUTE**).

routinism ▶ **noun** [mass noun] archaic the prevalence or domination of routine.
– DERIVATIVES **routinist** noun & adjective.

routinize (also **routinise**) ▶ **verb** [with obj.] make (something) into a matter of routine; subject to a routine: *communication was routinized to ensure consistency of information.*
– DERIVATIVES **routinization** noun.

roux /ruː/ ▶ **noun** (pl. **same**) Cookery a mixture of fat (especially butter) and flour used in making sauces.
– ORIGIN from French *(beurre) roux* 'browned (butter)'.

ROV ▶ **abbreviation** remotely operated vehicle.

Rovaniemi /ˈrəʊvəˌnɪəmi/ the principal town of Finnish Lapland; pop. 58,100 (est. 2007).

rove[1] ▶ **verb** [no obj., with adverbial of direction] travel constantly without a fixed destination; wander: *he spent most of the 1990s roving about the Caribbean.* ■ [with obj.] wander over or through in such a way: *children roving the streets.* ■ (usu. as adj. **roving**) travel for one's work, having no fixed base: *he trained as a roving reporter.* ■ (of a person's eyes) look in changing directions in order to see something thoroughly: *the policeman's eyes roved around the pub.*
▶ **noun** [in sing.] chiefly N. Amer. a journey, especially one with no specific destination; an act of wandering: *a new exhibit will electrify campuses on its national rove.*
– ORIGIN late 15th cent. (originally a term in archery in the sense 'shoot at a casual mark of undetermined range'): perhaps from dialect *rave* 'to stray', probably of Scandinavian origin.

rove[2] past of **REEVE**[2].

rove[3] ▶ **noun** a sliver of cotton, wool, or other fibre, drawn out and slightly twisted, especially preparatory to spinning.
▶ **verb** [with obj.] form (slivers of wool, cotton, or other fibre) into roves.
– ORIGIN late 18th cent.: of unknown origin.

rove[4] ▶ **noun** a small metal plate or ring for a rivet to pass through and be clenched over, especially in boatbuilding.
– ORIGIN Middle English: from Old Norse *ró*, with the addition of parasitic *-v-*.

rove beetle ▶ **noun** a long-bodied beetle with very short wing cases, typically found among decaying matter where it may scavenge or prey on other scavengers. ● Family Staphylinidae: numerous genera.

rover[1] ▶ **noun 1** a person who spends their time wandering: *they became rovers who departed further and further from civilization.*
2 (in various sports) a player not restricted to a particular position on the field. ■ Australian Rules one of the three players making up a ruck, typically one who is small, fast, and skilful at receiving the ball.

3 a vehicle for driving over rough terrain, especially one driven by remote control over extraterrestrial terrain.
4 Croquet a ball that has passed all the hoops but not pegged out. ■ a player who has such a ball.
5 Archery a mark for long-distance shooting. ■ a mark chosen at random and not at a determined range.
6 (**Rover** or **Rover Scout**) Brit. former term for VENTURE SCOUT.

rover[2] ▶ **noun** archaic a pirate.
– ORIGIN Middle English: from Middle Low German, Middle Dutch *rōver*, from *rōven* 'rob'; related to REAVE.

rover[3] ▶ **noun** a person or machine that makes roves of fibre (see ROVE[3]).

rover ticket ▶ **noun** Brit. a ticket permitting unlimited travel on buses, trains, or other public transport in an area for a specified period.

roving ▶ **noun** another term for ROVE[3]. ■ [mass noun] roves collectively.

roving commission ▶ **noun** Brit. an authorization given to someone conducting an inquiry to travel as is necessary.

roving eye ▶ **noun** a tendency to flirt or be constantly looking to start a new sexual relationship: *if his wife wasn't around, he had a roving eye.*

Rovno /ˈrɔvnə/ Russian name for RIVNE.

row[1] /rəʊ/ ▶ **noun** a number of people or things in a more or less straight line: *her villa stood in a row of similar ones.* ■ a line of seats in a theatre: *they sat in the front row.* ■ [often in place names] a street with a continuous line of houses along one or both of its sides: *he lives at 23 Saville Row.* ■ a horizontal line of entries in a table. ■ a complete line of stitches in knitting or crochet.
– PHRASES **a hard** (or **tough**) **row to hoe** a difficult task. **in a row** forming a line: *four chairs were set in a row.* ■ informal in succession: *he jumped nineteen clear rounds in a row.* **Row Z** Brit. informal the back row of seats in a concert hall, theatre, or stadium: *they could have snatched a late winner, but he struck his shot into row Z.*
– ORIGIN Old English *rāw*, of Germanic origin; related to Dutch *rij* and German *Reihe*.

row[2] /rəʊ/ ▶ **verb** [with obj.] propel (a boat) with oars: *out in the bay a small figure was rowing a rubber dinghy.* ■ [no obj., with adverbial of direction] travel by rowing a boat: *we rowed down the river all day.* ■ convey (a passenger) in a boat by rowing it: *her father was rowing her across the lake.* ■ [no obj.] engage in the sport of rowing, especially competitively: *he rowed for England* | [with complement] *he rowed stroke in the University Eight.*
▶ **noun** [in sing.] a spell of rowing.
– PHRASAL VERBS **row someone down** overtake a team in a rowing race, especially a bumping race. **row someone out** exhaust someone by rowing. **row over** complete the course of a boat race with little effort, owing to the absence or inferiority of competitors.
– DERIVATIVES **rower** noun.
– ORIGIN Old English *rōwan*, of Germanic origin; related to RUDDER; from an Indo-European root shared by Latin *remus* 'oar', Greek *eretmon* 'oar'.

row[3] /raʊ/ ▶ **noun** chiefly Brit. **1** a noisy acrimonious quarrel: *they had a row and she stormed out of the house.* ■ a serious dispute: *the director is at the centre of a row over policy decisions.* ■ informal a severe reprimand: *I always got a row if I left food on my plate.*
2 a loud noise or uproar: *if he's at home he must have heard that row.*
▶ **verb** [no obj.] have a quarrel: *they rowed about who would receive the money from the sale* | *she had rowed with her boyfriend the day before.* ■ [with obj.] Brit. rebuke severely: *she was rowed for leaving her younger brother alone.*
– PHRASES **make** (or **kick up**) **a row** informal, chiefly Brit. make a noise or commotion. ■ make a vigorous protest.
– ORIGIN mid 18th cent.: of unknown origin.

rowan /ˈrəʊən, ˈraʊən/ (also **rowan tree**) ▶ **noun** a small deciduous tree of the rose family, with compound leaves, white flowers, and red berries. Compare with MOUNTAIN ASH. ● Genus *Sorbus*, family Rosaceae: several species, in particular the European *S. aucuparia*, which is associated with much folklore.
– ORIGIN late 15th cent. (originally Scots and northern English): of Scandinavian origin; compare with Norwegian *rogn*.

rowboat ▶ **noun** North American term for ROWING BOAT.

rowdy ▶ **adjective** (**rowdier**, **rowdiest**) noisy and disorderly: *it was a rowdy but good-natured crowd.*
▶ **noun** (pl. **rowdies**) a noisy and disorderly person.
– DERIVATIVES **rowdily** adverb, **rowdiness** noun, **rowdyism** noun.
– ORIGIN early 19th cent. (originally US in the sense 'lawless backwoodsman'): of unknown origin.

Rowe, Nicholas (1674–1718), English dramatist. Notable works: *Tamerlane* (1701) and *The Fair Penitent* (1703).

rowel /ˈraʊ(ə)l/ ▶ **noun** a spiked revolving disc at the end of a spur.
▶ **verb** (**rowels**, **rowelling**, **rowelled**; US **rowels**, **roweling**, **roweled**) [with obj.] use a rowel to urge on (a horse): *he rowelled his horse on as fast as he could.*
– ORIGIN Middle English: from Old French *roel(e)*, from late Latin *rotella*, diminutive of Latin *rota* 'wheel'.

rowen /ˈraʊən/ ▶ **noun** US a second growth of grass or hay in one season.
– ORIGIN Middle English: from an Old Northern French variant of Old French *regain* 'an increase'.

row house ▶ **noun** N. Amer. a terraced house.

rowing ▶ **noun** [mass noun] the sport or pastime of propelling a boat by means of oars.

> Racing takes place in narrow, light boats (**shells**), between single rowers (**scullers**) with two oars, or between crews of two, four, or eight people with one oar each; crews are often steered by a coxswain.

rowing boat ▶ **noun** Brit. a small boat propelled by use of oars.

rowing machine ▶ **noun** an exercise machine with oars and a sliding seat, for exercising the muscles used in rowing.

Rowlandson /ˈrəʊlən(d)s(ə)n/, Thomas (1756–1827), English painter, draughtsman, and caricaturist. His best-known watercolours and drawings feature in a series of books known as *The Tours of Dr Syntax* (1812–21).

Rowling /ˈrəʊlɪŋ/, J. K. (b.1965), English novelist; full name *Joanne Kathleen Rowling*. She created the highly successful *Harry Potter* children's books, the first volume of which, *Harry Potter and the Philosopher's Stone*, was published in 1997.

rowlock /ˈrɒlək, ˈrʌlək/ ▶ **noun** Brit. a fitting on the gunwale of a boat which serves as a fulcrum for an oar and keeps it in place.
– ORIGIN mid 18th cent.: alteration of OARLOCK, influenced by the verb ROW[2].

Rowntree /ˈraʊntriː/, a family of English business entrepreneurs and philanthropists. **Joseph** (1801–59) was a grocer who established several Quaker schools. His son **Henry Isaac** (1838–83) founded the family cocoa and chocolate manufacturing firm in York, while his brother **Joseph** (1836–1925) became Henry's business partner in 1869 and founded three Rowntree trusts (1904) to support research into social welfare and policy.

row vector ▶ **noun** Mathematics a vector represented by a matrix consisting of a single row of elements.

Roxburghshire /ˈrɒksb(ə)rəʃɪə, -ʃə/ a former county of the Scottish Borders. Since 1975 it has been part of Borders region (now Scottish Borders).

royal ▶ **adjective** having the status of a king or queen or a member of their family: *contributors included members of the royal family.* ■ belonging to, carried out, or exercised by a king or queen: *the royal palace* | *the coalition obtained royal approval for the appointment.* ■ in the service or under the patronage of a king or queen: *a royal maid.* ■ of a quality or size suitable for a king or queen; splendid: *she received a royal welcome.* ■ [attrib.] Brit. informal real; utter (used for emphasis): *she's a* **right royal** *pain in the behind.*
▶ **noun 1** informal a member of the royal family.
2 short for ROYAL SAIL or ROYAL MAST.
3 short for ROYAL STAG.
4 (in full **metric royal**) [mass noun] a paper size, 636 × 480 mm. ■ (in full **royal octavo**) a book size, 234 × 156 mm. ■ (in full **royal quarto**) a book size, 312 × 237 mm.
5 Bell-ringing a system of change-ringing using ten bells.
– PHRASES **royal road to** a way of attaining or reaching something without trouble: *there is no royal road to teaching.*
– DERIVATIVES **royally** adverb.
– ORIGIN late Middle English: from Old French *roial*, from Latin *regalis* 'regal'.

Royal Academy of Arts (also **Royal Academy**) an institution established in London in 1768, whose purpose was to cultivate painting, sculpture, and architecture in Britain. Sir Joshua Reynolds was its first president and he instituted a highly influential series of annual lectures.

Royal Air Force (abbrev.: **RAF**) the British air force, formed in 1918 by amalgamation of the Royal Flying Corps (founded 1912) and the Royal Naval Air Service (founded 1914).

royal antelope ▶ **noun** a small West African antelope with an arched back, short neck, and a red and brown coat. ● *Neotragus pygmaeus*, family Bovidae.

royal assent ▶ **noun** [mass noun] assent of the sovereign to a Bill which has been passed by Parliament, and which thus becomes an Act of Parliament. Royal assent by the sovereign (in person or through commissioners of the Crown) is required before a Bill (or a Measure passed by the General Synod of the Church of England) can come into force as law, but it has not been withheld since 1707.

royal blue ▶ **noun** [mass noun] a deep, vivid blue.

Royal British Legion (in the UK) an association for the charitable support of ex-servicemen and -women and their immediate dependants, formed in 1921.

royal burgh ▶ **noun** historical (in Scotland) a burgh holding a charter from the Crown.

Royal Canadian Mounted Police the national police force of Canada, founded in 1873 as the North West Mounted Police. A member of the force is informally called a MOUNTIE.

Royal Commission ▶ **noun** (in the UK) a commission of inquiry appointed by the Crown on the recommendation of the government.

royal demesne ▶ **noun** chiefly historical an area of land owned by the Crown.

Royal Doulton ▶ **noun** see DOULTON.

royal duke ▶ **noun** a duke who is also a royal prince.

Royal Engineers the field engineering and construction corps of the British army.

royal fern ▶ **noun** a large pale green fern which has very long spreading fronds with widely spaced oblong lobes, occurring worldwide in wet habitats. ● *Osmunda regalis*, family Osmundaceae.

royal fish ▶ **noun** a whale, porpoise, or sturgeon caught near the British coast or cast ashore there. In these circumstances they belong to the Crown or, in the Duchy of Cornwall, to the Prince of Wales.

royal flush ▶ **noun** (in poker) a straight flush including ace, king, queen, jack, and ten all in the same suit, which is the hand of the highest possible value when wild cards are not in use.

Royal Gala ▶ **noun** a New Zealand dessert apple of a variety with red and yellow skin.
– ORIGIN 1960s: originally *Gala*, but renamed following a visit by Queen Elizabeth II, who was impressed by this variety.

Royal Greenwich Observatory the official astronomical institution of Great Britain. It was founded at Greenwich in London in 1675 by Charles II, and the old buildings now form part of the National Maritime Museum. The Observatory headquarters were moved to East Sussex in 1948 and to Cambridge in 1990.

royal icing ▶ **noun** [mass noun] chiefly Brit. hard white icing made from icing sugar and egg whites, typically used to decorate fruit cakes.

Royal Institution a British society founded in 1799 for the diffusion of scientific knowledge. It organizes educational events, promotes research, and maintains a museum, library, and information service.

royalist ▶ **noun** a person who supports the principle of monarchy or a particular monarchy. ■ (**Royalist**) a supporter of the King against Parliament in the English Civil War. ■ US a supporter of the British during the War of American Independence.
▶ **adjective** giving support to the monarchy: *the paper claims to be royalist.* ■ (**Royalist**) (in the English Civil War) supporting the King against Parliament: *the Royalist army.*
– DERIVATIVES **royalism** noun.

royal jelly ▶ **noun** [mass noun] a substance secreted by honeybee workers and fed by them to larvae which are being raised as potential queen bees.

Royal Leamington Spa official name for LEAMINGTON SPA.

R

Royal Marines a British armed service (part of the Royal Navy) founded in 1664, trained for service at sea, or on land under specific circumstances.

royal mast ▶ noun a section of a sailing ship's mast above the topgallant.

Royal Maundy ▶ noun see **MAUNDY**.

Royal Mint the establishment responsible for the manufacture of British coins. Set up in 1810 in London, it moved in 1968 to Llantrisant in South Wales.

Royal National Lifeboat Institution (abbrev.: **RNLI**) (in the UK) a voluntary organization formed in 1824 to operate an offshore rescue service with lifeboats.

Royal Navy (abbrev.: **RN**) the British navy. It was the most powerful navy in the world from the 17th century until the Second World War.

royal oak ▶ noun a sprig of oak worn on 29 May to commemorate the restoration of Charles II (1660), who hid in an oak tree after the battle of Worcester (1651).

royal palm ▶ noun a New World palm which is widely cultivated as an avenue tree. ● Genus *Roystonea*, family Palmae: several species, in particular *R. regia*.

royal plural ▶ noun another term for **ROYAL 'WE'**.

royal prerogative ▶ noun see **PREROGATIVE**.

royal purple ▶ noun [mass noun] a rich deep shade of purple.

royal sail ▶ noun a sail above a sailing ship's topgallant sail.

Royal Shakespeare Company (abbrev.: **RSC**) a British professional theatre company founded in 1961. It is based at Stratford-upon-Avon and at the Barbican Centre in London.

Royal Society (in full **Royal Society of London**) the oldest and most prestigious scientific society in Britain. It was formed by followers of Francis Bacon to promote scientific discussion especially in the physical sciences, and received its charter from Charles II in 1662.

Royal Society for the Prevention of Cruelty to Animals (abbrev.: **RSPCA**) (in the UK) a charitable organization formed in 1824 to safeguard the welfare of animals.

Royal Society for the Protection of Birds (abbrev.: **RSPB**) (in the UK) a charitable organization founded in 1889 for the conservation of wild birds.

Royal Society of Arts (abbrev.: **RSA**) an institution established in London in 1754 whose original purpose was to forge a link between art and commerce following a decline in craftsmanship after the onset of the Industrial Revolution. It now holds examinations for a wide range of vocational and professional qualifications.

royal stag ▶ noun Brit. a red deer stag with a head of twelve or more points.

royal standard ▶ noun a banner bearing the royal coat of arms, flown in the presence of royalty.

royal tennis ▶ noun another term for **REAL TENNIS**.

Royal Tunbridge Wells official name for **TUNBRIDGE WELLS**.

royalty ▶ noun (pl. **royalties**) **1** [mass noun] people of royal blood or status: *diplomats, heads of state, and royalty shared tables at the banquet.* ■ a member of a royal family: *she swept by as if she were royalty.* ■ the status or power of a king or queen: *the brilliance of her clothes, her jewels, all revealed her royalty.*
2 a sum paid to a patentee for the use of a patent or to an author or composer for each copy of a book sold or for each public performance of a work.
3 a royal right (now especially over minerals) granted by the sovereign to an individual or corporation. ■ a payment made by a producer of minerals, oil, or natural gas to the owner of the site or of the mineral rights over it.
– ORIGIN late Middle English: from Old French *roialte*, from *roial* (see **ROYAL**). The sense 'royal right (especially over minerals)' (late 15th cent.) developed into the sense 'payment made by a mineral producer to the site owner' (mid 19th cent.), which was then transferred to payments for the use of patents and published materials.

Royal Victorian Chain (in the UK) an order founded by Edward VII in 1902 and conferred by the sovereign on special occasions.

Royal Victorian Order (in the UK) an order founded by Queen Victoria in 1896 and typically conferred for great service rendered to the sovereign.

> It has five classes of membership, which are: Knight or Dame Grand Cross of the Royal Victorian Order (GCVO), Knight or Dame Commander (KCVO/DCVO), Commander (CVO), Lieutenant (LVO), and Member (MVO).

royal warrant ▶ noun a warrant issued by the sovereign, especially one authorizing a company to display the royal arms, indicating that goods or services are supplied to the sovereign or to a member of the royal family.

royal 'we' ▶ noun the use of 'we' instead of 'I' by a single person, as traditionally used by a sovereign.

Royal Worcester ▶ noun (trademark in the UK) see **WORCESTER**[2].

Royce, Sir (Frederick) Henry (1863–1933), English engine designer. He founded the company of Rolls-Royce Ltd with Charles Stewart Rolls in 1906, becoming famous as the designer of the Rolls-Royce Silver Ghost car and later also becoming known for his aircraft engines.

rozzer ▶ noun Brit. informal a police officer.
– ORIGIN late 19th cent.: of unknown origin.

RP ▶ abbreviation received pronunciation.

RPG ▶ abbreviation ■ report program generator, a high-level commercial computer programming language. ■ rocket-propelled grenade. ■ role-playing game.

RPI ▶ abbreviation retail price index.

rpm ▶ abbreviation ■ resale price maintenance. ■ revolutions per minute.

RPO ▶ abbreviation Royal Philharmonic Orchestra.

rpt ▶ abbreviation ■ repeat. ■ report.

RPV ▶ abbreviation remotely piloted vehicle.

RR ▶ abbreviation N. Amer. ■ railroad. ■ rural route.

-rrhoea ▶ combining form discharge; flow: *diarrhoea*.
– ORIGIN from Greek *rhoia* 'flow, flux'.

rRNA ▶ abbreviation Biochemistry ribosomal RNA.

RRP ▶ abbreviation Brit. recommended retail price.

RS ▶ abbreviation ■ (in the US) received standard. ■ (in the UK) Royal Scots.

Rs. ▶ abbreviation rupee(s).

RSA ▶ abbreviation ■ Republic of South Africa. ■ Royal Scottish Academy; Royal Scottish Academician. ■ (in the UK) Royal Society of Arts.

RSC ▶ abbreviation ■ Royal Shakespeare Company. ■ (in the UK) Royal Society of Chemistry.

RSE ▶ abbreviation Royal Society of Edinburgh.

RSFSR ▶ abbreviation historical Russian Soviet Federative Socialist Republic.

RSI ▶ abbreviation repetitive strain injury.

RSJ ▶ abbreviation rolled steel joist.

RSM ▶ abbreviation ■ (in the British army) Regimental Sergeant Major. ■ San Marino (international vehicle registration). [from Italian *Repubblica di San Marino*.]

RSNC ▶ abbreviation (in the UK) Royal Society for Nature Conservation.

RSPB ▶ abbreviation (in the UK) Royal Society for the Protection of Birds.

RSPCA ▶ abbreviation (in the UK) Royal Society for the Prevention of Cruelty to Animals.

RSS ▶ abbreviation Computing Really Simple Syndication, a standardized system for the distribution of content from an online publisher to Internet users.

RSV ▶ abbreviation Revised Standard Version (of the Bible).

RSVP ▶ abbreviation répondez s'il vous plaît; please reply (used at the end of invitations to request a response).
– ORIGIN French.

RT ▶ abbreviation ■ radio-telegraphy. ■ radio-telephony.

rt ▶ abbreviation right.

RTA ▶ abbreviation Brit. road traffic accident.

rte ▶ abbreviation route.

RTÉ ▶ abbreviation Radio Telefís Éireann, the official broadcasting organization of the Republic of Ireland.

RTF ▶ abbreviation Computing rich text format, developed to allow the transfer of graphics and formatted text between different applications and operating systems.

RTFM ▶ abbreviation Computing, vulgar slang read the fucking manual (used especially in email in reply to a question whose answer is patently obvious).

Rt Hon. ▶ abbreviation Brit. Right Honourable.

Rt Revd (also **Rt Rev.**) ▶ abbreviation Brit. Right Reverend.

RTW ▶ abbreviation round the world (denoting a type of plane ticket).

RU ▶ abbreviation ■ informal are you?: *where RU?* ■ Burundi (international vehicle registration). [from *Ruanda-Urundi* (now Rwanda and Burundi).] ■ rugby union.

Ru ▶ symbol the chemical element ruthenium.

RU486 ▶ noun trademark for **MIFEPRISTONE**.

rub ▶ verb (**rubs, rubbing, rubbed**) **1** [with obj.] apply firm pressure to the surface of (something), using a repeated back and forth motion: *she rubbed her arm, where she had a large bruise* | [no obj.] *he* **rubbed** *at the earth on his jeans.* ■ [with obj. and adverbial of direction] move (one's hand, a cloth, or another object) back and forth against a surface: *he rubbed a finger round the rim of his mug.* ■ [with obj. and adverbial] apply (ointment, polish, or a similar substance) with a back and forth motion: *she took out her suncream and rubbed some on her nose.* ■ make dry, clean, or smooth by rubbing: *she found a towel and began rubbing her hair* | [with obj. and complement] *I rubbed myself dry.* ■ (**rub something in/into/through**) work an ingredient into (a mixture) by breaking and blending it with firm movements of one's fingers: *sift the flour into a bowl and rub in the fat.* ■ reproduce the design of (a sepulchral brass or a stone) by rubbing paper laid on it with coloured wax, pencil, or chalk, etc.
2 (with reference to two things) move or cause to move to and fro against each other with a certain amount of friction: [with obj. and adverbial] *many insects make noises by rubbing parts of their bodies together* | [no obj., with adverbial] *the ice breaks into small floes that rub against each other.* ■ [no obj.] (of shoes or other hard items in contact with the skin) cause pain through friction: *badly fitting shoes can rub painfully.* ■ [no obj.] Bowls (of a bowl) be slowed or diverted by the unevenness of the ground.
▶ noun **1** an act of rubbing: *she pulled out a towel and gave her head a quick rub.* ■ an ointment designed to be rubbed on the skin to ease pain: *a muscle rub.*
2 (**the rub**) the central problem or difficulty in a situation: *that was the rub—she had not cared enough.* [from Shakespeare's *Hamlet* (III. i. 65).]
3 Bowls an inequality of the ground impeding or diverting a bowl; the diversion or hindering of a bowl by this.
– PHRASES **not have two pennies** (or **farthings** etc.) **to rub together** informal be very poor. **the rub of the green** Golf an accidental or unpredictable influence on the course or position of the ball. ■ good fortune, especially as determining events in a sporting match. **rub one's hands** rub one's hands together to show keen satisfaction. **rub it in** (or **rub someone's nose in something**) informal emphatically draw someone's attention to an embarrassing fact or mistake: *they don't just beat you, they rub it in.* **rub noses** rub one's nose against someone else's in greeting (especially as traditional among Maoris and some other peoples). **rub shoulders** (or N. Amer. **elbows**) associate or come into contact with another person: *he* **rubbed shoulders** *with TV stars at the party.* **rub someone** (or Brit. **rub someone up**) **the wrong way** irritate or repel someone (as by stroking a cat against the lie of its fur).
– PHRASAL VERBS **rub along** Brit. informal cope or manage without undue difficulty: *they rub along because their overheads are so low.* ■ have a satisfactorily friendly relationship. **rub something down** dry, smooth, or clean something by rubbing. ■ rub the sweat from a horse or one's own body after exercise. **rub off** be transferred by contact or association: *when parents are having a hard time, their tension can easily* **rub off** *on the kids.* **rub someone out** informal, chiefly N. Amer. kill someone. **rub something out** chiefly Brit. erase pencil marks with a rubber.
– ORIGIN Middle English (as a verb): perhaps from Low German *rubben*, of unknown ultimate origin. The noun dates from the late 16th cent.

Rub' al-Khali /ˌrʊb alˈkɑːli/ a vast desert in the Arabian peninsula, extending from central Saudi Arabia southwards to Yemen and eastwards to the United Arab Emirates and Oman. It is also known as the Great Sandy Desert and the Empty Quarter.

rubato /rʊˈbɑːtəʊ/ Music ▶ noun (pl. **rubatos** or **rubati** /-ti/) (also **tempo rubato**) the temporary disregarding of strict tempo to allow an expressive quickening or slackening, usually without altering the overall pace.
▶ adjective performed with rubato.
– ORIGIN Italian, literally 'robbed'.

rubber[1] ▸ **noun 1** [mass noun] a tough elastic polymeric substance made from the latex of a tropical plant or synthetically.
2 Brit. a piece of rubber used for erasing pencil or ink marks: *a pencil with a rubber at the end.*
3 (**rubbers**) N. Amer. rubber boots; galoshes.
4 N. Amer. informal a condom.
– DERIVATIVES **rubberiness** noun, **rubbery** adjective.
– ORIGIN mid 16th cent.: from the verb RUB + -ER[1]. The original sense was 'an implement (such as a hard brush) used for rubbing and cleaning'. Because an early use of the elastic substance (previously known as CAOUTCHOUC) was to rub out pencil marks, *rubber* gained the sense 'eraser' in the late 18th cent. The sense was subsequently (mid 19th cent.) generalized to refer to the substance in any form or use, at first often differentiated as INDIA RUBBER.

rubber[2] ▸ **noun** a contest consisting of a series of successive matches (typically three or five) between the same sides or people in cricket, tennis, and other games. ■ (also **rubber match** or **rubber game**) a deciding game in such a match. ■ Bridge a unit of play in which one side scores bonus points for winning the best of three games.
– ORIGIN late 16th cent.: of unknown origin; early use was as a term in bowls.

rubber band ▸ **noun** a loop of rubber for holding things together.

rubber boa ▸ **noun** a short snake with a stout shiny brown body that looks and feels like rubber, found in western North America. ● *Charina bottae*, family Boidae.

rubber bullet ▸ **noun** a large projectile made of rubber and shot from a firearm, used especially in riot control.

rubber cement ▸ **noun** [mass noun] a cement or adhesive containing rubber in a solvent.

rubber cheque ▸ **noun** informal, humorous a cheque that is returned unpaid.
– ORIGIN 1920s: by association with BOUNCE.

rubber-chicken ▸ **adjective** N. Amer. informal relating to a series of dinner and lunch appearances made by a politician or other public figures: *candidates pleading for money on the* ***rubber-chicken circuit.***
– ORIGIN 1950s: so called because of the mediocre food typically served at such functions.

rubber duck ▸ **noun** S. African informal an inflatable flat-bottomed rubber dinghy, typically motorized.
– DERIVATIVES **rubber ducker** noun.

rubberize (also **rubberise**) ▸ **verb** [with obj.] (usu. as adj. **rubberized**) treat or coat (something) with rubber.

rubber johnny ▸ **noun** another term for JOHNNY (sense 2).

rubberneck informal ▸ **verb** [no obj.] turn one's head to stare at something in a foolish manner: *a passer-by rubbernecking at the accident scene.*
▸ **noun** a person who rubbernecks.
– DERIVATIVES **rubbernecker** noun.

rubberoid ▸ **adjective** made of or resembling rubber.

rubber plant ▸ **noun 1** an evergreen tree of the fig family, which has large dark green shiny leaves and is widely cultivated as a houseplant. Native to SE Asia, it was formerly grown as a source of rubber. ● *Ficus elastica*, family Moraceae.
2 another term for RUBBER TREE.

rubber solution ▸ **noun** [mass noun] a liquid that dries to a rubber-like material, used especially as an adhesive in mending rubber articles.

rubber stamp ▸ **noun 1** a handheld device for inking and imprinting a message or design on a surface.
2 a person or organization that gives automatic approval or authorization to the decisions of others, without proper consideration: *the Commission were accused of being a rubber stamp for the police department.* ■ an indication of such an approval: *your application should get the rubber stamp from the residents' association.*
▸ **verb** (**rubber-stamp**) [with obj.] approve automatically without proper consideration: *parliament merely rubber-stamped the decisions of the party.*

rubber tree ▸ **noun** a tree that produces the latex from which rubber is manufactured, native to the Amazonian rainforest and widely cultivated elsewhere. ● *Hevea brasiliensis*, family Euphorbiaceae.

rubbing ▸ **noun 1** [mass noun] the action of rubbing something: *dab at the stain—vigorous rubbing could damage the carpet.*
2 an impression of a design on brass or stone, made by rubbing on paper laid over it with coloured wax, pencil, chalk, etc.

rubbing alcohol ▸ **noun** [mass noun] N. Amer. denatured alcohol, typically perfumed, used as an antiseptic or in massage.

rubbing strake ▸ **noun** a protective strip running along a boat's side below the gunwale to prevent damage when coming alongside something.

rubbing strip ▸ **noun** a raised strip fitted to a vehicle to protect the bodywork.

rubbish ▸ **noun** [mass noun] chiefly Brit. waste material; refuse or litter: *householders may be charged for the removal of non-recyclable rubbish.* ■ material that is considered unimportant or valueless: *she had to sift through the rubbish in every drawer.* ■ absurd, nonsensical, or worthless talk or ideas: *critics said their work was* ***a load of rubbish*** | [as exclamation] *some MPs yelled 'Rubbish!'*
▸ **verb** [with obj.] Brit. informal criticize severely and reject as worthless: *he rubbished the idea of a European Community-wide carbon tax.*
▸ **adjective** Brit. informal very bad; worthless or useless: *people might say I was a rubbish manager* | *she was rubbish at maths.*
– ORIGIN late Middle English: from Anglo-Norman French *rubbous*; perhaps related to Old French *robe* 'spoils'; compare with RUBBLE. The change in the ending was due to association with -ISH[1]. The verb (1950s) was originally Australian and New Zealand slang.

rubbishy ▸ **adjective** informal, chiefly Brit. of poor quality and little value: *rubbishy reality TV shows.*

rubble ▸ **noun** [mass noun] waste or rough fragments of stone, brick, concrete, etc., especially as the debris from the demolition of buildings: *two buildings collapsed, trapping scores of people in the rubble.* ■ pieces of rough or undressed stone used in building walls, especially as filling for cavities.
– DERIVATIVES **rubbly** adjective.
– ORIGIN late Middle English: perhaps from an Anglo-Norman French alteration of Old French *robe* 'spoils'; compare with RUBBISH.

rubbled ▸ **adjective** covered in rubble or reduced to rubble.

rub board ▸ **noun 1** a board fitted with teeth, used for making drawn work from linen.
2 N. Amer. another term for WASHBOARD (sense 1 of the noun).

rub-down ▸ **noun** an act of drying, smoothing down, or cleaning something by rubbing.

rube /ruːb/ ▸ **noun** N. Amer. informal a country bumpkin.
– ORIGIN late 19th cent.: abbreviation of the given name *Reuben.*

Rube Goldberg /ˌruːb ˈɡəʊl(d)bəːɡ/ ▸ **adjective** N. Amer. ingeniously or unnecessarily complicated in design or construction: *a Rube Goldberg machine.*
– ORIGIN 1950s: from the name of *Reuben Goldberg* (1883–1970), an American cartoonist whose illustrations often depicted devices with such a complicated design.

rubella /rʊˈbɛlə/ ▸ **noun** medical term for GERMAN MEASLES.
– ORIGIN late 19th cent.: modern Latin, neuter plural of Latin *rubellus* 'reddish'.

rubellite /ˈruːbəlʌɪt/ ▸ **noun** [mass noun] a red variety of tourmaline.
– ORIGIN late 18th cent.: from Latin *rubellus* 'reddish' + -ITE[1].

Rubens /ˈruːbənz/, Sir Peter Paul (1577–1640), Flemish painter. The foremost exponent of northern Baroque, he is best known for his portraits and mythological paintings featuring voluptuous female nudes, as in *Venus and Adonis* (*c.*1635).
– DERIVATIVES **Rubenesque** (also **Rubensesque**) adjective.

rubeola /rʊˈbiːələ/ ▸ **noun** medical term for MEASLES.
– ORIGIN late 17th cent.: from medieval Latin, diminutive (on the pattern of *variola*) of Latin *rubeus* 'red'.

rubescent /rʊˈbɛs(ə)nt/ ▸ **adjective** chiefly literary reddening; blushing.
– ORIGIN mid 18th cent.: from Latin *rubescent-* 'reddening', from the verb *rubescere*, from *ruber* 'red'.

Rubicon /ˈruːbɪk(ə)n, -kɒn/ a stream in NE Italy which marked the ancient boundary between Italy and Cisalpine Gaul. Julius Caesar led his army across it into Italy in 49 BC, breaking the law forbidding a general to lead an army out of his province, and so committing himself to war against the Senate and Pompey. The ensuing civil war resulted in victory for Caesar after three years. ■ [as noun] a point of no return: *on the way to political union we are now crossing the Rubicon.*

rubicon ▸ **noun** (in piquet) an act of winning a game against an opponent whose total score is less than 100, in which case the loser's score is added to rather than subtracted from the winner's.
▸ **verb** (**rubicons**, **rubiconing**, **rubiconed**) [with obj.] score a rubicon against (one's opponent).
– ORIGIN late 19th cent.: from RUBICON.

rubicund /ˈruːbɪk(ə)nd/ ▸ **adjective** (especially of someone's face) having a ruddy complexion.
– ORIGIN late Middle English (in the general sense 'red'): from Latin *rubicundus*, from *rubere* 'be red'.

rubidium /rʊˈbɪdɪəm/ ▸ **noun** [mass noun] the chemical element of atomic number 37, a rare soft silvery reactive metal of the alkali metal group. (Symbol: **Rb**)
– ORIGIN mid 19th cent.: modern Latin, from Latin *rubidus* 'red' (with reference to its spectral lines).

rubidium–strontium dating ▸ **noun** [mass noun] Geology a method of dating rocks from the relative proportions of rubidium-87 and its decay product, strontium-87.

rubiginous /rʊˈbɪdʒɪnəs/ ▸ **adjective** technical or literary rust-coloured.
– ORIGIN late 17th cent.: from Latin *rubigo*, *rubigin-* 'rust' + -OUS.

Rubik's cube /ˈruːbɪks/ ▸ **noun** trademark a puzzle in the form of a plastic cube covered with multi-coloured squares, which the player attempts to twist and turn so that all the squares on each face are of the same colour.
– ORIGIN 1980s: named after Erno *Rubik* (born 1944), its Hungarian inventor.

Rubinstein[1] /ˈruːbɪnstʌɪn/, Anton (Grigorevich) (1829–94), Russian composer and pianist. He composed symphonies, operas, songs, and piano music.

Rubinstein[2] /ˈruːbɪnstʌɪn/, Artur (1888–1982), Polish-born American pianist. He toured extensively in Europe and the US and among his many recordings are the complete works of Chopin.

Rubinstein[3] /ˈruːbɪnstʌɪn/, Helena (1882–1965), Polish-born American beautician and businesswoman. Her organization became an international cosmetics manufacturer and distributor.

rubisco /rʊˈbɪskəʊ/ ▸ **noun** [mass noun] Biochemistry an enzyme present in plant chloroplasts, involved in fixing atmospheric carbon dioxide during photosynthesis and in oxygenation of the resulting compound during photorespiration.
– ORIGIN 1980s: from *r(ib)u(lose)* + BIS- + *c(arb)o(xyl)*.

ruble ▸ **noun** variant spelling of ROUBLE.

rubredoxin /ˌruːbrɪˈdɒksɪn/ ▸ **noun** Biochemistry any of a class of iron-containing proteins involved in electron transfer processes within living cells.
– ORIGIN 1960s: from Latin *ruber*, *rubr-* 'red' + REDOX + -IN[1].

rubric /ˈruːbrɪk/ ▸ **noun 1** a heading on a document. ■ a category: *party policies on matters falling* ***under the rubric of*** *law and order.*
2 a set of instructions or rules. ■ a direction in a liturgical book as to how a church service should be conducted. ■ a statement of purpose or function: *art for a purpose, not for its own sake, was his rubric.*
– DERIVATIVES **rubrical** adjective.
– ORIGIN late Middle English *rubrish* (originally referring to a heading, section of text, etc. written in red for distinctiveness), from Old French *rubriche*, from Latin *rubrica* (*terra*) 'red (earth or ochre as writing material)', from the base of *rubeus* 'red'; the later spelling is influenced by the Latin form.

rubricate /ˈruːbrɪkeɪt/ ▸ **verb** chiefly historical add elaborate, typically red, capital letters or other decorations to (a manuscript).
– DERIVATIVES **rubrication** noun, **rubricator** noun.
– ORIGIN late 16th cent.: from Latin *rubricat-* 'marked in red', from the verb *rubricare*, from *rubrica* (see RUBRIC).

rub-up ▸ **noun** an act of polishing something.

ruby ▸ **noun** (pl. **rubies**) **1** a precious stone consisting of corundum in colour varieties varying from deep crimson or purple to pale rose. ■ [mass noun] an intense purplish-red colour: [as modifier] *the rich ruby liquid* | [in combination] *this wine has a youthful ruby-red colour.*
2 [mass noun] Printing an old type size equal to $5\frac{1}{2}$ points.
– ORIGIN Middle English: from Old French *rubi*, from medieval Latin *rubinus*, from the base of Latin *rubeus* 'red'.

R

ruby glass ▶ **noun** [mass noun] glass coloured red by the inclusion of specific impurities such as gold or metal oxides.

Ruby Murray ▶ **noun** Brit. rhyming slang a curry.
– ORIGIN the name of a Northern Irish singer (1935–96).

ruby port ▶ **noun** [mass noun] a deep red port, especially one matured in wood for only a few years and then fined.

ruby-tail (also **ruby-tail wasp**) ▶ **noun** a small metallic cuckoo wasp that is typically greenish-blue with an orange-red tip to the abdomen. Its larvae feed on the eggs and larvae of its host. ● Family Chrysididae: *Chrysis* and other genera, and many species, in particular *C. ignita*.

rubythroat ▶ **noun** a small thrush related to the robin, the male having a red throat and striped head, found from Siberia to China. ● Genus *Erithacus*, family Turdidae: three species.

ruby wedding ▶ **noun** Brit. the fortieth anniversary of a wedding.

RUC ▶ **abbreviation** historical Royal Ulster Constabulary.

ruche /ruːʃ/ ▶ **noun** a frill or pleat of fabric as decoration on a garment or soft furnishing.
– DERIVATIVES **ruched** adjective, **ruching** noun.
– ORIGIN early 19th cent.: from French, from medieval Latin *rusca* 'tree bark', of Celtic origin.

ruck[1] ▶ **noun 1** Rugby a loose scrum formed around a player with the ball on the ground. Compare with **MAUL**. ■ Australian Rules a group of three players who follow the play without fixed positions.
2 a tightly packed crowd of people: *Harry squeezed through the ruck to order another pint*. ■ (**the ruck**) the mass of ordinary people or things: *education was the key to success, a way out of the ruck*.
▶ **verb** [no obj.] Rugby & Australian Rules take part in a ruck.
– ORIGIN Middle English (in the sense 'stack of fuel, heap'): apparently of Scandinavian origin; compare with Norwegian *ruke* 'heap of hay'.

ruck[2] ▶ **verb** [with obj.] compress or move (cloth or clothing) so that it forms a number of untidy folds or creases: *her skirt was* **rucked up**. ■ [no obj.] (of cloth or clothing) form rucks: *Eleanor's dress* **rucked up** *at the front*.
▶ **noun** a crease or wrinkle.
– ORIGIN late 18th cent. (as a noun): from Old Norse *hrukka*.

ruck[3] Brit. informal ▶ **noun** a quarrel or fight, especially a brawl involving several people.
▶ **verb** [no obj.] engage in a ruck.
– ORIGIN 1950s: perhaps a shortened form of **RUCTION** or **RUCKUS**.

ruckle ▶ **verb & noun** Brit. another term for **RUCK**[2].

rucksack /ˈrʌksak, ˈrʊk-/ ▶ **noun** a bag with shoulder straps which allow it to be carried on someone's back, typically made of a strong, waterproof material and widely used by hikers.
– ORIGIN mid 19th cent.: from German, from *rucken* (dialect variant of *Rücken* 'back') + *Sack* 'bag, sack'.

ruckus /ˈrʌkəs/ ▶ **noun** a row or commotion: *a child is raising a ruckus in class* | [mass noun] *there's enough ruckus over identity cards*.
– ORIGIN late 19th cent.: perhaps related to **RUCTION** and **RUMPUS**.

rucola /ˈruːkələ/ ▶ **noun** another term for **ARUGULA**.

ruction ▶ **noun** informal a disturbance or quarrel. ■ (**ructions**) Brit. angry reactions, protests, or complaints: *if Mrs Salt catches her there'll be ructions*.
– ORIGIN early 19th cent.: of unknown origin.

rudaceous /ruːˈdeɪʃəs/ ▶ **adjective** Geology (of rock) composed of fragments of relatively large size (larger than sand grains).
– ORIGIN early 20th cent.: from Latin *rudus* 'rubble' + **-ACEOUS**.

rudbeckia /ruːdˈbɛkɪə, rʌd-/ ▶ **noun** a North American plant of the daisy family, with yellow or orange flowers and a dark cone-like centre. ● Genus *Rudbeckia*, family Compositae.
– ORIGIN modern Latin, named after Olaf *Rudbeck* (1660–1740), Swedish botanist.

Rudd, Kevin (Michael) (b.1957), Australian Labor statesman, Prime Minister 2007–10.

rudd ▶ **noun** (pl. **same**) a European freshwater fish of the carp family with a silvery body and red fins. ● *Scardinius erythrophthalmus*, family Cyprinidae.
– ORIGIN early 16th cent.: apparently related to archaic *rud* 'red colour'.

rudder ▶ **noun** a flat piece hinged vertically near the stern of a boat or ship for steering. ■ a vertical aerofoil pivoted from the tailplane of an aircraft, for controlling movement about the vertical axis. ■ [mass noun] application of a rudder in steering a boat, ship, or aircraft: *bring the aircraft to a stall and apply full rudder* | *a small amount of extra rudder*.
– ORIGIN Old English *rōther* 'paddle, oar', of West Germanic origin; related to Dutch *roer*, German *Ruder*, also to the verb **ROW**[2].

rudderless ▶ **adjective** lacking a rudder. ■ lacking a clear sense of one's aims or principles: *today's leadership is rudderless*.

ruddle ▶ **noun** [mass noun] another term for **REDDLE**. ■ a small block of reddle or a similar substance that is attached to the chest of a ram to mark the ewe that it tups.
– ORIGIN late Middle English: related to obsolete *rud* 'red colour' and **RED**; compare with **RADDLE**.

ruddy ▶ **adjective** (**ruddier**, **ruddiest**) **1** (of a person's face) having a healthy red colour: *a cheerful pipe-smoking man of ruddy complexion*. ■ having a reddish colour: *the ruddy evening light*.
2 Brit. informal, dated used as a euphemism for 'bloody'.
▶ **verb** (**ruddies**, **ruddying**, **ruddied**) [with obj.] make ruddy in colour: *a red flash ruddied the belly of a cloud*.
– DERIVATIVES **ruddily** adverb (rare), **ruddiness** noun.
– ORIGIN late Old English *rudig*, from the base of archaic *rud* 'red colour'; related to **RED**.

ruddy duck ▶ **noun** a New World stiff-tailed duck with a broad bill, naturalized in Britain, the male having mainly deep red-brown plumage and white cheeks. ● *Oxyura jamaicensis*, family Anatidae.

rude ▶ **adjective 1** offensively impolite or bad-mannered: *she had* **been rude to** *her boss* | *he is a rude and arrogant bully*.
2 referring to a taboo subject such as sex in a way considered embarrassing or offensive: *Graham giggled at every rude joke*.
3 [attrib.] having a startling abruptness: *the war came as a very* **rude awakening**.
4 [attrib.] chiefly Brit. vigorous or hearty: *Isabel had always been in* **rude health**.
5 dated roughly made or done; lacking sophistication: *a rude coffin*. ■ archaic ignorant and uneducated: *the new religion was first promulgated by rude men*.
– DERIVATIVES **rudely** adverb, **rudery** noun.
– ORIGIN Middle English (in sense 5, also 'uncultured'): from Old French, from Latin *rudis* 'unwrought' (referring to handicraft), figuratively 'uncultivated'; related to *rudus* 'broken stone'.

rude boy ▶ **noun** (in Jamaica) a lawless urban youth who likes ska or reggae music.

rudeness ▶ **noun** [mass noun] **1** lack of manners; discourteousness: *what I will not tolerate is rudeness*.
2 dated roughness or simplicity.

ruderal /ˈruːd(ə)r(ə)l/ Botany ▶ **adjective** (of a plant) growing on waste ground or among rubbish.
▶ **noun** a plant growing on waste ground or among rubbish.
– ORIGIN mid 19th cent.: from modern Latin *ruderalis*, from Latin *rudera*, plural of *rudus* 'rubble'.

rudiment /ˈruːdɪm(ə)nt/ ▶ **noun 1** (**the rudiments of**) the first principles of (a subject): *she taught the girls the rudiments of reading and writing*. ■ an elementary or primitive form of (something): *the rudiments of a hot-water system*.
2 Biology an undeveloped or immature part or organ, especially a structure in an embryo or larva which will develop into an organ, limb, etc.: *the fetal lung rudiment*.
3 Music a basic pattern used by drummers, such as the roll, the flam, and the paradiddle.
– ORIGIN mid 16th cent.: from French, or from Latin *rudimentum*, from *rudis* 'unwrought', on the pattern of *elementum* 'element'.

rudimentary /ˌruːdɪˈmɛnt(ə)ri/ ▶ **adjective** involving or limited to basic principles: *he received a rudimentary education*. ■ relating to an immature, undeveloped, or basic form: *a rudimentary stage of evolution*.
– DERIVATIVES **rudimentarily** adverb.

rudist /ˈruːdɪst/ (also **rudistid** /ruːˈdɪstɪd/) ▶ **noun** a cone-shaped fossil bivalve mollusc which formed colonies resembling reefs in the Cretaceous period. ● Superfamily Rudistacea, order Hippuritoida.
– ORIGIN late 19th cent.: from modern Latin *Rudista* (former group name), from Latin *rudis* 'rude'; for the variant spelling see **-ID**[3].

Rudolf, Lake former name (until 1979) for Lake Turkana (see **TURKANA, LAKE**).

Rudra /ˈrʊdrə/ Hinduism **1** (in the Rig Veda) a Vedic minor god, associated with the storm, father of the Maruts.
2 one of the names of **SHIVA**.

Rudras /ˈrʊdrəs/ another term for **MARUTS**.

rue[1] ▶ **verb** (**rues**, **rueing** or **ruing**, **rued**) [with obj.] bitterly regret (something one has done or allowed to happen) and wish it undone: *Ferguson will rue the day he turned down that offer* | *she might live to rue this impetuous decision*.
▶ **noun** [mass noun] archaic repentance; regret: *with rue my heart is laden*. ■ compassion; pity: *tears of pitying rue*.
– ORIGIN Old English *hrēow* 'repentance', *hrēowan* 'affect with contrition', of Germanic origin; related to Dutch *rouw* 'mourning' and German *Reue* 'remorse'.

rue[2] ▶ **noun** a perennial evergreen shrub with bitter strong-scented lobed leaves which are used in herbal medicine. ● *Ruta graveolens*, family Rutaceae.
■ used in names of other plants that resemble rue, especially in leaf shape, e.g. **goat's rue**, **meadow rue**, and **wall rue**.
– ORIGIN Middle English: from Old French, via Latin from Greek *rhutē*.

rueful ▶ **adjective** expressing sorrow or regret, especially in a wry or humorous way: *she gave a rueful grin*.
– DERIVATIVES **ruefully** adverb, **ruefulness** noun.
– ORIGIN Middle English (also in the sense 'pitiable'): from the noun **RUE**[1] + **-FUL**.

rufescent /rʊˈfɛs(ə)nt/ ▶ **adjective** chiefly literary tinged with red.
– ORIGIN early 19th cent.: from Latin *rufescent-* 'becoming reddish', from the verb *rufescere*, from *rufus* 'reddish'.

ruff[1] ▶ **noun 1** a projecting starched frill worn round the neck, characteristic of Elizabethan and Jacobean costume.
2 a projecting or conspicuously coloured ring of feathers or hair round the neck of a bird or mammal.
3 a pigeon of a domestic breed with a ruff of feathers on its neck.
4 (pl. **same** or **ruffs**) a North Eurasian wading bird, the male of which has a large variously coloured ruff and ear tufts in the breeding season, used in display. ● *Philomachus pugnax*, family Scolopacidae; the female is called a **reeve**.
– DERIVATIVES **ruffed** adjective.
– ORIGIN early 16th cent. (first used denoting a frill around a sleeve): probably from a variant of **ROUGH**.

ruff[2] ▶ **noun 1** (also **tommy ruff**) an edible marine fish of Australian inshore waters that is related to the Australian salmon. Also called **ROUGHY** in Australia. ● *Arripis georgianus*, family Arripidae.
2 variant spelling of **RUFFE**.
– ORIGIN late 19th cent.: from **RUFFE**.

ruff[3] ▶ **verb** [no obj.] (in bridge, whist, and similar card games) play a trump in a trick which was led in a different suit. ■ [with obj.] play a trump on (a card in another suit).
▶ **noun** an act of ruffing or opportunity to ruff.
– ORIGIN late 16th cent. (originally the name of a card game resembling whist): from Old French *rouffle*, a parallel formation to Italian *ronfa* (perhaps an alteration of *trionfo* 'a trump').

ruff[4] ▶ **noun** Music one of the basic patterns (rudiments) of drumming, consisting of a single note preceded by either two grace notes played with the other stick (**double-stroke ruff** or **drag**) or three grace notes played with alternating sticks (**four-stroke ruff**).
– ORIGIN late 17th cent.: probably imitative.

ruffe /rʌf/ (also **ruff**) ▶ **noun** a European freshwater fish of the perch family, with a greenish-brown back and yellow sides and underparts. ● *Gymnocephalus cernua*, family Percidae.
– ORIGIN late Middle English: probably from a variant of **ROUGH**.

ruffed grouse ▶ **noun** a North American woodland grouse which has a black ruff on the sides of the neck. ● *Bonasa umbellus*, family Tetraonidae (or Phasianidae).

ruffed lemur ▶ **noun** a lemur with a prominent muzzle and dense fur that forms a ruff around the neck, living in the Madagascan rainforest. ● *Varecia variegata*, family Lemuridae.

ruffian ▶ **noun** a violent person, especially one involved in crime.
– DERIVATIVES **ruffianism** noun, **ruffianly** adverb.
– ORIGIN late 15th cent.: from Old French *ruffian*, from Italian *ruffiano*, perhaps from dialect *rofia* 'scab, scurf', of Germanic origin.

ruffle ▶ **verb** [with obj.] **1** disorder or disarrange (someone's hair), typically by running one's hands through it: *he ruffled her hair affectionately*. ■ (of a bird)

erect (its feathers) in anger or display: *they warbled incessantly, their throat feathers ruffled.* ■ disturb the smoothness or tranquillity of: *the evening breeze ruffled the surface of the pond in the yard.* ■ disconcert or upset the composure of (someone): *Lancaster had been ruffled by her questions.*
2 (usu. as adj. **ruffled**) ornament with or gather into a frill: *a blouse with a high ruffled neck.*
▶ noun 1 an ornamental gathered or goffered frill of lace or other cloth on a garment, especially around the wrist or neck.
2 a vibrating drum beat.
– PHRASES **ruffle someone's feathers** cause someone to become annoyed or upset. **smooth someone's ruffled feathers** make someone less angry or irritated by using soothing words.
– ORIGIN Middle English (as a verb): of unknown origin. Current noun senses date from the late 17th cent.

rufiyaa /ˈruːfiːjɑː/ ▶ noun (pl. **same**) the basic monetary unit of the Maldives, equal to 100 laris.
– ORIGIN Maldivian.

rufous /ˈruːfəs/ ▶ adjective reddish brown in colour.
▶ noun [mass noun] a reddish-brown colour.
– ORIGIN late 18th cent.: from Latin *rufus* 'red, reddish' + **-OUS**.

rug ▶ noun a floor covering of thick woven material or animal skin, typically not extending over the entire floor. ■ Brit. a thick woollen coverlet or wrap, used especially when travelling. ■ a shaped garment worn by horses for protection or warmth. ■ informal, chiefly N. Amer. a toupee or wig.
– PHRASES **pull the rug (out) from under** abruptly withdraw support from (someone).
– ORIGIN mid 16th cent. (denoting a type of coarse woollen cloth): probably of Scandinavian origin; compare with Norwegian dialect *rugga* 'coverlet', Swedish *rugg* 'ruffled hair'; related to **RAG**[1]. The sense 'small carpet' dates from the early 19th cent.

Rugby /ˈrʌɡbi/ a town in central England, on the River Avon in Warwickshire; pop. 64,300 (est. 2009). Rugby School was founded there in 1567.

rugby (also **rugby football**) ▶ noun [mass noun] a team game played with an oval ball that may be kicked, carried, and passed from hand to hand. Points are scored by grounding the ball behind the opponents' goal line (thereby scoring a try) or by kicking it between the two posts and over the crossbar of the opponents' goal. See also **RUGBY LEAGUE** and **RUGBY UNION**.
– ORIGIN mid 19th cent.: named after *Rugby* School (see **RUGBY**), where the game was first played.

rugby league ▶ noun [mass noun] a form of rugby played in teams of thirteen, originally by a group of northern English clubs which separated from rugby union in 1895. Besides having somewhat different rules, the game differed from rugby union in always allowing professionalism.

rugby union ▶ noun [mass noun] a form of rugby played in teams of fifteen. Unlike rugby league, the game was originally strictly amateur, being opened to professionalism only in 1995.

Rügen /ˈruːɡ(ə)n/, German /ˈryːɡn/ an island in the Baltic Sea off the north coast of Germany, to which it is linked by a causeway. It forms part of the state of Mecklenburg-West Pomerania.

rugged /ˈrʌɡɪd/ ▶ adjective 1 (of ground or terrain) having a broken, rocky, and uneven surface: *a rugged coastline.* ■ (of a man) having attractively strong, rough-hewn features: *he was known for his rugged good looks.*
2 (of clothing, equipment, etc.) strongly made and capable of withstanding rough handling: *the binoculars are compact, lightweight, and rugged.* ■ having or requiring toughness and determination: *a week of rugged, demanding adventure at an outdoor training centre.*
– DERIVATIVES **ruggedly** adverb, **ruggedness** noun.
– ORIGIN Middle English (in the sense 'shaggy', also (of a horse) 'rough-coated'): probably of Scandinavian origin; compare with Swedish *rugga* 'roughen', also with **RUG**.

ruggedized (also **ruggedised**) ▶ adjective chiefly N. Amer. designed or improved to be hard-wearing or shock-resistant: *ruggedized computers suitable for use on the battlefield.*
– DERIVATIVES **ruggedization** noun.

rugger ▶ noun [mass noun] Brit. informal rugby.

rugger-bugger ▶ noun informal a boorish, aggressively masculine young man who is devoted to sport.
– ORIGIN 1970s (originally a South African usage): from **RUGGER** + *bugger* 'mate' (used freely and without sexual connotations in South African English).

rugola /ˈruːɡələ/ ▶ noun another term for **ARUGULA**.

rugosa /ruːˈɡəʊzə/ ▶ noun a SE Asian rose with dark green wrinkled leaves and deep pink flowers, widely used as a hedging plant. ● *Rosa rugosa*, family Rosaceae.
– ORIGIN late 19th cent.: feminine of Latin *rugosus* (see **RUGOSE**), used as a specific epithet.

rugose /ˈruːɡəʊs, rʊˈɡəʊs/ ▶ adjective chiefly Biology wrinkled; corrugated: *rugose corals.*
– DERIVATIVES **rugosity** noun.
– ORIGIN late Middle English: from Latin *rugosus*, from *ruga* 'wrinkle'.

rug rat ▶ noun N. Amer. informal a child.

Ruhr /rʊə/, German /ruːɐ/ a region of coal mining and heavy industry in North Rhine-Westphalia, western Germany. It is named after the River Ruhr, which flows through it, meeting the Rhine near Duisburg. The Ruhr was occupied by French troops 1923–4, after Germany defaulted on war reparation payments.

ruin ▶ noun [mass noun] the physical destruction or disintegration of something or the state of disintegrating or being destroyed: *a large white house* ***falling into gentle ruin.*** ■ [count noun] the remains of a building, typically an old one that has suffered much damage or disintegration: ***the ruins of*** *the castle | the church is a ruin now.* ■ the disastrous disintegration of someone's life: *the ruin and heartbreak wrought by alcohol, divorce, and violence.* ■ the cause of such disintegration: *they don't know how to say no, and that's been their ruin.* ■ the complete loss of one's money and other assets: *the financial cost could mean ruin.*
▶ verb 1 [with obj.] reduce (a building or place) to a state of decay, collapse, or disintegration: (as adj. **ruined**) *a ruined castle.* ■ cause great and usually irreparable damage or harm to; have a disastrous effect on: *a noisy motorway has ruined village life.* ■ reduce to a state of poverty: *they were ruined by the highest interest rates this century.*
2 [no obj.] literary fall headlong or with a crash: *carriages go ruining over the brink from time to time.*
– PHRASES **in ruins** in a state of complete disorder or disintegration: *the economy was in ruins.*
– ORIGIN Middle English (in the sense 'collapse of a building'): from Old French *ruine*, from Latin *ruina*, from *ruere* 'to fall'.

ruination ▶ noun [mass noun] the action or fact of ruining someone or something or of being ruined: *commercial malpractice causes the ruination of thousands of people.* ■ the state of being ruined: *the headquarters fell into ruination.*
– ORIGIN mid 17th cent.: from obsolete *ruinate* + **-ION**.

ruin marble ▶ noun [mass noun] marble having irregular markings said to resemble the outline of ruins.

ruinous ▶ adjective 1 disastrous or destructive: *a ruinous effect on the environment.* ■ costing far more than can be afforded: *the cost of their ransom might be ruinous.*
2 in ruins; dilapidated: *the castle is ruinous.*
– DERIVATIVES **ruinously** adverb.
– ORIGIN late Middle English (also in the sense 'falling down'): from Latin *ruinosus*, from *ruina* (see **RUIN**).

Ruisdael /ˈraʊsdɑːl, ˈrɔɪz-, -deɪl/ (also **Ruysdael**), Jacob van (*c.*1628–82), Dutch landscape painter. His work demonstrated the possibilities of investing landscape with subtle intimations of mood.

Ruiz de Alarcón y Mendoza /rʊˌiːθ deɪ ˌalɑːˈkɒn iː menˌdəʊsə/, Spanish /ˌrrwiθ de alarˈkon i menˌdoθa, ˌrrwis, menˌdosa/, Juan (1580–1639), Spanish dramatist, born in Mexico City. His most famous play, the moral comedy *La Verdad sospechosa*, was the basis of Corneille's *Le Menteur* (1642).

Rukh /ruːx/ the nationalist movement which established the independence of Ukraine in 1991.
– ORIGIN Ukrainian, 'people's movement'.

rukh /ruːk/ ▶ noun another term for **ROC**.
– ORIGIN from Hindi *rūkh*.

rule ▶ noun 1 one of a set of explicit or understood regulations or principles governing conduct or procedure within a particular area of activity: *the rules of cricket | those who did* ***break the rules*** *would be dealt with swiftly.* ■ a law or principle that operates within a particular sphere of knowledge, describing or prescribing what is possible or allowable: *the rules of grammar.* ■ a code of practice and discipline for a religious order or community: *the Rule of St Benedict.*
2 [mass noun] control of or dominion over an area or people: *the revolution brought an end to British rule.*
3 (**the rule**) the normal or customary state of things: *such accidents are the exception rather than the rule.*
4 a strip of wood or other rigid material used for measuring length or marking straight lines; a ruler. ■ a thin printed line or dash.
5 (**Rules**) Austral. short for **AUSTRALIAN RULES**.
▶ verb 1 [with obj.] exercise ultimate power or authority over (an area and its people): *Latin America today is ruled by elected politicians* | [no obj.] *the period in which Spain* ***ruled over*** *Portugal.* ■ (of a feeling) have a powerful and restricting influence on: *her whole life seemed to be ruled by fear.* ■ [no obj.] be a dominant or powerful factor: [with complement] *the black market rules supreme.* ■ [no obj.] informal be very good or the best: *Jackie tells me about Hanna's newest band, and says that it absolutely rules.* ■ Astrology (of a planet) have a particular influence over (a sign of the zodiac, house, etc.).
2 [with clause] pronounce authoritatively and legally to be the case: *an industrial tribunal ruled that he was unfairly dismissed from his job.*
3 [with obj.] make parallel lines across (paper): (as adj. **ruled**) *a sheet of ruled paper.*
4 [no obj., with adverbial] (of a price or a traded commodity with regard to its price) have a specified general level or strength: *in the jutes section Indus and Pak Jute ruled firm.*
– PHRASES **as a rule** usually, but not always. **by rule** in a regular manner according to a particular set of rules: *stress is not predictable by rule and must be learned word by word.* **make it a rule to do something** have it as a habit or general principle to do something: *I make it a rule never to mix business with pleasure.* **rule of law** the restriction of the arbitrary exercise of power by subordinating it to well-defined and established laws. **rule of the road** a custom or law regulating the direction in which two vehicles (or riders or ships) should move to pass one another on meeting, or which should give way to the other, so as to avoid collision. **rule of thumb** a broadly accurate guide or principle, based on practice rather than theory. **rule the roost** be in complete control. **run the rule over** Brit. examine cursorily for correctness or adequacy.
– PHRASAL VERBS **rule something out** (or **in**) exclude (or include) something as a possibility: *the prime minister ruled out a November election.*
– DERIVATIVES **ruleless** adjective.
– ORIGIN Middle English: from Old French *reule* (noun), *reuler* (verb), from late Latin *regulare*, from Latin *regula* 'straight stick'.

rule book ▶ noun the regulations or standards of behaviour that should be followed in a particular job, organization, or sphere: *a lot of bands decided they were going to tear up the rock rule book and start again.*

ruler ▶ noun 1 a person exercising government or dominion. ■ Astrology another term for **RULING PLANET**.
2 a straight strip or cylinder of plastic, wood, metal, or other rigid material, typically marked at regular intervals and used to draw straight lines or measure distances.
– DERIVATIVES **rulership** noun.

Rules Committee ▶ noun a house of a US federal or state legislature responsible for expediting the passage of bills.

ruling ▶ noun an authoritative decision or pronouncement, especially one made by a judge.
▶ adjective currently exercising authority or influence: *the ruling coalition.*

ruling elder ▶ noun a nominated or elected lay official of any of various Christian Churches, especially of a Presbyterian Church.

ruling passion ▶ noun an interest or concern that occupies a large part of someone's time and effort: *football remained their ruling passion.*

ruling planet ▶ noun Astrology a planet which is held to have a particular influence over a specific sign of the zodiac, house, aspect of life, etc.

Rum variant spelling of **RHUM**.

rum[1] ▶ noun [mass noun] an alcoholic spirit distilled from sugar-cane residues or molasses. ■ N. Amer. intoxicating drink.
– ORIGIN mid 17th cent.: perhaps an abbreviation of obsolete *rumbullion*, in the same sense.

rum[2] ▶ adjective (**rummer, rummest**) Brit. informal, dated odd; peculiar: *it's a rum business, certainly.*
– PHRASES **a rum go** dated a surprising occurrence or unforeseen turn of events.
– DERIVATIVES **rumness** noun.
– ORIGIN late 18th cent.: of unknown origin.

R

Rumania /ruːˈmeɪnɪə/ variant spelling of **ROMANIA**.

Rumanian /ruːˈmeɪnɪən/ ▶ adjective & noun variant spelling of **ROMANIAN**.

Rumansh /rʊˈmanʃ, -ˈmɑːnʃ/ ▶ adjective & noun variant of **ROMANSH**.

rumba /ˈrʌmbə/ (also **rhumba**) ▶ noun a rhythmic dance with Spanish and African elements, originating in Cuba. ■ a piece of music for the rumba or in a similar style. ■ a ballroom dance imitative of the rumba.
▶ verb (**rumbas**, **rumbaing** /-bə(r)ɪŋ/, **rumbaed** /-bəd/ or **rumba'd**) [no obj.] dance the rumba.
– ORIGIN 1920s: from Latin American Spanish.

rum baba ▶ noun see **BABA¹**.

rumble ▶ verb **1** [no obj.] make a continuous deep, resonant sound: *thunder rumbled, lightning flickered.* ■ [with adverbial of direction] (especially of a large vehicle) move with such a sound: *heavy lorries rumbled through the streets.* ■ [with obj.] utter in a deep, resonant voice: *the man's low voice rumbled an instruction.* ■ (of a person's stomach) make a deep, resonant sound due to hunger. ■ (**rumble on**) Brit. (of a dispute) continue in a persistent but low-key way: *the debate about television replays rumbles on.*
2 [with obj.] Brit. informal discover (an illicit activity or its perpetrator): *it wouldn't need a genius to rumble my little game.*
3 [no obj.] US informal take part in a street fight between gangs or large groups.
▶ noun **1** a continuous deep, resonant sound like distant thunder: *the continuous rumble of traffic* | figurative *there were of rumbles of discontent from small retailers.*
2 US informal a street fight between gangs or large groups.
– DERIVATIVES **rumbler** noun.
– ORIGIN late Middle English: probably from Middle Dutch *rommelen, rummelen*, of imitative origin. Sense 2 of the verb may be a different word.

rumble seat ▶ noun N. Amer. an uncovered folding seat in the rear of a car.

rumble strip ▶ noun a series of raised strips across a road or along its edge, changing the noise a vehicle's tyres make on the surface and so warning drivers of speed restrictions or of the edge of the road.

rumbling ▶ noun a continuous deep, resonant sound: *the rumbling of wheels in the distance.* ■ (often **rumblings**) an early indication or rumour of dissatisfaction or incipient change: *there are growing rumblings of discontent.*
▶ adjective making or constituting a deep resonant sound: *rumbling trams* | *a rumbling noise.* ■ (of dissatisfaction or a dispute) continuing in a persistent but low-key way: *a rumbling dispute about changes to working conditions.*

rumbustious /rʌmˈbʌstʃəs, -tɪəs/ ▶ adjective informal, chiefly Brit. boisterous or unruly.
– DERIVATIVES **rumbustiously** adverb, **rumbustiousness** noun.
– ORIGIN late 18th cent.: probably an alteration of archaic *robustious* 'boisterous, robust'.

R

rum butter ▶ noun [mass noun] a rich, sweet, rum-flavoured sauce of butter and sugar, served especially with mince pies or Christmas pudding.

rumdum /ˈrʌmdʌm/ ▶ noun N. Amer. informal a drunkard, especially a homeless alcoholic.
– ORIGIN late 19th cent.: from **RUM¹** + **DUMB**.

Rumelia /ruːˈmiːlɪə/ (also **Roumelia**) the territories in Europe which formerly belonged to the Ottoman Empire, including Macedonia, Thrace, and Albania.
– ORIGIN from Turkish *Rumeli*, 'land of the Romans'.

rumen /ˈruːmɛn/ ▶ noun (pl. **rumens** or **rumina** /-mɪnə/) Zoology the first stomach of a ruminant, which receives food or cud from the oesophagus, partly digests it with the aid of bacteria, and passes it to the reticulum.
– DERIVATIVES **ruminal** adjective.
– ORIGIN early 18th cent.: from Latin, literally 'throat'.

ruminant ▶ noun **1** an even-toed ungulate mammal that chews the cud regurgitated from its rumen. The ruminants comprise the cattle, sheep, antelopes, deer, giraffes, and their relatives. ● Suborder Ruminantia, order Artiodactyla: six families.
2 a contemplative person; a person given to meditation.
▶ adjective of or belonging to ruminants: *a ruminant animal.*
– ORIGIN mid 17th cent.: from Latin *ruminant-* 'chewing over again', from the verb *ruminari*, from *rumen* 'throat' (see **RUMEN**).

ruminate /ˈruːmɪneɪt/ ▶ verb [no obj.] **1** think deeply about something: *we sat ruminating on the nature of existence.*
2 (of a ruminant) chew the cud.
– DERIVATIVES **rumination** noun, **ruminative** adjective, **ruminatively** adverb, **ruminator** noun.
– ORIGIN mid 16th cent.: from Latin *ruminat-* 'chewed over', from the verb *ruminari*.

rummage ▶ verb [no obj.] search unsystematically and untidily through something: *he rummaged in his pocket for a handkerchief* | [with obj.] *he rummaged the drawer for his false teeth.* ■ [with obj.] find (something) by rummaging: *Mick **rummaged up** his skateboard.* ■ [with obj.] (of a customs officer) make a thorough search of (a vessel): *our brief was to rummage as many of the vessels as possible.*
▶ noun an unsystematic and untidy search. ■ a thorough search of a vessel by a customs officer.
– DERIVATIVES **rummager** noun.
– ORIGIN late 15th cent.: from Old French *arrumage*, from *arrumer* 'stow (in a hold)', from Middle Dutch *ruim* 'room'. In early use the word referred to the arranging of items such as casks in the hold of a ship, giving rise (early 17th cent.) to the verb sense 'make a search of (a vessel)'.

rummage sale ▶ noun chiefly N. Amer. a jumble sale.

rummer ▶ noun a large drinking glass.
– ORIGIN mid 17th cent.: of Low Dutch origin; related to Dutch *roemer*; the original meaning is perhaps 'Roman glass'.

rummy¹ ▶ noun [mass noun] a card game, sometimes played with two packs, in which the players try to form sets and sequences of cards.
– ORIGIN early 20th cent.: of unknown origin.

rummy² ▶ adjective (**rummier**, **rummiest**) another term for **RUM²**.

rumour (US **rumor**) ▶ noun a currently circulating story or report of uncertain or doubtful truth: *they were investigating rumours of a massacre* | [mass noun] ***rumour has it that** he will take a year off.*
▶ verb (**be rumoured**) be circulated as an unverified account: [with clause] ***it's rumoured that** he lives on a houseboat* | [with infinitive] *she is rumoured to have gone into hiding.*
– ORIGIN late Middle English: from Old French *rumur*, from Latin *rumor* 'noise'.

rumour-monger ▶ noun derogatory a person who spreads rumours.
– DERIVATIVES **rumour-mongering** noun.

rump ▶ noun **1** the hind part of the body of a mammal or the lower back of a bird. ■ chiefly humorous a person's buttocks.
2 a small or unimportant remnant of something originally larger: *once the profitable enterprises have been sold the unprofitable rump will be left* | [as modifier] *the rump Yugoslavia.* ■ (**the Rump**) short for **RUMP PARLIAMENT**.
– ORIGIN late Middle English: probably of Scandinavian origin; compare with Danish and Norwegian *rumpe* 'backside'.

rumple ▶ verb [with obj.] (usu. as adj. **rumpled**) give a creased, ruffled, or dishevelled appearance to: *a rumpled bed.*
▶ noun [in sing.] an untidy state.
– DERIVATIVES **rumply** adjective.
– ORIGIN early 16th cent. (as a noun in the sense 'wrinkle'): from Middle Dutch *rompel*.

rumpot ▶ noun informal, chiefly N. Amer. an alcoholic.

Rump Parliament the part of the Long Parliament which continued to sit after Pride's Purge in 1648 and voted for the trial which resulted in the execution of Charles I.
– ORIGIN origin uncertain: said to derive from *The Bloody Rump*, the name of a paper written before the trial, the word being popularized after a speech by Major General Brown, given at a public assembly; also said to have been coined by Clem Walker in his *History of Independency* (1648), as a term for those strenuously opposing the king.

rump steak ▶ noun a cut of beef from the animal's rump.

rumpus ▶ noun (pl. **rumpuses**) informal a noisy disturbance; a row: *he caused a rumpus with his flair for troublemaking.*
– ORIGIN mid 18th cent.: probably fanciful.

rumpus room ▶ noun N. Amer. & Austral./NZ a room for playing games, typically in the basement of a house.

rumpy pumpy ▶ noun [mass noun] informal, humorous sexual relations, especially when of a casual nature.
– ORIGIN 1960s: reduplication of **RUMP**.

run ▶ verb (**runs**, **running**; past **ran** /ran/; past participle **run**) **1** [no obj.] move at a speed faster than a walk, never having both or all the feet on the ground at the same time: *the dog ran across the road* | *she ran the last few yards, breathing heavily* | *he hasn't paid for his drinks—run and catch him.* ■ run as a sport or for exercise: *I run every morning.* ■ (of an athlete or a racehorse) compete in a race: *she ran in the 200 metres* | [with obj.] *Dave has run 42 marathons.* ■ [with obj.] enter (a racehorse) for a race. ■ Cricket (of a batsman) run from one wicket to the other in scoring or attempting to score a run. ■ [with obj.] W. Indian chase (someone) away: *Ah went tuh eat the mangoes but the people run mih.* ■ (of a boat) sail straight and fast directly before the wind. ■ (of a migratory fish) go upriver from the sea in order to spawn.
2 pass or cause to pass quickly in a particular direction: [no obj., with adverbial of direction] *the rumour ran through the pack of photographers* | [with obj. and adverbial of direction] *Helen ran her fingers through her hair.* ■ [no obj.] move about in a hurried and hectic way: *I've spent the whole day running round after the kids.* ■ move or cause to move forcefully or with a particular result: [no obj., with adverbial of direction] *the tanker **ran aground** off the Shetlands* | [with obj. and adverbial of direction] *a woman ran a pushchair into the back of my legs.* ■ [with obj.] informal fail to stop at (a red traffic light). ■ [with obj.] chiefly N. Amer. navigate (rapids or a waterfall) in a boat.
3 (with reference to a liquid) flow or cause to flow: [no obj., with adverbial of direction] *a small river runs into the sea at one side of the castle* | [with obj.] *she ran cold water into a basin.* ■ [with obj.] cause water to flow over: *I ran my hands under the tap.* ■ [with obj.] fill (a bath) with water: [with two objs] *I'll run you a nice hot bath.* ■ [no obj.] (**run with**) be covered or streaming with (a liquid): *his face was running with sweat.* ■ [no obj.] emit or exude a liquid: *she was weeping and her nose was running.* ■ [no obj.] (of a solid substance) melt and become fluid: *it was so hot that the butter ran.* ■ [no obj.] (of the sea, the tide, or a river) rise higher or flow more quickly: *there was still a heavy sea running.* ■ [no obj.] (of dye or colour in fabric or paper) dissolve and spread when the fabric or paper becomes wet: *the red dye ran when the socks were washed.*
4 extend or cause to extend in a particular direction: [no obj., with adverbial of direction] *cobbled streets run down to a tiny harbour* | [with obj. and adverbial of direction] *he ran a wire under the carpet.* ■ [no obj.] chiefly N. Amer. (of a stocking or pair of tights) develop a ladder.
5 [no obj.] (of a bus, train, ferry, or other form of transport) make a regular journey on a particular route: *buses run into town every half hour.* ■ [with obj.] put (a form of public transport) in service: *the group is drawing up plans to run trains on key routes.* ■ [with obj. and adverbial of direction] take (someone) somewhere in a car: *I'll run you home.*
6 [with obj.] be in charge of; manage: *Andrea runs her own catering business* | (as adj., in combination **-run**) *an attractive family-run hotel.* ■ [no obj., with adverbial] (of a system, organization, or plan) operate or proceed in a particular way: *everything's running according to plan.* ■ organize, implement, or carry out: *we decided to run a series of seminars.* ■ own, maintain, and use (a vehicle).
7 be in or cause to be in operation; function or cause to function: [no obj.] *the car **runs on** unleaded fuel* | [with obj.] *the modem must be **run off** a mains transformer.* ■ move or cause to move between the spools of a recording machine: [with obj.] *I ran the tape back.*
8 [no obj.] continue or be valid or operative for a particular period of time: *the course **ran for** two days* | *this particular debate will **run and run**.* ■ [with adverbial or complement] happen or arrive at the specified time: *the programme was running fifteen minutes late.* ■ (of a play or exhibition) be staged or presented: *the play ran at Stratford last year.*
9 [no obj.] pass into or reach a specified state or level: ***inflation is running at** 11 per cent* | [with complement] *the decision ran counter to previous government commitments.*
10 [no obj.] (**run in**) (of a quality, trait, or condition) be common or inherent in members of (a family), especially over several generations: *weight problems run in my family.*
11 [no obj.] stand as a candidate in an election: *he announced that he intended to **run for** President.* ■ [with obj.] (especially of a political party) sponsor (a candidate) in an election: *they ran their first independent candidate at the Bromley by-election.*
12 publish or be published in a newspaper or magazine: [with obj.] *the tabloid press ran the story* | [no obj.] *when the story ran, there was a big to-do.* ■ [no

obj.] (of a saying, argument, piece of writing, etc.) have a specified wording: *'Tapestries slashed!' ran the dramatic headline.*
13 [with obj.] bring (goods) into a country illegally and secretly; smuggle: *they run drugs for the cocaine cartels.*
14 [with two objs] N. Amer. cost (someone) (a specified amount): *a new photocopier will run us about $1,300.*
15 W. Indian provide: *the wait-and-see game continues until the government runs some ready cash.* ■ provide pasture for (sheep or cattle); raise (livestock).
▸ **noun 1** an act or spell of running: *I usually go for a run in the morning | a cross-country run.* ■ a running pace: *Rory set off **at a run**.* ■ an annual mass migration of fish up or down a river: *the annual salmon runs.*
2 a journey accomplished or route taken by a vehicle, aircraft, or boat, especially on a regular basis: *the London–Liverpool run.* ■ a short excursion made in a car: *we could take a run out to the country.* ■ the distance covered in a specified period, especially by a ship: *a record run of 398 miles from noon to noon.* ■ a short flight made by an aircraft on a straight and even course at a constant speed before or while dropping bombs.
3 an opportunity or attempt to achieve something: *their absence means the Russians will have **a clear run at** the title.* ■ a preliminary test of a procedure or system: *if you are styling your hair yourself, have a practice run.* ■ an attempt to secure election to political office: *his run for the Republican nomination.*
4 a continuous spell of a particular situation or condition: *he's had a run of bad luck.* ■ a continuous series of performances: *the play had a long run in the West End.* ■ a quantity or amount of something produced at one time: *a production run of only 150 cars.* ■ a continuous stretch or length of something: *long runs of copper piping.* ■ a rapid series of musical notes forming a scale. ■ a sequence of cards of the same suit.
5 (**a run on**) a widespread and sudden demand for (a commodity) or a widespread trading in (a currency): *there's been a big run on nostalgia toys this year.* ■ a sudden demand for repayment from (a bank) made by a large number of lenders: *growing nervousness among investors led to a run on some banks.*
6 (**the run**) the average or usual type of person or thing: *she stood out from **the general run of** Tory women.* ■ the general tendency of something: *quite against the run of play, Smith scored an early try.*
7 a sloping snow-covered course or track used for skiing, bobsleighing, or tobogganing: *a ski run.* ■ a track made or regularly used by a particular animal: *a badger run.*
8 an enclosed area in which domestic animals or birds may run freely in the open: *a chicken run.* ■ (**the run of**) free and unrestricted use of or access to: *her cats were given the run of the house.* ■ Austral./NZ a large open stretch of land used for pasture or the raising of stock.
9 Cricket a unit of scoring achieved by hitting the ball so that both batsmen are able to run between the wickets, or awarded in some other circumstances. ■ Baseball a point scored by the batter returning to home plate after touching the other bases.
10 chiefly N. Amer. a ladder in stockings or tights.
11 a downward trickle of paint or a similar substance when applied too thickly. ■ a small stream.
12 (**the runs**) informal diarrhoea.
13 Nautical the after part of a ship's bottom where it rises and narrows towards the stern.
– PHRASES **be run off one's feet** see FOOT. **come running** be eager to do what someone wants: *he had only to crook his finger and she would come running.* **give someone/thing a (good) run for their money** provide someone or something with challenging competition. **have a (good) run for one's money** derive reward or enjoyment in return for one's outlay or efforts. **on the run 1** trying to avoid being captured: *a criminal on the run from the FBI.* **2** while running: *he took a pass on the run.* ■ continuously busy: *I'm on the run every minute of the day.* **run before one can walk** attempt something difficult before one has grasped the basic skills. **run a blockade** see BLOCKADE. **run dry** (of a well or river) cease to flow or have any water. ■ (of a source or supply) be completely used up: *municipal relief funds had long since run dry.* **run an errand** carry out an errand for someone. **(make a) run for it** attempt to escape someone or something by running away. **run foul** (or chiefly N. Amer. **afoul**) **of 1** Nautical collide or become entangled with (an obstacle or another vessel): *another ship ran foul of us.* **2** come into conflict with; go against: *the act may run foul of data protection legislation.* **run the gauntlet** see GAUNTLET². **run someone close** almost defeat a person or team in a contest. **run high** see HIGH. **run oneself into the ground** see GROUND¹. **run into the sand** come to nothing: *the peace initiative now seems to be running into the sand.* **run its course** see COURSE. **run low** (or **short**) become depleted: *supplies had run short.* ■ have too little of something: *we're **running short of** time.* **run a mile** see MILE. **run off at the mouth** (or **run one's mouth**) N. Amer. informal talk excessively or indiscreetly. **run someone out of town** chiefly N. Amer. force someone to leave a place. **run rings round** see RING¹. **run riot** see RIOT. **run the risk** (or **run risks**) see RISK. **run the show** informal dominate or be in charge of an undertaking or area of activity. **run a temperature** be suffering from a high temperature. **run someone/thing to earth** (or **ground**) Hunting chase a quarry to its lair. ■ Brit. find someone or something after a long search. **run to ruin** archaic fall into disrepair. **run to seed** see SEED. **run wild** see WILD. **run with the hare and hunt with the hounds** see HARE.
– PHRASAL VERBS **run across** meet or find by chance: *I just thought you might have run across him before.* **run after** informal persistently seek to acquire or attain: *businesses which have spent years running after the baby boom market.* ■ seek the company of (a potential sexual or romantic partner). **run against** archaic collide with (someone). ■ happen to meet: *I ran against Flanagan the other day.* **run along** [in imperative] informal go away (used typically to address a child): *run along now, there's a good girl.* **run around with** (US also **run with**) informal associate habitually with (someone). **run at** rush towards (someone) to attack them. **run away** escape from a place, person, or situation: *children who **run away from** home normally go to London.* ■ (also informal **run off**) leave one's home or current partner in order to establish a relationship with someone else: *he **ran off with** his wife's best friend.* ■ try to avoid facing up to a difficult situation: *the government are **running away from** their responsibilities.* **run away with 1** (of one's imagination or emotions) escape the control of: *Susan's imagination was running away with her.* **2** accept (an idea) without thinking it through properly: *a lot of people ran away with the idea that they were pacifists.* **3** win (a competition or prize) easily: *Ipswich are running away with the championship.* **run something by** (or **past**) tell (someone) about something, especially in order to ascertain their opinion or reaction. **run someone/thing down 1** (of a vehicle or its driver) hit a person or animal and knock them to the ground. ■ (of a boat) collide with another vessel. **2** criticize someone or something unfairly or unkindly. **3** discover someone or something after a search: *she finally ran the professor down.* **run something down** (or **run down**) reduce (or become reduced) in size, numbers, or resources: *the government were reviled for running down the welfare state | hardwood stocks in some countries are rapidly running down.* ■ lose (or cause to lose) power; stop (or cause to stop) functioning: *the battery has run down.* ■ gradually deteriorate (or cause to deteriorate) in quality: *the property had been allowed to run down.* **run someone in** informal arrest someone. **run something in** Brit. prepare the engine of a new car for normal use by driving slowly for a period of time. ■ use something new in such a way as not to make maximum demands upon it: *whatever system you choose, you must run it in properly.* **run into 1** collide with: *he ran into a lamppost.* ■ meet by chance: *I ran into Moira on the way home.* ■ experience (a problem or difficulty): *the bank ran into financial difficulties.* **2** reach (a level or amount): *debts running into millions of dollars.* **3** blend into or appear to coalesce with: *her words ran into each other.* **run off** see RUN AWAY above. **run off with** informal steal: *the treasurer had run off with the pension funds.* **run something off 1** reproduce copies of a piece of writing on a machine. ■ write or recite something quickly and with little effort. **2** drain liquid from a container: *run off the water that has been standing in the pipes.* **run on 1** continue without stopping; go on longer than is expected: *the story ran on for months.* ■ talk incessantly. **2** (also **run upon**) (of a person's mind or a discussion) be preoccupied or concerned with: *my thoughts ran too much on death.* **3** Printing continue on the same line as the preceding matter. **run out 1** (of a supply of something) be used up: *our food is about to run out.* ■ use up one's supply of something: *we've **run out of** petrol.* ■ become no longer valid: *her contract runs out at the end of the year.* **2** (of rope) be paid out: *slowly, he let the cables run out.* **3** [with adverbial of direction] extend; project: *a row of buildings ran out to Whitehall Gate.* **4** [with complement] Brit. emerge from a contest in a specified position: *the team ran out 4–1 winners.* **run someone out** Cricket dismiss a batsman by dislodging the bails with the ball while the batsman is still running between the wickets. ■ (of a batsman) cause one's partner to be dismissed in this way by poor judgement. **run out on** informal abandon (someone). **run over 1** (of a container or its contents) overflow: *the bath's running over.* **2** exceed (an expected limit): *the film ran over schedule and budget.* **run someone/thing over** (of a vehicle or its driver) knock a person or animal down and pass over their body. **run over** go over (something) quickly as a reminder or rehearsal. **run through 1** be present in every part of; pervade: *a sense of personal loss runs through many of his lyrics.* **2** use or spend recklessly or rapidly: *her husband had long since run through her money.* **3** go over (something) quickly as a reminder or rehearsal: *I'll just run through the schedule for the weekend.* **run someone/thing through** stab a person or animal so as to kill them. **run to 1** extend to or reach (a specified amount or size): *the document ran to almost 100 pages.* ■ be enough to cover (a particular expense): *my income doesn't run to luxuries like taxis.* **2** (of a person) show a tendency to or inclination towards: *she was tall and running to fat.* **3** have recourse to (someone) for support: *don't come running to me for a handout.* **run something up 1** allow a debt or bill to accumulate: *he ran up debts of $153,000.* ■ achieve a particular score in a game or match: *they ran up 467 runs for the loss of eight wickets.* **2** make something quickly or hurriedly, especially a piece of clothing: *I'll run up a dress for you.* **3** raise a flag. **run up against** meet (a difficulty or problem): *the scheme could run up against European regulations.* **run with 1** proceed with; accept: *we do lots of tests before we run with a product.* **2** see RUN AROUND WITH above.
– DERIVATIVES **runnable** adjective.
– ORIGIN Old English *rinnan*, *irnan* (verb), of Germanic origin, probably reinforced in Middle English by Old Norse *rinna*, *renna*. The current form with *-u-* in the present tense is first recorded in the 16th cent.

> **USAGE** On the use of verbs used with **and** instead of a 'to' infinitive, as in *run and fetch the paper*, see **USAGE** at **AND**.

runabout ▸ **noun** a small car or light aircraft, especially one used for short journeys. ■ N. Amer. a small motor boat.

run-and-gun ▸ **adjective** US (in sport) denoting fast, free-flowing play without emphasis on set plays or defence.

runaround informal ▸ **noun 1** (**the runaround**) deceitful or evasive treatment: *they are being **given the runaround** by the Defence Ministry.*
2 a runabout. Computing.

runaway ▸ **noun 1** a person who has run away, especially from their family or an institution.
2 [often as modifier] an animal or vehicle that is running out of control: *a runaway train.* ■ [as modifier] denoting something happening or done very quickly, easily, or uncontrollably: *the runaway success of the book.*

runcible spoon /ˈrʌnsɪb(ə)l/ ▸ **noun** a fork curved like a spoon, with three broad prongs, one of which has a sharpened outer edge for cutting.
– ORIGIN late 19th cent.: used by Edward Lear, perhaps suggested by late 16th-cent. *rouncival*, denoting a large variety of pea.

Runcorn /ˈrʌŋkɔːn/ an industrial town in NW England, on the River Mersey in Cheshire; pop. 59,200 (est. 2009). It was developed as a new town from 1964.

rundown ▸ **noun 1** an analysis or summary of something by a knowledgeable person: *he gave his teammates **a rundown on** the opposition.*
2 a reduction in the productivity or activities of a company or institution: *a rundown in the business would be a devastating blow to the local economy.*
▸ **adjective** (usu. **run-down**) **1** (especially of a building or area) in a poor or neglected state after having been prosperous: *a run-down Edwardian villa.* ■ (of a company or industry) in a poor economic state.
2 tired and rather unwell, especially through overwork: *she felt tired and generally run-down.*

rune /ruːn/ ▸ **noun 1** a letter of an ancient Germanic alphabet, related to the Roman alphabet. ■ a similar mark of mysterious or magic significance. ■ (**runes**) small stones, pieces of bone, etc., bearing such marks, and used in divination: *the casting of the runes.* ■ a spell or incantation.

R

2 a section of the Kalevala or of an ancient Scandinavian poem.

> Runes were used by Scandinavians and Anglo-Saxons from about the 3rd century. They were formed mainly by modifying Roman or Greek characters to suit carving, and were used both in writing and in divination.

– PHRASES **read the runes** Brit. try to forecast the outcome of a situation by analysing all the significant factors involved.
– DERIVATIVES **runic adjective**.
– ORIGIN Old English *rūn* 'a secret, mystery'; not recorded between Middle English and the late 17th cent., when it was reintroduced under the influence of Old Norse *rúnir, rúnar* 'magic signs, hidden lore'.

rune stone ▸ noun 1 a large stone carved with runes by ancient Scandinavians or Anglo-Saxons.
2 a small stone, piece of bone, etc., marked with a rune and used in divination.

run-flat ▸ adjective relating to or denoting a kind of tyre which does not deflate after puncturing.
▸ noun a run-flat tyre.

rung¹ ▸ noun 1 a horizontal support on a ladder for a person's foot. ■ a level in a hierarchical structure, especially a class or career structure: *we must ensure that the low-skilled do not get trapped on the bottom rung.*
2 a strengthening crosspiece in the structure of a chair.
– ORIGIN Old English *hrung* (in sense 2); related to Dutch *rong* and German *Runge*.

rung² past participle of **RING²**.

run-in ▸ noun 1 Brit. the approach to an action or event: *the final run-in to the World Cup.* ■ the home stretch of a racecourse. ■ a period during which an engine or other device is run in.
2 informal a disagreement or fight, especially with someone in an official position: *a run-in with armed police in Rio.* ■ a collision: *a run-in with a parking meter.*

runlet ▸ noun a small stream.

runnel ▸ noun a gutter. ■ a brook or rill. ■ a small stream of a particular liquid: *a runnel of sweat.*
– ORIGIN late 16th cent. (denoting a brook or rill): variant of dialect *rindle*, influenced by the verb **RUN**.

runner ▸ noun 1 a person that runs, especially in a specified way: *Mary was a fast runner.* ■ a person who runs competitively as a sport or hobby: *a 400 metres runner.* ■ a horse that runs in a particular race: *there were only four runners.* ■ a vehicle or machine that operates in a satisfactory or specified way: *the van was a good and reliable runner.* ■ Brit. informal a contender for a job or position. ■ Brit. informal an idea that has a chance of being accepted; a practical suggestion: *trying to determine whether a tax on books is a runner.* ■ Cricket a person who runs between the wickets for an injured batsman. ■ a messenger, collector, or agent for a bank, bookmaker, or similar. ■ an orderly in the army. ■ Brit. informal a freelance antiques dealer.
2 [in combination] a person who smuggles specified goods into or out of a country or area: *a gun-runner.*
3 a rod, groove, or blade on which something slides. ■ each of the long pieces on the underside of a sledge that forms the contact in sliding. ■ (often **runners**) a roller for moving a heavy article. ■ a ring capable of slipping or sliding along a strap or rod or through which something may be passed or drawn. ■ Nautical a rope in a single block with one end round a tackle block and the other having a hook.
4 a shoot, typically leafless, which grows from the base of a plant along the surface of the ground and can take root at points along its length. ■ a plant that spreads by means of runners. ■ a twining plant.
5 a long, narrow rug or strip of carpet, especially for a hall or stairway.
6 (also **runner stone**) a revolving millstone.
7 archaic a police officer. See also **BOW STREET RUNNER**.
8 (also **runner duck**) see **INDIAN RUNNER**.
9 a fast-swimming fish of the jack family, occurring in tropical seas. ● Several species in the family Carangidae, in particular the **rainbow runner** and the **blue runner** (*Caranx crysos*) of the western Atlantic.
– PHRASES **do a runner** Brit. informal leave or escape hastily or furtively.

runner bean ▸ noun Brit. a Central American bean plant with scarlet flowers and very long flat edible pods. Also called **SCARLET RUNNER**. ● *Phaseolus coccineus*, family Leguminosae.
■ the pod and seed of the runner bean eaten as food.

R

runner-up ▸ noun (pl. **runners-up**) a competitor or team taking second place in a contest.

running ▸ noun [mass noun] 1 the action or movement of a runner. ■ the sport of racing on foot: *marathon running.*
2 the action of managing or operating something: *the day-to-day running of the office.*
▸ adjective 1 [attrib.] denoting something that runs, in particular: ■ (of water) flowing naturally or supplied to a building through pipes and taps: *hot and cold running water.* ■ (of a sore or a part of the body) exuding liquid or pus: *a running sore.*
2 done while running: *a running jump.*
3 continuous or recurring over a long period: *a running joke.* ■ [postpositive] consecutive; in succession: *he failed to produce an essay for the third week running.*
– PHRASES **in** (or **out of**) **the running** in (or no longer in) contention for an award, victory, or a place in a team: *he is in the running for an Oscar.* **make the running** Brit. set the pace in a race or activity. **take a running jump** [often as imperative] used as an expression of angry dismissal or rejection: *I hope you told that boss of yours to take a running jump.* **take up the running** take over as pacesetter in a race.

running back ▸ noun American Football an offensive player who specializes in carrying the ball.

running battle ▸ noun a military engagement which does not occur at a fixed location. ■ a confrontation which has gone on for a long time.

running belay ▸ noun Climbing a device attached to a rock face through which a climbing rope runs freely, acting as a pulley if the climber falls.

running board ▸ noun a footboard extending along the side of a vehicle, typically found on early models of car.

running commentary ▸ noun a verbal description of events, given as they occur.

running dog ▸ noun 1 informal a servile follower, especially of a political system: *the running dogs of capitalism.* [translating Chinese *zǒugǒu*.]
2 a dog bred to run, especially for racing or pulling a sled.

running fix ▸ noun a determination of one's position made by taking bearings at different times and allowing for the distance covered in the interval.

running gear ▸ noun [mass noun] the moving parts of a machine, especially the wheels, steering, and suspension of a vehicle. ■ the moving rope and tackle used in handling a boat.

running head (also **running headline**) ▸ noun a heading printed at the top of each page of a book or chapter.

running knot ▸ noun a knot that slips along the rope and changes the size of a noose.

running lights ▸ plural noun 1 another term for **NAVIGATION LIGHTS**.
2 small lights on a motor vehicle that remain illuminated while the vehicle is running.

running mate ▸ noun chiefly N. Amer. 1 an election candidate for the lesser of two closely associated political offices.
2 a horse entered in a race in order to set the pace for another horse from the same stable, which is intended to win.

running pine ▸ noun N. Amer. a clubmoss which has a ground-hugging habit and propagates by means of runners. ● Genus *Lycopodium*, family Lycopodiaceae, in particular *L. clavatum*.

running repairs ▸ plural noun Brit. minor or temporary repairs carried out on machinery while it is in use.

running rigging ▸ noun see **RIGGING** (sense 1).

running rope ▸ noun a rope that is able to move freely, especially through a pulley.

running stitch ▸ noun [mass noun] a simple needlework stitch consisting of a line of small even stitches which run back and forth through the cloth without overlapping.

running total ▸ noun a total that is continually adjusted to take account of further items.

runny ▸ adjective (**runnier, runniest**) 1 more liquid than is usual or expected: *the soufflé was hard on top and quite runny underneath.*
2 (of a person's nose) producing or discharging mucus.

Runnymede /ˈrʌnɪmiːd/ a meadow on the south bank of the Thames near Windsor. It is famous for its association with Magna Carta, which was signed by King John in 1215 there or nearby.

run-off ▸ noun 1 a further competition, election, race, etc., after a tie or inconclusive result.
2 [mass noun] the draining away of water (or substances carried in it) from the surface of an area of land, a building or structure, etc. ■ the water or other material that drains freely off the surface of something.
3 NZ a separate area of land where young animals are kept.

run-of-the-mill ▸ adjective lacking unusual or special aspects; ordinary: *a run-of-the-mill job.*

run-on ▸ adjective denoting a line of verse in which a sentence is continued without a pause beyond the end of a line, couplet, or stanza.

run-out ▸ noun 1 Cricket the dismissal of a batsman by being run out.
2 informal a short session of play, practice, or participation in sporting competition, especially at the beginning of a season or after a period of absence due to injury.
3 a slight error in a rotating tool, machine component, etc. such as being off-centre or not exactly round.
4 a length of time or stretch of ground over which something gradually ceases or is brought to an end or a halt: *the commission recommended abolition after a run-out of ten years.*

runt ▸ noun 1 a small pig or other animal, especially the smallest in a litter. ■ derogatory an undersized or weak person.
2 a pigeon of a large domestic breed.
3 a small ox or cow, especially one of various Scottish Highland or Welsh breeds.
– DERIVATIVES **runty adjective** (**runtier, runtiest**).
– ORIGIN early 16th cent. (in the sense 'old or decayed tree stump'): of unknown origin.

run-through ▸ noun 1 a rehearsal: *a run-through of the whole show.*
2 a brief outline or summary: *the textbooks provide a run-through of research findings.*

runtime ▸ noun 1 the time that a film or DVD lasts: *a thriller that is so well paced it seems a lot shorter than its three-hour runtime.*
2 Computing the length of time a program takes to run. ■ the time at or during which a program is run. ■ a cut-down version of a program that can be run but not changed.
▸ adjective (of software) in a reduced version that can be run but not changed.

run-up ▸ noun 1 the period preceding a notable event: *a programme aimed at lowering unemployment in the run-up to the next election.*
2 an act of running briefly to gain momentum before performing a jump in athletics, bowling in cricket, etc. ■ the strip of ground behind the wicket on which the bowler runs before bowling.
3 Golf a low approach shot that bounces and runs forward.
4 an act of running an engine or turbine to prepare it for use or to test it.
5 a marked rise in the value or level of something: *a sharp run-up of land and stock prices.*

runway ▸ noun 1 a strip of hard ground along which aircraft take off and land.
2 North American term for **CATWALK** (sense 1).
3 an animal run, especially one made by small mammals in grass, under snow, etc.
4 an incline or chute down which logs are slid.

Runyon /ˈrʌnjən/, (Alfred) Damon (1884–1946), American author and journalist. His short stories about New York's underworld characters are written in a highly individual style with much use of colourful slang.

rupee /ruːˈpiː, rʊˈpiː/ ▸ noun the basic monetary unit of India, Pakistan, Sri Lanka, Nepal, Mauritius, and the Seychelles, equal to 100 paise in India, Pakistan, and Nepal, and 100 cents in Sri Lanka, Mauritius, and the Seychelles.
– ORIGIN via Hindi from Sanskrit *rūpya* 'wrought silver'.

Rupert, Prince (1619–82), English Royalist general, son of Frederick V (elector of the Palatinate) and nephew of Charles I. The Royalist leader of cavalry, he initially won a series of victories, but was defeated by Parliamentarian forces at Marston Moor (1644) and Naseby (1645).

Rupert's Land (also **Prince Rupert's Land**) a historical region of northern and western Canada, roughly corresponding to what is now Manitoba,

Saskatchewan, Yukon, Alberta, and the southern part of the Northwest Territories. It was originally granted in 1670 by Charles II to the Hudson's Bay Company and named after Prince Rupert, the first governor of the Company; it was purchased by Canada in 1870.

rupestrian /ruːˈpɛstrɪən/ ▶ adjective (of art) done on rock or cave walls.
– ORIGIN late 18th cent.: from modern Latin *rupestris* 'found on rocks' (from Latin *rupes* 'rock') + -AN.

rupiah /ruːˈpiːə/ ▶ noun the basic monetary unit of Indonesia, equal to 100 sen.
– ORIGIN Indonesian, from Hindi *rūpyah* (see RUPEE).

rupture ▶ verb 1 [no obj.] (especially of a pipe or container, or bodily part such as an organ or membrane) break or burst suddenly: *if the main artery ruptures he could die.* ▪ [with obj.] cause to break or burst suddenly: *the impact ruptured both fuel tanks.* ▪ (**be ruptured** or **rupture oneself**) suffer an abdominal hernia: *one of the boys was ruptured and needed to be fitted with a truss.*
2 [with obj.] breach or disturb (a harmonious feeling or situation): *once trust and confidence has been ruptured it can be difficult to regain.*
▶ noun 1 an instance of breaking or bursting suddenly and completely: *a small hairline crack could develop into a rupture* | [mass noun] *the patient died after rupture of an aneurysm.* ▪ an abdominal hernia.
2 a breach of a harmonious relationship: *the rupture with his father would never be healed.*
– ORIGIN late Middle English (as a noun): from Old French *rupture* or Latin *ruptura*, from *rumpere* 'to break'. The verb dates from the mid 18th cent.

rupturewort ▶ noun a small Old World plant of the pink family, which was formerly believed to cure hernias. ● *Herniaria glabra*, family Caryophyllaceae.

rural ▶ adjective in, relating to, or characteristic of the countryside rather than the town: *remote rural areas.*
– DERIVATIVES **ruralism** noun, **ruralist** noun, **rurality** noun, **ruralization** noun, **rurally** adverb.
– ORIGIN late Middle English: from Old French, or from late Latin *ruralis*, from *rus, rur-* 'country'.

rural dean ▶ noun see DEAN[1] (sense 1).

rural district ▶ noun Brit. historical a group of country parishes governed by an elected council.

Rurik /ˈrʊərɪk/ (also **Ryurik**) ▶ noun a member of a dynasty that ruled Muscovy and much of Russia from the 9th century until the death of Fyodor, son of Ivan the Terrible, in 1598. It was reputedly founded by a Varangian chief who settled in Novgorod in 862.
▶ adjective relating to the Ruriks.

Ruritania /ˌrʊərɪˈteɪnɪə/ an imaginary kingdom in central Europe used as a fictional background for the adventure novels of courtly intrigue and romance written by Anthony Hope (1863–1933).
– DERIVATIVES **Ruritanian** adjective & noun.

rusa /ˈruːsə/ (also **rusa deer**) ▶ noun an Indonesian deer with a brown coat and branched antlers. ● *Cervus timorensis*, family Cervidae.
– ORIGIN late 18th cent.: modern Latin (former genus name), from Malay.

rusbank /ˈrəsbaŋk/ ▶ noun (pl. **rusbanks** or **rusbanke**) S. African a long wooden settle, typically with a back and seat made of woven leather thongs.
– ORIGIN Afrikaans, from *rus* 'rest' + *bank* 'bench'.

Ruse /ˈruːseɪ/ (also **Rousse**) an industrial city and the principal port of Bulgaria, on the Danube; pop. 156,959 (2008). Turkish during the Middle Ages, it was captured by Russia in 1877 and ceded to Bulgaria.

ruse /ruːz/ ▶ noun an action intended to deceive someone; a trick: *Emma tried to think of a ruse to get Paul out of the house.*
– ORIGIN late Middle English (as a hunting term): from Old French, from *ruser* 'use trickery', earlier 'drive back', perhaps based on Latin *rursus* 'backwards'.

rush[1] ▶ verb 1 [no obj., with adverbial of direction] move with urgent haste: *Oliver rushed after her* | *I rushed outside and hailed a taxi.* ▪ (of air or a liquid) flow strongly: *the water rushed in through the great oaken gates.* ▪ [no obj.] act with great haste: *as soon as the campaign started they **rushed into action*** | [with infinitive] *shoppers rushed to buy computers.* ▪ [with obj.] force (someone) to act hastily: *I don't want to **rush you into** something.* ▪ [with obj. and adverbial of direction] take (someone) somewhere with great haste: *an ambulance was waiting to rush him to hospital.* ▪ [with two objs] deliver (something) quickly to (someone): *we'll rush you a copy at once.* ▪ (**rush something out**) produce and distribute something very quickly: *a rewritten textbook was rushed out last autumn.* ▪ [with obj.] deal with (something) hurriedly: *panic measures were **rushed through parliament**.* ▪ [with obj.] dash towards (someone or something) in an attempt to attack or capture: *to rush the bank and fire willy-nilly could be disastrous for everyone.*
2 [with obj.] American Football advance towards (an opposing player, especially the quarterback). ▪ [no obj.] run from scrimmage with the ball.
3 [with obj.] US entertain (a new student) in order to assess suitability for membership of a college fraternity or sorority.
4 [with obj.] Brit. informal, dated overcharge (a customer): *They rushed you, all right! It's not worth a penny more than £120.*
▶ noun 1 a sudden quick movement towards something, typically by a number of people: *there was a **rush for** the door.* ▪ a sudden flow or flood: *she felt a rush of cold air.* ▪ a flurry of hasty activity: *the pre-Christmas rush* | [as modifier] *a rush job.* ▪ a sudden strong demand for a commodity: *there's been a **rush on** the Western News because of the murder.* ▪ a sudden intense feeling: *Mark felt **a rush of** anger.* ▪ informal a sudden thrill or feeling of euphoria such as experienced after taking certain drugs.
2 American Football an act of advancing forward, especially towards the quarterback.
3 (**rushes**) the first prints made of a film after a period of shooting.
– PHRASES **a rush of blood (to the head)** a sudden attack of wild irrationality.
– DERIVATIVES **rusher** noun, **rushingly** adverb.
– ORIGIN late Middle English: from an Anglo-Norman French variant of Old French *ruser* 'drive back', an early sense of the word in English (see RUSE).

rush[2] ▶ noun 1 a marsh or waterside plant with slender stem-like pith-filled leaves, widely distributed in temperate areas. Some kinds are used for matting, chair seats, and baskets. ● Genus *Juncus*, family Juncaceae. ▪ used in names of similar plants of wet habitats, e.g. **flowering rush**. ▪ a stem of a rush plant. ▪ [mass noun] rushes used as a material.
2 archaic a thing of no value (used for emphasis): *not one of them is **worth a rush**.*
– DERIVATIVES **rushlike** adjective, **rushy** adjective.
– ORIGIN Old English *risc, rysc*, of Germanic origin.

Rushdie /ˈrʌʃdi, ˈrʊʃ-/, Sir (Ahmed) Salman (b.1947), Indian-born British novelist. His work, chiefly associated with magic realism, includes *Midnight's Children* (Booker Prize, 1981) and *The Satanic Verses* (1988). The latter, regarded by Muslims as blasphemous, caused Ayatollah Khomeini to issue a fatwa in 1989 condemning Rushdie to death. In 1998 the Iranian government dissociated itself from the fatwa.

rushed ▶ adjective done or completed too hurriedly; hasty: *a rushed job.* ▪ (of a person) short of time; hurrying: *I'm too rushed to do it.*

rush hour ▶ noun a time during each day when traffic is at its heaviest.

rushlight ▶ noun historical a candle made by dipping the pith of a rush in tallow.

Rushmore, Mount a mountain in the Black Hills of South Dakota, noted for its giant relief carvings of four US Presidents—George Washington, Thomas Jefferson, Abraham Lincoln, and Theodore Roosevelt—carved (1927–41) under the direction of the sculptor Gutzon Borglum (1867–1941).

rus in urbe /ˌruːs ɪn ˈəːbeɪ/ ▶ noun literary an illusion of countryside created by a building or garden within a city.
– ORIGIN Latin, literally 'country in the city'.

rusk ▶ noun chiefly Brit. a light, dry biscuit or piece of twice-baked bread, especially one prepared for use as baby food. ▪ [mass noun] twice-baked bread used in foods such as sausages, and formerly as rations at sea.
– ORIGIN late 16th cent.: from Spanish or Portuguese *rosca* 'twist, coil, roll of bread', of unknown ultimate origin.

Ruskin, John (1819–1900), English art and social critic. His prolific writings on art and architecture include *Modern Painters* (five volumes, 1843–60), *The Seven Lamps of Architecture* (1849), and *The Stones of Venice* (three volumes, 1851–3). After 1860 he devoted himself to social and economic reform, campaigning for the recovery of medieval piety and Christian ideals and against the scientific advances of his times.

Russell[1], Bertrand (Arthur William), 3rd Earl Russell (1872–1970), British philosopher, mathematician, and social reformer. In *Principia Mathematica* (1910–13) he and A. N. Whitehead attempted to express all of mathematics in formal logic terms. He expounded logical atomism in *Our Knowledge of the External World* (1914) and neutral monism in *The Analysis of Mind* (1921). A conscientious objector during the First World War, he also campaigned for women's suffrage and against nuclear arms. Nobel Prize for Literature (1950).

Russell[2], George William (1867–1935), Irish poet and journalist. After the performance of his poetic drama *Deirdre* (1902) Russell became a leading figure in the Irish literary revival.

Russell[3], John, 1st Earl Russell (1792–1878), British Whig statesman, Prime Minister 1846–52 and 1865–6. He was responsible for introducing the Reform Bill of 1832 into Parliament and resigned his second premiership when his attempt to extend the franchise further was unsuccessful.

Russell's paradox ▶ noun a logical paradox stated in terms of set theory, concerning the set of all sets that do not contain themselves as members, namely that the condition for it to contain itself is that it should not contain itself.
– ORIGIN 1920s: named after Bertrand *Russell* (see RUSSELL[1]).

Russell's viper ▶ noun a large venomous Asian snake which has a yellow-brown body with black markings. ● *Daboia* (or *Vipera*) *russelli*, family Viperidae.
– ORIGIN early 20th cent.: named after Patrick *Russell* (1727–1805), Scottish physician and naturalist.

russet ▶ adjective 1 reddish brown in colour: *the russet bracken.*
2 archaic rustic; homely: *that terse and epigrammatic style, with its russet Saxon.*
▶ noun 1 [mass noun] a reddish-brown colour: *the woods in autumn are a riot of russet and gold.*
2 a dessert apple of a variety with a slightly rough brownish skin.
3 [mass noun] historical a coarse homespun reddish-brown or grey cloth used for simple clothing.
– DERIVATIVES **russety** adjective.
– ORIGIN Middle English: from an Anglo-Norman French variant of Old French *rousset*, diminutive of *rous* 'red', from Provençal *ros*, from Latin *russus* 'red'.

Russia /ˈrʌʃə/ a country in northern Asia and eastern Europe; pop. 140,041,200 (est. 2009); official language, Russian; capital, Moscow. Official name RUSSIAN FEDERATION.

The modern state originated from the expansion of the principality of Muscovy into a great empire. Russia played an increasing role in Europe from the time of Peter the Great in the early 18th century. Following the overthrow of the tsar in the Russian Revolution of 1917, Russia became the largest of the constituent republics of the Soviet Union, with more than three quarters of the area and over half of the population. On the break-up of the Soviet Union and the collapse of Communist control in 1991, Russia emerged as an independent state and a founder member of the Commonwealth of Independent States.

Russia leather ▶ noun [mass noun] a durable leather made from calfskins and impregnated with birch bark oil, used for bookbinding.

Russian ▶ adjective relating to Russia, its people, or their language.
▶ noun 1 a native or inhabitant of Russia, or a person of Russian descent. ▪ historical (in general use) a national of the former Soviet Union.
2 [mass noun] the language of Russia, an Eastern Slavic language written in the Cyrillic alphabet and spoken by over 130 million people.
– DERIVATIVES **Russianist** noun, **Russianization** noun, **Russianize** (also **Russianise**) verb, **Russianness** noun.
– ORIGIN mid 16th cent.: from medieval Latin *Russianus*.

Russian ballet ▶ noun [mass noun] a style of ballet developed at the Russian Imperial Ballet Academy, popularized in the West by Sergei Diaghilev's Ballets Russes from 1909.

Russian Blue ▶ noun a cat of a breed with short greyish-blue fur, green eyes, and large pointed ears.

Russian boot ▶ noun a boot that loosely encloses the wearer's calf.

Russian Civil War a conflict fought in Russia (1918–21) after the Revolution, between the Bolshevik Red Army and the counter-revolutionary White Russians. The Bolsheviks were ultimately victorious,

R

and the Union of Soviet Socialist Republics was established.

Russian doll ▶ noun each of a set of brightly painted hollow wooden dolls of varying sizes, designed to fit inside each other.

Russian Federation official name for **Russia**.

Russian olive ▶ noun North American term for **oleaster**.

Russian Orthodox Church the national Church of Russia. See **Orthodox Church**.

Russian Revolution the revolution in the Russian empire in 1917, in which the tsarist regime was overthrown and replaced by Bolshevik rule under Lenin.

> There were two phases to the Revolution: the first, in March (Old Style, February, whence **February Revolution**), was sparked off by food and fuel shortages during the First World War and began with strikes and riots in Petrograd (St Petersburg). The tsar abdicated, and a provisional government was set up. The second phase, in November 1917 (Old Style, October, whence **October Revolution**), was marked by the seizure of power by the Bolsheviks in a coup led by Lenin. After workers' councils or **soviets** took power in major cities, the new Soviet constitution was declared in 1918.

Russian Revolution of 1905 the uprising in Russia in 1905.

> Popular discontent, fuelled by heavy taxation and the country's defeat in the Russo-Japanese War, led to a peaceful demonstration in St Petersburg, which was fired on by troops. The crew of the battleship *Potemkin* mutinied and a soviet was formed in St Petersburg, prompting Tsar Nicholas II to make a number of short-lived concessions including the formation of an elected legislative body or Duma.

Russian roulette ▶ noun [mass noun] the practice of loading a bullet into one chamber of a revolver, spinning the cylinder, and then pulling the trigger while pointing the gun at one's own head. ■ an activity that is potentially very dangerous.

Russian salad ▶ noun Brit. a salad of mixed diced vegetables with mayonnaise.

Russian tea ▶ noun [mass noun] tea laced with rum and typically served with lemon.

Russian thistle ▶ noun N. Amer. a prickly tumbleweed which is an inland form of saltwort. Native to Eurasia, it was accidentally introduced into North America, where it has become a pest. ● *Salsola pestifera*, family Chenopodiaceae.

Russian vine ▶ noun an Asian climbing plant of the dock family, with long clusters of white or pink flowers, which is sometimes cultivated as a fast-growing screening plant. ● *Fallopia baldschuanica*, family Polygonaceae.

Russify /ˈrʌsɪfʌɪ/ ▶ verb (**Russifies, Russifying, Russified**) [with obj.] make Russian in character.
– DERIVATIVES **Russification** noun.

R

Russki /ˈrʌski/ (also **Russky**) ▶ noun (pl. **Russkis** or **Russkies**) informal, often offensive a Russian.
– ORIGIN mid 19th cent.: from Russian *russkiĭ* 'Russian', or from **Russian**, on the pattern of Russian surnames ending in *-skiĭ*.

Russo- ▶ combining form Russian; Russian and ...: *Russo-Japanese*. ■ relating to Russia.

Russo-Finnish War another term for **Winter War**.

Russo-Japanese War a war between the Russian empire and Japan 1904–5, caused by territorial disputes in Manchuria and Korea. Russia suffered a series of humiliating defeats and the peace settlement gave Japan the ascendancy in the disputed region.

Russophile /ˈrʌsə(ʊ)fʌɪl/ ▶ noun a person who is friendly towards or fond of Russia, especially someone who is sympathetic to the political system and customs of the former Soviet Union.
– DERIVATIVES **Russophilia** noun.

Russophobe /ˈrʌsə(ʊ)fəʊb/ ▶ noun a person who feels an intense dislike towards Russia and things Russian, especially the political system or customs of the former Soviet Union.
– DERIVATIVES **Russophobia** noun.

Russo-Turkish Wars a series of wars between Russia and the Ottoman Empire, fought largely in the Balkans, the Crimea, and the Caucasus in the 19th century. The treaty ending the war of 1877–8 freed the nations of Romania, Serbia, and Bulgaria from Turkish rule.

russula /ˈrʌsələ/ ▶ noun a widespread woodland toadstool that typically has a brightly coloured flattened cap and a white stem and gills. ● Genus *Russula*, family Russulaceae, class Hymenomycetes: numerous species. See also **sickener** (sense 2).
– ORIGIN modern Latin, from Latin *russus* 'red' (because many, such as the sickener, have a red cap).

rust ▶ noun [mass noun] **1** a reddish- or yellowish-brown flaking coating of iron oxide that is formed on iron or steel by oxidation, especially in the presence of moisture.
2 [usu. with adj. or noun modifier] a fungal disease of plants which results in reddish or brownish patches. ● The fungi belong to *Puccinia* and other genera, order Uredinales, class Teliomycetes.
3 a reddish-brown colour: [in combination] *her rust-coloured coat*.
▶ verb [no obj.] be affected with rust: *the blades had **rusted away*** | (as adj. **rusting**) *rusting machinery*.
– DERIVATIVES **rustless** adjective.
– ORIGIN Old English *rūst*, of Germanic origin; related to Dutch *roest*, German *Rost*, also to **red**.

rust belt ▶ noun [often as modifier] informal, chiefly N. Amer. a part of a country characterized by declining industry and a falling population, especially in the American Midwest and NE states: *a rust-belt town*.

rust bucket ▶ noun informal a car, ship, or other vehicle which is old and badly rusted.

rustic ▶ adjective **1** of or relating to the countryside; rural. ■ having a simplicity and charm that is considered typical of the countryside: *a party of Morris dancers decked out in rustic costume*. ■ lacking the sophistication of the city; backward and provincial: *you are a rustic halfwit*.
2 made in a plain and simple fashion, in particular: ■ made of untrimmed branches or rough timber: *a rustic oak bench*. ■ (of masonry) having a rough-hewn or roughened surface or deeply sunk joints. ■ denoting freely formed lettering, especially a relatively informal style of handwritten Roman capital letter.
▶ noun **1** often derogatory an unsophisticated country person.
2 a small brownish European moth. ● Several genera and species in the family Noctuidae.
– DERIVATIVES **rustically** adverb, **rusticity** noun.
– ORIGIN late Middle English (in the sense 'rural'): from Latin *rusticus*, from *rus* 'the country'.

rusticate /ˈrʌstɪkeɪt/ ▶ verb **1** [with obj.] Brit. suspend (a student) from a university as a punishment (used chiefly at Oxford and Cambridge).
2 [no obj.] dated go to, live in, or spend time in the country.
3 [with obj.] fashion (masonry) in large blocks with sunk joints and a roughened surface.
– DERIVATIVES **rustication** noun.
– ORIGIN late 15th cent. (in the sense 'countrify'): from Latin *rusticat-* '(having) lived in the country', from the verb *rusticari*, from *rusticus* (see **rustic**).

rustle ▶ verb **1** [no obj.] make a soft, muffled crackling sound like that caused by the movement of dry leaves or paper: *she came closer, her skirt swaying and rustling*. ■ [with adverbial of direction] move with a rustling sound: *a nurse rustled in*. ■ [with obj.] cause (something) to make a rustling sound: *Dolly rustled the paper irritably*.
2 [with obj.] round up and steal (cattle, horses, or sheep).
3 [no obj.] N. Amer. informal move or act quickly or energetically; hustle: *rustle around the kitchen, see what there is*.
▶ noun a soft, muffled crackling sound like that made by the movement of dry leaves or paper: *there was a rustle in the undergrowth behind her*.
– PHRASAL VERBS **rustle something up** informal produce something quickly when it is needed: *see if you can rustle up a cup of tea for Paula and me, please*.
– DERIVATIVES **rustler** noun (sense 2 of the verb).
– ORIGIN late Middle English (as a verb): imitative; compare with Flemish *rijsselen* and Dutch *ritselen*. The noun dates from the mid 18th cent.

rustproof ▶ adjective (of metal or a metal object) not susceptible to corrosion by rust.
▶ verb [with obj.] make resistant to corrosion by rust.

rusty ▶ adjective (**rustier, rustiest**) **1** (of a metal object) affected by rust: *a rusty hinge*. ■ rust-coloured: *green grass turning a rusty brown*. ■ (of black clothes) discoloured by age.
2 (of knowledge or a skill) impaired by lack of recent practice: *my typing is a little rusty*. ■ stiff with age or disuse: *it was my first race for three months and I felt a bit rusty*.
– DERIVATIVES **rustily** adverb, **rustiness** noun.
– ORIGIN Old English *rūstig* (see **rust, -y**[1]).

rusty dusty ▶ noun black English a person's buttocks.
– ORIGIN late 16th cent. (in the sense 'dusty, fusty'): reduplication of **rusty**. The current transferred use dates from the 1950s.

rut[1] ▶ noun **1** a long deep track made by the repeated passage of the wheels of vehicles.
2 a habit or pattern of behaviour that has become dull and unproductive but is hard to change: *the EC was stuck **in a rut** and was losing its direction*.
– DERIVATIVES **rutted** adjective, **rutty** adjective (**ruttier, ruttiest**).
– ORIGIN late 16th cent.: probably from Old French *rute* (see **route**).

rut[2] ▶ noun an annual period of sexual activity in deer and some other mammals, during which the males fight each other for access to the females: *a moose **in rut***.
▶ verb (**rutted, rutting**) [no obj.] (often as adj. **rutting**) engage in such activity: *a rutting stag*.
– DERIVATIVES **ruttish** adjective.
– ORIGIN late Middle English: from Old French, from Latin *rugitus*, from *rugire* 'to roar'.

rutabaga /ˌruːtəˈbeɪgə/ ▶ noun N. Amer. another term for **swede** (sense 1).
– ORIGIN late 18th cent.: from Swedish dialect *rotabagge*.

Ruth[1] a book of the Bible telling the story of Ruth, a Moabite woman, who married her deceased husband's kinsman Boaz and bore a son who became grandfather to King David.

Ruth[2], Babe (1895–1948), American baseball player; born *George Herman Ruth*. He played for the Boston Red Sox (1914–19) and the New York Yankees (1919–35), setting a record of 714 home runs which remained unbroken until 1974.

ruth ▶ noun [mass noun] archaic a feeling of pity, distress, or grief.
– ORIGIN Middle English: from the verb **rue**[1], probably influenced by Old Norse *hrygth*.

Ruthenia /ruːˈθiːnɪə/ a region of eastern Europe on the southern slopes of the Carpathian Mountains, now forming the Transcarpathian region of western Ukraine.
– DERIVATIVES **Ruthenian** adjective & noun.
– ORIGIN named after the *Ruthenes* (from medieval Latin *Rutheni*), a Slavic people, ancestors of the Ukrainians.

ruthenium /rʊˈθiːnɪəm/ ▶ noun [mass noun] the chemical element of atomic number 44, a hard silvery-white metal of the transition series. (Symbol: **Ru**)
– ORIGIN mid 19th cent.: modern Latin, from medieval Latin *Ruthenia* (see **Ruthenia**), so named because it was discovered in ores from the Urals.

Rutherford /ˈrʌðəfəd/, Sir Ernest, 1st Baron Rutherford of Nelson (1871–1937), New Zealand physicist, regarded as the founder of nuclear physics. As a result of his experiments on the scattering of alpha particles, he proposed that the positive charge in an atom, and virtually all its mass, is concentrated in a central nucleus. He also performed the first artificial transmutation of matter. Nobel Prize for Chemistry (1908).

rutherfordium /ˌrʌðəˈfɔːdɪəm/ ▶ noun [mass noun] the chemical element of atomic number 104, a very unstable element made by high-energy atomic collisions. (Symbol: **Rf**)
– ORIGIN 1960s: modern Latin, named after E. *Rutherford* (see **Rutherford**).

ruthless ▶ adjective having or showing no pity or compassion for others: *a ruthless manipulator*.
– DERIVATIVES **ruthlessly** adverb, **ruthlessness** noun.
– ORIGIN Middle English: from **ruth** + **-less**.

rutilant /ˈruːtɪl(ə)nt/ ▶ adjective literary glowing or glittering with red or golden light: *rutilant gems*.
– ORIGIN late Middle English: from Latin *rutilant-* 'glowing red', from the verb *rutilare*, from *rutilus* 'reddish'.

rutile /ˈruːtɪl, ˈruːtʌɪl/ ▶ noun [mass noun] a black or reddish-brown mineral consisting of titanium dioxide, typically occurring as needle-like crystals.
– ORIGIN early 19th cent.: from French, or from German *Rutil*, from Latin *rutilus* 'reddish'.

rutin /ˈruːtɪn/ ▶ noun [mass noun] Chemistry a compound of the flavonoid class found in common rue, buckwheat, capers, and other plants, and sometimes taken as a dietary supplement.

– ORIGIN mid 19th cent.: from Latin *ruta* 'rue' + -IN[1].

Rutland /'rʌtlənd/ a unitary authority in the east Midlands, formerly the smallest county in England; administrative centre, Oakham.

Ruwenzori /ˌruːɛn'zɔːri/ a mountain range in central Africa, on the border between Uganda and the Democratic Republic of the Congo (Zaire) between Lake Edward and Lake Albert, rising to 5,110 m (16,765 ft) at Margherita Peak on Mount Stanley. The range is generally thought to be the 'Mountains of the Moon' mentioned by Ptolemy, and as such the supposed source of the Nile.

Ruysdael variant spelling of **RUISDAEL**.

RV ▶ abbreviation ■ N. Amer. recreational vehicle (especially a motorized caravan). ■ a rendezvous point. ■ Revised Version (of the Bible).

RWA ▶ abbreviation Rwanda (international vehicle registration).

Rwanda /ruː'andə/ a landlocked country in central Africa, to the north of Burundi and the south of Uganda; pop. 10,746,300 (est. 2009); official languages, Rwanda (a Bantu language) and French; capital, Kigali. Official name **Rwandese Republic**.

> Inhabited largely by Hutu and Tutsi peoples, the area was claimed by Germany from 1890 and after the First World War became part of a Belgian trust territory. Rwanda became independent as a republic in 1962, shortly after the violent overthrow of the Tutsi monarchy by the majority Hutu people. In 1994 over 500,000 people, largely Tutsis, were slaughtered by predominantly Hutu supporters of the government, and over a million fled as refugees into Zaire (now the Democratic Republic of the Congo) and neighbouring countries. The Tutsi-dominated Rwandan Patriotic Front took power as the new government.

– DERIVATIVES **Rwandan** adjective & noun, **Rwandese** adjective & noun.

Rx ▶ noun N. Amer. a doctor's prescription.
– ORIGIN abbreviation of Latin *recipe!* 'take!'.

Ry ▶ abbreviation Railway.

-ry ▶ suffix a shortened form of **-ERY** (as in *devilry*, *rivalry*).

Ryazan /ˌrɪə'zaːn/ an industrial city in European Russia, situated to the south-east of Moscow; pop. 510,800 (est. 2008).

Rybinsk /'rɪbɪnsk/ a city in NW Russia, a port on the River Volga; pop. 211,000 (est. 2008). It was formerly known as Shcherbakov (1946–57) and, in honour of the former President of the Soviet Union, Yuri Andropov, as Andropov (1984–9).

Rydberg atom /'rɪdbəːg/ ▶ noun Physics an atom in a highly excited state in which one electron has almost sufficient energy to escape. Atoms, usually hydrogen atoms, in this **Rydberg state** are used in atomic research.
– ORIGIN named after J. R. *Rydberg* (see **RYDBERG CONSTANT**).

Rydberg constant ▶ noun Physics a constant, $1.097 \times 10^7\ m^{-1}$, which appears in the formulae for the wave numbers of lines in atomic spectra and is a function of the rest mass and charge of the electron, the speed of light, and Planck's constant.
– ORIGIN early 20th cent.: named after Johannes R. *Rydberg* (1854–1919), Swedish physicist.

Ryder Cup a golf tournament held every two years and played between teams of male professionals from the US and Europe (originally Great Britain), first held in 1927.
– ORIGIN so named because the trophy was donated by Samuel *Ryder* (1859–1936), English seed merchant.

rye ▶ noun [mass noun] **1** a wheat-like cereal plant which tolerates poor soils and low temperatures. ● *Secale cereale*, family Gramineae.
■ grains of rye, used mainly for making bread or whisky, and for fodder: [as modifier] *rye flour*.
2 (also **rye whisky**) whisky in which a significant amount of the grain used in distillation is fermented rye: *half a bottle of rye*.
3 chiefly N. Amer. short for **RYE BREAD**: *pastrami on rye*.
– ORIGIN Old English *ryge*, of Germanic origin; related to Dutch *rogge* and German *Roggen*.

rye bread ▶ noun [mass noun] bread made with rye flour, typically dark in colour and with a dense, chewy texture.

ryegrass ▶ noun [mass noun] a Eurasian grass which is a valuable fodder and lawn grass. ● Genus *Lolium*, family Gramineae: several species, in particular *L. perenne*.
– ORIGIN early 18th cent.: alteration of obsolete *ray-grass*, of unknown origin.

Ryle[1] /rʌɪl/, Gilbert (1900–76), English philosopher. In *The Concept of Mind* (1949) he attacks the mind–body dualism of Descartes. He was a cousin of the astronomer Sir Martin Ryle.

Ryle[2] /rʌɪl/, Sir Martin (1918–84), English astronomer. His demonstration that remote objects appeared to be different from closer ones helped to establish the Big Bang theory of the universe. Nobel Prize for Physics (1974). He was a cousin of the philosopher Gilbert Ryle.

ryokan /rɪ'əʊkan/ ▶ noun a traditional Japanese inn.
– ORIGIN Japanese.

ryot /'rʌɪət/ ▶ noun dated an Indian peasant or tenant farmer.
– ORIGIN from Urdu *raiyat*, from Arabic *ra'īyya* 'flock, subjects', from *ra'ā* 'to pasture'.

Rysy /'rɪsi/ a peak in the Tatra Mountains rising to a height of 2,499 m (8,197 ft).

ryu /rɪ'uː/ ▶ noun (pl. **same** or **ryus**) a Japanese school or style of art.
– ORIGIN Japanese.

Ryukyu Islands /rɪ'uːkjuː/ a chain of islands in the western Pacific, stretching for about 960 km (600 miles) from the southern tip of the island of Kyushu, Japan, to Taiwan. Part of China in the 14th century, the archipelago was incorporated into Japan by 1879 and was held under US military control between 1945 and 1972.

Ryurik variant spelling of **RURIK**.

R

S s

S[1] (also **s**) ▸ **noun** (pl. **Ss** or **S's**) **1** the nineteenth letter of the alphabet. ▪ denoting the next after R in a set of items, categories, etc.
2 a shape like that of a capital S: [in combination] *an S-bend.*

S[2] ▸ **abbreviation** ▪ (chiefly in Catholic use) Saint: *S Ignatius Loyola.* ▪ siemens. ▪ small (as a clothes size). ▪ South or Southern: *65° S.* ▪ Biochemistry Svedberg unit(s). ▪ Sweden (international vehicle registration).
▸ **symbol** ▪ the chemical element sulphur. ▪ Chemistry entropy.

s ▸ **abbreviation** ▪ second(s). ▪ Law section (of an act). ▪ shilling(s). ▪ Grammar singular. ▪ Chemistry solid. ▪ (in genealogies) son(s). ▪ succeeded. ▪ Chemistry denoting electrons and orbitals possessing zero angular momentum and total symmetry: *s-electrons.* [*s* from *sharp*, originally applied to lines in atomic spectra.]
▸ **symbol** (in mathematical formulae) distance.

's /s, z/ after a vowel sound or voiced consonant informal ▸ **contraction** is: *it's raining.* ▪ has: *she's gone.* ▪ us: *let's go.* ▪ does: *what's he do?*

's- /s, z/ before a voiced consonant ▸ **prefix** archaic (used chiefly in oaths) God's: *'sblood.*
– ORIGIN shortened form.

-s[1] /s, z/ after a vowel sound or voiced consonant ▸ **suffix** denoting the plurals of nouns (as in *apples*, *wagons*, etc.). Compare with **-ES**[1].
– ORIGIN Old English plural ending *-as.*

-s[2] /s, z/ after a vowel sound or voiced consonant ▸ **suffix** forming the third person singular of the present of verbs (as in *sews*, *runs*, etc.). Compare with **-ES**[2].
– ORIGIN Old English dialect.

-s[3] /s, z/ after a vowel sound or voiced consonant ▸ **suffix** **1** forming adverbs such as *besides.*
2 forming possessive pronouns such as *hers*, *ours.*
– ORIGIN Old English *-es*, masculine and neuter genitive singular ending.

-s[4] /s, z/ after a vowel sound or voiced consonant ▸ **suffix** forming nicknames or pet names: *ducks.*
– ORIGIN suggested by **-S**[1].

-s' /s/; /z/ after a vowel sound or voiced consonant ▸ **suffix** denoting possession in plural nouns and sometimes in singular nouns having a final *s*: *the girls' dormitories* | *Giles' sister.*
– ORIGIN Old English *-es.*

-'s[1] /s, z/ after a vowel sound or voiced consonant/ɪz/ after a sibilant ▸ **suffix** denoting possession in singular nouns, also in plural nouns not having a final *-s*: *the car's engine* | *Mrs Ross's son* | *the children's teacher.*
– ORIGIN Old English, masculine and neuter genitive singular ending.

-'s[2] /s, z/ after a vowel sound or voiced consonant/ɪz/ after a sibilant ▸ **suffix** denoting the plural of a letter or symbol: *T's* | *9's.*

> **USAGE** There are a few special instances in which it is acceptable to use an apostrophe to indicate plurals, as with letters and symbols where **s** added without punctuation could look odd or be undecipherable (*dot your i's and cross your t's; he rated a string of 9.9's from the jury*). However, when forming plurals of regular nouns it is wrong to use an apostrophe, e.g. *six pens* not *six pen's*. For further discussion, see **USAGE** at **APOSTROPHE**[1].

S & L ▸ **abbreviation** savings and loan.

SA ▸ **abbreviation** ▪ Salvation Army. ▪ informal, dated sex appeal. ▪ South Africa. ▪ South America. ▪ South Australia. ▪ historical Sturmabteilung.

Saadi variant spelling of **SADI**.

saag /sɑːg/ (also **sag**) ▸ **noun** Indian spinach or another leafy vegetable.
– ORIGIN from Hindi *sāg.*

Saale[1] /ˈsɑːlə/ a river of east central Germany. Rising in northern Bavaria near the border with the Czech Republic, it flows 425 km (265 miles) north to join the Elbe near Magdeburg.

Saale[2] /ˈzɑːlə/ ▸ **noun** [usu. as modifier] Geology the penultimate Pleistocene glaciation in northern Europe, corresponding to the Wolstonian of Britain (and possibly the Riss of the Alps). ▪ the system of deposits laid down in the Saale glaciation.
– DERIVATIVES **Saalian** /ˈzɑːlɪən/ **adjective & noun**.
– ORIGIN 1930s: from **SAALE**[1].

Saanen /ˈsɑːnən/ ▸ **noun** a dairy goat of a white hornless breed, first developed in the region of Saanen in Switzerland.

Saar /sɑː/, German /ˈzaːɐ/ a river of western Europe. Rising in the Vosges mountains in eastern France, it flows 240 km (150 miles) northwards to join the Mosel River in Germany, just east of the border with Luxembourg. French name **SARRE**. ▪ the Saarland.

Saarbrücken /sɑːˈbrʊkən/, German /ˌzaːɐˈbrYkn/ an industrial city in western Germany, the capital of Saarland, on the River Saar close to the border with France; pop. 177,900 (est. 2006).

Saarland /ˈsɑːland/, German /ˈzaːɐlant/ a state of western Germany, on the border with France; capital, Saarbrücken. Rich in coal and iron ore and historically dominated by France, the area was administered by the League of Nations from the end of the First World War until 1935; it became the tenth German state in 1957.

sab Brit. informal ▸ **noun** a hunt saboteur.
▸ **verb** (**sabs**, **sabbing**, **sabbed**) [no obj.] act as a hunt saboteur: *they travelled the country sabbing and demonstrating.*
– ORIGIN 1970s: abbreviation of **SABOTEUR**.

Saba /ˈsɑːbə/ **1** an island in the Netherlands Antilles, in the Caribbean; pop. 1,601 (2009). The smallest island in the group, it is situated to the north-west of St Kitts.
2 an ancient kingdom in SW Arabia, famous for its trade in gold and spices; the biblical Sheba.

sabadilla /ˌsabəˈdɪlə/ ▸ **noun** a Mexican plant of the lily family, whose seeds contain veratrine.
● *Schoenocaulon officinale*, family Liliaceae.
▪ [mass noun] a preparation of sabadilla seeds, used as an agricultural insecticide and in medicines.
– ORIGIN early 19th cent.: from Spanish *cebadilla*, diminutive of *cebada* 'barley'.

Sabaean /səˈbiːən/ ▸ **noun** a member of an ancient Semitic people who ruled Saba in SW Arabia until overrun by Persians and Arabs in the 6th century AD.
▸ **adjective** relating to the Sabaeans.
– ORIGIN from Latin *Sabaeus* (from Greek *Sabaios*) + **-AN**.

Sabah /ˈsɑːbɑː/ a state of Malaysia, comprising the northern part of Borneo and some offshore islands; capital, Kota Kinabalu. A British protectorate from 1888, it joined Malaysia in 1963.

Sabaoth /ˈsabeɪɒθ, saˈbeɪɒθ/ ▸ **plural noun** archaic the hosts of heaven (in the biblical title 'Lord (God) of Sabaoth').
– ORIGIN via Latin from Greek *Sabaōth*, from Hebrew *ṣĕḇā'ōṯ*, plural of *ṣāḇā'* 'host (of heaven)'.

sabayon /ˈsabʌɪjɒ̃/ ▸ **noun** French term for **ZABAGLIONE**.

sabbatarian /ˌsabəˈtɛːrɪən/ ▸ **noun** a Christian who strictly observes Sunday as the sabbath. ▪ a Jew who strictly observes the sabbath. ▪ a Christian belonging to a denomination or sect that observes Saturday as the sabbath.
▸ **adjective** relating to or upholding the observance of the sabbath.
– DERIVATIVES **sabbatarianism** **noun**.
– ORIGIN early 17th cent.: from late Latin *sabbatarius* (from Latin *sabbatum* 'sabbath') + **-AN**.

sabbath ▸ **noun** **1** (often **the Sabbath**) a day of religious observance and abstinence from work, kept by Jews from Friday evening to Saturday evening, and by most Christians on Sunday.
2 (also **witches' sabbath**) a supposed midnight meeting held by witches.
– ORIGIN Old English, from Latin *sabbatum*, via Greek from Hebrew *šabbāṯ*, from *šāḇaṯ* 'to rest'.

sabbatical /səˈbatɪk(ə)l/ ▸ **noun** a period of paid leave granted to a university teacher for study or travel, traditionally one year for every seven years worked: *she's away **on sabbatical**.*
▸ **adjective** **1** relating to a sabbatical.
2 archaic of or appropriate to the sabbath.
– ORIGIN late 16th cent.: via late Latin from Greek *sabbatikos* 'of the sabbath' + **-AL**.

sabbatical year ▸ **noun** **1** a year's sabbatical leave.
2 (in biblical times) a year observed every seventh year under the Mosaic law as a 'sabbath' during which the land was allowed to rest.

Sabellian[1] /səˈbɛlɪən/ ▸ **noun** a member of a group of Oscan-speaking peoples of ancient Italy, including the Sabines and Samnites.
▸ **adjective** relating to the Sabellians.
– ORIGIN from Latin *Sabellus* + **-IAN**.

Sabellian[2] /səˈbɛlɪən/ ▸ **adjective** relating to the teachings of Sabellius (*fl. c.*220 in North Africa), who developed a form of the modalist doctrine that the Father, Son, and Holy Spirit are not truly distinct but merely aspects of one divine being.
▸ **noun** a follower of the teachings of Sabellius.
– DERIVATIVES **Sabellianism** **noun**.

saber ▸ **noun & verb** US spelling of **SABRE**.

Sabian /ˈseɪbɪən/ ▸ **noun** a member of a non-Muslim sect classed in the Koran with Jews, Christians, and Zoroastrians as having a faith revealed by the true God. It is not known who the original Sabians were, but the name was adopted by some groups in order to give themselves legitimacy as People of the Book.
▸ **adjective** relating to the Sabians.
– ORIGIN early 17th cent.: from Arabic *ṣābi'* + **-AN**.

sabicu /ˌsabɪˈkuː/ ▸ **noun** a Caribbean tree of the pea family, with timber that resembles mahogany and is used chiefly in boatbuilding. ● *Lysiloma sabicu*, family Leguminosae.
– ORIGIN mid 19th cent.: from Cuban Spanish *sabicú.*

Sabine /ˈsabʌɪn/ ▸ **noun** a member of an ancient Oscan-speaking people of the central Apennines in Italy, north-east of Rome, who feature in early

Roman legends and were incorporated into the Roman state in 290 BC.
▶ adjective relating to the Sabines.
– ORIGIN from Latin *Sabinus*.

Sabin vaccine /ˈseɪbɪn/ ▶ noun a vaccine against poliomyelitis containing attenuated virus and given by mouth.
– ORIGIN 1950s: named after Albert B. *Sabin* (1906–93), American virologist.

sabji /ˈsʌbdʒiː/ ▶ noun (pl. **sabjis**) Indian variant spelling of SABZI.

sabkha /ˈsabkə, -xə/ ▶ noun an area of coastal flats subject to periodic flooding and evaporation which result in the accumulation of aeolian clays, evaporites, and salts, found in North Africa and Arabia.
– ORIGIN late 19th cent.: from Arabic *sabqa* 'salt flat'.

sable[1] /ˈseɪb(ə)l/ ▶ noun a marten with a short tail and dark brown fur, native to Japan and Siberia and valued for its fur. ● *Martes zibellina*, family Mustelidae.
■ [mass noun] the fur of the sable.
– ORIGIN late Middle English: from Old French, in the sense 'sable fur', from medieval Latin *sabelum*, of Slavic origin.

sable[2] /ˈseɪb(ə)l/ ▶ adjective literary or Heraldry black.
▶ noun 1 [mass noun] literary or Heraldry black. ■ **(sables)** archaic mourning garments.
2 (also **sable antelope**) a large African antelope with long curved horns, the male of which has a black coat and the female a russet coat, both having a white belly. ● *Hippotragus niger*, family Bovidae.
– ORIGIN Middle English: from Old French (as a heraldic term), generally taken to be identical with SABLE[1], although sable fur is dark brown.

sablefish ▶ noun (pl. **same** or **sablefishes**) a large commercially important fish with a slaty-blue to black back, occurring throughout the North Pacific. ● *Anoplopoma fimbria*, family Anoplopomatidae.

sabot /ˈsabəʊ/ ▶ noun 1 a kind of simple shoe, shaped and hollowed out from a single block of wood, traditionally worn by French and Breton peasants.
2 a device which ensures the correct positioning of a bullet or shell in the barrel of a gun, attached either to the projectile or inside the barrel and falling away as it leaves the muzzle.
3 a box from which cards are dealt at casinos in gambling games such as baccarat and chemin de fer. Also called SHOE. Austral.
– DERIVATIVES **saboted** /ˈsabəʊd/ adjective (sense 1).
– ORIGIN early 17th cent.: French, blend of *savate* 'shoe' and *botte* 'boot'.

sabotage /ˈsabətɑːʒ/ ▶ verb [with obj.] deliberately destroy, damage, or obstruct (something), especially for political or military advantage.
▶ noun [mass noun] the action of sabotaging something: *a coordinated campaign of sabotage*.
– ORIGIN early 20th cent.: from French, from *saboter* 'kick with sabots, wilfully destroy' (see SABOT).

saboteur /ˌsabəˈtəː/ ▶ noun a person who engages in sabotage.
– ORIGIN 1920s: French, from the verb *saboter* (see SABOTAGE).

sabra /ˈsabrə/ ▶ noun a Jew born in Israel (or before 1948 in Palestine).
– ORIGIN from modern Hebrew *ṣabbār* 'opuntia fruit' (opuntias being common in coastal regions of Israel).

Sabratha /ˈsabrəθə/ (also **Sabrata** /-brətə/) one of the three ancient cities of Tripolitania .

sabre /ˈseɪbə/ (US **saber**) ▶ noun 1 a heavy cavalry sword with a curved blade and a single cutting edge.
■ historical a cavalry soldier and horse.
2 a light fencing sword with a tapering, typically curved blade.
▶ verb [with obj.] archaic cut down or wound with a sabre.
– ORIGIN late 17th cent.: from French, alteration of obsolete *sable*, from German *Sabel* (local variant of *Säbel*), from Hungarian *szablya*.

sabre-rattling ▶ noun [mass noun] the display or threat of military force.

sabre saw ▶ noun a portable electric jigsaw.

sabretache /ˈsabətaʃ/ ▶ noun historical a flat satchel on long straps worn by some cavalry and horse artillery officers from the left of the waist-belt.
– ORIGIN early 19th cent.: from French, from German *Säbeltasche*, from *Säbel* 'sabre' + *Tasche* 'pocket'.

sabretooth ▶ noun 1 (also **sabre-toothed cat** or **tiger**) a large extinct carnivorous mammal of the cat family, with massive curved upper canine teeth. ● Several genera in the family Felidae, in particular *Smilodon* of the American Pleistocene and *Machairodus* of the Old World Pliocene.
2 a large extinct marsupial mammal with similar teeth, of the South American Pliocene. ● Genus *Thylacosmilus*, family Borhyaenidae.

sabreur /saˈbrəː/ ▶ noun a cavalryman or fencer using a sabre.
– ORIGIN French, from *sabrer* 'strike with a sabre'.

sabrewing ▶ noun a large tropical American hummingbird with a green back and long curved wings. ● Genus *Campylopterus*, family Trochilidae: several species.

sabzi /ˈsʌbziː/ (also **sabji** /ˈsʌbdʒiː/) ▶ noun (pl. **sabzis**) [mass noun] Indian vegetables, especially when cooked.
– ORIGIN from Persian *sabz* 'green'.

SAC ▶ abbreviation Senior Aircraftman.

sac /sak/ ▶ noun a hollow, flexible structure resembling a bag or pouch: *a fountain pen with an ink sac*. ■ a cavity within an organism, enclosed by a membrane and containing air, liquid, or solid structures. ■ the distended membrane surrounding a hernia, cyst, or tumour.
– DERIVATIVES **sac-like** adjective.
– ORIGIN mid 18th cent. (as a term in biology): from French *sac* or Latin *saccus* 'sack, bag'.

saccade /saˈkɑːd/ ▶ noun (usu. **saccades**) technical a rapid movement of the eye between fixation points.
– DERIVATIVES **saccadic** /saˈkadɪk/ adjective.
– ORIGIN early 18th cent. (in the sense 'jerking movement'): from French, literally 'violent pull', from Old French *saquer* 'to pull'.

saccate /ˈsakeɪt/ ▶ adjective Botany dilated to form a sac.

saccharide /ˈsakərʌɪd/ ▶ noun Biochemistry another term for SUGAR (sense 2 of the noun).
– ORIGIN mid 19th cent.: from modern Latin *saccharum* 'sugar' + -IDE.

saccharin /ˈsakərɪn/ ▶ noun [mass noun] a sweet-tasting synthetic compound used in food and drink as a substitute for sugar. ● Alternative name: **o-sulphobenzoic imide**; chem. formula: $C_7H_5NO_3S$.
– ORIGIN late 19th cent.: from modern Latin *saccharum* 'sugar' + -IN[1].

saccharine /ˈsakərʌɪn, -ɪn, -iːn/ ▶ noun another term for SACCHARIN.
▶ adjective 1 excessively sweet or sentimental: *saccharine music*.
2 dated relating to or containing sugar; sugary.
– ORIGIN late 17th cent.: from modern Latin *saccharum* + -INE[1].

saccharo- ▶ combining form relating to sugar: *saccharometer*.
– ORIGIN via Latin from Greek *sakkharon* 'sugar'.

saccharometer /ˌsakəˈrɒmɪtə/ ▶ noun a hydrometer for estimating the sugar content of a solution.

saccharose /ˈsakərəʊz, -s/ ▶ noun Chemistry another term for SUCROSE.
– ORIGIN late 19th cent.: from modern Latin *saccharum* 'sugar' + -OSE[2].

saccule /ˈsakjuːl/ ▶ noun Biology & Anatomy a small sac, pouch, or cyst. ■ another term for SACCULUS.
– DERIVATIVES **saccular** adjective, **sacculated** adjective, **sacculation** noun.
– ORIGIN mid 19th cent.: anglicized form of Latin *sacculus* (see SACCULUS).

sacculus /ˈsakjʊləs/ ▶ noun Anatomy the smaller of the two fluid-filled sacs forming part of the labyrinth of the inner ear (the other being the utriculus). It contains a region of hair cells and otoliths which send signals to the brain concerning the orientation of the head. ■ another term for SACCULE.
– ORIGIN mid 18th cent.: from Latin, diminutive of *saccus* 'sack'.

SACD ▶ abbreviation super audio CD, a type of compact disc that provides a sound quality superior to that of conventional discs.

sacerdotal /ˌsasəˈdəʊt(ə)l, ˌsakə-/ ▶ adjective relating to priests or the priesthood; priestly. ■ Theology relating to or denoting a doctrine which ascribes sacrificial functions and spiritual or supernatural powers to ordained priests.
– DERIVATIVES **sacerdotalism** noun.
– ORIGIN late Middle English: from Old French, or from Latin *sacerdotalis*, from *sacerdos*, *sacerdot-* 'priest'.

sachem /ˈseɪtʃəm, ˈsatʃəm/ ▶ noun (among some American Indian peoples) a chief. ■ N. Amer. informal a boss or leader.
– ORIGIN from Narragansett, 'chief, sagamore'.

Sachertorte /ˈzaxəˌtɔːtə/, German /ˈzaxɐˌtɔrtə/ ▶ noun (pl. **Sachertorten** /-ˌtɔːt(ə)n/, German /-ˌtɔrtn/) a chocolate gateau with apricot jam filling and chocolate icing.
– ORIGIN German, from the name of Franz *Sacher*, the pastry chef who created it, + *Torte* 'tart, pastry'.

sachet /ˈsaʃeɪ/ ▶ noun 1 Brit. a small sealed bag or packet containing a small quantity of something: *a sachet of sugar*.
2 a small bag containing dried scented material such as lavender, used to scent clothes. ■ [mass noun] archaic dried, scented material for use in scenting clothes.
– ORIGIN mid 19th cent. (in sense 2): from French, 'little bag', diminutive of *sac*, from Latin *saccus* 'sack, bag'.

Sachs /saks, zaks/, Hans (1494–1576), German poet and dramatist. Some of his poetry celebrated Luther and furthered the Protestant cause, while other pieces were comic verse dramas.

Sachsen /ˈzaksn/ German name for SAXONY.

Sachsen-Anhalt /ˌzaksnˈanhalt/ German name for SAXONY-ANHALT.

sack[1] ▶ noun 1 a large bag made of a strong material such as hessian, thick paper, or plastic, used for storing and carrying goods. ■ the contents of a sack or the amount it can contain: *a sack of flour*.
2 (also **sack dress**) a woman's short loose unwaisted dress, typically narrowing at the hem, popular especially in the 1950s. ■ historical a woman's long loose dress or gown. ■ a piece of dress material fastened to the shoulders of a woman's gown in loose pleats and forming a long train, fashionable in the 18th century.
3 **(the sack)** informal dismissal from employment: ***he got the sack for swearing | they were given the sack***.
4 **(the sack)** informal, chiefly N. Amer. bed, especially as regarded as a place for sex.
5 Baseball, informal a base.
6 American Football a tackle of a quarterback behind the line of scrimmage.
▶ verb [with obj.] 1 informal dismiss from employment: *any official found to be involved would be sacked on the spot*.
2 **(sack out)** N. Amer. informal go to bed, or go to sleep.
3 American Football tackle (a quarterback) behind the line of scrimmage.
4 rare put into a sack or sacks.
– PHRASES **hit the sack** informal go to bed. **a sack of potatoes** informal used in similes to refer to clumsiness, inertness, or unceremonious treatment of the person or thing in question.
– DERIVATIVES **sackable** adjective, **sack-like** adjective.
– ORIGIN Old English *sacc*, from Latin *saccus* 'sack, sackcloth', from Greek *sakkos*, of Semitic origin. Sense 1 of the verb dates from the mid 19th cent.

sack[2] ▶ verb [with obj.] (chiefly in historical contexts) plunder and destroy (a captured town or building).
▶ noun the pillaging of a town or city: *the sack of Rome*.
– ORIGIN mid 16th cent.: from French *sac*, in the phrase *mettre à sac* 'put to sack', on the model of Italian *fare il sacco*, *mettere a sacco*, which perhaps originally referred to filling a sack with plunder.

sack[3] ▶ noun [mass noun] historical a dry white wine formerly imported into Britain from Spain and the Canaries.
– ORIGIN early 16th cent.: from the phrase *wyne seck*, from French *vin sec* 'dry wine'.

sackbut /ˈsakbʌt/ ▶ noun an early form of trombone used in Renaissance music.
– ORIGIN late 15th cent.: from French *saquebute*, from obsolete *saqueboute* 'hook for pulling a man off a horse', from *saquer* 'to pull' + *bouter* 'to hit'.

sackcloth ▶ noun [mass noun] a very coarse, rough fabric woven from flax or hemp.
– PHRASES **sackcloth and ashes** used with allusion to the wearing of sackcloth and having ashes sprinkled on the head as a sign of penitence or mourning (Matt 11:21).

sack coat ▶ noun historical a loose-fitting coat hanging straight down from the shoulders, particularly as worn by men (sometimes as part of military uniform) in the 19th and early 20th centuries.

sackful ▶ noun (pl. **sackfuls**) the quantity of something held by a sack: ***a sackful of rice***.

sacking ▶ noun 1 informal an act of dismissing someone from employment: *the offence merited a written warning that could lead to a sacking*.
2 the pillaging of a town or city.
3 [mass noun] coarse material for making sacks; sackcloth.

sack lunch ▶ noun N. Amer. informal a packed lunch.

S

sack race ▶ **noun** a race in which competitors stand in sacks and jump forward.

sack suit ▶ **noun** chiefly N. Amer. a suit with a straight loose-fitting jacket.

Sackville-West, Vita (1892–1962), English novelist and poet; full name *Victoria Mary Sackville-West*. Her works include the novel *All Passion Spent* (1931). She is also known for the garden which she created at Sissinghurst in Kent and for her friendship with Virginia Woolf.

sacra plural form of SACRUM.

sacral /ˈseɪkr(ə)l, ˈsak-/ ▶ **adjective** [attrib.] **1** relating to sacred rites or symbols: *sacral horns of a Minoan type*.
2 Anatomy relating to the sacrum.
– DERIVATIVES **sacrality** noun (sense 1).

sacralize /ˈseɪkrəlʌɪz/ (also **sacralise**) ▶ **verb** [with obj.] chiefly N. Amer. imbue with or treat as having a sacred character or quality: *rural images that sacralize country life*.
– DERIVATIVES **sacralization** noun.

sacrament /ˈsakrəm(ə)nt/ ▶ **noun** (in the Christian Church) a ceremony regarded as imparting spiritual grace, in particular: ■ (in the Roman Catholic and many Orthodox Churches) the seven rites of baptism, confirmation, the Eucharist, penance, anointing of the sick, ordination, and matrimony. ■ (among Protestants) baptism and the Eucharist. ■ (also **the Blessed Sacrament** or **the Holy Sacrament**) (in Catholic use) the consecrated elements of the Eucharist, especially the bread or Host: *he heard Mass and received the sacrament*. ■ a thing of mysterious and sacred significance; a religious symbol.
– ORIGIN Middle English: from Old French *sacrement*, from Latin *sacramentum* 'solemn oath' (from *sacrare* 'to hallow', from *sacer* 'sacred'), used in Christian Latin as a translation of Greek *mustērion* 'mystery'.

sacramental ▶ **adjective** relating to or constituting a sacrament or the sacraments.
▶ **noun** an observance analogous to but not reckoned among the sacraments, such as the use of holy water or the sign of the cross.
– DERIVATIVES **sacramentalism** noun **sacramentality** noun, **sacramentalize** (also **sacramentalise**) verb, **sacramentally** adverb.

Sacramento /ˌsakrəˈmɛntəʊ/ **1** a river of northern California, which rises near the border with Oregon and flows some 611 km (380 miles) southwards to San Francisco Bay.
2 the state capital of California, situated on the Sacramento River to the north-east of San Francisco; pop. 463,794 (est. 2008).

sacrament of reconciliation (also **sacrament of penance**) ▶ **noun** (chiefly in the Roman Catholic Church) the practice of private confession of sins to a priest and the receiving of absolution.

sacrarium /səˈkrɛːrɪəm/ ▶ **noun** (pl. **sacraria** /-rɪə/) the sanctuary of a church. ■ (in the Roman Catholic Church) a piscina. ■ (in the ancient Roman world) a shrine, in particular the room in a house containing the penates.
– ORIGIN Latin, from *sacer*, *sacr-* 'holy'.

S

sacré bleu /ˌsakreɪ ˈbləː/, French /sakʀe blø/ ▶ **exclamation** a French expression of surprise, exasperation, or dismay.
– ORIGIN alteration of *sacré Dieu* 'holy God'.

sacred /ˈseɪkrɪd/ ▶ **adjective** connected with God or a god or dedicated to a religious purpose and so deserving veneration: *sacred rites | the site at Eleusis is sacred to Demeter*. ■ religious rather than secular: *sacred music*. ■ (of writing or text) embodying the laws or doctrines of a religion: *a sacred Hindu text*. ■ regarded with great respect and reverence by a particular religion, group, or individual: *cows are sacred and the eating of beef is taboo*. ■ regarded as too valuable to be interfered with; sacrosanct: *to a police officer nothing is sacred*.
– DERIVATIVES **sacredly** adverb, **sacredness** noun.
– ORIGIN late Middle English: past participle of archaic *sacre* 'consecrate', from Old French *sacrer*, from Latin *sacrare*, from *sacer*, *sacr-* 'holy'.

sacred bamboo ▶ **noun** another term for NANDINA.

Sacred College another term for COLLEGE OF CARDINALS.

sacred cow ▶ **noun** an idea, custom, or institution held to be above criticism (with reference to the Hindus' respect for the cow as a holy animal).

Sacred Heart ▶ **noun** the heart of Christ, especially as represented in an image and regarded as an object of devotion among Roman Catholics.

sacred ibis ▶ **noun** a mainly white ibis with a bare black head and neck and black plumes over the lower back, native to Africa and the Middle East, and venerated by the ancient Egyptians. ● *Threskiornis aethiopicus*, family Threskiornithidae.

sacred scarab ▶ **noun** see SCARAB.

sacrifice ▶ **noun** **1** an act of slaughtering an animal or person or surrendering a possession as an offering to a deity: *they offer sacrifices to the spirits* | [mass noun] *the ancient laws of animal sacrifice*. ■ an animal, person, or object offered in the act of sacrifice.
2 Christian Church Christ's offering of himself in the Crucifixion. ■ the Eucharist regarded either (in Catholic terms) as a propitiatory offering of the body and blood of Christ or (in Protestant terms) as an act of thanksgiving.
3 an act of giving up something valued for the sake of something else regarded as more important or worthy: *we must all be prepared to **make sacrifices***. ■ Chess a move intended to allow the opponent to win a pawn or piece, for strategic or tactical reasons. ■ (also **sacrifice bunt** or **sacrifice fly**) Baseball a bunted or fly ball which puts the batter out but allows a base runner to advance. ■ (also **sacrifice bid**) Bridge a bid made in the belief that it will be less costly to be defeated in the contract than to allow the opponents to make a contract.
▶ **verb** [with obj.] **1** offer or kill as a religious sacrifice: *the goat was sacrificed at the shrine*.
2 give up (something valued) for the sake of other considerations: *working hard doesn't mean sacrificing your social life*. ■ Chess deliberately allow one's opponent to win (a pawn or piece). ■ Baseball advance (a base runner) by a sacrifice. ■ [no obj.] Bridge make a sacrifice bid.
– ORIGIN Middle English: from Old French, from Latin *sacrificium*; related to *sacrificus* 'sacrificial', from *sacer* 'holy'.

sacrificial ▶ **adjective** relating to or constituting a sacrifice: *an altar for sacrificial offerings*. ■ technical designed to be used up or destroyed in fulfilling a purpose or function.
– DERIVATIVES **sacrificially** adverb.

sacrilege /ˈsakrɪlɪdʒ/ ▶ **noun** [mass noun] violation or misuse of what is regarded as sacred: *putting ecclesiastical vestments to secular use was considered sacrilege*.
– ORIGIN Middle English: via Old French from Latin *sacrilegium*, from *sacrilegus* 'stealer of sacred things', from *sacer*, *sacr-* 'sacred' + *legere* 'take possession of'.

sacrilegious /ˌsakrɪˈlɪdʒəs/ ▶ **adjective** involving or committing sacrilege: *a sacrilegious act*.
– DERIVATIVES **sacrilegiously** adverb.

sacring /ˈseɪkrɪŋ/ ▶ **noun** archaic or historical the consecration of a bishop, a sovereign, or the Eucharistic elements.
– ORIGIN Middle English: from the obsolete verb *sacre* 'consecrate'.

sacring bell ▶ **noun** a bell rung in some Christian churches at certain points during the Mass or Eucharist, especially at the elevation of the consecrated elements.

sacrist /ˈsakrɪst, ˈseɪ-/ ▶ **noun** chiefly historical another term for SACRISTAN.

sacristan /ˈsakrɪstən/ ▶ **noun** **1** a person in charge of a sacristy and its contents.
2 archaic the sexton of a parish church.
– ORIGIN Middle English: from medieval Latin *sacristanus*, based on Latin *sacer*, *sacr-* 'sacred'.

sacristy /ˈsakrɪsti/ ▶ **noun** (pl. **sacristies**) a room in a church where a priest prepares for a service, and where vestments and articles of worship are kept.
– ORIGIN late Middle English: from French *sacristie*, from medieval Latin *sacristia*, based on Latin *sacer*, *sacr-* 'sacred'.

sacro- /ˈseɪkrəʊ, ˈsakrəʊ-/ ▶ **combining form** relating to the sacrum: *sacroiliac*.
– ORIGIN from Latin (*os*) *sacrum* 'sacrum'.

sacroiliac /ˌseɪkrəʊˈɪlɪak, ˌsak-/ ▶ **adjective** Anatomy relating to the sacrum and the ilium. ■ denoting the rigid joint at the back of the pelvis between the sacrum and the ilium.

sacrosanct /ˈsakrə(ʊ)saŋ(k)t, ˈseɪk-/ ▶ **adjective** (especially of a principle, place, or routine) regarded as too important or valuable to be interfered with: *the individual's right to work has been upheld as sacrosanct*.
– DERIVATIVES **sacrosanctity** noun.
– ORIGIN late 15th cent.: from Latin *sacrosanctus*, from *sacro* 'by a sacred rite' (ablative of *sacrum*) + *sanctus* 'holy'.

sacrum /ˈseɪkrəm, ˈsak-/ ▶ **noun** (pl. **sacra** /-krə/ or **sacrums**) Anatomy a triangular bone in the lower back formed from fused vertebrae and situated between the two hip bones of the pelvis.
– ORIGIN mid 18th cent.: from Latin *os sacrum*, translation of Greek *hieron osteon* 'sacred bone' (from the belief that the soul resides in it).

SACW ▶ **abbreviation** Senior Aircraftwoman.

SAD ▶ **abbreviation** seasonal affective disorder.

sad ▶ **adjective** (**sadder**, **saddest**) **1** feeling or showing sorrow; unhappy: *I was sad and subdued | they looked at her with sad, anxious faces*. ■ causing or characterized by sorrow or regret; unfortunate and regrettable: *he told her the sad story of his life | a sad day for us all*.
2 informal pathetically inadequate or unfashionable: *the show is tongue-in-cheek—anyone who takes it seriously is a bit sad*.
3 (of dough) heavy through having failed to rise.
– PHRASES **sad to say** unfortunately, regrettably.
– ORIGIN Old English *sæd* 'sated, weary', also 'weighty, dense', of Germanic origin; related to Dutch *zat* and German *satt*, from an Indo-European root shared by Latin *satis* 'enough'. The original meaning was replaced in Middle English by the senses 'steadfast, firm' and 'serious, sober', and later 'sorrowful'.

Sadat /saˈdat/, (Muhammad) Anwar al- (1918–81), Egyptian statesman, President 1970–81. Sadat worked to achieve peace in the Middle East, visiting Israel (1977) and attending talks with Menachim Begin at Camp David in 1978, the year they shared the Nobel Peace Prize. He was assassinated by members of the Islamic Jihad.

SADC ▶ **abbreviation** Southern African Development Community.

Saddam Hussein /saˈdam/ see HUSSEIN[3].

sadden ▶ **verb** [with obj.] cause to feel sorrow; make unhappy: *he was greatly saddened by the death of his only son* | [with obj. and infinitive] *I was saddened to see their lack of commitment*.

saddle ▶ **noun** **1** a seat fastened on the back of a horse or other animal for riding, typically made of leather and raised at the front and rear. ■ a seat on a bicycle or motorcycle.
2 a shaped support on which a cable, wire, or pipe rests. ■ a fireclay bar for supporting ceramic ware in a kiln. ■ the part of a draught horse's harness which supports the straps to which the shafts are attached.
3 a low part of a ridge between two higher points or peaks. ■ Mathematics a low region of a curve between two high points, especially (in three dimensions) one representing the highest point of a curve in one direction and the lowest point in another direction.
4 the lower part of the back in a mammal or fowl, especially when distinct in shape or marking. ■ a joint of meat consisting of the two loins.
▶ **verb** [with obj.] **1** put a saddle on (a horse): *he was in the stable **saddling up** his horse*. ■ (of a trainer) enter (a horse) for a race.
2 (usu. **be saddled with**) burden (someone) with an onerous responsibility or task: *he's saddled with debts of $12 million*.
– PHRASES **in the saddle** on horseback. ■ in a position of control or responsibility.
– ORIGIN Old English *sadol*, *sadul*, of Germanic origin; related to Dutch *zadel* and German *Sattel*, perhaps from an Indo-European root shared by Latin *sella* 'seat' and SIT.

saddleback ▶ **noun** **1** Architecture a tower roof which has two opposite gables connected by a pitched section.
2 a hill with a ridge along the top that dips in the middle.
3 a pig of a black breed with a white stripe across the back.
4 a New Zealand wattlebird with mainly black plumage, a reddish-brown back, and two small red wattles under the bill. ● *Philesturnus carunculatus*, family Callaeidae.

saddlebag ▶ **noun** each of a pair of bags attached behind the saddle on a horse, bicycle, or motorcycle. ■ (**saddlebags**) US informal excess fat around the hips and thighs.

saddle-bow ▶ **noun** chiefly archaic the pommel of a saddle, or a similar curved part behind the rider.

saddlebred ▶ **noun** a horse bred to have the gait of an American Saddle Horse.

saddlecloth ▸ noun a cloth laid on a horse's back under the saddle.

saddle horse ▸ noun **1** a wooden frame or stand on which saddles are cleaned or stored.
2 chiefly N. Amer. a horse kept for riding only.

saddler ▸ noun someone who makes, repairs, or deals in saddlery.

saddlery ▸ noun (pl. **saddleries**) [mass noun] saddles, bridles, and other equipment for horses. ■ the making or repairing of saddlery. ■ a saddler's premises.

saddle shoe ▸ noun an oxford shoe with a piece of leather in a contrasting colour stitched across the instep, typically black or brown on a white shoe.

saddle soap ▸ noun [mass noun] soft soap containing neat's-foot oil, used for cleaning leather.

saddle-sore ▸ noun a bruise or sore on a horse's back, caused by pressure or chafing of an ill-fitting saddle.
▸ adjective chafed by riding on a saddle.

saddle stitch ▸ noun a stitch of thread or a wire staple passed through the fold of a magazine or booklet. ■ [mass noun] (in needlework) a decorative stitch made with long stitches on the upper side of the cloth alternated with short stitches on the underside.
▸ verb (**saddle-stitch**) [with obj.] sew with a saddle stitch.

saddle tank ▸ noun a small steam locomotive with a water tank that fits over the top and sides of the boiler like a saddle.

saddle tree ▸ noun a frame around which a saddle is built.

saddo ▸ noun (pl. **saddos**) Brit. informal a person perceived as contemptible or pathetically inadequate.
– ORIGIN 1990s: extension of SAD.

Sadducee /ˈsadjʊsiː/ ▸ noun a member of a Jewish sect or party of the time of Christ that denied the resurrection of the dead, the existence of spirits, and the obligation of oral tradition, emphasizing acceptance of the written Law alone. Compare with PHARISEE.
– DERIVATIVES **Sadducean** /-ˈsiːən/ adjective.
– ORIGIN Old English *sadducēas* (plural), via late Latin from Greek *Saddoukaios*, from Hebrew *ṣĕḏōqī* in the sense 'descendant of Zadok' (2 Sam. 8:17).

Sade /sɑːd/, Donatien Alphonse François, Comte de (1740–1814), French writer and soldier; known as **the Marquis de Sade**. His career as a cavalry officer was interrupted by periods of imprisonment for cruelty and debauchery. While in prison he wrote a number of sexually explicit works, including *Les 120 Journées de Sodome* (1784) and *Justine* (1791).

sadhana /ˈsɑːðənɑː/ ▸ noun [mass noun] Indian disciplined and dedicated practice or learning, especially in religion or music.
– ORIGIN from Sanskrit *sādhanā* 'dedication to an aim', from *sādh* 'bring about'.

sadhu /ˈsɑːduː/ ▸ noun Indian a holy man, sage, or ascetic.
– ORIGIN Sanskrit.

Sadi /ˈsɑːdi/ (also **Saadi**) (*c.*1213–*c.*1291), Persian poet; born *Sheikh Muslih Addin*. His principal works were the collections known as the *Bustan* (1257) and the *Gulistan* (1258).

sad-iron ▸ noun historical a solid iron for smoothing clothes.
– ORIGIN mid 18th cent.: from SAD, in the obsolete sense 'weighty'.

sadism ▸ noun [mass noun] the tendency to derive pleasure, especially sexual gratification, from inflicting pain, suffering, or humiliation on others.
– DERIVATIVES **sadist** noun.
– ORIGIN late 19th cent.: from French *sadisme*, from the name of the Marquis de SADE.

sadistic ▸ adjective deriving pleasure from inflicting pain, suffering, or humiliation on others: *she took a sadistic pleasure in tormenting him.*
– DERIVATIVES **sadistically** adverb.

Sadler's Wells Theatre /ˈsadləz/ a London theatre opened by Lilian Baylis in 1931, known for its ballet and opera companies.
– ORIGIN named after Thomas *Sadler*, who discovered a medicinal spring at the original site in 1683.

sadly ▸ adverb **1** in a sad manner: *he smiled sadly.*
2 [sentence adverb] it is a sad or regrettable fact that; unfortunately: *sadly, the forests of Sulawesi are now under threat.* ■ [as submodifier] to a regrettable extent; regrettably: *his schemes went sadly awry.*

sadness ▸ noun [mass noun] the condition or quality of being sad: *a source of great sadness.*

sadomasochism /ˌseɪdəʊˈmasəkɪz(ə)m/ ▸ noun [mass noun] psychological tendency or sexual practice characterized by both sadism and masochism.
– DERIVATIVES **sadomasochist** noun, **sadomasochistic** adjective.

sad sack ▸ noun informal, chiefly US an inept blundering person.

sadza /ˈsadzə/ ▸ noun [mass noun] (in southern and East Africa) porridge made of ground maize or millet.
– ORIGIN Shona.

sae[1] ▸ abbreviation Brit. stamped addressed envelope.

sae[2] /seɪ/ ▸ adverb non-standard spelling of **so**[1], used in representing Scottish speech.

Safaqis /səˈfɑːkɪs/ another name for SFAX.

safari ▸ noun (pl. **safaris**) an expedition to observe or hunt animals in their natural habitat, especially in East Africa: *one week **on safari**.*
– ORIGIN late 19th cent.: from Kiswahili, from Arabic *safara* 'to travel'.

safari jacket ▸ noun a belted lightweight jacket, typically of beige or khaki cotton or linen and having four patch pockets.

safari park ▸ noun an area of parkland where wild animals are kept in the open and may be observed by visitors driving through.

safari suit ▸ noun a lightweight suit consisting of a safari jacket with matching trousers, shorts, or skirt.

safari supper ▸ noun a social occasion at which the different courses of a meal are eaten at different people's houses.

Safavid /ˈsafəvɪd/ ▸ noun a member of a dynasty which ruled Persia from 1502 to 1736 and installed Shia rather than Sunni Islam as the state religion.
▸ adjective relating to the Safavid dynasty.
– ORIGIN from Arabic *ṣafawī* 'descended from the ruler Sophy'.

safe ▸ adjective **1** [predic.] protected from or not exposed to danger or risk; not likely to be harmed or lost: *eggs remain in the damp sand, **safe from** marine predators | she felt safe with him.*
2 not likely to cause or lead to harm or injury; not involving danger or risk: *we have to cross the river where it's safe for us to do so | a safe investment that produced regular income.* ■ (of a place) affording security or protection: *put it in a safe place.*
3 often derogatory cautious and unenterprising: *MacGregor would be a compromise, the safe choice.*
4 based on good reasons or evidence and not likely to be proved wrong: *the verdict is safe and satisfactory | his world, **it's safe to say**, will not fall apart.*
5 uninjured; with no harm done: *they had returned **safe and sound** | hopes of her safe return later faded.*
6 informal excellent (used to express approval or enthusiasm): *that shirt is real safe.*
▸ noun **1** a strong fireproof cabinet with a complex lock, used for the storage of valuables.
2 N. Amer. informal a condom.
– PHRASES **as safe as houses** see HOUSE. **in safe hands** see HAND. **safe in the knowledge that** confident because of the specified fact: *they used to recruit hundreds a year, safe in the knowledge that many would leave.* **a safe pair of hands** see HAND. **to be on the safe side** in order to have a margin of security against risks: *to be on the safe side, she had recorded everything.*
– DERIVATIVES **safely** adverb, **safeness** noun.
– ORIGIN Middle English (as an adjective): from Old French *sauf*, from Latin *salvus* 'uninjured'. The noun is from the verb SAVE[1], later assimilated to the adjectival form.

safe area ▸ noun an area not liable to attack, especially one designated as such by the United Nations.

safe bet ▸ noun a bet that is certain to succeed. ■ a thing in which confidence can be placed regarding a future outcome.

safe-breaker (also **safe-blower** or **safe-cracker**) ▸ noun informal a person who breaks open and robs safes.

safe conduct ▸ noun [mass noun] immunity from arrest or harm when passing through an area. ■ [count noun] a document securing such a privilege.

safe deposit (also **safety deposit**) ▸ noun [usu. as modifier] a strongroom or safe in which valuables may be securely stored, typically within a bank or hotel: *a safe-deposit box.*

safeguard ▸ noun a measure taken to protect someone or something or to prevent something undesirable: *the charity called for tougher safeguards to protect Britain's remaining natural forests.*
▸ verb [with obj.] protect from harm or damage with an appropriate measure: *a framework which safeguards employees from exploitation.*
– ORIGIN late Middle English (denoting protection or safe conduct): from Old French *sauve garde*, from *sauve* 'safe' + *garde* 'guard'. Compare with SAGGAR.

safe haven ▸ noun a place of refuge or security.

safe house ▸ noun a house in a secret location, used by spies or criminals in hiding.

safekeeping ▸ noun [mass noun] preservation in a safe place: *she'd put her wedding ring in her purse for safekeeping.*

safelight ▸ noun a light with a coloured filter that can be used in a darkroom without affecting photosensitive film or paper.

safe period ▸ noun the time during and near a woman's menstrual period when conception is least likely.

safe seat ▸ noun Brit. a parliamentary seat that is likely to be retained with a large majority in an election.

safe sex ▸ noun [mass noun] sexual activity in which people take precautions to protect themselves against sexually transmitted diseases such as AIDS.

safety ▸ noun (pl. **safeties**) **1** [mass noun] the condition of being protected from or unlikely to cause danger, risk, or injury: *they should leave for their own safety | the survivors were airlifted to safety.* ■ [as modifier] denoting something designed to prevent injury or damage: *a safety barrier | a safety helmet.* ■ [count noun] N. Amer. short for SAFETY CATCH.
2 American Football a defensive back who plays in a deep position. ■ a play in which the ball is downed by the offence in their own end zone, scoring two points to the defence.
3 US informal a condom.
– PHRASES **safety first** used to advise caution. **there's safety in numbers** proverb being in a group of people makes you feel more confident or secure about taking action.
– ORIGIN Middle English: from Old French *sauvete*, from medieval Latin *salvitas*, from Latin *salvus* 'safe'.

safety belt ▸ noun a belt or strap securing a person to prevent injury, especially in a vehicle or aircraft.

safety boat ▸ noun an accompanying boat providing support in case of emergency, especially in water sports or competitive situations.

safety cage ▸ noun a protective metal cage, in particular a framework of reinforced struts protecting a car's passenger cabin against crash damage.

safety catch ▸ noun chiefly Brit. a device that prevents a gun being fired or a machine being operated accidentally.

safety chain ▸ noun a chain fitted for security purposes, especially on a door, watch, or piece of jewellery.

safety-critical ▸ adjective designed or needing to be fail-safe for safety purposes.

safety curtain ▸ noun a fireproof curtain that can be lowered between the stage and the main part of a theatre to prevent the spread of fire.

safety deposit ▸ noun another term for SAFE DEPOSIT.

safety factor ▸ noun a margin of security against risks. ■ technical the ratio of a material's strength to an expected strain.

safety film ▸ noun [mass noun] fire-resistant cinema film.

safety fuse ▸ noun **1** a protective electric fuse.
2 a fuse that burns at a constant slow rate, used for the controlled firing of a detonator.

safety glass ▸ noun **1** [mass noun] glass that has been toughened or laminated so that it is less likely to splinter when broken.
2 (**safety glasses**) toughened glasses or goggles for protecting the eyes when using power tools or industrial or laboratory equipment.

safety harness ▸ noun a system of belts or restraints to hold a person to prevent falling or injury.

safety lamp ▸ noun historical a miner's portable lamp with a flame protected, typically by wire gauze, to reduce the risk of explosion from ignited methane (firedamp). The first to be introduced, in the early 19th century, was the Davy lamp.

safety match ▸ noun a match igniting only when struck on a specially prepared surface, especially the side of a matchbox.

safety net ▶ noun a net placed to catch an acrobat or similar performer in case of a fall. ■ a safeguard against possible hardship or adversity: *a safety net for workers who lose their jobs.*

safety pin ▶ noun a pin with a point that is bent back to the head and is held in a guard when closed.

safety razor ▶ noun a razor with a guard to reduce the risk of cutting the skin.

safety valve ▶ noun a valve that opens automatically to relieve excessive pressure. ■ a means of giving harmless vent to feelings of tension or stress.

safflower ▶ noun an orange-flowered thistle-like Eurasian plant with seeds that yield an edible oil and petals that were formerly used to produce a red or yellow dye. ● *Carthamus tinctorius*, family Compositae.
■ (**safflower oil**) [mass noun] the edible oil obtained from the seeds of this plant.
– ORIGIN late Middle English: from Dutch *saffloer* or German *Saflor*, via Old French and Italian from Arabic *aṣfar* 'yellow'. The spelling has been influenced by SAFFRON and FLOWER.

saffron ▶ noun 1 [mass noun] an orange-yellow flavouring, food colouring, and dye made from the dried stigmas of a crocus. ■ the orange-yellow colour of saffron.
2 (also **saffron crocus**) an autumn-flowering crocus with reddish-purple flowers, native to warmer regions of Eurasia. Enormous numbers of flowers are required to produce a small quantity of the large red stigmas used for the spice. ● *Crocus sativus*, family Iridaceae.
– ORIGIN Middle English: from Old French *safran*, based on Arabic *za'farān*.

safranine /ˈsafrəniːn/ (also **safranin** /-nɪn/) ▶ noun Chemistry any of a large group of synthetic azo dyes, mainly red, used as biological stains.
– ORIGIN mid 19th cent. (denoting the yellow colouring matter in saffron): from French.

sag¹ ▶ verb (**sags, sagging, sagged**) [no obj.] 1 sink, subside, or bulge downwards under weight or pressure or through lack of strength: *she let her head sag lower and lower | the bed sagged in the middle* | (as adj. **sagging**) *sagging shelves bearing rusty paint tins.*
■ hang down loosely or unevenly: *stockings which sagged at the knees.*
2 decline to a lower level, usually temporarily: *exports are forging ahead while home sales sag.*
▶ noun 1 a downward curve or bulge in a structure caused by weakness or excessive weight or pressure: *a sag in the middle necessitated a third set of wheels.*
■ [mass noun] Geometry the amount of a sag, measured as the perpendicular distance from the middle of the curve to the straight line between the two supporting points.
2 a decline, especially a temporary one.
– PHRASAL VERBS **sag off** N. English informal play truant from school.
– DERIVATIVES **saggy** adjective (**saggier, saggiest**).
– ORIGIN late Middle English (as a verb): apparently related to Middle Low German *sacken*, Dutch *zakken* 'subside'.

sag² ▶ noun variant spelling of SAAG.

saga /ˈsɑːɡə/ ▶ noun 1 a long story of heroic achievement, especially a medieval prose narrative in Old Norse or Old Icelandic.
2 a long, involved story, account, or series of incidents: *launching into the saga of her engagement.*
– ORIGIN early 18th cent.: from Old Norse, literally 'narrative'; related to SAW³.

saga boy ▶ noun informal, chiefly W. Indian a playboy.

sagacious /səˈɡeɪʃəs/ ▶ adjective having or showing keen mental discernment and good judgement; wise or shrewd: *they were sagacious enough to avoid any outright confrontation.*
– DERIVATIVES **sagaciously** adverb.
– ORIGIN early 17th cent.: from Latin *sagax, sagac-* 'wise' + -IOUS.

sagacity /səˈɡasɪti/ ▶ noun [mass noun] the quality of being sagacious: *a man of great political sagacity.*

sagamore /ˈsaɡəmɔː/ ▶ noun (among some American Indian peoples) a chief; a sachem.
– ORIGIN Eastern Abnaki.

Sagan¹ /ˈseɪɡ(ə)n/, Carl (Edward) (1934–96), American astronomer. Sagan showed that amino acids can be synthesized in an artificial primordial soup irradiated by ultraviolet light—a possible origin of life on the earth. He wrote several popular science books, and was co-producer of the television series *Cosmos* (1980).

Sagan² /saˈɡɒ̃/, French /saɡɑ̃/, Françoise (1935–2004), French novelist, dramatist, and short-story writer; pseudonym of *Françoise Quoirez*. She rose to fame with her first novel *Bonjour Tristesse* (1954); in this and subsequent novels she examined the transitory nature of love as experienced in brief liaisons.

saganaki /ˌsaɡəˈnɑːki/ ▶ noun [mass noun] a Greek dish consisting of breaded or floured cheese fried in butter, served as an appetizer.
– ORIGIN modern Greek, denoting a small two-handled frying pan, in which the dish is traditionally made.

sagar /ˈsɑːɡə/ ▶ noun Indian a sea or ocean. ■ a large lake.
– ORIGIN Hindi *sāgar*.

sage¹ ▶ noun [mass noun] 1 an aromatic plant whose greyish-green leaves are used as a culinary herb, native to southern Europe and the Mediterranean.
● *Salvia officinalis*, family Labiatae.
■ used in names of aromatic plants of the mint family that resemble sage, e.g. **wood sage**.
2 (also **white sage**) either of two bushy North American plants with silvery-grey leaves: ● an aromatic plant which was formerly burnt by the Cheyenne for its cleansing properties and as an incense (*Artemisia ludoviciana*, family Compositae). ● a plant of the goosefoot family (*Krascheninnikovia lanata*, family Chenopodiaceae).
– ORIGIN Middle English: from Old French *sauge*, from Latin *salvia* 'healing plant', from *salvus* 'safe'.

sage² ▶ noun (especially in ancient history or legend) a profoundly wise man.
▶ adjective profoundly wise: *they nodded in agreement with these sage remarks.*
– DERIVATIVES **sagely** adverb, **sageness** noun.
– ORIGIN Middle English (as an adjective): from Old French, from Latin *sapere* 'be wise'.

sagebrush ▶ noun [mass noun] a shrubby aromatic North American plant of the daisy family. ● Genus *Artemisia*, family Compositae: several species, in particular *A. tridentata*.
■ scrub which is dominated by sagebrush, occurring chiefly in semi-arid regions of western North America.

Sagebrush State informal name for NEVADA.

sage Derby (also **sage Derby cheese**) ▶ noun [mass noun] a firm cheese made with an infusion of sage which flavours it and gives it a mottled green colour.

sage green ▶ noun [mass noun] a greyish-green colour like that of sage leaves.

sage grouse ▶ noun a large grouse of western North America, with long pointed tail feathers, noted for the male's courtship display in which air sacs are inflated to make a popping sound. ● *Centrocercus urophasianus*, family Tetraonidae (or Phasianidae).

saggar /ˈsaɡə/ (also **sagger**) ▶ noun a protective fireclay box enclosing ceramic ware while it is being fired.
– ORIGIN mid 18th cent.: probably a contraction of the noun SAFEGUARD.

Sagitta /səˈdʒɪtə, -ˈɡɪtə/ Astronomy a small northern constellation (the Arrow), lying in the Milky Way north of Aquila.
– ORIGIN Latin.

sagittal /ˈsadʒɪt(ə)l, səˈdʒɪ-/ Anatomy ▶ adjective 1 relating to or denoting the suture on top of the skull which runs between the parietal bones in a front to back direction.
2 of or in a plane parallel to the sagittal suture, especially that dividing the body into left and right halves.
– DERIVATIVES **sagittally** adverb.
– ORIGIN late Middle English: from medieval Latin *sagittalis*, from Latin *sagitta* 'arrow'.

sagittal crest ▶ noun Zoology (in many mammals) a bony ridge on the top of the skull to which the jaw muscles are attached.

Sagittarius /ˌsadʒɪˈtɛːrɪəs/ 1 Astronomy a large constellation (the Archer), said to represent a centaur carrying a bow and arrow. The centre of the Galaxy is situated within it.
2 Astrology the ninth sign of the zodiac, which the sun enters about 22 November. ■ (**a Sagittarius**) a person born when the sun is in this sign.
– DERIVATIVES **Sagittarian** noun & adjective (sense 2).
– ORIGIN Latin, 'archer'.

sagittate /ˈsadʒɪteɪt/ ▶ adjective Botany & Zoology shaped like an arrowhead.
– ORIGIN mid 18th cent.: from Latin *sagitta* 'arrow' + -ATE².

sago /ˈseɪɡəʊ/ ▶ noun (pl. **sagos**) 1 [mass noun] edible starch which is obtained from a palm and is a staple food in parts of the tropics. The pith inside the trunk is scraped out, washed, and dried to produce a flour or processed to produce the granular sago used in the West. ■ (also **sago pudding**) a sweet dish made from sago and milk.
2 (**sago palm**) the palm from which most sago is obtained, growing in freshwater swamps in SE Asia.
● *Metroxylon sagu*, family Palmae.
■ any of a number of palms or cycads which yield a starch similar to sago.
– ORIGIN mid 16th cent.: from Malay *sagu* (originally via Portuguese).

saguaro /səˈɡwɑːrəʊ, -ˈwɑː-/ (also **saguaro cactus**) ▶ noun (pl. **saguaros**) a giant cactus which can grow to 20 metres in height and whose branches are shaped like candelabra, native to the SW United States and Mexico. The edible fruit was formerly a source of food and drink. ● *Carnegiea gigantea*, family Cactaceae.
– ORIGIN mid 19th cent.: from Mexican Spanish.

Saguia el-Hamra /səˌɡiːə ɛlˈhamrə/ an intermittent river in the north of Western Sahara. It flows into the Atlantic west of Laayoune. ■ the region through which this river flows. A territory of Spain from 1934, it united with Río de Oro in 1958 to become a part of Spanish Sahara.

Sahara Desert /səˈhɑːrə/ (also **the Sahara**) a vast desert in North Africa, extending from the Atlantic in the west to the Red Sea in the east, and from the Mediterranean and the Atlas Mountains in the north to the Sahel in the south. The largest desert in the world, it covers an area of about 9,065,000 sq. km (3,500,000 sq. miles). In recent years it has been extending southwards into the Sahel.
– DERIVATIVES **Saharan** adjective.
– ORIGIN *Sahara* from Arabic *ṣaḥrā'* 'desert'.

Sahel /səˈhɛl/ a vast semi-arid region of North Africa, to the south of the Sahara, which forms a transitional zone at the south of the desert and comprises the northern part of the region known as Sudan.
– DERIVATIVES **Sahelian** /-ˈhiːlɪən/ adjective & noun.

sahib /ˈsɑː(h)ɪb, sɑːb/ (also **sahab**) ▶ noun Indian a polite title or form of address for a man: *the Doctor Sahib.*
– ORIGIN Urdu, via Persian from Arabic *ṣāḥib* 'friend, lord'.

Sahin Line /saˈhɪn/ another term for ATTILA LINE.
– ORIGIN *Sahin*, the name of a town in Turkey.

sahitya /sɑːˈhɪtjəː/ ▶ noun [mass noun] Indian literature or lyrics.
– ORIGIN from Sanskrit *sāhitya*.

Sahiwal /ˈsɑːhɪvɑːl, -wɑːl/ ▶ noun an animal of a breed of cattle which originated in Pakistan but is now used in other tropical regions. Sahiwals have small horns and a hump on the back of the neck.
– ORIGIN early 20th cent.: from the name of a town in the central Punjab, Pakistan.

sahukar /ˈsaʊkɑː/ ▶ noun Indian a moneylender. ■ a banker.
– ORIGIN late 18th cent.: Hindi *sāhūkār* 'great merchant'.

sai /sʌɪ/ ▶ noun (pl. **same**) a dagger with two sharp prongs curving outward from the hilt, originating in Okinawa and sometimes used in pairs in martial arts.
– ORIGIN Japanese.

said past and past participle of SAY. ▶ adjective used in legal language or humorously to refer to someone or something already mentioned or named: *acting in pursuance of the said agreement.*

Saida /ˈsʌɪdə/ Arabic name for SIDON.

saiga /ˈseɪɡə, ˈsʌɪɡə/ (also **saiga antelope**) ▶ noun an Asian antelope which has a distinctive convex snout with the nostrils opening downwards, living in herds on the cold steppes. ● *Saiga tartarica*, family Bovidae.
– ORIGIN early 19th cent.: from Russian.

Saigon /sʌɪˈɡɒn/ a city and port on the south coast of Vietnam; pop. 5,929,500 (est. 2009). It was the capital of the French colony established in Vietnam in the 19th century, becoming capital of South Vietnam in the partition of 1954. Official name (since 1975) HO CHI MINH CITY.

sail ▶ noun 1 a piece of material extended on a mast to catch the wind and propel a boat or ship or other vessel: *all the sails were unfurled.* ■ [mass noun] the use of sailing ships as a means of transport: *this led to*

S

bigger ships as steam replaced sail. ■ archaic a sailing ship: *sail ahoy!*
2 something resembling a sail in shape or function, in particular: ■ a wind-catching apparatus attached to the arm of a windmill. ■ the broad fin on the back of a sailfish or of some prehistoric reptiles. ■ a structure by which an animal is propelled across the surface of water by the wind, e.g. the float of a Portuguese man-of-war.
3 a voyage or excursion in a ship, especially a sailing ship or boat: *they went for a sail.*
4 the conning tower of a submarine.
5 S. African a canvas sheet or tarpaulin. [loan translation, based on Dutch *seil* 'tarpaulin'.]
▸ verb [no obj.] 1 travel in a boat with sails, especially as a sport or recreation: *Ian took us out sailing on the lake.* ■ [with adverbial] travel in a ship or boat using sails or engine power: *the ferry caught fire sailing between Caen and Portsmouth.* ■ [with adverbial] begin a voyage; leave a harbour: *the catamaran sails at 3:30.* ■ [with obj.] travel by ship on or across (a sea) or on (a route): *plastic ships could be sailing the oceans soon.* ■ [with obj. and adverbial of direction] navigate or control (a boat or ship): *I stole a small fishing boat and sailed it to the Delta.*
2 [with adverbial of direction] move smoothly and rapidly or in a stately or confident manner: *the ball sailed inside the right-hand post.* ■ (**sail through**) informal succeed easily at (something, especially a test or examination): *Ali sailed through his exams.* ■ (**sail into**) informal attack physically or verbally with force.
– PHRASES **in** (or **under**) **full sail** with all the sails in position or fully spread: *a galleon in full sail.* **sail close to** (or **near**) **the wind** 1 come close to breaking a rule or the law; behave or operate in a risky way. 2 Nautical sail as nearly against the wind as possible. **take in sail** furl the sail or sails of a vessel. **under sail** with the sails hoisted: *at a speed of eight knots under sail.*
– DERIVATIVES **sailable** adjective, **sailed** adjective [in combination] *a black-sailed ship.*
– ORIGIN Old English *segel* (noun), *seglian* (verb), of Germanic origin; related to Dutch *zeil* and German *Segel* (nouns).

sailboard ▸ noun a board with a mast attached to it by a swivel joint, and a sail, used in windsurfing.
– DERIVATIVES **sailboarder** noun, **sailboarding** noun.

sailboat ▸ noun North American term for SAILING BOAT.

sailcloth ▸ noun [mass noun] canvas or other material used for making sails. ■ a canvas-like fabric used for making durable weatherproof clothes.

sailer ▸ noun a sailing boat or ship of specified power or manner of sailing.

sailfin molly ▸ noun a small brightly coloured freshwater fish, the male of which has a long high dorsal fin. Native to North and Central America, it is popular in aquaria. ● Genus *Poecilia*, family Poeciliidae: *P. latipinna* and *P. velifera*.
– ORIGIN *sailfin* with reference to the dorsal fin + MOLLY.

sailfish ▸ noun (pl. **same** or **sailfishes**) a fish with a high sail-like dorsal fin, in particular: ● an edible migratory billfish that is a prized game fish (genus *Istiophorus*, family Istiophoridae, in particular *I. platypterus*). ● (also **Celebes sailfish**) a small tropical freshwater fish of Sulawesi, popular in aquaria (*Telmatherina ladigesi*, family Atherinidae).

sail-fluke ▸ noun another term for MEGRIM[2].

sailing ▸ noun [mass noun] the action of sailing in a ship or boat: [as modifier] *a sailing club.* ■ [count noun] a voyage made by a ferry or cruise ship, especially according to a planned schedule: *the company operates five sailings a day from Ramsgate to Dunkirk.* ■ [in sing.] an act of beginning a voyage or of leaving a harbour.

sailing boat ▸ noun Brit. a boat propelled by sails.

sailing master ▸ noun an officer responsible for the navigation of a ship or yacht.

sailing orders ▸ plural noun instructions to the captain of a vessel regarding such matters as time of departure and destination.

sailing ship ▸ noun a ship driven by sails.

sailmaker ▸ noun a person who makes, repairs, or alters sails as a profession.
– DERIVATIVES **sailmaking** noun.

sail-off ▸ noun a sailing contest used to decide the final result of a competition or championship.

sailor ▸ noun a person whose job it is to work as a member of the crew of a commercial or naval ship or boat, especially one who is below the rank of officer. ■ [usu. with adj. or noun modifier] a person who goes sailing as a sport or recreation: *he is a keen sailor in his spare time.* ■ (**a good/bad sailor**) a person who rarely (or often) becomes sick at sea in rough weather.
– DERIVATIVES **sailorly** adjective.
– ORIGIN mid 17th cent.: variant of obsolete *sailer*.

sailor collar ▸ noun a collar cut deep and square at the back, tapering to a V-neck at the front.

sailor hat ▸ noun another term for BOATER (sense 1).

sailor suit ▸ noun a suit of blue and white material resembling the dress uniform of an ordinary seaman, especially as fashionable dress for young boys during the 19th century.

sail plan ▸ noun a scale diagram of the masts, spars, rigging, and sails of a sailing vessel.

sailplane ▸ noun a glider designed for sustained flight.

sainfoin /ˈseɪnfɔɪn, ˈsan-/ ▸ noun [mass noun] a pink-flowered plant of the pea family, which is native to Asia and grown widely for fodder. ● *Onobrychis viciifolia*, family Leguminosae.
– ORIGIN mid 17th cent.: from obsolete French *saintfoin*, from modern Latin *sanum foenum* 'wholesome hay' (with reference to its medicinal properties).

Sainsbury, John James (1844–1928), English grocer. He opened his first grocery store in London in 1875. After his death the business was continued by members of his family, developing into a large supermarket chain.

saint /seɪnt/ before a name usually /s(ə)nt/ ▸ noun
1 a person acknowledged as holy or virtuous and regarded in Christian faith as being in heaven after death. ■ a person of exalted virtue who is canonized by the Church after death and who may be the object of veneration and prayers for intercession. ■ (**Saint**) (abbrev.: **St** or **S**) used in titles of religious saints: *the epistles of Saint Paul | St Mary's Church.* ■ (**Saint**) a member of the Church of Jesus Christ of Latter-Day Saints; a Mormon. ■ (in biblical use) a Christian believer.
2 informal a very virtuous, kind, or patient person: *she's a saint to go on living with that man.*
▸ verb [with obj.] formally recognize as a saint; canonize. ■ (as adj. **sainted**) worthy of being a saint; very virtuous: *the story of his sainted sister Eileen.*
– PHRASES **my sainted aunt** see AUNT.
– DERIVATIVES **saintdom** noun, **sainthood** noun, **saintlike** adjective, **saintship** noun.
– ORIGIN Middle English, from Old French *seint*, from Latin *sanctus* 'holy', past participle of *sancire* 'consecrate'.

St Agnes, St Barnabas, etc. see AGNES, ST[1]; BARNABAS, ST; etc.

St Albans /ˈɔːlbənz/ a city in Hertfordshire, in SE England; pop. 80,200 (est. 2009). The city developed around an abbey, which was founded in Saxon times on the site of the martyrdom in the 3rd century of St Alban, a Christian Roman from the nearby Roman city of Verulamium.

St Andrews a town in east Scotland, in Fife, on the North Sea; pop. 17,100 (est. 2009). It is noted for its university, founded in 1410, and its championship golf courses.

St Andrew's cross ▸ noun a diagonal or X-shaped cross, especially white on a blue background (as a national emblem of Scotland). Also called SALTIRE.

St Anthony cross (also **St Anthony's cross**) ▸ noun a T-shaped cross.

St Anthony's fire ▸ noun 1 another term for ERYSIPELAS.
2 another term for ERGOTISM.

Saint-Barthélemy /sɑ̃,bɑːˈtɛlɛmi/ an island in the Caribbean, one of the Leeward Islands. Formerly part of the French department of Guadeloupe, it became an overseas department in its own right in 2007. Known informally in English as ST BARTS.

St Bartholomew's Day Massacre see MASSACRE OF ST BARTHOLOMEW.

St Barts informal English name for SAINT-BARTHÉLEMY.

St Bernard (also **St Bernard dog**) ▸ noun a very large dog of a breed originally kept to rescue travellers by the monks of the Hospice on the Great St Bernard.

St Bernard Pass either of two passes across the Alps in southern Europe. The **Great St Bernard Pass**, on the border between SW Switzerland and Italy, rises to 2,469 m (8,100 ft). The **Little St Bernard Pass**, on the French–Italian border south-east of Mont Blanc, rises to 2,188 m (7,178 ft).
– ORIGIN named after the hospices founded on their summits in the 11th century by the French monk *St Bernard*.

St Christopher and Nevis, Federation of official name for ST KITTS AND NEVIS.

St Clements ▸ noun a non-alcoholic cocktail of orange juice mixed with lemonade or bitter lemon.
– ORIGIN 1980s: the name of a London church, with reference to the first line of the children's song *Oranges and lemons, say the bells of St Clements*.

St Croix /krɔɪ/ an island in the Caribbean, the largest of the US Virgin Islands; chief town, Christiansted. Purchased by Denmark in 1753, it was sold to the US in 1917.

St David's a small city near the coast of SW Wales, in Pembrokeshire; pop. 1,600 (est. 2008). Its 12th-century cathedral houses the shrine of St David, the patron saint of Wales. Welsh name TYDDEWI.

Saint-Denis /ˌsɑ̃dəˈniː/, French /sɛ̃dəni/ 1 a municipality in France, now a northern suburb of Paris.
2 the capital of the French island of Réunion, a port on the north coast; pop. 143,000 (est. 2007).

Sainte-Beuve /sɑ̃tˈbəːv/, French /sɛ̃tbœv/, Charles Augustin (1804–69), French critic and writer. In his criticism he concentrated on the influence of social and other factors in the development of character.

St Elmo's fire /ˈɛlməʊz/ ▸ noun [mass noun] a phenomenon in which a luminous electrical discharge appears on a ship or aircraft during a storm.
– ORIGIN regarded as a sign of protection given by St Elmo, the patron saint of sailors.

St-Émilion /ˌsɑ̃t eɪˈmɪljɒ̃/, French /sɛ̃t emiljɔ̃/ a small town situated to the north of the Dordogne in SW France. It gives its name to a group of Bordeaux wines.

St-Étienne /ˌsɑ̃teɪˈtjɛn/ an industrial city in SE central France, south-west of Lyons; pop. 180,773 (2009).

St Eustatius /juːˈsteɪʃəs/ a small volcanic island in the Caribbean, in the Netherlands Antilles; pop. 2,768 (2009).

Saint-Exupéry /ˌsɑ̃tɪgˈzuːpɛri/, French /sɛ̃tegzypeʀi/, Antoine (Marie Roger) de (1900–44), French writer and aviator, best known for the fable *The Little Prince* (1943).

St George's the capital of Grenada in the Caribbean, a port in the south-west of the island; pop. 5,200 (est. 2009).

St George's Channel a channel between Wales and Ireland, linking the Irish Sea with the Celtic Sea.

St George's cross ▸ noun a +-shaped cross, red on a white background (especially as a national emblem of England).

St George's mushroom ▸ noun a common European mushroom with a creamy-white cap and white gills, growing typically in rings and first appearing around St George's Day (April 23). ● *Tricholoma gambosum*, family Tricholomataceae, class Hymenomycetes.

St Gotthard Pass /ˈgɒtɑːd/ a mountain pass in the Alps in southern Switzerland, situated at an altitude of 2,108 m (6,916 ft).
– ORIGIN named after a former chapel and hospice (14th cent.), dedicated to St Godehard or *Gotthard*, an 11th-cent. bishop of Hildesheim in Germany.

St Helena /hɪˈliːnə/ a solitary island in the South Atlantic, a British overseas territory; pop. 7,600 (est. 2009); official language, English; capital, Jamestown. It was administered by the East India Company from 1659 until 1834, when it became a British colony. Ascension, Tristan da Cunha, and Gough Island are dependencies of St Helena. It is famous as the place of Napoleon's exile (1815–21) and death.
– DERIVATIVES **St Helenian** adjective & noun.
– ORIGIN so named when it was first encountered by the Portuguese on the feast day of *St Helena*, 21 May, 1502.

St Helens an industrial town and metropolitan district in NW England, to the north-east of Liverpool; pop. 102,000 (est. 2009).

St Helens, Mount an active volcano in SW Washington, in the Cascade Range, rising to 2,560 m (8,312 ft). A dramatic eruption in May 1980 reduced its height by several hundred metres and spread volcanic ash and debris over a large area.

St Helier /ˈhɛlɪə/ the capital of Jersey, situated on the south coast; pop. 28,500 (est. 2009).

S

St James's Palace a royal palace in London, built by Henry VIII on the site of an earlier leper hospital dedicated to **St James the Less**.

St John 1 an island in the Caribbean, one of the three principal islands of the US Virgin Islands.
2 (usu. **Saint John**) a city in New Brunswick, eastern Canada, a port on the Bay of Fundy at the mouth of the St John River; pop. 68,043 (2006).

St John Ambulance a voluntary organization providing first aid, nursing, ambulance, and welfare services.

St John's 1 the capital of Antigua and Barbuda, situated on the NW coast of Antigua; pop. 26,000 (est. 2007).
2 the capital of the province of Newfoundland and Labrador, a port on the SE coast of the island; pop. 100,646 (2006).

St John's wort ▶ **noun** a herbaceous plant or shrub with distinctive yellow five-petalled flowers and paired oval leaves. ● Genus *Hypericum*, family Guttiferae: many species.
– ORIGIN so named because some species come into flower near the feast day of St John the Baptist (24 June).

St Kilda /ˈkɪldə/ a small island group of the Outer Hebrides, situated in the Atlantic 64 km (40 miles) west of Lewis and Harris. The islands are now uninhabited and are administered as a nature reserve.

St Kitts and Nevis a country in the Caribbean consisting of two adjoining islands of the Leeward Islands; pop. 40,100 (est. 2009); languages, English (official), Creole; capital, Basseterre (on St Kitts). Official name **Federation of St Christopher and Nevis**.

> St Kitts was visited in 1493 by Christopher Columbus. The islands were colonized by English settlers from 1623, becoming the first successful English colony in the West Indies. A self-governing union between St Kitts and Nevis (and briefly Anguilla) was created in 1967 and became a fully independent member of the Commonwealth in 1983.

– ORIGIN *St Kitts*, alteration (by settlers) of *St Christopher*, a name given to the island by Columbus; *Nevis* from Spanish *las nieves* 'the snows' (because of the 'snowy' clouds surrounding the peak).

Saint Laurent /ˌsã lɔːˈrɒ̃/, French /sɛ̃ lɔʀɑ̃/, Yves (Mathieu) (1936–2008), French couturier. He opened his own fashion house in 1962, later launching Rive Gauche boutiques to sell ready-to-wear garments and expanding the business to include perfumes.

St Lawrence River a river of North America, which flows for some 1,200 km (750 miles) from Lake Ontario along the border between Canada and the US to the Gulf of St Lawrence on the Atlantic coast.

St Lawrence Seaway a waterway in North America, which flows for 3,768 km (2,342 miles) through the Great Lakes and along the course of the St Lawrence River to the Atlantic. It is open along its entire length to ocean-going vessels.

St Leger /ˈlɛdʒə/ ▶ **noun** an annual flat horse race at Doncaster for three-year-olds, held in September.
– ORIGIN named after Colonel Anthony *St Leger* (1731–86), who instituted the race in 1776.

saintliness ▶ **noun** [mass noun] the quality or state of being saintly; holiness.

St Louis /ˈluːi/ a city and port in eastern Missouri, on the Mississippi just south of its confluence with the Missouri; pop. 354,361 (est. 2008). Founded as a French fur-trading post, it passed to the US as part of the Louisiana Purchase.

St Louis encephalitis ▶ **noun** [mass noun] a form of viral encephalitis which can be fatal and is transmitted by mosquitoes.

St Lucia /ˈluːʃə/ a country in the Caribbean, one of the Windward Islands; pop. 160,300 (est. 2009); languages, English (official), French Creole; capital, Castries.

> First encountered by Europeans around 1500, St Lucia was settled by both French and British in the 17th century. Possession of the island was long disputed until France ceded it to Britain in 1814. Since 1979 it has been an independent state within the Commonwealth.

– DERIVATIVES **St Lucian** adjective & noun.

St Luke's summer ▶ **noun** Brit. a period of fine weather around 18 October (the saint's feast day).

saintly ▶ adjective (**saintlier**, **saintliest**) very holy or virtuous: *a truly saintly woman*. ■ relating to a saint: *a crypt for some saintly relic*.

St Malo /sã ˈmɑːləʊ/ a walled town and port on the north coast of Brittany, in NW France; pop. 51,292 (2006).

St Mark's Cathedral the cathedral church of Venice since 1807. It was built in the 9th century to house relics of St Mark, and rebuilt in the 11th century.

St Mark's fly ▶ **noun** a dark European fly which first appears around St Mark's Day (April 25th). It drifts slowly over low vegetation with the legs hanging down. ● *Bibio marci*, family Bibionidae.

St Martin /ˌsã mɑːˈtã/ a small island in the Caribbean, one of the Leeward Islands; pop. 35,300 (est. 2006). The southern section of the island is administered by the Dutch, forming part of the Netherlands Antilles; the larger northern part of the island is part of the French overseas department of Guadeloupe. Dutch name **Sint Maarten**.

St Martin's summer ▶ **noun** Brit. dated a period of fine weather around 11 November (the feast day of St Martin of Tours).

St Moritz /san ˈmɒrɪts, məˈrɪts/ a resort and winter-sports centre in SE Switzerland.

St-Nazaire /ˌsãnaˈzɛː/, French /sɛ̃nazɛʀ/ a seaport and industrial town in NW France, on the Atlantic coast at the mouth of the Loire; pop. 71,373 (2006).

St Nicolas /sɛ̃ nikɔla/ French name for **Sint-Niklaas**.

St Patrick's cabbage ▶ **noun** a European saxifrage with a rosette of long-stalked leaves and branching clusters of small white flowers. ● *Saxifraga spathularis*, family Saxifragaceae.

St Paul the state capital of Minnesota, situated on the Mississippi adjacent to Minneapolis, with which it forms the Twin Cities metropolitan area; pop. 279,590 (est. 2008).

saintpaulia /s(ə)ntˈpɔːlɪə/ ▶ **noun** a plant of the genus *Saintpaulia* (family Gesneriaceae), especially (in gardening) an African violet.
– ORIGIN named after Baron W. von *Saint Paul* (1860–1910), the German explorer who discovered it.

St Paul's Cathedral a cathedral on Ludgate Hill, London, designed by Sir Christopher Wren and built between 1675 and 1711.

St Peter's Basilica a Roman Catholic basilica in the Vatican City. Built in the 16th century on the site of a structure erected by Constantine on the supposed site of St Peter's crucifixion, it is the largest Christian church.

St Petersburg /ˈpiːtəzbəːg/ **1** a city and seaport in NW Russia, situated on the delta of the River Neva, on the eastern shores of the Gulf of Finland; pop. 4,548,800 (est. 2008). Former names **Petrograd** (1914–24) and **Leningrad** (1924–91).

> Founded in 1703 by Peter the Great, St Petersburg was the capital of Russia from 1712 until the Russian Revolution. It was the scene in February and October 1917 of the events which triggered the Revolution. During the Second World War it was subjected by German and Finnish forces to a siege which lasted for more than two years (1941–4).

2 a resort city in western Florida, on the Gulf of Mexico; pop. 245,314 (est. 2008).

St Peter's fish ▶ **noun** a fish with a dark mark near each pectoral fin, in particular a widely farmed cichlid of Africa and the Middle East (also called **tilapia**). ● *Sarotherodon galileus*, family Cichlidae. Alternative name: **Galilee cichlid**.
– ORIGIN with biblical allusion to Matt. 17:27.

St Pierre and Miquelon /san ˈpjɛː, ˈmiːklɒn/ a group of eight small islands in the North Atlantic, off the south coast of Newfoundland; pop. 7,100 (est. 2009). An overseas territory of France, the islands form the last remaining French possession in North America.

St Pölten /ˈpəːlt(ə)n/ a city in NE Austria, capital of the state of Lower Austria; pop. 51,353 (2006).

Saint-Saëns /ˈsãsɒ̃/, French /sɛ̃sɑ̃s/, (Charles) Camille (1835–1921), French composer, pianist, and organist. His work, which is characterized by elegance of form and melodic invention rather than emotion, includes his Third Symphony (1886), the tone poem *Danse macabre* (1874), and the *Carnaval des animaux* (1886).

saint's day ▶ **noun** a day on which a saint is particularly commemorated in the Christian Church.

Saint-Simon¹ /ˌsãsiːˈmɒ̃/, Claude-Henri de Rouvroy, Comte de (1760–1825), French social reformer and philosopher. Later claimed as the founder of French socialism, he argued that society should be organized by leaders of industry and given spiritual direction by scientists.

Saint-Simon² /ˌsãsiːˈmɒ̃/, Louis de Rouvroy, Duc de (1675–1755), French writer. He is best known for his *Mémoires*, a detailed record of court life between 1694 and 1723, in the reigns of Louis XIV and XV.

St Sophia /səˈfiːə, -ˈfʌɪə/ the key monument of Byzantine architecture, originally a church, at Istanbul. Built by order of Justinian and inaugurated in 537, it was converted into a mosque after the Turkish invasion of 1453. In 1935 Atatürk declared it a museum. Also called **Hagia Sophia**, **Santa Sophia**.

St Stephens a name for the House of Commons.
– ORIGIN from *St Stephen*, the name of the ancient chapel in Westminster, in which the House used to sit (1537–1834).

St Stephen's Day ▶ **noun** Irish December 26; Boxing Day.

St Swithin's day ▶ **noun** 15 July, a Church festival commemorating St Swithin and popularly believed to be a day on which, if it rains, it will continue raining for the next forty days.

St Thomas an island in the Caribbean, the second-largest of the US Virgin Islands, situated to the east of Puerto Rico; pop. 53,700 (est. 2009); chief town, Charlotte Amalie. Settled by the Dutch in 1657, it passed nine years later to the Danes, who sold it to the US in 1917.

St Trinian's /ˈtrɪnɪənz/ a fictional girls' school invented by Ronald Searle in 1941, whose pupils are characterized by unruly behaviour and untidy school uniform.

St-Tropez /ˌsãtrə(ʊ)ˈpeɪ/ a fishing port and resort on the Mediterranean coast of southern France, south-west of Cannes; pop. 5,690 (2006).

St Valentine's Day Massacre the shooting on 14th February 1929 of seven members of the rival 'Bugsy' Moran's gang by some of Al Capone's men disguised as policemen.

St Vincent, Cape a headland in SW Portugal, which forms the south-westernmost tip of the country. It was the site of a sea battle in 1797 in which the British fleet under Admiral John Jervis defeated the Spanish. Portuguese name **São Vincente**.

St Vincent and the Grenadines /ˈvɪns(ə)nt, ˈgrɛnədiːnz/ an island state in the Windward Islands in the Caribbean, consisting of the mountainous island of St Vincent and some of the Grenadines; pop. 104,600 (est. 2009); languages, English (official), English-based Creole; capital, Kingstown.

> The French, Dutch, and British all made attempts at settlements in the 18th century, and the islands finally fell to British possession in 1783. The state obtained full independence with a limited form of membership of the Commonwealth in 1979.

St Vitus's dance /ˈvʌɪtəsɪz/ ▶ **noun** old-fashioned term for **Sydenham's chorea**.
– ORIGIN so named because a visit to *St Vitus*'s shrine was believed to alleviate the disease.

Saipan /sʌɪˈpan/ the largest of the islands comprising the Northern Marianas in the western Pacific.

saith /sɛθ/ archaic third person singular present of **say**.

saithe /seɪθ/ ▶ **noun** a commercially valuable food fish of the cod family, which occurs in the North Atlantic. Also called **coalfish**, **coley**, (N. Amer.) **pollock**.
● *Pollachius virens*, family Gadidae.
– ORIGIN mid 16th cent.: from Old Norse *seithr*.

Saiva /ˈsʌɪvə/ ▶ **noun** a member of one of the main branches of modern Hinduism, devoted to the worship of the god Shiva as the supreme being. Compare with **Vaishnava**.
– DERIVATIVES **Saivite** noun & adjective.
– ORIGIN from Sanskrit *śaiva* 'sacred to Shiva'.

sakabula /ˌsakəˈbuːlə/ ▶ **noun** S. African a widowbird of SE Africa, the mainly black male of which has a very long tail. ● *Euplectes progne*, family Ploceidae. Alternative name: **long-tailed widowbird**.
– ORIGIN late 19th cent.: from Xhosa and Zulu *isakabula*.

Sakai /sɑːˈkʌɪ/ an industrial city in Japan, on Osaka Bay just south of the city of Osaka; pop. 831,715 (2007).

sake[1] /seɪk/ ▶ **noun 1** (**for the sake of something** or **for something's sake**) for the purpose of; in the interest of; in order to achieve or preserve: *the couple moved to the coast for the sake of her health* | *let us say, for the sake of argument, that the plotter and the assassin are one and the same person.* ■ (**for its own sake** or **something for something's sake** or **for the sake of it**) used to indicate something that is done as an end in itself rather than to achieve some other purpose: *new ideas amount to change for change's sake.*
2 (**for the sake of someone** or **for someone's sake**) out of consideration for or in order to help or please someone: *I have to make an effort for John's sake.*
3 (**for God's** or **goodness'**, **Christ's**, **heaven's**, **Pete's** etc. **sake**) used to express impatience, annoyance, urgency, or desperation: *'Oh, for God's sake!' snarled Dyson* | *where did you get it, for heaven's sake?*
– PHRASES **for old times' sake** in memory of former times; in acknowledgement of a shared past: *they sat in the back seats for old times' sake.*
– ORIGIN Old English *sacu* 'contention, crime', of Germanic origin; related to Dutch *zaak* and German *Sache*, from a base meaning 'affair, legal action, thing'. The phrase *for the sake of* may be from Old Norse.

sake[2] /'sɑːki, 'sakeɪ/ ▶ **noun** [mass noun] a Japanese alcoholic drink made from fermented rice, traditionally drunk warm in small porcelain cups.
– ORIGIN Japanese.

saker /'seɪkə/ ▶ **noun 1** a large Eurasian falcon with a brown back and whitish head, used in falconry.
● *Falco cherrug*, family Falconidae.
2 an early form of cannon.
– ORIGIN late Middle English: from Old French *sacre*, from Arabic *ṣaqr* 'falcon'.

Sakha, Republic of /'sɑːkə/ official name for **YAKUTIA**.

Sakhalin /ˌsakə'liːn/ a large Russian island in the Sea of Okhotsk, situated off the coast of eastern Russia and separated from it by the Tartar Strait; capital, Yuzhno-Sakhalinsk. From 1905 to 1946 it was divided into the northern part, held by Russia, and the southern part (Karafuto), occupied by Japan.

Sakharov /'sakərɒf/, Andrei (Dmitrievich) (1921–89), Russian nuclear physicist and civil rights campaigner. Having helped to develop the Soviet hydrogen bomb, he campaigned against nuclear proliferation. He fought for reform and human rights in the USSR, for which he was awarded the Nobel Peace Prize in 1975 but was also sentenced to internal exile 1980–6.

Saki /'sɑːki/ (1870–1916), British short-story writer, born in Burma; pseudonym of *Hector Hugh Munro*. His stories encompass the satiric, comic, macabre, and supernatural, and frequently depict animals as agents seeking revenge on humankind.

saki /'sɑːki/ ▶ **noun** (pl. **sakis**) a tropical American monkey with coarse fur and a long bushy nonprehensile tail. ● Genera *Pithecia* and *Chiropotes*, family Cebidae: several species.
– ORIGIN late 18th cent.: via French from Tupi *saui*.

sakkie-sakkie /ˌsakɪ'saki/ ▶ **noun** [mass noun] S. African a simple, rhythmical style of Afrikaner music and dance.
– ORIGIN Afrikaans, probably symbolic of the repetitive rhythm (also expressing disparagement).

Sakti ▶ **noun** Hinduism variant spelling of **SHAKTI**.

sal /sɑːl/ ▶ **noun** a North Indian tree which yields teak-like timber and dammar resin. ● *Shorea robusta*, family Dipterocarpaceae.
– ORIGIN late 18th cent.: from Hindi *sāl*.

salaam /sə'lɑːm/ ▶ **exclamation** a common greeting in many Arabic-speaking and Muslim countries.
▶ **noun** a gesture of greeting or respect typically consisting of a low bow of the head and body with the hand or fingers touching the forehead. ■ (**salaams**) respectful compliments.
▶ **verb** [no obj.] make a salaam.
– ORIGIN early 17th cent.: from Arabic *(al-)salām (ʿalaikum)* 'peace (be upon you)'.

salable ▶ **adjective** variant spelling of **SALEABLE**.

salacious /sə'leɪʃəs/ ▶ **adjective** having or conveying undue or indecent interest in sexual matters: *salacious stories.*
– DERIVATIVES **salaciously** adverb, **salaciousness** noun, **salacity** noun (dated).
– ORIGIN mid 17th cent.: from Latin *salax*, *salac-* (from *salire* 'to leap') + **-IOUS**.

salad ▶ **noun** a cold dish of various mixtures of raw or cooked vegetables, usually seasoned with oil, vinegar, or other dressing and sometimes accompanied by meat, fish, or other ingredients: *a green salad* | [mass noun] *bowls of salad.* ■ [mass noun] [with modifier] a mixture containing a specified ingredient served with a dressing: *a red pepper filled with tuna salad.* ■ a vegetable suitable for eating raw.
– PHRASES **one's salad days** the period when one is young and inexperienced. ■ the peak or heyday of something. [from Shakespeare's *Antony and Cleopatra* I. v. 73.]
– ORIGIN late Middle English: from Old French *salade*, from Provençal *salada*, based on Latin *sal* 'salt'.

salad cream ▶ **noun** [mass noun] Brit. a creamy salad dressing resembling mayonnaise.

salad dressing ▶ **noun** see **DRESSING** (sense 1).

salade /sə'lɑːd/ ▶ **noun** another term for **SALLET**.

salade niçoise /ˌsalɑːd niː'swɑːz/ ▶ **noun** (pl. **salades niçoises** pronunc. **same**) [mass noun] a salad typically including tuna, black olives, hard-boiled eggs, and tomatoes.
– ORIGIN French, 'salad from Nice'.

Saladin /'salədɪn/ (1137–93), sultan of Egypt and Syria 1174–93; Arabic name *Salah-ad-Din Yusuf ibn-Ayyub*. Saladin reconquered Jerusalem from the Christians in 1187, but he was defeated by Richard the Lionheart at Arsuf (1191). He earned a reputation not only for military skill but also for honesty and chivalry.

Salafi /sə'lɑːfi/ ▶ **noun** (pl. **Salafis**) a member of a strictly orthodox Sunni Muslim sect advocating a return to the early Islam of the Koran and Sunna.
– ORIGIN Arabic, from *salaf* 'predecessors', 'forebears'.

salal /sə'lal/ ▶ **noun** a North American plant of the heather family, with clusters of pink or white flowers and edible purple-black berries. ● *Gaultheria shallon*, family Ericaceae.
– ORIGIN early 19th cent.: from Chinook Jargon *sallal*.

Salam /sə'lɑːm/, Abdus (1926–1996), Pakistani theoretical physicist. He independently developed a unified theory to explain electromagnetic interactions and the weak nuclear force. In 1979 he was awarded the Nobel Prize for Physics, shared with Sheldon Lee Glashow and Steven Weinberg.

Salamanca /ˌsalə'maŋkə/ a city in western Spain, in Castilla-León; pop. 155,740 (2008).

salamander /'saləˌmandə/ ▶ **noun 1** a newt-like amphibian that typically has bright markings, once thought able to endure fire. ● Order Urodela: four families, in particular Salamandridae, and numerous species.
2 a mythical lizard-like creature said to live in fire or to be able to withstand its effects. ■ an elemental spirit living in fire.
3 a metal plate heated and placed over food to brown it.
4 archaic a red-hot iron or poker.
– DERIVATIVES **salamandrine** /-'mandrɪn/ **adjective**.
– ORIGIN Middle English (in sense 2): from Old French *salamandre*, via Latin from Greek *salamandra*. Sense 1 dates from the early 17th cent.

salami /sə'lɑːmi/ ▶ **noun** (pl. **same** or **salamis**) [mass noun] a type of highly seasoned sausage, originally from Italy, usually eaten cold in slices.
– ORIGIN Italian, plural of *salame*, from a late Latin word meaning 'to salt'.

Salamis /'saləmɪs/ an island in the Saronic Gulf in Greece, to the west of Athens. The strait between the island and the mainland was the scene in 480 BC of a crushing defeat of the Persian fleet under Xerxes I by the Greeks under Themistocles.

sal ammoniac /ˌsal ə'məʊnɪak/ ▶ **noun** old-fashioned term for **AMMONIUM CHLORIDE**.
– ORIGIN Middle English: from Latin *sal ammoniacus* 'salt of Ammon' (see **AMMONIACAL**).

Salang Pass /'sɑːlaŋ/ a high-altitude route across the Hindu Kush in Afghanistan. A road and tunnel were built by the Soviet Union during the 1960s to improve the supply route to Kabul.

salariat /sə'lɛːrɪət/ ▶ **noun** (**the salariat**) salaried white-collar workers.
– ORIGIN early 20th cent.: from French, from *salaire* 'salary', on the pattern of *prolétariat* 'proletariat'.

salaried ▶ **adjective** receiving or recompensed by a salary rather than a wage: *salaried employees* | *he was in salaried employment.*

salary ▶ **noun** (pl. **salaries**) a fixed regular payment, typically paid on a monthly basis but often expressed as an annual sum, made by an employer to an employee, especially a professional or white-collar worker: *he received a salary of £24,000* | [as modifier] *a 15 per cent salary increase.* Compare with **WAGE**.
▶ **verb** (**salaries**, **salarying**, **salaried**) [with obj.] archaic pay a salary to.
– ORIGIN Middle English: from Anglo-Norman French *salarie*, from Latin *salarium*, originally denoting a Roman soldier's allowance to buy salt, from *sal* 'salt'.

salaryman ▶ **noun** (pl. **salarymen**) (especially in Japan) a white-collar worker.

salat /sa'lɑːt/ ▶ **noun** [mass noun] the ritual prayer of Muslims, performed five times daily in a set form, one of the Five Pillars of Islam.
– ORIGIN Arabic, plural of *salāh* 'prayer, worship'.

Salazar /ˌsalə'zɑː/, Antonio de Oliveira (1889–1970), Portuguese statesman, Prime Minister 1932–68. During his long premiership he ruled the country as a virtual dictator, enacting a new authoritarian constitution along Fascist lines. Salazar maintained Portugal's neutrality throughout the Spanish Civil War and the Second World War.

salbutamol /sal'bjuːtəmɒl/ ▶ **noun** [mass noun] Medicine a synthetic compound related to aspirin, used as a bronchodilator in the treatment of asthma and other conditions involving constriction of the airways.
– ORIGIN 1960s: from *sal(icylic acid)* + *but(yl)* + *am(ine)* + **-OL**.

salchow /'salkəʊ/ ▶ **noun** a jump in figure skating from the backward inside edge of one skate to the backward outside edge of the other, with one or more full turns in the air.
– ORIGIN early 20th cent.: named after Ulrich *Salchow* (1877–1949), Swedish skater.

sale ▶ **noun 1** [mass noun] the exchange of a commodity for money; the action of selling something: *we withdrew it from sale* | [count noun] *the sale has fallen through.* ■ (**sales**) a quantity or amount sold: *price cuts failed to boost sales.* ■ (**sales**) the activity or business of selling products: *director of sales and marketing.*
2 a period during which a shop sells goods at reduced prices: *the January sales got under way this week.* ■ a public or charitable event at which goods are sold or auctioned: *a bric-a-brac sale will be held at St Cuthbert's Church Centre.*
– PHRASES (**up**) **for sale** offered for purchase; to be bought: *cars for sale at reasonable prices.* **on sale 1** offered for purchase: *the November issue is on sale now.* **2** N. Amer. offered for purchase at a reduced price. **sale or return** Brit. an arrangement by which a purchaser takes a quantity of goods with the right of returning surplus goods without payment.
– ORIGIN late Old English *sala*, from Old Norse *sala*, of Germanic origin; related to **SELL**.

saleable (US also **salable**) ▶ **adjective** fit or able to be sold.
– DERIVATIVES **saleability** noun.

Salem /'seɪləm/ **1** the state capital of Oregon, situated on the Willamette River south-west of Portland; pop. 153,435 (est. 2008).
2 a city and port in NE Massachusetts, on the Atlantic coast north of Boston; pop. 41,256 (est. 2008). First settled in 1626, it was the scene in 1692 of a notorious series of witchcraft trials.
3 an industrial city in Tamil Nadu in southern India; pop. 872,400 (est. 2009).

sale of work ▶ **noun** Brit. an event where goods made by members of a parish or other organization are sold, typically to raise funds for charity.

salep /'saləp/ ▶ **noun** [mass noun] a starchy preparation of the dried tubers of various orchids, used as a thickener in cookery, and formerly in medicines and tonics.
– ORIGIN mid 18th cent.: from French, from Turkish *sālep*, from Arabic *(kuṣa-'t-) ṯaʿlab*, the name of an orchid (literally 'fox's testicles').

saleratus /ˌsalə'reɪtəs/ ▶ **noun** [mass noun] US sodium bicarbonate (or sometimes potassium bicarbonate) as the main ingredient of baking powder.
– ORIGIN mid 19th cent.: from modern Latin *sal aeratus* 'aerated salt'.

sale ring ▶ **noun** Brit. an enclosure around which a circle of buyers stands at an auction to view livestock offered for sale.

Salerno /sa'lɛːnəʊ/, Italian /sa'lɛrno/ a port on the west coast of Italy, on the Gulf of Salerno south-east of Naples; pop. 140,489 (2008).

saleroom ▶ **noun** Brit. a room in which items are sold at auction.

sales clerk ▶ **noun** N. Amer. a shop assistant.

sales engineer ▶ noun a salesperson with technical knowledge of the goods and their market.

salesgirl ▶ noun a female shop assistant.

Salesian /sə'liːzɪən, -ʒ(ə)n/ ▶ adjective relating to a Roman Catholic educational religious order founded near Turin in 1859 and named after St Francis de Sales.
▶ noun a member of this order.

saleslady ▶ noun (pl. **salesladies**) a saleswoman.

salesman ▶ noun (pl. **salesmen**) a man whose job involves selling or promoting commercial products, either in a shop or visiting locations to get orders: *an insurance salesman.*
– DERIVATIVES **salesmanship** noun.

salesperson ▶ noun (pl. **salespersons** or **salespeople**) a salesman or saleswoman (used as a neutral alternative).

salesroom ▶ noun another term for SALEROOM.

saleswoman ▶ noun (pl. **saleswomen**) a woman whose job involves selling or promoting commercial products.

Salford /'sɔːlfəd/ an industrial city and metropolitan district in NW England, near Manchester; pop. 69,600 (est. 2009).

Salian /'seɪlɪən/ ▶ noun a member of the Salii, a 4th-century Frankish people living near the River IJssel, from whom the Merovingians were descended.
▶ adjective relating to the Salii.

Salic /'salɪk, 'seɪ-/ ▶ adjective another term for SALIAN.

salicin /'salɪsɪn/ ▶ noun [mass noun] Chemistry a bitter compound present in willow bark. It is a glucoside related to aspirin, and accounts for the ancient use of willow bark as a pain-relieving drug.
– ORIGIN mid 19th cent.: from French *salicine*, from Latin *salix, salic-* 'willow'.

salicional /sə'lɪʃ(ə)n(ə)l/ ▶ noun an organ stop with a soft reedy tone.
– ORIGIN mid 19th cent.: from German *Salicional*, from Latin *salix, salic-* 'willow' + the obscurely derived suffix *-ional*.

Salic law historical ▶ noun **1** a law excluding females from dynastic succession, especially as the alleged fundamental law of the French monarchy.
2 a Frankish law book extant in Merovingian and Carolingian times.

salicylate /sə'lɪsɪlət/ ▶ noun Chemistry a salt or ester of salicylic acid.

salicylic acid /,salɪ'sɪlɪk/ ▶ noun [mass noun] Chemistry a bitter compound present in certain plants. It is used as a fungicide and in the manufacture of aspirin and dyestuffs. ● Alternative name: **o-hydroxybenzoic acid**; chem. formula: $C_6H_4(OH)(COOH)$.
– ORIGIN mid 19th cent.: *salicylic* from French *salicyle* (the radical of the acid), from Latin *salix, salic-* 'willow'.

salient /'seɪlɪənt/ ▶ adjective **1** most noticeable or important: *it succinctly covered all the salient points of the case.* ■ prominent; conspicuous: *the salient object in my view.*
2 (of an angle) pointing outwards. The opposite of RE-ENTRANT.
3 [postpositive] Heraldry (of an animal) standing on its hind legs with the forepaws raised, as if leaping.
▶ noun a piece of land or section of fortification that juts out to form an angle. ■ an outward bulge in a line of military attack or defence.
– DERIVATIVES **salience** noun, **saliency** noun, **saliently** adverb.
– ORIGIN mid 16th cent. (as a heraldic term): from Latin *salient-* 'leaping', from the verb *salire*. The noun dates from the early 19th cent.

Salientia /,seɪlɪ'ɛnʃɪə, -'ɛnt-/ ▶ plural noun Zoology another term for ANURA.
– ORIGIN modern Latin (plural), from Latin *salire* 'to leap'.

Salieri /,salɪ'ɛːri/, Antonio (1750–1825), Italian composer. His output includes over forty operas and four oratorios. Salieri lived in Vienna and taught Beethoven, Schubert, and Liszt. He was hostile to Mozart, whom he considered his rival, but a rumour that he poisoned him is now thought to be without foundation.

salina /sə'lʌɪnə/ ▶ noun (chiefly in the Caribbean or South America) a salt pan, salt lake, or salt marsh.
– ORIGIN late 16th cent.: from Spanish, from medieval Latin, 'salt pit', in Latin *salinae* (plural) 'salt pans'.

saline /'seɪlʌɪn/ ▶ adjective containing or impregnated with salt: *saline alluvial soils.* ■ chiefly Medicine (of a solution) containing sodium chloride and/or a salt or salts of magnesium or another alkali metal.
▶ noun [mass noun] a solution of salt in water. ■ a saline solution used in medicine.
– DERIVATIVES **salinity** noun, **salinization** (also **salinisation**) noun.
– ORIGIN late 15th cent.: from Latin *sal* 'salt' + -INE[1].

Salinger /'salɪndʒə/, J. D. (1919–2010), American novelist and short-story writer; full name *Jerome David Salinger*. He is best known for his novel of adolescence *The Catcher in the Rye* (1951).

salinometer /,salɪ'nɒmɪtə/ ▶ noun an instrument for measuring the salinity of water.

Salisbury[1] /'sɔːlzb(ə)ri/ **1** a city in southern England, in Wiltshire; pop. 42,900 (est. 2009). It is noted for its 13th-century cathedral, whose spire, at 123 m (404 ft), is the highest in England. Its diocese is known as Sarum, an old name for the city.
2 former name (until 1982) for HARARE.

Salisbury[2] /'sɔːlzb(ə)ri/, Robert Arthur Talbot Gascoigne-Cecil, 3rd Marquess of (1830–1903), British Conservative statesman, Prime Minister 1885–6, 1886–92, and 1895–1902. He supported the policies which resulted in the Second Boer War (1899–1902).

Salish /'seɪlɪʃ/ ▶ noun (pl. **same**) **1** a member of a group of American Indian peoples inhabiting areas of the north-western US and the west coast of Canada.
2 [mass noun] the group of related languages spoken by the Salish, now all extinct or nearly so.
▶ adjective relating to the Salish or their languages.
– DERIVATIVES **Salishan** adjective.
– ORIGIN a local name, literally 'Flatheads'.

saliva /sə'lʌɪvə/ ▶ noun [mass noun] watery liquid secreted into the mouth by glands, providing lubrication for chewing and swallowing, and aiding digestion.
– DERIVATIVES **salivary** /sə'lʌɪ-, 'salɪ-/ adjective.
– ORIGIN late Middle English: from Latin.

salivate /'salɪveɪt/ ▶ verb [no obj.] **1** secrete saliva, especially in anticipation of food. ■ [with obj.] technical cause (a person or animal) to produce an unusually copious secretion of saliva.
2 display great relish at the sight or prospect of something: *I was fairly **salivating at** the prospect of a $10 million loan.*
– DERIVATIVES **salivation** noun.
– ORIGIN mid 17th cent.: from Latin *salivat-* '(having) produced saliva', from the verb *salivare*, from *saliva* (see SALIVA).

Salk /sɔːlk/, Jonas Edward (1914–95), American microbiologist. He developed the standard **Salk vaccine** against polio, using virus inactivated by formalin, in the early 1950s, and later became the director of the institute in San Diego that now bears his name.

sallee ▶ noun variant spelling of SALLY[3].

sallet /'salɪt/ ▶ noun historical a light helmet with an outward curve extending over the back of the neck, worn as part of medieval armour.
– ORIGIN late Middle English: from French *salade*, based on Latin *caelare* 'engrave' (from *caelum* 'chisel').

sallow[1] ▶ adjective (of a person's face or complexion) of an unhealthy yellow or pale brown colour.
– DERIVATIVES **sallowness** noun.
– ORIGIN Old English *salo* 'dusky', of Germanic origin; related to Old Norse *sǫlr* 'yellow', from a base meaning 'dirty'.

sallow[2] ▶ noun **1** chiefly Brit. a willow tree, especially one of a low-growing or shrubby kind. Also called PUSSY WILLOW. ● Genus *Salix*, family Salicaceae: several species, in particular the **great sallow** (goat willow, *S. caprea*) and the **grey** (or **common**) **sallow** (grey willow, *S. cinerea*).
2 a European moth with dull yellow, orange, and brown patterned wings. ● Genus *Xanthia*, family Noctuidae: several species.
– ORIGIN Old English *salh*, of Germanic origin; related to Old Norse *selja*, and Latin *salix* 'willow'.

Sallust /'saləst/ (86–35 BC), Roman historian and politician; Latin name *Gaius Sallustius Crispus*. As a historian he was concerned with the political and moral decline of Rome after the fall of Carthage in 146 BC. His chief surviving works deal with the Catiline conspiracy and the Jugurthine War.

Sally (also **Sally Army** or **Sallies**) ▶ noun Brit. informal the Salvation Army.
– ORIGIN early 20th cent.: alteration of SALVATION.

sally[1] ▶ noun (pl. **sallies**) **1** a sudden charge out of a besieged place against the enemy; a sortie. ■ a brief journey or sudden start into activity.
2 a witty or lively remark, especially one made as an attack or as a diversion in an argument; a retort.
▶ verb (**sallies, sallying, sallied**) [no obj., with adverbial of direction] make a military sortie: *they sallied out to harass the enemy.* ■ formal or humorous set out from a place to do something: *I made myself presentable and sallied forth.*
– ORIGIN late Middle English: from French *saillie*, feminine past participle (used as a noun) of *saillir* 'come or jut out', from Old French *salir* 'to leap', from Latin *salire*.

sally[2] ▶ noun (pl. **sallies**) the part of a bell rope that has coloured wool woven into it to provide a grip for the bell-ringer's hands.
– ORIGIN mid 17th cent. (denoting the first movement of a bell when set for ringing): perhaps from SALLY[1] in the sense 'leaping motion'.

sally[3] (also **sallee**) ▶ noun (pl. **sallies** or **sallees**) Austral. any of a number of acacias and eucalyptuses that resemble willows. ● Several species, including **white sally** (*Eucalyptus pauciflora*, family Myrtaceae).
– ORIGIN late 19th cent.: dialect variant of SALLOW[2].

Sally Lightfoot ▶ noun (pl. **Sally Lightfoots**) a common active crab of rocky shores in the Caribbean, Central America, and the Galapagos Islands. ● *Grapsus grapsus*, family Grapsidae.

Sally Lunn ▶ noun a sweet, light teacake, typically served hot.
– ORIGIN said to be from the name of a woman selling such cakes in Bath *c.*1800.

sally port ▶ noun a small exit point in a fortification for the passage of troops when making a sally.

salmagundi /,salmə'gʌndi/ ▶ noun (pl. **salmagundis**) **1** a dish of chopped meat, anchovies, eggs, onions, and seasoning.
2 a general mixture; a miscellaneous collection.
– ORIGIN from French *salmigondis*, of unknown origin.

salmanazar /,salmə'neɪzə/ ▶ noun a wine bottle of approximately twelve times the standard size.
– ORIGIN 1930s: named after *Shalmaneser*, a king of Assyria (2 Kings 17–18).

salmi /'salmi/ ▶ noun (pl. **salmis**) a ragout or casserole of game stewed in a rich sauce: *a pheasant salmi.*
– ORIGIN French, abbreviation of *salmigondis* (see SALMAGUNDI).

salmon /'samən/ ▶ noun (pl. **same**) **1** a large edible fish that is a popular sporting fish, much prized for its pink flesh. Salmon mature in the sea but migrate to freshwater streams to spawn. ● Family Salmonidae (the **salmon family**): the **Atlantic salmon** (*Salmo salar*), which sometimes returns to spawn two or three times, and five species of Pacific salmon (genus *Oncorhynchus*), which always die after spawning. The salmon family also includes trout, charr, whitefish, and their relatives.
■ [mass noun] the flesh of the salmon as food.
2 [usu. with modifier] any of a number of fishes resembling the salmon, in particular: ● (**Australian salmon**) a large green and silver fish of Australasian inshore waters, popular as a game fish (*Arripis trutta*, family Arripidae). ● a prized food fish of the drum family (Sciaenidae), in particular the **Cape salmon** of the Indian Ocean (*Atractoscion aequidens*) and sea trouts of the western Atlantic (genus *Cynoscion*).
3 [mass noun] a pale pink colour.
– DERIVATIVES **salmony** adjective.
– ORIGIN Middle English *samoun*, from Anglo-Norman French *saumoun*, from Latin *salmo, salmon-*. The spelling with *-l-* is influenced by Latin.

salmonberry ▶ noun (pl. **salmonberries**) a North American bramble which bears pink raspberry-like fruit. ● Genus *Rubus*, family Rosaceae: several species, in particular *R. spectabilis*.
■ the edible fruit of the salmonberry.

salmonella /,salmə'nɛlə/ ▶ noun (pl. **salmonellae** /-liː/) [mass noun] a bacterium that occurs mainly in the gut, especially a serotype causing food poisoning. ● Genus *Salmonella*: numerous serotypes; Gram-negative rods. ■ food poisoning caused by infection with the salmonella bacterium: *an outbreak of salmonella.*
– DERIVATIVES **salmonellosis** /-'ləʊsɪs/ noun.
– ORIGIN modern Latin, named after Daniel E. *Salmon* (1850–1914), American veterinary surgeon.

salmonid /'salmənɪd, sal'mɒnɪd/ ▶ noun Zoology a fish of the salmon family (Salmonidae).
– ORIGIN mid 19th cent.: from modern Latin *Salmonidae* (plural), based on Latin *salmo, salmon-* 'salmon' + -ID[2].

salmon ladder (also **salmon leap**) ▶ noun a series of natural steps in a cascade or steeply sloping

S

riverbed, or a similar arrangement incorporated into a dam, allowing salmon to pass upstream.

salmonoid Zoology ▸ **noun** a fish of a group that includes the salmon family together with the pikes, smelts, and argentines. ● Superfamily Salmonoidea: several families.
▸ **adjective** relating to or denoting fish of the salmonoid group.

salmon run ▸ **noun** a migration of salmon up a river from the sea, in order to spawn.

salmon trout ▸ **noun** Brit. a sea trout. ■ N. Amer. a lake trout. ■ Austral. an Australian salmon.

Salome /sə'ləʊmi/ (in the New Testament) the daughter of Herodias, who danced before her stepfather Herod Antipas. Given a choice of reward for her dancing, she asked for the head of St John the Baptist and thus caused him to be beheaded.

salon ▸ **noun 1** an establishment where a hairdresser, beautician, or couturier conducts trade.
2 a reception room in a large house. ■ historical a regular social gathering, especially of writers and artists, at the house of a woman prominent in high society. ■ N. Amer. a meeting of intellectuals or other eminent people at the invitation of a celebrity or socialite.
3 (**Salon**) an annual exhibition of the work of living artists held by the Royal Academy of Painting and Sculpture in Paris from 1648, originally in the Salon d'Apollon in the Louvre.
– ORIGIN late 17th cent.: from French (see SALOON).

Salon des Refusés /,salɒ̃ deɪ 'rəfjʊːzeɪ/, French /salɔ̃ de ʀəfyze/ an exhibition in Paris ordered by Napoleon III in 1863 to display pictures rejected by the Salon. The artists represented included Manet, Cézanne, Pissarro, and Whistler.
– ORIGIN French, literally 'exhibition of the rejected (works)'.

Salonica /sə'lɒnɪkə/ former name for THESSALONÍKI.

salon music ▸ **noun** [mass noun] often derogatory light classical music originally considered suitable for playing in a salon.

saloon ▸ **noun 1** a public room or building used for a specified purpose. ■ (also **saloon bar**) Brit. another term for LOUNGE BAR. ■ N. Amer. historical or humorous a place where alcoholic drinks may be bought and drunk. ■ a large public room for use as a lounge on a ship. ■ (also **saloon car**) Brit. a luxurious railway carriage used as a lounge or restaurant or as private accommodation: *a dining saloon*.
2 (also **saloon car**) Brit. a car having a closed body and a closed boot separated from the part in which the driver and passengers sit.
– ORIGIN early 18th cent. (in the sense 'drawing room'): from French *salon*, from Italian *salone* 'large hall', augmentative of *sala* 'hall'.

saloon deck ▸ **noun** a deck on the same level as a ship's saloon, for the use of passengers.

saloon pistol (also **saloon rifle**) ▸ **noun** a gun adapted for firing at short range.

Salop /'saləp/ another name for SHROPSHIRE. It was the official name of the county 1974–80.
– DERIVATIVES **Salopian** /sə'ləʊpɪən/ **adjective & noun**.
– ORIGIN abbreviation of Anglo-Norman French *Salopesberie*, a corruption of Old English *Scrobbesbyrig* 'Shrewsbury'.

salopettes /,salə'pets/ ▸ **plural noun** trousers with a high waist and shoulder straps, typically made of a padded fabric and worn for skiing.
– ORIGIN 1970s: from French *salopette* in the same sense + *-s* by analogy with such words as *trousers*.

salotto /sa'lɒtəʊ/ ▸ **noun** (pl. **salotti** /sə'lɒti/) (especially in Italy) a reception room.
– ORIGIN Italian, diminutive of *sala* 'hall'.

salp /salp/ ▸ **noun** a free-swimming marine invertebrate related to the sea squirts, with a transparent barrel-shaped body. ● Several genera in the class Thaliacea, subphylum Urochordata.
– ORIGIN mid 19th cent.: from French *salpe*, based on Greek *salpē* 'fish'.

salpicon /'salpɪkɒn/ ▸ **noun** a mixture of finely chopped ingredients bound in a thick sauce and used as a filling or stuffing.
– ORIGIN via French from Spanish, from *salpicar* 'sprinkle (with salt)'.

salpiglossis /,salpɪ'glɒsɪs/ ▸ **noun** a South American plant of the nightshade family, with brightly patterned funnel-shaped flowers. ● Genus *Salpiglossis*, family Solanaceae.
– ORIGIN modern Latin, formed irregularly from Greek *salpinx* 'trumpet' + *glōssa* 'tongue'.

salpingectomy /,salpɪn'dʒɛktəmi/ ▸ **noun** (pl. **salpingectomies**) [mass noun] surgical removal of the fallopian tubes.

salpingitis /,salpɪn'dʒʌɪtɪs/ ▸ **noun** [mass noun] Medicine inflammation of the fallopian tubes.

salpingo- /'salpɪŋgəʊ/ (also **salping-** before a vowel) ▸ **combining form** relating to the fallopian tubes: *salpingostomy*.
– ORIGIN from Greek *salpinx*, *salping-* 'trumpet'.

salpingostomy /,salpɪŋ'gɒstəmi/ ▸ **noun** [mass noun] surgical unblocking of a blocked fallopian tube.

salsa /'salsə/ ▸ **noun** [mass noun] **1** a type of Latin American dance music incorporating elements of jazz and rock. ■ [count noun] a dance performed to salsa music.
2 (especially in Latin American cookery) a spicy tomato sauce.
– ORIGIN Spanish, literally 'sauce', extended in American Spanish to denote the dance.

salsa verde /,salsə 'vəːdeɪ, 'vəːdi/ ▸ **noun** [mass noun] **1** an Italian sauce made with olive oil, garlic, capers, anchovies, vinegar or lemon juice, and parsley.
2 a Mexican sauce of finely chopped onion, garlic, coriander, parsley, and hot peppers.
– ORIGIN Spanish, literally 'green sauce'.

salsero /sal'sɛːrəʊ/ ▸ **noun** (pl. **salseros**) a salsa musician or dancer.
– ORIGIN Spanish.

salsify /'salsɪfi/ ▸ **noun** [mass noun] an edible European plant of the daisy family, with a long root like that of a parsnip. ● *Tragopogon porrifolius*, family Compositae. ■ the root of the salsify used as a vegetable. Also called VEGETABLE OYSTER.
– ORIGIN late 17th cent.: from French *salsifis*, from obsolete Italian *salsefica*, of unknown ultimate origin.

SALT /sɔːlt, sɒlt/ ▸ **abbreviation** Strategic Arms Limitation Talks.

salt /sɔːlt, sɒlt/ ▸ **noun 1** (also **common salt**) [mass noun] a white crystalline substance which gives seawater its characteristic taste and is used for seasoning or preserving food. ● Alternative name: **sodium chloride**; chem. formula: NaCl. ■ literary something which adds freshness or piquancy: *he described danger as the salt of pleasure*.
2 Chemistry any chemical compound formed from the reaction of an acid with a base, with all or part of the hydrogen of the acid replaced by a metal or other cation.
3 (usu. **old salt**) informal an experienced sailor.
▸ **adjective** [attrib.] **1** impregnated with, treated with, or tasting of salt: *salt water* | *salt beef*.
2 (of a plant) growing on the coast or in salt marshes.
▸ **verb** [with obj.] **1** (usu. as adj. **salted**) season or preserve with salt: *cook the carrots in boiling salted water*. ■ make (something) piquant or more interesting: *there was good talk to salt the occasion*.
2 sprinkle (a road or path) with salt in order to melt snow or ice.
3 informal fraudulently make (a mine) appear to be a paying one by placing rich ore into it.
4 (as adj. **salted**) (of a horse) having developed a resistance to disease by surviving it.
– PHRASES **rub salt into the** (or **someone's**) **wound** make a painful experience even more painful for someone. **the salt of the earth** a person or group of people of great kindness, reliability, or honesty. [with biblical allusion to Matt 5:13.] **sit below the salt** be of lower social standing or worth. [from the former custom of placing a large salt cellar in the middle of a dining table with the host at one end.] **take something with a pinch** (or **grain**) **of salt** regard something as exaggerated; believe only part of something: *I take anything he says with a large pinch of salt*. **worth one's salt** good or competent at the job or profession specified: *any astrologer worth her salt would have predicted this*. **put salt on the tail of** capture (with reference to jocular directions given to children for catching a bird).
– PHRASAL VERBS **salt something away** informal secretly store or put by something, especially money: *they salted the money away in numbered bank accounts around the world*. **salt something out** cause soap to separate from lye by adding salt. ■ Chemistry cause an organic compound to separate from an aqueous solution by adding an electrolyte.
– DERIVATIVES **saltish** adjective, **saltless** adjective, **saltness** noun.
– ORIGIN Old English *sealt* (noun), *sealtan* (verb), of Germanic origin; related to Dutch *zout* and German *Salz* (nouns), from an Indo-European root shared by Latin *sal*, Greek *hals* 'salt'.

salt-and-pepper ▸ **adjective** another way of saying PEPPER-AND-SALT.

saltarello /,saltə'rɛləʊ/ ▸ **noun** (pl. **saltarellos** or **saltarelli** /-li/) an energetic Italian or Spanish dance for one couple, characterized by leaps and skips.
– ORIGIN early 18th cent.: Italian *salterello*, Spanish *saltarelo*, based on Latin *saltare* 'to dance'.

saltation /sal'teɪʃ(ə)n, sɔː-, sɒ-/ ▸ **noun** [mass noun] **1** Biology abrupt evolutionary change; sudden large-scale mutation.
2 Geology the transport of hard particles over an uneven surface in a turbulent flow of air or water.
3 archaic the action of leaping or dancing.
– DERIVATIVES **saltatory** /'saltət(ə)ri, 'sɔː-, 'sɒ-/ **adjective**.
– ORIGIN early 17th cent. (in sense 3): from Latin *saltatio(n-)*, from *saltare* 'to dance', frequentative of *salire* 'to leap'.

saltatorial /,saltə'tɔːrɪəl, sɔː-, sɒ-/ ▸ **adjective** chiefly Entomology (especially of grasshoppers or their limbs) adapted for leaping.

saltbox ▸ **noun** N. Amer. a frame house having up to three storeys at the front and one fewer at the back with a steeply pitched roof.

salt bridge ▸ **noun** Chemistry **1** a tube containing an electrolyte (typically in the form of a gel), providing electrical contact between two solutions.
2 a link between electrically charged acidic and basic groups, especially on different parts of a large molecule such as a protein.

saltbush ▸ **noun** a salt-tolerant orache plant sometimes used in the reclamation of saline soils or to provide grazing in areas of salty soil. ● Genus *Atriplex*, family Chenopodiaceae: several species, in particular the Australian *A. vesicaria*.

salt cellar ▸ **noun** a dish or container for storing salt, now typically a closed container with perforations in the lid for sprinkling. ■ informal a deep hollow that is sometimes evident above the collarbone.
– ORIGIN late Middle English: from SALT + obsolete *saler*, from Old French *salier* 'salt-box', from Latin *salarium* (see SALARY). The change in spelling of the second word was due to association with CELLAR.

salt dome ▸ **noun** a dome-shaped structure in sedimentary rocks, formed where a large mass of salt has been forced upwards. Such structures often form traps for oil or natural gas.

salter ▸ **noun** historical a person dealing in or employed in the production of salt. ■ a person whose work involved the preservation of meat or fish in salt. ■ another term for DRY-SALTER.
– ORIGIN Old English *sealtere* (see SALT, -ER[1]).

saltern /'sɔːltən, 'sɒ-/ ▸ **noun** a set of pools in which seawater is left to evaporate to make salt.
– ORIGIN Old English *sealtærn* 'salt building' (the original use denoting a salt works).

salt finger ▸ **noun** Oceanography one of several alternating columns of rising and descending water produced when a layer of water is overlain by a denser, saltier layer.
– DERIVATIVES **salt fingering** noun.

salt fish ▸ **noun** [mass noun] fish, especially cod, that has been preserved in salt.

salt flats ▸ **plural noun** areas of flat land covered with a layer of salt.

salt glaze ▸ **noun** Pottery a hard glaze with a pitted surface, produced on stoneware by adding salt to the kiln during firing.
– DERIVATIVES **salt-glazed** adjective, **salt glazing** noun.

salt horse ▸ **noun** [mass noun] Nautical slang, archaic salted beef.

Saltillo /sal'tiːjəʊ, -'tiːljəʊ/ a city in northern Mexico, capital of the state of Coahuila, situated in the Sierra Madre south-west of Monterrey; pop. 633,677 (2005).

saltimbocca /,saltɪm'bɒkə/ ▸ **noun** [mass noun] a dish consisting of rolled pieces of veal or poultry cooked with herbs, bacon, and other flavourings.
– ORIGIN Italian, literally 'leap into the mouth'.

saltine /sɔːl'tiːn, sɒ-/ ▸ **noun** N. Amer. a thin crisp savoury biscuit sprinkled with salt.
– ORIGIN from SALT + -INE[4].

salting ▸ **noun** (usu. **saltings**) Brit. an area of coastal land that is regularly covered by the tide.

saltire /'saltʌɪə, 'sɔː-/ ▸ **noun** Heraldry a diagonal cross as a heraldic ordinary. ■ [as modifier] (of a design) incorporating a motif based on such a diagonal cross.

S

– DERIVATIVES **saltirewise** adverb.
– ORIGIN late Middle English: from Old French *saultoir* 'stirrup cord, stile, saltire', based on Latin *saltare* 'to dance'.

salt lake ▶ noun a lake of salt water.

Salt Lake City the capital of Utah, situated near the south-eastern shores of the Great Salt Lake; pop. 181,698 (est. 2008). Founded in 1847 by Brigham Young, the city is the world headquarters of the Church of Jesus Christ of Latter-Day Saints (Mormons).

salt lick ▶ noun a place where animals go to lick salt from the ground. ■ a block of salt provided for animals to lick.

salt marsh ▶ noun an area of coastal grassland that is regularly flooded by seawater.

salt meadow ▶ noun chiefly N. Amer. a meadow that is subject to flooding by seawater; a salt marsh.

salt mine ▶ noun a mine yielding rock salt. ■ (usu. **salt mines**) humorous a job involving demanding or gruelling work: *so it's back to the salt mines here in Cambridge.*

salt pan ▶ noun a shallow container or depression in the ground in which salt water evaporates to leave a deposit of salt.

saltpetre /sɔːlt'piːtə, sɒ-/ (US **saltpeter**) ▶ noun another term for POTASSIUM NITRATE.
– ORIGIN late Middle English: from Old French *salpetre*, from medieval Latin *salpetra*, probably representing *sal petrae* 'salt of rock' (i.e. found as an encrustation). The change in the first element was due to association with SALT.

salt spoon ▶ noun a tiny spoon with a roundish deep bowl, used for serving oneself with salt.

saltus /'saltəs/ ▶ noun literary a sudden transition; a breach of continuity.
– ORIGIN mid 17th cent.: from Latin, literally 'leap'.

saltwater ▶ adjective [attrib.] of or found in salt water; living in the sea: *saltwater fish.*

saltwater crocodile ▶ noun a large and dangerous crocodile occurring in estuaries and coastal waters from SW India to northern Australia. ● *Crocodylus porosus*, family Crocodylidae.

saltwort ▶ noun a plant of the goosefoot family, which typically grows in salt marshes. It is rich in alkali and its ashes were formerly used in soap-making. ● Genus *Salsola*, family Chenopodiaceae.

salty ▶ adjective (**saltier**, **saltiest**) **1** tasting of, containing, or preserved with salt.
2 (of language or humour) down-to-earth; coarse: *her wild ways and salty language shocked the local gentry.*
3 informal tough or aggressive: *a salty campaign strategist.*
– DERIVATIVES **saltily** adverb, **saltiness** noun.

salubrious /sə'luːbrɪəs/ ▶ adjective health-giving; healthy: *odours of far less salubrious origin.* ■ (of a place) pleasant; not run-down.
– DERIVATIVES **salubriously** adverb, **salubriousness** noun, **salubrity** noun.
– ORIGIN mid 16th cent.: from Latin *salubris* (from *salus* 'health') + -OUS.

S

saluki /sə'luːki/ ▶ noun (pl. **salukis**) a tall, swift, slender dog of a silky-coated breed with large drooping ears and fringed feet.
– ORIGIN early 19th cent.: from Arabic *salūqī*.

salut /sa'luː/ ▶ exclamation used to express friendly feelings towards one's companions before drinking.
– ORIGIN French.

salutary /'saljʊt(ə)ri/ ▶ adjective (especially with reference to something unwelcome or unpleasant) producing good effects; beneficial: *it failed to draw salutary lessons from Britain's loss of its colonies.* ■ archaic health-giving: *the salutary Atlantic air.*
– ORIGIN late Middle English (as a noun in the sense 'remedy'): from French *salutaire* or Latin *salutaris*, from *salus, salut-* 'health'.

salutation ▶ noun a gesture or utterance made as a greeting or acknowledgement of another's arrival or departure: *we greeted them but no one returned our salutations* | [mass noun] *he raised his glass in salutation.* ■ a standard formula of words used in a letter to address the person being written to.
– ORIGIN late Middle English: from Old French, or from Latin *salutatio(n-)*, from *salutare* 'pay one's respects to' (see SALUTE).

salutatorian /sə,ljuːtə'tɔːrɪən/ ▶ noun N. Amer. the student ranking second highest in a graduating class who delivers the salutatory.

salutatory /sə'ljuːtət(ə)ri/ ▶ adjective chiefly N. Amer. (especially of an address) relating to or of the nature of a salutation.
▶ noun (pl. **salutatories**) N. Amer. an address of welcome, especially one given as an oration by the student ranking second highest in a graduating class at a university or college.
– ORIGIN late 17th cent. (as an adjective): from Latin *salutatorius*, from *salutare* 'pay one's respects to' (see SALUTE).

salute ▶ noun a gesture of respect or polite recognition, especially one made to or by a person when arriving or departing: *he raises his arms in a triumphant salute.* ■ a prescribed movement, typically a raising of a hand to the head, made by a member of a military or similar force as a formal sign of respect or recognition. ■ [often with modifier] the discharge of a gun or guns as a formal or ceremonial sign of respect or celebration: *a twenty-one-gun salute.* ■ Fencing the formal performance of certain guards or other movements by fencers before engaging.
▶ verb [with obj.] make a formal salute to: *don't you usually salute a superior officer?* | [no obj.] *he clicked his heels and saluted.* ■ greet: *he saluted her with a smile.* ■ show or express admiration and respect for: *we salute a truly great photographer.*
– PHRASES **salute the judge** Austral. informal (of a horse) win a race. **take the salute** (of a senior officer in the armed forces or other person of importance) acknowledge formally a salute given by a body of troops marching past.
– DERIVATIVES **saluter** noun.
– ORIGIN late Middle English: from Latin *salutare* 'greet, pay one's respects to', from *salus, salut-* 'health, welfare, greeting'; the noun partly from Old French *salut*.

Salvador /'salvədɔː/ a port on the Atlantic coast of eastern Brazil, capital of the state of Bahia; pop. 2,892,625 (2007). Founded in 1549, it was the capital of the Portuguese colony until 1763, when the seat of government was transferred to Rio de Janeiro. Former name BAHIA.

Salvadorean /,salvə'dɔːrɪən/ ▶ adjective relating to El Salvador.
▶ noun a native or inhabitant of El Salvador.

salvage ▶ verb [with obj.] rescue (a wrecked or disabled ship or its cargo) from loss at sea: *an emerald and gold cross was salvaged from the wreck.* ■ retrieve or preserve (something) from potential loss or adverse circumstances: *it was the only crumb of comfort he could salvage from the ordeal.*
▶ noun [mass noun] the rescue of a wrecked or disabled ship or its cargo from loss at sea: [as modifier] *a salvage operation was under way.* ■ the cargo saved from a wrecked or sunken ship: *salvage taken from a ship that had sunk in the river.* ■ the rescue of property or material from potential loss or destruction. ■ Law payment made or due to a person who has saved a ship or its cargo.
– DERIVATIVES **salvageable** adjective, **salvager** noun.
– ORIGIN mid 17th cent. (as a noun denoting payment for saving a ship or its cargo): from French, from medieval Latin *salvagium*, from Latin *salvare* 'to save'. The verb dates from the late 19th cent.

salvage yard ▶ noun N. Amer. a place where disused machinery is broken up.

Salvarsan /'salvəsan/ ▶ noun Medicine, historical another term for ARSPHENAMINE.
– ORIGIN early 20th cent.: from German, from Latin *salvare* 'save' + German *Arsenik* 'arsenic' + -AN.

salvation ▶ noun [mass noun] **1** preservation or deliverance from harm, ruin, or loss: *they try to sell it to us as economic salvation.* ■ (**one's salvation**) a source or means of being saved from harm, ruin, or loss: *his only salvation was to outfly the enemy.*
2 Theology deliverance from sin and its consequences, believed by Christians to be brought about by faith in Christ.
– ORIGIN Middle English: from Old French *salvacion*, from ecclesiastical Latin *salvation-* (from *salvare* 'to save'), translating Greek *sōtēria*.

Salvation Army (abbrev.: **SA**) a worldwide Christian evangelical organization on quasi-military lines. Established by William Booth, it is noted for its work with the poor and for its brass bands.

salvationist ▶ noun (**Salvationist**) a member of the Salvation Army.
▶ adjective relating to salvation. ■ (**Salvationist**) relating to the Salvation Army.
– DERIVATIVES **salvationism** noun.

salve[1] ▶ noun an ointment used to promote healing of the skin or as protection. ■ something that is soothing or consoling for wounded feelings or an uneasy conscience: *the idea provided him with a salve for his guilt.*
▶ verb [with obj.] **1** soothe (wounded pride or one's conscience): *charity salves our conscience.*
2 archaic apply salve to.
– ORIGIN Old English *sealfe* (noun), *sealfian* (verb), of Germanic origin; related to Dutch *zalf* and German *Salbe*.

salve[2] ▶ verb archaic term for SALVAGE.
– DERIVATIVES **salvable** adjective.
– ORIGIN early 18th cent.: back-formation from the noun SALVAGE.

salver ▶ noun a tray, typically one made of silver and used in formal circumstances.
– ORIGIN mid 17th cent.: from French *salve* 'tray for presenting food to the king', from Spanish *salva* 'sampling of food', from *salvar* 'make safe'.

Salve Regina /,salveɪ rə'dʒiːnə/ ▶ noun a Roman Catholic hymn or prayer said or sung after compline, and after the Divine Office from Trinity Sunday to Advent.
– ORIGIN the opening words in Latin, 'hail (holy) queen'.

salvia ▶ noun a widely distributed plant of a genus including the sages, especially (in gardening) a bedding plant cultivated for its spikes of bright flowers. ● Genus *Salvia*, family Labiatae: many species, in particular the scarlet-flowered *S. splendens*.
– ORIGIN modern Latin, from Latin *salvia* 'sage'.

salvific /sal'vɪfɪk/ ▶ adjective Theology leading to salvation.
– ORIGIN late 16th cent.: from Latin *salvificus* 'saving', from *salvus* 'safe'.

Salvo ▶ noun (pl. **Salvos**) Austral. informal a member of the Salvation Army.
– ORIGIN late 19th cent.: abbreviation of SALVATION.

salvo ▶ noun (pl. **salvos** or **salvoes**) a simultaneous discharge of artillery or other guns in a battle. ■ a number of weapons released from one or more aircraft in quick succession. ■ a sudden, vigorous, or aggressive act or series of acts: *the pardons provoked a salvo of accusations.*
– ORIGIN late 16th cent. (earlier as *salve*): from French *salve*, Italian *salva* 'salutation'.

sal volatile /,sal və'latɪli/ ▶ noun [mass noun] a scented solution of ammonium carbonate in alcohol, used as smelling salts.
– ORIGIN mid 17th cent.: modern Latin, literally 'volatile salt'.

salvor /'salvə, 'salvɔː/ ▶ noun a person engaged in salvage of a ship or items lost at sea.

salwar /sʌl'wɑː/ (also **shalwar**) ▶ noun a pair of light, loose, pleated trousers, usually tapering to a tight fit around the ankles, worn by women from South Asia typically with a kameez (the two together being a **salwar kameez**).
– ORIGIN from Persian and Urdu *šalwār*.

Salween /'salwiːn, sal'wiːn/ a river of SE Asia, which rises in Tibet and flows for 2,400 km (1,500 miles) south-east and south through Burma to the Gulf of Martaban, an inlet of the Andaman Sea.

Salyut /sa'ljuːt, 'saljuːt/ a series of seven Soviet manned orbiting space stations, launched between 1971 and 1982.
– ORIGIN Russian, used as a greeting; compare with French SALUT.

Salzburg /'saltsbəːg, 'sɔːlts-/, German /'zaltsbʊrk/ a city in western Austria, near the border with Germany, the capital of a state of the same name; pop 146,972 (2006). It is noted for its annual music festivals, one of which is dedicated to the composer Mozart, who was born in the city in 1756.

Salzgitter /'salts,gɪtə, 'sɔːlts-/, German /'zalts,gɪtɐ/ an industrial city in Germany, in Lower Saxony south-east of Hanover; pop. 106,700 (est. 2006).

Salzkammergut /'saltskamə,guːt, 'sɔːlts-/, German /'zaltskamɐ,guːt/ a resort area of lakes and mountains in the state of Salzburg in western Austria.

SAM ▶ abbreviation surface-to-air missile.

Sam. ▶ abbreviation Samuel (in biblical references).

samadhi /sʌ'mɑːdi/ ▶ noun (pl. **samadhis**) **1** [mass noun] Hinduism & Buddhism a state of intense concentra-

tion achieved through meditation. In yoga this is regarded as the final stage, at which union with the divine is reached (before or at death).
2 Indian a tomb.
– ORIGIN from Sanskrit *samādhi* 'contemplation'.

saman /sa'mɑːn/ (also **samaan, saman tree**) ▸ **noun** West Indian term for RAIN TREE.
– ORIGIN Latin American Spanish.

samango /sa'maŋgəʊ/ (also **samango monkey**) ▸ **noun** (pl. **samangos**) S. African an African guenon which has blue-grey fur with black markings.
• *Cercopithecus mitis*, family Cercopithecidae. Alternative name: **diademed monkey**.
– ORIGIN late 19th cent.: from Zulu *insimango*.

Samar /'sɑːmɑː/ an island in the Philippines, situated to the south-east of Luzon; pop. 1,650,000 (est. 2007). It is the third-largest island of the group.

Samara /sə'mɑːrə/ a city and river port in SW central Russia, situated on the Volga at its confluence with the River Samara; pop. 1,135,400 (est. 2008). Former name (1935–91) KUIBYSHEV.

samara /'samərə, sə'mɑːrə/ ▸ **noun** Botany a winged nut or achene containing one seed, as in ash and maple.
– ORIGIN late 16th cent.: modern Latin, from Latin, denoting an elm seed.

Samaria /sə'mɛːrɪə/ **1** an ancient city of central Palestine, founded in the 9th century BC as the capital of the northern Hebrew kingdom of Israel. The ancient site is situated in the modern West Bank, north-west of Nablus.
2 the region of ancient Palestine around Samaria, between Galilee in the north and Judaea in the south.

Samarinda /ˌsamə'rɪndə/ a city in Indonesia, in eastern Borneo; pop. 505,700 (est. 2005).

Samaritan ▸ **noun 1** (usu. **Good Samaritan**) a charitable or helpful person (with reference to Luke 10:33).
2 a member of a people inhabiting Samaria in biblical times, or of the modern community claiming descent from them, adhering to a form of Judaism accepting only its own ancient version of the Pentateuch as Scripture.
3 [mass noun] the dialect of Aramaic formerly spoken in Samaria.
4 (**the Samaritans**) (in the UK) an organization which counsels the suicidal and others in distress, mainly through a telephone service.
▸ **adjective** relating to Samaria or the Samaritans.
– DERIVATIVES **Samaritanism** noun.
– ORIGIN from late Latin *Samaritanus*, from Greek *Samareitēs*, from *Samareia* 'Samaria'. The New Testament parable of the Good Samaritan reflects a proverbial hostility between Jews and Samaritans.

samarium /sə'mɛːrɪəm/ ▸ **noun** [mass noun] the chemical element of atomic number 62, a hard silvery white metal of the lanthanide series. (Symbol: **Sm**)
– ORIGIN late 19th cent.: from *samar(skite)*, a mineral in which its spectrum was first observed (named after *Samarsky*, a 19th-cent. Russian official) + -IUM.

Samarkand /ˌsamɑː'kand, 'saməkand/ (also **Samarqand**) a city in eastern Uzbekistan; pop. 312,900 (est. 2007). One of the oldest cities of Asia, it was founded in the 3rd or 4th millennium BC. It grew to prominence as a prosperous centre of the silk trade, situated on the Silk Road, and in the 14th century became the capital of Tamerlane's Mongol empire.

Samarra /sə'mɑːrə/ a city in Iraq, on the River Tigris north of Baghdad; pop. 214,100 (est. 2004).

Sama Veda /sɑːmə 'veɪdə/ Hinduism one of the four Vedas, a collection of melodies and liturgical chants. Its material is drawn largely from the Rig Veda. See VEDA.
– ORIGIN from Sanskrit *sāmaveda*, from *sāman* 'chant' and *veda* '(sacred) knowledge'.

samba /'sambə/ ▸ **noun** a Brazilian dance of African origin. ▪ a piece of music for the samba. ▪ a lively modern ballroom dance imitating the samba.
▸ **verb** (**sambas, sambaing** /-bə(r)ɪŋ/, **sambaed** /-bəd/ or **samba'd**) [no obj.] dance the samba.
– ORIGIN late 19th cent.: from Portuguese, of African origin.

sambal /'sambal/ ▸ **noun** (in oriental cookery) hot relish made with vegetables or fruit and spices.
– ORIGIN Malay.

sambar¹ /'sambɑː/ ▸ **noun** a dark brown woodland deer with branched antlers, of southern Asia. • *Cervus unicolor*, family Cervidae.
– ORIGIN late 17th cent.: from Hindi *sābar*, from Sanskrit *śambara*.

sambar² (also **sambhar**) ▸ **noun** [mass noun] a spicy south Indian dish consisting of lentils and vegetables.
– ORIGIN from Tamil *cāmpār*, via Marathi from Sanskrit *sambhāra* 'collection, materials'.

Sambo ▸ **noun** (pl. **Sambos** or **Samboes**) **1** offensive a black person.
2 (**sambo**) historical a person of mixed race, especially of black and Indian or black and European blood.
– ORIGIN early 18th cent.: sense 1 perhaps from Fula *sambo* 'uncle'; sense 2 from American Spanish *zambo*, denoting a kind of yellow monkey.

Sam Browne (also **Sam Browne belt**) ▸ **noun** a leather belt with a supporting strap that passes over the right shoulder, worn by army and police officers.
– ORIGIN early 20th cent.: named after Sir *Sam* uel J. *Brown(e)* (1824–1901), the British military commander who invented it.

sambuca /sam'bʊkə/ ▸ **noun** [mass noun] an Italian aniseed-flavoured liqueur.
– ORIGIN Italian, from Latin *sambucus* 'elder tree'.

Samburu /sam'bʊruː/ ▸ **noun** (pl. **same**) **1** a member of a mainly pastoral people of northern Kenya.
2 [mass noun] the Nilotic language of the Samburu.
▸ **adjective** relating to the Samburu or their language.
– ORIGIN a local name.

same ▸ **adjective** (**the same**) **1** identical; not different: *she was saying the same thing over and over* | *I have never made the same mistake since* | *I'm* ***the same*** *age as you are* | ***the very same*** *people who practised all the rules are now the most sceptical* | [with clause] *he put on the same costume that he had worn in Ottawa.* | *she was still the* ***same old*** *Beth.* ▪ not having changed; unchanged: *he's worked at the same place for quite a few years.* ▪ used to emphasize that one is referring to a particular, unique person or thing: *people will always notice if you wear the same shirt two days running* | *they drank out of the same glass.* ▪ (**this/that same**) referring to a person or thing just mentioned: *that same year I went to Boston.*
2 of an identical type; exactly similar: *they all wore the same clothes.*
▸ **pronoun 1** (**the same**) the same thing as something previously mentioned: *I'll resign and encourage everyone else to do the same.* ▪ (chiefly in formal or legal use) the person or thing just mentioned: *put the tailboard up and secure same with a length of wire.*
2 people or things that are identical or share the same characteristics: *there are several brands and they're not all the same.*
▸ **adverb** similarly; in the same way: *treating women the* ***same as*** *men* | *he gave me five dollars,* ***same as*** *usual.*
– PHRASES **all** (or **just**) **the same** in spite of this; nevertheless: *she knew they had meant it kindly, but it had hurt all the same.* ▪ in any case; anyway: *thanks all the same, but I've something better to do.* **at the same time** see TIME. **be all the same to** be unimportant to (someone) what happens: *it was all the same to me where it was being sold.* **by the same token** see TOKEN. **one and the same** the same person or thing (used for emphasis). **same again** another drink of the same kind as the last (said as a request or offer). **same difference** informal used to express the speaker's belief that two or more things are essentially the same, in spite of apparent differences. **same here** informal the same applies to me. **same old, same old** used to convey that something is drearily predictable or familiar: *the game's fantasy setting is the same old, same old.* (**the**) **same to you!** may you do or have the same thing (a response to a greeting or insult).
– ORIGIN Middle English: from Old Norse *sami*, from an Indo-European root shared by Sanskrit *sama*, Greek *homos*.

sameness ▸ **noun** [mass noun] lack of variety; uniformity or monotony: *there is a sameness about all the political parties.* ▪ the quality of being the same; identity or similarity: *sameness of meaning across different languages.*

samey ▸ **adjective** (**samier, samiest**) Brit. informal lacking in variety; monotonous.
– DERIVATIVES **sameyness** noun.

samfi /'samfi/ (also **samfie**) ▸ **noun** W. Indian a swindler or confidence trickster: [as modifier] *a samfi man.*
– ORIGIN probably from an African language.

samfu /'samfuː/ ▸ **noun** a light suit consisting of a plain high-necked jacket and loose trousers, worn by women from China.
– ORIGIN 1950s: from Chinese (Cantonese dialect) *shaam foò*, from *shaam* 'coat' + *foò* 'trousers'.

Samhain /saʊn, 'saʊɪn, 'sawɪn/, Irish /'səʊnʲ/ ▸ **noun** the first day of November, celebrated by the ancient Celts as a festival marking the beginning of winter.
– ORIGIN Irish, from Old Irish *samain*.

Sam Hill ▸ **noun** N. Amer. informal used in exclamations as a euphemism for 'hell': *what in Sam Hill is that?*
– ORIGIN mid 19th cent.: of unknown origin.

Sami /'sɑːmi, sɑːm/ ▸ **plural noun** the Lapps of northern Scandinavia.
– ORIGIN Lappish, of unknown origin.

> **USAGE** Sami is the term by which the Lapps themselves prefer to be known. Its use is becoming increasingly common, although **Lapp** is still the main term in general use.

Samian /'seɪmɪən/ ▸ **noun** a native or inhabitant of Samos.
▸ **adjective** relating to Samos.

Samian ware ▸ **noun** [mass noun] a type of fine, glossy, reddish-brown pottery widely made in the Roman Empire. Also called TERRA SIGILLATA.

samisen /'samɪsɛn/ (also **shamisen** /'ʃamɪsɛn/) ▸ **noun** a traditional Japanese three-stringed lute with a square body, played with a large plectrum.
– ORIGIN early 17th cent.: Japanese, from Chinese *san-hsien*, from *san* 'three' + *hsien* 'string'.

samite /'samʌɪt, seɪ-/ ▸ **noun** [mass noun] historical a rich silk fabric interwoven with gold and silver threads, used for dressmaking and decoration in the Middle Ages.
– ORIGIN Middle English: from Old French *samit*, via medieval Latin from medieval Greek *hexamiton*, from Greek *hexa-* 'six' + *mitos* 'thread'.

samiti /'samɪti/ ▸ **noun** (pl. **samitis**) Indian a committee, society, or association.
– ORIGIN 1930s: Hindi, from Sanskrit, 'meeting, committee'.

samizdat /'samɪzdat, ˌsamɪz'dat/ ▸ **noun** [mass noun] the clandestine copying and distribution of literature banned by the state, especially formerly in the communist countries of eastern Europe.
– ORIGIN 1960s: Russian, literally 'self-publishing house'.

sammie ▸ **noun** Austral./NZ informal a sandwich.
– ORIGIN 1970s: representing a pronunciation of the first syllable of SANDWICH, modified by following *w*, + -IE.

Samnite /'samnʌɪt/ ▸ **noun** a member of an Oscan-speaking people of southern Italy in ancient times, who spent long periods at war with republican Rome in the 4th to 1st centuries BC.
▸ **adjective** relating to this people.
– ORIGIN from Latin *Samnites* (plural); related to *Sabinus* (see SABINE).

Samoa /sə'məʊə/ a group of islands in Polynesia, divided between American Samoa and the state of Samoa. ▪ a country consisting of the western islands of Samoa; pop. 220,000 (est. 2009); official languages, Samoan and English; capital, Apia.

> First visited by the Dutch in the early 18th century, the islands were divided administratively in 1899 into American Samoa in the east and German Samoa in the west. After the First World War the nine western islands were mandated to New Zealand, and became an independent republic within the Commonwealth in 1962, as Western Samoa. The country became known as Samoa in 1997.

S

Samoan ▸ **adjective** relating to Samoa, its people, or their language.
▸ **noun 1** a native or inhabitant of Samoa.
2 [mass noun] the Polynesian language of Samoa, which has over 300,000 speakers in Samoa, New Zealand, the US, and elsewhere.

Samos /'seɪmɒs/ a Greek island in the Aegean, situated close to the coast of western Turkey.

samosa /sə'məʊsə/ ▸ **noun** a triangular savoury pastry fried in ghee or oil, containing spiced vegetables or meat.
– ORIGIN from Persian and Urdu.

samovar /'saməvɑː, ˌsamə'vɑː/ ▸ **noun** a highly decorated tea urn used in Russia.
– ORIGIN Russian, literally 'self-boiler'.

Samoyed /'samәjɛd, ˌsamɔɪ'ɛd/ ▸ **noun 1** a member of a group of mainly nomadic peoples of northern Siberia, who traditionally live as reindeer herders.
2 [mass noun] any of several Samoyedic (Uralic) languages of the Samoyeds. ▪ another term for SAMOYEDIC.
3 a dog of a white Arctic breed.
– ORIGIN from Russian *samoed*.

Samoyedic /ˌsaməˈjɛdɪk, ˌsamɔɪ-/ ▶ **noun** [mass noun] a group of Uralic languages of northern Siberia, of which the most widely spoken is Nenets.
▶ **adjective** relating to the Samoyeds or their languages.

samp ▶ **noun** [mass noun] US & S. African coarsely ground Indian corn, or a kind of porridge made from it.
– ORIGIN mid 17th cent.: from Algonquian *nasamp* 'softened by water'.

sampan /ˈsampan/ ▶ **noun** a small boat of a kind used in East Asia, typically with an oar or oars at the stern.
– ORIGIN early 17th cent.: from Chinese *san-ban*, from *san* 'three' + *ban* 'board'.

samphire /ˈsamfʌɪə/ ▶ **noun** (also **rock samphire**) a European plant of the parsley family, which grows on rocks and cliffs by the sea. Its aromatic fleshy leaves are sometimes eaten as a vegetable. ● *Crithmum maritimum*, family Umbelliferae.
■ used in names of fleshy-leaved plants resembling samphire that grow near the sea, e.g. **golden samphire**.
– ORIGIN mid 16th cent. (earlier as *sampiere*): from French (*herbe de*) *Saint Pierre* 'St Peter('s herb)'.

sampladelic ▶ **adjective** denoting a type of dance music that is psychedelic or disorientating in nature and created using samples and other digital technology: *sampladelic and soulful jungle*.
– DERIVATIVES **sampladelia** noun.

sample ▶ **noun 1** a small part or quantity intended to show what the whole is like: *investigations involved analysing samples of handwriting*. ■ a small amount of a food or other commodity, especially one given to a prospective customer. ■ a specimen taken for scientific testing or analysis: *a urine sample*. ■ Statistics a portion drawn from a population, the study of which is intended to lead to statistical estimates of the attributes of the whole population.
2 a sound or piece of music created by sampling.
▶ **verb** [with obj.] **1** take a sample or samples of (something) for analysis: *bone marrow cells were sampled*. ■ try the qualities of (food or drink) by tasting it. ■ get a representative experience of: *sample some entertaining nights out in Liverpool*.
2 Electronics ascertain the momentary value of (an analogue signal) many times a second so as to convert the signal to digital form. ■ record or extract (a small piece of music or sound) digitally for reuse as part of a composition or song: *riffs sampled from other musicians* | (as noun **sampling**) *sampling is bringing older music to younger ears*.
– ORIGIN Middle English (as a noun): from an Anglo-Norman French variant of Old French *essample* 'example'. Current senses of the verb date from the mid 18th cent.

sample bag ▶ **noun** another term for **SHOW BAG**.

sample point ▶ **noun** Statistics a single possible observed value of a variable.

sampler ▶ **noun 1** a piece of embroidery worked in various stitches as a specimen of skill, typically containing the alphabet and some mottoes.
2 a representative collection or example of something: *a sampler of rock plants*.
3 a person or device that takes and analyses samples.
4 an electronic device for sampling music and sound.
– ORIGIN Middle English (denoting an example to be imitated): from Old French *essamplaire* 'exemplar'.

S

sample space ▶ **noun** Statistics the range of values of a random variable.

sampling error ▶ **noun** [mass noun] Statistics error in a statistical analysis arising from the unrepresentativeness of the sample taken.

sampling frame ▶ **noun** Statistics a list of the items or people forming a population from which a sample is taken.

samplist ▶ **noun** a musician or performer who samples music.

samsara /sʌmˈsɑːrə/ ▶ **noun** Hinduism & Buddhism the material world. ■ [mass noun] the cycle of death and rebirth to which life in the material world is bound.
– DERIVATIVES **samsaric** adjective.
– ORIGIN from Sanskrit *saṃsāra*.

samskara /sʌmˈskɑːrə/ ▶ **noun** Hinduism a purificatory ceremony or rite marking a major event in one's life.
– ORIGIN from Sanskrit *saṃskāra* 'an act of making perfect, preparation'.

Samson an Israelite leader (probably 11th century BC) famous for his strength (Judges 13–16). He fell in love with Delilah and confided to her that his strength lay in his uncut hair. She betrayed him to the Philistines who cut off his hair and blinded him, but his hair grew again, and he pulled down the pillars of a house, destroying himself and a large gathering of Philistines.

Samson post ▶ **noun** a strong pillar fixed to a ship's deck to act as a support for a tackle or other equipment.
– ORIGIN late 16th cent. (denoting a kind of mousetrap): probably with biblical allusion to **SAMSON**.

Samuel (in the Bible) a Hebrew prophet who rallied the Israelites after their defeat by the Philistines and became their ruler. ■ either of two books of the Bible covering the history of ancient Israel from Samuel's birth to the end of the reign of David.

samurai /ˈsam(j)ʊrʌɪ/ ▶ **noun** (pl. **same**) historical a member of a powerful military caste in feudal Japan.
– ORIGIN Japanese.

SAN ▶ **abbreviation** Computing storage area network.

San /sɑːn/ ▶ **noun** (pl. **same**) **1** a member of the aboriginal peoples of southern Africa commonly called Bushmen. See **BUSHMAN**.
2 [mass noun] the group of Khoisan languages spoken by the San. ■ any of the San languages.
▶ **adjective** relating to the San or their languages.
– ORIGIN from Nama *sān* 'aboriginals, settlers'.

san ▶ **noun** informal term for **SANATORIUM**.

-san ▶ **suffix** (in Japan) an honorific title added to a personal or family name as a mark of politeness: *Yamagouchi-san*.
– ORIGIN Japanese, contraction of more formal *sama*.

Sana'a /saˈnɑː, ˈsɑːnə/ (also **Sanaa**) the capital of Yemen; pop. 1,707,500 (est. 2004).

San Andreas fault /ˌsan anˈdreɪəs/ a fault line extending for some 965 km (600 miles) through the length of coastal California. Seismic activity is common along its course and is due to two crustal plates sliding past each other along the line of the fault.

San Antonio /san anˈtəʊnɪəʊ/ an industrial city in south central Texas; pop. 1,351,305 (est. 2008). It is the site of the Alamo mission.

sanative /ˈsanətɪv/ ▶ **adjective** archaic conducive to physical or spiritual health and well-being; healing.
– ORIGIN late Middle English: from Old French *sanatif* or late Latin *sanativus*, from Latin *sanare* 'to cure'.

sanatorium /ˌsanəˈtɔːrɪəm/ ▶ **noun** (pl. **sanatoriums** or **sanatoria** /-rɪə/) an establishment for the medical treatment of people who are convalescing or have a chronic illness. ■ Brit. a room or building for sick children in a boarding school.
– ORIGIN mid 19th cent.: modern Latin, based on Latin *sanare* 'heal'.

Sancerre /sɒ̃ˈsɛː/, French /sɑ̃sɛʀ/ ▶ **noun** [mass noun] a light wine, typically white, produced in the part of France around Sancerre.

Sanchi /ˈsɑːntʃi/ the site in Madhya Pradesh of several well-preserved ancient Buddhist stupas.

Sancho Panza /ˌsantʃəʊ ˈpanzə/ the squire of Don Quixote. He is an uneducated peasant but has a store of proverbial wisdom, and is thus a foil to his master.

sancoche /saŋˈkɒtʃ, -kɒʃ, -kɒtʃi/ (also **sancocho** /-ˈkɒtʃəʊ/) ▶ **noun** [mass noun] (in South America and the Caribbean) a thick soup consisting of meat and root vegetables.
– ORIGIN from Latin American Spanish *sancocho* 'a stew'.

sanctify /ˈsaŋ(k)tɪfʌɪ/ ▶ **verb** (**sanctifies**, **sanctifying**, **sanctified**) [with obj.] set apart as or declare holy; consecrate: *a small shrine was built to sanctify the site*. ■ make legitimate or binding by a religious ceremony: *their love is sanctified by the sacrament of marriage*. ■ free from sin; purify: *may God sanctify his soul*. ■ cause to be or seem morally right or acceptable: *ancient customs that are sanctified by tradition*.
– DERIVATIVES **sanctification** noun, **sanctifier** noun.
– ORIGIN late Middle English: from Old French *saintifier* (influenced later by *sanctifier*), from ecclesiastical Latin *sanctificare*, from Latin *sanctus* 'holy'.

sanctimonious /ˌsaŋ(k)tɪˈməʊnɪəs/ ▶ **adjective** derogatory making a show of being morally superior to other people: *what happened to all the sanctimonious talk about putting his family first?*
– DERIVATIVES **sanctimoniously** adverb, **sanctimoniousness** noun, **sanctimony** /ˈsaŋ(k)tɪməni/ noun.
– ORIGIN early 17th cent. (in the sense 'holy in character'): from Latin *sanctimonia* 'sanctity' (from *sanctus* 'holy') + **-OUS**.

sanction ▶ **noun 1** a threatened penalty for disobeying a law or rule: *a range of sanctions aimed at deterring insider abuse*. ■ (**sanctions**) measures taken by a state to coerce another to conform to an international agreement or norms of conduct, typically in the form of restrictions on trade or official sporting participation. ■ Philosophy a consideration operating to enforce obedience to any rule of conduct.
2 [mass noun] official permission or approval for an action: *he appealed to the bishop for his sanction*. ■ official confirmation or ratification of a law. ■ [count noun] Law, historical a law or decree, especially an ecclesiastical decree.
▶ **verb** [with obj.] **1** give official permission or approval for (an action): *the scheme was sanctioned by the court*.
2 impose a sanction or penalty on.
– DERIVATIVES **sanctionable** adjective.
– ORIGIN late Middle English (as a noun denoting an ecclesiastical decree): from French, from Latin *sanctio(n-)*, from *sancire* 'ratify'. The verb dates from the late 18th cent.

sanctitude ▶ **noun** [mass noun] formal the state or quality of being holy, sacred, or saintly.
– ORIGIN late Middle English: from Latin *sanctitudo*, from *sanctus* 'holy'.

sanctity ▶ **noun** (pl. **sanctities**) [mass noun] **1** the state or quality of being holy, sacred, or saintly: *the site of the tomb was a place of sanctity for the ancient Egyptians*.
2 ultimate importance and inviolability: *the sanctity of human life*.
– ORIGIN late Middle English (in the sense 'saintliness'): from Old French *saintite*, reinforced by Latin *sanctitas*, from *sanctus* 'holy'.

sanctuary ▶ **noun** (pl. **sanctuaries**) **1** [mass noun] refuge or safety from pursuit, persecution, or other danger: *his sons took sanctuary in the church* | [count noun] *she thought of her room as a sanctuary*.
2 a nature reserve: *a bird sanctuary*. ■ a place where injured or unwanted animals of a specified kind are cared for: *a donkey sanctuary*.
3 a holy place; a temple. ■ the inmost recess or holiest part of a temple. ■ the part of the chancel of a church containing the high altar.
– ORIGIN Middle English (in sense 3): from Old French *sanctuaire*, from Latin *sanctuarium*, from *sanctus* 'holy'. Early use in reference to a church or other sacred place where a fugitive was immune, by the law of the medieval Church, from arrest, gave rise to sense 1, sense 2.

sanctuary lamp ▶ **noun** a candle or small light left lit in the sanctuary of a church, especially (in Catholic churches) a red lamp indicating the presence of the reserved Sacrament.

sanctum /ˈsaŋ(k)təm/ ▶ **noun** (pl. **sanctums**) **1** a sacred place, especially a shrine within a temple or church.
2 a private place from which most people are excluded.
– ORIGIN late 16th cent.: from Latin, neuter of *sanctus* 'holy', from *sancire* 'consecrate'.

sanctum sanctorum /saŋ(k)ˈtɔːrəm/ ▶ **noun** (pl. **sancta sanctorum** or **sanctum sanctorums**) the holy of holies in the Jewish temple.
– ORIGIN late Middle English: Latin *sanctum* (see **SANCTUM**) + *sanctorum* 'of holy places', translating Hebrew *qōḏeš haqqŏḏāšîm* 'holy of holies'.

Sanctus /ˈsaŋ(k)təs/ ▶ **noun** Christian Church a hymn beginning *Sanctus, sanctus, sanctus* (Holy, holy, holy) forming a set part of the Mass.
– ORIGIN late Middle English: from Latin, literally 'holy'.

sanctus bell ▶ **noun** another term for **SACRING BELL**.

Sand /sɒ̃/, George (1804–76), French novelist; pseudonym of *Amandine-Aurore Lucille Dupin, Baronne Dudevant*. Her earlier novels, including *Lélia* (1833), portray women's struggles against conventional morals; she later wrote a number of pastoral novels, such as *La Mare au diable* (1846).

sand ▶ **noun** [mass noun] **1** a loose granular substance, typically pale yellowish brown, resulting from the erosion of siliceous and other rocks and forming a major constituent of beaches, river beds, the seabed, and deserts. ■ (**sands**) an expanse of sand, typically along a shore: [in place names] *Goodwin Sands*. ■ [count noun] a stratum of sandstone or compacted sand. ■ technical sediment whose particles are larger than silt (typically greater than 0.06 mm).
2 a light yellow-brown colour like that of sand.
3 N. Amer. informal firmness of purpose: *no one has the sand to stand against him*.
▶ **verb** [with obj.] **1** smooth or polish with sandpaper or a mechanical sander: *mask off the area to be painted*

and sand it down | (as noun **sanding**) *some recommend a light sanding between the second and third coats.*
2 sprinkle or overlay with sand, to give better purchase on a surface.
– PHRASES **drive** (or **run**) (**something**) **into the sand** come (or bring something) to a halt: *the initiative seems to be running into the sand.* **the sands** (**of time**) **are running out** the allotted time is nearly at an end. [with reference to the sand of an hourglass.]
– DERIVATIVES **sand-like** adjective.
– ORIGIN Old English, of Germanic origin; related to Dutch *zand* and German *Sand*.

sandal[1] ▶ noun a light shoe with either an openwork upper or straps attaching the sole to the foot.
– DERIVATIVES **sandalled** (US **sandaled**) adjective.
– ORIGIN late Middle English: via Latin from Greek *sandalion*, diminutive of *sandalon* 'wooden shoe', probably of Asiatic origin; compare with Persian *sandal*.

sandal[2] ▶ noun short for SANDALWOOD.

sandalwood ▶ noun (also **white sandalwood**) a widely cultivated Indian tree which yields fragrant timber and oil. ● *Santalum album*, family Santalaceae.
■ [mass noun] a perfume or incense derived from the timber of the sandalwood. ■ used in names of trees which yield timber similar to that of the sandalwood, e.g. **red sandalwood**.
– ORIGIN early 16th cent.: *sandal* from medieval Latin *sandalum* (based on Sanskrit *candana*) + WOOD.

Sandalwood Island another name for SUMBA.

sandarac /'sandərak/ (also **gum sandarac**) ▶ noun [mass noun] a gum resin obtained from the alerce (cypress) of Spain and North Africa, used in making varnish.
– ORIGIN late Middle English (denoting realgar): from Latin *sandaraca*, from Greek *sandarakē*, of Asiatic origin. The current sense dates from the mid 17th cent.

Sandawe /san'dɑːweɪ/ ▶ noun 1 (pl. **same** or **Sandawes**) a member of an indigenous people of Tanzania.
2 [mass noun] the Khoisan language of the Sandawe.
▶ adjective relating to the Sandawe or their language.

sandbag ▶ noun a bag filled with sand, typically used for defensive purposes or as ballast in a boat.
▶ verb (**sandbags**, **sandbagging**, **sandbagged**) [with obj.] 1 (usu. as adj. **sandbagged**) barricade using sandbags: *boarded-up shopfronts and sandbagged doorways.*
2 hit or knock over with or as if with a blow from a sandbag. ■ N. Amer. coerce or bully.
3 [no obj.] deliberately underperform in a race or competition to gain an unfair advantage.
– DERIVATIVES **sandbagger** noun.

sandbank ▶ noun a deposit of sand forming a shallow area in the sea or a river.

sandbar ▶ noun a long, narrow sandbank, especially at the mouth of a river.

sand bath ▶ noun a container of heated sand, used in a laboratory to supply uniform heating.

sandblast ▶ verb [with obj.] roughen or clean (a surface) with a jet of sand driven by compressed air or steam.
▶ noun such a jet of sand.
– DERIVATIVES **sandblaster** noun.

sandboard ▶ noun a long, narrow board, often a modified snowboard, used for sliding down sand dunes.
– DERIVATIVES **sandboarder** noun, **sandboarding** noun.

sandbox ▶ noun 1 a box containing sand, especially one kept on a train to hold sand for sprinkling on to slippery rails. ■ historical a perforated container for sprinkling sand on to wet ink in order to dry it. ■ N. Amer. a children's sandpit. ■ Computing a virtual space in which new or untested software can be run securely.
2 (also **sandbox tree**) a tropical American tree whose seed cases were formerly used to hold sand for blotting ink. ● *Hura crepitans*, family Euphorbiaceae.
Golf

sandboy ▶ noun (in phrase (**as**) **happy as a sandboy**) extremely happy or carefree.
– ORIGIN probably originally denoting a boy hawking sand for sale.

sandcastle ▶ noun a model of a castle built out of sand, typically by children.

sand cat ▶ noun a small wild cat with a plain yellow to greyish coat, a dark-ringed tail, and large eyes, of the deserts of North Africa and SW Asia. ● *Felis margarita*, family Felidae.

sand cherry ▶ noun a dwarf North American wild cherry tree. ● Genus *Prunus*, family Rosaceae: two species.
■ the fruit of the sand cherry.

sand crack ▶ noun a vertical fissure in the wall of a horse's hoof, originating at the top of the hoof.

sand dab ▶ noun a small flatfish which is found in the Pacific coastal waters of America. ● Genus *Citharichthys*, family Bothidae: several species.
■ another term for WINDOWPANE (sense 2).

sand dollar ▶ noun a flattened sea urchin which lives partly buried in sand, feeding on detritus. ● Order Clypeasteroida, class Echinoidea.

sand eel ▶ noun a small elongated marine fish which lives in shallow waters of the northern hemisphere, often found burrowing in the sand. ● Family Ammodytidae: several genera and species, including the European *Ammodytes tobianus*.

sander ▶ noun a power tool used for smoothing a surface with sandpaper or other abrasive material.

sanderling /'sandəlɪŋ/ ▶ noun a small migratory sandpiper of northern Eurasia and Canada, typically seen running after receding waves on the beach. ● *Calidris alba*, family Scolopacidae.
– ORIGIN early 17th cent.: of unknown origin.

sanders /'sɑːndəz, 'san-/ (also **sanderswood**) ▶ noun [mass noun] the timber of the red sandalwood, from which a red dye is obtained. ● This timber is obtained from *Pterocarpus santalinus*, family Leguminosae.
– ORIGIN Middle English: from Old French *sandre*, variant of *sandle* 'sandalwood'.

sandesh /sʌn'deɪʃ/ ▶ noun [mass noun] an Indian sweet made from paneer and sugar and cut into squares.
– ORIGIN from Bengali *sandeś*.

sand filter ▶ noun a filter used in water purification and consisting of layers of sand arranged with coarseness of texture increasing downwards.

sandfish ▶ noun (pl. **same** or **sandfishes**) 1 a small marine fish with fringed lips, which burrows in the sand, in particular: ● an elongated Australian fish (*Crapatulus arenarius*, family Leptoscopidae). ● a North Pacific fish (*Trichodon trichodon*, family Trichodontidae).
2 (**belted sandfish**) a small sea bass which lives only in shallow inshore waters around Florida. ● *Serranus subligarius*, family Serranidae.

sand flea ▶ noun 1 another term for CHIGGER (sense 1).
2 another term for SANDHOPPER.

sandfly ▶ noun (pl. **sandflies**) 1 a small hairy biting fly of tropical and subtropical regions, which transmits a number of diseases including leishmaniasis. ● Subfamily Phlebotominae, family Psychodidae: several genera, in particular *Phlebotomus*.
2 Austral./NZ another term for BLACKFLY (sense 2).

sandglass ▶ noun an hourglass measuring a fixed amount of time (not necessarily one hour).

Sandgroper ▶ noun Austral. informal a Western Australian.
– ORIGIN late 19th cent.: so named because of the large amount of sand in Western Australia.

sandgrouse ▶ noun (pl. **same**) a seed-eating ground-dwelling bird with brownish plumage, allied to the pigeons and found in the deserts and arid regions of the Old World. ● Family Pteroclididae, genera *Pterocles* and *Syrrhaptes*: several species.

sandhi /'sʌndi/ ▶ noun [mass noun] Grammar the process whereby the form of a word changes as a result of its position in an utterance (e.g. the change from *a* to *an* before a vowel).
– ORIGIN from Sanskrit *saṃdhi* 'putting together'.

sandhill ▶ noun a sand dune.

sandhill crane ▶ noun a chiefly migratory North American crane with greyish plumage and a red crown. ● *Grus canadensis*, family Gruidae.

sandhog ▶ noun N. Amer. a person who does construction work underground or under water.

sandhopper ▶ noun a small crustacean of the seashore which typically lives among seaweed and leaps when disturbed. Also called SAND FLEA. ● *Orchestia* and other genera, order Amphipoda.

Sandhurst a training college at Camberley, Surrey, for officers for the British army. It was formed in 1946 from an amalgamation of the Royal Military College at Sandhurst in Berkshire and the Royal Military Academy at Woolwich, London. Official name **Royal Military Academy, Sandhurst**.

San Diego /ˌsan dɪ'eɪɡəʊ/ an industrial city and naval port on the Pacific coast of southern California, just north of the border with Mexico; pop. 1,279,329 (est. 2008).

Sandinista /ˌsandɪ'niːstə/ ▶ noun a member of a left-wing Nicaraguan political organization, the Sandinista National Liberation Front (FSLN), which came to power in 1979 after overthrowing the dictator Anastasio Somoza. Opposed during most of their period of rule by the US-backed Contras, the Sandinistas were voted out of office in 1990.
– ORIGIN named after a similar organization founded by the nationalist leader Augusto César *Sandino* (1893–1934).

sand iron ▶ noun Golf a sand wedge.

sandiver /'sandɪvə/ ▶ noun [mass noun] a scum that forms on molten glass.
– ORIGIN late Middle English: apparently from Old French *suin de verre* 'exudation from glass', from *suer* 'to sweat' + *verre* 'glass'.

sand lance ▶ noun another term for SAND EEL.

sand lizard ▶ noun a small ground-dwelling Old World lizard favouring heathland or sandy areas. ● *Lacerta agilis* (of Eurasia), and genus *Pedioplanis* (of Africa), family Lacertidae.

sandlot ▶ noun N. Amer. a piece of unoccupied land used by children for games. ■ [as modifier] denoting or relating to sport played by amateurs: *sandlot baseball.*

sandman ▶ noun (**the sandman**) a fictional man supposed to make children sleep by sprinkling sand in their eyes.

sand martin ▶ noun a gregarious swallow-like bird with dark brown and white plumage, excavating nest holes in sandy banks and cliffs near water. ● Genus *Riparia*, family Hirundinidae: three species, in particular the widespread *R. riparia* (North American name: **bank swallow**).

sand painting ▶ noun [mass noun] an American Indian ceremonial art form using coloured sands, used in connection with healing ceremonies. ■ [count noun] an example of sand painting.

sandpaper ▶ noun [mass noun] paper with sand or another abrasive stuck to it, used for smoothing or polishing woodwork or other surfaces.
▶ verb [with obj.] smooth with sandpaper.
– DERIVATIVES **sandpapery** adjective.

sandpiper ▶ noun a wading bird with a long bill and typically long legs, nesting on the ground by water and frequenting coastal areas on migration. ● Family Scolopacidae (the **sandpiper family**): several genera, especially *Calidris*, *Tringa*, and *Actitis*, and numerous species. The sandpiper family also includes the godwits, curlews, redshanks, turnstones, phalaropes, woodcock, snipe, and ruff.

sandpit ▶ noun a quarry from which sand is excavated. ■ Brit. a shallow box or hollow in the ground, partly filled with sand for children to play in.

sand plover ▶ noun a migratory African and Asian plover, typically small in size and resembling a ringed plover without black on the breast. ● Genus *Charadrius*, family Charadriidae: several species.

Sandringham House /'sandrɪŋəm/ a country residence of the British royal family, north-east of King's Lynn in Norfolk.

sand shark ▶ noun a voracious brown-spotted shark of tropical Atlantic waters. ● *Odontaspis taurus*, family Odontaspididae.
■ any of a number of mainly harmless rays, dogfish, and sharks found in shallow coastal waters.

sandshoe ▶ noun chiefly Scottish & Austral./NZ another term for PLIMSOLL.

sandstone ▶ noun [mass noun] sedimentary rock consisting of sand or quartz grains cemented together, typically red, yellow, or brown in colour.

sandstorm ▶ noun a strong wind carrying clouds of sand with it, especially in a desert.

sand table ▶ noun a relief model in sand used to explain military tactics and plan campaigns.

sandveld /'sandfelt/ ▶ noun [mass noun] S. African land characterized by dry, sandy soil.
– ORIGIN Afrikaans, from Dutch *zand* 'sand' + *veld* 'terrain'.

sand wasp ▶ noun a digger wasp that excavates its burrow in sandy soil. Sand wasps typically have an abdomen with a very long and slender 'waist'.

S

● Subfamily Sphecinae, family Sphecidae: *Ammophila* and other genera.

sand wedge ▸ **noun** Golf a heavy, lofted iron with a flange on the bottom, used for hitting the ball out of sand.

sandwich /ˈsan(d)wɪdʒ, -wɪtʃ/ ▸ **noun 1** an item of food consisting of two pieces of bread with a filling between them, eaten as a light meal: *a ham sandwich*. ■ Brit. a sponge cake of two or more layers with jam or cream between. ■ something that is constructed like or has the form of a sandwich.
2 [as modifier] Brit. relating to a sandwich course: *the degree includes a sandwich year*.
▸ **verb** [with obj.] (usu. **be sandwiched between**) insert or squeeze (someone or something) between two other people or things, typically in a restricted space or so as to be uncomfortable: *the girl was sandwiched between two burly men in the back of the car*.
– PHRASES **the meat** (or **filling**) **in the sandwich** a person who is awkwardly caught between two opposing factions. **a sandwich** (or **two sandwiches**) **short of a picnic** see **SHORT**.
– ORIGIN mid 18th cent.: named after the 4th Earl of *Sandwich* (1718–92), an English nobleman said to have eaten food in this form so as not to leave the gaming table.

sandwich board ▸ **noun** a pair of advertisement boards connected by straps by which they are hung over a person's shoulders.

sandwich course ▸ **noun** Brit. a training course with alternate periods of formal instruction and practical experience.

sandwich generation ▸ **noun** a generation of people, typically in their thirties or forties, responsible both for bringing up their own children and for the care of their ageing parents.

Sandwich Islands former name for **HAWAII**.

sandwich tern ▸ **noun** a large crested tern found in both Europe and North and South America.
● *Thalassius sandvicensis*, family Sternidae (or Laridae).
– ORIGIN late 18th cent.: named after *Sandwich*, a town in Kent.

sandwort ▸ **noun** a widely distributed low-growing plant of the pink family, typically having small white flowers and growing in dry sandy ground. ● *Arenaria* and other genera, family Caryophyllaceae.

sandy ▸ **adjective** (**sandier**, **sandiest**) **1** covered in or consisting mostly of sand: *pine woods and a fine sandy beach*.
2 (especially of hair) light yellowish brown.
– DERIVATIVES **sandiness** noun.
– ORIGIN Old English *sandig* (see **SAND**, **-Y**[1]).

sand yacht ▸ **noun** a wind-driven three-wheeled vehicle with a sail, used for racing on beaches.

sandy blight ▸ **noun** [mass noun] Austral. an infection of the eyes, either conjunctivitis or trachoma, in which irritation is caused by granular inflammation of the eyelids.

sandy dog ▸ **noun** another term for **DOGFISH** (sense 1).

sane ▸ **adjective** (of a person) of sound mind; not mad or mentally ill: *hard work kept me sane*. ■ reasonable or sensible: *a sane discussion of the important social issues of our time*.
– DERIVATIVES **sanely** adverb, **saneness** noun.
– ORIGIN early 17th cent.: from Latin *sanus* 'healthy'.

S

Sanfilippo's syndrome /ˌsanfɪˈliːpəʊz/ ▸ **noun** [mass noun] Medicine a defect in metabolism similar to Hurler's syndrome.
– ORIGIN 1960s: named after Sylvester J. *Sanfilippo*, 20th-cent. American physician.

Sanforized /ˈsanfərʌɪzd/ (also **Sanforised**) ▸ **adjective** N. Amer. trademark (of cotton or other fabrics) pre-shrunk by a controlled compressive process; meeting certain standards of washing shrinkage.
– ORIGIN 1930s: from the name of *Sanford* L. Cluett (1874–1968), the American inventor of the process.

San Francisco /ˌsan franˈsɪskəʊ/ a city and seaport on the coast of California, situated on a peninsula between the Pacific and San Francisco Bay; pop. 808,976 (est. 2008). The city suffered severe damage from an earthquake in 1906, and has been frequently shaken by less severe earthquakes since.
– DERIVATIVES **San Franciscan** noun & adjective.

sang past of **SING**.

sangam /ˈsʌŋgʌm/ ▸ **noun** Indian a confluence of rivers, especially that of the Ganges and Jumna at Allahabad.
– ORIGIN from Sanskrit *saṃgama*.

sangar /ˈsaŋgə/ (also **sanga**) ▸ **noun** a small protected structure used for observing or firing from, which is built up from the ground.
– ORIGIN mid 19th cent.: from Pashto, probably from Persian *sang* 'stone'.

sangaree /ˌsaŋgəˈriː/ ▸ **noun** [mass noun] a cold drink of wine mixed with water and spices.
– ORIGIN from Spanish *sangría* (see **SANGRIA**).

sang-de-boeuf /ˌsɒ̃dəˈbəːf/ ▸ **noun** [mass noun] a deep red colour, typically found on old Chinese porcelain.
– ORIGIN French, literally 'ox blood'.

sangeet /sʌnˈgiːt/ ▸ **noun** a celebration held before a Hindu wedding ceremony for the bride-to-be and her female friends and relatives.
– ORIGIN from Sanskrit *saṃgīta* 'singing together, concert, music', from *saṃgāy-* 'sing together'.

Sanger /ˈsaŋə/, Frederick (b.1918), English biochemist. He determined the complete amino-acid sequence of insulin in 1955, and established the complete nucleotide sequence of a viral DNA in 1977. Nobel Prize for Chemistry (1958 and 1980).

sangfroid /sɒ̃ˈfrwɑː/ ▸ **noun** [mass noun] composure or coolness shown in danger or under trying circumstances.
– ORIGIN mid 18th cent.: from French *sang-froid*, literally 'cold blood'.

sangh /saŋ, sʌŋ/ ▸ **noun** Indian an organized group of people with a shared aim or interest; an association or other organization.
– ORIGIN Hindi *saṅgh*.

sangha /ˈsʌŋgə/ ▸ **noun** the Buddhist monastic order, including monks, nuns, and novices.
– ORIGIN from Sanskrit *saṃgha* 'community'.

Sangiovese /ˌsandʒɪə(ʊ)ˈveɪzi/ ▸ **noun** [mass noun] a variety of black wine grape used in making Chianti and other Italian red wines. ■ a red wine made from the Sangiovese grape.
– ORIGIN Italian.

Sango /ˈsaŋgəʊ/ ▸ **noun** [mass noun] a dialect of Ngbandi. ■ a lingua franca developed from Sango and related dialects, one of the national languages of the Central African Republic.
▸ **adjective** relating to Sango.
– ORIGIN the name in Ngbandi.

sangoma /saŋˈgɔːma/ ▸ **noun** (in southern Africa) a traditional healer or diviner.
– ORIGIN from Zulu *isangoma*.

sangrail /saŋˈgreɪl/ (also **sangreal**) ▸ **noun** another term for **GRAIL** (sense 1).
– ORIGIN late Middle English: from Old French *saint graal* 'Holy Grail'.

sangria /saŋˈgriːə/ ▸ **noun** [mass noun] a Spanish drink of red wine mixed with lemonade, fruit, and spices.
– ORIGIN Spanish, literally 'bleeding'; compare with **SANGAREE**.

sanguinary /ˈsaŋgwɪn(ə)ri/ ▸ **adjective** chiefly archaic involving or causing much bloodshed.
– ORIGIN Middle English (in the sense 'relating to blood'): from Latin *sanguinarius*, from *sanguis*, *sanguin-* 'blood'.

sanguine /ˈsaŋgwɪn/ ▸ **adjective 1** optimistic or positive, especially in an apparently bad or difficult situation: *he is sanguine about prospects for the global economy*. ■ (in medieval science and medicine) of or having the constitution associated with the predominance of blood among the bodily humours, supposedly marked by a ruddy complexion and an optimistic disposition. ■ archaic (of the complexion) florid or ruddy.
2 literary & Heraldry blood-red.
3 archaic bloody or bloodthirsty.
▸ **noun** [mass noun] a blood-red colour. ■ a deep red-brown crayon or pencil containing iron oxide. ■ Heraldry a blood-red stain used in blazoning.
– DERIVATIVES **sanguinely** adverb, **sanguineness** noun.
– ORIGIN Middle English: from Old French *sanguin(e)* 'blood red', from Latin *sanguineus* 'of blood', from *sanguis*, *sanguin-* 'blood'.

sanguineous /saŋˈgwɪnɪəs/ ▸ **adjective** archaic resembling or containing blood.

Sanhedrin /ˈsanɪdrɪn, sanˈhiːdrɪn, sanˈhedrɪn/ (also **Sanhedrim** /-rɪm/) the highest court of justice and the supreme council in ancient Jerusalem.
– ORIGIN from late Hebrew *sanhedrīn*, from Greek *sunedrion* 'council', from *sun-* 'with' + *hedra* 'seat'.

sanicle /ˈsanɪk(ə)l/ ▸ **noun** a plant of the parsley family which has burr-like fruit. ● Genus *Sanicula*, family Umbelliferae: several species, in particular the Eurasian **wood sanicle** (*S. europaea*).
– ORIGIN late Middle English: via Old French from medieval Latin *sanicula*, perhaps from Latin *sanus* 'healthy'.

sanidine /ˈsanɪdiːn/ ▸ **noun** [mass noun] a glassy mineral of the alkali feldspar group, typically occurring as tabular crystals.
– ORIGIN early 19th cent.: from Greek *sanis*, *sanid-* 'board' + **-INE**[4].

sanitarian ▸ **noun** chiefly archaic an official responsible for public health or a person in favour of public health reform.
– ORIGIN mid 19th cent.: from **SANITARY** + **-IAN**.

sanitarium /ˌsanɪˈtɛːrɪəm/ ▸ **noun** (pl. **sanitariums** or **sanitaria** /-rɪə/) North American term for **SANATORIUM**.
– ORIGIN mid 19th cent.: pseudo-Latin, from Latin *sanitas* 'health'.

sanitary ▸ **adjective** relating to the conditions that affect hygiene and health, especially the supply of sewage facilities and clean drinking water: *a sanitary engineer*. ■ hygienic and clean: *the most convenient and sanitary way to get rid of food waste from your kitchen*.
– DERIVATIVES **sanitarily** adverb.
– ORIGIN mid 19th cent.: from French *sanitaire*, from Latin *sanitas* 'health', from *sanus* 'healthy'.

sanitary engineer ▸ **noun** a person dealing with systems needed to maintain public health.

sanitary protection ▸ **noun** [mass noun] sanitary towels and tampons, considered collectively.

sanitary towel (also **sanitary pad**; N. Amer. **sanitary napkin** or **napkin**) ▸ **noun** an absorbent pad worn by women to absorb menstrual blood.

sanitaryware ▸ **noun** [mass noun] toilet bowls, cisterns, and other fittings.

sanitation ▸ **noun** [mass noun] conditions relating to public health, especially the provision of clean drinking water and adequate sewage disposal.
– ORIGIN mid 19th cent.: formed irregularly from **SANITARY**.

sanitize (also **sanitise**) ▸ **verb** [with obj.] make clean and hygienic: *new chemicals for sanitizing a pool*. ■ derogatory make (something) more palatable by removing elements that are likely to be unacceptable or controversial: (as adj. **sanitized**) *a sanitized version of his career*.
– DERIVATIVES **sanitization** noun, **sanitizer** noun.

sanity ▸ **noun** [mass noun] the ability to think and behave in a normal and rational manner; sound mental health: *I began to doubt my own sanity*. ■ reasonable and rational behaviour.
– ORIGIN late Middle English (in the sense 'health'): from Latin *sanitas* 'health', from *sanus* 'healthy'. Current senses date from the early 17th cent.

sanjak /ˈsandʒak/ ▸ **noun** (in the Ottoman Empire) one of the several administrative districts into which a larger district (vilayet) was divided.
– ORIGIN from Turkish *sancak*, literally 'banner'.

San Joaquin Valley fever /ˌsan wɑːˈkiːn/ ▸ **noun** see **VALLEY FEVER**.

San Jose /həʊˈzeɪ/ a city in western California, situated to the south of San Francisco Bay; pop. 948,279 (est. 2008).

San José /həʊˈzeɪ/ the capital of Costa Rica; pop. 350,535 (2007).

San Juan /ˈhwɑːn/ the capital and chief port of Puerto Rico, on the north coast of the island; pop. 426,600 (est. 2006).

sank past of **SINK**[1].

San Luis Potosí /san luːˌiːs ˌpɒtəʊˈsiː/ a state of central Mexico. ■ the capital of San Luis Potosí; pop. 685,934 (2005).

San Marino /məˈriːnəʊ/ a republic forming a small enclave in Italy, near Rimini; pop. 30,200 (est. 2009); official language, Italian; capital, the town of San Marino. It is perhaps Europe's oldest state, claiming to have been independent almost continuously since its foundation in the 4th century.
– ORIGIN said to be named after *Marino*, a Dalmatian stonecutter who fled there to escape the persecution of Christians under Diocletian.

San Martín /mɑːˈtiːn/, José de (1778–1850), Argentinian soldier and statesman. Having assisted in the liberation of his country from Spanish rule (1812–13), he went on to aid in the liberation of Chile (1817–18) and Peru (1820–4).

sannyasi /sənˈjɑːsi/ (also **sanyasi** or **sannyasin**) ▸ **noun** (pl. **same**) a Hindu religious mendicant.
– ORIGIN based on Sanskrit *saṃnyāsin* 'laying aside, ascetic', from *sam* 'together' + *ni* 'down' + *as* 'throw'.

San Pedro Sula /ˌpɛdrəʊ ˈsuːlə/ a city in northern Honduras, near the Caribbean coast; pop. 623,100 (est. 2008).

sanpro ▸ **noun** short for **SANITARY PROTECTION**, especially in commercial language.

sans /sanz/ ▸ **preposition** literary or humorous without: *a picture of Maughan sans specs*.
– ORIGIN Middle English: from Old French *sanz*, from a variant of Latin *sine* 'without', influenced by Latin *absentia* 'in the absence of'.

sansa /ˈsansə/ ▸ **noun** another term for **THUMB PIANO**.
– ORIGIN based on Arabic *ṣanj* 'cymbal'.

San Salvador /ˈsalvədɔː/, Spanish /salβaˈðəər/ the capital of El Salvador; pop. 316,090 (2007).

sans-culotte /ˌsan(z)kjʊˈlɒt/, French /sɑ̃kylɔt/ ▸ **noun** a lower-class Parisian republican in the French Revolution. ■ an extreme republican or revolutionary.
– DERIVATIVES **sans-culottism** noun.
– ORIGIN French, literally 'without knee breeches'.

San Sebastián /sɪˈbastɪən/, Spanish /seβasˈtjan/ a port and resort in northern Spain, situated on the Bay of Biscay close to the border with France; pop. 184,248 (2008).

sansei /ˈsanseɪ/ ▸ **noun** (pl. **same**) N. Amer. an American or Canadian whose grandparents were immigrants from Japan. Compare with **NISEI** and **ISSEI**.
– ORIGIN 1940s: Japanese, from *san* 'third' + *sei* 'generation'.

sansevieria /ˌsansɪˈvɪərɪə/ (also **sanseveria**) ▸ **noun** a plant of the genus *Sansevieria* in the agave family, especially (in gardening) mother-in-law's tongue.
– ORIGIN modern Latin, named after Raimondo di Sangro (1710–71), Prince of *Sanseviero* (now Sansevero), Italy.

Sanskrit /ˈsanskrɪt/ ▸ **noun** [mass noun] an ancient Indo-European language of India, in which the Hindu scriptures and classical Indian epic poems are written and from which many northern Indian (Indic) languages are derived.
▸ **adjective** relating to Sanskrit.

> Sanskrit was spoken in India roughly 1200–400 BC, and continues in use as a language of religion and scholarship. It is written from left to right in the Devanagari script. The suggestion by **Sir William Jones** (1746–94) of its common origin with Latin and Greek was a major advance in the development of historical linguistics.

– DERIVATIVES **Sanskritic** adjective, **Sanskritist** noun.
– ORIGIN from Sanskrit *saṃskṛta* 'composed, elaborated', from *sam* 'together' + *kṛ* 'make' + the past participle ending *-ta*.

Sansovino /ˌsansəˈviːnəʊ/, Jacopo Tatti (1486–1570), Italian sculptor and architect. He was city architect of Venice, where his buildings, including the Palazzo Corner (1533) and St Mark's Library (begun 1536), show the development of classical architectural style for contemporary use.

sans serif /san ˈsɛrɪf/ (also **sanserif**) Printing ▸ **noun** [mass noun] a style of type without serifs.
▸ **adjective** without serifs.
– ORIGIN mid 19th cent.: apparently from French *sans* 'without' + **SERIF**.

sant /sʌnt/ ▸ **noun** Hinduism & Sikhism a saint.
– ORIGIN from Hindi *santaḥ* 'venerable men'.

Santa Ana /ˌsantə ˈanə/ **1** a city in El Salvador, situated close to the border with Guatemala; pop. 245,421 (2007).
2 a volcano in El Salvador, situated south-west of the city of Santa Ana. It rises to a height of 2,381 m (7,730 ft).
3 a city in southern California, south-east of Los Angeles; pop. 339,100 (est. 2008).

Santa Barbara a resort city in California, on the Pacific coast north-west of Los Angeles; pop. 86,400 (est. 2008).

Santa Catarina /ˌkatəˈriːnə/ a state of southern Brazil, on the Atlantic coast; capital, Florianópolis.

Santa Claus (also informal **Santa**) another term for **FATHER CHRISTMAS**.
– ORIGIN originally a US usage, alteration of Dutch dialect *Sante Klaas* 'St Nicholas'.

Santa Cruz /kruːz/, Spanish /kruθ, krus/ **1** a city in the central region of Bolivia; pop. 1,561,061 (2009).
2 a port and the chief city of the island of Tenerife, in the Canary Islands; pop. 221,956 (2008). Full name **Santa Cruz de Tenerife**.

Santa Fe /ˈfeɪ/ (also **Santa Fé**) **1** the state capital of New Mexico; pop. 71,831 (est. 2008).
2 a city in northern Argentina, on the Salado River near its confluence with the Paraná; pop. 506,300 (est. 2009).

Santa Fé de Bogotá /ˌsantə feɪ deɪ bɒgəˈtɑː/ official name for **BOGOTÁ**.

Santal /ˈsantɑːl/ ▸ **noun** a member of the largest single indigenous group in India, spread over its eastern part and numbering about 5 million.
▸ **adjective** relating to the Santals.
– ORIGIN Bengali *sā̃otāl*, from *Saont*, a place in NE India.

Santali /sanˈtɑːli/ ▸ **noun** [mass noun] the Munda language of the Santals, with over 3 million speakers.
▸ **adjective** relating to the Santals or their language.

Santa Monica a resort city on the coast of SW California, situated on the west side of the Los Angeles conurbation; pop. 87,700 (est. 2008).

Santander /ˌsantanˈdɛː/ a port in northern Spain, on the Bay of Biscay, capital of Cantabria; pop. 182,302 (2008).

Santa Sophia another name for **ST SOPHIA**.

Santayana /ˌsantʌɪˈjɑːnə/, George (1863–1952), Spanish philosopher and writer; born *Jorge Augustin Nicolás Ruiz de Santayana*. His works include *The Realms of Being* (1924), poetry, and the novel *The Last Puritan* (1935).

santeria /ˌsanteˈriːə/ ▸ **noun** [mass noun] a pantheistic Afro-Cuban religious cult developed from the beliefs and customs of the Yoruba people and incorporating some elements of the Catholic religion.
– ORIGIN Spanish, literally 'holiness'.

santero /sanˈtɛːrəʊ/ ▸ **noun** (pl. **santeros**) **1** (in Mexico and Spanish-speaking areas of the south-western US) a person who makes religious images.
2 a priest of the santeria religious cult.
– ORIGIN Spanish.

Santiago /ˌsantɪˈɑːgəʊ/ the capital of Chile, situated to the west of the Andes in the central part of the country; pop. 4,985,900 (est. 2008).

Santiago de Compostela /deɪ ˌkɒmpɒˈstɛlə/ a city in NW Spain, capital of Galicia; pop. 94,339 (2008). The remains of St James the Great are said to have been brought there after his death; it is an important place of pilgrimage.

Santiago de Cuba /ˈkjuːbə/ a port on the coast of SE Cuba, the second-largest city on the island; pop. 426,679 (2008).

santim /ˈsantiːm/ ▸ **noun** a monetary unit of Latvia, equal to one hundredth of a lat.
– ORIGIN from Latvian *santims*, from French *centime* + the Latvian masculine ending *-s*.

santo /ˈsantəʊ/ ▸ **noun** (pl. **santos**) (in Mexico and Spanish-speaking areas of the south-western US) a religious symbol, especially a wooden representation of a saint.
– ORIGIN Spanish or Italian.

Santo Domingo /ˌsantəʊ dəˈmɪŋgəʊ/ the capital of the Dominican Republic, a port on the south coast; pop. 2,154,000 (est. 2007). From 1936 to 1961 it was called Ciudad Trujillo.

santolina /ˌsantəˈliːnə/ ▸ **noun** a plant of the genus *Santolina* in the daisy family, especially (in gardening) cotton lavender.
– ORIGIN modern Latin, perhaps an alteration of **SANTONICA**.

santon /ˈsantɒn/ ▸ **noun** (chiefly in Provence) a figurine adorning a representation of the manger in which Jesus was laid.
– ORIGIN French, from Spanish, from *santo* 'saint'.

santonica /sanˈtɒnɪkə/ ▸ **noun** [mass noun] the dried flower heads of a wormwood plant, containing the drug santonin. ● The plant is *Artemisia cina* (family Compositae) of Turkestan.
– ORIGIN mid 17th cent.: from Latin *Santonica* (*herba*) '(plant) of the Santoni', referring to a tribe of Aquitania (now **AQUITAINE**[1]).

santonin /ˈsantənɪn/ ▸ **noun** [mass noun] Chemistry a toxic crystalline compound present in santonica and related plants, used as an anthelmintic. ● Chem. formula: $C_{15}H_{18}O_3$.
– ORIGIN mid 19th cent.: from **SANTONICA** + **-IN**[1].

santoor /sʌnˈtʊə, sʌnˈtɔː/ ▸ **noun** an Indian musical instrument like a dulcimer, played by striking with a pair of small, spoon-shaped wooden hammers.
– ORIGIN from Arabic *santīr*, alteration of Greek *psaltērion* 'psaltery'.

Santorini /ˌsantɒˈriːni/ another name for **THERA**.

Santos /ˈsantɒs/ a port on the coast of Brazil, situated just south-east of São Paulo; pop. 418,288 (2007).

sanyasi ▸ **noun** variant spelling of **SANNYASI**.

São Francisco /ˌsaʊ franˈsɪskuː/ a river of eastern Brazil. It rises in Minas Gerais and flows for 3,200 km (1,990 miles) northwards then eastwards, meeting the Atlantic to the north of Aracajú.

saola /ˈʃaʊlɑː/ ▸ **noun** a small two-horned mammal discovered in Vietnam in 1992, with similarities to both antelopes and oxen. ● *Pseudoryx nghetinhensis*.
– ORIGIN 1990s: a local name, literally 'spindle horn'.

São Luís /luːˈiːs/ a port in NE Brazil, on the Atlantic coast, capital of the state of Maranhão; pop. 957,515 (2007).

Saône /səʊn/ a river of eastern France, which rises in the Vosges mountains and flows 480 km (298 miles) south-west to join the Rhône at Lyons.

São Paulo /ˈpaʊluː/ a state of southern Brazil, on the Atlantic coast. ■ the capital city of São Paulo; pop. 10,886,500 (est. 2007).

São Tomé and Príncipe /tʊˈmeɪ, ˈprɪnsɪpeɪ/ a country consisting of two main islands and several smaller ones in the Gulf of Guinea; pop. 212,700 (est. 2009); languages, Portuguese (official), Portuguese Creole; capital, São Tomé. The islands were settled by Portugal from 1493 and became an overseas province of that country. São Tomé and Príncipe became independent in 1975.

São Vincente /ˌsaʊ vɪnˈsent/ Portuguese name for Cape St Vincent (see **ST VINCENT, CAPE**).

sap[1] ▸ **noun** [mass noun] the fluid which circulates in the vascular system of a plant, consisting chiefly of water with dissolved sugars and mineral salts. ■ vigour or energy: *the hot, heady days of youth when the sap was rising*.
▸ **verb** (**saps, sapping, sapped**) [with obj.] gradually weaken or destroy (a person's strength or power): *our energy is being sapped by bureaucrats and politicians*. ■ (**sap someone of**) drain someone of (strength or power): *her illness had sapped her of energy and life*.
– DERIVATIVES **sapless** adjective.
– ORIGIN Old English *sæp*, probably of Germanic origin. The verb (dating from the mid 18th cent.) is often interpreted as a figurative use of the notion 'drain the sap from', but is derived originally from the verb **SAP**[2], in the sense 'undermine'.

sap[2] ▸ **noun** historical a tunnel or trench to conceal an assailant's approach to a fortified place.
▸ **verb** (**saps, sapping, sapped**) [no obj.] historical dig a sap or saps. ■ [with obj.] archaic make insecure by removing the foundations of: *a crazy building, sapped and undermined by the rats*. ■ [with obj.] Geography undercut by water or glacial action.
– ORIGIN late 16th cent. (as a verb in the sense 'dig a sap or covered trench'): from French *saper*, from Italian *zappare*, from *zappa* 'spade, spadework', probably from Arabic *sarab* 'underground passage', or *sabora* 'probe a wound, explore'.

S

sap[3] ▸ **noun** informal, chiefly N. Amer. a foolish and gullible person: *He fell for it! What a sap!*
– ORIGIN early 19th cent.: abbreviation of dialect *sapskull* 'person with a head like sapwood', from **SAP**[1] (in the sense 'sapwood') + **SKULL**.

sap[4] N. Amer. informal ▸ **noun** a bludgeon or club.
▸ **verb** (**saps, sapping, sapped**) [with obj.] hit with a bludgeon or club.
– ORIGIN late 19th cent. (as a noun): abbreviation of **SAPLING** (from which such a club was originally made).

sapele /səˈpiːli/ ▸ **noun** a large tropical African hardwood tree, with reddish-brown timber that resembles mahogany. ● Genus *Entandrophragma*, family Meliaceae.
– ORIGIN early 20th cent.: from the name of a port on the Benin River, Nigeria.

sap green ▸ **noun** [mass noun] a vivid yellowish-green pigment made from buckthorn berries.

saphenous /səˈfiːnəs/ ▸ **adjective** [attrib.] Anatomy relating to or denoting either of the two large superficial veins in the leg.
– ORIGIN mid 19th cent.: from medieval Latin *saphena* 'vein' + **-OUS**.

sapid /ˈsapɪd/ ▶ **adjective** having a strong, pleasant taste. ■ (of talk or writing) pleasant or interesting.
– DERIVATIVES **sapidity** /səˈpɪdɪti/ **noun**.
– ORIGIN early 17th cent.: from Latin *sapidus*, from *sapere* 'to taste'.

sapient /ˈseɪpɪənt/ ▶ **adjective 1** formal wise, or attempting to appear wise. ■ (chiefly in science fiction) intelligent: *sapient life forms*.
2 relating to the human species (*Homo sapiens*): *our sapient ancestors of 40,000 years ago*.
▶ **noun** a human of the species *Homo sapiens*.
– DERIVATIVES **sapience noun**, **sapiently adverb**.
– ORIGIN late Middle English: from Old French, or from Latin *sapient-* 'being wise', from the verb *sapere*.

sapiential ▶ **adjective** literary relating to wisdom.
– ORIGIN late 15th cent.: from Old French, or from ecclesiastical Latin *sapientialis*, from Latin *sapientia* 'wisdom'.

Sapir /səˈpɪə/, Edward (1884–1939), German-born American linguistics scholar and anthropologist. One of the founders of American structural linguistics, he carried out important research on American Indian languages and linguistic theory.

Sapir–Whorf hypothesis /ˈwɔːf/ Linguistics ▶ **noun** a hypothesis, first advanced by Edward Sapir in 1929 and subsequently developed by Benjamin Whorf, that the structure of a language determines a native speaker's perception and categorization of experience.

sapling ▶ **noun 1** a young tree, especially one with a slender trunk. ■ literary a young and slender or inexperienced person.
2 a greyhound in its first year.
– ORIGIN Middle English: from the noun SAP[1] + -LING.

sapodilla /ˌsapəˈdɪlə/ ▶ **noun** a large evergreen tropical American tree which has edible fruit and hard durable wood and yields chicle. ● *Manilkara zapota*, family Sapotaceae.
■ (also **sapodilla plum**) the sweet brownish bristly fruit of the sapodilla.
– ORIGIN late 17th cent.: from Spanish *zapotillo*, diminutive of *zapote*, from Nahuatl *tzápotl*.

saponaceous /ˌsapəˈneɪʃəs/ ▶ **adjective** of, like, or containing soap; soapy.
– ORIGIN early 18th cent.: from modern Latin *saponaceus* (from Latin *sapo, sapon-* 'soap') + -OUS.

saponify /səˈpɒnɪfʌɪ/ ▶ **verb** (**saponifies, saponifying, saponified**) [with obj.] Chemistry turn (fat or oil) into soap by reaction with an alkali. ■ convert (any ester) into an alcohol and a metal salt by alkaline hydrolysis.
– DERIVATIVES **saponification noun**.
– ORIGIN early 19th cent.: from French *saponifier*, from Latin *sapo, sapon-* 'soap'.

saponin /ˈsapənɪn/ ▶ **noun** [mass noun] Chemistry a toxic compound which is present in soapwort and makes foam when shaken with water. ■ [count noun] any of the class of steroid and terpenoid glycosides which foam when shaken with water, examples of which are used in detergents and foam fire extinguishers.
– ORIGIN mid 19th cent.: from French *saponine*, from Latin *sapo, sapon-* 'soap'.

S

sapper ▶ **noun** a military engineer who lays or detects and disarms mines. ■ Brit. a soldier in the Corps of Royal Engineers.
– ORIGIN early 17th cent.: from the verb SAP[2] + -ER[1].

sapphic /ˈsafɪk/ ▶ **adjective 1** formal or humorous relating to lesbians or lesbianism: *sapphic lovers*.
2 (**Sapphic**) relating to Sappho or her poetry.
▶ **plural noun** (**sapphics**) verse in a metre associated with Sappho.
– ORIGIN early 16th cent. (in sense 2 of the adjective): from French *saphique*, via Latin from Greek *Sapphikos*, from *Sapphō* (see SAPPHO).

sapphire /ˈsafʌɪə/ ▶ **noun 1** a transparent precious stone, typically blue, which is a variety of corundum (aluminium oxide): [as modifier] *a sapphire ring*. ■ [mass noun] a bright blue colour.
2 a small hummingbird with shining blue or violet colours in its plumage and a short tail. ● *Hylocharis* and other genera, family Trochilidae: several species.
– DERIVATIVES **sapphirine** /ˈsafɪrʌɪn/ **adjective**.
– ORIGIN Middle English: from Old French *safir*, via Latin from Greek *sappheiros*, probably denoting lapis lazuli.

sapphism /ˈsafɪz(ə)m/ ▶ **noun** [mass noun] formal or humorous lesbianism.
– ORIGIN late 19th cent.: from SAPPHO + -ISM.

Sappho /ˈsafəʊ/ (early 7th century BC), Greek lyric poet who lived on Lesbos. Many of her poems express her affection and love for women, and have given rise to her association with female homosexuality.

Sapporo /səˈpɔːrəʊ/ a city in northern Japan, capital of the island of Hokkaido; pop. 1,874,410 (2007).

sappy ▶ **adjective** (**sappier, sappiest**) **1** informal, chiefly N. Amer. mawkishly over-sentimental.
2 (of a plant) containing a lot of sap.
– DERIVATIVES **sappily adverb**, **sappiness noun**.

sapro- ▶ **combining form** Biology relating to putrefaction or decay: *saprogenic*.
– ORIGIN from Greek *sapros* 'putrid'.

saprolegnia /ˌsaprə(ʊ)ˈlɛgnɪə/ ▶ **noun** [mass noun] an aquatic fungus which can attack the bodies of fish and other aquatic animals. ● Genus *Saprolegnia*, subdivision Mastigomycotina.
– ORIGIN modern Latin, from SAPRO- 'of decay' + Greek *legnon* 'border'.

saprophagous /saˈprɒfəgəs/ ▶ **adjective** Biology (of an organism) feeding on or obtaining nourishment from decaying organic matter.

saprophyte /ˈsaprə(ʊ)fʌɪt/ ▶ **noun** Biology a plant, fungus, or microorganism that lives on dead or decaying organic matter.
– DERIVATIVES **saprophytic adjective**, **saprophytically adverb**.

saprotroph /ˈsaprə(ʊ)trəʊf, -trɒf/ ▶ **noun** Biology an organism that feeds on or derives nourishment from decaying organic matter.
– DERIVATIVES **saprotrophic adjective**.
– ORIGIN back-formation from *saprotrophic*.

sapsucker ▶ **noun** an American woodpecker that pecks rows of small holes in trees and visits them for sap and insects. ● *Sphyrapicus*, family Picidae: four species.

sapwood ▶ **noun** [mass noun] the soft outer layers of recently formed wood between the heartwood and the bark, containing the functioning vascular tissue.

Saqqara /səˈkɑːrə/ a vast necropolis at the ancient Egyptian city of Memphis, with monuments dating from the 3rd millennium BC to the Graeco-Roman age, notably a step pyramid which is the first known building made entirely of stone (*c.*2650 BC).

SAR ▶ **abbreviation** ■ search and rescue, an emergency service involving the detection and rescue of those who have met with an accident or mishap in dangerous or isolated locations. ■ Special Administrative Region (of the People's Republic of China).

saraband /ˈsarəband/ (also **sarabande**) ▶ **noun** a slow, stately Spanish dance in triple time. ■ a piece of music written for the saraband.
– ORIGIN early 17th cent.: from French *sarabande*, from Spanish and Italian *zarabanda*.

Saracen /ˈsarəs(ə)n/ ▶ **noun 1** an Arab or Muslim, especially at the time of the Crusades.
2 a nomad of the Syrian and Arabian desert at the time of the Roman Empire.
– DERIVATIVES **Saracenic adjective**.
– ORIGIN Middle English, from Old French *sarrazin*, via late Latin from late Greek *Sarakēnos*, perhaps from Arabic *šarqī* 'eastern'.

Saracen's head ▶ **noun** a conventionalized depiction of the head of a Saracen as a heraldic charge or inn sign.

Saragossa /ˌsarəˈgɒsə/ a city in northern Spain, capital of Aragon, situated on the River Ebro; pop. 666,129 (2008). Spanish name **ZARAGOZA**.
– ORIGIN alteration of *Caesaraugusta*, the name given to the ancient settlement on the site, taken by the Romans in the 1st cent. BC.

Sarah (in the Bible) the wife of Abraham and mother of Isaac (Gen. 17:15 ff.).

Sarajevo /ˌsarəˈjeɪvəʊ/ the capital of Bosnia and Herzegovina; pop. 304,600 (est. 2008).

> Taken by the Austro-Hungarians in 1878, it became a centre of Slav opposition to Austrian rule. It was the scene in June 1914 of the assassination by a Bosnian Serb named Gavrilo Princip of Archduke Franz Ferdinand (1863–1914), the heir to the Austrian throne, an event which triggered the outbreak of the First World War. The city suffered severely from the ethnic conflicts that followed the break-up of Yugoslavia in 1991, and was besieged by Bosnian Serb forces in the surrounding mountains from 1992 to 1994.

Saran /səˈran/ (also **Saran Wrap**) ▶ **noun** N. Amer. trademark for POLYVINYL CHLORIDE, especially as cling film.
– ORIGIN 1940s: of unknown origin.

sarangi /səˈraŋgi, sɑːˈrʌŋgi/ ▶ **noun** (pl. **sarangis**) an Indian bowed musical instrument about two feet high, with three or four main strings and up to thirty-five sympathetic strings.
– ORIGIN from Hindi *sāraṅgī*.

Saransk /səˈransk/ a city in European Russia, capital of the autonomous republic of Mordvinia, situated to the south of Nizhni Novgorod; pop. 295,300 (est. 2008).

sarape /sɛˈrɑːpeɪ/ ▶ **noun** variant spelling of SERAPE.

Saratoga, Battle of /ˌsarəˈtəʊgə/ either of two battles fought in 1777 during the War of American Independence, near the modern city of Saratoga Springs in New York State. The British defeats are conventionally regarded as the turning point in the war in favour of the American side.

Saratov /səˈrɑːtɒf/ a city in SW central Russia, situated on the River Volga north of Volgograd; pop. 836,100 (est. 2008).

Sarawak /səˈrɑːwək/ a state of Malaysia, comprising the north-western part of Borneo; capital, Kuching.

sarcasm ▶ **noun** [mass noun] the use of irony to mock or convey contempt: *she didn't like the note of sarcasm in his voice*.
– ORIGIN mid 16th cent.: from French *sarcasme*, or via late Latin from late Greek *sarkasmos*, from Greek *sarkazein* 'tear flesh', in late Greek 'gnash the teeth, speak bitterly' (from *sarx, sark-* 'flesh').

sarcastic ▶ **adjective** marked by or given to using irony in order to mock or convey contempt: *making sarcastic comments | I think they're being sarcastic*.
– DERIVATIVES **sarcastically adverb**.
– ORIGIN late 17th cent.: from French *sarcastique*, from *sarcasme* (see SARCASM), on the pattern of pairs such as *enthousiasme, enthousiastique*.

sarcenet ▶ **noun** variant spelling of SARSENET.

sarcococca /ˌsɑːkə(ʊ)ˈkɒksə/ ▶ **noun** a small East Asian winter-flowering shrub of the box family, with white or pink flowers and black or red berries. ● Genus *Sarcococca*, family Buxaceae.
– ORIGIN modern Latin, from Greek *sarx, sarc-* 'flesh' + *kokkos* 'berry'.

sarcoid /ˈsɑːkɔɪd/ Medicine ▶ **adjective** relating to, denoting, or suffering from sarcoidosis.
▶ **noun** a granuloma of the type present in sarcoidosis. ■ [mass noun] the condition and symptoms of sarcoidosis: *tissues affected by sarcoid*.
– ORIGIN mid 19th cent. (in the sense 'resembling flesh'): from Greek *sarx, sark-* 'flesh' + -OID.

sarcoidosis /ˌsɑːkɔɪˈdəʊsɪs/ ▶ **noun** [mass noun] Medicine a chronic disease of unknown cause characterized by the enlargement of lymph nodes in many parts of the body and the widespread appearance of granulomas derived from the reticuloendothelial system.

sarcolemma /ˈsɑːkəʊˌlɛmə/ ▶ **noun** Physiology the fine transparent tubular sheath which envelops the fibres of skeletal muscles.
– DERIVATIVES **sarcolemmal adjective**.
– ORIGIN mid 19th cent.: from Greek *sarx, sark-* 'flesh' + *lemma* 'husk'.

sarcoma /sɑːˈkəʊmə/ ▶ **noun** (pl. **sarcomas** or **sarcomata** /sɑːˈkəʊmətə/) Medicine a malignant tumour of connective or other non-epithelial tissue.
– DERIVATIVES **sarcomatosis** /sɑːˌkəʊməˈtəʊsɪs/ **noun**, **sarcomatous adjective** /sɑːˈkəʊmətəs/.
– ORIGIN early 19th cent.: modern Latin, from Greek *sarkōma*, from *sarkoun* 'become fleshy', from *sarx, sark-* 'flesh'.

sarcomere /ˈsɑːkə(ʊ)mɪə/ ▶ **noun** Anatomy a structural unit of a myofibril in striated muscle, consisting of a dark band and the nearer half of each adjacent pale band.
– ORIGIN late 19th cent.: from Greek *sarx, sark-* 'flesh' + *meros* 'part'.

sarcopenia /ˌsɑːkəʊˈpiːnɪə/ ▶ **noun** [mass noun] Medicine the loss of skeletal muscle mass and strength as a result of ageing.
– ORIGIN 1990s: from Greek *sarx, sark-* 'flesh' + *penia* 'poverty'.

sarcophagus /sɑːˈkɒfəgəs/ ▶ **noun** (pl. **sarcophagi** /-gʌɪ, -dʒʌɪ/) a stone coffin, typically adorned with a sculpture or inscription and associated with the ancient civilizations of Egypt, Rome, and Greece.
– ORIGIN late Middle English: via Latin from Greek *sarkophagos* 'flesh-consuming', from *sarx, sark-* 'flesh' + *-phagos* '-eating'.

sarcoplasm /ˈsɑːkə(ʊ)plaz(ə)m/ ▶ **noun** [mass noun] Physiology the cytoplasm of striated muscle cells.
– DERIVATIVES **sarcoplasmic adjective**.

– ORIGIN late 19th cent.: from Greek *sarx*, *sark-* 'flesh' + **PLASMA**.

sarcoptic mange /sɑːˈkɒptɪk/ ▸ **noun** [mass noun] a form of mange caused by the itch mite and tending to affect chiefly the abdomen and hindquarters. Compare with **DEMODECTIC MANGE**.
– ORIGIN late 19th cent.: *sarcoptic* from the modern Latin genus name *Sarcoptes* (from Greek *sarx*, *sark-* 'flesh') + **-IC**.

sarcosine /ˈsɑːkəsiːn/ ▸ **noun** [mass noun] Biochemistry a crystalline amino acid which occurs in the body as a product of the metabolism of creatine. ● Alternative name: ***N*-methylglycine**; chem. formula: CH_3NHCH_2COOH.
– ORIGIN mid 19th cent.: from Greek *sarx*, *sark-* 'flesh' + **-INE**[4].

Sard /sɑːd/ ▸ **adjective & noun** another term for **SARDINIAN**.

sard /sɑːd/ ▸ **noun** [mass noun] a yellow or brownish-red semi-precious stone consisting of a variety of chalcedony.
– ORIGIN late Middle English: from French *sarde* or Latin *sarda*, from Greek *sardios*, probably from *Sardō* 'Sardinia'.

Sardanapalus /ˌsɑːdəˈnapələs/ the name given by ancient Greek historians to the last king of Assyria (died before 600 BC), portrayed as being notorious for his wealth and sensuality. It may not represent a specific historical person.

sardar /ˈsəːdɑː/ (also **sirdar**) ▸ **noun** chiefly Indian
1 a leader (often used as a proper name).
2 a Sikh (often used as a title or form of address).
– ORIGIN from Persian and Urdu *sar-dār*.

Sardegna /sarˈdeɲɲa/ Italian name for **SARDINIA**.

sardelle /sɑːˈdɛl/ ▸ **noun** a sardine, anchovy, or other small fish similarly prepared for eating.
– ORIGIN late 16th cent.: from Italian *sardella*, diminutive of *sarda* (see **SARDINE**[1]).

sardine[1] /sɑːˈdiːn/ ▸ **noun 1** a young pilchard or other young or small herring-like fish.
2 (**sardines**) [treated as sing.] Brit. a children's game based on hide-and-seek, in which one child hides and the other children, as they find the hider, join him or her in the hiding place until just one child remains.
▸ **verb** [with obj.] informal pack closely together.
– PHRASES **packed like sardines** crowded very close together, as sardines are in tins.
– ORIGIN late Middle English: from French, or from Latin *sardina*, from *sarda*, from Greek, probably from *Sardō* 'Sardinia'.

sardine[2] /ˈsɑːdʌɪn/ ▸ **noun** another term for **SARDIUS**.
– ORIGIN late Middle English: via late Latin from Greek *sardinos*, variant of *sardios* (see **SARDIUS**).

Sardinia /sɑːˈdɪnɪə/ a large Italian island in the Mediterranean Sea to the west of Italy; pop. 1,671,001 (2008); capital, Cagliari. In 1720 it was joined with Savoy and Piedmont to form the kingdom of Sardinia; the kingdom formed the nucleus of the Risorgimento, becoming part of a unified Italy under Victor Emmanuel II of Sardinia in 1861. Italian name **SARDEGNA**.

Sardinian ▸ **adjective** relating to Sardinia, its people, or their language.
▸ **noun 1** a native or inhabitant of Sardinia.
2 [mass noun] the Romance language of Sardinia.

Sardis /ˈsɑːdɪs/ an ancient city of Asia Minor, the capital of Lydia, whose ruins lie near the west coast of modern Turkey, to the north-east of Izmir.

sardius /ˈsɑːdɪəs/ ▸ **noun** a red precious stone mentioned in the Bible (e.g. Exodus 28:17) and in classical writings, probably ruby or carnelian.
– ORIGIN late Middle English: via late Latin from Greek *sardios*.

sardonic /sɑːˈdɒnɪk/ ▸ **adjective** grimly mocking or cynical: *Starkey attempted a sardonic smile*.
– DERIVATIVES **sardonically** adverb, **sardonicism** noun.
– ORIGIN mid 17th cent.: from French *sardonique*, earlier *sardonien*, via Latin from Greek *sardonios* 'of Sardinia', alteration of *sardanios*, used by Homer to describe bitter or scornful laughter.

sardonyx /ˈsɑːdənɪks/ ▸ **noun** [mass noun] onyx in which white layers alternate with sard.
– ORIGIN Middle English: via Latin from Greek *sardonux*, probably from *sardios* 'sardius' + *onux* 'onyx'.

saree ▸ **noun** variant spelling of **SARI**.

sargasso /sɑːˈgasəʊ/ (also **sargasso weed**) ▸ **noun** another term for **SARGASSUM**.
– ORIGIN late 16th cent.: from Portuguese *sargaço*, of unknown origin.

Sargasso Sea a region of the western Atlantic Ocean between the Azores and the Caribbean, so called because of the prevalence in it of floating sargasso seaweed. It is the breeding place of eels from the rivers of Europe and eastern North America, and is known for its usually calm conditions.

sargassum /sɑːˈgasəm/ (also **sargassum weed**) ▸ **noun** [mass noun] a brown seaweed with berry-like air bladders, typically forming large floating masses. ● Genus *Sargassum*, class Phaeophyceae.
– ORIGIN modern Latin, from Portuguese *sargaço* (see **SARGASSO**).

sargassum fish ▸ **noun** a small toadfish which occurs worldwide, with a bizarre shape and intricate coloration to camouflage it among the floating sargassum weed that it frequents. ● *Histrio histrio*, family Antennariidae.

sarge ▸ **noun** informal sergeant.
– ORIGIN mid 19th cent.: abbreviation.

Sargent[1], John Singer (1856–1925), American painter. He is best known for his portraiture in a style noted for its bold brushwork. He was much in demand in Parisian circles, but following a scandal over the supposed eroticism of *Madame Gautreau* (1884), he moved to London.

Sargent[2], Sir (Henry) Malcolm (Watts) (1895–1967), English conductor and composer. In 1921 he made an acclaimed debut conducting his own *Impressions of a Windy Day*. He was responsible for the BBC Promenade Concerts from 1948.

Sargodha /səˈgəʊdə/ a city in north central Pakistan; pop. 586,900 (est. 2009).

Sargon /ˈsɑːgɒn/ (2334–2279 BC), the semi-legendary founder of the ancient kingdom of Akkad.

Sargon II /ˈsɑːgɒn/ (d.705 BC), king of Assyria 721–705 BC, probably a son of Tiglath-pileser III. He is famous for his conquest of cities in Syria and Palestine; he also took ten of the tribes of Israel into captivity in Assyria (see **LOST TRIBES**).

sari /ˈsɑːri/ (also **saree**) ▸ **noun** (pl. **saris** or **sarees**) a garment consisting of a length of cotton or silk elaborately draped around the body, traditionally worn by women from South Asia.
– ORIGIN late 18th cent.: from Hindi *sāṛī*.

sarin /ˈsɑːrɪn/ ▸ **noun** [mass noun] an organophosphorus nerve gas, developed in Germany during the Second World War.
– ORIGIN from German *Sarin*, of unknown origin.

Sark one of the Channel Islands, a small island lying to the east of Guernsey.

sark ▸ **noun** Scottish & N. English a shirt or chemise.
– ORIGIN Old English *serc*, of Germanic origin.

sarkar /səːˈkɑː/ ▸ **noun** Indian a man who is in a position of authority, especially one who owns land worked by tenant farmers (often used as a form of address).
– ORIGIN from Persian and Urdu *sarkār*, from *sar* 'chief' + *kār* agent, doer.

sarking ▸ **noun** [mass noun] boarding or building felt fixed over the rafters of a roof before the tiles or slates are added.
– ORIGIN late Middle English (originally Scots and northern English): from **SARK** + **-ING**[1].

Sarkozy /sɑːˈkəʊzi/, Nicolas (b.1955), French statesman, President since 2007.

sarky ▸ **adjective** (**sarkier**, **sarkiest**) Brit. informal sarcastic.
DERIVATIVES **sarkily** adverb, **sarkiness** noun.
– ORIGIN early 20th cent.: abbreviation.

Sarmatia /sɑːˈmeɪʃə/ an ancient region situated to the north of the Black Sea, extending originally from the Urals to the Don and inhabited by Slavic peoples.
– DERIVATIVES **Sarmatian** adjective & noun.

sarmie /ˈsɑːmi/ ▸ **noun** S. African informal a sandwich.

sarnie ▸ **noun** Brit. informal a sandwich.

sarod /səˈrəʊd/ ▸ **noun** a lute used in classical North Indian music, with four main strings.
– ORIGIN Urdu, from Persian *surod* 'song, melody'.

sarong /səˈrɒŋ/ ▸ **noun** a garment consisting of a long piece of cloth worn wrapped round the body and tucked at the waist or under the armpits, traditionally worn in SE Asia and now also by women in the West.
– ORIGIN mid 19th cent.: Malay, literally 'sheath'.

Saronic Gulf /səˈrɒnɪk/ an inlet of the Aegean Sea on the coast of SE Greece. Athens and the port of Piraeus lie on its northern shores.

saros /ˈsɛːrɒs/ ▸ **noun** Astronomy a period of about 18 years between repetitions of solar and lunar eclipses.
– ORIGIN early 19th cent.: from Greek, from Babylonian *šār(u)* '3,600 (years)', the sense apparently based on a misinterpretation of the number.

sarpanch /ˈsʌrpʌntʃ/ ▸ **noun** Indian the head of a village.
– ORIGIN from Urdu *sar-panch*, from *sar* 'head' + *panch* 'five'.

sarracenia /ˌsarəˈsiːnɪə/ ▸ **noun** a North American pitcher plant of marshy places, some kinds of which are cultivated as ornamentals. ● Genus *Sarracenia*, family Sarraceniaceae: several species, including the purple-flowered *S. purpurea*, which has become naturalized in Ireland.
– ORIGIN modern Latin, named after Michel *Sarrazin* (died 1734), Canadian botanist.

Sarre /saʀ/ French name for **SAAR**.

sarrusophone /səˈrʌsəfəʊn/ ▸ **noun** a member of a family of wind instruments similar to saxophones but with a double reed like an oboe.
– ORIGIN late 19th cent.: from the name of W. *Sarrus*, the 19th-cent. French bandmaster who invented it, + **-PHONE**.

SARS ▸ **abbreviation** severe acute respiratory syndrome.

sarsaparilla /ˌsɑːs(ə)pəˈrɪlə/ ▸ **noun** [mass noun] **1** a preparation of the dried rhizomes of various plants, especially smilax, used to flavour some drinks and medicines and formerly as a tonic. ■ a sweet drink flavoured with sarsaparilla.
2 the tropical American climbing plant from which sarsaparilla is generally obtained. ● Genus *Smilax*, family Liliaceae: several species, in particular *S. regelii*, which is the chief source of commercial sarsaparilla.
– ORIGIN late 16th cent.: from Spanish *zarzaparilla*, from *zarza* 'bramble' + a diminutive of *parra* 'vine'.

sarsen /ˈsɑːs(ə)n/ (also **sarsen stone**) ▸ **noun** Geology a silicified sandstone boulder of a kind which occurs on the chalk downs of southern England. Such stones were used in constructing Stonehenge and other prehistoric monuments.
– ORIGIN late 17th cent.: probably a variant of **SARACEN**.

sarsenet /ˈsɑːsnɪt/ (also **sarcenet**) ▸ **noun** [mass noun] a fine, soft silk fabric, used as a lining material and in dressmaking.
– ORIGIN late Middle English: from Anglo-Norman French *sarzinett*, perhaps a diminutive of *sarzin* 'Saracen', suggested by Old French *drap sarrasinois* 'Saracen cloth'.

Sarto /ˈsɑːtəʊ/, Italian /ˈsartəo/, Andrea del (1486–1531), Italian painter; born *Andrea d'Agnolo*. An important painter of the High Renaissance, his work includes a cycle of frescoes in the church of Santa Annunziata in Florence (1514–24).

sartorial /sɑːˈtɔːrɪəl/ ▸ **adjective** [attrib.] relating to tailoring, clothes, or style of dress: *sartorial elegance*.
– DERIVATIVES **sartorially** adverb.
– ORIGIN early 19th cent.: from Latin *sartor* 'tailor' (from *sarcire* 'to patch') + **-IAL**.

sartorius /sɑːˈtɔːrɪəs/ (also **sartorius muscle**) ▸ **noun** Anatomy a long, narrow muscle running obliquely across the front of each thigh from the hip bone to the inside of the leg below the knee.
– ORIGIN early 18th cent.: modern Latin, from Latin *sartor* 'tailor' (because the muscle is used when adopting a cross-legged position, earlier associated with a tailor's sewing posture).

Sartre /ˈsɑːtrə/, French /saʀtʀ/, Jean-Paul (1905–80), French philosopher, novelist, dramatist, and critic. A leading existentialist, he dealt in his work with the nature of human life and the structures of consciousness. He refused the Nobel Prize for Literature in 1964. Notable works: *Nausée* (novel, 1938), *Being and Nothingness* (treatise, 1943), and *Huis clos* (play, 1944).

Sarum /ˈsɛːrəm/ an old name for Salisbury, still used as the name of its diocese. See also **OLD SARUM**. ■ [as modifier] denoting the order of divine service used before the Reformation in the diocese of Salisbury and, by the 15th century, in most of England, Wales, and Ireland: *Sarum Use*.
– ORIGIN from medieval Latin, perhaps from an abbreviated form of Latin *Sarisburia* 'Salisbury'.

sarus crane /ˈsɛːrəs/ ▸ **noun** a large red-headed crane found from India to the Philippines. ● *Grus antigone*, family Gruidae.
– ORIGIN mid 19th cent.: *sarus* from Sanskrit *sārasa*.

sarvodaya /sɑːˈvəʊdəjə/ ▸ **noun** [mass noun] Indian the economic and social development of a community

S

as a whole, especially as advocated by Mahatma Gandhi.
– ORIGIN Sanskrit, from *sarva* 'all' + *udaya* 'prosperity'.

SAS ▶ abbreviation Special Air Service.

Sasanian ▶ adjective & noun variant of SASSANIAN.

sasanqua /sə'saŋkwə, -kə/ ▶ noun a Japanese camellia with fragrant white or pink flowers and seeds which yield tea oil. ● *Camellia sasanqua*, family Theaceae.
– ORIGIN mid 19th cent.: from Japanese *sasank(w)a*.

SASE ▶ abbreviation N. Amer. self-addressed stamped envelope.

sash[1] ▶ noun a long strip or loop of cloth worn over one shoulder or round the waist, especially as part of a uniform or official dress.
– DERIVATIVES **sashed** adjective, **sashless** adjective.
– ORIGIN late 16th cent. (earlier as *shash*, denoting fine fabric twisted round the head as a turban): from Arabic *šāš* 'muslin, turban'.

sash[2] ▶ noun a frame holding the glass in a window, typically one of two sliding frames in a sash window.
– DERIVATIVES **sashed** adjective.
– ORIGIN late 17th cent.: alteration of CHASSIS, interpreted as plural.

sashay /sa'ʃeɪ/ ▶ verb [no obj.] informal, chiefly N. Amer. **1** [with adverbial of direction] walk in an ostentatious yet casual manner, typically with exaggerated movements of the hips and shoulders: *Louise was sashaying along in a long black satin dress.*
2 perform the sashay.
▶ noun (in American square dancing) a figure in which partners circle each other by taking sideways steps.
– ORIGIN mid 19th cent. (as a verb): alteration of CHASSÉ.

sash cord ▶ noun a strong cord attaching either of the sash weights of a sash window to a sash.

sash cramp ▶ noun a tool used for clamping the sashes of a window together during gluing.

sashimi /'saʃɪmi/ ▶ noun [mass noun] a Japanese dish of bite-sized pieces of raw fish eaten with soy sauce and wasabi paste: *tuna sashimi.*
– ORIGIN Japanese.

sash weight ▶ noun a weight attached by a cord to each side of the sash of a sash window to balance it at any height.

sash window ▶ noun a window with one or two sashes which can be slid vertically to make an opening.

sasin /'sasɪn/ ▶ noun another term for BLACKBUCK.
– ORIGIN mid 19th cent.: from Nepali.

sasine /'seɪsɪn/ ▶ noun [mass noun] **1** Scots Law investment by registration of a deed transferring ownership of property. ■ [count noun] an act or record of sasine.
2 historical the conferring of possession of feudal property.
– ORIGIN mid 17th cent.: variant of SEISIN.

Sask. ▶ abbreviation Saskatchewan.

Saskatchewan /sə'skatʃɪwən/ **1** a province of central Canada; pop. 968,157 (2006); capital, Regina.
2 a river of Canada. Rising in two headstreams in the Rocky Mountains, it flows eastwards for 596 km (370 miles) to Lake Winnipeg.

Saskatoon /ˌsaskə'tuːn/ an industrial city in south central Saskatchewan, situated in the Great Plains on the South Saskatchewan River; pop. 202,340 (2006).

Sasquatch /'saskwatʃ, -wɒtʃ/ ▶ noun another term for BIGFOOT.
– ORIGIN early 20th cent.: Salish.

sass N. Amer. informal ▶ noun [mass noun] impudence; cheek: *the kind of boy that wouldn't give you any sass.*
▶ verb [with obj.] be cheeky or rude to (someone): *we wouldn't have dreamed of sassing our parents.*
– ORIGIN mid 19th cent.: variant of SAUCE.

sassaby /sə'seɪbi/ ▶ noun variant spelling of TSESSEBI.

sassafras /'sasəfras/ ▶ noun a deciduous North American tree with aromatic leaves and bark. The leaves are infused to make tea or ground into filé. ● *Sassafras albidum*, family Lauraceae.
■ [mass noun] an extract of the leaves or bark of the sassafras, used medicinally or in perfumery.
– ORIGIN late 16th cent.: from Spanish *sasafrás*, based on Latin *saxifraga* 'saxifrage'.

Sassanian /sa'seɪmɪən/ (also **Sasanian** or **Sassanid** /'sasənɪd/) ▶ adjective relating to a dynasty that ruled Persia from the early 3rd century AD until the Arab Muslim conquest of 651.
▶ noun a member of the Sassanian dynasty.
– ORIGIN from *Sasan* (the name of the grandfather or father of Ardashir, the first Sassanian) + -IAN.

Sassenach /'sasənax, -nak/ Scottish & Irish, derogatory ▶ noun an English person.
▶ adjective English.
– ORIGIN early 18th cent. (as a noun): from Scottish Gaelic *Sasunnoch*, Irish *Sasanach*, from Latin *Saxones* 'Saxons'.

Sassoon /sə'suːn/, Siegfried (Lorraine) (1886–1967), English poet and novelist. He is known for his starkly realistic poems written while serving in the First World War, expressing his contempt for war leaders as well as compassion for his comrades.

sassy ▶ adjective (**sassier**, **sassiest**) informal lively, bold, and full of spirit; cheeky: *Toni was smart and sassy and liked to pretend she was a hard nut.*
– DERIVATIVES **sassily** adverb, **sassiness** noun.
– ORIGIN mid 19th cent.: variant of SAUCY.

sastra ▶ noun variant spelling of SHASTRA.

sastrugi /sa'struːgi/ ▶ plural noun parallel wave-like ridges caused by winds on the surface of hard snow, especially in polar regions.
– ORIGIN mid 19th cent.: from Russian *zastrugi* 'small ridges'.

SAT ▶ abbreviation ■ trademark (in the US) Scholastic Aptitude Test, a test of a student's verbal and mathematical skills, used for admission to American colleges. ■ standard assessment task.

sat past and past participle of SIT.

Sat. ▶ abbreviation Saturday.

satai ▶ noun variant spelling of SATAY.

Satan the Devil; Lucifer.
– ORIGIN Old English, via late Latin and Greek from Hebrew *śāṭān*, literally 'adversary', from *śāṭan* 'plot against'.

satang /'sataŋ/ ▶ noun (pl. **same** or **satangs**) a monetary unit of Thailand, equal to one hundredth of a baht.
– ORIGIN Thai, from Pali *sata* 'hundred'.

satanic ▶ adjective of or characteristic of Satan. ■ connected with satanism: *a satanic cult.* ■ extremely evil or wicked.
– DERIVATIVES **satanically** adverb.

satanic abuse ▶ noun another term for RITUAL ABUSE.

satanism ▶ noun [mass noun] the worship of Satan, typically involving a travesty of Christian symbols and practices, such as placing a cross upside down.
– DERIVATIVES **satanist** noun & adjective.

satanize (also **satanise**) ▶ verb [with obj.] rare portray as satanic or evil.

satay /'sateɪ/ (also **satai** or **saté**) ▶ noun [mass noun] an Indonesian and Malaysian dish consisting of small pieces of meat grilled on a skewer and served with a spiced sauce that typically contains peanuts.
– ORIGIN from Malay *satai*, Indonesian *sate*.

SATB ▶ abbreviation soprano, alto, tenor, and bass (used to describe the constitution of a choir or to specify the singing voices required for a particular piece of music).

satchel ▶ noun a bag carried on the shoulder by a long strap and closed by a flap, used especially for school books.
– ORIGIN Middle English: from Old French *sachel*, from Latin *saccellus* 'small bag'.

satchel charge ▶ noun an explosive on a board fitted with a rope or wire loop for carrying and attaching.

satcom (also **SATCOM**) ▶ noun [mass noun] satellite communications.
– ORIGIN late 20th cent.: blend.

sate[1] ▶ verb [with obj.] satisfy (a desire or an appetite) to the full: *sate your appetite at the resort's restaurant.*
■ supply (someone) with as much as or more of something than is desired or can be managed: *he was sated with flying.*
– ORIGIN early 17th cent.: probably an alteration of dialect *sade*, from Old English *sadian* 'become sated or weary' (related to SAD). The change in the final consonant was due to association with SATIATE.

sate[2] ▶ verb archaic spelling of SAT.

saté ▶ noun variant spelling of SATAY.

sateen /sa'tiːn/ ▶ noun [mass noun] a cotton fabric woven like satin with a glossy surface.
– ORIGIN late 19th cent.: alteration of SATIN, on the pattern of *velveteen*.

satellite ▶ noun **1** an artificial body placed in orbit round the earth or another planet in order to collect information or for communication. ■ [as modifier] transmitted by satellite; using or relating to satellite technology: *satellite broadcasting.* ■ [mass noun] satellite television: *a news service on satellite.*
2 Astronomy a celestial body orbiting the earth or another planet.
3 [usu. as modifier] something that is separated from or on the periphery of something else but is nevertheless dependent on or controlled by it: *satellite offices in London and New York.* ■ a small country or state politically or economically dependent on another. ■ a community or town dependent on a nearby larger town.
4 Genetics a portion of the DNA of a genome with repeating base sequences and of different density from the main sequence.
– ORIGIN mid 16th cent. (in the sense 'follower, obsequious underling'): from French *satellite* or Latin *satelles, satellit-* 'attendant'.

satellite dish ▶ noun a bowl-shaped aerial with which signals are transmitted to or received from a communications satellite.

satellite feed ▶ noun a live broadcast via satellite forming part of another programme.

satellite television ▶ noun [mass noun] television broadcast using a satellite to relay signals to appropriately equipped customers in a particular area.

satellitium /ˌsatə'lɪtɪəm/ ▶ noun Astrology a grouping of several planets in a sign.

Sati /'sʌtiː/ Hinduism the wife of Shiva, reborn as Parvati. According to some accounts, she died by throwing herself into a sacred fire.

sati /'sʌtiː, sʌ'tiː/ (also **suttee**) ▶ noun (pl. **satis** or **suttees**) [mass noun] the former Hindu practice of a widow throwing herself on to her husband's funeral pyre. ■ [count noun] a widow who committed such an act.
– ORIGIN Hindi, from Sanskrit *satī* 'faithful wife', from *sat* 'good'.

satiate /'seɪʃɪeɪt/ ▶ verb another term for SATE[1]: *he folded up his newspaper, his curiosity satiated.*
▶ adjective archaic satisfied to the full; sated.
– DERIVATIVES **satiable** adjective (archaic), **satiation** noun.
– ORIGIN late Middle English: from Latin *satiatus*, past participle of *satiare*, from *satis* 'enough'.

Satie /'sati, 'sɑːti/, Erik (Alfred Leslie) (1866–1925), French avant-garde composer. He formed an irreverent avant-garde artistic set associated with Les Six, Dadaism, and surrealism. Notable works: *Gymnopédies* (1888).

satiety /sə'tʌɪɪti/ ▶ noun [mass noun] chiefly technical the feeling or state of being sated.
– ORIGIN mid 16th cent.: from Old French *saciete*, from Latin *satietas*, from *satis* 'enough'.

satiety centre ▶ noun Physiology an area of the brain situated in the hypothalamus and concerned with the regulation of food intake.

satin ▶ noun [mass noun] a smooth, glossy fabric, usually of silk, produced by a weave in which the threads of the warp are caught and looped by the weft only at certain intervals: [as modifier] *a blue satin dress.* ■ [as modifier] denoting or having a surface or finish resembling this fabric, produced on metal or other material: *an aluminium alloy with a black satin finish.*
▶ verb (**satins**, **satining**, **satined**) [with obj.] give a smooth, glossy surface to.
▶ adjective smooth like satin: *a luxurious satin look.*
– DERIVATIVES **satiny** adjective.
– ORIGIN late Middle English: via Old French from Arabic *zaytūnī* 'of Tsinkiang', a town in China.

satinette /ˌsatɪ'nɛt, 'satɪnɪt/ (also **satinet**) ▶ noun [mass noun] a fabric with a similar finish to satin, made partly or wholly of cotton or synthetic fibre.

satin paper ▶ noun fine glossy paper, used for writing or printmaking.

satin spar ▶ noun [mass noun] a fibrous variety of gypsum.

satin stitch ▶ noun [mass noun] a long straight embroidery stitch, giving the appearance of satin.

satin walnut ▶ noun see SWEET GUM.

satin weave ▶ noun [mass noun] a method of weaving fabric in which either the warp or the weft predominates on the surface.

satinwood ▶ noun **1** [mass noun] glossy yellowish timber from a tropical tree, valued for cabinetmaking.
2 the tropical hardwood tree that produces satinwood. ● Two species in the family Rutaceae: **Ceylon satinwood** (*Chloroxylon swietenia*), native to India and Sri Lanka,

and **West Indian** (or **Jamaican**) **satinwood** (*Zanthoxylum flava*), native to the Caribbean, Bermuda, and southern Florida. ■ used in names of trees which yield high-quality timber resembling satinwood, e.g. **Nigerian satinwood**.

satire /ˈsatʌɪə/ ▶ **noun** [mass noun] the use of humour, irony, exaggeration, or ridicule to expose and criticize people's stupidity or vices, particularly in the context of contemporary politics and other topical issues. ■ [count noun] a play, novel, film, or other work which uses satire: *a stinging* ***satire on*** *American politics.* ■ a genre of literature characterized by the use of satire. ■ [count noun] (in Latin literature) a literary miscellany, especially a poem ridiculing prevalent vices or follies.
– DERIVATIVES **satirist** noun.
– ORIGIN early 16th cent.: from French, or from Latin *satira*, later form of *satura* 'poetic medley'.

satiric /səˈtɪrɪk/ ▶ **adjective** another term for SATIRICAL.

satirical ▶ **adjective** containing or using satire: *a New York-based satirical magazine.* ■ sarcastic, critical, and mocking another's weaknesses: *his satirical sense of humour.*
– DERIVATIVES **satirically** adverb.
– ORIGIN early 16th cent.: from late Latin *satiricus* (from *satira* 'poetic medley': see SATIRE) + -AL.

satirize /ˈsatɪrʌɪz/ (also **satirise**) ▶ **verb** [with obj.] deride and criticize by means of satire: *the movie satirized the notion of national superiority.*
– DERIVATIVES **satirization** noun.

satisfaction ▶ **noun** [mass noun] **1** fulfilment of one's wishes, expectations, or needs, or the pleasure derived from this: *I looked round with satisfaction | managing directors seeking greater job satisfaction.* **2** Law the payment of a debt or fulfilment of an obligation or claim: *in* ***full and final satisfaction*** *of the claim.* ■ [with negative] what is felt to be owed or due to one, especially in reparation of an injustice or wrong: *the work will come to a halt if the electricity and telephone people* ***don't get satisfaction.*** ■ historical the opportunity to defend one's honour in a duel: *I* ***demand*** *the* ***satisfaction*** *of a gentleman.* **3** Christian Theology Christ's atonement for sin.
– PHRASES **to one's satisfaction** so that one is satisfied: *some amendments were made, not entirely to his satisfaction.*
– ORIGIN Middle English: from Old French, or from Latin *satisfactio(n-)*, from *satisfacere* 'satisfy, content' (see SATISFY). The earliest recorded use referred to the last part of religious penance after 'contrition' and 'confession': this involved fulfilment of the observance required by the confessor, in contrast with the current meaning 'fulfilment of one's own expectations'.

satisfactory ▶ **adjective** fulfilling expectations or needs; acceptable, though not outstanding or perfect: *he didn't get a satisfactory answer.* ■ (of a patient in a hospital) not deteriorating or likely to die. ■ Law (of evidence or a verdict) sufficient for the needs of the case: *the verdict is* ***safe and satisfactory.***
– DERIVATIVES **satisfactorily** adverb, **satisfactoriness** noun.
– ORIGIN late Middle English (in the sense 'leading to the atonement of sin'): from Old French *satisfactoire* or medieval Latin *satisfactorius*, from Latin *satisfacere* 'to content' (see SATISFY). The current senses date from the mid 17th cent.

satisfice /ˈsatɪsfʌɪs/ ▶ **verb** [no obj.] formal decide on and pursue a course of action that will satisfy the minimum requirements necessary to achieve a particular goal.
– ORIGIN mid 16th cent. (in the sense 'satisfy'): alteration of SATISFY, influenced by Latin *satisfacere*. The formal use dates from the 1950s.

satisfied ▶ **adjective** contented; pleased: *satisfied customers | she was very* ***satisfied with*** *the results.*

satisfy ▶ **verb** (**satisfies, satisfying, satisfied**) [with obj.] **1** meet the expectations, needs, or desires of (someone): *I have never been* ***satisfied with*** *my job.* ■ fulfil (a desire or need): *social services is trying to satisfy the needs of so many different groups.* ■ adequately meet or comply with (a condition, obligation, or demand): *the whole team is working flat out to satisfy demand.* ■ pay off (a debt or creditor): *there was insufficient collateral to satisfy the loan.* **2** provide (someone) with adequate or convincing information or proof about something: [with obj. and clause] *people need to be satisfied that the environmental assessments are accurate | the chief engineer* ***satisfied himself*** *that it was not a weapon.* **3** Mathematics (of a quantity) make (an equation) true.
– PHRASES **satisfy the examiners** Brit. reach the standard required to pass an examination.
– DERIVATIVES **satisfiability** noun, **satisfiable** adjective.
– ORIGIN late Middle English: from Old French *satisfier*, formed irregularly from Latin *satisfacere* 'to content', from *satis* 'enough' + *facere* 'make'.

satisfying ▶ **adjective** giving fulfilment or the pleasure associated with this: *these are very satisfying books.*
– DERIVATIVES **satisfyingly** adverb.

satnav /ˈsatnav/ ▶ **noun** [mass noun] navigation dependent on information received from satellites.
– ORIGIN 1970s: blend of SATELLITE and NAVIGATION.

satori /səˈtɔːri/ ▶ **noun** [mass noun] Buddhism sudden enlightenment: *the road that leads to satori.*
– ORIGIN Japanese, literally 'awakening'.

satphone ▶ **noun** a telephone that transmits its signal via a geostationary communications satellite.

satrap /ˈsatrap/ ▶ **noun** a provincial governor in the ancient Persian empire. ■ any subordinate or local ruler.
– ORIGIN late Middle English: from Old French *satrape* or Latin *satrapa*, based on Old Persian *kšathra-pāvan* 'country-protector'.

satrapy /ˈsatrəpi/ ▶ **noun** (pl. **satrapies**) a province governed by a satrap.

satsang /ˈsatsaŋ, ˈsʌtsʌŋ/ ▶ **noun** Indian a spiritual discourse or sacred gathering.
– ORIGIN from Sanskrit *satsaṅga* 'association with good men'.

Satsuma /ˈsatsʊmə/ a former province of SW Japan. It comprised the major part of the south-western peninsula of Kyushu island, also known as the Satsuma Peninsula.

satsuma /satˈsuːmə/ ▶ **noun 1** a tangerine of a hardy loose-skinned variety, originally grown in Japan. **2** also /ˈsatsʊmə, -sjʊ-/ (**Satsuma** or **Satsuma ware**) [mass noun] Japanese pottery from Satsuma, ranging from simple 17th-century earthenware to later work made for export to Europe, often elaborately painted, with a crackled cream-coloured glaze.
– ORIGIN late 19th cent.: named after the province SATSUMA.

saturate ▶ **verb** /ˈsatʃəreɪt/ [with obj.] cause (something) to become thoroughly soaked with water or other liquid so that no more can be absorbed: *the soil is saturated.* ■ cause (a substance) to combine with, dissolve, or hold the greatest possible quantity of another substance: *the groundwater is* ***saturated with*** *calcium hydroxide.* ■ magnetize or charge (a substance or device) fully. ■ Electronics put (a device) into a state in which no further increase in current is achievable. ■ fill (something or someone) with something until no more can be held or absorbed: *the air is* ***saturated with*** *the smells of food.* ■ supply (a market) beyond the point at which the demand for a product is satisfied: *Japan's electronics industry began to saturate the world markets.* ■ overwhelm (an enemy target area) by concentrated bombing.
▶ **noun** /ˈsatʃərət/ (usu. **saturates**) a saturated fat.
▶ **adjective** /ˈsatʃərət/ literary saturated with moisture.
– DERIVATIVES **saturable** adjective (technical).
– ORIGIN late Middle English (as an adjective in the sense 'satisfied'): from Latin *saturat-* 'filled, glutted', from the verb *saturare*, from *satur* 'full'. The early sense of the verb (mid 16th cent.) was 'satisfy'; the noun dates from the 1950s.

saturated ▶ **adjective 1** holding as much water or moisture as can be absorbed; thoroughly soaked. ■ Chemistry (of a solution) containing the largest possible amount of a particular solute. ■ [often in combination] having or holding as much as can be absorbed of something: *the glitzy, media-saturated plasticity of Los Angeles.* **2** Chemistry (of an organic molecule) containing the greatest possible number of hydrogen atoms, without carbon–carbon double or triple bonds. ■ denoting fats containing a high proportion of fatty acid molecules without double bonds, considered to be less healthy in the diet than unsaturated fats. **3** (of colour) very bright, full, and free from an admixture of white: *intense and saturated colour.*

saturation ▶ **noun** [mass noun] the state of being saturated or the action of saturating. ■ Chemistry the degree or extent to which something is dissolved or absorbed compared with the maximum possible, usually expressed as a percentage. ■ [as modifier] to a very full extent, especially beyond the point regarded as necessary or desirable: *the press provided saturation coverage of the hearings.* ■ (also **colour saturation**) (especially in photography) the intensity of a colour, expressed as the degree to which it differs from white.

saturation diving ▶ **noun** [mass noun] deep-sea diving in which the diver's bloodstream is saturated with helium or other suitable gas at the pressure of the surrounding water, so that the decompression time afterwards is independent of the duration of the dive.

saturation point ▶ **noun** [in sing.] Chemistry the stage at which no more of a substance can be absorbed into a vapour or dissolved into a solution. ■ the stage beyond which no more of something can be absorbed or accepted: *the market quickly reached saturation point.*

Saturday ▶ **noun** the day of the week before Sunday and following Friday, and (together with Sunday) forming part of the weekend: *the match will be held* ***on Saturday*** *| the counter is closed on Saturdays and Sundays |* [as modifier] *Saturday night.*
▶ **adverb** chiefly N. Amer. on Saturday: *he made his first appearance Saturday.* ■ (**Saturdays**) on Saturdays; each Saturday: *they sleep late Saturdays.*
– ORIGIN Old English *Sætern(es)dæg*, translation of Latin *Saturni dies* 'day of Saturn'; compare with Dutch *zaterdag*.

Saturday night special ▶ **noun** informal, chiefly N. Amer. a cheap low-calibre pistol or revolver, easily obtained and concealed.

Saturn 1 Roman Mythology an ancient god, regarded as a god of agriculture. Greek equivalent CRONUS. [from Latin *Saturnus*, perhaps from Etruscan.] **2** Astronomy the sixth planet from the sun in the solar system, circled by a system of broad flat rings.

> Saturn orbits between Jupiter and Uranus at an average distance of 1,427 million km from the sun. It is a gas giant with an equatorial diameter of 120,000 km, with a conspicuous ring system extending out to a distance twice as great. The planet has a dense hydrogen-rich atmosphere, similar to that of Jupiter but with less distinct banding. There are at least eighteen satellites, the largest of which is Titan, and including small shepherd satellites that orbit close to two of the rings.

3 a series of American space rockets, of which the very large *Saturn V* was used as the launch vehicle for the Apollo missions of 1968–72.

Saturnalia /ˌsatəˈneɪlɪə/ ▶ **noun** [treated as sing. or pl.] the ancient Roman festival of Saturn in December, a period of general merrymaking and the predecessor of Christmas. ■ (**saturnalia**) an occasion of wild revelry or indulgence: *a saturnalia of shopping.*
– DERIVATIVES **saturnalian** adjective.
– ORIGIN Latin, literally 'matters relating to Saturn', neuter plural of *Saturnalis*.

Saturnian ▶ **adjective 1** relating to the planet Saturn. **2** another term for SATURNINE.

saturniid /səˈtəːnɪɪd/ ▶ **noun** Entomology a silk moth of a family (Saturniidae) which includes the emperor moths and the giant Indian silk moths. They typically have prominent eyespots on the wings.
– ORIGIN late 19th cent.: from modern Latin *Saturniidae* (plural), from the genus name *Saturnia*.

saturnine /ˈsatənʌɪn/ ▶ **adjective 1** (of a person or their manner) gloomy: *a saturnine temperament.* ■ (of a person or their features) dark in colouring and moody or mysterious: *his saturnine face and dark, watchful eyes.* **2** archaic relating to lead.
– ORIGIN late Middle English (as a term in astrology): from Old French *saturnin*, from medieval Latin *Saturninus* 'of Saturn' (identified with lead by the alchemists and associated with slowness and gloom by astrologers).

saturnism ▶ **noun** archaic term for LEAD POISONING.
– ORIGIN mid 19th cent.: from SATURN in the obsolete alchemical sense 'lead' + -ISM.

satyagraha /sʌˈtjɑːgrəhɑː/ ▶ **noun** [mass noun] a policy of passive political resistance, especially that advocated by Mahatma Gandhi against British rule in India.
– ORIGIN Sanskrit, from *satya* 'truth' + *āgraha* 'obstinacy'.

satyr /ˈsatə/ ▶ **noun 1** Greek Mythology one of a class of lustful, drunken woodland gods. In Greek art they were represented as a man with a horse's ears and tail, but in Roman representations as a man with a goat's ears, tail, legs, and horns. ■ a man who has strong sexual desires.

S

2 a satyrid butterfly with chiefly dark brown wings. ● Tribes Satyrini (including the Eurasian genus *Satyrus*) and Euptychiini (the American **wood satyrs**), subfamily Satyrinae, family Nymphalidae.
– DERIVATIVES **satyric** adjective.
– ORIGIN late Middle English: from Old French *satyre*, or via Latin from Greek *saturos*.

satyriasis /ˌsatɪˈrʌɪəsɪs/ ▶ **noun** [mass noun] uncontrollable or excessive sexual desire in a man.
– ORIGIN late Middle English: via late Latin from Greek *saturiasis*, from *saturos* (see SATYR).

satyrid /səˈtɪrɪd/ ▶ **noun** Entomology a butterfly of a group which includes the browns, heaths, ringlets, and related species. They typically have brown wings with small eyespots and many live in woodland and breed on grasses. Also called BROWN. ● Subfamily Satyrinae, family Nymphalidae (formerly the family Satyridae).
– ORIGIN early 20th cent.: from modern Latin *Satyridae* (plural), from Latin *Satyrus* (see SATYR), used as a genus name.

sauce ▶ **noun** [mass noun] **1** a liquid or semi-liquid substance served with food to add moistness and flavour: *tomato sauce* | [count noun] *the stock cubes can be added to soups and sauces.* ■ N. Amer. stewed fruit, especially apples, eaten as dessert or used as a garnish.
2 (**the sauce**) informal alcoholic drink: *she's been on the sauce for years.*
3 informal, chiefly Brit. impertinence; cheek.
▶ **verb** [with obj.] **1** provide a sauce for (something); season with a sauce. ■ make more interesting and exciting.
2 informal be rude or impudent to (someone).
– PHRASES **what's sauce for the goose is sauce for the gander** proverb what is appropriate in one case is also appropriate in the other case in question.
– DERIVATIVES **sauceless** adjective.
– ORIGIN Middle English: from Old French, based on Latin *salsus* 'salted', past participle of *salere* 'to salt', from *sal* 'salt'. Compare with SALAD.

sauce boat ▶ **noun** a long, narrow jug used for serving sauce.

sauced ▶ **adjective** informal, chiefly N. Amer. drunk.

sauce mousseline ▶ **noun** see MOUSSELINE (sense 3).

saucepan ▶ **noun** a deep cooking pan, typically round, made of metal, and with one long handle and a lid.
– DERIVATIVES **saucepanful** noun (pl. **saucepanfuls**).

saucer ▶ **noun** a shallow dish, typically having a circular indentation in the centre, on which a cup is placed.
– PHRASES **have eyes like saucers** have one's eyes opened wide in amazement.
– DERIVATIVES **saucerful** noun (pl. **saucerfuls**), **saucerless** adjective.
– ORIGIN Middle English (denoting a condiment dish): from Old French *saussier(e)* 'sauce boat', probably suggested by late Latin *salsarium*.

saucer bug ▶ **noun** a disc-shaped predatory water bug which lives in muddy ponds and breathes by means of an air bubble around the body. ● *Ilyocoris cimicoides*, family Naucoridae, suborder Heteroptera.

saucier /ˈsəʊsɪeɪ/ ▶ **noun** a chef who prepares sauces.
– ORIGIN French.

saucisson /ˈsəʊsɪsɒ̃/, French /sosisɔ̃/ ▶ **noun** a large, thick French sausage, typically firm in texture and flavoured with herbs.
– ORIGIN French, literally 'large sausage'.

saucy ▶ **adjective** (**saucier**, **sauciest**) informal **1** chiefly Brit. sexually suggestive in a light-hearted and humorous way. ■ cheeky or impertinent.
2 chiefly N. Amer. having or expressing a bold, lively, or spirited manner.
– DERIVATIVES **saucily** adverb, **sauciness** noun.
– ORIGIN early 16th cent. (in the sense 'savoury, flavoured with sauce'): from SAUCE + -Y[1].

saudade /saʊˈdɑːdə/ ▶ **noun** [mass noun] (especially with reference to songs or poetry) a feeling of longing, melancholy, or nostalgia that is supposedly characteristic of the Portuguese or Brazilian temperament.
– ORIGIN Portuguese.

Saudi /ˈsaʊdi, ˈsɔːdi/ ▶ **adjective** relating to Saudi Arabia or its ruling dynasty.
▶ **noun** (pl. **Saudis**) a citizen of Saudi Arabia, or a member of its ruling dynasty.
– ORIGIN from the name of Abdul-Aziz ibn *Saud* (1880–1953), first king of Saudi Arabia.

Saudi Arabia a country in SW Asia occupying most of the Arabian peninsula; pop. 28,686,600 (est. 2009); official language, Arabic; capital, Riyadh.

> The birthplace of Islam in the 7th century, Saudi Arabia emerged from the Arab revolt against the Turks during the First World War to become an independent kingdom in 1932. Since the Second World War the economy has been revolutionized by the exploitation of the area's oil resources, and Saudi Arabia is the largest oil producer in the Middle East. It continues to be governed along traditional Islamic lines.

– DERIVATIVES **Saudi Arabian** adjective & noun.

sauerbraten /ˈsaʊəˌbrɑːt(ə)n/ ▶ **noun** [mass noun] chiefly N. Amer. a dish of German origin consisting of beef that is marinaded in vinegar with peppercorns, onions, and other seasonings before cooking.
– ORIGIN from German, from *sauer* 'sour' + *Braten* 'roast meat'.

sauerkraut /ˈsaʊəkraʊt/ ▶ **noun** [mass noun] a German dish of chopped pickled cabbage.
– ORIGIN from German, from *sauer* 'sour' + *Kraut* 'vegetable'.

sauger /ˈsɔːgə/ ▶ **noun** a slender North American pike-perch with silver eyes, which is active at twilight and at night. ● *Stizostedion canadense*, family Percidae.
– ORIGIN late 19th cent.: of unknown origin.

Saul (in the Bible) the first king of Israel (11th century BC).

Saul of Tarsus see PAUL, ST.

Sault Sainte Marie /ˌsuː seɪnt məˈriː/ two North American river ports which face each other across the falls of the St Mary's River, between Lakes Superior and Huron. The northern port (pop. 74,948, 2006) lies in Ontario, Canada, while the southern port (pop. 14,087, est. 2008) is in the US state of Michigan.

Saumur /ˈsəʊmjʊə/, French /somyʀ/ ▶ **noun** [mass noun] a French white wine resembling champagne.
– ORIGIN from the name of a town in the department of Maine-et-Loire.

sauna /ˈsɔːnə/ ▶ **noun** a small room used as a hot-air or steam bath for cleaning and refreshing the body: figurative *the air-con was broken—the place was like a sauna.* ■ a session in a sauna.
– ORIGIN late 19th cent.: from Finnish.

saunf /sɔ̃ːf/ ▶ **noun** Indian term for ANISEED, often served in the Indian subcontinent after meals, mixed with sugar.
– ORIGIN from Hindi *sаũph*.

saunter ▶ **verb** [no obj., with adverbial of direction] walk in a slow, relaxed manner: *Adam sauntered into the room.*
▶ **noun** a leisurely stroll: *a quiet saunter down the road.*
– DERIVATIVES **saunterer** noun.
– ORIGIN late Middle English (in the sense 'to muse, wonder'): of unknown origin. The current sense dates from the mid 17th cent.

-saur ▶ **combining form** forming names of reptiles, especially extinct ones: *ichthyosaur* | *stegosaur*.
– ORIGIN modern Latin, from Greek *sauros* 'lizard'; compare with -SAURUS, a suffix of modern Latin genus names.

Sauria /ˈsɔːrɪə/ ▶ **plural noun** Zoology former term for LACERTILIA.
– ORIGIN modern Latin (plural), from Greek *sauros* 'lizard'.

saurian /ˈsɔːrɪən/ ▶ **adjective** of or like a lizard.
▶ **noun** any large reptile, especially a dinosaur or other extinct form.
– ORIGIN early 19th cent.: from modern Latin *Sauria* (see SAURIA) + -AN.

saurischian /sɔːˈrɪskɪən, -ˈrɪʃɪən/ Palaeontology
▶ **adjective** relating to or denoting dinosaurs of an order distinguished by having a pelvic structure resembling that of lizards. Compare with ORNITHISCHIAN.
▶ **noun** a saurischian dinosaur. ● Order Saurischia, superorder Dinosauria; comprises the carnivorous theropods and the herbivorous sauropods.
– ORIGIN late 19th cent.: from the modern Latin plural *Saurischia* (from Greek *sauros* 'lizard' + *iskhion* 'hip joint') + -AN.

sauropod /ˈsɔːrəpɒd, ˈsaʊr-/ ▶ **noun** a very large quadrupedal herbivorous dinosaur with a long neck and tail, small head, and massive limbs. ● Infraorder Sauropoda, suborder Sauropodomorpha, order Saurischia; e.g. apatosaurus, brachiosaurus, and diplodocus.
– ORIGIN late 19th cent.: from modern Latin *Sauropoda* (plural), from Greek *sauros* 'lizard' + *pous, pod-* 'foot'.

-saurus ▶ **combining form** forming genus names of reptiles, especially extinct ones: *stegosaurus*.
– ORIGIN modern Latin.

saury /ˈsɔːri/ ▶ **noun** (pl. **sauries**) a long slender-bodied edible marine fish with an elongated snout. ● Family Scomberesocidae: four genera and species, including *Scomberesox saurus* of the Atlantic (also called SKIPPER[2]), and *Cololabis saira* of the Pacific.
– ORIGIN late 18th cent.: perhaps via late Latin from Greek *sauros* 'horse mackerel'.

sausage ▶ **noun** **1** a short cylindrical tube of minced pork, beef, or other meat encased in a skin, typically sold raw to be grilled or fried before eating. ■ [mass noun] a cylindrical tube of minced pork, beef, or other meat seasoned and cooked or preserved, sold mainly to be eaten cold in slices: *smoked German sausage.* ■ [usu. as modifier] an object shaped like a sausage.
2 Brit. used as an affectionate form of address, especially to a child: *'Silly sausage,' he teased.*
– PHRASES **not a sausage** Brit. informal nothing at all.
– ORIGIN late Middle English: from Old Northern French *saussiche*, from medieval Latin *salsicia*, from Latin *salsus* 'salted' (see SAUCE).

sausage dog ▶ **noun** informal British term for DACHSHUND.

sausage meat ▶ **noun** [mass noun] minced meat with spices and a binder such as cereal, used in sausages or as a stuffing.

sausage roll ▶ **noun** Brit. a piece of sausage meat wrapped in pastry and baked.

sausage tree ▶ **noun** a tropical African tree with red bell-shaped flowers and large pendulous sausage-shaped fruits. ● *Kigelia pinnata*, family Bignoniaceae.

Saussure /səʊˈsjʊə/, French /sosyʀ/, Ferdinand de (1857–1913), Swiss linguistics scholar. He was one of the founders of modern linguistics and his work is fundamental to the development of structuralism. Saussure made a distinction between *langue* and *parole*, and stressed that linguistic study should focus on the former.

sauté /ˈsəʊteɪ/ ▶ **adjective** [attrib.] fried quickly in a little hot fat: *sauté potatoes.*
▶ **noun** **1** a dish cooked in such a way.
2 Ballet a jump off both feet, landing in the same position.
▶ **verb** (**sautés**, **sautéing**, **sautéed** or **sautéd**) [with obj.] fry quickly in a little hot fat: *sauté the onions in the olive oil.*
– ORIGIN early 19th cent.: French, literally 'jumped', past participle of *sauter*.

Sauternes /sə(ʊ)ˈtəːn/, French /sotɛʀn/ ▶ **noun** [mass noun] a sweet white wine from Sauternes in the Bordeaux region of France.

sautoir /ˈsəʊtwɑː/ ▶ **noun** a long necklace consisting of a fine gold chain and typically set with jewels.
– ORIGIN 1930s: French, extended use of the original word which denoted a harness loop used as a stirrup for 'jumping' (from *sauter* 'to jump') into the saddle.

sauve qui peut /ˌsəʊv kiː ˈpəː/ ▶ **noun** archaic or literary a general stampede, panic, or disorder.
– ORIGIN French, literally 'save who can'.

Sauveterrian /səʊvˈtɛːrɪən/ ▶ **adjective** Archaeology relating to or denoting an early Mesolithic culture of western Europe, especially France, dated to about 9,500–7,500 years ago. ■ (as noun **the Sauveterrian**) the Sauveterrian culture or period.
– ORIGIN 1940s: *Sauveterre*-la-Lémance, France, the type site, + -IAN.

Sauvignon /ˈsəʊvɪnjɒ̃/ (also **Sauvignon Blanc**) ▶ **noun** [mass noun] a variety of white wine grape. ■ a white wine made from the Sauvignon grape.
– ORIGIN French.

Savage, Michael Joseph (1872–1940), New Zealand Labour statesman, Prime Minister 1935–40. New Zealand's first Labour Prime Minister, he introduced many reforms, including social security legislation which he dubbed 'applied Christianity'.

savage ▶ **adjective** **1** (of an animal or force of nature) fierce, violent, and uncontrolled: *packs of savage dogs roamed the streets.* ■ cruel and vicious; aggressively hostile: *a savage attack on the government.*
2 (of something bad or negative) very great; severe: *the decision was a savage blow for the town.*
3 (chiefly in historical or literary contexts) primitive; uncivilized. ■ (of a place) wild-looking and inhospitable; uncultivated.
▶ **noun** **1** (chiefly in historical or literary contexts) a member of a people regarded as primitive and uncivilized.
2 a brutal or vicious person: *the mother of one of the victims has described his assailants as savages.*
3 Heraldry a representation of a bearded and semi-naked man with a wreath of leaves.

▸ **verb** [with obj.] (especially of a dog or wild animal) attack ferociously and maul: *police are rounding up dogs after a girl was savaged.* ▪ subject to a vicious verbal attack; criticize brutally: *he savaged the government for wasting billions in their failed bid to prop up the pound.*
– DERIVATIVES **savagely** adverb, **savageness** noun.
– ORIGIN Middle English: from Old French *sauvage* 'wild', from Latin *silvaticus* 'of the woods', from *silva* 'a wood'.

savagery ▸ **noun** (pl. **savageries**) [mass noun] **1** the quality of being fierce or cruel: *a crime of the utmost savagery.*
2 (chiefly in historical or literary contexts) the condition of being primitive or uncivilized: *without adult society, the children descend into savagery.*

Savai'i /sɑːˈvʌɪi/ (also **Savaii**) a mountainous volcanic island in the SW Pacific, the largest of the Samoan islands.

SAVAK /ˈsavak/ ▸ **noun** the secret intelligence organization of Iran, established in 1957 and disbanded in 1979.
– ORIGIN acronym from Persian *Sāzmān-i-Attalāt Va Amnīyat-i-Keshvar* 'National Security and Intelligence Organization'.

Savannah /səˈvanə/ a port in Georgia, just south of the border with South Carolina, on the Savannah River close to its outlet on the Atlantic; pop. 132,410 (est. 2008).

savannah (also **savanna**) ▸ **noun** a grassy plain in tropical and subtropical regions, with few trees.
– ORIGIN mid 16th cent.: from Spanish *sabana*, from Taino *zavana*.

Savannakhet /ˌsavanəˈkɛt/ (also **Savannaket**) a town in southern Laos, on the Mekong River at the border with Thailand; pop. 76,200 (est. 2009).

savant /ˈsav(ə)nt/, French /savɑ̃/ ▸ **noun** a learned person, especially a distinguished scientist. See also IDIOT SAVANT.
– ORIGIN early 18th cent.: French, literally 'knowing (person)', present participle (used as a noun) of *savoir*.

savante /ˈsav(ə)nt/, French /savɑ̃t/ ▸ **noun** a female savant.
– ORIGIN mid 18th cent.: French, feminine of *savant* (see SAVANT).

savarin /ˈsavərɪn/ ▸ **noun** a light ring-shaped cake made with yeast and soaked in liqueur-flavoured syrup.
– ORIGIN named after Anthelme Brillat-*Savarin* (1755–1826), French gastronome.

savate /səˈvɑːt/ ▸ **noun** [mass noun] a French method of boxing in which feet and fists are used.
– ORIGIN French, originally denoting an ill-fitting shoe.

save[1] ▸ **verb** [with obj.] **1** keep safe or rescue (someone or something) from harm or danger: *they brought him in to help* **save** *the club* **from** *bankruptcy.* ▪ prevent (someone) from dying: *the doctors did everything they could to save him.* ▪ (in Christian use) preserve (a person's soul) from damnation. ▪ keep (someone) in health (used in exclamations and formulaic expressions): *God save the Queen.*
2 keep and store up (something, especially money) for future use: *she had never been able to save much from her salary* | [no obj.] *you can* **save up for** *retirement in a number of ways.* ▪ avoid the need to use up or spend (money, time, or other resources): *save £20* **on** *a new camcorder* | [with two objs] *an efficient dishwasher would save them one year and three months at the sink.* ▪ preserve (something) by not expending or using it: *save your strength till later.* ▪ (in imperative **save it**) N. Amer. informal stop talking: *save it, Joey—I'm in big trouble now.*
3 Computing keep (data) by moving a copy to a storage location: *save the instructions to a new file.*
4 avoid, lessen, or guard against: *this approach saves wear and tear on the books* | [with two objs] *the statement was made to save the government some embarrassment.*
5 prevent an opponent from scoring (a goal or point) in a game or from winning (the game): *the powerful German saved three match points.* ▪ Soccer (of a goalkeeper) stop (a shot) from entering the goal. ▪ Baseball (of a relief pitcher) preserve (a winning position) gained by another pitcher.
▸ **noun 1** chiefly Soccer an act of preventing an opponent's scoring: *the keeper made a great save.* ▪ Baseball an instance of preserving a winning position gained by another pitcher.
2 Computing an act of saving data to a storage location.
– PHRASES **save one's breath** [often in imperative] not bother to say something because it is pointless. **save the day** (or **situation**) find or provide a solution to a difficulty or disaster. **save face, save someone's face** see FACE. **save someone's life** prevent someone dying by taking specific action. ▪ (**cannot do something to save one's life**) used to indicate that the person in question is completely incompetent at a particular activity or task: *Adrian couldn't draw to save his life.* **save someone's skin** (or **neck** or **bacon**) rescue someone from danger or difficulty. **save the tide** Nautical, archaic get in and out of port while the tide lasts. **save someone the trouble** (or **bother**) avoid involving someone in useless or pointless effort: *write it down and save yourself the trouble of remembering.*
– DERIVATIVES **savable** (also **saveable**) adjective.
– ORIGIN Middle English: from Old French *sauver*, from late Latin *salvare*, from Latin *salvus* 'safe'. The noun dates from the late 19th cent.

save[2] ▸ **preposition & conjunction** formal or literary except; other than: *no one needed to know save herself* | *the kitchen was empty* **save for** *Boris.*
– ORIGIN Middle English: from Old French *sauf, sauve*, from Latin *salvo, salva* (ablative singular of *salvus* 'safe'), used in phrases such as *salvo jure, salva innocentia* 'with no violation of right or innocence'.

save as you earn (abbrev.: **SAYE**) ▸ **noun** (in the UK) a method of saving money that carries certain tax privileges.

saveloy /ˈsavəlɔɪ/ ▸ **noun** Brit. a seasoned red pork sausage, dried and smoked and sold ready to eat.
– ORIGIN mid 19th cent.: alteration of obsolete French *cervelat*, from Italian *cervellata*; compare with CERVELAT.

saver ▸ **noun 1** a person who regularly saves money through a bank or recognized scheme.
2 [in combination] an object, action, or process that prevents a particular resource from being used up or expended: *an annual check-up can be a significant money-saver.*
3 a travel fare offering reductions on the standard price: *a new saver from London to Edinburgh.*
4 Horse Racing, informal a hedging bet.

Savery /ˈseɪvəri/, Thomas (*c.*1650–1715), English engineer; known as **Captain Savery**. He patented an early steam engine that was later developed by Thomas Newcomen.

Save the Children Fund (in the UK) a charity founded in 1919 operating internationally to aid children. Princess Anne has been its president since 1971.

savin /ˈsavɪn/ ▸ **noun** a bushy Eurasian juniper which typically has horizontally spreading branches.
● *Juniperus sabina*, family Cupressaceae.
▪ [mass noun] an extract obtained from this plant, formerly used as an abortifacient.
– ORIGIN Old English, from Old French *savine*, from Latin *sabina* (*herba*) 'Sabine (herb)'.

saving ▸ **noun 1** an economy of or reduction in money, time, or another resource: *this resulted in a considerable* **saving in** *development costs.*
2 (usu. **one's savings**) the money one has saved, especially through a bank or official scheme: *the agents were cheating them out of their* **life savings**.
3 Law a reservation; an exception.
▸ **adjective** [in combination] preventing waste of a particular resource: *an energy-saving light bulb.*
▸ **preposition 1** with the exception of; except.
2 archaic with due respect to.
– ORIGIN Middle English: from SAVE[1]; the preposition probably from SAVE[2], on the pattern of *touching*.

saving clause ▸ **noun** Law a provision in a contract, statute, or other legal document containing an exemption from one or more of its conditions or obligations.

saving grace ▸ **noun** [mass noun] the redeeming grace of God. ▪ [count noun] a redeeming quality or characteristic.

savings account ▸ **noun** a deposit account.

savings and loan (also **savings and loan association**) ▸ **noun** (in the US) an institution which accepts savings at interest and lends money to savers for house or other purchases.

savings bank ▸ **noun** a non-profit-making financial institution receiving small deposits at interest.

Savings Bond ▸ **noun 1** another term for PREMIUM BOND.
2 (in the US) a government bond sold to the general public, yielding variable interest.

savings certificate ▸ **noun** (in the UK) a document issued to savers by the government guaranteeing fixed interest for five years on a deposit.

savings ratio ▸ **noun** Economics the ratio of personal savings to disposable income in an economy.

saviour (US **savior**) ▸ **noun** a person who saves someone or something from danger or difficulty. ▪ (**the/our Saviour**) (in Christianity) God or Jesus Christ as the redeemer of sin and saver of souls.
– ORIGIN Middle English: from Old French *sauveour*, from ecclesiastical Latin *salvator* (translating Greek *sōtēr*), from late Latin *salvare* 'to save'.

savoir faire /ˌsavwɑː ˈfɛː/, French /savwaʀ fɛʀ/ ▸ **noun** [mass noun] the ability to act or speak appropriately in social situations.
– ORIGIN early 19th cent.: French, literally 'know how to do'.

Savonarola /ˌsavɒnəˈrəʊlə/, Girolamo (1452–98), Italian preacher and religious reformer. A Dominican monk and strict ascetic, he became popular for his passionate preaching against immorality and corruption. Savonarola became virtual ruler of Florence (1494–5) but in 1497 he was excommunicated and later executed as a heretic.

Savonlinna /ˌsɑːvɒnˈlɪnə/ a town in SE Finland; pop. 27,755 (2009).

Savonnerie carpet /ˈsavɒ̃ri/ ▸ **noun** a hand knotted pile carpet, originally made in 17th-century Paris.
– ORIGIN late 19th cent.: French *savonnerie*, literally 'soap factory', referring to the original building on the site, converted to carpet manufacture.

savory ▸ **noun** [mass noun] an aromatic plant of the mint family, used as a culinary herb. ● Genus *Satureja*, family Labiatae: several species, in particular the annual **summer savory** (*S. hortensis*), which is traditionally used with beans, and the coarser flavoured perennial **winter savory** (*S. montana*).
– ORIGIN Middle English: perhaps from Old English *sætherie*, or via Old French, from Latin *satureia*.

savour (US **savor**) ▸ **verb 1** [with obj.] taste (good food or drink) and enjoy it to the full: *gourmets will want to savour our game specialities.* ▪ enjoy or appreciate (something pleasant) to the full, especially by lingering over it: *I wanted to savour every moment.*
2 [no obj.] (**savour of**) have a suggestion or trace of (a quality or attribute, typically one considered bad): *their genuflections savoured of superstition and popery.*
▸ **noun** [mass noun] a characteristic taste, flavour, or smell, especially a pleasant one: *the subtle savour of wood smoke.* ▪ a suggestion or trace, typically of something bad.
– DERIVATIVES **savourless** adjective.
– ORIGIN Middle English: from Old French, from Latin *sapor*, from *sapere* 'to taste'.

savoury (US **savory**) ▸ **adjective 1** (of food) belonging to the category which is salty or spicy rather than sweet.
2 [usu. with negative] morally wholesome or acceptable: *everyone knew it was a front for less savoury operations.*
▸ **noun** (pl. **savouries**) chiefly Brit. a savoury snack.
– DERIVATIVES **savourily** adverb, **savouriness** noun.
– ORIGIN Middle English (in the sense 'pleasing to the sense of taste or smell'): from Old French *savoure* 'tasty, fragrant', based on Latin *sapor* 'taste'.

Savoy an area of SE France bordering on NW Italy, a former duchy ruled by the counts of Savoy from the 11th century. In 1720 Savoy was joined with Sardinia and Piedmont to form the kingdom of Sardinia, but in 1861, when Sardinia became part of a unified Italy, Savoy was ceded to France.
– DERIVATIVES **Savoyard** adjective & noun.

savoy (also **savoy cabbage**) ▸ **noun** a cabbage of a hardy variety with densely wrinkled leaves.
– ORIGIN late 16th cent.: from SAVOY.

Savu Sea /ˈsɑːvuː/ a part of the Indian Ocean which is encircled by the islands of Sumba, Flores, and Timor.

savvy informal, chiefly N. Amer. ▸ **noun** [mass noun] shrewdness and practical knowledge, especially in politics or business: *the corporate-finance bankers lacked the necessary political savvy.*
▸ **verb** (**savvies, savvying, savvied**) [with clause] know or understand: *Tom would savvy what to do about her* | [no obj.] *I've been told, but I want to make sure. Savvy?*
▸ **adjective** (**savvier, savviest**) shrewd and knowledgeable about the realities of life: [in combination] *the city's young, media-savvy crowd.*
– ORIGIN late 18th cent.: originally black and pidgin English imitating Spanish *sabe usted* 'you know'.

saw[1] ▸ **noun** a hand tool for cutting wood or other hard materials, typically with a long, thin serrated blade and operated using a backwards and forwards movement. ■ a mechanical power-driven tool for cutting which has a toothed rotating disc or moving band. ■ Zoology a serrated organ or part, such as the toothed snout of a sawfish.
▸ **verb** (past participle chiefly Brit. **sawn** or chiefly N. Amer. **sawed**) **1** [with obj.] cut (something) using a saw: *the top of each post is **sawn off** at railing height* | [no obj.] *thieves escaped after **sawing through** iron bars on a window.* ■ make or form (something) using a saw: *the seats are sawn from well-seasoned elm planks.* ■ cut (something) as if with a saw, especially roughly or so as to leave rough or unfinished edges: *the woman who **sawed off** all my lovely hair.* ■ [no obj.] make rapid sawlike motions in cutting, or in playing a stringed instrument: *he was **sawing away** energetically at the loaf.*
2 [no obj.] (**saw off**) Canadian (of two or more people) compromise by making concessions to one another: *they sawed off over wages and concluded the deal.*
– DERIVATIVES **sawlike** adjective.
– ORIGIN Old English *saga*, of Germanic origin; related to Dutch *zaag*.

saw[2] past of **SEE**[1].

saw[3] ▸ **noun** a proverb or maxim.
– ORIGIN Old English *sagu* 'a saying, speech', of Germanic origin; related to German *Sage*, also to **SAY** and **SAGA**.

sawbench ▸ **noun** a circular saw mounted under a bench so that the blade projects up through a slot.

sawbill ▸ **noun** another term for **MERGANSER**.

sawbones ▸ **noun** (pl. **same**) informal a doctor or surgeon.

sawbuck ▸ **noun** N. Amer. **1** a sawhorse.
2 informal a $10 note. [by association of the X-shaped ends of a sawhorse with the Roman numeral X (= 10).]
– ORIGIN mid 19th cent.: from Dutch *zaagbok*, from *zaag* 'saw' + *bok* 'vaulting horse'.

saw doctor ▸ **noun** a specialist in the care and sharpening of saws.

sawdust ▸ **noun** [mass noun] powdery particles of wood produced by sawing.

saw-edged ▸ **adjective** with a jagged edge like a saw.

sawed-off ▸ **adjective & noun** North American term for **SAWN-OFF**.

sawfish ▸ **noun** (pl. **same** or **sawfishes**) a large, tropical, mainly marine fish related to the rays, with an elongated flattened snout that bears large blunt teeth along each side. ● Family Pristidae: two genera, in particular *Pristis*, and several species.

sawfly ▸ **noun** (pl. **sawflies**) an insect related to the wasps, with a sawlike egg-laying tube used to cut into plant tissue before depositing the eggs. The larvae resemble caterpillars and can be serious pests of crops and foliage. ● Suborder Symphyta, order Hymenoptera: many families.

saw frame ▸ **noun** a frame in which a saw blade is held taut.

S

saw gin ▸ **noun** Brit. another term for **COTTON GIN**.

sawgrass ▸ **noun** chiefly N. Amer. a sedge with spiny-edged leaves. ● *Cladium*, family Cyperaceae: two species, in particular the North American *C. jamaicensis*, which is a dominant plant in the Florida Everglades.

sawhorse ▸ **noun** N. Amer. a rack supporting wood for sawing.

sawlog ▸ **noun** a felled tree trunk suitable for cutting up into timber.

sawm /səʊm/ ▸ **noun** [mass noun] Islam fasting from dawn until dusk during Ramadan, one of the Five Pillars of Islam.
– ORIGIN Arabic *ṣawm*, from *ṣama* 'abstain from food, drink, and sexual intercourse'.

sawmill ▸ **noun** a factory in which logs are sawn into planks or boards by machine.

sawn past participle of **SAW**[1].

sawn-off (N. Amer. **sawed-off**) ▸ **adjective** [attrib.] (of a gun) having a specially shortened barrel to make handling easier and to give a wider field of fire. ■ informal (of an item of clothing) having been cut short. ■ US informal (of a person) short.
▸ **noun** informal a sawn-off shotgun.

saw palmetto ▸ **noun** a small palm with fan-shaped leaves that have sharply toothed stalks, native to the south-eastern US. ● Several species in the family Palmae, in particular *Serenoa repens*.

saw pit ▸ **noun** historical the pit in which the lower of two men working a pit saw stands.

saw set ▸ **noun** a tool for setting the teeth of a saw so that they point in alternate directions.

sawtooth (also **sawtoothed**) ▸ **adjective** shaped like the teeth of a saw with alternate steep and gentle slopes. ■ (of a waveform) showing a slow linear rise and rapid linear fall or vice versa.

saw-whet owl ▸ **noun** a small North and Central American owl with a call that resembles the sound of a saw blade being sharpened. ● Genus *Aegolius*, family Strigidae: two species, in particular the North American *A. acadicus*.

saw-wort ▸ **noun** a plant of the daisy family, with purple flowers and serrated leaves, native to Eurasia and North Africa. ● *Serratula tinctoria*, family Compositae.

sawyer ▸ **noun 1** a person who saws timber for a living.
2 US an uprooted tree floating in a river but held fast at one end. [with allusion to the trapped log's movement backwards and forwards.]
3 a large longhorn beetle whose larvae bore tunnels in the wood of injured or recently felled trees, producing an audible chewing sound. ● Genus *Monochamus*, family Cerambycidae.
■ NZ a large wingless bush cricket whose larvae bore in wood.
– ORIGIN Middle English (earlier as *sawer*): from the noun **SAW**[1] + **-YER**.

sax[1] ▸ **noun** informal a saxophone. ■ a saxophone player.
– DERIVATIVES **saxist** noun.
– ORIGIN early 20th cent.: abbreviation.

sax[2] (also **zax**) ▸ **noun** a small axe used for cutting roof slates, with a point for making nail holes.
– ORIGIN Old English *seax* 'knife', of Germanic origin, from an Indo-European root meaning 'cut'.

saxe (also **saxe blue**) ▸ **noun** [mass noun] a light blue colour with a greyish tinge.
– ORIGIN mid 19th cent.: from French, literally 'Saxony', the source of a dye of this colour.

Saxe-Coburg-Gotha /saks,kəʊbəːɡˈɡəʊtə, -ˈɡəʊθə/ the name of the British royal house 1901–17. The name dates from the accession of Edward VII, whose father Prince Albert was a prince of the German duchy of Saxe-Coburg and Gotha.

saxhorn ▸ **noun** a member of a family of brass instruments with valves and a funnel-shaped mouthpiece, used mainly in military and brass bands.
– ORIGIN from the name of Charles J. *Sax* (1791–1865) and his son Antoine-Joseph 'Adolphe' *Sax* (1814–94), Belgian instrument-makers, + **HORN**.

saxifrage /ˈsaksɪfreɪdʒ/ ▸ **noun** a low-growing plant of poor soils, bearing small white, yellow, or red flowers and forming rosettes of succulent leaves or hummocks of mossy leaves. Many are grown as alpines in rockeries. ● Genus *Saxifraga*, family Saxifragaceae.
– ORIGIN late Middle English: from Old French *saxifrage* or late Latin *saxifraga* (*herba*), from Latin *saxum* 'rock' + *frangere* 'break'.

Saxon ▸ **noun 1** a member of a people that inhabited parts of central and northern Germany from Roman times, many of whom conquered and settled in much of southern England in the 5th–6th centuries. ■ a native of modern Saxony in Germany.
2 [mass noun] the language of the Saxons, in particular: ■ (**Old Saxon**) the West Germanic language of the ancient Saxons. ■ another term for **OLD ENGLISH**. ■ the Low German dialect of modern Saxony.
▸ **adjective 1** relating to the Anglo-Saxons, their language (Old English), or their period of dominance in England (5th–11th centuries). ■ relating to or denoting the style of early Romanesque architecture preceding the Norman in England.
2 relating to Saxony or the continental Saxons or their language.
– ORIGIN Middle English: from Old French, from late Latin and Greek *Saxones* (plural), of West Germanic origin; related to Old English *Seaxan*, *Seaxe* (plural), perhaps from the base of **SAX**[2].

Saxony /ˈsaksəni/ a large region and former kingdom of Germany, including the modern states of Saxony in the south-east, Saxony-Anhalt in the centre, and Lower Saxony in the north-west. German name **SACHSEN**. ■ a state of eastern Germany, on the upper reaches of the River Elbe; capital, Dresden.
– ORIGIN from late Latin *Saxonia*, from Latin *Saxo*, *Saxon-* (see **SAXON**).

saxony /ˈsaks(ə)ni/ ▸ **noun** [mass noun] a fine kind of wool. ■ a fine-quality cloth made from saxony, chiefly used for making coats.
– ORIGIN mid 19th cent.: from **SAXONY**.

Saxony-Anhalt /ˌsaksənɪˈanhalt/ a state of Germany, on the plains of the Elbe and the Saale Rivers; capital, Magdeburg. It corresponds to the former duchy of Anhalt and the central part of the former kingdom of Saxony. German name **SACHSEN-ANHALT**.

saxophone /ˈsaksəfəʊn/ ▸ **noun** a member of a family of metal wind instruments with a reed like that of a clarinet, used especially in jazz and dance music.
– DERIVATIVES **saxophonic** /-ˈfɒnɪk/ adjective, **saxophonist** /sakˈsɒf(ə)nɪst, ˈsaksə,fəʊnɪst/ noun.
– ORIGIN from the name of Adolphe *Sax* (see **SAXHORN**) + **-PHONE**.

say ▸ **verb** (**says**; past and past participle **said**) **1** [reporting verb] utter words so as to convey information, an opinion, a feeling or intention, or an instruction: [with direct speech] *'Thank you,' he said* | [with clause] *he said the fund stood at £100,000* | [with obj.] *our parents wouldn't believe a word we said* | [with infinitive] *he said to come early.* ■ (of a text or a symbolic representation) convey specified information or instructions: [with clause] *the Act says such behaviour is an offence.* ■ [with obj.] enable a listener or reader to learn or understand something by conveying or revealing (information or ideas): *I don't want to say too much* | figurative *her rise and fall says a lot about our brutal political system* | *the film's title says it all.* ■ [with obj.] (of a clock or watch) indicate (a specified time): *the clock says ten past two.* ■ (**be said**) be asserted or reported: [with infinitive] *they were said to be training freedom fighters* | [with clause] *it is said that she lived to over a hundred.* ■ [with obj.] (**say something for**) present a consideration in favour of or excusing (someone or something): *all I can say for him is that he's a better writer than some.* ■ [with obj.] utter the whole of (a speech or other set of words, typically one learned in advance): *the padre finished saying the Nunc Dimittis.*
2 [with clause] assume something in order to work out what its consequences would be; make a hypothesis: *let's say we pay in five thousand pounds in the first year.* ■ used parenthetically to indicate that something is being suggested as possible or likely but not certain: *the form might include, say, a dozen questions.*
▸ **exclamation** N. Amer. informal used to express surprise or to draw attention to a remark or question: *say, did you notice any blood?*
▸ **noun** [in sing.] an opportunity for stating one's opinion or feelings: *she let him **have his say**.* ■ an opportunity to influence developments and policy: *the assessor will **have a say** in how the money is spent* | [mass noun] *the households concerned would still **have** some **say** in what happened.*
– PHRASES **go without saying** be obvious: *it goes without saying that lay appointees must be selected with care.* [translating French (*cela*) *va sans dire*.] **have something to say for oneself** contribute a specified amount to a conversation or discussion: *a dull girl with little to say for herself.* **how say you?** Law how do you find? (addressed to the jury when requesting its verdict). **I** (or **he**, **she**, etc.) **cannot** (or **could not**) **say** I (or he, she, etc.) do not know. **I'll say** informal used to express emphatic agreement: *'That was a good landing.' 'I'll say!'* **I must** (or **have to**) **say** I cannot refrain from saying (used to emphasize an opinion): *you have a nerve, I must say!* **I say!** Brit. dated used to express surprise or to draw attention to a remark: *I say, that's a bit much!* **I wouldn't say no** informal used to indicate that one would like something. **not to say** used to introduce a stronger alternative or addition to something already said: *it is easy to become sensitive, not to say paranoid.* **say no more** informal used to indicate that one understands what someone is trying to imply. **says I** (or **he**, **she** etc.) informal, chiefly Brit. used after direct speech in reporting someone's part in a conversation. **says you!** informal used in spoken English to express disagreement or disbelief: *'He's guilty.' 'Says you. I think he's innocent.'* **say when** informal said when helping someone to food or drink to instruct them to indicate when they have enough. **say the word** give permission or instructions to do something. **that is to say** used to introduce a clarification, interpretation, or correction of something already said. **there is no saying** it is impossible to know. **they say** it is rumoured. **to say nothing of** another way of saying **NOT TO MENTION** (see **MENTION**). **what do** (or **would**) **you say** used to make a suggestion or offer: *what do you say to a glass of wine?* **when all is said and done** when everything is taken into account (used to indicate that one is making a generalized

judgement). **you can say that again!** informal used to express emphatic agreement. **you don't say** (or **you don't say so**)! informal used to express amazement or disbelief. **you** (or **you've**) **said it!** informal used to express agreement with what someone has said.
– ORIGIN Old English *secgan*, of Germanic origin; related to Dutch *zeggen* and German *sagen*.
– DERIVATIVES **sayable** adjective, **sayer** noun [usu. in combination] *nay-sayers*.

SAYE ▶ abbreviation save as you earn.

Sayers, Dorothy L. (1893–1957), English novelist and dramatist; full name *Dorothy Leigh Sayers*. She is chiefly known for her detective fiction featuring the amateur detective Lord Peter Wimsey; titles include *The Nine Tailors* (1934).

saying ▶ noun a short, pithy, commonly known expression which generally offers advice or wisdom. ■ (**sayings**) a collection of such expressions identified with a particular person, especially a political or religious leader.
– PHRASES **as** (or **so**) **the saying goes** (or **is**) used to introduce or follow an expression, drawing attention to its status as a saying rather than part of one's normal language: *I am, as the saying goes, burnt out*.

sayonara /ˌsʌɪəˈnɑːrə/ ▶ exclamation informal, chiefly US goodbye.
– ORIGIN Japanese.

Say's law /ˈseɪz/ ▶ noun Economics a law stating that supply creates its own demand.
– ORIGIN 1930s: named after Jean Baptiste *Say* (1767–1832), French economist.

say-so ▶ noun [in sing.] informal the power or act of deciding or allowing something: *no new employees come into the organization without his say-so*. ■ (usu. **on someone's say-so**) a person's arbitrary or unauthorized assertion or instruction: *I don't stop on the say-so of anybody's assistant*.

sayyid /ˈseɪjɪd, ˈsʌɪɪd/ ▶ noun a Muslim claiming descent from Muhammad, especially through Husayn, the prophet's younger grandson. ■ a respectful Muslim form of address.
– ORIGIN Arabic, literally 'lord, prince'.

saz /saz/ ▶ noun a long-necked stringed instrument of the lute family, originating in the Ottoman Empire.
– ORIGIN late 19th cent.: from Turkish, from Persian *sāz* 'musical instrument'.

Sb ▶ symbol the chemical element antimony.
– ORIGIN from Latin *stibium*.

SBA ▶ abbreviation (in the US) Small Business Administration.

S-Bahn /ˈɛsbɑːn/ ▶ noun (in some German cities) a fast urban railway line or system.
– ORIGIN German, abbreviation of (*Stadt*) *Schnellbahn* '(urban) fast railway'.

SBF ▶ abbreviation single black female (used in personal advertisements).

SBM ▶ abbreviation single black male (used in personal advertisements).

SBS ▶ abbreviation **1** sick building syndrome. **2** Special Boat Service.

SC ▶ abbreviation ■ South Carolina (in official postal use). ■ (in the UK) special constable.

Sc ▶ symbol the chemical element scandium.

sc. ▶ abbreviation that is to say (introducing a word to be supplied or an explanation of an ambiguity).
– ORIGIN from SCILICET.

s.c. ▶ abbreviation small capitals (used as an instruction for a typesetter).

scab ▶ noun **1** a dry, rough protective crust that forms over a cut or wound during healing. **2** [mass noun] mange or a similar skin disease in animals. See also SHEEP SCAB. ■ [usu. with modifier] any of a number of fungal diseases of plants in which rough patches develop, especially on apples and potatoes. **3** informal a person or thing regarded with contempt. ■ derogatory a person who refuses to strike or join a trade union or who takes the place of a striking worker.
▶ verb (**scabs, scabbing, scabbed**) [no obj.] **1** (usu. as adj. **scabbed**) become encrusted or covered with a scab or scabs: *she rested her scabbed fingers on his arm*. **2** act or work as a scab. ■ [with obj.] Brit. informal scrounge.
– DERIVATIVES **scab-like** adjective.
– ORIGIN Middle English (as a noun): from Old Norse *skabb*; related to dialect *shab* (compare with SHABBY). The sense 'contemptible person' (dating from the late 16th cent.) was probably influenced by Middle Dutch *schabbe* 'slut'.

scabbard /ˈskabəd/ ▶ noun a sheath for the blade of a sword or dagger, typically made of leather or metal. ■ a sheath for a gun or other weapon or tool.
– ORIGIN Middle English: from Anglo-Norman French *escalberc*, from a Germanic compound of words meaning 'cut' (related to SHEAR) and 'protect' (related to the second element of HAUBERK).

scabbardfish ▶ noun (pl. **same** or **scabbardfishes**) an elongated marine fish with heavy jaws and large teeth, which occurs mostly in the deeper waters of warm seas. ● Several genera and species in the family Trichiuridae, including the edible silvery-white *Lepidopus caudatus*.

scabby ▶ adjective (**scabbier, scabbiest**) **1** covered in scabs. **2** informal, chiefly Irish & Scottish (of a person) loathsome; despicable.
– DERIVATIVES **scabbiness** noun.

scabies /ˈskeɪbiːz/ ▶ noun [mass noun] a contagious skin disease marked by itching and small raised red spots, caused by the itch mite.
– ORIGIN late Middle English (denoting various skin diseases): from Latin, from *scabere* 'to scratch'. The current sense dates from the early 19th cent.

scabious /ˈskeɪbɪəs/ ▶ noun a plant of the teasel family, with pink, white, or (most commonly) blue pincushion-shaped flowers. ● *Scabiosa*, *Knautia*, and other genera, family Dipsacaceae: several species, including the **devil's bit scabious** (see DEVIL'S BIT).
▶ adjective affected with mange; scabby.
– ORIGIN late Middle English: based on Latin *scabiosus* 'rough, scabby'; the noun is from medieval Latin *scabiosa* (*herba*) 'rough, scabby (plant)', formerly regarded as a cure for skin disease (see SCABIES).

scablands ▶ plural noun Geology flat elevated land deeply scarred by channels of glacial or fluvioglacial origin and with poor soil and little vegetation, especially in the Columbia Plateau, Washington State, US.

scabrous /ˈskeɪbrəs, ˈskabrəs/ ▶ adjective **1** rough and covered with, or as if with, scabs. ■ unpleasant; unattractive: *a scabrous hovel*. **2** indecent; salacious: *scabrous details included being regularly seen with a mistress*.
– DERIVATIVES **scabrously** adverb, **scabrousness** noun.
– ORIGIN late 16th cent. (first used to describe an author's style as 'harsh, unmusical, unpolished'): from French *scabreux* or late Latin *scabrosus*, from Latin *scaber* 'rough'.

scad ▶ noun another term for JACK[1] (sense 11).
– ORIGIN early 17th cent.: of unknown origin.

scads ▶ plural noun informal, chiefly N. Amer. a large number or quantity: *they raised scads of children*.
– ORIGIN mid 19th cent.: of unknown origin.

Scafell Pike /skɔːˈfɛl/ a mountain in the Lake District of NW England, in Cumbria. Rising to a height of 978 m (3,210 ft), it is the highest peak in England.

scaffold /ˈskafəʊld, -f(ə)ld/ ▶ noun **1** a raised wooden platform used formerly for the public execution of criminals. **2** a structure made using scaffolding.
▶ verb [with obj.] attach scaffolding to (a building): (as adj. **scaffolded**) *the soot-black scaffolded structure*.
– DERIVATIVES **scaffolder** noun.
– ORIGIN Middle English (denoting a temporary platform from which to repair or erect a building): from Anglo-Norman French, from Old French (*e*)*schaffaut*, from the base of CATAFALQUE.

scaffolding ▶ noun [mass noun] a temporary structure on the outside of a building, made of wooden planks and metal poles, used by workmen while building, repairing, or cleaning the building. ■ the materials used in scaffolding.

scag ▶ noun variant spelling of SKAG.

scagliola /skalˈjəʊlə/ ▶ noun [mass noun] imitation marble or other stone, made of plaster mixed with glue and dyes which is then painted or polished.
– ORIGIN mid 18th cent.: from Italian *scagliuola*, diminutive of *scaglia* 'a scale'.

scalable (also **scaleable**) ▶ adjective **1** able to be scaled or climbed. **2** able to be changed in size or scale: *scalable fonts*. ■ (of a computing process) able to be used or produced in a range of capabilities: *it is scalable across a range of systems*. **3** technical able to be measured or graded according to a scale.
– DERIVATIVES **scalability** noun.

scala media /ˌskeɪlə ˈmiːdɪə/ ▶ noun (pl. **scalae media** /ˌskeɪliː, ˌskeɪlʌɪ/) Anatomy the central duct of the cochlea in the inner ear, containing the sensory cells and separated from the scala tympani and scala vestibuli by membranes.
– ORIGIN late 19th cent.: from Latin, literally 'middle ladder'.

scalar /ˈskeɪlə/ Mathematics & Physics ▶ adjective (of a quantity) having only magnitude, not direction.
▶ noun a scalar quantity.
– ORIGIN mid 17th cent.: from Latin *scalaris*, from *scala* 'ladder' (see SCALE[3]).

scalar field ▶ noun Mathematics a function of a space whose value at each point is a scalar quantity.

scalariform /skəˈlarɪfɔːm/ ▶ adjective Botany (especially of the walls of water-conducting cells) having thickened bands arranged like the rungs of a ladder.
– ORIGIN mid 19th cent.: from Latin *scalaris* 'of a ladder' + -IFORM.

scalar product ▶ noun Mathematics a scalar function of two vectors, equal to the product of their magnitudes and the cosine of the angle between them. Also called DOT PRODUCT. Compare with VECTOR PRODUCT. ● Written as **a.b** or **ab**.

scala tympani /ˌskeɪlə tɪmˈpɑːni/ ▶ noun (pl. **scalae tympani** /ˌskeɪliː, ˌskeɪlʌɪ/) Anatomy the lower bony passage of the cochlea.
– ORIGIN early 18th cent.: from Latin, literally 'ladder of the tympanum'.

scala vestibuli /vɛˈstɪbjʊli/ ▶ noun (pl. **scalae vestibuli**) Anatomy the upper bony passage of the cochlea.
– ORIGIN early 18th cent.: from Latin, literally 'ladder of the vestibule'.

scalawag ▶ noun North American spelling of SCALLYWAG.

scald[1] ▶ verb [with obj.] injure with very hot liquid or steam: *the tea scalded his tongue*. ■ heat (milk or other liquid) to near boiling point. ■ immerse (something) briefly in boiling water for various purposes, such as to facilitate the removal of skin from fruit or to preserve meat. ■ cause to feel a searing sensation like that of boiling water on skin: *she fought to stave off the hot tears scalding her eyes*. ■ archaic rinse (a container) with boiling water.
▶ noun **1** a burn or other injury caused by hot liquid or steam. **2** [mass noun] any of a number of plant diseases which produce an effect similar to that of scalding, especially a disease of fruit marked by browning and caused by excessive sunlight, bad storage conditions, or atmospheric pollution.
– PHRASES **like a scalded cat** very quickly: *he took off like a scalded cat*.
– ORIGIN Middle English (as a verb): from Anglo-Norman French *escalder*, from late Latin *excaldare*, from Latin *ex-* 'thoroughly' + *calidus* 'hot'. The noun dates from the early 17th cent.

scald[2] ▶ noun variant spelling of SKALD.

scaldfish ▶ noun (pl. **same** or **scaldfishes**) a small edible European flatfish of inshore waters, the fragile scales of which are easily scraped off, giving the appearance of a scald. Also called MEGRIM[2]. ● *Arnoglossus laterna*, family Bothidae.

scalding ▶ adjective very hot; burning: *she took a sip of scalding tea* | [as submodifier] *the water was scalding hot*. ■ intense and painful or distressing: *a scalding tirade of abuse*.

scale[1] ▶ noun **1** each of the small, thin horny or bony plates protecting the skin of fish and reptiles, typically overlapping one another. **2** something resembling a fish scale in appearance or function, in particular: ■ a thick dry flake of skin. ■ a rudimentary leaf, feather, or bract. ■ each of numerous microscopic tile-like structures covering the wings of butterflies and moths. **3** [mass noun] a flaky deposit, in particular: ■ a white deposit formed in a kettle, boiler, etc. by the evaporation of water containing lime. ■ tartar formed on teeth. ■ a coating of oxide formed on heated metal. Botany
▶ verb **1** [with obj.] remove scale or scales from: *he scales the fish and removes the innards*. ■ remove tartar from (teeth) by scraping them. **2** [no obj.] (often as noun **scaling**) (especially of the skin) form scales: *moisturizers can ease off drying and scaling*. ■ come off in scales or thin pieces; flake off: *the paint was scaling from the brick walls*.
– PHRASES **the scales fall from someone's eyes** someone is no longer deceived. [with biblical reference to Acts 9:18.]

S

– DERIVATIVES **scaled** adjective [often in combination] *a rough-scaled fish*, **scaleless** adjective, **scaler** noun.
– ORIGIN Middle English: shortening of Old French *escale*, from the Germanic base of SCALE².

scale² ▶ noun **1** (usu. **scales**) an instrument for weighing, originally a simple balance (**a pair of scales**) but now usually a device with an electronic or other internal weighing mechanism. ■ (also **scale pan**) either of the dishes on a simple balance. ■ (**the Scales**) the zodiacal sign or constellation Libra.
2 S. African a large drinking container for beer or other alcoholic drink.
▶ verb weigh a specified weight: *some men scaled less than ninety pounds*.
– PHRASES **throw something on** (or **into**) **the scale** contribute something to one side of an argument or debate. **tip** (or **turn**) **the scales** see TIP².
– ORIGIN Middle English (in the sense 'drinking cup', surviving in South African English): from Old Norse *skál* 'bowl', of Germanic origin; related to Dutch *schaal*, German *Schale* 'bowl', also to English dialect *shale* 'dish'.

scale³ ▶ noun **1** a graduated range of values forming a standard system for measuring or grading something: *company employees have hit the top of their pay scales*. ■ the full range of different levels of people or things, from lowest to highest: *two men at opposite ends of the* ***social scale*** | *at the other end of the scale, premiership clubs are forced to pay huge wages*. ■ a series of marks at regular intervals in a line used in measuring something: *the mean delivery time is plotted against a scale on the right*. ■ a device having a series of marks at regular intervals for measuring: *she read the exact distance off a scale*. ■ a rule determining the distances between marks on a scale: *the vertical axis is given on a logarithmic scale*.
2 [in sing.] the relative size or extent of something: *no one foresaw the scale of the disaster* | *everything in the house is* ***on a grand scale***. ■ [often as modifier] a ratio of size in a map, model, drawing, or plan: *a one-fifth scale model of a seven-storey building* | *an Ordnance map* ***on a scale of*** *1:2500*.
3 Music an arrangement of the notes in any system of music in ascending or descending order of pitch: *the scale of C major*.
4 (in full **scale of notation**) Mathematics a system of numerical notation in which the value of a digit depends upon its position in the number, successive positions representing successive powers of a fixed base: *the conversion of the number to the binary scale*.
5 Photography the range of exposures over which a photographic material will give an acceptable variation in density.
▶ verb [with obj.] **1** climb up or over (something high and steep): *thieves scaled a high fence*.
2 represent in proportional dimensions; reduce or increase in size according to a common scale: (as adj. **scaled**) *scaled plans of the house*. ■ [no obj.] (of a quantity or property) be variable according to a particular scale.
3 N. Amer. estimate the amount of timber that will be produced from (a log or uncut tree).
– PHRASES **play** (or **sing** or **practise**) **scales** Music perform the notes of a scale as an exercise for the fingers or voice. **to scale** with a uniform reduction or enlargement: *it is hard to build models to scale from a drawing*. **in scale** (of a drawing or model) in proportion to the surroundings.
– PHRASAL VERBS **scale something back/down** (or **up**) reduce (or increase) something in size, number, or extent: *manufacturing capacity has been scaled down*.
– DERIVATIVES **scaler** noun.
– ORIGIN late Middle English: from Latin *scala* 'ladder' (the verb via Old French *escaler* or medieval Latin *scalare* 'climb'), from the base of Latin *scandere* 'to climb'.

S

scale armour ▶ noun [mass noun] historical armour consisting of small overlapping plates of metal, leather, or horn.

scale board ▶ noun [mass noun] very thin wood used (especially formerly) in bookbinding, making hatboxes, and backing pictures.

scale insect ▶ noun a small bug with a protective shield-like scale. It spends most of its life attached by its mouth to a single plant, sometimes occurring in such large numbers that it becomes a serious pest. ● Superfamily Coccoidea, suborder Homoptera: several families, in particular Coccidae.

scale leaf ▶ noun Botany a small modified leaf, especially a colourless membranous one, such as on a rhizome or forming part of a bulb.

scalene /ˈskeɪliːn/ ▶ adjective (of a triangle) having sides unequal in length.
▶ noun **1** (also **scalene muscle**) Anatomy another term for SCALENUS.
2 a scalene triangle.
– ORIGIN mid 17th cent.: via late Latin from Greek *skalēnos* 'unequal'; related to *skolios* 'bent'.

scalenus /skəˈliːnəs/ ▶ noun (pl. **scaleni** /-nʌɪ/) any of several muscles extending from the neck to the first and second ribs.
– ORIGIN early 18th cent.: modern Latin, from late Latin *scalenus (musculus)* 'unequal (muscle)' (see SCALENE).

scale of notation ▶ noun see SCALE³ (sense 4 of the noun).

scale pan ▶ noun see SCALE².

scale worm ▶ noun a marine bristle worm with scales on the upper surface which have a protective function, and in some species are able to luminesce. ● Family Aphroditidae: *Aphrodite* and other genera. See also SEA MOUSE.

Scaliger¹ /ˈskalɪdʒə/, Joseph Justus (1540–1609), French scholar, son of Julius Caesar Scaliger. His *De Emendatione Temporum* (1583) gave a more scientific foundation to the understanding of ancient chronology by comparing and revising the computations of time made by different civilizations, including those of the Babylonians and Egyptians.

Scaliger² /ˈskalɪdʒə/, Julius Caesar (1484–1558), Italian-born French classical scholar and physician. Besides polemical works directed against Erasmus (1531, 1536), he wrote treatises on poetics and philosophy, and commentaries on botanical works.

scaling ladder ▶ noun historical a ladder used for climbing fortress walls in an attempt to break a siege or for firefighting.

scallion /ˈskalɪən/ ▶ noun chiefly N. Amer. a long-necked onion with a small bulb, in particular a shallot or spring onion.
– ORIGIN late Middle English: from Anglo-Norman French *scaloun*, based on Latin *Ascalonia (caepa)* '(onion) of *Ascalon*', a port in ancient Palestine.

scallop /ˈskɒləp, ˈskaləp/ ▶ noun **1** an edible bivalve mollusc with a ribbed fan-shaped shell. Scallops swim by rapidly opening and closing the shell valves. ● Family Pectinidae: *Chlamys*, *Pecten*, and other genera. ■ short for SCALLOP SHELL. ■ a small pan or dish shaped like a scallop shell and used for baking or serving food.
2 (usu. **scallops**) each of a series of convex rounded projections forming an ornamental edging cut in material or worked in lace or knitting in imitation of the edge of a scallop shell.
3 another term for ESCALOPE.
▶ verb (**scallops**, **scalloping**, **scalloped**) **1** [with obj.] (usu. as adj. **scalloped**) ornament (an edge or material) with scallops: *a scalloped V-shaped neckline*. ■ cut, shape, or arrange in the form of a scallop shell: *he leaned against the scalloped seat of the limousine*.
2 [no obj.] (usu. as noun **scalloping**) N. Amer. gather or dredge for scallops.
3 [with obj.] bake with milk or a sauce: (as adj. **scalloped**) *scalloped potatoes*.
– DERIVATIVES **scalloper** noun.
– ORIGIN Middle English: shortening of Old French *escalope*, probably of Germanic origin. The verb dates from the mid 18th cent.

scallop shell ▶ noun a single valve from the shell of a scallop. ■ historical a representation of a scallop shell worn by a pilgrim as a souvenir of the shrine of St James at Santiago de Compostela in Spain.

scally ▶ noun (pl. **scallies**) informal (in the north-west of England, especially Liverpool) a roguish self-assured young person, typically a man, who is boisterous, disruptive, or irresponsible.
– ORIGIN 1980s: abbreviation of SCALLYWAG.

scallywag (N. Amer. also **scalawag**) ▶ noun informal **1** a person, typically a child, who behaves badly but in an amusingly mischievous rather than harmful way; a rascal.
2 US a white Southerner who collaborated with northern Republicans during the post-Civil War reconstruction period.
– ORIGIN mid 19th cent.: of unknown origin.

scaloppine /ˌskaləˈpiːneɪ, -ni/ (also **scallopini**) ▶ plural noun (in Italian cooking) thin, boneless slices of meat, typically veal, sautéed or fried.
– ORIGIN Italian, plural of *scaloppina*, diminutive of *scaloppa* 'envelope'.

scalp ▶ noun **1** the skin covering the head, excluding the face. ■ historical the scalp with the hair belonging to it, cut or torn away from an enemy's head as a battle trophy, a former practice among American Indians. ■ used with reference to the defeat of an opponent: *in rugby Gloucester* ***claimed the scalp*** *of would-be champions Bath*.
2 Scottish a bare rock projecting above surrounding water or vegetation.
▶ verb [with obj.] **1** historical take the scalp of (an enemy). ■ informal punish severely: *if I ever heard anybody doing that I'd scalp them*.
2 N. Amer. informal resell (shares or tickets) at a large or quick profit.
– DERIVATIVES **scalper** noun (sense 2 of the verb).
– ORIGIN Middle English (denoting the skull or cranium): probably of Scandinavian origin.

scalpel ▶ noun a knife with a small, sharp, sometimes detachable blade, as used by a surgeon.
– ORIGIN mid 18th cent.: from French, or from Latin *scalpellum*, diminutive of *scalprum* 'chisel', from *scalpere* 'to scratch'.

scalp lock ▶ noun historical a long lock of hair left on the shaved head by a North American Indian as a challenge to enemies.

scaly ▶ adjective (**scalier**, **scaliest**) covered in scales. ■ (of skin) dry and flaking.
– DERIVATIVES **scaliness** noun.

scaly anteater ▶ noun another term for PANGOLIN.

scalyfoot ▶ noun (pl. **scalyfoots**) a snake-like Australian legless lizard with a prehensile tail and the hindlimb remnants visible as scaly flaps. ● Genus *Pygopus*, family Pygopodidae: two species, in particular the common *P. lepidopodus*.

scaly-tailed squirrel ▶ noun a squirrel-like rodent with horny scales on the underside of the tail, native to west and central Africa. ● Family Anomaluridae: three genera and several species, in particular the **flightless scaly-tailed squirrel** (*Zenkerella insignis*); the remainder are all flying squirrels.

scam ▶ noun informal a dishonest scheme; a fraud: *an insurance scam*.
▶ verb (**scams**, **scamming**, **scammed**) [with obj.] swindle: *a guy that scams old pensioners out of their savings*.
– DERIVATIVES **scammer** noun.
– ORIGIN 1960s: of unknown origin.

scammony /ˈskaməni/ ▶ noun a plant of the convolvulus family, the dried roots of which yield a strong purgative. ● Two species in the family Convolvulaceae: *Convolvulus scammonia* of Asia, and *Ipomoea orizabensis* of Mexico.
– ORIGIN Old English, from Old French *escamonie* or Latin *scammonia*, from Greek *skammōnia*.

scamorza /skaˈmɔːtsə/ ▶ noun [mass noun] a mild white Italian cheese made from cow's or buffalo's milk, produced in small gourd-shaped balls.
– ORIGIN 1930s: Italian, from *scamozzare* 'cut off'; compare with MOZZARELLA.

scamp¹ ▶ noun informal **1** a person, especially a child, who is mischievous in a likeable or amusing way.
2 W. Indian a wicked or worthless person; a rogue.
– DERIVATIVES **scampish** adjective.
– ORIGIN mid 18th cent. (denoting a highwayman): from obsolete *scamp* 'rob on the highway', probably from Middle Dutch *schampen* 'slip away', from Old French *eschamper*. Early usage (still reflected in West Indian English) was derogatory.

scamp² ▶ verb [with obj.] dated do (something) in a perfunctory or inadequate way: *she had scamped her work*.
– ORIGIN mid 19th cent.: perhaps the same word as SCAMP¹, but associated in sense with the verb SKIMP.

scamper ▶ verb [no obj., with adverbial of direction] (especially of a small animal or child) run with quick light steps, especially through fear or excitement: *he scampered in like an overgrown puppy*.
▶ noun [in sing.] an act of scampering.
– ORIGIN late 17th cent. (in the sense 'run away'): probably from SCAMP².

scampi ▶ noun [treated as sing. or pl.] Norway lobsters when prepared or cooked.
– ORIGIN Italian.

scan ▶ verb (**scans**, **scanning**, **scanned**) [with obj.] **1** look at all parts of (something) carefully in order to detect some feature: *he raised his binoculars to scan the coast*. ■ look quickly but not very thoroughly through (a document or other text) in order to identify relevant information: *we scan the papers for news from the trouble spots* | [no obj.] ***I scanned through*** *the reference materials*.

2 cause (a surface, object, or part of the body) to be traversed by a detector or an electromagnetic beam: *their brains are scanned so that researchers can monitor the progress of the disease.* ▪ [with obj. and adverbial] cause (a beam) to traverse across a surface or object: *we scanned the beam over a sector of 120°.* ▪ resolve (a picture) into its elements of light and shade in a prearranged pattern for the purposes of television transmission. ▪ convert (a document or picture) into digital form for storage or processing on a computer: *text and pictures can be **scanned into** the computer.*
3 analyse the metre of (a line of verse) by reading with the emphasis on its rhythm or by examining the pattern of feet or syllables. ▪ [no obj.] (of verse) conform to metrical principles.
▶ **noun 1** an act of scanning someone or something: *a quick scan of the sports page.*
2 a medical examination using a scanner: *a brain scan.* ▪ an image obtained by scanning or with a scanner: *you can't predict anything until he has seen the scan.*
– DERIVATIVES **scannable** adjective.
– ORIGIN late Middle English (as a verb in sense 3 of the verb): from Latin *scandere* 'climb' (in late Latin 'scan (verses)'), by analogy with the raising and lowering of one's foot when marking rhythm. From 'analyse (metre)' arose the senses 'estimate the correctness of' and 'examine minutely', which led to 'look at searchingly' (late 18th cent.).

scandal ▶ **noun** an action or event regarded as morally or legally wrong and causing general public outrage: *a bribery scandal involving one of his key supporters.* ▪ [mass noun] the outrage or anger caused by a scandalous action or event: *divorce was cause for scandal in the island.* ▪ [mass noun] rumour or malicious gossip about scandalous events or actions: *I know that you would want no scandal attached to her name.* ▪ [in sing.] a state of affairs regarded as wrong or reprehensible and causing general public outrage or anger: *it's a scandal that many older patients are dismissed as untreatable.*
– ORIGIN Middle English (in the sense 'discredit to religion (by the reprehensible behaviour of a religious person)'): from Old French *scandale*, from ecclesiastical Latin *scandalum* 'cause of offence', from Greek *skandalon* 'snare, stumbling block'.

scandalize[1] (also **scandalise**) ▶ **verb** [with obj.] shock or horrify (someone) by a real or imagined violation of propriety or morality: *their lack of manners scandalized their hosts.*
– ORIGIN late 15th cent. (in the sense 'make a public scandal of'): from French *scandaliser* or ecclesiastical Latin *scandalizare*, from Greek *skandalizein*.

scandalize[2] (also **scandalise**) ▶ **verb** [with obj.] Sailing reduce the area of (a sail) by lowering the head or raising the boom.
– ORIGIN mid 19th cent.: alteration of obsolete *scantelize*, from *scantle* 'make small'.

scandalmonger ▶ **noun** a person who stirs up public outrage towards someone or their actions by spreading rumours or malicious gossip.
– DERIVATIVES **scandalmongering** noun.

scandalous ▶ **adjective** causing general public outrage by a perceived offence against morality or law: *a series of scandalous liaisons | a scandalous allegation.* ▪ (of a state of affairs) disgracefully bad: *a scandalous waste of ratepayers' money.*
– DERIVATIVES **scandalously** adverb, **scandalousness** noun.

scandal sheet ▶ **noun** derogatory a newspaper or magazine giving prominence to scandalous stories or gossip.

scandent /ˈskandənt/ ▶ **adjective** chiefly Palaeontology (especially of a graptolite) having a climbing habit.
– ORIGIN late 17th cent.: from Latin *scandent-* 'climbing', from the verb *scandere*.

Scandentia /skanˈdɛnʃə/ ▶ **plural noun** Zoology a small order of mammals which comprises the tree shrews.
– ORIGIN modern Latin (plural), from Latin *scandent-* 'climbing', from the verb *scandere*.

Scandinavia /ˌskandɪˈneɪvɪə/ a large peninsula in NW Europe, occupied by Norway and Sweden. It is bounded by the Arctic Ocean in the north, the Atlantic in the west, and the Baltic Sea in the south and east. ▪ a cultural region consisting of the countries of Norway, Sweden, and Denmark and sometimes also of Iceland, Finland, and the Faroe Islands.
– ORIGIN Latin.

Scandinavian ▶ **adjective** relating to Scandinavia, its people, or their languages.
▶ **noun 1** a native or inhabitant of Scandinavia, or a person of Scandinavian descent.
2 [mass noun] the northern branch of the Germanic languages, comprising Danish, Norwegian, Swedish, Icelandic, and Faroese, all descended from Old Norse.

scandium /ˈskandɪəm/ ▶ **noun** [mass noun] the chemical element of atomic number 21, a soft silvery-white metal resembling the rare earth elements. (Symbol: **Sc**)
– ORIGIN late 19th cent.: modern Latin, from *Scandia*, contraction of *Scandinavia* (where minerals are found containing this element).

scanner ▶ **noun** a device for examining, reading, or monitoring something, in particular: ▪ Medicine a machine that examines the body through the use of radiation, ultrasound, or magnetic resonance imaging, as a diagnostic aid. ▪ Electronics a device that scans documents and converts them into digital data.

scanning electron microscope (abbrev.: **SEM**) ▶ **noun** an electron microscope in which the surface of a specimen is scanned by a beam of electrons that are reflected to form an image.

scanning tunnelling microscope (abbrev.: **STM**) ▶ **noun** a high-resolution microscope using neither light nor an electron beam, but with an ultra-fine tip able to reveal atomic and molecular details of surfaces.

scansion /ˈskanʃ(ə)n/ ▶ **noun** [mass noun] the action of scanning a line of verse to determine its rhythm. ▪ the rhythm of a line of verse.
– ORIGIN mid 17th cent.: from Latin *scansio(n-)*, from *scandere* 'to climb'; compare with SCAN.

scant ▶ **adjective** barely sufficient or adequate: *companies with scant regard for the safety of future generations.* ▪ [attrib.] barely amounting to a specified number or quantity: *she weighed a scant two pounds.*
▶ **verb** [with obj.] chiefly N. Amer. provide grudgingly or in insufficient amounts: *he does not scant his attention to the later writings.* ▪ deal with inadequately; neglect: *the press regularly scants a host of issues relating to safety and health.*
– DERIVATIVES **scantly** adverb, **scantness** noun.
– ORIGIN Middle English: from Old Norse *skamt*, neuter of *skammr* 'short'.

scantling ▶ **noun 1** a timber beam of small cross section. ▪ the size to which a piece of timber or stone is measured and cut.
2 (often **scantlings**) a set of standard dimensions for parts of a structure, especially in shipbuilding.
3 archaic a specimen, sample, or small amount of something.
– ORIGIN early 16th cent. (denoting prescribed size, or a set of standard dimensions): alteration of obsolete *scantillon* (from Old French *escantillon* 'sample'), by association with the suffix -LING.

scanty ▶ **adjective** (**scantier**, **scantiest**) small or insufficient in quantity or amount: *they paid whatever they could out of their scanty wages to their families.* ▪ (of clothing) revealing; skimpy: *the women looked cold in their scanty bodices.*
▶ **plural noun** (**scanties**) informal women's skimpy knickers or pants.
– DERIVATIVES **scantily** adverb, **scantiness** noun.
– ORIGIN late 16th cent.: from SCANT + -Y[1].

Scapa Flow /ˈskɑːpə, ˈskapə/ a strait in the Orkney Islands, Scotland. It was an important British naval base, especially in the First World War. The German High Seas Fleet was interned there after its surrender, and was scuttled in 1919 as an act of defiance against the terms of the Versailles peace settlement.

scape ▶ **noun** Entomology the basal segment of an insect's antenna, especially when it is enlarged and lengthened (as in a weevil).
– ORIGIN early 19th cent.: via Latin from Greek *skapos* 'rod'; related to SCEPTRE.

-scape ▶ **combining form** denoting a specified type of scene: *moonscape.*
– ORIGIN on the pattern of *landscape*.

scapegoat ▶ **noun 1** a person who is blamed for the wrongdoings, mistakes, or faults of others, especially for reasons of expediency.
2 (in the Bible) a goat sent into the wilderness after the Jewish chief priest had symbolically laid the sins of the people upon it (Lev. 16).
▶ **verb** [with obj.] make a scapegoat of.
– ORIGIN mid 16th cent.: from archaic *scape* 'escape' + GOAT.

scapegrace ▶ **noun** archaic a mischievous or wayward person, especially a young person or child; a rascal.
– ORIGIN early 19th cent.: from *scape* (see SCAPEGOAT) + GRACE, literally denoting a person who escapes the grace of God.

scaphoid /ˈskafɔɪd/ ▶ **noun** Anatomy a large carpal bone articulating with the radius below the thumb.
– ORIGIN mid 18th cent. (in the sense 'boat-shaped'): from modern Latin *scaphoides*, from Greek *skaphoeidēs*, from *skaphos* 'boat'.

Scaphopoda /ˌskafəˈpəʊdə/ ▶ **plural noun** Zoology a class of molluscs that comprises the tusk shells.
– DERIVATIVES **scaphopod** noun.
– ORIGIN modern Latin (plural), from Greek *skaphē* 'boat' + *pous, pod-* 'foot'.

scapula /ˈskapjʊlə/ ▶ **noun** (pl. **scapulae** /-liː/ or **scapulas**) Anatomy technical term for SHOULDER BLADE.
– ORIGIN late 16th cent.: from late Latin, singular of Latin *scapulae* 'shoulder blades'.

scapular ▶ **adjective** Anatomy & Zoology relating to the shoulder or shoulder blade.
▶ **noun 1** a short monastic cloak covering the shoulders. ▪ a symbol of affiliation to an ecclesiastical order, consisting of two strips of cloth hanging down the breast and back and joined across the shoulders.
2 Medicine a bandage passing over and around the shoulders.
3 Ornithology a scapular feather.
– ORIGIN late 15th cent. (in sense 1 of the noun): from late Latin *scapulare*, from *scapula* 'shoulder'. The adjective (late 17th cent.) and the later senses of the noun are from SCAPULA + -AR[1].

scapular feather ▶ **noun** Ornithology a feather covering the shoulder, growing above the region where the wing joins the body.

scapulary ▶ **noun** (pl. **scapularies**) another term for SCAPULAR (sense 1 of the noun, sense 3 of the noun).
– ORIGIN Middle English: from an Anglo-Norman French variant of Old French *eschapeloyre*, based on late Latin *scapulare* (see SCAPULAR).

scapulimancy /ˈskapjʊlɪˌmansi/ ▶ **noun** [mass noun] Anthropology divination from the cracks in a burned animal shoulder blade, traditional among some North American hunting peoples.

scar ▶ **noun 1** a mark left on the skin or within body tissue where a wound, burn, or sore has not healed completely and fibrous connective tissue has developed: *a faint scar ran the length of his left cheek.* ▪ a lasting effect of grief, fear, or other emotion left on a person's character by an unpleasant experience: *the attack has left mental scars on Terry and his family.* ▪ a mark left on something following damage of some kind: *Max could see scars of the blast.* ▪ a mark left at the point of separation of a leaf, frond, or other part from a plant.
2 a steep high cliff or rock outcrop, especially of limestone. [Middle English: from Old Norse *sker* 'low reef'.]
▶ **verb** (**scars**, **scarring**, **scarred**) [with obj.] mark with a scar or scars: *he is likely to be **scarred for life** after injuries to his face, arms, and legs* | (as adj., in combination **-scarred**) *battle-scarred troops.* ▪ [no obj.] form or be marked with a scar.
– DERIVATIVES **scarless** adjective.
– ORIGIN late Middle English: from Old French *escharre*, via late Latin from Greek *eskhara* 'scab'.

scarab /ˈskarəb/ ▶ **noun** (also **sacred scarab**) a large dung beetle of the eastern Mediterranean area, regarded as sacred in ancient Egypt. ● *Scarabaeus sacer*, family Scarabaeidae (the **scarab family**). The scarab family also includes the smaller dung beetles and chafers, together with some very large tropical kinds such as Hercules, goliath, and rhinoceros beetles.
▪ an ancient Egyptian gem cut in the form of this beetle, sometimes depicted with the wings spread, and engraved with hieroglyphs on the flat underside. ▪ any scarabaeid beetle.
– ORIGIN late 16th cent. (originally denoting a beetle of any kind): from Latin *scarabaeus*, from Greek *skarabeios*.

scarabaeid /ˌskarəˈbiːɪd/ ▶ **noun** Entomology a beetle of the scarab family (Scarabaeidae), typically having strong spiky forelegs for burrowing.
– ORIGIN mid 19th cent.: from modern Latin *Scarabaeidae* (plural), from Latin *scarabaeus* (see SCARAB).

scarabaeoid /ˌskarəˈbiːəɔɪd/ ▶ **noun** Entomology a beetle of a large group that includes the scarabaeids, dor beetles, and stag beetles. Scarabaeoids include the largest known beetles, and are distinguished by having plate-like terminal segments in the antennae. Formerly called LAMELLICORN. ● Superfamily Scarabaeoidea (formerly Lamellicornia).

S

– ORIGIN late 19th cent.: from modern Latin *Scarabaeoidea* (plural), from Latin *scarabaeus* (see SCARAB).

scaramouch /ˈskarəmaʊtʃ, -muːtʃ/ ▶ **noun** archaic a boastful but cowardly person.
– ORIGIN mid 17th cent.: from Italian *Scaramuccia*, the name of a stock character in Italian farce, from *scaramuccia* 'skirmish'.

Scarborough /ˈskɑːb(ə)rə/ a fishing port and resort on the coast of North Yorkshire; pop. 39,600 (est. 2009).

scarce ▶ **adjective** (especially of food, money, or some other resource) insufficient for the demand: *as raw materials became scarce, synthetics were developed.* ■ occurring in small numbers or quantities; rare: *the freshwater shrimp becomes scarce in soft water.*
▶ **adverb** archaic scarcely: *a babe scarce two years old.*
– PHRASES **make oneself scarce** informal leave a place, especially so as to avoid a difficult situation.
– DERIVATIVES **scarceness** noun.
– ORIGIN Middle English (in the sense 'restricted in quantity or size', also 'parsimonious'): from a shortening of Anglo-Norman *escars*, from a Romance word meaning 'plucked out, selected'.

scarcely ▶ **adverb** only just; almost not: *her voice is so low I can scarcely hear what she is saying.* ■ only a very short time before: *she had scarcely dismounted before the door swung open.* ■ used to suggest that something is unlikely to be or certainly not the case: *they could scarcely all be wrong.*

scarcity ▶ **noun** (pl. **scarcities**) [mass noun] the state of being scarce or in short supply; shortage: *a time of scarcity | the growing scarcity of resources.*

scare /skɛː/ ▶ **verb** [with obj.] cause great fear or nervousness in; frighten: *the rapid questions were designed to* **scare** *her* **into** *blurting out the truth.* ■ [with obj. and adverbial] drive or keep (someone) away by frightening them: *the ugly scenes scared the holiday crowds away.* ■ [no obj.] become scared: *I don't think I scare easily.*
▶ **noun** a sudden attack of fright: *gosh, that gave me a scare!* ■ [usu. with modifier] a general feeling of anxiety or alarm about something: *bombs and bomb scares disrupted shopping.*
– PHRASAL VERBS **scare something up** informal, chiefly N. Amer. manage to find or obtain something: *for a price, the box office can usually scare up a pair of tickets.*
– DERIVATIVES **scarer** noun.
– ORIGIN Middle English: from Old Norse *skirra* 'frighten', from *skjarr* 'timid'.

scarecrow ▶ **noun** an object made to resemble a human figure, set up to scare birds away from a field where crops are growing. ■ informal a person who is very badly dressed, odd-looking, or thin. ■ archaic an object of baseless fear.

scared ▶ **adjective** fearful; frightened: *she's* **scared stiff** *of her dad* | [with clause] *I was scared I was going to kill myself* | [with infinitive] *he's scared to come to you and ask for help.*

scaredy-cat ▶ **noun** informal a timid person.

scaremonger ▶ **noun** a person who spreads frightening or ominous reports or rumours.
– DERIVATIVES **scaremongering** noun & adjective.

S

scare quotes ▶ **plural noun** quotation marks placed round a word or phrase to draw attention to an unusual or arguably inaccurate use.

scare tactics ▶ **plural noun** a strategy intended to influence public reaction by the exploitation of fear.

scarf¹ ▶ **noun** (pl. **scarves** or **scarfs**) a length or square of fabric worn around the neck or head.
– DERIVATIVES **scarfed** (also **scarved**) adjective.
– ORIGIN mid 16th cent. (in the sense 'sash (around the waist or over the shoulder)'): probably based on Old Northern French *escarpe*, probably identical with Old French *escharpe* 'pilgrim's scrip'.

scarf² ▶ **verb** [with obj.] **1** join the ends of (two pieces of timber or metal) by bevelling or notching them so that they fit over or into each other.
2 make an incision in the blubber of (a whale).
▶ **noun 1** a joint connecting two pieces of timber or metal in which the ends are bevelled or notched so that they fit over or into each other.
2 an incision made in the blubber of a whale.
– ORIGIN Middle English (as a noun): probably via Old French from Old Norse. The verb dates from the early 17th cent.

scarf³ ▶ **verb** [with obj.] N. Amer. informal eat or drink (something) hungrily or enthusiastically: *he scarfed down the waffles.*
– ORIGIN 1960s: variant of SCOFF².

scarf ring ▶ **noun** a ring through which the ends or corners of a scarf are threaded in order to hold the scarf in position.

scarf-skin ▶ **noun** [mass noun] archaic the thin outer layer of the skin; the epidermis.

scarifier /ˈskarɪfʌɪə, ˈskɛːrɪ-/ ▶ **noun** a tool with spikes or prongs used for breaking up matted vegetation in the surface of a lawn. ■ a machine with spikes used for breaking up the surface of a road. ■ chiefly Austral. a machine with spikes or prongs used for loosening soil.

scarify¹ /ˈskarɪfʌɪ, ˈskɛːrɪ-/ ▶ **verb** (**scarifies, scarifying, scarified**) [with obj.] **1** cut and remove debris from (a lawn) with a scarifier. ■ break up the surface of (soil or a road or pavement).
2 make shallow incisions in (the skin), especially as a medical procedure or traditional cosmetic practice: *she scarified the snakebite with a paring knife.*
3 criticize severely and hurtfully.
– DERIVATIVES **scarification** noun.
– ORIGIN late Middle English: from Old French *scarifier*, via late Latin from Greek *skariphasthai* 'scratch an outline', from *skariphos* 'stylus'.

scarify² /ˈskɛːrɪfʌɪ/ ▶ **verb** (**scarifies, scarifying, scarified**) [with obj.] (usu. as adj. **scarifying**) informal frighten: *a scarifying mix of extreme violence and absurdist humour.*
– ORIGIN late 18th cent.: formed irregularly from SCARE, perhaps on the pattern of *terrify*.

scarlatina /ˌskɑːləˈtiːnə/ (also **scarletina**) ▶ **noun** another term for SCARLET FEVER.
– ORIGIN early 19th cent.: modern Latin, from Italian *scarlattina* (feminine), based on *scarlatto* 'scarlet'.

Scarlatti /skɑːˈlati/ the name of two Italian composers. **(Pietro) Alessandro (Gaspare)** (1660–1725) was an important and prolific composer of operas which carried Italian opera through the baroque period and into the classical. His son **(Giuseppe) Domenico** (1685–1757) wrote over 550 sonatas for the harpsichord, and his work made an important contribution to the development of the sonata form.

scarlet ▶ **adjective** of a brilliant red colour: *a mass of scarlet berries.*
▶ **noun** [mass noun] a brilliant red colour: *papers lettered in scarlet and black.* ■ clothes or material of this colour.
– ORIGIN Middle English (originally denoting any brightly coloured cloth): shortening of Old French *escarlate*, from medieval Latin *scarlata*, via Arabic and medieval Greek from late Latin *sigillatus* 'decorated with small images', from *sigillum* 'small image'.

scarlet elf cup ▶ **noun** see ELF CUP.

scarlet fever ▶ **noun** [mass noun] an infectious bacterial disease affecting especially children, and causing fever and a scarlet rash. It is caused by streptococci.

scarletina ▶ **noun** variant spelling of SCARLATINA.

Scarlet Pimpernel the name assumed by the hero of a series of novels by Baroness Orczy. He was an English nobleman who rescued aristocrats during the French Revolution, always avoiding capture.

scarlet pimpernel ▶ **noun** a small European plant with scarlet flowers that close in rainy or cloudy weather. Also called POOR MAN'S WEATHER GLASS.
● *Anagallis arvensis arvensis*, family Primulaceae.

scarlet runner ▶ **noun** the runner bean.

scarlet woman ▶ **noun** a notoriously promiscuous or immoral woman.
– ORIGIN early 19th cent.: originally applied as a derogatory reference to the Roman Catholic Church, regarded as being devoted to showy ritual (Rev. 17).

scarp ▶ **noun** a very steep bank or slope; an escarpment. ■ the inner wall of a ditch in a fortification. Compare with COUNTERSCARP.
▶ **verb** [with obj.] cut or erode (a slope or hillside) so that it becomes steep, perpendicular, or precipitous. ■ provide (a ditch in a fortification) with a steep scarp and counterscarp.
– ORIGIN late 16th cent. (with reference to fortification): from Italian *scarpa*.

scarper ▶ **verb** [no obj.] Brit. informal run away: *they left the stuff where it was and scarpered.*
– ORIGIN mid 19th cent.: probably from Italian *scappare* 'to escape', influenced by rhyming slang *Scapa Flow* 'go'.

scarp slope ▶ **noun** a slope in the land that cuts across the underlying strata, especially the steeper slope of a cuesta. Often contrasted with DIP SLOPE.

Scart (also **SCART**) ▶ **noun** a 21-pin socket used to connect video equipment.
– ORIGIN 1980s: acronym from French *Syndicat des Constructeurs des Appareils Radiorécepteurs et Téléviseurs*, the committee which designed the connector.

scarves plural form of SCARF¹.

scary ▶ **adjective** (**scarier, scariest**) informal frightening; causing fear: *a scary movie.* ■ uncannily striking or surprising: *it was scary the way they bonded with each other.*
– DERIVATIVES **scarily** adverb, **scariness** noun.

scat¹ ▶ **verb** (**scats, scatting, scatted**) [no obj., usu. in imperative] informal go away; leave: *Scat! Leave me alone.*
– ORIGIN mid 19th cent.: perhaps an abbreviation of SCATTER, or perhaps from the sound of a hiss (used to drive an animal away) + *-cat*.

scat² ▶ **noun** (also **scat singing**) [mass noun] improvised jazz singing in which the voice is used in imitation of an instrument.
▶ **verb** (**scats, scatting, scatted**) [no obj.] sing using the voice in imitation of an instrument.
– ORIGIN 1920s: probably imitative.

scat³ ▶ **noun** [mass noun] droppings, especially those of carnivorous mammals.
– ORIGIN 1950s: from Greek *skōr*, *skat-* 'dung'.

scat⁴ ▶ **noun** a small deep-bodied silvery fish that lives in inshore and estuarine waters of the Indo-Pacific.
● Family Scatophagidae: several genera and species. See also ARGUS (sense 3).
– ORIGIN 1960s: abbreviation of modern Latin *Scatophagidae*, from Greek *skatophagos* 'dung-eating' (because the fish is often found beside sewage outlets).

scathe /skeɪð/ archaic ▶ **verb** [with obj. and usu. with negative] harm; injure: *he was barely scathed.* ■ literary damage or destroy by fire or lightning.
▶ **noun** [mass noun] harm; injury.
– DERIVATIVES **scatheless** adjective.
– ORIGIN Middle English: from Old Norse *skathi* (noun), *skatha* (verb); related to Dutch and German *schaden* (verb).

scathing ▶ **adjective** witheringly scornful; severely critical: *she launched* **a scathing attack on** *the Prime Minister.*
– DERIVATIVES **scathingly** adverb.

scatology /skaˈtɒlədʒi/ ▶ **noun** [mass noun] an interest in or preoccupation with excrement and excretion. ■ obscene literature that is concerned with excrement and excretion.
– DERIVATIVES **scatological** adjective.
– ORIGIN late 19th cent.: from Greek *skōr*, *skat-* 'dung' + -LOGY.

scatophagous /skaˈtɒfəgəs/ ▶ **adjective** Zoology (of an insect or other animal) feeding on dung; coprophagous.
– ORIGIN late 19th cent.: from modern Latin *scatophagus* (from Greek *skatophagos* 'dung-eating') + -OUS.

scatter ▶ **verb** [with obj.] **1** throw in various random directions: **scatter** *the coconut* **over** *the icing | his family are hoping to scatter his ashes at sea.* ■ cover (a surface) with objects thrown or spread randomly over it: *sandy beaches scattered with driftwood.* ■ (**be scattered**) [usu. with adverbial] occur or be found at intervals rather than all together: *there are many watermills scattered throughout the marshlands* | (as adj. **scattered**) *a scattered cliff-top community.*
2 [no obj.] (of a group of people or animals) separate and move off quickly in different directions: *the roar made the dogs scatter.* ■ [with obj.] cause (a group of people or animals) to move off quickly in different directions: *he charged across the foyer, scattering people.*
3 Physics deflect or diffuse (electromagnetic radiation or particles).
4 Baseball pitch (balls) effectively, allowing several hits but little or no scoring.
▶ **noun 1** a small, dispersed amount of something: *a* **scatter of** *boulders round the pothole mouth.*
2 [mass noun] Statistics the degree to which repeated measurements or observations of a quantity differ.
3 [mass noun] Physics the scattering of light, other electromagnetic radiation, or particles.
– DERIVATIVES **scatterer** noun.
– ORIGIN Middle English (as a verb): probably a variant of SHATTER.

scatterbrain ▶ **noun** a person who tends to be disorganized and lacking in concentration.

scatterbrained ▶ **adjective** (of a person) disorganized and lacking in concentration.

scatter cushion ▶ **noun** a small cushion designed to be placed randomly so as to create a casual effect and to be moved as required.

scatter diagram (also **scatter plot**) ▶ **noun** Statistics a graph in which the values of two variables are plotted along two axes, the pattern of the resulting points revealing any correlation present.

scattergram (also **scattergraph**) ▶ **noun** another term for SCATTER DIAGRAM.

scattergun ▶ **adjective** another term for SCATTERSHOT.
▶ **noun** N. Amer. a shotgun.

scattering ▶ **noun 1** an act of scattering something. ■ a small, dispersed amount of something: *the scattering of freckles across her cheeks and forehead.*
2 [mass noun] Physics the process in which electromagnetic radiation or particles are deflected or diffused.

scattering angle ▶ **noun** Physics the angle through which a scattered particle or beam is deflected.

scatter rug ▶ **noun** a small decorative rug designed to be placed with a casual effect and moved as required.

scattershot ▶ **adjective** denoting something that is broad but random and haphazard in its range: *you cannot take a scattershot approach to a public relations campaign.*

scatty ▶ **adjective** (**scattier**, **scattiest**) Brit. informal absent-minded and disorganized.
– DERIVATIVES **scattily** adverb, **scattiness** noun.
– ORIGIN early 20th cent.: abbreviation of SCATTER-BRAINED.

scaup /skɔːp/ ▶ **noun** a Eurasian, North American, and New Zealand diving duck, the male of which has a black head with a green or purple gloss. ● Family Anatidae: three species in the genus *Aythya*, in particular the widespread (**greater**) **scaup** (*A. marila*), with a black breast and white sides.
– ORIGIN late 17th cent.: Scots variant of Scots and northern English *scalp* 'mussel-bed', a feeding ground of the duck.

scauper ▶ **noun** variant of SCORP.

scaur ▶ **noun** archaic spelling of SCAR (sense 2 of the noun).

scavenge /ˈskavɪn(d)ʒ/ ▶ **verb** [with obj.] **1** search for and collect (anything usable) from discarded waste: *people sell junk* ***scavenged from*** *the garbage* | *the city dump where the squatters scavenge to survive.* ■ (of an animal) search for (carrion) as food. ■ search for discarded items or food in (a place): *the mink is still commonly seen scavenging the beaches of California.*
2 remove (combustion products) from an internal-combustion engine cylinder on the return stroke of the piston.
3 Chemistry combine with and remove (molecules, radicals, etc.) from a particular medium.
– ORIGIN mid 17th cent. (in the sense 'clean out (dirt)'): back-formation from SCAVENGER.

scavenger ▶ **noun 1** an animal that feeds on carrion, dead plant material, or refuse.
2 a person who searches for and collects discarded items.
3 archaic a person employed to clean the streets.
4 Chemistry a substance that reacts with and removes particular molecules, radicals, etc.
– ORIGIN mid 16th cent.: alteration of earlier *scavager*, from Anglo-Norman French *scawager*, from Old Northern French *escauwer* 'inspect', from Flemish *scauwen* 'to show'. The term originally denoted an officer who collected *scavage*, a toll on foreign merchants' goods offered for sale in a town, later a person who kept the streets clean.

scavenger cell ▶ **noun** another term for PHAGOCYTE.

scavenger hunt ▶ **noun** a game, typically played in an extensive outdoor area, in which participants have to collect a number of miscellaneous objects.

scazon /ˈskeɪz(ə)n, ˈska-/ ▶ **noun** Prosody a modification of the iambic trimeter, in which a spondee or trochee takes the place of the final iambus.
– ORIGIN late 17th cent.: via Latin from Greek *skazōn*, neuter present participle (used as a noun) of *skazein* 'to limp'.

ScD ▶ **abbreviation** Doctor of Science.
– ORIGIN from Latin *scientiae doctor*.

SCE ▶ **abbreviation** Scottish Certificate of Education.

scena /ˈʃeɪnə/ ▶ **noun** a scene in an opera. ■ an elaborate dramatic solo usually including recitative.
– ORIGIN Italian, from Latin, 'scene'.

scenario /sɪˈnɑːrɪəʊ/ ▶ **noun** (pl. **scenarios**) a written outline of a film, novel, or stage work giving details of the plot and individual scenes: *the scenarios for four short stories.* ■ a postulated sequence or development of events: *a possible scenario is that he was attacked after opening the front door.* ■ a setting, in particular for a work of art or literature: *the scenario is World War Two.*
– ORIGIN late 19th cent.: from Italian, from Latin *scena* 'scene'.

scenarist /sɪˈnɑːrɪst/ ▶ **noun** a screenwriter.

scend /sɛnd/ (also **send**) archaic ▶ **noun** the push or surge created by a wave. ■ a pitching or surging movement in a boat.
▶ **verb** [no obj.] (of a vessel) pitch or surge up in a heavy sea.
– ORIGIN late 15th cent. (as a verb): alteration of SEND[1] or DESCEND. The noun dates from the early 18th cent.

scene ▶ **noun 1** the place where an incident in real life or fiction occurs or occurred: *the emergency team were among the first* ***on the scene*** | *relatives left floral tributes* ***at the scene of*** *the crash.* ■ a place or setting regarded as having a particular character or making a particular impression: ***a scene of*** *carnage.* ■ a landscape: *thick snow had turned the scene outside into a picture postcard.* ■ an incident of a specified nature: *there had already been some scenes of violence.* ■ a representation of an incident, or the incident itself: *scenes of 1930s America.* ■ [with adj. or noun modifier] a specified area of activity or interest: *one of the biggest draws on the Irish music scene.* ■ (usu. **the scene**) informal a social environment frequented predominantly by homosexuals: *I don't go out into the scene now.* ■ [usu. in sing.] a public display of emotion or anger: *she was loath to* ***make a scene*** *in the office.*
2 a sequence of continuous action in a play, film, opera, or book: *a scene from Tarantino's latest movie.* ■ a subdivision of an act of a play in which the time is continuous and the setting fixed and which does not usually involve a change of characters: *beginning at Act One, Scene One.* ■ [mass noun] [usu. as modifier] the pieces of scenery used in a play or opera: *scene changes.*
– PHRASES **behind the scenes** out of sight of the public at a theatre or organization. ■ secretly: *diplomatic manoeuvres going on behind the scenes.* **change of scene** a move to different surroundings. **come** (or **appear** or **arrive**) **on the scene** arrive; appear: *the family had gone by the time I came on the scene.* **hit** (or US **make**) **the scene** informal arrive; appear. **not one's scene** informal not something one enjoys or is interested in: *as for that job you mention, not my scene.* **set the scene** describe a place or situation in which something is about to happen. ■ create the conditions for a future event: *she jumped a flawless round and* ***set the scene for*** *a hair-raising jump-off.*
– ORIGIN mid 16th cent. (denoting a subdivision of a play, or (a piece of) stage scenery): from Latin *scena*, from Greek *skēnē* 'tent, stage'.

scene dock ▶ **noun** a space in a theatre near the stage in which scenery is stored.

scene-of-crime (also **scenes-of-crime**) ▶ **adjective** Brit. relating to or denoting a civilian branch of the police force concerned with the collection of forensic evidence.

scenery ▶ **noun** [mass noun] **1** the natural features of a landscape considered in terms of their appearance, especially when picturesque: *spectacular views of mountain scenery.*
2 the painted background used to represent natural features or other surroundings on a theatre stage or film set.
– PHRASES **change of scenery** another way of saying CHANGE OF SCENE (see SCENE). **chew the scenery** informal, chiefly US (of an actor) overact.
– ORIGIN mid 18th cent. (earlier as *scenary*): from Italian *scenario* (see SCENARIO). The change in the ending was due to association with -ERY.

scene-shifter ▶ **noun** chiefly Brit. a person who moves the scenery on a stage between the scenes of a play.
– DERIVATIVES **scene-shifting** noun.

scene-stealer ▶ **noun** a person or thing taking more than their fair share of attention.

scenester /ˈsiːnstə/ ▶ **noun** informal, chiefly N. Amer. a person associated with or immersed in a particular fashionable cultural scene.

scenic ▶ **adjective 1** providing or relating to views of impressive or beautiful natural scenery: *the scenic route from Florence to Siena* | *scenic beauty.*
2 [attrib.] relating to theatrical scenery: *a scenic artist from the Royal Opera House.*
3 (of a picture) representing an incident: *the trend to scenic figural work.*
– DERIVATIVES **scenically** adverb.
– ORIGIN early 17th cent. (in the sense 'theatrical'): via Latin from Greek *skēnikos* 'of the stage', from *skēnē* (see SCENE).

scenic railway ▶ **noun** an attraction at a fair or in a park consisting of a miniature railway that runs past natural features and artificial scenery.

scenography ▶ **noun** [mass noun] the design and painting of theatrical scenery. ■ (in painting and drawing) the representation of objects in perspective.
– DERIVATIVES **scenographic** adjective.
– ORIGIN mid 17th cent.: from French *scénographie*, or via Latin from Greek *skēnographia* 'scene-painting', from *skēnē* (see SCENE).

scent ▶ **noun 1** a distinctive smell, especially one that is pleasant: *the scent of freshly cut hay.* ■ [mass noun] pleasant-smelling liquid worn on the skin; perfume: *she sprayed scent over her body.*
2 a trail indicated by the characteristic smell of an animal and perceptible to hounds or other animals: *the hound followed the scent.* ■ a trail of evidence or other signs assisting someone in a search or investigation: *once their interest is aroused they follow the scent with sleuth-like pertinacity.*
3 [mass noun] archaic the faculty or sense of smell.
▶ **verb** [with obj.] **1** (usu. **be scented with**) impart a pleasant scent to: *a glass of tea scented with a local herb.*
2 discern by the sense of smell: *a shark can scent blood from well over half a kilometre away.* ■ sense the presence, existence, or imminence of: *the Premier scented victory last night.* ■ sniff (the air) for a scent: *the bull advanced, scenting the breeze at every step.*
– PHRASES **on the scent** in possession of a useful clue in a search or investigation. **put** (or **throw**) **someone off the scent** mislead someone in the course of a search or investigation.
– DERIVATIVES **scentless** adjective.
– ORIGIN late Middle English (denoting the sense of smell): from Old French *sentir* 'perceive, smell', from Latin *sentire*. The addition of *-c-* (in the 17th cent.) is unexplained.

scented ▶ **adjective** having a pleasant scent: *scented soap.*

scent gland ▶ **noun** an animal gland that secretes an odorous pheromone or defensive substance, especially one under the tail of a carnivorous mammal such as a civet or skunk.

scent mark ▶ **noun** (also **scent marking**) an odorous substance containing a pheromone that is deposited by a mammal from a scent gland or in the urine or faeces, typically on prominent objects in an area.
▶ **verb** (**scent-mark**) [no obj.] (of a mammal) deposit a scent mark.

scepter ▶ **noun** US spelling of SCEPTRE.

sceptic (archaic & N. Amer. **skeptic**) ▶ **noun 1** a person inclined to question or doubt accepted opinions. ■ a person who doubts the truth of Christianity and other religions; an atheist.
2 Philosophy an ancient or modern philosopher who denies the possibility of knowledge, or even rational belief, in some sphere.

> The leading ancient sceptic was Pyrrho, whose followers at the Academy vigorously opposed Stoicism. Modern sceptics have held diverse views: the most extreme have doubted whether any knowledge at all of the external world is possible (see SOLIPSISM), while others have questioned the existence of objects beyond our experience of them.

▶ **adjective** another term for SCEPTICAL.
– ORIGIN late 16th cent. (in sense 2 of the noun): from French *sceptique*, or via Latin from Greek *skeptikos*, from *skepsis* 'inquiry, doubt'.

sceptical (US **skeptical**) ▶ **adjective 1** not easily convinced; having doubts or reservations: *the public were deeply sceptical about some of the proposals.*
2 Philosophy relating to the theory that certain knowledge is impossible.
– DERIVATIVES **sceptically** (US **skeptically**) adverb.

scepticism (archaic & N. Amer. **skepticism**) ▶ **noun** [mass noun] **1** a sceptical attitude; doubt as to the truth of something: *these claims were treated with scepticism.*
2 Philosophy the theory that certain knowledge is impossible.

sceptre (US **scepter**) ▶ **noun** an ornamented staff carried by rulers on ceremonial occasions as a symbol of sovereignty.
– DERIVATIVES **sceptred** adjective.

S

– ORIGIN Middle English: from Old French *ceptre*, via Latin from Greek *skēptron*, from *skēptein* (alteration of *skēptesthai*) 'lean on'.

sch. ▶ abbreviation ■ scholar. ■ school. ■ schooner.

schadenfreude /ˈʃɑːd(ə)n,frɔɪdə/, German /ˈʃaːdən,frɔydə/ ▶ noun [mass noun] pleasure derived by someone from another person's misfortune.
– ORIGIN German *Schadenfreude*, from *Schaden* 'harm' + *Freude* 'joy'.

schappe /ʃap, ˈʃapə/ ▶ noun [mass noun] fabric or yarn made from waste silk.
– ORIGIN late 19th cent.: from German *Schappe* 'waste silk'.

schedule /ˈʃɛdjuːl, ˈskɛd-/ ▶ noun **1** a plan for carrying out a process or procedure, giving lists of intended events and times: *we have drawn up an engineering schedule.* ■ (usu. **one's schedule**) one's day-to-day plans or timetable: *take a moment out of your busy schedule.* ■ a timetable: *information on airline schedules.*
2 chiefly Law an appendix to a formal document or statute, especially as a list, table, or inventory.
3 (with reference to the British system of income tax) any of the forms (named 'A', 'B', etc.) issued for completion and relating to the various classes into which taxable income is divided.
▶ verb [with obj.] **1** arrange or plan (an event) to take place at a particular time: *the release of the single is scheduled for April.* ■ make arrangements for (someone or something) to do something: [with obj. and infinitive] *he is scheduled to be released from prison this spring.*
2 Brit. include (a building or site) in a list for legal preservation or protection.
– PHRASES **ahead of** (or **behind**) **schedule** earlier (or later) than planned or expected. **to** (or **on** or **according to**) **schedule** on time; as planned or expected.
– DERIVATIVES **schedular** adjective.
– ORIGIN late Middle English (in the sense 'scroll, explanatory note, appendix'): from Old French *cedule*, from late Latin *schedula* 'slip of paper', diminutive of *scheda*, from Greek *skhedē* 'papyrus leaf'. The verb dates from the mid 19th cent.

scheduled ▶ adjective **1** included in or planned according to a schedule: *the bus makes one scheduled thirty-minute stop.* ■ (especially of an airline or flight) relating to or forming part of a regular service rather than specially chartered.
2 Brit. (of a building or other historic monument) included in a list for legal preservation and protection.

scheduled caste ▶ noun the official name given in India to the lowest caste, considered 'untouchable' in orthodox Hindu scriptures and practice, officially regarded as socially disadvantaged.

scheduled territories ▶ plural noun another term for STERLING AREA.

scheduled tribe ▶ noun (in India) an indigenous people officially regarded as socially disadvantaged.

scheduler ▶ noun a person or machine that organizes or maintains schedules. ■ Computing a program that arranges jobs or a computer's operations into an appropriate sequence.

S

scheelite /ˈʃiːlʌɪt/ ▶ noun [mass noun] a fluorescent mineral, white when pure, which consists of calcium tungstate and is an important ore of tungsten.
– ORIGIN mid 19th cent.: from the name of Carl W. *Scheele* (1742–86), Swedish chemist, + -ITE[1].

schefflera /ˈʃɛflərə/ ▶ noun an evergreen tropical or subtropical shrub or small tree which is widely grown as a pot plant for its decorative foliage.
● Genus *Schefflera*, family Araliaceae.
– ORIGIN modern Latin, named after J. C. *Scheffler*, 18th-cent. German botanist.

Scheherazade /ʃə,hɛrəˈzɑːd, -ˈzɑːdə/ the narrator of the *Arabian Nights*, a collection of stories written in Arabic. See ARABIAN NIGHTS.

Scheldt /skɛlt, ʃɛlt/ a river of northern Europe. Rising in northern France, it flows 432 km (270 miles) through Belgium and the Netherlands to the North Sea. Also called **Schelde** /ˈskɛldə/, /ˈʃɛl-/. French name ESCAUT.

schelly /ˈskɛli/ (also **skelly**) ▶ noun a powan (fish) of a variety occurring only in three lakes in the English Lake District.
– ORIGIN mid 18th cent.: a local name.

schema /ˈskiːmə/ ▶ noun (pl. **schemata** /-mətə/ or **schemas**) **1** technical a representation of a plan or theory in the form of an outline or model: *a schema of scientific reasoning.*
2 Logic a syllogistic figure.
3 (in Kantian philosophy) a conception of what is common to all members of a class; a general or essential type or form.
– ORIGIN late 18th cent. (as a term in philosophy): from Greek *skhēma* 'form, figure'.

schematic ▶ adjective (of a diagram or other representation) symbolic and simplified. ■ (of thought, ideas, etc.) simplistic or formulaic in character: *Freeman constructs a highly schematic reading of the play.*
▶ noun (in technical contexts) a schematic diagram, in particular of an electric or electronic circuit.
– DERIVATIVES **schematically** adverb.

schematism ▶ noun [mass noun] the arrangement or presentation of something according to a scheme or schema.
– ORIGIN early 17th cent.: from modern Latin *schematismus*, from Greek *skhēmatismos* 'assumption of a certain form', from *skhēma*, *skhēmat-* 'form'.

schematize (also **schematise**) ▶ verb [with obj.] arrange or represent in a schematic form.
– DERIVATIVES **schematization** noun.

scheme ▶ noun a large-scale systematic plan or arrangement for attaining some particular object or putting a particular idea into effect: *the occupational sick pay scheme.* ■ a secret or underhand plan; a plot: *police uncovered a scheme to steal paintings worth more than $250,000.* ■ a particular ordered system or arrangement: *a classical rhyme scheme.*
▶ verb **1** [no obj.] make plans, especially in a devious way or with intent to do something illegal or wrong: [with infinitive] *he schemed to bring about the collapse of the government.* ■ S. African informal think; suppose: [with clause] *I scheme it could work.*
2 [with obj.] arrange according to a colour scheme.
– PHRASES **the scheme of things** a supposed or apparent overall system, within which everything has a place and in relation to which individual details are ultimately to be assessed: *in the overall scheme of things, we didn't do badly.*
– ORIGIN mid 16th cent. (denoting a figure of speech): from Latin *schema*, from Greek (see SCHEMA). An early sense was 'diagram of the position of celestial objects', giving rise to 'diagram, outline', whence the current senses. The unfavourable notion 'plot' arose in the mid 18th cent.

schemer ▶ noun a person who is involved in making secret or underhand plans.

scheming ▶ adjective given to or involved in making secret and underhand plans: *they had mean, scheming little minds.*
▶ noun [mass noun] the activity or practice of making secret and underhand plans.
– DERIVATIVES **schemingly** adverb.

schemozzle ▶ noun variant spelling of SHEMOZZLE.

Schengen agreement /ˈʃɛŋən ə,griːmənt/ an intergovernmental agreement on the relaxation of border controls between participating European countries, first signed in Schengen, Luxembourg, in June 1985 by France, West Germany, Belgium, the Netherlands, and Luxembourg. A revised version of the agreement was incorporated into the European Union in 1999 and widened to include non-EU members of a similar Nordic union.

scherzando /skɛːtˈsandəʊ/ Music ▶ adverb & adjective (especially as a direction) in a playful manner.
– ORIGIN Italian, literally 'joking'.

scherzo /ˈskɛːtsəʊ/ ▶ noun (pl. **scherzos** or **scherzi** /-tsi/) Music a vigorous, light, or playful composition, typically comprising a movement in a symphony or sonata.
– ORIGIN Italian, literally 'jest'.

Schiaparelli /,ʃapəˈrɛli/, Italian /,skjapaˈreli/, Elsa (1896–1973), Italian-born French fashion designer. She introduced padded shoulders in 1932 and the vivid shade now known as 'shocking pink'.

Schick test /ʃɪk/ ▶ noun Medicine a test for previously acquired immunity to diphtheria, using an intradermal injection of diphtheria toxin.
– ORIGIN early 20th cent.: named after Bela *Schick* (1877–1967), Hungarian-born American paediatrician.

Schiele /ˈʃiːlə/, Egon (1890–1918), Austrian painter and draughtsman. His style is characterized by an aggressive linear energy and a neurotic intensity. Notable works: *The Cardinal and the Nun* (1912) and *Embrace* (1917).

Schiff base ▶ noun Chemistry an organic compound having the structure $R^1R^2C{=}NR^3$ (where $R^{1,2,3}$ are alkyl groups and R^1 may be hydrogen).
– ORIGIN late 19th cent.: named after Hugo *Schiff* (1834–1915), German chemist.

Schiff's reagent /ʃɪfs/ ▶ noun [mass noun] Chemistry an acid solution of fuchsin decolorized by sulphur dioxide or potassium metabisulphite, used in testing for aldehydes (which restore the magenta colour).
– ORIGIN late 19th cent.: see SCHIFF BASE.

Schiller /ˈʃɪlə/, German /ˈʃɪlɐ/, (Johann Christoph) Friedrich von (1759–1805), German dramatist, poet, historian, and critic. Initially influenced by the *Sturm und Drang* movement, he was later an important figure of the Enlightenment. His historical plays include the trilogy *Wallenstein* (1800), *Mary Stuart* (1800), and *William Tell* (1804). Among his best-known poems is 'Ode to Joy', which Beethoven set to music in his Ninth Symphony.

schilling /ˈʃɪlɪŋ/ ▶ noun (until the introduction of the euro in 2002) the basic monetary unit of Austria, equal to 100 groschen.
– ORIGIN from German *Schilling*; compare with SHILLING.

Schindler /ˈʃɪndlə/, German /ˈʃɪndlɐ/, Oskar (1908–74), German industrialist. He saved more than 1,200 Jews from concentration camps by employing them first in his enamelware factory in Cracow and then in an armaments factory that he set up in Czechoslovakia in 1944.

schipperke /ˈskɪpəki, ˈʃɪp-, -kə/ ▶ noun a small black tailless dog of a breed with a ruff of fur round its neck.
– ORIGIN late 19th cent.: from Dutch dialect, literally 'little boatman', with reference to its use as a watchdog on barges.

schism /ˈsɪz(ə)m, ˈskɪz(ə)m/ ▶ noun a split or division between strongly opposed sections or parties, caused by differences in opinion or belief. ■ the formal separation of a Church into two Churches or the secession of a group owing to doctrinal and other differences. See also GREAT SCHISM.
– ORIGIN late Middle English: from Old French *scisme*, via ecclesiastical Latin from Greek *skhisma* 'cleft', from *skhizein* 'to split'.

schismatic ▶ adjective characterized by or favouring schism.
▶ noun chiefly historical (especially in the Christian Church) a person who promotes schism; an adherent of a schismatic group.
– DERIVATIVES **schismatically** adverb.
– ORIGIN late Middle English: from Old French *scismatique*, via ecclesiastical Latin from ecclesiastical Greek *skhismatikos*, from *skhisma* (see SCHISM).

schist /ʃɪst/ ▶ noun [mass noun] Geology a coarse-grained metamorphic rock which consists of layers of different minerals and can be split into thin irregular plates.
– ORIGIN late 18th cent.: from French *schiste*, via Latin from Greek *skhistos* 'split', from the base of *skhizein* 'cleave'.

schistose /ˈʃɪstəʊs/ ▶ adjective (of metamorphic rock) having a laminar structure like that of schist.
– DERIVATIVES **schistosity** noun.

schistosome /ˈʃɪstə(ʊ),səʊm/ ▶ noun Zoology & Medicine a parasitic flatworm which needs two hosts to complete its life cycle. The immature form infests freshwater snails and the adult lives in the blood vessels of birds and mammals, causing bilharzia in humans. Also called BLOOD FLUKE. ● Genus *Schistosoma*, subclass Digenea, class Trematoda.
– ORIGIN early 20th cent.: from modern Latin *Schistosoma*, from Greek *skhistos* 'divided' + *sōma* 'body'.

schistosomiasis /,ʃɪstə(ʊ)səˈmʌɪəsɪs/ ▶ noun another term for BILHARZIA (the disease).

schizandra /skɪtˈsandrə/ ▶ noun [mass noun] a Chinese herb whose berries are credited with various stimulant or medicinal properties. ● *Schisandra chinensis*, family Schisandraceae.
– ORIGIN mid 19th cent.: modern Latin *Schisandra*, formed as SCHIZO- + Greek *andr-*, *anēr* man, on account of the divided stamens.

schizanthus /skɪtˈsanθəs/ ▶ noun a South American plant of the nightshade family, with irregularly lobed showy flowers marked with one or more contrasting colours. Also called POOR MAN'S ORCHID.
● Genus *Schizanthus*, family Solanaceae.

– ORIGIN modern Latin, from Greek *skhizein* 'to split' + *anthos* 'flower'.

schizo informal ▶ **adjective** (of a person or their behaviour) schizophrenic.
▶ **noun** (pl. **schizos**) a schizophrenic.
– ORIGIN 1940s: abbreviation.

schizo- ▶ **combining form** divided; split: *schizocarp*. ■ relating to schizophrenia: *schizotype*.
– ORIGIN from Greek *skhizein* 'to split'.

schizo-affective ▶ **adjective** (of a person or a mental condition) characterized by symptoms of both schizophrenia and manic-depressive psychosis.

schizocarp /ˈʃʌɪzə(ʊ)kɑːp, ˈskɪts-/ ▶ **noun** Botany a dry fruit that splits into single-seeded parts when ripe.
– ORIGIN 19th cent.: from SCHIZO- + Greek *karpos* 'fruit'.

schizogenous /ʃʌɪˈzɒdʒənəs, skɪts-/ ▶ **adjective** Botany (of an intercellular space in a plant) formed by the splitting of the common wall of contiguous cells.
– DERIVATIVES **schizogeny** noun.

schizogony /ʃʌɪˈzɒgəni, skɪts-/ ▶ **noun** [mass noun] Biology asexual reproduction by multiple fission, found in some protozoa, especially parasitic sporozoans.
– ORIGIN late 19th cent.: from SCHIZO- 'divided' + Greek *-gonia* 'production'.

schizoid /ˈskɪtsɔɪd, ˈskɪdz-/ ▶ **adjective** Psychiatry denoting or having a personality type characterized by emotional aloofness and solitary habits. ■ informal (in general use) resembling schizophrenia in having inconsistent or contradictory elements; mad or crazy: *it's a frenzied, schizoid place*.
▶ **noun** a schizoid person.

schizont /ˈʃʌɪzɒnt, ˈskɪ-/ ▶ **noun** Biology (in certain sporozoan protozoans) a cell that divides by schizogony to form daughter cells.
– ORIGIN early 20th cent.: from SCHIZO- 'divided' + -ONT.

schizophrenia /ˌskɪtsə(ʊ)ˈfriːnɪə/ ▶ **noun** [mass noun] a long-term mental disorder of a type involving a breakdown in the relation between thought, emotion, and behaviour, leading to faulty perception, inappropriate actions and feelings, withdrawal from reality and personal relationships into fantasy and delusion, and a sense of mental fragmentation. ■ (in general use) a mentality or approach characterized by inconsistent or contradictory elements.
– DERIVATIVES **schizophrenic** /-ˈfrɛnɪk/ **adjective & noun**.
– ORIGIN early 20th cent.: modern Latin, from Greek *skhizein* 'to split' + *phrēn* 'mind'.

schizostylis /ˌʃɪzə(ʊ)ˈstʌɪlɪs/ ▶ **noun** (pl. **same**) a plant of a genus that includes the Kaffir lily. ● Genus *Schizostylis*, family Iridaceae.
– ORIGIN modern Latin, from SCHIZO- 'divided' + Latin *stilus* 'style' (because of the split styles of the plant).

schizotype /ˈskɪtsəʊtʌɪp/ ▶ **noun** a personality type in which mild symptoms of schizophrenia are present.
– DERIVATIVES **schizotypal** adjective, **schizotypy** noun.

Schlegel /ˈʃleɪg(ə)l/, August Wilhelm von (1767–1845), German romantic poet and critic, who was among the founders of art history and comparative philology.

schlemiel /ʃləˈmiːl/ ▶ **noun** N. Amer. informal a stupid, awkward, or unlucky person.
– ORIGIN late 19th cent.: from Yiddish *shlemiel*.

schlenter /ˈʃlɛntə/ S. African ▶ **adjective** not genuine; counterfeit.
▶ **noun** a fake diamond. ■ an illegal or dishonest scheme. ■ a confidence trickster.
▶ **verb** [with obj.] informal achieve or acquire by underhand means: *I can always manage to schlenter a car*.
– ORIGIN from Dutch and Afrikaans *slenter* 'trick'. The *sch-* probably reflects Yiddish influence in the 19th cent. in diamond mining.

schlep /ʃlɛp/ (also **schlepp**) informal, chiefly N. Amer. ▶ **verb** (**schleps**, **schlepping**, **schlepped**) [with obj.] haul or carry (something heavy or awkward): *she schlepped her groceries home*. ■ [no obj., with adverbial of direction] (of a person) go or move reluctantly or with effort: *I would have preferred not to schlep all the way over there to run an errand*.
▶ **noun 1** a tedious or difficult journey.
2 another term for SCHLEPPER.
– ORIGIN early 20th cent. (as a verb): from Yiddish *shlepn* 'drag', from Middle High German *sleppen*.

schlepper /ˈʃlɛpə/ ▶ **noun** N. Amer. informal an inept or stupid person.
– ORIGIN 1930s: Yiddish, from *shlepn* (see SCHLEP).

Schleswig /ˈʃlɛsvɪg/, German /ˈʃleːsvɪç/ a former Danish duchy, situated in the southern part of the Jutland peninsula. Taken by Prussia in 1866, it was incorporated with the neighbouring duchy of Holstein as the province of Schleswig-Holstein. The northern part of Schleswig was returned to Denmark in 1920 after a plebiscite held in accordance with the Treaty of Versailles.

Schleswig-Holstein /ˈhɒlstʌɪn/, German /ˈhɔlʃtaın/ a state of NW Germany, occupying the southern part of the Jutland peninsula; capital, Kiel. It comprises the former duchies of Schleswig and Holstein.

Schlick /ʃlɪk/, Moritz (1882–1936), German philosopher and physicist, founder of the Vienna Circle. Notable works: *General Theory of Knowledge* (1918).

Schliemann /ˈʃliːman/, Heinrich (1822–90), German archaeologist. In 1871 he began excavating the mound of Hissarlik on the NE Aegean coast of Turkey, where he discovered the remains of nine superimposed cities, identifying the second oldest as Homer's Troy, although it was later found to be pre-Homeric. He subsequently undertook excavations at Mycenae (1876).

schlieren /ˈʃlɪərən/ ▶ **plural noun** technical discernible layers in a transparent material that differ from the surrounding material in density or composition. ■ Geology irregular streaks or masses in igneous rock that differ from the surrounding rock in texture or composition.
– ORIGIN late 19th cent.: from German *Schlieren*, plural of *Schliere* 'streak'.

schlimazel /ʃlɪˈmɒz(ə)l/ (also **schlemazel**) ▶ **noun** US informal a consistently unlucky or accident-prone person.
– ORIGIN Yiddish, from Middle High German *slim* 'crooked' + Hebrew *mazzāl* 'luck'.

schlock /ʃlɒk/ ▶ **noun** [mass noun] N. Amer. informal cheap or inferior goods or material; trash.
– DERIVATIVES **schlocky adjective** (**schlockier**, **schlockiest**).
– ORIGIN early 20th cent.: apparently from Yiddish *shlak* 'an apoplectic stroke', *shlog* 'wretch, untidy person, apoplectic stroke'.

schlockmeister /ˈʃlɒkˌmʌɪstə/ ▶ **noun** informal, chiefly N. Amer. a purveyor of cheap or trashy goods.
– ORIGIN early 20th cent.: from SCHLOCK + German *Meister* 'master'.

schloss /ʃlɒs/ ▶ **noun** (in Germany, Austria, or their former territories) a castle.
– ORIGIN early 19th cent.: from German *Schloss*.

schlub /ʃlʌb/ (also **shlub**) ▶ **noun** N. Amer. informal a talentless, unattractive, or boorish person.
– ORIGIN 1960s: Yiddish *shlub*, perhaps from Polish *żłób*.

schlump /ʃlʊmp/ ▶ **noun** N. Amer. informal a slow, slovenly, or inept person.
– ORIGIN 1940s: apparently related to Yiddish *shlumperdik* 'dowdy' and German *Schlumpe* 'slattern'.

schmaltz /ʃmɔːlts, ʃmalts/ ▶ **noun** [mass noun] informal excessive sentimentality, especially in music or films.
– ORIGIN 1930s: from Yiddish *shmaltz*, from German *Schmalz* 'dripping, lard'.

schmaltzy ▶ **adjective** (**schmaltzier**, **schmaltziest**) informal excessively sentimental: *schmaltzy ballads*.

schmatte /ˈʃmatə/ (also **shmatte**) ▶ **noun** US informal a rag; a ragged or shabby garment.
– ORIGIN 1970s: Yiddish *shmatte*, from Polish *szmata* 'rag'.

schmear /ʃmɪə/ (also **schmeer**, **shmeer**, or **shmear**) N. Amer. informal ▶ **noun 1** an underhand inducement.
2 a smear or spread: *a schmear of low-fat cream cheese*.
▶ **verb** [with obj.] flatter or ingratiate oneself with (someone): *he was buying us drinks and schmearing us up*.
– PHRASES **the whole schmear** everything possible or available; every aspect of the situation: *I'm going for the whole schmear*.
– ORIGIN 1960s: from Yiddish *shmirn* 'flatter, grease'.

Schmidt–Cassegrain telescope /ʃmɪtˈkasɪgreɪn/ ▶ **noun** a type of catadioptric telescope, using the correcting plate of a Schmidt telescope together with the secondary mirror and rear focus of a Cassegrain telescope.

Schmidt telescope (also **Schmidt camera**) ▶ **noun** a type of catadioptric telescope used solely for wide-angle astronomical photography, with a thin glass plate at the front to correct for spherical aberration. A curved photographic plate is placed at the prime focus inside the telescope.
– ORIGIN 1930s: named after Bernhard V. *Schmidt* (1879–1935), the German inventor.

Schmitt trigger ▶ **noun** Electronics a bistable circuit in which the output increases to a steady maximum when the input rises above a certain threshold, and decreases almost to zero when the input voltage falls below another threshold.
– ORIGIN 1940s: named after Otto H. *Schmitt* (born 1913), American electronics engineer.

schmo /ʃməʊ/ (also **shmo**) ▶ **noun** (pl. **schmoes**) N. Amer. informal a stupid person. ■ (also **Joe Schmo**) a hypothetical ordinary man: *a lot of Joe Schmoes make it to the big leagues*.
– ORIGIN 1940s: alteration of SCHMUCK.

schmooze /ʃmuːz/ chiefly N. Amer. ▶ **verb** [no obj.] talk intimately and cosily; gossip. ■ [with obj.] talk in a cosy and intimate manner to (someone), typically in order to manipulate them.
▶ **noun** a long and intimate conversation.
– DERIVATIVES **schmoozer noun**, **schmoozy adjective** (**schmoozier**, **schmooziest**).
– ORIGIN late 19th cent. (as a verb): from Yiddish *shmuesn* 'converse, chat'.

schmuck /ʃmʌk/ ▶ **noun** N. Amer. informal a foolish or contemptible person.
– ORIGIN late 19th cent.: from Yiddish *shmok* 'penis'.

schmutter /ˈʃmʌtə(r)/ ▶ **noun** [mass noun] informal
1 clothing; garments.
2 worthless material; rubbish.
– ORIGIN 1950s: from Yiddish *schmatte* 'rag'.

schnapps /ʃnaps/ ▶ **noun** [mass noun] a strong alcoholic drink resembling gin.
– ORIGIN from German *Schnaps*, literally 'dram of liquor', from Low German and Dutch *snaps* 'mouthful'.

schnauzer /ˈʃnaʊzə/ ▶ **noun** a dog of a German breed with a close wiry coat and heavy whiskers round the muzzle.
– ORIGIN 1920s: from German, from *Schnauze* 'muzzle, snout'.

schnitzel /ˈʃnɪtz(ə)l/ ▶ **noun** a thin slice of veal or other light meat, coated in breadcrumbs and fried.
– ORIGIN from German *Schnitzel*, literally 'slice'.

schnook /ʃnʊk/ ▶ **noun** US informal a fool.
– ORIGIN 1940s: perhaps from German *Schnucke* 'small sheep' or from Yiddish *shnuk* 'snout'.

schnorrer /ˈʃnɒrə, ˈʃnɔːrə/ ▶ **noun** informal, chiefly N. Amer. a beggar or scrounger; a layabout.
– ORIGIN late 19th cent.: from Yiddish *shnorrer*, variant of German *Schnurrer*.

schnozz /ʃnɒz/ (also **schnozzola**) ▶ **noun** N. Amer. informal a person's nose.
– ORIGIN 1940s: from Yiddish *shnoytz*, from German *Schnauze* 'snout'.

Schoenberg /ˈʃəːnbəːg/, Arnold (1874–1951), Austrian-born American composer and music theorist. His major contribution to modernism was the development of atonality and serialism. He introduced atonality into his second string quartet (1907–8), while *Serenade* (1923) is the first example of the technique of serialism.

scholar ▶ **noun** a specialist in a particular branch of study, especially the humanities. ■ chiefly archaic a person who is highly educated or has an aptitude for study: *Mr Bell declares himself no scholar*. ■ a university student holding a scholarship. ■ archaic a student or pupil.
– ORIGIN Old English *scol(i)ere* 'schoolchild, student', from late Latin *scholaris*, from Latin *schola* (see SCHOOL[1]).

scholarly ▶ **adjective** involving or relating to serious academic study: *scholarly journals | a scholarly career*. ■ having or showing knowledge, learning, or devotion to academic pursuits: *a scholarly account of the period | an earnest, scholarly man*.
– DERIVATIVES **scholarliness** noun.

scholarship ▶ **noun 1** [mass noun] academic study or achievement; learning at a high level.
2 a grant or payment made to support a student's education, awarded on the basis of academic or other achievement.

scholar's mate ▶ **noun** see MATE[2].

scholastic ▶ **adjective 1** of or concerning schools and education: *scholastic achievement*. ■ US relating to secondary schools.
2 relating to medieval scholasticism. ■ typical of scholasticism in being pedantic or overly subtle.
▶ **noun 1** Philosophy & Theology, historical an adherent of scholasticism; a schoolman.

S

2 (in the Roman Catholic Church) a member of a religious order, especially the Society of Jesus, who is between the novitiate and the priesthood.
– DERIVATIVES **scholastically** adverb.
– ORIGIN late 16th cent. (in sense 2 of the adjective): via Latin from Greek *skholastikos* 'studious', from *skholazein* 'be at leisure to study', from *skholē* (see SCHOOL[1]).

scholasticism /skəˈlastɪˌsɪz(ə)m/ ▶ noun [mass noun] the system of theology and philosophy taught in medieval European universities, based on Aristotelian logic and the writings of the early Christian Fathers and emphasizing tradition and dogma. ■ narrow-minded insistence on traditional doctrine.

scholiast /ˈskəʊlɪast/ ▶ noun historical a commentator on ancient or classical literature.
– DERIVATIVES **scholiastic** adjective.
– ORIGIN late 16th cent.: from medieval Greek *skholiastēs*, from *skholiazein* 'write scholia' (see SCHOLIUM).

scholium /ˈskəʊlɪəm/ ▶ noun (pl. **scholia** /-lɪə/) historical a marginal note or explanatory comment made by a scholiast.
– ORIGIN mid 16th cent.: modern Latin, from Greek *skholion*, from *skholē* 'learned discussion'.

school[1] ▶ noun 1 an institution for educating children: *Ryder's children did not go to school at all* | [as modifier] *school books*. ■ the buildings used by a school: *the cost of building a new school*. ■ [treated as pl.] the pupils and staff of a school: *the head addressed the whole school*. ■ [mass noun] a day's work at school: *school started at 7 a.m.*
2 any institution at which instruction is given in a particular discipline: *a dancing school*. ■ N. Amer. informal another term for UNIVERSITY. ■ a department or faculty of a university concerned with a particular subject of study: *the School of Medicine*.
3 a group of people, particularly writers, artists, or philosophers, sharing similar ideas or methods: *the Frankfurt school of critical theory*. ■ [with adj. or noun modifier] a style, approach, or method of a specified character: *film-makers are tired of the skin-deep school of cinema*.
4 (**schools**) Brit. (at Oxford University) the hall in which final examinations are held. ■ final examinations.
5 Brit. a group gambling together: *a poker school*. ■ a group of people drinking together in a bar and taking turns to buy the drinks.
▶ verb [with obj.] 1 chiefly formal or N. Amer. send to school; educate: *Taverier was born in Paris and schooled in Lyon*. ■ train or discipline (someone) in a particular skill or activity: *he **schooled** her **in** horsemanship* | *it's important to **school yourself to** be good at exams*.
2 Riding train (a horse) on the flat or over fences.
▶ adjective S. African (of a Xhosa) educated and westernized. Contrasted with RED (sense 4 of the adjective). ■ (of a name) of Western origin. [with reference to the mission schools, which encouraged westernized dress, language, and behaviour.]
– PHRASES **leave school** finish one's education: *he left school at 16*. **of** (or **from**) **the old school** see OLD SCHOOL. **the school of hard knocks** see KNOCK. **school of thought** a particular way of thinking, especially one not followed by the speaker: *there is a school of thought that says 1960s office blocks should be refurbished as residential accommodation*.
– ORIGIN Old English *scōl*, *scolu*, via Latin from Greek *skholē* 'leisure, philosophy, lecture place', reinforced in Middle English by Old French *escole*.

school[2] ▶ noun a large group of fish or sea mammals.
▶ verb [no obj.] (of fish or sea mammals) form a large group.
– ORIGIN late Middle English: from Middle Low German, Middle Dutch *schōle*, of West Germanic origin; related to Old English *scolu* 'troop'. Compare with SHOAL[1].

school age ▶ noun [mass noun] the age range of children normally attending school.

school board ▶ noun N. Amer. or historical a local board or authority responsible for the provision and maintenance of schools.

schoolbook ▶ noun a textbook used in a school.

schoolboy ▶ noun a boy attending school. ■ [as modifier] characteristic of or associated with schoolboys: *schoolboy humour*.

schoolboy error ▶ noun Brit. informal a very basic or foolish mistake.

School Certificate ▶ noun a qualification achieved by taking public examinations of proficiency for secondary-school pupils. These examinations existed between 1917 and 1951 in England and Wales, and are current in New Zealand. ■ School Certificate examinations.

schoolchild ▶ noun (pl. **schoolchildren**) a child attending school.

school colours ▶ plural noun see COLOUR (sense 4 of the noun).

schooldays ▶ plural noun the period in someone's life when they attended school: *a close friend from their schooldays*.

school dinner ▶ noun (usu. **school dinners**) Brit. a midday meal provided for a child at school.

school district ▶ noun N. Amer. a unit for the local administration of schools.

schooled ▶ adjective [often in combination] educated or trained in a specified activity or in a particular way: *a man well **schooled in** making money*.

schooler ▶ noun [in combination] chiefly N. Amer. a pupil attending a school of the specified kind or being educated in the specified way: *a high-schooler*.

schoolfellow ▶ noun more formal term for SCHOOLMATE.

schoolgirl ▶ noun a girl attending school. ■ [as modifier] characteristic of or associated with schoolgirls: *schoolgirl French*.

schoolhouse ▶ noun a building used as a school, especially in a small community or village. ■ Brit., chiefly historical a private house adjoining a small school, lived in by the school's teacher.

schoolie ▶ noun informal, Austral. & dialect a schoolteacher. ■ a school pupil.
– PHRASES **schoolies week** (in Australia) a week of celebrations to mark the end of the final year of senior school.

schooling ▶ noun [mass noun] 1 education received at school: *his parents paid for his schooling*.
2 Riding the training of a horse on the flat or over fences: [as modifier] *schooling fences*.

school inspector (also **schools inspector**) ▶ noun (in the UK) an official who reports on teaching standards in schools on behalf of Ofsted.

schoolkid ▶ noun informal a schoolchild.

school-leaver ▶ noun Brit. a young person who is about to leave or has just left school.

school-leaving age ▶ noun Brit. the minimum age at which a young person may legally leave school.

schoolman ▶ noun (pl. **schoolmen**) historical 1 a teacher in a university in medieval Europe.
2 a scholastic theologian.

schoolmarm ▶ noun chiefly N. Amer. a schoolmistress (typically used with reference to a woman regarded as prim, strict, and brisk in manner).
– DERIVATIVES **schoolmarmish** adjective.

schoolmaster ▶ noun chiefly Brit. 1 a male teacher in a school.
2 an experienced horse that is used to train or give confidence to inexperienced riders or horses.
– DERIVATIVES **schoolmasterly** adjective.

schoolmastering ▶ noun [mass noun] dated the profession of a schoolmaster; teaching.

schoolmate ▶ noun informal a person who attends or attended the same school as oneself.

schoolmistress ▶ noun chiefly Brit. a female teacher in a school.

schoolmistressy ▶ adjective informal having characteristics commonly associated with schoolmistresses, especially those of formality and briskness: *her crisp, rather schoolmistressy manner*.

school night ▶ noun a night before a morning on which one must get up for school or (informal) work: *I didn't mean to drink so much red wine on a school night*.

schoolroom ▶ noun a room used for lessons, especially the main classroom in a small school. ■ (**the schoolroom**) used to refer to school as an institution: *I was green as grass, straight out of the schoolroom*.

school ship ▶ noun a training ship.

schoolteacher ▶ noun a person who teaches in a school.
– DERIVATIVES **schoolteaching** noun.

schoolwork ▶ noun [mass noun] work that is done or to be done by school students.

schoolyard ▶ noun chiefly N. Amer. a school playground.

school year ▶ noun the period in the year during which pupils attend school, from the beginning of the autumn term to the end of the summer term.

schooner /ˈskuːnə/ ▶ noun 1 a sailing ship with two or more masts, typically with the foremast smaller than the mainmast.
2 Brit. a glass for drinking a large measure of sherry. ■ N. Amer. & Austral./NZ a tall beer glass.
– ORIGIN early 18th cent.: perhaps from dialect *scun* 'skim along', influenced by Dutch words beginning with *sch-*.

Schopenhauer /ˈʃəʊp(ə)nˌhaʊə, ˈʃɒp-/, Arthur (1788–1860), German philosopher. According to his philosophy, as expressed in *The World as Will and Idea*, the will is identified with ultimate reality and happiness is only achieved by abnegating the will (as desire).

schorl /ʃɔːl/ ▶ noun [mass noun] a black iron-rich variety of tourmaline.
– ORIGIN late 18th cent.: from German *Schörl*, of unknown origin.

schottische /ʃɒˈtiːʃ, ˈʃɒtɪʃ/ ▶ noun a slow polka.
– ORIGIN mid 19th cent.: from German *der schottische Tanz* 'the Scottish dance'.

Schottky barrier /ˈʃɒtki/ ▶ noun Electronics an electrostatic depletion layer formed at the junction of a metal and a semiconductor, which causes it to act as an electrical rectifier.
– ORIGIN 1940s: named after Walter *Schottky* (1886–1976), German physicist.

Schottky diode ▶ noun Electronics a solid-state diode having a metal-semiconductor junction, used in fast switching applications.
– ORIGIN 1960s: named after W. *Schottky* (see SCHOTTKY BARRIER).

Schottky effect ▶ noun Electronics the increase in thermionic emission from a solid surface due to the presence of an external electric field.
– ORIGIN 1920s: named after W. *Schottky* (see SCHOTTKY BARRIER).

Schreiner /ˈʃrʌɪnə/, Olive (Emilie Albertina) (1855–1920), South African novelist and feminist. Notable works: *The Story of an African Farm* (novel, 1883) and *Woman and Labour* (1911).

Schröder /ˈʃrəːdə/, Gerhard (b.1944), German Social Democratic Party statesman, Chancellor of Germany 1998–2005.

Schrödinger /ˈʃrəːdɪŋə/, Erwin (1887–1961), Austrian theoretical physicist. He founded the study of wave mechanics, deriving the equation whose roots define the energy levels of atoms. His general works influenced scientists of many different disciplines. Nobel Prize for Physics (1933).

Schrödinger equation Physics a differential equation which forms the basis of the quantum-mechanical description of matter in terms of the wave-like properties of particles in a field. Its solution is related to the probability density of a particle in space and time.

schtuck ▶ noun variant spelling of SHTOOK.

schtum /ʃtʊm/ ▶ adjective variant spelling of SHTUM.

schtup /ʃtʊp/ ▶ verb variant spelling of SHTUP.

Schubert /ˈʃuːbət/, Franz (1797–1828), Austrian composer. His music is associated with the romantic movement for its lyricism and emotional intensity, but belongs in formal terms to the classical age. His works include more than 600 songs, the 'Trout' piano quintet (1819), and nine symphonies.
– DERIVATIVES **Schubertian** adjective.

Schulz /ʃʊlts/, Charles (1922–2000), American cartoonist. He is remembered as the creator of the 'Peanuts' comic strip which features a range of characters including the boy Charlie Brown and the dog Snoopy.

Schumacher[1] /ˈʃuːmaxə/, E. F. (1911–77), German economist and conservationist; full name *Ernst Friedrich Schumacher*. His most famous work is *Small is Beautiful: Economics as if People Mattered* (1973), which argues that mass production needs to be replaced by smaller, more energy-efficient enterprises.

Schumacher[2] /ˈʃuːmakə/, German /ˈʃuːmaxɐ/, Michael (b.1969), German racing driver, winner of seven Formula One world championships and holder of the world record in his number of Grand Prix wins.

Schumann /ˈʃuːmən/, Robert (Alexander) (1810–56), German composer. He was a leading romantic composer, particularly noted for his songs (including settings of poems by Heinrich Heine and Robert

S

Burns) and piano music. His other works include four symphonies and much chamber music. His wife **Clara** (1819–96) was a noted pianist and composer.

schuss /ʃʊs/ ▸ **noun** a straight downhill run on skis. ▸ **verb** [no obj.] make a straight downhill run on skis.
– ORIGIN 1930s: from German *Schuss*, literally 'shot'.

Schütz /ʃʊts/, Heinrich (1585–1672), German composer and organist. He is regarded as the first German baroque composer, and composed what is thought to have been the first German opera (*Dafne*, 1627; now lost).

schwa /ʃwɑː/ ▸ **noun** Phonetics the unstressed central vowel (as in *a* moment *ago*), represented by the symbol /ə/ in the International Phonetic Alphabet.
– ORIGIN late 19th cent.: from German, from Hebrew *šəwā'*.

Schwaben /ˈʃvaːbn/ German name for **SWABIA**.

Schwäbisch Gmünd /ˌʃveɪbɪʃ ɡ(ə)ˈmʊntʃ/, German /ˌʃvɛːbɪʃ ˈɡmʏnt/ a city in SW Germany, situated to the east of Stuttgart; pop. 61,200 (est. 2006).

Schwann /ʃvan, ʃwɒn/, Theodor Ambrose Hubert (1810–82), German physiologist. He showed that animals (as well as plants) are made up of individual cells and that the egg begins life as a single cell. He is best known for discovering the cells forming the myelin sheaths of nerve fibres (Schwann cells).

Schwarzenegger /ˈʃwɔːtsəˌnɛɡə/, Arnold (b.1947), Austrian-born American actor and politician, noted for action roles, for instance in *The Terminator* (1984).

Schwarzkopf /ˈʃvɑːtskɒpf/, Dame (Olga Maria) Elisabeth (Friederike) (b.1915), German operatic soprano. She is especially famous for her roles in works by Richard Strauss, such as *Der Rosenkavalier*.

Schwarzschild black hole /ˈʃvɑːtsˌʃiːlt, ˈʃwɔːtsˌtʃʌɪld/ ▸ **noun** Physics a black hole of a kind supposed to result from the complete gravitational collapse of an electrically neutral and non-rotating body, having a physical singularity at the centre to which infalling matter inevitably proceeds and at which the curvature of space–time is infinite. A **Schwarzschild radius** is the radius of the boundary of a hole of this type.
– ORIGIN named after Karl *Schwarzschild* (1873–1916), German astronomer.

Schwarzwald /ˈʃvartsvalt/ German name for **BLACK FOREST**.

Schweinfurt /ˈʃvʌɪnfʊət/ a city in western Germany; pop. 54,000 (est. 2006). It became part of Bavaria in 1803.

Schweitzer /ˈʃwʌɪtsə, ˈʃvʌɪ-/, Albert (1875–1965), German theologian, musician, and medical missionary, born in Alsace. In 1913 he qualified as a doctor and went as a missionary to Gabon, where he established a hospital. Nobel Peace Prize (1952).

Schweiz /ʃvaɪts/ German name for **SWITZERLAND**.

Schwerin /ʃvɛˈriːn/ a city in NE Germany, capital of Mecklenburg-West Pomerania, situated on the south-western shores of Lake Schwerin; pop. 96,300 (est. 2006).

Schwyz /ʃviːts/ a city in central Switzerland, situated to the east of Lake Lucerne, the capital of a canton of the same name; pop. 14,193 (2007). The canton was one of the three original cantons of the Swiss Confederation, to which it gave its name.

sciaenid /sʌɪˈiːnɪd/ ▸ **noun** Zoology a fish of the drum family (Sciaenidae), whose members are mainly marine and important for food or sport.
– ORIGIN early 20th cent.: from modern Latin *Sciaenidae* (plural), from the genus name *Sciaena*, from Greek *skiaina*, denoting a kind of fish.

sciagraphy /sʌɪˈaɡrəfi/ (also **skiagraphy**) ▸ **noun** [mass noun] the use of shading and the projection of shadows to show perspective in architectural or technical drawing.
– DERIVATIVES **sciagraphic** adjective.
– ORIGIN late 16th cent.: from French *sciagraphie*, via Latin from Greek *skiagraphia*, from *skia* 'shadow'.

sciamachy /sʌɪˈaməki/ ▸ **noun** [mass noun] archaic sham fighting for exercise or practice. ■ argument or conflict with an imaginary opponent.
– ORIGIN early 17th cent.: from Greek *skiamakhia*, from *skia* 'shadow' + *-makhia* '-fighting'.

sciatic /sʌɪˈatɪk/ ▸ **adjective** relating to the hip. ■ of or affecting the sciatic nerve. ■ suffering from or liable to sciatica.
– ORIGIN early 16th cent. (as a noun denoting sciatica): from French *sciatique*, via late Latin from Greek *iskhiadikos* 'relating to the hips, subject to sciatica', from *iskhion* 'hip joint'.

sciatica ▸ **noun** [mass noun] pain affecting the back, hip, and outer side of the leg, caused by compression of a spinal nerve root in the lower back, often owing to degeneration of an intervertebral disc.
– ORIGIN late Middle English: from late Latin *sciatica (passio)* '(affliction) of sciatica', feminine of *sciaticus*, from Greek *iskhiadikos* (see **SCIATIC**).

sciatic nerve ▸ **noun** Anatomy a major nerve extending from the lower end of the spinal cord down the back of the thigh, and dividing above the knee joint. It is the nerve with the largest diameter in the human body.

SCID ▸ **abbreviation** severe combined immune deficiency, a rare genetic disorder in which affected children have no resistance to disease and must be kept isolated from infection from birth.

science ▸ **noun** [mass noun] the intellectual and practical activity encompassing the systematic study of the structure and behaviour of the physical and natural world through observation and experiment: *the world of science and technology*. ■ a particular area of science: *veterinary science* | [count noun] *the agricultural sciences*. ■ a systematically organized body of knowledge on a particular subject: *the science of criminology*. ■ archaic knowledge of any kind.
– ORIGIN Middle English (denoting knowledge): from Old French, from Latin *scientia*, from *scire* 'know'.

science fiction (abbrev.: **SF**) ▸ **noun** [mass noun] fiction based on imagined future scientific or technological advances and major social or environmental changes, frequently portraying space or time travel and life on other planets.

Science Museum a national museum of science, technology, and industry in South Kensington, London.

science park ▸ **noun** an area devoted to scientific research or the development of science-based or technological industries.

scienter /sʌɪˈɛntə/ ▸ **noun** [mass noun] Law the fact of an act having been done knowingly, especially as grounds for civil damages.
– ORIGIN Latin, from *scire* know.

sciential /sʌɪˈɛnʃ(ə)l/ ▸ **adjective** archaic concerning or having knowledge.
– ORIGIN late Middle English: from late Latin *scientialis*, from *scientia* 'knowledge' (see **SCIENCE**).

scientific ▸ **adjective 1** based on or characterized by the methods and principles of science: *the scientific study of earthquakes*. ■ relating to or used in science: *scientific instruments*.
2 informal systematic; methodical: *how many people buy food in an organized, scientific way?*
– DERIVATIVES **scientifically** adverb, **scientificity** noun.
– ORIGIN late 16th cent.: from French *scientifique* or late Latin *scientificus* 'producing knowledge', from *scientia* (see **SCIENCE**). Early use described the liberal arts as opposed to the 'mechanic' arts (i.e. arts requiring manual skill).

scientific management ▸ **noun** [mass noun] management of a business, industry, or economy, according to principles of efficiency derived from experiments in methods of work and production, especially from time-and-motion studies.

scientific method ▸ **noun** a method of procedure that has characterized natural science since the 17th century, consisting in systematic observation, measurement, and experiment, and the formulation, testing, and modification of hypotheses.

scientific misconduct ▸ **noun** [mass noun] action which wilfully compromises the integrity of scientific research, such as plagiarism or the falsification or fabrication of data.

scientifiction /saɪəntɪˈfɪkʃ(ə)n/ ▸ **noun** [mass noun] science fiction.
– ORIGIN early 20th cent.: blend of **SCIENTIFIC** and **FICTION**.

scientism ▸ **noun** [mass noun] rare thought or expression regarded as characteristic of scientists. ■ excessive belief in the power of scientific knowledge and techniques.
– DERIVATIVES **scientistic** adjective.

scientist ▸ **noun** a person who is studying or has expert knowledge of one or more of the natural or physical sciences.

Scientology ▸ **noun** [mass noun] trademark a religious system based on the seeking of self-knowledge and spiritual fulfilment through graded courses of study and training. It was founded by American science-fiction writer L. Ron Hubbard (1911–86) in 1955.
– DERIVATIVES **Scientologist** noun.
– ORIGIN from Latin *scientia* 'knowledge' + **-LOGY**.

sci-fi ▸ **noun** informal short for **SCIENCE FICTION**.

scilicet /ˈsɪlɪsɛt, ˈsʌɪlɪsɛt, ˈskiːlɪkɛt/ ▸ **adverb** that is to say; namely (introducing a word to be supplied or an explanation of an ambiguity).
– ORIGIN Latin, from *scire licet* 'one is permitted to know'.

scilla /ˈsɪlə/ ▸ **noun** a plant of the lily family which typically bears small blue star- or bell-shaped flowers and glossy strap-like leaves, native to Eurasia and temperate Africa. ● Genus *Scilla*, family Liliaceae.
– ORIGIN modern Latin, from Latin *scilla* 'sea onion', from Greek *skilla*.

Scilly Isles /ˈsɪli/ (also **Isles of Scilly** or **the Scillies** /ˈsɪlɪz/) a group of about 140 small islands (of which five are inhabited) off the south-western tip of England; pop. 2,200 (est. 2009); capital, Hugh Town (on St Mary's).
– DERIVATIVES **Scillonian** adjective & noun.

scimitar /ˈsɪmɪtə/ ▸ **noun** a short sword with a curved blade that broadens towards the point, used originally in Eastern countries.
– ORIGIN mid 16th cent.: from French *cimeterre* or Italian *scimitarra*, of unknown origin.

scimitarbill ▸ **noun** a long-tailed East African bird with a long slender downcurved bill and mainly black plumage with a purple gloss. ● Genus *Rhinopomastus* (or *Pheoniculus*), family Phoeniculidae: two species. Alternative name: **scimitar-billed wood-hoopoe**.

scimitar oryx (also **scimitar-horned oryx**) ▸ **noun** an oryx with scimitar-shaped horns, now living only along the southern edge of the Sahara. ● *Oryx dammah*, family Bovidae.

scintigram /ˈsɪntɪɡram/ ▸ **noun** Medicine an image of an internal part of the body produced by scintigraphy.
– ORIGIN 1950s: from **SCINTILLATION** + **-GRAM**[1].

scintigraphy /sɪnˈtɪɡrəfi/ ▸ **noun** [mass noun] Medicine a technique in which a scintillation counter or similar detector is used with a radioactive tracer to obtain an image of a bodily organ or a record of its functioning.
– DERIVATIVES **scintigraphic** adjective.
– ORIGIN 1950s: from **SCINTILLATION** + **-GRAPHY**.

scintilla /sɪnˈtɪlə/ ▸ **noun** [in sing.] a tiny trace or spark of a specified quality or feeling: ***a scintilla of doubt***.
– ORIGIN late 17th cent.: from Latin.

scintillate /ˈsɪntɪleɪt/ ▸ **verb** [no obj.] emit flashes of light; sparkle. ■ Physics fluoresce momentarily when struck by a charged particle or photon.
– DERIVATIVES **scintillant** adjective & noun.
– ORIGIN early 17th cent.: from Latin *scintillat-* 'sparkled', from the verb *scintillare*, from *scintilla* 'spark'.

scintillating ▸ **adjective 1** sparkling or shining brightly: *the scintillating sun*.
2 brilliantly and excitingly clever or skilful: *the audience loved his scintillating wit* | *the team produced a scintillating second-half performance*.
– DERIVATIVES **scintillatingly** adverb.

scintillation ▸ **noun** a flash or sparkle of light: *scintillations of diamond-hard light*. ■ [mass noun] the process or state of emitting flashes of light. ■ Physics a small flash of visible or ultraviolet light emitted by fluorescence in a phosphor when struck by a charged particle or high-energy photon. ■ [mass noun] Astronomy the twinkling of the stars, caused by the earth's atmosphere diffracting starlight unevenly.

scintillator ▸ **noun** Physics a material that fluoresces when struck by a charged particle or high-energy photon. ■ a detector for charged particles and gamma rays in which scintillations produced in a phosphor are detected and amplified by a photomultiplier, giving an electrical output signal.

scintiscan ▸ **noun** Medicine another term for **SCINTIGRAM**.
– ORIGIN 1960s: from **SCINTILLATION** + **SCAN**.

sciolist /ˈsʌɪəlɪst/ ▸ **noun** archaic a person who pretends to be knowledgeable and well informed.
– DERIVATIVES **sciolism** noun.
– ORIGIN early 17th cent.: from late Latin *sciolus* (diminutive of Latin *scius* 'knowing', from *scire* 'know') + **-IST**.

scion /ˈsʌɪən/ ▸ **noun 1** a young shoot or twig of a plant, especially one cut for grafting or rooting.
2 a descendant of a notable family: *he was the scion of a wealthy family*.

S

– ORIGIN Middle English: from Old French *ciun* 'shoot, twig', of unknown origin.

Scipio Aemilianus /ˌskɪpɪəʊ iːˌmɪlɪˈɑːnəs/ (*c.*185–129 BC), Roman general and politician; full name *Publius Cornelius Scipio Aemilianus Africanus Minor*, adoptive grandson of Scipio Africanus. He achieved distinction in the siege of Carthage (146) during the third Punic War and in his campaign in Spain (133).

Scipio Africanus /ˌafrɪˈkɑːnəs/ (236–*c.*184 BC), Roman general and politician; full name *Publius Cornelius Scipio Africanus Major*. He was successful in concluding the second Punic War, firstly by the defeat of the Carthaginians in Spain in 206 and then by the defeat of Hannibal in Africa in 202.

scire facias /ˌsʌɪriː ˈfeɪʃɪas/ ▶ **noun** US Law a writ requiring a person to show why a judgement regarding a record or patent should not be enforced or annulled.
– ORIGIN Latin, literally 'let (the person) know'.

scirocco ▶ **noun** variant spelling of **SIROCCO**.

scirrhus /ˈsɪrəs, ˈskɪ-/ ▶ **noun** (pl. **scirrhi** /-rʌɪ/) Medicine a carcinoma that is hard to the touch.
– DERIVATIVES **scirrhous** adjective.
– ORIGIN late Middle English: modern Latin, from Greek *skirros*, from *skiros* 'hard'.

scissel /ˈsɪs(ə)l/ ▶ **noun** [mass noun] clippings and strips of waste metal produced during the manufacture of coins.
– ORIGIN early 17th cent.: from French *cisaille*, from *cisailler* 'clip with shears'.

scissile /ˈsɪsʌɪl, -sɪl/ ▶ **adjective** chiefly Biochemistry (of a chemical bond) readily undergoing scission.
– ORIGIN early 17th cent.: from Latin *scissilis*, from *sciss-* 'cut, divided', from the verb *scindere*.

scission /ˈsɪʃ(ə)n/ ▶ **noun** [mass noun] technical the action or state of cutting or being cut, in particular: ■ chiefly Biochemistry breakage of a chemical bond, especially one in a long chain molecule so that two smaller chains result. ■ [count noun] a division or split between people or parties; a schism.
– ORIGIN late Middle English: from Old French, or from late Latin *scissio(n-)*, from *scindere* 'cut, cleave'.

scissor ▶ **verb 1** [with obj. and adverbial] cut (something) with scissors: *pages scissored out of a magazine*. **2** [with obj.] move (one's legs) back and forth in a way resembling the action of scissors: *he was still hanging on, scissoring his legs uselessly*. ■ [no obj.] (of a person's legs) move in a way resembling the action of scissors.
▶ **noun** see **SCISSORS**.
– ORIGIN early 17th cent.: from **SCISSORS**.

scissorbill ▶ **noun 1** another term for **SKIMMER** (sense 5).
2 N. Amer. informal an incompetent or objectionable person.

scissor hold (also **scissors hold**) ▶ **noun** Wrestling a hold in which the head or other part of the opponent's body is gripped between the legs which are then locked at the instep or ankles to apply pressure.

scissor kick (also **scissors kick**) ▶ **noun** (in various sports, particularly swimming and soccer) a kick in which the legs make a sharp snapping movement like that of a pair of scissors.

S **scissor lift** ▶ **noun** a surface raised or lowered by the closing or opening of crossed supports pivoted like the two halves of a pair of scissors.

scissors (also **a pair of scissors**) ▶ **plural noun** an instrument used for cutting cloth, paper, and other material, consisting of two blades laid one on top of the other and fastened in the middle so as to allow them to be opened and closed by a thumb and finger inserted through rings on the end of their handles. ■ (also **scissor**) [as modifier] denoting an action in which two things cross each other or open and close like the blades of a pair of scissors: *as the fish swims the tail lobes open and close in a slight scissor action*. ■ Rugby a tactical move in which a player running diagonally takes the ball from a teammate and changes the direction of the attack, or feints to do so.
– PHRASES **scissors and paste** another term for **CUT AND PASTE** (see **CUT**).
– ORIGIN late Middle English: from Old French *cisoires*, from late Latin *cisoria*, plural of *cisorium* 'cutting instrument', from *cis-*, variant of *caes-*, stem of *caedere* 'to cut'. The spelling with *sc-* (16th cent.) was by association with the Latin stem *sciss-* 'cut'.

scissortail ▶ **noun 1** (also **scissor-tailed flycatcher**) a tyrant flycatcher with a very long forked tail, found in the southern US and noted for its spectacular aerial display. ● *Tyrannus forficatus*, family Tyrannidae.
2 (also **scissors-tail**) a small SE Asian freshwater fish with a deeply forked tail. ● *Rasbora trilineata*, family Cyprinidae.

Sciuromorpha /skɪˌʊərə(ʊ)ˈmɔːfə/ ▶ **plural noun** Zoology a major division of the rodents that comprises the squirrels, prairie dogs, and marmots. ● Suborder Sciuromorpha, order Rodentia.
– ORIGIN modern Latin (plural), from Greek *skiouros* (from *skia* 'shadow' + *oura* 'tail') + *morphē* 'form'.

sclera /ˈsklɪərə/ ▶ **noun** Anatomy the white outer layer of the eyeball. At the front of the eye it is continuous with the cornea.
– DERIVATIVES **scleral** adjective.
– ORIGIN late 19th cent.: modern Latin, from Greek *sklēros* 'hard'.

Scleractinia /ˌsklɛrakˈtɪnɪə/ ▶ **plural noun** Zoology an order of coelenterates that comprises the stony corals. Also called **MADREPORARIA**.
– DERIVATIVES **scleractinian** noun & adjective.
– ORIGIN modern Latin (plural), from Greek *sklēros* 'hard' + *aktis, aktin-* 'ray'.

sclerenchyma /ˌsklɪəˈrɛŋkɪmə, sklə-/ ▶ **noun** [mass noun] Botany strengthening tissue in a plant, formed from cells with thickened, typically lignified, walls.
– DERIVATIVES **sclerenchymatous** adjective /ˌsklɪərɛŋˈkɪmətəs/.
– ORIGIN mid 19th cent.: modern Latin, from Greek *sklēros* 'hard' + *enkhuma* 'infusion', on the pattern of *parenchyma*.

sclerite /ˈsklɪərʌɪt, ˈsklɛ-/ ▶ **noun** Zoology a component section of an exoskeleton, especially each of the plates forming the skeleton of an arthropod.
– ORIGIN mid 19th cent.: from Greek *sklēros* 'hard' + **-ITE**[1].

scleritis /sklɪəˈrʌɪtɪs, sklə-/ ▶ **noun** [mass noun] Medicine inflammation of the sclera of the eye.

sclero- /ˈsklɪərəʊ/ ▶ **combining form** hard; hardened; hardening: *scleroderma* | *sclerotherapy*.
– ORIGIN from Greek *sklēros* 'hard'.

scleroderma /ˌsklɪərəˈdəːmə/ ▶ **noun** [mass noun] Medicine a chronic hardening and contraction of the skin and connective tissue, either locally or throughout the body.

sclerophyll /ˈsklɪərəfɪl, ˈsklɛ-/ ▶ **noun** Botany a woody plant with evergreen leaves that are tough and thick in order to reduce water loss.
– DERIVATIVES **sclerophyllous** /-ˈrɒfɪləs/ adjective.
– ORIGIN early 20th cent.: from Greek *sklēros* 'hard' + *phullon* 'leaf'.

scleroprotein /ˌsklɪərə(ʊ)ˈprəʊtiːn, ˌsklɛ-/ ▶ **noun** Biochemistry an insoluble structural protein such as keratin, collagen, or elastin.

Scleroscope /ˈsklɪərəskəʊp, ˈsklɛ-/ ▶ **noun** (trademark in the US) an instrument for determining the hardness of materials by measuring the height of rebound of a small diamond-tipped hammer dropped on to the material from a standard height.

sclerosed /sklɪəˈrəʊst, sklə-, ˈsklɪə-/ ▶ **adjective** Medicine (especially of blood vessels) affected by sclerosis.

sclerosing cholangitis /sklɪəˈrəʊsɪŋ ˌkɒlanˈgʌɪtɪs, sklə-/ ▶ **noun** [mass noun] Medicine a complication of ulcerative colitis in which the bile ducts develop irregularities and narrowing.
– ORIGIN 1980s: *sclerosing* from the verb *sclerose* (back-formation from **SCLEROSED**); *cholangitis* from Greek *kholē* 'bile' + *angeion* 'vessel' + **-ITIS**.

sclerosis /sklɪəˈrəʊsɪs, sklə-/ ▶ **noun** [mass noun] **1** Medicine abnormal hardening of body tissue. ■ (in full **multiple sclerosis**) a chronic, typically progressive disease involving damage to the sheaths of nerve cells in the brain and spinal cord, whose symptoms may include numbness, impairment of speech and of muscular coordination, blurred vision, and severe fatigue. Also called **DISSEMINATED SCLEROSIS**.
2 excessive resistance to change: *the challenge was to avoid institutional sclerosis*.
– ORIGIN late Middle English (originally denoting a hard external tumour): via medieval Latin from Greek *sklērōsis*, from *sklēroun* 'harden'.

sclerotherapy /ˌsklɪərə(ʊ)ˈθɛrəpi, ˌsklɛ-/ ▶ **noun** [mass noun] Medicine the treatment of varicose blood vessels by the injection of an irritant which causes inflammation, coagulation of blood, and narrowing of the blood vessel wall.

sclerotic /sklɪəˈrɒtɪk, sklə-/ ▶ **adjective 1** Medicine of or having sclerosis.
2 becoming rigid and unresponsive; losing the ability to adapt: *sclerotic management*.
3 Anatomy relating to the sclera.
▶ **noun** another term for **SCLERA**.

sclerotin /ˈsklɪərətɪn, ˈsklɛ-/ ▶ **noun** [mass noun] Biochemistry a structural protein which forms the cuticles of insects and is hardened and darkened by a natural tanning process in which protein chains are cross-linked by quinone groups.
– ORIGIN 1940s: from **SCLERO-** 'hardened', on the pattern of such words as *keratin*.

sclerotium /sklɪəˈrəʊtɪəm, sklə-/ ▶ **noun** (pl. **sclerotia** /-tɪə/) Botany the hard dark resting body of certain fungi, consisting of a mass of hyphal threads, capable of remaining dormant for long periods.
– ORIGIN mid 19th cent.: modern Latin (former genus name), from Greek *sklēros* 'hard'.

sclerotized /ˈsklɪərətʌɪzd, ˈsklɛ-/ (also **sclerotised**) ▶ **adjective** Entomology (of an insect's body, or part of one) hardened by conversion into sclerotin.
– DERIVATIVES **sclerotization** noun.

sclerotome /ˈsklɪərə(ʊ)təʊm, ˈsklɛ-/ ▶ **noun** Embryology the part of each somite in a vertebrate embryo giving rise to bone or other skeletal tissue. Compare with **DERMATOME**, **MYOTOME**.

sclerous /ˈsklɪərəs/ ▶ **adjective** (of tissue) hardened or bony.
– ORIGIN mid 19th cent.: from Greek *sklēros* 'hard' + **-OUS**.

SCM ▶ (in the UK) **abbreviation** ■ State Certified Midwife. ■ Student Christian Movement.

scoff[1] ▶ **verb** [no obj.] speak to someone or about something in a scornfully derisive or mocking way: *Patrick professed to scoff at soppy love scenes in films* | [with direct speech] *'You, a scientist?' he scoffed*.
▶ **noun** an expression of scornful derision. ■ archaic an object of ridicule: *his army was the scoff of all Europe*.
– DERIVATIVES **scoffer** noun, **scoffingly** adverb.
– ORIGIN Middle English (first used as a noun in the sense 'mockery, scorn'): perhaps of Scandinavian origin.

scoff[2] informal ▶ **verb** [with obj.] eat (something) quickly and greedily: *he can scoff a cannelloni faster than you can drink a pint*.
▶ **noun** [mass noun] food.
– ORIGIN late 18th cent. (as a verb): originally a variant of Scots and dialect *scaff*. The noun is from Afrikaans *schoff*, representing Dutch *schoft* 'quarter of a day', (by extension) 'meal'.

scofflaw ▶ **noun** N. Amer. informal a person who flouts the law, especially by failing to comply with a law that is difficult to enforce effectively.

scold ▶ **verb** [with obj.] remonstrate with or rebuke (someone) angrily: *Mum took Anna away, scolding her for her bad behaviour*.
▶ **noun** archaic a woman who nags or grumbles constantly.
– DERIVATIVES **scolder** noun.
– ORIGIN Middle English (as a noun): probably from Old Norse *skáld* 'skald'.

scolding ▶ **noun** an angry rebuke or reprimand: *she'd get a scolding from Victoria*.

scold's bridle ▶ **noun** another term for **BRANKS**.

scolex /ˈskəʊlɛks/ ▶ **noun** (pl. **scolices** /-lɪsiːz/) Zoology the anterior end of a tapeworm, bearing suckers and hooks for attachment.
– ORIGIN mid 19th cent.: modern Latin, from Greek *skōlēx* 'worm'.

scoliosis /ˌskɒlɪˈəʊsɪs, ˌskəʊ-/ ▶ **noun** [mass noun] Medicine abnormal lateral curvature of the spine.
– DERIVATIVES **scoliotic** adjective.
– ORIGIN early 18th cent.: modern Latin, from Greek, from *skolios* 'bent'.

scollop ▶ **noun & verb** archaic spelling of **SCALLOP**.

scombroid /ˈskɒmbrɔɪd/ Zoology ▶ **noun** a fish of the mackerel family, or one of a larger group that also includes the barracudas and billfishes. ● Family Scombridae or suborder Scombroidei.
▶ **adjective** relating to fish of this family or group.
– ORIGIN mid 19th cent.: from modern Latin *Scombroidea* (superfamily name), from Greek *skombros*, denoting a tuna or mackerel.

sconce[1] ▶ **noun** a candle holder that is attached to a wall with an ornamental bracket. ■ a flaming torch or candle secured in a sconce.
– ORIGIN late Middle English (originally denoting a portable lantern with a screen to protect the flame): shortening of Old French *esconse* 'lantern', or from medieval Latin *sconsa*, from Latin *absconsa (laterna)* 'dark (lantern)' (i.e. a lantern with a device for concealing the light), from *abscondere* 'to hide'.

sconce[2] ▶ **noun** archaic a small fort or earthwork defending a ford, pass, or castle gate. ■ a shelter or screen from fire or the weather.
– ORIGIN late Middle English: from Dutch *schans* 'brushwood', from Middle High German *schanze*. The earliest recorded sense 'screen, interior partition' derives perhaps from SCONCE[1]; the later senses date from the late 16th cent.

Scone /skuːn/ an ancient Scottish settlement to the north of Perth, where the kings of medieval Scotland were crowned on the Stone of Destiny.

scone /skɒn, skəʊn/ ▶ **noun** a small unsweetened or lightly sweetened cake made from flour, fat, and milk and sometimes having added fruit.
– ORIGIN early 16th cent. (originally Scots): perhaps from Middle Dutch *schoon(broot)* 'fine (bread)'.

scooch /skuːtʃ/ (also **scootch**) ▶ **verb** [no obj.] N. Amer. informal **1** crouch or squat: *he scooched down and rubbed the dog's head.*
2 move in or pass through a tight or narrow space: *waiters kept pressing against the table trying to scooch by.* ■ move a short distance, especially while seated: *she scooched over to make room, then leaned against me.*
– ORIGIN mid 19th cent.: origin unknown.

scoop ▶ **noun 1** a utensil resembling a spoon, with a short handle and a deep bowl, used for removing dry or semi-solid substances from a container. ■ a short-handled deep shovel used for moving grain, coal, etc. ■ a moving bowl-shaped part of a digging machine, dredger, or other mechanism into which material is gathered. ■ a long-handled spoon-like surgical instrument. ■ a quantity taken up by a scoop: *an apple pie with **scoops of** ice cream on top.*
2 informal a piece of news published by a newspaper or broadcast by a television or radio station in advance of its rivals. ■ (**the scoop**) N. Amer. the latest information about something.
3 an exaggerated upward slide or portamento in singing.
▶ **verb 1** [with obj. and adverbial] pick up and move (something) with a scoop: *I scooped the grain into the bag.* ■ create (a hollow or hole) with or as if with a scoop: *a hole was **scooped out** in the floor of the dwelling.* ■ pick up (someone or something) in a swift, fluid movement: *he laughed and **scooped** her **up** in his arms.*
2 [with obj.] informal publish a news story before (a rival reporter, newspaper, or broadcaster). ■ win (an amount of money, a prize, or a trophy).
3 [no obj.] (in singing) preface notes with an exaggerated upward slide or portamento.
– DERIVATIVES **scooper** noun, **scoopful** noun.
– ORIGIN Middle English (originally denoting a utensil for pouring liquids): from Middle Dutch, Middle Low German *schōpe* 'waterwheel bucket'; from a West Germanic base meaning 'draw water'; related to the verb SHAPE.

scoop neck ▶ **noun** a deeply curved wide neckline on a garment.

scoop net ▶ **noun** a fishing net on a long handle used for reaching to the bottom of a river or other shallow water.

scoosh (also **skoosh**) Scottish ▶ **verb** [with obj.] squirt or splash (liquid).
▶ **noun** a splash or squirt of liquid. ■ [mass noun] a fizzy drink such as lemonade.
– ORIGIN imitative.

scoot ▶ **verb** [no obj.] informal go or leave somewhere quickly: *they scooted off on their bikes.*
– ORIGIN mid 18th cent.: of unknown origin.

scooter ▶ **noun 1** (also **motor scooter**) a light two-wheeled open motor vehicle on which the driver sits over an enclosed engine with their legs together and their feet resting on a floorboard. ■ [often with modifier] any small, light, vehicle able to travel quickly across water, ice, or snow.
2 a child's toy consisting of a footboard mounted on two wheels and a long steering handle, propelled by resting one foot on the footboard and pushing the other against the ground.
▶ **verb** [no obj.] travel or ride on a scooter.
– DERIVATIVES **scooterist** noun.

scopa /ˈskəʊpə/ ▶ **noun** (pl. **scopae** /-piː/) Zoology a small brush-like tuft of hairs on some insects, especially that on which pollen collects on the leg of a bee.
– ORIGIN early 19th cent.: from Latin *scopae* (plural) 'twigs, broom'.

scope ▶ **noun** [mass noun] **1** the extent of the area or subject matter that something deals with or to which it is relevant: *we widened the scope of our investigation | such questions go beyond the scope of this book.*
2 the opportunity or possibility to do or deal with something: *the **scope for** major change is always limited by political realities.* ■ archaic a purpose, end, or intention: *Plato even maintains religion to be the chief aim and scope of human life.*
3 informal a telescope, microscope, or other device having a name ending in *-scope*: *infrared night scopes.*
4 Nautical the length of cable extended when a ship rides at anchor.
5 Linguistics & Logic the number of terms or arguments affected by an operator such as a quantifier or conjunction.
▶ **verb** [with obj.] **1** (**scope something out**) assess or investigate something: *they'd scoped out their market.* ■ set the scope of (a projected undertaking): *it is important that a project is scoped correctly to ensure the budget can be accurately defined.*
2 N. Amer. informal look at carefully; scan: *they watched him scoping the room, looking for Michael.*
– ORIGIN mid 16th cent. (in the sense 'target for shooting at'): from Italian *scopo* 'aim', from Greek *skopos* 'target', from *skeptesthai* 'look out'. Sense 3 of the noun is derived from -SCOPE.

-scope ▶ **combining form** denoting an instrument for observing, viewing, or examining: *microscope | telescope.*
– DERIVATIVES **-scopic** combining form in corresponding adjectives.
– ORIGIN from modern Latin *-scopium*, from Greek *skopein* 'look at'.

scopolamine /skə(ʊ)ˈpɒləmiːn/ ▶ **noun** another term for HYOSCINE.
– ORIGIN late 19th cent.: from *Scopolia* (genus name of the plants yielding it) + AMINE.

scopophilia /ˌskɒpə(ʊ)ˈfɪlɪə/ ▶ **noun** [mass noun] sexual pleasure derived chiefly from watching others when they are naked or engaged in sexual activity; voyeurism.
– ORIGIN 1920s: from Greek *skopein* 'look at' + -PHILIA.

scopophobia /ˌskɒpə(ʊ)ˈfəʊbɪə/ ▶ **noun** [mass noun] extreme or irrational fear of being looked at or seen.
– ORIGIN 1990s: from Greek *skopein* 'look at' + -PHOBIA.

scops owl /skɒps/ ▶ **noun** a small owl with distinctive ear tufts, found in Europe, Africa, and Asia.
● Genus *Otus*, family Strigidae: many species, in particular the widespread **Eurasian scops owl** (*O. scops*).
– ORIGIN early 18th cent.: *scops* from modern Latin *Scops* (former genus name), from Greek *skōps*.

scopula /ˈskɒpjʊlə/ ▶ **noun** (pl. **scopulae** /-liː/) Zoology a small brush-like structure on some insects, especially on the legs of spiders.
– ORIGIN early 19th cent.: from late Latin, diminutive of Latin *scopa* (see SCOPA).

-scopy ▶ **combining form** indicating viewing, observation, or examination, typically with an instrument having a name ending in *-scope*: *endoscopy | microscopy.*
– ORIGIN from Greek *skopia* 'observation', from *skopein* 'examine, look at'.

scorbutic /skɔːˈbjuːtɪk/ ▶ **adjective** relating to or affected with scurvy. See also ANTISCORBUTIC.
– ORIGIN mid 17th cent.: from modern Latin *scorbuticus*, from medieval Latin *scorbutus* 'scurvy', perhaps from Middle Low German *schorbūk* (from *schoren* 'to break' + *būk* 'belly').

scorch ▶ **verb 1** [with obj.] burn the surface of (something) with flame or heat: *surrounding houses were scorched by heat from the blast.* ■ [no obj.] become burnt when exposed to heat or a flame: *the meat had scorched.* ■ (often as adj. **scorched**) (of the heat of the sun) cause (vegetation or a place) to become dried out and lifeless: *a desolate, scorched landscape.*
2 [no obj., with adverbial of direction] informal (of a person or vehicle) move very fast: *a sports car scorching along the expressway.*
▶ **noun** [mass noun] the burning or charring of the surface of something: [as modifier] *a scorch mark.* ■ Botany a form of plant necrosis, typically of fungal origin, marked by browning of leaf margins.
– ORIGIN Middle English (as a verb): perhaps related to Old Norse *skorpna* 'be shrivelled'.

scorched earth policy ▶ **noun** a military strategy of burning or destroying crops or other resources that might be of use to an invading enemy force.

scorcher ▶ **noun** [usu. in sing.] informal **1** a day or period of very hot weather: *next week could be a real scorcher.*
2 Brit. a remarkable or extreme example of something, in particular: ■ a very powerfully struck shot or kick. ■ a sensational or very good book, film, or play. ■ a violent argument. ■ dated a person who drives or cycles very fast.

scorching ▶ **adjective** very hot: *the scorching July sun.* ■ (of criticism) harsh; severe. ■ informal very fast: *she set a scorching pace.*
– DERIVATIVES **scorchingly** adverb.

scordatura /ˌskɔːdəˈtjʊərə/ ▶ **noun** [mass noun] Music the technique of altering the normal tuning of a stringed instrument to produce particular effects.
– ORIGIN late 19th cent.: Italian, from *scordare* 'be out of tune'.

score ▶ **noun 1** the number of points, goals, runs, etc. achieved in a game or by a team or an individual: *the final score was 4–3 to Royston.* ■ informal an act of gaining a goal or point in a game. ■ a rating or grade, such as a mark achieved in a test: *an IQ score of 161.* ■ (**the score**) informal the state of affairs; the facts about the present situation: *'What's wrong Simon? What's the score?'* ■ informal an act of buying illegal drugs. ■ informal the proceeds of a crime.
2 (pl. **same**) a group or set of twenty or about twenty: *a score of men lost their lives in the battle | Doyle's success brought imitators **by the score**.* ■ (**scores of**) a large number of something: *he sent scores of enthusiastic letters to friends.*
3 a written representation of a musical composition showing all the vocal and instrumental parts arranged one below the other. ■ the music composed for a film or play.
4 a notch or line cut or scratched into a surface. ■ historical a running account kept by marks against a customer's name, typically in a public house.
▶ **verb** [with obj.] **1** gain (a point, goal, run, etc.) in a competitive game: *McCartney scored a fine goal* | [no obj.] *Wilson outstripped his marker to score.* ■ be worth (a number of points): *a yes answer scores ten points.* ■ [no obj.] record the score during a game; act as scorer. ■ Baseball cause (a teammate) to score. ■ informal secure (a success or an advantage): *the band scored a hit single.* ■ (**score off**) Brit. informal outdo or humiliate (someone) in an argument. ■ informal buy or acquire (something, typically illegal drugs): *Sally had scored some acid.* ■ [no obj.] informal succeed in attracting a sexual partner for a casual encounter.
2 orchestrate or arrange (a piece of music), typically for a specified instrument or instruments: *the Quartet Suite was scored for flute, violin, viola da gamba, and continuo.* ■ compose the music for (a film or play).
3 cut or scratch a notch or line on (a surface): *score the card until you cut through.* ■ (**score something out/through**) delete text by drawing a line through it. ■ historical record (a total owed) by making marks against a customer's name: *a slate on which the old man **scored up** vast accounts.*
4 Medicine & Biology examine (experimentally treated cells, bacterial colonies, etc.), making a record of the number showing a particular character.
– PHRASES **keep (the) score** register the score of a game as it is made. **know the score** informal be aware of the essential facts about a situation. **on the score of** Brit. because of: *power-driven hedge trimmers tend to get a bad press on the score of danger.* **on that** (or **this**) **score** so far as that (or this) is concerned: *my priority was to blend new faces into the team and we have succeeded on that score.* **score points** outdo another person, especially in an argument. **score points off** another way of saying SCORE OFF below. **settle** (or **pay**) **a** (or **the**) **score 1** take revenge on someone for something damaging that they have done in the past. **2** dated pay off a debt or other obligation.
– DERIVATIVES **scoreless** adjective.
– ORIGIN late Old English *scoru* 'set of twenty', from Old Norse *skor* 'notch, tally, twenty', of Germanic origin; related to SHEAR. The verb (late Middle English) is from Old Norse *skora* 'make an incision'.

scoreboard ▶ **noun** a large board on which the score in a game or match is displayed.

scorebox ▶ **noun** Cricket a room or hut in which the official scorers work and on which the score is displayed for spectators.

scorecard (also **scoresheet** or **scorebook**) ▶ **noun** (in sport) a card, sheet, or book in which scores are entered.

score draw ▶ **noun** a draw in soccer in which goals have been scored, especially as distinguished from a no-score draw in football pools.

scorekeeper ▶ **noun** an official who records the score at a sports match.
– DERIVATIVES **scorekeeping** noun.

S

scoreline ▶ noun Brit. the number of points or goals scored in a match; the score.
– ORIGIN 1960s: extension of the original use denoting a line in a newspaper giving the score in a sports contest.

scorer ▶ noun **1** a person who scores goals, points, etc. in a game.
2 a person who keeps a record of the score in a game.

scoria /ˈskɔːrɪə/ ▶ noun (pl. **scoriae** /-rɪiː/) [mass noun]
1 basaltic lava ejected as fragments from a volcano, typically with a frothy texture.
2 slag separated from molten metal during smelting.
– DERIVATIVES **scoriaceous** /-ˈeɪʃəs/ adjective.
– ORIGIN late Middle English (denoting slag from molten metal): via Latin from Greek *skōria* 'refuse', from *skōr* 'dung'. The geological term dates from the late 18th cent.

scorn ▶ noun [mass noun] a feeling and expression of contempt or disdain for someone or something: *I do not wish to become the object of scorn.* ■ [in sing.] archaic a person viewed with contempt or disdain: *a scandal and a scorn to all who look on thee.* ■ [count noun] archaic a statement or gesture indicating contempt.
▶ verb [with obj.] feel or express contempt or disdain for: *the minister scorned Labour's attempt to woo voters.* ■ reject (something) in a contemptuous way: *a letter scorning his offer of intimacy.* ■ [no obj., with infinitive] refuse to do something because one is too proud: *at her lowest ebb, she would have scorned to stoop to such tactics.*
– PHRASES **pour scorn on** speak with contempt or mockery of.
– DERIVATIVES **scorner** noun (rare).
– ORIGIN Middle English: shortening of Old French *escarn* (noun), *escharnir* (verb), of Germanic origin.

scornful ▶ adjective feeling or expressing contempt or derision: *the opposition were **scornful of** the Prime Minister's proposal | scornful laughter.*
– DERIVATIVES **scornfully** adverb, **scornfulness** noun.

scorp (also **scorper** or **scauper**) ▶ noun a drawknife with a circular blade and a single handle, used to scoop out wood when carving or engraving.
– ORIGIN mid 19th cent. (as *scorper*), based on Latin *scalper* 'knife'.

Scorpio Astrology the eighth sign of the zodiac (the Scorpion), which the sun enters about 23 October.
■ (**a Scorpio**) (pl. **Scorpios**) a person born when the sun is in this sign.
– DERIVATIVES **Scorpian** noun & adjective.
– ORIGIN Latin.

scorpioid ▶ adjective Zoology relating to or resembling a scorpion. ■ Botany (of a flower cluster) curled up at the end, and uncurling as the flowers develop.
– ORIGIN mid 19th cent.: from Greek *skorpioeidēs*, from *skorpios* 'scorpion'.

scorpion ▶ noun a terrestrial arachnid which has lobster-like pincers and a poisonous sting at the end of its jointed tail, which it can hold curved over its back. Most kinds live in tropical and subtropical areas. ● Order Scorpiones.
■ used in names of arachnids and insects resembling a scorpion, e.g. **false scorpion**, **water scorpion**. ■ (**the Scorpion**) the zodiacal sign Scorpio or the constellation Scorpius. ■ (**scorpions**) literary a whip with metal points. [with allusion to 1 Kings 12:11.]
– ORIGIN Middle English: via Old French from Latin *scorpio(n-)*, based on Greek *skorpios* 'scorpion'.

S

scorpionfish ▶ noun (pl. **same** or **scorpionfishes**) a chiefly bottom-dwelling marine fish which is typically red in colour and has spines on the head that are sometimes venomous. ● Family Scorpaenidae: many genera and numerous species, including the redfishes and rockfishes.

scorpion fly ▶ noun a slender predatory insect with membranous wings, long legs, and a downward-pointing beak. The terminal swollen section of the male's abdomen is carried curved up like a scorpion's sting. ● Order Mecoptera: several families, in particular Panorpidae.

Scorpius /ˈskɔːpɪəs/ Astronomy a large constellation (the Scorpion). It contains the red giant Antares.
– ORIGIN Latin.

Scorsese /skɔːˈseɪzi/, Martin (b.1942), American film director. Notable works: *Mean Streets* (1973), *Taxi Driver* (1976), and *The Last Temptation of Christ* (1988).

scorzonera /ˌskɔːzə(ʊ)ˈnɪərə/ ▶ noun a plant of the daisy family with tapering purple-brown edible roots. Also called BLACK SALSIFY, VIPER'S GRASS.
● *Scorzonera hispanica*, family Compositae.
■ [mass noun] the root of the scorzonera used as a vegetable.
– ORIGIN early 17th cent.: from Italian, from *scorzone*, from an alteration of medieval Latin *curtio(n-)* 'venomous snake' (against whose venom the plant may have been regarded as an antidote).

Scot ▶ noun a native of Scotland or a person of Scottish descent. ■ a member of a Gaelic people that migrated from Ireland to Scotland around the late 5th century.
– ORIGIN Old English *Scottas* (plural), from late Latin *Scottus*, of unknown ultimate origin.

> **USAGE** On the different uses of **Scot**, **Scottish**, and **Scotch**, see USAGE at SCOTTISH.

scot ▶ noun archaic a payment corresponding to a modern tax, rate, or other assessed contribution.
– PHRASES **scot and lot** historical a tax levied by a municipal corporation on its members.
– ORIGIN late Old English, from Old Norse *skot* 'a shot', reinforced by Old French *escot*, of Germanic origin; related to SHOT[1].

Scot. ▶ abbreviation ■ Scotland. ■ Scottish.

Scotch ▶ adjective old-fashioned term for SCOTTISH.
▶ noun **1** short for SCOTCH WHISKY.
2 (as plural noun **the Scotch**) dated the people of Scotland.
3 [mass noun] dated the form of English spoken in Scotland.
– ORIGIN late 16th cent.: contraction of SCOTTISH.

> **USAGE** The use of **Scotch** to mean 'relating to Scotland or its people' is disliked by Scottish people and is now uncommon, although it survives in fixed expressions like ***Scotch egg*** and ***Scotch whisky***. For more details, see USAGE at SCOTTISH.

scotch[1] ▶ verb **1** [with obj.] decisively put an end to: *a spokesman has scotched the rumours.* ■ archaic render (something regarded as dangerous) temporarily harmless: *feudal power in France was scotched, though far from killed.*
2 [with obj. and adverbial] wedge (someone or something) somewhere: *he soon scotched himself against a wall.*
■ [with obj.] archaic prevent (a wheel or other rolling object) from moving or slipping by placing a wedge underneath.
▶ noun archaic a wedge placed under a wheel or other rolling object to prevent it moving or slipping.
– ORIGIN early 17th cent. (as a noun): of unknown origin; perhaps related to SKATE[1]. The sense 'render temporarily harmless' is based on an emendation of Shakespeare's *Macbeth* III. ii. 13 as 'We have scotch'd the snake, not kill'd it', originally understood as a use of SCOTCH[2]; the sense 'put an end to' (early 19th cent.) results from the influence on this of the notion of wedging or blocking something so as to render it inoperative.

scotch[2] archaic ▶ verb [with obj.] cut or score the skin or surface of.
▶ noun a cut or score in skin or another surface.
– ORIGIN late Middle English: of unknown origin.

Scotch argus ▶ noun a brown Eurasian grassland butterfly marked with orange and a chain of eyespots near the wing margins, found chiefly in upland areas.
● *Erebia aethiops*, subfamily Satyrinae, family Nymphalidae.

Scotch bonnet ▶ noun a small chilli pepper which is the hottest variety available.

Scotch broth ▶ noun [mass noun] a traditional Scottish soup made from beef or mutton stock with pearl barley and vegetables.

Scotch cap ▶ noun another term for BONNET (sense 1).

Scotch catch ▶ noun another term for SCOTCH SNAP.

Scotch egg ▶ noun Brit. a hard-boiled egg enclosed in sausage meat, rolled in breadcrumbs, and fried.

Scotch fir ▶ noun old-fashioned term for SCOTS PINE.

Scotchgard ▶ noun [mass noun] trademark a preparation for giving a waterproof grease- and stain-resistant finish to textiles, leather, and other materials, based on organofluorine compounds.
▶ verb [with obj.] treat with such a substance.

Scotch glue ▶ noun [mass noun] an adhesive made from hide and other animal products, formerly used in carpentry.

Scotch kale ▶ noun [mass noun] kale of a variety with purplish leaves.

Scotchlite ▶ noun [mass noun] trademark a light-reflecting material containing a layer of minute glass lenses.

Scotchman ▶ noun (pl. **Scotchmen**) dated a Scotsman.

Scotch mist ▶ noun [mass noun] a thick drizzly mist of a kind common in the Scottish Highlands.

Scotch pancake ▶ noun another term for DROP SCONE.

Scotch pie ▶ noun a meat pie traditionally made with minced mutton, round in shape with a raised pastry rim.

Scotch snap (also **Scotch catch**) ▶ noun Music a rhythmic feature in which a dotted note is preceded by a stressed shorter note, characteristic of strathspeys.

Scotch tape trademark, chiefly N. Amer. ▶ noun [mass noun] transparent adhesive tape.
▶ verb (**Scotch-tape**) [with obj. and adverbial] stick with transparent adhesive tape.

Scotch whisky ▶ noun [mass noun] whisky distilled in Scotland, especially from malted barley.

Scotchwoman ▶ noun (pl. **Scotchwomen**) dated a Scotswoman.

scoter /ˈskəʊtə/ ▶ noun (pl. **same** or **scoters**) a northern diving duck that winters off the coast, the male of which has mainly black plumage. ● Genus *Melanitta*, family Anatidae: three species.
– ORIGIN late 17th cent.: perhaps an error for *sooter* (with reference to its black plumage).

scot-free ▶ adverb without suffering any punishment or injury: *the people who kidnapped you will **get off scot-free**.*
– ORIGIN from the early sense 'not subject to the payment of scot'.

scotia /ˈskəʊʃə/ ▶ noun (chiefly in classical architecture) a concave moulding, especially at the base of a column.
– ORIGIN mid 16th cent.: via Latin from Greek *skotia*, from *skotos* 'darkness', with reference to the shadow produced.

Scoticism ▶ noun variant spelling of SCOTTICISM.

Scotland a country forming the northernmost part of Great Britain and of the United Kingdom; pop. 5,169,000 (est. 2008); capital, Edinburgh.

> Scotland was settled by Celtic peoples during the Bronze and early Iron Age. An independent country in the Middle Ages, it was amalgamated with England as a result of the union of the Crowns in 1603 and of the Parliaments in 1707. The distinctive Celtic society of the Highlands, based on clans, was destroyed in the aftermath of the Jacobite uprisings of 1715 and 1745–6 and the Highland clearances of the 18th and 19th centuries. In 1997 the Scots voted in favour of the establishment of a devolved parliament with tax-raising powers, which was inaugurated in 2000.

Scotland Yard the headquarters of the London Metropolitan Police, situated from 1829 to 1890 in Great Scotland Yard off Whitehall, from 1890 until 1967 in New Scotland Yard on the Thames Embankment, and from 1967 in New Scotland Yard, Westminster. ■ used to allude to the Criminal Investigation Department of the London Metropolitan Police force.

scotoma /skɒˈtəʊmə, skə(ʊ)-/ ▶ noun (pl. **scotomas** or **scotomata** /-mətə/) Medicine a partial loss of vision or blind spot in an otherwise normal visual field.
– ORIGIN mid 16th cent. (denoting dizziness and dim vision): via late Latin from Greek *skotōma*, from *skotoun* 'darken', from *skotos* 'darkness'.

scotopic /skə(ʊ)ˈtɒpɪk/ ▶ adjective Physiology relating to or denoting vision in dim light, believed to involve chiefly the rods of the retina. Often contrasted with PHOTOPIC.
– ORIGIN early 20th cent.: from Greek *skotos* 'darkness' + -OPIA + -IC.

Scots ▶ adjective another term for SCOTTISH: *Scots law* | [postpositive] *a pound Scots*. [northern variant, originally as *Scottis*.]
▶ noun **1** plural form of SCOT.
2 [mass noun] the form of English used in Scotland.

> **USAGE** On the use of **Scots**, **Scottish**, and **Scotch**, see USAGE at SCOTTISH.

Scotsman (or **Scotswoman**) ▶ noun (pl. **Scotsmen** or **Scotswomen**) a native or inhabitant of Scotland, or a person of Scottish descent.

Scots pine (also **Scots fir**) ▶ noun a Eurasian pine tree which is extensively planted for its timber (deal) and other products. It is the dominant tree of the old Caledonian pine forest of the Scottish Highlands. ● *Pinus sylvestris*, family Pinaceae.

Scott[1] two English architects. **Sir George Gilbert** (1811–78) designed the Albert Memorial in London

(1863–72), which exemplifies the Gothic style that he favoured. His grandson **Sir Giles Gilbert** (1880–1960) is best known for the Gothic Anglican cathedral in Liverpool (begun in 1904, completed in 1978).

Scott², Sir Peter (Markham) (1909–89), English naturalist and artist, son of Sir Robert Scott. In 1946 he founded the Wildfowl Trust at Slimbridge in Gloucestershire.

Scott³, Sir Ridley (b.1937), English film director. Notable works: *Alien* (1979), *Blade Runner* (1982), and *Thelma and Louise* (1991).

Scott⁴, Sir Robert (Falcon) (1868–1912), English explorer and naval officer, father of Sir Peter Scott. In 1910–12 Scott and four companions made a journey to the South Pole by sledge, arriving there in January 1912 to discover that Roald Amundsen had beaten them by a month. Scott and his companions died on the journey back to base.

Scott⁵, Sir Walter (1771–1832), Scottish novelist and poet. He established the form of the historical novel in Britain and was influential in his treatment of rural themes and use of regional speech. Notable novels: *Waverley* (1814), *Ivanhoe* (1819), and *Kenilworth* (1821).

Scotticism /ˈskɒtɪsɪz(ə)m/ (also **Scoticism**) ▶ **noun** a characteristically Scottish phrase, word, or idiom.
– ORIGIN early 18th cent.: from late Latin *Scot(t)icus* + **-ISM**.

Scotticize /ˈskɒtɪsʌɪz/ (also **Scotticise**) ▶ **verb** [with obj.] rare make Scottish in character.

Scottie ▶ **noun** informal **1** (also **Scottie dog**) a Scottish terrier.
2 used as a nickname for a Scotsman.

Scottish ▶ **adjective** relating to Scotland or its people: *the Scottish Highlands* | *Scottish dancing*.
▶ **noun** (as plural noun **the Scottish**) the people of Scotland. See also **SCOTS**.
– DERIVATIVES **Scottishness** noun.

> **USAGE** The terms **Scottish**, **Scot**, **Scots**, and **Scotch** are all variants of the same word. They have had different histories, however, and in modern English they have developed different uses and connotations. The normal everyday word used to mean 'of or relating to Scotland or its people' is **Scottish**, as in ***Scottish** people*; ***Scottish** hills*; ***Scottish** Gaelic*; or *she's English, not **Scottish***. The normal, neutral word for 'a person from Scotland' is **Scot**, along with **Scotsman**, **Scotswoman**, and the plural form **the Scots** (or, less commonly, **the Scottish**). The word **Scotch**, meaning either 'of or relating to Scotland' or 'a person/the people from Scotland', was widely used in the past by Scottish writers such as Robert Burns and Sir Walter Scott. It is now less common, being disliked by many Scottish people (as being an 'English' invention) and now regarded as old-fashioned in most contexts. It survives in certain fixed phrases, as for example ***Scotch** broth*, ***Scotch** mist*, and ***Scotch** whisky*.
> **Scots** is used, like **Scottish**, as an adjective meaning 'relating to Scotland'. However, it tends to be used in a narrower sense to refer specifically to the form of English spoken and used in Scotland, as in *a **Scots** accent* or *the **Scots** word for 'night'*.

Scottish Blackface ▶ **noun** a long-coated sheep of a hardy breed developed in upland areas of northern Britain, with black legs and muzzle.

Scottish Borders a council area of southern Scotland; administrative centre, Melrose.

Scottish Nationalist ▶ **noun** a member or supporter of Scottish nationalism or of the Scottish National Party.

Scottish National Party (abbrev.: **SNP**) a political party formed in 1934, which seeks autonomous government for Scotland. It won its first parliamentary seat in 1945, and has since maintained a small group of MPs.

Scottish terrier ▶ **noun** a small terrier of a rough-haired short-legged breed.

scoundrel ▶ **noun** a dishonest or unscrupulous person; a rogue.
– DERIVATIVES **scoundrelism** noun, **scoundrelly** adjective.
– ORIGIN late 16th cent.: of unknown origin.

scour¹ ▶ **verb 1** [with obj.] clean or brighten the surface of (something) by rubbing it hard, typically with an abrasive or detergent: *she scoured the cooker* | *I was **scouring out** the pans*. ■ remove (dirt or unwanted matter) by scouring: *use an electric toothbrush to **scour off** plaque*. ■ (of water or a watercourse) make (a channel or pool) by flowing quickly over something and removing soil or rock: *a stream came crashing through a narrow cavern to **scour out** a round pool below*.
2 [no obj.] (of livestock) suffer from diarrhoea. ■ [with obj.] archaic administer a strong purgative to.
▶ **noun** [mass noun] **1** the action of scouring or the state of being scoured, especially by swift-flowing water. ■ [in sing.] an act of rubbing something hard to clean or brighten it: *give the floor a good scour*.
2 (also **scours**) diarrhoea in livestock, especially cattle and pigs.
– DERIVATIVES **scourer** noun.
– ORIGIN Middle English: from Middle Dutch, Middle Low German *schūren*, from Old French *escurer*, from late Latin *excurare* 'clean (off)', from *ex-* 'away' + *curare* 'to clean'.

scour² ▶ **verb** [with obj.] subject (a place, text, etc.) to a thorough search in order to locate something: *David **scoured** each newspaper **for** an article on the murder*. ■ [no obj., with adverbial of direction] move rapidly in a particular direction, especially in search or pursuit of someone or something: *he scoured up the ladder*.
– ORIGIN late Middle English: related to obsolete *scour* 'moving hastily', of unknown origin.

scourge ▶ **noun 1** historical a whip used as an instrument of punishment.
2 a person or thing that causes great trouble or suffering: *the scourge of mass unemployment*.
▶ **verb** [with obj.] **1** historical whip (someone) as a punishment.
2 cause great suffering to: *political methods used to scourge and oppress workers*.
– DERIVATIVES **scourger** noun (historical).
– ORIGIN Middle English: shortening of Old French *escorge* (noun), *escorgier* (verb), from Latin *ex-* 'thoroughly' + *corrigia* 'thong, whip'.

scouring rush ▶ **noun** a horsetail with a very rough ridged stem, formerly used for scouring and polishing. ● Genus *Equisetum*, family Equisetaceae, in particular *E. hyemale*.

Scouse /skaʊs/ Brit. informal ▶ **noun 1** [mass noun] the dialect or accent of people from Liverpool.
2 short for **SCOUSER**.
▶ **adjective** relating to Liverpool: *a Scouse accent*.
– ORIGIN mid 19th cent.: abbreviation of **LOBSCOUSE**.

Scouser ▶ **noun** Brit. informal a person from Liverpool.

scout¹ ▶ **noun 1** a soldier or other person sent out ahead of a main force so as to gather information about the enemy's position, strength, or movements. ■ [usu. in sing.] an instance of gathering information, especially by reconnoitring an area: *I returned from a lengthy scout round the area*. ■ a ship or aircraft employed for reconnaissance, especially a small, fast aircraft.
2 short for **TALENT SCOUT**.
3 (also **Scout** or **Boy Scout**) a member of the Scout Association.
4 (also **scout bee**) a honeybee that searches for a new site for a swarm to settle or for a new food source.
5 a domestic worker at a college at Oxford University.
6 informal, dated a man or boy: *I've got nothing against old Adrian—he's a **good scout***.
▶ **verb** [no obj.] make a search for someone or something in various places: *I was sent to **scout around** for a place to park the camper* | *we **scouted for** clues*. ■ (especially of a soldier) go ahead of a main force so as to gather information about an enemy's position, strength, or movements. ■ [with obj.] explore or examine (a place or area of business) so as to gather information about it: *American companies are keen to **scout out** business opportunities*. ■ look for suitably talented people for recruitment to one's own organization or sports team: *Butcher has been scouting for United*.
– PHRASES **Scout's honour** the oath taken by a Scout. ■ informal used to indicate that one has the honourable standards associated with Scouts, and so will stand by a promise or tell the truth.
– DERIVATIVES **scouter** noun.
– ORIGIN late Middle English (as a verb): from Old French *escouter* 'listen', earlier *ascolter*, from Latin *auscultare*. Sense 5 of the noun (early 18th cent.) is of uncertain origin.

scout² ▶ **verb** [with obj.] rare reject (a proposal or idea) with scorn.
– ORIGIN early 17th cent.: of Scandinavian origin; compare with Old Norse *skúta*, *skúti* 'a taunt'.

Scout Association a worldwide youth organization founded for boys in 1907 by Lord Baden-Powell with the aim of developing their character by training them in self-sufficiency and survival techniques in the outdoors. Called the Boy Scouts until 1967, the Scout Association admitted girls as members from 1990.

scout car ▶ **noun** chiefly US a fast armoured vehicle used for military reconnaissance and liaison.

Scouter ▶ **noun** an adult leader in the Scout Association.

scouting ▶ **noun** [mass noun] **1** the action of gathering information about enemy forces or an area. ■ the activity of a talent scout.
2 (also **Scouting**) the characteristic activity and occupation of a Scout; the Scout movement.

Scoutmaster ▶ **noun** a man in charge of a group of Scouts (in 1964 replaced in official use by **Scout leader**).

scow /skaʊ/ ▶ **noun** N. Amer. a wide-beamed sailing dinghy. ■ a flat-bottomed boat used for transporting cargo to and from ships in harbour.
– ORIGIN mid 17th cent.: from Dutch *schouw* 'ferry boat'.

scowl ▶ **noun** an angry or bad-tempered expression.
▶ **verb** [no obj.] frown in an angry or bad-tempered way: *she **scowled at** him defiantly*.
– DERIVATIVES **scowler** noun.
– ORIGIN late Middle English (as a verb): probably of Scandinavian origin; compare with Danish *skule* 'scowl'. The noun dates from the early 16th cent.

SCPO ▶ **abbreviation** Senior Chief Petty Officer.

SCPS ▶ **abbreviation** (in the UK) Society of Civil and Public Servants.

SCR ▶ **abbreviation** Brit. Senior Common (or Combination) Room.

scrabble ▶ **verb** [no obj.] scratch or grope around with one's fingers to find, collect, or hold on to something: *she scrabbled at the grassy slope, desperate for purchase*. ■ (of an animal) scratch at something with its claws: *a lonely dog was scrabbling at the door*. ■ [with adverbial of direction] scramble or crawl quickly: *lizards scrabbling across the walls*.
▶ **noun 1** [in sing.] an act of scratching or scrambling for something: *he heard the scrabble of claws behind him*.
2 (**Scrabble**) [mass noun] trademark a game in which players build up words on a board from small lettered squares or tiles.
– ORIGIN mid 16th cent. (in the sense 'make marks at random, scrawl'): from Middle Dutch *schrabbelen*, frequentative of *schrabben* 'to scrape'. The noun sense 'struggle to achieve something' is originally a North American usage dating from the late 18th cent.

scrag ▶ **verb** (**scrags**, **scragging**, **scragged**) [with obj.] **1** informal, chiefly Brit. handle roughly; beat up. ■ Rugby grasp (an opponent) by placing an arm around the neck.
2 archaic or US kill by strangling or hanging. ■ US informal, dated kill; murder.
▶ **noun 1** an unattractively thin person or animal.
2 archaic, informal a person's neck.
– ORIGIN mid 16th cent. (as a noun): perhaps an alteration of Scots and northern English *crag* 'neck'. The verb (mid 18th cent.) developed the sense 'handle roughly' from the early use 'hang, strangle'.

scrag-end ▶ **noun** [mass noun] Brit. the inferior end of a neck of mutton.

scraggy ▶ **adjective** (**scraggier**, **scraggiest**) (of a person or animal) thin and bony. ■ (also chiefly N. Amer. **scraggly**) ragged, thin, or untidy in form or appearance: *an old man with a scraggy beard*.
– DERIVATIVES **scraggily** adverb, **scragginess** noun.

scram ▶ **verb** (**scrams**, **scramming**, **scrammed**) [no obj., usu. in imperative] informal leave or go away from a place quickly: *get out of here, you miserable wretches—scram!*
– ORIGIN early 20th cent.: probably from the verb **SCRAMBLE**.

scramasax /ˈskraməsaks/ ▶ **noun** a large knife with a single-edged blade found among the grave goods in many Anglo-Saxon burials. Such knives were used in hunting and fighting.
– ORIGIN mid 19th cent.: of Germanic origin.

scramble ▶ **verb 1** [no obj., with adverbial of direction] make one's way quickly or awkwardly up a steep gradient or over rough ground by using one's hands as well as one's feet: *we scrambled over the damp boulders*. ■ move hurriedly or clumsily from or into a particular place or position: *she scrambled out of the car* | *I tried to scramble to my feet*. ■ (**scramble into**) put (clothes) on hurriedly: *Robbie scrambled*

S

into jeans and a T-shirt. ■ [with obj.] informal perform (an action) or achieve (a result) hurriedly, clumsily, or with difficulty: *Cork scrambled a 1–0 win over Monaghan.* ■ [with infinitive] struggle or compete with others for something in an eager or uncontrolled and undignified way: *firms scrambled to win public-sector contracts.*
2 [with obj.] order (a fighter aircraft or its pilot) to take off immediately in an emergency or for action: *the Hurricanes were scrambled again, this time meeting Italian fighters.* ■ [no obj.] (of a fighter aircraft or its pilot) take off for emergency action.
3 [with obj.] make (something) jumbled or muddled: *maybe the alcohol has scrambled his brains.* ■ cook (eggs) by beating them with a little liquid and then cooking and stirring them gently. ■ make (a broadcast transmission or telephone conversation) unintelligible unless received by an appropriate decoding device: *the signal is scrambled into code.*
4 [no obj.] American Football (of a quarterback) run with the ball behind the line of scrimmage, avoiding tackles.
▶ **noun** [usu. in sing.] **1** a difficult or hurried clamber up or over something: *an undignified scramble over the wall.* ■ a mountain walk up steep terrain involving the use of one's hands. ■ Brit. a motorcycle race over rough and hilly ground. ■ an eager or uncontrolled and undignified struggle with others to obtain or achieve something: *I lost Tommy in the* ***scramble for*** *a seat.*
2 an emergency take-off by fighter aircraft.
3 a disordered mixture of things.
– ORIGIN late 16th cent.: imitative; compare with the dialect words *scamble* 'stumble' and *cramble* 'crawl'.

scrambled egg ▶ **noun** [mass noun] **1** (also **scrambled eggs**) a dish of eggs prepared by beating them with a little liquid and then cooking and stirring them gently.
2 informal gold braid on a military officer's cap.

scrambler ▶ **noun 1** a device for scrambling a broadcast transmission or telephone conversation.
2 a person who walks over steep, mountainous terrain as a pastime. ■ Brit. a motorcycle for racing over rough and hilly ground.
3 a plant with long slender stems supported by other plants.
4 American Football a quarterback noted for scrambling.

scrambling ▶ **noun** [mass noun] **1** the action of scrambling up or over rough or steep ground, especially as a leisure activity. ■ Brit. the sport of racing motorcycles over rough and hilly ground.
2 the alteration of the speech frequency of a telephone conversation or broadcast transmission so as to make it unintelligible without a decoding device.

scramjet ▶ **noun** Aeronautics a ramjet in which combustion takes place in a stream of gas moving at supersonic speed.
– ORIGIN 1960s: from *s(upersonic)* + *c(ombustion)* + RAMJET.

scran ▶ **noun** [mass noun] dialect food.
– ORIGIN early 18th cent. (denoting a bill at an inn): of unknown origin.

Scranton an industrial city in NE Pennsylvania; pop. 72,233 (est. 2008).
– ORIGIN named after the *Scranton* family who established a steelworks on the site in 1840, around which the city developed.

S

scrap[1] ▶ **noun 1** a small piece or amount of something, especially one that is left over after the greater part has been used: *I scribbled her address on* ***a scrap of*** *paper* | ***scraps of*** *information.* ■ (**scraps**) bits of uneaten food left after a meal. ■ used to emphasize the lack or smallness of something: *there was not a* ***scrap of*** *aggression in him* | *every* ***scrap of*** *green land is up for grabs by development.* ■ a particularly small thing of its kind: *she was wearing a short black skirt and a tiny scrap of a top.*
2 (also **scrap metal**) [mass noun] discarded metal for reprocessing: *the steamer was eventually sold for scrap.* ■ [often as modifier] any waste articles or discarded material.
▶ **verb** (**scraps, scrapping, scrapped**) [with obj.] discard or remove from service (a redundant, old, or inoperative vehicle, vessel, or machine), especially so as to convert it to scrap metal: *a bold decision was taken to scrap existing plant.* ■ abolish or cancel (a plan, policy, or law): *he supports the idea that road tax should be scrapped.*
– ORIGIN late Middle English (as a plural noun denoting fragments of uneaten food): from Old Norse *skrap* 'scraps'; related to *skrapa* 'to scrape'. The verb dates from the late 19th cent.

scrap[2] informal ▶ **noun** a fight or quarrel, especially a minor or spontaneous one.
▶ **verb** (**scraps, scrapping, scrapped**) [no obj.] engage in a minor fight or quarrel. ■ compete fiercely: *the two drivers scrapped for the lead.*
– DERIVATIVES **scrapper** noun.
– ORIGIN late 17th cent. (as a noun in the sense 'sinister plot, scheme'): perhaps from the noun SCRAPE.

scrapbook ▶ **noun** a book of blank pages for sticking cuttings, drawings, or pictures in.

scrapbooking ▶ **noun** [mass noun] chiefly N. Amer. the activity or hobby of making scrapbooks.
– DERIVATIVES **scrapbooker** noun.

scrape ▶ **verb 1** [with obj.] drag or pull a hard or sharp implement across (a surface or object) so as to remove dirt or other matter: *remove the green tops from the carrots and scrape them* | [with obj. and complement] *we scraped the dishes clean.* ■ [with obj. and adverbial] use a sharp or hard implement to remove (dirt or unwanted matter) from something: *she scraped the mud off her shoes.* ■ [with obj. and adverbial] apply (a hard or sharp implement) to a surface so as to remove dirt or other matter: *he scraped the long-bladed razor across the stubble on his cheek.* ■ make (a hollow) by scraping away soil or rock: *he found a ditch, scraped a hole, and put the bag in it.*
2 rub or cause to rub by accident against a rough or hard surface, causing damage or injury: [no obj.] *he smashed into the wall and felt his teeth* ***scrape against*** *the plaster* | [with obj.] *she reversed in a reckless sweep, scraping the Range Rover.* ■ [with obj.] draw or move (something) along or over something else, making a harsh noise: *she* ***scraped back*** *her chair and stood up.* ■ [no obj.] move with or make a harsh scraping sound: *she lifted the gate to prevent it scraping along the ground.* ■ [no obj., with adverbial] narrowly pass by or through something: *there was only just room to* ***scrape through*** *between the tree and the edge of the stream.* ■ [no obj.] humorous play a violin tunelessly: *Olivia was scraping away at her violin.* ■ [with obj.] (**scrape something back**) draw one's hair tightly back off the forehead: *her hair* ***was scraped back into a bun.*** ■ [with obj. and adverbial] Brit. spread (butter or margarine) thinly over bread.
3 [with obj.] just manage to achieve; accomplish with great effort or difficulty: *Scotland scraped a lucky home draw with Portugal* | *for some years he* ***scraped a living*** *as a tutor.* ■ (**scrape something together/up**) collect or accumulate something with difficulty: *they could hardly scrape up enough money for one ticket, let alone two.* ■ [no obj.] try to save as much money as possible; economize: *they had scrimped and scraped and saved for years.* ■ [no obj.] (**scrape by/along**) manage to live with difficulty: *she has to* ***scrape by*** *on Social Security.* ■ [no obj., with adverbial] barely manage to succeed in a particular undertaking: *Bowden* ***scraped in*** *with 180 votes at the last election* | *he* ***scraped through*** *the entrance exam.*
4 [with obj.] copy (data) from a website using a computer program.
▶ **noun 1** an act or sound of scraping: *he heard the scrape of his mother's key in the lock.* ■ an injury or mark caused by scraping: *there was a long, shallow scrape on his shin.* ■ a place where soil has been scraped away, especially a shallow hollow formed in the ground by a bird during a courtship display or for nesting. ■ [in sing.] Brit. a thinly applied layer of butter or margarine on bread: *when making sandwiches, use only the thinnest scrape of fat.* ■ archaic an obsequious bow in which one foot is drawn backwards along the ground.
2 Medicine, informal a procedure of dilatation of the cervix and curettage of the uterus.
3 informal an embarrassing or difficult predicament caused by one's own unwise behaviour: *he'd been in worse scrapes than this before now.*
– PHRASES **scrape acquaintance with** dated contrive to get to know. **scrape the barrel** (or **the bottom of the barrel**) informal be reduced to using things or people of the poorest quality because there is nothing else available.
– ORIGIN Old English *scrapian* 'scratch with the fingernails', of Germanic origin, reinforced in Middle English by Old Norse *skrapa* or Middle Dutch *schrapen* 'to scratch'.

scraper ▶ **noun** a tool or device used for scraping, especially for removing dirt, paint, or other unwanted matter from a surface. ■ Archaeology a prehistoric flint implement with a sharpened edge used for scraping material such as hide or wood.

scraperboard ▶ **noun** [mass noun] Brit. cardboard or board with a blackened surface which can be scraped off for making white line drawings.

scrapheap ▶ **noun** a pile of discarded materials or articles: *cars on a scrapheap* | figurative *it should be consigned to the scrapheap of technological history.*

scrapie ▶ **noun** [mass noun] a disease of sheep involving the central nervous system, characterized by a lack of coordination causing affected animals to rub against trees and other objects for support, and thought to be caused by a virus-like agent such as a prion.
– ORIGIN early 20th cent.: from the verb SCRAPE + -IE.

scraping ▶ **noun** [mass noun] the action or sound of something scraping or being scraped: *the scraping of the spoon in the bowl* | [in sing.] *there was a loud scraping of chairs.* ■ [count noun] (usu. **scrapings**) a small amount of something that has been obtained by scraping it from a surface: *I got some scrapings from under the girl's fingernails.*

scrap merchant ▶ **noun** a person who deals in scrap metal or other waste articles.

scrap metal ▶ **noun** another term for SCRAP[1] (sense 2 of the noun).

scrappage /'skrapɪdʒ/ ▶ **noun** [mass noun] the action of scrapping old or inoperative vehicles, vessels, or machines. ■ [often as modifier] a government programme that gives drivers a financial incentive to replace old cars with newer, more fuel-efficient ones: *a car scrappage scheme.*

scrap paper ▶ **noun** [mass noun] odd bits of paper, used for making rough notes.

scrapple ▶ **noun** [mass noun] US scraps of pork or other meat stewed with maize meal and shaped into large cakes.
– ORIGIN mid 19th cent.: diminutive of the noun SCRAP[1].

scrappy ▶ **adjective** (**scrappier, scrappiest**) **1** consisting of disorganized, untidy, or incomplete parts: *scrappy lecture notes piled up unread.* [mid 19th cent.: derivative of SCRAP[1].]
2 N. Amer. informal determined, argumentative, or pugnacious: *he had a scrappy New York temperament.* [late 19th cent.: derivative of SCRAP[2].]
– DERIVATIVES **scrappily** adverb, **scrappiness** noun.

scrapyard ▶ **noun** a place where scrap is collected before being recycled or discarded.

scratch ▶ **verb 1** [with obj.] score or mark the surface of (something) with a sharp or pointed object: *the car's paintwork was battered and scratched* | [no obj.] *he scratched at a stain on his jacket.* ■ make a long, narrow superficial wound in the skin of: *her arms were scratched by the thorns* | *I scratched myself on the tree.* ■ rub (a part of one's body) with one's fingernails to relieve itching: *Jessica lifted her sunglasses and scratched her nose.* ■ [with obj. and adverbial] make (a mark or hole) by scoring a surface with a sharp or pointed object: *I found two names scratched on one of the windowpanes.* ■ write (something) hurriedly or awkwardly. ■ [with obj. and adverbial] remove (something) from something else by pulling a sharp implement over it: *he scratched away the plaster.* ■ [no obj.] make a rasping or grating noise by scraping something over a hard surface: *the dog scratched to be let in* | (as noun **scratching**) *there was a sound of scratching behind the wall.* ■ [no obj.] (of a bird or mammal, especially a chicken) rake the ground with the beak or claws in search of food. ■ [no obj.] (**scratch for**) search for (someone or something that is hard to locate or find): *he's still* ***scratching around for*** *a woman to share his life.* ■ accomplish (something) with great effort or difficulty: *Tabitha wondered how long the woman had been* ***scratching a living*** *on the waterways.* ■ [no obj.] (**scratch along**) make a living with difficulty: *many architects now scratch along doing loft conversions.*
2 [with obj.] cancel or strike out (writing) with a pen or pencil: *the name of Dr McNab was* ***scratched out*** *and that of Dr Dunstaple substituted.* ■ withdraw (a competitor) from a competition: *Jolie's Halo was* ***scratched from*** *a minor stakes race at Monmouth Park.* ■ [no obj.] (of a competitor) withdraw from a competition: *due to a knee injury she was forced to* ***scratch from*** *the race.* ■ cancel or abandon (an undertaking or project): *banks seem prepared to scratch stabilization charges.*
3 [no obj.] (often as noun **scratching**) play a record using the scratch technique (sense 2 of the noun).
▶ **noun 1** a mark or wound made by scratching: *the scratches on her arm were throbbing.* ■ [in sing.] informal a slight or insignificant wound or injury: *it's nothing—just a scratch.* ■ [in sing.] an act or spell of scratching oneself to relieve itching: *he gave his scalp a good scratch.* ■ a rasping or grating noise produced by something rubbing against a hard surface: *the*

scratch of a match lighting a cigarette. ■ [mass noun] a rough hiss, caused by the friction of the stylus in the groove, heard when a record is played.
2 [mass noun] a technique, used especially in rap music, of stopping a record by hand and moving it back and forwards to give a rhythmic scratching effect.
3 [mass noun] (in sport) the starting point in a race for a competitor that is not given a handicap or advantage. [originally denoting a boundary or starting line for sports competitors.] ■ Golf a handicap of zero, indicating that a player is good enough to achieve par on a course.
4 [mass noun] informal money: *he was working to get some scratch together.*
▶ **adjective** [attrib.] **1** assembled or made from whatever is available, and so unlikely to be of the highest quality: *City were fielding a scratch squad.*
2 (of a sports competitor or event) with no handicap given.
– PHRASES **from scratch** from the very beginning, especially without making use of or relying on any previous work for assistance: *he built his own computer company from scratch.* **scratch a —— and find a ——** used to suggest that an investigation of someone or something soon reveals their true nature: *they believe that if you scratch a homophobe, you'll probably find a racist.* **scratch one's head** informal think hard in order to find a solution to something. ■ feel or express bewilderment. **scratch the surface 1** deal with a matter only in the most superficial way: *research has only scratched the surface of the paranormal.* **2** initiate the briefest investigation to discover something concealed: *they have a boring image but scratch the surface and it's fascinating.* **up to scratch** up to the required standard; satisfactory: *her German was not up to scratch.* **you scratch my back and I'll scratch yours** proverb if you do me a favour, I'll return it.
– DERIVATIVES **scratcher** noun.
– ORIGIN late Middle English: probably a blend of the synonymous dialect words *scrat* and *cratch*, both of uncertain origin; compare with Middle Low German *kratsen* and Old High German *krazzōn*.

scratchboard ▶ **noun** another term for SCRAPERBOARD.

scratch card ▶ **noun** a card with a section or sections coated in an opaque waxy substance which may be scraped away to reveal a symbol indicating whether a prize has been won in a competition.

scratch coat ▶ **noun** N. Amer. a rough coating of plaster scratched before it is quite dry to ensure the adherence of the next coat.

scratchings (also **pork scratchings**) ▶ **plural noun** Brit. crisp pieces of pork fat left after rendering lard, eaten as a snack.

scratch pad ▶ **noun** chiefly N. Amer. a notepad. ■ Computing a small, fast memory for the temporary storage of data.

scratchplate ▶ **noun** a plastic or metal plate attached to the front of a guitar to protect it from being scratched by the plectrum.

scratch-resistant ▶ **adjective** (of a surface or hard material) not easily damaged by scratching.

scratchy ▶ **adjective** (**scratchier**, **scratchiest**) (especially of a fabric or garment) having a rough, uncomfortable texture and tending to cause itching or discomfort. ■ (of a voice or sound) rough; grating: *she dropped her voice to a scratchy whisper.* ■ (of a record) making a crackling or rough sound because of scratches on the surface. ■ (of writing or a drawing) done with quick and jagged strokes: *a scratchy ink sketch of a man on horseback.* ■ bad-tempered or irritable: *she was a little abrupt and scratchy.*
– DERIVATIVES **scratchily** adverb, **scratchiness** noun.

scrawl ▶ **verb** [with obj.] write (something) in a hurried, careless way: *Charlie scrawled his signature* | [no obj.] *he was scrawling on the back of a used envelope.*
▶ **noun** an example of hurried, careless writing: *the page was covered in scrawls and doodles* | [mass noun] *reams and reams of handwritten scrawl.*
– DERIVATIVES **scrawly** adjective.
– ORIGIN early 17th cent.: apparently an alteration of the verb CRAWL, perhaps influenced by obsolete *scrawl* 'sprawl'.

scrawny ▶ **adjective** (**scrawnier**, **scrawniest**) (of a person or animal) unattractively thin and bony. ■ (of vegetation) meagre or stunted.
– DERIVATIVES **scrawniness** noun.
– ORIGIN mid 19th cent.: variant of dialect *scranny*; compare with archaic *scrannel* 'weak, feeble' (referring to sound).

scream ▶ **verb** [no obj.] **1** give a long, loud, piercing cry or cries expressing extreme emotion or pain: *they could hear him screaming in pain* | (as adj. **screaming**) *a harassed mum with a screaming child.* ■ [reporting verb] cry something in a high-pitched, frenzied way: [no obj.] *I ran to the house screaming for help* | [with direct speech] *'Get out!' he screamed* | [with obj.] *he screamed abuse down the phone.* ■ urgently and vociferously call attention to one's views or feelings, especially ones of anger or distress: [with clause] *his supporters scream that he is being done an injustice* | figurative *the creative side of me is screaming out for attention.*
2 make a loud, high-pitched sound: *sirens were screaming from all over the city.* ■ [no obj., with adverbial of direction] move very rapidly with or as if with a loud, high-pitched sound: *a shell screamed overhead.*
3 informal, dated turn informer.
▶ **noun 1** a long, loud, piercing cry expressing extreme emotion or pain: *they were awakened by screams for help.* ■ a high-pitched cry made by an animal: *the screams of the seagulls.*
2 a loud, piercing sound: *the scream of a falling bomb.*
3 [in sing.] informal an irresistibly funny person, thing, or situation: *the movie's a scream.*
– ORIGIN Middle English: origin uncertain; perhaps from Middle Dutch.

screamer ▶ **noun 1** a person or thing that makes a screaming sound.
2 informal a thing remarkable for speed or impact: *he won a screamer of a 500 cc final.* ■ an extremely fast ball or shot: *he sent two screamers past the Oxford goalkeeper.* ■ chiefly US a sensational or very large headline: *his death caused a front-page screamer.* ■ dated a thing that causes screams of laughter.
3 a large goose-like South American waterbird with a short bill, a sharp bony spur on each wing, and a harsh honking call. ● Family Anhimidae: two genera and three species.
– PHRASES **two-pot screamer** Austral. informal a person who shows the effects of alcohol after drinking comparatively little.

screamingly ▶ **adverb** [as submodifier] to a very great extent; extremely: *a screamingly dull daily routine.*

scree ▶ **noun** [mass noun] a mass of small loose stones that form or cover a slope on a mountain. ■ [count noun] a slope covered with scree.
– ORIGIN early 18th cent.: probably a back-formation from the plural *screes*, from Old Norse *skritha* 'landslip'; related to *skrítha* 'glide'.

screech ▶ **verb** [no obj.] (of a person or animal) give a loud, harsh, piercing cry: *she hit her brother, causing him to screech with pain.* ■ make a loud, harsh, squealing sound: (as adj. **screeching**) *she brought the car to a screeching halt.* ■ [no obj., with adverbial of direction] move rapidly with a loud, harsh, squealing sound: *the van screeched round a bend at speed.*
▶ **noun** a loud, harsh, piercing cry. ■ a loud, harsh, squealing sound: *a screech of brakes.*
– DERIVATIVES **screecher** noun, **screechy** adjective (**screechier**, **screechiest**).
– ORIGIN mid 16th cent.: alteration of archaic *scritch*, of imitative origin.

screech beetle ▶ **noun** an oval convex water beetle with large eyes, which lives in muddy pools. When held it squeaks by rubbing the tip of the abdomen against the wing cases. ● *Hygrobia hermanni*, family Hygrobiidae.

screech owl ▶ **noun** an owl with a screeching call: ● a small American owl related to the scops owls (genus *Otus*, family Strigidae: in particular *Otus asio*). ● Brit. another term for BARN OWL.

screed ▶ **noun 1** a long speech or piece of writing, typically one regarded as tedious.
2 [mass noun] a levelled layer of material (e.g. cement) applied to a floor or other surface. ■ [count noun] a strip of plaster or other material placed on a surface as a guide to thickness.
▶ **verb** [with obj.] level (a floor or layer of concrete) with a straight edge using a back and forth motion while moving across the surface.
– ORIGIN Middle English: probably a variant of the noun SHRED. The early sense was 'fragment cut from a main piece', then 'torn strip', whence (via the notion of a long roll or list) sense 1 of the noun.

screeding ▶ **noun** [mass noun] a levelled layer of material (e.g. cement) applied to a floor or other surface.

screel /skriːl/ ▶ **verb** [no obj.] chiefly Scottish & W. Indian utter or emit a high-pitched or discordant cry or sound; screech.
– ORIGIN late 19th cent.: of imitative origin, or related to the verb SKIRL.

screen ▶ **noun 1** a fixed or movable upright partition used to divide a room, give shelter from draughts, heat, or light, or to provide concealment or privacy. ■ a thing providing concealment or protection: *his jeep was discreetly parked behind a screen of trees* | *the article is using science as a screen for unexamined prejudice.* ■ [often with modifier] Architecture a partition of carved wood or stone separating the nave of a church from the chancel, choir, or sanctuary. See also ROOD SCREEN. ■ a windscreen of a motor vehicle: *a branch whipped across the screen and tore off one of the wipers.* ■ a frame with fine wire netting used in a window or doorway to keep out mosquitoes and other flying insects.
2 the surface of a cathode ray tube or similar electronic device, especially that of a television, VDU, or monitor, on which images and data are displayed. ■ a blank, typically white or silver surface on which a photographic image is projected: *two historical swashbucklers are due to fill cinema screens this year.* ■ (**the screen**) films or television; the film industry: *she's a star of the track as well as the screen.* ■ the data or images displayed on a computer screen: *pressing the F1 key at any time will display a help screen.* ■ Photography a flat piece of ground glass on which the image formed by a camera lens is focused.
3 Printing a transparent finely ruled plate or film used in half-tone reproduction.
4 [in sing.] a system of checking a person or thing for the presence or absence of something, typically a disease: *services offered by the centre include a health screen for people who have just joined the company.*
5 a part of an electrical or other instrument which protects it from or prevents it causing electromagnetic interference. ■ Electronics (also **screen grid**) a grid placed between the control grid and the anode of a valve to reduce the capacitance between these electrodes.
6 Military a detachment of troops or ships detailed to cover the movements of the main body.
7 a large sieve or riddle, especially one for sorting substances such as grain or coal into different sizes.
▶ **verb** [with obj.] **1** conceal, protect, or shelter (someone or something) with a screen or something forming a screen: *her hair swung across to screen her face* | *a high hedge screened all of the front from passers-by.* ■ (**screen something off**) separate something from something else with or as if with a screen: *an area had been screened off as a waiting room.* ■ protect (someone) from something dangerous or unpleasant: *in my country a man of my rank would be screened completely from any risk of attack.* ■ prevent from causing or protect from electromagnetic interference: *ensure that your microphone leads are properly screened from hum pickup.*
2 show (a film or video) or broadcast (a television programme): *the show is to be screened by the BBC later this year.*
3 test (a person or substance) for the presence or absence of a disease: *outpatients were screened for cervical cancer.* ■ check on or investigate (someone), typically to ascertain whether they are suitable for or can be trusted in a particular situation or job: *all prospective presidential candidates would have to be screened by a preselection committee.* ■ evaluate or analyse (something) for its suitability for a particular purpose or application: *only one per cent of rainforest plants have been screened for medical use.* ■ (**screen someone/thing out**) exclude someone or something after evaluation or investigation: *anti-spam software can screen out large amounts of unwanted email.*
4 pass (a substance such as grain or coal) through a large sieve or screen, especially so as to sort it into different sizes.
5 Printing project (a photograph or other image) through a transparent ruled plate so as to be able to reproduce it as a half-tone.
– DERIVATIVES **screenable** adjective, **screener** noun, **screenful** noun.
– ORIGIN Middle English: shortening of Old Northern French *escren*, of Germanic origin.

screen door ▶ **noun** the outer door of a pair, used for protection against insects, weather, etc.

screen dump ▶ **noun** Computing the process or an instance of causing what is displayed on a screen to be printed out. ■ a resulting printout.

screening ▶ **noun 1** a showing of a film, video, or television programme.
2 [mass noun] the evaluation or investigation of something as part of a methodical survey, to assess suitability for a particular role or purpose.

S

3 the testing of a person or group of people for the presence of a disease or other condition: *prenatal screening for Down's syndrome.*
4 (**screenings**) refuse separated by sieving grain.

screen pass ▶ noun American Football a forward pass to a player protected by a screen of blockers.

screenplay ▶ noun the script of a film, including acting instructions and scene directions.

screen-print ▶ verb [with obj.] (often as adj. **screen-printed**) force ink or metal on to (a surface) through a prepared screen of fine material so as to create a picture or pattern.
▶ noun (**screen print**) a picture or design produced by screen-printing.

screen saver ▶ noun Computing a program which, after a set time, replaces an unchanging screen display with a moving image to prevent damage to the phosphor.

screen scraping ▶ noun [mass noun] the action of using a computer program to copy data from a website.

screenshot ▶ noun an image of the display on a computer screen.

screen test ▶ noun a filmed test to ascertain whether an actor is suitable for a film role.
▶ verb (**screen-test**) [with obj.] give a screen test to (an actor).

screen time ▶ noun [mass noun] **1** the time allotted to or occupied by a particular subject, actor, etc., on film or television: *these characters deserve more screen time.*
2 time spent using a device such as a computer, television, or games console.

screenwash ▶ noun [mass noun] a mixture of water, detergents, and sometimes antifreeze used to clean the windscreens of vehicles.

screenwriter ▶ noun a person who writes a screenplay.
– DERIVATIVES **screenwriting** noun.

screw ▶ noun **1** a short, slender, sharp-pointed metal pin with a raised helical thread running around it and a slotted head, used to join things together by being rotated so that it pierces wood or other material and is held tightly in place. ■ a cylinder with a helical ridge or thread running round the outside (a **male screw**) that can be turned to seal an opening, apply pressure, adjust position, etc., especially one fitting into a corresponding internal groove or thread (a **female screw**). ■ historical (**the screws**) an instrument of torture having the action of a screw. ■ (also **screw propeller**) a ship's or aircraft's propeller (considered as acting like a screw in moving through water or air).
2 an act of turning a screw or other object having a thread. ■ [mass noun] Billiards & Snooker, Brit. backspin given to the cue ball by hitting it below centre, intended to make it move backwards after striking the object ball. ■ [count noun] Brit. a small twisted-up piece of paper, typically containing a substance such as salt or tobacco.
3 informal a prisoner's derogatory term for a warder.
4 [in sing.] vulgar slang an act of sexual intercourse. ■ [with adj.] a sexual partner of a specified ability.
5 [in sing.] Brit. informal, dated an amount of salary or wages: *he's offered me the job with a jolly good screw.*
6 archaic, informal a mean or miserly person.
7 Brit. informal a worn-out horse.
▶ verb **1** [with obj. and adverbial] fasten or tighten with a screw or screws: *screw the hinge to your new door.* ■ rotate (something) so as to fit it into or on to a surface or object by means of a spiral thread: *Philip screwed the top on the flask.* ■ [no obj., with adverbial] (of an object) be attached or removed by being rotated by means of a spiral thread: *a connector which screws on to the gas cylinder.* ■ (**screw something around/round**) turn one's head or body round sharply: *he screwed his head around to try to find the enemy.*
2 [with obj.] informal cheat or swindle (someone), especially by charging them too much for something: *the loss of advertising contracts will amount to more than the few quid that they're trying to* **screw us for**. ■ (**screw something out of**) extort or force something, especially money, from (someone) by putting them under strong pressure: *your grandmother screwed cash out of him for ten years.* ■ (**be screwed**) be in serious trouble: *if you're colour-blind, you're screwed.*
3 [with obj.] vulgar slang have sexual intercourse with. ■ [no obj.] (of a couple) have sexual intercourse.
4 [with obj.] impart spin or curl to (a ball or shot). ■ [no obj.] Billiards & Snooker, Brit. play a shot with screw.
– PHRASES **have one's head screwed on (the right way)** informal have common sense. **have a screw loose** informal be slightly eccentric or mentally disturbed. **put the screws on** informal exert strong psychological pressure on (someone) so as to intimidate them into doing something. **a turn of the screw** informal an additional degree of pressure or hardship added to a situation that is already extremely difficult to bear. **turn** (or **tighten**) **the screw** (or **screws**) informal exert strong pressure on someone.
– PHRASAL VERBS **screw around 1** vulgar slang have many different sexual partners. **2** informal fool about. **screw someone over** informal treat someone unfairly; cheat or swindle someone. **screw up 1** (of the muscles of one's face or around one's eyes) contract, typically so as to express emotion or because of bright light. **2** informal, chiefly N. Amer. completely mismanage or mishandle a situation: *I'm sorry, Susan, I screwed up.* **screw someone up** informal cause someone to be emotionally or mentally disturbed: *this job can really screw you up.* **screw something up 1** crush a piece of paper or fabric into a tight mass. ■ tense the muscles of one's face or around one's eyes, typically so as to register an emotion or because of bright light. **2** informal cause something to fail or go wrong: *why are you trying to screw up your life?* **3** summon up one's courage: *now Stephen had to screw up his courage and confess.*
– DERIVATIVES **screwable** adjective, **screwer** noun.
– ORIGIN late Middle English (as a noun): from Old French *escroue* 'female screw, nut', from Latin *scrofa*, literally 'sow', later 'screw'. The early sense of the verb was 'contort (the features), twist around' (late 16th cent.).

screwball chiefly N. Amer. ▶ noun **1** Baseball a ball pitched with reverse spin as compared to a curve ball.
2 informal a crazy or eccentric person.
▶ adjective informal crazy; absurd. ■ relating to or denoting a style of fast-moving comedy film involving eccentric characters or ridiculous situations.
– DERIVATIVES **screwballer** noun (sense 1 of the noun).

screw cap ▶ noun a round cap or lid that can be screwed on to a bottle or jar.
– DERIVATIVES **screw-capped** adjective.

screw coupling ▶ noun a female screw with threads at both ends for joining lengths of piping or rods.

screw-down ▶ adjective adapted or designed to be closed by screwing: *the flex is held by a screw-down bar.*

screwdriver ▶ noun **1** a tool with a flattened or cross-shaped tip that fits into the head of a screw to turn it.
2 a cocktail made from vodka and orange juice.

screwed ▶ adjective **1** (of a bolt or other device) having a helical ridge or thread running around the outside.
2 informal in a difficult or hopeless situation; ruined or broken.
3 [predic.] archaic, informal drunk.

screwed-up ▶ adjective **1** informal (of a person) emotionally disturbed; neurotic: *the screwed-up children of wealthy parents.* ■ (of an event or a situation) spoiled by being badly managed or carried out: *that was the most screwed-up audition.*
2 chiefly Brit. (of paper or fabric) crumpled or crushed into a ball: *a screwed-up paper bag.* ■ (of a person's face or eyes) crumpled, especially because of worry or effort.

screw eye ▶ noun a screw with a loop for passing a cord through, instead of a slotted head.

screwgate (also **screwgate karabiner**) ▶ noun Climbing a type of lockable karabiner.

screw gear ▶ noun a gear consisting of an endless screw with a cogwheel or pinion.

screw hook ▶ noun a hook with a point and thread for fastening it to woodwork.

screw-in ▶ adjective adapted or designed to be attached by screwing into something.

screw jack ▶ noun a vehicle jack worked by a screw device.

screw-on ▶ adjective adapted or designed to be attached by screwing on to something.

screw pine ▶ noun another term for PANDANUS.

screw plate ▶ noun a steel plate with threaded holes for making male screws.

screw propeller ▶ noun see SCREW (sense 1 of the noun).

screw tap ▶ noun a tool for making female screws.

screw thread ▶ noun see THREAD (sense 3 of the noun).

screw top ▶ noun a round cap or lid that can be screwed on to a bottle or jar.
– DERIVATIVES **screw-topped** adjective.

screw-up ▶ noun informal, chiefly N. Amer. a situation that has been completely mismanaged or mishandled: *a massive bureaucratic screw-up.*

screw valve ▶ noun a stopcock opened and shut by a screw.

screw worm ▶ noun **1** a worm gear or other mechanical device bearing a screw.
2 a large American blowfly larva which enters the wounds of mammals and sometimes humans, developing under the skin and often causing death. The adult fly is called the **screw-worm fly**. • *Cochliomyia* (or *Callitroga*) *hominivorax*, family Calliphoridae.

screwy ▶ adjective (**screwier**, **screwiest**) informal, chiefly N. Amer. rather odd or eccentric.
– DERIVATIVES **screwiness** noun.

Scriabin /skrɪˈɑːbɪn/ (also **Skryabin**), Aleksandr (Nikolaevich) (1872–1915), Russian composer and pianist. He wrote symphonies, tone poems, and numerous pieces for the piano, including sonatas and preludes. Much of his later music reflects his interest in mysticism and theosophy, especially his third symphony. Notable works: *The Divine Poem* (symphony, 1903) and *Prometheus: The Poem of Fire* (tone poem, 1909–10).

scribble[1] ▶ verb [with obj.] write or draw (something) carelessly or hurriedly: *he took the clipboard and scribbled something illegible* | (as adj. **scribbled**) *scribbled notes* | [no obj.] *hastily he scribbled in the margin.* ■ [no obj.] informal write for a living or as a hobby: *they scribbled, potted, and painted.*
▶ noun a piece of writing or a picture produced carelessly or hurriedly: *illegible scribbles* | [mass noun] *the postman would never be able to decipher your scribble.*
– DERIVATIVES **scribbly** adjective (**scribblier**, **scribbliest**).
– ORIGIN late Middle English: from medieval Latin *scribillare*, diminutive of Latin *scribere* 'write'.

scribble[2] ▶ verb [with obj.] (often as noun **scribbling**) card (wool, cotton, etc.) coarsely.
– ORIGIN late 17th cent.: probably from Low German; compare with German *schrubbeln* (in the same sense), frequentative of Low German *schrubben* 'to scrub'.

scribbler ▶ noun informal a person who writes for a living or as a hobby.

scribe ▶ noun **1** historical a person who copies out documents, especially one employed to do this before printing was invented. ■ informal, often humorous a writer, especially a journalist.
2 historical a Jewish record-keeper or, later, a professional theologian and jurist.
3 (also **scribe awl**) a pointed instrument used for making marks on wood, bricks, etc., to guide a saw or in signwriting.
▶ verb [with obj.] **1** chiefly literary write: *he scribed a note that he passed to Dan.*
2 mark with a pointed instrument.
– DERIVATIVES **scribal** adjective.
– ORIGIN Middle English (in sense 2 of the noun): from Latin *scriba*, from *scribere* 'write'. The verb was first used in the sense 'write down'; in sense 2 it is perhaps partly a shortening of DESCRIBE.

scriber ▶ noun another term for SCRIBE (sense 3 of the noun).

scrim ▶ noun [mass noun] strong, coarse fabric, chiefly used for heavy-duty lining or upholstery. ■ [count noun] Theatre a piece of gauze cloth that appears opaque until lit from behind, used as a screen or backcloth. ■ [count noun] a type of heatproof gauze cloth put over film or television lamps to diffuse the light. ■ [count noun] N. Amer. a thing that conceals or obscures something: *a thin scrim of fog covered the island.*
– ORIGIN late 18th cent.: of unknown origin.

scrimmage ▶ noun **1** a confused struggle or fight.
2 [mass noun] American Football a sequence of play beginning with the placing of the ball on the ground with its longest axis at right angles to the goal line. ■ [count noun] chiefly American Football a session in which teams practise by playing a simulated game.
▶ verb [no obj.] chiefly American Football engage in a scrimmage. ■ [with obj.] put (the ball) into a scrimmage.
– DERIVATIVES **scrimmager** noun.
– ORIGIN late Middle English: alteration of dialect *scrimish*, variant of the noun SKIRMISH.

scrimp ▶ verb [no obj.] be thrifty or parsimonious; economize: *I have **scrimped and saved** to give you a good education.*
– ORIGIN mid 18th cent. (in the sense 'keep short of food'): from Scots *scrimp* 'meagre'; perhaps related to SHRIMP.

scrimshander /ˈskrɪm,ʃandə/ ▶ verb another term for SCRIMSHAW.
▶ noun a person who makes scrimshaws.
– ORIGIN mid 19th cent.: from a variant of SCRIMSHAW + -ER[1].

scrimshank /ˈskrɪmʃaŋk/ ▶ verb [no obj.] Brit. informal (especially of a person in the armed services) shirk one's duty.
– ORIGIN late 19th cent.: of unknown origin.

scrimshaw ▶ verb [with obj.] adorn ivory or shells with carved or coloured designs.
▶ noun [mass noun] scrimshawed ivory or shells.
– ORIGIN early 19th cent.: of unknown origin; perhaps influenced by the surname *Scrimshaw*.

scrip[1] ▶ noun **1** a provisional certificate of money subscribed to a bank or company, entitling the holder to a formal certificate and dividends. ■ [mass noun] scrip certificates collectively. ■ (also **scrip issue** or **dividend**) an issue of additional shares to shareholders in proportion to the shares already held.
2 (also **land scrip**) N. Amer. a certificate entitling the holder to acquire possession of certain portions of public land.
3 [mass noun] N. Amer. historical paper money in amounts of less than a dollar.
– ORIGIN mid 18th cent.: abbreviation of *subscription receipt*.

scrip[2] ▶ noun historical a small bag or pouch, typically one carried by a pilgrim, shepherd, or beggar.
– ORIGIN Middle English: probably a shortening of Old French *escrepe* 'purse'.

scrip[3] ▶ noun another term for SCRIPT[2].

scripophily /skrɪˈpɒfɪli/ ▶ noun [mass noun] the collection of old bond and share certificates as a pursuit or hobby. ■ old bond and share certificates collectively.
– ORIGIN 1970s: from SCRIP[1] + -PHILY.

script[1] ▶ noun **1** [mass noun] handwriting as distinct from print; written characters: *her neat, tidy script.* ■ printed type imitating handwriting. ■ [with adj.] writing using a particular alphabet: *Russian script.*
2 the written text of a play, film, or broadcast.
■ Computing an automated series of instructions carried out in a specific order.
3 Brit. a candidate's written answers in an examination.
▶ verb [with obj.] write a script for (a play, film, or broadcast).
– ORIGIN late Middle English (in the sense 'something written'): shortening of Old French *escript*, from Latin *scriptum*, neuter past participle (used as a noun) of *scribere* 'write'.

script[2] ▶ noun informal a doctor's prescription, especially one for narcotic drugs.
– ORIGIN 1950s: abbreviation.

script kiddie ▶ noun informal, derogatory a person who uses existing computer scripts or codes to hack into computers, lacking the expertise to write their own.

scriptorial ▶ adjective rare relating to writing.

scriptorium /skrɪpˈtɔːrɪəm/ ▶ noun (pl. **scriptoria** /-rɪə/ or **scriptoriums**) chiefly historical a room set apart for writing, especially one in a monastery where manuscripts were copied.
– ORIGIN late 18th cent.: from medieval Latin, from Latin *script-* 'written', from the verb *scribere*.

scriptural ▶ adjective from or relating to the Bible: *scriptural quotations from Genesis.*
– DERIVATIVES **scripturally** adverb.
– ORIGIN mid 17th cent.: from late Latin *scripturalis*, from Latin *scriptura* 'writings' (see SCRIPTURE).

scripture /ˈskrɪptʃə/ ▶ noun [mass noun] (also **scriptures**) the sacred writings of Christianity contained in the Bible: *passages of scripture | the fundamental teachings of the scriptures.* ■ the sacred writings of a religion other than Christianity.
– ORIGIN Middle English: from Latin *scriptura* 'writings', from *script-* 'written', from the verb *scribere*.

scriptwriter ▶ noun a person who writes a script for a play, film, or broadcast.
– DERIVATIVES **scriptwriting** noun.

scrivener /ˈskrɪv(ə)nə/ ▶ noun historical **1** a clerk, scribe, or notary.
2 a person who invested money at interest for clients and lent funds to those who wanted to raise money on security.
– ORIGIN Middle English (in sense 1): shortening of Old French *escrivein*, from Latin *scriba* (see SCRIBE). Sense 2 dates from the early 17th cent.

scrod /skrɒd/ ▶ noun N. Amer. a young cod, haddock, or similar fish, especially one prepared for cooking.
– ORIGIN mid 19th cent.: of unknown origin.

scrofula /ˈskrɒfjʊlə/ ▶ noun [mass noun] chiefly historical a disease with glandular swellings, probably a form of tuberculosis. Also formerly called KING'S EVIL.
– DERIVATIVES **scrofulous** adjective.
– ORIGIN late Middle English: from medieval Latin, diminutive of Latin *scrofa* 'breeding sow' (said to be subject to the disease).

scroggin ▶ noun [mass noun] Austral./NZ a mixture of dried fruit, nuts, and other food eaten as a snack by hikers.
– ORIGIN 1940s: of unknown origin.

scroll ▶ noun **1** a roll of parchment or paper for writing on. ■ an ancient book or document written on a scroll. ■ an ornamental design or carving resembling a partly unrolled scroll of parchment, e.g. on the capital of a column, or at the end of a stringed instrument. ■ Art & Heraldry a depiction of a narrow ribbon bearing a motto or inscription.
2 [mass noun] [usu. as modifier] the facility which moves a display on a computer screen in order to view new material.
▶ verb **1** [no obj., with adverbial] move displayed text or graphics in a particular direction on a computer screen in order to view different parts of them: *she scrolled through her file.* ■ (of displayed text or graphics) move up, down, or across a computer screen.
2 [with obj.] cause to move like paper rolling or unrolling: *the wind **scrolled back** the uppermost layer of loose dust.*
– DERIVATIVES **scrollable** adjective.
– ORIGIN late Middle English: alteration of obsolete *scrow* 'roll', shortening of ESCROW.

scroll bar ▶ noun a long thin section at the edge of a computer display by which material can be scrolled using a mouse.

scrolled ▶ adjective having an ornamental design or carving resembling a scroll of parchment.

scroller ▶ noun **1** a computer game in which the background scrolls past at a constant rate.
2 another term for SCROLL SAW.

scrolling ▶ noun [mass noun] the action of moving displayed text or graphics up, down, or across on a computer screen in order to view different parts of them.
▶ adjective [attrib.] (of an ornamental design or carving) made to resemble a partly unrolled scroll of parchment.

scroll saw ▶ noun a narrow-bladed saw for cutting decorative spiral lines or patterns.

scrollwork ▶ noun [mass noun] decoration consisting of spiral lines or patterns, especially as cut by a scroll saw.

scrooch ▶ verb [no obj.] informal, chiefly US crouch; bend.
– ORIGIN mid 19th cent.: dialect variant of US *scrouge* 'squeeze, crowd', perhaps reinforced by the verb CROUCH.

Scrooge, Ebenezer, a miserly curmudgeon in Charles Dickens's novel *A Christmas Carol* (1843). ■ (as noun **a Scrooge**) a person who is mean with money.

scrote ▶ noun Brit. informal a contemptible person.
– ORIGIN 1970s: from SCROTUM.

scrotum /ˈskrəʊtəm/ ▶ noun (pl. **scrota** /-tə/ or **scrotums**) a pouch of skin containing the testicles.
– DERIVATIVES **scrotal** adjective.
– ORIGIN late 16th cent.: from Latin.

scrounge informal ▶ verb [with obj.] seek to obtain (something, typically food or money) at the expense or through the generosity of others or by stealth: *he had managed to scrounge a free meal* | [no obj.] *we didn't scrounge off the social security.* ■ (often **scrounge something up**) N. Amer. search for or obtain by searching.
▶ noun [in sing.] an act of scrounging.
– PHRASES **on the scrounge** Brit. engaged in scrounging.
– ORIGIN early 20th cent.: variant of dialect *scrunge* 'steal'.

scrounger ▶ noun informal, derogatory a person who borrows from or lives off others.

scrub[1] ▶ verb (**scrubs, scrubbing, scrubbed**) [with obj.] **1** rub (someone or something) hard so as to clean them, typically with a brush and water: *he had to scrub the floor | she was **scrubbing herself down** at the sink* | [no obj.] *she **scrubbed** furiously **at** the plates.* ■ (**scrub something away/off**) remove dirt by rubbing hard: *it took ages to scrub off the muck.* ■ [no obj.] (**scrub up**) thoroughly clean one's hands and arms before performing surgery: *the doctor scrubbed up and donned a protective gown.* ■ [no obj.] (**scrub up well**) Brit. informal (of a person) have a smart and well-groomed appearance after making a deliberate effort: *the band scrub up well to play weddings and parties.*
2 informal cancel or abandon (something): *the first two races had to be scrubbed because of blustery winds and rough seas.*
3 use water to remove impurities from (gas or vapour).
4 Motor Racing (of a driver) allow (a tyre) to slide or scrape across the road surface so as to reduce speed. ■ (of a driver) reduce (speed) by allowing the tyres to slide or scrape across the road surface.
5 [no obj.] (of a rider) rub the arms and legs urgently on a horse's neck and flanks to urge it to move faster.
▶ noun **1** an act of scrubbing something or someone: ***give the floor a good scrub.***
2 a semi-abrasive cosmetic lotion applied to the face or body in order to cleanse the skin.
3 (**scrubs**) special hygienic clothing worn by surgeons during operations.
– ORIGIN late 16th cent.: probably from Middle Low German, Middle Dutch *schrobben, schrubben*.

scrub[2] ▶ noun **1** [mass noun] vegetation consisting mainly of brushwood or stunted forest growth. ■ (also **scrubs**) land covered with scrub vegetation.
2 [as modifier] denoting a shrubby or small form of a plant: *scrub apple trees.* ■ N. Amer. denoting an animal of inferior breed or physique: *a scrub bull.*
3 informal an insignificant or contemptible person.
■ N. Amer. a sports team or player not among the best or most skilled. ■ short for SCRUBBER (sense 2).
4 [mass noun] N. Amer. an informal team game played by children in a public area.
– DERIVATIVES **scrubby** adjective (**scrubbier, scrubbiest**).
– ORIGIN late Middle English (in the sense 'stunted tree'): variant of SHRUB[1].

scrubber ▶ noun **1** a brush or other object used to clean something. ■ a person who cleans something.
■ an apparatus using water or a solution for purifying gases or vapours.
2 Brit. informal, derogatory a promiscuous woman.
3 Austral./NZ an animal which lives in the scrub.
■ informal a person of unkempt appearance.

scrubbing brush (N. Amer. **scrub brush**) ▶ noun a hard brush for scrubbing floors.

scrub-bird ▶ noun a secretive Australian songbird with mainly brown plumage and a long tail, now rare. ● Family Atrichornithidae and genus *Atrichornis*: two species.

scrubfowl ▶ noun a small megapode with a short tail, typically having brown and grey plumage. ● Genera *Megapodius* and *Eulipoa*, family Megapodiidae: several species.

scrubland ▶ noun [mass noun] (also **scrublands**) land consisting of scrub vegetation.

scrub nurse ▶ noun a nurse who handles sterile equipment while assisting a surgeon during a surgical operation.

scrub oak ▶ noun N. Amer. a shrubby dwarf oak which forms thickets. ● Genus *Quercus*, family Fagaceae: several species, in particular *Q. ilicifolia*.

scrub suit ▶ noun N. Amer. a garment worn by surgeons and other theatre staff while performing or assisting at an operation.

scrub-turkey ▶ noun another term for BRUSH-TURKEY.

scrub typhus ▶ noun [mass noun] a rickettsial disease transmitted to humans by mites and found in parts of eastern Asia. Also called TSUTSUGAMUSHI DISEASE.

scrub wallaby ▶ noun another term for PADEMELON.

scruff[1] ▶ noun the back of a person's or animal's neck: *he grabbed him **by the scruff of** his **neck**.*
▶ verb [with obj.] grasp (an animal) by the scruff of its neck.
– ORIGIN late 18th cent.: alteration of dialect *scuff*, of obscure origin.

scruff[2] ▶ noun Brit. informal a person with a dirty or untidy appearance.

S

– ORIGIN early 16th cent. (in the sense 'scurf'): variant of **SCURF**. The word came to mean 'worthless thing', whence the current sense (mid 19th cent.).

scruffy ▶ adjective (**scruffier**, **scruffiest**) shabby and untidy or dirty: *a teenager in scruffy jeans and a baggy T-shirt.*
– DERIVATIVES **scruffily** adverb, **scruffiness** noun.

scrum ▶ noun Rugby an ordered formation of players, used to restart play, in which the forwards of a team form up with arms interlocked and heads down, and push forward against a similar group from the opposing side. The ball is thrown into the scrum and the players try to gain possession of it by kicking it backwards towards their own side. ■ Brit. informal a disorderly crowd of people or things: *there was quite a scrum of people at the bar.*
▶ verb (**scrums**, **scrumming**, **scrummed**) [no obj.] Rugby form or take part in a scrum. ■ informal jostle; crowd: *everyone was **scrumming around** behind him.*
– ORIGIN late 19th cent.: abbreviation of **SCRUMMAGE**.

scrum half ▶ noun Rugby a half back who puts the ball into the scrum and stands ready to receive it again.

scrummage ▶ noun & verb another term for **SCRUM**.
– DERIVATIVES **scrummager** noun.
– ORIGIN early 19th cent.: variant of **SCRIMMAGE**.

scrummy ▶ adjective (**scrummier**, **scrummiest**) informal delicious.
– ORIGIN early 20th cent.: from **SCRUMPTIOUS** + **-Y**[1].

scrump ▶ verb [with obj.] Brit. informal steal (fruit) from an orchard or garden.
– ORIGIN mid 19th cent.: from dialect *scrump* 'withered apple'.

scrumple ▶ verb [with obj.] Brit. crumple (paper or cloth): *she **scrumpled it up** and tossed it into the waste-paper basket.*
– ORIGIN early 16th cent.: alteration of **CRUMPLE**.

scrumptious ▶ adjective informal (of food) extremely appetizing or delicious. ■ (of a person) very attractive.
– DERIVATIVES **scrumptiously** adverb, **scrumptiousness** noun.
– ORIGIN mid 19th cent.: of unknown origin.

scrumpy ▶ noun [mass noun] Brit. rough strong cider, especially as made in the West Country of England.
– ORIGIN early 20th cent.: from dialect *scrump* 'withered apple'.

scrunch ▶ verb [no obj.] make a loud crunching noise: *crisp yellow leaves scrunched satisfyingly underfoot.* ■ [with obj. and adverbial] crush or squeeze (something) into a compact mass: *Flora scrunched the handkerchief into a ball.* ■ [no obj., with adverbial] become crushed or squeezed into a compact mass: *their faces **scrunch up** with concentration.* ■ [with obj.] style (hair) by squeezing or crushing it in the hands to give a tousled look.
▶ noun [in sing.] a loud crunching noise: *Charlotte heard the scrunch of boots on gravel.*
– ORIGIN late 18th cent. (in the sense 'eat or bite noisily'): probably imitative; compare with **CRUNCH**.

scrunch-dry ▶ verb [with obj.] dry (hair) while scrunching it to give a tousled look.

scrunchy ▶ adjective (**scrunchier**, **scrunchiest**) making a loud crunching noise when crushed or compressed: *scrunchy snow.*
▶ noun (also **scrunchie**) (pl. **scrunchies**) a circular band of fabric-covered elastic used for fastening the hair.

S

scruple ▶ noun **1** (usu. **scruples**) a feeling of doubt or hesitation with regard to the morality or propriety of a course of action: *I **had no scruples about** eavesdropping* | [mass noun] *without scruple, politicians use fear as a persuasion weapon.*
2 historical a unit of weight equal to 20 grains, used by apothecaries. ■ archaic a very small amount of something, especially a quality.
▶ verb [no obj., with infinitive] [usu. with negative] hesitate or be reluctant to do something that one thinks may be wrong: *she doesn't scruple to ask her parents for money.*
– ORIGIN late Middle English: from French *scrupule* or Latin *scrupulus*, from *scrupus*, literally 'rough pebble', (figuratively) 'anxiety'.

scrupulous ▶ adjective (of a person or process) diligent, thorough, and extremely attentive to details: *the research has been carried out with scrupulous attention to detail.* ■ very concerned to avoid doing wrong: *she's too scrupulous to have an affair with a married man.*
– DERIVATIVES **scrupulosity** noun, **scrupulously** adverb [as submodifier] *she was scrupulously polite*, **scrupulousness** noun.
– ORIGIN late Middle English (in the sense 'troubled with doubts'): from French *scrupuleux* or Latin *scrupulosus*, from *scrupulus* (see **SCRUPLE**).

scrutator /skruːˈteɪtə/ ▶ noun a person whose official duty it is to examine or investigate something. ■ historical a university official responsible for examining votes at university elections and announcing the result.
– ORIGIN late 16th cent.: from Latin, from *scrutari* 'search, examine'.

scrutineer ▶ noun a person who examines or inspects something closely and thoroughly. ■ chiefly Brit. a person who supervises the conduct of an election or competition.

scrutinize (also **scrutinise**) ▶ verb [with obj.] examine or inspect closely and thoroughly: *customers were warned to scrutinize the small print.*
– DERIVATIVES **scrutinization** noun, **scrutinizer** noun.

scrutiny ▶ noun (pl. **scrutinies**) [mass noun] critical observation or examination: *every aspect of local government was placed **under scrutiny**.*
– ORIGIN late Middle English: from Latin *scrutinium*, from *scrutari* 'to search' (originally 'sort rubbish', from *scruta* 'rubbish'). Early use referred to the taking of individual votes in an election procedure.

scry /skrʌɪ/ ▶ verb (**scries**, **scrying**, **scried**) [no obj.] foretell the future using a crystal ball or other reflective object or surface.
– DERIVATIVES **scryer** noun.
– ORIGIN early 16th cent.: shortening of **DESCRY**.

SCSI ▶ abbreviation Computing small computer system interface, a standard for connecting computers and their peripherals together.

scuba /ˈskuːbə, ˈskjuːbə/ ▶ noun an aqualung. ■ [mass noun] scuba diving.
– ORIGIN 1950s: acronym from *self-contained underwater breathing apparatus.*

scuba diving ▶ noun [mass noun] the sport or pastime of swimming underwater using a scuba.
– DERIVATIVES **scuba-dive** verb, **scuba diver** noun.

scud[1] ▶ verb (**scuds**, **scudding**, **scudded**) **1** [no obj., with adverbial of direction] move fast in a straight line because or as if driven by the wind: *we lie watching the clouds **scudding across the sky** | three small ships were **scudding before** a brisk breeze.*
2 [with obj.] chiefly Scottish slap, beat, or spank: *she scudded me across the head.*
▶ noun **1** chiefly literary a mass of vapoury clouds or spray driven fast by the wind. ■ a driving shower of rain or snow; a gust. ■ [mass noun] the action of moving fast in a straight line when driven by the wind: *the scud of the clouds before the wind.*
2 (**Scud** or **Scud missile**) a type of long-range surface-to-surface guided missile able to be fired from a mobile launcher. [a code name assigned by NATO to a series of such missiles developed by the former Soviet Union.]
– ORIGIN mid 16th cent. (as a verb): perhaps an alteration of the noun **SCUT**[1], thus reflecting the sense 'race like a hare'.

scud[2] ▶ noun (in phrase **in the scud** or **scuddy**) Scottish (of a person) naked.
– DERIVATIVES **scuddy** adjective.
– ORIGIN early 19th cent.: of uncertain origin.

scudo /ˈskuːdəʊ/ ▶ noun (pl. **scudi** /-di/) historical a coin, typically made of silver, formerly used in various Italian states.
– ORIGIN Italian, from Latin *scutum* 'shield'.

scuff ▶ verb [with obj.] scrape or brush the surface of (a shoe or other object) against something: *I accidentally scuffed the heel of one shoe on a paving stone.* ■ mark (a surface) by scraping or brushing it, especially with one's shoes: *the lino on the floor was scuffed.* ■ [no obj.] (of an object or surface) become marked by scraping or brushing: *for kids who play rough, shoes that won't scuff.* ■ drag (one's feet or heels) when walking: *he scuffed his feet boyishly.* ■ [no obj., with adverbial of direction] walk while dragging one's feet or heels: *she scuffed along in her carpet slippers.*
▶ noun a mark made by scraping or grazing a surface or object: *dark colours don't show scuffs.*
– ORIGIN early 18th cent.: perhaps of imitative origin.

scuffle ▶ noun **1** a short, confused fight or struggle at close quarters: *there were minor **scuffles with** police.*
2 an act or sound of moving in a hurried, confused, or shuffling manner: *he heard the scuffle of feet.*
▶ verb [no obj.] **1** engage in a short, confused fight or struggle at close quarters: *the teacher noticed two pupils scuffling in the corridor.*
2 [with adverbial of direction] move in a hurried, confused, or awkward way, making a rustling or shuffling sound: *a drenched woman scuffled through the doorway.* ■ [with obj.] (of an animal or person) move (something) in a scrambling or confused manner: *the rabbit struggled free, scuffling his front paws.*
– ORIGIN late 16th cent. (as a verb): probably of Scandinavian origin; compare with Swedish *skuffa* 'to push'; related to **SHOVE** and **SHUFFLE**.

scull[1] ▶ noun each of a pair of small oars used by a single rower. ■ an oar placed over the stern of a boat to propel it by a side to side motion, reversing the blade at each turn. ■ a light, narrow boat propelled with a scull or a pair of sculls. ■ (**sculls**) a race between boats in which each participant uses a pair of oars.
▶ verb [no obj.] propel a boat with sculls. ■ [with obj. and adverbial of direction] transport (someone) in a boat propelled with sculls. ■ [no obj., with adverbial of direction] (of an aquatic animal) propel itself with fins or flippers.
– ORIGIN Middle English: of unknown origin.

scull[2] ▶ noun Canadian a large group of fish which has migrated from the open sea to inshore waters. ■ the season when this happens.
– ORIGIN variant of **SCHOOL**[2].

scullcap ▶ noun variant spelling of **SKULLCAP** (sense 3).

sculler /ˈskʌlə/ ▶ noun a person who sculls a boat. ■ a boat propelled with a scull or pair of sculls.

scullery /ˈskʌl(ə)ri/ ▶ noun (pl. **sculleries**) chiefly historical a small kitchen or room at the back of a house used for washing dishes and other dirty household work.
– ORIGIN late Middle English (denoting the department of a household concerned with kitchen utensils): from Old French *escuelerie*, from *escuele* 'dish', from Latin *scutella* 'salver', diminutive of *scutra* 'wooden platter'.

scullion ▶ noun archaic a servant assigned the most menial kitchen tasks.
– ORIGIN late 15th cent.: of unknown origin but perhaps influenced by **SCULLERY**.

sculpin /ˈskʌlpɪn/ ▶ noun a chiefly marine fish of the northern hemisphere, with a broad flattened head and spiny scales and fins. ● Cottidae and related families: many genera and numerous species, including the bullheads.
– ORIGIN late 17th cent.: perhaps from obsolete *scorpene*, via Latin from Greek *skorpaina*, denoting a kind of fish.

sculpt (also **sculp**) ▶ verb [with obj.] create or represent (something) by carving, casting, or other shaping techniques: *sculpting human figures from ivory* | [no obj.] *she was teaching him how to sculpt.*
– ORIGIN mid 19th cent.: from French *sculpter*, from *sculpteur* 'sculptor'; later regarded as a back-formation from **SCULPTOR** or **SCULPTURE**.

Sculptor /ˈskʌlptə/ Astronomy a faint southern constellation (the Sculptor or Sculptor's Workshop), between Grus and Cetus.
– ORIGIN Latin.

sculptor ▶ noun an artist who makes sculptures.
– ORIGIN mid 17th cent.: from Latin, from *sculpt-* 'hollowed out', from the verb *sculpere*.

sculptress ▶ noun a female artist who makes sculptures.

sculptural ▶ adjective relating to or resembling sculpture: *sculptural decoration* | *sculptural works.*
– DERIVATIVES **sculpturally** adverb.

sculpture ▶ noun [mass noun] the art of making two- or three-dimensional representative or abstract forms, especially by carving stone or wood or by casting metal or plaster. ■ [count noun] a work of art made by sculpture: *a bronze sculpture* | [mass noun] *a collection of sculpture.* ■ Zoology & Botany raised or sunken patterns or texture on the surface of a shell, pollen grain, cuticle, or other biological specimen.
▶ verb [with obj.] make or represent (a form) by carving, casting, or other shaping techniques: *the choir stalls were each carefully sculptured.* ■ form or shape as if by sculpture, especially with strong, smooth curves: (as adj. **sculptured**) *he had an aquiline nose and sculptured lips.*
– ORIGIN late Middle English: from Latin *sculptura*, from *sculpere* 'carve'.

sculpturesque ▶ adjective old-fashioned term for **SCULPTURAL**.

sculpturing ▶ noun [mass noun] the action of forming or shaping something by or as if by sculpture: *the gadget is great for blow-drying, sculpturing, and moulding.* ■ a shape or outline produced by or as if by sculpture: *the mountain's graceful sculpturing.* ■ Zoology & Botany sculpture: *the external sculpturing consists of a series of corrugations.*

scum ▶ **noun** [mass noun] a layer of dirt or froth on the surface of a liquid: *green scum found on stagnant pools.* ■ informal a worthless or contemptible person or group of people: *you drug dealers are the scum of the earth.*
▶ **verb (scums, scumming, scummed)** [with obj.] form a layer of dirt or froth on (a liquid): *litter scummed the surface of the water.* ■ [no obj.] (of a liquid) become covered with a layer of dirt or froth: *the lagoon scummed over.*
– DERIVATIVES **scummy adjective (scummier, scummiest)**.
– ORIGIN Middle English: from Middle Low German, Middle Dutch *schūm*, of Germanic origin.

scumbag ▶ **noun** informal a contemptible or objectionable person.

scumble /'skʌmb(ə)l/ Art ▶ **verb** [with obj.] modify (a painting or colour) by applying a very thin coat of opaque paint to give a softer or duller effect. ■ modify (a drawing) with light shading in pencil or charcoal to give a softer effect.
▶ **noun** a thin, opaque coat of paint or layer of shading applied to give a softer or duller effect. ■ the effect produced by scumbling.
– ORIGIN late 17th cent. (as a verb): perhaps a frequentative of the verb SCUM.

scuncheon /'skʌn(t)ʃ(ə)n/ ▶ **noun** the inside face of a door jamb or window frame.
– ORIGIN Middle English: shortening of Old French *escoinson*, based on *coin* 'corner'.

scunge ▶ **noun** Austral./NZ informal dirt; scum: *this glass has scunge on it.* ■ a disagreeable person. ■ a person who is mean with money; a scrounger.
– ORIGIN early 19th cent. (originally Scots in the sense 'scrounger'): of unknown origin; compare with the verb SCROUNGE.

scungille /skʊn'dʒiːleɪ, -li/ (also **scungile**) ▶ **noun** (pl. **scungilli** /-li/) a mollusc (especially with reference to its meat eaten as a delicacy).
– ORIGIN from Italian dialect *scunciglio*, probably an alteration of Italian *conchiglia* 'seashell'.

scungy ▶ **adjective (scungier, scungiest)** Austral./NZ informal dirty and disagreeable.

scunner chiefly Scottish ▶ **noun** a strong dislike: *why have you a scunner against Esme?* ■ a source of irritation or strong dislike.
▶ **verb** [no obj.] feel disgust or strong dislike.
– ORIGIN late Middle English (first used in the sense 'shrink back with fear'): of unknown origin.

Scunthorpe /'skʌnθɔːp/ an industrial town in NE England, in North Lincolnshire; pop. 74,800 (est. 2009).

scup ▶ **noun** (pl. **same**) a common porgy (fish) with faint dark vertical bars, occurring off the coasts of the north-west Atlantic. ● *Stenotomus chrysops*, family Sparidae.
– ORIGIN mid 19th cent.: from Narragansett *mishcup*, from *mishe* 'big' + *cuppi* 'close together' (because of the shape of the scales).

scupper¹ ▶ **noun** (usu. **scuppers**) a hole in a ship's side to carry water overboard from the deck. ■ an outlet in the side of a building for draining water.
– ORIGIN late Middle English: perhaps via Anglo-Norman French from Old French *escopir* 'to spit'; compare with German *Speigatt*, literally 'spit hole'.

scupper² ▶ **verb** [with obj.] **1** chiefly Brit. sink (a ship or its crew) deliberately.
2 informal prevent from working or succeeding; thwart: *plans for a bypass were scuppered by a public inquiry.*
– ORIGIN late 19th cent. (as military slang in the sense 'kill, especially in an ambush'): of unknown origin. The sense 'sink' dates from the 1970s.

scuppernong /'skʌpəˌnɒŋ/ ▶ **noun** [mass noun] a variety of the muscadine grape native to the basin of the Scuppernong River in North Carolina. ■ wine made from the scuppernong grape.

scurf ▶ **noun** [mass noun] flakes on the surface of the skin that form as fresh skin develops below, occurring especially as dandruff. ■ a flaky deposit on a plant resulting from a fungal infection.
– DERIVATIVES **scurfy adjective**.
– ORIGIN late Old English *sceorf*, from the base of *sceorfan* 'gnaw', *sceorfian* 'cut to shreds'.

scurrility /skə'rɪlɪti/ ▶ **noun** (pl. **scurrilities**) [mass noun] the quality of being scurrilous: *a mixture of humour and mild scurrility.*

scurrilous /'skʌrɪləs/ ▶ **adjective** making or spreading scandalous claims about someone with the intention of damaging their reputation: *a scurrilous attack on his integrity.* ■ humorously insulting: *a very funny collection of bawdy and scurrilous writings.*
– DERIVATIVES **scurrilously adverb, scurrilousness noun.**
– ORIGIN late 16th cent.: from French *scurrile* or Latin *scurrilus* (from *scurra* 'buffoon') + **-ous**.

scurry ▶ **verb (scurries, scurrying, scurried)** [no obj., with adverbial of direction] (of a person or small animal) move hurriedly with short quick steps: *pedestrians scurried for cover.*
▶ **noun** [in sing.] **1** a situation of hurried and confused movement: *I was in such a scurry.*
2 a flurry of rain or snow.
– ORIGIN early 19th cent.: abbreviation of *hurry-scurry*, reduplication of HURRY.

scurvy ▶ **noun** [mass noun] a disease caused by a deficiency of vitamin C, characterized by swollen bleeding gums and the opening of previously healed wounds, which particularly affected poorly nourished sailors until the end of the 18th century.
▶ **adjective (scurvier, scurviest)** archaic worthless or contemptible: *that was a scurvy trick.*
– DERIVATIVES **scurvily adverb**.
– ORIGIN late Middle English (as an adjective meaning 'scurfy'): from SCURF + -Y¹. The noun use (mid 16th cent.) is by association with French *scorbut* (see SCORBUTIC).

scurvy grass ▶ **noun** [mass noun] a small cress-like European plant with fleshy tar-flavoured leaves, growing near the sea. It is rich in vitamin C and was formerly eaten, especially by sailors, to prevent scurvy. ● Genus *Cochlearia*, family Cruciferae: several species, in particular *C. officinalis*.

scut¹ ▶ **noun** the short tail of a hare, rabbit, or deer.
– ORIGIN late Middle English: of unknown origin; compare with obsolete *scut* 'short', also 'shorten'.

scut² ▶ **noun** informal, chiefly Irish a person perceived as foolish, contemptible, or objectionable.
– ORIGIN late 19th cent.: of unknown origin.

scuta plural form of SCUTUM.

scutage /'skjuːtɪdʒ/ ▶ **noun** [mass noun] (in a feudal society) money paid by a vassal to his lord in lieu of military service.
– ORIGIN late Middle English: from medieval Latin *scutagium*, from Latin *scutum* 'shield'.

Scutari /skuː'tɑːri/ **1** a former name for Üsküdar near Istanbul, site of a British army hospital in which Florence Nightingale worked during the Crimean War.
2 /sku'tari/ Italian name for SHKODËR.

scutch /skʌtʃ/ ▶ **verb** [with obj.] dress (fibrous material, especially retted flax) by beating it.
– DERIVATIVES **scutcher noun**.
– ORIGIN mid 18th cent.: from obsolete French *escoucher*, from Latin *excutere* 'shake out'.

scutcheon ▶ **noun** archaic spelling of ESCUTCHEON.

scute /skjuːt/ ▶ **noun** Zoology a thickened horny or bony plate on a turtle's shell or on the back of a crocodile, stegosaurus, etc.
– ORIGIN Middle English (denoting a coin): from Latin SCUTUM.

scutellum /skjʊ'tɛləm/ ▶ **noun** (pl. **scutella** /-lə/) Botany & Zoology a small shield-like structure, in particular: ■ a modified cotyledon in the embryo of a grass seed. ■ the third dorsal sclerite in each thoracic segment of an insect.
– DERIVATIVES **scutellar adjective**.
– ORIGIN mid 18th cent.: modern Latin, diminutive of Latin *scutum* 'shield'.

scutter chiefly Brit. ▶ **verb** [no obj., with adverbial of direction] (especially of a small animal) move hurriedly with short steps: *a little dog scuttered up from the cabin.*
▶ **noun** [in sing.] an act or sound of scuttering.

scuttle¹ ▶ **noun 1** a metal container with a handle, used to fetch and store coal for a domestic fire. ■ the amount of coal held in a scuttle: *carrying endless scuttles of coal up from the cellar.*
2 Brit. the part of a car's bodywork between the windscreen and the bonnet.
– ORIGIN late Old English *scutel* 'dish, platter', from Old Norse *skutill*, from Latin *scutella* 'dish'.

scuttle² ▶ **verb** [no obj., with adverbial of direction] run hurriedly or furtively with short quick steps: *a mouse scuttled across the floor.*
▶ **noun** [in sing.] an act or sound of scuttling: *I heard the scuttle of rats across the room.*
– ORIGIN late 15th cent.: compare with dialect *scuddle*, frequentative of SCUD¹.

scuttle³ ▶ **verb** [with obj.] **1** sink (one's own ship) deliberately by holing it or opening its seacocks to let water in.
2 deliberately cause (a scheme) to fail: *some of the stockholders are threatening to scuttle the deal.*
▶ **noun** an opening with a cover in a ship's deck or side.
– ORIGIN late 15th cent. (as a noun): perhaps from Old French *escoutille*, from the Spanish diminutive *escotilla* 'hatchway'. The verb dates from the mid 17th cent.

scuttlebutt ▶ **noun** [mass noun] N. Amer. informal rumour; gossip: *the scuttlebutt had it that he was a government spy.*
– ORIGIN early 19th cent. (denoting a water butt on the deck of a ship, providing drinking water): from *scuttled butt*.

Scutum /'skjuːtəm/ Astronomy a small constellation near the celestial equator (the Shield), lying in the Milky Way between Aquila and Serpens.
– ORIGIN Latin.

scutum /'skjuːtəm/ ▶ **noun** (pl. **scuta** /-tə/) Zoology another term for SCUTE. ■ Entomology the second dorsal sclerite in each thoracic segment of an insect.
– ORIGIN late 18th cent.: from Latin, literally 'oblong shield'.

scutwork ▶ **noun** [mass noun] informal, chiefly US tedious, menial work.
– ORIGIN 1970s: of unknown origin, compare with SCUT².

scuzz ▶ **noun** [mass noun] informal something regarded as disgusting or sordid: *you can whip all the scuzz into the spare room and shut the door.*
– ORIGIN 1960s: probably an informal abbreviation of DISGUSTING.

scuzzball (also **scuzzbag**) ▶ **noun** informal, chiefly N. Amer. a despicable or disgusting person.

scuzzy ▶ **adjective (scuzzier, scuzziest)** informal dirty and unpleasant: *a scuzzy flat | scuzzy sheets.*

Scylla /'sɪlə/ Greek Mythology a female sea monster who devoured sailors when they tried to navigate the narrow channel between her cave and the whirlpool Charybdis. In later legend Scylla was a dangerous rock, located on the Italian side of the Strait of Messina.
– PHRASES **Scylla and Charybdis** used to refer to a situation involving two dangers in which an attempt to avoid one increases the risk from the other.

scyphistoma /sʌɪ'fɪstəmə, skʌɪ-, skɪ-/ ▶ **noun** (pl. **scyphistomae** /-miː/ or **scyphistomas**) Zoology the fixed polyp-like stage in the life cycle of a jellyfish, which reproduces asexually by budding (strobilation).
– ORIGIN late 19th cent.: from Latin *scyphus* 'cup' + Greek *stoma* 'mouth'.

Scyphozoa /ˌsʌɪfə'zəʊə, ˌskʌɪf-, ˌskɪf-/ ▶ **plural noun** Zoology a class of marine coelenterates which comprises the jellyfishes.
– DERIVATIVES **scyphozoan noun & adjective**.
– ORIGIN modern Latin (plural), from Greek *skuphos* 'drinking cup' + Greek *zōion* 'animal'.

scythe ▶ **noun** a tool used for cutting crops such as grass or corn, with a long curved blade at the end of a long pole attached to one or two short handles.
▶ **verb** [with obj.] cut with a scythe. ■ [no obj., with adverbial] move through or penetrate something rapidly and forcefully: *attacking players can scythe through defences.*
– ORIGIN Old English *sīthe*, of Germanic origin; related to Dutch *zeis* and German *Sense*.

Scythia /'sɪðɪə/ an ancient region of SE Europe and Asia. The Scythian empire, which existed between the 8th and 2nd centuries BC, was centred on the northern shores of the Black Sea and extended from southern Russia to the borders of Persia.
– DERIVATIVES **Scythian adjective & noun**.

SD ▶ **abbreviation** ■ South Dakota (in official postal use). ■ Swaziland (international vehicle registration).

S. Dak. ▶ **abbreviation** South Dakota.

SDI ▶ **abbreviation** Strategic Defense Initiative.

SDLP ▶ **abbreviation** (in Northern Ireland) Social Democratic and Labour Party.

SDP ▶ **abbreviation** historical (in the UK) Social Democratic Party.

SDR ▶ **abbreviation** special drawing right (from the International Monetary Fund).

SE ▶ **abbreviation** south-east or south-eastern.

Se ▶ **symbol** the chemical element selenium.

se- ▶ prefix in words adopted from Latin originally meaning 'apart' (as in *separate*) or meaning 'without' (as in *secure*).
– ORIGIN from Latin *se-*, from the earlier preposition and adverb *se*.

SEA ▶ abbreviation Single European Act.

sea ▶ noun (often **the sea**) the expanse of salt water that covers most of the earth's surface and surrounds its land masses: *a ban on dumping radioactive wastes in the sea* | [as count noun] *the seas today swarm with crustacean arthropods.* ■ [often in place names] a roughly definable area of the sea: *the Black Sea.* ■ **(seas)** large waves: *the lifeboat met seas of thirty-five feet head-on.* ■ [count noun] a vast expanse or quantity of something: *she scanned the sea of faces for Stephen.*
– PHRASES **at sea** sailing on the sea. ■ (also **all at sea**) confused or unable to decide what to do: *he feels at sea with economics.* **by sea** by means of a ship or ships: *other army units were sent by sea.* **go to sea** set out on a voyage. ■ become a sailor in a navy or a merchant navy. **on the sea** situated on the coast. **put (out) to sea** leave land on a voyage.
– ORIGIN Old English *sǣ*, of Germanic origin; related to Dutch *zee* and German *See*.

sea anchor ▶ noun an object dragged in the water behind a boat in order to keep its bows pointing into the waves or to lessen leeway.

sea anemone ▶ noun a sedentary marine coelenterate with a columnar body which bears a ring of stinging tentacles around the mouth. ● Order Actiniaria, class Anthozoa.

sea-angel ▶ noun an angel shark.

seabag ▶ noun chiefly N. Amer. a sailor's travelling bag or trunk.

sea bass ▶ noun any of a number of marine fishes that are related to or resemble the common perch, in particular: ● a mainly tropical fish of a large family (Serranidae, the **sea bass family**), especially one of the genus *Centropristis*; the sea bass family also includes the groupers. ● (**white sea bass**) a large game fish of the Pacific coast of North America (*Cynoscion nobilis*, family Sciaenidae).

seabed ▶ noun the ground under the sea; the ocean floor.

Seabee ▶ noun a member of one of the construction battalions of the Civil Engineer Corps of the US Navy.
– ORIGIN representing a pronunciation of the letters *CB* (from *construction battalion*).

seabird ▶ noun a bird that frequents the sea or coast.

sea biscuit ▶ noun **1** another term for **SHIP'S BISCUIT**. **2** another term for **SAND DOLLAR**.

seaboard ▶ noun a region bordering the sea; the coastline: *the eastern seaboard of the United States.*

sea boat ▶ noun [usu. with adj.] a boat or ship considered in terms of its ability to cope with conditions at sea.

Seaborg /'siːbɔːg/, Glenn (Theodore) (1912–99), American nuclear chemist. During 1940–58 Seaborg and his colleagues produced nine of the transuranic elements (plutonium to nobelium) in a cyclotron. Seaborg and his early collaborator **Edwin McMillan** (1907–91) shared the Nobel Prize for Chemistry in 1951.

S

seaborgium /siː'bɔːgɪəm/ ▶ noun [mass noun] the chemical element of atomic number 106, a very unstable element made by high-energy atomic collisions. (Symbol: **Sg**)
– ORIGIN modern Latin, named after G. *Seaborg* (see **SEABORG**).

seaborne ▶ adjective transported or travelling by sea: *seaborne trade.*

sea bream ▶ noun a deep-bodied marine fish that resembles the freshwater bream, in particular: ● Several genera and species in the family Sparidae (the **sea bream family**), in particular the **red sea bream** (*Pagellus bogaraveo*), which is fished commercially, and the **black sea bream** (*Spondyliosoma cantharus*), a popular angling fish. ● a fish of Australasian coastal waters, with a purple back and silver underside (*Seriolella brama*, family Centrolophidae). Also called **WAREHOU** in New Zealand.

sea breeze ▶ noun **1** a breeze blowing towards the land from the sea, especially during the day owing to the relative warmth of the land.
2 a cocktail typically consisting of vodka, grapefruit juice, and cranberry juice.

sea buckthorn ▶ noun a bushy Eurasian shrub or small tree which typically grows on sandy coasts. It bears orange berries and some plants are spiny. ● *Hippophae rhamnoides*, family Elaeagnaceae.

sea butterfly ▶ noun a small mollusc with wing-like extensions to its body which it uses for swimming. ● Orders Thecosomata (with shells) and Gymnosomata (lacking shells), class Gastropoda.

sea captain ▶ noun a person who commands a ship, especially a merchant ship.

SeaCat ▶ noun trademark a large, high-speed catamaran used as a passenger and car ferry on short sea crossings.

sea change ▶ noun a profound or notable transformation.
– ORIGIN from Shakespeare's *Tempest* (I. ii. 403).

sea chest ▶ noun a sailor's storage chest.

sea coal ▶ noun [mass noun] archaic mineral coal, as distinct from other types of coal such as charcoal.

seacock ▶ noun a valve sealing off an opening through a ship's hull below or near to the waterline (e.g. one connecting a ship's sewage system to the sea).

sea cow ▶ noun a sirenian, especially a manatee.

sea cucumber ▶ noun an echinoderm which has a thick worm-like body with tentacles around the mouth. They typically have rows of tube feet along the body and breathe by means of a respiratory tree. ● Class Holothuroidea.

Sea Dayak ▶ noun another term for the **IBAN** people.
– ORIGIN so named because of their involvement in coastal raids on the neighbouring Land Dayaks.

sea dog ▶ noun **1** informal an old or experienced sailor.
2 Heraldry a mythical beast like a dog with fins, webbed feet, and a scaly tail.

sea duck ▶ noun any of a number of ducks that frequent the sea, especially the eiders, scoters, and long-tailed duck. ● Tribes Somateriini (and Mergini), family Anatidae: several genera.

sea eagle ▶ noun a large Eurasian fish-eating eagle that frequents coasts and wetlands. ● Genus *Haliaetus*, family Accipitridae: several species, in particular the widespread **white-tailed sea eagle** (*H. albicilla*), recently reintroduced to Scotland.

sea egg ▶ noun a sea urchin.

sea elephant ▶ noun another term for **ELEPHANT SEAL**.

sea fan ▶ noun a horny coral with a vertical tree- or fan-like skeleton, living chiefly in warmer seas. ● *Gorgonis* and other genera, order Gorgonacea.

seafaring ▶ adjective (of a person) regularly travelling by sea.
▶ noun [mass noun] the practice of regularly travelling by sea.
– DERIVATIVES **seafarer** noun.

sea-floor spreading ▶ noun [mass noun] Geology the formation of fresh areas of oceanic crust which occurs through the upwelling of magma at mid-ocean ridges and its subsequent outward movement on either side.

seafood ▶ noun [mass noun] shellfish and sea fish, served as food.

sea fret ▶ noun see **FRET**[4].

seafront ▶ noun the part of a coastal town next to and directly facing the sea.

sea-girt ▶ adjective literary surrounded by sea.

seagoing ▶ adjective (of a ship) suitable or designed for voyages on the sea. ■ characterized by or relating to travelling by sea, especially habitually: *a seagoing life.*

sea gooseberry ▶ noun a common comb jelly with a spherical body bearing two long retractile branching tentacles, typically occurring in swarms. ● *Pleurobrachia pileus*, class Tentaculata.

sea grape ▶ noun a salt-resistant tree of the dock family, bearing grape-like bunches of edible purple fruit and found on the Atlantic coasts of tropical America. ● *Coccoloba uvifera*, family Polygonaceae. ■ the fruit of the sea grape.

seagrass ▶ noun [mass noun] a grass-like plant that lives in or close to the sea, especially eelgrass. ● Genera *Cymodocea* (family Cymodoceaceae), *Zostera* (family Zosteraceae), and others.

sea green ▶ adjective of a pale bluish green colour.

seagull ▶ noun a popular name for a gull.

sea hare ▶ noun a large sea slug which has a minute internal shell and lateral extensions to the foot. Most species can swim, and many secrete distasteful chemicals to deter predators. ● *Aplysia* and other genera, order Anaspidea, class Gastropoda.

sea heath ▶ noun a small woody creeping plant of European salt marshes, bearing a superficial resemblance to heather. ● *Frankenia laevis*, family Frankeniaceae.

sea holly ▶ noun a spiny-leaved plant of the parsley family, with metallic blue teasel-like flowers, growing in sandy places by the sea and native to Europe. ● *Eryngium maritimum*, family Umbelliferae. See also **ERYNGIUM**.

seahorse ▶ noun **1** a small marine fish with segmented bony armour, an upright posture, a curled prehensile tail, a tubular snout, and a head and neck suggestive of a horse. The male has a brood pouch in which the eggs develop. ● Genus *Hippocampus*, family Syngnathidae: many species, including the European *H. ramulosus*.
2 a mythical creature with a horse's head and fish's tail.

Sea Island cotton ▶ noun [mass noun] a fine-quality long-stapled cotton grown on islands off the southern US.

seakale ▶ noun [mass noun] a maritime Eurasian plant of the cabbage family, sometimes cultivated for its edible young shoots. ● *Crambe maritima*, family Cruciferae.

seakeeping ▶ noun [mass noun] [usu. as modifier] the ability of a vessel to withstand rough conditions at sea.

sea-kindly ▶ adjective (of a ship) easy to handle at sea.

sea krait ▶ noun a venomous sea snake with a compressed tail, occurring in tropical coastal waters of the eastern Indian Ocean and western Pacific, coming ashore to bask and breed. ● Genus *Laticauda*, family Elapidae: two species.

SEAL (also **Seal**) ▶ noun a member of an elite force within the US Navy, specializing in guerrilla warfare and counter-insurgency.
– ORIGIN 1960s: abbreviation of 'sea, air, land (team)'.

seal[1] ▶ noun **1** a device or substance that is used to join two things together so as to prevent them coming apart or to prevent anything passing between them: *attach a draught seal to the door itself.* ■ [in sing.] the state or fact of being joined or rendered impervious with a seal: *many fittings have tapered threads for a better seal.* ■ the water standing in the trap of a drain to prevent foul air from rising, considered in terms of its depth.
2 a piece of wax, lead, or other material with an individual design stamped into it, attached to a document as a guarantee of authenticity. ■ a design resembling a seal embossed in paper as a guarantee of authenticity. ■ an engraved device used for stamping a seal. ■ a decorative adhesive stamp.
3 a thing regarded as a confirmation or guarantee of something: *the monarchy is the seal of the unbroached integrity of the Isles.*
4 (**the seal**) (also **the seal of confession** or **the seal of the confessional**) the obligation on a priest not to divulge anything said during confession: *I was told **under the seal**.*
▶ verb [with obj.] **1** fasten or close securely: *he folded it, sealed the envelope, and walked to the postbox.* ■ (**seal something in**) prevent something from escaping by closing a container or opening. ■ (**seal something off**) isolate an area by preventing or monitoring access to and from it: *anti-terrorist squad officers sealed off the area to search for possible bombs.*
2 apply a non-porous coating to (a surface) to make it impervious: *the pine boarding should be sealed with polyurethane.*
3 fry (food) briefly at a high temperature to prevent it from losing moisture during subsequent cooking: *heat the oil and seal the lamb on both sides.*
4 conclude, establish, or secure (something) definitively: *to seal the deal he offered Thornton a place on the board of the company.*
5 fix a piece of wax or lead stamped with a design to (a document) to authenticate it.
– PHRASES **my** (or **his** etc.) **lips are sealed** used to convey that one will not discuss or reveal something. **put** (or **set**) **the seal on** finally confirm or conclude; give final authorization to: *the UN envoy hopes to set the seal on a lasting peace.* **seal someone's fate** see **FATE**. **set** (or **put**) **one's seal to** (or **on**) mark with one's distinctive character: *it was the Stewart dynasty which most markedly set its seal on the place.*
– DERIVATIVES **sealable** adjective.
– ORIGIN Middle English (in sense 2 of the noun): from Old French *seel* (noun), *seeler* (verb), from Latin *sigillum* 'small picture', diminutive of *signum* 'a sign'.

seal² ▸ noun a fish-eating aquatic mammal with a streamlined body and feet developed as flippers, that returns to land to breed or rest. ● Families Phocidae (the **true seals**) and Otariidae (the **eared seals**, including the fur seals and sea lions). The latter have external ear flaps and are able to sit upright, and the males are much larger than the females.
■ another term for SEALSKIN.
▸ verb [no obj.] (usu. as noun **sealing**) hunt for seals.
– ORIGIN Old English *seolh*, of Germanic origin.

sea lane ▸ noun a route at sea designated for use or regularly used by shipping.

sealant ▸ noun [mass noun] material used for sealing something so as to make it airtight or watertight.

sea lavender ▸ noun a chiefly maritime plant with small pink or lilac funnel-shaped flowers. Several kinds are cultivated and some are used as everlasting flowers. ● Genus *Limonium* (formerly *Statice*), family Plumbaginaceae.

sea lawyer ▸ noun informal an eloquently and obstinately argumentative person.

sealed-beam ▸ adjective denoting a vehicle headlamp with a sealed unit consisting of the light source, reflector, and lens.

sealed book ▸ noun archaic term for CLOSED BOOK (see CLOSED).

sealed orders ▸ plural noun Military orders for procedure which are not to be opened before a specified time.

sea legs ▸ plural noun (**one's sea legs**) a person's ability to keep their balance and not feel seasick when on board a moving ship.

sea lemon ▸ noun a yellowish sea slug. ● *Archidoris* and other genera, order Nudibranchia, class Gastropoda.

sealer¹ ▸ noun **1** [usu. with modifier] a device or substance used to seal something.
2 (also **sealer jar**) Canadian a jar with a hermetic seal designed to preserve food such as fruit, pickles, and jams.

sealer² ▸ noun a ship or person engaged in hunting seals.

sea lettuce ▸ noun [mass noun] an edible seaweed with green fronds that resemble lettuce leaves. ● *Ulva lactuca*, division Chlorophyta.

sea level ▸ noun the level of the sea's surface, used in reckoning the height of geographical features such as hills and as a barometric standard: *it is only 500 feet above sea level*. Compare with MEAN SEA LEVEL.

sealift ▸ noun a large-scale transportation of troops, supplies, and equipment by sea.

sea lily ▸ noun a sedentary marine echinoderm which has a small body on a long jointed stalk, with feather-like arms to trap food. ● Class Crinoidea.

sealing wax ▸ noun [mass noun] a mixture of shellac and rosin with turpentine and pigment, softened by heating and used to make seals.

sea lion ▸ noun **1** an eared seal occurring mainly on Pacific coasts, the large male of which has a mane on the neck and shoulders. ● Five genera and species in the family Otariidae.
2 Heraldry a mythical beast formed of a lion's head and foreparts and a fish's tail.

sea loch ▸ noun see LOCH.

Sea Lord ▸ noun either of two senior officers in the Royal Navy (**First Sea Lord**, **Second Sea Lord**) serving originally as members of the Admiralty Board (now of the Ministry of Defence).

sealpoint ▸ noun a dark brown marking on the fur of the head, tail, and paws of a Siamese cat. ■ a cat with sealpoint markings.

seal ring ▸ noun chiefly historical a finger ring with a seal for impressing sealing wax.

sealskin ▸ noun [mass noun] [often as modifier] the skin or prepared fur of a seal, especially when made into a garment.

seals of office ▸ plural noun (in the UK) engraved seals held during tenure of an official position, especially that of Lord Chancellor or Secretary of State, and symbolizing the office held.

sealstone ▸ noun a gemstone bearing an engraved device for use as a seal.

seal-top ▸ adjective (of a spoon) having a flat design resembling an embossed seal at the end of its handle.
▸ noun a seal-top spoon.

Sealyham /ˈsiːlɪəm/ (in full **Sealyham terrier**) ▸ noun a terrier of a wire-haired short-legged breed.
– ORIGIN late 19th cent.: from *Sealyham*, the name of a village in SW Wales, where the dog was first bred.

seam ▸ noun **1** a line where two pieces of fabric are sewn together in a garment or other article. ■ a line where the edges of two pieces of wood, wallpaper, or another material touch each other. ■ a long thin indentation or scar: *the track cleaves a seam through corn*.
2 an underground layer of a mineral such as coal or gold. ■ a supply of something valuable: *Sunderland have a rich seam of experienced players*. ■ a trace or presence of something: *there is a seam of despondency in Stipe's words*.
▸ verb **1** join with a seam: *it can be used for seaming garments*.
2 (usu. as adj. **seamed**) make a long, narrow indentation in: *men in middle age have seamed faces*.
– PHRASES **bursting** (or **bulging**) **at the seams** informal (of a place or building) full to overflowing. **come** (or **fall**) **apart at the seams** informal (of a person or system) be in a very poor condition and near to collapse: *the attitude of the airport guard was symptomatic of a system falling apart at the seams*.
– ORIGIN Old English *sēam*, of Germanic origin; related to Dutch *zoom* and German *Saum*.

seaman ▸ noun (pl. **seamen**) a person who works as a sailor, especially one below the rank of officer. ■ the lowest rank in the US navy, below petty officer. ■ [with adj.] a person regarded in terms of their ability to captain or crew a boat or ship: *he's the best seaman on the coast*.
– DERIVATIVES **seamanlike** adjective, **seamanly** adjective.
– ORIGIN Old English *sǣman* (see SEA, MAN).

seamanship ▸ noun [mass noun] the skill, techniques, or practice of handling a ship or boat at sea.

seamark ▸ noun a conspicuous object distinguishable at sea, serving to guide or warn sailors in navigation.

sea mat ▸ noun a bryozoan, especially one which forms mat-like encrustations on underwater objects. ● *Membranipora* and other genera, class Gymnolaemata.

seam bowler ▸ noun Cricket a bowler, generally fast, who makes the ball deviate by bouncing on its seam.
– DERIVATIVES **seam bowling** noun.

seamer ▸ noun **1** Cricket another term for SEAM BOWLER. ■ a ball which deviates by bouncing on its seam.
2 a person who seams garments.

seamfree ▸ adjective (of a garment) having no seams: *seamfree socks*.

sea mile ▸ noun a unit of distance equal to a minute of arc of a great circle and varying (because the earth is not a perfect sphere) between approximately 2,014 yards (1,842 metres) at the equator and 2,035 yards (1,861 metres) at the pole. Compare with NAUTICAL MILE.

seamless ▸ adjective (of a fabric or surface) smooth and without seams or obvious joins: *seamless stockings*. ■ smooth and continuous, with no apparent gaps or spaces between one part and the next: *the seamless integration of footage from different sources*.
– DERIVATIVES **seamlessly** adverb.

sea-moth ▸ noun a small fish with bony plates covering the body and large pectoral fins which spread out horizontally like wings. It lives in the warmer waters of the Indo-Pacific. ● Family Pegasidae: several genera and species, including the widely distributed *Eurypegasus draconis*.

seamount ▸ noun a submarine mountain.

sea mouse ▸ noun a large marine bristle worm with a stout oval body which bears matted fur-like iridescent chaetae. ● Genus *Aphrodite*, class Polychaeta.

seamstress ▸ noun a woman who sews, especially one who earns her living by sewing.
– ORIGIN late 16th cent.: from archaic *seamster*, *sempster* 'tailor, seamstress' + -ESS¹.

seamy ▸ adjective (**seamier**, **seamiest**) sordid and disreputable: *a seamy sex scandal*.
– DERIVATIVES **seaminess** noun.

Seanad /ˈʃanəð, -d/, Irish /ˈsʲanad/ (also **Seanad Éireann** /ˈɛːrən/, Irish /ˈeːrʲən/) the upper house of Parliament in the Republic of Ireland, composed of sixty members, of whom eleven are nominated by the Taoiseach and forty-nine are elected by institutions.
– ORIGIN Irish, 'senate (of Ireland)'.

seance /ˈseɪɒns, -ɒ̃s, -ɑːns/ ▸ noun a meeting at which people attempt to make contact with the dead, especially through the agency of a medium.
– ORIGIN late 18th cent.: French *séance*, from Old French *seoir*, from Latin *sedere* 'sit'.

sea nettle ▸ noun a jellyfish with stinging tentacles. ● *Chrysaora* and other genera, class Scyphozoa.

Sea of Azov, Sea of Galilee, etc. see AZOV, SEA OF; GALILEE, SEA OF, etc.

sea otter ▸ noun an entirely aquatic marine otter of North Pacific coasts, formerly hunted for its dense fur. It is noted for its habit of floating on its back with a stone balanced on the abdomen, in order to crack open bivalve molluscs. ● *Enhydra lutris*, family Mustelidae.

sea pen ▸ noun a marine coelenterate related to the corals, forming a feather-shaped colony with a horny or calcareous skeleton. ● Order Pennatulacea, class Anthozoa.

Sea Peoples any or all of the groups of invaders, of uncertain identity, who encroached on Egypt and the eastern Mediterranean by land and sea in the late 13th century BC. The Egyptians were successful in driving them away, but some, including the Philistines, settled in Palestine. Also called PEOPLES OF THE SEA.

sea perch ▸ noun any of a number of marine fishes which typically have a long-based dorsal fin and which are popular as sporting fish, in particular:
● a fish of the snapper family (Lutjanidae: several genera).
● a surfperch.

sea pink ▸ noun another term for THRIFT (sense 2).

seaplane ▸ noun an aircraft with floats or skis instead of wheels, designed to land on and take off from water.

seaport ▸ noun a town or city with a harbour for seagoing ships.

sea potato ▸ noun a yellowish-brown European heart urchin. ● *Echinocardium cordatum*, class Echinoidea.

sea power ▸ noun [mass noun] a country's naval strength, especially as a weapon of war.

SEAQ ▸ abbreviation (in the UK) Stock Exchange Automated Quotations (the computer system on which dealers trade shares and seek or provide price quotations on the London Stock Exchange).

seaquake ▸ noun a sudden disturbance of the sea caused by a submarine eruption or earthquake.

sear ▸ verb [with obj.] **1** burn or scorch the surface of (something) with a sudden, intense heat: *the water got so hot that it seared our lips*. ■ fix (an image or memory) permanently in someone's mind or memory: *the unfortunate childhood encounter is **seared on** his memory*. ■ fry (food) quickly at a high temperature so that it will retain its juices in subsequent cooking: (as adj. **seared**) *seared chicken livers*.
2 [no obj., with adverbial of direction] (of pain) be experienced as a sudden, burning sensation: *a crushing pain seared through his chest*.
3 archaic cause to wither. ■ make (someone's conscience or feelings) insensitive.
▸ adjective variant spelling of SERE¹.
– ORIGIN Old English *sēar* (adjective), *sēarian* (verb), of Germanic origin.

search ▸ verb [no obj.] try to find something by looking or otherwise seeking carefully and thoroughly: *I searched among the rocks, but there was nothing* | *Daniel is then able to **search out** the most advantageous mortgage* | *Hugh will be **searching for** the truth*. ■ [with obj.] examine (a place, vehicle, or person) thoroughly in order to find something or someone: *she searched the house from top to bottom* | *the guards searched him for weapons*. ■ [with obj.] look for information or an item of interest in (a computer network or database) by keying words or other characters into a search engine. *I must search the Internet for one of his pictures*.
▸ noun an act of searching for someone or something: *the police carried out a thorough search of the premises* | *he plans to go to the Himalayas **in search of** a yeti*. ■ an act of searching a computer database or network: *time-consuming searches of the Internet*. ■ Computing the systematic retrieval of information, or the facility for this. ■ Law an investigation of public records to find if a property is subject to any liabilities or encumbrances.
– PHRASES **search me!** informal I do not know (used for emphasis).
– DERIVATIVES **searcher** noun.
– ORIGIN Middle English: from Old French *cerchier* (verb), from late Latin *circare* 'go round', from Latin *circus* 'circle'.

searchable ▸ adjective (of a database, website, etc.) capable of being computationally searched: *the archive is fully searchable*. ■ (of an item) able to be

located by a computational search: *numbers are not treated as searchable terms.*
– DERIVATIVES **searchability** noun.

search engine ▸ noun Computing a program that searches for and identifies items in a database that correspond to keywords or characters specified by the user, used especially for finding particular sites on the Internet.

search engine optimization ▸ noun [mass noun] the process of maximizing the number of visitors to a particular website by ensuring that the site appears high on the list of results returned by a search engine.

searching ▸ adjective thoroughly scrutinizing, especially in a disconcerting way: *you have to ask yourselves some searching questions.*
– DERIVATIVES **searchingly** adverb.

searchlight ▸ noun a powerful outdoor electric light with a concentrated beam that can be turned in the required direction.

search party ▸ noun a group of people organized to look for someone or something that is lost.

search warrant ▸ noun a legal document authorizing a police officer or other official to enter and search premises.

searing ▸ adjective extremely hot or intense: *the searing heat of the sun | a searing pain.* ■ severely critical: *a searing indictment of the government's performance.*
– DERIVATIVES **searingly** adverb.

sea robin ▸ noun a gurnard (fish), especially one of warm seas which has wing-like pectoral fins that are brightly coloured. ● Family Triglidae: several genera and many species.

sea room ▸ noun [mass noun] clear space at sea for a ship to turn or manoeuvre in.

Sears Tower /sɪəz/ a skyscraper in Chicago, the tallest building in the world when it was completed in 1973. It is 443 m (1,454 ft) high and has 110 floors.

sea-run ▸ adjective N. Amer. (of a migratory fish, especially a trout) having returned to the sea after spawning.

sea salt ▸ noun [mass noun] salt produced by the evaporation of seawater.

seascape ▸ noun a view of an expanse of sea. ■ a depiction of a seascape.

Sea Scout ▸ noun (especially in the UK) a member of the maritime branch of the Scout Association.

sea serpent ▸ noun a legendary serpent-like sea monster.

sea shanty ▸ noun British term for SHANTY².

seashell ▸ noun the shell of a marine mollusc.

seashore ▸ noun (usu. **the seashore**) an area of sandy, stony, or rocky land bordering and level with the sea. ■ Law the land between high- and low-water marks.

seasick ▸ adjective suffering from sickness or nausea caused by the motion of a ship at sea.
– DERIVATIVES **seasickness** noun.

seaside ▸ noun (usu. **the seaside**) a place by the sea, especially a beach area or holiday resort.

S

sea slater ▸ noun a common shore-dwelling crustacean which is related to the woodlouse. ● *Ligia oceanica*, order Isopoda.

sea slug ▸ noun a shell-less marine mollusc which is typically brightly coloured, with external gills and a number of appendages on the upper surface. ● Order Nudibranchia, class Gastropoda.

sea snail ▸ noun **1** a marine mollusc, especially one with a spiral shell. ● Subclass Prosobranchia, class Gastropoda.
2 another term for SNAILFISH.

sea snake ▸ noun a venomous marine snake with a flattened tail, which lives in the warm coastal waters of the Indian and Pacific oceans and does not come on to land. ● Subfamily Hydrophiinae, family Elapidae: several genera and species, including the **yellow-bellied sea snake** (*Pelamis platurus*), the only species found in the open ocean.

season ▸ noun **1** each of the four divisions of the year (spring, summer, autumn, and winter) marked by particular weather patterns and daylight hours, resulting from the earth's changing position with regard to the sun. ■ a period of the year characterized by a particular climatic feature or marked by a particular activity, event, or festivity: *the rainy season | the season for gathering pine needles.* ■ a fixed time in the year when a particular sporting activity is pursued: *the English cricket season is almost upon us.* ■ the time of year when a particular fruit, vegetable, or other food is plentiful and in good condition: *the pies are made with fruit that is **in season** | new season's lamb.* ■ (**the season**) a time of year traditionally adopted by the English upper classes for a series of fashionable social events. ■ archaic a proper or suitable time: *to everything there is a season.* ■ archaic an indefinite or unspecified period of time; a while: *this most beautiful soul; who walked with me for a season in this world.*
2 a period when a female mammal is ready to mate: *this system of communication works very well, especially when a female is **in season**.* Brit. informal
▸ verb [with obj.] **1** add salt, herbs, pepper, or other spices to (food): *season the soup to taste with salt and pepper.* ■ add a quality or feature to (something), especially so as to make it more lively or exciting: *his conversation is seasoned liberally with exclamation points and punch lines.*
2 make (wood) suitable for use as timber by adjusting its moisture content to that of the environment in which it will be used: *I collect and season most of my wood.*
– PHRASES **for all seasons** suitable in or appropriate for every kind of weather: *a coat for all seasons.* ■ adaptable to any circumstance: *a singer for all seasons.* **season's greetings** used as an expression of goodwill at Christmas or the New Year.
– ORIGIN Middle English: from Old French *seson*, from Latin *satio(n-)* 'sowing', later 'time of sowing', from the root of *serere* 'to sow'.

seasonable ▸ adjective **1** usual for or appropriate to a particular season of the year: *the seasonable temperatures.*
2 archaic coming at the right time or meeting the needs of the occasion; opportune.
– DERIVATIVES **seasonability** noun, **seasonableness** noun, **seasonably** adverb.

seasonal ▸ adjective relating to or characteristic of a particular season of the year: *a selection of seasonal fresh fruit.* ■ fluctuating or restricted according to the season or time of year: *there are companies whose markets are seasonal | seasonal rainfall.*
– DERIVATIVES **seasonality** noun, **seasonally** adverb.

> **USAGE** People sometimes confuse the words **seasonal** and **seasonable. Seasonal** means 'relating to a particular season' (*seasonal fresh fruit*) or 'fluctuating or restricted according to the season' (*there are companies whose markets are seasonal*), while **seasonable** is a rarer word which means 'usual for or appropriate to a particular season' (*in December the magazine carried cartoons and songs, including a seasonable Christmas carol*).

seasonal affective disorder ▸ noun [mass noun] depression associated with late autumn and winter and thought to be caused by a lack of light.

seasoned ▸ adjective **1** (of food) having had salt, pepper, herbs, or spices added: *seasoned flour.*
2 (of wood) made suitable for use as timber by adjusting its moisture content: *it was made from seasoned, untreated oak.*
3 accustomed to particular conditions; experienced: *she is a seasoned traveller.*

seasoning ▸ noun [mass noun] **1** salt, herbs, or spices added to food to enhance the flavour.
2 the process of adjusting the moisture content of wood to make it more suitable for use as timber.

season ticket ▸ noun a ticket for a period of travel or a series of events which costs less than purchasing a number of separate tickets.

sea spider ▸ noun a spider-like marine arachnid which has a narrow segmented body with a minute abdomen and long legs. ● Class Pycnogonida.

sea squill ▸ noun see SQUILL (sense 1).

sea squirt ▸ noun a marine tunicate which has a bag-like body with orifices through which water flows into and out of a central pharynx. ● Class Ascidiacea, subphylum Urochordata.

sea stack ▸ noun see STACK (sense 2 of the noun).

sea star ▸ noun a starfish.

sea state ▸ noun the degree of turbulence at sea, generally measured on a scale of 0 to 9 according to average wave height.

seat ▸ noun **1** a thing made or used for sitting on, such as a chair or stool. ■ the roughly horizontal part of a chair, on which one's weight rests directly. ■ a sitting place for a passenger in a vehicle or for a member of an audience: *a fairly small theatre with 1,300 seats.*
2 a person's buttocks. ■ the part of a garment that covers the buttocks. ■ a manner of sitting on a horse: *he's got the worst seat on a horse of anyone I've ever seen.*
3 a place in an elected legislative or other body: *he lost his seat in the 1997 election.* ■ Brit. a parliamentary constituency: *a safe Labour seat in the North-East.*
4 a principal site or location: *Parliament House was the seat of the Scots Parliament until the Union with England.* ■ Brit. short for COUNTRY SEAT.
5 a part of a machine that supports or guides another part.
▸ verb [with obj.] **1** arrange for (someone) to sit somewhere: *Owen seated his guests in the draughty baronial hall.* ■ (**seat oneself** or **be seated**) sit down: *she invited them to be seated* | (as adj. **seated**) *a dummy in a seated position.* ■ (of a vehicle or building) have seats for (a specified number of people): *the jet seats up to 175 passengers.*
2 [with obj. and adverbial of place] fit in position: *upper boulders were simply seated in the interstices below.*
– PHRASES **take one's seat** start to take part in the business of an assembly after being elected.
– DERIVATIVES **seatless** adjective.
– ORIGIN Middle English (as a noun): from Old Norse *sæti*, from the Germanic base of SIT. The verb dates from the late 16th cent.

seat belt ▸ noun a belt used to secure someone in the seat of a motor vehicle or aircraft.

-seater ▸ combining form denoting a vehicle, sofa, or building with a specified number of seats: *a six-seater.*

seating ▸ noun [mass noun] the seats with which a building or room is provided: *the restaurant has seating for 80.*

SEATO ▸ abbreviation South East Asia Treaty Organization.

sea trout ▸ noun **1** Brit. a European brown trout of a salmon-like migratory race. Also called SALMON TROUT. ● *Salmo trutta trutta*, family Salmonidae.
2 [with modifier] N. Amer. a trout-like marine fish of the drum family occurring in the western Atlantic. ● Genus *Cynoscion*, family Sciaenidae: several species, including the weakfish.

Seattle /sɪˈat(ə)l/ a port and industrial city in the state of Washington, on the eastern shores of Puget Sound; pop. 598,541 (est. 2008). First settled in 1852, it is now the largest city in the north-western US.

sea turtle ▸ noun see TURTLE (sense 1).

sea urchin ▸ noun a marine echinoderm which has a spherical or flattened shell covered in mobile spines, with a mouth on the underside and calcareous jaws. ● Class Echinoidea.

sea wall ▸ noun a wall or embankment erected to prevent the sea encroaching on or eroding an area of land.

seaward ▸ adverb (also **seawards**) towards the sea: *after about a mile they turned seaward.*
▸ adjective going or pointing towards the sea: *there was a seaward movement of water on the bottom.* ■ nearer or nearest to the sea: *the seaward end of the village.*
▸ noun [in sing.] the side that faces or is nearer to the sea: *breakwaters were extended further **to seaward**.*

sea wasp ▸ noun a box jelly which can inflict a dangerous sting.

seawater ▸ noun [mass noun] water in or taken from the sea: [as modifier] *a seawater swimming pool.*

seaway ▸ noun **1** an inland waterway capable of accommodating seagoing ships. ■ a natural channel connecting two areas of sea. ■ a route across the sea used by ships.
2 [in sing.] a rough sea in which to sail: *with the engine mounted amidship, the boat pitches less **in a seaway**.*

seaweed ▸ noun [mass noun] large algae growing in the sea or on rocks below the high-water mark.

sea wolf ▸ noun another term for WOLF FISH.

seaworthy ▸ adjective (of a boat) in a good enough condition to sail on the sea.
– DERIVATIVES **seaworthiness** noun.

sebaceous /sɪˈbeɪʃəs/ ▸ adjective technical relating to oil or fat. ■ relating to a sebaceous gland or its secretion.
– ORIGIN early 18th cent.: from Latin *sebaceus* (from *sebum* 'tallow') + -OUS.

sebaceous cyst ▸ noun a swelling in the skin arising in a sebaceous gland, typically filled with yellowish sebum. Also called WEN¹.

sebaceous gland ▸ noun a small gland in the skin which secretes a lubricating oily matter (sebum) into the hair follicles to lubricate the skin and hair.

Sebastian, St /sɪ'bastɪən/ (late 3rd century), Roman martyr. According to legend he was a soldier who was shot by archers on the orders of Diocletian, but who recovered, confronted the emperor, and was then clubbed to death. Feast day, 20 January.

Sebastopol /sɪ'bastəp(ə)l, -pɒl/ a fortress and naval base in Ukraine, near the southern tip of the Crimea; pop. 339,900 (est. 2009). The focal point of military operations during the Crimean War, it fell to Anglo-French forces in September 1855 after a year-long siege. Ukrainian and Russian name SEVASTOPOL.

Sebat /'si:bat/ (also **Shebat**, **Shevat**) ▸ noun (in the Jewish calendar) the fifth month of the civil and eleventh of the religious year, usually coinciding with parts of January and February.
– ORIGIN from Hebrew *šĕbaṭ*.

seborrhoea /,sɛbə'ri:ə/ (US **seborrhea**) ▸ noun [mass noun] Medicine excessive discharge of sebum from the sebaceous glands.
– DERIVATIVES **seborrhoeic** adjective.
– ORIGIN late 19th cent.: from SEBUM + -RRHOEA.

sebum /'si:bəm/ ▸ noun [mass noun] an oily secretion of the sebaceous glands.
– ORIGIN late 19th cent.: modern Latin, from Latin *sebum* 'grease'.

SEC ▸ abbreviation Securities and Exchange Commission, a US governmental agency which monitors trading in securities and company takeovers.

sec¹ ▸ abbreviation secant.

sec² ▸ noun (**a sec**) informal a second; a very short space of time: *stay put, I'll be back in a sec.*
– ORIGIN late 19th cent.: abbreviation.

sec³ ▸ adjective (of wine) dry.
– ORIGIN French, from Latin *siccus*.

Sec. ▸ abbreviation secretary.

sec. ▸ abbreviation second(s).

SECAM /'si:kam/ ▸ noun [mass noun] the television broadcasting system used in France and eastern Europe.
– ORIGIN from French *séquentiel couleur à mémoire* (so named because the colour information is transmitted in sequential blocks to a memory in the receiver).

secant /'si:k(ə)nt, 'sɛk-/ ▸ noun **1** (abbrev.: **sec**) Mathematics the ratio of the hypotenuse to the shorter side adjacent to an acute angle (in a right-angled triangle); the reciprocal of a cosine.
2 Geometry a straight line that cuts a curve in two or more parts.
– ORIGIN late 16th cent.; from French *sécante*, based on Latin *secare* 'to cut'.

secateurs /,sɛkə'tə:z, 'sɛkətə:z/ ▸ plural noun (also **a pair of secateurs**) Brit. a pair of pruning clippers for use with one hand.
– ORIGIN mid 19th cent.: plural of French *sécateur* 'cutter', formed irregularly from Latin *secare* 'to cut'.

Secchi disc /'sɛki/ ▸ noun an opaque disc, typically white, used to gauge the transparency of water by measuring the depth—known as the **Secchi depth**—at which the disc ceases to be visible from the surface.
– ORIGIN early 20th cent.: named after Angelo *Secchi* (1818–78), Italian astronomer.

secco /'sɛkəʊ/ (also **fresco secco**) ▸ noun [mass noun] the technique of painting on dry plaster with pigments mixed in water.
– ORIGIN mid 19th cent.: from Italian, literally 'dry', from Latin *siccus*.

secede /sɪ'si:d/ ▸ verb [no obj.] withdraw formally from membership of a federal union, an alliance, or a political or religious organization: *the kingdom of Belgium **seceded from** the Netherlands in 1830.*
– DERIVATIVES **seceder** noun.
– ORIGIN early 18th cent.: from Latin *secedere*, from *se-* 'apart' + *cedere* 'go'.

Secernentea /,sɪsə:'nɛntɪə/ ▸ plural noun Zoology another term for PHASMIDA (sense 2).
– ORIGIN modern Latin (plural), from Latin *secernent-* 'separating', from the verb *secernere*.

secession /sɪ'sɛʃ(ə)n/ ▸ noun [mass noun] the action of withdrawing formally from membership of a federation or body, especially a political state: *the republics want secession from the union.* ■ (**the Secession**) historical the withdrawal of eleven Southern states from the US Union in 1860, leading to the Civil War. ■ (**the Secession**) variant of SEZESSION.
– DERIVATIVES **secessional** adjective, **secessionism** noun, **secessionist** noun.
– ORIGIN mid 16th cent. (denoting the withdrawal of plebeians from ancient Rome in order to compel the patricians to redress their grievances): from French *sécession* or Latin *secessio(n-)*, from *secedere* 'go apart' (see SECEDE).

Sechuana /sɛ'tʃwɑ:nə/ dated ▸ noun & adjective variant spelling of SETSWANA.

Seckel /'sɛk(ə)l/ ▸ noun a pear of a small sweet juicy brownish-red variety, grown chiefly in the US.
– ORIGIN early 19th cent.: from the surname of an early grower.

seclude ▸ verb [with obj.] keep (someone) away from other people: *I secluded myself up here for a life of study and meditation.*
– ORIGIN late Middle English (in the sense 'obstruct access to'): from Latin *secludere*, from *se-* 'apart' + *claudere* 'to shut'.

secluded ▸ adjective (of a place) not seen or visited by many people; sheltered and private: *the gardens are quiet and secluded.*

seclusion ▸ noun [mass noun] the state of being private and away from other people: *they enjoyed ten days of peace and seclusion.* ■ [count noun] archaic a sheltered or private place.
– DERIVATIVES **seclusive** adjective.
– ORIGIN early 17th cent.: from medieval Latin *seclusio(n-)*, from *secludere* 'shut off' (see SECLUDE).

Seconal /'sɛk(ə)nal, -(ə)l/ ▸ noun [mass noun] trademark a barbiturate drug used as a sedative and hypnotic.
– ORIGIN 1930s: blend of SECONDARY and ALLYL.

second¹ /'sɛk(ə)nd/ ▸ ordinal number **1** constituting number two in a sequence; coming after the first in time or order; 2nd: *he married for a second time | Herbert was the second of their six children | the second of October | the second-youngest player.* ■ secondly (used to introduce a second point or reason): *second, they are lightly regulated; and third, they do business with non-resident clients.* ■ Music an interval spanning two consecutive notes in a diatonic scale. ■ the note which is higher by a second interval than the tonic of a diatonic scale or root of a chord. ■ the second in a sequence of a vehicle's gears: *he took the corner in second.* ■ Baseball second base. ■ chiefly Brit. the second form of a school or college. ■ (**seconds**) informal a second course or second helping of food at a meal. ■ denoting someone or something regarded as comparable to or reminiscent of a better-known predecessor: *a fear that the conflict would turn into a second Vietnam.*
2 subordinate or inferior in position, rank, or importance: *it was **second only to** Copenhagen among Baltic ports | he is a writer first and a scientist second.* ■ additional to that already existing, used, or possessed: *a second home | French as a second language.* ■ the second finisher or position in a race or competition: *he finished second.* ■ Brit. a place in the second grade in an examination, especially for a degree. ■ Music performing a lower or subordinate of two or more parts for the same instrument or voice: *the second violins.* ■ (**seconds**) goods of an inferior quality. ■ (**the seconds**) the reserve team of a sports club. ■ coarse flour, or bread made from it.
3 an assistant, in particular: ■ an attendant assisting a combatant in a duel or boxing match. ■ a Cub or Brownie chosen by their pack to assist the Sixer and replace them when they are absent.
▸ verb [with obj.] formally support or endorse (a nomination or resolution or its proposer) as a necessary preliminary to adoption or further discussion: *Bridgeman seconded Maxwell's motion calling for the reform.* ■ express agreement with: *her view is seconded by most Indian leaders today.* ■ archaic support; back up: *so well was he seconded by the multitude of labourers at his command.*
– PHRASES **every second** see EVERY OTHER at EVERY. **in the second place** as a second consideration or point. **second to none** the best, worst, fastest, etc.
– DERIVATIVES **seconder** noun.
– ORIGIN Middle English: via Old French from Latin *secundus* 'following, second', from the base of *sequi* 'follow'. The verb dates from the late 16th cent.

second² /'sɛk(ə)nd/ ▸ noun **1** (abbrev.: **s**) a sixtieth of a minute of time, which as the SI unit of time is defined in terms of the natural periodicity of the radiation of a caesium-133 atom. (Symbol: ″) ■ informal a very short time: *his eyes met Charlotte's for a second.*
2 (also **arc second** or **second of arc**) a sixtieth of a minute of angular distance. (Symbol: ″)
– ORIGIN late Middle English: from medieval Latin *secunda (minuta)* 'second (minute)', feminine (used as a noun) of *secundus*, referring to the 'second' operation of dividing an hour by sixty.

second³ /sɪ'kɒnd/ ▸ verb [with obj.] Brit. transfer (a military officer or other official or worker) temporarily to other employment or another position: *I was seconded to a public relations unit.*
– DERIVATIVES **secondee** /-'di:/ noun.
– ORIGIN early 19th cent.: from French *en second* 'in the second rank (of officers)'.

second Adam ▸ noun (**the second Adam**) (in Christian thought) Jesus Christ.
– ORIGIN with biblical allusion to 1 Cor. 15: 45–47.

Second Adar see ADAR.

Second Advent ▸ noun another term for SECOND COMING.

secondary ▸ adjective **1** coming after, less important than, or resulting from someone or something else that is primary: *luck plays a role, but it's ultimately **secondary to** local knowledge.* ■ relating to education for children from the age of eleven to sixteen or eighteen: *a secondary school.* ■ having a reversible chemical reaction and therefore able to store energy. ■ relating to or denoting the output side of a device using electromagnetic induction, especially in a transformer.
2 (**Secondary**) Geology former term for MESOZOIC.
3 Chemistry (of an organic compound) having its functional group located on a carbon atom which is bonded to two other carbon atoms. ■ (chiefly of amines) derived from ammonia by replacement of two hydrogen atoms by organic groups.
▸ noun (pl. **secondaries**) **1** short for: ■ Brit. a secondary school. ■ Ornithology a secondary feather. ■ a secondary coil or winding in an electrical transformer.
2 (**the Secondary**) Geology, dated the Secondary or Mesozoic era.
– DERIVATIVES **secondarily** adverb, **secondariness** noun.
– ORIGIN late Middle English: from Latin *secundarius* 'of the second quality or class', from *secundus* (see SECOND¹).

secondary articulation ▸ noun Phonetics an additional feature in the pronunciation of a consonant (besides the actual place of articulation), such as palatalization or lip-rounding.

secondary colour ▸ noun a colour resulting from the mixing of two primary colours.

secondary evidence ▸ noun [mass noun] Law something, in particular documentation, which confirms the existence of unavailable primary evidence.

secondary feather ▸ noun any of the flight feathers growing from the second joint of a bird's wing.

secondary industry ▸ noun [mass noun] Economics industry that converts the raw materials provided by primary industry into commodities and products for the consumer; manufacturing industry.

secondary modern school ▸ noun historical (in the UK) a secondary school of a kind offering a general education to children not selected for grammar or technical schools.

secondary picketing ▸ noun [mass noun] Brit. picketing by strikers of the premises of a firm that trades with their employer but is not otherwise involved in the dispute in question.

secondary planet ▸ noun a satellite of a planet.

secondary process ▸ noun Psychoanalysis a thought process connecting the preconscious and conscious, governed by the reality principle and reflecting the decision-making and problem-solving activity of the ego.

secondary sector ▸ noun Economics the sector of the economy concerned with or relating to secondary industry.

secondary sexual characteristics ▸ plural noun physical characteristics developed at puberty which distinguish between the sexes but are not involved in reproduction.

secondary smoke ▸ noun [mass noun] smoke inhaled involuntarily from tobacco being smoked by others.

secondary smoking ▸ noun another term for PASSIVE SMOKING.

secondary structure ▸ noun Biochemistry the local three-dimensional structure of sheets, helices, or other forms adopted by a polynucleotide or polypeptide chain, due to electrostatic attraction between neighbouring residues.

S

secondary thickening ▶ **noun** [mass noun] Botany (in the stem or root of a woody plant) the increase in girth resulting from the formation of new woody tissue by the cambium.

secondary treatment ▶ **noun** [mass noun] the further treatment of sewage effluent by biological methods following sedimentation.

second ballot ▶ **noun** a further ballot held to confirm the selection of a candidate where a previous ballot did not yield an absolute majority.

second best ▶ **adjective** next after the best: *his second-best suit*.
▶ **noun** a less adequate or less desirable alternative: *he would have to settle for second best*.
– PHRASES **come off second best** be defeated in a competition.

Second Boer War see **Boer Wars**.

second cause ▶ **noun** Logic a cause that is itself caused.

second childhood ▶ **noun** a period in someone's adult life when they act as a child, either for fun or as a consequence of reduced mental capabilities.

second class ▶ **noun** [in sing.] a set of people or things grouped together as the second best. ■ [mass noun] the second-best accommodation in an aircraft, train, or ship. ■ Brit. the second-highest division in the results of the examinations for a university degree: *he obtained a second class in modern history*.
▶ **adjective & adverb** of the second-best quality or in the second division: [as adj.] *until 1914 women were thought of as second-class citizens*. ■ relating to the second-best accommodation in an aircraft, train, or ship: [as adj.] *I want second-class tickets* | [as adv.] *they don't fly second class*. ■ relating to a class of mail having lower priority than first-class mail: [as adj.] *second-class postage stamps*. ■ (in North America) denoting a class of mail which includes newspapers and periodicals. ■ [as adj.] Brit. relating to the second-highest division in the results of the examinations for a university degree: *a respectable second-class degree*.

Second Coming ▶ **noun** Christian Theology the prophesied return of Christ to Earth at the Last Judgement.

second cousin ▶ **noun** see **cousin**.

second-cut ▶ **adjective** another term for **cross-cut**.

second-degree ▶ **adjective** [attrib.] **1** Medicine denoting burns that cause blistering but not permanent scars.
2 Law, chiefly N. Amer. denoting a category of a crime, especially murder, that is less serious than a first-degree crime.

seconde /sə'kɒ̃d/ ▶ **noun** Fencing the second of eight parrying positions.
– ORIGIN early 18th cent.: from French, feminine of *second* 'second'.

Second Empire the imperial government in France of Napoleon III, 1852–70. ■ the period of the Second Empire.

second floor ▶ **noun** Brit. the floor two levels above the ground floor. ■ N. Amer. the floor directly above the ground floor.

second-generation ▶ **adjective 1** denoting the offspring of parents who came to live in a particular country: *she was a second-generation American*.
2 of a more advanced stage of technology than previous models or systems.

second-guess ▶ **verb** [with obj.] **1** anticipate or predict (someone's actions or thoughts) by guesswork: *he had to second-guess what the environmental regulations would be in five years' time*.
2 chiefly N. Amer. criticize (someone or something) with hindsight: *no one should second-guess police officers whose lives are on the line*.

second hand ▶ **noun** an extra hand in some watches and clocks which moves round to indicate the seconds.

second-hand ▶ **adjective 1** (of goods) having had a previous owner; not new: *a second-hand car*. ■ denoting a shop where such goods can be bought: *a second-hand bookshop*.
2 (of information or experience) accepted on another's authority and not from original investigation: *second-hand knowledge of her country*.
▶ **adverb 1** on the basis that something has had a previous owner: *tips on the pitfalls to avoid when buying second-hand*.
2 on the basis of what others have said; indirectly: *I was discounting anything I heard second-hand*.
– PHRASES **at second hand** by hearsay rather than direct observation or experience.

second-hand smoke ▶ **noun** N. Amer. another term for **second smoke**.

second honeymoon ▶ **noun** a romantic holiday taken by a couple who have been married for some time.

second in command ▶ **noun** the officer next in authority to the commanding or chief officer.

second intention ▶ **noun** [mass noun] Medicine the healing of a wound in which the edges do not meet, and new epithelium must form across granulation tissue: *healing by second intention*.

Second International see **international** (sense 2 of the noun).

Second Isaiah another name for **Deutero-Isaiah**.

second lieutenant ▶ **noun** a rank of officer in the army and the US air force, above warrant officer or chief warrant officer and below lieutenant or first lieutenant.

second line ▶ **noun 1** a battle line behind the front line to support it and make good its losses.
2 [as modifier] ranking second in strength, effectiveness, ability, or value: *second-line American computer manufacturers*.
3 [usu. as modifier] a medical treatment or therapy used in support of another, or as a more drastic measure if the primary treatment is ineffective.

secondly ▶ **adverb** in the second place (used to introduce a second point or reason): *he was presented first of all as a hopelessly unqualified candidate and secondly as an extremist*.

second master ▶ **noun** a deputy headmaster.

second mate ▶ **noun** another term for **second officer**.

secondment ▶ **noun** [mass noun] Brit. the temporary transfer of an official or worker to another position or employment: *he spent two years* ***on secondment*** *to the Department of Industry*.

second messenger ▶ **noun** Physiology a substance whose release within a cell is promoted by a hormone and which brings about a response by the cell.

second mortgage ▶ **noun** a mortgage taken out on a property that is already mortgaged.

second name ▶ **noun** Brit. a surname.

second nature ▶ **noun** [mass noun] a tendency or habit that has become characteristic or instinctive: *deceit was becoming* ***second nature to*** *her*.

secondo /sɪ'kɒndəʊ/ ▶ **noun** (pl. **secondi** /-di/) Music the second or lower part in a duet.
– ORIGIN Italian.

second officer ▶ **noun** an assistant mate on a merchant ship.

second person ▶ **noun** see **person** (sense 2).

second position ▶ **noun 1** Ballet a posture in which the feet form a straight line, being turned out to either side with the heels separated by the distance of a small step. ■ a position of the arms in which they are held out to each side of the body, curving forwards and slightly upwards.
2 Music a position of the left hand on the fingerboard of a stringed instrument nearer to the bridge than the first position, enabling a higher-pitched set of notes to be played.

second-rate ▶ **adjective** of mediocre or inferior quality: *a second-rate theatre*.
– DERIVATIVES **second-rater** noun.

second reading ▶ **noun** a second presentation of a bill to a legislative assembly, in the UK to approve its general principles and in the US to debate committee reports.

Second Reich see **Reich**[1].

Second Republic the republican regime in France from the deposition of King Louis Philippe (1848) to the beginning of the Second Empire (1852).

second sight ▶ **noun** [mass noun] the supposed ability to perceive future or distant events; clairvoyance.
– DERIVATIVES **second-sighted** adjective.

second strike ▶ **noun** a retaliatory attack conducted with weapons designed to withstand an initial nuclear attack (a 'first strike').

second string ▶ **noun 1** (often in phrase **a second string to one's bow**) an alternative resource or course of action in case another one fails: *he was principally a batsman and bowling was the second string to his bow*.
2 (in sport) the second-choice players: *Mimms will play in goal for City 's second string*.

second teeth ▶ **plural noun** the set of permanent teeth that replace the milk teeth in humans and other mammals.

second thoughts (US also **second thought**) ▶ **plural noun** a change of opinion or resolve reached after considering something again: ***on second thoughts****, perhaps he was right*.

second wind ▶ **noun** [in sing.] a person's ability to breathe freely during exercise, after having been out of breath. ■ a new strength or energy to continue something that is an effort: *she gained a second wind during the campaign and turned the opinion polls around*.

Second World ▶ **noun** the former communist block consisting of the Soviet Union and some countries in eastern Europe.

Second World War a war (1939–45) in which the Axis Powers (Germany, Italy, and Japan) were defeated by an alliance eventually including the United Kingdom and its dominions, the Soviet Union, and the United States.

> Hitler's invasion of Poland in September 1939 led Great Britain and France to declare war on Germany. Germany defeated and occupied France the following year and soon overran much of Europe. Italy joined the war in 1940, and the US and Japan entered following the Japanese attack on the US fleet at Pearl Harbor. Italy surrendered in 1943 and the Allies launched a full-scale invasion in Normandy in June 1944. The war in Europe ended when Germany surrendered in May 1945; Japan surrendered after the US dropped atom bombs on Hiroshima and Nagasaki in August 1945. An estimated 55 million people were killed during the war, including a much higher proportion of civilians than in the First World War.

secrecy ▶ **noun** [mass noun] the action of keeping something secret or the state of being kept secret: *the bidding is conducted* ***in secrecy***.
– ORIGIN late Middle English: from **secret**, probably on the pattern of *privacy*.

secret ▶ **adjective** not known or seen or not meant to be known or seen by others: *how did you guess I'd got a secret plan?* | *the resupply effort was probably* ***kept secret from*** *Congress*. ■ [attrib.] not meant to be known as such by others: *a secret drinker*. ■ fond of or good at keeping things about oneself unknown: *he can be the most secret man*.
▶ **noun** something that is kept or meant to be kept unknown or unseen by others: *a state secret* | *at first I tried to* ***keep it a secret from*** *my wife*. ■ something that is not properly understood; a mystery: *I'm not trying to explain the secrets of the universe in this book*. ■ a valid but not commonly known or recognized method of achieving or maintaining something: *the secret of a happy marriage is compromise*. ■ a prayer said by the priest in a low voice after the offertory in a Roman Catholic Mass.
– PHRASES **be in (on) the secret** be among the small number of people who know something. **in secret** without others knowing. **make no secret of something** make something perfectly clear.
– ORIGIN late Middle English: from Old French, from Latin *secretus* (adjective) 'separate, set apart', from the verb *secernere*, from *se-* 'apart' + *cernere* 'sift'.

secret agent ▶ **noun** a spy acting for a country.

secretagogue /sɪ'kriːtəgɒg/ ▶ **noun** Physiology a substance which promotes secretion.
– ORIGIN early 20th cent.: from **secrete**[1] + Greek *agōgos* 'leading'.

secretaire /ˌsɛkrɪ'tɛː/ ▶ **noun** a small writing desk; an escritoire.
– ORIGIN late 18th cent.: from French *secrétaire*, literally 'secretary'.

secretariat /ˌsɛkrɪ'tɛːrɪət/ ▶ **noun** a permanent administrative office or department, especially a governmental one. ■ [treated as sing. or pl.] the staff working in a secretariat.
– ORIGIN early 19th cent.: from French *secrétariat*, from medieval Latin *secretariatus*, from *secretarius* (see **secretary**).

secretary /'sɛkrɪt(ə)ri/ ▶ **noun** (pl. **secretaries**) a person employed by an individual or in an office to assist with correspondence, make appointments, and carry out administrative tasks. ■ an official of a society or other organization who conducts its correspondence and keeps its records. ■ the principal assistant of a UK government minister or ambassador: [as title] *Chief Secretary to the Treasury*. ■ an official in charge of a US government department.
– DERIVATIVES **secretarial** adjective, **secretaryship** noun.

S

– ORIGIN late Middle English (originally in the sense 'person entrusted with a secret'): from late Latin *secretarius* 'confidential officer', from Latin *secretum* 'secret', neuter of *secretus* (see SECRET).

secretary bird ▸ noun a slender long-legged African bird of prey that feeds on snakes, having a crest likened to a quill pen stuck behind the ear. ● *Sagittarius serpentarius*, the only member of the family Sagittariidae.

secretary general ▸ noun (pl. **secretary generals**) a title given to the principal administrator of some organizations.

Secretary of State ▸ noun **1** (in the UK) the head of a major government department.
2 (in the US) the head of the State Department, responsible for foreign affairs.
3 (in Canada) a government minister responsible for a specific area within a department.

secret ballot ▸ noun a ballot in which votes are cast in secret.

secrete[1] /sɪˈkriːt/ ▸ verb [with obj.] (of a cell, gland, or organ) produce and discharge (a substance): *insulin is secreted in response to rising levels of glucose in the blood.*
– DERIVATIVES **secretor** noun, **secretory** adjective.
– ORIGIN early 18th cent.: back-formation from SECRETION.

secrete[2] /sɪˈkriːt/ ▸ verb [with obj.] conceal; hide: *the assets had been secreted in Swiss bank accounts.*
– ORIGIN mid 18th cent.: alteration of the obsolete verb *secret* 'keep secret'.

secretin /sɪˈkriːtɪn/ ▸ noun [mass noun] Biochemistry a hormone released into the bloodstream by the duodenum (especially in response to acidity) to stimulate secretion by the liver and pancreas.
– ORIGIN early 20th cent.: from SECRETION + -IN[1].

Secret Intelligence Service (abbrev.: **SIS**) official name for **MI6**.

secretion ▸ noun [mass noun] a process by which substances are produced and discharged from a cell, gland, or organ for a particular function in the organism or for excretion. ■ [count noun] a substance discharged by secretion.
– ORIGIN mid 17th cent.: from French *sécrétion* or Latin *secretio(n-)* 'separation', from *secret-* 'moved apart', from the verb *secernere*.

secretive ▸ adjective (of a person or an organization) inclined to conceal feelings and intentions or not to disclose information: *she was very secretive about her past.* ■ (of a state or activity) characterized by the concealment of intentions and information: *secretive deals.* ■ (of a person's expression or manner) having an enigmatic or conspiratorial quality: *a secretive smile.*
– DERIVATIVES **secretively** adverb, **secretiveness** noun.
– ORIGIN mid 19th cent.: back-formation from *secretiveness*, suggested by French *secrétivité*, from *secret* 'secret'.

secret list ▸ noun a register of research work or developments on sensitive military projects, the details of which may not be disclosed for reasons of national security.

secretly ▸ adverb in a secret way; without others knowing: *the two were secretly married in 1751 | I was embarrassed, but secretly pleased too.*

secret police ▸ noun [treated as pl.] a police force working in secret against a government's political opponents.

secret service ▸ noun **1** a government department concerned with espionage.
2 (**Secret Service**) (in the US) a branch of the Treasury Department dealing with counterfeiting and providing protection for the President.

secret society ▸ noun an organization whose members are sworn to secrecy about its activities.

sect ▸ noun a group of people with somewhat different religious beliefs (typically regarded as heretical) from those of a larger group to which they belong. ■ often derogatory a group that has separated from an established Church; a nonconformist Church. ■ a philosophical or political group, especially one regarded as extreme or dangerous.
– ORIGIN Middle English: from Old French *secte* or Latin *secta*, literally 'following', hence 'faction, party', from the stem of *sequi* 'follow'.

sect. ▸ abbreviation section.

sectarian ▸ adjective denoting or concerning a sect or sects: *the city's traditional sectarian divide.* ■ (of an action) carried out on the grounds of membership of a sect, denomination, or other group: *sectarian killings.* ■ rigidly following the doctrines of a sect or other group.
▸ noun a member of a sect. ■ a person who rigidly follows the doctrines of a sect or other group.
– DERIVATIVES **sectarianism** noun, **sectarianize** (also **sectarianise**) verb.
– ORIGIN mid 17th cent.: from SECTARY + -AN, reinforced by SECT.

sectary /ˈsɛktəri/ ▸ noun (pl. **sectaries**) a member of a religious or political sect.
– ORIGIN mid 16th cent.: from modern Latin *sectarius* 'schismatic', from medieval Latin *sectarius* 'adherent', from Latin *secta* (see SECT).

section ▸ noun **1** any of the more or less distinct parts into which something is or may be divided or from which it is made up. ■ a relatively distinct part of a book, newspaper, statute, or other document. ■ N. Amer. a measure of land, equal to one square mile. ■ chiefly N. Amer. a particular district of a town. ■ NZ a building plot.
2 a distinct group within a larger body of people or things: *the non-parliamentary section of the party.* ■ a group of players of a family of instruments within an orchestra: *the brass section.* ■ [in names] a specified military unit: *a GHQ Signals Section.* ■ a subdivision of an army platoon. ■ Biology a secondary taxonomic category, especially a subgenus.
3 [mass noun] the cutting of a solid by or along a plane. ■ the shape resulting from cutting a solid along a plane. ■ [count noun] a representation of the internal structure of something as if it has been cut through vertically or horizontally. ■ [count noun] Surgery a separation by cutting. ■ [count noun] Biology a thin slice of plant or animal tissue prepared for microscopic examination.
▸ verb [with obj.] **1** divide into sections: *she began to section the grapefruit.* ■ (**section something off**) separate an area from a larger one: *parts of the curved balcony had been sectioned off with wrought-iron grilles.* ■ Biology cut (animal or plant tissue) into thin slices for microscopic examination. ■ Surgery divide by cutting: *it is common veterinary practice to section the nerves to the hoof of a limping horse.*
2 Brit. commit (someone) compulsorily to a psychiatric hospital in accordance with a section of a mental health act: *should she be sectioned and forced back into hospital?*
– DERIVATIVES **sectioned** adjective [often in combination] *a square-sectioned iron peg.*
– ORIGIN late Middle English (as a noun): from French *section* or Latin *sectio(n-)*, from *secare* 'to cut'. The verb dates from the early 19th cent.

sectional ▸ adjective relating to a section or subdivision of a larger whole: *a sectional championship.* ■ relating to a section or group within a community: *the chairman of the commission looked on sectional interests as a danger to the common good.* ■ relating to a view of the structure of an object in section: *sectional drawings.* ■ made or supplied in sections: *sectional sills, made from more than one piece of timber.*
▸ noun N. Amer. a sofa made in sections that can be used separately as chairs.
– DERIVATIVES **sectionalize** (also **sectionalise**) verb, **sectionally** adverb.

sectionalism ▸ noun [mass noun] restriction of interest to a narrow sphere; undue concern with local interests or petty distinctions at the expense of general well-being.
– DERIVATIVES **sectionalist** noun & adjective.

section house ▸ noun chiefly Brit. a building providing residential accommodation for unmarried police officers.

section mark ▸ noun a sign (§) used as a reference mark or to indicate a section of a book.

sector ▸ noun **1** an area or portion that is distinct from others. ■ a distinct part or branch of a nation's economy or society or of a sphere of activity such as education. ■ Military a subdivision of an area for military operations. ■ Computing a subdivision of a track on a magnetic disk.
2 the plane figure enclosed by two radii of a circle or ellipse and the arc between them.
3 a mathematical instrument consisting of two arms hinged at one end and marked with sines, tangents, etc. for making diagrams.
– DERIVATIVES **sectoral** adjective.
– ORIGIN late 16th cent. (in sense 2, sense 3): from late Latin, a technical use of Latin *sector* 'cutter', from *sect-* 'cut off', from the verb *secare*.

sectorial /sɛkˈtɔːrɪəl/ ▸ adjective **1** of or like a sector: *sectorial boundaries.*
2 Zoology denoting a carnassial tooth, or a similar cutting tooth in mammals other than carnivores.

secular /ˈsɛkjʊlə/ ▸ adjective **1** not connected with religious or spiritual matters: *secular buildings | secular attitudes to death.* Contrasted with SACRED.
2 Christian Church (of clergy) not subject to or bound by religious rule; not belonging to or living in a monastic or other order. Contrasted with REGULAR.
3 Astronomy of or denoting slow changes in the motion of the sun or planets.
4 Economics (of a fluctuation or trend) occurring or persisting over an indefinitely long period: *there is evidence that the slump is not cyclical but secular.*
5 occurring once every century or similarly long period (used especially in reference to celebratory games in ancient Rome).
▸ noun a secular priest.
– DERIVATIVES **secularism** noun, **secularist** noun, **secularity** noun, **secularization** (also **secularisation**) noun, **secularize** (also **secularise**) verb, **secularly** adverb.
– ORIGIN Middle English: sense 1 of the adjective, sense 2 of the adjective from Old French *seculer*, from Latin *saecularis*, from *saeculum* 'generation, age', used in Christian Latin to mean 'the world' (as opposed to the Church); sense 3 of the adjective, sense 4 of the adjective, sense 5 of the adjective (early 19th cent.) from Latin *saecularis* 'relating to an age or period'.

secular arm ▸ noun (**the secular arm**) the legal authority of the civil power as invoked by the Church to punish offenders.

secular humanism ▸ noun [mass noun] liberalism, with regard in particular to the belief that religion should not be taught or practised within a publicly funded education system.
– DERIVATIVES **secular humanist** noun.

secund /sɪˈkʌnd/ ▸ adjective Botany arranged on one side only (such as the flowers of lily of the valley).
– ORIGIN late 18th cent.: from Latin *secundus* (see SECOND[1]).

secure ▸ adjective **1** fixed or fastened so as not to give way, become loose, or be lost: *check to ensure that all nuts and bolts are secure.* ■ (of a place of detention) having provisions against the escape of inmates: *a secure unit for young offenders.*
2 certain to remain safe and unthreatened: *his position as party leader was less than secure | a more competitive economy will lead to an increase in secure employment.* ■ protected against attack or other criminal activity: *no airport is totally secure.* ■ feeling confident and free from fear or anxiety: *everyone needs to have a home and to feel secure and wanted.* ■ (**secure of**) dated feeling no doubts about attaining: *she remained poised and complacent, secure of admiration.*
▸ verb [with obj.] **1** fix or attach (something) firmly so that it cannot be moved or lost: *pins **secure** the handle **to** the main body.* ■ make (a door or container) hard to open; fasten or lock: *doors are likely to be well secured at night.* ■ Surgery compress (a blood vessel) to prevent bleeding.
2 succeed in obtaining (something), especially with difficulty: *the division secured a major contract.* ■ seek to guarantee repayment of (a loan) by having a right to take possession of an asset in the event of non-payment: *a loan **secured on** your home.*
3 protect against threats; make safe: *the government is concerned to **secure** the economy **against** too much foreign ownership.*
– PHRASES **secure arms** Military hold a rifle with the muzzle downward and the lock in the armpit to guard it from rain.
– DERIVATIVES **securable** adjective, **securely** adverb, **securement** noun.
– ORIGIN mid 16th cent. (in the sense 'feeling no apprehension'): from Latin *securus*, from *se-* 'without' + *cura* 'care'.

Securitate /sɪˌkjʊərɪˈtɑːteɪ, sɪˌkjɔːrɪˈtɑːteɪ/ the internal security force of Romania, set up in 1948 and officially disbanded during the revolution of December 1989.
– ORIGIN Romanian, 'Security'.

securitize (also **securitise**) ▸ verb [with obj.] (often as adj. **securitized**) convert (an asset, especially a loan) into marketable securities, typically for the purpose of raising cash by selling them to other investors: *the use of securitized debt as a major source of corporate finance.*
– DERIVATIVES **securitization** noun.

S

security ▸ noun (pl. **securities**) **1** [mass noun] the state of being free from danger or threat: *the system is designed to provide maximum security against toxic spills* | *job security.* ▪ the safety of a state or organization against criminal activity such as terrorism, theft, or espionage: *a matter of national security.* ▪ procedures followed or measures taken to ensure the security of a state or organization: *amid tight security the presidents met in the Colombian resort.* ▪ the state of feeling safe, stable, and free from fear or anxiety: *this man could give her the emotional security she needed.*
2 a thing deposited or pledged as a guarantee of the fulfilment of an undertaking or the repayment of a loan, to be forfeited in case of default.
3 (often **securities**) a certificate attesting credit, the ownership of stocks or bonds, or the right to ownership connected with tradable derivatives.
– PHRASES **on security of something** using something as a guarantee.
– ORIGIN late Middle English: from Old French *securite* or Latin *securitas*, from *securus* 'free from care' (see **SECURE**).

security blanket ▸ noun **1** a blanket or other familiar object which is a comfort to someone, typically a child.
2 Brit. an official sanction imposed on information in order to maintain complete secrecy about something.

Security Council a permanent body of the United Nations seeking to maintain peace and security. It consists of fifteen members, of which five (China, France, the UK, the US, and Russia) are permanent and have the power of veto. The other members are elected for two-year terms.

security guard ▸ noun a person employed to protect a building against intruders or damage.

security risk ▸ noun a person or situation which poses a possible threat to the security of something.

Security Service official name for **MI5**.

securocrat /sɪˈkjʊərə(ʊ)krat, sɪˈkjɔːrə(ʊ)krat/ ▸ noun a military or police officer who holds an influential position in the government; an advocate of the close involvement of military and police officers in government.
– ORIGIN blend of **SECURITY** and **BUREAUCRAT**.

sedan /sɪˈdan/ ▸ noun **1** (also **sedan chair**) chiefly historical an enclosed chair for conveying one person, carried between horizontal poles by two porters.
2 chiefly N. Amer. a car for four or more people.
– ORIGIN perhaps an alteration of an Italian dialect word, based on Latin *sella* 'saddle', from *sedere* 'sit'.

Sedan, Battle of /sɪˈdan/ a battle fought in 1870 near the town of Sedan in NE France, in which the Prussian army defeated a smaller French army under Napoleon III, opening the way for a Prussian advance on Paris and marking the end of the French Second Empire.

sedate¹ ▸ adjective calm, dignified, and unhurried: *in the old days, business was carried on at a rather more sedate pace.* ▪ quiet and rather dull: *sedate suburban domesticity.*
– DERIVATIVES **sedately** adverb, **sedateness** noun.
– ORIGIN late Middle English (originally as a medical term meaning 'not sore or painful', also 'calm, tranquil'): from Latin *sedatus*, past participle of *sedare* 'settle', from *sedere* 'sit'.

S

sedate² ▸ verb [with obj.] calm (someone) or make them sleep by administering a sedative drug: *she was heavily sedated.*
– ORIGIN 1960s: back-formation from **SEDATION**.

sedation ▸ noun [mass noun] the action of administering a sedative drug to produce a state of calm or sleep: *he was distraught with grief and under* ***sedation.*** ▪ a state of calm or sleep produced by a sedative drug.
– ORIGIN mid 16th cent.: from French *sédation* or Latin *sedatio(n-)*, from *sedare* 'settle' (see **SEDATE¹**).

sedative ▸ adjective promoting calm or inducing sleep: *the seeds have a sedative effect.*
▸ noun a drug taken for its calming or sleep-inducing effect.
– ORIGIN late Middle English: from Old French *sedatif* or medieval Latin *sedativus*, from Latin *sedat-* 'settled', from the verb *sedare* (see **SEDATE¹**).

sedentary /ˈsɛd(ə)nt(ə)ri/ ▸ adjective (of a person) tending to spend much time seated; somewhat inactive. ▪ (of work or a way of life) characterized by much sitting and little physical exercise. ▪ (of a position) sitting; seated. ▪ Zoology & Anthropology inhabiting the same locality throughout life; not migratory or nomadic. ▪ Zoology (of an animal) sessile.
– DERIVATIVES **sedentariness** noun.
– ORIGIN late 16th cent. (in the sense 'not migratory'): from French *sédentaire* or Latin *sedentarius*, from *sedere* 'sit'.

Seder /ˈseɪdə/ ▸ noun a Jewish ritual service and ceremonial dinner for the first night or first two nights of Passover.
– ORIGIN from Hebrew *sēḏer* 'order, procedure'.

sederunt /sɪˈdɪərənt, -ˈdɛː-/ ▸ noun (in Scotland) a sitting of an ecclesiastical assembly or other body.
– ORIGIN early 17th cent.: from Latin, literally '(the following persons) sat', from *sedere* 'sit'.

sedge ▸ noun a grass-like plant with triangular stems and inconspicuous flowers, growing typically in wet ground. Sedges are widely distributed throughout temperate and cold regions. ● Family Cyperaceae: *Carex* and other genera.
– DERIVATIVES **sedgy** adjective.
– ORIGIN Old English *secg*, of Germanic origin, from an Indo-European root shared by Latin *secare* 'to cut'.

Sedgemoor, Battle of /ˈsɛdʒmɔː, -mʊə/ a battle fought in 1685 on the plain of Sedgemoor in Somerset. The forces of the rebel Duke of Monmouth, who had landed in Dorset as champion of the Protestant cause and pretender to the throne, were decisively defeated by James II's troops.

sedge warbler ▸ noun a common migratory Eurasian songbird with streaky brown plumage, frequenting marshes and reed beds. ● *Acrocephalus schoenobaenus*, family Sylviidae.

Sedgwick /ˈsɛdʒwɪk/, Adam (1785–1873), English geologist. He specialized in the fossil record of rocks from North Wales, assigning the oldest of these to a period that he named the Cambrian.

sedilia /sɪˈdɪlɪə/ ▸ plural noun (sing. **sedile** /sɪˈdʌɪli/) a group of stone seats for clergy in the south chancel wall of a church, usually three in number and often canopied and decorated.
– ORIGIN late 18th cent.: from Latin, 'seat', from *sedere* 'sit'.

sediment ▸ noun [mass noun] matter that settles to the bottom of a liquid; dregs. ▪ Geology particulate matter that is carried by water or wind and deposited on the surface of the land or the seabed, and may in time become consolidated into rock.
▸ verb [no obj.] settle as sediment. ▪ (of a liquid) deposit a sediment. ▪ [with obj.] deposit (something) as a sediment: *the DNA was* ***sedimented*** *by centrifugation* | (as adj. **sedimented**) *sedimented waste.*
– DERIVATIVES **sedimentation** noun.
– ORIGIN mid 16th cent.: from French *sédiment* or Latin *sedimentum* 'settling', from *sedere* 'sit'.

sedimentary ▸ adjective relating to sediment. ▪ Geology (of rock) that has formed from sediment deposited by water or air.

sedimentation coefficient (also **sedimentation constant**) ▸ noun Biochemistry a quantity related to the size of a microscopic particle, equal to the terminal outward velocity of the particle when centrifuged in a fluid medium divided by the centrifugal force acting on it, expressed in units of time.

sedition ▸ noun [mass noun] conduct or speech inciting people to rebel against the authority of a state or monarch.
– ORIGIN late Middle English (in the sense 'violent strife'): from Old French, or from Latin *seditio(n-)*, from *sed-* 'apart' + *itio(n-)* 'going' (from the verb *ire*).

seditious ▸ adjective inciting or causing people to rebel against the authority of a state or monarch: *the letter was declared seditious.*
– DERIVATIVES **seditiously** adverb.
– ORIGIN late Middle English: from Old French *seditieux* or Latin *seditiosus*, from *seditio* 'mutinous separation' (see **SEDITION**).

seditious libel ▸ noun Law a published statement which is seditious. ▪ [mass noun] the action or crime of publishing a seditious statement.

seduce ▸ verb [with obj.] attract (someone) to a belief or into a course of action that is inadvisable or foolhardy: *they should not be* ***seduced into*** *thinking that their success ruled out the possibility of a relapse.* ▪ entice into sexual activity. ▪ attract powerfully: *the melody seduces the ear with warm string tones.*
– DERIVATIVES **seducer** noun, **seducible** adjective.
– ORIGIN late 15th cent. (originally in the sense 'persuade (someone) to abandon their duty'): from Latin *seducere*, from *se-* 'away, apart' + *ducere* 'to lead'.

seduction ▸ noun [mass noun] the action of seducing someone: *if seduction doesn't work, she can play on his sympathy* | [count noun] *she was planning a seduction.* ▪ [count noun] (often **seductions**) a tempting or attractive thing: *the seductions of the mainland.*
– ORIGIN early 16th cent.: from French *séduction* or Latin *seductio(n-)*, from *seducere* 'draw aside' (see **SEDUCE**).

seductive ▸ adjective tempting and attractive; enticing: *a seductive voice.*
– DERIVATIVES **seductively** adverb, **seductiveness** noun.
– ORIGIN mid 18th cent.: from **SEDUCTION**, on the pattern of pairs such as *induction, inductive.*

seductress ▸ noun a woman who seduces someone, especially one who entices a man into sexual activity.
– ORIGIN early 19th cent.: from obsolete *seductor* 'male seducer', from *seducere* (see **SEDUCE**).

sedulous /ˈsɛdjʊləs/ ▸ adjective (of a person or action) showing dedication and diligence: *he watched himself with the most sedulous care.*
– DERIVATIVES **sedulity** /sɪˈdjuːlɪti/ noun, **sedulously** adverb, **sedulousness** noun.
– ORIGIN mid 16th cent.: from Latin *sedulus* 'zealous' + **-OUS**.

sedum /ˈsiːdəm/ ▸ noun a widely distributed fleshy-leaved plant with small star-shaped yellow, pink, or white flowers, grown as an ornamental. ● Genus *Sedum*, family Crassulaceae: many species, including the stonecrops.
– ORIGIN from modern Latin, denoting a houseleek.

see¹ ▸ verb (**sees, seeing, saw**; past participle **seen**) [with obj.] **1** perceive with the eyes; discern visually: *in the distance she could see the blue sea* | [no obj.] *Andrew couldn't see out of his left eye* | figurative *I can't see into the future.* ▪ [with clause] be or become aware of something from observation or from a written or other visual source: *I see from your appraisal report that you have asked for training.* ▪ be a spectator of (a film, game, or other entertainment); watch: *I went to see King Lear at the Old Vic.* ▪ [in imperative] refer to (a specified source) for further information (used as a direction in a text): *elements are usually classified as metals or non-metals (see chapter 11).*
2 discern or deduce after reflection or from information; understand: *I can't see any other way to treat it* | [with clause] *I saw that perhaps he was right* | *she could see what Rhoda meant.* ▪ [with clause] ascertain after inquiring, considering, or discovering an outcome: *I'll go along to the club and see if I can get a game.* ▪ [with obj. and adverbial] regard in a specified way: *he saw himself as a good teacher* | *you and I see things differently.* ▪ (**see something in**) find good or attractive qualities in (someone): *I don't know what I see in you.* ▪ view or predict as a possibility; envisage: *I can't see him earning any more anywhere else.* ▪ used to ascertain or express comprehension, agreement, or continued attention, or to emphasize that an earlier prediction was correct: *it has to be the answer, don't you see?* | *see, I told you I'd come.*
3 experience or witness (an event or situation): *I shall not live to see it* | [with obj. and complement] *I can't bear to see you so unhappy.* ▪ be the time or setting of (something): *the 1970s saw the beginning of a technological revolution.*
4 meet (someone one knows) socially or by chance: *I saw Colin last night.* ▪ visit (a person or place): *I went to see Caroline* | *see Alaska in style.* ▪ meet regularly as a boyfriend or girlfriend: *some guy she was seeing was messing her around.* ▪ consult (a specialist or professional): *you may need to see a solicitor.* ▪ give an interview or consultation to: *the doctor will see you now.*
5 [with obj. and adverbial of direction] escort or conduct (someone) to a specified place: *don't bother seeing me out.*
6 [no obj.] ensure: *Lucy* ***saw to it that*** *everyone got enough to eat* | [with clause] ***see that*** *no harm comes to him.*
7 (in poker or brag) equal the bet of (an opponent) and require them to reveal their cards in order to determine who has won the hand.
– PHRASES **as far as I can see** to the best of my understanding or belief. **as I see it** in my opinion. **be seeing things** see **THING**. **(I'll) be seeing you** another way of saying **SEE YOU**. **have seen better days** have declined from former prosperity or good condition: *this part of South London has seen better days.* **have seen it all before** be very worldly or very familiar with a particular situation. **let me see** said as an appeal for time to think before speaking: *Let me see, how old is he now?* **see a man about a dog** humorous said euphemistically when leaving to

go to the toilet or keep an undisclosed appointment. **see eye to eye, see fit** see EYE, FIT[1], etc. **see here!** said to emphasize a statement or command or to express a protest: *now see here, you're going to get it back for me!* **see one's way clear to do** (or **doing**) **something** find that it is possible or convenient to do something (often used in polite requests). **see someone coming** recognize a person who can be fooled or deceived. **see something coming** foresee or be prepared for an event, typically an unpleasant one. **see someone damned first** Brit. informal said when angrily refusing to do what a person wants. **see someone right** Brit. informal make sure that a person is appropriately rewarded or looked after. **see sense** (or **reason**) realize that one is wrong and start acting sensibly. **see the back of** informal be rid of (an unwanted person or thing): *we were always glad to see the back of her.* **see you** (**later**) informal said when parting from someone. **we'll see about that** said when angrily contradicting or challenging an assertion: *Oh, you think it's funny, do you? We'll see about that!*

– PHRASAL VERBS **see about** (or **see to**) attend to or deal with: *he had gone to see about a job he had heard of* | *I'll see to Dad's tea.* **see after** chiefly N. Amer. or archaic take care of; look after. **see something of** spend a specified amount of time with (someone) socially: *we saw a lot of the Bakers.* **see someone off 1** accompany a person who is leaving to their point of departure: *they came to the station to see him off.* **2** Brit. repel an invader or intruder: *the dogs saw them off in no time.* ■ informal deal with the threat posed by: *they saw off Cambridge in the FA Cup.* **see someone out** Brit. (of an article) last longer than the remainder of someone's life: *no point in fixing the gate, it'll see me out.* **see something out 1** come to the end of a period of time or undertaking: *I could well see out my career in Italy.* **2** continue to work on or be involved with a task or project until it is completed. **see over** tour and examine (a building or site): *Bridget asked if he'd like to see over the house.* **see through** not be deceived by; detect the true nature of: *he can see through her lies and deceptions.* **see someone through** support a person for the duration of a difficult time. **see something through** persist with an undertaking until it is completed.

– DERIVATIVES **seeable** adjective.

– ORIGIN Old English *sēon*, of Germanic origin; related to Dutch *zien* and German *sehen*, perhaps from an Indo-European root shared by Latin *sequi* 'follow'.

see[2] ▸ noun the place in which a cathedral church stands, identified as the seat of authority of a bishop or archbishop.

– ORIGIN Middle English: from Anglo-Norman French *sed*, from Latin *sedes* 'seat', from *sedere* 'sit'.

seed ▸ noun **1** the unit of reproduction of a flowering plant, capable of developing into another such plant. ■ [mass noun] a quantity of seeds: *grass seed* | *you can grow artichokes from seed.* ■ the cause or latent beginning of a feeling, process, or condition: *the conversation sowed a tiny seed of doubt in his mind.* **2** [mass noun] a man's semen. ■ archaic (chiefly in biblical use) a person's offspring or descendants. **3** any of a number of stronger competitors in a sports tournament who have been assigned a specified position in an ordered list with the aim of ensuring that they do not play each other in the early rounds: *he knocked the top seed out of the championships.* **4** (also **seed crystal**) a small crystal introduced into a liquid to act as a nucleus for crystallization. **5** a small container for radioactive material placed in body tissue during radiotherapy.

▸ verb **1** [with obj.] sow (land) with seeds: *the shoreline is seeded with a special grass.* ■ sow (seed). ■ cause (something) to begin to develop or grow: *his interest in public service was seeded when he was a child.* ■ place a crystal or crystalline substance in (something) in order to cause crystallization or condensation (especially in a cloud to produce rain). **2** [no obj.] (of a plant) produce or drop seeds: *mulches encourage many plants to seed freely.* ■ (**seed itself**) (of a plant) reproduce itself by means of its own seeds: *feverfew will seed itself readily.* **3** [with obj.] remove the seeds from (vegetables or fruit): *stem and seed the chillies.* **4** [with obj.] give (a competitor) the status of seed in a tournament: [with obj. and complement] *he was seeded second for the competition.*

– PHRASES **go** (or **run**) **to seed** (of a plant) cease flowering as the seeds develop. ■ deteriorate, especially through neglect: *Mark knows he has allowed himself to go to seed.*

– ORIGIN Old English *sǣd*, of Germanic origin; related to Dutch *zaad*, German *Saat*, also to the verb SOW[1].

seedbed ▸ noun a bed of fine soil in which seedlings are germinated.

seed cake ▸ noun [mass noun] cake containing caraway seeds as flavouring.

seed capital ▸ noun see SEED MONEY.

seed coat ▸ noun Botany the protective outer coat of a seed.

seed corn ▸ noun [mass noun] good-quality corn kept for seed. ■ Brit. assets set aside for the generation of profit or other benefit in the future.

seedeater ▸ noun a finch or related songbird that feeds mainly on seeds, in particular: ● a small American bunting (genus *Sporophila*, subfamily Emberizinae, family Emberizidae). ● an African finch related to the canary (genus *Serinus*, family Fringillidae).

seeded ▸ adjective **1** [in combination] (of a plant or fruit) having a seed or seeds of a specified kind or number: *a single-seeded fruit.* ■ (of land or an area of ground) having been sown with seed: *seeded lawns.* ■ Heraldry (of a flower) having seeds of a specified tincture. **2** (of a fruit or vegetable) having had the seeds removed: *seeded, chopped tomatoes.* **3** given the status of seed in a sports tournament: *Italy is one of the eight seeded teams.*

seeder ▸ noun **1** a machine for sowing seed mechanically. **2** a plant that produces seeds in a particular way or under particular conditions: *it has a reputation as a free seeder.*

seed fern ▸ noun another term for PTERIDOSPERM.

seed head ▸ noun a flower head in seed.

seed leaf ▸ noun Botany a cotyledon.

seedless ▸ adjective denoting a fruit that has no seeds: *seedless grapes.*

seedling ▸ noun a young plant, especially one raised from seed and not from a cutting.

seed-lip ▸ noun chiefly historical a basket for holding seed, used when sowing by hand.

seed money ▸ noun [mass noun] money allocated to initiate a project.

seed pearl ▸ noun a very small pearl.

seed plot ▸ noun old-fashioned term for SEEDBED.

seed potato ▸ noun a potato that is intended for replanting to produce a new plant and hence more tubers.

seedsman ▸ noun (pl. **seedsmen**) a person who deals in seeds as a profession.

seed time ▸ noun the sowing season.

seedy ▸ adjective (**seedier**, **seediest**) **1** sordid and disreputable: *his seedy affair with a soft-porn starlet.* ■ shabby and squalid: *an increasingly seedy and dilapidated property.* **2** dated unwell: *she felt weak and seedy.*

– DERIVATIVES **seedily** adverb, **seediness** noun.

Seeger /ˈsiːɡə/, Pete (b.1919), American folk musician and songwriter. Seeger was a prominent figure in the American folk revival. Notable songs: 'If I Had a Hammer' (*c.*1949) and 'Where Have All the Flowers Gone?' (1956).

seeing ▸ conjunction (**seeing as/that**) because; since: *seeing that I'm awake, I might as well come with you.*

▸ noun [mass noun] the action of seeing someone or something. ■ Astronomy the quality of observed images as determined by atmospheric conditions.

– PHRASES **seeing is believing** proverb you need to see something before you can accept that it really exists or occurs.

Seeing Eye dog ▸ noun N. Amer. trademark a guide dog trained to lead blind people.

seek ▸ verb (past and past participle **sought**) [with obj.] attempt to find (something): *they came here to seek shelter from biting winter winds.* ■ attempt or desire to obtain or achieve (something): *the new regime sought his extradition* | [no obj., with infinitive] *her parents had never sought to interfere with her freedom.* ■ ask for (something) from someone: *he sought help from the police.* ■ (**seek someone/thing out**) search for and find someone or something: *it's his job to seek out new customers.* ■ archaic go to (a place): *I sought my bedroom each night to brood over it.*

– PHRASES **seek dead** Brit. used to instruct a retriever to go and look for game that has been shot. **seek one's fortune** travel somewhere in the hope of achieving wealth and success. **to seek** archaic lacking; not yet found: *the end she knew, the means were to seek.* ■ (**far to seek**) out of reach; a long way off.

– DERIVATIVES **seeker** noun [often in combination] *a pleasure-seeker* | *a job-seeker.*

– ORIGIN Old English *sēcan*, of Germanic origin; related to Dutch *zieken* and German *suchen*, from an Indo-European root shared by Latin *sagire* 'perceive by scent'.

seek time ▸ noun Computing the time taken for a disk drive to locate the area on the disk where the data to be read is stored.

seel /siːl/ ▸ verb [with obj.] archaic close (a person's eyes); prevent (someone) from seeing: *the wise Gods seel our eyes in our own filth.*

– ORIGIN late 15th cent. (originally a term in falconry meaning 'stitch shut the eyelids of (a hawk)'): from French *ciller*, or medieval Latin *ciliare*, from Latin *cilium* 'eyelid'.

seem ▸ verb [no obj.] **1** give the impression of being something or having a particular quality: [with complement] *Dawn seemed annoyed* | *it seemed a dismal town* | [with infinitive] *there seems to be plenty to eat* | [with clause] *it seemed that he was determined to oppose her.* ■ [with infinitive] used to make a statement less forceful: *I seem to remember giving you very precise instructions.* ■ [with clause] (**it seems** or **it would seem**) used to suggest in a cautious or polite way that something is the case: *it would seem that he has been fooling us all.* **2** (**cannot seem to do something**) be unable to do something, despite having tried: *he couldn't seem to remember his lines.*

– ORIGIN Middle English (also in the sense 'suit, befit, be appropriate'): from Old Norse *sœma* 'to honour', from *sœmr* 'fitting'.

seeming ▸ adjective appearing to be real or true, but not necessarily being so; apparent: *Ellen's seeming indifference to the woman's fate.* ■ [in combination] giving the impression of having a specified quality: *an angry-seeming man.*

▸ noun [mass noun] literary the outward appearance or aspect of someone or something, especially when considered as deceptive or as distinguished from reality: *that dissidence between inward reality and outward seeming.*

seemingly ▸ adverb so as to give the impression of having a certain quality; apparently: *a seemingly competent and well-organized person.* ■ [sentence adverb] according to the facts as one knows them; as far as one knows: *it's touch-and-go, seemingly, and she's asking for you.*

seemly ▸ adjective (**seemlier**, **seemliest**) conforming to accepted notions of propriety or good taste; decorous: *I felt it was not seemly to observe too closely.*

– DERIVATIVES **seemliness** noun.

– ORIGIN Middle English: from Old Norse *sœmiligr*, from *sœmr* 'fitting' (see SEEM).

seen past participle of SEE[1]. ▸ exclamation W. Indian said as an expression of approval or agreement, or when seeking confirmation of an utterance: *you will get far, jus' stay on the right track, seen?*

See of Rome ▸ noun another term for HOLY SEE.

seep ▸ verb [no obj., with adverbial of direction] (of a liquid) flow or leak slowly through porous material or small holes: *water began to seep through the soles of his boots.*

▸ noun N. Amer. a place where petroleum or water oozes slowly out of the ground.

– ORIGIN late 18th cent.: perhaps a dialect form of Old English *sīpian* 'to soak'.

S

seepage ▸ noun [mass noun] the slow escape of a liquid or gas through porous material or small holes. ■ the quantity of liquid or gas that seeps out.

seer[1] /ˈsiːə, sɪə/ ▸ noun **1** a person of supposed supernatural insight who sees visions of the future. ■ an expert who provides forecasts of the economic or political future: *our seers have grown gloomier about prospects for growth.* **2** [usu. in combination] chiefly archaic a person who sees something specified: *a seer of the future* | *ghost-seers.*

– ORIGIN Middle English: from SEE[1] + -ER[1].

seer[2] /sɪə/ ▸ noun dated (in South Asia) a varying unit of weight (about one kilogram) or liquid measure (about one litre).

– ORIGIN from Hindi *ser.*

seersucker ▸ noun [mass noun] a lightweight fabric with a crimped or puckered surface.

– ORIGIN early 18th cent.: from Persian *šir o šakar*, literally 'milk and sugar', (by transference) 'striped cotton garment' because seersucker formerly was typically striped.

see-saw ▸ noun a long plank balanced in the middle on a fixed support, on each end of which children sit

and swing up and down by pushing the ground alternately with their feet. ■ a situation characterized by rapid, repeated changes from one state or condition to another: *the emotional see-saw of a first love affair* | [as modifier] *see-saw interest rates*.
▶ **verb** [no obj.] change rapidly and repeatedly from one position, situation, or condition to another and back again: *the market see-sawed as rumours spread of an imminent cabinet reshuffle*. ■ [with obj.] cause (something) to move back and forth or up and down rapidly and repeatedly: *Sybil see-sawed the car back and forth*.
– ORIGIN mid 17th cent. (originally used by sawyers as a rhythmical refrain): reduplication of the verb SAW[1] (symbolic of the sawing motion).

seethe ▶ **verb** [no obj.] **1** (of a liquid) boil or be turbulent as if boiling: *the grey ocean seethed*. ■ [with obj.] archaic cook (food) by boiling it in a liquid.
2 (of a person) be filled with intense but unexpressed anger: *inwardly he was seething at the slight to his authority*.
3 (of a place) be crowded with people or things moving about in a rapid or hectic way: *the entire cellar was seething with spiders*. ■ [with adverbial of direction] (of a crowd of people) move in a rapid or hectic way: *we cascaded down the stairs and seethed across the station* | (as adj. **seething**) *the seething mass of commuters*.
– DERIVATIVES **seethingly** adverb.
– ORIGIN Old English *sēothan* 'make or keep boiling', of Germanic origin; related to Dutch *zieden*.

see-through ▶ **adjective** (especially of clothing) translucent: *this shirt's a bit see-through when it's wet*.

Sefer /ˈseɪfə/ ▶ **noun** (pl. **Sifrei**) Judaism a book of Hebrew religious literature. ■ (usu. **Sefer Torah** /ˈtɔːrə, ˈtəʊrə/) a scroll containing the Torah or Pentateuch.
– ORIGIN from Hebrew *sēper tōrāh* 'book of (the) Law'.

segment /ˈsɛɡm(ə)nt/ ▶ **noun 1** each of the parts into which something is or may be divided. ■ a portion of time allocated to a particular broadcast item on radio or television. ■ a separate broadcast item, typically one of a number that make up a particular programme.
2 Geometry a part of a figure cut off by a line or plane intersecting it, in particular: ■ the part of a circle enclosed between an arc and a chord. ■ the part of a line included between two points. ■ the part of a sphere cut off by any plane not passing through the centre.
3 Zoology each of the series of similar anatomical units of which the body and appendages of some animals are composed, such as the visible rings of an earthworm's body.
4 Phonetics the smallest distinct part of a spoken utterance, especially with regard to vowel and consonant sounds rather than stress or intonation.
▶ **verb** usually /sɛɡˈmɛnt/ [with obj.] divide (something) into separate parts or sections: *the unemployed are segmented into two groups*. ■ [no obj.] divide into separate parts or sections: *the market is beginning to segment into a number of well-defined categories*. ■ [no obj.] Embryology (of a cell) undergo cleavage; divide into many cells.
– DERIVATIVES **segmentary** adjective, **segmentation** noun.
– ORIGIN late 16th cent. (as a term in geometry): from Latin *segmentum*, from *secare* 'to cut'. The verb dates from the mid 19th cent.

S

segmental ▶ **adjective 1** consisting of or divided into segments. ■ Phonetics denoting or relating to the division of speech into segments.
2 Architecture having the form of an arch of which the curved part forms a shallow arc of a circle, less than a semicircle.

segmented /ˈsɛɡm(ə)ntɪd, sɛɡˈmɛntɪd/ ▶ **adjective** consisting of or divided into segments: *segmented labour markets*. ■ Zoology (of an animal's body or appendage) formed of a longitudinal series of similar parts.

Segovia[1] /sɪˈɡəʊvɪə/, Spanish /seˈɣoβja/ a city in north central Spain, north-east of Madrid; pop. 56,858 (2008). Taken by the Moors in the 8th century, it was reclaimed by the king of Castile, Alfonso VI (d.1109), in 1079.

Segovia[2] /sɪˈɡəʊvɪə/, Spanish /seˈɣoβja/, Andrés (1893–1987), Spanish guitarist and composer. He was largely responsible for the revival of the classical guitar, elevating it to use as a concert instrument and making a large number of transcriptions of classical music to increase the repertoire of the instrument.

segregate ▶ **verb** /ˈsɛɡrɪɡeɪt/ **1** [with obj.] set apart from the rest or from each other; isolate or divide: *disabled people should not be segregated from the rest of society*. ■ separate or divide along racial, sexual, or religious lines: *blacks were segregated in churches, schools, and colleges* | (as adj. **segregated**) *segregated education systems*.
2 [no obj.] Genetics (of pairs of alleles) be separated at meiosis and transmitted independently via separate gametes.
▶ **noun** /ˈsɛɡrɪɡət/ **1** Genetics an allele that has undergone segregation.
2 Botany a species within an aggregate.
– DERIVATIVES **segregable** adjective, **segregative** adjective.
– ORIGIN mid 16th cent.: from Latin *segregat-* 'separated from the flock', from the verb *segregare*, from *se-* 'apart' + *grex, greg-* 'flock'.

segregation ▶ **noun 1** [mass noun] the action or state of setting someone or something apart from others: *the segregation of pupils with learning difficulties*. ■ the enforced separation of different racial groups in a country, community, or establishment: *an official policy of racial segregation*.
2 Genetics the separation of pairs of alleles at meiosis and their independent transmission via separate gametes.
– DERIVATIVES **segregational** adjective, **segregationist** adjective & noun (in the racial sense).

segue /ˈsɛɡweɪ/ ▶ **verb** (**segues, segueing, segued**) [no obj., with adverbial] (in music and film) move without interruption from one piece of music or scene to another: *allowing one song to segue into the next*.
▶ **noun** an uninterrupted transition from one piece of music or film scene to another.
– ORIGIN Italian, literally 'follows'.

seguidilla /ˌsɛɡɪˈdiːljə, -ˈdiːjə/ ▶ **noun** a Spanish dance in triple time.
– ORIGIN mid 18th cent.: Spanish, from *seguida* 'sequence', from *seguir* 'follow'.

Seguridad /sɪˌɡʊərɪˈdad/, Spanish /seˌɣuriˈðað/ the Spanish security service.
– ORIGIN Spanish, literally 'Security'.

Sehnsucht /ˈzeɪnzuːxt/, German /ˈzeːnzʊxt/ ▶ **noun** [mass noun] literary yearning; wistful longing.
– ORIGIN German.

sei ▶ **noun** another term for SEI WHALE.

seicento /seɪˈtʃɛntəʊ/ ▶ **noun** [mass noun] [often as modifier] the style of Italian art and literature of the 17th century: *Florentine seicento painting*.
– ORIGIN Italian, '600', shortened from *mille seicento* '1600', used with reference to the years 1600–99.

seiche /seɪʃ/ ▶ **noun** a temporary disturbance or oscillation in the water level of a lake or partially enclosed body of water, especially one caused by changes in atmospheric pressure.
– ORIGIN mid 19th cent.: from Swiss French, perhaps from German *Seiche* 'sinking (of water)'.

seidel /ˈzʌɪd(ə)l/ ▶ **noun** dated a beer mug or glass.
– ORIGIN early 20th cent.: from German *Seidel*, originally denoting a measure between a third and a half of a litre.

Seidlitz powder /ˈsɛdlɪts/ ▶ **noun** a laxative preparation containing tartaric acid, sodium potassium tartrate, and sodium bicarbonate which effervesces when mixed with water.
– ORIGIN late 18th cent.: named with reference to the mineral water of *Seidlitz*, a village in Bohemia.

seif /siːf, seɪf/ (also **seif dune**) ▶ **noun** a sand dune in the form of a long, narrow ridge.
– ORIGIN early 20th cent.: from Arabic *sayf* 'sword' (because of the shape).

seigneur /seɪˈnjəː/ (also **seignior** /ˈseɪnjə/) ▶ **noun** chiefly historical a feudal lord; the lord of a manor.
– DERIVATIVES **seigneurial** adjective.
– ORIGIN late 16th cent.: from Old French, from Latin *senior* 'older, elder'.

seigniorage /ˈseɪnjərɪdʒ/ (also **seignorage**) ▶ **noun 1** [mass noun] profit made by a government by issuing currency, especially the difference between the face value of coins and their production costs. ■ historical the Crown's right to a percentage on bullion brought to a mint for coining.
2 historical a thing claimed by a sovereign or feudal superior as a prerogative.
– ORIGIN late Middle English: from Old French *seignorage*, from *seigneur* (see SEIGNEUR).

seigniory /ˈseɪnjəri/ (also **seigneury**) ▶ **noun** (pl. **seigniories**) a feudal lordship; the position, authority, or domain of a feudal lord.
– ORIGIN Middle English: from Old French *seignorie*, from *seigneur* (see SEIGNEUR).

Seikan Tunnel /ˈseɪkan/ the world's longest underwater tunnel, linking the Japanese islands of Hokkaido and Honshu under the Tsungaru Strait. Completed in 1988, the tunnel is 51.7 km (32.3 miles) in length.

Seine /seɪn/, French /sɛn/ a river of northern France. Rising north of Dijon, it flows north-westwards for 761 km (473 miles), through the cities of Troyes and Paris to the English Channel near Le Havre.

seine /seɪn/ ▶ **noun** (also **seine net**) a fishing net which hangs vertically in the water with floats at the top and weights at the bottom edge, the ends being drawn together to encircle the fish.
▶ **verb** [with obj.] fish (an area) with a seine: *the fishermen then seine the weir*. ■ catch (fish) with a seine: *they seine whitefish and salmon*.
– DERIVATIVES **seiner** noun.
– ORIGIN Old English *segne*, of West Germanic origin, via Latin from Greek *sagēnē*; reinforced in Middle English by Old French *saine*.

seise ▶ **verb** see SEIZE (sense 6).

seisin /ˈsiːzɪn/ (also **seizin**) ▶ **noun** [mass noun] Law possession of land by freehold. ■ Brit. historical possession, especially of land: *Richard Fitzhugh did not take seisin of his lands until 1480*.
– ORIGIN Middle English: from Old French *seisine*, from *saisir* 'seize'.

seismic /ˈsʌɪzmɪk/ ▶ **adjective** relating to earthquakes or other vibrations of the earth and its crust. ■ relating to or denoting geological surveying methods involving vibrations produced artificially by explosions. ■ of enormous proportions or effect: *there are seismic pressures threatening American society*.
– DERIVATIVES **seismically** adverb.
– ORIGIN mid 19th cent.: from Greek *seismos* 'earthquake' (from *seien* 'to shake') + -IC.

seismicity /sʌɪzˈmɪsɪti/ ▶ **noun** [mass noun] Geology the occurrence or frequency of earthquakes in a region: *the high seismicity of the area*.

seismic reflection ▶ **noun** [mass noun] Geology the reflection of elastic waves at boundaries between different rock formations, especially as a technique for prospecting or research.

seismic refraction ▶ **noun** [mass noun] Geology the refraction of elastic waves on passing between formations of rock having different seismic velocities.

seismic velocity ▶ **noun** Geology the velocity of propagation of elastic waves in a particular rock.

seismic wave ▶ **noun** Geology an elastic wave in the earth produced by an earthquake or other means.

seismo- ▶ **combining form** of an earthquake; relating to earthquakes: *seismograph*.
– ORIGIN from Greek *seismos* 'earthquake'.

seismogram /ˈsʌɪzmə(ʊ)ɡram/ ▶ **noun** a record produced by a seismograph.

seismograph /ˈsʌɪzmə(ʊ)ɡrɑːf/ ▶ **noun** an instrument that measures and records details of earthquakes, such as force and duration.
– DERIVATIVES **seismographic** adjective.

seismology /sʌɪzˈmɒlədʒi/ ▶ **noun** [mass noun] the branch of science concerned with earthquakes and related phenomena.
– DERIVATIVES **seismological** adjective, **seismologically** adverb, **seismologist** noun.

seismometer /sʌɪzˈmɒmɪtə/ ▶ **noun** another term for SEISMOGRAPH.

seismosaurus /ˈsʌɪzmə(ʊ)sɔːrəs/ ▶ **noun** a huge late Jurassic dinosaur known from only a few bones, probably the longest ever animal with a length of up to 35–45 m, and one of the heaviest at up to 100 metric tons. ● Genus *Seismosaurus*, infraorder Sauropoda, order Saurischia.
– ORIGIN modern Latin, from SEISMO- 'of an earthquake' + Greek *sauros* 'lizard'.

seitan /ˈseɪtan/ ▶ **noun** [mass noun] a type of textured vegetable protein made from wheat gluten, used as a meat substitute.
– ORIGIN perhaps from Japanese *shokubutsusei tanpaku* 'vegetable protein'.

sei whale /seɪ/ ▶ **noun** a small rorqual with dark steely-grey skin and white grooves on the belly. ● *Balaenoptera borealis*, family Balaenopteridae.
– ORIGIN early 20th cent.: from Norwegian *sejhval*.

seiza /ˈseɪzə/ ▶ **noun** [in sing.] an upright kneeling position which is traditionally used in Japan in meditation and as part of the preparation in martial arts.

– ORIGIN Japanese, from *sei* 'correct' + *za* 'sitting'.

seize ▶ **verb 1** [with obj.] take hold of suddenly and forcibly: *she jumped up and seized his arm* | *he* ***seized hold of*** *the door handle.* ■ take forcible possession of: *army rebels seized an air force base* | *the current President seized power in a coup.* ■ (of the police or another authority) take possession of (something) by warrant or legal right: *police have seized 726 lb of cocaine.*
2 take (an opportunity) eagerly and decisively: *he seized his chance to attack as Carr hesitated.*
3 (of a feeling or pain) affect (someone) suddenly or acutely: *he was seized by the most dreadful fear.*
4 strongly appeal to or attract (the imagination or attention): *the story of the king's escape seized the public imagination.* ■ formal understand (something) quickly or clearly: *he always strains to seize the most sombre truths.* ■ (**be seized of**) be aware or informed of: *the judge was fully seized of the point.*
5 [no obj.] (of a machine with moving parts) become jammed: *the engine* ***seized up*** *after only three weeks.*
6 (also **seise**) (**be seized of**) English Law be in legal possession of: *the court is currently seized of custody applications.* ■ historical have or receive freehold possession of (property): *any person who is seized of land has a protected interest in that land.*
– PHRASES **seize the day** make the most of the present moment. [translating CARPE DIEM.]
– PHRASAL VERBS **seize on/upon** take eager advantage of (something): *any momentary upturn was seized upon as evidence of recovery.*
– DERIVATIVES **seizable** adjective, **seizer** noun.
– ORIGIN Middle English: from Old French *seizir* 'give seisin', from medieval Latin *sacire*, in the phrase *ad proprium sacire* 'claim as one's own', from a Germanic base meaning 'procedure'.

seizin ▶ noun variant spelling of SEISIN.

seizing ▶ noun Nautical, archaic a length of cord or rope used for fastening or tying.

seizure ▶ noun **1** [mass noun] the action of capturing someone or something using force: *the seizure of the Assembly building* | *the Nazi seizure of power.* ■ the action of confiscating or impounding property by warrant of legal right.
2 a sudden attack of illness, especially a stroke or an epileptic fit: *the patient* ***had a seizure.***

sejant /ˈsiːdʒ(ə)nt/ ▶ adjective [usu. postpositive] Heraldry (of an animal) sitting upright.
– ORIGIN late 15th cent.: alteration of an Old French variant of *seant* 'sitting', from the verb *seoir*, from Latin *sedere* 'sit'.

Sekhmet /ˈsɛkmɛt/ Egyptian Mythology a ferocious lioness-goddess, counterpart of the gentle cat-goddess Bastet and wife of Ptah at Memphis.

Sekt /zɛkt/ ▶ noun [mass noun] a German sparkling white wine.
– ORIGIN German.

selachian /sɪˈleɪkɪən/ Zoology ▶ noun an elasmobranch fish of a group that comprises the sharks and dogfishes. ● The former group Selachii, subclass Elasmobranchii: now treated as one, two, or three superorders.
▶ adjective relating to the selachians.
– ORIGIN mid 19th cent.: from modern Latin *Selachii* (from Greek *selakhos* 'shark') + -AN.

seladang /səˈlɑːdaŋ/ ▶ noun another term for GAUR.
– ORIGIN early 19th cent.: from Malay.

selaginella /ˌsɛlədʒɪˈnɛlə, sɪˌladʒɪˈnɛlə/ ▶ noun a creeping moss-like plant of a genus which includes the lesser clubmosses. ● Genus *Selaginella*, family Selaginellaceae.
– ORIGIN modern Latin, diminutive of Latin *selago* 'clubmoss'.

selah /ˈsiːlə, -lɑː/ ▶ exclamation (in the Bible) occurring frequently at the end of a verse in Psalms and Habakkuk, probably as a musical direction.
– ORIGIN from Hebrew *selāh*.

Selangor /səˈlaŋə/ a state of Malaysia, on the west coast of the Malay Peninsula; capital, Shah Alam.

Selcraig /ˈsɛlkreɪg/ see SELKIRK.

seldom ▶ adverb not often; rarely: *Islay is seldom visited by tourists* | *he was seldom absent* | [in combination] *an old seldom-used church.*
▶ adjective [attrib.] dated not common; infrequent: *a great but seldom pleasure.*
– ORIGIN Old English *seldan*, of Germanic origin; related to Dutch *zelden* and German *selten*, from a base meaning 'strange, wonderful'.

select ▶ verb [with obj.] carefully choose as being the best or most suitable: *children must select their GCSE subjects* | [with obj. and infinitive] *he has been selected to take part* | [no obj.] *you can* ***select from*** *a range of quality products.* ■ [no obj.] (**select for/against**) Biology (in terms of evolution) determine whether (a characteristic or organism) will survive: *the commonest phenotype in a population can be selected against.* ■ use a mouse or keystrokes to mark (something) on a computer screen for a particular operation.
▶ adjective (of a group of people or things) carefully chosen from a larger number as being the best or most valuable: *he joined his select team of young Intelligence operatives.* ■ (of a place or group of people) only used by or consisting of a wealthy or sophisticated elite; exclusive: *the opera was seen by a small and highly select audience.*
– DERIVATIVES **selectable** adjective, **selectness** noun.
– ORIGIN mid 16th cent.: from Latin *select-* 'chosen', from the verb *seligere*, from *se-* 'apart' + *legere* 'choose'.

select committee ▶ noun a small legislative committee appointed for a special purpose: [in titles] *the Commons Select Committee on the Environment.*

selectee ▶ noun a person who is selected. ■ US a conscript.

selection ▶ noun [mass noun] **1** the action or fact of carefully choosing someone or something as being the best or most suitable: *such men decided the selection of candidates* | *some local Tories objected to his selection.* ■ [count noun] a number of carefully chosen things: *the publication of a selection of his poems.* ■ [count noun] a range of things from which a choice may be made: *the restaurant offers a wide selection of hot and cold dishes.* ■ [count noun] a horse or horses tipped as worth bets in a race or meeting. ■ [count noun] data highlighted on a computer screen for a particular operation.
2 Biology a process in which environmental or genetic influences determine which types of organism thrive better than others, regarded as a factor in evolution. See also NATURAL SELECTION.
3 Austral./NZ historical the action of choosing and acquiring plots of land for small farming on terms favourable to the buyer. ■ [count noun] a plot of land acquired in such a way.
– ORIGIN early 17th cent.: from Latin *selectio(n-)*, from *seligere* 'select by separating off' (see SELECT).

selectional ▶ adjective Linguistics denoting or relating to the process by which only certain words or structures can occur naturally, normally, or correctly in the context of other words.
– DERIVATIVES **selectionally** adverb.

selection pressure ▶ noun Biology an agent of differential mortality or fertility that tends to make a population change genetically.

selection rule ▶ noun Physics a rule which describes whether particular quantum transitions in an atom or molecule are allowed or forbidden.

selective ▶ adjective relating to or involving the selection of the most suitable or best qualified: *the cow is the result of generations of selective breeding.* ■ (of a person) tending to choose carefully: *he is very* ***selective in*** *his reading.* ■ (of a process or agent) affecting some things and not others: *modern pesticides are more selective in effect.* ■ chiefly Electronics operating at or responding to a particular frequency.
– DERIVATIVES **selectively** adverb, **selectiveness** noun.

selective attention ▶ noun [mass noun] Psychology the capacity for or process of reacting to certain stimuli selectively when several occur simultaneously.

selective service ▶ noun [mass noun] N. Amer. service in the armed forces under conscription.

selectivity ▶ noun [mass noun] the quality of carefully choosing someone or something as the best or most suitable: *provision is organized on the principle of selectivity.* ■ the property of affecting some things and not others. ■ Electronics the ability of a device to respond to a particular frequency without interference from others.

selectman ▶ noun (pl. **selectmen**) a member of the local government board of a New England town.

selector ▶ noun a person or thing that selects something, in particular: ■ Brit. a person appointed to select a representative team in a sport. ■ (also **selecta**) Brit. informal a disc jockey (especially in the context of reggae and UK garage music). ■ a device for selecting a particular gear or other setting of a machine or device.

selenate /ˈsɛlɪneɪt/ ▶ noun Chemistry a salt or ester of selenic acid.

Selene /sɪˈliːni/ Greek Mythology the goddess of the moon, who fell in love with Endymion.
– ORIGIN from Greek *selēnē* 'moon'.

selenic acid /sɪˌlɛnɪk/ ▶ noun [mass noun] Chemistry a crystalline acid analogous to sulphuric acid, made by oxidizing some selenium compounds. ● Chem. formula: H_2SeO_4.

selenite /ˈsɛlɪnʌɪt/ ▶ noun [mass noun] a form of gypsum occurring as transparent crystals or thin plates.
– ORIGIN mid 17th cent.: via Latin from Greek *selēnitēs lithos* 'moonstone', from *selēnē* 'moon' + *lithos* 'stone'.

selenium /sɪˈliːnɪəm/ ▶ noun [mass noun] the chemical element of atomic number 34, a grey crystalline non-metal with semiconducting properties. (Symbol: **Se**)
– DERIVATIVES **selenide** noun.
– ORIGIN early 19th cent.: modern Latin, from Greek *selēnē* 'moon'.

selenium cell ▶ noun a photoelectric device containing a piece of selenium.

seleno- ▶ combining form relating to or shaped like the moon: *selenography.*
– ORIGIN from Greek *selēnē* 'moon'.

selenodont /sɪˈliːnə(ʊ)dɒnt/ ▶ adjective Zoology (of molar teeth) having crescent-shaped ridges on the grinding surfaces, characteristic of the ruminants. ■ (of an ungulate) having such teeth.
– ORIGIN late 19th cent.: from SELENO- 'moon-shaped' + Greek *odous, odont-* 'tooth'.

selenography /ˌsɛlɪˈnɒgrəfi, ˌsiː-/ ▶ noun [mass noun] the scientific mapping of the moon; lunar geography.
– DERIVATIVES **selenographer** noun, **selenographic** adjective.

selenology /ˌsɛlɪˈnɒlədʒi, ˌsiː-/ ▶ noun [mass noun] the scientific study of the moon.

Seleucid /sɪˈluːsɪd/ ▶ adjective relating to or denoting a dynasty ruling over Syria and a great part of western Asia from 311 to 65 BC. Its capital was at Antioch.
▶ noun a member of the Seleucid dynasty.
– ORIGIN from *Seleucus* Nicator (the founder, one of Alexander the Great's generals) + -ID[3].

self ▶ noun (pl. **selves**) a person's essential being that distinguishes them from others, especially considered as the object of introspection or reflexive action: *our alienation from our true selves* | *guilt can be turned against the self* | [mass noun] *language is an aspect of a person's sense of self.* ■ (**one's self**) one's particular nature or personality; the qualities that make one individual or unique: *by the end of the round he was* ***back to his old self*** | *Paula seemed to be her usual cheerful self.* ■ [mass noun] one's own interests or pleasure: *to love in an unpossessive way implies the total surrender of self.*
▶ pronoun (pl. **selves**) oneself, in particular: ■ (with adj. **one's self**) used ironically to refer to oneself or someone else: *an article with a picture of* ***my good self.*** ■ used on counterfoils, cheques, and other papers to refer to the holder or person who has signed.
▶ adjective [attrib.] (of a trimming or cover) of the same material and colour as the rest of the item: *a button-through style with self belt.*
▶ verb [with obj.] chiefly Botany self-pollinate; self-fertilize: (as noun **selfing**) *the flowers never open and pollination is normally by selfing.* ■ (usu. as adj. **selfed**) Genetics cause (an animal or plant) to breed with or fertilize one of the same hybrid origin or strain: *progeny were derived from selfed crosses.*
– ORIGIN Old English, of Germanic origin; related to Dutch *zelf* and German *selbe*. Early use was emphatic, expressing the sense '(I) myself', '(he) himself', etc. The verb dates from the early 20th cent.

self- ▶ combining form of or directed towards oneself or itself: *self-hatred.* ■ by one's own efforts; by its own action: *self-acting.* ■ on, in, for, or relating to oneself or itself: *self-adhesive.*

self-abandonment (also **self-abandon**) ▶ noun [mass noun] the action of completely surrendering oneself to a desire or impulse.
– DERIVATIVES **self-abandoned** adjective.

self-abasement ▶ noun [mass noun] the belittling or humiliation of oneself.

self-abnegation /sɛlfˌabnɪˈgeɪʃ(ə)n/ ▶ noun [mass noun] the denial or abasement of oneself: *she turned the letter into a grovelling form of self-abnegation.*

self-absorption ▶ noun [mass noun] **1** preoccupation with one's own emotions, interests, or situation.
2 Physics the absorption by a body of radiation which it has itself emitted.
– DERIVATIVES **self-absorbed** adjective.

S

self-abuse ▸ noun [mass noun] behaviour which causes damage or harm to oneself. ■ euphemistic masturbation.

self-accusation ▸ noun [mass noun] the action of accusing oneself, stemming from feelings of guilt.
– DERIVATIVES **self-accusatory** adjective.

self-acting ▸ adjective archaic (of a machine or operation) acting without external influence or control; automatic.

self-actualization (also **self-actualisation**) ▸ noun [mass noun] the realization or fulfilment of one's talents and potentialities, especially considered as a drive or need present in everyone.

self-addressed ▸ adjective (especially of an envelope) bearing one's own address: *enclose a self-addressed envelope.*

self-adhesive ▸ adjective coated with a sticky substance; adhering without requiring moistening.

self-adjusting ▸ adjective (chiefly of machinery) adjusting itself to meet varying requirements.
– DERIVATIVES **self-adjustment** noun.

self-advancement ▸ noun [mass noun] the advancement or promotion of oneself or one's interests: *a positive step in women's self-advancement.*

self-advertisement ▸ noun [mass noun] the active publicization of oneself: *he turned the group into a vehicle for self-advertisement.*
– DERIVATIVES **self-advertising** adjective.

self-advocacy ▸ noun [mass noun] the action of representing oneself or one's views or interests.

self-affirmation ▸ noun [mass noun] the recognition and assertion of the existence and value of one's individual self.

self-aggrandizement /ɪˈgrandɪzm(ə)nt/ (also **self-aggrandisement**) ▸ noun [mass noun] the action or process of promoting oneself as being powerful or important.
– DERIVATIVES **self-aggrandizing** adjective.

self-alienation ▸ noun [mass noun] the process of distancing oneself from one's own feelings or activities, such as may occur in mental illness or as a symptom of emotional distress.

self-aligning ▸ adjective (of a bearing or machine part) capable of aligning itself automatically.

self-analysis ▸ noun [mass noun] the analysis of oneself, in particular one's motives and character.
– DERIVATIVES **self-analysing** adjective.

self-annihilation ▸ noun [mass noun] the annihilation or obliteration of self, especially as a process of mystical contemplation.

self-appointed ▸ adjective having assumed a position or role without the endorsement of others: *self-appointed experts.*

self-approbation ▸ noun another term for SELF-APPROVAL.

self-approval ▸ noun [mass noun] approval or appreciation of oneself.
– DERIVATIVES **self-approving** adjective.

self-assembly ▸ noun [mass noun] the construction of an object, especially a piece of furniture, from materials sold in kit form: *you can buy it as a flat-pack for self-assembly.* ■ Biology the spontaneous formation of a ribosome, virus, or other body in a medium containing the appropriate components.
– DERIVATIVES **self-assemble** verb.

S

self-assertion ▸ noun [mass noun] the confident and forceful expression or promotion of oneself, one's views, or one's desires.
– DERIVATIVES **self-asserting** adjective, **self-assertive** adjective, **self-assertiveness** noun.

self-assessment ▸ noun [mass noun] assessment or evaluation of oneself or one's actions, attitudes, or performance. ■ Brit. calculation of one's own taxable liability.

self-assurance ▸ noun [mass noun] confidence in one's own abilities or character.

self-assured ▸ adjective confident in one's own abilities or character: *a self-assured 16-year-old.*
– DERIVATIVES **self-assuredly** adverb.

self-awareness ▸ noun [mass noun] conscious knowledge of one's own character, feelings, motives, and desires: *the process can be painful but it leads to greater self-awareness.*
– DERIVATIVES **self-aware** adjective.

self-balancing ▸ adjective (of a system) capable of achieving equilibrium or equality of its elements by processes inherent within it: *society is postulated as a self-balancing system based on consensus.* ■ (of an account record) having the debit side equal to the credit side.
▸ noun [mass noun] the process by which a system achieves and maintains a steady state by internal forces.

self-betrayal ▸ noun [mass noun] the intentional or inadvertent revelation of the truth about one's actions or thoughts.

self-build ▸ noun [mass noun] [often as modifier] Brit. the building of homes by their owners: *self-build schemes* | *self-build is the cheapest way to get a home to your specification.*
– DERIVATIVES **self-builder** noun.

self-cancelling ▸ adjective **1** having elements which contradict or negate one another.
2 (of a mechanical device) designed to stop working automatically when no longer required.

self-catering Brit. ▸ adjective (of a holiday or accommodation) offering facilities for people to cook their own meals: *guests stay in self-catering apartments.*
▸ noun [mass noun] the action of holidaying or staying in accommodation with facilities to cook one's own meals: *self-catering in southern Portugal is easy.*

self-censorship ▸ noun [mass noun] the exercising of control over what one says and does, especially to avoid criticism: *a climate of self-censorship, fear, and hypocrisy.*

self-centred ▸ adjective preoccupied with oneself and one's affairs: *he's far too self-centred to care what you do.*
– DERIVATIVES **self-centredly** adverb, **self-centredness** noun.

self-certification ▸ noun [mass noun] the practice of giving information about oneself or one's company in a formal statement rather than being obliged to ask a third party to do so: *the applicability of self-certification to aircraft safety tests.* ■ the practice, for the purpose of claiming sick pay, by which an employee rather than a doctor declares in writing that an absence was due to illness.
– DERIVATIVES **self-certificate** noun.

self-certify ▸ verb [with obj.] Brit. attest or confirm (one's financial standing) in a formal statement: *if you wish to self-certify your earnings, you will have to supply accounts for the year.* ■ (as adj. **self-certified**) (of a loan or mortgage) obtained as a result of attesting or confirming one's financial standing in this way.

self-cleaning ▸ adjective (of an object or apparatus) able to clean itself: *a self-cleaning oven.*

self-closing ▸ adjective (especially of a door or valve) closing automatically.

self-cocking ▸ adjective (of a gun) having a hammer that is raised by the trigger, not by hand.

self-coloured (also **self-colour**) ▸ adjective of a single uniform colour: *a self-coloured carpet.* ■ (of a trimming or accessory) of the same colour as the rest of the item: *self-coloured buttons.*

self-command ▸ noun the ability to control one's emotions; self-control.

self-compatible ▸ adjective Botany (of a plant or species) able to be fertilized by its own pollen.

self-conceit ▸ noun undue pride in oneself.
– DERIVATIVES **self-conceited** adjective.

self-concept ▸ noun Psychology an idea of the self constructed from the beliefs one holds about oneself and the responses of others.

self-condemnation ▸ noun [mass noun] the blaming of oneself for something. ■ the inadvertent revelation of one's wrongdoing.
– DERIVATIVES **self-condemned** adjective, **self-condemning** adjective.

self-confessed ▸ adjective [attrib.] having openly admitted to being a person with certain characteristics: *a self-confessed chocoholic.*
– DERIVATIVES **self-confessedly** adverb, **self-confession** noun, **self-confessional** adjective.

self-confidence ▸ noun [mass noun] a feeling of trust in one's abilities, qualities, and judgement.

self-confident ▸ adjective trusting in one's abilities, qualities, and judgement.
– DERIVATIVES **self-confidently** adverb.

self-congratulation ▸ noun [mass noun] undue complacency or pride regarding one's personal achievements or qualities; self-satisfaction: *a hefty dose of self-congratulation about how noble we are.*
– DERIVATIVES **self-congratulatory** adjective.

self-conscious ▸ adjective **1** feeling undue awareness of oneself, one's appearance, or one's actions: *I feel a bit self-conscious parking my scruffy old car* | *a self-conscious laugh.*
2 (especially of an action or intention) deliberate and with full awareness, especially affectedly so: *her self-conscious identification with the upper classes.* ■ Philosophy & Psychology having knowledge of one's own existence, especially the knowledge of oneself as a conscious being.
– DERIVATIVES **self-consciously** adverb, **self-consciousness** noun.

self-consistent ▸ adjective not having parts or aspects which are in conflict or contradiction with each other; consistent: *the theory is both rigorous and self-consistent.*
– DERIVATIVES **self-consistency** noun.

self-contained ▸ adjective **1** (of a thing) complete, or having all that is needed, in itself. ■ Brit. (of accommodation) having its own kitchen and bathroom, and typically its own private entrance: *a group of self-contained flats.*
2 (of a person) quiet and independent; not depending on or influenced by others.
– DERIVATIVES **self-containment** noun (sense 2).

self-contempt ▸ noun [mass noun] contempt or loathing for oneself or one's actions.
– DERIVATIVES **self-contemptuous** adjective.

self-contradiction ▸ noun [mass noun] inconsistency between aspects or parts of a whole.
– DERIVATIVES **self-contradicting** adjective, **self-contradictory** adjective.

self-control ▸ noun [mass noun] the ability to control oneself, in particular one's emotions and desires, especially in difficult situations: *Lucy silently struggled for self-control.*
– DERIVATIVES **self-controlled** adjective.

self-correcting ▸ adjective correcting oneself or itself without external help.
– DERIVATIVES **self-correct** verb, **self-correction** noun.

self-created ▸ adjective created by oneself or itself: *his self-created role as the bad boy of the music scene.*
– DERIVATIVES **self-creating** adjective, **self-creation** noun.

self-critical ▸ adjective critical of oneself or one's actions in a self-aware or unduly disapproving manner: *she felt miserably self-critical for her reluctance to go.*
– DERIVATIVES **self-criticism** noun.

self-deceit ▸ noun another term for SELF-DECEPTION.

self-deceiving ▸ adjective allowing oneself to believe that a false or unvalidated feeling, idea, or situation is true: *I prefer my cynicism to your self-deceiving optimism.*
– DERIVATIVES **self-deceiver** noun.

self-deception ▸ noun [mass noun] the action or practice of allowing oneself to believe that a false or unvalidated feeling, idea, or situation is true: *Jane remarked on men's capacity for self-deception.*
– DERIVATIVES **self-deceptive** adjective.

self-defeating ▸ adjective (of an action) preventing rather than achieving a desired result; futile.

self-defence ▸ noun [mass noun] the defence of one's person or interests, especially through the use of physical force, which is permitted in certain cases as an answer to a charge of violent crime: *he claimed self-defence in the attempted murder charge* | [as modifier] *self-defence classes.*
– DERIVATIVES **self-defensive** adjective.

self-definition ▸ noun [mass noun] definition of one's individuality and role in life: *the struggle for national self-definition.*

self-delusion ▸ noun [mass noun] the action of deluding oneself; failure to recognize reality: *he retreats into a world of fantasy and self-delusion.*

self-denial ▸ noun [mass noun] the denial of one's own interests and needs; self-sacrifice.
– DERIVATIVES **self-denying** adjective.

self-denying ordinance ▸ noun a resolution (1645) of the Long Parliament depriving members of parliament of civil and military office.

self-dependence ▸ noun [mass noun] reliance on one's own strengths rather than on others; independence.

self-deprecating ▸ adjective modest about or critical of oneself, especially humorously so: *self-deprecating jokes.*

– DERIVATIVES **self-deprecatingly** adverb, **self-deprecation** noun, **self-deprecatory** adjective.

self-depreciatory ▶ adjective another term for SELF-DEPRECATING.
– DERIVATIVES **self-depreciation** noun.

self-despair ▶ noun [mass noun] despair or dismay about oneself or one's actions.

self-destroying ▶ adjective destroying or capable of destroying oneself or itself; self-destructive.

self-destruct ▶ verb [no obj.] (of a thing) destroy itself by exploding or disintegrating automatically, having been preset to do so: *the tape would automatically self-destruct after twenty minutes.*
▶ adjective enabling a thing to self-destruct: *a self-destruct mechanism.*
– DERIVATIVES **self-destruction** noun.

self-destructive ▶ adjective destroying or causing harm to oneself.
– DERIVATIVES **self-destructively** adverb.

self-determination ▶ noun [mass noun] the process by which a country determines its own statehood and forms its own government: *the changes cannot be made until the country's right to self-determination is recognized.* ■ the process by which a person controls their own life.

self-development ▶ noun [mass noun] the process by which a person's character or abilities are gradually developed: *graduates have stressed the value of their courses for self-development.*

self-devotion ▶ noun [mass noun] the devotion of oneself to a person or cause.

self-diagnose ▶ verb [no obj.] diagnose oneself as having a particular medical condition: *many patients self-diagnose and do not seek medical attention for their symptoms.*

self-diffusion ▶ noun [mass noun] Chemistry the migration of constituent atoms or molecules within the bulk of a substance, especially in a crystalline solid.

self-directed ▶ adjective **1** (of an emotion, statement, or activity) directed at one's self: *she grimaces with a bitter self-directed humour.*
2 (of an activity) under one's own control: *this gives learners guidance in their self-directed learning.*
■ (of a person) showing initiative and the ability to organize oneself.
– DERIVATIVES **self-direction** noun.

self-discipline ▶ noun [mass noun] the ability to control one's feelings and overcome one's weaknesses.
– DERIVATIVES **self-disciplined** adjective.

self-discovery ▶ noun [mass noun] the process of acquiring insight into one's own character.

self-disgust ▶ noun [mass noun] profound revulsion at one's own character or actions: *his descent into drunkenness filled him with self-disgust.*

self-doubt ▶ noun [mass noun] lack of confidence in oneself and one's abilities: *his later years were plagued by self-doubt.*

self-dramatization (also **self-dramatisation**) ▶ noun [mass noun] dramatization of one's own situation or feelings for effect.

self-drive ▶ adjective Brit. **1** (of a hired vehicle) driven by the person who hires the vehicle, rather than a professional driver: *a self-drive removal van.*
2 (of a holiday) involving use of one's own car rather than transport arranged by the operator.

self-educated ▶ adjective educated largely through one's own efforts, rather than by formal instruction: *he was a self-made and almost self-educated businessman.*
– DERIVATIVES **self-education** noun.

self-effacing ▶ adjective not claiming attention for oneself; retiring and modest: *his demeanour was self-effacing, gracious, and polite.*
– DERIVATIVES **self-effacement** noun, **self-effacingly** adverb.

self-employed ▶ adjective working for oneself as a freelance or the owner of a business rather than for an employer: *a self-employed builder.* ■ relating to or designed for people working for themselves: *the rules for self-employed pension plans have been altered.*
– DERIVATIVES **self-employment** noun.

self-enclosed ▶ adjective not choosing to or able to communicate with others or with external systems: *the family is a self-enclosed unit.*

self-esteem ▶ noun [mass noun] confidence in one's own worth or abilities; self-respect: *assertiveness training for those with low self-esteem.*

self-evaluation ▶ noun another term for SELF-ASSESSMENT.

self-evident ▶ adjective not needing to be demonstrated or explained; obvious: *self-evident truths* | [with clause] *it is self-evident that childhood experiences must have a profound effect upon our beliefs about ourselves.*
– DERIVATIVES **self-evidence** noun, **self-evidently** adverb.

self-examination ▶ noun [mass noun] the study of one's own behaviour and motivations: *a period of considerable self-doubt and self-examination.* ■ the action of examining one's own body for signs of illness.

self-excited ▶ adjective Physics relating to or denoting a machine or system that generates or excites its own magnetic field.

self-existent ▶ adjective existing independently of other beings or causes.

self-explanatory ▶ adjective easily understood; not needing explanation: *the film's title is fairly self-explanatory.*

self-expression ▶ noun [mass noun] the expression of one's feelings, thoughts, or ideas, especially in writing, art, music, or dance.
– DERIVATIVES **self-expressive** adjective.

self-faced ▶ adjective (of stone) having an undressed surface.

self-feeder ▶ noun **1** a furnace or machine that renews its own fuel or material automatically.
2 a device for supplying food to farm animals automatically.
– DERIVATIVES **self-feeding** adjective.

self-fertile ▶ adjective Botany (of a plant) capable of self-fertilization.
– DERIVATIVES **self-fertility** noun.

self-fertilization (also **self-fertilisation**) ▶ noun [mass noun] Biology the fertilization of plants and some invertebrate animals by their own pollen or sperm rather than that of another individual.
– DERIVATIVES **self-fertilized** adjective, **self-fertilizing** adjective.

self-financing ▶ adjective (of an organization or enterprise) having or generating enough income to finance itself.
– DERIVATIVES **self-financed** adjective.

self-flagellation ▶ noun [mass noun] the action of flogging oneself, especially as a form of religious discipline. ■ excessive criticism of oneself.

self-flattery ▶ noun [mass noun] the holding of an unjustifiably high opinion of oneself or one's actions.
– DERIVATIVES **self-flattering** adjective.

self-forgetful ▶ adjective forgetful of one's self or one's needs.
– DERIVATIVES **self-forgetfulness** noun.

self-fulfilling ▶ adjective (of an opinion or prediction) bound to be proved correct or to come true as a result of behaviour caused by its being expressed: *expecting something to be bad can turn out to be a self-fulfilling prophecy.*

self-fulfilment (US **self-fulfillment**) ▶ noun [mass noun] the fulfilment of one's hopes and ambitions: *it is the striving for self-fulfilment which guides and gives consistency to our lives.*

self-generating ▶ adjective generated by itself, rather than by some external force: *the strident activity of the industrial scene seems to be self-generating.*

self-glorification ▶ noun [mass noun] exaltation of oneself and one's abilities: *they fought not merely for self-glorification but for the common good.*

self-governing ▶ adjective exercising control over one's own affairs, in particular: ■ (of a British hospital or school) having opted out of local authority control. ■ (of a former colony or dependency) administering its own affairs.

self-government ▶ noun [mass noun] **1** government of a country by its own people, especially after having been a colony.
2 old-fashioned term for SELF-CONTROL.
– DERIVATIVES **self-governed** adjective.

self-gravitation ▶ noun [mass noun] Astronomy the gravitational forces acting among the components of a massive body.

self-harm ▶ noun [mass noun] deliberate injury to oneself, typically as a manifestation of a psychological or psychiatric disorder.
▶ verb [no obj.] commit self-harm.
– DERIVATIVES **self-harmer** noun.

self-hatred (also **self-hate**) ▶ noun [mass noun] intense dislike of oneself.

self-heal ▶ noun a purple-flowered Eurasian plant of the mint family, which was formerly widely used for healing wounds. ● *Prunella vulgaris*, family Labiatae.

self-help ▶ noun [mass noun] the use of one's own efforts and resources to achieve things without relying on others: *a reduction in the role of the state and an increasing reliance on self-help.*

selfhood ▶ noun [mass noun] the quality that constitutes one's individuality; the state of having an individual identity.

self-identification ▶ noun [mass noun] the attribution of certain characteristics or qualities to oneself: *self-identification by the old person as sick or inadequate.*

self-identity ▶ noun [mass noun] the recognition of one's potential and qualities as an individual, especially in relation to social context: *caring can become the defining characteristic of women's self-identity.*

self-image ▶ noun the idea one has of one's abilities, appearance, and personality: *poverty causes lowered self-respect and self-image.*

self-immolation ▶ noun [mass noun] the offering of oneself as a sacrifice, especially by burning.

self-importance ▶ noun [mass noun] an exaggerated sense of one's own value or importance: *he was a big, blustering, opinionated cop, full of self-importance.*

self-important ▶ adjective having an exaggerated sense of one's own value or importance: *a self-important bureaucrat.*
– DERIVATIVES **self-importantly** adverb.

self-imposed ▶ adjective (of a task or circumstance) imposed on oneself, not by an external force: *he went into self-imposed exile.*

self-improvement ▶ noun [mass noun] the improvement of one's knowledge, status, or character by one's own efforts.

self-incompatible ▶ adjective Botany (of a plant or species) unable to be fertilized by its own pollen.
– DERIVATIVES **self-incompatibility** noun.

self-induced ▶ adjective **1** brought about by oneself: *self-induced vomiting.*
2 produced by electrical self-induction.

self-inductance ▶ noun Physics a measure or coefficient of self-induction in a circuit, usually measured in henries. ■ [mass noun] the property of an electric circuit that permits self-induction.

self-induction ▶ noun [mass noun] Physics the induction of an electromotive force in a circuit when the current in that circuit is varied. Compare with MUTUAL INDUCTION.

self-indulgence ▶ noun [mass noun] the quality of being self-indulgent. ■ [count noun] something done or allowed in a self-indulgent way: *simple-minded pleasures and self-indulgences.*

self-indulgent ▶ adjective characterized by doing or tending to do exactly what one wants, especially when this involves pleasure or idleness: *a self-indulgent extra hour of sleep.* ■ (of a creative work) lacking economy and control.
– DERIVATIVES **self-indulgently** adverb.

self-inflicted ▶ adjective (of a wound or other harm) inflicted on oneself.

self-insurance ▶ noun [mass noun] insurance of oneself or one's interests by maintaining a fund to cover possible losses rather than by purchasing an insurance policy.

self-interest ▶ noun [mass noun] one's personal interest or advantage, especially when pursued without regard for others.

self-interested ▶ adjective motivated by one's personal interest or advantage, especially without regard for others: *many groups pursue self-interested aims.*

self-involved ▶ adjective wrapped up in oneself or one's own thoughts.
– DERIVATIVES **self-involvement** noun.

selfish ▶ adjective (of a person, action, or motive) lacking consideration for other people; concerned chiefly with one's own personal profit or pleasure: *I joined them for selfish reasons.*
– DERIVATIVES **selfishly** adverb.

selfishness ▶ noun [mass noun] the quality or state of being selfish; lack of consideration for other people: *an act of pure selfishness.*

selfism ▶ noun [mass noun] concentration on one's own interests; self-centredness or self-absorption.

self-justification ▶ noun [mass noun] the justification or excusing of oneself or one's actions.
– DERIVATIVES **self-justificatory** adjective, **self-justifying** adjective.

self-knowledge ▶ noun [mass noun] understanding of oneself or one's own motives or character.
– DERIVATIVES **self-knowing** adjective.

selfless ▶ adjective concerned more with the needs and wishes of others than with one's own; unselfish: *an act of selfless devotion.*
– DERIVATIVES **selflessly** adverb, **selflessness** noun.

self-limiting ▶ adjective relating to or denoting something which limits itself, in particular: ■ Medicine (of a condition) ultimately resolving itself without treatment. ■ (in psychology) preventing the development or expression of the self.

self-liquidating ▶ adjective denoting an asset, project, etc. that earns sufficiently over a fixed period to pay for its cost.

self-loading ▶ adjective (especially of a gun) loading automatically: *a self-loading pistol.*
– DERIVATIVES **self-loader** noun.

self-loathing ▶ noun [mass noun] hatred of oneself.

self-locking ▶ adjective locking itself shut or in a fixed position: *self-locking screws.*

self-love ▶ noun [mass noun] regard for one's own well-being and happiness.

self-made ▶ adjective made by oneself: *his self-made fortune | a self-made kite.* ■ having become successful or rich by one's own efforts: *a self-made millionaire.*

self-management ▶ noun [mass noun] management of or by oneself; the taking of responsibility for one's own behaviour and well-being. ■ the distribution of political control to individual regions of a state, especially as a form of socialism practised by its own members.
– DERIVATIVES **self-managing** adjective.

self-mastery ▶ noun [mass noun] self-control.

selfmate ▶ noun [mass noun] Chess a problem in which the solver's task is to force the opponent to deliver checkmate.

self-medicate ▶ verb [no obj.] administer medication to oneself without medical supervision. ■ drink or take drugs to relieve stress or other conditions.
– DERIVATIVES **self-medication** noun.

self-mocking ▶ adjective mocking oneself: *a wry, self-mocking smile.*
– DERIVATIVES **self-mockery** noun, **self-mockingly** adverb.

self-mortification ▶ noun [mass noun] the subjugation of appetites or desires by self-denial or self-discipline as an aspect of religious devotion: *voluntary self-mortification such as fasting.*

self-motivated ▶ adjective motivated to do or achieve something because of one's own enthusiasm or interest, without needing pressure from others: *she's a very independent self-motivated individual.*
– DERIVATIVES **self-motivating** adjective, **self-motivation** noun.

S

self-mutilation ▶ noun [mass noun] the mutilation of oneself, especially as a symptom of mental or emotional disturbance.

self-neglect ▶ noun [mass noun] neglect of oneself, especially one's physical well-being

selfness ▶ noun [mass noun] **1** a person's essential individuality.
2 archaic selfishness; self-regard.

self-obsessed ▶ adjective excessively preoccupied with one's own life and circumstances; thinking only about oneself: *even self-obsessed pop stars don't want the rumour mill to overshadow their music.*
– DERIVATIVES **self-obsession** noun.

self-opinionated ▶ adjective having an arrogantly high regard for oneself or one's own opinions: *a pompous, self-opinionated bully.*
– DERIVATIVES **self-opinion** noun.

self-parodic ▶ adjective another term for **SELF-PARODYING**.

self-parody ▶ noun [mass noun] the intentional or inadvertent parodying or exaggeration of one's usual behaviour or speech: *they are soft-spoken and clean-cut to the point of self-parody.*

self-parodying ▶ adjective appearing to parody one's usual behaviour or speech, especially inadvertently: *pathetic, self-parodying former beauty queens propped up by surgery and cosmetics.*

self-perpetuating ▶ adjective perpetuating itself or oneself without external agency or intervention: *the self-perpetuating power of the bureaucracy.*
– DERIVATIVES **self-perpetuation** noun.

self-pity ▶ noun [mass noun] excessive, self-absorbed unhappiness over one's own troubles.

self-pitying ▶ adjective characterized by self-pity: *he was in one of his self-pitying moods.*
– DERIVATIVES **self-pityingly** adverb.

self-policing ▶ noun [mass noun] the process of keeping order or maintaining control within a community without accountability or reference to an external authority.
▶ adjective (of a community) independently responsible for keeping and maintaining order.

self-pollination ▶ noun [mass noun] Botany the pollination of a flower by pollen from the same flower or from another flower on the same plant.
– DERIVATIVES **self-pollinated** adjective, **self-pollinating** adjective, **self-pollinator** noun.

self-portrait ▶ noun a portrait that an artist produces of themselves.
– DERIVATIVES **self-portraiture** noun.

self-possessed ▶ adjective calm, confident, and in control of one's feelings; composed.

self-possession ▶ noun [mass noun] the state or feeling of being calm, confident, and in control of one's feelings; composure.

self-preservation ▶ noun [mass noun] the protection of oneself from harm or death, especially regarded as a basic instinct in human beings and animals.

self-proclaimed ▶ adjective [attrib.] described as or proclaimed to be such by oneself, without endorsement by others: *books written by self-proclaimed experts.*

self-promotion ▶ noun [mass noun] the action of promoting or publicizing oneself or one's activities, especially in a forceful way: *she's guilty of criminally bad taste and shameless self-promotion.*
– DERIVATIVES **self-promoter** noun, **self-promoting** adjective.

self-propagating ▶ adjective (especially of a plant) able to propagate itself.
– DERIVATIVES **self-propagation** noun.

self-propelled ▶ adjective moving or able to move without external propulsion or agency: *a self-propelled weapon.*
– DERIVATIVES **self-propelling** adjective.

self-protection ▶ noun [mass noun] protection of oneself or itself.
– DERIVATIVES **self-protective** adjective.

self-raising flour ▶ noun [mass noun] Brit. flour that has a raising agent already added.

self-rating ▶ noun [mass noun] evaluation of one's own character, feelings, or behaviour, used as a tool in psychology to quantify people's perception of themselves or assess mental health risks.

self-realization (also **self-realisation**) ▶ noun [mass noun] fulfilment of one's own potential.

self-referential ▶ adjective (especially of a literary or other creative work) making reference to itself, its author or creator, or their other work: *self-referential elements in Donne's poems.*
– DERIVATIVES **self-referentiality** noun, **self-referentially** adverb.

self-reflection ▶ noun [mass noun] serious thought about one's character and actions.
– DERIVATIVES **self-reflective** adjective.

self-reflexive ▶ adjective containing a reflection or image of itself; self-referential: *sociology's self-reflexive critique.*

self-regard ▶ noun [mass noun] regard or consideration for oneself; self-respect. ■ conceit; vanity.
– DERIVATIVES **self-regarding** adjective.

self-regulating ▶ adjective regulating itself without intervention from external bodies: *advertising is governed by a self-regulating system.*
– DERIVATIVES **self-regulation** noun, **self-regulatory** adjective.

self-reliance ▶ noun [mass noun] reliance on one's own powers and resources rather than those of others.

self-reliant ▶ adjective reliant on one's own powers and resources rather than those of others: *a self-reliant little girl.*
– DERIVATIVES **self-reliantly** adverb.

self-renewal ▶ noun [mass noun] the process of renewing oneself or itself.

self-report ▶ verb [with obj.] provide details about (one's circumstances, typically one's medical or psychological condition): *35% of participants self-reported a history of asthma.*

self-reproach ▶ noun [mass noun] reproach or blame directed at oneself: *the bitter tears of self-reproach.*
– DERIVATIVES **self-reproachful** adjective.

self-respect ▶ noun [mass noun] pride and confidence in oneself; a feeling that one is behaving with honour and dignity.

self-respecting ▶ adjective having self-respect: *proud, self-respecting mountain villagers.* ■ [attrib.] often humorous fully meriting a particular role or name: *no self-respecting editor would run such an article.*

self-restraint ▶ noun [mass noun] restraint imposed by oneself on one's own actions; self-control.
– DERIVATIVES **self-restrained** adjective.

self-revealing ▶ adjective revealing one's character or motives, especially inadvertently: *his most intimate and self-revealing book.*
– DERIVATIVES **self-revelation** noun, **self-revelatory** adjective.

Selfridge /ˈsɛlfrɪdʒ/, Harry Gordon (1858–1947), American-born British businessman. In 1906 he came to England and began to build the department store in Oxford Street, London, that bears his name; it opened in 1909.

self-righteous ▶ adjective having or characterized by a certainty, especially an unfounded one, that one is totally correct or morally superior: *self-righteous indignation and complacency.*
– DERIVATIVES **self-righteously** adverb.

self-righteousness ▶ noun [mass noun] the quality or state of being self-righteous.

self-righting ▶ adjective (of a boat) designed to right itself when capsized.

self-rising flour ▶ noun US term for **SELF-RAISING FLOUR**.

self-rule ▶ noun another term for **SELF-GOVERNMENT** (sense 1).

self-sacrifice ▶ noun [mass noun] the giving up of one's own interests or wishes in order to help others or advance a cause.
– DERIVATIVES **self-sacrificial** adjective, **self-sacrificing** adjective.

selfsame ▶ adjective [attrib.] exactly the same: *he was standing in the selfsame spot you're filling now.*

self-satisfaction ▶ noun [mass noun] excessive satisfaction with oneself or one's achievements; smug complacency: *a look of self-satisfaction.*

self-satisfied ▶ adjective excessively satisfied with oneself or one's achievements; smugly complacent: *a pompous, self-satisfied fool.*

self-sealing ▶ adjective sealing itself without the usual process or procedure, in particular: ■ (of a pneumatic tyre, fuel tank, etc.) able to seal small punctures automatically. ■ (of an envelope) self-adhesive.

self-seed ▶ verb [no obj.] (of a plant) propagate itself by seed: (as adj. **self-seeding**) *an early-blooming, self-seeding primrose.*
– DERIVATIVES **self-seeder** noun.

self-seeking ▶ adjective having concern for one's own welfare and interests before those of others: *the self-seeking aggrandizement of Party bosses.*
▶ noun [mass noun] concern for oneself before others.
– DERIVATIVES **self-seeker** noun.

self-selection ▶ noun [mass noun] **1** the action of putting oneself forward for something.
2 [often as modifier] the action of selecting something for oneself: *a self-selection buffet.*
– DERIVATIVES **self-select** verb, **self-selecting** adjective (sense 1).

self-service ▶ adjective denoting a shop, restaurant, etc. where customers select goods for themselves and pay at a checkout: *a self-service cafeteria.*
▶ noun [mass noun] the system whereby customers select goods for themselves and pay at a checkout: *providing quick self-service.*

self-serving ▶ adjective & noun another term for **SELF-SEEKING**.

self-shifter ▸ noun a car with an automatic gearbox.

self-similar ▸ adjective Mathematics (of an object or set of objects) similar to itself at a different time, or to a copy of itself on a different scale.
– DERIVATIVES **self-similarity** noun.

self-sow ▸ verb [no obj.] (of a plant) propagate itself by seed: (as adj. **self-sown**) *a batch of self-sown seedlings*.

self-starter ▸ noun **1** a person who is sufficiently motivated or ambitious to work on their own initiative without needing direction.
2 dated the starter of a motor-vehicle engine.
– DERIVATIVES **self-starting** adjective.

self-sterile ▸ adjective Biology incapable of self-fertilization.
– DERIVATIVES **self-sterility** noun.

self-stimulation ▸ noun [mass noun] Physiology a phenomenon which occurs in the hypothalamus and other areas of the brain, in which the propagation of electrical stimulation has positive reinforcing properties which act to maintain and perpetuate the impulses.

self-storage ▸ noun [mass noun] a system whereby individuals rent containers or units of space within a large warehouse to store possessions.

self-styled ▸ adjective [attrib.] using a description or title that one has given oneself: *self-styled experts* | *the self-styled President of Bougainville*.

self-subsistent ▸ adjective subsistent without dependence on or support from external agencies.

self-sufficiency ▸ noun [mass noun] the quality or condition of being self-sufficient: *a means of developing economic self-sufficiency*.

self-sufficient ▸ adjective needing no outside help in satisfying one's basic needs, especially with regard to the production of food: *I don't think the country could ever be self-sufficient in food*. ■ emotionally and intellectually independent: *their son was a little bit of a loner and very self-sufficient*.
– DERIVATIVES **self-sufficiently** adverb.

self-suggestion ▸ noun another term for AUTO-SUGGESTION.

self-supporting ▸ adjective **1** having the resources to be able to survive without outside assistance.
2 staying up or upright without being supported by something else: *arches were originally self-supporting structures*.
– DERIVATIVES **self-support** noun.

self-surrender ▸ noun [mass noun] the surrender of oneself or one's will to an external influence, an emotion, or another person.

self-sustaining ▸ adjective able to continue in a healthy state without outside assistance: *the studies throw doubt on whether these businesses are really self-sustaining*.
– DERIVATIVES **self-sustained** adjective.

self-system ▸ noun Psychology the complex of drives and responses relating to the self; the set of potentialities which develop in an individual's character in response to parental and other external influence.

self-tailing ▸ adjective (of a winch) designed to maintain constant tension in the rope round it so that it does not slip.

self-tanner ▸ noun a lotion containing ingredients that react with the skin to produce an artificial tan.
– DERIVATIVES **self-tanning** adjective.

self-tapping ▸ adjective (of a screw) able to cut a thread in the material into which it is inserted.

self-taught ▸ adjective having acquired knowledge or skill on one's own initiative rather than through formal instruction or training: *a self-taught artist*.

self-timer ▸ noun a mechanism in a camera that introduces a delay between the operation of the shutter release and the opening of the shutter, so that the photographer can be included in the photograph.

self-titled ▸ adjective (of an album, CD, etc.) having a title that is the same as the performer's name.

self-torture ▸ noun [mass noun] the inflicting of pain, especially mental pain, on oneself.

self-transcendence ▸ noun [mass noun] the overcoming of the limits of the individual self and its desires in spiritual contemplation and realization.

self-understanding ▸ noun [mass noun] awareness of and ability to understand one's own actions.

self-willed ▸ adjective obstinately doing what one wants in spite of the wishes or orders of others: *the child may be very obstinate and self-willed*.
– DERIVATIVES **self-will** noun.

self-winding ▸ adjective (chiefly of a watch) wound by some automatic means, such as an electric motor or the movement of the wearer, rather than by hand.

self-worth ▸ noun another term for SELF-ESTEEM.

Seljuk /ˈsɛldʒuːk/ ▸ noun a member of any of the Turkish dynasties which ruled Asia Minor in the 11th to 13th centuries, successfully invading the Byzantine Empire and defending the Holy Land against the Crusaders.
– DERIVATIVES **Seljukian** /-ˈdʒuːkɪən/ adjective & noun.
– ORIGIN from Turkish *seljūq*, the name of the reputed ancestor of the dynasty.

selkie (also **selky** or **silkie**) ▸ noun (pl. **selkies**) Scottish a mythical creature that resembles a seal in the water but assumes human form on land.
– ORIGIN from *selch*, variant of SEAL[1], + -IE.

Selkirk /ˈsɛlkəːk/, Alexander (1676–1721), Scottish sailor; also called *Alexander Selcraig*. While on a privateering expedition in 1704 Selkirk quarrelled with his captain and was put ashore, at his own request, on one of the uninhabited Juan Fernandez Islands, where he remained until 1709. His experiences formed the basis of Daniel Defoe's novel *Robinson Crusoe* (1719).

Selkirkshire a former county of SE Scotland. It was made a part of Borders region (now Scottish Borders) in 1975.

sell ▸ verb (past and past participle **sold**) [with obj.] **1** give or hand over (something) in exchange for money: *they had sold the car* | *the family business had been **sold off*** | [with two objs] *I was trying to sell him my butterfly collection*. ■ have a stock of (something) available for sale: *the store sells hi-fis, TVs, videos, and other electrical goods*. ■ [no obj.] be purchased in specified amounts or for a specified price: *the album sold 6 million copies in the United States* | *this magazine of yours won't sell* | *these antiques of the future **sell for** about £375*. ■ [no obj.] (**sell out**) sell all of one's stock of something: *they had nearly **sold out of** the initial run of 75,000 copies*. ■ [no obj.] (**sell out**) be all sold: *it was clear that the performances would not sell out*. ■ [no obj.] (**sell through**) (of a product) be purchased by a customer from a retail outlet. ■ [no obj.] (**sell up**) Brit. sell all of one's property, possessions, or assets: *Ernest sold up and retired*. ■ (**sell oneself**) have sex in exchange for money. ■ [no obj.] (**sell out**) abandon one's principles for reasons of expedience: *the prime minister has come under fire for **selling out to** the United States*. ■ (**sell someone out**) betray someone for one's own benefit: *the clansmen became tenants and the chiefs sold them out*. ■ archaic offer (something) dishonourably for money or other reward.
2 persuade someone of the merits of: *he sold the idea of making a film about Tchaikovsky* | *he just won't sell himself*. ■ (**sell someone on**) cause someone to become enthusiastic about: *I'm just not sold on the idea*.
3 archaic trick or deceive (someone).
▸ noun informal **1** an act of selling or attempting to sell something: *every other television commercial is a sell for Australian lager*.
2 Brit. a disappointment, typically one arising from being deceived as to the merits of something: *actually, Hawaii's a bit of a sell—not a patch on Corfu*.
– PHRASES **sell someone a bill of goods** see BILL OF GOODS. **sell someone down the river** see RIVER. **sell someone a** (or **the**) **dummy** see DUMMY. **sell the pass** see PASS[2]. **sell someone a pup** see PUP. **sell someone/thing short** see SHORT. **sell one's soul** (**to the devil**) do or be willing to do anything, no matter how wrong it is, in order to achieve one's objective: *it is very easy to get to the top of any employment structure if you are prepared to sell your soul*.
– DERIVATIVES **sellable** adjective.
– ORIGIN Old English *sellan* (verb), of Germanic origin; related to Old Norse *selja* 'give up, sell'. Early use included the sense 'give, hand (something) over voluntarily in response to a request'.

sella /ˈsɛlə/ (in full **sella turcica** /ˈtəːkɪkə/) ▸ noun (pl. **sellae** /ˈsɛliː/ or **sellae turcicae** /ˈtəːkɪkiː/) Anatomy a depression in the sphenoid bone, containing the pituitary gland.
– ORIGIN late 17th cent.: from Latin, 'saddle', (in full) 'Turkish saddle'.

Sellafield the site of a nuclear power station and reprocessing plant on the coast of Cumbria in NW England. It was the scene in 1957 of a fire which caused a serious escape of radioactive material. Former name (1947–81) WINDSCALE.

sell-by date ▸ noun Brit. a date marked on a perishable product indicating the recommended time by which it should be sold: *crisps past their sell-by date*. ■ informal a time after which something or someone is no longer considered desirable or effective: *do broadcasters have a sell-by date?*

selldown ▸ noun Austral./NZ the widespread selling of shares, resulting in falling prices.

seller ▸ noun **1** a person who sells something: *street sellers of newspapers, flowers, etc.*
2 [with adj.] a product that sells in some specified way: *the book became the biggest seller in the history of royal publishing*.
– PHRASES **seller's** (or **sellers'**) **market** an economic situation in which goods or shares are scarce and sellers can keep prices high.

Sellers, Peter (1925–80), English comic actor. He made his name in *The Goon Show*, a radio series of the 1950s, but is best known for the 'Pink Panther' series of films of the 1960s and 1970s, in which he played the French detective Inspector Clouseau.

sell-in ▸ noun [mass noun] the sale of goods to retail traders prior to public retailing.

selling point ▸ noun a feature of a product for sale that makes it attractive to customers.

selling race ▸ noun a horse race after which the winning horse must be auctioned.

sell-off ▸ noun a sale of assets, typically at a low price, carried out in order to dispose of them. ■ chiefly N. Amer. a sale of shares, bonds, or commodities, especially one that causes a fall in price.

Sellotape Brit. ▸ noun [mass noun] trademark transparent adhesive tape.
▸ verb [with obj. and adverbial] fasten or stick with transparent adhesive tape: *there was a note Sellotaped to my door*.
– ORIGIN 1940s: from an alteration of CELLULOSE + TAPE.

sell-out ▸ noun **1** an event for which all tickets are sold: *the game is sure to be a sell-out*.
2 a betrayal of one's principles for reasons of expedience: *one of the biggest political sell-outs in decades*.

sell-through ▸ noun [mass noun] the ratio of the quantity of goods sold by a retail outlet to the quantity distributed to it wholesale: *the sell-through was amazing, 60 per cent*.

seltzer /ˈsɛltsə/ (also **seltzer water**) ▸ noun [mass noun] dated soda water. ■ medicinal mineral water from Niederselters in Germany.
– ORIGIN mid 18th cent.: alteration of German *Selterser*, from (*Nieder*)*selters* (see above).

selva ▸ noun a tract of land covered by dense equatorial forest, especially in the Amazon basin.
– ORIGIN mid 19th cent.: from Spanish or Portuguese, from Latin *silva* 'wood'.

selvedge /ˈsɛlvɪdʒ/ (chiefly N. Amer. also **selvage**) ▸ noun **1** an edge produced on woven fabric during manufacture that prevents it from unravelling.
2 Geology a zone of altered rock, especially volcanic glass, at the edge of a rock mass.
– ORIGIN late Middle English: from an alteration of SELF + EDGE, on the pattern of early modern Dutch *selfegghe*. The geological term dates from the 1930s.

S

selves plural form of SELF.

Selznick /ˈsɛlznɪk/, David O. (1902–65), American film producer; full name *David Oliver Selznick*. He produced such films as *King Kong* (1933) for RKO and *Anna Karenina* (1935) for MGM before establishing his own production company in 1936 and producing such screen classics as *Gone with the Wind* (1939) and *Rebecca* (1940).

SEM ▸ abbreviation scanning electron microscope.

semanteme /sɪˈmantiːm/ ▸ noun Linguistics a minimal distinctive unit of meaning. Compare with SEMEME.
– ORIGIN early 20th cent.: from French *sémantème*, from *sémantique* (see SEMANTIC), on the pattern of words such as *morphème* 'morpheme'.

semantic /sɪˈmantɪk/ ▸ adjective relating to meaning in language or logic.
– DERIVATIVES **semantically** adverb.
– ORIGIN mid 17th cent.: from French *sémantique*, from Greek *sēmantikos* 'significant', from *sēmainein* 'signify', from *sēma* 'sign'.

semantic field ▸ noun Linguistics a lexical set of semantically related items, for example verbs of perception.

semanticity /ˌsɪmanˈtɪsɪti/ ▸ **noun** [mass noun] the quality that a linguistic system has of being able to convey meanings, in particular by reference to the world of physical reality.

semantics ▸ **plural noun** [usu. treated as sing.] the branch of linguistics and logic concerned with meaning. The two main areas are **logical semantics**, concerned with matters such as sense and reference and presupposition and implication, and **lexical semantics**, concerned with the analysis of word meanings and relations between them. ■ the meaning of a word, phrase, or text: *such quibbling over semantics may seem petty stuff.*
– DERIVATIVES **semanticist** noun.

semaphore ▸ **noun** [mass noun] a system of sending messages by holding the arms or two flags or poles in certain positions according to an alphabetic code. ■ [count noun] an apparatus for signalling in this way, consisting of an upright with movable parts. ■ [count noun] a signal sent by semaphore.
▸ **verb** [with obj.] send (a message) by semaphore or by signals resembling semaphore: *Josh stands facing the rear and semaphoring the driver's intentions to frustrated queues of following cars.*
– DERIVATIVES **semaphoric** adjective.
– ORIGIN early 19th cent. (denoting a signalling apparatus): from French *sémaphore*, formed irregularly from Greek *sēma* 'sign' + *-phoros*.

Semarang /səˈmɑːraŋ/ a port in Indonesia, on the north coast of Java; pop. 1,396,000 (est. 2007).

semasiology /sɪˌmeɪzɪˈɒlədʒi/ ▸ **noun** [mass noun] the branch of knowledge that deals with concepts and the terms that represent them. Compare with **ONOMASIOLOGY**.
– DERIVATIVES **semasiological** adjective.
– ORIGIN mid 19th cent.: from German *Semasiologie*, from Greek *sēmasia* 'meaning', from *sēmainein* 'signify'.

semblable /ˈsɛmbləb(ə)l/ ▸ **noun** literary a counterpart or equal to someone: *there was Dodge, her semblable, her conspirator.*
– ORIGIN Middle English (as an adjective meaning 'like, similar'): from Old French, from *sembler* 'seem'.

semblance ▸ **noun** [mass noun] the outward appearance or apparent form of something, especially when the reality is different: *she tried to force her thoughts back into some* **semblance of** *order.* ■ archaic resemblance; similarity: *it bears some* **semblance to** *the thing I have in mind.*
– ORIGIN Middle English: from Old French, from *sembler* 'seem', from Latin *similare*, *simulare* 'simulate'.

seme /siːm/ ▸ **noun** another term for **SEMANTEME**.
– ORIGIN mid 19th cent.: from Greek *sēma* 'sign'.

semé /ˈsɛmi, ˈsɛmeɪ/ (also **semée**) ▸ **adjective** Heraldry covered with small bearings of indefinite number (e.g. stars, fleurs-de-lis) arranged all over the field.
– ORIGIN late Middle English: French, literally 'sown', past participle of *semer*.

Semei /səˈmeɪ/ (also **Semey**) an industrial city and river port in eastern Kazakhstan, on the Irtysh River close to the border with Russia; pop. 281,814 (est. 2006). Founded in the 18th century, it was known as Semipalatinsk until 1991.

Semele /ˈsɛmɪli/ Greek Mythology the mother, by Zeus, of Dionysus. The fire of Zeus's thunderbolts killed her but made her child immortal.

sememe /ˈsiːmiːm, ˈsiːm-/ ▸ **noun** Linguistics the unit of meaning carried by a morpheme. Compare with **SEMANTEME**.
– ORIGIN early 20th cent.: from **SEME** + **-EME**.

semen /ˈsiːmən/ ▸ **noun** [mass noun] the male reproductive fluid, containing spermatozoa in suspension.
– ORIGIN late Middle English: from Latin, literally 'seed', from *serere* 'to sow'.

semester /sɪˈmɛstə/ ▸ **noun** a half-year term in a school or university, especially in North America, typically lasting for fifteen to eighteen weeks.
– ORIGIN early 19th cent.: from German *Semester*, from Latin *semestris* 'six-monthly', from *sex* 'six' + *mensis* 'month'.

Semey variant spelling of **SEMEI**.

semi ▸ **noun** (pl. **semis**) informal **1** Brit. a semi-detached house: *a three-bedroomed semi.*
2 a semi-final: *they defeated them in the semi.*
3 N. Amer. a semi-trailer: *she pulled into the path of a semi.*
– ORIGIN early 20th cent.: abbreviation.

semi- ▸ **prefix 1** half: *semicircular.* ■ occurring or appearing twice in a specified period: *semi-annual.*
2 partly; in some degree or particular: *semi-conscious.* ■ almost: *semi-darkness.*
– ORIGIN from Latin; related to Greek *hēmi-*.

semi-acoustic ▸ **adjective** (of a guitar) having one or more pickups and a hollow body, typically with f-holes.
▸ **noun** a semi-acoustic guitar.

semi-annual ▸ **adjective** occurring twice a year: *their semi-annual meetings.*
– DERIVATIVES **semi-annually** adverb.

semiaquatic ▸ **adjective** (of an animal) living partly on land and partly in water: *semiaquatic crocodiles.* ■ (of a plant) growing in very wet or waterlogged ground.

semi-autobiographical ▸ **adjective** (of a written work) dealing partly with the writer's own life but also containing fictional elements.

semi-automatic ▸ **adjective** partially automatic: *a semi-automatic gearbox.* ■ (of a firearm) having a mechanism for self-loading but not for continuous firing: *semi-automatic rifles.*
▸ **noun** a semi-automatic firearm.

semi-autonomous ▸ **adjective** acting independently to some degree: *semi-autonomous working groups.* ■ (of a country, state, or community) having a degree of, but not complete, self-government: *one of Spain's 17 semi-autonomous regions.*

semi-basement ▸ **noun** a storey of a building partly below ground level.

semibold ▸ **adjective** Printing printed in a typeface with thick strokes but not as thick as bold.

semibreve /ˈsɛmɪbriːv/ ▸ **noun** Music, Brit. a note having the time value of two minims or four crotchets, represented by a ring with no stem. It is the longest note now in common use. Also called **WHOLE NOTE**.

semicircle ▸ **noun** a half of a circle or of its circumference. ■ a set of objects arranged in a semicircle: *chairs were in a semicircle round the hearth.*
– ORIGIN early 16th cent.: from Latin *semicirculus* (see **SEMI-**, **CIRCLE**).

semicircular ▸ **adjective** forming or shaped like a semicircle: *a semicircular driveway.*

semicircular canals ▸ **plural noun** three fluid-filled bony channels in the inner ear. They are situated at right angles to each other and provide information about orientation to the brain to help maintain balance.

semi-classical ▸ **adjective** Physics (of a theory or method) intermediate between a classical or Newtonian description and one based on quantum mechanics or relativity.

semicolon /ˌsɛmɪˈkəʊlən, -ˈkəʊlɒn/ ▸ **noun** a punctuation mark (;) indicating a pause, typically between two main clauses, that is more pronounced than that indicated by a comma.

semiconducting ▸ **adjective** (of a material or device) having the properties of a semiconductor.

semiconductor ▸ **noun** a solid substance that has a conductivity between that of an insulator and that of most metals, either due to the addition of an impurity or because of temperature effects. Devices made of semiconductors, notably silicon, are essential components of most electronic circuits.

semi-conscious ▸ **adjective** only partially conscious: *he dragged out the semi-conscious pilot.*

semi-conservative ▸ **adjective** Biochemistry relating to or denoting replication of a nucleic acid in which one complete strand of each double helix is directly derived from the parent molecule.

semi-crystalline ▸ **adjective** Chemistry (of a solid) possessing crystalline character to some degree.

semi-cylinder ▸ **noun** Geometry half of a cylinder cut longitudinally.
– DERIVATIVES **semi-cylindrical** adjective.

semi-darkness ▸ **noun** [mass noun] a light level in which it is possible to see, but not clearly.

semidemisemiquaver ▸ **noun** Music, Brit. another term for **HEMIDEMISEMIQUAVER**.

semi-deponent ▸ **adjective** (of a Latin verb) having active forms in present tenses, and passive forms with active sense in perfect tenses.

semi-detached Brit. ▸ **adjective** (of a house) joined to another house on one side only by a common wall.
▸ **noun** a semi-detached house.

semidiameter /ˌsɛmɪdʌɪˈamɪtə/ ▸ **noun** Geometry half of a diameter.

semi-documentary ▸ **adjective** (of a film) having a factual background and a fictitious story.
▸ **noun** a semi-documentary film.

semi-dome ▸ **noun** Architecture a half-dome formed by vertical section.

semi-double ▸ **adjective** (of a flower) intermediate between single and double in having only the outer stamens converted to petals.

semi-elliptical ▸ **adjective** having the shape of half of an ellipse bisected by one of its diameters, especially the major axis.

semi-final ▸ **noun** a match or round immediately preceding the final, the winner of which goes on to the final.
– DERIVATIVES **semi-finalist** noun.

semi-finished ▸ **adjective** prepared for the final stage of manufacture: *crude steel and semi-finished metal products.*

semi-fitted ▸ **adjective** (of a garment) shaped to the body but not closely fitted: *a single-breasted semi-fitted jacket.*

semi-fluid ▸ **adjective** having a thick consistency between solid and liquid.
▸ **noun** a semi-fluid substance.

semifreddo /sɛmiˈfreɪdəʊ, -ˈfrɛdəʊ/ ▸ **noun** (pl. **semifreddos**) a light semi-frozen Italian dessert.
– ORIGIN Italian, from *semi-* **SEMI-** + *freddo* 'cold'.

semi-independent ▸ **adjective** partially free from outside control.

semi-infinite ▸ **adjective** Mathematics (of a line or solid) limited in one direction and stretching to infinity in the other.

semi-invalid ▸ **noun** a partially disabled or somewhat infirm person.

semi-lethal ▸ **adjective** Genetics relating to or denoting an allele or chromosomal abnormality which impairs the viability of most of the individuals homozygous for it.

semi-liquid ▸ **adjective & noun** another term for **SEMI-FLUID**.

semi-literate ▸ **adjective** unable to read or write with ease or fluency; poorly educated: *a high proportion of the population is still relatively poor and semi-literate.* ■ (of a text) poorly written: *the semi-literate glossies.*
– DERIVATIVES **semi-literacy** noun.

Sémillon /ˈsɛmɪjɒ̃/ ▸ **noun** [mass noun] a variety of white wine grape grown in France and elsewhere. ■ a white wine made from this grape.
– ORIGIN French dialect, based on Latin *semen* 'seed'.

semilunar ▸ **adjective** chiefly Anatomy shaped like a half-moon or crescent.
– ORIGIN late Middle English: from medieval Latin *semilunaris* (see **SEMI-**, **LUNAR**).

semilunar bone ▸ **noun** another term for **LUNATE BONE** (see **LUNATE**).

semilunar cartilage ▸ **noun** a crescent-shaped cartilage in the knee.

semilunar valve ▸ **noun** Anatomy each of a pair of valves in the heart, at the bases of the aorta and the pulmonary artery, consisting of three cusps or flaps which prevent the flow of blood back into the heart.

semimajor axis ▸ **noun** Geometry either of the halves of the major axis of an ellipse.

semimetal ▸ **noun** Chemistry an element (e.g. arsenic, antimony, or tin) whose properties are intermediate between those of metals and solid non-metals or semiconductors.
– DERIVATIVES **semimetallic** adjective.
– ORIGIN mid 17th cent.: from modern Latin *semimetallum* (see **SEMI-**, **METAL**).

semiminor axis ▸ **noun** Geometry either of the halves of the minor axis of an ellipse.

semi-modal ▸ **noun** a verb that functions to some extent like a modal verb, typically in the way it forms negative and interrogative constructions. English semi-modals include *need* and *dare*.

semi-monocoque ▸ **adjective** relating to or denoting aircraft or vehicle structures combining a load-bearing shell with integral frames.

semi-monthly ▸ **adjective** chiefly N. Amer. occurring or published twice a month: *semi-monthly pay days.*

seminal ▸ **adjective 1** strongly influencing later developments: *his seminal work on chaos theory.*
2 relating to or denoting semen. ■ Botany relating to or derived from the seed of a plant.
– DERIVATIVES **seminally** adverb.

– ORIGIN late Middle English (in sense 2): from Old French *seminal* or Latin *seminalis*, from *semen* 'seed'. Sense 1 dates from the mid 17th cent.

seminal vesicle ▶ noun Anatomy each of a pair of glands which open into the vas deferens near to its junction with the urethra and secrete many of the components of semen.

seminar /ˈsɛmɪnɑː/ ▶ noun a conference or other meeting for discussion or training. ■ a class at university in which a topic is discussed by a teacher and a small group of students.
– ORIGIN late 19th cent.: from German *Seminar*, from Latin *seminarium* (see SEMINARY).

seminary /ˈsɛmɪn(ə)ri/ ▶ noun (pl. **seminaries**) a training college for priests or rabbis.
– DERIVATIVES **seminarian** /-ˈnɛːrɪən/ noun, **seminarist** noun.
– ORIGIN late Middle English (denoting a seed plot): from Latin *seminarium* 'seed plot', neuter of *seminarius* 'of seed', from *semen* 'seed'.

seminiferous /ˌsɛmɪˈnɪf(ə)rəs/ ▶ adjective producing or conveying semen.
– ORIGIN late 17th cent.: from Latin *semen, semin-* 'seed' + -FEROUS.

Seminole /ˈsɛmɪnəʊl/ ▶ noun (pl. **same** or **Seminoles**) **1** a member of an American Indian people of the Creek confederacy, noted for resistance in the 19th century to encroachment on their land in Georgia and Florida. Many were resettled in Oklahoma.
2 [mass noun] the Muskogean language of the Seminoles, now with fewer than 10,000 speakers.
▶ adjective relating to the Seminoles or their language.
– ORIGIN via Creek from American Spanish *cimarrón* 'wild, untamed'.

semiochemical /ˌsiːmɪə(ʊ)ˈkɛmɪk(ə)l/ ▶ noun Biochemistry a pheromone or other chemical that conveys a signal from one organism to another so as to modify the behaviour of the recipient organism.
– ORIGIN 1970s: from Greek *sēmeion* 'sign' + CHEMICAL.

semi-official ▶ adjective having some, but not full, official authority or recognition: *a semi-official visit*.
– DERIVATIVES **semi-officially** adverb.

semiology /ˌsiːmɪˈɒlədʒi, ˌsɛmɪ-/ ▶ noun [mass noun] another term for SEMIOTICS.
– DERIVATIVES **semiological** adjective, **semiologist** noun.
– ORIGIN 1920s: from Greek *sēmeion* 'sign' (from *sēma* 'mark') + -LOGY.

semi-opaque ▶ adjective not fully clear or transparent.

semi-opera ▶ noun a drama or similar entertainment with a substantial proportion of vocal music in addition to instrumental movements.

semiosis /sɛmɪˈəʊsɪs, ˌsɛmɪ-/ ▶ noun [mass noun] Linguistics the process of signification in language or literature.
– ORIGIN early 20th cent.: from Greek *sēmeiosis* '(inference from) a sign'.

semiotics /ˌsiːmɪˈɒtɪks, ˌsɛmɪ-/ ▶ plural noun [treated as sing.] the study of signs and symbols and their use or interpretation.
– DERIVATIVES **semiotic** adjective **semiotically** adverb, **semiotician** /-ˈtɪʃ(ə)n/ noun.
– ORIGIN late 19th cent.: from Greek *sēmeiotikos* 'of signs', from *sēmeioun* 'interpret as a sign'.

Semipalatinsk /ˌsɛmɪpəˈlɑːtɪnsk/ former name (until 1991) for SEMEI.

semipalmated /ˌsɛmɪpalˈmeɪtɪd/ ▶ adjective used in names of wading birds that have toes webbed for part of their length, e.g. **semipalmated sandpiper**.

semi-Pelagian /ˌsɛmɪpɪˈleɪdʒɪən/ Christian Theology ▶ adjective denoting the doctrine that the first steps towards good can be taken by the human will, though supervening divine grace is needed for salvation. It was (questionably) attributed to John Cassian (d.435), and was generally held to be heretical. See also PELAGIUS.
▶ noun a holder of this doctrine.
– DERIVATIVES **semi-Pelagianism** noun.

semi-permanent ▶ adjective not permanent, but involving some stability or endurance: *the company employs him on a semi-permanent basis*.
– DERIVATIVES **semi-permanently** adverb.

semipermeable ▶ adjective (of a material or membrane) allowing certain substances to pass through it but not others, especially allowing the passage of a solvent but not of certain solutes.

semi-precious ▶ adjective denoting minerals which can be used as gems but are considered to be less valuable than precious stones.

semi-pro ▶ adjective & noun (pl. **semi-pros**) informal short for SEMI-PROFESSIONAL.

semi-professional ▶ adjective receiving payment for an activity but not relying entirely on it for a living: *a semi-professional musician*.
▶ noun a person who is engaged in an activity on such a basis.

semi-prone position ▶ noun another term for RECOVERY POSITION.

semiquaver /ˈsɛmɪˌkweɪvə/ ▶ noun Music, Brit. a note having the time value of a sixteenth of a semibreve or half a quaver, represented by a large dot with a two-hooked stem. Also called SIXTEENTH NOTE.

semiquinone /ˌsɛmɪˈkwɪnəʊn/ ▶ noun Chemistry a compound derived from a quinone, in which one of the two oxygen atoms is ionized or bonded to a hydrogen atom.

Semiramis /sɪˈmɪrəmɪs/ Greek Mythology the daughter of an Assyrian goddess who married an Assyrian king. After his death she ruled for many years and became one of the founders of Babylon. She is thought to have been based on the historical queen Sammuramat (*c*.800 BC).

semi-retired ▶ adjective having retired or withdrawn from employment or an occupation but continuing to work part-time or occasionally.
– DERIVATIVES **semi-retirement** noun.

semi-rigid ▶ adjective stiff and solid, but not inflexible: *a semi-rigid polyethylene hose*. ■ (of an airship) having a stiffened keel attached to a flexible gas container. ■ (of an inflatable boat) having a rigid hull and inflatable sponsons.

semi-skilled ▶ adjective (of work or a worker) having or needing some, but not extensive, training: *assembly lines of semi-skilled workers*.

semi-skimmed ▶ adjective Brit. (of milk) having had some of the cream removed.

semi-solid ▶ adjective highly viscous; slightly thicker than semi-fluid.

semi-submersible ▶ adjective denoting an oil or gas drilling platform or barge with submerged hollow pontoons able to be flooded with water when the vessel is anchored on site in order to provide stability.
▶ noun a semi-submersible oil rig.

semi-synthetic ▶ adjective Chemistry (of a substance) made by synthesis from a naturally occurring material.

Semite /ˈsiːmʌɪt, ˈsɛm-/ ▶ noun a member of any of the peoples who speak or spoke a Semitic language, including in particular the Jews and Arabs.
– ORIGIN from modern Latin *Semita*, via late Latin from Greek *Sēm* 'Shem', son of Noah in the Bible, from whom these peoples were traditionally supposed to be descended.

Semitic /sɪˈmɪtɪk/ ▶ adjective **1** relating to or denoting a family of languages that includes Hebrew, Arabic, and Aramaic and certain ancient languages such as Phoenician and Akkadian, constituting the main subgroup of the Afro-Asiatic family.
2 relating to the peoples who speak these languages, especially Hebrew and Arabic.

semitone ▶ noun Music, Brit. the smallest interval used in classical Western music, equal to a twelfth of an octave or half a tone; a half step.

semi-trailer ▶ noun chiefly N. Amer. a trailer having wheels at the back but supported at the front by a towing vehicle. ■ an articulated lorry.

semi-transparent ▶ adjective partially or imperfectly transparent.

semi-tropics ▶ plural noun another term for SUBTROPICS.
– DERIVATIVES **semi-tropical** adjective.

semivowel ▶ noun a speech sound intermediate between a vowel and a consonant, e.g. *w* or *y*.
– ORIGIN mid 16th cent.: from SEMI- + VOWEL, on the pattern of Latin *semivocalis*.

Semmelweis /ˈzɛm(ə)lvʌɪs/, Ignaz Philipp (1818–65), Hungarian obstetrician; Hungarian name *Ignác Fülöp Semmelweis*. He discovered the infectious character of puerperal fever and advocated rigorous cleanliness and the use of antiseptics by doctors examining patients.

semmit /ˈsɛmɪt/ ▶ noun Scottish an undershirt; a vest.
– ORIGIN late Middle English: of unknown origin.

semolina ▶ noun [mass noun] the hard grains left after the milling of flour, used in puddings and in pasta. ■ a pudding made of semolina.
– ORIGIN late 18th cent.: from Italian *semolino*, diminutive of *semola* 'bran', from Latin *simila* 'flour'.

semper fidelis /ˌsɛmpə fɪˈdeɪlɪs/ ▶ adjective always faithful (the motto of the US Marine Corps).
– ORIGIN Latin.

sempervivum /ˌsɛmpəˈvʌɪvəm/ ▶ noun a plant of a genus that includes the houseleek. ● Genus *Sempervivum*, family Crassulaceae.
– ORIGIN modern Latin, from Latin *semper* 'always' + *vivus* 'living'.

sempiternal /ˌsɛmpɪˈtəːn(ə)l/ ▶ adjective literary eternal and unchanging; everlasting: *the sempiternal sadness of the industrial background*.
– DERIVATIVES **sempiternally** adverb, **sempiternity** noun.
– ORIGIN late Middle English: from Old French *sempiternel* or late Latin *sempiternalis*, from Latin *sempiternus*, from *semper* 'always' + *aeternus* 'eternal'.

semplice /ˈsɛmplɪtʃeɪ/ ▶ adverb Music (as a direction) in a simple style of performance.
– ORIGIN Italian, literally 'simple'.

sempre /ˈsɛmpreɪ/ ▶ adverb Music (in directions) throughout; always: *sempre forte*.
– ORIGIN Italian.

sempstress /ˈsɛm(p)strɪs/ ▶ noun another term for SEAMSTRESS.

Semtex ▶ noun [mass noun] a very pliable, odourless plastic explosive.
– ORIGIN 1980s: probably a blend of *Semtin* (the name of a village in the Czech Republic near the place of production) and EXPLOSIVE.

SEN ▶ abbreviation (in the UK) State Enrolled Nurse.

sen /sɛn/ ▶ noun (pl. **same**) **1** a monetary unit of Brunei, Cambodia, Indonesia, and Malaysia, equal to one hundredth of a dollar in Brunei, one hundredth of a riel in Cambodia, one hundredth of a rupiah in Indonesia, and one hundredth of a ringgit in Malaysia.
2 a former monetary unit in Japan, equal to one hundredth of a yen.
– ORIGIN Sense 1 represents CENT; sense 2 is of Japanese origin.

Sen. ▶ abbreviation ■ N. Amer. Senate. ■ N. Amer. Senator. ■ Senior.

Senanayake /ˌsɛnəˈnʌɪəkə/, Don Stephen (1884–1952), Sinhalese statesman, Prime Minister of Ceylon 1947–52. As Prime Minister he presided over Ceylon's achievement of full dominion status within the Commonwealth.

senarius /sɪˈnɛːrɪəs/ ▶ noun (pl. **senarii** /-ɪiː, -ɪʌɪ/) Prosody a verse of six feet, especially an iambic trimeter.
– ORIGIN mid 16th cent.: from Latin (see SENARY).

senary /ˈsiːnəri, ˈsɛn-/ ▶ adjective rare relating to or based on the number six.
– ORIGIN late 16th cent.: from Latin *senarius* 'containing six', based on *sex* 'six'.

senate ▶ noun **1** the smaller upper assembly in the US, US states, France, and other countries. ■ the governing body of a university or college.
2 the state council of the ancient Roman republic and empire, which shared legislative power with the popular assemblies, administration with the magistrates, and judicial power with the knights.
– ORIGIN Middle English: from Old French *senat*, from Latin *senatus*, from *senex* 'old man'.

S

senator ▶ noun **1** a member of a senate, in particular a member of the US Senate: [as title] *Senator Vandenburg*.
2 Scots Law a Lord of Session.
– DERIVATIVES **senatorial** adjective, **senatorship** noun.
– ORIGIN Middle English (denoting a member of the ancient Roman senate): from Old French *senateur*, from Latin *senator* (see SENATE).

senatus consultum /sɛˌnɑːtuːs kɒnˈsʊltʊm/ ▶ noun (pl. **senatus consulta** /kɒnˈsʊltə/) a decree of the ancient Roman senate.
– ORIGIN Latin.

send[1] ▶ verb (past and past participle **sent**) **1** [with obj.] cause to go or be taken to a particular destination; arrange for the delivery of, especially by post: *we sent a reminder letter but received no reply* | [with two objs] *he sent her a nice little note*. ■ order or instruct to go to a particular destination or in a particular direction: *the BBC sent me to Washington to cover the trial*. ■ [no obj., with infinitive] send a message or letter: *he sent to invite her to supper*. ■ [with obj. and adverbial

of direction] cause to move sharply or quickly; propel: *the volcano sent clouds of ash up four miles into the air.* ■ (**send someone to**) arrange for someone to go to (an institution) and stay there for a particular purpose: *many parents prefer to send their children to single-sex schools.*
2 [with obj. and complement] cause to be in a specified state: *while driving in London I was sent crazy by roadworks.* ■ [with obj.] informal affect with powerful emotion; put into ecstasy: *it's the spectacle and music that send us, not the words.*
– PHRASES **send someone flying** cause someone to be knocked violently off balance or to the ground. **send someone packing** see PACK[1]. **send someone to Coventry** see COVENTRY. **send someone to the showers** see SHOWER. **send word** send a message: *he sent word that he was busy.*
– PHRASAL VERBS **send away for** order or request that (something) be sent to one: *you can send away for the recipe.* **send someone down** Brit. **1** expel a student from a university. **2** (US **send someone up**) informal sentence someone to imprisonment: *you're going to get sent down for possessing drugs.* **send something down** Cricket bowl a ball or an over: *Bainbridge sent down 25 overs and finished with 5 for 44.* **send for** order or instruct (someone) to come to one; summon: *if you don't go I shall send for the police.* ■ order by post: *send for our mail order catalogue.* **send something in** submit material to be considered for a competition or possible publication: *don't forget to send in your entries for our summer competition.* **send off for** another way of saying SEND AWAY FOR above. **send someone off** instruct someone to go; arrange for someone's departure: *she sent him off to a lecturing engagement.* ■ (of a referee, especially in soccer or rugby) order a player to leave the field and take no further part in the game: *the goalkeeper was sent off for a professional foul.* **send something off** dispatch something by post: *please take a moment or two to send off a cheque to a good cause.* **send something on** transmit mail or luggage to a further destination or in advance of one's own arrival. **send something out 1** produce, emit, or give out something: *radar signals were sent out in powerful pulses.* **2** dispatch items to a number of people: *the company sent out written information about the stock.* **send someone/thing up** informal **1** Brit. give an exaggerated imitation of someone or something in order to ridicule them: *we used to send him up something rotten.* **2** (**send someone up**) see SEND SOMEONE DOWN above.
– DERIVATIVES **sendable** adjective, **sender** noun.
– ORIGIN Old English *sendan*, of Germanic origin; related to Dutch *zenden* and German *senden*.

send² ▶ noun & verb variant spelling of SCEND.

Sendai /sɛn'dʌɪ/ a city in Japan, situated near the NE coast of the island of Honshu; pop. 1,001,387 (2007). It is the capital of the region of Tohoku.

Sendai virus /'sɛndʌɪ/ ▶ noun [mass noun] Biology a parainfluenza virus which causes disease of the upper respiratory tract in mice and is used in the laboratory to produce cell fusion.

Sendak /'sɛndak/, Maurice (Bernard) (b.1928), American children's author and illustrator. His books, which feature characters that are both frightening and comic, include *Where the Wild Things Are* (1963).

sendal /'sɛnd(ə)l/ ▶ noun [mass noun] historical a fine, rich silk material, chiefly used to make ceremonial robes and banners.
– ORIGIN Middle English: from Old French *cendal*, ultimately from Greek *sindōn*.

Sendero Luminoso /sɛn,ðɛrəʊ lumi'nəʊsəʊ/ Spanish name for SHINING PATH.

sending ▶ noun an unpleasant or evil thing or creature supposedly sent by someone with paranormal or magical powers to warn, punish, or take revenge on a person.
– ORIGIN mid 19th cent.: from Old Norse.

send-off ▶ noun a celebratory demonstration of goodwill at a person's departure: *I got an affectionate send-off from my colleagues.*

send-up ▶ noun informal an act of imitating someone or something in order to ridicule them; a parody: *a delicious send-up of a speech given by a trendy academic.*

sene /'sɛni/ ▶ noun (pl. **same** or **senes**) a monetary unit of Samoa, equal to one hundredth of a tala.
– ORIGIN Samoan.

Seneca¹ /'sɛnɪkə/, Lucius Annaeus (*c*.4 BC–AD 65), Roman statesman, philosopher, and dramatist; known as **Seneca the Younger**. Son of Seneca the Elder, he became tutor to Nero in 49 and was appointed consul in 57. His *Epistulae Morales* is a notable Stoic work.

Seneca² /'sɛnɪkə/, Marcus (or Lucius) Annaeus (*c*.55 BC–*c*.39 AD), Roman rhetorician, born in Spain; known as **Seneca the Elder**. Father of Seneca the Younger, he is best known for his works on rhetoric, only parts of which survive.

Seneca³ /'sɛnɪkə/ ▶ noun (pl. **same** or **Senecas**) **1** a member of an American Indian people that was one of the five nations comprising the original Iroquois confederacy.
2 [mass noun] the Iroquoian language of the Seneca, now with few speakers.
▶ adjective relating to the Seneca or their language.
– ORIGIN via Dutch from Algonquian.

senecio /sə'niːsɪəʊ, -ʃɪəʊ/ ▶ noun (pl. **senecios**) a plant of a genus that includes the ragworts and groundsels. Many kinds are cultivated as ornamentals and some are poisonous weeds of grassland. ● Genus *Senecio*, family Compositae.
– ORIGIN modern Latin, from Latin, literally 'old man, groundsel', with reference to the hairy white fruits.

Senegal /,sɛnɪ'gɔːl/ a country on the coast of West Africa; pop. 13,711,600 (est. 2009); languages, French (official), Wolof, and other West African languages; capital, Dakar.

> Part of the Mali empire in the 14th and 15th centuries, the area was colonized by the French and became part of French West Africa in 1895. Briefly a partner in the Federation of Mali (1959), Senegal withdrew and became a fully independent republic in 1960. The Gambia forms an enclave within Senegal.

– DERIVATIVES **Senegalese** /-gə'liːz/ adjective & noun.

Senegambia /,sɛnə'gambɪə/ a region of West Africa consisting of the Senegal and Gambia Rivers and the area between them. It lies mostly in Senegal and western Mali.

senesce /sɪ'nɛs/ ▶ verb [no obj.] Biology (of a living organism) deteriorate with age.
– ORIGIN mid 17th cent.: from Latin *senescere*, from *senex* 'old'.

senescence /sɪ'nɛs(ə)ns/ ▶ noun [mass noun] Biology the condition or process of deterioration with age. ■ loss of a cell's power of division and growth.
– DERIVATIVES **senescent** adjective.

seneschal /'sɛnɪʃ(ə)l/ ▶ noun **1** historical the steward or major-domo of a medieval great house.
2 chiefly historical a governor or other administrative or judicial officer.
– ORIGIN Middle English: from Old French, from medieval Latin *seniscalus*, from a Germanic compound of words meaning 'old' and 'servant'.

senex /'sɛnɛks/ ▶ noun (pl. **senes** /'sɛneɪs/) (in literature, especially comedy) an old man as a stock figure.
– ORIGIN from Latin, 'old man'.

senhor /sɛn'jɔː/ ▶ noun (in Portuguese-speaking countries) a man (often used as a title or polite form of address): *Senhor Emilio Sofia Rosa.*
– ORIGIN Portuguese, from Latin *senior* (see SENIOR).

senhora /sɛn'jɔːrə/ ▶ noun (in Portuguese-speaking countries) a woman, especially a married woman (often used as a title or polite form of address): *I look forward to hearing what Senhora Rocha decides.*
– ORIGIN Portuguese, feminine of SENHOR.

senhorita /,sɛnjə'riːtə/ ▶ noun (in Portuguese-speaking countries) a young woman, especially an unmarried one (often used as a title or polite form of address).
– ORIGIN Portuguese, diminutive of SENHORA.

senile ▶ adjective (of a person) having or showing the weaknesses or diseases of old age, especially a loss of mental faculties: *she couldn't cope with her senile husband.* ■ (of a condition) characteristic of or caused by old age: *senile decay.*
– ORIGIN mid 17th cent.: from French *sénile* or Latin *senilis*, from *senex* 'old man'.

senile dementia ▶ noun [mass noun] dementia occurring in old age as a result of progressive brain degeneration.

senile plaque ▶ noun Medicine a microscopic mass of fragmented and decaying nerve terminals around an amyloid core, numbers of which occur in the brains of people with Alzheimer's disease.

senility ▶ noun [mass noun] the condition of being senile: *the onset of senility.*

senior /'siːnɪə, 'siːnjə/ ▶ adjective **1** of a more advanced age: *he is 20 years senior to Leonard.*
2 of or for older or more experienced people. ■ Brit. for or denoting schoolchildren above a certain age, typically [illegible] ■ US of or for the final year at a university or high school. ■ relating to or denoting competitors of above a certain age or of the highest status in a particular sport. ■ (often **Senior**) [postpositive] (in names) denoting the elder of two who have the same name in a family, especially a father as distinct from his son: *Henry James senior.*
3 high or higher in rank or status: *he is a senior Finance Ministry official | the people senior to me in my department.*
▶ noun a person who is a specified number of years older than someone else: *she was only two years his senior.* ■ an elderly person, especially an old-age pensioner. ■ a student in one of the higher forms of a senior school. ■ a competitor of above a certain age or of the highest status in a particular sport: *at fourteen you move up to the seniors.*
– ORIGIN late Middle English: from Latin, literally 'older, older man', comparative of *senex*, *sen-* 'old man, old'.

senior aircraftman (or **senior aircraftwoman**) ▶ noun a rank in the RAF, above leading aircraftman and below junior technician.

senior chief petty officer ▶ noun a rank in the US navy, above chief petty officer and below master chief petty officer.

senior citizen ▶ noun an elderly person, especially an old-age pensioner.

senior combination room ▶ noun a term used at Cambridge University for SENIOR COMMON ROOM.

senior common room ▶ noun Brit. a room used for social purposes by fellows, lecturers, and other senior members of a college. ■ [treated as sing. or pl.] the senior members of a college regarded collectively.

senior high school ▶ noun N. Amer. a secondary school typically comprising the three highest grades.

seniority ▶ noun [mass noun] **1** the fact or state of being older or higher in rank or status than someone else: *26 archbishops and bishops in order of seniority.*
2 a privileged position earned by reason of longer service or higher rank: *pay and benefits rise with seniority.*

senior master sergeant ▶ noun a rank of non-commissioned officer in the US air force, above master sergeant and below chief master sergeant.

senior moment ▶ noun informal a temporary mental lapse (humorously attributed to the gradual loss of one's mental faculties as one grows older).

senior nursing officer ▶ noun Brit. the person in charge of nursing services in a hospital.

senior registrar ▶ noun Brit. a hospital doctor undergoing specialist training, one grade below that of consultant.

Senior Service ▶ noun Brit. the Royal Navy.

seniti /'sɛnɪti/ ▶ noun (pl. **same**) a monetary unit of Tonga, equal to one hundredth of a pa'anga.
– ORIGIN Tongan.

senna ▶ noun the cassia tree. ■ [mass noun] a laxative prepared from the dried pods of the cassia tree. ■ used in names of similar plants of the pea family, e.g. **bladder senna**.
– ORIGIN mid 16th cent.: from medieval Latin *sena*, from Arabic *sanā*.

Sennacherib /sɪ'nakərɪb/ (d.681 BC), king of Assyria 705–681, son of Sargon II. In 701 he put down a Jewish rebellion, laying siege to Jerusalem but sparing it from destruction (according to 2 Kings 19:35). He also rebuilt the city of Nineveh and made it his capital.

sennet /'sɛnɪt/ ▶ noun (in the stage directions of Elizabethan plays) a call on a trumpet or cornet to signal the ceremonial entrance or exit of an actor.
– ORIGIN late 16th cent.: perhaps a variant of SIGNET.

sennight /'sɛnʌɪt/ ▶ noun archaic a week.
– ORIGIN Old English *seofon nihta* 'seven nights'.

sennit ▶ noun [mass noun] plaited straw, hemp, or similar fibrous material used in making hats. ■ Nautical variant spelling of SINNET.

Senoi /sɛ'nɔɪ/ ▶ noun (pl. **same**) a member of an aboriginal people of western Malaysia.
▶ adjective relating to the Senoi.
– ORIGIN a local name.

Señor /sɛ'njɔː/ ▶ noun (pl. **Señores** /-reɪz/) a title or form of address used of or to a Spanish-speaking man, corresponding to *Mr* or *sir*: *he is certain his information is correct, Señor.*

– ORIGIN Spanish, from Latin *senior* (see SENIOR).

Señora /sɛˈnjɔːrə/ ▶ **noun** a title or form of address used of or to a Spanish-speaking woman, corresponding to *Mrs* or *madam*: *Señora Dolores*.
– ORIGIN Spanish, feminine of SEÑOR.

Señorita /ˌsɛnjəˈriːtə/ ▶ **noun** a title or form of address used of or to a Spanish-speaking unmarried woman, corresponding to *Miss*.
– ORIGIN Spanish, diminutive of SEÑORA.

Senr ▶ **abbreviation** Senior (in names).

sensate /ˈsɛnseɪt, -sət/ ▶ **adjective** perceiving or perceived by the senses: *you are immersed in an illusionary, yet sensate, world*.
– ORIGIN mid 17th cent.: from late Latin *sensatus* 'having senses', from *sensus* (see SENSE).

sensation ▶ **noun 1** a physical feeling or perception resulting from something that happens to or comes into contact with the body: *a burning sensation in the middle of the chest*. ■ [mass noun] the capacity to have such feelings or perceptions: *they had lost sensation in one or both forearms*. ■ an inexplicable awareness or impression: [with clause] *she had the eerie* ***sensation*** *that she was being watched*.
2 a widespread reaction of interest and excitement: *his arrest for poisoning* ***caused a sensation***. ■ a person, object, or event that arouses such interest and excitement: *she was a sensation, the talk of the evening*.
– ORIGIN early 17th cent.: from medieval Latin *sensatio(n-)*, from Latin *sensus* (see SENSE).

sensational ▶ **adjective 1** causing great public interest and excitement: *a sensational murder trial*. ■ presenting information in a way that is intended to provoke public interest and excitement, at the expense of accuracy: *cheap sensational periodicals*.
2 informal very good indeed; very impressive or attractive: *you look sensational | a sensational view*.
– DERIVATIVES **sensationally** adverb.

sensationalism ▶ **noun** [mass noun] **1** (especially in journalism) the presentation of stories in a way that is intended to provoke public interest or excitement, at the expense of accuracy: *media sensationalism*.
2 Philosophy another term for PHENOMENALISM.
– DERIVATIVES **sensationalist** noun & adjective, **sensationalistic** adjective.

sensationalize (also **sensationalise**) ▶ **verb** [with obj.] (especially of a newspaper) present information about (something) in a sensational way: *the papers want to sensationalize the tragedy that my family has suffered*.

sense ▶ **noun 1** a faculty by which the body perceives an external stimulus; one of the faculties of sight, smell, hearing, taste, and touch: *the bear has a keen sense of smell which enables it to hunt at dusk*.
2 a feeling that something is the case: *she had the sense of being a political outsider | you can improve your general health and sense of well-being*. ■ a keen intuitive awareness of or sensitivity to the presence or importance of something: *she had a fine sense of comic timing*.
3 [mass noun] a sane and realistic attitude to situations and problems: *he earned respect by the good sense he showed at meetings*. ■ a reasonable or comprehensible rationale: *I can't* ***see the sense*** *in leaving all the work to you*.
4 a way in which an expression or a situation can be interpreted; a meaning: *it is not clear which sense of the word 'characters' is intended in this passage*.
5 chiefly Mathematics & Physics a property (e.g. direction of motion) distinguishing a pair of objects, quantities, effects, etc. which differ only in that each is the reverse of the other. ■ [as modifier] Genetics relating to or denoting a coding sequence of nucleotides, complementary to an antisense sequence.
▶ **verb** [with obj.] **1** perceive by a sense or senses: *with the first frost, they could sense a change in the days*. ■ be aware of (something) without being able to define exactly how one knows: *she could sense her father's anger rising* | [with clause] *he could sense that he wasn't liked*.
2 (of a machine or similar device) detect: *an optical fibre senses a current flowing in a conductor*.
– PHRASES **bring someone to their** (or **come to one's**) **senses** restore someone to (or regain) consciousness. ■ cause someone to (or start to) think and behave reasonably after a period of folly or irrationality. **in a** (or **one**) **sense** by a particular interpretation of a statement or situation: *in a sense, behaviour cannot develop independently of the environment*. **in one's senses** fully aware and in control of one's thoughts and words; sane: *would any man in his senses invent so absurd a story?* **make sense** be intelligible, justifiable, or practicable. **make sense of** find meaning or coherence in: *she must try to make sense of what was going on*. **out of one's senses** in or into a state of madness. **take leave of one's senses** (in hyperbolic use) go mad.
– ORIGIN late Middle English (as a noun in the sense 'meaning'): from Latin *sensus* 'faculty of feeling, thought, meaning', from *sentire* 'feel'. The verb dates from the mid 16th cent.

sense datum ▶ **noun** Philosophy an immediate object of perception, which is not a material object; a sense impression.

sensei /sɛnˈseɪ/ ▶ **noun** (pl. **same**) (in martial arts) a teacher: [as title] *Sensei Ritchie began work*.
– ORIGIN Japanese, from *sen* 'previous' + *sei* 'birth'.

senseless ▶ **adjective 1** [often as complement] (of a person) unconscious: *the attack left a policeman beaten senseless*. ■ incapable of sensation: *she knocked the glass from the girl's senseless fingers*.
2 lacking common sense; wildly foolish: *it was as senseless as crossing Death Valley on foot*. ■ (especially of violent or wasteful action) without discernible meaning or purpose: *in Vietnam I saw the senseless waste of human beings*.
– DERIVATIVES **senselessly** adverb, **senselessness** noun.

sense organ ▶ **noun** an organ of the body which responds to external stimuli by conveying impulses to the sensory nervous system.

Sensex ▶ **noun** a figure indicating the relative prices of shares on the Mumbai (Bombay) Stock Exchange.
– ORIGIN 1990s: blend of SENSITIVE and INDEX.

sensibility ▶ **noun** (pl. **sensibilities**) [mass noun] **1** the quality of being able to appreciate and respond to complex emotional or aesthetic influences; sensitivity: *the study of literature leads to a growth of intelligence and sensibility*. ■ (**sensibilities**) a quality of delicate sensitivity that makes one liable to be offended or shocked: *the scale of the poverty revealed by the survey shocked people's sensibilities*.
2 Zoology, dated sensitivity to sensory stimuli.
– ORIGIN late Middle English (denoting the power of sensation): from late Latin *sensibilitas*, from *sensibilis* 'that can be perceived by the senses' (see SENSIBLE).

sensible ▶ **adjective 1** done or chosen in accordance with wisdom or prudence; likely to be of benefit: *I cannot believe that it is sensible to spend so much | a sensible diet*. ■ (of a person) possessing or displaying prudence: *he was a sensible and capable boy*.
2 (of an object) practical and functional rather than decorative: *Mum always made me have sensible shoes*.
3 archaic readily perceived; appreciable: *it will effect a sensible reduction in these figures*. ■ (**sensible of/to**) able to notice or appreciate; not unaware of: *we are sensible of the difficulties he faces*.
– DERIVATIVES **sensibleness** noun, **sensibly** adverb.
– ORIGIN late Middle English (also in the sense 'perceptible by the senses'): from Old French, or from Latin *sensibilis*, from *sensus* (see SENSE).

sensillum /sɛnˈsɪləm/ ▶ **noun** (pl. **sensilla** /sɛnˈsɪlə/) Zoology (in arthropods and some other invertebrates) a simple sensory receptor consisting of a modified cell or small group of cells of the cuticle or epidermis, typically hair- or rod shaped.
– ORIGIN early 20th cent.: modern Latin, diminutive of Latin *sensus* 'sense'.

sensitive ▶ **adjective 1** quick to detect or respond to slight changes, signals, or influences: *the new method of protein detection was more sensitive than earlier ones | spiders are* ***sensitive to*** *vibrations on their web*. ■ easily damaged, injured, or distressed by slight changes: *the committee called for improved protection of wildlife in environmentally sensitive areas*. ■ (of photographic materials) prepared so as to respond rapidly to the action of light. ■ (of a market) unstable and liable to quick changes of price because of outside influences.
2 having or displaying a quick and delicate appreciation of others' feelings: *I pay tribute to the Minister for his sensitive handling of the bill*. ■ easily offended or upset: *I suppose I shouldn't be so sensitive*.
3 kept secret or with restrictions on disclosure to avoid endangering security: *he was suspected of passing sensitive information to other countries*.
▶ **noun** a person who is believed to respond to paranormal influences.
– DERIVATIVES **sensitively** adverb, **sensitiveness** noun.
– ORIGIN late Middle English (in the sense 'sensory'): from Old French *sensitif, -ive* or medieval Latin *sensitivus*, formed irregularly from Latin *sentire* 'feel'. The current senses date from the early 19th cent.

sensitive period ▶ **noun** Psychology a time or stage in a person's development when they are more responsive to certain stimuli and quicker to learn particular skills.

sensitive plant ▶ **noun 1** a tropical American plant of the pea family, whose leaflets fold together and leaves bend down when touched. A common weed of sugar cane, it has become naturalized throughout the tropics. ● *Mimosa pudica*, family Leguminosae.
2 informal a delicate or sensitive person.

sensitivity ▶ **noun** (pl. **sensitivities**) [mass noun] the quality or condition of being sensitive: *a total lack of common decency and sensitivity* | [in sing.] *he has* ***a sensitivity to*** *cow's milk*. ■ (**sensitivities**) feelings liable to be offended or hurt; sensibilities: *the only rules that matter are practical ones that respect local sensitivities*.

sensitize (also **sensitise**) ▶ **verb** [with obj.] (often **sensitize someone/thing to**) cause (someone or something) to respond to certain stimuli; make sensitive: *the introductory section aims to sensitize students to the methodology of the course*. ■ make (photographic film) sensitive to light: *the kit sensitizes any 35 mm film in hours*. ■ make (an organism) abnormally sensitive to a foreign substance: *the workers had been immunologically sensitized to the enzyme*.
– DERIVATIVES **sensitization** noun, **sensitizer** noun.

sensitometer /ˌsɛnsɪˈtɒmɪtə/ ▶ **noun** Photography a device for measuring the sensitivity of photographic equipment to light.

sensor ▶ **noun** a device which detects or measures a physical property and records, indicates, or otherwise responds to it.
– ORIGIN 1950s: from SENSORY, on the pattern of *motor*.

sensorimotor /ˌsɛns(ə)rɪˈməʊtə/ ▶ **adjective** Physiology (of nerves or their actions) having or involving both sensory and motor functions or pathways.

sensorineural /ˌsɛns(ə)rɪˈnjʊər(ə)l/ ▶ **adjective** Medicine (of hearing loss) caused by a lesion or disease of the inner ear or the auditory nerve.

sensorium /sɛnˈsɔːrɪəm/ ▶ **noun** (pl. **sensoria** /-rɪə/ or **sensoriums**) the sensory apparatus or faculties considered as a whole: *virtual reality technology directed at recreating the human sensorium*.
– DERIVATIVES **sensorial** adjective, **sensorially** adverb.
– ORIGIN mid 17th cent.: from late Latin, from Latin *sens-* 'perceived', from the verb *sentire*.

sensory ▶ **adjective** relating to sensation or the physical senses; transmitted or perceived by the senses: *sensory input*.
– DERIVATIVES **sensorily** adverb.
– ORIGIN mid 18th cent.: from Latin *sens-* 'perceived' (from the verb *sentire*) or from the noun SENSE + -ORY[2].

sensory deprivation ▶ **noun** [mass noun] a process by which someone is deprived of normal external stimuli such as sight and sound for an extended period of time, especially as an experimental technique in psychology.

sensual /ˈsɛnsjʊəl, -ʃʊəl/ ▶ **adjective** of or arousing gratification of the senses and physical, especially sexual, pleasure: *the production of the ballet is sensual and passionate*.
– DERIVATIVES **sensualism** noun, **sensualize** (also **sensualise**) verb, **sensually** adverb.
– ORIGIN late Middle English (in the sense 'sensory'): from late Latin *sensualis*, from *sensus* (see SENSE).

> **USAGE** The words **sensual** and **sensuous** are frequently used interchangeably to mean 'gratifying the senses', especially in a sexual sense. Strictly speaking, this goes against a traditional distinction, by which **sensuous** is a more neutral term, meaning 'relating to the senses rather than the intellect', as in *swimming is a beautiful,* ***sensuous*** *experience*, while **sensual** relates to gratification of the senses, especially sexually, as in *a* ***sensual*** *massage*. In fact the word **sensuous** is thought to have been invented by Milton (1641) in a deliberate attempt to avoid the sexual overtones of **sensual**. In practice, the connotations are such that it is difficult to use **sensuous** in this sense. While traditionalists struggle to maintain a distinction, the evidence from the Oxford English Corpus and elsewhere suggests that the 'neutral' use of **sensuous** is rare in modern English. If a neutral use is intended it is advisable to use alternative wording.

sensualist ▶ **noun** a person devoted to physical, especially sexual, pleasure: *a dedicated sensualist*.

S

sensuality ▶ **noun** [mass noun] the enjoyment, expression, or pursuit of physical, especially sexual, pleasure: *he ate the grapes with surprising sensuality.* ■ the condition of being pleasing or fulfilling to the senses: *life can dazzle with its sensuality, its colour.*
– ORIGIN Middle English (denoting the animal side of human nature): from Old French *sensualite*, from late Latin *sensualitas*, from *sensualis* (see SENSUAL).

sensu lato /ˌsɛnsuː ˈlɑːtəʊ/ ▶ **adverb** formal in the broad sense.
– ORIGIN Latin.

sensum /ˈsɛnsəm/ ▶ **noun** (pl. **sensa** /-sə/) Philosophy a sense datum.
– ORIGIN mid 19th cent.: modern Latin, 'something sensed', neuter past participle of Latin *sentire* 'feel'.

sensuous /ˈsɛnsjʊəs, ˈsɛnʃʊəs/ ▶ **adjective 1** relating to or affecting the senses rather than the intellect: *the work showed a deliberate disregard of the more sensuous and immediately appealing aspects of painting.*
2 attractive or gratifying physically, especially sexually: *her voice was rather deep but very sensuous.*
– DERIVATIVES **sensuously** adverb, **sensuousness** noun.
– ORIGIN mid 17th cent.: from Latin *sensus* 'sense' + -OUS.

> **USAGE** On the use of the words **sensuous** and **sensual**, see USAGE at SENSUAL.

Sensurround /ˈsɛnsəraʊnd/ ▶ **noun** [mass noun] trademark a cinema special-effects technique whereby the audience is apparently surrounded by low-frequency sound: [as modifier] *Sensurround sound.*
– ORIGIN 1970s: blend of SENSE and SURROUND.

sensu stricto /ˌsɛnsuː ˈstrɪktəʊ/ ▶ **adverb** formal strictly speaking; in the narrow sense: *the process was one of substitution rather than change sensu stricto.*
– ORIGIN Latin, 'in the restricted sense'.

sent[1] past and past participle of SEND[1].

sent[2] /ˈsɛnt/ ▶ **noun** a monetary unit of Estonia, equal to one hundredth of a kroon.
– ORIGIN respelling of CENT.

sente /ˈsɛnti/ ▶ **noun** (pl. **lisente** /lɪˈsɛnti/) a monetary unit of Lesotho, equal to one hundredth of a loti.
– ORIGIN Sesotho.

sentence ▶ **noun 1** a set of words that is complete in itself, typically containing a subject and predicate, conveying a statement, question, exclamation, or command, and consisting of a main clause and sometimes one or more subordinate clauses. ■ Logic a series of signs or symbols expressing a proposition in an artificial or logical language.
2 the punishment assigned to a defendant found guilty by a court, or fixed by law for a particular offence: *her husband is **serving** a three-year sentence for fraud | slander of an official carried an eight-year prison sentence | he was **under sentence of** death.*
▶ **verb** [with obj.] declare the punishment decided for (an offender): *ten army officers were **sentenced to** life imprisonment.*
– ORIGIN Middle English (in the senses 'way of thinking, opinion', 'court's declaration of punishment', and 'gist (of a piece of writing)'): via Old French from Latin *sententia* 'opinion', from *sentire* 'feel, be of the opinion'.

S

sentence adverb ▶ **noun** Grammar an adverb or adverbial phrase that expresses a writer's or speaker's attitude to the content of the sentence in which it occurs (such as *frankly, obviously*), or places the sentence in a particular context (such as *technically, politically*).

> **USAGE** The traditional definition of an adverb is that it is a word that modifies the meaning of a verb, an adjective, or another adverb, as in, for example, *he shook his head **sadly***. However, another important function of some adverbs is to comment on a whole sentence, either expressing the speaker's attitude or classifying the discourse. For example, in ***sadly**, he is rather overbearing*, **sadly** does not mean that he is overbearing in a sad manner: it expresses the speaker's attitude to what is being stated. Traditionalists take the view that the use of sentence adverbs is inherently suspect and that they should always be paraphrased, e.g. using such wording as ***it is sad that** he is rather overbearing*. A particular objection is raised to the sentence adverbs **hopefully** and **thankfully**, since they cannot even be paraphrased in the usual way (see USAGE at HOPEFULLY and THANKFULLY). Nevertheless, there is overwhelming evidence that such usages are well established and widely accepted in everyday speech and writing.

sentential /sɛnˈtɛnʃ(ə)l/ ▶ **adjective** Grammar & Logic relating to a sentence: *sentential meaning.*

sententious /sɛnˈtɛnʃəs/ ▶ **adjective** given to moralizing in a pompous or affected manner: *he tried to encourage his men with sententious rhetoric.*
– DERIVATIVES **sententiously** adverb, **sententiousness** noun.
– ORIGIN late Middle English: from Latin *sententiosus*, from *sententia* 'opinion' (see SENTENCE). The original sense was 'full of meaning or wisdom', later becoming depreciatory.

sentient /ˈsɛnʃ(ə)nt/ ▶ **adjective** able to perceive or feel things: *she had been instructed from birth in the equality of all sentient life forms.*
– DERIVATIVES **sentience** noun **sentiently** adverb.
– ORIGIN early 17th cent.: from Latin *sentient-* 'feeling', from the verb *sentire*.

sentiment ▶ **noun 1** a view or opinion that is held or expressed: *I agree with your sentiments regarding the road bridge.* ■ [mass noun] general feeling or opinion: *the council sought steps to control the rise of racist sentiment.* ■ a feeling or emotion: *an intense sentiment of horror.* ■ archaic the expression of a view or desire especially as formulated for a toast.
2 [mass noun] exaggerated and self-indulgent feelings of tenderness, sadness, or nostalgia: *many of the appeals rely on treacly sentiment.*
– ORIGIN late Middle English (in the senses 'personal experience' and 'physical feeling, sensation'): from Old French *sentement*, from medieval Latin *sentimentum*, from Latin *sentire* 'feel'.

sentimental ▶ **adjective** of or prompted by feelings of tenderness, sadness, or nostalgia: *she felt a sentimental attachment to the place creep over her.* ■ having or arousing feelings of tenderness, sadness, or nostalgia, typically in an exaggerated and self-indulgent way: *a sentimental ballad | I'm a sentimental old fool.*
– DERIVATIVES **sentimentally** adverb.

sentimentalism ▶ **noun** [mass noun] excessively sentimental behaviour, writing, or speech.
– DERIVATIVES **sentimentalist** noun.

sentimentality ▶ **noun** (pl. **sentimentalities**) [mass noun] exaggerated and self-indulgent tenderness, sadness, or nostalgia: *there are passages which verge on sentimentality.*

sentimentalize (also **sentimentalise**) ▶ **verb** [with obj.] treat, regard, or portray in a sentimental way: (as adj. **sentimentalized**) *the impossibly sentimentalized and saintly ideal of the Virgin Mother.*
– DERIVATIVES **sentimentalization** noun.

sentimental value ▶ **noun** the value of an object deriving from personal or emotional associations rather than material worth.

sentinel /ˈsɛntɪn(ə)l/ ▶ **noun 1** a soldier or guard whose job is to stand and keep watch: *soldiers **stood sentinel** with their muskets.*
2 Medicine an indicator of the presence of disease.
▶ **verb** (**sentinels**, **sentinelling**, **sentinelled**; US **sentinels**, **sentineling**, **sentineled**) [with obj.] station a soldier or guard by (a place) to keep watch: *a wide course had been roped off and sentinelled with police.*
– ORIGIN late 16th cent.: from French *sentinelle*, from Italian *sentinella*, of unknown origin.

sentry ▶ **noun** (pl. **sentries**) a soldier stationed to keep guard or to control access to a place.
– PHRASES **stand sentry** keep guard or control access to a place.
– ORIGIN early 17th cent.: perhaps from obsolete *centrinel*, variant of SENTINEL.

sentry box ▶ **noun** a structure providing shelter for a standing sentry.

sentry-go ▶ **noun** [mass noun] Military the duty of being a sentry.

Senufo /səˈnuːfəʊ/ ▶ **noun 1** (pl. **same**) a member of a West African people inhabiting parts of Côte d'Ivoire (Ivory Coast), Mali, and Burkina.
2 [mass noun] the language of the Senufo, which belongs to the Gur group and has many different dialects.
▶ **adjective** relating to the Senufo or their language.
– ORIGIN Akan.

Senussi /sɛˈnuːsi/ ▶ **noun** (pl. **same** or **Senussis**) a member of a North African Muslim religious fraternity founded in 1837 by **Sidi Muhammad ibn Ali es-Senussi** (d.1859).

SEO ▶ **abbreviation** Computing search engine optimization.

Seoul /səʊl/ the capital of South Korea, situated in the north-west of the country on the Han River; pop. 10,456,000 (est. 2008). It was the capital of the Korean Yi dynasty from the late 14th century until 1910, when Korea was annexed by the Japanese. Extensively developed under Japanese rule, it became the capital of South Korea after the partition of 1945.

sepal /ˈsɛp(ə)l, ˈsiːp(ə)l/ ▶ **noun** Botany each of the parts of the calyx of a flower, enclosing the petals and typically green and leaf-like.
– ORIGIN early 19th cent.: from French *sépale*, modern Latin *sepalum*, from Greek *skepē* 'covering', influenced by French *pétale* 'petal'.

separable ▶ **adjective 1** able to be separated or treated separately: *body and soul are not separable.*
2 Grammar (of a verb) having a prefix that is written as a separate word in some circumstances. ■ (of an English phrasal verb) allowing the insertion of the direct object between the base verb and the particle, e.g. *look it over* as opposed to *go over it.*
– DERIVATIVES **separability** noun, **separableness** noun, **separably** adverb.
– ORIGIN late Middle English: from Latin *separabilis*, from *separare* 'disjoin, divide' (see SEPARATE).

separate ▶ **adjective** /ˈsɛp(ə)rət/ forming or viewed as a unit apart or by itself: *this raises two separate issues | he regards the study of literature as quite **separate from** life.* ■ not joined or touching physically: *a bathroom and separate toilet.* ■ different; distinct: *melt the white and plain chocolate in separate bowls.*
▶ **verb** /ˈsɛpəreɪt/ **1** [with obj.] cause to move or be apart: *police were trying to separate two rioting mobs | they were separated by the war.* ■ form a distinction or boundary between: *only a footpath **separated** their garden **from** the shore | six years separated the two brothers.* ■ [no obj.] become detached or disconnected; move apart: *the second stage of the rocket failed to separate | they separated at the corner, agreeing to meet within two hours.* ■ [no obj.] stop living together as a couple: *after her parents separated she was brought up by her mother* | (as adj. **separated**) *her parents are separated.* ■ US discharge or dismiss (someone) from service or employment.
2 divide into constituent or distinct elements: [no obj.] *the processed milk had **separated into** curds and whey* | [with obj.] *separate the eggs and beat the egg yolks | the organ loft **separating off** the choir.* ■ [with obj.] extract or remove for use or rejection: *the skins are **separated from** the juice before fermentation.* ■ [with obj.] distinguish between or from others; consider individually: *we cannot **separate** his thinking **from** his activity | his position **separates** him **from** those who might share his interests.*
▶ **plural noun** (**separates** /ˈsɛp(ə)rəts/) **1** individual items of clothing, such as skirts, jackets, or trousers, suitable for wearing in different combinations.
2 the self-contained, free-standing components of a sound-reproduction system.
3 portions into which a soil, sediment, etc. can be sorted according to particle size, mineral composition, or other criteria.
– PHRASES **go one's separate ways** leave in a different direction from someone with whom one has just travelled or spent time. ■ end a romantic, professional, or other relationship. **separate but equal** US historical racially segregated but ensuring equal opportunities to all races. **separate the men from the boys** see MAN. **separate the sheep from the goats** divide people or things into superior and inferior groups. [with biblical allusion to Matt. 25:33.] **separate the wheat from the chaff** see CHAFF[1].
– DERIVATIVES **separateness** noun, **separative** /ˈsɛp(ə)rətɪv/ adjective, **separator** /ˈsɛpəreɪtə/ noun, **separatory** /-rət(ə)ri/ adjective.
– ORIGIN late Middle English: from Latin *separat-* 'disjoined, divided', from the verb *separare*, from *se-* 'apart' + *parare* 'prepare'.

separately ▶ **adverb** as a separate entity or entities; not together: *they arrived together but left separately | I shall consider that figure separately from the prime costs.*

separate school ▶ **noun** Canadian a school receiving pupils from a particular religious group.

separation ▶ **noun** [mass noun] **1** the action or state of moving or being moved apart: *the damage that might arise from the separation of parents and children.* ■ the state in which a husband and wife remain married but live apart: *legal grounds for divorce or separation* | [count noun] *she and her husband have agreed to **a trial separation**.* See also LEGAL SEPARATION.

2 the division of something into constituent or distinct elements: *prose structured into short sentences with meaningful separation into paragraphs.* ■ the extraction or removal of a specified substance for use or rejection. ■ the process of distinguishing between two or more things: *religion involved the separation of the sacred and the profane.*
3 (also **stereo separation**) distinction or difference between the signals carried by the two channels of a stereophonic system.
4 short for COLOUR SEPARATION.
5 Physics & Aeronautics the generation of a turbulent boundary layer between the surface of a body and a moving fluid, or between two fluids moving at different speeds.
– PHRASES **separation of powers** the vesting of the legislative, executive, and judiciary powers of government in separate bodies.
– ORIGIN late Middle English: via Old French from Latin *separatio(n-)*, from *separare* 'disjoin, divide' (see SEPARATE).

separation anxiety ▶ **noun** [mass noun] Psychiatry anxiety provoked in a young child by separation or the threat of separation from its mother or main carer.

separation order ▶ **noun** a court order for the legal separation of a married couple.

separatism ▶ **noun** [mass noun] the advocacy or practice of separation of a certain group of people from a larger body on the basis of ethnicity, religion, or gender: *Basque separatism.*

separatist ▶ **noun** a person who supports the separation of a particular group of people from a larger body on the basis of ethnicity, religion, or gender: *religious separatists.*
▶ **adjective** relating to such separation or those supporting it: *a separatist rebellion.*

Sepedi /sɛˈpɛːdi/ ▶ **noun** [mass noun] a Bantu language of southern Africa, the main member of the North Sotho group and spoken by about 4 million people.

Sephadex /ˈsɛfədɛks/ ▶ **noun** [mass noun] trademark a preparation of dextran used as a gel in chromatography, electrophoresis, and other separation techniques.
– ORIGIN 1950s: of unknown origin.

Sephardi /sɪˈfɑːdi/ ▶ **noun** (pl. **Sephardim** /-dɪm/) a Jew of Spanish or Portuguese descent. They retain their own distinctive dialect of Spanish (Ladino), customs, and rituals, preserving Babylonian Jewish traditions rather than the Palestinian ones of the Ashkenazim. Compare with ASHKENAZI. ■ any Jew of the Middle East or North Africa.
– DERIVATIVES **Sephardic** adjective.
– ORIGIN modern Hebrew, from *sĕp̄ārad*, a country mentioned in Obad. 20 and taken to be Spain.

Sepharose /ˈsɛfərəʊz/ ▶ **noun** [mass noun] trademark a preparation of agarose used as a gel in chromatography, electrophoresis, and other separation techniques.
– ORIGIN 1960s: of unknown origin.

sephira /ˈsɛfɪrɑː/ ▶ **noun** (pl. **sephiroth** /ˈsɛfɪrəʊθ/) (in the Kabbalah) each of the ten attributes or emanations surrounding the infinite and by means of which it relates to the finite. They are represented as spheres on the Tree of Life.
– ORIGIN from Hebrew *sĕp̄īrāh*.

sepia /ˈsiːpɪə/ ▶ **noun** [mass noun] **1** a reddish-brown colour associated particularly with monochrome photographs of the 19th and early 20th centuries: [as modifier] *old sepia photographs.* ■ a brown pigment prepared from a black fluid secreted by cuttlefish, used in monochrome drawing and in watercolours. ■ [count noun] a drawing done with this pigment.
2 a blackish fluid secreted by a cuttlefish as a defensive screen.
– ORIGIN late Middle English (denoting a cuttlefish): via Latin from Greek *sēpia* 'cuttlefish'. The current senses date from the early 19th cent.

sepoy /ˈsiːpɔɪ, sɪˈpɔɪ/ ▶ **noun** historical an Indian soldier serving under British or other European orders. ■ (in South Asia) a police constable.
– ORIGIN from Urdu and Persian *sipāhī* 'soldier', from *sipāh* 'army'.

Sepoy Mutiny another term for INDIAN MUTINY.

seppuku /sɛˈpuːkuː/ ▶ **noun** another term for HARA-KIRI.
– ORIGIN Japanese, from *setsu* 'to cut' + *fuku* 'abdomen'.

seps /sɛps/ ▶ **noun** an African lizard with a snake-like body and very short or non-existent legs. ● Genera *Tetradactylus*, family Gerrhosauridae: several species, formerly regarded as skinks.
– ORIGIN mid 16th cent. (denoting a venomous serpent described by classical authors): via Latin from Greek *sēps*, from the base of *sēpein* 'make rotten'.

sepsis /ˈsɛpsɪs/ ▶ **noun** [mass noun] Medicine the presence in tissues of harmful bacteria and their toxins, typically through infection of a wound.
– ORIGIN late 19th cent.: modern Latin, from Greek *sēpsis*, from *sēpein* 'make rotten'.

sept ▶ **noun** a subdivision of a clan, originally one in Ireland.
– ORIGIN early 16th cent.: probably an alteration of SECT.

Sept. ▶ **abbreviation** ■ September. ■ Septuagint.

sept- ▶ **combining form** variant spelling of SEPTI- (as in *septcentenary*).

septa plural form of SEPTUM.

septage /ˈsɛptɪdʒ/ ▶ **noun** [mass noun] excrement and other waste material contained in or removed from a septic tank.
– ORIGIN 1970s: from SEPTIC, on the pattern of *sewage.*

septal[1] ▶ **adjective 1** Anatomy & Biology relating to a septum or septa.
2 Archaeology (of a stone or slab) separating compartments in a burial chamber.

septal[2] ▶ **adjective** relating to a sept or clan.

septarium /sɛpˈtɛːrɪəm/ ▶ **noun** (pl. **septaria** /-rɪə/) Geology a concretionary nodule, typically of ironstone, having radial cracks filled with calcite or another mineral.
– DERIVATIVES **septarian** adjective.
– ORIGIN late 18th cent.: modern Latin, from Latin *septum* 'enclosure'.

septate ▶ **adjective** Anatomy & Biology having or partitioned by a septum or septa.
– DERIVATIVES **septation** noun.

septcentenary /ˌsɛp(t)sɛnˈtiːn(ə)ri, -ˈtɛn-/ ▶ **noun** (pl. **septcentenaries**) the seven-hundredth anniversary of a significant event.
▶ **adjective** relating to a seven-hundredth anniversary.

September ▶ **noun** the ninth month of the year, in the northern hemisphere usually considered the first month of autumn: *sow the plants in early September* | *a course commencing this September.*
– ORIGIN late Old English, from Latin, from *septem* 'seven' (being originally the seventh month of the Roman year).

September 11 the date of an attack in 2001 in which two airliners were flown directly into the World Trade Center, causing the complete collapse of the twin towers, and a third airliner was flown into the Pentagon, causing a five-storey section of the building to collapse; a fourth airliner, believed also to have been targeted on Washington, was brought to the ground in Pennsylvania as a result of what is thought to be passenger intervention. The airliners were hijacked by Islamic fundamentalist terrorists believed to be involved with al-Qaeda. Also called **9/11**.

septenarius /ˌsɛptɪˈnɛːrɪəs/ ▶ **noun** (pl. **septenarii** /-rɪʌɪ/) Prosody a verse line of seven feet, especially a trochaic or iambic tetrameter catalectic.
– ORIGIN early 19th cent.: from Latin, from *septeni* 'in sevens', from *septem* 'seven'.

septenary /ˈsɛptɪn(ə)ri, -ˈtiːn(ə)ri/ ▶ **adjective** relating to or divided into seven.
▶ **noun** (pl. **septenaries**) a group or set of seven, in particular: ■ a period of seven years. ■ Music the seven notes of the diatonic scale. ■ a septenarius.
– ORIGIN late Middle English: from Latin *septenarius* (see SEPTENARIUS).

septennial ▶ **adjective** recurring every seven years. ■ lasting for or relating to a period of seven years.
– ORIGIN mid 17th cent.: from late Latin *septennis* (from Latin *septem* 'seven' + *annus* 'year') + -AL.

septennium /sɛpˈtɛnɪəm/ ▶ **noun** (pl. **septennia** /-nɪə/ or **septenniums**) rare a specified period of seven years.
– ORIGIN mid 19th cent.: from late Latin, from Latin *septem* 'seven' + *annus* 'year'.

septet /sɛpˈtɛt/ (also **septette**) ▶ **noun** a group of seven people playing music or singing together. ■ a composition for a septet.
– ORIGIN early 19th cent.: from German *Septett*, from Latin *septem* 'seven'.

septi- (also **sept-**) ▶ **combining form** seven; having seven: *septivalent.*
– ORIGIN from Latin *septem* 'seven'.

septic /ˈsɛptɪk/ ▶ **adjective 1** (chiefly of a wound or a part of the body) infected with bacteria: *his feet had gone septic.*
2 [attrib.] denoting a drainage system incorporating a septic tank.
▶ **noun** N. Amer. a drainage system incorporating a septic tank.
– DERIVATIVES **septically** adverb.
– ORIGIN early 17th cent.: via Latin from Greek *sēptikos*, from *sēpein* 'make rotten'.

septicaemia /ˌsɛptɪˈsiːmɪə/ (US **septicemia**) ▶ **noun** [mass noun] blood poisoning, especially that caused by bacteria or their toxins.
– DERIVATIVES **septicaemic** adjective.
– ORIGIN mid 19th cent.: modern Latin, from Greek *sēptikos* + *haima* 'blood'.

septic tank ▶ **noun** a tank, typically underground, in which sewage is collected and allowed to decompose through bacterial activity before draining by means of a soakaway.

septillion /sɛpˈtɪljən/ ▶ **cardinal number** (pl. **septillions** or (with numeral) **same**) a thousand raised to the eighth power (10^{24}). ■ dated, chiefly Brit. a million raised to the seventh power (10^{42}).
– ORIGIN late 17th cent.: from French, from *million*, by substitution of the prefix *septi-* 'seven' (from Latin *septimus* 'seventh') for the initial letters.

septimal /ˈsɛptɪm(ə)l/ ▶ **adjective** relating to the number seven.
– ORIGIN mid 19th cent.: from Latin *septimus* 'seventh' (from *septem* 'seven') + -AL.

septime /ˈsɛptɪm, -tiːm/ ▶ **noun** Fencing the seventh of the eight parrying positions.
– ORIGIN late 19th cent.: from Latin *septimus* 'seventh'.

septivalent /ˌsɛptɪˈveɪl(ə)nt/ ▶ **adjective** Chemistry another term for HEPTAVALENT.

septoria /sɛpˈtɔːrɪə/ ▶ **noun** [mass noun] a fungus of a genus that includes many kinds that cause diseases in plants. ● Genus *Septoria*, subdivision Deuteromycotina. ■ leaf spot disease caused by such a fungus.
– ORIGIN modern Latin, from Latin *septum* (see SEPTUM).

septuagenarian /ˌsɛptjʊədʒɪˈnɛːrɪən/ ▶ **noun** a person who is between 70 and 79 years old.
– ORIGIN late 18th cent.: from Latin *septuagenarius* (based on *septuaginta* 'seventy') + -AN.

Septuagesima /ˌsɛptjʊəˈdʒɛsɪmə/ (also **Septuagesima Sunday**) ▶ **noun** the Sunday before Sexagesima.
– ORIGIN late Middle English: from Latin, 'seventieth (day)', probably named by analogy with QUINQUAGESIMA.

Septuagint /ˈsɛptjʊədʒɪnt/ ▶ **noun** a Greek version of the Hebrew Bible (or Old Testament), including the Apocrypha, made for Greek-speaking Jews in Egypt in the 3rd and 2nd centuries BC and adopted by the early Christian Churches.
– ORIGIN mid 16th cent. (originally denoting the translators themselves): from Latin *septuaginta* 'seventy', because of the tradition that it was produced, under divine inspiration, by seventy-two translators working independently.

septum /ˈsɛptəm/ ▶ **noun** (pl. **septa** /-tə/) chiefly Anatomy & Biology a partition separating two chambers, such as that between the nostrils or the chambers of the heart.
– ORIGIN mid 17th cent.: from Latin *septum*, from *sepire* 'enclose', from *sepes* 'hedge'.

septuple /ˈsɛptjʊp(ə)l, sɛpˈtjuːp(ə)l/ rare ▶ **adjective** [attrib.] consisting of seven parts or elements. ■ consisting of seven times as much or as many as usual. ■ (of time in music) having seven beats in a bar.
▶ **verb** [with obj.] multiply (something) by seven; increase sevenfold.
– ORIGIN early 17th cent. (as a verb): from late Latin *septuplus*, from Latin *septem* 'seven'.

septuplet /ˈsɛptjʊplɪt, sɛpˈtjuːplɪt/ ▶ **noun 1** (usu. **septuplets**) each of seven children born at one birth.
2 Music a group of seven notes to be performed in the time of four or six.
– ORIGIN late 19th cent.: from late Latin *septuplus* (see SEPTUPLE), on the pattern of words such as *triplet.*

sepulchral /sɪˈpʌlkr(ə)l/ ▶ **adjective** relating to a tomb or interment: *sepulchral monuments.* ■ gloomy; dismal: *a speech delivered in sepulchral tones.*
– DERIVATIVES **sepulchrally** adverb.
– ORIGIN early 17th cent.: from French *sépulchral* or Latin *sepulchralis*, from *sepulcrum* (see SEPULCHRE).

sepulchre /ˈsɛp(ə)lkə/ (US **sepulcher**) ▸ **noun** a small room or monument, cut in rock or built of stone, in which a dead person is laid or buried.
▸ **verb** [with obj.] literary lay or bury in or as if in a sepulchre: *tomes are soon out of print and sepulchred in the dust of libraries*.
– ORIGIN Middle English: via Old French from Latin *sepulcrum* 'burial place', from *sepelire* 'bury'.

sepulture /ˈsɛp(ə)ltʃə/ ▸ **noun** [mass noun] archaic burial; interment: *the rites of sepulture*.
– ORIGIN Middle English: via Old French from Latin *sepultura*, from *sepelire* 'bury'.

seq. (also **seqq.**) ▸ **adverb** short for ET SEQ.

sequacious /sɪˈkweɪʃəs/ ▸ **adjective** formal (of a person) lacking independence or originality of thought.
– ORIGIN mid 17th cent.: from Latin *sequax*, *sequac-* 'following' (from *sequi* 'follow') + -IOUS.

sequel ▸ **noun** a published, broadcast, or recorded work that continues the story or develops the theme of an earlier one. ■ something that takes place after or as a result of an earlier event: *this encouragement to grow potatoes had a disastrous sequel some fifty years later*.
– PHRASES **in the sequel** Brit. formal as things develop.
– ORIGIN late Middle English (in the senses 'body of followers', 'descendants' and 'consequence'): from Old French *sequelle* or Latin *sequella*, from *sequi* 'follow'.

sequela /sɪˈkwiːlə/ ▸ **noun** (pl. **sequelae** /-liː/) (usu. **sequelae**) Medicine a condition which is the consequence of a previous disease or injury: *the long-term sequelae of infection*.
– ORIGIN late 18th cent.: from Latin, from *sequi* 'follow'.

sequence /ˈsiːkw(ə)ns/ ▸ **noun 1** a particular order in which related things follow each other: *the content of the programme should follow a logical sequence* | [mass noun] *the poems should be read in sequence*. ■ Music a repetition of a phrase or melody at a higher or lower pitch. ■ Biochemistry the order in which amino-acid or nucleotide residues are arranged in a protein, DNA, etc.
2 a set of related events, movements, or items that follow each other in a particular order: *a gruelling sequence of exercises* | *a sonnet sequence*. ■ a set of three or more playing cards of the same suit next to each other in value, for example 10, 9, 8. ■ Mathematics an infinite ordered series of numerical quantities.
3 a part of a film dealing with one particular event or topic: *the famous underwater sequence*.
4 (in the Eucharist) a hymn said or sung after the Gradual or Alleluia that precedes the Gospel.
▸ **verb** [with obj.] **1** arrange in a particular order: *trainee librarians decide how a set of misfiled cards could be sequenced*. ■ Biochemistry ascertain the sequence of amino-acid or nucleotide residues in (a protein, DNA, etc.).
2 play or record (music) with a sequencer.
– ORIGIN late Middle English (in sense 4 of the noun): from late Latin *sequentia*, from Latin *sequent-* 'following', from the verb *sequi* 'follow'.

sequence dancing ▸ **noun** [mass noun] a type of ballroom dancing in which the couples all perform the same steps and movements simultaneously.

S

sequence of tenses ▸ **noun** [mass noun] Grammar the dependence of the tense of a subordinate verb on the tense of the verb in the main clause (e.g. *I think that you* are *wrong*; *I thought that you* were *wrong*).

sequencer ▸ **noun 1** a programmable electronic device for storing sequences of musical notes, chords, or rhythms and transmitting them to an electronic musical instrument.
2 Biochemistry an apparatus for determining the sequence of amino acids or other monomers in a biological polymer.

sequent ▸ **adjective** archaic following in a sequence or as a logical conclusion.
– DERIVATIVES **sequently** adverb.
– ORIGIN mid 16th cent.: from Old French, or from Latin *sequent-* 'following' (see SEQUENCE).

sequential /sɪˈkwɛnʃ(ə)l/ ▸ **adjective** forming or following in a logical order or sequence: *a series of sequential steps*. ■ chiefly Computing performed or used in sequence: *sequential processing of data files*.
– DERIVATIVES **sequentiality** noun, **sequentially** adverb.
– ORIGIN early 19th cent. (as a medical term in the sense 'following as a secondary condition'): from SEQUENCE, on the pattern of *consequential*.

sequential access ▸ **noun** [mass noun] access to a computer data file that requires the user to read through the file from the beginning in the order in which it is stored. Compare with DIRECT ACCESS.

sequential circuit ▸ **noun** Electronics a circuit whose output depends on the order or timing of the inputs. Compare with COMBINATIONAL CIRCUIT.

sequester /sɪˈkwɛstə/ ▸ **verb** [with obj.] **1** isolate or hide away: *she is sequestered in deepest Dorset* | *the artist sequestered himself in his studio for two years*.
2 another term for SEQUESTRATE.
3 Chemistry form a chelate or other stable compound with (an ion, atom, or molecule) so that it is no longer available for reactions.
– ORIGIN late Middle English: from Old French *sequestrer* or late Latin *sequestrare* 'commit for safekeeping', from Latin *sequester* 'trustee'.

sequestered ▸ **adjective** (of a place) isolated and hidden away: *a wild sequestered spot*.

sequestrate /ˈsiːkwəstreɪt, ˈsiːkwɛs-/ ▸ **verb** [with obj.] take legal possession of (assets) until a debt has been paid or other claims have been met: *the power of courts to sequestrate the assets of unions*. ■ take forcible possession of (something); confiscate: *in November 1956 the property was sequestrated by the authorities*. ■ legally place (the property of a bankrupt) in the hands of a trustee for division among the creditors. ■ declare (someone) bankrupt: *two more poll tax rebels were sequestrated*.
– DERIVATIVES **sequestrator** /ˈsiːkwɪˌstreɪtə/ noun.
– ORIGIN late Middle English (in the sense 'separate from general access'): from late Latin *sequestrat-* 'given up for safekeeping', from the verb *sequestrare* (see SEQUESTER).

sequestration /ˌsiːkwəˈstreɪʃ(ə)n/ ▸ **noun** [mass noun] **1** the action of sequestrating or taking legal possession of assets.
2 the action of chemically sequestering a substance: *carbon sequestration*.

sequestrum /sɪˈkwɛstrəm/ ▸ **noun** (pl. **sequestra** /-trə/) Medicine a piece of dead bone tissue formed within a diseased or injured bone, typically in chronic osteomyelitis.
– DERIVATIVES **sequestrectomy** /ˌsiːkwɪˈstrɛktəmi/ noun (pl. **sequestrectomies**).
– ORIGIN mid 19th cent.: modern Latin, neuter of Latin *sequester* 'standing apart'.

sequin ▸ **noun 1** a small shiny disc sewn on to clothing for decoration.
2 historical a Venetian gold coin.
– DERIVATIVES **sequinned** (also **sequined**) adjective.
– ORIGIN late 16th cent. (in sense 2): from French, from Italian *zecchino*, from *zecca* 'a mint', from Arabic *sikka* 'a die for coining'. Sense 1 dates from the late 19th cent.

sequoia /sɪˈkwɔɪə/ ▸ **noun** a redwood tree, especially the California redwood.
– ORIGIN from modern Latin *Sequoia* (genus name), from *Sequoya*, the name of the Cherokee Indian who invented the Cherokee syllabary.

Sequoia National Park a national park in the Sierra Nevada of California, east of Fresno. It was established in 1890 to protect groves of giant sequoia trees, of which the largest, the General Sherman Tree, is thought to be between 3,000 and 4,000 years old.

sera plural form of SERUM.

serac /ˈsɛrak, sɛˈrak/ ▸ **noun** a pinnacle or ridge of ice on the surface of a glacier.
– ORIGIN mid 19th cent.: from Swiss French *sérac*, originally the name of a compact white cheese.

seraglio /sɛˈrɑːlɪəʊ, sɪ-/ ▸ **noun** (pl. **seraglios**) **1** the women's apartments (harem) in a Muslim palace. ■ another term for HAREM (sense 2).
2 historical a Turkish palace, especially the Sultan's court and government offices at Constantinople.
– ORIGIN late 16th cent.: from Italian *serraglio*, via Turkish from Persian *sarāy* 'palace'; compare with SERAI.

serai /səˈrʌɪ/ ▸ **noun** another term for CARAVANSERAI (sense 1).

Seraing /səˈraŋ/ an industrial town in Belgium, on the River Meuse just south-west of Liège; pop. 61,657 (2008).

Seram Sea variant spelling of CERAM SEA.

serang /səˈraŋ/ ▸ **noun** Indian an Asian head of a lascar crew.
– ORIGIN from Persian and Urdu *sar-hang* 'commander', from *sar* 'head' + *hang* 'authority'.

serape /sɛˈrɑːpeɪ/ (also **sarape**) ▸ **noun** a shawl or blanket worn as a cloak by people from Latin America.
– ORIGIN Mexican Spanish.

seraph /ˈsɛrəf/ ▸ **noun** (pl. **seraphim** /-fɪm/ or **seraphs**) an angelic being, regarded in traditional Christian angelology as belonging to the highest order of the ninefold celestial hierarchy, associated with light, ardour, and purity.
– ORIGIN Old English, back-formation from *seraphim* (plural), via late Latin and Greek from Hebrew *śĕrāpîm*. Compare with CHERUB.

seraphic /səˈrafɪk/ ▸ **adjective** characteristic of or resembling a seraph or seraphim; angelic: *a seraphic smile*.
– DERIVATIVES **seraphically** adverb.
– ORIGIN mid 17th cent.: from medieval Latin *seraphicus*, from late Latin *seraphim* (see SERAPH).

Seraphic Doctor the nickname of St Bonaventura.

Serapis /ˈsɛrəpɪs, səˈreɪp-/ Egyptian Mythology a god whose cult was developed by Ptolemy I at Memphis as a combination of Apis and Osiris, to unite Greeks and Egyptians in a common worship.

seraskier /ˌsɛrəˈskɪə/ ▸ **noun** historical the commander-in-chief and minister of war of the Ottoman Empire.
– ORIGIN Turkish, from Persian *sar'askar* 'head (of the) army'.

Serb ▸ **noun** a native or inhabitant of Serbia, or a person of Serbian descent.
▸ **adjective** relating to Serbia, the Serbs, or their language.
– ORIGIN Serbian *Srb*.

Serbia /ˈsəːbɪə/ a republic in the Balkans; pop. 7,379,300 (est. 2009); official language, Serbian; capital, Belgrade.

> Serbia was conquered by the Turks in the 14th century, regaining independence in 1878. Serbian rivalry with the Austro-Hungarian Empire contributed to the outbreak of the First World War, after which Serbia was absorbed into the kingdom of Serbs, Croats, and Slovenes (named Yugoslavia from 1929–2003). In 1991–2 four out of the six Yugoslav republics seceded; Serbia became involved in armed conflict with neighbouring Croatia, the civil war in Bosnia, and the suppression of Albanian nationalism in Kosovo. On the break-up of Yugoslavia it remained in federation with Montenegro until 2006.

Serbian ▸ **noun 1** [mass noun] the Southern Slavic language of the Serbs, almost identical to Croatian but written in the Cyrillic alphabet. See SERBO-CROAT.
2 another term for SERB.
▸ **adjective** relating to Serbia, the Serbs, or their language.

Serbo- ▸ **combining form** Serbian; Serbian and ...: *Serbo-Croat*. ■ relating to Serbia.

Serbo-Croat /ˌsəːbəʊˈkrəʊat/ (also **Serbo-Croatian** /-krəʊˈeɪʃ(ə)n/) ▸ **noun** [mass noun] a term for the Southern Slavic language spoken in Serbia, Croatia, and elsewhere in the former Yugoslavia. Serbo-Croat comprises two closely similar forms: Serbian, written in the Cyrillic alphabet, and Croat, written in the Roman alphabet. Since the break-up of Yugoslavia the names of the individual languages have generally been preferred.
▸ **adjective** relating to Serbo-Croat.

Sercial /ˈsəːsɪəl/ ▸ **noun** [mass noun] a variety of wine grape grown chiefly in Madeira. ■ a dry light Madeira made from this grape.
– ORIGIN Portuguese.

sere[1] (also **sear**) ▸ **adjective** literary (especially of vegetation) dry or withered.
– ORIGIN Old English *sēar*: see SEAR.

sere[2] /sɪə/ ▸ **noun** Ecology a natural succession of plant (or animal) communities, especially a full series from uncolonized habitat to the appropriate climax vegetation. Compare with SUCCESSION.
– ORIGIN early 20th cent.: from Latin *serere* 'join in a series'.

Seremban /səˈrɛmbən/ the capital of the state of Negri Sembilan in Malaysia, situated in the south-west of the Malay Peninsula; pop. 419,500 (est. 2009).

serenade ▸ **noun** a piece of music sung or played in the open air, typically by a man at night under the window of his beloved. ■ another term for SERENATA.
▸ **verb** [with obj.] entertain (someone) with a serenade: *a strolling guitarist serenades the diners*.
– DERIVATIVES **serenader** noun.

– ORIGIN mid 17th cent.: from French *sérénade*, from Italian *serenata*, from *sereno* 'serene'.

serenata /ˌsɛrəˈnɑːtə/ ▶ **noun** Music a cantata with a pastoral subject. ■ a simple form of suite for orchestra or wind band.
– ORIGIN Italian, 'serenade' (see SERENADE).

serendipitous /ˌsɛr(ə)nˈdɪpɪtəs/ ▶ **adjective** occurring or discovered by chance in a happy or beneficial way: *a serendipitous encounter*.
– DERIVATIVES **serendipitously adverb**.

serendipity /ˌsɛr(ə)nˈdɪpɪti/ ▶ **noun** [mass noun] the occurrence and development of events by chance in a happy or beneficial way: *a fortunate stroke of serendipity* | [count noun] *a series of small serendipities*.
– ORIGIN 1754: coined by Horace Walpole, suggested by *The Three Princes of Serendip*, the title of a fairy tale in which the heroes 'were always making discoveries, by accidents and sagacity, of things they were not in quest of'.

serene ▶ **adjective** calm, peaceful, and untroubled; tranquil: *her eyes were closed and she looked very serene* | *serene certainty*.
▶ **noun** (usu. **the serene**) archaic an expanse of clear sky or calm sea: *not a cloud obscured the deep serene*.
– DERIVATIVES **serenely adverb**.
– ORIGIN late Middle English (describing the weather or sky as 'clear, fine, and calm'): from Latin *serenus*.

Serengeti /ˌsɛrənˈgɛti/ a vast plain in Tanzania, to the west of the Great Rift Valley. In 1951 the Serengeti National Park was created to protect the area's large numbers of wildebeest, zebra, and Thomson's gazelle.

Serenissima /ˌsɛrəˈnɪsɪmə/ ▶ **noun** (**La Serenissima** or **the Serenissima**) a name for Venice: *the Serenissima's seafaring past*.
– ORIGIN Italian, feminine of *serenissimo* 'most serene'.

serenity ▶ **noun** (pl. **serenities**) [mass noun] the state of being calm, peaceful, and untroubled: *an oasis of serenity amidst the bustling city*.
– ORIGIN late Middle English: from Old French *serenite*, from Latin *serenitas*, from *serenus* 'clear, fair' (see SERENE).

serf ▶ **noun** an agricultural labourer bound by the feudal system who was tied to working on his lord's estate.
– DERIVATIVES **serfage noun**, **serfdom noun**.
– ORIGIN late 15th cent. (in the sense 'slave'): from Old French, from Latin *servus* 'slave'.

serge /səːdʒ/ ▶ **noun** [mass noun] a durable twilled woollen or worsted fabric.
– ORIGIN late Middle English: from Old French *sarge*, from a variant of Latin *serica (lana)* 'silken (wool)', from *sericus* (see SILK).

sergeant /ˈsɑːdʒ(ə)nt/ ▶ **noun** a rank of non-commissioned officer in the army or air force, above corporal and below staff sergeant. ■ Brit. a police officer ranking below an inspector. ■ US a police officer ranking below a lieutenant.
– ORIGIN Middle English: from Old French *sergent*, from Latin *servient-* 'serving', from the verb *servire*. Early use was as a general term meaning 'attendant, servant' and 'common soldier'; the term was later applied to specific official roles.

sergeant-at-arms ▶ **noun** variant spelling of SERJEANT-AT-ARMS.

Sergeant Baker ▶ **noun** Austral. a brightly coloured edible marine fish with two elongated dorsal fin rays, occurring in warm Australian coastal waters. ● *Aulopus purpurissatus*, family Aulopidae.
– ORIGIN late 19th cent.: of unknown origin.

sergeant fish ▶ **noun** another term for COBIA.

sergeant major ▶ **noun 1** a warrant officer in the British army whose job is to assist the adjutant of a regiment or battalion (**regimental sergeant major**) or a subunit commander (**company sergeant major, battery sergeant major**, etc.).
2 a high rank of non-commissioned officer in the US army, above master sergeant and below warrant officer.
3 a fish with boldly striped sides which lives in warm seas, typically on coral reefs. ● *Abudefduf saxatilis*, family Pomacentridae.

serger /ˈsəːdʒə/ ▶ **noun** a sewing machine used for overcasting to prevent material from fraying at the edge.

Sergipe /səːˈʒiːpi/ a state in eastern Brazil, on the Atlantic coast; capital, Aracajú.

Sergius, St /ˈsəːdʒɪəs/ (1314–92), Russian monastic reformer and mystic; Russian name *Svyatoi Sergi Radonezhsky*. He founded forty monasteries, re-establishing the monasticism which had been lost through the Tartar invasion, and inspired the resistance which saved Russia from the Tartars in 1380. Feast day, 25 September.

Sergt ▶ **abbreviation** Sergeant.

serial ▶ **adjective** [attrib.] **1** consisting of, forming part of, or taking place in a series: *a serial publication*. ■ Linguistics (of verbs) used in sequence to form a construction, as in *they wanted, needed, longed for peace*.
2 repeatedly committing the same offence and typically following a characteristic, predictable behaviour pattern: *a serial killer*. ■ repeatedly following the same behaviour pattern: *he was a serial adulterer* | *serial monogamy*.
3 Music using transformations of a fixed series of notes.
4 Computing (of a device) involving the transfer of data as a single sequence of bits. ■ (of a processor) running only a single task, as opposed to multitasking.
▶ **noun 1** a story or play appearing in regular instalments on television or radio or in a magazine or newspaper: *a new three-part drama serial*.
2 (usu. **serials**) (in a library) a periodical.
– DERIVATIVES **seriality noun**, **serially adverb**.
– ORIGIN mid 19th cent.: from SERIES + -AL, perhaps suggested by French *sérial*.

serial comma (also **Oxford comma**) ▶ **noun** a comma used after the penultimate item in a list of three or more items, before 'and' or 'or' (e.g. *an Italian painter, sculptor, and architect*).

serialism ▶ **noun** [mass noun] Music a compositional technique in which a fixed series of notes, especially the twelve notes of the chromatic scale, are used to generate the harmonic and melodic basis of a piece and are subject to change only in specific ways. The first fully serial movements appeared in 1923 in works by Arnold Schoenberg. See also TWELVE-NOTE.
– DERIVATIVES **serialist adjective & noun**.

serialize (also **serialise**) ▶ **verb** [with obj.] **1** publish or broadcast (a story or play) in regular instalments: *sections of the book were serialized in the Sunday Times*.
2 arrange (something) in a series.
3 Music compose according to the techniques of serialism.
– DERIVATIVES **serialization noun**.

serial monogamy ▶ **noun** [mass noun] the practice of engaging in a succession of monogamous sexual relationships.
– DERIVATIVES **serial monogamist noun**.

serial number ▶ **noun** an identification number showing the position of a printed or manufactured item in a series.

serial port ▶ **noun** Computing a connector by which a device that sends data one bit at a time may be connected to a computer.

serial section ▶ **noun** Biology each of a series of thin sections through tissue cut in successive parallel planes, especially for mounting on microscope slides.
– DERIVATIVES **serial sectioning noun**.

seriate technical ▶ **adjective** /ˈsɪərɪət/ arranged or occurring in one or more series.
▶ **verb** /ˈsɪərɪeɪt/ [with obj.] arrange (items) in a sequence according to prescribed criteria.
– DERIVATIVES **seriation noun**.
– ORIGIN mid 19th cent.: back-formation from *seriation*, from SERIES.

seriatim /ˌsɪərɪˈeɪtɪm, ˌsɛrɪ-/ ▶ **adverb** formal taking one subject after another in regular order; point by point: *it is proposed to deal with these matters seriatim*.
– ORIGIN late 15th cent.: from medieval Latin, from Latin *series*, on the pattern of Latin *gradatim* and *literatim*.

sericite /ˈsɛrɪsʌɪt/ ▶ **noun** [mass noun] a fine-grained fibrous variety of muscovite, found chiefly in schist.
– ORIGIN mid 19th cent.: from Latin *sericum* 'silk' + -ITE[1].

sericulture /ˈsɛrɪˌkʌltʃə/ ▶ **noun** [mass noun] the production of silk and the rearing of silkworms for this purpose.
– DERIVATIVES **sericultural adjective**.
– ORIGIN mid 19th cent.: abbreviation of French *sériciculture*, from late Latin *sericum* 'silk' + French *culture* 'cultivation'.

seriema /ˌsɛrɪˈiːmə/ (also **cariama**) ▶ **noun** a large ground-dwelling South American bird related to the bustards, with a long neck and legs and a crest above the bill. ● Family Cariamidae: two genera and species.
– ORIGIN mid 19th cent.: modern Latin, from Tupi *siriema* 'crested'.

series ▶ **noun** (pl. **same**) **1** a number of events, objects, or people of a similar or related kind coming one after another: *the explosion was the latest in **a series of** accidents* | *he gave **a series of** lectures on modern art*. ■ a set of books, periodicals, or other documents published in a common format or under a common title. ■ a set of games played between two teams: *the Test series against Australia*. ■ a set of stamps, banknotes, or coins issued at a particular time.
2 a set or sequence of related television or radio programmes: *a new drama series*.
3 Music another term for TONE ROW.
4 [as modifier] denoting electrical circuits or components arranged so that the current passes through each successively. The opposite of PARALLEL.
5 Geology (in chronostratigraphy) a range of strata corresponding to an epoch in time, being a subdivision of a system and itself subdivided into stages: *the Pliocene series*.
6 Chemistry a set of elements with common properties or of compounds related in composition or structure: *the metals of the lanthanide series*.
7 Mathematics a set of quantities constituting a progression or having the several values determined by a common relation.
8 Phonetics a group of speech sounds having at least one phonetic feature in common but distinguished in other respects.
– PHRASES **in series** (of a set of batteries or electrical components) arranged so that the current passes through each successively.
– ORIGIN early 17th cent.: from Latin, literally 'row, chain', from *serere* 'join, connect'.

serif /ˈsɛrɪf/ ▶ **noun** a slight projection finishing off a stroke of a letter, as in T contrasted with T.
– DERIVATIVES **seriffed adjective**.
– ORIGIN mid 19th cent.: perhaps from Dutch *schreef* 'dash, line', of Germanic origin.

serigraph /ˈsɛrɪgrɑːf/ ▶ **noun** chiefly N. Amer. a printed design produced by means of a silk screen.
– DERIVATIVES **serigrapher noun**, **serigraphy noun**.
– ORIGIN late 19th cent.: formed irregularly from Latin *sericum* 'silk' + -GRAPH.

serin /ˈsɛrɪn/ ▶ **noun** a small Eurasian and North African finch related to the canary, with a short bill and typically streaky plumage. ● Genus *Serinus*, family Fringillidae: several species, in particular the **European serin** (*S. serinus*).
– ORIGIN mid 16th cent. (denoting a canary): from French, 'canary', of unknown ultimate origin.

serine /ˈsɪəriːn, ˈsɛr-/ ▶ **noun** [mass noun] Biochemistry a hydrophilic amino acid which is a constituent of most proteins. ● Chem. formula: $CH_2OHCHNH_2COOH$
– ORIGIN late 19th cent.: from Latin *sericum* 'silk' + -INE[4].

serio-comic /sɪərɪəʊˈkɒmɪk/ ▶ **adjective** combining the serious and the comic; serious in intention but humorous in manner or vice versa: *a telling serio-comic critique*.

serious ▶ **adjective 1** demanding or characterized by careful consideration or application: *marriage is a serious matter* | *we give serious consideration to safety recommendations*. ■ solemn or thoughtful in character or manner: *her face grew serious*. ■ (of music, literature, or other art forms) requiring or meriting deep reflection: *he bridges the gap between serious and popular music*.
2 acting or speaking sincerely and in earnest, rather than in a joking or half-hearted manner: *actors who are serious about their work*.
3 significant or worrying because of possible danger or risk; not slight or negligible: *she escaped serious injury*.
4 [attrib.] informal substantial in terms of size, number, or quality: *he suddenly had serious money to spend*.
– ORIGIN late Middle English: from Old French *serieux* or late Latin *seriosus*, from Latin *serius* 'earnest, serious'.

seriously ▶ **adverb 1** in a solemn or considered manner: *the doctor looked seriously at him*.
2 with earnest intent; not lightly or superficially: *I seriously considered cancelling my subscription*. ■ really or sincerely: *do you seriously believe that I would jeopardize my career by such acts?* ■ [sentence adverb] used to add sincerity to a statement, especially after a facetious exchange of remarks: *seriously though, short cuts rarely work*.

3 to a degree that is significant or worrying: *the amount of fat you eat can seriously affect your health* | [as submodifier] *three men are seriously ill in hospital.*
4 [as submodifier] informal very; extremely: *he was seriously rich.*
– PHRASES **take someone/thing seriously** regard someone or something as important and worthy of attention.

seriousness ▶ **noun** [mass noun] the quality or state of being serious: *we are aware of the seriousness of the situation* | *she replied with deadly seriousness.*
– PHRASES **in all seriousness** very seriously; not as a joke: *I ask this question in all seriousness.*

serjeant ▶ **noun** (in official lists) a sergeant in the Foot Guards.
– ORIGIN Middle English: variant (commonly used in legal contexts) of **SERGEANT**.

serjeant-at-arms (N. Amer. **sergeant-at-arms**) ▶ **noun** (pl. **serjeants-at-arms**) an official of a legislative assembly whose duty includes maintaining order and security. ■ Brit. historical a knight or armed officer in the service of the monarch or a lord.

serjeant-at-law ▶ **noun** (pl. **serjeants-at-law**) historical a barrister of the highest rank.

serjeanty ▶ **noun** (pl. **serjeanties**) [mass noun] historical a form of feudal tenure conditional on rendering some specified personal service to the monarch.

sermon ▶ **noun 1** a talk on a religious or moral subject, especially one given during a church service and based on a passage from the Bible.
2 informal a long or tedious piece of admonition or reproof; a lecture.
– DERIVATIVES **sermonic** adjective.
– ORIGIN Middle English (also in the sense 'speech, discourse'): from Old French, from Latin *sermo(n-)* 'discourse, talk'.

sermonize (also **sermonise**) ▶ **verb** [no obj.] **1** compose or deliver a sermon.
2 deliver an opinionated and dogmatic talk to someone: *they confidently sermonize on the fixed nature of identity.*
– DERIVATIVES **sermonizer** noun.

Sermon on the Mount ▶ **noun** the discourse of Christ recorded in Matt. 5–7, including the Beatitudes and the Lord's Prayer.

sero- ▶ **combining form** relating to serum: *serotype.* ■ involving a serous membrane: *serositis.*
– ORIGIN representing **SERUM**.

seroconvert /ˌsɪərəʊkənˈvəːt/ ▶ **verb** [no obj.] Medicine (of a person) undergo a change from a seronegative to a seropositive condition.
– DERIVATIVES **seroconversion** noun.

serodiagnosis ▶ **noun** [mass noun] Medicine diagnosis based on the study of blood sera.
– DERIVATIVES **serodiagnostic** adjective.

serology /sɪəˈrɒlədʒi/ ▶ **noun** [mass noun] the scientific study or diagnostic examination of blood serum, especially with regard to the response of the immune system to pathogens or introduced substances.
– DERIVATIVES **serologic** adjective, **serological** adjective, **serologically** adverb, **serologist** noun.

S

seronegative ▶ **adjective** Medicine giving a negative result in a test of blood serum, e.g. for the presence of a virus.
– DERIVATIVES **seronegativity** noun.

seropositive ▶ **adjective** Medicine giving a positive result in a test of blood serum, e.g. for the presence of a virus.
– DERIVATIVES **seropositivity** noun.

seroprevalence /ˌsɪərəʊˈprɛvələns/ ▶ **noun** [mass noun] Medicine the level of a pathogen in a population, as measured in blood serum.

serosa /sɪˈrəʊsə/ ▶ **noun** [mass noun] Physiology the tissue of a serous membrane.
– DERIVATIVES **serosal** adjective.
– ORIGIN modern Latin, feminine of medieval Latin *serosus* 'serous'.

serositis /ˌsɪrəˈsʌɪtɪs/ ▶ **noun** [mass noun] Medicine inflammation of a serous membrane.

serotine /ˈsɛrətiːn/ ▶ **noun** a medium-sized insectivorous bat found in Eurasia and Africa: ● a chiefly Eurasian bat (genus *Eptesicus*, family Vespertilionidae, in particular the widespread *E. serotinus*). ● an African bat (genus *Pipistrellus*, family Vespertilionidae).
– ORIGIN late 18th cent.: from French *sérotine*, from Latin *serotinus* 'of the evening, late', from *serus* 'late'.

serotonergic /ˌsɛrətə(ʊ)ˈnɜːdʒɪk/ ▶ **adjective** Biochemistry denoting a nerve ending that releases and is stimulated by serotonin.

serotonin /ˌsɛrəˈtəʊnɪn/ ▶ **noun** Biochemistry a compound present in blood platelets and serum, which constricts the blood vessels and acts as a neurotransmitter. ● Alternative name: **5-hydroxytryptamine**; chem. formula: $C_{10}H_{12}N_2O$.
– ORIGIN 1940s: from **SERUM** + **TONIC** + **-IN**[1].

serotype /ˈsɪərə(ʊ)tʌɪp/ Microbiology ▶ **noun** a serologically distinguishable strain of a microorganism.
▶ **verb** [with obj.] assign (a microorganism) to a particular serotype.
– DERIVATIVES **serotypic** /ˌsɪərə(ʊ)ˈtɪpɪk/ adjective.

serous /ˈsɪərəs/ ▶ **adjective** Physiology of, resembling, or producing serum.
– DERIVATIVES **serosity** noun.
– ORIGIN late Middle English: from French *séreux* or medieval Latin *serosus*, from *serum* (see **SERUM**).

serous membrane ▶ **noun** a mesothelial tissue which lines certain internal cavities of the body, forming a smooth, transparent, two-layered membrane lubricated by a fluid derived from serum. The peritoneum, pericardium, and pleura are serous membranes.

serow /ˈsɛrəʊ/ ▶ **noun** a goat-antelope with short, sharp horns, long, coarse hair, and a beard, native to forested mountain slopes of SE Asia, Taiwan, and Japan. ● Genus *Capricornis*, family Bovidae: two species.
– ORIGIN mid 19th cent.: probably from Lepcha *sā-ro*.

Serpens /ˈsəːp(ə)nz/ Astronomy a large constellation (the Serpent) on the celestial equator, said to represent the snake coiled around Ophiuchus. It is divided into two parts by Ophiuchus, **Serpens Caput** (the 'head') and **Serpens Cauda** (the 'tail').
– ORIGIN Latin.

serpent ▶ **noun 1** chiefly literary a large snake. ■ (**the Serpent**) a biblical name for Satan (see Gen. 3, Rev. 20). ■ a dragon or other mythical snake-like reptile.
2 a sly or treacherous person, especially one who exploits a position of trust in order to betray it.
3 historical a bass wind instrument made of leather-covered wood in three U-shaped turns, with a cup-shaped mouthpiece and few keys.
– ORIGIN Middle English: via Old French from Latin *serpent-* 'creeping', from the verb *serpere*.

Serpentes /səːˈpɛntiːz/ ▶ **plural noun** Zoology another term for **OPHIDIA**.
– ORIGIN Latin, 'reptiles'.

serpentine /ˈsəːp(ə)ntʌɪn/ ▶ **adjective** of or like a serpent or snake: *serpentine coils.* ■ winding and twisting like a snake: *serpentine country lanes.* ■ complex, cunning, or treacherous: *his charm was too subtle and serpentine for me.*
▶ **noun 1** [mass noun] a dark green mineral consisting of hydrated magnesium silicate, sometimes mottled or spotted like a snake's skin.
2 (**the Serpentine**) a winding lake in Hyde Park, London, constructed in 1730.
3 a riding exercise consisting of a series of half-circles made alternately to right and left.
4 historical a kind of cannon, used especially in the 15th and 16th centuries.
▶ **verb** [no obj., with adverbial of direction] move or lie in a winding path or line.
– ORIGIN late Middle English: via Old French from late Latin *serpentinus* (see **SERPENT**).

serpentine verse ▶ **noun** Prosody a metrical line beginning and ending with the same word.

serpentinite /ˈsəːp(ə)ntɪˌnʌɪt/ ▶ **noun** [mass noun] Geology a dark, typically greenish metamorphic rock, consisting largely of serpentine or related minerals, formed when mafic igneous rocks are altered by water.
– ORIGIN 1930s: from **SERPENTINE** + **-ITE**[1].

serpentinize /ˈsəːp(ə)ntɪˌnʌɪz/ (also **serpentinise**) ▶ **verb** [with obj.] Geology convert into serpentine.
– DERIVATIVES **serpentinization** noun.

serpiginous /səːˈpɪdʒɪnəs/ ▶ **adjective** Medicine (of a skin lesion or ulcerated region) having a wavy margin.
– ORIGIN late Middle English: from medieval Latin *serpigo, serpigin-* 'ringworm' (from Latin *serpere* 'to creep') + **-OUS**.

SERPS /səːps/ ▶ **abbreviation** (in the UK) state earnings-related pension scheme.

serpulid /ˈsəːpjʊlɪd/ ▶ **noun** Zoology a small marine fan worm which lives in a twisted shell-like tube, typically in colonies, with retractable tentacles for filter-feeding. ● Family Serpulidae, class Polychaeta.
– ORIGIN late 19th cent.: from modern Latin *Serpulidae* (plural), from late Latin *serpula* 'small serpent', from Latin *serpere* 'to creep'.

serranid /səˈranɪd, ˈsɛrə-/ ▶ **noun** Zoology a fish of the sea bass family (Serranidae), whose members are predatory marine fish with a spiny dorsal fin.
– ORIGIN mid 20th cent.: from modern Latin *Serranidae* (plural), from the genus name *Serranus*, from Latin *serra* 'saw'.

serrano /səˈrɑːnəʊ/ ▶ **noun** (pl. **serranos**) a small green chilli pepper of a very hot variety.
– ORIGIN from Spanish, literally 'of the mountains, highlander'.

serrate /ˈsɛreɪt/ ▶ **adjective** chiefly Botany serrated: *leaves with serrate margins.*
– ORIGIN mid 17th cent.: from late Latin *serratus*, from Latin *serra* 'saw'.

serrated ▶ **adjective** having or denoting a jagged edge; sawlike: *a knife with a serrated edge.*

serration ▶ **noun** (usu. **serrations**) a tooth or point of a serrated edge or surface: *a heavy-duty knife with sawtooth serrations.*

serried ▶ **adjective** [attrib.] (of rows of people or things) standing close together: *serried ranks of soldiers* | *the serried rows of vines.*
– ORIGIN mid 17th cent.: past participle of *serry* 'press close', probably from French *serré* 'close together', based on Latin *sera* 'lock'.

sertão /ˈsɛːtɑ̃ːʊ/ ▶ **noun** (pl. **sertãos**) (in Brazil) an arid region of scrub.
– ORIGIN early 19th cent.: Portuguese.

Sertoli cell /səːˈtəʊli/ ▶ **noun** Anatomy a type of somatic cell around which spermatids develop in the tubules of the testis.
– ORIGIN late 19th cent.: named after Enrico *Sertoli* (1842–1910), Italian histologist.

serum /ˈsɪərəm/ ▶ **noun** (pl. **sera** /-rə/ or **serums**) [mass noun] **1** an amber-coloured, protein-rich liquid which separates out when blood coagulates.
2 the blood serum of an animal used to provide immunity to a pathogen or toxin by inoculation or as a diagnostic agent.
– ORIGIN late 17th cent.: from Latin, literally 'whey'.

serum hepatitis ▶ **noun** [mass noun] a viral form of hepatitis transmitted through infected blood products, causing fever, debility, and jaundice.

serum sickness ▶ **noun** [mass noun] an allergic reaction to an injection of serum, typically mild and characterized by skin rashes, joint stiffness, and fever.

serval /ˈsəːv(ə)l/ ▶ **noun** a slender African wild cat with long legs, large ears, and a black-spotted orange-brown coat. ● *Felis serval*, family Felidae.
– ORIGIN late 18th cent.: from French, from Portuguese *cerval* 'deer-like', from *cervo* 'deer', from Latin *cervus*.

servant ▶ **noun** a person who performs duties for others, especially a person employed in a house on domestic duties or as a personal attendant. ■ a person employed in the service of a government: *a government servant.* See also **CIVIL SERVANT**, **PUBLIC SERVANT**. ■ a devoted and helpful follower or supporter: *he was a great servant of the Labour Party.*
– ORIGIN Middle English: from Old French, literally '(person) serving', present participle (used as a noun) of *servir* 'to serve'.

serve ▶ **verb** [with obj.] **1** perform duties or services for (another person or an organization): *Malcolm has served the church very faithfully.* ■ provide (an area or group of people) with a product or service: *a hospital which serves a large area of Wales.* ■ [no obj.] be employed as a member of the armed forces: *he had hoped to serve with the Medical Corps.* ■ spend (a period) in office, in an apprenticeship, or in prison: *he is serving a ten-year jail sentence.*
2 present (food or drink) to someone: *they serve wine instead of beer* | *serve white wines chilled.* ■ present (someone) with food or drink: *the cafe refused to serve him with the tea* | [with two objs] *Peter served them generous portions of soup.* ■ (of food or drink) be enough for: *the recipe serves four people.* ■ chiefly Brit. attend to (a customer in a shop): *she turned to serve the impatient customer.* ■ supply (goods) to a customer. ■ [no obj.] Christian Church act as a server at the celebration of the Eucharist. ■ [with two objs] archaic play (a trick) on (someone): *I remember the trick you served me.*
3 Law deliver (a document such as a summons or writ) in a formal manner to the person to whom it is addressed: *the court then issues the summons and serves it on your debtor.* ■ deliver a document

to (someone) in such a way: *they were just about to serve him with a writ.*
4 be of use in achieving or satisfying: *this book will serve a useful purpose | the union came into existence to serve the interests of musicians.* ■ [no obj.] be of some specified use: *the square now **serves as** the town's chief car park* | [with infinitive] *sweat serves to cool down the body.* ■ [with obj. and adverbial] treat (someone) in a specified way: *Cornish homeowners wonder if they are being fairly served.* ■ (of a male breeding animal) copulate with (a female).
5 [no obj.] (in tennis and other racket sports) hit the ball or shuttlecock to begin play for each point of a game: *he tossed the ball up to serve* | [with obj.] *serve the ball on to the front wall.* ■ (**serve out**) win the final game of a set or match while serving.
6 Nautical bind (a rope) with thin cord to protect or strengthen it.
7 Military operate (a gun).
▶ **noun 1** (in tennis and other racket sports) an act of hitting the ball or shuttlecock to start play: *he was let down by an erratic serve.*
2 Austral. informal a reprimand: *he would be willing to give the country a serve in an English newspaper.*
– PHRASES **if my memory serves** (**me**) if I remember correctly: *if my memory serves me, this is not the first time.* **serve someone right** be someone's deserved punishment or misfortune: *it would serve you right if Jeff walked out on you.* **serve one's time** (chiefly US also **serve out one's time**) hold office for the normal period: *every sergeant had served his time as a constable.* ■ (also **serve time**) spend time in office, in an apprenticeship, or in prison: *he is serving time in Swansea Prison.* **serve one's/its turn** be useful or helpful. **serve two masters** take orders from two superiors or follow two conflicting or opposing principles or policies at the same time. [with biblical allusion to Matt. 6:24.]
– ORIGIN Middle English: from Old French *servir*, from Latin *servire*, from *servus* 'slave'.

serve-and-volley ▶ **adjective** Tennis denoting a style of play in which the server moves close to the net after serving, ready to play an attacking volley off the service return.
– DERIVATIVES **serve-and-volleyer** noun.

server ▶ **noun 1** a person or thing that serves. ■ N. Amer. a waiter or waitress. ■ Christian Church a person assisting the celebrant at the celebration of the Eucharist.
2 a computer or computer program which manages access to a centralized resource or service in a network.

server farm ▶ **noun** another term for DATA CENTRE.

servery ▶ **noun** (pl. **serveries**) Brit. a counter, service hatch, or room from which meals are served.

Servian[1] /'sə:vɪən/ ▶ **adjective** relating to Servius Tullius, the semi-legendary sixth king of ancient Rome (*fl.* 6th century BC).

Servian[2] /'sə:vɪən/ ▶ **noun & adjective** archaic variant of SERBIAN.

Servian wall a wall encircling the ancient city of Rome, said to have been built by Servius Tullius (see SERVIAN[1]).

service ▶ **noun 1** [mass noun] the action of helping or doing work for someone: *millions are involved in voluntary service.* ■ [count noun] an act of assistance: *he has done us a great service | he volunteered his services as a driver.* ■ assistance or advice given to customers during and after the sale of goods: *they aim to provide better quality of service.* ■ the action of serving food and drinks to customers: *they complained of poor bar service.* ■ short for SERVICE CHARGE: *service is included in the final bill.* ■ a period of employment with a company or organization: *he retired after 40 years' service.* ■ employment as a servant: *the pitifully low wages gained from domestic service.* ■ the use which can be made of a machine: *the computer should provide good service for years.*
2 a system supplying a public need such as transport, communications, or utilities such as electricity and water: *a regular bus service.* ■ a public department or organization run by the state: *the probation service.* ■ (**the services**) the armed forces: (as modifier **service**) *service personnel.* ■ (**services**) Brit. an area with parking beside a major road supplying petrol, refreshments, and other amenities to motorists.
3 a ceremony of religious worship according to a prescribed form: *a funeral service.*
4 a periodic routine inspection and maintenance of a vehicle or other machine: *he took his car in for a service.*
5 [with modifier] a set of matching crockery used for serving a particular meal: *a dinner service.*
6 [mass noun] (in tennis and other racket sports) the action or right of serving to begin play. ■ [count noun] a serve.
7 [mass noun] Law the formal delivery of a document such as a writ or summons.
▶ **verb** [with obj.] **1** perform routine maintenance or repair work on (a vehicle or machine): *ensure that gas appliances are serviced regularly.* ■ supply and maintain systems for public utilities and transport and communications in (an area): *the village is small and well serviced.* ■ perform a service or services for (someone): *her life is devoted to servicing others.* ■ pay interest on (a debt): *taxpayers are paying $250 million just to service that debt.*
2 (of a male animal) mate with (a female animal). ■ vulgar slang (of a man) have sexual intercourse with (a woman).
– PHRASES **be at someone's service** be ready to assist someone whenever possible. **be of service** be available to assist someone. **in service 1** in or available for use. **2** dated employed as a servant. **out of service** not available for use. **see service** serve in the armed forces: *he saw service in both world wars.* ■ be used: *the building later saw service as a blacksmith's shop.*
– ORIGIN Old English (denoting religious devotion or a form of liturgy), from Old French *servise* or Latin *servitium* 'slavery', from *servus* 'slave'. The early sense of the verb (mid 19th cent.) was 'be of service to, provide with a service'.

serviceable ▶ **adjective 1** fulfilling its function adequately; usable: *an ageing but still serviceable water supply system.* ■ in working order: *only twelve aircraft were fully serviceable this morning.*
2 functional and durable rather than attractive: *sturdy, serviceable laced-up shoes.*
– DERIVATIVES **serviceability** noun, **serviceably** adverb.
– ORIGIN Middle English (in the sense 'willing to be of service'): from Old French *servisable*, from *servise* (see SERVICE).

service area ▶ **noun 1** Brit. a roadside area where services are available to motorists.
2 the area transmitted to by a broadcasting station.

serviceberry ▶ **noun** (pl. **serviceberries**) **1** the fruit of the service tree.
2 another term for JUNEBERRY.

service book ▶ **noun** a book of authorized forms of worship used in a church.

service bureau ▶ **noun** an organization providing services such as scanning and colour printing.

service ceiling ▶ **noun** the maximum height at which a particular type of aircraft can sustain a specified rate of climb.

service charge ▶ **noun 1** an extra charge made for serving customers in a restaurant.
2 a charge made for maintenance on a property which has been leased.

service club ▶ **noun** N. Amer. an association of business or professional people with the aims of promoting community welfare and goodwill.

service dress ▶ **noun** [mass noun] Brit. military uniform worn on formal but not ceremonial occasions.

service flat ▶ **noun** Brit. a rented flat in which domestic service and sometimes meals are provided by the management.

service game ▶ **noun** (in tennis and other racket sports) a game in which a particular player serves.

service industry ▶ **noun** a business that does work for a customer, and occasionally provides goods, but is not involved in manufacturing.

service line ▶ **noun** (in tennis, badminton, and other sports) a line on a court marking the limit of the area into which the ball must be served.

serviceman (or **servicewoman**) ▶ **noun** (pl. **servicemen** or **servicewomen**) **1** a person serving in the armed forces.
2 a person providing maintenance on machinery, especially domestic machinery.

service mark ▶ **noun** a legally registered name or designation used in the manner of a trademark to distinguish an organization's services from those of its competitors.

service module ▶ **noun** a detachable compartment of a spacecraft carrying fuel and supplies.

service provider ▶ **noun** a company which allows its subscribers access to the Internet.

servicer ▶ **noun 1** a person or organization that services something: *you will have to go to your car servicer for this.*
2 N. Amer. an organization that collects debt payments on behalf of a lender.

service road ▶ **noun** a subsidiary road running parallel to a main road and giving access to houses, shops, or businesses.

service station ▶ **noun** an establishment beside a road selling petrol and oil and sometimes having the facilities to carry out maintenance.

service tree ▶ **noun** a Eurasian tree of the rose family, closely related to the rowan. ● Genus *Sorbus*, family Rosaceae: the southern European **true service tree** (*S. domestica*), with compound leaves and green-brown fruits that are edible when overripe, and the **wild service tree** (*S. torminalis*), with lobed leaves and brown berries.
– ORIGIN mid 16th cent.: *service* from an alteration of the plural of obsolete *serve*, from Old English *syrfe*, based on Latin *sorbus*.

serviette ▶ **noun** Brit. a table napkin.
– ORIGIN late 15th cent.: from Old French, from *servir* 'to serve'.

servile ▶ **adjective 1** having or showing an excessive willingness to serve or please others: *bowing his head in a servile manner.*
2 of or characteristic of a slave or slaves.
– DERIVATIVES **servilely** adverb.
– ORIGIN late Middle English (in the sense 'suitable for a slave or for the working class'): from Latin *servilis*, from *servus* 'slave'.

servility ▶ **noun** [mass noun] an excessive willingness to serve or please others: *a classic example of media servility.*

serving ▶ **noun** a quantity of food suitable for or served to one person: *a large **serving of** spaghetti.*

servingman (or **servingwoman**) ▶ **noun** (pl. **servingmen** or **servingwomen**) archaic a servant or attendant.

Servite /'sə:vʌɪt/ ▶ **noun** a friar or nun of the Catholic religious order of the Servants of Blessed Mary, founded in 1233.
▶ **adjective** relating to this order.
– ORIGIN from medieval Latin *Servitae* (plural), from Latin, from *Servi Beatae Mariae*, the formal title of the order (see above).

servitor /'sə:vɪtə/ ▶ **noun** archaic a person who serves or attends on a social superior. ■ historical an Oxford undergraduate performing menial duties in exchange for assistance from college funds.
– DERIVATIVES **servitorship** noun.
– ORIGIN Middle English: via Old French from late Latin, from *servit-* 'served', from the verb *servire* (see SERVE).

servitude /'sə:vɪtju:d/ ▶ **noun** [mass noun] **1** the state of being a slave or completely subject to someone more powerful.
2 Law, archaic the subjection of property to an easement.
– ORIGIN late Middle English: via Old French from Latin *servitudo*, from *servus* 'slave'.

servlet ▶ **noun** Computing an applet that runs on a server, typically within Java.
– ORIGIN 1990s: blend of APPLET and SERVER.

S

servo[1] ▶ **noun** (pl. **servos**) short for SERVOMECHANISM or SERVOMOTOR.
– ORIGIN late 19th cent.: from Latin *servus* 'slave'.

servo[2] ▶ **noun** (pl. **servos**) Austral. informal a service station.
– ORIGIN 1980s: abbreviation of SERVICE STATION + -O.

servomechanism ▶ **noun** a powered mechanism producing motion or forces at a higher level of energy than the input level, e.g. in the brakes and steering of large motor vehicles, especially where feedback is employed to make the control automatic.

servomotor ▶ **noun** the motive element in a servomechanism.

sesame /'sɛsəmi/ ▶ **noun** [mass noun] a tall annual herbaceous plant of tropical and subtropical areas of the Old World, cultivated for its oil-rich seeds. ● *Sesamum indicum*, family Pedaliaceae.
■ (**sesame seed**) the edible seeds of this plant, which are used whole or have the oil extracted.
– PHRASES **open sesame** a free or unrestricted means of admission or access: *academic success is not an automatic open sesame to the job market.* [from the magic formula in the tale of Ali Baba and the Forty Thieves (see ALI BABA).]

– ORIGIN late Middle English: via Latin from Greek *sēsamon, sēsamē*; compare with Arabic *simsim*.

sesamoid /ˈsɛsəmɔɪd/ (also **sesamoid bone**) ▶ **noun** a small independent bone or bony nodule developed in a tendon where it passes over an angular structure, typically in the hands and feet. The kneecap is a particularly large sesamoid bone.
– ORIGIN late 17th cent.: from **SESAME** (with reference to the similarity in shape of a sesame seed) + **-OID**.

sesamum /ˈsɛsəməm/ ▶ **noun** another term for **SESAME**.
– ORIGIN mid 16th cent.: via Latin from Greek.

sesh ▶ **noun** Brit. informal a session, especially a drinking session: *an all-day sesh*.

Sesotho /sɛˈsuːtuː/ ▶ **noun** [mass noun] the South Sotho language of the Basotho people, an official language in Lesotho and South Africa, with over 5 million speakers.
– ORIGIN the name in Sesotho.

sesqui- ▶ **combining form** denoting one and a half: *sesquicentenary*. ■ Chemistry (of a compound) in which a particular element or group is present in a ratio of 3:2 compared with another: *sesquioxide*.
– ORIGIN from Latin *semi-* (see **SEMI-**) + *que* 'and'.

sesquialtera /ˌsɛskwɪˈalt(ə)rə/ ▶ **adjective** Music relating to or denoting a ratio of 3:2, as in an interval of a fifth. ■ denoting a mixture stop in an organ, typically consisting of two ranks of narrow-scaled open flue pipes.
– ORIGIN late Middle English: from Latin, feminine of *sesquialter*, from *sesqui* (see **SESQUI-**) + *alter* 'second'.

sesquicentenary /ˌsɛskwɪsɛnˈtiːn(ə)ri, -ˈtɛn-/ ▶ **noun** (pl. **sesquicentenaries**) the one-hundred-and-fiftieth anniversary of a significant event.
▶ **adjective** relating to such an anniversary.

sesquicentennial /ˌsɛskwɪsɛnˈtɛnɪəl/ ▶ **adjective** relating to a sesquicentenary.
▶ **noun** a sesquicentenary.

sesquioxide /ˌsɛskwɪˈɒksʌɪd/ ▶ **noun** Chemistry an oxide in which oxygen is present in the ratio of three atoms to two of another element.

sesquipedalian /ˌsɛskwɪpɪˈdeɪlɪən/ ▶ **adjective** formal (of a word) polysyllabic; long: *sesquipedalian surnames*. ■ characterized by long words; long-winded: *the sesquipedalian prose of scientific journals*.
– ORIGIN mid 17th cent.: from Latin *sesquipedalis* 'a foot and a half long', from *sesqui-* (see **SESQUI-**) + *pes, ped-* 'foot'.

sesquiterpene /ˌsɛskwɪˈtəːpiːn/ ▶ **noun** Chemistry a terpene with the formula $C_{15}H_{24}$, or a simple derivative of such a compound.

sess ▶ **noun** variant spelling of **CESS**[1].

sessile /ˈsɛsʌɪl, ˈsɛsɪl/ ▶ **adjective** Biology (of an organism, e.g. a barnacle) fixed in one place; immobile. ■ Botany & Zoology (of a plant or animal structure) attached directly by its base without a stalk or peduncle.
– ORIGIN early 18th cent.: from Latin *sessilis*, from *sess-* 'seated', from the verb *sedere*.

sessile oak ▶ **noun** a Eurasian oak tree with stalkless egg-shaped acorns, common in hilly areas with poor soils. Also called **DURMAST OAK**. ● *Quercus petraea*, family Fagaceae.

S

session ▶ **noun** **1** a meeting of a deliberative or judicial body to conduct its business. ■ a period during which such meetings are regularly held: *legislation to curb wildcat strikes will be introduced during the coming parliamentary session*. ■ the part of a year or of a day during which teaching takes place in a school or college.
2 [often with modifier] a period devoted to a particular activity: *gym is followed by a training session*. ■ a period of recording music in a studio, especially by a session musician: *he did the sessions for a Great Country Hits album*. ■ informal a period of heavy or sustained drinking.
3 the governing body of a Presbyterian Church.
– PHRASES **in session** assembled for or proceeding with business.
– DERIVATIVES **sessional** adjective.
– ORIGIN late Middle English: from Old French, or from Latin *sessio(n-)*, from *sess-* 'seated' (see **SESSILE**).

session clerk ▶ **noun** a chief lay official in the session of a Presbyterian Church.

session musician ▶ **noun** a freelance musician hired to play on recording sessions.

sesterce /ˈsɛstəːs/ (also **sestertius** /sɛˈstəːʃəs/) ▶ **noun** (pl. **sesterces** /-siːz/ or **sestertii** /-ˈstəːʃiː/) an ancient Roman coin and monetary unit equal to one quarter of a denarius.
– ORIGIN from Latin *sestertius* (*nummus*) '(coin) that is two and a half (asses)'.

sestet /sɛsˈtɛt/ ▶ **noun** **1** Prosody the last six lines of a sonnet.
2 Music, rare a sextet.
– ORIGIN early 19th cent.: from Italian *sestetto*, from *sesto*, from Latin *sextus* 'a sixth'.

sestina /sɛˈstiːnə/ ▶ **noun** Prosody a poem with six stanzas of six lines and a final triplet, all stanzas having the same six words at the line ends in six different sequences.
– ORIGIN mid 19th cent.: from Italian, from *sesto* (see **SESTET**).

Set /sɛt/ variant spelling of **SETH**[2].

set[1] ▶ **verb** (**sets, setting**; past and past participle **set**)
1 [with obj. and usu. with adverbial] put, lay, or stand (something) in a specified place or position: *Delaney set the mug of tea down | Catherine set a chair by the bed*. ■ (**be set**) be situated or fixed in a specified place or position: *the village was set among olive groves on a hill*. ■ represent (a story, play, film, or scene) as happening at a specified time or in a specified place: *a private-eye novel set in Berlin*. ■ mount a precious stone in (something, typically a piece of jewellery): *a bracelet set with emeralds*. ■ mount (a precious stone) in something. ■ Printing arrange (type) as required. ■ Printing arrange the type for (a piece of text): *article headings will be set in Times fourteen point*. ■ prepare (a table) for a meal by placing cutlery, crockery, etc. on it in their proper places. ■ (**set something to**) provide (music) so that a written work can be produced in a musical form: *a form of poetry which can be set to music*. ■ Bell-ringing move (a bell) so that it rests in an inverted position ready for ringing. ■ cause (a hen) to sit on eggs. ■ put (a seed or plant) in the ground to grow. ■ Sailing put (a sail) up in position to catch the wind.
2 [with obj. and usu. with adverbial] put or bring into a specified state: *the Home Secretary set in motion a review of the law* | [with obj. and complement] *the hostages were set free*. ■ [with obj. and present participle] cause (someone or something) to start doing something: *the incident set me thinking*. ■ [with obj. and infinitive] instruct (someone) to do something: *he'll set a man to watch you*. ■ give someone (a task or test) to do: *schools will begin to set mock tests* | [with two objs] *the problem we have been set*. ■ establish as (an example) for others to follow, copy, or try to achieve: *the scheme sets a precedent for other companies*. ■ establish (a record): *his time in the 25 m freestyle set a national record*. ■ decide on and announce: *they set a date for a full hearing at the end of February*. ■ fix (a price, value, or limit) on something: *the unions had set a limit on the size of the temporary workforce*.
3 [with obj.] adjust (a clock or watch), typically to show the right time. ■ adjust (an alarm clock) to sound at the required time. ■ adjust (a device) so that it performs a particular operation: *you have to be careful not to set the volume too high*. ■ Electronics cause (a binary device) to enter the state representing the numeral 1.
4 [no obj.] harden into a solid or semi-solid state: *cook for a further thirty-five minutes until the filling has set*. ■ [with obj.] arrange (the hair) while damp so that it dries in the required style: *she had set her hair on small rollers*. ■ [with obj.] put parts of (a broken or dislocated bone or limb) into the correct position for healing. ■ (of a bone) be restored to its normal condition by knitting together again after being broken: *children's bones soon set*. ■ (with reference to a person's face) assume or cause to assume a fixed or rigid expression: [no obj.] *her features never set into a civil parade of attention* | [with obj.] *Travis's face was set as he looked up*. ■ (of a hunting dog) adopt a rigid attitude indicating the presence of game.
5 [no obj.] (of the sun, moon, or another celestial body) appear to move towards and below the earth's horizon as the earth rotates: *the sun was setting and a warm red glow filled the sky*.
6 [no obj., with adverbial of direction] (of a tide or current) take or have a specified direction or course: *a fair tide can be carried well past Land's End before the stream sets to the north*.
7 [with obj.] chiefly N. Amer. start (a fire).
8 [with obj.] (of blossom or a tree) form into or produce (fruit). ■ [no obj.] (of fruit) develop from blossom. ■ (of a plant) produce (seed): *the herb has flowered and started to set seed*.
9 [no obj.] dialect sit: *the rest of them people just set there goggle-eyed for a minute*.
– PHRASES **set one's heart** (or **hopes**) **on** have a strong desire for or to do: *she had her heart set on going to university*. **set sail** hoist the sails of a boat. ■ begin a voyage: *tomorrow we set sail for France*. **set one's teeth** clench one's teeth together. ■ become resolute: *they have set their teeth against a change which would undermine their prospects of forming a government*. **set the wheels in motion** do something to begin a process or put a plan into action.
– PHRASAL VERBS **set about 1** start doing something with vigour or determination: *it would be far better to admit the problem openly and set about tackling it*. **2** Brit. informal attack (someone). **set someone against** cause someone to be in opposition or conflict with: *he hadn't meant any harm but his few words had set her against him*. **set something against** offset something against: *wives' allowances can henceforth be set against investment income*. **set someone apart** give someone an air of unusual superiority: *his ability and self-effacing modesty have set him apart*. **set something apart** separate something and keep it for a special purpose: *there were books and rooms set apart as libraries*. **set something aside 1** save or keep something, typically money or time, for a particular purpose: *the bank expected to set aside about $700 million for restructuring*. ■ remove land from agricultural production. **2** annul a legal decision or process. **set someone/thing back 1** delay or impede the progress of someone or something: *this incident undoubtedly set back research*. **2** informal (of a purchase) cost someone a particular amount of money: *that must have set you back a bit*. **set something by** archaic or US save something for future use. **set someone down** Brit. stop and allow someone to alight from a vehicle. **set something down** record something in writing. ■ establish something as a rule or principle to be followed: *the Association set down codes of practice for all members to comply with*. **set forth** (or **forward**) archaic begin a journey. **set something forth** state or describe something in writing or speech: *the principles and aims set forth in the Social Charter*. **set in** (of something unpleasant or unwelcome) begin and seem likely to continue: *tables should be treated with preservative before the bad weather sets in*. **set something in** insert something, especially a sleeve, into a garment. **set off** begin a journey: *they set off together in the small car*. **set someone off** cause someone to start doing something, especially laughing or talking: *anything will set him off laughing*. **set something off 1** detonate a bomb. ■ cause an alarm to go off. ■ cause a series of things to occur: *the fear is that this could set off a chain reaction in other financial markets*. **2** serve as decorative embellishment to: *a pink carnation set off nicely by a red bow tie and cream shirt*. **set something off against** another way of saying **SET SOMETHING AGAINST** above. **set on** (or **upon**) attack (someone) violently: *he and his friends were set upon by a gang*. **set someone/thing on** (or **upon**) cause or urge a person or animal to attack: *I was asked to leave and threatened with having dogs set upon me*. **set out** begin a journey. ■ aim or intend to do something: *she drew up a grandiose statement of what her organization should set out to achieve*. **set something out** arrange or display something in a particular order or position. ■ present information or ideas in a well-ordered way in writing or speech: *this chapter sets out the debate surrounding pluralism*. **set to 1** begin doing something vigorously: *she set to with bleach and scouring pads to render the vases spotless*. **2** (of a dancer) acknowledge another dancer, typically one's partner, using the steps prescribed. **set someone up 1** establish someone in a particular capacity or role: *his father set him up in business*. ■ informal arrange a meeting between one person and another, with the aim of encouraging a romantic relationship between them: *Todd tried to set her up with one of his friends*. **2** restore or enhance the health of someone: *after my operation the doctor recommended a cruise to set me up again*. **3** informal make an innocent person appear guilty of something: *suppose Lorton had set him up for Newley's murder?* **set something up 1** place or erect something in position: *police set up a roadblock on Lower Thames Street*. **2** establish a business, institution, or other organization. ■ make the arrangements necessary for something: *he asked if I would like him to set up a meeting with the president*. **3** begin making a loud sound: *a colony of monkeys had set up a racket in the canopy*. **set oneself up as** establish oneself in (a particular occupation): *she set herself up as an acupuncturist in Leamington*. ■ claim to be or act like a specified kind of person:

he set himself up as a crusader for higher press and broadcasting standards.
– ORIGIN Old English *settan*, of Germanic origin; related to Dutch *zetten*, German *setzen*, also to SIT.

set² ▶ **noun 1** a group or collection of things that belong together or resemble one another or are usually found together: *a set of false teeth* | *a new cell with two sets of chromosomes* | *a spare set of clothes.* ■ a collection of implements, containers, or other objects customarily used together: *a fondue set.* ■ a group of people with common interests or occupations or of similar social status: *it was a fashionable haunt of the literary set.* ■ Brit. a group of pupils or students of the same average ability in a particular subject who are taught together: *the policy of allocating pupils to mathematics sets.* ■ (in tennis, darts, and other games) a group of games counting as a unit towards a match: *he took the first set 6–3.* ■ (in jazz or popular music) a sequence of songs or pieces performed together and constituting or forming part of a live show or recording: *a short four-song set.* ■ a group of people making up the required number for a square dance or similar country dance. ■ a fixed number of repetitions of a particular bodybuilding exercise. ■ Mathematics & Logic a collection of distinct entities regarded as a unit, being either individually specified or (more usually) satisfying specified conditions: *the set of all positive integers.*
2 [in sing.] the way in which something is set, disposed, or positioned: *the shape and set of the eyes.* ■ the posture or attitude of a part of the body, typically in relation to the impression this gives of a person's feelings or intentions: *the determined set of her upper torso.* ■ short for MINDSET. ■ Austral./NZ informal a grudge: *most of them hear a thing or two and then **get a set on** you.* ■ the flow of a current or tide in a particular direction: *the rudder kept the dinghy straight against the set of the tide.* ■ Bell-ringing the inverted position of a bell when it is ready for ringing. ■ (also **dead set**) a setter's pointing in the presence of game. ■ the inclination of the teeth of a saw in alternate directions. ■ a warp or bend in wood, metal, or another material caused by continued strain or pressure.
3 a radio or television receiver: *a TV set.*
4 a collection of scenery, stage furniture, and other articles used for a particular scene in a play or film. ■ the place or area in which filming is taking place or a play is performed: *the magazine has interviews **on set** with top directors.*
5 an arrangement of the hair when damp so that it dries in the required style: *a shampoo and set.*
6 a cutting, young plant, or bulb used in the propagation of new plants. ■ a young fruit that has just formed.
7 the last coat of plaster on a wall.
8 Printing the amount of spacing in type controlling the distance between letters. ■ the width of a piece of type.
9 variant spelling of SETT.
10 Snooker another term for PLANT (sense 4 of the noun).
▶ **verb** (**sets, setting, setted**) [with obj.] Brit. group (pupils or students) in sets according to ability.
– PHRASES **make a dead set at** Brit. make a determined attempt to win the affections of. [by association with hunting (see *dead set* above).]
– ORIGIN late Middle English: partly from Old French *sette*, from Latin *secta* 'sect', partly from SET¹.

set³ ▶ **adjective 1** fixed or arranged in advance: *try to feed the puppy at set times each day.* ■ (of a view or habit) unlikely to change: *I've been on my own a long time and I'm rather **set in my ways**.* ■ (of a person's expression) held for an unnaturally long time without changing, typically as a reflection of determination. ■ (of a meal or menu in a restaurant) offered at a fixed price with a limited choice of dishes. ■ (of a book) prescribed for study as part of a particular course or for an examination. ■ having a conventional or predetermined wording; formulaic: *witnesses often delivered their testimony according to a set speech.*
2 [predic.] ready, prepared, or likely to do something: *'All set for tonight?' he asked* | [with infinitive] *water costs look set to increase.* ■ (**set against**) firmly opposed to: *last night you were dead set against the idea.* ■ (**set on**) determined to do (something): *he's set on marrying that girl.*
– ORIGIN late Old English, past participle of SET¹.

seta /ˈsiːtə/ ▶ **noun** (pl. **setae** /-tiː/) chiefly Zoology a stiff hair-like or bristle-like structure, especially in an invertebrate. ■ Botany (in a moss or liverwort) the stalk supporting the capsule.
– DERIVATIVES **setal** adjective.
– ORIGIN late 18th cent.: from Latin, 'bristle'.

set-aside ▶ **noun 1** [mass noun] the policy of taking land out of production to reduce crop surpluses. ■ land taken out of production in this way: *he has fifty acres of set-aside.*
2 US a government contract awarded without competition to a minority-owned business.
3 US a portion of funds reserved for a particular purpose.

setback ▶ **noun 1** a reversal or check in progress: *a serious setback for the peace process.*
2 Architecture a plain, flat offset in a wall.
3 N. Amer. the distance by which a building or part of a building is set back from the property line.

se-tenant /siːˈtɛnənt/ ▶ **adjective** Philately (of stamps, especially stamps of different designs) joined together side by side as when printed: *a se-tenant block of four stamps.*
– ORIGIN early 20th cent.: from French, literally 'holding together'.

Seth¹ /sɛθ/, Vikram (b.1952), Indian novelist and poet. He is best known for the verse novel *The Golden Gate* (1986) and the novel *A Suitable Boy* (1993).

Seth² /sɛθ/ (also **Set**) Egyptian Mythology an evil god who murdered his brother Osiris and wounded Osiris's son Horus. Seth is represented as having the head of an animal with a long pointed snout.

seth /seɪt/ ▶ **noun** Indian a merchant or banker. ■ a rich man. ■ used as a title for a person of high social status: *'Have you come back happy and well, Sethji?'.*
– ORIGIN from Hindi *seṭh*, from Sanskrit *śreṣṭha* 'best, chief'.

SETI ▶ **abbreviation** search for extraterrestrial intelligence, the designation of a series of projects based mainly on attempts to detect artificial radio transmissions from outer space.

set-in ▶ **adjective** (of a sleeve) made separately and inset into a garment.

set list ▶ **noun** a list of the songs that a band or singer intends to perform at a particular concert.

set menu ▶ **noun** a limited menu offered for a set number of courses, at a fixed price.

set-net ▶ **noun** a fishing net fastened in position, into which fish are driven.

set-off ▶ **noun 1** an item or amount that is or may be set off against another in the settlement of accounts. ■ Law a counterbalancing debt pleaded by the defendant in an action to recover money due. ■ dated a counterbalancing or compensating circumstance or condition: *as a set-off against such discussions there had come an improvement in their pecuniary position.*
2 a step or shoulder at which the thickness of part of a building or machine is reduced.
3 [mass noun] Printing the unwanted transference of ink from one printed sheet or page to another before it has set.

seton /ˈsiːt(ə)n/ ▶ **noun** Medicine, historical a skein of cotton or other absorbent material passed below the skin and left with the ends protruding, to promote drainage of fluid or to act as a counterirritant.
– ORIGIN late Middle English: from medieval Latin *seto(n-)*, apparently from Latin *seta* 'bristle'.

setose /ˈsiːtəʊs, -z/ ▶ **adjective** chiefly Zoology bearing bristles or setae; bristly.
– ORIGIN mid 17th cent.: from Latin *seta* 'bristle' + -OSE¹.

set phrase ▶ **noun** an unvarying phrase having a specific meaning, such as 'raining cats and dogs', or being the only context in which a word appears, for example 'amends' in 'make amends'.

set piece ▶ **noun 1** a passage or section of a novel, play, film, or piece of music that is arranged in an elaborate or conventional pattern for maximum effect: *the film lurches from one comic set piece to another.* ■ a formal and carefully structured speech.
2 Brit. a carefully organized and practised move in a team game by which the ball is returned to play, as at a scrum or a free kick.

set play ▶ **noun** Sport a prearranged manoeuvre carried out from a restart by the team who have the advantage.

set point ▶ **noun** (in tennis and other sports) a point which if won by one of the players or sides will also win them a set.

set screw ▶ **noun** a screw for adjusting or clamping parts of a machine.

set scrum ▶ **noun** Rugby another term for SCRUM.

set shot ▶ **noun** Basketball a shot at the basket made without jumping.

set square ▶ **noun** Brit. a right-angled triangular plate for drawing lines, especially at 90°, 45°, 60°, or 30°. ■ a form of T-square with an additional arm turning on a pivot for drawing lines at fixed angles to the head.

Setswana /sɛˈtswɑːnə/ ▶ **noun** [mass noun] the Bantu language of the Tswana people, related to the Sotho languages and spoken by over 4 million people in southern Africa.
– ORIGIN the name in Setswana.

sett (also **set**) ▶ **noun 1** the earth or burrow of a badger.
2 a granite paving block.
3 the particular pattern of stripes in a tartan.
– ORIGIN Middle English: variant of SET², the spelling with *-tt* prevailing in technical senses.

settee ▶ **noun** Brit. a long upholstered seat for more than one person, typically with a back and arms.
– ORIGIN early 18th cent.: perhaps a fanciful variant of SETTLE².

setter ▶ **noun 1** a dog of a large long-haired breed trained to stand rigid when scenting game.
2 [usu. in combination] a person or thing that sets something: *the battle between wage-setters and policy-makers.*

set theory ▶ **noun** [mass noun] the branch of mathematics which deals with the formal properties of sets as units (without regard to the nature of their individual constituents) and the expression of other branches of mathematics in terms of sets.
– DERIVATIVES **set-theoretic** adjective, **set-theoretical** adjective.

setting /ˈsɛtɪŋ/ ▶ **noun 1** the place or type of surroundings where something is positioned or where an event takes place: *a romantic house in a wonderful setting beside the River Wye.* ■ the place and time at which a play, novel, or film is represented as happening: *short stories with a contemporary setting.* ■ N. Amer. the scenery and stage furniture used in a play or film.
2 a piece of metal in which a precious stone or gem is fixed to form a piece of jewellery.
3 a piece of vocal or choral music composed for particular words: *a setting of Yevtushenko's bleak poem.*
4 short for PLACE SETTING.
5 a speed, height, or temperature at which a machine or device can be adjusted to operate: *if you find the room getting too hot, check the thermostat setting.*

setting lotion ▶ **noun** [mass noun] lotion applied to damp hair prior to its being set, enabling it to keep its shape longer.

settle¹ ▶ **verb 1** [with obj.] resolve or reach an agreement about (an argument or problem): *the unions have settled their year-long dispute with Hollywood producers.* ■ end (a legal dispute) by mutual agreement: *if the dispute was not settled it was possible there would be strike action* | [no obj.] *he sued for libel and then settled out of court.* ■ reach a decision about; determine: *exactly what goes into the legislation has not been settled* | [no obj.] *they had not yet **settled on** a date for the wedding.* ■ [no obj.] (**settle for**) accept or agree to (something that one considers to be less than satisfactory): *it was too cold for champagne so they settled for a cup of tea.*
2 [with obj.] pay (a debt or account): *his bill was settled by charge card* | [no obj.] ***I settled up with your brother** for my board and lodging.* ■ (**settle something on**) give money or property to (someone) through a deed of settlement or a will.
3 [no obj.] adopt a more steady or secure style of life, especially in a permanent job and home: *one day I **will settle down** and raise a family.* ■ [with adverbial of place] make one's permanent home somewhere: *in 1863 the family settled in London.* ■ [with obj.] establish a colony in: *European immigrants settled much of Australia.* ■ begin to feel comfortable or established in a new situation: *he had **settled into** his new job.* ■ (**settle down to**) turn one's attention to; apply oneself to: *Catherine settled down to her studies.* ■ become or make calmer or quieter: [no obj.] *after a few months the controversy **settled down*** | [with obj.] *try to **settle your puppy down** before going to bed.* ■ [with obj.] dated silence (a troublesome person) by some means: *he told me to hold my tongue or he would find a way to settle me.*
4 [no obj., with adverbial of place] sit or come to rest in a comfortable position: *he settled into an armchair.* ■ [with obj. and adverbial of place] make (someone) comfortable in a particular place or position: *she allowed*

S

him to settle her in the taxi. ■ [with obj.] move or adjust (something) so that it rests securely: *she settled her bag on her shoulder.* ■ (especially of snow) fall on to a surface and remain there: *traffic came to a standstill after the snow began to settle | dust from the mill had settled on the roof.* ■ [no obj.] (of suspended particles) sink slowly in a liquid to form sediment. ■ (of a liquid) become clear or still through this process: *he watched his pint settling.* ■ [no obj.] (of an object or objects) gradually sink down under its or their own weight: *they listened to the soft ticking and creaking as the house settled.* ■ [no obj.] (of a ship) begin to sink.
– PHRASES **settle one's affairs** (or **estate**) make any necessary arrangements, such as writing a will, before one's death. **settle someone's hash** see HASH[1].
– DERIVATIVES **settleable** adjective.
– ORIGIN Old English *setlan* 'to seat, place', from SETTLE[2].

settle[2] ▸ noun a wooden bench with a high back and arms, typically incorporating a box under the seat.
– ORIGIN Old English *setl* 'a place to sit', of Germanic origin; related to German *Sessel* and Latin *sella* 'seat', also to SIT.

settlement ▸ noun **1** an official agreement intended to resolve a dispute or conflict: *unions succeeded in reaching a pay settlement* | [mass noun] *the settlement of the boundary disputes.* ■ a formal arrangement made between the parties to a lawsuit in order to resolve it, especially out of court: *the award was made as an out-of-court settlement by the driver's insurance firm.*
2 a place, typically one which has hitherto been uninhabited, where people establish a community: *the little settlement of Buttermere.* ■ [mass noun] the process of settling in such a place: *a continent where settlement is at the mercy of geography.* ■ [mass noun] the action of allowing or helping people to do this.
3 Law an arrangement whereby property passes to a succession of people as dictated by the settlor. ■ the amount or property given by such an arrangement. ■ short for MARRIAGE SETTLEMENT.
4 [mass noun] the action or process of settling an account.
5 [mass noun] subsidence of the ground or a structure built on it: *a boundary wall, which has cracked due to settlement, is to be replaced.*

Settlement, Act of a statute of 1701 that vested the British Crown in Sophia of Hanover (granddaughter of James I of England and VI of Scotland) and her Protestant heirs, so excluding Roman Catholics, including the Stuarts, from the succession. Sophia's son became George I.

settlement house ▸ noun an institution in an inner-city area, typically sponsored by a church or college, providing educational, recreational, and other social services to the community.

settler ▸ noun a person who settles in an area, typically one with no or few previous inhabitants.

settling time ▸ noun technical the time taken for a measuring or control instrument to get within a certain distance of a new equilibrium value without subsequently deviating from it by that amount.

S

settlor /ˈsɛtlə/ ▸ noun Law a person who makes a settlement, especially of property in establishing a trust.

set-to ▸ noun (pl. **set-tos**) informal a fight or argument: *we had a little set-to in the pub.*

set-top box ▸ noun a box-shaped device that converts a digital television signal to analogue for viewing on a conventional set, or that enables cable or satellite television to be viewed.

Setúbal /səˈtuːb(ə)l/ a port and industrial town on the coast of Portugal, south of Lisbon; pop. 123,564 (2007).

set-up ▸ noun [usu. in sing.] informal **1** the way in which something, especially an organization or equipment, is organized, planned, or arranged: *would you feel comfortable in a team-teaching set-up?* ■ an organization or arrangement: *a set-up called Film Education.* ■ a set of equipment needed for a particular activity or purpose: *I have a recording set-up in my house.*
2 a scheme or trick intended to incriminate or deceive someone: *Listen. He didn't die. It was a set-up.* ■ chiefly N. Amer. a contest with a prearranged outcome.
3 (in a ball game) a pass or play intended to provide an opportunity for another player to score.

Seurat /ˈsəːrʌ/, French /sœʀa/, Georges Pierre (1859–91), French painter. The founder of neo-Impressionism, he is chiefly associated with pointillism, which he developed during the 1880s. Among his major paintings using this technique is *Sunday Afternoon on the Island of La Grande Jatte* (1884–6).

sev /seɪv/ ▸ noun [mass noun] an Indian snack consisting of long, thin strands of gram flour, deep-fried and spiced.
– ORIGIN Hindi.

Sevastopol Russian /sʲivaˈstəpəlʲ/ Ukrainian and Russian name for SEBASTOPOL.

seven ▸ cardinal number equivalent to the sum of three and four; one more than six, or three less than ten; 7: *two sevens are fourteen | the remaining seven were sentenced to terms of imprisonment.* (Roman numeral: **vii** or **VII**) ■ a group or unit of seven people or things: *animals were offered for sacrifice in sevens.* ■ seven years old: *my mother died when I was seven.* ■ seven o'clock: *the meeting doesn't finish until seven.* ■ a size of garment or other merchandise denoted by seven. ■ a playing card with seven pips. ■ (**sevens**) seven-a-side rugby.
– PHRASES **the seven deadly sins** (in Christian tradition) the sins of pride, covetousness, lust, anger, gluttony, envy, and sloth. **the seven seas** all the oceans of the world (conventionally listed as the Arctic, Antarctic, North Pacific, South Pacific, North Atlantic, South Atlantic, and Indian Oceans). **the seven-year itch** a supposed tendency to infidelity after seven years of marriage.
– ORIGIN Old English *seofon*, of Germanic origin; related to Dutch *zeven* and German *sieben*, from an Indo-European root shared by Latin *septem* and Greek *hepta*.

sevenfold ▸ adjective seven times as great or as numerous: *profits have recorded a sevenfold increase to £218 million.* ■ having seven parts or elements: *the sevenfold purpose of religious education.*
▸ adverb by seven times; to seven times the number or amount: *his rent had gone up sevenfold.*

Seven Hills of Rome the seven hills on which the ancient city of Rome was built: Aventine, Caelian, Capitoline, Esquiline, Quirinal, Viminal, and Palatine.

Seven Sages seven wise Greeks of the 6th century BC, to each of whom a moral saying is attributed. The seven, named in a traditional list found in Plato, are Bias, Chilon, Cleobulus, Periander, Pittacus, Solon, and Thales.

Seven Sisters Astronomy the star cluster of the Pleiades.

Seven Sleepers (in early Christian legend) seven noble Christian youths of Ephesus who fell asleep in a cave while fleeing from the Decian persecution and awoke 187 years later.

seventeen ▸ cardinal number one more than sixteen, or seven more than ten; 17: *seventeen years later | a list of names, seventeen in all.* (Roman numeral **xvii** or **XVII**) ■ seventeen years old: *he joined the Marines at seventeen.* ■ a size of garment or other merchandise denoted by seventeen. ■ a set or team of seventeen individuals.
– DERIVATIVES **seventeenth** ordinal number.
– ORIGIN Old English *seofontiene*, from the Germanic base of SEVEN.

seventh ▸ ordinal number **1** constituting number seven in a sequence; 7th: *his seventh goal of the season | the seventh of June | he was the seventh of eight children.* ■ the seventh finisher or position in a race or competition: *Jo Richardson came seventh.* ■ seventhly (used to introduce a seventh point or reason). ■ Music an interval spanning seven consecutive notes in a diatonic scale. ■ Music the note which is higher by this interval than the tonic of a diatonic scale or root of a chord. ■ Music a chord in which the seventh note of the scale forms an important component.
2 each of seven equal parts into which something is or may be divided.
– PHRASES **in seventh heaven** see HEAVEN.
– DERIVATIVES **seventhly** adverb.

Seventh-Day Adventist ▸ noun a member of a strict Protestant sect which preaches the imminent return of Christ to Earth (originally expecting the Second Coming in 1844) and observes Saturday as the sabbath.

seventy ▸ cardinal number (pl. **seventies**) the number equivalent to the product of seven and ten; ten less than eighty; 70: *about seventy people attended | seventy were arrested.* (Roman numeral: **lxx** or **LXX**) ■ (**seventies**) the numbers from seventy to seventy-nine, especially the years of a century or of a person's life: *Dad was now in his seventies.* ■ seventy years old: *she was nearly seventy.* ■ seventy miles an hour: *doing about seventy.* ■ a size of garment or other merchandise denoted by seventy.
– DERIVATIVES **seventieth** ordinal number, **seventyfold** adjective & adverb.
– ORIGIN Old English *hundseofontig*, from *hund-* (of uncertain origin) + *seofon* 'seven' + *-tig* (see -TY[2]).

seventy-eight (usu. **78**) ▸ noun an old gramophone record designed to be played at 78 rpm.

Seven Wonders of the World the seven most spectacular man-made structures of the ancient world.

> Traditionally they comprise (1) the pyramids of Egypt, especially those at Giza; (2) the Hanging Gardens of Babylon; (3) the Mausoleum of Halicarnassus; (4) the temple of Artemis at Ephesus in Asia Minor; (5) the Colossus of Rhodes; (6) the huge ivory and gold statue of Zeus at Olympia in the Peloponnese, made by Phidias c.430 BC; (7) the Pharos of Alexandria (or in some lists, the walls of Babylon).

Seven Years War a war (1756–63) which ranged Britain, Prussia, and Hanover against Austria, France, Russia, Saxony, Sweden, and Spain.

> Its main issues were the struggle between Britain and France for supremacy overseas, and that between Prussia and Austria for the domination of Germany. The British made substantial gains over France abroad, capturing French Canada and undermining French influence in India. The war was ended by the Treaties of Paris and Hubertusburg in 1763, leaving Britain the supreme European naval and colonial power and Prussia in an appreciably stronger position than before in central Europe.

sever ▸ verb [with obj.] divide by cutting or slicing, especially suddenly and forcibly: *the head was severed from the body* | (as adj. **severed**) *severed limbs.* ■ put an end to (a connection or relationship); break off: *the notice itself may be sufficient to sever the joint tenancy.*
– DERIVATIVES **severable** adjective.
– ORIGIN Middle English: from Anglo-Norman French *severer*, from Latin *separare* 'disjoin, divide'.

several ▸ determiner & pronoun more than two but not many: [as determiner] *the author of several books* | [as pronoun] *the programme is one of several in the UK | several of his friends attended.*
▸ adjective separate or respective: *the two levels of government sort out their several responsibilities.* ■ Law applied or regarded separately. Often contrasted with JOINT.
– ORIGIN late Middle English: from Anglo-Norman French, from medieval Latin *separalis*, from Latin *separ* 'separate, different'.

severally ▸ adverb separately or individually; each in turn: *the partners are jointly and severally liable.*

severalty ▸ noun [mass noun] archaic the condition of being separate.
– PHRASES **in severalty** Law (of land) in one's own right as private property, rather than in interest with another.
– ORIGIN late Middle English: from Anglo-Norman French *severalte*, from *several* (see SEVERAL).

severance ▸ noun [mass noun] **1** the action of ending a connection or relationship: *the severance and disestablishment of the Irish Church* | [count noun] *a complete severance of links with the Republic.* ■ the state of being separated or cut off. ■ dismissal or discharge from employment: [as modifier] *employees were offered severance terms.* ■ short for SEVERANCE PAY.
2 division by cutting or slicing.
– ORIGIN late Middle English: from Anglo-Norman French, based on Latin *separare* (see SEVER).

severance pay ▸ noun an amount paid to an employee on the early termination of a contract.

severe ▸ adjective (**severer**, **severest**) **1** (of something bad or undesirable) very great; intense: *a severe shortage of technicians | a severe attack of asthma | the damage is not too severe.* ■ demanding great ability, skill, or resilience: *a severe test of stamina.*
2 (of punishment of a person) strict or harsh: *the charges would have warranted a severe sentence.* ■ (of a person) formal and unsmiling.
3 very plain in style or appearance: *she wore another severe suit, grey this time.*
– ORIGIN mid 16th cent. (in sense 2): from French *sévère* or Latin *severus*.

severely ▸ adverb **1** to an undesirably great or intense degree: *our business has been severely affected by the slowdown* | [as submodifier] *severely injured patients.*

2 strictly or harshly: *the culprits will be severely punished.* ■ in a formal and unsmiling way: *'I hope you're not trying to steal my girlfriend,' I said severely.*
3 in a very plain style: *her hair was severely pulled back into a bun.*

severity ▶ noun [mass noun] the fact or condition of being severe: *sentences should reflect the severity of the crime | hay fever symptoms vary in severity.*

Severn a river of SW Britain. Rising in central Wales, it flows north-east then south in a broad curve for some 290 km (180 miles) to its mouth on the Bristol Channel. The estuary is spanned by a suspension bridge north of Bristol, opened in 1966, and a second bridge a few miles to the south, opened in 1996.

Severnaya Zemlya /ˌsɛvɛːˌnʌɪə zɪmˈljɑː/ a group of uninhabited islands in the Arctic Ocean off the north coast of Russia, to the north of the Taimyr Peninsula.

Severodvinsk /ˌsɛvərəˈdvɪnsk/ a port in NW Russia, on the White Sea coast west of Archangel; pop. 191,400 (est. 2008).

Severus /sɪˈvɪərəs/, Septimius (146–211), Roman emperor 193–211; full name *Lucius Septimius Severus Pertinax*. He reformed the imperial administration and the army. In 208 he led an army to Britain to suppress a rebellion in the north of the country and later died at York.

severy /ˈsɛvəri/ ▶ noun (pl. **severies**) Architecture a bay or compartment in a vaulted ceiling.
– ORIGIN late Middle English: from Old French *civoire* 'ciborium' (see **CIBORIUM**).

seviche /sɛˈviːtʃeɪ/ ▶ noun variant spelling of **CEVICHE**.

Seville /səˈvɪl/ a city in southern Spain, the capital of Andalusia, situated on the Guadalquivir River; pop. 699,759 (2008). A leading cultural centre of Moorish Spain, it was reclaimed by the Spanish in 1248, and rapidly became prominent as a centre of trade with the colonies of the New World. Spanish name **Sevilla** /seˈβija/.

Seville orange /ˈsɛvɪl/ ▶ noun a bitter orange used for marmalade.

Sevin /ˈsɛvɪn/ ▶ noun trademark for **CARBARYL**.
– ORIGIN 1950s: of unknown origin.

Sèvres /ˈsɛvr(ə)/, French /sɛvʀ/ ▶ noun [mass noun] a type of fine porcelain characterized by elaborate decoration on backgrounds of intense colour, made at Sèvres in the suburbs of Paris.

sevruga /sɛvˈruːgə/ ▶ noun a migratory sturgeon found only in the basins of the Caspian and Black Seas, much fished for its caviar. ● *Acipenser stellatus*, family Acipenseridae.
■ [mass noun] caviar obtained from this fish.
– ORIGIN late 16th cent.: from Russian *sevryuga*.

sew ▶ verb (past participle **sewn** or **sewed**) [with obj.] join, fasten, or repair (something) by making stitches with a needle and thread or a sewing machine: *she sewed the seams and hemmed the border* | [no obj.] *I don't even sew very well.* ■ [with obj. and adverbial] attach (something) to something else by sewing: *she could sew the veil on properly in the morning.* ■ make (a garment) by sewing.
– PHRASAL VERBS **sew something up** informal bring something to a favourable conclusion: *they had the match sewn up by half-time.* ■ achieve exclusive control over something: *the courier market has been more or less sewn up by two companies.*
– ORIGIN Old English *siwan*, of Germanic origin, from an Indo-European root shared by Latin *suere* and Greek *suein*.

sewage /ˈsuːɪdʒ/ ▶ noun [mass noun] waste water and excrement conveyed in sewers.
– ORIGIN mid 19th cent.: from **SEWER**[1], by substitution of the suffix **-AGE**.

sewage farm ▶ noun Brit. a place where sewage is treated, especially for use as an agricultural fertilizer.

sewage works ▶ noun [treated as sing. or pl.] Brit. a place where sewage is treated so that the resultant effluent can be returned safely to a river, the sea, etc.

sewellel /sɪˈwɛləl/ ▶ noun another term for **MOUNTAIN BEAVER**.
– ORIGIN early 19th cent.: from Chinook Jargon *šwalál* 'robe of mountain-beaver skin'.

sewen ▶ noun variant spelling of **SEWIN**.

sewer[1] /ˈsuːə, ˈsjuːə/ ▶ noun an underground conduit for carrying off drainage water and waste matter.
– ORIGIN Middle English (denoting a watercourse to drain marshy land): from Old Northern French *seuwiere* 'channel to drain the overflow from a fish pond', based on Latin *ex-* 'out of' + *aqua* 'water'.

sewer[2] /ˈsəʊə/ ▶ noun a person that sews.

sewerage ▶ noun [mass noun] **1** the provision of drainage by sewers.
2 US term for **SEWAGE**.

sewer rat ▶ noun another term for **BROWN RAT**.

sewin /ˈsjuːɪn/ (also **sewen**) ▶ noun (in Wales) a sea trout.
– ORIGIN mid 16th cent.: of unknown origin.

sewing ▶ noun [mass noun] the action or activity of sewing. ■ work that is to be or is being sewn: *she put down her sewing.*

sewing machine ▶ noun a machine with a mechanically driven needle for sewing or stitching cloth.

sewn past participle of **SEW**.

sex ▶ noun **1** [mass noun] (chiefly with reference to people) sexual activity, including specifically sexual intercourse: *he enjoyed talking about sex | she didn't want to **have sex with** him.* ■ [in sing.] euphemistic a person's genitals.
2 either of the two main categories (male and female) into which humans and most other living things are divided on the basis of their reproductive functions: *adults of both sexes.* ■ [mass noun] the fact of belonging to one of these categories: *direct discrimination involves treating someone less favourably on the grounds of their sex.* ■ the group of all members of either of these categories: *she was well known for her efforts to improve the social condition of her sex.*
▶ verb [with obj.] **1** determine the sex of.
2 (**sex something up**) informal present something in a more interesting or lively way.
3 (**sex someone up**) informal arouse or attempt to arouse someone sexually.
– DERIVATIVES **sexer** noun.
– ORIGIN late Middle English (denoting the two categories, male and female): from Old French *sexe* or Latin *sexus*.

> **USAGE** On the difference in use between the words **sex** (in sense 2 above) and **gender**, see **USAGE** at **GENDER**.

sex- ▶ combining form variant spelling of **SEXI-**, shortened before a vowel (as in *sexennial*), or shortened before a consonant (as in *sexfoil*).

sex act ▶ noun a sexual act. ■ (**the sex act**) the act of sexual intercourse.

sexagenarian /ˌsɛksədʒɪˈnɛːrɪən/ ▶ noun a person who is between 60 and 69 years old.
– ORIGIN mid 18th cent.: from Latin *sexagenarius* (based on *sexaginta* 'sixty') + **-AN**.

Sexagesima /ˌsɛksəˈdʒɛsɪmə/ (also **Sexagesima Sunday**) ▶ noun the Sunday before Quinquagesima.
– ORIGIN late Middle English: from ecclesiastical Latin, literally 'sixtieth (day)', probably named by analogy with **QUINQUAGESIMA**.

sexagesimal /ˌsɛksəˈdʒɛsɪm(ə)l/ ▶ adjective **1** relating to or reckoning by sixtieths.
2 relating to the number sixty.
▶ noun (also **sexagesimal fraction**) a fraction based on sixtieths (i.e. with a denominator equal to a power of sixty), as in the divisions of the degree and hour.
– DERIVATIVES **sexagesimally** adverb.
– ORIGIN late 17th cent.: from Latin *sexagesimus* 'sixtieth' + **-AL**.

sex appeal ▶ noun [mass noun] the quality of being attractive in a sexual way: *she just oozes sex appeal.*

sex bomb ▶ noun informal a woman who is very sexually attractive.

sexcapade ▶ noun informal, chiefly US a sexual escapade; an illicit affair.
– ORIGIN 1960s: blend of **SEX** and **ESCAPADE**.

sexcentenary /ˌsɛk(s)sɛnˈtiːn(ə)ri, -ˈtɛn-/ ▶ noun (pl. **sexcentenaries**) the six-hundredth anniversary of a significant event.
▶ adjective relating to a six-hundredth anniversary.

sex change ▶ noun a change in a person's physical sexual characteristics, typically by surgery and hormone treatment.

sex chromatin ▶ noun [mass noun] Biology material found only in the nuclei of female cells (especially as the Barr body) and believed to represent the inactivated X chromosome.

sex chromosome ▶ noun a chromosome concerned in determining the sex of an organism, typically one of two kinds.

> In humans and other mammals females have two similar sex chromosomes (XX) while males have dissimilar ones (XY). In birds and some other animals, females have dissimilar sex chromosomes (ZW) and males similar ones (WW). Some other organisms have a sex chromosome present only in one sex.

sex crime ▶ noun informal a crime involving sexual assault or having a sexual motive.

sex discrimination (also **sexual discrimination**) ▶ noun [mass noun] discrimination in employment and opportunity against a person (typically a woman) on grounds of sex.

sex drive ▶ noun a person's urge to seek satisfaction of their sexual needs.

sexed ▶ adjective **1** [with submodifier] having specified sexual appetites: *highly sexed heterosexual males.*
2 having sexual characteristics.

sexennial /sɛkˈsɛnɪəl/ ▶ adjective recurring every six years. ■ lasting for or relating to a period of six years.
– ORIGIN mid 17th cent.: from **SEXENNIUM** + **-AL**.

sexennium /sɛkˈsɛnɪəm/ ▶ noun (pl. **sexennia** /-nɪə/ or **sexenniums**) rare a specified period of six years.
– ORIGIN Latin, from *sex* 'six' + *annus* 'year'.

sexfoil ▶ noun (especially in architecture) an ornamental design having six leaves or petals radiating from a common centre.
– ORIGIN late 17th cent.: from **SEXI-** 'six', on the pattern of words such as *trefoil*.

sex hormone ▶ noun a hormone, such as oestrogen or testosterone, affecting sexual development or reproduction.

sexi- (also **sex-** before a vowel) ▶ combining form six; having six: *sexivalent*.
– ORIGIN from Latin *sex* 'six'.

sex industry ▶ noun (**the sex industry**) prostitution and pornography viewed as an industry.

sexism ▶ noun [mass noun] prejudice, stereotyping, or discrimination, typically against women, on the basis of sex.
– DERIVATIVES **sexist** adjective & noun.

sexivalent /ˌsɛksɪˈveɪl(ə)nt/ ▶ adjective Chemistry another term for **HEXAVALENT**.

sex kitten ▶ noun informal a young woman who asserts or exploits her sexual attractiveness.

sexless ▶ adjective **1** lacking in sexual desire, activity, or attractiveness: *I've no patience with pious, sexless females.*
2 neither male nor female: *a stylized and sexless falsetto.*
– DERIVATIVES **sexlessly** adverb, **sexlessness** noun.

sex life ▶ noun a person's sexual activity and relationships considered as a whole.

sex-linked ▶ adjective chiefly Biology tending to be associated with one sex or the other. ■ (of a gene or heritable characteristic) carried by a sex chromosome.
– DERIVATIVES **sex linkage** noun.

sex maniac ▶ noun informal a person whose need for sexual gratification is excessive or obsessive.

sex object ▶ noun a person regarded by another only in terms of their sexual attractiveness or availability: *we're now in a period when it is permissible for women to make men into sex objects.*

sex offender ▶ noun a person who commits a crime involving a sexual act.

sexology ▶ noun [mass noun] the study of human sexual life or relationships.
– DERIVATIVES **sexological** adjective, **sexologist** noun.

sexpartite /sɛksˈpɑːtʌɪt/ ▶ adjective divided or involving division into six parts: *the sexpartite vault is of 12th-century construction.*
– ORIGIN mid 18th cent.: from **SEXI-** 'six' + **PARTITE**, on the pattern of words such as *bipartite*.

sexpert ▶ noun informal an expert in sexual matters.

sexploitation ▶ noun informal the commercial exploitation of sex, sexual attractiveness, or sexually explicit material.
– ORIGIN 1940s: blend of **SEX** and *exploitation* (see **EXPLOIT**).

sexpot ▶ noun informal a sexy person.

sex role ▶ noun the role or behaviour learned by a person as appropriate to their sex, determined by the prevailing cultural norms.

S

sex-starved ▶ adjective lacking and strongly desiring sexual gratification.

sex symbol ▶ noun a person widely noted for their sexual attractiveness.

sext ▶ noun a service forming part of the Divine Office of the Western Christian Church, traditionally said (or chanted) at the sixth hour of the day (i.e. noon).
– ORIGIN late Middle English: from Latin *sexta (hora)* 'sixth (hour)', from *sextus* 'sixth'.

Sextans /ˈsɛkst(ə)nz/ Astronomy a faint constellation (the Sextant), lying on the celestial equator between Leo and Hydra.
– ORIGIN Latin.

sextant /ˈsɛkst(ə)nt/ ▶ noun an instrument with a graduated arc of 60° and a sighting mechanism, used for measuring the angular distances between objects and especially for taking altitudes in navigation and surveying.
– ORIGIN late 16th cent. (denoting the sixth part of a circle): from Latin *sextans, sextant-* 'sixth part', from *sextus* 'sixth'.

sextet (also **sextette**) ▶ noun a group of six people playing music or singing together. ▪ a composition for a sextet. ▪ a set of six people or things: *a sextet of new releases*.
– ORIGIN mid 19th cent.: alteration of **SESTET**, suggested by Latin *sex* 'six'.

sex therapy ▶ noun [mass noun] counselling or other therapy which addresses a person's psychological or physical sexual problems.
– DERIVATIVES **sex therapist** noun.

sextile /ˈsɛkstʌɪl, -tɪl/ ▶ noun [mass noun] Astrology an aspect of 60° (one sixth of a circle): *the Jupiter–Saturn cycle is now in sextile to its most difficult period*.
– ORIGIN late Middle English: from Latin *sextilis*, from *sextus* 'sixth'.

sextillion /sɛksˈtɪljən/ ▶ cardinal number (pl. **sextillions** or (with numeral) **same**) a thousand raised to the seventh power (10^{21}). ▪ dated, chiefly Brit. a million raised to the sixth power (10^{36}).
– DERIVATIVES **sextillionth** ordinal number.
– ORIGIN late 17th cent.: from French, from *million*, by substitution of the prefix *sexti-* 'six' (from Latin *sextus* 'sixth') for the initial letters.

sextodecimo /ˌsɛkstə(ʊ)ˈdɛsɪməʊ/ (abbrev.: **16mo**) ▶ noun (pl. **sextodecimos**) a size of book page that results from folding each printed sheet into sixteen leaves (thirty-two pages). ▪ a book of sextodecimo size.
– ORIGIN late 17th cent.: from Latin *sexto decimo*, ablative of *sextus decimus* 'sixteenth'.

sexton ▶ noun a person who looks after a church and churchyard, typically acting as bell-ringer and gravedigger.
– ORIGIN Middle English: from Anglo-Norman French *segrestein*, from medieval Latin *sacristanus* (see **SACRISTAN**).

sexton beetle ▶ noun another term for **BURYING BEETLE**.

sex tourism ▶ noun [mass noun] the organization of holidays with the purpose of taking advantage of the lack of restrictions imposed on sexual activity and prostitution by some foreign countries.
– DERIVATIVES **sex tourist** noun.

sextuple /ˈsɛkstjʊp(ə)l, sɛksˈtjuːp(ə)l/ ▶ adjective [attrib.] consisting of six parts or things. ▪ six times as much or as many.
▶ noun a sixfold number or amount.
▶ verb [with obj.] multiply by six; increase sixfold.
– DERIVATIVES **sextuply** adverb.
– ORIGIN early 17th cent.: from medieval Latin *sextuplus*, formed irregularly from Latin *sex* 'six', on the pattern of late Latin *quintuplus* 'quintuple'.

sextuplet /ˈsɛkstjʊplɪt, sɛksˈtjuːplɪt/ ▶ noun **1** each of six children born at one birth.
2 Music a group of six notes to be performed in the time of four.
– ORIGIN mid 19th cent.: from **SEXTUPLE**, on the pattern of words such as *triplet*.

sex typing ▶ noun [mass noun] **1** Psychology & Sociology the stereotypical categorization of people, or their appearance or behaviour, according to conventional perceptions of what is typical of each sex.
2 Biology the process of determining the sex of a person or other organism, especially in difficult cases where special tests are necessary.
– DERIVATIVES **sex-typed** adjective.

sexual /ˈsɛkʃʊəl, -sjʊəl/ ▶ adjective **1** relating to the instincts, physiological processes, and activities connected with physical attraction or intimate physical contact between individuals: *she had felt the thrill of a sexual attraction*.
2 relating to the two sexes or to gender: *sensitivity about sexual stereotypes*. ▪ of or characteristic of one sex or the other: *the hormones which control the secondary sexual characteristics*.
3 Biology (of reproduction) involving the fusion of gametes. ▪ being of one sex or the other; capable of sexual reproduction.
– DERIVATIVES **sexually** adverb.
– ORIGIN mid 17th cent.: from late Latin *sexualis*, from Latin *sexus* 'sex'.

sexual dimorphism ▶ noun [mass noun] Zoology distinct difference in size or appearance between the sexes of an animal in addition to the sexual organs themselves.

sexual harassment ▶ noun [mass noun] harassment (typically of a woman) in a workplace, or other professional or social situation, involving the making of unwanted sexual advances or obscene remarks.

sexual intercourse ▶ noun [mass noun] sexual contact between individuals involving penetration, especially the insertion of a man's erect penis into a woman's vagina, typically culminating in orgasm and the ejaculation of semen.

sexual inversion ▶ noun see **INVERSION** (sense 4).

sexuality /sɛkʃʊˈalɪti, ˌsɛksjʊ-/ ▶ noun (pl. **sexualities**) [mass noun] capacity for sexual feelings: *she began to understand the power of her sexuality*. ▪ [count noun] a person's sexual orientation or preference: *people with proscribed sexualities*. ▪ sexual activity.

sexualize (also **sexualise**) ▶ verb [with obj.] make sexual; attribute sex or a sex role to: (as adj. **sexualized**) *sexualized images of women*.
– DERIVATIVES **sexualization** noun.

sexual orientation ▶ noun [mass noun] a person's sexual identity in relation to the gender to which they are attracted; the fact of being heterosexual, homosexual, or bisexual.

sexual politics ▶ plural noun [usu. treated as sing.] the principles determining the relationship of the sexes; relations between the sexes regarded in terms of power.

sexual relations ▶ plural noun sexual intercourse.

sexual reproduction ▶ noun [mass noun] Biology the production of new living organisms by combining genetic information from two individuals of different types (sexes). In most higher organisms, one sex (male) produces a small motile gamete which travels to fuse with a larger stationary gamete produced by the other (female).

sexual revolution ▶ noun the liberalization of established social and moral attitudes to sex, particularly that occurring in western countries during the 1960s, as the women's movement and developments in contraception instigated changes in attitudes towards sex and women's sexuality, and sexual equality became an aim of society.

sexual selection ▶ noun [mass noun] Biology natural selection arising through preference by one sex for certain characteristics in individuals of the other sex.

sex worker ▶ noun a prostitute.

sexy ▶ adjective (**sexier**, **sexiest**) **1** sexually attractive or exciting: *sexy French underwear*. ▪ sexually aroused: *neither of them was feeling sexy*.
2 informal very exciting or appealing: *business magazines might not seem like the sexiest career choice*.
– DERIVATIVES **sexily** adverb, **sexiness** noun.

Seychelles /seɪˈʃɛlz, -ˈʃɛl/ (also **the Seychelles**) a country consisting of a group of about ninety islands in the Indian Ocean, about 1,000 km (600 miles) NE of Madagascar; pop. 87,500 (est. 2009); languages, French Creole (official), English, French; capital, Victoria.

> The islands were uninhabited until the mid 18th century, when the French annexed them. The Seychelles were captured by Britain during the Napoleonic Wars and administered from Mauritius before becoming a separate colony in 1903 and an independent republic within the Commonwealth in 1976.

– DERIVATIVES **Seychellois** /ˌseɪʃɛlˈwʌ/ adjective & noun (pl. **same**).

Seyfert galaxy /ˈseɪfəːt/ ▶ noun Astronomy a galaxy of a type characterized by a bright compact core that shows strong infrared emission.
– ORIGIN named after Carl K. *Seyfert* (1911–60), American astronomer.

Seymour[1] /ˈsiːmɔː/, Jane (*c.*1509–37), third wife of Henry VIII and mother of Edward VI. She married Henry in 1536 and finally provided the king with the male heir he wanted, although she died twelve days afterwards.

Seymour[2] /ˈsiːmɔː/, Lynn (b.1939), Canadian ballet dancer; born *Lynn Springbett*. From 1957 she danced for the Royal Ballet. Her most acclaimed roles came in Frederick Ashton's *Five Brahms Waltzes in the Manner of Isadora Duncan* and *A Month in the Country* (both 1976).

sez ▶ verb non-standard spelling of 'says', used in representing uneducated speech: *'I've got a paper 'ere that sez they can't come in.'*.

Sezession /ˌzeɪzɛtsɪˈəʊn/, German /ˌzetsɛˈsi̯oːn/ (also **Secession** /sɪˈsɛʃ(ə)n/) ▶ noun (**the Sezession**) a radical movement involving groups of avant-garde German and Austrian artists who, from 1892, organized exhibitions independently of the traditional academies. The **Vienna Secession** founded by Gustav Klimt in 1897 helped to launch the Jugendstil.
– ORIGIN German, literally 'secession'.

SF ▶ abbreviation ▪ Finland (international vehicle registration). [from Finnish *Suomi* + Swedish *Finland*.] ▪ science fiction. ▪ Sinn Fein.

sf ▶ abbreviation Music sforzando.

SFA ▶ abbreviation ▪ Scottish Football Association. ▪ (in the UK) Securities and Futures Authority.

Sfax /sfaks/ (also **Safaqis**) a port on the east coast of Tunisia; pop. 265,100 (est. 2004). It is a centre for the region's phosphate industry.

SFO ▶ abbreviation (in the UK) Serious Fraud Office.

sforzando /sfɔːˈtsandəʊ/ (also **sforzato** /-ˈtsɑːtəʊ/) Music ▶ adverb & adjective (especially as a direction) with sudden emphasis.
▶ noun (pl. **sforzandos** or **sforzandi** /-di/) a sudden or marked emphasis.
– ORIGIN Italian, literally 'using force'.

sfumato /sfʊˈmɑːtəʊ/ ▶ noun [mass noun] Art the technique of allowing tones and colours to shade gradually into one another, producing softened outlines or hazy forms.
– ORIGIN mid 19th cent.: Italian, literally 'shaded off', past participle of *sfumare*.

SFX ▶ abbreviation special effects.
– ORIGIN *FX* representing a pronunciation of *effects*.

sfz ▶ abbreviation Music sforzando.

SG ▶ abbreviation ▪ Law Solicitor General. ▪ Physics specific gravity.

Sg ▶ symbol the chemical element seaborgium.

sgd ▶ abbreviation signed.

SGML ▶ abbreviation Computing Standard Generalized Markup Language, an international standard for defining methods of encoding electronic texts to describe layout, structure, syntax, etc., which can then be used for analysis or to display the text in any desired format.

SGP ▶ abbreviation Singapore (international vehicle registration).

sgraffito /sgraˈfiːtəʊ/ ▶ noun (pl. **sgraffiti** /-ti/) [mass noun] a form of decoration made by scratching through a surface to reveal a lower layer of a contrasting colour, typically done in plaster or stucco on walls, or in slip on ceramics before firing.
– ORIGIN mid 18th cent.: Italian, literally 'scratched away', past participle of *sgraffiare*.

's-Gravenhage /ˌsxraːvənˈhaːxə/ Dutch name for The Hague (see **HAGUE**).

Sgt ▶ abbreviation Sergeant.

sh. ▶ abbreviation Brit. shilling(s).

shaadi /ˈʃadi, ˈʃɑːdi/ ▶ noun (pl. **shaadis** /ˈʃadiz, ˈʃɑːdiz/) (in South Asia) a wedding.
– ORIGIN Urdu and Persian *šādī*.

Shaanxi /ʃɑːnˈʃiː/ (also **Shensi**) a mountainous province of central China; capital, Xian. It is the site of the earliest settlements of the ancient Chinese civilizations. Compare with **SHANXI**.

Shaba /ˈʃɑːbə/ the name by which the copper-mining region of Katanga in the south-east of the Democratic Republic of the Congo (Zaire) was known between 1972 and 1997.

Shabaka /ˈʃabəkə/ (d.698 BC), Egyptian pharaoh, founder of the 25th dynasty, reigned 712–698 BC; known as **Sabacon**. He promoted the cult of Amun and revived the custom of pyramid burial in his own death arrangements.

shabash /ˈʃɑːbɑːʃ/ ▶ **exclamation** Indian well done!
– ORIGIN from Urdu and Persian *šābāš*, from *šād* 'joyful' + *bāš!* (imperative) 'be!'.

Shabbat /ʃaˈbat/ ▶ **noun** (among Sephardic Jews and in Israel) the Sabbath. Compare with **SHABBOS**.
– ORIGIN from Hebrew *šabbāṯ*.

Shabbos /ˈʃabəs/ (also **Shabbes**) ▶ **noun** (among Ashkenazic Jews) the Sabbath. Compare with **SHABBAT**.
– ORIGIN Yiddish, from Hebrew *šabbāṯ*.

shabby ▶ **adjective** (**shabbier**, **shabbiest**) **1** in poor condition through long use or lack of care: *a conscript in a shabby uniform saluted the car.* ■ dressed in old or worn clothes: *a shabby fellow in slippers and an undershirt.*
2 (of behaviour) mean and unfair: *Snooping, was he? That's a shabby trick.*
– DERIVATIVES **shabbily** adverb, **shabbiness** noun.
– ORIGIN mid 17th cent.: from dialect *shab* 'scab' (from a Germanic base meaning 'itch') + **-Y**[1].

shabrack /ˈʃabrak/ ▶ **noun** historical a cavalry saddle-cloth used in European armies.
– ORIGIN early 19th cent.: from German *Schabracke*, of east European origin; compare with Russian *shabrak*.

shabti /ˈʃabti/ (also **ushabti**) ▶ **noun** (pl. **shabtis**) each of a set of wooden, stone, or faience figurines, in the form of mummies, placed in an ancient Egyptian tomb to do any work that the dead person might be called upon to do in the afterlife.
– ORIGIN from Egyptian *šbty*, literally 'answerer'.

shabu-shabu /ˌʃabuːˈʃabuː/ ▶ **noun** [mass noun] a Japanese dish of pieces of thinly sliced beef or pork cooked quickly with vegetables in boiling water and then dipped in sauce.
– ORIGIN Japanese.

shack ▶ **noun** a roughly built hut or cabin.
▶ **verb** [no obj.] (**shack up**) informal move in or live with someone as a lover.
– ORIGIN late 19th cent.: perhaps from Mexican *jacal*, Nahuatl *xacatli* 'wooden hut'. The early sense of the verb was 'live in a shack' (originally a US usage).

shackland ▶ **noun** (in South Africa) a hastily erected urban shack settlement, not officially proclaimed as a residential area.

shackle ▶ **noun 1** (**shackles**) a pair of fetters connected together by a chain, used to fasten a prisoner's wrists or ankles together. ■ a situation or factor that restrains or restricts someone or something: *society is going to* **throw off the shackles of** *racism and colonialism.*
2 a metal link, typically U-shaped, closed by a bolt, used to secure a chain or rope to something. ■ a pivoted link connecting a spring in a vehicle's suspension to the body of the vehicle.
▶ **verb** [with obj.] chain with shackles. ■ restrain; limit: *they seek to shackle the oil and gas companies by imposing new controls.*
– ORIGIN Old English *sc(e)acul* 'fetter', of Germanic origin; related to Dutch *schakel* 'link, coupling'.

shackle lock ▶ **noun** another term for **D-LOCK**.

Shackleton, Sir Ernest Henry (1874–1922), British explorer. During one of his Antarctic expeditions (1914–16), Shackleton's ship *Endurance* was crushed in the ice. Shackleton and his crew eventually reached an island, from where he and five others set out in an open boat on a 1,300-km (800-mile) voyage to South Georgia to get help.

shacky ▶ **adjective** N. Amer. informal (of a building) dilapidated or ramshackle.

shad ▶ **noun** (pl. **same** or **shads**) a herring-like fish that spends much of its life in the sea, typically entering rivers to spawn. It is an important food fish in many regions. ● Genera *Alosa* and *Caspialosa*, family Clupeidae: several species. See **ALLIS SHAD** and **TWAITE SHAD**.
– ORIGIN Old English *sceadd*, of unknown origin.

shadbush (also **shadblow**) ▶ **noun** North American term for **JUNEBERRY**.
– ORIGIN early 19th cent.: so named because it flowers at the same time as shad are found in the rivers.

shadchan /ˈʃadxən, ˈʃɒd-/ (also **shadkhan**) ▶ **noun** (pl. **same** /ˈʃadxɛn/, **shadchanim** /ˈʃadxənɪm/, or **shadchans**) a Jewish professional matchmaker or marriage broker.
– ORIGIN from Yiddish *shadkhn*, based on Hebrew *šiddēḵ* 'negotiate'.

Shaddai /ˈʃadʌɪ/ ▶ **noun** one of the names given to God in the Hebrew Bible.
– ORIGIN Hebrew, translated as 'Almighty' in English versions of the Bible, but of uncertain meaning.

shaddock /ˈʃadək/ ▶ **noun** another term for **POMELO**.
– ORIGIN late 17th cent.: named after Captain *Shaddock*, who introduced it to the West Indies in the 17th cent.

shaddup /ʃʌˈdʌp/ ▶ **exclamation** informal be quiet!: *'Shaddup! If he wants to confess, let him.'.*
– ORIGIN 1950s: representing a pronunciation of *shut up*.

shade ▶ **noun 1** [mass noun] comparative darkness and coolness caused by shelter from direct sunlight: *sitting in the shade | this area will be* **in shade** *for much of the day.* ■ the darker part of a picture. ■ a position of relative inferiority or obscurity: *her elegant pink and black ensemble would* **put** *most outfits* **in the shade**. ■ (usu. **shades**) literary a shadow or area of darkness: *the shades of evening drew on.* ■ historical a portrait in silhouette.
2 a colour, especially with regard to how light or dark it is or as distinguished from one nearly like it: *various shades of blue* | [mass noun] *Maria's eyes darkened* **in shade**. ■ Art a slight degree of difference between colours. ■ a slightly differing variety of something: *politicians of all shades of opinion.* ■ [in sing.] a slight amount of something: *the goal had more than* **a shade of** *good fortune about it.*
3 a lampshade. ■ (often **shades**) N. Amer. a screen or blind on a window. ■ an eyeshade. ■ (**shades**) informal sunglasses.
4 literary a ghost. ■ (**the Shades**) the underworld; Hades.
▶ **verb** [with obj.] **1** screen from direct light: *she shaded her eyes against the sun.* ■ cover, moderate, or exclude the light of: *he shaded the torch with his hand.*
2 darken or colour (an illustration or diagram) with parallel pencil lines or a block of colour: *she* **shaded in** *the outline of a chimney.* ■ [no obj., with adverbial] (of a colour or something coloured) gradually change into another colour: *the sky shaded from turquoise to night blue.*
3 Brit. informal narrowly win or gain an advantage in (a contest): *the Welsh side shaded a tight, tough first half.*
4 make a slight reduction in the amount, rate, or price of: *banks may shade the margin over base rate they charge customers.* ■ [no obj.] decline slightly in price, amount, or rate: [with complement] *their shares shaded 10p to 334p.*
– PHRASES **a shade ——** a little ——: *he was a shade hung-over.* **shades of ——** used to suggest reminiscence of or comparison with someone or something specified: *a long, drawn-out orchestral climax (shades of Wagner or Strauss).*
– DERIVATIVES **shadeless** adjective, **shader** noun.
– ORIGIN Old English *sc(e)adu*, of Germanic origin. Compare with **SHADOW**.

shading ▶ **noun 1** [mass noun] the darkening or colouring of an illustration or diagram with parallel lines or a block of colour.
2 a very slight variation: *the shadings of opinion even among those who are in broad agreement.*
3 [mass noun] a layer of paint or material used to provide shade, especially for plants: *liquid greenhouse shading.*

shadkhan ▶ **noun** variant spelling of **SHADCHAN**.

shadoof /ʃəˈduːf/ ▶ **noun** a pole with a bucket and counterpoise used especially in Egypt for raising water.
– ORIGIN mid 19th cent.: from Egyptian Arabic *šādūf*.

shadow ▶ **noun 1** a dark area or shape produced by a body coming between rays of light and a surface: *trees cast long shadows.* ■ [mass noun] partial or complete darkness, especially as produced in this way: *the north side of the cathedral was deep in shadow* | (**shadows**) *a stranger slowly approached from the shadows.* ■ [mass noun] the shaded part of a picture. ■ a dark patch or area on a surface: *her face was pale and there were shadows under her eyes.* ■ a region of opacity on a radiograph: *shadows on his lungs.*
2 used in reference to proximity, ominous oppressiveness, or sadness and gloom: *the shadow of war fell across Europe | only one shadow lay over Sally's life.* ■ used in reference to something insubstantial or fleeting: *a freedom that was more shadow than substance.* ■ used in reference to a position of relative inferiority or obscurity: *he* **lived in the shadow of** *his father.* ■ [with negative] the slightest trace of something: *she knew* **without a shadow of a doubt** *that he was lying.* ■ a weak or inferior remnant or version of something: *this fine-looking, commanding man had become* **a shadow of** *his former self.* ■ an expression of perplexity or sadness: *a shadow crossed Maria's face.*
3 an inseparable attendant or companion: *her faithful shadow, a Yorkshire terrier called Heathcliffe.* ■ a person secretly following and observing another. ■ a person that accompanies someone in their daily activities at work in order to gain experience at or insight into a job. ■ [usu. as modifier] Brit. the opposition counterpart of a government minister or ministry: *the shadow Chancellor.*
4 short for **EYESHADOW**.
▶ **verb** [with obj.] **1** envelop in shadow; cast a shadow over: *the market is shadowed by St Margaret's church | a hood shadowed her face.*
2 follow and observe (someone) closely and secretly: *he had been up all night shadowing a team of poachers.* ■ Brit. (of an opposition politician) be the counterpart of (a government minister or a ministry). ■ accompany (someone) in their daily activities at work in order to gain experience at or insight into a job.
– PHRASES **be frightened of one's shadow** be very timid or nervous. **wear oneself to a shadow** completely exhaust oneself through overwork.
– DERIVATIVES **shadower** noun, **shadowless** adjective.
– ORIGIN Old English *scead(u)we* (noun), oblique case of *sceadu* (see **SHADE**), *sceadwian* 'screen or shield from attack', of Germanic origin; related to Dutch *schaduw* and German *Schatten* (nouns), from an Indo-European root shared by Greek *skotos* 'darkness'.

shadow-box ▶ **verb** [no obj.] (often as noun **shadow-boxing**) spar with an imaginary opponent as a form of training. ■ make a show of tackling a problem or opponent while avoiding any direct engagement: *a fortnight of political shadow-boxing.*

shadow economy ▶ **noun** illicit economic activity existing alongside a country's official economy, e.g. black market transactions and undeclared work.

shadowgraph ▶ **noun** an image formed by the shadow of an object on a surface. ■ an image formed when light shone through a fluid is refracted differently by regions of different density. ■ a radiograph.

shadowland ▶ **noun** literary a place in shadow. ■ (usu. **shadowlands**) an indeterminate borderland between places or states, typically represented as an abode of ghosts and spirits.

shadow mask ▶ **noun** a perforated metal screen situated directly behind the phosphor screen in certain types of colour television tube, having a pattern of precisely located holes through which the electron beams pass so as to strike the correct dots on the phosphor screen.

shadow price ▶ **noun** Economics the estimated price of a good or service for which no market price exists.

shadow stitch ▶ **noun** [mass noun] a criss-cross embroidery stitch used on sheer materials for filling in spaces, worked on the reverse side so as to show through in a shadowy way with an outline resembling a backstitch.

shadow theatre ▶ **noun** a display in which the shadows of flat jointed puppets are cast on a screen which is viewed by the audience from the other side. Such shows originated in East Asia, and were popular in London and Paris in the 18th and 19th centuries; they survive in traditional form in Java and Bali.

shadow work ▶ **noun** [mass noun] embroidery done in shadow stitch.

shadowy ▶ **adjective** (**shadowier**, **shadowiest**) full of shadows: *a long, shadowy, cobbled passage.* ■ of uncertain identity or nature: *a shadowy figure appeared through the mist | the shadowy world of covert operations.*
– DERIVATIVES **shadowiness** noun.

shady ▶ **adjective** (**shadier**, **shadiest**) **1** situated in or full of shade: *shady woods.* ■ giving shade from sunlight: *they sprawled under a shady carob tree.*
2 informal of doubtful honesty or legality: *he was involved in his grandmother's shady deals.*
– DERIVATIVES **shadily** adverb, **shadiness** noun.

shaft ▶ **noun 1** a long, narrow part or section forming the handle of a tool or club, the body of a spear or arrow, or similar: *the shaft of a golf club | the shaft of a feather.* ■ an arrow or spear. ■ a column, especially the main part between the base and capital. ■ a long cylindrical rotating rod for the transmission of motive power in a machine. ■ each of the pair of poles between which a horse is harnessed to a vehicle.
2 a ray of light or bolt of lightning: *a shaft of sunlight.* ■ a sudden flash of a quality or feeling: *a shaft of inspiration.* ■ a remark intended to be witty,

S

wounding, or provoking: *he directs his shafts against her*.
3 a long, narrow, typically vertical hole that gives access to a mine, accommodates a lift in a building, or provides ventilation.
4 vulgar slang a man's penis. ■ (**the shaft**) N. Amer. informal harsh or unfair treatment: *the executives continue to raise their pay while the workers get the shaft*.
▶ **verb 1** [no obj., with adverbial of direction] (of light) shine in beams: *brilliant sunshine shafted through the skylight*.
2 [with obj.] vulgar slang (of a man) have sexual intercourse with (a woman). ■ informal treat (someone) harshly or unfairly: *I suppose she'll get a lawyer and I'll be shafted*.
– DERIVATIVES **shafted adjective** [in combination] *a long-shafted harpoon*.
– ORIGIN Old English *scæft, sceaft* 'handle, pole', of Germanic origin; related to Dutch *schaft*, German *Schaft*, and perhaps also to SCEPTRE. Early senses of the verb (late Middle English) were 'fit with a handle' and 'send out shafts of light'.

shaft drive ▶ **noun** a mechanism in which power is transmitted from an engine by means of a driveshaft, especially to the wheels of a vehicle or a boat's propeller.
– DERIVATIVES **shaft-driven adjective**.

Shaftesbury /ˈʃɑːftsb(ə)ri/, Anthony Ashley Cooper, 7th Earl of (1801–85), English philanthropist and social reformer. A dominant figure of the 19th-century social reform movement, he inspired much of the legislation designed to improve conditions for the large working class created as a result of the Industrial Revolution. His reforms included the introduction of the ten-hour working day (1847).

shaft grave ▶ **noun** a type of grave found in late Bronze Age Greece and Crete in which the burial chamber is approached by a vertical shaft sometimes lined with stones and roofed over with beams.

shaft horsepower ▶ **noun** [mass noun] the power delivered to a propeller or turbine shaft.

shafting ▶ **noun 1** [mass noun] a system of connected shafts for transmitting motive power in a machine.
2 vulgar slang an act of sexual intercourse.

shag[1] ▶ **noun 1** [usu. as modifier] a carpet or rug with a long, rough pile: *wall-to-wall shag carpet*. ■ [as modifier] (of a pile) long and rough: *a shag pile*. ■ [mass noun] cloth with a velvet nap on one side.
2 a thick, tangled hairstyle or mass of hair.
3 (also **shag tobacco**) [mass noun] a coarse kind of cut tobacco.
– ORIGIN late Old English *sceacga* 'rough matted hair', of Germanic origin; related to Old Norse *skegg* 'beard' and SHAW[2].

shag[2] ▶ **noun** a western European and Mediterranean cormorant with greenish-black plumage and a long curly crest in the breeding season. ● *Phalacrocorax aristotelis*, family Phalacrocoracidae.
■ chiefly NZ any cormorant.
– PHRASES **like a shag on a rock** Austral. informal in an isolated or exposed position.
– ORIGIN mid 16th cent.: perhaps a use of SHAG[1], with reference to the bird's 'shaggy' crest.

shag[3] Brit. vulgar slang ▶ **verb** (**shags, shagging, shagged**) [with obj.] have sexual intercourse with (someone). ■ [no obj.] (of two people) have sexual intercourse.
▶ **noun** an act of sexual intercourse. ■ [with adj.] a sexual partner of a specified ability.
– DERIVATIVES **shaggable adjective**, **shagger noun**.
– ORIGIN late 18th cent.: of unknown origin.

shag[4] ▶ **noun** a dance originating in the US in the 1930s and 1940s, characterized by vigorous hopping from one foot to the other.
– ORIGIN of obscure derivation; perhaps from obsolete *shag* 'waggle'.

shag[5] ▶ **verb** [with obj.] Baseball chase or catch (fly balls) for practice.
– ORIGIN early 20th cent.: of unknown origin.

shagged (also **shagged out**) ▶ **adjective** Brit. informal exhausted: *they were too shagged to do any cleaning*. ■ damaged, ruined, or useless: *I thought my hearing was shagged because I play the drums*.

shaggy ▶ **adjective** (**shaggier, shaggiest**) (of hair or fur) long, thick, and unkempt: *the mountain goat has a long, shaggy coat*. ■ having long, thick, unkempt hair or fur: *a huge shaggy Alsatian*. ■ having a covering resembling rough, thick hair.
– PHRASES **shaggy-dog story** a long, rambling story or joke, typically one that is amusing only because it is absurdly inconsequential or pointless. [from an anecdote of this type, about a shaggy-haired dog (1945).]
– DERIVATIVES **shaggily** adverb, **shagginess** noun.

shaggy ink cap ▶ **noun** a common mushroom which has a tall, narrow white cap covered with shaggy scales, occurring worldwide and edible when young. ● *Coprinus comatus*, family Coprinaceae, class Hymenomycetes.

shagpile (also **shagpile carpet**) ▶ **noun** [mass noun] carpet with a long, rough pile.

shagreen /ʃaˈgriːn/ ▶ **noun** [mass noun] **1** sharkskin used as a decorative material or, due to its natural rough surface of pointed scales, as an abrasive.
2 a kind of untanned leather with a rough granulated surface.
– ORIGIN late 17th cent.: variant of CHAGRIN in the literal sense 'rough skin'.

Shah[1] /ʃɑː/, Karim Al-Hussain, see AGA KHAN.

Shah[2] /ʃɑː/, Reza, see PAHLAVI[1].

shah /ʃɑː/ ▶ **noun** historical a title of the former monarch of Iran.
– ORIGIN mid 16th cent.: from Persian *šāh*, from Old Persian *kšāyaṯiya* 'king'.

shahada /ʃaˈhɑːdɑ/ (also **shahadah**) ▶ **noun** the Muslim profession of faith ('there is no god but Allah, and Muhammad is the messenger of Allah'), one of the Five Pillars of Islam.
– ORIGIN from Arabic *šahāda* 'testimony, evidence'.

Shah Alam /ˈɑːləm/ the capital of the state of Selangor in Malaysia, near the west coast of the Malay Peninsula; pop. 617,100 (est. 2009).

shahid /ʃəˈhiːd/ (also **shaheed**) ▶ **noun** a Muslim martyr.
– ORIGIN via Urdu from Arabic *šahīd* 'witness, martyr'.

shahtoosh /ʃɑːˈtuːʃ/ ▶ **noun** [mass noun] high-quality wool from the neck hair of the Himalayan ibex. ■ fabric woven from this. ■ [count noun] a shawl made from this fabric.
– ORIGIN mid 19th cent.: via Punjabi from Persian *šāh* 'king' + Kashmiri *tośa* 'fine shawl material'.

shaikh ▶ **noun** variant spelling of SHEIKH.

Shaitan /ʃeɪˈtɑːn/ (also **Shaytan**) ▶ **noun** (in Muslim countries) the Devil or an evil spirit. ■ (**shaitan**) an evilly disposed, vicious, or cunning person or animal.
– ORIGIN Arabic *šayṭān* from Hebrew *śāṭān*. Compare with SATAN.

Shaka /ˈʃakə/ (also **Chaka**) (*c.*1787–1828), Zulu chief 1816–28. He reorganized his forces and waged war against many Nguni clans, subjugating them and forming a Zulu empire in SE Africa.

shake ▶ **verb** (past **shook**; past participle **shaken**) **1** [no obj.] (of a structure or area of land) tremble or vibrate: *buildings shook in Sacramento and tremors were felt in Reno*. ■ [with obj.] cause to tremble or vibrate: *a severe earthquake shook the area*. ■ (of a person, part of the body, or the voice) tremble uncontrollably from a strong emotion: *Luke was **shaking with** rage | her voice **shook with** passion*.
2 [with obj.] move (an object) up and down or from side to side with rapid, forceful, jerky movements: *she stood in the hall and shook her umbrella*. ■ [with obj. and adverbial] remove (an object or substance) from something by movements of this kind: *they shook the sand out of their shoes*. ■ grasp (someone) and move them roughly to and fro, either in anger or to rouse them from sleep: [with obj. and complement] *he gently shook the driver awake and they set off*. ■ brandish in anger or as a warning; make a threatening gesture with: *men shook their fists and shouted*. ■ informal get rid of or put an end to: *I couldn't shake the feeling that everyone was laughing at me*.
3 [with obj.] upset the composure or confidence of; shock or astonish: *rumours of a further loss shook the market* | (as adj. **shaken**) *the boy was visibly shaken*. ■ [with obj. and adverbial] cause a change of mood or attitude by shocking or disturbing (someone): *if the bombing cannot shake the government out of its complacency, what will?*
▶ **noun 1** an act of shaking: *she gave her red curls a vehement shake*. ■ an amount of something that is sprinkled by shaking a container: *add a few **shakes of** sea salt and black pepper*.
2 (**the shakes**) informal a fit of trembling or shivering: *I wouldn't go in there, it gives me the shakes*.
3 short for MILKSHAKE.
4 informal an earth tremor.
5 Music a trill.
6 N. Amer. a kind of rough wooden shingle, used especially on rustic buildings: *cedar shakes*.
– PHRASES **get** (or **give someone**) **a fair shake** N. Amer. informal get (or give someone) just treatment or a fair chance: *I do not believe he gave the industry a fair shake*. **in two shakes** (**of a lamb's tail**) informal very quickly. **more —— than one can shake a stick at** informal used to emphasize the largeness of an amount: *a team with more experience than you can shake a stick at*. **no great shakes** informal not very good or significant: *it is no great shakes as a piece of cinema*. **shake the dust off one's feet** leave indignantly or disdainfully. **shake hands** (**with someone**) (or **shake someone by the hand** or **shake someone's hand**) clasp someone's right hand in one's own at meeting or parting, in reconciliation or congratulation, or as a sign of agreement. **shake one's head** turn one's head from side to side in order to indicate refusal, denial, disapproval, or incredulity: *she shook her head in disbelief*. **shake** (or **quake**) **in one's shoes** (or **boots**) tremble with apprehension. **shake a leg** [as imperative] informal make a start; rouse oneself.
– PHRASAL VERBS **shake down** become established in a new place or situation; settle down: *it was disruptive to the industry as it was shaking down after deregulation*. **shake someone down** N. Amer. informal extort money from someone. **shake someone off** manage to evade or outmanoeuvre someone who is following or pestering one: *he thought he had shaken off his pursuer*. **shake something off** successfully deal with or recover from: *Sheedy has shaken off a calf injury*. **shake on** informal confirm (an agreement) by shaking hands: *they shook on the deal*. **shake something out 1** get rid of or abandon an attitude or practice: *we are going to shake out the old attitudes*. **2** Sailing unwind or untie a reef to increase the area of a sail. **shake someone up** rouse someone from lethargy, apathy, or complacency: *he had to do something to shake the team up—we lacked spark*. **shake something up 1** mix ingredients by shaking: *use soap flakes shaken up in the water to make bubbles*. **2** make radical changes to the organization or structure of an institution or system: *he presented plans to shake up the legal profession*.
– DERIVATIVES **shakeable** (also **shakable**) **adjective**.
– ORIGIN Old English *sc(e)acan* (verb), of Germanic origin.

shakedown ▶ **noun** informal, chiefly N. Amer. **1** another term for SHAKE-UP.
2 a thorough search of a person or place.
3 an act of swindling someone or extorting money.
4 a test of a new product or model, especially a vehicle or ship.
5 a makeshift bed.

shake hole ▶ **noun** another term for SINKHOLE.

shaken past participle of SHAKE.

shaken baby syndrome ▶ **noun** [mass noun] a condition characterized by cranial injury, retinal haemorrhage, etc. observed in infants who have been violently jolted.

shake-out ▶ **noun** informal an upheaval in or radical reorganization of a business, market, or organization, typically involving streamlining and redundancies.

shaker ▶ **noun 1** [with modifier] a container used for mixing ingredients by shaking: *a cocktail shaker*. ■ a container with a pierced top from which a powdered substance such as flour or salt is poured by shaking.
2 (**Shaker**) a member of an American religious sect, the United Society of Believers in Christ's Second Coming, established in England *c.*1750 and living simply in celibate mixed communities. [so named from the wild, ecstatic movements engaged in during worship.] ■ [as modifier] denoting a style of elegantly functional furniture traditionally produced by Shaker communities.
– DERIVATIVES **Shakerism noun** (sense 2).

Shakespeare, William (1564–1616), English dramatist.

> His plays are written mostly in blank verse and include comedies, such as *A Midsummer Night's Dream* and *As You Like It*; historical plays, including *Richard III* and *Henry V*; the Greek and Roman plays, which include *Julius Caesar* and *Antony and Cleopatra*; enigmatic comedies such as *All's Well that Ends Well* and *Measure for Measure*; the great tragedies, *Hamlet*, *Othello*, *King Lear*, and *Macbeth*; and the group of tragicomedies with which he ended his career, such as *The Winter's Tale* and *The Tempest*. He also wrote more than 150 sonnets, published in 1609.

– DERIVATIVES **Shakespearean** /ʃeɪkˈspɪərɪən/ (also **Shakespearian**) **noun & adjective**.

shake-up ▶ **noun** informal a radical reorganization.

S

Shakhty /ˈʃɑːkti/ a coal-mining city in SW Russia, situated in the Donets Basin north-east of Rostov; pop. 244,400 (est. 2008).

shako /ˈʃeɪkəʊ, ˈʃakəʊ/ ▶ noun (pl. **shakos**) a cylindrical or conical military hat with a peak and a plume or pom-pom.
– ORIGIN early 19th cent.: via French from Hungarian *csákó (süveg)* 'peaked (cap)', from *csák* 'peak', from German *Zacken* 'spike'.

Shakti /ʃʌkˈtiː/ (also **Sakti**) ▶ noun [mass noun] Hinduism the female principle of divine energy, especially when personified as the supreme deity. See also **DEVI** and **PARVATI**.
– ORIGIN from Sanskrit *śakti* 'power, divine energy'.

shakudo /ˈʃakuːdəʊ/ ▶ noun [mass noun] a Japanese alloy of copper and gold, typically having a blue patina.
– ORIGIN mid 19th cent.: Japanese, from *shaku* 'red' + *dō* 'copper'.

shakuhachi /ˌʃakʊˈhatʃi/ ▶ noun (pl. **shakuhachis**) a Japanese bamboo flute, held vertically when played.
– ORIGIN late 19th cent.: Japanese, from *shaku*, a measure of length (approx. 0.33 metre) + *hachi* 'eight (tenths)'.

shaky ▶ adjective (**shakier**, **shakiest**) shaking or trembling: *she managed a shaky laugh.* ■ unstable because of poor construction or heavy use: *a cracked, dangerously shaky table.* ■ not safe or reliable; liable to fail or falter: *thoroughly shaky evidence | after a shaky start the Scottish team made superb efforts.*
– DERIVATIVES **shakily** adverb, **shakiness** noun.

shale ▶ noun [mass noun] soft finely stratified sedimentary rock that formed from consolidated mud or clay and can be split easily into fragile plates.
– DERIVATIVES **shaly** (also **shaley**) adjective (**shalier**, **shaliest**).
– ORIGIN mid 18th cent.: probably from German *Schale*; related to English dialect *shale* 'dish' (see **SCALE**[2]).

shale oil ▶ noun [mass noun] oil obtained from bituminous shale.

shall ▶ modal verb (3rd sing. present **shall**) **1** (in the first person) expressing the future tense: *this time next week I shall be in Scotland | we shan't be gone long.*
2 expressing a strong assertion or intention: *they shall succeed | you shall not frighten me out of this.*
3 expressing an instruction or command: *you shall not steal.*
4 used in questions indicating offers or suggestions: *shall I send you the book? | shall we go?*
– ORIGIN Old English *sceal*, of Germanic origin; related to Dutch *zal* and German *soll*, from a base meaning 'owe'.

USAGE There is considerable confusion about when to use **shall** and **will**. The traditional rule in standard British English is that **shall** is used with first person pronouns (**I** and **we**) to form the future tense, while **will** is used with second and third persons (**you, he, she, it, they**), e.g. *I shall be late; she will not be there.* To express a strong determination to do something these positions are reversed, with **will** being used with the first person and **shall** with the second and third persons, e.g. *I will not tolerate this; you shall go to school.* In practice, however, **shall** and **will** are today used more or less interchangeably in statements (though not in questions). Given that the forms are frequently contracted (**we'll, she'll**, etc.) there is often no need to make a choice between **shall** and **will**, another factor no doubt instrumental in weakening the distinction. The interchangeable use of **shall** and **will** is now part of standard British and US English.

shallop /ˈʃaləp/ ▶ noun chiefly historical a light sailing boat used mainly for coastal fishing or as a tender. ■ a large, heavy boat with one or more masts and carrying fore-and-aft or lug sails, sometimes equipped with guns.
– ORIGIN late 16th cent.: from French *chaloupe*, from Dutch *sloep* 'sloop'.

shallot /ʃəˈlɒt/ ▶ noun **1** a small bulb which resembles an onion and is used for pickling or as a substitute for onion.
2 the plant which produces these bulbs, each mature bulb producing a cluster of smaller bulbs. ● *Allium ascalonicum*, family Liliaceae (or Alliaceae).
– ORIGIN mid 17th cent.: shortening of *eschalot*, from French *eschalotte*, alteration of Old French *eschaloigne* (in Anglo-Norman French *scaloun*: see **SCALLION**).

shallow ▶ adjective **1** of little depth: *serve the noodles in a shallow bowl | being fairly shallow, the water was warm.* ■ situated at no great depth: *the shallow bed of the North Sea.* ■ varying only slightly from a specified or understood line or direction, especially the horizontal: *a shallow roof.* ■ (of breathing) taking in little air.
2 not exhibiting, requiring, or capable of serious thought: *a shallow analysis of contemporary society.*
▶ noun (**shallows**) an area of the sea, a lake, or a river where the water is not very deep.
▶ verb [no obj.] (of the sea, a lake, or a river) become less deep over time or in a particular place: *the boat ground to a halt where the water shallowed.*
– DERIVATIVES **shallowly** adverb, **shallowness** noun.
– ORIGIN late Middle English: obscurely related to **SHOAL**[2].

Shalmaneser III /ˌʃalməˈniːzə/ (d.824 BC), king of Assyria 859–824. Most of his reign was devoted to the expansion of his kingdom and the conquest of neighbouring lands. According to Assyrian records he defeated an alliance of Syrian kings and the king of Israel in a battle at Qarqar on the Orontes in 853 BC.

shalom /ʃəˈlɒm/ ▶ exclamation used as salutation by Jews at meeting or parting, meaning 'peace'.
– ORIGIN from Hebrew *šālōm*.

shalt archaic second person singular of **SHALL**.

shalwar /ʃʌlˈwɑː/ ▶ noun variant spelling of **SALWAR**.

sham ▶ noun **1** a thing that is not what it is purported to be: *our current free health service is a sham.* ■ [mass noun] pretence: *George abhorred sham and affectation.* ■ a person who pretends to be someone or something they are not: *he was a sham, totally unqualified for his job as a senior doctor.*
2 N. Amer. short for **PILLOW SHAM**.
▶ adjective bogus; false: *a clergyman who arranged a sham marriage.*
▶ verb (**shams, shamming, shammed**) [no obj.] falsely present something as the truth: *was he ill or was he shamming?* ■ [with obj.] pretend to be or to be experiencing: *she shams indifference* | [no obj., with complement] *the opossum escapes danger by shamming dead.*
– DERIVATIVES **shammer** noun.
– ORIGIN late 17th cent.: perhaps a northern English dialect variant of the noun **SHAME**.

shama /ˈʃɑːmə/ ▶ noun a long-tailed forest thrush of southern Asia, typically having blackish plumage with a reddish-brown belly. ● Genus *Copsychus*, family Turdidae: five species.
– ORIGIN mid 19th cent.: from Hindi *śyāma*, from Sanskrit.

shamal /ʃəˈmɑːl/ ▶ noun a hot, dry north-westerly wind blowing across the Persian Gulf in summer, typically causing sandstorms.
– ORIGIN late 17th cent.: from Arabic *šamāl* 'north (wind)'.

shaman /ˈʃamən, ˈʃeɪm-/ ▶ noun (pl. **shamans**) a person regarded as having access to, and influence in, the world of good and evil spirits, especially among some peoples of northern Asia and North America. Typically such people enter a trance state during a ritual, and practise divination and healing.
– DERIVATIVES **shamanic** /ʃəˈmanɪk/ adjective, **shamanism** noun, **shamanist** noun & adjective, **shamanistic** adjective.
– ORIGIN late 17th cent.: from German *Schamane* and Russian *shaman*, from Tungus *šaman*.

shamateur ▶ noun derogatory a sports player who makes money from sporting activities though classified as amateur.
– DERIVATIVES **shamateurism** noun.
– ORIGIN late 19th cent.: blend of **SHAM** and **AMATEUR**.

shamba /ˈʃambə/ ▶ noun (in East Africa) a cultivated plot of ground; a farm or plantation.
– ORIGIN Kiswahili.

shamble ▶ verb [no obj., with adverbial of direction] (of a person) move with a slow, shuffling, awkward gait: *he shambled off down the corridor.*
▶ noun [in sing.] a slow, shuffling, awkward gait.
– DERIVATIVES **shambly** adjective.
– ORIGIN late 16th cent.: probably from dialect *shamble* 'ungainly', perhaps from the phrase *shamble legs*, with reference to the legs of trestle tables (such as would be used in a meat market: see **SHAMBLES**).

shambles ▶ plural noun [treated as sing.] **1** informal a state of total disorder: *my career was* **in a shambles**.
2 a butcher's slaughterhouse (archaic except in place names).

shambling ▶ adjective moving with a slow, shuffling, awkward gait: *a big, shambling, shy man.*

shambolic ▶ adjective informal, chiefly Brit. chaotic, disorganized, or mismanaged: *the department's shambolic accounting.*
– DERIVATIVES **shambolically** adverb.
– ORIGIN 1970s: from **SHAMBLES**, probably on the pattern of *symbolic*.

shame ▶ noun [mass noun] **1** a painful feeling of humiliation or distress caused by the consciousness of wrong or foolish behaviour: *she was hot with shame | he felt a pang of shame at telling Alice a lie.* ■ a loss of respect or esteem; dishonour: *the incident had brought shame on his family.* ■ [count noun] a person, action, or situation that brings a loss of respect or honour: *ignorance of Latin would be a disgrace and a* ***shame to*** *any public man.*
2 [in sing.] a regrettable or unfortunate situation or action: *what a shame Ellie won't be here | it is a shame that they are not better known.*
▶ verb [with obj.] make (someone) feel ashamed: *I tried to* ***shame him into*** *giving some away | legal action must be taken and companies* ***named and shamed***. ■ bring shame to: *the entire debacle has shamed Scotland.* ■ cause (someone) to feel inadequate by outdoing or surpassing them: *she shames me with her eighty-year-old energy.*
▶ exclamation S. African used to express sentimental pleasure, especially at something small and endearing: *look at the foals—shame, aren't they sweet?*
– PHRASES **put someone to shame** make someone feel inadequate by greatly outdoing or surpassing them: *she puts me to shame, she's so capable.* **shame on you** used to reprove someone for something of which they should be ashamed: ***shame on you*** *for hitting a woman.*
– ORIGIN Old English *sc(e)amu* (noun), *sc(e)amian* 'feel shame', of Germanic origin; related to Dutch *schamen* (verb) and German *Scham* (noun), *schämen* (verb).

shame culture ▶ noun Anthropology a culture in which conformity of behaviour is maintained through the individual's fear of being shamed. Compare with **GUILT CULTURE**.

shamefaced ▶ adjective feeling or expressing shame or embarrassment: *all the boys looked shamefaced.*
– DERIVATIVES **shamefacedly** adverb, **shamefacedness** noun.
– ORIGIN mid 16th cent. (in the sense 'modest, shy'): alteration of archaic *shamefast*, by association with **FACE**.

shameful ▶ adjective worthy of or causing shame or disgrace: *a shameful accusation.*
– DERIVATIVES **shamefully** adverb [as submodifier] *record companies are shamefully slow in fulfilling orders,* **shamefulness** noun.
– ORIGIN Old English *sc(e)amful* 'modest, shamefaced' (see **SHAME, -FUL**).

shameless ▶ adjective (of a person or their conduct) characterized by or showing a lack of shame; barefaced or brazen: *his shameless hypocrisy.*
– DERIVATIVES **shamelessly** adverb, **shamelessness** noun.
– ORIGIN Old English *sc(e)amlēas* (see **SHAME, -LESS**).

shamiana /ˈʃɑːmɪɑːnə/ ▶ noun Indian a marquee.
– ORIGIN via Urdu from Persian *shāmiyāna*.

Shamir /ʃaˈmɪə/, Yitzhak (b.1915), Polish-born Israeli statesman, Prime Minister 1983–4 and 1986–92; Polish name *Yitzhak Jazernicki*. Under his leadership Israel did not retaliate when attacked by Iraqi missiles during the Gulf War, thereby possibly averting an escalation of the conflict.

S

shamisen ▶ noun variant spelling of **SAMISEN**.

shammy (also **shammy leather**) ▶ noun (pl. **shammies**) informal term for **CHAMOIS** (sense 2).
– ORIGIN early 18th cent.: a phonetic spelling.

shampoo ▶ noun [mass noun] a liquid preparation containing soap for washing the hair: *he smelt clean, of soap and shampoo* | [count noun] *an anti-dandruff shampoo.* ■ a similar substance for cleaning a carpet, soft furnishings, or a car. ■ [count noun] an act of washing or cleaning something, especially the hair, with shampoo: *a shampoo and set.*
▶ verb (**shampoos, shampooing, shampooed**) [with obj.] wash or clean (something, especially the hair) with shampoo: *Dolly was sitting in the bath shampooing her hair.*
– ORIGIN mid 18th cent. (in the sense 'massage (as part of a Turkish bath process)'): from Hindi *cāmpo!* 'press!', imperative of *cāmpnā*.

shamrock ▶ noun a low-growing clover-like plant with three-lobed leaves, used as the national emblem of Ireland. ● The shamrock of legend has been identified with a number of different plants in the family Leguminosae, in particular the lesser yellow trefoil (*Trifolium minus*). ■ a spray or leaf of this plant.

– ORIGIN late 16th cent.: from Irish *seamróg* 'trefoil' (diminutive of *seamar* 'clover').

shamus /ˈʃeɪməs/ ▶ **noun** N. Amer. informal a private detective.
– ORIGIN 1920s: of unknown origin.

Shan /ʃɑːn/ ▶ **noun** (pl. **same** or **Shans**) **1** a member of a people living mainly in northern Burma (Myanmar) and adjacent parts of southern China.
2 [mass noun] the language of the Shan, related to Thai and having about 2.5 million speakers.
▶ **adjective** relating to the Shan or their language.
– ORIGIN Burmese.

Shandong /ʃanˈdʊŋ/ (also **Shantung**) a coastal province of eastern China; capital, Jinan. It occupies the Shandong Peninsula, separating southern Bo Hai from the Yellow Sea.

shandy ▶ **noun** (pl. **shandies**) [mass noun] Brit. beer mixed with a non-alcoholic drink (typically lemonade).
– ORIGIN late 19th cent.: abbreviation of *shandygaff*, in the same sense, of unknown origin.

Shang /ʃaŋ/ a dynasty which ruled China during part of the 2nd millennium BC, probably the 16th–11th centuries. The period encompassed the invention of Chinese ideographic script and the discovery and development of bronze casting.

Shangaan /ˈʃaŋgɑːn/ ▶ **noun** (pl. **same** or **Shangaans**) **1** a member of the Tsonga people of southern Africa.
2 [mass noun] the Bantu language of the Shangaan.
▶ **adjective** relating to the Shangaan or their language.
– ORIGIN probably named after the founding chief *Soshangane*.

Shanghai /ʃaŋˈhʌɪ/ a city on the east coast of China, a port on the estuary of the Yangtze; pop. 11,283,700 (est. 2006). Opened for trade with the west in 1842, Shanghai contained until the Second World War areas of British, French, and American settlement. It was the site in 1921 of the founding of the Chinese Communist Party.

shanghai[1] /ʃaŋˈhʌɪ/ ▶ **verb** (**shanghais**, **shanghaiing**, **shanghaied**) [with obj.] historical force (someone) to join a ship lacking a full crew by drugging them or using other underhand means. ■ informal coerce or trick (someone) into a place or position or into doing something: *Brady shanghaied her into his Jaguar and roared off.*
– ORIGIN late 19th cent.: from SHANGHAI.

shanghai[2] /ʃaŋˈhʌɪ/ Austral./NZ ▶ **noun** (pl. **shanghais**) a catapult.
▶ **verb** (**shanghais**, **shanghaiing**, **shanghaied**) [with obj.] shoot with a catapult. ■ [with obj. and adverbial of direction] catapult in a particular direction: *the springy, resilient saplings would shanghai him backwards.*
– ORIGIN mid 19th cent.: probably an alteration of Scots dialect *shangan* 'a stick cleft at one end'.

Shango /ˈʃaŋgəʊ/ ▶ **noun** [mass noun] a religious cult originating in western Nigeria and now practised chiefly in parts of the Caribbean. ■ (also **Shangor**) an African god of thunder significant to this cult. ■ [count noun] a dance associated with this cult.
– ORIGIN from Yoruba.

Shangri-La /ˌʃaŋgrɪˈlɑː/ a Tibetan utopia in James Hilton's novel *Lost Horizon* (1933). ■ (as noun **a Shangri-La**) a place regarded as an earthly paradise, especially when involving a retreat from the pressures of modern civilization.
– ORIGIN from *Shangri* (an invented name) + Tibetan *la* 'mountain pass'.

S

shank ▶ **noun 1** (often **shanks**) a person's leg, especially the part from the knee to the ankle: *the old man's thin, bony shanks showed through his trousers.* ■ the lower part of an animal's foreleg. ■ this part of an animal's leg as a cut of meat.
2 the shaft or stem of a tool or implement, in particular: ■ a long, narrow part of a tool connecting the handle to the operational end. ■ the cylindrical part of a bit by which it is held in a drill. ■ the long stem of a key, spoon, anchor, etc. ■ the straight part of a fish hook.
3 a part or appendage by which something is attached to something else, especially a wire loop attached to the back of a button. ■ the band of a ring rather than the setting or gemstone.
4 the narrow middle of the sole of a shoe.
▶ **verb** [with obj.] Golf strike (the ball) with the heel of the club: *I shanked a shot and hit a person on a shoulder.*
– DERIVATIVES **shanked adjective** [usu. in combination] *a long-shanked hook.*
– ORIGIN Old English *sceanca*, of West Germanic origin; related to Dutch *schenk* 'leg bone' and High German *Schenkel* 'thigh'. The use of the verb as a golfing term dates from the 1920s.

Shankar[1] /ˈʃaŋkə/, Ravi (b.1920), Indian sitar player and composer. From the mid 1950s he toured Europe and the US giving sitar recitals, doing much to stimulate contemporary Western interest in Indian music.

Shankar[2] /ˈʃaŋkə/, Uday (1900–77), Indian dancer, brother of Ravi Shankar. He introduced Anna Pavlova to Indian dance and performed with her in his ballet *Krishna and Radha* (1923). He later toured the world with his own company, introducing Indian dance to European audiences.

shanking ▶ **noun** [mass noun] **1** Golf the action of striking the ball with the heel of the club.
2 any of a number of plant diseases resulting in the darkening and shrivelling of a plant or fruit from the base of a stem or stalk.

Shankly, Bill (1913–81), Scottish footballer and manager; full name *William Shankly*. He was a renowned manager of Liverpool (1960–74), with whom he had great success in Britain and Europe.

Shanks's pony (N. Amer. also **Shanks's mare**) ▶ **noun** used to refer to one's own legs and the action of walking as a means of conveyance.
– ORIGIN late 18th cent.: first recorded as *shanks-nag* in R. Fergusson's *Poems* (1785).

Shannon[1] the longest river of Ireland. It rises in County Leitrim near Lough Allen and flows 390 km (240 miles) south and west to its estuary on the Atlantic. ■ an international airport in the Republic of Ireland, situated on the River Shannon west of Limerick. ■ a shipping forecast area in the NE Atlantic to the south-west of Ireland.

Shannon[2], Claude Elwood (1916–2001), American engineer. He was the pioneer of mathematical communication theory, which has become vital to the design of both communication and electronic equipment. He also investigated digital circuits, and was the first to use the term *bit* to denote a unit of information.

Shannon's theorem (also **Shannon's information theorem**) ▶ **noun** a theorem defining the maximum capacity of a communication channel to carry information with no more than an arbitrary error rate, given the bandwidth and signal-to-noise ratio.
– ORIGIN mid 20th cent.: named after C. E. Shannon (see SHANNON[2]).

shanny ▶ **noun** (pl. **shannies**) a small greenish-brown European blenny (fish) of the shoreline and intertidal waters. ● *Blennius pholis*, family Blenniidae.
– ORIGIN mid 19th cent.: of unknown origin; compare with earlier *shan*, in the same sense.

Shansi /ʃanˈsiː/ variant spelling of SHANXI.

shan't ▶ **contraction** shall not.

shanti /ˈʃɑːnti/ ▶ **noun** [mass noun] Indian peace: [as exclamation] *'Shanti! Shanti! You must not let anger possess you like that.'*
– ORIGIN from Sanskrit *śānti* 'peace, tranquillity'.

Shantou /ʃanˈtaʊ/ a port in the province of Guangdong in SE China, situated on the South China Sea at the mouth of the Han River; pop. 4,840,500 (est. 2006). It was designated a treaty port in 1869. Former name SWATOW.

Shantung /ʃanˈtʊŋ/ variant spelling of SHANDONG.

shantung /ʃanˈtʌŋ/ ▶ **noun** [mass noun] a dress fabric spun from tussore silk with random irregularities in the surface texture.
– ORIGIN late 19th cent.: from SHANTUNG, where it was originally made.

shanty[1] ▶ **noun** (pl. **shanties**) a small, crudely built shack.
– ORIGIN early 19th cent. (originally a North American usage): perhaps from Canadian French *chantier* 'lumberjack's cabin, logging camp'.

shanty[2] (Brit. also **sea shanty**; archaic or US **chantey** or **chanty**) ▶ **noun** (pl. **shanties**) a song with alternating solo and chorus, of a kind originally sung by sailors while performing physical labour together.
– ORIGIN mid 19th cent.: probably from French *chantez!* 'sing!', imperative plural of *chanter*.

shantyman ▶ **noun** (pl. **shantymen**) N. Amer. a lumberjack.

shanty town ▶ **noun** a deprived area on the outskirts of a town consisting of large numbers of shanty dwellings.

Shanxi /ʃanˈʃiː/ (also **Shansi**) a province of north central China, to the south of Inner Mongolia; capital, Taiyuan. Compare with SHAANXI.

Shaolin /ˈʃaʊlɪn/ ▶ **noun** [mass noun] [usu. as modifier] any of various styles or schools of Chinese martial arts developed by the monks of the Shaolin Temple, a Buddhist monastery in China.
– ORIGIN from Chinese *Shàolínsì*, literally 'young forest temple'.

SHAPE ▶ **abbreviation** Supreme Headquarters Allied Powers Europe.

shape ▶ **noun 1** the external form, contours, or outline of someone or something: *she liked the shape of his nose | houseplants come in all shapes and sizes |* [mass noun] *the stones are irregular in shape.* ■ a person or thing that is difficult to see and identify clearly: *he saw a shape through the mist.* ■ a specific form or guise assumed by someone or something: *a fiend in human shape.*
2 a geometric figure such as a square, triangle, or rectangle. ■ a piece of material, paper, etc., made or cut in a particular form: *stick paper shapes on for the puppet's eyes and nose.*
3 [mass noun] the correct or original form or contours of something: *her skirt had lost its shape long ago | the lid had been battered* ***out of shape.*** ■ definite or orderly arrangement: *check that your structure will* ***give shape to*** *your essay.* ■ the distinctive nature or qualities of something: *debates about the future shape of British society.*
4 [mass noun] good physical condition: *she has to work hard to* ***keep in shape*** *| I trained with the featherweight champion of Europe to* ***get in shape.*** ■ [with adj.] the specified condition or state of someone or something: *he was in no shape to drive | the company came through a difficult period in excellent financial shape.*
▶ **verb** [with obj.] **1** give a particular shape or form to: *most caves are shaped by the flow of water through limestone | shape the dough into two-inch balls.* ■ form or produce (a sound or words). ■ make (something) fit the form of something else: [with obj. and infinitive] *suits have been shaped to fit so snugly that no curve is undefined.* ■ determine the nature of; have a great influence on: *his childhood was shaped by a loving relationship with his elder brother.*
2 [no obj.] (of a sports player or athlete) take up a stance or set oneself to perform a particular action: [with infinitive] *I had plenty of time and shaped to kick to the near touchline.*
– PHRASES **in any shape or form** (or **in any way, shape, or form**) in any manner or under any circumstances: *96 per cent of the electorate voted against Europeanization in any shape or form.* **in the shape of** represented or embodied by: *retribution arrived in the shape of my irate father.* ■ by way of; in the nature of: *there had been little or nothing in the shape of academic planning.* **lick** (or **knock** or **whip**) **someone/thing into shape** act forcefully to bring someone or something into a fitter, more efficient, or better-organized state: *the bank were eager to whip the company into shape for eventual sale.* **the shape of things to come** the way the future is likely to develop. [the title of a novel by H. G. Wells (1933).] **shape up or ship out** informal, chiefly N. Amer. used as an ultimatum to someone to improve their performance or behaviour or face being made to leave. **take shape** assume a distinct form; develop into something definite or tangible: *the past few months have seen the state's health insurance legislation begin to take shape.*
– PHRASAL VERBS **shape up** develop or progress in a particular way: *I wanted to see how things had been shaping up in my absence | it was shaping up to be another bleak year.* ■ become physically fit: *she was looking for a way to shape up after the birth of her second son.* ■ informal improve one's behaviour or performance to the required standard: *the manager has ordered his goal-shy strike force to shape up.*
– DERIVATIVES **shapable** (also **shapeable**) **adjective**, **shaped adjective** [usu. in combination] *egg-shaped | X-shaped*, **shaper noun**.
– ORIGIN Old English *gesceap* 'external form', also 'creation', *sceppan* 'create', of Germanic origin.

shaped charge ▶ **noun** an explosive charge with a cavity which causes the blast to be concentrated into a small area.

shapeless ▶ **adjective** (especially of a garment) lacking a distinctive or attractive shape: *she wore a shapeless frock and no make-up.*
– DERIVATIVES **shapelessly adverb**, **shapelessness noun**.

shapely ▶ **adjective** (**shapelier**, **shapeliest**) (especially of a woman or part of her body) having an attractive or well-proportioned shape: *however much she ate it made no difference to her shapely figure.*
– DERIVATIVES **shapeliness noun**.

shape memory ▶ **noun** [mass noun] Metallurgy a property exhibited by certain alloys of recovering their initial shape when they are heated after having been plastically deformed.

shape-shifter ▶ **noun** (chiefly in science fiction or mythology) a person or being with the ability to change their physical form at will.
– DERIVATIVES **shape-shifting** noun & adjective.

shapewear ▶ **noun** [mass noun] women's tight-fitting underwear intended to control and shape the figure.

shapka /ˈʃapkə/ ▶ **noun** a brimless Russian hat of fur or sheepskin.
– ORIGIN Russian, literally 'hat'.

sharara /ʃʌˈrɑːrə/ ▶ **noun** a pair of loose pleated trousers worn by women from South Asia, typically with a kameez and dupatta.
– ORIGIN from Urdu.

shard ▶ **noun** a piece of broken ceramic, metal, glass, or rock, typically having sharp edges: *shards of glass flew in all directions.*
– ORIGIN Old English *sceard* 'gap, notch, potsherd', of Germanic origin; related to Dutch *schaarde* 'notch', also to SHEAR.

share[1] ▶ **noun 1** a part or portion of a larger amount which is divided among a number of people, or to which a number of people contribute: *under the proposals, investors would pay a greater share of the annual fees required | we gave them all the chance to have a share in the profits.* ■ each of the notional parts into which property held by joint owners is divided: *Jake had a share in a large, seagoing vessel.* ■ [in sing.] the allotted or due amount of something that a person expects to have or to do, or that is expected to be accepted or done by them: *she's done more than her* ***fair share of*** *globetrotting.* ■ [in sing.] a person's part in or contribution to something: *she can't take a share in childcare — she's a nervous wreck.*
2 one of the equal parts into which a company's capital is divided, entitling the holder to a proportion of the profits: *he's selling his shares in BT.*
▶ **verb** [with obj.] have a portion of (something) with another or others: *he* ***shared*** *the pie* ***with*** *her | all members of the band equally share the band's profits.* ■ [with obj. and adverbial] give a portion of (something) to another or others: *they* ***shared out*** *the peanuts.* ■ use, occupy, or enjoy (something) jointly with another or others: *they once shared a flat in Chelsea* | [no obj.] *there weren't enough plates so we had to share* | (as adj. **shared**) *a shared bottle of wine.* ■ possess (a view or quality) in common with others: *other countries don't share our reluctance to eat goat meat.* ■ [no obj.] (**share in**) (of a number of people or organizations) have a part in (something, especially an activity): *UK companies would share in the development of three oil platforms.* ■ tell someone about (something, especially something personal): *she had never* ***shared*** *the secret* ***with*** *anyone before.*
– PHRASES **share and share alike** have or receive an equal share: *we all share and share alike in camp.* **share a moment** see MOMENT.
– DERIVATIVES **shareable** (also **sharable**) adjective, **sharer** noun.
– ORIGIN Old English *scearu* 'division, part into which something may be divided', of Germanic origin; related to Dutch *schare* and German *Schar* 'troop, multitude', also to SHEAR. The verb dates from the late 16th cent.

share[2] ▶ **noun** short for PLOUGHSHARE.

share capital ▶ **noun** [mass noun] the part of the capital of a company that comes from the issue of shares.

sharecropper ▶ **noun** chiefly N. Amer. a tenant farmer who gives a part of each crop as rent.
– DERIVATIVES **sharecrop** verb (**sharecrops**, **sharecropping**, **sharecropped**).

shared care ▶ **noun** [mass noun] (in the UK) an arrangement between a welfare agency and the family of a mentally or physically ill person for the provision of respite care or emergency assistance.

shared ownership ▶ **noun** [mass noun] (in Britain) a system by which the occupier of a dwelling buys a proportion of the property and pays rent on the remainder, typically to a local authority or housing association.

share-farmer ▶ **noun** chiefly Austral./NZ a tenant farmer who receives an agreed share of the profits from the owner.
– DERIVATIVES **share-farming** noun.

shareholder ▶ **noun** an owner of shares in a company.
– DERIVATIVES **shareholding** noun.

share milker ▶ **noun** NZ a person who works another's dairy farm for a share of the profits, often owning all or part of the herd of cows.

share option ▶ **noun** a benefit in the form of an option given by a company to an employee to buy a share in the company at a discount or at a stated fixed price.

share-out ▶ **noun** Brit. an act of sharing something out, especially money.

share premium ▶ **noun** Finance the amount by which the amount received by a company for a stock issue exceeds its face value.

shareware ▶ **noun** [mass noun] Computing software that is available free of charge and often distributed informally for evaluation, after which a fee may be requested for continued use.

sharia /ʃəˈriːə/ (also **shariah** or **shariat** /ʃəˈriːət/) ▶ **noun** [mass noun] Islamic canonical law based on the teachings of the Koran and the traditions of the Prophet (Hadith and Sunna), prescribing both religious and secular duties and sometimes retributive penalties for lawbreaking. It has generally been supplemented by legislation adapted to the conditions of the day, though the manner in which it should be applied in modern states is a subject of dispute between Muslim traditionalists and reformists.
– ORIGIN from Arabic *šarī'a*; the variant *shariat* from Urdu and Persian.

sharif /ʃəˈriːf/ (also **shereef** or **sherif**) ▶ **noun 1** a descendant of Muhammad through his daughter Fatima.
2 a Muslim ruler, magistrate, or religious leader.
– DERIVATIVES **sharifian** adjective.
– ORIGIN from Arabic *šarīf* 'noble', from *šarafa* 'be exalted'.

Sharjah /ˈʃɑːdʒə/ one of the seven member states of the United Arab Emirates; pop. 934,400 (est. 2009). Arabic name ASH SHARIQAH. ■ its capital city, situated on the Persian Gulf; pop. 845,600 (est. 2009).

shark[1] ▶ **noun 1** a long-bodied chiefly marine fish with a cartilaginous skeleton, a prominent dorsal fin, and tooth-like scales. Most sharks are predatory, though the largest kinds feed on plankton, and some can grow to a large size. ● Several orders (or superorders) of the subclass Elasmobranchii: many families.
2 a small SE Asian freshwater fish with a shark-like tail, popular in aquaria. ● Two species in the family Cyprinidae: the small **red-tailed black shark** (*Labeo bicolor*), and the larger **black shark** (*Morulius chrysophekadion*).
3 a light greyish-brown European moth, the male of which has pale silvery hindwings. ● Genus *Cucullia*, family Noctuidae: several species.
▶ **verb** [no obj.] Brit. informal (typically of a man at a social gathering) be in active pursuit of a sexual partner: *as soon as he arrived he was sharking among the women.*
– ORIGIN late Middle English: of unknown origin.

shark[2] ▶ **noun** informal **1** a person who unscrupulously exploits or swindles others: *property sharks want to develop 200 acres around the site.*
2 US an expert in a specified field: *a pool shark.*
– ORIGIN late 16th cent.: perhaps from German *Schurke* 'worthless rogue', influenced by SHARK[1].

sharkskin ▶ **noun** [mass noun] the rough scaly skin of a shark, sometimes used as shagreen. ■ a stiff, slightly lustrous synthetic fabric.

shark-sucker ▶ **noun** another term for REMORA.

Sharon[1] /ˈʃɑr(ə)n/ a fertile coastal plain in Israel, lying between the Mediterranean Sea and the hills of Samaria.

Sharon[2] /ʃəˈrɒn/, Ariel (b.1928), Israeli general and Likud statesman, Prime Minister 2001–6.

sharon fruit /ˈʃɛːr(ə)n, ˈʃar(ə)n/ ▶ **noun** a persimmon, especially one of an early-fruiting orange variety grown in Israel.
– ORIGIN from SHARON[1].

Sharp, Cecil (James) (1859–1924), English collector of folk songs and folk dances. From 1904 onwards he published a number of collections of songs and dances, stimulating a revival of interest in English folk music. Sharp also founded the English Folk Dance Society in 1911.

sharp ▶ **adjective 1** (of an object) having an edge or point that is able to cut or pierce something: *cut the cake with a very sharp knife | keep tools sharp.* ■ tapering to a point or edge: *a sharp pencil | her face was thin and her nose sharp.* ■ (of sand or gravel) composed of angular grains.
2 producing a sudden, piercing physical sensation or effect: *I suddenly felt a sharp pain in my back.* ■ (of a food, taste, or smell) acidic and intense: *fresh goats' milk cheese has a slightly sharper flavour than fromage frais.* ■ (of a sound) sudden and penetrating: *there was a sharp crack of thunder.* ■ (of words or a speaker) critical or hurtful: *she feared his sharp tongue | he could be very sharp with her.* ■ (of an emotion or experience) felt acutely or intensely; painful: *her sharp disappointment was tinged with embarrassment.*
3 distinct in outline or detail; clearly defined: *the job was a sharp contrast from her past life | the scene was as sharp and clear in his mind as a film.*
4 (of an action or change) sudden and marked: *there was a sharp increase in interest rates | he heard her sharp intake of breath.* ■ (of a bend, angle, or turn) making a sudden change of direction: *the bus creaked round a sharp hairpin bend.*
5 having or showing speed of perception, comprehension, or response: *her sharp eyes missed nothing | his old mind was not so sharp as it once was.* ■ quick to take advantage, especially in an unscrupulous or dishonest way: *Paul's a sharp operator.*
6 (of musical sound) above true or normal pitch. ■ [postpositive] (of a note) a semitone higher than a specified note: *F sharp.* ■ (of a key) having a sharp or sharps in the signature.
7 informal (of clothes or their wearer) smart and stylish: *they were greeted by a young man in a sharp suit.*
▶ **adverb 1** precisely (used after an expression of time): *the meeting starts at 7.30 sharp.*
2 in a sudden or abrupt way: *turn sharp right at the corner | he was brought up sharp by Helen's voice.*
3 above the true or normal pitch of musical sound: *he heard him playing a little sharp on the high notes.*
▶ **noun 1** a musical note raised a semitone above natural pitch. ■ the sign (♯) indicating this.
2 a long, sharply pointed needle used for general sewing. ■ (usu. **sharps**) a thing with a sharp edge, such as a blade or a fragment of glass: *the safe disposal of sharps and clinical waste.*
3 informal a swindler or cheat. See also CARD SHARP.
▶ **verb** [with obj.] **1** (usu. as adj. **sharped**) Music, US raise the pitch of (a note).
2 archaic cheat or swindle (someone), especially at cards. [late 17th cent.: from SHARPER; compare with SHARK[2].]
– PHRASES **sharp as a tack** N. Amer. extremely clever or astute. **the sharp end** see END.
– DERIVATIVES **sharply** adverb.
– ORIGIN Old English *sc(e)arp*, of Germanic origin; related to Dutch *scherp* and German *scharf*.

Shar Pei /ʃɑː ˈpeɪ/ ▶ **noun** (pl. **Shar Peis**) a compact squarely built dog of a breed of Chinese origin, with a characteristic wrinkly skin and short bristly coat of a fawn, cream, black, or red colour.
– ORIGIN from Chinese *shā pí*, literally 'sand skin'.

sharpen ▶ **verb 1** make or become sharp or sharper: [with obj.] *she sharpened her pencil* | [no obj.] *her tone sharpened.*
2 (**sharpen up** or **sharpen something up**) improve or cause to improve: *they've got to* ***sharpen up*** *in front of the goal | students will* ***sharpen up*** *their reading skills.*
– DERIVATIVES **sharpener** noun.

sharper ▶ **noun** informal a swindler, especially at cards.

S

Sharpeville massacre the killing of sixty-nine anti-apartheid demonstrators by security forces at Sharpeville, a black township south of Johannesburg, on 21 March 1960. Following the massacre, the South African government banned the African National Congress and the Pan-Africanist Congress.

sharp-eyed ▶ **adjective** quick to notice things; observant: *sharp-eyed readers may have already spotted this.*

sharp-featured ▶ **adjective** (of a person) having well-defined facial features.

sharpie ▶ **noun** (pl. **sharpies**) **1** a sharp-prowed, flat-bottomed New England sailing boat, with one or two masts each rigged with a triangular sail.
2 informal, chiefly N. Amer. another term for SHARPER.
3 Austral. informal (in the 1960s and 1970s) a young person resembling a skinhead, with close-cropped hair and distinctive dress.

sharpish informal ▶ **adjective** fairly sharp.
▶ **adverb** Brit. quickly; soon: *I'd slip away sharpish if I were you.*

sharpness ▶ **noun** [mass noun] the quality or state of being sharp: *the sweet flavour contrasts with the sharpness of the lemon | his health and mental sharpness declined.*

sharp practice ▶ noun [mass noun] dishonest or barely honest dealings.

sharp-set ▶ adjective dated very hungry.

sharpshooter ▶ noun a person who is very skilled in shooting.
– DERIVATIVES **sharpshooting** noun & adjective.

sharp-tongued ▶ adjective (of a person) given to using cutting, harsh, or critical language.

sharp-witted ▶ adjective (of a person) quick to notice and understand things.
– DERIVATIVES **sharp-wittedly** adverb, **sharp-wittedness** noun.

shashlik /ˈʃaʃlɪk/ ▶ noun (pl. **same** or **shashliks**) (in Asia and eastern Europe) a mutton kebab.
– ORIGIN from Russian *shashlyk*, based on Turkish *şiş* 'spit, skewer'; compare with SHISH KEBAB.

Shasta daisy /ˈʃastə/ ▶ noun a tall Pyrenean plant which bears a single large white daisy-like flower. ● *Leucanthemum maximum* or its hybrids, family Compositae.
– ORIGIN mid 19th cent.: named after Mount *Shasta* in California.

shastra /ˈʃɑːstrə/ (also **sastra**) ▶ noun (in Hinduism and some forms of Buddhism) a work of sacred scripture.
– ORIGIN from Sanskrit *śāstra*.

shat past and past participle of SHIT.

Shatt al-Arab /ˌʃat al ˈarəb/ a river of SW Asia, formed by the confluence of the Tigris and Euphrates Rivers and flowing 195 km (120 miles) through SE Iraq to the Persian Gulf. Its lower course forms the border between Iraq and Iran.

shatter ▶ verb **1** break or cause to break suddenly and violently into pieces: [no obj.] *bullets riddled the bar top, glasses shattered, bottles exploded* | [with obj.] *the window was shattered by a stone*. ■ [with obj.] damage or destroy (something abstract): *the crisis will shatter their confidence*.
2 [with obj.] upset (someone) greatly: *everyone was shattered by the news*.
– DERIVATIVES **shatterer** noun, **shatterproof** adjective.
– ORIGIN Middle English (in the sense 'scatter, disperse'): perhaps imitative; compare with SCATTER.

shatter cone ▶ noun Geology a fluted conical structure produced in rock by intense mechanical shock, such as that associated with meteoritic impact.

shattered ▶ adjective Brit. informal exhausted: *I usually feel too shattered to do more than crawl into bed*.

shattering ▶ adjective very shocking or upsetting: *he found it a shattering experience*.
– DERIVATIVES **shatteringly** adverb.

shauri /ˈʃaʊriː/ ▶ noun (pl. **shauris** or **shauries**) (in East Africa) a debate, argument, or problematic issue.
– ORIGIN Kiswahili.

shave ▶ verb **1** [no obj.] (of a man) cut the hair off the face with a razor: *he washed, shaved, and had breakfast*. ■ [with obj.] cut the hair off (a part of the body) with a razor: *she shaved her legs*. ■ [with obj.] cut the hair off the face or another part of the body of (someone) with a razor: *his wife washed and shaved him*. ■ cut (hair) off with a razor: *professional male swimmers* ***shave off*** *their body hair*.
S
2 [with obj.] cut (a thin slice or slices) from the surface of something: *scrape a large sharp knife across the surface,* ***shaving off*** *rolls of very fine chocolate*. ■ take (a small amount) from something: *she* ***shaved*** *0.5 seconds* ***off*** *the British junior record*. ■ reduce by a small amount: *they shaved profit margins*.
3 [with obj.] pass or send something close to (something else), missing it narrowly: *Scott shaved the post in the 29th minute*.
▶ noun an act of shaving hair from the face or a part of the body: *you need a shave*.
– ORIGIN Old English *sc(e)afan* 'scrape away the surface of (something) by paring', of Germanic origin; related to Dutch *schaven* and German *schaben*.

shavehook ▶ noun a tool used to remove paint from moulded areas.

shaveling /ˈʃeɪvlɪŋ/ ▶ noun archaic, derogatory a clergyman or priest with a tonsured head.

shaven ▶ adjective shaved: *a boy with a shaven head* | [in combination] *shaven-headed monks*.

shaver ▶ noun **1** an electric razor.
2 informal a young lad.

shavetail ▶ noun US military slang, often derogatory a newly commissioned officer, especially a second lieutenant. ■ informal an inexperienced person.
– ORIGIN figuratively, from the early sense 'untrained pack animal' (identified by a shaven tail).

Shavian /ˈʃeɪvɪən/ ▶ adjective relating to or in the manner of George Bernard Shaw or his writings or ideas.
▶ noun an admirer of Shaw or his work.
– ORIGIN from *Shavius* (Latinized form of *Shaw*) + -AN.

shaving ▶ noun **1** a thin strip cut off a surface: *she brushed wood shavings from her knees*.
2 [mass noun] the action of shaving.

Shavuoth /ʃəˈvuːəs, ʃɑːvʊˈɒt/ (also **Shavuot**) ▶ noun a major Jewish festival held on the 6th (and usually the 7th) of Sivan, fifty days after the second day of Passover. It was originally a harvest festival, but now also commemorates the giving of the Law (the Torah). Also called PENTECOST, FEAST OF WEEKS.
– ORIGIN from Hebrew *šāḇūʿōṯ* 'weeks', with reference to the weeks between Passover and Pentecost.

Shaw, George Bernard (1856–1950), Irish dramatist and writer. His best-known plays combine comedy with a questioning of conventional morality and thought; they include *Man and Superman* (1903), *Pygmalion* (1913), and *St Joan* (1923). A socialist, he became an active member of the Fabian Society. Nobel Prize for Literature (1925).

shaw[1] ▶ noun Farming, chiefly Scottish the parts of a potato plant that appear above the ground.
– ORIGIN early 19th cent.: perhaps a variant of the noun SHOW.

shaw[2] ▶ noun archaic, chiefly Scottish a small group of trees; a thicket.
– ORIGIN Old English *sceaga*, of Germanic origin; related to SHAG[1].

shawarma /ʃəˈwɔːmə/ ▶ noun (in some Arabic-speaking countries) a doner kebab.
– ORIGIN colloquial Arabic *šāwirma*, from Turkish *çevirme* 'sliced meat roasted on a spit' from *çevirmek* 'turn, rotate'.

shawl ▶ noun a piece of fabric worn by women over the shoulders or head or wrapped round a baby.
– DERIVATIVES **shawled** adjective.
– ORIGIN early 17th cent.: from Urdu and Persian *šāl*, probably from *Shāliāt*, the name of a town in India.

shawl collar ▶ noun a rounded turned-down collar, without lapel notches, that extends down the front of a garment.

shawlie ▶ noun Scottish, Irish, & N. English, dated a poor working-class woman (traditionally wearing a shawl).

shawm /ʃɔːm/ ▶ noun a medieval and Renaissance wind instrument, forerunner of the oboe, with a double reed enclosed in a wooden mouthpiece, and having a penetrating tone.
– ORIGIN Middle English: from Old French *chalemel*, via Latin from Greek *kalamos* 'reed'.

Shawnee /ʃɔːˈniː/ ▶ noun (pl. **same** or **Shawnees**) **1** a member of an American Indian people living formerly in the eastern US and now chiefly in Oklahoma.
2 [mass noun] the Algonquian language of the Shawnee, now with few speakers.
▶ adjective relating to the Shawnee or their language.
– ORIGIN the name in Delaware.

shay ▶ noun informal term for CHAISE (sense 1).
– ORIGIN early 18th cent.: back-formation from CHAISE, interpreted as plural.

shaykh ▶ noun variant spelling of SHEIKH.

shazam /ʃəˈzam/ ▶ exclamation used to introduce an extraordinary deed, story, or transformation: *She prayed for his arrival and shazam! There he was*.
– ORIGIN 1940s: an invented word, used by conjurors.

Shcherbakov /ˌʃtʃəːbəˈkɒf/ former name (1946–57) for RYBINSK.

shchi /ʃtʃiː/ ▶ noun [mass noun] a type of Russian cabbage soup.
– ORIGIN Russian.

she ▶ pronoun [third person singular] used to refer to a woman, girl, or female animal previously mentioned or easily identified: *my sister told me that she was not happy*. ■ used to refer to a ship, vehicle, country, or other inanimate thing regarded as female: *I was aboard the St Roch shortly before she sailed for the Northwest Passage*. ■ used to refer to a person or animal of unspecified sex: *only include your child if you know she won't distract you*. ■ any female person: *she who rocks the cradle rules the world*. ■ W. Indian her or hers: *give she lavender oil*. ■ Austral./NZ it (used to refer to something not usually regarded as female): *reckon some decent weather and she'll be right*.
▶ noun [in sing.] a female; a woman: *society would label him a slut if he were a she*. ■ [in combination] female: *a she-bear* | *a she-wolf*.
– PHRASES **who's she—the cat's mother?** Brit. informal **1** used as a mild reproof, especially to a child, for impolite use of the pronoun *she* rather than a person's name. **2** expressing the belief that a woman or girl has a high opinion of herself or is putting on airs.
– ORIGIN Middle English: probably a phonetic development of the Old English feminine personal pronoun *hēo*, *hīe*.

> **USAGE** **1** For a discussion of whether to say *I am older than* **she** or *I am older than* **her**, see USAGE at PERSONAL PRONOUN and THAN.
> **2** The use of the pronoun **he** to refer to a person of unspecified sex, once quite acceptable, has become problematic in recent years and is now usually regarded as old-fashioned or sexist. One of the responses to this has been to use **she** in the way that **he** has been used, as in *only include your* **child** *if you know* **she** *won't distract you*. In some types of writing, for example books on childcare or child psychology, this use of **she** has become quite common. In most contexts, however, it is likely to be distracting in the same way that he now is, and alternatives such as 'he or she' or 'they' are preferable. See USAGE at HE and THEY.

s/he ▶ pronoun a written representation of 'he or she' used as a neutral alternative to indicate someone of either sex.

shea /ʃiː, ˈʃiːə/ ▶ noun a small tropical African tree which bears oily nuts from which shea butter is obtained. ● *Vitellaria paradoxa* (or *Butyrospermum parkii*), family Sapotaceae.
– ORIGIN late 18th cent.: from Mande *sye*.

shea butter ▶ noun [mass noun] a fatty substance obtained from the nuts of the shea tree, used in cosmetic skin preparations and food.

sheading /ˈʃiːdɪŋ/ ▶ noun each of the six administrative divisions of the Isle of Man.
– ORIGIN late 16th cent.: variant of *shedding* (see SHED[2]).

sheaf ▶ noun (pl. **sheaves**) a bundle of grain stalks laid lengthways and tied together after reaping. ■ a bundle of objects of one kind, especially papers: *he waved* ***a sheaf of*** *papers in the air*.
▶ verb [with obj.] bundle into sheaves.
– ORIGIN Old English *scēaf*, of Germanic origin; related to Dutch *schoof* 'sheaf' and German *Schaub* 'wisp of straw', also to the verb SHOVE.

shealing ▶ noun variant spelling of SHIELING.

shear ▶ verb (past participle **shorn** or **sheared**) **1** [with obj.] cut the wool off (a sheep or other animal). ■ cut off (something such as hair, wool, or grass), with scissors or shears: *I'll* ***shear off*** *all that fleece*. ■ (**be shorn of**) have something cut off: *they were shorn of their hair* | figurative *the richest man in the US was shorn of nearly $2 billion*.
2 break off or cause to break off, owing to a structural strain: [no obj.] *the gear sheared and jammed in the rear wheel* | [with obj.] *the left wing had been almost completely* ***sheared off***.
▶ noun [mass noun] a strain produced by pressure in the structure of a substance, when its layers are laterally shifted in relation to each other. See also WIND SHEAR.
– DERIVATIVES **shearer** noun.
– ORIGIN Old English *sceran* (originally in the sense 'cut through with a weapon'), of Germanic origin; related to Dutch and German *scheren*, from a base meaning 'divide, shear, shave'.

> **USAGE** The two verbs **shear** and **sheer** are sometimes confused: see USAGE at SHEER[2].

shearling ▶ noun a sheep that has been shorn once: [as modifier] *a group of shearling rams*. ■ [mass noun] wool or fleece from such a sheep. ■ chiefly US a coat made from or lined with such wool.

shears (also **a pair of shears**) ▶ plural noun a cutting instrument in which two blades move past each other, like scissors but typically larger: *garden shears*.
– ORIGIN Old English *scēara* (plural) 'scissors, cutting instrument', of Germanic origin; related to Dutch *schaar* and German *Schere*, also to SHEAR.

shearwater ▶ noun **1** a long-winged seabird related to the petrels, often flying low over the surface of the water far from land. ● Family Procellariidae: three genera, in particular *Puffinus*, and many species.
2 North American term for SKIMMER (sense 5).

sheatfish /ˈʃiːtfɪʃ/ ▶ noun (pl. **same** or **sheatfishes**) another term for WELS.

– ORIGIN late 16th cent.: from an alteration of **SHEATH** + **FISH**[1].

sheath ▸ **noun** (pl. **sheaths** /ʃiːðz, ʃiːθs/) a close-fitting cover for the blade of a knife or sword. ■ a structure in living tissue which closely envelops another: *the fatty sheath around nerve fibres.* ■ a protective covering around an electric cable. ■ (also **sheath dress**) a woman's close-fitting dress. ■ chiefly Brit. a condom.
– DERIVATIVES **sheathless** adjective.
– ORIGIN Old English *scæth, scēath* 'scabbard', of Germanic origin; related to Dutch *schede*, German *Scheide*, also to the verb **SHED**[2].

sheathbill ▸ **noun** a mainly white pigeon-like bird with a horny sheath around the base of the bill, breeding on the coasts of sub-Antarctic islands and feeding by scavenging. ● Family Chionididae and genus *Chionis*: two species.

sheathe /ʃiːð/ ▸ **verb 1** [with obj.] put (a weapon such as a knife or sword) into a sheath.
2 (often **be sheathed in**) encase (something) in a close-fitting or protective covering: *her legs were sheathed in black stockings.*
– ORIGIN late Middle English: from **SHEATH**.

sheathing /ˈʃiːðɪŋ/ ▸ **noun** [mass noun] protective casing or covering.

sheath knife ▸ **noun** a short knife similar to a dagger, carried in a sheath.

sheave[1] ▸ **verb** another term for **SHEAF**.
– ORIGIN late 16th cent.: from **SHEAVES**.

sheave[2] ▸ **noun** a wheel with a groove for a rope to run on, as in a pulley block.
– ORIGIN Middle English: from a Germanic base meaning 'wheel, pulley'.

sheaves plural form of **SHEAF**.

Sheba /ˈʃiːbə/ the biblical name of Saba in SW Arabia. The queen of Sheba visited King Solomon in Jerusalem (1 Kings 10).
– ORIGIN from Hebrew *šəḇā'*.

shebang /ʃɪˈbaŋ/ ▸ **noun 1** [in sing.] informal a matter, operation, or set of circumstances: *the Mafia boss who's running **the whole shebang**.*
2 N. Amer. archaic a rough hut or shelter.
– ORIGIN mid 19th cent.: of unknown origin.

Shebat /ˈʃiːbat/ ▸ **noun** variant spelling of **SEBAT**.

shebeen /ʃɪˈbiːn/ ▸ **noun** (especially in Ireland, Scotland, and South Africa) an unlicensed establishment or private house selling alcohol and typically regarded as slightly disreputable. ■ (in South Africa) an informal licensed drinking place in a township.
– ORIGIN late 18th cent.: from Anglo-Irish *síbín*, from *séibe* 'mugful'.

shed[1] ▸ **noun** a simple roofed structure used for garden storage, to shelter animals, or as a workshop. ■ a larger structure for storing or maintaining vehicles or other machinery: *a shed is required for the three engines.* ■ Austral./NZ a building for shearing sheep or milking cattle.
▸ **verb** (**sheds, shedding, shedded**) [with obj.] park (a vehicle) in a depot.
– ORIGIN late 15th cent.: apparently a variant of the noun **SHADE**.

shed[2] ▸ **verb** (**sheds, shedding**; past and past participle **shed**) [with obj.] **1** (of a tree or other plant) allow (leaves or fruit) to fall to the ground: *both varieties shed leaves in winter.* ■ (of a reptile, insect, etc.) allow (its skin or shell) to come off, to be replaced by another one that has grown underneath. ■ (of a mammal) lose (hair) as a result of moulting, disease, or age. ■ take off (clothes). ■ have the property of repelling (water or a similar substance).
2 discard (something undesirable, superfluous, or outdated): *many firms use relocation as an opportunity to shed jobs.*
3 cast or give off (light): *the full moon shed a watery light on the scene.*
4 Brit. accidentally allow (something) to fall off or spill: *a lorry shed its load of steel bars.*
5 eliminate part of (an electrical power load) by disconnecting circuits.
– PHRASES **shed (someone's) blood** be injured or killed (or kill or injure someone). **shed light on** see **LIGHT**[1]. **shed tears** weep; cry.
– ORIGIN Old English *sc(e)ādan* 'separate out (one selected group), divide', also 'scatter', of Germanic origin; related to Dutch and German *scheiden*. Compare with **SHEATH**.

she'd ▸ **contraction** she had; she would.

shedder ▸ **noun 1** a person or thing that sheds something.
2 a female salmon after spawning.

she-devil ▸ **noun** a malicious or spiteful woman.

shedhand ▸ **noun** Austral./NZ a labourer employed to do unskilled work in a shearing shed.

shedload ▸ **noun** Brit. informal a large amount or number.
– ORIGIN 1990s: from **SHED**[1] + **LOAD**; perhaps euphemistic after **SHITLOAD**.

Sheela-na-gig /ˌʃiːlənəˈɡɪɡ/ ▸ **noun** a medieval stone figure of a naked female with the legs wide apart and the hands emphasizing the genitals, found in churches in Britain and Ireland.
– ORIGIN from Irish *Síle na gcíoch* 'Julia of the breasts'.

sheen ▸ **noun** [in sing.] a soft lustre on a surface: *black crushed velvet with a slight sheen* | figurative *he seemed to shine with that unmistakable showbiz sheen.*
▸ **verb** literary shine or cause to shine softly: [with obj.] *men entered with rain sheening their steel helms* | [no obj.] *her black hair sheened in the sun.*
– ORIGIN early 17th cent.: from obsolete *sheen* 'beautiful, resplendent'; apparently related to the verb **SHINE**.

sheeny[1] ▸ **adjective** (**sheenier, sheeniest**) having a sheen; lustrous or shining: *a woman with sheeny hair.*

sheeny[2] ▸ **noun** (pl. **sheenies**) N. Amer. informal, offensive a Jewish person.
– ORIGIN early 19th cent.: origin unknown.

sheep ▸ **noun** (pl. **same**) **1** a domesticated ruminant mammal with a thick woolly coat and (typically only in the male) curving horns. It is kept in flocks for its wool or meat, and is proverbial for its tendency to follow others in the flock. ● *Ovis aries*, family Bovidae, descended from the wild mouflon.
■ a wild mammal related to this, such as the argali, bighorn, bharal, and urial.
2 used with reference to people who are too easily influenced or led: *party members should not follow their leader like sheep.*
3 a person regarded as a protected follower of God. [with biblical allusion to Luke 15:6.] ■ a member of a minister's congregation.
– PHRASES **count sheep** count imaginary sheep jumping over a fence one by one in an attempt to send oneself to sleep. **make sheep's eyes at someone** look at someone in a foolishly amorous way.
– DERIVATIVES **sheeplike** adjective.
– ORIGIN Old English *scēp, scǣp, scēap*, of West Germanic origin; related to Dutch *schaap* and German *Schaf*.

sheep bot ▸ **noun** see **NOSTRIL FLY**.

sheep dip ▸ **noun** [mass noun] a liquid preparation for cleansing sheep of parasites or preserving their wool. ■ [count noun] a place where sheep are dipped in such a preparation.

sheepdog ▸ **noun** a dog trained to guard and herd sheep. ■ a dog of a breed suitable for this.

sheepdog trials ▸ **plural noun** a public competitive display of the skills of sheepdogs.

sheepfold ▸ **noun** a sheep pen.

sheepish ▸ **adjective** showing or feeling embarrassment from shame or a lack of self-confidence: *a sheepish grin.*
– DERIVATIVES **sheepishly** adverb, **sheepishness** noun.

sheep laurel ▸ **noun** a North American kalmia which is sometimes cultivated as an ornamental. ● *Kalmia angustifolia*, family Ericaceae.

sheeple /ˈʃiːp(ə)l/ ▸ **plural noun** derogatory people compared to sheep in being docile, foolish, or easily led: *by the time the sheeple wake up and try to change things, it will be too late.*
– ORIGIN 1940s: blend of **SHEEP** and **PEOPLE**.

sheep run ▸ **noun** (especially in Australia) an extensive tract of land on which sheep are pastured.

sheep's-bit ▸ **noun** a blue-flowered European plant which resembles a scabious. ● *Jasione montana*, family Campanulaceae.

sheep scab ▸ **noun** [mass noun] an intensely itching skin disease of sheep caused by a parasitic mite. ● The mite is *Psoroptes communis*, family Psoroptidae.

sheepshank ▸ **noun** a kind of knot used to shorten a rope temporarily, made by taking two bights of rope and securing them to the standing rope with two half hitches.

sheepshead ▸ **noun** (pl. **same**) any of a number of boldly marked edible game fishes which live in warm American waters. ● a black-and-silver-striped porgy of Atlantic coastal and brackish waters (*Archosargus probatocephalus*, family Sparidae). ● (**California sheepshead**) a black and red wrasse of Californian coastal waters (*Semicossyphus pulcher*, family Labridae).

sheepskin ▸ **noun 1** a sheep's skin with the wool on, especially when made into a garment or rug: [as modifier] *a sheepskin coat.* ■ [mass noun] leather from a sheep's skin used in bookbinding.
2 (in South Africa) a party with country dancing. [originally held to celebrate sheep shearing.]

sheep tick ▸ **noun** a large tick that infests many mammals, including humans, and frequently transmits diseases. ● *Ixodes ricinus*, family Ixodidae.

sheep walk ▸ **noun** Brit. a tract of land on which sheep are pastured.

sheer[1] ▸ **adjective 1** [attrib.] nothing other than; unmitigated (used for emphasis): *she giggled with sheer delight* | *it's been sheer hard work.*
2 (especially of a cliff or wall) perpendicular or nearly so: *the sheer ice walls.*
3 (of a fabric) very thin; diaphanous: *sheer white silk chiffon.*
▸ **adverb 1** perpendicularly: *the ridge fell sheer, in steep crags.*
2 archaic completely; right: *she went sheer forward when the door was open.*
▸ **noun** a very fine or diaphanous fabric or article.
– DERIVATIVES **sheerly** adverb, **sheerness** noun.
– ORIGIN Middle English (in the sense 'exempt, cleared'): probably an alteration of dialect *shire* 'pure, clear', from the Germanic base of the verb **SHINE**. In the mid 16th cent. the word was used to describe clear, pure water, and also in sense 3 of the adjective.

sheer[2] ▸ **verb** [no obj., with adverbial] (typically of a boat) swerve or change course quickly: *the boat sheered off to beach further up the coast.* ■ avoid or move away from an unpleasant topic: *her mind **sheered away** from images she didn't want to dwell on.*
▸ **noun** a sudden deviation from a course, especially by a boat.
– ORIGIN early 17th cent.: perhaps from Middle Low German *scheren* 'to shear'.

> **USAGE** The two verbs **sheer** and **shear** have a similar origin but do not have identical meanings. **Sheer**, the less common verb, means 'swerve or change course quickly', as in *the boat **sheers off** the bank.* **Shear**, on the other hand, usually means 'cut the wool off a sheep' and can also mean 'break off', as in *the pins broke and the wing part **sheared off**.*

sheer[3] ▸ **noun** [mass noun] the upward slope of a ship's lines towards the bow and stern.
– ORIGIN late 17th cent.: probably from the noun **SHEAR**.

sheerlegs ▸ **plural noun** [treated as sing.] a hoisting apparatus made from poles joined at or near the top and separated at the bottom, used for masting ships, installing engines, and hauling heavy objects.

sheesh /ʃiːʃ/ ▸ **exclamation** used to express disbelief or exasperation.
– ORIGIN 1950s: probably an alteration of **JEEZ**.

sheet[1] ▸ **noun 1** a large rectangular piece of cotton or other fabric, used on a bed to cover the mattress and as a layer beneath blankets when these are used.
2 a rectangular piece of paper, especially one of a standard size produced commercially and used for writing and printing on: *a **sheet of** unmarked **paper**.* ■ a quantity of text or other information contained on such a piece of paper: *he produced yet another sheet of figures.* ■ Printing a flat piece of paper as opposed to a reel of continuous paper, the bound pages of a book, or a folded map. ■ all the postage stamps printed on one piece of paper: *a sheet of 1p stamps.* ■ a map, especially one part of a series covering a larger area.
3 a broad flat piece of material such as metal or glass: *the small pipe has been formed from a flat sheet of bronze.* ■ an extensive unbroken surface area of something: *Loch Affric is a lovely **sheet of** water among trees* | [as modifier] *sheet ice.* ■ a broad moving mass of flames or water: *the rain was still falling in sheets.*
▸ **verb 1** [with obj.] cover with or wrap in a sheet of cloth: *lorry drivers don't sheet their loads.*
2 [no obj., with adverbial of direction] (of rain) fall in large quantities: *rain sheeted down.*
– PHRASES **(as) white as a sheet** (of a person) very pale, especially from shock.

S

– ORIGIN Old English *scēte, scīete*, of Germanic origin; related to the verb SHOOT in its primary sense 'to project'.

sheet[2] Nautical ▶ **noun 1** a rope attached to the lower corner of a sail for securing or extending the sail or for altering its direction.
2 (**sheets**) the space at the bow or stern of an open boat.
▶ **verb** [with obj.] (**sheet something in/out**) make a sail more or less taut. ■ (**sheet something home**) extend a sail by tightening the sheets so that the sail is set as flat as possible.
– PHRASES **two** (or **three**) **sheets to the wind** informal drunk.
– ORIGIN Old English *scēata* 'lower corner of a sail', of Germanic origin; related to Old Norse *skauti* 'kerchief' (see also SHEET[1]).

sheet anchor ▶ **noun 1** an additional anchor for use in emergencies.
2 a very dependable person or thing.
– ORIGIN late 15th cent.: perhaps related to obsolete *shot*, denoting two cables spliced together, later influenced by SHEET[2].

sheet bend ▶ **noun** a method of temporarily fastening one rope through the loop of another.

sheeted ▶ **adjective 1** covered with or enveloped in a sheet of cloth: *the sheeted body*.
2 Geology (of rock) fissured or divided into layers, especially by faulting.

sheet feeder ▶ **noun** a device for feeding paper into a computer printer a sheet at a time.

sheeting ▶ **noun** [mass noun] material formed into or used as a sheet: *a window covered with plastic sheeting*.

sheetlet ▶ **noun** a small unseparated sheet of postage stamps.

sheet lightning ▶ **noun** [mass noun] lightning with its brightness diffused by reflection within clouds.

sheet metal ▶ **noun** [mass noun] metal formed into thin sheets, typically by rolling or hammering.

sheet music ▶ **noun** [mass noun] printed music, as opposed to performed or recorded music. ■ music published in single or interleaved sheets, not bound.

Sheetrock ▶ **noun** [mass noun] trademark, chiefly US a plasterboard made of gypsum layered between sheets of heavy paper.

Sheffield an industrial city in South Yorkshire, northern England; pop. 417,700 (est. 2009). Sheffield is famous for the manufacture of cutlery and silverware and for the production of steel.

Sheffield plate ▶ **noun** [mass noun] copper plated with silver by rolling and edging with silver film and ribbon, especially as produced in Sheffield between 1760 and 1840.

sheikh /ʃeɪk, ʃiːk/ (also **shaikh, shaykh,** or **sheik**) ▶ **noun 1** an Arab leader, in particular the chief or head of an Arab tribe, family, or village.
2 a leader in a Muslim community or organization.
– DERIVATIVES **sheikhdom** noun.
– ORIGIN late 16th cent.: based on Arabic *šayḵ* 'old man, sheikh', from *šāḵa* 'be or grow old'.

S

sheila ▶ **noun** Austral./NZ informal a girl or woman.
– ORIGIN mid 19th cent. (originally as *shaler*): of unknown origin, later assimilated to the given name *Sheila*.

sheitel /ˈʃeɪt(ə)l/ ▶ **noun** (among orthodox Ashkenazic Jews) a wig worn by a married woman.
– ORIGIN late 19th cent.: from Yiddish *sheytl*, from a Germanic base meaning 'crown of the head'.

shekel /ˈʃɛk(ə)l/ ▶ **noun** the basic monetary unit of modern Israel, equal to 100 agorot. ■ historical a silver coin and unit of weight used in ancient Israel and the Middle East. ■ (**shekels**) informal money; wealth.
– ORIGIN from Hebrew *šeqel*, from *šāqal* 'weigh'.

Shekinah /ʃɪˈkʌɪnə/ (also **Shekhinah**) ▶ **noun** [mass noun] (in Jewish and Christian theology) the glory of the divine presence, conventionally represented as light or interpreted symbolically (in Kabbalism as a divine feminine aspect).
– ORIGIN mid 17th cent.: from late Hebrew, from *šākan* 'dwell, rest'.

shelduck /ˈʃɛldʌk/ (male also **sheldrake** /-dreɪk/) ▶ **noun** (pl. **same** or **shelducks**) a large goose-like Old World duck with brightly coloured plumage, typically showing black and white wings in flight.
● Genus *Tadorna*, family Anatidae: several species, in particular *T. tadorna* of Eurasian coasts, with white, greenish-black, and chestnut plumage.
– ORIGIN Middle English (as *sheldrake*): probably from dialect *sheld* 'pied' (related to Middle Dutch *schillede* 'variegated') + DUCK[1]. The form *shelduck* dates from the early 18th century.

shelf[1] ▶ **noun** (pl. **shelves**) **1** a flat length of wood or rigid material, attached to a wall or forming part of a piece of furniture, that provides a surface for the storage or display of objects.
2 a ledge of rock or protruding strip of land. ■ a submarine bank, or a part of the continental shelf.
– PHRASES **off the shelf** not designed or made to order but taken from existing stock or supplies: *off-the-shelf software packages*. **on the shelf 1** informal no longer useful or desirable: *an injury which has kept him on the shelf*. **2** (especially of a woman) past an age when one might expect to have the opportunity to marry.
– DERIVATIVES **shelf-ful** noun (pl. **shelf-fuls**), **shelf-like** adjective.
– ORIGIN Middle English: from Middle Low German *schelf*; related to Old English *scylfe* 'partition', *scylf* 'crag'.

shelf[2] Austral./NZ informal ▶ **noun** (pl. **shelfs**) an informer.
▶ **verb** [with obj.] inform on (someone).
– ORIGIN 1930s (as a noun): probably from the phrase *on the shelf* 'out of the way'.

shelf life ▶ **noun** the length of time for which an item remains usable, fit for consumption, or saleable.

shelf mark ▶ **noun** a notation on a book showing its place in a library.

shelf room ▶ **noun** [mass noun] the amount of available space on a shelf.

shell ▶ **noun 1** the hard protective outer case of a mollusc or crustacean: *cowrie shells* | [mass noun] *the technique of carving shell*. ■ the thin outer covering of an animal's egg, which is hard and fragile in that of a bird but leathery in that of a reptile. ■ the outer case of a nut kernel or seed. ■ the carapace of a tortoise, turtle, or terrapin. ■ the wing cases of a beetle. ■ the integument of an insect pupa or chrysalis. ■ (**one's shell**) used with reference to a state of shyness or introversion: *she'll soon **come out of her shell** with the right encouragement*.
2 an explosive artillery projectile or bomb: *the sound of the shell passing over, followed by the explosion* | [as modifier] *shell holes*. ■ a hollow metal or paper case used as a container for fireworks, explosives, or cartridges. ■ N. Amer. a cartridge.
3 something resembling or likened to a shell because of its shape or its function as an outer case: *pasta shells* | *baked pastry shells filled with cheese*. ■ the walls of an unfinished or gutted building or other structure: *the hotel was a shell, the roof having collapsed completely*. ■ an outer form without substance: *he was a shell of the man he had been previously*.
4 the metal framework of a vehicle body. ■ a light racing boat. ■ an inner or roughly made coffin. ■ the hand guard of a sword.
5 Physics each of a set of orbitals around the nucleus of an atom, occupied or able to be occupied by electrons of similar energies.
6 Computing short for SHELL PROGRAM.
▶ **verb** [with obj.] **1** bombard with shells: *several villages north of the security zone were shelled*. ■ Baseball score heavily against (an opposing pitcher or team).
2 remove the shell or pod from (a nut or seed): *they were shelling peas* | (as adj. **shelled**) *shelled Brazil nuts*.
– PHRASAL VERBS **shell something out** (also **shell out**) informal pay (a specified amount of money, especially one regarded as excessive): *he has had to shell out £500 a week hiring a bodyguard* | *she ended up **shelling out** for two rooms*.
– DERIVATIVES **shelled** adjective, **shell-less** adjective, **shelly** adjective.
– ORIGIN Old English *scell* (noun), of Germanic origin; related to Dutch *schel* 'scale, shell', also to SCALE[1]. The verb dates from the mid 16th cent. in sense 2 of the verb.

she'll ▶ **contraction** she shall; she will.

shellac /ʃəˈlak/ ▶ **noun** [mass noun] lac resin melted into thin flakes, used for making varnish.
▶ **verb** (**shellacks, shellacking, shellacked**) [with obj.]
1 [often as adj.] varnish (something) with shellac.
2 N. Amer. informal defeat or beat (someone) decisively: *they were shellacked in the 1982 election*.
– ORIGIN mid 17th cent.: from SHELL + LAC[1], translating French *laque en écailles* 'lac in thin plates'.

shellback ▶ **noun** N. Amer. informal an old or experienced sailor, especially one who has crossed the equator.

shell bit ▶ **noun** a gouge-shaped boring bit.

shell company ▶ **noun** a non-trading company used as a vehicle for various financial manoeuvres or kept dormant for future use in some other capacity.

shell egg ▶ **noun** an egg bought or sold in its natural state in the shell.

Shelley[1], Mary (Wollstonecraft) (1797–1851), English writer, daughter of William Godwin and Mary Wollstonecraft. She eloped with Percy Bysshe Shelley in 1814 and married him in 1816. She is chiefly remembered as the author of the Gothic novel *Frankenstein, or the Modern Prometheus* (1818).

Shelley[2], Percy Bysshe (1792–1822), English poet. He was a leading figure of the romantic movement with radical political views. Notable works include *Queen Mab* (political poems, 1813), *Prometheus Unbound* (lyrical drama, 1820), *The Defence of Poetry* (essay, 1821), and *Adonais* (1821), an elegy on the death of Keats.

shellfire ▶ **noun** [mass noun] bombardment by shells.

shellfish ▶ **noun** (pl. **same**) an aquatic shelled mollusc (e.g. an oyster or cockle) or a crustacean (e.g. a crab or shrimp), especially one that is edible. ■ [mass noun] such molluscs or crustaceans as food.

shell game ▶ **noun** N. Amer. another term for THIMBLE-RIG. ■ a deceptive and evasive action or ploy, especially a political one: *he **played a shell game**, misleading the tax department about his real worth*.

shell heap ▶ **noun** Archaeology a mound of domestic waste consisting mainly of shells, common at prehistoric sites.

shell jacket ▶ **noun 1** an army officer's tight-fitting undress jacket reaching to the waist.
2 the jacket of a shell suit.

shell-like ▶ **adjective** resembling a shell in shape or appearance: *a creature with a shell-like carapace*.
▶ **noun** Brit. informal a person's ear: *Prentice had a word in somebody's shell-like*.

shell lime ▶ **noun** [mass noun] fine-quality lime produced by roasting seashells.

shell money ▶ **noun** [mass noun] chiefly historical shells used as a medium of exchange, especially wampum.

shell mound ▶ **noun** another term for SHELL HEAP.

shell pink ▶ **noun** [mass noun] a delicate pale pink.

shell program ▶ **noun** Computing a program which provides an interface between the user and the operating system.

shell shock ▶ **noun** [mass noun] psychological disturbance caused by prolonged exposure to active warfare, especially being under bombardment. Also called COMBAT FATIGUE.
– ORIGIN First World War: with reference to exposure to shellfire.

shell-shocked ▶ **adjective** suffering from shell shock. ■ shocked or confused because of a sudden alarming experience: *he told shell-shocked investors that the company needed still more money to survive the year*.

shell suit ▶ **noun** Brit. a casual outfit consisting of a loose jacket and trousers with elasticated waist, having a soft lining and a shiny polyester outer shell.

shell top ▶ **noun** a short sleeveless top, typically having button fastenings down the back and a simple shape with a high neckline.

shellwork ▶ **noun** [mass noun] ornamentation consisting of shells cemented on to a surface.

Shelta /ˈʃɛltə/ ▶ **noun** [mass noun] an ancient secret language used by Irish and Welsh Travellers and Gypsies, and based largely on altered Irish or Gaelic words.
– ORIGIN late 19th cent.: of unknown origin.

shelter ▶ **noun 1** a place giving temporary protection from bad weather or danger. ■ a place providing food and accommodation for the homeless. ■ an animal sanctuary.
2 [mass noun] a shielded or safe condition; protection: *he hung back in the shelter of a rock* | *you're welcome to **take shelter** from the storm*.
▶ **verb** [with obj.] protect or shield from something harmful, especially bad weather: *the hut sheltered him from the cold wind*. ■ [no obj., with adverbial of place] find refuge or take cover from bad weather or danger: *people were sheltering under store canopies and trees*. ■ prevent (someone) from having to do or face something difficult or unpleasant: *we are sheltered from the awfulness of reality*. ■ protect (income) from taxation: *only your rental income can be sheltered*.
– DERIVATIVES **shelterer** noun, **shelterless** adjective.

– ORIGIN late 16th cent.: perhaps an alteration of *sheld*, an old spelling of SHIELD, + -URE.

shelter belt ▸ noun a line of trees or shrubs planted to protect an area, especially a field of crops, from fierce weather.

sheltered ▸ adjective (of a place) protected from bad weather: *the plants need a shady, sheltered spot in the garden.* ■ protected from difficulties or unpleasant realities: *I was a mathematics don at Cambridge living a rather sheltered life* | *a sheltered childhood.*

sheltered housing (also **sheltered accommodation**) ▸ noun [mass noun] Brit. accommodation for elderly or disabled people consisting of private independent units with some shared facilities and a warden.

shelterwood ▸ noun [mass noun] mature trees left standing to provide shelter in which saplings can grow.

sheltie (also **shelty**) ▸ noun (pl. **shelties**) a Shetland pony or sheepdog.
– ORIGIN early 17th cent.: probably representing an Orkney pronunciation of Old Norse *Hjalti* 'Shetlander'.

shelve[1] ▸ verb [with obj.] **1** place or arrange (items, especially books) on a shelf.
2 decide not to proceed with (a project or plan), either temporarily or permanently: *plans to reopen the school have been shelved.*
3 fit with shelves: *one whole long wall was shelved.*
– DERIVATIVES **shelver** noun.
– ORIGIN late 16th cent. (in the sense 'project like a shelf' (Shakespearean usage)): from *shelves*, plural of SHELF[1].

shelve[2] ▸ verb [no obj., with adverbial] (of ground) slope downwards in a specified manner or direction: *the ground shelved gently down to the water.*
– ORIGIN late Middle English: origin uncertain; perhaps from SHELF[1].

shelves plural form of SHELF[1].

shelving ▸ noun [mass noun] **1** shelves collectively: *a lack of shelving and cupboards.*
2 the action of shelving something.

Shem /ʃɛm/ (in the Bible) a son of Noah (Gen. 10:21), traditional ancestor of the Semites.

Shema /ʃɛˈmɑː/ a Hebrew text consisting of three passages from the Pentateuch (Deuteronomy 6:4, 11:13–21; Numbers 15:37–41) and beginning 'Hear O Israel, the Lord our God is one Lord'. It forms an important part of Jewish evening and morning prayer and is used as a Jewish confession of faith.
– ORIGIN Hebrew, literally 'hear', the first word of Deut. 6:4.

she-male ▸ noun informal a transvestite or transsexual.

shemozzle /ʃɪˈmɒz(ə)l/ (also **schemozzle**) ▸ noun informal a state of chaos and confusion; a muddle.
– ORIGIN late 19th cent.: Yiddish, suggested by late Hebrew *šel-lō'-mazzāl* 'of no luck'.

shen /ʃɛn/ ▸ noun (pl. **same**) (in Chinese thought) the spiritual element of a person's psyche.
– ORIGIN from Chinese *shén*.

Shenandoah /ˌʃɛnənˈdəʊə/ a river of Virginia. Rising in two headstreams, one on each side of the Blue Ridge Mountains, it flows some 240 km (150 miles) northwards to join the Potomac at Harpers Ferry.

Shenandoah National Park a national park in the Blue Ridge Mountains of northern Virginia, situated to the south-east of the Shenandoah River. It was established in 1935.

shenanigans /ʃɪˈnanɪɡ(ə)nz/ ▸ plural noun informal secret or dishonest activity or manoeuvring: *the chairman was accused of financial shenanigans.* ■ silly or high-spirited behaviour; mischief.
– ORIGIN mid 19th cent.: of unknown origin.

sheng /ʃʌŋ/ ▸ noun (pl. **same**) a Chinese form of mouth organ with about seventeen reed pipes of bamboo set in a rounded windchest.
– ORIGIN late 18th cent.: from Chinese *shēng*.

Shensi /ʃɛnˈsiː/ variant of SHAANXI.

Shenyang /ʃɛnˈjaŋ/ a city in NE China; pop. 4,101,200 (est. 2006). An important Manchurian city between the 17th and early 20th centuries, it is now the capital of the province of Liaoning. Former name MUKDEN.

Shenzhen /ʃɛnˈʒɛn/ an industrial city in southern China, just north of Hong Kong; pop. 1,819,300 (est. 2006).

she-oak ▸ noun another term for CASUARINA.

Sheol /ˈʃiːəʊl, ˈʃiːɒl/ the Hebrew underworld, abode of the dead.
– ORIGIN Hebrew.

shepherd ▸ noun a person who tends and rears sheep. ■ a member of the clergy who provides spiritual care and guidance for a congregation.
▸ verb [with obj.] **1** (usu. as noun **shepherding**) tend (sheep) as a shepherd. ■ give guidance to (someone), especially on spiritual matters.
2 [with obj. and adverbial of direction] guide or direct in a particular direction: *I shepherded them through the door.*
– ORIGIN Old English *scēaphierde*, from SHEEP + obsolete *herd* 'herdsman'.

shepherd dog ▸ noun a sheepdog.

shepherdess /ˈʃɛpədɪs, ˌʃɛpəˈdɛs/ ▸ noun a female shepherd. ■ an idealized or romanticized rustic young woman in pastoral literature.

shepherd satellite (also **shepherd moon**) ▸ noun Astronomy a small moon orbiting close to a planetary ring, especially of Saturn, and whose gravitational field confines the ring within a narrow band.

shepherd's crook ▸ noun a staff with a hook at one end used by shepherds.

shepherd's needle ▸ noun a white-flowered Eurasian plant of the parsley family, with long needle-shaped fruit. ● *Scandix pecten-veneris*, family Umbelliferae.

shepherd's pie ▸ noun Brit. a dish of minced meat under a layer of mashed potato.

shepherd's plaid ▸ noun a small black-and-white check pattern. ■ [mass noun] woollen cloth with this pattern.

shepherd's purse ▸ noun a widely distributed white-flowered weed of the cabbage family, with triangular or heart-shaped seed pods. ● *Capsella bursa-pastoris*, family Cruciferae.

sher /ʃɛː/ ▸ noun Indian a lion or tiger. ■ a courageous person.
– ORIGIN Urdu *śer* 'lion, tiger'.

sherardize /ˈʃɛrədʌɪz/ (also **sherardise**) ▸ verb [with obj.] coat (iron or steel) with zinc by heating it in contact with zinc dust.
– ORIGIN early 20th cent.: from the name of *Sherard* Cowper-Coles (1867–1936), English inventor, + -IZE.

Sheraton /ˈʃɛrət(ə)n/ ▸ adjective (of furniture) designed, made by, or in the simple, delicate, and graceful style of the English furniture-maker Thomas Sheraton (1751–1806).

sherbet ▸ noun **1** [mass noun] Brit. a flavoured sweet effervescent powder eaten alone or made into a drink.
2 (especially in Arab countries) a cooling drink of sweet diluted fruit juices.
3 N. Amer. water ice; sorbet.
4 Austral. humorous beer.
– ORIGIN early 17th cent.: from Turkish *şerbet*, Persian *šerbet*, from Arabic *šarba* 'drink', from *šariba* 'to drink'. Compare with SYRUP.

> **USAGE** The tendency to insert an **r** into the second syllable of **sherbet** is common: the misspelling **sherbert** accounts for around a quarter of the citations for the word in the Oxford English Corpus.

sherd /ʃəːd/ ▸ noun another term for POTSHERD.

shereef (also **sherif**) ▸ noun variant spelling of SHARIF.

Sheridan /ˈʃɛrɪd(ə)n/, Richard Brinsley (1751–1816), Irish dramatist and Whig politician. His plays are comedies of manners; they include *The Rivals* (1775) and *The School for Scandal* (1777). In 1780 he entered Parliament, becoming a celebrated orator and holding senior government posts.

sheriff ▸ noun **1** (also **high sheriff**) (in England and Wales) the chief executive officer of the Crown in a county, having various administrative and judicial functions. ■ an honorary officer elected annually in some English towns.
2 (in Scotland) a judge.
3 US an elected officer in a county, responsible for keeping the peace.
4 Austral. an officer of the Supreme Court who enforces judgements and the execution of writs.
– DERIVATIVES **sheriffdom** noun.
– ORIGIN Old English *scīrgerēfa* (see SHIRE, REEVE[1]).

sheriff clerk ▸ noun (in Scotland) the clerk of a sheriff's court.

sheriff court ▸ noun (in Scotland) a judicial court for civil cases, equivalent to a county court.

sheriff-depute ▸ noun (pl. **sheriffs-deputes**) historical (in Scotland) the chief judge of a county or district.

sheriff principal ▸ noun (pl. **sheriffs principal**) (in Scotland) each of six chief judges.

Sherlock ▸ noun informal a person who investigates mysteries or shows great perceptiveness: *it doesn't take a Sherlock to figure out that she's lying to me.*
– DERIVATIVES **Sherlockian** noun & adjective.
– ORIGIN early 20th cent.: from *Sherlock* Holmes (see HOLMES[2]).

Sherman, William Tecumseh (1820–91), American general. In 1864 in the American Civil War he became chief Union commander in the west. He set out with 60,000 men on a march through Georgia, during which he crushed Confederate forces and broke civilian morale by his policy of deliberate destruction of the territory he passed through.

Sherpa /ˈʃəːpə/ ▸ noun (pl. **same** or **Sherpas**) a member of a Himalayan people living on the borders of Nepal and Tibet, renowned for their skill in mountaineering. ■ informal a civil servant or diplomat who undertakes preparatory work prior to a summit conference.
– ORIGIN from Tibetan *sharpa* 'inhabitant of an eastern country'.

sherry ▸ noun (pl. **sherries**) [mass noun] a fortified wine originally and mainly from southern Spain.
– DERIVATIVES **sherried** adjective.
– ORIGIN late 16th cent.: alteration of archaic *sherris*, interpreted as plural, from Spanish (*vino de*) *Xeres* 'Xeres (wine)' (Xeres being the former name of JEREZ).

's-Hertogenbosch /ˌs(h)ɛːtəʊxənˈbɒs/ a city in the southern Netherlands, the capital of North Brabant; pop. 136,481 (2008).

sherwani /ʃəˈwɑːni/ ▸ noun (pl. **sherwanis**) a knee-length coat buttoning to the neck, worn by men from South Asia.
– ORIGIN from Urdu and Persian *širwānī* 'from Shirvan' (referring to a town in NE Persia).

she's ▸ contraction she is; she has.

Shetland Islands /ˈʃɛtlənd/ (also **Shetland** or **the Shetlands**) a group of about 100 islands off the north coast of Scotland, north-east of the Orkneys, constituting a council area of Scotland; pop. 21,800 (est. 2009); chief town, Lerwick. Together with the Orkney Islands the Shetland Islands became a part of Scotland in 1472, having previously been ruled by Norway and Denmark.
– DERIVATIVES **Shetlander** noun.

Shetland lace ▸ noun [mass noun] a black or white bobbin lace made from Shetland wool. ■ knitwear made using openwork stitches to give a lacy effect.

Shetland pony ▸ noun a pony of a small hardy rough-coated breed.

Shetland sheep ▸ noun a sheep of a hardy short-tailed breed native to Shetland and bred especially for its fine wool.

Shetland sheepdog ▸ noun a small dog of a collie-like breed.

Shetland wool ▸ noun [mass noun] a type of fine loosely twisted wool from Shetland sheep.

Shevat /ˈʃiːvat/ ▸ noun variant spelling of SEBAT.

shew /ʃəʊ/ ▸ verb old-fashioned spelling of SHOW.

shewbread /ˈʃəʊbrɛd/ ▸ noun [mass noun] twelve loaves placed every Sabbath in the Jewish Temple and eaten by the priests at the end of the week.
– ORIGIN mid 16th cent.: suggested by German *Schaubrot*, representing Hebrew *leḥem pānīm*, literally 'bread of the face (of God)'.

shh (also **sh**) ▸ exclamation used to call for silence: *'Shh! Keep your voice down!'.*
– ORIGIN mid 19th cent.: variant of HUSH.

Shia /ˈʃɪə/ (also **Shi'a**) ▸ noun (pl. **same** or **Shias**) [mass noun] one of the two main branches of Islam, followed by about a tenth of Muslims, especially in Iran, that rejects the first three Sunni caliphs and regards Ali, the fourth caliph, as Muhammad's first true successor. Compare with SUNNI. ■ [count noun] a Muslim who adheres to this branch of Islam.
– ORIGIN from Arabic *šī'a* 'party (of Ali)'.

shiatsu /ʃɪˈatsuː/ ▸ noun [mass noun] a form of therapy of Japanese origin based on the same principles as acupuncture, in which pressure is applied to certain points on the body using the hands.
– ORIGIN Japanese, literally 'finger pressure'.

shibboleth /ˈʃɪbəlɛθ/ ▸ noun a custom, principle, or belief distinguishing a particular class or group of people, especially a long-standing one regarded as

S

outmoded or no longer important: *liberal shibboleths about education.*
– ORIGIN mid 17th cent.: from Hebrew *šibbōleṯ* 'ear of corn', used as a test of nationality by its difficult pronunciation (Judg. 12:6).

shicer /ˈʃʌɪsə/ ▸ **noun** Austral./NZ informal, dated a worthless thing or person, especially a swindler. ▪ Mining an unproductive claim or mine.
– ORIGIN mid 19th cent.: from German *Scheisser* 'contemptible person'.

shicker /ˈʃɪkə/ (also **shikker**) US & Austral./NZ informal
▸ **adjective** (also **shickered**) [predic.] drunk: *they got shickered, talked cars and deals.*
▸ **noun** a drunk.
– ORIGIN late 19th cent.: from Yiddish *shiker*, from Hebrew *šikkōr*, from *šākar* 'be drunk'.

shidduch /ˈʃɪdəx/ ▸ **noun** (pl. **shidduchim**) a Jewish arranged marriage.
– ORIGIN Yiddish, from Hebrew *šiddūḵ* 'negotiation (of a marriage)'.

shied past and past participle of SHY².

shield ▸ **noun 1** a broad piece of metal or another suitable material, held by straps or a handle attached on one side, used as a protection against blows or missiles. ▪ a sporting trophy shaped like a shield, consisting of an engraved metal plate mounted on a piece of wood. ▪ a US police officer's badge. ▪ Heraldry a stylized representation of a shield used for displaying a coat of arms.
2 a person or thing providing protection: *a coating of grease provides a shield against abrasive dirt.* ▪ a protective plate or screen on machinery or equipment. ▪ a device or material that prevents or reduces the emission of light or other radiation. ▪ a hard flat or convex part of an animal, especially a shell.
3 Geology a large rigid area of the earth's crust, typically of Precambrian rock, which has been unaffected by later orogenic episodes, e.g. the Canadian Shield.
▸ **verb** [with obj.] protect from a danger, risk, or unpleasant experience: *he pulled the cap lower to shield his eyes from the glare | these people have been completely shielded from economic forces.* ▪ prevent from being seen: *the rocks she sat behind shielded her from the lodge.* ▪ enclose or screen (a piece of machinery) to protect the user. ▪ prevent or reduce the escape of sound, light, or other radiation from (something): *uranium shutters shield the cobalt radioactive source.*
– DERIVATIVES **shieldless** adjective.
– ORIGIN Old English *scild* (noun), *scildan* (verb), of Germanic origin; related to Dutch *schild* and German *Schild*, from a base meaning 'divide, separate'.

shield bug ▸ **noun** a broad shield-shaped bug which is typically brightly coloured or boldly marked. It emits a foul smell when handled or molested. Also called STINK BUG. ● Pentatomidae and other families, suborder Heteroptera.

shield fern ▸ **noun** any of a number of ferns that have circular shield-like scales protecting the spore cases: ● a European fern of damp woodland (genus *Polystichum*, family Dryopteridaceae). ● N. Amer. an evergreen fern (genus *Thelypteris*, family Thelypteridaceae). ● Austral./NZ a fern of forested country (family Aspidiaceae).

S

shield volcano ▸ **noun** Geology a broad domed volcano with gently sloping sides, characteristic of the eruption of fluid, basaltic lava.

shieling /ˈʃiːlɪŋ/ (also **shealing**) ▸ **noun** Scottish a roughly constructed hut used while pasturing animals. ▪ an area of pasture.
– ORIGIN mid 16th cent.: from Scots *shiel* 'hut' (of unknown origin) + -ING¹.

shift /ʃɪft/ ▸ **verb 1** move or cause to move from one place to another, especially over a small distance: [with obj.] *a team from the power company came to shift the cables away from the house* | [no obj.] *the roof cracked and shifted.* ▪ [no obj.] change the position of one's body, especially because one is nervous or uncomfortable: *he shifted a little in his chair.* ▪ [with obj.] change the emphasis, direction, or focus of: *she's shifting the blame on to me.* ▪ [no obj.] change in emphasis, direction, or focus: *the wind had shifted to the east | the balance of power shifted abruptly.* ▪ [no obj.] Brit. informal move quickly: *you'll have time for a bite if you shift.* ▪ (in imperative **shift oneself**) Brit. informal move from a place or rouse oneself from a state of inactivity: *shift yourself, Ruby, do something useful and get the plates.* ▪ [with obj.] Computing move (data) to the right or left in a register: *the partial remainder is shifted left.* ▪ [with obj.] Brit. informal remove (a stain). ▪ [with obj.] informal sell (something): *a lot of high-priced product you simply don't know how to shift.* ▪ [with obj.] Brit. informal eat or drink (something) hastily or in large amounts.
2 [no obj.] chiefly N. Amer. change gear in a vehicle: *she shifted down to fourth.*
3 [no obj.] archaic be evasive or indirect: *they know not how to shift and rob as the old ones do.*
▸ **noun 1** a slight change in position, direction, or tendency: *a shift in public opinion.* ▪ [mass noun] Astronomy the displacement of spectral lines. See also RED SHIFT. ▪ (also **shift key**) a key on a typewriter or computer keyboard used to switch between two sets of characters or functions, principally between lower- and upper-case letters. ▪ short for SOUND SHIFT. ▪ N. Amer. the gear lever or gear-changing mechanism in a vehicle. ▪ [mass noun] Building the positioning of successive rows of bricks so that their ends do not coincide. ▪ Computing a movement of the digits of a word in a register one or more places to left or right, equivalent to multiplying or dividing the corresponding number by a power of whatever number is the base. ▪ American Football a change of position by two or more players before the ball is put into play.
2 each of two or more recurring periods in which different groups of workers do the same jobs in relay: *Anne was on the night shift.* ▪ a group of workers who work in this way.
3 (also **shift dress**) a woman's straight unwaisted dress. ▪ historical a long, loose-fitting undergarment.
4 archaic an ingenious or devious device or stratagem: *the thousand shifts and devices of which Hannibal was a master.*
– PHRASES **get a shift on** Brit. informal hurry up: *it's quite a drive to London, so we should really get a shift on.* **make shift** do what one wants to do in spite of not having ideal conditions. **shift for oneself** manage as best one can without help. **shift one's ground** say or write something that contradicts something one has previously written or said. **shifting sands** something that is constantly changing, especially unpredictably: *whether something is accepted depends upon the shifting sands of taste.*
– DERIVATIVES **shiftable** adjective.
– ORIGIN Old English *sciftan* 'arrange, divide, apportion', of Germanic origin; related to German *schichten* 'to layer, stratify'. A common Middle English sense 'change, replace' gave rise to sense 3 of the noun (via the notion of changing one's clothes) and sense 2 of the noun (via the concept of relays of workers).

shifter ▸ **noun** [usu. in combination] **1** a person or thing that shifts something: *each morning the rock-shifters travel by donkey cart to start work.*
2 N. Amer. a gearbox of a motor vehicle or a set of gear levers on a bicycle: *a new, improved five-speed shifter.*

shifting cultivation (also **shifting agriculture**) ▸ **noun** [mass noun] a form of agriculture, used especially in tropical Africa, in which an area of ground is cleared of vegetation and cultivated for a few years and then abandoned for a new area until its fertility has been naturally restored.

shiftless ▸ **adjective** characterized by laziness, indolence, and a lack of ambition: *a shiftless lot of good-for-nothings.*
– DERIVATIVES **shiftlessly** adverb, **shiftlessness** noun.

shift lever ▸ **noun** N. Amer. another term for GEAR LEVER.

shift register ▸ **noun** Computing a register that is designed to allow the bits of its contents to be moved to left or right.

shift work ▸ **noun** [mass noun] work comprising recurring periods in which different groups of workers do the same jobs in relay.

shifty ▸ **adjective** (**shiftier**, **shiftiest**) informal **1** (of a person or their manner) appearing deceitful or evasive: *he had a shifty look about him.*
2 constantly changing; shifting: *it was a close race in a shifty wind on smooth water.*
– DERIVATIVES **shiftily** adverb, **shiftiness** noun.

shigella /ʃɪˈɡɛlə/ ▸ **noun** (pl. **same** or **shigellae**) a bacterium that is an intestinal pathogen of humans and other primates, some kinds of which cause dysentery. ● Genus *Shigella*; Gram-negative rods.
– ORIGIN modern Latin, from the name of Kiyoshi *Shiga* (1870–1957), Japanese bacteriologist, + the diminutive suffix *-ella*.

shih-tzu /ʃiːˈtsuː/ ▸ **noun** a dog of a breed with long silky erect hair and short legs.
– ORIGIN 1920s: from Chinese *shīzi* 'lion'.

shiitake /ʃɪˈtɑːkeɪ, ʃɪɪ-/ (also **shitake**, **shiitake mushroom**) ▸ **noun** an edible mushroom which grows on fallen timber, cultivated in Japan and China. ● *Lentinus edodes*, family Pleurotaceae, class Hymenomycetes.
– ORIGIN late 19th cent.: from Japanese, from *shii*, denoting a kind of oak, + *take* 'mushroom'.

Shiite /ˈʃiːʌɪt/ (also **Shi'ite**) ▸ **noun** an adherent of the Shia branch of Islam.
▸ **adjective** relating to Shia.
– DERIVATIVES **Shiism** /ˈʃiːɪz(ə)m/ (also **Shi'ism**) **noun**.

Shijiazhuang /ˌʃiːdʒɪəˈʒwaŋ/ a city in NE central China, capital of Hebei province; pop. 2,241,500 (est. 2006).

shikar /ʃɪˈkɑː/ ▸ **noun** [mass noun] Indian hunting as a sport.
– ORIGIN from Urdu and Persian *šikār*.

shikara /ʃɪˈkɑːrə/ ▸ **noun** Indian (in Kashmir) a houseboat. ▪ (also **shikari**) a light, flat-bottomed boat.
– ORIGIN via Kashmiri from Persian *šikārī* 'of hunting'.

shikari /ʃɪˈkɑːriː/ ▸ **noun** (pl. **shikaris**) Indian a hunter. ▪ a guide on hunting expeditions.
– ORIGIN via Urdu from Persian *šikārī* 'of hunting'.

shikhara /ʃɪˈkɑːrə/ (also **shikara**) ▸ **noun** Indian a spire on a Hindu temple.
– ORIGIN from Sanskrit *śikhara* 'peak, spire'.

shikker ▸ **adjective & noun** variant spelling of SHICKER.

Shikoku /ʃɪˈkəʊkuː/ the smallest of the four main islands of Japan, constituting an administrative region; pop. 4,142,000 (est. 2005); capital, Matsuyama. It is divided from Kyushu to the west and southern Honshu to the north by the Inland Sea.

shikra /ˈʃɪkrə/ ▸ **noun** a small stocky sparrowhawk found in Africa and central and southern Asia. ● Genus *Accipiter*, family Accipitridae: two species, in particular the widespread *A. badius*.
– ORIGIN mid 19th cent.: from Persian and Urdu *šikara*.

shiksa /ˈʃɪksə/ ▸ **noun** often derogatory (used especially by Jews) a gentile girl or woman.
– ORIGIN late 19th cent.: from Yiddish *shikse*, from Hebrew *šiqṣāh* (from *šeqeṣ* 'detested thing' + the feminine suffix *-āh*).

shill N. Amer. informal ▸ **noun** an accomplice of a hawker, gambler, or swindler who acts as an enthusiastic customer to entice or encourage others.
▸ **verb** [no obj.] act or work as such a person.
– ORIGIN early 20th cent.: probably from earlier *shillaber*, of unknown origin.

shillelagh /ʃɪˈleɪlə, -li/ ▸ **noun** a thick stick of blackthorn or oak used in Ireland, typically as a weapon.
– ORIGIN late 18th cent.: from the name of the town *Shillelagh*, in Co. Wicklow, Ireland.

shilling ▸ **noun 1** a former British coin and monetary unit equal to one twentieth of a pound or twelve pence.
2 the basic monetary unit in Kenya, Tanzania, and Uganda, equal to 100 cents.
– PHRASES **not the full shilling** Brit. informal very unintelligent or slow. **take the King's** (or **Queen's**) **shilling** Brit. enlist as a soldier. [with reference to the former practice of paying a shilling to a soldier who enlisted.]
– ORIGIN Old English *scilling*, of Germanic origin; related to Dutch *schelling* and German *Schilling*.

Shillong /ʃɪˈlɒŋ/ a city in the far north-east of India, capital of the state of Meghalaya; pop. 141,700 (est. 2009).

Shilluk /ʃɪˈluːk/ ▸ **noun** (pl. **same** or **Shilluks**) **1** a member of a Sudanese people living mainly on the west bank of the Nile.
2 [mass noun] the Nilotic language of the Shilluk.
▸ **adjective** relating to the Shilluk or their language.
– ORIGIN the name in Shilluk.

shilly-shally ▸ **verb** (**shilly-shallies**, **shilly-shallying**, **shilly-shallied**) [no obj.] fail to act resolutely or decisively: *the government shilly-shallied about the matter.*
▸ **noun** [mass noun] indecisive behaviour.
– ORIGIN mid 18th cent.: originally as *shill I, shall I*, reduplication of *shall I?*

Shilton, Peter (b.1949), English footballer. He played in goal for a number of clubs and made a record 1,000th league appearance in 1996. For England he won a record 125 caps (1970–90).

shim ▸ **noun** a washer or thin strip of material used to align parts, make them fit, or reduce wear.
▸ **verb** (**shims, shimming, shimmed**) [with obj.] wedge (something) or fill up (a space) with a shim.
– ORIGIN early 18th cent.: of unknown origin.

shimiyana /ʃɪmɪˈjɑːnə/ ▸ **noun** [mass noun] S. African a home-brewed liquor of sugar or treacle and water, fermented in the sun.
– ORIGIN from Zulu *isishimeyana*.

Shimla /ˈʃɪmlə/ (also **Simla**) a city in NE India, capital of the state of Himachal Pradesh; pop. 208,600 (est. 2009).

shimmer ▸ **verb** [no obj.] shine with a soft tremulous light: *the sea shimmered in the sunlight* | (as adj. **shimmering**) *shimmering candlelight*.
▸ **noun** [in sing.] a light with such qualities: *a pale shimmer of moonlight*.
– DERIVATIVES **shimmeringly** adverb, **shimmery** adjective.
– ORIGIN late Old English *scymrian*, of Germanic origin; related to German *schimmern*, also to SHINE. The noun dates from the early 19th cent.

shimmy ▸ **noun** (pl. **shimmies**) **1** a kind of ragtime dance in which the whole body shakes or sways.
2 [mass noun] shaking, especially abnormal vibration of the wheels of a motor vehicle: *steering stabilizers reduce shimmy even from oversized tyres*.
3 archaic informal term for CHEMISE.
▸ **verb** (**shimmies, shimmying, shimmied**) [no obj.]
1 dance the shimmy.
2 [with adverbial of direction] move effortlessly; glide with a swaying motion: *her hair swung in waves as she shimmied down the catwalk*.
3 shake or vibrate abnormally: *he braked hard and felt the car shimmy dangerously*.
– ORIGIN early 20th cent.: of unknown origin.

shin ▸ **noun** the front of the leg below the knee. ■ a cut of beef from the lower part of a cow's leg.
▸ **verb** (**shins, shinning, shinned**) [no obj.] (**shin up/down**) climb quickly up or down by gripping with one's arms and legs: *he shinned up a tree*.
– ORIGIN Old English *scinu*, probably from a Germanic base meaning 'narrow or thin piece'; related to German *Schiene* 'thin plate' and Dutch *scheen*. The verb was originally in nautical use (early 19th cent.).

Shin Bet /ʃɪn ˈbɛt/ (also **Shin Beth**) the principal security service of Israel, concerned primarily with counter-espionage.
– ORIGIN modern Hebrew, the initial letters of the first two words of *šērūṯ biṭṭāhōn kĕlālī* '(general) security service'.

shin bone ▸ **noun** the tibia.

shindig ▸ **noun** informal a large, lively party, especially one celebrating something. ■ a noisy disturbance or quarrel.
– ORIGIN mid 19th cent.: probably from the nouns SHIN and DIG, influenced later by SHINDY.

shindy ▸ **noun** (pl. **shindies**) informal a noisy disturbance or quarrel: *there were plenty of gulls **kicking up a shindy***. ■ a large, lively party.
– ORIGIN early 19th cent.: perhaps an alteration of SHINTY.

shine ▸ **verb** (past and past participle **shone** or **shined**) [no obj.] **1** (of the sun or another source of light) give out a bright light: *the sun shone through the window*. ■ glow or be bright with reflected light: *she brushed her hair until it shone*. ■ (of a person's eyes) be bright with emotion: *his eyes **shone with** excitement*. ■ [with obj. and adverbial of direction] direct (a torch or other light) somewhere in order to see something in the dark: *he shone the torch around the room before entering*.
2 be very talented or perform very well: *a boy who shone at nothing*.
3 (past and past participle **shined**) [with obj.] make (an object made of leather, metal, or wood) bright by rubbing it; polish: *his shoes were shined to perfection*.
▸ **noun** [in sing.] a quality of brightness produced when light is reflected on something: *my hair has lost its shine*. ■ an act of rubbing something to give it a shiny surface: *Archie's shoes got a quick shine from a boy with a cloth*.
– PHRASES **take the shine off** spoil the brilliance or excitement of: *these concerns are taking the shine off Britain's economic recovery*. **take a shine to** informal develop a liking for.
– PHRASAL VERBS **shine through** (of a good quality or skill) be clearly evident: *at Murrayfield his talent shone through*.
– ORIGIN Old English *scīnan*, of Germanic origin; related to Dutch *schijnen* and German *scheinen*.

shiner ▸ **noun 1** a thing that shines or reflects light. ■ [in combination] a person or thing that polishes something: *shoeshiners*.
2 informal a black eye.
3 a small silvery North American freshwater fish which typically has colourful markings. ● *Notropis* and other genera, family Cyprinidae: several species.

shingle[1] ▸ **noun** [mass noun] a mass of small rounded pebbles, especially on a seashore.
– DERIVATIVES **shingly** adjective.
– ORIGIN late Middle English: of unknown origin.

shingle[2] ▸ **noun 1** a rectangular wooden tile used on walls or roofs.
2 dated a woman's short haircut in which the hair tapers from the back of the head to the nape of the neck. [so named because of the layering.]
3 N. Amer. a small signboard, especially one found outside a doctor's or lawyer's office.
▸ **verb** [with obj.] **1** roof or clad with shingles: (as adj. **shingled**) *a tower surmounted by a shingled spire*.
2 dated cut (a woman's hair) in a shingle.
– PHRASES **hang out one's shingle** N. Amer. begin to practise a profession.
– ORIGIN Middle English (as a noun): apparently from Latin *scindula*, earlier *scandula* 'a split piece of wood'.

shingles ▸ **plural noun** [treated as sing.] Medicine a painful acute inflammation of the nerve ganglia, with a skin eruption often forming a girdle around the middle of the body. It is caused by the same virus as chickenpox. Also called HERPES ZOSTER.
– ORIGIN late Middle English: representing medieval Latin *cingulus*, variant of Latin *cingulum* 'girdle', from *cingere* 'gird'.

shin guard ▸ **noun** another term for SHIN PAD.

shining ▸ **adjective 1** giving out or reflecting bright light: *a shining expanse of water*.
2 brilliant or excellent at something: *he has set a **shining example** with his model behaviour*.
– DERIVATIVES **shiningly** adverb.

Shining Path a Peruvian Maoist revolutionary movement and terrorist organization, founded in 1970 and led by Abimael Guzmán (b.1934) until his capture and imprisonment in 1992.
– ORIGIN translating Spanish SENDERO LUMINOSO.

Shinkansen /ˈʃiːnkɑːnˌsɛn/ ▸ **noun** (pl. **same**) (in Japan) a railway system carrying high-speed passenger trains. ■ a train operating on such a system.
– ORIGIN Japanese, from *shin* 'new' + *kansen* 'main line'.

Shinner ▸ **noun** Irish informal, chiefly derogatory a member or supporter of Sinn Fein.

shinny[1] ▸ **verb** (**shinnies, shinnying, shinnied**) North American term for SHIN: *he loved to shinny up that tree*.
– ORIGIN late 19th cent.: from the noun SHIN + -Y[2].

shinny[2] (also **shinny hockey**) ▸ **noun** [mass noun] N. Amer. an informal form of ice hockey played especially by children, on the street or on ice, often with a ball or other object in place of a puck.
– ORIGIN variant of SHINTY.

Shinola /ʃʌɪˈnəʊlə/ ▸ **noun** [mass noun] US trademark a brand of boot polish. ■ informal used as a euphemism for 'shit': *there'll be the same old Shinola on television*.
– PHRASES **neither shit nor Shinola** vulgar slang neither one thing nor the other. **not know shit from Shinola** vulgar slang used to indicate that someone is ignorant or innocent.
– ORIGIN early 20th cent.: from SHINE + *-ola* (suffix chiefly in US usage).

shin pad ▸ **noun** a pad worn to protect the shins when playing soccer, hockey, and other sports.

shin splints ▸ **plural noun** [treated as sing. or pl.] acute pain in the shin and lower leg caused by prolonged running, typically on hard surfaces.

Shinto /ˈʃɪntəʊ/ ▸ **noun** [mass noun] a Japanese religion dating from the early 8th century and incorporating the worship of ancestors and nature spirits and a belief in sacred power (**kami**) in both animate and inanimate things. It was the state religion of Japan until 1945. See also AMATERASU.
– DERIVATIVES **Shintoism** noun, **Shintoist** noun.
– ORIGIN Japanese, from Chinese *shen dao* 'way of the gods'.

shinty ▸ **noun** (pl. **shinties**) [mass noun] a Scottish twelve-a-side game resembling hockey, played with curved sticks and taller goalposts and derived from the Irish game of hurling.
– ORIGIN mid 18th cent. (earlier as *shinny*): apparently from the cry *shin ye, shin you, shin t' ye*, used in the game, of unknown origin; compare with SHINNY[2].

shiny ▸ **adjective** (**shinier, shiniest**) (of a smooth surface) reflecting light, typically because very clean or polished: *shiny hair* | *shiny black shoes*.
– DERIVATIVES **shinily** adverb, **shininess** noun.

ship ▸ **noun 1** a large boat for transporting people or goods by sea. ■ a sailing vessel with a bowsprit and three or more square-rigged masts. ■ informal any boat, especially a racing boat.
2 a spaceship.
3 N. Amer. an aircraft.
▸ **verb** (**ships, shipping, shipped**) **1** [with obj. and adverbial of direction] transport (goods or people) on a ship: *the wounded soldiers were shipped home*. ■ send by some other means of transport or by mail: *he was captured and **shipped off** to a labour camp* | *the freight would be shipped by rail* | *spare parts were quickly **shipped out***. ■ [no obj.] (**ship out**) (of a naval force) go to sea from a home port: *Bob got sick a week before we shipped out*. ■ [no obj.] dated embark on a ship: *people wishing to get from London to New York ship at Liverpool*. ■ (of a sailor) take service on a ship: *Jack, you shipped with the Admiral once, didn't you?*
2 [no obj.] (of a product) be made available for purchase: *the cellular phone is expected to ship at about $500 sometime this summer*.
3 [with obj.] (of a boat) take in (water) over the side.
4 [with obj.] take (oars) from the rowlocks and lay them inside a boat. ■ fix (something such as a rudder or mast) in its place on a boat or ship.
– PHRASES **a sinking ship** used with reference to a situation in which people are deserting an organization or enterprise that is failing: *they have fled like rats from a sinking ship*. **ship a sea** Brit. (of a boat) be flooded by a wave. **take ship** set off on a voyage by ship; embark: *they were due to take ship for Rhodes*. **when one's ship comes in** (or **home**) when one's fortune is made.
– DERIVATIVES **shipless** adjective, **shippable** adjective.
– ORIGIN Old English *scip* (noun), late Old English *scipian* (verb), of Germanic origin; related to Dutch *schip* and German *Schiff*.

-ship ▸ **suffix** forming nouns: **1** denoting a quality or condition: *companionship* | *friendship*.
2 denoting status, office, or honour: *ambassadorship* | *citizenship*. ■ denoting a tenure of office: *chairmanship*.
3 denoting a skill in a certain capacity: *workmanship*.
4 denoting the collective individuals of a group: *membership*.
– ORIGIN Old English *-scipe, scype*, of Germanic origin.

shipboard ▸ **noun** [as modifier] used or occurring on board a ship: *shipboard life*.
– PHRASES **on shipboard** on board a ship.

ship-breaker ▸ **noun** a contractor who breaks up old ships for scrap.

shipbroker ▸ **noun** a broker who specializes in arranging charters, cargo space, and passenger bookings on ships.

shipbuilder ▸ **noun** a person or company whose job or business is the design and construction of ships.
– DERIVATIVES **shipbuilding** noun.

ship burial ▸ **noun** Archaeology a burial in a wooden ship under a mound. The custom was reserved for those who were particularly honoured in Scandinavia and parts of the British Isles in the pagan Anglo-Saxon and Viking periods (6th–11th centuries AD).

ship canal ▸ **noun** a canal wide and deep enough for ships to travel along it.

ship chandler ▸ **noun** see CHANDLER.

shiplap ▸ **verb** [with obj.] fit (boards) together by halving so that each overlaps the one below: (as adj. **shiplapped**) *shiplapped pine used as facing for the first floor*.
▸ **noun** [mass noun] boards which have been fitted together in this way, typically used for cladding. ■ [count noun] [usu. as modifier] a joint between boards made by halving: *a shiplap joint*.

Shipley, Jenny (b.1952), New Zealand National Party stateswoman, Prime Minister 1997–9; full name *Jennifer Mary Shipley*.

shipload ▸ **noun** as much cargo or as many people as a ship can carry.

shipmaster ▸ **noun** a ship's captain.

shipmate ▸ **noun** a fellow member of a ship's crew.

shipment ▸ **noun** [mass noun] the action of shipping goods: *logs waiting for shipment*. ■ [count noun] a quantity of goods shipped; a consignment.

ship money ▸ noun [mass noun] historical a tax raised in England in medieval times to provide ships for the navy.

ship of the desert ▸ noun literary a camel.

ship of the line ▸ noun historical a sailing warship of the largest size, used in the line of battle.

shipowner ▸ noun a person owning a ship or shares in a ship.

shippen /ˈʃɪp(ə)n/ ▸ noun variant spelling of SHIPPON.

shipper ▸ noun a person or company that transports or receives goods by sea, land, or air.
– ORIGIN late Old English *scipere* 'sailor'. Current senses date from the mid 18th cent.

shipping ▸ noun [mass noun] ships considered collectively, especially those in a particular area or belonging to a particular country: *the volume of shipping using these ports*. ■ the transport of goods by sea or some other means.

shipping agent ▸ noun a licensed agent in a port who transacts a ship's business, such as insurance or documentation, for the owner.

shipping bill ▸ noun (in the UK) a form used by Customs and Excise before goods can be exported from the country or removed from a bonded warehouse.

shipping master ▸ noun Brit. an official presiding over the signing-on and discharging of seamen.

shipping office ▸ noun the office of a shipping agent or shipping master.

shippon /ˈʃɪp(ə)n/ (also **shippen**) ▸ noun dialect a cattle shed.
– ORIGIN Old English *scypen*, of Germanic origin.

ship rat ▸ noun another term for BLACK RAT.

ship-rigged ▸ adjective (of a sailing ship) square-rigged.

ship's biscuit ▸ noun [mass noun] a very hard, coarse kind of biscuit formerly taken on sea voyages.

ship's boat ▸ noun a small boat carried on board a ship.

ship's company ▸ noun the crew of a ship.

ship's corporal ▸ noun see CORPORAL[1] (sense 2).

shipshape ▸ adjective in good order; trim and neat: *he checked that everything was shipshape*.

ship's husband ▸ noun an agent responsible for providing maintenance and supplies for a ship in port.
– DERIVATIVES **ship's husbandry** noun.

ship-to-shore ▸ adjective from a ship to land: *ship-to-shore phone calls*.
▸ noun a radio-telephone connecting a ship to land, or connecting a train or other vehicle to a control centre.

shipway ▸ noun a slope on which a ship is built and down which it slides to be launched.

shipworm ▸ noun another term for TEREDO.

shipwreck ▸ noun the destruction of a ship at sea by sinking or breaking up, for example in a storm or after striking a rock. ■ a ship so destroyed: *the detritus of a forgotten shipwreck*.
▸ verb (**be shipwrecked**) (of a person or ship) suffer a shipwreck.

shipwright ▸ noun a shipbuilder.

shipyard ▸ noun an enclosed area of land where ships are built and repaired.

shiralee /ˈʃɪrəliː/ ▸ noun Austral. informal, dated a bundle of personal belongings or blankets carried by a tramp.
– ORIGIN late 19th cent.: of unknown origin.

Shiraz[1] /ˈʃɪəraz, ʃɪˈraz/ a city in SW central Iran; pop. 1,227,331 (2006). The city is noted for the school of miniature painting based there between the 14th and 16th centuries, and for the manufacture of carpets.

Shiraz[2] /ˈʃɪəraz, ʃɪˈraz/ ▸ noun [mass noun] a variety of black wine grape. ■ a red wine made from this grape.
– ORIGIN from SHIRAZ[1], apparently an alteration of French *syrah*, influenced by the belief that the vine was brought from Iran by the Crusades.

shire /ˈʃʌɪə/ ▸ noun **1** Brit. a county, especially in England. ■ (**the Shires**) used in reference to parts of England regarded as strongholds of traditional rural culture, especially the rural Midlands. ■ historical an administrative district in medieval times ruled jointly by an alderman and a sheriff.
2 Austral. a rural area with its own elected council.
– ORIGIN Old English *scīr* 'care, official charge, county', of Germanic origin.

-shire /ʃɪə, ʃə/ ▸ combining form forming the names of counties: *Oxfordshire* | *South Yorkshire*.

shire county ▸ noun (in the UK) a non-metropolitan county (in existence since 1974).

shire horse ▸ noun a heavy, powerful horse of a draught breed, originally from the English Midlands.

shirk ▸ verb [with obj.] avoid or neglect (a duty or responsibility): *I do not shirk any responsibility in this matter* | [no obj.] *she is neither shirking nor lying*. ■ [no obj.] [usu. with negative] (**shirk from**) be unwilling to do (something difficult): *we will not shirk from closing a school if the evidence should justify it*.
▸ noun archaic a person who shirks.
– DERIVATIVES **shirker** noun.
– ORIGIN mid 17th cent. (in the sense 'practise fraud or trickery'): from obsolete *shirk* 'sponger', perhaps from German *Schurke* 'scoundrel'.

shirr /ʃəː/ ▸ verb [with obj.] **1** gather (an area of fabric or part of a garment) by means of drawn or elasticized threads in parallel rows: (as adj. **shirred**) *a swimsuit with a shirred front*.
2 US bake (an egg without its shell).
– ORIGIN mid 19th cent.: of unknown origin.

shirt ▸ noun a garment for the upper body made of cotton or a similar fabric, with a collar and sleeves, and with buttons down the front. ■ [usu. with modifier] a similar garment of stretchable material without full fastenings, worn as casual wear or for sports: *a rugby shirt*. ■ [with modifier] Brit. used to refer to membership of a particular sports team: *Smith increased his chances of a Great Britain shirt with a penalty shot save*.
– PHRASES **keep your shirt on** informal don't lose your temper; stay calm. **lose one's shirt** informal lose all one's possessions. **put one's shirt on** Brit. informal bet all one has on; be sure of: *they'll confirm it's him, I'll put my shirt on it*. **the shirt off** (or **on**) **one's back** informal used to refer to someone's last remaining possessions: *he had fled to France with nothing but the shirt on his back*.
– DERIVATIVES **shirted** adjective [often in combination] *white-shirted bouncers*, **shirtless** adjective.
– ORIGIN Old English *scyrte*, of Germanic origin; related to Old Norse *skyrta* (compare with SKIRT), Dutch *schort*, German *Schürze* 'apron', also to SHORT; probably from a base meaning 'short garment'.

shirt dress ▸ noun a dress with a collar and button fastening in the style of a shirt, typically cut without a seam at the waist.

shirt front ▸ noun the breast of a shirt, in particular that of a stiffened evening shirt.

shirting ▸ noun [mass noun] a material for making shirts, especially a fine cotton in plain colours or incorporating a traditional woven stripe.

shirtlifter ▸ noun Brit. informal, derogatory a homosexual.

shirtsleeve ▸ noun (usu. **shirtsleeves**) the sleeve of a shirt: *he rolled up his shirtsleeves*.
– PHRASES **in (one's) shirtsleeves** wearing a shirt with nothing over it.
– DERIVATIVES **shirtsleeved** adjective.

shirt tail ▸ noun the lower, typically curved, part of a shirt which comes below the waist.

shirtwaist ▸ noun N. Amer. a woman's blouse resembling a shirt. ■ (also **shirtwaist dress**) another term for SHIRTWAISTER.

shirtwaister ▸ noun a woman's dress with a seam at the waist, its bodice incorporating a collar and button fastening in the style of a shirt.

shirty ▸ adjective (**shirtier**, **shirtiest**) Brit. informal bad-tempered or annoyed: *she got quite shirty*.
– DERIVATIVES **shirtily** adverb, **shirtiness** noun.

shisha /ˈʃiːʃə/ ▸ noun (in Egypt and other Arabic-speaking countries) a hookah. ■ [mass noun] tobacco for smoking in a hookah, especially when mixed with flavourings such as mint.
– ORIGIN Egyptian Arabic *šīša*, from Turkish *şişe*.

shisham /ˈʃɪʃəm/ (also **shisham tree**) ▸ noun an Indian tree of the pea family, which produces useful timber. ● *Dalbergia sissoo*, family Leguminosae.
– ORIGIN mid 19th cent.: from Persian and Urdu *šīšam*.

shish kebab /ˌʃɪʃ kɪˈbab/ ▸ noun a dish of pieces of marinated meat and vegetables cooked and served on skewers.
– ORIGIN from Turkish *şiş kebap*, from *şiş* 'skewer' + *kebap* 'roast meat'.

shiso /ˈʃiːsəʊ/ ▸ noun [mass noun] a plant of the mint family, native to eastern Asia, used as a herb in Japanese cookery. ● *Perilla frutescens*, family Labiatae (or Lamiaceae): many varieties.
– ORIGIN Japanese.

shit vulgar slang ▸ noun [mass noun] **1** faeces. ■ [in sing.] an act of defecating. ■ (**the shits**) diarrhoea.
2 [count noun] a contemptible or worthless person.
3 something worthless; rubbish; nonsense. ■ unpleasant experiences or treatment.
4 personal belongings; stuff. ■ an intoxicating drug, especially cannabis.
▸ verb (**shits, shitting**; past and past participle **shitted** or **shit** or **shat**) **1** [no obj.] expel faeces from the body. ■ [with obj.] (**shit oneself**) soil one's clothes as a result of expelling faeces accidentally. ■ [with obj.] (**shit oneself**) be very frightened.
2 [with obj.] tease or try to deceive (someone).
▸ exclamation an exclamation of disgust, anger, or annoyance.
– PHRASES **beat** (or **kick**) **the shit out of** beat (someone) very severely. **be shitting bricks** be extremely nervous or frightened. **do bears shit in the woods?** used to indicate that something is blatantly obvious. **get one's shit together** organize oneself so as to be able to deal with or achieve something. **give someone the shits** chiefly Austral./NZ make someone annoyed or angry. **in the shit** in trouble. **no shit** used as a way of confirming or seeking confirmation of the truth of a statement. **not give a shit** not care at all. **not know shit** not know anything. **shit for brains** chiefly N. Amer. a stupid person. **be up shit creek** (also **be up shit creek without a paddle**) be in an awkward predicament. **when the shit hits the fan** when the disastrous consequences of something become public.
– ORIGIN Old English *scitte* 'diarrhoea', of Germanic origin; related to Dutch *schijten*, German *scheissen* (verb). The term was originally neutral and used without vulgar connotation.

shitake ▸ noun variant spelling of SHIITAKE.

shitbag ▸ noun vulgar slang a contemptible person.

shitcan ▸ verb (**shitcans, shitcanning, shitcanned**) [with obj.] US vulgar slang throw (something) away. ■ discard or reject (someone or something).

shite ▸ noun & exclamation Brit. vulgar slang another term for SHIT.

shit-eating ▸ adjective vulgar slang, chiefly US smug; self-satisfied.

shitepoke ▸ noun N. Amer. informal any of a number of birds of the heron family. ● Several species in the family Ardeidae, in particular the green-backed *Butorides striatus*.
– ORIGIN late 18th cent.: from SHITE (because of the bird's habit of defecating when disturbed) + the noun POKE[1].

shitface ▸ noun vulgar slang an obnoxious person.

shit-faced ▸ adjective [predic.] vulgar slang drunk or under the influence of drugs.

shithead ▸ noun vulgar slang a contemptible person.

shithole ▸ noun vulgar slang an extremely dirty, shabby, or otherwise unpleasant place.

shit-hot ▸ adjective vulgar slang excellent or highly skilled.

shithouse ▸ noun vulgar slang a toilet. ■ an extremely unpleasant place.
– PHRASES **be built like a brick shithouse** (of a person) have a very solid physique.

shitkicker ▸ noun N. Amer. vulgar slang **1** an unsophisticated or oafish person, especially one from a rural area.
2 (**shitkickers**) substantially made boots with thick soles and typically with reinforced toes.

shitless ▸ adjective (in phrase **be scared** (or **bored**) **shitless**) vulgar slang be extremely frightened (or bored).

shitlist ▸ noun N. Amer. vulgar slang a list of those whom one dislikes or plans to harm.

shitload ▸ noun vulgar slang a large amount or number.

shit-scared ▸ adjective vulgar slang terrified.

shit-stirrer ▸ noun vulgar slang a person who takes pleasure in causing trouble or discord.
– DERIVATIVES **shit-stirring** noun.

shitstorm ▸ noun vulgar slang a situation marked by violent controversy.

shitty ▸ adjective (**shittier, shittiest**) vulgar slang **1** (of a person or action) contemptible; worthless. ■ (of an experience or situation) unpleasant; awful.
2 covered with excrement.

shitwork ▸ noun [mass noun] vulgar slang work considered to be menial or routine.

shiur /ˈʃiːʊə/ ▸ **noun** (pl. **shiurim** /-rɪm/) Judaism a Talmudic study session, usually led by a rabbi.
– ORIGIN from Hebrew *šiʿūr* 'measure, portion'.

shiv /ʃɪv/ ▸ **noun** N. Amer. informal a knife or razor used as a weapon.
– ORIGIN probably from Romany *chiv* 'blade'.

Shiva /ˈʃiːvə, ˈʃɪvə/ (also **Siva**) Hinduism a god associated with the powers of reproduction and dissolution.

> Shiva is regarded by some as the supreme being and by others as forming a triad with Brahma and Vishnu. He is worshipped in many aspects: as destroyer, ascetic, lord of the cosmic dance, and lord of beasts, and through the symbolic lingam. His wife is Parvati.

– ORIGIN from Sanskrit *Śiva*, literally 'the auspicious one'.

shiva /ˈʃɪvə/ (also **shivah**) ▸ **noun** [mass noun] Judaism a period of seven days' formal mourning for the dead, beginning immediately after the funeral.
– ORIGIN from Hebrew *šiḇʿāh* 'seven'.

Shivaji /ʃɪˈvɑːdʒi/ (also **Sivaji**) (1627–80), Indian raja of the Marathas 1674–80. He raised a successful Hindu revolt against Muslim rule in 1659 and expanded Maratha territory. After being crowned raja he blocked Mogul expansionism by forming an alliance with the sultans in the south.

shivaree /ˌʃɪvəˈriː/ ▸ **noun** chiefly US variant spelling of CHARIVARI.

shive /ʃʌɪv/ ▸ **noun** a broad bung hammered into a hole in the top of a cask when the cask has been filled.
– ORIGIN Middle English: related to SHEAVE[2]. The original sense was 'slice (of bread)', later 'piece of split wood'; the current sense dates from the mid 19th cent.

shiver[1] ▸ **verb** [no obj.] shake slightly and uncontrollably as a result of being cold, frightened, or excited: *they shivered in the damp foggy cold.*
▸ **noun** a momentary trembling movement: *she gave a little shiver as the wind flicked at her bare arms | the way he looked at her sent* ***shivers down her spine.*** ■ (**the shivers**) a spell or an attack of trembling, typically as a result of fear or horror: *a look that gave him the shivers.*
– DERIVATIVES **shiverer** noun, **shiveringly** adverb.
– ORIGIN Middle English *chivere*, perhaps an alteration of dialect *chavele* 'to chatter', from Old English *ceafl* 'jaw'.

shiver[2] ▸ **noun** (usu. **shivers**) each of the small fragments into which something such as glass is shattered when broken; a splinter.
▸ **verb** [no obj.] break into such splinters or fragments: *the world seemed to shiver into a million splinters of prismatic colour.*
– PHRASES **shiver my timbers** a mock oath attributed to sailors.
– ORIGIN Middle English: from a Germanic base meaning 'to split'; related to German *Schiefer* 'slate'.

shivery ▸ **adjective** shaking or trembling as a result of cold, illness, fear, or excitement: *he felt cold and shivery.*

shivoo /ʃɪˈvuː/ ▸ **noun** Austral./NZ informal, dated a party or celebration; a revel.
– ORIGIN late 19th cent.: from obsolete *shiveau*, of unknown origin.

Shiv Sena /ʃɪv ˈseɪnə/ a Hindu nationalist organization centred in Maharashtra.
– ORIGIN from Sanskrit *Śiva* 'Shiva' + *sena* 'army'.

Shizuoka /ˌʃɪzuːˈəʊkə/ a city in the south of the island of Honshu in Japan; pop. 711,882 (2007).

Shkodër /ˈʃkəʊdə/ a city in NW Albania, near the border with Montenegro; pop. 91,300 (est. 2009). Italian name **Scutari**.

shlub /ʃlʌb/ ▸ **noun** variant spelling of SCHLUB.

SHM ▸ **abbreviation** simple harmonic motion.

shmatte /ˈʃmatə/ ▸ **noun** variant spelling of SCHMATTE.

shmear /ʃmiːə/ (also **schmeer**) ▸ **noun & verb** variant spelling of SCHMEAR.

shmo ▸ **noun** (pl. **shmoes**) variant spelling of SCHMO.

sho ▸ **adverb** non-standard spelling of SURE, representing its pronunciation in the southern US: *ah sho is glad tuh have yuh.*

Shoah /ˈʃəʊə/ ▸ **noun** (**the Shoah**) another term for THE HOLOCAUST (see HOLOCAUST).
– ORIGIN modern Hebrew, literally 'catastrophe'.

shoal[1] ▸ **noun** a large number of fish swimming together: *a shoal of bream.* Compare with SCHOOL[2]. ■ informal, chiefly Brit. a large number of people or things: *shoals of people were coming up the drive.*
▸ **verb** [no obj.] (of fish) form shoals.
– ORIGIN late 16th cent.: probably from Middle Dutch *schōle* 'troop'. Compare with SCHOOL[2].

shoal[2] ▸ **noun** an area of shallow water. ■ a submerged sandbank visible at low water. ■ (usu. **shoals**) a hidden danger or difficulty: *he alone could safely guide them through Hollywood's treacherous shoals.*
▸ **verb** [no obj.] (of water) become shallower.
▸ **adjective** dialect or N. Amer. (of water) shallow.
– ORIGIN Old English *sceald* (adjective), of Germanic origin; related to SHALLOW.

shoat /ʃəʊt/ (also **shote**) ▸ **noun** N. Amer. a young pig, especially one which is newly weaned.
– ORIGIN late Middle English: of unknown origin; compare with West Flemish *schote*.

shochet /ˈʃɒkɛt, -x-/ ▸ **noun** (pl. **shochetim** /-ɪm/) a person officially certified as competent to kill cattle and poultry in the manner prescribed by Jewish law.
– ORIGIN late 19th cent.: from Hebrew *šōḥēṭ* 'slaughtering'.

shochu /ˈʃəʊtʃuː/ ▸ **noun** [mass noun] a rough Japanese spirit distilled from any of various ingredients, including sake dregs.
– ORIGIN from Japanese *shōchū*.

shock[1] ▸ **noun 1** a sudden upsetting or surprising event or experience: *it was a shock to face such hostile attitudes.* ■ a feeling of disturbed surprise resulting from a sudden upsetting event: *her death gave us all a terrible shock* | [mass noun] *her eyes opened wide* ***in shock.*** ■ a disturbance causing instability in an economy: *trading imbalances caused by the two oil shocks.* ■ short for ELECTRIC SHOCK.
2 [mass noun] an acute medical condition associated with a fall in blood pressure, caused by such events as loss of blood, severe burns, allergic reaction, or sudden emotional stress, and marked by cold, pallid skin, irregular breathing, rapid pulse, and dilated pupils: *he died of shock due to massive abdominal haemorrhage.*
3 a violent shaking movement caused by an impact, explosion, or tremor: *earthquake shocks* | [mass noun] *rackets today don't bend or absorb shock the way wooden rackets do.*
4 short for SHOCK ABSORBER.
▸ **verb 1** [with obj.] cause (someone) to feel surprised and upset: *she was shocked at the state of his injuries.* ■ offend the moral feelings of; outrage: *the revelations shocked the nation.* ■ [no obj.] experience outrage: *he shocked so easily.*
2 affect with physiological shock, or with an electric shock.
3 [no obj.] archaic collide violently: *carriage after carriage shocked fiercely against the engine.*
– PHRASES **short, sharp shock** Brit. a brief but harsh custodial sentence intended to discourage an offender from committing further offences.
– DERIVATIVES **shockability** noun, **shockable** adjective.
– ORIGIN mid 16th cent.: from French *choc* (noun), *choquer* (verb), of unknown origin. The original senses were 'throw (troops) into confusion by charging at them' and 'an encounter between charging forces', giving rise to the notion of 'sudden violent blow or impact'.

shock[2] ▸ **noun** a group of twelve sheaves of grain placed upright and supporting each other to allow the grain to dry and ripen.
▸ **verb** [with obj.] arrange (sheaves of grain) in such a group.
– ORIGIN Middle English: perhaps from Middle Dutch, Middle Low German *schok*, of unknown origin.

shock[3] ▸ **noun** an unkempt or thick mass of hair: *a man with a shock of ginger hair.*
– ORIGIN mid 17th cent.: origin uncertain; compare with obsolete *shough*, denoting a breed of lapdog. The word originally denoted a dog with long shaggy hair, and was then used as an adjective meaning 'unkempt, shaggy'. The current sense dates from the early 19th cent.

shock absorber ▸ **noun** a device for absorbing jolts and vibrations, especially on a vehicle.

shock brigade ▸ **noun** (in the former Soviet Union) a body of workers who exceeded production quotas and were assigned to an especially urgent or arduous task.

shock cord ▸ **noun** [mass noun] heavy elasticated cord; bungee cord.

shocker ▸ **noun** informal **1** something that shocks, especially through being unacceptable or sensational: *the play's penultimate sequence is a shocker.* ■ a person who behaves badly or acts in a sensational manner: *I was a shocker when I was younger.*
2 Brit. a shock absorber.

shock-headed ▸ **adjective** having thick, shaggy, and unkempt hair.

shock-horror ▸ **adjective** Brit. informal causing great public outrage: *a shock-horror TV advertising campaign.*

shocking ▸ **adjective** causing indignation or disgust; offensive: *shocking behaviour.* ■ causing a feeling of surprise and dismay: *she brought shocking news.* ■ Brit. informal very bad: *I've got a shocking cold.*
– DERIVATIVES **shockingly** adverb, **shockingness** noun.

shocking pink ▸ **noun** [mass noun] a vibrant shade of pink.

shock jock ▸ **noun** informal a disc jockey on a talk-radio show who expresses opinions in a deliberately offensive or provocative way.

Shockley, William (Bradford) (1910–89), British-born American physicist. Shockley and his researchers at Bell Laboratories developed the transistor in 1948 and in 1958 he shared with them the Nobel Prize for Physics. He later became a controversial figure because of his views on a supposed connection between race and intelligence.

shockproof ▸ **adjective 1** designed to resist damage when dropped or knocked: *a shockproof watch.*
2 not easily shocked: *fifth-form grammar-school boys consider themselves a rather shockproof lot.*

shock stall ▸ **noun** [mass noun] a marked increase in drag and a loss of lift and control on an aircraft approaching the speed of sound.

shock tactics ▸ **plural noun** a strategy using sudden violent or extreme action to shock someone into doing something.

shock therapy (also **shock treatment**) ▸ **noun** [mass noun] treatment of chronic mental conditions by electroconvulsive therapy or by inducing physiological shock. ■ sudden and drastic measures taken to solve an intractable problem.

shock troops ▸ **plural noun** troops trained specially for carrying out a sudden assault.

shockumentary ▸ **noun** (pl. **shockumentaries**) a documentary film or programme that deals with subjects such as death or violence in a graphic and often sensationalized way.
– ORIGIN 1970s: blend of SHOCK[1] and DOCUMENTARY.

shock wave ▸ **noun** a sharp change of pressure in a narrow region travelling through a medium, especially air, caused by explosion or by a body moving faster than sound. ■ (usu. **shock waves**) a widespread feeling of shock caused by an unexpected event: *the oil embargo* ***sent shock waves through*** *the American economy.*

shock worker ▸ **noun** (in the former Soviet Union) a member of a shock brigade.

shod past and past participle of SHOE.

shoddy ▸ **adjective** (**shoddier**, **shoddiest**) badly made or done: *we're not paying good money for shoddy goods.* ■ lacking moral principle; sordid: *a shoddy misuse of the honours system.*
▸ **noun** [mass noun] an inferior quality yarn or fabric made from the shredded fibre of waste woollen cloth or clippings.
– DERIVATIVES **shoddily** adverb, **shoddiness** noun.
– ORIGIN mid 19th cent.: of unknown origin.

shoe ▸ **noun 1** a covering for the foot, typically made of leather, having a sturdy sole and not reaching above the ankle. ■ a horseshoe.
2 something resembling a shoe in shape or use, in particular: ■ a drag for a wheel. ■ short for BRAKE SHOE. ■ a socket, especially on a camera, for fitting a flash unit or other accessory. ■ a metal rim or ferrule, especially on the runner of a sledge. ■ a step for a mast. ■ a box from which cards are dealt in casinos at baccarat or some other card games.
▸ **verb** (**shoes**, **shoeing**; past and past participle **shod**)
1 [with obj.] fit (a horse) with a shoe or shoes. ■ (**be shod**) be wearing shoes of a specified kind: *his large feet were shod in trainers.*
2 protect (the end of an object such as a pole) with a metal shoe: *the four wooden baulks were each shod with heavy iron heads.* ■ fit a tyre to (a wheel).
– PHRASES **be** (or **put oneself**) **in another person's shoes** be (or put oneself) in another person's

S

situation or predicament: *if I'd been in your shoes I'd have walked out on him.* **dead men's shoes** property or a position coveted by a prospective successor but available only on a person's death. **if the shoe fits, wear it** N. Amer. see IF THE CAP FITS, WEAR IT (at CAP[1]). **shoe leather** informal used in reference to the wear on shoes through walking: *you can save on shoe leather by giving us your instructions over the telephone.* **wait for the other shoe to drop** N. Amer. informal be prepared for a further or consequential event or complication to occur.
– DERIVATIVES **shoeless** adjective.
– ORIGIN Old English *scōh* (noun), *scōg(e)an* (verb), of Germanic origin; related to Dutch *schoen* and German *Schuh*.

shoebill (also **shoe-billed stork**) ▶ noun another term for WHALE-HEADED STORK.

shoeblack ▶ noun dated, chiefly Brit. a person who cleans the shoes of passers-by for payment.

shoebox ▶ noun a box in which a pair of shoes is delivered or sold. ■ informal a very small room or space: *a shoebox of a room.*

shoegazing ▶ noun [mass noun] a style of rock music characterized by a sound in which the distinctions between separate instruments and vocals are blurred.
– ORIGIN 1990s: from the supposed tendency of the performers to look down, rather than at the audience.

shoehorn ▶ noun a curved instrument used for easing one's heel into a shoe.
▶ verb [with obj. and adverbial] force into an inadequate space: *people were shoehorned into cramped corners.*

shoelace ▶ noun a cord or leather strip passed through eyelets or hooks on opposite sides of a shoe and pulled tight and fastened.

shoemaker ▶ noun a person who makes shoes and other footwear as a profession.
– DERIVATIVES **shoemaking** noun.

Shoemaker–Levy 9 /ˈliːvi/ a comet discovered in March 1993, when it had just broken up as a result of passing very close to Jupiter. In July 1994 more than twenty separate fragments impacted successively on Jupiter, causing large explosions in its atmosphere.
– ORIGIN named after Carolyn (born 1929) and Eugene *Shoemaker* (1928–97), American astronomers, and David *Levy* (born 1948), Canadian astronomer, discoverers of the comet.

shoepack ▶ noun N. Amer. an oiled leather boot, typically having a rubber sole.
– ORIGIN mid 18th cent.: from Delaware (Unami) *sippack* 'shoes', from *čípahkpo* 'moccasins', later assimilated to SHOE and PACK[1].

shoeshine ▶ noun chiefly N. Amer. an act of polishing someone's shoes, especially for payment: [as modifier] *a shoeshine boy.*
– DERIVATIVES **shoeshiner** noun.

shoestring ▶ noun **1** informal a small or inadequate budget: *many early studies were done* ***on a shoestring*** | [as modifier] *a shoestring budget.*
2 N. Amer. a shoelace.
▶ adjective N. Amer. (of a save or tackle in sport) near or around the ankles or feet, or just above the ground.

S

shoestring potatoes ▶ plural noun N. Amer. potatoes cut into long, thin strips and deep-fried.

shoe tree ▶ noun a shaped block inserted into a shoe when it is not being worn to keep the shoe in shape.

shofar /ˈʃəʊfə/ ▶ noun (pl. **shofars** or **shofroth** /ˈʃəʊfrəʊt/) a ram's-horn trumpet formerly used by Jews as an ancient battle signal and now used in Jewish religious ceremonies.
– ORIGIN from Hebrew *šōpār*, (plural) *šōpārōṯ*.

shogun /ˈʃəʊgʊn/ ▶ noun a hereditary commander-in-chief in feudal Japan. Because of the military power concentrated in his hands and the consequent weakness of the nominal head of state (the mikado or emperor), the shogun was generally the real ruler of the country until feudalism was abolished in 1867.
– DERIVATIVES **shogunate** /-nət/ noun.
– ORIGIN Japanese, from Chinese *jiāng jūn* 'general'.

shoji /ˈʃəʊdʒi/ (also **shoji screen**) ▶ noun (pl. **same** or **shojis**) (in Japan) a sliding outer or inner door made of a latticed screen covered with white paper.
– ORIGIN from Japanese *shōji*.

Sholapur variant spelling of SOLAPUR.

Shona /ˈʃəʊnə/ ▶ noun (pl. **same** or **Shonas**) **1** a member of a group of peoples inhabiting parts of southern Africa. The Shona comprise over three quarters of the population of Zimbabwe, and smaller groups live in South Africa, Zambia, and Mozambique. See also MASHONA.
2 [mass noun] any of the closely related Bantu languages spoken by the Shona, with over 5 million speakers altogether.
▶ adjective relating to the Shona or their languages.
– ORIGIN a local name.

shone past and past participle of SHINE.

shongololo ▶ noun variant spelling of SONGOLOLO.

shonky Austral./NZ informal ▶ adjective (**shonkier**, **shonkiest**) dishonest, unreliable, or illegal, especially in a devious way: *shonky political goings-on.*
▶ noun (also **shonk**) a person engaged in suspect business activities.
– ORIGIN 1970s: perhaps from English dialect *shonk* 'smart'.

shoo ▶ exclamation a word said to frighten or drive away a person or animal.
▶ verb (**shoos**, **shooing**, **shooed**) [with obj. and adverbial of direction] make (a person or animal) go away by waving one's arms at them, saying 'shoo', or otherwise acting in a discouraging manner: *I went to comfort her but she shooed me away.*
– ORIGIN a natural exclamation: first recorded in late Middle English. The verb use dates from the early 17th cent.

shoo-fly pie ▶ noun N. Amer. a rich tart made of treacle baked in a pastry case with a crumble topping.
– ORIGIN from the US interjection *shoo-fly* (referring to the need to wave flies away from the sweet treacle).

shoogly /ˈʃʊgli/ ▶ adjective Scottish unsteady; wobbly.
– ORIGIN Middle English: probably of imitative origin.

shoo-in ▶ noun informal a person or thing that is certain to succeed, especially someone who is certain to win a competition: *he was* ***a shoo-in for*** *re-election.*
– ORIGIN 1930s: from the earlier use of the term denoting the winner of a rigged horse race.

shook[1] past of SHAKE. ▶ adjective informal **1** (**shook up**) emotionally or physically disturbed; upset: *she looks pretty shook up from the letter.*
2 (**shook on**) Austral./NZ keen on; enthusiastic about: *those stories you read about where two blokes get shook on the same sheila.*

shook[2] ▶ noun N. Amer. a set of components ready for assembly into a box or cask.
– ORIGIN late 18th cent.: of unknown origin.

shoot ▶ verb (past and past participle **shot**) **1** [with obj.] kill or wound (a person or animal) with a bullet or arrow: *he was shot in the leg during an armed robbery* | [with obj. and complement] *troops* ***shot dead*** *29 people.* ■ [no obj.] fire a bullet from a gun or discharge an arrow from a bow: *he* ***shot at*** *me twice* | *the troops were ordered to* ***shoot to kill*** | [with obj.] *they shot a volley of arrows into the village.* ■ [no obj., with adverbial] use a firearm with a specified degree of skill: *we shot well against Spain.* ■ cause (a gun) to fire. ■ [no obj.] hunt game with a gun: *we go to Scotland to shoot every autumn.*
2 move or cause to move suddenly and rapidly in a particular direction: [no obj., with adverbial of direction] *the car shot forward* | *Ward's hand shot out, grabbing his arm* | [with obj. and adverbial of direction] *he would have fallen if Marc hadn't shot out a hand to stop him.* ■ [no obj.] (of a pain) move with a sharp stabbing sensation: *Claudia felt a pain shoot through her chest* | figurative *a pang of regret shot through her.* ■ [no obj.] extend sharply in a particular direction: *a road that seemed to just shoot upwards at a terrifying angle.* ■ [with obj.] move (a bolt) to fasten or unfasten a door. ■ [with obj.] (of a boat) sweep swiftly down or under (rapids, a waterfall, or a bridge). ■ [with obj.] informal (of a motor vehicle) pass (a traffic light at red). ■ [no obj.] Cricket (of a ball) dart along the ground after pitching.
3 [no obj.] (in football, hockey, basketball, etc.) kick, hit, or throw the ball or puck in an attempt to score a goal: *Williams twice shot wide* | [with obj.] *after school, we'd go straight out in the alley to shoot baskets.* ■ [with obj.] informal make (a specified score) for a round of golf: *in the second round he shot a 65.* ■ [with obj.] N. Amer. informal play a game of (pool, dice, or cards).
4 [with obj.] direct (a glance, question, or remark) at someone: [with two objs] *Luke shot her a quick glance* | [with direct speech] *'I can't believe what I'm hearing,' she* ***shot back.*** ■ [no obj., in imperative] used to invite a comment or question: *'May I just ask you one more question?' 'Shoot.'.*
5 [with obj.] film or photograph (a scene, film, etc.): *she has just been commissioned to shoot a video.*
6 [no obj.] (of a plant or seed) send out buds or shoots; germinate. ■ (of a bud or shoot) appear; sprout.
7 [with obj.] informal inject oneself or another person with (a narcotic drug): *he shot dope into his arm.*
8 [with obj.] plane (the edge of a board) accurately.
▶ noun **1** a young branch or sucker springing from the main stock of a tree or other plant: *he nipped off the new shoots that grew where the leaves joined the stems.*
2 an occasion when a group of people hunt and shoot game for sport: *a grouse shoot.* ■ Brit. an area of land used for shooting game. ■ a shooting match: *activities include a weekly rifle shoot.*
3 an occasion when a professional photographer takes photographs or when a film or video is being made: *a photo shoot* | *a fashion shoot.*
4 variant spelling of CHUTE[1].
5 a rapid in a stream: *follow the portages that skirt all nine shoots of whitewater.*
▶ exclamation N. Amer. informal used as a euphemism for 'shit': *shoot, it was a great day to be alive.*
– PHRASES **have shot one's bolt** see BOLT[1]. **shoot the breeze** (or **the bull**) N. Amer. informal have a casual conversation. **shoot one's cuffs** pull one's shirt cuffs out to project beyond the cuffs of one's jacket or coat. **shoot from the hip** informal react without careful consideration of one's words or actions. **shoot oneself in the foot** informal inadvertently make a situation worse for oneself. **shoot it out** informal engage in a decisive confrontation, typically a gun battle. **shoot a line** Brit. informal describe something in an exaggerated or untruthful way: *he never shot a line about his escapades.* **shoot one's mouth off** informal talk boastfully or indiscreetly.
– PHRASAL VERBS **shoot someone/thing down** bring down an aircraft or missile by shooting at it: *their helicopter was shot down by an air-to-air missile.* ■ kill or wound someone by shooting them, esp. in a ruthless way: *troops shot down 28 demonstrators.* ■ crush someone or their opinions by forceful criticism: *she tried to argue and got* ***shot down in flames*** *for her trouble.* **shoot through** Austral./NZ informal leave, typically to escape from or avoid someone or something: *me wife's shot through and I can't pay the rent.* [1940s: from *shoot through like a Bondi tram* (Bondi being a Sydney suburb).] **shoot up** (especially of a child) grow taller rapidly. ■ (of a price or amount) rise suddenly. **shoot someone/thing up 1** cause great damage to something by shooting: *the police shot up our building.* **2** (also **shoot up**) informal inject oneself (or someone else) with a narcotic drug: *she went home and shot up alone in her room* | *shoot people up with the new chemical and see what happens.*
– DERIVATIVES **shootable** adjective.
– ORIGIN Old English *scēotan*, of Germanic origin; related to Dutch *schieten* and German *schiessen*, also to SHEET[1], SHOT[1], and SHUT.

shoot-'em-up ▶ noun informal a fast-moving story or film of which gunfire is a dominant feature. ■ a simple computer game in which the sole objective is to kill as many enemies as possible.

shooter ▶ noun **1** a person who uses a gun either regularly or on a particular occasion. ■ informal a gun.
2 a member of a team in games such as netball and basketball whose role is to attempt to score goals. ■ a person who throws a dice.
3 Cricket a bowled ball that moves rapidly along the ground after pitching.
4 informal, chiefly N. Amer. a small alcoholic drink, especially of spirits: *geez, he could use a shooter of whiskey.*

shooting ▶ noun [mass noun] the action or practice of shooting: *the unprovoked shooting of civilians by soldiers* | [count noun] *20,000 fatal shootings a year.* ■ the sport or pastime of shooting with a gun. ■ the right of shooting game over an area of land. ■ [count noun] an estate or other area rented to shoot over.
▶ adjective moving or growing quickly: *shooting beams of light played over the sea.* ■ (of a pain) sudden and piercing.
– PHRASES **the whole shooting match** informal everything: *the whole shooting match is being computerized.*

shooting board ▶ noun a board with a step-shaped profile used to guide the motion of a plane relative to a workpiece to ensure accurate planing.

shooting box ▶ noun Brit. a lodge used by hunters in the shooting season.

shooting brake ▶ noun Brit. dated an estate car.

shooting coat ▶ noun a padded waterproof coat with large pockets, worn when shooting game. ■ archaic term for MORNING COAT.

shooting gallery ▶ noun a room or fairground booth used for recreational shooting at targets with guns or airguns. ■ N. Amer. informal a place used for taking drugs, especially injecting heroin.

shooting iron ▸ noun informal, chiefly US a firearm.

shooting jacket ▸ noun another term for SAFARI JACKET.

shooting range ▸ noun an area provided with targets for the controlled practice of shooting.

shooting star ▸ noun **1** a small, rapidly moving meteor burning up on entering the earth's atmosphere.
2 a North American plant with white, pink, or purple hanging flowers with backward-curving petals. The flowers are carried above the leaves on slender stems and turn to face up following fertilization. ● Genus *Dodecatheon*, family Primulaceae.

shooting stick ▸ noun a walking stick with a handle that unfolds to form a seat and a sharpened end which can be stuck firmly in the ground.

shooting war ▸ noun a war in which there is armed conflict as opposed to mere threats, propaganda, or sanctions.

shootist ▸ noun N. Amer. informal a person who shoots, especially a marksman.
– ORIGIN mid 19th cent.: from SHOOT + -IST.

shoot-out ▸ noun informal a decisive gun battle. ■ (also **penalty shoot-out**) Soccer a tiebreaker decided by each side taking a specified number of penalty kicks.

shop ▸ noun **1** a building or part of a building where goods or services are sold: *a video shop | a barber's shop.* ■ [in sing.] informal an act of going shopping: *she slogged her way round the supermarket doing the weekly shop.*
2 [usu. with modifier] a place where things are manufactured or repaired; a workshop: *an auto repair shop.* ■ a room or department in a factory where a particular stage of production is carried out: *the machine shop.* ■ (**the shop**) informal the place where one works: *she pointed to the classroom ceiling—'I live here, over the shop.'*
▸ verb (**shops, shopping, shopped**) **1** [no obj.] go to a shop or shops to buy goods: *she **shopped for** groceries twice a week.* ■ (**shop around**) look for the best available price or rate for something: *they shopped around for cheaper food.* ■ N. Amer. short for WINDOW-SHOP.
2 [with obj.] Brit. informal inform on (someone): *she shopped her husband to bosses for taking tools home.*
– PHRASES **all over the shop** see ALL. **set up shop** establish oneself in a business: *he set up shop as a hairdresser in Soho.* **shut up shop** cease trading. ■ informal cease doing something: *flowers that come in one great burst, then shut up shop for the rest of the year.* **talk shop** discuss matters concerning one's work, especially at a social occasion when this is inappropriate.
– ORIGIN Middle English: shortening of Old French *eschoppe* 'lean-to booth', of West Germanic origin; related to German *Schopf* 'porch' and English dialect *shippon* 'cattle shed'. The verb is first recorded (mid 16th cent.) in the sense 'imprison' (from an obsolete slang use of the noun for 'prison'), hence sense 2 of the verb.

shopaholic ▸ noun informal a compulsive shopper.
– ORIGIN 1980s: blend of SHOP and ALCOHOLIC.

shop assistant ▸ noun Brit. a person who serves customers in a shop.

shop-bought ▸ adjective (especially of an item of food) bought in a shop as opposed to being homemade: *shop-bought pasta sauces.*

shop boy ▸ noun dated a male shop assistant.

shop class ▸ noun N. Amer. a class in which practical skills such as carpentry or engineering are taught: *back in high school I made a wooden dummy in shop class.*

shopfitter ▸ noun a person whose job it is to fit the counters, shelves, etc. with which a shop is equipped.
– DERIVATIVES **shopfitting** noun.

shop floor ▸ noun Brit. the part of a workshop or factory where production as distinct from administrative work is carried out: *working conditions on the shop floor.*

shopfront ▸ noun Brit. the facade of a shop.

shop girl ▸ noun dated a female shop assistant.

shophouse ▸ noun (in SE Asia) a shop opening on to the pavement and also used as the owner's residence.

shopkeeper ▸ noun the owner and manager of a shop.
– DERIVATIVES **shopkeeping** noun.

shoplifting ▸ noun [mass noun] the action of stealing goods from a shop while pretending to be a customer.
– DERIVATIVES **shoplift** verb, **shoplifter** noun.

shoplot ▸ noun SE Asian the area occupied by a shop.

shopman ▸ noun (pl. **shopmen**) Brit. dated a male shop assistant or shopkeeper.

shoppe /ʃɒp, ˈʃɒpi/ ▸ noun a shop with spurious old-fashioned charm or quaintness: *the mishmash of the usual Tourist Gift Shoppe.*

shopper ▸ noun a person who is shopping. ■ Brit. a bag for holding shopping, that is attached to wheels and pushed or pulled along: *a four-wheeled tartan shopper.* ■ a small-wheeled bicycle with a basket, designed for use while shopping.

shopping ▸ noun [mass noun] [often as modifier] the purchasing of goods from shops: *a busy shopping area.* ■ goods bought from shops, especially food and household goods: *a bag of shopping.*

shopping cart ▸ noun North American term for SHOPPING TROLLEY.

shopping centre ▸ noun an area or complex of shops.

shopping list ▸ noun a list of purchases to be made. ■ a list of items to be considered or acted on: *a lengthy shopping list of detailed proposals.*

shopping mall ▸ noun see MALL (sense 1)

shopping trolley ▸ noun Brit. a bag or basket on wheels for carrying shopping, in particular a large wire basket on wheels provided for the use of supermarket customers.

shopping village ▸ noun an upmarket out-of-town shopping centre.

shop-soiled ▸ adjective Brit. (of an article) made dirty or imperfect by being displayed or handled in a shop.

shop steward ▸ noun a person elected by workers, for example in a factory, to represent them in dealings with management.

shop talk ▸ noun [mass noun] conversation about one's occupation or business at an informal or social occasion.

shopwalker ▸ noun Brit. dated a senior employee in a large shop who supervises assistants, directs customers, and answers queries.

shop window ▸ noun a window of a shop, in which goods are displayed: *looking in a shop window.* ■ (**the shop window**) a position that allows a person or organization to demonstrate their strengths: *he is keen to put himself **in the shop window**.*

shopworker ▸ noun Brit. a person who works in a shop.

shopworn ▸ adjective N. Amer. another term for SHOP-SOILED.

shore[1] ▸ noun the land along the edge of a sea, lake, or other large body of water: *I made for the shore.* ■ Law the land between ordinary high- and low-water marks. ■ (usu. **shores**) a country or other geographic area bounded by a coast: *record companies have been anxious to import the music to American shores.*
– PHRASES **in shore** on the water near land or nearer to land. **on shore** ashore; on land: *are any of the crew left on shore?*
– DERIVATIVES **shoreless** adjective, **shoreward** adjective & adverb, **shorewards** adverb.
– ORIGIN Middle English: from Middle Dutch, Middle Low German *schōre*; perhaps related to the verb SHEAR.

shore[2] ▸ noun a prop or beam set obliquely against something weak or unstable as a support.
– PHRASAL VERBS **shore something up** support or hold up something with props or beams: *rescue workers had to shore up the building, which was in danger of collapse.* ■ support or assist something that would otherwise fail or decline: *Congress approved a $700 billion plan to shore up the financial industry.*
– ORIGIN Middle English: from Middle Dutch, Middle Low German *schore* 'prop', of unknown origin.

shore[3] archaic past of SHEAR.

shore-based ▸ adjective operating from or based on a shore or land: *shore-based guns.*

shorebird ▸ noun a bird that frequents the shore. ■ chiefly N. Amer. a wader of the order Charadriiformes, such as a sandpiper.

shorelark ▸ noun a widespread lark of open country, especially the Arctic and mountains, the male having a black and white head pattern and two small black horn-like crests. ● Genus *Eremophila*, family Alaudidae: two species, in particular *E. alpestris*. North American name: **horned lark**.

shore leave ▸ noun [mass noun] leisure time spent ashore by a sailor: *the hall was full of sailors **on shore leave**.*

shoreline ▸ noun the line along which a large body of water meets the land: *he walked along the shoreline.*

shoreside ▸ noun the edge of a shore: [as modifier] *a shoreside restaurant.* ■ the side of something nearest the shore: *men on the shoreside of each boat were poling it upriver.*

shoreweed ▸ noun [mass noun] a small European plant with grass-like leaves, growing in mud and shallow water at the edge of ponds. ● *Littorella uniflora*, family Plantaginaceae.

shoring ▸ noun [mass noun] shores or props used to support or hold up something weak or unstable.

shorn past participle of SHEAR.

short ▸ adjective **1** measuring a small distance from end to end: *short dark hair | a short flight of steps | the bed was too short for him.* ■ (of a journey) covering a small distance: *the hotel is a short walk from the sea.* ■ (of a garment or sleeves on a garment) only covering the top part of a person's arms or legs: *a short skirt.* ■ (of a person) small in height: *he is short and tubby.* ■ (of a ball in cricket, a shot in tennis, etc.) travelling only a small distance before bouncing: *he uses his opportunities to attack every short ball.* ■ Cricket denoting fielding positions relatively close to the batsman: *short midwicket.*
2 lasting or taking a small amount of time: *visiting London for a short break | a short conversation.* ■ [attrib.] seeming to last less time than is the case; passing quickly: *in 10 short years all this changed.* ■ (of a person's memory) retaining things for only a small amount of time: *he has a short memory for past misdeeds.* ■ Stock Exchange (of stocks or other securities or commodities) sold in advance of being acquired, with reliance on the price falling so that a profit can be made. ■ Stock Exchange (of a broker, position in the market, etc.) buying or based on such stocks or other securities or commodities. ■ denoting or having a relatively early date for the maturing of a bill of exchange.
3 relatively small in extent: *a short speech | he wrote a short book.* ■ (**short of/on**) not having enough of (something); lacking or deficient in: *they were very short of provisions | I know you're short on cash.* ■ [predic.] in insufficient supply: *food is short.*
4 Phonetics (of a vowel) categorized as short with regard to quality and length (e.g. in standard British English the vowel /ʊ/ in *good* is short as distinct from the long vowel /uː/ in *food*). ■ Prosody (of a vowel or syllable) having the lesser of the two recognized durations.
5 [predic.] (of a person) terse; uncivil: *he was often sharp and rather **short with** her.*
6 (of odds or a chance) reflecting or representing a high level of probability: *they have been backed at short odds to win thousands of pounds.*
7 (of pastry) containing a high proportion of fat to flour and therefore crumbly. ■ (of clay) having poor plasticity.
▸ adverb (chiefly in sport) at, to, or over a relatively small distance: *you go deep and you go short.* ■ not as far as the point aimed at; not far enough: *all too often you pitch the ball short.*
▸ noun **1** Brit. a drink of spirits served in a small measure.
2 a short film as opposed to a feature film.
3 a short sound such as a short signal in Morse code or a short vowel or syllable: *her call was two longs and a short.*
4 a short circuit.
5 Stock Exchange a person who sells short. ■ (**shorts**) Stock Exchange short-dated stocks.
6 (**shorts**) a mixture of bran and coarse flour.
▸ verb **1** short-circuit or cause to short-circuit: [no obj.] *the electrical circuit had **shorted out** |* [with obj.] *if the contact terminals are shorted, the battery quickly overheats.*
2 ■ [with obj.] Stock Exchange sell (stocks or other securities or commodities) in advance of acquiring them, with the aim of making a profit when the price falls.
– PHRASES **be caught** (or Brit. **taken**) **short** be put at a disadvantage: *he encouraged young people to build up a range of skills so they are not caught short when employment ends suddenly.* ■ Brit. informal urgently need to urinate or defecate. **a brick short of a load** (or **two sandwiches short of a picnic**, etc.) informal (of a person) stupid or slightly mad: *she's two bricks short of a load.* **bring** (or **pull**) **someone up short**

S

make someone check or pause abruptly: *he was entering the office when he was brought up short by the sight of John.* **come short** fail to reach a goal or standard: *we're so close to getting the job done, but we keep **coming up** short.* ■ S. African get into trouble: *if you try to trick him you'll come short.* **for short** as an abbreviation or nickname: *the File Transfer Protocol, or FTP for short.* **get** (or **have**) **someone by the short and curlies** (or **short hairs**) informal have complete control of a person. [from military slang, referring to pubic hair.] **go short** not have enough of something, especially food: *you won't go short when I die.* **in short** to sum up; briefly: *we hope, in short, to bring theory and practice together in each session.* **in short order** chiefly N. Amer. immediately; rapidly: *after the killing the camp had been shut down in short order.* **in the short run** (or **term**) in the near future. **in short supply** (of a commodity) scarce. **little** (or **nothing**) **short of** almost (or equal to); little (or nothing) less than: *he regarded the cost of living as little short of scandalous.* **make short work of** accomplish, consume, or destroy quickly: *we made short work of our huge portions.* **sell short** Stock Exchange sell stock or other securities or commodities which one does not own at the time, in the hope of buying at a lower price before the delivery time. **sell someone/thing short** fail to recognize or state the true value of: *don't sell yourself short—you've got what it takes.* **short and sweet** brief but pleasant or relevant: *his comments were short and sweet.* **the short end of the stick** N. Amer. an outcome in which one has less advantage than others. **short for** an abbreviation or nickname for: *I'm Robbie—short for Roberta.* **short of** less than: *he died at sixty-one, four years short of his pensionable age.* ■ not reaching as far as. ■ without going so far as (some extreme action): *short of putting out an all-persons alert, there's little else we can do.* **short of breath** panting; short-winded. **short, sharp shock** see SHOCK[1]. **stop short** stop suddenly or abruptly. **stop short of** not go as far as (some extreme action): *the measures stopped short of establishing direct trade links.*

– DERIVATIVES **shortish** adjective, **shortness** noun.

– ORIGIN Old English *sceort*, of Germanic origin; related to SHIRT and SKIRT.

short-acting ▸ adjective (chiefly of a drug) having effects that only last for a short time.

shortage ▸ noun a state or situation in which something needed cannot be obtained in sufficient amounts: *a **shortage of** hard cash | food shortages |* [mass noun] *the problems of land shortage in the countryside.*

short-arm ▸ adjective denoting a blow or throw executed with the arm not fully extended or with motion from the elbow only.

short-arse ▸ noun informal, derogatory a person of small stature.

short back and sides ▸ noun Brit. a haircut in which the hair is cut short at the back and the sides.

shortbread ▸ noun [mass noun] a crisp, rich, crumbly type of biscuit made with butter, flour, and sugar.

shortcake ▸ noun [mass noun] **1** Brit. shortbread.
2 N. Amer. a rich dessert made from short pastry and topped with fruit and whipped cream.

S

short-change ▸ verb [with obj.] cheat (someone) by giving insufficient money as change: *I'm sure I was short-changed at the bar.* ■ treat unfairly by withholding something of value: (as adj. **short-changed**) *I felt short-changed when United left five of their stars at home.*

▸ noun (**short change**) [mass noun] insufficient money given as change.

short circuit ▸ noun an electrical circuit in a device of lower resistance than that of a normal circuit, especially one resulting from the unintended contact of components and consequent accidental diversion of the current.

▸ verb (**short-circuit**) (with reference to an electrical device) malfunction or fail, or cause to do this, as a result of a short circuit: [no obj.] *the birds caused the electricity supply to short-circuit* | [with obj.] *water had leaked into the washing machine's motor, short-circuiting it.* ■ [with obj.] shorten (a process or activity) by using a more direct (but often improper) method: *the normal processes of a democracy should not be short-circuited.*

shortcoming ▸ noun (usu. **shortcomings**) a fault or failure to meet a certain standard, typically in a person's character, a plan, or a system: *he discussed the shortcomings of his wife.*

short commons ▸ plural noun see COMMONS.

short corner ▸ noun (in field hockey) a penalty hit taken from a spot on the goal line relatively close to the goalposts (but not within ten yards).

short covering ▸ noun [mass noun] Stock Exchange the buying in of stocks or other securities or commodities that have been sold short, typically to avoid loss when prices move upwards.

shortcrust (also **shortcrust pastry**) ▸ noun [mass noun] Brit. crumbly pastry made with flour, fat, and a little water, typically used for pies, flans, and tarts.

shortcut ▸ noun an alternative route that is shorter than the one usually taken: *they were **taking a shortcut** to town.* ■ an accelerated way of doing or achieving something: *teaching no longer offered **a shortcut to** secure employment.* ■ Computing a record of the address of a file, website, or other data made to enable quick access.

short-dated ▸ adjective (of a stock or bond) due for early payment or redemption.

short-day ▸ adjective denoting a plant that needs a daily period of darkness of more than a certain length to initiate flowering, which therefore happens naturally as the days shorten in the autumn.

short division ▸ noun [mass noun] arithmetical division in which the quotient is written directly without a succession of intermediate workings.

short-eared owl ▸ noun a migratory day-flying owl that frequents open country, found in northern Eurasia and North and South America. ● *Asio flammeus*, family Strigidae.

shorten ▸ verb **1** make or become shorter: [with obj.] *he shortened his stride | patients whose waiting time had been shortened* | [no obj.] *as skirts shortened, so heels rose | around mid September, days shorten and temperatures dip.* ■ (with reference to gambling odds) make or become shorter; decrease: [with obj.] *Ladbrokes shortened Nashwan's odds from 2–1 to 7–4* | [no obj.] *the odds had shortened to 14–1.* ■ [with obj.] Prosody & Phonetics make (a vowel or syllable) short.
2 [with obj.] Sailing reduce the amount of (sail spread).

short end ▸ noun (**the short end**) the part of a stock market which deals in short-term stocks or other securities or commodities.

shortening ▸ noun [mass noun] fat used for making pastry.

shortfall ▸ noun a deficit of something required or expected: *they are facing an expected $10 billion **shortfall in** revenue.*

short field ▸ noun Baseball the part of the outfield nearest the infield: *he hit the next hard into short field.*

short-fused ▸ adjective informal quick-tempered.

shorthair ▸ noun a cat of a short-haired breed.

shorthand ▸ noun [mass noun] a method of rapid writing by means of abbreviations and symbols, used especially for taking dictation. The major systems of shorthand currently in use are those devised in 1837 by Sir Isaac Pitman and (in the US) in 1888 by John R. Gregg (1867–1948). ■ [in sing.] a short and simple way of expressing or referring to something: *poetry for him is simply a **shorthand for** literature that has aesthetic value.*

short-handed ▸ adjective not having enough or the usual number of staff or crew: *the kitchen was a bit short-handed* | [as adv.] *the management worked short-handed.* ■ Ice Hockey (of a goal) scored by a team playing with fewer players on the ice than their opponent. ■ Ice Hockey (of a situation) occurring while or because a team has fewer than six players on the ice.

shorthand typist ▸ noun Brit. a typist qualified to take and transcribe shorthand.

short haul ▸ noun a relatively short distance in terms of travel or the transport of goods: *it is only a short haul over the mountains to Los Angeles* | [as modifier] *short-haul routes.*

short head Horse Racing, Brit. ▸ noun a length less than that of a horse's head (used in referring to the distance by which a horse wins or loses): *he lost **by a short head**.*

▸ verb (**short-head**) [with obj.] narrowly beat.

shorthold ▸ adjective English Law relating to or denoting a tenancy whereby the tenant agrees to rent a property for a stated term, at the end of which the landlord may recover it.

shorthorn ▸ noun an animal of a breed of cattle with short horns.

short hundredweight ▸ noun see HUNDREDWEIGHT.

shortie ▸ noun variant spelling of SHORTY.

short leet ▸ noun & verb Scottish term for SHORTLIST.

shortlist ▸ noun a list of selected candidates from which a final choice is made: *a shortlist of four companies.*

▸ verb [with obj.] put (someone or something) on a shortlist: *the novel was **shortlisted for** the Booker Prize.*

short-lived ▸ adjective lasting only a short time: *a short-lived romance | these benefits are likely to be short-lived.*

shortly ▸ adverb **1** in a short time; soon: *the new database will shortly be available for consultation | the flight was hijacked **shortly after** takeoff.*
2 in a few words; briefly: *they received a letter shortly outlining the proposals.* ■ abruptly, sharply, or curtly: *'Do you like cricket?' 'I do not,' she said shortly.*

– ORIGIN Old English *scortlice* (see SHORT, -LY[2]).

short mark ▸ noun informal term for BREVE (sense 2).

short measure ▸ noun an amount, especially of alcohol, less than that which is declared or paid for.

short metre ▸ noun a metrical pattern for hymns in which the stanzas have four lines with 6, 6, 8, and 6 syllables.

short order ▸ noun N. Amer. an order or dish of food which can be quickly prepared and served: *a short order of souvlaki* | [as modifier] *I'm a short-order cook.*

– PHRASES **in short order** see SHORT.

Short Parliament the first of two parliaments summoned by Charles I in 1640 (the other being the Long Parliament). Due to its insistence on seeking a general redress of grievances against him before granting the money he required, Charles dismissed it after only three weeks.

short-pitched ▸ adjective Cricket (of a delivery) bowled so that the ball bounces relatively near the bowler: *fast, short-pitched bowling.*

short-range ▸ adjective **1** (especially of a vehicle or missile) only able to be used or be effective over short distances: *short-range nuclear weapons.*
2 of or over a short period of future time: *short-range schemes | short-range forecasting.*

short rib ▸ noun **1** Brit. another term for FLOATING RIB.
2 (**short ribs**) N. Amer. a narrow cut of beef containing the ends of the ribs near to the breastbone.

short-run ▸ adjective taken or considered on a short timescale; short-term: *periods of often violent short-run price volatility.*

shorts ▸ plural noun short trousers that reach only to the knees or thighs: *cycling shorts.* ■ N. Amer. men's underpants.

short score ▸ noun Music a score in which the parts are condensed on to a small number of staves.

short-sheet ▸ verb [with obj.] N. Amer. informal make (a bed) as an apple-pie bed. ■ give an apple-pie bed to (someone). ■ cheat or treat unjustly: *we retirees have been short-sheeted for a long time.*

short shrift ▸ noun [mass noun] **1** rapid and unsympathetic dismissal; curt treatment: *the judge **gave short shrift to** an argument based on the right to free speech.*
2 archaic little time between condemnation and execution or punishment.

short sight ▸ noun [mass noun] the inability to see things clearly unless they are relatively close to the eyes, owing to the focusing of rays of light by the eye at a point in front of the retina. Also called MYOPIA.

short-sighted ▸ adjective Brit. having short sight. ■ lacking imagination or foresight: *a short-sighted government.*

– DERIVATIVES **short-sightedly** adverb, **short-sightedness** noun.

short-sleeved ▸ adjective having sleeves that do not reach below the elbow: *a short-sleeved silk top.*

short-staffed ▸ adjective having too few or fewer than the usual number of staff.

short-stay ▸ adjective denoting or relating to people staying somewhere for only a short period: *short-stay accommodation.*

shortstop /ˈʃɔːtstɒp/ ▸ noun Baseball a fielder positioned between second and third base.

short story ▸ noun a story with a fully developed theme but significantly shorter and less elaborate than a novel.

short subject ▸ noun chiefly US a short film, typically one shown before the screening of a feature film.

short suit ▸ noun (in bridge or whist) a holding of only one or two cards of one suit in a hand.

short-tailed vole ▸ noun another term for **FIELD VOLE**.

short temper ▸ noun a tendency to lose one's temper quickly.

short-tempered ▸ adjective quick to lose one's temper.

short tennis ▸ noun [mass noun] tennis played on a small court with a small racket and a soft ball, used especially as an introduction to the game for children.

short-term ▸ adjective occurring in or relating to a relatively short period of future time: *it might be a wise short-term investment.*

short-termism ▸ noun [mass noun] concentration on short-term projects or objectives for immediate profit at the expense of long-term security.

short time ▸ noun [mass noun] Brit. the condition of working fewer than the regular hours per day or days per week: *staff have agreed to work on short time.*

short-timer ▸ noun US military slang a person nearing the end of their period of military service.

short title ▸ noun an abbreviated form of a title of a book or document.

short ton ▸ noun see **TON**[1].

short trousers ▸ plural noun trousers reaching only to the knee, as worn typically by young boys.

short view ▸ noun (**the short view**) consideration of the present and immediate future only: *you will say I was taking the short view.*

short waist ▸ noun a high waist on a woman's dress or a person's body.
– DERIVATIVES **short-waisted** adjective.

short wave ▸ noun a radio wave of a wavelength between about 10 and 100 m (and a frequency of about 3 to 30 MHz): [as modifier] *a short-wave transmitter.* ▪ [mass noun] broadcasting using radio waves of this wavelength: [as modifier] *short-wave radio.*

short weight ▸ noun [mass noun] weight that is less than that declared: *unscrupulous retailers give short weight by including an excessive amount of packaging.*

short-winded ▸ adjective (of a person) out of breath or quickly becoming so.

shorty (also **shortie**) ▸ noun (pl. **shorties**) informal a person who is shorter than average (often used as a nickname). ▪ [often as modifier] a short garment, especially a short dress, nightdress, or raincoat: *she pulled on a shorty nightshirt.*

Shoshone /ʃəˈʃəʊni/ ▸ noun (pl. **same** or **Shoshones**)
1 a member of an American Indian people living chiefly in Wyoming, Idaho, and Nevada.
2 [mass noun] the Uto-Aztecan language of the Shoshone.
▸ adjective relating to the Shoshone or their language.
– ORIGIN of unknown origin.

Shoshonean ▸ noun [mass noun] a branch of the Uto-Aztecan language family that includes Comanche and Shoshone.
▸ adjective relating to or denoting this group of languages.

Shostakovich /ˌʃɒstəˈkəʊvɪtʃ/, Dmitri (Dmitrievich) (1906–75), Russian composer. He developed a highly personal style and, although he experimented with atonality and twelve-note techniques, his music always returned to a basic tonality. He is best known for his fifteen symphonies.

shot[1] ▸ noun **1** the firing of a gun or cannon: *Mulder killed him with a single shot* | figurative *they have* ***fired the opening shot*** *in what's expected to be a savage price war.* ▪ an attempt to hit a target by shooting: *he asked me if I would like to* ***have a shot at*** *a pheasant.* ▪ [with adj.] a person with a specified level of ability in shooting: *Roy was a very good shot.* ▪ a critical or hostile remark: *Paul tried one last shot—'You realize what you want will cost more money?'.*
2 a hit, stroke, or kick of the ball in sports such as football, tennis, or golf: *his partner pulled off a winning backhand shot.* ▪ an attempt to score a goal: *he took a shot that the goalie stopped.* ▪ informal an attempt to do something: *several of the competitors will* ***have a shot at*** *the all-round title.*
3 (pl. **same**) a ball of stone or metal used as a missile shot from a large gun or cannon. ▪ (also **lead shot**) [mass noun] tiny lead pellets used in quantity in a single charge or cartridge in a shotgun. ▪ a heavy ball thrown by a shot-putter.
4 a photograph: *a group shot of all the family.* ▪ a film sequence photographed continuously by one camera: *the movie's opening shot is of a character walking across a featureless landscape.* ▪ [mass noun] the range of a camera's view: *a prop man was standing just* ***out of shot.***
5 informal a small drink of spirits: *he took a shot of whisky.* ▪ an injection of a drug or vaccine: *a shot of impure heroin.*
6 [usu. with modifier] the launch of a space rocket: *a moon shot.*
– PHRASES **give it one's best shot** informal do the best that one can. **like a shot** informal without hesitation; willingly: *'Would you go back?' 'Like a shot.'.* **not have a shot in one's locker** Brit. have no money or chances left. **a shot across the bows** see **BOW**[3]. **a shot in the arm** informal an encouraging stimulus: *the movie was a real shot in the arm for our crew.* **a shot in the dark** see **DARK**.
– ORIGIN Old English *sc(e)ot, gesc(e)ot* of Germanic origin; related to German *Geschoss*, from the base of the verb **SHOOT**.

shot[2] past and past participle of **SHOOT**. ▸ adjective
1 (of coloured cloth) woven with a warp and weft of different colours, giving a contrasting effect when looked at from different angles: *a dress of shot silk.* ▪ interspersed with a different colour: *dark hair shot with silver.* ▪ (**shot through with**) suffused with (a particular feature or quality): *the mist was shot through with orange spokes of light.*
2 informal ruined or worn out: *a completely shot engine will put you out of the race* | *my nerves are shot.* ▪ [predic.] US & Austral./NZ drunk.
– PHRASES **get** (or **be**) **shot of** Brit. informal get (or be) rid of. **shot to pieces** (or **to hell**) informal ruined.

shot[3] ▸ noun [in sing.] Brit. informal, dated a bill or one's share of it, especially in a pub: *he had paid her shot.*
– ORIGIN late Middle English: from **SHOT**[1]; compare with Old English *scēotan* 'shoot, pay, contribute' and **SCOT**.

shot-blast ▸ verb [with obj.] clean or strip (a metal or other surface) by directing a high-speed stream of steel particles at it.

shotcrete ▸ noun another term for **GUNITE**.
– ORIGIN 1950s: from **SHOT**[2] + **CONCRETE**.

shote ▸ noun variant spelling of **SHOAT**.

shot-firer ▸ noun a person who fires a blasting charge, for example in mining.

shot glass ▸ noun a small glass used for serving spirits.

shotgun ▸ noun a smooth-bore gun for firing small shot at short range.

shotgun cloning ▸ noun [mass noun] the artificial insertion of random fragments of DNA from a donor organism into a recipient by genetic engineering.

shotgun marriage (also **shotgun wedding**) ▸ noun informal an enforced or hurried wedding, especially because the bride is pregnant.

shotgun microphone ▸ noun another term for **GUN MICROPHONE**.

shot hole ▸ noun **1** a hole made by the passage of a shot.
2 a hole bored in rock for the insertion of a blasting charge.
3 a small round hole made in a leaf by a fungus or bacterium, especially in a fruit tree following an attack of leaf spot: [as modifier] *shot-hole disease.* ▪ a small hole made in wood by a boring beetle: [as modifier] *a shot-hole borer.*

shotmaking ▸ noun [mass noun] the playing of aggressive or decisive strokes in tennis, golf, and other games.
– DERIVATIVES **shotmaker** noun.

Shotokan /ʃə(ʊ)ˈtəʊkan/ ▸ noun [mass noun] the style of karate which is the most widespread in the UK and a number of other countries.
– ORIGIN Japanese, from *shō* 'right, true' + *to* 'way' + *kan* 'mansion'.

shot-peen ▸ verb shape (sheet metal) by bombarding it with a stream of metal shot.

shot-put (also **shot-putting**) ▸ noun an athletic contest in which a very heavy round ball is thrown as far as possible.
– DERIVATIVES **shot-putter** noun.

shotted ▸ adjective filled or weighted with shot.

shotten herring /ˈʃɒt(ə)n/ ▸ noun a herring that has spawned. ▪ archaic a weakened or dispirited person.
– ORIGIN Middle English: *shotten*, archaic past participle of **SHOOT**, in the specialized sense 'discharge (spawn)'.

shottist ▸ noun S. African a person who is skilled in shooting and takes part in shooting competitions.

shot tower ▸ noun historical a tower in which shot was made from molten lead poured through sieves at the top and falling into water at the bottom.

should ▸ modal verb (3rd sing. **should**) **1** used to indicate obligation, duty, or correctness, typically when criticizing someone's actions: *he should have been careful* | *I think we should trust our people more* | *you shouldn't have gone.* ▪ indicating a desirable or expected state: *by now pupils should be able to read with a large degree of independence.* ▪ used to give or ask advice or suggestions: *you should go back to bed* | *what should I wear?* ▪ (**I should**) used to give advice: *I should hold out if I were you.*
2 used to indicate what is probable: *£348 m should be enough to buy him out* | *the bus should arrive in a few minutes.*
3 formal expressing the conditional mood: ▪ (in the first person) indicating the consequence of an imagined event: *if I were to obey my first impulse, I should spend my days writing letters.* ▪ referring to a possible event or situation: *if you should change your mind, I'll be at the hotel* | *should anyone arrive late, admission is likely to be refused.*
4 used in a clause with 'that' after a main clause describing feelings: *it is astonishing that we should find violence here.*
5 used in a clause with 'that' expressing purpose: *in order that training should be effective it must be planned systematically.*
6 (in the first person) expressing a polite request or acceptance: *I should like some more, if I may* | *we should be grateful for your advice.*
7 (in the first person) expressing a conjecture or hope: *he'll have a sore head, I should imagine* | *'It won't happen again.' 'I should hope not.'.*
8 used to emphasize to a listener how striking an event is or was: *you should have seen Marge's face.* ▪ (**who/what should —— but**) emphasizing how surprising an event was: *I was in this shop when who should I see across the street but Tobias.*
– ORIGIN Old English *sceolde*: past of **SHALL**.

> **USAGE** As with **shall** and **will**, there is confusion about when to use **should** and **would**. The traditional rule is that **should** is used with first person pronouns (**I** and **we**), as in *I said I* ***should*** *be late*, and **would** is used with second and third persons (**you, he, she, it, they**), as in *you didn't say you* ***would*** *be late.* In practice, **would** is normally used instead of **should** in reported speech and conditional clauses: *I said I* ***would*** *be late; if we had known we* ***would*** *have invited her.* In spoken and informal contexts the issue rarely arises, since the distinction is obscured by the use of the contracted forms **I'd, we'd**, etc.
> In modern English uses of **should** are dominated by the senses relating to obligation (for which **would** cannot be substituted), as in *you* ***should*** *go out more often*, and for related emphatic uses, as in *you* ***should*** *have seen her face!*
> For a discussion on the use of **should of** instead of **should have**, see **USAGE** at **HAVE**.

shoulder ▸ noun **1** the upper joint of each of a person's arms and the part of the body between this and the neck. ▪ (in quadrupeds) the joint of the upper forelimb and the adjacent part of the back. ▪ the part of a bird or insect at which the wing is attached. ▪ a joint of meat from the upper foreleg and shoulder blade of an animal: *a shoulder of lamb.* ▪ a part of a garment covering the shoulder: *a jacket with padded shoulders.* ▪ (**shoulders**) the upper part of the back and arms: *a tall youth with broad shoulders.* ▪ (**shoulders**) this part of the body regarded as bearing responsibility or hardship or providing strength: *all accounts place the blame squarely on his shoulders.*
2 a part of something resembling a shoulder in shape, position, or function: *the shoulder of a pulley.* ▪ a point at which a steep slope descends from a plateau or highland area: *the shoulder of the hill sloped down* | *a resort sheltered by the shoulder of Ben Nevis.*
3 another term for **HARD SHOULDER**.
▸ verb **1** [with obj.] put (something heavy) over one's shoulder or shoulders to carry: *we shouldered our crippling backpacks and set off slowly up the hill.* ▪ take on (a burden or responsibility): *the day-to-day work will be shouldered by an action group.*
2 [with obj. and adverbial of direction] push (someone or something) out of one's way with one's shoulder: *she shouldered him brusquely aside.* ▪ [no obj., with adverbial of direction] move in this way: *he shouldered past a*

woman with a baby | *he* ***shouldered his way*** *through the seething mass of children.*

– PHRASES **be looking over one's shoulders** be anxious or insecure about a possible danger: *takeovers are the thing that keeps suppliers looking over their shoulders.* **put one's shoulder to the wheel** set to work vigorously. **rub shoulders with** see RUB. **shoulder arms** hold a rifle against the right side of the body, barrel upwards. **a shoulder to cry on** someone who listens sympathetically to someone's problems. **shoulder to shoulder** side by side: *everyone is bunched together shoulder to shoulder.* ■ acting together towards a common aim; with united effort: *we fought shoulder to shoulder with the rest of the country.* **straight from the shoulder** see STRAIGHT.

– DERIVATIVES **shouldered adjective** [in combination] *broad-shouldered.*

– ORIGIN Old English *sculdor*, of West Germanic origin; related to Dutch *schouder* and German *Schulter*.

shoulder bag ▶ **noun** a bag with a long strap that is hung over the shoulder.

shoulder belt ▶ **noun** a bandolier or other strap passing over one shoulder and under the opposite arm.

shoulder blade ▶ **noun** either of the large, flat triangular bones which lie against the ribs in the upper back and provide attachments for the bone and muscles of the upper arm. Also called SCAPULA.

shoulder charge ▶ **noun** a charge made leading with the shoulder.

▶ **verb** (**shoulder-charge**) [with obj.] charge at (a person or obstacle) with the shoulder first.

shoulder-high ▶ **adjective & adverb** up to or at the height of the shoulders: [as adj.] *a glade of shoulder-high grass* | [as adv.] *he was lifted shoulder-high.*

shoulder holster ▶ **noun** a gun holster worn under the armpit.

shoulder-in ▶ **noun** (in dressage) a movement in which the horse moves parallel to the side of the arena, with its hindquarters carried closer to the wall than its shoulders and its body curved towards the centre.

shoulder joint ▶ **noun** the joint connecting an upper limb or forelimb to the body. It is a ball-and-socket joint in which the head of the humerus fits into the socket of the scapula.

shoulder knot ▶ **noun** a knot of ribbon, metal, or lace worn as part of a ceremonial dress.

shoulder-length ▶ **adjective** (of hair) reaching down to the shoulders.

shoulder pad ▶ **noun** a shaped pad sewn into the shoulder of a garment to provide bulk and shape. ■ a hard protective pad for the shoulders used in certain sports, such as ice hockey and American football.

shoulder season (also **shoulder period**) ▶ **noun** a travel period between peak and off-peak seasons.

shoulder stand ▶ **noun** a gymnastic movement in which, starting from a supine position, the torso and legs are raised vertically over the head and supported on the shoulders and arms.

shoulder strap ▶ **noun** a narrow strip of material going over the shoulder from front to back of a garment. ■ a long strap attached to a bag for carrying it over the shoulder. ■ a strip of cloth from shoulder to collar on a military uniform, bearing a symbol of rank.

S

shoulder-surfing ▶ **noun** [mass noun] the practice of spying on the user of a cash-dispensing machine or other electronic device in order to obtain their personal identification number, password, etc.

shouldn't ▶ **contraction** should not.

shout ▶ **verb 1** [no obj.] (of a person) utter a loud cry, typically as an expression of a strong emotion: *she shouted for joy.* ■ [reporting verb] say something very loudly: [with obj.] *he leant out of his window and shouted abuse at them* | *I* ***shouted out*** *a warning* | [with direct speech] *'Come back!' she shouted.* ■ (**shout at**) speak loudly and angrily to: *he apologized because he had shouted at her in front of them all.* ■ [with obj.] (**shout someone down**) prevent someone from speaking or being heard by shouting: *he was shouted down as he tried to explain the decision.* ■ [with obj.] indicate or express (a particular quality) unequivocally or powerfully: *from crocodile handbag to gold-trimmed shoes she shouted money.*
2 [with two objs] Austral./NZ informal treat (someone) to (something, especially a drink): *I'll shout you a beer.* ■ [no obj.] buy a round of drinks: *anyone shooting a hole in one must* ***shout for*** *all players present on the course.*

▶ **noun 1** a loud cry expressing a strong emotion or calling attention: *his words were interrupted by warning shouts.* ■ Brit. informal a call-out for one of the emergency services.
2 (**one's shout**) Brit. informal one's turn to buy a round of drinks: *'Do you want another drink? My shout.'*

– PHRASES **all over bar the shouting** Brit. informal (of a contest) almost finished and therefore virtually decided. **give someone a shout** informal call on or get in touch with someone. **in with a shout** informal having a good chance: *they were definitely in with a shout of bringing off a victory.* **shout something from the rooftops** talk openly about something personal or secret. **shout the odds** talk in a loud and opinionated way.

– DERIVATIVES **shouter noun**, **shouty adjective** (informal).

– ORIGIN late Middle English: perhaps related to SHOOT; compare with Old Norse *skúta* 'a taunt', also with the verb SCOUT[2].

shouting match ▶ **noun** a loud quarrel.

shout-out ▶ **noun** informal (especially in hip-hop or dance music) a mention, credit, or greeting, typically one made over the radio or during a live performance.

shove ▶ **verb** [with obj.] push (someone or something) roughly: *police started* ***pushing and shoving*** *people down the street* | [no obj.] *kids pushed, kicked, and shoved.* ■ [no obj., with adverbial of direction] make one's way by pushing someone or something: *Woolley shoved past him.* ■ [with obj. and adverbial of place] put (something) somewhere carelessly or roughly: *she shoved the books into her briefcase.* ■ (**shove it**) informal used to express angry dismissal of something: *I told the selectors to shove it.*

▶ **noun** a strong push: *she gave him a hefty shove and he nearly fell.*

– PHRASAL VERBS **shove off 1** [usu. in imperative] informal go away: *shove off—you're bothering the customers.* **2** push away from the shore in a boat. **shove up** Brit. informal move oneself to make room for someone.

– ORIGIN Old English *scūfan* (verb), of Germanic origin; related to Dutch *schuiven* and German *schieben*, also to SHUFFLE.

shove-halfpenny ▶ **noun** [mass noun] a game in which coins are struck so that they slide across a marked board on a table.

shovel ▶ **noun** a tool resembling a spade with a broad blade and typically upturned sides, used for moving coal, earth, snow, or other material. ■ a machine or part of a machine having a similar shape or function. ■ an amount of something carried or moved with a shovel: *a few shovels of earth.*

▶ **verb** (**shovels**, **shovelling**, **shovelled**; US **shovels**, **shoveling**, **shoveled**) [with obj. and adverbial] move (coal, earth, snow, or similar) with a shovel: *she shovelled coal on the fire.* ■ informal put or push (something, typically food) somewhere quickly and in large quantities: *Dave was shovelling pasta into his mouth.*

– DERIVATIVES **shovelful noun** (pl. **shovelfuls**).

– ORIGIN Old English *scofl*, of Germanic origin; related to Dutch *schoffel*, German *Schaufel*, also to the verb SHOVE.

shovelboard ▶ **noun** [mass noun] Brit. a game played by pushing discs with the hand or with a long-handled shovel over a marked surface.

– ORIGIN mid 16th cent.: alteration of obsolete *shove-board*, from SHOVE + BOARD.

shoveler (also **shoveller**) ▶ **noun 1** a dabbling duck with a long broad bill. ● Genus *Anas*, family Anatidae: four species, in particular *A. clypeata* of Eurasia and North America.
2 (Brit. usu. **shoveller**) a person or thing that shovels something: *a snow shoveller.*

– ORIGIN late Middle English (denoting a spoonbill): alteration of earlier *shovelard*, from SHOVEL, perhaps influenced by *mallard*.

shovel hat ▶ **noun** a black felt hat with a low round crown and a broad brim turned up at the sides, formerly worn especially by clergymen.

shovelhead (also **shovelhead shark**) ▶ **noun** another term for BONNETHEAD.

shovel pass ▶ **noun** American Football an underarm pass made with a shovelling movement of the arms.

shovelware ▶ **noun** [mass noun] Computing software or online content that has been added to a CD or placed on the Internet without having been altered so as to suit the new medium.

– ORIGIN 1980s: from the notion of 'shovelling' the information on to a CD or the Internet indiscriminately.

show ▶ **verb** (past participle **shown** or **showed**) **1** be, allow, or cause to be visible: [no obj.] *wrinkles were starting to show on her face* | *the glow of a city skyline* ***showed up*** *ahead* | [no obj., with complement] *the muscles of her jaws showed white through the skin* | [with obj.] *a white blouse will show the blood* | *a rising moon* ***showed up*** *the wild seascape.* ■ [with obj.] offer, exhibit, or produce (something) for inspection: *an alarm salesperson should show an ID card* | [with two objs] *he wants to show you all his woodwork stuff.* ■ [with obj.] put on display in an exhibition or competition: *he ceased rather early in his career to show his work* | [no obj.] *other artists who showed there included Robert Motherwell.* ■ [with obj.] present (a film or television programme) on a screen for viewing. ■ [no obj.] (of a film) be presented for viewing: *a movie showing at the Venice Film Festival.* ■ [with obj.] indicate (a particular time, measurement, etc.): *a travel clock showing the time in different cities.* ■ [with obj.] represent or depict in art: *a postcard showing the Wicklow Mountains.* ■ (**show oneself**) allow oneself to be seen; appear in public: *he was amazed that she would have the gall to show herself.* ■ [no obj.] informal arrive for an appointment or at a gathering: *only two waitresses* ***showed up*** *for work* | *her date failed to show.*
2 [with obj.] allow (a quality or emotion) to be perceived; display: *it was Frank's turn to show his frustration* | *a wife who showed increasing signs of mental instability.* ■ accord or treat someone with (a specified quality): *he urged his soldiers to show no mercy* | [with two objs] *he has learned to show women some respect.* ■ [no obj.] (of an emotion) be noticeable: *he tried not to let his relief show.* ■ [no obj.] informal (of a woman) be visibly pregnant: *Shirl was four months gone and just starting to show.*
3 [with obj.] demonstrate or prove: *experts say this shows the benefit of regular inspections* | [with clause] *the figures show that the underlying rate of inflation continues to fall.* ■ (**show oneself**) prove or demonstrate oneself to be: [with infinitive] *she showed herself to be a harsh critic* | [with complement] *the youth soon showed himself a canny batsman.* ■ explain or demonstrate something to: [with clause] *he showed the boy how to operate the machine.* ■ [with obj. and adverbial of direction] conduct or lead: *show them in, please.*
4 [no obj.] N. Amer. finish third or in the first three in a race.

▶ **noun 1** a spectacle or display, typically an impressive one: *spectacular shows of bluebells.*
2 a play or other stage performance, especially a musical. ■ a light entertainment programme on television or radio. ■ [usu. with adj. or noun modifier] an event or competition involving the public display of animals, plants, or products: *a dog show.* ■ informal an undertaking, project, or organization: *I man a desk in a little office. I don't run the show.*
3 an outward appearance or display of a quality or feeling: *Joanie was frightened of any* ***show of*** *affection.* ■ an outward display intended to give a false impression: *Drew* ***made a show of*** *looking around for firewood* | [mass noun] *they are all show.* ■ informal a ludicrous spectacle: *now don't* ***make a show of*** *yourself in front of him.*
4 Medicine a discharge of blood and mucus from the vagina at the onset of labour or menstruation.
5 US & Austral./NZ an opportunity for doing something; a chance: *I didn't have a show.*

– PHRASES **all over the show** another way of saying ALL OVER THE PLACE (see ALL). **for show** for the sake of appearance rather than for use. **get** (or **keep**) **the show on the road** informal begin (or continue with) an undertaking or enterprise: *'Let's get this show on the road—we're late already.'* **give the** (**whole**) **show away** demonstrate the inadequacies or reveal the truth of something. **good** (or **bad** or **poor**) **show!** Brit. informal, dated used to express approval (or disapproval or dissatisfaction). **have something** (or **nothing**) **to show for** have a (or no) visible result of (one's work or experience): *a year later, he had nothing to show for his efforts.* **on show** being exhibited. **show one's cards** another way of saying SHOW ONE'S HAND below. **show cause** Law produce satisfactory grounds for application of (or exemption from) a procedure or penalty. **show (someone) a clean pair of heels** informal run away (from someone) extremely fast. **show someone the door** dismiss or eject someone from a place. **show one's face** appear in public: *she was so ashamed she could hardly show her face.* **show the flag** see FLAG[1]. **show one's hand** (in a card game) reveal one's cards. ■ disclose one's plans: *he needed hard evidence, and to get it he would have to show his hand.* **show a leg** [in imperative] Brit. informal, dated get out of bed; get up. **show of force** a demonstration of the forces at one's command and of

one's readiness to use them. **show of hands** a vote carried out among a group by the raising of hands, with numbers typically being estimated rather than counted. **show one's teeth** Brit. demonstrate or use one's power or authority in an aggressive or intimidating way: *the council showed its teeth for the first time by imposing an economic embargo.* **show the way** indicate what can or should be done by doing it first: *Morgan showed the way by becoming Deputy Governor of Jamaica.* **show willing** Brit. display a willingness to help.
– PHRASAL VERBS **show something forth** archaic exhibit something: *the heavens show forth the glory of God.* **show off** informal boastfully display one's abilities or accomplishments. **show someone/thing off** display someone or something that is a source of pride: *his jeans were tight-fitting, showing off his compact figure.* **show out** Bridge reveal that one has no cards of a particular suit. **show someone round** (or chiefly N. Amer. **around**) point out interesting features in a place or building to someone. **show someone/thing up** expose someone or something as being bad or faulty: *it's a pity they haven't showed up the authorities for what they are.* ■ (**show someone up**) informal embarrass or humiliate someone: *she says I showed her up in front of her friends.*
– ORIGIN Old English *scēawian* 'look at, inspect', from a West Germanic base meaning 'look'; related to Dutch *schouwen* and German *schauen*.

Showa /ˈʃəʊwə/ ▶ **noun** the period when Japan was ruled by the emperor Hirohito.
– ORIGIN Japanese, from *shō* 'bright, clear' + *wa* 'harmony'.

show-and-tell ▶ **noun** [mass noun] chiefly N. Amer. a teaching method, used especially in teaching young children, in which pupils are encouraged to bring items they have selected to class and describe them to their classmates.

show bag ▶ **noun** Austral. a bag of goods, especially trade samples or publicity material, available at events such as annual shows.

showband ▶ **noun** a band which plays cover versions of popular songs. ■ a band, especially a jazz band, which performs with theatrical extravagance.

showbiz ▶ **noun** informal term for **SHOW BUSINESS**.
– DERIVATIVES **showbizzy** adjective.

showboat ▶ **noun** (in the US) a river steamer on which theatrical performances are given. ■ informal, chiefly N. Amer. a show-off; an exhibitionist.
▶ **verb** [no obj.] informal, chiefly N. Amer. show off: (as adj. **showboating**) *a lot of showboating politicians.*
– DERIVATIVES **showboater** noun.

show business ▶ **noun** [mass noun] the theatre, films, television, and pop music as a profession or industry.

showcard ▶ **noun** a large card bearing a conspicuous design, used especially in advertising, market research, and teaching.

showcase ▶ **noun** a glass case used for displaying articles in a shop or museum. ■ a place or occasion for presenting something favourably to general attention: *the gallery will provide **a showcase for** Scotland's young photographers.*
▶ **verb** [with obj.] exhibit; display: *the albums showcase his production skills.*

showdown ▶ **noun 1** a final test or confrontation intended to settle a dispute.
2 (in poker or brag) the requirement at the end of a round that the players who remain in should show their cards to determine which is the strongest hand.

shower /ˈʃaʊə/ ▶ **noun 1** a brief and usually light fall of rain, hail, sleet, or snow. ■ a mass of small things falling or moving at the same time: ***a shower of** dust sprinkled his face.* ■ a group of particles produced by a cosmic-ray particle in the earth's atmosphere.
2 a cubicle or bath in which a person stands under a spray of water to wash. ■ the apparatus that produces such a spray of water. ■ (US also **shower bath**) an act of washing oneself in a shower.
3 a large number of things happening or given at the same time: ***a shower of** awards.* ■ [often with modifier] N. Amer. a party at which presents are given to someone, typically a woman who is about to get married or have a baby: *she loved going to baby showers.*
4 [in sing.] Brit. informal a group of people perceived as incompetent or worthless: *look at this lot—what a shower!*
▶ **verb 1** [no obj., with adverbial of direction] (of a mass of small things) fall or be thrown in a shower: *bits of broken glass showered over me.* ■ [with obj. and adverbial of direction] cause (a mass of small things) to fall in a shower: *his hooves showered sparks across the concrete floor.* ■ [with obj.] (**shower someone with**) throw (a number of things) all at once towards someone: *hooligans showered him with rotten eggs.*
2 [with obj.] (**shower someone with**) give someone a great number of (things): *he showered her with kisses.* ■ (**shower something on/upon**) give a great number of things to (someone): *senior officers showered praise on their young policewomen.*
3 [no obj.] wash oneself in a shower.
– ORIGIN Old English *scūr* 'light fall of rain, hail, etc.', of Germanic origin; related to Dutch *schoer* and German *Schauer*.

showerproof ▶ **adjective** (of a garment) resistant to light rain.
▶ **verb** [with obj.] make showerproof.

showery ▶ **adjective** (of weather or a period of time) characterized by frequent showers of rain.

showgirl ▶ **noun** an actress who sings and dances in musicals, variety acts, and similar shows.

showground ▶ **noun** an area of land on which a show takes place.

show house (also **show home**) ▶ **noun** Brit. a house on a newly built estate which is furnished and decorated to be shown to prospective buyers.

showing ▶ **noun** [mass noun] the action of showing something, or the fact of being shown: *Alsatian dog, championship quality, excellent results in showing.* ■ [count noun] a presentation of a cinema film or television programme: *another showing of the three-part series.* ■ [count noun] [with adj.] a performance of a specified quality: *despite poor opinion poll showings, the party selected him as its candidate.* ■ the way in which something is argued or represented: ***on her own showing** she would make a more suitable wife for him than her twin.*
– ORIGIN Old English *scēawung*.

showjumping ▶ **noun** [mass noun] the competitive sport of riding horses over a course of fences and other obstacles in an arena, with penalty points for errors.
– DERIVATIVES **showjump** verb, **showjumper** noun.

showman ▶ **noun** (pl. **showmen**) a person who produces or presents shows as a profession, especially the proprietor, manager, or MC of a circus, fair, or other variety show. ■ a person skilled at entertaining, theatrical presentation or performance.
– DERIVATIVES **showmanship** noun.

Show Me State informal name for **MISSOURI**.

shown past participle of **SHOW**.

show-off ▶ **noun** informal a person who acts pretentiously or who publicly parades themselves, their possessions, or their accomplishments.

showpiece ▶ **noun 1** something which attracts attention or admiration as an outstanding example of its type: *the factory has expanded and become a showpiece of British industry.* ■ something which offers a particular opportunity for a display of skill: *the serenade was a showpiece for the wind section.*
2 an item of work presented for exhibition or display.

showplace ▶ **noun** a place of beauty or interest attracting many visitors.

show pony ▶ **noun** Brit. informal a stylish or flamboyant person, especially a performer, who enjoys being in the limelight.

showreel ▶ **noun** a short videotape containing examples of an actor's or director's work for showing to potential employers.

showroom ▶ **noun** a room used to display goods for sale, such as appliances, cars, or furniture.

show-stopper ▶ **noun** informal a performance or item receiving prolonged applause. ■ something that is striking or has great popular appeal: *the brilliant orange flowers against the bronze-green foliage were a show-stopper.*
– DERIVATIVES **show-stopping** adjective.

show time ▶ **noun** the time at which a play, film, or concert is scheduled to begin. ■ used to signal the beginning of an event or process that is expected to be dramatic, decisive, or otherwise significant.

show trial ▶ **noun** a judicial trial held in public with the intention of influencing or satisfying public opinion, rather than of ensuring justice.

show tune ▶ **noun** a song from a musical that has become popular in its own right.

show window ▶ **noun** a shop window looking on to a street, used for exhibiting goods.

showy ▶ **adjective** (**showier**, **showiest**) having a striking appearance or style, typically by being excessively bright, colourful, or ostentatious: *showy flowers | she wore a great deal of showy costume jewellery.*
– DERIVATIVES **showily** adverb, **showiness** noun.

shoyu /ˈʃəʊjuː/ ▶ **noun** [mass noun] a type of Japanese soy sauce.
– ORIGIN from Japanese *shōyu*.

s.h.p. ▶ **abbreviation** shaft horsepower.

shrank past of **SHRINK**.

shrapnel /ˈʃrapn(ə)l/ ▶ **noun** [mass noun] **1** fragments of a bomb, shell, or other object thrown out by an explosion.
2 informal small change: *little more than a few pounds and a handful of shrapnel.*
– ORIGIN early 19th cent.: named after General Henry *Shrapnel* (1761–1842), the British soldier who invented the shell.

shred ▶ **noun** (usu. **shreds**) a strip of material, such as paper, cloth, or food, that has been torn, cut, or scraped from something larger: *her dress was **torn to shreds**.* ■ [often with negative] a very small amount: *we have not **a shred of** evidence to go on.*
▶ **verb** (**shreds**, **shredding**, **shredded**) [with obj.] tear or cut into shreds: (as adj. **shredded**) *shredded cabbage.*
– PHRASES **in shreds** very badly damaged; destroyed or ruined: *my reputation will be in shreds.* **tear someone/thing to shreds** informal criticize someone or something aggressively.
– ORIGIN late Old English *scrēad* 'piece cut off', *scrēadian* 'trim, prune', of West Germanic origin; related to **SHROUD**.

shredder ▶ **noun 1** a machine or other device for shredding something, especially documents.
2 informal a snowboarder.

Shreveport /ˈʃriːvpɔːt/ an industrial city in NW Louisiana, on the Red River near the border with Texas; pop. 199,729 (est. 2008).

shrew ▶ **noun 1** a small mouse-like insectivorous mammal with a long pointed snout and tiny eyes. ● Family Soricidae: many genera, in particular *Sorex* and *Crocidura*, and numerous species.
2 a bad-tempered or aggressively assertive woman.
– ORIGIN Old English *scrēawa*, *scrǣwa*, of Germanic origin; related words in Germanic languages have senses such as 'dwarf', 'devil', or 'fox'.

shrewd ▶ **adjective 1** having or showing sharp powers of judgement; astute: *she was shrewd enough to guess the motive behind his gesture | a shrewd career move.*
2 archaic (especially of weather) piercingly cold: *a shrewd east wind.* ■ (of a blow) severe: *a bayonet's shrewd thrust.* ■ mischievous; malicious.
– DERIVATIVES **shrewdly** adverb, **shrewdness** noun.
– ORIGIN Middle English (in the sense 'evil in nature or character'): from **SHREW** in the sense 'evil person or thing', or as the past participle of obsolete *shrew* 'to curse'. The word developed the sense 'cunning', and gradually gained a favourable connotation during the 17th cent.

shrewish ▶ **adjective** (of a woman) bad-tempered or aggressively assertive: *his shrewish wife.*
– DERIVATIVES **shrewishly** adverb, **shrewishness** noun.

shrew-mole ▶ **noun** a small shrew-like mole with a long tail, native to Asia and North America. ● *Neurotrichus* and other genera, family Talpidae: five species.

S

Shrewsbury /ˈʃrəʊzb(ə)ri, ˈʃruːz-/ a town in western England, the county town of Shropshire, situated on the River Severn near the border with Wales; pop. 65,500 (est. 2009).

Shri /ʃriː/ (also **Sri** /sri/) ▶ **noun** Indian a title of respect used before the name of a man, a god, or a sacred book: *Shri Chaudhuri.*
– ORIGIN from Sanskrit *Śrī* 'beauty, fortune', used as an honorific title.

shriek ▶ **verb** [no obj.] utter a high-pitched piercing sound or words, especially as an expression of terror, pain, or excitement: *the audience **shrieked with laughter** |* [with direct speech] *'There it is!' she shrieked |* [with obj.] *she was shrieking abuse at a taxi.* ■ (of something inanimate) make a high-pitched screeching sound: *the wheels shrieked as the car sped away.* ■ be very obvious or strikingly discordant: *the answer **shrieked at** her all too clearly | the patterned carpets **shrieked at** Blanche from the shabby store.*
▶ **noun 1** a high-pitched piercing cry or sound; a scream: *shrieks of laughter.*
2 informal an exclamation mark.
– DERIVATIVES **shrieker** noun, **shrieking** adjective, **shriekingly** adverb.

– ORIGIN late 15th cent. (as a verb): imitative; compare with dialect *screak*, Old Norse *skrækja*, also with SCREECH.

shrieval /ˈʃriːv(ə)l/ ▶ **adjective** chiefly historical relating to a sheriff.
– ORIGIN late 17th cent.: from *shrieve*, obsolete variant of SHERIFF.

shrievalty ▶ **noun** (pl. **shrievalties**) chiefly historical the office, jurisdiction, or tenure of a sheriff.

shrift ▶ **noun** [mass noun] archaic confession, especially to a priest: *go to shrift*. See also SHORT SHRIFT. ■ absolution by a priest.
– ORIGIN Old English *scrift* 'penance imposed after confession', from SHRIVE.

shrike ▶ **noun** a songbird with a strong sharply hooked bill, often impaling its prey of small birds, lizards, and insects on thorns. Also called BUTCHER-BIRD. ● Family Laniidae: several genera and numerous species, especially in Africa, e.g. the **great grey shrike** (*Lanius excubitor*), of both Eurasia and North America.
■ used in names of similar birds of other families, e.g. **cuckoo-shrike**, **pepper-shrike**.
– ORIGIN mid 16th cent.: perhaps related to Old English *scrīc* 'thrush' and Middle Low German *schrīk* 'corncrake', of imitative origin.

shrill ▶ **adjective** (of a voice or sound) high-pitched and piercing: *a shrill laugh*. ■ derogatory (especially of a complaint or demand) loud and forceful: *a concession to their shrill demands*.
▶ **verb** [no obj.] make a shrill noise: *a piercing whistle shrilled through the night air*. ■ speak or cry with a shrill voice: [with direct speech] *'How dare you!' she shrilled*.
▶ **noun** [in sing.] a shrill sound or cry: *the rising shrill of women's voices*.
– DERIVATIVES **shrillness** noun, **shrilly** adverb.
– ORIGIN late Middle English: of Germanic origin; related to Low German *schrell* 'sharp in tone or taste'.

shrimati /ˈʃriːmʌti/ ▶ **noun** Indian used as a title of respect for a woman, especially a married woman.
– ORIGIN Hindi.

shrimp ▶ **noun** (pl. **same** or **shrimps**) a small free-swimming crustacean with an elongated body, typically marine and frequently of commercial importance as food. ● *Pandalus*, *Crangon*, and other genera, order Decapoda.
■ informal, derogatory a small, physically weak person.
▶ **verb** [no obj.] fish for shrimps: (as modifier **shrimping**) *a shrimping net*.
– ORIGIN Middle English: probably related to Middle Low German *schrempen* 'to wrinkle', Middle High German *schrimpfen* 'to contract', also to SCRIMP.

shrimper ▶ **noun 1** a boat designed or used for catching shrimps.
2 a person who fishes for shrimps.

shrimp plant ▶ **noun** an evergreen Mexican shrub with clusters of small flowers in pinkish-brown bracts that are said to resemble shrimps, widely grown as a houseplant. ● *Justicia brandegeana*, family Acanthaceae.

shrine ▶ **noun** a place regarded as holy because of its associations with a divinity or a sacred person or relic, marked by a building or other construction. ■ a place associated with or containing memorabilia of a particular revered person or thing: *her grave has become a shrine for fans from all over the world*. ■ a casket containing sacred relics; a reliquary. ■ a niche or enclosure containing a religious statue or other object.
▶ **verb** [with obj.] literary enshrine.
– ORIGIN Old English *scrīn* 'cabinet, chest, reliquary', of Germanic origin; related to Dutch *schrijn* and German *Schrein*, from Latin *scrinium* 'chest for books'.

S

Shriner /ˈʃrʌɪnə/ ▶ **noun** a member of the Order of Nobles of the Mystic Shrine, a charitable society founded in the US in 1872.

shrink ▶ **verb** (past **shrank**; past participle **shrunk** or (especially as adj.) **shrunken**) **1** become or make smaller in size or amount: [no obj.] *the workforce shrank to a thousand* | [with obj.] *the sun had shrunk and dried the wood* | (as adj. **shrinking**) *the shrinking market has provoked a massive price war*. ■ [no obj.] (of clothes or material) become smaller as a result of being immersed in water. ■ (as adj. **shrunken**) (of a person's face or other part of the body) wrinkled or shrivelled through old age or illness: *a tiny shrunken face and enormous eyes*.
2 [no obj., with adverbial of direction] move back or away, especially because of fear or disgust: *she shrank away from him, covering her face* | *he shrank back against the wall*. ■ [often with negative] (**shrink from**) be averse to or unwilling to do (something difficult or unappealing): *I don't shrink from my responsibilities*. ■ [no obj.] (**shrink into oneself**) become withdrawn.
▶ **noun** informal a psychiatrist: *you should see a shrink*. [from *headshrinker*.]
– DERIVATIVES **shrinkable** adjective, **shrinker** noun, **shrinkingly** adverb.
– ORIGIN Old English *scrincan*, of Germanic origin; related to Swedish *skrynka* 'to wrinkle'.

shrinkage ▶ **noun** [mass noun] the process, fact, or amount of shrinking: *give long curtains good hems to allow for shrinkage*. ■ an allowance made for reduction in the takings of a business due to wastage or theft.

shrink-fit ▶ **adjective** denoting clothing, especially denim jeans, designed to shrink to the desired size after initial washing.

shrinking violet ▶ **noun** [often with negative] informal an exaggeratedly shy person: *Dorothy is no shrinking violet when it comes to expressing her views*.

shrink-resistant ▶ **adjective** (of textiles or garments) resistant to shrinkage.

shrink-wrap ▶ **verb** [with obj.] package (an article) by enclosing it in clinging transparent plastic film that shrinks tightly on to it: (as adj. **shrink-wrapped**) *shrink-wrapped blocks of cheese*. ■ (as adj. **shrink-wrapped**) Computing (of a product) sold commercially as a ready-made software package.
▶ **noun** [mass noun] clinging transparent plastic film used to enclose an article as packaging.

shrive /ʃrʌɪv/ ▶ **verb** (past **shrove**; past participle **shriven**) [with obj.] archaic (of a priest) hear the confession of, assign penance to, and absolve. ■ (**shrive oneself**) present oneself to a priest for confession, penance, and absolution.
– ORIGIN Old English *scrīfan* 'impose as a penance', of Germanic origin; related to Dutch *schrijven* and German *schreiben* 'write', from Latin *scribere* 'write'.

shrivel ▶ **verb** (**shrivels**, **shrivelling**, **shrivelled**; US **shrivels**, **shriveling**, **shriveled**) wrinkle and contract or cause to wrinkle and contract, especially due to loss of moisture: [no obj.] *the flowers simply shrivelled up* | [with obj.] *a heatwave so intense that it shrivelled the grapes in every vineyard*. ■ [no obj.] lose momentum, will, or desire: *as American interest shrivelled, so did the government's*. ■ [with obj.] cause to feel worthless or insignificant: *she shrivelled him with one glance*.
– ORIGIN mid 16th cent.: perhaps of Scandinavian origin; compare with Swedish dialect *skryvla* 'to wrinkle'.

shrivelled (US **shriveled**) ▶ **adjective** wrinkled and shrunken, especially as a result of loss of moisture or old age: *a handful of shrivelled leaves* | *his shrivelled limbs*.

shriven past participle of SHRIVE.

shroff /ʃrɒf/ ▶ **noun 1** Indian a banker or money changer.
2 SE Asian a cashier.
– ORIGIN Persian and Urdu *saraf*, from Arabic *ṣarrāf*, from *ṣarafa* 'exchange money'.

shroom ▶ **noun** informal, chiefly US a mushroom, especially one with hallucinogenic properties.
– ORIGIN 1970s: shortening of MUSHROOM.

Shropshire a county of England, situated on the border with Wales; county town, Shrewsbury.

shroud ▶ **noun 1** a length of cloth or an enveloping garment in which a dead person is wrapped for burial: *he was buried in a linen shroud*. ■ technical a protective casing or cover.
2 a thing that envelops or obscures something: *a shroud of mist* | *they operate behind a shroud of secrecy*.
3 (**shrouds**) a set of ropes forming part of the standing rigging of a sailing boat and supporting the mast or topmast. ■ (also **shroud line**) each of the lines joining the canopy of a parachute to the harness.
▶ **verb** [with obj.] **1** wrap or dress (a body) in a shroud for burial.
2 cover or envelop so as to conceal from view: *mountains shrouded by cloud* | *the mystery which shrouds the origins of the universe*.
– ORIGIN late Old English *scrūd* 'garment, clothing', of Germanic origin, from a base meaning 'cut'; related to SHRED. An early sense of the verb (Middle English) was 'cover so as to protect'.

shroud-laid ▶ **adjective** (of rope) made of four strands laid right-handed on a core.

shrove past of SHRIVE.

Shrovetide ▶ **noun** Shrove Tuesday and the two days preceding it, when it was formerly customary to attend confession.
– ORIGIN late Middle English: of obscure origin; the first element related to SHRIVE.

Shrove Tuesday ▶ **noun** the day before Ash Wednesday. Though named for its former religious significance, it is chiefly marked by feasting and celebration, which traditionally preceded the observance of the Lenten fast. Compare with MARDI GRAS.

shrub[1] ▶ **noun** a woody plant which is smaller than a tree and has several main stems arising at or near the ground.
– DERIVATIVES **shrubby** adjective (**shrubbier**, **shrubbiest**).
– ORIGIN Old English *scrubb*, *scrybb* 'shrubbery'; compare with West Flemish *schrobbe* 'vetch', Norwegian *skrubba* 'dwarf cornel', also with SCRUB[2].

shrub[2] ▶ **noun** [mass noun] **1** a drink made of sweetened fruit juice and spirits, typically rum or brandy.
2 N. Amer. a slightly acid cordial made from fruit juice and water.
– ORIGIN early 18th cent.: from Arabic *šurb*, *šarāb*, from *šariba* 'to drink'; compare with SHERBET and SYRUP.

shrubbery ▶ **noun** (pl. **shrubberies**) an area in a garden planted with shrubs.

shrug ▶ **verb** (**shrugs**, **shrugging**, **shrugged**) [with obj.] raise (one's shoulders) slightly and momentarily to express doubt, ignorance, or indifference: *Jimmy looked enquiringly at Pete, who shrugged his shoulders* | [no obj.] *he just shrugged and didn't look interested*. ■ (**shrug something off**) dismiss something as unimportant: *the managing director shrugged off the criticism*.
▶ **noun 1** an act or instance of shrugging one's shoulders: *she lifted her shoulders in a dismissive shrug*.
2 a woman's close-fitting cardigan or jacket, cut short at the front and back so that only the arms and shoulders are covered.
– ORIGIN late Middle English (in the sense 'fidget'): of unknown origin.

shrunk (also **shrunken**) past participle of SHRINK.

shtetl /ˈʃtɛt(ə)l/ ▶ **noun** (pl. **shtetlach** /ˈʃtɛtlɑːx/ or **shtetls**) historical a small Jewish town or village in eastern Europe.
– ORIGIN Yiddish, 'little town'.

shtick /ʃtɪk/ ▶ **noun** informal an attention-getting or theatrical routine, gimmick, or talent.
– ORIGIN 1960s: Yiddish, from German *Stück* 'piece'.

shtook /ʃtʊk/ (also **schtuck**) ▶ **noun** [mass noun] informal trouble: *I'm in shtook with my boss*.
– ORIGIN 1930s: of unknown origin.

shtum /ʃtʊm/ (also **schtum**) informal ▶ **adjective** silent; non-communicative: *he kept shtum about the fact that he was sent down for fraud*.
▶ **verb** (**shtums**, **shtumming**, **shtummed**) [no obj.] be or become quiet and non-communicative: *you start to say something and then just when it's getting interesting you **shtum up***.
– ORIGIN 1950s: Yiddish, from German *stumm*.

shtup /ʃtʊp/ (also **schtup**) vulgar slang ▶ **verb** (**shtups**, **shtupping**, **shtupped**) [with obj.] have sexual intercourse with (someone).
▶ **noun** an act of sexual intercourse.
– ORIGIN 1960s: Yiddish.

shubunkin /ʃʊˈbʌŋkɪn/ ▶ **noun** a goldfish of an ornamental variety, having black spots, red patches, and long fins and tail.
– ORIGIN early 20th cent.: from Japanese.

shuck /ʃʌk/ chiefly N. Amer. ▶ **noun 1** an outer covering such as a husk or pod, especially the husk of an ear of maize. ■ the shell of an oyster or clam. ■ the integument of certain insect pupae or larvae.
2 informal a person or thing regarded as worthless or contemptible: *he said the idea was a shuck*.
▶ **exclamation** (**shucks**) informal used to express surprise, regret, irritation, or, in response to praise, self-deprecation: *'Thank you for getting it.' 'Oh, shucks, it was nothing.'* See also AW-SHUCKS.
▶ **verb** [with obj.] **1** remove the shucks from maize or shellfish: *shuck and drain the oysters*. ■ informal take off (a garment): *she **shucked off** her nightdress and started dressing*. ■ informal abandon; get rid of: *the regime's ability to **shuck off** its totalitarian characteristics*.
2 informal cause (someone) to believe something that is not true; fool or tease.
– DERIVATIVES **shucker** noun.
– ORIGIN late 17th cent.: of unknown origin.

shudder ▶ verb [no obj.] (of a person) tremble convulsively, typically as a result of fear or revulsion: *she still shuddered at the thought of him* | *I shuddered with horror.* ■ (especially of a vehicle, machine, or building) shake or vibrate deeply: *the train shuddered and edged forward.* ■ (usu. as adj. **shuddering**) (of a person's breathing) be unsteady, especially as a result of emotional disturbance: *he drew a deep, shuddering breath.*
▶ noun an act of shuddering: *the elevator rose with a shudder* | figurative *the pound's devaluation sent shudders through the market.*
– PHRASES **give someone the shudders** informal cause someone to feel repugnance or fear. **I shudder to think** used to convey that something is too unpleasant to contemplate: *I shudder to think what might have happened if he hadn't woken you up.*
– DERIVATIVES **shudderingly** adverb, **shuddery** adjective.
– ORIGIN Middle English (as a verb): from Middle Dutch *schūderen*, from a Germanic base meaning 'shake'.

shuffle /ˈʃʌf(ə)l/ ▶ verb 1 [no obj., with adverbial] walk by dragging one's feet along or without lifting them fully from the ground: *I stepped into my skis and shuffled to the edge of the steep slope* | (as adj. **shuffling**) *she heard Gran's shuffling steps.* ■ shift one's position while sitting or move one's feet while standing, typically because of boredom, nervousness, or embarrassment: *Christine shuffled uneasily in her chair* | [with obj.] *Ben shuffled his feet in the awkward silence.*
2 [with obj.] rearrange (a pack of cards) by sliding them over each other quickly. ■ move (people or things) around so as to occupy different positions or to be in a different order. ■ [no obj.] (**shuffle through**) sort or look through (a number of things) hurriedly: *he shuffled through the papers.*
3 [with obj.] (**shuffle something into**) put part of one's body into (an item of clothing), typically in a clumsy way: *she shuffled her feet into a pair of shoes.* ■ (**shuffle something off**) get out of or avoid a responsibility or obligation: *some hospitals can shuffle off their responsibilities by claiming to have no suitable facilities.* ■ [no obj.] archaic behave in a shifty or evasive manner: *Mr Milles did not frankly own it, but seem'd to shuffle about it.* ■ [no obj.] (**shuffle out of**) archaic get out of (a difficult situation) in an underhand way: *he shuffles out of the consequences by vague charges of undue influence.*
▶ noun 1 [in sing.] a shuffling movement, walk, or sound: *there was a shuffle of approaching feet.* ■ a quick dragging or scraping movement of the feet in dancing. ■ a dance performed with such steps. ■ a piece of music for or in the style of such a dance. ■ a rhythmic motif based on such a dance step and typical of early jazz, consisting of alternating crotchets and quavers in a triplet pattern.
2 an act of shuffling a pack of cards. ■ a change of order or relative positions; a reshuffle: *the Prime Minister may have to consider a cabinet shuffle in the spring.* ■ a facility on a CD player for playing tracks in an arbitrary order: [as modifier] *a shuffle facility.*
3 archaic a piece of equivocation or subterfuge.
– PHRASES **be** (or **get**) **lost in the shuffle** N. Amer. informal be overlooked or missed in a confused or crowded situation. **shuffle off this mortal coil** see COIL[2].
– DERIVATIVES **shuffler** noun.
– ORIGIN mid 16th cent.: perhaps from Low German *schuffeln* 'walk clumsily', also 'deal dishonestly, shuffle (cards)', of Germanic origin; related to SHOVE and SCUFFLE.

shuffleboard ▶ noun North American term for SHOVELBOARD.

shufti /ˈʃʊfti/ ▶ noun (pl. **shuftis**) Brit. informal a look or reconnoitre, especially a quick one: *I'll take a shufti round the wood while I'm about it.*
– ORIGIN 1940s (originally military slang): from Arabic *šāfa* 'try to see'.

shul /ʃuːl/ ▶ noun a synagogue.
– ORIGIN late 19th cent.: Yiddish, from German *Schule* 'school'.

Shumen /ˈʃuːmən/ an industrial city in NE Bulgaria; pop. 86,978 (2008).

shun ▶ verb (**shuns, shunning, shunned**) [with obj.] persistently avoid, ignore, or reject (someone or something) through antipathy or caution: *he shunned fashionable society* | (as adj. **shunned**) *the shunned wife's quiet divorce.*
– ORIGIN Old English *scunian* 'abhor, shrink back with fear, seek safety from an enemy', of unknown origin.

shunt ▶ verb 1 [with obj. and adverbial of direction] push or pull (a train or part of a train) from the main line to a siding or from one line of rails to another: *their train had been shunted into a siding.* ■ push or shove (someone or something): *chairs were being shunted to and fro.* ■ direct or divert to a less important place or position: *amateurs were gradually being shunted to filing jobs.*
2 [with obj.] provide (an electrical current) with a conductor joining two points of a circuit, through which more or less of the current may be diverted.
▶ noun 1 an act of pushing or shoving something. ■ Brit. informal a motor accident, especially a collision of vehicles travelling one close behind the other.
2 an electrical conductor joining two points of a circuit, through which more or less of a current may be diverted. ■ Surgery an alternative path for the passage of the blood or other body fluid: [as modifier] *shunt surgery.*
– ORIGIN Middle English (in the sense 'move suddenly aside'): perhaps from SHUN.

shunter ▶ noun a small locomotive used for shunting. ■ a railway worker engaged in such work.

shura /ˈʃʊərə/ ▶ noun [mass noun] Islam the principle of consultation, in particular as applied to government. ■ [count noun] a consultative council.
– ORIGIN from Arabic *šūrā* 'consultation'.

shuriken /ˈʃʊərɪkɛn/ ▶ noun a weapon in the form of a star with projecting blades or points, used as a missile in some martial arts.
– ORIGIN Japanese, literally 'dagger in the hand'.

shush /ʃʊʃ, ʃʌʃ/ ▶ exclamation be quiet: *Shush! Do you want to wake everyone?*
▶ noun 1 an utterance of 'shush': *the thumps were followed by shushes from the aunts.*
2 a soft swishing or rustling sound.
▶ verb 1 [with obj.] tell or signal (someone) to be silent: *she shushed him with a wave.* ■ [no obj.] become or remain silent: *Beth told her to shush.*
2 [no obj., usu. with adverbial of direction] move with or make a soft swishing or rustling sound: *I stood to watch a big liner shushing slowly past* | (as noun **shushing**) *she could hear the gentle shushing of the waves.*
– ORIGIN 1920s: imitative.

shu-shu /ˈʃuːʃuː/ W. Indian ▶ noun [mass noun] rumour; gossip: *the shu-shu is that he is being paid his full salary ever since he was ordered back to work.*
▶ verb [no obj.] speak at close range in a low tone, typically to exchange gossip.
– ORIGIN from French *chuchoter* 'to whisper'.

shut ▶ verb (**shuts, shutting**; past and past participle **shut**) [with obj.] 1 move (something) into position so as to block an opening; close: *shut the window, please* | *she shut her lips tight* | (as adj. **shut**) *she slammed the door shut.* ■ [no obj.] move or be able to be moved so as to block an opening: *the door shut behind him.* ■ block an opening into (something) by moving something into position: *he shut the box and locked it.* ■ [with obj. and adverbial] keep in a place by closing something such as a door: *it was his own dog which he had accidentally shut outside.*
2 fold or bring together the sides of (something) so as to close it: *he shut his book.*
3 prevent access to or along: *they ought to shut the path up to that terrible cliff.* ■ make or become unavailable for business or service, either permanently or until due to be open again: [with obj.] *we shut the shop for lunch* | [no obj.] *the accident and emergency departments will shut.*
4 [no obj.] (**shut it**) [in imperative] informal stop talking; be quiet.
– PHRASES **be** (or **get**) **shut of** informal be (or get) rid of: *I'd be glad to be shut of him.* **shut the door on** (or **to**) see DOOR. **shut one's eyes to** see EYE. **shut one's mind to** see MIND. **shut the stable door after the horse has bolted** see STABLE[1]. **shut up shop** see SHOP. **shut your face** (or **mouth** or **trap**)**!** informal used as a rude or angry way of telling someone to be quiet.
– PHRASAL VERBS **shut someone/thing away** keep someone or something inside a place so as not to be seen or contacted by other people: *she supposes that Mrs Tilney was shut away in her bedroom chamber.*
shut down (or **shut something down**) cease (or cause something to cease) business or operation: *the plant's operators decided to shut down the reactor.*
shut someone/thing in keep someone or something inside a place by closing something such as a door: *her parents shut her in an upstairs room.* ■ enclose or surround a place: *the village is shut in by the mountains on either side.* ■ trap something by shutting a door or drawer on it: *you shut your finger in the door.*
shut off (or **shut something off**) (especially in relation to water, electricity, or gas) stop (or cause to stop) flowing: *he was about to shut off the power.* ■ stop (or cause to stop) working: *the engines shut off automatically.* ■ (**shut something off**) block the entrances and exits of something: *the six compartments were being shut off from each other.* **shut oneself off** isolate oneself from other people. **shut someone/thing out 1** screen someone or something from view: *clouds shut out the stars.* ■ block something from the mind: *anything he didn't like he shut out.* **2** prevent something from occurring or someone from doing something: *there was a high-mindedness which shut out any consideration of alternatives.* **shut up** (or **shut someone up**) [often in imperative] informal stop (or cause someone to stop) talking: *just shut up and listen.* **shut something up** close all doors and windows of a building or room, typically because it will be unoccupied for some time.
– ORIGIN Old English *scyttan* 'put (a bolt) in position to hold fast', of West Germanic origin; related to Dutch *schutten* 'shut up, obstruct', also to SHOOT.

shutdown ▶ noun a closure of a factory or system, typically a temporary closure due to a fault or for maintenance. ■ a turning off of a computer or computer system.

shut-eye ▶ noun [mass noun] informal sleep: *we'd better get some shut-eye.*

shut-in ▶ noun 1 N. Amer. a person confined indoors, especially as a result of either physical or mental disability.
2 a state or period in which an oil or gas well has available but unused capacity.

shut-off ▶ noun [usu. as modifier] a device used for stopping a supply or operation: *a shut-off valve.* ■ [mass noun] the cessation of flow, supply, or activity.

shutout ▶ noun a play, game, or inning in which the opposition is prevented from scoring.

shut-out bid ▶ noun Bridge a high bid intended to end the auction; a pre-emptive bid.

shutter ▶ noun 1 each of a pair of hinged panels fixed inside or outside a window that can be closed for security or privacy or to keep out the light.
2 Photography a device that opens and closes to expose the film in a camera.
3 Music the blind enclosing the swell box in an organ, used for controlling the volume of sound.
▶ verb [with obj.] close the shutters of (a window or building): *the windows were shuttered against the afternoon heat* | (as adj. **shuttered**) *barred and shuttered shops.*
– PHRASES **put up the shutters** Brit. (of a business) cease trading for the day or permanently.
– DERIVATIVES **shutterless** adjective.

shutterbug ▶ noun informal, chiefly N. Amer. an enthusiastic photographer.

shuttering ▶ noun [mass noun] wood in planks or strips used as a temporary structure to contain setting concrete, to support the sides of earth trenches, or similar. ■ [count noun] a temporary structure of this kind.

shutter priority ▶ noun [mass noun] Photography a system used in some automatic cameras in which the shutter speed is selected by the user and the appropriate aperture is then set by the camera. Compare with APERTURE PRIORITY.

S

shutter release ▶ noun the button on a camera that is pressed to make the shutter open.

shutter speed ▶ noun Photography the nominal time for which a shutter is open at a given setting.

shuttle ▶ noun 1 a form of transport that travels regularly between two places: *the nine o'clock shuttle from Edinburgh* | [as modifier] *a shuttle bus departs every 30 minutes.* ■ short for SPACE SHUTTLE.
2 a bobbin with two pointed ends used for carrying the weft thread across between the warp threads in weaving. ■ a bobbin carrying the lower thread in a sewing machine.
3 short for SHUTTLECOCK.
▶ verb [no obj., with adverbial of direction] travel regularly between two or more places: *the Secretary of State shuttled to and fro seeking compromise.* ■ [with obj. and adverbial of direction] transport in a shuttle: *the river taxi shuttled employees between the newspaper's offices and the capital.*
– ORIGIN Old English *scytel* 'dart, missile', of Germanic origin; compare with Old Norse *skutill* 'harpoon'; related to SHOOT. Sense 1 and the verb are from the movement of the bobbin from one side of the loom to the other and back.

shuttlecock ▶ **noun** a cork to which feathers are attached to form a cone shape, or a similar object of plastic, struck with rackets in the games of badminton and battledore.

shuttle diplomacy ▶ **noun** [mass noun] negotiations conducted by a mediator who travels between two or more parties that are reluctant to hold direct discussions.

shuttler ▶ **noun** informal, chiefly Indian a badminton player.

shuttle service ▶ **noun** a transport service operating to and fro over a short route.

shy[1] ▶ **adjective** (**shyer**, **shyest**) **1** nervous or timid in the company of other people: *I was pretty shy at school | a shy smile.* ■ (**shy of/about**) slow or reluctant to do (something): *the wealthy have become less shy of displaying their privilege.* ■ [in combination] having a dislike of or aversion to a specified thing: *they were a little camera-shy.* ■ (of a wild mammal or bird) reluctant to remain in sight of humans.
2 (**shy of**) informal less than; short of: *the shares are 29p shy of their flotation price.* ■ before: *he left school just shy of his fourteenth birthday.*
3 (of a plant) not bearing flowers or fruit well or prolifically.
▶ **verb** (**shies**, **shying**, **shied**) [no obj.] (especially of a horse) start suddenly aside in fright at an object, noise, or movement. ■ (**shy from**) avoid doing or becoming involved in (something) due to nervousness or a lack of confidence: *don't shy away from saying what you think.*
▶ **noun** a sudden startled movement, especially of a frightened horse.
– DERIVATIVES **shyer** noun, **shyly** adverb.
– ORIGIN Old English *scēoh* '(of a horse) easily frightened', of Germanic origin; related to German *scheuen* 'shun', *scheuchen* 'scare'; compare with **ESCHEW**. The verb dates from the mid 17th cent.

shy[2] dated ▶ **verb** (**shies**, **shying**, **shied**) [with obj.] fling or throw (something) at a target: *he tore the spectacles off and shied them at her.*
▶ **noun** (pl. **shies**) an act of flinging or throwing something at a target.
– PHRASES **have a shy at** try to hit something, especially with a ball or stone. ■ archaic attempt to do or obtain something. ■ archaic jeer at: *you are always having a shy at Lady Ann and her relations.*
– ORIGIN late 18th cent.: of unknown origin.

Shylock a Jewish moneylender in Shakespeare's *Merchant of Venice*, who lends money to Antonio but demands in return a pound of Antonio's own flesh should the debt not be repaid on time. ■ (as noun **a Shylock**) a moneylender who charges extremely high rates of interest.

shyness ▶ **noun** [mass noun] the quality or state of being shy: *gradually he overcame his natural shyness.*

shyster ▶ **noun** informal a person, especially a lawyer, who uses unscrupulous, fraudulent, or deceptive methods in business.
– ORIGIN mid 19th cent.: said to be from *Scheuster*, the name of a lawyer whose behaviour provoked accusations of 'scheuster' practices, perhaps reinforced by German *Scheisser* 'worthless person'.

SI ▶ **abbreviation** ■ the international system of units of measurement. [from French *Système International*.] ■ Law statutory instrument.

S

Si ▶ **symbol** the chemical element silicon.

si /siː/ ▶ **noun** Music another term for **TE**.
– ORIGIN early 18th cent.: from the initial letters of *Sancte Iohannes*, the closing words of a Latin hymn (see **SOLMIZATION**).

Siachen Glacier /sɪˈɑːtʃən/ a glacier in the Karakoram mountains in NW India, situated at an altitude of some 5,500 m (17,800 ft). Extending over 70 km (44 miles), it is one of the world's longest glaciers.

sial /ˈsʌɪəl/ ▶ **noun** [mass noun] Geology, dated the material of the upper or continental part of the earth's crust, characterized as relatively light and rich in silica and alumina. Contrasted with **SIMA**.
– ORIGIN 1920s: from the initial letters of **SILICA** and **ALUMINA**.

sialagogue /ˈsʌɪələɡɒɡ/ ▶ **noun** Medicine a drug that promotes the secretion of saliva.
– ORIGIN late 18th cent.: from French, from Greek *sialon* 'saliva' + *agōgos* 'leading'.

sialic acid /sʌɪˈalɪk/ ▶ **noun** [mass noun] Biochemistry a substance present in saliva which consists of acyl derivatives of neuraminic acid.
– ORIGIN 1950s: *sialic* from Greek *sialon* 'saliva' + **-IC**.

sialidase /sʌɪˈalɪdeɪz/ ▶ **noun** another term for **NEURAMINIDASE**.
– ORIGIN 1950s: from Greek *sialon* 'saliva' + **-IDE** + **-ASE**.

Sialkot /sɪˈɑːlkɒt/ an industrial city in the province of Punjab, in Pakistan; pop. 502,700 (est. 2009).

Siam /sʌɪˈam/ former name (until 1939) for **THAILAND**.

Siam, Gulf of former name for the Gulf of Thailand (see **THAILAND, GULF OF**).

siamang /ˈsʌɪəmaŋ, ˈsiːə-/ ▶ **noun** a large black gibbon native to Sumatra and Malaya. ● *Hylobates syndactylus*, family Hylobatidae.
– ORIGIN early 19th cent.: from Malay.

Siamese /ˌsʌɪəˈmiːz/ ▶ **noun** (pl. **same**) **1** dated a native of Siam (now Thailand) in SE Asia.
2 old-fashioned term for **THAI** (the language).
3 (also **Siamese cat**) a cat of a lightly built short-haired breed characterized by slanting blue eyes and typically pale fur with darker points.
▶ **adjective** dated of or concerning Siam, its people, or language.

Siamese fighting fish ▶ **noun** see **FIGHTING FISH**.

Siamese twins ▶ **plural noun** dated term for **CONJOINED TWINS**.
– ORIGIN with reference to the *Siamese* men Chang and Eng (1811–74), who, despite being joined at the waist, led an active life.

Sian variant of **XIAN**.

SIB ▶ **abbreviation** Securities and Investment Board, a regulatory body that oversees London's financial markets.

sib ▶ **noun 1** chiefly Zoology a brother or sister; a sibling.
2 Anthropology a group of people recognized by an individual as his or her kindred.
– ORIGIN Old English 'related by birth or descent', of unknown origin. Modern senses date from the late 19th and early 20th cents.

Sibelius /sɪˈbeɪlɪəs/, Jean (1865–1957), Finnish composer; born *Johan Julius Christian Sibelius*. His affinity with his country's landscape and legends, especially the epic *Kalevala*, is expressed in a series of tone poems including *The Swan of Tuonela* (1893), *Finlandia* (1899), and *Tapiola* (1925).

Šibenik /ˈʃɪbɛnɪk/ an industrial city and port in Croatia, on the Adriatic coast; pop. 37,200 (est. 2009).

Siberia /sʌɪˈbɪərɪə/ a vast region of Russia, extending from the Urals to the Pacific and from the Arctic coast to the northern borders of Kazakhstan, Mongolia, and China. Noted for the severity of its winters, it was traditionally used as a place of exile; it is now a major source of minerals and hydroelectric power.
– DERIVATIVES **Siberian** adjective & noun.

Siberian tiger ▶ **noun** a tiger of a large and threatened race with a long thick coat, found in SE Siberia and NE China.

sibia /ˈsɪbɪə/ ▶ **noun** a southern Asian songbird of the babbler family, typically having a blackish or greyish head and a long tail. ● Genus *Heterophasia* (and *Crocias*), family Timaliidae: several species.
– ORIGIN Nepalese *sibya*.

sibilant ▶ **adjective 1** making or characterized by a hissing sound: *his sibilant whisper.*
2 Phonetics (of a speech sound) sounded with a hissing effect, for example *s*, *sh*.
▶ **noun** Phonetics a sibilant speech sound.
– DERIVATIVES **sibilance** noun, **sibilantly** adverb.
– ORIGIN mid 17th cent.: from Latin *sibilant-* 'hissing', from the verb *sibilare*.

sibilate /ˈsɪbɪleɪt/ ▶ **verb** [with obj.] literary utter with a hissing sound.
– DERIVATIVES **sibilation** noun.
– ORIGIN mid 17th cent.: from Latin *sibilat-* 'hissed, whistled', from the verb *sibilare*.

Sibiu /siːˈbjuː/ an industrial city in central Romania; pop. 154,452 (2006).

siblicide /ˈsɪblɪsʌɪd/ ▶ **noun** [mass noun] Zoology the killing of a sibling or siblings, as a behaviour pattern typical in various animal groups.

sibling ▶ **noun** each of two or more children or offspring having one or both parents in common; a brother or sister.
– ORIGIN Old English, in the sense 'relative' (see **SIB**, **-LING**). The current sense dates from the early 20th cent.

sibship ▶ **noun 1** chiefly Zoology a group of offspring having the same two parents.
2 [mass noun] Anthropology the state of belonging to a sib or the same sib.

sibyl /ˈsɪbɪl/ ▶ **noun** a woman in ancient times who was thought to utter the prophecies of a god. ■ literary a woman able to foretell the future.
– ORIGIN from Old French *Sibile* or medieval Latin *Sibilla*, via Latin from Greek *Sibulla*.

sibylline /ˈsɪbɪlʌɪn/ ▶ **adjective** chiefly literary relating to or characteristic of a sibyl; prophetic and mysterious.
– ORIGIN late 16th cent.: from Latin *Sibillinus*, from *Sibylla* **SIBYL**.

Sibylline books ▶ **plural noun** a collection of oracles belonging to the ancient Roman state and used for guidance by magistrates and others.

sic[1] /sɪk/ ▶ **adverb** used in brackets after a copied or quoted word that appears odd or erroneous to show that the word is quoted exactly as it stands in the original, as in *a story must hold a child's interest and 'enrich his (sic) life'.*
– ORIGIN Latin, literally 'so, thus'.

sic[2] ▶ **verb** (**sics**, **sicking**, **sicked**) variant of **SICK**[2].

sic bo /sɪk ˈbəʊ/ ▶ **noun** [mass noun] a Chinese game in which bets are placed on the outcome of the roll of three dice.
– ORIGIN from Chinese, literally 'dice pair'.

siccative /ˈsɪkətɪv/ ▶ **noun** a drying agent used as a component of paint.
– ORIGIN late Middle English: from late Latin *siccativus*, from *siccare* 'to dry'.

sice[1] /sʌɪs/ ▶ **noun** (especially in gambling) the six on a dice.
– ORIGIN late Middle English: from Old French *sis*, from Latin *sex* 'six'.

sice[2] ▶ **noun** variant spelling of **SYCE**.

Sichuan /sɪˈtʃwɑːn/ (also **Szechuan** or **Szechwan**) a province of west central China; capital, Chengdu.

Sicilia /siˈtʃilja/ Italian name for **SICILY**.

siciliano /sɪˌtʃɪlɪˈɑːnəʊ, -ˌsɪlɪ-/ (also **siciliana**) ▶ **noun** (pl. **sicilianos**) a dance, song, or instrumental piece in 6/8 or 12/8 time, typically in a minor key, and evoking a pastoral mood.
– ORIGIN Italian, literally 'Sicilian'.

Sicilian Vespers a massacre of French inhabitants of Sicily, which began near Palermo at the time of vespers on Easter Monday in 1282. The ensuing war resulted in the replacement of the unpopular French Angevin dynasty by the Spanish House of Aragon.

Sicily a large Italian island in the Mediterranean, off the south-western tip of Italy; capital, Palermo. It is separated from the Italian mainland by the Strait of Messina and its highest point is the volcano Mount Etna. Italian name **SICILIA**.
– DERIVATIVES **Sicilian** /sɪˈsɪlɪən/ adjective & noun.

sick[1] ▶ **adjective 1** affected by physical or mental illness: *nursing very sick children | half my staff were off sick* | (as plural noun **the sick**) *visiting the sick and the elderly.* ■ relating to those who are ill: *the company organized a sick fund for its workers.* ■ (of an organization, system, or society) suffering from serious problems: *the British economy remains sick.*
2 [predic.] feeling nauseous and wanting to vomit: *he was starting to feel sick | Mark felt sick with fear.* ■ [attrib.] (of an emotion) so intense as to cause one to feel unwell or nauseous: *he had a sick fear of returning.* ■ informal disappointed, mortified, or miserable: *he looked pretty sick at that, but he eventually agreed.* ■ archaic pining or longing for someone or something: *he was sick for a sight of her.*
3 (**sick of**) intensely annoyed with or bored by (someone or something) as a result of having had too much of them: *I'm absolutely sick of your moods.*
4 informal (especially of humour) having something unpleasant such as death or misfortune as its subject and dealing with it in an offensive way: *this was someone's idea of a sick joke.* ■ (of a person) having abnormal or unnatural tendencies; perverted: *he is a deeply sick man from whom society needs to be protected.*
5 informal excellent.
▶ **noun** [mass noun] Brit. informal vomit.
▶ **verb** [with obj.] (**sick something up**) Brit. informal bring something up by vomiting.
– PHRASES **be sick 1** be ill. **2** Brit. vomit. **get sick 1** be ill. **2** N. Amer. vomit. **make someone sick** cause someone to vomit or feel nauseous or unwell. ■ cause someone to feel intense annoyance or disgust: *you're so damned self-righteous you make me sick!* —— **oneself sick** do something to such an extent that one feels nauseous or unwell (often used for emphasis): *she was worrying herself sick about Mike.* **on the sick** Brit. informal receiving sickness benefit. **sick and**

tired of informal annoyed about or bored with (someone or something) and unwilling to put up with them any longer: *I am sick and tired of all the criticism.* **(as) sick as a dog** informal extremely ill. **(as) sick as a parrot** Brit. informal extremely disappointed. **the sick man of ——** a country that is politically or economically unsound, especially in comparison with its neighbours: *the country had been the sick man of Europe for too long.* [applied in the late 19th cent. to the Sultan of Turkey, later extended to Turkey and other countries.] **sick to death of** informal another way of saying SICK AND TIRED OF above. **sick to one's stomach** nauseous. ■ disgusted.

– DERIVATIVES **sickish** adjective.

– ORIGIN Old English *sēoc* 'affected by illness', of Germanic origin; related to Dutch *ziek* and German *siech*.

> **WORD TRENDS** A common trick of slang is to invert meanings, so that seemingly negative words are used as terms of approval—**bad** and **wicked** are two established examples, with positive uses dating back to 1897 and 1920 respectively. **Sick** is a more recent arrival, first seen as a US synonym for 'excellent' or 'very impressive' in 1983: *it was a sick party and there were tons of cool people there.* It is particularly common in skateboard and snowboard culture, where it can be used to imply an element of risk and danger: *Shawn is a badass skater. He busts some sick tricks.*

sick² (also **sic**) ▶ **verb** [with obj.] **(sick something on)** set a dog on: *the plan was to surprise the heck out of the grizzly by sicking the dog on him.* ■ **(sick someone on)** informal set someone to pursue, keep watch on, or accompany (another).

– ORIGIN mid 19th cent.: dialect variant of SEEK.

sick bag ▶ **noun** a paper bag provided in an aircraft or ship as a receptacle for vomit.

sickbay ▶ **noun** a room or building set aside for the treatment or accommodation of the sick, especially within a military base, ship, or school.

sickbed ▶ **noun** an invalid's bed (often used to refer to the state or condition of being an invalid): *he had climbed from his sickbed to help the club.*

sick benefit ▶ **noun** informal short for SICKNESS BENEFIT.

sick building syndrome ▶ **noun** [mass noun] a condition affecting office workers, typically marked by headaches and respiratory problems, attributed to unhealthy or stressful factors in the working environment such as poor ventilation.

sick call ▶ **noun 1** a visit to a sick person, typically one made by a doctor or priest.
2 Military a summons for those reporting sick to attend for treatment.

sicken ▶ **verb 1** [with obj.] make (someone) feel disgusted or appalled: *she was sickened by the bomb attack.* ■ [no obj.] archaic feel disgust or horror: *he sickened at the thought.*
2 [no obj.] become ill: *Dawson sickened unexpectedly and died in 1916.* ■ **(sicken for)** begin to show symptoms of (a particular illness): *I hope I'm not sickening for a cold.*

sickener ▶ **noun 1** informal something which causes disgust or severe disappointment.
2 **(the sickener)** a poisonous toadstool with a red cap and a white or cream-coloured stem and gills, found in both Eurasia and North America. ● Genus *Russula*, family Russulaceae, class Hymenomycetes, in particular *R. emetica*.

sickening ▶ **adjective** causing or liable to cause a feeling of nausea or disgust: *a sickening stench of blood* | *she hit the ground with a sickening thud.* ■ informal causing great annoyance or disappointment.

– DERIVATIVES **sickeningly** adverb.

Sickert /ˈsɪkət/, Walter Richard (1860–1942), British painter, of Danish and Anglo-Irish descent. His subjects are mainly urban scenes and figure compositions, particularly pictures of the theatre and music hall, and drab domestic interiors.

sick headache ▶ **noun** a headache accompanied by nausea, particularly a migraine.

sickie ▶ **noun** informal **1** Brit. a day taken as sick leave when one is not actually ill: *she* **took a sickie** *only last week and enjoyed a morning in bed.*
2 another word for SICKO.

sickle ▶ **noun** a short-handled farming tool with a semicircular blade, used for cutting corn, lopping, or trimming.

– ORIGIN Old English *sicol, sicel*, of Germanic origin; related to Dutch *sikkel* and German *Sichel*, based on Latin *secula*, from *secare* 'to cut'.

sick leave ▶ **noun** [mass noun] leave of absence granted because of illness.

sicklebill ▶ **noun** any of a number of birds with a long, narrow downcurved bill: ● a tropical American hummingbird (genus *Eutoxeres*, family Trochilidae: two species). ● a New Guinea bird of paradise (two genera in the family Paradisaeidae).

sickle-cell anaemia (also **sickle-cell disease**) ▶ **noun** [mass noun] a severe hereditary form of anaemia in which a mutated form of haemoglobin distorts the red blood cells into a crescent shape at low oxygen levels. It is commonest among those of African descent.

sickle-cell trait ▶ **noun** [mass noun] a relatively mild condition caused by the presence of a single gene for sickle-cell anaemia, producing a smaller amount of abnormal haemoglobin and conferring some resistance to malaria.

sickle feather ▶ **noun** each of the long middle feathers of a cock's tail.

sick list ▶ **noun** a list, especially in the army or navy, of people who are ill and unable to work.

sickly ▶ **adjective** (**sicklier**, **sickliest**) **1** often ill; in poor health: *she was a thin, sickly child.* ■ (of a person's complexion or expression) indicative of poor health: *his usual sickly pallor.* ■ literary (of a place or climate) causing or characterized by unhealthiness: *a sickly vaporous swamp.*
2 (of a flavour, smell, colour, etc.) unpleasant in a way that induces discomfort or nausea: *the walls were painted a sickly green* | *she liked her coffee sweet and sickly.* ■ excessively sentimental or mawkish: *a sickly fable of delicate young lovers.*

– DERIVATIVES **sickliness** noun.

– ORIGIN late Middle English: probably suggested by Old Norse *sjúkligr*.

sick-making ▶ **adjective** informal nauseatingly unpleasant or shocking: *a sick-making stench.* ■ overly sentimental, coy, or trite.

sickness ▶ **noun** [mass noun] **1** the state of being ill: *she was absent through sickness* | [as modifier] *a sickness allowance.* ■ [often with adj. or noun modifier] a particular type of illness or disease: *botulism causes fodder sickness of horses* | [count noun] *a woman suffering an incurable sickness.*
2 the feeling or fact of being affected with nausea or vomiting: *she felt a wave of sickness wash over her* | *travel sickness.*

– ORIGIN Old English *sēocnesse* (see SICK¹, -NESS).

sickness benefit ▶ **noun** [mass noun] (in the UK) benefit paid weekly by the state to an individual for sickness which interrupts paid employment.

sick note ▶ **noun** a note to be given to an employer, teacher, or person in authority confirming that an absence was due to sickness.

sick nurse ▶ **noun** dated a nurse who looks after the sick and infirm (as distinct from a children's nurse).

sicko ▶ **noun** (pl. **sickos**) informal a mentally ill or perverted person, especially one who is sadistic.

sick-out ▶ **noun** N. Amer. informal a period of unwarranted sick leave taken as a form of group industrial action.

sick pay ▶ **noun** [mass noun] Brit. pay given to an employee on sick leave.

sickroom ▶ **noun** a room in a school or place of work occupied by or set apart for people who are unwell.

sida /ˈsʌɪdə/ ▶ **noun** a plant of the mallow family, native to tropical and warm regions. ● Genus *Sida*, family Malvaceae.

– ORIGIN modern Latin, from Greek *sidē* 'pomegranate tree', also 'water lily'.

sidalcea /sɪˈdalsɪə/ ▶ **noun** a herbaceous North American plant of the mallow family, several kinds of which are cultivated as ornamentals. ● Genus *Sidalcea*, family Malvaceae.

– ORIGIN modern Latin, from *Sida* + *Alcea*, names of related genera.

siddha /ˈsɪdʌ/ ▶ **noun** Hinduism an ascetic who has achieved enlightenment.

– ORIGIN Sanskrit.

Siddhartha Gautama /sɪˌdɑːtə ˈɡaʊtəmə/ see BUDDHA.

siddhi /ˈsɪdi/ ▶ **noun** (pl. **siddhis**) Hinduism **1** [mass noun] complete understanding; enlightenment.
2 a paranormal power possessed by a siddha.

– ORIGIN Sanskrit.

Siddons /ˈsɪd(ə)nz/, Mrs Sarah (1755–1831), English actress, sister of John Kemble; born *Sarah Kemble*. She was an acclaimed tragic actress, noted particularly for her role as Lady Macbeth.

siddur /ˈsɪdʊə/ ▶ **noun** (pl. **siddurim** /-rɪm/) a Jewish prayer book containing prayers and other information relevant to the daily liturgy.

– ORIGIN Hebrew *siddūr*, literally 'order'.

side ▶ **noun 1** a position to the left or right of an object, place, or central point: *a town on the other side of the river* | *on either side of the entrance was a garden* | *Rona tilted her head to one side* | [in combination] *stream-side plants.* ■ either of the two halves of an object, surface, or place regarded as divided by an imaginary central line: *she lay on her side of the bed* | *the left side of the brain.* ■ the right or the left part of a person's or animal's body, especially of the human torso: *he has been paralysed down his right side since birth.* ■ either of the lateral halves of the body of a butchered animal, or of an animal or fish prepared for eating: *a side of beef.*
2 an upright or sloping surface of a structure or object that is not the top or bottom and generally not the front or back: *a car crashed into the side of the house* | *line the sides of the cake tin* | [as modifier] *a side entrance.* ■ each of the flat surfaces of a solid object. ■ either of the two surfaces of something flat and thin, such as paper. ■ the amount of writing needed to fill one side of a sheet of paper: *do not write more than three sides.* ■ either of the two faces of a record or of the two separate tracks on a length of recording tape.
3 **(one's side)** a place or position closely adjacent to someone: *his wife stood* **at his side**.
4 a part or region near the edge and away from the middle of something: *a minibus was parked at the side of the road* | *cottages on the south side of the green.* ■ each of the lines forming the boundary of a plane rectilinear figure: *the farm buildings formed three sides of a square.*
5 a person or group opposing another or others in a dispute, contest, or debate: *the two sides agreed to resume border trade* | *whose side are you on?* ■ Brit. a sports team. ■ the position, interests, or attitude of one person or group, especially when regarded as being in opposition to another or others: *Mrs Burt hasn't kept her side of the bargain* | *I would have loved to have heard his side of the argument.*
6 a particular aspect of a situation or a person's character: *her ability to put up with his disagreeable side.* ■ a person's kinship or line of descent as traced through either their father or mother: *Richard was of French descent on his mother's side.*
7 Brit. informal a television channel considered as one of two or more that are available: *what's on the other side?*
8 [as modifier] subsidiary to or less important than something: *a side dish of fresh vegetables.* ■ chiefly N. Amer. a dish served as subsidiary to the main one: *sides of German potato salad and red cabbage.*
9 (also **sidespin**) [mass noun] horizontal spinning motion given to a ball. ■ chiefly Brit. spin given to the cue ball in snooker and billiards by hitting it on one side.
10 [mass noun] [usu. with negative] Brit. informal boastful or pretentious manner or attitude: *there was absolutely no side to him.*
11 W. Indian either of a pair of things: *a pair of shoes, one side winged by a bullet.*
▶ **verb 1** [no obj.] **(side with/against)** support or oppose in a conflict, dispute, or debate: *he felt that Max had betrayed him by siding with Beatrice.*
2 [with obj.] provide with a side or sides; form the side of: *the hills that side a long valley.*

– PHRASES **by** (or **at**) **someone's side** close to someone, especially so as to give them comfort or moral support: *a stepson who stayed by your side when your own son deserted you.* **from side to side 1** alternately left and right from a central point: *I shook my head frantically from side to side.* **2** across the entire width; right across: *the fleet stretched four miles from side to side.* **have something on one's side** (or **something is on one's side**) have something operating to one's advantage: *now he had time on his side, Thomas relaxed a little.* **let the side down** Brit. fail to meet the expectations of one's colleagues or friends, especially by mismanaging something. **on/from every side** (or **on/from all sides**) in or from all directions; everywhere: *there were shouts now from all sides.* **on** (or **to**) **one side** out of one's way; aside. ■ to be dealt with or considered later: *before the kick-off a player has to set his frustrations to one side.* **on the —— side** tending towards being ——; rather ——: *these boots are a bit on the tight side.* **on the side 1** in addition to one's regular job or as a subsidiary source of income: *his main job was a cop*

S

but on the side he sold water purifiers. **2** secretly, especially with regard to an illicit sexual relationship: *Brian had a mistress on the side.* **3** N. Amer. served separately from the main dish: *a club sandwich with French fries on the side.* **side by side** (of two or more people or things) close together and facing the same way: *on we jogged, side by side, for a mile.* ■ together: *the two institutions worked side by side in complete harmony.* **side of the fence** see FENCE. **take sides** support one person or cause against another or others in a dispute or contest: *I do not want to take sides in this matter.* **take** (or **draw**) **someone to/on one side** speak to someone in private, especially so as to advise or warn them about something. **this side of 1** before (a particular time, date, or event): *this side of midnight.* ■ yet to reach (a particular age): *I'm this side of forty-five.* **2** informal used to convey that something is comparable with a paragon or model of its kind: *the finest coffee this side of Brazil.* (**on**) **this side of the grave** in life.
– DERIVATIVES **sideless** adjective.
– ORIGIN Old English *side* 'left or right part of the body', of Germanic origin; related to Dutch *zijde* and German *Seite*, probably from a base meaning 'extending lengthways'.

sidearm /ˈsʌɪdɑːm/ ▶ noun a weapon worn at a person's side, such as a pistol or formerly a sword.
▶ adjective (of a throw, pitch, or cast) performed or delivered with a sweeping motion of the arm from the side of the body at or below shoulder level: *a sidearm delivery* | [as adv.] *I could throw sidearm.*
▶ verb [with obj.] chiefly Baseball throw or pitch a ball to (someone) with such a sweeping motion of the arm. ■ throw or pitch (a ball or other object) in this way.
– DERIVATIVES **sidearmer** noun.

sideband ▶ noun Telecommunications each of two frequency bands either side of the carrier wave, which contain the modulated signal.

sidebar ▶ noun chiefly N. Amer. a short article in a newspaper or magazine placed alongside a main article and containing additional or explanatory material. ■ a secondary, additional, or incidental thing; a side issue. ■ (also **sidebar conference**) (in a court of law) a discussion between the lawyers and the judge held out of earshot of the jury.

side bet ▶ noun a bet over and above a main bet, especially on a subsidiary issue.

sideboard ▶ noun **1** a flat-topped piece of furniture with cupboards and drawers, used for storing crockery, glasses, and table linen.
2 (usu. **sideboards**) Brit. a sideburn.
3 a board forming the side, or a part of the side, of a structure, especially a removable board at the side of a cart or lorry.

sideburn ▶ noun (usu. **sideburns**) a strip of hair grown by a man down each side of the face in front of his ears.
– ORIGIN late 19th cent.: originally *burnside*, from the name of General *Burnside* (1824–81), who wore sideburns.

sidecar ▶ noun **1** a small, low vehicle attached to the side of a motorcycle for carrying passengers.
2 a cocktail of brandy and lemon juice with orange liqueur.
3 another term for JAUNTING CAR.

S

side chain ▶ noun Chemistry a group of atoms attached to the main part of a molecule with a ring or chain structure.

side chair ▶ noun an upright wooden chair without arms.

side chapel ▶ noun a subsidiary chapel opening off the side aisle in a large church.

sidecut ▶ noun a curve in the side of a ski or snowboard which allows it to turn more smoothly.

sided ▶ adjective [in combination] having sides of a specified number or type: *narrow, steep-sided canyons.*
– DERIVATIVES **sidedly** adverb [in combination], **sidedness** noun.

side door ▶ noun a door at the side of a building.

side drum ▶ noun a small drum in the form of a short cylinder with a membrane at each end, the upper one being struck with hard sticks and the lower one often fitted with rattling cords or wires (snares).
– ORIGIN late 18th cent.: so named because it was originally played suspended from the drummer's side.

side effect ▶ noun a secondary, typically undesirable effect of a drug or medical treatment: *many anti-cancer drugs now in use have toxic side effects.*

side-foot ▶ verb [with obj.] kick (a ball) with the inside of the foot, especially in soccer.

side glance ▶ noun a sideways or brief glance.

sidehill ▶ noun N. Amer. a hillside.

side issue ▶ noun a point or topic connected to or raised by some other issue, but not as important, especially one that distracts attention from that which is important.

sidekick ▶ noun informal a person's assistant or close associate, especially one who has less authority than that person.

sidelight ▶ noun **1** a light placed at the side of something. ■ Brit. a small light on either side of the front of a motor vehicle, used in poor light when full headlights are not required. ■ (**sidelights**) a ship's navigation lights. ■ [mass noun] natural light coming from the side.
2 a narrow window or pane of glass set alongside a door or larger window.
3 a piece of incidental information that helps to clarify or enliven a subject.

sideline ▶ noun **1** an activity done in addition to one's main job, especially to earn extra income: [as modifier] *a sideline career as a stand-up comic.* ■ an auxiliary line of goods or trade: *electronic handbooks are a lucrative sideline for the firm.*
2 either of the two lines bounding the longer sides of a football field, basketball court, or similar. ■ (**the sidelines**) the area immediately outside such lines as a place for non-players, substitutes, or spectators. ■ (**the sidelines**) a position where one is observing a situation rather than directly involved in it: *we are not just watching* ***from the sidelines****, we are rolling our sleeves up and getting involved.*
▶ verb [with obj.] cause (a player) to be unable to play in a team or game: *an ankle injury has sidelined him for two weeks.* ■ remove from the centre of activity or attention; place in a less influential position: *backbench MPs have been sidelined and excluded from decision-making.*

sidelong ▶ adjective & adverb directed to or from one side; sideways: [as adj.] *Steve gave her a sidelong glance* | [as adv.] *he looked sidelong at her with a quick smile.*
– ORIGIN late Middle English: alteration of earlier *sideling*, from SIDE + the adverbial suffix *-ling*.

sideman ▶ noun (pl. **sidemen**) a supporting musician in a jazz band or rock group.

sidemeat ▶ noun [mass noun] N. Amer. salt pork or bacon, typically cut from the side of the pig.

side-necked turtle ▶ noun a freshwater turtle with a relatively long head and neck that is retracted sideways into the shell for defence. ● Suborder Pleurodira: families Chelidae (South America and Australasia) and Pelomedusidae (South America and southern Africa), and several genera.

side note ▶ noun a marginal note in a text.

side-on ▶ adverb with the side of someone or something towards something else: *the ship was wallowing side-on to the swell.*
▶ adjective directed from or towards a side: *a shot of the crowd from the side-on camera.* ■ (of a collision) involving the side of a vehicle.

side plate ▶ noun a plate smaller than a dinner plate, used for bread or other accompaniments to a meal.

side pond ▶ noun a pond positioned beside a canal lock in such a way that water can flow into or out of it when the lock is operated.

sidereal /sʌɪˈdɪərɪəl/ ▶ adjective of or with respect to the distant stars (i.e. the constellations or fixed stars, not the sun or planets).
– ORIGIN mid 17th cent.: from Latin *sidereus* (from *sidus, sider-* 'star') + -AL.

sidereal clock ▶ noun Astronomy a clock measuring sidereal time in terms of 24 equal divisions of a sidereal day.

sidereal day ▶ noun Astronomy the time between two consecutive transits of the First Point of Aries. It represents the time taken by the earth to rotate on its axis relative to the stars, and is almost four minutes shorter than the solar day because of the earth's orbital motion.

sidereal month ▶ noun Astronomy the time it takes the moon to orbit once around the earth with respect to the stars (approximately 27¹/₄ days).

sidereal period ▶ noun Astronomy the period of revolution of one body about another with respect to the distant stars.

sidereal time ▶ noun [mass noun] Astronomy time reckoned from the motion of the earth (or a planet) relative to the distant stars (rather than with respect to the sun).

sidereal year ▶ noun Astronomy the orbital period of the earth around the sun, taking the stars as a reference frame. It is 20 minutes longer than the tropical year because of precession.

siderite /ˈsʌɪdərʌɪt, ˈsɪd-/ ▶ noun **1** [mass noun] a brown mineral consisting of ferrous carbonate, occurring as the main component of some kinds of ironstone or as rhombohedral crystals in mineral veins.
2 a meteorite consisting mainly of nickel and iron.
– DERIVATIVES **sideritic** adjective.
– ORIGIN late 16th cent. (denoting lodestone): from Greek *sidēros* 'iron' + -ITE¹.

sidero-¹ ▶ combining form relating to the stars: *siderostat.*
– ORIGIN from Latin *sidus, sider-* 'star'.

sidero-² ▶ combining form relating to iron: *siderophore.*
– ORIGIN from Greek *sidēros* 'iron'.

side road ▶ noun a minor or subsidiary road, especially one joining or diverging from a main road.

siderophore /ˈsɪdərə(ʊ),fɔː, ˈsʌɪ-/ ▶ noun Biochemistry a molecule which binds and transports iron in micro-organisms.

siderostat /ˈsɪd(ə)rə(ʊ)stat, ˈsʌɪ-/ ▶ noun Astronomy an instrument used for keeping the image of a celestial object in a fixed position.

side-saddle ▶ noun a saddle in which the rider has both feet on the same side of the horse, typically used by a woman rider wearing a skirt.
▶ adverb sitting in this position on a horse.

side salad ▶ noun a salad served as a side dish.

side shoot ▶ noun a shoot growing from the side of a plant's stem.

sideshow ▶ noun a small show or stall at an exhibition, fair, or circus. ■ a minor or diverting incident or issue, especially one which distracts attention from something more important.

side-slip ▶ noun a sideways skid or slip. ■ Aeronautics a sideways movement of an aircraft, especially downwards towards the inside of a turn. ■ (in skiing and surfing) an act of travelling down a slope or wave in a direction not in line with one's skis or board.
▶ verb [no obj.] skid or slip sideways: *the weight counteracts the tyre's tendency to side-slip.* ■ Aeronautics move in a side-slip. ■ (in skiing and surfing) travel sideways or in any direction not in line with one's skis or board.

sidesman ▶ noun (pl. **sidesmen**) Brit. a churchwarden's assistant, who performs such duties as showing worshippers to their seats and taking the collection during a church service.

sidespin ▶ noun see SIDE (sense 9 of the noun).

side split ▶ noun Canadian a split-level house with fewer storeys on one side than the other.

side-splitting ▶ adjective informal extremely amusing: *side-splitting anecdotes.*
– DERIVATIVES **side-splittingly** adverb.

sidestep ▶ verb (**sidesteps, sidestepping, sidestepped**) [with obj.] avoid (someone or something) by stepping sideways: *he sidestepped a defender and crossed the ball.* ■ avoid dealing with or discussing (something problematic or disagreeable): *he neatly sidestepped the questions about riots.* ■ [no obj.] Skiing climb or descend by lifting alternate skis while facing sideways on the slope.
▶ noun a step taken sideways, typically to avoid someone or something.

side stream ▶ noun a tributary stream.

sidestream smoke ▶ noun [mass noun] smoke that passes from a cigarette into the surrounding air, rather than into the smoker's lungs.

side street ▶ noun a minor or subsidiary street.

sidestroke ▶ noun a swimming stroke similar to the breaststroke in which the swimmer lies on their side.

side suit ▶ noun Bridge a suit other than the trump suit.

sideswipe ▶ noun **1** a passing critical remark about someone or something.
2 chiefly N. Amer. a glancing blow from or on the side of something, especially a motor vehicle.
▶ verb [with obj.] chiefly N. Amer. strike with a glancing blow: *Curtis jerked the wheel hard over and sideswiped the other car.*

side table ▶ noun a table placed at the side of a room or apart from the main table.

side tone ▶ noun [mass noun] feedback in a telephone receiver, in particular the reproduction of the user's own voice.

sidetrack ▶ verb [with obj.] **1** cause (someone) to be distracted from an immediate or important issue: *he does not let himself get sidetracked by fads and trends.* ■ divert (a project or debate) away from a central issue or previously determined plan: *the effort at reform has been sidetracked for years.*
2 chiefly N. Amer. direct (a train) into a branch line or siding. ■ divert (a well or borehole) to reach a productive deposit or to avoid an obstruction.
▶ noun a minor path or track. ■ chiefly N. Amer. a railway branch line or siding. ■ a well or borehole which runs partly to one side of the original line of drilling.

side trip ▶ noun a minor excursion during a voyage or trip.

side valve ▶ noun a valve in an internal-combustion engine mounted alongside the cylinder.

side view ▶ noun a view from the side.

sidewalk ▶ noun N. Amer. a pavement.

sidewall ▶ noun the side of a tyre, typically marked or coloured distinctively.

sideward ▶ adjective & adverb (also **sidewards**) another term for SIDEWAYS.

sideways ▶ adverb & adjective **1** to, towards, or from the side: [as adv.] *she tilted her body sideways* | [as adj.] *he hurried towards his office without a sideways glance.* ■ [as adv.] with one side facing forward: *the lorry slid sideways across the road.* ■ so as to occupy a job or position at the same level as one previously held rather than be promoted or demoted: [as adj.] *after the reshuffle there were sideways moves for ministers.*
2 by an indirect way: [as adv.] *he came into politics sideways, as campaign manager for Ronald Reagan.* ■ [as adj.] from an unconventional or unorthodox viewpoint: *take a* ***sideways look at*** *daily life.*
– PHRASES **knock someone sideways** see KNOCK. **sideways on** from the side; side-on.

side-wheeler ▶ noun N. Amer. a steamer with paddle wheels on either side.

side whiskers ▶ plural noun whiskers or sideburns on a man's cheeks.

sidewind /ˈsʌɪdwʌɪnd/ ▶ verb [no obj.] (often as noun **sidewinding**) (of a sidewinder or other snake) move sideways in a series of S-shaped curves.

side wind ▶ noun a wind blowing predominantly from one side.

sidewinder[1] /ˈsʌɪdˌwʌɪndə/ ▶ noun a pale-coloured, nocturnal, burrowing rattlesnake that moves sideways over sand by throwing its body into S-shaped curves. It is found in the deserts of North America.
● *Crotalus cerastes*, family Viperidae.

sidewinder[2] /ˈsʌɪdˌwɪndə/ ▶ noun N. Amer. a heavy blow with the fist delivered from or on the side.

sidewise ▶ adverb & adjective US another term for SIDEWAYS.

Sidhe /ʃiː/ ▶ plural noun the fairy people of Irish folklore, said to live beneath the hills and often identified as the remnant of the ancient Tuatha Dé Danann.
– ORIGIN from Irish *aos sidhe* 'people of the fairy mound'.

Sidi bel Abbès /ˌsɪdɪ bɛl əˈbɛs/ a town in northern Algeria, situated to the south of Oran; pop. 197,600 (est. 2009).

siding ▶ noun **1** a short track at the side of and opening on to a railway line, used chiefly for shunting or stabling trains. ■ N. Amer. a loop line. ■ S. African a scheduled stop on a railway line, often in open country, for farming produce to be loaded and passengers taken on board.
2 [mass noun] N. Amer. cladding material for the outside of a building.

sidle ▶ verb [no obj., with adverbial of direction] walk in a furtive, unobtrusive, or timid manner, especially sideways or obliquely: *I* ***sidled up to*** *her.*
▶ noun [in sing.] an instance of walking in this way.
– ORIGIN late 17th cent.: back-formation from *sideling* (see SIDELONG).

Sidney, Sir Philip (1554–86), English poet, courtier, and soldier. His best-known work is *Arcadia* (published posthumously in 1590), a pastoral prose romance including poems in a wide variety of verse forms.

Sidon /ˈsʌɪd(ə)n/ a city in Lebanon, on the Mediterranean coast south of Beirut; pop. 58,400 (est. 2009). Founded in the 3rd millennium BC, it was a Phoenician seaport and city-state. Arabic name **SAIDA**.

Sidra, Gulf of /ˈsɪdrə/ (also **Gulf of Sirte**) a broad inlet of the Mediterranean on the coast of Libya, between the towns of Benghazi and Misratah.

SIDS ▶ abbreviation sudden infant death syndrome, a technical term for COT DEATH.

Siebengebirge /ˈziːb(ə)ngəˌbɪəgə/, German /ˈziːbŋgəˌbɪrgə/ a range of hills in western Germany, on the right bank of the Rhine south-east of Bonn.

siege ▶ noun a military operation in which enemy forces surround a town or building, cutting off essential supplies, with the aim of compelling those inside to surrender: *Verdun had withstood a siege of ten weeks* | [as modifier] *siege warfare.* ■ a similar operation by a police or other force to compel an armed person to surrender.
– PHRASES **lay siege to** conduct a siege of (a place): *government forces laid siege to the building* | figurative *the press laid siege to her flat.* **under siege** (of a place) undergoing a siege: *the fort had been under siege by guerrillas since June* | figurative *we are* ***under siege from*** *budget cuts.*
– ORIGIN Middle English: from Old French *sege*, from *asegier* 'besiege'.

siege economy ▶ noun an economy in which import controls are imposed and the export of capital is curtailed.

siege gun ▶ noun a heavy gun used in attacking a place under siege.

siege mentality ▶ noun a defensive or paranoid attitude based on the belief that others are hostile towards one.

Siegfried /ˈsiːgfriːd/ the hero of the first part of the Nibelungenlied. A prince of the Netherlands, Siegfried obtains a hoard of treasure by killing the dragon Fafner. He marries Kriemhild, and helps Gunther to win Brunhild before being killed by Hagen.

Siegfried Line 1 the line of defence constructed by the Germans along the western frontier of Germany before the Second World War.
2 another term for **HINDENBURG LINE**.

Sieg Heil /ziːk ˈhʌɪl/ ▶ exclamation a victory salute used originally by Nazis at political rallies.
– DERIVATIVES **Sieg-Heiling** adjective.
– ORIGIN German, literally 'hail victory!'

Siemens /ˈsiːmənz/ a German family of scientific entrepreneurs and engineers. **Ernst Werner von Siemens** (1816–92) was an electrical engineer who developed the process of electroplating, devised an electric generator which used an electromagnet, and pioneered electrical traction. His brother **Karl Wilhelm** (1823–83) (also known as *Sir Charles William Siemens*) moved to England, where he developed the open-hearth steel furnace and designed the cable-laying steamship *Faraday*. Their brother **Friedrich** (1826–1904) applied the principles of the open-hearth furnace to glass-making.

siemens /ˈsiːmənz/ (abbrev.: **S**) ▶ noun Physics the SI unit of conductance, equal to one reciprocal ohm.
– ORIGIN 1930s: named after K. W. von SIEMENS.

Siena /sɪˈɛnə/ a city in west central Italy, in Tuscany; pop. 54,159 (2008). In the 13th and 14th centuries it was the centre of a flourishing school of art. Its central square is the venue for the noted Palio horse race.
– DERIVATIVES **Sienese** /sɪəˈniːz/ adjective & noun.

sienna ▶ noun [mass noun] a kind of ferruginous earth used as a pigment in painting, normally yellowish-brown in colour (**raw sienna**) or deep reddish-brown when roasted (**burnt sienna**). ■ the colour of this pigment.
– ORIGIN late 18th cent.: from Italian *(terra di) Sienna* '(earth of) Siena'.

Sierpinski triangle /ʃɪəˈpɪnski/ (also **Sierpinski gasket**) ▶ noun Mathematics a fractal based on a triangle with four equal triangles inscribed in it. The central triangle is removed and each of the other three treated as the original was, and so on, creating an infinite regression in a finite space.
– ORIGIN 1970s: named after Wacław *Sierpiński* (1882–1969), Polish mathematician.

sierra /sɪˈɛrə, sɪˈɛːrə/ ▶ noun **1** (especially in Spanish-speaking countries or the western US) a long jagged mountain chain.
2 a code word representing the letter S, used in radio communication.
– ORIGIN mid 16th cent.: Spanish, from Latin *serra* 'saw'.

Sierra Club a North American environmental group, founded in 1892. The pioneering naturalist John Muir was its first president.

Sierra Leone /lɪˈəʊn/ a country on the coast of West Africa; pop. 5,132,100 (est. 2009); languages, English (official), English Creole, Temne, and other West African languages; capital, Freetown.

An area of British influence from the late 18th century, the district around Freetown on the coast became a colony in 1807, serving as a centre for operations against slave traders. The large inland territory was not declared a protectorate until 1896. Sierra Leone achieved independence within the Commonwealth in 1961 but was suspended from the organization between 1997 and 2001 following military coups in 1992 and 1997.

– DERIVATIVES **Sierra Leonean** adjective & noun.

Sierra Madre /ˈmɑːdreɪ/ a mountain system in Mexico, extending from the border with the US in the north to the southern border with Guatemala.

Sierra Nevada /nəˈvɑːdə/ **1** a mountain range in southern Spain, in Andalusia, south-east of Granada.
2 a mountain range in eastern California. Rising sharply from the Great Basin in the east, it descends more gently to California's Central Valley in the west.

siesta /sɪˈɛstə/ ▶ noun an afternoon rest or nap, especially one taken during the hottest hours of the day in a hot climate.
– ORIGIN mid 17th cent.: Spanish, from Latin *sexta (hora)* 'sixth hour'.

sieve /sɪv/ ▶ noun a utensil consisting of a wire or plastic mesh held in a frame, used for straining solids from liquids, for separating coarser from finer particles, or for reducing soft solids to a pulp. ■ used figuratively with reference to the fact that a sieve does not hold all its contents: *she's forgotten all the details already, she's got* ***a mind like a sieve.***
▶ verb [with obj.] put (a food substance or other material) through a sieve. ■ (usu. **sieve something out**) remove (unwanted items): *filters sieve large particles out of the water to prevent them from harming the pumps.* ■ [no obj.] (**sieve through**) examine in detail: *lawyers had sieved through her contract.*
– DERIVATIVES **sieve-like** adjective.
– ORIGIN Old English *sife* (noun), of West Germanic origin; related to Dutch *zeef* and German *Sieb*.

sieve cell ▶ noun Botany a sieve element of a primitive type present in ferns and gymnosperms, with narrow pores and no sieve plate.

sieve element ▶ noun Botany an elongated cell in the phloem of a vascular plant, in which the primary wall is perforated by pores through which water is conducted.

sieve plate ▶ noun Botany an area of relatively large pores present in the common end walls of sieve tube elements. ■ Zoology a perforated plate in the integument of an invertebrate, especially the madreporite of an echinoderm.

sievert /ˈsiːvət/ (abbrev.: **Sv**) ▶ noun Physics the SI unit of dose equivalent (the biological effect of ionizing radiation), equal to an effective dose of a joule of energy per kilogram of recipient mass.
– ORIGIN 1940s: named after Rolf M. *Sievert* (1896–1966), Swedish physicist.

sieve tube ▶ noun Botany a series of sieve tube elements placed end to end to form a continuous tube.

sieve tube element (also **sieve tube member**) ▶ noun Botany a sieve element of a type present in angiosperms, a series of which are joined end to end to form sieve tubes, with sieve plates between the elements.

sifaka /sɪˈfakə/ ▶ noun a large gregarious lemur which leaps from tree to tree in an upright position. ● Genus *Propithecus*, family Indriidae: two species.
– ORIGIN mid 19th cent.: from Malagasy.

sift ▶ verb [with obj.] **1** put (a fine or loose substance) through a sieve so as to remove lumps or large particles: *sift the flour into a large bowl.* ■ cause to flow or pass as through a sieve: *Miranda sifted the warm sand through her fingers.* ■ [no obj., with adverbial of direction] (of snow, ash, etc.) descend lightly or sparsely as if sprinkled from a sieve: *ash began to sift down round them.*
2 examine (something) thoroughly so as to isolate that which is most important: *until we sift the*

S

evidence ourselves, we can't comment objectively | [no obj.] *the fourth stage involves **sifting through** the data and evaluating it.* ■ (**sift something out**) separate something, especially something to be discarded, from something else: *he asked for streamlined procedures to sift out frivolous applications.*
▶ **noun** [usu. in sing.] an act of sifting something, especially so as to isolate that which is most important: *a careful archaeological sift must be made through the debris.* ■ an amount of sifted material: *the floor was dusted with a fine sift of flour.*
– DERIVATIVES **sifted** adjective, **sifter** noun, **sifting** noun.
– ORIGIN Old English *siftan*, of West Germanic origin; related to Dutch *ziften*, also to SIEVE.

SIG ▶ **abbreviation** Computing special interest group, a type of newsgroup.

sig ▶ **noun** Computing, informal a short personalized message at the end of an email.
– ORIGIN 1990s: abbreviation of SIGNATURE.

Sig. ▶ **abbreviation** Signor.

Sigatoka /ˌsɪɡəˈtəʊkə/ ▶ **noun** [mass noun] a fungal disease of banana plants characterized by elongated spots on the leaves, which then rot completely. ● The fungus is *Mycosphaerella musicola*, subdivision Ascomycotina.
– ORIGIN 1920s: named after a district in Fiji.

sigh ▶ **verb** [no obj.] emit a long, deep audible breath expressing sadness, relief, tiredness, or similar: *Harry sank into a chair and sighed with relief.* ■ (of the wind or something through which the wind blows) make a sound resembling this: *a breeze made the treetops sigh.* ■ (**sigh for**) literary feel a deep yearning for (someone or something lost, unattainable, or distant): *he sighed for days gone by.*
▶ **noun** a long, deep audible exhalation expressing sadness, relief, tiredness, or similar: *she let out a long sigh of despair* | figurative *the councils **heaved a sigh of relief** when they saved over £6m between them.* ■ a gentle sound resembling a sigh, especially one made by the wind.
– ORIGIN Middle English (as a verb): probably a back-formation from *sighte*, past tense of *siche, sike*, from Old English *sīcan*.

sight ▶ **noun 1** [mass noun] the faculty or power of seeing: *Joseph lost his sight as a baby* | [as modifier] *a sight test.* ■ the action or fact of seeing someone or something: *I've always been scared of the sight of blood.* ■ the area or distance within which someone can see or something can be seen: *he now refused to let Rose out of his sight.* ■ dated a person's view or consideration: *we are all equal **in the sight of** God.*
2 a thing that one sees or that can be seen: *John was a familiar sight in the bar for many years* | *he was getting used to seeing unpleasant sights.* ■ (**sights**) places of interest to tourists and visitors in a city, town, or other place: *she offered to show me the sights.* ■ (**a sight**) informal a person or thing having a ridiculous, repulsive, or dishevelled appearance: *'I must look a frightful sight,' she said.*
3 (usu. **sights**) a device on a gun or optical instrument used for assisting a person's precise aim or observation.
▶ **verb 1** [with obj.] manage to see or observe (someone or something); catch an initial glimpse of: *tell me when you sight London Bridge.*
2 [no obj., with adverbial of direction] take aim by looking through the sights of a gun: *she sighted down the barrel.* ■ take a detailed visual measurement of something with or as with a sight. ■ [with obj.] adjust the sight of (a firearm or optical instrument).
– PHRASES **at first sight** on first seeing or meeting someone: *it was **love at first sight**.* ■ from an initial impression: *the debate is more complex than it seems at first sight.* **catch** (or **get a**) **sight of** glimpse for a moment; suddenly notice: *when she caught sight of him she smiled.* **in sight** visible: *no other vehicle was in sight.* ■ near at hand; close to being achieved or realized: *the minister insisted that agreement was in sight.* **in** (or **within**) **sight of** so as to see or be seen from: *I climbed the hill and came in sight of the house.* ■ within reach of; close to attaining: *he was safe for the moment and in sight of victory.* **in** (or **within**) **one's sights** visible, especially through the sights of one's gun. ■ within the scope of one's ambitions or expectations: *he had the prize firmly in his sights.* **lose sight of** be no longer able to see. ■ fail to consider, be aware of, or remember: *we should not lose sight of the fact that the issues involved are moral ones.* **not a pretty sight** informal not a pleasant spectacle or situation. **on** (or **at**) **sight** as soon as someone or something has been seen: *in Africa, paramilitary game wardens shoot poachers on sight.* **out of sight 1** not visible: *she saw them off, waving until the car was out of sight.* **2** (also **outasight**) [often as exclamation] informal extremely good; excellent. **out of sight, out of mind** proverb you soon forget people or things that are no longer visible or present. (**get**) **out of my sight!** go away at once! **raise** (or **lower**) **one's sights** become more (or less) ambitious; increase (or lower) one's expectations. **set one's sights on** have as an ambition; hope strongly to achieve or reach: *Katherine set her sights on university.* **a sight ——** informal much; to a considerable extent: *the old lady is a sight cleverer than Sarah* | *he's a sight too full of himself.* **a sight for sore eyes** informal a person or thing that one is extremely pleased or relieved to see. **a sight to behold** a person or thing that is particularly impressive or worth seeing.
– DERIVATIVES **sighter** noun.
– ORIGIN Old English *(ge)sihth* 'something seen', of West Germanic origin; related to Dutch *zicht* and German *Gesicht* 'sight, face, appearance'. The verb dates from the mid 16th cent. (in sense 2 of the verb).

USAGE On the confusion of sight and site, see USAGE at SITE.

sight deposit ▶ **noun** a bank deposit that can be withdrawn immediately without notice or penalty.

sighted ▶ **adjective** (of a person) having the ability to see; not blind: *a sighted guide is needed* | (as plural noun **the sighted**) *both the sighted and the visually impaired.* ■ [in combination] having a specified kind of sight: *the keen-sighted watcher may catch a glimpse.*

sight gag ▶ **noun** informal a visual joke.

sight glass ▶ **noun** a transparent tube or window through which the level of liquid in a reservoir or supply line can be checked visually.

sighthound ▶ **noun** a hound originally bred to hunt independently from humans, such as a greyhound or a whippet.

sighting ▶ **noun** an instance of seeing or catching sight of something, typically something unusual or rare: *the reported sightings of a UFO near a Suffolk airbase.*

sighting shot ▶ **noun** an experimental shot to guide shooters in adjusting their sights.

sightless ▶ **adjective** unable to see; blind: *blank, sightless eyes.* ■ literary invisible.
– DERIVATIVES **sightlessly** adverb, **sightlessness** noun.

sight line ▶ **noun** a hypothetical line from someone's eye to what is seen (used especially with reference to good or bad visibility): *the authorities require good sight lines at road junctions.*

sightly ▶ **adjective** pleasing to the eye: *metal guards can also be used but are less sightly.*
– DERIVATIVES **sightliness** noun.

sight-read ▶ **verb** [with obj.] read and perform (music) from sheet music, without preparation.
– DERIVATIVES **sight-reader** noun.

sight screen ▶ **noun** Cricket a large white screen placed near the boundary in line with the wicket to help the batsman see the ball.

sightseeing ▶ **noun** [mass noun] the activity of visiting places of interest in a particular location: [as modifier] *a sightseeing tour.*
– DERIVATIVES **sightsee** verb.

sightseer ▶ **noun** a person who goes sightseeing: *hordes of sightseers.*

sight-sing ▶ **verb** [with obj.] sing (music) at sight, without preparation.

sight unseen ▶ **adverb** without the opportunity to look at the object in question beforehand: *they bought their computers sight unseen through the mail.* ■ without being seen: *what other treasures remain sight unseen?*

sigil /ˈsɪdʒɪl/ ▶ **noun** an inscribed or painted symbol considered to have magical power. ■ archaic a seal: *the supply wains bore the High King's sigil.* ■ literary a sign or symbol.
– ORIGIN late Middle English: from late Latin *sigillum* 'sign'.

SIGINT /ˈsɪɡɪnt/ ▶ **abbreviation** signals intelligence.

siglum /ˈsɪɡləm/ ▶ **noun** (pl. **sigla** /-lə/) a letter or symbol which stands for a word or name, especially to denote a particular manuscript or edition of a text.
– ORIGIN early 18th cent.: from late Latin *sigla* (plural), perhaps from *singula*, neuter plural of *singulus* 'single'.

sigma /ˈsɪɡmə/ ▶ **noun** the eighteenth letter of the Greek alphabet (Σ, σ), transliterated as 's'. ● The form ς is used instead of σ at the end of a word. The uncial form, resembling the letter *c*, is also sometimes used.
■ (**Sigma**) [followed by Latin genitive] Astronomy the eighteenth star in a constellation: *Sigma Octantis.*
■ Chemistry & Physics relating to or denoting an electron or orbital with zero angular momentum about an internuclear axis.
▶ **symbol** ■ (Σ) mathematical sum. ■ (σ) standard deviation.
– ORIGIN Greek.

sigmate /ˈsɪɡmeɪt/ ▶ **adjective** having the shape of a Σ or a letter S.

sigmoid /ˈsɪɡmɔɪd/ ▶ **adjective 1** curved like the uncial sigma; crescent-shaped.
2 S-shaped.
▶ **noun** Anatomy short for SIGMOID COLON.
– DERIVATIVES **sigmoidal** adjective.
– ORIGIN late 17th cent.: from Greek *sigmoeidēs*, from *sigma* (see SIGMA).

sigmoid colon ▶ **noun** Anatomy the S-shaped last part of the large intestine, leading into the rectum.

sigmoidoscopy /ˌsɪɡmɔɪˈdɒskəpi/ ▶ **noun** [mass noun] examination of the sigmoid colon by means of a flexible tube inserted through the anus.
– DERIVATIVES **sigmoidoscope** noun, **sigmoidoscopic** adjective.

sign ▶ **noun 1** an object, quality, or event whose presence or occurrence indicates the probable presence or occurrence of something else: *flowers are often given as a sign of affection* | [with clause] *the shops are full, which is a sign that the recession is past its worst.* ■ something regarded as an indication of what is happening or going to happen: ***the signs are that** counterfeiting is growing at an alarming rate.* ■ [with negative] used to indicate that someone or something is not where they should be or are expected to be: *there was still no sign of her.* ■ Medicine an indication of a disease detectable by a medical practitioner even if not apparent to the patient. Compare with SYMPTOM. ■ a miracle regarded as evidence of supernatural power (chiefly in biblical and literary use). ■ [mass noun] N. Amer. the trail of a wild animal: *wolverine sign.*
2 a gesture or action used to convey information or an instruction: *she gave him the thumbs-up sign.* ■ an action or reaction that conveys something about someone: *she gave no sign of having seen him.* ■ a gesture used in a system of sign language. ■ [mass noun] short for SIGN LANGUAGE. ■ a symbol or word used to represent an operation, instruction, concept, or object in algebra, music, or other subjects.
3 a notice on public display that gives information or instructions in a written or symbolic form: *I didn't see the 'Stop' sign.*
4 (also **zodiacal sign**) Astrology each of the twelve equal sections into which the zodiac is divided, named from the constellations formerly situated in each, and associated with successive periods of the year according to the position of the sun on the ecliptic: *a sign of the Zodiac* | *a person born **under the sign of** Virgo.*
5 Mathematics the positiveness or negativeness of a quantity.
▶ **verb 1** [with obj.] write one's name on (a letter, card, document, etc.) to identify oneself as the writer or sender: *the card was signed by the whole class.* ■ authorize (a document or other written or printed material) by attaching a signature: *the two countries signed a non-aggression treaty.* ■ write (one's name) for purposes of identification or authorization: *she signed her name in the book* | [with obj. and complement] *she **signed herself** Imogen* | [no obj.] *he signed on the dotted line.* ■ engage (someone, typically a sports player or a musician) to work for one by signing a contract with them: *the manager plans to sign a new goalkeeper.* ■ [no obj.] commit oneself to work by signing a contract: *a new striker has **signed for** Blackburn.*
2 [no obj.] use gestures to convey information or instructions: [with infinitive] *she signed to her husband to leave the room.* ■ communicate in sign language: *she was learning to sign.* ■ [with obj.] express or perform (something) in sign language.
3 [with obj.] indicate with signposts or other markers: *the footpath is signed by the gate.*
4 [with obj.] archaic mark or consecrate with the sign of the cross.
– PHRASES **sign of the cross** a Christian sign made in blessing or prayer by tracing a cross from the forehead to the chest and to each shoulder, or in the air. **sign of the times** something judged to indicate the nature of a particular period, typically something undesirable: *the theft was a sign of the times.* **signed,**

sealed, and delivered (or **signed and sealed**) formally and officially agreed and in effect.
– PHRASAL VERBS **sign something away/over** officially relinquish rights or property by signing a deed: *I have no intention of signing away my inheritance.* **sign for** sign a receipt to confirm that one has received (something delivered). **sign in** (or **out**) sign a register on arrival (or departure), typically in a hotel. **sign someone in** (or **out**) record someone's arrival (or departure) in a register. **sign off 1** conclude a letter, broadcast, or other message: *he signed off with a few words of advice.* ■ conclude an activity: *he **signed off from** school athletics with a double in the shot.* ■ sign to record that one is leaving work for the day. ■ Bridge indicate by a conventional bid that one is seeking to end the bidding. **2** Brit. register to stop receiving unemployment benefit after finding work. **sign someone off** record that someone is entitled to miss work, typically because of illness. **sign off on** US informal give one's approval to: *it was hard to get celebrities to sign off on those issues.* **sign on 1** commit oneself to employment, membership of a society, or some other undertaking: *I'll **sign on with** a nursing agency.* **2** Brit. register as unemployed. **sign someone on** take someone into one's employment. **sign something out** sign to indicate that one has borrowed or hired something: *I signed out the keys.* **sign up** commit oneself to a period of employment, education, or in the armed forces: *he **signed up for** a ten-week course.* ■ (also **sign something up**) conclude a business deal: *the firm has signed up with a new Russian company.* **sign someone up** formally engage someone in employment.
– DERIVATIVES **signable** adjective, **signer** noun.
– ORIGIN Middle English: from Old French *signe* (noun), *signer* (verb), from Latin *signum* 'mark, token'.

Signac /ˈsiːnjak/, Paul (1863–1935), French neo-Impressionist painter. A pointillist painter, he had a technique that was freer than Seurat's and was characterized by the use of small dashes and patches of pure colour rather than dots.

signage ▶ noun [mass noun] signs collectively, especially commercial or public display signs.

signal[1] ▶ noun **1** a gesture, action, or sound that is used to convey information or instructions, typically by prearrangement between the parties concerned: *the firing of the gun was the **signal for** a chain of beacons to be lit* | [with infinitive] *the policeman raised his hand as a signal to stop.* ■ an indication of a situation: *the markets are waiting for a clear signal about the direction of policy.* ■ an event or statement that provides the impulse for an occurrence: *the champion's announcement that he was retiring was the **signal for** scores of journalists to gather at his last match.* ■ Bridge a prearranged convention of bidding or play intended to convey information to one's partner.
2 an electrical impulse or radio wave transmitted or received: *equipment for receiving TV signals.*
3 an apparatus on a railway, typically a coloured light or a semaphore, giving indications to train drivers of whether or not the line is clear.
▶ verb (**signals, signalling, signalled**; US **signals, signaling, signaled**) [no obj.] convey information or instructions by means of a gesture, action, or sound: *hold your fire until I signal.* ■ [with obj. and infinitive] instruct (someone) to do something by means of gestures or signs: *she signalled Charlotte to be silent.* ■ (of a cyclist, motorist, or vehicle) indicate an intention to turn in a specified direction using an extended arm or flashing indicator: [with complement] *Stone signalled right* | [with infinitive] *the truck signalled to turn left.* ■ [with obj.] indicate the existence or occurrence of (something) by actions or sounds: *the Community could signal displeasure by refusing to cooperate* | [with clause] *she gave a glance which signalled that her father was being secretive.*
– DERIVATIVES **signaller** noun.
– ORIGIN late Middle English: from Old French, from medieval Latin *signale*, neuter of late Latin *signalis*, from Latin *signum* 'mark, token' (see **SIGN**). The verb dates from the early 19th cent.

signal[2] ▶ adjective [attrib.] striking in extent, seriousness, or importance; outstanding: *he attacked the government for their signal failure of leadership.*
– DERIVATIVES **signally** adverb.
– ORIGIN early 17th cent.: from French *signalé*, from the Italian past participle *segnalato* 'distinguished, made illustrious', from *segnale* 'a signal'.

signal box (chiefly US also **signal tower**) ▶ noun Brit. a building beside a railway track from which signals, points, and other equipment are controlled.

signal-caller ▶ noun American Football a player who signals the next play or formation to other team members.

signalize (also **signalise**) ▶ verb [with obj.] **1** mark or indicate (something), especially in a striking or conspicuous manner: *people seek to change their name to signalize a change in status that has taken place.* ■ archaic make (something) noteworthy or remarkable: *a little flower with not much to signalize it.*
2 US & Austral. provide (an intersection) with traffic signals.

signalman ▶ noun (pl. **signalmen**) a railway worker responsible for operating signals and points. ■ a person responsible for sending and receiving naval or military signals.

signals intelligence ▶ noun [mass noun] the branch of military intelligence concerned with the monitoring, interception, and interpretation of radio and radar signals.

signal-to-noise ratio ▶ noun the ratio of the strength of an electrical or other signal carrying information to that of unwanted interference. ■ informal a measure of how much useful information there is in a system, such as the Internet, as a proportion of the entire contents.

signary /ˈsɪgnəri/ ▶ noun (pl. **signaries**) the signs constituting the syllabic or alphabetic symbols of a language.
– ORIGIN early 20th cent.: from Latin *signum* 'mark, token' + **-ARY[1]**, on the pattern of *syllabary*.

signatory /ˈsɪgnət(ə)ri/ ▶ noun (pl. **signatories**) a party that has signed an agreement, especially a state that has signed a treaty: *Britain is a **signatory to** the convention* | [as modifier] *the signatory states.*
– ORIGIN late 19th cent.: from Latin *signatorius* 'of sealing', from *signat-* 'marked (with a cross)', from the verb *signare*.

signature ▶ noun **1** a person's name written in a distinctive way as a form of identification in authorizing a cheque or document or concluding a letter. ■ [mass noun] the action of signing a document: *the licence was sent to the customer for signature.* ■ a distinctive pattern, product, or characteristic by which someone or something can be identified: *the chef produced the pâté that was his signature* | [as modifier] *his signature dish.*
2 Music short for **KEY SIGNATURE** or **TIME SIGNATURE**.
3 Printing a letter or figure printed at the foot of one or more pages of each sheet of a book as a guide in binding. ■ a printed sheet after being folded to form a group of pages.
4 N. Amer. the part of a medical prescription that gives instructions about the use of the medicine or drug prescribed.
– ORIGIN mid 16th cent. (as a Scots legal term, denoting a document presented by a writer to the Signet): from medieval Latin *signatura* 'sign manual' (in late Latin denoting a marking on sheep), from Latin *signare* 'to sign, mark'.

signature tune ▶ noun chiefly Brit. a distinctive piece of music associated with a particular programme or performer on television or radio.

signboard ▶ noun a board displaying the name or logo of a business or product. ■ chiefly N. Amer. a board displaying a sign to direct traffic or travellers.

signed-rank test ▶ noun Statistics a non-parametric test for comparing two sets of values by calculating the distribution of positive or negative differences in ranking of corresponding pairs.

signee ▶ noun a person who has signed a contract or other official document.

signet ▶ noun historical a small seal, especially one set in a ring, used instead of or with a signature to give authentication to an official document. ■ (usu. **the Signet**) the royal seal formerly used for special purposes in England and Scotland, and in Scotland later as the seal of the Court of Session.
– ORIGIN late Middle English: from Old French, or from medieval Latin *signetum*, diminutive of *signum* 'token, seal'.

signet ring ▶ noun a ring with letters or a design carved on it.

signifiant /ˌsiːnjiːˈfjɒ̃/ ▶ noun another term for **SIGNIFIER**.
– ORIGIN French.

significance ▶ noun [mass noun] **1** the quality of being worthy of attention; importance: *adolescent education was felt to be a social issue of some significance.*
2 the meaning to be found in words or events: *the significance of what was happening was clearer to me than to her.*
3 (also **statistical significance**) the extent to which a result deviates from that expected to arise simply from random variation or errors in sampling.
– ORIGIN late Middle English (denoting unstated meaning): from Old French, or from Latin *significantia*, from *significare* 'indicate, portend'.

significant ▶ adjective **1** sufficiently great or important to be worthy of attention; noteworthy: *a significant increase in sales.*
2 having a particular meaning; indicative of something: *in times of stress her dreams seemed to her especially significant.* ■ suggesting a meaning or message that is not explicitly stated: *she gave him a significant look.*
3 Statistics relating to or having significance.
– ORIGIN late 16th cent. (in sense 2): from Latin *significant-* 'indicating', from the verb *significare* (see **SIGNIFY**).

significant figure ▶ noun Mathematics each of the digits of a number that are used to express it to the required degree of accuracy, starting from the first non-zero digit.

significantly ▶ adverb **1** in a sufficiently great or important way as to be worthy of attention: *energy bills have increased significantly this year* | [as submodifier] *their situation is significantly different from ours.*
2 in a way that has a particular meaning: [as sentence adverb] *significantly, he has refused to give a straight answer to this question.* ■ in a manner that suggests a meaning or message that is not explicitly stated: *he paused significantly.*

significant other ▶ noun a person with whom someone has an established romantic or sexual relationship.

signification ▶ noun [mass noun] the representation or conveying of meaning. ■ [count noun] an exact meaning or sense.
– ORIGIN Middle English: via Old French from Latin *significatio(n-)*, from *significare* 'indicate' (see **SIGNIFY**).

significative /sɪgˈnɪfɪkətɪv/ ▶ adjective rare being a symbol or sign of something; having a meaning.

significator ▶ noun Astrology (in a horary chart) the planet which signifies the inquirer, or the subject of the question. ■ a card chosen to represent the inquirer in a tarot reading.

signifié /ˌsiːnjiːˈfjeɪ/ ▶ noun another term for **SIGNIFIED**.
– ORIGIN French.

signified ▶ noun Linguistics the meaning or idea expressed by a sign, as distinct from the physical form in which it is expressed. Compare with **SIGNIFIER**.

signifier ▶ noun Linguistics a sign's physical form (such as a sound, printed word, or image) as distinct from its meaning. Compare with **SIGNIFIED**.

signify ▶ verb (**signifies, signifying, signified**)
1 [with obj.] be an indication of: *this decision signified a fundamental change in their priorities.* ■ be a symbol of; have as meaning: *the church used this image to signify the Holy Trinity.* ■ (of a person) indicate or declare (a feeling or intention): *signify your agreement by signing the letter below.* ■ [no obj.] [with negative] be of importance: *the locked door doesn't necessarily signify.*
2 [no obj.] US informal (among black Americans) exchange boasts or insults as a game or ritual.
– ORIGIN Middle English: from Old French *signifier*, from Latin *significare* 'indicate, portend', from *signum* 'token'.

signing ▶ noun [mass noun] **1** the action of writing one's signature on an official document: *the signing of the Anglo-French agreement to build Concorde.* ■ the action of recruiting someone, especially to a professional sports team or record company: *the signing of overseas players.* ■ [count noun] Brit. a person who has recently been recruited, especially to join a professional sports team or record company: *Manchester United's latest signing.* ■ [count noun] an event in a bookshop or other place at which an author signs a number of books to gain publicity and sales.
2 sign language.
3 the provision of signs in a street or other place.

sign language ▶ noun [mass noun] a system of communication using visual gestures and signs, as used by deaf people.

sign-off ▶ noun **1** the conclusion of a letter, broadcast, etc.

S

2 Bridge a bid indicating that the bidder wishes to end bidding.

Signor /ˈsiːnjɔː, siːˈnjɔː/ (also **Signore** /siːˈnjɔːreɪ/) ▸ **noun** (pl. **Signori** /-ˈnjɔːri/) a title or form of address used of or to an Italian-speaking man, corresponding to *Mr* or *sir*: *Signor Ugolotti* | *I am a man of honour, Signor*.
– ORIGIN Italian, from Latin *senior* (see **SENIOR**).

Signora /siːˈnjɔːrə/ ▸ **noun** a title or form of address used of or to an Italian-speaking married woman, corresponding to *Mrs* or *madam*: *good night, Signora*.
– ORIGIN Italian, feminine of *signor* (see **SIGNOR**).

Signorina /ˌsiːnjəˈriːnə/ ▸ **noun** a title or form of address used of or to an Italian-speaking unmarried woman, corresponding to *Miss*: *Signorina Rosalba*.
– ORIGIN Italian, diminutive of *signora* (see **SIGNORA**).

signory /ˈsiːnjəri/ ▸ **noun** (pl. **signories**) **1** another term for **SEIGNIORY**.
2 historical the governing body of a medieval Italian republic. [influenced by Italian *signoria*.]

signpost ▸ **noun** a sign giving information such as the direction and distance to a nearby town, typically found at a road junction. ■ something that acts as a guide or indicator: *shorts remain the fashion signpost of summer's arrival*.
▸ **verb** [with obj.] provide (an area) with a signpost or signposts: *most of the walks were well signposted*. ■ chiefly Brit. indicate (a place) with a signpost: *Battle is clearly signposted off all the main roads*.

sign-up ▸ **noun** [mass noun] [usu. as modifier] the action of enrolling for something or of enrolling or employing someone: *a sign-up fee of £29.95*.

signwriter (also **sign painter**) ▸ **noun** a person who paints commercial signs and advertisements.
– DERIVATIVES **signwriting** noun.

sigri /ˈsiːgri/ ▸ **noun** (pl. **sigris**) (in South Asia) a type of brazier.
– ORIGIN from Punjabi *sagṛī*.

Sigurd /ˈsɪgʊəd/ (in Norse legend) the Norse equivalent of Siegfried, husband of Gudrun.

Sihanouk /ˈsiənʊk/, Norodom (b.1922), Cambodian king 1941–55 and 1993–2004, Prime Minister 1955–60, and head of state 1960–70 and 1975–6. After Cambodian independence in 1953, Sihanouk abdicated in favour of his father in order to become Prime Minister. On his father's death Sihanouk proclaimed himself head of state. He was ousted in a US-backed coup and was briefly reinstated by the Khmer Rouge. Sihanouk reigned as king for the second time from 1993 until 2004.

sika /ˈsiːkə/ (also **sika deer**) ▸ **noun** a forest-dwelling deer with a greyish winter coat that turns yellowish-brown with white spots in summer. It is native to Japan and SE Asia and naturalized in Britain and elsewhere. ● *Cervus nippon*, family Cervidae.
– ORIGIN late 19th cent.: from Japanese *shika*.

sike /sʌɪk/ ▸ **noun** Scottish & N. English a small stream or rill, typically one that flows through marshy ground and is often dry in summer.
– ORIGIN Old English *sīc*.

Sikh /siːk/ ▸ **noun** an adherent of Sikhism.
▸ **adjective** relating to Sikhs or Sikhism.
– ORIGIN from Punjabi 'disciple', from Sanskrit *śiṣya*.

S

Sikhism /ˈsiːkɪz(ə)m, ˈsɪk-/ ▸ **noun** [mass noun] a monotheistic religion founded in Punjab in the 15th century by Guru Nanak.

> Sikh teaching centres on spiritual liberation and social justice and harmony, though the community took on a militant aspect during early conflicts. The last guru, Gobind Singh (1666–1708), passed his authority to the scripture, the Guru Granth Sahib, and to the Khalsa, the body of initiated Sikhs.

Sikh Wars a series of wars between the Sikhs and the British in 1845 and 1848–9, culminating in the British annexation of Punjab.

Siking /ʃiːˈkɪŋ/ former name for **XIAN**.

Sikkim /ˈsɪkɪm/ a state of NE India, in the eastern Himalayas between Bhutan and Nepal, on the border with Tibet; capital, Gangtok. After British rule it became an Indian protectorate, becoming a state of India in 1975.
– DERIVATIVES **Sikkimese** adjective & noun.

Sikorsky /sɪˈkɔːski/, Igor (Ivanovich) (1889–1972), Russian-born American aircraft designer. He built the first large four-engined aircraft, the Grand (1913), in his native country and went on to establish the Sikorsky company in the US. In 1939 he developed the first mass-produced helicopter.

Siksika /ˈsɪksɪkə/ ▸ **plural noun** the northernmost of the three peoples forming the Blackfoot confederacy.
– ORIGIN from Blackfoot *siksi-* 'black' + *ka-* 'foot'.

silage /ˈsʌɪlɪdʒ/ ▸ **noun** [mass noun] grass or other green fodder compacted and stored in airtight conditions, typically in a silo, without first being dried, and used as animal feed in the winter.
▸ **verb** [no obj.] (often as noun **silaging**) make silage. ■ [with obj.] preserve (grass and other green fodder) as silage.
– ORIGIN late 19th cent.: alteration of **ENSILAGE**, influenced by **SILO**.

silane /ˈsʌɪleɪn/ ▸ **noun** [mass noun] Chemistry a colourless gaseous compound of silicon and hydrogen which has strong reducing properties and is spontaneously flammable in air. ● Chem. formula: SiH_4. ■ [count noun] any of the large class of hydrides of silicon analogous to the alkanes.
– ORIGIN early 20th cent.: from **SILICON** + **-ANE**[2].

silastic /sɪˈlastɪk/ ▸ **noun** [mass noun] trademark silicone rubber.
– ORIGIN 1940s: blend of **SILICON** and **ELASTIC**.

Silat /sɪˈlat/ ▸ **noun** [mass noun] the Malay art of self-defence, practised as a martial art or accompanied by drums as a ceremonial display or dance.
– ORIGIN Malay.

Silbury Hill /ˈsɪlb(ə)ri/ a Neolithic monument near Avebury in Wiltshire, a flat-topped conical mound more than 40 m (130 ft) high, which is the largest man-made prehistoric mound in Europe.

Silchester /ˈsɪltʃɪstə/ a village in Hampshire, situated to the south-west of Reading. It is the site of an important town of pre-Roman and Roman Britain, known to the Romans as Calleva Atrebatum.

sild ▸ **noun** (pl. **same**) a small immature herring, especially one caught in northern European seas.
– ORIGIN 1920s: from Danish and Norwegian.

silence ▸ **noun** [mass noun] complete absence of sound: *sirens pierce the silence of the night* | [count noun] *an eerie silence descended over the house*. ■ the fact or state of abstaining from speech: *Karen had withdrawn into sullen silence* | *she was **reduced to silence** for a moment* | *we finished our meal **in silence***. ■ the avoidance of mentioning or discussing something: *politicians keep their silence on the big questions*. ■ [count noun] a short appointed period of time during which people stand still and do not speak as a sign of respect for a dead person or group of people: *the game was preceded by a two-minute silence in his memory*.
▸ **verb** [with obj.] cause to become silent; prohibit or prevent from speaking: *she was silenced by the Inspector's stern look* | *the team's performance silenced their critics*. ■ (usu. as adj. **silenced**) fit (a gun or an exhaust system) with a silencer: *a silenced .22 rifle*.
– PHRASES **silence is golden** proverb it's often wise to say nothing.
– ORIGIN Middle English: from Old French, from Latin *silentium*, from *silere* 'be silent'.

silencer ▸ **noun 1** Brit. a device fixed to the exhaust of a motor vehicle to reduce engine noise.
2 a device used to reduce the sound of a gun as it is fired.

silent ▸ **adjective** not making or accompanied by any sound: *the wood was still and silent*. ■ (of a person) not speaking: *she fell silent for a moment*. ■ not expressed aloud: *a silent prayer*. ■ (of a letter) written but not pronounced, e.g. *b* in *doubt*. ■ (of a film) without an accompanying soundtrack. ■ saying or recording nothing on a particular subject: *the poems are silent on the question of marriage*. ■ (of a person) not prone to speak much; taciturn: *I'm the strong, silent type*.
– PHRASES **(as) silent as the grave** see **GRAVE**[1]. **the silent majority** the majority of people, regarded as holding moderate opinions but rarely expressing them. **the silent treatment** a stubborn refusal to talk to someone, especially after a recent argument or disagreement.
– DERIVATIVES **silently** adverb.
– ORIGIN late 15th cent. (in the sense 'not speaking'): from Latin *silent-* 'being silent', from the verb *silere*.

silent partner ▸ **noun** North American term for **SLEEPING PARTNER**.

Silenus /sʌɪˈliːnəs/ Greek Mythology an aged woodland deity, one of the sileni, who was entrusted with the education of Dionysus. He is depicted either as dignified and musical, or as an old drunkard. ■ (as noun **silenus**) (pl. **sileni** /-nʌɪ/) a woodland spirit, usually depicted in art as old and having ears like those of a horse.

Silesia /sʌɪˈliːzɪə, -ˈliːʒə/ a region of central Europe, centred on the upper Oder valley, now largely in SW Poland. It was partitioned at various times between the states of Prussia, Austria–Hungary, Poland, and Czechoslovakia.
– DERIVATIVES **Silesian** adjective & noun.

silex /ˈsʌɪlɛks/ ▸ **noun** [mass noun] silica, especially quartz or flint.
– ORIGIN late 16th cent.: from Latin, 'flint'.

silhouette /ˌsɪlʊˈɛt/ ▸ **noun** the dark shape and outline of someone or something visible in restricted light against a brighter background. ■ a representation of someone or something showing the shape and outline only, typically coloured in solid black.
▸ **verb** [with obj.] cast or show (someone or something) as a dark shape and outline against a brighter background: *the castle was **silhouetted against** the sky*.
– PHRASES **in silhouette** seen or placed as a silhouette.
– ORIGIN late 18th cent.: named (although the reason remains obscure) after Étienne de *Silhouette* (1709–67), French author and politician.

silica /ˈsɪlɪkə/ ▸ **noun** [mass noun] a hard, unreactive, colourless compound which occurs as the mineral quartz and as a principal constituent of sandstone and other rocks. ● Alternative name: **silicon dioxide**; chem. formula: SiO_2.
– DERIVATIVES **siliceous** /-ˈlɪʃəs/ (also **silicious**) adjective.
– ORIGIN early 19th cent.: from Latin *silex*, *silic-* 'flint', on the pattern of words such as *alumina*.

silica gel ▸ **noun** [mass noun] hydrated silica in a hard granular hygroscopic form used as a desiccant.

silicate /ˈsɪlɪkeɪt, -kət/ ▸ **noun** Chemistry a salt in which the anion contains both silicon and oxygen, especially one of the anion SiO_4^{2-}. ■ any of the many minerals consisting of silica combined with metal oxides, forming a major component of the rocks of the earth's crust.

silicic /sɪˈlɪsɪk/ ▸ **adjective** Geology (of rocks) rich in silica.

silicic acid ▸ **noun** [mass noun] Chemistry a weakly acidic colloidal hydrated form of silica made by acidifying solutions of alkali metal silicates.

siliciclastic /sɪˌlɪsɪˈklastɪk/ ▸ **adjective** Geology relating to or denoting clastic rocks consisting largely of silica or silicates.

silicide /ˈsɪlɪsʌɪd/ ▸ **noun** Chemistry a binary compound of silicon with another element or group.

silicify /sɪˈlɪsɪfʌɪ/ ▸ **verb** (**silicifies**, **silicifying**, **silicified**) [with obj.] convert into or impregnate with silica.
– DERIVATIVES **silicification** noun.

silicon /ˈsɪlɪk(ə)n/ ▸ **noun** [mass noun] the chemical element of atomic number 14, a non-metal with semiconducting properties, used in making electronic circuits. Pure silicon exists in a shiny dark grey crystalline form and as an amorphous powder. (Symbol: **Si**)
– ORIGIN early 19th cent.: alteration of earlier *silicium*, from Latin *silex*, *silic-* 'flint', on the pattern of *carbon* and *boron*.

silicon carbide ▸ **noun** [mass noun] a hard refractory crystalline compound of silicon and carbon; carborundum. ● Chem. formula: SiC.

silicon chip ▸ **noun** a microchip.

silicone /ˈsɪlɪkəʊn/ ▸ **noun** any of a class of synthetic materials which are polymers with a chemical structure based on chains of alternate silicon and oxygen atoms, with organic groups attached to the silicon atoms. Such compounds are typically resistant to chemical attack and insensitive to temperature changes and are used to make rubber and plastics and in polishes and lubricants.
▸ **verb** [with obj.] join or otherwise treat (something) with a silicone.

siliconize /ˈsɪlɪkənʌɪz/ (also **siliconise**) ▸ **verb** [with obj.] (often as adj. **siliconized**) coat or otherwise treat (something) with silicone.

Silicon Valley a name given to an area between San Jose and Palo Alto in Santa Clara County, California, US, noted for its computing and electronics industries.

silicosis /ˌsɪlɪˈkəʊsɪs/ ▸ **noun** [mass noun] Medicine lung fibrosis caused by the inhalation of dust containing silica.
– DERIVATIVES **silicotic** adjective.

siliqua /ˈsɪlɪkwə/ (also **silique** /sɪˈliːk/) ▸ noun (pl. **siliquae** /-kwiː/ or **siliques** /sɪˈliːks/) **1** Botany the long, narrow seed pod of many plants of the cabbage family, splitting open when mature.
2 a Roman silver coin of the 4th and 5th centuries AD, worth 1/24 solidus.
– ORIGIN Latin, literally 'pod'.

silk ▸ noun **1** [mass noun] a fine, strong, soft lustrous fibre produced by silkworms in making cocoons and collected to make thread and fabric. ■ thread or fabric made from the fibre produced by the silkworm: [as modifier] *a silk shirt.* ■ (**silks**) garments made from such fabric, especially as worn by a jockey in the colours of a particular horse owner. ■ [count noun] Riding a cover worn over a riding hat made from a silk-like fabric. ■ (**silks**) the silky styles of the female maize flower.
2 Brit. informal a Queen's (or King's) Counsel. [so named because of the right accorded to wear a gown made of silk.]
– PHRASES **take silk** Brit. become a Queen's (or King's) Counsel.
– DERIVATIVES **silk-like** adjective.
– ORIGIN Old English *sioloc*, *seolec*, from late Latin *sericum*, neuter of Latin *sericus*, based on Greek *Sēres*, the name given to the inhabitants of the Far Eastern countries from which silk first came overland to Europe.

silk cotton ▸ noun another term for KAPOK.

silk-cotton tree ▸ noun a tree which produces silk cotton. ● Two species in the family Bombacaceae: the **Indian silk-cotton tree** (*Bombax ceiba*) and the ceiba.

silk dupion ▸ noun see DUPION.

silken ▸ adjective made of silk: *a silken ribbon.* ■ soft or lustrous like silk: *silken hair.*
– ORIGIN Old English *seolcen* (see SILK, -EN²).

silk gland ▸ noun a gland in a silkworm, spider, or other arthropod that secretes the substance which hardens as threads of silk or web.

silk hat ▸ noun a man's tall cylindrical hat covered with black silk plush.

silkie ▸ noun (pl. **silkies**) **1** a small chicken of a breed characterized by long soft plumage.
2 variant spelling of SELKIE.

silk moth ▸ noun a large moth with a caterpillar that spins a protective silken cocoon: ● (**the silk moth**) a domesticated Asian moth whose larva is the chief commercial silkworm (*Bombyx mori*, family Bombycidae). ● (also **giant silk moth**) a saturniid moth.

Silk Road (also **Silk Route**) an ancient caravan route linking Xian in central China with the eastern Mediterranean. It was established during the period of Roman rule in Europe, and took its name from the silk which was brought to the west from China.

silk screen ▸ noun a screen of fine mesh used in screen printing. ■ a print made by screen printing.
▸ verb (**silk-screen**) [with obj.] print, decorate, or reproduce using a silk screen.

silk-stocking ▸ adjective N. Amer. wealthy; aristocratic: *a silk-stocking district | a silk-stocking crowd.*

silkworm ▸ noun the commercially bred caterpillar of the domesticated silk moth (*Bombyx mori*), which spins a silk cocoon that is processed to yield silk fibre. ■ [with modifier] a commercial silk-yielding caterpillar of a saturniid moth.
– ORIGIN Old English *seolcwyrm* (see SILK, WORM).

silky ▸ adjective (**silkier**, **silkiest**) of or resembling silk, especially in being soft, fine, and lustrous: *the fur felt silky and soft.* ■ (of a person or their speech or manner) suave and smooth, especially in a way intended to be persuasive: *a silky, seductive voice.*
– DERIVATIVES **silkily** adverb, **silkiness** noun.

silky oak ▸ noun a tall Australian tree which yields silky-textured timber similar to oak. ● Several species in the family Proteaceae, in particular *Cardwellia sublimis* and the frequently cultivated *Grevillea robusta*.

sill (also chiefly Building **cill**) ▸ noun a shelf or slab of stone, wood, or metal at the foot of a window opening or doorway. ■ a strong horizontal beam forming a base in the frame of a timber-framed building. ■ each of the lower horizontal members of the frame of a cart or motor or rail vehicle. ■ Geology a tabular sheet of igneous rock intruded between and parallel with the existing strata. Compare with DYKE¹. ■ an underwater ridge or rock ledge extending across the bed of a body of water.
– ORIGIN Old English *syll*, *sylle* 'horizontal beam forming a foundation', of Germanic origin; related to German *Schwelle* 'threshold'.

sillabub ▸ noun archaic spelling of SYLLABUB.

sillimanite /ˈsɪlɪmənʌɪt/ ▸ noun [mass noun] an aluminosilicate mineral typically occurring as fibrous masses, commonly in schist or gneiss.
– ORIGIN mid 19th cent.: from the name of Benjamin *Silliman* (1779–1864), American chemist + -ITE¹.

Sillitoe /ˈsɪlɪtəʊ/, Alan (b.1928), English writer, noted for his novels about working-class provincial life, such as *Saturday Night and Sunday Morning* (1958) and *The Loneliness of the Long-Distance Runner* (1959).

silly ▸ adjective (**sillier**, **silliest**) **1** having or showing a lack of common sense or judgement; absurd and foolish: *another of his silly jokes | 'Don't be silly!' she said.* ■ ridiculously trivial or frivolous: *he would brood about silly things.* ■ [as complement] used to convey that an activity or process has been engaged in to such a degree that someone is no longer capable of thinking or acting sensibly: *he often drank himself silly | his mother worried herself silly over him.*
2 archaic (especially of a woman, child, or animal) helpless; defenceless.
3 [attrib.] Cricket denoting fielding positions very close to the batsman: *silly mid-on.*
▸ noun (pl. **sillies**) informal a foolish person (often used as a form of address): *come on, silly.*
– PHRASES **the silly season** high summer regarded as the season when newspapers often publish trivial material because of a lack of important news.
– DERIVATIVES **sillily** adverb, **silliness** noun.
– ORIGIN late Middle English (in the sense 'deserving of pity or sympathy'): alteration of dialect *seely* 'happy', later 'innocent, feeble', from a West Germanic base meaning 'luck, happiness'. The sense 'foolish' developed via the stages 'feeble' and 'unsophisticated, ignorant'.

silly billy ▸ noun informal, chiefly Brit. a silly or foolish person.

silo /ˈsʌɪləʊ/ ▸ noun (pl. **silos**) **1** a tall tower or pit on a farm used to store grain. ■ a pit or other airtight structure in which green crops are compressed and stored as silage.
2 an underground chamber in which a guided missile is kept ready for firing.
3 a system, process, department, etc. that operates in isolation from others: *it's vital that team members step out of their silos and start working together.*
– ORIGIN mid 19th cent.: from Spanish, via Latin from Greek *siros* 'corn pit'.

Siloam /sʌɪˈləʊəm/ (in the New Testament) a spring and pool of water near Jerusalem, where a man born blind was told by Jesus to wash, thereby gaining sight (John 9:7).

siloxane /sɪˈlɒkseɪn/ ▸ noun Chemistry a compound having a molecular structure based on a chain of alternate silicon and oxygen atoms, especially (as in silicone) with organic groups attached to the silicon atoms.
– ORIGIN early 20th cent.: blend of SILICON and OXYGEN + -ANE².

silt ▸ noun [mass noun] fine sand, clay, or other material carried by running water and deposited as a sediment, especially in a channel or harbour. ■ [count noun] a bed or layer of such material. ■ technical sediment whose particles are between clay and sand in size (typically 0.002–0.06 mm).
▸ verb [no obj.] become filled or blocked with silt: *the river's mouth had silted up* | (as noun **silting**) *the silting of the river estuary.* ■ [with obj.] fill or block with silt.
– DERIVATIVES **siltation** noun, **silty** adjective (**siltier**, **siltiest**).
– ORIGIN late Middle English: probably originally denoting a salty deposit and of Scandinavian origin, related to Danish and Norwegian *sylt* 'salt marsh', also to SALT.

siltstone ▸ noun [mass noun] fine-grained sedimentary rock consisting of consolidated silt.

Silurian /sʌɪˈljʊərɪən, sɪ-/ ▸ adjective Geology relating to or denoting the third period of the Palaeozoic era, between the Ordovician and Devonian periods. ■ (as noun **the Silurian**) the Silurian period or the system of rocks deposited during it.

> The Silurian lasted from about 439 to 409 million years ago. The first true fish and land plants appeared, and the end of the period is marked by the climax of the Caledonian orogeny.

– ORIGIN early 18th cent.: from Latin *Silures* (denoting a people of ancient SE Wales) + -IAN.

siluroid /sɪˈljʊərɔɪd/ Zoology ▸ noun a fish of an order (Siluriformes) that comprises the catfishes.
▸ adjective relating to fish of this order.
– ORIGIN mid 19th cent.: from *Silurus* (genus name) + -OID.

silvan ▸ adjective variant spelling of SYLVAN.

Silvanus /sɪlˈveɪnəs, sɪlˈvɑːnəs/ Roman Mythology an Italian woodland deity identified with Pan.

silver ▸ noun [mass noun] **1** a precious shiny greyish-white metal, the chemical element of atomic number 47. (Symbol: **Ag**)
2 a shiny grey-white colour or appearance like that of silver: *the dark hair was now highlighted with silver.*
3 silver dishes, containers, or cutlery: *thieves stole £5,000 worth of silver | the family silver.* ■ household cutlery of any material.
4 coins made from silver or from a metal that resembles silver. ■ chiefly Scottish money.
5 [count noun] short for SILVER MEDAL.
▸ verb [with obj.] (often as adj. **silvered**) coat or plate with silver: *large silvered candlesticks.* ■ provide (mirror glass) with a backing of a silver-coloured material in order to make it reflective. ■ literary (especially of the moon) give a silvery appearance to: *the brilliant moon silvered the turf.* ■ turn (a person's hair) grey or white. ■ [no obj.] (of a person's hair) turn grey or white.
– PHRASES **be born with a silver spoon in one's mouth** be born into a wealthy family of high social standing. **every cloud has a silver lining** proverb every difficult or sad situation has a comforting or more hopeful aspect, even though this may not be immediately apparent. **the silver screen** the cinema industry; cinema films collectively: *stars of the silver screen.*
– ORIGIN Old English *seolfor*, of Germanic origin; related to Dutch *zilver* and German *Silber*.

silver age ▸ noun a period regarded as notable but inferior to a golden age, such as that of so-called silver Latin literature.

silverback ▸ noun a mature male mountain gorilla, which is distinguished by an area of white or silvery hair across the back and is the dominant member of its social group.

silver band ▸ noun Brit. a brass band playing silver-plated instruments.

silver beet ▸ noun Australian and New Zealand term for CHARD.

silverberry ▸ noun (pl. **silverberries**) a North American shrub related to the oleaster, with red-brown stems and silvery leaves, flowers, and berries. ● *Elaeagnus commutata*, family Elaeagnaceae.

silver birch ▸ noun a Eurasian birch with silver-grey bark, common on poorer soils to the northern limit of tree growth. ● *Betula pendula*, family Betulaceae. ■ N. Amer. another term for PAPER BIRCH.

silver bullet ▸ noun a bullet made of silver, supposedly the only weapon that could kill a werewolf. ■ chiefly N. Amer. a simple and seemingly magical solution to a complicated problem.

silver disc ▸ noun a framed silver-coloured disc awarded to a recording artist or group for sales of a recording exceeding a specified figure (lower than those required for a gold disc).

silver drummer ▸ noun see DRUMMER (sense 3).

silver-eared mesia ▸ noun see MESIA.

silvereye ▸ noun an Australasian songbird of the white-eye family, with mainly greenish plumage and a white ring round the eye. ● Genus *Zosterops*, family Zosteropidae: two or three species.

silver fern ▸ noun **1** another term for PONGA.
2 a stylized fern leaf in silver, as an emblem of New Zealand.

silver fir ▸ noun a fir tree with foliage that appears silvery or bluish because of whitish lines on the undersides of the needles. ● Genus *Abies*, family Pinaceae: several species, in particular *A. alba*.

silverfish ▸ noun (pl. **same** or **silverfishes**) **1** a silvery bristletail that lives in houses and other buildings, chiefly nocturnal and feeding on starchy materials. ● *Lepisma saccharina*, family Lepismatidae.
2 a silver-coloured fish, especially a variety of goldfish.

silver fox ▸ noun a red fox of a North American variety which has black fur with white tips. ■ [mass noun] the fur of this animal.

S

silver gilt ▶ **noun** [mass noun] gilded silver. ■ an imitation gilding of yellow lacquer over silver leaf.

silvering ▶ **noun** [mass noun] silver-coloured material used to coat glass in order to make it reflective.

silver iodide ▶ **noun** [mass noun] a yellow insoluble powder that darkens on exposure to light. It is used in photography and artificial rainmaking.

silver jubilee ▶ **noun** the twenty-fifth anniversary of a significant event.

silver Latin ▶ **noun** [mass noun] literary Latin from the death of Augustus (AD 14) to the mid second century.

silver leaf ▶ **noun** [mass noun] **1** a fungal disease of ornamental and fruit trees, especially plum trees, resulting in silvery discoloration of the leaves. ● The fungus is *Chondrostereum purpureum*, family Stereaceae, class Hymenomycetes.
2 silver that has been beaten into a very thin sheet, suitable for applying to surfaces as a decoration.

silver-line ▶ **noun** either of two European moths with two or three whitish lines on the forewing: ● (**brown silver-line**) a light brown moth whose larvae feed on bracken (*Petrophora chlorosata*, family Geometridae). ● (**silver-lines**) a moth with mainly green forewings (genera *Pseudoips* and *Bena*, family Noctuidae).

silver medal ▶ **noun** a medal made of or coloured silver, customarily awarded for second place in a race or competition.

silvern /ˈsɪlv(ə)n/ ▶ **adjective** archaic made of or coloured silver.
– ORIGIN Old English *seolfren*, *silfren* (see SILVER, -N[1]).

silver nitrate ▶ **noun** [mass noun] a colourless solid, soluble in water, formerly used in photography. ● Chem. formula: $AgNO_3$.

silver paper ▶ **noun** [mass noun] **1** chiefly Brit. foil made of aluminium or other silver-coloured metal.
2 archaic fine white tissue paper.

silver plate ▶ **noun** [mass noun] a thin layer of silver electroplated or otherwise applied as a coating to another metal. ■ objects coated with silver. ■ plates, dishes, etc. made of silver.
▶ **verb** (**silver-plate**) [with obj.] cover (something) with a thin layer of silver.

silverpoint ▶ **noun** [mass noun] the art of drawing with a silver-pointed instrument on paper prepared with a coating of powdered bone or zinc white, creating a fine indelible line composed of metal fragments.

silver salmon ▶ **noun** another term for COHO.

silver sand ▶ **noun** [mass noun] Brit. a fine white sand used in gardening.

silver service ▶ **noun** [mass noun] a style of serving food at formal meals in which the server uses a silver spoon and fork in one hand to serve the food item by item on to the diner's plate.

silverside ▶ **noun 1** [mass noun] Brit. the upper side of a round of beef from the outside of the leg.
2 (also **silversides**) a small, slender, chiefly marine fish with a bright silver line along its sides. ● Family Atherinidae: several genera and species.

silversmith ▶ **noun** a person who makes silver articles.
– DERIVATIVES **silversmithing** noun.

S

silver solder ▶ **noun** [mass noun] a brazing alloy consisting largely of copper and silver.

silver standard ▶ **noun** historical a system by which the value of a currency is defined in terms of silver, for which the currency may be exchanged.

Silver State informal name for NEVADA.

Silverstone a motor-racing circuit near Towcester in Northamptonshire.

silver surfer ▶ **noun** informal an elderly person who is a regular or enthusiastic user of the Internet.

silversword ▶ **noun** a Hawaiian plant of the daisy family, which has long, narrow leaves with silvery hairs and clusters of purplish flowers. ● Genus *Argyroxiphium*, family Compositae.

silver thaw ▶ **noun** a glassy coating of ice formed on the ground or an exposed surface by freezing rain or the refreezing of thawed ice.

silver tongue ▶ **noun** a tendency to be eloquent and persuasive in speaking.
– DERIVATIVES **silver-tongued** adjective.

silver tree ▶ **noun** a South African tree which has light silvery-green leaves covered with very fine down. ● *Leucadendron argenteum*, family Proteaceae.

silverware ▶ **noun** [mass noun] dishes, containers, or cutlery made of or coated with silver, or made of a material resembling silver.

silver wedding ▶ **noun** Brit. the twenty-fifth anniversary of a wedding.

silverweed ▶ **noun** [mass noun] a yellow-flowered herbaceous potentilla with silvery compound leaves, a common grassland weed of north temperate regions. ● *Potentilla anserina*, family Rosaceae.

silvery ▶ **adjective 1** like silver in colour or appearance; shiny and grey-white: *shoals of silvery fish*. ■ (of a person's hair) grey-white and lustrous.
2 (of a sound) gentle, clear, and melodious: *a little silvery laugh*.
– DERIVATIVES **silveriness** noun.

silver Y ▶ **noun** a greyish-brown European moth that has purple-tinged wings with a white Y-shaped mark on the forewings. ● *Autographa gamma*, family Noctuidae.

silviculture /ˈsɪlvɪˌkʌltʃə/ ▶ **noun** [mass noun] the growing and cultivation of trees.
– DERIVATIVES **silvicultural** adjective, **silviculturist** noun.
– ORIGIN late 19th cent.: from French *sylviculture*, from Latin *silva* 'wood' + French *culture* 'cultivation'.

SIM (also **SIM card**) ▶ **noun** a smart card inside a mobile phone, carrying an identification number unique to the owner, storing personal data, and preventing operation if removed.
– ORIGIN 1980s: acronym from *subscriber identification module*.

sim ▶ **noun** informal a video game that simulates an activity such as flying an aircraft or playing a sport.
– ORIGIN late 20th cent.: abbreviation of *simulation* (see SIMULATE).

sima /ˈsʌɪmə/ ▶ **noun** [mass noun] Geology, dated the material of the lower part of the earth's crust, underlying both the ocean and the continents, characterized as relatively heavy and rich in silica and magnesia. Contrasted with SIAL.
– ORIGIN early 20th cent.: blend of SILICA + MAGNESIUM.

simazine /ˈsɪməziːn, ˈsʌɪ-/ ▶ **noun** [mass noun] a synthetic compound derived from triazine and used as a herbicide, especially to kill broadleaved weeds and grasses before they emerge.
– ORIGIN 1950s: blend of SYMMETRICAL and TRIAZINE.

Simbirsk /sɪmˈbɪəsk/ a city in European Russia, a port on the River Volga south-east of Nizhni Novgorod; pop. 607,000 (est. 2008). Between 1924 and 1992 it was called Ulyanovsk, in honour of Lenin (Vladimir Ilich Ulyanov), who was born there in 1870.

simcha /ˈsɪmtʃə, -xa/ ▶ **noun** a Jewish private party or celebration.
– ORIGIN from Hebrew *śimḥāh* 'rejoicing'.

Simenon /ˈsiːmənɒ̃/, Georges (Joseph Christian) (1903–89), Belgian-born French novelist. He is best known for his series of detective novels featuring Commissaire Maigret.

Simeon /ˈsɪmɪən/ (in the Bible) a Hebrew patriarch, son of Jacob and Leah (Gen. 29:33). ■ the tribe of Israel traditionally descended from Simeon.

Simeon Stylites, St /stʌɪˈlʌɪtiːz/ (c.390–459), Syrian monk. After living in a monastic community he became the first to practise an extreme form of asceticism which involved living on top of a pillar.

Simferopol /ˌsɪmfəˈrɒp(ə)l/ a city in the Crimea; pop. 337,100 (est. 2009). It was settled by the Tartars in the 16th century, when it was known as Ak-Mechet, and was seized in 1736 by the Russians.

simian /ˈsɪmɪən/ ▶ **adjective** relating to or affecting apes or monkeys: *simian immunodeficiency virus*. Compare with PROSIMIAN. ■ derogatory resembling a monkey: *his simian features*.
▶ **noun** an ape or monkey.
– ORIGIN early 17th cent.: from Latin *simia* 'ape', perhaps via Latin from Greek *simos* 'flat-nosed'.

similar ▶ **adjective** having a resemblance in appearance, character, or quantity, without being identical: *a soft cheese **similar to** Brie | northern India and similar areas*. ■ Geometry (of geometrical figures) having the same shape, with the same angles and proportions, though of different sizes.
▶ **noun 1** chiefly archaic a person or thing similar to another.
2 (usu. **similars**) a substance that produces effects resembling the symptoms of particular diseases (the basis of homeopathic treatment): *the principle of treatment by similars*.
– ORIGIN late 16th cent. (also as a term in anatomy meaning 'homogeneous'): from French *similaire* or medieval Latin *similaris*, from Latin *similis* 'like'.

> **USAGE** The standard construction for **similar** is with **to**, as in *I've had problems **similar to** yours*. However, in British English, the construction **similar as** is sometimes used instead, as in *I've had **similar** problems **as** yourself*. This is not accepted as correct in standard English.

similarity ▶ **noun** (pl. **similarities**) the state or fact of being similar: *the similarity of symptoms makes them hard to diagnose*. ■ (usu. **similarities**) a similar feature or aspect: *the **similarities between** people of different nationalities*.

similarly ▶ **adverb** [usu. as submodifier] in a similar way: *a similarly priced property*. ■ [sentence adverb] used to indicate a similarity between two facts or events: *The diaries of politicians tend to be self-justificatory. Similarly, autobiographies may be idealized*.

simile /ˈsɪmɪli/ ▶ **noun** a figure of speech involving the comparison of one thing with another thing of a different kind, used to make a description more emphatic or vivid (e.g. *as brave as a lion*). ■ [mass noun] the use of such a method of comparison.
– ORIGIN late Middle English: from Latin, neuter of *similis* 'like'.

similitude /sɪˈmɪlɪtjuːd/ ▶ **noun** [mass noun] the quality or state of being similar to something. ■ [count noun] archaic a comparison between two things. ■ [count noun] archaic a person or thing resembling someone or something else.
– ORIGIN late Middle English: from Old French, from Latin *similitudo*, from *similis* 'like'.

Simla /ˈsɪmlə/ variant spelling of SHIMLA.

SIMM ▶ **abbreviation** Computing single in-line memory module, containing RAM chips.

Simmental /ˈsɪm(ə)ntɑːl/ ▶ **noun** an animal of a red and white breed of cattle farmed for both meat and milk.
– ORIGIN 1950s: named after a valley in central Switzerland.

simmer ▶ **verb** [no obj.] (of water or food that is being heated) stay just below boiling point while bubbling gently: *the goulash was simmering slowly in the oven*. ■ [with obj.] keep (something) at such a point when cooking or heating it: *simmer the sauce gently until thickened*. ■ exist in a suppressed state: *the disagreement simmered for years and eventually boiled over*. ■ show or feel barely suppressed anger or other strong emotion: *she was simmering with resentment*. ■ (**simmer down**) become calmer and quieter.
▶ **noun** [in sing.] a state or temperature just below boiling point: *bring the water to a simmer*.
– ORIGIN mid 17th cent.: alteration of dialect *simper* (in the same sense), perhaps imitative.

Simnel /ˈsɪmn(ə)l/, Lambert (c.1475–1525), English pretender and rebel. He was trained by Yorkists to impersonate firstly one of the Princes in the Tower and subsequently the Earl of Warwick in an attempt to overthrow Henry VII.

simnel cake /ˈsɪmn(ə)l/ ▶ **noun** chiefly Brit. a rich fruit cake, typically with a marzipan covering and decoration, eaten especially at Easter or during Lent.
– ORIGIN mid 17th cent.: *simnel* from Old French *simenel*, based on Latin *simila* or Greek *semidalis* 'fine flour'.

simoleon /sɪˈməʊlɪɒn/ ▶ **noun** US informal a dollar.
– ORIGIN late 19th cent.: perhaps on the pattern of *napoleon*.

Simon[1], (Marvin) Neil (b.1927), American dramatist. Most of his plays are wry comedies portraying aspects of middle-class life; they include *Barefoot in the Park* (1963) and *The Odd Couple* (1965).

Simon[2], Paul (b.1942), American singer and songwriter. He achieved fame with **Art Garfunkel** (b.1941) for the albums *Sounds of Silence* (1966) and *Bridge Over Troubled Water* (1970). The duo split up in 1970 and Simon went on to pursue a successful solo career, recording albums such as *Graceland* (1986).

Simon, St an Apostle; known as **Simon the Zealot**. According to one tradition he preached and was martyred in Persia along with St Jude. Feast day (with St Jude), 28 October.

Simonides /sʌɪˈmɒnɪdiːz/ (c.556–468 BC), Greek lyric poet. Much of his poetry, which includes elegies, odes, and epigrams, celebrates the heroes of the Persian Wars.

simonize /ˈsʌɪmənʌɪz/ ▶ **verb** [with obj.] US polish (a motor vehicle).
– ORIGIN 1930s: *Simoniz*, the proprietary name of a type of polish, + -IZE.

Simon Peter another name for PETER, ST.

simon-pure ▶ **adjective** completely genuine, authentic, or honest.
– ORIGIN late 18th cent.: from (*the real*) *Simon Pure*, a character in Centlivre's *Bold Stroke for a Wife* (1717), who for part of the play is impersonated by another character.

Simon Says ▶ **noun** [mass noun] a children's game in which players must obey the leader's instructions if (and only if) they are prefaced with the words 'Simon says'.

simony /ˈsʌɪməni, ˈsɪm-/ ▶ **noun** [mass noun] chiefly historical the buying or selling of ecclesiastical privileges, for example pardons or benefices.
– DERIVATIVES **simoniac** /-ˈməʊnɪak/ **adjective & noun**, **simoniacal** /-ˈnʌɪək(ə)l/ **adjective**.
– ORIGIN Middle English: from Old French *simonie*, from late Latin *simonia*, from *Simon* Magus (Acts 8:18).

simoom /sɪˈmuːm/ (also **simoon** /-muːn/) ▶ **noun** a hot, dry, dust-laden wind blowing in the desert, especially in Arabia.
– ORIGIN late 18th cent.: from Arabic *samūm*, from *samma* 'to poison'.

simp ▶ **noun** N. Amer. informal a silly or foolish person.
– ORIGIN early 20th cent.: abbreviation of SIMPLETON.

simpatico /sɪmˈpatɪkəʊ/ ▶ **adjective** (of a person) likeable and easy to get on with. ▪ having or characterized by shared attributes or interests; compatible: *a simpatico relationship*.
– ORIGIN Italian and Spanish.

simper ▶ **verb** [no obj.] smile in an affectedly coquettish, coy, or ingratiating manner: *she simpered, looking pleased with herself*.
▶ **noun** an affectedly coquettish, coy, or ingratiating smile or gesture: *an exaggerated simper*.
– DERIVATIVES **simperingly** **adverb**.
– ORIGIN mid 16th cent.: of unknown origin; compare with German *zimpfer* 'elegant, delicate'.

simple ▶ **adjective** (**simpler**, **simplest**) **1** easily understood or done; presenting no difficulty: *a simple solution | camcorders are now so simple to operate*. ▪ [attrib.] used to emphasize the fundamental and straightforward nature of something: *the simple truth*.
2 plain, basic, or uncomplicated in form, nature, or design; without much decoration or ornamentation: *a simple white blouse | the house is furnished in a simple country style*. ▪ humble and unpretentious: *a quiet unassuming man with simple tastes*.
3 composed of a single element; not compound. ▪ Mathematics denoting a group that has no proper normal subgroup. ▪ Botany (of a leaf or stem) not divided or branched. ▪ (of a lens, microscope, etc.) consisting of a single lens or component. ▪ (in English grammar) denoting a tense formed without an auxiliary, for example *sang* as opposed to *was singing*. ▪ (of interest) payable on the sum loaned only. Compare with COMPOUND¹.
4 of very low intelligence.
▶ **noun** chiefly historical a medicinal herb, or a medicine made from one: *the gatherers of simples*.
– DERIVATIVES **simpleness** **noun**.
– ORIGIN Middle English: from Old French, from Latin *simplus*. The noun sense (mid 16th cent.) originally referred to a medicine made from one constituent, especially from one plant.

simple eye ▶ **noun** a small eye of an insect or other arthropod which has only one lens, typically present in one or more pairs. Also called OCELLUS. Contrasted with COMPOUND EYE.

simple fracture ▶ **noun** a fracture of the bone only, without damage to the surrounding tissues or breaking of the skin.

simple harmonic motion ▶ **noun** [mass noun] Physics oscillatory motion under a retarding force proportional to the amount of displacement from an equilibrium position.

simple interval ▶ **noun** Music an interval of one octave or less.

simple machine ▶ **noun** Mechanics any of the basic mechanical devices for applying a force, such as an inclined plane, wedge, or lever.

simple majority ▶ **noun** a majority in which the highest number of votes cast for any one candidate, issue, or item exceeds the second-highest number, while not constituting an absolute majority.

simple-minded ▶ **adjective** having or showing very little intelligence or judgement.
– DERIVATIVES **simple-mindedly** **adverb**, **simple-mindedness** **noun**.

simple sentence ▶ **noun** a sentence consisting of only one clause, with a single subject and predicate.

Simple Simon ▶ **noun** a foolish or gullible person.
– ORIGIN probably from the name of a character who features in various nursery rhymes.

simple time ▶ **noun** [mass noun] musical rhythm or metre in which each beat in a bar may be subdivided simply into halves or quarters. Compare with COMPOUND TIME.

simpleton ▶ **noun** a foolish or gullible person.
– ORIGIN mid 17th cent.: from SIMPLE, on the pattern of surnames derived from place names ending in *-ton*.

simplex ▶ **adjective** technical composed of or characterized by a single part or structure. ▪ (of a communication system, computer circuit, etc.) only allowing transmission of signals in one direction at a time.
▶ **noun** a simple or uncompounded word.
– ORIGIN late 16th cent.: from Latin, literally 'single', variant of *simplus* 'simple'.

simplex method ▶ **noun** Mathematics a standard method of maximizing a linear function of several variables under several constraints on other linear functions.

simpliciter /sɪmˈplɪsɪtə/ ▶ **adverb** chiefly Law simply; unconditionally.
– ORIGIN Latin, literally 'simply'.

simplicity ▶ **noun** [mass noun] **1** the quality or condition of being easy to understand or do: *for the sake of simplicity, this chapter will concentrate upon one theory*.
2 the quality or condition of being plain or uncomplicated in form or design: *the grandeur and simplicity of Roman architecture*. ▪ [count noun] a thing that is plain or uncomplicated: *the simplicities of pastoral living*.
– PHRASES **be simplicity itself** be extremely easy.
– ORIGIN late Middle English: from Old French *simplicite* or Latin *simplicitas*, from *simplex* (see SIMPLEX).

simplify ▶ **verb** (**simplifies**, **simplifying**, **simplified**) [with obj.] make (something) simpler or easier to do or understand: *an overhaul of court procedure to simplify litigation*.
– DERIVATIVES **simplification** **noun**.
– ORIGIN mid 17th cent.: from French *simplifier*, from medieval Latin *simplificare*, from Latin *simplus* (see SIMPLE).

simplism /ˈsɪmplɪz(ə)m/ ▶ **noun** [mass noun] the oversimplification of an issue.

simplistic ▶ **adjective** treating complex issues and problems as if they were much simpler than they really are: *simplistic solutions*.
– DERIVATIVES **simplistically** **adverb**.

Simplon /ˈsɪmplɒn/ a pass in the Alps in southern Switzerland, consisting of a road built by Napoleon in 1801–5 at an altitude of 2,028 m (6,591 ft) and a railway tunnel (built in 1922) which links Switzerland and Italy.

simply ▶ **adverb** **1** in a straightforward or plain manner: *she spoke simply and from the heart*.
2 merely; just: *simply complete the application form*. ▪ [as submodifier] absolutely; completely (used for emphasis): *it makes Trevor simply furious*. ▪ [sentence adverb] used to introduce a short summary of a situation: *quite simply, some things have to be taught*.

Simpson¹, Sir James Young (1811–71), Scottish surgeon and obstetrician. He discovered the usefulness of chloroform as an anaesthetic shortly after the first use of ether.

Simpson², Wallis (1896–1986), American wife of Edward, Duke of Windsor (Edward VIII); born *Wallis Warfield*. Her relationship with the king caused a scandal in view of her impending second divorce and forced the king's abdication in 1936.

Simpson Desert a desert in central Australia, situated between Alice Springs and the Channel Country to the east.
– ORIGIN named in 1929 after A. A. *Simpson*, then president of the Royal Geographical Society of Australia.

Simpson's rule ▶ **noun** Mathematics an arithmetical rule for estimating the area under a curve where the values of an odd number of ordinates, including those at each end, are known.
– ORIGIN late 19th cent.: named after Thomas *Simpson* (1710–61), English mathematician.

simul /ˈsɪm(ə)l/ ▶ **noun** Chess a display in which a player plays a number of games simultaneously against different opponents.
– ORIGIN 1960s: abbreviation of SIMULTANEOUS.

simulacrum /ˌsɪmjʊˈleɪkrəm/ ▶ **noun** (pl. **simulacra** /-krə/ or **simulacrums**) an image or representation of someone or something: *a small-scale simulacrum of a skyscraper*. ▪ an unsatisfactory imitation or substitute: *a bland simulacrum of American soul music*.
– ORIGIN late 16th cent.: from Latin, from *simulare* (see SIMULATE).

simulant ▶ **noun** a thing which simulates or resembles something else: *jade simulants*.
– ORIGIN mid 18th cent.: from Latin *simulant-* 'copying, representing', from the verb *simulare*.

simulate /ˈsɪmjʊleɪt/ ▶ **verb** [with obj.] imitate the appearance or character of: *red ochre intended to simulate blood*. ▪ pretend to have or feel (an emotion): *it was impossible to force a smile, to simulate pleasure*. ▪ produce a computer model of: *future population changes were simulated by computer*.
– DERIVATIVES **simulation** **noun**, **simulative** **adjective**.
– ORIGIN mid 17th cent. (earlier (Middle English) as *simulation*): from Latin *simulat-* 'copied, represented', from the verb *simulare*, from *similis* 'like'.

simulated ▶ **adjective** manufactured in imitation of some other material: *a simulated leather handbag*. ▪ (of an emotion) pretended or feigned: *she howled in simulated anguish*. ▪ imitating the conditions of something, especially as a training exercise: *a simulated terrorist attack*.

simulator ▶ **noun** a machine designed to provide a realistic imitation of the controls and operation of a vehicle, aircraft, or other complex system, used for training purposes. ▪ (also **simulator program**) a program enabling a computer to execute programs written for a different operating system.

simulcast /ˈsɪm(ə)lkɑːst/ ▶ **noun** a simultaneous transmission of the same programme on radio and television, or on two or more channels. ▪ N. Amer. a live transmission of a public celebration or sports event: *simulcasts of live races*.
▶ **verb** (past and past participle **simulcast**) [with obj.] broadcast (a simulcast transmission): *it will be simulcast live to 201 countries*.
– ORIGIN 1940s: blend of SIMULTANEOUS and BROADCAST.

simultaneous /ˌsɪm(ə)lˈteɪnɪəs/ ▶ **adjective** occurring, operating, or done at the same time: *a simultaneous withdrawal of troops | simultaneous translation*.
– DERIVATIVES **simultaneity** /-təˈniːɪti, -təˈneɪɪti/ **noun**, **simultaneousness** **noun**.
– ORIGIN mid 17th cent.: based on Latin *simul* 'at the same time', probably influenced by late Latin *momentaneus*.

simultaneous equations ▶ **plural noun** equations involving two or more unknowns that are to have the same values in each equation.

simultaneously ▶ **adverb** at the same time: *the telethon was broadcast simultaneously on 31 US networks*.

simurg /sɪˈməːg/ ▶ **noun** (in Persian mythology) a large mythical bird of great age, believed to have the power of reasoning and speech.
– ORIGIN from Persian *sīmurğ*, from Pahlavi *sēn* 'eagle' + *murğ* 'bird'.

sin¹ /sɪn/ ▶ **noun** an immoral act considered to be a transgression against divine law: *a sin in the eyes of God* | [mass noun] *the human capacity for sin*. ▪ an act regarded as a serious or regrettable fault, offence, or omission: *he committed the unforgivable sin of refusing to give interviews*.
▶ **verb** (**sins**, **sinning**, **sinned**) [no obj.] commit a sin: *I sinned and brought shame down on us*. ▪ (**sin against**) offend against (God, a person, or a principle): *Lord, we have sinned against you*.
– PHRASES (**as**) —— **as sin** informal having a particular undesirable quality to a high degree: *as ugly as sin | miserable as sin*. **for one's sins** humorous, chiefly Brit. used to suggest that a task or duty is so onerous or unpleasant that it must be a punishment. **live in sin** informal, dated live together as though married. **sin of commission** a sinful action. **sin of omission** a sinful failure to perform an action.
– ORIGIN Old English *synn* (noun), *syngian* (verb); probably related to Latin *sons*, *sont-* 'guilty'.

sin² /sʌɪn/ ▶ **abbreviation** sine.

Sinai /ˈsʌɪnʌɪ, -nɪʌɪ/ an arid mountainous peninsula in NE Egypt, extending into the Red Sea between the

S

Gulf of Suez and the Gulf of Aqaba. It was occupied by Israel between 1967 and 1982. In the south is Mount Sinai, where, according to the Bible, Moses received the Ten Commandments (Exod. 19–34).

Sinaitic /ˌsʌɪneɪˈɪtɪk/ ▶ adjective relating to Mount Sinai or the Sinai peninsula.

Sinaloa /ˌsiːnəˈləʊə/ a state on the Pacific coast of Mexico; capital, Culiacán Rosales.

Sinanthropus /sɪˈnanθrəpəs/ ▶ noun a former genus name applied to some fossil hominids found in China in 1926. See **Peking man**.
– ORIGIN modern Latin, from **Sino-** 'Chinese' (because remains were found near Beijing) + Greek *anthrōpos* 'man'.

Sinatra /sɪˈnɑːtrə/, Frank (1915–98), American singer and actor; full name *Francis Albert Sinatra*. His many hits include 'Night and Day' and 'My Way'. He won an Oscar for his role in the film *From Here to Eternity* (1953).

Sinbad the Sailor (also **Sindbad**) the hero of one of the tales in the *Arabian Nights*, who relates the fantastic adventures he has during his voyages.

sin bin informal ▶ noun (in sport) a box or bench to which offending players can be sent for a period as a penalty during a game, especially in ice hockey. ■ Brit. a place where offenders are sent for detention, punishment, or rehabilitation.
▶ verb (**sin-bin**) [with obj.] send (a player) to a sin bin as a penalty.

since ▶ preposition, conjunction, & adverb **1** in the intervening period between (the time mentioned) and the time under consideration, typically the present: [as prep.] *she has suffered from depression since she was sixteen* | *the worst property slump since the war* | *I've felt better since I've been here* | [as adv.] *she ran away on Friday and we haven't seen her since.*
2 [conjunction] for the reason that; because: *delegates were delighted, since better protection of rhino reserves will help protect other rare species.*
3 [adverb] ago: *the settlement had vanished* ***long since.***
– ORIGIN late Middle English: contraction of obsolete *sithence*, or from dialect *sin* (both from dialect *sithen* 'thereupon, afterwards, ever since').

sincere ▶ adjective (**sincerer**, **sincerest**) free from pretence or deceit; proceeding from genuine feelings: *they offer their sincere thanks to Paul.* ■ (of a person) saying what they genuinely feel or believe; not dishonest or hypocritical.
– DERIVATIVES **sincereness** noun.
– ORIGIN mid 16th cent. (also in the sense 'not falsified, unadulterated'): from Latin *sincerus* 'clean, pure'.

sincerely ▶ adverb in a sincere or genuine way: *I sincerely hope that we shall have a change of government* | *a sincerely held belief.*
– PHRASES **yours sincerely** (US also **sincerely yours**) a formula used to end a letter, typically a formal one in which the recipient is addressed by name.

sincerity ▶ noun [mass noun] the absence of pretence, deceit, or hypocrisy: *the sincerity of his beliefs is unquestionable.*

sinciput /ˈsɪnsɪpʌt/ ▶ noun Anatomy the front of the skull from the forehead to the crown.
– DERIVATIVES **sincipital** /-ˈsɪpɪt(ə)l/ adjective.
– ORIGIN late 16th cent.: from Latin, from *semi-* 'half' + *caput* 'head'.

S

Sinclair[1] /ˈsɪŋklɛː/, Sir Clive (Marles) (b.1940), English electronics engineer and entrepreneur. In the 1970s and early 1980s he pioneered innovative products such as the pocket calculator and personal computer.

Sinclair[2] /ˈsɪŋklɛː/, Upton (Beall) (1878–1968), American novelist and social reformer. He agitated for social justice in seventy-nine books, including *The Jungle* (1906) and the eleven-volume 'Lanny Budd' series (1940–53).

Sind /sɪnd/ a province of SE Pakistan, traversed by the lower reaches of the Indus; capital, Karachi.

Sindebele /sɪnˈdeɪbeli, ˌsɪndɛˈbeɪli/ ▶ noun another term for **Ndebele** (the language).

Sindhi /ˈsɪndi/ ▶ noun (pl. **Sindhis**) **1** a native or inhabitant of Sind.
2 [mass noun] the Indic language of Sind, used also in western India and having about 18 million speakers.
▶ adjective relating to the province of Sind or its people, or the Sindhi language.
– ORIGIN from Persian and Urdu *sindī*, from Sanskrit *sindhu* 'river' (specifically the Indus).

sindoor /ˈsɪndʊə/ (also **sindur**) ▶ noun [mass noun] red pigment made from powdered red lead, especially as applied as a dot on the forehead or in the parting of the hair of married Hindu women.
– ORIGIN Hindi *sindur*, from Sanskrit *sindura* 'red lead'.

sine /sʌɪn/ ▶ noun Mathematics the trigonometric function that is equal to the ratio of the side opposite a given angle (in a right-angled triangle) to the hypotenuse.
– ORIGIN late 16th cent.: from Latin *sinus* 'curve', used in medieval Latin as a translation of Arabic *jayb* 'pocket, sine'.

sinecure /ˈsʌɪnɪkjʊə, ˈsɪn-/ ▶ noun a position requiring little or no work but giving the holder status or financial benefit.
– DERIVATIVES **sinecurism** noun, **sinecurist** noun.
– ORIGIN mid 17th cent.: from Latin *sine cura* 'without care'.

sine curve (also **sine wave**) ▶ noun a curve representing periodic oscillations of constant amplitude as given by a sine function. Also called **sinusoid**.

sine die /ˌsiːneɪ ˈdiːeɪ, ˌsʌɪni ˈdʌɪiː/ ▶ adverb (with reference to business or proceedings that have been adjourned) with no appointed date for resumption: *the case was adjourned sine die.*
– ORIGIN Latin, literally 'without a day'.

sine qua non /ˌsɪni kwɑː ˈnəʊn, ˌsʌɪni kweɪ ˈnɒn/ ▶ noun an essential condition; a thing that is absolutely necessary: *grammar and usage are the sine qua non of language teaching and learning.*
– ORIGIN Latin, literally '(cause) without which not'.

sinew ▶ noun a piece of tough fibrous tissue uniting muscle to bone; a tendon or ligament. ■ (usu. **sinews**) the parts of a structure, system, or organization that give it strength or bind it together: *the sinews of government.*
▶ verb [with obj.] (usu. as adj. **sinewed**) literary strengthen with or as if with sinews: *the sinewed shape of his back.*
– ORIGIN Old English *sin(e)we* 'tendon', of Germanic origin; related to Dutch *zeen* and German *Sehne*.

sinewy ▶ adjective consisting of or resembling sinews. ■ (of a person or animal) lean and muscular: *a short, sinewy, sunburnt man* | figurative *the language is spare and sinewy.*

sinfonia /sɪnˈfəʊnɪə, ˌsɪnfəˈniːə/ ▶ noun Music a symphony. ■ (in baroque music) an orchestral piece used as an introduction to an opera, cantata, or suite. ■ a small symphony orchestra.
– ORIGIN Italian.

sinfonia concertante ▶ noun a piece of music for orchestra with one or (usually) more soloists, typically from the 18th century.
– ORIGIN Italian, literally 'harmonizing symphony'.

sinfonietta /ˌsɪnfəʊnɪˈɛtə/ ▶ noun Music a short or simple symphony. ■ a small symphony orchestra.
– ORIGIN Italian, diminutive of *sinfonia* (see **sinfonia**).

sinful ▶ adjective wicked and immoral; committing or characterized by the committing of sins: *sinful men* | *a sinful way of life.* ■ highly reprehensible: *a sinful waste.*
– DERIVATIVES **sinfully** adverb, **sinfulness** noun.
– ORIGIN Old English *synfull* (see **sin**[1], **-ful**).

sing ▶ verb (past **sang**; past participle **sung**) **1** [no obj.] make musical sounds with the voice, especially words with a set tune: *Bella sang to the baby.* ■ [with obj.] perform (a song, words, or tune) by making musical sounds with the voice: *I asked her to sing some carols* | (as noun **singing**) *the singing of hymns in Latin.* ■ (**sing along**) sing in accompaniment to a song or piece of music. ■ [with obj.] (**sing something out**) call something out loudly: *he sang out a greeting.* ■ (of a bird) make characteristic melodious whistling and twittering sounds: *the birds were singing in the trees.*
2 [no obj.] make a high-pitched whistling or buzzing sound: *the kettle was beginning to sing.* ■ (of a person's ear) be affected with a continuous buzzing sound, especially as the after-effect of a blow or loud noise: *a stinging slap that made my ear sing.*
3 [no obj.] informal act as an informer to the police: *as soon as he got put under pressure, he* ***sang like a canary.***
4 [with obj.] recount or celebrate in poetry or other literature: *poetry should sing the variety of the human race* | [no obj.] *these poets sing of the American experience.* ■ [no obj.] archaic compose poetry.
▶ noun informal an act or spell of singing. ■ US a meeting for amateur singing.
– PHRASES **all-singing, all-dancing** Brit. informal having a large number and variety of impressive features. **sing a different tune** (or **song**) change one's opinion about or attitude towards someone or something. **sing for one's supper** see **supper**. **sing from the same hymn** (or **song**) **sheet** Brit. informal present a united front in public by not disagreeing with one another. **sing in** (or **out**) **the new** (or **old**) **year** celebrate the new year (or the end of the previous year) with singing. **sing the praises of** see **praise**. **sing someone to sleep** cause someone to fall asleep by singing gently to them.
– DERIVATIVES **singable** adjective.
– ORIGIN Old English *singan* (verb), of Germanic origin; related to Dutch *zingen* and German *singen.*

sing. ▶ abbreviation singular.

singalong ▶ noun an informal occasion when people sing together in a group. ■ [usu. as modifier] a light popular song or tune to which one can easily sing along in accompaniment: *an album featuring simple, singalong tunes.*

Singapore /ˌsɪŋəˈpɔː/ a country in SE Asia consisting of the island of Singapore (linked by a causeway to the southern tip of the Malay Peninsula) and some fifty-four smaller islands; pop. 4,657,500 (est. 2009); official languages, Malay, Chinese, Tamil, and English; capital, Singapore City.

> Established as a trading post under the East India Company in 1819, Singapore came under British colonial rule in 1867 as part of the Straits Settlements with Penang and Malacca. Singapore rapidly grew to become the most important commercial centre and naval base in SE Asia. After the Second World War it became first a British Crown Colony in 1946 and then a self-governing state within the Commonwealth in 1959. Federated with Malaysia in 1963, it declared full independence two years later.

– DERIVATIVES **Singaporean** /-ˈpɔːrɪən/ adjective & noun.

Singapore sling ▶ noun a cocktail made from gin and cherry brandy.

singe ▶ verb (**singes**, **singeing**, **singed**) [with obj.] burn (something) superficially or lightly: *the fire had singed his eyebrows* | (as adj. **singed**) *a smell of singed feathers.* ■ [no obj.] be burnt in this way: *the heat was so intense I could feel the hairs on my hands singe.* ■ burn the bristles or down off (the carcass of a pig or fowl) to prepare it for cooking.
▶ noun a superficial burn.
– ORIGIN Old English *sencgan*, of West Germanic origin; related to Dutch *zengen.*

Singer[1], Isaac Bashevis (1904–91), Polish-born American novelist and short-story writer. His work blends realistic detail and elements of fantasy, mysticism, and magic to portray the lives of Polish Jews from many periods. Nobel Prize for Literature (1978).

Singer[2], Isaac Merrit (1811–75), American inventor. In 1851 he designed and built the first commercially successful sewing machine.

singer ▶ noun a person who sings, especially professionally: *a pop singer.*

singer-songwriter ▶ noun a person who sings and writes popular songs, especially professionally.

Singh /sɪŋ/ ▶ noun a title or surname adopted by certain warrior castes of northern India, especially by male members of the Sikh Khalsa.
– ORIGIN from Punjabi *siṅgh* 'lion', from Sanskrit *siṃha* 'lion'.

Singhalese /ˌsɪŋgəˈliːz/ ▶ noun & adjective variant spelling of **Sinhalese**.

singing hinny ▶ noun a kind of currant cake baked on a griddle, originating in northern England.

singing saw ▶ noun another term for **musical saw**.

sing-jay ▶ noun a DJ who raps and sings as part of their performance.

single ▶ adjective **1** [attrib.] only one; not one of several: *a single red rose* | *the kingdom was ruled over by a single family.* ■ regarded as distinct from each other or others in a group: *she wrote down every single word* | *alcohol is the single most important cause of violence.* ■ [with negative] even one (used for emphasis): *they didn't receive a single reply.* ■ designed or suitable for one person: *a single bed.* ■ archaic not accompanied by others; alone.
2 unmarried or not involved in a stable sexual relationship: *a single mother.*
3 [attrib.] consisting of one part: *the studio was a single large room.* ■ Brit. (of a ticket) valid for an outward journey only, not for the return. ■ (of a flower) having only one whorl of petals. ■ denoting an alcoholic

drink that consists of one measure of spirits: *a single whisky*.
4 archaic free from duplicity or deceit; ingenuous: *a pure and single heart*.
▶ **noun 1** an individual person or thing rather than part of a pair or a group. ■ a short record or CD featuring one main song or track. ■ (**singles**) people who are unmarried or not involved in a stable sexual relationship: *the divorce rate is rising so you'll see more singles in their late 30s and early 40s* | [as modifier] *a singles holiday*. ■ Brit. a ticket that is valid only for an outward journey. ■ a single measure of spirits. ■ US informal a one-dollar note.
2 a play that scores one point, in particular: ■ Cricket a hit for one run. ■ Baseball a hit which allows the batter to proceed safely to first base.
3 (**singles**) (especially in tennis and badminton) a game or competition for individual players, not pairs or teams.
4 (usu. **singles**) Bell-ringing a system of change-ringing in which one pair of bells changes places at each round.
▶ **verb** [with obj.] **1** (**single someone/thing out**) choose someone or something from a group for special treatment: *one newspaper was singled out for criticism*.
2 thin out (seedlings or saplings).
3 reduce (a railway track) to a single line.
4 [no obj.] Baseball hit a single. ■ [with obj.] cause (a run) to be scored by hitting a single. ■ [with obj.] advance (a runner) by hitting a single.
– DERIVATIVES **singledom** noun, **singleness** noun.
– ORIGIN Middle English: via Old French from Latin *singulus*, related to *simplus* 'simple'.

single acrostic ▶ **noun** an acrostic using the first letter only of each line.

single-acting ▶ **adjective** (of an engine) having pressure applied only to one side of the piston.

single-action ▶ **adjective** (of a gun) needing to be cocked by hand before it can be fired.

single-blind ▶ **adjective** denoting a test or experiment in which information that may bias the results is concealed from either tester or subject.

single bond ▶ **noun** a chemical bond in which one pair of electrons is shared between two atoms.

single-breasted ▶ **adjective** (of a jacket or coat) showing only one row of buttons at the front when fastened.

single carriageway ▶ **noun** a road with only one lane in each direction.

single-cell protein ▶ **noun** [mass noun] protein derived from a culture of single-celled organisms, used especially as a food supplement.

single combat ▶ **noun** [mass noun] fighting between two people: *he defeated the enemy champion in single combat*.

single-copy ▶ **adjective** Genetics (of a gene or genetic sequence) present in a genome in only one copy.

single cream ▶ **noun** [mass noun] Brit. thin cream with a relatively low fat content.

single currency ▶ **noun** a currency used by all the members of an economic federation. ■ (also **single European currency**) the currency (the euro) which replaced the national currencies of twelve member states of the European Union in 2002.

single-cut ▶ **adjective** (of a file) having grooves cut in one direction only, not crossing each other.

single-decker ▶ **noun** chiefly Brit. a bus having only one floor or level.

single digging ▶ **noun** [mass noun] (in gardening) digging in which only the topsoil is turned over, to the depth of one spit.

single end ▶ **noun** Scottish a single room.

single-ended ▶ **adjective** (of an electronic device) designed for use with unbalanced signals and therefore having one input and one output terminal connected to earth.

single-entry ▶ **adjective** denoting a system of bookkeeping in which each transaction is entered in one account only.

Single European Act a treaty providing for the establishment of a single European market from 1 January 1993, and giving greater powers to the European Parliament. It came into force on 1 July 1987.

single file ▶ **noun** [in sing.] a line of people or things arranged one behind another: *we trooped along in single file* | [as modifier] *a single-file column*.
▶ **adverb** one behind another: *we walked single file*.

single-foot ▶ **verb** [no obj.] N. Amer. (of a horse) walk by moving both legs on each side in alternation, each foot falling separately.

single-lens reflex ▶ **adjective** denoting a reflex camera in which the lens that forms the image on the film also provides the image in the viewfinder.

single malt (also **single malt whisky**) ▶ **noun** [mass noun] whisky unblended with any other malt.

single market ▶ **noun** an association of countries trading with each other without restrictions or tariffs. The European single market came into effect on 1 January 1993.

single-minded ▶ **adjective** concentrating on only one aim: *the single-minded pursuit of profit*.
– DERIVATIVES **single-mindedly** adverb, **single-mindedness** noun.

single parent ▶ **noun** a person bringing up a child or children without a partner.

singles bar ▶ **noun** a bar frequented by single people who are seeking a romantic or sexual partner.

single-seater ▶ **noun** a vehicle or aircraft for one person.

single-source ▶ **verb** [with obj.] give a franchise to a single supplier for (a particular product).

single stick ▶ **noun** Fencing a stick of about a sword's length. ■ [mass noun] fencing with a single stick.

singlet ▶ **noun 1** chiefly Brit. a sleeveless garment worn under or instead of a shirt; a vest.
2 Physics a single unresolvable line in a spectrum, not part of a multiplet. ■ a state or energy level with zero spin, giving a single value for a particular quantum number.
3 Chemistry an atomic or molecular state in which all electron spins are paired.
– ORIGIN mid 18th cent. (originally denoting a man's short jacket): from SINGLE (because the garment was unlined) + -ET[1], on the pattern of *doublet*.

singleton ▶ **noun** a single person or thing of the kind under consideration: *splitting the clumps of plants into singletons*. ■ [often as modifier] a child or animal born singly, rather than one of a multiple birth: *singleton boys*. ■ informal a person who is not married or in a long-term relationship. ■ (in card games, especially bridge) a card that is the only one of its suit in a hand. ■ Mathematics & Logic a set which contains exactly one element.
– ORIGIN late 19th cent.: from SINGLE, on the pattern of *simpleton*.

single transferable vote ▶ **noun** an electoral system of proportional representation in which a person's vote can be transferred to a second or further competing candidate (according to the voter's stated order of preference) if the candidate of first choice is eliminated during a succession of counts or has more votes than are needed for election.

singletree ▶ **noun** North American term for SWINGLETREE.

single-vision ▶ **adjective** denoting glasses of which each lens is a single optical element; not bifocal.

Singlish ▶ **noun** [mass noun] **1** a variety of English spoken in Singapore, incorporating elements of Chinese and Malay.
2 a variety of English spoken in Sri Lanka, incorporating elements of Sinhala.

singly ▶ **adverb** one at a time; separately or individually: *he talked to the players singly and in groups*.

Sing Sing a New York State prison, built in 1825–8 at Ossining village on the Hudson River and formerly notorious for its severe discipline. Official name OSSINING CORRECTIONAL FACILITY.

sing-song ▶ **adjective** (of a person's voice) having a repeated rising and falling rhythm: *the sing-song voices of children reciting tables*.
▶ **noun 1** Brit. informal an informal gathering for singing.
2 [in sing.] a sing-song way of speaking.
▶ **verb** (**sing-songs, sing-songing, sing-songed**) [no obj.] speak or recite something in a sing-song manner.

singsong girl ▶ **noun** (in China) a female entertainer. ■ informal a prostitute.

Singspiel /ˈzɪŋʃpiːl/ ▶ **noun** (pl. **Singspiele** /-ə/) a form of German light opera, typically with spoken dialogue, popular especially in the late 18th century.
– ORIGIN from German *singen* 'sing' + *Spiel* 'play'.

singular ▶ **adjective 1** Grammar (of a word or form) denoting or referring to just one person or thing. ■ single; unique: *she always thought of herself as singular, as his only daughter*.
2 exceptionally good or great; remarkable: *he had the singular good fortune not to die in the trenches*. ■ strange or eccentric in some respect: *no explanation accompanied this rather singular statement*.
3 Mathematics (of a square matrix) having a zero determinant.
4 Physics & Mathematics relating to or of the nature of singularity.
▶ **noun** Grammar a singular word or form. ■ (**the singular**) the singular number: *a word in the singular*.
– ORIGIN Middle English (in the sense 'solitary, single', also 'beyond the average'): from Old French *singuler*, from Latin *singularis*, from *singulus* (see SINGLE).

singularity ▶ **noun** (pl. **singularities**) **1** [mass noun] the state, fact, quality, or condition of being singular: *he believed in the singularity of all cultures*. ■ [count noun] a peculiarity or odd trait.
2 Physics & Mathematics a point at which a function takes an infinite value, especially in space–time when matter is infinitely dense, such as at the centre of a black hole.
– ORIGIN Middle English: from Old French *singularite*, from late Latin *singularitas*, from *singularis* 'alone (of its kind)' (see SINGULAR).

singularize (also **singularise**) ▶ **verb** [with obj.] rare
1 make distinct or conspicuous.
2 give a singular form to (a word).
– DERIVATIVES **singularization** noun.

singularly ▶ **adverb** in a remarkable or noticeable way: *you have singularly failed to live up to your promises* | [as submodifier] *a singularly unattractive colour*. ■ in a strange or eccentric way: *Charlotte thought her very singularly dressed*.

sinh /ʃʌɪn, sɪntʃ, sʌɪˈneɪtʃ/ ▶ **abbreviation** Mathematics hyperbolic sine.
– ORIGIN late 19th cent.: from *sin(e)* + *h(yperbolic)*.

Sinhalese /ˌsɪnhəˈliːz, ˌsɪnə-/ (also **Singhalese**, **Sinhala** /sɪnˈhɑːlə/) ▶ **noun** (pl. **same**) **1** a member of a people originally from northern India, now forming the majority of the population of Sri Lanka.
2 [mass noun] an Indic language spoken by the Sinhalese, descended from Sanskrit. It has about 13 million speakers.
▶ **adjective** relating to the Sinhalese or their language.
– ORIGIN from Sanskrit *Siṅhala* 'Sri Lanka' + -ESE.

Sining variant of XINING.

sinister ▶ **adjective 1** giving the impression that something harmful or evil is happening or will happen: *there was something sinister about that murmuring voice*. ■ evil or criminal: *there might be a more sinister motive behind the government's actions*.
2 [attrib.] archaic & Heraldry of, on, or towards the left-hand side (in a coat of arms, from the bearer's point of view, i.e. the right as it is depicted). The opposite of DEXTER[1].
– DERIVATIVES **sinisterly** adverb, **sinisterness** noun.
– ORIGIN late Middle English (in the sense 'malicious, underhand'): from Old French *sinistre* or Latin *sinister* 'left'.

sinistral /ˈsɪnɪstr(ə)l/ ▶ **adjective** of or on the left side or the left hand (the opposite of DEXTRAL). ■ left-handed. ■ Geology relating to or denoting a strike-slip fault in which the motion of the block on the further side of the fault from an observer is towards the left. ■ Zoology (of a spiral mollusc shell) with whorls rising to the left and coiling in a clockwise direction.
▶ **noun** a left-handed person.
– DERIVATIVES **sinistrality** noun, **sinistrally** adverb.

Sinitic /sɪˈnɪtɪk/ ▶ **adjective** relating to or denoting the division of the Sino-Tibetan language family that includes the many forms of Chinese.
– ORIGIN late 19th cent.: via late Latin from Greek *sinai* 'the Chinese', from Arabic *ṣīn*, denoting the Chinese empire.

sink[1] ▶ **verb** (past **sank**; past participle **sunk**) **1** [no obj.] go down below the surface of something, especially of a liquid; become submerged: *he saw the coffin sink below the surface of the waves*. ■ (of a ship) go to the bottom of the sea or some other body of water because of damage or a collision: *the trawler sank with the loss of all six crew*. ■ [with obj.] cause (a ship) to sink: *a freak wave sank their boat near the shore*. ■ fail and not be seen or heard of again: *the film sank virtually without trace*. ■ [with obj.] cause to fail: *this pledge could sink the government*. ■ [with obj.] conceal, keep in the background, or ignore: *they agreed to sink their differences*.
2 [no obj.] descend from a higher to a lower position; drop downwards: *you can relax on the veranda as the sun sinks low*. ■ (of a person) lower oneself or drop

S

down gently: *she sank back on to her pillow.* ■ [with adverbial of direction] gradually penetrate into the surface of something: *her feet sank into the thick pile of the carpet.*
3 [no obj.] gradually decrease or decline in value, amount, quality, or intensity: *their output sank to a third of the pre-war figure.* ■ lapse or fall into a particular state or condition: *he **sank into** a coma after suffering a brain haemorrhage.* ■ approach death: *the doctor concluded that the lad was sinking fast.*
4 [with obj.] insert beneath a surface: *rails fixed in place with screws sunk below the surface of the wood.* ■ (**sink something into**) cause something sharp to penetrate (a surface): *the dog sank its teeth into her arm.* ■ [with obj. and adverbial] push or thrust (an object) into something: *Kelly stood watching, her hands sunk deep into her pockets.* ■ excavate (a well) or bore (a shaft) vertically downwards: *they planned to sink a gold mine in Oklahoma.* ■ hit (a ball) into a hole in golf or snooker. ■ (in golf) hit the ball into the hole with (a putt or other shot): *he sank a four-foot birdie putt at the fifth hole.*
5 [with obj.] Brit. informal rapidly consume (an alcoholic drink): *English players sinking a few post-match lagers.*
– PHRASES **a** (or **that**) **sinking feeling** an unpleasant feeling caused by the realization that something unpleasant or undesirable has happened or is about to happen. **sink or swim** fail or succeed entirely by one's own efforts.
– PHRASAL VERBS **sink in** (of words or facts) be fully understood or realized: *Peter read the letter twice before its meaning sank in.* **sink something in/into** put money or energy into (something); invest something in: *many investors sank their life savings into the company.*
– DERIVATIVES **sinkable** adjective, **sinkage** noun.
– ORIGIN Old English *sincan*, of Germanic origin; related to Dutch *zinken* and German *sinken*.

> **USAGE** Historically, the past tense of **sink** has been both **sank** and **sunk** (*the boat **sank**; the boat **sunk***) and the past participle has been both **sunk** and **sunken** (*the boat had already **sunk**; the boat had already **sunken***). In modern English the past is generally **sank** and the past participle is **sunk**, with the form **sunken** now surviving only as an adjective, as in *a **sunken** garden* or ***sunken** cheeks.*

sink² ▶ noun **1** a fixed basin with a water supply and outflow pipe.
2 a pool or marsh in which a river's water disappears by evaporation or percolation. ■ technical a body or process which acts to absorb or remove energy or a particular component from a system: *a heat sink* | *the oceans can act as a sink for CO_2.* The opposite of **SOURCE**.
3 short for **SINKHOLE**.
4 [usu. as modifier] Brit. a school or estate situated in a socially deprived area: *the local sink school* | *a sink estate.*
– ORIGIN Middle English: from **SINK¹**.

sinker ▶ noun **1** a weight used to sink a fishing line or sounding line.
2 (also **sinker ball**) Baseball a pitch which drops markedly as it nears home plate.
3 a type of windsurfing board of insufficient buoyancy to support its crew unless moving fast.
4 US a doughnut.

sinkhole ▶ noun a cavity in the ground, especially in a limestone formation, caused by water erosion and providing a route for surface water to disappear underground.

Sinkiang /sɪn'kjaŋ/ variant of **XINJIANG**.

sinking fund ▶ noun a fund formed by periodically setting aside money for the gradual repayment of a debt or replacement of a wasting asset.

sinless ▶ adjective free from sin: *the sinless life of Christ.*
– DERIVATIVES **sinlessly** adverb, **sinlessness** noun.

sinner ▶ noun a person who transgresses against divine law by committing an immoral act or acts.

sinnet /'sɪnɪt/ (also **sennit**) ▶ noun [mass noun] Nautical braided cordage in flat, round, or square form, made from three to nine cords.
– ORIGIN early 17th cent.: of unknown origin.

Sinn Fein /ʃɪn 'feɪn/, Irish /ˌʃʲinʲ 'fʲeːnʲ/ a political movement and party seeking a united republican Ireland.

> Founded in 1905, Sinn Fein became increasingly committed to Republicanism after the failure of the Home Rule movement. Having won a majority of Irish seats in the 1918 general election, its members refused to go to Westminster and set up their own parliament in Ireland in 1919. After a split in the 1920s the party began to function as the political wing of the IRA. It now sends representatives to the Northern Ireland Assembly and the Irish Dáil; Sinn Fein MPs elected to the House of Commons do not take up their seats.

– DERIVATIVES **Sinn Feiner** noun.
– ORIGIN from Irish *sinn féin* 'we ourselves'.

Sino- /'sʌɪnəʊ/ ▶ combining form Chinese; Chinese and ...: *Sino-American.* ■ relating to China.
– ORIGIN from late Latin *Sinae* (see **SINITIC**).

sino-atrial /ˌsʌɪnəʊ'eɪtrɪəl/ ▶ adjective Anatomy relating to or denoting a small body of specialized muscle tissue (the **sino-atrial node**) in the wall of the right atrium of the heart, whose contractions regulate the heartbeat.
– ORIGIN early 20th cent.: from **SINUS** + *atrial* (see **ATRIUM**).

sin offering ▶ noun (in traditional or ancient Judaism) an offering made as an atonement for sin.

Sino-Japanese Wars two wars (1894–5, 1937–45) fought between China and Japan.

> The first war, caused by rivalry over Korea, was ended by a treaty in Japan's favour and led to the eventual overthrow of the Manchus in 1912. In the second war Japanese expansionism led to trouble in Manchuria in 1931 and to the establishment of a Japanese puppet state (Manchukuo) a year later.

Sinology /sʌɪ'nɒlədʒi, sɪ-/ ▶ noun [mass noun] the study of Chinese language, history, customs, and politics.
– DERIVATIVES **Sinological** adjective, **Sinologist** noun.

Sino-Tibetan ▶ adjective relating to or denoting a large language family of eastern Asia which includes Chinese, Burmese, Tibetan, and (in some classifications) Thai. They are tonal languages, but the exact relationships between them are far from clear.
▶ noun [mass noun] the Sino-Tibetan language family.

sinsemilla /ˌsɪnsə'mɪlə/ ▶ noun [mass noun] cannabis of a variety which has a particularly high concentration of narcotic agents.
– ORIGIN 1970s: from American Spanish, literally 'without seed'.

sin tax ▶ noun informal a tax on items such as alcohol or tobacco.

sinter /'sɪntə/ ▶ noun [mass noun] **1** Geology a hard siliceous or calcareous deposit precipitated from mineral springs.
2 solid material which has been sintered, especially a mixture of iron ore and other materials prepared for smelting.
▶ verb [with obj.] make (a powdered material) coalesce into a solid or porous mass by heating it (and usually also compressing it) without liquefaction. ■ [no obj.] coalesce in this way.
– ORIGIN late 18th cent. (as a noun): from German *Sinter*; compare with **CINDER**.

Sint Maarten /sɪnt 'maːrtə(n)/ Dutch name for **ST MARTIN**.

Sint-Niklaas /ˌsɪnt 'nɪkla:s/ an industrial town in northern Belgium, south-west of Antwerp; pop. 70,450 (2008). French name **ST NICOLAS**.

Sintra /'si:ntrə/ (also **Cintra**) a small town in western Portugal, situated in a mountainous area to the north-west of Lisbon; pop. 28,400 (est. 2009).

Sintu /'sɪntu:/ ▶ adjective & noun S. African another term for **BANTU** (the language family).
– ORIGIN 1970s: from the Bantu elements *(i)si-* denoting language or culture, and *-ntu* '(African) person'.

sinuate /'sɪnjʊət/ ▶ adjective Botany & Zoology having a wavy or sinuous margin; with alternate rounded notches and lobes.
– ORIGIN late 17th cent.: from Latin *sinuatus*, past participle of *sinuare* 'to bend'.

Sinuiju /'ʃɪnədʒu:/ a city and port in North Korea, situated on the Yalu River near its mouth on the Yellow Sea; pop. 383,200 (est. 2003).

sinuosity /ˌsɪnjʊ'ɒsɪti/ ▶ noun (pl. **sinuosities**) [mass noun] the ability to curve or bend easily and flexibly. ■ [count noun] a bend, especially in a stream or road.
– ORIGIN late 16th cent.: from French *sinuosité* or medieval Latin *sinuositas*, from *sinuosus* (see **SINUOUS**).

sinuous /'sɪnjʊəs/ ▶ adjective having many curves and turns: *the river follows a sinuous trail through the dale.* ■ lithe and supple: *the sinuous grace of a cat.*
– DERIVATIVES **sinuously** adverb, **sinuousness** noun.
– ORIGIN late 16th cent.: from French *sinueux* or Latin *sinuosus*, from *sinus* 'a bend'.

sinus /'sʌɪnəs/ ▶ noun **1** (often **sinuses**) Anatomy & Zoology a cavity within a bone or other tissue, especially one in the bones of the face or skull connecting with the nasal cavities. ■ an irregular venous or lymphatic cavity, reservoir, or dilated vessel. ■ Medicine an infected tract leading from a deep-seated infection and discharging pus to the surface. ■ Botany a rounded notch between two lobes on the margin of a leaf or petal.
2 [as modifier] Physiology relating to or denoting the sino-atrial node of the heart or its function of regulating the heartbeat: *sinus rhythm* | *sinus tachycardia.*
– ORIGIN late Middle English (in the medical sense): from Latin, literally 'a recess, bend'.

sinusitis /ˌsʌɪnə'sʌɪtɪs/ ▶ noun [mass noun] Medicine inflammation of a nasal sinus.

sinusoid /'sʌɪnəsɔɪd/ ▶ noun **1** another term for **SINE CURVE**.
2 Anatomy a small irregularly shaped blood vessel found in certain organs, especially the liver.
– DERIVATIVES **sinusoidal** adjective, **sinusoidally** adverb.
– ORIGIN early 19th cent.: from French *sinusoïde*, from Latin *sinus* (see **SINUS**).

sinus venosus /vi:'nəʊsəs/ ▶ noun (pl. **sinus venosi**) Zoology the first chamber of the heart in fish, amphibians, and reptiles, emptying into the right atrium.
– ORIGIN early 19th cent.: modern Latin, literally 'venous cavity'.

Sion /'sʌɪən/ ▶ noun variant spelling of **ZION**.

-sion ▶ suffix forming nouns such as *mansion, persuasion.*
– ORIGIN from Latin participial stems ending in *-s* + **-ION**.

Siouan /'su:ən/ ▶ noun [mass noun] a family of North American Indian languages spoken by the Sioux and related people, including Dakota, Hidatsa, and Crow.
▶ adjective relating to or denoting the Siouan language family.

Sioux /su:/ ▶ noun (pl. **same**) another term for the Dakota people of North America or their language. See **DAKOTA²**.
▶ adjective relating to the Sioux or their language.
– ORIGIN North American French, from *Nadouessioux* from Ojibwa (Ottawa dialect) *nātowēssiwak*, by substitution of the French plural ending *-x* for the Ojibwa plural *-ak*.

sip ▶ verb (**sips, sipping, sipped**) [with obj.] drink (something) by taking small mouthfuls: *I sat sipping coffee* | [no obj.] *she sipped at her tea.*
▶ noun a small mouthful of liquid: *she took a **sip of** the red wine.*
– DERIVATIVES **sipper** noun.
– ORIGIN late Middle English: perhaps a modification of **SUP¹**, as symbolic of a less vigorous action.

sipe /sʌɪp/ ▶ noun a groove or channel in the tread of a tyre to improve its grip.
– ORIGIN 1950s: from dialect *sipe* 'oozing, trickling', of unknown origin.

siphon /'sʌɪf(ə)n/ (also **syphon**) ▶ noun a tube used to convey fluid upwards from a reservoir and then down to a lower level by gravity. Once the fluid has been forced into the tube, typically by suction or immersion, flow is maintained by the different fluid pressures at the tube openings. ■ Zoology a tubular organ in an aquatic animal, especially a mollusc, through which water is drawn in or expelled.
▶ verb [with obj.] draw off or convey (liquid) by means of a siphon. ■ draw off or transfer over a period of time, especially illegally or unfairly: *he's been **siphoning** money **off** the firm.*
– DERIVATIVES **siphonal** adjective (Zoology), **siphonic** /-'fɒnɪk/ adjective.
– ORIGIN late Middle English: from French, or via Latin from Greek *siphōn* 'pipe'. The verb dates from the mid 19th cent.

Siphonaptera /ˌsʌɪfə'napt(ə)rə/ ▶ plural noun Entomology an order of insects that comprises the fleas.
– DERIVATIVES **siphonapteran** noun & adjective.
– ORIGIN modern Latin (plural), from Greek *siphōn* 'tube' + *apteros* 'wingless'.

Siphonophora /ˌsʌɪfə'nɒf(ə)rə/ ▶ plural noun Zoology an order of colonial marine coelenterates that includes the Portuguese man-of-war, having a float or swimming bell for drifting or swimming on the open sea.
– ORIGIN modern Latin (plural), from Greek *siphōn* 'tube' + *pherein* 'to bear'.

siphonophore /sʌɪˈfɒnəfɔː/ ▶ **noun** Zoology a colonial marine coelenterate of the order Siphonophora, such as a Portuguese man-of-war.

siphuncle /ˈsʌɪfʌŋk(ə)l/ ▶ **noun** Zoology (in shelled cephalopods such as nautiloids and ammonoids) a calcareous tube containing living tissue running through all the shell chambers, serving to pump fluid out of vacant chambers in order to adjust buoyancy.
ORIGIN mid 18th cent.: from Latin *siphunculus* 'small tube'.

Siphunculata /sʌɪˌfʌŋkjʊˈlɑːtə/ ▶ **plural noun** Entomology another term for **ANOPLURA**.
– ORIGIN modern Latin (plural), from Latin *siphunculus* 'small tube'.

SIPP ▶ **noun** (in the UK) a self-invested personal pension, a pension plan that enables the holder to choose and manage the investments made.

sippet ▶ **noun** a small piece of bread or toast, used to dip into soup or sauce or as a garnish.
– ORIGIN mid 16th cent.: apparently a diminutive of **SOP**.

sippy cup ▶ **noun** US a small beaker with a lid and a spout, for an infant or young child to drink from.

Sipuncula /sʌɪˈpʌŋkjʊlə/ ▶ **plural noun** Zoology a small phylum that comprises the peanut worms. Also called **Sipunculida**.
– DERIVATIVES **sipunculan** noun & adjective, **sipunculid** noun & adjective.
– ORIGIN modern Latin (plural), from *Sipunculus* (genus name), based on a variant of Latin *siphunculus* 'small tube'.

sir (also **Sir**) ▶ **noun** used as a polite or respectful way of addressing a man, especially one in a position of authority: *excuse me, sir.* ■ used to address a man at the beginning of a formal or business letter: *Dear Sir.* ■ used as a title before the forename of a knight or baronet. ■ another expression for **SIREE**.
– ORIGIN Middle English: reduced form of **SIRE**.

Sir. ▶ **abbreviation** (in biblical references) Sirach (Apocrypha).

Siracusa /ˌsɪrəˈkuzə/ Italian name for **SYRACUSE** (sense 1).

sirdar ▶ **noun** variant spelling of **SARDAR**.

Sirdaryo /ˌsɪədɑːˈjəʊ/ a river of central Asia. Rising in two headstreams in the Tien Shan mountains in eastern Uzbekistan, it flows for some 2,220 km (1,380 miles) west and north-west through southern Kazakhstan to the Aral Sea. Russian name **SYR-DARYA**.

sire /sʌɪə/ ▶ **noun 1** the male parent of an animal, especially a stallion or bull kept for breeding.
2 archaic a respectful form of address for someone of high social status, especially a king. ■ a father or other male forebear.
▶ **verb** [with obj.] be the male parent of (an animal). ■ literary (of a person) be the father of.
– ORIGIN Middle English (in sense 2 of the noun): from Old French, from an alteration of Latin *senior* (see **SENIOR**). Sense 1 of the noun dates from the early 16th cent.

siree /sɪˈriː/ (also **sirree**) ▶ **exclamation** N. Amer. informal used for emphasis, especially after *yes* and *no*: *he's not the type to treat young employees like mud, no siree.*
– ORIGIN early 19th cent.: from **SIR** + the emphatic suffix *-ee*.

siren ▶ **noun 1** a device that makes a loud prolonged signal or warning sound: *ambulance sirens.*
2 Greek Mythology each of a number of women or winged creatures whose singing lured unwary sailors on to rocks. ■ a woman who is considered to be alluring or fascinating but also dangerous in some way.
3 an eel-like American amphibian with tiny forelimbs, no hindlimbs, small eyes, and external gills, typically living in muddy pools. ● Family Sirenidae: genera *Siren* and *Pseudobranchus*, and three species, including the **greater siren** (*S. lacertina*).
– PHRASES **siren song** (or **call**) used in reference to the appeal of something that is alluring but also potentially harmful or dangerous: *a mountaineer who hears the siren song of K2.*
– ORIGIN Middle English (denoting an imaginary type of snake): from Old French *sirene*, from late Latin *Sirena*, feminine of Latin *Siren*, from Greek *Seirēn*.

Sirenia /sʌɪˈriːnɪə/ ▶ **plural noun** Zoology an order of large aquatic plant-eating mammals which includes the manatees and dugong. They live chiefly in tropical coastal waters and are distinguished by paddle-like forelimbs and a tail flipper replacing hindlimbs. ● Order Sirenia: two families and four living species.
– ORIGIN modern Latin (see **SIREN**).

sirenian Zoology ▶ **noun** a large aquatic plant-eating mammal of the order Sirenia, such as a manatee or dugong.
▶ **adjective** relating to or denoting sirenians.

siren suit ▶ **noun** a one-piece garment for the whole body which is easily put on or taken off, originally designed for use in air-raid shelters.

Sir Galahad ▶ **noun** see **GALAHAD**.

Sirius /ˈsɪrɪəs/ Astronomy the brightest star in the sky, south of the celestial equator in the constellation Canis Major. It is a binary star with a dim companion, which is a white dwarf. Also called **DOG STAR**.
– ORIGIN Latin, from Greek *seirios astēr* 'scorching star'.

sirloin ▶ **noun** [mass noun] good-quality beef cut from the loin: [as modifier] *fresh sirloin steaks.*
– ORIGIN late Middle English: from Old French (see **SUR-**[1], **LOIN**).

sirocco /sɪˈrɒkəʊ/ (also **scirocco**) ▶ **noun** (pl. **siroccos**) a hot wind, often dusty or rainy, blowing from North Africa across the Mediterranean to southern Europe.
– ORIGIN early 17th cent.: via French from Italian *scirocco*, based on Spanish Arabic *šalūq* 'east wind'.

sirrah /ˈsɪrə/ ▶ **noun** archaic used as a term of address for a man or boy, especially one younger or of lower status than the speaker.
– ORIGIN early 16th cent.: probably from **SIRE**, when still two syllables in Middle English, with the second syllable assimilated to **AH**.

sirtaki /səːˈtaki/ ▶ **noun** variant spelling of **SYRTAKI**.

Sirte, Gulf of /ˈsəːti/ another name for **SIDRA, GULF OF**.

sirup ▶ **noun** US spelling of **SYRUP**.

sirupy ▶ **adjective** US spelling of **SYRUPY**.

SIS ▶ **abbreviation** (in the UK) Secret Intelligence Service. See **MI6**.

sis[1] /sɪs/ ▶ **noun** informal a person's sister (often used as a form of address): *where are you going, sis?*
– ORIGIN mid 17th cent.: abbreviation.

sis[2] /sɪs, səs/ ▶ **exclamation** S. African informal used to express disappointment, disgust, or contempt.
– ORIGIN from Afrikaans *sies*.

sisal /ˈsʌɪs(ə)l/ ▶ **noun** [mass noun] a Mexican agave with large fleshy leaves, cultivated for fibre production. ● *Agave sisalana*, family Agavaceae.
■ the fibre made from the sisal plant, used especially for ropes or matting.
– ORIGIN mid 19th cent.: from *Sisal*, the name of a port in Yucatán, Mexico.

siskin ▶ **noun** a small songbird related to the goldfinch, with yellow and black in the plumage. ● Genus *Carduelis* (and *Serinus*), family Fringillidae: the North Eurasian **(spruce) siskin** (*C. spinus*), with dark-streaked greenish-yellow plumage, and several species in the New World.
– ORIGIN mid 16th cent.: from Middle Dutch *siseken*, a diminutive related to German *Zeisig*, of Slavic origin.

Sisley /ˈsɪsli, ˈsɪzli/, Alfred (1839–99), French Impressionist painter, of English descent. He is chiefly remembered for his paintings of the countryside around Paris in the 1870s, with their concentration on reflecting surfaces and fluid brushwork.

sissy (Brit. also **cissy**) informal ▶ **noun** (pl. **sissies**) a person regarded as effeminate or cowardly.
▶ **adjective** (**sissier**, **sissiest**) feeble and cowardly.
– DERIVATIVES **sissified** adjective, **sissiness** noun, **sissyish** adjective.
– ORIGIN mid 19th cent. (in the sense 'sister'): from **SIS**[1] + **-Y**[2].

sister ▶ **noun 1** a woman or girl in relation to other daughters and sons of her parents.
2 a female friend or associate, especially a female fellow member of a trade union or other organization. ■ a fellow woman seen in relation to feminist issues. ■ informal, chiefly N. Amer. a fellow black woman.
3 (often **Sister**) a member of a religious order of women.
4 (often **Sister**) Brit. a senior female nurse, typically in charge of a ward.
5 [as modifier] denoting an organization or place which bears a relationship to another of common origin or allegiance or mutual association: *Securicor and its sister company Securicor Services | a sister ship.*
– DERIVATIVES **sisterliness** noun, **sisterly** adjective.
– ORIGIN Old English, of Germanic origin; related to Dutch *zuster* and German *Schwester*, from an Indo-European root shared by Latin *soror*.

sister city ▶ **noun** a city that is twinned with another.

sister-german ▶ **noun** (pl. **sisters-german**) archaic a sister sharing both parents with another.

sisterhood ▶ **noun 1** [mass noun] the relationship between sisters. ■ the feeling of kinship with and closeness to a group of women or all women.
2 (often **Sisterhood**) an association, society, or community of women linked by a common interest, religion, or trade.

sister-in-law ▶ **noun** (pl. **sisters-in-law**) the sister of one's wife or husband. ■ the wife of one's brother or brother-in-law.

Sister of Mercy ▶ **noun** a member of an order of women founded for educational or charitable purposes, especially that founded in Dublin in 1827.

Sistine /ˈsɪstiːn, -tʌɪn/ ▶ **adjective** relating to any of the popes called Sixtus, especially Sixtus IV.
– ORIGIN from Italian *Sistino*, from *Sisto* 'Sixtus'.

Sistine Chapel a chapel in the Vatican, built in the late 15th century by Pope Sixtus IV, containing a painted ceiling and fresco of the Last Judgement by Michelangelo and also frescoes by Botticelli.

sistrum /ˈsɪstrəm/ ▶ **noun** (pl. **sistra** /-trə/) a musical instrument of ancient Egypt consisting of a metal frame with transverse metal rods which rattled when the instrument was shaken.
– ORIGIN late Middle English: via Latin from Greek *seistron*, from *seiein* 'to shake'.

Siswati /sɪˈswɑːti/ ▶ **noun** another term for **SWAZI** (the language).

Sisyphean /ˌsɪsɪˈfiːən/ ▶ **adjective** denoting a task that can never be completed.
– ORIGIN late 16th cent.: from Latin *Sisypheius* (based on Greek *Sisuphos*: see **SISYPHUS**) + **-AN**.

Sisyphus /ˈsɪsɪfəs/ Greek Mythology the son of Aeolus, punished in Hades for his misdeeds in life by being condemned to the eternal task of rolling a large stone to the top of a hill, from which it always rolled down again.

sit ▶ **verb** (**sits**, **sitting**; past and past participle **sat** /sat/)
1 [no obj.] adopt or be in a position in which one's weight is supported by one's buttocks rather than one's feet and one's back is upright: *you'd better sit down | I sat next to him at dinner.* ■ [with obj.] cause to adopt or be in such a position: *I sat the baby on my lap.* ■ [no obj.] (of an animal) rest with the hind legs bent and the body close to the ground: *it is important for a dog to sit when instructed.* ■ [with obj.] ride or keep one's seat on (a horse). ■ [with obj.] (of a table, room, or building) be large enough for (a specified number of seated people): *the chapel sat about 3,000 people.* ■ (**sit for**) pose, typically in a seated position, for (an artist or photographer): *Walter Deverell asked her to sit for him.* ■ [with obj.] N. Amer. not use (a player) in a game: *the manager must decide who to sit in the World Series.*
2 [no obj., with adverbial of place] be or remain in a particular position or state: *the fridge was sitting in a pool of water.* ■ [with adverbial] (of an item of clothing) fit a person well or badly as specified: *the blue uniform sat well on his big frame.* ■ (**sit with**) be harmonious with: *his shyness doesn't sit easily with Hollywood tradition.*
3 [no obj.] (of a parliament, committee, court of law, etc.) be engaged in its business: *Parliament continued sitting until March 16.* ■ serve as a member of a council, jury, or other official body: *they were determined that women jurists should sit on the tribunal.* ■ (**sit for**) Brit. be the Member of Parliament for (a particular constituency).
4 [with obj.] Brit. take (an examination): *pupils are required to sit nine subjects at GCSE | [no obj.] he was about to sit for his Cambridge entrance exam.*
5 [no obj., in combination] live in someone's house while they are away and look after their pet or pets: *Fenella had been cat-sitting for me.* See also **BABYSIT**.
6 [no obj.] (of a bird) rest on a branch; perch. ■ (of a bird) remain on its nest to incubate its egg: (as adj. **sitting**) *a sitting hen.*
▶ **noun** [in sing.] **1** a period of sitting: *a sit in the shade.*
2 archaic the way in which an item of clothing fits someone: *the sit of her frock.*
– PHRASES **sit at someone's feet** be someone's pupil or follower. **sit in judgement** see **JUDGEMENT**. **sit on the fence** see **FENCE**. **sit on one's arse** vulgar slang do nothing; fail to take action. **sit on one's hands** take no action. **sit (heavy) on the stomach** (of food) take a long time to be digested. **sit on someone's tail** drive extremely close behind another vehicle, typically while waiting for a chance to overtake. **sit tight** informal remain firmly in one's place. ■ refrain from taking action or changing one's mind: *we're*

S

advising our clients to sit tight and neither to buy nor sell. **sit up (and take notice)** informal suddenly start paying attention or have one's interest aroused.
– PHRASAL VERBS **sit back** relax: *sit back and enjoy the music.* ■ take no action; choose not to become involved: *I can't just sit back and let Liz get on with it.* **sit by** take no action in order to prevent something undesirable from occurring: *I'm not going to sit by and let an innocent man go to jail.* **sit down 1** archaic encamp outside a city in order to besiege it: *with a large force he* ***sat down before*** *Ravenna.* **2** Brit. accept or put up with an unwelcome situation or development: *if they think I'm going to* ***sit down under*** *it, they can think again.* **sit in 1** (of a group of people) occupy a place as a form of protest. **2** attend a meeting or discussion without taking an active part in it: *I sat in on a training session for therapists.* **sit in for** temporarily carry out the duties of (another person). **sit on** informal **1** fail to deal with: *she sat on the article until a deadline galvanized her into putting words to paper.* **2** subdue (someone), typically by saying something intended to discomfit or embarrass them. ■ suppress (something): *I want this story sat on.* **sit something out** not take part in a particular event or activity: *he had to sit out Sheffield Wednesday's UEFA Cup game.* ■ wait without moving or taking action until a particular unwelcome situation or process is over: *most of the workers seem to be sitting the crisis out, waiting to see what will happen.* **sit through** stay until the end of (a tedious or lengthy meeting or performance). **sit up** (or **sit someone up**) **1** move (or cause someone to move) from a lying or slouching to a sitting position: *Amy sat up and rubbed her eyes | I'll sit you up on the pillows.* **2** refrain from going to bed until a later time than usual: *we sat up late to watch a horror film.*
– ORIGIN Old English *sittan*, of Germanic origin; related to Dutch *zitten*, German *sitzen*, from an Indo-European root shared by Latin *sedere* and Greek *hezesthai*.

USAGE In sentences such as *we were* ***sat*** *there for hours* the use of the past participle **sat** with the verb 'to be' is informal and not part of standard English. Originally only in dialect, it is now common in British (though not US) English. Standard English uses the present participle **sitting** in similar contexts, as in *we were* ***sitting*** *there for hours.*

Sita /ˈsiːtɑː/ (in the Ramayana) the wife of Rama. She is the Hindu model of the ideal woman, an incarnation of Lakshmi.
– ORIGIN from Sanskrit *Sītā*, literally 'furrow'.

sitar /ˈsɪtɑː, sɪˈtɑː/ ▶ **noun** a large, long-necked Indian lute with movable frets, played with a wire pick.
– DERIVATIVES **sitarist** /sɪˈtɑːrɪst/ **noun**.
– ORIGIN via Urdu from Persian *sitār*, from *sih* 'three' + *tār* 'string'.

sitatunga /ˌsɪtəˈtʌŋgə/ ▶ **noun** a brown or greyish antelope with splayed hoofs and, in the male, spiral horns, inhabiting swampy areas in central and East Africa. ● *Tragelaphus spekii*, family Bovidae.
– ORIGIN late 19th cent.: from Kiswahili.

sitcom ▶ **noun** informal a situation comedy.
– ORIGIN 1960s: abbreviation.

S

sit-down ▶ **adjective** denoting a meal eaten sitting at a table. ■ denoting a protest in which demonstrators occupy their workplace or sit down on the ground in a public place, refusing to leave until their demands are met.
▶ **noun** a period of sitting down; a short rest. ■ a sit-down protest.

site ▶ **noun** an area of ground on which a town, building, or monument is constructed: *the proposed site of a hydroelectric dam | the concrete is mixed* ***on site.*** ■ a place where a particular event or activity is occurring or has occurred: *the site of the Battle of Flodden.* ■ short for **BUILDING SITE**. ■ short for **CAMPSITE** or **CARAVAN SITE**. ■ short for **WEBSITE**.
▶ **verb** [with obj. and adverbial of place] fix or build (something) in a particular place: *the rectory is sited behind the church* | (as noun **siting**) *decisions concerning the siting of nuclear power plants.*
– ORIGIN late Middle English (as a noun): from Anglo-Norman French, or from Latin *situs* 'local position'. The verb dates from the late 16th cent.

USAGE Many people confuse the words **site** and **sight**. As a noun, **site** means 'a place where something is constructed or has occurred' (*the site of the battle; the concrete is mixed on site*), while **sight** chiefly means 'the faculty or power of seeing' (*he lost his sight as a baby*).

sitella ▶ **noun** variant spelling of **SITTELLA**.

sit-in ▶ **noun** a form of protest in which demonstrators occupy a place, refusing to leave until their demands are met.

Sitka /ˈsɪtkə/ (also **Sitka spruce**) ▶ **noun** a fast-growing North American spruce tree, widely cultivated for its strong lightweight timber. ● *Picea sitchensis*, family Pinaceae.
– ORIGIN late 19th cent.: named after *Sitka*, a town in Alaska.

sitkamer /ˈsɪtkamər/ ▶ **noun** South African term for **SITTING ROOM**.
– ORIGIN Afrikaans.

sitrep ▶ **noun** informal a report on the current military situation in a particular area.
– ORIGIN 1940s: from *sit(uation) rep(ort)*.

sits vac ▶ **plural noun** Brit. informal situations vacant (see **SITUATION**).
– ORIGIN 1960s: abbreviation.

Sittang /ˈsɪtaŋ/ a river of southern Burma (Myanmar). Rising in the Pegu mountains, it flows some 560 km (350 miles) south into the Bay of Bengal at the Gulf of Martaban.

sittella /sɪˈtɛlə/ (also **sitella**) ▶ **noun** a small Australasian songbird of the nuthatch family, typically having a black cap or head. ● Genus *Neositta*, family Sittidae: two species, in particular the **varied sittella** (*N. chrysoptera*) of Australia.
– ORIGIN mid 19th cent.: from modern Latin *Sittella* (former genus name), from Greek *sittē* 'nuthatch'.

sitter ▶ **noun 1** a person who sits, especially for a portrait or examination. ■ a sitting hen.
2 [usu. in combination] a person who looks after children, pets, or a house while the parents or owners are away: *a house-sitter.* ■ a person who provides care and companionship for people who are ill.
3 Brit. informal (in sport) an easy catch or shot.

sitting ▶ **noun 1** a continuous period of being seated, especially when engaged in a particular activity: *twenty pieces of music is a bit much to take in at one sitting.* ■ a period of time spent as a model for an artist or photographer.
2 a scheduled period of time when a number of people are served a meal, especially in a restaurant: *there will be two sittings for Christmas lunch.*
3 a period of time during which a committee or parliament is engaged in its normal business. ■ Law, Brit. a period of time when a law court holds sessions: *a special sitting of Basildon magistrates.*
▶ **adjective** [attrib.] **1** in a seated position. ■ (of an animal or bird) not running or flying.
2 (of an MP or other elected representative) current; present: *the resignation of the sitting member.*
3 (of a hen or other bird) settled on eggs for the purpose of incubating them.

Sitting Bull (*c.*1831–90), Sioux chief; Sioux name *Tatanka Iyotake*. As the main chief of the Sioux peoples from about 1867, Sitting Bull led the Sioux in the fight to retain their lands; this resulted in the massacre of General Custer and his men at Little Bighorn.

sitting duck (also **sitting target**) ▶ **noun** informal a person or thing with no protection against an attack or other source of danger.

sitting room ▶ **noun** chiefly Brit. a room in a house in which people can sit down and relax.

sitting tenant ▶ **noun** Brit. a tenant already in occupation of premises, especially when there is a change of owner.

sitting trot ▶ **noun** Riding a style of riding in which a rider remains seated while a horse is trotting, rather than rising from the saddle on alternate strides.

situate ▶ **verb** /ˈsɪtʃʊeɪt, -tjʊ-/ [with obj. and adverbial of place] fix or build (something) in a certain place or position: *the pilot light is usually situated at the front of the boiler* | (as adj., with submodifier **situated**) *a conveniently situated hotel.* ■ put in context; describe the circumstances surrounding (something): *it is necessary to situate these ideas in the wider context of the class structure.* ■ (**be situated**) [with adverbial] be in a specified financial or marital position: *Amy is now comfortably situated.*
▶ **adjective** /ˈsɪtʃʊət, -tjʊət/ Law or archaic situated.
– ORIGIN late Middle English: from medieval Latin *situat-* 'placed', from the verb *situare*, from Latin *situs* 'site'.

situation ▶ **noun 1** a set of circumstances in which one finds oneself; a state of affairs: *the situation between her and Jake had come to a head | the political situation in Russia.*
2 the location and surroundings of a place: *the situation of the town is pleasant.*
3 formal a position of employment; a job.
– PHRASES **situations vacant** (or **wanted**) chiefly Brit. lists of jobs offered (or sought), especially in a newspaper.
– DERIVATIVES **situational adjective**, **situationally adverb**.
– ORIGIN late Middle English (in sense 2): from French, or from medieval Latin *situatio(n-)*, from *situare* 'to place' (see **SITUATE**). Sense 1 dates from the early 18th cent.

situation comedy ▶ **noun** a television or radio series in which the same set of characters are involved in various amusing situations.

situation ethics ▶ **plural noun** [treated as sing.] Philosophy the doctrine of flexibility in the application of moral laws according to circumstances.

situationism ▶ **noun** [mass noun] **1** the theory that human behaviour is determined by surrounding circumstances rather than by personal qualities.
2 a revolutionary political theory which regards modern industrial society as being inevitably oppressive and exploitative.
– DERIVATIVES **situationist noun & adjective**.

sit-up ▶ **noun** a physical exercise designed to strengthen the abdominal muscles, in which a person sits up from a supine position without using the arms for leverage.

sit-up-and-beg ▶ **adjective** Brit. denoting a bicycle with relatively high handlebars ridden in an upright sitting position.

sit-upon ▶ **noun** informal, humorous a person's buttocks.

situs /ˈsʌɪtəs/ ▶ **noun** Law, chiefly US the place to which for purposes of legal jurisdiction or taxation a property belongs.

situs inversus /ˌsʌɪtəs ɪnˈvəːsəs, ˌsiːtəs/ ▶ **noun** [mass noun] Medicine an uncommon condition in which the heart and other organs of the body are transposed through the sagittal plane to lie on the opposite (left or right) side from the usual.
– ORIGIN late 19th cent.: from Latin *situs inversus viscerum* 'inverted placing of the internal organs'.

Sitwell, Dame Edith (Louisa) (1887–1964), English poet and critic. Her early verse, with that of her brothers **Osbert** (1892–1969) and **Sacheverell** (1897–1988), marked a revolt against the prevailing Georgian style of the day. In 1923 she attracted attention with *Façade*, a group of poems in notated rhythm recited to music by William Walton.

sitz bath /sɪts/ ▶ **noun** a bath in which only the buttocks and hips are immersed in water.
– ORIGIN mid 19th cent.: partial translation of German *Sitzbad*, from *sitzen* 'sit' + *Bad* 'bath'.

sitzfleisch /ˈzɪtsflʌɪʃ/ ▶ **noun** [mass noun] informal, chiefly US a person's buttocks. ■ power to endure or to persevere in an activity; stamina.
– ORIGIN from German, from *sitzen* 'sit' + *Fleisch* 'flesh'.

sitzkrieg /ˈzɪtskriːg/ ▶ **noun** a war, or a phase of a war, in which there is little or no active warfare.
– ORIGIN 1940s: suggested by **BLITZKRIEG**, from German *sitzen* 'sit'.

Siva /ˈsiːvə, ˈʃiːvə/ variant spelling of **SHIVA**.
– DERIVATIVES **Sivaism noun**.

Sivaji variant spelling of **SHIVAJI**.

Sivan /ˈsiːvɑːn/ ▶ **noun** (in the Jewish calendar) the ninth month of the civil and third of the religious year, usually coinciding with parts of May and June.
– ORIGIN from Hebrew *sīwān*.

Siwalik Hills /sɪˈwɑːlɪk/ a range of foothills in the southern Himalayas, extending from NE India across Nepal to Sikkim.

Siwash /ˈsʌɪwɒʃ/ ▶ **noun** derogatory **1** an American Indian of the northern Pacific coast.
2 another term for **CHINOOK JARGON**.
▶ **adjective** derogatory relating to American Indians of the northern Pacific coast.
▶ **verb** (**siwash**) [no obj.] N. Amer. informal camp without a tent.
– ORIGIN Chinook Jargon, from Canadian French *sauvage* 'wild'.

Siwash sweater ▶ **noun** Canadian a thick sweater made by Siwash Indians and decorated with symbols from their mythology.

six ▶ **cardinal number** equivalent to the product of two and three; one more than five, or four less than ten; 6: *she's lived here six months | six of the people*

arrested have been charged | *a six-week tour.* (Roman numeral: **vi** or **VI**) ■ a group or unit of six people or things. ■ six years old: *a child of six.* ■ six o'clock: *it's half past six.* ■ Cricket a hit that reaches the boundary without first striking the ground, scoring six runs. Compare with FOUR. ■ a size of garment or other merchandise denoted by six. ■ a playing card or domino with six pips. ■ a group of six Brownies or Cubs. ■ (**the Six**) another name for LES SIX.
– PHRASES **at sixes and sevens** in a state of total confusion or disarray. **knock** (or **hit**) **someone for six** Brit. informal utterly surprise or overcome someone. [with allusion to a forceful hit that scores six runs in cricket.] **six feet under** informal dead and buried. **six of one and half a dozen of the other** used to convey that there is little real difference between two alternatives.
– ORIGIN Old English *siex, six, syx*, of Germanic origin; related to Dutch *zes* and German *sechs*, from an Indo-European root shared by Latin *sex* and Greek *hex*.

Six, Les see LES SIX.

sixain /ˈsɪkseɪn/ ▶ noun a six-line stanza.
– ORIGIN late 16th cent.: from French, from *six* 'six'.

Six Counties the counties of Northern Ireland. Compare with TWENTY-SIX COUNTIES.

Six Day War a war, 5–10 June 1967, in which Israel occupied Sinai, the Old City of Jerusalem, the West Bank, and the Golan Heights and defeated an Egyptian, Jordanian, and Syrian alliance. Arab name JUNE WAR.

sixer ▶ noun **1** the leader of a group of six Brownies or Cubs.
2 Cricket, chiefly Indian a hit for six runs.
3 US a six-pack.

sixfold ▶ adjective six times as great or as numerous: *a sixfold increase in their overheads.* ■ having six parts or elements: *a sixfold plan of action.*
▶ adverb by six times; to six times the number or amount: *coal prices have risen sixfold.*

six-gun ▶ noun another term for SIX-SHOOTER.

Six Nations ▶ plural noun **1** [treated as sing.] an annual international rugby union championship involving England, France, Ireland, Scotland, and Wales. It was known as the Five Nations until Italy joined in 2000.
2 the peoples of the Iroquois confederacy. Compare with FIVE NATIONS (sense 2).

six-pack ▶ noun **1** a pack of six cans of beer held together with a plastic fastener.
2 informal a man's set of visibly well-developed abdominal muscles.

sixpence ▶ noun Brit. a coin worth six old pence ($2\frac{1}{2}$p), withdrawn in 1980. ■ the sum of six pence, especially before decimalization (1971).
– PHRASES **on a sixpence** Brit. informal used to refer to a manoeuvre that can be performed by a moving vehicle or person within a small area or short distance: *the car stops on a sixpence.*

sixpenny ▶ adjective [attrib.] Brit. costing or worth six pence, especially before decimalization (1971).

six-pounder ▶ noun a gun discharging a shot that weighs six pounds.

six-shooter ▶ noun a revolver with six chambers.

sixte /sɪkst/ ▶ noun Fencing the sixth of the eight parrying positions.
– ORIGIN late 19th cent.: French, from Latin *sextus* 'sixth'.

sixteen ▶ cardinal number equivalent to the product of four and four; one more than fifteen, or six more than ten; 16: *sixteen miles east of Dublin* | *sixteen of our eighteen patients.* (Roman numeral: **xvi** or **XVI**) ■ a size of garment or other merchandise denoted by sixteen. ■ sixteen years old: *a daughter of sixteen.*
– DERIVATIVES **sixteenth** ordinal number.
– ORIGIN Old English *siextiene* (see SIX, -TEEN).

sixteenmo ▶ noun (pl. **sixteenmos**) another term for SEXTODECIMO.

sixteenth note ▶ noun Music, N. Amer. a semiquaver.

sixth ▶ ordinal number **1** constituting number six in a sequence; 6th: *her sixth novel* | *the sixth of the month* | *to the original five categories we add a sixth.* ■ the sixth finisher or position in a race or competition: *he could only finish sixth.* ■ chiefly Brit. the sixth form of a school or college. ■ sixthly (used to introduce a sixth point or reason): *sixth, given all the facts there is no logical reason why we can't make a decision.* ■ Music an interval spanning six consecutive notes in a diatonic major or minor scale, e.g. C to A (**major sixth**) or A to F (**minor sixth**). ■ Music the note which is higher by this interval than the tonic of a scale or root of a chord.
2 each of six equal parts into which something is or may be divided: *a sixth of the total population.*
– DERIVATIVES **sixthly** adverb.

sixth form ▶ noun Brit. the two final years at school for students between the ages of 16 and 18 who are preparing for A or AS levels.
– DERIVATIVES **sixth-former** noun.

sixth-form college ▶ noun Brit. a college for pupils in their final years of secondary education, starting at the age of 16.

sixth sense ▶ noun a supposed intuitive faculty giving awareness not explicable in terms of normal perception: *some sixth sense told him he was not alone.*

sixty ▶ cardinal number (pl. **sixties**) the number equivalent to the product of six and ten; ten more than fifty; 60: *a crew of sixty* | *sixty bedrooms* | *sixty per cent of the children.* (Roman numeral: **lx** or **LX**) ■ (**sixties**) the numbers from sixty to sixty-nine, especially the years of a century or of a person's life: *Morris was in his early sixties* | *the flower children of the sixties.* ■ sixty miles an hour: *they were doing sixty.* ■ sixty years old: *he retired at sixty.* ■ a size of garment or other merchandise denoted by sixty.
– DERIVATIVES **sixtieth** ordinal number, **sixtyfold** adjective & adverb.
– ORIGIN Old English *siextig* (see SIX, -TY[2]).

sixty-fourmo ▶ noun (pl. **sixty-fourmos**) a size of book in which each leaf is one sixty-fourth the size of a printing sheet. ■ a book of this size.

sixty-fourth note ▶ noun Music, N. Amer. a hemidemisemiquaver.

sixty-four thousand dollar question ▶ noun informal something that is not known and on which a great deal depends.
– ORIGIN 1940s: originally *sixty-four dollar question*, from a question posed for the top prize in a broadcast quiz show.

sixty-nine ▶ noun another term for SOIXANTE-NEUF.

sizable ▶ adjective variant spelling of SIZEABLE.

sizar /ˈsʌɪzə/ ▶ noun an undergraduate at Cambridge University or at Trinity College, Dublin, receiving financial help from the college and formerly having certain menial duties.
– DERIVATIVES **sizarship** noun.
– ORIGIN late 16th cent.: from obsolete *size* 'ration of bread, beer, etc.' + -AR[2].

size[1] ▶ noun **1** [mass noun] the relative extent of something; a thing's overall dimensions or magnitude; how big something is: *the schools varied in size* | *a forest the size of Wales* | [count noun] *firms of all sizes.* ■ extensive dimensions or magnitude: *she seemed slightly awed by the size of the building.*
2 each of the classes, typically numbered, into which garments or other articles are divided according to how large they are: *I can never find anything in my size.* ■ a person or garment corresponding to such a numbered class: *she's a size 10.*
▶ verb [with obj.] **1** alter or sort in terms of size or according to size: *twist drills are sized in millimetres.*
2 (**size something up**) estimate or measure something's dimensions: *she was trying to size up a room with a tape measure.* ■ (**size someone/thing up**) informal form an estimate or rough judgement of someone or something: *the two men sized each other up.*
▶ adjective [in combination] having a specified size; sized: *marble-size chunks of hail.*
– PHRASES **of a size** (of two or more people or things) having the same dimensions. **of some size** fairly large. **that's about the size of it** informal said to confirm someone's assessment of a situation, especially of one regarded as bad. **to size** to the dimensions wanted: *the PVC sheet is easily cut to size.*
– DERIVATIVES **sized** adjective [usu. in combination] *a pocket-sized computer*, **sizer** noun.
– ORIGIN Middle English (also in the sense 'assize, ordinance fixing a rate of payment'): from Old French *sise*, from *assise* 'ordinance', or a shortening of ASSIZE.

size[2] ▶ noun [mass noun] a gelatinous solution used in glazing paper, stiffening textiles, and preparing plastered walls for decoration.
▶ verb [with obj.] treat with size to glaze or stiffen.
– ORIGIN Middle English: perhaps the same word as SIZE[1].

sizeable (also **sizable**) ▶ adjective fairly large: *a sizeable proportion of the population* | *a sizeable apartment.*
– DERIVATIVES **sizeably** adverb.

sizeism ▶ noun [mass noun] prejudice or discrimination on the grounds of a person's size.
– DERIVATIVES **sizeist** adjective.

Sizewell a village on the Suffolk coast, the site of two nuclear power stations including a pressurized-water reactor.

size zero ▶ noun a very small size of women's clothing, especially a US size equivalent to a UK size 4.

sizzle ▶ verb [no obj.] **1** (of food) make a hissing sound when frying or cooking: *the bacon began to sizzle in the pan.*
2 informal be very hot: *we sizzled in blazing sunshine this week.* ■ be very exciting or passionate: *they simply sizzle as their affair develops.*
▶ noun **1** [in sing.] a hissing sound, as of food frying or cooking: *the sizzle of hot dogs.*
2 [mass noun] informal a state or quality of great excitement or passion: *it would be a waste not to cast him in roles requiring some sexual sizzle.*
– DERIVATIVES **sizzler** noun.
– ORIGIN early 17th cent.: imitative.

sizzling ▶ adjective informal very hot: *the sizzling summer temperatures.* ■ very exciting or passionate: *that was the start of a sizzling affair.*

SJ ▶ abbreviation Society of Jesus.

Sjælland /ˈsjɛlan/ Danish name for ZEALAND.

sjambok /ˈʃambɒk/ ▶ noun (in South Africa) a long, stiff whip, originally made of rhinoceros hide.
▶ verb (**sjamboks, sjambokking, sjambokked**) [with obj.] flog with a sjambok.
– ORIGIN from South African Dutch *tjambok*, via Malay from Urdu *chābuk*.

SJC ▶ abbreviation (in the US) Supreme Judicial Court.

Sjögren's syndrome /ˈʃəːɡrən/ (also **Sjögren's disease**) ▶ noun [mass noun] Medicine a chronic autoimmune condition characterized by degeneration of the salivary and lachrymal glands, causing dryness of the mouth and eyes.
– ORIGIN 1930s: named after Henrik S. C. *Sjögren* (1899–1986), Swedish physician.

SK ▶ abbreviation Saskatchewan (in official postal use).

ska /skɑː/ ▶ noun [mass noun] a style of fast popular music having a strong offbeat and originating in Jamaica in the 1960s, a forerunner of reggae.
– ORIGIN 1960s: of unknown origin.

skaapsteker /ˈskɑːpˌsteɪkə/ ▶ noun S. African a greyish-brown snake of southern Africa, which is venomous but rarely dangerous. ● Genus *Psammophylax*, family Colubridae: two species.
– ORIGIN early 19th cent.: via Afrikaans from Dutch *schaap* 'sheep' + *steker* 'stinger'.

skag (also **scag**) ▶ noun [mass noun] informal, chiefly N. Amer. heroin.
– ORIGIN early 20th cent. (in sense 'cigarette'): of unknown origin.

Skagerrak /ˈskaɡəræk/ a strait separating southern Norway from the NW coast of Denmark.

skald /skɔːld, skald/ (also **scald**) ▶ noun historical (in ancient Scandinavia) a composer and reciter of poems honouring heroes and their deeds.
– DERIVATIVES **skaldic** adjective.
– ORIGIN from Old Norse *skáld*, of unknown origin.

S

Skanda /ˈskandə/ Hinduism the Hindu war god, first son of Shiva and Parvati and brother of Ganesha. He is depicted as a boy or youth, sometimes with six heads and often with his mount, a peacock.

skank /skaŋk/ ▶ noun **1** a steady-paced dance performed to reggae music, characterized by rhythmically bending forward, raising the knees, and extending the hands palms-downwards. ■ [mass noun] reggae music suitable for such dancing.
2 N. Amer. informal a sleazy or unpleasant person. ■ derogatory a promiscuous woman: *the office skank.*
▶ verb **1** [no obj.] (often as adj. **skanking**) play reggae music or dance in this style. ■ informal walk or move in a sexually suggestive way.
2 [with obj.] informal swindle or deceive: *they made a tidy sum skanking the tourists.* ■ obtain by deception or theft: *I skanked the poster off some wall.*
– ORIGIN 1970s: of unknown origin.

skanky ▶ adjective (**skankier, skankiest**) informal, chiefly N. Amer. (esp. of a person) dirty and unpleasant: *the skanky folk who populate LA's film scene.*

Skara Brae /ˌskɑːrə ˈbreɪ, ˌskarə/ a late Neolithic (3rd millennium BC) settlement on Mainland in the Orkney Islands.

skarn /skɑːn/ ▶ **noun** [mass noun] Geology lime-bearing siliceous rock produced by the metamorphic alteration of limestone or dolomite.
– ORIGIN early 20th cent.: from Swedish, literally 'dung, filth'.

skat ▶ **noun** [mass noun] a three-handed trick-taking card game with bidding, originating in Germany.
– ORIGIN mid 19th cent.: from German, from Italian *scarto* 'a discard', from *scartare* 'discard'.

skate[1] ▶ **noun** an ice skate or roller skate. ■ short for SKATEBOARD. ■ a device, typically with wheels on the underside, used to move a heavy or unwieldy object.
▶ **verb** [no obj.] **1** move on ice skates or roller skates in a gliding fashion: *the boys were skating on the ice.* ■ [with obj.] perform (a specified figure) on skates: *double-eight figures skated entirely on one foot.* ■ ride on a skateboard.
2 (**skate over/round/around**) pass over or refer only fleetingly to (a subject or problem): *she seemed to skate over the next part of her story.*
3 (**skate through**) make quick and easy progress through: *he admits he had expected to skate through the system.*
– PHRASES **get one's skates on** Brit. informal hurry up.
– DERIVATIVES **skater** noun.
– ORIGIN mid 17th cent. (originally as the plural *scates*): from Dutch *schaats* (singular but interpreted as plural), from Old French *eschasse* 'stilt'.

skate[2] ▶ **noun** (pl. **same** or **skates**) a typically large marine fish of the ray family with a cartilaginous skeleton and a flattened diamond-shaped body.
● Family Rajidae: numerous species, in particular the commercially valuable *Raja batis.*
■ [mass noun] the flesh of a skate or thornback used as food.
– ORIGIN Middle English: from Old Norse *skata*.

skate[3] ▶ **noun** informal, dated or S. African an uncouth and disreputable man.
– ORIGIN late 19th cent.: of uncertain origin.

skateboard ▶ **noun** a short narrow board with two small wheels fixed to the bottom of either end, on which a person can ride in a standing or crouching position, propelling themselves by occasionally pushing one foot against the ground.
▶ **verb** [no obj.] (often as noun **skateboarding**) ride on a skateboard.
– DERIVATIVES **skateboarder** noun.

skatepark ▶ **noun** an area designated and equipped for skateboarding.

skating ▶ **noun** [mass noun] the action or activity of skating on ice skates, roller skates, or a skateboard as a sport or pastime.

skating rink ▶ **noun** an expanse of ice artificially made for skating, or a floor used for roller skating.

skean /skiːn, 'skiːən/ ▶ **noun** a dagger formerly used in Ireland and Scotland.
– ORIGIN late Middle English: from Irish and Scottish Gaelic *sgian* 'knife'.

skean dhu /'duː/ ▶ **noun** a dagger worn in the stocking as part of Highland dress.
– ORIGIN early 19th cent.: from SKEAN + Scottish Gaelic *dubh* 'black'.

S

skebenga /skə'bɛŋgə/ ▶ **noun** S. African a gangster; a bandit.
– ORIGIN from Zulu *isigebengu* 'bandit, plunderer'.

sked informal, chiefly N. Amer. ▶ **noun** short for SCHEDULE.
▶ **verb** (**skeds, skedding, skedded**) short for SCHEDULE.

skedaddle /skɪ'dad(ə)l/ ▶ **verb** [no obj.] informal depart quickly or hurriedly; run away.
– ORIGIN mid 19th cent.: of unknown origin.

skedonk /skə'dɒŋk/ ▶ **noun** S. African informal an old, battered car.
– ORIGIN of unknown origin.

skeet (also **skeet shooting**) ▶ **noun** [mass noun] N. Amer. a shooting sport in which a clay target is thrown from a trap to simulate the flight of a bird.
– ORIGIN 1920s: apparently a pseudo-archaic alteration of the verb SHOOT.

skeeter[1] ▶ **noun** informal, chiefly N. Amer. & Austral. a mosquito.
– ORIGIN mid 19th cent.: shortened form, representing a casual pronunciation.

skeeter[2] ▶ **verb** variant spelling of SKITTER.

skeevy /'skiːvi/ ▶ **adjective** US informal unpleasant, squalid, or distasteful: *a skeevy Vegas motel.*
– ORIGIN 1970s: from Italian *schifo* 'repugnance, disgust'.

skeg ▶ **noun** a tapering or projecting after section of a vessel's keel. ■ a fin underneath the rear of a surfboard.
– ORIGIN early 17th cent.: from Old Norse *skegg* 'beard', perhaps from Dutch *scheg.*

skein /skeɪn/ ▶ **noun 1** a length of thread or yarn, loosely coiled and knotted. ■ an element that forms part of a complex or complicated whole: *he weaves together the skeins of philosophy, ecology, folklore, and history.*
2 a flock of wild geese or swans in flight, typically in a V-shaped formation.
– ORIGIN Middle English: shortening of Old French *escaigne*, of unknown origin.

skeletal /'skɛlɪt(ə)l, skə'liːt(ə)l/ ▶ **adjective 1** relating to or functioning as a skeleton: *the skeletal remains of aquatic organisms.* ■ very thin; emaciated: *a small, skeletal boy clothed in rags.*
2 existing only in outline or as a framework of something: *a skeletal plot for a novel.*
– DERIVATIVES **skeletally** adverb.

skeletal muscle ▶ **noun** a muscle which is connected to the skeleton to form part of the mechanical system which moves the limbs and other parts of the body. ■ another term for STRIATED MUSCLE.

skeleton ▶ **noun 1** an internal or external framework of bone, cartilage, or other rigid material supporting or containing the body of an animal or plant. ■ used in reference to a very thin or emaciated person or animal: *she was no more than a skeleton at the end.* ■ the remaining part of something after its life or usefulness is gone: *the chapel was stripped to a skeleton of its former self.*
2 the supporting framework, basic structure, or essential part of something: *the concrete skeleton of an unfinished building | the skeleton of a report.* ■ [as modifier] denoting the essential or minimum number of people, things, or parts necessary for something: *there was only a skeleton staff on duty.*
– PHRASES **skeleton in the cupboard** (N. Amer. **skeleton in the closet**) a discreditable or embarrassing fact that someone wishes to keep secret.
– DERIVATIVES **skeletonize** (also **skeletonise**) verb.
– ORIGIN late 16th cent.: modern Latin, from Greek, neuter of *skeletos* 'dried up', from *skellein* 'dry up'.

Skeleton Coast an arid coastal area in Namibia. Comprising the northern part of the Namib desert, it extends from Walvis Bay in the south to the border with Angola.

skeleton key ▶ **noun** a key designed to fit many locks by having the interior of the bit hollowed.

skelf /skɛlf/ ▶ **noun** Scottish **1** a splinter or sliver of wood.
2 informal a troublesome or annoying person.
– ORIGIN late Middle English (in the sense 'shelf'): probably from Middle Low German *schelf*; compare with SHELF[1]. Sense 1 dates from the early 17th cent.

skell ▶ **noun** US informal (in New York) a tramp or homeless person.
– ORIGIN 1950s: perhaps a shortening of SKELETON.

skelly[1] /'skɛli/ ▶ **adjective** Scottish cross-eyed.
– ORIGIN late 18th cent.: based on Old Norse *skjálgr* 'wry, oblique'.

skelly[2] ▶ **noun** variant spelling of SCHELLY.

skelm /'skɛl(ə)m/ S. African ▶ **noun** a scoundrel.
▶ **adjective** (of a person) sly; wicked.
– ORIGIN early 17th cent.: from Dutch *schelm*, from German.

skelp /skɛlp/ ▶ **verb** [with obj.] Scottish & N. English strike, slap, or smack.
– ORIGIN late Middle English: probably imitative.

Skelton, John (*c.*1460–1529), English poet. Court poet to Henry VIII, he wrote verse consisting of short irregular rhyming lines with rhythms based on colloquial speech.

skene /'skiːni/ ▶ **noun** (in ancient Greek theatre) a three-dimensional structure which formed part of the stage or set.
– ORIGIN from Greek *skēnē* 'hut, tent'.

skep (also **skip**) ▶ **noun** a straw or wicker beehive. ■ archaic a wooden or wicker basket.
– ORIGIN late Old English *sceppe* 'basket', from Old Norse *skeppa* 'basket, bushel'.

skeptic ▶ **noun** US spelling of SCEPTIC.

skeptical ▶ **adjective** US spelling of SCEPTICAL.

skerm /'skɛr(ə)m/ ▶ **noun** (in southern Africa) a temporary dwelling for nomads or travellers. ■ a screen or hide for hunters or game watchers.
– ORIGIN Afrikaans.

skerrick /'skɛrɪk/ ▶ **noun** [usu. with negative] Austral./NZ informal the smallest bit: *there's not a skerrick of food in the house.*
– ORIGIN early 19th cent.: of unknown origin. The word is also recorded as an English slang term meaning 'halfpenny'.

skerry /'skɛri/ ▶ **noun** (pl. **skerries**) Scottish a reef or rocky island.
– ORIGIN early 17th cent.: Orkney dialect, from Old Norse *sker*.

sketch ▶ **noun 1** a rough or unfinished drawing or painting, often made to assist in making a more finished picture: *a charcoal sketch.* ■ a brief written or spoken account or description, giving only basic details: *a biographical sketch of Ernest Hemingway.* ■ a rough or unfinished version of any creative work.
2 a short humorous play or performance, consisting typically of one scene in a revue or comedy programme.
3 informal, dated a comical or amusing person or thing.
▶ **verb** [with obj.] make a rough drawing of: *as they talked, Modigliani began to sketch her* | [no obj.] *Jeanne sketched and painted whenever she had the time.* ■ (**sketch something out/in**) give a brief account or general outline of something: *they sketched out the prosecution case.* ■ perform (a gesture) with one's hands or body: *he sketched a graceful bow in her direction.*
– DERIVATIVES **sketcher** noun.
– ORIGIN mid 17th cent.: from Dutch *schets* or German *Skizze*, from Italian *schizzo*, from *schizzare* 'make a sketch', based on Greek *skhedios* 'done extempore'.

sketchbook (also **sketch pad**) ▶ **noun** a pad of drawing paper for sketching on.

sketch map ▶ **noun** a roughly drawn map that shows only basic details.

sketchy ▶ **adjective** (**sketchier, sketchiest**) not thorough or detailed: *the information they had was sketchy.* ■ (of a picture) resembling a sketch; consisting of outline without much detail.
– DERIVATIVES **sketchily** adverb, **sketchiness** noun.

skeuomorph /'skjuːə(ʊ)mɔːf/ ▶ **noun** an object or feature which imitates the design of a similar artefact in another material.
– ORIGIN late 19th cent.: from Greek *skeuos* 'container, implement' + *morphē* 'form'.

skew ▶ **adjective 1** neither parallel nor at right angles to a specified or implied line; askew; crooked: *his hat looked slightly skew | a skew angle.*
2 Mathematics (of a pair of lines) neither parallel nor intersecting. ■ (of a curve) not lying in a plane.
3 Statistics (of a statistical distribution) not symmetrical.
▶ **noun 1** an oblique angle; a slant.
2 a bias towards one particular group or subject: *the paper had a working-class skew.*
3 [mass noun] Statistics the state of not being symmetrical.
▶ **verb 1** [no obj., with adverbial] suddenly change direction or position: *the car had skewed across the track.* ■ twist or turn or cause to do this: *he skewed around in his saddle* | [with obj.] *his leg was skewed in and pushed against the other one.*
2 [with obj.] make biased or distorted in a way that is regarded as inaccurate, unfair, or misleading: *the curriculum is skewed towards the practical subjects.*
3 [with obj.] Statistics cause (a distribution) to be asymmetrical.
– PHRASES **on the skew** neither parallel nor at right angles to a specified or implied line; askew.
– DERIVATIVES **skewness** noun.
– ORIGIN late Middle English (as a verb in the sense 'move obliquely'): shortening of Old Northern French *eskiuwer*, variant of Old French *eschiver* 'eschew'. The adjective and noun (early 17th cent.) are from the verb.

skew arch (also **skew bridge**) ▶ **noun** an arch (or bridge) with the line of the arch not at right angles to the abutment.

skewback ▶ **noun** the sloping face of the abutment on which an extremity of an arch rests.

skewbald ▶ **adjective** (of an animal) having irregular patches of white and another colour (properly not black). Compare with PIEBALD.
▶ **noun** a skewbald animal, especially a horse.
– ORIGIN mid 17th cent.: from obsolete *skewed* 'skewbald' (of uncertain origin), on the pattern of *piebald.*

skewer ▶ **noun** a long piece of wood or metal used for holding pieces of food, typically meat, together during cooking.
▶ **verb** [with obj.] fasten together or pierce with a pin or skewer: (as adj. **skewered**) *skewered meat and fish.*

■ informal subject to sharp criticism or critical analysis: *politicians are used to being skewered.*
– ORIGIN late Middle English: of unknown origin.

skew gear ▶ **noun** a gear consisting of two cogwheels having non-parallel, non-intersecting axes.

skew-symmetric ▶ **adjective** Mathematics (of a matrix) having all the elements of the principal diagonal equal to zero, and each of the remaining elements equal to the negative of the element in the corresponding position on the other side of the diagonal.

skew-whiff ▶ **adverb & adjective** Brit. informal not straight; askew: [as adv.] *he knocked my wig skew-whiff.*

ski ▶ **noun** (pl. **skis**) each of a pair of long, narrow pieces of hard, flexible material, typically pointed and turned up at the front, fastened under the feet for travelling over snow. ■ a similar device fitted to the underside of a vehicle or aircraft to enable it to travel or land on snow or ice. ■ [as modifier] relating to or used for skiing: *a ski instructor | ski boots.* ■ another term for **WATERSKI**.
▶ **verb** (**skis, skiing, skied**) [no obj.] travel over snow on skis; take part in the sport or recreation of skiing: *they skied down the mountain.* ■ [with obj.] ski on (a particular ski run or type of snow): *off-piste spring snow is easy to ski.*
– DERIVATIVES **skiable** adjective.
– ORIGIN mid 18th cent.: from Norwegian, from Old Norse *skíth* 'billet, snowshoe'.

skiagraphy /skʌɪˈagrəfi/ ▶ **noun** variant spelling of **SCIAGRAPHY**.

Skiathos /skiːˈaθɒs/ a Greek island in the Aegean Sea, the most westerly of the Northern Sporades group, Greek name **Skíathos** /ˈskiaθɔs/.

ski binding ▶ **noun** see **BINDING** (sense 3 of the noun).

ski boat ▶ **noun 1** a small powerboat used for towing waterskiers.
2 S. African a boat with an outboard motor, designed for offshore angling.

ski-bob ▶ **noun** a device resembling a bicycle with skis instead of wheels, used for sliding down snow-covered slopes.
▶ **verb** [no obj.] ride a ski-bob.

skid ▶ **verb** (**skids, skidding, skidded**) **1** [no obj.] (of a vehicle) slide, typically sideways or obliquely, on slippery ground or as a result of stopping or turning too quickly: *her car skidded and hit the grass verge | the taxi cab skidded to a halt.* ■ slip; slide: *Barbara's foot skidded and she fell to the floor.* ■ [with obj.] cause to skid: *he skidded his car.* ■ [with obj.] N. Amer. move a heavy object on skids: *they skidded the logs down the hill to the waterfront.*
2 [with obj.] fasten a skid to (a wheel) as a brake.
▶ **noun 1** an act of skidding or sliding: *the Volvo went into a skid.*
2 a runner attached to the underside of an aircraft for use when landing on snow or grass. ■ N. Amer. each of a set of wooden rollers used for moving a log or other heavy object.
3 a braking device consisting of a wooden or metal shoe preventing a wheel from revolving.
4 a beam or plank of wood used to support a ship under construction or repair.
– PHRASES **hit the skids** informal begin a rapid decline or deterioration. **on the skids** informal (of a person or their career) in a bad state; failing. **put the skids under** informal hasten the decline or failure of.
– DERIVATIVES **skiddy** adjective.
– ORIGIN late 17th cent. (as a noun in the sense 'supporting beam'): perhaps related to Old Norse *skíth* (see **SKI**).

skid lid ▶ **noun** Brit. informal a crash helmet.

Skidoo /skɪˈduː/ (also **skidoo**) trademark, chiefly N. Amer. ▶ **noun** a motorized toboggan.
▶ **verb** (**skidoos, skidooing, skidooed**) [no obj.] (usu. as noun **skidooing**) ride on a Skidoo.
– ORIGIN 1960s: an arbitrary formation from **SKI**.

skidoo /skɪˈduː/ (also **skiddoo**) ▶ **verb** (**skidoos, skidooing, skidooed**) [no obj.] N. Amer. informal, dated leave somewhere quickly.
– PHRASES **twenty-three skidoo** a hasty departure.
– ORIGIN early 20th cent.: perhaps from **SKEDADDLE**. The term is said to have been used originally in reference to male onlookers chased by police from the Flatiron Building, 23rd Street, New York, where the skirts of female passers-by were raised by winds intensified by the building's design.

skidpan (N. Amer. **skidpad**) ▶ **noun** a slippery road surface prepared for drivers to practise control of skidding.

skid road ▶ **noun** N. Amer. **1** a road formed of skids along which logs were hauled. ■ historical a part of a town frequented by loggers.
2 another term for **SKID ROW**.

skid row ▶ **noun** informal, chiefly N. Amer. a run-down part of a town frequented by vagrants and alcoholics. ■ a desperately unfortunate or difficult situation: *with no money to spend, the club are on skid row.*
– ORIGIN 1930s: alteration of **SKID ROAD**.

skidsteer loader ▶ **noun** a small highly manoeuvrable farm vehicle with a large bucket or fork at the front end.

skier[1] ▶ **noun** a person who skis.

skier[2] ▶ **noun** variant spelling of **SKYER**.

skiff ▶ **noun** a light rowing boat or sculling boat, typically for one person.
– ORIGIN late 15th cent.: from French *esquif*, from Italian *schifo*, of Germanic origin; related to **SHIP**.

skiffle ▶ **noun** [mass noun] **1** Brit. a kind of folk music with a blues or jazz flavour that was popular in the 1950s, played by a small group and often incorporating improvised instruments such as washboards.
2 US a style of 1920s and 1930s jazz deriving from blues, ragtime, and folk music, using both improvised and conventional instruments.
– ORIGIN 1920s: perhaps imitative.

ski-flying ▶ **noun** [mass noun] a form of ski jumping from a higher slope so that the skier jumps further.

skiing ▶ **noun** [mass noun] the action of travelling over snow on skis, especially as a sport or recreation. Competitive skiing falls into two categories: **Nordic** (cross-country racing and jumping) and **Alpine** (downhill or straight racing, and slalom racing round a series of markers).

skijoring /ˈskiːdʒɔːrɪŋ, -ˈdʒɔː-/ ▶ **noun** [mass noun] the action of being pulled over snow or ice on skis by a horse or dog, as a sport or recreation activity.
– ORIGIN 1920s: from Norwegian *skikjøring*, from *ski* 'ski' + *kjøre* 'to drive'.

ski jump ▶ **noun** a steep slope levelling off before a sharp drop to allow a skier to leap through the air. ■ a leap made from a ski jump.
– DERIVATIVES **ski jumper** noun, **ski jumping** noun.

skilfish ▶ **noun** (pl. **same** or **skilfishes**) a large fish of the North Pacific which is an important food fish in Japan. ● *Erilepis zonifer*, family Anoplopomatidae.
– ORIGIN late 19th cent.: from Haida *sqil*.

skilful (also chiefly N. Amer. **skillful**) ▶ **adjective** having or showing skill: *a skilful midfielder.*
– DERIVATIVES **skilfully** adverb, **skilfulness** noun.

ski lift ▶ **noun** a system used to transport skiers up a slope to the top of a run, typically consisting of moving seats attached to an overhead cable.

skill ▶ **noun** [mass noun] the ability to do something well; expertise: *difficult work, taking great skill.* ■ [count noun] a particular ability: *the skills of cookery.*
▶ **verb** [with obj.] (usu. as noun **skilling**) train (a worker) to do a particular task.
– DERIVATIVES **skilless** adjective (archaic).
– ORIGIN late Old English *scele* 'knowledge', from Old Norse *skil* 'discernment, knowledge'.

skilled ▶ **adjective** having or showing the knowledge, ability, or training to perform a certain activity or task well: *a lab technician skilled in electronics | skilled draughtsmen.* ■ based on such training or experience; showing expertise: *skilled legal advice.* ■ (of work) requiring special abilities or training: *a highly skilled job.*

skillet ▶ **noun 1** Brit. historical a small metal cooking pot with a long handle, typically having legs.
2 N. Amer. a frying pan.
– ORIGIN Middle English: perhaps from Old French *escuelete*, diminutive of *escuele* 'platter', from late Latin *scutella*.

skillful ▶ **adjective** chiefly N. Amer. variant spelling of **SKILFUL**.

skill set ▶ **noun** a person's range of skills or abilities.

skilly ▶ **noun** [mass noun] Brit., chiefly historical thin broth, typically made from oatmeal and water and flavoured with meat.
– ORIGIN mid 19th cent.: abbreviation of archaic *skilligalee*, a fanciful formation.

skim ▶ **verb** (**skims, skimming, skimmed**) **1** [with obj.] remove (a substance) from the surface of a liquid: *as the scum rises, skim it off.* ■ remove a substance from the surface of (a liquid): *bring the stock to the boil, then skim it to remove any foam.* ■ informal steal or embezzle (money), especially in small amounts over a period of time: *she was skimming money from the household kitty.* ■ (often as noun **skimming**) fraudulently copy (credit or debit card details) with a card swipe or other device.
2 [no obj., with adverbial of direction] go or move quickly and lightly over or on a surface or through the air: *he let his fingers skim across her shoulders.* ■ [with obj.] pass over (a surface), nearly or lightly touching it in the process: *we stood on the bridge, watching swallows skimming the water.* ■ [with obj.] throw (a flat stone) low over an expanse of water so that it bounces on the surface several times.
3 [with obj.] read (something) quickly so as to note only the important points: *he skimmed the report* | [no obj.] *she skimmed through the newspaper.* ■ (**skim over**) deal with or treat (a subject) briefly or superficially.
▶ **noun 1** a thin layer of a substance on the surface of a liquid: ***a skim of*** *ice.*
2 an act of reading something quickly or superficially: *a quick skim through the pamphlet.*
– ORIGIN Middle English (in the sense 'remove scum from (a liquid)'): back-formation from **SKIMMER**, or from Old French *escumer*, from *escume* 'scum, foam'.

ski mask ▶ **noun** a protective covering for the head and face, with holes for the eyes, nose, and mouth.

skimboard ▶ **noun** a type of surfboard, typically round or short, used for riding shallow water.
– DERIVATIVES **skimboarder** noun, **skimboarding** noun.

skimmed milk (N. Amer. also **skim milk**) ▶ **noun** [mass noun] milk from which the cream has been removed.

skimmel /ˈskɪm(ə)l/ (also **schimmel** /ˈʃɪm(ə)l/) ▶ **noun** S. African a roan or dapple-grey horse.
– ORIGIN mid 19th cent.: Afrikaans, from Dutch *schimmel* 'mildew, mottled, grey horse'.

skimmer ▶ **noun 1** a person or thing that skims. ■ a utensil or device for removing a substance from the surface of a liquid.
2 a hydroplane, hydrofoil, hovercraft, or other vessel that has little or no displacement at speed.
3 informal a close-fitting dress.
4 chiefly N. Amer. a flat, broad-brimmed straw hat.
5 a long-winged seabird related to the terns, feeding by flying low over the water surface with its knife-like extended lower mandible immersed. ● Genus *Rynchops*, family Rynchopidae (or Laridae): three species, one each in Africa, Asia, and America.
6 North American term for **DARTER** (sense 3).
– ORIGIN Middle English: from Old French *escumoir*, from *escumer* 'skim', from *escume* 'scum'.

skimmia /ˈskɪmɪə/ ▶ **noun** an evergreen East Asian shrub with creamy-white flowers and red berries. ● Genus *Skimmia*, family Rutaceae.
– ORIGIN modern Latin, from Japanese.

skimmington ▶ **noun** historical a procession made through a village intended to bring ridicule on and make an example of a nagging wife or an unfaithful husband.
– PHRASES **ride skimmington** hold such a procession.
– ORIGIN early 17th cent.: perhaps from *skimming ladle*, used as a thrashing instrument during the procession.

skimobile /ˈskiːməbiːl/ ▶ **noun** N. Amer. a motor vehicle for travelling over snow, with caterpillar tracks at the back and steerable skis in front.

S

skimp ▶ **verb** [no obj.] expend or use less time, money, or material on something than is necessary in an attempt to economize: ***don't skimp on*** *insurance when you book your holidays.*
▶ **noun** informal a fashionably short or revealing garment.
– ORIGIN late 18th cent.: of unknown origin; compare with **SCAMP**[2] and **SCRIMP**.

skimpy ▶ **adjective** (**skimpier, skimpiest**) **1** (of clothes) short and revealing: *a skimpy dress.*
2 providing or consisting of less than is needed; meagre: *my knowledge of music is extremely skimpy.*
– DERIVATIVES **skimpily** adverb, **skimpiness** noun.

skin ▶ **noun 1** the thin layer of tissue forming the natural outer covering of the body of a person or animal: *I use body lotion to keep my skin supple* | [mass noun] *a flap of skin.* ■ the skin of a dead animal with or without the fur, used as material for clothing or other items: [mass noun] *is this real crocodile skin?* ■ a container made from the skin of an animal such as a goat, used for holding liquids.
2 an outer layer or covering, in particular: ■ the peel or outer layer of certain fruits or vegetables. ■ the thin outer covering of a sausage. ■ a thin layer forming on the surface of certain hot liquids, such as milk, as they cool. ■ informal a cigarette paper. ■ the

outermost layer of a structure such as a building or aircraft. ■ (usu. **skins**) a strip of sealskin or other material attached to the underside of a ski to prevent a skier slipping backwards during climbing.
3 Brit. informal a skinhead.
4 (usu. **skins**) informal (especially in jazz) a drum or drum head.
5 [as modifier] informal relating to or denoting pornographic literature or films: *the skin trade*.
6 [mass noun] US a card game in which each player has one card which they bet will not be the first to be matched by a card dealt from the pack.
7 Computing a customized graphic user interface for an application or operating system.
▶ **verb** (**skins, skinning, skinned**) [with obj.] **1** remove the skin from (an animal or a fruit or vegetable).
2 graze (a part of one's body): *he scrambled down from the tree with such haste that he skinned his knees*.
3 [no obj.] (of a wound) form new skin: *the hole in his skull **skinned over***. ■ [with obj.] archaic cover with skin: *the wound was skinned, but the strength of his thigh was not restored*.
4 informal take money from or swindle (someone).
5 Soccer, informal (of a player) take the ball past (a defender) with ease.
6 [no obj.] (**skin up**) Brit. informal make a cannabis cigarette.
– PHRASES **be skin and bone** (of a person or animal) be very thin. **by the skin of one's teeth** by a very narrow margin; only just: *I only got away by the skin of my teeth*. [from a misquotation of Job 19:20: 'I am escaped with the skin of my teeth' (i.e. and nothing else).] **get under someone's skin** informal **1** annoy or irritate someone intensely: *it was the sheer effrontery of them which got under my skin*. **2** fill someone's mind in a compelling and persistent way. **3** reach or display a deep understanding of someone: *movies that get under the skin of the British national character*. **give someone (some) skin** US black slang shake or slap hands together as a gesture or friendship or solidarity. **have skin in the game** US informal have a personal investment in an organization or undertaking, and therefore a vested interest in its success. **have a thick** (or **thin**) **skin** be insensitive (or oversensitive) to criticism or insults. **it's no skin off my nose** (or US **off my back**) informal used to indicate that one is not offended or adversely affected by something: *'I've not much appetite, I'm afraid.' 'No skin off my nose.'* **keep** (or **sleep in**) **a whole skin** archaic escape being wounded or injured. **skin and blister** Brit. rhyming slang one's sister. **skin (one's) teeth** W. Indian laugh or smile. **there's more than one way to skin a cat** proverb there's more than one way of achieving one's aim. **under the skin** in reality, as opposed to superficial appearances: *he still believes that all women are goddesses under the skin*.
– DERIVATIVES **skinless** adjective, **skin-like** adjective.
– ORIGIN late Old English *scinn*, from Old Norse *skinn*; related to Dutch *schinden* 'flay, peel' and German *schinden*.

skin beetle ▶ **noun** chiefly N. Amer. a beetle that feeds on carrion, hide, or similar material, and is sometimes a serious pest of stored goods. ● Several species in the families Dermestidae and Trogidae.

skincare ▶ **noun** [mass noun] the use of cosmetics to care for the skin: [as modifier] *skincare products*.

skin-deep ▶ **adjective** not deep or lasting; superficial: *their left-wing attitudes were only skin-deep*.

skinder /ˈskənə, ˈskɪnə/ (also **skinner**) S. African informal ▶ **noun** [mass noun] gossip: *we can catch up on the skinder*.
▶ **verb** [no obj.] engage in gossip.
– ORIGIN from Afrikaans *skinder* 'to slander, gossip'.

skin diving ▶ **noun** [mass noun] the action or sport of swimming under water without a diving suit, typically in deep water using an aqualung and flippers.
– DERIVATIVES **skin-dive** verb, **skin-diver** noun.

skin effect ▶ **noun** Physics the tendency of a high-frequency alternating current to flow through only the outer layer of a conductor.

skin flick ▶ **noun** informal, chiefly Brit. a pornographic film.

skinflint ▶ **noun** informal a person who spends as little money as possible; a miser.

skinfold ▶ **noun** a fold of skin and underlying fat formed by pinching, the thickness of which is a measure of nutritional status.

skin friction ▶ **noun** [mass noun] Physics friction at the surface of a solid and a fluid in relative motion.

skinful ▶ **noun** Brit. informal enough alcoholic drink to make one drunk: *he **had a skinful** on New Year's Eve*.

skin game ▶ **noun** N. Amer. informal a rigged gambling game; a swindle.

skin graft ▶ **noun** a surgical operation in which a piece of healthy skin is transplanted to a new site or to a different individual. ■ a piece of skin transferred in this way.

skinhead ▶ **noun** a young man of a subculture characterized by close-cropped hair and heavy boots, often perceived as aggressive, violent, and racist.

skink ▶ **noun** a smooth-bodied lizard with short or absent limbs, typically burrowing in sandy ground, and occurring throughout tropical and temperate regions. ● Family Scincidae: numerous genera and species.
– ORIGIN late 16th cent.: from French *scinc* or Latin *scincus*, from Greek *skinkos*.

skinned ▶ **adjective** [in combination] having a skin of a specified type: *a fair-skinned woman*.

Skinner, Burrhus Frederic (1904–90), American behaviourist psychologist. He promoted the view that the proper aim of psychology should be to predict behaviour, and hence be able to control it.

skinner ▶ **noun 1** a person who skins animals or prepares skins. ■ a person who deals in animal skins; a furrier.
2 Horse Racing, Austral./NZ informal a horse that wins a race at very long odds. ■ a result that is very profitable to bookmakers.
3 variant spelling of SKINDER.

Skinner box ▶ **noun** Psychology an apparatus for studying instrumental conditioning in animals (typically rats or pigeons) in which the animal is isolated and provided with a lever or switch which it learns to use to obtain a reward, such as a food pellet, or to avoid a punishment, such as an electric shock.

skinny ▶ **adjective** (**skinnier, skinniest**) **1** (of a person or part of their body) unattractively thin: *his skinny arms*.
2 (of a garment) tight-fitting: *a skinny jumper*.
3 informal (of coffee) made with skimmed or semi-skimmed milk: *one skinny latte to go, please*.
▶ **noun** informal **1** (pl. **skinnies**) a skinny person.
2 (**the skinny**) US confidential information on a particular person or topic: *net managers who want the skinny on the latest in computer security*.
– DERIVATIVES **skinniness** noun.

skinny-dip ▶ **verb** [no obj.] informal swim naked.
▶ **noun** a naked swim.
– DERIVATIVES **skinny-dipper** noun.

skinnymalinks /ˈskɪnɪməlɪŋks/ (also **skinny-malink**) ▶ **noun** Scottish a very thin person.
– ORIGIN late 19th cent.: origin uncertain; a Scottish children's song related the adventures of a thin man known as 'Skinamalinky Long Leg'.

skinny-rib ▶ **noun** a tightly fitting sweater or cardigan.

skin-pop informal, chiefly N. Amer. ▶ **verb** [with obj.] inject (a drug, typically a narcotic) subcutaneously.
▶ **noun** a subcutaneous injection of a drug, typically a narcotic.

skins game ▶ **noun** N. Amer. a form of a sport, especially golf, in which the winner of each hole or similar stage is awarded a 'skin' or financial prize, the value of which increases as the game progresses.

skint ▶ **adjective** Brit. informal (of a person) having little or no money available: *I'm a bit skint just now*.
– ORIGIN 1920s: variant of colloquial *skinned*, in the same sense, past participle of SKIN.

skin test ▶ **noun** a test to determine whether an immune reaction is elicited when a substance is applied to or injected into the skin.
▶ **verb** (**skin-test**) [with obj.] (usu. as noun **skin-testing**) perform such a test on (someone).

skintight ▶ **adjective** (of a garment) very close-fitting.

skip[1] ▶ **verb** (**skips, skipping, skipped**) **1** [no obj., with adverbial of direction] move along lightly, stepping from one foot to the other with a hop or bounce: *she began to skip down the path*.
2 [no obj.] Brit. jump over a rope which is held at both ends by oneself or two other people and turned repeatedly over the head and under the feet, as a game or for exercise. ■ [with obj.] N. Amer. jump over (a rope that is being turned). ■ [with obj.] jump lightly over: *the children used to skip the puddles*.
3 [with obj.] omit (part of a book that one is reading, or a stage in a sequence that one is following): *the video manual allows the viewer to skip sections he's not interested in*. ■ [no obj.] move quickly and in an unmethodical way from one point or subject to another: *Marian skipped half-heartedly through the book*.
4 [with obj.] fail to attend or deal with as appropriate; miss: *I wanted to skip my English lesson to visit my mother | try not to skip breakfast*. ■ [no obj.] (**skip it**) informal abandon an undertaking, conversation, or activity: *after several wrong turns in our journey, we almost decided to skip it*. ■ [no obj.] informal run away; disappear: *I'm not giving them a chance to skip off again*. ■ informal depart quickly and secretly from: *she skipped her home amid rumours of a romance*.
5 [with obj.] throw (a stone) so that it ricochets off the surface of water.
▶ **noun 1** a light, bouncing step; a skipping movement: *he moved with a strange, dancing skip*.
2 Computing an act of passing over part of a sequence of data or instructions.
3 N. Amer. informal a person who defaults or absconds.
– ORIGIN Middle English: probably of Scandinavian origin.

skip[2] ▶ **noun 1** Brit. a large transportable open-topped container for building and other refuse.
2 a cage or bucket in which men or materials are lowered and raised in mines and quarries. ■ variant spelling of SKEP.

skip[3] ▶ **noun** the captain or director of a side at bowls or curling.
▶ **verb** (**skips, skipping, skipped**) [with obj.] act as skip of (a side).
– ORIGIN early 19th cent. (originally Scots): abbreviation of SKIPPER[1].

ski pants ▶ **plural noun** trousers worn for skiing. ■ women's trousers imitating a style of these, made of stretchy fabric with tapering legs and an elastic stirrup under each foot.

skipjack ▶ **noun 1** (also **skipjack tuna**) a small tuna with dark horizontal stripes, widely distributed throughout tropical and temperate seas. Also called BONITO or OCEANIC BONITO. ● *Katsuwonus* (or *Euthynnus*) *pelamis*, family Scombridae.
2 another term for CLICK BEETLE.
3 a sloop-rigged sailing boat of a kind used off the east coast of the US.
– ORIGIN early 18th cent.: from the verb SKIP[1] + JACK[1]. Sense 1 is from the fish's habit of jumping out of the water; sense 2, sense 3 arose in the 19th cent.

ski-plane ▶ **noun** an aeroplane having its undercarriage fitted with skis for landing on snow or ice.

ski pole ▶ **noun** either of two light metal poles held by a skier to assist in balance or propulsion.

skipper[1] informal ▶ **noun** the captain of a ship or boat, especially a small trading or fishing vessel. ■ the captain of a side in a game or sport. ■ the captain of an aircraft.
▶ **verb** [with obj.] act as captain of.
– ORIGIN late Middle English: from Middle Dutch, Middle Low German *schipper*, from *schip* 'ship'.

skipper[2] ▶ **noun 1** a person or thing that skips. ■ used in the names of small insects and crustaceans that skip or hop, e.g. **cheese-skipper**.
2 a small brownish moth-like butterfly with rapid darting flight. ● Family Hesperiidae: numerous genera.
3 the Atlantic saury (fish) (see SAURY).

skipper[3] ▶ **noun** S. African a long-sleeved sweatshirt or T-shirt.
– ORIGIN of unknown origin.

skippet ▶ **noun** chiefly historical a small round wooden box used to preserve documents and seals.
– ORIGIN late Middle English: of unknown origin.

skipping rope ▶ **noun** Brit. a length of rope used for skipping, typically with a handle at each end.

skip zone ▶ **noun** the annular region round a broadcasting station where neither direct nor reflected waves are received.

skirl /skəːl/ ▶ **noun** a shrill sound, especially that of bagpipes.
▶ **verb** [no obj.] (of bagpipes) make such a sound.
– ORIGIN late Middle English (as a verb): probably of Scandinavian origin; ultimately imitative.

skirmish ▶ **noun** an episode of irregular or unpremeditated fighting, especially between small or outlying parts of armies or fleets. ■ a short argument: *there was a skirmish over the budget*.
▶ **verb** [no obj.] (often as noun **skirmishing**) engage in a skirmish: *reports of skirmishing along the border*.
– DERIVATIVES **skirmisher** noun.
– ORIGIN Middle English (as a verb): from Old French *eskirmiss-*, lengthened stem of *eskirmir*, from a Germanic verb meaning 'defend'.

skirr /skəː/ ▶ **verb** [no obj., with adverbial of direction] rare move rapidly, especially with a whirring sound: *five dark birds rose skirring away*.

– ORIGIN mid 16th cent.: perhaps related to SCOUR[1] or SCOUR[2].

skirret /ˈskɪrɪt/ ▶ noun an East Asian plant of the parsley family, formerly cultivated in Europe for its edible carrot-like root. ● *Sium sisarum*, family Umbelliferae.
– ORIGIN Middle English *skirwhit(e)*, perhaps from Scots *skire* 'bright, clear' + WHITE.

skirt ▶ noun **1** a woman's outer garment fastened around the waist and hanging down around the legs. ■ the part of a coat or dress that hangs below the waist.
2 [mass noun] informal women regarded as objects of sexual desire: *so, Sandro, off to chase some skirt?*
3 a surface that conceals or protects the wheels or underside of a vehicle or aircraft. ■ the curtain that hangs round the base of a hovercraft to contain the air cushion.
4 [mass noun] an animal's diaphragm and other membranes as food: *bits of beef skirt.* ■ [count noun] Brit. a cut of meat from the lower flank.
5 a small flap on a saddle, covering the bar from which the stirrup leather hangs.
▶ verb [with obj.] **1** go round or past the edge of: *he did not go through the city but skirted it.* ■ be situated along or around the edge of: *the fields that skirted the highway were full of cattle.* ■ [no obj.] (**skirt along/around**) go along or around (something) rather than directly through or across it: *the river valley skirts along the northern slopes of the hills.*
2 attempt to ignore; avoid dealing with: *they are both skirting the issue* | [no obj.] *the treaty skirted around the question of political cooperation.*
– DERIVATIVES **skirted** adjective [in combination] *a full-skirted dress.*
– ORIGIN Middle English: from Old Norse *skyrta* 'shirt'; compare with synonymous Old English *scyrte*, also with SHORT. The verb dates from the early 17th cent.

skirt-chaser ▶ noun informal a man who pursues women amorously and is fickle in his affections.
– DERIVATIVES **skirt-chasing** noun.

skirting (also **skirting board**) ▶ noun Brit. a wooden board running along the base of an interior wall.

ski run ▶ noun a track on a slope for skiing.

ski stick ▶ noun old-fashioned term for SKI POLE.

skit ▶ noun a short comedy sketch or piece of humorous writing, especially a parody: *a skit on daytime magazine programmes.*
– ORIGIN early 18th cent. (in the sense 'satirical comment or attack'): related to the rare verb *skit* 'move lightly and rapidly', perhaps from Old Norse (compare with *skjóta* 'shoot').

skite /skʌɪt/ informal ▶ verb [no obj.] **1** Austral./NZ boast: *she did it just so that she could skite about it.*
2 [with adverbial of direction] move quickly and forcefully, especially when glancing off a surface: *rain skited off her coat.*
▶ noun **1** Austral./NZ a boaster. [mid 19th cent.: from Scots and northern English dialect, denoting a person regarded with contempt; compare with BLATHERSKITE.] ■ [mass noun] boasting; boastfulness.
2 Scottish a period of heavy drinking: *he only drank brandy when he was on a skite.*
– ORIGIN early 18th cent. (in sense 2 of the verb): perhaps of Old Norse origin; compare with SKIT.

ski touring ▶ noun [mass noun] a form of skiing in which people travel across mountainous terrain, both skiing downhill and climbing using skins.
– DERIVATIVES **ski tour** noun, **ski tourer** noun.

ski tow ▶ noun **1** a type of ski lift, with a moving rope or bars suspended from a moving overhead cable.
2 a tow rope for waterskiers.

skitter (also **skeeter**) ▶ verb **1** [no obj., with adverbial of direction] move lightly and quickly or hurriedly: *the girls skittered up the stairs* | figurative *her mind skittered back to that day at the office.*
2 [with obj.] draw (bait) jerkily across the surface of the water as a technique in fishing.
– ORIGIN mid 19th cent.: apparently a frequentative of SKITE.

skittery ▶ adjective restless; skittish: *a skittery horse.*

skittish ▶ adjective (of an animal, especially a horse) nervous or excitable; easily scared: *a skittish chestnut mare* | figurative *skittish investors withdrew their money from equity markets.* ■ (of a person) playfully frivolous or unpredictable: *my skittish and immature mother.*
– DERIVATIVES **skittishly** adverb, **skittishness** noun.
– ORIGIN late Middle English: perhaps from the rare verb *skit* 'move lightly and rapidly'.

skittle ▶ noun **1** (**skittles**) [treated as sing.] a game played with wooden pins, typically nine in number, set up at the end of an alley to be bowled down with a wooden ball or disc. ■ (in full **table skittles**) a game played with similar pins set up on a board to be knocked down by swinging a suspended ball. ■ Brit. informal chess that is not played seriously.
2 a pin used in the game of skittles.
▶ verb [with obj.] knock over as if in a game of skittles: *she put her hand out and skittled a row of bottles.* ■ Cricket get (batsmen) out in rapid succession: *Pakistan were skittled out for 93.*
– ORIGIN mid 17th cent.: of unknown origin. The word *skyttel* exists in Danish and Swedish in the sense 'shuttle, child's marble', but there is no evidence to connect this with the game of skittles.

skive[1] /skʌɪv/ Brit. informal ▶ verb [no obj.] avoid work or a duty by staying away or leaving early; shirk: *I skived off school* | [with obj.] *she used to skive lessons.*
▶ noun [in sing.] an instance of avoiding work or a duty by staying away or leaving early. ■ an easy option.
– DERIVATIVES **skiver** noun.
– ORIGIN early 20th cent.: perhaps from French *esquiver* 'slink away'.

skive[2] /skʌɪv/ ▶ verb [with obj.] technical pare (the edge of a piece of leather or other material) so as to reduce its thickness.
– ORIGIN early 19th cent.: from Old Norse *skífa*; related to SHIVE.

skivvy ▶ noun (pl. **skivvies**) **1** Brit. informal a female domestic servant who performs menial tasks. ■ a person doing work that is poorly paid and considered menial.
2 (also **skivvy shirt**) US & Austral. a lightweight high-necked long-sleeved garment. ■ a T-shirt or short-sleeved vest.
3 (**skivvies**) N. Amer. underwear consisting of a vest and underpants. [originally a US navy term.]
▶ verb (**skivvies, skivvying, skivvied**) [no obj.] Brit. informal do menial household tasks; work as a skivvy.
– ORIGIN early 20th cent.: of unknown origin.

skiwear ▶ noun [mass noun] clothing suitable for wearing while skiing.

skof /skɒf/ ▶ noun S. African **1** a period of work; a shift.
2 a stage of a journey.
– ORIGIN late 18th cent. (in sense 2): from Afrikaans, from Dutch *schoft*: see SCOFF[2].

skokiaan /ˈskɒkɪɑːn/ ▶ noun [mass noun] S. African an illicit home-brewed liquor made of yeast, sugar, and water.
– ORIGIN perhaps from Zulu *isikokeyana* 'small enclosure', referring to the practice of hiding illicit liquor in holes in the ground.

skol /skɒl, skəʊl/ (also **skoal**) ▶ exclamation used to express friendly feelings towards one's companions before drinking.
– ORIGIN early 17th cent. (a Scots use): from Danish and Norwegian *skaal*, Swedish *skål*, from Old Norse *skál* 'bowl'; perhaps introduced through the visit of James VI to Denmark in 1589.

skolly /ˈskɒli/ ▶ noun (pl. **skollies**) S. African informal a petty criminal of mixed ethnic origin; a hooligan.
– ORIGIN Afrikaans, probably from Dutch *schoelje* 'rogue'.

skookum /ˈskuːkəm/ N. Amer. ▶ adjective informal (of a person or animal) strong, brave, or impressive.
▶ noun archaic a street party or trade fair.
– ORIGIN mid 19th cent.: from Chinook Jargon.

skookum house ▶ noun N. Amer. informal a jail.

skoosh ▶ verb variant spelling of SCOOSH.

Skopje /ˈskɒpjeɪ/ the capital of the republic of Macedonia, situated in the north on the Vardar River; pop. 522,200 (est. 2006). Founded by the Romans, it became the capital of Macedonia in 1945.

skort /skɔːt/ (also **skorts**) ▶ noun chiefly N. Amer. a pair of shorts with a flap across the front (and sometimes also the back) to give the appearance of a skirt.
– ORIGIN 1990s: blend of SKIRT and SHORTS.

skosh /skəʊʃ/ ▶ noun US informal a small amount; a little: *the car could do with a skosh more room in the back.*
– ORIGIN 1950s: from Japanese *sukoshi*.

Skraeling /ˈskreɪlɪŋ/ ▶ noun an Inuit or other indigenous inhabitant of Greenland or Vinland (on the NE coast of North America) at the time of early Norse settlement.
– ORIGIN from Old Norse *Skrælingjar* (plural).

Skryabin variant spelling of SCRIABIN.

skua /ˈskjuːə/ ▶ noun a large brownish predatory seabird related to the gulls, pursuing other birds to make them disgorge fish they have caught. ● Family Stercorariidae: genera *Catharacta* (four larger species) and *Stercorarius* (three smaller species, North American name: **jaeger**).
– ORIGIN late 17th cent.: modern Latin, from Faroese *skúvur*, from Old Norse *skúfr* (apparently imitative).

skulduggery /skʌlˈdʌɡ(ə)ri/ (also **skullduggery**) ▶ noun [mass noun] underhand, unscrupulous, or dishonest behaviour or activities: *a firm that investigates commercial skulduggery.*
– ORIGIN mid 19th cent.: alteration of Scots *sculduddery*, of unknown origin.

skulk ▶ verb [no obj.] keep out of sight, typically with a sinister or cowardly motive: *don't skulk outside the door like a spy!* ■ [with adverbial of direction] move stealthily or furtively: *he spent most of his time skulking about the corridors.*
▶ noun a group of foxes.
– DERIVATIVES **skulker** noun.
– ORIGIN Middle English: of Scandinavian origin; compare with Norwegian *skulka* 'lurk', and Danish *skulke*, Swedish *skolka* 'shirk'.

skull ▶ noun a bone framework enclosing the brain of a vertebrate; the skeleton of a person's or animal's head. ■ informal a person's head or brain: *a skull crammed with too many thoughts.*
▶ verb [with obj.] informal hit (someone) on the head.
– PHRASES **out of one's skull** informal **1** out of one's mind; crazy. **2** very drunk. **skull and crossbones** a representation of a skull with two thigh bones crossed below it as an emblem of piracy or death.
– DERIVATIVES **skulled** adjective [in combination] *long-skulled.*
– ORIGIN Middle English *scolle*; of unknown origin; compare with Old Norse *skoltr*.

skullcap ▶ noun **1** a small close-fitting peakless cap. ■ a protective helmet, in particular one worn by jockeys or horse riders.
2 the top part of the skull.
3 a widely distributed plant of the mint family, whose tubular flowers have a helmet-shaped cup at the base. ● Genus *Scutellaria*, family Labiatae.

skull session ▶ noun US informal a discussion or conference.

skunk ▶ noun **1** a cat-sized American mammal of the weasel family, with distinctive black-and-white striped fur. When threatened it squirts a fine spray of foul-smelling irritant liquid from its anal glands towards its attacker. ● *Mephitis* and other genera, family Mustelidae: several species, in particular the **striped skunk** (*M. mephitis*).
■ [mass noun] the fur of the skunk. ■ informal a contemptible person.
2 informal short for SKUNKWEED.
▶ verb [with obj.] N. Amer. informal **1** defeat (someone) overwhelmingly in a game or contest, especially by preventing them from scoring at all.
2 dated fail to pay (a bill or creditor).
– ORIGIN mid 17th cent.: from Abnaki *segankw*; variants occur in many other American Indian dialects.

skunk cabbage ▶ noun a North American plant of the arum family, the flower of which has a distinctive unpleasant smell. ● Two species in the family Araceae: the western *Lysichiton americanum*, with a stalked yellow flower, and the eastern *Symplocarpus foetidus*, with a greenish purple flower.

skunkweed ▶ noun [mass noun] cannabis of a variety which has a high concentration of narcotic agents.

skunkworks ▶ plural noun [usu. treated as sing.] US informal an experimental laboratory or department of a company or institution, typically smaller than and independent of its main research division.
– ORIGIN 1970s: allegedly from an association with the *Skonk Works*, an illegal still in the 'Li'l Abner' comic strip.

skutterudite /ˈskʊt(ə)rəˌdʌɪt/ ▶ noun [mass noun] a grey metallic mineral, typically forming cubic or octahedral crystals, consisting chiefly of an arsenide of cobalt and nickel.
– ORIGIN mid 19th cent.: from *Skutterud* (now Skuterud), a village in SE Norway, + -ITE[1].

sky ▶ noun (pl. **skies**) (often **the sky**) the region of the atmosphere and outer space seen from the earth: *hundreds of stars were shining in the sky* | [mass noun] *Dorcas had never seen so much sky.* ■ literary heaven; heavenly power: *the just vengeance of incensed skies.*
▶ verb (**skies, skying, skied**) [with obj.] informal hit (a ball) high into the air: *he skied his tee shot.* ■ hang (a picture) very high on a wall, especially in an exhibition.

S

– PHRASES **out of a clear blue sky** see BLUE[1]. **the sky is the limit** informal there is practically no limit (to something such as a price that can be charged or the opportunities afforded to someone). **to the skies** very highly; enthusiastically: *he wrote to his sister praising Lizzie to the skies.* **under the open sky** out of doors.
– DERIVATIVES **skyey** adjective, **skyless** adjective.
– ORIGIN Middle English (also in the plural denoting clouds), from Old Norse *ský* 'cloud'. The verb dates from the early 19th cent.

sky blue ▶ noun [mass noun] a bright clear blue.

sky-blue pink ▶ noun [mass noun] humorous a non-existent colour.

skybox ▶ noun N. Amer. a luxurious enclosed seating area high up in a sports arena.

sky burial ▶ noun a Tibetan funeral ritual involving the exposure of a dismembered corpse to sacred vultures.

skycap ▶ noun N. Amer. a porter at an airport.

sky-clad ▶ adjective naked (used especially in the context of modern pagan ritual).
– ORIGIN early 20th cent.: probably a translation of Sanskrit *Digambara* (see DIGAMBARA).

sky cloth ▶ noun a backdrop painted or coloured to represent the sky.

skydiving ▶ noun [mass noun] the sport of jumping from an aircraft and performing acrobatic manoeuvres in the air under free fall before landing by parachute.
– DERIVATIVES **skydive** verb, **skydiver** noun.

Skye a mountainous island of the Inner Hebrides, now linked to the west coast of Scotland by a bridge; chief town, Portree. It is the largest and most northerly island of the group.

skyer (also **skier**) ▶ noun Cricket a hit which goes very high.

Skye terrier ▶ noun a small long-haired terrier of a slate-coloured or fawn-coloured Scottish breed.

skyflower ▶ noun a shrub of the verbena family, with clusters of lilac flowers and yellow berries, native to Central and South America. ● *Duranta erecta*, family Verbenaceae.

skyglow ▶ noun [mass noun] brightness of the night sky in a built-up area as a result of light pollution.

sky-high ▶ adverb & adjective as if reaching the sky; very high: [as adv.] *they were blown sky-high.* ■ at or to a very high level; very great: [as adj.] *sky-high premiums.*

skyhook ▶ noun 1 Climbing a small flattened hook, with an eye for attaching a rope, fixed temporarily into a rock face.
2 Basketball a very high-arcing hook shot.
3 dated used humorously to refer to the apparent means by which an aircraft remains airborne.

skyjack ▶ verb [with obj.] hijack (an aircraft).
▶ noun an act of skyjacking.
– DERIVATIVES **skyjacker** noun.
– ORIGIN 1960s: blend of SKY and HIJACK.

Skylab an American orbiting space laboratory launched in 1973, used for experiments in zero gravity and for astrophysical studies until 1974.

S

skylark ▶ noun a common Eurasian and North African lark of farmland and open country, noted for its prolonged song given in hovering flight. ● Genus *Alauda*, family Alaudidae: two species, in particular the widespread *A. arvensis*.
▶ verb [no obj.] pass time by playing tricks or practical jokes; indulge in horseplay: *he was skylarking with a friend when he fell into a pile of boxes.* [late 17th cent. (originally in nautical use): by association with the verb LARK[2].]

skylight ▶ noun a window set in a roof or ceiling at the same angle.

skylight filter ▶ noun Photography a very slightly pink filter that reduces haze and excessive blueness of the sky in photographs by absorbing ultraviolet light.

skyline ▶ noun an outline of land and buildings defined against the sky: *the skyline of the city.*

skylit (also **skylighted**) ▶ adjective fitted with or lit by a skylight or skylights.

sky marshal ▶ noun an armed guard who travels incognito on certain international flights, trained to take action in the event of a hijack or other terrorist action.

sky pilot ▶ noun informal a clergyman.

skyr /skɪə/ ▶ noun [mass noun] an Icelandic dish consisting of curdled milk.
– ORIGIN Icelandic.

skyrocket ▶ noun a rocket designed to explode high in the air as a signal or firework.
▶ verb (**skyrockets, skyrocketing, skyrocketed**) [no obj.] informal (of a price, rate, or amount) increase very steeply or rapidly: *the cost of the welfare system has skyrocketed.*

skysail /ˈskʌɪseɪl, -s(ə)l/ ▶ noun a light sail above the royal in a square-rigged ship.

skyscape ▶ noun a view of an expanse of sky. ■ a picture of such a view.

skyscraper ▶ noun a very tall building of many storeys.

sky surfing ▶ noun [mass noun] the sport of jumping from an aircraft and surfing through the air on a board before landing by parachute.

skywalk ▶ noun another term for SKYWAY (sense 2).

skyward ▶ adverb (also **skywards**) towards the sky: *flames were now shooting skyward.*
▶ adjective moving or directed towards the sky: *the city was heavily guarded by skyward laser batteries.*

skywatch ▶ verb [no obj.] informal observe or monitor the sky, especially for celestial objects or aircraft.
– DERIVATIVES **skywatcher** noun.

sky wave ▶ noun a radio wave reflected from the ionosphere.

skyway ▶ noun chiefly N. Amer. 1 a recognized route followed by aircraft.
2 a covered overhead walkway between buildings.
3 a raised motorway.

skywriting ▶ noun [mass noun] words in the form of smoke trails made by an aeroplane, especially for advertising.
– DERIVATIVES **skywriter** noun.

SLA ▶ abbreviation Computing service level agreement.

slab ▶ noun 1 a large, thick, flat piece of stone or concrete, typically square or rectangular in shape: *paving slabs | she settled on a slab of rock.* ■ a flat, heavy table top or counter, used during the preparation or display of food: *a fishmonger's slab.* ■ Brit. a table used for laying a body on in a mortuary. ■ Climbing a large, smooth body of rock lying at a sharp angle to the horizontal.
2 a large, thick slice or piece of cake, bread, chocolate, etc.: *a slab of bread and cheese.*
3 an outer piece of timber sawn from a log.
4 Austral./NZ informal a pack containing 24 bottles or cans of beer.
▶ verb (**slabs, slabbing, slabbed**) [with obj.] (often as noun **slabbing**) remove slabs from (a log or tree) to prepare it for sawing into planks.
– DERIVATIVES **slabby** adjective.
– ORIGIN Middle English: of unknown origin.

slab avalanche ▶ noun an avalanche formed by a sheet of snow breaking along a fracture line.

slabbed ▶ adjective covered with slabs: *a slabbed patio area.*

slabber chiefly Scottish & Irish ▶ verb 1 [no obj.] dribble at the mouth; slaver: *he was slabbering like a child.* ■ [with obj.] splatter or splash (something): *his trouser legs were slabbered with mud.*
2 [no obj.] chatter, especially about matters of little importance.
▶ noun a dribble of saliva.
– ORIGIN mid 16th cent. (in the sense 'dribble on'): related to dialect *slab* 'muddy place, puddle'.

slack[1] ▶ adjective 1 not taut or held tightly in position; loose: *a slack rope | her mouth went slack.*
2 having or showing laziness or negligence: *slack accounting procedures.*
3 slow or sluggish: *they were working at a slack pace.* ■ (of business or trade) characterized by a lack of work or activity; quiet: *business was rather slack.*
4 W. Indian lewd: *the veteran king of slack chat.* ■ (of a person, typically a woman) promiscuous.
5 (of a tide) neither ebbing nor flowing.
▶ noun 1 the part of a rope or line which is not held taut; the loose or unused part: *I picked up the rod and wound in the slack.*
2 (**slacks**) casual trousers.
3 informal a spell of inactivity or laziness: *he slept deeply, refreshed by a little slack in the daily routine.*
▶ verb 1 [with obj.] loosen (something, especially a rope).
2 decrease or reduce in intensity, quantity, or speed: [no obj.] *the flow of blood slacked off* | [with obj.] *the horse slacked his pace.*
3 [no obj.] Brit. informal work slowly or lazily: *she ticked off her girls if they were slacking.*
4 [with obj.] slake (lime).
– PHRASES **cut someone some slack** N. Amer. informal allow someone some leeway in their conduct. **take** (or **pick**) **up the slack** 1 improve the use of resources to avoid an undesirable lull in business: *as domestic demand starts to flag, foreign demand will help pick up the slack.* 2 pull on the loose end or part of a rope in order to make it taut.
– DERIVATIVES **slackly** adverb, **slackness** noun.
– ORIGIN Old English *slæc* 'inclined to be lazy, unhurried', of Germanic origin; related to Latin *laxus* 'loose'.

slack[2] ▶ noun [mass noun] coal dust or small pieces of coal.
– ORIGIN late Middle English: probably from Low German or Dutch.

slacken ▶ verb 1 make or become slack: [with obj.] *he slackened his grip* | [no obj.] *suddenly the line slackens and flutters in the wind.*
2 reduce or decrease in speed or intensity: [no obj.] *the pace never slackens.*

slacker ▶ noun informal a person who avoids work or effort. ■ US a person who evades military service. ■ chiefly N. Amer. a young person (especially in the 1990s) of a subculture characterized by apathy and aimlessness.

slack water ▶ noun the state of the tide when it is turning, especially at low tide.

slag ▶ noun 1 [mass noun] stony waste matter separated from metals during the smelting or refining of ore. ■ similar material produced by a volcano; scoria.
2 Brit. informal, derogatory a promiscuous woman. ■ a contemptible or insignificant person.
▶ verb (**slags, slagging, slagged**) 1 [no obj.] (usu. as noun **slagging**) produce deposits of slag.
2 [with obj.] Brit. informal criticize (someone) in an abusive and insulting manner: *my girlfriend was always slagging him off.*
– DERIVATIVES **slaggy** adjective (**slaggier, slaggiest**).
– ORIGIN mid 16th cent.: from Middle Low German *slagge*, perhaps from *slagen* 'strike', with reference to fragments formed by hammering. The verb sense 'criticize' dates from the 1970s.

slag heap ▶ noun Brit. a hill or area of refuse from a mine or industrial site.

slag wool ▶ noun [mass noun] mineral wool made from blast-furnace slag.

slain past participle of SLAY[1].

slainte /ˈslɑːntʃə/ ▶ exclamation used to express friendly feelings towards one's companions before drinking.
– ORIGIN from Scottish Gaelic *slàinte*, literally 'health'.

slake ▶ verb [with obj.] 1 quench or satisfy (one's thirst): *slake your thirst with citron pressé.* ■ satisfy (desires): *restaurants worked to slake the Italian obsession with food.*
2 combine (quicklime) with water to produce calcium hydroxide.
– ORIGIN Old English *slacian* 'become less eager', also 'slacken', from the adjective *slæc* 'slack'; compare with Dutch *slaken* 'diminish, relax'.

slaked lime ▶ noun see LIME[1].

slalom /ˈslɑːləm/ ▶ noun a ski race down a winding course marked out by poles. ■ a sporting event on water with a winding course marked out by obstacles, typically a canoe or sailing race.
▶ verb [no obj., with adverbial of direction] move or race in a winding path, avoiding obstacles: *she drove with reckless speed, slaloming in and out of the stalled cars.*
– ORIGIN 1920s: from Norwegian, literally 'sloping track'.

slam[1] ▶ verb (**slams, slamming, slammed**) [with obj.] 1 shut (a door, window, or lid) forcefully and loudly: *he slams the door behind him as he leaves.* ■ [no obj.] be closed forcefully and loudly: *she heard a car door slam.* ■ [with obj. and adverbial] push or put something somewhere with great force: *Charlie slammed down the phone.* ■ [no obj.] (**slam into**) crash into; collide heavily with: *the car mounted the pavement, slamming into a lamp post.* ■ [with obj. and adverbial of direction] informal hit (something) with great force in a particular direction: *he slammed a shot into the net.* ■ put (something) into action suddenly or forcefully: *I slammed on the brakes.* ■ [no obj., with adverbial of direction] move violently or loudly: *he slammed out of the room.* ■ informal, chiefly N. Amer. score points against or gain a victory over (someone) easily. ■ short for SLAM-DANCE.
2 informal criticize severely: *the new TV soap was slammed as being cynical and irresponsible.*

3 (usu. as noun **slamming**) (of a telephone company) take over the account of (a telephone customer) without their permission.
▶ noun 1 a loud bang caused by the forceful shutting of something such as a door: *the door closed with a slam.*
2 (usu. **the slam**) N. Amer. informal prison. [abbreviation of SLAMMER.]
3 chiefly US a poetry contest in which competitors recite their entries and are judged by members of the audience, the winner being elected after several elimination rounds.
– ORIGIN late 17th cent.: probably of Scandinavian origin; compare with Old Norse *slam(b)ra.*

slam² ▶ noun Bridge a grand slam (all thirteen tricks) or small slam (twelve tricks), for which bonus points are scored if bid and made.
– ORIGIN early 17th cent. (originally the name of a card game): perhaps from obsolete *slampant* 'trickery'.

slam-bang informal, chiefly N. Amer. ▶ adjective exciting and energetic: *a slam-bang action cartoon.* ■ with no niceties, subtleties, or restraints; direct and forceful: *the slam-bang world of daily journalism.*
▶ adverb suddenly and forcefully or violently: *I walked slam-bang into this character.*

slam-dance ▶ verb [no obj.] (usu. as noun **slam-dancing**) chiefly N. Amer. take part in a form of dancing to rock music in which people deliberately collide with one another.
– DERIVATIVES **slam dancer** noun.

slam dunk ▶ noun Basketball a shot in which a player thrusts the ball down through the basket. ■ [usu. as modifier] N. Amer. informal something reliable or unfailing; a foregone conclusion or certainty: *the film season's one slam-dunk hit.*
▶ verb (**slam-dunk**) [with obj.] Basketball thrust (the ball) down through the basket. ■ N. Amer. informal defeat or dismiss decisively: *they continue to slam-dunk every proposal we make.*

slammer ▶ noun 1 (usu. **the slammer**) informal prison.
2 chiefly N. Amer. a person who deliberately collides with others when slam-dancing.
3 (also **tequila slammer**) a cocktail made with tequila and champagne or another fizzy drink, which is covered, slammed on the table, and then drunk in one.

slamming ▶ noun [mass noun] the practice of switching a customer from one telephone service provider to another without the customer's authorization.

slander ▶ noun [mass noun] Law the action or crime of making a false spoken statement damaging to a person's reputation: *he is suing the TV company for slander.* Compare with LIBEL. ■ [count noun] a false and malicious spoken statement: *I've had just about all I can stomach of your slanders.*
▶ verb [with obj.] make false and damaging statements about (someone): *they were accused of slandering the head of state.*
– DERIVATIVES **slanderer** noun.
– ORIGIN Middle English: from Old French *esclandre*, alteration of *escandle*, from late Latin *scandalum* (see SCANDAL).

slanderous ▶ adjective (of a spoken statement) false and malicious: *slanderous allegations.*
– DERIVATIVES **slanderously** adverb.

slang ▶ noun [mass noun] a type of language consisting of words and phrases that are regarded as very informal, are more common in speech than writing, and are typically restricted to a particular context or group of people: *grass is slang for marijuana | army slang* | [as modifier] *slang terms.*
▶ verb [with obj.] informal attack (someone) using abusive language: *he watched ideological groups slanging one another.*
– ORIGIN mid 18th cent.: of unknown origin.

slanging match ▶ noun Brit. a prolonged exchange of insults.

slanguage ▶ noun [mass noun] a form of slang; slangy speech: *weird and wonderful teen slanguage.*
– ORIGIN late 19th cent.: blend of SLANG and LANGUAGE.

slangy ▶ adjective (**slangier**, **slangiest**) using or denoting slang: *the style is so slangy as to be incomprehensible.*
– DERIVATIVES **slangily** adverb, **slanginess** noun.

slant ▶ verb 1 [usu. with adverbial of direction] slope or lean in a particular direction; diverge or cause to diverge from the vertical or horizontal: [no obj.] *a ploughed field slanted up to the skyline* | [with obj.] *slant your skis as you turn.* ■ (especially of light or shadow) fall in an oblique direction: *the early sun slanted across the mountains.*
2 [with obj.] (often as adj. **slanted**) present or view (information) from a particular angle, especially in a biased or unfair way: *slanted news coverage.*
▶ noun 1 [in sing.] a sloping position: *the hedge grew at a slant | cut flower stems on the slant.*
2 a particular point of view from which something is seen or presented: *a new slant on science.*
▶ adjective [attrib.] sloping: *slant pockets.*
– ORIGIN late Middle English: variant of dialect *slent*, of Scandinavian origin, probably influenced by ASLANT.

slant-eyed ▶ adjective (of a person) having slanting eyes (often used as an insult towards people of Japanese or Chinese origin).

slant height ▶ noun the height of a cone from the vertex to the periphery (rather than the centre) of the base.

slanting ▶ adjective positioned or directed in a sloping or oblique direction: *the slanting beams of the roof | the slanting rays of the evening sun.*

slantwise ▶ adjective & adverb at an angle or in a sloping direction: [as adj.] *a slantwise glance* | [as adv.] *the bird veers and drops slantwise towards the wood.*

slap¹ ▶ verb (**slaps**, **slapping**, **slapped**) 1 [with obj.] hit or strike with the palm of the hand or a flat object: *my sister slapped my face.* ■ [no obj., with adverbial] hit against or into something with the sound of such an action: *water slapped against the boat.* ■ (**slap someone down**) informal reprimand someone forcefully.
2 [with obj. and adverbial] put or apply (something) somewhere quickly, carelessly, or forcefully: *slap on a bit of make-up | he slapped a copy of the paper onto her desk.* ■ (**slap something on**) informal impose a fine or other penalty on: *the government had slapped an embargo on imports.*
▶ noun 1 a blow with the palm of the hand or a flat object: *he gave her a slap across her cheek.* ■ a sound made or as if made by a slap: *she heard the slap of water against the harbour wall.*
2 [mass noun] informal make-up, especially when applied thickly or carelessly.
▶ adverb (also **slap bang**) informal suddenly and directly, especially with great force: *storming out of her room, she went slap into Luke.* ■ exactly; right: *the parador is slap bang in the middle of the Alhambra.*
– PHRASES **a slap in the face** an unexpected rejection or affront. **a slap on the back** congratulations or commendations: *they deserve a hearty slap on the back for their efforts.* **slap someone on the back** congratulate someone. **a slap on the wrist** a mild reprimand or punishment.
– ORIGIN late Middle English (as a verb): probably imitative. The noun dates from the mid 17th cent.

slap² ▶ adjective S. African 1 lacking strength, energy, or discipline; ineffectual.
2 (of food) soft or runny.
– ORIGIN Afrikaans, literally 'dangling, flabby'.

slap and tickle ▶ noun [mass noun] Brit. informal playful sexual activity.

slap bass ▶ noun [mass noun] a style of playing double bass or bass guitar by pulling and releasing the strings sharply against the fingerboard, used for effect in jazz or popular music.

slapdash ▶ adjective done too hurriedly and carelessly: *he gave a slapdash performance.*
▶ adverb dated hurriedly and carelessly.

slap-happy ▶ adjective informal 1 cheerfully casual, often in a careless or irresponsible way: *he possessed sauntering slap-happy courage.* ■ (of an action or operation) unmethodical; poorly thought out: *slap-happy surveying methods.*
2 chiefly N. Amer. dazed or stupefied from happiness or relief: *she's a bit slap-happy after such a narrow escape.*

slaphead ▶ noun Brit. informal a bald or balding man.

slapjack ▶ noun N. Amer. a kind of pancake cooked on a griddle.

slapper ▶ noun 1 Brit. informal, derogatory a promiscuous or vulgar woman.
2 informal term for SLAP SHOT.

slap shot ▶ noun Ice Hockey a hard shot made by raising the stick just above or below the waist before striking the puck with a sharp slapping motion.

slapstick ▶ noun 1 [mass noun] comedy based on deliberately clumsy actions and humorously embarrassing events: *slapstick humour.*
2 a device consisting of two flexible pieces of wood joined together at one end, used by clowns and in pantomime to produce a loud slapping noise.

slap-up ▶ adjective [attrib.] Brit. informal (of a meal or celebration) large and sumptuous: *a slap-up dinner.*

slash ▶ verb [with obj.] 1 cut with a wide, sweeping movement, typically using a knife or sword: *she tried to kill herself by slashing her wrists | a tyre was slashed on my car* | [no obj.] *the man slashed at him with a sword.* ■ informal reduce (a price, quantity, etc.) greatly: *the workforce has been slashed by 2,000.* ■ (as adj. **slashing**) informal vigorously incisive or effective: *a slashing magazine attack on her.*
2 archaic lash, whip, or thrash. ■ crack (a whip). ■ criticize severely.
▶ noun 1 a cut made with a wide, sweeping stroke: *the man took a mighty slash at his head with a large sword.* ■ a wound or gash made by such an action: *he staggered over with a crimson slash across his temple.* ■ a bright patch or flash of colour or light: *the foliage is handsome—yellow and gold with the odd slash of red.*
2 an oblique stroke (/) in print or writing, used between alternatives (e.g. *and/or*), in fractions (e.g. *3/4*), in ratios (e.g. *miles/day*), or between separate elements of a text. ■ [as modifier] denoting or belonging to a genre of fiction, chiefly published in fanzines, in which any of various male pairings from the popular media is portrayed as having a homosexual relationship. [1980s: from the use of an oblique stroke to link adjoining names or initials (as in *Kirk/Spock*).]
3 Brit. informal an act of urinating.
4 [mass noun] N. Amer. debris resulting from the felling or destruction of trees.
– ORIGIN late Middle English: perhaps imitative, or from Old French *esclachier* 'break in pieces'. The noun dates from the late 16th cent.

slash-and-burn ▶ adjective [attrib.] relating to or denoting a method of agriculture in which existing vegetation is cut down and burned off before new seeds are sown, typically used as a method for clearing forest land for farming. ■ aggressive, drastic, or ruthless: *her slash-and-burn campaigning style.*

slashed ▶ adjective (of a garment) having slits to show the lining material or skin beneath: *she wore slashed jeans.*

slasher ▶ noun informal 1 any of various tools for cutting wood.
2 (also **slasher film**) a horror film, especially one depicting a series of violent murders or assaults by an attacker armed with a knife or razor.
3 US a sporting competitor who is quick and agile.

slash pine ▶ noun a pine growing in a low-lying coastal region of the south-eastern US, Central America, and the Caribbean. ● Genus *Pinus*, family Pinaceae: several species, in particular *P. caribaea.*
– ORIGIN from *slash*, a US term for swampy ground.

slash pocket ▶ noun a pocket set in a garment with a diagonal slit for the opening.

slasto /'slastəʊ/ ▶ noun [mass noun] S. African trademark a slate-like shale used for flooring and tiling.
– ORIGIN blend of SLATE and STONE.

slat ▶ noun a thin, narrow piece of wood, plastic, or metal, especially one of a series which overlap or fit into each other, as in a fence or a Venetian blind.
– ORIGIN late Middle English (in the sense 'roofing slate'): shortening of Old French *esclat* 'splinter', from *esclater* 'to split'. The current sense dates from the mid 18th cent.

slate ▶ noun 1 [mass noun] a fine-grained grey, green, or bluish-purple metamorphic rock easily split into smooth, flat plates.
2 a flat plate of slate used as roofing material. ■ a flat plate of slate formerly used for writing on in schools. ■ Brit. a record of a person's debit or credit (in pubs and shops formerly written on a slate): *'Five quid,' said the barman. 'Put it on my slate,' I suggested.*
3 [mass noun] [usu. as modifier] a bluish-grey colour: *suits of slate grey.*
4 a list of candidates for election to a post or office, typically a group sharing a set of political views: *candidates on the left's slate won 74 per cent of constituency votes.* ■ chiefly N. Amer. a range of something on offer: *the company has revealed details of a $60m slate of film productions.*
5 a board showing the identifying details of a take in a film, held in front of the camera at the beginning and end of the take.
▶ verb [with obj.] 1 cover (something, especially a roof) with slates.

S

2 Brit. informal criticize severely: *his work was slated by the critics.*
3 chiefly N. Amer. schedule; plan: *London shows are slated for late June* | [with infinitive] *construction is slated to begin late next year.* ■ nominate (someone) as a candidate for an office or post: *I understand that I am being slated for promotion.*
4 identify (a take in a film) using a slate.
– DERIVATIVES **slaty** adjective.
– ORIGIN Middle English *sclate, sklate*, shortening of Old French *esclate*, feminine synonymous with *esclat* 'piece broken off' (see SLAT).

slate-coloured ▸ adjective of a dark bluish or greenish grey.

slate pencil ▸ noun chiefly historical a pencil made of soft slate used for writing on slate.

slater ▸ noun **1** a person who slates roofs for a living.
2 a woodlouse or similar isopod crustacean. ● Several species in the order Isopoda. See also SEA SLATER.

slather /'slaðə/ ▸ verb [with obj.] informal spread or smear (a substance) thickly or liberally: *slather on some tanning lotion.* ■ spread or smear a substance thickly or liberally on: *scones* ***slathered with*** *clotted cream.*
▸ noun (often **slathers**) N. Amer. informal a large amount.
– PHRASES **open slather** Austral./NZ informal freedom to act without restriction; free rein: *you've got open slather here, lad—do what you like.*
– ORIGIN early 19th cent.: of unknown origin.

slatted ▸ adjective having slats: *a slatted bench.*

slattern /'slat(ə)n/ ▸ noun dated a dirty, untidy woman.
– ORIGIN mid 17th cent.: related to *slattering* 'slovenly', from dialect *slatter* 'to spill, slop', frequentative of *slat* 'strike', of unknown origin.

slatternly ▸ adjective dated (of a woman or her appearance) dirty and untidy.
– DERIVATIVES **slatternliness** noun.

slaughter /'slɔːtə/ ▸ verb [with obj.] kill (animals) for food. ■ kill (people or animals) in a cruel or violent way, typically in large numbers: *innocent civilians are being slaughtered.* ■ informal defeat (an opponent) thoroughly: *the first team were slaughtered.*
▸ noun [mass noun] the killing of animals for food. ■ the killing of a large number of people or animals in a cruel or violent way: *the slaughter of 20 peaceful demonstrators.* ■ [count noun] informal a thorough defeat: *a magnificent 5–0 slaughter of Coventry.*
– DERIVATIVES **slaughterer** noun, **slaughterous** adjective.
– ORIGIN Middle English (as a noun): from Old Norse *slátr* 'butcher's meat'; related to SLAY¹. The verb dates from the mid 16th cent.

slaughtered ▸ adjective Brit. informal extremely drunk.

slaughterhouse ▸ noun a place where animals are slaughtered for food.

Slav /slɑːv/ ▸ noun a member of a group of peoples in central and eastern Europe speaking Slavic languages.
▸ adjective another term for SLAVIC.
– DERIVATIVES **Slavist** noun.
– ORIGIN from medieval Latin *Sclavus*, late Greek *Sklabos*, later also from medieval Latin *Slavus*.

S

slave ▸ noun (especially in the past) a person who is the legal property of another and is forced to obey them. ■ a person who works very hard without proper remuneration or appreciation: *by the time I was ten, I had become her slave, doing all the housework.* ■ a person who is excessively dependent upon or controlled by something: *the poorest people of the world are* ***slaves to*** *the banks* | *she was no* ***slave to*** *fashion.* ■ a device, or part of one, directly controlled by another: [as modifier] *a slave cassette deck.* Compare with MASTER¹.
▸ verb [no obj.] work excessively hard: *after* ***slaving away*** *for fourteen years all he gets is two thousand.* ■ [with obj.] subject (a device) to control by another: *should the need arise, the two channels can be slaved together.*
– ORIGIN Middle English: shortening of Old French *esclave*, equivalent of medieval Latin *sclava* (feminine) 'Slavonic (captive)': the Slavonic peoples had been reduced to a servile state by conquest in the 9th cent.

slave bangle (also **slave bracelet**) ▸ noun a bangle or bracelet worn above the elbow.

slave bell ▸ noun (in South Africa) a large bell hung between two whitewashed pillars, formerly used to summon slaves and mark the beginning and end of work periods.

Slave Coast a part of the west coast of Africa, between the Volta River and Mount Cameroon, from which slaves were exported in the 16th–19th centuries.

slave-driver ▸ noun informal a person who works others very hard.
– DERIVATIVES **slave-drive** verb.

slaveholder ▸ noun historical a person who owned slaves.
– DERIVATIVES **slaveholding** noun.

slave labour ▸ noun [mass noun] labour which is coerced and inadequately rewarded, or people that do it: *most of production is carried out by slave labour.*

slave-making ant (also **slave-maker ant**) ▸ noun an ant that raids the nests of other ant species and steals the pupae, which later become workers in the new colony. ● Several species in the family Formicidae, in particular the European *Formica sanguinea*. See also AMAZON ANT.

slaver¹ /'sleɪvə/ ▸ noun historical a person who dealt in or owned slaves. ■ a ship used for transporting slaves.

slaver² /'slavə, 'sleɪvə/ ▸ noun [mass noun] **1** saliva running from the mouth.
2 archaic excessive or obsequious flattery.
▸ verb [no obj.] let saliva run from the mouth: *the Labrador was slavering at the mouth.* ■ show excessive admiration or desire: *suburbanites* ***slavering over*** *drop-dead models.*
– ORIGIN Middle English: probably from Low German; compare with SLOBBER.

slavery ▸ noun [mass noun] the state of being a slave: *thousands had been sold into slavery.* ■ the practice or system of owning slaves. ■ a condition of having to work very hard without proper remuneration or appreciation: *female domestic slavery.* ■ excessive dependence on or devotion to something: ***slavery to*** *tradition.*

slave ship ▸ noun historical a ship transporting slaves, especially one carrying slaves from Africa.

Slave State (also **slave state**) ▸ noun historical any of the Southern states of the US in which slavery was legal before the Civil War.

slave trade ▸ noun [mass noun] historical the procuring, transporting, and selling of human beings as slaves, in particular the former trade in black Africans as slaves by European countries and North America.
– DERIVATIVES **slave trader** noun.

Slavey /'sleɪvi/ ▸ noun (pl. **same** or **Slaveys**) **1** a member of a Dene people of NW Canada.
2 [mass noun] either of the two languages (**North** and **South Slavey**) spoken by the Slavey.
▸ adjective relating to the Slavey or their languages.
– ORIGIN translating Cree *awahkān* 'captive, slave'.

slavey ▸ noun (pl. **slaveys**) Brit. informal, dated a maidservant, especially a hard-worked one.

Slavic /'slɑːvɪk, 'slavɪk/ ▸ adjective relating to or denoting the branch of the Indo-European language family that includes Russian, Ukrainian, and Belorussian (**Eastern Slavic**), Polish, Czech, Slovak, and Sorbian (**Western Slavic**), and Bulgarian, Serbian, Croatian, Macedonian, and Slovene (**Southern Slavic**). ■ relating to or denoting the peoples of central and eastern Europe who speak any of these languages.
▸ noun [mass noun] the Slavic languages collectively. See also SLAVONIC.

slaving ▸ noun [mass noun] [usu. as modifier] historical the action of enslaving people: *a slaving expedition.*

slavish ▸ adjective servile or submissive: *he noted the slavish, feudal respect they had for her.* ■ showing no attempt at originality: *a slavish adherence to protocol.*
– DERIVATIVES **slavishly** adverb, **slavishness** noun.

Slavonian grebe /slə'vəʊnɪən/ ▸ noun a North Eurasian and North American grebe with reddish underparts and a black and gold crest. ● *Podiceps auritus*, family Podicipedidae.
– ORIGIN *Slavonian* from medieval Latin *S(c)lavonia* 'country of the Slavs'.

Slavonic /slə'vɒnɪk/ ▸ adjective & noun another term for SLAVIC. See also CHURCH SLAVONIC.
– ORIGIN from medieval Latin *S(c)lavonicus*, from *S(c)lavonia* 'country of the Slavs', from *Sclavus* (see SLAV).

Slavophile ▸ noun a person who greatly admires the Slavic peoples or their languages.

slaw ▸ noun [mass noun] N. Amer. coleslaw.
– ORIGIN late 18th cent.: from Dutch *sla*, shortened from *salade* 'salad'.

slay¹ ▸ verb (past **slew**; past participle **slain**) [with obj.] archaic or literary kill (a person or animal) in a violent way: *St George slew the dragon.* ■ chiefly N. Amer. murder (someone) (used chiefly in journalism): *a man was slain with a shotgun.* ■ informal greatly impress or amuse (someone): *you slay me, you really do.*
– DERIVATIVES **slayer** noun.
– ORIGIN Old English *slēan* 'strike, kill', of Germanic origin; related to Dutch *slaan* and German *schlagen*.

slay² ▸ noun variant spelling of SLEY.

slaying ▸ noun [mass noun] archaic or literary the killing of a person or animal: *the slaying of a dragon.* ■ chiefly N. Amer. the murder of someone (used chiefly in journalism): [count noun] *a gangland slaying.*

SLBM ▸ abbreviation submarine-launched ballistic missile.

SLD ▸ abbreviation Social and Liberal Democrats.

SLE ▸ abbreviation systemic lupus erythematosus.

sleaze ▸ noun [mass noun] Brit. immoral, sordid, and corrupt behaviour or activities: *political campaigns that are long on sleaze and short on substance.* ■ [count noun] informal, chiefly N. Amer. a sordid, corrupt, or immoral person.
▸ verb [no obj., with adverbial] informal behave in an immoral, corrupt, or sordid way: *you're the last person who has to sleaze around bars.*
– ORIGIN 1960s: back-formation from SLEAZY.

sleazeball (also **sleazebag**) ▸ noun informal, chiefly N. Amer. a disreputable, disgusting, or despicable person (also used as a general term of abuse).

sleazoid (also **sleazo**) informal, chiefly US ▸ adjective sleazy, sordid, or despicable: *a sleazoid lawyer.*
▸ noun a sleazy, sordid, or despicable person.

sleazy ▸ adjective (**sleazier**, **sleaziest**) **1** (of a person or situation) sordid, corrupt, or immoral: *a sleazy private detective.* ■ (of a place) squalid and seedy: *a sleazy all-night cafe.*
2 dated (of textiles and clothing) flimsy.
– DERIVATIVES **sleazily** adverb, **sleaziness** noun.
– ORIGIN mid 17th cent.: of unknown origin.

sleb ▸ noun informal a celebrity.
– ORIGIN 1990s: representing a colloquial pronunciation of CELEB.

sled ▸ noun & verb (**sleds**, **sledding**, **sledded**) North American term for SLEDGE¹.
– ORIGIN Middle English: from Middle Low German *sledde*; related to the verb SLIDE.

sledge¹ chiefly Brit. ▸ noun a vehicle on runners for conveying loads or passengers over snow or ice, often pulled by draught animals. ■ a toboggan.
▸ verb [no obj., with adverbial of direction] ride on a sledge: *they sledged down the slopes in the frozen snow* | (as noun **sledging**) *I love sledging.* ■ [with obj. and adverbial of direction] carry (passengers or a load) on a sledge: *the task of sledging 10-metre lifeboats across tundra.*
– DERIVATIVES **sledger** noun.
– ORIGIN late 16th cent. (as a noun): from Middle Dutch *sleedse*; related to SLED. The verb dates from the early 18th cent.

sledge² ▸ noun a sledgehammer.
▸ verb [with obj.] (usu. as noun **sledging**) Cricket (of a fielder) make offensive remarks to (an opposing batsman) in order to break their concentration.
– DERIVATIVES **sledger** noun.
– ORIGIN Old English *slecg* (noun), from a Germanic base meaning 'to strike', related to SLAY¹. The current sense of the verb dates from the late 20th cent.

sledgehammer ▸ noun a large, heavy hammer used for such jobs as breaking rocks and driving in fence posts. ■ [as modifier] powerful; forceful: *sledgehammer blows.* ■ [as modifier] ruthless, insensitive, or using unnecessary force: *under his sledgehammer direction, anything of subtlety is swamped.*
▸ verb [with obj.] hit with a sledgehammer.

sleek ▸ adjective (of hair, fur, or skin) smooth and glossy: *he was tall, with sleek, dark hair.* ■ (of an animal) having smooth, glossy hair or fur: *a sleek black cat.* ■ (of a person) having a wealthy and well-groomed appearance: *a sleek and ambitious junior Minister.* ■ (of an object) having an elegant, streamlined shape or design: *his sleek black car slid through the traffic.* ■ ingratiating; unctuous: *she gave Guy a sleek smile to underline her words.*
▸ verb [with obj. and adverbial of direction] make (hair) smooth and glossy: *her black hair was sleeked down.*
– DERIVATIVES **sleekly** adverb, **sleekness** noun, **sleeky** adjective (**sleekier**, **sleekiest**).
– ORIGIN late Middle English: a later variant of SLICK (adjective and verb).

sleekit /'sliːkɪt/ ▸ adjective **1** Scottish artfully flattering or ingratiating. ■ sly or cunning: *his sleekit public*

image is going to make permanent fame a daunting challenge.
2 literary having a glossy skin or surface.
– ORIGIN early 16th cent.: from SLEEK.

sleep ▶ noun [mass noun] **1** a condition of body and mind which typically recurs for several hours every night, in which the nervous system is inactive, the eyes closed, the postural muscles relaxed, and consciousness practically suspended: *I was on the verge of sleep* | [in sing.] *a good night's sleep.* ■ chiefly literary a state compared to or resembling sleep, such as death or complete silence or stillness: *a photograph of the poet in his last sleep.* ■ [count noun] informal (typically in the context of anticipating a forthcoming event) a night, or a night's sleep: *two more sleeps till I fly to LA.*
2 a gummy secretion found in the corners of the eyes after sleep: *she sat up, rubbing the sleep from her eyes.*
▶ verb (past and past participle **slept** /slɛpt/) **1** [no obj.] be in a state of sleep: *she slept for half an hour* | (as adj. **sleeping**) *he looked at the sleeping child.* ■ be inactive or dormant: *Copenhagen likes to be known as the city that never sleeps.* ■ literary be at peace in death; lie buried: *he sleeps in Holywell cemetery.*
2 [with obj.] provide (a specified number of people) with beds, rooms, or places to stay the night: *studios sleeping two people cost £70 a night.*
3 [no obj., with adverbial] have sexual intercourse or be involved in a sexual relationship: *I won't sleep with a man who doesn't respect me.*
– PHRASES **one could do something in one's sleep** informal one could do something with no effort or conscious thought. **get to sleep** manage to fall asleep: *he got to sleep eventually.* **go to sleep** fall asleep. ■ (of a limb) become numb as a result of prolonged pressure. **let sleeping dogs lie** proverb avoid interfering in a situation that is currently causing no problems but may well do so as a result of such interference. **put someone to sleep** make someone unconscious by using drugs, alcohol, or an anaesthetic. ■ (also **send someone to sleep**) bore someone greatly. **put something to sleep** kill an animal, especially an old or badly injured one, painlessly (used euphemistically). **sleep easy** see EASY. **sleep like a log** (or **top**) sleep very soundly. **sleep on it** informal delay making a decision until the following day. **the sleep of the just** a deep, untroubled sleep. **sleep rough** see ROUGH. **sleep tight** [usu. in imperative] sleep well. **sleep with one eye open** sleep very lightly, aware of what is happening around one.
– PHRASAL VERBS **sleep around** informal have many casual sexual partners. **sleep in** remain asleep or in bed later than usual in the morning: *life assumes a different rhythm on the weekend; we sleep in, cut the grass, wash the car.* **sleep something off** dispel the effects of or recover from something by going to sleep: *she thought it wise to let him sleep off his hangover.* **sleep out** sleep outdoors: *they slept out all night by the river.* **sleep over** N. Amer. spend the night at a place other than one's own home: *Katie was asked to sleep over with Jenny.*
– ORIGIN Old English *slēp, slǣp* (noun), *slēpan, slǣpan* (verb), of Germanic origin; related to Dutch *slapen* and German *schlafen.*

sleeper ▶ noun **1** a person or animal who is asleep or who sleeps in a specified way: *he was a light sleeper, for long periods an insomniac.*
2 a thing used for or connected with sleeping, in particular: ■ a train carrying sleeping cars. ■ a sleeping car, or a berth in one. ■ informal a sleeping pill ■ (usu. **sleepers**) chiefly N. Amer. a sleepsuit for a baby or small child. ■ N. Amer. a sofa or chair that converts into a bed.
3 a film, book, play, etc. that eventually achieves unexpected success after initially attracting very little attention. ■ an antique whose true value goes unrecognized for some time. ■ (also **sleeper agent**) a secret agent who remains inactive for a long period while establishing a secure position.
4 Brit. a ring or post worn in a pierced ear to keep the hole from closing.
5 Brit. a wooden or concrete beam laid transversely under railway track to support it.
6 a stocky fish with mottled coloration which occurs widely in warm seas and fresh water. ● *Dormitator* and other genera, family Gobiidae (or Eleotridae): many species. See also COCKABULLY.

sleeper cell ▶ noun a group of secret agents that have remained inactive for a long period.

sleep-in ▶ adjective [attrib.] (of a domestic employee) resident in an employer's house: *a sleep-in babysitter.*
▶ noun **1** an instance of remaining asleep or in bed longer than usual in the morning: *a well-deserved sleep-in.*
2 a form of protest in which the participants sleep overnight in premises which they have occupied: *a student sleep-in began last night.*

sleepiness ▶ noun [mass noun] the state of being sleepy: *long road trips cause fatigue and sleepiness.*

sleeping bag ▶ noun a warm lined padded bag to sleep in, especially when camping.

sleeping car (Brit. also **sleeping carriage**) ▶ noun a railway carriage provided with beds or berths.

sleeping draught ▶ noun Brit. dated a drink or drug intended to induce sleep.

sleeping partner ▶ noun Brit. a partner not sharing in the actual work of a firm.

sleeping pill ▶ noun a tablet of a drug which helps to induce sleep, such as chloral hydrate or a barbiturate sedative.

sleeping policeman ▶ noun Brit. a hump in the road intended to cause traffic to reduce speed.

sleeping sickness ▶ noun [mass noun] **1** a tropical disease caused by parasitic protozoans (trypanosomes) which are transmitted by the bite of the tsetse fly. It causes fever, chills, pain in the limbs, and anaemia, and eventually affects the nervous system causing extreme lethargy and death. Also called TRYPANOSOMIASIS.
2 US term for SLEEPY SICKNESS.

sleep-learning ▶ noun [mass noun] learning by hearing while asleep, typically by playing a tape recording of what is to be learned.

sleepless ▶ adjective characterized by or experiencing lack of sleep: *another sleepless night* | *Lisa lay sleepless.* ■ chiefly literary continually active or moving: *the sleepless river.*
– DERIVATIVES **sleeplessly** adverb, **sleeplessness** noun.

sleep mode ▶ noun Electronics a power-saving mode of operation in which devices or parts of devices are switched off until needed.

sleep-out ▶ noun an occasion of sleeping outdoors. ■ Austral./NZ a veranda, porch, or outbuilding providing sleeping accommodation.

sleepover ▶ noun a night spent by children or young people at a friend's house.

sleepsuit ▶ noun Brit. a young child's one-piece garment, typically worn as nightwear.

sleepwalk ▶ verb [no obj.] walk around and sometimes perform other actions while asleep. ■ engage in an activity without interest, enthusiasm, or awareness of the possible consequences: *we are sleepwalking into a surveillance society.*
▶ noun an instance of sleepwalking.
– DERIVATIVES **sleepwalker** noun.

sleepwear ▶ noun [mass noun] clothing suitable for wearing in bed.

sleepy ▶ adjective (**sleepier**, **sleepiest**) needing or ready for sleep: *the wine had made her sleepy.* ■ showing the effects of sleep: *she rubbed her sleepy eyes.* ■ inducing sleep; soporific: *the sleepy heat of the afternoon.* ■ (of a place) without much activity: *he turned off the road into a sleepy little town.* ■ (of a business or organization) lacking the ability or will to respond to change; not dynamic: *the one-time sleepy world of pensions.*
– DERIVATIVES **sleepily** adverb.

sleepyhead ▶ noun a sleepy or inattentive person (usually as a form of address): *come on, sleepyhead, time to get up.*

sleepy sickness ▶ noun [mass noun] Brit. encephalitis lethargica, a brain infection causing drowsiness and sometimes coma. See also SLEEPING SICKNESS.

sleet ▶ noun [mass noun] rain containing some ice, as when snow melts as it falls. ■ US a thin coating of ice formed by sleet or rain freezing on coming into contact with a cold surface.
▶ verb [no obj.] (**it sleets, it is sleeting**, etc.) sleet falls: *it was sleeting so hard we could barely see.*
– DERIVATIVES **sleety** adjective.
– ORIGIN Middle English: of Germanic origin; probably related to Middle Low German *slōten* (plural) 'hail' and German *Schlosse* 'hailstone'.

sleeve ▶ noun **1** the part of a garment that wholly or partly covers a person's arm: *a shirt with the sleeves rolled up.*
2 a protective paper or cardboard cover for a record, CD, or DVD: *an album sleeve.* ■ a protective or connecting tube fitting over or enclosing a rod, spindle, or smaller tube.
3 a windsock. ■ a drogue towed by an aircraft.
– PHRASES **up one's sleeve** (of a strategy, idea, or resource) kept secret and in reserve for use when needed: *he was new to the game but had a few tricks up his sleeve.* **wear one's heart on one's sleeve** see HEART.
– DERIVATIVES **sleeved** adjective [often in combination] *a cap-sleeved shirt*, **sleeveless** adjective.
– ORIGIN Old English *slēfe, slief(e), slȳf*; related to Middle Dutch *sloove* 'covering'.

sleeve board ▶ noun a small ironing board over which a sleeve is pulled for pressing.

sleeveen /ˈsliːviːn, sliːˈviːn/ ▶ noun Irish informal an untrustworthy or cunning person.
– ORIGIN mid 19th cent.: from Irish *slíbhín* 'trickster'.

sleeve link ▶ noun Brit. dated a cufflink.

sleeve note ▶ noun Brit. an article printed on a record or CD sleeve giving information about the music or musician.

sleeve nut ▶ noun a long nut with right-hand and left-hand screw threads for drawing together conversely threaded pipes or shafts.

sleeve valve ▶ noun a valve in the form of a cylinder which slides to cover and uncover an inlet or outlet.

sleeving ▶ noun [mass noun] Brit. tubular covering for electrical or other cables.

sleigh /sleɪ/ ▶ noun a sledge drawn by horses or reindeer, especially one used for passengers.
▶ verb [no obj.] (usu. as noun **sleighing**) ride on a sleigh.
– ORIGIN early 17th cent. (originally a North American usage): from Dutch *slee*; related to SLED.

sleigh bed ▶ noun chiefly N. Amer. a bed resembling a sleigh, with outward curving head- and footboards.

sleigh bell ▶ noun a tinkling bell attached to the harness of a sleigh horse.

sleight /slʌɪt/ ▶ noun [mass noun] literary the use of dexterity or cunning, especially so as to deceive.
– PHRASES **sleight of hand** manual dexterity, typically in performing conjuring tricks: *a nifty bit of sleight of hand got the ashtray into the correct position.* ■ skilful deception: *this is financial sleight of hand of the worst sort.*
– ORIGIN Middle English *sleghth* 'cunning, skill', from Old Norse *slœgth*, from *slœgr* 'sly'.

slender ▶ adjective (**slenderer, slenderest**) **1** (of a person or part of the body) gracefully thin: *her slender neck.* ■ (especially of a rod or stem) of small girth or breadth: *slender iron railings.*
2 (of something abstract) barely sufficient in amount or basis: *people of slender means* | *a slender majority of four.*
– DERIVATIVES **slenderize** (also **slenderise**) verb (chiefly N. Amer.), **slenderly** adverb, **slenderness** noun.
– ORIGIN late Middle English: of unknown origin.

slender loris ▶ noun see LORIS.

slept past and past participle of SLEEP.

sleuth /sluːθ/ informal ▶ noun a detective.
▶ verb [no obj.] (often as noun **sleuthing**) carry out a search or investigation in the manner of a detective: *scientists began their genetic sleuthing for honey mushrooms four years ago.* ■ [with obj.] dated investigate (someone or something).
– ORIGIN Middle English (originally in the sense 'track', in SLEUTH-HOUND): from Old Norse *slóth*; compare with SLOT². Current senses date from the late 19th cent.

sleuth-hound ▶ noun dated a bloodhound. ■ informal an eager investigator; a detective.

slew¹ (also **slue**) ▶ verb **1** [no obj., with adverbial of direction] turn or slide violently or uncontrollably: [no obj.] *the Renault slewed from side to side in the snow* | [with obj.] *he slewed the aircraft round before it settled on the runway.*
2 [no obj.] (of an electronic device) undergo slewing.
▶ noun [in sing.] a violent or uncontrollable sliding movement.
– ORIGIN mid 18th cent. (originally in nautical use): of unknown origin.

slew² past of SLAY¹.

slew³ ▶ noun informal, chiefly N. Amer. a large number or quantity of something: *he asked me a slew of questions.*
– ORIGIN mid 19th cent.: from Irish *sluagh.*

slewing ▶ noun [mass noun] Electronics the response of an electronic device to a sudden large increase in input, especially one that causes the device to respond at its maximum rate.

S

slew rate ▸ noun Electronics the maximum rate at which an amplifier can respond to an abrupt change of input level.

sley /sleɪ/ (also **slay**) ▸ noun a tool used in weaving to force the weft into place.
– ORIGIN Old English *slege*; related to SLAY[1].

slice ▸ noun **1** a thin, broad piece of food, such as bread, meat, or cake, cut from a larger portion: *four slices of bread* | *potato slices*. ■ a portion or share of something: *local authorities control a huge slice of public spending*.
2 a utensil with a broad, flat blade for lifting foods such as cake and fish.
3 Golf a stroke which makes the ball curve away to the right (for a left-handed player, the left). ■ (in other sports) a shot or stroke made with glancing contact so that the ball travels forward spinning.
▸ verb [with obj.] **1** cut (something, especially food) into slices: *slice the onion into rings* | (as adj. **sliced**) *a sliced loaf*. ■ (**slice something off/from**) cut something from (something larger) with a sharp implement: *he sliced a corner from a fried egg* | figurative *he sliced 70 seconds off the record*. ■ cut with or as if with a sharp implement: *the bomber's wings were slicing the air with some efficiency* | [no obj.] *the blade sliced into his palm*. ■ [no obj., with adverbial of direction] move easily and quickly: *Grimsby sliced through Swindon's defence*.
2 Golf strike (the ball) or play (a stroke) so that the ball curves away to the right (for a left-handed player, the left). ■ (in other sports) propel (the ball) with a glancing contact so that it travels forward spinning: *Evans went and sliced a corner into his own net*.
– PHRASES **slice and dice** divide a quantity of information up into smaller parts, especially in order to analyse it more closely or in different ways. **a slice of the action** see A PIECE OF THE ACTION at PIECE. **a slice of life** a realistic representation of everyday experience in a film, play, or book.
– DERIVATIVES **sliceable** adjective, **slicer** noun [often in combination] *a bacon-slicer*.
– ORIGIN Middle English (in the sense 'fragment, splinter'): shortening of Old French *esclice* 'splinter', from the verb *esclicier*, of Germanic origin; related to German *schleissen* 'to slice', also to SLIT.

slick ▸ adjective **1** done or operating in an impressively smooth and efficient way: *Rangers have been entertaining crowds with a slick passing game*. ■ smooth and superficially impressive but insincere or shallow: *the brands are backed by slick advertising* | *a salesperson may be viewed as a slick confidence trickster*.
2 (of skin or hair) smooth and glossy: *a dandy-looking dude with a slick black ponytail*. ■ (of a surface) smooth, wet, and slippery: *she tumbled back against the slick, damp wall*.
▸ noun **1** an oil slick.
2 an application or amount of a glossy or oily substance: *a slick of lip gloss*.
3 (usu. **slicks**) a racing-car or bicycle tyre without a tread, for use in dry weather conditions.
4 N. Amer. informal a glossy magazine.
5 N. Amer. informal a smooth but insincere or shallow person.
▸ verb **1** [with obj. and adverbial] make (one's hair) flat, smooth, and glossy by applying water, oil, or gel to it: *his damp hair was slicked back*. ■ cover with a film of liquid; make wet or slippery: *she woke to find her body slicked with sweat*.
2 (**slick someone/thing up**) N. Amer. make someone or something smart, tidy, or stylish.
– DERIVATIVES **slickly** adverb, **slickness** noun.
– ORIGIN Middle English (in the senses 'glossy' and 'make smooth or glossy'): probably from Old English and related to Old Norse *slíkr* 'smooth'; compare with SLEEK.

slickenside ▸ noun (usu. **slickensides**) Geology a polished and striated rock surface that results from friction along a fault or bedding plane.
– ORIGIN mid 18th cent.: from a dialect variant of the adjective SLICK + SIDE.

slicker ▸ noun N. Amer. **1** informal a cheat or swindler. ■ short for CITY SLICKER.
2 a raincoat made of smooth material.

slide ▸ verb (past and past participle **slid**) [no obj., with adverbial of direction] move along a smooth surface while maintaining continuous contact with it: *she slid down the bank into the water* | (as adj. **sliding**) *the tank should have a sliding glass cover*. ■ [with obj. and adverbial of direction] move (something) along a surface in such a way: *she slid the keys over the table*. ■ move smoothly, quickly, or unobtrusively: [no obj.] *I quickly slid into a seat at the back of the hall* | [with obj.] *she slid the bottle into her pocket*. ■ change gradually to a worse condition or lower level: *the country faces the prospect of sliding from recession into slump*.
▸ noun **1** a structure with a smooth sloping surface for children to slide down. ■ a smooth stretch or slope of ice or packed snow for sliding or tobogganing on.
2 an act of sliding along a smooth surface: *use an ice axe to halt a slide on ice and snow*. ■ Baseball a sliding approach made to a base along the ground. ■ [usu. in combination or with noun modifier] (in skateboarding and snowboarding) a manoeuvre in which the board slides along an obstacle such as a rail or the edge of a ramp.
3 a decline in value or quality: *the current slide in house prices*.
4 a part of a machine or instrument that slides. ■ the place on a machine or instrument where a sliding part operates. ■ [mass noun] slide guitar: *I'd been playing slide for years*.
5 a rectangular piece of glass on which an object is mounted or placed for examination under a microscope. ■ a mounted transparency, especially one placed in a projector for viewing on a screen: [as modifier] *a slide show*.
6 Brit. a hairslide.
7 a sandal or light shoe without a back.
– PHRASES **let something slide** negligently allow something to deteriorate: *Papa had let the business slide after Mama's death*.
– DERIVATIVES **slidable** adjective, **slidably** adverb.
– ORIGIN Old English *slīdan* (verb); related to SLED and SLEDGE[1]. The noun, first in the sense 'act of sliding', is recorded from the late 16th cent.

slide duplicator (also **slide copier**) ▸ noun Photography an optical device attached to the front of a camera lens for rephotographing a transparency.

slide fastener ▸ noun N. Amer. a zip fastener or similar fastening device.

slide guitar ▸ noun [mass noun] a style of guitar playing in which a glissando effect is produced by moving a bottleneck or similar device over the strings, used especially in blues.

slide projector ▸ noun a piece of equipment used for displaying photographic slides on a screen.

slider ▸ noun **1** a knob or lever which is moved horizontally or vertically to control a variable, such as the volume of a radio.
2 Baseball a pitch that moves laterally as it nears home plate.
3 a North American freshwater turtle with a red or yellow patch on the side of the head. ● Genus *Trachemys* (or *Pseudemys*), family Emydidae: several species, in particular the **pond slider** (*T. scripta*).

slide rule ▸ noun a ruler with a sliding central strip, marked with logarithmic scales and used for making rapid calculations, especially multiplication and division.

slide show ▸ noun a presentation supplemented by or based on a display of projected images or photographic slides.

slide valve ▸ noun a piece that opens and closes an aperture by sliding across it.

slideway ▸ noun a part or parts of a machine on or between which a sliding part works.

sliding door ▸ noun a door drawn across an aperture on a groove or suspended from a track, rather than turning on hinges.

sliding scale ▸ noun a scale of fees, taxes, wages, etc. that varies in accordance with the variation of a particular standard.

sliding seat ▸ noun a seat able to slide to and fro on runners, especially one in a racing rowing boat used to adjust the length of a stroke.

slight ▸ adjective **1** small in degree; inconsiderable: *a slight increase* | *a slight ankle injury* | *the chance of success is very slight*. ■ (especially of a creative work) not profound or substantial; rather trivial or superficial: *a slight romantic comedy*.
2 (of a person or their build) not sturdy; thin or slender: *she was slight and delicate-looking*.
▸ verb [with obj.] **1** insult (someone) by treating or speaking of them without proper respect or attention: *he was desperate not to slight a guest*.
2 archaic raze or destroy (a fortification).
▸ noun an insult caused by a failure to show someone proper respect or attention: *an unintended slight can create grudges* | *he was seething at the slight to his authority*.
– PHRASES **not in the slightest** not at all: *he didn't mind in the slightest*. **the slightest ——** [usu. with negative] any —— whatsoever: *I don't have the slightest idea*.
– DERIVATIVES **slightness** noun.
– ORIGIN Middle English; the adjective from Old Norse *sléttr* 'smooth' (an early sense in English), of Germanic origin; related to Dutch *slechts* 'merely' and German *schlicht* 'simple', *schlecht* 'bad'; the verb (originally in the sense 'make smooth or level'), from Old Norse *slétta*. The sense 'treat with disrespect' dates from the late 16th cent.

slighting ▸ adjective showing a lack of respect; insulting or disparaging: *slighting references to Roman Catholics*.
– DERIVATIVES **slightingly** adverb.

slightly ▸ adverb **1** to a small degree; not considerably: *he lowered his voice slightly* | [as submodifier] *they are all slightly different*.
2 (with reference to a person's build) in a slender way: *a slightly built girl*.

Sligo /ˈslʌɪɡəʊ/ a county of the Republic of Ireland, in the west in the province of Connacht. ■ the county town of Sligo, a seaport on Sligo Bay, an inlet of the Atlantic; pop. 17,892 (2006).

slily ▸ adverb variant spelling of SLYLY (see SLY).

slim ▸ adjective (**slimmer**, **slimmest**) **1** (of a person or their build) gracefully thin; slender: *her slim figure* | *the girls were tall and slim*. ■ (of a thing) small in width and typically long and narrow in shape: *a slim gold band encircled her wrist*. ■ (of a garment) cut on slender lines; designed to make the wearer appear slim: *a pair of slim, immaculately cut trousers*. ■ (of a business or other organization) reduced to a smaller size in the hope that it will become more efficient.
2 (of something abstract, especially a chance or margin) very small: *there was just a slim chance of success* | *a slim majority of sixteen*.
3 S. African crafty, sly, or unscrupulous. [Dutch.]
▸ verb (**slims**, **slimming**, **slimmed**) [no obj.] Brit. make oneself thinner by dieting and sometimes exercising: *if he's overweight, he should slim* | (as noun **slimming**) *an aid to slimming*. ■ [with obj.] make (a person or part of the body) thinner in such a way: *how can I slim down my hips?* ■ [with obj.] reduce (a business or other organization) to a smaller size in the hope of making it more efficient: *restructuring and slimming down the organization*.
▸ noun **1** [in sing.] a course or period of slimming: *a sponsored slim*.
2 (also **slim disease**) African term for **AIDS**.
– DERIVATIVES **slimly** adverb, **slimmer** noun, **slimness** noun.
– ORIGIN mid 17th cent.: from Low German or Dutch (from a base meaning 'slanting, cross, bad'), of Germanic origin. The pejorative sense found in Dutch and German existed originally in the English noun *slim* 'lazy or worthless person'; compare with the South African usage 'crafty, sly' (sense 3 of the adjective).

slime ▸ noun [mass noun] un unpleasantly thick and slippery liquid substance: *the cold stone was wet with slime*.
▸ verb [with obj.] cover with slime: *what grass remained was slimed over with pale brown mud*.
– ORIGIN Old English *slīm*, of Germanic origin; related to Dutch *slijm* and German *Schleim* 'mucus, slime', Latin *limus* 'mud', and Greek *limnē* 'marsh'.

slimeball ▸ noun informal a repulsive or despicable person.

slime mould ▸ noun a simple organism that consists of an acellular mass of creeping jelly-like protoplasm containing nuclei, or a mass of amoeboid cells. When it reaches a certain size it forms a large number of spore cases. ● Division Myxomycota, kingdom Fungi, in particular the class Myxomycetes; also treated as protozoan (phylum Gymnomyxa, kingdom Protista).

slim jim ▸ noun informal a very slim person or thing. ■ (**slim jims**) long, narrow trousers. ■ a long, thin variety of smoked sausage. ■ (trademark in the US) a long flexible metal strip with a hooked end, used to unlock a car door without using a key.

slimline ▸ adjective **1** slender in design or build. ■ stripped of unnecessary elements; economical: *a slimline orchestra*.
2 Brit. (of food or drink) low in calories: *slimline tonic*.

slimy ▸ adjective (**slimier**, **slimiest**) **1** covered by or resembling slime: *thick, slimy mud*.
2 informal repellently smooth and obsequious: *a slimy, cigar-puffing political fixer*.
– DERIVATIVES **slimily** adverb, **sliminess** noun.

sling[1] ▸ noun **1** a flexible strap or belt used in the form of a loop to support or raise a hanging weight: *the*

S

horse had to be supported by a sling fixed to the roof. ▪ a bandage or soft strap looped round the neck to support an injured arm: *she had her arm in a sling.* ▪ a pouch or frame for carrying a baby, supported by a strap round the neck or shoulders. ▪ a short length of rope used to provide additional support for the body in abseiling or climbing.
2 a simple weapon in the form of a strap or loop, used to hurl stones or other small missiles.
3 Austral./NZ informal a bribe or gratuity.
▸ **verb** (past and past participle **slung**) **1** [with obj. and adverbial of place] suspend or arrange (something), especially with a strap or straps, so that it hangs loosely in a particular position: *a hammock was slung between two trees.* ▪ carry (something, especially a garment) loosely and casually about one's person: *he had his jacket* ***slung over*** *one shoulder.* ▪ hoist or transfer (something) with a sling: *horse after horse was slung up from the barges.*
2 [with obj. and adverbial of direction] Brit. informal casually throw or fling: *sling a few things into your knapsack.* ▪ hurl (a stone or other missile) from a sling or similar weapon. ▪ [no obj.] (**sling off**) Austral./NZ informal mock; make fun: *I wasn't slinging off at your religion.*
3 [no obj.] Austral./NZ informal pay a bribe or gratuity.
– PHRASES **put someone's** (or **have one's**) **ass in a sling** N. Amer. vulgar slang cause someone to be (or be) in trouble. **sling beer** N. Amer. informal work as a bartender. **sling hash** (or **plates**) N. Amer. informal serve food in a cafe or diner. **sling one's hook** see HOOK. **slings and arrows** used with reference to adverse factors or circumstances: *the slings and arrows of outrageous critics.* [with reference to Shakespeare's *Hamlet* III. i. 58.]
– DERIVATIVES **slinger** noun.
– ORIGIN Middle English: probably from Low German, of symbolic origin; compare with German *Schlinge* 'noose, snare'. Sense 2 of the verb is from Old Norse *slyngva*.

sling² ▸ **noun** a sweetened drink of spirits, especially gin, and water. See also SINGAPORE SLING.
– ORIGIN mid 18th cent.: of unknown origin.

slingback ▸ **noun** a shoe held in place by a strap around the ankle above the heel: [as modifier] *high-heeled slingback shoes.*

sling bag ▸ **noun** an unstructured fabric shoulder bag.

slingshot ▸ **noun 1** chiefly N. Amer. a hand-held catapult. ▪ a shot from a hand-held catapult.
2 [mass noun] [often as modifier] the effect of the gravitational pull of a celestial object in accelerating and changing the course of another object or a spacecraft.
▸ **verb** (**slingshots, slingshotting**; past and past participle **slingshot** or **slingshotted**) forcefully accelerate through the effect of gravity: [no obj.] *the car would hit the first dip, then slingshot off the second rise.*

slink ▸ **verb** (past and past participle **slunk**) [no obj., with adverbial of direction] move smoothly and quietly with gliding steps, in a stealthy or sensuous manner: *the fox came slinking through the bracken.* ▪ come or go unobtrusively or furtively: *all the staff have slunk off home.*
▸ **noun** [in sing.] a slinking movement or walk: *she moved with a sensuous slink.*
– ORIGIN Old English *slincan* 'crawl, creep'; compare with Middle Dutch and Middle Low German *slinken* 'subside, sink'.

slinky ▸ **adjective** (**slinkier, slinkiest**) informal (of a garment) fitting closely to the lines of the body: *a slinky black evening dress.* ▪ graceful and sinuous or seductive in movement: *slinky models sashayed down the catwalk.*
– DERIVATIVES **slinkily** adverb, **slinkiness** noun.

slip¹ ▸ **verb** (**slips, slipping, slipped**) [no obj.] **1** lose one's footing and slide unintentionally for a short distance: *I slipped over on the ice | he kept slipping in the mud.* ▪ [with adverbial of direction] (of an object) accidentally slide or move out of position or from someone's grasp: *the envelope slipped through Luke's fingers | a wisp of hair had slipped down over her face.* ▪ fail to grip or make proper contact with a surface: *the front wheels began to slip* | (as adj. **slipping**) *a badly slipping clutch.*
2 [with adverbial of direction] go or move quietly or quickly, without attracting notice: *we slipped out by a back door.* ▪ [with obj. and adverbial of direction] put (something) in a particular place or position quietly, quickly, or stealthily: *she slipped the map into her pocket* | [with two objs] *I slipped him a tenner to keep quiet.* ▪ (**slip into/out of**) put on or take off (a garment) quickly and easily.
3 pass or change to a lower, worse, or different condition, typically in a gradual or imperceptible way: *many people feel standards have slipped* | [with complement] *the bank's shares slipped 1.5p to 227p.* ▪ (**be slipping**) informal be behaving in a way that is not up to one's usual level of performance: *you're slipping, Doyle—you need a holiday.*
4 [with obj.] escape or get loose from (a means of restraint): *the giant balloon slipped its moorings.* ▪ (of a thought or fact) fail to be remembered by (one's mind or memory); elude (one's notice): *a beautiful woman's address was never likely to slip his mind.* ▪ release (an animal, typically a hunting dog) from restraint. ▪ Knitting move (a stitch) to the other needle without knitting it. ▪ release (the clutch of a motor vehicle) slightly or for a moment. ▪ disengage (a ship's anchor) when leaving a port in haste. ▪ (of an animal) produce (dead young) prematurely; abort.
▸ **noun 1** an act of sliding unintentionally for a short distance: *a single slip could send them plummeting down the mountainside.* ▪ [mass noun] relative movement of an object or surface and a solid surface in contact with it. ▪ a reduction in the movement of a pulley or other mechanism due to slipping of the belt, rope, etc. ▪ a sideways movement of an aircraft in flight, typically downwards towards the centre of curvature of a turn. ▪ [mass noun] Geology the extent of relative horizontal displacement of corresponding points on either side of a fault plane.
2 a fall to a lower level or standard: *a continued slip in house prices.* ▪ (also **slip-up**) a minor or careless mistake: *the judge made a slip in his summing up.*
3 a loose-fitting garment, typically a short petticoat: *a silk slip* | [as modifier] *a slip dress.*
4 Cricket a fielding position (often one of two or more in an arc) close behind the batsman on the off side, for catching balls edged by the batsman: *he was caught* ***in the slips*** *for 32 | King is at* ***first slip***. ▪ a fielder at this position.
5 short for SLIPWAY.
6 (usu. **slips**) a leash which enables a dog to be released quickly.
7 Knitting short for SLIP STITCH.
– PHRASES **give someone the slip** informal evade or escape from someone. **let something slip 1** reveal something inadvertently in the course of a conversation: [with clause] *Clive had let slip he was married.* **2** archaic release a hound from the leash so as to begin the chase: *let slip the dogs of war.* **let something slip through one's fingers** (or **grasp**) lose hold or possession of something. **slip of the pen** (or **the tongue**) a minor mistake in writing (or speech). **slip through the net** see NET¹. **there's many a slip 'twixt cup and lip** proverb many things can go wrong between the start of a project and its completion; nothing is certain until it has happened.
– PHRASAL VERBS **slip away 1** depart without saying goodbye; leave quietly or surreptitiously. ▪ slowly disappear; recede or dwindle: *his ability to concentrate is slipping away.* ▪ die peacefully (used euphemistically): *he lay there and quietly slipped away.* **2** (also **slip by**) (of time) elapse: *the night was slipping away.* **slip something in** insert a remark smoothly or adroitly into a conversation: *she slipped in a question about the length of time he'd been working on the assignment.* **slip out** (of a remark) be uttered inadvertently: *the question slipped out before I'd considered the wisdom of it.* **slip up** informal make a careless error: *they often slipped up when it came to spelling.*
– ORIGIN Middle English (in the sense 'move quickly and softly'): probably from Middle Low German *slippen* (verb); compare with SLIPPERY.

slip² ▸ **noun 1** a small piece of paper, typically a form for writing on or one giving printed information: *his monthly salary slip | complete the tear-off slip below.* ▪ Printing a printer's proof on a long piece of paper; a galley proof. ▪ a long, narrow strip of a thin material such as wood.
2 a cutting taken from a plant for grafting or planting; a scion.
– PHRASES **a slip of a ——** used to denote a small, slim person: *you are little more than a slip of a girl.*
– ORIGIN late Middle English: probably from Middle Dutch, Middle Low German *slippe* 'cut, strip'.

slip³ ▸ **noun** [mass noun] a creamy mixture of clay, water, and typically a pigment of some kind, used especially for decorating earthenware.
– ORIGIN mid 17th cent.: of obscure origin; compare with Norwegian *slip(a)* 'slime'.

slip-carriage (also **slip-coach**) ▸ **noun** Brit. historical a railway carriage on an express which could be detached so as to come to rest at a station where the rest of the train did not stop.

slipcase ▸ **noun** a close-fitting case open at one side or end for an object such as a book, CD, or DVD.

slip casting ▸ **noun** [mass noun] the manufacture of ceramic ware by allowing slip to solidify in a mould.
– DERIVATIVES **slip-cast** adjective.

slipcover ▸ **noun** chiefly N. Amer. a loose cover, in particular a detachable cover for a chair or sofa. ▪ a jacket or slip case for a book, CD, or DVD.

slip form ▸ **noun** a mould in which a concrete structure of uniform cross section is cast by filling the mould with liquid concrete and then continuously moving and refilling it at a sufficiently slow rate for the emerging part to have partially set.

slip knot ▸ **noun 1** a knot that can be undone by a pull.
2 a running knot.

slip-on ▸ **adjective** (especially of shoes or clothes) having no (or few) fastenings and therefore able to be put on and taken off quickly.
▸ **noun** a slip-on shoe or garment.

slipover ▸ **noun** a pullover, typically one without sleeves.
▸ **adjective** (**slip-over**) denoting a garment designed to be put on over the head: *a slip-over sweater.*

slippage ▸ **noun** [mass noun] the action or process of slipping or subsiding. ▪ failure to meet a standard or deadline; the extent of this: *slippage on any job will entail slippage on the overall project.*

slipped ▸ **adjective** Heraldry (of a flower or leaf) depicted with a stalk.

slipped disc ▸ **noun** a cartilaginous disc between vertebrae in the spine that is displaced or partly protruding, pressing on nearby nerves and causing back pain or sciatica.

slipper ▸ **noun** a comfortable slip-on shoe that is worn indoors. ▪ a light slip-on shoe, especially one used for dancing.
▸ **verb** [with obj.] beat (someone) with a slipper.
– DERIVATIVES **slippered** adjective.

slipper bath ▸ **noun** Brit., chiefly historical a bath with one high end to lean against and the other end covered over.

slipper flower ▸ **noun** another term for CALCEOLARIA.

slipperiness ▸ **noun** [mass noun] the quality or state of being slippery: *a play about the slipperiness of language.*

slipper limpet ▸ **noun** a mollusc which has an oval shell with an internal ledge, giving the empty shell a slipper-like appearance. ● Genus *Crepidula*, family Crepidulidae, class Gastropoda: many species, especially the North American *C. fornicata*, which has become a serious pest of oyster beds in Europe.

slipper orchid ▸ **noun** another term for LADY'S SLIPPER.

slipper satin ▸ **noun** [mass noun] a fine-quality semi-glossy satin, used in dressmaking and for dancing slippers.

slipper sock ▸ **noun** a thick sock, typically with a leather sole, for use as a slipper.

slippery ▸ **adjective** (**slipperier, slipperiest**) (of a surface or object) difficult to hold firmly or stand on because it is smooth, wet, or slimy: *slippery ice | her hand was slippery with sweat.* ▪ (of a person) evasive and unpredictable; not to be relied on: *Martin's a slippery customer.* ▪ (of a word or concept) elusive in meaning because changing according to one's point of view: *the word 'intended' is a decidedly slippery one.* **S**
– PHRASES **slippery slope** a course of action likely to lead to something bad or disastrous: *he is on the slippery slope towards a life of crime.*
– DERIVATIVES **slipperily** adverb.
– ORIGIN late 15th cent.: from dialect *slipper* 'slippery', probably suggested by Luther's *schlipfferig*.

slippery dip ▸ **noun** Austral. a children's slide in a playground or park.

slippery elm ▸ **noun** a North American elm with coarsely textured leaves and rough outer bark. The mucilaginous inner bark has long been used medicinally. ● *Ulmus fulva*, family Ulmaceae.

slippery hitch ▸ **noun** a kind of knot made fast by catching part of the rope beneath the loop, released by pulling on the free end.

slippy ▸ **adjective** (**slippier, slippiest**) informal slippery: *the towpath was slippy with mud | slippy tyres.*
– PHRASES **look** (or **be**) **slippy** Brit. dated be quick.
– DERIVATIVES **slippiness** noun.

slip rail ▶ noun Austral./NZ a rail in a fence which can be removed to provide an opening.

slip ring ▶ noun a ring in a dynamo or electric motor which is attached to and rotates with the shaft, passing an electric current to a circuit via a fixed brush pressing against it.

slip road ▶ noun Brit. a road entering or leaving a motorway or dual carriageway.

slip rope ▶ noun a mooring rope with both ends on board ship, enabling the crew to cast off without disembarking.

slip sheet ▶ noun Printing a sheet of paper placed between newly printed sheets to prevent set-off or smudging.

slipshod ▶ adjective **1** characterized by a lack of care, thought, or organization: *he'd caused many problems with his slipshod management.*
2 archaic (of shoes) worn down at the heel.
– ORIGIN late 16th cent. (originally in the sense 'wearing slippers or loose shoes'): from the verb SLIP[1] + SHOD.

slip-slop ▶ noun South African term for FLIP-FLOP.

slip stitch ▶ noun **1** (in sewing) a loose stitch joining layers of fabric and not visible externally.
2 [mass noun] [often as modifier] Knitting a type of stitch in which the stitches are moved from one needle to the other without being knitted: *a slip stitch pattern.*
▶ verb (**slip-stitch**) [with obj.] sew or knit with slip stitches.

slipstone ▶ noun a shaped oilstone used to sharpen gouges.

slipstream ▶ noun **1** a current of air or water driven back by a revolving propeller or jet engine. ■ the partial vacuum created in the wake of a moving vehicle, often used by other vehicles in a race to assist in overtaking.
2 an assisting force regarded as drawing something along behind something else: *when the US economy booms, the rest of the world is pulled along in the slipstream.*
▶ verb [no obj.] (especially in motor racing) follow closely behind another vehicle, travelling in its slipstream and awaiting an opportunity to overtake.

slipware ▶ noun [mass noun] pottery decorated with slip (see SLIP[3]).

slipway ▶ noun a slope built leading down into water, used for launching and landing boats and ships or for building and repairing them.

slit ▶ noun a long, narrow cut or opening: *make a slit in the stem under a bud* | *arrow slits.*
▶ verb (**slits, slitting, slit**) [with obj.] **1** make a long, narrow cut in: *give me the truth or I will slit your throat* | [with obj. and complement] *he slit open the envelope.* ■ cut (something) into strips: *a wide recording head magnetizes the tape before it is slit to domestic size.*
2 (past and past participle **slitted**) form (one's eyes) into slits; squint.
– DERIVATIVES **slitter** noun.
– ORIGIN late Old English *slite* (noun); related to Old English *slītan* 'split, rend' (of Germanic origin).

slit-eyed ▶ adjective having long, narrow eyes, or eyes narrowed by squinting.

slither ▶ verb [no obj., with adverbial of direction] move smoothly over a surface with a twisting or oscillating motion: *I spied a baby adder slithering away.* ■ slide or slip unsteadily on a loose or slippery surface: *we slithered down a snowy mountain track.*
▶ noun **1** [in sing.] a slithering movement: *a snake-like slither across the grass.*
2 a sliver: *a slither of bacon.*
– DERIVATIVES **slithery** adjective.
– ORIGIN Middle English: alteration of the dialect verb *slidder*, frequentative from the base of SLIDE.

slit lamp ▶ noun Medicine a lamp which emits a narrow but intense beam of light, used for examining the interior of the eye.

slit pocket ▶ noun a side pocket with a vertical opening.

slit trench ▶ noun a narrow trench for a soldier or a small group of soldiers and their equipment.

slitty ▶ adjective (**slittier, slittiest**) chiefly derogatory (of the eyes) long and narrow.

Sliven /'sliːv(ə)n/ a commercial city in east central Bulgaria, in the foothills of the Balkan Mountains; pop. 94,456 (2008).

sliver /'slɪvə, 'slʌɪ-/ ▶ noun **1** a small, thin, narrow piece of something cut or split off a larger piece: *a sliver of cheese* | figurative *there was a sliver of light under his door.*
2 a strip of loose untwisted textile fibres produced by carding.
▶ verb **1** [with obj.] (usu. as adj. **slivered**) cut or break (something) into small, thin, narrow pieces: *slivered almonds.*
2 convert (textile fibres) into slivers.
– ORIGIN late Middle English: from dialect *slive* 'cleave'.

slivovitz /'slɪvəvɪts/ ▶ noun [mass noun] a type of plum brandy made chiefly in the former Yugoslavia and in Romania.
– ORIGIN Croatian *šljivovica*, from *šljiva* 'plum'.

Sloane[1], Sir Hans (1660–1753), Irish physician and naturalist. He endowed the Chelsea Physic Garden, and his books and specimens formed the basis of the British Museum Library and the Natural History Museum in London.

Sloane[2] (also **Sloane Ranger**) ▶ noun Brit. informal a fashionable upper-class young woman, especially one living in London.
– DERIVATIVES **Sloaney** adjective (**Sloanier, Sloaniest**).
– ORIGIN 1970s: from *Sloane* Square, London (+ Lone *Ranger*, the name of a fictitious cowboy hero).

slob ▶ noun **1** Brit. informal a lazy and slovenly person.
2 [mass noun] Irish muddy land.
▶ verb [no obj.] Brit. informal behave in a lazy and slovenly manner: *he spent his life watching television and generally* ***slobbing around****.*
– DERIVATIVES **slobbish** adjective, **slobbishness** noun, **slobby** adjective (**slobbier, slobbiest**).
– ORIGIN late 18th cent.: from Irish *slab* 'mud', from Anglo-Irish *slab* 'ooze, sludge', probably of Scandinavian origin.

slobber ▶ verb [no obj.] have saliva dripping copiously from the mouth: *Fido tended to slobber* | (as adj. **slobbering**) *big slobbering kisses.* ■ (**slobber over**) show excessive enthusiasm for: *news executives slobbered over him for autographs.*
▶ noun [mass noun] saliva dripping copiously from the mouth.
– DERIVATIVES **slobbery** adjective.
– ORIGIN late Middle English: probably from Middle Dutch *slobberen* 'walk through mud', also 'feed noisily', of imitative origin.

sloe ▶ noun another term for BLACKTHORN. ■ the small bluish-black fruit of the blackthorn, with a sharp sour taste.
– ORIGIN Old English *slā(h)*, of Germanic origin; related to Dutch *slee* and German *Schlehe*, from an Indo-European root probably shared by Latin *livere* 'be blue' and Croatian *šljiva* 'plum'.

sloe-eyed ▶ adjective having attractive dark eyes, typically almond-shaped.

sloe gin ▶ noun [mass noun] a liqueur made by steeping sloes in gin.

slog informal ▶ verb (**slogs, slogging, slogged**) **1** [no obj.] work hard over a period of time: *they were slogging away to meet a deadline.* ■ [with adverbial of direction] walk or move with difficulty or effort: *I slogged through the heather in the heat.*
2 [with obj.] hit (someone or something) forcefully and typically wildly, especially in boxing or cricket: *batsmen careering down the pitch to slog the ball up in the air.* ■ (**slog it out**) Brit. fight or compete fiercely: *they'll be slogging it out in the first round of the cup next Sunday.*
▶ noun **1** [usu. in sing.] a spell of difficult, tiring work or travelling: *it would be a* ***hard slog*** *back to the camp* | [mass noun] *it wasn't all slog during those years.*
2 a forceful and uncontrolled hit, especially in cricket: *a slog hit the fielder on the helmet.*
– DERIVATIVES **slogger** noun.
– ORIGIN early 19th cent.: of unknown origin; compare with SLUG[2].

slogan ▶ noun **1** a short and striking or memorable phrase used in advertising. ■ a motto associated with a political party or movement or other group.
2 historical a Scottish Highland war cry.
– ORIGIN early 16th cent.: from Scottish Gaelic *sluagh-ghairm*, from *sluagh* 'army' + *gairm* 'shout'.

sloganeer ▶ verb (usu. as noun **sloganeering**) [no obj.] employ or invent slogans, typically in a political context.
▶ noun a person who sloganeers.

sloka /'ʃləʊkə/ ▶ noun a couplet of Sanskrit verse, especially one in which each line contains sixteen syllables.
– ORIGIN from Sanskrit *śloka* 'noise, praise'.

slo-mo ▶ noun informal short for SLOW MOTION.

sloop ▶ noun a one-masted sailing boat with a mainsail and jib rigged fore and aft. ■ (also **sloop of war**) historical a small square-rigged sailing warship with two or three masts. ■ historical a small anti-submarine warship used for convoy escort in the Second World War.
– ORIGIN early 17th cent.: from Dutch *sloep(e)*, of unknown origin.

sloosh Brit. informal ▶ noun a rush of water or an energetic rinsing: *a sloosh with this mouthwash helps loosen plaque.* ■ [mass noun] the noise of heavy splashing or rushing water: *the sloosh of water in the culverts.*
▶ verb [no obj., with adverbial] (of liquid) flow or pour with a rush: *she gazed at the torrent of water slooshing downstream.* ■ [with obj.] rinse (something) with a rush of water: ***sloosh down*** *the changing-room floor.*
– ORIGIN early 20th cent.: imitative.

sloot /sluːt/ (also **sluit**) ▶ noun S. African a deep gully eroded by rainfall. ■ historical a narrow water channel constructed for irrigation.
– ORIGIN Afrikaans, from Dutch *sloot* 'ditch'.

slop[1] ▶ verb (**slops, slopping, slopped**) **1** [no obj., with adverbial of direction] (of a liquid) spill or flow over the edge of a container, typically as a result of careless handling: *water slopped over the edge of the sink.* ■ [with obj.] cause (a liquid) to spill or overflow in such a way: *in spite of his care he slopped some water.* ■ (of liquid) move within a container, noisily slapping against the sides. ■ [with obj. and adverbial] apply or pour (a liquid substance) in a casual or careless manner: *they spent their weekend slopping on paint.* ■ (**slop through**) wade through (a wet or muddy area): *they were slopping through paddy fields.*
2 [no obj.] (**slop about/around**) chiefly Brit. dress in an untidy or casual manner: *at weekends he would slop about in his oldest clothes.*
3 [no obj.] (**slop out**) Brit. (especially in prison) empty the contents of a chamber pot: (as noun **slopping out**) *the indignity of slopping out.*
4 [with obj.] feed slops to (an animal).
5 [no obj.] chiefly N. Amer. speak or write in a sentimentally effusive manner; gush: *she* ***slopped over*** *her dog.*
▶ noun **1** (**slops**) waste water from a kitchen, bathroom, or chamber pot that has to be emptied by hand: *sink slops.* ■ semi-liquid kitchen refuse, often used as animal food. ■ unappetizing semi-liquid food.
2 [mass noun] chiefly N. Amer. sentimental language or material: *country music is not all commercial slop.*
3 Nautical a choppy sea.
– ORIGIN mid 16th cent. (in the sense 'to spill, splash'): probably related to SLIP[3]. Early use of the noun denoted 'slushy mud', the first of the current senses ('unappetizing food') dating from the mid 17th cent.

slop[2] ▶ noun archaic **1** a workman's loose outer garment.
2 (**slops**) wide, baggy trousers common in the 16th and early 17th centuries, especially as worn by sailors. ■ clothes and bedding supplied to sailors by the navy. ■ ready-made or cheap clothing.
– ORIGIN late Middle English (in sense 1): from the second element of Old English *oferslop* 'surplice', of Germanic origin.

slop basin (N. Amer. also **slop bowl**) ▶ noun Brit. a bowl for the dregs of cups of tea or coffee.

slop bucket ▶ noun a bucket for removing waste from a kitchen or chamber pot.

slope ▶ noun **1** a surface of which one end or side is at a higher level than another; a rising or falling surface: *he slithered helplessly down the slope.* ■ a difference in level or sideways position between the two ends or sides of a thing: *the roof should have a slope sufficient for proper drainage* | [mass noun] *the backward slope of the chair.* ■ (often **slopes**) a part of the side of a hill or mountain, especially as a place for skiing: *a ten-minute cable car ride delivers you to the slopes.* ■ the gradient of a graph at any point. ■ Electronics the mutual conductance of a valve, numerically equal to the gradient of one of the characteristic curves of the valve.
2 US informal, offensive a person from East Asia, especially Vietnam.
▶ verb **1** [no obj.] (of a surface or line) be inclined from a horizontal or vertical line; slant up or down: *the garden* ***sloped down*** *to a stream* | *the ceiling sloped.* ■ [with obj.] place or arrange in such a position or inclination: *Poole sloped his shoulders* | (as adj. **sloped**) *a sloped leather writing surface.*
2 [no obj., with adverbial of direction] Brit. informal move in an idle or aimless manner: *I had seen Don sloping about the beach.* ■ (**slope off**) leave unobtrusively, typi-

cally in order to evade work or duty: *the men sloped off looking ashamed of themselves.*
– PHRASES **at the slope** Military (of a rifle) held with the barrel on the left shoulder and the butt in the left hand. **slope arms** Military hold a rifle at the slope.
– ORIGIN late 16th cent. (as a verb): from the obsolete adverb *slope*, a shortening of ASLOPE. The use of the verb with reference to aimless or unobtrusive movement may be related to LOPE.

sloping ▸ adjective inclined from a horizontal or vertical line: *a sloping floor.*

sloppy ▸ adjective (**sloppier**, **sloppiest**) **1** (of semi-fluid matter) containing too much liquid; watery: *do not make the concrete too sloppy.*
2 careless and unsystematic; excessively casual: *we gave away a goal through sloppy defending.*
3 (of a garment) casual and loose-fitting: *she wore a sloppy sweater and jeans.*
4 informal (of literature or behaviour) weakly or foolishly sentimental: *lovers of sloppy romance.*
– DERIVATIVES **sloppily** adverb, **sloppiness** noun.

sloppy joe ▸ noun informal **1** a long, loose-fitting sweater.
2 N. Amer. a hamburger in which the minced-beef filling is made into a kind of meat sauce, typically with tomatoes and spices.

slosh ▸ verb **1** [no obj., with adverbial of direction] (of liquid in a container) move irregularly with a splashing sound: *water in the boat sloshed about under our feet* | figurative *there is so much money now **sloshing around** in professional tennis.* ■ move through liquid with a splashing sound: *they sloshed up the tracks in the dank woods.* ■ [with obj. and adverbial of direction] pour (liquid) clumsily: *she sloshed coffee into a cracked cup.*
2 [with obj.] Brit. informal hit (someone) hard.
▸ noun **1** an act or sound of splashing: *the distant slosh of the washing machine in the basement.* ■ a quantity of liquid that is poured out: *I gave Michael and myself another **slosh of** rye.*
2 Brit. informal a heavy blow.
– ORIGIN early 19th cent.: variant of the noun SLUSH.

sloshed ▸ adjective informal drunk: *I drank a lot of wine and got sloshed.*

sloshy ▸ adjective (**sloshier**, **sloshiest**) **1** wet and sticky; slushy: *the sloshy mud.*
2 informal excessively sentimental; sloppy: *the programme is a sloshy and patronizing affair.*

slot[1] ▸ noun **1** a long, narrow aperture or slit in a machine for something to be inserted: *he slid a coin into the slot of the jukebox.* ■ a groove or channel into which something fits or in which something works, such as one in the head of a screw.
2 an allotted place in an arrangement or scheme such as a broadcasting schedule: *a late-night television slot* | *landing slots at Heathrow airport.*
▸ verb (**slots**, **slotting**, **slotted**) [with obj. and adverbial of direction] place (something) into a long, narrow aperture: *he slotted a cassette into the tape machine* | *the plates come in sections that can be **slotted together***
■ [no obj.] be placed or able to be placed into such an aperture: *the processors will slot into a personal computer.* ■ Brit. informal (of a soccer player) score (a goal) with a precise shot: *he slotted in the opening goal.*
■ [no obj.] (**slot in/into**) (of a person) fit easily into (a new role or situation): *employers look for someone who will slot into the office culture.*
– DERIVATIVES **slotted** adjective.
– ORIGIN late Middle English (in the sense 'slight depression running down the middle of the chest', surviving as a Scots term): from Old French *esclot*, of obscure origin.

slot[2] ▸ noun (usu. **slots**) the track of a deer, as visible in soft ground.
– ORIGIN late 16th cent.: from Old French *esclot* 'hoof print of a horse', probably from Old Norse *slóth* 'trail'; compare with SLEUTH.

slotback ▸ noun American Football a back between the tackle and the split end.

slot car ▸ noun N. Amer. an electrically driven miniature racing car which travels in a slot in a track.

sloth /sləʊθ/ ▸ noun **1** [mass noun] reluctance to work or make an effort; laziness: *he should overcome his natural sloth and complacency.*
2 a slow-moving tropical American mammal that hangs upside down from the branches of trees using its long limbs and hooked claws. ● Families Bradypodidae (three species of **three-toed sloth** in genus *Bradypus*) and Megalonychidae (two species of **two-toed sloth** in genus *Choloepus*), order Xenarthra (or Edentata).
– ORIGIN Old English: from SLOW + -TH[2].

sloth bear ▸ noun a shaggy-coated nocturnal Indian bear which uses its long curved claws for hanging upside down like a sloth and for opening termite mounds to feed on the insects. ● *Melursus ursinus*, family Ursidae.

slothful ▸ adjective lazy: *fatigue made him slothful.*
– DERIVATIVES **slothfully** adverb, **slothfulness** noun.

slot machine ▸ noun Brit. a vending machine selling small items. ■ chiefly N. Amer. a fruit machine.

slotted spoon ▸ noun a large spoon with slots for straining food.

slouch ▸ verb **1** [no obj., with adverbial] stand, move, or sit in a lazy, drooping way: *he slouched against the wall* | (**be slouched**) *he was slouched in his chair.*
2 [with obj.] dated bend one side of the brim of (a hat) downwards.
▸ noun [in sing.] **1** a lazy, drooping posture or movement: *his stance was a round-shouldered slouch.*
2 [usu. with negative] informal an incompetent person: *my brother was **no slouch at** making a buck.*
3 a downward bend of a hat brim.
– DERIVATIVES **slouchy** adjective (**slouchier**, **slouchiest**).
– ORIGIN early 16th cent. (in the sense 'lazy, slovenly person'): of unknown origin. *Slouching* was used to mean 'hanging down, drooping' (specifically describing a hat with a brim hanging over the face), and 'having an awkward posture' from the 17th cent.

slouch hat ▸ noun a hat with a wide flexible brim.

Slough /slaʊ/ a town in SE England to the west of London; pop. 119,400 (est. 2009).

slough[1] /slaʊ/ ▸ noun **1** a swamp. ■ N. Amer. a muddy side channel or inlet.
2 a situation characterized by lack of progress or activity: *the economic slough of the interwar years.*
– DERIVATIVES **sloughy** adjective.
– ORIGIN Old English *slōh*, *slō(g)*, of unknown origin.

slough[2] /slʌf/ ▸ verb **1** [with obj.] (usu. **slough something off**) shed or remove (a layer of dead skin): *a snake sloughs off its old skin* | *exfoliate once a week to slough off any dry skin.* ■ get rid of (something undesirable or no longer required): *he is concerned to slough off the country's bad environmental image.*
■ [no obj.] (**slough off**) (of dead skin) drop off; be shed.
2 [no obj.] (**slough away/down**) (of soil or rock) collapse or slide into a hole or depression.
▸ noun [mass noun] the dropping off of dead tissue from living flesh: *the drugs can cause blistering and slough.*
– DERIVATIVES **sloughy** adjective.
– ORIGIN Middle English (as a noun denoting a skin, especially the outer skin shed by a snake): perhaps related to Low German *slu(we)* 'husk, peel'. The verb dates from the early 18th cent.

Slough of Despond /slaʊ/ a deep boggy place in John Bunyan's *The Pilgrim's Progress* between the City of Destruction and the gate at the beginning of Christian's journey. ■ a state of hopeless depression: *while everyone is having a blast I am sinking into the Slough of Despond.*

Slovak /ˈsləʊvak/ ▸ noun **1** a native or inhabitant of Slovakia, or a person of Slovak descent.
2 [mass noun] the Western Slavic language of Slovakia, with about 5 million speakers.
▸ adjective relating to the Slovaks or their language.
– ORIGIN the name in Slovak, from a Slavic root shared with SLOVENE and perhaps related to *slovo* 'word'.

Slovakia /sləˈvakɪə, -ˈvɑːkɪə/ a country in central Europe; pop. 5,463,000 (est. 2009); official language, Slovak; capital, Bratislava.

> Slovakia was dominated by Hungary until it declared independence in 1918 and united with the Czech-speaking areas of Bohemia and Moravia to form Czechoslovakia. The eastern of the two constituent republics of Czechoslovakia, Slovakia became independent on the partition of that country on 1 January 1993.

– DERIVATIVES **Slovakian** adjective & noun.

sloven /ˈslʌv(ə)n/ ▸ noun dated a person who is habitually untidy or careless.
– ORIGIN late 15th cent. (in the sense 'person with base manners'): perhaps from Flemish *sloef* 'dirty' or Dutch *slof* 'careless, negligent'.

Slovene /ˈsləʊviːn, sləʊˈviːn/ ▸ noun **1** a native or inhabitant of Slovenia, or a person of Slovene descent.
2 [mass noun] the Southern Slavic language of the Slovenes, with about 2 million speakers.
▸ adjective relating to Slovenia, its people, or their language.
– ORIGIN from Slovene *Slovenec*, from a Slavic root shared with SLOVAK and perhaps related to *slovo* 'word'.

Slovenia /sləˈviːnɪə/ a country in SE Europe, formerly a constituent republic of Yugoslavia; pop. 2,005,700 (est. 2009); official language, Slovene; capital, Ljubljana.

> Slovenia formed part of the Austrian empire and in 1919 was ceded to the kingdom of Serbs, Croats, and Slovenes (named Yugoslavia from 1929), of which it remained a constituent republic until it declared its independence in 1991.

Slovenian ▸ noun & adjective another term for SLOVENE.

slovenly ▸ adjective (especially of a person or their appearance) untidy and dirty: *a fat, slovenly ex-rock star.* ■ (especially of a person or action) careless; excessively casual: *slovenly speech.*
– DERIVATIVES **slovenliness** noun.

slow ▸ adjective **1** moving or operating, or designed to do so, only at a low speed; not quick or fast: *until recently diesel cars were slow and noisy* | *a slow dot-matrix printer.* ■ taking a long time to perform a specified action: *she was rather a slow reader* | [with infinitive] *large organizations can be slow to change.*
■ lasting or taking a long time: *a slow process* | *the journey home was slow.* ■ not allowing or intended for fast travel: *the slow lane.* ■ (of a sports field or ground) likely to make the ball bounce or run slowly or to prevent competitors from travelling fast.
2 [predic. or as complement] (of a clock or watch) showing a time earlier than the correct time: *the clock was five minutes slow.*
3 not prompt to understand, think, or learn: *he's so slow, so unimaginative.*
4 uneventful and rather dull: *a slow and mostly aimless narrative.* ■ (of business) with little activity; slack: *sales were slow.*
5 Photography (of a film) needing long exposure. ■ (of a lens) having a small aperture.
6 (of a fire or oven) burning or giving off heat gently: *bake the dish in a preheated slow oven.*
▸ adverb at a slow pace; slowly: *the train went slower and slower* | [in combination] *a slow-moving river.*
▸ verb [no obj.] reduce one's speed or the speed of a vehicle or process: *the train slowed to a halt* | *investment has slowed down* | [with obj.] *he slowed the car.* ■ (**slow down/up**) live or work less actively or intensely: *I wasn't feeling well and had to slow down.*
– PHRASES **slow but** (or **and**) **sure** not quick but achieving the required result eventually: *I am making good progress—slow but sure.*
– DERIVATIVES **slowish** adjective, **slowness** noun.
– ORIGIN Old English *slāw* 'slow-witted, sluggish', of Germanic origin.

> **USAGE** The word **slow** is normally used as an adjective (*a **slow** learner; the journey was **slow***). It is also used as an adverb in certain specific contexts, including compounds such as **slow-acting** and **slow-moving** and in the expression **go slow**. Other adverbial use is informal and usually regarded as non-standard, as for example in *he drives too **slow** and go as **slow** as you can*. In such contexts standard English uses **slowly** instead. The use of **slow** and **slowly** in this respect contrasts with the use of **fast**, which is completely standard in use as both an adjective and an adverb; there is no word 'fastly'.

slowcoach ▸ noun Brit. informal a person who acts or moves slowly: *'Come on, slowcoach,' urged George.*

slow cooker ▸ noun a large electric pot used for cooking food, especially stews, very slowly.

slowdown ▸ noun an act of slowing down: *a traffic slowdown in the passing lane.* ■ a decline in economic activity.

slow drag ▸ noun a slow blues rhythm or piece of music.
▸ verb (**slow-drag**) [no obj.] dance to such a rhythm.

slow handclap ▸ noun an instance of slow, rhythmic clapping by an audience as a sign of displeasure or impatience.

slow loris ▸ noun see LORIS.

slowly ▸ adverb at a slow speed; not quickly: *they moved forward slowly.*
– PHRASES **slowly but surely** achieving the desired results gradually and reliably rather than quickly and spectacularly: *the new church began, slowly but surely, to grow.*

slow march ▸ noun a military marching pace approximately half the speed of the quick march.

slow match ▸ noun [mass noun] historical a slow-burning wick or cord for lighting explosives.

slow motion ▸ noun [mass noun] the action of showing film or playing back video more slowly than it was made or recorded, so that the action appears much slower than in real life: *the scene was shown in slow motion* | [as modifier] *a slow-motion sequence.*

slow neutron ▸ noun a neutron with low kinetic energy especially after moderation.

slowpoke ▸ noun informal North American term for SLOWCOACH.

slow puncture ▸ noun chiefly Brit. a puncture causing only gradual deflation of a tyre.

slow reactor ▸ noun Physics a nuclear reactor using mainly slow neutrons.

slow-scan ▸ adjective Telecommunications scanning at a much slower rate than usual, so that the resulting signal has a much smaller bandwidth: *a slow-scan transmission.*

slow-twitch ▸ adjective Physiology (of a muscle fibre) contracting slowly, providing endurance rather than strength.

slow virus ▸ noun a virus or virus-like organism that multiplies slowly in the host organism and has a long incubation period.

slow-witted ▸ adjective slow to understand, think, or learn; stupid: *the slow-witted interviewer failed to pounce on his remarks.*
– DERIVATIVES **slow-wittedness** noun.

slow-worm ▸ noun a small snake-like Eurasian legless lizard that is typically brownish or copper-coloured and which gives birth to live young. Also called BLINDWORM. ● *Anguis fragilis*, family Anguidae.
– ORIGIN Old English *slāwyrm*, from *slā-* (of uncertain origin) + *wyrm* 'snake'.

SLR ▸ abbreviation ■ self-loading rifle. ■ single-lens reflex.

slub[1] ▸ noun a lump or thick place in yarn or thread. ■ [mass noun] fabric woven from yarn or thread containing lumps or thick places.
▸ adjective denoting fabric having an irregular appearance caused by uneven thickness of the warp.
– DERIVATIVES **slubbed** adjective.
– ORIGIN early 19th cent.: of unknown origin.

slub[2] ▸ noun [mass noun] wool that has been slightly twisted in preparation for spinning.
▸ verb (**slubs, slubbing, slubbed**) [with obj.] twist (wool) in this way.
– ORIGIN late 18th cent.: of unknown origin.

sludge ▸ noun [mass noun] **1** thick, soft, wet mud or a similar viscous mixture of liquid and solid components, especially the product of an industrial or refining process. ■ dirty oil, especially in the sump of an internal-combustion engine.
2 [usu. as modifier] an unattractive muddy shade of brown or green: *a sludge green.*
3 sea ice newly formed in small pieces.
– DERIVATIVES **sludgy** adjective (**sludgier, sludgiest**).
– ORIGIN early 17th cent.: of uncertain origin; compare with SLUSH.

S

slue ▸ verb & noun variant spelling of SLEW[1].

slug[1] ▸ noun **1** a tough-skinned terrestrial mollusc which typically lacks a shell and secretes a film of mucus for protection. It can be a serious plant pest. ● Order Stylommatophora, class Gastropoda.
2 a slow, lazy person.
3 an amount of liquor that is gulped or poured: *he took a* **slug of** *whisky.*
4 an elongated, typically rounded piece of metal: *the reactor uses embedded* **slugs of** *uranium.* ■ chiefly N. Amer. a bullet, especially a lead one. ■ a missile for an airgun.
5 a line of type in Linotype printing.
▸ verb (**slugs, slugging, slugged**) [with obj.] drink (something, typically alcohol) in a large draught; swig: *she picked up her drink and slugged it straight back.*
– DERIVATIVES **slugger** noun.
– ORIGIN late Middle English (in the sense 'sluggard'): probably of Scandinavian origin; compare with Norwegian dialect *slugg* 'large heavy body'. Sense 1 dates from the early 18th cent.

slug[2] informal, chiefly N. Amer. ▸ verb (**slugs, slugging, slugged**) [with obj.] strike (someone) with a hard blow: *he was the one who'd get slugged.* ■ (**slug it out**) settle a dispute or contest by fighting or competing fiercely: *they went outside to slug it out.*
▸ noun a hard blow.
– DERIVATIVES **slugger** noun.
– ORIGIN mid 19th cent.: of unknown origin; compare with the verb SLOG.

slugabed ▸ noun chiefly N. Amer. or archaic a lazy person who stays in bed late.
– ORIGIN late 16th cent.: from the rare verb *slug* 'be lazy or slow' + ABED.

slugfest ▸ noun N. Amer. informal a tough and challenging contest, especially in sports such as boxing and baseball.
– ORIGIN early 20th cent.: from SLUG[2] + -FEST.

sluggard ▸ noun a lazy, sluggish person.
– DERIVATIVES **sluggardly** adjective.
– ORIGIN Middle English: from the rare verb *slug* 'be lazy or slow' + -ARD.

sluggish ▸ adjective slow-moving or inactive: *a sluggish stream.* ■ lacking energy or alertness: *Alex woke late feeling tired and sluggish.* ■ slow to respond or make progress: *the car had been sluggish all morning.*
– DERIVATIVES **sluggishly** adverb, **sluggishness** noun.
– ORIGIN late Middle English: from the noun SLUG[1] or the verb *slug* (see SLUGGARD) + -ISH[1].

slug pellet ▸ noun a pellet containing a substance poisonous to slugs, placed among growing plants to prevent them being damaged.

sluice /sluːs/ ▸ noun **1** (also **sluice gate**) a sliding gate or other device for controlling the flow of water, especially one in a lock gate. ■ (also **sluiceway**) an artificial water channel for carrying off overflow or surplus water. ■ (in gold mining) a channel or trough constructed with grooves into which a current of water is directed in order to separate gold from the ore containing it.
2 an act of rinsing or showering with water: *a sluice with cold water.*
▸ verb [with obj.] wash or rinse freely with a stream or shower of water: *she sluiced her face in cold water* | *crews* **sluiced down** *the decks of their ship.* ■ [no obj., with adverbial of direction] (of water) pour or flow freely: *the waves sluiced over them.*
– ORIGIN Middle English (as a noun): from Old French *escluse* 'sluice gate', based on Latin *excludere* 'exclude'. The verb dates from the late 16th cent.

sluit /sluːt, ˈsluːɪt/ ▸ noun variant spelling of SLOOT.

slum ▸ noun a squalid and overcrowded urban street or district inhabited by very poor people. ■ a house or building unfit for human habitation.
▸ verb (**slums, slumming, slummed**) [no obj.] informal spend time at a lower social level than one's own through curiosity or for charitable purposes: *day trippers slumming among the natives.* ■ (**slum it**) put up with conditions that are less comfortable or of a lower quality than one is used to: *businessmen are having to slum it in aircraft economy class seats.*
– ORIGIN early 19th cent. (originally slang, in the sense 'room'): of unknown origin.

slumber literary ▸ verb [no obj.] sleep: *Sleeping Beauty slumbered in her forest castle* | figurative *the village street slumbered under the afternoon sun.*
▸ noun (often **slumbers**) a sleep: *scaring folk from their slumbers.*
– DERIVATIVES **slumberer** noun, **slumberous** (also **slumbrous**) adjective.
– ORIGIN Middle English: alteration of Scots and northern English *sloom*, in the same sense. The *-b-* was added for ease of pronunciation.

slumberland ▸ noun [mass noun] literary or humorous the state of being asleep.

slumber party ▸ noun N. Amer. a party for teenagers, typically girls, in which all the guests stay the night at the house where the party is held.

slumgullion /slʌmˈɡʌljən/ ▸ noun [mass noun] US informal cheap or insubstantial stew.
– ORIGIN late 19th cent.: probably an invented word.

slumlord ▸ noun N. Amer. informal a landlord of slum property, typically one who charges extortionate rents.

slummock Brit. informal ▸ noun a dirty, untidy, or slovenly person.
▸ verb [no obj.] behave in a lazy, indolent, or clumsy way: *you've slummocked in bed for weeks.*
– ORIGIN mid 19th cent.: of unknown origin.

slummy ▸ adjective (**slummier, slummiest**) full of slums, or resembling a slum: *a slummy neighbourhood.*
– DERIVATIVES **slumminess** noun.

slump ▸ verb [no obj.] **1** [with adverbial] sit, lean, or fall heavily and limply: *she slumped against the cushions* | (**be slumped**) *Denis was slumped in his seat.*
2 undergo a sudden severe or prolonged fall in price, value, or amount: *land prices slumped.* ■ fail or decline substantially: *United* **slumped to** *another one–nil defeat.*
▸ noun a sudden severe or prolonged fall in the price, value, or amount of something: *a slump in profits.* ■ a prolonged period of abnormally low economic activity, typically bringing widespread unemployment. ■ a period of substantial failure or decline: *Arsenal's recent slump.*
– DERIVATIVES **slumpy** adjective.
– ORIGIN late 17th cent. (in the sense 'fall into a bog'): probably imitative and related to Norwegian *slumpe* 'to fall'.

slung past and past participle of SLING[1].

slung shot ▸ noun a hard object, such as a metal ball, attached by a strap or thong to the wrist and used as a weapon.

slunk past and past participle of SLINK.

slur ▸ verb (**slurs, slurring, slurred**) [with obj.] **1** speak (words) indistinctly so that the sounds run into one another: *he was slurring his words like a drunk.* ■ [no obj.] (of words or speech) be spoken in this way: *his speech was beginning to slur.* ■ pass over (a fact or aspect) so as to conceal or minimize it: *essential attributes are being* **slurred over** *or ignored.*
2 Music perform (a group of two or more notes) legato: (as adj. **slurred**) *a group of slurred notes.* ■ mark (notes) with a slur.
3 chiefly US make damaging or insulting insinuations or allegations about: *try and slur the integrity of the police to secure an acquittal.*
▸ noun **1** an insinuation or allegation about someone that is likely to insult them or damage their reputation: *the comments were a* **slur on** *staff at the hospital.*
2 an act of speaking indistinctly so that sounds or words run into one another or a tendency to speak in such a way: *there was a trace of a slur in his voice.*
3 Music a curved line used to show that a group of two or more notes are to be sung to one syllable or played or sung legato.
– ORIGIN Middle English: originally as noun in sense 'thin, fluid mud', later as verb meaning 'smear, smirch', 'disparage (a person)', 'gloss over (a fault)'.

slurp ▸ verb [with obj.] drink or eat (something) with a loud sucking noise: *she slurped her coffee* | [no obj.] *he slurped noisily from a wine glass.*
▸ noun a loud sucking sound made while drinking or eating: *she drank it down with a loud slurp.* ■ a mouthful of liquid drunk with a loud sucking sound: *he took a noisy* **slurp of** *his beer.*
– DERIVATIVES **slurpy** adjective.
– ORIGIN mid 17th cent.: from Dutch *slurpen*.

slurry ▸ noun (pl. **slurries**) [mass noun] a semi-liquid mixture, typically of fine particles of manure, cement, or coal and water.
– ORIGIN late Middle English: related to dialect *slur* 'thin mud', of unknown origin.

slush ▸ noun [mass noun] **1** partially melted snow or ice: *the snow was turning into brown slush in the gutters.* ■ watery mud.
2 informal excessive sentiment: *the slush of Hollywood's romantic fifties films.*
▸ verb [no obj.] make a squelching or splashing sound: *there was water slushing around in the galley.*
– ORIGIN mid 17th cent.: probably imitative; compare with SLOSH.

slush fund ▸ noun a reserve of money used for illicit purposes, especially political bribery.
– ORIGIN mid 19th cent.: originally nautical slang denoting money collected to buy luxuries, from the sale of watery food known as *slush*.

slush pile ▸ noun informal a stack of unsolicited manuscripts that have been sent to a publishing company for consideration.

slushy ▸ adjective (**slushier, slushiest**) **1** resembling, consisting of, or covered with slush: *slushy snow.*
2 informal excessively sentimental: *slushy novels.*
– DERIVATIVES **slushiness** noun.

slut ▸ noun a slovenly or promiscuous woman.
– DERIVATIVES **sluttish** adjective, **sluttishness** noun, **slutty** adjective.
– ORIGIN Middle English: of unknown origin.

sly ▸ adjective (**slyer, slyest**) having or showing a cunning and deceitful nature: *a sly, manipulative woman.* ■ showing in an insinuating way that one has some secret knowledge that may be harmful or embarrassing: *he gave a sly grin.* ■ (of an action) surreptitious: *a sly sip of water.*

– PHRASES **on the sly** in a secretive fashion: *she was drinking on the sly*.
– DERIVATIVES **slyly** (also **slily**) adverb, **slyness** noun.
– ORIGIN Middle English (also in the sense 'dexterous'): from Old Norse *slægr* 'cunning', originally 'able to strike' from the verb *slá*; compare with SLEIGHT.

slyboots ▶ noun informal a sly person.

sly grog ▶ noun [mass noun] Austral./NZ informal liquor sold illicitly.

slype /slʌɪp/ ▶ noun a covered way between a cathedral transept and the chapter house or deanery.
– ORIGIN mid 19th cent.: perhaps a variant of dialect *slipe* 'long narrow piece of ground'.

SM ▶ abbreviation ■ sadomasochism. ■ Sergeant Major. ■ short metre.

Sm ▶ symbol the chemical element samarium.

smack[1] ▶ noun a sharp slap or blow, typically one given with the palm of the hand: *she gave Mark a smack across the face*. ■ a loud, sharp sound made by such a blow or a similar action: *she closed the ledger with a smack*. ■ a loud kiss: *I was saluted with two hearty smacks on my cheeks*.
▶ verb [with obj.] **1** strike (someone or something), typically with the palm of the hand and as a punishment: *Jessica smacked his face, quite hard*. ■ [with obj. and adverbial of place] smash, drive, or put forcefully into or on to something: *he smacked a fist into the palm of a black-gloved hand*.
2 part (one's lips) noisily in eager anticipation or enjoyment of food or drink.
3 archaic crack (a whip).
▶ adverb (also **smack bang**) informal **1** in a sudden and violent way: *I ran smack into the back of a parked truck*.
2 exactly; precisely: *our mother's house was smack in the middle of the city*.
– PHRASES **a smack in the face** (or **eye**) informal a strong rebuff.
– ORIGIN mid 16th cent. (in the sense 'part (one's lips) noisily'): from Middle Dutch *smacken*, of imitative origin; compare with German *schmatzen* 'eat or kiss noisily'.

smack[2] ▶ verb [no obj.] (**smack of**) have a flavour of; taste of: *the tea smacked strongly of tannin*. ■ suggest the presence or effects of (something wrong or unpleasant): *the whole thing smacks of a cover-up*.
▶ noun (**a smack of**) a flavour or taste of: *anything with even a modest smack of hops dries the palate*. ■ a trace or suggestion of: *I hear the smack of collusion between them*.
– ORIGIN Old English *smæc* 'flavour, smell', of Germanic origin; related to Dutch *smaak* and German *Geschmack*.

smack[3] ▶ noun Brit. a single-masted sailing boat used for coasting or fishing.
– ORIGIN early 17th cent.: from Dutch *smak*, of unknown ultimate origin.

smack[4] ▶ noun [mass noun] informal heroin.
– ORIGIN 1940s: probably an alteration of Yiddish *shmek* 'a sniff'.

smack dab ▶ adverb N. Amer. informal exactly; precisely: *I'm in Bolivia, smack dab in the heart of South America*.

smackdown ▶ noun informal, chiefly US **1** a bitter contest or confrontation: *the famously crusty Democrat had a series of smackdowns with the Governor*.
2 a decisive or humiliating defeat or setback.
– ORIGIN 1990s: from SMACK[1].

smacker (also **smackeroo**) ▶ noun informal **1** a loud kiss.
2 Brit. one pound sterling: *300,000 smackers*. ■ N. Amer. one dollar.

small ▶ adjective **1** of a size that is less than normal or usual: *the room was small and quiet | the small hill that sheltered the house*. ■ not great in amount, number, strength, or power: *a rather small amount of money*. ■ not fully grown or developed; young: *as a small boy, he spent his days either reading or watching cricket*. ■ used of the first letter of a word that has both a general and a specific use to show that in this case the general use is intended: *they are diehard conservatives, with a small c*.
2 insignificant; unimportant: *these are small points*. ■ (of a business or its owner) operating on a modest scale: *a small farmer*. ■ archaic low or inferior in rank or position; socially undistinguished.
▶ plural noun (**smalls**) **1** Brit. informal small items of clothing, especially underwear.
2 [treated as sing.] W. Indian a gratuity or small gift of money.
▶ adverb into small pieces: *cut the okra up small*. ■ in a small size: *you shouldn't write so small*.
– PHRASES **feel** (or **look**) **small** feel (or look) contemptibly weak or insignificant. **in a small way** on a small scale: *in a small way his life has been improved*. **it is** (or **what**) **a small world** used to express surprise at meeting an acquaintance or discovering a personal connection in a distant place or an unexpected context. **no small ——** a good deal of ——: *a matter of no small consequence*. **small is beautiful** used, especially in environmentalism, to express the belief that something small-scale is better than a large-scale equivalent. [the title of a book by E. F. Schumacher (1973).] **the small of the back** the part of a person's back where the spine curves in at the level of the waist. **small potatoes** informal something insignificant or unimportant: *her business was small potatoes beside his empire*. **the small screen** television as a medium. **small wonder** not very surprising: *it's small wonder that her emotions had see-sawed*.
– DERIVATIVES **smallish** adjective, **smallness** noun.
– ORIGIN Old English *smæl*, of Germanic origin; related to Dutch *smal* and German *schmal*.

small ad ▶ noun Brit. a small advertisement in a newspaper, typically one inserted by a private individual in a classified section.

small arms ▶ plural noun portable firearms, especially rifles, pistols, and light machine guns.

small beer ▶ noun [mass noun] **1** Brit. a thing that is considered unimportant: *even with £10,000 to invest, you are still small beer for most stockbrokers*.
2 archaic weak beer.

small-bore ▶ adjective denoting a firearm with a narrow bore, in international and Olympic shooting generally .22 inch calibre (5.6 millimetre bore). ■ N. Amer. informal trivial; unimportant: *small-bore economic issues*.

small bower ▶ noun see BOWER[2].

small calorie ▶ noun see CALORIE.

small capital ▶ noun a capital letter which is of the same height as a lower-case x in the same typeface, AS THIS.

small change ▶ noun [mass noun] coins of low value. ■ something trivial: *his wrongdoings were small change compared to a lot of happenings in the city*.

small circle ▶ noun a circle on the surface of a sphere whose plane does not pass through the sphere's centre.

small claims court ▶ noun a local court in which claims for small sums of money can be heard and decided quickly and cheaply, without legal representation.

small clause ▶ noun Linguistics a clause which contains neither a finite verb nor the infinitive marker 'to', for example *him groan* in *I heard him groan*.

small coal ▶ noun another term for SLACK[2].

small end ▶ noun (in a piston engine) the end of the connecting rod connected to the piston.

small forward ▶ noun Basketball a versatile forward who is effective outside the key as well as near the net.

small fry ▶ plural noun **1** insignificant people or things: *he was small fry and privy to nothing*. **2** young fish.

smallgoods ▶ plural noun Austral./NZ cooked meats and meat products.

smallholding ▶ noun Brit. an agricultural holding smaller than a farm. ■ [mass noun] the practice of farming smallholdings: *cooperation with neighbours is the key to successful smallholding*.
– DERIVATIVES **smallholder** noun.

small hours ▶ plural noun (**the small hours**) the early hours of the morning after midnight: *she returned in the small hours*.

small intestine ▶ noun the part of the intestine that runs between the stomach and the large intestine; the duodenum, jejunum, and ileum collectively.

small letter ▶ noun a lower-case letter, as distinct from a capital letter.

small-minded ▶ adjective having or showing rigid opinions or a narrow outlook; petty: *my family are small-minded provincials*.
– DERIVATIVES **small-mindedly** adverb, **small-mindedness** noun.

smallmouth ▶ noun N. Amer. the smallmouth bass. See BLACK BASS.

smallpox ▶ noun [mass noun] an acute contagious viral disease, with fever and pustules that usually leave permanent scars. It was effectively eradicated through vaccination by 1979. Also called VARIOLA.

small print ▶ noun [mass noun] Brit. printed matter in small type. ■ inconspicuous details or conditions printed in an agreement or contract, especially ones that may prove unfavourable: *check the small print and make sure you know your rights*.

small-reed ▶ noun a reed-like grass which grows in damp woods and marshes in temperate regions.
● Genus *Calamagrostis*, family Gramineae.

small-scale ▶ adjective of limited size or extent: *a small-scale research project | small-scale manufacturing*.

small screen ▶ noun (**the small screen**) television as a medium: *transplanting the timeless values of good literature to the small screen*.

small slam ▶ noun Bridge the bidding and winning of twelve of the thirteen tricks.

small stores ▶ plural noun small items for personal use on a sea voyage.

small-sword ▶ noun chiefly historical a light tapering sword used for duelling.

small talk ▶ noun [mass noun] polite conversation about unimportant or uncontroversial matters, especially as engaged in on social occasions: *propriety required that he face these people and **make small talk***.

small-time ▶ adjective informal unimportant; minor: *a small-time gangster*.
– DERIVATIVES **small-timer** noun.

small-town ▶ adjective relating to or characteristic of a small town, especially as considered to be unsophisticated or petty: *small-town gossip*.

smalt /smɔːlt, smɒlt/ ▶ noun [mass noun] chiefly historical glass coloured blue with cobalt oxide. ■ a pigment made by pulverizing smalt glass.
– ORIGIN mid 16th cent.: from French, from Italian *smalto*, of Germanic origin; related to SMELT[1].

smaltite /ˈsmɔːltʌɪt, ˈsmɒl-/ ▶ noun [mass noun] a grey metallic mineral consisting chiefly of cobalt arsenide, typically occurring as cubic or octahedral crystals.
– ORIGIN mid 19th cent.: from *smaltine* (a rare word with the same sense) + -ITE[1].

smarm informal ▶ verb **1** [no obj.] chiefly Brit. behave in an ingratiating way in order to gain favour: *she had smarmed up to him in order to entrap him*.
2 [with obj.] smooth down (one's hair) with water, oil, or gel: *he had **smarmed his hair down***.
▶ noun [mass noun] ingratiating behaviour: *it takes a combination of smarm and confidence to persuade them*.
– ORIGIN mid 19th cent. (originally dialect in the sense 'smear, bedaub'): of unknown origin.

smarmy ▶ adjective (**smarmier**, **smarmiest**) informal ingratiating and wheedling in a way that is regarded as insincere or excessive: *a smarmy, unctuous reply*.
– DERIVATIVES **smarmily** adverb, **smarminess** noun.

smart ▶ adjective **1** (of a person) clean, tidy, and well dressed: *you look very smart*. ■ (of clothes) attractively neat and stylish: *a smart blue skirt*. ■ (of an object) bright and fresh in appearance: *a smart green van*. ■ (of a place) fashionable and upmarket: *a smart restaurant*.
2 informal having or showing a quick-witted intelligence: *if he was that smart he would never have been tricked*. ■ (of a device) programmed so as to be capable of some independent action: *hi-tech smart weapons*. ■ chiefly N. Amer. showing impertinence by making clever or sarcastic remarks: *don't get smart or I'll whack you one*.
3 quick; brisk: *he set off at a smart pace*.
▶ verb [no obj.] (of part of the body) feel a sharp stinging pain: *her legs were scratched and smarting* | (as adj. **smarting**) *Susan rubbed her smarting eyes*. ■ feel upset and annoyed: *defence chiefs are still smarting from the government's cuts*.
▶ noun **1** [mass noun] sharp stinging pain: *the smart of the recent cuts*. ■ archaic mental pain or suffering: *sorrow is the effect of smart, and smart the effect of faith*.
2 (**smarts**) N. Amer. informal intelligence; acumen: *I don't think I have the smarts for it*.
– PHRASES **look smart** chiefly Brit. be quick: *come up here, and look smart about it!*
– DERIVATIVES **smartly** adverb, **smartness** noun.
– ORIGIN Old English *smeortan* (verb), of West Germanic origin; related to German *schmerzen*; the adjective is related to the verb, the original sense (late Old English) being 'causing sharp pain'; from

S

this arose 'keen, brisk', whence the current senses of 'mentally sharp' and 'neat in a brisk, sharp style'.

WORD TRENDS It may be time to worry when your fridge has a higher IQ than you do. The use of **smart** to refer to devices capable of seemingly intelligent and independent action was first seen in 1972, with *smart bomb* one of the earliest combinations. *Smart cards* followed in 1980, and have become such a part of modern life that, after *people*, *card* is the word most often modified by **smart**, according to the Oxford English Corpus. In recent years even the most everyday objects have become **smart**: there are *smart plasters* that wirelessly monitor a patient's vital signs, and *smart fridges* that tell you when your milk is about to go off. **Smart** now also refers to things done efficiently and with careful planning: *understanding how organizations create smart strategies for change | unless the city council develops a land use plan to ensure smart growth, urban sprawl could cripple the city.*

smart alec (chiefly N. Amer. also **smart aleck**) informal ▶ **noun** a person who is irritating because they behave as if they know everything.
▶ **adjective** irritating as a result of behaving as if one knows everything: *a smart-alec answer.*
– DERIVATIVES **smart-alecky** adjective.
– ORIGIN mid 19th cent.: from SMART + *Alec*, diminutive of the given name *Alexander*.

smart-arse (US **smart-ass**) ▶ **noun** informal another term for SMART ALEC.

smart bomb ▶ **noun** a radio-controlled or laser-guided bomb.

smart card ▶ **noun** a plastic card with a built-in microprocessor, used typically to perform financial transactions.

smarten ▶ **verb** (**smarten up** or **smarten someone/thing up**) **1** make or become smarter in appearance: [with obj.] *he spent part of the proceeds on smartening up his flat* | [no obj.] *if there was water to spare I would smarten up and shave.*
2 [no obj.] behave more wisely: *if you don't smarten up soon, you'll find yourself out on the street.*

smartish ▶ **adverb** informal, chiefly Brit. quickly; briskly: *get over here smartish!*

smart money ▶ **noun** [mass noun] money bet or invested by people with expert knowledge: *the smart money in entertainment is invested in copyright.* ■ knowledgeable people collectively: *the smart money in music programming is abandoning pop.*

smart mouth N. Amer. informal ▶ **noun** an ability or tendency to make cheeky retorts; impudence: *why do you hide behind that smart mouth all the time?*
▶ **verb** (**smart-mouth**) [no obj.] make impudent remarks to someone.
– DERIVATIVES **smart-mouthed** adjective.

smartphone ▶ **noun** a mobile phone which incorporates a palmtop computer or PDA.

smart quotes ▶ **plural noun** Computing quotation marks which, although all keyed the same, are automatically interpreted and set as opening or closing marks (inverted or raised commas) rather than vertical lines.

smart set ▶ **noun** (**the smart set**) fashionable people considered as a group.

smartweed ▶ **noun** [mass noun] chiefly N. Amer. a plant of the dock family, typically having slender leaves and a short spike of tiny compact flowers. ● Genus *Polygonum*, family Polygonaceae: several species.

smarty ▶ **noun** (pl. **smarties**) informal **1** a know-all.
2 dated a smart or fashionable person.

smarty-pants (Brit. also **smarty-boots**) ▶ **noun** another term for SMARTY (sense 1).

smash ▶ **verb 1** [with obj.] violently break (something) into pieces: *the thief smashed a window to get into the car | gone are the days when he* ***smashed up*** *hotels.* ■ [no obj.] be violently broken into pieces; shatter: *the glass ball smashed instantly on the pavement.* ■ violently knock down or crush inwards: *soldiers* ***smashed down*** *doors.* ■ crash and severely damage (a vehicle): *my Land Rover's been* ***smashed up****.* ■ hit or attack (someone) very violently: *Donald smashed him over the head.* ■ easily or comprehensively beat (a record): *he smashed the course record.* ■ completely defeat, destroy, or foil (something regarded as hostile or dangerous): *a deliberate attempt to smash the trade union movement.* ■ [no obj.] informal, dated (of a business) go bankrupt; fail financially.
2 [no obj., with adverbial of direction] move so as to hit or collide with something with great force and impact: *their plane smashed into a mountainside.* ■ [with obj. and adverbial of direction] (in sport) strike (the ball) or score (a goal, run, etc.) with great force: *he smashed home the Tranmere winner.* ■ [with obj.] (in tennis, badminton, and similar sports) strike (the ball or shuttlecock) downwards with a hard overarm volley.
▶ **noun 1** an act or sound of something smashing: *he heard the smash of glass.* ■ Brit. a violent collision or impact between vehicles: *a car smash.* ■ a violent blow: *a forearm smash.* ■ a stroke in tennis, badminton, and similar sports in which the ball or shuttlecock is hit downwards with a hard overarm volley.
2 (also **smash hit**) informal a very successful song, film, show, or performer: *a box office smash.*
3 a mixture of spirits (typically brandy) with flavoured water and ice.
4 informal, dated a bankruptcy or financial failure.
▶ **adverb** with a sudden, violent shattering: *they were together for an instant, and then smash it was all gone.*
– PHRASES **go to smash** informal, dated be ruined or destroyed: *he sees the community going to smash.*
– ORIGIN early 18th cent. (as a noun): probably imitative, representing a blend of words such as *smack*, *smite* with *bash*, *mash*, etc.

smash-and-grab Brit. ▶ **adjective** denoting a robbery in which the thief smashes a shop window and seizes goods: *a smash-and-grab raid on a jeweller.*
▶ **noun** a robbery of this type.

smashed ▶ **adjective 1** violently or badly broken or shattered: *a smashed collar bone.*
2 [predic.] informal very drunk: *when they go back to the barracks, the single men get smashed.*

smasher ▶ **noun 1** Brit. informal a very attractive or impressive person or thing: *the night nurse was a smasher.*
2 [usu. in combination] a person or device that breaks something up: *riot police had clashed with window-smashers.*

smashing ▶ **adjective** Brit. informal excellent; wonderful: *you look smashing!*
– DERIVATIVES **smashingly** adverb.

smash-mouth ▶ **adjective** N. Amer. Sport (of a style of play) aggressive and confrontational.

smash-up ▶ **noun** informal a violent collision, especially of cars.

smattering (also **smatter**) ▶ **noun** a slight superficial knowledge of a language or subject: *Edward had only* ***a smattering of*** *Welsh.* ■ a small amount of something: ***a smattering of*** *snow.*
– ORIGIN mid 16th cent.: from *smatter* 'talk ignorantly, prate' (surviving in Scots), of unknown origin.

smaze ▶ **noun** [mass noun] a mixture of smoke and haze.

SME ▶ **abbreviation** ■ small to medium-sized enterprise, a company with no more than 500 employees. ■ Suriname (international vehicle registration).

smear ▶ **verb** [with obj.] **1** coat or mark (something) messily or carelessly with a greasy or sticky substance: *his face was* ***smeared with*** *dirt.* ■ [with obj. and adverbial] spread (a greasy or sticky substance) over something: *she smeared sunblock on her skin.* ■ messily blur the outline of (something such as writing or paint); smudge: *her lipstick was smeared.*
2 damage the reputation of (someone) by false accusations; slander: *someone was trying to smear her by faking letters.*
▶ **noun 1** a mark or streak of a greasy or sticky substance: *there was an oil smear on his jacket.*
2 a sample of tissue or other material taken from part of the body, spread thinly on a microscope slide for examination, typically for medical diagnosis: *the smears were stained for cryptosporidium.* ■ Brit. short for SMEAR TEST.
3 a false accusation intended to damage someone's reputation: *the popular press were indulging in unwarranted smears.*
4 Climbing an insecure foothold.
– DERIVATIVES **smearer** noun, **smeary** adjective (**smearier**, **smeariest**).
– ORIGIN Old English *smierwan* (verb), *smeoru* 'ointment, grease', of Germanic origin; related to German *schmieren* (verb), *Schmer* (noun).

smear campaign ▶ **noun** a plan to discredit a public figure by making false accusations.

smear test ▶ **noun** Brit. a test to detect signs of cervical cancer. See CERVICAL SMEAR.

smectic /ˈsmɛktɪk/ ▶ **adjective** denoting or involving a state of a liquid crystal in which the molecules are oriented in parallel and arranged in well-defined planes. Compare with NEMATIC.
▶ **noun** a smectic substance.
– ORIGIN late 17th cent.: via Latin from Greek *smēktikos* 'cleansing' (because of the soap-like consistency).

smectite /ˈsmɛktʌɪt/ ▶ **noun** [mass noun] a clay mineral (e.g. bentonite) which undergoes reversible expansion on absorbing water.
– ORIGIN early 19th cent.: from Greek *smēktis* 'fuller's earth' + -ITE[1].

smegma /ˈsmɛgmə/ ▶ **noun** [mass noun] a sebaceous secretion in the folds of the skin, especially under a man's foreskin.
– ORIGIN early 19th cent.: via Latin from Greek *smēgma* 'soap', from *smēkhein* 'cleanse'.

smell ▶ **noun** [mass noun] the faculty or power of perceiving odours or scents by means of the organs in the nose: *a highly developed sense of smell | dogs locate the bait by smell.* ■ [count noun] a quality in something that is perceived by this faculty; an odour or scent: *lingering kitchen smells | a smell of coffee.* ■ an unpleasant odour: *twenty-seven cats lived there—you can imagine the smell!* ■ an act of inhaling in order to ascertain an odour or scent: *have a smell of this.*
▶ **verb** (past and past participle **smelt** or **smelled**) **1** [with obj.] perceive or detect the odour or scent of (something): *I think I can smell something burning* | [no obj.] *becoming deaf or blind or unable to smell.* ■ sniff at (something) in order to perceive or detect its odour or scent: *the dogs smell each other.* ■ (**smell something out**) detect or discover something by the faculty of smell: *his nose can smell out an animal from ten miles away.* ■ detect or suspect (something) by means of instinct or intuition: *he can smell trouble long before it gets serious | he can* ***smell out*** *weakness in others.*
2 [no obj.] emit an odour or scent of a specified kind: *the place smelled of damp* | [with complement] *the food smelt and tasted good* | (as adj., in combination **-smelling**) *a strong-smelling herb.* ■ have a strong or unpleasant odour: *if I don't get a bath soon I'll start to smell | it smells in here.* ■ appear in a certain way; be suggestive of something: *it* ***smells like a hoax*** *to me.*
– PHRASES **smell blood** discern weakness or vulnerability in an opponent. **smell a rat** informal begin to suspect trickery or deception. **smell the roses** N. Amer. informal enjoy or appreciate what is often ignored.
– DERIVATIVES **smellable** adjective, **smeller** noun.
– ORIGIN Middle English: of unknown origin.

smelling bottle ▶ **noun** chiefly historical a small bottle containing smelling salts or perfume.

smelling salts ▶ **plural noun** chiefly historical a pungent substance sniffed as a restorative in cases of faintness or headache, typically consisting of ammonium carbonate mixed with perfume.

smelly ▶ **adjective** (**smellier**, **smelliest**) having a strong or unpleasant smell: *smelly feet.*
– DERIVATIVES **smelliness** noun.

smelt[1] ▶ **verb** [with obj.] (often as noun **smelting**) extract (metal) from its ore by a process involving heating and melting: *tin smelting.* ■ extract a metal from (ore) in this way.
– DERIVATIVES **smelter** noun, **smeltery** noun (pl. **smelteries**).
– ORIGIN mid 16th cent.: from Middle Dutch, Middle Low German *smelten*; related to the verb MELT.

smelt[2] past and past participle of SMELL.

smelt[3] ▶ **noun** (pl. **same** or **smelts**) a small silvery fish which lives in both marine and fresh water and is sometimes fished commercially, in particular: ● a fish of the northern hemisphere (family Osmeridae: *Osmerus* and other genera). ● a fish of Australasian waters (family Retropinnidae: several genera).
– ORIGIN Old English; obscurely related to various European names of fish; compare with SMOLT.

Smersh /smɔːʃ/ historical the popular name for the Russian counter-espionage organization responsible for maintaining security within the Soviet armed and intelligence services.
– ORIGIN abbreviation of Russian *Smert' shpionam*, literally 'death to spies'.

Smetana /ˈsmɛtənə/, Bedřich (1824–84), Czech composer. Regarded as the founder of Czech music, he was dedicated to the cause of Czech nationalism, as is apparent in his operas, such as *The Bartered Bride* (1866) and in the cycle of tone poems *Ma Vlast ('My Country'*, 1874–9).

smetana /ˈsmɛtənə/ ▶ **noun** [mass noun] sour cream.
– ORIGIN Russian, from *smetat'* 'sweep off'.

smew /smjuː/ ▶ **noun** a small migratory merganser (diving duck) of northern Eurasia, the male of which has white plumage with a crest and fine black markings. ● *Mergus albellus*, family Anatidae.

– ORIGIN late 17th cent.: obscurely related to Dutch *smient* 'wigeon' and German *Schmeiente* 'small wild duck'.

smidge ▶ noun informal another term for SMIDGEN: *a smidge over five foot two.*

smidgen (also **smidgeon** or **smidgin**) ▶ noun informal a small amount of something: *add a smidgen of cayenne.*
– ORIGIN mid 19th cent.: perhaps from Scots *smitch* in the same sense.

smilax /ˈsmʌɪlaks/ ▶ noun **1** a widely distributed climbing shrub with hooks and tendrils. Several South American species yield sarsaparilla from their roots, and some are cultivated as ornamentals.
● Genus *Smilax*, family Liliaceae.
2 a climbing asparagus, the decorative foliage of which is used by florists. ● *Asparagus* (or *Myrsiphyllum*) *asparagoides*, family Liliaceae.
– ORIGIN late 16th cent.: via Latin from Greek, literally 'bindweed'.

smile ▶ verb [no obj.] form one's features into a pleased, kind, or amused expression, typically with the corners of the mouth turned up and the front teeth exposed: *she was smiling broadly | he smiled at Shelley* | (as adj. **smiling**) *smiling faces.* ■ [with obj.] express (a feeling) by smiling: *he smiled his admiration of the great stone circle.* ■ (**smile at/on/upon**) regard favourably or indulgently: *at first fortune smiled on him.* ■ (often as adj. **smiling**) literary (especially of landscape) have a bright or pleasing aspect: *smiling groves and terraces.*
▶ noun a pleased, kind, or amused facial expression, typically with the corners of the mouth turned up and the front teeth exposed: *he flashed his most winning smile | she greeted us all with a smile.*
– PHRASES **be all smiles** informal look very cheerful and pleased, especially in contrast to a previous mood. **come up smiling** informal recover from adversity and cheerfully face what is to come.
– DERIVATIVES **smiler** noun, **smilingly** adverb.
– ORIGIN Middle English: perhaps of Scandinavian origin; related to SMIRK.

smiley (also **smily**) ▶ adjective (**smilier**, **smiliest**) informal smiling; cheerful: *he drew a smiley face.*
▶ noun (pl. **smileys** or **smilies**) (in electronic communications) a symbol that represents a smiling face, typically formed by the characters :-) and used to indicate that the writer is pleased or joking.

smilodon /ˈsmʌɪlədɒn/ ▶ noun a large sabre-toothed cat of the Pleistocene epoch (see SABRETOOTH).
● *Smilodon fatalis* of North America and *Smilodon populator* of South America.
– ORIGIN modern Latin, from Greek *smilē* 'knife' + *odous, odont-* 'tooth'.

smirch /sməːtʃ/ ▶ verb [with obj.] make (something) dirty; soil: *the window was smirched by heat and smoke.* ■ discredit (a person or their reputation); taint: *I am not accustomed to having my honour smirched*
▶ noun a dirty mark or stain. ■ a blot on someone's character; a flaw.
– ORIGIN late 15th cent.: probably symbolic.

smirk ▶ verb [no obj.] smile in an irritatingly smug, conceited, or silly way: *he smirked in triumph.*
▶ noun a smug, conceited, or silly smile: *Gloria pursed her mouth in a self-satisfied smirk.*
– DERIVATIVES **smirker** noun, **smirkily** adverb, **smirkingly** adverb, **smirky** adjective (**smirkier**, **smirkiest**).
– ORIGIN Old English *sme(a)rcian*, from a base shared by SMILE. The early sense was 'to smile'; it later gained a notion of smugness or silliness.

smit /smɪt/ archaic past participle of SMITE.

smite ▶ verb (past **smote**; past participle **smitten**) **1** [with obj.] literary strike with a firm blow: *he smites the water with his sword.* ■ archaic defeat or conquer (a people or land): *he may smite our enemies.* ■ (especially of disease) attack or affect severely: *various people had been smitten with untimely summer flu.*
2 (**be smitten**) be strongly attracted to someone or something: *she was smitten with the boy.*
▶ noun archaic a heavy blow or stroke with a weapon or the hand: *the kirk rang with slaps and smites.*
– DERIVATIVES **smiter** noun.
– ORIGIN Old English *smītan* 'to smear, blemish', of Germanic origin; related to Dutch *smijten* and German *schmeissen* 'to fling'.

Smith[1], Adam (1723–90), Scottish economist and philosopher. Often regarded as the founder of modern economics, he advocated minimal state interference in economic matters and discredited mercantilism. Notable works: *Inquiry into the Nature and Causes of the Wealth of Nations* (1776).

Smith[2], Bessie (1894–1937), American blues singer. She made over 150 recordings, including some with Benny Goodman and Louis Armstrong.

Smith[3], Ian (Douglas) (1919–2007), Rhodesian statesman, Prime Minister 1964–79. In 1965 he issued a unilateral declaration of independence from Britain (UDI) because he would not agree to black majority rule. He eventually resigned in 1979.

Smith[4], Joseph (1805–44), American religious leader and founder of the Church of Jesus Christ of Latter-Day Saints (the Mormons).

Smith[5], Stevie (1902–71), English poet and novelist; pseudonym of *Florence Margaret Smith*. She is mainly remembered for her witty, caustic, and enigmatic verse; collections include *A Good Time was Had By All* (1937) and *Not Waving But Drowning* (1957).

Smith[6], Sydney (1771–1845), English Anglican churchman, essayist, and wit. He is notable for his *Letters of Peter Plymley* (1807), which defended Catholic Emancipation.

Smith[7], William (1769–1839), English land surveyor and geologist, known as the father of English geology. He produced the first geological map of England and Wales, based on his discovery that rock strata found in different places could be distinguished on the basis of their characteristic assemblages of fossils.

smith ▶ noun a worker in metal. ■ short for BLACKSMITH.
▶ verb [with obj.] treat (metal) by heating, hammering, and forging it: *tin-bronze was cast into ingots before being smithed into bracelets.*
– ORIGIN Old English, of Germanic origin; related to Dutch *smid* and German *Schmied.*

-smith ▶ combining form denoting a person skilled in creating something with a specified material: *goldsmith | wordsmith.*

smithereens /ˌsmɪðəˈriːnz/ (also **smithers** /ˈsmɪðəz/) ▶ plural noun informal small pieces: *a grenade blew him to smithereens.*
– ORIGIN early 19th cent.: probably from Irish *smidirín.*

smithery ▶ noun [mass noun] the work of or goods made by a smith.

Smithfield a part of London containing the city's principal meat market.

Smithsonian Institution /smɪθˈsəʊnɪən/ a US foundation for education and scientific research in Washington DC, opened in 1846 and now responsible for administering many museums, art galleries, and other establishments. It originated in a £100,000 bequest in the will of the English chemist and mineralogist James Smithson (1765–1829).

smithsonite /ˈsmɪθsənʌɪt/ ▶ noun [mass noun] a yellow, grey, or green mineral consisting of zinc carbonate typically occurring as crusts or rounded masses.
– ORIGIN mid 19th cent.: from the name *Smithson* (see SMITHSONIAN INSTITUTION) + -ITE[1].

smithy /ˈsmɪði/ ▶ noun (pl. **smithies**) a blacksmith's workshop; a forge.
– ORIGIN Middle English, from Old Norse *smithja.*

smitten past participle of SMITE.

smock ▶ noun a loose dress or blouse for a woman or child, with the upper part closely gathered in smocking. ■ a loose overall worn to protect one's clothes: *an artist's smock.* ■ (also **smock-frock**) historical a smocked linen overgarment worn by an agricultural worker.
▶ verb [with obj.] (usu. as adj. **smocked**) decorate (a garment) with smocking: *smocked dresses.*
– DERIVATIVES **smocked** adjective [usu. in combination] *blue-smocked schoolgirls.*
– ORIGIN Old English *smoc* 'woman's loose-fitting undergarment'; probably related to Old English *smūgan* 'to creep' and Old Norse *smjúga* 'put on a garment, creep into'.

smocking ▶ noun [mass noun] decoration on a garment created by gathering a section of the material into tight pleats and holding them together with parallel stitches in an ornamental pattern.

smog ▶ noun [mass noun] fog or haze intensified by smoke or other atmospheric pollutants.
– DERIVATIVES **smoggy** adjective (**smoggier**, **smoggiest**).
– ORIGIN early 20th cent.: blend of SMOKE and FOG[1].

smoke ▶ noun **1** [mass noun] a visible suspension of carbon or other particles in air, typically one emitted from a burning substance: *bonfire smoke.*
2 an act of smoking tobacco: *I'm dying for a smoke.* ■ informal a cigarette or cigar.
3 (**the Smoke** or **the Big Smoke**) Brit. informal a big city, especially London: *she was offered a job in the Smoke.*
▶ verb **1** [no obj.] emit smoke or visible vapour: *heat the oil until it just smokes.*
2 [no obj.] inhale and exhale the smoke of tobacco or a drug: *Janine was sitting at the kitchen table smoking* | [with obj.] *he smoked forty cigarettes a day.*
3 [with obj.] treat, fumigate, or cleanse by exposure to smoke. ■ (often as adj. **smoked**) cure or preserve (meat or fish) by exposure to smoke: *smoked salmon.* ■ (usu. as adj. **smoked**) treat (glass) so as to darken it: *the smoked glass of his lenses.* ■ subdue (insects, especially bees) by exposing them to smoke. ■ (**smoke someone/thing out**) drive someone or something out of a place by using smoke: *we will fire the roof and smoke him out.* ■ (**smoke someone out**) force someone to make something known: *as the press smokes him out on other human rights issues, he will be revealed as a social conservative.*
4 [with obj.] N. Amer. informal kill (someone) by shooting. ■ defeat overwhelmingly in a fight or contest.
5 [with obj.] archaic make fun of (someone).
– PHRASES **go up in smoke** informal be destroyed by fire. ■ (of a plan) come to nothing: *more than one dream is about to go up in smoke.* **no smoke without fire** (N. Amer. also **where there's smoke there's fire**) proverb there's always some reason for a rumour. **smoke and mirrors** N. Amer. the obscuring or embellishing of the truth of a situation with misleading or irrelevant information: *the budget process is an exercise in smoke and mirrors.* [with reference to illusion created by conjuring tricks.] **smoke like a chimney** smoke tobacco incessantly.
– DERIVATIVES **smokable** (also **smokeable**) adjective.
– ORIGIN Old English *smoca* (noun), *smocian* (verb), from the Germanic base of *smēocan* 'emit smoke'; related to Dutch *smook* and German *Schmauch.*

smoke alarm ▶ noun a fire-protection device that automatically detects and gives a warning of the presence of smoke.

smoke ball ▶ noun a projectile filled with material which emits dense smoke on ignition, used to conceal military operations.

smoke bomb ▶ noun a bomb that emits dense smoke as it explodes.

smokebox ▶ noun **1** an oven for smoking food.
2 the chamber in a steam engine or boiler between the flues and the funnel or chimney stack.
3 another term for SMOKER (sense 4).

smoke bush ▶ noun another term for SMOKE TREE.

smoke-dry ▶ verb [with obj.] cure (meat or fish) by exposing it to smoke.

smoke-free ▶ adjective without smoke: *a smoke-free environment.* ■ where smoking is not permitted: *a smoke-free train.*

smoke-ho ▶ noun variant of SMOKO.

smokehouse ▶ noun chiefly N. Amer. a shed or room for curing food by exposure to smoke.

S

smokejumper ▶ noun N. Amer. a firefighter who arrives by parachute to extinguish a forest fire.

smokeless ▶ adjective producing or emitting little or no smoke: *smokeless fuel.*

smokeless zone ▶ noun Brit. a district in which it is illegal to create smoke and where only smokeless fuel may be used.

smoker ▶ noun **1** a person who smokes tobacco regularly.
2 a person or device that smokes fish or meat.
3 chiefly N. Amer. an informal social gathering for men.
4 a device which emits smoke for subduing bees in a hive.

smoke ring ▶ noun a ring-shaped puff of smoke exhaled by a smoker.

smoke room ▶ noun Brit. another term for SMOKING ROOM.

smoker's cough ▶ noun a persistent cough caused by excessive smoking.

smokescreen ▶ noun a cloud of smoke created to conceal military operations. ■ a ruse designed to disguise someone's real intentions or activities: *he tried to create a smokescreen by quibbling about the statistics.*

smoke shop ▶ **noun** N. Amer. a shop selling tobacco products and smoking equipment.

smoke signal ▶ **noun** a column of smoke used as a way of conveying a message to a distant person. ■ an indication of someone's intentions or views: *a series of political smoke signals has aroused hopes for a fresh initiative on Northern Ireland.*

smokestack ▶ **noun** a chimney or funnel for discharging smoke from a locomotive, ship, factory, etc.

smokestone ▶ **noun** another term for **SMOKY QUARTZ**.

smoke tree ▶ **noun** a Eurasian shrub or small tree which bears feathery plumes of purple or reddish flowers and fruit, giving it a smoky appearance. ● *Cotinus coggygria* (formerly *Rhus cotinus*), family Anacardiaceae.

smoke tunnel ▶ **noun** a form of wind tunnel using thin jets of smoke to show the motion of air.

smokie ▶ **noun** Scottish a smoked haddock.

smoking ▶ **noun** [mass noun] the action or habit of inhaling and exhaling the smoke of tobacco or a drug: *the effect of smoking on health.*
▶ **adjective 1** emitting smoke or visible vapour: *they huddled round his smoking fire in the winter damp.*
2 (often **smokin'**) informal lively and exciting: *Wow! This band is really smokin'!*

smoking gun ▶ **noun** a piece of incontrovertible incriminating evidence.

smoking jacket ▶ **noun** a man's comfortable jacket, typically made of velvet, formerly worn while smoking after dinner.

smoking room ▶ **noun** a room set aside for smoking in a hotel or other public building.

smoko /ˈsməʊkəʊ/ (also **smoke-ho**) ▶ **noun** (pl. **smokos**) Austral./NZ informal a rest from work for a smoke; a tea break.

smoky (also **smokey**) ▶ **adjective** (**smokier**, **smokiest**) **1** filled with or smelling of smoke: *a smoky office.* ■ producing or obscured by a great deal of smoke: *smoky factory chimneys.*
2 like smoke in colour or appearance: *her wide smoky eyes.*
3 having the taste or aroma of smoked food: *smoky bacon.*
– DERIVATIVES **smokily** adverb, **smokiness** noun.

smoky quartz ▶ **noun** [mass noun] a semi-precious variety of quartz ranging in colour from light greyish brown to nearly black.

smolder ▶ **verb** US spelling of **SMOULDER**.

Smolensk /sməˈljɛnsk/ a city in western European Russia, on the River Dnieper close to the border with Belarus; pop. 316,500 (est. 2008).

Smollett /ˈsmɒlɪt/, Tobias (George) (1721–71), Scottish novelist. His humorous and fast-moving picaresque novels include *The Adventures of Roderick Random* (1748) and *The Adventures of Peregrine Pickle* (1751).

smolt /sməʊlt/ ▶ **noun** a young salmon (or trout) after the parr stage, when it becomes silvery and migrates to the sea for the first time.
– ORIGIN late Middle English (originally Scots and northern English): of unknown origin; compare with **SMELT³**.

S

smooch informal ▶ **verb** [no obj.] kiss and cuddle amorously: *the young lovers smooched in their car.* ■ Brit. dance slowly in a close embrace.
▶ **noun** a kiss or a spell of amorous kissing and cuddling: *he moved in for a big smooch.* ■ Brit. a period of slow dancing in a close embrace: *they suggest a dance but it turns into a smooch.*
– DERIVATIVES **smoocher** noun, **smoochy** adjective (**smoochier**, **smoochiest**).
– ORIGIN 1930s: from dialect *smouch*, of imitative origin.

smoodge (also **smooge**) Austral./NZ informal ▶ **verb** [no obj.] behave in an ingratiating manner: *he used to hang around here smoodging to Mum.*
▶ **noun** [mass noun] affectionate flattery: *what's wrong with a bit of smoodge between friends?*
– ORIGIN early 20th cent.: probably an alteration of dialect *smouch* 'kiss, sidle up to'.

smoor /smʊə/ S. African ▶ **noun** [mass noun] a Malay stew typically made with fish.
▶ **verb** [with obj.] braise or stew (meat or fish).
– ORIGIN Afrikaans.

smooth ▶ **adjective 1** having an even and regular surface; free from perceptible projections, lumps, or indentations: *smooth flat rocks | his face was curiously smooth and youthful.* ■ (of a liquid) with an even consistency; without lumps: *cook gently until the sauce is smooth.* ■ (of the sea or another body of water) without heavy waves; calm: *the smooth summer sea.* ■ denoting the face of a tennis or squash racket without the projecting loops from the stringing process (used as a call when the racket is spun to decide the right to serve first or to choose ends).
2 (of movement) without jerks: *the trucks gave a smooth ride | graphics are excellent, with fast, smooth scrolling.* ■ (of an action, event, or process) without problems or difficulties: *the group's expansion into the US market was not quite so smooth.*
3 (of a person or their manner) suavely charming in a way regarded as possibly insincere: *his voice was infuriatingly smooth.*
4 (of food or drink) without harshness or bitterness: *a lovely, smooth, very fruity wine.*
▶ **verb** (also **smoothe**) [with obj.] **1** give (something) a flat, regular surface or appearance: *she smoothed out the newspaper | you can use glasspaper to smooth the joint.* ■ modify (a graph, curve, etc.) so as to lessen irregularities: *values are collected over a long period of time so that fluctuations are smoothed out.*
2 deal successfully with (a problem or difficulty): *these doctrinal disputes were smoothed over.* ■ free (a course of action) from difficulties or problems: *a conference would be held to smooth the way for the establishment of the provisional government.*
▶ **adverb** archaic in a way that is without difficulties: *the course of true love never did run smooth.*
– DERIVATIVES **smoother** noun, **smoothish** adjective.
– ORIGIN Old English *smōth*, probably of Germanic origin, though no cognates are known. The verb dates from Middle English.

smooth-bore ▶ **noun** [often as modifier] a gun with an unrifled barrel: *smooth-bore muskets.*

smooth breathing ▶ **noun** see **BREATHING** (sense 2).

smooth-faced ▶ **adjective 1** concealing one's true feelings by a show of friendliness.
2 clean-shaven.

smooth hound ▶ **noun** a small European shark which typically lives close to the bottom in shallow waters. ● Genus *Mustelus*, family Triakidae: two species.

smoothie ▶ **noun 1** informal a man with a smooth, suave manner: *a smoothie with an eye for a pretty girl.*
2 a thick, smooth drink of fresh fruit puréed with milk, yogurt, or ice cream.

smoothing iron ▶ **noun** historical a flat iron.

smoothing plane ▶ **noun** a small plane for finishing the surface of wood.

smoothly ▶ **adverb 1** in a smooth way: *the bust is smoothly carved in white marble | traffic was soon flowing smoothly again.*
2 without problems or difficulties: *everything seemed to be going smoothly.*

smooth muscle ▶ **noun** [mass noun] Physiology muscle tissue in which the contractile fibrils are not highly ordered, occurring in the gut and other internal organs and not under voluntary control. Often contrasted with **STRIATED MUSCLE**.

smoothness ▶ **noun** [mass noun] the quality or state of being smooth: *the smoothness of her skin | the evacuation went off with remarkable smoothness.*

smooth newt ▶ **noun** a small yellowish-brown smooth-skinned newt that is widely distributed throughout Europe and western Asia. ● *Triturus vulgaris*, family Salamandridae.

smooth snake ▶ **noun** a harmless Eurasian snake which is grey to reddish in colour, typically living in heathy country where it feeds on lizards. ● *Coronella austriaca*, family Colubridae.

smooth talk ▶ **noun** [mass noun] charming or flattering language, especially when used to persuade someone to do something.
▶ **verb** (**smooth-talk**) [with obj.] informal use charming or flattering language to persuade (someone) to do something: *don't try to smooth-talk me.*
– DERIVATIVES **smooth-talker** noun.

smooth-talking ▶ **adjective** using charming or flattering language to persuade someone to do something: *a smooth-talking salesman.*

smooth tongue ▶ **noun** the ability or tendency to use insincere flattery or persuasion: *your smooth tongue could even turn your mistakes to your advantage.*
– DERIVATIVES **smooth-tongued** adjective.

smorgasbord /ˈsmɔːɡəsbɔːd/ ▶ **noun** a range of open sandwiches and delicacies served as hors d'oeuvres or a buffet. ■ a wide range of something; a variety: *the album is a smorgasbord of different musical styles.*
– ORIGIN Swedish, from *smörgås* '(slice of) bread and butter' (from *smör* 'butter' + *gås* 'goose, lump of butter') + *bord* 'table'.

smorzando /smɔːˈtsandəʊ/ Music ▶ **adverb & adjective** (especially as a direction) dying away.
– ORIGIN Italian, literally 'extinguishing'.

smote past of **SMITE**.

smother ▶ **verb** [with obj.] **1** kill (someone) by covering their nose and mouth so that they suffocate. ■ make (someone) feel trapped and oppressed by acting in an overly protective manner towards them.
2 extinguish (a fire) by covering it. ■ suppress (a feeling or action): *she smothered a sigh.* ■ (in sport) stop the motion of (the ball or a shot): *the goalkeeper was able to smother the ball.*
3 (**smother someone/thing in/with**) cover someone or something entirely with: *rich orange sorbets smothered in fluffy whipped cream.* ■ cook in a covered container: (as adj. **smothered**) *smothered fried chicken.*
▶ **noun** a mass of something that stifles or obscures: *all this vanished in a smother of foam.*
– ORIGIN Middle English (as a noun in the sense 'stifling smoke'): from the base of Old English *smorian* 'suffocate'.

smothered mate ▶ **noun** [mass noun] Chess checkmate in which the king has no vacant square to move to and is checkmated by a knight.

smoulder (US also **smolder**) ▶ **verb** [no obj.] burn slowly with smoke but no flame: *the bonfire still smouldered, the smoke drifting over the paddock.* ■ show or feel barely suppressed anger, hatred, or another powerful emotion: *Anna smouldered with indignation* | (as adj. **smouldering**) *he met her smouldering eyes.* ■ exist in a suppressed or concealed state: *the controversy smouldered on for several years* | (as adj. **smouldering**) *smouldering rage.*
▶ **noun** [mass noun] smoke coming from a smouldering fire: *the last acrid smoulder of his cigarette.*
– DERIVATIVES **smoulderingly** adverb.
– ORIGIN late Middle English: related to Dutch *smeulen*.

SMPTE ▶ **abbreviation** Society of Motion Picture and Television Engineers (used to denote a time coding system for synchronizing video and audio tapes).

smriti /ˈsmrɪti/ ▶ **noun** (pl. **smritis**) a Hindu religious text containing traditional teachings on religion, such as the Mahabharata.
– ORIGIN from Sanskrit *smṛti* 'remembrance'.

SMS ▶ **abbreviation** Short Message (or Messaging) Service, a system that enables mobile phone users to send and receive text messages.
▶ **noun** (pl. **SMSs**) a text message that is sent or received using SMS.
▶ **verb** (**SMSs**, **SMSing**, **SMSed**) [no obj.] send someone a text message using SMS: *I'm SMSing more than speaking on my mobile phone these days* | [with obj.] *SMS me or send me an email.*

SMSgt ▶ **abbreviation** Senior Master Sergeant.

SMTP ▶ **abbreviation** Simple Mail Transfer (or Transport) Protocol, a standard for the transmission of email on a computer network.

smudge¹ ▶ **verb** [with obj.] cause (something) to become messily smeared by rubbing it: *she dabbed her eyes, careful not to smudge her make-up.* ■ [no obj.] become smeared when rubbed: *mascaras that smudge or flake around the eyes.* ■ make blurred or indistinct: *the photograph had been smudged by the photocopier and was by no means as clear as the original.*
▶ **noun** a blurred or smeared mark on the surface of something: *a smudge of blood on the floor.* ■ an indistinct or blurred view or image: *the low smudge of hills on the horizon.*
– DERIVATIVES **smudgily** adverb, **smudginess** noun, **smudgy** adjective (**smudgier**, **smudgiest**).
– ORIGIN late Middle English (as a verb in the sense 'soil, stain'): of unknown origin. The noun dates from the late 18th cent.

smudge² ▶ **noun** N. Amer. a smoky outdoor fire that is lit to keep off insects or protect plants against frost.
– ORIGIN mid 18th cent. (in the sense 'suffocating smoke'): related to obsolete *smudge* 'cure herring by smoking', of obscure origin.

smudge pot ▶ **noun** N. Amer. a container for a smudge (see **SMUDGE²**).

smug ▶ **adjective** (**smugger**, **smuggest**) having or showing an excessive pride in oneself or one's achievements: *he was feeling smug after his win.*

– DERIVATIVES **smugly** adverb, **smugness** noun.
– ORIGIN mid 16th cent. (originally in the sense 'neat, spruce'): from Low German *smuk* 'pretty'.

smuggle ▶ verb [with obj.] move (goods) illegally into or out of a country: *he's been smuggling cigarettes from Gibraltar into Spain* | (as noun **smuggling**) *cocaine smuggling has increased alarmingly*. ■ [with obj. and adverbial of direction] convey (someone or something) somewhere secretly and illicitly: *he smuggled out a message*.
– ORIGIN late 17th cent.: from Low German *smuggelen*, of unknown ultimate origin.

smuggler ▶ noun a person who smuggles goods: *drug smugglers*.

smush /smʌʃ/ ▶ verb [with obj.] N. Amer. informal crush or smash: *they smushed marshmallows in their mouths*.
– ORIGIN early 19th cent.: alteration of MUSH¹.

smut ▶ noun **1** a small flake of soot or other dirt or a mark left by one: *all those black smuts from the engine*.
2 [mass noun] a fungal disease of cereals in which parts of the ear change to black powder. ● The fungi belong to *Ustilago* and other genera, order Ustilaginales, class Teliomycetes.
3 [mass noun] obscene or lascivious talk, writing, or pictures: *porn, in his view, is far from being harmless smut*.
▶ verb (**smuts, smutting, smutted**) [with obj.] (often as adj. **smutted**) **1** mark with flakes or soot or other dirt: *the smutted sky*.
2 infect (a plant) with smut: *smutted wheat*.
– ORIGIN late Middle English (in the sense 'defile, corrupt, make obscene'): related to German *schmutzen*; compare with SMUDGE¹. The noun dates from the mid 17th cent.

smut ball ▶ noun a grain of wheat or another cereal affected by smut.

smut mill ▶ noun a machine for removing smut from cereal grain.

Smuts /smʌts/, Jan (Christiaan) (1870–1950), South African statesman and soldier, Prime Minister 1919–24 and 1939–48. He led Boer forces during the Second Boer War, but afterwards supported the policy of Anglo-Boer cooperation. He commanded Allied troops against German East Africa (1916) and later helped to found the League of Nations.

smutty ▶ adjective (**smuttier, smuttiest**) (of talk, writing, or pictures) obscene or lascivious: *smutty jokes*.
– DERIVATIVES **smuttily** adverb, **smuttiness** noun.

Smyrna /ˈsməːnə/ an ancient city on the west coast of Asia Minor, on the site of modern Izmir in Turkey.

SN ▶ abbreviation Senegal (international vehicle registration).

Sn ▶ symbol the chemical element tin.
– ORIGIN from late Latin *stannum* 'tin'.

snack ▶ noun a small amount of food eaten between meals. ■ a light meal that is eaten in a hurry or in a casual manner. ■ Austral. informal a thing that is easy to accomplish: *it'll be a snack*.
▶ verb [no obj.] eat a snack: *she likes to* **snack on** *yogurt*.
– ORIGIN Middle English (originally in the sense 'snap, bite'): from Middle Dutch *snac(k)*, from *snacken* 'to bite', variant of *snappen*. Senses relating to food date from the late 17th cent.

snack bar ▶ noun a place where snacks are sold.

snackette ▶ noun **1** a very small amount of food.
2 W. Indian a small shop selling snacks, cigarettes, and minor groceries.

snaffle ▶ noun (also **snaffle bit**) (on a bridle) a simple bit, typically a jointed one, used with a single set of reins. ■ (also **snaffle bridle**) a bridle with a snaffle bit.
▶ verb [with obj.] Brit. informal take (something) for oneself, typically quickly or without permission: *shall we snaffle some of Bernard's sherry?*
– ORIGIN mid 16th cent. (denoting a bridle bit): probably from Low German or Dutch; compare with Middle Low German, Middle Dutch *snavel* 'beak, mouth'. The verb (mid 19th cent.) is perhaps a different word.

snafu /snaˈfuː, ˈsnafuː/ N. Amer. informal ▶ noun a confused or chaotic state; a mess: *an enormous amount of my time was devoted to untangling snafus*.
▶ adjective in utter confusion or chaos: *our refrigeration plant is snafu*.
▶ verb [with obj.] throw (a situation) into chaos: *you ignored his orders and snafued everything*.
– ORIGIN 1940s: acronym from *situation normal: all fouled* (or *fucked*) *up*.

snag¹ ▶ noun **1** an unexpected or hidden obstacle or drawback: *there's one small snag*.
2 a sharp, angular, or jagged projection: *keep an emery board handy in case of nail snags*. ■ a rent or tear in fabric caused by a snag.
3 N. Amer. a dead tree.
▶ verb (**snags, snagging, snagged**) [with obj.] **1** catch or tear (something) on a sharp projection: *thorns snagged his sweater*. ■ [no obj.] become caught on a sharp projection: *radio aerials* **snagged on** *bushes and branches*.
2 N. Amer. informal catch or obtain: *it's the first time they've snagged the star for a photo*.
– DERIVATIVES **snaggy** adjective (sense 2 of the noun).
– ORIGIN late 16th cent. (in sense 2 of the noun): probably of Scandinavian origin. The early sense 'stump sticking out from a tree trunk' gave rise to a US sense 'submerged piece of timber obstructing navigation', of which sense 1 is originally a figurative use. Current verb senses arose in the 19th cent.

snag² ▶ noun Austral./NZ informal a sausage.
– ORIGIN 1940s: of unknown origin.

snagging ▶ noun [mass noun] Brit. the process of checking a new building for minor faults that need to be rectified.
– ORIGIN from SNAG¹.

snaggle ▶ noun a tangled or knotted mass.
▶ verb [no obj.] become knotted or tangled.
– ORIGIN early 20th cent.: from the noun SNAG¹ + -LE².

snaggle-tooth ▶ noun **1** (pl. **snaggle-teeth**) an irregular or projecting tooth.
2 (pl. **snaggle-tooths**) a small deep-sea fish with large fangs at the front of the jaws and a number of light-emitting organs on the body. ● Family Astronesthidae: several genera and species.
– DERIVATIVES **snaggle-toothed** adjective.

snail ▶ noun a mollusc with a single spiral shell into which the whole body can be withdrawn. ● Many species in the class Gastropoda.
■ used in reference to something very slow: *he drove* **at a snail's pace**.
– DERIVATIVES **snail-like** adjective.
– ORIGIN Old English *snæg(e)l*, of Germanic origin; related to German *Schnecke*.

snailfish ▶ noun (pl. **same** or **snailfishes**) a small fish of cool or cold seas, with loose jelly-like skin and typically a ventral sucker. Also called SEA SNAIL. ● *Liparis* and other genera, family Cyclopteridae: several species, including *L. liparis* of the North Atlantic.

snail mail ▶ noun [mass noun] informal the ordinary postal system as opposed to email.

snake ▶ noun **1** a long limbless reptile which has no eyelids, a short tail, and jaws that are capable of considerable extension. Some snakes have a venomous bite. ● Suborder Ophidia (or Serpentes), order Squamata: many families.
2 (also **snake in the grass**) a treacherous or deceitful person: *that man is a cold-blooded snake*.
3 (**the snake**) a former system of interconnected exchange rates for the currencies of EC countries.
4 (in full **plumber's snake**) a long flexible wire for clearing obstacles in piping.
▶ verb [no obj., with adverbial of direction] move or extend with the twisting motion of a snake: *a rope snaked down*.
– DERIVATIVES **snake-like** adjective.
– ORIGIN Old English *snaca*, of Germanic origin.

snakebark maple ▶ noun a maple tree with longitudinal pale stripes on the bark. ● Genus *Acer*, family Aceraceae: several species, in particular *A. davidii* (of eastern Asia) and the moosewood.

snakebird ▶ noun another term for DARTER (sense 1).

snakebite ▶ noun [mass noun] **1** the bite of a snake, especially a venomous one.
2 Brit. a drink consisting of draught cider and lager in equal proportions.

snakebitten ▶ adjective N. Amer. informal doomed to misfortune; unlucky: *the snakebitten space shuttle chalked up a fourth launch delay*.

snakeboard ▶ noun trademark a type of skateboard consisting of two footplates joined by a bar, allowing for greater speed and manoeuvrability than with a standard skateboard.
– DERIVATIVES **snakeboarder** noun, **snakeboarding** noun.
– ORIGIN 1990s: blend of SNAKE and SKATEBOARD.

snake charmer ▶ noun an entertainer who appears to make snakes move by playing music.

snake dance ▶ noun a dance in which the performers handle live snakes or imitate the motions of snakes, in particular a ritual dance of the North American Hopi Indians involving the handling of live rattlesnakes.
▶ verb (**snake-dance**) [no obj.] perform a snake dance.

snake eyes ▶ plural noun [treated as sing.] N. Amer. informal a throw of two ones with a pair of dice. ■ the worst possible result; a complete lack of success: *his elegant, amusing book sadly* **came up snake eyes**.

snake fence (also **snake-rail fence**) ▶ noun N. Amer. a fence made of roughly split rails or poles joined in a zigzag pattern with their ends crossing.

snakefish ▶ noun (pl. **same** or **snakefishes**) see CUTLASSFISH, LIZARDFISH.

snake fly ▶ noun a slender woodland insect with transparent wings and a long 'neck' which allows the head to be raised above the body. ● Family Raphidiidae, order Neuroptera: *Raphidia* and other genera.

snakehead ▶ noun **1** a freshwater fish with a broad, heavily scaled head and a long cylindrical body, native to tropical Africa and Asia. ● Family Channidae: several genera and species.
2 a member of a Chinese criminal network chiefly engaged in smuggling illegal immigrants to the West. [translation of Chinese *shétóu*.]

snake-hipped ▶ adjective (of a person) having very slender hips and moving in a sinuous way.

snake lizard ▶ noun a nocturnal legless lizard native to Australia and New Guinea. ● *Delma*, *Lialis*, and other genera, family Pygopodidae: many species, in particular *D. nasuta* and *L. burtonis*.

snakelocks anemone ▶ noun a sea anemone of cool seas, with long snake-like tentacles. It has symbiotic algae living in its cells which give it a green colour. ● *Anemonia viridis*, order Actiniaria.

snake mackerel ▶ noun another term for ESCOLAR.

snake oil ▶ noun [mass noun] informal, chiefly N. Amer. a substance with no real medicinal value sold as a remedy for all diseases. ■ a product, policy, etc. of little real worth or value that is promoted as the solution to a problem: *the new tax plan was denounced as snake oil*.

snake pit ▶ noun a pit containing poisonous snakes. ■ a scene of vicious behaviour or ruthless competition: *the literary snake pits of New York*.

snake-rail fence ▶ noun another term for SNAKE FENCE.

Snake River a river of the north-western US. Rising in Yellowstone National Park in Wyoming, it flows for 1,670 km (1,038 miles) through Idaho into the state of Washington, where it joins the Columbia River.

snakeroot ▶ noun **1** any of a number of North American plants reputed to contain an antidote to snake poison, in particular: ● (**Virginian snakeroot**) a birthwort with long heart-shaped leaves and curved tubular flowers (*Aristolochia serpentaria*, family Aristolochiaceae). ● (**white snakeroot**) a poisonous plant which causes milk sickness in livestock (*Eupatorium rugosum*, family Compositae).
2 any of a number of plants thought to resemble a snake in shape, in particular **Indian snakeroot** (see RAUWOLFIA).

S

snakes and ladders ▶ plural noun [treated as sing.] Brit. a children's game in which players move counters along a board, gaining an advantage by moving up pictures of ladders or a disadvantage by moving down pictures of snakes.

snake's head ▶ noun a Eurasian fritillary with flowers chequered in red and purple, typically growing in damp hay meadows and water meadows. ● *Fritillaria meleagris*, family Liliaceae.

snakeskin ▶ noun [mass noun] [often as modifier] the skin of a snake: *snakeskin boots*.

snakeweed ▶ noun [mass noun] old-fashioned term for BISTORT.

snakewood ▶ noun **1** a tree or shrub which has timber from which a snakebite antidote or other medicinal extract is obtained. ● Several species, in particular the tree *Strychnos minor* (or *colubrina*) (family Loganiaceae), of the Indian subcontinent.
2 a tropical American tree which has timber with a snakeskin pattern, used for decorative work. ● *Brosimum rubescens*, family Moraceae.

snaky (also **snakey**) ▶ adjective (**snakier, snakiest**) **1** like a snake in appearance; long and sinuous: *a long snaky whip*. ■ of the supposed nature of a snake in showing coldness, venom, or cunning: *a snaky friend*.

2 Austral./NZ informal angry; irritable: *what are you snaky about?*
– DERIVATIVES **snakily** adverb.

snap ▶ verb (**snaps**, **snapping**, **snapped**) **1** break suddenly and completely, typically with a sharp cracking sound: [no obj.] *guitar strings kept snapping* | [with obj.] *dead twigs can be **snapped off**.* ■ [no obj.] emit a sudden, sharp cracking sound: *banners snapping in the breeze.* ■ [with complement or adverbial] move or alter with a brisk movement and typically a sharp sound: [with obj.] *Rosa snapped her bag shut* | [no obj.] *his mouth snapped into a tight, straight line.* ■ [no obj.] suddenly lose one's self-control: *she claims she snapped after years of violence.*
2 [no obj.] (of an animal) make a sudden audible bite: *a dog was **snapping at** his heels.*
3 [reporting verb] say something quickly and irritably: [no obj.] *McIlvanney **snapped at** her* | [with direct speech] *'I really don't much care,' she snapped.*
4 [with obj.] take a snapshot of: *he planned to spend the time snapping rare wildlife* | [no obj.] *photographers were **snapping away at** her.*
5 [with obj.] American Football put (the ball) into play by a quick backward movement.
▶ noun **1** a sudden, sharp cracking sound or movement: *she closed her purse with a snap.* ■ [mass noun] vigour or liveliness of style or action; zest: *the snap of the dialogue.*
2 [in sing.] a hurried, irritable tone or manner: *'I'm still waiting,' he said with a snap.*
3 a snapshot: *holiday snaps.*
4 [mass noun] Brit. a card game in which cards from two piles are turned over simultaneously and players call 'snap' as quickly as possible when two similar cards are exposed. ■ [as exclamation] said when one notices that one has or does the identical thing to someone else: *'Snap!' They looked at each other's ties with a smile.*
5 a sudden brief spell of cold or otherwise distinctive weather: *a cold snap.*
6 [mass noun] N. English food, especially food taken to work to be eaten during a break.
7 [in sing.] N. Amer. informal an easy task: *a control panel that makes operation a snap.*
8 (usu. **snaps**) N. Amer. a press stud.
▶ adjective [attrib.] done or taken on the spur of the moment, unexpectedly, or without notice: *a snap decision* | *he could call a snap election.*
– PHRASES **in a snap** informal, chiefly N. Amer. in a moment; almost immediately: *gourmet-quality meals are ready in a snap.* **snap one's fingers** see FINGER. **snap someone's head off** see HEAD.
– PHRASAL VERBS **snap out of** [often in imperative] informal get out of (a bad or unhappy mood) by a sudden effort: *come on, Fran—snap out of it!* **snap something up** quickly and eagerly buy or secure something that is in short supply or being sold cheaply: *all the tickets have been snapped up.*
– DERIVATIVES **snappable** adjective, **snappingly** adverb.
– ORIGIN late 15th cent. (in the senses 'make a sudden audible bite' and 'quick sharp biting sound'): probably from Middle Dutch or Middle Low German *snappen* 'seize'; partly imitative.

snap-action ▶ adjective **1** denoting a switch or relay that makes and breaks contact rapidly, whatever the speed of the activating mechanism.
2 denoting a gun whose hinged barrel is secured by a spring catch.

S

snap bean ▶ noun N. Amer. a bean of a variety grown for its edible pods.
– ORIGIN late 18th cent.: so named because the pods are broken into pieces to be eaten.

snap-brim ▶ adjective (of a hat) with a brim that can be turned up and down at opposite sides.

snapdragon ▶ noun a plant bearing spikes of brightly coloured two-lobed flowers which gape like a mouth when a bee lands on the curved lip.
● *Antirrhinum majus*, family Scrophulariaceae.

snap fastener ▶ noun another term for PRESS STUD.

snap hook (also **snap link**) ▶ noun a hook with a spring allowing the entrance but preventing the escape of a cord, link, etc.

snap-lock ▶ adjective denoting a device or component which is fastened automatically when pushed into position: *the top is secured by snap-lock buckles.*

snap-on (also **snap-in**) ▶ adjective denoting a cover or attachment that is attached or secured with a snap.

snap pea ▶ noun another term for SUGAR SNAP.

snapper ▶ noun **1** a marine fish that is typically reddish and is valued as food, in particular: ● a fish of a widespread tropical family (Lutjanidae, the **snapper family**), which snaps its toothed jaws. See also RED SNAPPER. ● a fish of Australasian coastal waters (*Chrysophrys auratus*, family Sparidae).
2 another term for SNAPPING TURTLE.
3 informal a photographer.
4 N. Amer. a paper cracker, or the part of a cracker that makes a bang.
5 American Football a centre player.

snapping turtle ▶ noun a large American freshwater turtle with a long neck and strong hooked jaws.
● Family Chelydridae: *Chelydra serpentina* and the alligator snapper.

snappish ▶ adjective (of a dog) irritable and inclined to bite. ■ irritable and curt: *she was often snappish with the children.*
– DERIVATIVES **snappishly** adverb, **snappishness** noun.

snappy ▶ adjective (**snappier**, **snappiest**) informal **1** irritable and inclined to speak sharply; snappish: *anything unusual made her snappy and nervous.*
2 cleverly concise; neat: *snappy catchphrases.* ■ neat and elegant: *a snappy dresser.*
– PHRASES **make it snappy** be quick about it: *into bed and make it snappy!*
– DERIVATIVES **snappily** adverb, **snappiness** noun.

snap roll ▶ noun a manoeuvre in which an aircraft makes a single quick revolution about its longitudinal axis while flying horizontally.

snapshot ▶ noun **1** an informal photograph taken quickly, typically with a small hand-held camera. ■ a brief look or summary: *this excellent book can only be a snapshot of a complex industry.* ■ Computing a record of the contents of a storage location or data file at a given time.
2 (**snap shot**) a shot in soccer or hockey taken quickly with little backlift.

snare ▶ noun **1** a trap for catching birds or mammals, typically one having a noose of wire or cord. ■ a thing likely to lure or tempt someone into harm or error: *seducers laid their snares for innocent provincials.*
2 a length of wire, gut, or hide stretched across a drumhead to produce a rattling sound. ■ (also **snare drum**) a drum fitted with snares; a side drum.
3 Surgery a wire loop for severing polyps or other growths.
▶ verb [with obj.] catch (a bird or mammal) in a snare. ■ catch or trap (someone): *five blackmailers were snared in a police sting.*
– DERIVATIVES **snarer** noun.
– ORIGIN late Old English *sneare*, from Old Norse *snara*. Sense 2 of the noun is probably from Middle Low German, Middle Dutch *snare* 'harp string'.

snarf ▶ verb [with obj.] informal, chiefly N. Amer. eat or drink quickly or greedily: *they **snarfed up** frozen yogurt.*
– ORIGIN 1950s: perhaps imitative.

snark ▶ noun an imaginary animal (used typically with reference to a task or goal that is elusive or impossible to achieve): *pinning down the middle classes is like the hunting of the snark.*
– ORIGIN 1876: nonsense word coined by Lewis Carroll in *The Hunting of the Snark*.

snarky ▶ adjective (**snarkier**, **snarkiest**) N. Amer. informal sharply critical: *snarky remarks.*
– ORIGIN early 20th cent.: from dialect verb *snark* 'snore, snort', 'find fault'.

snarl[1] ▶ verb [no obj.] (of an animal such as a dog) make an aggressive growl with bared teeth: (as adj. **snarling**) *snarling alsatians.* ■ [reporting verb] (of a person) say something in an angry, bad-tempered voice: *I used to **snarl at** anyone I disliked* | [with direct speech] *'Shut your mouth!' he snarled* | [with obj.] *he snarled a few choice remarks at them.*
▶ noun an act or sound of snarling: *a snarl of rage.*
– DERIVATIVES **snarler** noun, **snarlingly** adverb, **snarly** adjective (**snarlier**, **snarliest**).
– ORIGIN late 16th cent.: extension of obsolete *snar*, of Germanic origin; related to German *schnarren* 'rattle, snarl', probably imitative.

snarl[2] ▶ verb [with obj.] **1** (**snarl something up**) entangle something: *the trailing lead got snarled up in a bramble bush.* ■ hinder or impede something: *the coach became snarled up in traffic* | *a heavy backlog of cases has snarled up the court process.*
2 decorate (metalwork) with raised shapes by hammering the underside.
▶ noun a knot or tangle: *snarls of wild raspberry plants.*
– ORIGIN late Middle English (in the senses 'snare, noose' and 'catch in a snare'): from SNARE.

snarling iron ▶ noun a tool struck with a hammer to create decorative raised work on metal.

snarl-up ▶ noun Brit. informal a traffic jam. ■ a muddle or mistake: *there's a snarl-up in editing.*

snash ▶ noun [mass noun] Scottish insolence; abuse: *he did not have to take this snash.*
– ORIGIN late 18th cent.: probably imitative.

snatch ▶ verb [with obj.] quickly seize (something) in a rude or eager way: *she snatched a biscuit from the plate* | figurative *a victory snatched from the jaws of defeat* | [no obj.] *she **snatched at** the handle.* ■ informal steal (something) or kidnap (someone) by seizing or grabbing suddenly: *the baby was snatched from a shopping centre last night.* ■ quickly secure or obtain (something) when a chance presents itself: *we snatched a few hours' sleep.* ■ [no obj.] (**snatch at**) eagerly take or accept (an offer or opportunity): *I snatched at the chance.*
▶ noun **1** an act of snatching or quickly seizing something: *a quick snatch of breath.* ■ informal a kidnapping or theft.
2 a short spell of doing something: *brief snatches of sleep.* ■ a fragment of song or talk: *picking up snatches of conversation.*
3 Weightlifting the rapid raising of a weight from the floor to above the head in one movement.
4 vulgar slang a woman's genitals.
– DERIVATIVES **snatcher** noun [in combination] *a bag-snatcher*, **snatchy** adjective.
– ORIGIN Middle English *sna(c)che* (verb) 'suddenly snap at', (noun) 'a snare'; perhaps related to SNACK.

snatch squad ▶ noun a group of police officers or soldiers detailed to seize troublemakers in a crowd.

snavel /ˈsnav(ə)l/ (also **snavle** or **snavvle**) ▶ verb [with obj.] Austral. informal steal; grab: *they'll snavel all the land.*
– ORIGIN late 18th cent. (originally English slang): perhaps a variant of SNAFFLE.

snazzy ▶ adjective (**snazzier**, **snazziest**) informal stylish and attractive: *snazzy little silk dresses.*
– DERIVATIVES **snazzily** adverb, **snazziness** noun.
– ORIGIN 1960s: of unknown origin.

sneak ▶ verb (past and past participle **sneaked** or informal, chiefly N. Amer. **snuck**) **1** [no obj., with adverbial of direction] move or go in a furtive or stealthy manner: *I sneaked out by the back exit.* ■ [with obj. and adverbial of direction] convey (someone or something) in such a way: *someone sneaked a camera inside.* ■ [with obj.] do or obtain (something) in a stealthy or furtive way: *she sneaked a glance at her watch.* ■ (**sneak up on**) creep up on (someone) without being detected: *he sneaks up on us slyly.*
2 [no obj.] Brit. informal (especially in children's use) inform an adult or person in authority of a companion's misdeeds; tell tales: *she **sneaked on** us.*
▶ noun informal **1** Brit. (especially in children's use) someone who informs an adult or person in authority of a companion's misdeeds; a telltale. ■ a furtive and contemptible person: *he was branded a prying sneak for eavesdropping on intimate conversation.*
2 (usu. **sneaks**) N. Amer. short for SNEAKER.
▶ adjective [attrib.] acting or done surreptitiously, unofficially, or without warning: *a sneak thief* | *a sneak preview.*
– ORIGIN late 16th cent.: probably dialect; perhaps related to obsolete *snike* 'to creep'.

USAGE The traditional standard past form of **sneak** is **sneaked** (*she sneaked round the corner*). An alternative past form, **snuck** (*she snuck past me*), arose in the US in the 19th century. Until very recently **snuck** was confined to US dialect use and was regarded as non-standard. However, in the last few decades its use has spread in the US, where it is now regarded as a standard alternative to **sneaked** in all but the most formal contexts. In the Oxford English Corpus there are now more US citations for **snuck** than there are for **sneaked**, and there is evidence of **snuck** gaining ground in British English also.

sneakbox ▶ noun US a small, flat boat masked with brush or weeds, used in wildfowl shooting.

sneaker ▶ noun chiefly N. Amer. a soft shoe worn for sports or casual occasions.

sneaking ▶ adjective [attrib.] **1** (of a feeling) persistent in one's mind but reluctantly held or not fully recognized: *I've a sneaking suspicion they'll do well.*
2 informal furtive and contemptible: *an unpleasant, sneaking habit.*
– DERIVATIVES **sneakingly** adverb.

sneaky ▶ adjective (**sneakier**, **sneakiest**) **1** furtive; sly: *sneaky, underhand tactics.*

2 (of a feeling) persistent but reluctantly held; sneaking: *I developed a sneaky fondness for the old lady.*
– DERIVATIVES **sneakily** adverb, **sneakiness** noun.

sneck Scottish & N. English ▶ **noun** a latch on a door or window.
▶ **verb** [with obj.] close or fasten (a door or window) with a latch.
– ORIGIN Middle English: obscurely related to SNATCH.

sneer ▶ **noun** a contemptuous or mocking smile, remark, or tone: *he acknowledged their presence with a condescending sneer.*
▶ **verb** [no obj.] smile or speak in a contemptuous or mocking manner: *she had **sneered at** their bad taste* | [with direct speech] *'I see you're conservative in your ways,' David sneered.*
– DERIVATIVES **sneerer** noun, **sneeringly** adverb.
– ORIGIN late Middle English: probably of imitative origin.

sneeze ▶ **verb** [no obj.] make a sudden involuntary expulsion of air from the nose and mouth due to irritation of one's nostrils: *the smoke made her sneeze.*
▶ **noun** an act or the sound of expelling air from the nose in such a way: *he stopped a sudden sneeze.*
– PHRASES **not to be sneezed at** informal not to be rejected without careful consideration; worth having or taking into account: *a saving of £550 was not to be sneezed at.*
– DERIVATIVES **sneezer** noun, **sneezy** adjective (**sneezier**, **sneeziest**).
– ORIGIN Middle English: apparently an alteration of Middle English *fnese* due to misreading or misprinting (after initial *fn-* had become unfamiliar), later adopted because it sounded appropriate.

sneezeweed ▶ **noun** [mass noun] a yellow-flowered North American plant of the daisy family. Some kinds are toxic to grazing animals and some are used by American Indians in the treatment of colds. ● Genus *Helenium*, family Compositae.

sneezewort ▶ **noun** a Eurasian plant related to the yarrow, whose dried leaves induce sneezing. ● *Achillea ptarmica*, family Compositae.

snell N. Amer. ▶ **noun** a short line of gut or horsehair by which a fish hook is attached to a longer line.
▶ **verb** [with obj.] tie or fasten (a hook) to a line.
– ORIGIN mid 19th cent.: of unknown origin.

Snellen test /ˈsnɛlən/ ▶ **noun** an eyesight test using rows of letters printed in successively decreasing sizes (the **Snellen scale**) of which patients are asked to read as many as they can.
– ORIGIN mid 19th cent.: named after Hermann *Snellen* (1834–1908), Dutch ophthalmologist.

Snell's law ▶ **noun** Physics a law stating that the ratio of the sines of the angles of incidence and refraction of a wave are constant when it passes between two given media.
– ORIGIN late 19th cent.: named after Willebrord van Roijen *Snell* (1591–1626), Dutch mathematician.

snib chiefly Scottish & Irish ▶ **noun** a lock, latch, or fastening for a door or window. ■ the small catch on a Yale lock which holds the bolt in or out.
▶ **verb** (**snibs**, **snibbing**, **snibbed**) [with obj.] bolt, fasten, or lock (a door).
– ORIGIN early 19th cent.: perhaps from Low German *snibbe* 'beak-like point'.

snick ▶ **verb** [with obj.] **1** cut a small notch or incision in (something): *the stem can be carefully snicked to allow the bud to swell.* ■ Cricket deflect (the ball) slightly with the edge of the bat; deflect a ball delivered by (a bowler) in this way.
2 cause (something) to make a sharp clicking sound: [with obj. and complement] *he placed the pen in the briefcase and snicked it shut.* ■ [no obj.] make such a sound: *the bolt snicked into place.*
▶ **noun 1** a small notch or cut: *he had several shaving snicks.* ■ Cricket a slight deflection of the ball by the bat.
2 a sharp click: *he heard the snick of the latch.*
– ORIGIN late 17th cent.: probably from obsolete *snick or snee* 'fight with knives'.

snicker ▶ **verb** [no obj.] give a smothered or half-suppressed laugh; snigger. ■ (of a horse) whinny.
▶ **noun** a smothered laugh; a snigger. ■ a whinny.
– DERIVATIVES **snickeringly** adverb.
– ORIGIN late 17th cent.: imitative.

snicket ▶ **noun** chiefly N. English a narrow passage between houses; an alleyway.
– ORIGIN late 19th cent.: of unknown origin.

snide ▶ **adjective 1** derogatory or mocking in an indirect way: *snide remarks about my mother.*
2 chiefly N. Amer. (of a person) devious and underhand: *a snide divorce lawyer.*
3 informal, chiefly Brit. counterfeit; inferior: *snide Rolex watches.*
▶ **noun** informal an unpleasant or underhand person.
– DERIVATIVES **snidely** adverb, **snideness** noun, **snidey** adjective.
– ORIGIN mid 19th cent. (in sense 3 of the adjective): of unknown origin.

sniff ▶ **verb** [no obj.] draw up air audibly through the nose to detect a smell, to stop it running, or to express contempt: *his dog **sniffed at** my trousers* | [with direct speech] *'You're behaving in an unladylike fashion,' sniffed Mother.* ■ [with obj.] draw in (a scent, substance, or air) through the nose: *Miranda sniffed the heavy perfume of the lilies.* ■ (**sniff around/round**) informal investigate covertly, especially in an attempt to find out confidential or incriminating information about someone. ■ [with obj.] (**sniff something out**) informal discover something by investigation: *he made millions sniffing out tax loopholes for companies.*
▶ **noun** an act or sound of sniffing: *he gave a sniff of disapproval.* ■ an amount of air or other substance taken up by sniffing: *his drug use was confined to a sniff of amyl nitrite.* ■ [in sing.] informal a hint or sign: *they're off at the first **sniff of** trouble.* ■ [in sing.] informal a small chance: *the Olympic hosts will at least **get a sniff at** a medal.*
– PHRASES **not to be sniffed at** informal worth having, accepting, or taking into account: *the price is not to be sniffed at.*
– ORIGIN Middle English: imitative.

sniffer ▶ **noun 1** a person who sniffs something: *a glue sniffer.* ■ informal a device for detecting an invisible and dangerous substance, such as gas or radiation.
2 informal a person's nose.
3 (also **sniffer program**) a computer program that detects and records a variety of restricted information, especially the secret passwords needed to gain access to files or networks.

sniffer dog ▶ **noun** a dog trained to find drugs or explosives by smell.

sniffle ▶ **verb** [no obj.] sniff slightly or repeatedly, typically because of a cold or fit of crying.
▶ **noun** an act or sound of sniffing: *he was restraining his sniffles rather well.* ■ a head cold causing a running nose and sniffing: *she had a slight cough and a sniffle.*
– DERIVATIVES **sniffly** adjective.
– ORIGIN mid 17th cent.: imitative; compare with SNIVEL.

sniffy ▶ **adjective** (**sniffier**, **sniffiest**) informal scornful; contemptuous: *some people are sniffy about tea bags.*
– DERIVATIVES **sniffily** adverb, **sniffiness** noun.

snifter ▶ **noun 1** Brit. informal a small quantity of an alcoholic drink: *care to join me for a snifter?*
2 N. Amer. a balloon glass for brandy.
– ORIGIN mid 19th cent.: imitative; compare with dialect *snift* 'to snort'.

snifter valve (also **snifting valve**) ▶ **noun** a valve on a steam engine that allows air in or out.

snig ▶ **verb** (**snigs**, **snigging**, **snigged**) [with obj.] Austral./NZ drag (a heavy load, especially timber) using ropes or chains: *bullock teams would snig the logs to the winder.*
– ORIGIN late 18th cent.: of unknown origin.

snigger Brit. ▶ **verb** [no obj.] laugh in a half-suppressed, typically scornful way: *the boys at school were sure to **snigger at** him behind his back* | [with direct speech] *'Doesn't he look a fool?' they sniggered.*
▶ **noun** a half-suppressed, typically scornful laugh.
– DERIVATIVES **sniggerer** noun, **sniggeringly** adverb.
– ORIGIN early 18th cent.: later variant of SNICKER.

sniggery ▶ **adjective** informal characterized by or liable to cause sniggering: *sniggery jokes.*

snigging chain ▶ **noun** Austral./NZ a chain used to move logs.

sniggle ▶ **verb** [no obj.] fish for eels by pushing a baited hook into holes in which they are hiding.
– ORIGIN mid 17th cent.: frequentative, based on earlier *snig* 'small eel', of unknown origin.

snip ▶ **verb** (**snips**, **snipping**, **snipped**) [with obj.] cut (something) with scissors or shears, typically with small quick strokes: *she was snipping a few dead heads off the roses* | [no obj.] *she inspected the embroidery, **snipping at** loose threads.*
▶ **noun 1** an act of cutting something in such a way: *he took a snip at a dandelion on the grass.* ■ a small piece of something that has been cut off: *the collage consists of snips of wallpaper.*
2 Brit. informal a surprisingly cheap item; a bargain: *the wine is a snip at £3.65.* ■ dated a thing that is easily achieved.
3 (**snips**) shears for cutting metal: *tin snips.*
4 N. Amer. informal a small or insignificant person: *imagine that little snip telling me I was wrong!*
– ORIGIN mid 16th cent. (in the sense 'a shred'): from Low German *snip* 'small piece', of imitative origin.

snipe /snʌɪp/ ▶ **noun** (pl. **same** or **snipes**) a wading bird of marshes and wet meadows, with brown camouflaged plumage, a long straight bill, and typically a drumming display flight. ● *Gallinago* and other genera, family Scolopacidae: several species, e.g. the **common snipe** (*G. gallinago*).
▶ **verb** [no obj.] **1** shoot at someone from a hiding place, especially accurately and at long range: *the soldiers in the trench sniped at us.*
2 make a sly or petty verbal attack: *the state governor constantly **sniped at** the president* | (as noun **sniping**) *there has been some sniping about inept leadership.*
– DERIVATIVES **sniper** noun.
– ORIGIN Middle English: probably of Scandinavian origin; compare with Icelandic *mýrisnípa*; obscurely related to Dutch *snip* and German *Schnepfe*.

snipe eel ▶ **noun** a slender marine eel with a long, thin beak-like snout, typically occurring in deep water. ● Family Nemichthyidae: several genera and species.

snipefish ▶ **noun** (pl. **same** or **snipefishes**) a marine fish that has a long, slender snout with the mouth at the tip. ● Family Macrorhamphosidae: several genera and species.

snipe fly ▶ **noun** a slender, long-legged predatory fly. ● Family Rhagionidae: many genera and species.

snippet ▶ **noun** a small piece or brief extract: ***snippets of** information about the war.*
– DERIVATIVES **snippety** adjective.

snippy ▶ **adjective** (**snippier**, **snippiest**) informal, chiefly N. Amer. curt or sharp, especially in a condescending way: *a snippy note from our landlord.*
– DERIVATIVES **snippily** adverb, **snippiness** noun.

snit ▶ **noun** N. Amer. informal a fit of irritation; a sulk: *the ambassador and delegation had withdrawn in a snit.*
– ORIGIN 1930s: of unknown origin.

snitch informal ▶ **verb 1** [with obj.] steal.
2 [no obj.] inform on someone: *she wouldn't tell who **snitched on** me.*
▶ **noun** an informer.
– ORIGIN late 17th cent.: of unknown origin.

snivel ▶ **verb** (**snivels**, **snivelling**, **snivelled**; US **snivels**, **sniveling**, **sniveled**) [no obj.] cry and sniffle: *Kate started to snivel, looking sad and stunned.* ■ complain in a whining or tearful way: *he shouldn't snivel about his punishment* | (as adj. **snivelling**) *you snivelling little brat!*
▶ **noun** an act or sound of snivelling: *Lucy's torrent of howls weakened to a snivel.*
– DERIVATIVES **sniveller** noun.
– ORIGIN late Old English (recorded only in the verbal noun *snyflung* 'mucus'), from *snofl*, in the same sense; compare with SNUFFLE.

snob ▶ **noun** a person with an exaggerated respect for high social position or wealth who seeks to associate with social superiors and looks down on those regarded as socially inferior. ■ [with adj. or noun modifier] a person who believes that their tastes in a particular area are superior to those of other people: *a musical snob.*
– DERIVATIVES **snobbism** noun, **snobby** adjective (**snobbier**, **snobbiest**).
– ORIGIN late 18th cent. (originally dialect in the sense 'cobbler'): of unknown origin; early senses conveyed a notion of 'lower status or rank', later denoting a person seeking to imitate those of superior social standing or wealth. Folk etymology connects the word with Latin *sine nobilitate* 'without nobility' but the first recorded sense has no connection with this.

snobbery ▶ **noun** (pl. **snobberies**) [mass noun] the character or quality of being a snob: *the worst aspects of English class snobbery.*

snobbish ▶ **adjective** relating to, characteristic of, or like a snob: *the writer takes a rather snobbish tone.*
– DERIVATIVES **snobbishly** adverb, **snobbishness** noun.

SNOBOL /ˈsnəʊbɒl/ ▶ **noun** [mass noun] a high-level computer programming language used especially in manipulating textual data.
– ORIGIN 1960s: formed from letters taken from *string-oriented symbolic language*, on the pattern of *COBOL*.

S

snob value ▸ **noun** [mass noun] value attached to something for its power to indicate supposed social superiority: *the 'Lancashire' coffin was more expensive and carried snob value.*

sno-cone ▸ **noun** variant spelling of **SNOW CONE**.

snoek /snuːk/ ▸ **noun** South African term for **BARRACOUTA**.
– ORIGIN Afrikaans from Dutch, 'pike'; compare with **SNOOK²**.

snog Brit. informal ▸ **verb** (**snogs, snogging, snogged**) [no obj.] kiss and cuddle amorously: *the pair were snogging on the sofa* | [with obj.] *he snogged my girl at a party.*
▸ **noun** a long kiss or a period of amorous kissing and cuddling: *he gave her a proper snog, not just a peck.*
– DERIVATIVES **snogger** noun.
– ORIGIN 1940s: of unknown origin.

snood /snuːd/ ▸ **noun 1** an ornamental hairnet or fabric bag worn over the hair at the back of a woman's head. ■ historical a ribbon or band worn by unmarried women in Scotland to confine their hair.
2 a wide ring of knitted material worn as a hood or scarf.
3 a short line attaching a hook to a main line in sea fishing.
– ORIGIN Old English *snōd*, of unknown origin.

snook¹ /snuːk/ ▸ **noun** (in phrase **cock a snook**) informal, chiefly Brit. place one's hand so that the thumb touches one's nose and the fingers are spread out, in order to express contempt. ■ openly show contempt or a lack of respect for someone or something: *he spent a lifetime cocking a snook at the art world.*
– ORIGIN late 18th cent.: of unknown origin.

snook² /snuːk/ ▸ **noun** a large edible game fish of the Caribbean which is sometimes found in brackish water. ● *Centropomus undecimalis*, family Centropomidae.
– ORIGIN late 17th cent.: from Dutch *snoek* (see **SNOEK**).

snooker ▸ **noun** [mass noun] a game played with cues on a billiard table in which the players use a cue ball (white) to pocket the other balls (fifteen red and six coloured) in a set order. ■ [count noun] a position in a game of snooker or pool in which a player cannot make a direct shot at any permitted ball: *he needed a snooker to have a chance of winning the frame.*
▸ **verb** [with obj.] subject (oneself or one's opponent) to a snooker. ■ Brit. leave (someone) in a difficult position; thwart: *I managed to lose my flat keys—that was me snookered.* ■ US trick, entice, or trap: *they were snookered into buying books at prices that were too high.*
– ORIGIN late 19th cent.: of unknown origin.

snoop informal ▸ **verb** [no obj.] investigate or look around furtively in an attempt to find out something, especially information about someone's private affairs: *your sister might find the ring if she goes **snooping** about* | (as adj. **snooping**) *snooping neighbours.*
▸ **noun** [in sing.] an act of looking around in such a way: *I could go back to her cottage and have another snoop.* ■ a person who investigates in such a way.
– DERIVATIVES **snooper** noun, **snoopy** adjective.
– ORIGIN mid 19th cent.: from Dutch *snœpen* 'eat on the sly'.

snooperscope ▸ **noun** a device which converts infrared radiation into a visible image, used for seeing in the dark.

S

snoot ▸ **noun 1** informal a person's nose.
2 informal a person who shows contempt for those considered to be of a lower social class: *the snoots complain that the paper has lowered its standards.*
3 a tubular or conical attachment used to produce a narrow beam from a spotlight.
▸ **adjective** informal stylish and sophisticated: *a snoot silk shirt.*
– ORIGIN mid 19th cent.: variant of **SNOUT**.

snootful ▸ **noun** informal as much as one can take of something, especially alcoholic drink: *for a hundred kopecks, you get a snootful of vodka.*

snooty ▸ **adjective** (**snootier, snootiest**) informal showing disapproval or contempt towards others, especially those considered to belong to a lower social class: *snooty neighbours.*
– DERIVATIVES **snootily** adverb, **snootiness** noun.
– ORIGIN early 20th cent.: from **SNOOT** + **-Y¹**; compare with **SNOTTY**.

snooze informal ▸ **noun 1** a short, light sleep, especially during the day: *he settled in the grass for a snooze.*
2 N. Amer. something boring or tedious.
▸ **verb** [no obj.] have a short, light sleep: *the children play beach games while the adults snooze in the sun.*
– DERIVATIVES **snoozer** noun, **snoozy** adjective (**snoozier, snooziest**).
– ORIGIN late 18th cent.: of unknown origin.

snooze button ▸ **noun** a control on a clock which sets an alarm to repeat after a short interval, allowing time for a little more sleep.

snore ▸ **noun** a snorting or grunting sound in a person's breathing while they are asleep: *she lay on the mattress listening to Sally's snores.* ■ informal a thing that is extremely boring: *she sings a version of 'Passionate Kisses' that's a certified snore.*
▸ **verb** [no obj.] make a snorting or grunting sound while asleep: *he was snoring loudly* | (as noun **snoring**) *you keep me awake all night with your snoring.*
– DERIVATIVES **snorer** noun.
– ORIGIN Middle English (in the sense 'a snort, snorting'): probably imitative; compare with **SNORT**.

snorkel /ˈsnɔːk(ə)l/ ▸ **noun 1** a tube for a swimmer to breathe through while under water.
2 (**Snorkel**) trademark a type of hydraulically elevated platform for firefighting.
▸ **verb** (**snorkels, snorkelling, snorkelled**; US **snorkels, snorkeling, snorkeled**) [no obj.] (often as noun **snorkelling**) swim using a snorkel: *the sea is incredibly clear—ideal for snorkelling* | *snorkel around the unspoilt coral reefs.*
– DERIVATIVES **snorkeller** noun.
– ORIGIN 1940s: from German *Schnorchel*.

Snorri Sturluson /ˌsnɒːrɪ ˈstəːləs(ə)n/ (1178–1241), Icelandic historian and poet. A leading figure of medieval Icelandic literature, he wrote the *Younger Edda* or *Prose Edda* and the *Heimskringla*, a history of the kings of Norway from mythical times to the year 1177.

snort ▸ **noun** an explosive sound made by the sudden forcing of breath through one's nose, used to express indignation, derision, or incredulity: *he gave a snort of disgust.* ■ a similar sound made by an animal, typically when excited or frightened. ■ informal a quantity of an illegal drug, especially cocaine, inhaled in powdered form through the nose: *they were high on a few snorts.* ■ informal a measure of an alcoholic drink: *a bottle of rum was opened and they took a good long snort.*
▸ **verb** [no obj.] make a sudden explosive sound through one's nose, especially to express indignation or derision: *she snorted with laughter* | [with direct speech] *'How perfectly ridiculous!' he snorted.* ■ (of an animal) make such a sound, especially when excited or frightened. ■ [with obj.] informal inhale (the powdered form of an illegal drug, especially cocaine) through the nose.
– ORIGIN late Middle English (as a verb, also in the sense 'snore'): probably imitative; compare with **SNORE**. The noun dates from the early 19th cent.

snorter ▸ **noun** informal **1** a person or thing that snorts, especially someone who inhales cocaine.
2 Brit. dated a thing that is an extreme or remarkable example of its kind, especially for its strength or severity: *the opening batsman fended off a snorter.*

snot ▸ **noun** informal **1** [mass noun] nasal mucus.
2 a contemptible or worthless person.
– ORIGIN late Middle English: probably from Middle Dutch, Middle Low German; related to **SNOUT**.

snot-nosed ▸ **adjective** informal **1** childish and inexperienced: *what would I be doing with a snot-nosed kid like him?*
2 considering oneself superior; conceited: *a snot-nosed snob.*

snot rag ▸ **noun** informal a handkerchief.

snotter¹ ▸ **noun** (usu. **snotters**) informal, chiefly Scottish a piece or drop of nasal mucus.

snotter² ▸ **noun** Nautical a fitting which holds the heel of a sprit close to the mast. ■ a length of rope with an eye spliced in each end.
– ORIGIN mid 18th cent.: of unknown origin.

snotty ▸ **adjective** (**snottier, snottiest**) informal **1** full of or covered with nasal mucus: *a snotty nose.*
2 having or showing a superior or conceited attitude: *a snotty letter.*
– DERIVATIVES **snottily** adverb, **snottiness** noun.

snotty-nosed ▸ **adjective** informal another term for **SNOT-NOSED**.

snout ▸ **noun 1** the projecting nose and mouth of an animal, especially a mammal. ■ informal a person's nose. ■ the projecting front or end of something such as a pistol.
2 Brit. informal a cigarette. ■ [mass noun] tobacco.
3 Brit. informal a police informer.
4 (also **snout moth**) a European moth with long palps that extend in front of the head like a snout. ● *Hypsena* and other genera, family Noctuidae, in particular **the snout** (*H. proboscidalis*).
– DERIVATIVES **snouted** adjective [often in combination] *long-snouted baboons*, **snouty** adjective.
– ORIGIN Middle English: from Middle Dutch, Middle Low German *snūt*; related to **SNOT**.

snout beetle ▸ **noun** N. Amer. a weevil.

snout butterfly ▸ **noun** a butterfly with long palps that extend in front of the head like a snout. ● Subfamily Libytheinae, family Nymphalidae: several species.

Snow, C. P., 1st Baron Snow of Leicester (1905–80), English novelist and scientist; full name *Charles Percy Snow*. He is best known for his sequence of eleven novels *Strangers and Brothers*, which deals with moral dilemmas in the academic world, and for his lecture *Two Cultures* (1959).

snow ▸ **noun** [mass noun] **1** atmospheric water vapour frozen into ice crystals and falling in light white flakes or lying on the ground as a white layer: *we were trudging through deep snow.* ■ (**snows**) falls of snow: *the first snows of winter.*
2 something resembling snow, in particular: ■ a mass of flickering white spots on a television or radar screen, caused by interference or a poor signal. ■ informal cocaine. ■ a dessert or other dish resembling snow: *vanilla snow.* ■ [with modifier] a frozen gas resembling snow: *carbon dioxide snow.*
▸ **verb 1** [no obj.] (**it snows, it is snowing**, etc.) snow falls: *it's not snowing so heavily now.* ■ (**be snowed in/up**) be confined or blocked by a large quantity of snow: *I was snowed in for a week.*
2 [with obj.] N. Amer. informal mislead or charm (someone) with elaborate and insincere words: *they would snow the public into believing that all was well.*
– PHRASAL VERBS **be snowed under** be overwhelmed with a very large quantity of something, especially work: *he's been **snowed under with** urgent cases.*
– DERIVATIVES **snowless** adjective, **snowlike** adjective.
– ORIGIN Old English *snāw*, of Germanic origin; related to Dutch *sneeuw* and German *Schnee*, from an Indo-European root shared by Latin *nix*, *niv-* and Greek *nipha*.

snowball ▸ **noun 1** a ball of packed snow, especially one made for throwing at other people for fun. ■ a thing that grows rapidly in size, intensity, or importance: *a public-debt snowball that could grow to American proportions* | [as modifier] *the closures are expected to have a snowball effect, impacting jobs and tax revenues.*
2 a cocktail containing advocaat and lemonade.
3 a dessert resembling a ball of snow, especially one containing or covered in ice cream.
▸ **verb 1** [with obj.] throw snowballs at: *I made sure the other kids stopped snowballing Celia.*
2 [no obj.] increase rapidly in size, intensity, or importance: *the campaign was snowballing.*
– PHRASES **a snowball's chance (in hell)** informal no chance at all: *the scheme has a snowball's chance in hell of being accepted.*

snowball tree (also **snowball bush**) ▸ **noun** a guelder rose of a sterile variety which produces large globular white flower heads.

snowbell ▸ **noun** an Asian tree related to the storax, bearing clusters of fragrant white hanging flowers at midsummer. ● *Styrax japonica*, family Styracaceae.

snowberry ▸ **noun** (pl. **snowberries**) a North American shrub of the honeysuckle family, bearing white berries and often cultivated as an ornamental or for hedging. ● *Symphoricarpos albus*, family Caprifoliaceae.

snowbird ▸ **noun 1** N. Amer. informal a northerner who moves to a warmer Southern state in the winter.
2 a widespread and variable junco (songbird) with grey or brown upper parts and a white belly. ● *Junco hyemalis*, family Emberizidae (subfamily Emberizinae). Alternative name: **dark-eyed junco**. ■ the snow bunting.

snowblade ▸ **noun** a type of short ski about a metre in length, used without ski sticks.
– DERIVATIVES **snowblader** noun, **snowblading** noun.

snow-blind ▸ **adjective** temporarily blinded by the glare of light reflected by a large expanse of snow.
– DERIVATIVES **snow blindness** noun.

snowblink ▸ **noun** a white reflection in the sky of snow or ice on the ground.

snowblower ▸ **noun** a machine that clears fallen snow from a pavement, road, or other area by blowing it out to the side.

snowboard ▸ **noun** a board resembling a short, broad ski, used for sliding downhill on snow.

soda lake ▸ noun a salt lake with a high content of sodium salts.

soda lime ▸ noun [mass noun] a mixture of calcium oxide and sodium hydroxide.

sodalite /ˈsəʊdəlʌɪt/ ▸ noun [mass noun] a blue mineral consisting chiefly of an aluminosilicate and chloride of sodium, occurring chiefly in alkaline igneous rocks.
– ORIGIN early 19th cent.: from **SODA** + **-LITE**.

sodality /səʊˈdalɪti/ ▸ noun (pl. **sodalities**) a confraternity or association, especially a Roman Catholic religious guild or brotherhood.
– ORIGIN early 17th cent.: from French *sodalité* or Latin *sodalitas*, from *sodalis* 'comrade'.

soda pop ▸ noun [mass noun] US informal a sweet carbonated drink.

soda siphon ▸ noun a bottle from which carbonated water is dispensed by allowing the gas pressure to force it out.

soda water ▸ noun see **SODA** (sense 1).

sodbuster ▸ noun N. Amer. informal a farmer or farm worker who ploughs the land.

sodden ▸ adjective saturated with liquid, especially water; soaked through: *his clothes were sodden.* ■ [in combination] having drunk an excessive amount of a particular alcoholic drink: *a whisky-sodden criminal.*
▸ verb [with obj.] archaic saturate (something) with water.
– DERIVATIVES **soddenly** adverb, **soddenness** noun.
– ORIGIN Middle English (in the sense 'boiled, cooked by boiling'): archaic past participle of **SEETHE**.

Soddy, Frederick (1877–1956), English physicist. He assisted William Ramsay in the discovery of helium and formulated a theory of isotopes, the word *isotope* being coined by him in 1913, after work on radioactive decay. Nobel Prize for Chemistry (1921).

sodger /ˈsəʊdʒə/ ▸ noun non-standard spelling of **SOLDIER**, used to represent regional pronunciation.

sodium ▸ noun [mass noun] the chemical element of atomic number 11, a soft silver-white reactive metal of the alkali-metal group. (Symbol: **Na**)
– DERIVATIVES **sodic** adjective (Mineralogy).
– ORIGIN early 19th cent.: from **SODA** + **-IUM**.

sodium amytal ▸ noun see **AMYTAL**.

sodium bicarbonate ▸ noun [mass noun] a soluble white powder used in fire extinguishers and effervescent drinks and as a raising agent in baking. Also called **BAKING SODA**. ● Chem. formula: $NaHCO_3$.

sodium carbonate ▸ noun [mass noun] a white alkaline compound with many commercial applications including the manufacture of soap and glass. Also called **WASHING SODA**. ● Chem. formula: Na_2CO_3.

sodium chloride ▸ noun [mass noun] a colourless crystalline compound occurring naturally in seawater and halite; common salt. ● Chem. formula: NaCl.

sodium cromoglycate ▸ noun see **CROMOGLYCATE**.

sodium hydroxide ▸ noun [mass noun] a strongly alkaline white deliquescent compound used in many industrial processes, e.g. the manufacture of soap and paper. Also called **CAUSTIC SODA**. ● Chem. formula: NaOH.

sodium nitrate ▸ noun [mass noun] a white powdery compound used mainly in the manufacture of fertilizers. ● Chem. formula: $NaNO_3$.

sodium thiosulphate ▸ noun [mass noun] a white soluble compound used in photography as a fixer to dissolve unchanged silver halides. Also called **HYPO**[1]. ● Chem. formula: $Na_2S_2O_3$.

sodium-vapour lamp (also **sodium lamp**) ▸ noun a lamp in which an electrical discharge in sodium vapour gives a yellow light, typically used in street lighting.

Sodom /ˈsɒdəm/ a town in ancient Palestine, probably south of the Dead Sea. According to Gen. 19:24 it was destroyed by fire from heaven, together with Gomorrah, for the wickedness of its inhabitants.
■ (as noun **a Sodom**) a wicked or depraved place.

sodomite /ˈsɒdəmʌɪt/ ▸ noun a person who engages in anal intercourse.
– DERIVATIVES **sodomitic** adjective, **sodomitical** adjective.
– ORIGIN Middle English (in the sense 'sodomy'): via Old French from late Latin *Sodomita*, from Greek *Sodomitēs* 'inhabitant of Sodom'.

sodomy ▸ noun [mass noun] anal intercourse.
– DERIVATIVES **sodomize** (also **sodomise**) verb.
– ORIGIN Middle English: from medieval Latin *sodomia*, from late Latin *peccatum Sodomiticum* 'sin of Sodom' (after Gen. 19:5, which implies that the men of Sodom practised homosexual rape) (see **SODOM**).

Sodor /ˈsəʊdə/ a medieval diocese comprising the Hebrides and the Isle of Man. **Sodor and Man** has been the official name for the Anglican diocese of the Isle of Man since 1684.
– ORIGIN from Norse *Sudhr-eyjar* 'southern isles'; the islands belonged formerly to Norway.

Sod's Law ▸ noun Brit. another term for **MURPHY'S LAW**.

SOE ▸ abbreviation Special Operations Executive.

soever ▸ adverb archaic or literary of any kind; to any extent: *how great soever the assurance is.*

-soever ▸ combining form of any kind; to any extent: *whatsoever | whosoever.*
– ORIGIN Middle English: originally as the phrase *so ever.*

sofa ▸ noun a long upholstered seat with a back and arms, for two or more people.
– ORIGIN early 17th cent.: from French, based on Arabic *ṣuffa*.

sofa bed ▸ noun a sofa that can be converted into a bed, typically for occasional use.

Sofar /ˈsəʊfɑː/ (also **SOFAR**) ▸ noun [mass noun] a system in which the sound waves from an underwater explosion are detected and located by three or more listening stations, useful in determining the position at sea of survivors of a disaster.
– ORIGIN 1940s: from *So(und) f(ixing) a(nd) r(anging)*.

soffit /ˈsɒfɪt/ ▸ noun the underside of an architectural structure such as an arch, a balcony, or overhanging eaves.
– ORIGIN early 17th cent.: from French *soffite* or Italian *soffitto*, based on Latin *suffixus* 'fastened below'.

Sofia /ˈsəʊfɪə, səˈfiːə/ the capital of Bulgaria; pop. 1,162,898 (2008). An ancient Thracian settlement, it became a province of Rome in the first century AD. It was held by the Turks between the late 14th and late 19th centuries and became the capital of Bulgaria in 1879.

sofrito /sɒˈfriːtəʊ/ (also **soffritto**) ▸ noun [mass noun] (in Spanish and Italian cooking) a mixture of lightly fried onions and garlic, usually with tomatoes and other vegetables, used as a base for soups and stews.
– ORIGIN Spanish *sofrito*, Italian *soffritto*, literally 'lightly fried'.

S. of S. ▸ abbreviation Song of Songs (in biblical references).

soft ▸ adjective **1** easy to mould, cut, compress, or fold; not hard or firm to the touch: *soft margarine | the ground was soft beneath their feet.* ■ having a smooth surface or texture; not rough or coarse: *soft crushed velvet | her hair felt very soft.* ■ (of a person) weak and lacking courage: *soft southerners.* ■ (of a market, currency, or commodity) falling or likely to fall in value.
2 having a pleasing quality involving a subtle effect or contrast rather than sharp definition: *the soft glow of the lamps | the moon's pale light cast soft shadows.* ■ (of a voice or sound) quiet and gentle: *they spoke in soft whispers.* ■ not strong or violent: *a soft breeze rustled the trees.* ■ dialect (of the weather) rainy, moist, or thawing.
3 sympathetic, lenient, or compassionate, especially to a degree perceived as excessive; not strict or sufficiently strict: *the government is not becoming **soft on** crime | Julia's soft heart was touched by his grief.* ■ (of words or language) not harsh or angry; conciliatory; soothing: *he was no good with soft words, gentle phrases.* ■ willing to compromise in political matters: *candidates ranging from far right to soft left.* ■ informal (of a job or way of life) requiring little effort.
4 (of a drink) not alcoholic. ■ (of a drug) not likely to cause addiction. ■ (of radiation) having little penetrating power. ■ (of a detergent) biodegradable. ■ (also **soft-core**) (of pornography) suggestive or erotic but not explicit.
5 (of water) free from mineral salts that make lathering difficult.
6 informal foolish; silly: *he must be going soft in the head.* ■ (**soft on**) informal infatuated with: *was Brendan soft on her?*
7 (of a consonant) pronounced as a fricative (as *c* in *ice*).
▸ adverb **1** in a quiet or gentle way: *I can just speak soft and she'll hear me.*
2 informal in a weak or foolish way: *don't talk soft.*
– PHRASES **have a soft spot** (Indian also **soft corner**) **for** be fond of or affectionate towards. **soft option** an easier alternative: *probation should in no sense be seen as a soft option by the judiciary.* **soft touch** (also **easy touch**) informal a person who readily gives or does something if asked.
– DERIVATIVES **softish** adjective, **softly** adverb, **softness** noun.
– ORIGIN Old English *sōfte* 'agreeable, calm, gentle', of West Germanic origin; related to Dutch *zacht* and German *sanft*.

softa /ˈsɒftə/ ▸ noun a Muslim student of sacred law and theology.
– ORIGIN Turkish, from Persian, 'severe, hard'.

softback ▸ adjective & noun another term for **PAPERBACK**.

softball ▸ noun [mass noun] a modified form of baseball played on a smaller field with a larger, softer ball, seven rather than nine innings, and underarm pitching. The game evolved in the US during the late 19th century from a form of indoor baseball. ■ [count noun] a ball used in softball.

soft-boiled ▸ adjective (of an egg) boiled for a short time, leaving the yolk soft or liquid.

soft box ▸ noun Photography a frame with a cloth covering used to diffuse the light from a flash or floodlight.

soft-centred ▸ adjective (of a sweet) having a soft filling. ■ (of a person) having a compassionate or sentimental nature.

soft clam ▸ noun another term for **SOFTSHELL CLAM**.

soft coal ▸ noun [mass noun] bituminous coal.

soft copy ▸ noun Computing a legible version of a piece of information not printed on a physical medium, especially as stored or displayed on a computer.

soft-core ▸ adjective see **SOFT** (sense 4 of the adjective).

softcover ▸ adjective & noun another term for **PAPERBACK**.

soft crab ▸ noun another term for **SOFTSHELL CRAB**.

soften ▸ verb **1** make or become soft or softer: [with obj.] *plant extracts to soften and moisturize the skin* | [no obj.] *let the vegetables soften over a low heat.* ■ [with obj.] (of a market, currency, or commodity) fall in value: *the share price has softened recently.*
2 make or become less severe: [with obj.] *a major injection of private cash could **soften the blow** for the taxpayer* | [no obj.] *her expression softened at the sight of Diane's white face.* ■ [with obj.] undermine the resistance of (someone): *the blockade appears a better weapon with which to **soften** them **up** for eventual surrender.*
3 [with obj.] remove mineral salts from (water).
– DERIVATIVES **softener** noun.

softening of the brain ▸ noun [mass noun] informal or archaic mental deterioration, especially senile dementia, supposedly resulting from degeneration of the brain tissue.

soft focus ▸ noun [mass noun] deliberate slight blurring or lack of definition in a photograph or film.
▸ adjective (**soft-focus**) characterized by or producing such a lack of definition.

soft fruit ▸ noun Brit. a small stoneless fruit, such as a strawberry or a blackcurrant.

soft furnishings ▸ plural noun Brit. items made of cloth, such as curtains, chair coverings, etc., used to decorate a room.

S

soft goods ▸ plural noun Brit. textiles.

soft-headed ▸ adjective lacking wisdom or intelligence.
– DERIVATIVES **soft-headedness** noun.

soft-hearted ▸ adjective kind and compassionate.
– DERIVATIVES **soft-heartedness** noun.

soft hyphen ▸ noun a hyphen inserted into a word not otherwise hyphenated, to be displayed or typeset only if it falls at the end of a line of text.

softie (also **softy**) ▸ noun (pl. **softies**) informal a soft-hearted, weak, or sentimental person.

soft iron ▸ noun [mass noun] iron that has a low carbon content and is easily magnetized and demagnetized, used to make the cores of solenoids and other electrical equipment.

soft landing ▸ noun a controlled landing of a spacecraft during which no serious damage is incurred. ■ the slowing down of economic growth at an acceptable degree relative to inflation and unemployment.
– DERIVATIVES **soft-land** verb.

soft loan ▸ noun a loan, typically one to a developing country, made on terms very favourable to the borrower.

softly-softly ▸ adjective [attrib.] Brit. cautious and patient: *he urged the president to use a softly-softly approach to the crisis.*

soft-nosed ▸ adjective (of a bullet) expanding on impact.

soft palate ▸ noun the fleshy, flexible part towards the back of the roof of the mouth.

soft-paste ▸ adjective denoting artificial porcelain, typically made with white clay and ground glass and fired at a comparatively low temperature.

soft pedal ▸ noun a pedal on a piano that can be pressed to make the tone softer.
▸ verb (**soft-pedal**) [with obj.] refrain from emphasizing the more unpleasant aspects of; play down: *the administration's decision to soft-pedal the missile program.*

softphone ▸ noun a piece of software that allows the user to make telephone calls over the Internet.

soft power ▸ noun [mass noun] a persuasive approach to international relations, typically involving the use of economic or cultural influence. Compare with HARD POWER.

soft rock ▸ noun [mass noun] a style of rock music with a less persistent beat and more emphasis on lyrics and melody than hard rock.

soft roe ▸ noun see ROE[1].

soft rot ▸ noun [mass noun] any of a number of bacterial and fungal diseases of fruit and vegetables in which the tissue becomes soft and slimy. ■ any of a number of fungal conditions affecting timber, which becomes soft and friable.

soft sell ▸ noun (often **the soft sell**) a method of salesmanship or advertising that uses subtle persuasion.
▸ verb (**soft-sell**) [with obj.] sell (something) by using such a method.

softshell (also **softshell turtle**) ▸ noun a freshwater turtle with a flattened leathery shell, native to Asia, Africa, and North America. ● Family Trionychidae: several genera and many species, including the **spiny softshell** (*Apalone* (or *Trionyx*) *spinifera*) of North America.

softshell clam ▸ noun a marine bivalve mollusc with a thin shell and a long siphon, valued as food on the east coast of North America. Also called SOFT CLAM, STEAMER CLAM. ● Genus *Mya*, family Myidae, especially *M. arenaria*.

softshell crab ▸ noun chiefly N. Amer. a crab, especially a blue crab, that has recently moulted and has a new shell that is still soft and edible. Also called SOFT CRAB.

soft-shoe ▸ noun a kind of tap dance performed in soft-soled shoes.
▸ verb [no obj.] perform a dance of this kind. ■ [with adverbial of direction] move quietly and carefully so as not to draw attention to oneself: *I soft-shoed after him* | figurative *he soft-shoed into a safer topic of conversation.*

soft shoulder ▸ noun N. Amer. an unmetalled strip of land at the side of a road.

soft skills ▸ plural noun personal attributes that enable someone to interact effectively and harmoniously with other people.

S

soft soap ▸ noun [mass noun] **1** a semi-fluid soap, especially one made with potassium rather than sodium salts.
2 informal persuasive flattery.
▸ verb (**soft-soap**) [with obj.] informal use flattery in order to persuade or cajole (someone) to do something.

soft sore ▸ noun another term for CHANCROID.

soft-spoken ▸ adjective speaking or said with a gentle, quiet voice.

soft sugar ▸ noun [mass noun] Brit. granulated or powdered sugar.

soft tack ▸ noun [mass noun] archaic bread or other nourishing food, especially as eaten by sailors or soldiers.

soft target ▸ noun a person or thing that is relatively unprotected or vulnerable, especially to military or terrorist attack.

soft-top ▸ noun a motor vehicle having a roof that can be folded back. ■ (**soft top**) a roof of this type.

soft toy ▸ noun Brit. a children's toy, typically a toy animal, made of fabric stuffed with a soft filling.

software ▸ noun [mass noun] the programs and other operating information used by a computer. Compare with HARDWARE.

soft wheat ▸ noun [mass noun] wheat of a variety having a soft grain rich in starch.

softwood ▸ noun [mass noun] **1** the wood from a conifer (such as pine, fir, or spruce) as distinguished from that of broadleaved trees. ■ [count noun] a tree producing softwood.
2 (in gardening) young pliable growth on shrubs and other plants from which cuttings can be taken.

softy ▸ noun variant spelling of SOFTIE.

soggy ▸ adjective (**soggier**, **soggiest**) very wet and soft: *we squelched through the soggy ground.*
– DERIVATIVES **soggily** adverb, **sogginess** noun.
– ORIGIN early 18th cent. (in the sense 'boggy'): from dialect *sog* 'a swamp' + -Y[1].

Sogne Fjord /ˈsɒŋə/ a fjord on the west coast of Norway. The longest and deepest fjord in the country, it extends inland for some 200 km (125 miles), with a maximum depth of 1,308 m (4,291 ft). Norwegian name **Sognafjorden** /ˈsɔŋnəˌfjuːrən/.

sogo shosha /ˌsəʊgəʊ ˈʃəʊʃə/ ▸ noun (pl. **same**) a very large Japanese company that trades internationally in a wide range of goods and services.
– ORIGIN Japanese, from *sōgō* 'comprehensive' + *shōsha* 'mercantile society'.

soh /səʊ/ (also **so** or **sol**) ▸ noun Music (in tonic sol-fa) the fifth note of a major scale. ■ the note G in the fixed-doh system.
– ORIGIN Middle English *sol*: representing (as an arbitrary name for the note) the first syllable of *solve*, taken from a Latin hymn (see SOLMIZATION).

SOHO ▸ adjective relating to a market for cheap consumer electronics used by individuals and small companies.
– ORIGIN 1990s: acronym from *small office home office*.

soi-disant /ˌswɑːdiːˈzɒ̃/ ▸ adjective self-styled; so-called: *a soi-disant novelist.*
– ORIGIN French, from *soi* 'oneself' + *disant* 'saying'.

soigné /ˈswʌnjeɪ/ ▸ adjective (fem. **soignée** pronunc. **same**) dressed very elegantly; well groomed: *she was dark, petite, and soignée.*
– ORIGIN past participle of French *soigner* 'take care of', from *soin* 'care'.

soigneur /swʌnˈjəː/ ▸ noun Cycling a person who gives training, massage, and other assistance to a team, especially during a race.
– ORIGIN French, from *soigner* 'take care of'.

soil[1] ▸ noun [mass noun] the upper layer of earth in which plants grow, a black or dark brown material typically consisting of a mixture of organic remains, clay, and rock particles. ■ the territory of a particular nation: *the stationing of US troops on Japanese soil.*
– DERIVATIVES **soil-less** adjective.
– ORIGIN late Middle English: from Anglo-Norman French, perhaps representing Latin *solium* 'seat', by association with *solum* 'ground'.

soil[2] ▸ verb [with obj.] make dirty: *he might soil his expensive suit* | (as adj. **soiled**) *a soiled T-shirt.* ■ make dirty by defecating in or on. ■ bring discredit to; tarnish: *what good is there in soiling your daughter's reputation?*
▸ noun [mass noun] waste matter, especially sewage containing excrement. See also NIGHT SOIL. ■ [count noun] archaic a stain or discolouring mark.
– ORIGIN Middle English (as a verb): from Old French *soiller*, based on Latin *sucula*, diminutive of *sus* 'pig'. The earliest use of the noun (late Middle English) was 'muddy wallow for wild boar'; current noun senses date from the early 16th cent.

soil[3] ▸ verb [with obj.] rare feed (cattle) on fresh-cut green fodder (originally for the purpose of purging them).
– ORIGIN early 17th cent.: perhaps from SOIL[2].

soil mechanics ▸ plural noun [usu. treated as sing.] the branch of science concerned with the properties and behaviour of soil as they affect its use in civil engineering.

soil pipe ▸ noun a sewage or waste-water pipe.

soil science ▸ noun [mass noun] the branch of science concerned with the formation, nature, ecology, and classification of soil.

soil stack ▸ noun the pipe which takes all the waste water from the upstairs plumbing system of a building.

soirée /ˈswɑːreɪ/ ▸ noun an evening party or gathering, typically in a private house, for conversation or music.
– ORIGIN French, from *soir* 'evening'.

soixante-neuf /ˌswasɒntˈnəːf/ ▸ noun [mass noun] informal sexual activity between two people involving mutual oral stimulation of each other's genitals.
– ORIGIN French, literally 'sixty-nine', from the position of the couple.

sojourn /ˈsɒdʒ(ə)n, -dʒəːn/ formal ▸ noun a temporary stay: *her sojourn in Rome.*
▸ verb [no obj., with adverbial of place] stay somewhere temporarily: *she had sojourned once in Egypt.*
– DERIVATIVES **sojourner** noun.
– ORIGIN Middle English: from Old French *sojourner*, based on Latin *sub-* 'under' + late Latin *diurnum* 'day'.

Soka Gakkai /ˌsəʊkə ˈgakʌɪ/ a political and lay religious organization founded in Japan in 1930, based on the teachings of the Nichiren Buddhist sect.
– ORIGIN Japanese, from *sō* 'create' + *ka* 'value' + *gakkai* '(learned) society'.

sokaiya /ˈsəʊkʌɪjə/ ▸ noun (pl. **same**) a holder of shares in a Japanese company who tries to extort money from it by threatening to cause trouble for executives at a general meeting of the shareholders.
– ORIGIN Japanese, from *sōkai* 'general meeting' + *-ya* 'dealer'.

soke ▸ noun Brit. historical a right of local jurisdiction. ■ a district under a particular jurisdiction; a minor administrative district.
– ORIGIN late Old English, back-formation from obsolete *soken* 'habitual visiting of a place'.

Sokol /ˈsɒkɒl/ ▸ noun a Slav gymnastic society aiming to promote a communal spirit and physical fitness, originating in Prague in 1862.
– ORIGIN Czech, literally 'falcon' (the emblem of the society).

Sol /sɒl/ Roman Mythology the sun, especially when personified as a god.
– ORIGIN Latin.

sol[1] /sɒl/ ▸ noun variant of SOH.

sol[2] /sɒl/ ▸ noun Chemistry a fluid suspension of a colloidal solid in a liquid.
– ORIGIN late 19th cent.: abbreviation of SOLUTION.

sol[3] /sɒl/ (also **nuevo sol**) ▸ noun (pl. **soles** /ˈsɒlɛz, ˈsəʊlɛz/) the basic monetary unit of Peru, equal to 100 cents. It replaced the inti in 1991.
– ORIGIN Spanish, literally 'sun'.

-sol ▸ combining form in nouns denoting different kinds and states of soil: *histosol* | *vertisol*.
– ORIGIN from Latin *solum* 'soil'.

sola[1] /ˈsəʊlə/ ▸ noun an Indian swamp plant of the pea family, with stems that yield the pith that is used to make sola topis. ● *Aeschynomene indica*, family Leguminosae.
– ORIGIN mid 19th cent.: from Bengali *solā*, Hindi *śolā*.

sola[2] ▸ noun feminine form of SOLUS.

solace /ˈsɒlɪs/ ▸ noun [mass noun] comfort or consolation in a time of great distress or sadness: *she sought solace in her religion.*
▸ verb [with obj.] give solace to.
– ORIGIN Middle English: from Old French *solas* (noun), *solacier* (verb), based on Latin *solari* 'to console'.

solan /ˈsəʊlən/ (also **solan goose**) ▸ noun the northern gannet. See GANNET (sense 1).
– ORIGIN late Middle English: probably from Old Norse *súla* 'gannet' + *and-* 'duck'.

solanaceous /ˌsɒləˈneɪʃəs/ ▸ adjective Botany relating to or denoting plants of the nightshade family (Solanaceae).
– ORIGIN early 19th cent.: from modern Latin *Solanaceae* (plural), based on Latin *solanum* 'nightshade' + -OUS.

solander /səˈlandə/ (also **solander box**) ▸ noun a protective box made in the form of a book, for holding such items as botanical specimens, maps, papers, etc.
– ORIGIN late 18th cent.: named after Daniel C. *Solander* (1736–82), Swedish botanist.

solanine /ˈsɒləniːn/ ▸ noun [mass noun] Chemistry a poisonous compound which is present in green potatoes and in related plants. It is a steroid glycoside of the saponin group.
– ORIGIN mid 19th cent.: from French, from the genus name *Solanum* + -INE[4].

solanum /səˈleɪnəm/ ▸ noun a plant of a genus that includes the potato and woody nightshade. ● Genus *Solanum*, family Solanaceae.
– ORIGIN Latin.

Solapur /ˈʃəʊləpʊə/ (also **Sholapur**) a city in western India, on the Deccan plateau in the state of Maharashtra; pop. 1,128,900 (est. 2009).

solar[1] /ˈsəʊlə/ ▸ adjective relating to or determined by the sun: *solar radiation.* ■ relating to or denoting energy derived from the sun's rays: *solar heating.*

– ORIGIN late Middle English: from Latin *solaris*, from *sol* 'sun'.

solar[2] /ˈsɒlə, ˈsəʊlə/ ▸ noun Brit. an upper chamber in a medieval house.
– ORIGIN Middle English: from Anglo-Norman French *soler*, from Latin *solarium* 'gallery, terrace'.

solar battery (also **solar cell**) ▸ noun a device converting solar radiation into electricity.

solar constant ▸ noun Physics the rate at which energy reaches the earth's surface from the sun, usually taken to be 1,388 watts per square metre.

solar day ▸ noun the time between successive meridian transits of the sun at a particular place.

solar eclipse ▸ noun an eclipse in which the sun is obscured by the moon.

solar energy ▸ noun [mass noun] radiant energy emitted by the sun. ■ another term for SOLAR POWER.

solar flare ▸ noun Astronomy a brief eruption of intense high-energy radiation from the sun's surface, associated with sunspots and causing radio and magnetic disturbances on the earth.

solarium /səˈlɛːrɪəm/ ▸ noun (pl. **solariums** or **solaria** /-rɪə/) **1** a room equipped with sunlamps or sunbeds which can be used to acquire an artificial suntan.
2 a room fitted with extensive areas of glass to admit sunlight.
– ORIGIN mid 19th cent.: from Latin, literally 'sundial, place for sunning oneself', from Latin *sol* 'sun'.

solarize (also **solarise**) ▸ verb [with obj.] Photography change the relative darkness of (a part of an image) by overexposure to light.
– DERIVATIVES **solarization** noun.

solar mass ▸ noun Astronomy the mass of the sun used as a unit of mass, equal to 1.989×10^{30} kg.

solar myth ▸ noun a myth ascribing the sun's course or attributes to a particular god or hero.

solar panel ▸ noun a panel designed to absorb the sun's rays as a source of energy for generating electricity or heating.

solar plexus ▸ noun a complex of ganglia and radiating nerves of the sympathetic system at the pit of the stomach.

solar pond ▸ noun a pool of very salty water in which convection is inhibited, allowing accumulation of energy from solar radiation in the lower layers.

solar power ▸ noun [mass noun] power obtained by harnessing the energy of the sun's rays.

solar system ▸ noun Astronomy the collection of eight planets and their moons in orbit round the sun, together with smaller bodies in the form of asteroids, meteoroids, and comets.

solar wind ▸ noun the continuous flow of charged particles from the sun which permeates the solar system.

solar year ▸ noun see YEAR (sense 1).

SOLAS /ˈsəʊləs/ ▸ noun [mass noun] [usu. as modifier] the provisions made during a series of international conventions governing maritime safety.
– ORIGIN 1960s: acronym from *safety of life at sea*.

solatium /səˈleɪʃɪəm/ ▸ noun (pl. **solatia** /-ʃɪə/) formal a thing given to someone as a compensation or consolation: *a suitable solatium in the form of an apology was offered to him.*
– ORIGIN early 19th cent.: from Latin, literally 'solace'.

sola topi ▸ noun a sun hat made from the pith of the stems of sola plants, formerly worn in India.

sold past and past participle of SELL.

soldanella /ˌsɒldəˈnɛlə/ ▸ noun a dwarf European alpine plant with bell-shaped flowers that have fringed petals and often appear in snow. ● Genus *Soldanella*, family Primulaceae.
– ORIGIN modern Latin, from Italian, of unknown ultimate origin.

solder /ˈsəʊldə, ˈsɒldə/ ▸ noun [mass noun] a low-melting alloy, especially one based on lead and tin or (for higher temperatures) on brass or silver, used for joining less fusible metals.
▸ verb [with obj.] join with solder.
– DERIVATIVES **solderable** adjective, **solderer** noun.
– ORIGIN Middle English: from Old French *soudure*, from the verb *souder*, from Latin *solidare* 'fasten together', from *solidus* 'solid'.

soldering iron ▸ noun an electrical tool used for melting solder and applying it to metals that are to be joined.

soldi plural form of SOLDO.

soldier ▸ noun **1** a person who serves in an army. ■ (also **common soldier** or **private soldier**) a private in an army.
2 Entomology a wingless caste of ant or termite with a large specially modified head and jaws, involved chiefly in defence.
3 Brit. informal a strip of bread or toast, used for dipping into a soft-boiled egg.
4 [usu. as modifier] an upright brick, timber, or other building element.
▸ verb [no obj.] **1** serve as a soldier: (as noun **soldiering**) *soldiering was what the Colonel understood.*
2 (**soldier on**) informal carry on doggedly; persevere: *Graham wasn't enjoying this, but he soldiered on.*
– DERIVATIVES **soldierly** adjective, **soldiership** noun (archaic).
– ORIGIN Middle English: from Old French *soldier*, from *soulde* '(soldier's) pay', from Latin *solidus* (see SOLIDUS). The verb dates from the early 17th cent.

soldier beetle ▸ noun an elongated flying beetle with soft downy wing cases, typically found on flowers, where it hunts other insects. ● Family Cantharidae: several genera.

soldierfish ▸ noun (pl. **same** or **soldierfishes**) a squirrelfish that is typically bright red in colour. ● Several genera and species in the family Holocentridae.

soldier fly ▸ noun a bright metallic fly with a flattened body, which frequently basks in the sun with its wings folded flat over the body. ● Family Stratiomyidae: many genera.

soldier of Christ ▸ noun an active or proselytizing Christian.

soldier of fortune ▸ noun a person who works as a soldier for any country or group that will pay them; a mercenary.

soldiery ▸ noun [treated as sing. or pl.] soldiers collectively: *the town was filled with disbanded soldiery.* ■ [mass noun] military training or knowledge: *the arts of soldiery.*

soldo /ˈsɒldəʊ/ ▸ noun (pl. **soldi** /ˈsɒldi/) a former Italian coin and monetary unit worth the twentieth part of a lira.
– ORIGIN Italian, from Latin *solidus* (see SOLIDUS).

Sole a shipping forecast area in the NE Atlantic, covering the western approaches to the English Channel.

sole[1] ▸ noun the undersurface of a person's foot: *the soles of their feet were nearly black with dirt.* ■ the section forming the underside of a piece of footwear (typically excluding the heel when this forms a distinct part). ■ the part of the undersurface of a person's foot between the toes and the instep. ■ the undersurface of a tool or implement such as a plane or the head of a golf club. ■ the floor of a ship's cabin or cockpit.
▸ verb [with obj.] put a new sole on to (a shoe).
– DERIVATIVES **soled** adjective [in combination] *rubber-soled shoes.*
– ORIGIN Middle English: from Old French, from Latin *solea* 'sandal, sill', from *solum* 'bottom, pavement, sole'; compare with Dutch *zool* and German *Sohle*.

sole[2] ▸ noun (pl. **same**) a marine flatfish of almost worldwide distribution, important as a food fish. ● Several species in the families Soleidae, Pleuronectidae, and Bothidae. See DOVER SOLE, LEMON SOLE.
– ORIGIN Middle English: from Old French, from Provençal *sola*, from Latin *solea* (see SOLE[1]), named from its shape.

sole[3] ▸ adjective **1** [attrib.] one and only: *my sole aim was to contribute to the national team.* ■ belonging or restricted to one person or group of people: *the health club is for the sole use of our guests.*
2 archaic (especially of a woman) unmarried. ■ alone; unaccompanied.
– ORIGIN late Middle English (also in the senses 'secluded' and 'unrivalled'): from Old French *soule*, from Latin *sola*, feminine of *solus* 'alone'.

solebar ▸ noun a longitudinal structural piece forming part of the underframe of a railway vehicle.

solecism /ˈsɒlɪsɪz(ə)m/ ▸ noun a grammatical mistake in speech or writing. ■ a breach of good manners; an instance of incorrect behaviour.
– DERIVATIVES **solecistic** /-ˈsɪstɪk/ adjective.
– ORIGIN mid 16th cent.: from French *solécisme*, or via Latin from Greek *soloikismos*, from *soloikos* 'speaking incorrectly'.

solely /ˈsəʊlli/ ▸ adverb not involving anyone or anything else; only: *he is solely responsible for any debts the company may incur* | *people are appointed solely on the basis of merit.*

solemn ▸ adjective **1** formal and dignified: *a solemn procession.* ■ not cheerful or smiling; serious: *Tim looked very solemn.*
2 characterized by deep sincerity: *he swore a solemn oath to keep faith.*
– DERIVATIVES **solemnly** adverb, **solemnness** noun.
– ORIGIN Middle English (in the sense 'associated with religious rites'): from Old French *solemne*, from Latin *sollemnis* 'customary, celebrated at a fixed date', from *sollus* 'entire'.

solemnity /səˈlɛmnɪti/ ▸ noun (pl. **solemnities**) [mass noun] the state or quality of being serious and dignified: *his ashes were laid to rest with great solemnity.* ■ [count noun] (usu. **solemnities**) a formal, dignified rite or ceremony: *the ritual of the Church was observed in all its solemnities.*
– ORIGIN Middle English (in the sense 'observance of formality and ceremony', frequently in the phrases *in solemnity, with solemnity*): from Old French *solemnite*, from Latin *sollemnitas*, from *sollemnis* (see SOLEMN).

solemnize /ˈsɒləmnʌɪz/ (also **solemnise**) ▸ verb [with obj.] duly perform (a ceremony, especially that of marriage). ■ mark (an event) with a formal ceremony.
– DERIVATIVES **solemnization** noun.
– ORIGIN late Middle English: from Old French *solemniser*, from medieval Latin *solemnizare*, from Latin *sollemnis* (see SOLEMN).

Solemn League and Covenant an agreement made in 1643 between the English Parliament and the Scottish Covenanters during the English Civil War, by which the Scots would provide military aid in return for the establishment of a Presbyterian system in England, Scotland, and Ireland. Although the Scottish support proved crucial in the Parliamentary victory, the principal Presbyterian leaders were expelled from Parliament in 1647 and the covenant was never honoured.

Solemn Mass ▸ noun another term for HIGH MASS.

solenodon /səˈlɛnədən/ ▸ noun a forest-dwelling mammal with a long flexible snout and a stiff muscular tail, occurring only in Cuba and Hispaniola. ● Family Solenodontidae and genus *Solenodon*: two species.
– ORIGIN modern Latin, from Greek *sōlēn* 'channel, pipe' + *odō* (variant of *odous, odont-*) 'tooth'.

solenoid /ˈsɒlənɔɪd, ˈsəʊl-/ ▸ noun a cylindrical coil of wire acting as a magnet when carrying electric current.
– DERIVATIVES **solenoidal** adjective.
– ORIGIN early 19th cent.: from French *solénoïde*, from Greek *sōlēn* 'channel, pipe'.

Solent /ˈsəʊlənt/ a channel between the NW coast of the Isle of Wight and the mainland of southern England.

soleplate ▸ noun **1** a metal plate forming the base of an electric iron, machine saw, or other machine.
2 a horizontal timber at the base of a wall frame.

solera /səˈlɛːrə/ ▸ noun (also **solera system**) [mass noun] a Spanish method of producing wine, especially sherry and Madeira, whereby small amounts of younger wines stored in an upper tier of casks are systematically blended with the more mature wine in the casks below. ■ (also **solera wine**) [count noun] a blend of sherry or Malaga wine produced by the solera system. ■ [count noun] a wine cask, typically one with a capacity of four hogsheads, on the bottom tier of the solera system and containing the oldest wine.
– ORIGIN Spanish, literally 'cross-beam, stone base'.

Soleure /sɔlœʀ/ French name for SOLOTHURN.

soleus /sə(ʊ)ˈliːəs/ (also **soleus muscle**) ▸ noun Anatomy a broad muscle in the lower calf, below the gastrocnemius, which flexes the foot to point the toes downwards.
– ORIGIN late 17th cent.: modern Latin, from Latin *solea* 'sole'.

sol-fa /ˈsɒlfɑː/ ▸ noun short for TONIC SOL-FA.
▸ verb (**sol-fas, sol-faing, sol-faed**) [with obj.] sing a tune using the sol-fa syllables.

solfatara /ˌsɒlfəˈtɑːrə/ ▸ noun Geology a volcanic crater emitting sulphurous and other gases.
– ORIGIN late 18th cent.: from the name of a volcano near Naples, from Italian *solfo* 'sulphur'.

solfège /ˈsɒlfɛʒ/ ▸ noun another term for SOLFEGGIO.
– ORIGIN French.

S

solfeggio /sɒlˈfɛdʒɪəʊ/ ▶ **noun** (pl. **solfeggi** /-dʒi/) Music an exercise in singing using sol-fa syllables.
■ [mass noun] solmization.
– ORIGIN Italian.

soli plural form of SOLO.

solicit ▶ **verb** (**solicits, soliciting, solicited**) **1** [with obj.] ask for or try to obtain (something) from someone: *he called a meeting to solicit their views* | [no obj.] *don't solicit for money*. ■ ask (someone) for something: *historians and critics are solicited for opinions by the auction houses*.
2 [no obj.] accost someone and offer one's or someone else's services as a prostitute: (as noun **soliciting**) *although prostitution was not itself an offence, soliciting was*.
– DERIVATIVES **solicitation** noun.
– ORIGIN late Middle English: from Old French *solliciter*, from Latin *sollicitare* 'agitate', from *sollicitus* 'anxious', from *sollus* 'entire' + *citus* (past participle of *ciere* 'set in motion').

solicitor ▶ **noun 1** Brit. a member of the legal profession qualified to deal with conveyancing, the drawing up of wills, and other legal matters. A solicitor may also instruct barristers and represent clients in some courts. Compare with BARRISTER, ATTORNEY.
■ N. Amer. the chief law officer of a city, town, or government department.
2 N. Amer. a person who tries to obtain business orders, advertising, etc.; a canvasser.
– ORIGIN late Middle English (denoting an agent or deputy): from Old French *solliciteur*, from *solliciter* (see SOLICIT).

solicitor general ▶ **noun** (pl. **solicitors general**) (in the UK) the Crown law officer below the Attorney General or (in Scotland) below the Lord Advocate.
■ (in the US) the law officer below the Attorney General.

solicitous ▶ **adjective** characterized by or showing interest or concern: *she was always solicitous about the welfare of her students* | *a solicitous enquiry*.
■ archaic eager or anxious to do something: *he was solicitous to cultivate her mamma's good opinion*.
– DERIVATIVES **solicitously** adverb, **solicitousness** noun.
– ORIGIN mid 16th cent.: from Latin *sollicitus* (see SOLICIT) + -OUS.

solicitude ▶ **noun** [mass noun] care or concern for someone or something: *I was touched by his solicitude*.
– ORIGIN late Middle English: from Old French *sollicitude*, from Latin *sollicitudo*, from *sollicitus* (see SOLICITOUS).

solid ▶ **adjective** (**solider, solidest**) **1** firm and stable in shape; not liquid or fluid: *the stream was frozen solid* | *solid fuels*. ■ strongly built or made of strong materials; not flimsy or slender: *a solid door with good, secure locks*.
2 having three dimensions: *a solid figure with six plane faces*. ■ [attrib.] concerned with objects having three dimensions: *solid geometry*.
3 not hollow or containing spaces or gaps: *a sculpture made out of solid rock* | *a solid mass of flowers* | *the shops were packed solid*. ■ consisting of the same substance throughout: *solid silver cutlery*. ■ (of typesetting) without extra space between the lines of characters. ■ (of a line or surface) without spaces; unbroken: *the solid outline encloses the area within which we measured*. ■ (of time) uninterrupted; continuous: [postpositive] *it poured for two hours solid*.
■ unanimous or undivided: *they received solid support from their teammates*.
4 dependable; reliable: *the defence is solid* | *there is solid evidence of lower inflation*. ■ sound but without any special qualities or flair: *the rest of the acting is solid*.
5 (**solid with**) US informal on good terms with: *he thought he could put himself* ***in solid with*** *you by criticizing her*.
6 Austral. informal severe; unfair: *they'll* ***be solid on*** *him for that mistake*.
▶ **noun 1** a substance or object that is solid rather than liquid or fluid. ■ (**solids**) food that is not liquid: *she drinks only milk and rarely eats solids*.
2 Geometry a body or geometric figure having three dimensions.
– PHRASES **the solid South** chiefly historical the politically united Southern states of America, traditionally regarded as giving unwavering electoral support to the Democratic Party.
– DERIVATIVES **solidly** adverb, **solidness** noun.
– ORIGIN late Middle English: from Latin *solidus*; related to *salvus* 'safe' and *sollus* 'entire'.

solidago /ˌsɒlɪˈdeɪɡəʊ/ ▶ **noun** (pl. **solidagos**) a plant of the genus *Solidago* in the daisy family, especially (in gardening) goldenrod.
– ORIGIN modern Latin, from a medieval Latin alteration of late Latin *consolida* 'comfrey'.

solid angle ▶ **noun** a three-dimensional analogue of an angle, such as that subtended by a cone or formed by planes meeting at a point. It is measured in steradians.

solidarity ▶ **noun 1** [mass noun] unity or agreement of feeling or action, especially among individuals with a common interest; mutual support within a group: *factory workers voiced solidarity with the striking students*.
2 (**Solidarity**) an independent trade union movement in Poland which developed into a mass campaign for political change and inspired popular opposition to Communist regimes across eastern Europe. Formed in 1980 under the leadership of Lech Wałęsa, it was banned in 1981 following the imposition of martial law. Legalized again in 1989, it won a majority in the elections of that year. [translating Polish *Solidarność*.]
– ORIGIN mid 19th cent.: from French *solidarité*, from *solidaire* 'solidary'.

solidary ▶ **adjective** (of a group or community) characterized by solidarity or coincidence of interests.
– ORIGIN early 19th cent.: from French *solidaire*, from *solide* 'solid'.

solid-body ▶ **adjective** denoting an electric guitar without a soundbox, the strings being mounted on a solid shaped block forming the guitar body.

solid-drawn ▶ **adjective** (of a tube) pressed or drawn out from a solid bar of metal.

solidi plural form of SOLIDUS.

solidify ▶ **verb** (**solidifies, solidifying, solidified**) make or become hard or solid: [no obj.] *the magma slowly solidifies and forms crystals*. ■ [with obj.] make stronger; reinforce: *social and political pressures helped to solidify national identities*.
– DERIVATIVES **solidification** noun, **solidifier** noun.

solidity ▶ **noun** [mass noun] the quality or state of being firm or strong in structure: *the sheer strength and solidity of Romanesque architecture*. ■ the quality of being reliable in character: *he exuded an aura of reassuring solidity*.

solid solution ▶ **noun** Chemistry a solid mixture containing a minor component uniformly distributed within the crystal lattice of the major component.

solid state ▶ **noun** [mass noun] the state of matter in which materials are not fluid but retain their boundaries without support, the atoms or molecules occupying fixed positions with respect to each other and unable to move freely.
▶ **adjective** (**solid-state**) (of a device) making use of the electronic properties of solid semiconductors (as opposed to valves).

solidus /ˈsɒlɪdəs/ ▶ **noun** (pl. **solidi** /-dʌɪ/) **1** chiefly Brit. another term for SLASH (sense 2 of the noun).
2 (also **solidus curve**) Chemistry a curve in a graph of the temperature and composition of a mixture, below which the substance is entirely solid.
3 historical a gold coin of the later Roman Empire. [from Latin *solidus* (*nummus*).]
– ORIGIN Latin, literally 'solid'.

solifluction /ˌsɒlɪˈflʌkʃ(ə)n, ˌsəʊlɪ-/ ▶ **noun** [mass noun] Geology the gradual movement of wet soil or other material down a slope, especially where frozen subsoil acts as a barrier to the percolation of water.
– ORIGIN early 20th cent.: from Latin *solum* 'soil' + *fluctio(n-)* 'flowing', from the verb *fluere* 'to flow'.

solifuge /ˈsɒlɪfjuːdʒ/ (also **solifugid** /sɒˈlɪfjʊdʒɪd/) ▶ **noun** Zoology a sun spider.
– ORIGIN mid 17th cent.: from Latin *solifuga*.

Solihull /ˈsɒlɪhʌl, ˌsəʊlɪˈhʌl/ a town in the Midlands, forming part of the conurbation of Birmingham; pop. 92,600 (est. 2009).

soliloquy /səˈlɪləkwi/ ▶ **noun** (pl. **soliloquies**) an act of speaking one's thoughts aloud when by oneself or regardless of any hearers, especially by a character in a play. ■ a part of a play involving a soliloquy.
– DERIVATIVES **soliloquist** noun, **soliloquize** (also **soliloquise**) verb.
– ORIGIN Middle English: from late Latin *soliloquium*, from Latin *solus* 'alone' + *loqui* 'speak'.

Soliman /ˈsɒlɪmən/ variant spelling of SULEIMAN I.

solipsism /ˈsɒlɪpsɪz(ə)m/ ▶ **noun** [mass noun] the view or theory that the self is all that can be known to exist.
■ the quality of being self-centred or selfish.
– DERIVATIVES **solipsist** noun, **solipsistic** adjective, **solipsistically** adverb.
– ORIGIN late 19th cent.: from Latin *solus* 'alone' + *ipse* 'self' + -ISM.

solitaire /ˈsɒlɪtɛː, ˌsɒlɪˈtɛː/ ▶ **noun 1** [mass noun] Brit. a game for one player played by removing pegs one at a time from a board by jumping others over them from adjacent holes, the object being to be left with only one peg. ■ N. Amer. the card game patience.
2 a diamond or other gem set in a piece of jewellery by itself. ■ a ring set with such a gem.
3 either of two large extinct flightless birds related to the dodo, found on two of the Mascarene Islands until they were exterminated in the 18th century.
● Family Raphidae: the **Rodriguez solitaire** (*Pezophaps solitaria*), and the poorly known **Réunion solitaire** (*Ornithaptera solitaria*).
4 a large American thrush with mainly grey plumage and a short bill. ● Genus *Myadestes*, family Turdidae: several species.
– ORIGIN early 18th cent.: from French, from Latin *solitarius* (see SOLITARY).

solitary ▶ **adjective 1** done or existing alone: *I live a pretty solitary life* | *tigers are essentially solitary*.
■ (of a place) secluded or isolated: *solitary farmsteads*. ■ (of a bird, mammal, or insect) living alone or in pairs, especially in contrast to related social forms: *a solitary wasp*. ■ (of a flower or other part) borne singly.
2 [attrib.] [often with negative] single; only: *we have not a solitary shred of evidence to go on*.
▶ **noun** (pl. **solitaries**) **1** a recluse or hermit.
2 informal short for SOLITARY CONFINEMENT.
– DERIVATIVES **solitarily** adverb, **solitariness** noun.
– ORIGIN Middle English: from Latin *solitarius*, from *solus* 'alone'.

solitary confinement ▶ **noun** the isolation of a prisoner in a separate cell as a punishment.

solitary wave ▶ **noun** another term for SOLITON.

soliton /ˈsɒlɪtɒn/ ▶ **noun** Physics a quantum or quasiparticle propagated as a travelling non-dissipative wave which is neither preceded nor followed by another such disturbance.
– ORIGIN 1960s: from SOLITARY + -ON.

solitude ▶ **noun 1** [mass noun] the state or situation of being alone: *she savoured her few hours of freedom and solitude*.
2 a lonely or uninhabited place.
– ORIGIN Middle English: from Old French, or from Latin *solitudo*, from *solus* 'alone'.

solmization /ˌsɒlmɪˈzeɪʃ(ə)n/ (also **solmisation**) ▶ **noun** [mass noun] Music a system of associating each note of a scale with a particular syllable, especially to teach singing.

> The commonest European system, still in use, originally named the notes *ut, re, mi, fa, sol, la* in groups of six (hexachords) beginning on G, C, or F, using syllables from a Latin hymn for St John the Baptist's Day in which each phrase begins on the next note in the scale: '*Ut* queant laxis *re*sonare fibris *Mi*ra gestorum *fa*muli tuorum, *Sol*ve polluti *la*bili reatum, Sancte Iohannes'. A seventh note *si* was added later (from the initials of Sancte Iohannes). Modern systems typically use the sequence as arbitrarily adapted in the 19th century: *doh, ray, me, fah, soh, la, te*, with doh being C in the fixed-doh system and the keynote in the movable-doh or tonic sol-fa system.

– ORIGIN mid 18th cent.: from French *solmisation*, based on *sol* 'soh' + *mi* (see ME²).

Solnhofen /ˈzəʊlnˌhəʊf(ə)n/, German /ˈzoːlnˌhoːfn/ a village in Bavaria, Germany, near which there are extensive, thinly stratified beds of lithographic limestone dating from the Upper Jurassic period. These beds are noted as the chief source of archaeopteryx fossils.

solo ▶ **noun** (pl. **solos**) **1** a thing done by one person unaccompanied, in particular: ■ (pl. **solos** or **soli**) a piece of vocal or instrumental music or a dance, or a part or passage in one, for one performer. ■ an unaccompanied flight by a pilot in an aircraft.
2 (also **solo whist**) [mass noun] a card game resembling whist in which the players make bids and the highest bidder plays against the others in an attempt to win a specified number of tricks. ■ [count noun] a bid by which a player undertakes to win five tricks in solo whist.
3 a motorbike without a sidecar.

▸ **adjective & adverb** for or done by one person alone; unaccompanied: [as adj.] *a solo album* | [as adv.] *she'd spent most of her life flying solo.* ■ [as adj.] (of a motorbike) without a sidecar: *a solo machine.*
▸ **verb** (**soloes, soloing, soloed**) [no obj.] perform something unaccompanied, in particular: ■ perform an unaccompanied piece of music or a part or passage in one. ■ fly an aircraft unaccompanied. ■ undertake solo climbing.
– ORIGIN late 17th cent. (as a musical term): from Italian, from Latin *solus* 'alone'.

solo climbing ▸ **noun** [mass noun] the sport of climbing unaided by ropes and other equipment, and without the assistance of other people.
– DERIVATIVES **solo climber** noun.

soloist ▸ **noun** a musician or singer who performs a solo.

Solomon /ˈsɒləmən/, son of David, king of ancient Israel *c.*970–*c.*930 BC. In the Bible Solomon is traditionally associated with the Song of Songs, Ecclesiastes, and Proverbs, while his wisdom is illustrated by the Judgement of Solomon. Discontent with his rule, however, led to the secession of the northern tribes in the reign of his son Rehoboam. ■ (as noun usu. **a Solomon**) a very wise person.
– DERIVATIVES **Solomonic** /sɒləˈmɒnɪk/ adjective.

Solomon Gundy ▸ **noun** West Indian and Canadian term for **SALMAGUNDI**.
– ORIGIN alteration.

Solomon Islands (also **the Solomons**) **1** a country consisting of a group of islands in the SW Pacific, to the east of New Guinea; pop. 595,600 (est. 2009); languages, English (official), Pidgin, local Austronesian and Papuan languages; capital, Honiara.

> The islands were divided between Britain and Germany in the late 19th century; the southern islands became a British protectorate in 1893 while the north remained German until mandated to Australia in 1920. With the exception of the northern part of the chain (now part of Papua New Guinea), the Solomons became self-governing in 1976 and fully independent within the Commonwealth two years later.

2 a large archipelago in the SW Pacific comprising a double chain of islands, of which those in the north-west form part of Papua New Guinea, the rest constituting the country of the Solomon Islands.
– DERIVATIVES **Solomon Islander** noun.

Solomon's seal ▸ **noun 1** a figure like the Star of David.
2 a widely distributed plant of the lily family, having arching stems that bear a double row of broad leaves with drooping green and white flowers in their axils.
• Genus *Polygonatum*, family Liliaceae: many species.

Solon /ˈsəʊlɒn/ (*c.*630–*c.*560 BC), Athenian statesman and lawgiver. One of the Seven Sages, he revised the code of laws established by Draco, making it less severe. His division of the citizens into four classes based on wealth rather than birth laid the foundations of Athenian democracy.

solo stop ▸ **noun** an organ stop especially suitable for imitating a solo performance on another instrument.

Solothurn /ˈzəʊləʊˌtʊən/, German /ˈzoːloːˌtʊrn/ a canton in NW Switzerland, in the Jura mountains. French name **SOLEURE**. ■ its capital, a town on the River Aare; pop. 15,364 (2007).

solo whist ▸ **noun** see **SOLO** (sense 2 of the noun).

solstice /ˈsɒlstɪs/ ▸ **noun** either of the two times in the year, the **summer solstice** and the **winter solstice**, when the sun reaches its highest or lowest point in the sky at noon, marked by the longest and shortest days.
– DERIVATIVES **solstitial** adjective.
– ORIGIN Middle English: from Old French, from Latin *solstitium*, from *sol* 'sun' + *stit-* 'stopped, stationary' (from the verb *sistere*).

Solti /ˈʃɒlti/, Sir Georg (1912–97), Hungarian-born British conductor. He revivified Covent Garden as musical director (1961–71) and was conductor of the Chicago Symphony Orchestra (1969–91) and the London Philharmonic Orchestra (1979–83).

solubilize /ˈsɒljʊbɪlʌɪz/ (also **solubilise**) ▸ **verb** [with obj.] technical make (a substance) soluble or more soluble.
– DERIVATIVES **solubilization** noun.

soluble ▸ **adjective 1** (of a substance) able to be dissolved, especially in water: *the poison is soluble in alcohol.*
2 (of a problem) able to be solved.
– DERIVATIVES **solubility** noun.
– ORIGIN late Middle English: from Old French, from late Latin *solubilis*, from *solvere* (see **SOLVE**).

soluble glass ▸ **noun** another term for **WATER GLASS** (sense 1).

solunar /sɒˈluːnə/ ▸ **adjective** relating to the combined influence or conjunction of the sun and moon.
– ORIGIN late 18th cent.: blend of **SOL** and **LUNAR**.

solus /ˈsəʊləs/ ▸ **adjective** (fem. **sola** /-lə/) alone or unaccompanied (used especially as a stage direction).
– ORIGIN Latin.

solute /ˈsɒljuːt, sɒˈljuːt/ ▸ **noun** the minor component in a solution, dissolved in the solvent.
– ORIGIN late 19th cent.: from Latin *solutum*, neuter of *solutus* 'loosened', past participle of the verb *solvere*.

solution ▸ **noun 1** a means of solving a problem or dealing with a difficult situation: *there are no easy solutions to financial and marital problems.* ■ the correct answer to a puzzle: *the solution to this month's crossword.* ■ (**solutions**) products or services designed to meet a particular need: *an Internet marketing firm specializing in e-commerce solutions.*
2 a liquid mixture in which the minor component (the solute) is uniformly distributed within the major component (the solvent). ■ [mass noun] the process or state of being dissolved in a solvent.
3 [mass noun] archaic the action of separating or breaking down; dissolution: *the solution of British supremacy in South Africa.*
– ORIGIN late Middle English: from Old French, from Latin *solutio(n-)*, from *solvere* 'loosen' (see **SOLVE**).

> **WORD TRENDS** Everyone is familiar with signs and adverts offering all manner of **solutions**: *high-end storage solutions* | *a leading provider of payment solutions.* The usage began during the 1990s in the computer industry, where **solutions** were packages of software and hardware put together by IT companies to do a particular job for their customers. It is now an all-purpose word in commercial language for products, services, or companies, and is sometimes almost meaningless: *frozen meal solutions* are just frozen meals, after all. The term's overuse perhaps implies a stressed, anxious society, where everyday needs are marketed as problems that require solving. See also **ISSUE**.

solution set ▸ **noun** Mathematics the set of all the solutions of an equation or condition.

Solutrean /səˈluːtrɪən/ ▸ **adjective** Archaeology relating to or denoting an Upper Palaeolithic culture of central and SW France and parts of Iberia. It is dated to about 21,000–18,000 years ago, following the Aurignacian and preceding the Magdalenian. ■ (as noun **the Solutrean**) the Solutrean culture or period.
– ORIGIN late 19th cent.: from *Solutré*, the site of a cave in eastern France, where objects from this culture were found, + **-AN**.

solvate Chemistry ▸ **verb** /sɒlˈveɪt/ [with obj.] (of a solvent) enter into reversible chemical combination with (a dissolved molecule, ion, etc.).
▸ **noun** /ˈsɒlveɪt/ a more or less loosely bonded complex formed between a solvent and a dissolved species.
– DERIVATIVES **solvation** noun.
– ORIGIN early 20th cent.: formed irregularly from **SOLVE** + **-ATE**[1].

Solvay process /ˈsɒlveɪ/ ▸ **noun** [mass noun] Chemistry an industrial process for obtaining sodium carbonate from limestone, ammonia, and brine.
– ORIGIN late 19th cent.: named after Ernest Solvay (1838–1922), Belgian chemist.

solve ▸ **verb** [with obj.] find an answer to, explanation for, or means of effectively dealing with (a problem or mystery): *the policy could solve the town's housing crisis* | *a murder investigation that has never been solved.*
– DERIVATIVES **solvable** adjective, **solver** noun.
– ORIGIN late Middle English (in the sense 'loosen, dissolve, untie'): from Latin *solvere* 'loosen, unfasten'.

solvent ▸ **adjective 1** having assets in excess of liabilities; able to pay one's debts: *interest rate rises have very severe effects on normally solvent companies.*
2 [attrib.] able to dissolve other substances: *osmotic, chemical, or solvent action.*
▸ **noun** the liquid in which a solute is dissolved to form a solution. ■ a liquid, typically one other than water, used for dissolving other substances. ■ something that acts to weaken or dispel a particular attitude or situation: *an unrivalled solvent of social prejudices.*
– DERIVATIVES **solvency** noun (sense 1 of the adjective).
– ORIGIN mid 17th cent.: from Latin *solvent-* 'loosening, unfastening, paying', from the verb *solvere*.

solvent abuse ▸ **noun** [mass noun] the use of certain volatile organic solvents as intoxicants by inhalation, e.g. glue-sniffing.

solvent extraction ▸ **noun** [mass noun] Chemistry the partial removal of a substance from a solution or mixture by dissolving it in another, immiscible solvent in which it is more soluble.

Solway Firth an inlet of the Irish Sea, separating Cumbria (in England) from Dumfries and Galloway (in Scotland).

Solyman variant spelling of **SULEIMAN I**.

Solzhenitsyn /ˌsɒlʒəˈnɪtsɪn/, Alexander (1918–2008), Russian novelist; Russian name *Aleksandr Isaevich Solzhenitsyn*. He spent eight years in a labour camp for criticizing Stalin and began writing on his release. From 1963 his books were banned in the Soviet Union, and he was exiled in 1974, eventually returning to Russia in 1994. Notable works: *One Day in the Life of Ivan Denisovich* (1962) and *The Gulag Archipelago* (1973). Nobel Prize for Literature (1970).

som /səʊm/ ▸ **noun** (pl. **same**) the basic monetary unit of Kyrgyzstan and Uzbekistan, equal to 100 tiyin.
– ORIGIN Kyrgyz and Uzbek, literally 'rouble'.

Som. ▸ **abbreviation** Somerset.

soma[1] /ˈsəʊmə/ ▸ **noun 1** Biology the parts of an organism other than the reproductive cells.
2 the body as distinct from the soul, mind, or psyche.
– ORIGIN late 19th cent.: from Greek *sōma* 'body'.

soma[2] /ˈsəʊmə/ ▸ **noun** [mass noun] Hinduism an intoxicating drink prepared from a plant and used in Vedic ritual, believed to be the drink of the gods. See also **HOM**. ■ (also **soma plant**) [count noun] a plant used to make this. ■ (in Aldous Huxley's novel *Brave New World*) a narcotic drug which produces euphoria and hallucination, distributed by the state in order to promote content and social harmony.
– ORIGIN Sanskrit *sōma*.

somaesthetic /ˌsəʊmiːsˈθɛtɪk/ (US **somesthetic**) ▸ **adjective** another term for **SOMATOSENSORY**.
– ORIGIN late 19th cent.: from Greek *sōma* 'body' + **AESTHETIC**.

Somali /səˈmɑːli/ ▸ **noun** (pl. **same** or **Somalis**) a member of a mainly Muslim people of Somalia. ■ [mass noun] the Cushitic language of the Somalis, the official language of Somalia, also spoken in Djibouti and parts of Kenya and Ethiopia, and having over 6 million speakers. ■ a native or inhabitant of Somalia.
▸ **adjective** relating to Somalia, the Somalis, or their language.
– DERIVATIVES **Somalian** adjective & noun.
– ORIGIN the name in Somali.

Somalia /səˈmɑːlɪə/ a country in the Horn of Africa; pop. 9,832,000 (est. 2009); official languages, Somali and Arabic; capital, Mogadishu.

> The area of the Horn of Africa was divided between British and Italian spheres of influence in the late 19th century, and the modern republic of Somalia became independent in 1960 following the unification of the former British Somaliland and Italian Somalia. Civil war broke out in Somalia in 1988 and led to the overthrow of the government in 1991; in that year northern Somalia declared itself independent as the Somaliland Republic, and central government in the country remains weak.

Somali Peninsula another name for **HORN OF AFRICA**.

soman /ˈsəʊmən/ ▸ **noun** [mass noun] a lethal organophosphorus nerve gas, developed in Germany during the Second World War.
– ORIGIN 1950s: from German, of unknown origin.

somatic /səˈmatɪk/ ▸ **adjective** relating to the body, especially as distinct from the mind. ■ Biology relating to the soma.
– DERIVATIVES **somatically** adverb.
– ORIGIN late 18th cent.: from Greek *sōmatikos*, from *sōma* 'body'.

somatic cell ▸ **noun** Biology any cell of a living organism other than the reproductive cells.

somatic mutation ▸ **noun** [mass noun] Biology the occurrence of a mutation in the somatic tissue of an organism, resulting in a genetically mosaic individual.

somatization /ˌsəʊmətʌɪˈzeɪʃ(ə)n/ (also **somatisation**) ▸ **noun** [mass noun] Psychiatry the manifestation of

S

psychological distress by the presentation of bodily symptoms: [as modifier] *somatization disorder*.
– DERIVATIVES **somatize** verb.

somato- ▶ combining form relating to the human or animal body: *somatotype*.
– ORIGIN from Greek *sōma, sōmat-* 'body'.

somatomedin /ˌsəʊmətə(ʊ)ˈmiːdɪn/ ▶ noun [mass noun] Biochemistry a hormone which acts as an intermediate in the stimulation of tissue growth by growth hormone.
– ORIGIN 1970s: from **SOMATO-** 'of the body' + *(inter) med(iary)* + **-IN**[1].

somatopleure /ˌsəʊmətə(ʊ)ˈplʊə/ ▶ noun Embryology a layer of tissue in a vertebrate embryo comprising the ectoderm and the outer layer of mesoderm, and giving rise to the amnion, chorion, and part of the body wall. Often contrasted with **SPLANCHNOPLEURE**.
– ORIGIN late 19th cent.: from **SOMATO-** 'of the body' + Greek *pleura* 'side'.

somatosensory ▶ adjective Physiology relating to or denoting a sensation (such as pressure, pain, or warmth) which can occur anywhere in the body, in contrast to one localized at a sense organ (such as sight, balance, or taste). Also called **SOMAESTHETIC**.

somatostatin /ˌsəʊmətə(ʊ)ˈstatɪn/ ▶ noun [mass noun] Biochemistry a hormone secreted in the pancreas and pituitary gland which inhibits gastric secretion and somatotrophin release.

somatotrophin /ˌsəʊmətə(ʊ)ˈtrəʊfɪn/ ▶ noun [mass noun] Biochemistry a growth hormone secreted by the anterior pituitary gland.

somatotype ▶ noun a category to which people are assigned according to the extent to which their bodily physique conforms to a basic type (usually endomorphic, mesomorphic, or ectomorphic).
– ORIGIN 1940s: coined by W. H. Sheldon in *Varieties of Human Physique*.

sombre (US also **somber**) ▶ adjective **1** dark or dull in colour or tone: *the night skies were sombre and starless*.
2 having or conveying a feeling of deep seriousness and sadness: *he looked at her with a sombre expression*.
– DERIVATIVES **sombrely** adverb, **sombreness** noun.
– ORIGIN mid 18th cent.: from French, based on Latin *sub* 'under' + *umbra* 'shade'.

sombrero /sɒmˈbrɛːrəʊ/ ▶ noun (pl. **sombreros**) a broad-brimmed felt or straw hat, typically worn in Mexico and the south-western US.
– ORIGIN Spanish, from *sombra* 'shade' (see **SOMBRE**).

some ▶ determiner **1** an unspecified amount or number of: *I made some money running errands | he played some records for me*.
2 used to refer to someone or something that is unknown or unspecified: *she married some newspaper magnate twice her age | there must be some mistake | he's in* **some kind of** *trouble*.
3 (used with a number) approximately: *some thirty different languages are spoken*.
4 (pronounced stressing 'some') a considerable amount or number of: *he went to some trouble | I've known you for some years now*.
5 (pronounced stressing 'some') at least a small amount or number of: *he liked some music but generally wasn't musical*.
6 (pronounced stressing 'some') expressing admiration of something notable: *that was some goal*. ■ used ironically to express disapproval or disbelief: *Mr Power gave his stock reply. Some help! | not that Jennifer would ever be on the dole. Some chance of that*.
▶ pronoun **1** an unspecified number or amount of people or things: *here are* **some of** *our suggestions | if you want whisky I'll give you some*.
2 (pronounced stressing 'some') at least a small amount or number of people or things: *surely some have noticed*.
▶ adverb N. Amer. informal to some extent; quite a lot: *he needs feeding up some*.
– PHRASES **and then some** informal and plenty more than that: *we got our money's worth and then some*. **some few** see **FEW**. **some little** a considerable amount of: *she lingered for some little time*.
– ORIGIN Old English *sum*, of Germanic origin, from an Indo-European root shared by Greek *hamōs* 'somehow' and Sanskrit *sama* 'any, every'.

-some[1] ▶ suffix forming adjectives meaning: **1** productive of: *loathsome*.
2 characterized by being: *wholesome*. ■ apt to: *tiresome*.
– ORIGIN Old English *-sum*.

-some[2] ▶ suffix (forming nouns) denoting a group of a specified number: *foursome*.
– ORIGIN Old English *sum* 'some'.

-some[3] ▶ combining form denoting a portion of a body, especially a particle of a cell: *chromosome*.
– ORIGIN from Greek *sōma* 'body'.

somebody ▶ pronoun **1** some person; someone.
2 a person of importance or authority: *I'd like to be somebody* | [as noun] *nobodies who want to become somebodies*.

some day (also **someday**) ▶ adverb at some time in the future: *some day I'll live in the countryside*.

somehow ▶ adverb in some way; by some means: *somehow I managed to get the job done*. ■ for a reason that is not known or specified: *he looked different somehow*.

someone ▶ pronoun **1** an unknown or unspecified person; some person: *there's someone at the door | someone from the audience shouted out*.
2 a person of importance or authority: *a small-time lawyer keen to be someone*.

someplace ▶ adverb & pronoun N. Amer. informal another term for **SOMEWHERE**.

somersault /ˈsʌməsɒlt, -sɔːlt/ ▶ noun an acrobatic movement in which a person turns head over heels in the air or on the ground and lands or finishes on their feet: *a backward somersault* | figurative *Paula's stomach* ***turned a somersault***.
▶ verb [no obj.] perform a somersault, or make a similar movement accidentally: *his car somersaulted into a ditch*.
– ORIGIN mid 16th cent. (as a noun): from Old French *sombresault*, from Provençal *sobresaut*, from *sobre* 'above' + *saut* 'leap'.

Somerset /ˈsʌməsɛt/ a county of SW England, on the Bristol Channel; county town, Taunton.

somesthetic ▶ adjective US spelling of **SOMAESTHETIC**.

something ▶ pronoun **1** a thing that is unspecified or unknown: *we stopped for something to eat | I knew something terrible had happened | something about her frightened me*.
2 used in various expressions indicating that a description or amount being stated is not exact: *a wry look,* ***something between*** *amusement and regret | grassland totalling* ***something over*** *three hundred acres | there were* ***something like*** *fifty applications*.
▶ adverb [as submodifier] **1** informal used for emphasis with a following adjective functioning as an adverb: *my back hurts something terrible | he used to take the mickey out of me something awful*.
2 archaic or dialect to some extent; somewhat: *the people were something scared*.
– PHRASES **or something** informal added as a reference to an unspecified alternative similar to the thing mentioned: *you look like you just climbed a mountain or something*. **quite** (or **really**) **something** informal something considered impressive or notable. **something else** informal an exceptional person or thing: *the reaction from the crowd was something else*. **something like 1** an amount in the region of: *there were something like 50 applications*. **2** rather like: *they taste something like swordfish*. **something of** to some degree: *Richard was something of an expert at the game*. **something or other** see **OTHER**. **there is something in —— ——** is worth considering; there is some truth in ——: *people think I'm stupid because I think there's something in this alien business*. **thirty-something** (**forty-something**, etc.) informal an unspecified age between thirty and forty (or forty and fifty, etc.): *a forty-something has-been rock star* | [as noun] *she writes a column geared to twenty- and thirty-somethings*.
– ORIGIN Old English *sum thing* (see **SOME, THING**).

sometime ▶ adverb at some unspecified or unknown time: *you must come and have supper sometime | sometime after six everybody left*. ■ archaic at one time; formerly: *the Emperor Constantine used this speech sometime unto his bishops*.
▶ adjective **1** former: *the sometime editor of the paper*.
2 N. Amer. occasional: *a sometime contributor*.

sometimes ▶ adverb occasionally, rather than all of the time: *sometimes I want to do things on my own*.

someway ▶ adverb (often **someways**) informal, chiefly N. Amer. in some way or manner; by some means: *we've got to make money someway*.

somewhat ▶ adverb to a moderate extent or by a moderate amount; rather: *matters have improved somewhat since then* | [as submodifier] *a somewhat thicker book*.
– PHRASES **more than somewhat** informal very or very much: *it must have changed more than somewhat since then*. **somewhat of** something of: *it was somewhat of a disappointment*.

somewhen ▶ adverb informal at some time: *somewhen between 1918 and 1930*.

somewhere ▶ adverb in or to some place: *I've seen you somewhere before | can we go somewhere warm?* ■ used to indicate an approximate amount: *it cost* ***somewhere around*** *two thousand dollars*.
▶ pronoun some unspecified place: *in search of somewhere to live*.
– PHRASES **get somewhere** informal make progress; achieve success.

somite /ˈsəʊmʌɪt/ ▶ noun Zoology each of a number of body segments containing the same internal structures, clearly visible in invertebrates such as earthworms but also present in the embryonic stages of vertebrates. Also called **METAMERE**.
– ORIGIN mid 19th cent.: from Greek *sōma* 'body' + **-ITE**[1].

Somme /sɒm/ a river of northern France. Rising east of Saint-Quentin, it flows through Amiens to the English Channel north-east of Dieppe. The upper valley of the Somme was the scene of heavy fighting in the First World War.

Somme, Battle of the a major battle of the First World War between the British and the Germans, on the Western Front in northern France July–November 1916. More than a million men on both sides were killed or wounded.

sommelier /sɒˈmɛljeɪ/ ▶ noun a wine waiter.
– ORIGIN early 19th cent.: French, literally 'butler'.

sommer /ˈsɒmə/ ▶ adverb S. African informal just; simply: *I used to just sommer sit there*.
– ORIGIN Afrikaans.

somnambulism /sɒmˈnambjʊlɪz(ə)m/ ▶ noun [mass noun] sleepwalking.
– DERIVATIVES **somnambulant** adjective, **somnambulantly** adverb, **somnambulist** noun, **somnambulistic** adjective, **somnambulistically** adverb.
– ORIGIN late 18th cent.: from French *somnambulisme*, from Latin *somnus* 'sleep' + *ambulare* 'to walk'.

somniferous /sɒmˈnɪf(ə)rəs/ ▶ adjective tending to induce sleep; soporific.
– ORIGIN early 17th cent.: from Latin *somnifer* (from *somnium* 'dream') + **-OUS**.

somnolent /ˈsɒmnəl(ə)nt/ ▶ adjective sleepy; drowsy. ■ causing or suggestive of drowsiness: *a somnolent summer day*.
– DERIVATIVES **somnolence** noun, **somnolency** noun, **somnolently** adverb.
– ORIGIN late Middle English (in the sense 'causing sleepiness'): from Old French *sompnolent* or Latin *somnolentus*, from *somnus* 'sleep'.

somoni /sɒˈməʊni/ ▶ noun (pl. **same** or **somonis**) the basic monetary unit of Tajikistan, equal to one hundred dirams.
– ORIGIN Tajik, from the name of Ismail *Samani*, the 9th-century founder of the Tajik nation.

Somoza /səˈməʊzə/ the name of a family of Nicaraguan statesmen: ■ **Anastasio** (1896–1956), President 1937–47 and 1951–6; full name *Anastasio Somoza García*. He took presidential office following a military coup in 1936. Somoza ruled Nicaragua as a virtual dictator and was assassinated. ■ **Luis** (1922–67), President 1957–63, son of Anastasio; full name *Luis Somoza Debayle*. ■ **Anastasio** (1925–80), President 1967–79, younger brother of Luis; full name *Anastasio Somoza Debayle*. His dictatorial regime was overthrown by the Sandinistas and he was assassinated while in exile in Paraguay.

son ▶ noun a boy or man in relation to either or both of his parents. ■ a male offspring of an animal. ■ a male descendant: *the sons of Adam*. ■ (**the Son**) (in Christian belief) the second person of the Trinity; Christ. ■ a man considered in relation to his native country or area: *one of Norfolk's most famous sons*. ■ a man regarded as the product of a particular person, influence, or environment: *sons of the church*. ■ (also **my son**) used by an older person as a form of address for a boy or young man: *you're on private land, son*.
– PHRASES **son of a bitch** (pl. **sons of bitches**) informal used as a general term of contempt or abuse. **son of a gun** (pl. **sons of guns**) informal, chiefly N. Amer. a jocular or affectionate way of addressing or referring to someone. [with reference to the guns carried aboard ships: the epithet is said to have been applied originally to babies born at sea to women allowed to accompany their husbands.]
– DERIVATIVES **sonship** noun.

S

– ORIGIN Old English *sunu*, of Germanic origin; related to Dutch *zoon* and German *Sohn*, from an Indo-European root shared by Greek *huios*.

sonar /ˈsəʊnɑː/ ▶ **noun** [mass noun] a system for the detection of objects under water by emitting sound pulses and detecting or measuring their return after being reflected. ■ [count noun] an apparatus used in this system. ■ the method of echolocation used in air or water by animals such as whales and bats.
– ORIGIN 1940s: from *so(und) na(vigation and) r(anging)*, on the pattern of *radar*.

sonata /səˈnɑːtə/ ▶ **noun** a composition for an instrumental soloist, often with a piano accompaniment, typically in several movements with one or more in sonata form.
– ORIGIN late 17th cent.: Italian, literally 'sounded' (originally as distinct from 'sung'), feminine past participle of *sonare*.

sonata form ▶ **noun** [mass noun] a type of composition in three sections (exposition, development, and recapitulation) in which two themes or subjects are explored according to set key relationships. It forms the basis for much classical music, including the sonata, symphony, and concerto.

sonatina /ˌsɒnəˈtiːnə/ ▶ **noun** a simple or short sonata.
– ORIGIN mid 18th cent.: Italian, diminutive of SONATA.

sonde /sɒnd/ ▶ **noun** an instrument probe that automatically transmits information about its surroundings underground, under water, in the atmosphere, etc.
– ORIGIN early 20th cent.: from French, literally 'sounding (line)'.

Sondheim /ˈsɒndhʌɪm/, Stephen (Joshua) (b.1930), American composer and lyricist. He became famous with his lyrics for Leonard Bernstein's *West Side Story* (1957). He has since written a number of musicals, including *A Little Night Music* (1973) and *Sweeney Todd* (1979).

sone /səʊn/ ▶ **noun** a unit of subjective loudness, equal to 40 phons.
– ORIGIN 1930s: from Latin *sonus* 'a sound'.

son et lumière /ˌsɒn eɪ ˈluːmjɛː/, French /sɔ̃ e lymjɛʀ/ ▶ **noun** an entertainment held by night at a historic monument or building, telling its history by the use of lighting effects and recorded sound.
– ORIGIN French, literally 'sound and light'.

Song /sɒŋ/ (also **Sung**) a dynasty that ruled in China AD 960–1279.

> The **Northern Song** was ousted in 1127 by Mongolian tribes who absorbed it within their newly founded Jin dynasty. The **Southern Song** continued to flourish until it finally fell to the Mongols, led by the grandsons of Genghis Khan, in 1279. Both the Northern and Southern Song dynasties were marked by prosperity, cultural flowering, and technological advances.

song ▶ **noun 1** a short poem or other set of words set to music or meant to be sung: *a pop song*. ■ [mass noun] singing or vocal music: *the pilgrims **broke into song***. ■ a musical composition suggestive of a song. ■ a poem, especially one in rhymed stanzas: *The Song of Hiawatha*. ■ [mass noun] archaic poetry.
2 [mass noun] the musical phrases uttered by some birds, whales, and insects, typically forming a recognizable and repeated sequence and used chiefly for territorial defence or for attracting mates.
– PHRASES **for a song** informal very cheaply: *the place was going for a song*. **on song** Brit. informal performing well: *will Swindon be on song for the new season?* **a song and dance** informal, chiefly Brit. a fuss or commotion: *she would be sure to **make a song and dance about** her aching feet*. ■ N. Amer. a long explanation that is pointless or deliberately evasive.
– ORIGIN Old English *sang*, of Germanic origin; related to Dutch *zang* and German *Sang*, also to SING.

songbird ▶ **noun 1** a bird with a musical song.
2 Ornithology a perching bird of an advanced group distinguished by having the muscles of the syrinx attached to the bronchial semi-rings; an oscine passerine. ● Suborder Oscines, order Passeriformes; in Europe 'songbird' is effectively synonymous with 'passerine' or 'perching bird'.
3 informal a female singer.

songbook ▶ **noun** a book containing a collection of songs with music.

songcraft ▶ **noun** [mass noun] the art or skill of writing or composing songs.

song cycle ▶ **noun** a set of related songs, often on a romantic theme, intended to form a single musical entity.

song flight ▶ **noun** [mass noun] territorial display flight that involves song, as in the skylark.

song form ▶ **noun** a form used in the composition of a song, in particular a simple melody and accompaniment or a three-part work in which the third part is a repetition of the first.

Songhai /sɒŋˈɡʌɪ/ ▶ **noun** (pl. **same** or **Songhais**) **1** a member of a people of West Africa living mainly in Niger and Mali.
2 [mass noun] the Nilo-Saharan language of the Songhai, with about 2 million speakers.
▶ **adjective** relating to the Songhai or their language.
– ORIGIN the name in Songhai.

Song Hong /sɒŋ ˈhɒŋ/ Vietnamese name for RED RIVER (sense 1).

Songkran /ˈsɒŋkrɑːn/ ▶ **noun** a festival celebrating the traditional Thai New Year, held in April and marked by the throwing and sprinkling of water.
– ORIGIN Thai.

Song of Solomon see SONG OF SONGS.

Song of Songs a book of the Bible containing an anthology of Hebrew love poems traditionally ascribed to Solomon but in fact dating from a much later period. Jewish and Christian writers have interpreted the book allegorically as representing God's relationship with his people, or with the soul. Also called SONG OF SOLOMON, CANTICLES.

Song of the Three Holy Children a book of the Apocrypha, telling of three Hebrew exiles thrown into a furnace by Nebuchadnezzar.

songololo /ˌsɒŋɡɒˈlɒlɒ/ (also **shongololo**) ▶ **noun** (pl. **songololos**) S. African a millipede which curls up into a pinwheel-shaped coil when disturbed. ● *Julus terrestris*, class Diplopoda.
– ORIGIN early 20th cent.: from Xhosa *i-songololo*, Zulu *i-shongololo* (from *ukus(h)onga* 'roll up').

songsmith ▶ **noun** informal a person who writes popular songs.

song sparrow ▶ **noun** a sparrow-like North American bird related to the buntings, noted for its constant and characteristic song. ● *Melospiza melodia*, family Emberizidae (subfamily Emberizinae).

songster ▶ **noun** a person who sings, especially fluently and skilfully. ■ a person who writes songs or verse. ■ a songbird.
– ORIGIN Old English *sangestre* (see SONG, -STER).

songstress ▶ **noun** a female songster.

song thrush ▶ **noun** a common European and central Asian thrush with a buff spotted breast, having a loud song in which each phrase is repeated two or three times. ● *Turdus philomelos*, family Turdidae.

songwriter ▶ **noun** a person who writes popular songs or the music for them.
– DERIVATIVES **songwriting** noun.

sonic ▶ **adjective** relating to or using sound waves. ■ denoting or having a speed equal to that of sound.
– DERIVATIVES **sonically** adverb.
– ORIGIN 1920s: from Latin *sonus* 'sound' + -IC.

sonicate /ˈsɒnɪkeɪt/ Biochemistry ▶ **verb** [with obj.] subject (a biological sample) to ultrasonic vibration so as to fragment the cells, macromolecules, and membranes.
▶ **noun** a biological sample which has been sonicated.
– DERIVATIVES **sonication** noun.
– ORIGIN 1950s: from SONIC + -ATE².

sonic barrier ▶ **noun** another term for SOUND BARRIER.

sonic boom ▶ **noun** a loud explosive noise caused by the shock wave from an aircraft or other object travelling faster than the speed of sound.

sonics ▶ **plural noun** musical sounds artificially produced or reproduced.

Soninke /sɒˈniːŋkeɪ/ ▶ **noun** (pl. **same** or **Soninkes**) **1** a member of a West African people living in Mali and Senegal.
2 [mass noun] the language of the Soninke, which belongs to the Mande group and has about 1 million speakers.
▶ **adjective** relating to the Soninke or their language.
– ORIGIN the name in Soninke.

son-in-law ▶ **noun** (pl. **sons-in-law**) the husband of one's daughter.

sonnet ▶ **noun** a poem of fourteen lines using any of a number of formal rhyme schemes, in English typically having ten syllables per line.
▶ **verb** (**sonnets**, **sonneting**, **sonneted**) [no obj.] archaic compose sonnets. ■ [with obj.] celebrate in a sonnet.
– ORIGIN mid 16th cent.: from French, or from Italian *sonetto*, diminutive of *suono* 'a sound'.

sonneteer /ˌsɒnɪˈtɪə/ ▶ **noun** a writer of sonnets.

sonny ▶ **noun** informal used by an older person as a familiar form of address for a young boy. ■ (also **Sonny Jim**) used as a humorous or patronizing way of addressing a man: *look, sonny Jim, that's all I can tell you*.

sono- /ˈsəʊnəʊ, ˈsɒnəʊ/ ▶ **combining form** relating to sound: *sonometer*.
– ORIGIN from Latin *sonus* 'sound'.

sonobuoy ▶ **noun** a buoy equipped to detect underwater sounds and transmit them by radio.

sonofabitch ▶ **noun** non-standard spelling of SON OF A BITCH (see SON), used in representing informal American speech.

Son of Man ▶ **noun** Jesus Christ.

sonogram ▶ **noun 1** a graph representing a sound, showing the distribution of energy at different frequencies.
2 a visual image produced from an ultrasound examination.

sonography /səˈnɒɡrəfi/ ▶ **noun** [mass noun] **1** the analysis of sound using an instrument which produces a graphical representation of its component frequencies.
2 another term for ULTRASONOGRAPHY.
– DERIVATIVES **sonograph** noun, **sonographic** adjective.

sonoluminescence ▶ **noun** [mass noun] Physics luminescence excited in a substance by the passage of sound waves through it.
– DERIVATIVES **sonoluminescent** adjective.

sonometer /səˈnɒmɪtə/ ▶ **noun** another term for MONOCHORD.

Sonora /səˈnɒrə/ a state of NW Mexico, on the Gulf of California; capital, Hermosillo.

Sonora Desert an arid region of North America, comprising SE California and SW Arizona in the US and, in Mexico, much of Baja California and the western part of Sonora.

Sonoran /səˈnɔːrən/ ▶ **adjective** relating to, denoting, or characteristic of a biogeographical region including desert areas of the south-western US and central Mexico.
– ORIGIN late 19th cent.: from SONORA + -AN.

sonorant /ˈsɒn(ə)r(ə)nt, səˈnɔːr(ə)nt/ ▶ **noun** Phonetics a sound produced with the vocal cords so positioned that spontaneous voicing is possible; a vowel, a glide, or a liquid or nasal consonant.
– ORIGIN 1930s: from SONOROUS + -ANT.

sonority /səˈnɒrɪti/ ▶ **noun** [mass noun] the quality or fact of being sonorous. ■ Phonetics the relative loudness of a speech sound.

sonorous /ˈsɒn(ə)rəs, səˈnɔːrəs/ ▶ **adjective** (of a person's voice or other sound) imposingly deep and full. ■ capable of producing a deep or ringing sound: *the alloy is sonorous and useful in making bells*. ■ (of a speech or style) using imposing language: *he relished the sonorous words of condemnation*.
– DERIVATIVES **sonorously** adverb, **sonorousness** noun.
– ORIGIN early 17th cent.: from Latin *sonorus* (from *sonor* 'sound') + -OUS.

sonsy /ˈsɒnsi/ (also **sonsie**) ▶ **adjective** (**sonsier**, **sonsiest**) Scottish literary having an attractive and healthy appearance.
– ORIGIN mid 16th cent. (also in the sense 'lucky'): from Irish and Scottish Gaelic *sonas* 'good fortune' (from *sona* 'fortunate') + -Y¹.

Sontag /ˈsɒntaɡ/, Susan (1933–2004), American writer and critic. She established her reputation as a radical intellectual with *Against Interpretation* (essays, 1966). Other notable works: *On Photography* (1976) and *Illness as Metaphor* (1979).

Soochow /suːˈtʃaʊ/ variant of SUZHOU.

sook /suːk, sʊk/ ▶ **noun** informal, chiefly Austral./NZ & Canadian **1** a person lacking spirit or self-confidence.
2 a hand-reared calf.
– DERIVATIVES **sooky** adjective.
– ORIGIN mid 19th cent.: dialect variant of the noun SUCK.

sool /suːl/ ▶ **verb** [with obj.] chiefly Austral./NZ (of a dog) attack or worry (an animal). ■ urge or goad (someone) into doing something.

S

– ORIGIN late 19th cent.: variant of dialect *sowl* 'seize by the ears', of unknown origin.

soon ▸ adverb **1** in or after a short time: *everyone will soon know the truth | he'll be home soon | they arrived soon after 7.30.* ■ early: *how soon can you get here? | it's a pity you have to leave so soon | I wish you'd told me sooner | it was too soon to know.*
2 used to indicate one's preference in a particular matter: *I'd just as soon Tim did it | I'd sooner stay where I am.*
– PHRASES **no sooner —— than** used to convey that the second event mentioned happens immediately after the first: *she had no sooner spoken than the telephone rang.* **sooner or later** at some future time; eventually: *you'll have to tell him sooner or later.* **sooner rather than later** before much time has gone by: *I would be grateful if you would come to your senses sooner rather than later.*
– DERIVATIVES **soonish** adverb.
– ORIGIN Old English *sōna* 'immediately', of West Germanic origin.

USAGE In standard English the phrase **no sooner** is followed by **than**, as in *we had* ***no sooner*** *arrived* ***than*** *we had to leave*. This is because **sooner** is a comparative, and comparatives are followed by **than** (*earlier* **than**; *better* **than**, and so on). It is incorrect to follow **no sooner** with **when** rather than **than**, as in *we had* ***no sooner*** *arrived* ***when*** *we had to leave*.

Sooner State informal name for **OKLAHOMA**.
– ORIGIN *Sooner* in the sense 'one who acts prematurely', i.e. a person who tried to get into the frontier territory of Oklahoma before the US government opened it to settlers in 1889.

soot ▸ noun [mass noun] a deep black powdery or flaky substance consisting largely of amorphous carbon, produced by the incomplete burning of organic matter.
▸ verb [with obj.] cover or clog (something) with soot.
– ORIGIN Old English *sōt*, of Germanic origin; related to German dialect *Sott*, from an Indo-European root shared by the verb **SIT**.

sooth /suːθ/ ▸ noun [mass noun] archaic truth.
– PHRASES **in sooth** in truth; really.
– ORIGIN Old English *sōth* (originally as an adjective in the sense 'genuine, true'), of Germanic origin.

soothe ▸ verb [with obj.] gently calm (a person or their feelings): *a shot of brandy might soothe his nerves.* ■ reduce pain or discomfort in (a part of the body): *to soothe the skin try chamomile or thyme.* ■ relieve or ease (pain): *it contains a mild anaesthetic to soothe the pain.*
– DERIVATIVES **soother** noun.
– ORIGIN Old English *sōthian* 'verify, show to be true', from *sōth* 'true' (see **SOOTH**). In the 16th cent. the verb passed through the senses 'corroborate (a statement)', 'humour (a person) by expressing assent' and 'flatter by one's assent', whence 'mollify, appease' (late 17th cent.).

soothing ▸ adjective having a gently calming effect: *she put on some soothing music.* ■ reducing pain or discomfort: *almond oil is renowned for its soothing properties.*
– DERIVATIVES **soothingly** adverb.

S

soothsayer ▸ noun a person supposed to be able to foresee the future.
– DERIVATIVES **soothsaying** noun.
– ORIGIN Middle English (in the sense 'person who speaks the truth'): see **SOOTH**.

sooty ▸ adjective (**sootier**, **sootiest**) covered with or coloured like soot: *his olive skin and sooty eyes.* ■ used in names of birds and other animals that are mainly blackish or brownish black, e.g. **sooty tern**.

sooty mould ▸ noun [mass noun] a black velvety mould that grows on the surfaces of leaves and stems affected by honeydew. ● Family Capnodiaceae, subdivision Ascomycotina.

sop ▸ noun **1** a thing of no great value given or done as a concession to appease someone whose main concerns or demands are not being met: *my agent telephones as a sop but never finds me work.*
2 a piece of bread dipped in gravy, soup, or sauce.
▸ verb (**sops**, **sopping**, **sopped**) [with obj.] (**sop something up**) soak up liquid using an absorbent substance: *he used some bread to sop up the sauce.* ■ archaic wet thoroughly; soak.
– ORIGIN Old English *soppian* 'dip (bread) in liquid', *sopp* (noun), probably from the base of Old English *sūpan* 'sup'. Sense 1 (mid 17th cent.) alludes to the sop used by Aeneas on his visit to Hades to appease Cerberus.

sopaipilla /ˌsɒpʌɪˈpiːljə, -ˈpiːjə/ ▸ noun (especially in New Mexico) a deep-fried pastry, typically square, eaten with honey or sugar or as a bread.
– ORIGIN American Spanish.

sophism /ˈsɒfɪz(ə)m/ ▸ noun a clever but false argument, especially one used deliberately to deceive.
– ORIGIN late Middle English: from Old French *sophime*, via Latin from Greek *sophisma* 'clever device', from *sophizesthai* 'become wise' (see **SOPHIST**).

sophist /ˈsɒfɪst/ ▸ noun a paid teacher of philosophy and rhetoric in the Classical and Hellenistic periods, associated in popular thought with moral scepticism and specious reasoning. ■ a person who reasons with clever but false arguments.
– DERIVATIVES **sophistic** /səˈfɪstɪk/ adjective, **sophistical** /səˈfɪstɪk(ə)l/ adjective, **sophistically** adverb.
– ORIGIN mid 16th cent.: via Latin from Greek *sophistēs*, from *sophizesthai* 'devise, become wise', from *sophos* 'wise'.

sophisticate ▸ verb /səˈfɪstɪkeɪt/ [with obj.] **1** make (someone or something) more sophisticated: *readers who have been sophisticated by modern literary practice.*
2 [no obj.] archaic talk or reason in an impressively complex and educated manner. ■ mislead or corrupt by sophistry: *books of casuistry, which sophisticate the understanding and defile the heart.*
▸ adjective /səˈfɪstɪkət/ archaic sophisticated.
▸ noun /səˈfɪstɪkət/ a person with much worldly experience and knowledge of fashion and culture: *he is still the butt of jokes made by New York sophisticates.*
– ORIGIN late Middle English (as an adjective in the sense 'adulterated', and as a verb in the sense 'mix with a foreign substance'): from medieval Latin *sophisticatus* 'tampered with', past participle of the verb *sophisticare*, from *sophisticus* 'sophistic'. The shift of sense probably occurred first in the adjective *unsophisticated*, from 'uncorrupted' via 'innocent' to 'inexperienced, uncultured'. The noun dates from the early 20th cent.

sophisticated ▸ adjective **1** having, revealing, or proceeding from a great deal of worldly experience and knowledge of fashion and culture: *a chic, sophisticated woman | a young man with sophisticated tastes.* ■ appealing to people with such knowledge or experience: *a sophisticated restaurant.*
2 (of a machine, system, or technique) developed to a high degree of complexity: *highly sophisticated computer systems.* ■ (of a person or their thoughts, reactions, and understanding) aware of and able to interpret complex issues; subtle: *discussion and reflection are necessary for a sophisticated response to a text.*
– DERIVATIVES **sophisticatedly** adverb.

sophistication ▸ noun [mass noun] the quality of being sophisticated: *her air of sophistication and confidence | the technological sophistication of their products.*

sophistry /ˈsɒfɪstri/ ▸ noun (pl. **sophistries**) [mass noun] the use of clever but false arguments, especially with the intention of deceiving. ■ [count noun] a fallacious argument.

Sophocles /ˈsɒfəkliːz/ (*c.*496–406 BC), Greek dramatist. His seven surviving plays are notable for their complexity of plot and depth of characterization, and for their examination of the relationship between mortals and the divine order. Notable plays: *Antigone* and *Oedipus Rex* (also called *Oedipus Tyrannus*).

sophomore /ˈsɒfəmɔː/ ▸ noun US a second-year university or high-school student.
– ORIGIN mid 17th cent.: perhaps from earlier *sophumer*, from *sophum*, *sophom* (obsolete variants of **SOPHISM**) + **-ER**¹.

sophomoric /ˌsɒfəˈmɒrɪk/ ▸ adjective relating to or characteristic of a sophomore: *my sophomoric years.* ■ pretentious or juvenile: *sophomoric double entendres.*

Sophy /ˈsəʊfi/ ▸ noun (pl. **Sophies**) historical a former title for the ruler of Persia, associated especially with the Safavid dynasty.
– ORIGIN from Arabic *ṣafī-al-dīn* 'pure of religion'.

soporific /ˌsɒpəˈrɪfɪk/ ▸ adjective tending to induce drowsiness or sleep: *the motion of the train had a somewhat soporific effect.* ■ sleepy or drowsy: *some medicine made her soporific.* ■ tediously boring or monotonous: *a libel trial is in large parts intensely soporific.*
▸ noun a drug or other substance that induces drowsiness or sleep.
– DERIVATIVES **soporifically** adverb.
– ORIGIN mid 17th cent.: from Latin *sopor* 'sleep' + **-IFIC**.

sopping ▸ adjective saturated with liquid; wet through: *get those sopping clothes off* | [as submodifier] *the handkerchief was sopping wet.*
– ORIGIN mid 19th cent.: present participle of **SOP**.

soppy ▸ adjective (**soppier**, **soppiest**) Brit. informal
1 self-indulgently sentimental: *I look at babies with a soppy smile on my face.*
2 lacking spirit and strength of character; feeble: *my little sisters were too soppy for our adventurous games.*
– DERIVATIVES **soppily** adverb, **soppiness** noun.
– ORIGIN early 19th cent. (in the sense 'soaked with water'): from **SOP** + **-Y**¹.

sopranino /ˌsɒprəˈniːnəʊ/ ▸ noun Music (pl. **sopraninos**) an instrument, especially a recorder or saxophone, higher than soprano.
– ORIGIN early 20th cent.: Italian, diminutive of **SOPRANO**.

soprano /səˈprɑːnəʊ/ ▸ noun (pl. **sopranos**) **1** the highest singing voice. ■ a female or boy singer with a soprano voice. ■ a part written for a soprano voice.
2 [usu. as modifier] an instrument of a high or the highest pitch in its family: *a soprano saxophone.*
– ORIGIN mid 18th cent.: Italian, from *sopra* 'above', from Latin *supra*.

soprano clef ▸ noun Music an obsolete clef placing middle C on the lowest line of the stave.

soprano recorder ▸ noun North American term for **DESCANT RECORDER**.

Sopwith /ˈsɒpwɪθ/, Sir Thomas (Octave Murdoch) (1888–1989), English aircraft designer. During the First World War he designed the fighter biplane the Sopwith Camel, while in the Second World War, as chairman of the Hawker Siddeley company, he was responsible for the production of aircraft such as the Hurricane fighter.

sora /ˈsɔːrə, ˈsəʊrə/ (also **sora crake** or **rail**) ▸ noun a common small brown and grey American crake (bird), frequenting marshes. ● *Porzana carolina*, family Rallidae.
– ORIGIN early 18th cent.: probably from an American Indian language.

Sorb /sɔːb/ ▸ noun a member of a Slavic people living in parts of SE Brandenburg and eastern Saxony. Also called **WEND**.
– ORIGIN from German *Sorbe*.

sorb /sɔːb/ ▸ noun the fruit of the true service tree.
– ORIGIN early 16th cent.: from French *sorbe* or Latin *sorbus* 'service tree', *sorbum* 'serviceberry'.

sorbent /ˈsɔːb(ə)nt/ ▸ noun Chemistry a substance which has the property of collecting molecules of another substance by sorption.
– ORIGIN early 20th cent.: from *sorb* 'take up by sorption', on the pattern of *absorbent*.

sorbet /ˈsɔːbeɪ, -bɪt/ ▸ noun **1** a water ice.
2 archaic an Arabian sherbet.
– ORIGIN late 16th cent.: from French, from Italian *sorbetto*, from Turkish *şerbet*, based on Arabic *šariba* 'to drink'; compare with **SHERBET**.

Sorbian /ˈsɔːbɪən/ ▸ adjective relating to the Sorbs or their language.
▸ noun the traditional language of the Sorbs, a Slavic language related to Polish and Czech. It has been revived from near extinction and has around 70,000 speakers. Also called **WENDISH** or **LUSATIAN**.

sorbitan /ˈsɔːbɪtan/ ▸ noun [usu. as modifier] Chemistry any of a group of compounds which are cyclic ethers derived from sorbitol or its derivatives.
– ORIGIN 1930s: blend of **SORBITOL** and **ANHYDRIDE**.

sorbitol /ˈsɔːbɪtɒl/ ▸ noun [mass noun] Chemistry a sweet-tasting crystalline compound found in some fruit. ● A hexahydric alcohol; chem. formula: $CH_2OH(CHOH)_4CH_2OH$.
– ORIGIN late 19th cent.: from **SORB** + **-ITE**¹ + **-OL**.

Sorbonne /sɔːˈbɒn/, French /sɔrbɔn/ the seat of the faculties of science and literature of the University of Paris.
– ORIGIN originally a theological college founded by Robert de Sorbon, chaplain to Louis IX, *c.*1257.

sorbus /ˈsɔːbəs/ ▸ noun a tree or shrub of a genus which includes the rowan, service tree, and whitebeam. ● Genus *Sorbus*, family Rosaceae: many species.
– ORIGIN modern Latin, from Latin *sorbus* 'service tree'.

sorcerer ▸ noun a person who claims or is believed to have magic powers; a wizard.
– ORIGIN late Middle English: from *sorser* (from Old French *sorcier*, based on Latin *sors*, *sort-* 'lot') + **-ER**¹.

sorceress ▸ noun a female sorcerer; a witch.

sorcery ▸ noun [mass noun] the use of magic, especially black magic.
– DERIVATIVES **sorcerous** adjective.

sordid ▸ adjective **1** involving immoral or dishonourable actions and motives; arousing moral distaste and contempt: *the story paints a sordid picture of bribes and scams.*
2 dirty or squalid: *the overcrowded housing conditions were sordid and degrading.*
– DERIVATIVES **sordidly** adverb, **sordidness** noun.
– ORIGIN late Middle English (as a medical term in the sense 'purulent'): from French *sordide* or Latin *sordidus*, from *sordere* 'be dirty'. The current senses date from the early 17th cent.

sordino /sɔːˈdiːnəʊ/ ▸ noun (pl. **sordini** /-ni/) Music a mute for a musical instrument. ▪ (**sordini**) (on a piano) the dampers.
– ORIGIN late 16th cent.: from Italian, from *sordo* 'mute', from Latin *surdus*.

sordor /ˈsɔːdə/ ▸ noun [mass noun] chiefly literary physical or moral sordidness.
– ORIGIN early 19th cent.: from **SORDID**, on the pattern of the pair *squalid, squalor*.

sore ▸ adjective **1** (of a part of one's body) painful or aching: *she had a sore throat.* ▪ suffering pain from a part of one's body: *he was sore from the long ride.*
2 [predic.] informal, chiefly N. Amer. upset and angry: *I didn't even know they were sore at us.*
3 [attrib.] severe; urgent: *we're in sore need of him.*
▸ noun a raw or painful place on the body: *all of us had sores and infections on our hands.* ▪ a cause or source of distress or annoyance: *there's no point raking over the past and opening old sores.*
▸ adverb archaic extremely; severely: *they were sore afraid.*
– PHRASES **sore point** an issue about which someone feels distressed or annoyed and which it is therefore advisable to avoid raising with them. **stand** (or **stick**) **out like a sore thumb** be very obviously different from the surrounding people or things.
– DERIVATIVES **soreness** noun.
– ORIGIN Old English *sār* (noun and adjective), *sāre* (adverb), of Germanic origin; related to Dutch *zeer* 'sore' and German *sehr* 'very'. The original sense was 'causing intense pain, grievous', whence the adverbial use.

sorehead ▸ noun N. Amer. informal a person who is in a bad temper or easily irritated.

sorel /ˈsɒr(ə)l/ ▸ noun Brit. a male fallow deer in its third year.
– ORIGIN late 15th cent.: variant of **SORREL²**.

sorely ▸ adverb to a very high degree or level of intensity: *she would sorely miss his company* | *help was sorely needed.*
– ORIGIN Old English *sārlīce* (see **SORE**, **-LY²**).

sorghum /ˈsɔːgəm/ ▸ noun [mass noun] a cereal which is native to warm regions of the Old World and is a major source of grain and stockfeed. ● Genus *Sorghum*, family Gramineae: many species, in particular *S. bicolor* and its cultivars.
– ORIGIN late 16th cent.: modern Latin, from Italian *sorgo*, perhaps based on a variant of Latin *syricum* 'Syrian'.

sori plural form of **SORUS**.

Soroptimist /səˈrɒptɪmɪst/ ▸ noun a member of an international association of clubs for professional and business women founded in California in 1921.
– ORIGIN 1920s: from Latin *soror* 'sister' + *optimist* (see **OPTIMISM**).

sororal /səˈrɔːr(ə)l/ ▸ adjective formal of or like a sister or sisters.
– ORIGIN mid 17th cent.: from Latin *soror* 'sister' + **-AL**.

sorority /səˈrɒrɪti/ ▸ noun (pl. **sororities**) N. Amer. a society for female students in a university or college.
– ORIGIN mid 16th cent.: from medieval Latin *sororitas*, or from Latin *soror* 'sister' (on the pattern of *fraternity*).

sorosis /səˈrəʊsɪs/ ▸ noun (pl. **soroses** /-siːz/) Botany a fleshy multiple fruit, e.g. a pineapple or mulberry, derived from the ovaries of several flowers.
– ORIGIN mid 19th cent.: modern Latin, from Greek *sōros* 'heap'.

sorption /ˈsɔːpʃ(ə)n/ ▸ noun [mass noun] Chemistry absorption and adsorption considered as a single process.
– ORIGIN early 20th cent.: back-formation from **ABSORPTION** and **ADSORPTION**.

sorrel¹ /ˈsɒr(ə)l/ ▸ noun **1** a European plant of the dock family, with arrow-shaped leaves that are used in salads and cookery for their acidic flavour. See also **WOOD SORREL**. ● Genus *Rumex*, family Polygonaceae: several species, including the **English sorrel** (*R. acetosa*) and the more slender-leaved **French sorrel** (*R. scutatus*).
2 (also **red sorrel**) a tall annual Caribbean hibiscus with red flowers and stems. ● *Hibiscus sabdariffa*, family Malvaceae.
▪ [mass noun] a sweet red drink made from the sepals of these flowers.
– ORIGIN late Middle English: from Old French *sorele*, of Germanic origin; related to **SOUR**.

sorrel² /ˈsɒr(ə)l/ ▸ noun a horse with a light reddish-brown coat. ▪ [mass noun] [usu. as modifier] a light reddish-brown colour: *a sorrel mare with four white socks.*
– ORIGIN Middle English: from Old French *sorel*, from *sor* 'yellowish', from a Germanic adjective meaning 'dry'.

sorrel tree ▸ noun another term for **SOURWOOD**.

Sorrento /səˈrɛntəʊ/ a town on the west coast of central Italy, situated on a peninsula separating the Bay of Naples, which it faces, from the Gulf of Salerno; pop. 16,583 (2008).

sorrow ▸ noun [mass noun] a feeling of deep distress caused by loss, disappointment, or other misfortune suffered by oneself or others: *a bereaved person needs time to work through their sorrow.* ▪ [count noun] an event or circumstance that causes sorrow: *it was a great sorrow to her when they separated.* ▪ the outward expression of grief; lamentation.
▸ verb [no obj.] feel or display deep distress: (as adj. **sorrowing**) *the sorrowing widower found it hard to relate to his sons.*
– ORIGIN Old English *sorh, sorg* (noun), *sorgian* (verb), of Germanic origin; related to Dutch *zorg* and German *Sorge*.

sorrowful ▸ adjective feeling or showing grief: *she looked at him with sorrowful eyes.* ▪ causing grief: *the sorrowful news of his father's death.*
– DERIVATIVES **sorrowfully** adverb, **sorrowfulness** noun.
– ORIGIN Old English *sorhful* (see **SORROW**, **-FUL**).

sorry ▸ adjective (**sorrier**, **sorriest**) **1** [predic.] feeling sad or distressed through sympathy with someone else's misfortune: *I was sorry to hear about what happened to your family.* ▪ (**sorry for**) filled with compassion for: *I felt sorry for the poor boys working for him.*
2 [predic.] feeling regret or penitence: *he said he was sorry he had upset me* | *I'm sorry if I was a bit brusque.* ▪ used to express apology: *sorry—I was trying not to make a noise.* ▪ used as a polite request that someone should repeat something that one has failed to hear or understand: *I'm sorry—you were saying?*
3 [attrib.] in a poor or pitiful state: *he looks a sorry sight with his broken jaw.* ▪ unpleasant and regrettable, especially on account of incompetence or misbehaviour: *we feel so ashamed that we keep quiet about the whole sorry business.*
– PHRASES **sorry for oneself** sad and self-pitying.
– DERIVATIVES **sorrily** adverb, **sorriness** noun.
– ORIGIN Old English *sārig* 'pained, distressed', of West Germanic origin, from the base of the noun **SORE**. The shortening of the root vowel has given the word an apparent connection with the unrelated **SORROW**.

sort ▸ noun **1** a category of things or people with a common feature; a type: *if only we knew the sort of people she was mixing with* | *a radical change poses **all sorts of** questions.* ▪ [with adj.] informal a person of a specified nature: *Frank was a genuinely friendly sort.*
2 [mass noun] Computing the arrangement of data in a prescribed sequence.
3 archaic a manner or way: *in law also the Judge is **in a sort** superior to his King.*
▸ verb [with obj.] **1** arrange systematically in groups; separate according to type: *the mail was sorted* | *she **sorted out** the clothes, some to be kept, some to be thrown away.* ▪ [no obj.] (**sort through**) look at (a group of things) in succession in order to classify them or make a selection: *she sat down and sorted through her mail.*
2 resolve (a problem or difficulty): *the teacher helps the children to **sort out** their problems.* ▪ resolve the problems or difficulties of: *I need time to **sort** myself **out**.*
– PHRASES **after a sort** dated after a fashion. **in some sort** dated to a certain extent: *I am in some sort indebted to you.* **it takes all sorts to make a world** proverb people vary greatly in character, tastes, and abilities (often used as a comment on what the speaker feels to be strange behaviour): *he was wearing make-up—well, it takes all sorts.* **nothing of the sort** used as an emphatic way of denying permission or refuting an earlier statement: *'I'll pay.' 'You'll do nothing of the sort.'.* **of a sort** (or **of sorts**) informal of a somewhat unusual or inferior kind: *the training camp actually became a tourist attraction of sorts.* **out of sorts** slightly unwell. ▪ in low spirits; irritable: *the trying events of the day had put him out of sorts.* **sort of** informal to some extent; in some way or other: *'Do you see what I mean?' 'Sort of,' answered Jean cautiously.* **sort out the men from the boys** show or prove who is the best at a particular activity. **the — sort** the kind of person likely to do or be involved with the thing specified: *she'd never imagined Steve to be the marrying sort.*
– PHRASAL VERBS **sort someone out** informal deal with a troublesome person, typically by reprimanding or punishing them: *if he can't pay you, I'll sort him out.* **sort something out 1** separate something from a mixed group: *she **sorted out** the lettuce **from** the spinach.* **2** arrange or organize something: *they are anxious to sort out travelling arrangements.*
– DERIVATIVES **sortable** adjective, **sorter** noun.
– ORIGIN late Middle English: from Old French *sorte*, from an alteration of Latin *sors, sort-* 'lot, condition'.

> **USAGE** The construction **these sort of**, as in *I don't want to answer **these sort of** questions*, is technically ungrammatical. This is because **these** is plural and needs to agree with a plural noun (in this case **sorts** rather than **sort**). The construction is undoubtedly common and has been used for hundreds of years, but is best avoided in formal writing. See also **USAGE** at **KIND¹**.

sorta ▸ contraction informal sort of: *I did sorta like the movie.*

sortal /ˈsɔːt(ə)l/ Linguistics & Philosophy ▸ adjective denoting or relating to a term representing a semantic feature that applies to an entity as long as it exists, classifying it as being of a particular kind.
▸ noun a term of this kind, for example *human* as opposed to *engineer*.

sorted ▸ adjective Brit. informal organized, arranged, or dealt with satisfactorily: *'And your social commitments?' 'They're well sorted'* | *he's working on that old car he's been trying to get sorted.* ▪ (of a person) confident, organized, and emotionally well balanced: *after a while, you realize they're not as sorted as they seem* | *a pretty sorted kind of bloke.* ▪ (of a person) prepared for something or provided with something, especially illegal drugs.

sortes /ˈsɔːtiːz, ˈsɔːteɪz/ (also **sortes Biblicae** /ˈbɪblɪkiː/) ▸ plural noun [treated as sing.] divination, or the seeking of guidance, by chance selection of a passage in the Bible or another text regarded as authoritative.
– ORIGIN Latin, 'chance selections (of the Bible)'.

sortie ▸ noun an attack made by troops coming out from a position of defence. ▪ an operational flight by a single military aircraft. ▪ a short trip or journey: *an early-morning sortie into the garden of our hotel.* ▪ an attempt to participate in a new activity or sphere: *this latest book is the author's first **sortie into** non-fiction.*
▸ verb (**sorties**, **sortieing**, **sortied**) [no obj.] come out from a defensive position to make an attack.
– ORIGIN late 18th cent.: from French, feminine past participle of *sortir* 'go out'.

S

sortilege /ˈsɔːtɪlɪdʒ/ ▸ noun [mass noun] chiefly historical the practice of foretelling the future from a card or other item drawn at random from a collection.
– ORIGIN late Middle English: via Old French from medieval Latin *sortilegium* 'sorcery', from Latin *sortilegus* 'sorcerer', from Latin *sors, sort-* 'lot, chance' + *legere* 'choose'.

sorting office ▸ noun an office in which mail is sorted according to its destination.

sortition ▸ noun [mass noun] the action of selecting or determining something by the casting or drawing of lots.
– ORIGIN late 16th cent.: from Latin *sortitio(n-)*, from *sortire* 'divide or obtain by lot'.

sort-out ▸ noun Brit. an act of tidying or organizing things by separating them into categories: *start your kitchen reorganization with a sort-out.*

sorus /ˈsɔːrəs/ ▸ noun (pl. **sori** /-rʌɪ/) Botany a cluster of spore-producing receptacles on the underside of a fern frond. ▪ a gamete-producing or fruiting body in certain algae and fungi.
– ORIGIN mid 19th cent.: modern Latin, from Greek *sōros* 'heap'.

SOS ▸ noun (pl. **SOSs**) an international code signal of extreme distress, used especially by ships at sea. ▪ an

urgent appeal for help. ■ Brit. a message broadcast in an emergency in an attempt to contact a person whose whereabouts are not known.
– ORIGIN early 20th cent.: letters chosen as being easily transmitted and recognized in Morse code; by folk etymology an abbreviation of *save our souls*.

sosatie /sə'sɑ:ti/ ▶ **noun** (pl. **sosaties**) a South African dish of cubes of curried or spiced meat grilled on a skewer.
– ORIGIN Afrikaans; compare with **SATAY**.

Sosnowiec /sɒs'nɒvjɛts/ an industrial mining town in SW Poland, west of Cracow; pop. 223,284 (2007).

so-so ▶ **adjective** neither very good nor very bad: *a happy ending to a so-so season* | *'How are you?' 'So-so.'*

sostenuto /,sɒstə'nu:təʊ/ Music ▶ **adjective** (of a passage of music) to be played in a sustained or prolonged manner.
▶ **noun** (pl. **sostenutos**) a passage to be played in a sustained and prolonged manner. ■ [mass noun] performance in this manner.
– ORIGIN Italian, 'sustained'.

sot ▶ **noun** a habitual drunkard.
▶ **verb** (**sots, sotting, sotted**) [no obj.] archaic drink alcohol habitually.
– DERIVATIVES **sottish** adjective.
– ORIGIN late Old English *sott* 'foolish person', from medieval Latin *sottus*, reinforced by Old French *sot* 'foolish'. The current sense of the noun dates from the late 16th cent.

soteriology /sə(ʊ),tɪərɪ'ɒlədʒi, sɒ-/ ▶ **noun** [mass noun] Theology the doctrine of salvation.
– DERIVATIVES **soteriological** adjective.
– ORIGIN mid 19th cent.: from Greek *sōtēria* 'salvation' + **-LOGY**.

Sothic /'səʊθɪk, 'sɒθ-/ ▶ **adjective** relating to Sirius (the Dog Star), especially with reference to the ancient Egyptian year fixed by its heliacal rising.
– ORIGIN early 19th cent.: from Greek *Sōthis* (from an Egyptian name of the Dog Star) + **-IC**.

Sotho /'su:tu:/ ▶ **noun** (pl. **same** or **Sothos**) **1** a member of a group of peoples living chiefly in Botswana, Lesotho, and northern South Africa.
2 [mass noun] the group of Bantu languages spoken by the Sotho peoples, of which the most important are Sepedi (also called **North Sotho**) and Sesotho (also called **South Sotho**). The term **Western Sotho** is sometimes used of the related language Setswana.
▶ **adjective** relating to the Sotho peoples or their languages.
– ORIGIN the stem of **BASOTHO** and **SESOTHO**.

sotol /'səʊtəʊl/ ▶ **noun** [mass noun] a North American desert plant of the agave family, with spiny-edged leaves and small white flowers. ● Genus *Dasylirion*, family Agavaceae: several species.
■ an alcoholic drink made from the sap of the sotol plant.
– ORIGIN late 19th cent.: via American Spanish from Nahuatl *tzotolli*.

sotto voce /,sɒtəʊ 'vəʊtʃeɪ/ ▶ **adverb & adjective** (of singing or a spoken remark) in a quiet voice: [as adv.] *'It won't be cheap,' he added sotto voce* | [as adj.] *a sotto voce remark*.
– ORIGIN from Italian *sotto* 'under' + *voce* 'voice'.

S

sou /su:/ ▶ **noun** historical a former French coin of low value. ■ [usu. with negative] informal a very small amount of money: *he didn't have a sou*.
– ORIGIN French, originally as *sous* (plural), from Old French *sout* from Latin *solidus* (see **SOLIDUS**).

sou' ▶ **abbreviation** (especially in compounds) south.

soubise /su:'bi:z/ ▶ **noun** [mass noun] a thick white sauce made with onion purée and often served with fish or eggs.
– ORIGIN named after Charles de Rohan *Soubise* (1715–87), French general and courtier.

soubresaut /'su:brəsəʊ/ ▶ **noun** (pl. pronunc. **same**) Ballet a straight-legged jump from both feet with the toes pointed and feet together, one behind the other.
– ORIGIN French.

soubrette /su:'brɛt/ ▶ **noun** a minor female role in a comedy, typically that of a pert maidservant.
– ORIGIN mid 18th cent.: French, from Provençal *soubreto*, feminine of *soubret* 'coy', from *sobrar*, from Latin *superare* 'be above'.

soubriquet /'su:brɪkeɪ/ ▶ **noun** variant spelling of **SOBRIQUET**.

souchong /'su:ʃɒŋ/ ▶ **noun** [mass noun] a fine black variety of China tea.
– ORIGIN mid 18th cent.: from Chinese *siú* 'small' + *chúng* 'sort'.

soucouyant /,su:ku:'jɒ̃/ ▶ **noun** (in eastern Caribbean folklore) a malignant witch believed to shed her skin by night and suck the blood of her victims.
– ORIGIN West Indian creole.

souffle /'su:f(ə)l/ ▶ **noun** Medicine a low murmuring or blowing sound heard through a stethoscope.
– ORIGIN late 19th cent.: from French, from *souffler* 'to blow', from Latin *sufflare*.

soufflé /'su:fleɪ/ ▶ **noun** a light, spongy baked dish made typically by adding flavoured egg yolks to stiffly beaten egg whites. ■ any of various light sweet or savoury dishes made with beaten egg whites.
– ORIGIN French, literally 'blown', past participle of *souffler* (see **SOUFFLE**).

Soufrière /,su:frɪ'ɛ:/ **1** a dormant volcano on the French island of Guadeloupe in the Caribbean. Rising to 1,468 m (4,813 ft), it is the highest peak in the Lesser Antilles.
2 an active volcanic peak on the island of St Vincent in the Caribbean. It rises to a height of 1,234 m (4,006 ft).
– ORIGIN French, from *soufre* 'sulphur'.

sough /saʊ, sʌf/ ▶ **verb** [no obj.] (of the wind in trees, the sea, etc.) make a moaning, whistling, or rushing sound.
▶ **noun** [in sing.] a sound of this type.
– ORIGIN Old English *swōgan*, of Germanic origin.

sought past and past participle of **SEEK**.

sought after ▶ **adjective** much in demand; generally desired: *the most expensive and sought-after perfume*.

souk /su:k/ (also **suk, sukh,** or **suq**) ▶ **noun** an Arab market or marketplace; a bazaar.
– ORIGIN from Arabic *sūq*.

soukous /'su:ku:s/ ▶ **noun** [mass noun] a style of African popular music characterized by syncopated rhythms and intricate contrasting guitar melodies, originating in the Democratic Republic of the Congo (Zaire).
– ORIGIN perhaps from French *secouer* 'to shake'.

soul ▶ **noun 1** the spiritual or immaterial part of a human being or animal, regarded as immortal. ■ a person's moral or emotional nature or sense of identity: *in the depths of her soul, she knew he would betray her*.
2 [mass noun] emotional or intellectual energy or intensity, especially as revealed in a work of art or an artistic performance: *their interpretation lacked soul*. ■ black American culture or ethnic pride. ■ short for **SOUL MUSIC**.
3 the essence or embodiment of a specified quality: *he was **the soul of** discretion* | *brevity is the soul of wit*. ■ an individual person: *I'll never tell a soul* | *it was bad news for some poor soul*. ■ a person regarded with affection or pity: *she's a nice old soul*.
– PHRASES **lost soul** a soul that is damned. ■ chiefly humorous a person who seems unable to cope with everyday life. **upon my soul!** dated an exclamation of surprise.
– DERIVATIVES **souled** adjective.
– ORIGIN Old English *sāwol, sāw(e)l*, of Germanic origin; related to Dutch *ziel* and German *Seele*.

soul case ▶ **noun** N. Amer. & W. Indian informal the body.

soul catcher ▶ **noun** (among various North American Indian peoples) a hollowed bone tube used by a medicine man to contain the soul of a sick person.

soul-destroying ▶ **adjective** (of an activity) unbearably monotonous.

soul food ▶ **noun** [mass noun] food traditionally associated with black people of the southern US.

soulful ▶ **adjective** expressing or appearing to express deep and often sorrowful feeling: *she gave him a soulful glance*.
– DERIVATIVES **soulfully** adverb, **soulfulness** noun.

soul kiss ▶ **noun** another term for **FRENCH KISS**.

soulless ▶ **adjective** (especially of a place) lacking character and individuality: *she found the apartment beautiful but soulless*. ■ (of an activity) tedious and uninspiring: *soulless, non-productive work*. ■ lacking or suggesting the lack of human feelings and qualities: *two soulless black eyes were watching her*.
– DERIVATIVES **soullessly** adverb, **soullessness** noun.

soulmate ▶ **noun** a person ideally suited to another as a close friend or romantic partner.

soul music ▶ **noun** [mass noun] a kind of music incorporating elements of rhythm and blues and gospel music, popularized by American black people. Characterized by an emphasis on vocals and an impassioned improvisatory delivery, it is associated with performers such as Marvin Gaye, Aretha Franklin, James Brown, and Otis Redding.

soul-searching ▶ **noun** [mass noun] deep and anxious consideration of one's emotions and motives or of the correctness of a course of action.
▶ **adjective** involving or expressing such consideration: *long, soul-searching conversations about religion*.

soulster ▶ **noun** informal a singer of soul music.

Soumak /'su:mak/ ▶ **noun** a rug or carpet made in the neighbourhood of Shemakha in Azerbaijan, distinguished by a flat, napless surface and loose threads at the back.
– ORIGIN early 20th cent.: perhaps an alteration of *Shemakha* (see above).

sound[1] ▶ **noun** [mass noun] **1** vibrations that travel through the air or another medium and can be heard when they reach a person's or animal's ear: *light travels faster than sound*. ■ [count noun] a thing that can be heard: *she heard the sound of voices in the hall* | *don't make a sound*. ■ the area or distance within which something can be heard: *we were always **within sound of** the train whistles*.
2 (also **musical sound**) sound produced by continuous and regular vibrations, as opposed to noise.
3 music, speech, and sound effects when recorded and used to accompany a film, video, or broadcast: [as modifier] *a sound studio*. ■ broadcasting by radio as distinct from television. ■ the distinctive quality of the music of a particular composer or performer or of the sound produced by a particular instrument: *the sound of the Beatles*. ■ (**sounds**) informal popular music: *sounds of the Sixties*.
4 [in sing.] an idea or impression conveyed by words: *you've had a hard day, **by the sound of it***.
▶ **verb 1** emit or cause to emit sound: [no obj.] *a loud buzzer sounded* | [with obj.] *she sounded the horn*. ■ [with obj.] give an audible signal to indicate (something): *a different bell begins to sound midnight*. ■ [with obj.] express or convey (a warning): *pharmaceutical companies are **sounding the alarm** about counterfeit drugs*. ■ [with obj.] pronounce: *sound the rhymes clearly*. ■ [with obj.] test (the lungs or another body cavity) by noting the sound they produce: *the doctor sounded her chest*.
2 [no obj.] convey a specified impression when heard: [with complement] *he sounded worried*. ■ (of something or someone that has been described to one) convey a specified impression: ***it sounds as though** you really do believe that* | [with complement] *the house sounds lovely*.
– PHRASAL VERBS **sound off** express one's opinions in a loud or forceful manner: *Pietro started sounding off to the press*.
– DERIVATIVES **soundless** adjective, **soundlessly** adverb, **soundlessness** noun.
– ORIGIN Middle English *soun*, from Anglo-Norman French *soun* (noun), *suner* (verb), from Latin *sonus*. The form with *-d* was established in the 16th cent.

sound[2] ▶ **adjective 1** in good condition; not damaged, injured, or diseased: *they returned **safe and sound*** | *he was not of sound mind*. ■ financially secure: *she could get her business on a sound footing for the first time*. ■ Brit. informal excellent: *He ate his lasagne with relish. 'It's sound, this.'*.
2 based on valid reason or good judgement: *sound advice for healthy living* | *the scientific content is sound*. ■ competent, reliable, or holding acceptable views: *he's very **sound on** his law*.
3 (of sleep) deep and undisturbed. ■ (of a person) tending to sleep deeply.
4 (of a beating) severe: *such people should be given a sound thrashing*.
▶ **adverb** soundly: *he was sound asleep*.
– PHRASES **(as) sound as a bell** in perfect condition.
– DERIVATIVES **soundly** adverb, **soundness** noun.
– ORIGIN Middle English: from Old English *gesund*, of West Germanic origin; related to Dutch *gezond* and German *gesund*.

sound[3] ▶ **verb** [with obj.] **1** ascertain (the depth of water in the sea, a lake, or a river), typically by means of a line or pole or using sound echoes. ■ find the depth of water in (a ship's hold).
2 question (someone) discreetly or cautiously so as to ascertain their opinions on a subject: *we'll **sound out** parliament first*. ■ inquire into (someone's opinions) discreetly or cautiously: *officials arrived to **sound out** public opinion at meetings in factories*.
3 Medicine examine (a person's bladder or other internal cavity) with a long surgical probe.
4 [no obj.] (especially of a whale) dive down steeply to a great depth.
▶ **noun** a long surgical probe, typically with a curved, blunt end.
– DERIVATIVES **sounder** noun.

– ORIGIN late Middle English: from Old French *sonder*, based on Latin *sub-* 'below' + *unda* 'wave'.

sound[4] ▸ **noun** a narrow stretch of water forming an inlet or connecting two wider areas of water such as two seas or a sea and a lake. ■ (**the Sound**) another name for **ØRESUND**.
– ORIGIN Middle English: from Old Norse *sund* 'swimming, strait'; related to **SWIM**.

soundalike ▸ **noun** a person or thing that closely resembles another in sound, especially someone whose voice or style of speaking or singing is very similar to that of a famous person.

sound barrier ▸ **noun** (**the sound barrier**) the increased drag, reduced controllability, and other effects which occur when an aircraft approaches the speed of sound, formerly regarded as an obstacle to supersonic flight.

sound bite ▸ **noun** a short extract from a recorded interview or speech, chosen for its succinctness or concision.

soundboard (also **sounding board**) ▸ **noun** a thin sheet of wood over which the strings of a piano or similar instrument are positioned to increase the sound produced.

soundbox ▸ **noun** the hollow chamber forming the body of a stringed musical instrument and providing resonance.

sound card ▸ **noun** a device which can be slotted into a computer to allow the use of audio components for multimedia applications.

soundcheck ▸ **noun** a test of sound equipment before a musical performance or recording to check that the desired sound is being produced.

soundclash ▸ **noun 1** a head-to-head competition between DJs.
2 a piece of popular music that features a mixture or clash of very different styles.

sound conditioner ▸ **noun** a device designed to mask or block out undesirable sounds by generating white noise or some other continuous, unobtrusive sound.

sound effect ▸ **noun** a sound other than speech or music made artificially for use in a play, film, or other broadcast production.

sound engineer ▸ **noun** a technician dealing with acoustics for a broadcast or musical performance.

soundhole ▸ **noun** an aperture in the belly of a stringed instrument.

sounding[1] ▸ **noun 1** [mass noun] the action of measuring the depth of a body of water. ■ a measurement taken by sounding. ■ the determination of any physical property at a depth in the sea or at a height in the atmosphere. ■ (**soundings**) archaic the area of sea close to the shore which is shallow enough for the bottom to be reached by means of a sounding line.
2 (**soundings**) information or evidence ascertained as a preliminary step before taking action: *he took soundings about the possibility of moving offices.*

sounding[2] ▸ **adjective** archaic giving forth sound, especially loud or resonant sound: *he went in with a sounding plunge.* ■ having an imposing sound but little substance: *the orator has been apt to deal in sounding commonplaces.*

sounding board ▸ **noun 1** a board or screen placed over or behind a pulpit or stage to reflect a speaker's voice forward. ■ another term for **SOUNDBOARD**.
2 a person or group whose reactions to suggested ideas are used as a test of their validity or likely success before they are made public. ■ a channel through which ideas are disseminated.

sounding line ▸ **noun** a weighted line with distances marked off at regular intervals, used to measure the depth of water under a boat.

sounding rod ▸ **noun** a rod used to measure the depth of water under a boat or in a ship's hold or other container.

sound post ▸ **noun** a small wooden rod wedged between the front and back surfaces of a violin or similar instrument and modifying its vibrations.

sound pressure ▸ **noun** [mass noun] Physics the difference between the instantaneous pressure at a point in the presence of a sound wave and the static pressure of the medium.

soundproof ▸ **adjective** preventing, or constructed of material that prevents, the passage of sound.
▸ **verb** [with obj.] make (a room or building) resistant to the passage of sound.

soundscape ▸ **noun** a piece of music considered in terms of its component sounds: *his lush keyboard soundscapes.*

sound shift ▸ **noun** Linguistics a systematic change in the pronunciation of a set of speech sounds as a language evolves.

sound spectrograph ▸ **noun** an instrument for analysing sound into its frequency components.

sound stage ▸ **noun** an area of a film studio with acoustic properties suitable for the recording of sound, typically used to record dialogue.

sound symbolism ▸ **noun** [mass noun] the partial representation of the sense of a word by its sound, as in *bang*, *fizz*, and *slide*. See also **ONOMATOPOEIA**.

sound system ▸ **noun** a set of equipment for the reproduction and amplification of sound.

soundtrack ▸ **noun** a recording of the musical accompaniment of a film. ■ a strip on the edge of a film on which the sound component is recorded.
▸ **verb** [with obj.] provide (a film) with a soundtrack: *it is soundtracked by the great Ennio Morricone.*

sound wave ▸ **noun** Physics a wave of compression and rarefaction, by which sound is propagated in an elastic medium such as air.

soup ▸ **noun** [mass noun] **1** a liquid dish, typically savoury and made by boiling meat, fish, or vegetables etc. in stock or water: *a bowl of tomato soup.*
2 a substance or mixture regarded as resembling soup in appearance or consistency: *the waves and the water beyond have become a thick brown soup.* ■ informal the chemicals in which film is developed.
3 US informal nitroglycerine or gelignite, especially as used for safe-breaking.
▸ **verb** [with obj.] (**soup something up**) (often as adj. **souped-up**) informal increase the power and efficiency of an engine or other machine: *a souped-up Ford with big rear wheels.* [1930s, perhaps influenced by **SUPER-**.] ■ make something more elaborate or impressive: *we had to soup up the show for the new venue.*
– PHRASES **from soup to nuts** N. Amer. informal from beginning to end; completely: *I know all about that game from soup to nuts.* **in the soup** informal in trouble.
– ORIGIN Middle English: from Old French *soupe* 'sop, broth (poured on slices of bread)', from late Latin *suppa*, of Germanic origin.

soup and fish ▸ **noun** Brit. informal, dated men's evening dress.
– ORIGIN so named from the traditional first two courses of a formal dinner.

soupçon /ˈsuːpsɒn, -sɔ̃/ ▸ **noun** a very small quantity of something: *a soupçon of mustard.*
– ORIGIN mid 18th cent.: French, from Old French *souspeçon*, from medieval Latin *suspectio* (see **SUSPICION**).

soup kitchen ▸ **noun** a place where free food is served to those who are homeless or destitute.

soup plate ▸ **noun** a deep, wide-rimmed plate in which soup is served.

soup spoon ▸ **noun** a large spoon with a round bowl, used for eating soup.

soupy ▸ **adjective** (**soupier**, **soupiest**) having the appearance or consistency of soup: *a soupy stew.* ■ (of the air or climate) humid. ■ informal mawkishly sentimental: *soupy nostalgia.*
– DERIVATIVES **soupily** adverb, **soupiness** noun.

sour ▸ **adjective 1** having an acid taste like lemon or vinegar: *she sampled the wine and found it was sour.* ■ (of food, especially milk) having gone bad because of fermentation. ■ having a rancid smell: *her breath was always sour.*
2 feeling or expressing resentment, disappointment, or anger: *he gave her a sour look | the meeting ended on a sour note.*
3 (of soil) deficient in lime and usually dank.
4 (of petroleum or natural gas) containing a relatively high proportion of sulphur.
▸ **noun** [with modifier] a drink made by mixing a spirit with lemon or lime juice: *a rum sour.*
▸ **verb** make or become sour: [with obj.] *water soured with tamarind* | (as adj. **soured**) *soured cream.* ■ make or become unpleasant, acrimonious, or difficult: [with obj.] *a dispute soured relations between the two countries* | [no obj.] *many friendships have soured over borrowed money.*
– PHRASES **go** (or **turn**) **sour** become less pleasant; turn out badly: *their relationship began to turn sour.* **sour grapes** used to refer to an attitude in which someone adopts a negative attitude to something because they cannot have it themselves. [with allusion to Aesop's fable *The Fox and the Grapes*.]
– DERIVATIVES **sourish** adjective, **sourly** adverb, **sourness** noun.
– ORIGIN Old English *sūr*, of Germanic origin; related to Dutch *zuur* and German *sauer*.

source ▸ **noun 1** a place, person, or thing from which something originates or can be obtained: *mackerel is a good source of fish oil.* ■ a spring or fountain head from which a river or stream issues: *the source of the Nile.* ■ a person who provides information: *military sources announced a reduction in strategic nuclear weapons.* ■ a book or document used to provide evidence in research.
2 technical a body or process by which energy or a particular component enters a system. The opposite of **SINK**[2]. ■ Electronics a part of a field-effect transistor from which carriers flow into the inter-electrode channel.
▸ **verb** [with obj.] obtain from a particular source: *each type of coffee is sourced from one country.* ■ find out where (something) can be obtained: *she was called upon to source a supply of carpet.*
– PHRASES **at source** at the point of origin or issue: *reduction of pollution at source.* ■ used to show that a sum is deducted from earnings or other payments before they are made: *your pension contribution will be deducted at source.*
– ORIGIN late Middle English: from Old French *sours(e)*, past participle of *sourdre* 'to rise', from Latin *surgere*.

sourcebook ▸ **noun** a collection of writings and articles on a particular subject, especially one used as a basic introduction to that subject.

source code ▸ **noun** [mass noun] Computing a text listing of commands to be compiled or assembled into an executable computer program.

source criticism ▸ **noun** [mass noun] the analysis and study of the sources used by biblical authors.

source program ▸ **noun** Computing a program written in a language other than machine code, typically a high-level language.

source rock ▸ **noun** Geology a rock formation from which later sediments are derived or in which a particular mineral originates. ■ a sediment containing sufficient organic matter to be a future source of hydrocarbons.

sour cream ▸ **noun** [mass noun] cream which has been deliberately fermented by the addition of certain bacteria.

sourdough ▸ **noun 1** [mass noun] leaven for making bread, consisting of fermenting dough, originally that left over from a previous baking. ■ bread made using sourdough.
2 N. Amer. historical an experienced prospector in the western US or Canada.

sour grass ▸ **noun** [mass noun] grass which is coarse, unpalatable, or of very low nutritional value.
● Species in several genera of the family Gramineae, in particular *Elionurus* (in South Africa), and *Andropogon* and *Valota* (in the Caribbean).

sour mash ▸ **noun** [mass noun] US a mash used in distilling certain malt whiskeys. ■ whiskey distilled using sour mash.

sourpuss ▸ **noun** informal a bad-tempered or habitually sullen person.
– ORIGIN 1930s (originally US): from **SOUR** + **PUSS**[2].

soursop ▸ **noun 1** a large acidic custard apple with white fibrous flesh.
2 the evergreen tropical American tree which bears soursops. ● *Annona muricata*, family Annonaceae.

sourveld /ˈsaʊəvɛlt/ ▸ **noun** [mass noun] S. African land covered with coarse vegetation, or the vegetation itself.
– ORIGIN partial translation of South African Dutch *zuurveld*.

sourwood ▸ **noun** a North American tree of the heather family, which has acid-tasting leaves. Also called **SORREL TREE**. ● *Oxydendrum arboreum*, family Ericaceae.

sous- /suː(z)/ ▸ **prefix** (in words adopted from French) subordinate: *sous-chef.*
– ORIGIN from French *sous* 'under'.

Sousa /ˈsuːzə/, John Philip (1854–1932), American composer and conductor. His works include more than a hundred marches, for example *The Stars and Stripes*.

S

sousaphone /ˈsuːzəfəʊn/ ▸ **noun** an American form of tuba with a wide bell pointing forward above the player's head, used in marching bands.
– DERIVATIVES **sousaphonist** /-ˈzɒf(ə)nɪst/ **noun**.
– ORIGIN 1920s: named after J. P. **Sousa**, on the pattern of *saxophone*.

souse /saʊs/ ▸ **verb** [with obj.] soak in or drench with liquid: *the chips were well soused with vinegar*.
▸ **noun 1** [mass noun] liquid used for pickling. ■ N. Amer. & W. Indian food, especially a pig's head, in pickle.
2 informal a drunkard. ■ dated a period of heavy drinking.
– ORIGIN late Middle English (as a noun denoting pickled meat): from Old French *sous* 'pickle', of Germanic origin; related to **salt**.

soused ▸ **adjective 1** (of food, especially fish) preserved in pickle or a marinade: *soused herring*.
2 informal drunk: *I was soused to the eyeballs*.

souslik /ˈsuːslɪk/ (also **suslik**) ▸ **noun** a short-tailed ground squirrel native to Eurasia and the Arctic.
● Genus *Spermophilus*, family Sciuridae: several species, in particular the **European souslik** (*S. citellus*).
– ORIGIN late 18th cent.: from Russian.

sou-sou /ˈsuːsuː/ ▸ **noun** W. Indian a cooperative savings system in which each person contributes the same fixed amount each week, and the whole amount is taken by a different member each time.
– ORIGIN from Yoruba.

Sousse /suːs/ (also **Susah**, **Susa**) a port and resort on the east coast of Tunisia; pop. 173,000 (est. 2004).

sous vide /suː ˈviːd/ ▸ **noun** [mass noun] a method of treating food by partial cooking followed by vacuum-sealing and chilling.
▸ **adjective & adverb** (of food or cooking) involving such preparation: [as adj.] *a convection oven can be used in sous vide operations* | [as adv.] *cooking sous vide*.
– ORIGIN French, literally 'under vacuum'.

soutache /suːˈtaʃ/ ▸ **noun** a narrow, flat ornamental braid used to trim garments.
– ORIGIN mid 19th cent.: from French, from Hungarian *sujtás*.

soutane /suːˈtɑːn/ ▸ **noun** a type of cassock worn by Roman Catholic priests.
– ORIGIN mid 19th cent.: from French, from Italian *sottana*, from *sotto* 'under', from Latin *subtus*.

souteneur /ˌsuːtəˈnəː/ ▸ **noun** a pimp.
– ORIGIN French, literally 'protector'.

souter /ˈsuːtə/ (also **soutar**) ▸ **noun** Scottish & N. English a shoemaker.
– ORIGIN Old English *sūtere*, from Latin *sutor*, from *suere* 'sew'.

souterrain /ˈsuːtəreɪn/ ▸ **noun** chiefly Archaeology an underground chamber or passage.
– ORIGIN mid 18th cent.: from French, from *sous* 'under' + *terre* 'earth'.

south ▸ **noun** (usu. **the south**) **1** the direction towards the point of the horizon 90° clockwise from east: *the breeze came from the south* | *they trade with the countries to the south*. ■ the compass point corresponding to this.
2 the southern part of the world or of a specified country, region, or town: *he was staying in the south of France*. ■ (usu. **the South**) the southern part of England. ■ (usu. **the South**) the Southern states of the United States. ■ (usu. **the South**) the less industrialized and economically advanced nations of the world.
3 (**South**) [as name] Bridge the player sitting opposite and partnering North.
▸ **adjective** [attrib.] **1** lying towards, near, or facing the south: *the south coast*. ■ (of a wind) blowing from the south.
2 of or denoting the southern part of an area, city, or country or its inhabitants: *South America*.
▸ **adverb 1** to or towards the south: *they journeyed south along the valley* | *the village is a few miles south of Cambridge*.
2 (**south of**) below (a particular amount, cost, etc.): *media spending last year was south of $1 million*.
▸ **verb** [no obj.] move towards the south: *the wind southed a point or two*. ■ (of a celestial object) cross the meridian.
– PHRASES **down south** informal to or in the south of a country. **go south** informal, chiefly N. Amer. fall in value, deteriorate, or fail. **south by east** (or **west**) between south and south-south-east (or south-south-west).
– ORIGIN Old English *sūth*, of Germanic origin; related to Low German *sud*.

S

South Africa a country occupying the southernmost part of the continent of Africa; pop. 49,052,500 (est. 2009); languages: official languages, English, Afrikaans, Zulu, Xhosa, and other languages; administrative capital, Pretoria; seat of legislature, Cape Town.

> Inhabited by Khoisan people in the south and south-east and various Bantu-speaking peoples in the eastern, central, and northern areas, the region was settled by the Dutch in the 17th century, the area of the Cape coming under British administration in 1806. There followed inland expansion and British dominance of local populations, culminating in victory in the Zulu and Boer Wars at the end of the 19th century. The colonies of Natal, the Cape, Transvaal, and Orange Free State joined to form the self-governing Union of South Africa in 1910. In 1961 South Africa became a republic and left the Commonwealth. From 1948 it pursued a policy of white minority rule (apartheid), which led to international diplomatic isolation. A gradual dismantling of apartheid began in 1990 following the release of the African National Congress leader Nelson Mandela. Majority rule was achieved after the country's first democratic elections in April 1994, won by the ANC. South Africa rejoined the Commonwealth in 1994.

South African ▸ **noun** a native or inhabitant of South Africa.
▸ **adjective** relating to South Africa. ■ Botany relating to or denoting a phytogeographical kingdom comprising only the Cape region.

South African Dutch ▸ **noun** [mass noun] the Afrikaans language from the 17th to the 19th centuries, during its development from Dutch.
▸ **adjective** dated or derogatory relating to Afrikaans-speaking South Africans.

South America a continent comprising the southern half of the American land mass, connected to North America by the Isthmus of Panama. It includes the Falkland Islands, the Galapagos Islands, and Tierra del Fuego (See also **America**.).
– DERIVATIVES **South American adjective & noun**.

Southampton /saʊθˈ(h)am(p)tə()n, saʊˈθam(p)t(ə)n/ an industrial city and seaport on the south coast of England, in Hampshire; pop. 234,800 (est. 2009). It lies at the end of Southampton Water, an inlet of the English Channel opposite the Isle of Wight.

South Asia the southern part of Asia, in particular India, Pakistan, Bangladesh, Nepal, and Sri Lanka.
– DERIVATIVES **South Asian noun & adjective**.

South Atlantic Ocean see **Atlantic Ocean**.

South Australia a state comprising the central southern part of Australia; pop. 1,603,361 (2008); capital, Adelaide. Constituted as a semi-independent colony in 1836, it became a Crown Colony in 1841 and was federated with the other states of Australia in 1901.

South Bank the area adjacent to the southern bank of the River Thames in London, especially the cultural complex located between Westminster and Blackfriars Bridges.

southbound ▸ **adjective** travelling or leading towards the south: *southbound traffic* | *the southbound carriageway of the A1*.

South Carolina a state of the US on the Atlantic coast; pop. 4,479,800 (est. 2008); capital, Columbia. The region was permanently settled by the English from 1663. Separated from North Carolina in 1729, South Carolina became one of the original thirteen states of the Union (1788). In 1860 it was the first state to secede from the Union, precipitating the American Civil War.
– DERIVATIVES **South Carolinian noun & adjective**.

South China Sea see **China Sea**.

South Dakota a state in the north central US; pop. 804,194 (est. 2008); capital, Pierre. Acquired partly by the Louisiana Purchase in 1803, it became a part of the former Dakota Territory in 1861. It separated from North Dakota in 1889, becoming the 40th state of the US.
– DERIVATIVES **South Dakotan noun & adjective**.

South Devon ▸ **noun** an animal of a breed of large light red or fawn cattle.

Southdown ▸ **noun** a sheep of a breed raised especially for mutton, originally on the South Downs of Hampshire and Sussex.

south-east ▸ **noun 1** (usu. **the south-east**) the direction towards the point of the horizon midway between south and east: *a ship was coming in from the south-east*. ■ the compass point corresponding to this.
2 the south-eastern part of a country, region, or town.
▸ **adjective** [attrib.] **1** lying towards, near, or facing the south-east: *a table stood in the south-east corner*. ■ (of a wind) blowing from the south-east.
2 of or denoting the south-eastern part of a specified country, region, or town or its inhabitants: *South East Asia*.
▸ **adverb** to or towards the south-east: *turn south-east to return to your starting point*.
– DERIVATIVES **south-eastern adjective**.

South East Asia the part of south-eastern Asia that includes the countries of Cambodia, Indonesia, Laos, Malaysia, Burma (Myanmar), the Philippines, Singapore, Thailand, and Vietnam.

South East Asia Treaty Organization (abbrev.: **SEATO**) a defence alliance which existed between 1954 and 1977 for countries of SE Asia and part of the SW Pacific, to further a US policy of containing Communism. Its members were Australia, Britain, France, New Zealand, Pakistan, the Philippines, Thailand, and the US.

southeaster ▸ **noun** a wind blowing from the south-east.

south-easterly ▸ **adjective & adverb** another term for **south-east**.
▸ **noun** another term for **southeaster**.

South-East Iceland a shipping forecast area covering part of the NE Atlantic between Iceland and the Faroes.

south-eastward ▸ **adverb** (also **south-eastwards**) towards the south-east: *he walked south-eastwards from the river*.
▸ **adjective** situated in, directed toward, or facing the south-east.

Southend-on-Sea a resort town in Essex, SE England, on the Thames estuary east of London; pop. 156,400 (est. 2009).

South Equatorial Current an ocean current that flows westwards across the Pacific Ocean just south of the equator.

southerly /ˈsʌðəli/ ▸ **adjective & adverb** in a southward position or direction: *the most southerly of the Greek islands* | [as adv.] *they made off southerly*. ■ (of a wind) blowing from the south.
▸ **noun** (often **southerlies**) a wind blowing from the south.

southern /ˈsʌð(ə)n/ ▸ **adjective 1** [attrib.] situated in the south or directed towards or facing the south: *the southern hemisphere*. ■ (of a wind) blowing from the south.
2 living in or originating from the south: *the southern rural poor*. ■ relating to or characteristic of the south or its inhabitants: *a faintly southern accent*.
– DERIVATIVES **southernmost adjective**.
– ORIGIN Old English *sūtherne* (see **south**, **-ern**).

Southern Alps a mountain range in the South Island, New Zealand. Running roughly parallel to the west coast, it extends for almost the entire length of the island. At Aoraki/Mount Cook, its highest peak, it rises to 3,764 m (12,349 ft).

Southern Baptist ▸ **noun** a member of a large convention of Baptist churches established in the US in 1845, typically having a fundamentalist and evangelistic approach to Christianity.

Southern blot ▸ **noun** Biology a procedure for identifying specific sequences of DNA, in which fragments separated on a gel are transferred directly to a second medium on which assay by hybridization may be carried out.
– ORIGIN late 20th cent.: named after Edwin M. *Southern* (born 1938), British biochemist.

Southern Comfort ▸ **noun** [mass noun] trademark a whisky-based alcoholic drink of US origin.

Southern Cone ▸ **noun** the region of South America comprising the countries of Paraguay, Uruguay, Argentina, Chile, and southern Brazil.

Southern Cross Astronomy the constellation Crux.

southerner ▸ **noun** a native or inhabitant of the south, especially of the southern United States or southern England.

southern-fried ▸ **adjective** chiefly N. Amer. (of food, especially chicken) coated in flour, egg, and breadcrumbs and then deep-fried.

southern hemisphere the half of the earth that is south of the equator.

Southern Lights another name for the aurora australis. See **AURORA**.

Southern Ocean the expanse of ocean surrounding Antarctica.

Southern Paiute ▸ noun & adjective see **PAIUTE**.

Southern Rhodesia see **ZIMBABWE**.

southernwood ▸ noun a bushy artemisia of southern Europe. Also called **LAD'S LOVE**. ● *Artemisia abrotanum*, family Compositae.

Southey /ˈsʌði, ˈsaʊði/, Robert (1774–1843), English poet. Associated with the Lake Poets, he is best known for his shorter poems, such as the 'Battle of Blenheim' (1798). He was made Poet Laureate in 1813.

South Georgia a British overseas territory in the South Atlantic, a barren island situated 1,120 km (700 miles) east of the Falkland Islands. It was first explored in 1775 by Captain James Cook, who named the island after George III.

South Glamorgan a former county of South Wales, on the Bristol Channel, dissolved in 1996.

southing ▸ noun [mass noun] distance travelled or measured southward, especially at sea. ■ [count noun] a figure or line representing southward distance on a map. ■ Astronomy the transit of a celestial object, especially the sun, across the meridian due south of the observer. ■ [count noun] Astronomy the angular distance of a star or other object south of the celestial equator.

South Island the more southerly and larger of the two main islands of New Zealand, separated from the North Island by Cook Strait.

South Korea a country in East Asia, occupying the southern part of the peninsula of Korea; pop. 48,509,000 (est. 2009); official language, Korean; capital, Seoul. Official name **KOREA, REPUBLIC OF**.

> South Korea was formed in 1948, when Korea was partitioned along the 38th parallel. The Korean War (1950–3) was followed by decades of hostility between North and South Korea, but a summit meeting of the two leaders was held in 2000. An emerging industrial power, South Korea has had one of the world's fastest-growing economies since the 1960s.

– DERIVATIVES **South Korean** adjective & noun.

South Orkney Islands a group of uninhabited islands in the South Atlantic, lying to the north-east of the Antarctic Peninsula. Discovered in 1821, the islands are administered as part of the British Antarctic Territory.

South Ossetia an autonomous region of Georgia, situated in the Caucasus on the border with Russia; capital, Tskhinvali. See also **OSSETIA**.

South Pacific Commission an agency established in 1947 to promote the economic and social stability of the islands in the South Pacific, having twenty-seven member governments and administrations.

southpaw ▸ noun a left-handed boxer who leads with the right hand. ■ Baseball a left-handed pitcher. ■ informal, chiefly N. Amer. a left-hander in any sphere.
– ORIGIN mid 19th cent. (denoting the left hand or a punch with the left hand): the usage in baseball is from the orientation of the diamond to the same points of the compass, causing the pitcher to have his left hand on the south side of his body.

South Pole ▸ noun see **POLE²**.

Southport a resort town in NW England, on the Irish Sea coast north of Liverpool; pop. 88,000 (est. 2009).

South Sandwich Islands a group of uninhabited volcanic islands in the South Atlantic, lying 480 km (300 miles) south-east of South Georgia. They are administered from the Falkland Islands.

South Sea (also **South Seas**) archaic the southern Pacific Ocean.

South Sea Bubble a speculative boom in the shares of the South Sea Company in 1720 which ended with the failure of the company and a general financial collapse.

South Shetland Islands a group of uninhabited islands in the South Atlantic, lying north of the Antarctic Peninsula. Discovered in 1819, the islands are administered as part of the British Antarctic Territory.

South Shields a port on the coast of NE England, at the mouth of the Tyne opposite North Shields; pop. 79,200 (est. 2009).

south-south-east ▸ noun the compass point or direction midway between south and south-east.

south-south-west ▸ noun the compass point or direction midway between south and south-west.

South Uist see **UIST**.

South Utsire see **UTSIRE**.

southward /ˈsaʊθwəd/, Nautical /ˈsʌðəd/ ▸ adjective in a southerly direction: *people began a southward drift.*
▸ adverb (also **southwards**) towards the south: *the village stretches southwards across the plain.*
▸ noun (**the southward**) the direction or region to the south: *cool air from the ocean to the southward.*
– DERIVATIVES **southwardly** adjective & adverb.

south-west ▸ noun **1** (usu. **the south-west**) the direction towards the point of the horizon midway between south and west: *clouds uncoiled from the south-west.* ■ the compass point corresponding to this.
2 the south-western part of a country, region, or town.
▸ adjective [attrib.] **1** lying towards, near, or facing the south-west: *the south-west tower collapsed in a storm.* ■ (of a wind) blowing from the south-west.
2 of or denoting the south-western part of a specified country, region, or town or its inhabitants: *south-west London.*
▸ adverb to or towards the south-west: *they drove directly south-west.*
– DERIVATIVES **south-western** adjective.

South West Africa former name for **NAMIBIA**.

South West Africa People's Organization (abbrev.: **SWAPO**) a nationalist organization formed in Namibia in 1964–6 to oppose the illegitimate South African rule over the region. It waged a guerrilla campaign, operating largely from Angola; it eventually gained UN recognition, and won elections in 1989.

southwester ▸ noun a wind blowing from the south-west.

south-westerly ▸ adjective & adverb another term for **SOUTH-WEST**.
▸ noun another term for **SOUTHWESTER**.

south-westward ▸ adverb (also **south-westwards**) towards the south-west: *the governor sent two companies of foot soldiers south-westwards.*
▸ adjective situated in, directed toward, or facing the south-west: *the south-westward extension of the valley.*

South Yorkshire a metropolitan county of northern England.

Soutine /suːˈtiːn/, Chaim (1893–1943), French painter, born in Lithuania. A major exponent of expressionism, he produced pictures of grotesque figures during the 1920s, while from 1925 he increasingly painted still lifes.

souvenir /ˌsuːvəˈnɪə/ ▸ noun a thing that is kept as a reminder of a person, place, or event.
▸ verb [with obj.] informal take as a memento: *many parts of the aircraft have been souvenired.*
– ORIGIN late 18th cent.: from French, from *souvenir* 'remember', from Latin *subvenire* 'occur to the mind'.

souvlaki /suːˈvlɑːki/ ▸ noun (pl. **souvlakia** /-kɪə/ or **souvlakis**) [mass noun] a Greek dish of pieces of meat grilled on a skewer.
– ORIGIN modern Greek.

sou'wester /saʊˈwɛstə/ ▸ noun a waterproof hat with a broad flap covering the neck.

sov ▸ noun Brit. informal a pound sterling.
– ORIGIN early 19th cent.: abbreviation of **SOVEREIGN**.

sovereign ▸ noun **1** a supreme ruler, especially a monarch.
2 a former British gold coin worth one pound sterling, now only minted for commemorative purposes.
▸ adjective **1** possessing supreme or ultimate power: *in modern democracies the people's will is in theory sovereign.* ■ [attrib.] (of a nation or its affairs) acting or done independently and without outside interference: *a sovereign, democratic republic.* ■ [attrib.] archaic or literary possessing royal power and status: *our most sovereign lord the King.*
2 [attrib.] dated very good or effective: *a sovereign remedy for all ills.*
– DERIVATIVES **sovereignly** adverb.
– ORIGIN Middle English: from Old French *soverain*, based on Latin *super* 'above'. The change in the ending was due to association with **REIGN**.

sovereign good ▸ noun (**the sovereign good**) the greatest good, especially that of a state or its people.

sovereign pontiff ▸ noun see **PONTIFF**.

sovereigntist ▸ noun Canadian a person who supports Quebec's right to self-government or full independence.

sovereignty ▸ noun (pl. **sovereignties**) [mass noun] supreme power or authority: *the sovereignty of Parliament.* ■ the authority of a state to govern itself or another state: *national sovereignty.* ■ [count noun] a self-governing state.
– ORIGIN late Middle English: from Old French *sovereinete*, from *soverain* (see **SOVEREIGN**).

sovereign wealth fund ▸ noun a state-owned investment fund.

soviet /ˈsəʊvɪət, ˈsɒv-/ ▸ noun **1** an elected local, district, or national council in the former Soviet Union. ■ a revolutionary council of workers or peasants in Russia before 1917.
2 (**Soviet**) a citizen of the former Soviet Union.
▸ adjective (**Soviet**) of or concerning the former Soviet Union: *the Soviet leader.*
– DERIVATIVES **Sovietism** noun, **Sovietization** noun, **Sovietize** (also **Sovietise**) verb.
– ORIGIN early 20th cent.: from Russian *sovet* 'council'.

Sovietologist /ˌsəʊvɪəˈtɒlədʒɪst, ˌsɒ-/ ▸ noun a person who studies the former Soviet Union.
– DERIVATIVES **Sovietological** adjective, **Sovietology** noun.

Soviet Union a former federation of Communist republics occupying the northern half of Asia and part of eastern Europe; capital, Moscow. Full name **UNION OF SOVIET SOCIALIST REPUBLICS**.

> Created from the Russian empire in the aftermath of the 1917 Russian Revolution, the Soviet Union was the largest country in the world. It comprised fifteen republics: Russia, Belarus, Ukraine, Georgia, Armenia, Moldova, Azerbaijan, Kazakhstan, Kyrgyzstan, Turkmenistan, Tajikistan, Uzbekistan, and the three Baltic states Estonia, Latvia, and Lithuania (annexed in 1940). After the Second World War, the Soviet Union emerged as a superpower in rivalry with the US, leading to the Cold War. Decades of repression and economic failure eventually led to attempts at liberalization and economic reform under President Mikhail Gorbachev during the 1980s. The Soviet Union was formally dissolved in 1991, some of its constituents joining a looser confederation, the Commonwealth of Independent States.

sovkhoz /ˈsɒvkɒz, sʌvˈkɔːz/ ▸ noun (pl. **same**, **sovkhozes** /ˈsɒvkɒzɪz, sʌvˈkɔːzɪz/, or **sovkhozy** /ˈsɒvkɒzi, sʌvˈkɔːzi/) a state-owned farm in the former Soviet Union.
– ORIGIN Russian, from *sov(etskoe) khoz(yaĭstvo)* 'Soviet farm'.

sow¹ /səʊ/ ▸ verb (past **sowed** /səʊd/; past participle **sown** /səʊn/ or **sowed**) [with obj.] **1** plant (seed) by scattering it on or in the earth: *fill a pot with compost and sow a thin layer of seeds on top.* ■ plant the seeds of (a plant or crop): *catch crops should be sown after minimal cultivation.* ■ plant (a piece of land) with seed: *the field used to be sown with oats.* ■ (**be sown with**) be thickly covered with: *the night sky was sown with stars.* ■ lay or plant (an explosive mine) or cover (territory) with mines.
2 disseminate or introduce (something undesirable): *the new policy has sown confusion and doubt.*
– PHRASES **sow the seed** (or **seeds**) **of** do something which will eventually bring about (a particular result): *the seeds of dissension had been sown.* **sow one's wild oats** see **OAT**.
– DERIVATIVES **sower** noun.
– ORIGIN Old English *sāwan*, of Germanic origin; related to Dutch *zaaien* and German *säen*.

sow² /saʊ/ ▸ noun **1** an adult female pig, especially one which has farrowed. ■ the female of certain other mammals, e.g. the guinea pig.
2 a large block of metal (larger than a 'pig') made by smelting.
– PHRASES **you can't make a silk purse out of a sow's ear** proverb you can't create a fine product from inferior materials.
– ORIGIN Old English *sugu*; related to Dutch *zeug*, German *Sau*, from an Indo-European root shared by Latin *sus* and Greek *hus* 'pig'.

sowback /ˈsaʊbak/ ▸ noun a low ridge of sand.

sowbread /ˈsaʊbrɛd/ ▸ noun a cyclamen with pale pink or white flowers and leaves that do not appear until late summer after flowering, native to southern Eurasia. ● *Cyclamen hederifolium*, family Primulaceae.
– ORIGIN mid 16th cent.: so named because the roots are reputedly eaten by wild boars in Sicily.

S

sowbug /ˈsaʊbʌɡ/ ▸ **noun** chiefly N. Amer. another term for **WOODLOUSE**.

Soweto /səˈwɛtəʊ, -ˈweɪtəʊ/ a large urban area, consisting of several townships, in South Africa south-west of Johannesburg. In 1976 demonstrations against the compulsory use of Afrikaans in schools resulted in violent police activity and the deaths of hundreds of people.
– DERIVATIVES **Sowetan** noun & adjective.
– ORIGIN from *So(uth) We(stern) To(wnships)*.

sown past participle of **SOW**[1].

sowthistle /ˈsaʊθɪs(ə)l/ ▸ **noun** a Eurasian plant with yellow flowers, thistle-like leaves, and milky sap. Also called **MILK THISTLE**. ● Genus *Sonchus*, family Compositae.

sox ▸ **noun** chiefly N. Amer. non-standard plural spelling of **SOCK** (sense 1 of the noun).

Soxhlet /ˈsɒkslət/ ▸ **noun** [as modifier] Chemistry denoting a form of condensing apparatus used for the continuous solvent extraction of a solid.
– ORIGIN late 19th cent.: named after Franz *Soxhlet* (1848–1926), Belgian chemist.

soy ▸ **noun 1** (also **soy sauce**) [mass noun] a sauce made with fermented soya beans, used in Chinese and Japanese cooking.
2 another term for **SOYA**.
– ORIGIN from Japanese *shō-yu*, from Chinese *shi-yu*, from *shi* 'salted beans' + *yu* 'oil'.

soya ▸ **noun** [mass noun] Brit. **1** protein derived from the beans of an Asian plant, used as a replacement for animal protein in certain foods. ■ (also **soya sauce**) soy sauce.
2 the widely cultivated plant of the pea family which produces soya beans. ● *Glycine max*, family Leguminosae.
– ORIGIN late 17th cent.: from Dutch *soja*, from Malay *soi* (see **SOY**).

soya meal ▸ **noun** [mass noun] the residue of soya bean seeds after the extraction of their oil, used as animal feed.

soya milk ▸ **noun** [mass noun] the liquid obtained by suspending soya bean flour in water, used as a fat-free substitute for milk, particularly by vegans.

soybean (also **soya bean**) ▸ **noun** a bean of the soya plant.

Soyinka /ʃɔɪˈɪŋkə/, Wole (b.1934), Nigerian dramatist, novelist, and critic. In 1986 he became the first African to receive the Nobel Prize for Literature. Notable works: *The Lion and the Jewel* (play, 1959) and *The Interpreters* (novel, 1965).

Soyuz /sɔɪˈjuːz, ˈsɔɪjʊz/ a series of manned Soviet orbiting spacecraft, used to investigate the operation of orbiting space stations.

sozzled ▸ **adjective** informal very drunk.
– ORIGIN late 19th cent.: past participle of dialect *sozzle* 'mix sloppily', probably of imitative origin.

SP ▸ **abbreviation** starting price.

sp. ▸ **abbreviation** species (usually singular).

Spa /spɑː/ a small town in eastern Belgium, south-east of Liège; pop. 10,549 (2008). It has been celebrated since medieval times for the curative properties of its mineral springs.

spa ▸ **noun 1** a mineral spring considered to have health-giving properties. ■ a place or resort with such a spring. ■ a commercial establishment offering health and beauty treatment through such means as steam baths, exercise equipment, and massage.
2 (also **spa bath** or **pool**) a bath containing hot aerated water.
– ORIGIN early 17th cent.: from **SPA**.

space ▸ **noun** [mass noun] **1** a continuous area or expanse which is free, available, or unoccupied: *a table took up much of the space* | [count noun] *we shall all be living together in a small space* | *he reversed out of the parking space*. ■ [count noun] an area of land which is not occupied by buildings: *she had a love of open spaces*. ■ (also **commercial space**) an area rented or sold as business premises. ■ [count noun] a blank between printed, typed, or written words, characters, numbers, etc. ■ [count noun] Music each of the four gaps between the five lines of a stave.
2 the dimensions of height, depth, and width within which all things exist and move: *the work gives the sense of a journey in space and time*. ■ (also **outer space**) the physical universe beyond the earth's atmosphere. ■ the near-vacuum extending between the planets and stars, containing small amounts of gas and dust. ■ Mathematics a mathematical concept generally regarded as a set of points having some specified structure.
3 an interval of time (often used to suggest that the time is short considering what has happened or been achieved in it): *both their cars were stolen in the space of three days*.
4 the amount of paper used or needed to write about a subject: *there is no space to give further details*. ■ pages in a newspaper, or time between television or radio programmes, available for advertising.
5 the freedom to live, think, and develop in a way that suits one: *a teenager needing her own space*.
6 Telecommunications one of two possible states of a signal in certain systems. The opposite of **MARK**[1].
▸ **verb 1** [with obj.] position (two or more items) at a distance from one another: *the poles are spaced 3m apart*. ■ (in printing or writing) put blanks between (words, letters, or lines): (as noun **spacing**) *the default setting is single line spacing*.
2 (**be spaced out** or chiefly N. Amer. **space out**) informal be or become euphoric or unaware of one's surroundings, especially from taking drugs: *I was so tired that I began to feel totally spaced out* | *I kind of space out for a few minutes*.
– PHRASES **watch this space** informal further developments are expected and more information will be given later.
– DERIVATIVES **spacer** noun.
– ORIGIN Middle English: shortening of Old French *espace*, from Latin *spatium*. Current verb senses date from the late 17th cent.

space age ▸ **noun** (**the space age**) the era starting when the exploration of space became possible.
▸ **adjective** (**space-age**) very modern; technologically advanced: *a space-age control room*.

space bar ▸ **noun** a long key on a typewriter or computer keyboard for making a space between words.

space blanket ▸ **noun** a light metal-coated sheet designed to retain heat, originally developed for use in space travel.

space cadet ▸ **noun 1** a trainee astronaut.
2 informal a person regarded as being out of touch with reality.

space capsule ▸ **noun** a small spacecraft or the part of a larger one that contains the instruments or crew.

space charge ▸ **noun** Physics a collection of particles with a net electric charge occupying a region, either in free space or in a device.

spacecraft ▸ **noun** (pl. **same** or **spacecrafts**) a vehicle used for travelling in space.

space density ▸ **noun** Astronomy the frequency of occurrence of stars, particles, or other celestial objects, per specified volume of space.

spacefaring ▸ **noun** [mass noun] the action or activity of travelling in space.
– DERIVATIVES **spacefarer** noun.

space flight ▸ **noun** a journey through space. ■ [mass noun] space travel.

space frame ▸ **noun** a three-dimensional structural framework which is designed to behave as an integral unit and to withstand loads applied at any point.

space group ▸ **noun** Crystallography any of 230 symmetry groups used to classify crystal structures.

space heater ▸ **noun** a self-contained appliance for heating an enclosed space within a building.
– DERIVATIVES **space heating** noun.

spacehopper ▸ **noun** Brit. trademark a toy for sitting on and bouncing around, consisting of a large plastic orange ball with horn-like projections at the top to hold on to.

space lattice ▸ **noun** Crystallography a regular, indefinitely repeated array of points in three dimensions in which the points lie at the intersections of three sets of parallel equidistant planes.

spaceman (or **spacewoman**) ▸ **noun** (pl. **spacemen** or **spacewomen**) an astronaut.

space opera ▸ **noun** informal, chiefly N. Amer. a novel, film, or television programme set in outer space, typically of a simplistic and melodramatic nature.

spaceplane ▸ **noun** an aircraft that takes off and lands conventionally but is capable of entry into orbit or travel through space.

spaceport ▸ **noun** a base from which spacecraft are launched.

space probe ▸ **noun** see **PROBE**.

space race ▸ **noun** (**the space race**) the competition between nations regarding achievements in the field of space exploration.

space rocket ▸ **noun** a rocket designed to travel through space or to launch a spacecraft.

space-saving ▸ **adjective** occupying little space; enabling the available space to be used economically: *a space-saving flat LCD screen*.

spaceship ▸ **noun** a spacecraft, especially one controlled by a crew.

Spaceship Earth ▸ **noun** the world considered as possessing finite resources common to all humankind.

space shot ▸ **noun** the launch of a spacecraft and its subsequent progress in space.

space shuttle ▸ **noun** a rocket-launched spacecraft able to land like an unpowered aircraft, used to make repeated journeys between the earth and space.

space station ▸ **noun** a large artificial satellite used as a long-term base for manned operations in space.

spacesuit ▸ **noun** a garment designed to allow an astronaut to survive in space.

space telescope ▸ **noun** an astronomical telescope that operates in space by remote control, to avoid interference by the earth's atmosphere.

space–time ▸ **noun** [mass noun] Physics the concepts of time and three-dimensional space regarded as fused in a four-dimensional continuum.

space travel ▸ **noun** [mass noun] travel through outer space.
– DERIVATIVES **space traveller** noun.

space vehicle ▸ **noun** a spacecraft.

spacewalk ▸ **noun** a period of physical activity engaged in by an astronaut in space outside a spacecraft.
▸ **verb** undertake a spacewalk.
– DERIVATIVES **spacewalker** noun.

space warp ▸ **noun** an imaginary or hypothetical distortion of space–time that enables space travellers to travel faster than light or otherwise make journeys contrary to the laws of physics.

spacey (also **spacy**) ▸ **adjective** (**spacier**, **spaciest**) informal unaware of one's surroundings or in a state of euphoria, especially as a result of taking drugs. ■ (of popular, especially electronic music) drifting and ethereal.

spacial ▸ **adjective** variant spelling of **SPATIAL**.

spacious ▸ **adjective** (especially of a room or building) having ample space.
– DERIVATIVES **spaciously** adverb, **spaciousness** noun.
– ORIGIN late Middle English: from Old French *spacios* or Latin *spatiosus*, from *spatium* (see **SPACE**).

spackle /ˈspak(ə)l/ ▸ **noun** [mass noun] N. Amer. trademark a compound used to fill cracks in plaster and produce a smooth surface before decoration.
▸ **verb** [with obj.] repair (a surface) or fill (a hole or crack) with spackle.
– ORIGIN 1920s: perhaps a blend of **SPARKLE** and German *Spachtel* 'putty knife, mastic'.

SPAD ▸ **abbreviation** Brit. (on a railway) signal passed at danger.

spade[1] ▸ **noun** a tool with a sharp-edged, typically rectangular, metal blade and a long handle, used for digging or cutting earth, sand, turf, etc. ■ a tool of a similar shape for another purpose, especially one for removing the blubber from a whale. ■ [as modifier] shaped like a spade: *a spade bit*.
▸ **verb** [with obj.] dig over (ground) with a spade: *while spading the soil, I think of the flowers*. ■ [with obj. and adverbial of direction] move (soil) with a spade: *earth is spaded into the grave*.
– PHRASES **call a spade a spade** speak plainly without avoiding unpleasant or embarrassing issues.
– DERIVATIVES **spadeful** noun (pl. **spadefuls**).
– ORIGIN Old English *spadu*, *spada*, of Germanic origin; related to Dutch *spade*, German *Spaten*, also to Greek *spathē* 'blade, paddle'.

spade[2] ▸ **noun 1** (**spades**) one of the four suits in a conventional pack of playing cards, denoted by a black inverted heart-shaped figure with a small stalk. ■ (**a spade**) a card of the suit of spades.
2 informal, offensive a black person.
– PHRASES **in spades** informal to a very high degree: *he got his revenge now in spades*.
– ORIGIN late 16th cent.: from Italian *spade*, plural of *spada* 'sword', via Latin from Greek *spathē*; compare with **SPADE**[1].

spade beard ▸ **noun** an oblong-shaped beard.

spadefish ▸ **noun** (pl. **same** or **spadefishes**) a marine fish with an almost disc-shaped body. It lives in tropical inshore waters, where it often forms schools. ● *Chaetodipterus* and other genera, family Ephippidae: several species, including the western Atlantic *C. faber*.

spadefoot (also **spadefoot toad**) ▸ **noun** (pl. **spadefoots**) a plump, short-legged burrowing toad with a prominent sharp-edged tubercle on the hind feet, native to North America and Europe. ● Family Pelobatidae: several genera, including *Scaphiophus* (of America) and *Pelobates* (of Europe), and several species, in particular *P. fuscus*.

spade foot ▸ **noun** a square enlargement at the end of a chair leg.

spade guinea ▸ **noun** a guinea of George III's reign with a spade-shaped shield on the reverse.

spadework ▸ **noun** [mass noun] hard or routine preparatory work.

spadille /spəˈdɪl/ ▸ **noun** (in the card games ombre and quadrille) the ace of spades.
– ORIGIN late 17th cent.: from French, from Spanish *espadilla*, diminutive of *espada* 'sword' (see SPADE[2]).

spadix /ˈspeɪdɪks/ ▸ **noun** (pl. **spadices** /-siːz/) **1** Botany a spike of minute flowers closely arranged round a fleshy axis and typically enclosed in a spathe, characteristic of the arums.
2 Zoology (in certain invertebrates) a part or organ which is more or less conical in shape, e.g. a group of connected tentacles in a nautiloid.
– ORIGIN mid 18th cent.: via Latin from Greek, literally 'palm branch'.

spae /speɪ/ ▸ **verb** [with obj.] Scottish predict; foretell.
– ORIGIN Middle English: from Old Norse *spá*, of unknown origin.

spaetzle /ˈʃpɛtslə, ˈʃpɛts(ə)l/ (also **spätzle**) ▸ **plural noun** [treated as sing. or pl.] small dumplings of a type made in southern Germany and Alsace, consisting of seasoned dough poached in boiling water.
– ORIGIN from German dialect *Spätzle*, literally 'little sparrows'.

spaewife ▸ **noun** Scottish a woman who is believed to be able to predict the future.

spag bol ▸ **noun** informal, chiefly Brit. spaghetti Bolognese.

spaghetti /spəˈɡɛti/ ▸ **plural noun** pasta made in solid strings, between macaroni and vermicelli in thickness.
– ORIGIN Italian, plural of the diminutive of *spago* 'string'.

spaghetti bolognese /spəˌɡɛti bɒləˈneɪz/ ▸ **noun** [mass noun] spaghetti served with a sauce of minced beef, tomato, onion, and herbs.
– ORIGIN Italian, literally 'spaghetti of Bologna'.

spaghettification ▸ **noun** [mass noun] Physics the process by which (in some theories) an object would be stretched and ripped apart by gravitational forces on falling into a black hole.

spaghettini /ˌspaɡeˈtiːni/ ▸ **plural noun** pasta in the form of strings of thin spaghetti.
– ORIGIN Italian, diminutive of *spaghetti* 'little strings' (see SPAGHETTI).

spaghetti squash ▸ **noun** another term for VEGETABLE SPAGHETTI.

spaghetti strap ▸ **noun** a thin shoulder strap on an item of women's clothing.

spaghetti western ▸ **noun** informal a western film made cheaply in Europe by an Italian director.

spagyric /spəˈdʒɪrɪk/ archaic or literary ▸ **adjective** relating to alchemy.
▸ **noun** an alchemist.
– ORIGIN late 16th cent.: modern Latin *spagiricus*, used and probably invented by Paracelsus.

spahi /ˈspɑːhiː/ ▸ **noun** historical **1** a member of the Turkish irregular cavalry.
2 a member of the Algerian cavalry in French service.
– ORIGIN mid 16th cent.: from Turkish *sipahi*, from Persian *sipāhī* (see SEPOY).

Spain a country in SW Europe, occupying the greater part of the Iberian peninsula; pop. 40,525,000 (est. 2009); languages, Spanish (official), Catalan; capital, Madrid. Spanish name **España**.

> Spain was dominated by the Moors from about 718 until the rise of independent Christian kingdoms, notably Aragon and Castile; the last Moorish stronghold, Granada, was won back in the late 15th century. Under the Habsburg kings of the 16th century Spain became the dominant European power, building up a huge empire in America and elsewhere; most of this was lost in the early 19th century. The Spanish Civil War (1936–9) was followed by the establishment of a Fascist dictatorship under General Franco; after his death in 1975 a constitutional monarchy was re-established. Spain became a member of the EC in 1986.

spake archaic or literary past of SPEAK.

spall /spɔːl/ ▸ **verb** [with obj.] break (ore, rock, or stone) into smaller pieces, especially in preparation for sorting. ■ [no obj.] (of ore, rock, or stone) break off in fragments: *cracks below the surface cause slabs of material to spall off*.
▸ **noun** a splinter or chip, especially of rock.
– ORIGIN late Middle English (as a noun): of unknown origin. The verb dates from the mid 18th cent.

spallation /spɔːˈleɪʃ(ə)n/ ▸ **noun** [mass noun] **1** Physics the break-up of a bombarded nucleus into several parts.
2 Geology separation of fragments from the surface of a rock, especially by interaction with a compression wave.

spalpeen /spalˈpiːn/ ▸ **noun** Irish a rascal.
– ORIGIN late 18th cent. (denoting a migratory farm worker): from Irish *spailpín*, of unknown origin.

spalted /ˈspɔːltɪd/ ▸ **adjective** denoting wood containing blackish irregular lines as a result of fungal decay, sometimes used to produce a decorative surface.
– ORIGIN 1970s: from dialect *spalt* 'to split, splinter' + -ED[1].

spam ▸ **noun** [mass noun] **1** irrelevant or inappropriate messages sent on the Internet to a large number of users.
2 (**Spam**) trademark a tinned meat product made mainly from ham.
▸ **verb** [with obj.] send the same message indiscriminately to (a large numbers of Internet users).
– DERIVATIVES **spammer** noun.
– ORIGIN 1930s: apparently from *sp(iced h)am*. The Internet sense appears to derive from a sketch by the British 'Monty Python' comedy group, set in a cafe in which every item on the menu includes spam.

span[1] ▸ **noun 1** the full extent of something from end to end; the amount of space that something covers: *a warehouse with a clear span of 28 feet*. ■ the wingspan of an aircraft or a bird. ■ an arch or part of a bridge between piers or supports. ■ (also **handspan**) the maximum distance between the tips of the thumb and little finger, taken as the basis of a measurement equal to 9 inches.
2 the length of time for which something lasts: *a short concentration span*. ■ archaic a short distance or time.
▸ **verb** (**spans, spanning, spanned**) **1** [with obj.] (of a bridge, arch, etc.) extend from side to side of: *the stream was spanned by a narrow bridge*. ■ cover or enclose with the length of one's hand: *her waist was slender enough for him to span with his hands*.
2 extend across (a period of time or a range of subjects): *their interests span almost all the conventional disciplines*.
– ORIGIN Old English, 'distance between the tips of the thumb and little finger', of Germanic origin; reinforced in Middle English by Old French *espan*.

span[2] ▸ **noun 1** Nautical a rope with its ends fastened at different points to a spar or other object in order to provide a purchase.
2 a team of people or animals, in particular: ■ N. Amer. a matched pair of horses, mules, or oxen. ■ S. African a team of two or more pairs of oxen. ■ S. African a work gang, especially of prisoners.
3 (**a span**) S. African informal, dated a lot: *thanks a span*.
▸ **verb** [with obj.] S. African yoke (an animal): *he spanned his donkeys to the cart*.
– ORIGIN mid 16th cent. (as a verb): from Dutch or Low German *spannen*. The noun (originally in nautical use) dates from the mid 18th cent.

span[3] ▸ **adjective** see SPICK AND SPAN.

span[4] chiefly archaic past of SPIN.

spanakopita /ˌspanəˈkɒpɪtə/ ▸ **noun** (in Greek cooking) a filo pastry stuffed with spinach and feta cheese.
– ORIGIN modern Greek, literally 'spinach pie'.

spandex ▸ **noun** [mass noun] a type of stretchy polyurethane fabric.
– ORIGIN 1950s: an arbitrary formation from EXPAND.

spandrel /ˈspandrɪl/ ▸ **noun** Architecture the almost triangular space between one side of the outer curve of an arch, a wall, and the ceiling or framework. ■ the space between the shoulders of adjoining arches and the ceiling or moulding above.
– ORIGIN late Middle English: perhaps from Anglo-Norman French *spaund(e)re*, or from *espaundre* 'expand'.

spandrel wall ▸ **noun** a wall built on the curve of an arch, filling in the spandrel.

spang ▸ **adverb** US informal directly; completely: *looking the General right spang in the eye*.
– ORIGIN mid 19th cent.: of unknown origin.

spangle ▸ **noun** a small thin piece of glittering material, typically sewn as one of many on clothing for decoration; a sequin. ■ a spot of bright colour or light.
▸ **verb** [with obj.] (usu. as adj. **spangled**) cover with spangles or other small sparkling objects: *a spangled dress*.
– DERIVATIVES **spangly** adjective (**spanglier, spangliest**).
– ORIGIN late Middle English: diminutive from obsolete *spang* 'glittering ornament', from Middle Dutch *spange* 'buckle'.

spangle gall ▸ **noun** a reddish disc-shaped gall that forms on the undersides of oak leaves in response to the developing larva of a gall wasp. It results from eggs laid in the summer and alternates with the currant gall within the annual cycle. ● The wasp is *Neuroterus quercusbaccarum*, family Cynipidae.

Spanglish /ˈspaŋɡlɪʃ/ ▸ **noun** [mass noun] a hybrid language combining words and idioms from both Spanish and English.

Spaniard /ˈspanjəd/ ▸ **noun 1** a native or inhabitant of Spain, or a person of Spanish descent.
2 a spiny rock plant of the parsley family, native to New Zealand. ● Genus *Aciphylla*, family Umbelliferae.
– ORIGIN Middle English: shortening of Old French *Espaignart*, from *Espaigne* 'Spain'.

spaniel ▸ **noun** a dog of a breed with a long silky coat and drooping ears. ■ used as a symbol of devotion or obsequiousness: [as modifier] *oh stop looking at me with those spaniel eyes*.
– ORIGIN Middle English: from Old French *espaigneul* 'Spanish (dog)', from Latin *Hispaniolus* 'Spanish'.

Spanish ▸ **adjective** relating to Spain, its people, or its language.
▸ **noun 1** (as plural noun **the Spanish**) the people of Spain.
2 [mass noun] the main language of Spain and of much of Central and South America (except Brazil) and several other countries. It is a Romance language with over 300 million speakers worldwide.
– DERIVATIVES **Spanishness** noun.
– ORIGIN Middle English: from SPAIN + -ISH[1], with later shortening of the first vowel.

Spanish America the parts of America once colonized by Spaniards and in which Spanish is still generally spoken, including most of Central and South America (except Brazil) and part of the Caribbean.

Spanish-American ▸ **noun** a native or inhabitant of the Spanish-speaking countries of Central and South America.
▸ **adjective** of or relating to the Spanish-speaking countries or peoples of Central and South America.

Spanish-American War a war between Spain and the United States in the Caribbean and the Philippines in 1898. American public opinion having been aroused by alleged Spanish atrocities in Cuba and the destruction of the warship *Maine* in Havana harbour, the US declared war and successfully invaded Cuba, Puerto Rico, and the Philippines, all of which Spain gave up by the Treaty of Paris (1898).

Spanish Armada see ARMADA.

Spanish bayonet ▸ **noun** a yucca with long stiff sword-shaped leaves and tall, slender spikes of white flowers, found from the southern US to the Caribbean. ● *Yucca aloifolia*, family Agavaceae.

Spanish broom ▸ **noun** a Mediterranean broom with fragrant yellow flowers and almost leafless stems which were formerly used in basketry. ● *Spartium junceum*, family Leguminosae.

Spanish chestnut ▸ **noun** see CHESTNUT (sense 2).

Spanish Civil War the conflict (1936–9) between Nationalist forces (including monarchists and members of the Falange Party) and Republicans (including socialists and Communists and Catalan and Basque separatists) in Spain.

> It began with a military uprising against the leftist Republican Popular Front government in July 1936. In bitter fighting the Nationalists, led by General Franco, gradually gained control of the countryside but failed to capture the capital, Madrid. After periods of prolonged stalemate,

S

Franco finally succeeded in capturing Barcelona and Madrid in early 1939. He established a Fascist dictatorship that lasted until his death in 1975.

Spanish-Colonial ▶ adjective denoting a style of architecture characteristic of Spanish America.

Spanish flu (also **Spanish influenza**) ▶ noun [mass noun] influenza caused by an influenza virus of type A, in particular that of the pandemic which began in 1918.

Spanish fly ▶ noun a bright green European blister beetle with a mousy smell. ● *Lytta vesicatoria*, family Meloidae.
■ [mass noun] a toxic preparation of the dried bodies of these beetles, formerly used in medicine as a counter-irritant and sometimes taken as an aphrodisiac. Also called CANTHARIDES.

Spanish guitar ▶ noun the standard six-stringed acoustic guitar, used especially for classical and folk music.

Spanish ibex (also **Spanish goat**) ▶ noun see IBEX.

Spanish Inquisition an ecclesiastical court established in 1478 and directed originally against converts from Judaism and Islam but later also against Protestants. It operated with great severity and was not suppressed until the early 19th century.

Spanish mackerel ▶ noun a large edible game fish related to the mackerel. ● Genus *Scomberomorus*, family Scombridae: several species, in particular *S. maculatus* of the tropical Atlantic, and *S. commerson* of the Indo-Pacific.

Spanish Main the former name for the north coast of South America between the Orinoco River and Panama, and adjoining parts of the Caribbean Sea.

Spanish Mission ▶ noun [as modifier] denoting a style of architecture characteristic of the Catholic missions in Spanish America.

Spanish moss ▶ noun [mass noun] a tropical American plant which grows as silvery-green festoons on trees, obtaining water and nutrients directly through its surface. ● *Tillandsia usneoides*, family Bromeliaceae. See also AIR PLANT.

Spanish omelette ▶ noun an omelette containing chopped vegetables, especially potatoes, often served open rather than folded.

Spanish onion ▶ noun a large onion with a mild flavour.

Spanish practice ▶ noun another term for OLD SPANISH CUSTOM.

Spanish rice ▶ noun [mass noun] a dish of rice with onions, peppers, tomatoes, and other vegetables, often coloured and flavoured with saffron.

Spanish Sahara former name (1958–75) for WESTERN SAHARA.

Spanish Succession, War of the a European war (1701–14), provoked by the death without issue of the Spanish king Charles II. The Grand Alliance of Britain, the Netherlands, and the Holy Roman emperor threw back a French invasion of the Low Countries, and, although the Peace of Utrecht confirmed the accession of a Bourbon king in Spain, prevented Spain and France from being united under one crown.

S

Spanish Town a town in Jamaica, west of Kingston, the second-largest town and a former capital of Jamaica; pop. 148,800 (est. 2006).

Spanish windlass ▶ noun a device for tightening a rope or cable by twisting it using a stick as a lever.

spank ▶ verb [with obj.] slap with one's open hand or a flat object, especially on the buttocks as a punishment: *she was spanked for spilling ink on the carpet*.
▶ noun a slap or series of slaps of this type.
– ORIGIN early 18th cent.: perhaps imitative.

spanker ▶ noun **1** a fore-and-aft sail set on the after side of a ship's mast, especially the mizzenmast.
2 informal, dated a very fine person or thing.

spanking ▶ adjective **1** (especially of a horse or its gait) lively; brisk: *a spanking trot*.
2 informal very good: *we had a spanking time*. ■ fine and impressive: *a spanking white Rolls Royce* | [as submodifier] *a spanking new conference centre*.
▶ noun an act of slapping, especially on the buttocks as a punishment for children.

spanner ▶ noun chiefly Brit. a tool with a shaped opening or jaws for gripping and turning a nut or bolt.
– PHRASES **spanner in the works** see WORK.
– ORIGIN late 18th cent.: from German *spannen* 'draw tight' + -ER[1].

span of control ▶ noun the area of activity and number of functions, people, or things for which an individual or organization is responsible.

spanspek /ˈspanspɛk/ ▶ noun South African term for CANTALOUPE.
– ORIGIN Afrikaans.

spansule /ˈspansjuːl/ ▶ noun trademark a capsule which when swallowed releases one or more medicinal drugs over a set period.
– ORIGIN 1950s: blend of the noun SPAN[1] and CAPSULE.

span-worm ▶ noun North American term for LOOPER.

spar[1] ▶ noun a thick, strong pole such as is used for a mast or yard on a ship. ■ the main longitudinal beam of an aeroplane wing.
– ORIGIN Middle English: shortening of Old French *esparre*, or from Old Norse *sperra*; related to Dutch *spar* and German *Sparren*.

spar[2] ▶ verb (**spars, sparring, sparred**) [no obj.] **1** make the motions of boxing without landing heavy blows, as a form of training: *one contestant broke his nose while sparring*. ■ argue with someone without marked hostility: *mother and daughter spar regularly over drink, drugs, and career*.
2 (of a gamecock) fight with the feet or spurs.
▶ noun **1** a period or bout of sparring.
2 informal a close friend.
– ORIGIN Old English *sperran, spyrran* 'strike out', of unknown origin; compare with Old Norse *sperrask* 'kick out'.

spar[3] ▶ noun [usu. in combination or with modifier] a crystalline, easily cleavable, translucent or transparent mineral.
– DERIVATIVES **sparry** adjective.
– ORIGIN late 16th cent.: from Middle Low German; related to Old English *spærstān* 'gypsum'.

sparable /ˈsparəb(ə)l/ ▶ noun a headless nail used for the soles and heels of shoes.
– ORIGIN early 17th cent.: contraction of *sparrow-bill* (in the same sense), with reference to the nail's shape.

sparagmos /spəˈragməs/ ▶ noun [mass noun] the dismemberment of a victim, forming a part of some ancient rituals and represented in Greek myths and tragedies.
– ORIGIN Greek, literally 'tearing'.

sparaxis /spəˈraksɪs/ ▶ noun a South African plant of the iris family, with slender sword-shaped leaves and showy multicoloured flowers. ● Genus *Sparaxis*, family Iridaceae.
– ORIGIN modern Latin, from Greek, literally 'laceration', from *sparassein* 'to tear'.

spar buoy ▶ noun a buoy made of a spar with one end moored so that the other stands up.

spar deck ▶ noun the light upper deck of a vessel.

spare ▶ adjective **1** additional to what is required for ordinary use: *few people had spare cash for inessentials*. ■ not currently in use or occupied: *a spare seat*. ■ (of time) not taken up by one's usual duties or activities; available for leisure: *he tried to write poetry in his spare time*.
2 with no excess fat; thin: *a spare, bearded figure*.
3 elegantly simple: *her clothes are smart and spare in style*.
▶ noun **1** an item kept in case another item of the same type is lost, broken, or worn out.
2 (in tenpin bowling) an act of knocking down all the pins with two balls.
▶ verb **1** [with two objs] give (something of which one has enough) to (someone): *she asked if I could spare her a bob or two*. ■ make free or available: *I'm sure you can spare me a moment*.
2 [with obj.] refrain from killing, injuring, or distressing: *there was no way the men would spare her*. ■ [with two objs] refrain from inflicting (something unpleasant) on (someone): *the country had until now been spared the violence occurring elsewhere*.
3 (**spare oneself**) [with negative] try to ensure or satisfy one's own comfort or needs: *in her concern to help others, she has never spared herself*.
4 [no obj.] archaic be frugal: *but some will spend, and some will spare*.
– PHRASES **go spare** Brit. informal become extremely angry or distraught. **spare someone's blushes** see BLUSH. **spare no effort** do everything one possibly can in order to achieve something: *we will spare no effort to secure the release of the captives*. **spare no expense** (or **no expense spared**) pay any amount of money in order to achieve something. **spare the rod and spoil the child** see ROD. **spare a thought for** remember: *spare a thought for our volunteer group at Christmas*. **to spare** left over: *that turkey will feed ten people with some to spare*.
– DERIVATIVES **sparely** adverb, **spareness** noun, **sparer** noun (rare).
– ORIGIN Old English *spær* 'not plentiful, meagre', *sparian* 'refrain from injuring', 'refrain from using', of Germanic origin; related to Dutch and German *sparen* 'to spare'.

spare part ▶ noun a duplicate part to replace a lost or damaged part of a machine.

spare-part surgery ▶ noun [mass noun] informal the treatment of organ failure by surgical transplantation or the insertion of artificial replacements.

spare rib ▶ noun (usu. **spare ribs**) a closely trimmed rib of pork.
– ORIGIN late 16th cent.: probably from Middle Low German *ribbesper* (by transposition of the syllables), and associated with the adjective SPARE.

spare tyre ▶ noun **1** an extra tyre carried in a motor vehicle for use in case of a puncture.
2 informal a roll of fat round a person's waist.

sparge /spɑːdʒ/ chiefly technical ▶ verb [with obj.] moisten by sprinkling with water, especially in brewing.
▶ noun [mass noun] the action of sprinkling or splashing. ■ [count noun] a spray of hot water, especially water sprinkled over malt when brewing.
– DERIVATIVES **sparger** noun.
– ORIGIN late 16th cent. (as a verb in the sense 'sprinkle (water) about'): apparently from Latin *spargere* 'to sprinkle'. The current senses date from the early 19th cent.

sparid /ˈsparɪd, ˈspɛːrɪd/ ▶ noun Zoology a fish of the sea bream family (Sparidae), whose members are marine and have deep bodies with long spiny dorsal fins.
– ORIGIN 1960s: from modern Latin *Sparidae* (plural), via Latin from Greek *sparos* 'sea bream'.

sparing ▶ adjective moderate; economical: *physicians advised sparing use of the ointment*.
– DERIVATIVES **sparingly** adverb, **sparingness** noun.

Spark, Dame Muriel (1918–2006), Scottish novelist. Notable works: *The Prime of Miss Jean Brodie* (1961) and *The Mandelbaum Gate* (1965).

spark[1] ▶ noun **1** a small fiery particle thrown off from a fire, alight in ashes, or produced by striking together two hard surfaces such as stone or metal. ■ a small flash of light produced by a sudden disruptive electrical discharge through the air. ■ a discharge such as this serving to ignite the explosive mixture in an internal-combustion engine.
2 a small amount of a quality or intense feeling: *a tiny spark of anger flared within her*. ■ a sense of liveliness and excitement: *there was a spark between them at their first meeting*.
3 (also **Sparks**) informal used as a nickname for a radio operator or an electrician, especially in the armed forces.
▶ verb **1** [no obj.] emit sparks of fire or electricity: *the ignition sparks as soon as the gas is turned on*. ■ produce sparks at the point where an electric circuit is interrupted.
2 [with obj.] ignite: *the explosion sparked a fire*.
■ provide the stimulus for (an event or process): *the trial sparked a furious row* | *the severity of the plan **sparked off** street protests*.
– PHRASES **spark out** Brit. informal completely unconscious: *I think he would knock Bowe spark out*. **sparks fly** an encounter becomes heated or lively. **strike sparks off each other** (or **one another**) (of two or more people) creatively inspire each other while working on something.
– DERIVATIVES **sparkless** adjective.
– ORIGIN Old English *spærca, spearca*, of unknown origin.

spark[2] archaic ▶ noun a lively young man.
▶ verb [no obj.] engage in courtship.
– ORIGIN early 16th cent.: probably a figurative use of SPARK[1].

spark chamber ▶ noun Physics an apparatus designed to show ionizing particles.

spark gap ▶ noun a space between electrical terminals across which a transient discharge passes.

sparking plug ▶ noun Brit. another term for SPARK PLUG.

sparkle ▶ verb [no obj.] **1** shine brightly with flashes of light: *her earrings sparkled as she turned her head*.
2 be vivacious and witty: *after a glass of wine, she began to sparkle*.
▶ noun **1** a glittering flash of light: *there was a sparkle in his eyes*.

2 [mass noun] vivacity and wit: *she's got a kind of sparkle.*
– DERIVATIVES **sparkly** adjective (**sparklier**, **sparkliest**).
– ORIGIN Middle English: frequentative (verb) or diminutive (noun) of SPARK[1].

sparkler ▸ noun **1** a hand-held firework that emits sparks.
2 informal a gemstone, especially a diamond.
3 informal a sparkling wine.
4 a nozzle attached to the spout on a beer pump to give the beer a frothy head.

sparkling ▸ adjective **1** shining brightly with flashes of light: *her sparkling blue eyes.* ■ lively and witty: *sparkling dialogue.*
2 (of a drink) effervescent; fizzy: *sparkling wine.*
– DERIVATIVES **sparklingly** adverb.

spark plug ▸ noun a device for firing the explosive mixture in an internal-combustion engine.

sparky ▸ adjective (**sparkier**, **sparkiest**) lively and high-spirited: *her sparky personality.*
▸ noun Brit. informal an electrician.

sparling ▸ noun an edible European smelt (fish) which migrates into fresh water to spawn. ● *Osmerus eperlanus*, family Osmeridae.
– ORIGIN Middle English: shortening of Old French *esperlinge*, of Germanic origin.

sparring partner ▸ noun a boxer employed to engage in sparring with another as training. ■ a person with whom one continually argues or contends.

sparrow ▸ noun **1** a small finch-like Old World bird related to the weaver birds, typically with brown and grey plumage. ● Family Passeridae (or Ploceidae): four genera, in particular *Passer*, and many species, e.g. the cosmopolitan **house sparrow** (*P. domesticus*).
2 [usu. with modifier] any of a number of birds that resemble true sparrows in size or colour: ● an American bunting (many genera in the subfamily Emberizinae, family Emberizidae). ● a waxbill, in particular the Java sparrow. ● see HEDGE SPARROW.
– ORIGIN Old English *spearwa*, of Germanic origin.

sparrow fart ▸ noun (in phrase **at sparrow fart**) informal very early in the morning.

sparrow grass ▸ noun dialect term for ASPARAGUS.
– ORIGIN mid 17th cent.: corruption (by folk etymology) of obsolete *sparagus* 'asparagus'.

sparrowhawk ▸ noun a small Old World woodland hawk that preys on small birds. ● Genus *Accipiter*, family Accipitridae: many species, in particular the widespread **northern sparrowhawk** (*A. nisus*).
■ N. Amer. the American kestrel (see KESTREL).

sparse ▸ adjective thinly dispersed or scattered: *areas of sparse population.* ■ scanty; in short supply: *information on earnings is sparse.*
– DERIVATIVES **sparsely** adverb, **sparseness** noun, **sparsity** noun.
– ORIGIN early 18th cent. (used to describe writing in the sense 'widely spaced'): from Latin *sparsus*, past participle of *spargere* 'scatter'.

Sparta /'spɑːtə/ a city in the southern Peloponnese in Greece, capital of the department of Laconia; pop. 14,400 (est. 2009). It was a powerful city-state in the 5th century BC, defeating its rival Athens in the Peloponnesian War to become the leading city of Greece.

Spartacist /'spɑːtəsɪst, -təkɪst/ ▸ noun a member of the Spartacus League.

Spartacus /'spɑːtəkəs/ (died *c.*71 BC), Thracian slave and gladiator. He led a revolt against Rome in 73, but was eventually defeated by Crassus in 71 and killed in battle.

Spartacus League a German revolutionary socialist group founded in 1916 by Rosa Luxemburg and Karl Liebknecht (1871–1919). At the end of 1918 the group became the German Communist Party, which in 1919 organized an uprising in Berlin that was brutally crushed.
– ORIGIN *Spartacus* was adopted as a pseudonym by Karl Liebknecht.

Spartan[1] ▸ adjective relating to Sparta in ancient Greece.
▸ noun a citizen of Sparta.

Spartan[2] ▸ noun a Canadian dessert apple of a variety with crisp white flesh and maroon-flushed yellow skin.

spartan ▸ adjective showing or characterized by austerity or a lack of comfort or luxury: *the accommodation was fairly spartan.*
– ORIGIN mid 17th cent.: from SPARTAN[1], because the inhabitants of Sparta were traditionally held to be indifferent to comfort or luxury.

spartina /spɑː'tʌɪnə, -'tiːnə/ (also **spartina grass**) ▸ noun a plant of a genus that comprises the cordgrasses. ● Genus *Spartina*, family Gramineae.
– ORIGIN modern Latin, from Greek *spartinē* 'rope'.

spar tree ▸ noun Forestry a tree or other tall structure to which cables are attached for hauling logs.

spasm ▸ noun a sudden involuntary muscular contraction or convulsive movement. ■ a sudden and brief spell of an activity or sensation: *a spasm of coughing woke him.* ■ [mass noun] prolonged involuntary muscle contraction: *the airways in the lungs go into spasm.*
– ORIGIN late Middle English: from Old French *spasme*, or via Latin from Greek *spasmos*, *spasma*, from *span* 'pull'.

spasmodic ▸ adjective **1** occurring or done in brief, irregular bursts: *spasmodic fighting continued.*
2 caused by, subject to, or in the nature of a spasm or spasms: *a spasmodic cough.*
– DERIVATIVES **spasmodically** adverb.
– ORIGIN late 17th cent.: from modern Latin *spasmodicus*, from Greek *spasmōdēs*, from *spasma* (see SPASM).

spasmolytic /ˌspazmə(ʊ)'lɪtɪk/ Medicine ▸ adjective (of a drug or treatment) able to relieve spasm of smooth muscle.
▸ noun a spasmolytic drug.

spasmophilia /ˌspazmə(ʊ)'fɪlɪə/ ▸ noun [mass noun] Medicine undue tendency of the muscles to contract, caused by ionic imbalance in the blood, or associated with anxiety disorders.

Spassky /'spaski/, Boris (Vasilevich) (b.1937), Russian chess player, world champion 1969–72. He lived in Paris from 1975 and played for France in the 1984 Olympics.

spastic ▸ adjective **1** relating to or affected by muscle spasm. ■ relating to or denoting a form of muscular weakness (**spastic paralysis**) typical of cerebral palsy, caused by damage to the brain or spinal cord and involving reflex resistance to passive movement of the limbs and difficulty in initiating and controlling muscular movement. ■ (of a person) having cerebral palsy.
2 informal, offensive incompetent or uncoordinated.
▸ noun **1** a person with cerebral palsy.
2 informal, offensive an incompetent or uncoordinated person.
– DERIVATIVES **spastically** adverb, **spasticity** noun.
– ORIGIN mid 18th cent.: via Latin from Greek *spastikos* 'pulling', from *span* 'pull'.

> **USAGE** The word **spastic** has been used in medical senses since the 18th century. In the 1970s and 1980s it became a term of abuse, used mainly by schoolchildren, directed towards any person regarded as incompetent or physically uncoordinated. Nowadays, the use of the word **spastic**, whether as a noun or as an adjective, is likely to cause offence, and it is preferable to use phrasing such as *a person with **cerebral palsy*** instead.

spat[1] past and past participle of SPIT[1].

spat[2] ▸ noun **1** (usu. **spats**) historical a short cloth gaiter covering the instep and ankle.
2 a cover for the upper part of an aircraft wheel.
– ORIGIN early 19th cent.: abbreviation of SPATTERDASH.

spat[3] informal ▸ noun a quarrel about an unimportant matter.
▸ verb (**spats**, **spatting**, **spatted**) [no obj.] quarrel about an unimportant matter.
– ORIGIN early 19th cent. (originally a US colloquial usage): probably imitative.

spat[4] ▸ noun [mass noun] the spawn or larvae of shellfish, especially oysters.
– ORIGIN mid 17th cent.: from Anglo-Norman French, of unknown ultimate origin.

spatchcock ▸ noun a chicken or game bird split open and grilled.
▸ verb [with obj.] split open (a poultry or game bird) ready for grilling. ■ informal, chiefly Brit. add (a phrase, sentence, clause, etc.) in a context where it is inappropriate: *a new clause has been spatchcocked into the Bill.*
– ORIGIN late 18th cent. (originally an Irish usage): perhaps related to the noun DISPATCH + COCK[1], but compare with SPITCHCOCK.

spate ▸ noun **1** a large number of similar things coming in quick succession: ***a spate of** attacks on holidaymakers.*
2 chiefly Brit. a sudden flood in a river.
– PHRASES **in (full) spate** (of a river) overflowing due to a sudden flood. ■ used to refer to a person or action that is continuing with vigour and without pause: *the headmaster was in full spate.*
– ORIGIN late Middle English (originally Scots and northern English in the sense 'flood, inundation'): of unknown origin.

spathe /speɪð/ ▸ noun Botany a large sheathing bract enclosing the flower cluster of certain plants, especially the spadix of arums and palms.
– ORIGIN late 18th cent.: via Latin from Greek *spathē* 'broad blade'.

spathic iron ore /'spaθɪk/ ▸ noun another term for SIDERITE (sense 1).
– ORIGIN mid 19th cent.: *spathic* from *spath*, a rare variant of SPAR[3], + -IC.

spathulate /'spatjʊlət/ ▸ adjective Botany & Zoology variant spelling of SPATULATE.

spatial /'speɪʃ(ə)l/ (also **spacial**) ▸ adjective relating to space: *the spatial distribution of population.*
– DERIVATIVES **spatiality** noun, **spatialization** (also **spatialisation**) noun, **spatialize** (also **spatialise**) verb, **spatially** adverb.
– ORIGIN mid 19th cent.: from Latin *spatium* 'space' + -AL.

spatio-temporal /ˌspeɪʃɪəʊ'tɛmp(ə)r(ə)l/ ▸ adjective Physics & Philosophy belonging to both space and time or to space time.
– DERIVATIVES **spatio-temporally** adverb.

Spätlese /'ʃpɛtˌleɪzə/ ▸ noun (pl. **Spätleses** or **Spätlesen** /-ˌleɪz(ə)n/) [mass noun] a white wine of German origin or style made from grapes harvested late in the season.
– ORIGIN from German, from *spät* 'late' + *Lese* 'picking, vintage'.

spatter ▸ verb [with obj.] cover with drops or spots of something: *passing vehicles **spattered** his shoes and trousers **with** mud.* ■ scatter or splash (liquid, mud, etc.) over a surface: *he spatters grease all over the cooker.* ■ [no obj.] fall so as to be scattered over an area: *she watched the raindrops spatter down.*
▸ noun a spray or splash of something. ■ a sprinkling: *there was **a spatter of** freckles over her nose.* ■ a short outburst of sound: *the sharp spatter of shots.*
– ORIGIN mid 16th cent. (in the sense 'splutter while speaking'): frequentative, from a base shared by Dutch, Low German *spatten* 'burst, spout'.

spatterdash ▸ noun (usu. **spatterdashes**) historical a long gaiter or legging worn to keep stockings or trousers clean, especially when riding.

spatterdock ▸ noun N. Amer. a yellow-flowered water lily. ● Genus *Nuphar*, family Nymphaeaceae: several species, in particular *N. advena*.

spatterware ▸ noun [mass noun] pottery decorated by sponging it with colour; sponged ware.

spatula ▸ noun **1** an implement with a broad, flat, blunt blade, used for mixing and spreading things, especially in cooking and painting. ■ US a fish slice.
2 Brit. a thin, flat wooden or metal instrument used in medical examinations e.g. for holding down the tongue or taking cell samples.
– ORIGIN early 16th cent.: from Latin, variant of *spathula*, diminutive of *spatha* (see SPATHE).

spatulate /'spatjʊlət/ ▸ adjective having a broad, rounded end: *his thick, spatulate fingers.* ■ (also **spathulate**) Botany & Zoology broad at the apex and tapered to the base: *large spatulate leaves.*

spätzle ▸ plural noun variant spelling of SPAETZLE.

spavin /'spavɪn/ ▸ noun a disorder of a horse's hock. See BOG SPAVIN, BONE SPAVIN.
– DERIVATIVES **spavined** adjective.
– ORIGIN late Middle English: shortening of Old French *espavin*, variant of *esparvain*, of Germanic origin.

spawn ▸ verb **1** [no obj.] (of a fish, frog, mollusc, crustacean, etc.) release or deposit eggs: *the fish spawn among fine-leaved plants.* ■ (**be spawned**) (of a fish, frog, etc.) be laid as eggs.
2 [with obj.] often derogatory (of a person) produce (offspring): *why had she married a man who could spawn a boy like that?* ■ produce or generate a large number of: *the decade spawned a bewildering variety of books on the forces.*
▸ noun [mass noun] **1** the eggs of fish, frogs, etc.: *the fish covers its spawn with gravel.* ■ the process of producing spawn.
2 chiefly derogatory the product or offspring of a person or place: *the spawn of Satan.*
3 the mycelium of a fungus, especially a cultivated mushroom.

S

– DERIVATIVES **spawner** noun.
– ORIGIN late Middle English: shortening of Anglo-Norman French *espaundre* 'to shed roe', variant of Old French *espandre* 'pour out', from Latin *expandere* 'expand'.

spay ▶ verb [with obj.] sterilize (a female animal) by removing the ovaries.
– ORIGIN late Middle English: shortening of Old French *espeer* 'cut with a sword', from *espee* 'sword', from Latin *spatha* (see SPATHE).

spaz (also **spazz**) offensive ▶ noun (pl. **spazzes**) short for SPASTIC.
▶ verb (**spazzes, spazzing, spazzed**) [no obj.] (**spaz out**) chiefly US lose physical or emotional control.
– ORIGIN 1960s: abbreviation of SPASTIC.

spaza /ˈspɑːzə/ ▶ noun (in South Africa) a small unofficial store in a township, often based in a private house.
– ORIGIN township slang, literally 'camouflaged', of unknown origin.

SPCK ▶ abbreviation Society for Promoting Christian Knowledge.

speak ▶ verb (past **spoke**; past participle **spoken**) [no obj.] **1** say something in order to convey information or to express a feeling: *in his agitation he was unable to speak | she refused to speak about the incident.* ■ have a conversation: *last time we spoke, you told me you couldn't do the job | I'll* ***speak to*** *him if he rings up.* ■ [with obj.] utter (a word, message, etc.): *patients copy words spoken by the therapist.* ■ [with obj.] communicate in or be able to communicate in (a specified language): *my mother spoke Russian.* ■ make a speech or contribute to a debate: *twenty thousand people attended to hear him speak.* ■ (**speak for**) express the views or position of (another): *he claimed to speak for the majority of local people.* ■ convey one's views or position indirectly: ***speaking through*** *his solicitor, he refused to join the debate.* ■ (**speak to**) answer (a question) or address (an issue or problem): *we should be disappointed if the report did not speak to the issue of literacy.* ■ (**speak of**) mention or discuss in speech or writing: *the books speak of betrayal.*
2 (**speak to**) talk to in order to reprove or advise: *she tried to speak to Seb about his drinking.* ■ talk to in order to give or obtain information: *he had spoken to the police.* ■ appeal or relate to: *the story spoke to him directly.*
3 (of behaviour, an object, etc.) serve as evidence for something: *everything in the house* ***spoke of*** *hard times and neglect* | [with obj.] *his frame spoke tiredness.* ■ [with obj. and infinitive or adverbial] archaic show (someone or something) to be in a particular state or to possess a certain quality: *she had seen nothing that spoke him of immoral habits.*
4 (of a musical instrument or other object) make a sound when functioning: *the gun spoke again | insufficient air circulates for the pipes to speak.* ■ (of a hound) bark.
– PHRASES **not to speak of** used in introducing a further factor to be considered: *the rent had to be paid, not to speak of school fees.* **something speaks for itself** the implications of something are so clear that no supporting evidence is needed: *the figures speak for themselves.* **speak for oneself** give one's own opinions. **speak for yourself** [in imperative] used to tell someone that an opinion they have expressed is not shared by oneself: *'This is such a boring place.' 'Speak for yourself—I like it.'.* **speak in tongues** speak in an unknown language during religious worship, regarded as one of the gifts of the Holy Spirit (Acts 2). **speak one's mind** express one's opinions frankly. **speak volumes** (of a gesture, circumstance, etc.) convey a great deal without using words: *a look that spoke volumes | his record* ***speaks volumes for*** *his determination.* **speak well** (or **ill**) **of** praise (or criticize). —— **to speak of** [with negative] used to indicate that there is so little of something that it is hardly worth mentioning: *I've no capital—well, none to speak of.*
– PHRASAL VERBS **speak out** (or **up**) express one's opinions frankly and publicly: *the government will be forthright in speaking out against human rights abuses.* **speak up** speak more loudly: *We can't hear you. Speak up!* **speak up for** speak in support of: *there was no independent body to speak up for press freedoms.*
– DERIVATIVES **speakable** adjective.
– ORIGIN Old English *sprecan*, later *specan*, of West Germanic origin; related to Dutch *spreken* and German *sprechen*.

-speak ▶ combining form forming nouns denoting a manner of speaking, characteristic of a specified field or group: *technospeak.*
– ORIGIN on the pattern of *(New)speak.*

speakeasy ▶ noun (pl. **speakeasies**) informal (in the US during Prohibition) an illicit liquor shop or drinking club.

speaker ▶ noun **1** a person who speaks. ■ a person who delivers a speech or lecture. ■ [usu. with modifier or in combination] a person who speaks a specified language: *he is a fluent English and French speaker.*
2 (**Speaker**) the presiding officer in a legislative assembly, especially the House of Commons.
3 short for LOUDSPEAKER.
– DERIVATIVES **speakership** noun (sense 2).

speakerphone ▶ noun chiefly N. Amer. a telephone with a loudspeaker and microphone, which does not need to be held in the hand.

speaking ▶ noun [mass noun] the action of conveying information or expressing one's feelings in speech. ■ the activity of delivering speeches: *public speaking.*
▶ adjective [attrib.] used for or engaged in speech: *you have a clear speaking voice.* ■ [in combination] able to communicate in a specified language: *an English-speaking guide.* ■ conveying meaning as though in words: *she gave him a speaking look.* ■ (of a portrait) so lifelike as to seem to be capable of speech: *a speaking likeness.*
– PHRASES **on speaking terms** polite or friendly towards someone, especially after an argument: *Maisie wasn't on speaking terms with any of her family.* —— **speaking** used to indicate the degree of accuracy intended in a statement or the point of view from which it is made: *generally speaking, I got on well with most of the playing staff.* **speaking of** used to introduce a remark about a topic recently alluded to: *speaking of cost, can I afford to buy it?*

speaking clock ▶ noun Brit. a telephone service giving the correct time in recorded speech.

speaking trumpet ▶ noun historical an instrument for making the voice carry, especially at sea.

speaking tube ▶ noun a pipe for conveying a person's voice from one room or building to another.

spear ▶ noun **1** a weapon with a pointed tip, typically of steel, and a long shaft, used for thrusting or throwing. ■ a similar barbed instrument used for catching fish. ■ archaic a spearman.
2 a plant shoot, especially a pointed stem of asparagus or broccoli.
▶ verb [with obj.] pierce or strike with a spear or other pointed object: *she speared her last chip with her fork.*
– PHRASES **the spear side** the male side or members of a family. The opposite of THE DISTAFF SIDE.
– ORIGIN Old English *spere*, of Germanic origin; compare with Dutch *speer* and German *Speer.*

spear carrier ▶ noun an actor with a walk-on part. ■ an unimportant participant in something.

spearfish ▶ noun (pl. **same** or **spearfishes**) a billfish that resembles the marlin. ● Genus *Tetrapturus*, family Istiophoridae: several species.
▶ verb [no obj.] (often as noun **spearfishing**) fish using a spear.

speargrass ▶ noun [mass noun] **1** any of a number of grasses with hard pointed seed heads, some of which are sharp enough to harm livestock. ● *Heteropogon, Stipa*, and other genera, family Gramineae.
2 chiefly NZ any of a number of spiny or prickly plants, in particular the piripiri and the Spaniard.

speargun ▶ noun a gun used to propel a spear in underwater fishing.

spearhead ▶ noun **1** the point of a spear.
2 an individual or group chosen to lead an attack or movement: *she became the* ***spearhead of*** *a health education programme.*
▶ verb [with obj.] lead (an attack or movement): *he's spearheading a campaign to reduce the number of accidents at work.*

spearman ▶ noun (pl. **spearmen**) chiefly historical a man, especially a soldier, who uses a spear.

Spearman's rank correlation ▶ noun a product–moment correlation coefficient devised as a measure of the degree of agreement between two rankings. (Symbol: ρ)
– ORIGIN early 20th cent.: named after Charles E. *Spearman* (1863–1945), English psychologist.

spearmint ▶ noun [mass noun] the common garden mint, which is used as a culinary herb and to flavour chewing gum. ● *Mentha spicata*, family Labiatae.

spearwort ▶ noun a European buttercup of marshes and ditches, with thick hollow stems and long, narrow spear-shaped leaves. ● Genus *Ranunculus*, family Ranunculaceae: the **lesser spearwort** (*R. flammula*) and the less common **greater spearwort** (*R. lingua*).

spec[1] ▶ noun (in phrase **on spec**) informal in the hope of success but without any specific plan or instructions: *he built the factory on spec and hoped someone would buy it.*
– ORIGIN late 18th cent.: abbreviation of SPECULATION.

spec[2] ▶ noun (US also **specs**) short for SPECIFICATION (sense 2): *a camera with a very basic spec.*
▶ verb (**specs, specing, specced**) [with obj.] give (something) a particular specification; construct to a specified standard: *the range allows buyers to spec their truck to their needs.*

speccy ▶ adjective variant spelling of SPECKY.

special ▶ adjective **1** better, greater, or otherwise different from what is usual: *they always made a special effort at Christmas.* ■ exceptionally good or pleasant: *she's a very special person.* ■ (of a subject) studied in particular depth.
2 belonging specifically to a particular person or place: *we want to preserve our town's special character.* ■ designed or organized for a particular person, purpose, or occasion: *we will return by special coaches.* ■ used to denote education for children with particular needs, especially those with learning difficulties.
3 Mathematics denoting a group consisting of matrices of unit determinant.
▶ noun a thing, such as a product or broadcast, that is designed or organized for a particular occasion or purpose: *television's election night specials.* ■ a dish not on the regular menu at a restaurant but served on a particular day. ■ a person assigned to a special duty; a special constable or special correspondent. ■ informal a product or service offered at a temporarily reduced price.
– DERIVATIVES **specialness** noun.
– ORIGIN Middle English: shortening of Old French *especial* 'especial' or Latin *specialis*, from *species* 'appearance' (see SPECIES).

Special Air Service (abbrev.: **SAS**) (in the UK) a specialist army regiment trained in commando techniques of warfare, formed during the Second World War and used in clandestine operations, frequently against terrorists.

Special Boat Service (abbrev.: **SBS**) (in the UK) a nautical counterpart of the SAS, provided by the Royal Marines.

Special Branch (in the UK) the police department dealing with political security.

special case ▶ noun **1** a situation or person that has unusual qualities or needs.
2 Law a written statement of fact presented by litigants to a court.

special constable ▶ noun (in the UK) a person who is trained to act as a police officer on particular occasions, especially in times of emergency.

special correspondent ▶ noun a journalist writing for a newspaper on special events or a special area of interest.

special delivery ▶ noun [mass noun] (in the UK) guaranteed delivery of a letter within the UK the day after posting. ■ (in the US) delivery of mail outside normal hours on payment of an additional fee. ■ [count noun] a letter or parcel sent by a special-delivery service.

special development area (also **special area**) ▶ noun (in the UK) a district for which special economic provision is made in legislation.

special drawing rights (abbrev.: **SDR**) ▶ plural noun a form of international money, created by the International Monetary Fund, and defined as a weighted average of various convertible currencies.

special edition ▶ noun an edition of a newspaper, magazine, television programme, etc. which differs from the usual format, especially in concentrating on one particularly important story.

special effect ▶ noun an illusion created for films and television by props, camerawork, computer graphics, etc.: *a non-stop action film filled with amazing stunts and spectacular special effects.*

special forces ▶ plural noun the units of a country's armed forces that undertake covert, counterterrorist, and other specialized operations.

S

special intention ▶ **noun** (in the Roman Catholic Church) a special aim or purpose for which a mass is celebrated or prayers are said.

special interest group ▶ **noun** a group of people or an organization seeking or receiving special advantages, typically through political lobbying.

specialist ▶ **noun** a person who concentrates primarily on a particular subject or activity; a person highly skilled in a specific and restricted field. ■ a person highly trained in a particular branch of medicine.
▶ **adjective** possessing or involving detailed knowledge or study of a restricted topic: *you may require specialist financial advice.* ■ [attrib.] concentrating on a restricted field, market, or area of activity: *a specialist electrical shop.*
– DERIVATIVES **specialism** noun.

speciality /ˌspɛʃɪˈalɪti/ (chiefly N. Amer. & Medicine also **specialty**) ▶ **noun** (pl. **specialities**) **1** a pursuit, area of study, or skill to which someone has devoted much time and effort and in which they are expert: *his speciality was watercolours.* ■ a product, especially a type of food, which a person or region is famous for making well: *a restaurant serving freshly made local specialities.* ■ [as modifier] meeting particular tastes or needs: *speciality potatoes for salads.*
2 (often **specialty**) a branch of medicine or surgery.
– ORIGIN late Middle English (denoting the quality of being special or distinctive): from Old French *especialite* or late Latin *specialitas*, from Latin *specialis* (see **SPECIAL**).

specialize (also **specialise**) ▶ **verb** [no obj.] concentrate on and become expert in a particular subject or skill: *he could **specialize in** tropical medicine.* ■ confine oneself to providing a particular product or service: *the firm **specialized in** commercial brochures.* ■ make a habit of engaging in a particular activity: *a group of writers have **specialized in** attacking the society they live in.* ■ [with obj.] Biology adapt or set apart (an organ or part) to serve a special function or to suit a particular way of life: *zooids specialized for different functions.*
– DERIVATIVES **specialization** noun.
– ORIGIN early 17th cent.: from French *spécialiser*, from *spécial* 'special'.

specialized (also **specialised**) ▶ **adjective** requiring or involving detailed and specific knowledge or training: *employees with specialized skills.* ■ concentrating on a small area of a subject: *periodicals have become more and more specialized.* ■ designed for a particular purpose: *specialized software.*

special jury ▶ **noun** Brit. historical a jury with members of a particular social standing. Compare with **COMMON JURY**.

special licence ▶ **noun** Brit. a licence allowing a marriage to take place at a time or place not normally permitted.

specially ▶ **adverb** for a special purpose: *a new coat and hat, bought specially* | [as submodifier] *a specially commissioned report.*

> **USAGE** On the differences between **specially** and **especially**, see **USAGE** at **ESPECIALLY**.

special needs ▶ **plural noun** (in the context of children at school) particular educational requirements resulting from learning difficulties, physical disability, or emotional and behavioural difficulties.

Special Operations Executive (abbrev.: **SOE**) a secret British military service during the Second World War, set up in 1940 to carry out clandestine operations and coordinate with resistance movements in Europe and later East Asia.

special pleading ▶ **noun** [mass noun] argument in which the speaker deliberately ignores aspects that are unfavourable to their point of view.

special school ▶ **noun** (in the UK) a school catering for children with special needs.

special sort ▶ **noun** Printing a character, such as an accented letter or a symbol, that is not normally included in any font.

special team ▶ **noun** American Football a squad that is used for kick-offs, punts, and other special plays.

specialty /ˈspɛʃ(ə)lti/ ▶ **noun** (pl. **specialties**) **1** chiefly N. Amer. & Medicine another term for **SPECIALITY**.
2 Law a contract under seal.
– ORIGIN Middle English (denoting special affection or attachment): shortening of Old French *especialte*, from *especial* (see **SPECIAL**).

special verdict ▶ **noun** Law a verdict that requires an answer to one or more specific detailed questions, with the application of the law left up to the judge. ■ a verdict that an accused person is not guilty by reason of insanity.

speciation /ˌspiːʃɪˈeɪʃ(ə)n, ˌspiːs-/ ▶ **noun** [mass noun] Biology the formation of new and distinct species in the course of evolution.
– DERIVATIVES **speciate** verb.

specie /ˈspiːʃiː, ˈspiːʃi/ ▶ **noun** [mass noun] money in the form of coins rather than notes.
– PHRASES **in specie** Law in the real, precise, or actual form specified: *the plaintiff could not be sure of recovering his goods in specie.*
– ORIGIN mid 16th cent.: from Latin, ablative of *species* 'form, kind', in the phrase *in specie* 'in the actual form'.

species /ˈspiːʃiːz, -ʃɪz, ˈspiːs-/ ▶ **noun** (pl. **same**) **1** (abbrev.: **sp., spp.**) Biology a group of living organisms consisting of similar individuals capable of exchanging genes or interbreeding. The species is the principal natural taxonomic unit, ranking below a genus and denoted by a Latin binomial, e.g. *Homo sapiens*. ■ Logic a group subordinate to a genus and containing individuals agreeing in some common attributes and called by a common name.
2 a kind or sort: *a species of invective at once tough and suave.* ■ used humorously to refer to people who share a characteristic or occupation: *a political species that is becoming more common, the environmental statesman.* ■ Chemistry & Physics a particular kind of atom, molecule, ion, or particle: *a new molecular species.*
3 Christian Church the visible form of each of the elements of consecrated bread and wine in the Eucharist.
– ORIGIN late Middle English: from Latin, literally 'appearance, form, beauty', from *specere* 'to look'.

species barrier ▶ **noun** the natural mechanisms that prevent a virus or disease from spreading from one species to another.

speciesism /ˈspiːʃiːˌzɪz(ə)m, ˈspiːs-/ ▶ **noun** [mass noun] the assumption of human superiority leading to the exploitation of animals.
– DERIVATIVES **speciesist** adjective & noun.

species rose ▶ **noun** a rose belonging to a distinct species and not to one of the many varieties produced by hybridization.

specific /spəˈsɪfɪk/ ▶ **adjective** **1** clearly defined or identified: *savings were made by increasing the electricity supply only until it met specific development needs.* ■ precise and clear in making statements or issuing instructions: *when ordering goods be specific.* ■ belonging or relating uniquely to a particular subject: *information needs are often very **specific to** individuals.*
2 Biology relating to species or a species.
3 (of a duty or a tax) levied at a fixed rate per physical unit of the thing taxed, regardless of its price.
4 Physics of or denoting a number equal to the ratio of the value of some property of a given substance to the value of the same property of some other substance used as a reference, such as water, or of a vacuum, under equivalent conditions. ■ of or denoting a physical quantity expressed in terms of a unit mass, volume, or other measure, in order to give a value independent of the properties or scale of the particular system studied.
▶ **noun** **1** chiefly dated a medicine or remedy effective in treating a particular disease or part of the body.
2 (usu. **specifics**) a precise detail: *I wish I'd put more thought into the specifics.*
– DERIVATIVES **specifically** adverb *they don't talk specifically about education* | [sentence adverb] *these are war, or more specifically anti-war, novels*, **specificity** /ˌspɛsɪˈfɪsɪti/ noun, **specificness** noun.
– ORIGIN mid 17th cent. (originally in the sense 'having a special determining quality'): from late Latin *specificus*, from Latin *species* (see **SPECIES**).

specific activity ▶ **noun** Physics the activity of a given radioisotope per unit mass.

specification /ˌspɛsɪfɪˈkeɪʃ(ə)n/ ▶ **noun** **1** an act of identifying something precisely or of stating a precise requirement: *give a full specification of the job advertised* | [mass noun] *there was no clear specification of objectives.*
2 (usu. **specifications**) a detailed description of the design and materials used to make something. ■ a standard of workmanship or materials required to be met in a piece of work: *everything was built to a higher specification.* ■ a description of an invention accompanying an application for a patent.
– ORIGIN late 16th cent.: from medieval Latin *specificatio(n-)*, from late Latin *specificare* (see **SPECIFY**).

specific charge ▶ **noun** Physics the ratio of the charge of an ion or subatomic particle to its mass.

specific disease ▶ **noun** a disease caused by a particular and characteristic organism.

specific epithet ▶ **noun** chiefly Botany & Microbiology the second element in the Latin binomial name of a species, which follows the generic name and distinguishes the species from others in the same genus. Compare with **SPECIFIC NAME, TRIVIAL NAME**.

specific gravity ▶ **noun** another term for **RELATIVE DENSITY**.

specific heat capacity ▶ **noun** Physics the heat required to raise the temperature of the unit mass of a given substance by a given amount (usually one degree).

specific name ▶ **noun** chiefly Botany & Microbiology the Latin binomial name of a species, consisting of the generic name followed by the specific epithet. ■ chiefly Zoology another term for **SPECIFIC EPITHET**.

specific performance ▶ **noun** [mass noun] Law the performance of a contractual duty, as ordered in cases where damages would not be adequate remedy.

specify ▶ **verb** (**specifies, specifying, specified**) [with obj.] identify clearly and definitely: *the coup leader promised an election but did not specify a date.* ■ [with clause] state a fact or requirement clearly and precisely: *the agency failed to **specify that** the workers were not their employees.* ■ include in an architect's or engineer's specifications: *naval architects specified circular portholes.*
– DERIVATIVES **specifiable** adjective, **specifier** noun.
– ORIGIN Middle English: from Old French *specifier* or late Latin *specificare* (see **SPECIFIC**).

specimen /ˈspɛsɪmɪn/ ▶ **noun** **1** an individual animal, plant, piece of a mineral, etc. used as an example of its species or type for scientific study or display. ■ an example of something regarded as typical of its class or group: [as modifier] *a specimen paper of the new test.* ■ a sample for medical testing, especially of urine.
2 informal used to refer humorously to a person or animal: *Carla could not help feeling a degree of reluctant admiration for this odd female specimen.*
– ORIGIN early 17th cent. (in the sense 'pattern, model'): from Latin, from *specere* 'to look'.

specimen plant (also **specimen tree**) ▶ **noun** an unusual or impressive plant or tree grown as a focus of interest in a garden.

specious /ˈspiːʃəs/ ▶ **adjective** superficially plausible, but actually wrong: *a specious argument.* ■ misleading in appearance, especially misleadingly attractive: *the music trade gives Golden Oldies a specious appearance of novelty.*
– DERIVATIVES **speciously** adverb, **speciousness** noun.
– ORIGIN late Middle English (in the sense 'beautiful'): from Latin *speciosus* 'fair', from *species* (see **SPECIES**).

speck[1] ▶ **noun** a tiny spot: *the figure in the distance had become a mere speck.* ■ a small particle of a substance: ***specks of** dust.* ■ a rotten spot in fruit.
▶ **verb** [with obj.] mark with small spots: *their skin was specked with goose pimples.*
– DERIVATIVES **speckless** adjective.
– ORIGIN Old English *specca*; compare with the noun **SPECKLE**.

speck[2] ▶ **noun** [mass noun] a smoked ham of a type produced in NE Italy.
– ORIGIN via Italian from Dutch *spek*, German *Speck* 'fat bacon, whale blubber' (in which sense it was formerly used in English): related to Old English *spec*.

speckle ▶ **noun** (usu. **speckles**) a small spot or patch of colour.
▶ **verb** [with obj.] mark with a large number of small spots or patches of colour: *gulls whirled round the masts, speckling the docks with guano.*
– ORIGIN late Middle English (as a noun): from Middle Dutch *spekkel*; the verb (late 16th cent.) from the noun or a back-formation from *speckled*.

speckled ▶ **adjective** covered or marked with a large number of small spots or patches of colour: *a large speckled brown egg* | *a fine waxy film **speckled with** yeast cells.*

speckled trout ▶ **noun** N. Amer. the brook charr. See **CHARR**.

speckled wood ▶ **noun** a brown Eurasian butterfly with cream or orange markings, favouring light

S

woodland habitats. ● *Pararge aegeria*, subfamily Satyrinae, family Nymphalidae.

specky (also **speccy**) ▶ adjective informal (of a person) wearing spectacles.

specs ▶ plural noun **1** informal a pair of spectacles. **2** US term for SPEC².
– ORIGIN early 19th cent.: abbreviation.

spect ▶ verb non-standard form of EXPECT representing childish pronunciation: *I spect they've been to a party.*

spectacle ▶ noun a visually striking performance or display: *the acrobatic feats make a good spectacle* | [mass noun] *the show is pure spectacle.* ■ an event or scene regarded in terms of its visual impact: *the spectacle of a city's mass grief.*
– PHRASES **make a spectacle of oneself** draw attention to oneself by behaving in a ridiculous way in public.
– ORIGIN Middle English: via Old French from Latin *spectaculum* 'public show', from *spectare*, frequentative of *specere* 'to look'.

spectacled ▶ adjective wearing spectacles. ■ used in names of animals with markings on the face or elsewhere that resemble spectacles.

spectacled bear ▶ noun a South American bear with a black or dark brown coat and white markings around the eyes. ● *Tremarctos ornatus*, family Ursidae.

spectacled caiman ▶ noun a small South American caiman with a bony ridge between the eyes which gives the appearance of spectacles. ● *Caiman sclerops*, family Alligatoridae.

spectacled cobra ▶ noun an Asian cobra with a marking on the hood that resembles spectacles. Also called INDIAN COBRA. ● *Naja naja*, family Elapidae.

spectacles ▶ plural noun Brit. a pair of glasses.

spectacular ▶ adjective beautiful in a dramatic and eye-catching way: *spectacular mountain scenery.* ■ strikingly large or obvious: *the party suffered a spectacular loss in the election.*
▶ noun an event such as a pageant or musical, produced on a large scale and with striking effects.
– DERIVATIVES **spectacularly** adverb.
– ORIGIN late 17th cent.: from SPECTACLE, on the pattern of words such as *oracular.*

spectate ▶ verb [no obj.] be a spectator, especially at a sporting event: *the two of us spectated at the first race.*
– ORIGIN early 18th cent.: back-formation from SPECTATOR.

spectator ▶ noun a person who watches at a show, game, or other event.
– DERIVATIVES **spectatorial** adjective, **spectatorship** noun.
– ORIGIN late 16th cent.: from French *spectateur* or Latin *spectator*, from *spectare* 'gaze at, observe' (see SPECTACLE).

spectator sport ▶ noun a sport that many people find entertaining to watch.

specter ▶ noun US spelling of SPECTRE.

spectinomycin /ˌspɛktɪnə(ʊ)ˈmʌɪsɪn/ ▶ noun [mass noun] Medicine a bacterial antibiotic used as an alternative to penicillin. ● The drug is obtained from the bacterium *Streptomyces spectabilis*.
– ORIGIN 1960s: from the specific epithet *spectabilis* (see above), literally 'visible, remarkable' + -MYCIN.

Spector /ˈspɛktə/, Phil (b.1940), American record producer and songwriter; born *Harvey Phillip Spector*. He pioneered a 'wall of sound' style, using echo and tape loops, and had a succession of hit recordings in the 1960s with groups such as the Ronettes and the Crystals. In 2009 he was convicted of murdering the actress Lana Clarkson.

spectra plural form of SPECTRUM.

spectral¹ ▶ adjective of or like a ghost: *a spectral, menacing face.*
– DERIVATIVES **spectrally** adverb.
– ORIGIN early 19th cent.: from SPECTRE + -AL.

spectral² ▶ adjective of or concerning spectra or the spectrum.
– DERIVATIVES **spectrally** adverb.
– ORIGIN mid 19th cent.: from SPECTRUM + -AL.

spectral index ▶ noun an exponential factor relating the flux density of a radio source to its frequency.

spectral tarsier ▶ noun a tarsier which has a tail with a long bushy tuft and a scaly base, native to Sulawesi. ● *Tarsius spectrum*, family Tarsiidae.

spectral type (also **spectral class**) ▶ noun the group in which a star is classified according to its spectrum, especially using the Harvard classification.

spectre (US **specter**) ▶ noun a ghost. ■ something widely feared as a possible unpleasant or dangerous occurrence: *the spectre of nuclear holocaust.*
– ORIGIN early 17th cent.: from French *spectre* or Latin *spectrum* (see SPECTRUM).

spectro- ▶ combining form representing SPECTRUM.

spectrochemistry ▶ noun [mass noun] chemistry based on the study of the spectra of substances.

spectrogram ▶ noun a photographic or other visual or electronic representation of a spectrum.

spectrograph ▶ noun an apparatus for photographing or otherwise recording spectra.
– DERIVATIVES **spectrographic** adjective, **spectrographically** adverb, **spectrography** noun.

spectroheliograph /ˌspɛktrə(ʊ)ˈhiːlɪəgrɑːf/ ▶ noun an instrument for taking photographs of the sun in light of one wavelength only.

spectrohelioscope /ˌspɛktrə(ʊ)ˈhiːlɪəskəʊp/ ▶ noun a device similar to a spectroheliograph which produces a directly observable monochromatic image of the sun.

spectrolite /ˈspɛktrə(ʊ)lʌɪt/ ▶ noun [mass noun] the mineral labradorite, especially when used as a gemstone.

spectrometer /spɛkˈtrɒmɪtə/ ▶ noun an apparatus used for recording and measuring spectra, especially as a method of analysis.
– DERIVATIVES **spectrometric** adjective, **spectrometry** noun.

spectrophotometer /ˌspɛktrə(ʊ)fəʊˈtɒmɪtə/ ▶ noun an apparatus for measuring the intensity of light in a part of the spectrum, especially as transmitted or emitted by particular substances.
– DERIVATIVES **spectrophotometric** /-təˈmɛtrɪk/ adjective, **spectrophotometrically** adverb, **spectrophotometry** noun.

spectroscope ▶ noun an apparatus for producing and recording spectra for examination.

spectroscopy /spɛkˈtrɒskəpi/ ▶ noun [mass noun] the branch of science concerned with the investigation and measurement of spectra produced when matter interacts with or emits electromagnetic radiation.
– DERIVATIVES **spectroscopic** adjective, **spectroscopically** adverb, **spectroscopist** noun.

spectrum ▶ noun (pl. **spectra** /-trə/) **1** a band of colours, as seen in a rainbow, produced by separation of the components of light by their different degrees of refraction according to wavelength. ■ (**the spectrum**) the entire range of wavelengths of electromagnetic radiation. ■ a characteristic series of frequencies of electromagnetic radiation emitted or absorbed by a substance. ■ the components of a sound or other phenomenon arranged according to such characteristics as frequency, charge, and energy.
2 used to classify something in terms of its position on a scale between two extreme points: *the left or the right of the political spectrum.* ■ a wide range: *self-help books are covering a broader and broader spectrum.*
– ORIGIN early 17th cent. (in the sense 'spectre'): from Latin, literally 'image, apparition', from *specere* 'to look'.

spectrum analyser ▶ noun a device for analysing a system of oscillations, especially sound, into its separate components.

specula plural form of SPECULUM.

specular /ˈspɛkjʊlə/ ▶ adjective relating to or having the properties of a mirror.
– ORIGIN late 16th cent. (in *specular stone*, a substance formerly used as glass): from Latin *specularis*, from *speculum* (see SPECULUM).

speculate /ˈspɛkjʊleɪt/ ▶ verb [no obj.] **1** form a theory or conjecture about a subject without firm evidence: *my colleagues speculate about my private life* | [with clause] *observers **speculated that** the authorities wished to improve their image.*
2 invest in stocks, property, or other ventures in the hope of gain but with the risk of loss: *he didn't look as though he had the money to **speculate in** shares.*
– DERIVATIVES **speculator** noun.
– ORIGIN late 16th cent.: from Latin *speculat-* 'observed from a vantage point', from the verb *speculari*, from *specula* 'watchtower', from *specere* 'to look'.

speculation ▶ noun [mass noun] **1** the forming of a theory or conjecture without firm evidence: *there has been widespread speculation that he plans to quit* | [count noun] *these are only speculations.*
2 investment in stocks, property, etc. in the hope of gain but with the risk of loss: *the company's move into property speculation.*

speculative ▶ adjective **1** engaged in, expressing, or based on conjecture rather than knowledge: *he gave her a speculative glance.*
2 (of an investment) involving a high risk of loss. ■ (of a business venture) undertaken on the chance of success, without a pre-existing contract.
– DERIVATIVES **speculatively** adverb, **speculativeness** noun.

speculative builder ▶ noun a person who has houses erected without securing buyers in advance.

speculum /ˈspɛkjʊləm/ ▶ noun (pl. **specula** /-lə/)
1 Medicine a metal instrument that is used to dilate an orifice or canal in the body to allow inspection.
2 Ornithology a bright patch of plumage on the wings of certain birds, especially a strip of metallic sheen on the secondary flight feathers of many ducks.
3 a mirror or reflector of glass or metal, especially (formerly) a metallic mirror in a reflecting telescope. ■ short for SPECULUM METAL.
– ORIGIN late Middle English: from Latin, literally 'mirror', from *specere* 'to look'.

speculum metal ▶ noun [mass noun] an alloy of copper and tin used to make mirrors, especially formerly for telescopes.

sped past and past participle of SPEED.

speech ▶ noun **1** [mass noun] the expression of or the ability to express thoughts and feelings by articulate sounds: *he was born deaf and without the power of speech.* ■ a person's style of speaking: *she wouldn't accept his correction of her speech.*
2 a formal address or discourse delivered to an audience: *he gave a speech about the company.* ■ a sequence of lines written for one character in a play.
– ORIGIN Old English *sprǣc*, *sprēc*, later *spēc*, of West Germanic origin: related to Dutch *spraak*, German *Sprache*, also to SPEAK.

speech act ▶ noun Linguistics & Philosophy an utterance considered as an action, particularly with regard to its intention, purpose, or effect.

speech centre (also **speech area**) ▶ noun a region of the brain involved in the comprehension or production of speech.

speech community ▶ noun a group of people sharing a common language or dialect.

speech day ▶ noun Brit. an annual celebration held at some schools, especially public schools, at which speeches are made and prizes are presented.

speechify ▶ verb (**speechifies**, **speechifying**, **speechified**) [no obj.] (often as noun **speechifying**) deliver a speech, especially in a tedious or pompous way: *the after-dinner speechifying begins.*
– DERIVATIVES **speechification** noun, **speechifier** noun.

speechless ▶ adjective unable to speak, especially as the temporary result of shock or strong emotion: *he was speechless with rage.*
– DERIVATIVES **speechlessly** adverb, **speechlessness** noun.
– ORIGIN Old English *spǣclēas* (see SPEECH, -LESS).

speech pathology ▶ noun another term for SPEECH THERAPY.
– DERIVATIVES **speech pathologist** noun.

speech-reading ▶ noun [mass noun] lip-reading.

speech recognition ▶ noun [mass noun] the process of enabling a computer to identify and respond to the sounds produced in human speech.

speech sound ▶ noun a phonetically distinct unit of speech.

speech synthesis ▶ noun [mass noun] the process of generating spoken language by machine on the basis of written input.

speech therapy ▶ noun [mass noun] training to help people with speech and language problems to speak more clearly.
– DERIVATIVES **speech therapist** noun.

speech-writer ▶ noun a person employed to write speeches for others to deliver.

speed ▶ noun **1** [mass noun] the rate at which someone or something moves or operates or is able to move or operate: *we turned on to the runway and began to **gather speed*** | *an engine running **at full speed*** | [count noun] *the car has a top speed of 147 mph.* ■ rapidity of movement or action: *the accident was due to excessive*

S

speed. ■ the rate at which something happens or is done: *they were bemused by the speed of events | the course is delivered on CDROM so students can progress at their own speed.*
2 each of the possible gear ratios of a bicycle. ■ US or dated each of the possible gear ratios of a motor vehicle.
3 the light-gathering power or f number of a camera lens. ■ the duration of a photographic exposure. ■ the sensitivity of photographic film to light.
4 [mass noun] informal an amphetamine drug, especially methamphetamine.
5 [mass noun] archaic success; prosperity: *wish me good speed.*
▶ verb (past and past participle **sped**) **1** [no obj., with adverbial of direction] move quickly: *I got into the car and home we sped.* ■ (past and past participle **speeded**) [no obj.] (of a motorist or vehicle) travel at a speed that is greater than the legal limit: *the car that crashed was speeding.* ■ (past and past participle **speeded**) (**speed up**) move or work more quickly: *you force yourself to speed up because you don't want to keep others waiting.* ■ (past and past participle **speeded**) [with obj.] cause to move or happen more quickly: *they sought to* **speed up** *decision-making.*
2 [with obj.] archaic make prosperous or successful: *may God speed you.*
3 [no obj.] informal take or be under the influence of an amphetamine drug: *more kids than ever are speeding, tripping, and getting stoned.*
– PHRASES **at speed** quickly: *a car flashed past them at speed.* **up to speed 1** operating at full speed or at an expected rate or level. **2** informal fully informed or up to date: *his secretary's up to speed on IT.*
– DERIVATIVES **speeder** noun.
– ORIGIN Old English *spēd* (noun), *spēdan* (verb), from the Germanic base of Old English *spōwan* 'prosper, succeed', a sense reflected in early usage.

speed bag ▶ noun N. Amer. a small punchbag used by boxers for practising quick punches.

speedball ▶ noun **1** informal a mixture of cocaine with heroin.
2 a small punchball used by boxers for practising quick punches.
3 [mass noun] US a ball game resembling soccer but in which the ball may be handled.

speedboat ▶ noun a motor boat designed for high speed.

speed bump (also **speed hump**) ▶ noun a ridge set at intervals in a road surface to control the speed of vehicles.

speed camera ▶ noun a roadside camera triggered by speeding vehicles, taking either video footage or a photograph of the vehicle with a record of its speed.

speed dating (US trademark **SpeedDating**) ▶ noun [mass noun] an organized social activity in which people seeking romantic relationships have a series of short conversations with potential partners in order to determine whether there is mutual interest.

speed dial ▶ noun a function on some telephones which allows numbers to be entered into a memory and dialled with the push of a single button.
▶ verb (**speed-dial**) (**speed-dials, speed-dialling, speed-dialled**) [with obj.] dial (a telephone number) by using a speed dial function.

speedily ▶ adverb quickly or promptly: *your claim will be dealt with as speedily as possible.*

speed limit ▶ noun the maximum speed at which a vehicle may legally travel on a particular stretch of road.

speed limiter ▶ noun see LIMITER.

speed merchant ▶ noun informal **1** a motorist who enjoys driving fast.
2 Cricket & Baseball a fast bowler or pitcher.

speedo ▶ noun (pl. **speedos**) **1** informal short for SPEEDOMETER.
2 (**Speedos**) trademark men's brief, tight swimming trunks.

speedometer /spiːˈdɒmɪtə/ ▶ noun an instrument on a vehicle's dashboard indicating its speed.

speed-read ▶ verb [with obj.] read rapidly by assimilating several phrases or sentences at once.
– DERIVATIVES **speed-reader** noun.

speedster ▶ noun informal a person or thing that operates well at high speed, for example a fast car.

speed trap ▶ noun a radar trap.

speed-up ▶ noun an increase in speed, especially in a person's or machine's rate of working.

speedway ▶ noun [mass noun] **1** Brit. a form of motorcycle racing in which the riders race several laps around an oval dirt track, typically in a stadium. ■ [count noun] a stadium or track used for speedway racing.
2 N. Amer. a road or track used for motor-car racing. ■ a highway for fast motor traffic.

speedwell ▶ noun a small creeping herbaceous plant of north temperate regions, with small blue or pink flowers. ● Genus *Veronica*, family Scrophulariaceae: several species, including the **germander speedwell**.

speedwriting ▶ noun [mass noun] trademark a form of shorthand using the letters of the alphabet.

speedy ▶ adjective (**speedier, speediest**) **1** done or occurring quickly: *a speedy recovery.*
2 moving quickly: *a speedy winger.*
– DERIVATIVES **speediness** noun.

speedy trial ▶ noun chiefly US Law a criminal trial held after minimal delay, as considered to be a citizen's constitutional right.

Speenhamland system /ˈspiːnəmland/ ▶ noun historical a system of poor relief first adopted in the late 18th century and established throughout rural England in succeeding years.
– ORIGIN first adopted in *Speenhamland*, an English village near Newbury, Berks.

Speer /spɪə/, German /ʃpeːɐ/, Albert (1905–81), German architect and Nazi government official, designer of the Nuremberg stadium for the 1934 Nazi Party congress. He was also Minister for Armaments and Munitions. Following the Nuremberg trials, he served twenty years in Spandau prison.

speiss /spʌɪs/ ▶ noun [mass noun] a mixture of impure compounds of arsenic and antimonium with nickel, cobalt, iron, and other metals, produced in the smelting of cobalt and other ores.
– ORIGIN late 18th cent.: from German *Speise* 'food, amalgam'.

spekboom /ˈspɛkbʊəm/ ▶ noun a South African shrub with succulent leaves, which is used for fodder during times of drought. ● *Portulacaria afra*, family Portulacaceae.
– ORIGIN mid 19th cent.: from Afrikaans, from *spek* 'bacon' + *boom* 'tree'.

Speke /spiːk/, John Hanning (1827–64), English explorer. With Sir Richard Burton, he became the first European to discover Lake Tanganyika (1858). He also discovered Lake Victoria, naming it in honour of the queen.

speleology /ˌspiːlɪˈɒlədʒi, ˌspɛl-/ ▶ noun [mass noun] the study or exploration of caves.
– DERIVATIVES **speleological** adjective, **speleologist** noun.
– ORIGIN late 19th cent.: from French *spéléologie*, via Latin from Greek *spēlaion* 'cave'.

speleothem /ˈspiːlɪə(ʊ)θɛm/ ▶ noun Geology a structure formed in a cave by the deposition of minerals from water, e.g. a stalactite or stalagmite.
– ORIGIN 1950s: from Greek *spēlaion* 'cave' + *thema* 'deposit'.

spell[1] ▶ verb (past and past participle **spelled** or chiefly Brit. **spelt**) [with obj.] **1** write or name the letters that form (a word) in correct sequence: *Dolly spelled her name* | [no obj.] *journals have a house style about how to spell.* ■ (of letters) make up or form (a word).
2 be a sign or characteristic of: *she had the chic, efficient look that spells Milan.* ■ mean or have as a result: *the plans would spell disaster for the economy.*
– PHRASAL VERBS **spell something out** explain something in detail: *I'll spell out the problem again.*
– ORIGIN Middle English: shortening of Old French *espeller*, from the Germanic base of SPELL[2].

spell[2] ▶ noun a form of words used as a magical charm or incantation. ■ a state of enchantment caused by a magic spell: *the magician may* **cast a spell on** *himself.* ■ an ability to control or influence people as though one had magical power over them: *he woke from her spell.*
– PHRASES **under a spell** not fully in control of one's thoughts and actions. **under someone's spell** so devoted to someone that they seem to have magic power over one.
– ORIGIN Old English *spel(l)* 'narration', of Germanic origin.

spell[3] ▶ noun a short period: *I want to get away from racing for a spell.* ■ a period spent in an activity: *a spell of greenhouse work.* ■ Austral./NZ a period of rest from work. ■ Cricket a series of overs during a session of play in which a particular bowler bowls.
▶ verb [with obj.] chiefly N. Amer. allow (someone) to rest briefly by taking their place in an activity: *I got sleepy and needed her to spell me for a while at the wheel.* ■ [no obj.] Austral./NZ take a brief rest: *I'll spell for a bit.*
– ORIGIN late 16th cent.: variant of dialect *spele* 'take the place of', of unknown origin. The early sense of the noun was 'shift of relief workers'.

spell[4] ▶ noun a splinter of wood.
– ORIGIN late Middle English: perhaps a variant of obsolete *speld* 'chip, splinter'.

spellbind ▶ verb (past and past participle **spellbound**) [with obj.] hold the complete attention of (someone) as though by magic; fascinate: *the singer* **held** *the audience* **spellbound.**
– DERIVATIVES **spellbinder** noun.

spellbinding ▶ adjective holding one's attention completely as though by magic; fascinating: *a place of spellbinding beauty.*
– DERIVATIVES **spellbindingly** adverb.

spellcheck ▶ noun [often as modifier] a check of the spelling in a file of text using a spellchecker. ■ a spellchecker.
▶ verb [with obj.] check the spelling in (a text) using a spellchecker.

spellchecker ▶ noun a computer program which checks the spelling of words in files of text, typically by comparison with a stored list of words.

speller ▶ noun [with adj.] a person who spells with a specified ability: *a very weak speller.* ■ chiefly N. Amer. a book for teaching spelling. ■ another term for SPELLCHECKER.

spelling ▶ noun [mass noun] the process or activity of writing or naming the letters of a word. ■ [count noun] the way a word is spelled: *the spelling of his name was influenced by French.* ■ a person's ability to spell words: *her spelling was deplorable.*

spelling bee ▶ noun a spelling competition.

spelling checker ▶ noun a spellchecker.

spelt[1] past and past participle of SPELL[1].

spelt[2] ▶ noun [mass noun] an old kind of wheat with bearded ears and spikelets that each contain two narrow grains, not widely grown but favoured as a health food. Compare with EINKORN, EMMER. ● *Triticum spelta*, family Gramineae.
– ORIGIN late Old English, from Old Saxon *spelta*. The word was rare until the 16th cent., when it was readopted from Middle Dutch.

spelter /ˈspɛltə/ ▶ noun [mass noun] commercial crude smelted zinc. ■ a solder or other alloy in which zinc is the main constituent.
– ORIGIN mid 17th cent.: compare with Old French *espeautre*, Middle Dutch *speauter*; related to PEWTER.

spelunking /spɪˈlʌŋkɪŋ/ ▶ noun [mass noun] N. Amer. the exploration of caves, especially as a hobby.
– DERIVATIVES **spelunker** noun.
– ORIGIN 1940s: from obsolete *spelunk* 'cave' (from Latin *spelunca*) + -ING[1].

Spence, Sir Basil (Urwin) (1907–76), British architect, born in India. He designed the new Coventry cathedral (1962).

spence ▶ noun archaic a larder.
– ORIGIN late Middle English: shortening of Old French *despense*, from Latin *dispensa*, feminine past participle of *dispendere* (see DISPENSE).

Spencer[1], Herbert (1820–1903), English philosopher and sociologist. He sought to apply the theory of natural selection to human societies, developing social Darwinism and coining the phrase the 'survival of the fittest' (1864).

Spencer[2], Sir Stanley (1891–1959), English painter. He is best known for his religious and visionary works in the modern setting of his native village of Cookham in Berkshire.

spencer[1] ▶ noun a short, close-fitting jacket, worn by women and children in the early 19th century. ■ a thin woollen vest, worn by women for extra warmth in winter.
– ORIGIN probably named after the second Earl *Spencer* (1758–1834), English politician.

spencer[2] ▶ noun Sailing a trysail.
– ORIGIN mid 19th cent.: of unknown origin.

Spencerian /spɛnˈsɪərɪən/ ▶ adjective relating to a style of sloping handwriting widely taught in American schools from around 1850.
– ORIGIN mid 19th cent.: named after the US calligrapher Platt Rogers *Spencer* (1800–64), who devised it.

spend ▶ verb (past and past participle **spent**) [with obj.] **1** give (money) to pay for goods, services, or so as

S

to benefit someone or something: *the firm has spent £100,000 **on** hardware.* ■ use or give out the whole of; exhaust: *she couldn't buy any more because she had already spent her money | the initial surge of interest had spent itself.*
2 pass (time) in a specified way or in a particular place: *she spent a lot of time travelling.*
▸ **noun** informal an amount of money paid out: *the average spend at the cafe is £10 a head.*
– PHRASES **spend a penny** Brit. informal used euphemistically to refer to a need to urinate. [with reference to the coin-operated locks of public toilets.]
– DERIVATIVES **spendable** adjective, **spender** noun.
– ORIGIN Old English *spendan*, from Latin *expendere* 'pay out'; partly also a shortening of obsolete *dispend*, from Latin *dispendere* 'pay out'.

Spender, Sir Stephen (1909–95), English poet and critic. In his critical work *The Destructive Element* (1935) Spender defended the importance of political subject matter in literature.

spending money ▸ **noun** [mass noun] money available to be spent on pleasures and entertainment.

spendthrift ▸ **noun** a person who spends money in an extravagant, irresponsible way.

spendy ▸ **adjective** informal, chiefly US costing a great deal; expensive. ■ spending a great deal of money; extravagant: *that's not a real spendy crowd—they eat fast food.*

Spengler /ˈspɛŋɡlə/, German /ˈʃpɛŋlɐ/, Oswald (1880–1936), German philosopher. In his book *The Decline of the West* (1918–22) he argues that civilizations undergo a seasonal cycle of a thousand years and are subject to growth and decay analogous to biological species.

Spenser, Edmund (*c.*1552–99), English poet. He is best known for his allegorical romance *The Faerie Queene* (1590; 1596), celebrating Queen Elizabeth I and written in the Spenserian stanza.
– DERIVATIVES **Spenserian** adjective.

Spenserian stanza /spɛnˈsɪərɪən/ ▸ **noun** the stanza used by Spenser in *The Faerie Queene*, consisting of eight iambic pentameters and an alexandrine, with the rhyming scheme *ababbcbcc*.

spent past and past participle of **SPEND**. ▸ **adjective** having been used and unable to be used again: *a spent matchstick.* ■ having no power or energy left: *the movement has become a spent force.*

spent tan ▸ **noun** see **TAN**[1] (sense 3 of the noun).

sperm ▸ **noun** (pl. **same** or **sperms**) **1** [mass noun] semen. ■ [count noun] a spermatozoon.
2 short for **SPERM WHALE**. ■ [mass noun] short for **SPERMACETI** or **SPERM OIL**.
– ORIGIN late Middle English: via late Latin from Greek *sperma* 'seed', from *speirein* 'to sow'.

spermaceti /ˌspəːməˈsiːti, -ˈsɛti/ ▸ **noun** [mass noun] a white waxy substance produced by the sperm whale, formerly used in candles and ointments. It is present in a rounded organ in the head, where it focuses acoustic signals and aids in the control of buoyancy.
– ORIGIN late 15th cent.: from medieval Latin, from late Latin *sperma* 'sperm' + *ceti* 'of a whale' (genitive of *cetus*, from Greek *kētos* 'whale'), from the belief that it was whale spawn.

spermatheca /ˌspəːməˈθiːkə/ ▸ **noun** (pl. **spermathecae** /-ˈθiːkiː/) Zoology (in a female or hermaphrodite invertebrate) a receptacle in which sperm is stored after mating.
– ORIGIN early 19th cent.: from late Latin *sperma* 'sperm' + **THECA**.

spermatic ▸ **adjective** relating to sperm or semen.
– ORIGIN late Middle English: via late Latin from Greek *spermatikos*, from *sperma* (see **SPERM**).

spermatic cord ▸ **noun** a bundle of nerves, ducts, and blood vessels connecting the testicles to the abdominal cavity.

spermatid /ˈspəːmətɪd/ ▸ **noun** Biology an immature male sex cell formed from a spermatocyte, which may develop into a spermatozoon without further division.

spermato- ▸ **combining form** Biology relating to sperm or seeds: *spermatophore | spermatozoid.*
– ORIGIN from Greek *sperma*, *spermat-* 'sperm'.

spermatocyte /ˈspəːmətə(ʊ)sʌɪt, spəˈmat-/ ▸ **noun** Biology a cell produced at the second stage in the formation of spermatozoa, formed from a spermatogonium and dividing by meiosis into spermatids.

spermatogenesis /ˌspəːmətə(ʊ)ˈdʒɛnɪsɪs, spəˌmatə(ʊ)-/ ▸ **noun** [mass noun] Biology the production or development of mature spermatozoa.

spermatogonium /ˌspəːmətə(ʊ)ˈɡəʊnɪəm, spəˌmatə(ʊ)-/ ▸ **noun** (pl. **spermatogonia** /-nɪə/) Biology a cell produced at an early stage in the formation of spermatozoa, formed in the wall of a seminiferous tubule and giving rise by mitosis to spermatocytes.
– DERIVATIVES **spermatogonial** adjective.
– ORIGIN late 19th cent.: from **SPERM** + modern Latin *gonium* (from Greek *gonos* 'offspring, seed').

spermatophore /ˈspəːmətə(ʊ)fɔː, spəˈmat-/ ▸ **noun** Zoology a protein capsule containing a mass of spermatozoa, transferred during mating in various insects, arthropods, cephalopod molluscs, etc.

spermatophyte /ˈspəːmətə(ʊ)ˌfʌɪt, spəˈmat-/ ▸ **noun** Botany a plant of a large division that comprises those that bear seeds, including the gymnosperms and angiosperms. ● Division Spermatophyta.

spermatozoid /ˌspəːmətə(ʊ)ˈzəʊɪd, spəˌmat-/ ▸ **noun** Botany a motile male gamete produced by a lower plant or a gymnosperm. Also called **ANTHEROZOID**.

spermatozoon /ˌspəːmətə(ʊ)ˈzəʊɒn, spəˌmat-/ ▸ **noun** (pl. **spermatozoa** /-ˈzəʊə/) Biology the mature motile male sex cell of an animal, by which the ovum is fertilized, typically having a compact head and one or more long flagella for swimming.
– DERIVATIVES **spermatozoal** adjective, **spermatozoan** adjective.
– ORIGIN mid 19th cent.: from Greek *sperma*, *spermat-* 'seed' + *zōion* 'animal'.

sperm bank ▸ **noun** a place where semen is kept in cold storage for use in artificial insemination.

sperm count ▸ **noun** a measure of the number of spermatozoa per ejaculation or per measured amount of semen, used as an indication of a man's fertility.

spermicide ▸ **noun** a substance that kills spermatozoa, used as a contraceptive.
– DERIVATIVES **spermicidal** adjective, **spermicidally** adverb.

spermidine /ˈspəːmɪdiːn/ ▸ **noun** [mass noun] Biochemistry a colourless compound with a similar distribution and effect to spermine. ● A polyamine; chem. formula: $H_2N(CH_2)_3NH(CH_2)_4NH_2$.
– ORIGIN 1920s: from **SPERM** + **-IDE** + **-INE**[4].

spermine /ˈspəːmiːn/ ▸ **noun** [mass noun] Biochemistry a deliquescent compound which acts to stabilize various components of living cells and is widely distributed in living and decaying tissues. ● A polyamine; chem. formula: $(H_2N(CH_2)_3NH(CH_2)_2)_2$.

spermo- ▸ **combining form** equivalent to **SPERMATO-**.

sperm oil ▸ **noun** [mass noun] an oil found with spermaceti in the head of the sperm whale, used formerly as a lubricant.

sperm whale ▸ **noun** a toothed whale with a massive head, typically feeding at great depths on squid, formerly valued for the spermaceti and sperm oil in its head and the ambergris in its intestines. ● Family Physeteridae: two genera and three species, in particular the very large *Physeter macrocephalus* (also called **CACHALOT**).
– ORIGIN mid 19th cent.: *sperm*, abbreviation of **SPERMACETI**.

spessartine /ˈspɛsətiːn/ ▸ **noun** [mass noun] a form of garnet containing manganese and aluminium, occurring as orange-red to dark brown crystals.
– ORIGIN mid 19th cent.: from French, from *Spessart*, the name of a district in NW Bavaria, + **-INE**[4].

spew ▸ **verb** [with obj.] expel large quantities of (something) rapidly and forcibly: *buses were spewing out black clouds of exhaust.* ■ [no obj., with adverbial of direction] be poured or forced out in large quantities: *great screeds of paper spewed out of the computer.* ■ [no obj.] informal vomit.
▸ **noun** [mass noun] informal vomit.
– DERIVATIVES **spewer** noun.
– ORIGIN Old English *spīwan*, *spēowan*, of Germanic origin; related to German *speien*.

Spey /speɪ/ a river of east central Scotland. Rising in the Grampian Mountains east of the Great Glen, it flows 171 km (108 miles) north-eastwards to the North Sea.

SPF ▸ **abbreviation** sun protection factor (indicating the effectiveness of protective skin preparations).

sphagnum /ˈsfaɡnəm/ ▸ **noun** [mass noun] a plant of a genus that comprises the peat mosses. ● Genus *Sphagnum*, family Sphagnaceae.
– ORIGIN mid 18th cent.: modern Latin, from Greek *sphagnos*, denoting a kind of moss.

sphalerite /ˈsfaləraɪt/ ▸ **noun** [mass noun] a shiny mineral, yellow to dark brown or black in colour, consisting of zinc sulphide.
– ORIGIN mid 19th cent.: from Greek *sphaleros* 'deceptive' + **-ITE**[1]. Compare with **BLENDE**.

sphene /sfiːn/ ▸ **noun** [mass noun] a greenish-yellow or brown mineral consisting of a silicate of calcium and titanium, occurring in granitic and metamorphic rocks in wedge-shaped crystals.
– ORIGIN early 19th cent.: from French *sphène*, from Greek *sphēn* 'wedge'.

sphenoid /ˈsfiːnɔɪd/ Anatomy ▸ **noun** (also **sphenoid bone**) a compound bone which forms the base of the cranium, behind the eye and below the front part of the brain. It has two pairs of broad lateral 'wings' and a number of other projections, and contains two air-filled sinuses.
▸ **adjective** relating to the sphenoid bone.
– DERIVATIVES **sphenoidal** adjective.
– ORIGIN mid 18th cent.: from modern Latin *sphenoides*, from Greek *sphēnoeidēs*, from *sphēn* 'wedge'.

Sphenopsida /sfɛˈnɒpsɪdə/ ▸ **plural noun** Botany a class of pteridophyte plants that comprises the horsetails and their extinct relatives.
– DERIVATIVES **sphenopsid** noun & adjective.
– ORIGIN modern Latin (plural), from Greek *sphēn* 'wedge' + *opsis* 'appearance'.

sphere ▸ **noun 1** a round solid figure, or its surface, with every point on its surface equidistant from its centre. ■ a spherical object; a ball or globe. ■ a globe representing the earth. ■ chiefly literary a celestial body. ■ literary the sky perceived as a vault upon or in which celestial bodies are represented as lying. ■ each of a series of revolving concentrically arranged spherical shells in which celestial bodies were formerly thought to be set in a fixed relationship.
2 an area of activity, interest, or expertise; a section of society or an aspect of life distinguished and unified by a particular characteristic: *political reforms to match those in the economic sphere.*
▸ **verb** [with obj.] archaic enclose in or as if in a sphere. ■ form into a rounded or perfect whole.
– PHRASES **music** (or **harmony**) **of the spheres** the natural harmonic tones supposedly produced by the movement of the celestial spheres or the bodies fixed in them. **sphere of influence** (or **interest**) a country or area in which another country has power to affect developments though it has no formal authority. ■ a field or area in which an individual or organization has power to affect events and developments.
– ORIGIN Middle English: from Old French *espere*, from late Latin *sphera*, earlier *sphaera*, from Greek *sphaira* 'ball'.

-sphere ▸ **combining form** denoting a structure or region of spherical form, especially a region round the earth: *ionosphere.*
– ORIGIN from **SPHERE**, on the pattern of *(atmo)sphere*.

spheric /ˈsfɛrɪk/ ▸ **adjective** spherical.
– DERIVATIVES **sphericity** noun.

spherical ▸ **adjective** shaped like a sphere: *spherical pearls.* ■ relating to the properties of spheres. ■ formed inside or on the surface of a sphere.
– DERIVATIVES **spherically** adverb.
– ORIGIN late 15th cent.: via late Latin from Greek *sphairikos*, from *sphaira* (see **SPHERE**).

spherical aberration ▸ **noun** a loss of definition in the image arising from the surface geometry of a spherical mirror or lens.

spherical angle ▸ **noun** an angle formed by the intersection of two great circles of a sphere.

spherical coordinates (also **spherical polar coordinates**) ▸ **plural noun** three coordinates that define the location of a point in three-dimensional space. They are the length of its radius vector r, the angle θ between the vertical plane containing this vector and the x-axis, and the angle φ between this vector and the horizontal x–y plane. ● Usually written (r, θ, φ).

spherical triangle ▸ **noun** a triangle formed by three arcs of great circles on a sphere.

spherical trigonometry ▸ **noun** [mass noun] the branch of trigonometry concerned with the measurement of the angles and sides of spherical triangles.

spheroid /ˈsfɪərɔɪd/ ▸ **noun** a sphere-like but not perfectly spherical body. ■ a solid generated by a half-revolution of an ellipse about its major axis (**prolate spheroid**) or minor axis (**oblate spheroid**).
– DERIVATIVES **spheroidal** adjective.

spheroplast /ˈsfɪərəʊplast, -plɑːst/ ▸ **noun** Biology a bacterium or plant cell bound by its plasma membrane, the cell wall being deficient or lacking and the whole having a spherical form.

spherule /ˈsfɛrjuːl/ ▸ **noun** a small sphere.

– ORIGIN mid 17th cent.: from late Latin *sphaerula*, diminutive of Latin *sphaera* (see SPHERE).

spherulite /ˈsfɛrjʊlʌɪt/ ▶ **noun** chiefly Geology a small spheroidal mass of crystals (especially of a mineral) grouped radially around a point.
– DERIVATIVES **spherulitic** adjective.
– ORIGIN early 19th cent.: from SPHERULE + -ITE¹.

sphincter /ˈsfɪŋktə/ ▶ **noun** Anatomy a ring of muscle surrounding and serving to guard or close an opening or tube, such as the anus or the openings of the stomach.
– DERIVATIVES **sphincteral** adjective, **sphincteric** adjective.
– ORIGIN late 16th cent.: via Latin from Greek *sphinktēr*, from *sphingein* 'bind tight'.

sphingid /ˈsfɪndʒɪd/ ▶ **noun** Entomology a moth of the hawkmoth family (Sphingidae).
– ORIGIN early 20th cent.: from modern Latin *Sphingidae* (plural), from Greek *Sphinx* (see SPHINX).

sphingo- ▶ **combining form** used in the names of various related compounds isolated from the brain and nervous tissue: *sphingomyelin*.
– ORIGIN from Greek *Sphinx*, *Sphing-* 'Sphinx', originally in *sphingosine*, with reference to the enigmatic nature of the compound.

sphingolipid /ˌsfɪŋɡə(ʊ)ˈlɪpɪd/ ▶ **noun** Biochemistry any of a class of compounds which are fatty acid derivatives of sphingosine and occur chiefly in the cell membranes of the brain and nervous tissue.

sphingomyelin /ˌsfɪŋɡə(ʊ)ˈmʌɪəlɪn/ ▶ **noun** [mass noun] Biochemistry a substance which occurs widely in brain and nervous tissue, consisting of complex phosphoryl derivatives of sphingosine and choline.

sphingosine /ˈsfɪŋɡə(ʊ)sʌɪn/ ▶ **noun** [mass noun] Biochemistry a basic compound which is a constituent of a number of substances important in the metabolism of nerve cells, especially sphingomyelins. ● A crystalline alcohol; chem. formula: $C_{18}H_{37}NO_2$.

sphinx ▶ **noun 1** (**Sphinx**) Greek Mythology a winged monster of Thebes, having a woman's head and a lion's body. It propounded a riddle about the three ages of man, killing those who failed to solve it, until Oedipus was successful, whereupon the Sphinx committed suicide. ■ an ancient Egyptian stone figure having a lion's body and a human or animal head, especially the huge statue near the Pyramids at Giza. ■ an enigmatic or inscrutable person.
2 North American term for HAWKMOTH.
– ORIGIN late Middle English: via Latin from Greek *Sphinx*, apparently from *sphingein* 'draw tight'.

sphygmo- /ˈsfɪɡməʊ/ ▶ **combining form** Physiology relating to the pulse or pulsation: *sphygmograph*.
– ORIGIN from Greek *sphugmos* 'pulse'.

sphygmograph ▶ **noun** an instrument which produces a line recording the strength and rate of a person's pulse.

sphygmomanometer /ˌsfɪɡməʊməˈnɒmɪtə/ ▶ **noun** an instrument for measuring blood pressure, typically consisting of an inflatable rubber cuff which is applied to the arm and connected to a column of mercury next to a graduated scale, enabling the determination of systolic and diastolic blood pressure by increasing and gradually releasing the pressure in the cuff.
– DERIVATIVES **sphygmomanometry** noun.

Sphynx /sfɪŋks/ ▶ **noun** a cat of a hairless breed, originally from North America.

spic ▶ **noun** US informal, offensive a Spanish-speaking person from Central or South America or the Caribbean, especially a Mexican.
– ORIGIN early 20th cent.: abbreviation of US slang *spiggoty*, in the same sense, of uncertain origin: perhaps an alteration of *speak the* in 'no speak the English'.

Spica /ˈspiːkə/ Astronomy the brightest star in the constellation Virgo.
– ORIGIN Latin, literally 'ear of wheat (in the hand of the goddess)'.

spica /ˈspʌɪkə/ ▶ **noun** Medicine a bandage folded into a spiral arrangement resembling an ear of wheat or barley.
– ORIGIN late 17th cent.: from Latin, literally 'spike, ear of corn'; related to *spina* 'spine'. The current sense is influenced by Greek *stakhus* 'ear of wheat'.

spic and span ▶ **adjective** variant spelling of SPICK AND SPAN.

spiccato /spɪˈkɑːtəʊ/ Music ▶ **noun** [mass noun] a style of staccato playing on stringed instruments involving bouncing the bow on the strings.
▶ **adjective & adverb** performed or to be performed in this style.
– ORIGIN Italian, literally 'detailed, distinct'.

spice ▶ **noun 1** an aromatic or pungent vegetable substance used to flavour food, e.g. cloves, pepper, or cumin: *the cake is packed with spices* | [mass noun] *sift together flour, baking powder, and mixed spice*. ■ [mass noun] an element providing interest and excitement: *healthy rivalry adds spice to the game*.
2 [mass noun] a russet or ginger colour.
3 [mass noun] N. English sweets; confectionery.
▶ **verb** [with obj.] (often as adj. **spiced**) flavour with spice: *turbot with a spiced sauce*. ■ make more interesting or exciting: *she was probably adding details to spice up the story*.
– ORIGIN Middle English: shortening of Old French *espice*, from Latin *species* 'sort, kind', in late Latin 'wares'.

spicebush ▶ **noun** a North American shrub with aromatic leaves, bark, and fruit. The leaves were formerly used for a tea and the fruit as an allspice substitute. ● *Lindera benzoin*, family Lauraceae.

Spice Islands former name for MOLUCCA ISLANDS.

spick and span (also **spic and span**) ▶ **adjective** neat, clean, and well looked after: *my little house is spick and span*.
– ORIGIN late 16th cent. (in the sense 'brand new'): from *spick and span new*, emphatic extension of dialect *span new*, from Old Norse *spán-nýr*, from *spánn* 'chip' + *nýr* 'new'; *spick* influenced by Dutch *spiksplinternieuw*, literally 'splinter new'.

spicule /ˈspɪkjuːl/ ▶ **noun 1** technical a minute sharp-pointed object or structure that is typically present in large numbers, such as a fine particle of ice. ■ Zoology each of the small needle-like or sharp-pointed structures of calcite or silica which make up the skeleton of a sponge.
2 Astronomy a short-lived, relatively small radial jet of gas in the chromosphere or lower corona of the sun.
– DERIVATIVES **spicular** adjective, **spiculate** /-lət/ adjective, **spiculation** noun.
– ORIGIN late 18th cent.: from modern Latin *spicula*, *spiculum*, diminutives of *spica* 'ear of grain'.

spicy ▶ **adjective** (**spicier**, **spiciest**) flavoured with or fragrant with spice: *pasta in a spicy tomato sauce*. ■ exciting or entertaining, especially through being mildly indecent: *spicy jokes and suggestive songs*.
– DERIVATIVES **spicily** adverb, **spiciness** noun.

spider ▶ **noun 1** an eight-legged predatory arachnid with an unsegmented body consisting of a fused head and thorax and a rounded abdomen. Spiders have fangs which inject poison into their prey, and most kinds spin webs in which to capture insects. ● Order Araneae, class Arachnida. ■ used in names of similar or related arachnids, e.g. **sea spider**, **sun spider**.
2 an object resembling a spider, especially one having numerous or prominent legs or radiating spokes. ■ Brit. a set of radiating elastic ties used to hold a load in place on a vehicle. ■ a long-legged rest for a billiard cue that can be placed over a ball without touching it.
3 another term for CRAWLER (in the computing sense).
▶ **verb** [no obj., with adverbial of direction] move in a scuttling manner suggestive of a spider: *a treecreeper spidered head first down the tree trunk*. ■ form a pattern suggestive of a spider or its web.
– DERIVATIVES **spiderish** adjective.
– ORIGIN late Old English *spīthra*, from *spinnan* (see SPIN).

spider beetle ▶ **noun** a small long-legged scavenging beetle, the female of which has a rounded body that gives it a spider-like appearance. ● Family Ptinidae: *Ptinus* and other genera.

spider crab ▶ **noun** a crab with long thin legs and a compact pear-shaped body, which is camouflaged in some kinds by attached sponges and seaweed. ● Majidae and other families, order Decapoda: *Macropodia* and other genera.

spider flower ▶ **noun** a plant with clusters of flowers which have long protruding stamens or styles. ● a South American plant (genus *Cleome*, family Capparidaceae, in particular *C. hassleriana*). ● an Australian grevillea.

spider-hunting wasp ▶ **noun** a fast-moving digger wasp that provisions its nest burrow with spiders that it has caught and paralysed. ● Family Pompilidae: many genera.

spider lily ▶ **noun** a lily that typically has long slender petals or elongated petal-like parts around the flower. ● *Hymenocallis* and other genera, family Liliaceae (or Amaryllidaceae).

spiderling ▶ **noun** a young spider.

spiderman ▶ **noun** (pl. **spidermen**) Brit. informal a person who works at great heights in building work.

spider mite ▶ **noun** an active plant-feeding mite which resembles a minute spider and is frequently a serious garden and greenhouse pest. ● Family Tetranychidae: many species, in particular the **red spider mite** (*Tetranychus urticae*).

spider monkey ▶ **noun** a South American monkey with very long limbs and a long prehensile tail. ● Genus *Brachyteles*, family Cebidae: four species.

spider naevus ▶ **noun** a cluster of minute red blood vessels visible under the skin, occurring typically during pregnancy or as a symptom of certain diseases (e.g. cirrhosis or acne rosacea).

spider orchid ▶ **noun** an orchid with a flower that is said to resemble a spider. ● Several genera in the family Orchidaceae, in particular *Ophrys* of Europe, related to the bee orchid, *Caladenia* of Australia, with long, narrow petals and sepals, and the epiphytic **tree spider orchids** (*Dendrobium*) of Australia.

spider plant ▶ **noun** a plant of the lily family which has long, narrow leaves with a central yellow stripe, native to southern Africa and popular as a houseplant. ● *Chlorophytum comosum*, family Liliaceae.

spider vein ▶ **noun** another term for THREAD VEIN.

spiderweb ▶ **noun** a web made by a spider. ■ a thing resembling a spider's web: *the spiderweb of overhead transmission lines*. ■ a type of turquoise criss-crossed with fine dark lines.
▶ **verb** (**spiderwebs**, **spiderwebbing**, **spiderwebbed**) [with obj.] cover with a pattern resembling a spiderweb: *a glass block spiderwebbed with cracks*.

spiderwort ▶ **noun** an American plant whose flowers bear long hairy stamens. ● Genus *Tradescantia*, family Commelinaceae: several species, including the blue-flowered North American *T. virginiana*, from which many cultivars have been derived.

spidery ▶ **adjective** resembling a spider, especially having long, thin, angular lines like a spider's legs: *the letters were written in a spidery hand*.

spiegeleisen /ˈspiːɡ(ə)lˌʌɪz(ə)n/ ▶ **noun** [mass noun] an alloy of iron and manganese, used in steel-making.
– ORIGIN mid 19th cent.: from German, from *Spiegel* 'mirror' + *Eisen* 'iron'.

spiel /ʃpiːl, spiːl/ informal ▶ **noun** an elaborate or glib speech or story, typically one used by a salesperson.
▶ **verb** [with obj.] reel off; recite: *he solemnly spieled all he knew*. ■ [no obj.] speak glibly or at length.
– ORIGIN late 19th cent.: from German *Spiel* 'a game'.

Spielberg /ˈspiːlbəːɡ/, Steven (b.1947), American film director and producer. His science-fiction and adventure films such as *ET* (1982) and *Jurassic Park* (1993) broke box office records, while *Schindler's List* (1993) won seven Oscars.

spieler /ˈʃpiːlə, ˈspiːlə/ informal ▶ **noun 1** a glib or voluble speaker.
2 Austral./NZ a gambler or swindler.
3 a gambling club.
– ORIGIN mid 19th cent.: from German *Spieler* 'player' (see SPIEL).

S

spiff ▶ **verb** [with obj.] (**spiff someone/thing up**) N. Amer. informal make someone or something attractive, smart, or stylish: *he arrived all spiffed up in a dinner jacket*.
– ORIGIN late 19th cent.: perhaps from dialect *spiff* 'well dressed'.

spiffing ▶ **adjective** Brit. informal, dated excellent; splendid. *it's a frightfully spiffing idea*.
– ORIGIN late 19th cent.: of unknown origin.

spifflicate /ˈspɪflɪkeɪt/ (also **spiflicate**) ▶ **verb** [with obj.] informal, humorous treat roughly or severely; destroy: *the mosquito was spifflicated*.
– ORIGIN mid 18th cent.: a fanciful formation.

spiffy ▶ **adjective** (**spiffier**, **spiffiest**) N. Amer. informal smart in appearance: *a spiffy new outfit*.
– DERIVATIVES **spiffily** adverb.
– ORIGIN mid 19th cent.: of unknown origin.

spignel /ˈspɪɡn(ə)l/ ▶ **noun** an aromatic plant of the parsley family with white flowers, found on mountains in Europe. ● *Meum athamanticum*, family Umbelliferae.
– ORIGIN early 16th cent.: perhaps from Anglo-Norman French *spigurnelle*, the name of an unidentified plant.

spigot /ˈspɪɡət/ ▶ **noun 1** a small peg or plug, especially for insertion into the vent of a cask.

2 US a tap. ▪ a device for controlling the flow of liquid in a tap.
3 the plain end of a section of a pipe fitting into the socket of the next one.
– ORIGIN Middle English: perhaps an alteration of Provençal *espigou(n)*, from Latin *spiculum*, diminutive of *spicum*, variant of *spica* (see SPICA).

spike[1] ▸ **noun 1** a thin, pointed piece of metal, wood, or another rigid material. ▪ a large stout nail, especially one used to fasten a rail to a railway sleeper. ▪ each of several metal points set into the sole of a running shoe to prevent slipping. ▪ (**spikes**) a pair of running shoes with such metal points. ▪ chiefly Brit. a pointed metal rod standing on a base and used for filing paper items such as bills, or journalistic material considered for publication and rejected. ▪ informal a hypodermic needle.
2 a sharp increase in the magnitude or concentration of something: *the oil price spike*. ▪ Electronics a pulse of very short duration in which a rapid increase in voltage is followed by a rapid decrease.
3 Brit. informal a hostel ward offering temporary accommodation for the homeless.
▸ **verb** [with obj.] **1** impale on or pierce with a sharp point: *she spiked another oyster*. ▪ (of a newspaper editor) reject (a story) by or as if by filing it on a spike: *the editors deemed the article in bad taste and spiked it*. ▪ stop the progress of (a plan or undertaking); put an end to: *he doubted they would spike the entire effort over this one negotiation*. ▪ historical render (a gun) useless by plugging up the vent with a spike.
2 form into or cover with sharp points: *his hair was matted and spiked with blood*. ▪ [no obj.] take on a sharp, pointed shape: *lightning spiked across the sky*. ▪ [no obj.] increase and then decrease sharply; reach a peak: *oil prices would spike and fall again*.
3 informal add alcohol or a drug to contaminate (drink or food) surreptitiously: *she bought me an orange juice and spiked it with vodka*. ▪ add sharp or pungent flavouring to (food or drink): *spike the liquid with lime or lemon juice*. ▪ enrich (a nuclear reactor or its fuel) with a particular isotope.
4 (in volleyball) hit (the ball) forcefully from a position near the net so that it moves downward into the opposite court. ▪ American Football fling (the ball) forcefully to the ground, typically in celebration of a touchdown or victory.
– PHRASES **spike someone's guns** Brit. thwart someone's plans.
– ORIGIN Middle English: perhaps from Middle Low German, Middle Dutch *spiker*, related to SPOKE[1]. The verb dates from the early 17th cent.

spike[2] ▸ **noun** Botany a flower cluster formed of many flower heads attached directly to a long stem. Compare with CYME, RACEME.
– ORIGIN late Middle English (denoting an ear of corn): from Latin *spica* (see SPICA).

spike heel ▸ **noun** a high tapering heel on a woman's shoe.

spikelet ▸ **noun** Botany the basic unit of a grass flower, consisting of two glumes or outer bracts at the base and one or more florets above.

spikemoss ▸ **noun** a chiefly tropical creeping clubmoss which has branching stems with hair-like spines on the leaf margins, small spore-bearing cones, and typically a mat-like growth. ● Genus *Selaginella* and family Selaginellaceae, class Lycopsida.

spikenard /ˈspʌɪknɑːd/ ▸ **noun 1** [mass noun] historical a costly perfumed ointment much valued in ancient times.
2 the Himalayan plant of the valerian family that produces the rhizome from which spikenard was prepared. See also PLOUGHMAN'S SPIKENARD. ● *Nardostachys grandiflora*, family Valerianaceae.
– ORIGIN Middle English: from medieval Latin *spica nardi* (see SPIKE[2], NARD), translating Greek *nardostakhus*.

spiky ▸ **adjective** (**spikier**, **spikiest**) like a spike or spikes or having many spikes: *he has short spiky hair*. ▪ informal easily offended or annoyed.
– DERIVATIVES **spikily** adverb, **spikiness** noun.

spile /spʌɪl/ ▸ **noun 1** a small wooden peg or spigot for stopping a cask. ▪ N. Amer. a small wooden or metal spout for tapping the sap from a sugar maple.
2 a large, heavy timber driven into the ground to support a superstructure.
▸ **verb** [with obj.] chiefly US or dialect broach (a cask) with a peg in order to draw off liquid.
– ORIGIN early 16th cent.: from Middle Dutch, Middle Low German, 'wooden peg'; in sense 2 of the noun apparently an alteration of PILE[2].

spilite /ˈspʌɪlʌɪt, ˈspɪl-/ ▸ **noun** [mass noun] Geology an altered form of basalt, rich in albite and commonly amygdaloidal in texture, typical of basaltic lava solidified under water.
– ORIGIN mid 19th cent.: from French *spillite*, from Greek *spilos* 'spot, stain'.

spill[1] ▸ **verb** (past and past participle **spilt** or **spilled**) [with obj.] **1** cause or allow (liquid) to flow over the edge of its container, especially unintentionally: *you'll spill that tea if you're not careful* | figurative *azaleas spilled cascades of flowers over the pathways*. ▪ [no obj.] (of liquid) flow over the edge of its container: *some of the wine spilled on to the floor* | figurative *light spilled into the room from the landing*. ▪ (with reference to the contents of something) empty out or be emptied out on to a surface: [with obj.] *the bag fell to the floor, **spilling out** its contents* | [no obj.] *passengers' baggage had **spilled out** of the hold*. ▪ [no obj., with adverbial of direction] (of a number of people) move out of somewhere quickly: *students began to spill out of the building*. ▪ (in the context of ball games) drop (the ball). ▪ Sailing let (wind) out of a sail, typically by slackening the sheets.
2 informal reveal (confidential information) to someone: *she ought not to be **spilling out** her troubles to you*.
3 cause to fall off a horse or bicycle: *the horse was wrenched off course, spilling his rider*.
▸ **noun 1** a quantity of liquid that has spilled or been spilt: *wipe up spills immediately*. ▪ an instance of a liquid spilling or being spilt: *he was absolved from any blame for the oil spill*.
2 a fall from a horse or bicycle.
3 Austral. a vacating of all or several posts in a cabinet or parliamentary party to allow reorganization after one important change of office.
– PHRASES **spill the beans** informal reveal secret information unintentionally or indiscreetly. **spill (someone's) blood** kill or wound people. **spill one's guts** informal reveal copious information to someone in an uninhibited way.
– PHRASAL VERBS **spill over** (of a bad situation or strong emotion) reach a point at which it can no longer be controlled or contained: *years of frustration spilled over into violence*.
– ORIGIN Old English *spillan* 'kill, destroy, waste, shed (blood)'; of unknown origin.
– DERIVATIVES **spillage** noun, **spiller** noun.

spill[2] ▸ **noun** a thin strip of wood or paper used for lighting a fire, candle, pipe, etc.
– ORIGIN Middle English (in the sense 'sharp fragment of wood'): obscurely related to SPILE. The current sense dates from the early 19th cent.

Spillane /spɪˈleɪn/, Mickey (1918–2006), American writer; pseudonym of *Frank Morrison Spillane*. His popular detective novels include *My Gun Is Quick* (1950) and *The Big Kill* (1951).

spillikin /ˈspɪlɪkɪn/ ▸ **noun 1** (**spillikins**) [treated as sing.] a game played with a heap of small rods of wood, bone, or plastic, in which players try to remove one at a time without disturbing the others.
2 a splinter or fragment.
– ORIGIN mid 18th cent.: from SPILL[2] + -KIN.

spillover ▸ **noun** an instance of overflowing or spreading into another area: *there has been a spillover into state schools of the ethos of independent schools*. ▪ a thing that spreads or has spread into another area: *the village was a spillover from a neighbouring, larger village*. ▪ [usu. as modifier] an unexpected consequence or repercussion: *the spillover effect of the quarrel*.

spillway ▸ **noun** a passage for surplus water from a dam. ▪ a natural drainage channel cut by water from melting glaciers or ice fields.

spilt past and past participle of SPILL[1].

spilth ▸ **noun** [mass noun] archaic the action of spilling; material that is spilt.

spin ▸ **verb** (**spins**, **spinning**, **spun**) **1** turn or whirl round quickly: [no obj.] *the girl **spun round** in alarm* | *the rear wheels spun violently* | [with obj.] *he fiddled with the radio, spinning the dial*. ▪ [no obj.] (of a person's head) give a sensation of dizziness: *the figures were enough to make her head spin*. ▪ [with obj.] toss (a coin). ▪ chiefly Cricket (with reference to a ball) move or cause to move through the air with a revolving motion. ▪ [with obj.] spin-dry (clothes). ▪ [with obj.] play (a record). ▪ [with obj.] shape (sheet metal) by pressure applied during rotation on a lathe: (as adj. **spun**) *spun metal components*.
2 [with obj.] draw out and twist (the fibres of wool, cotton, or other material) to convert them into yarn, either by hand or with machinery: *they **spin** wool **into** the yarn for weaving* | (as adj. **spun**) *spun glass*. ▪ make (threads) in this way: *this method is used to spin filaments from syrups*. ▪ (of a spider or a silkworm or other insect) produce (gossamer or silk) or construct (a web or cocoon) by extruding a fine viscous thread from a special gland.
3 [with obj.] give (a news story) a particular emphasis or bias.
4 [no obj.] fish with a spinner: *they were spinning for salmon in the lake*.
▸ **noun 1** a rapid turning or whirling motion: *he concluded the dance with a double spin*. ▪ [mass noun] revolving motion imparted to a ball in a game, especially cricket, tennis, or snooker: *this racket enables the player to impart more spin to the ball*. ▪ [usu. in sing.] an uncontrolled fast revolving descent of an aircraft, resulting from a stall: *he tried to stop the plane from **going into a spin***. ▪ Physics the intrinsic angular momentum of a subatomic particle.
2 [in sing.] informal a brief trip in a vehicle for pleasure: *a spin around town*.
3 [in sing.] the presentation of information in a particular way; a slant, especially a favourable one: *he tried to put a positive spin on the president's campaign* | [mass noun] *he was sick and tired of the Government's control freakery and spin*.
4 [with adj.] [in sing.] Austral./NZ informal a piece of good or bad luck: *Kevin had had a rough spin*.
– PHRASES **spin one's wheels** N. Amer. informal waste one's time or efforts. **spin a yarn** tell a long, far-fetched story.
– PHRASAL VERBS **spin something off** (of a parent company) turn a subsidiary into a new and separate company. **spin out** N. Amer. (of a driver or car) lose control, especially in a skid. **spin something out 1** make something last as long as possible: *they tried to spin out the debate through their speeches and interventions*. ▪ spend or occupy time aimlessly: *Shane and Mary played games to spin out the afternoon*. **2** (**spin someone out**) Cricket dismiss a batsman or side by spin bowling.
– ORIGIN Old English *spinnan* 'draw out and twist (fibre)'; related to German *spinnen*. The noun dates from the mid 19th cent.

spina bifida /ˌspʌɪnə ˈbɪfɪdə/ ▸ **noun** [mass noun] a congenital defect of the spine in which part of the spinal cord and its meninges are exposed through a gap in the backbone. It often causes paralysis of the lower limbs, and sometimes learning difficulties.
– ORIGIN early 18th cent.: modern Latin (see SPINE, BIFID).

spinach /ˈspɪnɪdʒ, -ɪtʃ/ ▸ **noun** an edible Asian plant of the goosefoot family, with large dark green leaves which are widely eaten as a vegetable. ● *Spinacia oleracea*, family Chenopodiaceae.
– DERIVATIVES **spinachy** adjective.
– ORIGIN Middle English: probably from Old French *espinache*, via Arabic from Persian *aspānāk*.

spinach beet ▸ **noun** beet of a variety which is cultivated for its leaves, which resemble spinach in taste and appearance. ● *Beta vulgaris* subsp. (or var.) *cicla*, family Chenopodiaceae.

spinal ▸ **adjective** relating to the spine: *spinal injuries*. ▪ relating to or forming the central axis or backbone of something: *the building of a new spinal road*.
– DERIVATIVES **spinally** adverb.
– ORIGIN late 16th cent.: from late Latin *spinalis*, from Latin *spina* (see SPINE).

spinal canal ▸ **noun** a cavity which runs successively through each of the vertebrae and encloses the spinal cord.

spinal column ▸ **noun** the spine; the backbone.

spinal cord ▸ **noun** the cylindrical bundle of nerve fibres and associated tissue which is enclosed in the spine and connects nearly all parts of the body to the brain, with which it forms the central nervous system.

spinal tap ▸ **noun** North American term for LUMBAR PUNCTURE.

spin bowler ▸ **noun** Cricket an expert at bowling with spin.

spindle ▸ **noun 1** a slender rounded rod with tapered ends used in hand spinning to twist and wind thread from a mass of wool or flax held on a distaff. ▪ a pin or rod used on a spinning wheel to twist and wind the thread. ▪ a pin bearing the bobbin of a spinning machine. ▪ a measure of length for yarn, equal to 15,120 yards (13,826 metres) for cotton or 14,400 yards (13,167 metres) for linen. ▪ a turned piece of wood used as a banister or chair leg. ▪ N. Amer.

S

a pointed metal rod on a base, used for filing paper items.
2 a rod or pin serving as an axis that revolves or on which something revolves. ■ the vertical rod at the centre of a record turntable which keeps the record in place during play.
3 Biology a slender mass of microtubules formed when a cell divides. At metaphase the chromosomes become attached to it by their centromeres before being pulled towards its ends.
4 (also **spindle tree** or **bush**) a Eurasian shrub or small tree with slender toothed leaves and pink capsules containing bright orange seeds. Its hard timber was formerly used for making spindles.
● Genus *Euonymus*, family Celastraceae: several species, in particular *E. europaea*.
– ORIGIN Old English *spinel*, from the base of the verb SPIN.

spindle-back ▸ adjective (of a chair) with a back consisting of framed cylindrical bars.

spindle cell ▸ noun Medicine a narrow, elongated cell indicating the presence of a type of sarcoma. ■ Zoology a narrow, elongated cell present in the blood of most non-mammalian vertebrates, functioning as a platelet.

spindle-shanks ▸ plural noun informal, dated long thin legs. ■ [treated as sing.] a person with long thin legs.
– DERIVATIVES **spindle-shanked** adjective.

spindle-shaped ▸ adjective having a circular cross section and tapering towards each end.

spindle shell ▸ noun a predatory marine mollusc which has a shell that forms a long slender spiral with a narrow canal extending downwards from the aperture. ● *Neptunea antiqua* (family Buccinidae) of northern seas, and *Fusinus* and other genera (family Fasciolariidae) of tropical and temperate seas, class Gastropoda.

spindle whorl ▸ noun chiefly Archaeology a whorl or small pulley used to weight a spindle.

spindly ▸ adjective (**spindlier**, **spindliest**) long or tall and thin: *spindly arms and legs*. ■ weak or insubstantial in construction: *spindly chairs*.

spin doctor ▸ noun informal a spokesperson employed to give a favourable interpretation of events to the media, especially on behalf of a political party.

spin-down ▸ noun [mass noun] a decrease in the speed of rotation of a spinning object, in particular a celestial object or computer disc.

spindrift ▸ noun [mass noun] spray blown from the crests of waves by the wind. ■ driving snow or sand.
– ORIGIN early 17th cent. (originally Scots): variant of *spoondrift*, from archaic *spoon* 'run before wind or sea' + the noun DRIFT.

spin dryer ▸ noun Brit. a machine for extracting water from wet clothes by spinning them in a revolving perforated drum.
– DERIVATIVES **spin-dry** verb (**spin-dries**, **spin-drying**, **spin-dried**).

spine ▸ noun **1** a series of vertebrae extending from the skull to the small of the back, enclosing the spinal cord and providing support for the thorax and abdomen; the backbone. ■ the central feature or main source of strength of something: *players of high quality who will form the spine of our side | Puerto Rico's mountainous spine*. ■ [mass noun] resolution or strength of character.
2 the part of a book's jacket or cover that encloses the inner edges of the pages, facing outwards when the book is on a shelf and typically bearing the title and the author's name.
3 Zoology & Botany any hard, pointed defensive projection or structure, such as a prickle of a hedgehog, a spike-like projection on a sea urchin, a sharp ray in a fish's fin, or a spike on the stem of a plant.
4 (also **pay spine**) a linear pay scale operated by some large organizations that allows flexibility for local and specific conditions.
5 Geology a tall mass of viscous lava extruded from a volcano.
– DERIVATIVES **spined** adjective.
– ORIGIN late Middle English: shortening of Old French *espine*, or from Latin *spina* 'thorn, prickle, backbone'.

spine-chiller ▸ noun a story or film that inspires terror and excitement.

spine-chilling ▸ adjective (of a story or film) inspiring terror and excitement: *a spine-chilling tale*.

spinel /spɪˈnɛl, ˈspɪn(ə)l/ ▸ noun [mass noun] a hard glassy mineral occurring as octahedral crystals of variable colour and consisting chiefly of magnesium and aluminium oxides. ■ [count noun] Chemistry any of a class of oxides including spinel, containing aluminium and another metal and having the general formula MAl_2O_4.
– ORIGIN early 16th cent.: from French *spinelle*, from Italian *spinella*, diminutive of *spina* 'thorn'.

spineless ▸ adjective **1** having no spine or backbone; invertebrate.
2 weak and purposeless: *a spineless coward*.
3 (of an animal or plant) lacking spines.
– DERIVATIVES **spinelessly** adverb, **spinelessness** noun.

spinel ruby ▸ noun [mass noun] a deep red variety of spinel, often of gem quality.

spinet /spɪˈnɛt, ˈspɪnɪt/ ▸ noun **1** historical a small harpsichord with the strings set obliquely to the keyboard, popular in the 18th century.
2 US a type of small upright piano.
– ORIGIN mid 17th cent.: shortening of obsolete French *espinette*, from Italian *spinetta* 'virginal, spinet', diminutive of *spina* 'thorn' (see SPINE), the strings being plucked by quills.

spinetail ▸ noun any of a number of birds with pointed feather tips projecting beyond the tail: ● (also **spine-tailed swift**) a mainly African and Asian swift (several genera in the family Apodidae). ● a small tropical American ovenbird (*Synallaxis* and other genera, family Furnariidae).

spine-tingling ▸ adjective informal thrilling or pleasurably frightening: *a spine-tingling adventure*.

spinifex /ˈspɪnɪfɛks/ ▸ noun a grass with coarse spiny leaves and spiny flower heads which break off and are blown about like tumbleweed, occurring from East Asia to Australia. ● Genus *Spinifex*, family Gramineae.
– ORIGIN early 19th cent.: modern Latin, from Latin *spina* 'thorn' + *-fex* from *facere* 'make'.

spinifexbird ▸ noun a secretive warbler that frequents thickets of spinifex in central Australia. ● *Eremiornis carteri*, family Sylviidae.

spinmeister /ˈspɪnmʌɪstə/ ▸ noun informal an accomplished or politically powerful spin doctor.
– ORIGIN 1990s: from SPIN + -MEISTER.

spinnaker /ˈspɪnəkə/ ▸ noun a large three-cornered sail, typically bulging when full, set forward of the mainsail of a racing yacht when running before the wind.
– ORIGIN mid 19th cent.: apparently a fanciful formation from *Sphinx*, the name of the yacht first using it, perhaps influenced by SPANKER.

spinner ▸ noun **1** a person occupied in making thread by spinning.
2 Cricket a bowler who is expert in spinning the ball. ■ a spun ball.
3 (also **spinnerbait**) Fishing a lure designed to revolve when pulled through the water. ■ a type of fishing fly, used chiefly for trout.
4 a metal fairing that is attached to and revolves with the propeller boss of an aircraft in order to streamline it.

spinneret /ˈspɪnərɛt/ ▸ noun Zoology any of a number of different organs through which the silk, gossamer, or thread of spiders, silkworms, and certain other insects is produced. ■ (in the production of man-made fibres) a cap or plate with a number of small holes through which a fibre-forming solution is forced.

spinney ▸ noun (pl. **spinneys**) Brit. a small area of trees and bushes.
– ORIGIN late 16th cent.: shortening of Old French *espinei*, from an alteration of Latin *spinetum* 'thicket', from *spina* 'thorn'.

spinning[1] ▸ noun [mass noun] the action or process of spinning; the conversion of fibres into yarn.

spinning[2] ▸ noun [mass noun] trademark an intense form of aerobic exercise performed on stationary exercise bikes and led by an instructor who sets the constantly varying pace.

spinning jenny ▸ noun historical a machine for spinning with more than one spindle at a time, patented by James Hargreaves in 1770.

spinning mule ▸ noun see MULE[1] (sense 3).

spinning top ▸ noun see TOP[2] (sense 1).

spinning wheel ▸ noun a household machine for spinning yarn with a spindle driven by a wheel attached to a crank or treadle.

spinny ▸ adjective Canadian informal mad; crazy.

spin-off ▸ noun a by-product or incidental result of a larger project: *the commercial spin-off from defence research*. ■ a product marketed by its association with a popular television programme, film, personality, etc.: [as modifier] *spin-off merchandising*. ■ a subsidiary of a parent company that has been sold off, creating a new company.

Spinone /spɪˈnəʊni/ ▸ noun (pl. **Spinoni**) a wire-haired gun dog of an Italian breed, typically white with brown markings, drooping ears, and a docked tail.
– ORIGIN 1940s: Italian.

spinose /ˈspʌɪnəʊs, spʌɪˈnəʊs/ (also **spinous** /ˈspʌɪnəs/) ▸ adjective chiefly Botany & Zoology having spines; spiny: *spinose forms will need care in collecting*.

spin-out ▸ noun N. Amer. informal **1** a spin-off.
2 a skidding spin by a vehicle out of control.

Spinoza /spɪˈnəʊzə/, Baruch (or Benedict) de (1632–77), Dutch philosopher, of Portuguese-Jewish descent. Spinoza espoused a pantheistic system, seeing 'God or nature' as a single infinite substance, with mind and matter being two incommensurable ways of conceiving the one reality.
– DERIVATIVES **Spinozism** noun, **Spinozist** noun & adjective, **Spinozistic** adjective.

spin-stabilized (also **spin-stabilised**) ▸ adjective (of a satellite or spacecraft) stabilized in a desired orientation by being made to rotate about an axis.
– DERIVATIVES **spin-stabilization** noun.

spinster ▸ noun an unmarried woman, typically an older woman beyond the usual age for marriage.
– DERIVATIVES **spinsterhood** noun, **spinsterish** adjective.
– ORIGIN late Middle English (in the sense 'woman who spins'): from the verb SPIN + -STER; in early use the term was appended to names of women to denote their occupation. The current sense dates from the early 18th cent.

USAGE The development of the word **spinster** is a good example of the way in which a word acquires strong connotations to the extent that it can no longer be used in a neutral sense. From the 17th century the word was appended to names as the official legal description of an unmarried woman: *Elizabeth Harris of London, **Spinster***. This type of use survives today in some legal and religious contexts. In modern everyday English, however, **spinster** cannot be used to mean simply 'unmarried woman'; it is now always a derogatory term, referring or alluding to a stereotype of an older woman who is unmarried, childless, prissy, and repressed.

spinthariscope /spɪnˈθarɪskəʊp/ ▸ noun Physics an instrument that shows the incidence of alpha particles by flashes on a fluorescent screen.
– ORIGIN early 20th cent.: formed irregularly from Greek *spintharis* 'spark' + -SCOPE.

spinto /ˈspɪntəʊ/ ▸ noun (pl. **spintos**) a lyric soprano or tenor voice of powerful dramatic quality. ■ a singer with a spinto voice.
– ORIGIN 1950s: Italian, literally 'pushed', past participle of *spingere* 'push'.

spinulose /ˈspɪnjʊləʊs/ ▸ adjective Botany & Zoology having small spines.
– ORIGIN early 19th cent.: from modern Latin *spinulosus*, from *spinula*, diminutive of *spina* 'thorn, spine'.

spiny ▸ adjective (**spinier**, **spiniest**) full of or covered with prickles: *a spiny cactus*. ■ informal difficult to understand or handle: *a spiny problem*.
– DERIVATIVES **spininess** noun.

spiny anteater ▸ noun another term for ECHIDNA.

spiny dogfish ▸ noun another term for SPUR-DOG.

spiny-headed worm ▸ noun another term for THORNY-HEADED WORM.

spiny lobster ▸ noun a large edible crustacean with a spiny shell and long heavy antennae, but lacking the large claws of true lobsters. ● Family Palinuridae: several genera and species, in particular *Palinuris vulgaris* of European waters, and the American genus *Panulirus*.

spiny mouse ▸ noun a mouse that has spines mixed with the hair on its back, native to Africa and SW Asia. ● Genus *Acomys*, family Muridae: several species.

spiracle /ˈspʌɪrək(ə)l/ ▸ noun Zoology an external respiratory opening, especially each of a number of pores on the body of an insect, or each of a pair of vestigial gill slits behind the eye of a cartilaginous fish.
– DERIVATIVES **spiracular** adjective.
– ORIGIN late 18th cent.: from Latin *spiraculum*, from *spirare* 'breathe'.

spiraea /spʌɪˈriːə/ (chiefly US also **spirea**) ▸ noun a shrub of the rose family, with clusters of small white or pink flowers. Found throughout the northern

S

hemisphere, it is widely cultivated as a garden ornamental. ● Genus *Spiraea*, family Rosaceae.
– ORIGIN modern Latin, from Greek *speiraia*, from *speira* 'a coil'.

spiral ▶ **adjective** winding in a continuous and gradually widening (or tightening) curve, either around a central point on a flat plane or about an axis so as to form a cone: *a spiral pattern*. ■ winding in a continuous curve of constant diameter about a central axis, as though along a cylinder; helical. ■ (of a stairway) constantly turning in one direction as it rises, around a solid or open centre: *a wrought-iron spiral staircase*. ■ Medicine (of a fracture) curving round a long bone lengthwise. ■ short for SPIRAL-BOUND: *a spiral notebook*.
▶ **noun 1** a spiral curve, shape, pattern, or object: *a spiral of smoke*. ■ Astronomy short for SPIRAL GALAXY.
2 a progressive rise or fall of prices, wages, etc., each responding to an upward or downward stimulus provided by a previous one: *an inflationary spiral*. ■ a process of deterioration through the continuous increase or decrease of a specified feature: *this spiral of deprivation and environmental degradation*.
▶ **verb** (**spirals, spiralling, spiralled**; US **spirals, spiraling, spiraled**) **1** [no obj., with adverbial of direction] move in a spiral course: *a wisp of smoke spiralled up from the trees*. ■ [with obj. and adverbial] cause to have a spiral shape or follow a spiral course: *spiral the bandage round the limb*.
2 [no obj.] show a continuous and dramatic increase: *inflation continued to spiral* | (as adj. **spiralling**) *he needed to relax after the spiralling tensions of the day*. ■ (**spiral down/downward**) decrease or deteriorate continuously: *he expects the figures to spiral down further*.
– DERIVATIVES **spirally** adverb.
– ORIGIN mid 16th cent. (as an adjective): from medieval Latin *spiralis*, from Latin *spira* 'coil' (see SPIRE²).

spiral-bound ▶ **adjective** (of a book or notepad) bound with a wire or plastic spiral threaded through a row of holes along one edge.

spiral galaxy ▶ **noun** a galaxy in which the stars and gas clouds are concentrated mainly in one or more spiral arms.

spirant /ˈspʌɪr(ə)nt/ Phonetics ▶ **adjective** (of a consonant) uttered with a continuous expulsion of breath.
▶ **noun** a spirant consonant; a fricative.
– ORIGIN mid 19th cent.: from Latin *spirant-* 'breathing', from the verb *spirare*.

spire¹ ▶ **noun** a tapering conical or pyramidal structure on the top of a building, typically a church tower. ■ the continuation of a tree trunk above the point where branching begins, especially in a tree of a tapering form. ■ a long tapering object: *spires of delphiniums*.
– DERIVATIVES **spired** adjective, **spiry** adjective.
– ORIGIN Old English *spīr* 'tall slender stem of a plant'; related to German *Spier* 'tip of a blade of grass'.

spire² ▶ **noun** Zoology the upper tapering part of the spiral shell of a gastropod mollusc, comprising all but the whorl containing the body.
– ORIGIN mid 16th cent. (in the general sense 'a spiral'): from French, or via Latin from Greek *speira* 'a coil'.

S

spirea ▶ **noun** US variant spelling of SPIRAEA.

spire shell ▶ **noun** a marine or freshwater mollusc with a long conical spiral shell. ● Hydrobiidae and related families, class Gastropoda.

spirillum /spʌɪˈrɪləm/ ▶ **noun** (pl. **spirilla** /-lə/) a bacterium with a rigid spiral structure, found in stagnant water and sometimes causing disease. ● Genus *Spirillum*; Gram-negative.
– ORIGIN modern Latin, irregular diminutive of Latin *spira* 'a coil'.

spirit ▶ **noun 1** the non-physical part of a person which is the seat of emotions and character; the soul: *we seek a harmony between body and spirit*. ■ such a part regarded as a person's true self and as capable of surviving physical death or separation: *a year after he left, his spirit is still present*. ■ such a part manifested as an apparition after a person's death; a ghost. ■ a supernatural being: *shrines to nature spirits*. ■ (**Spirit**) short for HOLY SPIRIT.
2 [in sing.] the prevailing or typical quality, mood, or attitude of a person, group, or period of time: *I hope the team will build on this spirit of confidence* | *the university is a symbol of the nation's egalitarian spirit*. ■ [with adj.] a person identified with their most prominent quality or with their role in a group or movement: *he was a leading spirit in the conference*. ■ (often **spirits**) a person's mood or attitude: *the warm weather lifted everyone's spirits* | *he confessed in a spirit of self-respect*. ■ [mass noun] the quality of courage, energy, and determination: *his visitors admired his spirit and good temper*.
3 the real meaning or the intention behind something as opposed to its strict verbal interpretation: *the rule had been broken in spirit if not in letter*.
4 (usu. **spirits**) chiefly Brit. strong distilled liquor such as brandy, whisky, gin, or rum. ■ [mass noun] [with modifier] a volatile liquid, especially a fuel, prepared by distillation: *aviation spirit*. ■ archaic a solution of volatile components extracted from something, typically by distillation or by solution in alcohol: *spirits of turpentine*.
5 archaic a highly refined substance or fluid thought to govern vital phenomena.
▶ **verb** (**spirits, spiriting, spirited**) [with obj. and adverbial of direction] convey rapidly and secretly: *stolen cows were* **spirited away** *some distance to prevent detection*.
– PHRASES **enter into the spirit** join wholeheartedly in an event, especially one of celebration and festivity: *he* **entered into the spirit of** *the occasion by dressing as a pierrot*. **in** (or **in the**) **spirit** in thought or intention though not physically: *he couldn't be here in person, but he is with us in spirit*. **the spirit is willing but the flesh is weak** proverb someone has good intentions but fails to live up to them. [with biblical allusion to Matt. 26:41.] **when the spirit moves someone** when someone feels inclined to do something: *he can be quite candid when the spirit moves him*. [a phrase originally in Quaker use, with reference to the Holy Spirit.] **the spirit world** (in animistic and occult belief) the non-physical realm in which disembodied spirits have their existence.
– PHRASAL VERBS **spirit someone up** archaic stimulate, animate, or cheer up someone.
– ORIGIN Middle English: from Anglo-Norman French, from Latin *spiritus* 'breath, spirit', from *spirare* 'breathe'.

spirited ▶ **adjective 1** full of energy, enthusiasm, and determination: *a spirited campaigner for women's rights*.
2 [in combination] having a specified character, attitude, or mood: *a warm-hearted, generous-spirited man*.
– DERIVATIVES **spiritedly** adverb, **spiritedness** noun.

spirit gum ▶ **noun** [mass noun] a quick-drying solution of gum, chiefly used by actors to attach false hair to their faces.

spiritism ▶ **noun** another term for SPIRITUALISM (sense 1).
– DERIVATIVES **spiritist** adjective & noun, **spiritistic** adjective.

spirit lamp ▶ **noun** a lamp burning volatile spirits, especially methylated spirits, instead of oil.

spiritless ▶ **adjective** lacking courage, vigour, or vivacity: *Ruth and I played a spiritless game of Scrabble*.
– DERIVATIVES **spiritlessly** adverb, **spiritlessness** noun.

spirit level ▶ **noun** a device consisting of a sealed glass tube partially filled with alcohol or other liquid, containing an air bubble whose position reveals whether a surface is perfectly level.

spirit of hartshorn ▶ **noun** see HARTSHORN.

spirit of wine (also **spirits of wine**) ▶ **noun** [mass noun] archaic purified alcohol.

spiritous ▶ **adjective** another term for SPIRITUOUS.

spirits of salt ▶ **noun** archaic term for HYDROCHLORIC ACID.

spiritual /ˈspɪrɪtʃʊəl, -tjʊəl/ ▶ **adjective 1** relating to or affecting the human spirit or soul as opposed to material or physical things: *I'm responsible for his spiritual welfare*. ■ having a relationship based on a profound level of mental or emotional communion: *he never forgot his spiritual father*. ■ (of a person) not concerned with material values or pursuits.
2 relating to religion or religious belief: *the country's spiritual leader*.
▶ **noun** (also **Negro spiritual**) a religious song of a kind associated with black Christians of the southern US, and thought to derive from the combination of European hymns and African musical elements by black slaves.
– PHRASES **one's spiritual home** a place in which one feels a strong sense of belonging: *I had always thought of Italy as my spiritual home*.
– DERIVATIVES **spirituality** noun, **spiritually** adverb.
– ORIGIN Middle English: from Old French *spirituel*, from Latin *spiritualis*, from *spiritus* (see SPIRIT).

spiritualism ▶ **noun** [mass noun] **1** a system of belief or religious practice based on supposed communication with the spirits of the dead, especially through mediums.
2 Philosophy the doctrine that the spirit exists as distinct from matter, or that spirit is the only reality.
– DERIVATIVES **spiritualist** noun, **spiritualistic** adjective.

spiritualize (also **spiritualise**) ▶ **verb** [with obj.] elevate to a spiritual level.
– DERIVATIVES **spiritualization** noun.

spirituous /ˈspɪrɪtjʊəs/ ▶ **adjective** formal or archaic containing much alcohol; distilled: *spirituous beverages*.
– ORIGIN late 16th cent. (in the sense 'spirited, lively'): from Latin *spiritus* 'spirit' + **-ous**, or from French *spiritueux*.

spiritus /ˈspɪrɪtʊs/ ▶ **noun** literary a particular spirit or quality.
– ORIGIN Latin, 'breath, spirit'.

spiritus rector /ˈrɛktɔː/ ▶ **noun** [mass noun] a ruling or guiding spirit.
– ORIGIN Latin.

spiro-¹ ▶ **combining form 1** spiral; in a spiral: *spirochaete*.
2 Chemistry denoting a molecule with two rings with one atom common to both: *spironolactone*.
– ORIGIN from Latin *spira*, Greek *speira* 'a coil'.

spiro-² ▶ **combining form** relating to breathing: *spirometer*.
– ORIGIN formed irregularly from Latin *spirare* 'breathe'.

spirochaete /ˈspʌɪrə(ʊ)kiːt/ (US **spirochete**) ▶ **noun** a flexible spirally twisted bacterium, especially one that causes syphilis. ● *Treponema* and other genera, order Spirochaetales; Gram-negative.
– ORIGIN late 19th cent.: from SPIRO-¹ 'in a spiral' + Greek *khaitē* 'long hair'.

spirograph ▶ **noun 1** an instrument for recording breathing movements.
2 (**Spirograph**) trademark a toy which is used to draw intricate curved patterns using interlocking plastic cogs and toothed rings of different sizes.
– DERIVATIVES **spirographic** adjective (sense 1).

spirogyra /ˌspʌɪrə(ʊ)ˈdʒʌɪrə/ ▶ **noun** Botany a filamentous green alga of a genus that includes blanket weed. ● Genus *Spirogyra*, division Chlorophyta.
– ORIGIN modern Latin, from SPIRO-¹ 'spiral' + Greek *guros, gura* 'round'.

spirometer /spʌɪˈrɒmɪtə/ ▶ **noun** an instrument for measuring the air capacity of the lungs.
– DERIVATIVES **spirometry** noun.

spironolactone /ˌspʌɪrənə(ʊ)ˈlaktəʊn/ ▶ **noun** [mass noun] Medicine a steroid drug which promotes sodium excretion and is used in the treatment of certain types of oedema and hypertension.
– ORIGIN 1960s: from SPIRO-¹ (sense 2) + LACTONE, with the insertion of **-ONE**.

spirt ▶ **verb & noun** old-fashioned spelling of SPURT.

spirulina /ˌspɪrʊˈlʌɪnə, ˌspʌɪrʊ-/ ▶ **noun** [mass noun] filamentous cyanobacteria which form tangled masses in warm alkaline lakes in Africa and Central and South America. ● Genus *Spirulina*, division Cyanobacteria. ■ (usu. **Spirulina**) the substance of such growths dried and prepared as a food or food additive, which is a rich source of many vitamins and minerals.
– ORIGIN modern Latin, from *spirula* 'small spiral (shell)'.

spit¹ ▶ **verb** (**spits, spitting**; past and past participle **spat** or **spit**) [no obj.] **1** eject saliva forcibly from one's mouth, sometimes as a gesture of contempt or anger: *Todd spat in Hugh's face*. ■ [with obj.] forcibly eject (food or liquid) from one's mouth: *the baby* **spat out** *its porridge*. ■ (**spit up**) N. Amer. (especially of a baby) vomit or regurgitate food. ■ [with obj.] utter in a hostile or aggressive way: *she spat abuse at the jury* | [with direct speech] *'Go to hell!' she spat*. ■ black English perform rap music. ■ (of a fire or something being cooked) emit small bursts of sparks or hot fat with a series of short, explosive noises. ■ (of a cat) make a hissing noise as a sign of anger or hostility.
2 (**it spits, it is spitting**, etc.) Brit. light rain falls: *it began to spit*.
▶ **noun 1** [mass noun] saliva, typically that which has been ejected from a person's mouth.
2 an act of spitting.
– PHRASES **be the spit** (or **the dead spit**) **of** informal look exactly like: *Felix is the spit of Rosa's brother*. [see SPITTING IMAGE.] **spit-and-sawdust** Brit. informal used to describe an old-fashioned or simple pub or bar, of a type whose floor was originally covered with sawdust. **spit blood** informal be very angry. **spit** (**out**)

the dummy Austral. informal behave in a bad-tempered or petulant way. **spit feathers** (or **tacks** or Austral. **chips**) informal, chiefly Brit. **1** be very thirsty. **2** be very angry. **spit in the eye** (or **face**) **of** show contempt or scorn for. **spitting distance** see **WITHIN SPITTING DISTANCE** at **DISTANCE**. **spit in** (or **into**) **the wind** do something futile or pointless. **spit it out** informal used to urge someone to say or confess something quickly: *spit it out, man, I haven't got all day.*
– DERIVATIVES **spitty** adjective.
– ORIGIN Old English *spittan*, of imitative origin.

spit² ▶ noun **1** a long, thin metal rod pushed through meat in order to hold and turn it while it is roasted over an open fire: *chicken cooked on a spit.*
2 a narrow point of land projecting into the sea: *a narrow spit of land shelters the bay.*
▶ verb (**spits, spitting, spitted**) [with obj.] put a spit through (meat) in order to roast it over an open fire: *he spitted the rabbit and cooked it.*
– DERIVATIVES **spitty** adjective.
– ORIGIN Old English *spitu*, of West Germanic origin; related to Dutch *spit* and German *Spiess*.

spit³ ▶ noun (pl. **same** or **spits**) a layer of earth whose depth is equal to the length of the blade of a spade: *break up the top spit with a fork.*
– ORIGIN early 16th cent.: from Middle Dutch and Middle Low German; probably related to **SPIT²**.

spit and polish ▶ noun [mass noun] thorough or exaggerated cleaning and polishing, especially by a soldier: *they gave the dining room some extra spit and polish.*

spitball N. Amer. ▶ noun **1** a piece of paper that has been chewed and shaped into a ball for use as a missile.
2 Baseball an unlawful pitch made with a ball moistened with saliva or sweat to make it move erratically.
▶ verb [with obj.] informal throw out (a suggestion) for discussion: *I'm just spitballing a few ideas.*
– DERIVATIVES **spitballer** noun.

spitchcock ▶ noun an eel that has been split and grilled or fried.
▶ verb [no obj.] split and grill or fry (an eel or other fish).
– ORIGIN late 15th cent.: of unknown origin; compare with **SPATCHCOCK**.

spit curl ▶ noun North American term for **KISS-CURL**.

spit dog ▶ noun a firedog with a hook on its upright for supporting a spit.

spite ▶ noun [mass noun] a desire to hurt, annoy, or offend someone: *he'd think I was saying it out of spite.* ■ [count noun] archaic a grudge: *it seemed as if the wind had a spite at her.*
▶ verb [with obj.] deliberately hurt, annoy, or offend (someone): *he put the house up for sale to spite his family.*
– PHRASES **in spite of** without being affected by the particular factor mentioned: *he was suddenly cold in spite of the sun.* **in spite of oneself** although one did not want or expect to do so: *Oliver smiled in spite of himself.*
– ORIGIN Middle English: shortening of Old French *despit* 'contempt', *despiter* 'show contempt for'.

spiteful ▶ adjective showing or caused by malice: *the teachers made spiteful little jokes about me.*
– DERIVATIVES **spitefully** adverb, **spitefulness** noun.

spitfire ▶ noun a person with a fierce temper.

Spithead /spɪt'hɛd/ a channel between the NE coast of the Isle of Wight and the mainland of southern England. It offers sheltered access to Southampton Water and deep anchorage.

spit-roast ▶ verb [with obj.] (usu. as adj. **spit-roasted**) cook (a piece of meat) on a spit: *spit-roasted lamb.*

Spitsbergen /'spɪts,bəːg(ə)n/ a Norwegian island in the Svalbard archipelago, in the Arctic Ocean north of Norway; principal settlement, Longyearbyen.

spitter ▶ noun **1** a person who spits.
2 another term for **SPITBALL** (sense 2 of the noun).

spitting cobra ▶ noun an African cobra that defends itself by spitting venom from the fangs, typically at the aggressor's eyes. ● Genera *Naja* and *Hemachatus*, family Elapidae: three species, in particular the **black-necked spitting cobra** (*N. nigricollis*).

spitting image ▶ noun informal the exact double of (another person or thing): *she's the spitting image of her mum.*
– ORIGIN late 19th cent.: originally as *the spit of* or *the spit and image of*; perhaps from the idea of a person apparently being formed from the spit of another, so great is the similarity between them.

spittle ▶ noun [mass noun] saliva, especially as ejected from the mouth.
– DERIVATIVES **spittly** adjective.
– ORIGIN late 15th cent.: alteration of dialect *spattle*, by association with **SPIT¹**.

spittlebug ▶ noun another term for **FROGHOPPER**.

spittoon /spɪ'tuːn/ ▶ noun a metal or earthenware pot typically having a funnel-shaped top, used for spitting into.

Spitz, Mark (Andrew) (b.1950), American swimmer. He won seven gold medals in the 1972 Olympic Games at Munich and set twenty-seven world records for free style and butterfly (1967–72).

spitz ▶ noun a dog of a small breed with a pointed muzzle, especially a Pomeranian.
– ORIGIN mid 19th cent.: from German *Spitz(hund)*, from *spitz* 'pointed' + *Hund* 'dog'.

spiv ▶ noun Brit. informal a man, typically a flashy dresser, who makes a living by disreputable dealings.
– DERIVATIVES **spivvish** adjective, **spivvy** adjective (**spivvier, spivviest**).
– ORIGIN 1930s: perhaps related to **SPIFFY**.

splake /spleɪk/ ▶ noun a hybrid trout of North American lakes. ● Produced by crossing the speckled trout (*S. fontinalis*) with the lake trout (*Salvelinus namaycush*).
– ORIGIN 1950s: blend of *speckled* and **LAKE¹**.

splanchnic /'splaŋknɪk/ ▶ adjective Anatomy relating to the viscera or internal organs, especially those of the abdomen.
– ORIGIN late 17th cent.: from modern Latin *splanchnicus*, from Greek *splankhnikos*, from *splankhna* 'entrails'.

splanchnopleure /,splaŋknə(ʊ)'plʊə/ ▶ noun Embryology a layer of tissue in a vertebrate embryo comprising the endoderm and the inner layer of mesoderm, and giving rise to the gut, lungs, and yolk sac. Often contrasted with **SOMATOPLEURE**.
– ORIGIN late 19th cent.: from Greek *splankhna* 'entrails' + *pleura* 'side'.

splash ▶ verb **1** [with obj. and adverbial of direction] cause (liquid) to strike or fall on something in irregular drops: *she splashed cold water on to her face.* ■ [with obj.] make wet by splashing: *they splashed each other with water.* ■ [no obj., with adverbial of direction] (of a liquid) fall or be scattered in irregular drops: *a tear fell and splashed on to the pillow.* ■ [no obj., with adverbial] strike or move around in a body of water, causing it to fly about noisily: *a stone splashed into the water* | *she splashed up the path.* ■ (**be splashed with**) be decorated with scattered patches of: *a field splashed with purple clover.*
2 [with obj.] print (a story or photograph, especially a sensational one) in a prominent place in a newspaper or magazine: *the story was* ***splashed across*** *the front pages.*
▶ noun **1** a sound made by something striking or falling into liquid: *we hit the water with a mighty splash.* ■ a spell of moving about in water energetically: *the girls joined them for a final splash in the pool.* ■ a small quantity of liquid that has fallen or been dashed against a surface: ***a splash of*** *gravy.* ■ a small quantity of liquid added to a drink: ***a splash of*** *lemonade.* ■ a bright patch of colour: *add a red scarf to give* ***a splash of*** *colour.*
2 informal a prominent or sensational news feature or story: *a front-page splash.*
– PHRASES **make a splash** informal attract a great deal of attention.
– PHRASAL VERBS **splash down** (of a spacecraft) land on water. **splash out** Brit. informal spend money freely: *she* ***splashed out on*** *a Mercedes.*
– ORIGIN early 18th cent. (as a verb): alteration of **PLASH¹**.

splashback ▶ noun Brit. a panel behind a sink or cooker that protects the wall from splashes.

splashboard ▶ noun a screen designed to protect the passengers of a vehicle or boat from splashes.

splashdown ▶ noun the alighting of a returning spacecraft on the sea, with the assistance of parachutes.

splashy ▶ adjective (**splashier, splashiest**) **1** characterized by water splashing about: *a splashy waterfall.* ■ characterized by irregular patches of bright colour: *splashy floral silks.*
2 informal attracting a great deal of attention; ostentatiously impressive: *I don't care for splashy Hollywood parties.*

splat¹ ▶ noun a piece of thin wood in the centre of a chair back.
– ORIGIN mid 19th cent.: from obsolete *splat* 'split up'; related to **SPLIT**.

splat² informal ▶ noun a sound of something soft and wet or heavy striking a surface: *the goblin makes a huge splat as he hits the ground.*
▶ adverb with a splat: *he lands splat on his right elbow.*
▶ verb (**splats, splatting, splatted**) [with obj.] crush or squash with a splat: *he was splatting a bug.* ■ [no obj.] land or be squashed with a splat.
– ORIGIN late 19th cent.: abbreviation of **SPLATTER**.

splatter ▶ verb **1** [with obj.] splash with a liquid, typically a thick or viscous one: *a passing cart rolled by, splattering him with mud.* ■ splash (a liquid) over a surface or object. ■ [no obj., with adverbial] (of a liquid) splash: *heavy droplets of rain splatter on to the windscreen.*
2 informal prominently or sensationally publish (a story) in a newspaper: *the story is* ***splattered over*** *pages two and three.*
▶ noun **1** a spot or trail of a thick or viscous liquid splashed over a surface or object: *each puddle we crossed threw* ***a splatter of*** *mud on the windshield.*
2 [as modifier] informal denoting or referring to films featuring many violent and gruesome deaths: *a splatter movie.*
– ORIGIN late 18th cent.: imitative.

splatterpunk ▶ noun [mass noun] informal a literary genre characterized by the explicit description of horrific, violent, or pornographic scenes.

splay ▶ verb [with obj.] thrust or spread (things, especially limbs or fingers) out and apart: *her hands were splayed across his broad shoulders* | *he stood with his legs and arms* ***splayed out***. ■ [no obj.] (especially of limbs or fingers) be thrust or spread out and apart: *his legs* ***splayed out*** *in front of him.* ■ [no obj.] become wider or more separated: *the river* ***splayed out***, *deepening to become an estuary.* ■ (usu. as adj. **splayed**) construct (a window, doorway, or other aperture) so that it diverges or is wider at one side of the wall than the other: *the walls are pierced by splayed window openings.*
▶ noun **1** a tapered widening of a road at an intersection to increase visibility.
2 a surface making an oblique angle with another, especially a splayed window or other aperture.
■ [mass noun] the degree of bevel or slant of a surface.
▶ adjective [usu. in combination] turned outward or widened: *the girls were sitting splay-legged.*
– ORIGIN Middle English (in the sense 'unfold to view, display'): shortening of the verb **DISPLAY**.

splay-foot ▶ noun a broad flat foot turned outward.
– DERIVATIVES **splay-footed** adjective.

spleen ▶ noun **1** Anatomy an abdominal organ involved in the production and removal of blood cells in most vertebrates and forming part of the immune system.
2 [mass noun] bad temper; spite: *he could* ***vent his spleen*** *on the institutions which had duped him.*
– DERIVATIVES **spleenful** adjective.
– ORIGIN Middle English: shortening of Old French *esplen*, via Latin from Greek *splēn*; sense 2 derives from the earlier belief that the spleen was the seat of bad temper.

spleenwort ▶ noun a small fern which grows in rosettes on rocks and walls, typically with rounded or triangular lobes on a slender stem. Spleenworts were formerly used to treat disorders of the spleen.
● Genus *Asplenium*, family Aspleniaceae.

splen- ▶ combining form Anatomy relating to the spleen: *splenectomy.*
– ORIGIN from Greek *splēn* 'spleen'.

splendent ▶ adjective archaic shining brightly. ■ illustrious; great.
– ORIGIN late 15th cent.: from Latin *splendent-* 'shining', from the verb *splendere*.

splendid ▶ adjective magnificent; very impressive: *a splendid view of Windsor Castle* | *his robes were splendid.* ■ informal excellent; very good: *a splendid fellow* | [as exclamation] *'Is your family well? Splendid!'.*
– PHRASES **splendid isolation** used to emphasize the isolation of a person or thing: *the stone stands in* ***splendid isolation*** *near the moorland road.* [late 19th cent.: first applied to the period of 1890–1907 when Britain pursued a policy of diplomatic and commercial non-involvement.]
– DERIVATIVES **splendidly** adverb [as submodifier] *a splendidly ornate style*, **splendidness** noun.
– ORIGIN early 17th cent.: from French *splendide* or Latin *splendidus*, from *splendere* 'shine, be bright'.

splendiferous /splɛn'dɪf(ə)rəs/ ▶ adjective informal, humorous splendid: *a splendiferous Sunday dinner.*

S

– DERIVATIVES **splendiferously** adverb, **splendiferousness** noun.
– ORIGIN mid 19th cent.: formed irregularly from SPLENDOUR.

splendour (US **splendor**) ▸ noun [mass noun] magnificent and splendid appearance; grandeur: *the barren splendour of the Lake District.* ■ (**splendours**) magnificent features or qualities: *the splendours of the imperial court.*
– ORIGIN late Middle English: from Anglo-Norman French *splendur* or Latin *splendor*, from *splendere* 'shine, be bright'.

splenectomy /splɪˈnɛktəmi/ ▸ noun (pl. **splenectomies**) a surgical operation involving removal of the spleen.

splenetic /splɪˈnɛtɪk/ ▸ adjective **1** bad-tempered; spiteful: *a splenetic rant.*
2 archaic term for SPLENIC.
– DERIVATIVES **splenetically** adverb (sense 1).
– ORIGIN late Middle English (as a noun denoting a person with a diseased spleen): from late Latin *spleneticus*, from Greek *splēn* (see SPLEEN).

splenic /ˈsplɛnɪk, ˈspliːnɪk/ ▸ adjective relating to the spleen: *the splenic artery.*
– ORIGIN early 17th cent.: from French *splénique*, or via Latin from Greek *splēnikos*, from *splēn* (see SPLEEN).

splenitis /splɪˈnʌɪtɪs/ ▸ noun [mass noun] Medicine inflammation of the spleen.

splenium /ˈspliːnɪəm/ ▸ noun Anatomy the thick posterior part of the corpus callosum of the brain.
– DERIVATIVES **splenial** adjective.
– ORIGIN mid 19th cent.: from Latin.

splenius /ˈspliːnɪəs/ (also **splenius muscle**) ▸ noun (pl. **splenii** /-nɪʌɪ/) Anatomy either of two muscles attached to the vertebrae in the neck and upper back which draw back the head.
– ORIGIN mid 18th cent.: modern Latin, from Greek *splēnion* 'bandage'.

splenomegaly /ˌspliːnə(ʊ)ˈmɛg(ə)li/ ▸ noun [mass noun] abnormal enlargement of the spleen.
– ORIGIN early 20th cent.: from SPLEN- 'spleen' + Greek *megas, megal-* 'great'.

splice ▸ verb [with obj.] join or connect (a rope or ropes) by interweaving the strands at the ends: *we learned how to weave and splice ropes* | figurative *the work splices detail and generalization.* ■ join (pieces of timber, film, or tape) at the ends: *commercials can be* ***spliced in*** *later* | *he had to* ***splice*** *the short music films* ***together.*** ■ Genetics join or insert (a gene or gene fragment).
▸ noun a join consisting of two ropes, pieces of tape or timber, etc. joined together at the ends. ■ the wedge-shaped tang of a cricket-bat handle, forming a joint with the blade.
– PHRASES **get** (or **be**) **spliced** Brit. informal get married. **splice the main brace** Brit. historical (in the navy) serve out an extra tot of rum. [perhaps arising from the issue of a tot of rum as a reward for the actual splicing of the main brace, which would be a rare and difficult operation.]
– DERIVATIVES **splicer** noun.
– ORIGIN early 16th cent.: probably from Middle Dutch *splissen*, of unknown origin.

spliff ▸ noun Brit. informal a cannabis cigarette. ■ [mass noun] cannabis.
– ORIGIN 1930s (originally West Indian): of unknown origin.

spline /splʌɪn/ ▸ noun **1** a rectangular key fitting into grooves in the hub and shaft of a wheel, especially one formed integrally with the shaft which allows movement of the wheel on the shaft. ■ a corresponding groove in a hub along which the key may slide.
2 a slat of wood, metal, etc. ■ a flexible wood or rubber strip used especially in drawing large curves.
3 (also **spline curve**) Mathematics a continuous curve constructed so as to pass through a given set of points and have a certain number of continuous derivatives.
▸ verb [with obj.] secure (a part) by means of a spline. ■ (usu. as adj. **splined**) fit with a spline: *splined freewheels.*
– ORIGIN mid 18th cent. (originally East Anglian dialect): perhaps related to SPLINTER.

splint ▸ noun **1** a strip of rigid material used for supporting and immobilizing a broken bone when it has been set: *she had to wear splints on her legs.*
2 a long, thin strip of wood used to light a fire. ■ a rigid or flexible strip, especially of wood, used in basketwork.
3 a bony enlargement on the inside of a horse's leg, on the splint bone.
4 S. African a fragment of diamond.
▸ verb [with obj.] secure (a broken limb) with a splint or splints: *his leg was splinted.*
– ORIGIN Middle English (in sense 2 of the noun; also denoting a section of armour): from Middle Dutch, Middle Low German *splinte* 'metal plate or pin'; related to SPLINTER.

splint bone ▸ noun either of two small bones in the foreleg of a horse or other large quadruped, lying behind and close to the cannon bone.

splinter ▸ noun a small, thin, sharp piece of wood, glass, or similar material broken off from a larger piece: *a splinter of ice.*
▸ verb break or cause to break into small sharp fragments: [no obj.] *the soap box splintered* | [with obj.] *he crashed into a fence, splintering the wooden barricade.* ■ (of a group or organization) separate into smaller units, typically as a result of disagreement: *the party had begun to splinter into factions.*
– DERIVATIVES **splintery** adjective.
– ORIGIN Middle English: from Middle Dutch *splinter*, *splenter*; related to SPLINT.

splinter bar ▸ noun Brit. another term for SWINGLETREE.

splinter group (also **splinter party**) ▸ noun a small organization, typically a political party, that has broken away from a larger one.

splinter-proof ▸ adjective **1** capable of withstanding splinters from bursting shells or bombs: *splinter-proof shutters.*
2 not producing splinters when broken: *splinter-proof glass.*

Split /splɪt/ a seaport on the coast of southern Croatia; pop. 177,500 (est. 2009). Founded as a Roman colony in 78 BC, it contains the ruins of the palace of the emperor Diocletian, built in about AD 300.

split ▸ verb (**splits, splitting, split**) **1** break or cause to break forcibly into parts, especially into halves or along the grain: [no obj.] *the ice cracked and split* | [with obj.] *split and toast the muffins.* ■ remove or be removed by breaking, separating, or dividing: [no obj.] *a group of Nottinghamshire miners* ***split away*** *to create a separate union.* ■ divide or cause to divide into parts or elements: [no obj.] *the river had* ***split into*** *a number of channels* | ***splitting*** *water* ***into*** *oxygen and hydrogen.* ■ [with obj.] divide and share (something, especially resources or responsibilities): *they met up and split the booty.* ■ [with obj.] cause the fission of (an atom).
2 (with reference to a group of people) divide into two or more groups: [no obj.] *let's* ***split up*** *and find the other two* | [with obj.] *once again the family was* ***split up.*** ■ [no obj.] end a marriage or an emotional or working relationship: *after the band* ***split up*** *Tex became a railway clerk.* ■ [with obj.] (of an issue) cause (a group) to be divided because of opposing views: *the party was deeply* ***split over*** *its future direction.*
3 [no obj.] informal (of one's head) suffer great pain from a headache: *my head is splitting* | (as adj. **splitting**) *a splitting headache.*
4 [no obj.] Brit. informal betray the secrets of or inform on someone: *I told him I wouldn't* ***split on*** *him.*
5 [no obj.] informal leave a place, especially suddenly: *'Let's split,' Harvey said.*
▸ noun **1** a tear, crack, or fissure in something, especially down the middle or along the grain: *splits appeared in the decaying planks* | *light squeezed through a small split in the curtain.* ■ an instance or act of splitting or being split; a division: *a 75–25 split of proceeds* | *the split between the rich and the poor.* ■ a separation into parties or within a party; a schism: *the accusations caused a split in the party.* ■ an ending of a marriage or other relationship: *a much-publicized split with his wife.*
2 (**the splits** or US also **a split**) (in gymnastics and dance) an act of leaping in the air or sitting down with the legs straight and at right angles to the body, one in front and the other behind, or one at each side: *I could never* ***do the splits*** *before.*
3 a thing that is divided or split, in particular: ■ a bun, roll, or cake that is split or cut in half. ■ a split osier used in basketwork. ■ each strip of steel or cane that makes up the reed in a loom. ■ half a bottle of champagne. ■ a single thickness of split hide. ■ (in tenpin bowling) a formation of standing pins after the first ball in which there is a gap between two pins or groups of pins, making a spare unlikely. ■ US a split-level house.
4 the time taken to complete a recognized part of a race, or the point in the race where such a time is measured.
5 N. Amer. a drawn match or series.
– PHRASES **split the difference** take the average of two proposed amounts. **split hairs** see HAIR. **split one's sides** (N. Amer. also **split a gut**) informal be convulsed with laughter. **split the ticket** (or **one's vote**) US vote for candidates of more than one party. **split the vote** (of a candidate or minority party) attract votes from another candidate or party with the result that both are defeated by a third.
– ORIGIN late 16th cent. (originally in the sense 'break up a ship', describing the force of a storm or rock): from Middle Dutch *splitten*, of unknown ultimate origin.

split-brain ▸ adjective [attrib.] Psychiatry having the corpus callosum severed or absent, so as to eliminate the main connection between the two hemispheres of the brain.

split decision ▸ noun a decision based on a majority verdict rather than on a unanimous one, especially as to the winner on points of a boxing match.

split end ▸ noun **1** (usu. **split ends**) a tip of a person's hair which has split from dryness or ill-treatment.
2 American Football an offensive end positioned on the line of scrimmage but some distance away from the other linemen.

split-half ▸ adjective [attrib.] Statistics relating to or denoting a technique of splitting a body of supposedly homogeneous data into two halves and calculating the results separately for each to assess their reliability.

split image ▸ noun an image in a rangefinder or camera focusing system that has been bisected by optical means, the halves being aligned only when the system is in focus.

split infinitive ▸ noun a construction consisting of an infinitive with an adverb or other word inserted between *to* and the verb, e.g. *she seems to really like it.*

> **USAGE** *You have* **to** *really* **watch** *him;* **to** *boldly* **go** *where no man has gone before.* It is still widely held that splitting infinitives—separating the infinitive marker **to** from the verb, as in the above examples—is wrong. The dislike of split infinitives is long-standing but is not well founded, being based on an analogy with Latin. In Latin, infinitives consist of only one word (e.g. *crescere* 'to grow'; *amare* 'to love'), which makes them impossible to split: therefore, so the argument goes, they should not be split in English either. But English is not the same as Latin. In particular, the placing of an adverb in English is extremely important in giving the appropriate emphasis: *you really have* **to watch** *him* and **to go** *boldly where no man has gone before*, examples where the infinitive is not split, convey a different emphasis or sound awkward. In the modern context, some traditionalists may continue to hold up the split infinitive as an error in English. However, in standard English the principle of allowing split infinitives is broadly accepted as both normal and useful.

split-level ▸ adjective **1** (of a building) having a room or rooms higher than others by less than a whole storey: *a large split-level house.* ■ (of a room) having its floor on two levels.
2 (of a cooker) having the oven and hob in separately installed units.
▸ noun a split-level building.

split pea ▸ noun a pea dried and split in half for cooking.

split-personality disorder ▸ noun less common term for MULTIPLE-PERSONALITY DISORDER.

split-phase ▸ adjective denoting or relating to an induction motor or other device utilizing two or more voltages at different phases produced from a single-phase supply.

split pin ▸ noun a metal cotter pin with two arms passed through a hole, held in place by the springing apart of the arms.

split-rail ▸ adjective denoting a fence or enclosure made from pieces of wood split lengthwise from logs.

split ring ▸ noun a small steel ring with two spiral turns, such as a key ring.

split run ▸ noun a print run of a newspaper during which some articles or advertisements are changed so as to produce different editions.

split screen ▸ noun a cinema, television, or computer screen on which two or more separate images are displayed.

split second ▸ noun a very brief moment of time: *for a split second, I hesitated.*

▸ adjective very rapid or accurate: *split-second timing is crucial.*

split shift ▸ noun a working shift comprising two or more separate periods of duty in a day.

split shot ▸ noun **1** [mass noun] small pellets used to weight a fishing line.
2 Croquet a stroke driving two touching balls in different directions.

splitsville ▸ noun informal the termination of a relationship, especially a romantic one: *it's splitsville for Steve and Nikki.*
– ORIGIN 1980s: from SPLIT + -*s*- + -VILLE.

splitter ▸ noun **1** a person or thing occupied in or designed for splitting something: *a log splitter.*
2 a person, especially a taxonomist, who attaches more importance to differences than to similarities in classification. Contrasted with LUMPER.
3 informal a severe headache.

splittism ▸ noun [mass noun] (among communists, or in communist countries) the pursuance of factional interests in opposition to official Communist Party policy.
– DERIVATIVES **splittist** noun.

splodge ▸ noun & verb Brit. another term for SPLOTCH.
– DERIVATIVES **splodgy** adjective (**splodgier**, **splodgiest**).

splosh informal ▸ verb [no obj., with adverbial of direction] make a soft splashing sound as one moves: *he sploshed across the road.*
▸ noun **1** a soft splashing sound: *a quiet splosh.* ■ a splash of liquid: *sploshes of wine.*
2 [mass noun] dated money.
– ORIGIN mid 19th cent.: imitative.

splotch informal ▸ noun a daub, blot, or smear of something, typically a liquid: ***a splotch of** red in a larger area of yellow.*
▸ verb [with obj.] make a daub, blot, or smear on: *a rag splotched with grease.*
– DERIVATIVES **splotchy** adjective (**splotchier**, **splotchiest**).
– ORIGIN early 17th cent.: perhaps a blend of SPOT and obsolete *plotch* 'blotch'.

splurge informal ▸ noun an act of spending money freely or extravagantly: *the annual pre-Christmas splurge.* ■ a large or excessive amount of something: *there has recently been a splurge of teach-yourself books.*
▸ verb [with obj.] spend (money) freely or extravagantly: *I'd **splurged** about £2,500 **on** clothes* | [no obj.] *we **splurged on** T-bone steaks.*
– ORIGIN early 19th cent. (originally US): probably imitative.

splurt informal ▸ noun a sudden gush of liquid. ■ a sudden brief outburst of something: *I let out **a splurt of** laughter.*
▸ verb [with obj.] push out with force; spit out: *the rear wheels splurted gravel.*
– ORIGIN late 18th cent.: imitative.

splutter ▸ verb [no obj.] make a series of short explosive spitting or choking sounds: *she coughed and spluttered, tears coursing down her face.* ■ [reporting verb] say something rapidly, indistinctly, and with a spitting sound, as a result of anger, embarrassment, or another strong emotion: [with obj.] *he began to splutter excuses* | [with direct speech] *'How dare you?' she spluttered.* ■ [with obj.] spit (something) out from one's mouth noisily and in small splashes: *spluttering brackish water, he struggled to regain his feet.*
▸ noun a short explosive spitting or choking noise.
– ORIGIN late 17th cent.: imitative; compare with SPUTTER.

Spock, Benjamin McLane (1903–98), American paediatrician and writer; known as **Dr Spock**. His influential manual *The Common Sense Book of Baby and Child Care* (1946) challenged traditional ideas in child-rearing in favour of a psychological approach.

spod ▸ noun Brit. informal a dull or socially inept person, especially someone who is excessively studious.
– DERIVATIVES **spoddy** adjective (**spoddier**, **spoddiest**).
– ORIGIN 1980s: of unknown origin.

Spode /spəʊd/ ▸ noun [mass noun] trademark fine pottery or porcelain made at the factories of the English potter Josiah Spode (1755–1827) or his successors, characteristically consisting of ornately decorated and gilded services and large vases.

spodic /ˈspɒdɪk/ ▸ adjective Soil Science denoting a soil horizon rich in aluminium oxide and organic matter and typically also containing iron oxide, produced by percolating water.
– ORIGIN 1960s: from Greek *spodos* 'ashes' + -IC.

spodosol /ˈspɒdə(ʊ)sɒl/ ▸ noun Soil Science a soil of an order characterized by a spodic horizon and including most podzols.
– ORIGIN 1960s: from Greek *spodos* 'ashes' + -SOL + Latin *solum* 'soil'.

spodumene /ˈspɒdjʊmiːn/ ▸ noun [mass noun] a translucent, typically greyish-white aluminosilicate mineral which is an important source of lithium.
– ORIGIN early 19th cent.: from French *spodumène*, from Greek *spodoumenos* 'burning to ashes', present participle of *spodousthai*, from *spodos* 'ashes'.

spoil ▸ verb (past and past participle **spoilt** (chiefly Brit.) or **spoiled**) [with obj.] **1** diminish or destroy the value or quality of: *I wouldn't want to spoil your fun* | *a series of political blunders spoilt their chances of being re-elected.* ■ prevent someone from enjoying (an occasion or event): *she was afraid of spoiling Christmas for the rest of the family.* ■ mark (a ballot paper) incorrectly so as to make one's vote invalid, especially as a gesture of protest. ■ [no obj.] (of food) become unfit for eating: *I've got some ham that'll spoil if we don't eat it tonight.*
2 harm the character of (a child) by being too lenient or indulgent: *the last thing I want to do is spoil Thomas* | (as adj. **spoilt** or **spoiled**) *a spoilt child.* ■ treat with great or excessive kindness, consideration, or generosity: *breakfast in bed—you're spoiling me!*
3 [no obj.] (**be spoiling for**) be extremely or aggressively eager for: *Cooper was spoiling for a fight.*
4 archaic rob (a person or a place) of goods or possessions by force or violence.
▸ noun **1** (usu. **spoils**) goods stolen or taken forcibly from a person or place: *the looters carried their spoils away.*
2 [mass noun] waste material brought up during the course of an excavation or a dredging or mining operation: *colliery spoil.*
– PHRASES **be spoilt for choice** Brit. have so many options that it is difficult to make a choice.
– ORIGIN Middle English (in the sense 'to plunder'): shortening of Old French *espoille* (noun), *espoillier* (verb), from Latin *spoliare*, from *spolium* 'plunder, skin stripped from an animal', or a shortening of DESPOIL.

spoilage ▸ noun [mass noun] **1** the action or process of spoiling, especially the deterioration of food and other perishable goods.
2 waste produced by material being spoilt, especially paper that is spoilt in printing.

spoiler ▸ noun **1** a person or thing that spoils something. ■ (especially in a political context) a person who obstructs or prevents an opponent's success while having no chance of winning a contest themselves. ■ a news story published to divert attention from and reduce the impact of a similar item published elsewhere. ■ a description of an important plot development in a television programme, film, etc. before it is shown to the public.
2 a flap on the wing of an aircraft which can be projected in order to create drag and so reduce speed. ■ a similar device on a motor vehicle intended to improve roadholding when travelling at very high speeds.
3 an electronic device for preventing unauthorized copying of sound recordings by means of a disruptive signal inaudible on the original.

spoiling tactics ▸ plural noun a strategy designed to obstruct or prevent the success of a project, opponent, etc.: *the home side, frustrated by the Wasps' strong defence, resorted to spoiling tactics.*

spoilsman ▸ noun (pl. **spoilsmen**) US a person who supports or seeks to profit by the spoils system.

spoilsport ▸ noun a person who behaves in a way that spoils others' pleasure, especially by not joining in an activity.

spoils system ▸ noun chiefly US the practice of a successful political party giving public office to its supporters.

spoilt chiefly Brit. past and past participle of SPOIL.

Spokane /spə(ʊ)ˈkeɪn/ a city in eastern Washington, situated on the falls of the Spokane River, near the border with Idaho; pop. 202,319 (est. 2008).

spoke[1] ▸ noun each of the bars or wire rods connecting the centre of a wheel to its outer edge. ■ each of a set of radial handles projecting from a ship's wheel. ■ each of the metal rods in an umbrella to which the material is attached.
– PHRASES **put a spoke in someone's wheel** Brit. prevent someone from carrying out a plan.
– DERIVATIVES **spoked** adjective [in combination] *a wire-spoked wheel.*
– ORIGIN Old English *spāca*, of West Germanic origin; related to Dutch *speek*, German *Speiche*, from the base of SPIKE[1].

spoke[2] past of SPEAK.

spoken past participle of SPEAK. ▸ adjective [in combination] speaking in a specified way: *a blunt-spoken man.*
– PHRASES **be spoken for** be already claimed, owned, or reserved. ■ already have a romantic commitment: *he knows Claudine is spoken for.*

spokeshave /ˈspəʊkʃeɪv/ ▸ noun a small plane with a handle on each side of its blade, used for shaping curved surfaces (originally wheel spokes).
▸ verb [with obj.] shape with a spokeshave.

spokesman (or **spokeswoman**) ▸ noun (pl. **spokesmen** or **spokeswomen**) a person who makes statements on behalf of a group: *a spokesman for Greenpeace.*
– ORIGIN early 16th cent.: formed irregularly from SPOKE[2], on the pattern of words such as *craftsman*.

spokesmodel ▸ noun N. Amer. informal an attractive and stylishly dressed person, especially a young woman, who advertises or promotes something.

spokesperson ▸ noun (pl. **spokespersons** or **spokespeople**) a spokesman or spokeswoman (used as a neutral alternative).

Spoleto /spəˈleɪtəʊ/ a town in Umbria, in central Italy; pop. 39,164 (2008). It was one of Italy's principal cities from the 6th to the 8th century AD.

spoliation /ˌspəʊlɪˈeɪʃ(ə)n/ ▸ noun [mass noun] **1** the action of ruining or destroying something: *the spoliation of the countryside.*
2 the action of taking goods or property from somewhere by violent means: *the spoliation of the Church.*
– DERIVATIVES **spoliator** noun.
– ORIGIN late Middle English (denoting pillaging): from Latin *spoliatio(n-)*, from the verb *spoliare* 'strip, deprive' (see SPOIL).

spondaic /spɒnˈdeɪɪk/ ▸ adjective Prosody of or concerning spondees. ■ (of a hexameter) having a spondee as its fifth foot.
– ORIGIN late 16th cent.: via French or late Latin from Greek *spondeiakos*, from *spondeios* (see SPONDEE).

spondee /ˈspɒndiː/ ▸ noun Prosody a foot consisting of two long (or stressed) syllables.
– ORIGIN late Middle English: from Old French, or via Latin from Greek *spondeios* (*pous*) '(foot) of a libation', from *spondē* 'libation' (being characteristic of music accompanying libations).

spondulicks /spɒnˈd(j)uːlɪks/ (also **spondulix**) ▸ plural noun Brit. informal money.
– ORIGIN mid 19th cent.: of unknown origin.

spondylitis /ˌspɒndɪˈlʌɪtɪs/ ▸ noun [mass noun] Medicine inflammation of the joints of the backbone. See also ANKYLOSING SPONDYLITIS.
– ORIGIN mid 19th cent.: from Latin *spondylus* 'vertebra' (from Greek *spondulos*) + -ITIS.

spondylosis /ˌspɒndɪˈləʊsɪs/ ▸ noun [mass noun] Medicine a painful condition of the spine resulting from the degeneration of the intervertebral discs.
– ORIGIN early 20th cent.: from Greek *spondulos* 'vertebra' + -OSIS.

sponge ▸ noun **1** a primitive sedentary aquatic invertebrate with a soft porous body that is typically supported by a framework of fibres or calcareous or glassy spicules. Sponges draw in a current of water to extract nutrients and oxygen. ● Phylum Porifera: several classes.
2 a piece of a soft, light, porous absorbent substance originally consisting of the fibrous skeleton of such an invertebrate but now usually made of synthetic material, used for washing and cleaning. ■ [in sing.] an act of wiping or cleaning with a sponge: *they gave him a quick **sponge down**.* ■ [mass noun] such a substance used as padding or insulating material: *the headguard is padded with sponge.* ■ a piece of sponge impregnated with spermicide and inserted into a woman's vagina as a form of barrier contraceptive. ■ [mass noun] [with modifier] metal in a porous form, typically prepared by reduction without fusion or by electrolysis: *platinum sponge.*
3 (also **sponge cake**) Brit. a very light cake made with eggs, sugar, and flour but little or no fat: *a chocolate sponge* | [mass noun] *the gateau is made with moist sponge.* ■ short for SPONGE PUDDING.
4 informal a person who lives at someone else's expense.
5 informal a heavy drinker.
▸ verb (**sponges**, **sponging** or **spongeing**, **sponged**) **1** [with obj.] wipe or clean with a wet sponge or cloth: *she sponged him down in an attempt to cool his fever.*

S

■ remove or wipe away (liquid or a mark) with a sponge or cloth: *I'll go and **sponge** this orange juice **off** my dress.* ■ give a decorative effect to (a painted surface) by applying a different shade of paint with a sponge. ■ decorate (pottery) using a sponge.
2 [no obj.] informal obtain or accept money or food from other people without doing or intending to do anything in return: *they found they could earn a perfectly good living by **sponging off** others.* ■ [with obj.] obtain (something) in such a way: *he edged closer, clearly intending to sponge money from her.*
– DERIVATIVES **spongeable** adjective, **sponge-like** adjective.
– ORIGIN Old English (in sense 2 of the noun), via Latin from Greek *spongia*, later form of *spongos*, reinforced in Middle English by Old French *esponge*.

sponge bag ▶ noun Brit. a toilet bag.

sponge bath ▶ noun North American term for **BLANKET BATH**.

sponge cloth ▶ noun [mass noun] soft, lightly woven cloth with a slightly wrinkled surface.

sponge pudding ▶ noun Brit. a steamed or baked pudding of fat, flour, and eggs.

sponger ▶ noun **1** informal a person who lives at others' expense.
2 a person who applies decoration to pottery with a sponge.

sponge rubber ▶ noun [mass noun] rubber latex processed into a sponge-like substance.

sponge tree ▶ noun another term for **OPOPANAX** (sense 1).

spongiform /ˈspʌndʒɪfɔːm/ ▶ adjective chiefly Veterinary Medicine having or denoting a porous structure or consistency resembling that of a sponge.

spongin /ˈspʌn(d)ʒɪn/ ▶ noun [mass noun] Biochemistry the horny or fibrous substance found in the skeleton of many sponges.

spongy /ˈspʌn(d)ʒi/ (also **spongey**) ▶ adjective (**spongier**, **spongiest**) like a sponge, especially in being porous, compressible, or absorbent: *a soft, spongy blanket of moss.* ■ (of metal) having an open, porous structure: *spongy platinum.* ■ (chiefly of a motor vehicle's braking system) lacking firmness.
– DERIVATIVES **sponginess** noun.

sponson /ˈspɒns(ə)n/ ▶ noun a projection on the side of a boat, ship, or seaplane, in particular: ■ a gun platform standing out from a warship's side. ■ a short subsidiary wing that serves to stabilize a seaplane. ■ a buoyancy chamber fitted to a boat's hull, especially on a canoe. ■ a triangular platform supporting the wheel on a paddle steamer.
– ORIGIN mid 19th cent.: of unknown origin.

sponsor ▶ noun **1** a person or organization that pays for or contributes to the costs involved in staging a sporting or artistic event in return for advertising. ■ a person who pledges to donate a certain amount of money to another person after they have participated in a fundraising event organized on behalf of a charity. ■ chiefly US a business or organization that pays for or contributes to the costs of a radio or television programme in return for advertising.
2 a person who introduces and supports a proposal for legislation: *a leading sponsor of the bill.* ■ a person taking official responsibility for the actions of another: *they act as sponsors and contacts for new immigrants.* ■ a godparent at a child's baptism. ■ (especially in the Roman Catholic Church) a person presenting a candidate for confirmation.
▶ verb [with obj.] **1** provide funds for (a project or activity or the person carrying it out): *Joe is being sponsored by a government training scheme.* ■ pay some or all of the costs involved in staging (a sporting or artistic event) in return for advertising. ■ pledge to donate a certain sum of money to (someone) after they have participated in a fund-raising event for charity. ■ (often as adj. **sponsored**) pledge to donate money to a participant in (a fund-raising event): *they raised £70 by a sponsored walk.*
2 introduce and support (a proposal) in a legislative assembly: *a Labour MP sponsored the bill.* ■ propose and organize (negotiations or talks) between other people or groups: *the USA sponsored negotiations between the two sides.*
– ORIGIN mid 17th cent. (as a noun): from Latin, from *spondere* 'promise solemnly'. The verb dates from the late 19th cent.

sponsorship ▶ noun [mass noun] the position of being a sponsor: *the company's sponsorship of the tournament.* ■ financial support received from a sponsor: *we raised about £6,000 in sponsorship.*

spontaneity /ˌspɒntəˈneɪɪti/ ▶ noun [mass noun] the condition of being spontaneous; spontaneous behaviour or action: *she occasionally tore up her usual schedule in favour of spontaneity.*

spontaneous /spɒnˈteɪnɪəs/ ▶ adjective performed or occurring as a result of a sudden impulse or inclination and without premeditation or external stimulus: *the audience broke into spontaneous applause* | *a spontaneous display of affection.* ■ having an open, natural, and uninhibited manner. ■ (of a process or event) occurring without apparent external cause: *spontaneous miscarriages.* ■ Biology (of movement or activity in an organism) instinctive or involuntary: *the spontaneous mechanical activity of circular smooth muscle.* ■ archaic (of a plant) growing naturally and without being tended or cultivated.
– DERIVATIVES **spontaneously** adverb.
– ORIGIN mid 17th cent.: from late Latin *spontaneus* (from (*sua*) *sponte* 'of (one's) own accord') + **-ous**.

spontaneous combustion ▶ noun [mass noun] the ignition of organic matter (e.g. hay or coal) without apparent cause, typically through heat generated internally by rapid oxidation.

spontaneous generation ▶ noun [mass noun] historical the supposed production of living organisms from non-living matter, as inferred from the apparent appearance of life in some infusions.

spoof informal ▶ noun **1** a humorous imitation of something, typically a film or a particular genre of film, in which its characteristic features are exaggerated for comic effect: *a Robin Hood spoof.*
2 a trick played on someone as a joke.
▶ verb [with obj.] **1** imitate (something) while exaggerating its characteristic features for comic effect: *it is a movie that spoofs other movies.*
2 hoax or trick (someone): *they proceeded to spoof Western intelligence with false information.* ■ interfere with (radio or radar signals) so as to make them useless.
– DERIVATIVES **spoofer** noun, **spoofery** noun.
– ORIGIN late 19th cent.: coined by Arthur Roberts (1852–1933), English comedian.

spook informal ▶ noun **1** a ghost.
2 chiefly N. Amer. a spy: *a CIA spook.*
3 offensive, dated, chiefly US a black person.
▶ verb [with obj.] frighten; unnerve: *they spooked a couple of grizzly bears.* ■ [no obj.] (especially of an animal) take fright suddenly: *he'll spook if we make any noise.*
– ORIGIN early 19th cent.: from Dutch, of unknown origin.

spooky ▶ adjective (**spookier**, **spookiest**) informal
1 sinister or ghostly in a way that causes fear and unease: *I bet this place is really spooky late at night.*
2 chiefly N. Amer. easily frightened; nervous.
– DERIVATIVES **spookily** adverb, **spookiness** noun.

spool ▶ noun a cylindrical device on which film, magnetic tape, thread, or other flexible materials can be wound; a reel: *spools of electrical cable.* ■ a cylindrical device attached to a fishing rod and used for winding and unwinding the line as required. ■ [as modifier] denoting furniture of a style popular in England in the 17th century and North America in the 19th century, typically ornamented with a series of small knobs resembling spools: *a narrow spool bed.*
▶ verb **1** [with obj. and adverbial] wind (magnetic tape, thread, etc.) on to a spool: *he was trying to spool his tapes back into the cassettes with a pencil eraser.* ■ [no obj., with adverbial] be wound on or off a spool: *the plastic reel allows the line to run free as it spools out.*
2 [with obj.] Computing send (data that is intended for printing or processing on a peripheral device) to an intermediate store: *users can set which folder they wish to spool files to.* [acronym from *simultaneous peripheral operation online*.]
3 [no obj.] (of an engine) increase its speed of rotation, typically to that required for operation: *a jet engine can take up to six seconds to **spool up**.*
– ORIGIN Middle English (denoting a spool for thread): shortening of Old French *espole* or from Middle Low German *spōle*, of West Germanic origin; related to Dutch *spoel* and German *Spule*. The verb dates from the early 17th cent.

spoon ▶ noun **1** an implement consisting of a small, shallow oval or round bowl on a long handle, used for eating, stirring, and serving food. ■ the contents of a spoon: *three spoons of sugar.* ■ (**spoons**) a pair of spoons held in the hand and beaten together rhythmically as a percussion instrument.
2 a thing resembling a spoon in shape, in particular: ■ (also **spoon bait**) a fishing lure designed to wobble when pulled through the water. ■ an oar with a broad curved blade. ■ Golf, dated a club with a slightly concave wooden head.
▶ verb **1** [with obj. and adverbial of direction] put (food) into or on something with a spoon: *Rosie spooned sugar into her mug.*
2 [no obj.] informal, dated (of two people) behave in an amorous way; kiss and cuddle: *I saw them spooning on the beach.* ■ (of two people) lie close together sideways and front to back, so as to fit together like spoons.
3 [with obj.] hit (a ball) up into the air with a soft or weak stroke: *he spooned his shot high over the bar.*
– DERIVATIVES **spooner** noun, **spoonful** noun (pl. **spoonfuls**).
– ORIGIN Old English *spōn* 'chip of wood', of Germanic origin; related to German *Span* 'shaving'. Sense 1 of the noun is of Scandinavian origin. The verb dates from the early 18th cent.

spoonbill ▶ noun a tall mainly white or pinkish wading bird related to ibises, having a long bill with a very broad flat tip. ● Genera *Platalea* and *Ajaia*, family Threskiornithidae: several species.

spoon bread ▶ noun [mass noun] US soft maize bread.

spoonerism ▶ noun a verbal error in which a speaker accidentally transposes the initial sounds or letters of two or more words, often to humorous effect, as in the sentence *you have hissed the mystery lectures.*
– ORIGIN early 20th cent.: named after the Revd W. A. *Spooner* (1844–1930), an English scholar who reputedly made such errors in speaking.

spoon-feed ▶ verb [with obj.] feed with a spoon. ■ provide (someone) with so much help or information that they do not need to think for themselves.

spoonworm ▶ noun an unsegmented worm-like marine invertebrate that lives in burrows, crevices, or discarded shells. They typically have a sausage-shaped body with a long proboscis that can be extended over the seabed. ● Phylum Echiura.

spoony informal ▶ adjective (**spoonier**, **spooniest**) dated sentimentally or foolishly amorous: *I was spoony over Miss Talmadge to the point of idolatry.* ■ archaic foolish; silly.
▶ noun (pl. **spoonies**) archaic a silly or foolish person.
– DERIVATIVES **spooniness** noun.

spoor /spʊə, spɔː/ ▶ noun the track or scent of an animal: *they searched around the hut for a spoor* | [mass noun] *the trail is marked by wolf spoor.* ■ S. African the track of a wagon or motor vehicle.
▶ verb [with obj.] follow the track or scent of (an animal or person): *taking the spear, he set off to spoor the man.*
– ORIGIN early 19th cent.: from Afrikaans, from Middle Dutch *spor*, of Germanic origin.

Sporades /ˈspɒrədiːz/ two groups of Greek islands in the Aegean Sea. The **Northern Sporades**, which lie close to the east coast of mainland Greece, include the islands of Euboea, Skiros, Skiathos, and Skopelos. The **Southern Sporades**, situated off the west coast of Turkey, include Rhodes and the other islands of the Dodecanese.

sporadic /spəˈradɪk/ ▶ adjective occurring at irregular intervals or only in a few places; scattered or isolated: *sporadic fighting broke out.*
– DERIVATIVES **sporadically** adverb.
– ORIGIN late 17th cent.: via medieval Latin from Greek *sporadikos*, from *sporas*, *sporad-* 'scattered'; related to *speirein* 'to sow'.

sporangiophore /spəˈran(d)ʒɪə(ʊ)ˌfɔː/ ▶ noun Botany (in a fungus) a specialized hypha bearing sporangia.

sporangium /spəˈran(d)ʒɪəm/ ▶ noun (pl. **sporangia** /-dʒɪə/) Botany (in ferns and lower plants) a receptacle in which asexual spores are formed.
– DERIVATIVES **sporangial** adjective.
– ORIGIN early 19th cent.: modern Latin, from Greek *spora* 'spore' + *angeion* 'vessel'.

spore ▶ noun Biology a minute, typically one-celled, reproductive unit capable of giving rise to a new individual without sexual fusion, characteristic of lower plants, fungi, and protozoans. ■ Botany (in a plant exhibiting alternation of generations) a haploid reproductive cell which gives rise to a gametophyte. ■ Microbiology (in bacteria) a rounded resistant form adopted by a bacterial cell in adverse conditions.
– ORIGIN mid 19th cent.: from modern Latin *spora*, from Greek *spora* 'sowing, seed', from *speirein* 'to sow'.

spork /spɔːk/ ▶ noun a spoon-shaped eating utensil with short tines at the tip.
– ORIGIN early 20th cent.: blend of **SPOON** and **FORK**.

S

sporo- ▸ combining form Biology relating to spores: *sporogenesis*.
– ORIGIN from Greek *spora* 'spore'.

sporocyst ▸ noun Zoology a parasitic fluke in the initial stage of infection in a snail host, developed from a miracidium. ■ (in parasitic sporozoans) an encysted zygote in an invertebrate host.

sporogenesis /ˌspɒrə(ʊ)ˈdʒɛnɪsɪs, ˌspɔːrə(ʊ)-/ ▸ noun [mass noun] chiefly Botany the process of spore formation.

sporogenous /spəˈrɒdʒɪnəs/ ▸ adjective chiefly Botany (of an organism or tissue) producing spores.

sporogony /spəˈrɒɡəni/ ▸ noun [mass noun] Zoology the asexual process of spore formation in parasitic sporozoans.

sporophore /ˈspɒrəfɔː, ˈspɔː-/ ▸ noun Botany the spore-bearing structure of a fungus.

sporophyte /ˈspɒrəfʌɪt, ˈspɔː-/ ▸ noun Botany (in the life cycle of plants with alternating generations) the asexual and usually diploid phase, producing spores from which the gametophyte arises. It is the dominant form in vascular plants, e.g. the frond of a fern.
– DERIVATIVES **sporophytic** adjective.

Sporozoa /ˌspɒrəˈzəʊə/ ▸ plural noun Zoology & Medicine a phylum of mainly parasitic spore-forming protozoans that have a complex life cycle with sexual and asexual generations. They include the organisms that cause malaria, babesiosis, coccidiosis, and toxoplasmosis. Also called **APICOMPLEXA**.
– ORIGIN modern Latin (plural), from **SPORE** + Greek *zōia* 'animals'.

sporozoan Zoology & Medicine ▸ noun a protozoan of the phylum Sporozoa.
▸ adjective relating to or denoting sporozoans.

sporozoite /ˌspɒrə(ʊ)ˈzəʊʌɪt, ˌspɔː-/ ▸ noun Zoology & Medicine a motile spore-like stage in the life cycle of some parasitic sporozoans (e.g. the malaria organism), which is typically the infective agent introduced into a host.
– ORIGIN late 19th cent.: from **SPORO-** 'relating to spores' + Greek *zōion* 'animal' + **-ITE**[1].

sporran /ˈspɒr(ə)n/ ▸ noun a small pouch worn around the waist so as to hang in front of the kilt as part of men's Scottish Highland dress.
– ORIGIN mid 18th cent.: from Scottish Gaelic *sporan*.

sport ▸ noun **1** an activity involving physical exertion and skill in which an individual or team competes against another or others for entertainment: *team sports such as soccer and rugby* | [mass noun] *I used to play a lot of sport* | (as modifier **sports**) *a sports centre*. ■ (**sports**) Brit. an occasion on which people compete in various athletic activities: *I won the 200 metres in the school sports*. ■ [mass noun] [usu. with adj.] success or pleasure derived from an activity such as hunting or fishing: *I have heard there is good sport to be had in Buttermere*. ■ [mass noun] dated entertainment; fun: *it was considered great sport to catch him out*. ■ archaic a source of amusement or entertainment: *I do not wish to show myself the sport of a man like Wildeve*.
2 informal a person who behaves in a good or specified way in response to teasing, defeat, or a similarly trying situation: *go on, be a sport!* | *Angela's a bad sport*. ■ chiefly Austral./NZ used as a friendly form of address, especially between men who do not know each other: *hold on, sport!*
3 Biology an animal or plant showing abnormal or striking variation from the parent type, especially in form or colour, as a result of spontaneous mutation. US
▸ verb **1** [with obj.] wear or display (a distinctive item): *he was sporting a huge handlebar moustache*.
2 [no obj.] play in a lively, energetic way: *the children sported in the water*.
– PHRASES **in sport** for fun: *I have assumed the name was given more or less in sport*. **make sport of** dated make fun of. **the sport of kings** horse racing.
– DERIVATIVES **sporter** noun.
– ORIGIN late Middle English (in the sense 'pastime, entertainment'): shortening of **DISPORT**.

sportif /spɔːˈtiːf/ ▸ adjective interested in athletic sports. ■ (of a garment or style of dress) suitable for sport or informal wear; casually stylish.
– ORIGIN French.

sporting ▸ adjective **1** [attrib.] connected with or interested in sport: *a major sporting event*.
2 fair and generous in one's behaviour or treatment of others, especially in a contest: *it was jolly sporting of you to let me have first go*.
– DERIVATIVES **sportingly** adverb (sense 2).

sporting chance ▸ noun [in sing.] a reasonable chance of winning or succeeding.

sportive ▸ adjective playful; light-hearted. ■ archaic amorous; lustful.
– DERIVATIVES **sportively** adverb, **sportiveness** noun.

sports bar ▸ noun a bar where televised sport is shown continuously.

sports car ▸ noun a low-built car designed for performance at high speeds, often having a roof that can be folded back.

sportscast ▸ noun N. Amer. a broadcast of sports news or a sports event.
– DERIVATIVES **sportscaster** noun.

sports day ▸ noun Brit. an occasion on which the pupils of a school compete in various races and athletic events.

sports finder ▸ noun Photography a direct-vision viewfinder typically consisting of a simple frame which allows action outside the field of view of the camera to be seen.

sports ground ▸ noun a piece of land used for sports.

sports jacket (US also **sport jacket** or **sports coat**) ▸ noun a man's jacket resembling a suit jacket, for informal wear.

sportsman ▸ noun (pl. **sportsmen**) **1** a man who takes part in a sport, especially as a professional. ■ dated a man who hunts or shoots wild animals as a pastime.
2 a person who behaves sportingly.
– DERIVATIVES **sportsmanlike** adjective, **sportsmanship** noun.

sportsperson ▸ noun (pl. **sportspersons** or **sportspeople**) a sportsman or sportswoman (used as a neutral alternative).

sportster ▸ noun a sports car.

sportswear ▸ noun [mass noun] clothes worn for sport or for casual outdoor use.

sportswoman ▸ noun (pl. **sportswomen**) a woman who takes part in sport, especially professionally.

sportswriter ▸ noun a journalist who writes about sport.

sport utility (also **sport utility vehicle**) ▸ noun a high-performance four-wheel-drive vehicle.

sporty ▸ adjective (**sportier**, **sportiest**) informal fond of or good at sport: *tracksuits don't necessarily mean you're sporty*. ■ (of clothing) casual yet attractively stylish: *a sporty outfit*. ■ (of a car) compact and with fast acceleration: *the sporty 1.5 litre coupe*.
– DERIVATIVES **sportily** adverb, **sportiness** noun.

sporulate /ˈspɒrjʊleɪt/ ▸ verb [no obj.] Biology produce or form a spore or spores.
– DERIVATIVES **sporulation** noun.

spot ▸ noun **1** a small round or roundish mark, differing in colour or texture from the surface around it: *ladybirds have black spots on their red wing covers*. ■ a small mark or stain: *a spot of mildew on the wall*. ■ a blemish on someone's character or reputation. ■ chiefly N. Amer. a pip on a domino, playing card, or dice.
2 a particular place or point: *a nice secluded spot* | *an ideal picnic spot*. ■ [with adj. or noun modifier] a small feature or part of something with a particular quality: *his bald spot* | *there was one bright spot in a night of dismal failure*. ■ short for **PENALTY SPOT**. ■ a ranking: *the runner-up spot*. ■ a place for an individual item within a show: *she couldn't do her usual singing spot in the club*.
3 a pimple.
4 informal, chiefly Brit. a small amount of something: *a spot of rain* | *a spot of bother flared up*. ■ dated a small alcoholic drink: *may I offer you a spot?*
5 [as modifier] denoting a system of trading in which commodities or currencies are delivered and paid for immediately after a sale: *trading in the spot markets* | *the current spot price*.
6 short for **SPOTLIGHT**.
7 (also **spot board**) a board for working plaster before application.
8 [in combination] informal, chiefly N. Amer. a banknote of a specified value: *a ten-spot*.
▸ verb (**spots**, **spotting**, **spotted**) [with obj.] **1** see, notice, or recognize (someone or something) that is difficult to detect or that one is searching for: *Andrew spotted the advert in the paper* | *the men were spotted by police*. ■ recognize that (someone) has a particular talent, especially for sport or show business: *we were spotted by a talent scout*. ■ Brit. observe and note the details of (a certain class of thing) as a hobby: *women don't collect stamps or spot trains*. ■ [no obj.] Military locate an enemy's position, typically from the air: *they were spotting for enemy aircraft*. ■ (in weight training, gymnastics, etc.) observe (a performer) in order to minimize the risk of accidents or injuries.
2 mark or become marked with spots: [with obj.] *the velvet was spotted with stains*. ■ [with obj.] cover (a surface or area) thinly: *thorn trees spotted the land*. ■ [with obj.] archaic stain or sully the moral character or qualities of.
3 [no obj.] (**it spots**, **it is spotting**, etc.) rain slightly: *it was still spotting with rain*.
4 place (a ball) on its designated starting point on a billiard table.
5 [with two objs] N. Amer. informal give or lend (money) to (someone): *I'll spot you $300*. ■ allow (an advantage) to (someone) in a game or sport: *the higher-rated team spots the lower-rated team the difference in their handicaps*.
– PHRASES **hit the spot** informal be exactly what is required: *the cup of coffee hit the spot*. **in a spot** informal in a difficult situation. **on the spot 1** without any delay; immediately: *he offered me the job on the spot*. **2** at the scene of an event: *journalists on the spot reported no progress*. **3** Brit. (with reference to an action) performed without moving from one's original position: *running on the spot*. **put someone on the spot** informal force someone into a situation in which they must make a difficult decision or answer a difficult question.
– ORIGIN Middle English: perhaps from Middle Dutch *spotte*. The sense 'notice, recognize' arose from the early 19th-cent. slang use 'note as a suspect or criminal'.

spot advertising ▸ noun [mass noun] television advertising occupying a short break during or between programmes.

spot ball ▸ noun Billiards one of two white cue balls, distinguished from the other by two black spots.

spot-buy ▸ verb [with obj.] Stock Exchange pay for (a currency or commodity) immediately after a sale is made.

spot check ▸ noun a test made without warning on a randomly selected subject.
▸ verb (**spot-check**) [with obj.] subject to a spot check.

spot height ▸ noun the altitude of a point, especially as shown on a map.

spot kick ▸ noun another term for **PENALTY KICK**.

spotlamp ▸ noun another term for **SPOTLIGHT**.

spotless ▸ adjective absolutely clean or pure; immaculate: *a spotless white apron*. ■ without faults or moral blemishes; pure: *spotless behaviour is seemingly the norm in his organization*.
– DERIVATIVES **spotlessly** adverb, **spotlessness** noun.

spotlight ▸ noun a lamp projecting a narrow, intense beam of light directly on to a place or person, especially a performer on stage. ■ a beam of light from a lamp of this kind: *the knife flashed in the spotlight*. ■ (**the spotlight**) intense scrutiny or public attention: *she was constantly **in the media spotlight***.
▸ verb (past and past participle **spotlighted** or **spotlit**) [with obj.] illuminate with a spotlight: *the dancers are spotlighted from time to time throughout the evening*. ■ direct attention to (a problem or situation): *the protest spotlighted the overcrowding in British prisons*.

S

spot meter ▸ noun Photography a photometer that measures the intensity of light received within a cone of small angle, usually 2° or less.

spot on ▸ adjective & adverb Brit. informal completely accurate or accurately: [as adj.] *your reviews are spot on*.

spotted ▸ adjective marked or decorated with spots: *a red spotted handkerchief*.
– DERIVATIVES **spottedness** noun.

spotted deer ▸ noun another term for **CHITAL**.

spotted dick ▸ noun [mass noun] Brit. a suet pudding containing currants.

spotted dog ▸ noun **1** a Dalmatian dog.
2 Brit. another term for **SPOTTED DICK**.

spotted fever ▸ noun [mass noun] any of a number of diseases characterized by fever and skin spots, in particular: ■ cerebrospinal meningitis. ■ typhus. ■ (also **Rocky Mountain spotted fever**) a rickettsial disease transmitted by ticks.

spotted flycatcher ▸ noun a common migratory Old World flycatcher with grey-brown plumage.
● *Muscicapa striata*, family Muscicapidae.

spotted hyena ▸ noun a southern African hyena which has a greyish-yellow to reddish coat with irregular dark spots, and a loud laughing call. ● *Crocuta crocuta*, family Hyaenidae.

spotted orchid ▸ **noun** a common Eurasian orchid with spotted leaves and flowers varying from purple to white, with darker markings on the lip. ● Genus *Dactylorhiza*, family Orchidaceae: several species, in particular the **common spotted orchid** (*D. fuchsii*), which grows chiefly on calcareous soils, and the **heath spotted orchid** (*D. maculata*), of damp acid soils.

spotter ▸ **noun** [often in combination] a person who looks for or observes a particular thing as a hobby or job: *plane-spotters*. ■ an aviator or aircraft employed in locating or observing enemy positions: [as modifier] *spotter planes*. ■ (in gymnastics, weight training, etc.) a person stationed to observe the performer and minimize the risk of accidents or injuries. ■ US informal a person employed by a company or business to keep watch on employees or customers.

spotty ▸ **adjective** (**spottier**, **spottiest**) marked with spots: *a spotty purple flower*. ■ Brit. having pimples: *a spotty youth*. ■ N. Amer. of uneven quality; patchy: *his spotty record on the environment*.
– DERIVATIVES **spottily** adverb, **spottiness** noun.

spot-weld ▸ **verb** [with obj.] join by welding at a number of separate points: *the wire was spot-welded in place*.
▸ **noun** (**spot weld**) a weld made by spot-welding.

spousal /ˈspaʊz(ə)l/ ▸ **adjective** [attrib.] Law, chiefly N. Amer. relating to marriage or to a husband or wife: *the spousal benefits of married couples*.

spouse /spaʊz, -s/ ▸ **noun** a husband or wife, considered in relation to their partner.
– ORIGIN Middle English: from Old French *spous(e)*, variant of *espous(e)*, from Latin *sponsus* (masculine), *sponsa* (feminine), past participles of *spondere* 'betroth'.

spout ▸ **noun 1** a tube or lip projecting from a container, through which liquid can be poured: *a teapot with a chipped spout*.
2 a stream of liquid issuing from somewhere with great force: *the tall spouts of geysers*. ■ the plume of water vapour ejected from the blowhole of a whale: *the spout of an occasional whale*.
3 a pipe or trough through which water may be carried away or from which it can flow out. ■ a sloping trough for conveying grain, coal, etc. to a lower level; a chute. ■ historical a lift in a pawnshop used to convey pawned items up for storage.
▸ **verb** [with obj.] **1** send out (liquid) forcibly in a stream: *volcanoes spouted ash and lava*. ■ [no obj., with adverbial] (of a liquid) flow out forcibly in a stream: *blood was spouting from the cuts on my hand*. ■ (of a whale or dolphin) eject (water vapour and air) through its blowhole.
2 express (one's views or ideas) in a lengthy, declamatory, and unreflecting way: *he was spouting platitudes about our furry friends*.
– PHRASES **put something up the spout** Brit. informal, dated pawn something. **up the spout** Brit. informal **1** no longer working or likely to be useful or successful. **2** (of a woman) pregnant. **3** (of a bullet or cartridge) in the barrel of a gun and ready to be fired.
– DERIVATIVES **spouted** adjective, **spouter** noun.
– ORIGIN Middle English (as a verb): from Middle Dutch *spouten*, from an imitative base shared by Old Norse *spýta* 'to spit'.

spp. ▸ **abbreviation** species (plural).

SPQR ▸ **abbreviation** ■ historical the Senate and people of Rome. [from Latin *Senatus Populusque Romanus*.] ■ humorous small profits and quick returns.

Spr ▸ **abbreviation** (in the UK) Sapper.

Sprachgefühl /ˈʃprɑːxɡəˌfuːl/, German /ˈʃpraːxɡəˌfyːl/ ▸ **noun** [mass noun] intuitive feeling for the natural idiom of a language. ■ the essential character of a language.
– ORIGIN German, from *Sprache* 'speech, a language' + *Gefühl* 'feeling'.

spraddle ▸ **verb** [with obj.] (usu. as adj. **spraddled**) chiefly W. Indian & N. Amer. spread (one's legs) far apart: *the cat's spraddled hind legs*.
– ORIGIN mid 17th cent. (in the sense 'sprawl'): probably from *sprad*, dialect past participle of **SPREAD**.

sprag ▸ **noun 1** a simple brake on a vehicle, especially a stout stick or bar inserted between the spokes of a wheel to check its motion.
2 a prop in a coal mine.
– ORIGIN mid 19th cent.: of unknown origin.

sprain ▸ **verb** [with obj.] wrench or twist the ligaments of (an ankle, wrist, or other joint) violently so as to cause pain and swelling but not dislocation: *he left in a wheelchair after spraining an ankle*.
▸ **noun** the result of spraining a joint.
– ORIGIN early 17th cent.: of unknown origin.

spraing /spreɪŋ/ ▸ **noun** [mass noun] a viral disease of potatoes characterized by curved lesions inside the tubers and rings or lesions on the leaves.
– ORIGIN early 16th cent. (originally Scots, denoting a brightly coloured stripe): apparently of Scandinavian origin; compare with Norwegian *sprang* 'lace, fringe'.

spraint /spreɪnt/ (also **spraints**) ▸ **noun** [mass noun] the droppings of an otter.
– ORIGIN late Middle English: from Old French *espreintes*, from *espraindre* 'squeeze out', based on Latin *exprimere* 'to express'.

sprang past of **SPRING**.

sprat ▸ **noun** a small marine fish of the herring family, widely caught for food and fish products. ● *Sprattus* and other genera, family Clupeidae: several species, in particular *S. sprattus* of European inshore waters.
■ any of a number of small fishes that resemble the true sprats, e.g. the sand eel.
▸ **verb** (**sprats**, **spratting**, **spratted**) [no obj.] fish for sprats.
– PHRASES **a sprat to catch a mackerel** Brit. a small outlay or risk ventured in the hope of a significant return.
– ORIGIN late 16th cent.: variant of Old English *sprot*, of unknown origin.

Spratly Islands /ˈspratli/ a group of small islands and coral reefs in the South China Sea, between Vietnam and Borneo. Dispersed over a distance of some 965 km (600 miles), the islands are variously claimed by China, Taiwan, Vietnam, the Philippines, and Malaysia.

sprauncy /ˈsprɔːnsi/ ▸ **adjective** (**sprauncier**, **spraunciest**) Brit. informal smart or showy in appearance: *a sprauncy little street*.
– ORIGIN 1950s: perhaps related to dialect *sprouncey* 'cheerful'.

sprawl ▸ **verb** [no obj., with adverbial] sit, lie, or fall with one's arms and legs spread out in an ungainly way: *the door shot open, sending him sprawling across the pavement* | *she lay sprawled on the bed*. ■ spread out over a large area in an untidy or irregular way: *the town sprawled along several miles of cliff top* | (as adj. **sprawling**) *the sprawling suburbs*.
▸ **noun** [usu. in sing.] an ungainly or carelessly relaxed position in which one's arms and legs are spread out: *she fell into a sort of luxurious sprawl*. ■ a group or mass of something that has spread out in an untidy or irregular way: *a sprawl of buildings*. ■ [mass noun] the disorganized and unattractive expansion of an urban or industrial area into the adjoining countryside: *the growth of urban sprawl*.
– DERIVATIVES **sprawlingly** adverb.
– ORIGIN Old English *spreawlian* 'move the limbs convulsively'; related to Danish *sprælle* 'kick or splash about'. The noun dates from the early 18th cent.

spray[1] ▸ **noun** [mass noun] liquid that is blown or driven through the air in the form of tiny drops: *a torrent of white foam and spray* | [count noun] *a fine spray of mud*.
■ a liquid preparation which can be forced out of a can or other container in tiny drops: *a can of insect spray*. ■ [count noun] a can or container holding a spray. ■ [count noun] an act of spraying something: *refresh your flowers with a quick spray*.
▸ **verb** [with obj. and adverbial of direction] apply (liquid) to someone or something in the form of tiny drops: *the product can be sprayed on to wet or dry hair*.
■ [with obj.] sprinkle or cover with tiny drops of liquid: *she sprayed herself with perfume*. ■ [no obj., with adverbial of direction] (of liquid) be driven through the air or forced out of something in tiny drops: *water sprayed into the air*. ■ [with obj.] scatter (something) somewhere with great force: *the truck shuddered to a halt, spraying gravel from under its wheels*. ■ [with obj.] (of a male cat) direct a stream of urine over (an object or area) to mark a territory. ■ [with obj.] (in sport) kick, hit, or throw (the ball) in an unpredictable way.
– DERIVATIVES **sprayable** adjective, **sprayer** noun.
– ORIGIN early 17th cent. (earlier as *spry*): related to Middle Dutch *spra(e)yen* 'sprinkle'.

spray[2] ▸ **noun** a stem or small branch of a tree or plant, bearing flowers and foliage: *a spray of honeysuckle*. ■ a bunch of cut flowers arranged in an attractive way. ■ a brooch in the form of a bouquet of flowers.
– ORIGIN Middle English: representing late Old English *(e)sprei*, recorded in personal and place names, of unknown origin.

spraydeck ▸ **noun** a flexible cover which is fitted to the opening in the top of a kayak to form a waterproof seal around the canoeist's body.

spray-dry ▸ **verb** [with obj.] dry (a foodstuff or a ceramic material) by spraying particles of it into a current of hot air, the water in the particles being rapidly evaporated.

spray gun ▸ **noun** a device resembling a gun which is used to spray a liquid such as paint or pesticide under pressure.

spray-paint ▸ **verb** [with obj.] paint (an image or message) on to a surface with a spray. ■ paint (a surface) with a spray: *they were spray-painting sidewalks and buildings*.

sprayskirt ▸ **noun** another term for **SPRAYDECK**.

spread ▸ **verb** (past and past participle **spread**) **1** [with obj.] open out (something) so as to extend its surface area, width, or length: *I spread a towel on the sand and sat down* | *she helped Colin to* ***spread out*** *the map*.
■ stretch out (arms, legs, hands, fingers, or wings) so that they are far apart: [with obj. and complement] *Bobby spread his arms wide*.
2 [no obj., with adverbial] extend over a large or increasing area: *rain over north-west Scotland will spread south-east during the day*. ■ (**spread out**) (of a group of people) move apart so as to cover a wider area: *the Marines spread out across the docks*. ■ [with obj. and adverbial] distribute or disperse (something) over an area: *volcanic eruptions spread dust high into the stratosphere*. ■ gradually reach or cause to reach a wider area or more people: [no obj.] *the violence spread from the city centre to the suburbs* | [with obj.] *she's always spreading rumours*. ■ (of people, animals, or plants) become distributed over a large or larger area: *the owls have spread as far north as Kuala Lumpur*. ■ [with obj. and adverbial] distribute in a specified way: *you can* ***spread*** *the payments* ***over*** *as long a period as you like*.
3 [with obj. and adverbial] apply (a substance) to an object or surface in an even layer: *he sighed, spreading jam on a croissant*. ■ cover (a surface) with a substance in an even layer: *spread each slice thinly with mayonnaise*. ■ [no obj., with adverbial] be able to be applied in an even layer: *a tub of unsalted butter that spreads so well*.
4 [with obj.] archaic lay (a table) for a meal.
▸ **noun 1** [mass noun] the fact or process of spreading over an area: *the spread of AIDS* | *the spread of the urban population into rural areas*.
2 the extent, width, or area covered by something: *the male's antlers can attain a spread of six feet*. ■ the wingspan of a bird. ■ an expanse or amount of something: *the green spread of the park*.
3 the range or variety of something: *a wide spread of ages*. ■ the difference between two rates or prices: *the very narrow spread between borrowing and deposit rates*. ■ short for **POINT SPREAD**.
4 a soft paste that can be applied in a layer to bread or other food.
5 an article or advertisement covering several columns or pages of a newspaper or magazine, especially one on two facing pages: *a double-page spread*.
6 informal a large and impressively elaborate meal.
7 N. Amer. a large farm or ranch.
8 N. Amer. a bedspread.
– PHRASES **spread like wildfire** see **WILDFIRE**. **spread oneself too thin** be involved in so many different activities that one's time and energy are not used to good effect. **spread one's wings** see **WING**.
– DERIVATIVES **spreadable** adjective.
– ORIGIN Old English *-sprǣdan* (used in combinations), of West Germanic origin; related to Dutch *spreiden* and German *spreiten*.

spread betting ▸ **noun** [mass noun] a form of betting in which the bettor wins or loses money according to the margin by which the value of a particular outcome varies from the spread of expected values quoted by the bookmaker.

spreadeagle ▸ **verb** [with obj.] stretch (someone) out with their arms and legs extended: *he lay spreadeagled in the road*. ■ [no obj.] Skating perform a spread eagle. ■ informal utterly defeat (an opponent in a sporting contest).
▸ **noun** (**spread eagle**) an emblematic representation of an eagle with its legs and wings extended, used especially as an emblem of the United States.
■ Skating a straight glide made with the feet in a line, with the heels touching, and the arms stretched out to either side.

▶ adjective US **1** stretched out with one's arms and legs extended: *prisoners are chained to their beds, spreadeagle, for days at a time*.
2 dated loudly or aggressively patriotic about the United States: *spreadeagle oratory*.

spreader ▶ noun **1** a device used for spreading or scattering a substance over a wide area. ■ a plant that grows over a wide area. ■ a bar attached to the mast of a yacht in order to spread the angle of the upper shrouds.
2 a person who spreads or disseminates something: *kids are the biggest spreaders of the virus*.

spreadsheet ▶ noun a computer program in which figures arranged in the rows and columns of a grid can be manipulated and used in calculations.
▶ verb [no obj.] (usu. as noun **spreadsheeting**) use a spreadsheet.

Sprechgesang /ˈʃprɛxgəˌzaŋ/, German /ˈʃprɛçgəˌzaŋ/ ▶ noun [mass noun] Music a style of dramatic vocalization intermediate between speech and song.
– ORIGIN German, literally 'speech song'.

Sprechstimme /ˈʃprɛxˌʃtɪmə/, German /ˈʃprɛçˌʃtɪmə/ ▶ noun [mass noun] Music another term for SPRECHGESANG. ■ the kind of voice used in Sprechgesang.
– ORIGIN German, literally 'speech voice'.

spree ▶ noun a spell or sustained period of unrestrained activity of a particular kind: *he went on a six-month crime spree | a shopping spree*. ■ dated a spell of unrestrained drinking
▶ verb (**sprees, spreeing, spreed**) [no obj.] dated take part in a spree.
– ORIGIN late 18th cent.: of unknown origin.

spreite /ˈʃprʌɪtə/ ▶ noun (pl. **spreiten** or **spreites**) Palaeontology a banded pattern of uncertain origin found in the infill of the burrows of certain fossil invertebrates.
– ORIGIN 1960s: from German *Spreite* 'layer, lamina'.

sprezzatura /ˌspretsəˈt(j)ʊərə/ ▶ noun [mass noun] studied carelessness, especially as a characteristic quality or style of art or literature.
– ORIGIN Italian.

sprig[1] ▶ noun **1** a small stem bearing leaves or flowers, taken from a plant: *a sprig of holly*.
2 a descendant or younger member of a family or social class: *a sprig of the French nobility*. ■ archaic, chiefly derogatory a young man.
3 a small moulded decoration applied to a piece of pottery before firing.
▶ verb (**sprigs, sprigging, sprigged**) **1** decorate (pottery) with small, separately moulded designs.
2 (as adj. **sprigged**) (chiefly of fabric or paper) decorated with a design of sprigs of leaves or flowers: *a sprigged cotton dress*.
– DERIVATIVES **spriggy** adjective.
– ORIGIN Middle English: from or related to Low German *sprick*.

sprig[2] ▶ noun **1** a small tapering tack with no head, used chiefly to hold glass in a window frame until the putty dries.
2 (usu. **sprigs**) Austral./NZ a stud on the sole of a shoe or boot.
– ORIGIN Middle English: of unknown origin.

sprightly (also **spritely**) ▶ adjective (**sprightlier, sprightliest; spritelier, spriteliest**) (especially of an old person) lively; full of energy: *she was quite sprightly for her age*.
– DERIVATIVES **sprightliness** noun.
– ORIGIN late 16th cent.: from *spright* (rare variant of SPRITE) + -LY[1].

spring ▶ verb (past **sprang** or chiefly N. Amer. **sprung** ; past participle **sprung**) **1** [no obj., with adverbial of direction] move or jump suddenly or rapidly upwards or forwards: *I sprang out of bed* | figurative *they sprang to her defence*. ■ [no obj., with complement or adverbial] move rapidly or suddenly from a constrained position by or as if by the action of a spring: *the drawer sprang open*. ■ operate suddenly by means of a mechanism: *the engine sprang into life*. ■ [with obj.] cause (a game bird) to rise from cover. ■ [with obj.] informal bring about the escape or release of (a prisoner): *the president sought to spring the hostages*.
2 [no obj.] (**spring from**) originate or arise from: *madness and creativity could spring from the same source*. ■ appear suddenly or unexpectedly from: *tears sprang from his eyes*. ■ (**spring up**) suddenly develop or appear: *a terrible storm sprang up*. ■ [with obj.] (**spring something on**) present or propose something suddenly or unexpectedly to (someone): *we decided to spring a surprise on them*.
3 [with obj.] (usu. as adj. **sprung**) cushion or fit (a vehicle or item of furniture) with springs: *a fully sprung bed*.
4 [no obj.] (especially of wood) become warped or split. ■ [with obj.] (of a boat) suffer splitting of (a mast or other part).
5 [no obj.] (**spring for**) N. Amer. informal pay for: *don't spring for the album until you've heard it*. ■ [with obj.] archaic spend (money): *he might spring a few shillings more*.
6 [with obj.] Austral. informal come upon (an illicit activity or its perpetrator): *our science teacher sprung me acting the goat*.
▶ noun **1** the season after winter and before summer, in which vegetation begins to appear, in the northern hemisphere from March to May and in the southern hemisphere from September to November: *in spring the garden is a feast of blossom* | [as modifier] *spring rain*. ■ Astronomy the period from the vernal equinox to the summer solstice. ■ short for SPRING TIDE.
2 an elastic device, typically a helical metal coil, that can be pressed or pulled but returns to its former shape when released, used chiefly to exert constant tension or absorb movement. ■ [mass noun] the ability to spring back strongly; elasticity: *the mattress has lost its spring*.
3 [in sing.] a sudden jump upwards or forwards: *with a sudden spring, he leapt on to the table*. ■ informal, dated an escape or release from prison.
4 a place where water or oil wells up from an underground source, or the basin or flow formed in such a way: *the well is fed by mountain springs*. ■ (usu. **springs**) the origin or a source of something: *the springs of his own emotions*.
5 an upward curvature of a ship's deck planking from the horizontal. ■ a split in a wooden plank or spar under strain.
6 Nautical a hawser laid out diagonally aft from a ship's bow or forward from a ship's stern and secured to a fixed point in order to prevent movement or assist manoeuvring.
– PHRASES **spring a leak** (of a boat or container) develop a leak. [originally in nautical use, referring to timbers springing out of position.] **spring a trap** cause a trap for catching animals to close suddenly. ■ trick someone into doing something: *she decided to spring the trap after noticing that her husband was behaving erratically*.
– DERIVATIVES **springless** adjective, **springlike** adjective.
– ORIGIN Old English *spring* (noun), *springan* (verb), of Germanic origin; related to Dutch and German *springen*. Early use in the senses 'head of a well' and 'rush out in a stream' gave rise to the figurative use 'originate'.

USAGE In British English the standard past tense is **sprang** (*she sprang forward*), while in US English the past can be either **sprang** or **sprung** (*I sprung out of bed*).

spring balance ▶ noun a balance that measures weight by the tension of a spring.

spring beauty ▶ noun a spring-flowering succulent plant. ● Genera *Claytonia* and *Montia*, family Portulacaceae: several species, in particular the American *M. perfoliata*, naturalized in Britain, and *C. virginica*, sometimes cultivated as an ornamental.

springboard ▶ noun **1** a strong, flexible board from which someone may jump in order to gain added impetus when performing a dive or a gymnastic movement. ■ a thing that lends impetus or assistance to a particular action, enterprise, or development: *an economic plan that may be the springboard for recovery*.
2 Canadian & Austral. a platform fixed to the side of a tree and used by a lumberjack when working at some height from the ground.

springbok /ˈsprɪŋbɒk/ ▶ noun **1** (S. African also **springbuck**) a gazelle with a characteristic habit of leaping (pronking) when disturbed, forming large herds on plains in southern Africa. ● *Antidorcas marsupialis*, family Bovidae.
2 (**the Springboks**) the South African international rugby union team.
– ORIGIN late 18th cent.: from Afrikaans, from Dutch *springen* 'to spring' + *bok* 'antelope'.

spring break ▶ noun N. Amer. a week's holiday for school and college students at Easter.
– DERIVATIVES **spring breaker** noun.

spring chicken ▶ noun **1** [usu. with negative] informal a young person: *you're no spring chicken yourself any more*.
2 a young chicken for eating (originally available only in spring).

spring clean ▶ noun Brit. a thorough cleaning of a house or room, typically undertaken in spring.
▶ verb (**spring-clean**) [with obj.] clean (a home or room) thoroughly.

springe /sprɪn(d)ʒ/ ▶ noun a noose or snare for catching small game.
– ORIGIN Middle English: from the base of SPRING.

spring equinox ▶ noun the equinox in spring, on about 20 March in the northern hemisphere and 22 September in the southern hemisphere. ■ Astronomy the equinox in March. Also called VERNAL EQUINOX.

springer ▶ noun **1** (also **springer spaniel**) a small spaniel of a breed originally used to spring game. There are two main breeds, the **English springer**, typically black and white or brown and white, and the less common red and white **Welsh springer**.
2 Architecture the lowest stone in an arch, where the curve begins.
3 a cow or heifer near to calving.
4 S. African any of a number of fish noted for leaping out of the water, in particular: ■ the tenpounder or ladyfish. ■ the skipjack tuna.

spring fever ▶ noun [mass noun] a feeling of restlessness and excitement felt at the beginning of spring.

Springfield 1 the state capital of Illinois; pop. 117,352 (est. 2008). It was the home and burial place of Abraham Lincoln.
2 a city in SW Massachusetts, on the Connecticut River; pop. 150,640 (est. 2008). It was first settled in 1636.
3 a city in SW Missouri, on the northern edge of the Ozark Mountains; pop. 156,206 (est. 2008).

spring greens ▶ plural noun the leaves of young cabbage plants of a variety that does not develop a heart.

springhare /ˈsprɪŋhɛː/ (also **springhaas** /ˈsprɪŋhɑːs/) ▶ noun (pl. **springhares** or **springhaas**) a large nocturnal burrowing rodent resembling a miniature kangaroo, with a rabbit-like head, a long bushy tail, and long hindlimbs, native to southern Africa. ● *Pedetes capensis*, the only member of the family Pedetidae.

spring-loaded ▶ adjective containing a compressed or stretched spring pressing one part against another: *a spring-loaded clothes peg*.

spring lock ▶ noun a type of lock with a spring-loaded bolt which requires a key only to open it, as distinct from a deadlock.

spring mattress ▶ noun a mattress containing springs in a frame.

spring onion ▶ noun Brit. an onion taken from the ground before the bulb has formed, typically eaten raw in salad.

spring peeper ▶ noun see PEEPER[2].

spring roll ▶ noun a Chinese snack consisting of a pancake filled with vegetables and sometimes meat, rolled into a cylinder and deep-fried.

Springsteen, Bruce (b.1949), American rock singer, songwriter, and guitarist, noted for his songs about working-class life in the US. Notable albums: *Born to Run* (1975) and *Born in the USA* (1984).

springtail ▶ noun a minute primitive wingless insect which has a springlike organ under the abdomen that enables it to leap when disturbed. Springtails are abundant in the soil and leaf litter. ● Order Collembola: many families.

springtide ▶ noun literary term for SPRINGTIME.

spring tide ▶ noun a tide just after a new or full moon, when there is the greatest difference between high and low water.

springtime ▶ noun the season of spring.

spring water ▶ noun [mass noun] water from a spring, as opposed to river water or rainwater.

springy ▶ adjective (**springier, springiest**) springing back quickly when squeezed or stretched; elastic: *the springy turf*. ■ (of movements) light and confident: *he left the room with a springy step*.
– DERIVATIVES **springily** adverb, **springiness** noun.

sprinkle ▶ verb **1** [with obj. and adverbial] cover (an object or surface) with small drops or particles of a substance: *I sprinkled the floor with water*. ■ scatter or pour (small drops or particles of a substance) over an object or surface: *sprinkle sesame seeds over the top*. ■ distribute or disperse something randomly or irregularly throughout (something): *he sprinkled his conversation with quotations*. ■ place or attach (a

S

number of things) at irregularly spaced intervals: *a dress with little daisies sprinkled all over it*.
2 [no obj.] (**it sprinkles, it is sprinkling**, etc.) N. Amer. rain very lightly: *it began to sprinkle*.
▸ **noun 1** a small quantity or amount of something scattered over an object or surface: ***a generous sprinkle of pepper*** | figurative ***fiction with a sprinkle of fact***.
2 [in sing.] N. Amer. a light rain.
3 (**sprinkles**) chiefly N. Amer. tiny sugar strands and balls used for decorating cakes and desserts.
– ORIGIN late Middle English: perhaps from Middle Dutch *sprenkelen*.

sprinkler ▸ **noun** a device that sprays water. ■ a device used for watering lawns. ■ an automatic fire extinguisher installed in the ceilings of a building.

sprinkling ▸ **noun** a small thinly distributed amount of something: ***a sprinkling of*** *grey in his hair*.

sprint ▸ **verb** [no obj., with adverbial of direction] run at full speed over a short distance: *I saw Charlie sprinting through the traffic towards me*.
▸ **noun** an act or short spell of running at full speed. ■ a short, fast race in which the competitors run a distance of 400 metres or less: *the 100 metres sprint*. ■ a short, fast race in cycling, swimming, etc.
– DERIVATIVES **sprinter** noun.
– ORIGIN late 18th cent. (as a dialect term meaning 'a bound or spring'): related to Swedish *spritta*.

sprinting ▸ **noun** [mass noun] the competitive athletic sport of running distances of 400 metres or less.

sprit ▸ **noun** Sailing a small spar reaching diagonally from a mast to the upper outer corner of a sail.
– ORIGIN Old English *sprēot* '(punting) pole'; related to SPROUT.

sprite ▸ **noun 1** an elf or fairy.
2 a computer graphic which may be moved on-screen and otherwise manipulated as a single entity.
3 a faint flash, typically red, sometimes emitted in the upper atmosphere over a thunderstorm owing to the collision of high-energy electrons with air molecules.
– ORIGIN Middle English: alteration of *sprit*, a contraction of SPIRIT.

spritely ▸ **adjective** variant spelling of SPRIGHTLY.

spritsail /ˈsprɪts(ə)l, -seɪl/ ▸ **noun** a sail extended by a sprit. ■ a sail extended by a yard set under a ship's bowsprit.

spritz ▸ **verb** [with obj.] squirt or spray a liquid at or on to (something) in quick short bursts: *she spritzed her neck with cologne*. ■ spray (a liquid) in this way: *she spritzed some perfume behind her ears*.
▸ **noun** an act of squirting or spraying liquid in short bursts or the liquid sprayed.
– ORIGIN early 20th cent.: from German *spritzen* 'to squirt'.

spritzer ▸ **noun** a mixture of wine and soda water.
– ORIGIN 1960s: from German *Spritzer* 'a splash'.

sprocket ▸ **noun** each of several projections on the rim of a wheel that engage with the links of a chain or with holes in film, tape, or paper. ■ (also **sprocket wheel**) a wheel with sprockets.
– ORIGIN mid 16th cent. (denoting a triangular piece of timber used in a roof): of unknown origin.

sprog Brit. informal, humorous ▸ **noun 1** a child.
2 a military recruit or trainee.
▸ **verb** (**sprogs, sprogging, sprogged**) [no obj.] have a baby.
– ORIGIN 1940s (originally services' slang): perhaps from obsolete *sprag* 'lively young man', of unknown origin.

sprosser /ˈsprɒsə/ ▸ **noun** another term for THRUSH NIGHTINGALE.
– ORIGIN late 19th cent.: from German.

sprout ▸ **verb** [no obj.] (of a plant) put out shoots: *the weeds begin to sprout*. ■ [with obj.] grow (plant shoots or hair): *many black cats sprout a few white hairs*. ■ [no obj.] (of a plant, flower, or hair) start to grow; spring up: *crocuses sprouted up from the grass*. ■ [no obj.] appear or develop suddenly and in large numbers: *plush new hotels are* ***sprouting up*** *everywhere*.
▸ **noun 1** a shoot of a plant. ■ (**sprouts**) young shoots, especially of alfalfa, mung beans, or soybeans, eaten as a vegetable.
2 short for BRUSSELS SPROUT.
– ORIGIN Middle English: of West Germanic origin; related to Dutch *spruiten* and German *spriessen*.

spruce¹ ▸ **adjective** neat in dress and appearance: *Angela was a very spruce and tidy person*.
▸ **verb** [with obj.] (**spruce someone/thing up**) make someone or something smarter or tidier: *the fund will be used to spruce up historic buildings*.
– DERIVATIVES **sprucely** adverb, **spruceness** noun.
– ORIGIN late 16th cent.: perhaps from SPRUCE² in the obsolete sense 'Prussian', in the phrase *spruce (leather) jerkin*.

spruce² ▸ **noun** a widespread coniferous tree which has a distinctive conical shape and hanging cones, widely grown for timber, pulp, and Christmas trees.
● Genus *Picea*, family Pinaceae: many species.
– ORIGIN late Middle English (denoting Prussia or something originating in Prussia): alteration of obsolete *Pruce* 'Prussia'. The application to the tree dates from the early 17th cent.

spruce³ ▸ **verb** [no obj.] Brit. informal, dated engage in pretence or deception, especially by feigning illness: *he's no fool; he'd have known if she was sprucing*. ■ [with obj.] deceive: *they spruced you proper*.
– DERIVATIVES **sprucer** noun.
– ORIGIN early 20th cent.: of unknown origin.

spruce beer ▸ **noun** [mass noun] a fermented drink using spruce twigs and needles as flavouring.

spruce budworm ▸ **noun** the brown caterpillar of a small North American moth which is a serious pest of spruce and other conifers. ● *Choristoneura fumiferana*, family Tortricidae.

sprue¹ /spruː/ ▸ **noun** a channel through which metal or plastic is poured into a mould. ■ a piece of metal or plastic which has solidified in a sprue, especially one joining a number of small moulded plastic items.
– ORIGIN early 19th cent.: of unknown origin.

sprue² /spruː/ ▸ **noun** [mass noun] disease of the small intestine causing malabsorption of food, in particular: ■ (also **tropical sprue**) a disease characterized by ulceration of the mouth and chronic enteritis, suffered by visitors to tropical regions from temperate countries. ■ (also **non-tropical sprue**) another term for COELIAC DISEASE.
– ORIGIN late 19th cent.: from Dutch *spruw* 'thrush'; perhaps related to Flemish *spruwen* 'sprinkle'.

spruik /spruːk/ ▸ **verb** [no obj.] Austral. informal speak in public, especially to advertise a show: *men who spruik outside striptease joints*. ■ promote or publicize: *the company forked out $15 million to spruik its digital revolution*.
– DERIVATIVES **spruiker** noun.
– ORIGIN early 20th cent.: of unknown origin.

spruit /spreɪt/ ▸ **noun** S. African a small watercourse, typically dry except during the rainy season.
– ORIGIN Dutch; related to SPROUT.

sprung past participle and (especially in North America) past of SPRING.

sprung rhythm ▸ **noun** [mass noun] a poetic metre approximating to speech, each foot having one stressed syllable followed by a varying number of unstressed ones.
– ORIGIN late 19th cent.: coined by G. M. Hopkins, who used the metre.

spry ▸ **adjective** (**spryer, spryest**) (especially of an old person) active; lively: *he continued to look spry and active well into his eighties*.
– DERIVATIVES **spryly** adverb, **spryness** noun.
– ORIGIN mid 18th cent.: of unknown origin.

spud ▸ **noun 1** informal a potato.
2 a small, narrow spade for cutting the roots of plants, especially weeds.
3 [often as modifier] a short length of pipe that is used to connect two components or that takes the form of a projection from a fitting to which a pipe may be screwed: *a spud washer*.
4 a type of ice chisel.
▸ **verb** (**spuds, spudding, spudded**) [with obj.] **1** dig up or cut (plants, especially weeds) with a small spade.
2 make the initial drilling for (an oil well).
– ORIGIN late Middle English (denoting a short knife): of unknown origin. The sense 'potato' (dating from the mid 19th cent.) was originally slang and dialect.

spud-bashing ▸ **noun** [mass noun] Brit. informal the chore of peeling potatoes, especially as a punishment in the army.

spud wrench ▸ **noun** a long bar with a socket on the end for tightening bolts.

spue ▸ **verb** archaic spelling of SPEW.

spumante /spuːˈmanteɪ, -ˈmanti/ ▸ **noun** [mass noun] an Italian sparkling white wine.
– ORIGIN Italian, literally 'sparkling'.

spume /spjuːm/ literary ▸ **noun** [mass noun] froth or foam, especially that found on waves.
▸ **verb** [no obj.] form or produce a mass of froth or foam: *water was spuming under the mill*.
– DERIVATIVES **spumous** adjective, **spumy** adjective.
– ORIGIN late Middle English: from Old French *(e)spume* or Latin *spuma*.

spumoni /spuːˈməʊni/ (also **spumone**) ▸ **noun** [mass noun] N. Amer. a kind of ice-cream dessert with different colours and flavours in layers.
– ORIGIN from Italian *spumone*, from *spuma* 'foam'.

spun past and past participle of SPIN.

spunk ▸ **noun** [mass noun] informal **1** courage and determination: *she's got no spunk, or she'd have left him long ago*.
2 Brit. vulgar slang semen.
3 [count noun] Austral. a sexually attractive person.
– ORIGIN mid 16th cent. (in the sense 'a spark, vestige'): of unknown origin; perhaps a blend of SPARK¹ and obsolete *funk* 'spark'.

spunky ▸ **adjective** (**spunkier, spunkiest**) informal
1 courageous and determined: *a spunky performance*.
2 chiefly Austral. sexually attractive: *a top chick with a spunky boyfriend*.
– DERIVATIVES **spunkily** adverb, **spunkiness** noun.

spun silk ▸ **noun** [mass noun] a cheap material made of short-fibred and waste silk.

spun sugar ▸ **noun** [mass noun] hardened sugar syrup drawn out into long filaments and used to make candyfloss or as a decoration for sweet dishes.

spun yarn ▸ **noun** [mass noun] Nautical cord made by twisting loose strands of rope together.

spur ▸ **noun 1** a device with a small spike or a spiked wheel that is worn on a rider's heel and used for urging a horse forward. ■ a horny spike on the back of the leg of a cock or male game bird, used in fighting. ■ a steel point fastened to the leg of a gamecock. ■ Medicine a short pointed growth or process on a part of the body.
2 a thing that prompts or encourages someone; an incentive: *wars act as* ***a spur to*** *practical invention*.
3 a thing that projects or branches off from a main body, in particular: ■ a projection from a mountain or mountain range. ■ a short branch road or railway line. ■ Botany a slender tubular projection from the base of a flower, e.g. a honeysuckle or orchid, typically containing nectar. ■ a short fruit-bearing side shoot.
4 a small, single-pointed support for ceramic ware in a kiln.
▸ **verb** (**spurs, spurring, spurred**) [with obj.] **1** urge (a horse) forward by digging one's spurs into its sides: *she spurred her horse towards the hedge*. ■ give an incentive or encouragement to (someone): *her sons' passion for computer games* ***spurred her on*** *to set up a software shop*. ■ promote the development of; stimulate: *governments cut interest rates to spur demand*.
2 prune in (a side shoot of a plant) so as to form a spur close to the stem: ***spur back*** *the lateral shoots*.
– PHRASES **on the spur of the moment** on impulse; without planning in advance: *I don't generally do things on the spur of the moment* | [as modifier] *a spur-of-the-moment decision*.
– DERIVATIVES **spurless** adjective, **spurred** adjective.
– ORIGIN Old English *spora, spura*, of Germanic origin; related to Dutch *spoor* and German *Sporn*, also to SPURN.

spur-dog ▸ **noun** a large white-spotted grey dogfish with venomous spines in front of the dorsal fins. It occurs in the North Atlantic and the Mediterranean, often in large shoals. ● *Squalus acanthias*, family Squalidae.

spurfowl ▸ **noun** an Asian and African game bird related to the partridges, with spurs on the legs.
● Genus *Galloperdix* of Asia (three species), and the **red-necked spurfowl** or francolin (*Francolinus afer*) of Africa, family Phasianidae.

spurge /spəːdʒ/ ▸ **noun** a herbaceous plant or shrub with milky latex and very small, typically greenish, flowers. Many kinds are cultivated as ornamentals and some are of commercial importance. ● Genus *Euphorbia*, family Euphorbiaceae: numerous species.
– ORIGIN late Middle English: shortening of Old French *espurge*, from *espurgier*, from Latin *expurgare* 'cleanse' (because of the purgative properties of the milky latex).

spur gear ▸ **noun** a gearwheel with teeth projecting parallel to the wheel's axis.

spurge laurel ▸ **noun** a low-growing evergreen Eurasian shrub with leathery leaves, small green flowers, and black poisonous berries. ● *Daphne laureola*, family Thymelaeaceae.

spurious /ˈspjʊərɪəs/ ▸ **adjective** not being what it purports to be; false or fake: *separating authentic and*

S

spurious claims. ■ (of a line of reasoning) apparently but not actually valid: *this spurious reasoning results in nonsense.* ■ archaic (of offspring) illegitimate.
– DERIVATIVES **spuriously** adverb, **spuriousness** noun.
– ORIGIN late 16th cent. (in the sense 'born out of wedlock'): from Latin *spurius* 'false' + **-OUS**.

spurn ▶ verb [with obj.] reject with disdain or contempt: *he spoke gruffly, as if afraid that his invitation would be spurned.* ■ archaic strike, tread, or push away with the foot: *with one touch of my feet, I spurn the solid Earth.*
▶ noun archaic an act of spurning.
– DERIVATIVES **spurner** noun.
– ORIGIN Old English *spurnan, spornan*; related to Latin *spernere* 'to scorn'; compare with **SPUR**.

spurrey /ˈspʌri/ (also **spurry**) ▶ noun (pl. **spurreys** or **spurries**) a small widely distributed plant of the pink family, with pink or white flowers. ● Genera *Spergula* and *Spergularia*, family Caryophyllaceae: several species, in particular **corn spurrey** (*Spergula arvensis*), a spindly weed of cornfields, and **sand spurrey** (*Spergularia rubra*), of sandy and gravelly soils.
– ORIGIN late 16th cent.: from Dutch *spurrie*; probably related to medieval Latin *spergula*.

spurrier /ˈspʌrɪə, ˈspəː-/ ▶ noun rare a person who makes spurs.

spur royal ▶ noun historical a gold coin worth fifteen shillings, made chiefly in the reign of James I and bearing a representation of a sun with rays.

spurt ▶ verb [no obj., with adverbial of direction] **1** gush out in a sudden and forceful stream: *he cut his finger, and blood spurted over the sliced potatoes.* ■ [with obj. and adverbial of direction] cause to gush out suddenly: *the kettle boiled and spurted scalding water.*
2 move with a sudden burst of speed: *the other car had spurted to the top of the ramp.*
▶ noun **1** a sudden gushing stream: *a sudden spurt of blood gushed into her eyes.*
2 a sudden marked burst or increase of activity or speed: *late in the race he* ***put on a spurt*** *and reached second place | a growth spurt.*
– ORIGIN mid 16th cent.: of unknown origin.

spur wheel ▶ noun another term for **SPUR GEAR**.

sputnik /ˈspʊtnɪk, ˈspʌt-/ ▶ noun each of a series of Soviet artificial satellites, the first of which (launched on 4 October 1957) was the first satellite to be placed in orbit.
– ORIGIN Russian, literally 'fellow-traveller'.

sputter ▶ verb **1** [no obj.] make a series of soft explosive or spitting sounds: *the engine spluttered and stopped.* ■ [reporting verb] speak in a series of incoherent bursts as a result of strong emotion: [with direct speech] *'But ... but ...' she sputtered.* ■ [with obj.] emit with a spitting sound: *the goose is in the oven, sputtering fat.* ■ [with adverbial] proceed in a spasmodic and feeble way: *strikes in the public services sputtered on.*
2 [with obj.] Physics deposit (metal) on a surface by using fast ions to eject particles of it from a target. ■ cover (a surface) with metal by this method.
▶ noun a series of soft explosive or spitting sounds: *the sputter of the motor died away.*
– DERIVATIVES **sputterer** noun.
– ORIGIN late 16th cent. (as a verb): from Dutch *sputteren*, of imitative origin.

sputum /ˈspjuːtəm/ ▶ noun [mass noun] a mixture of saliva and mucus coughed up from the respiratory tract, typically as a result of infection or other disease and often examined microscopically to aid medical diagnosis.
– ORIGIN late 17th cent.: from Latin, neuter past participle of *spuere* 'to spit'.

spy ▶ noun (pl. **spies**) a person employed by a government or other organization to secretly obtain information on an enemy or competitor. ■ a person who keeps watch on others secretly: [as modifier] *a spy camera.*
▶ verb (**spies, spying, spied**) **1** [no obj.] work for a government or other organization by secretly obtaining information about enemies or competitors: *he agreed to spy for the West.* ■ (**spy on**) observe (someone) furtively: *the couple were spied on by reporters.* ■ [with obj.] (**spy something out**) collect information about something to use in deciding how to act: *he would go and spy out the land.*
2 [with obj.] discern or make out, especially by careful observation: *he could spy a figure in the distance.*
– ORIGIN Middle English: shortening of Old French *espie* 'espying', *espier* 'espy', of Germanic origin, from an Indo-European root shared by Latin *specere* 'behold, look'.

spyglass ▶ noun a small telescope.

spyhole ▶ noun Brit. a peephole, especially one in a door for observing callers before opening.

spymaster ▶ noun the head of an organization of spies.

spyware ▶ noun [mass noun] software that enables a user to obtain covert information about another's computer activities by transmitting data covertly from their hard drive.

sq. ▶ abbreviation square: *51,100 sq. km.*

SQL ▶ abbreviation Computing Structured Query Language, an international standard for database manipulation.

Sqn Ldr ▶ abbreviation Squadron Leader.

squab /skwɒb/ ▶ noun **1** a young unfledged pigeon.
2 Brit. the padded back or side of a vehicle seat. ■ a thick stuffed cushion, especially one covering the seat of a chair or sofa.
▶ adjective archaic (of a person) short and fat.
– ORIGIN mid 17th cent. (in the sense 'inexperienced person'): of unknown origin; compare with obsolete *quab* 'shapeless thing' and Swedish dialect *skvabba* 'fat woman'.

squabble ▶ noun a noisy quarrel about something trivial: *family squabbles.*
▶ verb [no obj.] quarrel noisily over a trivial matter: *the boys were squabbling over a ball.*
– DERIVATIVES **squabbler** noun.
– ORIGIN early 17th cent.: probably imitative; compare with Swedish dialect *skvabbel* 'a dispute'.

squab pie ▶ noun Brit. **1** pigeon pie.
2 archaic a pie with a thick crust containing mutton, pork, onions, and apples. [early 18th cent.: regional use.]

squacco heron /ˈskwakəʊ/ ▶ noun a small crested buff and white heron found in southern Europe, the Middle East, and Africa. ● *Ardeola ralloides*, family Ardeidae.
– ORIGIN mid 18th cent.: *squacco* from Italian dialect *sguacco*.

squad ▶ noun [treated as sing. or pl.] a small group of people having a particular task: *an assassination squad.* ■ a small number of soldiers assembled for drill or assigned to a special task. ■ a group of sports players from which a team is chosen: *Ireland's World Cup squad.* ■ a division of a police force dealing with a particular type of crime: *the vice squad.*
– ORIGIN mid 17th cent.: shortening of French *escouade*, variant of *escadre*, from Italian *squadra* 'square'.

squad car ▶ noun a police patrol car.

squaddie (also **squaddy**) ▶ noun (pl. **squaddies**) Brit. informal a private soldier.

squadron ▶ noun an operational unit in an air force consisting of two or more flights of aircraft and the personnel required to fly them. ■ a principal division of an armoured or cavalry regiment, consisting of two or more troops. ■ a group of warships detached on a particular duty or under the command of a flag officer. ■ informal a large group of people or things: *he immediately commissioned a squadron of architects.*
– ORIGIN mid 16th cent. (originally denoting a group of soldiers in square formation): from Italian *squadrone*, from *squadra* 'square'.

squadron leader ▶ noun a rank of officer in the RAF, above flight lieutenant and below wing commander.

squalamine /ˈskweɪləmiːn/ ▶ noun [mass noun] Biochemistry a compound of the steroid type found in sharks, which has antibiotic properties.
– ORIGIN 1990s: from Latin *squalus* (denoting a kind of marine fish and used as a rare term in English for 'shark') + **AMINE**.

squalene /ˈskweɪliːn/ ▶ noun [mass noun] Biochemistry an oily liquid hydrocarbon which occurs in shark liver oil and human sebum, and is a metabolic precursor of sterols. ● A triterpenoid; chem. formula: $C_{30}H_{50}$.
– ORIGIN early 20th cent.: from Latin *squalus* (see **SQUALAMINE**) + **-ENE**.

squalid ▶ adjective (of a place) extremely dirty and unpleasant, especially as a result of poverty or neglect: *the squalid, overcrowded prison.* ■ showing or involving a contemptible lack of moral standards: *a squalid attempt to save themselves from electoral embarrassment.*
– DERIVATIVES **squalidly** adverb **squalidness** noun.
– ORIGIN late 16th cent.: from Latin *squalidus*, from *squalere* 'be rough or dirty'.

squall /skwɔːl/ ▶ noun **1** a sudden violent gust of wind or localized storm, especially one bringing rain, snow, or sleet: *low clouds and squalls of driving rain.*
2 a loud cry: *he emitted a short mournful squall.*
▶ verb [no obj.] (of a baby or small child) cry noisily and continuously: *Sarah was squalling in her crib.*
ORIGIN mid 17th cent.: probably an alteration of **SQUEAL**, influenced by **BAWL**.

squall line ▶ noun Meteorology a narrow band of high winds and storms associated with a cold front.

squally ▶ adjective (**squallier, squalliest**) (of weather) characterized by squalls: *squally showers.*

squalor /ˈskwɒlə/ ▶ noun [mass noun] the state of being extremely dirty and unpleasant, especially as a result of poverty or neglect: *they lived in squalor and disease.*
– ORIGIN early 17th cent.: from Latin, from *squalere* 'be dirty'.

Squamata /skwəˈmɑːtə/ ▶ plural noun Zoology a large order of reptiles which comprises the snakes, lizards, and worm lizards.
– ORIGIN modern Latin (plural), from Latin *squama* 'scale'.

squamate Zoology ▶ noun a reptile of the large order Squamata; a snake, lizard, or worm lizard.
▶ adjective relating to or denoting squamates.

squamocolumnar /ˌskweɪmə(ʊ)kəˈlʌmnə/ ▶ adjective Anatomy relating to or denoting a junction between layers of stratified squamous cells and columnar cells in epithelial tissue.

squamosal /skwəˈməʊs(ə)l/ ▶ noun Zoology the squamous portion of the temporal bone, especially when this forms a separate bone which, in mammals, articulates with the lower jaw.
– ORIGIN mid 19th cent.: from Latin *squamosus* (from *squama* 'scale') + **-AL**.

squamous /ˈskweɪməs/ ▶ adjective covered with or characterized by scales: *a squamous black hide.* ■ Anatomy relating to, consisting of, or denoting a layer of epithelium that consists of very thin flattened cells: *squamous cell carcinoma.* ■ [attrib.] Anatomy denoting the flat portion of the temporal bone which forms part of the side of the skull.
– ORIGIN late Middle English: from Latin *squamosus*, from *squama* 'scale'.

squamule /ˈskweɪmjuːl/ ▶ noun Botany & Zoology a small scale.
– DERIVATIVES **squamulose** adjective.
– ORIGIN mid 18th cent.: from Latin *squamula*, diminutive of *squama* 'scale'.

squander ▶ verb [with obj.] waste (something, especially money or time) in a reckless and foolish manner: *£100m of taxpayers' money has been* ***squandered on*** *administering the tax.* ■ allow (an opportunity) to pass or be lost: *the team squandered several good scoring chances.*
– DERIVATIVES **squanderer** noun.
– ORIGIN late 16th cent.: of unknown origin.

square ▶ noun **1** a plane figure with four equal straight sides and four right angles. ■ a thing that is square or approximately square in shape: *she tore a bit of cloth into a four-inch square.* ■ a thing having the shape or approximate shape of a cube: *a small square of chocolate.* ■ a small square area on the board used in a game. ■ historical a body of infantry drawn up in rectangular form. ■ a unit of 100 square ft used as a measure of flooring, roofing, etc. ■ a square scarf. ■ Brit. a mortar board. ■ the portion of the cover of a bound book which projects beyond the pages.
2 an open, typically four-sided, area surrounded by buildings in a village, town, or city: *a market square |* [in place names] *Leicester Square.* ■ an open area at the meeting of streets. ■ Cricket a closer-cut area at the centre of a ground, any strip of which may be prepared as a wicket. ■ an area within a military barracks or camp used for drill. ■ US a block of buildings bounded by four streets.
3 the product of a number multiplied by itself: *a circle's area is proportional to the square of its radius.*
4 an L-shaped or T-shaped instrument used for obtaining or testing right angles: *a carpenter's square.* ■ [mass noun] Astrology an aspect of 90° (one quarter of a circle): *Venus* ***in square to*** *Jupiter.*
5 informal a person considered to be old-fashioned or boringly conventional in attitude or behaviour.
6 N. Amer. informal a square meal: *three squares a day.*
▶ adjective **1** having the shape or approximate shape of a square: *a square table.* ■ having the shape or approximate shape of a cube: *a square block of flats.* ■ having or in the form of two right angles: *a suitable*

S

length of wood with square ends. ■ having an outline resembling two corners of a square: *his square jaw.* ■ broad and solid in shape: *he was short and square.*
2 denoting a unit of measurement equal to the area of a square whose side is of the unit specified: *30,000 square feet of new gallery space.* ■ [postpositive] denoting the length of each side of a square shape or object: *the office was fifteen feet square.*
3 at right angles; perpendicular: *these lines must be* ***square to*** *the top and bottom marked edges.* ■ Cricket & Soccer in a direction transversely across the field or pitch. ■ Astrology having or denoting an aspect of 90°: *Jupiter is square to the Sun.*
4 level or parallel: *place two pieces of wood one on top of the other, ensuring that they are exactly square.* ■ properly arranged; in good order: *we should get everything square before we leave.* ■ compatible or in agreement: *he wanted to make sure we were* ***square with*** *the court's decision and not subject to a lawsuit.* ■ fair and honest: *she'd been as square with him as anybody could be.*
5 (of two people) owing nothing to each other: *an acknowledgement that we are square.* ■ with both players or sides having equal scores in a game: *the goal brought the match* ***all square*** *once again.*
6 informal old-fashioned or boringly conventional: *Elvis was anything but square.*
7 (of rhythm) simple and straightforward.
▶ **adverb 1** directly; straight: *the ball hit me square in the forehead.* ■ informal fairly; honestly: *I'd acted square with him.*
2 Cricket & Soccer in a direction transversely across the field or pitch: *the ball bounced almost square to the left.*
▶ **verb** [with obj.] **1** make square or rectangular; give a square or rectangular cross section to: *you can* ***square off*** *the other edge.* ■ (usu. as adj. **squared**) mark out in squares: *a sheet of squared paper.*
2 multiply (a number) by itself: *5 squared equals 25.* ■ [usu. as postpositive adj.] (**squared**) convert (a linear unit of measurement) to a unit of area equal to a square whose side is of the unit specified: *there were only three people per kilometre squared.*
3 make compatible; reconcile: *I'm able to* ***square*** *my profession* ***with*** *my religious beliefs.* ■ [no obj.] be compatible: *do those announcements really* ***square with*** *the facts?*
4 balance (an account): *institutions are anxious to square their books before the election.* ■ settle or pay (a bill or debt): *would you* ***square up*** *the bill?* ■ make the score of (a match or game) even: [with obj. and complement] *his goal squared the match 1–1.*
5 bring (one's shoulders) into a position in which they appear square and broad, typically to prepare oneself for a difficult task or event: *chin up, shoulders squared, she stepped into the room.*
6 informal secure the help or acquiescence of (someone), especially by offering an inducement: *trying to square the press.*
7 Soccer pass (a ball) across the field, especially towards the centre.
8 Sailing set (a yard or other part of a ship) at right angles to the keel or other point of reference.
9 Astrology (of a planet) have a square aspect with (another planet or position): *Saturn squares the Sun on the 17th.*
– PHRASES **back to** (or **at**) **square one** informal back to where one started, with no progress having been made. **on the square 1** informal honest; straightforward. **2** having membership of the Freemasons. **out of square** not at right angles. **square accounts with** see ACCOUNT. **square the circle** construct a square equal in area to a given circle (a problem incapable of a purely geometrical solution). ■ do something that is considered to be impossible. **a square deal** see DEAL[1]. **a square peg in a round hole** see PEG.
– PHRASAL VERBS **square something away** N. Amer. arrange or deal with something in a satisfactory way: *don't you worry, we'll get things squared away.* **square off 1** N. Amer. another way of saying SQUARE UP below. **2** Austral./NZ settle a difference. **square someone off** Austral. placate someone. **square up** assume the attitude of a person about to fight: *he has been known to* ***square up to*** *people who have enraged him.* ■ (**square up to**) face and tackle (a difficulty or problem) resolutely: *the Party squared up to the necessity of facing fascism with military sanctions.*
– DERIVATIVES **squareness** noun, **squarer** noun, **squarish** adjective.
– ORIGIN Middle English: shortening of Old French *esquare* (noun), *esquarre* (past participle, used as an adjective), *esquarrer* (verb), based on Latin *quadra* 'square'.

square-bashing ▶ **noun** [mass noun] Brit. informal military drill performed repeatedly on a barrack square.

square brackets ▶ **plural noun** Brit. brackets of the form [ ].

square-built ▶ **adjective** broad or square in shape: *the embassy was a square-built Victorian affair.*

square cut ▶ **noun** Cricket a cut hit square on the offside.
▶ **verb** (**square-cut**) [with obj.] hit (the ball) with a square cut.

square dance ▶ **noun** a country dance of US origin that starts with four couples facing one another in a square, with the steps and movements shouted out by a caller.
▶ **verb** (**square-dance**) [no obj.] (often as noun **square-dancing**) participate in a square dance.
– DERIVATIVES **square dancer** noun.

square eyes ▶ **plural noun** Brit. humorous eyes supposedly affected by excessive television viewing: *he watched so much TV he'd got square eyes.*
– DERIVATIVES **square-eyed** adjective.

square go ▶ **noun** Scottish an unarmed brawl.

squarehead ▶ **noun** N. Amer. informal **1** a stupid or inept person.
2 offensive a person of Germanic or Scandinavian origin.

square knot ▶ **noun** US term for REEF KNOT.

square law ▶ **noun** Physics a law relating two variables one of which varies (directly or inversely) as the square of the other. See also INVERSE SQUARE LAW.

square leg ▶ **noun** Cricket a fielding position level with the batsman approximately halfway towards the boundary on the leg side. ■ a fielder at square leg.

squarely ▶ **adverb** directly, without deviating to one side: *Ashley looked at him squarely.* ■ in a direct and uncompromising manner: *they placed the blame squarely on the president.*

square meal ▶ **noun** a substantial, satisfying, and balanced meal: *three square meals a day.*
– ORIGIN said to derive from nautical use, with reference to the square platters on which meals were served on board ship.

square measure ▶ **noun** a unit of measurement relating to area.

Square Mile an informal name for the City of London.

square number ▶ **noun** the product of a number multiplied by itself, e.g. 1, 4, 9, 16.

square perch ▶ **noun** see PERCH[3] (sense 2).

square piano ▶ **noun** an early type of piano, small and oblong in shape.

square pole ▶ **noun** another term for PERCH[3] (sense 2).

square-rigged ▶ **adjective** (of a sailing ship) having the principal sails at right angles to the length of the ship, supported by horizontal yards attached to the mast or masts.

square-rigger ▶ **noun** a square-rigged sailing ship.

square rod ▶ **noun** another term for PERCH[3] (sense 2).

square root ▶ **noun** a number which produces a specified quantity when multiplied by itself.

square sail ▶ **noun** a four-cornered sail supported by a yard attached to a mast.

square-shouldered ▶ **adjective** (of a person or garment) having broad, square shoulders that do not slope.

square-toed ▶ **adjective** (of shoes or boots) having broad, square toes. ■ archaic old-fashioned or formal.

square wave ▶ **noun** Electronics a periodic wave that varies abruptly in amplitude between two fixed values, spending equal times at each.

squark /skwɑːk/ ▶ **noun** Physics the supersymmetric counterpart of a quark, with spin 0 instead of $^1/_2$.
– ORIGIN 1980s: from *s(uper)* + QUARK[1].

squash[1] ▶ **verb** [with obj.] **1** crush or squeeze (something) with force so that it becomes flat, soft, or out of shape: *wash and squash the cans before depositing them* | (as adj. **squashed**) *a squashed packet of cigarettes.* ■ [with obj. and adverbial] squeeze or force into a small or restricted space: *she squashed some of her clothes inside the bag.* ■ [no obj., with adverbial of direction] make one's way into a small or restricted space: *I squashed into the middle of the crowd.*
2 suppress or subdue (a feeling or action): *the mournful sound did nothing to squash her high spirits.* ■ firmly reject (an idea or suggestion): *the proposal was immediately squashed by the Heritage Department.* ■ silence or discomfit (someone), typically by making a humiliating remark: *she needled him with such venom that Seb was visibly squashed.*
▶ **noun 1** [in sing.] a state of being squeezed or forced into a small or restricted space: *it was a bit of a squash but he didn't seem to mind.* ■ [count noun] dated a social gathering or informal meeting: *a poetry squash in London.*
2 [mass noun] Brit. a concentrated liquid made from fruit juice and sugar, which is diluted to make a drink: *orange squash.*
3 (also **squash rackets**) [mass noun] a game in which two players use rackets to hit a small, soft rubber ball against the walls of a closed court.
4 Biology a preparation of softened tissue that has been made thin for microscopic examination by gently compressing or tapping it.
– ORIGIN mid 16th cent. (as a verb): alteration of QUASH.

squash[2] ▶ **noun** (pl. **same** or **squashes**) **1** an edible gourd, the flesh of which may be cooked and eaten as a vegetable.
2 the trailing plant of the gourd family which produces the squash. ● Genus *Cucurbita*, family Cucurbitaceae: many species and varieties, including the **winter squashes** and **summer squashes**.
– ORIGIN mid 17th cent.: abbreviation of Narragansett *asquutasquash*.

squashberry ▶ **noun** (pl. **squashberries**) a North American viburnum which bears edible berries. ● *Viburnum edule*, family Caprifoliaceae.

squash blossom ▶ **noun** [as modifier] denoting a type of silver jewellery made by Navajos and characterized by designs resembling the flower of the squash plant.

squash bug ▶ **noun** a bug which resembles a shield bug, several American kinds being serious pests of squashes and similar fruit. ● Family Coreidae, suborder Heteroptera: many species, in particular the North American *Anasasa tristis*.

squashy ▶ **adjective** (**squashier**, **squashiest**) easily crushed or squeezed into a different shape; having a soft consistency: *a big, squashy leather chair.*
– DERIVATIVES **squashily** adverb, **squashiness** noun.

squat ▶ **verb** (**squats**, **squatting**, **squatted**) **1** [no obj.] crouch or sit with one's knees bent and one's heels close to or touching one's buttocks or the back of one's thighs: *I* ***squatted down*** *in front of him.* ■ [with obj.] Weightlifting crouch down in such a way and rise again while holding (a specified weight) across one's shoulders: *he can squat 850 pounds.*
2 [no obj.] unlawfully occupy an uninhabited building or settle on a piece of land: *eight families are squatting in the house.* ■ [with obj.] unlawfully occupy (an uninhabited building).
▶ **adjective** (**squatter**, **squattest**) short and thickset; disproportionately broad or wide: *he was muscular and squat* | *a squat grey house.*
▶ **noun 1** [in sing.] a squatting position. ■ Weightlifting an exercise in which a person squats down and rises again while holding a barbell across one's shoulders. ■ (in gymnastics) an exercise involving a squatting movement or action.
2 a building occupied by people living in it without the legal right to do so. ■ an unlawful occupation of an uninhabited building.
3 N. Amer. informal short for DIDDLY-SQUAT.
– DERIVATIVES **squatly** adverb, **squatness** noun.
– ORIGIN Middle English (in the sense 'thrust down with force'): from Old French *esquatir* 'flatten', based on Latin *coactus*, past participle of *cogere* 'compel' (see COGENT). The current sense of the adjective dates from the mid 17th cent.

squatt ▶ **noun** the larva of the common housefly, used by anglers as bait.
– ORIGIN 1930s: perhaps from the adjective SQUAT.

squatter ▶ **noun 1** a person who unlawfully occupies an uninhabited building or unused land. ■ N. Amer. & Austral./NZ historical a settler with no legal title to the land occupied, typically one on land not yet allocated by a government.
2 Austral./NZ a large-scale sheep or cattle farmer. ■ historical a person occupying a tract of pastoral land as a tenant of the Crown.

squatter camp ▶ **noun** S. African another term for SHACKLAND.

squat thrust ▶ **noun** an exercise in which the legs are thrust backwards to their full extent from a squatting position with the hands on the floor.

S

squaw /skwɔː/ ▸ **noun** offensive an American Indian woman or wife. ■ N. Amer. offensive a woman or wife.
– ORIGIN mid 17th cent.: from Narragansett *squaws* 'woman', with related forms in many Algonquin dialects.

USAGE Until relatively recently, the word **squaw** was used neutrally in anthropological and other contexts to mean 'an American Indian woman or wife'. With changes in the political climate in the second half of the 20th century, however, the derogatory attitudes of the past towards American Indian women have meant that, in modern North American English, the word cannot be used in any sense without being offensive. In British English the word has not acquired offensive connotations to the same extent, but it is nevertheless uncommon and now regarded as old-fashioned.

squawfish ▸ **noun** (pl. **same** or **squawfishes**) a large predatory freshwater fish of the carp family, with a slender body and large mouth, found in western North America. ● Genus *Ptychocheilus*, family Cyprinidae: several species, in particular the **northern squawfish** (*P. oregonensis*).
– ORIGIN late 19th cent.: the word derives from the former importance to American Indians of such fish, as food.

squawk ▸ **verb** [no obj.] (of a bird) make a loud, harsh noise: *the geese flew upriver, squawking.* ■ [with direct speech] (of a person) say something in a loud, discordant tone: *'What are you doing?' she squawked.* ■ complain or protest about something.
▸ **noun** a loud, harsh, or discordant noise made by a bird or a person. ■ a complaint or protest: *her plan provoked a loud squawk from her friends.*
– DERIVATIVES **squawker** noun.
– ORIGIN early 19th cent.: imitative.

squawk box ▸ **noun** informal, chiefly N. Amer. a loudspeaker, in particular one that is part of an intercom system.

squaw man ▸ **noun** N. Amer. offensive a white or black man married to an American Indian woman.

squawroot ▸ **noun** either of two North American plants: ● a yellow-brown parasitic plant related to the broomrape (*Conopholis americana*, family Orobanchaceae). ● the blue cohosh. See **COHOSH**.

squeak ▸ **noun** a short, high-pitched sound or cry: *the door opened with a slight squeak.* ■ [with negative] a single remark or communication: *I didn't hear a squeak from him for months.*
▸ **verb** [no obj.] **1** make a high-pitched sound or cry: *he oiled the hinges to stop them squeaking.* ■ [with direct speech] say something in a nervous or excited high-pitched tone: *'You're scaring me,' she squeaked.* ■ informal inform on someone.
2 [with adverbial] informal succeed in achieving something by a very narrow margin: *the bill squeaked through with just six votes to spare.*
– ORIGIN late Middle English (as a verb): imitative; compare with Swedish *skväka* 'croak', also with **SQUEAL** and **SHRIEK**. The noun dates from the early 17th cent.

squeaker ▸ **noun 1** a person or thing that squeaks: *children blowing party squeakers.* ■ chiefly Brit. a young pigeon.
2 informal, chiefly N. Amer. a competition or election won or likely to be won by a narrow margin.

squeaky ▸ **adjective** (**squeakier**, **squeakiest**) having or making a high-pitched sound or cry: *a high, squeaky voice.*
– DERIVATIVES **squeakily** adverb, **squeakiness** noun.

squeaky clean ▸ **adjective** informal completely clean: *squeaky clean babies.* ■ beyond reproach; without vice: *politicians who are less than squeaky clean.*

squeal ▸ **noun** a long, high-pitched cry or noise: *they drew up with a squeal of brakes.*
▸ **verb** [no obj.] **1** make a squeal: *the girls squealed with delight.* ■ [with direct speech] say something in a high-pitched, excited tone: *'Don't you dare!' she squealed.* ■ informal complain or protest about something: *the bookies only squealed because we beat them.*
2 informal inform on someone to the police or a person in authority: *she feared they would victimize her for squealing on their pals.*
– DERIVATIVES **squealer** noun.
– ORIGIN Middle English (as a verb): imitative. The noun dates from the mid 18th cent.

squeamish ▸ **adjective** easily made to feel sick or disgusted: *I've always been squeamish about bugs.* ■ having fastidious moral views; scrupulous: *she was not squeamish about using her social influence in support of her son.*
– DERIVATIVES **squeamishly** adverb, **squeamishness** noun.
– ORIGIN late Middle English: alteration of dialect *squeamous*, from Anglo-Norman French *escoymos*, of unknown origin.

squeegee /ˈskwiːdʒiː/ ▸ **noun** a scraping implement with a rubber-edged blade set on a handle, typically used for cleaning windows. ■ a similar small instrument or roller used especially in photography for squeezing water out of prints. ■ [as modifier] informal denoting a person who cleans the windscreen of a car stopped in traffic and then demands payment from the driver: *squeegee merchants at every road junction.*
▸ **verb** (**squeegees**, **squeegeeing**, **squeegeed**) [with obj.] clean or scrape with a squeegee: *squeegee the shower doors while the surfaces are still wet.*
– ORIGIN mid 19th cent.: from archaic *squeege* 'to press', strengthened form of **SQUEEZE**.

squeeze ▸ **verb** [with obj.] **1** firmly press (something soft or yielding), typically with one's fingers: *Kate squeezed his hand affectionately* | [no obj.] *he squeezed with all his strength.* ■ [with obj. and adverbial] extract (liquid or a soft substance) from something by compressing or twisting it firmly: ***squeeze out** as much juice as you can* | (as adj., with submodifier **squeezed**) *freshly squeezed orange juice.*
2 [no obj., with adverbial of direction] manage to get into or through a narrow or restricted space: *Sarah squeezed in beside her* | *he found a hole in the hedge and squeezed his way through.* ■ [with obj. and adverbial of direction] manage to force into or through a narrow or restricted space: *she squeezed herself into her tightest pair of jeans.* ■ [with obj.] (**squeeze someone/thing in**) manage to find time for someone or something: *she may be able to squeeze you in, if you play your cards right.*
3 [with obj. and adverbial] obtain (something) from someone with difficulty: *councils will want to **squeeze** as much money **out of** taxpayers as they can.* ■ [with obj.] informal pressurize (someone) in order to obtain something from them: *she used the opportunity to squeeze him for information.* ■ [with obj.] (**squeeze someone/thing out**) force someone or something out of an activity or post: *workers have been squeezed out of their jobs.* ■ [with obj.] Bridge force (an opponent) to discard a guarding or potentially winning card. ■ [with obj.] (especially in a financial or commercial context) have a damaging or restricting effect on: *the economy is being squeezed by foreign debt repayments.*
4 (**squeeze something off**) informal shoot a round or shot from a gun: *squeeze off a few well-aimed shots.* ■ take a photograph: *he squeezed off a half-dozen Polaroids.*
▸ **noun 1** an act of squeezing something: *a gentle squeeze of the trigger.* ■ a hug. ■ a state of being forced into a small or restricted space: *it was **a tight squeeze** in the tiny hall.* ■ dated a crowded social gathering. ■ a small amount of liquid extracted from something by squeezing: *a squeeze of lemon juice.*
2 a strong financial demand or pressure, typically a restriction on borrowing, spending, or investment in a financial crisis: *industry faced higher costs and a **squeeze on** profits.* ■ [mass noun] informal money illegally extorted or exacted from someone: *he was out to extract some squeeze from her.* ■ Bridge a tactic that forces an opponent to discard an important card.
3 a moulding or cast of an object, or an impression or copy of a design, obtained by pressing a pliable substance round or over it.
4 N. Amer. informal a person's girlfriend or boyfriend: *the poor guy just lost his **main squeeze**.*
5 (also **squeeze play**) Baseball an act of hitting a ball short to the infield to enable a runner on third base to start for home as soon as the ball is pitched.
– PHRASES **put the squeeze on** informal coerce or pressurize (someone). **squeeze one's eyes shut** (or **closed**) close one's eyes tightly.
– DERIVATIVES **squeezable** adjective, **squeezer** noun.
– ORIGIN mid 16th cent.: from earlier *squise*, from obsolete *queise*, of unknown origin.

squeeze bottle ▸ **noun** a container made of flexible plastic which is squeezed to extract the contents.

squeeze box ▸ **noun** informal an accordion or concertina.

squeezy ▸ **adjective 1** (especially of a container) flexible and able to be squeezed to force out the contents.
2 archaic having a restricted or confined character: *a squeezy little room.*

squelch ▸ **verb** [no obj.] make a soft sucking sound such as that made by treading heavily through mud: *bedraggled guests squelched across the lawns.* ■ informal forcefully silence or suppress: *property developers tried to squelch public protest.*
▸ **noun 1** a soft sucking sound made when pressure is applied to liquid or mud: *the squelch of their feet.*
2 (also **squelch circuit**) Electronics a circuit that suppresses the output of a radio receiver if the signal strength falls below a certain level.
– DERIVATIVES **squelcher** noun, **squelchy** adjective (**squelchier**, **squelchiest**).
– ORIGIN early 17th cent. (originally denoting a heavy crushing fall on to something soft): imitative.

squib ▸ **noun 1** a small firework that burns with a hissing sound before exploding.
2 a short piece of satirical writing. ■ N. Amer. a short news item or filler in a newspaper.
3 informal a small, slight, or weak person, especially a child.
4 American Football a short kick on a kick-off.
▸ **verb** (**squibs**, **squibbing**, **squibbed**) **1** [with obj.] American Football kick (the ball) a comparatively short distance on a kick-off; execute (a kick) in this way.
2 [no obj.] archaic utter, write, or publish a satirical or sarcastic attack. ■ [with obj.] lampoon: *the mendicant parson, whom I am so fond of squibbing.*
– ORIGIN early 16th cent. (in sense 1 of the noun): of unknown origin; perhaps imitative of a small explosion. The verb was first recorded in sense 2 of the verb (late 16th cent.).

SQUID ▸ **noun** Physics a device used in particular in sensitive magnetometers, which consists of a superconducting ring containing one or more Josephson junctions. A change by one flux quantum in the ring's magnetic flux linkage produces a sharp change in its impedance.
– ORIGIN 1960s: acronym from *superconducting quantum interference device*.

squid ▸ **noun** (pl. **same** or **squids**) an elongated, fast-swimming cephalopod mollusc with eight arms and two long tentacles, typically able to change colour. ● Order Teuthoidea and Vampyromorpha, class Cephalopoda, in particular the common genus *Loligo*. See also **GIANT SQUID**. ■ [mass noun] the squid used as food. ■ an artificial bait for fish imitating a squid in form.
▸ **verb** (**squids**, **squidding**, **squidded**) [no obj.] fish using squid as bait.
– ORIGIN late 16th cent.: of unknown origin.

squidge ▸ **verb** [with obj.] informal squash or crush. ■ [no obj.] make a squelching noise.
– ORIGIN late 19th cent.: perhaps imitative.

squidgy ▸ **adjective** (**squidgier**, **squidgiest**) informal, chiefly Brit. soft, spongy, and moist: *a squidgy cream cake.*

squiffed ▸ **adjective** N. Amer. informal slightly drunk.
– ORIGIN late 19th cent.: variant of **SQUIFFY**.

squiffy ▸ **adjective** (**squiffier**, **squiffiest**) Brit. informal **1** slightly drunk: *I feel quite squiffy.*
2 askew; awry: *the graphics make your eyes go squiffy.*
– ORIGIN mid 19th cent.: of unknown origin.

squiggle ▸ **noun** a short line that curls and loops in an irregular way: *some prescriptions are a series of meaningless squiggles.*
▸ **verb** [no obj.] chiefly N. Amer. wriggle; squirm: *a thin worm that squiggled in his palm.*
– DERIVATIVES **squiggly** adjective (**squigglier**, **squiggliest**).
– ORIGIN early 19th cent.: perhaps a blend of **SQUIRM** and **WIGGLE** or **WRIGGLE**.

S

squill ▸ **noun 1** (also **sea squill**) a coastal Mediterranean plant of the lily family, with broad leaves, white flowers, and a very large bulb. ● *Drimia* (or *Urginea*) *maritima*, family Liliaceae.
■ (also **squills**) [mass noun] an extract of the bulb of the squill, which is poisonous and has medicinal and other uses.
2 [usu. with modifier] a small plant of the lily family, which resembles a hyacinth and has slender strap-like leaves and small clusters of violet-blue or blue-striped flowers. ● Several species in the family Liliaceae: genus *Scilla*, including the **spring squill** (*S. verna*), and the **striped squill** (*Puschkinia scilloides*).
– ORIGIN late Middle English: via Latin from Greek *skilla*.

squillion /ˈskwɪljən/ ▸ **cardinal number** (pl. **squillions** or (with numeral) **same**) informal an indefinite very large number: ***squillions of** pounds.*
– ORIGIN 1940s: fanciful formation on the pattern of *billion* and *trillion*.

squinancywort /ˈskwɪnənsɪˌwəːt/ ▸ **noun** a small Eurasian plant of delicate appearance, with fine narrow leaves and scented white or lilac flowers. It was formerly used in the treatment of quinsy. ● *Asperula cynanchica*, family Rubiaceae.

– ORIGIN early 18th cent.: from medieval Latin *squinantia* (apparently formed by confusion of Greek *sunankhē* with *kunankhē* 'cynanche', both denoting throat diseases) + WORT.

squinch¹ ▸ noun a straight or arched structure across an interior angle of a square tower to carry a superstructure such as a dome.

– ORIGIN late 15th cent.: alteration of obsolete *scunch*, abbreviation of SCUNCHEON.

squinch² ▸ verb [with obj.] chiefly N. Amer. **1** tense up the muscles of (one's eyes or face): *Gina **squinched** her face **up**.* ■ [no obj.] (of a person's eyes) narrow so as to be almost closed, typically in reaction to strong light: *he flicked on the inside light, which made my eyes **squinch up**.*
2 [no obj.] crouch down in order to make oneself seem smaller or to occupy less space: *I squinched down under the sheet.*

– ORIGIN early 19th cent.: perhaps a blend of the verbs SQUEEZE and PINCH.

squint ▸ verb **1** [no obj.] look at someone or something with one or both eyes partly closed in an attempt to see more clearly or as a reaction to strong light: *the bright sun made them squint.* ■ [with obj.] partly close (one's eyes) for such reasons.
2 [no obj.] have eyes that look in different directions: *Melanie did not squint.* ■ (of a person's eye) have a deviation in the direction of its gaze: *her left eye squinted slightly.*
▸ noun **1** [in sing.] a permanent deviation in the direction of the gaze of one eye: *I had a bad squint.*
2 [in sing.] informal a quick or casual look: *let me have a squint.*
3 an oblique opening through a wall in a church permitting a view of the altar from an aisle or side chapel.
▸ adjective chiefly Scottish not straight or level.

– DERIVATIVES **squinty** adjective (**squintier**, **squintiest**) [often in combination] *squinty-eyed.*

– ORIGIN mid 16th cent. (in the sense 'squinting', as in SQUINT-EYED): shortening of ASQUINT.

squint-eyed ▸ adjective **1** derogatory having a squint.
2 archaic spiteful.

squire ▸ noun **1** a man of high social standing who owns and lives on an estate in a rural area, especially the chief landowner in such an area: *the squire of Radbourne Hall* | [as title] *Squire Trelawny.* ■ Brit. informal used by a man as a friendly or humorous form of address to another man. ■ US archaic a title given to a magistrate, lawyer, or judge in some rural districts.
2 historical a young nobleman acting as an attendant to a knight before becoming a knight himself.
3 Austral. a subadult snapper fish (*Chrysophrys auratus*).
▸ verb [with obj.] (of a man) accompany or escort (a woman): *she was squired around Rome by a reporter.* ■ dated (of a man) have a romantic relationship with (a woman).

– DERIVATIVES **squireship** noun.

– ORIGIN Middle English (in sense 2 of the noun): shortening of Old French *esquier* 'esquire'.

squirearch /ˈskwʌɪəˌrɑːk/ ▸ noun a member of the squirearchy.

– DERIVATIVES **squirearchical** adjective.

– ORIGIN mid 19th cent.: back-formation from SQUIREARCHY, on the pattern of words such as *monarch.*

squirearchy /ˈskwʌɪəˌrɑːki/ ▸ noun (pl. **squirearchies**) landowners collectively, especially when considered as a class having political or social influence.

– ORIGIN late 18th cent.: from SQUIRE, on the pattern of words such as *hierarchy.*

squireen /ˌskwʌɪəˈriːn/ ▸ noun Brit. a minor landowner, especially one in Ireland.

– ORIGIN early 19th cent.: from SQUIRE + *-een* (representing the Irish diminutive suffix *-ín*).

squirl ▸ noun informal an ornamental flourish or curve, especially in handwriting.

– ORIGIN mid 19th cent.: perhaps a blend of SQUIGGLE and TWIRL or WHIRL.

squirm ▸ verb [no obj.] wriggle or twist the body from side to side, especially as a result of nervousness or discomfort: *he looked uncomfortable and squirmed in his chair.* ■ show or feel embarrassment or shame: *he squirmed as he recalled the phrases he had used.*
▸ noun [in sing.] a wriggling movement.

– DERIVATIVES **squirmer** noun, **squirmy** adjective.

– ORIGIN late 17th cent.: symbolic of writhing movement; probably associated with WORM.

squirrel ▸ noun an agile tree-dwelling rodent with a bushy tail, typically feeding on nuts and seeds.
● Family Sciuridae: several genera, in particular *Sciurus*, and numerous species.
■ a related rodent of the squirrel family. See GROUND SQUIRREL, FLYING SQUIRREL. ■ [mass noun] the fur of the squirrel.
▸ verb (**squirrels**, **squirrelling**, **squirrelled**; US **squirrels**, **squirreling**, **squirreled**) **1** [with obj.] (**squirrel something away**) hide money or something of value in a safe place: *the money was squirrelled away in foreign bank accounts.*
2 [no obj., with adverbial of direction] move in an inquisitive and restless manner: *they were squirrelling around in the woods in search of something.*

– ORIGIN Middle English: shortening of Old French *esquireul*, from a diminutive of Latin *sciurus*, from Greek *skiouros*, from *skia* 'shade' + *oura* 'tail'. Current verb senses date from the early 20th cent.

squirrel cage ▸ noun a rotating cylindrical cage in which a small captive animal can exercise as on a treadmill. ■ a monotonous or repetitive activity or way of life: *running madly about in a squirrel cage of activity.* ■ a form of rotor used in small electric motors, resembling a cylindrical cage.

squirrelfish ▸ noun (pl. **same** or **squirrelfishes**) a large-eyed, chiefly nocturnal marine fish that is typically brightly coloured and lives around rocks or coral reefs in warm seas. ● Family Holocentridae: several genera and species.

squirrelly ▸ adjective **1** relating to or resembling a squirrel.
2 N. Amer. informal restless, nervous, or unpredictable: *I got all squirrelly after you left.* ■ eccentric or mad.

squirrel monkey ▸ noun a small South American monkey with a non-prehensile tail, typically moving through trees by leaping. ● Genus *Saimiri*, family Cebidae: five species, in particular *S. sciureus.*

squirrel-tail grass ▸ noun [mass noun] a kind of barley with bushy spikelets, sometimes cultivated as an ornamental grass. ● *Hordeum jubatum*, family Gramineae.

squirt ▸ verb [with obj. and adverbial of direction] **1** cause (a liquid) to be ejected from a small opening in a thin, fast stream or jet: *she squirted soda into a glass.* ■ cause (a container of liquid) to eject its contents in a thin, fast stream: *some youngsters squirted a water pistol in her face.* ■ [with obj.] wet with a jet or stream of liquid: *she squirted me with scent.* ■ [no obj., with adverbial of direction] (of a liquid) be ejected from something in a thin, fast stream. ■ [no obj., with adverbial of direction] (of an object) move suddenly and unpredictably: *he got his glove on the ball but it squirted away.*
2 transmit (information) in highly compressed or speeded-up form.
▸ noun **1** a thin stream or small quantity of liquid squirted from something: ***a squirt of** perfume.* ■ a small device from which a liquid may be squirted.
2 informal a puny or insignificant person: *what did he see in this patronizing little squirt?*
3 a compressed radio signal transmitted at high speed.

– DERIVATIVES **squirter** noun.

– ORIGIN Middle English (as a verb): imitative.

squirt boat ▸ noun a small, highly manoeuvrable kayak.

squirt gun ▸ noun N. Amer. a water pistol.

squirting cucumber ▸ noun a Mediterranean plant of the gourd family, bearing a small cucumber-like fruit which falls readily when ripe and forcibly expels an irritant pulp containing its seeds. ● *Ecballium elaterium*, family Cucurbitaceae.

squish ▸ verb make a soft squelching sound when walked on or in: *the mud squished under my shoes.* ■ informal yield or cause to yield easily to pressure; squash: [no obj.] *strawberries so ripe that they squished if picked too firmly* | [with obj.] *Naomi was furiously squishing her ice cream in her bowl.*
▸ noun [in sing.] a soft squelching sound.

– DERIVATIVES **squishy** adjective (**squishier**, **squishiest**).

– ORIGIN mid 17th cent.: imitative.

squit ▸ noun **1** Brit. informal a small or insignificant person.
2 (**the squits**) diarrhoea.

– ORIGIN early 19th cent.: perhaps related to dialect *squit* 'to squirt'.

squitters ▸ plural noun informal diarrhoea.

– ORIGIN mid 17th cent.: perhaps from dialect *squit* 'to squirt'.

squiz Austral./NZ informal ▸ noun a look or glance.
▸ verb [with obj.] look or glance at.

– ORIGIN early 20th cent.: probably a blend of QUIZ² and SQUINT.

SR ▸ abbreviation historical (in the UK) Southern Railway.

Sr ▸ abbreviation ■ senior (in names): *E. T. Krebs Sr.* ■ Señor. ■ Signor. ■ Sister (in a religious order): [as a title] *Sr Agatha.*
▸ symbol the chemical element strontium.

sr ▸ abbreviation steradian(s).

SRA ▸ abbreviation (in the UK) Strategic Rail Authority.

SRAM ▸ noun Electronics a type of memory chip which is faster and requires less power than dynamic memory.

– ORIGIN abbreviation of *static random-access memory.*

Sranan /ˈsrɑːnən/ ▸ noun another term for TAKI-TAKI.

– ORIGIN from Taki-Taki *Sranan tongo*, literally 'Suriname tongue'.

Srebrenica /ˌsrɛbrɛˈniːtsə/ a town in eastern Bosnia and Herzegovina; pop. 4,500 (est. 2009). The town was the scene of a massacre of thousands of Muslim men by Serb forces in 1995. It was finally included in Serb-held territory in the 1995 partition of Bosnia and Herzegovina.

Sri ▸ noun Indian variant spelling of SHRI.

Sri Lanka /sriː ˈlaŋkə, ʃriː/ an island country off the SE coast of India; pop. 21,324,800 (est. 2009); languages, Sinhalese (official), Tamil; capital, Colombo. Former name (until 1972) CEYLON.

> The island was ruled by a strong native dynasty from the 12th century but was successively dominated by the Portuguese, Dutch, and British from the 16th century and finally annexed by the British in 1815. A Commonwealth state from 1948, the country became an independent republic in 1972. Since 1981 there has been fighting between government forces and Tamil separatist guerrillas.

– DERIVATIVES **Sri Lankan** adjective & noun.

Srinagar /sriːˈnʌɡə/ a city in NW India, the summer capital of the state of Jammu and Kashmir, situated on the Jhelum River in the foothills of the Himalayas; pop. 1,060,900 (est. 2009).

SRN ▸ abbreviation State Registered Nurse.

SRO ▸ abbreviation ■ (in the UK) self-regulatory organization, a body that regulates the activities of investment businesses. ■ N. Amer. single room occupancy. ■ standing room only.

SS¹ ▸ abbreviation ■ Saints: *the Church of SS Peter and Paul.* ■ Baseball shortstop. ■ social security. ■ steamship: *the SS Canberra.*

SS² the Nazi special police force. Founded in 1925 by Hitler as a personal bodyguard, the SS provided security forces (including the Gestapo) and administered the concentration camps.

– ORIGIN abbreviation of German *Schutzstaffel* 'defence squadron'.

SSAFA ▸ abbreviation (in the UK) Soldiers', Sailors', and Airmen's Families Association.

SSB ▸ abbreviation single sideband transmission, a type of amplitude modulation in which the carrier wave and one sideband are suppressed in order to occupy less bandwidth.

SSC ▸ abbreviation ■ (in Scotland) Solicitor in the Supreme Court. ■ Physics superconducting super collider.

SSE ▸ abbreviation south-south-east.

SSL ▸ abbreviation Secure Sockets Layer, a computing protocol that ensures the security of data sent via the Internet by using encryption.

SSP ▸ abbreviation (in the UK) statutory sick pay.

ssp. ▸ abbreviation subspecies (usually singular).

sspp. ▸ abbreviation subspecies (plural).

SSR ▸ abbreviation historical Soviet Socialist Republic.

SSRC ▸ abbreviation (in the UK) Social Science Research Council.

SSRI ▸ noun Medicine selective serotonin reuptake inhibitor, any of a group of antidepressant drugs (including Prozac) which inhibit the uptake of serotonin in the brain.

SSSI ▸ abbreviation (in the UK) Site of Special Scientific Interest.

SST ▸ abbreviation supersonic transport.

SSW ▸ abbreviation south-south-west.

St ▸ abbreviation ■ Saint: *St George*. ■ (usu. **St.**) Street: *10 Downing St*. ■ (also **ST**) Physics stokes.

st ▸ abbreviation ■ stone (in weight). ■ Cricket (on scorecards) stumped by.

-st ▸ suffix variant spelling of **-EST**[2].

Sta. ▸ abbreviation railway station.

stab ▸ verb (**stabs, stabbing, stabbed**) [with obj.] thrust a knife or other pointed weapon into (someone) so as to wound or kill: *he stabbed her in the stomach*. ■ [no obj.] make a thrusting gesture or movement at something with a pointed object: *she stabbed at the earth with the fork* | [with obj.] *she stabbed the air with her forefinger*. ■ [no obj.] (**stab into/through**) (of a sharp or pointed object) violently pierce: *a sharp end of wicker stabbed into his sole*. ■ [no obj.] (of a pain or painful thing) cause a sudden sharp sensation: *a stitch stabbed at her side* | (as adj. **stabbing**) *I felt a stabbing pain in my chest*.
▸ noun **1** a thrust with a knife or other pointed weapon: [as modifier] *multiple stab wounds*. ■ a wound made by stabbing: *she had a deep stab in the back*. ■ a thrusting movement with a finger or other pointed object: *impatient stabs of his finger*. ■ a sudden sharp feeling or pain: *she felt a stab of jealousy*.
2 (**stab at**) informal an attempt to do (something): *Meredith made a feeble stab at joining in*.
– PHRASES **stab someone in the back** betray someone. **a stab in the dark** see **DARK**.
– DERIVATIVES **stabber** noun.
– ORIGIN late Middle English: of unknown origin.

Stabat Mater /ˌstɑːbat ˈmɑːtə, ˈmeɪtə/ ▸ noun a medieval Latin hymn on the suffering of the Virgin Mary at the Crucifixion.
– ORIGIN from the opening words *Stabat mater dolorosa* 'Stood the mother, full of grief'.

stabbing ▸ noun an act or instance of wounding or killing someone with a knife: *the fatal stabbings of four women*.

stabilator /ˈsteɪbɪleɪtə/ ▸ noun a combined stabilizer and elevator at the tail of an aircraft.

stabile /ˈsteɪbʌɪl/ ▸ noun Art a free-standing abstract sculpture or structure, typically of wire or sheet metal, in the style of a mobile but rigid and stationary.
– ORIGIN 1940s: from Latin *stabilis* 'stable', influenced by **MOBILE**.

stability ▸ noun [mass noun] the state of being stable: *there are fears for the political stability of the area*.
– ORIGIN Middle English: from Old French *stablete*, from Latin *stabilitas*, from *stabilis* 'stable'.

stabilize (also **stabilise**) ▸ verb make or become unlikely to give way or overturn: [with obj.] *the craft was stabilized by throwing out the remaining ballast*. ■ make or become unlikely to change, fail, or decline: [with obj.] *an emergency program designed to stabilize the economy* | [no obj.] *his condition appears to have stabilized*.
– DERIVATIVES **stabilization** noun.

stabilizer (also **stabiliser**) ▸ noun **1** a thing used to keep something steady or stable, in particular: ■ the horizontal tailplane of an aircraft. ■ a gyroscopic device used to reduce the rolling of a ship. ■ (**stabilizers**) Brit. a pair of small supporting wheels fitted on either side of the rear wheel of a child's bicycle.
2 a substance which prevents the breakdown of emulsions, especially in foods and paints.

stable[1] ▸ adjective (**stabler, stablest**) (of an object or structure) not likely to give way or overturn; firmly fixed: *specially designed dinghies that are very stable*. ■ (of a patient or their medical condition) not deteriorating in health after an injury or operation: *he is now in a stable condition in hospital*. ■ sane and sensible; not easily upset or disturbed: *the officer concerned is mentally and emotionally stable*. ■ not likely to change or fail; firmly established: *a stable relationship* | *prices have remained relatively stable*. ■ not liable to undergo chemical decomposition, radioactive decay, or other physical change.
– DERIVATIVES **stably** adverb.
– ORIGIN Middle English: from Anglo-Norman French, from Latin *stabilis*, from the base of *stare* 'to stand'.

stable[2] ▸ noun a building set apart and adapted for keeping horses. ■ an establishment where racehorses are kept and trained. ■ the racehorses of a particular training establishment. ■ an organization or establishment training or producing a particular type of person or product: *the player comes from the same stable as Agassi*.
▸ verb [with obj.] put or keep (a horse) in a stable. ■ put or base (a train) in a depot.
– PHRASES **shut** (or **bolt**) **the stable door after the horse has bolted** Brit. try to avoid or prevent something undesirable when it is already too late to do so.
– DERIVATIVES **stableful** noun (pl. **stablefuls**).
– ORIGIN Middle English: shortening of Old French *estable* 'stable, pigsty', from Latin *stabulum*, from the base of *stare* 'to stand'.

stable boy ▸ noun a boy or man employed in a stable.

stable companion ▸ noun another term for **STABLEMATE**.

stable equilibrium ▸ noun a state in which a body tends to return to its original position after being disturbed.

stable fly ▸ noun a bloodsucking fly related to the housefly, that bites large mammals including humans. ● *Stomoxis calcitrans*, family Muscidae.

Stableford /ˈsteɪb(ə)lfəd/ ▸ noun [mass noun] [usu. as modifier] a form of stroke-play golf in which points are awarded according to the number of strokes taken to complete each hole: *a Stableford competition*.
– ORIGIN named after Frank B. *Stableford* (1870–1959), the American doctor who devised it.

stable girl ▸ noun a girl or woman employed in a stable.

stable lad ▸ noun Brit. a person employed in a stable.

stableman ▸ noun (pl. **stablemen**) chiefly US a person employed in a stable.

stablemate ▸ noun a horse, especially a racehorse, from the same establishment as another. ■ a person or product from the same organization or background as another: *the Daily Mirror and its Scottish stablemate the Daily Record*.

stable vice ▸ noun see **VICE**[1].

stabling ▸ noun [mass noun] accommodation for horses.

stablish ▸ verb archaic form of **ESTABLISH**.

stab stitch ▸ noun [mass noun] a needlework stitch in which the stitches on the visible surface of the cloth are smaller than those underneath.

staccato /stəˈkɑːtəʊ/ chiefly Music ▸ adverb & adjective with each sound or note sharply detached or separated from the others: [as adj.] *a staccato rhythm*. Compare with **LEGATO, MARCATO**.
▸ noun (pl. **staccatos**) a piece or passage marked to be performed staccato. ■ a series of short, sharp sounds or words: *her heels made a rapid staccato on the polished boards*.
– ORIGIN Italian, literally 'detached'.

staccato mark ▸ noun a dot or stroke above or below a note indicating that it is to be played staccato.

stack ▸ noun **1** a pile of objects, typically one that is neatly arranged: *a stack of boxes*. ■ (**a stack of/stacks of**) informal a large quantity of something: *there's stacks of work for me now*. ■ a rectangular or cylindrical pile of hay or straw or of grain in sheaf. ■ a vertical arrangement of hi-fi or guitar amplification equipment. ■ a number of aircraft flying in circles at different altitudes around the same point while waiting for permission to land at an airport. ■ a pyramidal group of rifles. ■ (**the stacks**) units of shelving in part of a library normally closed to the public, used to store books compactly. ■ Computing a set of storage locations which store data in such a way that the most recently stored item is the first to be retrieved.
2 a chimney, especially one on a factory, or a vertical exhaust pipe on a vehicle. ■ (also **sea stack**) Brit. a column of rock standing in the sea, remaining after erosion of cliffs.
3 Brit. a measure for a pile of wood of 108 cu. ft (3.06 cubic metres).
▸ verb [with obj.] **1** arrange (a number of things) in a pile, typically a neat one: *the books had been stacked up in neat piles* | *she stood up, beginning to stack the plates*. ■ fill or cover (a place or surface) with stacks of things: *he spent most of the time stacking shelves*. ■ cause (an aircraft) to fly in circles while waiting for permission to land at an airport: *I hope we aren't stacked for hours over Kennedy*.
2 shuffle or arrange (a pack of cards) dishonestly so as to gain an unfair advantage. ■ (**be stacked against/in favour of**) used to refer to a situation which is such that an unfavourable or a favourable outcome is overwhelmingly likely: *the odds were stacked against Fiji in the World Cup*.
3 [no obj.] (in snowboarding) fall over.
– PHRASAL VERBS **stack up 1** (or **stack something up**) form or cause to form a large quantity; build up: *cars stack up behind every bus*. **2** N. Amer. informal measure up; compare: *our rural schools stack up well against their urban counterparts*. ■ [usu. with negative] make sense: *to blame the debacle on the antics of a rogue trader is not credible—it doesn't stack up*.
– DERIVATIVES **stackable** adjective, **stacker** noun.
– ORIGIN Middle English: from Old Norse *stakkr* 'haystack', of Germanic origin.

stacked ▸ adjective **1** (of a number of things) put or arranged in a stack or stacks: *the stacked chairs*. ■ (of a place or surface) filled or covered with goods: *the stacked shelves*. ■ having sections that are arranged vertically: *full-sized washer/dryers are replacing stacked units*. ■ (of a heel) made from thin layers of material glued one on top of the other.
2 (of a pack of cards) shuffled or arranged dishonestly so as to gain an unfair advantage.
3 informal (of a woman) having large breasts.
4 Computing (of a task) placed in a queue for subsequent processing. ■ (of a stream of data) stored in such a way that the most recently stored item is the first to be retrieved.

stackyard ▸ noun a farmyard or enclosure where stacks of hay, straw, or grain in sheaf are stored.

staddle ▸ noun a platform or framework supporting a stack or rick. ■ (also **staddle stone**) a stone, especially one resembling a mushroom in shape, supporting a framework or rick.
– ORIGIN Old English *stathol* 'base, support', of Germanic origin; related to the verb **STAND**.

stadium ▸ noun (pl. **stadiums** or **stadia** /ˈsteɪdɪə/)
1 an athletic or sports ground with tiers of seats for spectators. ■ (in ancient Rome or Greece) a track for a foot race or chariot race.
2 (pl. **stadia**) an ancient Roman or Greek measure of length, about 185 metres (originally the length of a stadium).
– ORIGIN late Middle English (in sense 2): via Latin from Greek *stadion*. Sense 1 dates from the mid 19th cent.

stadtholder /ˈstadˌhəʊldə, ˈstat-/ (also **stadholder**) ▸ noun (from the 15th century to the late 18th century) the chief magistrate of the United Provinces of the Netherlands.
– DERIVATIVES **stadtholdership** noun.
– ORIGIN mid 16th cent.: from Dutch *stadhouder* 'deputy', from *stad* 'place' + *houder* 'holder', translating medieval Latin *locum tenens*.

Staël, Mme de, see **DE STAËL**.

staff[1] ▸ noun **1** [treated as sing. or pl.] all the people employed by a particular organization: *a staff of 600* | *hospital staff were not to blame*. ■ the teachers in a school or college: [as modifier] *a staff meeting*.
2 [treated as sing. or pl.] a group of officers assisting an officer in command of an army formation or administration headquarters. ■ (usu. **Staff**) short for **STAFF SERGEANT**.
3 a long stick used as a support when walking or climbing or as a weapon. ■ a rod or sceptre held as a sign of office or authority. ■ short for **FLAGSTAFF**. ■ Surveying a rod for measuring distances or heights. ■ Brit. a spindle in a watch. ■ Brit. a token in the form of a rod given to a train driver as authority to proceed over a single-track line.
4 Music another term for **STAVE** (sense 2 of the noun).
▸ verb [with obj.] provide (an organization, business, etc.) with staff: *legal advice centres are staffed by volunteer lawyers* | (as adj. **staffed**) *all units are fully staffed*.
– PHRASES **the staff of life** a staple food, especially bread.
– ORIGIN Old English *stæf* (in sense 3 of the noun), of Germanic origin; related to Dutch *staf* and German *Stab*.

staff[2] ▸ noun [mass noun] a mixture of plaster of Paris, cement, or a similar material, used for temporary building work.
– ORIGIN late 19th cent.: of unknown origin.

Staffa /ˈstafə/ a small uninhabited island of the Inner Hebrides, west of Mull. It is the site of Fingal's Cave and is noted for its basalt columns .

staffage /stəˈfɑːʒ/ ▸ noun [mass noun] accessory items in a painting, especially figures or animals in a landscape picture.
– ORIGIN late 19th cent.: from German, from *staffieren* 'decorate', perhaps from Old French *estoffer*, from *estoffe* 'stuff'.

staff association ▸ noun an association of employees performing some of the functions of a trade union, such as representing its members in discussions with management.

staff college ▸ noun a college at which military officers are trained for staff duties.

S

staffer ▶ noun chiefly N. Amer. a member of the staff of an organization, especially of a newspaper.

staff notation ▶ noun [mass noun] Music notation by means of a stave, especially as distinct from the tonic sol-fa.

staff nurse ▶ noun Brit. an experienced nurse less senior than a sister or charge nurse.

staff officer ▶ noun a military officer serving on the staff of a military headquarters or government department.

Stafford /ˈstafəd/ an industrial town in central England, to the south of Stoke-on-Trent, the county town of Staffordshire; pop. 63,700 (est. 2009).

Staffordshire a county of central England; county town, Stafford.

Staffordshire bull terrier ▶ noun a dog of a small stocky breed of terrier, with a short, broad head and dropped ears.

staffroom ▶ noun chiefly Brit. a common room for teachers in a school or college.

Staffs. ▶ abbreviation Staffordshire.

staff sergeant ▶ noun a rank of non-commissioned officer in the army, above sergeant and below warrant officer. ■ a rank of non-commissioned officer in the US air force, above airman and below technical sergeant.

stag ▶ noun **1** a male deer, especially a male red deer after its fifth year. ■ a turkeycock over one year old.
2 [usu. as modifier] a social gathering attended by men only: *a stag event.* ■ chiefly N. Amer. a man who attends a social gathering unaccompanied by a female partner.
3 Stock Exchange, Brit. a person who applies for shares in a new issue with a view to selling at once for a profit.
▶ adverb N. Amer. without a female partner at a social gathering: *a lot of boys went stag.*
▶ verb (**stags, stagging, stagged**) [with obj.] **1** Stock Exchange, Brit. buy (shares in a new issue) and sell them at once for a profit.
2 N. Amer. informal roughly cut (a garment, especially a pair of trousers) to make it shorter: (as adj. **stagged**) *stagged jeans.*
– ORIGIN Middle English (as a noun): related to Old Norse *steggr* 'male bird', Icelandic *steggi* 'tomcat'.

stag beetle ▶ noun a large dark beetle, the male of which has large branched jaws that resemble a stag's antlers. ● Family Lucanidae: several species, including the European *Lucanus cervus.*

stage ▶ noun **1** a point, period, or step in a process or development: *there is no need at this stage to give explicit details | I was in the early stages of pregnancy.* ■ a section of a journey or race: *the final stage of the journey is made by coach.* ■ each of two or more sections of a rocket or spacecraft that have their own engines and are jettisoned in turn when their propellant is exhausted. ■ [with modifier] Electronics a specified part of a circuit, typically one consisting of a single amplifying transistor or valve with the associated equipment.
2 a raised floor or platform, typically in a theatre, on which actors, entertainers, or speakers perform: *there are only two characters* ***on stage.*** ■ (**the stage**) the acting or theatrical profession: *I've always wanted to* ***go on the stage.*** ■ [in sing.] a scene of action or forum of debate, especially in a particular political context: *Britain is playing a leading role on the international stage.*
3 a floor or level of a building or structure: *the upper stage was added in the 17th century.* ■ (on a microscope) a raised and usually movable plate on which a slide or object is placed for examination.
4 Geology (in chronostratigraphy) a range of strata corresponding to an age in time, forming a subdivision of a series. ■ (in palaeoclimatology) a period of time marked by a characteristic climate: *the Boreal stage.*
5 historical a stagecoach.
▶ verb [with obj.] **1** present a performance of (a play or other show): *the show is being staged at the Grand Opera House in Belfast.* ■ organize and participate in (a public event): *UDF supporters staged a demonstration in Sofia.* ■ cause (something dramatic or unexpected) to happen: *the President's attempt to stage a comeback | the dollar staged a partial recovery.*
2 Medicine diagnose or classify (a disease or patient) as having reached a particular stage in the expected progression of the disease.
– PHRASES **hold the stage** dominate a scene of action or forum of debate. **set the stage for** prepare the conditions for (the occurrence or beginning of something): *these churchmen helped to set the stage for popular reform.* **stage left** (or **right**) on the left (or right) side of a stage from the point of view of a performer facing the audience.
– DERIVATIVES **stageable** adjective.
– ORIGIN Middle English (denoting a floor of a building, platform, or stopping place): shortening of Old French *estage* 'dwelling', based on Latin *stare* 'to stand'. Current senses of the verb date from the early 17th cent.

stagecoach ▶ noun a large closed horse-drawn vehicle formerly used to carry passengers and often mail along a regular route between two places.

stagecraft ▶ noun [mass noun] skill or experience in writing or staging plays.

stage direction ▶ noun an instruction in the text of a play indicating the movement, position, or tone of an actor, or the sound effects and lighting.

stage-diving ▶ noun [mass noun] the practice (typically among audience members) of jumping from the stage at a rock concert or other event to be caught and carried aloft by the crowd below.
– DERIVATIVES **stage-dive** verb, **stage-diver** noun.

stage door ▶ noun an actors' and workmen's entrance from the street to the area of a theatre behind the stage.

stage fright ▶ noun [mass noun] nervousness before or during an appearance before an audience.

stagehand ▶ noun a person who moves scenery or props before or during the performance of a play.

stage-manage ▶ verb [with obj.] be responsible for the lighting and other technical arrangements for (a stage play). ■ arrange and control (something) carefully in order to create a certain effect: *he stage-managed his image with astounding success.*
– DERIVATIVES **stage management** noun, **stage manager** noun.

stage name ▶ noun a name assumed for professional purposes by an actor or other performer.

stage play (also **stage production**) ▶ noun a play performed on stage rather than broadcast or made into a film.

stage presence ▶ noun [mass noun] the ability to command the attention of a theatre audience by the impressiveness of one's manner or appearance.

stager ▶ noun archaic an actor.

stage-struck ▶ adjective having a passionate desire to become an actor.

stage whisper ▶ noun a loud whisper uttered by an actor on stage, intended to be heard by the audience but supposedly unheard by other characters in the play.

stagey ▶ adjective variant spelling of STAGY.

stagflation ▶ noun [mass noun] Economics persistent high inflation combined with high unemployment and stagnant demand in a country's economy.
– ORIGIN 1960s: blend of *stagnation* (see STAGNATE) and INFLATION.

stagger ▶ verb **1** [no obj.] walk or move unsteadily, as if about to fall: *he staggered to his feet, swaying a little.* ■ [with obj. and adverbial of direction] continue in existence or operation uncertainly or precariously: *the treasury staggered from one crisis to the next.* ■ archaic waver in purpose; hesitate. ■ archaic (of a blow) cause (someone) to walk or move unsteadily, as if about to fall: *the collision staggered her and she fell.*
2 [with obj.] astonish or deeply shock: *I was staggered to find it was six o'clock* | (as adj. **staggering**) *the staggering bills for maintenance and repair.*
3 [with obj.] arrange (events, payments, hours, etc.) so that they do not occur at the same time: *meetings are staggered throughout the day.* ■ arrange (objects or parts) in a zigzag formation or so that they are not in line: *stagger the screws at each joint.*
▶ noun [in sing.] **1** an unsteady walk or movement: *she walked with a stagger.*
2 an arrangement of things in a zigzag formation or so that they are not in line. ■ the arrangement of the runners in lanes on a running track at the start of a race, so that the runner in the inside lane is positioned behind those in the next lane and so on until the outside lane.
– DERIVATIVES **staggerer** noun, **staggeringly** adverb [as submodifier] *a staggeringly unjust society.*
– ORIGIN late Middle English (as a verb): alteration of dialect *stacker*, from Old Norse *stakra*, frequentative of *staka* 'push, stagger'. The noun dates from the late 16th cent.

staggers ▶ plural noun [usu. treated as sing.] any of several parasitic or acute deficiency diseases of farm animals characterized by staggering or loss of balance. ■ the inability to stand or walk steadily, especially as a result of giddiness.

staghorn (also **stag's horn**) ▶ noun [mass noun] the antler of a stag, used to make handles for knives and walking sticks.

staghorn coral ▶ noun a large stony coral with antler-like branches. ● Genus *Acropora*, order Scleractinia, in particular *A. cervicornis.*

staghorn fern (also **stag's-horn fern**) ▶ noun a fern which has fronds that resemble antlers, occurring in tropical rainforests where it typically grows as an epiphyte. ● Genus *Platycerium*, family Polypodiaceae.

staghound ▶ noun a large dog of a breed used for hunting deer by sight or scent.

staging ▶ noun [mass noun] **1** the method of presenting a play or other dramatic performance: *the quality of staging and design* | [count noun] *one of the better stagings of Hamlet.* ■ the organizing of a public event or protest: *the staging of the Norfolk Festival of Movement.*
2 a stage or set of stages or temporary platforms arranged as a support for performers or between different levels of scaffolding. ■ Brit. a shelving unit for plants in a greenhouse.
3 Medicine diagnosis or classification of the particular stage reached by a progressive disease.
4 the arrangement of stages in a rocket or spacecraft. ■ the separation and jettisoning of a stage from the remainder of a rocket when its propellant is spent.

staging area (also **staging point**) ▶ noun a stopping place or assembly point en route to a destination.

staging post ▶ noun a place at which people, vehicles, or aircraft regularly stop when making a particular journey.

stagnant /ˈstagnənt/ ▶ adjective (of a body of water or the atmosphere of a confined space) having no current or flow and often having an unpleasant smell as a consequence: *a stagnant ditch.* ■ showing no activity; dull and sluggish: *a stagnant economy.*
– DERIVATIVES **stagnancy** noun, **stagnantly** adverb.
– ORIGIN mid 17th cent.: from Latin *stagnant-* 'forming a pool of standing water', from the verb *stagnare*, from *stagnum* 'pool'.

stagnate /stagˈneɪt, ˈstagneɪt/ ▶ verb [no obj.] (of water or air) cease to flow or move; become stagnant. ■ cease developing; become inactive or dull: *teaching can easily stagnate into a set of routines* | (as adj. **stagnating**) *stagnating consumer confidence.*
– DERIVATIVES **stagnation** noun.
– ORIGIN mid 17th cent.: from Latin *stagnat-* 'settled as a still pool', from the verb *stagnare*, from *stagnum* 'pool'.

stag night (also **stag party**) ▶ noun Brit. a celebration held for a man shortly before his wedding, attended by his male friends only. ■ N. Amer. any party attended by men only.

stag's horn ▶ noun variant form of STAGHORN.

stag's-horn fungus (also **staghorn fungus**) ▶ noun a small fungus of dead wood, which forms black velvety antler-shaped fruiting bodies with white tips, common in both Eurasia and North America. ● *Xylaria hypoxylon*, family Xylariaceae, subdivision Ascomycotina.

stagy /ˈsteɪdʒi/ (also **stagey**) ▶ adjective (**stagier, stagiest**) excessively theatrical; exaggerated: *a stagy melodramatic voice.*
– DERIVATIVES **stagily** adverb, **staginess** noun.

staid ▶ adjective sedate, respectable, and unadventurous: *staid law firms.*
– DERIVATIVES **staidly** adverb, **staidness** noun.
– ORIGIN mid 16th cent.: archaic past participle of STAY[1].

stain ▶ verb [with obj.] **1** mark or discolour with something that is not easily removed: *her clothing was stained with blood* | (as adj. **stained**) *a stained beer mat* | [no obj.] *red powder paint can stain.* ■ [no obj.] be marked or be liable to be marked with a stain. ■ damage or bring disgrace to (the reputation or image of someone or something): *the awful events would unfairly stain the city's reputation.*
2 colour (a material or object) by applying a penetrative dye or chemical: *wood can always be stained to a darker shade.*
▶ noun **1** a coloured patch or dirty mark that is difficult to remove: *there were mud stains on my shoes.* ■ a thing that damages or brings disgrace to someone or something's reputation: *he regarded his time in gaol as a stain on his character.*

S

2 a penetrative dye or chemical used in colouring a material or object. ■ Biology a special dye used to colour organic tissue so as to make the structure visible for microscopic examination. ■ Heraldry any of the minor colours used in blazoning and liveries, especially tenné and sanguine.
– DERIVATIVES **stainable** adjective, **stainer** noun.
– ORIGIN late Middle English (as a verb): shortening of archaic *distain*, from Old French *desteindre* 'tinge with a colour different from the natural one'. The noun was first recorded (mid 16th cent.) in the sense 'defilement, disgrace'.

stained glass ▸ noun [mass noun] coloured glass used to form decorative or pictorial designs, typically by setting contrasting pieces in a lead framework like a mosaic and used for church windows.

stainless ▸ adjective unmarked by or resistant to stains or discoloration. ■ (of a person or their reputation) free from wrongdoing or disgrace: *her supposedly stainless past.*

stainless steel ▸ noun [mass noun] a form of steel containing chromium, resistant to tarnishing and rust.

stair ▸ noun (usu. **stairs**) a set of steps leading from one floor of a building to another, typically inside the building: *he came up the stairs.* ■ a single step in such a set: *the bottom stair.*
– ORIGIN Old English *stǣger*, of Germanic origin; related to Dutch *steiger* 'scaffolding', from a base meaning 'climb'.

staircase ▸ noun a set of stairs and its surrounding walls or structure. ■ Brit. a set of stairs and the rooms leading off it in a large building, especially a school or college.

staircase shell ▸ noun another term for WENTLETRAP.

stairclimber ▸ noun an exercise machine on which the user simulates the action of climbing a staircase.

stairhead ▸ noun chiefly Brit. a landing at the top of a set of stairs.

stairlift ▸ noun a lift in the form of a chair that can be raised or lowered at the edge of a domestic staircase, used for carrying a person with walking difficulties.

stair rod ▸ noun a rod for securing a carpet in the angle between two steps.
– PHRASES **rain** (or **come down in**) **stair rods** Brit. informal rain very heavily.

stairway ▸ noun a set of steps or stairs and its surrounding walls or structure.

stairwell ▸ noun a shaft in a building in which a staircase is built.

staithe /steɪð/ ▸ noun (in the north and east of England) a landing stage for loading or unloading cargo boats.
– ORIGIN Middle English: from Old Norse *stǫth* 'landing stage'.

stake¹ ▸ noun 1 a strong wooden or metal post with a point at one end, driven into the ground to support a plant, form part of a fence, mark a boundary, etc. ■ (**the stake**) historical a wooden post to which a person was tied before being burned alive as a punishment. ■ a long vertical rod used in basket-making.
2 a metalworker's small anvil, typically with a projection for fitting into a socket on a bench.
3 a territorial division of the Mormon Church under the jurisdiction of a president.
▸ verb [with obj.] 1 support (a plant) with a stake or stakes.
2 (**stake something out**) mark an area with stakes so as to claim ownership of it: *the boundary between the two manors was properly staked out.* ■ be assertive in defining and defending a position or policy: *Elena was staking out a role for herself as a formidable political force.*
– PHRASES **go to the stake for** used to emphasize that one would do anything to defend a particular belief, opinion, or person. **pull up stakes** N. Amer. move or go to live elsewhere. **stake a claim** assert one's right to something.
– PHRASAL VERBS **stake someone/thing out** informal keep a person or place under surveillance: *they'd staked out Culley's flat for a day.*
– ORIGIN Old English *staca*, of West Germanic origin; related to Dutch *staak*, also to STICK².

stake² ▸ noun a sum of money or something else of value gambled on the outcome of a risky game or venture: *playing dice for high stakes* | figurative *the opposition **raised the stakes** in the battle for power* | *the **stakes are high** with a six-figure bonanza in television rights in the balance.* ■ a share or interest in a business, situation, or system: *GM acquired a 50 per cent stake in Saab.* ■ (**stakes**) prize money, especially in horse racing. ■ [in names] (**Stakes**) a horse race in which all the owners of the racehorses running contribute to the prize money: *the horse is to run in the Craven Stakes.* ■ (with modifier **stakes**) a situation involving competition in a specified area: *we will keep you one step ahead in the fashion stakes.*
▸ verb [with obj.] 1 gamble (money or something else of value) on the outcome of a race or game: *one gambler staked everything he'd got and lost* | figurative *it was risky to **stake** his reputation **on** one big success.*
2 N. Amer. informal give financial or other support to: *he **staked** him **to** an education at the École des Beaux-Arts.*
– PHRASES **at stake** 1 at risk: *people's lives could be at stake.* 2 at issue or in question: *the logical response is to give up, but there's more at stake than logic.*
– ORIGIN late Middle English: perhaps a specialized usage of STAKE¹, from the notion of an object being placed as a wager on a post or stake.

stake boat ▸ noun an anchored boat used to mark the course for a boat race.

stake body ▸ noun US a body for a lorry having a flat open platform with removable posts along the sides.

stakebuilding ▸ noun [mass noun] Finance the building up of a holding of shares in a company.

stakeholder ▸ noun 1 (in gambling) an independent party with whom each of those who make a wager deposits the money or counters wagered.
2 a person with an interest or concern in something, especially a business. ■ [as modifier] denoting a type of organization or system in which all the members or participants are seen as having an interest in its success: *a stakeholder economy.*
– DERIVATIVES **stakeholding** noun & adjective.

stakeholder pension ▸ noun (in the UK) a pension plan, intended primarily for those who do not belong to a company pension scheme or who are self-employed, which invests the money a person saves and uses the fund on retirement to buy a pension from a pension provider.

stake net ▸ noun a fishing net hung on stakes.

stake-out ▸ noun informal a period of secret surveillance of a building or an area by police in order to observe someone's activities.

staker ▸ noun 1 a person who gambles money on the outcome of a game or race.
2 Canadian a person who makes a mining claim.

Stakhanovite /stəˈkɑːnəvʌɪt, -ˈkanə-/ ▸ noun a worker in the former Soviet Union who was exceptionally hard-working and productive. ■ an exceptionally hard-working or zealous person.
– DERIVATIVES **Stakhanovism** noun, **Stakhanovist** noun & adjective.
– ORIGIN 1930s: from the name of Aleksei Grigorevich *Stakhanov* (1906–1977), Russian coal miner.

stalactite /ˈstaləktʌɪt/ ▸ noun a tapering structure hanging like an icicle from the roof of a cave, formed of calcium salts deposited by dripping water.
– DERIVATIVES **stalactitic** adjective.
– ORIGIN late 17th cent.: from modern Latin *stalactites*, from Greek *stalaktos* 'dripping', based on *stalassein* 'to drip'.

Stalag /ˈstalag, ˈʃtalag/ ▸ noun (in the Second World War) a German prison camp, especially for non-commissioned officers and privates.
– ORIGIN German, contraction of *Stammlager*, from *Stamm* 'base, main stock' + *Lager* 'camp'.

stalagmite /ˈstaləgmʌɪt/ ▸ noun a mound or tapering column rising from the floor of a cave, formed of calcium salts deposited by dripping water and often uniting with a stalactite.
– DERIVATIVES **stalagmitic** adjective.
– ORIGIN late 17th cent.: from modern Latin *stalagmites*, from Greek *stalagma* 'a drop', based on *stalassein* (see STALACTITE).

stale¹ ▸ adjective (**staler, stalest**) (of food) no longer fresh and pleasant to eat; hard, musty, or dry: *stale bread.* ■ no longer new and interesting or exciting: *their marriage had gone stale.* ■ [predic.] (of a person) no longer able to perform well or creatively because of having done something for too long: *a top executive tends to get stale.* ■ (of a cheque or legal claim) invalid because out of date.
▸ verb make or become stale: [no obj.] *she would cut up yesterday's leftover bread, staling now.*
– DERIVATIVES **stalely** adverb, **staleness** noun.
– ORIGIN Middle English (describing beer in the sense 'clear from long standing, strong'): probably from Anglo-Norman French and Old French, from *estaler* 'to halt'; compare with the verb STALL.

stale² ▸ verb [no obj.] (of an animal, especially a horse) urinate.
– ORIGIN late Middle English: perhaps from Old French *estaler* 'come to a stand, halt' (compare with STALE¹).

stalemate ▸ noun [mass noun] Chess a position counting as a draw, in which a player is not in check but cannot move except into check. ■ a situation in which further action or progress by opposing or competing parties seems impossible: *the war had again reached stalemate.*
▸ verb [with obj.] bring to or cause to reach stalemate: (as adj. **stalemated**) *the currently stalemated peace talks.*
– ORIGIN mid 18th cent.: from obsolete *stale* (from Anglo-Norman French *estale* 'position', from *estaler* 'be placed') + MATE².

Stalin¹ /ˈstɑːlɪn/ (also **Stalino**) former name (1924–61) for DONETSK.

Stalin² /ˈstɑːlɪn/, Joseph (1879–1953), Soviet statesman, General Secretary of the Communist Party of the USSR 1922–53; born *Iosif Vissarionovich Dzhugashvili.*

His adoptive name Stalin means 'man of steel'. Having isolated his political rival Trotsky, by 1927 Stalin was the uncontested leader of the Communist Party. In 1928 he launched a succession of five-year plans for rapid industrialization and the enforced collectivization of agriculture; as a result of this process some 10 million peasants are thought to have died. His large-scale purges of the intelligentsia in the 1930s were equally ruthless. After the victory over Hitler in 1945 he maintained a firm grip on neighbouring Communist states.

Stalinabad /ˈstɑːlɪnəbad/ former name (1929–61) for DUSHANBE.

Stalingrad /ˈstɑːlɪngrad/ former name (1925–61) for VOLGOGRAD.

Stalingrad, Battle of a long and bitterly fought battle of the Second World War, in which the German advance into the Soviet Union was turned back at Stalingrad in 1942–3. The Germans surrendered after suffering more than 300,000 casualties.

Stalinism ▸ noun [mass noun] the ideology and policies adopted by Stalin, based on centralization, totalitarianism, and the pursuit of communism.
– DERIVATIVES **Stalinist** noun & adjective.

Stalino /ˈstɑːlɪnəʊ/ see STALIN¹.

Stalin Peak former name (1933–1962) for ISMAIL SAMANI PEAK.

stalk¹ ▸ noun the main stem of a herbaceous plant: *he chewed a stalk of grass.* ■ the slender attachment or support of a leaf, flower, or fruit: *the acorns grow on stalks.* ■ a similar support for a sessile animal, or for an organ in an animal. ■ a slender support or stem of an object: *drinking glasses with long stalks.* ■ (in a vehicle) a lever on the steering column controlling the indicators, lights, etc.
– DERIVATIVES **stalked** adjective [in combination] *rough-stalked meadow grass*, **stalkless** adjective, **stalk-like** adjective, **stalky** adjective (**stalkier, stalkiest**).
– ORIGIN Middle English: probably a diminutive of dialect *stale* 'rung of a ladder, long handle'.

stalk² ▸ verb 1 [with obj.] pursue or approach stealthily: *a cat stalking a bird.* ■ harass or persecute (someone) with unwanted and obsessive attention: *for five years she was stalked by a man who would taunt and threaten her.* ■ chiefly literary move silently or threateningly through (a place): *the tiger stalks the jungle* | figurative *fear stalked the camp.*
2 [no obj., with adverbial of direction] stride somewhere in a proud, stiff, or angry manner: *without another word she turned and stalked out.*
▸ noun 1 a stealthy pursuit of someone or something.
2 a stiff, striding gait.
– DERIVATIVES **stalker** noun.
– ORIGIN late Old English *-stealcian* (in *bistealcian* 'walk cautiously or stealthily'), of Germanic origin; related to STEAL.

stalk-eyed ▸ adjective (of a crustacean) having eyes mounted on stalks.

stalking horse ▸ noun 1 a person or thing that is used to conceal someone's real intentions. ■ a candidate in an election for the leadership of a political party who stands only in order to provoke the election and thus allow a stronger candidate to come forward.
2 a screen traditionally made in the shape of a horse behind which a hunter may stay concealed when stalking prey.

S

– ORIGIN early 16th cent.: from the former practice of using a horse trained to allow a fowler to hide behind it, or under its coverings, until within easy range of prey.

stall ▶ **noun 1** a stand, booth, or compartment for the sale of goods in a market or large covered area: *fruit and vegetable stalls.*
2 an individual compartment for an animal in a stable or cowshed, enclosed on three sides. ■ a stable or cowshed. ■ N. Amer. a marked-out parking space for a vehicle. ■ (also **starting stall**) a cage-like compartment in which a horse is held immediately prior to the start of a race. ■ a compartment for one person in a set of toilets, shower cubicles, etc.
3 a fixed seat in the choir or chancel of a church, enclosed at the back and sides and often canopied, typically reserved for a particular member of the clergy.
4 (**stalls**) Brit. the seats on the ground floor in a theatre.
5 an instance of an engine, vehicle, aircraft, or boat stalling.
▶ **verb 1** [no obj.] (of a motor vehicle or its engine) stop running, typically because of an overload on the engine: *her car stalled at the crossroads.* ■ (of an aircraft) stop flying and begin to fall because the speed is too low or the angle of attack too large to maintain adequate lift. ■ Sailing have insufficient wind power in the sails to give controlled motion. ■ [with obj.] cause to stall.
2 stop or cause to stop making progress: [no obj.] *his career had stalled, hers taken off* | [with obj.] *the government has stalled the much-needed project.*
3 [no obj.] speak or act in a deliberately vague way in order to gain more time to deal with something; prevaricate: *she was* ***stalling for time.*** ■ [with obj.] delay or divert (someone) by prevarication: *stall him until I've had time to take a look.*
4 [with obj.] put or keep (an animal) in a stall, especially in order to fatten it.
– PHRASES **set out one's stall** Brit. display or assert one's abilities or position: *he has set out his stall as a strong supporter of free trade.*
– ORIGIN Old English *steall* 'stable or cattle shed', of Germanic origin; related to Dutch *stal*, also to STAND. Early senses of the verb included 'reside, dwell' and 'bring to a halt'.

stallage /ˈstɔːlɪdʒ/ ▶ **noun** [mass noun] Brit., chiefly historical rental, taxation, or fees charged for the holding of a stall in a market. ■ the right to hold a stall in a market.
– ORIGIN Middle English: shortening of Old French *estalage*, from *estal* 'stall'.

stall-feed ▶ **verb** [with obj.] feed and keep (an animal) in a stall, especially in order to fatten it.

stallholder ▶ **noun** Brit. a person owning or running a stall at a market.

stallion ▶ **noun** an uncastrated adult male horse.
– ORIGIN Middle English: from an Anglo-Norman French variant of Old French *estalon*, from a derivative of a Germanic base shared by STALL.

stall turn ▶ **noun** an aerobatic manoeuvre in which the aircraft climbs vertically before being stalled, when it turns on one wing into a dive.

stalwart /ˈstɔːlwət, ˈstal-/ ▶ **adjective** loyal, reliable, and hard-working: *he remained a stalwart supporter of the cause.* ■ dated strongly built and sturdy: *he was of stalwart build.*
▶ **noun** a loyal, reliable, and hard-working supporter of or participant in an organization or team: *the stalwarts of the Labour Party.*
– DERIVATIVES **stalwartly** adverb, **stalwartness** noun.
– ORIGIN late Middle English: Scots variant of obsolete *stalworth*, from Old English *stǣl* 'place' + *weorth* 'worth'.

Stamboul /stamˈbuːl/ archaic name for ISTANBUL.

stamen /ˈsteɪmən/ ▶ **noun** Botany the male fertilizing organ of a flower, typically consisting of a pollen-containing anther and a filament.
– ORIGIN mid 17th cent.: from Latin, literally 'warp in an upright loom, thread'.

stamina ▶ **noun** [mass noun] the ability to sustain prolonged physical or mental effort: *their secret is stamina rather than speed.*
– ORIGIN late 17th cent. (in the sense 'rudiments, essential elements of something'): from Latin, plural of STAMEN in the sense 'threads spun by the Fates'.

staminate /ˈstamɪnət/ ▶ **adjective** Botany (of a plant or flower) having stamens but no pistils. Compare with PISTILLATE.

staminode /ˈstamɪnəʊd/ ▶ **noun** Botany a sterile or abortive stamen, frequently resembling a stamen without its anther.

stammer ▶ **verb** [no obj.] speak with sudden involuntary pauses and a tendency to repeat the initial letters of words. ■ [with obj.] utter (words) in such a way: *I* ***stammered out*** *my history* | [with direct speech] *'I ... I can't,' Isabel stammered.*
▶ **noun** [in sing.] a tendency to stammer: *as a young man, he had a dreadful stammer.*
– DERIVATIVES **stammerer** noun, **stammering** noun & adjective, **stammeringly** adverb.
– ORIGIN late Old English *stamerian*, of West Germanic origin; related to STUMBLE. The noun dates from the late 18th cent.

stamp ▶ **verb** [with obj.] **1** bring down (one's foot) heavily on the ground or on something on the ground: *he stamped his foot in frustration* | [no obj.] *he threw his cigarette down and stamped on it* | figurative *Robertson stamped on all these suggestions.* ■ [with obj. and adverbial] crush, flatten, or remove with a heavy blow from one's foot: *she stamped the snow from her boots.* ■ [no obj., with adverbial of direction] walk with heavy, forceful steps: *John stamped off, muttering.*
2 impress a pattern or mark on (a surface, object, or document) using an engraved or inked block or die: *the woman stamped my passport.* ■ impress (a pattern or mark) with an engraved or inked block or die: *a key with a number* ***stamped on*** *the shaft* | figurative *it's one of those records that has 'classic' stamped all over it.* ■ make (something) by cutting it out with a die or mould: *the knives are* ***stamped out from*** *a flat strip of steel.* ■ reveal or mark out as having a particular quality or ability: *his style* ***stamps*** *him* ***as*** *a player to watch.*
3 fix a postage stamp or stamps on to (a letter): *Annie stamped the envelope for her.*
4 crush or pulverize (ore).
▶ **noun 1** an instrument for stamping a pattern or mark, in particular an engraved or inked block or die. ■ a mark or pattern made by a stamp, especially one indicating official validation: *passports with visa stamps* | figurative *the emperor gave them his* ***stamp of approval.*** ■ a characteristic or distinctive impression or quality: *the whole project has the stamp of authority* | *even the least expensive movie* ***bore the stamp*** *of the studio's plush style.* ■ a particular class or type of person or thing: *empiricism of this stamp has been especially influential in British philosophy.*
2 a small adhesive piece of paper stuck to something to show that an amount of money has been paid, in particular a postage stamp: *a first-class stamp* | *TV licence stamps.*
3 an act or sound of stamping with the foot: *the stamp of boots on the bare floor.*
4 a block for crushing ore in a stamp mill.
– PHRASES **stamp one's authority** (or **personality** or **style** etc.) **on** have a strong or permanent influence on: *he must be able to stamp his authority on the team.*
– PHRASAL VERBS **stamp something out 1** extinguish a fire by stamping on it: *he stamped out the flames before they could grow.* **2** suppress or put an end to something by taking decisive action: *urgent action is required to stamp out corruption.*
– DERIVATIVES **stamper** noun.
– ORIGIN Middle English (in the sense 'crush to a powder'): of Germanic origin; related to German *stampfen* 'stamp with the foot'; reinforced by Old French *estamper* 'to stamp'. Compare with STOMP.

Stamp Act ▶ **noun** an act regulating stamp duty.

stamp collecting ▶ **noun** [mass noun] the collection and study of postage stamps as objects of interest or value; philately.
– DERIVATIVES **stamp collector** noun.

stamp duty ▶ **noun** a duty levied on the legal recognition of certain documents.

stamped addressed envelope ▶ **noun** Brit. a self-addressed envelope with a stamp affixed, typically enclosed with a letter for an expected reply.

stampede ▶ **noun** a sudden panicked rush of a number of horses, cattle, or other animals. ■ a sudden rapid movement or reaction of a mass of people in response to a particular circumstance or stimulus: *a stampede of bargain hunters.* ■ [often in names] (in North America) a rodeo: *the Calgary Stampede.*
▶ **verb** [no obj.] (of horses, cattle, or other animals) rush wildly in a sudden mass panic: *the nearby sheep stampeded as if they sensed impending danger.* ■ [no obj., with adverbial of direction] (of people) move rapidly in a mass: *the children stampeded through the kitchen, playing tag or hide-and-seek.* ■ [with obj.] cause (people or animals) to stampede: *the raiders stampeded 200 mules* | figurative *don't let them* ***stampede*** *us* ***into*** *anything.*
– DERIVATIVES **stampeder** noun.
– ORIGIN early 19th cent.: Mexican Spanish use of Spanish *estampida* 'crash, uproar', of Germanic origin; related to the verb STAMP.

stamp hinge ▶ **noun** a small piece of gummed transparent paper used for fixing postage stamps in an album.

stamping ground (N. Amer. also **stomping ground**) ▶ **noun** a place where someone regularly spends time; a favourite haunt.

stamp mill ▶ **noun** a mill for crushing ore.

stamp office ▶ **noun** Brit. an office for the issue of government stamps and the receipt of stamp duty.

stamp paper ▶ **noun** [mass noun] the gummed marginal paper at the edge of a sheet of postage stamps.

stance /stɑːns, stans/ ▶ **noun 1** the way in which someone stands, especially when deliberately adopted (as in cricket, golf, and other sports); a person's posture: *she altered her stance, resting all her weight on one leg.* ■ the attitude of a person or organization towards something; a standpoint: *the party is changing its* ***stance on*** *Europe.*
2 Scottish a site on a street for a market, street vendor's stall, or taxi rank.
3 Climbing a ledge or foothold on which a belay can be secured.
– ORIGIN Middle English (denoting a standing place): from French, from Italian *stanza*.

stanch[1] /stɔːn(t)ʃ, stɑːn(t)ʃ/ ▶ **verb** chiefly US variant spelling of STAUNCH[2].

stanch[2] /stɔːn(t)ʃ/ ▶ **adjective** variant spelling of STAUNCH[1] (sense 2).

stanchion /ˈstanʃ(ə)n/ ▶ **noun** an upright bar, post, or frame forming a support or barrier.
– DERIVATIVES **stanchioned** adjective.
– ORIGIN Middle English: from Anglo-Norman French *stanchon*, from Old French *estanchon*, from *estance* 'a support', probably based on Latin *stant-* 'standing', from the verb *stare*.

stand ▶ **verb** (past and past participle **stood**) **1** [no obj., usu. with adverbial of place] have or maintain an upright position, supported by one's feet: *Lionel stood in the doorway* | *she stood still, heart hammering.* ■ rise to one's feet: *the two men* ***stood up*** *and shook hands.* ■ [no obj., with adverbial of direction] move somewhere in an upright position: *she stood aside to let them enter.* ■ [with obj. and adverbial of place] place or set in an upright or specified position: *don't stand the plant in direct sunlight.*
2 [no obj., with adverbial of place] (of an object, building, or settlement) be situated in a particular place or position: *the town stood on a hill* | *the hotel stands in three acres of gardens.* ■ (of a building or other vertical structure) remain upright and entire rather than fall into ruin or be destroyed: *after the storms only one house was left standing.* ■ remain valid or unaltered: *my decision stands* | *he won 31 caps–a record which stood for 42 years.* ■ (especially of a vehicle) remain stationary: *the train now standing at platform 3.* ■ (of a liquid) collect and remain motionless: *soil where water stands in winter.* ■ (especially of food) rest without disturbance, typically so as to infuse or marinate: *pour boiling water over the fruit and leave it to stand for 5 minutes.* ■ [no obj., with adverbial of direction] (of a ship) remain on a specified course: *the ship was standing north.*
3 [no obj., with complement] be in a specified state or condition: *since mother's death the house had stood empty* | *sorry, darling—I stand corrected.* ■ adopt a particular attitude towards a matter or issue: *students should consider where they stand on this issue.* ■ be of a specified height: *Sampson was a small man, standing 5 ft 4 in tall.* ■ (**stand at**) be at (a particular level or value): *the budget stood at £2,000 million per annum.* ■ [no obj., with infinitive] be in a situation where one is likely to do something: *investors stood to lose heavily.* ■ act in a specified capacity: *he stood security for the government's borrowings.* ■ (also **stand at stud**) [no obj.] (of a stallion) be available for breeding.
4 [with obj. and often modal] withstand (an experience or test) without being damaged: *small, stable boats that could stand the punishment of heavy seas* | *will your cooker stand the strain of the festive season?* ■ [with modal and usu. negative] informal be able to endure or tolerate: *I can't stand the way Mum talks to him* | *I can't stand brandy.*
5 [no obj.] Brit. be a candidate in an election: *he stood for parliament in 1968.*
6 [no obj.] act as umpire in a cricket match.

7 [usu. with two objs] provide (food or drink) for (someone) at one's own expense: *somebody in the bar would stand him a coffee.*

▸ **noun 1** [usu. in sing.] an attitude towards a particular issue: *the party's tough stand on immigration | his traditionalist stand.* ▪ a determined effort to resist or fight for something: *this was not the moment to* ***make a stand for*** *independence | we have to* ***take a stand against*** *racism.* ▪ an act of holding one's ground against or halting to resist an opposing force: *Custer's legendary last stand.* ▪ Cricket another term for PARTNERSHIP: *they shared a second-wicket stand of 135.*

2 a rack, base, or piece of furniture for holding, supporting, or displaying something: *a microphone stand.* ▪ a small stall or booth in a street, market, or public building from which goods are sold: *a hot-dog stand.* ▪ chiefly Brit. an upright structure on which an organization displays promotional material at an exhibition. ▪ a raised platform for a band, orchestra, or speaker.

3 the place where someone typically stands or sits: *she took her stand in front of the desks.* ▪ a place where vehicles, typically taxis, wait for passengers. ▪ (also **witness stand**) a witness box: *Sergeant Harris took the stand.*

4 a large raised tiered structure for spectators, typically at a sporting venue: *United's manager watched from the stands.*

5 [usu. in sing.] a cessation from motion or progress: *the train drew to a stand by the signal box.* ▪ the mean sea level at a particular period in the past. ▪ the state of the tide at high or low water when there is little change in water level. ▪ each halt made on a touring theatrical production to give one or more performances.

6 a group of growing plants of a specified kind, especially trees: *a stand of poplars.*

7 S. African a plot of land. [perhaps from Afrikaans *standplaas* 'standing place'.]

– PHRASES **as it stands** in its present condition: *there are no merits in the Bill as it stands.* ▪ (also **as things stand**) in the present circumstances: *the country would struggle, as it stands, to host the next World Cup.* **be at a stand** archaic be perplexed and unable to take action. **it stands to reason** see REASON. **stand and deliver!** historical a highwayman's order to hand over money and valuables. **stand a chance** see CHANCE. **stand easy!** see EASY. **stand one's ground** maintain one's position, typically in the face of opposition: *she stood her ground, refusing to let him intimidate her.* **stand someone in good stead** see STEAD. **stand on me** informal, dated rely on me; believe me. **stand on one's own (two) feet** be or become self-reliant or independent. **stand out a mile** see MILE. **stand out like a sore thumb** see SORE. **stand pat** see PAT². **stand treat** dated bear the expense of treating someone to something. **stand trial** be tried in a court of law. **stand up and be counted** state publicly one's support for someone or something. **will the real —— please stand up** informal used rhetorically to indicate that the specified person should clarify their position or reveal their true character: *he was so different from the unhappy man of a week ago—would the real Jack Lawrence please stand up?*

– PHRASAL VERBS **stand alone** be unequalled: *when it came to fun Fergus stood alone.* **stand aside** take no action to prevent, or not involve oneself in, something that is happening: *the army had stood aside as the monarchy fell.* ▪ another way of saying STAND DOWN (sense 1) below. **stand back** withdraw from a situation emotionally in order to view it more objectively. ▪ another way of saying STAND ASIDE above. **stand by 1** be present while something bad is happening but fail to take any action to stop it: *he was beaten to the ground as onlookers stood by.* **2** support or remain loyal to (someone), typically in a time of need: *she had stood by him during his years in prison.* ▪ adhere to or abide by (something promised, stated, or decided): *the government must stand by its pledges.* **3** be ready to deal or assist with something: *two battalions were on their way, and a third was standing by.* **stand down 1** withdraw or resign from a position or office: *he stood down as leader of the party.* **2** (**stand down** or **stand someone down**) relax or cause to relax after a state of readiness: *if something doesn't happen soon, I reckon they'll stand us down.* **3** (of a witness) leave the witness box after giving evidence. **stand for 1** be an abbreviation of or symbol for: *BBC stands for British Broadcasting Corporation.* **2** [with negative] informal refuse to endure or tolerate: *I won't stand for any nonsense.* **3** support (a cause or principle): *we stand for animal welfare.* **stand in 1** deputize: *Brown* ***stood in for*** *the injured Simpson.* **2** Nautical sail closer to the shore. **stand in with** dated be in league or partnership with. **stand off 1** move or keep away: *the women stood off at a slight distance.* **2** Nautical sail further away from the shore. **stand someone off 1** keep someone away; repel someone. **2** Brit. another way of saying LAY SOMEONE OFF (see LAY¹). **stand on 1** be scrupulous in the observance of: *call me Alexander—don't let's stand on formality.* **2** Nautical continue on the same course. **stand out 1** project from a surface: *the veins in his neck stood out.* ▪ be easily noticeable: *he was one of those men who stood out in a crowd.* ▪ be clearly better or more significant than someone or something: *four issues stand out as being of crucial importance.* **2** persist in opposition or support of something: *she* ***stood out against*** *public opinion.* **stand over 1** stand close to (someone) so as to watch, supervise, or intimidate them. **2** (**stand over** or **stand something over**) be postponed or postpone to be dealt with at a later date: *a number of points were stood over to a further meeting.* **stand to** [often in imperative] Military stand ready for an attack, especially one before dawn or after dark. **stand up** (of an argument, claim, evidence, etc.) remain valid after close scrutiny or analysis. **stand someone up** informal fail to keep an appointment with a boyfriend or girlfriend. **stand up for** speak or act in support of: *she learned to* ***stand up for herself.*** **stand up to 1** make a spirited defence against: *giving workers the confidence to stand up to their employers.* **2** be resistant to the harmful effects of (prolonged use).

– DERIVATIVES **stander** noun.

– ORIGIN Old English *standan* (verb), *stand* (noun), of Germanic origin, from an Indo-European root shared by Latin *stare* and Greek *histanai*, also by the noun STEAD.

> **USAGE** The use of the past participle **stood** with the verb 'to be', as in *we were* ***stood*** *in a line for hours,* is not acceptable in standard English, where the present participle **standing** should be used instead. See also **USAGE** at **SIT**.

stand-alone ▸ **adjective** (of computer hardware or software) able to operate independently of other hardware or software.

standard ▸ **noun 1** a level of quality or attainment: *their restaurant offers a high standard of service | the government's ambition to raise standards in schools.* ▪ a required or agreed level of quality or attainment: *half of the beaches fail to comply with European standards |* [mass noun] *their tap water was not* ***up to standard.*** ▪ Brit. historical (in elementary schools) a grade of proficiency tested by examination or the form or class preparing pupils for such a grade.

2 something used as a measure, norm, or model in comparative evaluations: *the wages are low by today's standards | the system had become an industry standard.* ▪ (**standards**) principles of conduct informed by notions of honour and decency: *a decline in moral standards.* ▪ the prescribed weight of fine metal in gold or silver coins: *the sterling standard for silver.* ▪ a system by which the value of a currency is defined in terms of gold or silver or both. ▪ a measure for timber, equivalent to 165 cu. ft (4.67 cubic metres).

3 (especially with reference to jazz or blues) a tune or song of established popularity.

4 a military or ceremonial flag carried on a pole or hoisted on a rope. ▪ used in names of newspapers: *a report in the Evening Standard.*

5 a tree or shrub that grows on an erect stem of full height. ▪ a shrub grafted on an erect stem and trained in tree form. ▪ Botany the large, frequently erect uppermost petal of a papilionaceous flower. Also called VEXILLUM. ▪ Botany one of the inner petals of an iris flower, frequently erect.

6 an upright water or gas pipe.

▸ **adjective 1** used or accepted as normal or average: *the standard rate of income tax | it is standard practice in museums to register objects as they are acquired.* ▪ (of a size, measure, design, etc.) regularly used or produced; not special or exceptional: *all these doors come in a range of standard sizes.* ▪ (of a work, repertoire, or writer) viewed as authoritative or of permanent value and so widely read or performed: *his essays on the interpretation of reality became a standard text.* ▪ denoting or relating to the form of a language widely accepted as the usual correct form: *speakers of standard English.*

2 [attrib.] (of a tree or shrub) growing on an erect stem of full height. ▪ (of a shrub) grafted on an erect stem and trained in tree form: *standard roses.*

– PHRASES **raise one's** (or **the**) **standard** take up arms; oppose: *he is the only one who has dared raise his standard against her.*

– DERIVATIVES **standardly** adverb.

– ORIGIN Middle English (denoting a flag raised on a pole as a rallying point, the authorized exemplar of a unit of measurement, or an upright timber): shortening of Old French *estendart*, from *estendre* 'extend'; in sense 4 of the noun, sense 5 of the noun, sense 6 of the noun, influenced by the verb STAND.

standard assessment task (abbrev.: **SAT**) ▸ **noun** (in the UK) a standard test given to schoolchildren to assess their progress in a core subject of the national curriculum.

standard-bearer ▸ **noun** a soldier who is responsible for carrying the distinctive flag of a unit, regiment, or army. ▪ a leading figure in a cause or movement: *the announcement made her a standard-bearer for gay rights.*

Standardbred ▸ **noun** N. Amer. a horse of a breed able to attain a specified speed, developed especially for trotting.

standard cost ▸ **noun** the estimated cost of a process, resource, or item used in a manufacturing enterprise, entered in an account and compared with the actual cost so that anomalies are readily detectable.

– DERIVATIVES **standard costing** noun.

standard deviation ▸ **noun** Statistics a quantity expressing by how much the members of a group differ from the mean value for the group.

standard error ▸ **noun** Statistics a measure of the statistical accuracy of an estimate, equal to the standard deviation of the theoretical distribution of a large population of such estimates.

standard gauge ▸ **noun** a railway gauge of 4 ft 8½ inches (1.435 m), standard in Britain and many other parts of the world.

Standard Grade ▸ **noun** (in Scotland) an examination equivalent to the GCSE.

standardize (also **standardise**) ▸ **verb** [with obj.] cause (something) to conform to a standard: *in quoting from the letters, I have standardized the spelling and punctuation.* ▪ [no obj.] (**standardize on**) adopt (something) as one's standard: *we could standardize on US equipment.* ▪ determine the properties of (something) by comparison with a standard.

– DERIVATIVES **standardizable** adjective, **standardization** noun, **standardizer** noun.

standard lamp ▸ **noun** Brit. a lamp with a tall stem whose base stands on the floor.

standard lens ▸ **noun** a camera lens with a focal length approximately equal to the diagonal of the negative (taken as 50 mm for a 35 mm camera), giving a field of view similar to that of the naked eye.

standard model ▸ **noun** (**the standard model**) Physics a mathematical description of the elementary particles of matter and the electromagnetic, weak, and strong forces by which they interact.

standard of living ▸ **noun** the degree of wealth and material comfort available to a person or community.

standard time ▸ **noun** [mass noun] a uniform time for places in approximately the same longitude, established in a country or region by law or custom.

standard wire gauge ▸ **noun** see WIRE GAUGE.

standby ▸ **noun** (pl. **standbys**) [mass noun] **1** readiness for duty or immediate deployment: *buses were placed* ***on standby*** *for the journey to London.* ▪ [count noun] a person or thing ready to be deployed immediately, especially if needed as backup in an emergency: *a generator was kept as a standby in case of power failure |* [as modifier] *a standby rescue vessel.* ▪ an operational mode of an electrical appliance in which the power is switched on but the appliance is not actually functioning: *switch off the TV at night instead of leaving it* ***on standby.*** ▪ [as modifier] denoting an economic or financial measure prepared for implementation in specified circumstances: *a standby credit facility.*

2 the state of waiting to secure an unreserved place for a journey or performance, allocated on the basis of earliest availability: *passengers were obliged to go* ***on standby.*** ▪ [count noun] a person waiting to secure an unreserved place for a journey or performance.

stand-down ▸ **noun** Military a period of relaxation after a state of alert.

standee /stanˈdiː/ ▸ **noun** a person who is standing rather than seated, especially in a passenger vehicle.

S

stand-in ▸ noun a person who stands in for another, especially in a match or performance; a substitute: [as modifier] *a stand-in goalkeeper.*

standing ▸ noun [mass noun] **1** position, status, or reputation: *their standing in the community | a man of high social standing.* ■ **(standings)** the table of scores indicating the relative positions of competitors in a sporting contest: *she heads the world championship standings.*
2 the length of time that something has lasted or that someone has fulfilled a role; duration: *an interdepartmental squabble of long standing.*
3 a stall for cattle and horses.
▸ adjective [attrib.] **1** (of a jump or a start in a running race) performed from rest or an upright position, without a run-up or the use of starting blocks.
2 remaining in force or use; permanent: *he has a standing invitation to visit them | a standing army.*
3 (of water) stagnant or still.
4 Printing (of metal type) kept set up after use.
– PHRASES **all standing** Sailing (chiefly with reference to a boat's stopping) without time to lower the sails. **in good standing** in favour or on good terms with someone: *the companies wanted to stay in good standing with the government.* **leave someone/thing standing** informal be much better or make much faster progress than someone or something else: *in the personal fitness stakes he left her standing.*

standing committee ▸ noun a permanent committee that meets regularly.

standing count (also **standing eight count**) ▸ noun Boxing a count of eight taken on a boxer who has not been knocked down but who appears temporarily unfit to continue fighting.

standing crop ▸ noun **1** a growing crop, especially of a cereal.
2 Ecology the total biomass of an ecosystem or any of its components at a given time.

standing joke ▸ noun something that regularly causes amusement or provokes ridicule.

standing order ▸ noun **1** Brit. an instruction to a bank by an account holder to make regular fixed payments to a particular person or organization.
2 Brit. an order for a commodity placed on a regular basis with a retailer such as a newsagent.
3 an order or ruling governing the procedures of a parliament or other society or council.
4 a military order or ruling that is retained irrespective of changing conditions.

standing ovation ▸ noun a period of prolonged applause during which the crowd or audience rise to their feet.

standing part ▸ noun the end of a rope or sheet in a ship's rigging which is made fast, as distinct from the end to be hauled on.

standing rigging ▸ noun see RIGGING (sense 1).

standing room ▸ noun [mass noun] space available for people to stand rather than sit in a passenger vehicle or building.

standing stone ▸ noun another term for MENHIR.

standing wave ▸ noun Physics a vibration of a system in which some particular points remain fixed while others between them vibrate with the maximum amplitude. Compare with TRAVELLING WAVE.

S

standish ▸ noun chiefly historical a stand for holding pens, ink, and other writing equipment.
– ORIGIN Middle English: commonly held to be from the verb STAND + DISH, but evidence of such a use of *dish* is lacking.

stand of arms ▸ noun archaic a complete set of weapons for one man.

stand of colours ▸ noun Brit. a battalion's flags.

stand-off ▸ noun **1** a deadlock between two equally matched opponents in a dispute or conflict: *the 16-day-old stand-off was no closer to being resolved.*
2 Rugby short for STAND-OFF HALF.

stand-off half ▸ noun Rugby a half back who forms a link between the scrum half and the three-quarters.

stand-offish ▸ adjective informal distant and cold in manner; unfriendly: *he was an arrogant, stand-offish prig.*
– DERIVATIVES **stand-offishly** adverb, **stand-offishness** noun.

stand oil ▸ noun [mass noun] linseed oil or another drying oil thickened by heating, used in paints, varnishes, and printing inks.

standout informal ▸ noun a person or thing of exceptional quality or ability: *standouts include the homemade ravioli and the pizzas.*
▸ adjective [attrib.] exceptionally good: *he became a standout quarterback in the NFL.*

standpipe ▸ noun a vertical pipe extending from a water supply, especially one connecting a temporary tap to the mains.

standpoint ▸ noun an attitude to a particular issue: *she writes on religion* ***from the standpoint of*** *a believer.* ■ the position from which someone is able to view a scene or an object.

standstill /ˈstan(d)stɪl/ ▸ noun [in sing.] a situation or condition in which there is no movement or activity at all: *the traffic* ***came to a standstill.***

standstill agreement ▸ noun Finance an agreement to maintain the present state of affairs, especially one made between two countries in which a debt owed by one to the other is held in abeyance for a specified period.

stand-to ▸ noun [mass noun] Military the state of readiness for action or attack. ■ the formal start to a day of military operations.

stand-up ▸ adjective [attrib.] **1** involving, done by, or engaged in by people standing up: *a stand-up party.* ■ (of comedy or a comedian) performed or performing by standing in front of an audience and telling jokes: *a stand-up comic | his stand-up routine depends on improvised observations.*
2 (of a fight or argument) involving direct confrontation: *she had a stand-up row with her husband.* ■ US informal courageous and loyal in a combative way.
3 designed to stay upright or erect.
▸ noun **1** a comedian who performs by standing in front of an audience and telling jokes. ■ [mass noun] stand-up comedy: *he began doing stand-up when he was fifteen.* ■ a brief monologue by a television news reporter.
2 a fight or argument involving direct confrontation.

Stanhope /ˈstanəp/, Lady Hester Lucy (1776–1839), English traveller. Granted a pension on the death of her uncle, Pitt the Younger, she settled in a ruined convent in the Lebanon Mountains in 1814 and participated in Middle Eastern politics for several years.

stanhope /ˈstanəp, -həʊp/ ▸ noun historical a light open horse-drawn carriage for one person, with two or four wheels.
– ORIGIN early 19th cent.: named after Fitzroy *Stanhope* (1787–1864), an English clergyman for whom the first one was made.

Stanier /ˈstanɪə/, Sir William (Arthur) (1876–1965), English railway engineer. He is chiefly remembered for his standard locomotive designs for the London Midland and Scottish Railway.

Stanislaus, St /ˈstanɪslɔːs/ (1030–79), patron saint of Poland; Polish name *Stanisław* /staˈniswaf/; known as **St Stanislaus of Cracow**. As bishop of Cracow (1072–79) he excommunicated King Boleslaus II. According to tradition Stanislaus was murdered by Boleslaus while taking Mass. Feast day, 11 April (formerly 7 May).

Stanislavsky /ˌstanɪsˈlafski/, Konstantin (Sergeevich) (1863–1938), Russian theatre director and actor; born *Konstantin Sergeevich Alekseev*. Stanislavsky trained his actors to take a psychological approach and use latent powers of self-expression when taking on roles; his theory and technique were later developed into method acting.

stank past of STINK.

Stanley[1] (also **Port Stanley**) the chief port and town of the Falkland Islands, situated on the island of East Falkland; pop. 2,115 (2006).

Stanley[2], Sir Henry Morton (1841–1904), Welsh explorer; born *John Rowlands*. As a newspaper correspondent he was sent in 1869 to central Africa to find David Livingstone; two years later he found him at Lake Tanganyika. After Livingstone's death in 1873 Stanley continued his explorations in Africa, charting Lake Victoria, tracing the course of the Congo, and mapping Lake Albert.

Stanley, Mount a mountain in the Ruwenzori range in central Africa, on the border between the Democratic Republic of the Congo (Zaire) and Uganda. Its highest peak, Margherita Peak, which rises to 5,110 m (16,765 ft), is the third-highest peak in Africa. African name NGALIEMA, MOUNT.
– ORIGIN named after Sir Henry M. STANLEY[2], the first European to reach it (1889).

Stanley crane ▸ noun another term for BLUE CRANE.

Stanley Cup a trophy awarded annually to the North American ice-hockey team that wins the championship in the National Hockey League.
– ORIGIN named after Lord *Stanley* of Preston (1841–1908), the Governor General of Canada who donated the trophy in 1893.

Stanley knife ▸ noun Brit. trademark a utility knife with a short, strong replaceable blade.
– ORIGIN late 19th cent.: named after the manufacturer, The *Stanley* Rule and Level Company (now The Stanley Works).

Stanleyville /ˈstanlɪvɪl/ former name (1882–1966) for KISANGANI.

stannary /ˈstan(ə)ri/ ▸ noun (pl. **stannaries**) (usu. **the stannaries**) Brit., chiefly historical a tin-mining district in Cornwall or Devon.
– ORIGIN late Middle English: from medieval Latin *stannaria* (plural), from late Latin *stannum* 'tin'.

stannary court ▸ noun Brit. historical a legal body for the regulation of tin miners in the stannaries.

stannic /ˈstanɪk/ ▸ adjective Chemistry of tin with a valency of four; of tin(IV). Compare with STANNOUS.
– ORIGIN late 18th cent.: from late Latin *stannum* 'tin' + -IC.

stannous /ˈstanəs/ ▸ adjective Chemistry of tin with a valency of two; of tin(II). Compare with STANNIC.
– ORIGIN mid 19th cent.: from late Latin *stannum* 'tin' + -OUS.

Stansted /ˈstanstɪd/ an international airport in Essex, north-east of London.

stanza /ˈstanzə/ ▸ noun a group of lines forming the basic recurring metrical unit in a poem; a verse. ■ a group of four lines in some Greek and Latin metres.
– DERIVATIVES **stanzaed** adjective, **stanzaic** /-ˈzeɪɪk/ adjective.
– ORIGIN late 16th cent.: from Italian, literally 'standing place', also 'stanza'.

stapedial /stəˈpiːdɪəl/ ▸ adjective [attrib.] Anatomy & Zoology relating to the stapes.
– ORIGIN late 19th cent.: from modern Latin *stapedius* (denoting the muscle attached to the neck of the stapes) + -AL.

stapelia /stəˈpiːlɪə/ ▸ noun a succulent African plant with large star-shaped fleshy flowers that have bold markings and a fetid carrion-like smell which attracts pollinating flies. Also called CARRION FLOWER.
● Genus *Stapelia*, family Asclepiadaceae.
– ORIGIN modern Latin, named after Jan Bode von *Stapel* (died 1636), Dutch botanist.

stapes /ˈsteɪpiːz/ ▸ noun (pl. **same**) Anatomy a small stirrup-shaped bone in the middle ear, transmitting vibrations from the incus to the inner ear. Also called STIRRUP.
– ORIGIN mid 17th cent.: modern Latin, from medieval Latin *stapes* 'stirrup'.

staph /staf/ ▸ noun informal short for STAPHYLOCOCCUS.

staphylinid /ˌstafɪˈlɪnɪd, -ˈlʌɪn-/ ▸ noun Entomology a beetle of a family (Staphylinidae) that comprises the rove beetles.
– ORIGIN late 19th cent.: from modern Latin *Staphylinidae* (plural), from the genus name *Staphylinus*, from Greek *staphulinos*, denoting a kind of insect.

staphylococcus /ˌstafɪlə(ʊ)ˈkɒkəs/ ▸ noun (pl. **staphylococci** /-ˈkɒk(s)ʌɪ, -ˈkɒk(s)iː/) a bacterium of a genus that includes many pathogenic kinds that cause pus formation, especially in the skin and mucous membranes. ● Genus *Staphylococcus*; Gram-positive cocci in clusters.
– DERIVATIVES **staphylococcal** adjective.
– ORIGIN modern Latin, from Greek *staphulē* 'bunch of grapes' + *kokkos* 'berry'.

staple[1] ▸ noun a piece of thin wire with two short right-angled end pieces which are driven by a stapler through sheets of paper to fasten them together. ■ a U-shaped metal bar with pointed ends for driving into wood to hold things such as wires in place.
▸ verb [with obj. and adverbial of place] attach or secure with a staple or staples: *Merrill stapled a batch of papers together.*
– ORIGIN Old English *stapol*, of Germanic origin; related to Dutch *stapel* 'pillar' (a sense reflected in English in early use).

staple[2] ▸ noun **1** a main or important element of something: *bread, milk, and other staples | Greek legend was the staple of classical tragedy.* ■ a main item of trade or production: *rubber became the staple of the Malayan economy.*

2 [mass noun] the fibre of cotton or wool considered with regard to its length and degree of fineness.
3 [often with modifier] historical a centre of trade, especially in a specified commodity: *proposals were made for a wool staple at Pisa.*
▸ **adjective** [attrib.] main or important, especially in terms of consumption: *the staple foods of the poor* | figurative *violence is the staple diet of the video generation.* ■ most important in terms of trade or production: *rice was the staple crop grown in most villages.*
– ORIGIN Middle English (in sense 3 of the noun): from Old French *estaple* 'market', from Middle Low German, Middle Dutch *stapel* 'pillar, emporium'; related to STAPLE[1].

staple gun ▸ **noun** a hand-held mechanical tool for driving staples into a hard surface.

stapler ▸ **noun** a device for fastening together sheets of paper with a staple or staples.

star ▸ **noun 1** a fixed luminous point in the night sky which is a large, remote incandescent body like the sun.

> True stars were formerly known as the **fixed stars**, to distinguish them from the planets or **wandering stars**. They are gaseous spheres consisting primarily of hydrogen and helium, there being an equilibrium between the compressional force of gravity and the outward pressure of radiation resulting from internal thermonuclear fusion reactions. Some six thousand stars are visible to the naked eye, but there are actually more than a hundred thousand million in our own Galaxy, while billions of other galaxies are known.

2 a conventional or stylized representation of a star, typically having five or more points: *the walls were painted with silver moons and stars.* ■ a star-shaped symbol used to indicate a category of excellence: *the hotel has three stars* | [as modifier] *MPs suggested giving ferries star ratings.* ■ an asterisk. ■ a white patch on the forehead of a horse or other animal. ■ (also **star connection**) [usu. as modifier] a Y-shaped arrangement of three-phase electrical windings. ■ (also **star network**) [usu. as modifier] a data or communication network in which all nodes are independently connected to one central unit.
3 a very famous or talented entertainer or sports player: *a pop star* | [as modifier] *she got star treatment.* ■ an outstandingly successful person or thing in a group: *he's a **rising star** in the party* | [as modifier] *Elinor was a star pupil.*
4 Astrology a planet, constellation, or configuration regarded as influencing a person's fortunes or personality: *his golf destiny was written in the stars.* ■ (**stars**) informal a horoscope published in a newspaper or magazine: *what do my stars say?*
5 used in names of starfishes and similar echinoderms with five or more radiating arms, e.g. **cushion star**, **brittlestar**.
▸ **verb** (**stars**, **starring**, **starred**) [with obj.] **1** (of a film, play, or other show) have (someone) as a principal performer: *a film starring Liza Minnelli.* ■ [no obj.] (of a performer) have a principal role in a film, play, or other show: *McQueen had **starred in** such epics as The Magnificent Seven* | (as adj. **starring**) *his first starring role.* ■ [no obj.] perform exceptionally in a game or other event: *Beckham **starred in** the win over Leeds.*
2 decorate or cover with star-shaped marks or objects: *thick grass **starred with** flowers.* ■ mark (something) for special notice or recommendation with an asterisk or other star-shaped symbol: *the activities listed below are starred according to their fitness ratings* | (as adj., in combination **-starred**) *Michelin-starred restaurants.*
– PHRASES **have stars in one's eyes** be idealistically hopeful about one's future: *a singer selected from hundreds of applicants with stars in their eyes.* **my stars!** informal, dated an expression of astonishment. **reach for the stars** have high or ambitious aims. **see stars** seem to see flashes of light, especially as a result of being hit on the head. **you're a star!** informal used to praise someone's efforts, especially by way of thanks.
– DERIVATIVES **starless** adjective, **starlike** adjective.
– ORIGIN Old English *steorra*, of Germanic origin; related to Dutch *ster*, German *Stern*, from an Indo-European root shared by Latin *stella* and Greek *astēr*.

star anise ▸ **noun** [mass noun] **1** a small star-shaped fruit with one seed in each arm. It has an aniseed flavour and is used unripe in Asian cookery.
2 the small Chinese evergreen tree from which star anise is obtained. ● *Illicium verum*, family Illiciaceae.

star apple ▸ **noun** an edible purple fruit with a star-shaped cross section. ● This is produced by the evergreen tropical American tree *Chrysophyllum cainito* (family Sapotaceae).

Stara Zagora /ˌstɑːrə zəˈɡɔːrə/ a city in east central Bulgaria; pop. 140,710 (2008). It was held by the Turks from 1370 until 1877, when it was destroyed by them during the Russo-Turkish War. It has since been rebuilt as a modern planned city.

starboard /ˈstɑːbɔːd, -bəd/ ▸ **noun** the side of a ship or aircraft that is on the right when one is facing forward. The opposite of PORT[3].
▸ **verb** [with obj.] turn (a ship or its helm) to starboard.
– ORIGIN Old English *stēorbord* 'rudder side' (see STEER[1], BOARD), because early Teutonic sailing vessels were steered with a paddle over the right side.

starboard watch ▸ **noun** see WATCH (sense 2 of the noun).

starburst ▸ **noun 1** a pattern of lines or rays radiating from a central object or source of light: [as modifier] *a starburst pattern.* ■ a camera lens attachment that produces a pattern of rays around the image of a source of light.
2 a period of intense activity in a galaxy involving the formation of stars.

starch ▸ **noun** [mass noun] **1** an odourless, tasteless white substance occurring widely in plant tissue and obtained chiefly from cereals and potatoes. It is a polysaccharide which functions as a carbohydrate store and is an important constituent of the human diet. ■ food containing starch.
2 powder or spray made from starch and used before ironing to stiffen fabric or clothing.
3 stiffness of manner or character: *the starch in her voice.*
▸ **verb** [with obj.] **1** stiffen (fabric or clothing) with starch: (as adj. **starched**) *his immaculately starched shirt.*
2 N. Amer. informal (of a boxer) defeat (an opponent) by a knockout.
– PHRASES **take the starch out of** US deflate or humiliate (someone).
– DERIVATIVES **starcher** noun.
– ORIGIN Old English (recorded only in the past participle *sterced* 'stiffened'), of Germanic origin; related to Dutch *sterken*, German *stärken* 'strengthen', also to STARK.

Star Chamber an English court of civil and criminal jurisdiction that developed in the late 15th century, trying especially those cases affecting the interests of the Crown. It was noted for its arbitrary and oppressive judgements and was abolished in 1641.

starchy ▸ **adjective** (**starchier**, **starchiest**) **1** (of food or diet) containing a lot of starch.
2 (of clothing) stiff with starch.
3 informal very stiff, formal, or prim in manner or character: *the manager is usually a bit starchy.*
– DERIVATIVES **starchily** adverb, **starchiness** noun.

star cloud ▸ **noun** a region where stars appear to be especially numerous and close together.

star connection ▸ **noun** see STAR (sense 2 of the noun).
– DERIVATIVES **star-connected** adjective.

star-crossed ▸ **adjective** literary thwarted by bad luck: *star-crossed lovers.*
– ORIGIN first used by Shakespeare in *Romeo and Juliet* (1597).

stardom ▸ **noun** [mass noun] the state or status of being a very famous or talented entertainer or sports player.

stardust ▸ **noun** [mass noun] a magical or charismatic quality or feeling: *he slipped past four defenders as though stardust had been sprinkled in his boots.*

stare ▸ **verb** [no obj.] look fixedly or vacantly at someone or something with one's eyes wide open: *he stared at her in amazement* | *Robyn sat staring into space, her mind numb.* ■ (of a person's eyes) be wide open, with a fixed or vacant expression: *her grey eyes stared back at him.* ■ [no obj., with adverbial of direction] be unpleasantly prominent or striking: *the obituaries stared out at us.*
▸ **noun** a long fixed or vacant look: *she gave him a cold stare.*
– PHRASES **be staring one in the face** be glaringly apparent or obvious: *the answer had been staring him in the face.* **be staring something in the face** be on the verge of defeat, death, or another unpleasant fate: *Everton were staring defeat in the face.* **stare someone in the eye** (or **face**) look fixedly or boldly at someone: *I stared him straight in the eye but he didn't recognize me.*
– PHRASAL VERBS **stare someone out** (or **down**) look fixedly at someone until they feel forced to look away: *Vi hissed, meeting his gaze, preparing to stare him out.*
– DERIVATIVES **starer** noun.
– ORIGIN Old English *starian*, of Germanic origin, from a base meaning 'be rigid'.

stare decisis /ˌstɛːrɪ dɪˈsʌɪzɪs, ˌstɑːreɪ dɪˈsiːsɪs/ ▸ **noun** [mass noun] Law the legal principle of determining points in litigation according to precedent.
– ORIGIN Latin, literally 'stand by things decided'.

starfish ▸ **noun** (pl. **same** or **starfishes**) a marine echinoderm (invertebrate) with five or more radiating arms. The undersides of the arms bear tube feet for locomotion and, in predatory species, for opening the shells of molluscs. ● Class Asteroidea.

starflower ▸ **noun** a plant with starlike flowers, in particular: ● a small North American woodland plant (*Trientalis borealis*, family Primulaceae). ● a star of Bethlehem.

star fruit ▸ **noun 1** another term for CARAMBOLA.
2 a small European plant with tiny white flowers and six-pointed star-shaped fruit, found in or close to shallow fresh water. ● *Damasonium alisma*, family Alismataceae.

stargazer ▸ **noun 1** informal an astronomer or astrologer.
2 Austral. informal a horse that turns its head when galloping.
3 a fish of warm seas that normally lies buried in the sand with only its eyes, which are on top of the head, protruding: ● a widely distributed fish that has electric organs (family Uranoscopidae: several genera). ● (**sand stargazer**) a western Atlantic fish (family Dactyloscopidae: several genera).
– DERIVATIVES **stargaze** verb.

stargazy pie /ˈstɑːɡeɪzi/ ▸ **noun** [mass noun] a kind of fish pie traditionally made in Cornwall, with the heads of the fish appearing through the crust.

stark ▸ **adjective 1** severe or bare in appearance or outline: *the ridge formed a stark silhouette against the sky.* ■ unpleasantly or sharply clear: *his position is **in stark contrast to** that of Curran* | *the **stark reality** of life for deprived minorities.*
2 [attrib.] complete; sheer: *he came running back in stark terror.* ■ rare completely naked.
3 archaic or literary stiff, rigid, or incapable of movement: *a human body lying stiff and stark by the stream.* ■ physically strong or powerful: *the dragoons were stark fellows.*
– PHRASES **stark naked** completely naked. **stark raving** (or **staring**) **mad** informal completely crazy.
– DERIVATIVES **starkly** adverb [as submodifier] *the reality is starkly different*, **starkness** noun.
ORIGIN Old English *stearc* 'unyielding, severe', of Germanic origin; related to Dutch *sterk* and German *stark* 'strong'.

Stark effect ▸ **noun** Physics the splitting of a spectrum line into several components by the application of an electric field.
– ORIGIN early 20th cent.: named after Johannes *Stark* (1874–1957), German physicist.

starkers ▸ **adjective** [predic.] Brit. informal completely naked: *he ran starkers across the pitch.*

starlet ▸ **noun 1** informal a young actress with aspirations to become a star: *a Hollywood starlet.* ■ a promising young sports player.
2 another term for CUSHION STAR.

S

starlight ▸ **noun** [mass noun] the light that comes from the stars.

starling[1] ▸ **noun** a gregarious Old World songbird with a straight bill, typically with dark lustrous or iridescent plumage but sometimes brightly coloured. ● Family Sturnidae (the **starling family**): many genera and numerous species, in particular the speckled **common** (or **European**) **starling** (*Sturnus vulgaris*), widely introduced elsewhere. The starling family also includes the mynahs, grackles, and (usually) the oxpeckers.
– ORIGIN Old English *stærlinc*, from *stær* 'starling' (of Germanic origin) + -LING.

starling[2] ▸ **noun** a wooden pile erected with others around or just upstream of a bridge or pier to protect it from the current or floating objects.
– ORIGIN late 17th cent.: perhaps a corruption of dialect *staddling* 'staddle'.

starlit ▸ **adjective** lit or made brighter by stars: *a clear starlit night.*

star network ▸ **noun** see STAR (sense 2 of the noun).

star-nosed mole ▸ **noun** a mole with a number of fleshy radiating tentacles around its nostrils, native to north-eastern North America. ● *Condylura cristata*, family Talpidae.

star of Bethlehem ▶ **noun** a plant of the lily family with star-shaped flowers which typically have green stripes on the outer surface, found in temperate regions of the Old World. ● Genera *Ornithogalum* and *Gagea*, family Liliaceae: several species, including the white-flowered *O. umbellatum* and the yellow-flowered *G. luteum*.

Star of David ▶ **noun** a six-pointed figure consisting of two interlaced equilateral triangles, used as a Jewish and Israeli symbol.

Starr, Ringo (b.1940), English rock and pop drummer; born *Richard Starkey*. He replaced Pete Best in the Beatles in 1962.

starrer ▶ **noun** informal a film which provides a starring role for a particular actor or actress: *the Julia Roberts starrer seized pole position in Italy*.

star route ▶ **noun** US a postal delivery route served by a private contractor.

star ruby ▶ **noun** a cabochon ruby reflecting an opalescent starlike image owing to its regular internal structure.

starry ▶ **adjective** (**starrier**, **starriest**) **1** full of or lit by stars: *a starry sky*. ■ resembling a star in brightness or shape: *tiny white starry flowers*.
2 informal relating to stars in the world of entertainment: *the series had the benefit of a starry cast*.
– DERIVATIVES **starrily adverb**, **starriness noun**.

starry-eyed ▶ **adjective** naively enthusiastic or idealistic: *starry-eyed romantics*.

Stars and Bars ▶ **plural noun** [treated as sing.] historical the flag of the Confederate States of America.

Stars and Stripes ▶ **plural noun** [treated as sing.] the national flag of the US.

star sapphire ▶ **noun** a cabochon sapphire that reflects a starlike image resulting from its regular internal structure.

star shell ▶ **noun** an explosive projectile designed to burst in the air and light up an enemy's position.

starship ▶ **noun** (in science fiction) a large manned spaceship used for interstellar travel.

star sign ▶ **noun** a sign of the zodiac.

star-spangled ▶ **adjective** literary covered, glittering, or decorated with stars: *the star-spangled horizon*. ■ impressively successful: *a star-spangled career*. ■ used humorously with reference to the American national flag and a perceived American identity: *star-spangled decency*.

Star-spangled Banner a song written in 1814 with words composed by Francis Scott Key (1779–1843) and a tune adapted from that of a popular English drinking song, *To Anacreon in Heaven*. It was officially adopted as the US national anthem in 1931.

star stream ▶ **noun** Astronomy a systematic drift of stars in the same general direction within a galaxy.

star-struck ▶ **adjective** fascinated or greatly impressed by famous people, especially those connected with the cinema or the theatre: *I was a star-struck cinema-goer*.

star-studded ▶ **adjective 1** (of the night sky) filled with stars.
2 informal featuring a number of famous people, especially actors or sports players: *a star-studded cast*.

S

star system ▶ **noun** a large number of stars with a perceptible structure; a galaxy.

START ▶ **abbreviation** Strategic Arms Reduction Talks.

start ▶ **verb 1** [no obj.] begin or be reckoned from a particular point in time or space; come into being: *the season starts in September | we ate before the film started | below Roaring Springs the real desert starts*. ■ embark on a continuing action or a new venture: *I'm **starting on** a new book* | [with infinitive or present participle] *I started to chat to him | we plan to start building in the autumn*. ■ use a particular point, action, or circumstance as an opening for a course of action: *the teacher can **start by** capitalizing on children's curiosity | I shall **start with** the case you mention first*. ■ [no obj., with adverbial of direction] begin to move or travel: *we started out into the snow | he started for the door*. ■ [with obj.] begin to engage in (an occupation), live through (a period), or attend (an educational establishment): *she will start school today | he started work at a travel agent | they started their married life*. ■ begin one's working life: *he started as a mess orderly | he **started off** as doctor in the house*. ■ cost at least a specified amount: *fees **start at** £300*.
2 [with obj.] cause to happen or begin: *two men started the blaze | those women started all the trouble | I'm starting a campaign to get the law changed*. ■ cause (a machine) to begin to work: *we had trouble starting the car | he **starts up** his van*. ■ [no obj.] (of a machine) begin operating or being used: *the noise of a lorry **starting up** | there was a moment of silence before the organ started*. ■ cause or enable to begin doing something: *his father **started** him **off** in business* | [with obj. and present participle] *what he said started me thinking*. ■ give a signal to (competitors) to start in a race.
3 [no obj.] jerk or give a small jump from surprise or alarm: *'Oh my!' she said, starting*. ■ [no obj., with adverbial of direction] literary move or appear suddenly: *she had seen Meg start suddenly from a thicket*. ■ (of eyes) bulge so as to appear to burst out of their sockets: *his eyes **started out of** his head like a hare's*. ■ be displaced or displace by pressure or shrinkage: [no obj.] *the mortar in the joints had started*. ■ [with obj.] rouse (game) from its lair.
▶ **noun** [usu. in sing.] **1** the point in time or space at which something has its origin; the beginning: *he takes over as chief executive at the start of next year | the event was a shambles from start to finish | his bicycle was found close to the start of a forest trail*. ■ the point or moment at which a race begins. ■ an act of beginning to do or deal with something: *I can **make a start on** cleaning up | an early start enabled us to avoid the traffic*. ■ used to indicate that a useful initial contribution has been made but that more remains to be done: *if he would tell her who had put him up to it, it would be a start*. ■ a person's position or circumstances at the beginning of their life: *she's anxious to give her baby the best **start in life***. ■ an advantage consisting in having set out in a race or on a journey earlier than one's rivals: *he had a ninety-minute start **on** them*.
2 a sudden movement of surprise or alarm: *she awoke **with a start** | the woman **gave a** nervous **start***. ■ dated a surprising occurrence: *you hear of some rum starts there*.
– PHRASES **don't start** (or **don't you start**) informal used to tell someone not to grumble or criticize: *don't start—I do my fair share*. **for a start** informal used to introduce the first or most important of a number of considerations: *this side are at an advantage—for a start, there are more of them*. **get the start of** dated gain an advantage over. **start a family** conceive one's first child. **start a hare** see **HARE**. **start something** informal cause trouble. **to start with** at first: *she wasn't very keen on the idea to start with*. ■ as the first thing to be taken into account: *to start with, I was feeling down*.
– PHRASAL VERBS **start again** chiefly Brit. abandon what one is doing and make a new beginning: *while I was writing this essay my computer froze and I had to start again*. **start in** informal begin doing something, especially talking: *people groan when she starts in about her acting ambitions*. ■ (**start in on**) N. Amer. begin to do or deal with: *she started in on her face*. ■ (**start in on**) N. Amer. attack verbally; begin to criticize. **start off** (or **start someone/thing off**) begin (or cause someone or something to begin) to operate or do something: *treatment should start off with attention to diet | what started you off on this search?* **start on** informal begin to criticize someone: *she started on about my not having proper furniture*. **start over** North American way of saying **START AGAIN**: *could you face going back to school and starting over?* **start out** (or **up**) embark on a venture or undertaking, especially a commercial one: *the company will start out with a hundred employees*.
– ORIGIN Old English *styrtan* 'to caper, leap', of Germanic origin; related to Dutch *storten* 'push' and German *stürzen* 'fall headlong, fling'. From the sense 'sudden movement' arose the sense 'initiation of movement, setting out on a journey' and hence 'beginning of a process, etc.'.

starter ▶ **noun 1** a person or thing that starts in a specified way: *I'm just a slow starter*. ■ a person who gives the signal for the start of a race. ■ [with adj.] a horse, competitor, or player taking part in a race or game at the start: *the trainer has confirmed Cool Ground as a definite starter*. ■ Baseball the pitcher who starts the game. ■ a topic, question, or other item with which to start a group discussion or course of study: *material to act as a **starter for** discussion*.
2 an automatic device for starting a machine, especially the engine of a vehicle. ■ a railway signal controlling the starting of trains from a station or other location.
3 chiefly Brit. the first course of a meal.
4 informal a plan or idea that has a chance of succeeding and is therefore worthy of consideration: *she began to think that she must move away, yet she knew that it was not even a starter*.
5 (also **starter culture**) a bacterial culture used to initiate souring in making yogurt, cheese, or butter. ■ a preparation of chemicals to initiate the breakdown of vegetable matter in making compost.
– PHRASES **for starters** informal first of all; to start with. **under starter's orders** (of horses, runners, or other competitors) ready to start a race and just waiting for the signal.

starter home ▶ **noun** a compact house or flat specifically designed and built to meet the requirements of young people buying their first home.

starter kit (also **starter pack**) ▶ **noun** a set of articles or equipment providing the items and instructions essential for someone taking up a particular activity or starting a process for the first time.

starting block ▶ **noun** (usu. **starting blocks**) a shaped rigid block for bracing the feet of a runner at the start of a race.

starting gate ▶ **noun** (usu. **the starting gate**) a restraining structure incorporating a barrier that is raised at the start of a race, typically in horse racing and skiing, to ensure a simultaneous start.

starting handle ▶ **noun** chiefly historical a crank for starting the engine of a car.

starting pistol ▶ **noun** a pistol used to give the signal for the start of a race.

starting point ▶ **noun** a place that marks the beginning of a journey. ■ a basis for or introduction to study, discussion, or further development.

starting post ▶ **noun** a post or other marker indicating the place at which a race is to start.

starting price ▶ **noun** the final odds at the start of a horse race.

starting stall ▶ **noun** see **STALL** (sense 2 of the noun).

startle ▶ **verb** [with obj.] cause to feel sudden shock or alarm: *a sudden sound in the doorway startled her* | [with infinitive] *he was startled to see a column of smoke* | (as adj. **startled**) *her startled eyes met his*.
– ORIGIN Old English *steartlian* 'kick, struggle', from the base of **START**. The early sense gave rise to 'move quickly, caper' (typically said of cattle), whence 'cause to react with fear' (late 16th cent.).

startling ▶ **adjective** very surprising, astonishing, or remarkable: *he bore a startling likeness to their father | she had startling blue eyes*.
– DERIVATIVES **startlingly adverb** [as submodifier] *a startlingly good memory*.

Start Point a headland on the south coast of Devon, to the south-west of Torquay.

start-up ▶ **noun** [mass noun] the action or process of setting something in motion: *the start-up of marketing in Europe* | [as modifier] *start-up costs*. ■ [count noun] a newly established business: ***problems facing start-ups** and small firms in rural areas*.

star turn ▶ **noun** the person or act that gives the most heralded or impressive performance in a programme.

starvation ▶ **noun** [mass noun] suffering or death caused by lack of food: *thousands died of starvation*.

starve ▶ **verb 1** suffer or die or cause to suffer or die from hunger: [no obj.] *she left her animals to starve | seven million **starved to death*** | (as adj. **starving**) *the world's starving children* | [with obj.] *for a while she had considered starving herself*. ■ (**be starving** or **starved**) informal feel very hungry: *I don't know about you, but I'm starving*. ■ [with obj.] (**starve someone out** or **into**) force someone out of (a place) or into (a specified state) by starvation: *the Royalists were starved out after eleven days | German U-boats hoping to starve Britain into submission*. ■ [with obj.] (usu. **be starved of** or US **for**) deprive of something necessary: *the arts are being starved of funds*.
2 [no obj.] archaic or dialect be freezing cold: *pull down that window for we are perfectly starving here*.
– ORIGIN Old English *steorfan* 'to die', of Germanic origin, probably from a base meaning 'be rigid' (compare with **STARE**); related to Dutch *sterven* and German *sterben*.

starveling /ˈstɑːvlɪŋ/ archaic ▶ **noun** an undernourished or emaciated person or animal.
▶ **adjective** lacking enough food; emaciated: *a starveling child*.

Star Wars popular name for **STRATEGIC DEFENSE INITIATIVE**.

starwort ▶ **noun** any of a number of plants with star-like flowers or leaves. ● *Stellaria* (family Caryophyllaceae), *Callitriche* (family Callitrichaceae), and other genera: several species, including the greater stitchwort.

stash[1] informal ▶ **verb** [with obj. and adverbial of place] store (something) safely in a secret place: *their wealth had been **stashed away** in Swiss banks*.

▶ **noun 1** a secret store of something: *the man grudgingly handed over **a stash of** notes.* ■ a quantity of an illegal drug, especially one kept for personal use: *one prisoner tried to swallow his stash.*
2 dated a hiding place or hideout.
– ORIGIN late 18th cent.: of unknown origin.

stash[2] ▶ **noun** US informal a moustache.
– ORIGIN 1940s: shortened form.

Stasi /ˈʃtɑːzi, ˈʃtɑː-/ the internal security force of the former German Democratic Republic, abolished in 1989.
– ORIGIN German, from *Sta(ats)si(cherheitsdienst)* 'state security service'.

stasis /ˈsteɪsɪs, ˈsta-/ ▶ **noun** [mass noun] formal or technical
1 a period or state of inactivity or equilibrium.
■ Medicine a stoppage of flow of a body fluid.
2 civil strife.
– ORIGIN mid 18th cent.: modern Latin, from Greek, literally 'standing, stoppage', from *sta-* base of *histanai* 'to stand'.

-stasis ▶ **combining form** (pl. **-stases**) Physiology slowing down; stopping: *haemostasis.*
– DERIVATIVES **-static combining form** in corresponding adjectives.
– ORIGIN from Greek *stasis* 'standing, stoppage'.

stat[1] /stat/ ▶ **abbreviation** informal ■ photostat. ■ statistic. ■ thermostat.

stat[2] /stat/ ▶ **adverb** (in a medical direction or prescription) immediately.
– ORIGIN late 19th cent.: abbreviation of Latin *statim.*

-stat ▶ **combining form** denoting instruments, substances, etc. maintaining a controlled state: *thermostat* | *haemostat.*
– ORIGIN partly from *(helio)stat*, partly a back-formation from **STATIC**.

statant /ˈsteɪtənt/ ▶ **adjective** [usu. postpositive] Heraldry (of an animal) standing with all four paws on the ground.
– ORIGIN late 15th cent.: formed irregularly from Latin *stat-* 'fixed, stationary' (from the verb *stare* 'to stand') + **-ANT**.

state ▶ **noun 1** the particular condition that someone or something is in at a specific time: *the state of the company's finances* | *we're worried about her **state of mind**.* ■ a physical condition as regards internal or molecular form or structure: *water in a liquid state.* ■ **(a state)** informal an agitated or anxious condition: *don't **get into a state**.* ■ informal a dirty or untidy condition: *look at the state of you—what a mess!* ■ Physics short for **QUANTUM STATE**.
2 a nation or territory considered as an organized political community under one government: *Germany, Italy, and other European states.* ■ an organized political community or area forming part of a federal republic: *the German state of Bavaria.* ■ **(the States)** informal term for **UNITED STATES**.
3 the civil government of a country: *services provided by the state* | [in combination] *state-owned companies* | [mass noun] *a minister engaged in **matters of state*** | [as modifier] *state education.* ■ **(the States)** the legislative body in Jersey, Guernsey, and Alderney.
4 [mass noun] pomp and ceremony associated with monarchy or high levels of government: *he was **buried in state**.* ■ [as modifier] involving the ceremony associated with a head of state: *the Queen paid a state visit to Malaysia.*
5 a specified impression taken from an etched or engraved plate at a particular stage. ■ a particular printed version of the first edition of a book, distinguished from others by prepublication changes.
▶ **verb 1** [reporting verb] express something definitely or clearly in speech or writing: [with clause] *the report stated that more than 51 per cent of voters failed to participate* | [with direct speech] *'Money hasn't changed me,' she stated firmly* | [with obj.] *people will be invited to state their views.* ■ [with obj.] chiefly Law specify the facts of (a case) for consideration: *judges must give both sides an equal opportunity to state their case.*
2 [with obj.] Music present or introduce (a theme or melody) in a composition.
– PHRASES **state of affairs** (or **things**) a situation or set of circumstances: *the survey revealed a sorry state of affairs in schools.* **state of the art** the most recent stage in the development of a product, incorporating the newest ideas and features: [as modifier] *a new state-of-the-art hospital.* **state of emergency** a situation of national danger or disaster in which a government suspends normal constitutional procedures in order to regain control: *the government has declared a state of emergency.* **state of grace** Theology a condition of being free from sin. **state of life** (in religious contexts) a person's occupation, calling, or status. **state of play** Brit. the score at a particular time in a cricket or football match. ■ the current situation in an ongoing process. **state of war** a situation when war has been declared or is in progress.
– DERIVATIVES **statable adjective**.
– ORIGIN Middle English (as a noun): partly a shortening of **ESTATE**, partly from Latin *status* 'manner of standing, condition' (see **STATUS**). The current verb senses date from the mid 17th cent.

state capitalism ▶ **noun** [mass noun] a political system in which the state has control of production and the use of capital.

statecraft ▶ **noun** [mass noun] the skilful management of state affairs; statesmanship: *issues of statecraft require great deliberation.*

stated ▶ **adjective** clearly expressed or identified; specified: *the stated aim of the programme* | *do not exceed the stated dose.*

State Department (in the US) the department in the government dealing with foreign affairs.

State Enrolled Nurse (abbrev.: **SEN**) ▶ **noun** (in the UK) a nurse enrolled on a state register and having a qualification lower than that of a State Registered Nurse.

state function ▶ **noun** Physics a quantity in thermodynamics, such as entropy or enthalpy, that has a unique value for each given state of a system.

statehood ▶ **noun** [mass noun] the status of being a recognized independent nation: *their aspirations for independent statehood have been consistently frustrated.*

state house ▶ **noun 1** (in the US) the building where the legislature of a state meets.
2 NZ a private house that is owned and let by the government.

stateless ▶ **adjective** (of a person) not recognized as a citizen of any country.
– DERIVATIVES **statelessness noun**.

statelet ▶ **noun** a small state, especially one that is closely affiliated to or has emerged from the break-up of a larger state.

stately ▶ **adjective** (**statelier**, **stateliest**) impressive or grand in size, appearance, or manner: *a stately 19th-century mansion.* ■ slow, formal, and dignified: *a stately procession.*
– DERIVATIVES **stateliness noun**.

stately home ▶ **noun** Brit. a large and impressive house that is occupied or was formerly occupied by an aristocratic family.

state machine ▶ **noun** Electronics a device which can be in one of a set number of stable conditions depending on its previous condition and on the present values of its inputs.

statement ▶ **noun** a definite or clear expression of something in speech or writing: *do you agree with this statement?* | *this is correct as **a statement of fact*** | [mass noun] *Minton's love of clear statement.* ■ an official account of facts, views, or plans, especially one for release to the media: *the ministers issued a joint statement calling for negotiations.* ■ a formal account of events given by a witness, defendant, or other party to the police or in a court of law: *she **made a statement** to the police.* ■ a document setting out items of debit and credit between a bank or other organization and a customer. ■ Music a presentation of a theme or melody within a composition. ■ (in the UK) an official assessment made by a local education authority concerning a child's special educational needs.
▶ **verb** [with obj.] Brit. officially assess (a child) as having special educational needs.

statement of claim ▶ **noun** English Law a pleading served by the plaintiff in a High Court action, containing the allegations made against the defendant and the relief sought by the plaintiff. See also **CLAIM** (sense 1 of the noun).

Staten Island /ˈstat(ə)n/ an island borough of New York City, in the south-west of the city; pop. 487,407 (2008).
– ORIGIN named by early Dutch settlers after the *Staten* or States General of the Netherlands.

State of the Union message (also **State of the Union address**) ▶ **noun** a yearly address delivered in January by the President of the US to Congress, giving the administration's view of the state of the nation and plans for legislation.

state pension ▶ **noun** see **PENSION**[1].

state prisoner ▶ **noun** another term for **PRISONER OF STATE**.

stater /ˈsteɪtə/ ▶ **noun** an ancient Greek gold or silver coin.
– ORIGIN via late Latin from Greek *statēr*, from a base meaning 'weigh'.

State Registered Nurse (abbrev.: **SRN**) ▶ **noun** (in the UK) a nurse enrolled on a state register and more highly qualified than a State Enrolled Nurse.

stateroom /ˈsteɪtruːm, -rʊm/ ▶ **noun** a large room in a palace or public building, for use on formal occasions. ■ a captain's or superior officer's room on a ship. ■ a private compartment on a ship. ■ N. Amer. a private compartment on a train.

state's attorney ▶ **noun** US a lawyer representing a state in court, especially in a criminal proceeding.

state school ▶ **noun** Brit. a school that is funded and controlled by the state and for which no fees are charged.

state secret ▶ **noun** a sensitive issue or piece of information which is kept secret by the government. ■ humorous an important and closely guarded piece of information: *her marriage was on the rocks, which was hardly a state secret at the time.*

state's evidence ▶ **noun** [mass noun] US Law evidence for the prosecution given by a participant in or accomplice to the crime being tried.

States General (also **Estates General**) ▶ **noun** the legislative body in the Netherlands from the 15th to 18th centuries, and in France until 1789, representing the three estates of the realm (i.e. the clergy, the nobility, and the commons).

stateside /ˈsteɪtsʌɪd/ ▶ **adjective & adverb** informal, chiefly N. Amer. of, in, or towards the US (used in reference to the US from elsewhere or from the geographically separate states of Alaska and Hawaii): [as adj.] *stateside police departments* | *they were headed stateside.*

statesman /ˈsteɪtsmən/ (or **stateswoman**) ▶ **noun** (pl. **statesmen** or **stateswomen**) a skilled, experienced, and respected political leader or figure.
– DERIVATIVES **statesmanlike adjective**, **statesmanship noun**.
– ORIGIN late 16th cent.: from *state's man*, translating French *homme d'état.*

state socialism ▶ **noun** [mass noun] a political system in which the state has control of industries and services.

statesperson ▶ **noun** (pl. **statespersons** or **statespeople**) a statesman or stateswoman (used as a neutral alternative).

states' rights ▶ **plural noun** (in the US) the rights and powers held by individual states rather than by the federal government.

state trial ▶ **noun** a trial in which prosecution is made by the state.

state university ▶ **noun** (in the US) a university managed by the public authorities of a particular state.

state vector ▶ **noun** Physics a vector in a space whose dimensions correspond to all the independent wave functions of a system, the instantaneous value of the vector conveying all possible information about the state of the system at that instant.

statewide ▶ **adjective & adverb** extending throughout a particular state in the US: [as adj.] *a statewide health system.*

static /ˈstatɪk/ ▶ **adjective 1** lacking in movement, action, or change, especially in an undesirable or uninteresting way: *demand has grown in what was a fairly static market* | *the whole ballet appeared too static.* ■ Computing (of a process or variable) not able to be changed during a set period, for example while a program is running.
2 Physics concerned with bodies at rest or forces in equilibrium. Often contrasted with **DYNAMIC**. ■ acting as weight but not moving. ■ relating to statics.
3 (of an electric charge) having gathered on or in an object that cannot conduct a current.
4 Computing (of a memory or store) not needing to be periodically refreshed by an applied voltage.
▶ **noun** [mass noun] crackling or hissing noises on a telephone, radio, or other telecommunication system. ■ short for **STATIC ELECTRICITY**. ■ N. Amer. informal angry or critical talk or behaviour: *the reception was going sour, breaking up into static.*
– DERIVATIVES **statically adverb**.
– ORIGIN late 16th cent. (denoting the science of weight and its effects): via modern Latin from Greek *statikē (tekhnē)* 'science of weighing'; the adjective

S

from modern Latin *staticus*, from Greek *statikos* 'causing to stand', from the verb *histanai*. Sense 1 of the adjective dates from the mid 19th cent.

static cling ▸ **noun** [mass noun] the adhering of a garment to the wearer's body or to another garment, caused by a build-up of static electricity.

statice /ˈstatɪsi/ ▸ **noun** another term for SEA LAVENDER.
– ORIGIN mid 18th cent.: from modern Latin *statice* (former genus name), based on Greek, feminine of *statikos* 'causing to stand still' (with reference to medicinal use of the plant to staunch blood).

static electricity ▸ **noun** [mass noun] a stationary electric charge, typically produced by friction, which causes sparks or crackling or the attraction of dust or hair.

static line ▸ **noun** a length of cord used instead of a rip cord for opening a parachute, attached at one end to the aircraft and temporarily snapped to the parachute at the other.

static pressure ▸ **noun** [mass noun] Physics the pressure of a fluid on a body when the latter is at rest relative to it.

statics ▸ **plural noun 1** [usu. treated as sing.] the branch of mechanics concerned with bodies at rest and forces in equilibrium. Compare with DYNAMICS (sense 1).
2 another term for STATIC.

statin /ˈstatɪn/ ▸ **noun** Medicine any of a group of drugs which act to reduce levels of cholesterol in the blood.
– ORIGIN 1980s: from *stat-* as in -STAT + -IN[1].

station ▸ **noun 1** a place where passenger trains stop on a railway line, typically with platforms and buildings: *a railway station* | [in names] *Paddington Station.* ■ a bus or coach station.
2 [usu. with modifier] a place or building where a specified activity or service is based: *a research station in the rainforest* | *coastal radar stations.* ■ a small military base, especially of a specified kind: *a naval station.* ■ N. Amer. a subsidiary post office. ■ Austral./NZ a large sheep or cattle farm.
3 [with modifier] a company involved in broadcasting of a specified kind: *a radio station.*
4 the place where someone or something stands or is placed on military or other duty: *the lookout resumed his station in the bow.* ■ [count noun] dated one's social rank or position: *Karen was getting ideas* **above her station***.*
5 Botany a particular site at which an interesting or rare plant grows.
6 short for STATIONS OF THE CROSS.
▸ **verb** [with obj. and adverbial of place] put in or assign to a specified place for a particular purpose, especially a military one: *troops* **were stationed in** *the town* | *a young girl had* **stationed herself** *by the door.*
– ORIGIN Middle English (as a noun): via Old French from Latin *statio(n-)*, from *stare* 'to stand'. Early use referred generally to 'position', especially 'position in life, status', and specifically, in ecclesiastical use, to 'a holy place of pilgrimage (visited as one of a succession'). The verb dates from the late 16th cent.

stationary ▸ **adjective** not moving or not intended to be moved: *a car collided with a stationary vehicle.* ■ Astronomy (of a planet) having no apparent motion in longitude. ■ not changing in quantity or condition: *a stationary population.*
– ORIGIN late Middle English: from Latin *stationarius* (originally in the sense 'belonging to a military station'), from *statio(n-)* 'standing' (see STATION).

> **USAGE** The words **stationary** and **stationery** are often confused. **Stationary** is an adjective which means 'not moving or not intended to be moved', as in *a car collided with a stationary vehicle*, whereas **stationery** is a noun which means 'writing and other office materials', as in *I wrote to my father on the hotel stationery.*

stationary bicycle (also **stationary bike**) ▸ **noun** an exercise bike.

stationary engine ▸ **noun** an engine that remains in a fixed position, especially one that drives generators or other machinery in a building.

stationary point ▸ **noun** Mathematics a point on a curve where the gradient is zero.

stationary state ▸ **noun** an unvarying condition in a physical process.

stationary wave ▸ **noun** Physics another term for STANDING WAVE.

station break ▸ **noun** N. Amer. a pause between broadcast programmes for an announcement of the identity of the station transmitting them.

stationer ▸ **noun** a person or shop selling paper, pens, and other writing and office materials.
– ORIGIN Middle English (in the sense 'bookseller'): from medieval Latin *stationarius* 'tradesman (at a fixed location, i.e. not itinerant)'. Compare with STATIONARY.

stationery ▸ **noun** [mass noun] writing and other office materials: *a range of stationery* | [as modifier] *a stationery supplier.*

> **USAGE** On the confusion of **stationery** and **stationary**, see **USAGE** at **STATIONARY**.

Stationery Office ▸ **noun** (in the UK) a government department that publishes governmental publications and provides stationery for government offices.

station hand ▸ **noun** Austral./NZ a worker on a large sheep or cattle farm.

station house ▸ **noun** N. Amer. a police or fire station.

station-keeping ▸ **noun** [mass noun] the maintenance of a ship's proper position relative to others in a fleet.

stationmaster ▸ **noun** Brit. an official in charge of a railway station.

station pointer ▸ **noun** a navigational instrument that fixes a ship's position on a chart by determining its place relative to two landmarks or conspicuous objects at sea.

station sergeant ▸ **noun** Brit. a sergeant in charge of a police station.

Stations of the Cross ▸ **plural noun** a series of fourteen pictures or carvings representing successive incidents during Jesus's progress from his condemnation by Pilate to his crucifixion and burial, before which devotions are performed in some Churches.

station wagon ▸ **noun** chiefly N. Amer. an estate car.

statism /ˈsteɪtɪz(ə)m/ ▸ **noun** [mass noun] a political system in which the state has substantial centralized control over social and economic affairs: *the rise of authoritarian statism.*
– DERIVATIVES **statist noun & adjective.**

statistic ▸ **noun** a fact or piece of data obtained from a study of a large quantity of numerical data: *the statistics show that the crime rate has increased.* ■ an event or person regarded as no more than such a piece of data (used to suggest an inappropriately impersonal approach): *he was just another statistic.*
▸ **adjective** another term for STATISTICAL.
– ORIGIN late 18th cent.: from German *statistisch* (adjective), *Statistik* (noun).

statistical ▸ **adjective** relating to the use of statistics: *a statistical comparison.*
– DERIVATIVES **statistically adverb** [sentence adverb] *these differences were not statistically significant.*

statistical inference ▸ **noun** [mass noun] the theory, methods, and practice of forming judgements about the parameters of a population and the reliability of statistical relationships, typically on the basis of random sampling.

statistical linguistics ▸ **plural noun** [treated as sing.] the application of statistical techniques to language analysis, typically using a large machine-readable corpus, in order to discover general principles of linguistic behaviour, genre difference, etc.

statistical mechanics ▸ **plural noun** [treated as sing.] the description of physical phenomena in terms of a statistical treatment of the behaviour of large numbers of atoms or molecules, especially as regards the distribution of energy among them.

statistical physics ▸ **plural noun** [treated as sing.] a branch of physics concerned with large numbers of particles to which statistics can be applied.

statistical significance ▸ **noun** see SIGNIFICANCE.

statistical tables ▸ **plural noun** the values of the cumulative distribution functions, probability functions, or probability density functions of certain common distributions presented as reference tables for different values of their parameters.

statistician ▸ **noun** an expert in the preparation and analysis of statistics.

statistics ▸ **plural noun** [treated as sing.] the practice or science of collecting and analysing numerical data in large quantities, especially for the purpose of inferring proportions in a whole from those in a representative sample.

Statius /ˈsteɪʃəs/, Publius Papinius (*c.*45–96 AD), Roman poet. He is best known for the *Silvae*, a miscellany of poems addressed to friends, and the *Thebais*, an epic concerning the bloody quarrel between the sons of Oedipus.

stative /ˈsteɪtɪv/ Linguistics ▸ **adjective** (of a verb) expressing a state or condition rather than an activity or event, such as *be* or *know*, as opposed to *run* or *grow*. Contrasted with DYNAMIC.
▸ **noun** a stative verb.
– ORIGIN mid 17th cent.: from Latin *stativus*, from *stat-* 'stopped, standing', from the verb *stare*.

stato- ▸ **combining form** relating to statics: *statocyst.*
– ORIGIN from Greek *statos* 'standing'.

statoblast /ˈstatə(ʊ)blast/ ▸ **noun** Zoology (in bryozoans) a resistant reproductive body produced asexually.

statocyst ▸ **noun** Zoology a small organ of balance and orientation in some aquatic invertebrates, consisting of a sensory vesicle or cell containing statoliths. Also called OTOCYST.

statolith ▸ **noun** Zoology a calcareous particle in the statocysts of invertebrates, which stimulates sensory receptors in response to gravity, so enabling balance and orientation. ■ another term for OTOLITH.

stator /ˈsteɪtə/ ▸ **noun** the stationary portion of an electric generator or motor, especially of an induction motor. ■ a row of small stationary aerofoils fixed to the casing of an axial-flow turbine, positioned between the rotors.
– ORIGIN late 19th cent.: from STATIONARY, on the pattern of *rotor*.

statoscope ▸ **noun** a form of aneroid barometer for measuring minute variations of pressure, used especially to indicate the altitude of an aircraft.
– ORIGIN early 20th cent.: from Greek *statos* 'standing' + -SCOPE.

stats ▸ **plural noun** informal short for STATISTICS.

statuary /ˈstatjʊəri, -tʃʊə-/ ▸ **noun** [mass noun] statues regarded collectively: *classical statuary.* ■ archaic the art or practice of making statues. ■ [count noun] archaic a sculptor.
– ORIGIN mid 16th cent.: from Latin *statuarius*, from *statua* (see STATUE).

statuary marble ▸ **noun** [mass noun] fine-grained white marble suitable for making statues.

statue /ˈstatjuː, -tʃuː/ ▸ **noun** a carved or cast figure of a person or animal, especially one that is life-size or larger.
– DERIVATIVES **statued adjective.**
– ORIGIN Middle English: from Old French, from Latin *statua*, from *stare* 'to stand'.

Statue of Liberty see LIBERTY, STATUE OF.

statuesque /ˌstatjʊˈɛsk, -tʃʊ-/ ▸ **adjective 1** (of a woman) attractively tall, graceful, and dignified: *her statuesque beauty.*
2 reminiscent of a statue in size, posture, or stillness: *frozen, statuesque attitudes.*
– DERIVATIVES **statuesquely adverb, statuesqueness noun.**
– ORIGIN late 18th cent.: from STATUE, on the pattern of *picturesque*.

statuette ▸ **noun** a small statue or figurine, especially one that is smaller than life-size.
– ORIGIN mid 19th cent.: from French, diminutive of *statue*.

stature ▸ **noun** [mass noun] a person's natural height: *a man of short stature* | *she was small in stature.* ■ importance or reputation gained by ability or achievement: *an architect of international stature.*
– DERIVATIVES **statured adjective** [in combination] *a short-statured fourteen-year-old.*
– ORIGIN Middle English: via Old French from Latin *statura*, from *stare* 'to stand'. The sense 'importance' dates from the mid 19th cent.

status ▸ **noun 1** relative social or professional position; standing: *an improvement in the status of women.* ■ [mass noun] high rank or social standing: *those who enjoy wealth and status.* ■ the official classification given to a person, country, or organization, determining their rights or responsibilities: *the duchy had been elevated to the status of a principality.*
2 the situation at a particular time during a process: *an update on the status of the bill.*
– ORIGIN late 18th cent. (as a legal term meaning 'legal standing'): from Latin, literally 'standing', from *stare* 'to stand'.

status asthmaticus /ˌsteɪtəs asˈmatɪkəs/ ▸ **noun** [mass noun] Medicine a severe condition in which asthma attacks follow one another without pause.
– ORIGIN modern Latin.

S

status bar ▸ **noun** Computing a horizontal bar, usually at the bottom of the screen or window, showing information about a document being edited or a program running.

status epilepticus /ˌɛpɪˈlɛptɪkəs/ ▸ **noun** [mass noun] Medicine a dangerous condition in which epileptic fits follow one another without recovery of consciousness between them.
– ORIGIN modern Latin.

status quo /ˈkwəʊ/ ▸ **noun** (usu. **the status quo**) the existing state of affairs, especially regarding social or political issues: *they have a vested interest in maintaining the status quo.*
– ORIGIN Latin, literally 'the state in which'.

status quo ante /kwəʊ ˈanti/ ▸ **noun** (usu. **the status quo ante**) the previously existing state of affairs.
– ORIGIN Latin, literally 'the state in which before'.

status symbol ▸ **noun** a possession that is taken to indicate a person's wealth or high social or professional status.

statute /ˈstatjuːt, -tʃuːt/ ▸ **noun** a written law passed by a legislative body: *the Act consolidated statutes dealing with non-fatal offences* | [mass noun] *immunities granted to trade unions* ***by statute***. ■ a rule of an organization or institution: *the appointment will be subject to the statutes of the university.* ■ archaic (in biblical use) a law or decree made by a sovereign, or by God.
– ORIGIN Middle English: from Old French *statut*, from late Latin *statutum*, neuter past participle of Latin *statuere* 'set up' from *status* 'standing' (see **STATUS**).

statute-barred ▸ **adjective** English Law (especially of a debt claim) no longer legally enforceable owing to a prescribed period of limitation having lapsed.

statute book ▸ **noun** a book in which laws are written. ■ (**the statute book**) a nation's laws regarded collectively: *the bill failed to* ***reach the statute book.***

statute law ▸ **noun** [mass noun] the body of principles and rules of law laid down in statutes. Compare with **COMMON LAW**, **CASE LAW**.

statute mile ▸ **noun** see **MILE**.

statute of limitations ▸ **noun** Law a statute prescribing a period of limitation for the bringing of actions of certain kinds.

statutes at large ▸ **plural noun** chiefly N. Amer. a country's statutes in their original version, regardless of later modifications.

statutory /ˈstatjʊt(ə)ri, -tʃʊ-/ ▸ **adjective** required, permitted, or enacted by statute: *statutory controls over prices.* ■ having come to be required or expected through being done or made regularly: *the statutory Christmas phone call to his mother.*
– DERIVATIVES **statutorily adverb**.

statutory declaration ▸ **noun** Law a prescribed declaration, made under statutory authority, which may in certain cases be substituted for a statement on oath.

statutory instrument ▸ **noun** Law a government or executive order of subordinate legislation.

statutory order ▸ **noun** Law former term for **STATUTORY INSTRUMENT**.

statutory rape ▸ **noun** [mass noun] US Law sexual intercourse with a minor.

statutory tenant ▸ **noun** Law a person who is legally entitled to remain in a property although their original tenancy has expired.

staunch[1] /stɔːn(t)ʃ/ ▸ **adjective 1** very loyal and committed in attitude: *a staunch supporter of the anti-nuclear lobby* | *a staunch Catholic.*
2 (of a wall) of strong or firm construction. ■ (also **stanch**) archaic (of a ship) watertight.
– DERIVATIVES **staunchly adverb** [as submodifier] *a staunchly Royalist county*, **staunchness noun**.
– ORIGIN late Middle English (in the sense 'watertight'): from Old French *estanche*, feminine of *estanc*, from a Romance base meaning 'dried up, weary'. Sense 1 dates from the early 17th cent.

staunch[2] /stɔːn(t)ʃ, stɑːn(t)ʃ/ (chiefly US also **stanch**) ▸ **verb** [with obj.] stop or restrict (a flow of blood) from a wound: *he staunched the blood with whatever came to hand* | figurative *the company did nothing to staunch the tide of rumours.* ■ stop the flow of blood from (a wound).
– ORIGIN Middle English: from Old French *estanchier*, from the base of **STAUNCH**[1].

staurolite /ˈstɔːrəlʌɪt/ ▸ **noun** [mass noun] a brown glassy mineral that occurs as hexagonal prisms often twinned in the shape of a cross. It consists of a silicate of aluminium and iron.
– ORIGIN early 19th cent.: from Greek *stauros* 'cross' + **-LITE**.

Stavanger /stəˈvaŋə/ a seaport in SW Norway; pop. 119,586 (2008). It is an important centre servicing offshore oilfields in the North Sea.

stave ▸ **noun 1** a vertical wooden post or plank in a building or other structure. ■ any of the lengths of wood fixed side by side to make a barrel, bucket, or other container. ■ a strong wooden stick or iron pole used as a weapon.
2 (also **staff**) Music, Brit. a set of five parallel lines on any one or between any adjacent two of which a note is written to indicate its pitch.
3 a verse or stanza of a poem.
▸ **verb** [with obj.] **1** (past and past participle **staved** or **stove**) (**stave something in**) break something by forcing it inwards or piercing it roughly: *the door was staved in.*
2 (past and past participle **staved**) (**stave something off**) avert or delay something bad or dangerous: *a reassuring presence can stave off a panic attack.*
– ORIGIN Middle English: back-formation from *staves*, archaic plural of **STAFF**[1]. Current senses of the verb date from the early 17th cent.

stave church ▸ **noun** a church of a type built in Norway from the 11th to the 13th century, the walls of which were constructed of upright planks or staves.

stave rhyme ▸ **noun** [mass noun] alliteration, especially in old Germanic poetry.

stavesacre /ˈsteɪvˌzeɪkə/ ▸ **noun** a southern European larkspur whose seeds were formerly used as an insecticide. ● *Delphinium staphisagria*, family Ranunculaceae.
– ORIGIN late Middle English: via Latin from Greek *staphis agria* 'wild raisin'.

Stavropol /ˈstavrəpɒl, stavˈrɒp(ə)l/ **1** a krai (administrative territory) in southern Russia, in the northern Caucasus. ■ its capital city; pop. 363,700 (est. 2008).
2 former name (until 1964) for **TOGLIATTI**.

stay[1] ▸ **verb 1** [no obj., usu. with adverbial] remain in the same place: *you stay here and I'll be back soon* | *Jenny decided to stay at home with their young child* | *he stayed with the firm as a consultant.* ■ (**stay for/to**) delay leaving so as to join in (an activity): *why not stay to lunch?*
2 [no obj., with complement or adverbial] remain in a specified state or position: *her ability to stay calm* | *tactics used to stay in power* | *I managed to stay out of trouble.*
3 [no obj.] (of a person) live somewhere temporarily as a visitor or guest: *the girls had gone to stay with friends* | *Minton invited him to* ***stay the night.*** ■ Scottish & S. African live permanently: *where do you stay?*
4 [with obj.] stop, delay, or prevent (something), in particular suspend or postpone (judicial proceedings) or refrain from pressing (charges). ■ assuage (hunger) for a short time: *I grabbed something to stay the pangs of hunger.* ■ literary curb; check: *he tries to stay the destructive course of barbarism.* ■ [no obj., in imperative] archaic wait a moment in order to allow someone time to think or speak: *stay, stand apart, I know not which is which.*
5 [with obj.] literary support or prop up.
▸ **noun 1** a period of staying somewhere, in particular of living somewhere temporarily as a visitor or guest: *an overnight stay at a luxury hotel.*
2 literary a curb or check: *there is likely to be a good public library as a stay against boredom.* ■ Law a suspension or postponement of judicial proceedings: *a stay of prosecution.*
3 a device used as a brace or support. ■ (**stays**) historical a corset made of two pieces laced together and stiffened by strips of whalebone.
4 [mass noun] archaic power of endurance.
– PHRASES **be here** (or **have come**) **to stay** informal be permanent or widely accepted: *the private sector is here to stay and likely to expand.* **stay the course** (or **distance**) keep going strongly to the end of a race or contest. ■ pursue a difficult task to the end. **stay of execution** a delay in carrying out a court order. **stay put** remain somewhere without moving or being moved. **stay well** S. African said as an expression of good wishes by a person leaving.
– PHRASAL VERBS **stay behind** remain in a classroom or school at the end of teaching, especially to receive punishment: *please stay behind after class – I would like to talk to you regarding your lateness.* **stay on** continue to study, work, or be somewhere after others have left: *75 per cent of sixteen-year-olds stay on in full-time education.* **stay over** (of a guest or visitor) sleep somewhere, especially at someone's home, for the night: *children stay over at each other's houses more often than they did.* **stay up** not go to bed: *they stayed up all night.* **stay with 1** remain in the mind or memory of: *Gary's words stayed with her all evening.* **2** continue or persevere with (an activity or task): *the incentive needed to stay with a healthy diet.* **3** (of a competitor or player) keep up with (another) during a race or match.
– ORIGIN late Middle English (as a verb): from Anglo-Norman French *estai-*, stem of Old French *ester*, from Latin *stare* 'to stand'; in the sense 'support' (sense 5 of the verb and sense 3 of the noun), partly from Old French *estaye* (noun), *estayer* (verb), of Germanic origin.

stay[2] ▸ **noun** a large rope, wire, or rod used to support a ship's mast, leading from the masthead to another mast or spar or down to another part of the ship. ■ a guy or rope supporting a flagstaff or other upright pole. ■ a supporting wire or cable on an aircraft.
▸ **verb** [with obj.] secure or steady (a mast) by means of stays.
– PHRASES **be in stays** (of a sailing ship) be head to the wind while tacking. **miss stays** (of a sailing ship) fail in an attempt to go about from one tack to another.
– ORIGIN Old English *stæg*, of Germanic origin; related to Dutch *stag*, from a base meaning 'be firm'.

stay-at-home ▸ **noun** informal a person who prefers to be at home rather than to travel, socialize, or go out to work: *her son was a real stay-at-home* | [as modifier] *working and stay-at-home mums.*

stay bar ▸ **noun** a support used in building or in machinery.

staycation /steɪˈkeɪʃ(ə)n/ ▸ **noun** informal a holiday spent in one's home country rather than abroad, or one spent at home and involving day trips to local attractions.
– ORIGIN early 21st cent.: blend of **STAY**[1] and **VACATION**.

stayer ▸ **noun 1** Brit. a tenacious person or thing, especially a horse able to hold out to the end of a race.
2 a person who lives somewhere temporarily as a visitor or guest.

staying power ▸ **noun** [mass noun] informal the ability to maintain an activity or commitment despite fatigue or difficulty; stamina: *do you have the staying power to study alone at home?*

stay rod ▸ **noun** another term for **STAY BAR**.

staysail /ˈsteɪseɪl, -s(ə)l/ ▸ **noun** a triangular fore-and-aft sail extended on a stay.

stay stitching ▸ **noun** [mass noun] stitching placed along a bias or curved seam to prevent the fabric of a garment from stretching while the garment is being made.

stay-up ▸ **noun** (usu. **stay-ups**) a stocking that has an elasticated top and stays in position without a need for suspenders.

STD ▸ **abbreviation** ■ Doctor of Sacred Theology. [from Latin *Sanctae Theologiae Doctor*.] ■ sexually transmitted disease. ■ Brit. subscriber trunk dialling.

stead ▸ **noun** the place or role that someone or something should have or fill (used in referring to a substitute): *you wish to have him superseded and to be appointed* ***in his stead.***
– PHRASES **stand someone in good stead** be advantageous or useful to someone in the future: *his early training stood him in good stead.*
– ORIGIN Old English *stede* 'place', of Germanic origin; related to Dutch *stad* 'town', German *Statt* 'place', *Stadt* 'town', from an Indo-European root shared by the verb **STAND**.

steadfast /ˈstɛdfɑːst, -fəst/ ▸ **adjective** resolutely or dutifully firm and unwavering: *steadfast loyalty.*
– DERIVATIVES **steadfastly adverb**, **steadfastness noun**.
– ORIGIN Old English *stedefæst* 'standing firm' (see **STEAD**, **FAST**[1]).

Steadicam ▸ **noun** trademark a lightweight mounting for a film camera which keeps it steady for filming when hand-held or moving.

steading ▸ **noun** Scottish & N. English a farm and its buildings; a farmstead.

steady ▸ **adjective** (**steadier**, **steadiest**) **1** firmly fixed, supported, or balanced; not shaking or moving: *the lighter the camera, the harder it is to hold steady* | *he refilled her glass with a steady hand.* ■ not faltering or wavering; controlled: *a steady gaze* | *she tried to keep her voice steady.* ■ (of a person) sensible, reliable, and self-restrained: *a solid, steady young man.*

S

2 regular, even, and continuous in development, frequency, or intensity: *a steady decline in the national birth rate* | *sales remain steady*. ■ not changing; regular and established: *I thought I'd better get a steady job* | *a steady boyfriend*. ■ (of a ship) moving without deviation from its course.

▸ verb (**steadies**, **steadying**, **steadied**) make or become steady: [with obj.] *I took a deep breath to steady my nerves* | (as adj. **steadying**) *she's the one steadying influence in his life* | [no obj.] *by May prices had steadied*.

▸ exclamation used as a warning to someone to keep calm or take care: *Steady now! We don't want you hurting yourself*.

▸ noun (pl. **steadies**) **1** informal a person's regular boyfriend or girlfriend: *his steady chucked him two weeks ago*.
2 a strut for stabilizing a caravan or other vehicle when stationary.

– PHRASES **go steady** informal have a regular romantic or sexual relationship with someone. **steady on!** Brit. used as a way of exhorting someone to calm down or be more reasonable.

– DERIVATIVES **steadier** noun, **steadily** adverb, **steadiness** noun.

– ORIGIN Middle English (in the sense 'unwavering, without deviation'): from STEAD + -Y[1]. The verb dates from the mid 16th cent.

steady-going ▸ adjective (of a person) moderate and sensible in behaviour; level-headed.

steady state ▸ noun an unvarying condition in a physical process, especially as in the theory that the universe is eternal and maintained by constant creation of matter.

> The steady state theory postulates that the universe maintains a constant average density, with more matter continuously created to fill the void left by galaxies that are receding from one another. The theory has now largely been abandoned in favour of the Big Bang theory and an evolving universe.

steak ▸ noun [mass noun] high-quality beef taken from the hindquarters of the animal, typically cut into thick slices that are cooked by grilling or frying. ■ [count noun] a thick slice of steak or other high-quality meat or fish: *a fillet steak* | *a salmon steak*. ■ poorer-quality beef that is cubed or minced and cooked by braising or stewing: *braising steak* | [as modifier] *steak and kidney pie*.

– ORIGIN Middle English: from Old Norse *steik*; related to *steikja* 'roast on a spit' and *stikna* 'be roasted'.

steak au poivre /əʊ ˈpwɑːvr(ə)/ ▸ noun [mass noun] steak coated liberally with crushed peppercorns before cooking.

– ORIGIN French, literally 'steak with pepper'.

steak Diane ▸ noun [mass noun] a dish consisting of thin slices of steak fried with seasonings, especially Worcestershire sauce.

steakhouse ▸ noun a restaurant that specializes in serving steaks.

steak knife ▸ noun a knife with a serrated blade for use when eating steak.

steak tartare ▸ noun [mass noun] a dish consisting of raw minced steak mixed with raw egg, onion, and seasonings and shaped into small cakes or patties.

S

steal ▸ verb (past **stole**; past participle **stolen**) **1** [with obj.] take (another person's property) without permission or legal right and without intending to return it: *thieves stole her bicycle* | (as adj. **stolen**) *stolen goods* | [no obj.] *she was found guilty of stealing from her employers*. ■ dishonestly pass off (another person's ideas) as one's own: *accusations that one group had stolen ideas from the other were soon flying*. ■ take the opportunity to give or share (a kiss) when it is not expected or when people are not watching: *he stole kisses in shop doorways*. ■ (in various sports) gain (an advantage, a run, or possession of the ball) unexpectedly or by exploiting the temporary distraction of an opponent. ■ Baseball run to (a base) while the pitcher is in the act of delivery.
2 [no obj., with adverbial of direction] move somewhere quietly or surreptitiously: *he stole down to the kitchen* | *she disobeyed a court order and* **stole away** *with the children* | figurative *a delicious languor was stealing over her*. ■ [with obj. and adverbial of direction] direct (a look) quickly and unobtrusively: *he stole a furtive glance at her*.

▸ noun [in sing.] **1** informal a bargain: *at £59.95 it's an absolute steal*.
2 chiefly N. Amer. an act of stealing something: *New York's biggest art steal*. ■ an idea taken from another work: *the chorus is a steal from The Smiths' 'London'*. ■ Baseball an act of stealing a base.

– PHRASES **steal someone blind** informal rob or cheat someone in a comprehensive or merciless way. **steal a march on** gain an advantage over (someone) by acting before they do: *stores that open on Sunday are stealing a march on their competitors*. **steal someone's heart** win someone's love. **steal the show** attract the most attention and praise. **steal someone's thunder** win praise for oneself by pre-empting someone else's attempt to impress. [from an exclamation by the English dramatist John Dennis (1657–1734), who invented a method of simulating the sound of thunder as a theatrical sound effect and used it in an unsuccessful play. Shortly after his play came to the end of its short run he heard his new thunder effects used at a performance of *Macbeth*, whereupon he is said to have exclaimed: 'Damn them! They will not let my play run, but they steal my thunder!'.]

– DERIVATIVES **stealable** adjective, **stealer** noun [in combination] *a sheep-stealer*.

– ORIGIN Old English *stelan* (verb), of Germanic origin; related to Dutch *stelen* and German *stehlen*.

stealth ▸ noun **1** [mass noun] cautious and surreptitious action or movement: *the silence and stealth of a hungry cat* | *privatization* **by stealth**.
2 [as modifier] (chiefly of aircraft) designed in accordance with technology which makes detection by radar or sonar difficult: *a stealth bomber*.

– ORIGIN Middle English (in the sense 'theft'): probably representing an Old English word related to STEAL, + -TH[2].

stealth tax ▸ noun a form of taxation levied in a covert or indirect manner.

stealthy ▸ adjective (**stealthier**, **stealthiest**) behaving or done in a cautious and surreptitious manner, so as not to be seen or heard: *stealthy footsteps*.

– DERIVATIVES **stealthily** adverb, **stealthiness** noun.

steam ▸ noun [mass noun] the vapour into which water is converted when heated, forming a white mist of minute water droplets in the air. ■ the invisible gaseous form of water, formed by boiling, from which this vapour condenses. ■ the expansive force of this vapour used as a source of power for machines: *the equipment was originally powered by steam* | [as modifier] *a steam locomotive*. ■ locomotives and railway systems powered in this way: *we were trainspotters in the last years of steam*. ■ energy and momentum or impetus: *the anti-corruption drive* **gathered steam**.

▸ verb **1** [no obj.] give off or produce steam: *a mug of coffee was steaming at her elbow*. ■ (**steam up** or **steam something up**) become or cause something to become covered or misted over with steam: [no obj.] *the glass keeps steaming up* | [with obj.] *the warm air had begun to steam up the windows*.
2 [with obj.] cook (food) by heating it in steam from boiling water: *steam the vegetables until just tender*. ■ [no obj.] (of food) cook by heating in steam: *leave the mussels to steam*. ■ clean or otherwise treat with steam: *he steamed his shirts to remove the odour*. ■ [with obj. and complement or adverbial] apply steam to (something fixed with adhesive) so as to open or loosen it: *he'd steamed the letter open and then resealed it*.
3 [no obj., with adverbial of direction] (of a ship or train) travel somewhere under steam power: *the 11.54 steamed into the station*. ■ informal come, go, or move somewhere rapidly or in a forceful way: *Jeremy steamed in ten minutes late* | figurative *the company has steamed ahead with its investment programme*. ■ [no obj.] (**steam in**) Brit. informal start or join a fight. ■ [no obj.] (often as noun **steaming**) informal (of a gang of thieves) move rapidly through a public place, stealing things or robbing people on the way.
4 [no obj.] (often **be/get steamed up**) informal be or become extremely agitated or angry: *you got all steamed up over nothing!* | *after steaming behind the closed door in his office, he came out and screamed at her*.
5 [with obj.] generate steam in and operate (a steam locomotive).

– PHRASES **get up** (or **pick up**) **steam 1** generate enough pressure to drive a steam engine. **2** (of a project in its early stages) gradually gain more impetus: *his campaign steadily picked up steam*. **have steam coming out of one's ears** informal be extremely angry or irritated. **in steam** (of a steam locomotive) ready for work, with steam in the boiler. **let** (or **blow**) **off steam** informal get rid of pent-up energy or strong emotion. **run out of steam** informal lose impetus or enthusiasm: *a rebellion that had run out of steam*. **under one's own steam** Brit. (with reference to travel) without assistance from others: *we're going to have to get there under our own steam*. **under steam** (of a machine) being operated by steam.

– ORIGIN Old English *stēam* 'vapour', *stēman* 'emit a scent, be exhaled', of Germanic origin; related to Dutch *stoom* 'steam'.

steam age ▸ noun the time when trains were drawn by steam locomotives.

steam bath ▸ noun a room that is filled with hot steam for the purpose of cleaning and refreshing the body and for relaxation. ■ a session in a steam bath.

steam beer ▸ noun [mass noun] US trademark an effervescent beer brewed chiefly in the western US.

steamboat ▸ noun a boat that is propelled by a steam engine, especially (in the US) a paddle-wheel craft of a type used on rivers in the 19th century.

steam distillation ▸ noun [mass noun] Chemistry distillation of a liquid in a current of steam, used especially to purify liquids that are not very volatile and are immiscible with water.

steamed ▸ adjective **1** [predic.] Brit. informal extremely drunk: *we went out and got steamed*.
2 [predic.] informal, chiefly N. Amer. angry; upset: *I was steamed*.
3 (of food) cooked by steaming: *steamed couscous*.

steam engine ▸ noun an engine that uses the expansion or rapid condensation of steam to generate power. ■ a steam locomotive.

steamer ▸ noun **1** a ship, boat, or locomotive powered by steam.
2 a type of saucepan in which food can be steamed.
3 a device used to direct a jet of hot steam on to a garment in order to remove creases.
4 informal a wetsuit.

steamer clam ▸ noun another term for SOFTSHELL CLAM.

steamer duck ▸ noun a sturdily built greyish duck which churns the water with its wings when fleeing danger, typically flightless and native to southern South America. ● Genus *Tachyeres*, family Anatidae: several species, including the flightless *T. brachypterus* of the Falkland Islands.

steamer rug ▸ noun US dated a travelling rug, especially for use on board a passenger ship for keeping warm on deck.

steamer trunk ▸ noun a sturdy trunk designed or intended for use on board a steamship.

steam gauge ▸ noun a pressure gauge attached to a steam boiler.

steam hammer ▸ noun a large steam-powered hammer used in forging.

steam heat ▸ noun [mass noun] heat produced by steam, especially by a central heating system in a building or on a train or ship that uses steam.

▸ verb [with obj.] (**steam-heat**) heat (something) by passing hot steam through it, especially at high pressure.

steamie ▸ noun (pl. **steamies**) Scottish informal a communal wash house.

steaming ▸ adjective **1** giving off steam: *a basin of steaming water*.
2 Brit. informal extremely drunk.
3 Brit. informal very angry.

▸ adverb (as submodifier **steaming hot**) extremely hot.

steam iron ▸ noun an electric iron that emits steam from holes in its flat surface, as an aid to ironing articles that are completely dry.

steam jacket ▸ noun a steam-filled casing that is fitted around a cylinder in order to heat its contents.

steam organ ▸ noun a fairground pipe organ that is driven by a steam engine and played by means of a keyboard or a system of punched cards.

steampunk ▸ noun [mass noun] a genre of science fiction that typically features steam-powered machinery rather than advanced technology.

steamroll ▸ verb chiefly N. Amer. another term for STEAMROLLER.

steamroller ▸ noun a heavy, slow-moving vehicle with a roller, used to flatten the surfaces of roads during construction. ■ an oppressive and relentless power or force: *victims of an ideological steamroller*.

▸ verb [with obj.] (of a government or other authority) forcibly pass (a measure) by restricting debate or otherwise overriding opposition: *the government's trying to* **steamroller** *a law* **through**. ■ force (someone) into doing or accepting something: *an attempt to* **steamroller** *the country* **into** *political reforms*.

steamship ▶ noun a ship that is propelled by a steam engine.

steam shovel ▶ noun an excavator that is powered by steam.

steam table ▶ noun N. Amer. (in a cafeteria or restaurant) a table with slots to hold food containers which are kept hot by steam circulating beneath them.

steam-tight ▶ adjective not allowing steam to pass through: *steam-tight joints.*

steam train ▶ noun a train that is powered by a steam engine.

steam turbine ▶ noun a turbine in which a high-velocity jet of steam rotates a bladed disc or drum.

steamy ▶ adjective (**steamier, steamiest**) **1** producing, filled with, or clouded with steam: *a small steamy kitchen.* ■ (of a place) hot and humid: *the hot, steamy jungle.*
2 informal depicting or involving passionate sexual activity: *steamy sex scenes* | *a steamy affair.*
– DERIVATIVES **steamily** adverb, **steaminess** noun.

stearate /ˈstɪəreɪt/ ▶ noun Chemistry a salt or ester of stearic acid.

stearic acid /ˈstɪərɪk, stɪˈarɪk/ ▶ noun Chemistry a solid saturated fatty acid obtained from animal or vegetable fats. ● Chem. formula: $CH_3(CH_2)_{16}COOH$.
– ORIGIN mid 19th cent.: *stearic* from French *stéarique*, from Greek *stear* 'tallow'.

stearin /ˈstɪərɪn/ ▶ noun [mass noun] a white crystalline substance which is the main constituent of tallow and suet. It is a glyceryl ester of stearic acid. ■ a mixture of fatty acids used in candle-making.
– ORIGIN early 19th cent.: from French *stéarine*, from Greek *stear* 'tallow'.

steatite /ˈstɪətʌɪt/ ▶ noun [mass noun] the mineral talc occurring in consolidated form, especially as soapstone.
– ORIGIN mid 18th cent.: via Latin from Greek *steatītēs*, from *stear, steat-* 'tallow'.

steato- ▶ combining form relating to fatty matter or tissue: *steatosis.*
– ORIGIN from Greek *stear, steat-* 'tallow, fat'.

steatopygia /ˌstɪətə(ʊ)ˈpɪdʒɪə/ ▶ noun [mass noun] accumulation of large amounts of fat on the buttocks, especially as a normal condition in the Khoikhoi and other peoples of arid parts of Southern Africa.
– DERIVATIVES **steatopygous** /ˌstɪətə(ʊ)ˈpʌɪɡəs, ˌstɪəˈtɒpɪɡəs/ adjective.
– ORIGIN early 19th cent.: modern Latin, from Greek *stear, steat-* 'tallow' + *pugē* 'rump'.

steatorrhoea /ˌstɪətə(ʊ)ˈriːə/ ▶ noun [mass noun] Medicine the excretion of abnormal quantities of fat with the faeces owing to reduced absorption of fat by the intestine.

steatosis /ˌstɪəˈtəʊsɪs/ ▶ noun [mass noun] Medicine infiltration of liver cells with fat, associated with disturbance of the metabolism by, for example, alcoholism, malnutrition, pregnancy, or drug therapy.

Stedman /ˈstɛdmən/ ▶ adjective [attrib.] Bell-ringing relating to or denoting a method of change-ringing: *Stedman triples.*
– ORIGIN mid 18th cent.: named after Fabian *Stedman*, the English printer (*fl.* 1670) who devised it.

steed ▶ noun archaic or literary a horse being ridden or available for riding.
– ORIGIN Old English *stēda* 'stallion'; related to STUD².

steel ▶ noun [mass noun] a hard, strong grey or bluish-grey alloy of iron with carbon and usually other elements, used as a structural and fabricating material: [as modifier] *steel girders.* ■ used as a symbol or embodiment of strength and firmness: *nerves of steel* | [as modifier] *a steel will.* ■ [count noun] a rod of roughened steel on which knives are sharpened.
▶ verb [with obj.] mentally prepare (oneself) to do or face something difficult: *his team were steeling themselves for disappointment* | [with infinitive] *she steeled herself to remain calm.*
– ORIGIN Old English *stýle, stēli*, of Germanic origin; related to Dutch *staal*, German *Stahl*, also to STAY². The verb dates from the late 16th cent.

steel band ▶ noun a band that plays music on steel drums.

steel blue ▶ noun [mass noun] a dark bluish-grey colour.

steel drum (also **steel pan**) ▶ noun a percussion instrument originating in Trinidad, made out of an oil drum with one end beaten down and divided by grooves into sections to give different notes.

Steele, Sir Richard (1672–1729), Irish essayist and dramatist. He founded and wrote for the periodicals the *Tatler* (1709–11) and the *Spectator* (1711–12), the latter in collaboration with Joseph Addison.

steel engraving ▶ noun [mass noun] the process or action of engraving a design into a steel plate. ■ [count noun] a print made from an engraved steel plate.

steel grey ▶ noun [mass noun] a dark purplish-grey colour: [as modifier] *the steel-grey November sky.*

steelhead (also **steelhead trout**) ▶ noun a rainbow trout of a large migratory race.

steel pan ▶ noun another term for STEEL DRUM.

steel wool ▶ noun [mass noun] fine strands of steel matted together into a mass, used as an abrasive.

steelwork ▶ noun [mass noun] articles of steel.

steelworks ▶ plural noun [usu. treated as sing.] a factory where steel is manufactured.
– DERIVATIVES **steelworker** noun.

steely ▶ adjective (**steelier, steeliest**) **1** resembling steel in colour, brightness, or strength: *a steely blue.*
2 coldly determined; hard: *there was a steely edge to his questions.*
– DERIVATIVES **steeliness** noun.

steelyard /ˈstiːljɑːd, ˈstɪljəd/ ▶ noun an apparatus for weighing that has a short arm taking the item to be weighed and a long graduated arm along which a weight is moved until it balances.

steen /stɪən, stiːn/ (also **stein**) ▶ noun [mass noun] a variety of white grape grown in South Africa. ■ the wine made from the steen grape. ■ (**stein**) a blended semi-sweet white wine, typically containing steen grapes.
– ORIGIN South African Dutch, elliptically from *steendruiven*, literally 'stone grapes'.

steenbok /ˈstiːnbɒk, ˈsteɪn-/ (also **steinbok** or **steenbuck**) ▶ noun a small African antelope with large ears, a small tail, and smooth upright horns. ● *Raphiceros campestris*, family Bovidae.
– ORIGIN late 18th cent.: from Dutch, from *steen* 'stone' + *bok* 'buck'.

steenbras /ˈstiːnbras, -brɑːs/ ▶ noun (pl. **same**) an edible South African sea bream of shallow waters. ● *Sparodon* and other genera, family Sparidae.
– ORIGIN early 17th cent.: from Afrikaans, from Dutch *steen* 'stone' + *brasen* 'bream'.

steep¹ ▶ adjective **1** (of a slope, flight of stairs, or angle) rising or falling sharply; almost perpendicular: *she pushed the bike up the steep hill.* ■ (of a rise or fall in an amount) very large or rapid: *the steep rise in unemployment.*
2 informal (of a price or demand) not reasonable; excessive: *a steep membership fee.* ■ dated (of a claim or account) exaggerated or incredible: *this is a rather steep statement.*
▶ noun chiefly Skiing or literary a steep mountain slope: *hair-raising steeps.*
– DERIVATIVES **steepish** adjective, **steeply** adverb, **steepness** noun.
– ORIGIN Old English *stēap* 'extending to a great height', of West Germanic origin; related to STEEPLE and STOOP¹.

steep² ▶ verb [with obj.] **1** soak (food or tea) in water or other liquid so as to extract its flavour or to soften it: *the chillies are steeped in olive oil* | [no obj.] *the noodles should be left to steep for 3–4 minutes.* ■ soak or saturate (cloth) in water or other liquid.
2 (usu. **be steeped in**) surround or fill with a quality or influence: *a city steeped in history.*
– ORIGIN Middle English: of Germanic origin; related to STOUP.

steepen ▶ verb become or cause to become steeper: [no obj.] *the snow improved as the slope steepened.*

steeple ▶ noun a church tower and spire. ■ a spire on the top of a church tower or roof. ■ archaic a tall tower of a church or other building.
▶ verb [with obj.] place (the fingers or hands) together so that they form an upward-pointing V-shape.
– DERIVATIVES **steepled** adjective.
– ORIGIN Old English *stēpel*, of Germanic origin; related to STEEP¹.

steeplechase ▶ noun a horse race run on a racecourse having ditches and hedges as jumps. ■ a running race in which runners must clear hurdles and water jumps.
– DERIVATIVES **steeplechaser** noun, **steeplechasing** noun.
– ORIGIN late 18th cent.: from STEEPLE (because originally a steeple marked the finishing point across country) + CHASE¹.

steeple-crowned ▶ adjective (of a hat) having a tall, pointed crown.

steeplejack ▶ noun a person who climbs tall structures such as chimneys and steeples in order to carry out repairs.

steer¹ ▶ verb [with obj.] guide or control the movement of (a vehicle, vessel, or aircraft), for example by turning a wheel or operating a rudder: *he steered the boat slowly towards the busy quay* | [no obj.] *he let Lily steer.* ■ [no obj., with adverbial of direction] (of a vehicle, vessel, or aircraft) be guided in a specified direction: *the ship steered into port.* ■ [with obj. and adverbial of direction] follow (a course) in a specified direction: *the fishermen were steering a direct course for Koepang.* ■ [with obj. and adverbial of direction] guide the movement or course of: *he had steered her to a chair* | figurative *he made an attempt to steer the conversation back to Heather.*
▶ noun **1** [mass noun] the type of steering of a vehicle: *some cars boast four-wheel steer.*
2 informal a piece of advice or information concerning the development of a situation: *the need for the NHS to be given a clear steer as to its future direction.*
– PHRASES **steer clear of** take care to avoid or keep away from: *steer clear of fatty food.* **steer a middle course** see MIDDLE.
– DERIVATIVES **steerable** adjective.
– ORIGIN Old English *stīeran*, of Germanic origin; related to Dutch *sturen* and German *steuern*.

steer² ▶ noun another term for BULLOCK.
– ORIGIN Old English *stēor*, of Germanic origin; related to Dutch *stier* and German *Stier*.

steerage ▶ noun [mass noun] **1** historical the part of a ship providing the cheapest accommodation for passengers: *poor emigrants in steerage.*
2 archaic or literary the action of steering a boat.

steerage way ▶ noun [mass noun] the rate of headway required if a ship is to be controlled by the helm.

steer-by-wire ▶ noun another term for DRIVE-BY-WIRE.

steerer ▶ noun a person or mechanism that steers a vehicle or vessel. ■ US informal a person who takes or entices someone to meet a racketeer or swindler.

steering ▶ noun [mass noun] the action of steering a vehicle, vessel, or aircraft. ■ the mechanism in a vehicle, vessel, or aircraft which makes it possible to steer it in different directions.

steering column ▶ noun a shaft that connects the steering wheel of a vehicle to the rest of the steering mechanism.

steering committee (also **steering group**) ▶ noun a committee that decides on the priorities or order of business of an organization and manages the general course of its operations.

steering wheel ▶ noun a wheel that a driver rotates in order to steer a vehicle.

steersman ▶ noun (pl. **steersmen**) a person who is steering a boat or ship.

steeve¹ ▶ noun (in a sailing ship) the angle of the bowsprit in relation to the horizontal.
▶ verb [with obj.] give (the bowsprit of a sailing ship) a specified inclination.
– ORIGIN mid 17th cent.: of unknown origin.

steeve² ▶ noun a derrick consisting of a long pole with a block at the end.
– ORIGIN late 15th cent. (as a verb): from Old French *estiver* or Spanish *estibar*, from Latin *stipare* 'pack tight'. The noun is first recorded as a 19th-cent. US term.

Stefan–Boltzmann law /ˌʃtɛfanˈbəʊltsmən/ ▶ noun Physics a law stating that the total radiation emitted by a black body is proportional to the fourth power of its absolute temperature.
– ORIGIN late 19th cent.: named after Josef *Stefan* (1835–93), Austrian physicist, and L. BOLTZMANN.

steganography /ˌstɛɡəˈnɒɡrəfi/ ▶ noun [mass noun] the practice of concealing messages or information within other non-secret text or data.
– ORIGIN late 16th cent.: modern Latin *steganographia*, from Greek *steganos* 'covered' + -GRAPHY.

stegosaur /ˈstɛɡəsɔː/ (also **stegosaurus** /ˌstɛɡəˈsɔːrəs/) ▶ noun a small-headed quadrupedal herbivorous dinosaur of the Jurassic and early Cretaceous periods, with a double row of large bony plates or spines along the back. ● Infraorder Stegosauria, order Ornithischia: several genera, including *Stegosaurus*.
– ORIGIN modern Latin, from Greek *stegē* 'covering' + *sauros* 'lizard'.

Steiermark /ˈʃtʌɪə‚mark/ German name for STYRIA.

Stein /stʌɪn/, Gertrude (1874–1946), American writer. Stein developed an esoteric stream-of-consciousness style, notably in *The Autobiography of Alice B.*

S

Toklas (1933). Her home in Paris became a focus for the avant-garde during the 1920s and 1930s.

stein¹ /stʌɪn/ ▶ **noun** a large earthenware beer mug.
– ORIGIN mid 19th cent.: from German *Stein*, literally 'stone'.

stein² ▶ **noun** variant spelling of **STEEN**.

Steinbeck /'stʌɪnbɛk/, John (Ernst) (1902–68), American novelist. His work, for example *Of Mice and Men* (1937) and *The Grapes of Wrath* (1939), is noted for its sympathetic and realistic portrayal of the migrant agricultural workers of California. Nobel Prize for Literature (1962).

steinbock /'stʌɪnbɒk/ ▶ **noun** (pl. **same** or **steinbocks**) an ibex, especially one living in the Alps.
– ORIGIN late 17th cent.: from German, from *Stein* 'stone' + *Bock* 'buck'.

steinbok /'stʌɪnbɒk/ ▶ **noun** variant spelling of **STEENBOK**.

Steiner /'ʃtʌɪnə, 'st-/, Rudolf (1861–1925), Austrian philosopher, founder of anthroposophy. He founded the Anthroposophical Society in 1912, aiming to integrate the practical and psychological in education. The society has contributed to child-centred education, especially with its Steiner schools.

Steinway /'stʌɪnweɪ/ ▶ **noun** a piano manufactured by the German piano-builder Henry Engelhard Steinway (1797–1871), or by the firm which he founded in New York in 1853.

stela /'sti:lə/ ▶ **noun** (pl. **stelae** /-li:/) Archaeology an upright stone slab or column typically bearing a commemorative inscription or relief design, often serving as a gravestone.
– ORIGIN late 18th cent.: via Latin from Greek (see **STELE**).

Stelazine /'stɛləzi:n/ ▶ **noun** trademark for **TRIFLUOPERAZINE**.
– ORIGIN 1950s: of unknown origin.

stele /sti:l, 'sti:li/ ▶ **noun 1** Botany the central core of the stem and root of a vascular plant, consisting of the vascular tissue (xylem and phloem) and associated supporting tissue. Also called **VASCULAR CYLINDER**.
2 Archaeology another term for **STELA**.
– DERIVATIVES **stelar adjective** (sense 1).
– ORIGIN early 19th cent.: from Greek *stēlē* 'standing block'.

Stella Maris /,stɛlə 'marɪs/ ▶ **noun** chiefly literary a female protector or guiding spirit at sea (a title sometimes given to the Virgin Mary).
– ORIGIN Latin, literally 'star of the sea'.

stellar /'stɛlə/ ▶ **adjective 1** relating to a star or stars: *stellar structure and evolution*.
2 informal featuring or having the quality of a star performer or performers: *a stellar cast had been assembled*. ■ exceptionally good; outstanding: *his restaurant has received stellar ratings in the guides*.
– DERIVATIVES **stelliform adjective**.
– ORIGIN mid 17th cent.: from late Latin *stellaris*, from Latin *stella* 'star'.

stellarator /'stɛləreɪtə/ ▶ **noun** Physics a toroidal apparatus for producing controlled fusion reactions in hot plasma, where all the controlling magnetic fields inside it are produced by external windings.
– ORIGIN 1950s: from **STELLAR** (with reference to the fusion processes in stars), on the pattern of *generator*.

S

stellar wind ▶ **noun** Astronomy a continuous flow of charged particles from a star.

stellate /'stɛleɪt, -lət/ ▶ **adjective** technical arranged in a radiating pattern like that of a star.
– DERIVATIVES **stellated adjective**.
– ORIGIN mid 17th cent.: from Latin *stellatus*, from *stella* 'star'.

Stellenbosch /'stɛlənbɒs/ a university town in SW South Africa, just east of Cape Town; pop. 99,000 (est. 2009).

Steller /'stɛlə/, Georg Wilhelm (1709–46), German naturalist and geographer. Steller was a research member of Vitus Bering's second expedition to Kamchatka and Alaska and described many new birds and mammals, several of which now bear his name.

Steller's sea cow ▶ **noun** a very large relative of the dugong that was formerly found in the area of the Bering Sea and Kamchatka Peninsula, discovered and hunted to extinction in the 18th century.
● *Hydrodamalis gigas*, family Dugongidae.

stellium /'stɛlɪəm/ ▶ **noun** Astrology another term for **SATELLITIUM**.

stem¹ ▶ **noun 1** the main body or stalk of a plant or shrub, typically rising above ground but occasionally subterranean. ■ the stalk supporting a fruit, flower, or leaf, and attaching it to a larger branch, twig, or stalk.
2 a long, thin supportive or main section of something: *the main stem of the wing feathers*. ■ the slender part of a wine glass between the base and the bowl. ■ the tube of a tobacco pipe. ■ a rod or cylinder in a mechanism, for example the sliding shaft of a bolt or the winding pin of a watch. ■ a vertical stroke in a letter or musical note.
3 Grammar the root or main part of a word, to which inflections or formative elements are added. ■ archaic or literary the main line of descent of a family or nation: *the Hellenic tribes were derived from the Aryan stem*.
4 the main upright timber or metal piece at the bow of a ship, to which the ship's sides are joined at the front end.
5 US informal a pipe used for smoking crack or opium.
▶ **verb** (**stems, stemming, stemmed**) **1** [no obj.] (**stem from**) originate in or be caused by: *many of the universities' problems stem from rapid expansion*.
2 [with obj.] remove the stems from (fruit or tobacco leaves).
3 [with obj.] (of a boat) make headway against (the tide or current).
– PHRASES **from stem to stern** from the front to the back, especially of a ship.
– DERIVATIVES **stemmed adjective** [in combination] *red-stemmed alder bushes*, **stemless adjective**, **stem-like adjective**.
– ORIGIN Old English *stemn, stefn*, of Germanic origin; related to Dutch *stam* and German *Stamm*. Sense 4 of the noun is related to Dutch *steven*, German *Steven*.

stem² ▶ **verb** (**stems, stemming, stemmed**) **1** [with obj.] stop or restrict (the flow of something): *a nurse did her best to stem the bleeding*. ■ stop the spread or development of (something undesirable): *an attempt to stem the rising tide of unemployment*.
2 [no obj.] Skiing slide the tail of one ski or both skis outwards in order to turn or slow down.
– ORIGIN Middle English (in the sense 'to stop, delay'): from Old Norse *stemma*, of Germanic origin. The skiing term (early 20th cent.) is from the German verb *stemmen*.

stem cell ▶ **noun** Biology an undifferentiated cell of a multicellular organism which is capable of giving rise to indefinitely more cells of the same type, and from which certain other kinds of cell arise by differentiation.

stem ginger ▶ **noun** [mass noun] a superior grade of crystallized or preserved ginger.

stemma /'stɛmə/ ▶ **noun** (pl. **stemmata** /-mətə/) a recorded genealogy of a family; a family tree. ■ a diagram showing the relationship between a text and its various manuscript versions.
– ORIGIN mid 17th cent.: via Latin from Greek *stemma* 'wreath', from *stephein* 'wreathe, crown'.

stemmatics /stɛ'matɪks/ ▶ **plural noun** [treated as sing.] the branch of study concerned with analysing the relationship of surviving variant versions of a text to each other, especially so as to reconstruct a lost original.

stemple ▶ **noun** archaic each of a number of crossbars in a mineshaft, serving as supports or steps.
– ORIGIN mid 17th cent.: perhaps related to German *Stempel*.

stem stitch ▶ **noun** [mass noun] an embroidery stitch forming a continuous line of long, overlapped stitches, typically used to represent narrow stems.

stem turn ▶ **noun** Skiing a turn made by stemming with the upper ski and lifting the lower one parallel to it towards the end.

stemware ▶ **noun** [mass noun] N. Amer. goblets and stemmed glasses regarded collectively.

stem-winder ▶ **noun** US **1** informal an entertaining and rousing speech: *a stem-winder of a speech*.
2 dated a watch wound by turning a knob on the end of a stem.
– ORIGIN Sense 1 from the notion of 'winding up' or causing a lively reaction from those listening.

stench ▶ **noun** a strong and very unpleasant smell: *the stench of rotting fish*.
– ORIGIN Old English *stenc* 'smell', of Germanic origin; related to Dutch *stank*, German *Gestank*, also to the verb **STINK**.

stencil ▶ **noun** a thin sheet of card, plastic, or metal with a pattern or letters cut out of it, used to produce the cut design on the surface below by the application of ink or paint through the holes. ■ a design produced by a stencil: *a floral stencil around the top of the room*.
▶ **verb** (**stencils, stencilling, stencilled**; US **stencils, stenciling, stenciled**) [with obj.] decorate (a surface) with a stencil: *the walls had been stencilled with designs* | (as noun **stencilling**) *the art of stencilling*. ■ produce (a design) with a stencil: *stencil a border around the door* | (as adj. **stencilled**) *the stencilled letters*.
– ORIGIN early 18th cent.: from earlier *stansel* 'ornament with various colours' (based on Latin *scintilla* 'spark').

Stendhal /'stɒ̃dɑ:l/, French /stɛ̃dal/ (1783–1842), French novelist; pseudonym of *Marie Henri Beyle*. His two best-known novels are *Le Rouge et le noir* (1830), relating the rise and fall of a young man from the provinces, and *La Chartreuse de Parme* (1839).

Sten gun ▶ **noun** a type of lightweight British submachine gun.
– ORIGIN 1940s: from the initials of the inventors' surnames, *S*hepherd and *T*urpin, suggested by **BREN**.

Steno /'sti:nəʊ/, Nicolaus (1638–86), Danish anatomist and geologist; Danish name *Niels Steensen*. His ideas on the geological history of the earth are now regarded as fundamental—that fossils are the petrified remains of living organisms, that many rocks arise from consolidation of sediments, and that such rocks occur in layers in the order in which they were laid down.

steno /'stɛnəʊ/ ▶ **noun** (pl. **stenos**) N. Amer. informal a shorthand typist: *it was written by the little steno herself*. ■ [as modifier] short for **STENOGRAPHY**.

stenography /stɪ'nɒgrəfi/ ▶ **noun** [mass noun] N. Amer. the action or process of writing in shorthand and transcribing the shorthand on a typewriter.
– DERIVATIVES **stenographer noun**, **stenographic adjective**.
– ORIGIN early 17th cent.: from Greek *stenos* 'narrow' + **-GRAPHY**.

stenohaline /,stɛnəʊ'heɪlʌɪn, -li:n/ ▶ **adjective** Ecology (of an aquatic organism) able to tolerate only a narrow range of salinity. Often contrasted with **EURYHALINE**.
– ORIGIN 1930s: from Greek *stenos* 'narrow' + *halinos* 'of salt'.

stenosis /stɪ'nəʊsɪs/ ▶ **noun** (pl. **stenoses**) [mass noun] Medicine the abnormal narrowing of a passage in the body.
– DERIVATIVES **stenosed adjective**, **stenosing adjective**, **stenotic adjective**.
– ORIGIN late 19th cent.: modern Latin, from Greek *stenōsis* 'narrowing', from *stenoun* 'make narrow', from *stenos* 'narrow'.

stenothermal /,stɛnə(ʊ)'θə:m(ə)l/ ▶ **adjective** Ecology (of an organism) able to tolerate only a small range of temperature. Often contrasted with **EURYTHERMAL**.
– ORIGIN late 19th cent.: from Greek *stenos* 'narrow' + **THERMAL**.

stenotopic /,stɛnə(ʊ)'tɒpɪk/ ▶ **adjective** Ecology (of an organism) able to tolerate only a restricted range of habitats or ecological conditions. Often contrasted with **EURYTOPIC**.
– ORIGIN 1940s: from Greek *stenos* 'narrow' + *topos* 'place' + **-IC**.

stenotype ▶ **noun** a machine resembling a typewriter that is used for recording speech in syllables or phonemes.
– DERIVATIVES **stenotypist noun**.
– ORIGIN late 19th cent.: from **STENOGRAPHY** + **TYPE**.

stent¹ ▶ **noun 1** Medicine a splint placed temporarily inside a duct, canal, or blood vessel to aid healing or relieve an obstruction. ■ an impression or cast of a part or body cavity, used to maintain pressure so as to promote healing, especially of a skin graft.
2 [mass noun] (also **Stents**) trademark a substance used in dentistry for taking impressions of the teeth.
– ORIGIN late 19th cent.: from the name of Charles T. *Stent* (1807–85), English dentist. The sense 'splint' dates from the 1960s.

stent² historical, chiefly Scottish ▶ **noun** an assessment of property made for purposes of taxation. ■ the amount or value assessed; a tax.
▶ **verb** [with obj.] assess and charge (a person or a community) for purposes of taxation.
– ORIGIN Middle English: from Old French *estente* 'valuation', related to Anglo-Norman French *extente* (see **EXTENT**).

stenter ▶ **noun** another term for **TENTER¹**.

– ORIGIN from Scots *stent* 'set up a tent' (perhaps a shortening of **EXTEND**) + **-ER**[1].

stentor /ˈstɛntə/ ▶ **noun 1** literary a person with a powerful voice.
2 Zoology a sedentary trumpet-shaped single-celled animal that is widespread in fresh water. ● Genus *Stentor*, phylum Ciliophora, kingdom Protista.
– ORIGIN early 17th cent.: from Greek *Stentōr*, the name of a herald in the Trojan War.

stentorian /stɛnˈtɔːrɪən/ ▶ **adjective** (of a person's voice) loud and powerful: *a stentorian roar.*

step ▶ **noun 1** an act or movement of putting one leg in front of the other in walking or running: *Ron took a step back | she turned and retraced her steps.* ■ the distance covered by a step: *Richard came a couple of steps nearer.* ■ [usu. in sing.] a person's particular way of walking: *she left the room with a springy step.* ■ each of the sequences of movement of the feet which make up a dance. ■ a short or easily walked distance: *the market is only a short step from the lake.*
2 a flat surface, especially one in a series, on which to place one's foot when moving from one level to another: *the bottom step of the staircase | a flight of marble steps.* ■ a doorstep: *there was a pint of milk on the step.* ■ a rung of a ladder. ■ (**steps** or **a pair of steps**) Brit. a stepladder. ■ [mass noun] step aerobics: [as modifier] *a step class.* ■ Climbing a foothold cut in a slope of ice.
3 a measure or action, especially one of a series taken in order to deal with or achieve a particular thing: *the government must **take steps** to discourage age discrimination | a major step forward in the fight against terrorism.* ■ a stage in a gradual process: *sales are up, which is a step in the right direction.* ■ a particular position or grade on an ascending or hierarchical scale: *the first step on the managerial ladder.*
4 Music, N. Amer. an interval in a scale; a tone (whole step) or semitone (half step).
5 Physics an abrupt change in the value of a quantity, especially voltage.
6 a block fixed to a boat's keel in order to take the base of a mast or other fitting.
▶ **verb** (**steps, stepping, stepped**) **1** [no obj., with adverbial] lift and set down one's foot or one foot after the other in order to walk somewhere or move to a new position: *Claudia tried to step back | I accidentally stepped on his foot.* ■ [as imperative] used as a polite or deferential way of asking someone to walk a short distance for a particular purpose: *please step this way.* ■ (**step it**) dated perform a dance: *they stepped it down the room between the lines of dancers.* ■ take a particular course of action: *he stepped out of retirement to answer an SOS call from his old club.*
2 [with obj.] Nautical set up (a mast) in its step.
– PHRASES **break step** stop walking or marching in step with others. **fall into step** change the way one is walking so that one is walking in step with another person. **in** (or **out of**) **step** putting (or not putting) one's feet forward alternately in the same rhythm as the people one is walking, marching, or dancing with. ■ conforming (or not conforming) to what others are doing or thinking: *the party is clearly **out of step with** voters.* ■ Physics (of two or more oscillations or other cyclic phenomena) having (or not having) the same frequency and always in the same phase. **follow** (or **tread**) **in someone's steps** do as someone else did, especially in making a journey or following a career. **keep step** remain walking, marching, or dancing in step. **mind** (or **watch**) **one's step** used as a warning to someone to walk or act carefully. **one step ahead** managing to avoid competition or danger from someone or something: *I try to keep one step ahead of the rest of the staff.* **step by step** so as to progress gradually and carefully from one stage to the next: *I'll explain it to you step by step* | [as modifier] *a step-by-step guide.* **step into the breach** see **BREACH**. **step into someone's shoes** take control of a task or job from another person. **step on it** (or **step on the gas**) informal go faster, typically in a motor vehicle. **step on someone's toes** see **TREAD ON SOMEONE'S TOES** at **TREAD**. **step out of line** behave inappropriately or disobediently. **step up to the plate** N. Amer. take action in response to an opportunity or crisis.
– PHRASAL VERBS **step aside** another way of saying **STEP DOWN**. **step back** mentally withdraw from a situation in order to consider it objectively. **step down** withdraw or resign from an important position or office: *he stepped down as party leader.* **step something down** decrease voltage by using a transformer. **step forward** offer one's help or services: *a company has stepped forward to sponsor the team.* **step in** become involved in a difficult situation, especially in order to help. ■ act as a substitute for someone: *Lucy stepped in at very short notice to take Joan's place.* **step out 1** leave a room or building for a short time. **2** N. Amer. informal go out with: *he was stepping out with a redheaded waitress.* **3** walk with long or vigorous steps: *she enjoyed the outing, stepping out manfully.* **step out on** US informal be sexually unfaithful to. **step something up 1** increase the amount, speed, or intensity of something: *police decided to step up security plans for the match.* **2** increase voltage using a transformer.
– DERIVATIVES **step-like** adjective.
– ORIGIN Old English *stæpe*, *stepe* (noun), *stæppan*, *steppan* (verb), of Germanic origin; related to Dutch *steppen* and German *stapfen*.

step- ▶ **combining form** denoting a relationship resulting from a remarriage: *stepmother.*
– ORIGIN Old English *stēop-*, from a Germanic base meaning 'bereaved, orphaned'.

step aerobics ▶ **plural noun** [mass noun] a type of aerobics that involves stepping up on to and down from a portable block.

Stepanakert /stʲɪpanəˈkʲɛrt/ Russian name for **XANKÄNDI**.

stepbrother ▶ **noun** a son of one's step-parent by a marriage other than that with one's own father or mother.

step change ▶ **noun** (in business or politics) a significant change in policy or attitude, especially one that results in an improvement or increase.

stepchild ▶ **noun** (pl. **stepchildren**) a child of one's husband or wife by a previous marriage.

step-cut ▶ **adjective** (of a gem) cut in straight facets round the centre.

stepdad ▶ **noun** informal term for **STEPFATHER**.

stepdaughter ▶ **noun** a daughter of one's husband or wife by a previous marriage.

stepfamily ▶ **noun** (pl. **stepfamilies**) a family that is formed on the remarriage of a divorced or widowed person and that includes a child or children.

stepfather ▶ **noun** a man who is married to one's mother after the divorce of one's parents or the death of one's father.

Stepford ▶ **noun** [as modifier] denoting someone who is regarded as robotically conformist or obedient: *it seems that colleges want to produce a generation of PC-driven Stepford students.*
– ORIGIN from *The Stepford Wives*, the title of a 1972 novel by the American writer Ira Levin (1929–2007), in which *Stepford* is the name of a fictional idyllic suburb where the men have replaced their wives with robots.

step function ▶ **noun** Mathematics & Electronics a function that increases or decreases abruptly from one constant value to another.

stephanotis /ˌstɛfəˈnəʊtɪs/ ▶ **noun** a Madagascan climbing plant which is cultivated for its fragrant waxy white flowers. ● Genus *Stephanotis*, family Asclepiadaceae.
– ORIGIN modern Latin, from Greek, literally 'fit for a wreath', from *stephanos* 'wreath'.

Stephen (*c.*1097–1154), grandson of William the Conqueror, king of England 1135–54. Stephen seized the throne from Matilda after the death of Henry I. Civil war followed until Matilda was defeated and forced to leave England in 1148.

Stephen, St[1] (died *c.*35), Christian martyr. One of the original seven deacons in Jerusalem appointed by the Apostles, he was charged with blasphemy and stoned, thus becoming the first Christian martyr. Feast day (in the Western Church) 26 December; (in the Eastern Church) 27 December.

Stephen, St[2] (*c.*977–1038), king and patron saint of Hungary, reigned 1000–38. The first king of Hungary, he took steps to Christianize the country. Feast day, 2 September or (in Hungary) 20 August.

Stephenson, George (1781–1848), English engineer, a pioneer of steam locomotives and railways. He built his first locomotive in 1814 and by 1825 had designed and driven an engine for the Stockton and Darlington Railway. With his son **Robert** (1803–59) he built the famous *Rocket* (1829), the prototype for all future steam locomotives. Robert is also famous as a bridge designer.

step-in ▶ **adjective** [attrib.] denoting a garment or pair of shoes that is put on by being stepped into and has no need for fastenings.
▶ **noun** (**step-ins**) **1** a pair of step-in shoes; slip-ons.
2 dated, chiefly N. Amer. a pair of women's briefs.

stepladder ▶ **noun** a short folding ladder with flat steps and a small platform.

stepmother ▶ **noun** a woman who is married to one's father after the divorce of one's parents or the death of one's mother.

stepmum ▶ **noun** informal term for **STEPMOTHER**.

step-parent ▶ **noun** a stepfather or stepmother.

steppe /stɛp/ ▶ **noun** (often **steppes**) a large area of flat unforested grassland in SE Europe or Siberia.
– ORIGIN late 17th cent.: from Russian *step'*.

stepped ▶ **adjective 1** having or formed into a step or series of steps: *a building with stepped access.*
2 carried out or occurring in stages or with pauses rather than continuously: *a stepped scale of discounts.*

stepper ▶ **noun 1** an electric motor or other device which moves or rotates in a series of small discrete steps.
2 a portable block used in step aerobics.

stepping stone ▶ **noun** a raised stone used singly or in a series as a place on which to step when crossing a stream or muddy area. ■ an action or event that helps one to make progress towards a specified goal: *the school championships are a **stepping stone to** international competition.*

step response ▶ **noun** Electronics the output of a device in response to an abrupt change in voltage.

stepsister ▶ **noun** a daughter of one's step-parent by a marriage other than with one's own father or mother.

stepson ▶ **noun** a son of one's husband or wife by a previous marriage.

step wedge ▶ **noun** Photography a series of contiguous uniformly shaded rectangles, growing progressively darker from white (or light grey) at one end to black (or dark grey) at the other.

stepwise ▶ **adverb & adjective** in a series of distinct stages; not continuously: [as adv.] *concentrations of the acid tend to decrease stepwise.*

-ster ▶ **suffix 1** denoting a person engaged in or associated with a particular activity or thing: *maltster | songster.*
2 denoting a person having a particular quality: *youngster.*
– ORIGIN Old English *-estre*, *-istre*, etc., of Germanic origin.

steradian /stəˈreɪdɪən/ (abbrev.: **sr**) ▶ **noun** the SI unit of solid angle, equal to the angle at the centre of a sphere subtended by a part of the surface equal in area to the square of the radius.
– ORIGIN late 19th cent.: from Greek *stereos* 'solid' + **RADIAN**.

sterane /ˈstɪəreɪn, ˈstɛreɪn/ ▶ **noun** Chemistry any of a class of saturated polycyclic hydrocarbons which are found in crude oils and are derived from the sterols of ancient organisms.
– ORIGIN 1950s: from **STEROID** + **-ANE**[2].

stercoraceous /ˌstəːkəˈreɪʃəs/ ▶ **adjective** technical consisting of or resembling dung or faeces.
– ORIGIN mid 18th cent.: from Latin *stercus*, *stercor-* 'dung' + **-ACEOUS**.

stere /stɪə/ ▶ **noun** a unit of volume equal to one cubic metre.
– ORIGIN late 18th cent.: from French *stère*, from Greek *stereos* 'solid'.

stereo /ˈstɛrɪəʊ, ˈstɪərɪəʊ/ ▶ **noun** (pl. **stereos**) **1** [mass noun] sound that is directed through two or more speakers so that it seems to surround the listener and to come from more than one source; stereophonic sound. ■ [count noun] a CD or record player that has two or more speakers and produces stereo sound.
2 Photography another term for **STEREOSCOPE**.
3 Printing short for **STEREOTYPE**.
▶ **adjective 1** short for **STEREOPHONIC**: *stereo equipment.*
2 Photography short for **STEREOSCOPIC** (see **STEREOSCOPE**).

stereo- ▶ **combining form** relating to solid forms having three dimensions: *stereography.* ■ relating to a three-dimensional effect, arrangement, etc.: *stereochemistry | stereophonic | stereoscope.*
– ORIGIN from Greek *stereos* 'solid'.

stereobate /ˈstɛrɪə(ʊ)beɪt, ˈstɪə-/ ▶ **noun** Architecture a solid mass of masonry serving as a foundation for a wall or row of columns.
– ORIGIN mid 19th cent.: from French *stéréobate*, via Latin from Greek *stereobatēs*, from Greek *stereos* 'solid' + *batēs* 'base' (from *bainein* 'to walk').

stereocamera ▸ noun a camera for simultaneously taking two photographs of the same thing from adjacent viewpoints, so that they will form a stereoscopic pair.

stereochemistry ▸ noun [mass noun] the branch of chemistry concerned with the three-dimensional arrangement of atoms and molecules and the effect of this on chemical reactions.
– DERIVATIVES **stereochemical** adjective, **stereochemically** adverb.

stereognosis /ˌstɛrɪə(ʊ)ˈnəʊsɪs, ˌstɪə-/ ▸ noun [mass noun] Psychology the mental perception of depth or three-dimensionality by the senses, usually in reference to the ability to perceive the form of solid objects by touch.
– ORIGIN early 20th cent.: from Greek *stereos* 'solid' + *gnōsis* 'knowledge'.

stereogram ▸ noun **1** a diagram or computer-generated image giving a three-dimensional representation of a solid object or surface.
2 a stereo radiogram.

stereography ▸ noun [mass noun] the depiction or representation of three-dimensional things by projection on to a two-dimensional surface, e.g. in cartography.
– DERIVATIVES **stereograph** noun, **stereographic** adjective, **stereographically** adverb.

stereoisomer /ˌstɛrɪəʊˈʌɪsəmə, ˌstɪə-/ ▸ noun Chemistry each of two or more compounds differing only in the spatial arrangement of their atoms.
– DERIVATIVES **stereoisomeric** adjective, **stereoisomerism** noun.

stereolithography ▸ noun [mass noun] a technique or process for creating three-dimensional objects, in which a computer-controlled moving laser beam is used to build up the required structure, layer by layer, from a liquid polymer that hardens on contact with laser light.
– DERIVATIVES **stereolithographic** adjective.

stereometry ▸ noun [mass noun] Geometry the measurement of solid bodies.

stereomicroscope ▸ noun a binocular microscope that gives a relatively low-power stereoscopic view of the subject.

stereophonic /ˌstɛrɪə(ʊ)ˈfɒnɪk, ˌstɪərɪə(ʊ)-/ ▸ adjective (of sound recording and reproduction) using two or more channels of transmission and reproduction so that the reproduced sound seems to surround the listener and to come from more than one source.
– DERIVATIVES **stereophonically** adverb, **stereophony** /-ˈɒf(ə)ni/ noun.

stereopsis /ˌstɛrɪˈɒpsɪs, ˌstɪərɪ-/ ▸ noun [mass noun] the perception of depth produced by the reception in the brain of visual stimuli from both eyes in combination; binocular vision.
– ORIGIN early 20th cent.: from **STEREO-** 'three-dimensional' + Greek *opsis* 'sight'.

stereopticon /ˌstɛrɪˈɒptɪk(ə)n, ˌstɪərɪ-/ ▸ noun a slide projector that combines two images to create a three-dimensional effect, or makes one image dissolve into another.
– ORIGIN mid 19th cent.: from **STEREO-** 'three-dimensional' + Greek *optikon*, neuter of *optikos* 'relating to vision'.

S

stereoscope /ˈstɛrɪə(ʊ)skəʊp, ˈstɪə-/ ▸ noun a device by which two photographs of the same object taken at slightly different angles are viewed together, creating an impression of depth and solidity.
– DERIVATIVES **stereoscopic** adjective, **stereoscopically** adverb, **stereoscopy** noun.

stereoselective /ˌstɛrɪəʊsɪˈlɛktɪv, ˌstɪə-/ ▸ adjective Chemistry (of a reaction) preferentially producing a particular stereoisomeric form of the product, irrespective of the configuration of the reactant.
– DERIVATIVES **stereoselectivity** noun.

stereo separation ▸ noun see **SEPARATION** (sense 3).

stereospecific ▸ adjective Chemistry another term for **STEREOSELECTIVE**.
– DERIVATIVES **stereospecifically** adverb, **stereospecificity** noun.

stereospondyl /ˌstɛrɪə(ʊ)ˈspɒndɪl, ˌstɪə-/ ▸ noun a fossil amphibian with a broad flat head, occurring in the Permian and Triassic periods. ● Suborder Stereospondyli, order Temnospondyli: several families.
– ORIGIN early 20th cent.: from modern Latin *Stereospondyli* (plural), from Greek *stereos* 'solid' + *spondulos* 'vertebra'.

stereotactic /ˌstɛrɪə(ʊ)ˈtaktɪk, ˌstɪərɪə(ʊ)-/ (also **stereotaxic** /-ˈtaksɪk/) ▸ adjective relating to or denoting techniques for surgical treatment or scientific investigation that permit the accurate positioning of probes inside the brain or other parts of the body.

stereotaxis /ˌstɛrɪə(ʊ)ˈtaksɪs, ˌstɪərɪə(ʊ)-/ (also **stereotaxy** /-ˈtaksi/) ▸ noun [mass noun] the use of stereotactic instruments or devices in surgery or research.
– ORIGIN late 19th cent.: from **STEREO-** *three-dimensional* + Greek *taxis* 'orientation'.

stereotype ▸ noun **1** a widely held but fixed and oversimplified image or idea of a particular type of person or thing: *the stereotype of the woman as the carer* | *sexual and racial stereotypes*. ■ a person or thing that conforms to such an image: *don't treat anyone as a stereotype*.
2 a relief printing plate cast in a mould made from composed type or an original plate.
▸ verb [with obj.] view or represent as a stereotype: *the city is too easily stereotyped as an industrial wasteland*.
– DERIVATIVES **stereotypic** adjective, **stereotypical** adjective, **stereotypically** adverb.
– ORIGIN late 18th cent.: from French *stéréotype* (adjective).

stereotyped ▸ adjective viewed or represented as a stereotype: *the film is weakened by its stereotyped characters*.

stereotypy /ˈstɛrɪə(ʊ)ˌtʌɪpi, ˈstɪə-/ ▸ noun [mass noun] the persistent repetition of an act, especially by an animal, for no obvious purpose.

steric /ˈstɛrɪk, ˈstɪərɪk/ ▸ adjective Chemistry relating to the spatial arrangement of atoms in a molecule, especially as it affects chemical reactions.
– DERIVATIVES **sterically** adverb.
– ORIGIN late 19th cent.: formed irregularly from Greek *stereos* 'solid' + **-IC**.

sterigma /stəˈrɪgmə/ ▸ noun (pl. **sterigmata** /stəˈrɪgmətə/) Botany (in some fungi) a spore-bearing projection from a cell.
– ORIGIN mid 19th cent.: modern Latin, from Greek *stērigma* 'a support', from *stērizein* 'to support'.

sterilant /ˈstɛrɪl(ə)nt/ ▸ noun an agent used to destroy microorganisms; a disinfectant. ■ a chemical agent used to destroy pests and diseases in the soil, especially fungi and nematodes.

sterile ▸ adjective **1** not able to produce children or young: *the disease had made him sterile*. ■ (of a plant) not able to produce fruit or seeds. ■ (of land or soil) too poor in quality to produce crops. ■ lacking in imagination, creativity, or excitement; uninspiring or unproductive: *he found the fraternity's teachings sterile*.
2 free from bacteria or other living microorganisms; totally clean: *a sterile needle and syringes*.
– DERIVATIVES **sterilely** adverb.
– ORIGIN late Middle English: from Old French, or from Latin *sterilis*; related to Greek *steira* 'barren cow'. Sense 2 dates from the late 19th cent.

sterility ▸ noun [mass noun] the quality or condition of being sterile: *the disease can cause sterility in males* | *the sterility of debate in the party*.

sterilize (also **sterilise**) ▸ verb [with obj.] **1** make (something) free from bacteria or other living microorganisms: *babies' feeding equipment can be cleaned and sterilized* | (as adj. **sterilized**) *sterilized jars*.
2 deprive (a person or animal) of the ability to produce offspring, typically by removing or blocking the sex organs. ■ make (land or water) unable to produce crops or support life.
– DERIVATIVES **sterilizable** adjective, **sterilization** noun, **sterilizer** noun.

sterlet /ˈstəːlɪt/ ▸ noun a small sturgeon of the Danube basin and Caspian Sea area, farmed and commercially fished for its flesh and caviar. ● *Acipenser ruthenus*, family Acipenseridae.
– ORIGIN late 16th cent.: from Russian *sterlyad'*.

sterling ▸ noun [mass noun] **1** British money: *prices in sterling are shown* | [as modifier] *issues of sterling bonds*.
2 short for **STERLING SILVER**: [as modifier] *a sterling spoon*.
▸ adjective (of a person or their work or qualities) excellent or valuable: *this organization does sterling work for youngsters*.
– ORIGIN Middle English: probably from *steorra* 'star' + **-LING** (because some early Norman pennies bore a small star). Until recently one popular theory was that the coin was originally made by *Easterling* moneyers (from the 'eastern' Hanse towns), but the stressed first syllable would not have been dropped.

sterling area a group of countries, most belonging to the British Commonwealth, that formerly pegged their exchange rates to sterling or kept their reserves in sterling rather than gold or dollars.

sterling silver ▸ noun [mass noun] silver of 92½ per cent purity.

Sterlitamak /ˌstɛːlɪtəˈmɑːk/ an industrial city in southern Russia, situated on the Belaya River to the north of Orenburg; pop. 268,300 (est. 2008).

stern[1] ▸ adjective (of a person or their manner) serious and unrelenting, especially in the assertion of authority and exercise of discipline: *a smile transformed his stern face* | *Mama looked stern*. ■ (of an act or statement) strict and severe: *stern measures to restrict vehicle growth*. ■ (of competition or opposition) putting someone or something under extreme pressure: *the past year has been a stern test of the ability of British industry*.
– PHRASES **be made of sterner stuff** have a stronger character and be more able to overcome problems than others: *whereas James was deeply wounded by the failure, George was made of sterner stuff*. [from Shakespeare's *Julius Caesar* (III. 2. 93).] **the sterner sex** archaic men regarded in contrast to women.
– DERIVATIVES **sternly** adverb, **sternness** noun.
– ORIGIN Old English *styrne*, probably from the West Germanic base of the verb **STARE**.

stern[2] ▸ noun the rearmost part of a ship or boat: *he stood at the stern of the yacht*. ■ humorous a person's bottom: *my stern can't take too much sun*.
– DERIVATIVES **sterned** adjective [in combination] *a square-sterned vessel*, **sternmost** adjective, **sternwards** adverb.
– ORIGIN Middle English: probably from Old Norse *stjórn* 'steering', from *stýra* 'to steer'.

sternal ▸ adjective relating to the sternum: *the sternal area* | *sternal muscles*.

sternal rib ▸ noun another term for **TRUE RIB**.

sterndrive ▸ noun an inboard engine connected to an outboard drive unit at the rear of a powerboat.

Sterne /stəːn/, Laurence (1713–68), Irish novelist. He is best known for his nine-volume work *The Life and Opinions of Tristram Shandy* (1759–67), which parodied the developing conventions of the novel form.

Stern Gang the British name for a militant Zionist group that campaigned in Palestine during the 1940s for the creation of a Jewish state. Founded by Avraham Stern (1907–42) as an offshoot of Irgun, the group assassinated the British Minister for the Middle East, Lord Moyne, and Count Bernadotte, the UN mediator for Palestine.

sternite ▸ noun Entomology (in an insect) a sclerotized plate forming the sternum of a segment. Compare with **TERGITE**.

Sterno /ˈstəːnəʊ/ ▸ noun [mass noun] US trademark flammable hydrocarbon jelly supplied in cans for use as fuel for cooking stoves.
– ORIGIN early 20th cent.: from the name of *Sternau* and Co., New York, + **-O**.

sternocleidomastoid /ˌstəːnə(ʊ)ˌklʌɪdə(ʊ)ˈmastɔɪd/ (also **sternocleidomastoid muscle**) ▸ noun Anatomy each of a pair of long muscles which connect the sternum, clavicle, and mastoid process of the temporal bone and serve to turn and nod the neck.

sternomastoid /ˌstəːnə(ʊ)ˈmastɔɪd/ ▸ noun another term for **STERNOCLEIDOMASTOID**.

sternpost ▸ noun the central upright support at the stern of a boat, traditionally bearing the rudder.

sternsheets ▸ plural noun the flooring planks in a boat's after section, or the seating in this section of an open boat.

sternum /ˈstəːnəm/ ▸ noun (pl. **sternums** or **sterna** /-nə/) Anatomy the breastbone. ■ Zoology a thickened ventral plate on each segment of the body of an arthropod.
– ORIGIN mid 17th cent.: modern Latin, from Greek *sternon* 'chest'.

sternutation /ˌstəːnjʊˈteɪʃ(ə)n/ ▸ noun [mass noun] formal the action of sneezing.
– ORIGIN late Middle English: from Latin *sternutatio(n-)*, from the verb *sternutare*, frequentative of *sternuere* 'to sneeze'.

sternutator /ˈstəːnjʊˌteɪtə/ ▸ noun an agent that causes sneezing, especially one used in chemical warfare that causes irritation to the nose and eyes, pain in the chest, and nausea.

sternway ▸ noun [mass noun] backward movement of a ship: *we begin making sternway towards the shoal*.

sternwheeler ▸ noun a steamer propelled by a paddle wheel positioned at the stern.

steroid /ˈstɪərɔɪd, ˈstɛrɔɪd/ ▸ **noun** Biochemistry any of a large class of organic compounds with a characteristic molecular structure containing four rings of carbon atoms (three six-membered and one five). They include many hormones, alkaloids, and vitamins. ■ short for **ANABOLIC STEROID**.
– DERIVATIVES **steroidal** adjective.
– ORIGIN 1930s: from **STEROL** + **-OID**.

sterol /ˈstɪərɒl, ˈstɛrɒl/ ▸ **noun** Biochemistry any of a group of naturally occurring unsaturated steroid alcohols, typically waxy solids.
– ORIGIN early 20th cent.: independent usage of the ending of words such as **CHOLESTEROL**.

stertorous /ˈstəːt(ə)rəs/ ▸ **adjective** (of breathing) noisy and laboured.
– DERIVATIVES **stertorously** adverb.
– ORIGIN early 19th cent.: from modern Latin *stertor* 'snoring sound' (from Latin *stertere* 'to snore') + **-OUS**.

stet ▸ **verb** (**stets, stetting, stetted**) [no obj., in imperative] let it stand (used as an instruction on a printed proof to indicate that an alteration should be ignored). ■ [with obj.] write such an instruction against (something altered).
▸ **noun** such an instruction made on a printed proof.
– ORIGIN Latin, 'let it stand', from *stare* 'to stand'.

stethoscope /ˈstɛθəskəʊp/ ▸ **noun** a medical instrument for listening to the action of someone's heart or breathing, typically having a small disc-shaped resonator that is placed against the chest, and two tubes connected to earpieces.
– DERIVATIVES **stethoscopic** adjective.
– ORIGIN early 19th cent.: from French *stéthoscope*, from Greek *stēthos* 'breast' + *skopein* 'look at'.

Stetson /ˈstɛts(ə)n/ ▸ **noun** (trademark in the US) a hat with a high crown and a very wide brim, traditionally worn by cowboys and ranchers in the US.
– ORIGIN late 19th cent.: named after John B. *Stetson* (1830–1906), American hat manufacturer.

Stettin /ʃtɛˈtiːn/ German name for **SZCZECIN**.

steups /stʃuːps/ W. Indian ▸ **verb** [no obj.] make a noise by sucking air and saliva through the teeth, typically to express annoyance or derision.
▸ **noun** an expression of annoyance or derision made by sucking air and saliva through the teeth.
– ORIGIN imitative.

stevedore /ˈstiːvədɔː/ ▸ **noun** a person employed at a dock to load and unload ships.
– ORIGIN late 18th cent.: from Spanish *estivador*, from *estivar* 'stow a cargo', from Latin *stipare* (see **STEEVE²**).

Stevenage /ˈstiːvənɪdʒ/ a town in Hertfordshire, SE England; pop. 79,600 (est. 2009). It was designated a planned urban centre in 1946 and was developed as a new town.

Stevengraph /ˈstiːv(ə)ngrɑːf/ ▸ **noun** a type of small picture made from brightly coloured woven silk, produced during the late 19th century.
– ORIGIN named after Thomas Stevens (1828–88), English weaver, whose firm made them.

Stevens, Wallace (1879–1955), American poet. He wrote poetry privately and mostly in isolation from the literary community, developing an original and colourful style. His *Collected Poems* (1954) won a Pulitzer Prize.

Stevenson, Robert Louis (Balfour) (1850–94), Scottish novelist, poet, and travel writer. Stevenson made his name with the adventure story *Treasure Island* (1883). Other notable works: *The Strange Case of Dr Jekyll and Mr Hyde* and *Kidnapped* (both 1886).

stevia /ˈstɛvɪə, ˈstiːvɪə/ ▸ **noun** a shrub native to tropical and subtropical America, whose leaves may be used as a calorie-free substitute for sugar. ● Genus *Stevia*, family Compositae, in particular *S. rebaudiana*.
– ORIGIN modern Latin (genus name), named after Pedro Jaime *Esteve* (1500–66), Spanish physician and botanist.

stevioside /ˈstiːvɪə(ʊ)sʌɪd/ ▸ **noun** [mass noun] a sweet compound of the glycoside class obtained from the leaves of a Paraguayan shrub and used as a food sweetener. ● The shrub is *Stevia rebaudiana* (family Compositae).
– ORIGIN 1930s: from the genus name *Stevia* (see **STEVIA**).

stew¹ ▸ **noun 1** [mass noun] a dish of meat and vegetables cooked slowly in liquid in a closed dish or pan: *lamb stew* | [count noun] *add to casseroles, stews, and sauces.*
2 [in sing.] informal a state of great anxiety or agitation: ***she's in a right old stew.***
3 archaic a heated public room used for steam baths. ■ a brothel.
▸ **verb 1** (with reference to meat, fruit, or other food) cook or be cooked slowly in liquid in a closed dish or pan: [with obj.] *beef stewed in wine.* ■ [no obj.] Brit. (of tea) become strong and bitter with prolonged brewing.
2 [no obj.] informal remain in a heated or stifling atmosphere: *sweaty clothes left to stew in a plastic bag.* ■ worry about something, especially on one's own: *James will be expecting us, so we will let him stew a bit.*
– PHRASES **stew in one's own juice** informal be left to suffer the consequences of one's own actions.
– ORIGIN Middle English (in the sense 'cauldron'): from Old French *estuve* (related to *estuver* 'heat in steam'), probably based on Greek *tuphos* 'smoke, steam'. Sense 1 of the noun (mid 18th cent.) is directly from the verb (dating from late Middle English).

stew² ▸ **noun** Brit. a pond or large tank for keeping fish for eating. ■ an artificial oyster bed.
– ORIGIN Middle English: from Old French *estui*, from *estoier* 'confine'.

stew³ ▸ **noun** N. Amer. informal a flight attendant.
– ORIGIN 1970s: abbreviation of **STEWARDESS**.

steward ▸ **noun 1** a person who looks after the passengers on a ship, aircraft, or train.
2 a person responsible for supplies of food to a college, club, or other institution.
3 an official appointed to supervise arrangements or keep order at a large public event, for example a race, match, or demonstration.
4 short for **SHOP STEWARD**.
5 a person employed to manage another's property, especially a large house or estate. ■ Brit., chiefly historical an officer of the royal household, especially an administrator of Crown estates: [in titles] *Chief Steward of the Duchy of Lancaster.* ■ a person whose responsibility it is to take care of something: *farmers pride themselves on being stewards of the countryside.*
▸ **verb** [with obj.] **1** (of an official) supervise arrangements or keep order at (a large public event): *the event was organized and stewarded properly.*
2 manage or look after (another's property).
– DERIVATIVES **stewardship** noun.
– ORIGIN Old English *stīweard*, from *stig* (probably in the sense 'house, hall') + *weard* 'ward'. The verb dates from the early 17th cent.

stewardess /ˈstjuːədɪs, ˌstjuːəˈdɛs/ ▸ **noun** a woman who is employed to look after the passengers on a ship or aircraft.

Stewart¹ ▸ **adjective & noun** variant spelling of **STUART⁵**.

Stewart², Sir Jackie (b.1939), British motor-racing driver; born *John Young Stewart*. He was three times Formula One world champion (1969; 1971; 1973).

Stewart³, James (Maitland) (1908–97), American actor, famous for roles in which he embodied the all-American hero. His films include *The Philadelphia Story* (1940), which earned him an Oscar, *It's a Wonderful Life* (1946), *Vertigo* (1958), and westerns such as *The Man from Laramie* (1955).

Stewart Island an island of New Zealand, situated off the south coast of the South Island, from which it is separated by the Foveaux Strait; chief settlement, Oban.
– ORIGIN named after Captain William *Stewart*, a whaler and sealer who made a survey of the island in 1809.

stewartry (also **stewardry**) ▸ **noun** (pl. **stewartries**) a former territorial division of Scotland (abolished in 1747) under the jurisdiction of a steward. ■ (**The Stewartry**) the Kirkcudbright district of Galloway.

stewbum ▸ **noun** US informal an alcoholic, especially one who is homeless.

stewed ▸ **adjective 1** (of food) cooked slowly in liquid in a closed dish or pan: *stewed apple.* ■ Brit. (of tea) tasting strong and bitter because of prolonged brewing.
2 informal drunk.

stewing ▸ **adjective** [attrib.] (of meat or other food) suitable for stewing: *a pound of stewing steak.*

stewpot ▸ **noun** a large pot in which stews are cooked.

stg ▸ **abbreviation** sterling.

Sth ▸ **abbreviation** south.

sthenic /ˈsθɛnɪk/ ▸ **adjective** Medicine, dated of or having a high or excessive level of strength and energy.
– ORIGIN late 18th cent.: from Greek *sthenos* 'strength', on the pattern of *asthenic*.

STI ▸ **abbreviation** sexually transmitted infection.

stibnite /ˈstɪbnʌɪt/ ▸ **noun** [mass noun] a lead-grey mineral, typically occurring as striated prismatic crystals, which consists of antimony sulphide and is the chief ore of antimony.
– ORIGIN mid 19th cent.: from Latin *stibium* 'black antimony' + **-INE⁴** + **-ITE¹**.

stichomythia /ˌstɪkə(ʊ)ˈmɪθɪə/ ▸ **noun** [mass noun] dialogue in which two characters speak alternate lines of verse, used as a stylistic device in ancient Greek drama.
– ORIGIN mid 19th cent.: modern Latin, from Greek *stikhomuthia*, from *stikhos* 'row, line of verse' + *muthos* 'speech, talk'.

stick¹ ▸ **noun 1** a thin piece of wood that has fallen or been cut off a tree. ■ a long, thin piece of wood used for support in walking or as a weapon. ■ (in hockey, polo, and other games) a long, thin implement, typically made of wood, with a curved head or angled blade that is used to hit or direct the ball or puck. ■ (**sticks**) (in field hockey) the foul play of raising the stick above the shoulder. ■ [usu. with modifier] a short, thin piece of wood used to impale food: *lolly sticks.* ■ (**the sticks**) informal goalposts or cricket stumps. ■ Nautical, archaic a mast or spar. ■ a piece of basic furniture: *every* ***stick of furniture*** *just vanished.*
2 something resembling or likened to a stick, in particular: ■ a long, thin piece of something: ***a stick of*** *dynamite | cinnamon sticks.* ■ used to refer to a very thin person or limb: *the girl was a stick | her arms were like sticks.* ■ [as modifier] (of a figure) drawn with short, thin, straight lines: *stick drawings of a man and girl.* ■ a conductor's baton. ■ a gear or control lever. ■ US a quarter-pound pack of butter or margarine. ■ a number of bombs or paratroopers dropped rapidly from an aircraft. ■ a small group of soldiers assigned to a particular duty: ***a stick of*** *heavily armed guards.*
3 a threat of punishment or unwelcome measures (often contrasted with the offer of reward as a means of persuasion): *training that relies more on the carrot than on the stick.* Compare with **CARROT** (sense 3). ■ [mass noun] Brit. informal severe criticism or treatment: *I* ***took a lot of stick*** *from the press.*
4 (**the sticks**) informal, derogatory rural areas far from cities or civilization: *he felt hard done by living* ***out in the sticks.***
5 [with adj.] informal, dated a person of a specified kind: *Janet's not such a bad* ***old stick*** *sometimes.*
6 Stock Exchange a large quantity of unsold stock, especially the proportion of shares which must be taken up by underwriters after an unsuccessful issue.
– PHRASES **over the sticks** Horse Racing in steeplechasing and hurdles. **sticks and stones may break my bones but names (or words) will never hurt me** proverb used to express indifference to an insult or abuse: *all that flies back and forth, really, is words—sticks and stones, y'know?* **up the stick** Brit. informal pregnant. **up sticks** Brit. informal go to live elsewhere. [from nautical slang *to up sticks* 'set up a boat's mast' (ready for departure).]
– DERIVATIVES **sticklike** adjective.
– ORIGIN Old English *sticca* 'peg, stick, spoon', of West Germanic origin; related to Dutch *stek* 'cutting from a plant' and German *Stecken* 'staff, stick'.

stick² ▸ **verb** (past and past participle **stuck**) **1** [with obj.] (**stick something in/into/through**) push a sharp or pointed object into or through (something): *he stuck his fork into the sausage | she stuck her finger in his eye.* ■ (**stick something on**) fix something on (a point or pointed object): *stick the balls of wool on knitting needles.* ■ [no obj.] (**stick in/into/through**) (of a pointed object) be or remain fixed with its point embedded in (something): *there was a slim rod sticking into the ground beside me.* ■ stab or pierce with a sharp object: (as adj. **stuck**) *he screamed like a stuck pig.*
2 [with obj. and adverbial] insert, thrust, or push: *a youth with a cigarette stuck behind one ear | she stuck out her tongue at him.* ■ [no obj., with adverbial of direction] protrude or extend in a certain direction: *his front teeth stick out | Sue's hair was sticking up at all angles.* ■ [with obj. and adverbial of place] put somewhere, typically in a quick or careless way: *just stick that sandwich on my desk.* ■ informal used to express angry dismissal: *he told them they could stick the job—he didn't want it anyway.* ■ informal cause to incur an expense or loss: *she stuck me for last month's rent.*
3 [no obj.] adhere or cling to something: *the plastic seats stuck to my skin | if you heat the noodles in the microwave, they tend to stick together.* ■ [with obj. and adverbial of place] fasten or cause to adhere to something: *she stuck the stamp on the envelope.* ■ informal be or become convincing, established, or regarded as

S

valid: *the authorities couldn't make the charges stick* | *the name stuck and Anastasia she remained.* ■ (in pontoon and similar card games) decline to add to one's hand.

4 (**be/get stuck**) be fixed in a particular position or unable to move or be moved: *Sara tried to open the window but it was stuck* | *we got stuck in a traffic jam* | *the cat's stuck up a tree.* ■ [no obj.] be or become fixed or jammed as a result of an obstruction: *he drove into a bog, where his wheels stuck fast.* ■ (**be/get stuck**) be unable to progress with a task or find the answer or solution to something: *I'm doing the crossword and I've got stuck.* ■ [no obj.] remain in a static condition; fail to progress: *he lost a lot of weight but had stuck at 15 stone.* ■ [with adverbial of place] (**be stuck**) informal be or remain in a specified place or situation, typically one perceived as tedious or unpleasant: *I don't want to be stuck in an office all my life.* ■ (**be stuck for**) be at a loss for or in need of: *I'm not usually stuck for words.* ■ (**be stuck with**) informal be unable to get rid of or escape from: *like it or not, she and Grant were stuck with each other.* ■ (**be stuck on**) informal be infatuated with: *he's too good for Jenny, even though she's so stuck on him.*

5 [often with negative] Brit. informal accept or tolerate (an unpleasant or unwelcome person or situation): *I can't stick Geoffrey—he's a real old misery.* ■ (**stick it out**) informal put up with or persevere with something difficult or disagreeable.

– PHRASES **get stuck in** (or **into**) Brit. informal start doing (something) with enthusiasm or determination: *we got stuck into the decorating.* **stick at nothing** allow nothing to deter one from achieving one's aim, however wrong or dishonest: *he would stick at nothing to preserve his privileges.* **stick 'em up!** informal hands up! (spoken by a person threatening someone else with a gun). **stick in one's mind** (or **memory**) be remembered clearly and for a long time: *one particular incident sticks in my mind.* **stick in one's throat** (or **craw**) (of words) be difficult or impossible to say. ■ be difficult or impossible to accept: *the thing that sticks in your throat is that we were successful and you weren't.* **stick it to** informal, chiefly N. Amer. treat harshly or severely. **stick one** (or **it**) **on** Brit. informal hit (someone). **stick one's neck out** informal risk incurring criticism or anger by acting or speaking boldly. **stick out a mile** see MILE. **stick out like a sore thumb** see SORE. **stick to one's guns** see GUN. **stick to one's ribs** (of food) be filling and nourishing: *a bowl of soup that will stick to your ribs.*

– PHRASAL VERBS **stick around** informal remain in or near a place: *I'd like to stick around and watch the game.* **stick at** informal persevere with (a task or endeavour) in a determined way. **stick by 1** continue to support or be loyal to (someone), typically during difficult times: *I love him and whatever happens I'll stick by him.* **2** another way of saying STICK TO (sense 2) below. **stick something on** informal place the blame for a mistake or wrongdoing on (someone). **stick out** be extremely noticeable: *many important things had happened to him, but one stuck out.* **stick out for** refuse to accept less than (what one has asked for): *they offered him a Rover but Vic stuck out for a Jaguar.* **stick to 1** continue or confine oneself to doing or using (a particular thing): *I'll stick to bitter lemon, thanks.* ■ not move or digress from (a path or a subject). **2** adhere to (a commitment, belief, or rule): *the government stuck to their election pledges.* **stick together** informal remain united or mutually loyal: *we Europeans must stick together.* **stick someone/thing up** informal, chiefly N. Amer. rob someone or something at gunpoint. **stick up for** support or defend (a person or cause). **stick with** informal **1** persevere or continue with: *I'm happy to stick with the present team.* **2** another way of saying STICK BY above.

– ORIGIN Old English *stician*, of Germanic origin; related to German *sticken* 'embroider', from an Indo-European root shared by Greek *stizein* 'to prick', *stigma* 'a mark' and Latin *instigare* 'spur on'. Early senses included 'pierce' and 'remain fixed (by its embedded pointed end)'.

stickability ▶ **noun** [mass noun] informal a person's ability to persevere with something; staying power: *the secret of success is stickability.*

stickball ▶ **noun** [mass noun] N. Amer. an informal game played with a stick and a ball, derived from the rules of baseball or lacrosse.

sticker ▶ **noun 1** an adhesive label or notice, generally printed or illustrated.
2 informal a determined or persistent person.

sticker price ▶ **noun** N. Amer. the advertised retail price of an article.

sticker shock ▶ **noun** [mass noun] N. Amer. informal shock or dismay experienced by the potential buyers of a particular product on discovering its high or increased price.

stick-handle ▶ **verb** [no obj.] (usu. as noun **stick-handling**) Ice Hockey control the puck with one's stick.

sticking plaster ▶ **noun** Brit. a piece of flexible material with an adhesive backing for covering cuts or small wounds. ■ [often as modifier] a temporary and inadequate solution to a serious problem: *speed cameras may help, but this is a sticking-plaster solution.*

sticking point ▶ **noun** an obstacle to progress towards an agreement or goal: *safety issues have been a sticking point in the negotiations.*

stick insect ▶ **noun** a long, slender, slow-moving insect that resembles a twig. Many species appear to lack males and the females lay fertile eggs without mating. ● Family Phasmatidae, order Phasmida: many genera.

stick-in-the-mud ▶ **noun** informal a person who is dull and unadventurous and who resists change.

stickleback ▶ **noun** a small fish with sharp spines along its back, able to live in both salt and fresh water and found in both Eurasia and North America.
● Family Gasterosteidae: several genera and species, including the common and widespread **three-spined stickleback** (*Gasterosteus aculeatus*).

– ORIGIN late Middle English: from Old English *sticel* 'thorn, sting' + *bæc* 'back'.

stickler ▶ **noun** a person who insists on a certain quality or type of behaviour: *he's **a stickler for** accuracy* | *I'm a stickler when it comes to timekeeping.*

– ORIGIN mid 16th cent. (in the sense 'umpire'): from obsolete *stickle* 'be umpire', alteration of obsolete *stightle* 'to control', frequentative of Old English *stiht(i)an* 'set in order'.

stick-nest rat ▶ **noun** a fluffy-haired gregarious Australian rat which builds nests of interwoven sticks. ● Genus *Leporillus*, family Muridae: two species, in particular *L. conditor*.

stickpin ▶ **noun** N. Amer. a straight pin with an ornamental head, worn to keep a tie in place or as a brooch.

stickseed ▶ **noun** a plant of the borage family which bears small barbed seeds. ● Genera *Hackelia* and *Lappula*, family Boraginaceae: several species, in particular *H. floribunda*, which resembles a forget-me-not.

stick shift ▶ **noun** N. Amer. a gear lever or manual transmission.

stick-to-it-iveness ▶ **noun** [mass noun] N. Amer. informal perseverance; persistence.

stickum /ˈstɪkəm/ ▶ **noun** [mass noun] informal, chiefly N. Amer. a sticky or adhesive substance; gum or paste.

– ORIGIN early 20th cent.: from the verb STICK[2] + *-um* (representing the pronoun *them*).

stick-up ▶ **noun** informal, chiefly US an armed robbery in which a gun is used to threaten people.

stickweed ▶ **noun** [mass noun] US any of a number of North American plants with hooked or barbed seeds, e.g. ragweed.

sticky ▶ **adjective** (**stickier, stickiest**) **1** tending or designed to stick to things on contact: *sticky cakes and pastries* | *a sticky label.* ■ (of a substance) glutinous; viscous: *the dough should be moist but not sticky.* ■ (of prices, interest rates, or wages) slow to change or react to change.
2 (of the weather) hot and humid; muggy: *it was an unusually hot and sticky summer.* ■ damp with sweat: *she felt hot and sticky and changed her clothes.*
3 informal involving problems; difficult or awkward: *the relationship is going through a sticky patch.*
4 (of a website) attracting a long visit or repeat visits from users: *make your site as sticky as possible to keep visitors there longer.*
▶ **noun 1** a piece of yellow paper with an adhesive strip on one side, used for leaving messages or reminders.
2 (on an Internet message board) a thread set to remain at the top of the list of threads regardless of when it was last updated.

– PHRASES **come to a sticky end** see END. **sticky fingers** informal a propensity to steal. **a sticky wicket** see WICKET.

– DERIVATIVES **stickily** adverb, **stickiness** noun.

stickybeak Austral./NZ informal ▶ **noun** an inquisitive and prying person. ■ [in sing.] an inquisitive or prying look or investigation: *guests were invited to have a good old stickybeak around.*
▶ **verb** [no obj.] pry into other people's affairs: *I don't mean to stickybeak, but when is he going to leave?*

sticky end ▶ **noun** Biochemistry an end of a DNA double helix at which a few unpaired nucleotides of one strand extend beyond the other.

sticky-fingered ▶ **adjective** informal given to stealing: *a sticky-fingered con artist.*

sticky tape ▶ **noun** [mass noun] Brit. transparent adhesive tape.

stiction /ˈstɪkʃ(ə)n/ ▶ **noun** [mass noun] Physics the friction which tends to prevent stationary surfaces from being set in motion.

Stieglitz /ˈstiːɡlɪts/, Alfred (1864–1946), American photographer, husband of Georgia O'Keefe. He was important for his pioneering work to establish photography as a fine art in the US.

stifado /stɪˈfɑːdəʊ/ ▶ **noun** [mass noun] a Greek dish of meat stewed with onions and sometimes tomatoes.

– ORIGIN from modern Greek *stiphado*.

stiff ▶ **adjective 1** not easily bent or changed in shape; rigid: *a stiff black collar* | *stiff cardboard.* ■ (of a semi-liquid substance) viscous; thick: *add wheat until the mixture is quite stiff.* ■ not moving as freely as is usual or desirable; difficult to turn or operate: *a stiff drawer* | *the shower tap is a little stiff.* ■ (of a person or part of the body) unable to move easily and without pain: *he was stiff from sitting on the desk* | *a stiff back.* ■ (of a person or their manner) not relaxed or friendly; constrained: *she greeted him with stiff politeness.*
2 severe or strong: *they face stiff fines and a possible jail sentence* | *a stiff increase in taxes.* ■ (of a wind) blowing strongly: *a stiff breeze stirring the lake.* ■ requiring strength or effort; difficult: *a long stiff climb up the bare hillside.* ■ (of an alcoholic drink) strong: *a stiff measure of brandy.*
3 (**stiff with**) informal full of: *the place is stiff with alarm systems.*
4 (**—— stiff**) informal having a specified unpleasant feeling to an extreme extent: *she was scared stiff* | *I was bored stiff with my project.*
▶ **noun** informal **1** a dead body.
2 chiefly N. Amer. a boring, conventional person: *ordinary working stiffs in respectable offices.*
3 (**the stiffs**) Brit. a sports club's reserve team.
▶ **verb** [with obj.] informal **1** N. Amer. cheat (someone) out of something, especially money. ■ fail to leave (someone) a tip.
2 N. Amer. ignore (someone) deliberately; snub.
3 kill (someone): *the girl was found stiffed in an air-conditioning duct.* ■ [no obj.] (of a commercial venture or product) be unsuccessful: *as soon as he began singing about the wife and kids, his albums stiffed.*

– PHRASES **stiff as a board** informal (of a person or part of the body) extremely stiff. **a stiff upper lip** a quality of uncomplaining stoicism: *senior managers had to keep a stiff upper lip and remain optimistic.*

– DERIVATIVES **stiffish** adjective, **stiffly** adverb, **stiffness** noun.

– ORIGIN Old English *stīf*, of Germanic origin; related to Dutch *stijf*.

stiff-arm ▶ **verb** [with obj.] tackle or fend off (a person) by extending an arm rigidly (illegal in rugby).

stiffen ▶ **verb** make or become stiff or rigid: [with obj.] *he stiffened his knees in an effort to prevent them trembling* | [no obj.] *my back **stiffens up** and I can't bend.* ■ [with obj.] support or strengthen (a garment or fabric), typically by adding tape or an adhesive layer. ■ make or become stronger or more steadfast: [with obj.] *outrage over the murders stiffened the government's resolve to confront the Mafia* | [no obj.] *the regime's resistance stiffened.*

– DERIVATIVES **stiffener** noun.

stiffening ▶ **noun** [mass noun] material used to stiffen a garment, fabric, or other object.

stiff-necked ▶ **adjective** haughty and stubborn: *stiff-necked pride.*

stifftail (also **stiff-tailed duck**) ▶ **noun** a diving duck with a stiff tail of pointed feathers, often held up at an angle. ● Family Anatidae: four genera, in particular *Oxyura*, and several species, e.g. the ruddy duck.

stiffy (also **stiffie**) ▶ **noun** (pl. **stiffies**) vulgar slang an erection of a man's penis.

stifle[1] ▶ **verb** [with obj.] **1** make (someone) unable to breathe properly; suffocate: *those in the streets were stifled by the fumes.*
2 restrain (a reaction) or stop oneself acting on (an emotion): *she stifled a giggle.* ■ prevent or constrain (an activity or idea): *high taxes were stifling private enterprise.*

– DERIVATIVES **stifler** noun.

– ORIGIN late Middle English: perhaps from a frequentative of Old French *estouffer* 'smother, stifle'.

stifle[2] (also **stifle joint**) ▶ noun a joint in the legs of horses, dogs, and other animals, equivalent to the knee in humans.
– ORIGIN Middle English: of unknown origin.

stifle bone ▶ noun the bone in front of a stifle.

stifling ▶ adjective 1 (of heat, air, or a room) very hot and causing difficulties in breathing; suffocating: *stifling heat | the loft is stifling in summer.*
2 making one feel constrained or oppressed: *the stifling formality of her family life.*
– DERIVATIVES **stiflingly** adverb [as submodifier] *a stiflingly hot day.*

stigma /ˈstɪɡmə/ ▶ noun (pl. **stigmas** or especially in sense 2 **stigmata** /-mətə, -ˈmɑːtə/) 1 a mark of disgrace associated with a particular circumstance, quality, or person: *the stigma of mental disorder | to be a non-reader carries a social stigma.*
2 (**stigmata**) (in Christian tradition) marks corresponding to those left on Christ's body by the Crucifixion, said to have been impressed by divine favour on the bodies of St Francis of Assisi and others.
3 Medicine a visible sign or characteristic of a disease. ■ a mark or spot on the skin.
4 Botany (in a flower) the part of a pistil that receives the pollen during pollination.
– ORIGIN late 16th cent. (denoting a mark made by pricking or branding): via Latin from Greek *stigma* 'a mark made by a pointed instrument, a dot'; related to STICK[1].

stigmaria /stɪɡˈmɛːrɪə/ ▶ noun (pl. **stigmariae** /-ˈmɛːrɪiː/) Palaeontology a fossilized root of a giant lycopod, common in Carboniferous coal measures. ● Class Lycopsida, in particular the genera *Lepidodendron* and *Sigillaria*.
– DERIVATIVES **stigmarian** adjective.
– ORIGIN mid 19th cent.: modern Latin, from Greek *stigma*, with reference to the scars where rootlets were attached, covering the fossils.

stigmatic ▶ adjective 1 relating to a stigma or stigmas, in particular constituting or conveying a mark of disgrace: *the less stigmatic offence of manslaughter.*
2 another term for ANASTIGMATIC.
▶ noun a person bearing stigmata.
– DERIVATIVES **stigmatically** adverb.
– ORIGIN late 16th cent. (in the sense '(person) marked with a blemish or deformity'): from Latin *stigma, stigmat-* + -IC.

stigmatist ▶ noun another term for STIGMATIC.

stigmatize (also **stigmatise**) ▶ verb [with obj.]
1 describe or regard as worthy of disgrace or great disapproval: *the institution was stigmatized as a last resort for the destitute.*
2 mark with stigmata.
– DERIVATIVES **stigmatization** noun.
– ORIGIN late 16th cent. (in the sense 'mark with a brand'): from French *stigmatiser* or medieval Latin *stigmatizare*, from Greek *stigmatizein*, from *stigma* (see STIGMA).

Stijl see DE STIJL.

stilb ▶ noun a unit of luminance equal to one candela per square centimetre.
– ORIGIN 1940s: from French, from Greek *stilbein* 'to glitter'.

stilbene /ˈstɪlbiːn/ ▶ noun [mass noun] Chemistry a synthetic aromatic hydrocarbon which forms phosphorescent crystals and is used in dye manufacture. ● Alternative name: *trans*-**1,2-diphenylethene**; chem. formula: $C_6H_5CH{=}CHC_6H_5$.
– ORIGIN mid 19th cent.: from Greek *stilbein* 'to glitter' + -ENE.

stilboestrol /stɪlˈbiːstrɒl/ (US **stilbestrol**) ▶ noun [mass noun] Biochemistry a powerful synthetic oestrogen used in hormone therapy, as a post-coital contraceptive, and as a growth-promoting agent for livestock.
– ORIGIN 1930s: from STILBENE + OESTRUS + -OL.

stile[1] ▶ noun an arrangement of steps that allows people but not animals to climb over a fence or wall.
– ORIGIN Old English *stigel*, from a Germanic root meaning 'to climb'.

stile[2] ▶ noun a vertical piece in the frame of a panelled door or sash window. Compare with RAIL[1] (sense 3 of the noun).
– ORIGIN late 17th cent.: probably from Dutch *stijl* 'pillar, doorpost'.

stiletto ▶ noun (pl. **stilettos**) 1 chiefly Brit. a woman's shoe with a thin, high tapering heel. ■ (also **stiletto heel**) a heel on a stiletto shoe.
2 a short dagger with a tapering blade. ■ a sharp-pointed tool for making eyelet holes.
– ORIGIN early 17th cent.: from Italian, diminutive of *stilo* 'dagger'.

still[1] ▶ adjective not moving or making a sound: *the still body of the young man | the sheriff commanded him to **stand still** and drop the gun | she sat very still, her eyes closed.* ■ (of air, water, or the weather) undisturbed by wind, sound, or current; calm and tranquil: *her voice carried on the still air | a still autumn day.* ■ chiefly Brit. (of a drink) not effervescent.
▶ noun 1 [mass noun] deep silence and calm; stillness: *the still of the night.*
2 an ordinary static photograph as opposed to a motion picture, especially a single shot from a cinema film: *film stills* | [as modifier] *stills photography.*
▶ adverb 1 up to and including the present or the time mentioned; even now (or then) as formerly: *he still lives with his mother | it was still raining.* ■ referring to something that will or may happen in the future: *we could still win.*
2 nevertheless; all the same: *I'm afraid he's crazy. Still, he's harmless.*
3 even (used with comparatives for emphasis): *write, or better still, type, captions for the pictures | Hank, already sweltering, began to sweat still more profusely.*
▶ verb make or become still; quieten: [with obj.] *she raised her hand, stilling Erica's protests* | [no obj.] *the din in the hall stilled.*
– PHRASES **still and all** informal nevertheless; even so. **still small voice** the voice of one's conscience (with reference to 1 Kings 19:12). **still waters run deep** proverb a quiet or placid manner may conceal a passionate nature.
– DERIVATIVES **stillness** noun.
– ORIGIN Old English *stille* (adjective and adverb), *stillan* (verb), of West Germanic origin, from a base meaning 'be fixed, stand'.

still[2] ▶ noun an apparatus for distilling alcoholic drinks such as whisky.
– ORIGIN mid 16th cent.: from the rare verb *still* 'extract by distillation', shortening of DISTIL.

stillage ▶ noun a wooden rack or pallet for holding stored goods off the floor or separating goods in transit.
– ORIGIN late 16th cent. (originally denoting a stand for casks): apparently from Dutch *stellagie* 'scaffold', from *stellen* 'to place'.

stillbirth ▶ noun the birth of an infant that has died in the womb (strictly, after having survived through at least the first 28 weeks of pregnancy, earlier instances being regarded as abortion or miscarriage).

stillborn ▶ adjective (of an infant) born dead. ■ (of a proposal or plan) having failed to develop or be realized: *the proposed wealth tax was stillborn.*

still-hunt chiefly N. Amer. ▶ verb [no obj.] (often as noun **still-hunting**) hunt game stealthily; stalk.
▶ noun a stealthy hunt for game.

still life ▶ noun (pl. **still lifes**) a painting or drawing of an arrangement of objects, typically including fruit and flowers and objects contrasting with these in texture, such as bowls and glassware. ■ [mass noun] this type or genre of painting or drawing.

still room ▶ noun Brit. historical a room in a large house used by the housekeeper for the storage of preserves, cakes, and liqueurs and the preparation of tea and coffee.
– ORIGIN early 18th cent.: a term used earlier for a room in a house where a still was kept for the distillation of perfumes and cordials.

Stillson /ˈstɪls(ə)n/ (also **Stillson wrench**) ▶ noun a large wrench with jaws that tighten as pressure is increased.
– ORIGIN early 20th cent.: named after Daniel C. Stillson (1830–99), its American inventor.

stilly literary ▶ adverb quietly and with little movement: *the birds rested stilly.*
▶ adjective still and quiet: *the stilly night.*

stilt ▶ noun 1 (usu. **stilts**) either of a pair of upright poles with supports for the feet enabling the user to walk at a distance above the ground. ■ each of a set of posts or piles supporting a building. ■ a small, flat, three-pointed support for ceramic ware in a kiln.
2 a long-billed wading bird with predominantly black and white plumage and very long slender reddish legs. ● Family Recurvirostridae: two genera, in particular *Himantopus*, and several species.
– ORIGIN Middle English: of Germanic origin; related to Dutch *stelt* and German *Stelze*. Sense 2 dates from the late 18th cent.

stilt bug ▶ noun a plant bug with very long slender legs. ● Family Berytidae, suborder Heteroptera: many genera.

stilted ▶ adjective 1 (of a manner of talking or writing) stiff and self-conscious or unnatural: *we made stilted conversation.*
2 standing on stilts: *villages of stilted houses.* ■ Architecture (of an arch) with pieces of upright masonry between the imposts and the springers.
– DERIVATIVES **stiltedly** adverb, **stiltedness** noun.

Stilton ▶ noun [mass noun] trademark a kind of strong rich cheese, often with blue veins, originally made at various places in Leicestershire.
– ORIGIN so named because it was formerly sold to travellers at a coaching inn in Stilton (now in Cambridgeshire).

stimulant ▶ noun a substance that raises levels of physiological or nervous activity in the body. ■ something that increases activity, interest, or enthusiasm in a specified field: *population growth is a major stimulant to industrial development.*
▶ adjective raising levels of physiological or nervous activity in the body: *caffeine has stimulant effects on the heart.*
– ORIGIN early 18th cent.: from Latin *stimulant-* 'urging, goading', from the verb *stimulare*.

stimulate ▶ verb [with obj.] raise levels of physiological or nervous activity in (the body or any biological system): *the women are given fertility drugs to stimulate their ovaries.* ■ encourage or arouse interest or enthusiasm in: *the reader could not fail to be stimulated by the ideas presented.* ■ encourage development of or increased activity in (a state or process): *the courses stimulate a passion for learning.*
– DERIVATIVES **stimulation** noun, **stimulative** adjective, **stimulator** noun, **stimulatory** adjective.
– ORIGIN mid 16th cent. (in the sense 'sting, afflict'): from Latin *stimulat-* 'urged, goaded', from the verb *stimulare*.

stimulating ▶ adjective encouraging or arousing interest or enthusiasm: *a rich and stimulating working environment.*
– DERIVATIVES **stimulatingly** adverb.

stimulus /ˈstɪmjʊləs/ ▶ noun (pl. **stimuli** /-lʌɪ, -liː/) a thing or event that evokes a specific functional reaction in an organ or tissue: *areas of the brain which respond to auditory stimuli.* ■ a thing that arouses activity or energy in someone or something; a spur or incentive: *if the tax were abolished, it would act as a stimulus to exports.* ■ [in sing.] an interesting and exciting quality: *she loved the stimulus of the job.*
– ORIGIN late 17th cent.: from Latin, 'goad, spur, incentive'.

sting ▶ noun 1 a small sharp-pointed organ at the end of the abdomen of bees, wasps, ants, and scorpions, capable of inflicting a painful or dangerous wound by injecting poison. ■ any of a number of minute hairs or other organs of plants, jellyfishes, etc., which inject a poisonous or irritating fluid when touched. ■ a wound from a sting: *a wasp or bee sting.* ■ a sharp tingling or burning pain or sensation: *she felt the sharp sting of tears behind her eyelids.* ■ [in sing.] a hurtful quality or effect: *I recalled the sting of his betrayal | she smiled to **take the sting out of** her words.*
2 informal a carefully planned operation, typically one involving deception: *five blackmailers were jailed last week after they were snared in a police sting.* S
▶ verb (past and past participle **stung**) 1 [with obj.] wound or pierce with a sting: *he was stung by a jellyfish* | [no obj.] *a nettle stings if you brush it lightly.* ■ feel or cause to feel a sharp tingling or burning pain or sensation: [no obj.] *her eyes stung as if she might cry again* | [with obj.] *the brandy stung his throat* | (as adj. **stinging**) *a stinging pain.* ■ [with obj.] (typically of something said) hurt or upset (someone): *stung by her mockery, Frank hung his head.* ■ (**sting someone into**) provoke someone to do (something) by causing annoyance or offence: *he was stung into action by an article in the paper.*
2 [with obj.] informal swindle or exorbitantly overcharge (someone): *I had to buy some boxer shorts at the last minute and got stung for £42.50!*
– PHRASES **sting in the tail** an unexpected, typically unpleasant or problematic end to something: *the Budget comes with a sting in the tail—future tax increases.*
– DERIVATIVES **stingingly** adverb, **stingless** adjective.
– ORIGIN Old English *sting* (noun), *stingan* (verb), of Germanic origin.

stingaree /ˌstɪŋəˈriː, ˈstɪŋəriː/ ▶ noun a cinnamon-brown stingray occurring on sand flats in shallow

Australian waters. ● *Urolophus testaceus*, family Urolophidae.
■ US & Austral./NZ informal any stingray.
– ORIGIN mid 19th cent.: alteration of STINGRAY.

stinge ▶ noun informal a mean or ungenerous person.
– ORIGIN early 20th cent.: back-formation from STINGY.

stinger ▶ noun **1** an insect or animal that stings, such as a bee or jellyfish. ■ the part of an insect or animal that holds a sting. ■ informal a painful blow: *he suffered a stinger on his right shoulder.*
2 (**Stinger**) (trademark in the US) a device consisting of a spiked metal ribbon that is placed across a road to stop vehicles by puncturing their tyres.

stinging nettle ▶ noun a Eurasian nettle covered in minute hairs that inject irritants such as histamine and acetylcholine when they are touched. ● Genus *Urtica*, family Urticaceae: several species, in particular *U. dioica*.

stingray ▶ noun a bottom-dwelling marine ray with a flattened diamond-shaped body and a long poisonous serrated spine at the base of the tail. ● Families Dasyatidae (the **long-tailed stingrays**) and Urolophidae (the **short-tailed stingrays**): several species.

stingy /ˈstɪn(d)ʒi/ ▶ adjective (**stingier**, **stingiest**) informal mean; ungenerous: *his boss is stingy and idle.*
– DERIVATIVES **stingily** adverb, **stinginess** noun.
– ORIGIN mid 17th cent.: perhaps a dialect variant of the noun STING + -Y[1].

stink ▶ verb (past **stank** or **stunk** ; past participle **stunk**) [no obj.] **1** have a strong unpleasant smell: *the place stank like a sewer* | *his breath stank of drink.* ■ [with obj.] (**stink somewhere out/up**) informal fill somewhere with a strong unpleasant smell: *her perfume stank the place out.*
2 informal be very unpleasant, contemptible, or scandalous: *he thinks the values of our society stink.* ■ (**stink of**) be highly suggestive of (something regarded with disapproval): *the whole affair stinks of a set-up.* ■ (**stink of**) have or appear to have a scandalously large amount of (something, especially money): *the whole place was luxurious and stank of money.*
▶ noun [in sing.] **1** a strong unpleasant smell; a stench: *the stink of the place hit me as I went in.*
2 informal a row or fuss: *a silly move now would **kick up a stink** we couldn't handle.*
▶ adjective W. Indian **1** having a strong unpleasant smell: *'What you doing with that stink dog?'.*
2 contemptible; corrupt: *the whole episode is so stink that the principal asked for an immediate transfer of the teacher.*
– PHRASES **like stink** informal extremely hard or intensely: *she's working like stink to get everything ready.*
– DERIVATIVES **stinky** adjective (**stinkier**, **stinkiest**) informal.
– ORIGIN Old English *stincan*, of West Germanic origin; related to Dutch and German *stinken*, also to STENCH.

stinkard /ˈstɪŋkəd/ ▶ noun archaic a smelly or despicable person.

stink badger ▶ noun a SE Asian badger with a long mobile snout, short stout limbs, and anal glands that contain a foul-smelling liquid which can be squirted at an attacker. ● Genus *Mydaus*, family Mustelidae: two species, including the teledu.

S

stink bomb ▶ noun a small glass container holding a sulphurous compound that is released when the container is thrown to the ground and broken, emitting a strong and very unpleasant smell.

stink bug ▶ noun another term for SHIELD BUG.

stinker ▶ noun informal a person or thing that smells very bad. ■ a contemptible or very unpleasant person or thing: *have those little stinkers been bullying you?* ■ a difficult task: *Tackled the crossword yet? It's a stinker.*

stinkhorn ▶ noun a widely distributed fungus which has a tall whitish stem with a rounded greenish-brown gelatinous head that turns into a foul-smelling slime containing the spores. ● Family Phallaceae, class Gasteromycetes: many species, including the common European *Phallus impudicus*.

stinking ▶ adjective foul-smelling: *he was locked in a stinking cell.* ■ informal very bad or unpleasant: *a stinking cold.*
▶ adverb [as submodifier] informal extremely: *she is obviously stinking rich.*
– DERIVATIVES **stinkingly** adverb.

stinking cedar ▶ noun a tree of the yew family found only in Florida, with fetid leaves, branches, and timber. ● *Torreya taxifolia*, family Taxaceae. Alternative name: **Florida torreya**.

stinking dungworm ▶ noun another term for BRANDLING.

stinking hellebore ▶ noun a European hellebore with greenish purple-tipped flowers. ● *Helleborus foetidus*, family Ranunculaceae.

stinking iris ▶ noun another term for GLADDON.

stinking smut ▶ noun another term for BUNT[2].

stinko ▶ adjective informal extremely drunk.

stinkpot ▶ noun **1** informal, chiefly US a contemptible or foul-smelling person or thing.
2 (also **stinkpot turtle**) an American musk turtle with a domed shell, typically living in muddy-bottomed waters and producing a strong unpleasant smell when disturbed. ● *Kinosternon odoratum* (or *Sternotherus odoratus*), family Kinosternidae.

stinkweed ▶ noun [mass noun] any of a number of plants with a strong or foetid smell, e.g. (N. Amer.) jimson weed.

stinkwood ▶ noun any of a number of trees that yield timber with an unpleasant odour, in particular: ● (**black stinkwood**) a South African tree (*Ocotea bullata*, family Lauraceae). ● a New Zealand tree (*Coprosoma foetidissima*, family Rubiaceae).

stint[1] ▶ verb [with obj.] [often with negative] supply a very ungenerous or inadequate amount of (something): *stowage room hasn't been stinted.* ■ restrict (someone) in the amount of something, especially money, given or permitted: *to avoid having to stint yourself, budget in advance.* ■ [no obj.] be very economical or mean about spending or providing something: *he doesn't **stint on** wining and dining.*
▶ noun **1** a person's fixed or allotted period of work: *his varied career included a stint as a magician.*
2 [mass noun] limitation of supply or effort: *a collector with an eye for quality and the means to indulge it **without stint**.*
– ORIGIN Old English *styntan* 'make blunt', of Germanic origin; related to STUNT[1].

stint[2] ▶ noun a small short-legged sandpiper of northern Eurasia and Alaska, with a brownish back and white underparts. ● Genus *Calidris*, family Scolopacidae: four species.
– ORIGIN Middle English: of unknown origin.

stipe /stʌɪp/ ▶ noun Botany a stalk or stem, especially the stem of a seaweed or fungus or the stalk of a fern frond.
– ORIGIN late 18th cent.: from French, from Latin *stipes* (see STIPES).

stipend /ˈstʌɪpɛnd/ ▶ noun a fixed regular sum paid as a salary or as expenses to a clergyman, teacher, or public official.
– ORIGIN late Middle English: from Old French *stipendie* or Latin *stipendium*, from *stips* 'wages' + *pendere* 'to pay'.

stipendiary /stʌɪˈpɛndɪəri, stɪ-/ ▶ adjective receiving a stipend; working for payment rather than voluntarily: *stipendiary clergy* | *a stipendiary magistrate.* ■ relating to or of the nature of a stipend: *stipendiary obligations.*
▶ noun (pl. **stipendiaries**) a person receiving a stipend.
– ORIGIN late Middle English (as a noun): from Latin *stipendiarius*, from *stipendium* (see STIPEND).

stipes /ˈstʌɪpiːz/ ▶ noun (pl. **stipites** /ˈstɪpɪtiːz/) Zoology a part or organ resembling a stalk, especially the second joint of the maxilla of an insect. ■ Botany more technical term for STIPE.
– ORIGIN mid 18th cent.: from Latin, literally 'log, tree trunk'.

stipitate ▶ adjective chiefly Botany (especially of a fungus) having a stipe or a stipes.

stipple ▶ verb [with obj.] (in drawing, painting, and engraving) mark (a surface) with numerous small dots or specks: (as noun **stippling**) *the miniaturist's use of stippling.* ■ produce a decorative effect on (paint or other material) by roughening its surface when it is wet.
▶ noun [mass noun] the process or technique of stippling a surface, or the effect so created.
– ORIGIN mid 17th cent.: from Dutch *stippelen*, frequentative of *stippen* 'to prick', from *stip* 'a point'.

stipulate[1] /ˈstɪpjʊleɪt/ ▶ verb [with obj.] demand or specify (a requirement), typically as part of an agreement: *he stipulated certain conditions before their marriage* | (as adj. **stipulated**) *the stipulated time has elapsed.*
– ORIGIN early 17th cent.: from Latin *stipulat-* 'demanded as a formal promise', from the verb *stipulari*.

stipulate[2] /ˈstɪpjʊlət/ ▶ adjective Botany (of a leaf or plant) having stipules.
– ORIGIN late 18th cent.: from Latin *stipula* (see STIPULE) + -ATE[2].

stipulation ▶ noun a condition or requirement that is specified or demanded as part of an agreement: *they donated their collection of prints with the stipulation that they never be publicly exhibited.*

stipule /ˈstɪpjuːl/ ▶ noun Botany a small leaf-like appendage to a leaf, typically borne in pairs at the base of the leaf stalk.
– DERIVATIVES **stipular** adjective.
– ORIGIN late 18th cent.: from French *stipule* or Latin *stipula* 'straw'.

stir[1] ▶ verb (**stirs**, **stirring**, **stirred**) **1** [with obj.] move a spoon or other implement round and round in (a liquid or other substance) in order to mix it thoroughly: *Desmond stirred his tea and ate a biscuit* | [no obj.] *pour in the cream and stir well.* ■ (**stir something in/into**) add an ingredient to (a liquid or other substance) in such a way: *stir in the flour and cook gently for two minutes.*
2 move or cause to move slightly: [no obj.] *nothing stirred except the wind* | [with obj.] *a gentle breeze stirred the leaves* | *cloudiness is caused by the fish **stirring up** mud.* ■ [no obj.] rise or wake from sleep: *no one else had stirred yet.* ■ (**stir from/out of**) leave or go out of (a place): *as he grew older, he seldom stirred from his club.* ■ begin or cause to begin to be active or to develop: [no obj.] *the 1960s, when the civil rights movement stirred* | [with obj.] *a voice **stirred her from** her reverie* | *he even **stirred himself** to play an encore.*
3 [with obj.] arouse strong feeling in (someone); move or excite: *they will be **stirred to** action by what is written* | *he **stirred up** the sweating crowd.* ■ arouse or prompt (a feeling or memory) or inspire (the imagination): *the story stirred many memories of my childhood* | *the rumours had **stirred up** his anger.* ■ [no obj.] Brit. informal deliberately cause trouble by spreading rumours or gossip: *Francis was always stirring, trying to score off people.*
▶ noun [in sing.] **1** a slight physical movement: *I stood, straining eyes and ears for the faintest stir.* ■ an initial sign of a specified feeling: *Caroline felt a stir of anger deep within her breast.*
2 a commotion: *the event caused quite a stir.*
3 an act of stirring food or drink: *he gives his Ovaltine a stir.*
– PHRASES **stir the blood** make someone excited or enthusiastic. **stir one's stumps** [often in imperative] Brit. informal, dated (of a person) begin to move or act.
– PHRASAL VERBS **stir something up** cause or provoke trouble or bad feeling: *he accused me of trying to stir up trouble.*
– ORIGIN Old English *styrian*, of Germanic origin; related to German *stören* 'disturb'.

stir[2] ▶ noun informal prison: *I've spent twenty-eight years in stir.*
– ORIGIN mid 19th cent.: perhaps from Romany *sturbin* 'jail'.

stirabout ▶ noun [mass noun] chiefly Irish porridge made by stirring oatmeal in boiling water or milk.

stir-crazy ▶ adjective informal, chiefly N. Amer. psychologically disturbed, especially as a result of being confined or imprisoned.

stir-fry ▶ verb [with obj.] fry (meat, fish, or vegetables) rapidly over a high heat while stirring briskly: (as adj. **stir-fried**) *stir-fried beef.*
▶ noun a dish cooked by stir-frying.

stirk /stəːk/ ▶ noun dialect a yearling bullock or heifer.
– ORIGIN Old English *stirc*, perhaps from *stēor* 'steer' + *-oc* (see -OCK).

Stirling[1] a city and administrative region in central Scotland, on the River Forth; pop. 32,000 (est. 2009).

Stirling[2], James (1692–1770), Scottish mathematician. His main work, *Methodus Differentialis* (1730), was concerned with summation and interpolation. A formula named after him, giving the approximate value of the factorial of large numbers, was actually first worked out by the French-born mathematician **Abraham de Moivre** (1667–1754).

Stirling[3], Robert (1790–1878), Scottish engineer and Presbyterian minister. In 1816 he invented (with the help of his brother James) a type of external-combustion engine using heated air.

Stirling engine ▶ noun a machine used to provide power or refrigeration, operating on a closed cycle in

which a working fluid is cyclically compressed and expanded at different temperatures.
– ORIGIN mid 19th cent.: named after Robert **Stirling**[1].

stirrer ▸ noun **1** an object or mechanical device used for stirring something.
2 Brit. informal a person who deliberately causes trouble between others by spreading rumours or gossip.

stirring ▸ adjective **1** causing excitement or strong emotion; rousing: *stirring songs*.
2 archaic moving briskly; active.
▸ noun an initial sign of activity, movement, or emotion: *the first stirrings of anger*.
– DERIVATIVES **stirringly** adverb.

stirrup ▸ noun **1** each of a pair of devices attached to each side of a horse's saddle, in the form of a loop with a flat base to support the rider's foot.
2 (**stirrups** or **lithotomy stirrups**) a pair of metal supports in which a woman's ankles may be placed during gynaecological examinations and childbirth, to hold her legs in a position which will facilitate medical examination or intervention.
3 (also **stirrup bone**) another term for **stapes**.
– ORIGIN Old English *stigrāp*, from the Germanic base of obsolete *sty* 'climb' + **rope**.

stirrup cup ▸ noun a cup of wine or other alcoholic drink offered to a person on horseback who is about to depart on a journey.

stirrup iron ▸ noun the metal loop of a stirrup, in which the rider's foot rests.

stirrup leather ▸ noun the strap attaching a stirrup iron to a saddle.

stirrup pants ▸ plural noun a pair of women's stretch trousers having a band of elastic at the bottom of each leg which passes under the arch of the foot.

stirrup pump ▸ noun chiefly historical a portable hand-operated water pump with a footrest resembling a stirrup, used to extinguish small fires.

stishovite /ˈstɪʃəvʌɪt/ ▸ noun [mass noun] a mineral that is a dense polymorph of silica and is formed at very high pressures, especially in meteorite craters.
– ORIGIN 1960s: from the name of Sergei M. *Stishov*, 20th-cent. Russian chemist, + **-ite**[1].

stitch ▸ noun **1** a loop of thread or yarn resulting from a single pass or movement of the needle in sewing, knitting, or crocheting. ■ a loop of thread used to join the edges of a wound or surgical incision: *he had to have sixteen stitches to his head*. ■ [usu. with modifier] a method of sewing, knitting, or crocheting producing a particular pattern or design: *basic embroidery stitches*. ■ [in sing., usu. with negative] informal the smallest item of clothing: *nymphs with come-hither looks and not a stitch on*.
2 a sudden sharp pain in the side of the body, caused by strenuous exercise: *he was panting and had a stitch*.
▸ verb [with obj.] **1** make, mend, or join (something) with stitches: *stitch a plain seam with right sides together* | *they stitched the cut on her face* | (as adj. in combination **-stitched**) *hand-stitched dresses*.
2 (**stitch someone up**) Brit. informal manipulate a situation so that someone is placed at a disadvantage or wrongly blamed for something: *he was stitched up by outsiders and ousted as chairman*. ■ (**stitch something up**) arrange or secure a deal or agreement to one's advantage: *the company has stitched up major deals all over the world to boost sales*.
– PHRASES **in stitches** informal laughing uncontrollably: *his droll self-mockery* ***had us in stitches***. **a stitch in time saves nine** proverb if you sort out a problem immediately it may save extra work later.
– DERIVATIVES **stitcher** noun, **stitchery** noun, **stitchless** adjective.
– ORIGIN Old English *stice* 'a puncture, stabbing pain', of Germanic origin; related to German *Stich* 'a sting, prick', also to **stick**[2]. The sense 'loop' (in sewing etc.) arose in Middle English.

stitchbird ▸ noun a rare New Zealand honeyeater with mainly dark brown or blackish plumage and a sharp call that resembles the word 'stitch'.
● *Notiomystis cincta*, family Meliphagidae.

stitching ▸ noun [mass noun] a row of stitches sewn on to cloth: *the gloves were white with black stitching*.

stitch-up ▸ noun Brit. informal an act of placing someone in a position in which they will be wrongly blamed for something, or of manipulating a situation to one's advantage.

stitchwort ▸ noun a straggling European plant of the pink family with a slender stem and white starry flowers. It was formerly thought to cure a stitch in the side. ● Genus *Stellaria*, family Caryophyllaceae: several species, in particular **greater stitchwort** (*S. holostea*).

stiver /ˈstʌɪvə/ ▸ noun a small coin formerly used in the Netherlands, equal to one twentieth of a guilder. ■ archaic any coin of low value. ■ [with negative] archaic a very small or insignificant amount: *they didn't care a stiver*.
– ORIGIN from Dutch *stuiver*, denoting a small coin; probably related to the noun **stub**.

STM ▸ abbreviation scanning tunnelling microscope.

stoa /ˈstəʊə/ ▸ noun a classical portico or roofed colonnade. ■ (**the Stoa**) the great hall in Athens in which the ancient Greek philosopher Zeno gave the founding lectures of the Stoic school of philosophy.
– ORIGIN Greek.

stoat ▸ noun a small carnivorous mammal of the weasel family which has chestnut fur with white underparts and a black-tipped tail. It is native to both Eurasia and North America and in northern areas the coat turns white in winter. Compare with **ermine**, **weasel**. ● *Mustela erminea*, family Mustelidae. North American name: **short-tailed weasel**.
– ORIGIN late Middle English: of unknown origin.

stob /stɒb/ ▸ noun dialect, chiefly Scottish & US a broken branch or a stump. ■ a stake used for fencing.
– ORIGIN Middle English: variant of **stub**.

stochastic /stəˈkastɪk/ ▸ adjective technical having a random probability distribution or pattern that may be analysed statistically but may not be predicted precisely.
– DERIVATIVES **stochastically** adverb.
– ORIGIN mid 17th cent.: from Greek *stokhastikos*, from *stokhazesthai* 'aim at, guess', from *stokhos* 'aim'.

stocious /ˈstəʊʃəs/ ▸ adjective Irish informal drunk; intoxicated.
– ORIGIN 1930s: of unknown origin.

stock ▸ noun **1** [mass noun] the goods or merchandise kept on the premises of a shop or warehouse and available for sale or distribution: *the store has a very low turnover of stock* | [count noun] *buy now, while stocks last!* | [as modifier] *stock shortages*. ■ a supply or quantity of something accumulated or available for future use: *I need to replenish my* ***stock of*** *wine* | [count noun] *fish stocks are being dangerously depleted*. ■ farm animals such as cattle, pigs, and sheep, bred and kept for their meat or milk; livestock. ■ short for **rolling stock**. ■ (also **film stock**) photographic film that has not been exposed or processed. ■ (in some card games) the cards that have not yet been dealt, left on the table to be drawn.
2 [mass noun] the capital raised by a business or corporation through the issue and subscription of shares: *between 1982 and 1986 the value of the company's stock rose by 86%*. ■ (usu. **stocks**) a portion of this as held by an individual or group as an investment: *she owned £3000 worth of stocks and shares*. ■ (usu. **stocks**) the shares of a particular company, type of company, or industry: *blue-chip stocks*. ■ (in the UK) securities issued by the government in fixed units with a fixed rate of interest: *government gilt-edged stock*. ■ a person's reputation or popularity: *I felt I was right, but my stock was low with this establishment*.
3 [mass noun] liquid made by cooking bones, meat, fish, or vegetables slowly in water, used as a basis for the preparation of soup, gravy, or sauces: *a pint of chicken stock*. ■ [with modifier] the raw material from which a specified commodity can be manufactured: *the fat can be used as soap stock*.
4 [mass noun] [usu. with adj. or noun modifier] a person's ancestry or line of descent: *her mother was of French stock*. ■ a breed, variety, or population of an animal or plant.
5 the trunk or woody stem of a living tree or shrub, especially one into which a graft (scion) is inserted. ■ the perennial part of a herbaceous plant, especially a rhizome.
6 a herbaceous European plant that is cultivated for its fragrant lilac, pink, or white flowers. [mid 17th cent.: from *stock-gillyflower*.] ● Genus *Matthiola*, family Cruciferae: several species, in particular the **Brompton stock** (*M. incana*) and the **night-scented stock** (*M. bicornis*).
7 (**the stocks**) [treated as sing. or pl.] historical an instrument of punishment consisting of an adjustable wooden structure with holes for securing a person's feet and hands, in which criminals were locked and exposed to public ridicule or assault.
8 the part of a rifle or other firearm to which the barrel and firing mechanism are attached, held against one's shoulder when firing the gun. ■ the crossbar of an anchor. ■ the handle of something such as a whip or fishing rod. ■ short for **headstock** (sense 1). ■ short for **tailstock**.
9 a band of white material tied like a cravat and worn as a part of formal horse-riding dress. ■ a piece of black material worn under a clerical collar.
10 (**stocks**) a frame used to support a ship or boat out of water, especially when under construction.
▸ adjective [attrib.] **1** (of a product or type of product) usually kept in stock and thus regularly available for sale: *25 per cent off stock items*.
2 (of a phrase or expression) so regularly used as to be automatic or hackneyed: *she faltered momentarily and then resorted to the teenager's favourite stock response 'whatever'*. ■ denoting a conventional character type or situation that recurs in a particular genre of literature, theatre, or film: *the stock characters in every cowboy film*. ■ denoting or relating to cinematic footage that can be regularly used in different productions, typically that of outdoor scenes used to add realism to a production shot in an indoor set.
▸ verb [with obj.] **1** have or keep a supply of (a particular product or type or product) available for sale: *most supermarkets now stock a range of organic produce*. ■ provide or fill with goods, items, or a supply of something: *I must* ***stock up*** *the fridge* | (as adj., with submodifier or in combination **stocked**) *a well-stocked shop*. ■ [no obj.] (**stock up**) amass supplies of something, typically for a particular occasion or purpose: *I'm stocking up for Christmas* | *you'd better* ***stock up with*** *fuel*.
2 fit (a rifle or other firearm) with a stock.
– PHRASES **in** (or **out of**) **stock** (of goods) available (or unavailable) for immediate sale in a shop. **on the stocks** in construction or preparation: *also on the stocks is a bill to bring about tax relief for these businesses*. **put stock in** [often with negative] have a specified amount of belief or faith in: *I don't put much stock in modern medicine*. **stock and station** Austral./NZ denoting a firm or agent dealing in farm products and supplies. **take stock** make an overall assessment of a particular situation, typically before making a decision: *he needed a period of peace and quiet in order to* ***take stock of*** *his life*.
– DERIVATIVES **stockless** adjective.
– ORIGIN Old English *stoc(c)* 'trunk, block of wood, post', of Germanic origin; related to Dutch *stok* and German *Stock* 'stick'. The notion 'store, fund' (sense 1 of the noun and sense 2 of the noun) arose in late Middle English and is of obscure origin, perhaps expressing 'growth from a central stem' or 'firm foundation'.

stockade ▸ noun a barrier formed from upright wooden posts or stakes, especially as a defence against attack or as a means of confining animals. ■ an enclosure bound by a stockade: *we got ashore and into the stockade*. ■ chiefly N. Amer. a military prison.
▸ verb [with obj.] (usu. as adj. **stockaded**) enclose (an area) by erecting a stockade.
– ORIGIN early 17th cent.: shortening of obsolete French *estocade*, alteration of *estacade*, from Spanish *estacada*, from the Germanic base of the noun **stake**[1].

stock book ▸ noun a book used by a business to keep records of quantities of goods acquired, held in stock, and disposed of.

stockbreeder ▸ noun a farmer who breeds livestock.
– DERIVATIVES **stockbreeding** noun.

stock brick ▸ noun a hard solid brick pressed in a mould.

stockbroker ▸ noun a broker who buys and sells securities on a stock exchange on behalf of clients.
– DERIVATIVES **stockbrokerage** noun, **stockbroking** noun.

stockbroker belt ▸ noun Brit. an affluent residential area outside a large city.

stock car ▸ noun **1** an ordinary car that has been strengthened for use in a type of race in which competing cars collide with each other.
2 N. Amer. a railway wagon for transporting livestock.

stock company ▸ noun N. Amer. a repertory company that is largely based in one theatre.

stock control ▸ noun [mass noun] the regulation of the stock-in-trade of a company so that all items are available without delay but without tying up unnecessarily large sums of money.

stock cube ▸ noun a cube of concentrated dehydrated meat, vegetable, or fish stock for use in cooking.

stock dove ▸ noun a grey Eurasian and North African pigeon, resembling a small wood pigeon, and nesting in holes in trees. ● *Columba oenas*, family Columbidae.

S

stocker ▸ noun **1** N. Amer. a farm animal, typically a young steer or heifer, destined for slaughter but kept until matured or fattened.
2 a person whose job is to fill the shelves of a shop or supermarket with merchandise.
3 N. Amer. informal a stock car.

stock exchange ▸ noun a market in which securities are bought and sold: *the company was floated on the Stock Exchange.* ■ (**the Stock Exchange**) the level of prices in such a market: *a plunge in the Stock Exchange during the election campaign.*

stockfeed ▸ noun [mass noun] food for livestock.

stockfish ▸ noun (pl. **same** or **stockfishes**) **1** a commercially valuable hake of coastal waters of southern Africa. ● *Merluccius capensis*, family Merlucciidae.
2 [mass noun] cod or a similar fish split and dried in the open air without salt.
– ORIGIN Middle English (in sense 2): from Middle Low German, Middle Dutch *stokvisch*, of unknown origin; sense 1 (early 19th cent.) from South African Dutch.

Stockhausen /ˈstɒkˌhaʊz(ə)n, ˈʃtɒk-/, Karlheinz (1928–2007), German composer. An important avant-garde composer and exponent of serialism, he co-founded an electronic music studio for West German radio, and in 1977 embarked on his *Licht* cycle of musical ceremonies, completed in 2003.

stockholder ▸ noun **1** chiefly N. Amer. a shareholder.
2 a holder of supplies for manufacturers.
– DERIVATIVES **stockholding** noun.

Stockholm /ˈstɒkhəʊm/ the capital of Sweden, a seaport on the east coast, situated on the mainland and on numerous adjacent islands; pop. 810,120 (2008).

Stockholm syndrome ▸ noun [mass noun] feelings of trust or affection felt in many cases of kidnapping or hostage-taking by a victim towards a captor.
– ORIGIN 1970s: with reference to a bank robbery in Stockholm.

Stockholm tar ▸ noun [mass noun] a kind of tar prepared from resinous pinewood and used in particular in shipbuilding and as an ingredient of ointments.

stock horse ▸ noun Austral./NZ a stockman's horse.

stockinet (also **stockinette**) ▸ noun [mass noun] a soft, loosely knitted stretch fabric, formerly used for making underwear and now used for cleaning, wrapping, or bandaging.
– ORIGIN late 18th cent.: probably an alteration of *stocking-net*.

stocking ▸ noun a women's garment, typically made of translucent nylon or silk, that fits closely over the foot and is held up by suspenders or an elasticated strip at the upper thigh. ■ short for CHRISTMAS STOCKING. ■ US or archaic a long sock worn by men. ■ [usu. with modifier] a cylindrical bandage or other medical covering for the leg resembling a stocking, especially an elasticated support used in the treatment of disorders of the veins. ■ a white marking of the lower part of a horse's leg, extending as far as, or just beyond, the knee or hock.
– PHRASES **in (one's) stockinged feet** without shoes: *she stood five feet ten in her stockinged feet.*
– DERIVATIVES **stockinged** adjective [in combination] *her black-stockinged legs*, **stockingless** adjective.
– ORIGIN late 16th cent.: from STOCK in the dialect sense 'stocking' + -ING[1].

stocking cap ▸ noun a knitted conical hat with a long tapered end, often bearing a tassel, that hangs down.

stocking filler (N. Amer. **stocking stuffer**) ▸ noun a small present suitable for putting in a Christmas stocking.

stocking mask ▸ noun a nylon stocking pulled over the face to disguise the features, used by criminals.

stocking stitch ▸ noun [mass noun] a knitting stitch consisting of alternate rows of plain and purl stitch.

stock-in-trade ▸ noun [mass noun] **1** the typical subject or commodity a person, company, or profession uses or deals in: *information is our stock-in-trade.* ■ qualities, ideas, or behaviour characteristic of a person or their work: *flippancy is his stock-in-trade.*
2 the goods kept in hand by a business for the purposes of its trade.

stockist ▸ noun Brit. a retailer that stocks goods of a particular type for sale: *one of the country's largest stockists of Italian designer labels.*

stockjobber ▸ noun **1** Brit. another term for JOBBER (sense 1).
2 N. Amer. derogatory a stockbroker.
– DERIVATIVES **stockjobbing** noun.

stocklist ▸ noun Brit. a publication listing a retailer's stock of goods with current prices.

stockman ▸ noun (pl. **stockmen**) **1** a person who looks after livestock. ■ US an owner of livestock.
2 US a person who looks after a stockroom or warehouse.

stock market ▸ noun (usu. **the stock market**) a stock exchange.

stock option ▸ noun another term for SHARE OPTION.

stock-out ▸ noun a situation in which an item is out of stock.

stockpile ▸ noun a large accumulated stock of goods or materials, especially one held in reserve for use at a time of shortage or other emergency.
▸ verb [with obj.] accumulate a large stock of (goods or materials): *he claimed that the weapons were being stockpiled.*
– DERIVATIVES **stockpiler** noun.

Stockport an industrial town and metropolitan district in NW England, near Manchester; pop. 133,400 (est. 2009).

stockpot ▸ noun a pot in which stock for soup is prepared by long, slow cooking.

stock-proof ▸ adjective (of a fence or other barrier) effective in preventing livestock from straying.

stockroom ▸ noun a room in which quantities of goods are stored.

stock split ▸ noun N. Amer. an issue of new shares in a company to existing shareholders in proportion to their current holdings.

stock-still ▸ adverb without any movement; completely still: *he stood stock-still.*

stocktaking ▸ noun [mass noun] the action or process of recording the amount of stock held by a business: *the shop is closed for stocktaking.* ■ the action of reviewing and assessing one's situation and options.
– DERIVATIVES **stocktake** noun & verb, **stocktaker** noun.

Stockton-on-Tees an industrial town in NE England, a port on the River Tees near its mouth on the North Sea; pop. 80,600 (est. 2009). The town developed after the opening in 1825 of the Stockton and Darlington Railway, the first passenger rail service in the world.

stock whip ▸ noun a whip used for driving cattle.

stocky ▸ adjective (**stockier**, **stockiest**) broad and sturdily built: *he had a short, stocky body.*
– DERIVATIVES **stockily** adverb, **stockiness** noun.

stockyard ▸ noun N. Amer. a large yard containing pens and sheds in which livestock is kept and sorted.

stodge ▸ noun [mass noun] Brit. informal food that is heavy, filling, and high in carbohydrates: *she ate her way through a plateful of stodge.* ■ dull and uninspired material or work.
– ORIGIN late 17th cent. (as a verb in the sense 'stuff to stretching point'): symbolic, suggested by STUFF and PODGE.

stodgy ▸ adjective (**stodgier**, **stodgiest**) Brit. (of food) heavy, filling, and high in carbohydrates. ■ dull and uninspired; lacking originality or excitement: *some of the material is rather stodgy and top-heavy with facts.* ■ chiefly US bulky or heavy in appearance: *this stodgy three-storey building.*
– DERIVATIVES **stodginess** noun, **stodgily** adverb.

stoep /stuːp/ ▸ noun S. African a veranda in front of a house.
– ORIGIN Afrikaans, from Dutch; related to STEP.

stog ▸ verb (**be stogged**) dialect or US be stuck or bogged down: *people are stogged in their misery.*
– ORIGIN early 19th cent.: perhaps symbolic and suggested by STICK[2] and BOG.

stogy /ˈstəʊgi/ (also **stogie**) ▸ noun (pl. **stogies**) N. Amer. a long, thin, cheap cigar.
– ORIGIN mid 19th cent. (originally as *stoga*): short for *Conestoga* in Pennsylvania.

stoic /ˈstəʊɪk/ ▸ noun **1** a person who can endure pain or hardship without showing their feelings or complaining.
2 (**Stoic**) a member of the ancient philosophical school of Stoicism.
▸ adjective **1** another term for STOICAL.
2 (**Stoic**) of or belonging to the Stoics or their school of philosophy.
– ORIGIN late Middle English: via Latin from Greek *stōïkos*, from STOA (with reference to Zeno's teaching in the *Stoa Poikilē* or Painted Porch, at Athens).

stoical /ˈstəʊɪk(ə)l/ ▸ adjective enduring pain and hardship without showing one's feelings or complaining: *he taught a stoical acceptance of suffering.*
– DERIVATIVES **stoically** adverb.

stoichiometric /ˌstɔɪkɪə(ʊ)ˈmɛtrɪk/ ▸ adjective Chemistry relating to stoichiometry. ■ relating to or denoting quantities of reactants in simple integral ratios, as prescribed by an equation or formula.
– DERIVATIVES **stoichiometrically** adverb.

stoichiometry /ˌstɔɪkɪˈɒmɪtri/ ▸ noun [mass noun] Chemistry the relationship between the relative quantities of substances taking part in a reaction or forming a compound, typically a ratio of whole integers.
– ORIGIN early 19th cent.: from Greek *stoikheion* 'element' + -METRY.

stoicism /ˈstəʊɪsɪz(ə)m/ ▸ noun [mass noun] **1** the endurance of pain or hardship without the display of feelings and without complaint.
2 (**Stoicism**) an ancient Greek school of philosophy founded at Athens by Zeno of Citium. The school taught that virtue, the highest good, is based on knowledge; the wise live in harmony with the divine Reason (also identified with Fate and Providence) that governs nature, and are indifferent to the vicissitudes of fortune and to pleasure and pain.

stoke ▸ verb [with obj.] add coal or other solid fuel to (a fire, furnace, boiler, etc.): *he stoked up the barbecue.* ■ encourage or incite (a strong emotion or tendency): *his composure had the effect of stoking her anger | the Chancellor was stoking up a consumer boom.* ■ [no obj.] informal consume a large quantity of food or drink to give one energy: *Carol was at the coffee machine, stoking up for the day.*
– ORIGIN mid 17th cent.: back-formation from STOKER.

stoked ▸ adjective informal, chiefly N. Amer. excited or euphoric: *when they told me I was on the team, I was stoked.*

stokehold ▸ noun a compartment in a steamship in which the boilers and furnace are housed.

stokehole ▸ noun a space in front of a furnace in which a stoker works.

Stoke-on-Trent a city on the River Trent in Staffordshire, central England; pop. 248,300 (est. 2009). It has long been the centre of the Staffordshire pottery industries.

Stoker, Bram (1847–1912), Irish novelist and theatre manager; full name *Abraham Stoker*. He was secretary and touring manager to the actor Henry Irving but is chiefly remembered as the author of the vampire story *Dracula* (1897).

stoker ▸ noun a person who tends the furnace on a steamship or steam train. ■ a mechanical device for supplying fuel to a firebox or furnace, especially on a steam locomotive.
– ORIGIN mid 17th cent.: from Dutch, from *stoken* 'stoke a furnace', from Middle Dutch *stoken* 'push, poke'; related to STICK[1].

stokes (abbrev.: **ST**) ▸ noun (pl. **same**) Physics the cgs unit of kinematic viscosity, corresponding to a dynamic viscosity of 1 poise and a density of 1 gram per cubic centimetre, equivalent to 10^{-4} square metres per second.
– ORIGIN mid 20th cent.: from the name of Sir G. Stokes (see STOKES' LAW).

Stokes' law ▸ noun Physics **1** a law stating that in fluorescence the wavelength of the emitted radiation is longer than that of the radiation causing it. This is not true in all cases.
2 an expression describing the resisting force on a particle moving through a viscous fluid and showing that a maximum velocity is reached in such cases, e.g. for an object falling under gravity through a fluid.
– ORIGIN late 19th cent.: named after Sir George *Stokes* (1819–1903), British physicist.

Stokes' theorem ▸ noun Mathematics a theorem proposing that the surface integral of the curl of a function over any surface bounded by a closed path is equal to the line integral of a particular vector function round that path.
– ORIGIN late 19th cent.: named after Sir G. *Stokes* (see STOKES' LAW).

Stokowski /stɒˈkɒfski/, Leopold (1882–1977), British-born American conductor, of Polish descent. He is best known for arranging and conducting the music for Walt Disney's film *Fantasia* (1940), which sought to bring classical music to cinema audiences by means of cartoons.

stokvel /ˈstɒkfɛl/ ▸ noun (in South Africa) a savings or investment society to which members regularly contribute an agreed amount and from which they

S

receive a lump sum payment. ■ (in South Africa) a society formed to hold regular parties that are funded by the members and generate profits for the hosts. ■ a party held by a stokvel.
– ORIGIN from an Africanized pronunciation of *stock-fair*, denoting a periodical gathering of buyers and sellers of livestock.

STOL ▸ **abbreviation** Aeronautics short take-off and landing.

stole[1] ▸ **noun** a woman's long scarf or shawl, especially of fur or similar material, worn loosely over the shoulders. ■ a priest's silk vestment worn over the shoulders and hanging down to the knee or below.
– ORIGIN Old English (in the senses 'long robe' and 'priest's vestment'), via Latin from Greek *stolē* 'clothing', from *stellein* 'array'.

stole[2] past of **STEAL**.

stolen past participle of **STEAL**.

stolen generation ▸ **noun** Austral. the Aboriginal people forcibly removed from their families as children between the 1900s and the 1960s, to be brought up by white foster families or in institutions.

stolid ▸ **adjective** calm, dependable, and showing little emotion or animation: *a stolid bourgeois gent*.
– DERIVATIVES **stolidity** noun, **stolidly** adverb, **stolidness** noun.
– ORIGIN late 16th cent.: from obsolete French *stolide* or Latin *stolidus* (perhaps related to *stultus* 'foolish').

stollen /'stɒlən, 'ʃtɒ-/ ▸ **noun** a rich German fruit and nut loaf.
– ORIGIN from German *Stollen*.

stolon /'stəʊlɒn/ ▸ **noun 1** Botany a creeping horizontal plant stem or runner that takes root at points along its length to form new plants. ■ an arching stem of a plant that roots at the tip to form a new plant, as in the bramble.
2 Zoology the branched stem-like structure of some colonial hydroid coelenterates, attaching the colony to the substrate.
– DERIVATIVES **stoloniferous** adjective.
– ORIGIN early 17th cent.: from Latin *stolo*, *stolon-* 'shoot, scion'.

stoma /'stəʊmə/ ▸ **noun** (pl. **stomas** or **stomata** /-mətə/) **1** Botany any of the minute pores in the epidermis of the leaf or stem of a plant, forming a slit of variable width which allows movement of gases in and out of the intercellular spaces. Also called **STOMATE**. ■ Zoology a small mouth-like opening in some lower animals.
2 Medicine an artificial opening made into a hollow organ, especially one on the surface of the body leading to the gut or trachea.
– DERIVATIVES **stomal** adjective (Medicine).
– ORIGIN late 17th cent.: modern Latin, from Greek *stoma* 'mouth'.

stomach ▸ **noun 1** the internal organ in which the first part of digestion occurs, being (in humans and many mammals) a pear-shaped enlargement of the alimentary canal linking the oesophagus to the small intestine. ■ each of four stomachs in a ruminant (the rumen, reticulum, omasum, and abomasum). ■ any of a number of organs analogous to the stomach in lower animals. ■ the front part of the body between the chest and thighs; the belly: *Blake hit him in the stomach*. ■ [in sing.] the stomach viewed as the seat of hunger, nausea, anxiety, or other unsettling feelings: *Virginia had a sick feeling in her stomach*.
2 [in sing.] [usu. with negative] an appetite for food or drink: *she doesn't have the stomach to eat anything*. ■ a desire or inclination for something involving conflict or difficulty: *the teams proved to have no stomach for a fight*.
▸ **verb** [with obj.] (usu. **cannot stomach**) consume (food or drink) without feeling or being sick: *if you cannot stomach orange juice, try apple juice*. ■ endure or accept (an obnoxious thing or person): *I can't stomach the self-righteous attitude of some managers*.
– PHRASES **on a full** (or **an empty**) **stomach** after having eaten (or having not eaten): *I always think better on a full stomach*. **a strong stomach** an ability to see or do unpleasant things without feeling sick or squeamish.
– DERIVATIVES **stomachful** noun (pl. **stomachfuls**).
– ORIGIN Middle English: from Old French *estomac*, *stomaque*, via Latin from Greek *stomakhos* 'gullet', from *stoma* 'mouth'. The early sense of the verb was 'be offended at, resent' (early 16th cent.).

stomach ache ▸ **noun** a pain in a person's stomach or belly.

stomacher ▸ **noun** historical a V-shaped piece of decorative cloth, worn over the chest and stomach by men and women in the 16th century, later only by women.
– ORIGIN late Middle English: probably a shortening of Old French *estomachier*, from *estomac* (see **STOMACH**).

stomachic /stə'makɪk/ dated ▸ **adjective** promoting the appetite or assisting digestion.
▸ **noun** a stomachic medicine or tonic.

stomach muscles ▸ **plural noun** the muscles constituting the front wall of the abdomen.

stomach pump ▸ **noun** a syringe attached to a long tube, used for extracting the contents of a person's stomach (for example, if they have taken poison).

stomach tube ▸ **noun** a tube passed into the stomach via the gullet for cleansing or emptying it or for introducing food.

stomata plural form of **STOMA**.

stomatal /'stəʊmət(ə)l, 'stɒ-/ ▸ **adjective** chiefly Botany relating to a stoma or stomata.

stomate /'stəʊmeɪt/ ▸ **noun** Botany another term for **STOMA**.
– ORIGIN mid 19th cent.: apparently an English singular of **STOMATA**.

stomatitis /ˌstəʊmə'tʌɪtɪs, ˌstɒ-/ ▸ **noun** [mass noun] Medicine inflammation of the mucous membrane of the mouth.
– ORIGIN mid 19th cent.: modern Latin, from *stoma*, *stomat-* 'mouth' + **-ITIS**.

stomatogastric /ˌstəʊmətə(ʊ)'gastrɪk, ˌstɒmətə(ʊ)-, stəˌmatə(ʊ)-/ ▸ **adjective** chiefly Zoology relating to or connected with the mouth and stomach.
– ORIGIN mid 19th cent.: from Greek *stoma*, *stomat-* 'mouth' + **GASTRIC**.

stomp ▸ **verb** [no obj., with adverbial of direction] tread heavily and noisily, typically in order to show anger: *Martin stomped off to the spare room*. ■ [no obj.] (**stomp on**) tread heavily or stamp on: *I stomped on the accelerator*. ■ [with obj.] chiefly US deliberately trample or tread heavily on: *Cobb proceeded to kick and stomp him viciously*. ■ [with obj.] stamp (one's feet). ■ [no obj.] dance with heavy stamping steps.
▸ **noun** informal (in jazz or popular music) a tune or song with a fast tempo and a heavy beat. ■ a lively dance performed to music with a fast tempo and heavy beat, involving stamping.
– DERIVATIVES **stomper** noun, **stompy** adjective (**stompier**, **stompiest**).
– ORIGIN early 19th cent. (originally US dialect): variant of the verb **STAMP**.

stompie /'stɒmpi/ ▸ **noun** (pl. **stompies**) S. African informal a cigarette butt. ■ a half-smoked cigarette kept for later use.
– PHRASES **pick up stompies** break into a conversation of which one has heard only the end.
– ORIGIN Afrikaans, diminutive of *stomp* 'stump'.

stomping ▸ **adjective** (of popular music) having a fast tempo and a heavy beat.

stomping ground ▸ **noun** N. Amer. another term for **STAMPING GROUND**.

stone ▸ **noun 1** [mass noun] hard solid non-metallic mineral matter of which rock is made, especially as a building material. ■ used in similes and metaphors to refer to weight or lack of feeling, expression, or movement: *Isabel stood as if* ***turned to stone*** | *the elevator* ***dropped like a stone***. ■ [count noun] a small piece of rock found on the ground. ■ [count noun] Astronomy a meteorite made of rock, as opposed to metal. ■ [count noun] Medicine a calculus; a gallstone or kidney stone.
2 a piece of stone shaped for a purpose, especially one of commemoration, ceremony, or demarcation: *a memorial stone* | *boundary stones*. ■ a gem or jewel. ■ short for **CURLING STONE**. ■ a round piece or counter, originally made of stone, used in various board games, especially the Japanese game of go. ■ a large flat table or sheet, originally made of stone and now usually of metal, on which pages of type are made up.
3 a hard seed in a cherry, plum, peach, and some other fruits.
4 (pl. **same**) Brit. a unit of weight equal to 14 lb (6.35 kg): *I weighed 10 stone*.
5 [mass noun] a natural shade of whitish or brownish-grey: [as modifier] *stone stretch trousers*.
▸ **verb** [with obj.] **1** throw stones at: *policemen were stoned by the crowd* | *two people were stoned to death*.
2 remove the stone from (a fruit): (as adj. **stoned**) *add 50 g of stoned black olives*.
3 build, face, or pave with stone.
– PHRASES **be written** (or **engraved** or **set**) **in stone** used to emphasize that something is fixed and unchangeable: *anything can change—nothing is written in stone*. **cast** (or **throw**) **the first stone** be the first to make an accusation (used to emphasize that a potential critic is not wholly blameless). [with biblical allusion to John 8:7.] **leave no stone unturned** try every possible course of action in order to achieve something. **stone me!** (or **stone the crows!**) Brit. informal an exclamation of surprise or shock. **a stone's throw** a short distance: *the Sea Life Centre is just a stone's throw from the sea itself*.
– DERIVATIVES **stoneless** adjective.
– ORIGIN Old English *stān* (noun), of Germanic origin; related to Dutch *steen* and German *Stein*. The verb dates from Middle English (first recorded in sense 1 of the verb).

Stone Age a prehistoric period when weapons and tools were made of stone or of organic materials such as bone, wood, or horn.

> The Stone Age covers a period of about 2.5 million years, from the first use of tools by the ancestors of humankind (*Australopithecus*) to the introduction of agriculture and the first towns. It is subdivided into the Palaeolithic, Mesolithic, and Neolithic periods, and is succeeded in Europe by the Bronze Age (or, sometimes, the Copper Age) about 5,000–4,000 years ago.

stone boat ▸ **noun** N. Amer. a flat-bottomed sled used for transporting stones and other heavy objects.

stone broke ▸ **adjective** North American term for **STONY BROKE**.

stonechat ▸ **noun** a small Old World songbird of the thrush family, having bold markings and a call like two stones being knocked together. ● Genus *Saxicola*, family Turdidae: three or four species, in particular the widespread *S. torquata*, the male of which has a black head and orange breast.

stone china ▸ **noun** [mass noun] a kind of very hard earthenware resembling porcelain.

stone circle ▸ **noun** a megalithic monument of a type found mainly in western Europe, consisting of stones, typically standing stones, arranged more or less in a circle.

> The earliest stone circles date from the Neolithic period. In the early Bronze Age many hundreds of small circles were constructed in western Britain, often from quite small stones. Circles often appear to be aligned astronomically, especially with particular sunrise or sunset positions, and it is generally agreed that they had a ritual function.

stone cold ▸ **adjective** completely cold.
▸ **adverb** (**stone-cold**) [as submodifier] completely: *stone-cold sober*.

stonecrop ▸ **noun** a small fleshy-leaved plant which typically has star-shaped yellow or white flowers and grows among rocks or on walls. ● Genus *Sedum*, family Crassulaceae: many species, including **yellow** (or **biting**) **stonecrop** (*S. acre*), whose tiny leaves have a bitter, peppery taste.

stone curlew ▸ **noun** a large-eyed bird resembling a plover with mottled brownish plumage, inhabiting open stony or sandy country. Also called **THICK-KNEE**. ● Family Burhinidae; two genera and several species, in particular *Burhinus oedicnemus* of Eurasia and Africa.

S

stonecutter ▸ **noun** a person who cuts stone from a quarry or who shapes and carves it for use.

stoned ▸ **adjective** informal under the influence of drugs, especially cannabis. ■ very drunk.

stone dead ▸ **adjective** [predic.] completely dead.

stone deaf ▸ **adjective** completely deaf.

stonefish ▸ **noun** (pl. **same** or **stonefishes**) a chiefly marine fish of bizarre appearance which lives in the tropical Indo-Pacific. It rests motionless in the sand with its venomous dorsal spines projecting and is a frequent cause of injury to swimmers. ● Family Synanceiidae: several genera and species, including *Synanceia verrucosa* (also called **DEVILFISH**).

stonefly ▸ **noun** (pl. **stoneflies**) a slender insect with transparent membranous wings, the larvae of which live in clean running water. The adults are used as bait by fly fishermen. ● Order Plecoptera: many families.

stone fruit ▸ **noun** a fruit with flesh or pulp enclosing a stone, such as a peach, plum, or cherry.

stoneground ▸ **adjective** (of flour) ground with millstones.

stonehatch ▸ **noun** dialect the ringed plover, which lines its nest with tiny pebbles.

Stonehenge a megalithic monument on Salisbury Plain in Wiltshire. Completed in several constructional phases from c.2950 BC, it is composed of a circle of sarsen stones surrounded by a bank and ditch and enclosing a circle of smaller bluestones. Within this inner circle is a horseshoe arrangement of five trilithons with the axis aligned on the midsummer sunrise, an orientation that was probably for ritual purposes.
– ORIGIN from Old English *stān* 'stone' + an element related to *hengan* 'to hang'.

stone marten ▶ **noun** a Eurasian marten that has chocolate-brown fur with a white throat. Also called **BEECH MARTEN**. ● *Martes foina*, family Mustelidae.

stonemason ▶ **noun** a person who cuts, prepares, and builds with stone.
– DERIVATIVES **stonemasonry** noun.

Stone of Scone /sku:n/ the stone on which medieval Scottish kings were crowned. It was brought to England by Edward I and preserved in the coronation chair in Westminster Abbey, and returned to Scotland in 1996. Also called **Coronation stone**, **Stone of Destiny**.

stone pine ▶ **noun** an umbrella-shaped southern European pine tree with large needles, very large glossy brown cones, and edible seeds (pine nuts). Also called **UMBRELLA PINE**. ● *Pinus pinea*, family Pinaceae. See also **AROLLA**.

stoner ▶ **noun 1** informal a person who regularly takes drugs, especially cannabis.
2 [in combination] Brit. a person or thing that weighs a specified number of stone: *a couple of 16-stoners*.

stonewall ▶ **verb** [with obj.] delay or obstruct (a request, process, or person) by refusing to answer questions or by being evasive: *she has also stonewalled queries about her love life* | (as noun **stonewalling**) *a master in the art of stonewalling and political intimidation*. ■ [no obj.] Cricket bat extremely defensively.
▶ **noun** an act of delaying or obstructing a person, request, or process.
– DERIVATIVES **stonewaller** noun.

stoneware ▶ **noun** [mass noun] a type of pottery which is impermeable and partly vitrified but opaque.

stonewashed (also **stonewash**) ▶ **adjective** (of a garment or fabric, especially denim) washed with abrasives to produce a worn or faded appearance.

stonework ▶ **noun** [mass noun] the parts of a building that are made of stone. ■ the work of a mason: *a masterpiece of clever stonework*.
– DERIVATIVES **stoneworker** noun.

stonewort ▶ **noun** a freshwater plant with whorls of slender leaves, related to green algae. Many kinds become encrusted with chalky deposits, giving them a stony feel. ● *Chara* and other genera in the class Charophyceae, division Chlorophyta; sometimes placed in its own division (Charophyta).

stonk military slang ▶ **noun** a concentrated artillery bombardment.
▶ **verb** [with obj.] bombard with concentrated artillery fire.
– ORIGIN 1940s: said to be formed from elements of the artillery term *Standard Regimental Concentration*.

S

stonker ▶ **noun** Brit. informal something which is very large or impressive of its kind: *it's a real stonker of a plan*.

stonkered ▶ **adjective** [predic.] Austral./NZ informal utterly exhausted or defeated. ■ drunk.
– ORIGIN 1920s: from Scots and northern English *stonk* 'game of marbles', perhaps of imitative origin.

stonking ▶ **adjective** Brit. informal used to emphasize something impressive, exciting, or very large: *a stonking 207 mph maximum speed* | [as submodifier] *a stonking good model*.
– ORIGIN 1980s: from the verb **STONK**.

stony ▶ **adjective** (**stonier**, **stoniest**) **1** covered with or full of small pieces of rock: *rough stony paths*. ■ made of or resembling stone: *stony steps*. ■ Astronomy (of a meteorite) consisting mostly of rock, as opposed to metal.
2 not having or showing feeling or sympathy: *Lucenzo's hard, stony eyes* | [in combination] *he walked away, stony-faced*.
– PHRASES **fall on stony ground** (of words or a suggestion) be ignored or badly received. [with biblical reference to the parable of the sower (Matt. 13:5).]
– DERIVATIVES **stonily** adverb, **stoniness** noun.
– ORIGIN Old English *stānig* (see **STONE**, **-Y¹**).

stony broke ▶ **adjective** Brit. informal entirely without money.

stony-hearted ▶ **adjective** very cruel or unfeeling.

stony-iron Astronomy ▶ **adjective** (of a meteorite) containing appreciable quantities of both rock and iron.
▶ **noun** a stony-iron meteorite.

stood past and past participle of **STAND**.

stooge ▶ **noun 1** derogatory a subordinate used by another to do unpleasant routine work: *party stooges put there to do a job on behalf of central office*.
2 a performer whose act involves being the butt of a comedian's jokes.
▶ **verb** [no obj.] **1** informal move about aimlessly; drift or cruise: *she **stooged around** in the bathroom for a while*.
2 perform a role that involves being the butt of a comedian's jokes.
– ORIGIN early 20th cent.: of unknown origin.

stook /stʊk, stu:k/ Brit. ▶ **noun** a group of sheaves of grain stood on end in a field.
▶ **verb** [with obj.] arrange (sheaves) in stooks.
– ORIGIN Middle English (as a noun): from or related to Middle Low German *stūke*.

stool ▶ **noun 1** a seat without a back or arms, typically resting on three or four legs or on a single pedestal.
2 a piece of faeces.
3 a root or stump of a tree or plant from which shoots spring.
4 US a decoy bird in hunting.
▶ **verb** [no obj.] (of a plant) throw up shoots from the root. ■ [with obj.] cut back (a plant) to or near ground level in order to induce new growth.
– PHRASES **at stool** Medicine when defecating. **fall between two stools** Brit. fail to be or take one of two satisfactory alternatives.
– ORIGIN Old English, of Germanic origin; related to Dutch *stoel*, German *Stuhl*, also to **STAND**. Current senses of the verb date from the late 18th cent.

stoolball ▶ **noun** [mass noun] (in the UK) a team game resembling cricket, with a board (originally a stool) as a wicket, played chiefly by women and girls.

stoolie ▶ **noun** N. Amer. informal short for **STOOL PIGEON**.

stool pigeon ▶ **noun** informal **1** a police informer.
2 a person acting as a decoy.
– ORIGIN late 19th cent.: so named from the original use of a pigeon fixed to a stool as a decoy.

stoop¹ ▶ **verb** [no obj.] **1** bend one's head or body forwards and downwards: *he **stooped down** and reached towards the coin* | *Linda stooped to pick up the bottles* | [with obj.] *the man stoops his head*. ■ have the head and shoulders habitually bent forwards: *he tends to stoop when he walks* | (as adj. **stooping**) *a thin, stooping figure* | (as adj. **stooped**) *a stooped old man*.
2 lower one's moral standards so far as to do something reprehensible: *Craig wouldn't **stoop to** thieving* | *she was unwilling to believe that anyone could **stoop so low** as to steal from a dead woman*.
■ [with infinitive] archaic condescend to do something: *the princes now and then stooped to pay a nominal homage*.
3 (of a bird of prey) swoop down on a quarry.
▶ **noun 1** [in sing.] a posture in which the head and shoulders are habitually bent forwards: *a tall, thin man with a stoop*.
2 the downward swoop of a bird of prey.
– ORIGIN Old English *stūpian* (verb), of Germanic origin; related to the adjective **STEEP¹**. Both senses of the noun date from the late 16th cent.

stoop² ▶ **noun** N. Amer. a porch with steps in front of a house or other building.
– ORIGIN mid 18th cent.: from Dutch *stoep* (see **STOEP**).

stoop ball ▶ **noun** [mass noun] N. Amer. a ball game resembling baseball in which the ball is thrown against a building rather than to a batter.

stoop labour ▶ **noun** [mass noun] N. Amer. agricultural labour performed in a stooping or squatting position.

stoor ▶ **noun** variant of **STOUR**.

stoosh ▶ **adjective** variant spelling of **STUSH**.

stooshie /ˈstʊʃi/ (also **stushie**) ▶ **noun** Scottish informal a row or fracas.
– ORIGIN early 19th cent.: of unknown origin.

stop ▶ **verb** (**stops**, **stopping**, **stopped**) **1** [no obj.] (of an event, action, or process) come to an end; cease to happen: *his laughter stopped as quickly as it had begun* | *the rain had stopped and the clouds had cleared*. ■ [with present participle] cease to perform a specified action or have a specified experience: *she stopped giggling* | [with obj.] *he stopped work for tea*. ■ [with present participle] abandon a specified practice or habit: *I've stopped eating meat*. ■ stop moving or operating: *he stopped to look at the view* | *my watch has stopped*.
■ (of a bus or train) call at a designated place to pick up or set down passengers: *main-line trains stop at platform 7*. ■ Brit. informal stay somewhere for a short time: *you'll have to **stop the night***.
2 [with obj.] cause (an action, process, or event) to come to an end: *this harassment has got to be stopped*.
■ prevent (an action or event) from happening: *a security guard was killed trying to stop a raid*.
■ prevent or dissuade (someone) from continuing in an activity or achieving an aim: *a campaign is under way to stop the bombers*. ■ [with obj. and present participle] prevent (someone or something) from performing a specified action or undergoing a specified experience: *several attempts were made to stop him giving evidence* | *you can't **stop** me **from** getting what I want*.
■ cause or order to cease moving or operating: *he stopped his car by the house* | *police were given powers to stop and search suspects*. ■ informal be hit by (a bullet). ■ instruct a bank to withhold payment on (a cheque). ■ refuse to supply as usual; withhold or deduct: *they stopped the strikers' wages*. ■ Boxing defeat (an opponent) by a knockout: *he was stopped in the sixth by Tyson*. ■ pinch back (a plant).
3 [with obj.] block or close up (a hole or leak): *he tried to stop the hole with the heel of his boot* | *the stile has been **stopped up***. ■ Brit. dated put a filling in (a tooth).
■ block the mouth of (a fox's earth) prior to a hunt.
■ plug the upper end of (an organ pipe), giving a note an octave lower. ■ obtain the required pitch from (the string of a violin or similar instrument) by pressing at the appropriate point with the finger.
■ make (a rope) fast with a stopper.
4 [no obj.] W. Indian be or behave in a particular way: *'Why was she so?' 'I don't know, you know how dem old people stop.'*. ■ [with complement] remain in a particular state or condition: *he said I mustn't stop barefooted, so I had to buy a pair of new shoes*.
▶ **noun 1** a cessation of movement or operation: *all business **came to a stop*** | *there were constant stops and changes of pace*. ■ a break or halt during a journey: *allow an hour or so for driving and as long as you like for stops* | *the flight landed for a refuelling stop*. ■ a place designated for a bus or train to halt and pick up or set down passengers: *the bus was pulling up at her stop*. ■ an object or part of a mechanism which is used to prevent something from moving: *the shelves have special stops to prevent them from being pulled out too far*. ■ Brit. dated a punctuation mark, especially a full stop. ■ used in telegrams to indicate a full stop: *MEET YOU AT THE AIRPORT STOP*. ■ Phonetics a consonant produced with complete closure of the vocal tract. ■ Bridge a high card that prevents the opponents from establishing a particular suit; a control.
■ Nautical a short length of rope used to secure something; a stopper.
2 a set of organ pipes of a particular tone and range of pitch. ■ (also **stop knob**) a knob, lever, or similar device in an organ or harpsichord which brings into play a set of pipes or strings of a particular tone and range of pitch.
3 Photography the effective diameter of a lens. ■ a device for reducing the effective diameter of a lens.
■ a unit of change of relative aperture or exposure (with a reduction of one stop equivalent to halving it).
– PHRASES **pull out all the stops** make a very great effort to achieve something: *we pulled out all the stops to meet the deadline*. ■ do something very elaborately or on a grand scale: *they gave a Christmas party and pulled out all the stops*. [with reference to the stops of an organ.] **put a stop to** cause to end: *she would have to put a stop to all this nonsense*. **stop at nothing** be utterly ruthless or determined in one's attempt to achieve something: *he would stop at nothing to retain his power*. **stop dead** (or **short**) suddenly cease moving, speaking, or acting. **stop one's ears** put one's fingers in one's ears to avoid hearing something. **stop someone's mouth** induce someone to keep silent about something. **stop payment** instruct a bank to withhold payment on a cheque.
stop the show (of a performer) provoke prolonged applause or laughter, causing an interruption.
– PHRASAL VERBS **stop by** (or **in**) call briefly and informally as a visitor. **stop something down** Photography reduce the aperture of a lens with a diaphragm. **stop off** (or **over**) pay a short visit en route to one's ultimate destination: *I stopped off to visit him and his wife*. **stop out** Brit. informal stay out, especially longer or later than might be expected.
stop something out cover an area that is not to be printed or etched when making a print or etching.
stop up Brit. informal refrain from going to bed; stay up.
– DERIVATIVES **stoppable** adjective.

– ORIGIN Old English (*for*)*stoppian* 'block up (an aperture)', of West Germanic origin; related to German *stopfen*, from late Latin *stuppare* 'to stuff'.

stopband ▶ noun Electronics a band of frequencies which are attenuated by a filter.

stopbank ▶ noun NZ an embankment built to prevent a river flooding.

stop bath ▶ noun Photography a bath for stopping the action of a preceding bath by neutralizing any of its chemical still present.

stop bead ▶ noun a bead or narrow moulding to stop movement, e.g. to prevent a sash window swinging back into the room.

stop bit ▶ noun Telecommunications (in asynchronous data transfers) one of a pattern of bits which indicate the end of a character or of the whole transmission.

stopcock ▶ noun an externally operated valve regulating the flow of a liquid or gas through a pipe, in particular one on the water main supplying a house.

stope /stəʊp/ ▶ noun (usu. **stopes**) a step-like working in a mine.
▶ verb [no obj.] (usu. as noun **stoping**) (in mining) excavate a series of steps or layers in (the ground or rock). ■ (as noun **stoping**) Geology the process by which country rock is broken up and removed by the upward movement of magma.
– ORIGIN mid 18th cent.: apparently related to the noun STEP.

Stopes /stəʊps/, Marie (Charlotte Carmichael) (1880–1958), Scottish birth-control campaigner. Her book *Married Love* (1918) was a frank treatment of sexuality within marriage. In 1921 she founded the pioneering Mothers' Clinic for Birth Control in London.

stopgap ▶ noun a temporary way of dealing with a problem or satisfying a need: *transplants are only a stopgap until more sophisticated alternatives can work*.

stop-go ▶ adjective alternately stopping and starting: *stop-go driving*. ■ Brit. of or relating to the alternate restriction and stimulation of economic demand by a government: *stop-go policies*.

stop knob ▶ noun the knob controlling a stop on an organ or harpsichord.

stop light ▶ noun **1** a red traffic signal. ■ N. Amer. a set of traffic lights.
2 (also Brit. **stop lamp**) a brake light.

stop list ▶ noun **1** a list of people deprived of particular rights, privileges, or services, in particular a list of people with whom members of an association are forbidden to do business.
2 a list of words automatically omitted from a computer-generated concordance or index, typically the most frequent words, which would slow down processing unacceptably.

stop-loss ▶ adjective **1** Finance denoting or relating to an order to sell a security or commodity at a specified price in order to limit a loss.
2 Military, US denoting or relating to a policy of forcibly retaining members of the armed forces on active duty beyond their original agreed period of enlistment.

stop-motion ▶ noun [mass noun] [usu. as modifier] a cinematographic technique whereby the camera is repeatedly stopped and started, for example to give animated figures the impression of movement.

stop-off ▶ noun another term for STOPOVER.

stop-out ▶ noun Brit. informal a person who stays out late at night.

stopover ▶ noun a break in a journey: *a brief stopover at Shannon Airport*. ■ a place where a journey is broken.

stoppage ▶ noun **1** an instance of movement, activity, or supply stopping or being stopped: *a power stoppage*. ■ a cessation of work by employees in protest at the terms set by their employers. ■ Boxing a knockout.
2 a blockage in a narrow passage, such as the barrel of a gun.
3 (**stoppages**) Brit. deductions from one's wages by an employer for the payment of tax, National Insurance, and other costs: *£6.40 an hour before stoppages*.

stoppage time ▶ noun another term for INJURY TIME.

Stoppard /ˈstɒpɑːd/, Sir Tom (b.1937), British dramatist, born in Czechoslovakia; born *Thomas Straussler*. His best-known plays are comedies, often dealing with metaphysical and ethical questions, for example *Rosencrantz and Guildenstern are Dead* (1966), which is based on the characters in *Hamlet*.

stopper ▶ noun **1** a plug for sealing a hole, especially in the neck of a bottle or other container.
2 [in combination] a person or thing that halts or obstructs a specified thing: *a crime-stopper*. ■ (in soccer or American football) a player whose function is to block attacks on goal from the middle of the field. ■ Baseball a starting pitcher depended on to win a game or reverse a losing streak, or a relief pitcher who prevents the opposing team from scoring highly. ■ (in sailing or climbing) a rope or clamp for preventing a rope or cable from being run out. ■ Bridge another term for CONTROL.
▶ verb [with obj.] (usu. as adj. **stoppered**) use a stopper to seal (a bottle or other container): *a small stoppered jar*.
– PHRASES **put a** (or **the**) **stopper on** informal prevent from happening or continuing.

stopping ▶ noun Brit. dated a filling for a tooth.

stopping train ▶ noun Brit. a train which stops at most or all intermediate stations on a line.

stopple N. Amer. ▶ noun a stopper or plug.
▶ verb [with obj.] seal with a stopper.
– ORIGIN Middle English: partly a shortening of Old French *estoupail* 'bung', reinforced by the verb STOP.

stop press ▶ noun [mass noun] Brit. late news inserted in a newspaper or periodical either at the last moment before printing or after printing has begun (especially as a heading): [as modifier] *stop-press news*.

stop-start (also **stop-and-start**) ▶ adjective informal alternately stopping and starting; progressing with interruptions: *stop-start journeys*.

stopstreet ▶ noun S. African an intersection at which there is a sign instructing drivers to stop before proceeding across.

stop time ▶ noun [mass noun] (in jazz) a rhythmic device whereby a chord or accent is played only on the first beat of every bar or every other bar, typically accompanying a solo.

stop valve ▶ noun a valve used to stop the flow of liquid in a pipe.

stop volley ▶ noun Tennis a volley played close to the net whereby the player allows the racket to be knocked backwards by the ball and sends it only just back over the net.

stopwatch ▶ noun a special watch with buttons that start, stop, and then zero the hands, used to time races.

stopword ▶ noun a word that is automatically omitted from a computer-generated concordance or index.

storage ▶ noun [mass noun] the action or method of storing something for future use: *the chair can be folded flat for easy storage* | [as modifier] *the room lacked storage space*. ■ the retention of retrievable data on a computer or other electronic system. ■ space available for storing something, in particular allocated space in a warehouse: *Cooper had put much of the furniture into storage*. ■ the cost of storing something in a warehouse.

storage battery (also **storage cell**) ▶ noun a battery (or cell) used for storing electrical energy.

storage device ▶ noun a piece of computer equipment on which information can be stored.

storage heater ▶ noun Brit. an electric heater that accumulates heat in water or bricks during the night (when electricity is cheaper) and releases it during the day.

storage ring ▶ noun Physics an approximately circular accelerator in which particles can be effectively stored by being made to circulate continuously at high energy.

storax /ˈstɔːraks/ (also **styrax**) ▶ noun **1** [mass noun] a rare fragrant gum resin obtained from an East Mediterranean tree, sometimes used in medicine, perfumery, and incense. ■ (**Levant** or **liquid storax**) a liquid balsam obtained from the Asian liquidambar tree.
2 a tropical or subtropical tree or shrub with showy white flowers in drooping clusters. ● Genus *Styrax*, family Styracaceae: several species, in particular *S. officinalis*, from which storax resin is obtained.
– ORIGIN late Middle English: from Latin, from a variant of Greek *sturax*.

store ▶ noun **1** a quantity or supply of something kept for use as needed: *the squirrel has a store of food* | figurative *her vast store of knowledge*. ■ a place where things are kept for future use or sale: *a grain store*. ■ (**stores**) supplies of equipment and food kept for use by members of an army, navy, or other institution, or the place where they are kept. ■ Brit. a computer memory.
2 chiefly N. Amer. a shop of any size or kind: *a health-food store*. ■ Brit. a large shop selling different types of goods. ■ (also **stores**) Brit. a shop selling basic necessities: *a well-stocked village store*.
3 a sheep, steer, cow, or pig acquired or kept for fattening.
▶ verb [with obj.] keep or accumulate (something) for future use: *a small room used for storing furniture*. ■ retain or enter (information) for future electronic retrieval: *the data is stored on disk*. ■ (**be stored with**) have a supply of (something useful): *a mind well stored with esoteric knowledge*.
– PHRASES **in store 1** in a safe place while not being used or displayed: *items held in store*. **2** coming in the future; about to happen: *he did not yet know what lay in store for him*. **set** (or **lay** or **put**) **store by** (or **on**) consider to be of a particular degree of importance or value: *many people set much store by privacy*.
– PHRASES **store something up** create problems for the future by failing to address a particular situation adequately at the time: *they're storing up trouble by denying opportunities to younger players*.
– DERIVATIVES **storable** adjective, **storer** noun.
– ORIGIN Middle English: shortening of Old French *estore* (noun), *estorer* (verb), from Latin *instaurare* 'renew'; compare with RESTORE.

store-and-forward ▶ adjective [attrib.] Telecommunications relating to or denoting a data network in which messages are routed to one or more intermediate stations where they may be stored before being forwarded to their destinations.

store card ▶ noun a credit card that can be used only in one store or chain of stores.

storefront ▶ noun N. Amer. **1** another term for SHOPFRONT.
2 a room or set of rooms facing the street on the ground floor of a commercial building, typically used as a shop: [as modifier] *a bright storefront eatery*.

storehouse ▶ noun a building used for storing goods. ■ a large supply of something: *an enormous storehouse of facts*.

storekeeper ▶ noun **1** a person responsible for stored goods.
2 N. Amer. a shopkeeper.

storeman ▶ noun (pl. **storemen**) Brit. a man responsible for stored goods.

storeroom ▶ noun a room in which items are stored.

storey (N. Amer. also **story**) ▶ noun (pl. **storeys** or **stories**) a part of a building comprising all the rooms that are on the same level: [in combination] *a three-storey building*.
– DERIVATIVES **storeyed** (N. Amer. also **storied**) adjective [in combination] *four-storeyed houses*.
– ORIGIN late Middle English: shortening of Latin *historia* 'history, story', a special use in Anglo-Latin, perhaps originally denoting a tier of painted windows or sculptures on the front of a building (representing a historical subject).

storiated /ˈstɔːrɪeɪtɪd/ ▶ adjective rare decorated with historical, legendary, or emblematic designs.
– ORIGIN late 19th cent.: compare with HISTORIATED.

storied[1] ▶ adjective literary celebrated in or associated with stories or legends: *the island's storied past*.

storied[2] ▶ adjective N. Amer. variant form of STOREYED (see STOREY).

stork ▶ noun a very tall long-legged wading bird with a long heavy bill and typically with white and black plumage. ● Family Ciconiidae: several genera and species, in particular the **white stork** (*Ciconia ciconia*), with black wing tips and a reddish bill and legs, often nesting on tall buildings in Europe.
■ the white stork as the supposed bringer of newborn babies.
– ORIGIN Old English *storc*, of Germanic origin; probably related to STARK (because of its rigid stance).

storksbill ▶ noun a European plant related to the cranesbill, with small pink flowers and fruits that have long twisted beaks. ● Genus *Erodium*, family Geraniaceae.

storm ▶ noun **1** a violent disturbance of the atmosphere with strong winds and usually rain, thunder, lightning, or snow. ■ (also **storm system**) an intense low-pressure weather system; a cyclone. ■ a wind of force 10 on the Beaufort scale (48–55 knots or

S

88–102 kph). ▪ a heavy discharge of missiles or blows: *two men were taken by a* ***storm of*** *bullets.*
2 a tumultuous reaction; an uproar or controversy: *the book caused a storm in America | the manager is at the centre of a drugs storm in Germany.* ▪ a vehement outburst of a specified feeling or reaction: *the disclosure raised* ***a storm of protest.***
3 (**storms**) N. Amer. storm windows.
4 a direct assault by troops on a fortified place.
▸ **verb 1** [no obj., with adverbial of direction] move angrily or forcefully in a specified direction: *she burst into tears and stormed off | he stormed out of the house.* ▪ [with direct speech] shout (something) angrily; rage: *'Don't patronize me!' she stormed.* ▪ move forcefully and decisively to a specified position in a game or contest: *Chester stormed back with two goals in five minutes.*
2 [with obj.] (of troops) suddenly attack and capture (a building or other place) by means of force: *commandos stormed a hijacked plane early today* | (as noun **storming**) *the storming of the Bastille.*
3 [no obj.] (**it storms, it is storming**, etc.) (of the weather) be violent, with strong winds and usually rain, thunder, lightning, or snow.
– PHRASES **go down a storm** be enthusiastically received by an audience. **the lull** (or **calm**) **before the storm** a period of unusual tranquillity or stability that seems likely to presage difficult times. **storm and stress** another term for **STURM UND DRANG**. **a storm in a teacup** Brit. great outrage or excitement about a trivial matter. **take something by storm** (of troops) capture a place by a sudden and violent attack. ▪ have great and rapid success in a particular place or with a particular group of people: *his first collection took the fashion world by storm.* **—— up a storm** chiefly N. Amer. perform the specified action with great enthusiasm and energy: *the band could really* ***play up a storm.***
– DERIVATIVES **stormproof** adjective.
– ORIGIN Old English, of Germanic origin; related to Dutch *storm* and German *Sturm*, probably also to the verb **STIR**[1]. The verb dates from late Middle English in sense 3 of the verb.

storm beach ▸ noun an expanse of sand or gravel thrown up on the coast by storms.

stormbound ▸ adjective prevented by storms from starting or continuing a journey.

storm centre ▸ noun the central point around which controversy or trouble happens: *Lusignan seems to have been the storm centre of the revolt.*

storm cloud ▸ noun a heavy, dark rain cloud. ▪ (**storm clouds**) used in reference to a threatening or ominous state of affairs: *the beginning of the decade saw* ***storm clouds gathering*** *over Europe.*

stormcock ▸ noun dialect the mistle thrush.

storm collar ▸ noun a high coat collar that can be turned up and fastened.

storm cuff ▸ noun a tight-fitting inner cuff which prevents rain or wind from getting inside a coat.

storm door ▸ noun chiefly N. Amer. an additional outer door for protection in bad weather or winter.

storm drain (US **storm sewer**) ▸ noun a drain built to carry away excess water in times of heavy rain.

S

stormer ▸ noun [usu. in sing.] Brit. informal something particularly impressive or good of its kind: *a stormer of an album | the engine is a real stormer.*

storm flap ▸ noun a piece of material designed to protect an opening or fastening on a tent or coat from the effects of rain.

storm glass ▸ noun historical a sealed tube containing a liquid, the clarity of which was thought to change when storms approach.

storming ▸ adjective [attrib.] Brit. informal (of a performance, especially in sport or music) outstandingly vigorous or impressive: *his storming finish carried him into third place.* ▪ excellent: *I think this is a storming book.*

storm jib ▸ noun Sailing a small heavy jib for use in a high wind.

storm lantern ▸ noun chiefly Brit. a hurricane lamp.

Stormont Castle /'stɔːmɒnt/ a castle in Belfast which was, until 1972, the seat of the Parliament of Northern Ireland and is now the headquarters of the Northern Ireland Assembly.

storm petrel ▸ noun a small seabird of the open ocean, typically having blackish plumage and a white rump, and formerly believed to be a harbinger of bad weather. ● Family Hydrobatidae: several genera and many species, e.g. *Hydrobates pelagicus* of the NE Atlantic and Mediterranean.

storm sail ▸ noun a sail of smaller size and stronger material than the corresponding one used in ordinary weather.

storm sewer ▸ noun US term for **STORM DRAIN**.

storm signal ▸ noun a lamp, flag, or other device used to give a visible warning of an approaching storm.

storm surge ▸ noun a rising of the sea as a result of wind and atmospheric pressure changes associated with a storm.

storm system ▸ noun see **STORM** (sense 1 of the noun).

storm troops ▸ plural noun another term for **SHOCK TROOPS**. ▪ (**Storm Troops**) historical the Nazi political militia; the Brownshirts.
– DERIVATIVES **storm trooper** noun.

storm water ▸ noun [mass noun] surface water in abnormal quantity resulting from heavy falls of rain or snow.

storm window ▸ noun chiefly N. Amer. a window fixed on the outside of a normal window for protection and insulation in bad weather or winter.

stormy ▸ adjective (**stormier, stormiest**) (of weather) characterized by strong winds and usually rain, thunder, lightning, or snow: *a dark and stormy night.* ▪ (of the sea or sky) having large waves or dark clouds because of windy or rainy conditions: *grey and stormy skies.* ▪ full of angry or violent outbursts of feeling: *a long and stormy debate | a stormy relationship.*
– DERIVATIVES **stormily** adverb, **storminess** noun.

stormy petrel ▸ noun **1** dated term for **STORM PETREL**.
2 a person who delights in conflict or attracts controversy.

Stornoway /'stɔːnəweɪ/ a port on the east coast of Lewis, in the Outer Hebrides; pop. 5,700 (est. 2009). The administrative centre of the Western Isles, it is noted for the manufacture of Harris tweed.

Storting /'stɔːtɪŋ/ the Norwegian parliament.
– ORIGIN Norwegian, from *stor* 'great' + *ting* 'assembly'.

story[1] ▸ noun (pl. **stories**) **1** an account of imaginary or real people and events told for entertainment: *an adventure story | I'm going to tell you a story.* ▪ a plot or storyline: *the novel has a good story.* ▪ a piece of gossip; a rumour: *there have been lots of stories going around, as you can imagine.* ▪ informal a false statement; a lie: *Ellie never* ***told stories****—she had always believed in the truth.*
2 a report of an item of news in a newspaper, magazine, or broadcast: *stories in the local papers.*
3 an account of past events in someone's life or in the development of something: *the story of modern farming | the film is based on a true story.* ▪ a particular person's representation of the facts of a matter: *during police interviews, Harper changed his story.* ▪ [in sing.] a situation viewed in terms of the information known about it or its similarity to another: *having such information is useful, but it is not the whole story | United kept on trying but it was* ***the same old story****—no luck.* ▪ (**the story**) informal the facts about the present situation: *What's the story on this man? Is he from around here?*
4 the commercial prospects or circumstances of a particular company: *the investors' flight to profitable businesses with solid stories.*
– PHRASES **but that's another story** informal used after raising a matter to indicate that one does not want to expand on it for now. **end of story** informal used to emphasize that there is nothing to add on a matter just mentioned: *Men don't cry in public. End of story.* **it's a long story** informal used to indicate that, for now, one does not want to talk about something that is too painful or complicated. **it's** (or **that's**) **the story of one's life** informal used as a resigned acknowledgement that one has experienced a particular misfortune too often. **the story goes** it is said or rumoured: ***the story goes that*** *he's fallen out with his friends.* **to cut** (or N. Amer. **make**) **a long story short** used to end an account of events quickly: *to cut a long story short, I married Stephen.*
– ORIGIN Middle English (denoting a historical account or representation): shortening of Anglo-Norman French *estorie*, from Latin *historia* (see **HISTORY**).

story[2] ▸ noun N. Amer. variant spelling of **STOREY**.

storyboard ▸ noun a sequence of drawings, typically with some directions and dialogue, representing the shots planned for a film or television production.

storybook ▸ noun a book containing a story or collection of stories intended for children. ▪ [as modifier] denoting something that is as idyllic or perfect as things typically are in children's stories: *it was a storybook finish to an illustrious career.*

story editor ▸ noun an editor who advises on the content and form of film or television scripts.

storyline ▸ noun the plot of a novel, play, film, or other narrative form.

storyteller ▸ noun a person who tells stories.
– DERIVATIVES **storytelling** noun & adjective.

stot ▸ verb (**stots, stotting, stotted**) **1** /stəʊt, stɒt/ Scottish bounce or cause to bounce against a surface: [with obj.] *I stotted the ball off the back wall.* ▪ [no obj.] move unsteadily; stagger or lurch: *he's been up there stotting aboot the mountain.*
2 /stɒt/ [no obj.] another term for **PRONK**.
– ORIGIN early 16th cent.: of unknown origin.

stotin /stɒ'tiːn/ ▸ noun a former monetary unit of Slovenia, equal to one hundredth of a tolar.
– ORIGIN Slovene.

stotinka /stɒ'tɪŋkə/ ▸ noun (pl. **stotinki** /stɒ'tɪŋki/) a monetary unit of Bulgaria, equal to one hundredth of a lev.
– ORIGIN Bulgarian, literally 'one hundredth'.

stotty /'stɒti/ (also **stottie, stotty cake**) ▸ noun (pl. **stotties**) [mass noun] N. English a kind of coarse bread made from spare scraps of white dough. ▪ [count noun] a soft roll made from coarse bread.
– ORIGIN of unknown origin.

stoup /stuːp/ ▸ noun a basin for holy water, especially on the wall near the door of a Roman Catholic church for worshippers to dip their fingers in before crossing themselves. ▪ archaic a flagon or beaker for drink.
– ORIGIN Middle English (in the sense 'pail, small cask'): from Old Norse *staup*, of Germanic origin; related to the verb **STEEP**[2].

Stour /'staʊə/ **1** a river of southern England which rises in west Wiltshire and flows south-east to meet the English Channel east of Bournemouth.
2 (also /stʊə/) a river of eastern England which rises south-east of Cambridge and flows south-eastwards to the North Sea.
3 a river of central England which rises west of Wolverhampton and flows south-westwards through Stourbridge and Kidderminster to meet the Severn at Stourport-on-Severn.

stour /stʊə/ (also **stoor**) ▸ noun [mass noun] Scottish & N. English dust forming a cloud or deposited in a mass.
– ORIGIN late Middle English: of uncertain origin.

stoush /staʊʃ/ Austral./NZ informal ▸ verb [with obj.] hit; fight with: *get out of that car while I stoush you.*
▸ noun a brawl or other fight.
– ORIGIN late 19th cent.: of unknown origin.

stout ▸ adjective **1** (of a person) rather fat or of heavy build: *stout middle-aged men.*
2 (of an object) strong and thick: *Billy had armed himself with a stout stick | stout walking boots.*
3 having or showing courage and determination: *he put up a stout defence in court.*
▸ noun [mass noun] a kind of strong, dark beer brewed with roasted malt or barley.
– DERIVATIVES **stoutish** adjective, **stoutly** adverb, **stoutness** noun.
– ORIGIN Middle English: from Anglo-Norman French and Old French dialect, of West Germanic origin; perhaps related to **STILT**. The noun (late 17th cent.) originally denoted any strong beer and is probably elliptical for *stout ale*.

stout-hearted ▸ adjective courageous or determined.
– DERIVATIVES **stout-heartedly** adverb, **stout-heartedness** noun.

stove[1] ▸ noun **1** an apparatus for cooking or heating that operates by burning fuel or using electricity.
2 Brit. a hothouse for plants.
▸ verb [with obj.] **1** fumigate or disinfect (a house) with sulphur or other fumes.
2 treat (an object) by heating it in a stove in order to apply a desired surface coating.
3 Brit. force or raise (plants) in a hothouse.
– ORIGIN Middle English (in the sense 'sweating room'): from Middle Dutch or Middle Low German *stove*; perhaps related to the noun **STEW**[1]. Current verb senses date from the early 17th cent.

stove[2] past and past participle of **STAVE**.

stoved ▶ **adjective** [attrib.] Scottish & N. English (of vegetables or meat) stewed.

stove enamel Brit. ▶ **noun** [mass noun] a heatproof enamel produced by heat treatment in a stove, or a paint imitating it.
▶ **verb** [with obj.] (usu. as adj. **stove-enamelled**) give (something) a stove-enamel finish.

stovepipe ▶ **noun** the pipe taking the smoke and gases from a stove up through a roof or to a chimney.

stovepipe hat ▶ **noun** a silk hat resembling a top hat but much taller.

stovies /ˈstəʊvɪz/ ▶ **plural noun** Scottish a dish of potatoes stewed in a pot.
– ORIGIN late 19th cent.: from Scots *stove* 'stew meat or vegetables', perhaps partly from Dutch *stoven*.

stow ▶ **verb** [with obj. and adverbial] pack or store (an object) carefully and neatly in a particular place: *Barney began stowing her luggage into the boot*.
– PHRASES **stow it!** informal used to tell someone to be quiet.
– PHRASAL VERBS **stow away** conceal oneself on a ship, aircraft, or other passenger vehicle in order to travel secretly or without paying the fare: *he stowed away on a ship bound for South Africa*.
– ORIGIN late Middle English: shortening of BESTOW.

stowage ▶ **noun** [mass noun] the action of stowing something. ■ space for stowing something in: *there is plenty of stowage beneath the berth*.

stowaway ▶ **noun** a person who stows away on a passenger vehicle.

Stowe, Harriet (Elizabeth) Beecher (1811–96), American novelist. She won fame with her anti-slavery novel *Uncle Tom's Cabin* (1852), which strengthened the contemporary abolitionist cause with its descriptions of the sufferings caused by slavery.

STP ▶ **abbreviation** ■ Physiology short-term potentiation. ■ Chemistry standard temperature and pressure. ■ Professor of Sacred Theology. [from Latin *Sanctae Theologiae Professor*.]

Str. ▶ **abbreviation** ■ Strait. ■ (**str.**) Rowing stroke.

strabismus /strəˈbɪzməs/ ▶ **noun** [mass noun] chiefly Medicine abnormal alignment of the eyes; the condition of having a squint.
– DERIVATIVES **strabismic** adjective.
– ORIGIN late 17th cent.: modern Latin, from Greek *strabismos*, from *strabizein* 'to squint', from *strabos* 'squinting'.

Strabo /ˈstreɪbəʊ/ (*c*.63 BC–*c*.23 AD), historian and geographer, of Greek descent. His only extant work, *Geographica*, in seventeen volumes, provides a detailed physical and historical geography of the ancient world during the reign of Augustus.

stracciatella /ˌstratʃəˈtɛlə/ ▶ **noun** [mass noun] an Italian soup containing eggs and cheese.
– ORIGIN Italian.

Strachey /ˈstreɪtʃi/, (Giles) Lytton (1880–1932), English biographer. A prominent member of the Bloomsbury Group, he achieved recognition with *Eminent Victorians* (1918), which attacked the literary Establishment through its satirical biographies of Florence Nightingale, General Gordon, and others.

Strad ▶ **noun** informal a Stradivarius.
– ORIGIN late 19th cent.: abbreviation.

straddle ▶ **verb** [with obj.] sit or stand with one leg on either side of: *he turned the chair round and straddled it*. ■ place (one's legs) wide apart: *he shifted his legs, straddling them to keep his balance*. ■ [no obj.] archaic stand, walk, or sit with one's legs wide apart. ■ extend across or be situated on both sides of: *a mountain range straddling the Franco-Swiss border*. ■ N. Amer. take up or maintain an equivocal position with regard to (a political issue): *a man who had straddled the issue of taxes*. ■ fire at (a target) with shots or bombs so that they fall short of and beyond it.
▶ **noun 1** an act of sitting or standing with one's legs wide apart.
2 Stock Exchange a simultaneous purchase of options to buy and to sell a security or commodity at a fixed price, allowing the purchaser to make a profit whether the price of the security or commodity goes up or down.
– DERIVATIVES **straddler** noun.
– ORIGIN mid 16th cent.: alteration of dialect *striddle*, back-formation from dialect *striddling* 'astride', from STRIDE + the adverbial suffix *-ling*.

Stradivari /ˌstradɪˈvɑːri/, Antonio (*c*.1644–1737), Italian violin-maker. He devised the proportions of the modern violin, giving a more powerful and rounded sound than earlier instruments possessed. About 650 of his celebrated violins, violas, and violoncellos are still in existence.

Stradivarius /ˌstradɪˈvɛːrɪəs/ ▶ **noun** a violin or other stringed instrument made by Antonio Stradivari or his followers.
– ORIGIN mid 19th cent.: Latinized form of STRADIVARI.

strafe /strɑːf, streɪf/ ▶ **verb** [with obj.] attack repeatedly with bombs or machine-gun fire from low-flying aircraft: *military aircraft strafed the village*.
▶ **noun** an attack from low-flying aircraft.
– ORIGIN early 20th cent.: humorous adaptation of the German First World War catchphrase *Gott strafe England* 'may God punish England'.

straggle ▶ **verb** [no obj., usu. with adverbial of direction] (of an irregular group of people) move along slowly so as to remain some distance behind the person or people in front: *the children straggled behind them* | (as adj. **straggling**) *the straggling crowd of refugees*. ■ grow, spread, or be laid out in an irregular, untidy way: *her hair was straggling over her eyes*.
▶ **noun** an untidy or irregularly arranged mass or group: *a straggle of cottages*.
– DERIVATIVES **straggler** noun.
– ORIGIN late Middle English: perhaps from dialect *strake* 'go'.

straggly ▶ **adjective** (**stragglier**, **straggliest**) growing or spreading in an irregular, untidy way: *his straggly dark hair*.

straight ▶ **adjective 1** extending or moving uniformly in one direction only; without a curve or bend: *a long, straight road*. ■ (of hair) not curly or wavy. ■ (of a garment) not flared or fitted closely to the body: *a straight skirt*. ■ (of an aim, blow, or course) going direct to the intended target: *a straight punch to the face*. ■ Geometry (of a line) lying on the shortest path between any two of its points. ■ (of an arch) flat-topped.
2 properly positioned so as to be level, upright, or symmetrical: *he made sure his tie was straight*. ■ [predic.] in proper order or condition: *it'll take a long time to get the place straight*.
3 not evasive; honest: *a straight answer* | *thank you for being straight with me*. ■ simple; straightforward: *a straight choice between nuclear power and penury*. ■ (of a look) bold and steady: *he gave her a straight, no-nonsense look*. ■ (of thinking) clear, logical, and unemotional.
4 [attrib.] in continuous succession: *he scored his fourth straight win*.
5 (of an alcoholic drink) undiluted; neat: *straight brandy*.
6 (especially of drama) serious as opposed to comic or musical: *a straight play*.
7 informal (of a person) conventional or respectable: *she looked pretty straight in her school clothes*. ■ heterosexual.
▶ **adverb 1** in a straight line; directly: *he was gazing straight at her* | *keep **straight on***. ■ with no delay or diversion; directly or immediately: *after dinner we went straight back to our hotel* | *I fell into bed and went straight to sleep*. ■ archaic at once; immediately: *I'll fetch up the bath to you straight*.
2 in or into a level, even, or upright position: *he pulled his clothes straight* | *sit up straight!*
3 correctly; clearly: *I'm so tired I can hardly think straight*. ■ honestly and directly; in a straightforward manner: *I told her straight—the kid's right*.
4 without a break; continuously: *he remembered working sixteen hours straight*.
▶ **noun 1** a part of something that is not curved or bent, especially the concluding stretch of a racecourse: *he pulled away in the straight to win by half a second*. ■ archaic a form or position that is not curved or bent: *the rod flew back to the straight*.
2 (in poker) a continuous sequence of five cards.
3 informal a conventional person. ■ a heterosexual person.
4 S. African informal (in township slang) a 750 ml bottle of liquor. [perhaps a transferred sense of US slang *straight* 'unadulterated whisky'.]
– PHRASES **get something straight** make a situation clear, especially by reaching an understanding. **go straight** live an honest life after being a criminal. **a straight face** a blank or serious facial expression, especially when trying not to laugh: *my father kept a straight face when he joked*. **the straight and narrow** the honest and morally acceptable way of living: *he's making a real effort to get back on the straight and narrow*. [a misinterpretation of Matt. 7:14, 'Strait is the gate, and narrow is the way which leadeth unto life, and few there be that find it'.] **straight away** immediately. **a straight fight** Brit. a contest between just two opponents, especially in an election. **straight from the shoulder 1** dated (of a blow) swift and well delivered. **2** (of words) frank or direct: *sometimes he spoke straight from the shoulder and sometimes in puzzles*. **straight off** (or **out**) informal without hesitation or deliberation: *Wendy drank half the bottle straight off*. **straight up** informal **1** Brit. truthfully; honestly: *come on, Bert, I won't hurt you—straight up*. **2** chiefly N. Amer. unmixed; unadulterated: *a dry martini served straight up*.
– DERIVATIVES **straightish** adjective, **straightly** adverb, **straightness** noun.
– ORIGIN Middle English (as an adjective and adverb): archaic past participle of STRETCH.

straight-ahead ▶ **adjective** (especially of popular music) straightforward or simple.

straight angle ▶ **noun** Mathematics an angle of 180°.

straight-arm ▶ **verb** [with obj.] N. Amer. informal ward off (an opponent) or remove (an obstacle) with the arm straight: *I straight-armed the woman leaning in on her*.

straight arrow N. Amer. informal ▶ **noun** an honest, morally upright person.
▶ **adjective** (**straight-arrow**) honest and morally upright: *the straight-arrow head coach found himself answering for their crimes*.

straightaway ▶ **adverb** variant spelling of STRAIGHT AWAY at STRAIGHT.
▶ **adjective** N. Amer. extending or moving in a straight line.
▶ **noun** N. Amer. a straight section of a road or racetrack.

straight chain ▶ **noun** Chemistry a chain of atoms in a molecule, usually carbon atoms, that is neither branched nor formed into a ring.

straight chair ▶ **noun** a straight-backed side chair.

straight-cut ▶ **adjective** (of tobacco) cut lengthwise into long silky fibres.

straight edge ▶ **noun** a bar with one accurately straight edge, used for testing whether something else is straight.
▶ **adjective** chiefly US (especially among fans of hardcore punk music) having an ascetic or abstinent lifestyle: *he's so straight-edge that he won't even take Tylenol when he has a headache*.

straight-eight ▶ **noun** an internal-combustion engine with eight cylinders in line. ■ a vehicle with a straight-eight engine.

straighten ▶ **verb 1** make or become straight: [with obj.] *she helped him straighten his tie* | [no obj.] *here the road straightens and its verges widen*. ■ [no obj.] stand or sit erect after bending: *he slowly **straightened up**, using the table for support*. ■ [no obj.] (**straighten up**) (of a vehicle, ship, or aircraft) stop turning and move in a straight line.
2 [with obj.] make tidy or put in order again: *he sat down at his desk, straightening his things that Lee had moved* | *they are asking for help in **straightening out** their lives*.
– DERIVATIVES **straightener** noun.

straight-faced ▶ **adjective** with a blank or serious facial expression.

straight flush ▶ **noun** (in poker or brag) a hand of cards all of one suit and in a continuous sequence (for example, the seven, eight, nine, ten, and jack of spades).

straightforward ▶ **adjective** uncomplicated and easy to do or understand: *in a straightforward case no fees will be charged*. ■ (of a person) honest and frank: *a straightforward young man*.
DERIVATIVES **straightforwardly** adverb, **straightforwardness** noun.

straightjacket ▶ **noun & verb** variant spelling of STRAITJACKET.

straight-laced ▶ **adjective** variant spelling of STRAIT-LACED.

straight-line ▶ **adjective 1** containing, characterized by, or relating to straight lines or motion in a straight line: *a straight-line graph* | *the Porsche's straight-line stability*.
2 Finance relating to a method of depreciation allocating a given percentage of the cost of an asset each year for a fixed period.

straight man ▶ **noun** the person in a comedy duo who speaks lines which give a comedian the opportunity to make jokes.

straight razor ▶ **noun** North American term for CUT-THROAT RAZOR.

S

straight shooter ▸ noun informal, chiefly N. Amer. an honest and forthright person.
– DERIVATIVES **straight-shooting** adjective.

straight-six ▸ noun an internal-combustion engine with six cylinders in line. ▪ a vehicle with a straight-six engine.

straight stitch ▸ noun a single short separate embroidery stitch.

straight time ▸ noun [mass noun] chiefly US normal working hours, paid at a regular rate.

straight-up ▸ adjective N. Amer. informal honest and trustworthy: *you sounded like a straight-up guy.* ▪ truly so called; genuine: *a straight-up suspense tale.*

straightway ▸ adverb archaic form of STRAIGHT AWAY (see STRAIGHT).

strain[1] ▸ verb **1** [with obj.] force (a part of one's body or oneself) to make an unusually great effort: *I stopped and listened, straining my ears for any sound.* ▪ [no obj.] make an unusually great effort: *his voice was so quiet that I had to strain to hear it.* ▪ injure (a limb, muscle, or organ) by overexerting it: *on cold days you are more likely to strain a muscle | glare from the screen can strain your eyes.* ▪ make severe or excessive demands on: *he strained her tolerance to the limit.* ▪ [no obj.] pull or push forcibly at something: *the bear **strained at** the chain around its neck | his stomach was swollen, **straining against** the thin shirt.* ▪ stretch (something) tightly: *the barbed wire fence was strained to posts six feet high.* ▪ archaic embrace (someone) tightly: *she strained the infant to her bosom again.*
2 [with obj.] pour (a mainly liquid substance) through a porous or perforated device or material in order to separate out any solid matter: *strain the custard into a bowl.* ▪ cause liquid to drain off (food which has been boiled, soaked, or canned) by using a porous or perforated device: *she turned to the sink to strain the noodles.* ▪ drain off (liquid) in this way: ***strain off** the surplus fat.*
▸ noun **1** a force tending to pull or stretch something to an extreme or damaging degree: *the usual type of chair puts an enormous strain on the spine | [mass noun] aluminium may bend under strain.* ▪ an injury to a part of the body caused by overexertion: *he has a slight groin strain.* ▪ Physics the magnitude of a deformation, equal to the change in the dimension of a deformed object divided by its original dimension.
2 a severe or excessive demand on the strength, resources, or abilities of someone or something: *the accusations **put a strain on** relations between the two countries | [mass noun] she's **under** considerable **strain**.* ▪ [mass noun] a state of tension or exhaustion resulting from severe demands on one's strength or resources: *the telltale signs of nervous strain.*
3 (usu. **strains**) the sound of a piece of music: *the distant strains of the brass band grew louder.*
– PHRASES **at (full) strain** archaic using the utmost effort. **strain every nerve** see NERVE. **strain at the leash** see LEASH.
– ORIGIN Middle English (as a verb): from Old French *estreindre*, from Latin *stringere* 'draw tight'. Current senses of the noun arose in the mid 16th cent.

S

strain[2] ▸ noun **1** a particular breed, stock, or variety of an animal or plant. ▪ a natural or cultured variety of a microorganism with a distinct form, biochemistry, or virulence. ▪ a variety of something abstract: *a strain of feminist thought.*
2 a particular tendency as part of a person's character: *there was a powerful strain of insanity on her mother's side of the family.*
– ORIGIN Old English *strīon* 'acquisition, gain', of Germanic origin; related to Latin *struere* 'to build up'.

strained ▸ adjective **1** showing signs of nervous tension or tiredness: *Jean's pale, strained face.* ▪ not relaxed or comfortable; tense or uneasy: *there was a strained silence | relations between the two countries were strained.* ▪ produced by deliberate effort rather than spontaneously; artificial or forced: *she gave a strained laugh.* ▪ far-fetched; laboured: *my example may seem a little strained.*
2 (of a limb or muscle) injured by overexertion or twisting.
3 (of a mainly liquid substance) having been strained to separate out any solid matter.

strain energy ▸ noun [mass noun] Mechanics energy stored in an elastic body under loading.

strainer ▸ noun a device having holes punched in it or made of crossed wires for separating solid matter from a liquid: *a tea strainer.*

strain gauge ▸ noun a device for indicating the strain of a material or structure at the point of attachment.

strait ▸ noun **1** (also **straits**) a narrow passage of water connecting two seas or two other large areas of water: [in place names] *the Straits of Gibraltar.*
2 (**straits**) used in reference to a situation characterized by a specified degree of trouble or difficulty: *the economy is **in dire straits** | redundancy left him in severe financial straits.*
▸ adjective archaic (of a place) of limited spatial capacity; narrow or cramped: *the road was so strait that a handful of men might have defended it.* ▪ close, strict, or rigorous: *my captivity was strait as ever.*
– DERIVATIVES **straitly** adverb, **straitness** noun.
– ORIGIN Middle English: shortening of Old French *estreit* 'tight, narrow', from Latin *strictus* 'drawn tight' (see STRICT).

straiten ▸ verb archaic make or become narrow: [with obj.] *the passage was straitened by tables.*

straitened ▸ adjective **1** characterized by poverty: *they lived in straitened circumstances.*
2 restricted in range or scope: *their straitened horizons.*

straitjacket (also **straightjacket**) ▸ noun a strong garment with long sleeves which can be tied together to confine the arms of a violent prisoner or mental patient. ▪ a severe restriction on freedom of action, development, or expression: *the government is operating in an economic straitjacket.*
▸ verb (**straitjackets, straitjacketing, straitjacketed**) [with obj.] restrain with a straitjacket. ▪ impose severely restrictive measures on (a person or activity): *the treaty should not be used as a tool to straitjacket international trade.*

strait-laced (also **straight-laced**) ▸ adjective having or showing very strict moral attitudes: *his strait-laced parents were horrified.*

> **USAGE** As an adjective **strait** means 'narrow or cramped' and 'strict or rigorous': the idea behind **strait-laced** and **straitjacket** is of being tightly laced or confined. As **strait** is now old-fashioned and unfamilar, however, people often interpret it as the more usual word **straight**. **Straight-laced** and **straightjacket** are now generally accepted in standard English, and the spelling **straight-laced** is more common than **strait-laced** in the Oxford English Corpus.

Straits Settlements a former British Crown Colony in SE Asia. Established in 1867, it comprised Singapore, Penang, and Malacca, and later included Labuan, Christmas Island, and the Cocos Islands. It was disbanded in 1946.

strake ▸ noun **1** a continuous line of planking or plates from the stem to the stern of a ship or boat.
2 a protruding ridge fitted to an aircraft or other structure to improve aerodynamic stability.
– ORIGIN Middle English: from Anglo-Latin *stracus*, *straca*; probably from the Germanic base of the verb STRETCH.

Stralsund /ˈstrɑːlzʊnt/ a town and fishing port in northern Germany, on the Baltic coast opposite the island of Rügen; pop. 58,300 (est. 2006).

stramash /strəˈmaʃ/ ▸ noun Scottish & N. English an uproar; a row.
– ORIGIN late 18th cent.: apparently imitative.

stramonium /strəˈməʊnɪəm/ ▸ noun [mass noun] a preparation of the dried leaves or poisonous seeds of the thorn apple, with medical and other uses.
– ORIGIN mid 17th cent.: modern Latin (part of the plant's binomial), perhaps an alteration of Tartar *turman* 'horse medicine'.

strand[1] ▸ verb [with obj.] drive or leave (a boat, sailor, or sea creature) aground on a shore: *the ships were stranded in shallow water* | (as adj. **stranded**) *a stranded whale.* ▪ leave (someone) without the means to move from somewhere: *two of the firm's lorries are stranded in France.*
▸ noun literary or Irish the shore of a sea, lake, or large river: *a heron glided to rest on a pebbly strand.*
– ORIGIN Old English (as a noun), of unknown origin. The verb dates from the early 17th cent.

strand[2] ▸ noun a single thin length of something such as thread, fibre, or wire, especially as twisted together with others: *strands of coloured wool.* ▪ a single hair or thin lock of hair. ▪ a string of beads or pearls. ▪ an element that forms part of a complex whole: *the journal has carried articles representing many different strands of opinion on the left.*
– ORIGIN late 15th cent.: of unknown origin.

stranded ▸ adjective [attrib.] (of thread, rope, or similar) arranged in single thin lengths twisted together: *stranded cotton* | [in combination] figurative *the many-stranded passions of the country.*

strandloper /ˈstrantˌlʊəpə/ (also **strandlooper**) ▸ noun **1** (**Strandloper**) a member of a Khoisan people who lived on the southern shores of southern Africa from prehistoric times until the second millennium AD.
2 S. African a person who collects items on the shore; a beachcomber.
– ORIGIN Afrikaans, from *strand* 'seashore' + *loper* 'runner'.

strandwolf /ˈstrantvɒlf, ˈstrandwʊlf/ ▸ noun S. African the brown hyena, which often frequents the shore, where it scavenges dead fish and birds. • *Hyaena brunnea*, family Hyaenidae.
– ORIGIN late 18th cent.: from South African Dutch, from *strand* 'seashore' + *wolf* 'wolf'.

strange ▸ adjective **1** unusual or surprising; difficult to understand or explain: *children have some strange ideas | he's a very strange man* | [with clause] ***it is strange how** things change.* ▪ slightly or undefinably unwell or ill at ease: *her head still felt strange.*
2 not previously visited, seen, or encountered; unfamiliar or alien: *she was lost in a strange country | a harsh accent that was **strange to** his ears.* ▪ (**strange to/at/in**) archaic unaccustomed to or unfamiliar with: *I am strange to the work.*
3 Physics (of a subatomic particle) having a non-zero value for strangeness.
– PHRASES **strange to say** (or literary **tell**) it is surprising or unusual that: *strange to say, I didn't really like carol singers.*
– DERIVATIVES **strangely** adverb [as submodifier] *the house was strangely quiet* | [sentence adverb] ***strangely enough**, people were able to perform this task without difficulty.*
– ORIGIN Middle English: shortening of Old French *estrange*, from Latin *extraneus* 'external, strange'.

strange attractor ▸ noun Mathematics an equation or fractal set representing a complex pattern of behaviour in a chaotic system.

strangeness ▸ noun [mass noun] **1** the state or fact of being strange.
2 Physics one of six flavours of quark.

strange particle ▸ noun Physics a subatomic particle classified as having a non-zero value for strangeness.

stranger ▸ noun a person whom one does not know or with whom one is not familiar: *don't talk to strangers | she remained **a stranger to** him.* ▪ a person who does not know, or is not known in, a particular place or community: *I'm **a stranger in** these parts | he must have been **a stranger to** the village.* ▪ (**stranger to**) a person entirely unaccustomed to (a feeling, experience, or situation): ***he is no stranger to** controversy.* ▪ a person who is not a member or official of the House of Commons.
– ORIGIN late Middle English: shortening of Old French *estrangier*, from Latin *extraneus* (see STRANGE).

strangle ▸ verb [with obj.] squeeze or constrict the neck of (a person or animal), especially so as to cause death: *the victim was strangled with a scarf.* ▪ (as adj. **strangled**) sounding as though the utterer's throat is constricted: *a series of strangled gasps.* ▪ suppress (an impulse, action, or sound): *she strangled a sob.* ▪ hamper or hinder the development or activity of: *they allowed bureaucracy to strangle initiative.*
– DERIVATIVES **strangler** noun.
– ORIGIN Middle English: shortening of Old French *estrangler*, from Latin *strangulare*, from Greek *strangalan*, from *strangalē* 'halter', related to *strangos* 'twisted'.

stranglehold ▸ noun [in sing.] a grip around the neck of another person that can kill by asphyxiation if held for long enough. ▪ complete or overwhelming control: *in France, supermarkets have less of a **stranglehold on** food supplies.*

strangles ▸ plural noun [usu. treated as sing.] a bacterial infection of the upper respiratory tract of horses, causing enlargement of the lymph nodes in the throat, which may impair breathing. • This disease is caused by the bacterium *Streptococcus equi*.
– ORIGIN early 17th cent.: plural of obsolete *strangle* 'strangulation', from STRANGLE.

strangulate /ˈstraŋgjʊleɪt/ ▸ verb [with obj.] (often as adj. **strangulated**) **1** Medicine prevent circulation of the blood supply through (a part of the body, especially a hernia) by constriction: *a strangulated hernia.*

2 informal strangle; throttle: *the poor woman died strangulated.* ■ (as adj. **strangulated**) sounding as though the utterer's throat is constricted: *a strangulated cry.*
– ORIGIN mid 17th cent. (in the sense 'suffocate'): from Latin *strangulat-* 'choked', from the verb *strangulare* (see STRANGLE).

strangulation ▸ noun [mass noun] **1** the action or state of strangling or being strangled: *death due to strangulation.*
2 Medicine the condition in which circulation of blood to a part of the body (especially a hernia) is cut off by constriction.

strangury /ˈstraŋɡjʊri/ ▸ noun [mass noun] Medicine a condition caused by blockage or irritation at the base of the bladder, resulting in severe pain and a strong desire to urinate.
– ORIGIN late Middle English: via Latin from Greek *strangouria*, from *stranx, strang-* 'drop squeezed out' + *ouron* 'urine'.

Stranraer /stranˈrɑː/ a port and market town in SW Scotland, in Dumfries and Galloway; pop. 10,300 (est. 2009). It is the terminus of a ferry service from Northern Ireland.

strap ▸ noun a strip of leather, cloth, or other flexible material, used to fasten, secure, or carry something or to hold on to something: *her bra strap | the strap of his shoulder bag.* ■ a strip of metal, often hinged, used to fasten or secure something. ■ (**the strap**) punishment by beating with a strip of leather.
▸ verb (**straps, strapping, strapped**) **1** [with obj. and adverbial of place] fasten or secure in a specified place or position with a strap: *I had to strap the bag to my bicycle | the children were strapped into their car seats.* ■ [with obj.] Brit. bind (an injured part of the body) with adhesive plaster: *the goalkeeper's knee was strapped up.*
2 [with obj.] beat (someone) with a strip of leather: *I expected when my dad walked in that he'd strap him.*
– ORIGIN late 16th cent. (denoting a trap for birds, also a piece of timber fastening two objects together): dialect form of STROP[1].

straphanger ▸ noun informal a standing passenger in a bus or train. ■ chiefly US a person who commutes to work by public transport.
– DERIVATIVES **strap-hang** verb.

strap hinge ▸ noun a hinge with long leaves or flaps for screwing on to the surface of a door or gate.

strapless ▸ adjective (especially of a dress or bra) without shoulder straps.

strapline ▸ noun a subsidiary heading or caption in a newspaper or magazine.

strap-on ▸ adjective able to be attached by a strap or straps.

strappado /strəˈpɑːdəʊ, -ˈeɪdəʊ/ ▸ noun (pl. **strappados**) (usu. **the strappado**) historical a form of punishment or torture in which the victim was secured to a rope and made to fall from a height almost to the ground before being stopped with an abrupt jerk. ■ the instrument used for inflicting the punishment or torture of strappado.
– ORIGIN mid 16th cent.: from French *(e)strapade*, from Italian *strappata*, from *strappare* 'to snatch'.

strapped ▸ adjective informal short of money: *I'm constantly strapped for cash.*

strapper ▸ noun chiefly Austral. a person who grooms racehorses.

strapping[1] ▸ adjective (especially of a young person) big and strong: *they had three strapping sons.*

strapping[2] ▸ noun [mass noun] adhesive plaster for binding injured parts of the body. ■ strips of leather or pliable metal used to hold, strengthen, or fasten something.

strappy ▸ adjective (**strappier strappiest**) (of shoes or clothes) having straps: *white strappy sandals.*

strapwork ▸ noun [mass noun] ornamentation imitating pierced and interlaced straps.

Strasberg /ˈstrazbəːɡ/, Lee (1901–82), American actor, director, and drama teacher, born in Austria; born *Israel Strassberg*. As artistic director of the Actors' Studio in New York City (1948–82) he was the leading figure in the development of method acting in the US.

Strasbourg /ˈstrazbəːɡ/, French /strasbuʀ/ a city in NE France, in Alsace, close to the border with Germany; pop. 276,867 (2006). Annexed by Germany in 1870, it was returned to France after the First World War. It is the headquarters of the Council of Europe and of the European Parliament.

Strat ▸ noun trademark a Fender Stratocaster electric guitar.

strata plural form of STRATUM.

stratagem /ˈstratədʒəm/ ▸ noun a plan or scheme, especially one used to outwit an opponent or achieve an end: *a series of devious stratagems.* ■ [mass noun] archaic skill in devising plans or schemes; cunning.
– ORIGIN late 15th cent. (originally denoting a military ploy): from French *stratagème*, via Latin from Greek *stratēgēma*, from *stratēgein* 'be a general', from *stratēgos*, from *stratos* 'army' + *agein* 'to lead'.

stratal ▸ adjective relating or belonging to strata or a stratum.

strategic /strəˈtiːdʒɪk/ ▸ adjective **1** relating to the identification of long-term or overall aims and interests and the means of achieving them: *strategic planning for the organization is the responsibility of top management.* ■ designed or planned to serve a particular purpose: *alarms are positioned at strategic points around the prison.*
2 relating to the gaining of overall or long-term military advantage: *Newark Castle was of strategic importance | British strategic and commercial interests.* ■ (of human or material resources) essential in fighting a war: *a large strategic air force.* ■ (of bombing or weapons) done or for use against industrial areas and communication centres of enemy territory as a long-term military objective: *strategic nuclear missiles.* Often contrasted with TACTICAL.
– DERIVATIVES **strategical** adjective, **strategically** adverb [as submodifier] *a strategically placed mirror.*
– ORIGIN early 19th cent.: from French *stratégique*, from Greek *stratēgikos*, from *stratēgos* (see STRATAGEM).

Strategic Arms Limitation Talks (abbrev.: **SALT**) a series of negotiations between the US and the Soviet Union aimed at the limitation or reduction of nuclear armaments, which produced the Strategic Arms Limitation Treaty. The talks were organized from 1968 onwards and held in stages until superseded by the START negotiations in 1983.

Strategic Arms Reduction Talks (abbrev.: **START**) a series of arms-reduction negotiations between the US and the Soviet Union begun in 1983. The Intermediate Nuclear Forces (INF) treaty was signed in 1987 and the Strategic Arms Reduction Treaty in 1991.

Strategic Defense Initiative (abbrev.: **SDI**) a projected US system of defence against nuclear weapons, using satellites armed with lasers to intercept and destroy intercontinental ballistic missiles. The project was renamed the BALLISTIC MISSILE DEFENSE ORGANIZATION in 1993. Popularly known as STAR WARS.

strategist ▸ noun a person skilled in planning action or policy, especially in war or politics.

strategize (also **strategise**) ▸ verb [no obj.] N. Amer. devise a strategy or strategies.

strategy /ˈstratɪdʒi/ ▸ noun (pl. **strategies**) **1** a plan of action designed to achieve a long-term or overall aim: *time to develop a coherent economic strategy* | [mass noun] *shifts in marketing strategy.*
2 [mass noun] the art of planning and directing overall military operations and movements in a war or battle. Often contrasted with TACTICS (see TACTIC). ■ [count noun] a plan for directing overall military operations and movements: *non-provocative defence strategies.*
– ORIGIN early 19th cent.: from French *stratégie*, from Greek *stratēgia* 'generalship', from *stratēgos* (see STRATAGEM).

Stratford-upon-Avon a town in Warwickshire, on the River Avon; pop. 23,100 (est. 2009). Famous as the birth and burial place of William Shakespeare, it is the site of the Royal Shakespeare Theatre.
– DERIVATIVES **Stratfordian** noun.

strath /straθ/ ▸ noun Scottish a broad mountain valley.
– ORIGIN mid 16th cent.: from Scottish Gaelic *srath*.

Strathclyde /straθˈklʌɪd/ a former local government region in west central Scotland, dissolved in 1996.

strathspey /straθˈspeɪ/ ▸ noun a slow Scottish dance. ■ a piece of music for a strathspey, typically in four-four time.
– ORIGIN mid 18th cent.: from *Strathspey*, the name of the valley of the River Spey.

stratified sample ▸ noun Statistics a sample that is drawn from a number of separate strata of the population, rather than at random from the whole population, in order that it should be representative.

stratiform /ˈstratɪfɔːm/ ▸ adjective technical arranged in layers: *stratiform clouds.* ■ Geology (of a mineral deposit) formed parallel to the bedding planes of the surrounding rock.

stratify /ˈstratɪfʌɪ/ ▸ verb (**stratifies, stratifying, stratified**) [with obj.] (usu. as adj. **stratified**) form or arrange into strata: *socially stratified cities* | [no obj.] *the residues have begun to stratify.* ■ arrange or classify: *stratifying patients into well-defined risk groups.* ■ place (seeds) close together in layers in moist sand or peat to preserve them or to help them germinate.
– DERIVATIVES **stratification** noun.

stratigraphy /strəˈtɪɡrəfi/ ▸ noun [mass noun] the branch of geology concerned with the order and relative position of strata and their relationship to the geological timescale. ■ the analysis of the order and position of layers of archaeological remains. ■ the structure of a particular set of strata.
– DERIVATIVES **stratigrapher** noun, **stratigraphic** adjective, **stratigraphical** adjective, **stratigraphically** adverb.
– ORIGIN mid 19th cent.: from STRATUM + -GRAPHY.

stratocumulus /ˌstratə(ʊ)ˈkjuːmjʊləs, ˌstreɪ-, ˌstrɑː-/ ▸ noun [mass noun] cloud forming a low layer of clumped or broken grey masses.

stratopause /ˈstratə(ʊ)pɔːz, ˌstreɪ-, ˌstrɑː-/ ▸ noun the interface between the stratosphere and the ionosphere.
ORIGIN 1950s: from STRATOSPHERE, suggested by TROPOPAUSE.

stratosphere /ˈstratəˌsfɪə/ ▸ noun the layer of the earth's atmosphere above the troposphere, extending to about 50 km above the earth's surface (the lower boundary of the mesosphere). ■ informal the very highest levels of something: *her next big campaign launched her into the fashion stratosphere.*
– DERIVATIVES **stratospheric** /-ˈsfɛrɪk/ adjective, **stratospherically** adverb.

stratovolcano /ˌstratəʊvɒlˈkeɪnəʊ/ ▸ noun (pl. **stratovolcanoes**) a volcano built up of alternate layers of lava and ash.

stratum /ˈstrɑːtəm, ˈstreɪtəm/ ▸ noun (pl. **strata** /-tə/) **1** a layer or a series of layers of rock in the ground: *a stratum of flint.* ■ a thin layer within any structure: *thin strata of air.*
2 a level or class to which people are assigned according to their social status, education, or income: *members of other social strata.* ■ Statistics a group into which members of a population are divided in stratified sampling.
– ORIGIN late 16th cent. (in the sense 'layer or coat of a substance'): modern Latin, from Latin, literally 'something spread or laid down', neuter past participle of *sternere* 'strew'.

> **USAGE** In Latin the word **stratum** is singular and its plural form is **strata**. In English this distinction is maintained—it is incorrect to use **strata** as a singular or to create the form **stratas** as the plural: *a series of overlying* ***strata*** *not a series of overlying* ***stratas***, *and a new* ***stratum*** *was uncovered not a new* ***strata*** *was uncovered.*

stratum corneum /ˌstrɑːtəm ˈkɔːnɪəm/ ▸ noun Anatomy the outermost layer of the skin, consisting of keratinized cells.
– ORIGIN Latin, literally 'horny layer'.

stratus /ˈstrɑːtəs, ˈstreɪtəs/ ▸ noun [mass noun] cloud forming a continuous horizontal grey sheet, often with rain or snow.
– ORIGIN early 19th cent.: modern Latin, from Latin, literally 'strewn', past participle of *sternere*.

Strauss[1] /straʊs, ʃt-/ the name of two Austrian composers: ■ **Johann** (1804–49), a leading composer of waltzes; known as **Strauss the Elder**. His best-known work is the *Radetzky March* (1838). ■ **Johann** (1825–99), son of Strauss the Elder; known as **Strauss the Younger**. He became known as 'the waltz king', composing many famous waltzes, such as *The Blue Danube* (1867). He is also noted for the operetta *Die Fledermaus* (1874).

Strauss[2] /straʊs, ʃt-/, Richard (1864–1949), German composer. With the librettist Hugo von Hofmannsthal he produced operas such as *Der Rosenkavalier* (1911). Often regarded as the last of the 19th-century romantic composers, Strauss is also known for the tone poem *Also Sprach Zarathustra* (1896).

stravaig /strəˈveɪɡ/ (also **stravage**) ▸ verb [no obj., with adverbial of direction] chiefly Scottish & Irish wander about aimlessly: *stravaiging about the roads.*
– ORIGIN late 18th cent.: probably a shortening of obsolete *extravage* 'digress, ramble'.

S

Stravinsky /strəˈvɪnski/, Igor (Fyodorovich) (1882–1971), Russian-born composer, resident in the US from 1939. He made his name with the ballets *The Firebird* (1910) and *The Rite of Spring* (1913); both shocked Paris audiences with their irregular rhythms and frequent dissonances. Stravinsky later developed a neoclassical style typified by *The Rake's Progress* (opera, 1948–51) and experimented with serialism in *Threni*.
– DERIVATIVES **Stravinskyian** adjective.

straw ▸ noun **1** [mass noun] dried stalks of grain, used especially as fodder or as material for thatching, packing, or weaving: [as modifier] *a straw hat*. ■ [count noun] a single dried stalk of grain: *the tramp sat chewing a straw*. ■ a pale yellow colour like that of straw.
2 a thin hollow tube of paper or plastic for sucking drink from a glass or bottle.
– PHRASES **clutch** (or **grasp** or **catch**) **at straws** be in such a desperate situation as to resort to even the most unlikely means of salvation. [from the proverb *a drowning man will clutch at a straw*.] **draw the short straw** be the unluckiest of a group of people, especially in being chosen to perform an unpleasant task. **draw straws** draw lots. **the last** (or **final**) **straw** a further difficulty or annoyance, typically minor in itself but coming on top of a series of difficulties, that makes a situation unbearable: *his affair was the last straw*. [from the proverb *the last straw breaks the (laden) camel's back*.] **not care** (or **give**) **a straw** (or **two straws**) not have the slightest concern about: *you don't care a straw what I think*. **a straw in the wind** chiefly Brit. a slight hint of future developments.
– DERIVATIVES **strawy** adjective.
– ORIGIN Old English *strēaw*, of Germanic origin; related to Dutch *stroo* and German *Stroh*, also to **STREW**.

strawberry ▸ noun (pl. **strawberries**) **1** a sweet soft red fruit with a seed-studded surface.
2 the low-growing plant which produces the strawberry, having white flowers, lobed leaves, and runners, and found throughout north temperate regions. ● Genus *Fragaria*, family Rosaceae; the commercial strawberry is usually *F.* × *ananassa*.
3 [mass noun] a deep pinkish-red colour.
– ORIGIN Old English *strēa(w)berige*, *strēowberige* (see **STRAW**, **BERRY**).

strawberry blonde (also **strawberry blond**) ▸ adjective denoting hair of a light reddish-blonde colour.
▸ noun a woman with light reddish-blonde hair.

strawberry mark ▸ noun a soft red birthmark.

strawberry roan ▸ adjective denoting an animal's coat which is chestnut mixed with white or grey.
▸ noun a strawberry roan animal.

strawberry tree ▸ noun a small evergreen European tree which bears clusters of whitish flowers late in the year, often at the same time as the strawberry-like fruit from the previous season's flowers.
● *Arbutus unedo*, family Ericaceae.

strawboard ▸ noun [mass noun] board made of straw pulp, used in building (faced with paper) and in book covers.

straw boss ▸ noun N. Amer. informal a junior supervisor with some responsibility but little authority.

S

strawflower ▸ noun an everlasting flower of the daisy family. ● Several species in the family Compositae, in particular the Australian *Helichrysum bracteatum* and plants of the genus *Helipterum*.

straw man ▸ noun another term for **MAN OF STRAW** (see **MAN**).

straw mushroom ▸ noun a small edible mushroom which grows on rice straw, cultivated in South East Asia. ● *Volvariella volvacea*, family Agaricaceae, class Hymenomycetes.

straw poll (N. Amer. also **straw vote**) ▸ noun an unofficial ballot conducted as a test of opinion: *I took a straw poll among my immediate colleagues*.

straw potatoes ▸ plural noun very thinly cut potato chips.

stray ▸ verb [no obj.] move away aimlessly from a group or from the right course or place: *dog owners are urged not to allow their dogs to stray* | *the military arrested anyone who strayed into the exclusion zone*. ■ [no obj., with adverbial of direction] (of the eyes or a hand) move idly or casually: *her eyes strayed to the telephone*. ■ be unfaithful to a spouse or partner: *men who stray are seen as more exciting and desirable*. ■ [no obj., with adverbial of direction] literary wander or roam: *over these mounds the shepherd strays*.
▸ adjective [attrib.] **1** not in the right place; separated from the group or target: *he pushed a few stray hairs from her face* | *she was killed by a stray bullet*. ■ (of a domestic animal) having no home or having wandered away from home: *stray dogs*.
2 Physics (of a physical quantity) arising as a consequence of the laws of physics, but unwanted and usually having a detrimental effect on the operation of equipment: *stray capacitance*.
▸ noun **1** a stray person or thing, especially a domestic animal.
2 (**strays**) electrical phenomena interfering with radio reception.
– ORIGIN Middle English: shortening of Anglo-Norman French and Old French *estrayer* (verb), Anglo-Norman French *strey* (noun), partly from **ASTRAY**.

streak ▸ noun **1** a long, thin line or mark of a different substance or colour from its surroundings: *a streak of oil*. ■ Microbiology a narrow line of bacteria smeared on the surface of a solid culture medium.
2 an element of a specified kind in someone's character: *there's a streak of insanity in the family* | *Lucy had a ruthless streak*. ■ [usu. with adj.] a continuous period of specified success or luck: *the theatre is **on a winning streak***.
3 informal an act of running naked in a public place so as to shock or amuse others: *a streak for charity*.
▸ verb **1** [with obj.] cover (a surface) with streaks: *tears streaking her face, Cynthia looked up* | *his beard was **streaked with** grey*. ■ dye (hair) with long, thin lines of a different colour to that of one's natural hair colour: [with obj. and complement] *hair that was streaked blonde*. ■ Microbiology smear (a needle, swab, etc.) over the surface of a solid culture medium to initiate a culture.
2 [no obj., with adverbial of direction] move very fast in a specified direction: *the cat streaked across the street*.
3 [no obj.] informal run naked in a public place so as to shock or amuse others.
– PHRASES **like a streak** informal very fast: *he is off like a streak*. **streak of lightning** a flash of lightning.
– DERIVATIVES **streaker** noun (sense 3 of the verb).
– ORIGIN Old English *strica*, of Germanic origin; related to Dutch *streek* and German *Strich*, also to **STRIKE**. The sense 'run naked' was originally US slang.

streaking ▸ noun [mass noun] long, thin lines of a different colour from their surroundings, especially on dyed hair.

streaky ▸ adjective (**streakier**, **streakiest**) **1** having streaks of different colours or textures: *streaky blond hair*. ■ Brit. (of bacon) cut from the belly and having alternate strips of fat and lean.
2 informal, chiefly N. Amer. variable in quality; not predictable or reliable.
3 Brit. informal lucky: *Wise's rather streaky opening goal for Chelsea*.
– DERIVATIVES **streakily** adverb, **streakiness** noun.

stream ▸ noun **1** a small, narrow river.
2 a continuous flow of liquid, air, or gas: *Frank blew out **a stream of** smoke* | *the blood gushed out in scarlet streams*. ■ a mass of people or things moving continuously in the same direction: *there is **a steady stream of** visitors*. ■ a large number of things that happen or come one after the other: *a woman screamed **a stream of** abuse*.
3 Computing a continuous flow of data or instructions, typically one having a constant or predictable rate. ■ a continuous flow of video and audio material relayed over the Internet.
4 Brit. a group in which schoolchildren of the same age and ability are taught: *children in the top streams*.
▸ verb **1** [no obj., with adverbial of direction] (of liquid, air, gas, etc.) run or flow in a continuous current in a specified direction: *she sat with tears **streaming down** her face* | *sunlight **streamed through** the windows*. ■ (of a mass of people or things) move in a continuous flow in a specified direction: *he was watching the taxis **streaming past***. ■ [no obj.] run with tears, sweat, or other liquid: *my eyes were streaming* | *I woke up in the night, **streaming with** sweat* | [with obj.] *his mouth was streaming blood*. ■ [no obj.] (of hair, clothing, etc.) float or wave at full extent in the wind: *her black cloak **streamed behind** her*.
2 [with obj.] (often as noun **streaming**) Computing relay (data, especially video and audio material) over the Internet as a steady, continuous flow.
3 [with obj.] Brit. put (schoolchildren) in groups of the same age and ability to be taught together: (as noun **streaming**) *streaming within comprehensive schools is common practice*.
– PHRASES **against** (or **with**) **the stream** against (or with) the prevailing view or tendency: *a world in which the demand for quality does not run against the stream*. **on stream** in or into operation or existence; available: *more jobs are **coming on stream***.
– DERIVATIVES **streamlet** noun.
– ORIGIN Old English *strēam* (noun), of Germanic origin; related to Dutch *stroom*, German *Strom*, from an Indo-European root shared by Greek *rhein* 'to flow'.

streamer ▸ noun **1** a long, narrow strip of material used as a decoration or symbol: *plastic party streamers* | figurative *a streamer of smoke*. ■ [usu. as modifier] a banner headline in a newspaper: *a streamer head in the student paper*. ■ [usu. as modifier] Fishing a fly with feathers attached: *a streamer fly*. ■ Astronomy an elongated mass of luminous matter, e.g. in aurorae or the sun's corona.
2 Computing short for **TAPE STREAMER**.

streamer weed ▸ noun [mass noun] a freshwater plant with long fronds that stream and wave in the current, especially water crowfoot.

streamflow ▸ noun the flow of water in a stream or river.

streaming ▸ adjective [attrib.] **1** Brit. (of a cold) accompanied by copious running of the nose and eyes: *she's got a streaming cold*.
2 Computing relating to or making use of a form of tape transport in which data may be transferred in bulk while the tape is in motion. ■ (of data) transmitted in a continuous stream while earlier parts are being used.

streamline ▸ verb [with obj.] **1** (usu. as adj. **streamlined**) design or provide with a form that presents very little resistance to a flow of air or water, increasing speed and ease of movement: *streamlined passenger trains*.
2 make (an organization or system) more efficient and effective by employing faster or simpler working methods: *the company streamlined its operations by removing whole layers of management*.
▸ noun a line along which the flow of a moving fluid is least turbulent.
▸ adjective **1** (of fluid flow) free from turbulence.
2 dated having a streamlined shape: *a streamline aeroplane*.

stream of consciousness ▸ noun Psychology a person's thoughts and conscious reactions to events, perceived as a continuous flow. The term was introduced by William James in his *Principles of Psychology* (1890). ■ a literary style in which a character's thoughts, feelings, and reactions are depicted in a continuous flow uninterrupted by objective description or conventional dialogue. James Joyce, Virginia Woolf, and Marcel Proust are among its notable early exponents.

streel /striːl/ Irish ▸ noun a disreputable, untidy person, especially a woman.
▸ verb [no obj., with adverbial of direction] wander aimlessly: *youngsters streeling through the house*. ■ [with obj.] trail or drag (something): *children streeling bits of coloured cloth*.
– ORIGIN early 19th cent.: from Irish *s(t)raoill(e)* 'untidy or awkward person'.

Streep, Meryl (b.1949), American actress; born *Mary Louise Streep*. She won Oscars for her parts in *Kramer vs Kramer* (1980) and *Sophie's Choice* (1982).

street ▸ noun **1** a public road in a city, town, or village, typically with houses and buildings on one or both sides: *the narrow, winding streets of Edinburgh* | [in place names] *45 Lake Street*. ■ (**the Street**) US Wall Street. ■ (**the street**/**streets**) the roads or public areas of a city or town: *every week, fans stop me in the street*. ■ [as modifier] denoting someone who is homeless: *the street kids of the city*.
2 [as modifier] relating to the outlook, values, or lifestyle of those young people who are perceived as composing a fashionable urban subculture: *London street style*.
– PHRASES **not in the same street** Brit. informal far inferior in terms of ability. **on the streets 1** homeless. **2** working as a prostitute. **streets ahead** Brit. informal greatly superior: *the restaurant is streets ahead of its local rivals*.
– DERIVATIVES **streeted** adjective, **streetward** adjective & adverb.
– ORIGIN Old English *strǣt*, of West Germanic origin, from late Latin *strāta (via)* 'paved (way)', feminine past participle of *sternere* 'lay down'.

street Arab ▸ noun archaic a raggedly dressed homeless child wandering the streets.

streetcar ▸ noun N. Amer. a tram.

street credibility (also informal **street cred**) ▸ **noun** [mass noun] acceptability among fashionable young urban people.

street cries ▸ **plural noun** the cries used by street traders to advertise their wares.

street door ▸ **noun** the main door of a house opening on to the street.

street entertainer ▸ **noun** a person who entertains the public in the street, especially with music, acting, or juggling.
– DERIVATIVES **street entertainment** noun.

street furniture ▸ **noun** [mass noun] objects placed or fixed in the street for public use, such as postboxes, road signs, and benches.

street jewellery ▸ **noun** [mass noun] Brit. enamel advertising plates as collectors' items.

street-legal ▸ **adjective** (of a vehicle) meeting all legal requirements for use on ordinary roads.

street light (also **street lamp**) ▸ **noun** a light illuminating a road, typically mounted on a tall post.
– DERIVATIVES **street lighting** noun.

street name ▸ **noun 1** an informal term for something, typically an illegal drug: *Special K is the street name for ketamine.*
2 N. Amer. the name of a stockbroking firm, bank, or dealer in which stock is held on behalf of a purchaser.

streetscape ▸ **noun** a view or scene of streets, especially in a city.

street-smart ▸ **adjective** N. Amer. another term for STREETWISE.

street theatre ▸ **noun** [mass noun] drama performed on the streets, typically in an informal or improvised manner.

street trader ▸ **noun** a person who sells something in the street, either from a stall or van or with their goods laid out on the pavement.
– DERIVATIVES **street trading** noun.

street value ▸ **noun** the price for which something, especially an amount of drugs, that is illegal or has been obtained illicitly can be sold: *detectives seized drugs with a street value of £300,000.*

streetwalker ▸ **noun** a prostitute who seeks clients in the street.
– DERIVATIVES **streetwalking** noun & adjective.

streetwise ▸ **adjective** informal having the skills and knowledge necessary for dealing with modern urban life: *I wasn't streetwise enough to figure out what he had in mind.* ▪ reflective of modern urban life, especially that of urban youth: *streetwise fashion.*

Strega /ˈstreɪɡə/ ▸ **noun** [mass noun] trademark a kind of orange-flavoured Italian liqueur.
– ORIGIN Italian, literally 'witch'.

Streisand /ˈstrʌɪs(ə)nd, -sand/, Barbra (Joan) (b.1942), American singer, actress, and film director. She won an Oscar for her performance in *Funny Girl* (1968). She later played the lead in *A Star is Born* (1976); the film's song 'Evergreen', composed by Streisand, won an Oscar.

strelitzia /strəˈlɪtsɪə/ ▸ **noun** a southern African plant of the genus *Strelitzia* (family Strelitziaceae), especially (in gardening) a bird of paradise flower.
– ORIGIN named after Charlotte of Mecklenburg-*Strelitz* (1744–1818), queen of George III.

strength /strɛŋθ, strɛŋkθ/ ▸ **noun** [mass noun] **1** the quality or state of being physically strong: *cycling can help you build up your strength.* ▪ the influence or power possessed by a person, organization, or country: *the political and military strength of European governments.* ▪ the degree of intensity of a feeling or belief: *street protests demonstrated the strength of feeling against the president.* ▪ the extent to which an argument or case is sound or convincing: *the strength of the argument for property taxation.* ▪ the potency, intensity, or speed of a force or natural agency: *the wind had markedly increased in strength.* ▪ Bridge the potential of a hand to win tricks, arising from the number and type of high cards it contains.
2 the capacity of an object or substance to withstand great force or pressure: *they were taking no chances with the strength of the retaining wall.* ▪ the emotional or mental qualities necessary in dealing with difficult or distressing situations: *many people find strength in religion | it takes strength of character to admit one needs help.*
3 the potency or degree of concentration of a drug, chemical, or drink: *it's double the strength of your average beer* | [count noun] *the solution comes in two strengths.*
4 [count noun] a good or beneficial quality or attribute of a person or thing: *the strengths and weaknesses of their sales and marketing operation | his strength was his obsessive single-mindedness.* ▪ literary a person or thing perceived as a source of mental or emotional support: *he was my closest friend, my strength and shield.*
5 the number of people comprising a group, typically a team or army: *the peacetime strength of the army was 415,000.* ▪ a number of people required to make such a group complete: *we are now more than 100 officers* ***below strength*** *| some units will be maintained* ***at full strength*** *while others will rely on reserves* | [in combination] *an under-strength side.*
– PHRASES **give me strength!** used as an expression of exasperation or annoyance. **go from strength to strength** develop or progress with increasing success. **in strength** in large numbers: *security forces were out in strength.* **on the strength of** on the basis or with the justification of: *I joined the bank on the strength of an MA in English.* **the strength of** chiefly Austral./NZ the point or meaning of; the truth about: *you've about got the strength of it, Mick.* **tower** (or **pillar**) **of strength** a person who can be relied upon to give a great deal of support and comfort to others.
– DERIVATIVES **strengthless** adjective.
– ORIGIN Old English *strengthu*, from the Germanic base of STRONG.

strengthen /ˈstrɛŋθ(ə)n, -ŋkθ(ə)n/ ▸ **verb** make or become stronger: [with obj.] *he advises an application of fluoride to strengthen the teeth* | [no obj.] *the wind won't strengthen until after dark.*
– PHRASES **strengthen someone's hand** (or **hands**) enable or encourage a person to act more vigorously or effectively.
– DERIVATIVES **strengthener** noun.

strenuous /ˈstrɛnjʊəs/ ▸ **adjective** requiring or using great effort or exertion: *the government made strenuous efforts to upgrade the quality of the teaching profession.*
– DERIVATIVES **strenuously** adverb, **strenuousness** noun.
– ORIGIN early 17th cent.: from Latin *strenuus* 'brisk' + -OUS.

strep ▸ **noun** Medicine, informal short for STREPTOCOCCUS.

Strepsiptera /strɛpˈsɪptərə/ ▸ **plural noun** Entomology an order of minute parasitic insects which comprises the stylops.
– DERIVATIVES **strepsipteran** noun & adjective.
– ORIGIN modern Latin (plural), from Greek *strepsi-* (combining form of *strephein* 'to turn') + *pteron* 'wing'.

strep throat ▸ **noun** [mass noun] N. Amer. a sore throat with fever caused by streptococcal infection.

strepto- ▸ **combining form** twisted; in the form of a twisted chain: *streptomycete.* ▪ associated with streptococci or streptomycetes: *streptokinase.*
– ORIGIN from Greek *streptos* 'twisted', from *strephein* 'to turn'.

streptocarpus /ˌstrɛptə(ʊ)ˈkɑːpəs/ ▸ **noun** an African plant with funnel-shaped flowers which are typically pink, white, or violet, cultivated as indoor or greenhouse plants. Also called CAPE PRIMROSE. ● Genus *Streptocarpus*, family Gesneriaceae.
– ORIGIN modern Latin, from STREPTO- 'twisted' + Greek *karpos* 'fruit'.

streptococcus /ˌstrɛptə(ʊ)ˈkɒkəs/ ▸ **noun** (pl. **streptococci** /-ˈkɒk(s)ʌɪ, -ˈkɒk(s)iː/) a bacterium of a genus that includes the agents of souring of milk and dental decay, and haemolytic pathogens causing various infections such as scarlet fever and pneumonia. ● Genus *Streptococcus*; Gram-positive cocci in pairs and chains.
– DERIVATIVES **streptococcal** adjective.

streptokinase /ˌstrɛptə(ʊ)ˈkʌɪneɪz/ ▸ **noun** [mass noun] Biochemistry an enzyme produced by some streptococci which is involved in breaking down red blood cells. It is used to treat blood clots and inflammation.

streptomycete /ˌstrɛptə(ʊ)ˈmʌɪsiːt/ ▸ **noun** (pl. **streptomycetes** /-ˈmʌɪsiːts, -mʌɪˈsiːtiːz/) a bacterium which occurs chiefly in soil as aerobic saprophytes resembling moulds, several of which are important sources of antibiotics. ● *Streptomyces* and related genera, order Actinomycetales; Gram-positive filaments forming chains of spores.
– ORIGIN 1950s: anglicized singular of modern Latin *Streptomyces*, from STREPTO- 'twisted' + Greek *mukēs*, *mukēt-* 'fungus'.

streptomycin /ˌstrɛptə(ʊ)ˈmʌɪsɪn/ ▸ **noun** [mass noun] Medicine an antibiotic that was the first drug to be successful against tuberculosis but is now chiefly used with other drugs because of its toxic side effects. ● This antibiotic is produced by the bacterium *Streptomyces griseus*.

stress ▸ **noun** [mass noun] **1** pressure or tension exerted on a material object: *the distribution of stress is uniform across the bar.* ▪ the degree of stress measured in units of force per unit area.
2 a state of mental or emotional strain or tension resulting from adverse or demanding circumstances: *he's obviously* ***under a lot of stress*** | [in combination] *stress-related illnesses.* ▪ [count noun] something that causes a state of strain or tension: *the stresses and strains of public life.*
3 particular emphasis or importance: *he has started to* ***lay greater stress on*** *the government's role in industry.* ▪ emphasis given to a particular syllable or word in speech, typically through a combination of relatively greater loudness, higher pitch, and longer duration: *normally, the stress falls on the first syllable.*
▸ **verb 1** [reporting verb] give particular emphasis or importance to (a point, statement, or idea) made in speech or writing: [with obj.] *they stressed the need for reform* | [with clause] *she was anxious to stress that her daughter's safety was her only concern* | [with direct speech] *'I want it done very, very neatly,' she stressed.* ▪ [with obj.] give emphasis to (a syllable or word) when pronouncing it.
2 [with obj.] subject to pressure or tension: *this type of workout does stress the shoulder and knee joints.*
3 [with obj.] cause mental or emotional strain or tension in: *I avoid many of the things that used to stress me before* | (as adj. **stressed**) *she should see a doctor if she is feeling particularly* ***stressed out.*** ▪ [no obj.] informal become tense or anxious; worry: *don't stress—there's plenty of time to get a grip on the situation.*
– DERIVATIVES **stressless** adjective, **stressor** noun (sense 3 of the verb).
– ORIGIN Middle English (denoting hardship or force exerted on a person for the purpose of compulsion): shortening of DISTRESS, or partly from Old French *estresse* 'narrowness, oppression', based on Latin *strictus* 'drawn tight' (see STRICT).

stress fracture ▸ **noun** a fracture of a bone caused by repeated (rather than sudden) mechanical stress.

stressful ▸ **adjective** causing mental or emotional stress: *corporate finance work can be stressful.*
– DERIVATIVES **stressfully** adverb, **stressfulness** noun.

stress incontinence ▸ **noun** [mass noun] a condition (found chiefly in women) in which there is involuntary emission of urine when pressure within the abdomen increases suddenly, as in coughing or jumping.

stress-timed ▸ **adjective** (of a language) characterized by a rhythm in which primary stresses occur at roughly equal intervals, irrespective of the number of unstressed syllables in between. English is a stress-timed language. Contrasted with SYLLABLE-TIMED.

stretch ▸ **verb** [no obj.] **1** (of something soft or elastic) be made or be capable of being made longer or wider without tearing or breaking: *my jumper stretched in the wash | rubber will stretch easily when pulled.* ▪ [with obj.] cause (something) to stretch by pulling it: *stretch the elastic | small squares of canvas were* ***stretched over*** *the bamboo frame.*
2 straighten or extend one's body or a part of one's body to its full length, typically so as to tighten one's muscles or in order to reach something: *the cat yawned and stretched* | [with obj.] *I* ***stretched out*** *a weary arm to turn on my radio | stretching my cramped legs | we lay* ***stretched out*** *on the sand.*
3 [no obj., with adverbial] extend or spread over an area or period of time: *the beach stretches for over four miles | the long hours of night stretched ahead of her.* ▪ last or cause to last longer than expected: [no obj.] *her nap had stretched to two hours* | [with obj.] *stretch your weekend into a mini summer vacation.* ▪ [no obj.] (of finances or resources) be sufficient or adequate for a certain purpose: *my budget won't* ***stretch to*** *a weekend at a health farm.*
4 [with obj.] make great demands on the capacity or resources of: *the cost of the court case has* ***stretched*** *their finances* ***to the limit.*** ▪ cause (someone) to make maximum use of their talents or abilities: *it's too easy—it doesn't stretch me.* ▪ informal adapt or extend the scope of (something) in a way that exceeds a reasonable or acceptable limit: *to describe her as sweet would be* ***stretching it a bit.***
▸ **noun 1** an act of stretching one's limbs or body: *I got up and had a stretch.* ▪ [mass noun] the fact or condition of a muscle being stretched. ▪ [mass noun] [usu. as modifier]

S

the capacity of a material or garment to stretch or be stretched; elasticity: *stretch jeans.* ▪ informal a difficult or demanding task: *it was a stretch for me to come up with the rent.*
2 a continuous area or expanse of land or water: *a treacherous stretch of road.* ▪ a continuous period of time: *long stretches of time.* ▪ informal a period of time spent in prison: *a four-year stretch for tax fraud.* ▪ chiefly N. Amer. a straight part of a racetrack, typically the home straight: *he made a promising start, but faded down the stretch.* ▪ Sailing the distance covered on one tack.
3 informal a stretch limo: *a chauffeur-driven stretch.*
– PHRASES **at full stretch** with a part of one's body fully extended. ▪ using the maximum amount of one's resources or energy: *increased export business kept our production plants at full stretch.* **at a stretch 1** in one continuous period: *I often had to work for over twenty hours at a stretch.* **2** only with difficulty or in extreme circumstances: *it is aimed at one age group, adults, or, at a stretch, business studies students.* **by no** (or **not by any**) **stretch of the imagination** used to emphasize that something is definitely not the case: *by no stretch of the imagination could Carl ever be called good-looking.* **stretch one's legs** go for a short walk after sitting in one place for some time. **stretch a point** allow or do something not usually acceptable: *since your daughter is one of my regular patients, I'm stretching a point.* **stretch one's wings** see WING.
– DERIVATIVES **stretchability** noun, **stretchable** adjective.
– ORIGIN Old English *streccan*, of West Germanic origin; related to Dutch *strekken* and German *strecken*. The noun dates from the late 16th cent.

stretcher ▸ noun **1** a framework of two poles with a long piece of canvas slung between them, used for carrying sick, injured, or dead people.
2 a wooden frame over which a canvas is spread and tautened ready for painting. ▪ [with modifier] a rod or frame used for expanding or tautening a specified thing: *sail stretchers.*
3 a rod or bar joining and supporting chair legs. ▪ a board in a boat against which a rower presses the feet for support.
4 a brick or stone laid with its long side along the face of a wall. Compare with HEADER (sense 3).
5 archaic, informal an exaggeration or lie.
▸ verb [with obj.] carry (a sick or injured person) somewhere on a stretcher: *their striker had to be stretchered off following a tackle.*

stretcher-bearer ▸ noun a person who helps to carry the sick or injured on stretchers, especially in time of war or at the scene of an accident.

stretcher party ▸ noun a group of stretcher-bearers.

stretch limo (also **stretch limousine**) ▸ noun a limousine that has an extended seating area.

stretch marks ▸ plural noun streaks or stripes on the skin, especially on the abdomen, caused by distension of the skin from obesity or during pregnancy.

stretch receptor ▸ noun Physiology a sensory receptor that responds to the stretching of surrounding muscle tissue and so contributes to the coordination of muscle activity.

stretchy ▸ adjective (**stretchier**, **stretchiest**) (especially of material or a garment) able to stretch or be stretched easily: *stretchy miniskirts.*
– DERIVATIVES **stretchiness** noun.

stretto /ˈstrɛtəʊ/ Music ▸ noun (pl. **stretti**) a passage, especially at the end of an aria or movement, to be performed in quicker time. ▪ a section at the end of a fugue in which successive introductions of the theme follow at shorter intervals than before, increasing the sense of excitement.
▸ adverb (as a direction) in quicker time.
– ORIGIN Italian, literally 'narrow'.

streusel /ˈstrɔɪz(ə)l, ˈstruːz(ə)l/ ▸ noun a crumbly topping or filling made from fat, flour, sugar, and often cinnamon. ▪ a cake or pastry with a streusel topping.
– ORIGIN from German *Streusel*, from *streuen* 'sprinkle'.

strew ▸ verb (past participle **strewn** or **strewed**) [with obj.] scatter or spread (things) untidily over a surface or area: *a small room with newspapers **strewn all over** the floor.* ▪ (usu. **be strewn with**) cover (a surface or area) with untidily scattered things: *the table was strewn with books and papers* | (as adj., in combination **strewn**) *boulder-strewn slopes.* ▪ be scattered or spread untidily over (a surface or area): *leaves strewed the path.*
– ORIGIN Old English *stre(o)wian*, of Germanic origin; related to Dutch *strooien*, German *streuen*, from an Indo-European root shared by Latin *sternere* 'lay flat'.

strewn field ▸ noun Geology a region of the earth's surface over which tektites of a similar age and presumed origin are found.

strewth (also **struth**) ▸ exclamation Brit. informal used to express surprise or dismay.
– ORIGIN late 19th cent.: contraction of *God's truth*.

stria /ˈstrʌɪə/ ▸ noun (pl. **striae** /-iː/) **1** technical a linear mark, slight ridge, or groove on a surface, often one of a number of similar parallel features.
2 Anatomy any of a number of longitudinal collections of nerve fibres in the brain.
– ORIGIN late 17th cent. (as a scientific term): from Latin, literally 'furrow'.

striate technical ▸ adjective /ˈstrʌɪət, ˈstrʌɪeɪt/ marked with striae: *the striate cortex.*
▸ verb /strʌɪˈeɪt/ [with obj.] mark with striae.
– DERIVATIVES **striation** noun.

striated /strʌɪˈeɪtɪd/ ▸ adjective striped or streaked. ▪ technical marked with striae.

striated muscle ▸ noun [mass noun] Physiology muscle tissue in which the contractile fibrils in the cells are aligned in parallel bundles, so that their different regions form stripes visible in a microscope. Muscles of this type are attached to the skeleton by tendons and are under voluntary control. Also called SKELETAL MUSCLE. Often contrasted with SMOOTH MUSCLE.

striatum /strʌɪˈeɪtəm/ ▸ noun (pl. **striata** /strʌɪˈeɪtə/) Anatomy short for CORPUS STRIATUM.
– DERIVATIVES **striatal** adjective.

stricken North American or archaic past participle of STRIKE. ▸ adjective seriously affected by an undesirable condition or unpleasant feeling: *the pilot landed the stricken aircraft* | *Raymond was **stricken with** grief* | [in combination] *the farms were drought-stricken.* ▪ (of a person's face or look) showing great distress: *she looked at Anne's stricken face, contorted with worry.*
– PHRASES **stricken in years** archaic old and feeble.

strickle ▸ noun **1** a rod used to level off a heaped measure.
2 a whetting tool.
– ORIGIN Old English *stricel* (in sense 1); related to STRIKE. Sense 2 dates from the mid 17th cent.

strict ▸ adjective **1** demanding that rules concerning behaviour are obeyed and observed: *my father was very strict* | *a strict upbringing.* ▪ (of a rule or discipline) demanding total obedience or observance; rigidly enforced: *civil servants are bound by strict rules on secrecy.*
2 (of a person) following rules or beliefs exactly: *a strict vegetarian.*
3 exact in correspondence or adherence to something; not allowing or admitting deviation or relaxation: *a strict interpretation of the law.*
– ORIGIN late Middle English (in the sense 'restricted in space or extent'): from Latin *strictus*, past participle of *stringere* 'tighten, draw tight'.

strict construction ▸ noun Law a literal interpretation of a statute or document by a court.

strict liability ▸ noun [mass noun] Law liability which does not depend on actual negligence or intent to harm.

strictly ▸ adverb **1** in a way that involves rigid enforcement or that demands obedience: *he's been brought up strictly.*
2 used to indicate that one is applying words or rules exactly or rigidly: [sentence adverb] ***strictly speaking**, ham is a cured, cooked leg of pork* | [as submodifier] *to be strictly accurate, there are two Wolvertons.* ▪ with no exceptions; completely or absolutely: *these foods are strictly forbidden.* ▪ no more than; purely: *that visit was strictly business* | *his attitude and manner were strictly professional.*

strictness ▸ noun [mass noun] the quality or condition of being strict: *the strictness of his upbringing.*

stricture /ˈstrɪktʃə/ ▸ noun **1** a restriction on a person or activity: *the strictures imposed by the British Board of Film Censors.*
2 a sternly critical or censorious remark or instruction: *his strictures on their lack of civic virtue.*
3 Medicine abnormal narrowing of a canal or duct in the body: *a colonic stricture* | [mass noun] *jaundice caused by bile duct stricture.*
– DERIVATIVES **strictured** adjective.
– ORIGIN late Middle English (in sense 3): from Latin *strictura*, from *stringere* 'draw tight' (see STRICT). Another sense of the Latin verb, 'touch lightly', gave rise to sense 2 via an earlier meaning 'incidental remark'.

stride ▸ verb (past **strode**; past participle **stridden**) **1** [no obj., with adverbial of direction] walk with long, decisive steps in a specified direction: *he strode across the road* | figurative *we are striding confidently towards the future.* ▪ [with obj.] walk about or along (a street or other place) in this way: *a woman striding the cobbled streets.*
2 [no obj.] (**stride across/over**) cross (an obstacle) with one long step. ▪ [with obj.] literary bestride: *new wealth enabled Britain to stride the world once more.*
▸ noun **1** a long, decisive step: *he crossed the room in a couple of strides.* ▪ [in sing.] the length of a step or manner of taking steps in walking or running: *the horse shortened its stride* | *he followed her with an easy stride.*
2 (usu. **strides**) a step or stage in progress towards an aim: *great strides have been **made** towards equality.* ▪ (**one's stride**) a good or regular rate of progress, especially after a slow or hesitant start: *the speaker was **getting into his stride**.*
3 (**strides**) Brit. informal trousers.
4 [as modifier] denoting or relating to a rhythmic style of jazz piano playing in which the left hand alternately plays single bass notes on the downbeat and chords an octave higher on the upbeat: *he's a noted stride pianist.*
– PHRASES **break** (**one's**) **stride** slow or interrupt the pace at which one walks or moves. **match someone stride for stride** manage to keep up with a competitor. **take something in one's stride** (US also **take something in stride**) deal with something difficult or unpleasant in a calm and accepting way: *I told her what had happened and she took it all in her stride.*
– DERIVATIVES **strider** noun.
– ORIGIN Old English *stride* (noun) 'single long step', *strīdan* (verb) 'stand or walk with the legs wide apart', probably from a Germanic base meaning 'strive, quarrel'; related to Dutch *strijden* 'fight' and German *streiten* 'quarrel'.

strident ▸ adjective **1** (of a sound) loud and harsh; grating: *his voice had become increasingly strident.* ▪ Phonetics another term for SIBILANT.
2 presenting a point of view, especially a controversial one, in an excessively forceful way: *public pronouncements on the crisis became less strident.*
– DERIVATIVES **stridency** noun, **stridently** adverb.
– ORIGIN mid 17th cent.: from Latin *strident-* 'creaking', from the verb *stridere*.

stridor /ˈstrʌɪdə/ ▸ noun [mass noun] a harsh or grating sound: *the engines' stridor increased.* ▪ Medicine a harsh vibrating noise when breathing, caused by obstruction of the windpipe or larynx.
– ORIGIN mid 17th cent.: from Latin, from *stridere* 'to creak'.

stridulate /ˈstrɪdjʊleɪt/ ▸ verb [no obj.] (of an insect, especially a male cricket or grasshopper) make a shrill sound by rubbing the legs, wings, or other parts of the body together.
– DERIVATIVES **stridulation** noun, **stridulatory** adjective.
– ORIGIN mid 19th cent.: from French *striduler*, from Latin *stridulus* 'creaking', from the verb *stridere*.

strife ▸ noun [mass noun] angry or bitter disagreement over fundamental issues; conflict: *strife within the community* | *decades of civil strife.* ▪ Austral./NZ trouble or difficulty of any kind.
– ORIGIN Middle English: shortening of Old French *estrif* (related to Old French *estriver* 'strive').

strigil /ˈstrɪdʒɪl/ ▸ noun **1** an instrument with a curved blade used, especially by ancient Greeks and Romans, to scrape sweat and dirt from the skin in a hot-air bath or after exercise; a scraper.
2 Entomology a comb-like structure on the forelegs of some insects, used chiefly for grooming.
– ORIGIN from Latin *strigilis*, from *stringere* 'touch lightly'. The term in entomology dates from the late 19th cent.

strigose /ˈstrʌɪɡəʊs/ ▸ adjective **1** Botany covered with short, stiff adpressed hairs.
2 Entomology finely grooved or furrowed.
– ORIGIN late 18th cent.: from Latin *striga* 'swathe, furrow' + -OSE[1].

strike ▸ verb (past and past participle **struck** /strʌk/) **1** [with obj.] hit forcibly and deliberately with one's hand or a weapon or other implement: *he raised his hand, as if to strike me* | *one man was struck on the head with a stick* | [no obj.] *Ewan **struck out at** her.* ▪ inflict (a blow): [with two objs] *he struck her two blows on the leg.* ▪ accidentally hit (a part of one's body) against something: *she fell, striking her head against the side*

of the boat. ■ come into forcible contact or collision with: *he was struck by a car in Whitepark Road.* ■ (of a beam or ray of light or heat) fall on (an object or surface): *the light struck her ring, reflecting off the diamond.* ■ (in sporting contexts) hit or kick (a ball): *he struck the ball into the back of the net.* ■ produce (a musical note) by pressing or hitting a key.
2 [with obj.] (of a disaster, disease, or other unwelcome phenomenon) occur suddenly and have harmful or damaging effects on: *a major earthquake struck the island* | [no obj.] *tragedy struck when Nick was killed in a car crash* | (as adj., in combination **struck**) *storm-struck areas.* ■ [no obj.] carry out an aggressive or violent action, typically without warning: *it was eight months before the murderer struck again.* ■ (usu. **be struck down**) kill or seriously incapacitate (someone): *he was struck down by a mystery virus.* ■ (**strike something into**) cause or create a particular strong emotion in (someone): *drugs—a subject guaranteed to strike fear into parents' hearts.* ■ [with obj. and complement] cause (someone) to be in a specified state: *he was struck dumb.*
3 [with obj.] (of a thought or idea) come into the mind of (someone) suddenly or unexpectedly: *a disturbing thought struck Melissa.* ■ cause (someone) to have a particular impression: [with clause] *it struck him that Marjorie was unusually silent* | *the idea* ***struck her as*** *odd.* ■ (**be struck by/with**) find particularly interesting, noticeable, or impressive: *Lucy was struck by the ethereal beauty of the scene.* ■ (**be struck on**) informal be deeply fond of or infatuated with: *she was rather struck on Angus, wasn't she?*
4 [no obj.] (of a clock) indicate the time by sounding a chime or stroke: [with complement] *the church clock struck twelve.* ■ (of time) be indicated by a clock sounding a chime or stroke: *eight o'clock struck.*
5 [with obj.] ignite (a match) by rubbing it briskly against an abrasive surface. ■ produce (fire or a spark) as a result of friction: *his iron stick struck sparks from the pavement.* ■ bring (an electric arc) into being.
6 [no obj.] (of employees) refuse to work as a form of organized protest, typically in an attempt to obtain a particular concession or concessions from their employer: *workers may strike over threatened job losses.* ■ [with obj.] N. Amer. undertake strike action against (an employer).
7 [with obj.] cancel, remove, or cross out with or as if with a pen: *I will* ***strike*** *his name* ***from*** *the list* | *the Court of Appeal* ***struck out*** *the claim for exemplary damages* | *she was* ***striking*** *words* ***through*** *with a pen.* ■ (**strike someone off**) officially remove someone from membership of a professional group: *he was struck off by the Law Society and will never practise as a solicitor again.* ■ (**strike something down**) N. Amer. abolish a law or regulation.
8 [with obj.] make (a coin or medal) by stamping metal. ■ (in cinematography) make (another print) of a film.
9 [with obj.] reach, achieve, or agree to (something involving agreement, balance, or compromise): *the team has* ***struck a deal*** *with a sports marketing agency* | *you have to* ***strike a happy medium.*** ■ (in financial contexts) reach (a figure) by balancing an account: *last year's loss was struck after allowing for depreciation of £67 million.* ■ Canadian form (a committee).
10 [with obj.] discover (gold, minerals, or oil) by drilling or mining. ■ come to or reach: *several days out of the village, we struck the Gilgit Road.* ■ [no obj.] (**strike on/upon**) discover or think of, especially unexpectedly or by chance: *pondering, she struck upon a brilliant idea.*
11 [no obj., with adverbial of direction] move or proceed vigorously or purposefully: *she struck out into the lake with a practised crawl* | *he struck off down the track.* ■ (**strike out**) start out on a new or independent course or endeavour: *after two years he was able to strike out on his own* | *he's struck out as a private eye.*
12 [with obj.] take down (a tent or the tents of an encampment): *it took ages to strike camp.* ■ dismantle (theatrical scenery): *the minute we finish this evening, they'll start striking the set.* ■ lower or take down (a flag or sail), especially as a salute or to signify surrender.
13 [with obj.] insert (a cutting of a plant) in soil to take root. ■ [no obj.] (of a plant or cutting) develop roots: *small conifers will strike from cuttings.* ■ [no obj.] (of a young oyster) attach itself to a bed.
14 [no obj.] Fishing secure a hook in the mouth of a fish by jerking or tightening the line after it has taken the bait or fly.
▶ **noun 1** a refusal to work organized by a body of employees as a form of protest, typically in an attempt to gain a concession or concessions from their employer: *dockers voted for an all-out strike* | [mass noun] *local government workers* ***went on strike*** | [as modifier] *strike action.* ■ [with modifier] an organized refusal to do something expected or required, with a similar aim: *a rent strike.*
2 a sudden attack, typically a military one: *the threat of nuclear strikes.* ■ (in sporting contexts) an act of hitting or kicking a ball: *his 32nd-minute strike helped the team to end a run of three defeats.* ■ (in tenpin bowling) an act of knocking down all the pins with one's first ball. ■ Fishing an act or instance of jerking or tightening the line to secure a fish that has already taken the bait or fly.
3 a discovery of gold, minerals, or oil by drilling or mining: *the Lena goldfields strike of 1912.*
4 Baseball a batter's unsuccessful attempt to hit a pitched ball. ■ a pitch that passes through the strike zone. ■ N. Amer. something to one's discredit: *when they returned from Vietnam they had* ***two strikes against them.***
5 the horizontal or compass direction of a stratum, fault, or other geological feature.
– PHRASES **strike an attitude** (or **pose**) hold one's body in a particular position to create an impression: *striking a dramatic pose, Antonia announced that she was leaving.* **strike a balance** see BALANCE. **strike a blow for** (or **at/against**) do something to help (or hinder) a cause, belief, or principle: *just by finishing the race, she hopes to strike a blow for womankind.* **strike a chord** see CHORD². **strike at the root** (or **roots**) **of** see ROOT¹. **strike hands** archaic (of two people) clasp hands to seal a deal or agreement. **strike home** see HOME. **strike (it) lucky** Brit. informal have good luck in a particular matter. **strike it rich** informal acquire a great deal of money, typically in a sudden or unexpected way. **strike a light** Brit. informal, dated used as an expression of surprise, dismay, or alarm. **strike me pink** Brit. informal, dated used to express astonishment or indignation. **strike while the iron is hot** make use of an opportunity immediately.
– PHRASAL VERBS **strike back 1** retaliate: *he* ***struck back at*** *critics who claim he is too negative.* **2** (of a gas burner) burn from an internal point before the gas has become mixed with air. **strike in** archaic intervene in a conversation or discussion. **strike someone out** (or **strike out**) Baseball dismiss someone (or be dismissed) by means of three strikes. ■ (**strike out**) N. Amer. informal fail or be unsuccessful: *the company struck out the first time it tried to manufacture personal computers.* **strike up** (or **strike something up**) (of a band or orchestra) begin to play a piece of music: *they struck up the 'Star-Spangled Banner'.* ■ (**strike something up**) begin a friendship or conversation with someone, typically in a casual way.
– ORIGIN Old English *strīcan* 'go, flow' and 'rub lightly', of West Germanic origin; related to German *streichen* 'to stroke', also to STROKE. The sense 'deliver a blow' dates from Middle English.

strike-breaker ▶ **noun** a person who works or is employed in place of others who are on strike, thereby making the strike ineffectual.

strike force ▶ **noun** [treated as sing. or pl.] a military force equipped and organized for sudden attack. ■ informal the forwards in a soccer team.

strikeout ▶ **noun** Baseball an out called when a batter has made three strikes.
▶ **adjective** Computing (of text) having a horizontal line through the middle; crossed out.

strike pay ▶ **noun** [mass noun] money paid to strikers by their trade union.

strike price ▶ **noun** Finance **1** the price fixed by the seller of a security after receiving bids in a tender offer, typically for a sale of gilt-edged securities or a new stock market issue.
2 the price at which a put or call option can be exercised.

striker ▶ **noun 1** an employee on strike.
2 the player who is to strike the ball in a game; a player considered in terms of ability to strike the ball: *a gifted striker of the ball.* ■ (chiefly in soccer) a forward or attacker.
3 Brit. a device striking the primer in a gun.

strike rate ▶ **noun** the success rate of a sports team, typically in scoring goals or runs.

striker plate ▶ **noun** a metal plate attached to a door jamb or lidded container, against which the end of a spring-lock bolt strikes when the door or lid is closed.

strike-slip fault ▶ **noun** Geology a fault in which rock strata are displaced mainly in a horizontal direction, parallel to the line of the fault.

strike zone ▶ **noun** Baseball an imaginary area over home plate extending from the armpits to the knees of a batter in the batting position.

striking ▶ **adjective 1** attracting attention by reason of being unusual, extreme, or prominent: *the murder bore a striking similarity to an earlier shooting* | [with clause] *it is* ***striking that*** *no research into the problem is being carried out.* ■ dramatically good-looking or beautiful: *she is naturally striking* | *a striking landscape.*
2 (of an employee) on strike: *striking mineworkers.*
▶ **noun** [mass noun] the action of striking: *substantial damage was caused by the striking of a submerged object.*
– PHRASES **within striking distance** see DISTANCE.
– DERIVATIVES **strikingly adverb** [as submodifier] *a strikingly beautiful girl.*

striking circle ▶ **noun** an elongated semicircle on a hockey field in front of the goal, from within which the ball must be hit in order to score.

striking plate ▶ **noun** another term for STRIKER PLATE.

striking price ▶ **noun** another term for STRIKE PRICE.

strimmer ▶ **noun** Brit. trademark a powered grass trimmer with a nylon cutting cord which rotates rapidly on a spindle.
– ORIGIN 1970s: probably a blend of STRING and TRIMMER.

Strindberg /ˈstrɪndbəːɡ/, (Johan) August (1849–1912), Swedish dramatist and novelist. His satire *The Red Room* (1879) is regarded as Sweden's first modern novel. His later plays are typically tense, psychic dramas, such as *A Dream Play* (1902).
– DERIVATIVES **Strindbergian adjective.**

Strine /strʌɪn/ informal ▶ **noun** [mass noun] the English language as spoken by Australians; the Australian accent, especially when considered pronounced or uneducated. ■ [count noun] an Australian.
▶ **adjective** relating to Australians or Australian English: *he spoke with a broad Strine accent.*
– ORIGIN 1960s: representing *Australian* in Strine.

string ▶ **noun 1** [mass noun] material consisting of threads of cotton, hemp, or other material twisted together to form a thin length. ■ [count noun] a piece of string used to tie round or attach to something. ■ [count noun] a piece of catgut or similar material interwoven with others to form the head of a sports racket. ■ [count noun] a length of catgut or wire on a musical instrument, producing a note by vibration. ■ (**strings**) the stringed instruments in an orchestra. ■ [as modifier] relating to or consisting of stringed instruments: *a string quartet.*
2 a set of things tied or threaded together on a thin cord: *she wore* ***a string of*** *agates round her throat.* ■ a sequence of similar items or events: ***a string of*** *burglaries.* ■ Computing a linear sequence of characters, words, or other data. ■ a group of racehorses trained at one stable. ■ a reserve team or player holding a specified position in an order of preference: *the village team held Rangers' second string to a 0–0 draw.* ■ a player assigned a specified rank in a team in an individual sport such as squash: *Taylor lost to third string Baines.*
3 a tough piece of fibre in vegetables, meat, or other food, such as a tough elongated piece connecting the two halves of a bean pod.
4 a G-string or thong.
5 short for STRINGBOARD.
6 Physics a hypothetical one-dimensional subatomic particle having the dynamical properties of a flexible loop. ■ (also **cosmic string**) a hypothetical thread-like concentration of energy within the structure of space–time.
▶ **verb** (past and past participle **strung**) **1** [with obj. and adverbial] hang (something) so that it stretches in a long line: *lights were strung across the promenade.* ■ thread (a series of small objects) on a string: *he collected stones with holes in them and strung them on a strong cord.* ■ (**be strung**) be arranged in a long line: *the houses were strung along the road.* ■ (**string something together**) add items to one another to form a series or coherent whole: *he can't string two sentences together.*
2 [with obj.] fit a string or strings to (a musical instrument, a racket, or a bow): *the harp had been newly strung.*
3 [with obj.] remove the strings from (a bean).
4 [with obj.] N. Amer. informal hoax or trick (someone): *I'm not stringing you—I'll eat my shirt if it's not true.*

S

5 [no obj.] informal work as a stringer in journalism: *he strings for almost every French radio service.*
6 [no obj.] Billiards determine the order of play by striking the cue ball from baulk to rebound off the top cushion, first stroke going to the player whose ball comes to rest nearer the bottom cushion.
– PHRASES **have many strings to one's bow** see BOW[1]. **how long is a piece of string?** Brit. used to indicate that something cannot be given a finite measurement. **no strings attached** informal used to show that an offer or opportunity carries no special conditions or restrictions. **on a string** under one's control or influence: *I keep all three men on a string and never make a choice.*
– PHRASAL VERBS **string along** Brit. informal stay with or accompany a person or group casually or as long as it is convenient. **string someone along** informal mislead someone deliberately over a length of time, especially about one's intentions: *she had no plans to marry him—she was just stringing him along.* **string something out** prolong something. ■ **(string out)** stretch out into a long line: *the runners string out in a line across the road.* **be strung out** informal be nervous or tense: *I often felt strung out by daily stresses.* ■ N. Amer. be under the influence of alcohol or drugs: *he died, strung out on booze.* **string someone/thing up 1** hang something up on strings. ■ kill someone by hanging. **2 (be strung up)** Brit. informal be tense or nervous.
– DERIVATIVES **stringless** adjective, **string-like** adjective.
– ORIGIN Old English *streng* (noun), of Germanic origin; related to German *Strang*, also to STRONG. The verb (dating from late Middle English) is first recorded in the senses 'arrange in a row' and 'fit with a string'.

string bass ▸ noun (especially among jazz musicians) a double bass.

string bean ▸ noun **1** any of various beans eaten in their fibrous pods, especially runner beans or French beans.
2 informal a tall, thin person.

string bed ▸ noun (in India) a charpoy.

stringboard ▸ noun a supporting timber or skirting in which the ends of the steps in a staircase are set. Also called STRINGER.

string course ▸ noun a raised horizontal band or course of bricks on a building.

stringed ▸ adjective (of a musical instrument) having strings: [in combination] *a three-stringed fiddle.*

stringendo /strɪnˈdʒɛndəʊ/ Music ▸ adverb & adjective (especially as a direction) with increasing speed.
▸ noun (pl. **stringendos** or **stringendi**) a passage performed or marked to be performed with increasing speed.
– ORIGIN Italian, literally 'squeezing, binding together'.

stringent /ˈstrɪn(d)ʒ(ə)nt/ ▸ adjective (of regulations, requirements, or conditions) strict, precise, and exacting: *stringent guidelines on air pollution.*
– DERIVATIVES **stringency** noun, **stringently** adverb.
– ORIGIN mid 17th cent. (in the sense 'compelling, convincing'): from Latin *stringent-* 'drawing tight', from the verb *stringere.*

S

stringer ▸ noun **1** a longitudinal structural piece in a framework, especially that of a ship or aircraft.
2 informal a newspaper correspondent who is retained on a part-time basis to report on events in a particular place.
3 [in combination] a reserve sports player holding a specified position in an order of preference: *six of the team's 24 first-stringers are Canadian.*
4 N. Amer. a chain with hooks on which caught fish are strung.
5 a stringboard.

stringhalt /ˈstrɪŋhɔːlt/ ▸ noun [mass noun] a condition affecting one or both of a horse's hind legs, causing exaggerated bending of the hock.

string line ▸ noun Billiards another term for BAULK LINE.

string orchestra ▸ noun an orchestra consisting only of string instruments of the violin family.

stringpiece ▸ noun a long piece supporting and connecting the parts of a wooden framework.

string quartet ▸ noun a chamber music ensemble consisting of first and second violins, viola, and cello. ■ a piece of music for a string quartet.

string theory ▸ noun [mass noun] a cosmological theory based on the existence of cosmic strings. See STRING (sense 6 of the noun).

string tie ▸ noun a very narrow necktie.

string vest ▸ noun a vest made of a meshed fabric, typically worn by men as underwear.

stringy ▸ adjective (**stringier**, **stringiest**) (especially of hair) resembling string in being long and thin. ■ (of a person) tall, wiry, and thin. ■ (of food) containing tough fibres and so hard to eat. ■ (of a liquid) viscous; forming strings.
– DERIVATIVES **stringiness** noun.

stringybark ▸ noun an Australian eucalyptus with tough fibrous bark. ● Several species in the genus *Eucalyptus*, family Myrtaceae.

strip[1] ▸ verb (**strips**, **stripping**, **stripped**) [with obj.] **1** remove all coverings from: *they stripped the bed.* ■ remove the clothes from (someone): [with obj. and complement] *the man had been stripped naked.* ■ [no obj.] take off one's clothes: *I was tempted to **strip off** for a swim | she **stripped down to** her underwear.* ■ pull or tear off (a garment or covering): *she **stripped off** her shirt* | figurative *strip away the hype and you'll find original thought.* ■ remove bark and branches from (a tree). ■ remove (paint or varnish) from (a surface): *the floorboards can be stripped, sanded, and polished | strip off the existing paint.* ■ remove the stems from (tobacco). ■ milk (a cow) to the last drop.
2 leave bare of accessories or fittings: *thieves **stripped** the room **of** luggage.* ■ remove the accessory fittings of or take apart (a machine, motor vehicle, etc.) to inspect or adjust it: *the tank was stripped down piece by piece.*
3 (strip someone of) deprive someone of (rank, power, or property): *the lieutenant was stripped of his rank.*
4 sell off (the assets of a company) for profit. ■ Finance divest (a bond) of its interest coupons so that it and they may be sold separately.
5 tear the thread or teeth from (a screw, gearwheel, etc.). ■ [no obj.] (of a screw, gearwheel, etc.) lose its thread or teeth.
6 [no obj.] (of a bullet) be fired from a rifled gun without spin owing to a loss of surface.
▸ noun **1** an act of undressing, especially in a striptease: *she got drunk and did a strip on top of the piano.* ■ [as modifier] used for or involving the performance of stripteases: *a campaigner against strip joints.*
2 Brit. the identifying outfit worn by the members of a sports team while playing.
– ORIGIN Middle English (as a verb): of Germanic origin; related to Dutch *stropen.* Sense 2 of the noun arose in the late 20th cent., possibly from the notion of clothing to which a player 'strips' down.

strip[2] ▸ noun **1** a long, narrow piece of cloth, paper, plastic, or some other material: *a **strip of** linen.* ■ a long, narrow area of land. ■ chiefly N. Amer. a main road in or leading out of a town that is lined with shops, restaurants, and other facilities. ■ [mass noun] steel or other metal in the form of narrow flat bars.
2 a comic strip: [as modifier] *a strip cartoon.*
3 Brit. a programme broadcast regularly at the same time: *he hosts a weekly two-hour advice strip.*
– ORIGIN late Middle English: from or related to Middle Low German *strippe* 'strap, thong', probably also to STRIPE.

strip club ▸ noun a club at which striptease performances are given in front of an audience.

strip cropping ▸ noun [mass noun] US cultivation in which different crops are sown in alternate strips to prevent soil erosion.

stripe ▸ noun **1** a long, narrow band or strip differing in colour or texture from the surface on either side of it: *a pair of blue shorts with pink stripes.* ■ archaic a blow with a scourge or lash.
2 a chevron sewn on to a uniform to denote military rank.
3 chiefly N. Amer. a type or category: *entrepreneurs **of** all **stripes** are joining in the offensive.*
▸ verb [with obj.] mark with stripes: *her body was striped with bands of sunlight.*
– PHRASES **earn one's stripes** gain a higher rank in the military. ■ deserve a position, status or reputation through work or achievements: *she's earning her stripes by showing how hard she's willing to work.*
– ORIGIN late Middle English: perhaps a back-formation from STRIPED, of Dutch or Low German origin; compare with Middle Dutch and Middle Low German *stripe.*

striped ▸ adjective marked with or having stripes: [in combination] *a green-striped coat.*

striped bass ▸ noun a large bass of North American coastal waters, with dark horizontal stripes along the upper sides, migrating up streams to breed. ● *Morone* (or *Roccus*) *saxatilis*, family Perchichthyidae.

striped hyena ▸ noun a hyena with numerous black stripes on the body and legs, living in steppe and desert areas from NE Africa to India. ● *Hyaena hyaena*, family Hyaenidae.

striped muscle ▸ noun another term for STRIATED MUSCLE.

striped polecat ▸ noun another term for ZORILLA.

striper ▸ noun another term for STRIPED BASS.

stripey ▸ adjective variant spelling of STRIPY.

strip light ▸ noun Brit. a tubular fluorescent lamp.

stripling ▸ noun archaic or humorous a young man.
– ORIGIN Middle English: probably from STRIP[2] (from the notion of 'narrowness', i.e. slimness) + -LING.

strip mall ▸ noun N. Amer. a shopping mall located on a busy main road.

strip mill ▸ noun a mill in which steel slabs are rolled into strips.

strip mine chiefly N. Amer. ▸ noun an opencast mine.
▸ verb (**strip-mine**) [with obj.] obtain (ore or coal) by opencast mining: *lignite coal is strip-mined at depths of 15 to 35 metres* | (as noun **strip-mining**) *protected lands opened up to strip-mining for coal.* ■ subject (an area of land) to opencast mining.

stripped-down ▸ adjective reduced to essentials: *a pretty, stripped-down ballad.*

stripper ▸ noun **1** a device used for stripping something: *a wire stripper removes insulation from flex.* ■ [mass noun] solvent for removing paint: *paint stripper.*
2 a striptease performer.

strippergram ▸ noun a novelty greetings message delivered by a person who accompanies it with a striptease act.

strip poker ▸ noun [mass noun] a form of poker in which a player with a losing hand takes off an item of clothing as a forfeit.

strip-search ▸ verb [with obj.] search (someone) for concealed items, typically drugs or weapons, in a way that involves the removal of all their clothes.
▸ noun an act of strip-searching someone.

striptease ▸ noun a form of entertainment in which a performer gradually undresses to music in a way intended to be sexually exciting: [as modifier] *a striptease act.*
– DERIVATIVES **stripteaser** noun.

stripy (also **stripey**) ▸ adjective (**stripier**, **stripiest**) Brit. striped: *a stripy T-shirt.*

strive ▸ verb (past **strove** or **strived**; past participle **striven** or **strived**) [no obj.] make great efforts to achieve or obtain something: *national movements were **striving for** independence* | [with infinitive] *we must strive to secure steady growth.* ■ struggle or fight vigorously: *scholars must **strive against** bias.*
– DERIVATIVES **striver** noun.
– ORIGIN Middle English: shortening of Old French *estriver*; related to *estrif* 'strife'.

strobe ▸ noun **1** a stroboscope. ■ a stroboscopic lamp: [as modifier] *strobe lights.*
2 N. Amer. an electronic flash for a camera.
▸ verb [no obj.] **1** flash intermittently: *the light of the fireworks strobed around the room.*
2 exhibit or give rise to strobing: *he explained that the stripes I was wearing would strobe.*
– ORIGIN 1940s: abbreviation of *stroboscopic* (see STROBOSCOPE).

strobila /strəˈbʌɪlə/ ▸ noun (pl. **strobilae** /-lʌɪ, -liː/) Zoology **1** the segmented part of the body of a tapeworm that consists of a long chain of proglottids.
2 a stack of immature larval jellyfish formed on a sessile polyp-like form by budding.
– DERIVATIVES **strobilation** noun.
– ORIGIN mid 19th cent.: modern Latin, from Greek *strobilē* 'twisted plug of lint', from *strephein* 'to twist'.

strobilus /ˈstrəʊbɪləs/ ▸ noun (pl. **strobili** /-lʌɪ, -liː/) Botany the cone of a pine, fir, or other conifer. ■ a cone-like structure, such as the flower of the hop.
– ORIGIN mid 18th cent.: from late Latin, from Greek *strobilos*, from *strephein* 'to twist'.

strobing /ˈstrəʊbɪŋ/ ▸ noun [mass noun] **1** irregular movement and loss of continuity sometimes seen in lines and stripes in a television picture.
2 jerkiness in what should be a smooth movement of an image on a screen.

stroboscope /ˈstrəʊbəskəʊp/ ▸ **noun** Physics an instrument for studying periodic motion or determining speeds of rotation by shining a bright light at intervals so that a moving or rotating object appears stationary. ■ a lamp made to flash intermittently, especially for this purpose.
– DERIVATIVES **stroboscopic** adjective, **stroboscopically** adverb.
– ORIGIN mid 19th cent.: from Greek *strobos* 'whirling' + -SCOPE.

strode past of STRIDE.

stroganoff /ˈstrɒɡənɒf/ ▸ **noun** [mass noun] a dish in which the central ingredient, typically strips of beef, is cooked in a sauce containing sour cream.
– ORIGIN named after Count Pavel *Stroganov* (1772–1817), Russian diplomat.

stroke ▸ **noun 1** an act of hitting or striking someone or something; a blow: *he received three strokes of the cane.* ■ a method of striking the ball in sports or games. ■ Golf an act of hitting the ball with a club, as a unit of scoring: *he won by two strokes.* ■ the sound made by a striking clock.
2 a mark made by drawing a pen, pencil, or paintbrush in one direction across paper or canvas: *the paint had been applied in careful, regular strokes.* ■ a line forming part of a written or printed character. ■ a short printed or written diagonal line typically separating characters or figures.
3 an act of moving one's hand across a surface with gentle pressure: *massage the cream into your skin using light upward strokes.*
4 each of a series of movements in which something moves out of its position and back into it: *the ray swam with effortless strokes of its huge wings.* ■ the whole motion of a piston in either direction. ■ the rhythm to which a series of repeated movements is performed: *the rowers sing to keep their stroke.* ■ a movement of the arms and legs forming one of a series in swimming. ■ a particular style of moving the arms and legs in swimming: *front crawl is a popular stroke.* ■ (in rowing) the mode or action of moving the oar. ■ (also **stroke oar**) the oar or oarsman nearest the stern of a boat, setting the timing for the other rowers.
5 a sudden disabling attack or loss of consciousness caused by an interruption in the flow of blood to the brain, especially through thrombosis.
▸ **verb** [with obj.] **1** move one's hand with gentle pressure over (a surface), typically repeatedly; caress: *he put his hand on her hair and stroked it.* ■ [with obj. and adverbial of place] apply (something) to a surface using a gentle movement: *she strokes blue eyeshadow on her eyelids.* ■ N. Amer. informal reassure or flatter (someone), especially in order to gain their cooperation: *production executives were expert at stroking stars and brokering talent.*
2 act as the stroke of (a boat or crew): *he stroked the coxed four to victory.*
3 hit or kick (a ball) smoothly and deliberately: *Markwick stroked the ball home.*
– PHRASES **at a** (or **one**) **stroke** by a single action having immediate effect: *attitudes cannot be changed at a stroke.* **not** (or **never**) **do a stroke of work** do no work at all. **on the stroke of ——** precisely at the specified time: *he arrived on the stroke of two.* **put someone off their stroke** disconcert someone so that they do not work or perform as well as they might. **stroke of genius** an outstandingly brilliant and original idea. **stroke of** (**good**) **luck** a fortunate occurrence that could not have been predicted or expected.
– DERIVATIVES **strokeable** adjective, **stroker** noun.
– ORIGIN Old English *strācian* 'caress lightly', of Germanic origin; related to Dutch *streek* 'a stroke', German *streichen* 'to stroke', also to STRIKE. The earliest noun sense 'blow' is first recorded in Middle English.

stroke play ▸ **noun** [mass noun] play in golf in which the score is reckoned by counting the number of strokes taken overall. Compare with MATCH PLAY.

stroll ▸ **verb** [no obj., with adverbial of direction] **1** walk in a leisurely way: *I strolled around the city.*
2 achieve a sporting victory without effort: *the horse strolled home by 12 lengths.*
▸ **noun 1** a short leisurely walk.
2 a victory or objective that is easily achieved.
– ORIGIN early 17th cent. (in the sense 'roam as a vagrant'): probably from German *strollen*, *strolchen*, from *Strolch* 'vagabond', of unknown ultimate origin.

stroller ▸ **noun 1** a person taking a leisurely walk: *shady gardens where strollers could relax.*
2 N. Amer. a pushchair.
3 S. African a young urban vagrant; a street child.

strolling players ▸ **plural noun** historical a troupe of itinerant actors.

stroma /ˈstrəʊmə/ ▸ **noun** (pl. **stromata** /-mətə/)
1 [mass noun] Anatomy & Biology the supportive tissue of an epithelial organ, tumour, gonad, etc., consisting of connective tissues and blood vessels. ■ the spongy framework of protein fibres in a red blood cell or platelet. ■ Botany the matrix of a chloroplast, in which the grana are embedded.
2 Botany a cushion-like mass of fungal tissue, having spore-bearing structures either embedded in it or on its surface.
– DERIVATIVES **stromal** adjective (chiefly Anatomy), **stromatic** adjective (chiefly Botany).
– ORIGIN mid 19th cent.: modern Latin, via late Latin from Greek *strōma* 'coverlet'.

stromatolite /strə(ʊ)ˈmatəlʌɪt/ ▸ **noun** a calcareous mound built up of layers of lime-secreting cyanobacteria and trapped sediment, found in Precambrian rocks as the earliest known fossils, and still being formed in lagoons in Australasia.
– ORIGIN 1930s: from modern Latin *stroma*, *stromat-* 'layer, covering' + -LITE.

stromatoporoid /ˌstrəʊməˈtɒpərɔɪd/ ▸ **noun** an extinct sessile coral-like marine organism of uncertain relationship which built up calcareous masses composed of laminae and pillars, occurring from the Cambrian to the Cretaceous.
– ORIGIN late 19th cent.: from modern Latin *Stromatopora* (genus name), from *stroma*, *stromat-* 'layer, covering' + *-pora*.

Stromboli /ˈstrɒmbəli, strɒmˈbəʊli/ a volcanic island in the Mediterranean, the most north-easterly of the Lipari Islands.

Strombolian /strɒmˈbəʊlɪən/ ▸ **adjective** Geology denoting volcanic activity of the kind typified by Stromboli, with continual mild eruptions in which lava fragments are ejected.

strong ▸ **adjective** (**stronger**, **strongest**) **1** having the power to move heavy weights or perform other physically demanding tasks: *she cut through the water with her strong arms.* ■ [attrib.] able to perform a specified action well and powerfully: *he was not a strong swimmer.* ■ exerting great force: *a strong current.* ■ powerful and difficult to resist or defeat: *a strong leader | the competition was too strong | the company was in a strong position to negotiate a deal.* ■ (of an argument or case) likely to succeed because of sound reasoning or convincing evidence: *there is a strong argument for decentralization.* ■ powerfully affecting the mind, senses, or emotions: *his imagery made a strong impression on the critics.* ■ (of language or actions) forceful and extreme, especially excessively or unacceptably so: *the government were urged to take strong measures against the perpetrators of violence | a play full of strong language.*
2 able to withstand force, pressure, or wear: *cotton is strong, hard-wearing, and easy to handle.* ■ not easily affected by disease or hardship. ■ not easily disturbed, upset, or affected: *driving on these motorways requires strong nerves | only a strong will enabled him to survive.* ■ firmly held or established: *he was a man of strong, though unconventional, religious beliefs | they had established a strong and trusting relationship.* ■ (of a market) having steadily high or rising prices.
3 very intense: *a strong smell.* ■ (of something seen or heard) not soft or muted; clear or prominent: *she should wear strong colours.* ■ (of food or its flavour) distinctive and pungent: *strong cheese.* ■ (of a solution or drink) containing a large proportion of a particular substance; concentrated: *a cup of strong coffee | strong lager.* ■ Chemistry (of an acid or base) fully ionized into cations and anions in solution; having (respectively) a very low or a very high pH.
4 used after a number to indicate the size of a group: *a hostile crowd several thousands strong.*
5 Grammar denoting a class of verbs in Germanic languages that form the past tense and past participle by a change of vowel within the stem rather than by addition of a suffix (e.g. *swim, swam, swum*).
6 Physics relating to or denoting the strongest of the known kinds of force between particles, which acts between nucleons and other hadrons when closer than about 10^{-13} cm (so binding protons in a nucleus despite the repulsion due to their charge), and which conserves strangeness, parity, and isospin.
– PHRASES **come on strong** informal **1** behave aggressively or assertively, especially in making sexual advances to someone. **2** improve one's position considerably: *he came on strong towards the end of the round.* **going strong** informal continuing to be healthy, vigorous, or successful: *the programme is still going strong after twelve series.* **strong on** good at: *he is strong on comedy.* ■ possessing large quantities of: *our pizza wasn't strong on pine nuts.* **strong meat** Brit. ideas or language likely to be found unacceptably forceful or extreme. **one's strong point** something at which one excels: *arithmetic had never been my strong point.*
– DERIVATIVES **strongish** adjective, **strongly** adverb.
– ORIGIN Old English, of Germanic origin; related to Dutch and German *streng*, also to STRING.

strong-arm ▸ **adjective** [attrib.] using or characterized by force or violence: *they were furious at what they said were government strong-arm tactics.*
▸ **verb** [with obj.] use force or violence against: *the culprit shouted before being strong-armed out of the door.*

strongbox ▸ **noun** a small lockable box, typically made of metal, in which valuables may be kept.

strong breeze ▸ **noun** a wind of force 6 on the Beaufort scale (22–27 knots or 40–50 kph).

strong drink ▸ **noun** [mass noun] alcohol, especially spirits.

strong gale ▸ **noun** a wind of force 9 on the Beaufort scale (41–47 knots or 75–87 kph).

stronghold ▸ **noun 1** a place where a particular cause or belief is strongly defended or upheld: *a Labour stronghold.*
2 a place that has been fortified so as to protect it against attack.

strong interaction ▸ **noun** Physics interaction at short distances between certain subatomic particles mediated by the strong force.

strongman ▸ **noun** (pl. **strongmen**) a man of great physical strength, especially one who performs feats of strength as a form of entertainment. ■ a leader who rules by the exercise of threats, force, or violence.

strong-minded ▸ **adjective** not easily influenced by others; resolute and determined.
– DERIVATIVES **strong-mindedness** noun.

strongpoint ▸ **noun** a specially fortified defensive position.

strongroom ▸ **noun** a room, typically one in a bank, designed to protect valuable items against fire and theft.

strong safety ▸ **noun** American Football a defensive back positioned opposite the strong side who usually covers the tight end.

strong suit ▸ **noun** (in bridge or whist) a holding of a number of high cards of one suit in a hand. ■ (**one's strong suit**) something at which one excels: *compassion is not Jack's strong suit.*

strong-willed ▸ **adjective** determined to do as one wants even if other people advise against it.

strongyle /ˈstrɒndʒɪl/ ▸ **noun** a nematode worm of a group that includes several common disease-causing parasites of mammals and birds. ● Genus *Strongylus* or family Strongylidae, class Phasmida. See also REDWORM (sense 2).
– ORIGIN mid 19th cent.: from modern Latin *Strongylus*, from Greek *strongulos* 'round'.

strongyloidiasis /ˌstrɒndʒɪlɔɪˈdʌɪəsɪs/ ▸ **noun** [mass noun] infestation with threadworms of a type found in tropical and subtropical regions, chiefly affecting the small intestine and causing ulceration and diarrhoea. ● The worms belong to the genus *Strongyloides*, class Phasmida, in particular *S. stercoralis*.

strontia /ˈstrɒnʃ(ɪ)ə/ ▸ **noun** [mass noun] Chemistry strontium oxide, a white solid resembling quicklime. ● Chem. formula: SrO.
– ORIGIN early 19th cent.: from earlier *strontian*, denoting native strontium carbonate from *Strontian*, a parish in the Highland region of Scotland, where it was discovered.

strontianite /ˈstrɒnʃ(ə)nʌɪt/ ▸ **noun** [mass noun] a rare pale greenish-yellow or white mineral consisting of strontium carbonate.
– ORIGIN late 18th cent.: from *strontian* (see STRONTIA) + -ITE[1].

strontium /ˈstrɒntɪəm, ˈstrɒnʃ(ɪ)əm/ ▸ **noun** [mass noun] the chemical element of atomic number 38, a soft silver-white metal of the alkaline earth series. Its salts are used in fireworks and flares because they give a brilliant red light. (Symbol: **Sr**)
– ORIGIN early 19th cent.: from STRONTIA + -IUM.

strop[1] ▸ **noun** a device, typically a strip of leather, for sharpening razors.

S

▶ **verb** (**strops, stropping, stropped**) [with obj.] sharpen on or with a strop: *he stropped a knife razor-sharp on his belt.*
– ORIGIN late Middle English (in the sense 'thong', also as a nautical term): probably a West Germanic adoption of Latin *stroppus* 'thong'.

strop[2] ▶ **noun** [usu. in sing.] Brit. informal a bad mood; a temper: *Nathalie gets in a strop and makes to leave.*
– ORIGIN 1970s: probably a back-formation from STROPPY.

strophanthin /strə(ʊ)ˈfanθɪn/ ▶ **noun** [mass noun] Medicine a poisonous substance of the glycoside class, obtained from certain African trees and used as a heart stimulant. ● This substance is obtained from trees of the genera *Strophanthus* and *Acokanthera* (family Apocynaceae).
– ORIGIN late 19th cent.: from modern Latin *strophanthus* (from Greek *strophos* 'twisted cord' + *anthos* 'flower', referring to the long segments of the corolla) + -IN[1].

strophe /ˈstrəʊfi/ ▶ **noun** the first section of an ancient Greek choral ode or of one division of it. ■ a group of lines forming a section of a lyric poem.
– DERIVATIVES **strophic** adjective.
– ORIGIN early 17th cent.: from Greek *strophē*, literally 'turning', from *strephein* 'to turn': the term originally denoted a movement from right to left made by a Greek chorus, or lines of choral song recited during this.

stroppy ▶ **adjective** (**stroppier, stroppiest**) Brit. informal bad-tempered and argumentative.
– DERIVATIVES **stroppily** adverb, **stroppiness** noun.
– ORIGIN 1950s: perhaps an abbreviation of OBSTREPEROUS.

stroud /straʊd/ ▶ **noun** [mass noun] Canadian coarse woollen fabric of a kind used in the manufacture of blankets.
– ORIGIN late 17th cent.: perhaps from the name of *Stroud* in Gloucestershire.

strove past of STRIVE.

strow /strəʊ/ ▶ **verb** (past participle **strown** /strəʊn/ or **strowed**) archaic variant of STREW.

struck past and past participle of STRIKE.

struck joint ▶ **noun** a masonry joint in which the mortar between two courses of bricks is sloped inwards so as to be flush with the surface of one but below that of the other.

structural ▶ **adjective** relating to or forming part of the structure of a building or other item: *the blast left ten buildings with major structural damage.* ■ relating to the arrangement of and relations between the parts or elements of a complex whole: *there have been structural changes in the industry.*
– DERIVATIVES **structurally** adverb.

structural engineering ▶ **noun** [mass noun] the branch of civil engineering that deals with large modern buildings and similar structures.
– DERIVATIVES **structural engineer** noun.

structural formula ▶ **noun** Chemistry a formula which shows the arrangement of atoms in the molecule of a compound.

structuralism ▶ **noun** [mass noun] a method of interpretation and analysis of aspects of human cognition, behaviour, culture, and experience, which focuses on relationships of contrast between elements in a conceptual system. ■ the doctrine that structure is more important than function.

Originating in the structural linguistics of Ferdinand de Saussure, and extended into anthropology by Claude Lévi-Strauss, structuralism was adapted to a wide range of social and cultural studies, especially in the 1960s, by writers such as Roland Barthes, Louis Althusser, and Jacques Lacan.

– DERIVATIVES **structuralist** noun & adjective.

structural linguistics ▶ **plural noun** [treated as sing.] the branch of linguistics that deals with language as a system of interrelated structures, in particular the theories and methods of Leonard Bloomfield, emphasizing the accurate identification of syntactic and lexical form as opposed to meaning and historical development.

structural steel ▶ **noun** [mass noun] strong mild steel in shapes suited to construction work.

structural unemployment ▶ **noun** [mass noun] unemployment resulting from industrial reorganization, typically due to technological change, rather than fluctuations in supply or demand.

structuration ▶ **noun** [mass noun] the state or process of organization in a structured form.

structure ▶ **noun 1** the arrangement of and relations between the parts or elements of something complex: *the two sentences have equivalent structures | the company's weakness is the inflexibility of its management structure.* ■ [mass noun] the quality of being organized: *we shall use three headings to give some structure to the discussion.*
2 a building or other object constructed from several parts: *the station is a magnificent structure and should not be demolished.*
▶ **verb** [with obj.] construct or arrange according to a plan; give a pattern or organization to: *services must be structured so as to avoid pitfalls.*
– DERIVATIVES **structureless** adjective.
– ORIGIN late Middle English (denoting the process of building): from Old French, or from Latin *structura*, from *struere* 'to build'. The verb is rarely found before the 20th cent.

structure plan ▶ **noun** a plan drawn up by a local planning authority for the use of a prescribed area of land.

strudel /ˈstruːd(ə)l, ˈʃtruː-/ ▶ **noun** a dessert of thin pastry rolled up round a fruit filling and baked.
– ORIGIN from German *Strudel*, literally 'whirlpool'.

struggle ▶ **verb** [no obj.] make forceful or violent efforts to get free of restraint or constriction: *before she could struggle, he lifted her up* | [with infinitive] *he struggled to break free.* ■ engage in conflict: *politicians continued to struggle over familiar issues.* ■ strive to achieve or attain something in the face of difficulty or resistance: *new authors are struggling in the present climate | many families on income support have to struggle to make ends meet* | (as adj. **struggling**) *a struggling team.* ■ (**struggle with**) have difficulty handling or coping with: *passengers struggle with bags and briefcases.* ■ [no obj., with adverbial of direction] make one's way with difficulty: *it took us all day to struggle back to our bivouac.*
▶ **noun** a forceful or violent effort to get free of restraint or resist attack: *there were signs of a struggle and there was a lot of blood around.* ■ a conflict or contest: *a power struggle for the leadership.* ■ a determined effort under difficulties: *with a struggle, she pulled the pram up the slope | the centre is the result of the scientists' struggle to realize their dream.* ■ a very difficult task: *it was a struggle to make herself understood.*
– PHRASES **the struggle for existence** (or **life**) the competition between organisms, especially as an element in natural selection, or between people seeking a livelihood.
– DERIVATIVES **struggler** noun.
– ORIGIN late Middle English: frequentative, perhaps of imitative origin. The noun dates from the late 17th cent.

strum ▶ **verb** (**strums, strumming, strummed**) [with obj.] play (a guitar or similar instrument) by sweeping the thumb or a plectrum up or down across the strings. ■ play (a tune) in such a way: *he strummed a few chords.* ■ [no obj.] play casually or unskilfully on a stringed or keyboard instrument.
▶ **noun** a sound made by strumming: *the brittle strum of acoustic guitars.* ■ an instance or spell of strumming.
– DERIVATIVES **strummer** noun.
– ORIGIN late 18th cent.: imitative; compare with THRUM[1].

struma /ˈstruːmə/ ▶ **noun** (pl. **strumae** /-miː/) Medicine a swelling of the thyroid gland; a goitre.
– ORIGIN mid 16th cent. (in the Latin sense): modern Latin, from Latin, 'scrofulous tumour'.

strumous /ˈstruːməs/ ▶ **adjective** archaic scrofulous.
– ORIGIN late 16th cent.: from Latin *strumosus*, from *struma* (see STRUMA).

strumpet ▶ **noun** archaic or humorous a female prostitute or a promiscuous woman.
– ORIGIN Middle English: of unknown origin.

strung past and past participle of STRING.

strut ▶ **noun 1** a rod or bar forming part of a framework and designed to resist compression.
2 [in sing.] a stiff, erect, and apparently arrogant or conceited gait: *that old confident strut and swagger has returned.*
▶ **verb** (**struts, strutting, strutted**) **1** [no obj., with adverbial] walk with a stiff, erect, and apparently arrogant or conceited gait: *peacocks strut through the grounds | she strutted down the catwalk.*
2 [with obj.] brace (something) with a strut or struts: *the holes were close-boarded and strutted.*
– PHRASES **strut one's stuff** informal dance or behave in a confident and expressive way.
– DERIVATIVES **strutter** noun, **struttingly** adverb.
– ORIGIN Old English *strūtian* 'protrude stiffly', of Germanic origin. Current senses date from the late 16th cent.

struth ▶ **exclamation** variant spelling of STREWTH.

strychnine /ˈstrɪkniːn, -nɪn/ ▶ **noun** [mass noun] a bitter and highly poisonous compound obtained from nux vomica and related plants. An alkaloid, it has occasionally been used as a stimulant.
– ORIGIN early 19th cent.: from French, via Latin from Greek *strukhnos*, denoting a kind of nightshade.

Sts ▶ **abbreviation** Saints.

Stuart[1], Charles Edward (1720–88), son of James Stuart, pretender to the British throne; known as **the Young Pretender** or **Bonnie Prince Charlie**. He led the Jacobite uprising of 1745–6. However, he was driven back to Scotland and defeated at the Battle of Culloden (1746).

Stuart[2], James (Francis Edward) (1688–1766), son of James II (James VII of Scotland), pretender to the British throne; known as **the Old Pretender**. He arrived in Scotland too late to alter the outcome of the 1715 Jacobite uprising and left the leadership of the 1745–6 uprising to his son Charles Edward Stuart.

Stuart[3], John McDouall (1815–66), Scottish explorer. He was a member of Charles Sturt's third expedition to Australia (1844–6) and subsequently crossed Australia from south to north and back again, at his sixth attempt (1860–2).

Stuart[4], Mary, see MARY, QUEEN OF SCOTS.

Stuart[5] (also **Stewart**) ▶ **adjective** relating to the royal family ruling Scotland 1371–1714 and Britain 1603–1649 and 1660–1714.
▶ **noun** a member of the Stuart family.

stub ▶ **noun 1** the truncated remnant of a pencil, cigarette, or similar-shaped object after use. ■ a truncated or unusually short thing: *he wagged his little stub of tail.* ■ [as modifier] denoting a projection or hole that goes only part of the way through a surface: *a stub tenon.*
2 the counterfoil of a cheque, receipt, ticket, or other document.
▶ **verb** (**stubs, stubbing, stubbed**) [with obj.] **1** accidentally strike (one's toe) against something: *I stubbed my toe, swore, and tripped.*
2 extinguish (a lighted cigarette) by pressing the lighted end against something: *she stubbed out her cigarette in the overflowing ashtray.*
3 grub up (a plant) by the roots: *he was found to have stubbed up a hedge.*
– ORIGIN Old English *stub(b)* 'stump of a tree', of Germanic origin. The verb is first recorded (late Middle English) in sense 3; sense 1 of the verb (mid 19th cent.) was originally a US usage.

stub axle ▶ **noun** an axle supporting only one wheel of a pair on opposite sides of a vehicle.

stubble ▶ **noun** [mass noun] **1** the cut stalks of cereal plants left sticking out of the ground after the grain is harvested.
2 short, stiff hairs growing on a man's face when he has not shaved for a while.
– DERIVATIVES **stubbled** adjective.
– ORIGIN Middle English: from Anglo-Norman French *stuble*, from Latin *stupla*, *stupula*, variants of *stipula* 'straw'.

stubbly ▶ **adjective** (**stubblier, stubbliest**) covered with stubble: *a stubbly chin.*

stubborn ▶ **adjective** having or showing dogged determination not to change one's attitude or position on something, especially in spite of good reasons to do so: *you're a silly, stubborn old woman.* ■ difficult to move, remove, or cure: *the removal of stubborn screws.*
– PHRASES **(as) stubborn as a mule** informal extremely stubborn.
– DERIVATIVES **stubbornly** adverb, **stubbornness** noun.
– ORIGIN Middle English (originally in the sense 'untameable, implacable'): of unknown origin.

Stubbs, George (1724–1806), English painter and engraver. He is particularly noted for his sporting scenes and paintings of horses and lions, such as the *Mares and Foals in a Landscape* series (*c.*1760–70).

stubby ▶ **adjective** (**stubbier, stubbiest**) short and thick: *Bob pointed with a stubby finger.*
▶ **noun** (pl. **stubbies**) Austral./NZ informal **1** a squat bottle of beer normally holding 375 cl.

2 (**Stubbies**) trademark a pair of men's brief shorts.
– DERIVATIVES **stubbiness** noun.

stucco /'stʌkəʊ/ ▶ noun [mass noun] fine plaster used for coating wall surfaces or moulding into architectural decorations.
▶ verb (**stuccoes, stuccoing, stuccoed**) [with obj.] (usu. as adj. **stuccoed**) coat or decorate with stucco: *a stuccoed house*.
– ORIGIN late 16th cent. (as a noun): from Italian, of Germanic origin.

stuck past participle of STICK².

stuck-up ▶ adjective informal staying aloof from others because one thinks one is superior.

stud¹ ▶ noun 1 a large-headed piece of metal that pierces and projects from a surface, especially for decoration. ■ a small, simple piece of jewellery for wearing in pierced ears or nostrils. ■ a fastener consisting of two buttons joined with a bar, used in formal wear to fasten a shirt front or to fasten a collar to a shirt. ■ (usu. **studs**) Brit. a small projection fixed to the base of footwear, especially sports boots, to allow the wearer to grip the ground. ■ (usu. **studs**) a small metal piece set into the tyre of a motor vehicle to improve roadholding in slippery conditions. ■ a small object projecting slightly from a road surface as a marker.
2 an upright timber in the wall of a building to which laths and plasterboard are nailed. ■ US the height of a room as indicated by the length of a timber wall stud.
3 a rivet or crosspiece in each link of a chain cable.
▶ verb (**studs, studding, studded**) [with obj.] decorate or augment (something) with many studs or similar small objects: *a dagger* ***studded with*** *precious diamonds*. ■ scatter or cover (something) with many small objects or features: *the sky was clear and studded with stars*.
– ORIGIN Old English *studu, stuthu* 'post, upright prop'; related to German *stützen* 'to prop'. The sense 'ornamental metal knob' arose in late Middle English.

stud² ▶ noun 1 an establishment where horses or other domesticated animals are kept for breeding: [as modifier] *a stud farm* | [mass noun] *the horse was retired to stud*. ■ a collection of horses or other domesticated animals belonging to one person. ■ (also **stud horse**) a stallion.
2 informal a young man thought to be very active sexually or regarded as a good sexual partner.
3 (also **stud poker**) [mass noun] a form of poker in which the first card of a player's hand is dealt face down and the others face up, with betting after each round of the deal.
– ORIGIN Old English *stōd*, of Germanic origin; related to German *Stute* 'mare', also to STAND.

stud book ▶ noun a book containing the pedigrees of horses.

studded ▶ adjective decorated or augmented with studs: *a studded leather belt*.

studding ▶ noun [mass noun] timber wall studs collectively.

studdingsail /'stʌns(ə)l/ ▶ noun (on a square-rigged sailing ship) an additional sail set at the end of a yard in light winds.
– ORIGIN mid 16th cent.: *studding* perhaps from Middle Low German, Middle Dutch *stōtinge* 'a thrusting'.

student ▶ noun a person who is studying at a university or other place of higher education. ■ a school pupil. ■ [as modifier] denoting someone who is studying in order to enter a particular profession: *a group of student nurses*. ■ a person who takes an interest in a particular subject: ***a student of*** *the free market*.
– DERIVATIVES **studentship** noun (Brit.), **studenty** adjective (Brit. informal).
– ORIGIN late Middle English: from Latin *student-* 'applying oneself to', from the verb *studere*, related to *studium* 'painstaking application'.

student-at-law ▶ noun Canadian a law student who is undergoing training with a firm.

Student's t-test ▶ noun a test for statistical significance that uses tables of a statistical distribution called **Student's *t*-distribution**, which is that of a fraction (*t*) whose numerator is drawn from a normal distribution with a mean of zero, and whose denominator is the root mean square of *k* terms drawn from the same normal distribution (where *k* is the number of degrees of freedom).
– ORIGIN early 20th cent.: *Student*, the pseudonym of William Sealy Gosset (1876–1937), English brewery employee.

stud horse ▶ noun see STUD².

studied ▶ adjective (of a quality or result) achieved or maintained by careful and deliberate effort: *he treated them with studied politeness*.
– DERIVATIVES **studiedly** adverb, **studiedness** noun.

studio ▶ noun (pl. **studios**) 1 a room where an artist, photographer, sculptor, etc. works. ■ a place where cinema films are made or produced. ■ a place where musical or sound recordings are made. ■ a room from which television programmes are broadcast, or in which they are recorded. ■ a place where performers, especially dancers, practise and exercise.
2 a film or television production company.
3 a studio flat.
– ORIGIN early 19th cent.: from Italian, from Latin *studium* (see STUDY).

studio couch ▶ noun chiefly N. Amer. a sofa bed.

studio flat ▶ noun (N. Amer. also **studio apartment**) Brit. a flat containing one main room.

studio portrait ▶ noun a large photograph for which the sitter is posed, typically taken in the photographer's studio.

studio theatre ▶ noun a small theatre where experimental and innovative productions are staged.

studious ▶ adjective 1 spending a lot of time studying or reading: *he was quiet and studious*.
2 done deliberately or with a purpose in mind: *his studious absence from public view*. ■ showing great care or attention: *he made a studious inspection of the buffet*.
– DERIVATIVES **studiously** adverb, **studiousness** noun.
– ORIGIN Middle English: from Latin *studiosus*, from *studium* 'painstaking application'.

studly ▶ adjective (**studlier, studliest**) informal (of a man) sexually attractive in a strongly masculine way: *a coterie of studly factory workers*.
– ORIGIN 1960s: from STUD².

studmuffin ▶ noun N. Amer. informal a man perceived as sexually attractive, typically one with well-developed muscles.

stud poker ▶ noun see STUD² (sense 3).

study ▶ noun (pl. **studies**) 1 [mass noun] the devotion of time and attention to acquiring knowledge on an academic subject, especially by means of books: *the study of English* | *an application to continue full-time study*. ■ (**studies**) activity of this type as pursued by one person: *some students may not be able to resume their studies*. ■ [count noun] an academic book or article on a particular topic: *a study of Jane Austen's novels*. ■ (**studies**) used in the title of an academic subject: *an undergraduate course in transport studies*.
2 a detailed investigation and analysis of a subject or situation: *a study of a sample of 5,000 children* | [mass noun] *the study of global problems*. ■ a portrayal in literature or another art form of an aspect of behaviour or character: *a complex study of a gay teenager*. ■ archaic a thing that is or deserves to be investigated; the subject of an individual's study: *I have made it my study to examine the nature and character of the Indians*. ■ archaic the object or aim of someone's endeavours: *the acquisition of a fortune is the study of all*. ■ [with adj.] theatrical slang a person who memorizes a role at a specified speed: *I'm a quick study*.
3 a room used or designed for reading, writing, or academic work.
4 a piece of work, especially a drawing, done for practice or as an experiment. ■ a musical composition designed to develop a player's technical skill.
5 a thing or person that is an embodiment or good example of something: *he perched on the edge of the bed, a study in confusion and misery*. ■ informal an amusing or remarkable thing or person: *Ira's face was a study as he approached the car*.
▶ verb (**studies, studying, studied**) [with obj.] 1 devote time and attention to acquiring knowledge on (an academic subject), especially by means of books: *students studying A-level drama*. ■ investigate and analyse (a subject or situation) in detail: *he has been studying mink for many years*. ■ [no obj.] apply oneself to study: *he spent his time listening to the radio rather than studying*. ■ [no obj.] acquire academic knowledge at an educational establishment: *he studied at the Kensington School of Art*. ■ [no obj.] (**study up**) US learn intensively about something, especially in preparation for a test of knowledge: *schoolchildren* ***studying up on*** *their forebears' games and chores*. ■ (of an actor) try to learn (the words of one's role). ■ W. Indian give serious thought or consideration to: *the people here don't make so much noise, so the government don't have us to study*.
2 look at closely in order to observe or read: *she bent her head to study the plans*.
3 archaic make an effort to achieve (a result) or take into account (a person or their wishes): *with no husband to study, housekeeping is mere play*.
– PHRASES **in a brown study** absorbed in one's thoughts. [apparently from *brown* in the sense 'gloomy'.]
– ORIGIN Middle English: shortening of Old French *estudie* (noun), *estudier* (verb), both based on Latin *studium* 'zeal, painstaking application'.

study-bedroom ▶ noun Brit. a room used both as a bedroom and as a study, typically by a student who is resident at a university.

study group ▶ noun a group of people who meet to study a particular subject and then report their findings or recommendations.

study hall ▶ noun [mass noun] N. Amer. the period of time in a school curriculum set aside for the preparation of schoolwork. ■ a schoolroom used for such work.

stuff ▶ noun [mass noun] 1 matter, material, articles, or activities of a specified or indeterminate kind that are being referred to, indicated, or implied: *I prefer to buy stuff in sales* | *we all offer to do stuff for each other* | *green stuff in stagnant water* | *a girl who's good at the technical stuff* | *all that running and swimming and stuff*. ■ a person's belongings, equipment, or baggage: *he took his stuff and went*. ■ Brit. informal, dated worthless or foolish ideas, speech, or writing; rubbish: [as exclamation] *stuff and nonsense!* ■ informal drink or drugs. ■ (**one's stuff**) things in which one is knowledgeable and experienced; one's area of expertise: *he* ***knows his stuff*** *and can really write*.
2 the basic constituents or characteristics of something or someone: *Healey was made of sterner stuff* | *such a trip was the stuff of his dreams*.
3 Brit. dated woollen fabric, especially as distinct from silk, cotton, and linen: [as modifier] *her dark stuff gown*.
4 N. Amer. (in sport) spin given to a ball to make it vary its course. ■ a player's ability to produce such spin or control the speed of delivery of a ball.
▶ verb [with obj.] 1 fill (a receptacle or space) tightly with something: *an old teapot* ***stuffed full of*** *cash* | figurative *his head has been* ***stuffed with*** *myths and taboos*. ■ force or cram (something) tightly into a receptacle or space: *he stuffed a thick wad of notes into his jacket pocket*. ■ informal hastily force (something) into a space: *Sadie took the coin and stuffed it in her coat pocket*. ■ fill out the skin of (a dead animal or bird) with material to restore the original shape and appearance: *he took the bird to a taxidermist to be stuffed* | (as adj. **stuffed**) *a stuffed parrot*. ■ fill (the cavity of an item of food) with a savoury or sweet mixture, especially before cooking: *chicken stuffed with mushrooms and breadcrumbs*. ■ informal fill (oneself) with large amounts of food: *he* ***stuffed himself with*** *Parisian chocolates*. ■ informal fill (envelopes) with identical copies of printed matter: *they spent the whole time in a back room stuffing envelopes*. ■ N. Amer. place bogus votes in (a ballot box).
2 [usu. in imperative] Brit. informal used to express indifference towards or rejection of (something): *stuff the diet!*
3 Brit. informal defeat heavily in sport: *Town got stuffed every week*.
4 Brit. vulgar slang (of a man) have sexual intercourse with (a woman).
– PHRASES **be stuffed up** informal have one's nose blocked up with catarrh as a result of a cold. **get stuffed** [usu. in imperative] Brit. informal said in anger to tell someone to go away or as an expression of contempt. **not give a stuff** Brit. informal not care at all: *I couldn't give a stuff what they think*. **stuff it** informal said to express indifference, resignation, or rejection: *Stuff it, I'm 61, what do I care?* **that's the stuff** Brit. informal said in approval of what has just been done or said.
– DERIVATIVES **stuffer** noun [in combination] *a sausage-stuffer*.
– ORIGIN Middle English (denoting material for making clothes): shortening of Old French *estoffe* 'material, furniture', *estoffer* 'equip, furnish', from Greek *stuphein* 'draw together'.

WORD TRENDS The e-commerce site Amazon has a section labelled 'Where's My Stuff?' to help customers find out about undelivered orders. The use of such a vague, casual term in an official context is an example of the informality of Internet language and, increasingly, of English in general. Though first found in Middle English, the noun **stuff** can also be seen as a very 21st century word, with the Oxford English Corpus showing that it's become steadily commoner since 2000. It tends now to refer to objects or material (*we*

S

began writing new stuff straight away; techniques for getting us to buy new stuff) or to actions and events in general (*interesting stuff is happening*) rather than to physical matter (*a girl with red and green stuff in her hair*), and generally has positive connotations (it's usually found attached to words like *good*, *new*, *great*, *interesting*, and *cool*).

stuffed shirt ▶ noun informal a conservative, pompous person.

stuff gown ▶ noun Brit. a gown worn by a barrister who is not a Queen's (or King's) Counsel.

stuffing ▶ noun [mass noun] **1** a mixture used to stuff poultry or meat before cooking.
2 padding used to stuff cushions, furniture, or soft toys.
3 [count noun] informal a heavy defeat in sport.
– PHRASES **knock** (or **take**) **the stuffing out of** informal severely impair the confidence or strength of (someone).

stuffing box ▶ noun a casing in which material such as greased wool is compressed around a shaft or axle to form a seal against gas or liquid, used for instance where the propeller shaft of a boat passes through the hull.

stuff sack ▶ noun a bag into which a sleeping bag, clothing, etc. can be packed.

stuffy ▶ adjective (**stuffier**, **stuffiest**) **1** (of a place) lacking fresh air or ventilation: *a stuffy, overcrowded office.* ■ (of a person's nose) blocked up and making breathing difficult.
2 (of a person) not receptive to new or unusual ideas; conventional and narrow-minded: *he was steady and rather stuffy.*
– DERIVATIVES **stuffily** adverb, **stuffiness** noun.

Stuka /'stu:kə, 'ʃt-/ ▶ noun a type of German military aircraft (the Junkers Ju 87) designed for dive-bombing, much used in the Second World War.
– ORIGIN contraction of German *Sturzkampfflugzeug* 'dive-bomber'.

stultify /'stʌltɪfʌɪ/ ▶ verb (**stultifies**, **stultifying**, **stultified**) [with obj.] **1** (usu. as adj. **stultifying**) cause to lose enthusiasm and initiative, especially as a result of a tedious or restrictive routine: *the stultifying conformity of provincial life.*
2 cause (someone) to appear foolish or absurd.
– DERIVATIVES **stultification** noun, **stultifier** noun, **stultifyingly** adverb.
– ORIGIN mid 18th cent.: from late Latin *stultificare*, from Latin *stultus* 'foolish'.

stum /stʌm/ ▶ noun [mass noun] unfermented grape juice.
▶ verb (**stums**, **stumming**, **stummed**) [with obj.] **1** prevent or stop the fermentation of (wine) by fumigating a cask with burning sulphur.
2 renew the fermentation of (wine) by adding stum.
– ORIGIN mid 17th cent.: from Dutch *stom* (noun), *stommen* (verb), from *stom* 'dumb'.

stumble ▶ verb [no obj.] trip or momentarily lose one's balance; almost fall: *her foot caught in the rug and she stumbled.* ■ [with adverbial of direction] trip repeatedly as one walks: *his legs still weak, he stumbled after them.* ■ make a mistake or repeated mistakes in speaking: *she stumbled over the words.* ■ (**stumble across/on/upon**) find or encounter by chance: *a policeman had stumbled across a gang of youths.*
▶ noun an act of stumbling. ■ a stumbling walk: *he parodied my groping stumble across the stage.*
– DERIVATIVES **stumbler** noun, **stumbling** adjective, **stumblingly** adverb.
– ORIGIN Middle English (as a verb): from Old Norse, from the Germanic base of STAMMER.

S

stumblebum ▶ noun N. Amer. informal a clumsy or inept person.

stumbling block ▶ noun a circumstance that causes difficulty or hesitation: *the country's water shortage was a stumbling block to investors.*

stumer /'stju:mə/ ▶ noun Brit. informal **1** a worthless cheque or a counterfeit coin or note.
2 a failure: *his piece was a stumer, a complete flop.*
– ORIGIN late 19th cent.: of unknown origin.

stump ▶ noun **1** the bottom part of a tree left projecting from the ground after most of the trunk has fallen or been cut down. ■ the small projecting remnant of something that has been cut or broken off or worn away: *the stump of an amputated arm.*
2 Cricket each of the three upright pieces of wood which form a wicket. ■ (**stumps**) close of play in a cricket match.
3 Art a cylinder with conical ends made of rolled paper or other soft material, used for softening or blending marks made with a crayon or pencil.
4 chiefly N. Amer. used in relation to political campaigning: *his jibes at his opponents may have won him some support* ***on the stump*** *early in his campaign* | [as modifier] *an inspiring stump speaker.* [referring to the use of a tree stump, from which an orator would speak.]
▶ verb [with obj.] **1** informal (of a question or problem) be too hard for; baffle: *education chiefs were stumped by some of the exam questions.* ■ (**be stumped**) be at a loss; not know what to do or say: *detectives are* ***stumped for*** *a reason for the attack.*
2 [no obj., with adverbial of direction] walk stiffly and noisily: *he stumped away on short thick legs.*
3 Cricket (of a wicketkeeper) dismiss (a batsman) by dislodging the bails with the ball while the batsman is out of the crease but not running.
4 N. Amer. travel around (a district) making political speeches: *there is no chance that he will be well enough to stump the country.*
5 Art use a stump on (a drawing, line, etc.).
– PHRASES **up a stump** N. Amer. informal in a situation too difficult to manage.
– PHRASAL VERBS **stump something up** Brit. informal pay a sum of money: *a buyer would have to stump up at least £8.5 million for the site.*
– ORIGIN Middle English (denoting a part of a limb remaining after an amputation): from Middle Low German *stump(e)* or Middle Dutch *stomp*. The early sense of the verb was 'stumble'.

stumper ▶ noun informal **1** chiefly N. Amer. a puzzling question.
2 Cricket a wicketkeeper.

stumpnose ▶ noun (pl. **same**) chiefly S. African a southern African sea bream, popular with anglers.
● *Rhabdosargus* and other genera, family Sparidae: several species, in particular the **white stumpnose** (*R. globiceps*), which is of commercial importance.

stump work ▶ noun [mass noun] a type of raised embroidery popular between the 15th and 17th centuries and characterized by elaborate designs padded with wool or hair.

stumpy ▶ adjective (**stumpier**, **stumpiest**) short and thick; squat: *weak stumpy legs.*
– DERIVATIVES **stumpiness** noun.

stun ▶ verb (**stuns**, **stunning**, **stunned**) [with obj.]
1 knock unconscious or into a semi-conscious state: *the man was stunned by a blow to the head.*
2 astonish or shock (someone) so that they are temporarily unable to react: *the community was stunned by the tragedy* | (as adj. **stunned**) *she stared at him in stunned disbelief.*
– ORIGIN Middle English: shortening of Old French *estoner* 'astonish'.

stung past and past participle of STING.

stun grenade ▶ noun a grenade that stuns people with its sound and flash, without causing serious injury.

stun gun ▶ noun a device used to immobilize an attacker without causing serious injury, typically by administering an electric shock.

stunk past and past participle of STINK.

stunner ▶ noun informal a strikingly beautiful or impressive person or thing: *the girl was a stunner.* ■ an amazing turn of events.

stunning ▶ adjective extremely impressive or attractive: *she looked stunning.*
– DERIVATIVES **stunningly** adverb.

stunsail /'stʌns(ə)l/ (also **stuns'l**) ▶ noun another term for STUDDINGSAIL.
– ORIGIN mid 18th cent.: contraction.

stunt[1] ▶ verb [with obj.] prevent from growing or developing properly: *some weeds produce chemicals that stunt the plant's growth* | figurative *the recovery of our industries is stunted by lack of funds* | (as adj. **stunted**) *an emotionally stunted young woman.*
– DERIVATIVES **stuntedness** noun.
– ORIGIN late 16th cent. (in the sense 'bring to an abrupt halt'): from dialect *stunt* 'foolish, stubborn', of Germanic origin; perhaps related to STUMP.

stunt[2] ▶ noun an action displaying spectacular skill and daring. ■ something unusual done to attract attention: *the story was spread as a publicity stunt to help sell books.*
▶ verb [no obj.] perform stunts, especially aerobatics: *agile terns are stunting over the water.*
– ORIGIN late 19th cent. (originally US college slang): of unknown origin.

stuntman (or **stuntwoman**) ▶ noun (pl. **stuntmen** or **stuntwomen**) a person employed to take an actor's place in performing dangerous stunts.

stupa /'stu:pə/ ▶ noun a dome-shaped building erected as a Buddhist shrine.
– ORIGIN from Sanskrit *stūpa*.

stupe[1] /stju:p/ archaic ▶ noun a piece of soft cloth or cotton wool dipped in hot water and used to make a poultice.
▶ verb [with obj.] treat with such a poultice.
– ORIGIN late Middle English (as a noun): via Latin from Greek *stupē*.

stupe[2] /stju:p/ ▶ noun informal a stupid person.
– ORIGIN mid 18th cent.: abbreviation of STUPID.

stupefacient /ˌstju:pɪ'feɪs(ə)nt/ Medicine ▶ adjective (chiefly of a drug) causing semi-consciousness.
▶ noun a stupefacient drug.
– ORIGIN mid 17th cent.: from Latin *stupefacient-* 'stupefying', from the verb *stupefacere*.

stupefaction ▶ noun [mass noun] the state of being stupefied: *salesmen stood in bored stupefaction.*

stupefy /'stju:pɪfʌɪ/ ▶ verb (**stupefies**, **stupefying**, **stupefied**) [with obj.] make (someone) unable to think or feel properly: *the offence of administering drugs to a woman with intent to stupefy her.* ■ astonish and shock: *the amount they spend on clothes would appal their parents and stupefy their grandparents.*
– DERIVATIVES **stupefier** noun, **stupefying** adjective, **stupefyingly** adverb [as submodifier] *a stupefyingly tedious task.*
– ORIGIN late Middle English: from French *stupéfier*, from Latin *stupefacere*, from *stupere* 'be struck senseless'.

stupendous /stju:'pɛndəs/ ▶ adjective extremely impressive: *the most stupendous views.*
– DERIVATIVES **stupendously** adverb [as submodifier] *a stupendously talented player*, **stupendousness** noun.
– ORIGIN mid 16th cent.: from Latin *stupendus* 'to be wondered at' (gerundive of *stupere*) + -ous.

stupid ▶ adjective (**stupider**, **stupidest**) lacking intelligence or common sense: *I was stupid enough to think she was perfect.* ■ dazed and unable to think clearly: *apprehension was numbing her brain and making her stupid.* ■ informal used to express exasperation or boredom: *she told him to stop messing about with his stupid painting.*
▶ noun informal a stupid person (often used as a term of address): *you're not a coward, stupid!*
– DERIVATIVES **stupidly** adverb.
– ORIGIN mid 16th cent.: from French *stupide* or Latin *stupidus*, from *stupere* 'be amazed or stunned'.

stupidity ▶ noun [mass noun] behaviour that shows a lack of good sense or judgement: *I can't believe my own stupidity* | [count noun] *one of the stupidities of our age.* ■ the quality of being stupid or unintelligent: *a comedy of infantile stupidity.*

stupidness ▶ noun [mass noun] chiefly W. Indian foolish or nonsensical talk or behaviour: *girl, what stupidness are you talking?*

stupor /'stju:pə/ ▶ noun [in sing.] a state of near-unconsciousness or insensibility: *a drunken stupor.*
– DERIVATIVES **stuporous** adjective.
– ORIGIN late Middle English: from Latin, from *stupere* 'be amazed or stunned'.

sturdy ▶ adjective (**sturdier**, **sturdiest**) (of a person or their body) strongly and solidly built: *he had a sturdy, muscular physique.* ■ strong enough to withstand rough work or treatment: *the bike is sturdy enough to cope with bumpy tracks.* ■ showing confidence and determination: *the townspeople have a sturdy independence.*
▶ noun [mass noun] vertigo in sheep caused by a tapeworm larva encysted in the brain.
– DERIVATIVES **sturdily** adverb, **sturdiness** noun.
– ORIGIN Middle English (in the senses 'reckless, violent' and 'intractable, obstinate'): shortening of Old French *esturdi* 'stunned, dazed'. The derivation remains obscure; thought by some to be based on Latin *turdus* 'a thrush' (compare with the French phrase *soûl comme une grive* 'drunk as a thrush').

sturgeon /'stə:dʒ(ə)n/ ▶ noun a very large primitive fish with bony plates on the body. It occurs in temperate seas and rivers of the northern hemisphere, especially central Eurasia, and is of commercial importance for its caviar and flesh. ● Family Acipenseridae: several genera and species.
– ORIGIN Middle English: from Anglo-Norman French, of Germanic origin; related to Dutch *steur* and German *Stör*.

Sturmabteilung /ˈʃtʊəmab,tʌɪlʊŋ/, German /ˈʃtʊrmap,taɪlʊŋ/ (abbrev.: **SA**) see **BROWNSHIRT**.
– ORIGIN German, literally 'storm division'.

Sturmer /ˈstəːmə/ (also **Sturmer pippin**) ▸ **noun** an eating apple of a late-ripening variety with a mainly yellowish-green skin and firm yellowish flesh.
– ORIGIN mid 19th cent.: named after the village of *Sturmer*, on the Essex–Suffolk border, where it was first grown.

Sturm und Drang /ˌʃtʊəm ʊnt ˈdraŋ/, German /ˌʃtʊrm ʊnt ˈdraŋ/ ▸ **noun** [mass noun] a literary and artistic movement in Germany in the late 18th century, influenced by Jean-Jacques Rousseau and characterized by the expression of emotional unrest and a rejection of neoclassical literary norms. ▪ turbulent emotion or stress: *that casual morning meeting dragged into a brawling afternoon of Sturm und Drang*.
– ORIGIN German, literally 'storm and stress'.

Sturt /stəːt/, Charles (1795–1869), English explorer. He led three expeditions into the Australian interior, becoming the first European to discover the Darling River (1828) and the source of the Murray (1830).

Sturt's desert rose ▸ **noun** see **DESERT ROSE** (sense 3).

stush /stʊʃ/ (also **stoosh**) ▸ **adjective** black slang smart, wealthy, or snobbish: *the stush journalists in attendance failed to understand the ghetto humour*.
– ORIGIN perhaps a corruption of **OSTENTATIOUS**.

stutter ▸ **verb** [no obj.] talk with continued involuntary repetition of sounds, especially initial consonants: *the child was stuttering in fright*. ▪ [with obj.] utter in such a way: *he shyly **stuttered out** an invitation to the cinema* | [with direct speech] *'W-what's happened?' she stuttered*. ▪ (of a machine or gun) produce a series of short, sharp sounds: *she flinched as a machine gun stuttered nearby*. ▪ (often as adj. **stuttering**) progress in an irregular way: *the stuttering economy*.
▸ **noun** a tendency to stutter while speaking. ▪ a series of short, sharp sounds produced by a machine or gun.
– DERIVATIVES **stutterer** noun, **stutteringly** adverb.
– ORIGIN late 16th cent. (as a verb): frequentative of dialect *stut*, of Germanic origin; related to German *stossen* 'strike against'.

Stuttgart /ˈʃtʊtɡɑːt/, German /ˈʃtʊtɡart/ an industrial city in western Germany, the capital of Baden-Württemberg, on the Neckar River; pop. 593,900 (est. 2006).

sty[1] ▸ **noun** (pl. **sties**) a pigsty.
▸ **verb** (**sties**, **stying**, **stied**) [with obj.] archaic keep (a pig) in a sty: *the most beggarly place that ever pigs were stied in*.
– ORIGIN Old English *stī-* (in *stīfearh* 'sty pig'), probably identical with *stig* 'hall' (see **STEWARD**), of Germanic origin.

sty[2] (also **stye**) ▸ **noun** (pl. **sties** or **styes**) an inflamed swelling on the edge of an eyelid, caused by bacterial infection of the gland at the base of an eyelash.
– ORIGIN early 17th cent.: from dialect *styany*, from *styan* (from Old English *stīgend* 'riser') + **EYE**.

Stygian /ˈstɪdʒɪən/ ▸ **adjective** relating to the River Styx in Greek mythology. ▪ literary very dark: *the Stygian crypt*.

stylar /ˈstʌɪlə/ ▸ **adjective** Botany relating to the style or styles of a flower.

style ▸ **noun 1** a particular procedure by which something is done; a manner or way: *different styles of management*. ▪ a way of painting, writing, composing, building, etc., characteristic of a particular period, place, person, or movement. ▪ a way of using language: *he never wrote in a journalistic style* | [mass noun] *students should pay attention to style and idiom*. ▪ [usu. with negative] (**one's style**) one's usual way of behaving or approaching situations: *backing out isn't my style*. ▪ an official or legal title: *the partnership traded **under the style of** Storr and Mortimer*.
2 a distinctive appearance, typically determined by the principles according to which something is designed: *the pillars are no exception to the general style*. ▪ a particular design of clothing. ▪ a way of arranging the hair.
3 [mass noun] elegance and sophistication: *a sophisticated nightspot with style and taste*.
4 Botany (in a flower) a narrow, typically elongated extension of the ovary, bearing the stigma.
5 Zoology (in an invertebrate) a small, slender pointed appendage; a stylet.
6 archaic term for **STYLUS** (sense 2).
▸ **verb** [with obj.] **1** design or make in a particular form: *the yacht is well proportioned and conservatively styled*. ▪ arrange (hair) in a particular way: *he styled her hair by twisting it up to give it body*.
2 [with obj. and complement] designate with a particular name, description, or title: *the official is styled principal and vice chancellor of the university*.
– PHRASES **in style** (or **in grand style**) in an impressive, grand, or luxurious way.
– DERIVATIVES **styleless** adjective, **stylelessness** noun, **styler** noun.
– ORIGIN Middle English (denoting a stylus, also a literary composition, an official title, or a characteristic manner of literary expression): from Old French *stile*, from Latin *stilus*. The verb dates (first in sense 2 of the verb) from the early 16th cent.

-style ▸ **suffix** (forming adjectives and adverbs) in a manner characteristic of: *family-style* | *church-style*.

style sheet ▸ **noun** Computing a type of template file consisting of font and layout settings to give a standardized look to certain documents.

stylet /ˈstʌɪlɪt/ ▸ **noun 1** Medicine a slender probe. ▪ a wire or piece of plastic run through a catheter or cannula in order to stiffen it or to clear it.
2 Zoology (in an invertebrate) a small style, especially a piercing mouthpart of an insect.
– ORIGIN late 17th cent.: from French *stilet*, from Italian *stiletto* (see **STILETTO**).

styli plural form of **STYLUS**.

styling ▸ **noun** [mass noun] the way in which something is made, designed, or performed: *the car's subtle European styling* | [count noun] *the musical stylings on his solo album*. ▪ the action or process of arranging hair in a particular way: [as modifier] *styling gel*.

stylish ▸ **adjective** having or displaying a good sense of style: *these are elegant and stylish performances*. ▪ fashionably elegant: *a stylish range of jewellery*.
– DERIVATIVES **stylishly** adverb, **stylishness** noun.

stylist ▸ **noun 1** a designer of fashionable styles of clothing. ▪ a hairdresser.
2 a person whose job is to arrange and coordinate food, clothes, etc. in a stylish and attractive way in photographs or films.
3 a writer noted for taking great pains over their writing style. ▪ (in sport or music) a person who performs with style.

stylistic ▸ **adjective** of or concerning style, especially literary style: *the stylistic conventions of magazine stories*.
– DERIVATIVES **stylistically** adverb.
– ORIGIN mid 19th cent.: from **STYLIST**, suggested by German *stilistisch*.

stylistics ▸ **plural noun** [treated as sing.] the study of the distinctive styles found in particular literary genres and in the works of individual writers.

stylite /ˈstʌɪlʌɪt/ ▸ **noun** historical an ascetic living on top of a pillar, especially in ancient or medieval Syria, Turkey, and Greece in the 5th century AD.
– ORIGIN mid 17th cent.: from ecclesiastical Greek *stulitēs*, from *stulos* 'pillar'.

stylize (also **stylise**) ▸ **verb** [with obj.] (usu. as adj. **stylized**) depict or treat in a mannered and non-realistic style: *gracefully shaped vases decorated with stylized but recognizable white lilies*.
– DERIVATIVES **stylization** noun.
– ORIGIN late 19th cent.: from **STYLE**, suggested by German *stilisiren*.

stylo /ˈstʌɪləʊ/ ▸ **noun** (pl. **stylos**) informal short for **STYLOGRAPH**.

stylobate /ˈstʌɪlə(ʊ)beɪt/ ▸ **noun** a continuous base supporting a row of columns in classical Greek architecture.
– ORIGIN late 17th cent.: via Latin from Greek *stulobatēs*, from *stulos* 'pillar' + *batēs* 'base' (from *bainein* 'to walk').

stylograph ▸ **noun** a kind of fountain pen having a fine perforated tube instead of a split nib.
– DERIVATIVES **stylographic** adjective.
– ORIGIN mid 19th cent.: from **STYLUS** + **-GRAPH**.

styloid ▸ **adjective** technical resembling a stylus or pen.
▸ **noun** short for **STYLOID PROCESS**.

styloid process ▸ **noun** Anatomy a slender projection of bone, such as that from the lower surface of the temporal bone of the skull, or those at the lower ends of the ulna and radius.

stylolite /ˈstʌɪlə(ʊ)lʌɪt/ ▸ **noun** Geology an irregular surface or seam within a limestone or other sedimentary rock, characterized by irregular interlocking pegs and sockets around 1 cm in depth and a concentration of insoluble minerals. ▪ a grooved peg forming part of such a seam.
– ORIGIN mid 19th cent.: from Greek *stulos* 'column' + **-LITE**.

stylometry /stʌɪˈlɒmɪtri/ ▸ **noun** [mass noun] the statistical analysis of variations in literary style between one writer or genre and another.
– DERIVATIVES **stylometric** /ˌstʌɪləˈmɛtrɪk/ adjective.

stylophone ▸ **noun** (trademark in the US) a miniature electronic musical instrument producing a distinctive buzzing sound when a stylus is drawn along its metal keyboard.

stylopized /ˈstʌɪləpʌɪzd/ (also **stylopised**) ▸ **adjective** Entomology (of a bee or other insect) parasitized by a stylops.

stylops /ˈstʌɪlɒps/ ▸ **noun** (pl. **same**) a minute insect that spends part or all of its life as an internal parasite of other insects, especially bees or wasps. The males are winged and the females typically retain a grub-like form and remain parasitic. • Order Strepsiptera, in particular genus *Stylops*, family Stylopidae.
– ORIGIN late 19th cent.: modern Latin, from Greek *stulos* 'column' + *ōps* 'eye, face'.

stylus /ˈstʌɪləs/ ▸ **noun** (pl. **styli** /-lʌɪ, -liː/ or **styluses**)
1 a hard point, typically of diamond or sapphire, following a groove in a record and transmitting the recorded sound for reproduction. ▪ a similar point producing a groove in a record when recording sound.
2 an ancient writing implement, consisting of a small rod with a pointed end for scratching letters on wax-covered tablets, and a blunt end for obliterating them. ▪ an implement of similar shape used especially for engraving and tracing. ▪ a pen-like device used to input handwritten text or drawings directly into a computer.
– ORIGIN early 18th cent. (as a modern Latin term in botany: see **STYLE**): erroneous spelling of Latin *stilus*.

stymie /ˈstʌɪmi/ ▸ **verb** (**stymies**, **stymieing**, **stymied**) [with obj.] informal prevent or hinder the progress of: *the changes must not be allowed to stymie new medical treatments*.
– ORIGIN mid 19th cent. (originally a golfing term, denoting a situation on the green where a ball obstructs the shot of another player): of unknown origin.

styptic /ˈstɪptɪk/ Medicine ▸ **adjective** (of a substance) capable of causing bleeding to stop when it is applied to a wound.
▸ **noun** a styptic substance.
– ORIGIN late Middle English: via Latin from Greek *stuptikos*, from *stuphein* 'to contract'.

styptic pencil ▸ **noun** a stick of a styptic substance, used to treat small cuts.

styrax /ˈstʌɪraks/ ▸ **noun** variant of **STORAX**.

styrene /ˈstʌɪriːn/ ▸ **noun** [mass noun] Chemistry an unsaturated liquid hydrocarbon obtained as a petroleum by-product. It is easily polymerized and is used to make plastics and resins. • Chem. formula: $C_6H_5CH{=}CH_2$.
– ORIGIN late 19th cent.: from **STYRAX** + **-ENE**.

Styria /ˈstɪrɪə/ a mountainous state of SE Austria; capital, Graz. German name **STEIERMARK**.
– DERIVATIVES **Styrian** noun & adjective.

styrofoam ▸ **noun** [mass noun] (trademark in the US) a kind of expanded polystyrene used especially for making food containers.
– ORIGIN 1950s: from **POLYSTYRENE** + **FOAM**.

Styx /stɪks/ Greek Mythology one of the nine rivers in the underworld, over which Charon ferried the souls of the dead.
– ORIGIN from Greek *Stux*, from *stugnos* 'hateful, gloomy'.

suasion /ˈsweɪʒ(ə)n/ ▸ **noun** [mass noun] formal persuasion as opposed to force or compulsion.
– ORIGIN late Middle English: from Old French, or from Latin *suasio(n-)*, from *suadere* 'to urge'.

suasive /ˈsweɪsɪv/ ▸ **adjective** formal serving to persuade. ▪ Grammar denoting a class of English verbs, for example *insist*, whose meaning includes the notion of persuading and which take a subordinate clause whose verb may either be in the subjunctive or take a modal.

suave /swɑːv/ ▸ **adjective** (**suaver**, **suavest**) (especially of a man) charming, confident, and elegant: *all the waiters were suave and deferential*.
– DERIVATIVES **suavely** adverb, **suaveness** noun.
– ORIGIN late Middle English (in the sense 'gracious, agreeable'): from Old French, or from Latin *suavis* 'agreeable'. The current sense dates from the mid 19th cent.

S

suavity /ˈswɑːvɪti/ ▶ **noun** (pl. **suavities**) [mass noun] the quality of being suave in manner.

sub informal ▶ **noun 1** a submarine. ■ N. Amer. short for SUBMARINE SANDWICH.
2 Brit. a subscription.
3 a substitute, especially in a sporting team.
4 Brit. a subeditor.
5 Brit. an advance or loan against expected income.
▶ **verb** (**subs**, **subbing**, **subbed**) [with obj.] **1** replace or be replaced; substitute: *he got a lot of applause when he was subbed* | [no obj.] *he* ***subbed for*** *Armstrong at some gigs.*
2 Brit. lend or advance a sum to (someone) against expected income: *who'll sub me till Thursday?*
3 subedit: *his copy was mercilessly subbed and rewritten.*

sub- ▶ **prefix 1** at, to, or from a lower level or position: *subalpine.* ■ lower in rank: *subaltern* | *subdeacon.* ■ of a smaller size; of a subordinate nature: *subculture.*
2 somewhat; nearly; more or less: *subantarctic.*
3 denoting subsequent or secondary action of the same kind: *sublet* | *subdivision.*
4 denoting support: *subvention.*
5 Chemistry in names of compounds containing a relatively small proportion of a component: *suboxide.*
– ORIGIN from Latin *sub* 'under, close to'.

subacid ▶ **adjective** (of a fruit) moderately sharp to the taste.

subacute ▶ **adjective 1** Medicine (of a condition) between acute and chronic.
2 moderately acute in shape or angle.

subadult ▶ **noun** Zoology an animal that is not fully adult.

subaerial ▶ **adjective** Geology existing, occurring, or formed in the open air or on the earth's surface, not under water or underground.
– DERIVATIVES **subaerially** adverb.

subagency ▶ **noun** (pl. **subagencies**) a subordinate commercial, political, or other agency.
– DERIVATIVES **subagent** noun.

subalpine ▶ **adjective** of or situated on the higher slopes of mountains just below the treeline.

subaltern /ˈsʌb(ə)lt(ə)n/ ▶ **noun** an officer in the British army below the rank of captain, especially a second lieutenant.
▶ **adjective 1** of lower status: *the private tutor was a recognized subaltern part of the bourgeois family.*
2 Logic, dated (of a proposition) implied by another proposition (e.g. as a particular affirmative is by a universal one), but not implying it in return.
– ORIGIN late 16th cent. (as an adjective): from late Latin *subalternus*, from Latin *sub-* 'next below' + *alternus* 'every other'.

subantarctic ▶ **adjective** relating to the region immediately north of the Antarctic Circle.

sub-aqua ▶ **adjective** relating to swimming or exploring under water, especially with an aqualung: *sub-aqua equipment.*
▶ **noun** [mass noun] underwater swimming or exploration with an aqualung.
– ORIGIN 1950s: from SUB- 'under' + Latin *aqua* 'water'.

sub-aquatic ▶ **adjective** underwater: *a narrow sub-aquatic microclimate.*

subaqueous ▶ **adjective** existing, formed, or taking place under water.

subarachnoid ▶ **adjective** Anatomy denoting or occurring in the fluid-filled space around the brain between the arachnoid membrane and the pia mater, through which major blood vessels pass.

subarctic ▶ **adjective** relating to the region immediately south of the Arctic Circle.

sub-assembly ▶ **noun** (pl. **sub-assemblies**) a unit assembled separately but designed to be incorporated with other units into a larger manufactured product.

Sub-Atlantic ▶ **adjective** Geology relating to or denoting the fifth climatic stage of the postglacial period in northern Europe, following the Sub-Boreal stage (from about 2,800 years ago to the present day). The climate has been cooler and wetter than in the earlier postglacial periods. ■ (as noun **the Sub-Atlantic**) the Sub-Atlantic climatic stage.

subatomic ▶ **adjective** smaller than or occurring within an atom.

subatomic particle ▶ **noun** see PARTICLE (sense 1).

subaudition ▶ **noun** a thing that is not stated, only implied or inferred.
– ORIGIN late 18th cent.: from late Latin *subauditio(n-)*, from *subaudire* 'understand'.

sub-basement ▶ **noun** a storey below a basement.

Sub-Boreal /ˈbɔːrɪəl/ ▶ **adjective** Geology relating to or denoting the fourth climatic stage of the postglacial period in northern Europe, between the Atlantic and Sub-Atlantic stages (about 5,000 to 2,800 years ago). The stage corresponds to the Neolithic period and Bronze Age, and the climate was cooler and drier than previously but still warmer than today. ■ (as noun **the Sub-Boreal**) the Sub-Boreal climatic stage.

sub-breed ▶ **noun** a minor variant of a breed; a secondary breed.

Subbuteo /sʌˈbjuːtɪəʊ/ ▶ **noun** [mass noun] trademark a tabletop version of soccer in which players use their fingers to flick miniature figures of footballers at the ball in order to strike it towards the goal.
– ORIGIN 1940s: punningly from Latin *Falco subbuteo* 'hobby falcon', represented on Subbuteo products.

subcarrier ▶ **noun** Telecommunications a carrier wave modulated by a signal wave and then used with other subcarriers to modulate the main carrier wave.

subcategory ▶ **noun** (pl. **subcategories**) a secondary or subordinate category.
– DERIVATIVES **subcategorization** (also **subcategorisation**) noun, **subcategorize** (also **subcategorise**) verb.

subclass ▶ **noun** a secondary or subordinate class. ■ Biology a taxonomic category that ranks below class and above order.

subclause ▶ **noun 1** chiefly Law a subsidiary section of a clause in a bill, contract, or treaty.
2 Grammar a subordinate clause.

subclavian /sʌbˈkleɪvɪən/ ▶ **adjective** Anatomy relating to or denoting an artery or vein which serves the neck and arm on the left or right side of the body.
– ORIGIN mid 17th cent.: from modern Latin *subclavius*, from *sub* 'under' + *clavis* 'key' (see CLAVICLE), + -IAN.

subclinical ▶ **adjective** Medicine relating to or denoting a disease which is not severe enough to present definite or readily observable symptoms.

subcommittee ▶ **noun** a committee composed of some members of a larger committee, board, or other body and reporting to it.

subcompact ▶ **noun** N. Amer. a motor vehicle which is smaller than a compact.

subconical ▶ **adjective** approximately conical.

subconscious ▶ **adjective** of or concerning the part of the mind of which one is not fully aware but which influences one's actions and feelings: *my subconscious fear.*
▶ **noun** (**one's/the subconscious**) the subconscious part of the mind (not in technical use in psychoanalysis, where *unconscious* is preferred).
– DERIVATIVES **subconsciously** adverb, **subconsciousness** noun.

subcontinent ▶ **noun** a large distinguishable part of a continent, such as North America or southern Africa. See also INDIAN SUBCONTINENT.
– DERIVATIVES **subcontinental** adjective.

subcontract ▶ **verb** /sʌbkənˈtrakt/ [with obj.] employ a firm or person outside one's company to do (work) as part of a larger project: *we would* ***subcontract*** *the translation* ***work out.*** ■ [no obj.] carry out work for a company as part of a larger project.
▶ **noun** /sʌbˈkɒntrakt/ a contract for a company or person to do work for another company as part of a larger project.

subcontractor ▶ **noun** a firm or person that carries out work for a company as part of a larger project.

subcontrary /sʌbˈkɒntrəri/ Logic, dated ▶ **adjective** denoting propositions which can both be true, but cannot both be false (e.g. *some X are Y* and *some X are not Y*).
▶ **noun** (pl. **subcontraries**) a subcontrary proposition.
– ORIGIN late 16th cent.: from late Latin *subcontrarius*, translation of Greek *hupenantios.*

subcortical ▶ **adjective** below the cortex. ■ Anatomy relating to or denoting the region of the brain below the cortex.

subcostal ▶ **adjective** Anatomy beneath a rib; below the ribs.

subcritical ▶ **adjective** Physics below a critical threshold, in particular: ■ (in nuclear physics) containing or involving less than the critical mass. ■ (of a flow of fluid) slower than the speed at which waves travel in the fluid.

subculture ▶ **noun** a cultural group within a larger culture, often having beliefs or interests at variance with those of the larger culture.
– DERIVATIVES **subcultural** adjective.

subcutaneous ▶ **adjective** Anatomy & Medicine situated or applied under the skin: *subcutaneous fat.*
– DERIVATIVES **subcutaneously** adverb.

subdeacon ▶ **noun** (in some Christian Churches) a minister of an order ranking below deacon.
– DERIVATIVES **subdiaconate** noun.

subdirectory ▶ **noun** (pl. **subdirectories**) Computing a directory below another directory in a hierarchy.

subdivide ▶ **verb** [with obj.] divide (something that has already been divided or that is a separate unit): *the heading was* ***subdivided into*** *eight separate sections.*
– ORIGIN late Middle English: from Latin *subdividere* (see SUB-, DIVIDE).

subdivision ▶ **noun 1** [mass noun] the action of subdividing or being subdivided. ■ [count noun] a secondary or subordinate division. ■ [count noun] Biology any taxonomic subcategory, especially (in botany) one that ranks below division and above class.
2 N. Amer. & Austral./NZ an area of land divided into plots for sale. ■ an area of housing.

subdominant ▶ **noun** Music the fourth note of the diatonic scale of any key.

subduction /səbˈdʌkʃ(ə)n/ ▶ **noun** [mass noun] Geology the sideways and downward movement of the edge of a plate of the earth's crust into the mantle beneath another plate.
– DERIVATIVES **subduct** verb.
– ORIGIN 1970s: via French from Latin *subductio(n-)*, from *subduct-* 'drawn from below', from the verb *subducere.*

subdue ▶ **verb** (**subdues**, **subduing**, **subdued**) [with obj.] overcome, quieten, or bring under control (a feeling or person): *she managed to subdue an instinct to applaud.* ■ bring (a country or people) under control by force: *Charles went on a campaign to subdue the Saxons.*
– DERIVATIVES **subduer** noun.
– ORIGIN late Middle English: from Anglo-Norman French *suduire*, from Latin *subducere*, literally 'draw from below'.

subdued ▶ **adjective 1** (of a person or their manner) quiet and rather reflective or depressed: *I felt strangely subdued as I drove home.*
2 (of colour or lighting) soft and restrained: *a subdued glow came through the curtains.*

subdural /sʌbˈdjʊər(ə)l/ ▶ **adjective** Anatomy situated or occurring between the dura mater and the arachnoid membrane of the brain and spinal cord.

subedit ▶ **verb** (**subedits**, **subediting**, **subedited**) [with obj.] chiefly Brit. check and correct (the text of a newspaper or magazine before printing), typically also writing headlines and captions: *he wrote articles on sport while subediting the Oxford Magazine.*
– DERIVATIVES **subeditor** noun, **subeditorial** adjective.

suberin /ˈsjuːb(ə)rɪn/ ▶ **noun** [mass noun] Botany an inert impermeable waxy substance present in the cell walls of corky tissues.
– ORIGIN mid 19th cent.: from Latin *suber* 'cork' + -IN[1].

suberize /ˈsjuːb(ə)rʌɪz/ (also **suberise**) ▶ **verb** [with obj.] (usu. as adj. **suberized**) Botany impregnate (the wall of a plant cell) with suberin: *suberized cell walls.*
– DERIVATIVES **suberization** noun.

subfamily ▶ **noun** (pl. **subfamilies**) a subdivision of a group. ■ Biology a taxonomic category that ranks below family and above tribe or genus, usually ending in *-inae* (in zoology) or *-oideae* (in botany).

subfloor ▶ **noun** the foundation for a floor in a building.

subform ▶ **noun** a subordinate or secondary form.

subframe ▶ **noun** a supporting frame, especially one into which a window or door is set, or one to which the engine or suspension of a car without a true chassis is attached.

subfusc /ˈsʌbfʌsk, sʌbˈfʌsk/ ▶ **adjective** literary dull; gloomy: *the light was subfusc and aqueous.*
▶ **noun** [mass noun] Brit. the dark formal clothing worn for examinations and formal occasions at some universities.
– ORIGIN early 18th cent.: from Latin *subfuscus*, from *sub-* 'somewhat' + *fuscus* 'dark brown'.

subgenre ▶ **noun** a subdivision of a genre of literature, music, film, etc.

subgenus ▸ noun (pl. **subgenera**) Biology a taxonomic category that ranks below genus and above species.
– DERIVATIVES **subgeneric** adjective.

subglacial ▸ adjective Geology situated or occurring underneath a glacier or ice sheet.

subgroup ▸ noun a subdivision of a group. ■ Mathematics a group whose members are all members of another group, both being subject to the same operations.

subharmonic ▸ noun an oscillation with a frequency equal to an integral submultiple of another frequency.
▸ adjective denoting or involving a subharmonic.

subheading (also **subhead**) ▸ noun a heading given to a subsection of a piece of writing.

subhuman ▸ adjective of a lower order of being than humans. ■ Zoology (of a primate) closely related to humans. ■ not worthy of a human being; debased or depraved: *he regards all PR people as subhuman.*
▸ noun a subhuman creature or person.

subjacent /səbˈdʒeɪs(ə)nt/ ▸ adjective technical situated below something else.
– DERIVATIVES **subjacency** noun.
– ORIGIN late 16th cent.: from Latin *subjacent-* 'lying underneath', from *sub-* 'under' + *jacere* 'to lie'.

subject ▸ noun /ˈsʌbdʒɛkt, ˈsʌbdʒɪkt/ **1** a person or thing that is being discussed, described, or dealt with: *I've said all there is to be said on the subject | he's the subject of a major new biography.* ■ a person or circumstance giving rise to a specified feeling, response, or action: *the incident was the **subject of** international condemnation.* ■ a person who is the focus of scientific or medical attention or experiment. ■ Logic the part of a proposition about which a statement is made. ■ Music a theme of a fugue or of a piece in sonata form; a leading phrase or motif.
2 a branch of knowledge studied or taught in a school, college, or university.
3 a member of a state other than its ruler, especially one owing allegiance to a monarch or other supreme ruler.
4 Grammar a noun or noun phrase functioning as one of the main components of a clause, being the element about which the rest of the clause is predicated.
5 Philosophy a thinking or feeling entity; the conscious mind; the ego, especially as opposed to anything external to the mind. ■ the central substance or core of a thing as opposed to its attributes.
▸ adjective /ˈsʌbdʒɪkt/ (**subject to**) **1** likely or prone to be affected by (a particular condition or occurrence, typically an unwelcome or unpleasant one): *he was subject to bouts of manic depression.*
2 dependent or conditional upon: *the proposed merger is subject to the approval of the shareholders.*
3 under the authority of: *ministers are subject to the laws of the land.* ■ [attrib.] under the control or domination of another ruler, country, or government: *the Greeks were the first subject people to break free from Ottoman rule.*
▸ adverb /ˈsʌbdʒɪkt/ (**subject to**) conditionally upon: *subject to the EC's agreement, we intend to set up an enterprise zone in the area.*
▸ verb /səbˈdʒɛkt/ [with obj.] **1** (**subject someone/thing to**) cause or force someone or something to undergo (a particular experience or form of treatment, typically an unwelcome or unpleasant one): *he'd subjected her to a terrifying ordeal.*
2 bring (a person or country) under one's control or jurisdiction, typically by using force: *the city had **been subjected to** Macedonian rule.*
– DERIVATIVES **subjectless** adjective.
– ORIGIN Middle English (in the sense '(person) owing obedience'): from Old French *suget*, from Latin *subjectus* 'brought under', past participle of *subicere*, from *sub-* 'under' + *jacere* 'throw'. Senses relating to philosophy, logic, and grammar are derived ultimately from Aristotle's use of *to hupokeimenon* meaning 'material from which things are made' and 'subject of attributes and predicates'.

subject catalogue ▸ noun a catalogue, especially in a library, that is arranged according to the subjects treated.

subjection ▸ noun [mass noun] the action of subjecting a country or person to one's control, or the fact of being subjected: *the country's subjection to European colonialism.*

subjective ▸ adjective **1** based on or influenced by personal feelings, tastes, or opinions: *his views are highly subjective | there is always the danger of making a subjective judgement.* Contrasted with OBJECTIVE. ■ dependent on the mind or on an individual's perception for its existence.
2 Grammar relating to or denoting a case of nouns and pronouns used for the subject of a sentence.
▸ noun (**the subjective**) Grammar the subjective case.
– DERIVATIVES **subjectively** adverb, **subjectiveness** noun, **subjectivity** noun.
– ORIGIN late Middle English (originally in the sense 'characteristic of a political subject, submissive'): from Latin *subjectivus*, from *subject-* 'brought under' (see SUBJECT).

subjective case ▸ noun Grammar the nominative.

subjectivism ▸ noun [mass noun] Philosophy the doctrine that knowledge is merely subjective and that there is no external or objective truth.
– DERIVATIVES **subjectivist** noun & adjective.

subject matter ▸ noun [mass noun] the topic dealt with or the subject represented in a debate, exposition, or work of art.

subjoin ▸ verb [with obj.] formal add (comments or supplementary information) at the end of a speech or text.
– ORIGIN late 16th cent.: from obsolete French *subjoindre*, from Latin *subjungere*, from *sub-* 'in addition' + *jungere* 'to join'.

sub judice /sʌb ˈdʒuːdɪsi, sʊb ˈjuːdɪkeɪ/ ▸ adjective Law under judicial consideration and therefore prohibited from public discussion elsewhere: *the cases were still sub judice.*
– ORIGIN Latin, literally 'under a judge'.

subjugate /ˈsʌbdʒʊgeɪt/ ▸ verb [with obj.] bring under domination or control, especially by conquest: *the invaders had soon subjugated most of the population.* ■ (**subjugate someone/thing to**) make someone or something subordinate to: *the new ruler firmly subjugated the Church to the state.*
– DERIVATIVES **subjugation** noun **subjugator** noun.
– ORIGIN late Middle English: from late Latin *subjugat-* 'brought under a yoke', from the verb *subjugare*, based on *jugum* 'yoke'.

subjunct /ˈsʌbjʌŋ(k)t/ ▸ noun Grammar an adverb or prepositional phrase used in a role that does not form part of the basic clause structure, for example *kindly* in *he kindly offered to help.*
– ORIGIN early 20th cent.: from Latin *subjunctus*, past participle of *subjungere* (see SUBJOIN).

subjunctive /səbˈdʒʌŋ(k)tɪv/ Grammar ▸ adjective relating to or denoting a mood of verbs expressing what is imagined or wished or possible. Compare with INDICATIVE.
▸ noun a verb in the subjunctive mood. ■ (**the subjunctive**) the subjunctive mood.
– DERIVATIVES **subjunctively** adverb.
– ORIGIN mid 16th cent.: from French *subjonctif, -ive* or late Latin *subjunctivus*, from *subjungere* (see SUBJOIN), rendering Greek *hupotaktikos* 'subjoined'.

USAGE *if I **were** you; the report recommends that he **face** the tribunal; it is important that they **be** aware of the provisions of the act.* These sentences all contain a verb in the **subjunctive mood**. The subjunctive is used to express situations which are hypothetical or not yet realized, and is typically used for what is imagined, hoped for, demanded, or expected. In English the subjunctive mood is fairly uncommon (especially in comparison with other languages such as French and Spanish), mainly because most of the functions of the subjunctive are covered by modal verbs such as **might**, **could**, and **should**. In fact, in English the subjunctive is often indistinguishable from the ordinary **indicative mood**, since its form in most contexts is identical. It is distinctive only in the third person singular, where the normal indicative **-s** ending is absent (*he **face*** rather than *he **faces*** in the example above), and in the verb 'to be' (*I **were*** rather than *I **was*** and *they **be*** rather than *they **are*** in the examples above). In modern English the subjunctive mood still exists but is regarded in many contexts as optional. Use of the subjunctive tends to convey a more formal tone but there are few people who would regard its absence as actually wrong. Today it survives mostly in fixed expressions, as in ***be** that as it may; God **help** you; **perish** the thought*; and ***come** what may.*

subkingdom ▸ noun Biology a taxonomic category that ranks below kingdom and above phylum or division.

sublanguage ▸ noun a specialized language or jargon associated with a specific group or context.

sublate /səˈbleɪt/ ▸ verb [with obj.] Philosophy assimilate (a smaller entity) into a larger one: *fragmented aspects of the self the subject is unable to sublate.*
– DERIVATIVES **sublation** noun.
– ORIGIN mid 19th cent. (earlier (mid 16th cent.) as *sublation*): from Latin *sublat-* 'taken away', from *sub-* 'from below' + *lat-* (from the stem of *tollere* 'take away').

sublateral ▸ noun a side shoot developing from a lateral shoot or branch of a plant.

sublease ▸ noun & verb another term for SUBLET.

sub-lessee ▸ noun a person who holds a sublease.

sub-lessor ▸ noun a person who grants a sublease.

sublet ▸ verb /sʌbˈlɛt/ (**sublets**, **subletting**; past and past participle **sublet**) [with obj.] lease (a property) to a subtenant: *I quit my job and sublet my apartment.*
▸ noun /ˈsʌblɛt/ a lease of a property by a tenant to a subtenant. ■ informal a property that has been subleased.

sublethal ▸ adjective having an effect less than lethal.

sub lieutenant ▸ noun a rank of officer in the Royal Navy, above midshipman and below lieutenant.

sublimate /ˈsʌblɪmeɪt/ ▸ verb **1** [with obj.] (in psychoanalytic theory) divert or modify (an instinctual impulse) into a culturally higher or socially more acceptable activity: *people who **sublimate** sexuality into activities which help to build up and preserve civilization.* ■ transform (something) into a purer or idealized form: *attractive rhythms are **sublimated** into a much larger context.*
2 Chemistry another term for SUBLIME.
▸ noun also /ˈsʌblɪmət/ Chemistry a solid deposit of a substance which has sublimed.
– DERIVATIVES **sublimation** noun.
– ORIGIN late Middle English (in the sense 'raise to a higher status'): from Latin *sublimat-* 'raised up', from the verb *sublimare*.

sublime ▸ adjective (**sublimer**, **sublimest**) **1** of very great excellence or beauty: *Mozart's sublime piano concertos* | (as noun **the sublime**) *experiences that ranged from the sublime to the ridiculous.* ■ producing an overwhelming sense of awe or other high emotion through being vast or grand: (as noun **the sublime**) *a sense of the sublime.*
2 (of a person's attitude or behaviour) extreme or unparalleled: *he had the sublime confidence of youth.*
▸ verb **1** [no obj.] Chemistry (of a solid substance) change directly into vapour when heated, typically forming a solid deposit again on cooling. ■ [with obj.] cause (a substance) to do this: *these crystals could be sublimed under a vacuum.*
2 [with obj.] archaic elevate to a high degree of moral or spiritual purity or excellence.
– DERIVATIVES **sublimely** adverb, **sublimity** noun.
– ORIGIN late 16th cent. (in the sense 'dignified, aloof'): from Latin *sublimis*, from *sub-* 'up to' + a second element perhaps related to *limen* 'threshold', *limus* 'oblique'.

Sublime Porte ▸ noun see PORTE.

subliminal /səˈblɪmɪn(ə)l/ ▸ adjective Psychology (of a stimulus or mental process) below the threshold of sensation or consciousness; perceived by or affecting someone's mind without their being aware of it.
– DERIVATIVES **subliminally** adverb.
– ORIGIN late 19th cent.: from SUB- 'below' + Latin *limen, limin-* 'threshold' + -AL.

subliminal advertising ▸ noun [mass noun] the use by advertisers of images and sounds to influence consumers' responses without their being consciously aware of it.

S

sublingual ▸ adjective Anatomy & Medicine situated or applied under the tongue. ■ denoting a pair of small salivary glands beneath the tongue.
– DERIVATIVES **sublingually** adverb.

sublittoral /sʌbˈlɪt(ə)r(ə)l/ chiefly Ecology ▸ adjective living, growing, or accumulating near to or just below the shore. ■ relating to or denoting a biogeographic zone extending (in the sea) from the average line of low tide to the edge of the continental shelf or (in a large lake) beyond the littoral zone but still well lit.
▸ noun the sublittoral zone.

Sub-Lt. ▸ abbreviation Sub Lieutenant.

sublunar ▸ adjective Astronomy within the moon's orbit and subject to its influence.

sublunary /sʌbˈluːn(ə)ri/ ▸ adjective literary belonging to this world as contrasted with a better or more spiritual one: *the concept was irrational to sublunary minds.*
– ORIGIN late 16th cent. (in the sense 'terrestrial'): from modern Latin *sublunaris*.

subluxation /ˌsʌblʌkˈseɪʃ(ə)n/ ▸ noun Medicine a partial dislocation. ■ a slight misalignment of the vertebrae, regarded in chiropractic theory as the cause of many health problems.

– ORIGIN late 17th cent.: from modern Latin *subluxatio(n-)* (see SUB-, LUXATE).

sub-machine gun ▸ noun a handheld lightweight machine gun.

subman ▸ noun (pl. **submen**) a subhuman person.

submandibular /ˌsʌbmanˈdɪbjʊlə/ ▸ adjective Anatomy situated beneath the jaw or mandible. ■ relating to or affecting a submandibular gland.

submandibular gland ▸ noun Anatomy either of a pair of salivary glands situated below the parotid glands. Also called SUBMAXILLARY GLAND.

submarginal ▸ adjective (of land) not allowing profitable farming or cultivation.

submarine /ˈsʌbməriːn, sʌbməˈriːn/ ▸ noun **1** a warship with a streamlined hull designed to operate completely submerged in the sea for long periods, equipped with a periscope and typically armed with torpedoes or missiles. ■ a submersible craft of any kind.
2 (also **submarine sandwich**) N. Amer. another term for HOAGIE.
▸ adjective existing, occurring, or used under the surface of the sea: *submarine volcanic activity*.
– DERIVATIVES **submariner** /sʌbˈmarɪnə/ noun.

submaxillary gland /ˌsʌbmakˈsɪləri/ ▸ noun another term for SUBMANDIBULAR GLAND.

submediant ▸ noun Music the sixth note of the diatonic scale of any key.

submenu ▸ noun Computing a menu accessed from a more general menu.

submerge ▸ verb [with obj.] cause (something) to be under water: *houses had been flooded and cars submerged.* ■ [no obj.] descend below the surface of an area of water: *the U-boat had had time to submerge.* ■ completely cover or obscure: *the tensions submerged earlier in the campaign now came to the fore.*
– DERIVATIVES **submergence** noun, **submergible** adjective.
– ORIGIN early 17th cent.: from Latin *submergere*, from *sub-* 'under' + *mergere* 'to dip'.

submerse /səbˈməːs/ ▸ verb [with obj.] submerge: *pellets were then submersed in agar.*
▸ adjective Botany denoting or characteristic of a plant growing entirely under water. Contrasted with EMERSE.
– ORIGIN late Middle English: from Latin *submers-* 'plunged below', from the verb *submergere* (see SUBMERGE).

submersible ▸ adjective designed to operate while submerged.
▸ noun a small submersible boat or other craft, especially one designed for research and exploration.

submersion ▸ noun [mass noun] the action or state of submerging or being submerged: *five small islands threatened by submersion.*

submicroscopic ▸ adjective too small to be seen by an ordinary light microscope.

subminiature ▸ adjective of greatly reduced size. ■ (of a camera) very small and using 16-mm film.

submission ▸ noun [mass noun] **1** the action of accepting or yielding to a superior force or to the will or authority of another person: *they were forced into submission.* ■ [count noun] Wrestling an act of surrendering to a hold by one's opponent. ■ archaic humility; meekness: *servile flattery and submission.*
2 the action of presenting a proposal, application, or other document for consideration or judgement: *reports should be prepared for submission at partners' meetings.* ■ [count noun] a proposal, application, or other document presented for consideration or judgement. ■ [count noun] Law a proposition or argument presented by counsel to a judge or jury.
– ORIGIN late Middle English: from Old French, or from Latin *submissio(n-)*, from the verb *submittere* (see SUBMIT).

submissive ▸ adjective ready to conform to the authority or will of others; meekly obedient or passive: *a submissive, almost sheeplike people.*
– DERIVATIVES **submissively** adverb.
– ORIGIN late 16th cent.: from SUBMISSION, on the pattern of pairs such as *remission, remissive*.

submissiveness ▸ noun [mass noun] the quality of being submissive: *he didn't confuse respect with submissiveness.*

submit ▸ verb (**submits, submitting, submitted**) **1** [no obj.] accept or yield to a superior force or to the authority or will of another person: *the original settlers were forced to **submit to** Bulgarian rule.* ■ (**submit oneself**) consent to undergo a certain treatment: *he **submitted himself** to a body search.* ■ agree to refer a matter to a third party for decision or adjudication: *the United States refused to **submit to** arbitration.*
2 [with obj.] subject to a particular process, treatment, or condition: *samples **submitted** to low pressure while being airfreighted.*
3 [with obj.] present (a proposal, application, or other document) to a person or body for consideration or judgement: *the panel's report was **submitted to** a parliamentary committee.* ■ [with clause] (especially in judicial contexts) suggest; argue: *he submitted that such measures were justified.*
– DERIVATIVES **submitter** noun.
– ORIGIN late Middle English: from Latin *submittere*, from *sub-* 'under' + *mittere* 'send, put'. Sense 3 'present for judgement' dates from the mid 16th cent.

submodifier ▸ noun Grammar an adverb used in front of an adjective or another adverb to modify its meaning, for example *very* in *very cold* or *unusually* in *an unusually large house*.
– DERIVATIVES **submodification** noun, **submodify** verb (**submodifies, submodifying, submodified**).

submontane /ˌsʌbˈmɒnteɪn/ ▸ adjective passing under or through mountains. ■ situated in the foothills or lower slopes of a mountain range.

submucosa /ˌsʌbmjuːˈkəʊsə/ ▸ noun (pl. **submucosae**) Physiology the layer of areolar connective tissue lying beneath a mucous membrane.
– DERIVATIVES **submucosal** adjective.
– ORIGIN late 19th cent.: from modern Latin *submucosa (membrana)*, feminine of *submucosus* 'submucous'.

submultiple ▸ noun a number that can be divided exactly into a specified number.
▸ adjective denoting such a number.

submunition /ˌsʌbmjuːˈnɪʃ(ə)n/ ▸ noun a small weapon or device that is part of a larger warhead and separates from it prior to impact.

subnetwork (also **subnet**) ▸ noun Computing a part of a larger network such as the Internet.

subnormal ▸ adjective not meeting standards or reaching a level regarded as usual, especially with respect to intelligence or development.
– DERIVATIVES **subnormality** noun.

subnuclear ▸ adjective Physics occurring in or smaller than an atomic nucleus.

suboptimal ▸ adjective technical of less than the highest standard or quality.

suborbital ▸ adjective **1** situated below or behind the orbit of the eye.
2 relating to or denoting a trajectory that does not complete a full orbit of the earth or other celestial body.

suborder ▸ noun Biology a taxonomic category that ranks below order and above family.

subordinary ▸ noun (pl. **subordinaries**) Heraldry a simple device or bearing that is less common than the ordinaries (e.g. roundel, orle, lozenge).

subordinate ▸ adjective /səˈbɔːdɪnət/ lower in rank or position: *his subordinate officers.* ■ of less or secondary importance: *in adventure stories, character must **be subordinate to** action.*
▸ noun /səˈbɔːdɪnət/ a person under the authority or control of another within an organization.
▸ verb /səˈbɔːdɪneɪt/ [with obj.] treat or regard as of lesser importance than something else: *practical considerations were **subordinated to** political expediency.* ■ make subservient to or dependent on something else.
– DERIVATIVES **subordinately** adverb.
– ORIGIN late Middle English: from medieval Latin *subordinatus* 'placed in an inferior rank', from Latin *sub-* 'below' + *ordinare* 'ordain'.

subordinate clause ▸ noun a clause, typically introduced by a conjunction, that forms part of and is dependent on a main clause (e.g. 'when it rang' in 'she answered the phone when it rang').

subordinated debt ▸ noun Finance a debt owed to an unsecured creditor that in the event of a liquidation can only be paid after the claims of secured creditors have been met.

subordinate legislation ▸ noun [mass noun] Law law which is enacted under delegated powers, such as statutory instruments.

subordinating conjunction ▸ noun a conjunction that introduces a subordinating clause, e.g. *although, because*. Contrasted with COORDINATING CONJUNCTION.

subordination ▸ noun [mass noun] the action of subordinating or the state of being subordinate: *the subordination of medicine to political expediency.*

suborn /səˈbɔːn/ ▸ verb [with obj.] bribe or otherwise induce (someone) to commit an unlawful act such as perjury: *he was accused of conspiring to suborn witnesses.*
– DERIVATIVES **subornation** noun, **suborner** noun.
– ORIGIN mid 16th cent.: from Latin *subornare* 'incite secretly', from *sub-* 'secretly' + *ornare* 'equip'.

suboscine /sʌbˈɒsʌɪn, -sɪn/ Ornithology ▸ adjective relating to or denoting passerine birds of a division that includes those other than songbirds, found chiefly in America. Compare with OSCINE. ● Suborder Deutero-Oscines, order Passeriformes.
▸ noun a bird of this division.

suboxide ▸ noun Chemistry an oxide containing the lowest or an unusually small proportion of oxygen.

subparallel ▸ adjective chiefly Geology almost parallel.

subphylum ▸ noun (pl. **subphyla**) Zoology a taxonomic category that ranks below phylum and above class.

subplot ▸ noun a subordinate plot in a play, novel, or similar work.

subpoena /səˈpiːnə/ Law ▸ noun (in full **subpoena ad testificandum**) a writ ordering a person to attend a court: *a subpoena may be issued to compel their attendance* | [mass noun] *they were all **under subpoena** to appear.*
▸ verb (**subpoenas, subpoenaing, subpoenaed** or **subpoena'd**) [with obj.] summon (someone) with a subpoena: *the Queen is above the law and cannot be subpoenaed.* ■ require (a document or other evidence) to be submitted to a court of law: *the decision to subpoena government records.*
– ORIGIN late Middle English (as a noun): from Latin *sub poena* 'under penalty' (the first words of the writ). Use as a verb dates from the mid 17th cent.

subpoena duces tecum /ˌdjuːsiːz ˈtiːkəm/ ▸ noun Law a writ ordering a person to attend a court and bring relevant documents.
– ORIGIN Latin, literally 'under penalty you shall bring with you'.

sub-postmaster (or **sub-postmistress**) ▸ noun chiefly Brit. a person in charge of a sub-post office.

sub-post office ▸ noun (in the UK) a small local post office offering fewer services than a main post office.

sub-prime ▸ adjective denoting or relating to credit or loan arrangements for borrowers with a poor credit history, typically having unfavourable conditions such as high interest rates: *the sub-prime mortgage market.*

subprogram ▸ noun Computing another term for SUBROUTINE.

subregion ▸ noun a division of a region.
– DERIVATIVES **subregional** adjective.

subrogation /ˌsʌbrəˈɡeɪʃ(ə)n/ ▸ noun [mass noun] Law the substitution of one person or group by another in respect of a debt or insurance claim, accompanied by the transfer of any associated rights and duties.
– DERIVATIVES **subrogate** /ˈsʌbrəɡeɪt/ verb.
– ORIGIN late Middle English (in the general sense 'substitution'): from late Latin *subrogatio(n-)*, from *subrogare* 'choose as substitute', from *sub-* 'in place of another' + *rogare* 'ask'.

sub rosa /sʌb ˈrəʊzə/ ▸ adjective & adverb formal happening or done in secret: [as adv.] *the committee operates sub rosa* | [as adj.] *sub rosa inspections.*
– ORIGIN Latin, literally 'under the rose', as an emblem of secrecy.

subroutine ▸ noun Computing a set of instructions designed to perform a frequently used operation within a program.

sub-Saharan ▸ adjective from or forming part of the African regions south of the Sahara desert.

subsample ▸ noun a sample drawn from a larger sample.
▸ verb [with obj.] take a subsample from.

subscribe ▸ verb **1** [no obj.] arrange to receive something, typically a publication, regularly by paying in advance: ***subscribe to** the magazine for twelve months and receive a free limited-edition T-shirt.* ■ arrange for access to an electronic mailing list or online service: *some 40,000 users have **subscribed to** the service.* ■ contribute or undertake to contribute a certain sum of money to a fund, project, or cause, typically on a regular basis: *he is one of the millions who **subscribe to** the NSPCC* | [with obj.] *he **subscribed** £400*

S

to the campaign. ■ [with obj.] apply to participate in: *the course has been fully subscribed.* ■ apply for or undertake to pay for an issue of shares: *they **subscribed** to the July rights issue at 300p a share* | [with obj.] *the issue was fully subscribed.* ■ [with obj.] (of a bookseller) agree before publication to take (a certain number of copies of a book): *most of the first print run of 15,000 copies has been subscribed.*
2 [no obj.] (**subscribe to**) express or feel agreement with (an idea or proposal): *we prefer to subscribe to an alternative explanation.*
3 [with obj.] formal sign (a will, contract, or other document): *he subscribed the will as a witness.* ■ sign (one's name) on such a document. ■ [with complement] (**subscribe oneself**) archaic sign oneself as: *he ventured still to subscribe himself her most obedient servant.*
– ORIGIN late Middle English (in the sense 'sign at the bottom of a document'): from Latin *subscribere*, from *sub-* 'under' + *scribere* 'write'.

subscriber ▸ **noun** a person who receives a publication regularly by paying in advance: *I am a new subscriber to Saga magazine.* ■ a person who pays to receive or access a service: *the company has 2.6 million subscribers to its digital service.* ■ a person who regularly contributes money to a fund, project, or cause.

subscriber trunk dialling ▸ **noun** [mass noun] Brit. the automatic connection of trunk calls by dialling without the assistance of an operator.

subscript ▸ **adjective** (of a letter, figure, or symbol) written or printed below the line.
▸ **noun** a subscript letter, figure, or symbol. ■ Computing a symbol (notionally written as a subscript but in practice usually not) used in a program, alone or with others, to specify one of the elements of an array.
– ORIGIN early 18th cent.: from Latin *subscript-* 'written below', from the verb *subscribere* (see SUBSCRIBE).

subscription ▸ **noun 1** [mass noun] the action of making or agreeing to make an advance payment in order to receive or participate in something or as a donation: *the newsletter is available only on subscription* | [count noun] *take out a one-year subscription.* ■ an arrangement by which access is granted to an online service. ■ [count noun] an advance payment made to receive or participate in something: *membership of the club is available at an annual subscription of £300.* ■ a system in which the production of a book is wholly or partly financed by advance orders.
2 formal a signature or short piece of writing at the end of a document: *he signed the letter and added a subscription.* ■ archaic a signed declaration or agreement.
– ORIGIN late Middle English (in sense 2): from Latin *subscriptio(n-)*, from *subscribere* 'write below' (see SUBSCRIBE).

subscription concert ▸ **noun** each of a series of concerts for which tickets are sold mainly in advance.

subsea ▸ **adjective** (especially of processes or equipment used in the oil industry) situated or occurring beneath the surface of the sea.

subsection ▸ **noun** a division of a section.

subsense ▸ **noun** a subsidiary sense of a word defined in a dictionary.

subsequence[1] /ˈsʌbsɪkw(ə)ns/ ▸ **noun** [mass noun] formal the state of following something, especially as a result or effect: *an affair which appeared in due subsequence in the newspapers.*

subsequence[2] /ˈsʌbˌsiːkw(ə)ns/ ▸ **noun** a sequence contained in or forming part of another sequence. ■ Mathematics a sequence derived from another by the omission of a number of terms.

subsequent ▸ **adjective** coming after something in time; following: *the theory was developed **subsequent** to the earthquake of 1906.* ■ Geology (of a stream or valley) having a direction or character determined by the resistance to erosion of the underlying rock, and typically following the strike of the strata.
– ORIGIN late Middle English: from Old French, or from Latin *subsequent-* 'following after' (from the verb *subsequi*).

subsequently ▸ **adverb** after a particular thing has happened; afterwards: *many of the Scots who voted for Union subsequently changed their minds.*

subserve ▸ **verb** [with obj.] help to further or promote: *they extended the uses of writing to subserve their political interest.*
– ORIGIN mid 17th cent.: from Latin *subservire* (see SUB-, SERVE).

subservient ▸ **adjective** prepared to obey others unquestioningly: *she was **subservient** to her parents.* ■ less important; subordinate: *he expected her career to become **subservient** to his.* ■ serving as a means to an end: *the whole narration is **subservient** to the moral plan of exemplifying twelve virtues in twelve knights.*
– DERIVATIVES **subservience** noun, **subserviency** noun, **subserviently** adverb.
– ORIGIN mid 17th cent.: from Latin *subservient-* 'subjecting to, complying with', from the verb *subservire* (see SUBSERVE).

subset ▸ **noun** a part of a larger group of related things. ■ Mathematics a set of which all the elements are contained in another set.

subshrub ▸ **noun** Botany a dwarf shrub, especially one that is woody only at the base.
– DERIVATIVES **subshrubby** adjective.

subside ▸ **verb** [no obj.] **1** become less intense, violent, or severe: *I'll wait a few minutes until the storm subsides.* ■ lapse into silence or inactivity: *Fergus opened his mouth to protest again, then subsided.* ■ (**subside in/into**) give way to (an overwhelming feeling, especially laughter): *Anthony and Mark subsided into mirth.*
2 (of water) go down to a lower or the normal level: *the floods subside almost as quickly as they arise.* ■ (of the ground) cave in; sink: *the island is subsiding.* ■ (of a building or other structure) sink lower into the ground: *a ditch which caused the tower to subside slightly.* ■ (of a swelling) reduce until gone: *it took seven days for the swelling to subside completely.* ■ [no obj., with adverbial] sink into a sitting, kneeling, or lying position: *Patrick subsided into his seat.*
– ORIGIN late 17th cent.: from Latin *subsidere*, from *sub-* 'below' + *sidere* 'settle' (related to *sedere* 'sit').

subsidence /səbˈsʌɪd(ə)ns, ˈsʌbsɪd(ə)ns/ ▸ **noun** [mass noun] the gradual caving in or sinking of an area of land.
– ORIGIN mid 17th cent.: from Latin *subsidentia* 'sediment', from the verb *subsidere* (see SUBSIDE).

subsidiarity /səbˌsɪdɪˈarɪti/ ▸ **noun** [mass noun] (in politics) the principle that a central authority should have a subsidiary function, performing only those tasks which cannot be performed at a more local level.

subsidiary ▸ **adjective** less important than but related or supplementary to something: *a subsidiary flue of the main chimney* | *many argue that the cause of animal rights is **subsidiary** to that of protecting the environment.* ■ (of a company) controlled by a holding or parent company.
▸ **noun** (pl. **subsidiaries**) a company controlled by a holding company.
– DERIVATIVES **subsidiarily** adverb.
– ORIGIN mid 16th cent. (in the sense 'serving to help or supplement'): from Latin *subsidiarius*, from *subsidium* 'support, assistance' (see SUBSIDY).

subsidize (also **subsidise**) ▸ **verb** [with obj.] support (an organization or activity) financially: *the mining industry continues to be subsidized.* ■ pay part of the cost of producing (something) to keep the selling price low: (as adj. **subsidized**) *subsidized food.*
– DERIVATIVES **subsidization** noun, **subsidizer** noun.

subsidy ▸ **noun** (pl. **subsidies**) **1** a sum of money granted by the state or a public body to help an industry or business keep the price of a commodity or service low: *a farm subsidy* | [mass noun] *the rail service now operates without subsidy.* ■ a sum of money granted to support an undertaking held to be in the public interest. ■ a grant or contribution of money.
2 historical a parliamentary grant to the sovereign for state needs. ■ a tax levied on a particular occasion.
– ORIGIN late Middle English: from Anglo-Norman French *subsidie*, from Latin *subsidium* 'assistance'.

subsist ▸ **verb** [no obj.] **1** maintain or support oneself, especially at a minimal level: *he **subsisted** on welfare and casual labour.* ■ [with obj.] archaic provide sustenance for: *the problem of subsisting the poor in a period of high bread prices.*
2 chiefly Law remain in force or effect. ■ (**subsist in**) be attributable to: *the effect of genetic maldevelopment may subsist in chromosomal mutation.*
– DERIVATIVES **subsistent** adjective.
– ORIGIN mid 16th cent. (in the sense 'continue to exist'): from Latin *subsistere* 'stand firm', from *sub-* 'from below' + *sistere* 'set, stand'.

subsistence ▸ **noun** [mass noun] **1** the action or fact of maintaining or supporting oneself at a minimal level: *the minimum income needed for subsistence.* ■ the means of doing this: *the garden provided not only subsistence but a little cash crop.* ■ [as modifier] denoting or relating to production at a level sufficient only for one's own use or consumption, without any surplus for trade: *subsistence agriculture.*
2 chiefly Law the state of remaining in force or effect: *rights of occupation normally only continue during the subsistence of the marriage.*

subsistence allowance (also **subsistence money**) ▸ **noun** chiefly Brit. an allowance or advance on someone's pay.

subsistence level (also **subsistence wage**) ▸ **noun** a standard of living (or wage) that provides only the bare necessities of life.

subsoil ▸ **noun** [mass noun] the soil lying immediately under the surface soil.
▸ **verb** [with obj.] (usu. as noun **subsoiling**) plough (land) so as to cut into the subsoil.

subsoiler ▸ **noun** a kind of plough with no mouldboard, used to loosen the soil at some depth below the surface without turning it over.

subsong ▸ **noun** [mass noun] Ornithology birdsong that is softer and less well defined than the usual territorial song, sometimes heard only at close quarters as a quiet warbling.

subsonic ▸ **adjective** relating to or flying at a speed or speeds less than that of sound.
– DERIVATIVES **subsonically** adverb.

subspace ▸ **noun 1** Mathematics a space that is wholly contained in another space, or whose points or elements are all in another space.
2 [mass noun] (in science fiction) a hypothetical space–time continuum used for communication at a speed faster than that of light.

sub specie aeternitatis /sʌb ˈspiːʃiː ɪˌtəːnɪˈtɑːtɪs/ ▸ **adverb** literary viewed in relation to the eternal; in a universal perspective: *sub specie aeternitatis the authors have got it about right.*
– ORIGIN Latin, literally 'under the aspect of eternity'.

subspecies (abbrev.: **subsp.** or **ssp.**) ▸ **noun** (pl. **same**) Biology a taxonomic category that ranks below species, usually a fairly permanent geographically isolated race. Subspecies are designated by a Latin trinomial, e.g. (in zoology) *Ursus arctos horribilis* or (in botany) *Beta vulgaris crassa.*
– DERIVATIVES **subspecific** adjective.

substage ▸ **noun** [usu. as modifier] an apparatus fixed beneath the ordinary stage of a compound microscope to support mirrors and other accessories.

substance ▸ **noun 1** a particular kind of matter with uniform properties: *a steel tube coated with a waxy substance.* ■ an intoxicating, stimulating, or narcotic chemical or drug, especially an illegal one: *he was suspended for using a banned substance* | [as modifier] *substance abuse.*
2 [mass noun] the real physical matter of which a person or thing consists and which has a tangible, solid presence: *proteins compose much of the actual substance of the body.* ■ the most important or essential part of something; the real or essential meaning: *the substance of the Maastricht Treaty.* ■ the subject matter of a text, speech, or work of art, especially as contrasted with the form or style in which it is presented.
3 [mass noun] the quality of having a solid basis in reality or fact: *the claim has no substance.* ■ the quality of being dependable or stable: *some were inclined to knock her for her lack of substance.* ■ the quality of being important, valid, or significant: *he had yet to accomplish anything of substance.* ■ wealth and possessions: *a woman of substance.*
4 [mass noun] Philosophy the essential nature underlying phenomena, which is subject to changes and accidents.
– PHRASES **in substance** essentially: *basic rights are equivalent in substance to human rights.*
– ORIGIN Middle English (denoting the essential nature of something): from Old French, from Latin *substantia* 'being, essence', from *substant-* 'standing firm', from the verb *substare.*

substance P ▸ **noun** [mass noun] Biochemistry a compound thought to be involved in the synaptic transmission of pain and other nerve impulses. It is a polypeptide with eleven amino-acid residues.

substandard ▸ **adjective 1** below the usual or required standard: *substandard housing.*
2 another term for NON-STANDARD.

substantial ▸ **adjective 1** of considerable importance, size, or worth: *a substantial amount of cash.* ■ strongly built or made: *a row of substantial Victorian villas.* ■ (of a meal) large and filling. ■ important in

S

material or social terms; wealthy: *a substantial Devon family.*
2 concerning the essentials of something: *there was substantial agreement on changing policies.*
3 real and tangible rather than imaginary: *spirits are shadowy, human beings substantial.*
– DERIVATIVES **substantiality** noun.
– ORIGIN Middle English: from Old French *substantiel* or Christian Latin *substantialis*, from *substantia* 'being, essence' (see SUBSTANCE).

substantialism ▶ noun [mass noun] Philosophy the doctrine that behind phenomena there are substantial realities.
– DERIVATIVES **substantialist** noun & adjective.

substantialize (also **substantialise**) ▶ verb [with obj.] give (something) substance or actual existence.

substantially ▶ adverb **1** to a great or significant extent: *profits grew substantially* | [as submodifier] *substantially higher pension costs.*
2 for the most part; essentially: *things will remain substantially the same over the next ten years.*

substantiate /səbˈstanʃɪeɪt/ ▶ verb [with obj.] provide evidence to support or prove the truth of: *they had found nothing to substantiate the allegations.*
– DERIVATIVES **substantiation** noun.
– ORIGIN mid 17th cent.: from medieval Latin *substantiat-* 'given substance', from the verb *substantiare*.

substantive /ˈsʌbst(ə)ntɪv/ ▶ adjective also /səbˈstantɪv/ **1** having a firm basis in reality and so important, meaningful, or considerable: *there is no substantive evidence for the efficacy of these drugs.*
2 having a separate and independent existence. ■ (of a rank or appointment) not acting or temporary; permanent. ■ (of an enactment, motion, or resolution) made in due form as such; not amended.
3 (of law) defining rights and duties, as opposed to giving the procedural rules by which those rights and duties are enforced.
4 (of a dye) not needing a mordant.
▶ noun (also **noun substantive**) Grammar, dated a noun.
– DERIVATIVES **substantival** /-ˈtʌɪv(ə)l/ adjective, **substantively** adverb.
– ORIGIN late Middle English (in the sense 'having an independent existence'): from Old French *substantif, -ive* or late Latin *substantivus*, from *substantia* 'essence' (see SUBSTANCE).

substation ▶ noun **1** a set of equipment reducing the high voltage of electrical power transmission to that suitable for supply to consumers.
2 a subordinate station for the police or fire service. ■ N. Amer. a small post office, for example one situated within a larger shop.

substellar ▶ adjective Astronomy relating to or denoting a body much smaller than a typical star whose mass is not great enough to support main sequence hydrogen burning.

substituent /səbˈstɪtjʊənt/ ▶ noun Chemistry an atom or group of atoms taking the place of another atom or group or occupying a specified position in a molecule.
– ORIGIN late 19th cent.: from Latin *substituent-* 'standing in place of', from the verb *substituere* (see SUBSTITUTE).

S

substitute ▶ noun **1** a person or thing acting or serving in place of another: *soya milk is used as a* ***substitute for*** *dairy milk.* ■ a person or thing that becomes the object of love or another emotion which is deprived of its natural outlet: *a father substitute.*
2 a sports player nominated as eligible to replace another after a match has begun.
3 Scots Law a deputy: *a sheriff substitute.*
▶ verb [with obj.] **1** use or add in place of: *dried rosemary can be* ***substituted for*** *the fresh herb.* ■ [no obj.] act or serve as a substitute: *I found someone to* ***substitute for*** *me.* ■ replace (someone or something) with another: ***customs officers substituted the drugs with another substance*** | *this was substituted by a new clause.* ■ Chemistry replace (an atom or group in a molecule, especially a hydrogen atom) with another. ■ (as adj. **substituted**) Chemistry (of a compound) in which one or more hydrogen atoms have been replaced by other atoms or groups: *a substituted terpenoid.*
2 replace (a sports player) with a substitute during a match: *he was substituted eleven minutes from time.*
– DERIVATIVES **substitutability** noun, **substitutable** adjective, **substitutive** adjective.
– ORIGIN late Middle English (denoting a deputy or delegate): from Latin *substitutus* 'put in place of', past participle of *substituere*, based on *statuere* 'set up'.

> **USAGE** Traditionally, the verb **substitute** is followed by **for** and means 'put someone or something in place of another', as in *she* ***substituted*** *the fake vase* ***for*** *the real one.* From the late 17th century **substitute** has also been used to mean 'replace someone or something with something else', as in *she* ***substituted*** *the real vase* ***with*** *the fake one.* This can be confusing, since the two sentences shown above mean the same thing, yet the object of the verb and the object of the preposition have swapped positions. Despite the potential confusion, the second, newer use is well established, especially in some scientific contexts and in sport (*the top scorer was substituted with almost half an hour still to play*), and is now generally regarded as part of normal standard English.

substitution ▶ noun [mass noun] the action of replacing someone or something with another person or thing: ***the substitution of*** *rail services* ***with*** *buses* | [count noun] *a tactical substitution.*
– DERIVATIVES **substitutional** adjective, **substitutionary** adjective.

substorm ▶ noun a localized disturbance of the earth's magnetic field in high latitudes, typically manifested as an aurora.

substrain ▶ noun a strain of a virus derived from another strain.

substrate /ˈsʌbstreɪt/ ▶ noun an underlying substance or layer. ■ the surface or material on or from which an organism lives, grows, or obtains its nourishment. ■ the substance on which an enzyme acts. ■ a material which provides the surface on which something is deposited or inscribed, for example the silicon wafer used to manufacture integrated circuits.
– ORIGIN early 19th cent.: anglicized form of SUBSTRATUM.

substratum /sʌbˈstrɑːtəm, -ˈstreɪtəm/ ▶ noun (pl. **substrata**) an underlying layer or substance, in particular a layer of rock or soil beneath the surface of the ground. ■ a foundation or basis of something: *there is a broad* ***substratum of*** *truth in her story.*
– ORIGIN mid 17th cent.: modern Latin, neuter past participle (used as a noun) of Latin *substernere*, from *sub-* 'below' + *sternere* 'strew'. Compare with STRATUM.

substructure ▶ noun an underlying or supporting structure.
– DERIVATIVES **substructural** adjective.

subsume /səbˈsjuːm/ ▶ verb [with obj.] include or absorb (something) in something else: *most of these phenomena can be* ***subsumed under*** *two broad categories.*
– DERIVATIVES **subsumable** adjective, **subsumption** noun.
– ORIGIN mid 16th cent. (in the sense 'subjoin, add'): from medieval Latin *subsumere*, from *sub-* 'from below' + *sumere* 'take'. The current sense dates from the early 19th cent.

subsurface ▶ noun the stratum or strata below the earth's surface.

subsystem ▶ noun a self-contained system within a larger system.

subtenant ▶ noun a person who leases property from a tenant.
– DERIVATIVES **subtenancy** noun.

subtend /sʌbˈtɛnd/ ▶ verb [with obj.] **1** Geometry (of a line, arc, or figure) form (an angle) at a particular point when straight lines from its extremities are joined at that point. ■ (of an angle or chord) have bounding lines or points that meet or coincide with those of (a line or arc).
2 Botany (of a bract) extend under (a flower) so as to support or enfold it.
– ORIGIN late 16th cent. (in sense 1): from Latin *subtendere*, from *sub-* 'under' + *tendere* 'stretch'. Sense 2 dates from the late 19th cent.

subtense ▶ noun Geometry a subtending line, especially the chord of an arc. ■ the angle subtended by a line at a point.
– ORIGIN early 17th cent.: from modern Latin *subtensa (linea)*, feminine past participle of *subtendere* (see SUBTEND).

subterfuge /ˈsʌbtəfjuːdʒ/ ▶ noun [mass noun] deceit used in order to achieve one's goal: *he had to use subterfuge and bluff on many occasions* | [count noun] *I hated all the subterfuges, I hated lying to you.*
– ORIGIN late 16th cent.: from French, or from late Latin *subterfugium*, from Latin *subterfugere* 'escape secretly', from *subter-* 'beneath' + *fugere* 'flee'.

subterminal ▶ adjective technical near the end of a chain or other structure.

subterranean /ˌsʌbtəˈreɪnɪən/ ▶ adjective existing, occurring, or done under the earth's surface. ■ secret; concealed: *the subterranean world of the behind-the-scenes television power brokers.*
– DERIVATIVES **subterraneous** adjective, **subterraneously** adverb.
– ORIGIN early 17th cent.: from Latin *subterraneus* (from *sub-* 'below' + *terra* 'earth') + -AN.

subterranean clover ▶ noun a European clover, naturalized as a weed of pastures in Australia, whose fruiting heads bury themselves in the ground. ● *Trifolium subterraneum*, family Leguminosae.

subtext ▶ noun an underlying and often distinct theme in a piece of writing or conversation.
– DERIVATIVES **subtextual** adjective.

subtilize /ˈsʌtɪlʌɪz/ (also **subtilise**) ▶ verb [with obj.] archaic make more subtle; refine.
– DERIVATIVES **subtilization** noun.

subtitle ▶ noun **1** (**subtitles**) captions displayed at the bottom of a cinema or television screen that translate or transcribe the dialogue or narrative.
2 a subordinate title of a published work or article giving additional information about its content.
▶ verb [with obj.] **1** provide (a film or programme) with subtitles: *much of the film is subtitled.*
2 provide (a published work or article) with a subtitle: *the novel was aptly subtitled.*

subtle /ˈsʌt(ə)l/ ▶ adjective (**subtler**, **subtlest**)
1 (especially of a change or distinction) so delicate or precise as to be difficult to analyse or describe: *his language expresses rich and subtle meanings.* ■ (of a mixture or effect) delicately complex and understated: *subtle lighting.* ■ capable of making fine distinctions: *a subtle mind.* ■ arranged in an ingenious and elaborate way.
2 making use of clever and indirect methods to achieve something: *he tried a more subtle approach.*
3 archaic crafty; cunning: *the subtle fiend dissembled.*
– DERIVATIVES **subtleness** noun, **subtly** adverb.
– ORIGIN Middle English (also in the sense 'not easily understood'): from Old French *sotil*, from Latin *subtilis*.

subtlety /ˈsʌt(ə)lti/ ▶ noun (pl. **subtleties**) [mass noun] the quality or state of being subtle: *the textural subtlety of Degas.* ■ [count noun] a subtle distinction, feature, or argument: *the subtleties of English grammar.*
– ORIGIN Middle English: from Old French *soutilte*, from Latin *subtilitas*, from *subtilis* 'fine, delicate' (see SUBTLE).

subtonic ▶ noun Music the note below the tonic, the seventh note of the diatonic scale of any key.

subtopia ▶ noun [mass noun] Brit. unsightly, sprawling suburban development.
– ORIGIN 1950s: blend of SUBURB and UTOPIA.

subtotal ▶ noun the total of one set of a larger group of figures to be added.
▶ verb (**subtotals**, **subtotalling**, **subtotalled**; US **subtotals**, **subtotaling**, **subtotaled**) [with obj.] add (numbers) so as to obtain a subtotal.
▶ adjective Medicine (of an injury or a surgical operation) partial; not total.

subtract ▶ verb [with obj.] take away (a number or amount) from another to calculate the difference: *subtract 43 from 60.* ■ take away (something) from something else so as to decrease the size, number, or amount: ***programs were added and subtracted as called for.***
– DERIVATIVES **subtracter** (also **subtractor**) noun, **subtractive** adjective.
– ORIGIN mid 16th cent.: from Latin *subtract-* 'drawn away', from *sub-* 'from below' + *trahere* 'to draw'.

subtraction ▶ noun [mass noun] the process or skill of taking one number or amount away from another: ***subtraction of*** *this figure* ***from*** *the total.* ■ Mathematics the process of taking a matrix, vector, or other quantity away from another under specific rules to obtain the difference.

subtrahend /ˈsʌbtrəˌhɛnd/ ▶ noun Mathematics a quantity or number to be subtracted from another.
– ORIGIN late 17th cent.: from Latin *subtrahendus* 'to be taken away', gerundive of *subtrahere* (see SUBTRACT).

subtropics ▶ plural noun (**the subtropics**) the regions adjacent to or bordering on the tropics.
– DERIVATIVES **subtropical** adjective.

subtype ▶ noun a secondary or subordinate type. ■ a subdivision of a type of microorganism.

Subud /sʊˈbuːd/ a movement, founded in 1947 and led by the Javanese mystic Pak Muhammad Subuh,

based on a system of exercises by which the individual seeks to approach a state of perfection through divine power.
– ORIGIN contraction of Javanese *susila budhi dharma*, from Sanskrit *suśīla* 'good disposition' + *buddhi* 'understanding' + *dharma* 'religious duty'.

subulate /ˈsjuːbjʊlət, -leɪt/ ▸ adjective Botany & Zoology (of a part) slender and tapering to a point; awl-shaped.
– ORIGIN mid 18th cent.: from Latin *subula* 'awl' + **-ATE**[2].

subumbrella ▸ noun Zoology the concave inner surface of the umbrella of a jellyfish or other medusa.
– DERIVATIVES **subumbrellar** adjective.

sub-underwrite ▸ verb [with obj.] Finance underwrite (part of a liability underwritten by another).
– DERIVATIVES **sub-underwriter** noun.

subungulate /sʌbˈʌŋgjʊlət, -leɪt/ ▸ noun Zoology a mammal of a diverse group that probably evolved from primitive ungulates, comprising the elephants, hyraxes, sirenians, and perhaps the aardvark.

subunit ▸ noun a distinct component of something: *chemical subunits of human DNA*.

suburb ▸ noun an outlying district of a city, especially a residential one.
– ORIGIN Middle English: from Old French *suburbe* or Latin *suburbium*, from *sub-* 'near to' + *urbs, urb-* 'city'.

suburban ▸ adjective of or characteristic of a suburb: *suburban life*. ■ contemptibly dull and ordinary: *Elizabeth despised Ann's house-proudness as deeply suburban*.
– DERIVATIVES **suburbanite** noun, **suburbanization** (also **suburbanisation**) noun, **suburbanize** (also **suburbanise**) verb.

suburbia ▸ noun [mass noun] the suburbs or their inhabitants viewed collectively.

subvent ▸ verb [with obj.] formal support or assist by the payment of a subvention.
– ORIGIN early 20th cent.: from Latin *subvent-* 'assisted', from the verb *subvenire* (see **SUBVENTION**).

subvention ▸ noun a grant of money, especially from a government.
– ORIGIN late Middle English (in the sense 'provision of help'): from Old French, from late Latin *subventio(n-)*, from Latin *subvenire* 'assist', from *sub-* 'from below' + *venire* 'come'.

subversive ▸ adjective seeking or intended to subvert an established system or institution: *subversive literature*.
▸ noun a subversive person.
– DERIVATIVES **subversively** adverb, **subversiveness** noun.
– ORIGIN mid 17th cent.: from medieval Latin *subversivus*, from the verb *subvertere* (see **SUBVERT**).

subvert ▸ verb [with obj.] undermine the power and authority of (an established system or institution): *an attempt to subvert democratic government*.
– DERIVATIVES **subversion** noun, **subverter** noun.
– ORIGIN late Middle English: from Old French *subvertir* or Latin *subvertere*, from *sub-* 'from below' + *vertere* 'to turn'.

subvocal ▸ adjective Psychology & Philosophy relating to or denoting an unarticulated level of speech comparable to thought.
– DERIVATIVES **subvocally** adverb.

subvocalize (also **subvocalise**) ▸ verb [with obj.] utter or form (words or sounds) with the lips silently or with barely audible sound, especially when talking to oneself, memorizing something, or reading.

subway ▸ noun **1** Brit. a tunnel under a road for use by pedestrians.
2 N. Amer. an underground railway.

subway series ▸ noun (in the US) a series of baseball games played between two teams in the same city, especially New York.

subwoofer ▸ noun a loudspeaker component designed to reproduce very low bass frequencies.

sub-zero ▸ adjective (of temperature) lower than zero; below freezing.

suc- ▸ prefix variant spelling of **SUB-** assimilated before *c* (as in *succeed, succussion*).

succah /ˈsʊkə/ (also **sukkah**) ▸ noun a booth in which a practising Jew spends part of Succoth.
– ORIGIN late 19th cent.: from Hebrew *sukkāh* 'hut'.

succedaneum /ˌsʌksɪˈdeɪnɪəm/ ▸ noun (pl. **succedanea** /-nɪə/) dated or literary a substitute, especially for a medicine or drug.
– ORIGIN early 17th cent.: modern Latin, neuter of Latin *succedaneus* 'following after', from *succedere* 'come close after' (see **SUCCEED**).

succeed ▸ verb **1** [no obj.] achieve the desired aim or result: *he **succeeded in** winning a pardon | a mission which could not possibly succeed*. ■ attain fame, wealth, or social status: *the management and business skills you need to succeed*.
2 [with obj.] take over a throne, office, or other position from: *he would succeed Hawke as Prime Minister*. ■ [no obj.] become the new rightful holder of an office, title, or property: *he **succeeded to** his father's kingdom*. ■ come after and take the place of: *her embarrassment was succeeded by fear*.
– PHRASES **nothing succeeds like success** proverb success leads to opportunities for further and greater successes.
– DERIVATIVES **succeeder** noun (archaic).
– ORIGIN late Middle English: from Old French *succeder* or Latin *succedere* 'come close after', from *sub-* 'close to' + *cedere* 'go'.

succeeding ▸ adjective [attrib.] coming after something in time; subsequent: *over the succeeding decades, recording equipment got cheaper*.

succentor /səkˈsɛntə/ ▸ noun Christian Church a precentor's deputy in some cathedrals.
– ORIGIN early 17th cent.: from late Latin, from Latin *succinere* 'sing to, chime in', from *sub-* 'subordinately' + *canere* 'sing'.

succès de scandale /sʊkˌseɪ də skɒnˈdɑːl/, French /syksɛ də skɑ̃dal/ ▸ noun a success due to notoriety or a thing's scandalous nature.
– ORIGIN French, literally 'success of scandal'.

succès d'estime /sʊkˌseɪ dɛˈstiːm/, French /syksɛ dɛstim/ ▸ noun (pl. **same**) a success in terms of critical appreciation, as opposed to popularity or commercial gain.
– ORIGIN French, literally 'success of opinion'.

success ▸ noun [mass noun] **1** the accomplishment of an aim or purpose: *the president had some success in restoring confidence*. ■ the attainment of fame, wealth, or social status: *the success of his play*. ■ [count noun] a person or thing that achieves desired aims or attains fame, wealth, etc.: *to judge from league tables, the school is a success | I must **make a success of** my business*.
2 archaic the good or bad outcome of an undertaking: *the good or ill success of their maritime enterprises*.
– ORIGIN mid 16th cent.: from Latin *successus*, from the verb *succedere* 'come close after' (see **SUCCEED**).

successful ▸ adjective accomplishing a desired aim or result: *a successful attack on the town | marketing of Japanese products has been highly successful*. ■ having achieved fame, wealth, or social status: *a successful actor*.
– DERIVATIVES **successfully** adverb, **successfulness** noun.

succession ▸ noun **1** a number of people or things of a similar kind following one after the other: *she had been secretary to a succession of board directors*. ■ Geology a group of strata representing a single chronological sequence.
2 [mass noun] the action or process of inheriting a title, office, property, etc.: *the new king was already elderly at the time of his succession*. ■ the right or sequence of inheriting a position, title, etc.: *the succession to the Crown was disputed*. ■ Ecology the process by which a plant or animal community successively gives way to another until a stable climax is reached. Compare with **SERE**[2].
– PHRASES **in quick** (or **rapid**) **succession** following one another at short intervals. **in succession** following one after the other without interruption: *she won the race for the second year in succession*. **in succession to** inheriting or elected to the place of: *he was elevated to the Lords in succession to his father*.
– DERIVATIVES **successional** adjective.
– ORIGIN Middle English (denoting legal transmission of an estate or the throne to another, also in the sense 'successors, heirs'): from Old French, or from Latin *successio(n-)*, from the verb *succedere* (see **SUCCEED**).

Succession, Act of (in English history) each of three Acts of Parliament passed during the reign of Henry VIII regarding the succession of his children.

> The first (1534) declared Henry's marriage to Catherine of Aragon to be invalid, fixing the succession on any child born to Henry's new wife Anne Boleyn. The second (1536) cancelled this, asserting the rights of Jane Seymour and her issue, while the third (1544) determined the order of succession of Henry's three children, the future Edward VI, Mary I, and Elizabeth I.

succession state ▸ noun a country resulting from the partition of another one.

successive ▸ adjective [attrib.] following one another or following others: *they were looking for their fifth successive win*.
– DERIVATIVES **successively** adverb, **successiveness** noun.
– ORIGIN late Middle English: from medieval Latin *successivus*, from *success-* 'followed closely', from the verb *succedere* (see **SUCCEED**).

successor ▸ noun a person or thing that succeeds another: *Schoenberg saw himself as a natural successor to the German romantic school*.

success story ▸ noun informal a successful person or thing.

succinate /ˈsʌksɪneɪt/ ▸ noun Chemistry a salt or ester of succinic acid.

succinct /səkˈsɪŋ(k)t/ ▸ adjective (especially of something written or spoken) briefly and clearly expressed: *use short, succinct sentences*.
– DERIVATIVES **succinctly** adverb, **succinctness** noun.
– ORIGIN late Middle English (in the sense 'encircled'): from Latin *succinctus* 'tucked up', past participle of *succingere*, from *sub-* 'from below' + *cingere* 'gird'.

succinic acid /sʌkˈsɪnɪk/ ▸ noun [mass noun] Biochemistry a crystalline organic acid which occurs in living tissue as an intermediate in glucose metabolism. ● Chem. formula: $HOOC(CH_2)_2COOH$.
– ORIGIN late 18th cent.: *succinic* from French *succinique*, from Latin *succinum* 'amber' (from which it was first derived).

succinylcholine /ˌsʌksɪnʌɪlˈkəʊliːn/ ▸ noun [mass noun] Medicine a synthetic compound used as a short-acting muscle relaxant and local anaesthetic. It is an ester of choline with succinic acid.

succor ▸ noun & verb US spelling of **SUCCOUR**.

succory /ˈsʌk(ə)ri/ ▸ noun another term for **CHICORY** (sense 1).
– ORIGIN mid 16th cent.: alteration of obsolete French *cicorée*.

succotash /ˈsʌkətaʃ/ ▸ noun [mass noun] US a dish of maize and lima beans boiled together.
– ORIGIN mid 18th cent.: from Narragansett *msiquatash* (plural).

Succoth /sʊˈkəʊt, ˈsʌkəθ/ (also **Sukkot, Sukkoth**) ▸ noun a major Jewish festival held in the autumn (beginning on the 15th day of Tishri) to commemorate the sheltering of the Israelites in the wilderness. It is marked by the erection of small booths covered in natural materials. Also called **FEAST OF TABERNACLES**.
– ORIGIN from Hebrew *sukkōṯ*, plural of *sukkāh* 'thicket, hut'.

succour /ˈsʌkə/ (US **succor**) ▸ noun [mass noun] assistance and support in times of hardship and distress. ■ (**succours**) archaic reinforcements of troops.
▸ verb [with obj.] give assistance or aid to: *prisoners of war were liberated and succoured*.
– DERIVATIVES **succourless** adjective.
– ORIGIN Middle English: via Old French from medieval Latin *succursus*, from Latin *succurrere* 'run to the help of', from *sub-* 'from below' + *currere* 'run'.

succubous /ˈsʌkjʊbəs/ ▸ adjective Botany (of a liverwort) having leaves obliquely inserted on the stem so that their upper edges are overlapped by the lower edges of the leaves above. Often contrasted with **INCUBOUS**.
– ORIGIN mid 19th cent.: from late Latin *succubare* 'lie under' + **-OUS**.

succubus /ˈsʌkjʊbəs/ ▸ noun (pl. **succubi** /-bʌɪ/) a female demon believed to have sexual intercourse with sleeping men.
– ORIGIN late Middle English: from medieval Latin *succubus* 'prostitute', from *succubare*, from *sub-* 'under' + *cubare* 'to lie'.

succulent ▸ adjective **1** (of food) tender, juicy, and tasty: *a succulent steak*.
2 Botany (of a plant, especially a xerophyte) having thick fleshy leaves or stems adapted to storing water.
▸ noun Botany a succulent plant.
– DERIVATIVES **succulence** noun, **succulently** adverb.
– ORIGIN early 17th cent.: from Latin *succulentus*, from *succus* 'juice'.

succumb ▸ verb [no obj.] fail to resist pressure, temptation, or some other negative force: *we cannot merely*

S

give up and succumb to despair. ■ die from the effect of a disease or injury.
– ORIGIN late 15th cent. (in the sense 'bring low, overwhelm'): from Old French *succomber* or Latin *succumbere*, from *sub-* 'under' + a verb related to *cubare* 'to lie'.

succursal /sə'kəːs(ə)l/ ▸ adjective (of a religious establishment such as a monastery) subsidiary to a principal establishment.
– ORIGIN mid 19th cent.: from French *succursale*, from medieval Latin *succursus*, from the verb *succurrere* (see SUCCOUR).

succuss /sə'kʌs/ ▸ verb [with obj.] (in preparing homeopathic remedies) shake (a solution) vigorously.
– DERIVATIVES **succussion** noun.
– ORIGIN mid 19th cent.: from Latin *succuss-* 'shaken', from the verb *succutere*, from *sub-* 'away' + *quatere* 'to shake'.

such ▸ determiner, predeterminer, & pronoun **1** of the type previously mentioned: *I have been involved in many such courses* | [as predeterminer] *I longed to find a kindred spirit, and in him I thought I had found such a person* | *we were second-class citizens and they treated us as* **such**.
2 (**such —— as/that**) of the type about to be mentioned: *there is no such thing as a free lunch* | [as predeterminer] *the farm is organized in such a way that it can be run by two adults* | *the wound was such that I had to have stitches.*
3 to so high a degree; so great (often used to emphasize a quality): *this material is of* **such** *importance* **that** *it has a powerful bearing on the case* | [as predeterminer] *autumn's such a beautiful season* | [as pronoun] **such** *is the elegance of his typeface* **that** *it is still a favourite of designers.*
– PHRASES **and such** and similar things: *he had activities like the scouts and Sunday school and such.* **as such** [often with negative] in the exact sense of the word: *it is possible to stay overnight here although there is no guest house as such.* **such-and-such** used to refer vaguely to a person or thing that does not need to be specified: *so many enterprises to be sold by such-and-such a date.* **such as 1** for example: *wild flowers such as mountain pansy and wild thyme.* **2** of a kind that; like: *an event such as we've shared.* **3** archaic those who: *such as alter in a moment, win not credit in a month.* **such as it is** (or **they are**) what little there is; for what it's worth: *the plot, such as it is, takes road movie form.* **such a one** such a person or thing: *what was the reward for* **such a one** *as Fox?* **such that** to the extent that: *the linking of sentences such that they constitute a narrative.*
– ORIGIN Old English *swilc, swylc*; related to Dutch *zulk*, German *solch*, from the Germanic bases of SO[1] and ALIKE.

suchlike ▸ pronoun things of the type mentioned: *carpets, old chairs, tables, and suchlike.*
▸ determiner of the type mentioned: *food, drink, clothing, and suchlike provisions.*

Suchou variant of SUZHOU.

Suchow /suː'tʃaʊ/ variant of XUZHOU.

suck ▸ verb **1** [with obj.] draw into the mouth by contracting the muscles of the lips and mouth to make a partial vacuum: *they suck mint juleps through straws* | *he* **sucked in** *air between sentences.* ■ hold (something) in the mouth and draw at it by contracting the lip and cheek muscles: *she sucked a mint* | [no obj.] *the child* **sucked on** *her thumb.* ■ draw fluid from (something) into the mouth by suction: *she sucked each segment of the orange carefully.* ■ [with obj. and adverbial of direction] draw in a specified direction by creating a vacuum: *he was sucked under the surface of the river.* ■ [no obj.] (of a pump) make a gurgling sound as a result of drawing air instead of water.
2 [with obj.] involve (someone) in something without their choosing: *I didn't want to be* **sucked into** *the role of dutiful daughter.*
3 [no obj.] N. Amer. informal be very bad or unpleasant: *I love your country but your weather sucks.* [by association with vulgar slang SUCKHOLE.]
▸ noun an act of sucking something. ■ the sound made by water retreating and drawing at something: *the soft suck of the sea against the sand.*
▸ exclamation (**sucks**) Brit. informal used to express derision and defiance: *sucks to them!*
– PHRASES **give suck** archaic give milk from the breast or teat; suckle. **suck someone dry** exhaust someone's physical, material, or emotional resources. **suck it and see** Brit. informal used to suggest that the only way to know if something will work or be suitable is to try it. **suck it up** US informal accept something unpleasant or difficult.
– PHRASAL VERBS **suck someone in** cheat or deceive someone: *we were sucked in by his charm and good looks.* **suck someone off** vulgar slang perform fellatio on someone. **suck up** informal behave obsequiously, especially for one's own advantage: *he has risen to where he is mainly by* **sucking up to** *the president.*
– ORIGIN Old English *sūcan* (verb), from an Indo-European imitative root; related to SOAK.

sucker ▸ noun **1** a person or thing that sucks, in particular: ■ a rubber cup that adheres to a surface by suction. ■ a flat or concave organ enabling an animal to cling to a surface by suction. ■ the piston of a suction pump. ■ a pipe through which liquid is drawn by suction.
2 informal a gullible or easily deceived person. ■ (**a sucker for**) a person especially susceptible to or fond of (a specified thing): *I always was a sucker for a good fairy tale.*
3 N. Amer. informal a thing or person not specified by name: *he's one strong sucker.*
4 Botany a shoot springing from the base of a tree or other plant, especially one arising from the root below ground level at some distance from the main stem or trunk. ■ a side shoot from an axillary bud, as in tomato plants or maize.
5 a freshwater fish with thick lips that are used to suck up food from the bottom, native to North America and Asia. ● Family Catostomidae: many genera and species.
6 N. Amer. informal a lollipop.
▸ verb **1** [no obj.] Botany (of a plant) produce suckers: *it spread rapidly after being left undisturbed to sucker.*
2 [with obj.] N. Amer. informal fool or trick (someone): *they got* **suckered into** *accepting responsibility.*

suckerfish ▸ noun (pl. **same** or **suckerfishes**) another term for REMORA.

sucker punch informal ▸ noun an unexpected punch or blow.
▸ verb (**sucker-punch**) [with obj.] hit (someone) with an unexpected punch or blow: *his father sucker-punched him and knocked him out.*

sucket spoon /'sʌkɪt/ (also **sucket fork**) ▸ noun a utensil for eating fruit, having a two-pronged fork at one end and a spoon at the other.
– ORIGIN late 15th cent.: *sucket*, alteration of obsolete *succate*, variant of *succade* 'sweetmeats', of unknown origin.

suckhole ▸ noun **1** US informal a whirlpool.
2 Canadian & Austral. vulgar slang a sycophant.
▸ verb [no obj.] Canadian & Austral. vulgar slang behave in a sycophantic way towards someone.

sucking ▸ adjective (of a child or animal) not yet weaned.

sucking disc ▸ noun Zoology an animal's sucker, especially one on the end of each tube foot of an echinoderm.

suckle ▸ verb [with obj.] feed (a baby or young animal) from the breast or teat: *a mother pig was suckling a huge litter.* ■ [no obj.] (of a baby or young animal) feed by sucking the breast or teat: *the infant's biological need to suckle.*
– ORIGIN late Middle English: probably a back-formation from SUCKLING.

suckler ▸ noun an unweaned animal, especially a calf. ■ a cow used to breed and suckle calves for beef.

Suckling, Sir John (1609–42), English poet, dramatist, and Royalist leader. His poems include 'Ballad upon a Wedding', published in the collection *Fragmenta Aurea* (1646).

suckling ▸ noun an unweaned child or animal: [as modifier] *roast suckling pig.*
– ORIGIN Middle English: from the verb SUCK + -LING.

suck-up ▸ noun N. Amer. informal a person who behaves obsequiously, especially for their own advantage.

sucky ▸ adjective (**suckier**, **suckiest**) N. Amer. informal
1 very bad or unpleasant: *her sucky state job.*
2 ingratiating and obsequious: *Tommy immediately put on his sucky expression.*

sucralfate /'s(j)uːkr(ə)lˌfeɪt/ ▸ noun [mass noun] Medicine a drug used in the treatment of gastric and duodenal ulcers. It is a complex of aluminium hydroxide and a sulphate derivative of sucrose.
– ORIGIN 1960s: blend of SUCROSE, ALUMINIUM, and *sulfate* (see SULPHATE).

sucralose /'s(j)uːkrələʊz/ ▸ noun [mass noun] a very sweet synthetic compound derived from sucrose and unable to be metabolized by the body, used as an artificial sweetener.
– ORIGIN 1970s: alteration of SUCROSE.

sucrase /'s(j)uːkreɪz/ ▸ noun another term for INVERTASE.

Sucre[1] /'suːkreɪ/ the legal capital and seat of the judiciary of Bolivia; pop. 274,576 (2009). It is situated in the Andes, at an altitude of 2,700 m (8,860 ft). Named Chuquisaca by the Spanish in 1539, the city was renamed in 1825 in honour of Antonio José de Sucre.

Sucre[2] /'suːkreɪ/, Antonio José de (1795–1830), Venezuelan revolutionary and statesman, President of Bolivia 1826–8. He served as Simón Bolívar's Chief of Staff, liberating Ecuador, Peru, and Bolivia from the Spanish, and was the first President of Bolivia.

sucre /'suːkreɪ/ ▸ noun the basic monetary unit of Ecuador until 2000, equal to 100 centavos.
– ORIGIN named after A. J. de *Sucre* (see SUCRE[2]).

sucrier /'s(j)uːkrɪeɪ/ ▸ noun a sugar bowl, typically one made of porcelain and with a cover.
– ORIGIN mid 19th cent.: French, from *sucre* 'sugar'.

sucrose /'s(j)uːkrəʊz, -əʊs/ ▸ noun [mass noun] Chemistry a compound which is the chief component of cane or beet sugar. ● A disaccharide containing glucose and fructose units; chem. formula: $C_{12}H_{22}O_{11}$.
– ORIGIN mid 19th cent.: from French *sucre* 'sugar' + -OSE[2].

suction ▸ noun [mass noun] the production of a partial vacuum by the removal of air in order to force fluid into a vacant space or procure adhesion.
▸ verb [with obj. and adverbial of direction] remove (something) using suction: *physicians used a tube to suction out the gallstones.*
– ORIGIN early 17th cent.: from late Latin *suctio(n-)*, from Latin *sugere* 'suck'.

suction pump ▸ noun a pump for drawing liquid through a pipe into a chamber emptied by a piston.

suctorial /sʌk'tɔːrɪəl/ ▸ adjective chiefly Zoology adapted for sucking (as, for example, the mouthparts of some insects). ■ (of an animal) having a sucker for feeding or adhering to something.
– DERIVATIVES **suctorially** adverb.
– ORIGIN mid 19th cent.: from modern Latin *suctorius* (from Latin *sugere* 'suck') + -AL.

Sudan /suː'dɑːn, -'dan/ **1** a country in NE Africa south of Egypt, with a coastline on the Red Sea; pop. 41,087,800 (est. 2009); languages, Arabic (official), Dinka, Hausa, and others; capital, Khartoum.

> Under Arab rule from the 13th century, Sudan was conquered by Egypt in 1820–2. It was separated from its northern neighbour by the Mahdist revolt of 1881–98 and administered after the reconquest of 1898 as an Anglo-Egyptian condominium. It became an independent republic in 1956, but has suffered severely as a result of protracted civil war between the Islamic government in the north and separatist forces in the south and west.

2 a vast region of North Africa, extending across the width of the continent from the southern edge of the Sahara to the tropical equatorial zone in the south.
– DERIVATIVES **Sudanese** /ˌsuːdə'niːz/ adjective & noun.
– ORIGIN from Arabic *sūdān*, literally 'country of the blacks'.

sudan grass ▸ noun [mass noun] a Sudanese sorghum cultivated for fodder in dry regions of the US. ● *Sorghum sudanense*, family Gramineae.

sudarium /s(j)uː'dɛːrɪəm/ ▸ noun (pl. **sudaria** /-rɪə/) (in the Roman Catholic Church) another term for VERONICA (sense 2).
– ORIGIN early 17th cent.: from Latin, literally 'napkin', from *sudor* 'sweat'.

sudatorium /ˌs(j)uːdə'tɔːrɪəm/ ▸ noun (pl. **sudatoria** /-rɪə/) a room, especially in ancient Roman times, used for hot-air or steam baths.
– ORIGIN Latin, neuter of *sudatorius*, from *sudare* 'to sweat'.

Sudbury /'sʌdb(ə)ri/ a city in SW central Ontario; pop. 157,857 (2006). It lies at the centre of Canada's largest mining region.

sudd /sʌd/ ▸ noun (**the sudd**) an area of floating vegetation in a stretch of the White Nile, thick enough to impede navigation.
– ORIGIN Arabic, literally 'obstruction'.

sudden ▸ adjective occurring or done quickly and unexpectedly or without warning: *a sudden bright flash.*
▸ adverb literary or informal suddenly: *sudden there swooped an eagle downward.*
– PHRASES **(all) of a sudden** suddenly: *I feel really tired all of a sudden.* **on a sudden** archaic way of saying ALL OF A SUDDEN.

S

– DERIVATIVES **suddenness** noun.
– ORIGIN Middle English: from Anglo-Norman French *sudein*, from an alteration of Latin *subitaneus*, from *subitus* 'sudden'.

sudden death ▸ noun [mass noun] informal a means of deciding the winner in a tied match, in which play continues and the winner is the first side or player to score: [as modifier] *a sudden-death play-off.*

sudden infant death syndrome ▸ noun technical term for COT DEATH.

suddenly ▸ adverb quickly and unexpectedly: *George II died suddenly | suddenly I heard a loud scream.*

Sudetenland /suːˈdeɪt(ə)nˌland/ an area in the north-west part of the Czech Republic, on the border with Germany. Allocated to Czechoslovakia after the First World War, it became an object of Nazi expansionist policies and was ceded to Germany as a result of the Munich Agreement of September 1938. In 1945 the area was returned to Czechoslovakia. Czech name **Sudety** /ˈsuːdɛtiː/.

sudoku /suːˈdəʊkuː, -ˈdɒ-/ ▸ noun a puzzle in which players insert the numbers one to nine into a grid consisting of nine squares subdivided into a further nine smaller squares in such a way that every number appears once in each horizontal line, vertical line, and square.
– ORIGIN early 21st cent.: from Japanese *sūdoku*, from *sū(ji)* 'number' + *doku(shin)* 'single status' after *sūji wa dokushin ni kagiru*, literally 'the numbers are restricted to single status', former name of the puzzle.

sudoriferous /ˌs(j)uːdəˈrɪf(ə)rəs/ ▸ adjective (of a gland) secreting sweat.
– ORIGIN late 16th cent. (in the sense 'sudorific'): from late Latin *sudorifer* (from Latin *sudor* 'sweat') + **-ous**.

sudorific /ˌs(j)uːdəˈrɪfɪk/ Medicine ▸ adjective relating to or causing sweating.
▸ noun a drug that induces sweating.
– ORIGIN early 17th cent.: from modern Latin *sudorificus*, from Latin *sudor* 'sweat'.

Sudra /ˈsuːdrə, ˈʃuːdrə/ ▸ noun a member of the worker caste, lowest of the four Hindu castes.
– ORIGIN from Sanskrit *śūdra*.

suds ▸ plural noun froth made from soap and water.
■ N. Amer. informal beer.
▸ verb [with obj.] chiefly N. Amer. lather, cover, or wash in soapy water: *Martha sudsed my back.* ■ [no obj.] form suds: *soft baby soap that sudsed.*
– DERIVATIVES **sudsy** adjective (**sudsier**, **sudsiest**).
– ORIGIN mid 19th cent.: of uncertain sense development but perhaps originally denoting the floodwater of the fens; compare with Middle Low German *sudde*, Middle Dutch *sudse* 'marsh, bog'; probably related to SEETHE.

sudser /ˈsʌdzə/ ▸ noun N. Amer. informal a soap opera.

sue ▸ verb (**sues**, **suing**, **sued**) **1** [with obj.] institute legal proceedings against (a person or institution), typically for redress: *she is to sue the baby's father* | [no obj.] *I sued for breach of contract.*
2 [no obj.] formal appeal formally to a person for something: *the rebels were forced to sue for peace.*
– DERIVATIVES **suable** adjective, **suer** noun.
– ORIGIN Middle English: from Anglo-Norman French *suer*, based on Latin *sequi* 'follow'. Early senses were very similar to those of the verb *follow*.

suede ▸ noun [mass noun] leather with the flesh side rubbed to make a velvety nap.
– ORIGIN mid 17th cent.: from French (*gants de*) *Suède* '(gloves of) Sweden'.

suedehead ▸ noun chiefly Brit. a young person of a subculture characterized by an appearance similar to that of skinheads but generally with slightly longer hair and smarter clothes.

suerte /ˈsweːteɪ/ ▸ noun an action or pass performed by a bullfighter. ■ each of the three stages of a bullfight.
– ORIGIN Spanish, literally 'chance, fate'.

suet /ˈs(j)uːɪt/ ▸ noun [mass noun] the hard white fat on the kidneys and loins of cattle, sheep, and other animals, used to make foods such as puddings, pastry, and mincemeat.
– DERIVATIVES **suety** adjective.
– ORIGIN Middle English: from Anglo-Norman French, from the synonymous word *su*, from Latin *sebum* 'tallow'.

Suetonius /swiːˈtəʊnɪəs/ (*c.*69–*c.*150 AD), Roman biographer and historian; full name *Gaius Suetonius Tranquillus*. His surviving works include *Lives of the Caesars*.

suet pudding ▸ noun a pudding of suet and flour, typically boiled or steamed.

Suez, Isthmus of /ˈsuːɪz/ an isthmus between the Mediterranean and the Red Sea, connecting Egypt and Africa to the Sinai peninsula and Asia. The port of Suez lies in the south. The isthmus is traversed by the Suez Canal.

Suez Canal a shipping canal connecting the Mediterranean at Port Said with the Red Sea. It was constructed between 1859 and 1869 by Ferdinand de Lesseps. From 1888 it was a neutral zone under British protection; its nationalization by Egypt in 1956 prompted the Suez crisis.

Suez crisis a short conflict following the nationalization of the Suez Canal by President Nasser of Egypt in 1956. Britain and France made a military alliance with Israel to regain control of the canal, but international criticism forced the withdrawal of forces.

suf- ▸ prefix variant spelling of SUB- assimilated before *f* (as in *suffocate*, *suffuse*).

suffer ▸ verb [with obj.] **1** experience or be subjected to (something bad or unpleasant): *he suffered intense pain* | [no obj.] *he'd suffered a great deal since his arrest.* ■ [no obj.] (**suffer from**) be affected by or subject to (an illness or ailment): *his daughter suffered from agoraphobia.* ■ [no obj.] become or appear worse in quality: *his relationship with Anne did suffer.* ■ [no obj.] archaic undergo martyrdom or execution.
2 archaic tolerate: *France will no longer suffer the existing government.* ■ [with obj. and infinitive] allow (someone) to do something: *my conscience would not suffer me to accept any more.*
– PHRASES **not suffer fools gladly** be impatient or intolerant towards people one regards as foolish or unintelligent. [with biblical allusion to 2 Cor. 11–19.]
– DERIVATIVES **sufferable** adjective, **sufferer** noun.
– ORIGIN Middle English: from Anglo-Norman French *suffrir*, from Latin *sufferre*, from *sub-* 'from below' + *ferre* 'to bear'.

sufferance ▸ noun [mass noun] **1** absence of objection rather than genuine approval; toleration: *Charles was only here **on sufferance**.* ■ Law the condition of the holder of an estate who continues to hold it after the title has ceased, without the express permission of the owner: *an estate at sufferance.* ■ archaic patient endurance.
2 archaic the suffering or undergoing of something bad or unpleasant.
– ORIGIN Middle English (in sense 2): from Anglo-Norman French *suffraunce*, from late Latin *sufferentia*, from *sufferre* (see SUFFER).

sufferation ▸ noun [mass noun] W. Indian unpleasant experiences; suffering: *our sufferation shall be no more.*

suffering ▸ noun [mass noun] the state of undergoing pain, distress, or hardship: *weapons that cause unnecessary suffering* | [count noun] *his disregard for the sufferings of his fellow countrymen.*

suffice /səˈfʌɪs/ ▸ verb [no obj.] be enough or adequate: *a quick look should suffice* | [with infinitive] *two examples should suffice to prove the contention.* ■ [with obj.] meet the needs of: *simple mediocrity cannot suffice them.*
– PHRASES **suffice (it) to say** used to indicate that one is saying enough to make one's meaning clear while withholding something for reasons of discretion or brevity: *suffice it to say that they were not considered suitable for this project.*
– ORIGIN Middle English: from Old French *suffis-*, stem of *suffire*, from Latin *sufficere* 'put under, meet the need of', from *sub-* 'under' + *facere* 'make'.

sufficiency ▸ noun (pl. **sufficiencies**) [mass noun] the condition or quality of being adequate or sufficient. ■ [in sing.] an adequate amount of something, especially of something essential: ***a sufficiency of** good food.* ■ archaic self-sufficiency or independence of character, especially of an arrogant or imperious sort.
– ORIGIN late 15th cent. (denoting sufficient means or wealth): from late Latin *sufficientia*, from the verb *sufficere* (see SUFFICE).

sufficient ▸ adjective & determiner enough; adequate: [as adj.] *he had a small private income which was sufficient for her needs* | [as determiner] *they had sufficient resources to survive.*
– DERIVATIVES **sufficiently** adverb.
– ORIGIN Middle English (in the sense 'legally satisfactory'): from Old French, or from Latin *sufficient-* 'meeting the need of' (see SUFFICE).

sufficient reason ▸ noun [mass noun] Philosophy the principle (associated particularly with G.W. Leibniz) that all events must ultimately be explicable in terms of the reasons a divine being would have had for choosing one alternative rather than another.

suffix /ˈsʌfɪks/ ▸ noun **1** a morpheme added at the end of a word to form a derivative (e.g. *-ation*, *-fy*, *-ing*, *-itis*).
2 Mathematics another term for SUBSCRIPT.
▸ verb also /səˈfɪks/ [with obj.] append (something), especially as a suffix.
– DERIVATIVES **suffixation** noun.
– ORIGIN late 18th cent. (as a noun): from modern Latin *suffixum*, neuter past participle (used as a noun) of Latin *suffigere*, from *sub-* 'subordinately' + *figere* 'fasten'.

suffocate ▸ verb die or cause to die from lack of air or inability to breathe: [no obj.] *ten detainees suffocated in an airless police cell* | [with obj.] *she was suffocated by fumes from the boiler.* ■ have or cause to have difficulty in breathing: [no obj.] *he was suffocating, his head jammed up against the back of the sofa* | [with obj.] *you're suffocating me—I can scarcely breathe* | (as adj. **suffocating**) *the suffocating heat.* ■ feel or cause to feel trapped and oppressed: (as adj. **suffocated**) *I felt suffocated by London.*
– DERIVATIVES **suffocatingly** adverb, **suffocation** noun.
– ORIGIN late 15th cent. (earlier (late Middle English) as *suffocation*): from Latin *suffocat-* 'stifled', from the verb *suffocare*, from *sub-* 'below' + *fauces* 'throat'.

Suffolk[1] /ˈsʌfək/ a county of eastern England, on the coast of East Anglia; county town, Ipswich.

Suffolk[2] /ˈsʌfək/ (also **Suffolk sheep**) ▸ noun a sheep of a large black-faced breed with a short fleece.

Suffolk punch ▸ noun see PUNCH[4] (sense 2).

suffragan /ˈsʌfrəg(ə)n/ (also **suffragan bishop** or **bishop suffragan**) ▸ noun a bishop appointed to help a diocesan bishop. ■ a bishop in relation to his archbishop or metropolitan.
– ORIGIN late Middle English: from Anglo-Norman French and Old French, representing medieval Latin *suffraganeus* 'assistant (bishop)', from Latin *suffragium* (see SUFFRAGE).

suffrage /ˈsʌfrɪdʒ/ ▸ noun **1** [mass noun] the right to vote in political elections. ■ [count noun] archaic a vote given in assent to a proposal or in favour of the election of a particular person.
2 (usu. **suffrages**) (in the Book of Common Prayer) the intercessory petitions pronounced by a priest in the Litany. ■ a series of petitions pronounced by the priest with the responses of the congregation. ■ archaic intercessory prayers, especially those for the dead.
– ORIGIN late Middle English (in the sense 'intercessory prayers', also 'assistance'): from Latin *suffragium*, reinforced by French *suffrage*. The modern sense of 'right to vote' was originally US (dating from the late 18th cent.).

suffragette /ˌsʌfrəˈdʒɛt/ ▸ noun historical a woman seeking the right to vote through organized protest.

In the UK in the early 20th century the suffragettes initiated a campaign of demonstrations and militant action, under the leadership of the Pankhursts, after the repeated defeat of women's suffrage bills in Parliament. In 1918 they won the vote for women over the age of 30, and ten years later were given full equality with men in voting rights.

suffragi /sʊˈfrɑːgi/ ▸ noun (pl. **suffragis**) (in Arabic-speaking countries) a waiter or butler.
– ORIGIN via Egyptian from Turkish *sofracı*, based on Arabic *sufra* 'food'.

suffragist ▸ noun chiefly historical a person advocating the extension of suffrage, especially to women.
– DERIVATIVES **suffragism** noun.

suffuse /səˈfjuːz/ ▸ verb [with obj.] gradually spread through or over: *her cheeks were suffused with colour | the first half of the poem is suffused with idealism.*
– DERIVATIVES **suffusion** noun.
– ORIGIN late 16th cent.: from Latin *suffus-* 'poured into', from *sub-* 'below, from below' + *fundere* 'pour'.

Sufi /ˈsuːfi/ ▸ noun (pl. **Sufis**) a Muslim ascetic and mystic.
– DERIVATIVES **Sufic** adjective.
– ORIGIN mid 17th cent.: from Arabic *ṣūfī*, perhaps from *ṣūf* 'wool' (referring to the woollen garment worn).

S

Sufism ▶ **noun** [mass noun] the mystical system of the Sufis.

> Sufism is the esoteric dimension of the Islamic faith, the spiritual path to mystical union with God. A reaction against the strict formality of orthodox teaching, it reached its peak in the 13th century. There are many Sufi orders, the best known being the dervishes of Turkey.

sug /sʌg/ ▶ **verb** (**sugs, sugging, sugged**) [no obj.] informal sell or attempt to sell a product under the guise of conducting market research: *a market researcher claims the firm is sugging.*
– ORIGIN 1980s: acronym from *sell under the guise*.

sug- ▶ **prefix** variant spelling of **SUB-** assimilated before *g* (as in *suggest*).

sugan /ˈsuːg(ə)n/ ▶ **noun** Irish a straw rope. ■ (also **sugan chair**) a chair with a seat made from woven straw ropes.
– ORIGIN late 17th cent.: from Irish *súgán*.

sugar ▶ **noun 1** [mass noun] a sweet crystalline substance obtained from various plants, especially sugar cane and sugar beet, consisting essentially of sucrose, and used as a sweetener in food and drink. ■ [count noun] a lump or teaspoonful of sugar, used to sweeten tea or coffee: *I'll have mine black with two sugars.*
2 Biochemistry any of the class of soluble, crystalline, typically sweet-tasting carbohydrates found in living tissues and exemplified by glucose and sucrose.
3 informal, chiefly N. Amer. used as a term of endearment: *what's wrong, sugar?*
4 [as exclamation] informal used as a euphemism for 'shit'.
5 informal a narcotic drug, especially heroin or LSD.
▶ **verb** [with obj.] **1** sweeten, sprinkle, or coat with sugar: *Mother absent-mindedly sugared her tea* | (as adj. **sugared**) *sugared almonds.* ■ [no obj.] (usu. as noun **sugaring**) Entomology spread a mixture of sugar, treacle, beer, etc., on a tree trunk in order to catch moths.
2 make more agreeable or palatable: *the novel was preachy but sugared heavily with jokes.*
– PHRASES **sugar the pill** see **PILL**[1].
– DERIVATIVES **sugarless** adjective.
– ORIGIN Middle English: from Old French *sukere*, from Italian *zucchero*, probably via medieval Latin from Arabic *sukkar*.

sugar apple ▶ **noun** another term for **SWEETSOP**.

sugar bean ▶ **noun** a French bean of a reddish mottled variety widely eaten in South Africa.

sugar beet ▶ **noun** [mass noun] beet of a variety from which sugar is extracted. It provides an important alternative sugar source to cane, and the pulp which remains after processing is used as stockfeed.

sugarbird ▶ **noun 1** a southern African songbird with a long, fine bill and very long tail, feeding on nectar and insects. ● Genus *Promerops*, family Promeropidae (or Meliphagidae): two species.
2 W. Indian another term for **BANANAQUIT**.

sugar bush ▶ **noun 1** a plantation of sugar maples.
2 South African term for **PROTEA**.

sugar candy ▶ **noun** another term for **CANDY**.

sugar cane ▶ **noun** [mass noun] a perennial tropical grass with tall stout jointed stems from which sugar is extracted. The fibrous residue can be used as fuel, in fibreboard, and for a number of other purposes. ● Genus *Saccharum*, family Gramineae: several species, in particular *S. officinarum* and its hybrids.

sugar-coat ▶ **verb** [with obj.] **1** coat (an item of food) with sugar: (as adj. **sugar-coated**) *sugar-coated almonds.*
2 make superficially attractive or acceptable: *you won't see him sugar-coat the truth.* ■ make excessively sentimental: *the film-makers' proficiency is overpowered by their tendency to sugar-coat the material.*

sugarcraft ▶ **noun** [mass noun] the art of creating confectionery or cake decorations from sugar paste.

sugar cube ▶ **noun** a sugar lump.

sugar daddy ▶ **noun** informal a rich older man who lavishes gifts on a young woman in return for her company or sexual favours.

sugar glider ▶ **noun** a flying phalanger that feeds on wattle gum and eucalyptus sap, native to Australia, New Guinea, and Tasmania. ● *Petaurus breviceps*, family Petauridae.

sugar gum ▶ **noun** an Australian eucalyptus with sweet foliage which is attractive to cattle and sheep. ● Genus *Eucalyptus*, family Myrtaceae: several species, in particular *E. cladocalyx*.

sugaring ▶ **noun** [mass noun] **1** (also **sugaring off**) N. Amer. the boiling down of maple sap until it thickens into syrup or crystallizes into sugar.
2 a method of removing unwanted hair by applying a mixture of lemon juice, sugar, and water to the skin and then peeling it off together with the hair.

sugar kelp ▶ **noun** [mass noun] a large brown seaweed with a long crinkly blade-like frond that grows up to 3 m in length and young stems that are edible. ● *Lactaria saccharina*, class Phaeophyceae.

sugarloaf ▶ **noun** a conical moulded mass of sugar. ■ something of this shape: [as modifier] *a sugarloaf hat.*

Sugar Loaf Mountain a rocky peak situated to the north-east of Copacabana Beach, in Rio de Janeiro, Brazil. It rises to a height of 390 m (1,296 ft).

sugar lump ▶ **noun** Brit. a small cube of compacted sugar used for sweetening hot drinks.

sugar maple ▶ **noun** a North American maple, from the sap of which maple sugar and maple syrup are made. ● *Acer saccharum*, family Aceraceae.

sugar of lead ▶ **noun** [mass noun] Chemistry, dated lead acetate, a soluble white crystalline salt. ● Chem. formula: $Pb(CH_3CO_2)_2$.
– ORIGIN mid 17th cent.: so named because of its sweet taste.

sugarplum ▶ **noun** chiefly archaic a crystallized plum. ■ a small round sweet of flavoured boiled sugar.

sugar snap (also **sugar snap pea, sugar pea**) ▶ **noun** mangetout, especially of a variety with thicker and more rounded pods.

sugar soap ▶ **noun** [mass noun] Brit. an alkaline preparation containing washing soda and soap, used for cleaning surfaces or removing paint.

sugary ▶ **adjective 1** containing much sugar: *energy-restoring, sugary drinks.* ■ resembling or coated in sugar: *a sugary texture.*
2 excessively sentimental: *sugary romance.*
– DERIVATIVES **sugariness** noun.

suggest ▶ **verb 1** [reporting verb] put forward for consideration: [with clause] *I suggest that we wait a day or two* | [with direct speech] *'Maybe you ought to get an expert,' she suggested* | [with obj.] *Ruth suggested a holiday.*
2 [with obj.] cause one to think that (something) exists or is the case: *finds of lead coffins suggested a cemetery north of the river* | [with clause] *the temperature wasn't as tropical as the bright sunlight may have suggested.* ■ state or express indirectly: [with clause] *are you suggesting that I should ignore her?* | [with obj.] *the seduction scenes suggest his guilt and her loneliness.* ■ evoke: *the theatrical interpretation of weather and water almost suggests El Greco.* ■ (**suggest itself**) (of an idea) come into one's mind.
– DERIVATIVES **suggester** noun.
– ORIGIN early 16th cent.: from Latin *suggest-* 'suggested, prompted', from the verb *suggerere*, from *sub-* 'from below' + *gerere* 'bring'.

suggestible ▶ **adjective** open to suggestion; easily swayed: *a suggestible client would comply.*
– DERIVATIVES **suggestibility** noun.

suggestion ▶ **noun 1** an idea or plan put forward for consideration: *here are some **suggestions for** tackling the problem.* ■ [mass noun] the action of suggesting something: ***at my suggestion**, the museum held an exhibition of his work.*
2 something that implies or indicates a certain fact or situation: *there is no suggestion that he was involved in any wrongdoing.* ■ a slight indication of something: *there was a suggestion of a smile on his lips.*
3 [mass noun] the action of calling up an idea in someone's mind by associating it with other things: *the power of suggestion.* ■ Psychology the action of influencing a person to accept an idea, belief, or impulse uncritically, especially as a technique in hypnosis. ■ [count noun] Psychology a belief or impulse of this type.
– ORIGIN Middle English (in the sense 'an incitement to evil'): via Old French from Latin *suggestio(n-)*, from the verb *suggerere* (see **SUGGEST**).

suggestive ▶ **adjective** tending to suggest an idea: *there were various suggestive pieces of evidence.* ■ indicative or evocative: *flavours **suggestive of** coffee and blackberry.* ■ making someone think of sexual matters: *a suggestive remark.*
– DERIVATIVES **suggestively** adverb, **suggestiveness** noun.

suh /sʌ/ ▶ **noun** non-standard spelling of **SIR**, used in representing British dialect or southern US or black speech.

Suharto /suːˈhɑːtəʊ/, Raden (1921–2008), Indonesian statesman, President 1968–98.

Sui /sweɪ/ a dynasty which ruled in China AD 581–618 and reunified the country.

suicidal ▶ **adjective** deeply unhappy or depressed and likely to commit suicide: *far from being suicidal, he was clearly enjoying life.* ■ relating to or likely to lead to suicide: *I began to take her suicidal tendencies seriously.* ■ likely to have a disastrously damaging effect on oneself or one's interests: *a suicidal career move.*
– DERIVATIVES **suicidality** noun, **suicidally** adverb.

suicide /ˈs(j)uːɪsʌɪd/ ▶ **noun** [mass noun] the action of killing oneself intentionally: *he **committed suicide** at the age of forty* | [count noun] *drug-related suicides.* ■ [count noun] a person who commits suicide. ■ a course of action which is disastrously damaging to oneself or one's interests: *it would be political suicide to restrict criteria for unemployment benefit.* ■ [as modifier] relating to or denoting a military or terrorist operation carried out by people who do not expect to survive it: *a suicide bomber.*
▶ **verb** [no obj.] intentionally kill oneself: *she suicided in a very ugly manner.*
– ORIGIN mid 17th cent.: from modern Latin *suicida* 'act of suicide', *suicidium* 'person who commits suicide', from Latin *sui* 'of oneself' + *caedere* 'kill'.

suicide pact ▶ **noun** an agreement between two or more people to commit suicide together.

suicide squeeze ▶ **noun** Baseball an act of running for home by a runner on third base as the ball is pitched.

sui generis /ˌsuːiː ˈdʒɛn(ə)rɪs, suːʌɪ, ˈgɛn-/ ▶ **adjective** unique: *the sui generis nature of animals.*
– ORIGIN Latin, literally 'of its own kind'.

sui juris /ˈdʒʊərɪs, ˌsuːiː ˈdʒʊərɪs/ ▶ **adjective** Law of age; independent: *the beneficiaries are all sui juris.*
– ORIGIN Latin, literally 'of one's own right'.

suint /swɪnt/ ▶ **noun** [mass noun] a natural greasy substance in sheep's wool, from which lanolin is obtained.
– ORIGIN late 18th cent.: from French, from *suer* 'sweat'.

Suisse /swiːs, sHis/ French name for **SWITZERLAND**.

suit ▶ **noun 1** a set of outer clothes made of the same fabric and designed to be worn together, typically consisting of a jacket and trousers or a jacket and skirt. ■ a set of clothes to be worn for a particular activity: *a jogging suit.* ■ a complete set of pieces of armour for covering the whole body. ■ informal a high-ranking executive in an organization, typically one regarded as exercising influence in an impersonal way: *maybe now the suits in Washington will listen.*
2 any of the sets into which a pack of playing cards is divided (in conventional packs comprising spades, hearts, diamonds, and clubs).
3 a lawsuit.
4 the process of trying to win a woman's affection with a view to marriage: *he could not compete with John in Marian's eyes and his suit came to nothing.* ■ literary a petition or entreaty made to a person in authority.
5 a complete set of sails required for a ship or for a set of spars.
▶ **verb** [with obj.] **1** be convenient for or acceptable to: *what time would suit you?* | [no obj.] *the flat has two bedrooms—if it suits, you can have one of them.* ■ (**suit oneself**) [often in imperative] act entirely according to one's own wishes (often used to express the speaker's annoyance): *'I'm not going to help you.' 'Suit yourself.'.* ■ (**suit something to**) archaic adapt something to: *they took care to suit their answers to the questions put to them.*
2 enhance the features, figure, or character of (someone): *the dress didn't suit her.*
3 [no obj.] N. Amer. put on clothes, especially for a particular activity: *I **suited up** and entered the water.*
– PHRASES **suit the action to the word** carry out one's stated intentions. **suit someone's book** Brit. informal be convenient or acceptable to someone. **suit someone down to the ground** Brit. be extremely convenient or appropriate for someone.
– ORIGIN Middle English: from Anglo-Norman French *siwte*, from a feminine past participle of a Romance verb based on Latin *sequi* 'follow'. Early senses included 'attendance at a court' and 'legal process'; sense 1 of the noun and sense 2 of the noun derive from an earlier meaning 'set of things to be used together'. The verb sense 'make appropriate' dates from the late 16th cent.

suitable ▶ **adjective** right or appropriate for a particular person, purpose, or situation: *these toys are not **suitable for** children under five.*

– DERIVATIVES **suitability** noun, **suitableness** noun, **suitably** adverb.
– ORIGIN late 16th cent.: from the verb SUIT, on the pattern of *agreeable*.

suitcase ▶ noun a case with a handle and a hinged lid, used for carrying clothes and other personal possessions.

suite /swiːt/ ▶ noun **1** a set of rooms designated for one person's or family's use or for a particular purpose. ■ a set of furniture of the same design.
2 Music a set of instrumental compositions, originally in dance style, to be played in succession. ■ a set of selected pieces from an opera or musical, arranged to be played as one instrumental work.
3 a group of people in attendance on a monarch or other person of high rank.
4 Computing a set of programs with a uniform design and the ability to share data.
5 Geology a group of minerals, rocks, or fossils occurring together and characteristic of a location or period.
– ORIGIN late 17th cent.: from French, from Anglo-Norman French *siwte* (see SUIT).

suited ▶ adjective **1** [predic.] right or appropriate for a particular person, purpose, or situation: *the task is ideally **suited to** a computer* | *the job is **well suited** to your abilities and experience.*
2 [in combination] wearing a suit of clothes of a specified type, fabric, or colour: *a dark-suited man* | *sober-suited lawyers.*

suiting ▶ noun [mass noun] fabric of a suitable quality for making suits, trousers, jackets, and skirts. ■ suits collectively.

suitor /ˈs(j)uːtə/ ▶ noun **1** a man who pursues a relationship with a particular woman, with a view to marriage.
2 a prospective buyer of a business or corporation.
– ORIGIN late Middle English (in the sense 'member of a retinue'): from Anglo-Norman French *seutor*, from Latin *secutor*, from *sequi* 'follow'.

suk (also **sukh**) ▶ noun variant spelling of SOUK.

Sukarno /suːˈkɑːnəʊ/, Achmad (1901–70), Indonesian statesman, President 1945–67. He led the struggle for independence, which was formally granted in 1949, but lost power in the 1960s after having been implicated in the abortive communist coup of 1965.

Sukhotai /ˌsʊkəˈtʌɪ/ (also **Sukhothai**) a town in NW central Thailand; pop. 34,800 (est. 2009). It was formerly the capital of an independent state of the same name, which flourished from the mid 13th to the mid 14th centuries.

sukiyaki /ˌsʊkɪˈjaki, -ˈjɑːki/ ▶ noun [mass noun] a Japanese dish of sliced meat, especially beef, fried rapidly with vegetables and sauce.
– ORIGIN Japanese.

sukkah ▶ noun variant spelling of SUCCAH.

Sukkot (also **Sukkoth**) ▶ noun variant form of SUCCOTH.

Sukkur /ˈsʌkə/ a city in SE Pakistan, on the Indus River; pop. 476,800 (est. 2009). Nearby is the Sukkur Barrage, a dam constructed across the Indus which directs water through irrigation channels to a large area of the Indus valley.

Sukuma /sʊˈkuːmə, sʊˈkjuːmə/ ▶ noun (pl. **same** or **Sukumas**) **1** a member of a people inhabiting west central Tanzania.
2 [mass noun] the Bantu language of the Sukuma, related to Nyamwezi and having around 4 million speakers.
▶ adjective relating to the Sukuma or their language.
– ORIGIN a local name.

Sulawesi /ˌsʊləˈweɪsi/ a mountainous island in the Greater Sunda group in Indonesia, situated to the east of Borneo; chief town, Ujung Pandang. It is noted as the habitat of numerous endemic species. Former name CELEBES.

Sulaymaniyah /ˌsʊlɪməˈniːə/ (also **Sulaimaniya**) a town in NE Iraq, in the mountainous region of southern Kurdistan; pop. 759,500 (est. 2009). Full name AS SULAYMANIYAH.

sulcate /ˈsʌlkeɪt/ ▶ adjective Botany & Zoology marked with parallel grooves.
– ORIGIN mid 18th cent.: from Latin *sulcatus* 'furrowed', past participle of *sulcare*.

sulcus /ˈsʌlkəs/ ▶ noun (pl. **sulci** /-sʌɪ/) Anatomy a groove or furrow, especially one on the surface of the brain.
– ORIGIN mid 17th cent.: from Latin, 'furrow, wrinkle'.

Suleiman I /ˈsuːlɪmən, ˌsuːleɪˈmɑːn/ (also **Soliman** or **Solyman**) (c.1494–1566), sultan of the Ottoman Empire 1520–66; also known as **Suleiman the Magnificent** or **Suleiman the Lawgiver**. The Ottoman Empire reached its fullest extent under his rule.

sulfa- ▶ combining form US spelling of SULPHA-.

sulfate ▶ noun US spelling of SULPHATE.

sulfur etc. ▶ noun US spelling of SULPHUR etc.

sulk ▶ verb [no obj.] be silent, morose, and bad-tempered out of annoyance or disappointment: *he was sulking over the break-up of his band.*
▶ noun a period of sulking: *she was in a fit of **the sulks**.*
– DERIVATIVES **sulker** noun.
– ORIGIN late 18th cent.: perhaps a back-formation from SULKY.

sulky ▶ adjective (**sulkier**, **sulkiest**) morose, bad-tempered, and resentful; refusing to be cooperative or cheerful: *disappointment was making her sulky.* ■ expressing or suggesting gloom and bad temper: *she had a sultry, sulky mouth.*
▶ noun (pl. **sulkies**) a light two-wheeled horse-drawn vehicle for one person, used chiefly in trotting races.
– DERIVATIVES **sulkily** adverb, **sulkiness** noun.
– ORIGIN mid 18th cent.: perhaps from obsolete *sulke* 'hard to dispose of', of unknown origin.

sull /sʌl/ ▶ verb [no obj.] US dialect (of an animal) refuse to advance. ■ (of a person) become sullen, sulk. *don't sull up on me, let's get it aired.*
– ORIGIN mid 19th cent.: back-formation from SULLEN.

Sulla /ˈsʌlə/ (138–78 BC), Roman general and politician; full name *Lucius Cornelius Sulla Felix*. After a victorious campaign against Mithridates VI, Sulla invaded Italy in 83. He was elected dictator in 82 and implemented constitutional reforms in favour of the Senate.

sullage /ˈsʌlɪdʒ/ ▶ noun [mass noun] waste water from household sinks, showers, and baths, but not waste liquid or excreta from toilets. ■ archaic refuse, especially sewage.
– ORIGIN mid 16th cent.: perhaps from Anglo-Norman French *suillage*, from *suiller* 'to soil'.

sullen ▶ adjective bad-tempered and sulky: *a sullen pout.* ■ (of the sky) full of dark clouds: *a sullen sunless sky.*
▶ noun (**the sullens**) archaic a sulky or depressed mood.
– DERIVATIVES **sullenly** adverb, **sullenness** noun.
– ORIGIN Middle English (in the senses 'solitary, averse to company', and 'unusual'): from Anglo-Norman French *sulein*, from *sol* 'sole'.

Sullivan, Sir Arthur (Seymour) (1842–1900), English composer. His fame rests on the fourteen light operas which he wrote in collaboration with the librettist W. S. Gilbert.

sully /ˈsʌli/ ▶ verb (**sullies**, **sullying**, **sullied**) [with obj.] literary damage the purity or integrity of: *they were outraged that anyone should sully their good name.* ■ make dirty: *she wondered if she dared sully the gleaming sink.*
– ORIGIN late 16th cent.: perhaps from French *souiller* 'to soil'.

sulpha /ˈsʌlfə/ (US **sulfa**) ▶ noun [mass noun] [usu. as modifier] the sulphonamide family of drugs: *a succession of life saving sulpha drugs.*
– ORIGIN 1940s: abbreviation (see SULPHA-).

sulpha- (US **sulfa-**) ▶ combining form in names of drugs derived from sulphanilamide.
– ORIGIN abbreviation of SULPHANILAMIDE.

sulphadiazine /ˌsʌlfəˈdʌɪəziːn/ (US **sulfadiazine**) ▶ noun [mass noun] Medicine a sulphonamide antibiotic used to treat meningococcal meningitis.

sulphamate /ˈsʌlfəmeɪt/ (US **sulfamate**) ▶ noun Chemistry a salt or ester of sulphamic acid.

sulphamethoxazole /ˌsʌlfəmɪˈθɒksəzəʊl/ (US **sulfamethoxazole**) ▶ noun [mass noun] Medicine a sulphonamide antibiotic used to treat respiratory and urinary tract infections, and as a component of the preparation co-trimoxazole.

sulphamic acid /sʌlˈfamɪk/ (US **sulfamic acid**) ▶ noun [mass noun] Chemistry a strongly acid crystalline compound used in cleaning agents and to make weedkiller. ● Chem. formula: $HOSO_2NH_2$.
– ORIGIN mid 19th cent.: *sulphamic* from SULPHUR + AMIDE + -IC.

sulphanilamide /ˌsʌlfəˈnɪləmʌɪd/ (US **sulfanilamide**) ▶ noun Medicine a synthetic compound with antibacterial properties which is the basis of the sulphonamide drugs. ● Alternative name: ***p*-aminobenzenesulphonamide**; chem. formula: $(H_2N)C_6H_4(SO_2NH_2)$.
– ORIGIN 1930s: from *sulphanilic* (from SULPHUR + ANILINE + -IC) + AMIDE.

sulphapyridine /ˌsʌlfəˈpɪrɪdiːn/ (US **sulfapyridine**) ▶ noun [mass noun] Medicine a sulphonamide antibiotic used to treat some forms of dermatitis.

sulphasalazine /ˌsʌlfəˈsaləziːn/ (US **sulfasalazine**) ▶ noun [mass noun] Medicine a sulphonamide antibiotic used to treat ulcerative colitis and Crohn's disease.
– ORIGIN 1960s: from SULPHA- + *sal(icylic acid)* + AZINE.

sulphate /ˈsʌlfeɪt/ (US **sulfate**) ▶ noun Chemistry a salt or ester of sulphuric acid, containing the anion SO_4^{2-} or the divalent group $-OSO_2O-$.
– ORIGIN late 18th cent.: from French *sulfate*, from Latin *sulphur* (see SULPHUR).

sulphide /ˈsʌlfʌɪd/ (US **sulfide**) ▶ noun Chemistry a binary compound of sulphur with another element or group.

sulphite /ˈsʌlfʌɪt/ (US **sulfite**) ▶ noun Chemistry a salt of sulphurous acid, containing the anion SO_3^{2-}.
– ORIGIN late 18th cent.: from French *sulfite*, alteration of *sulfate* (see SULPHATE).

sulphonamide /sʌlˈfɒnəmʌɪd/ (US **sulfonamide**) ▶ noun Medicine any of a class of synthetic drugs, derived from sulphanilamide, which are able to prevent the multiplication of some pathogenic bacteria.
– ORIGIN late 19th cent.: from SULPHONE + AMIDE.

sulphonate /ˈsʌlfəneɪt/ (US **sulfonate**) Chemistry ▶ noun a salt or ester of a sulphonic acid.
▶ verb [with obj.] convert (a compound) into a sulphonate, typically by reaction with sulphuric acid.
– DERIVATIVES **sulphonation** noun.

sulphone /ˈsʌlfəʊn/ (US **sulfone**) ▶ noun Chemistry an organic compound containing a sulphonyl group linking two organic groups.
– ORIGIN late 19th cent.: from German *Sulfon*, from *Sulfur* (see SULPHUR).

sulphonic acid (US **sulfonic acid**) ▶ noun Chemistry an organic acid containing the group $-SO_2OH$.

sulphonyl /ˈsʌlfənʌɪl, -nɪl/ (US **sulfonyl**) ▶ noun [as modifier] Chemistry of or denoting a divalent radical, $-SO_2-$, derived from a sulphonic acid group.

sulphur (US & Chemistry **sulfur**) ▶ noun **1** [mass noun] the chemical element of atomic number 16, a yellow combustible non-metal. (Symbol: **S**) ■ the material of which hellfire and lightning were formerly believed to consist. ■ a pale greenish-yellow colour: [as modifier] *the bird's **sulphur-yellow** throat.*

Sulphur occurs in volcanic and sedimentary deposits, as well as being a constituent of many minerals and petroleum. It is normally a bright yellow crystalline solid, but several other allotropic forms can be made. Sulphur is an ingredient of gunpowder, and is used in making matches and as an antiseptic and fungicide.

2 an American butterfly with predominantly yellow wings that may bear darker patches. ● *Colias*, *Phoebis*, and other genera, family Pieridae.
▶ verb [with obj.] disinfect or fumigate with sulphur.
– DERIVATIVES **sulphury** adjective.
– ORIGIN Middle English: from Anglo-Norman French *sulfre*, from Latin *sulfur*, *sulphur*.

USAGE In general use the standard British spelling is **sulphur** and the standard US spelling is **sulfur**. In chemistry, however, the **-f-** spelling is now the standard form in all related words in the field in both British and US contexts.

sulphurated /ˈsʌlfjʊreɪtɪd/ (US **sulfurated**) ▶ adjective impregnated or treated with sulphur.

sulphur candle ▶ noun a candle containing sulphur, burnt to produce sulphur dioxide for fumigation.

sulphur dioxide ▶ noun [mass noun] Chemistry a colourless pungent toxic gas formed by burning sulphur in air. ● Chem. formula: SO_2.

sulphureous /sʌlˈfjʊərɪəs/ (US **sulfureous**) ▶ adjective of, like, or containing sulphur.
– ORIGIN early 16th cent.: from Latin *sulphureus* (from SULPHUR) + -OUS.

sulphuretted hydrogen /ˌsʌlfjʊˈretɪd/ (US **sulfuretted hydrogen**) ▶ noun Chemistry archaic term for HYDROGEN SULPHIDE.

sulphuric /sʌlˈfjʊərɪk/ (US **sulfuric**) ▶ adjective containing sulphur or sulphuric acid: *the sulphuric by-products of wood fires.*
– ORIGIN late 18th cent.: from French *sulfurique*, from Latin (as SULPHUR).

sulphuric acid ▶ noun [mass noun] a strong acid made by oxidizing solutions of sulphur dioxide and used in large quantities as an industrial and laboratory

S

reagent. The concentrated form is an oily, dense, corrosive liquid. ● Chem. formula: H_2SO_4.

sulphurized /ˈsʌlfjʊrʌɪzd/ (also **sulphurised**, US **sulfurized**) ▸ **adjective** another term for **SULPHURATED**.
– DERIVATIVES **sulphurization** /-ˈzeɪʃ(ə)n/ **noun**.

sulphurous /ˈsʌlf(ə)rəs/ (US **sulfurous**) ▸ **adjective** 1 (chiefly of vapour) containing or derived from sulphur: *wafts of sulphurous fumes*. ■ like sulphur in colour; pale yellow.
2 marked by anger or profanity: *a sulphurous glance*.
– ORIGIN late Middle English: from Latin *sulphurosus*, from *sulphur* (see **SULPHUR**).

sulphurous acid ▸ **noun** [mass noun] Chemistry an unstable weak acid formed when sulphur dioxide dissolves in water. It is used as a reducing and bleaching agent. ● Chem. formula: H_2SO_3.

sulphur spring ▸ **noun** a spring of which the water contains sulphur or its compounds.

Sulpician /sʌlˈpɪʃɪən, sʌlˈpɪʃ(ə)n/ ▸ **noun** a member of a congregation of secular Roman Catholic priests founded in 1642 by a priest of St Sulpice, Paris, mainly to train candidates for holy orders.
▸ **adjective** relating to or denoting the Sulpicians.

sultan ▸ **noun** 1 a Muslim sovereign. ■ (**the Sultan**) historical the sultan of Turkey.
2 a bird of a breed of white domestic chicken from Turkey.
– DERIVATIVES **sultanate** **noun**.
– ORIGIN mid 16th cent.: from French, or from medieval Latin *sultanus*, from Arabic *sulṭān* 'power, ruler'.

sultana ▸ **noun** 1 Brit. a small, light brown, seedless raisin used in foods such as puddings and cakes.
2 a wife or concubine of a sultan. ■ any other woman in a sultan's family.
– ORIGIN late 16th cent. (in sense 2): from Italian, feminine of *sultano* (see **SULTAN**). Sense 1 dates from the mid 19th cent.

sultry /ˈsʌltri/ ▸ **adjective** (**sultrier**, **sultriest**) 1 (of the air or weather) hot and humid.
2 (especially of a woman or her behaviour) displaying or suggesting a strongly sexual nature: *a sultry French au pair*.
– DERIVATIVES **sultrily** **adverb**, **sultriness** **noun**.
– ORIGIN late 16th cent.: from obsolete *sulter* 'swelter'.

sulu /ˈsuːluː/ ▸ **noun** (pl. **sulus**) a length of cotton or other light fabric wrapped about the body as a sarong, worn from the waist by men and full-length by women from the Melanesian Islands.
– ORIGIN Fijian.

Sulu Sea /ˈsuːluː/ a sea in the Malay Archipelago, encircled by the NE coast of Borneo and the western islands of the Philippines.

sum ▸ **noun** 1 a particular amount of money: *they could not afford such a sum*.
2 (**the sum of**) the total amount resulting from the addition of two or more numbers, amounts, or items: *the sum of two prime numbers*. ■ the total amount of something that exists: *the sum of his own knowledge*.
3 an arithmetical problem, especially at an elementary level.
▸ **verb** (**sums**, **summing**, **summed**) [with obj.] technical find the sum of (two or more amounts): *if we sum these equations we obtain X*.
– PHRASES **in sum** to sum up: *this interpretation does little, in sum, to add to our understanding*.
– PHRASAL VERBS **sum up** give a brief summary: *Gerard will open the debate and I will sum up*. ■ Law (of a judge) review the evidence at the end of a case and direct the jury regarding points of law. **sum someone/thing up** concisely describe of the nature or character of someone or something: *selfish—that summed her up*.
– ORIGIN Middle English: via Old French from Latin *summa* 'main part, sum total', feminine of *summus* 'highest'.

sumac /ˈs(j)uːmak, ˈʃuː-/ (also **sumach**) ▸ **noun** a shrub or small tree with compound leaves, reddish hairy fruits in conical clusters, and bright autumn colours. ● Genera *Rhus* and *Cotinus*, family Anacardiaceae: several species, including the Mediterranean *R. coriaria* and the North American **staghorn sumac** (*R. typhina*), often grown as an ornamental.
■ the fruits of the Mediterranean sumac, used as a spice, especially in Middle Eastern cuisine.
– ORIGIN Middle English (denoting the dried and ground leaves of *R. coriaria* used in tanning and dyeing): from Old French *sumac* or medieval Latin *sumac(h)*, from Arabic *summāq*.

Sumatra /sʊˈmɑːtrə/ a large island of Indonesia, situated to the south-west of the Malay Peninsula, from which it is separated by the Strait of Malacca; chief city, Medan.
– DERIVATIVES **Sumatran** **adjective & noun**.

Sumatran rhinoceros ▸ **noun** a rare hairy two-horned rhinoceros found in montane rainforests from Malaysia to Borneo. ● *Dicerorhinus sumatrensis*, family Rhinocerotidae.

Sumba /ˈsʊmbə/ an island of the Lesser Sunda group in Indonesia, lying to the south of the islands of Flores and Sumbawa; chief town, Waingapu. Also called **SANDALWOOD ISLAND**.

Sumbawa /sʊmˈbɑːwə/ an island in the Lesser Sunda group in Indonesia, situated between Lombok and Flores.

Sumer /ˈsuːmə/ an ancient region of SW Asia in present-day Iraq, comprising the southern part of Mesopotamia. From the 4th millennium BC it was the site of city-states which became part of ancient Babylonia.

Sumerian /sʊˈmɪərɪən, sjuː-/ ▸ **adjective** relating to Sumer, its ancient language, or the element it contributed to Babylonian civilization.
▸ **noun** 1 a member of the indigenous non-Semitic people of ancient Babylonia.
2 [mass noun] the Sumerian language.

> The Sumerians had the oldest known written language, whose relationship to any other language is unclear. Theirs is the first historically attested civilization and they invented cuneiform writing, the sexagesimal system of mathematics, and the sociopolitical institution of the city-state. Their art, literature, and theology had a profound influence long after their demise *c.*2000 BC.

Sumgait /sumgaˈjit/ Russian name for **SUMQAYIT**.

sumi /ˈsuːmi/ ▸ **noun** [mass noun] a type of black Japanese ink prepared in solid sticks and used for painting and writing.
– ORIGIN Japanese, literally 'ink, blacking'.

sumi-e /ˈsuːmɪeɪ/ ▸ **noun** [mass noun] Japanese ink painting using sumi.
– ORIGIN from **SUMI** + Japanese *e* 'painting'.

summa /ˈsʊmə, ˈsʌmə/ ▸ **noun** (pl. **summae** /-miː/) chiefly archaic a summary of a subject.
– ORIGIN early 18th cent.: from Latin, literally 'sum total' (a sense reflected in Middle English).

summa cum laude /ˌsʌmə kʌm ˈlɔːdiː, ˌsʊmə kʊm ˈlaʊdeɪ/ ▸ **adverb & adjective** chiefly N. Amer. with the highest distinction: [as adv.] *he graduated summa cum laude* | [as adj.] *three scientific degrees, all summa cum laude*.
– ORIGIN Latin, literally 'with highest praise'.

summand /ˈsʌmand/ ▸ **noun** Mathematics a quantity to be added to another.
– ORIGIN mid 19th cent.: from Latin *summandus* 'to be added', gerundive of *summare*.

summarily ▸ **adverb** in a summary manner; without the customary formalities: *she was summarily dismissed*.

summarize (also **summarise**) ▸ **verb** [with obj.] give a brief statement of the main points of (something): *these results can be summarized in the following table* | [no obj.] *to summarize, there are three main categories*.
– DERIVATIVES **summarization** **noun**, **summarizer** **noun**.

summary ▸ **noun** (pl. **summaries**) a brief statement or account of the main points of something: *a summary of Chapter Three*.
▸ **adjective** 1 not including needless details or formalities; brief: *summary financial statements*.
2 Law (of a judicial process) conducted without the customary legal formalities: *summary arrest*. ■ (of a conviction) made by a judge or magistrate without a jury.
– PHRASES **in summary** in short: *in summary, there is no clear case for one tax system compared to another*.
– DERIVATIVES **summariness** **noun**.
– ORIGIN late Middle English (as an adjective): from Latin *summarius*, from *summa* 'sum total' (see **SUM**).

summary jurisdiction ▸ **noun** [mass noun] Law the authority of a court to use summary proceedings and arrive at a judgement.

summary offence ▸ **noun** Law an offence within the scope of a summary court.

summat /ˈsʌmət/ ▸ **pronoun** N. English non-standard form of **SOMETHING**.

summation /sʌˈmeɪʃ(ə)n/ ▸ **noun** [mass noun] 1 the process of adding things together: *the summation of numbers of small pieces of evidence*. ■ [count noun] a sum total of things added together.
2 the process of summing something up: *these will need summation in a single document*. ■ [count noun] a summary.
– DERIVATIVES **summational** **adjective**, **summative** **adjective**.

summer¹ ▸ **noun** the warmest season of the year, in the northern hemisphere from June to August and in the southern hemisphere from December to February: *this plant flowers in late summer* | *a long hot summer* | [as modifier] *summer holidays* | figurative *the golden summer of her life*. ■ Astronomy the period from the summer solstice to the autumnal equinox. ■ (**summers**) literary years, especially of a person's age: *a girl of sixteen or seventeen summers*.
▸ **verb** [no obj., with adverbial of place] spend the summer in a particular place: *well over 100 birds summered there in 1976*. ■ [with obj.] pasture (cattle) for the summer.
– DERIVATIVES **summery** **adjective**.
– ORIGIN Old English *sumor*, of Germanic origin; related to Dutch *zomer*, German *Sommer*, also to Sanskrit *samā* 'year'.

summer² (also **summer tree**) ▸ **noun** a horizontal bearing beam, especially one supporting joists or rafters.
– ORIGIN Middle English: from Old French *somier* 'packhorse', from late Latin *sagmarius*, from Greek *sagma* 'packsaddle'.

summer camp ▸ **noun** (especially in North America) a camp providing recreational and sporting facilities for children during the summer holiday period.

summer cypress ▸ **noun** another term for **KOCHIA**.

summer house ▸ **noun** a small building in a garden, used for sitting in during fine weather.

summer lightning ▸ **noun** [mass noun] distant sheet lightning without audible thunder, typically occurring on a summer night.

Summer Palace a palace (now in ruins) of the former Chinese emperors near Beijing.

summer pudding ▸ **noun** [mass noun] Brit. a pudding of soft summer fruit encased in bread or sponge.

summersault ▸ **noun & verb** archaic spelling of **SOMERSAULT**.

summer sausage ▸ **noun** [mass noun] N. Amer. a type of hard dried and smoked sausage which is similar to salami in preparation and can be made in winter to keep until summer.

summer school ▸ **noun** a course of lectures held during school and university summer vacations, taken as part of an academic course or as an independent course of study for professional or personal purposes.

summer solstice ▸ **noun** the solstice at midsummer, at the time of the longest day, about 21 June in the northern hemisphere and 22 December in the southern hemisphere. ■ Astronomy the solstice in June.

summer squash ▸ **noun** a squash which is eaten before the seeds and rind have hardened and which does not keep. ● Cultivars of *Cucurbita pepo* var. *melopepo*, family Cucurbitaceae.

summer stock ▸ **noun** [mass noun] chiefly N. Amer. theatrical productions by a repertory company organized for the summer season, especially at holiday resorts.

summertime ▸ **noun** the season or period of summer: *in summertime trains run every ten minutes*.

summer time ▸ **noun** [mass noun] Brit. time as adjusted to achieve longer evening daylight in summer by setting clocks an hour ahead of the standard time. Compare with **DAYLIGHT SAVING TIME**.

summer tree ▸ **noun** see **SUMMER²**.

summer-weight ▸ **adjective** (of clothes) made of light fabric and therefore cool to wear.

summing-up ▸ **noun** a restatement of the main points of an argument, case, etc. ■ Law a judge's review of evidence at the end of a case, with a direction to the jury regarding points of law.

summit ▸ **noun** 1 the highest point of a hill or mountain. ■ the highest attainable level of achievement: *the dramas are considered to form one of the summits of world literature*.
2 a meeting between heads of government.
– ORIGIN late Middle English (in the general sense 'top part'): from Old French *somete*, from *som* 'top', from Latin *summum*, neuter of *summus* 'highest'.

S

summiteer ▸ noun **1** a participant in a meeting between heads of government.
2 a climber who has reached the summit of a mountain.

summon ▸ verb [with obj.] **1** order (someone) to be present: *a waiter was summoned.* ■ authoritatively call on (someone) to be present as a defendant or witness in a law court. ■ urgently demand (help): *she summoned medical assistance.* ■ call people to attend (a meeting): *he summoned a meeting of head delegates.*
2 make an effort to produce (a particular quality or reaction) from within oneself: *she managed to **summon up** a smile.* ■ (**summon something up**) call an image to mind: *names that summon up images of far-off places.*
– DERIVATIVES **summonable** adjective, **summoner** noun.
– ORIGIN Middle English: from Old French *somondre*, from Latin *summonere* 'give a hint', later 'call, summon', from *sub-* 'secretly' + *monere* 'warn'.

summons ▸ noun (pl. **summonses**) an order to appear before a judge or magistrate, or the writ containing such an order: *a summons for non-payment of a parking ticket.* ■ an authoritative or urgent call to someone to be present or to do something: [with infinitive] *they might receive a summons to fly to France next day.*
▸ verb [with obj.] chiefly Law serve (someone) with a summons: [with obj. and infinitive] *he has been summonsed to appear in court next month.*
– ORIGIN Middle English: from Old French *sumunse*, from an alteration of Latin *summonita*, feminine past participle of *summonere* (see SUMMON).

summum bonum /ˌsʊməm ˈbɒnəm, ˌsʌməm ˈbəʊnəm/ ▸ noun the highest good, especially as the ultimate goal according to which values and priorities are established in an ethical system.
– ORIGIN Latin.

sumo /ˈsuːməʊ/ ▸ noun (pl. **sumos**) [mass noun] a Japanese form of heavyweight wrestling, in which a wrestler wins a bout by forcing his opponent outside a marked circle or by making him touch the ground with any part of his body except the soles of his feet. ■ [count noun] a sumo wrestler.
– ORIGIN from Japanese *sūmo*.

sump ▸ noun **1** a hollow or depression in which liquid collects, especially one in the floor of a mine or cave. ■ a cesspool.
2 the base of an internal-combustion engine, which serves as a reservoir of oil for the lubrication system.
– ORIGIN Middle English (in the sense 'marsh'): from Middle Dutch or Low German *sump*, or (in the mining sense) from German *Sumpf*; related to SWAMP.

sumph /sʌmf/ ▸ noun Scottish a stupid or clumsy person.
– ORIGIN early 18th cent.: of unknown origin.

sumpter /ˈsʌm(p)tə/ ▸ noun archaic a pack animal.
– ORIGIN Middle English: from Old French *sommetier*, via late Latin from Greek *sagma*, *sagmat-* 'pack-saddle'; compare with SUMMER[2].

sumptuary /ˈsʌm(p)tjʊəri/ ▸ adjective [attrib.] chiefly historical relating to or denoting laws that limit private expenditure on food and personal items.
– ORIGIN early 17th cent.: from Latin *sumptuarius*, from *sumptus* 'cost, expenditure', from *sumere* 'take'.

sumptuous ▸ adjective splendid and expensive-looking: *the banquet was a sumptuous, luxurious meal.*
– DERIVATIVES **sumptuosity** noun, **sumptuously** adverb, **sumptuousness** noun.
– ORIGIN late Middle English (in the sense 'made or produced at great cost'): from Old French *somptueux*, from Latin *sumptuosus*, from *sumptus* 'expenditure' (see SUMPTUARY).

Sumqayit /ˌsʊmkɑːˈiːt/ an industrial city in eastern Azerbaijan, on the Caspian Sea; pop. 299,700 (est. 2008). Russian name **Sumgait**.

sum total ▸ noun another term for SUM (sense 2 of the noun).

Sumy /ˈsuːmi/ an industrial city in NE Ukraine, near the border with Russia; pop. 273,900 (est. 2009).

sun ▸ noun **1** (also **Sun**) the star round which the earth orbits. ■ any similar star in the universe, with or without planets.

> The sun is the central body of the solar system. It provides the light and energy that sustains life on earth, and its changing position relative to the earth's axis determines the terrestrial seasons. The sun is a star of a type known as a G2 dwarf, a sphere of hydrogen and helium 1.4 million km in diameter which obtains its energy from nuclear fusion reactions deep within its interior, where the temperature is about 15 million degrees. The surface is a little under 6,000°C.

2 [mass noun] (usu. **the sun**) the light or warmth received from the earth's sun: *we sat outside in the sun.* ■ literary a person or thing regarded as a source of glory, inspiration, etc.: *the rhetoric faded before the sun of reality.* ■ literary used with reference to someone's success or prosperity: *the sun of the Plantagenets went down in clouds.*
3 literary a day or a year: *after going so many suns without food, I was sleeping.*
▸ verb (**suns, sunning, sunned**) (**sun oneself**) sit or lie in the sun: *Buzz could see Clare sunning herself on the terrace below.* ■ [with obj.] expose (something) to the sun, especially to warm or dry it: *the birds are sunning their wings.*
– PHRASES **against the sun** Nautical against the direction of the sun's apparent movement (in the northern hemisphere); from right to left or anticlockwise. **catch the sun** see CATCH. **make hay while the sun shines** see HAY[1]. **on which the sun never sets** (of an empire) worldwide. [applied in the 17th cent. to the Spanish dominions, later to the British Empire.] **shoot the sun** Nautical ascertain the altitude of the sun with a sextant in order to determine one's latitude. **under the sun** on earth; in existence (used in expressions emphasizing the large number of something). *they exchanged views on every subject under the sun.* **with the sun** Nautical in the direction of the sun's apparent movement (in the northern hemisphere); from left to right or clockwise.
– DERIVATIVES **sunlike** adjective, **sunward** adjective & adverb, **sunwards** adverb.
– ORIGIN Old English *sunne*, of Germanic origin; related to Dutch *zon* and German *Sonne*, from an Indo-European root shared by Greek *hēlios* and Latin *sol*.

Sun. ▸ abbreviation Sunday.

sun-and-planet gear ▸ noun a system of gear-wheels consisting of a central wheel (a **sun gear** or **sun wheel**) around which one or more outer wheels (**planet gears** or **planet wheels**) travel.

sunbake ▸ verb [no obj.] Austral./NZ sunbathe.

sun-baked ▸ adjective (especially of the ground) dry and hard from exposure to the sun's heat.

sunbath ▸ noun a period of sunbathing: *an upstairs deck on which you could take a sunbath.*

sunbathe ▸ verb [no obj.] sit or lie in the sun, especially to tan the skin: (as noun **sunbathing**) *it was too hot for sunbathing.*
– DERIVATIVES **sunbather** noun.

sunbeam ▸ noun a ray of sunlight.

sun bear (also **Malayan sun bear**) ▸ noun a small, mainly nocturnal bear which has a brownish-black coat with a light-coloured mark on the chest, native to SE Asia. ● *Helarctos malayanus*, family Ursidae.

sunbed ▸ noun Brit. a lounger used for sunbathing. ■ an apparatus used for acquiring a tan, consisting of two banks of lamps between which one lies or stands.

sunbelt ▸ noun a strip of territory receiving a high amount of sunshine, especially the southern US from California to Florida.

sunbird ▸ noun a small, brightly coloured Old World songbird with a long downcurved bill, feeding on nectar and resembling a hummingbird (but not able to hover). ● Family Nectariniidae: four genera, in particular *Nectarinia*, and numerous species.

sunbittern ▸ noun a tropical American wading bird with a long bill, neck, and legs, having mainly greyish plumage but showing chestnut and orange on the wings when they are spread in display. ● *Eurypyga helias*, the only member of the family Eurypygidae.
– ORIGIN late 19th cent.: so named because the pattern on the spread wings resembles a sunset.

sunblind ▸ noun Brit. an awning erected over a window in sunny weather.

sunblock ▸ noun [mass noun] a cream or lotion for protecting the skin from the sun and preventing sunburn.

sun bonnet ▸ noun a child's close-fitting peaked cotton hat that protects the head and neck from the sun.

sunbow ▸ noun a spectrum of colours like a rainbow produced by the sun shining on spray.

sunburn ▸ noun [mass noun] reddening, inflammation, and, in severe cases, blistering and peeling of the skin caused by overexposure to the ultraviolet rays of the sun.
▸ verb (**sunburns, sunburning**, past and past participle **sunburned** or **sunburnt**) (**be** (or **get**) **sunburned**) suffer from sunburn: *most of us managed to get sunburnt.* ■ (as adj. **sunburned** or **sunburnt**) tanned; brown from exposure to the sun: *a handsome sunburned face.* ■ [no obj.] suffer from sunburn: *a complexion that sunburnt easily.*

sunburst ▸ noun a sudden brief appearance of the full sun from behind clouds. ■ a decoration or ornament resembling the sun and its rays: [as modifier] *a pair of sunburst diamond earrings.* ■ a pattern of irregular concentric bands of colour with the brightest at the centre.

suncream ▸ noun [mass noun] a creamy preparation spread over a person's skin to protect it from sunburn and often to promote a suntan.

sundae ▸ noun a dish of ice cream with added ingredients such as fruit, nuts, and syrup.
– ORIGIN late 19th cent. (originally US): perhaps an alteration of SUNDAY, either because the dish was made with ice cream left over from Sunday and sold cheaply on the Monday, or because it was sold only on Sundays, a practice devised (according to some accounts) to circumvent Sunday legislation.

Sunda Islands /ˈsʌndə/ a chain of islands in the south-western part of the Malay Archipelago, consisting of two groups: the **Greater Sunda Islands**, which include Sumatra, Java, Borneo, and Sulawesi, and the **Lesser Sunda Islands**, which lie to the east of Java and include Bali, Sumbawa, Flores, Sumba, and Timor.

sun dance ▸ noun a dance performed by North American Indians in honour of the sun.

Sundanese /ˌsʌndəˈniːz/ ▸ noun (pl. **same**) **1** a member of a mainly Muslim people of western Java.
2 [mass noun] the Indonesian language of the Sundanese, with around 25 million speakers.
▸ adjective relating to the Sundanese or their language.
– ORIGIN from Sundanese *Sunda*, the western part of Java, + -ESE.

Sundarbans /ˈsʊndəbʌnz/ a region of swampland in the Ganges delta, extending from the mouth of the River Hooghly in West Bengal to that of the Tetulia in Bangladesh.

Sunday ▸ noun the day of the week before Monday and following Saturday, observed by Christians as a day of rest and religious worship and (together with Saturday) forming part of the weekend: *they left town on Sunday | many people work on Sundays* | [as modifier] *Sunday evening.* ■ (**the Sundays**) Brit. informal the newspapers published each Sunday.
▸ adverb chiefly N. Amer. on Sunday: *the concert will be held Sunday.* ■ (**Sundays**) on Sundays; each Sunday: *the programme is repeated Sundays at 9 p.m.*
– ORIGIN Old English *Sunnandæg* 'day of the sun', translation of Latin *dies solis*; compare with Dutch *zondag* and German *Sonntag*.

Sunday best ▸ noun (**one's Sunday best**) a person's best clothes, worn on Sundays or special occasions.

Sunday driver ▸ noun a person perceived as driving in a slow and unskilful way.

Sunday lunch ▸ noun [mass noun] a large meal served in the middle of the day on Sunday, traditionally featuring roast meat.

Sunday observance ▸ noun [mass noun] the Christian principle of keeping Sunday as a day of rest and worship.

Sunday painter ▸ noun an amateur painter, especially one with little training.

Sunday punch ▸ noun informal, chiefly US a powerful or devastating punch or other attacking action.

Sunday school ▸ noun a class held on Sundays to teach children about Christianity or Judaism.

sun deck ▸ noun **1** the deck, or part of a deck, of a yacht or cruise ship that is open to the sky.
2 N. Amer. a terrace or balcony positioned to catch the sun.

sunder ▸ verb [with obj.] literary split apart: *a universe sundered ages ago in a divine war.*
– PHRASES **in sunder** apart or into pieces: *hew their bones in sunder!*
– ORIGIN late Old English *sundrian*; related to German *sondern*.

Sunderland an industrial city and metropolitan district in NE England, a port at the mouth of the River Wear; pop. 171,300 (est. 2009).

S

sundew ▶ **noun** a small carnivorous plant of boggy places, with rosettes of leaves that bear sticky glandular hairs for trapping insects, which are then digested. ● Genus *Drosera*, family Droseraceae: many species, including the common European *D. rotundifolia*.

sundial ▶ **noun 1** an instrument showing the time by the shadow of a pointer cast by the sun on to a plate marked with the hours of the day.
2 (also **sundial shell**) a mollusc with a flattened spiral shell that is typically patterned in shades of brown, living in tropical and subtropical seas. ● Family Architectonicidae, class Gastropoda.

sun disc ▶ **noun** (especially in ancient Egypt) a winged disc representing a sun god.

sun dog ▶ **noun** another term for **PARHELION**.

sundown ▶ **noun** chiefly N. Amer. the time in the evening when the sun disappears or daylight fades.

sundowner ▶ **noun 1** Brit. informal an alcoholic drink taken at sunset.
2 Austral./NZ informal, dated a tramp arriving at a sheep station in the evening under the pretence of seeking work, so as to obtain food and shelter.

sun-drenched ▶ **adjective** (of a place) receiving a great deal of sunlight: *the sun-drenched beaches of Southern California*.

sundress ▶ **noun** a light, loose, sleeveless dress, typically having a wide neckline and thin shoulder straps.

sundrops ▶ **noun** a day-flowering North American plant with yellow flowers, related to the evening primrose. ● Genera *Oenothera* and *Calylophus*, family Onagraceae.

sundry ▶ **adjective** [attrib.] of various kinds; several: *prawn and garlic vol-au-vents and sundry other delicacies*.
▶ **noun** (pl. **sundries**) **1** (**sundries**) various items not important enough to be mentioned individually: *a drugstore selling magazines, newspapers, and sundries*.
2 Cricket Australian term for **EXTRA**.
– ORIGIN Old English *syndrig* 'distinct, separate'; related to **SUNDER**.

sun-dry ▶ **verb** [with obj.] (usu. as adj. **sun-dried**) dry (something, especially food) in the sun, as opposed to using artificial heat: *sun-dried tomatoes*.

sunfast ▶ **adjective** US (of a dye or fabric) not prone to fade in sunlight.

sun filter ▶ **noun** another term for **SUNSCREEN**.

sunfish ▶ **noun** (pl. **same** or **sunfishes**) **1** a large deep-bodied marine fish of warm seas, with tall dorsal and anal fins near the rear of the body and a very short tail. Also called **MOLA**. ● Family Molidae: three genera and several species, in particular the very large **ocean sunfish** (*Mola mola*).
2 a nest-building freshwater fish that is native to North America and popular in aquaria, e.g. the pumpkinseed. ● Several genera and species in the family Centrarchidae (the **sunfish family**). This family also includes sporting fish such as the black basses, rock bass, bluegill, and crappies.

S

sunflower ▶ **noun** a tall North American plant of the daisy family, with very large golden-rayed flowers. Sunflowers are cultivated for their edible seeds, which are an important source of oil for cooking and margarine. ● *Helianthus annus*, family Compositae.

Sunflower State informal name for **KANSAS**.

Sung /sʊŋ/ variant spelling of **SONG**.

sung past participle of **SING**.

sungazer ▶ **noun** a burrowing colonial girdled lizard native to Africa, noted for apparently staring at the sun while basking. Also called **GIANT ZONURE**. ● *Cordylus giganteus*, family Cordylidae.

sun gear ▶ **noun** see **SUN-AND-PLANET GEAR**.

sunglasses ▶ **plural noun** glasses tinted to protect the eyes from sunlight or glare.

sun-grazing ▶ **adjective** Astronomy (of a comet) having an orbit which passes close to the sun.

sungrebe ▶ **noun** a grebe-like tropical American waterbird of the finfoot family, with a striped head and black-spotted yellow feet. ● *Heliornis fulica*, family Heliornithidae. Alternative name: **American finfoot**.

sun hat ▶ **noun** a broad-brimmed hat that protects the head and neck from the sun.

sun helmet ▶ **noun** chiefly historical a rigid hat made of cork or a similar material, worn in tropical climates.

suni /ˈsuːni/ ▶ **noun** a dark brown dwarf antelope native to southern Africa. ● *Neotragus moschatus*, family Bovidae.
– ORIGIN late 19th cent.: a local word.

sun in splendour ▶ **noun** Heraldry the sun as heraldically blazoned, depicted with rays and often a human face.

sunk past participle of **SINK**[1].

sunken ▶ **adjective 1** having sunk or been submerged in water: *the wreck of a sunken ship*.
2 at a lower level than the surrounding area: *a sunken garden*. ■ (of a person's eyes or cheeks) deeply recessed, especially as a result of illness, hunger, or stress: *her face was white, with sunken cheeks*.
– ORIGIN late Middle English: past participle of **SINK**[1].

sunk fence ▶ **noun** a ditch with one side formed by a wall or with a fence running along the bottom.

Sun King the nickname of Louis XIV of France (see **LOUIS**[1]).

sun-kissed ▶ **adjective** made warm or brown by the sun: *the sun-kissed resort of Acapulco* | *her sun-kissed shoulders*.

sunlamp ▶ **noun 1** a lamp emitting ultraviolet rays used as a substitute for sunlight, typically to produce an artificial suntan or in therapy.
2 a large lamp with a parabolic reflector used in film-making.

sunless ▶ **adjective** without any sun: *a sunless winter day*. ■ (of a place) receiving no sunlight: *the windowless, sunless headquarters*.

sunlight ▶ **noun** [mass noun] light from the sun: *a shaft of sunlight*.

sunlit ▶ **adjective** illuminated by direct light from the sun: *clear sunlit waters*.

sun lounge ▶ **noun** Brit. a room with large windows and sometimes a glass roof, designed to allow in a lot of sunlight.

sunlounger ▶ **noun** Brit. a lounger used for sunbathing.

Sunna /ˈsʊnə, ˈsʌnə/ ▶ **noun** the traditional portion of Muslim law based on Muhammad's words or acts, accepted (together with the Koran) as authoritative by Muslims and followed particularly by Sunni Muslims.
– ORIGIN Arabic, literally 'form, way, course, rule'.

Sunni /ˈsʊni, ˈsʌni/ ▶ **noun** (pl. **same** or **Sunnis**) [mass noun] one of the two main branches of Islam, commonly described as orthodox, and differing from Shia in its understanding of the Sunna and in its acceptance of the first three caliphs. Compare with **SHIA**. ■ [count noun] a Muslim who adheres to this branch of Islam.
– DERIVATIVES **Sunnite** adjective & noun.
– ORIGIN Arabic, literally 'custom, normative rule'.

sunnies ▶ **plural noun** Austral./NZ informal sunglasses.

sunny ▶ **adjective** (**sunnier**, **sunniest**) bright with sunlight: *a sunny day*. ■ (of a place) receiving much sunlight: *Seefeld is set high on a sunny plateau*. ■ (of a person or their temperament) cheery and bright: *he had a sunny disposition*.
– PHRASES **sunny side up** N. Amer. (of an egg) fried on one side only.
– DERIVATIVES **sunnily** adverb, **sunniness** noun.

sunray ▶ **noun** a ray of sunlight. ■ a radiating line or broadening stripe resembling a ray of the sun.

sunray pleats ▶ **plural noun** widening pleats radiating out from a skirt's waistband.

sunrise ▶ **noun** the time in the morning when the sun appears or full daylight arrives: *an hour before sunrise*. ■ the colours and light visible in the sky on an occasion of the sun's first appearance in the morning, considered as a view or spectacle: *a spectacular sunrise over the summit of the mountain*.

sunrise industry ▶ **noun** a new and growing industry, especially in electronics or telecommunications.

sunroof ▶ **noun** a panel in the roof of a car that can be opened for extra ventilation.

sunroom ▶ **noun** chiefly N. Amer. another term for **SUN LOUNGE**.

sun rose ▶ **noun** another term for **ROCK ROSE**.

sun scald ▶ **noun** [mass noun] damage to plant tissue, especially bark or fruit, caused by exposure to excessive sunlight.

sunscreen ▶ **noun** [mass noun] a cream or lotion rubbed on to the skin to protect it from the sun. ■ [count noun] an active ingredient of creams and lotions of this kind and other preparations for the skin.

sunset ▶ **noun** the time in the evening when the sun disappears or daylight fades: *sunset was still a couple of hours away*. ■ the colours and light visible in the sky on an occasion of the sun's disappearance in the evening, considered as a view or spectacle: *a blue and gold sunset*. ■ a period of decline, especially the last years of a person's life: *the sunset of his life*.

sunset industry ▶ **noun** an old and declining industry.

sunset provision ▶ **noun** N. Amer. a stipulation that an agency or programme be disbanded or terminated at the end of a fixed period unless it is formally renewed.

sunset shell ▶ **noun** a burrowing bivalve mollusc with a long oval shell which (in some kinds) is pinkish with ray-like markings. ● Genus *Gari*, family Psammobiidae (or Sanguinolariidae).

sunshade ▶ **noun** a parasol, awning, or other device giving protection from the sun.

sunshine ▶ **noun** [mass noun] **1** direct sunlight unbroken by cloud, especially over a comparatively large area: *we walked in the warm sunshine*. ■ cheerfulness; happiness: *their colourful music can bring a ray of sunshine*.
2 Brit. informal used as a friendly or sometimes threatening form of address: *hand it over, sunshine*.
– DERIVATIVES **sunshiny** adjective.

sunshine law ▶ **noun** US a law requiring certain proceedings of governmental agencies to be open or available to the public.

sunshine roof ▶ **noun** Brit. old-fashioned term for **SUNROOF**.

Sunshine State ▶ **noun** any of the states of New Mexico, South Dakota, California, and Florida.

sun sign ▶ **noun** Astrology another term for **BIRTH SIGN**.

sunspace ▶ **noun** N. Amer. a room or area in a building having a glass roof and walls and intended to maximize the power of the sun's rays.

sun spider ▶ **noun** a fast-moving predatory arachnid with a pair of massive vertical pincers (chelicerae). Sun spiders live chiefly in warm deserts; many are active by day, and some grow to a large size. ● Order Solifugae (or Solpugida).

sunspot ▶ **noun** Astronomy a spot or patch that appears from time to time on the sun's surface, appearing dark by contrast with its surroundings.

Sunspots are regions of lower surface temperature and are believed to form where loops in the sun's magnetic field intersect the surface; an individual spot may persist for several weeks. The number of sunspots on the solar surface fluctuates according to a regular cycle, with times of maximum sunspot activity recurring every eleven years.

sun squirrel ▶ **noun** an African tree squirrel that typically has a dark ringed tail, noted for basking in the sun, which often causes bleaching of the fur. ● Genus *Heliosciurus*, family Sciuridae: five species.

sunstar ▶ **noun** a widely distributed starfish with a large number of arms. ● Genus *Solaster*, class Asteroidea.

sunstone ▶ **noun** a chatoyant gem consisting of feldspar, with a red or gold lustre.

sunstroke ▶ **noun** [mass noun] heatstroke brought about by excessive exposure to the sun.

sunsuit ▶ **noun** a child's suit of clothes, typically consisting of shorts and top, worn in hot sunny weather.

suntan ▶ **noun** a golden-brown colouring of the skin caused by exposure to the sun: *he had acquired quite a suntan*.
▶ **verb** [with obj.] (usu. as adj. **suntanned**) expose to the sun in order to achieve a tan: *a suntanned face*.

suntrap ▶ **noun** Brit. a place sheltered from the wind and positioned to receive much sunshine.

sunup ▶ **noun** chiefly N. Amer. the time in the morning when the sun appears or full daylight arrives: *they worked from sunup to sundown*.

sun visor ▶ **noun** a small screen above a vehicle's windscreen, attached by a hinge so that it can be lowered to protect the occupants' eyes from bright sunlight.

sun wheel ▶ **noun** see **SUN-AND-PLANET GEAR**.

sunyata /ˈʃuːnjətɑː, ˈsuː-/ ▶ **noun** [mass noun] Buddhism the doctrine that phenomena are devoid of an immutable or determinate intrinsic nature. It is often regarded as a means of gaining an intuition of ultimate reality. Compare with **TATHATA**.
– ORIGIN from Sanskrit *śūnyatā* 'emptiness'.

Sun Yat-sen /ˌsʊn jatˈsɛn/ (also **Sun Yixian** /ˌsʊn jiːʃiːˈan/) (1866–1925), Chinese Kuomintang statesman, provisional President of the Republic of China 1911–12 and President of the Southern Chinese Republic 1923–5. He organized the Kuomintang force and played a vital part in the revolution of 1911 which overthrew the Manchu dynasty. Following opposition, however, he resigned as President to establish a secessionist government at Guangzhou.

Suomi /ˈsuɔmi/ Finnish name for **FINLAND**.

sup[1] ▶ **verb** (**sups, supping, supped**) [with obj.] dated or N. English take (drink or liquid food) by sips or spoonfuls: *she* ***supped up*** *her soup delightedly* | [no obj.] *he was supping straight from the bottle.*
▶ **noun** a sip of liquid: *he took another sup of wine.* ■ [mass noun] N. English & Irish alcoholic drink.
– ORIGIN Old English *sūpan* (verb), *sūpa* (noun), of Germanic origin; related to Dutch *zuipen*, German *saufen* 'to drink'.

sup[2] ▶ **verb** (**sups, supping, supped**) [no obj.] dated eat supper: *you'll* ***sup on*** *seafood delicacies.*
– PHRASES **he who sups with the devil should have a long spoon** proverb a person who has dealings with a dangerous or wily person should be cautious.
– ORIGIN Middle English: from Old French *super*, of Germanic origin; related to **SUP**[1].

sup- ▶ **prefix** variant spelling of **SUB-** assimilated before *p* (as in *suppurate*).

Supadriv /ˈsuːpədrʌɪv/ ▶ **noun** trademark a type of cross head screwdriver with extra ridges between the arms of the cross.

super ▶ **adjective 1** informal very good or pleasant; excellent: *Julie was a super girl* | [as exclamation] *You're both coming in? Super!*
2 (of a manufactured product) very good; superfine: *a super quality binder.*
3 Building, chiefly Brit. short for **SUPERFICIAL** (used in expressing quantities of material).
▶ **adverb** [as submodifier] informal especially; particularly: *he's been super understanding.*
▶ **noun** informal **1** a superintendent.
2 archaic an extra, unwanted, or unimportant person; a supernumerary. ■ theatrical slang, dated or N. Amer. an extra.
3 [mass noun] superphosphate.
4 [mass noun] superfine fabric or manufacture.
– ORIGIN mid 19th cent.: abbreviation.

super- ▶ **combining form** above; over; beyond: *superlunary* | *superstructure.* ■ to a great or extreme degree: *superabundant* | *supercool.* ■ extra large of its kind: *supercontinent.* ■ having greater influence, capacity, etc. than another of its kind: *superbike* | *superpower.* ■ of a higher kind (especially in names of classificatory divisions): *superfamily.*
– ORIGIN from Latin *super-*, from *super* 'above, beyond'.

superable /ˈsuːp(ə)rəb(ə)l/ ▶ **adjective** able to be overcome.
– ORIGIN early 17th cent.: from Latin *superabilis*, from *superare* 'overcome'.

superabound ▶ **verb** [no obj.] archaic be very or too abundant: *the capitalists do not need to combine when labour superabounds.*
– ORIGIN late Middle English (in the sense 'be more abundant'): from late Latin *superabundare* (see **SUPER-**, **ABOUND**).

superabundant ▶ **adjective** more formal or literary term for **OVER-ABUNDANT**.
– DERIVATIVES **superabundance** noun, **superabundantly** adverb.
– ORIGIN late Middle English (in the sense 'very plentiful'): from late Latin *superabundant-* 'abounding to excess', from the verb *superabundare*.

superacid ▶ **noun** Chemistry a solution of a strong acid in a very acidic (usually non-aqueous) solvent, functioning as a powerful protonating agent.
– DERIVATIVES **superacidity** noun.

superadd ▶ **verb** [with obj.] rare add (something) to what has already been added: (as adj. **superadded**) *the presence of superadded infection by bacteria.*
– ORIGIN late Middle English: from Latin *superaddere* (see **SUPER-**, **ADD**).

superadiabatic /ˌsuːpəreɪdɪəˈbatɪk, -adɪə-/ ▶ **adjective** chiefly Meteorology relating to or denoting a temperature gradient which is steeper than that occurring in adiabatic conditions.

superalloy ▶ **noun** an alloy capable of withstanding high temperatures, high stresses, and often highly oxidizing atmospheres.

superaltar ▶ **noun** a portable slab of stone consecrated for use where there is no consecrated altar.
– ORIGIN Middle English: from medieval Latin *superaltare*, from *super-* 'over' + late Latin *altar(e)* 'altar'.

superannuate /ˌsuːpəˈranjʊeɪt/ ▶ **verb** [with obj.] retire (someone) with a pension: *his pilot's licence was withdrawn and he was superannuated.*
– DERIVATIVES **superannuable** adjective.
– ORIGIN mid 17th cent.: back-formation from *superannuated*, from medieval Latin *superannuatus*, from Latin *super-* 'over' + *annus* 'year'.

superannuated /suːpəˈranjʊeɪtɪd/ ▶ **adjective 1** (of a post or employee) belonging to a superannuation scheme: *she is not superannuated and has no paid holiday.*
2 outdated or obsolete through age or new developments: *superannuated computing equipment* | *a superannuated hippy.*

superannuation ▶ **noun** [mass noun] [usu. as modifier] regular payment made into a fund by an employee towards a future pension: *a superannuation fund.* ■ a pension of this type paid to a retired person. ■ the process of superannuating an employee.

superb ▶ **adjective 1** very good; excellent: *a superb performance.*
2 impressively splendid: *the Bey of Tunis was building himself a superb mausoleum.* ■ used in names of birds with attractive or colourful plumage, e.g. **superb lyrebird**.
– DERIVATIVES **superbly** adverb, **superbness** noun.
– ORIGIN mid 16th cent. (in sense 2): from Latin *superbus* 'proud, magnificent'.

superbike ▶ **noun** a high-performance motorcycle.

Super Bowl ▶ **noun** (in the US) the National Football League championship game played annually between the champions of the National and the American Football Conferences.

superbug ▶ **noun 1** a bacterium that is useful in biotechnology, typically one that has been genetically engineered to enhance its usefulness for a particular purpose.
2 a strain of bacteria that has become resistant to antibiotic drugs. ■ an insect that is difficult to control or eradicate, especially because it has become immune to insecticides.

supercalender ▶ **verb** [with obj.] give a highly glazed finish to (paper) by calendering it more than calendered paper: (as adj. **supercalendered**) *a supercalendered art paper.*

supercar ▶ **noun** a high-performance sports car.

supercargo ▶ **noun** (pl. **supercargoes** or **supercargos**) a representative of the ship's owner on board a merchant ship, responsible for overseeing the cargo and its sale.
– ORIGIN late 17th cent.: alteration of earlier *supracargo*, from Spanish *sobrecargo*, from *sobre* 'over' + *cargo* 'cargo'.

supercede ▶ **verb** see **SUPERSEDE**.

USAGE The spelling **supercede** is generally regarded as an error: see **USAGE** at **SUPERSEDE**.

supercell ▶ **noun** Meteorology a large slow-moving area of updraught and downdraught which causes violent thunderstorms, heavy hail, and tornadoes.

supercharge ▶ **verb** [with obj.] (usu. as adj. **supercharged**) fit or design (an internal-combustion engine) with a supercharger: *a supercharged 3.8-litre V6.* ■ supply with extra energy or power: *a supercharged computer.* ■ (as adj. **supercharged**) having powerful emotional overtones or associations: *appeasement is one of those supercharged words, like terrorism and fascism.*

supercharger ▶ **noun** a device that increases the pressure of the fuel–air mixture in an internal-combustion engine, fitted in order to achieve greater efficiency.

superciliary /ˌsuːpəˈsɪlɪəri/ ▶ **adjective** Anatomy relating to the eyebrow or the region over the eye.
– ORIGIN mid 18th cent.: from Latin *supercilium* 'eyebrow' (from *super-* 'above' + *cilium* 'eyelid') + **-ARY**[1].

supercilious ▶ **adjective** behaving or looking as though one thinks one is superior to others: *a supercilious lady's maid.*
– DERIVATIVES **superciliously** adverb, **superciliousness** noun.
– ORIGIN early 16th cent.: from Latin *superciliosus* 'haughty', from *supercilium* 'eyebrow'.

superclass ▶ **noun** Biology a taxonomic category that ranks above class and below phylum.

supercluster ▶ **noun** Astronomy a cluster of galaxies which themselves occur as clusters.

supercoil Biochemistry ▶ **noun** another term for **SUPERHELIX**.
▶ **verb** [with obj.] form (a substance) into a superhelix: (as adj. **supercoiled**) *a supercoiled circular DNA molecule.*

supercollider ▶ **noun** Physics a collider in which superconducting magnets are used to accelerate particles to energies of millions of megavolts.

supercomputer ▶ **noun** a particularly powerful mainframe computer.
– DERIVATIVES **supercomputing** noun.

superconductivity ▶ **noun** [mass noun] Physics the property of zero electrical resistance in some substances at very low absolute temperatures.
– DERIVATIVES **superconduct** verb, **superconducting** adjective, **superconductive** adjective.

superconductor ▶ **noun** Physics a substance capable of becoming superconducting at sufficiently low temperatures. ■ a substance in the superconducting state.

superconscious ▶ **adjective** transcending human or normal consciousness: *the superconscious, universal mind of God.*
– DERIVATIVES **superconsciousness** noun.

supercontinent ▶ **noun** each of several large land masses (notably Pangaea, Gondwana, and Laurasia) thought to have divided to form the present continents in the geological past.

supercool ▶ **verb** [with obj.] Chemistry cool (a liquid) below its freezing point without solidification or crystallization. ■ [no obj.] Biology (of a living organism) survive body temperatures below the freezing point of water.
▶ **adjective** informal extremely attractive, impressive, or calm: *the supercool tracks in this collection.*

supercritical ▶ **adjective** Physics above a critical threshold, in particular: ■ (in nuclear physics) containing or involving more than the critical mass. ■ (of a flow of fluid) faster than the speed at which waves travel in the fluid. ■ denoting an aerofoil or aircraft wing designed to tolerate shock-wave formation at transonic speeds. ■ relating to or denoting a fluid at a temperature and pressure greater than its critical temperature and pressure.

superdelegate ▶ **noun** US (in the Democratic Party) an unelected delegate who is free to support any candidate for the presidential nomination at the party's national convention.

super-duper ▶ **adjective** informal, humorous very good; marvellous: *a super-duper, plush touring bus.*

superego ▶ **noun** (pl. **superegos**) Psychoanalysis the part of a person's mind that acts as a self-critical conscience, reflecting social standards learned from parents and teachers. Compare with **EGO** and **ID**.

superelevation ▶ **noun** [mass noun] the amount by which the outer edge of a curve on a road or railway is banked above the inner edge.

supereminent ▶ **adjective** old-fashioned term for **PRE-EMINENT**.
– DERIVATIVES **supereminence** noun, **supereminently** adverb.
– ORIGIN mid 16th cent.: from Latin *supereminent-* 'rising above', from the verb *supereminere* 'rise above' (see **SUPER-**, **EMINENT**).

supererogation /ˌsuːpərɛrəˈɡeɪʃ(ə)n/ ▶ **noun** [mass noun] the performance of more work than duty requires.
– PHRASES **works of supererogation** (in the Roman Catholic Church) actions believed to form a reserve fund of merit that can be drawn on by prayer in favour of sinners.
– DERIVATIVES **supererogatory** /-ɪˈrɒɡət(ə)ri/ adjective.
– ORIGIN early 16th cent.: from late Latin *supererogatio(n-)*, from *supererogare* 'pay in addition', from *super-* 'over' + *erogare* 'pay out'.

superette ▶ **noun** US a small supermarket.
– ORIGIN 1930s: from **SUPERMARKET** + **-ETTE**.

superfamily ▶ **noun** (pl. **superfamilies**) Biology a taxonomic category that ranks above family and below order.

superfatted ▶ **adjective** (of soap) containing excess fats compared with its alkali content.

superfecundation /ˌsuːpəfɛk(ə)nˈdeɪʃ(ə)n, -fiːk-/ ▶ **noun** [mass noun] Medicine & Zoology fertilization of a second ovum during the same oestrus cycle as a result of a second mating, leading to fetuses of the same age but different parentage.

S

superfetation /ˌsuːpəfiːˈteɪʃ(ə)n/ ▶ noun [mass noun] Medicine & Zoology the occurrence of a second conception during pregnancy, giving rise to embryos of different ages in the uterus. ■ the accretion of one thing on another: *the superfetation of ideas*.
– ORIGIN early 17th cent.: from French *superfétation* or modern Latin *superfetatio(n-)*, from Latin *superfetare*, from *super-* 'above' + *fetus* 'fetus'.

superficial ▶ adjective 1 existing or occurring at or on the surface: *the building suffered only superficial damage*. ■ situated or occurring on the skin or immediately beneath it: *the superficial muscle groups*.
2 appearing to be true or real only until examined more closely: *the resemblance between the breeds is superficial*.
3 not thorough, deep, or complete; cursory: *he had only the most superficial knowledge of foreign countries*. ■ lacking depth of character or understanding: *perhaps I was a superficial person*.
4 Brit. Building denoting a quantity of a material expressed in terms of area covered rather than linear dimension or volume.
– DERIVATIVES **superficiality** /-ʃɪˈalɪti/ noun (pl. **superficialities**), **superficialness** noun.
– ORIGIN late Middle English: from late Latin *superficialis*, from Latin *superficies* (see SUPERFICIES).

superficially ▶ adverb 1 as to the outward appearance only; on the surface: [as submodifier] *the theory is superficially attractive* | [sentence adverb] *superficially, they have little in common*.
2 not thoroughly or deeply: *I understood the issue only superficially*.
3 at or on the surface or skin: *he was superficially wounded in the neck*.

superficies /ˌsuːpəˈfɪʃiːz/ ▶ noun (pl. **same**) archaic a surface: *the superficies of a sphere*. ■ literary an outward part or appearance: *the superficies of life*.
– ORIGIN mid 16th cent.: from Latin, from *super-* 'above' + *facies* 'face'.

superfine ▶ adjective 1 of especially high quality: *superfine cotton shirtings*.
2 (of fibres or an instrument) very thin: *superfine tweezers*. ■ consisting of especially small particles: *superfine face powder*.
– ORIGIN late 16th cent. (in the sense 'excessively elegant'): from SUPER- 'to a high degree' + FINE[1].

superfluidity ▶ noun [mass noun] Physics the property of flowing without friction or viscosity, as shown by liquid helium below about 2.18 kelvins.
– DERIVATIVES **superfluid** noun & adjective.

superfluity /ˌsuːpəˈfluːɪti/ ▶ noun (pl. **superfluities**) an unnecessarily or excessively large amount or number of something: ***a superfluity of** unoccupied time*. ■ an unnecessary thing: *they thought the garrison a superfluity*. ■ [mass noun] the state of being superfluous: *servants who had nothing to do but to display their own superfluity*.
– ORIGIN late Middle English: from Old French *superfluite*, from late Latin *superfluitas*, from Latin *superfluus* 'running over' (see SUPERFLUOUS).

superfluous /suːˈpəːflʊəs/ ▶ adjective unnecessary, especially through being more than enough: *the purchaser should avoid asking for superfluous information*.
– DERIVATIVES **superfluously** adverb, **superfluousness** noun.
– ORIGIN late Middle English: from Latin *superfluus*, from *super-* 'over' + *fluere* 'to flow'.

S

superfly US informal ▶ adjective (of clothing or a person's appearance) ostentatiously fashionable.
▶ noun (pl. **superflies**) an ostentatious, self-confident person.
– ORIGIN 1970s: the adjective from SUPER- + FLY[3]; the noun from the name of a character in the blaxploitation film *Superfly* (1972).

superfood ▶ noun a nutrient-rich food considered to be especially beneficial for health and well-being.

superfusion ▶ noun [mass noun] Physiology the technique of running a stream of liquid over the surface of a piece of suspended tissue, keeping it viable and allowing observation of the interchange of substances.

supergalaxy ▶ noun (pl. **supergalaxies**) another term for SUPERCLUSTER.

supergene[1] ▶ adjective Geology relating to or denoting the deposition or enrichment of mineral deposits by solutions moving downward through the rocks.
– ORIGIN early 20th cent.: from SUPER- + Greek *genēs* '-born, of a certain kind'.

supergene[2] ▶ noun Genetics a group of closely linked genes, typically having related functions.

supergiant ▶ noun Astronomy a very large star that is even brighter than a giant, often despite being relatively cool.

superglue ▶ noun a very strong quick-setting adhesive, based on cyanoacrylates or similar polymers.
▶ verb (**superglues**, **supergluing** or **superglueing**, **superglued**) [with obj.] stick with superglue: *he superglued his hands together*.

supergrass ▶ noun Brit. informal a police informer who implicates a large number of people.

supergravity ▶ noun [mass noun] Physics gravity as described or predicted by a supersymmetric quantum field theory.

supergroup ▶ noun an exceptionally successful rock group or one formed by musicians already famous from playing in other groups.

superheat Physics ▶ verb [with obj.] heat (a liquid) under pressure above its boiling point without vaporization. ■ heat (a vapour) above its temperature of saturation. ■ heat to a very high temperature.
▶ noun [mass noun] the excess of temperature of a vapour above its temperature of saturation.
– DERIVATIVES **superheater** noun.

superheavy ▶ adjective Physics relating to or denoting an element with an atomic mass or atomic number greater than those of the naturally occurring elements, especially one belonging to a group above atomic number 110 having proton/neutron ratios which in theory confer relatively long half-lives.

superheavyweight ▶ noun [mass noun] a weight above heavyweight in boxing and other sports. In the amateur boxing scale it begins at 91 kg. ■ [count noun] a superheavyweight boxer or other competitor.

superhelix ▶ noun (pl. **superhelices**) Biochemistry a helical structure formed from a number of protein or nucleic acid chains which are individually helical.
– DERIVATIVES **superhelical** adjective.

superhero ▶ noun (pl. **superheroes**) a benevolent fictional character with superhuman powers, such as Superman.

superhet ▶ noun informal short for SUPERHETERODYNE.

superheterodyne /ˌsuːpəˈhɛt(ə)rə(ʊ)dʌɪn/ ▶ adjective denoting or using a system of radio and television reception in which the receiver produces a tunable signal which is combined with the incoming signal to produce a predetermined intermediate frequency, on which most of the amplification is formed.
▶ noun a superheterodyne receiver.
– ORIGIN 1920s: from SUPERSONIC + HETERODYNE.

superhighway ▶ noun 1 N. Amer. a dual carriageway with controlled access.
2 (also **information superhighway**) an extensive electronic network such as the Internet, used for the rapid transfer of information such as sound, video, and graphics in digital form.

superhuman ▶ adjective having or showing exceptional ability or powers: *the pilot made one last superhuman effort not to come down right on our heads*.
– DERIVATIVES **superhumanly** adverb.
– ORIGIN mid 17th cent.: from late Latin *superhumanus* (see SUPER-, HUMAN).

superimpose ▶ verb [with obj.] place or lay (one thing) over another, typically so that both are still evident: *the number will appear on the screen, **superimposed on** a flashing button* | (as adj. **superimposed**) *different stone tools were found in superimposed layers*.
– DERIVATIVES **superimposable** adjective, **superimposition** noun.

superincumbent /ˌsuːp(ə)rɪnˈkʌmb(ə)nt/ ▶ adjective literary lying on something else: *the crushing effect of the superincumbent masonry*.

superinduce ▶ verb [with obj.] introduce or induce in addition.
– ORIGIN mid 16th cent.: from Latin *superinducere* 'cover over, bring from outside' (see SUPER-, INDUCE).

superinfection ▶ noun [mass noun] Medicine infection occurring after or on top of an earlier infection, especially following treatment with broad-spectrum antibiotics.

superintend ▶ verb [with obj.] be responsible for the management or arrangement of (an activity or organization); oversee: *he superintended a land reclamation scheme*.
– DERIVATIVES **superintendence** noun, **superintendency** noun.
– ORIGIN early 17th cent.: from ecclesiastical Latin *superintendere*, translating Greek *episkopein*.

superintendent ▶ noun a person who manages or superintends an organization or activity. ■ (in the UK) a police officer ranking above chief inspector. ■ (in the US) a high-ranking official, especially the chief of a police department. ■ N. Amer. the caretaker of a building.
– ORIGIN mid 16th cent.: from ecclesiastical Latin *superintendent-* 'overseeing', from the verb *superintendere* (see SUPERINTEND).

superior ▶ adjective 1 higher in rank, status, or quality: *a superior officer* | *the new model is **superior to** every other car on the road*. ■ of high standard or quality: *superior malt whiskies*. ■ greater in size or power: *deploying superior force*. ■ (**superior to**) above yielding to or being influenced by: *I felt superior to any accusation of anti-Semitism*.
2 having or showing an overly high opinion of oneself; conceited: *that girl was frightfully superior*.
3 (of a letter, figure, or symbol) written or printed above the line.
4 chiefly Anatomy further above or out; higher in position. ■ Botany (of the ovary of a flower) situated above the sepals and petals.
▶ noun 1 a person superior to another in rank or status, especially a colleague in a higher position: *obeying their superiors' orders*. ■ the head of a monastery or other religious institution.
2 Printing a superior letter, figure, or symbol.
– DERIVATIVES **superiorly** adverb.
– ORIGIN late Middle English: from Old French *superiour*, from Latin *superior*, comparative of *superus* 'that is above', from *super* 'above'.

Superior, Lake the largest of the five Great Lakes of North America, on the border between Canada and the US. With an area of 82,350 sq. km (31,800 sq. miles), it is the largest freshwater lake in the world.

superior conjunction ▶ noun Astronomy a conjunction of Mercury or Venus with the sun, when the planet and the earth are on opposite sides of the sun.

superior court ▶ noun Law 1 (in England) a higher court whose decisions have weight as precedents and which is not subject to control by any other court except by way of appeal.
2 (in some states of the US) a court of appeals or a court of general jurisdiction.

superiority ▶ noun [mass noun] 1 the state of being superior: *an attempt to establish **superiority over** others* | *the allies have achieved air superiority*.
2 a supercilious manner or attitude: *he attacked the media's smug superiority*.

superiority complex ▶ noun an attitude of superiority which conceals actual feelings of inferiority and failure.

superior planet ▶ noun Astronomy any of the planets Mars, Jupiter, Saturn, Uranus, and Neptune, whose orbits are further from the sun than the earth's.

superius /suːˈpɪərɪəs/ ▶ noun [mass noun] the highest voice part in early choral music; the cantus.
– ORIGIN late 18th cent.: from Latin, neuter (used as a noun) of *superior* (see SUPERIOR).

superjacent /ˌsuːpəˈdʒeɪs(ə)nt/ ▶ adjective technical lying over or above something else; overlying.
– ORIGIN late 16th cent.: from Latin *superjacent-*, from *super-* 'over' + *jacere* 'to lie'.

superlative /suːˈpəːlətɪv/ ▶ adjective 1 of the highest quality or degree: *a superlative piece of skill*.
2 Grammar (of an adjective or adverb) expressing the highest or a very high degree of a quality (e.g. *bravest*, *most fiercely*). Contrasted with POSITIVE and COMPARATIVE.
▶ noun 1 Grammar a superlative adjective or adverb. ■ (**the superlative**) the highest degree of comparison.
2 (usu. **superlatives**) an exaggerated or hyperbolical expression of praise: *the critics ran out of superlatives to describe him*.
– DERIVATIVES **superlatively** adverb [as submodifier] *he was superlatively fit*, **superlativeness** noun.
– ORIGIN late Middle English: from Old French *superlatif, -ive*, from late Latin *superlativus*, from Latin *superlatus* 'carried beyond', past participle of *superferre*.

superlattice ▶ noun Metallurgy & Physics an ordered arrangement of certain atoms in a solid solution which is superimposed on the solvent crystal lattice.

superluminal /ˌsuːpəˈluːmɪn(ə)l/ ▶ adjective Physics denoting or having a speed greater than that of light.
– ORIGIN 1950s: from SUPER- 'above' + Latin *lumen*, *lumin-* 'a light' + -AL.

superlunary /ˌsuːpəˈluːnəri/ ▶ **adjective** literary belonging to a higher world; celestial.
– ORIGIN early 17th cent.: from medieval Latin *superlunaris* (see SUPER-, LUNAR).

supermajority ▶ **noun** (pl. **supermajorities**) a number that is much more than half of a total, especially in a vote.

superman ▶ **noun** (pl. **supermen**) **1** another term for ÜBERMENSCH.
2 (**Superman**) a US cartoon character having great strength, the ability to fly, and other extraordinary powers. ■ (**a superman**) informal a man with exceptional physical or mental ability.
– ORIGIN early 20th cent.: from SUPER- 'exceptional' + MAN, coined by G. B. Shaw in imitation of German *Übermensch* (used by Nietzsche).

supermarket ▶ **noun** a large self-service shop selling foods and household goods.

supermassive ▶ **adjective** Astronomy having a mass many times (typically between 10^6 and 10^9 times) that of the sun: *a supermassive star.*

supermax ▶ **adjective** denoting or relating to an extremely high-security prison or part of a prison, intended for particularly dangerous prisoners.
▶ **noun** a supermax prison.
– ORIGIN 1970s: shortened from *super-maximum*, i.e. 'greater than the expected or conventional maximum'.

supermini ▶ **noun** (pl. **superminis**) **1** a type of small car with a relatively powerful engine.
2 a microcomputer with the capabilities of a mainframe.

supermodel ▶ **noun** a successful fashion model who has reached the status of a celebrity.

supermundane /ˌsuːpəˈmʌndeɪn/ ▶ **adjective** rare above or superior to the earth or worldly affairs.

supernal /suːˈpəːn(ə)l/ ▶ **adjective** chiefly literary relating to the sky or the heavens; celestial. ■ of exceptional quality or extent: *he is the supernal poet of our age* | *supernal erudition.*
– DERIVATIVES **supernally** adverb.
– ORIGIN late Middle English: from Old French, or from medieval Latin *supernalis*, from Latin *supernus*, from *super* 'above'.

supernatant /ˌsuːpəˈneɪt(ə)nt/ technical ▶ **adjective** denoting the liquid lying above a solid residue after crystallization, precipitation, centrifugation, or other process.
▶ **noun** a volume of supernatant liquid.

supernatural ▶ **adjective** (of a manifestation or event) attributed to some force beyond scientific understanding or the laws of nature: *a supernatural being.* ■ unnaturally or extraordinarily great: *a woman of supernatural beauty.*
▶ **noun** (**the supernatural**) manifestations or events considered to be of supernatural origin, such as ghosts.
– DERIVATIVES **supernaturalism** noun, **supernaturalist** noun, **supernaturally** adverb [as submodifier] *the monster was supernaturally strong.*

supernormal ▶ **adjective** exceeding or beyond the normal; exceptional: *a supernormal human.*
– DERIVATIVES **supernormality** noun.

supernova /ˌsuːpəˈnəʊvə/ ▶ **noun** (pl. **supernovae** /-viː/ or **supernovas**) Astronomy a star that suddenly increases greatly in brightness because of a catastrophic explosion that ejects most of its mass.

supernumerary /ˌsuːpəˈnjuːm(ə)r(ə)ri/ ▶ **adjective** present in excess of the normal or requisite number, in particular: ■ (of a person) not belonging to a regular staff but engaged for extra work. ■ not wanted or needed; redundant: *books were obviously supernumerary, and he began jettisoning them.* ■ (of an actor) appearing on stage but not speaking. ■ Botany & Zoology denoting a structure or organ occurring in addition to the normal ones: *a pair of supernumerary teats.*
▶ **noun** (pl. **supernumeraries**) a supernumerary person or thing.
– ORIGIN early 17th cent.: from late Latin *supernumerarius* '(soldier) added to a legion after it is complete', from Latin *super numerum* 'beyond the number'.

superorder ▶ **noun** Biology a taxonomic category that ranks above order and below class.

superordinate /ˌsuːpərˈɔːdɪnət/ ▶ **noun** **1** a thing that represents a superior order or category within a system of classification. ■ Linguistics a word whose meaning includes the meaning of one or more other words: *'bird' is the superordinate of 'canary'.*
2 a person of superior rank or status.
▶ **adjective** superior in rank or status: *senior staff's superordinate position.*
– ORIGIN early 17th cent.: from SUPER- 'above', on the pattern of *subordinate*.

superoxide ▶ **noun** Chemistry an oxide containing the anion O_2^-.

superphosphate ▶ **noun** [mass noun] a fertilizer made by treating phosphate rock with sulphuric or phosphoric acid.

superplastic Metallurgy ▶ **adjective** (of a metal or alloy) capable of extreme plastic extension under load.
▶ **noun** a superplastic metal or alloy.
– DERIVATIVES **superplasticity** noun.

superpose ▶ **verb** [with obj.] place (something) on or above something else, especially so that they coincide: (as adj. **superposed**) *a border of superposed triangles.*
– DERIVATIVES **superposition** noun.
– ORIGIN early 19th cent.: from French *superposer*, from *super-* 'above' + *poser* 'to place'.

superpower ▶ **noun** a very powerful and influential nation (used especially with reference to the US and the former Soviet Union when these were perceived as the two most powerful nations in the world).

supersaturate ▶ **verb** [with obj.] Chemistry increase the concentration of (a solution) beyond saturation point.
– DERIVATIVES **supersaturation** noun.

superscalar ▶ **adjective** Computing denoting a microprocessor architecture where several instructions are loaded at once and, as far as possible, are executed simultaneously, shortening the time taken to run the whole program.

superscribe ▶ **verb** [with obj.] write or print (an inscription) at the top of or on the outside of a document. ■ write or print (a letter, word, symbol, or line of writing or printing) above an existing letter, word, or line.
– DERIVATIVES **superscription** noun.
– ORIGIN late 15th cent.: from Latin *superscribere*, from *super-* 'over' + *scribere* 'write'.

superscript ▶ **adjective** (of a letter, figure, or symbol) written or printed above the line.
▶ **noun** a superscript letter, figure, or symbol.
– ORIGIN late 19th cent. (as an adjective): from Latin *superscriptus* 'written above', past participle of *superscribere*.

supersede /ˌsuːpəˈsiːd/ ▶ **verb** [with obj.] take the place of (a person or thing previously in authority or use); supplant: *the older models of car have now been superseded.*
– DERIVATIVES **supersession** noun.
– ORIGIN late 15th cent. (in the sense 'postpone, defer'): from Old French *superseder*, from Latin *supersedere* 'be superior to', from *super-* 'above' + *sedere* 'sit'. The current sense dates from the mid 17th cent.

> **USAGE** The standard spelling is **supersede** rather than **supercede**. The word is derived from the Latin verb *supersedere* but has been influenced by the presence of other words in English spelled with a **c**, such as **intercede** and **accede**. The **c** spelling is recorded as early as the 16th century; although still generally regarded as incorrect, it is now entered without comment in some modern dictionaries.

superset ▶ **noun** Mathematics a set which includes another set or sets.

supersize ▶ **adjective** larger than average or standard sizes; extremely large.
▶ **verb** [with obj.] (often as adj. **supersized**) greatly increase the size of: *supersized suitcases on wheels.*

supersonic ▶ **adjective** involving or denoting a speed greater than that of sound.
– DERIVATIVES **supersonically** adverb.

supersonics ▶ **plural noun** [treated as sing.] another term for ULTRASONICS.

superspace ▶ **noun** [mass noun] Physics a concept of space–time in which points are defined by more than four coordinates. ■ a space of infinitely many dimensions postulated to contain actual space–time and all possible spaces.

superspecies ▶ **noun** (pl. **same**) Biology a group of largely allopatric species which are descended from a common evolutionary ancestor and are closely related but too distinct to be regarded as subspecies of one species.

superstar ▶ **noun** an extremely famous and successful performer or sports player: *he became a superstar overnight* | [as modifier] *despite their superstar status the band refuse to change their lifestyle.*
– DERIVATIVES **superstardom** noun.

superstate ▶ **noun** a large and powerful state formed from a federation or union of nations: *we are not advocates of a European superstate.*

superstation ▶ **noun** N. Amer. a television station using satellite technology to broadcast over a very large area, especially an entire continent.

superstition ▶ **noun** [mass noun] excessively credulous belief in and reverence for the supernatural: *he dismissed the ghost stories as mere superstition.* ■ [count noun] a widely held but irrational belief in supernatural influences, especially as leading to good or bad luck, or a practice based on such a belief: *she touched her locket for luck, a superstition she'd had since childhood.*
– ORIGIN Middle English: from Old French, or from Latin *superstitio(n-)*, from *super-* 'over' + *stare* 'to stand' (perhaps from the notion of 'standing over' something in awe).

superstitious ▶ **adjective** having or showing a belief in superstitions: *many superstitious beliefs and practices are connected with sneezing.*
– DERIVATIVES **superstitiously** adverb, **superstitiousness** noun.

superstore ▶ **noun** a very large out-of-town supermarket.

superstratum /ˈsuːpəstrɑːtəm, -ˈstreɪtəm/ ▶ **noun** (pl. **superstrata** /-tə/) an overlying stratum.

superstring ▶ **noun** Physics a subatomic particle in a version of string theory that incorporates supersymmetry.

superstructure ▶ **noun** a structure built on top of something else. ■ the parts of a ship, other than masts and rigging, built above its hull and main deck. ■ the part of a building above its foundations. ■ a concept or idea based on others. ■ (in Marxist theory) the institutions and culture considered to result from or reflect the economic system underlying a society.
– DERIVATIVES **superstructural** adjective.

supersymmetry ▶ **noun** [mass noun] Physics a very general type of mathematical symmetry which relates fermions and bosons.
– DERIVATIVES **supersymmetric** adjective.

supertanker ▶ **noun** a very large oil tanker.

supertaster ▶ **noun** a person who has more taste buds than normal and is very sensitive to particular tastes.

supertax ▶ **noun** [mass noun] an additional tax on something already taxed.

supertitle ▶ **noun & verb** North American term for SURTITLE.

supertonic ▶ **noun** Music the second note of the diatonic scale of any key; the note above the tonic.

Super Tuesday ▶ **noun** US informal a day on which several states hold primary elections.

supertwist ▶ **adjective** denoting a type of liquid crystal display used in portable computers, in which to change state the plane of polarized light passing through the display is rotated by at least 180 degrees.

S

superunleaded ▶ **adjective** denoting unleaded petrol with a higher octane rating than that of regular unleaded petrol, achieved by the addition of aromatic hydrocarbons.
▶ **noun** [mass noun] superunleaded petrol.

superuser ▶ **noun** a user of a computer system with special privileges needed to administer and maintain the system; a system administrator.

supervene /ˌsuːpəˈviːn/ ▶ **verb** [no obj.] occur as an interruption or change to an existing situation: *he had appendicitis and as complications supervened, refrained from work for months* | (as adj. **supervening**) *any plan is liable to be disrupted by supervening events.* ■ Philosophy (of a fact or property) be entailed by or consequent on the existence or establishment of another: *the view that mental events supervene upon physical ones.*
– DERIVATIVES **supervenient** adjective, **supervention** noun.
– ORIGIN mid 17th cent.: from Latin *supervenire*, from *super-* 'in addition' + *venire* 'come'.

supervise ▶ **verb** [with obj.] observe and direct the execution of (a task or activity): *the sergeant left to supervise the loading of the lorries.* ■ observe and

direct the work of (someone): *nurses were supervised by a consultant psychiatrist.* ■ keep watch over (someone) in the interest of their or others' security: *the prisoners were supervised by two officers.*
– ORIGIN late 15th cent. (in the sense 'survey, peruse'): from medieval Latin *supervis-* 'surveyed, supervised', from *supervidere*, from *super-* 'over' + *videre* 'to see'.

supervision ▸ **noun** [mass noun] the action of supervising someone or something: *he was placed* ***under the supervision of*** *a probation officer.*

supervision order ▸ **noun** English Law a court order placing a child or young person under the supervision of a local authority or a probation officer in a case of delinquency or where care proceedings are appropriate.

supervisor ▸ **noun** a person who supervises a person or an activity. ■ a person who directs and oversees the work of a postgraduate research student.
– DERIVATIVES **supervisory** adjective.

supervoltage ▸ **noun** [usu. as modifier] Medicine a voltage in excess of 200 kV used in X-ray radiotherapy.

superweed ▸ **noun** a weed which is extremely resistant to herbicides, especially one created by the transfer of genes from genetically modified crops into wild plants.

superwoman ▸ **noun** (pl. **superwomen**) informal a woman with exceptional physical or mental ability, especially one who successfully manages a home, brings up children, and has a full-time job.

supinate /ˈsuːpɪneɪt/ ▸ **verb** [with obj.] Anatomy turn or hold (a hand, foot, or limb) so that the palm or sole is facing upwards or outwards: (as adj. **supinated**) *a supinated foot.* Compare with **PRONATE.** ■ [no obj.] walk or run with most of the weight on the outside of the feet.
– DERIVATIVES **supination** noun.
– ORIGIN mid 19th cent. (earlier (mid 17th cent.) as *supination*): back-formation from *supination*, from Latin *supinatio(n-)*, from *supinare* 'lay backwards', from *supinus* (see **SUPINE**).

supinator ▸ **noun** Anatomy **1** a muscle whose contraction produces or assists in the supination of a limb or part of a limb.
2 a person who supinates when walking or running.

supine /ˈsuːpʌɪn/ ▸ **adjective 1** (of a person) lying face upwards . ■ technical having the front or ventral part upwards. ■ (of the hand) with the palm upwards.
2 failing to act or protest as a result of moral weakness or indolence: *the government was supine in the face of racial injustice.*
▸ **noun** Grammar a Latin verbal noun used only in the accusative and ablative cases, especially to denote purpose (e.g. ***mirabile dictu*** 'wonderful to relate').
– DERIVATIVES **supinely** adverb, **supineness** noun.
– ORIGIN late Middle English: the adjective from Latin *supinus* 'bent backwards' (related to *super* 'above'); the noun from late Latin *supinum*, neuter of *supinus*.

supper ▸ **noun** an evening meal, typically a light or informal one: *we had a delicious cold supper* | [mass noun] *I was sent to bed without any supper.* ■ [with modifier] Scottish & N. English a meal consisting of the specified food with chips: *a fish supper.*
– PHRASES **sing for one's supper** earn a favour or benefit by providing a service in return: *the cruise lecturers are academics singing for their supper.*
– DERIVATIVES **supperless** adjective.
– ORIGIN Middle English: from Old French *super* 'to sup' (used as a noun) (see **SUP²**).

supper club ▸ **noun** a restaurant or nightclub serving suppers and usually providing entertainment.

supplant ▸ **verb** [with obj.] supersede and replace: *domestic production has been supplanted by imports and jobs have been lost.*
– DERIVATIVES **supplanter** noun.
– ORIGIN Middle English: from Old French *supplanter* or Latin *supplantare* 'trip up', from *sub-* 'from below' + *planta* 'sole'.

supple ▸ **adjective** (**suppler, supplest**) bending and moving easily and gracefully; flexible: *her supple fingers* | figurative *my mind is becoming more supple.* ■ not stiff or hard; easily manipulated: *this body oil leaves your skin feeling deliciously supple.*
▸ **verb** [with obj.] make more flexible.
– DERIVATIVES **supplely** (also **supply**) adverb, **suppleness** noun.
– ORIGIN Middle English: from Old French *souple*, from Latin *supplex, supplic-* 'submissive', from *sub-* 'under' + *placere* 'propitiate'.

supplejack ▸ **noun** any of a number of tropical and subtropical climbing plants with tough, supple stems: ● a tall North American climber (*Berchemia scandens*, family Rhamnaceae). ● a plant of the Caribbean and tropical America (*Paullinia plumieri*, family Sapindaceae). ● an Australasian plant (*Ripogonum scandens*, family Liliaceae).

supplement ▸ **noun 1** a thing added to something else in order to complete or enhance it: *the handout* ***is a supplement to*** *the official manual.* ■ a substance taken to remedy the deficiencies in a person's diet: *multivitamin supplements.* ■ a separate section, especially a colour magazine, added to a newspaper or periodical. ■ a sum of money paid to increase a person's income. ■ an additional charge payable for an extra service or facility: *the single room supplement is £2 per night.*
2 Geometry the amount by which an angle is less than 180°.
▸ **verb** [with obj.] add an extra element or amount to: *she took the job to supplement her husband's income.*
– DERIVATIVES **supplemental** adjective, **supplementally** adverb, **supplementation** noun.
– ORIGIN late Middle English: from Latin *supplementum*, from *supplere* 'fill up, complete' (see **SUPPLY¹**).

supplementary ▸ **adjective** completing or enhancing something: *the programme offers supplementary information about the news* | *the development of databases* ***supplementary to*** *existing ones.*
▸ **noun** (pl. **supplementaries**) a supplementary person or thing. ■ Brit. a question asked in parliament following the answer to a tabled one.
– DERIVATIVES **supplementarily** adverb.

supplementary angle ▸ **noun** Mathematics either of two angles whose sum is 180°.

supplementary benefit ▸ **noun** [mass noun] (in the UK) a weekly allowance formerly paid by the state to those with an income below a certain level, now replaced by **INCOME SUPPORT**.

suppletion /səˈpliːʃ(ə)n/ ▸ **noun** [mass noun] Linguistics the occurrence of an unrelated form to fill a gap in a conjugation (e.g. *went* as the past tense of *go*).
– DERIVATIVES **suppletive** adjective.
– ORIGIN Middle English: from Old French, from medieval Latin *suppletio(n-)*, from *supplere* 'fill up, make full' (see **SUPPLY¹**).

Supplex /ˈsʌplɛks/ ▸ **noun** [mass noun] trademark a synthetic stretchable fabric which is permeable to air and water vapour, used in sports and outdoor clothing.

suppliant /ˈsʌplɪənt/ ▸ **noun** a person making a humble or earnest plea to someone in power or authority.
▸ **adjective** making or expressing a plea, especially to someone in power or authority: *their faces were wary and suppliant.*
– DERIVATIVES **suppliantly** adverb.
– ORIGIN late Middle English (as a noun): from French, 'beseeching', present participle of *supplier*, from Latin *supplicare* (see **SUPPLICATE**).

supplicate /ˈsʌplɪkeɪt/ ▸ **verb** [no obj.] ask or beg for something earnestly or humbly: [with infinitive] *the plutocracy supplicated to be made peers.*
– DERIVATIVES **supplicant** adjective & noun, **supplicatory** adjective.
– ORIGIN late Middle English: from Latin *supplicat-* 'implored', from the verb *supplicare*, from *sub-* 'from below' + *placere* 'propitiate'.

supplication ▸ **noun** [mass noun] the action of asking or begging for something earnestly or humbly: *he fell to his knees in supplication.*

supply¹ /səˈplʌɪ/ ▸ **verb** (**supplies, supplying, supplied**) [with obj.] **1** make (something needed or wanted) available to someone; provide: *the farm supplies apples to cider makers.* ■ provide with something needed or wanted: *make sure the workers* ***are supplied with*** *enough building materials .* ■ be adequate to satisfy (a requirement or demand): *the two reservoirs supply about 1% of the city's needs.*
2 archaic take over (a vacant place or role): *when she died, no one could supply her place.*
▸ **noun** (pl. **supplies**) **1** a stock or amount of something supplied or available for use: *a farm with good water supply* | *the demand for tickets greatly exceeds the supply.* ■ [mass noun] the action of providing what is needed or wanted: *the deal involved the supply of forty fighter aircraft.* ■ [mass noun] Economics the amount of a good or service offered for sale. ■ (**supplies**) the provisions and equipment necessary for an army or for people engaged in a particular project or expedition. ■ [as modifier] providing necessary goods and equipment: *a supply ship.* ■ (**supplies**) Brit. a grant of money by Parliament for the costs of government.
2 [usu. as modifier] a person, especially a schoolteacher, acting as a temporary substitute for another.
– PHRASES **in short supply** not easily obtainable; scarce: *he meant to go, but time and petrol were in short supply.* **on supply** (of a schoolteacher) acting as a temporary substitute for another. **supply and demand** the amount of a commodity, product, or service available and the desire of buyers for it, considered as factors regulating its price: *by the law of supply and demand the cost of health care will plummet.*
– DERIVATIVES **supplier** noun.
– ORIGIN late Middle English: from Old French *soupleer*, from Latin *supplere* 'fill up', from *sub-* 'from below' + *plere* 'fill'. The early sense of the noun was 'assistance, relief' (chiefly a Scots use).

supply² /ˈsʌpli/ ▸ **adverb** variant spelling of **SUPPLELY** (see **SUPPLE**).

supply chain ▸ **noun** the sequence of processes involved in the production and distribution of a commodity.

supply-side ▸ **adjective** Economics denoting or relating to a policy designed to increase output and employment by changing the conditions under which goods and services are supplied, especially by measures which reduce government involvement in the economy and allow the free market to operate.
– DERIVATIVES **supply-sider** noun.

support ▸ **verb** [with obj.] **1** bear all or part of the weight of; hold up: *the dome was supported by a hundred white columns.*
2 give assistance to, especially financially: *the government gives £2,500 million a year to support the voluntary sector.* ■ provide with a home and the necessities of life: *my main concern was to support my family.* ■ give approval, comfort, or encouragement to: *the proposal was supported by many delegates.* ■ be actively interested in and concerned for the success of (a particular sports team). ■ (as adj. **supporting**) (of an actor or role) of secondary importance to the leading roles in a play or film. ■ (of a pop or rock group or performer) function as a secondary act to (another) at a concert.
3 suggest the truth of; corroborate: *the studies support our findings.*
4 produce enough food and water for; be capable of sustaining: *the land had lost its capacity to support life.*
5 endure; tolerate: *at work during the day I could support the grief.*
6 (of a computer or operating system) allow the use or operation of (a program, language, or device): *the new versions do not support the graphical user interface standard.*
▸ **noun 1** a thing that bears the weight of something or keeps it upright: *the best support for a camera is a tripod.* ■ [mass noun] the action of supporting something or someone or the state of being supported: *she clutched the sideboard for support.*
2 [mass noun] material assistance: *the bank provided unstinting financial support* | *air operations in support of British forces.* ■ approval, encouragement, or comfort: *the paper printed many letters in support of the government* | *she's been through a bad time and needs our support.* ■ technical help given to the user of a computer or other product.
3 [mass noun] evidence that serves to corroborate something: *the study provides support for both theories.*
4 a secondary act at a pop or rock concert: [as modifier] *a support band.*
– DERIVATIVES **supportability** noun, **supportable** adjective **supportless** adjective.
– ORIGIN Middle English (originally in the sense 'tolerate'): from Old French *supporter*, from Latin *supportare*, from *sub-* 'from below' + *portare* 'carry'.

supporter ▸ **noun 1** a person who approves of and encourages a public figure, political party, policy, etc.: *Labour supporters.* ■ a person who is actively interested in and wishes success for a particular sports team: *an Oxford United supporter.*
2 Heraldry a representation of an animal or other figure, typically one of a pair, holding up or standing beside an escutcheon.

supportive ▸ **adjective** providing encouragement or emotional help: *the staff are extremely supportive of each other.*

– DERIVATIVES **supportively** adverb, **supportiveness** noun.

supportive therapy ▸ noun [mass noun] treatment designed to improve, reinforce, or sustain a patient's physiological well-being or psychological self-esteem and self-reliance.

support price ▸ noun a minimum price guaranteed to a farmer for agricultural produce and maintained by subsidy or the buying in of surplus stock.

suppose ▸ verb **1** [with clause] think or assume that something is true or probable but lack proof or certain knowledge: *I suppose I got there about noon* | [with obj.] *he* **supposed** *the girl* **to be** *about twelve.* ▪ used to make a suggestion or a hesitant admission: [in imperative] *suppose we leave this to the police* | *I'm quite a good actress, I suppose.* ▪ used to introduce a hypothesis and imagine its development: *suppose he had been murdered—what then?* ▪ (of a theory or argument) assume or require that something is the case as a precondition: *the procedure supposes that a will has already been proved* | [with obj.] *the theory supposes a predisposition to interpret utterances.*
2 (**be supposed to do something**) be required to do something because of the position one is in or an agreement one has made: *I'm supposed to be meeting someone at the airport.* ▪ [with negative] be forbidden to do something: *I shouldn't have been in the study—I'm not supposed to go in there.*
– PHRASES **I suppose so** used to express hesitant agreement.
– DERIVATIVES **supposable** adjective.
– ORIGIN Middle English: from Old French *supposer*, from Latin *supponere* (from *sub-* 'from below' + *ponere* 'to place'), but influenced by Latin *suppositus* 'set under' and Old French *poser* 'to place'.

supposed ▸ adjective [attrib.] generally assumed or believed to be the case, but not necessarily so: *people admire their supposed industriousness.*

supposedly ▸ adverb [sentence adverb] according to what is generally assumed or believed (often used to indicate that the speaker doubts the truth of the statement): *the adverts are aimed at women, supposedly because they do the shopping.*

supposition ▸ noun a belief held without proof or certain knowledge; an assumption or hypothesis: *they were working on the supposition that his death was murder* | [mass noun] *their outrage was based on supposition and hearsay.*
– DERIVATIVES **suppositional** adjective.
– ORIGIN late Middle English (as a term in scholastic logic): from Old French, or from late Latin *suppositio(n-)* (translating Greek *hupothesis* 'hypothesis'), from the verb *supponere* (see **SUPPOSE**).

suppositious ▸ adjective based on assumption rather than fact: *most of the evidence is purely suppositious.*
– ORIGIN early 17th cent. (in the sense 'supposititious'): partly a contraction of **SUPPOSITITIOUS**, reinforced by **SUPPOSITION**.

supposititious /sə,pɒzɪ'tɪʃəs/ ▸ adjective substituted for the real thing; not genuine: *the supposititious heir to the throne.*
– DERIVATIVES **supposititiously** adverb.
– ORIGIN early 17th cent.: from Latin *supposititius* (from *supponere* 'to substitute') + **-ous**.

suppository ▸ noun (pl. **suppositories**) a solid medical preparation in a roughly conical or cylindrical shape, designed to be inserted into the rectum or vagina to dissolve.
– ORIGIN late Middle English: from medieval Latin *suppositorium*, neuter (used as a noun) of late Latin *suppositorius* 'placed underneath'.

suppress ▸ verb [with obj.] forcibly put an end to: *the rising was savagely suppressed.* ▪ prevent the development, action, or expression of (a feeling, impulse, idea, etc.); restrain: *she could not suppress a rising panic.* ▪ prevent the dissemination of (information): *the report had been suppressed.* ▪ prevent or inhibit (a process or reaction): *use of the drug suppressed the immune response.* ▪ partly or wholly eliminate (electrical interference). ▪ Psychoanalysis consciously inhibit (an unpleasant idea or memory) to avoid considering it.
– DERIVATIVES **suppressible** adjective, **suppressive** adjective, **suppressor** noun.
– ORIGIN late Middle English: from Latin *suppress-* 'pressed down', from the verb *supprimere*, from *sub-* 'down' + *premere* 'to press'.

suppressant ▸ noun a drug or other substance which acts to suppress or restrain something: *an appetite suppressant.*

suppression ▸ noun [mass noun] the action of suppressing something such as an activity or publication: *the heavy-handed suppression of political dissent.* ▪ Medicine stoppage or reduction of a discharge or secretion. ▪ Biology the absence or non-development of a part or organ that is normally present. ▪ Genetics the cancelling of the effect of one mutation by a second mutation. ▪ Psychology the restraint or repression of an idea, activity, or reaction by something more powerful. ▪ Psychoanalysis the conscious inhibition of unacceptable memories, impulses, or desires. ▪ prevention of electrical interference.

suppressor cell (also **suppressor T cell**) ▸ noun Physiology a lymphocyte which can suppress antibody production by other lymphoid cells.

suppurate /'sʌpjʊreɪt/ ▸ verb [no obj.] undergo the formation of pus; fester.
– DERIVATIVES **suppuration** noun, **suppurative** /-rətɪv/ adjective.
– ORIGIN late Middle English (in the sense 'cause to form pus'): based on Latin *sub-* 'below' + *pus, pur-* 'pus'.

supra /'su:prə/ ▸ adverb formal used in academic or legal texts to refer to someone or something mentioned above or earlier: *the recent work by McAuslan and others (supra).*
– ORIGIN Latin.

supra- /'su:prə/ ▸ prefix **1** above: *suprarenal.*
2 beyond; transcending: *supranational.*
– ORIGIN from Latin *supra* 'above, beyond, before in time'.

suprachiasmatic nucleus /,su:prə,kʌɪəz'matɪk/ ▸ noun Anatomy each of a pair of small nuclei in the hypothalamus of the brain, above the optic chiasma, thought to be concerned with the regulation of physiological circadian rhythms.

supramolecular ▸ adjective Biochemistry relating to or denoting structures composed of several or many molecules.

supramundane /su:prə'mʌndeɪn/ ▸ adjective transcending or superior to the physical world.

supranational ▸ adjective having power or influence that transcends national boundaries or governments: *supranational law.*
– DERIVATIVES **supranationalism** noun, **supranationality** noun.

supranuclear ▸ adjective Anatomy situated, occurring, or originating above a nucleus of the central nervous system.

supraoptic ▸ adjective Anatomy situated above the optic chiasma.

supraorbital ▸ adjective Anatomy situated above the orbit of the eye.

suprarenal ▸ adjective Anatomy another term for **ADRENAL**.

suprasegmental Linguistics ▸ adjective denoting a feature of an utterance other than the consonantal and vocalic components, for example (in English) stress and intonation.
▸ noun a suprasegmental feature.

supremacist ▸ noun an advocate of the supremacy of a particular group, especially one determined by race or sex: *a white supremacist.*
▸ adjective relating to or advocating such supremacy.
– DERIVATIVES **supremacism** noun.

supremacy /su:'prɛməsi/ ▸ noun [mass noun] the state or condition of being superior to all others in authority, power, or status: *the supremacy of the king.*

Supremacy, Act of (in English history) either of two Acts of Parliament of 1534 and 1559 (particularly the former), which established Henry VIII and Elizabeth I as supreme heads of the Church of England and excluded the authority of the Pope.

suprematism ▸ noun [mass noun] the Russian abstract art movement developed by Kazimir Malevich *c.*1915, characterized by simple geometrical shapes and associated with ideas of spiritual purity.
– DERIVATIVES **suprematist** noun.

supreme /su:'pri:m/ ▸ adjective **1** highest in rank or authority: *a unified force with a supreme commander.* ▪ most important or powerful: *on the race track he reigned supreme.*
2 very great or the greatest: *he was nerving himself for a supreme effort.* ▪ [postpositive] very good at or well known for a specified activity: *people expected the marathon runner supreme to win.* ▪ (of a penalty or sacrifice) involving death: *our comrades who made the supreme sacrifice.*
▸ noun (also **suprême** /su:'prɛm/) [mass noun] a rich cream sauce. ▪ a dish served in a supreme sauce: *chicken supreme.* [from French *suprême*.]
– PHRASES **the Supreme Being** a name for God.
– DERIVATIVES **supremely** adverb.
– ORIGIN late 15th cent. (in the sense 'highest'): from Latin *supremus*, superlative of *superus* 'that is above', from *super* 'above'.

supreme court ▸ noun the highest judicial court in a country or state. ▪ (in full **Supreme Court of the United Kingdom**) the final court of appeal in the UK for civil cases, which also hears appeals in criminal cases from England, Wales, and Northern Ireland. It was established in 2009 to take over the judicial functions of the House of Lords. ▪ (in full **US Supreme Court**) the highest federal court in the US, consisting of nine justices.

supreme pontiff ▸ noun see **PONTIFF**.

Supreme Soviet ▸ noun the governing council of the former Soviet Union or one of its constituent republics. That of the Soviet Union was its highest legislative authority and was composed of two equal chambers: the Soviet of Union and the Soviet of Nationalities.

supremo /su:'pri:məʊ/ ▸ noun (pl. **supremos**) Brit. informal a person in overall charge of an organization or activity: *the Channel Four supremo.* ▪ a person with great authority or skill in a certain area: *an interior by design supremo Kelly.*
– ORIGIN Spanish, literally 'supreme'.

supremum /su:'pri:məm/ ▸ noun Mathematics the smallest quantity that is greater than or equal to each of a given set or subset of quantities. The opposite of **INFIMUM**.
– ORIGIN 1940s: from Latin *supremum* 'highest part'.

Supt ▸ abbreviation Superintendent.

suq ▸ noun variant spelling of **SOUK**.

sur-[1] ▸ prefix equivalent to **SUPER-**.
– ORIGIN from French.

sur-[2] ▸ prefix variant spelling of **SUB-** assimilated before *r* (as in *surrogate*).

sura /'sʊərə/ (also **surah**) ▸ noun a chapter or section of the Koran.
– ORIGIN from Arabic *sūra*.

Surabaya /,sʊərə'bʌɪə/ a seaport in Indonesia, on the north coast of Java; pop. 2,336,800 (est. 2009). It is Indonesia's principal naval base and its second-largest city.

surah /'sʊərə/ ▸ noun [mass noun] a soft twilled silk fabric used in dressmaking.
– ORIGIN late 19th cent.: representing the French pronunciation of **SURAT**, where it was originally made.

surahi /sʊ'rɑ:hi/ ▸ noun (pl. **surahis**) an Indian clay pot with a long neck, used for storing water.
– ORIGIN via Urdu from Arabic *ṣurāḥiya* 'pure wine'.

sural /'sʊər(ə)l/ ▸ adjective Anatomy relating to the calf of the leg.
– ORIGIN early 17th cent.: from modern Latin *suralis*, from Latin *sura* 'calf'.

suramin /'sʊərəmɪn/ ▸ noun [mass noun] Medicine a synthetic compound derived from urea, used to treat trypanosomiasis, onchocerciasis, and filariasis.
– ORIGIN 1940s: of unknown origin.

Surat /'sʊərət, sʊ'rat/ a city in the state of Gujarat in western India, a port on the Tapti River near its mouth on the Gulf of Cambay; pop. 3,234,000 (est. 2009). It was the site of the first trading post of the East India Company, established in 1612.

surcease ▸ noun [mass noun] archaic or N. Amer. ending; cessation: *he teased us without surcease.* ▪ relief or consolation: *drugs are taken to provide surcease from intolerable psychic pain.*
▸ verb [no obj.] archaic stop; cease.
– ORIGIN late Middle English (as a verb): from Old French *sursis*, past participle of Old French *surseoir* 'refrain, delay', from Latin *supersedere* (see **SUPERSEDE**). The change in the ending was due to association with **CEASE**; the noun dates from the late 16th cent.

surcharge ▸ noun **1** an additional charge or payment: *we guarantee that no surcharges will be added to the cost of your holiday.* ▪ a charge made by assessors as a penalty for false returns of taxable property. ▪ Brit. an amount in an official account not passed by the auditor and having to be refunded by the person responsible. ▪ the showing of an omission in an account for which credit should have been given.
2 a mark printed on a postage stamp changing its value.

S

▸ **verb** [with obj.] **1** exact an additional charge or payment from: *retailers will be able to surcharge credit-card users.*
2 mark (a postage stamp) with a surcharge.
– ORIGIN late Middle English (as a verb): from Old French *surcharger* (see SUR-¹, CHARGE). The early sense of the noun (late 15th cent.) was 'excessive load'.

surcingle /ˈsəːsɪŋɡ(ə)l/ ▸ **noun** a wide strap which runs over the back and under the belly of a horse, used to keep a rug or other equipment in place.
– ORIGIN Middle English: from Old French *surcengle*, based on *cengle* 'girth', from Latin *cingula*, from *cingere* 'gird'.

surcoat /ˈsəːkəʊt/ ▸ **noun** historical a loose robe worn over armour. ■ a similar sleeveless garment worn as part of the insignia of an order of knighthood. ■ an outer coat of rich material.
– ORIGIN Middle English: from Old French *surcot*, from *sur* 'over' + *cot* 'coat'.

surd /səːd/ ▸ **adjective 1** Mathematics (of a number) irrational.
2 Phonetics (of a speech sound) uttered with the breath and not the voice (e.g. *f, k, p, s, t*).
▸ **noun 1** Mathematics a surd number, especially the irrational root of an integer.
2 Phonetics a surd consonant.
– ORIGIN mid 16th cent.: from Latin *surdus* 'deaf, mute'; as a mathematical term, translating Greek (Euclid) *alogos* 'irrational, speechless', apparently via Arabic *jiḏr aṣamm*, literally 'deaf root'. Sense 2 of the adjective dates from the mid 18th cent.

sure /ʃɔː, ʃʊə/ ▸ **adjective 1** [predic.] [often with clause] completely confident that one is right: *I'm sure I've seen that dress before | she had to check her diary to be sure of the day of the week.*
2 (**sure of/to do something**) certain to receive, get, or do something: *United are sure of a UEFA Cup place | it's sure to rain before morning.*
3 true beyond any doubt: *what is sure is that learning is a complex business.* ■ [attrib.] able to be relied on or trusted: *her neck was red—a sure sign of agitation.*
4 showing confidence or assurance: *the drawings impress by their sure sense of rhythm.*
▸ **adverb** informal, chiefly N. Amer. certainly (used for emphasis): *Texas sure was a great place to grow up.* ■ [as exclamation] used to show assent: *'Are you serious?' 'Sure.'*
– PHRASES **be sure** [usu. in imperative] do not fail (used to emphasize an instruction): [with infinitive] *be sure to pop in* | [with clause] *be sure that you know what is required.* **for sure** informal without doubt: *I can't say for sure what Giles really wanted.* **make sure** [usu. with clause] establish that something is definitely so; confirm: *go and make sure she's all right.* ■ ensure that something is done or happens: *he made sure that his sons were well educated.* (**as**) **sure as eggs is eggs** (also **as sure as fate**) without any doubt. **sure enough** informal used to introduce a statement that confirms something previously predicted: *when X-rays were taken, sure enough, there was the needle.* **sure of oneself** very confident of one's own abilities or views: *he's very sure of himself.* **sure thing** informal a certainty. ■ [as exclamation] chiefly N. Amer. certainly; of course: *'Can I watch?' 'Sure thing.'*. **to be sure** used to concede the truth of something that conflicts with another point that one wishes to make: *the ski runs are very limited, to be sure, but excellent for beginners.* ■ used for emphasis: *what an extraordinary woman she was, to be sure.*
– DERIVATIVES **sureness** noun.
– ORIGIN Middle English: from Old French *sur*, from Latin *securus* 'free from care'.

sure-fire ▸ **adjective** [attrib.] informal certain to succeed: *bad behaviour is a sure-fire way of getting attention.*

sure-footed ▸ **adjective** unlikely to stumble or slip: *tough, sure-footed hill ponies.* ■ confident and competent: *the challenges of the 1990s demand a responsible and sure-footed government.*
– DERIVATIVES **sure-footedly** adverb, **sure-footedness** noun.

surely ▸ **adverb 1** [sentence adverb] used to emphasize the speaker's firm belief that what they are saying is true and often their surprise that there is any doubt of this: *if there is no will, then surely the house goes automatically to you.* ■ without doubt; certainly: *if he did not heed the warning, he would surely die.* ■ [as exclamation] N. Amer. informal of course; yes: *'You'll wait for me?' 'Surely.'*.
2 with assurance or confidence: *no one knows how to move the economy quickly and surely in that direction.*

Sûreté /ˈsjʊəteɪ/, French /syʀte/ (also **Sûreté nationale** /ˌnasjəˈnɑːl/, French /nasjɔnal/) the French police department of criminal investigation.
– ORIGIN French, literally '(National) Security'.

surety /ˈʃʊərɪti, ˈʃʊəti/ ▸ **noun** (pl. **sureties**) **1** a person who takes responsibility for another's performance of an undertaking, for example their appearing in court or paying a debt. ■ money given to support an undertaking that someone will perform a duty, pay their debts, etc.; a guarantee: *the magistrate granted bail with a surety of £500.*
2 [mass noun] the state of being sure or certain of something: *the surety of my impending fatherhood.*
– PHRASES **of** (or **for**) **a surety** archaic for certain: *who can tell that for a surety?* **stand surety** become a surety; stand bail: *Alfonso agreed to stand surety for his friend's behaviour.*
– DERIVATIVES **suretyship** noun.
– ORIGIN Middle English (in the sense 'something given to support an undertaking that someone will fulfil an obligation'): from Old French *surte*, from Latin *securitas* (see SECURITY).

surf ▸ **noun 1** [mass noun] the mass or line of foam formed by waves breaking on a seashore or reef: *the roar of the surf.*
2 [in sing.] a spell of surfing: *he went for an early surf.*
▸ **verb 1** [no obj.] stand or lie on a surfboard and ride on the crest of a wave towards the shore: *he's learning to surf.* ■ [with obj.] ride (a wave) on a surfboard. ■ informal ride on the roof or outside of a fast-moving vehicle, typically a train, for excitement: *he fell to his death while surfing on a 70 mph train.*
2 [with obj.] move from site to site on (the Internet): *the device allows you to surf the Net and send emails.* ■ another term for CHANNEL-SURF.
– DERIVATIVES **surfer** noun, **surfy** adjective.
– ORIGIN late 17th cent.: apparently from obsolete *suff*, of unknown origin, perhaps influenced by the spelling of *surge*.

surface ▸ **noun 1** the outside part or uppermost layer of something: *the earth's surface | poor road surfaces.* ■ the level top of something: *roll out the dough on a floured surface.* ■ (also **surface area**) the area of such an outer part or uppermost layer: *the surface area of a cube.* ■ the upper limit of a body of liquid: *fish floating on the surface of the water.* ■ [in sing.] the outward appearance of someone or something, especially as distinct from less obvious aspects: *Tom was a womanizer, but on the surface he remained respectable* | [as modifier] *surface appearances.*
2 Geometry a continuous set of points that has length and breadth but no thickness.
▸ **adjective** [attrib.] relating to or found on the surface of something: *surface layers.* ■ denoting ships which travel on the surface of the water as distinct from submarines: *the surface fleet.* ■ carried by or denoting transportation by sea or overland rather than by air: *surface mail.*
▸ **verb 1** [no obj.] rise or come up to the surface of the water or the ground: *he surfaced from his dive.* ■ come to people's attention; become apparent: *the row first surfaced two years ago.* ■ informal (of a person) appear after having been asleep: *it was almost 11.30 before Anthony surfaced.*
2 [with obj.] provide (something, especially a road) with a particular surface: *a small path surfaced with terracotta tiles.*
– DERIVATIVES **surfaced** adjective [often in combination] *a smooth-surfaced cylinder*, **surfacer** noun.
– ORIGIN early 17th cent.: from French (see SUR-¹, FACE), suggested by Latin *superficies*.

surface-active ▸ **adjective** (of a substance, such as a detergent) tending to reduce the surface tension of a liquid in which it is dissolved.

surface chemistry ▸ **noun** [mass noun] the branch of chemistry concerned with the processes occurring at interfaces between phases, especially that between liquid and gas.

surface-mount ▸ **adjective** (of an electronic component) having leads that are designed to be soldered on the side of a circuit board that the body of the component is mounted on. Often contrasted with THROUGH-HOLE.

surface noise ▸ **noun** [mass noun] extraneous noise heard when a record is played, caused by imperfections in the grooves of the record or in the pickup system.

surface structure ▸ **noun** [mass noun] (in transformational grammar) the structure of a well-formed phrase or sentence in a language, as opposed to its underlying logical form. Contrasted with DEEP STRUCTURE.

surface tension ▸ **noun** [mass noun] the tension of the surface film of a liquid caused by the attraction of the particles in the surface layer by the bulk of the liquid, which tends to minimize surface area.

surface-to-air ▸ **adjective** (of a missile) designed to be fired from the ground or a vessel at an aircraft.

surface-to-surface ▸ **adjective** (of a missile) designed to be fired from one point on the ground or a vessel at another such point or vessel.

surface water ▸ **noun** [mass noun] **1** water that collects on the surface of the ground.
2 (also **surface waters**) the top layer of a body of water: *the surface water of a pond or lake.*

surfactant /səˈfakt(ə)nt/ ▸ **noun** a substance which tends to reduce the surface tension of a liquid in which it is dissolved.
– ORIGIN 1950s: from *surf(ace)-act(ive)* + -ANT.

surfbird ▸ **noun** a small migratory wader of the sandpiper family, with mainly dark grey plumage and a short bill and legs, breeding in Alaska. ● *Aphriza virgata*, family Scolopacidae.

surfboard ▸ **noun** a long, narrow shaped board used in surfing.

surfcasting ▸ **noun** [mass noun] fishing by casting a line into the sea from the shore.
– DERIVATIVES **surfcaster** noun.

surf club ▸ **noun** Austral./NZ an organization of lifeguards in charge of safety on a particular beach.

surfeit ▸ **noun** [usu. in sing.] an excessive amount of something: *a surfeit of food and drink.* ■ archaic an illness caused or regarded as being caused by excessive eating or drinking: *he died of a surfeit.*
▸ **verb** (**surfeits, surfeiting, surfeited**) [with obj.] (usu. **be surfeited with**) cause (someone) to desire no more of something as a result of having consumed or done it to excess: *I am surfeited with shopping.* ■ [no obj.] archaic consume too much of something: *he never surfeited on rich wine.*
– ORIGIN Middle English: from Old French, based on Latin *super-* 'above, in excess' + *facere* 'do'.

surficial /səˈfɪʃ(ə)l/ ▸ **adjective** Geology relating to the earth's surface: *surficial deposits.*
– DERIVATIVES **surficially** adverb.
– ORIGIN late 19th cent.: from SURFACE, on the pattern of *superficial*.

surfie ▸ **noun** Austral./NZ informal a surfing enthusiast, especially a young man.

surfing ▸ **noun** [mass noun] **1** the sport or pastime of being carried to the shore on the crest of large waves while standing or lying on a surfboard.
2 the activity of moving from site to site on the Internet.

surf lifesaver ▸ **noun** see LIFESAVER (sense 2).

surf music ▸ **noun** [mass noun] a style of popular music originating in the US in the early 1960s, characterized by high harmony vocals and typically having lyrics relating to surfing.

surf 'n' turf (also **surf and turf**) ▸ **noun** [mass noun] chiefly N. Amer. a dish containing both seafood and meat, typically shellfish and steak.

surfperch ▸ **noun** (pl. **same** or **surfperches**) a deep-bodied live-bearing fish of the North Pacific, living chiefly in coastal waters. Also called SEA PERCH.
● Family Embiotocidae: several genera and species.

surf-riding ▸ **noun** another term for SURFING (sense 1).

surge ▸ **noun** a sudden powerful forward or upward movement, especially by a crowd or by a natural force such as the tide: *flooding caused by tidal surges.* ■ a sudden large increase, typically a temporary one: *the firm predicted a 20% surge in sales.* ■ a major deployment of military forces to reinforce those already in a particular area. ■ a powerful rush of an emotion or feeling: *Sophie felt a surge of anger.* ■ a sudden marked increase in voltage or current in an electric circuit.
▸ **verb** [no obj., usu. with adverbial] **1** (of a crowd or a natural force) move suddenly and powerfully forward or upward: *the journalists surged forward.* ■ increase suddenly and powerfully: *shares surged to a record high.* ■ (of an emotion or feeling) affect someone powerfully and suddenly: *indignation surged up within her.* ■ (of an electric voltage or current) increase suddenly.
2 Nautical (of a rope, chain, or windlass) slip back with a jerk.

S

– ORIGIN late 15th cent. (in the sense 'fountain, stream'): the noun (in early use) from Old French *sourgeon*; the verb partly from the Old French stem *sourge-*, based on Latin *surgere* 'to rise'. Early senses of the verb included 'rise and fall on the waves' and 'swell with great force'.

surge chamber ▶ noun another term for SURGE TANK.

surgeon ▶ noun a medical practitioner qualified to practise surgery. ■ a doctor in the navy.
– ORIGIN Middle English: from Anglo-Norman French *surgien*, contraction of Old French *serurgien*, based on Latin *chirurgia*, from Greek *kheirourgia* 'handiwork, surgery', from *kheir* 'hand' + *ergon* 'work'.

surgeonfish ▶ noun (pl. **same** or **surgeonfishes**) a deep-bodied and typically brightly coloured tropical marine fish with a scalpel-like spine on each side of the tail. ● Family Acanthuridae: several genera and many species. See also TANG[3], UNICORN FISH.

surgeon general ▶ noun (pl. **surgeons general**) (chiefly in the US) the head of a public health service or of the medical service of an army, navy, or air force.

surgeon's knot ▶ noun a reef knot with one or more extra turns in the first half knot.
– ORIGIN from the use of such a knot to tie a ligature in surgery.

surgery ▶ noun (pl. **surgeries**) **1** [mass noun] the treatment of injuries or disorders of the body by incision or manipulation, especially with instruments: *cardiac surgery* | *he had surgery on his ankle.*
2 Brit. a place where a doctor, dentist, or other medical practitioner treats or advises patients. ■ [in sing.] an occasion on which such treatment or consultation occurs: *Doctor Bailey had finished his evening surgery.* ■ an occasion on which an MP, lawyer, or other professional person gives advice.
– ORIGIN Middle English: from Old French *surgerie*, contraction of *serurgerie*, from *serurgien* (see SURGEON).

surge tank ▶ noun a tank connected to a pipe carrying a liquid and intended to neutralize sudden changes of pressure in the flow by filling when the pressure increases and emptying when it drops.

surgical ▶ adjective **1** relating to or used in surgery: *a surgical dressing* | *a surgical ward.* ■ (of a special garment or appliance) worn to correct or relieve an injury, illness, or deformity: *surgical stockings.*
2 done with great precision, especially with reference to a swift and highly accurate military attack from the air: *surgical bombing.*
– DERIVATIVES **surgically** adverb.
– ORIGIN late 18th cent. (earlier as *chirurgical*): from French *cirurgical*, from Old French *sirurgie* (see SURGERY).

surgical spirit ▶ noun [mass noun] Brit. methylated spirit (often with other ingredients such as oil of wintergreen) used in medical practice, especially for cleansing the skin before injections or surgery.

suricate /'s(j)ʊərɪkeɪt/ ▶ noun a gregarious burrowing meerkat with dark bands on the back and a black-tipped tail, native to southern Africa. ● *Suricata suricatta*, family Herpestidae.
– ORIGIN late 18th cent.: via French from a local African word.

surimi /sʊ'riːmi/ ▶ noun [mass noun] a relatively tasteless and odourless paste made from minced fish, used especially to produce imitation crabmeat and lobster meat.
– ORIGIN Japanese, literally 'minced flesh'.

Suriname /ˌsʊərɪ'nam, -'naːmə/ (also **Surinam** /-'nam/) a country on the NE coast of South America; pop. 481,300 (est. 2009); languages, Dutch (official), Creoles, Hindi; capital, Paramaribo. Former name (until 1948) DUTCH GUIANA.

> Colonized by the Dutch and the English from the 17th century, Suriname became fully independent in 1975. The population is descended largely from African slaves and Asian workers brought in to work on sugar plantations; there is also a small American Indian population.

– DERIVATIVES **Surinamer** noun, **Surinamese** /-nə'miːz/ adjective & noun.

Suriname toad ▶ noun an aquatic South American toad with a flat body and long webbed feet, the female of which carries the eggs and tadpoles in pockets on her back. ● *Pipa pipa*, family Pipidae.

surjection /səː'dʒɛkʃ(ə)n/ ▶ noun Mathematics an onto mapping (see ONTO).
– DERIVATIVES **surjective** adjective.
– ORIGIN 1960s: from SUR-[1], after *injection*.

surly ▶ adjective (**surlier**, **surliest**) bad-tempered and unfriendly: *the porter left with a surly expression.*
– DERIVATIVES **surlily** adverb, **surliness** noun.
– ORIGIN mid 16th cent. (in the sense 'lordly, haughty, arrogant'): alteration of obsolete *sirly* (see SIR, -LY[1]).

surmise /sə'mʌɪz/ ▶ verb [no obj.] [usu. with clause] suppose that something is true without having evidence to confirm it: *he surmised that something must be wrong* | [with direct speech] *'I don't think they're locals,' she surmised.*
▶ noun a supposition that something may be true, even though there is no evidence to confirm it: *Charles was glad to have his surmise confirmed* | [mass noun] *all these observations remain surmise.*
– ORIGIN late Middle English (in the senses 'formal allegation' and 'allege formally'): from Anglo-Norman French and Old French *surmise*, feminine past participle of *surmettre* 'accuse', from late Latin *supermittere* 'put in afterwards', from *super-* 'over' + *mittere* 'send'.

surmount ▶ verb [with obj.] **1** overcome (a difficulty or obstacle): *all manner of cultural differences were surmounted.*
2 stand or be placed on top of: *the tomb was surmounted by a sculptured angel.*
– DERIVATIVES **surmountable** adjective.
– ORIGIN late Middle English (also in the sense 'surpass, be superior to'): from Old French *surmonter* (see SUR-[1], MOUNT[1]).

surmullet ▶ noun a red mullet that is widely distributed in the tropical Indo-Pacific. ● *Pseudupeneus fraterculus*, family Mullidae.
– ORIGIN late 17th cent.: from French *surmulet*, from Old French *sor* 'red' + *mulet* 'mullet'.

surname ▶ noun a hereditary name common to all members of a family, as distinct from a forename or given name. ■ archaic a name, title, or epithet added to a person's name, especially one indicating their birthplace or a particular quality or achievement: *Simeon of the pillar, by surname Stylites.*
▶ verb [with obj.] give a surname to: *Eddie Penham, so aptly surnamed, had produced a hand-painted sign for us.*
– ORIGIN Middle English: partial translation of Anglo-Norman French *surnoun*, suggested by medieval Latin *supernomen*.

surpass ▶ verb [with obj.] exceed; be greater than: *pre-war levels of production were surpassed in 1929.* ■ be better than: *he continued to surpass me at all games.* ■ (**surpass oneself**) do or be better than ever before: *the organist was surpassing himself.*
– DERIVATIVES **surpassable** adjective.
– ORIGIN mid 16th cent.: from French *surpasser*, from *sur-* 'above' + *passer* 'to pass'.

surpassing ▶ adjective dated or literary incomparable or outstanding: *a picture of surpassing beauty.*
– DERIVATIVES **surpassingly** adverb.

surplice /'səːplɪs/ ▶ noun a loose white linen vestment varying from hip-length to calf-length, worn over a cassock by clergy and choristers at Christian church services.
– DERIVATIVES **surpliced** adjective.
– ORIGIN Middle English: from Old French *sourpelis*, from medieval Latin *superpellicium*, from *super-* 'above' + *pellicia* 'fur garment'.

surplus ▶ noun an amount of something left over when requirements have been met; an excess of production or supply: *exports of food surpluses.* ■ an excess of income or assets over expenditure or liabilities in a given period, typically a financial year: *a trade surplus of $1,395 million.* ■ the excess value of a company's assets over the face value of its stock.
▶ adjective more than what is needed or used; excess: *make the most of your surplus cash* | *the firm told 284 employees that they were* ***surplus to requirements.*** ■ denoting a shop selling excess or outdated military equipment or clothing: *she had picked up her boots in an army surplus store.*
– ORIGIN late Middle English: from Old French *sourplus*, from medieval Latin *superplus*, from *super-* 'in addition' + *plus* 'more'.

surplus value ▶ noun [mass noun] Economics (in Marxist theory) the excess of value produced by the labour of workers over the wages they are paid.

surprise ▶ noun **1** an unexpected or astonishing event, fact, etc.: *the announcement came as a complete surprise.* ■ [mass noun] a feeling of mild astonishment or shock caused by something unexpected: *much to her surprise, she'd missed him.* ■ [as modifier] denoting something done or happening unexpectedly: *a surprise attack.*
2 [as modifier] Bell-ringing denoting a complex method of change-ringing: *surprise major.*
▶ verb [with obj.] (of something unexpected) cause (someone) to feel mild astonishment or shock: *I* ***was surprised at*** *his statement* | [with obj. and clause] *Joe was surprised that he enjoyed the journey.* ■ capture, attack, or discover suddenly and unexpectedly: *he surprised a gang stealing scrap metal.*
– PHRASES **surprise, surprise** informal said when giving someone a surprise. ■ said ironically when one believes that something was entirely predictable: *we entrust you with Jason's care and, surprise surprise, you make a mess of it.* **take someone/thing by surprise** attack or capture someone or something unexpectedly. ■ (**take someone by surprise**) happen when someone is not prepared: *the question took David by surprise.*
– ORIGIN late Middle English (in the sense 'unexpected seizure of a place, or attack on troops'): from Old French, feminine past participle of *surprendre*, from medieval Latin *superprehendere* 'seize'.

surprised ▶ adjective feeling or showing surprise: *there was a surprised silence.*
– DERIVATIVES **surprisedly** adverb.

surprising ▶ adjective causing surprise; unexpected: *a surprising sequence of events.*
– DERIVATIVES **surprisingly** adverb [as submodifier] *the profit margin in advertising is surprisingly low* | [sentence adverb] *not surprisingly, his enthusiasm knew no bounds*, **surprisingness** noun.

surra /'sʊərə, 'sʌrə/ ▶ noun [mass noun] a parasitic disease of camels and other mammals caused by trypanosomes, transmitted by biting flies and occurring chiefly in North Africa and Asia.
– ORIGIN late 19th cent.: from Marathi *sūra* 'air breathed through the nostrils'.

surreal ▶ adjective having the qualities of surrealism; bizarre: *a surreal mix of fact and fantasy.*
– DERIVATIVES **surreality** noun, **surreally** adverb.
– ORIGIN 1930s: back-formation from SURREALISM.

surrealism ▶ noun [mass noun] a 20th-century avant-garde movement in art and literature which sought to release the creative potential of the unconscious mind, for example by the irrational juxtaposition of images.

> Launched in 1924 by a manifesto of André Breton and having a strong political content, the movement grew out of symbolism and Dada and was strongly influenced by Sigmund Freud. In the visual arts its most notable exponents were André Masson, Jean Arp, Joan Miró, René Magritte, Salvador Dalí, Max Ernst, Man Ray, and Luis Buñuel.

– DERIVATIVES **surrealist** noun & adjective, **surrealistic** adjective, **surrealistically** adverb.
– ORIGIN early 20th cent.: from French *surréalisme* (see SUR-[1], REALISM).

surrebuttal /ˌsʌrɪ'bʌtəl/ ▶ noun another term for SURREBUTTER.

surrebutter /ˌsʌrɪ'bʌtə/ ▶ noun Law, archaic a plaintiff's reply to the defendant's rebutter.
– ORIGIN late 16th cent.: from SUR-[1] 'in addition' + REBUTTER, on the pattern of *surrejoinder*.

surrejoinder /ˌsʌrɪ'dʒɔɪndə/ ▶ noun Law, archaic a plaintiff's reply to the defendant's rejoinder.
– ORIGIN mid 16th cent.: from SUR-[1] 'in addition' + REJOINDER.

S

surrender ▶ verb **1** [no obj.] stop resisting to an enemy or opponent and submit to their authority: *over 140 rebels surrendered to the authorities.* ■ [with obj.] (in sport) lose (a point, game, or advantage) to an opponent: *she surrendered only twenty games in her five qualifying matches.* ■ (**surrender to**) give in to (a powerful emotion or influence): *the president has surrendered to panic and is making things worse* | *he* ***surrendered himself to*** *the mood of the hills.*
2 [with obj.] give up or hand over (a person, right, or possession), typically on compulsion or demand: *in 1815 Denmark* ***surrendered*** *Norway* ***to*** *Sweden* | *the UK is opposed to surrendering its monetary sovereignty.* ■ (of a person assured) cancel (a life insurance policy) and receive back a proportion of the premiums paid. ■ give up (a lease) before its expiry.
▶ noun [mass noun] **1** the action of surrendering to an opponent or powerful influence: *the final surrender of Germany on 8 May 1945* | [count noun] *the colonel was anxious to negotiate a surrender.*
2 the action of surrendering a lease or life insurance policy.
– PHRASES **surrender to bail** Law duly appear in court after release on bail.

– ORIGIN late Middle English (chiefly in legal use): from Anglo-Norman French (see SUR-¹, RENDER).

surrender value ▸ noun the amount payable to a person who surrenders a life insurance policy.

surreptitious /ˌsʌrəpˈtɪʃəs/ ▸ adjective kept secret, especially because it would not be approved of: *low wages were supplemented by surreptitious payments from tradesmen.*
– DERIVATIVES **surreptitiously** adverb, **surreptitiousness** noun.
– ORIGIN late Middle English (in the sense 'obtained by suppression of the truth'): from Latin *surreptitius* (from the verb *surripere*, from *sub-* 'secretly' + *rapere* 'seize') + -OUS.

Surrey a county of SE England; county town, Kingston upon Thames.

surrey ▸ noun (pl. **surreys**) historical (in the US) a light four-wheeled carriage with two seats facing forwards.
– ORIGIN late 19th cent.: originally denoting a *Surrey cart*, first made in SURREY, from which the carriage was later adapted.

surrogacy /ˈsʌrəgəsi/ ▸ noun [mass noun] the action or state of being a surrogate. ▪ the process of giving birth as a surrogate mother or of arranging such a birth.

surrogate /ˈsʌrəgət/ ▸ noun a substitute, especially a person deputizing for another in a specific role or office: *wives of MPs are looked on as **surrogates for** their husbands while the latter are at Westminster.* ▪ (in the Christian Church) a bishop's deputy who grants marriage licences. ▪ (in the US) a judge in charge of probate, inheritance, and guardianship.
– ORIGIN early 17th cent.: from Latin *surrogatus*, past participle of *surrogare* 'elect as a substitute', from *super-* 'over' + *rogare* 'ask'.

surrogate mother ▸ noun **1** a person or animal which takes on all or part of the role of mother to another person or animal.
2 a woman who bears a child on behalf of another woman, either from her own egg fertilized by the other woman's partner, or from the implantation in her womb of a fertilized egg from the other woman.

surround ▸ verb [with obj.] be all round (someone or something): *the hotel is surrounded by its own gardens* | figurative *he loves to **surround himself with** family and friends.* ▪ (of troops, police, etc.) encircle (someone or something) so as to cut off communication or escape: *troops surrounded the parliament building.* ▪ be associated with: *the killings were surrounded by controversy.*
▸ noun a thing that forms a border or edging around an object: *an oak fireplace surround.* ▪ (usu. **surrounds**) the area encircling something; surroundings: *the beautiful surrounds of Connemara.*
– ORIGIN late Middle English (in the sense 'overflow'): from Old French *souronder*, from late Latin *superundare*, from *super-* 'over' + *undare* 'to flow' (from *unda* 'a wave'); later associated with ROUND. Current senses of the noun date from the late 19th cent.

surrounding ▸ adjective [attrib.] all round a particular place or thing: *Cardiff and the surrounding area.*

S

surroundings ▸ plural noun the things and conditions around a person or thing: *I took up the time admiring my surroundings.*

surround sound ▸ noun [mass noun] a system of stereophony involving three or more speakers surrounding the listener so as to give a more realistic effect.

surtax ▸ noun an additional tax on something already taxed, especially a higher rate of tax on incomes above a certain level.
– ORIGIN late 19th cent.: from French *surtaxe* (see SUR-¹, TAX).

Surtees /ˈsəːtiːz/, Robert Smith (1805–64), English journalist and novelist. He is best remembered for his comic sketches of Mr Jorrocks, the sporting Cockney grocer, collected in *Jorrocks's Jaunts and Jollities* (1838).

surtitle ▸ noun (usu. **surtitles**) a caption projected on a screen above the stage in an opera, translating the text being sung.
▸ verb [with obj.] provide (an opera production) with surtitles.

surtout /ˈsəːtuː, səːˈtuː(t)/ ▸ noun historical a man's greatcoat of a similar style to a frock coat.
– ORIGIN late 17th cent.: from French, from *sur* 'over' + *tout* 'everything'.

Surtsey /ˈsəːtsi/ a small island to the south of Iceland, formed by a volcanic eruption in 1963.

surveillance /səˈveɪl(ə)ns, -ˈveɪəns/ ▸ noun [mass noun] close observation, especially of a suspected spy or criminal: *he found himself put **under surveillance** by British military intelligence.*
– ORIGIN early 19th cent.: from French, from *sur-* 'over' + *veiller* 'watch' (from Latin *vigilare* 'keep watch').

survey ▸ verb /səˈveɪ/ [with obj.] **1** look closely at or examine (someone or something): *her green eyes surveyed him coolly* | *I surveyed the options.*
2 examine and record the area and features of (an area of land) so as to construct a map, plan, or description: *he surveyed the coasts of New Zealand.* ▪ Brit. examine and report on the condition of (a building), especially for a prospective buyer: *the cottage didn't look unsafe, but he had it surveyed.*
3 investigate the opinions or experience of (a group of people) by asking them questions: *95 per cent of patients surveyed were satisfied with the health service.* ▪ investigate (behaviour or opinions) by questioning a group of people: *the investigator surveyed the attitudes and beliefs held by residents.*
▸ noun /ˈsəːveɪ/ **1** a general view, examination, or description of someone or something: *the author provides a survey of the relevant literature.* ▪ an investigation of the opinions or experience of a group of people, based on a series of questions.
2 Brit. an act of surveying a building: *the building society will insist that you have a survey done.* ▪ a written report detailing the findings of a building survey.
3 an act of surveying an area of land: *the flight involved a detailed aerial survey of military bases.* ▪ a map, plan, or detailed description obtained by surveying an area. ▪ a department carrying out the surveying of land: *the British Geological Survey.*
– ORIGIN late Middle English (in the sense 'examine and ascertain the condition of'): from Anglo-Norman French *surveier*, from medieval Latin *supervidere*, from *super-* 'over' + *videre* 'to see'. The early sense of the noun (late 15th cent.) was 'supervision'.

Surveyor a series of unmanned American spacecraft sent to the moon between 1966 and 1968, five of which successfully made soft landings.

surveyor ▸ noun a person who examines the condition of land and buildings professionally. ▪ Brit. an official inspector of something, especially for measurement and valuation purposes. ▪ a person who investigates or examines something, especially boats for seaworthiness.
– DERIVATIVES **surveyorship** noun.
– ORIGIN late Middle English (denoting a supervisor): from Anglo-Norman French *surveiour*, from the verb *surveier* (see SURVEY).

surveyor general ▸ noun (pl. **surveyors general** or **surveyor generals**) historical a chief supervisor in certain departments of the British government.

survivable ▸ adjective (of an accident or ordeal) able to be survived; not fatal: *air crashes are becoming more survivable.*
– DERIVATIVES **survivability** noun.

survival ▸ noun [mass noun] the state or fact of continuing to live or exist, typically in spite of an accident, ordeal, or difficult circumstances: *the animal's chances of survival were pretty low* | figurative *he was fighting for his political survival.* ▪ [count noun] an object or practice that has continued to exist from an earlier time: *his shorts were a survival from his army days.*
– PHRASES **survival of the fittest** Biology the continued existence of organisms which are best adapted to their environment, with the extinction of others, as a concept in the Darwinian theory of evolution. Compare with NATURAL SELECTION.

survival bag ▸ noun a large bag made of plastic or metal foil, used in an emergency by climbers and others as a protection against exposure.

survival curve ▸ noun a graph showing the proportion of a population living after a given age, or at a given time after contracting a serious disease or receiving a radiation dose.

survivalism ▸ noun [mass noun] **1** the practising of outdoor survival skills as a sport or hobby.
2 the policy of trying to ensure one's own survival or that of one's social or national group.
– DERIVATIVES **survivalist** noun & adjective.

survival kit ▸ noun a pack of emergency equipment, including food, medical supplies, and tools, especially as carried by members of the armed forces.

survival value ▸ noun [mass noun] the property of an ability, faculty, or characteristic that makes individuals possessing it more likely to survive, thrive, and reproduce: *everyone knows that a bad smell is of survival value to the skunk.*

survive ▸ verb [no obj.] continue to live or exist, especially in spite of danger or hardship: *against all odds the child survived.* ▪ [with obj.] continue to live or exist in spite of (an accident or ordeal): *he has survived several assassination attempts.* ▪ [with obj.] remain alive after the death of (a particular person): *he was survived by his wife and six children* | (as adj. **surviving**) *there were no surviving relatives.* ▪ manage to keep going in difficult circumstances: *she had to work day and night and **survive on** two hours' sleep.*
– ORIGIN late Middle English: from Old French *sourvivre*, from Latin *supervivere*, from *super-* 'in addition' + *vivere* 'live'.

survivor ▸ noun a person who survives, especially a person remaining alive after an event in which others have died: *he was the sole survivor of the massacre.* ▪ the remainder of a group of people or things: *a survivor from last year's team.* ▪ a person who copes well with difficulties in their life: *she is a born survivor.* ▪ Law a joint tenant who has the right to the whole estate on the other's death.

survivorship ▸ noun [mass noun] the state or condition of being a survivor; survival. ▪ chiefly Zoology the proportion of a population surviving to a given age.

survivorship curve ▸ noun chiefly Zoology a survival curve.

Surya /ˈsuːrɪə/ Hinduism the sun god of later Hindu mythology, originally one of several solar deities in the Vedic religion.
– ORIGIN from Sanskrit *sūrya* 'sun'.

sus /sʌs/ Brit. informal ▸ noun [mass noun] suspicion of having committed a crime: *he was picked **up on sus**.* ▪ [as modifier] historical relating to or denoting a law under which a person could be arrested on suspicion of having committed an offence: *the sus law.*

Sus. ▸ abbreviation (in biblical references) Susanna (Apocrypha).

sus- ▸ prefix variant spelling of SUB- before *c*, *p*, *t* (as in *susceptible*, *suspend*, *sustain*).

Susa /ˈsuːsə/ **1** an ancient city of SW Asia, one of the chief cities of the kingdom of Elam and later capital of the Persian Achaemenid dynasty.
2 another name for SOUSSE.

Susah /ˈsuːsə/ another name for SOUSSE.

Susanna (in the Apocrypha) a woman of Babylon falsely accused of adultery by two elders but saved by the sagacity of Daniel. ▪ the book of the Apocrypha telling the story of Susanna.

susceptibility ▸ noun (pl. **susceptibilities**) **1** [mass noun] the state or fact of being likely or liable to be influenced or harmed by a particular thing: *lack of exercise increases **susceptibility to** disease.*
2 (**susceptibilities**) a person's feelings, typically considered as being easily hurt: *I was so careful not to offend their susceptibilities.*
3 Physics the ratio of magnetization produced in a material to the magnetizing force.

susceptible /səˈsɛptɪb(ə)l/ ▸ adjective **1** likely or liable to be influenced or harmed by a particular thing: *patients with liver disease may be **susceptible to** infection.* ▪ (of a person) easily influenced by feelings or emotions; sensitive: *they only do it to tease him—he's too susceptible.*
2 (**susceptible of**) capable or admitting of: *the problem is not susceptible of a simple solution.*
– DERIVATIVES **susceptibly** adverb.
– ORIGIN early 17th cent.: from late Latin *susceptibilis*, from Latin *suscipere* 'take up, sustain', from *sub-* 'from below' + *capere* 'take'.

susceptive ▸ adjective archaic receptive or sensitive to something; susceptible.
– ORIGIN late Middle English: from late Latin *susceptivus*, from *suscept-* 'taken up', from the verb *suscipere* (see SUSCEPTIBLE).

sushi /ˈsuːʃi, ˈsʊʃi/ ▸ noun [mass noun] a Japanese dish consisting of small balls or rolls of vinegar-flavoured cold rice served with a garnish of vegetables, egg, or raw seafood.
– ORIGIN Japanese.

suslik /ˈsʌslɪk/ ▸ noun variant spelling of SOUSLIK.

suspect ▸ verb /səˈspɛkt/ [with obj.] **1** have an idea or impression of the existence, presence, or truth of (something) without certain proof: *if you suspect a gas leak, do not turn on an electric light* | [with clause]

she suspected that he might be bluffing | (as adj. **suspected**) *a suspected heart condition.* ▪ believe or feel that (someone) is guilty of an illegal, dishonest, or unpleasant act, without certain proof: *parents* ***suspected of*** *child abuse.*
2 doubt the genuineness or truth of: *a broker whose honesty he had no reason to suspect.*
▸ **noun** /ˈsʌspɛkt/ a person thought to be guilty of a crime or offence: *the police have arrested a suspect.*
▸ **adjective** /ˈsʌspɛkt/ not to be relied on or trusted; possibly dangerous or false: *a suspect package was found on the platform.*
– ORIGIN Middle English (originally as an adjective): from Latin *suspectus* 'mistrusted', past participle of *suspicere*, from *sub-* 'from below' + *specere* 'to look'.

suspend ▸ **verb** [with obj.] **1** temporarily prevent from continuing or being in force or effect: *work on the dam was suspended.* ▪ officially prohibit (someone) from holding their usual post or carrying out their usual role for a particular length of time: *two officers were* ***suspended from*** *duty pending the outcome of the investigation.* ▪ defer or delay (an action, event, or judgement): *the judge suspended judgement until January 15.* ▪ Law (of a judge or court) cause (an imposed sentence) not to be enforced as long as no further offence is committed within a specified period: *the sentence was suspended for six months* | (as adj. **suspended**) *a suspended jail sentence.*
2 hang (something) from somewhere: *the light was* ***suspended from*** *the ceiling.*
3 (**be suspended**) (of solid particles) be dispersed throughout the bulk of a fluid: *the paste contains collagen suspended in a salt solution.*
4 Music prolong (a note of a chord) into a following chord, usually so as to produce a temporary discord.
– PHRASES **suspend disbelief** temporarily allow oneself to believe something that is not true, especially in order to enjoy a work of fiction. **suspend payment** (of a company) cease to meet its financial obligations as a result of insolvency or insufficient funds.
– ORIGIN Middle English: from Old French *suspendre* or Latin *suspendere*, from *sub-* 'from below' + *pendere* 'hang'.

suspended animation ▸ **noun** [mass noun] the temporary cessation of most vital functions without death, as in a dormant seed or a hibernating animal.

suspended ceiling ▸ **noun** a ceiling with a space between it and the floor above from which it hangs.

suspender ▸ **noun 1** (usu. **suspenders**) Brit. an elastic strap attached to a belt or garter, fastened to the top of a stocking to hold it up.
2 (**suspenders**) N. Amer. a pair of braces for holding up trousers.

suspender belt ▸ **noun** Brit. a woman's undergarment consisting of a decorative belt and elastic suspenders to which the tops of stockings are fastened.

suspense ▸ **noun** [mass noun] **1** a state or feeling of excited or anxious uncertainty about what may happen: *come on, Fran, don't keep me in suspense!* ▪ a quality in a work of fiction that arouses excited expectation or uncertainty about what may happen: *a tale of mystery and suspense.*
2 chiefly Law the temporary cessation or suspension of something.
– DERIVATIVES **suspenseful** adjective.
– ORIGIN late Middle English: from Old French *suspens* 'abeyance', based on Latin *suspensus* 'suspended, hovering, doubtful', past participle of *suspendere* (see SUSPEND).

suspense account ▸ **noun** an account in the books of an organization in which items are entered temporarily before allocation to the correct or final account.

suspension ▸ **noun 1** [mass noun] the action of suspending someone or something or the condition of being suspended: *the suspension of military action* | *the investigation led to the suspension of several officers.*
2 [mass noun] the system of springs and shock absorbers by which a vehicle is supported on its wheels: *modifications have been made to the car's rear suspension.*
3 a mixture in which particles are dispersed throughout the bulk of a fluid: *a suspension of maize starch in arachis oil.* ▪ [mass noun] the state of being dispersed in such a way: *the agitator in the vat keeps the slurry* ***in suspension.***
4 Music a discord made by prolonging a note of a chord into the following chord.
– ORIGIN late Middle English: from French, or from Latin *suspensio(n-)*, from the verb *suspendere* (see SUSPEND).

suspension bridge ▸ **noun** a bridge in which the weight of the deck is supported by vertical cables suspended from further cables that run between towers and are anchored in abutments at each end.

suspension feeder ▸ **noun** Zoology an aquatic animal which feeds on particles of organic matter suspended in the water, especially a bottom-dwelling filter feeder.

suspensive ▸ **adjective 1** relating to the deferral or suspension of an event, action, or legal obligation.
2 archaic causing suspense.

suspensory ▸ **adjective 1** holding and supporting an organ or part: *a suspensory ligament.*
2 relating to the deferral or suspension of an event, action, or legal obligation: *a suspensory requirement.*
– ORIGIN late Middle English: from medieval Latin *suspensorius* 'used for hanging something up', from Latin *suspendere* (see SUSPEND).

suspicion ▸ **noun 1** a feeling or thought that something is possible, likely, or true: *she had a sneaking* ***suspicion that*** *he was laughing at her.* ▪ a feeling or belief that someone is guilty of an illegal, dishonest, or unpleasant action: *police would not say what aroused their suspicions* | [mass noun] *he was arrested* ***on suspicion of*** *murder.*
2 [mass noun] cautious distrust: *her activities were regarded with suspicion by the headmistress.*
3 a very slight trace: ***a suspicion of*** *a smile.*
– PHRASES **above suspicion** too obviously good or honest to be thought capable of wrongdoing. **under suspicion** thought to be guilty of wrongdoing.
– ORIGIN Middle English: from Anglo-Norman French *suspeciun*, from medieval Latin *suspectio(n-)*, from *suspicere* 'mistrust'. The change in the second syllable was due to association with Old French *suspicion* (from Latin *suspicio(n-)* 'suspicion').

suspicious ▸ **adjective** having or showing a cautious distrust of someone or something: *he was* ***suspicious of*** *her motives* | *she gave him a suspicious look.* ▪ causing one to have the idea or impression that someone or something is questionable, dishonest, or dangerous: *they are not treating the fire as suspicious.* ▪ having the belief or impression that someone is involved in an illegal or dishonest activity: *police were called when staff became suspicious.*
– DERIVATIVES **suspiciously** adverb, **suspiciousness** noun.
– ORIGIN Middle English: from Old French *suspicious*, from Latin *suspiciosus*, from *suspicio(n-)* (see SUSPICION).

suspire /səˈspʌɪə/ ▸ **verb** [no obj.] literary breathe.
– DERIVATIVES **suspiration** noun.
– ORIGIN late Middle English (in the sense 'yearn after'): from Latin *suspirare*, from *sub-* 'from below' + *spirare* 'breathe'.

Susquehanna /ˌsʌskwəˈhanə/ a river of the north-eastern US. It has two headstreams, one rising in New York State and one in Pennsylvania, which meet in central Pennsylvania. The river then flows 240 km (150 miles) south to Chesapeake Bay.

suss Brit. informal ▸ **verb** (**susses, sussing, sussed**) [with obj.] realize; grasp: *he's sussed it* | [with clause] *she* ***sussed out*** *right away that there was something fishy going on.* ▪ discover the true character or nature of: *I reckon I've got him sussed.*
▸ **noun** [mass noun] [with adj. or noun modifier] knowledge or awareness of a specified kind: *his lack of business suss.*
▸ **adjective** shrewd and wary: *he is too suss a character to fall into that trap.*
– ORIGIN 1930s: abbreviation of SUSPECT, SUSPICION.

sussed ▸ **adjective** Brit. informal shrewd and well informed: *the band were sussed and streetwise.*

Sussex[1] a former county of southern England. It was divided in 1974 into the counties of **East Sussex** and **West Sussex**.

Sussex[2] ▸ **noun** a speckled or red bird of a domestic English breed of chicken.

sustain ▸ **verb** [with obj.] **1** strengthen or support physically or mentally: *this thought had sustained him throughout the years* | (as adj. **sustaining**) *a sustaining breakfast of bacon and eggs.* ▪ bear (the weight of an object) without breaking or falling: *he sagged against her so that she could barely sustain his weight* | figurative *his health will no longer enable him to sustain the heavy burdens of office.*
2 undergo or suffer (something unpleasant, especially an injury): *he sustained severe head injuries.*
3 cause to continue for an extended period or without interruption: *he cannot sustain a normal conversation.* ▪ (of a performer) represent (a part or character) convincingly: *he sustained the role of Creon with burly resilience.*
4 uphold, affirm, or confirm the justice or validity of: *the allegations of discrimination were sustained.*
▸ **noun** [mass noun] Music an effect or facility on a keyboard or electronic instrument whereby a note can be sustained after the key is released.
– DERIVATIVES **sustainer** noun, **sustainment** noun.
– ORIGIN Middle English: from Old French *soustenir*, from Latin *sustinere*, from *sub-* 'from below' + *tenere* 'hold'.

sustainable ▸ **adjective 1** able to be maintained at a certain rate or level: *sustainable economic growth.* ▪ conserving an ecological balance by avoiding depletion of natural resources: *our fundamental commitment to sustainable development.*
2 able to be upheld or defended: *sustainable definitions of good educational practice.*
– DERIVATIVES **sustainability** noun, **sustainably** adverb.

sustained ▸ **adjective** continuing for an extended period or without interruption: *several years of sustained economic growth.*
– DERIVATIVES **sustainedly** adverb.

sustained-release ▸ **adjective** Medicine denoting a drug preparation in a capsule containing numerous tiny pellets with different coatings that release their contents steadily over a long period.

sustained yield ▸ **noun** [mass noun] a level of exploitation or crop production which is maintained by restricting the quantity harvested to avoid long-term depletion.

sustenance ▸ **noun** [mass noun] food and drink regarded as a source of strength; nourishment: *poor rural economies turned to potatoes for sustenance.* ▪ the maintaining of someone or something in life or existence: *he kept two or three cows for the sustenance of his family* | *the sustenance of parliamentary democracy.*
– ORIGIN Middle English: from Old French *soustenance*, from the verb *soustenir* (see SUSTAIN).

sustentation /ˌsʌst(ə)nˈteɪʃ(ə)n/ ▸ **noun** [mass noun] formal the support or maintenance of someone or something, especially through the provision of money: *provision is made for the sustentation of preachers.*
– ORIGIN late Middle English: from Old French, or from Latin *sustentatio(n-)*, from *sustentare* 'uphold, sustain', frequentative of *sustinere* (see SUSTAIN).

Susu /ˈsuːsuː/ ▸ **noun** (pl. **same**) **1** a member of a West African people of NW Sierra Leone and the southern coast of Guinea.
2 the language of the Susu, which belongs to the Mande group and has about 700,000 speakers.
▸ **adjective** relating to the Susu or their language.
– ORIGIN the name in Susu.

susurration /ˌs(j)uːsʌˈreɪʃ(ə)n/ (also **susurrus** /s(j)uːˈsʌrəs/) ▸ **noun** [mass noun] literary whispering or rustling: *the susurration of the river.*
– ORIGIN late Middle English: from late Latin *susurratio(n-)*, from Latin *susurrare* 'to murmur, hum'.

Sutherland[1] /ˈsʌðələnd/ a former county of Scotland, which became part of Highland region in 1975.

Sutherland[2] /ˈsʌðələnd/, Graham (Vivian) (1903–80), English painter. During the Second World War he was an official war artist. His post-war work included the tapestry *Christ in Majesty* (1962) in Coventry cathedral.

Sutherland[3] /ˈsʌðələnd/, Dame Joan (b.1926), Australian operatic soprano, noted for her dramatic coloratura roles, particularly the title role in Donizetti's *Lucia di Lammermoor*.

Sutlej /ˈsʌtlɪdʒ/ a river of northern India and Pakistan which rises in the Himalayas in SW Tibet, and flows for 1,450 km (900 miles) westwards through India into Punjab province in Pakistan, where it joins the Chenab River to form the Panjnad and eventually join the Indus. It is one of the five rivers that gave Punjab its name.

sutler /ˈsʌtlə/ ▸ **noun** historical a person who followed an army and sold provisions to the soldiers.
– ORIGIN late 16th cent.: from obsolete Dutch *soeteler*, from *soetelen* 'perform mean duties'.

sutra /ˈsuːtrə/ (also **sutta**) ▸ **noun 1** a rule or aphorism in Sanskrit literature, or a set of these on grammar or Hindu law or philosophy. See also **KAMA SUTRA**.
2 a Buddhist or Jainist scripture.
– ORIGIN from Sanskrit *sūtra* 'thread, rule', from *siv* 'sew'.

S

suttee /sʌˈtiː, ˈsʌti/ ▶ **noun** variant spelling of **SATI**.

Sutton Coldfield a town in the West Midlands, just north of Birmingham; pop. 108,600 (est. 2009).

Sutton Hoo the site in Suffolk of a Saxon ship burial of the 7th century AD, containing magnificent grave goods including jewellery and gold coins.

suture /ˈsuːtʃə/ ▶ **noun 1** a stitch or row of stitches holding together the edges of a wound or surgical incision. ■ a thread or wire used for suturing a wound or incision. ■ [mass noun] the action of stitching together the edges of a wound or incision.
2 a seam-like immovable junction between two bones, such as those of the skull. ■ Zoology a similar junction, such as between the sclerites of an insect's body. ■ Geology a line of junction formed by two crustal plates which have collided.
▶ **verb** [with obj.] stitch up (a wound or incision) with a suture: *the small incision was sutured.*
– DERIVATIVES **sutural adjective.**
– ORIGIN late Middle English: from French, or from Latin *sutura*, from *suere* 'sew'.

SUV ▶ **abbreviation** sport utility vehicle.

Suva /ˈsuːvə/ the capital of Fiji, situated on the SE coast of the island of Viti Levu; pop. 224,000 (est. 2007).

Suwannee /sʊˈwɒni/ (also **Swanee**) a river of the south-eastern US. Rising in SE Georgia, it flows for some 400 km (250 miles) south-west through northern Florida to the Gulf of Mexico.

suxamethonium /ˌsʌksəmɪˈθəʊnɪəm/ ▶ **noun** another term for **SUCCINYLCHOLINE**.
– ORIGIN 1950s: from *sux-* (representing the pronunciation of *succ-* in **SUCCINIC ACID**) + *methonium*, a complex cation.

suzerain /ˈsuːzəreɪn/ ▶ **noun** a sovereign or state having some control over another state that is internally autonomous. ■ historical a feudal overlord.
– DERIVATIVES **suzerainty noun.**
– ORIGIN early 19th cent.: from French, apparently from *sus* 'above' (from Latin *su(r)sum* 'upward'), suggested by *souverain* 'sovereign'.

Suzhou /suːˈdʒəʊ/ (also **Suchou** or **Soochow**) a city in eastern China, in the province of Jiangsu, situated west of Shanghai on the Grand Canal; pop. 1,416,200 (est. 2006). Founded in the 6th century BC, it was the capital of the ancient Wu kingdom.

Suzman /ˈsʊzmən/, Helen (1917–2009), South African politician, of Lithuanian-Jewish descent. From 1961 to 1974 she was the sole MP opposed to apartheid.

Suzuki /sʊˈzuːki/ ▶ **noun** [as modifier] denoting a method of teaching the violin, typically to very young children in large groups, developed by Shin'ichi Suzuki (1898–1998), Japanese educationalist and violin teacher.

Sv ▶ **abbreviation** sievert(s).

s.v. ▶ **abbreviation** (in textual references) under the given word or heading: *the dictionary lists 'rural policeman' s.v. 'rural'.*
– ORIGIN from Latin *sub voce* or *sub verbo*, literally 'under the word or voice'.

Svalbard /ˈsvɑːlbɑː/ a group of islands in the Arctic Ocean about 640 km (400 miles) north of Norway; pop. 2,100 (est. 2009). They came under Norwegian sovereignty in 1925. The chief settlement (on Spitsbergen) is Longyearbyen.

Svedberg /ˈsvɛdbəːg/ (also **Svedberg unit**) (abbrev.: **S**) ▶ **noun** Biochemistry a unit of time equal to 10^{-13} seconds, used in expressing sedimentation coefficients.
– ORIGIN 1940s: named after Theodor S. *Svedberg* (1884–1971), Swedish chemist.

svelte ▶ **adjective** (of a person) slender and elegant.
– ORIGIN early 19th cent.: from French, from Italian *svelto*.

Sven /svɛn/ variant spelling of **SWEYN I**.

Svengali /svɛnˈgɑːli/ ▶ **noun** a person who exercises a controlling or mesmeric influence on another, especially for a sinister purpose.
– ORIGIN early 20th cent.: the name of a musician in George du Maurier's novel *Trilby* (1894), who controls Trilby's stage singing hypnotically.

Sverdlovsk /svɛːdˈlɒfsk/ former name (1924–91) for **YEKATERINBURG**.

Sverige /ˈsvarjə/ Swedish name for **SWEDEN**.

Svetambara /sweˈtɑːmbərə/ ▶ **noun** a member of one of the two principal sects of Jainism, which was formed *c.*80 AD and survives today in parts of India. Ascetic adherents of the sect traditionally wear white clothing. See also **DIGAMBARA**.
– ORIGIN from Sanskrit *śvetāmbara*, literally 'white-clad'.

Sveti Konstantin /ˌsvɛti ˌkɒnstanˈtiːn/ another name for **DROUZHBA**.

SVGA ▶ **abbreviation** super video graphics array, a high-resolution standard for monitors and screens.

S-video ▶ **noun** [mass noun] a method of transmitting high-quality television signals from a video recorder, video camera, etc. by sending the signals for chrominance and luminance separately.
– ORIGIN from the initial letter of *separated* + **VIDEO**.

Svizzera /ˈzvittsera/ Italian name for **SWITZERLAND**.

SW ▶ **abbreviation** ■ south-west. ■ south-western.

SWA ▶ **abbreviation** Namibia (international vehicle registration).
– ORIGIN from *South West Africa*.

swab ▶ **noun 1** an absorbent pad or piece of material used in surgery and medicine for cleaning wounds, applying medication, or taking specimens. ■ a specimen of a secretion taken with a swab for examination: *he had taken throat swabs.*
2 a mop or other absorbent device for cleaning or mopping up a floor or other surface.
3 archaic a contemptible person. ■ US another term for **SWABBIE**.
▶ **verb** (**swabs, swabbing, swabbed**) [with obj.] clean (a wound or surface) with a swab: *the crew were* ***swabbing down*** *the decks | swab a patch of skin with alcohol.* ■ [with adverbial] absorb or clear (moisture) with a swab: *the blood was swabbed away.*
– ORIGIN mid 17th cent. (in the sense 'mop for cleaning the decks'): back-formation from *swabber* 'sailor detailed to swab decks', from early modern Dutch *zwabber*, from a Germanic base meaning 'splash' or 'sway'.

swabbie ▶ **noun** (pl. **swabbies**) US Nautical slang a member of the navy, typically one who is of low rank.

Swabia /ˈsweɪbɪə/ a former duchy of medieval Germany, now divided between SW Germany, Switzerland, and France. German name **SCHWABEN**.
– DERIVATIVES **Swabian adjective & noun.**

swacked ▶ **adjective** N. Amer. informal drunk.
– ORIGIN 1930s: past participle of Scots *swack* 'fling, strike heavily'.

swaddle ▶ **verb** [with obj.] wrap (someone, especially a baby) in garments or cloth: *she swaddled the baby tightly* | figurative *they have grown up swaddled in consumer technology.*
– ORIGIN Middle English: frequentative of **SWATHE[2]**.

swaddling clothes ▶ **plural noun** narrow bands of cloth formerly wrapped round a newborn child to restrain its movements and quieten it.

swadeshi /swaˈdɛʃi/ ▶ **adjective** Indian (of manufactured goods) made in India from Indian-produced materials.
– ORIGIN via Hindi from Sanskrit *svadeśīya* 'of one's own country', from *sva* 'own' + *deśa* 'country'; used originally with reference to a nationalist movement advocating Indian-made products.

swag ▶ **noun 1** an ornamental festoon of flowers, fruit, and greenery: *garlands and swags of foliage.* ■ a carved or painted representation of such a festoon. ■ a curtain or piece of fabric fastened so as to hang in a drooping curve.
2 [mass noun] informal money or goods taken by a thief or burglar: *garden machinery is the most popular swag.*
3 Austral./NZ a traveller's or miner's bundle of personal belongings. ■ informal a large number or amount: *Howard has promised me* ***a swag of*** *goodies.*
▶ **verb** (**swags, swagging, swagged**) [with obj.]
1 arrange in or decorate with a swag or swags of fabric: *swag the fabric gracefully over the curtain tie-backs* | (as adj. **swagged**) *the swagged contours of nomads' tents.*
2 [no obj.] Austral./NZ travel with one's personal belongings in a bundle: *we were* ***swagging it*** *in Queensland |* ***swagging my way*** *up to the Northern Territory.*
3 [no obj.] chiefly literary hang heavily: *the crinkly old hide swags here and there.* ■ sway from side to side: *the stout chief sat swagging from one side to the other of the carriage.*
– ORIGIN Middle English (in the sense 'bulging bag'): probably of Scandinavian origin. The original sense of the verb (early 16th cent.) was 'cause to sway or sag'.

swage /sweɪdʒ/ ▶ **noun 1** a shaped tool or die for giving a desired form to metal by hammering or pressure.
2 a groove, ridge, or other moulding on an object.
▶ **verb** [with obj.] shape (metal) using a swage, especially in order to reduce its cross section. ■ join (metal pieces) together by this process.
– ORIGIN late Middle English (in sense 2 of the noun): from Old French *souage* 'decorative groove', of unknown origin.

swage block ▶ **noun** a grooved or perforated block for shaping metal.

swagger ▶ **verb** [no obj., with adverbial of direction] walk or behave in a very confident and arrogant or self-important way: *he swaggered along the corridor* | (as adj. **swaggering**) *a swaggering gait.*
▶ **noun** [in sing.] a very confident and arrogant or self-important gait or manner: *they strolled around the camp with an exaggerated swagger.*
▶ **adjective 1** [attrib.] denoting a coat or jacket cut with a loose flare from the shoulders.
2 Brit. informal, dated smart or fashionable: *I'll take you somewhere swagger.*
– DERIVATIVES **swaggerer noun, swaggeringly adverb.**
– ORIGIN early 16th cent.: apparently a frequentative of the verb **SWAG**.

swagger stick ▶ **noun** a short cane carried by a military officer.

swagman ▶ **noun** (pl. **swagmen**) Austral./NZ a person carrying a swag or bundle of belongings.

Swahili /swəˈhiːli, swɑː-/ ▶ **noun** (pl. **same**) **1** [mass noun] a Bantu language widely used as a lingua franca in East Africa and having official status in several countries. There are probably fewer than 2 million native speakers, but it is in everyday use by over 20 million. Also called **KISWAHILI**.
2 a member of a people of Zanzibar and nearby coastal regions, descendants of the original speakers of Swahili.
▶ **adjective** relating to Swahili or to its native speakers.
– ORIGIN from Arabic *sawāḥil*, plural of *sāḥil* 'coast'.

swain ▶ **noun 1** literary a young lover or suitor.
2 archaic a country youth.
– ORIGIN late Old English (denoting a young man attendant on a knight), from Old Norse *sveinn* 'lad'.

swale ▶ **noun** chiefly N. Amer. & dialect a low or hollow place, especially a marshy depression between ridges.
– ORIGIN early 16th cent.: of unknown origin; probably taken to America from eastern England, where it is still in use.

Swaledale ▶ **noun** a sheep of a small hardy breed with long, coarse wool.
– ORIGIN early 20th cent.: from the name of a region in North Yorkshire.

swallow[1] ▶ **verb** [with obj.] **1** cause or allow (something, especially food or drink) to pass down the throat: *she swallowed a mouthful slowly.* ■ [no obj.] perform the muscular movement of the oesophagus required to do this, especially through fear or nervousness: *she swallowed hard, sniffing back her tears.* ■ put up with or meekly accept (something unwelcome): *he seemed ready to swallow any insult.* ■ believe unquestioningly (a lie or unlikely assertion): *she had swallowed his story hook, line, and sinker.* ■ resist expressing (a feeling) or uttering (words): *he swallowed his pride.*
2 take in and cause to disappear; engulf: *the dark mist* ***swallowed her up****.* ■ completely use up (money or resources): *debts* ***swallowed up*** *most of the money he had got for the house.*
▶ **noun** an act of swallowing something, especially food or drink: *he downed his drink in one swallow.* ■ an amount of something swallowed in one action: ***a swallow of*** *beer.*
– DERIVATIVES **swallowable adjective.**
– ORIGIN Old English *swelgan*, of Germanic origin; related to Dutch *zwelgen* and German *schwelgen*.

swallow[2] ▶ **noun** a migratory swift-flying songbird with a forked tail and long pointed wings, feeding on insects in flight. Compare with **WOODSWALLOW**.
● Family Hirundinidae: several genera, in particular *Hirundo*, and numerous species, e.g. the widespread *H. rustica* (North American name: **barn swallow**).
– PHRASES **one swallow does not make a summer** proverb a single fortunate event doesn't mean that what follows will also be good.
– ORIGIN Old English *swealwe*, of Germanic origin; related to Dutch *zwaluw* and German *Schwalbe*.

swallow dive Brit. ▶ **noun** a dive performed with one's arms outspread until close to the water.
▶ **verb** [no obj.] (**swallow-dive**) perform a swallow dive.

swallower ▶ **noun 1** [usu. in combination] a person or thing that swallows something: *pill-swallowers.*

2 a slender deep-sea fish with very large jaws and a distensible stomach, enabling it to swallow very large prey. ● Family Chiasmodontidae: *Chiasmodon* and other genera.

swallow hole ▶ **noun** another term for SINKHOLE.

swallowtail ▶ **noun 1** (also **swallowtail butterfly**) a large brightly coloured butterfly with tail-like projections on the hindwings. ● Family Papilionidae: many species, including the European *Papilio machaon*, of fenland country.
2 [usu. as modifier] a deeply forked tail. ■ a thing resembling a deeply forked tail in shape: *a black swallowtail coat.*
– DERIVATIVES **swallow-tailed** adjective.

swallow-wort ▶ **noun 1** a plant of the milkweed family, the follicles of which suggest a swallow with outstretched wings, often becoming a weed. ● Several species in the family Asclepiadaceae, in particular the European **black swallow-wort** (*Cynanchum* (or *Vincetoxicum*) *nigrum*), and the American *Asclepias curassavica*.
2 Brit. the greater celandine, formerly believed to be used by swallows to restore their sight.

swam past of SWIM.

swami /ˈswɑːmi/ ▶ **noun** (pl. **swamis**) a Hindu male religious teacher: [as title] *Swami Satchidananda.*
– ORIGIN from Hindi *swāmī* 'master, prince', from Sanskrit *svāmin*.

Swammerdam /ˈswaməd am/, Jan (1637–80), Dutch naturalist and microscopist. He classified insects into four groups and was the first to observe red blood cells.

swamp ▶ **noun** an area of low-lying, uncultivated ground where water collects; a bog or marsh. ■ an area of waterlogged ground: *the ceaseless deluge had turned the lawn into a swamp.*
▶ **verb** [with obj.] overwhelm or flood with water: *a huge wave swamped the canoes.* ■ [no obj.] (of a boat) become overwhelmed with water and sink. ■ overwhelm with an excessive amount of something; inundate: *the country was* ***swamped with*** *goods from abroad | feelings of guilt suddenly swamped her.*
– ORIGIN early 17th cent.: probably ultimately from a Germanic base meaning 'sponge' or 'fungus'.

swamp cabbage ▶ **noun** the skunk cabbage of western North America (*Lysichiton americanum*), the leaves of which are sometimes used in cooking.

swamp cypress ▶ **noun** a deciduous North American conifer with exposed root buttresses, typically growing in swamps and on water margins. Also called BALD CYPRESS. ● *Taxodium distichum*, family Taxodiaceae.

swamp deer ▶ **noun** a deer that inhabits swamps and grassy plains in India and Nepal. Also called BARASINGHA. ● *Cervus duvaucelli*, family Cervidae.

swamper ▶ **noun** informal, dated **1** N. Amer. an assistant to the captain of a riverboat or to a lorry driver.
2 N. Amer. a worker who trims felled trees and clears a road for lumberers in a forest.
3 US a native or inhabitant of a swampy region.

swamp fever ▶ **noun** [mass noun] **1** a contagious viral disease of horses that causes anaemia and emaciation and is usually fatal.
2 dated malaria.

swamphen /ˈswɒmphɛn/ (also **purple swamphen**) ▶ **noun** a marshbird of the rail family, with a purplish-blue head and breast and a large red bill, found throughout the Old World. ● *Porphyrio porphyrio*, family Rallidae.

swampland ▶ **noun** [mass noun] (also **swamplands**) land consisting of swamps.

swamp mahogany ▶ **noun** an Australian eucalyptus with long leaves and dark fibrous bark, grown elsewhere as an ornamental and as a shelter-belt tree. ● *Eucalyptus robusta*, family Myrtaceae.

swamp rat ▶ **noun** an African rodent that frequents dense vegetation on swampy ground. ● Three genera in the family Muridae, in particular the vole-like *Otomys* (also called VLEI RAT) and the slender *Malacomys*: several species.

swamp snake ▶ **noun** an olive-coloured venomous snake living in marshy and wet country on the east coast of Australia. ● *Hemiaspis signata*, family Elapidae.

swampy ▶ **adjective** (**swampier**, **swampiest**) characteristic of or resembling a swamp: *a swampy area.*

Swan, Sir Joseph Wilson (1828–1914), English physicist and chemist. He devised an electric light bulb in 1860 and in 1883 he formed a partnership with Thomas Edison to manufacture it.

swan ▶ **noun** a large waterbird with a long flexible neck, short legs, webbed feet, a broad bill, and typically all-white plumage. ● Genus *Cygnus* (and *Coscoroba*): several species.
▶ **verb** (**swans**, **swanning**, **swanned**) [no obj., with adverbial of direction] Brit. informal move about or go somewhere in a casual, irresponsible, or ostentatious way: *swanning around Europe nowadays are we?*
– DERIVATIVES **swanlike** adjective.
ORIGIN Old English, of Germanic origin; related to Dutch *zwaan* and German *Schwan*. The current sense of the verb originated as military slang, referring to the free movement of armoured vehicles.

swan dive N. Amer. ▶ **noun** a swallow dive.
▶ **verb** [no obj.] (**swan-dive**) perform a swan dive.

Swanee /ˈswɒni/ variant spelling of SUWANNEE.

Swanee whistle ▶ **noun** a musical instrument (often a toy) in the form of a pipe with a plunger instead of finger holes, so that the player slides from note to note.

swank informal, chiefly Brit. ▶ **verb** [no obj.] display one's wealth, knowledge, or achievements in a way that is intended to impress others: *he was* ***swanking about***, *playing the dashing young master spy.*
▶ **noun** [mass noun] behaviour, talk, or display intended to impress others: *a little money will buy you a good deal of swank.*
▶ **adjective** North American term for SWANKY.
– ORIGIN early 19th cent.: of unknown origin.

swankpot ▶ **noun** Brit. informal, dated a person attempting to impress others.

swanky ▶ **adjective** (**swankier**, **swankiest**) informal stylishly luxurious and expensive: *directors with swanky company cars.* ■ using one's wealth, knowledge, or achievements to try to impress others.
– DERIVATIVES **swankily** adverb, **swankiness** noun.

swan mussel ▶ **noun** a large European freshwater mussel of still or slow-moving water, the larvae of which parasitize fish. ● *Anodonta cygnea*, family Unionidae.

swan neck ▶ **noun** a curved structure shaped like a swan's neck: [as modifier] *a small swan-neck dispenser.*
– DERIVATIVES **swan-necked** adjective.

swannery ▶ **noun** (pl. **swanneries**) Brit. a place set aside for swans to breed.

Swan River a river of Western Australia. Rising as the Avon to the south-east of Perth, it flows north and west through Perth to the Indian ocean at Fremantle. It was the site of the first free European settlement in Western Australia.

swansdown ▶ **noun** [mass noun] **1** the fine down of a swan, used for trimmings and powder puffs.
2 a thick cotton fabric with a soft nap on one side. ■ a soft, thick fabric made from wool mixed with a little silk or cotton.

Swansea /ˈswɒnzi/ a city in South Wales, on the Bristol Channel; pop. 173,500 (est. 2009). Welsh name ABERTAWE.

Swanson, Gloria (1899–1983), American actress; born *Gloria May Josephine Svensson*. She was a major star of silent films such as *Sadie Thompson* (1928) but is now chiefly known for her performance as the fading movie star in *Sunset Boulevard* (1950).

swansong ▶ **noun** the final performance or activity of a person's career: *he has decided to make this tour his swansong.*
– ORIGIN early 19th cent.: suggested by German *Schwanengesang*, a song like that fabled to be sung by a dying swan.

swan-upping ▶ **noun** the annual practice of catching the swans on the River Thames and marking them to indicate ownership by the Crown or a corporation.

swap (also **swop**) ▶ **verb** (**swaps**, **swapping**, **swapped**) [with obj.] take part in an exchange of: *we swapped phone numbers | I'd* ***swap*** *places* ***with*** *you any day |* [no obj.] *I was wondering if you'd like to* ***swap with*** *me.* ■ give (one thing) and receive something else in exchange: ***swap*** *one of your sandwiches* ***for*** *a cheese and pickle?* ■ substitute (one thing) for another: *I* ***swapped*** *my busy life in London* ***for*** *a peaceful village retreat.*
▶ **noun** an act of exchanging one thing for another: *let's* ***do a swap.*** ■ a thing that has been or may be given in exchange for something else: *I've got one already, but I'll keep this as a swap.* ■ Finance an exchange of liabilities between two borrowers, either so that each acquires access to funds in a currency they need or so that a fixed interest rate is exchanged for a floating rate.
– DERIVATIVES **swappable** adjective, **swapper** noun.
– ORIGIN Middle English (originally in the sense 'throw forcibly'): probably imitative of a resounding blow. Current senses have arisen from an early use meaning 'strike hands as a token of agreement'.

swapfile ▶ **noun** Computing a file on a hard disk used to provide space for programs which have been transferred from the processor's memory.

swap meet ▶ **noun** chiefly N. Amer. **1** a gathering at which enthusiasts or collectors trade or exchange items of common interest: *a computer swap meet.*
2 a flea market.

SWAPO /ˈswɑːpəʊ/ ▶ **abbreviation** South West Africa People's Organization.

swap shop ▶ **noun** informal an agency which puts people with articles to exchange or trade in touch with each other.

swaption ▶ **noun** Finance an option giving the right but not the obligation to engage in a swap.
– ORIGIN 1980s: blend of SWAP and OPTION.

Swaraj /swəˈrɑːdʒ/ ▶ **noun** [mass noun] historical self-government or independence for India.
– DERIVATIVES **Swarajist** noun.
– ORIGIN from Sanskrit *svarājya*, from *sva* 'own' + *rājya* 'rule'; compare with RAJ.

sward /swɔːd/ ▶ **noun 1** literary an expanse of short grass.
2 Farming the upper layer of soil, especially when covered with grass.
– DERIVATIVES **swarded** adjective.
– ORIGIN Old English *sweard* 'skin'. The sense 'upper layer of soil' developed in late Middle English (at first in phrases such as *sward of the earth*).

sware archaic past of SWEAR.

swarf /swɑːf/ ▶ **noun** [mass noun] fine chips or filings of stone, metal, or other material produced by a machining operation.
– ORIGIN mid 16th cent.: either from Old English *geswearf* 'filings' or from Old Norse *svarf* 'file dust'.

swarm ▶ **noun** a large or dense group of flying insects: ***a swarm of*** *locusts.* ■ a large number of honeybees that leave a hive en masse with a newly fertilized queen in order to establish a new colony. ■ (**a swarm/swarms of**) a large number of people or things: *a swarm of journalists.* ■ a series of similar-sized earthquakes occurring together, typically near a volcano. ■ Astronomy a large number of minor celestial objects occurring together in space, especially a dense shower of meteors.
▶ **verb** [no obj.] **1** (of flying insects) move in or form a swarm: (as adj. **swarming**) *swarming locusts.* ■ (of honeybees, ants, or termites) issue from the nest in large numbers in order to mate and found new colonies: *the bees had swarmed and left the hive.*
2 [no obj., with adverbial] move somewhere in large numbers: *protesters were swarming into the building.* ■ (**swarm with**) be crowded or overrun with (moving people or things): *the place was swarming with police.*
– PHRASAL VERBS **swarm up** climb (something) rapidly by gripping it with one's hands and feet, alternately hauling and pushing oneself upwards: *I swarmed up the mast.*
– ORIGIN Old English *swearm* (noun), of Germanic origin; related to German *Schwarm*, probably also to the base of Sanskrit *svarati* 'it sounds'.

swarmer (also **swarmer cell**) ▶ **noun** Biology another term for ZOOSPORE.

swart /swɔːt/ ▶ **adjective** archaic or literary swarthy.
– ORIGIN Old English *sweart*, of Germanic origin; related to Dutch *zwart* and German *schwarz*.

swart gevaar /ˌswart xəˈfɑː/ ▶ **noun** historical (in South Africa under apartheid) a threat perceived as being posed by black people to whites.
– ORIGIN Afrikaans, literally 'black danger'.

swarthy ▶ **adjective** (**swarthier**, **swarthiest**) dark-complexioned: *swarthy men with gleaming teeth.*
– DERIVATIVES **swarthiness** noun.
– ORIGIN late 16th cent.: alteration of obsolete *swarty* (see SWART).

swash[1] ▶ **verb** [no obj.] **1** (of water or an object in water) move with a splashing sound: *the water swashed and rippled around the car wheels.*
2 archaic (of a person) flamboyantly swagger about or wield a sword: *he swashed about self-confidently.*
▶ **noun** the rush of seawater up the beach after the breaking of a wave. ■ archaic the motion or sound of water dashing or washing against something.
– ORIGIN mid 16th cent. (in the sense 'make a noise like swords clashing or beating on shields'): imitative.

S

swash[2] ▶ **adjective** Printing denoting an ornamental written or printed character, typically a capital letter.
– ORIGIN late 17th cent.: of unknown origin.

swashbuckle ▶ **verb** [no obj.] (usu. as adj. **swashbuckling**) engage in daring and romantic adventures with bravado or flamboyance: *a crew of swashbuckling buccaneers*.
– ORIGIN late 19th cent.: back-formation from SWASHBUCKLER.

swashbuckler ▶ **noun** a swashbuckling person. ■ a film or book portraying a swashbuckling person.
– ORIGIN mid 16th cent.: from SWASH[1] + BUCKLER.

swash plate ▶ **noun** an inclined disc revolving on an axle and giving reciprocating motion to a part in contact with it.

swastika /ˈswɒstɪkə/ ▶ **noun** an ancient symbol in the form of an equal-armed cross with each arm continued at a right angle, used (in clockwise form) as the emblem of the German Nazi party.
– ORIGIN late 19th cent.: from Sanskrit *svastika*, from *svasti* 'well-being', from *su* 'good' + *asti* 'being'.

swat ▶ **verb** (**swats**, **swatting**, **swatted**) [with obj.] hit or crush (something, especially an insect) with a sharp blow from a flat object: *I swatted a mosquito that had landed on my wrist* | [no obj.] *she was **swatting at** a fly*. ■ hit (someone) with a sharp blow: *she swatted him over the head with a rolled-up magazine*.
▶ **noun** a sharp blow: *the dog gave the hedgehog a sideways swat*.
– ORIGIN early 17th cent. (in the sense 'sit down'): northern English dialect and US variant of SQUAT.

swatch ▶ **noun** a sample, especially of fabric. ■ a collection of fabric samples, especially in the form of a book. ■ a patch or area of a material or surface: *the sunset had filled the sky with swatches of deep orange*.
– ORIGIN early 16th cent. (originally Scots and northern English, denoting the counterfoil of a tally, and later a tally fixed to a piece of cloth before dyeing): of unknown origin.

swathe[1] /sweɪð/ (chiefly N. Amer. also **swath** /sweɪð, swɒθ/) ▶ **noun** (pl. **swathes** /sweɪðz/ or **swaths** /sweɪðz, swɒθs/) **1** a row or line of grass, corn, or other crop as it falls or lies when mown or reaped. ■ a strip left clear by the passage of a mowing machine or scythe: *the combine had cut a deep swathe around the border of the fields*.
2 a broad strip or area of something: *vast swathes of countryside* | figurative *a significant **swathe of** popular opinion*.
– PHRASES **cut a swathe through** pass through (something) causing great damage, destruction, or change: *AIDS has cut a swathe through battalions of ordinary people*. **cut a wide swath** N. Amer. attract a great deal of attention by trying to impress others.
– ORIGIN Old English *swæth*, *swathu* 'track, trace', of West Germanic origin; related to Dutch *zwad(e)* and German *Schwade*. In Middle English the term denoted a measure of the width of grassland, probably reckoned by a sweep of the mower's scythe.

swathe[2] /sweɪð/ ▶ **verb** [with obj.] (usu. **be swathed in**) wrap in several layers of fabric: *his hands were swathed in bandages*.
▶ **noun** a piece or strip of material in which something is wrapped.
– ORIGIN late Old English *swath-* (noun), *swathian* (verb); compare with SWADDLE.

S

swather /ˈswɔːθə, ˈswɒθə/ ▶ **noun** a device on a mowing machine for raising uncut fallen grain and marking the line between cut and uncut grain.

Swatow /swɒˈtaʊ/ former name for SHANTOU.

SWAT team /swɒt/ ▶ **noun** (in the US) a group of elite police marksmen who specialize in high-risk tasks such as hostage rescue. ■ any group of specialists brought in to solve a difficult or urgent problem.
– ORIGIN 1980s: acronym from *Special Weapons and Tactics*.

sway ▶ **verb 1** move or cause to move slowly or rhythmically backwards and forwards or from side to side: [no obj.] *he swayed slightly on his feet* | (as adj. **swaying**) *swaying palm trees* | [with obj.] *wind rattled and swayed the trees*.
2 [with obj.] control or influence (a person or course of action): *he's easily swayed by other people*. ■ literary rule; govern: *now let the Lord forever reign and sway us as he will*.
▶ **noun** [mass noun] **1** a rhythmical movement from side to side: *the easy sway of her hips*.
2 rule; control: *the country was **under the sway of** rival warlords*.
– PHRASES **hold sway** have great power or influence over a particular person, place, or domain.
– ORIGIN Middle English: corresponding in sense to Low German *swājen* 'be blown to and fro' and Dutch *zwaaien* 'swing, walk in a tottering way'.

swayback ▶ **noun** [mass noun] an abnormally hollowed back, especially in a horse; lordosis.
– DERIVATIVES **sway-backed** adjective.

sway bar ▶ **noun** N. Amer. another term for ANTI-ROLL BAR.

Swazi /ˈswɑːzi/ ▶ **noun** (pl. **same** or **Swazis**) **1** a member of a people traditionally inhabiting Swaziland and Mpumalanga province in South Africa. ■ a native or inhabitant of Swaziland.
2 [mass noun] the Nguni language of the Swazi, an official language in Swaziland and South Africa with about 1.6 million speakers. Also called SISWATI.
▶ **adjective** relating to Swaziland, the Swazis, or their language.
– ORIGIN from the name of *Mswati*, a 19th-century king of the Swazis.

Swaziland a small landlocked kingdom in southern Africa, bounded by South Africa and Mozambique; pop. 1,337,200 (est. 2009); official languages, Swazi and English; capital, Mbabane.

> Swaziland was a South African protectorate from 1894 and came under British rule in 1902 after the Second Boer War. In 1968 it became a fully independent Commonwealth state.

SWB ▶ **abbreviation** short wheelbase.

swear ▶ **verb** (**swears**, **swearing**, past **swore**; past participle **sworn**) **1** [reporting verb] make a solemn statement or promise undertaking to do something or affirming that something is the case: [with clause] *Maria made me swear I would never tell anyone* | *I **swear by** all I hold dear that I had nothing to do with it* | [with direct speech] *'Never again,' she swore, 'will I be short of money'* | [with obj.] *they were reluctant to swear allegiance*. ■ [with obj.] take (an oath): *he forced them to swear an oath of loyalty to him*. ■ [with obj.] take a solemn oath as to the truth of (a statement): *I asked him if he would swear a statement to this effect*. ■ [with obj.] make (someone) promise to observe a certain course of action: *I've been **sworn to** secrecy*.
2 [no obj.] use offensive language, especially as an expression of anger: *Peter swore under his breath*.
– PHRASES **swear blind** (or N. Amer. **swear up and down**) informal affirm something emphatically: *his informant swore blind that the weapons were still there*.
– PHRASAL VERBS **swear by** informal have or express great confidence in the use, value, or effectiveness of: *Iris swears by her yoga*. **swear someone in** admit someone to a particular office or position by directing them to take a formal oath: *he was sworn in as president on 10 July*. **swear off** informal promise to abstain from: *I'd sworn off alcohol*. **swear something out** US Law obtain the issue of a warrant for arrest by making a charge on oath. **swear to** [usu. with negative] express one's assurance that something is the case: *I couldn't swear to it, but I'm pretty sure it's his writing*.
– DERIVATIVES **swearer** noun, **sweary** adjective (informal).
– ORIGIN Old English *swerian* of Germanic origin; related to Dutch *zweren*, German *schwören*, also to ANSWER.

swearing ▶ **noun** [mass noun] the use of offensive language: *there's a lot of swearing in the show*.

swear word ▶ **noun** an offensive word, used especially as an expression of anger.

sweat ▶ **noun 1** [mass noun] moisture exuded through the pores of the skin, typically in profuse quantities as a reaction to heat, physical exertion, fever, or fear: *beads of sweat broke out on her brow*. ■ [count noun] an instance or period of being covered with sweat: *even thinking about him made me **break out in a sweat*** | *we'd all **worked up a sweat** in spite of the cold*. ■ [count noun] informal a state of flustered anxiety or distress: *I don't believe he'd **get into** such **a sweat** about a girl*. ■ informal hard work; effort: *computer graphics take a lot of the sweat out of animation*. ■ [in sing.] informal a laborious task or undertaking: *helping to run the meeting was a bit of a sweat*.
2 (**sweats**) chiefly N. Amer. informal term for SWEATSUIT or SWEATPANTS. ■ [as modifier] denoting loose casual garments made of thick, fleecy cotton: *sweat tops and bottoms*.
▶ **verb** (**sweats**, **sweating**; past and past participle **sweated** or N. Amer. **sweat**) **1** [no obj.] exude sweat: *he was sweating profusely*. ■ [with obj.] (**sweat something out/off**) get rid of something from the body by exuding sweat: *a well-hydrated body sweats out waste products more efficiently*. ■ [with obj.] cause (a person or animal) to exude sweat by exercise or exertion: *cold as it was, the climb had sweated him*. ■ (of food or an object) ooze or exude beads of moisture on to its surface: *cheese stored at room temperature will quickly begin to sweat*. ■ (of a person) exert a great deal of strenuous effort: *I've **sweated over** this for six months*. ■ (of a person) be or remain in a state of extreme anxiety, typically for a prolonged period: *I let her sweat for a while, then I asked her out again*. ■ [with obj.] N. Amer. informal worry about (something): *he's not going to have a lot of time to sweat the details*.
2 [with obj.] heat (chopped vegetables) slowly in a pan with a small amount of fat, so that they cook in their own juices: *sweat the celery and onions with olive oil and seasoning*. ■ [no obj.] (of chopped vegetables) be cooked in this way: *let the chopped onion sweat gently for five minutes*.
3 [with obj. and adverbial] subject (metal) to surface melting, especially to fasten or join by solder without a soldering iron: *the tyre is sweated on to the wooden parts*.
– PHRASES **break sweat** (or US **break a sweat**) informal exert oneself physically. **by the sweat of one's brow** by one's own hard work, typically manual labour. **no sweat** informal used to convey that something is not difficult or problematic: *'We haven't any decaf, I'm afraid.' 'No sweat.'*. **sweat blood** informal make an extraordinarily strenuous effort to do something: *she's sweated blood to support her family*. ■ be extremely anxious: *we've been sweating blood over the question of what is right*. **sweat buckets** informal sweat profusely. **sweat bullets** N. Amer. informal be extremely anxious or nervous. **sweat it out** informal endure prolonged heat or exertion: *about 1,500 runners are expected to sweat it out in this year's run*. ■ wait in a state of extreme anxiety for something to happen or be resolved: *he sweated it out until the lab report was back*. **sweat the small stuff** US informal worry about trivial things.
– ORIGIN Old English *swāt* (noun), *swǣtan* (verb), of Germanic origin; related to Dutch *zweet* and German *Schweiss*, from an Indo-European root shared by Latin *sudor*.

sweatband ▶ **noun** a band of absorbent material worn around the head or wrist to soak up sweat, especially by participants in sport. ■ a band of absorbent material lining a hat.

sweated ▶ **adjective** relating to or denoting manual workers employed at very low wages for long hours and under poor conditions: *the use of sweated labour by unscrupulous employers*.

sweat equity ▶ **noun** [mass noun] N. Amer. informal an interest in a property earned by a tenant in return for labour towards upkeep or restoration.

sweater ▶ **noun 1** a knitted garment worn on the upper body, typically with long sleeves, put on over the head.
2 dated an employer who works employees hard in poor conditions for low pay.

sweat gland ▶ **noun** a small gland that secretes sweat, situated in the dermis of the skin. Such glands are found over most of the body, and have a simple coiled tubular structure.

sweating sickness ▶ **noun** any of various fevers with intense sweating, epidemic in England in the 15th–16th centuries.

sweat lodge ▶ **noun** a hut, typically dome-shaped, used by North American Indians for ritual steam baths as a means of purification.

sweatpants ▶ **plural noun** loose, warm trousers with an elasticated or drawstring waist, worn when exercising or as leisurewear.

sweatshirt ▶ **noun** a loose, warm sweater, typically made of cotton, worn when exercising or as leisurewear.

sweatshop ▶ **noun** a factory or workshop, especially in the clothing industry, where manual workers are employed at very low wages for long hours and under poor conditions.

sweat sock ▶ **noun** N. Amer. a thick, absorbent calf-length sock, often worn with trainers.

sweatsuit ▶ **noun** a suit consisting of a sweatshirt and sweatpants, worn when exercising or as leisurewear.

sweaty ▸ adjective (**sweatier, sweatiest**) exuding, soaked in, or inducing sweat: *my feet got so hot and sweaty.*
– DERIVATIVES **sweatily** adverb, **sweatiness** noun.

Swede ▸ noun a native or inhabitant of Sweden, or a person of Swedish descent.
– ORIGIN from Middle Low German and Middle Dutch *Swēde*, probably from Old Norse *Svíthjóth*, from *Svíar* 'Swedes' + *thjóth* 'people'.

swede ▸ noun **1** Brit. a large, round yellow-fleshed root which is eaten as a vegetable. Also called RUTABAGA in North America.
2 the European plant of the cabbage family which produces the swede. ● *Brassica napus*, family Cruciferae: 'napobrassica' group.
– ORIGIN early 19th cent.: from SWEDE, being first introduced into Scotland from Sweden in 1781–2.

Sweden a country occupying the eastern part of the Scandinavian peninsula; pop. 9,059,700 (est. 2009); official language, Swedish; capital, Stockholm. Swedish name SVERIGE.

> Originally united in the 12th century, Sweden formed part of the Union of Kalmar with Denmark and Norway from 1397 until its re-emergence as an independent kingdom in 1523. Between 1814 and 1905 it was united with Norway. A constitutional monarchy, Sweden has pursued a policy of non-alignment, and it remained neutral in the two world wars. Sweden joined the European Union in 1995.

Swedenborg /ˈswiːd(ə)nbɔːɡ/, Emanuel (1688–1772), Swedish scientist, philosopher, and mystic. The spiritual beliefs which he expounded after a series of mystical experiences blended Christianity with pantheism and theosophy.
– DERIVATIVES **Swedenborgian** /ˌswiːd(ə)nˈbɔːɡɪən/ adjective & noun.

Swede saw ▸ noun chiefly Canadian a type of saw with a bow-like tubular frame and many cutting teeth.

swedge /swɛdʒ/ Scottish informal ▸ noun a fight or brawl.
▸ verb [no obj.] fight or brawl.
– ORIGIN perhaps related to dialect *swag* 'sway heavily'.

Swedish ▸ adjective relating to Sweden, its people, or their language.
▸ noun [mass noun] the Scandinavian language of Sweden, also spoken in parts of Finland. It has over 8 million speakers.

Swedish massage ▸ noun [mass noun] a popular general-purpose system of massage, devised in Sweden.

Sweeney ▸ noun (**the Sweeney**) Brit. informal the members of a police flying squad.
– ORIGIN 1930s: from rhyming slang *Sweeney* Todd, a barber who murdered his customers (see TODD).

sweep ▸ verb (**sweeps, sweeping**; past and past participle **swept**) [with obj.] **1** clean (an area) by brushing away dirt or litter: *I've swept the floor* | *Greg **swept out** the kitchen.* ■ [with obj. and adverbial of direction] move or remove (dirt or litter) in such a way: *she swept the tea leaves into a dustpan.* ■ [with obj. and adverbial of direction] move or push (someone or something) with great force: *I was swept along by the crowd* | figurative *Nahum's smile swept away the air of apprehensive gloom.* ■ [with obj. and adverbial of direction] brush (hair) back from one's face or upwards: *long hair swept up into a high chignon.* ■ Cricket hit (the ball) on the leg side by bringing the bat across the body from a half-kneeling position; hit a ball delivered by (a bowler) with such a stroke.
2 [no obj., with adverbial of direction] move swiftly and smoothly: *a large black car swept past the open windows* | figurative *his cool grey eyes swept over her.* ■ (of a person) move in a confident and stately manner: *she swept magnificently from the hall.* ■ affect (an area or place) swiftly and widely: *the rebellion had swept through all four of the country's provinces* | [with obj.] *violence swept the country.* ■ (of a geographical or natural feature) extend continuously in a particular direction, especially in a curve: *green forests swept down the hillsides.* ■ [with obj.] N. Amer. win all the games in (a series); take each of the winning or main places in (a contest or event): *we knew we had to sweep these three home games.*
3 search (an area) for something: *the detective swept the room for hair and fingerprints.* ■ examine (something) for electronic listening devices: *the line is swept every fifteen minutes.* ■ cover (an entire area) with a gun: *they were trying to get the Lewis gun up behind some trees from where they would sweep the trench.*
▸ noun **1** an act of sweeping something with a brush: *I was giving the floor a quick sweep.* ■ short for CHIMNEY SWEEP.
2 a long, swift curving movement: *a grandiose sweep of his hand.* ■ Electronics the movement of a beam across the screen of a cathode ray tube. ■ Cricket an attacking stroke in which the bat is brought across the body from a half-kneeling position to hit the ball to leg.
3 a comprehensive search or survey of a place or area: *the police finished their sweep through the woods.* ■ (often **sweeps**) N. Amer. a survey of the ratings of television stations, carried out at regular intervals to determine advertising rates.
4 a long, typically curved stretch of road, river, country, etc.: *we could see a wide sweep of country perhaps a hundred miles across.* ■ a curved part of a drive in front of a building: *one fork of the drive continued on to the gravel sweep.* ■ the range or scope of something: *the whole sweep of the history of the USSR.*
5 informal a sweepstake.
6 N. Amer. an instance of winning every event, award, or place in a contest: *a World Series sweep.*
7 a long, heavy oar used to row a barge or other vessel: [as modifier] *a big, heavy sweep oar.*
8 a sail of a windmill.
9 a long pole mounted as a lever for raising buckets from a well.
– PHRASES **make a clean sweep** see CLEAN. **sweep the board** win every event or prize in a contest. **sweep someone off their feet** see FOOT. **sweep something under the carpet** see CARPET.
– ORIGIN Old English *swāpan* (verb), of Germanic origin; related to German *schweifen* 'sweep in a curve'.

sweepback ▸ noun [mass noun] the angle at which an aircraft's wing is set back from a right angle to the body.

sweeper ▸ noun **1** a person or device that cleans a floor or road by sweeping.
2 Soccer a player stationed behind the other defenders, free to defend at any point across the field and sometimes initiating and supporting attacks.
3 a small nocturnal shoaling fish of reefs and coastal waters, occurring chiefly in the tropical Indo-Pacific. ● Family Pempheridae: several genera and species, including the western Atlantic **glassy sweeper** (*Pempheris schomburgki*), with transparent young.

sweeping ▸ adjective **1** extending or performed in a long, continuous curve: *sweeping, desolate moorlands* | *a smooth sweeping motion.*
2 wide in range or effect: *we cannot recommend any sweeping alterations.* ■ (of a statement) taking no account of particular cases or exceptions; too general: *a sweeping assertion.*
▸ noun (**sweepings**) dirt or refuse collected by sweeping: *the sweepings from the house.*
– DERIVATIVES **sweepingly** adverb, **sweepingness** noun.

sweep second hand ▸ noun a second hand on a clock or watch, moving on the same dial as the other hands.

sweepstake ▸ noun (also **sweepstakes**) a form of gambling, especially on horse races, in which all the stakes are divided among the winners. ■ a race on which money is bet in this way. ■ a prize or prizes won in a sweepstake.

sweet ▸ adjective **1** having the pleasant taste characteristic of sugar or honey; not salt, sour, or bitter: *a cup of hot sweet tea.* ■ (of air, water, or food) fresh, pure, and untainted: *lungfuls of the clean, sweet air.* ■ [often in combination] smelling pleasant like flowers or perfume; fragrant: *a bunch of sweet-smelling flowers.* ■ (of sound) melodious or harmonious: *the sweet notes of the flute.* ■ chiefly US denoting music, especially jazz, played at a steady tempo without improvisation.
2 pleasing in general; delightful: *it was the sweet life he had always craved.* ■ highly satisfying or gratifying: *some sweet, short-lived revenge.* ■ working, moving, or done smoothly or easily: *the sweet handling of this motorcycle.*
3 (of a person or action) pleasant and kind or thoughtful: *a very sweet nurse came along* | *it was **sweet of** you to come.* ■ charming and endearing: *a sweet little cat.* ■ dear; beloved: *my sweet love.* ■ archaic used as a respectful form of address: *go to thy rest, sweet sir.*
4 (**sweet on**) informal, dated infatuated or in love with: *she seemed quite sweet on him.*
5 used for emphasis in various phrases and exclamations: *What had happened? Sweet nothing.*
▸ noun **1** Brit. a small shaped piece of confectionery made with sugar: *a bag of sweets.*
2 Brit. a sweet dish forming a course of a meal; a pudding or dessert.
3 used as an affectionate form of address: *hello, my sweet.*
4 (**the sweet**) archaic or literary the sweet part or element of something: *you have had the bitter, now comes the sweet.* ■ (**sweets**) the pleasures or delights found in something: *the sweets of office.*
– PHRASES **keep someone sweet** informal keep someone well disposed towards oneself, especially by favours or bribery. **in one's own sweet time** (or **way**) when (or how) one wants to, regardless of the possible inconvenience caused to others. **she's sweet** Austral./NZ informal all is well. **sweet dreams** used to express good wishes to a person going to bed. **sweet sixteen** sixteen regarded as the characteristic age of prettiness and innocence in a girl.
– DERIVATIVES **sweetish** adjective, **sweetly** adverb.
– ORIGIN Old English *swēte*, of Germanic origin; related to Dutch *zoet*, German *süss*, from an Indo-European root shared by Latin *suavis* and Greek *hēdus*.

sweet alyssum ▸ noun see ALYSSUM.

sweet-and-sour ▸ adjective (especially of Chinese-style food) cooked in a sauce containing sugar and either vinegar or lemon.

sweet balm ▸ noun see BALM (sense 3).

sweet basil ▸ noun see BASIL.

sweet bay ▸ noun see BAY².

sweetbread ▸ noun the thymus gland (or, rarely, the pancreas) of an animal, especially as used for food.

sweet briar ▸ noun **1** a Eurasian wild rose with fragrant leaves and flowers. ● *Rosa rubiginosa*, family Rosaceae.
2 W. Indian a spiny acacia with fragrant yellow flowers. ● Genus *Acacia*, family Leguminosae: *A. farnesiana*, an Old World tree which is grown throughout the tropics and yields an essential oil used in perfumery, and the tropical American *A. tortuosa*.

sweet butter ▸ noun [mass noun] a type of unsalted butter made from fresh pasteurized cream.

sweet chestnut ▸ noun see CHESTNUT.

sweet cicely ▸ noun a white-flowered European plant of the parsley family, with large fern-like leaves and a scent which resembles aniseed. ● *Myrrhis odorata*, family Umbelliferae.

sweetcorn ▸ noun [mass noun] maize of a variety with kernels that have a high sugar content. It is grown for human consumption and is harvested while slightly immature. ■ the kernels of sweetcorn eaten as a vegetable.

sweeten ▸ verb make or become sweet or sweeter, especially in taste: [with obj.] *a cup of coffee sweetened with saccharin* | [no obj.] *her smile sweetened.* ■ [with obj.] make more agreeable or acceptable: *there is no way to sweeten the statement.* ■ [with obj.] informal induce (someone) to be well disposed or helpful to oneself: *I am in the process of sweetening him up.*
– PHRASES **sweeten the pill** see PILL¹.

sweetener ▸ noun a substance used to sweeten food or drink, especially one other than sugar. ■ informal, chiefly Brit. an inducement, typically in the form of money or a concession: *a sweetener may persuade them to sell.*

sweet Fanny Adams ▸ noun see FANNY ADAMS (sense 1).

sweet fennel ▸ noun see FENNEL.

sweet flag ▸ noun an Old World waterside plant of the arum family, with leaves that resemble those of the iris. It is used medicinally and as a flavouring. Also called CALAMUS. ● *Acorus calamus*, family Araceae.

sweet gale ▸ noun another term for BOG MYRTLE.
– ORIGIN mid 17th cent.: *gale* from Old English *gagel*, *gagelle*, of Germanic origin; related to Dutch *gagel*, German *Gagel*.

sweetgrass ▸ noun [mass noun] any of a number of grasses which possess a sweet flavour, making them attractive to livestock, or a sweet smell, resulting in their former use as herbs for strewing or burning. ● *Glyceria*, *Hierochloe*, and other genera, family Gramineae.

sweet gum ▸ noun the North American liquidambar, which yields a balsam and decorative heartwood which is marketed as satin walnut. ● *Liquidambar styraciflua*, family Hamamelidaceae.

sweetheart ▸ noun a person that one is in love with: *the pair were childhood sweethearts.* ■ used as a

S

term of endearment or affectionate form of address: *don't worry, sweetheart, I've got it all worked out.* ■ a particularly lovable or pleasing person or thing: *he is an absolute sweetheart.* ■ [as modifier] informal denoting an arrangement reached privately by two sides, especially an employer and a trade union, in their own interests: *a sweetheart deal.*

sweetheart neckline ▶ noun a neckline on a dress or blouse that is low at the front and shaped like the top of a heart.

sweetheart rose ▶ noun N. Amer. a rose with small pink, white, or yellow flowers that are particularly attractive as buds.

sweetie ▶ noun informal **1** Brit. a sweet.
2 (also **sweetie-pie**) used as a term of endearment.

sweeting ▶ noun **1** an apple of a sweet-flavoured variety.
2 archaic darling.

sweetlips (also **sweetlip**) ▶ noun (pl. **same**) a patterned grunt (fish) that changes its colour and markings with age, occurring in the Indo-Pacific.
● *Plectorhynchus* and other genera, family Pomadasyidae: several species, including the **oriental sweetlips** (*P. orientalis*).

sweetmeal ▶ noun [mass noun] [usu. as modifier] Brit. sweetened wholemeal: *a sweetmeal biscuit.*

sweetmeat ▶ noun archaic an item of confectionery or sweet food.

sweet milk ▶ noun [mass noun] fresh whole milk, as opposed to buttermilk.

sweetness ▶ noun [mass noun] the quality of being sweet. ■ used as an affectionate form of address, though often ironically: *I've just got to go, sweetness.*
– PHRASES **sweetness and light** social or political harmony: *the relationship was by no means all sweetness and light.* ■ good-natured benevolence: *when he's around she's all sweetness and light.* [taken from Swift and used with aesthetic or moral reference, first by Arnold in *Culture and Anarchy* (1869).]

sweet pea ▶ noun a climbing plant of the pea family, widely cultivated for its colourful fragrant flowers.
● Genus *Lathyrus*, family Leguminosae: several species, in particular *L. odoratus*, which originated in southern Italy and Sicily.

sweet pepper ▶ noun a large green, yellow, orange, or red variety of capsicum which has a mild or sweet flavour and is often eaten raw. Also called BELL PEPPER in North America. ● *Capsicum annuum* var. *annuum*, 'grossum' group (or var. *grossum*).

sweet potato ▶ noun **1** an edible tropical tuber with white slightly sweet flesh.
2 the Central American climbing plant which yields sweet potatoes, widely cultivated in warm countries.
● *Ipomoea batatas*, family Convolvulaceae.

sweet rocket ▶ noun a herbaceous plant of the cabbage family, cultivated for its long spikes of mauve or white flowers which are fragrant in the evening.
● *Hesperis matronalis*, family Cruciferae.

sweetsop ▶ noun **1** a round or heart-shaped custard apple which has a green scaly rind and a sweet pulp. Also called SUGAR APPLE.
2 the tropical American evergreen shrub which yields sweetsops. ● *Annona squamosa*, family Annonaceae.

S

sweet spot ▶ noun informal the point or area on a bat, club, or racket at which it makes most effective contact with the ball.

sweet sultan ▶ noun a Near Eastern plant of the daisy family, with sweet-scented flowers, slender stems, and narrow grey-green leaves. ● *Centaurea moschata*, family Compositae.

sweet talk informal ▶ verb (**sweet-talk**) [with obj.] insincerely praise (someone) in order to persuade them to do something: *detectives **sweet-talked** them **into** confessing.*
▶ noun [mass noun] insincere praise used to persuade someone to do something.

sweet tooth ▶ noun (pl. **sweet tooths**) a great liking for sweet-tasting foods.
– DERIVATIVES **sweet-toothed** adjective.

sweetveld /ˈswiːtfɛlt/ ▶ noun [mass noun] S. African land on which plants providing nutritious grazing grow.
■ nutritious vegetation.
– ORIGIN probably partly translating Dutch *zoeteveld*; compare with SOURVELD.

sweet vernal grass ▶ noun see VERNAL GRASS.

sweet violet ▶ noun a sweet-scented Old World violet with heart-shaped leaves, used in perfumery and as a flavouring. ● *Viola odorata*, family Violaceae.

sweet william ▶ noun a fragrant European garden pink with flattened clusters of vivid red, pink, or white flowers. ● *Dianthus barbatus*, family Caryophyllaceae.

sweet woodruff ▶ noun see WOODRUFF.

swell ▶ verb (**swells, swelling, swelled**; past participle **swollen** or **swelled**) **1** [no obj.] (especially of a part of the body) become larger or rounder in size, typically as a result of an accumulation of fluid: *her bruised knee was already **swelling up*** | figurative *the sky was black and swollen with rain* | (as adj. **swollen**) *swollen glands.* ■ be intensely affected or filled with a particular emotion: *she felt herself **swell with** pride.*
2 become or make greater in intensity, number, amount, or volume: [no obj.] *the low murmur swelled to a roar* | (as adj. **swelling**) *the swelling ranks of Irish singer-songwriters* | [with obj.] *the city's population was swollen by refugees.*
▶ noun **1** [in sing.] a full or gently rounded shape or form: *the soft swell of her breast.*
2 a gradual increase in amount, intensity, or volume: *a huge swell in the popularity of one-day cricket.* ■ a welling up of a feeling: *a swell of pride swept over George.*
3 a slow, regular movement of the sea in rolling waves that do not break: *there was a heavy swell.*
4 a mechanism for producing a crescendo or diminuendo in an organ or harmonium.
5 informal, dated a fashionable or stylish person of wealth or high social position: *a crowd of city swells.*
▶ adjective N. Amer. informal, dated excellent; very good: *you're looking swell.* ■ archaic smart; fashionable: *a swell boulevard.*
▶ adverb N. Amer. informal, dated excellently; very well: *everything was just going swell.*
– PHRASES **one's head swells** one becomes conceited: *I am not saying this to make your head swell* | *if I say this, you'll get **swollen-headed**.*
– ORIGIN Old English *swellan* (verb), of Germanic origin; related to German *schwellen*. Current senses of the noun date from the early 16th cent.; the informal adjectival use derives from noun sense 5 of the noun (late 18th cent.).

swell box ▶ noun a part of a large organ in which some of the pipes are enclosed, with a movable shutter for controlling the sound level.

swelling ▶ noun an abnormal enlargement of a part of the body, typically as a result of an accumulation of fluid. ■ a natural rounded protuberance: *the lobes are prominent swellings on the base of the brain.*

swell organ ▶ noun a section of a large organ consisting of pipes enclosed in a swell box, usually played with an upper keyboard.

swelter ▶ verb [no obj.] be uncomfortably hot: *Barney sweltered in his doorman's uniform.*
▶ noun [in sing.] an uncomfortably hot atmosphere: *the swelter of the afternoon had cooled.*
– ORIGIN Middle English: from the base of dialect *swelt* 'perish', of Germanic origin.

sweltering ▶ adjective uncomfortably hot: *a sweltering English summer* | *the sweltering heat outside.*
– DERIVATIVES **swelteringly** adverb.

swept past and past participle of SWEEP.

swept-back ▶ adjective (of an aircraft wing) positioned to point somewhat backwards.

swept-up ▶ adjective another term for UPSWEPT.

swept volume ▶ noun the volume through which a piston or plunger moves as it makes a stroke.

swept-wing ▶ adjective (of an aircraft) having swept-back wings.

swerve ▶ verb change or cause to change direction abruptly: *a lorry swerved across her path* | [with obj.] *O'Hara swerved the motorcycle round the corner.*
▶ noun an abrupt change of direction: *do not make sudden swerves, particularly around parked vehicles.*
■ [mass noun] divergence from a straight course imparted to a ball or other object, especially in soccer, cricket, or snooker.
– DERIVATIVES **swerver** noun.
– ORIGIN Old English *sweorfan* 'depart, leave, turn aside', of Germanic origin; related to Middle Dutch *swerven* 'to stray'.

Sweyn I /sweɪn/ (also **Sven**) (d.1014), king of Denmark *c.*985–1014; known as **Sweyn Forkbeard**. From 1003 he launched a series of attacks on England, finally driving Ethelred the Unready to flee to Normandy at the end of 1013. Sweyn then became king of England but died five weeks later.

SWF ▶ abbreviation single white female (used in personal advertisements).

SWG ▶ abbreviation (in the UK) standard wire gauge, denoting a series of standard sizes in which wire is made.

swidden /ˈswɪd(ə)n/ ▶ noun an area of land cleared for cultivation by slashing and burning vegetation.
■ [mass noun] the method of clearing land by slashing and burning vegetation: *the practice of swidden.*
▶ verb [with obj.] clear (land) by slashing and burning vegetation.
– ORIGIN late 18th cent. (as a verb, originally dialect): variant of dialect *swithen* 'to burn'.

Swift, Jonathan (1667–1745), Irish satirist, poet, and Anglican cleric; known as **Dean Swift**. He is best known for *Gulliver's Travels* (1726), a satire on human society in the form of a fantastic tale of travels in imaginary lands.

swift ▶ adjective happening quickly or promptly: *a remarkably swift recovery.* ■ moving or capable of moving at high speed: *the water was very swift* | *the swiftest horse in his stable.*
▶ adverb literary except in combination swiftly: *streams which ran swift and very clear* | *a swift-acting poison.*
▶ noun **1** a swift-flying insectivorous bird with long, slender wings and a superficial resemblance to a swallow, spending most of its life on the wing.
● Family Apodidae: several genera and numerous species, in particular the common **Eurasian swift** (*Apus apus*).
2 (also **swift moth**) a moth, typically yellow-brown in colour, with fast darting flight. The eggs are scattered in flight and the larvae live underground feeding on roots, where they can be a serious pest.
● Family Hepialidae: *Hepialus* and other genera.
3 a light, adjustable reel for holding a skein of silk or wool.
– DERIVATIVES **swiftly** adverb, **swiftness** noun.
– ORIGIN Old English (as an adjective), from the Germanic base of Old English *swifan* 'move in a course, sweep'. The bird name dates from the mid 17th cent.

swift fox ▶ noun a small fox with a yellowish-buff coat and a black-tipped tail, living on the plains of North America. ● *Vulpes velox*, family Canidae.

swiftlet ▶ noun a small swift found in southern Asia and Australasia. ● Genera *Aerodramus* and *Collocalia*, family Apodidae: many species.

swifty (also **swiftie**) ▶ noun (pl. **swifties**) informal **1** Brit. an alcoholic drink consumed swiftly.
2 chiefly Austral./NZ a deceptive trick: *they had hoped to **pull a swifty**.*
3 chiefly Austral./NZ a person who acts or thinks quickly: *boy, are you a swifty.*

swig informal ▶ verb (**swigs, swigging, swigged**) [with obj.] drink in large draughts: *Dave swigged the wine in five gulps* | [no obj.] *Ratagan **swigged at** his beer.*
▶ noun a large draught of drink: *he took a swig of tea.*
– ORIGIN mid 16th cent. (as a noun in the obsolete sense 'liquor'): of unknown origin.

swill ▶ verb [with obj.] **1** Brit. wash or rinse out (an area or container) by pouring large amounts of water or other liquid over or into it: *I **swilled out** the mug.*
■ cause (liquid) to swirl round in a container or cavity: *she gently **swilled** her brandy **round** her glass.*
■ [no obj., with adverbial] (of a liquid) move or splash about over a surface: *the icy water swilled round us.*
2 informal drink (something) greedily or in large quantities: *they whiled away their evening swilling pints of bitter* | (as adj., in combination **swilling**) *his beer-swilling pals.* ■ accompany (food) with large quantities of drink: *a feast **swilled down** with pints of cider.*
▶ noun **1** [mass noun] kitchen refuse and scraps of waste food mixed with water for feeding to pigs. ■ informal alcohol of inferior quality.
2 informal a large mouthful of a drink: *a swill of ale.*
– DERIVATIVES **swiller** noun [usu. in combination] *beer-swillers.*
– ORIGIN Old English *swillan, swilian* (verb), of unknown origin. The noun dates from the mid 16th cent.

swim ▶ verb (**swims, swimming**; past **swam**; past participle **swum**) [no obj.] **1** propel the body through water by using the limbs, or (in the case of a fish or other aquatic animal) by using fins, tail, or other bodily movement: *they swam ashore* | *he swims thirty lengths twice a week.* ■ [with obj.] cross (a particular stretch of water) in this way: *she swam the Channel.* ■ float on or at the surface of a liquid. ■ [with obj.] cause to float or move across water: *the Russians were able to swim their infantry carriers across.*
2 be immersed in or covered with liquid: *mashed potatoes **swimming in** gravy.*
3 appear to reel or whirl before one's eyes: *Emily rubbed her eyes as the figures swam before her eyes.*

■ experience a dizzily confusing sensation in one's head: *the drink made his head swim.*
▶ **noun 1** an act or period of swimming: *we went for a swim in the river.*
2 a pool in a river which is a particularly good spot for fishing: *he landed two 5lb chub from the same swim.*
– PHRASES **in the swim** involved in or aware of current affairs or events. **swim with** (or **against**) **the tide** act in accordance with (or against) the prevailing opinion or tendency.
– DERIVATIVES **swimmable** adjective, **swimmer** noun.
– ORIGIN Old English *swimman* (verb), of Germanic origin; related to Dutch *zwemmen* and German *schwimmen.*

> **USAGE** In standard English the past tense of **swim** is **swam** (*she* **swam** *to the shore*) and the past participle is **swum** (*she had never* **swum** *there before*). In the 17th and 18th centuries **swam** and **swum** were used interchangeably for the past participle, but this is not acceptable in standard modern English.

swim bladder ▶ **noun** Zoology a gas-filled sac present in the body of many bony fishes, used to maintain and control buoyancy.

swimfeeder ▶ **noun** Fishing a small perforated container for bait which is cast into the water or attached to a lure to attract fish.

swimmeret /ˈswɪmərɛt/ ▶ **noun** another term for **PLEOPOD.**

swimming ▶ **noun** [mass noun] the sport or activity of propelling oneself through water using the limbs.

swimming bath (also **swimming baths**) ▶ **noun** Brit. a swimming pool, especially a public indoor one.

swimming costume ▶ **noun** Brit. a garment worn for swimming, especially a woman's one-piece swimsuit.

swimming crab ▶ **noun** a coastal crab which has paddle-like rear legs for swimming. ● Family Portunidae: many species, including the **velvet swimming crab** (*Macropipus puber*).

swimming hole ▶ **noun** chiefly N. Amer. a bathing place in a stream or river.

swimmingly ▶ **adverb** smoothly and satisfactorily: *things are going swimmingly.*

swimming pool ▶ **noun** an artificial pool for swimming in.

swimming trunks (also **swim trunks**) ▶ **plural noun** shorts worn by men for swimming.

swimsuit ▶ **noun** a woman's one-piece swimming costume.
– DERIVATIVES **swimsuited** adjective.

swimwear ▶ **noun** [mass noun] clothing worn for swimming.

Swinburne, Algernon Charles (1837–1909), English poet and critic. Associated as a poet with the Pre-Raphaelites, he also contributed to the revival of interest in Elizabethan and Jacobean drama and produced influential studies of William Blake and the Brontës.

swindle ▶ **verb** [with obj.] use deception to deprive (someone) of money or possessions: *a businessman swindled investors* **out of** *millions of pounds.* ■ obtain (money) fraudulently: *he was said to have swindled £62.5 million from the state-owned cement industry.*
▶ **noun** a fraudulent scheme or action: *he is mixed up in a £10 million insurance swindle.*
– DERIVATIVES **swindler** noun.
– ORIGIN late 18th cent.: back-formation from *swindler*, from German *Schwindler* 'extravagant maker of schemes, swindler', from *schwindeln* 'be giddy', also 'tell lies'.

Swindon a town in Wiltshire, central England; pop. 158,400 (est. 2009). An old market town, Swindon developed rapidly after railway engineering works were established there in 1841 and again in the 1950s as an overspill town for London.

swine ▶ **noun 1** (pl. **same**) chiefly formal or N. Amer. a pig.
2 (pl. **same** or **swines**) informal a contemptible or unpleasant person: *what an arrogant, unfeeling swine!* ■ a thing that is very difficult or unpleasant to deal with: *mist is a swine in unfamiliar country.*
– DERIVATIVES **swinish** adjective, **swinishly** adverb, **swinishness** noun.
– ORIGIN Old English *swīn*, of Germanic origin; related to Dutch *zwijn* and German *Schwein*, also to **sow**[2].

swine fever ▶ **noun** [mass noun] an intestinal viral disease of pigs.

swine flu ▶ **noun** [mass noun] a form of influenza which affects pigs, or a form of human influenza caused by a related virus.

swineherd ▶ **noun** chiefly historical a person who tends pigs.
– ORIGIN Old English, from **SWINE** + obsolete *herd* 'herdsman'.

swine vesicular disease ▶ **noun** [mass noun] an infectious viral disease of pigs causing mild fever and blisters around the mouth and feet.

swing ▶ **verb** (**swings, swinging**; past and past participle **swung**) **1** move or cause to move back and forth or from side to side while suspended or on an axis: [no obj.] *her long black skirt swung about her legs* | *the door swung shut behind him* | [with obj.] *a priest began swinging a censer* | (as adj. **swinging**) *local girls with their castanets and their swinging hips.* ■ [no obj.] informal be executed by hanging: *now he was going to swing for it.* ■ [with obj.] turn (a ship or aircraft) to all compass points in succession, in order to test compass error.
2 [no obj., with adverbial of direction] move by grasping a support from below and leaping: *we swung across like two trapeze artists* | (**swing oneself**) *the Irishman swung himself into the saddle.* ■ move quickly round to the opposite direction: *Ronni had swung round to face him.* ■ move with a rhythmic swaying gait: *the riflemen swung along smartly.*
3 [with adverbial of direction] move or cause to move in a smooth, curving line: [with obj.] *she swung her legs to the side of the bed* | [no obj.] *the cab swung into the car park.* ■ [with obj.] bring down (something held) with a curving movement, typically in order to hit an object: *I swung the club and missed the ball.* ■ [no obj.] (**swing at**) attempt to hit or punch, typically with a wide curving movement of the arm: *he swung at me with the tyre wrench.* ■ throw (a punch) with such a movement: *she swung a punch at him.* ■ [with obj.] Cricket (of a bowler) make a delivery of (a ball) deviate sideways from a regular course in the air. ■ [no obj.] Cricket (of a ball) deviate in such a way.
4 shift or cause to shift from one opinion, mood, or state of affairs to another: [no obj.] *opinion swung in the Chancellor's favour* | [with obj.] *the failure to seek peace could swing sentiment the other way.* ■ [with obj.] have a decisive influence on (something, especially a vote or election): *an attempt to swing the vote in their favour.* ■ [with obj.] informal succeed in bringing about: *what swung it was the £17,000 she offered the panel to let her win.*
5 [no obj.] play music with an easy flowing but vigorous rhythm: *the band swung on.* ■ (of music) be played with such a rhythm.
6 [no obj.] informal (of an event, place, or way of life) be lively, exciting, or fashionable.
7 [no obj.] informal be promiscuous, especially by engaging in group sex or swapping sexual partners.
▶ **noun 1** a seat suspended by ropes or chains, on which someone may sit and swing back and forth. ■ a spell of swinging on such an apparatus.
2 an act of swinging: *with the swing of her arm, the knife flashed through the air.* ■ the manner in which a golf club or a bat is swung: *the flaws in his swing weren't evident when he was an amateur.* ■ [mass noun] the motion of swinging: *this short cut gave her hair new movement and swing.* ■ an attempted blow or punch: *Neil took a swing at her.* ■ [mass noun] Cricket sideways deviation of the ball from a regular path: [as modifier] *a swing bowler.*
3 a discernible change in opinion, especially the amount by which votes or points scored change from one side to another: *a five per cent swing to Labour.*
4 [mass noun] a style of jazz or dance music with an easy flowing but vigorous rhythm. ■ the rhythmic feeling or drive of such music.
5 N. Amer. a swift tour involving a number of stops, especially one undertaken as part of a political campaign.
– PHRASES **get (back) into the swing of things** informal become accustomed to (or return to) an activity or routine. **go with a swing** Brit. informal (of a party or other event) be lively and enjoyable. **in full swing** at the height of activity: *by nine-thirty the dance was in full swing.* **swing the lead** Brit. informal shirk one's duty; malinger. [with nautical allusion to the lump of lead suspended by a string, slowly lowered to ascertain the depth of water.] **swings and roundabouts** Brit. a situation in which different actions or options result in no eventual gain or loss. [from the phrase *to gain on the swings and lose on the roundabouts.*] **swing into action** quickly begin acting or operating.
– DERIVATIVES **swinger** noun.
– ORIGIN Old English *swingan* 'to beat, whip', also 'rush', *geswing* 'a stroke with a weapon', of Germanic origin; related to German *schwingen* 'brandish'.

swingback ▶ **adjective** (of a coat) cut to swing as the wearer moves.

swingbin ▶ **noun** Brit. a rubbish bin with a lid that swings shut after being pushed open.

swingboat ▶ **noun** chiefly Brit. a boat-shaped swing with seats for several people at fairs.

swing bridge ▶ **noun** a bridge over water that can be rotated horizontally to allow ships through.

swingby /ˈswɪŋbʌɪ/ ▶ **noun** (pl. **swingbys**) a change in the flight path of a spacecraft using the gravitational pull of a celestial body. Compare with **SLINGSHOT.**

swing coat ▶ **noun** a coat cut so as to swing when the wearer moves.

swing door (N. Amer. also **swinging door**) ▶ **noun** a door that can be opened in either direction and is closed by a spring device when released.

swinge /swɪn(d)ʒ/ ▶ **verb** (**swinges, swingeing, swinged**) [with obj.] literary strike hard; beat.
– ORIGIN Old English *swengan* 'shake, shatter, move violently', of Germanic origin.

swingeing /ˈswɪn(d)ʒɪŋ/ ▶ **adjective** Brit. severe or extreme in size, amount, or effect: *swingeing cuts in public expenditure.*
– DERIVATIVES **swingeingly** adverb.

swinging ▶ **adjective** informal lively, exciting, and fashionable: *a swinging resort* | *the Swinging Sixties.* ■ sexually liberated or promiscuous.
– DERIVATIVES **swingingly** adverb.

swingle ▶ **noun 1** a wooden tool for beating flax and removing the woody parts from it.
2 the swinging part of a flail.
▶ **verb** [with obj.] beat (flax) with a swingle.
– ORIGIN Middle English: from Middle Dutch *swinghel*, from the base of the verb **SWING.**

swingletree /ˈswɪŋ(ə)ltriː/ ▶ **noun** chiefly Brit. a crossbar pivoted in the middle, to which the traces are attached in a horse-drawn cart or plough.

swingman ▶ **noun** (pl. **swingmen**) Basketball a player who can play both guard and forward.

swingometer /swɪŋˈɒmɪtə/ ▶ **noun** informal a device or computerized display used to demonstrate the effect of a political swing on an election.

swing set ▶ **noun** N. Amer. a frame for children to play on, typically including one or more swings and a slide.

swing shift ▶ **noun** N. Amer. a work shift from afternoon to late evening.

swing state ▶ **noun** a marginal US state where voters are liable to swing from one political party to another, important in determining the overall result of an election.

swing ticket ▶ **noun** an information tag attached by a string to an article for sale.

swing vote ▶ **noun** chiefly US a vote that has a decisive influence on the result of a poll.
– DERIVATIVES **swing voter** noun.

swing-wing ▶ **noun** [usu. as modifier] an aircraft wing that can move from a right-angled to a swept-back position: *swing-wing fighter bombers.*

S

swingy ▶ **adjective** (**swingier, swingiest**) **1** (of music) characterized by an easy flowing but vigorous rhythm.
2 (of a skirt, coat, or other garment) cut so as to swing as the wearer moves.

swipe informal ▶ **verb** [with obj.] **1** hit or try to hit with a swinging blow: *she swiped me right across the nose* | [no obj.] *Lola stood on the balcony, swiping at the moths.*
2 steal: *someone swiped one of his sausages.*
3 pass (a swipe card) through the electronic device that reads it.
▶ **noun** a sweeping blow: *he missed the ball with his first swipe.* ■ an attack or criticism: *he* **took a swipe at** *his critics.*
– DERIVATIVES **swiper** noun.
– ORIGIN mid 18th cent.: perhaps a variant of **SWEEP.**

swipe card ▶ **noun** a plastic card such as a credit card or ID card bearing magnetically encoded information which is read when the edge of the card is slid through an electronic device.

swipple ▶ **noun** dialect the swinging part of a flail.
– ORIGIN late Middle English: probably based on the verb **SWEEP.**

swirl ▶ **verb** [no obj.] move in a twisting or spiralling pattern: *the smoke was swirling around him* | (as adj.

swirling) figurative *a flood of swirling emotions.* ■ [with obj.] cause to move in such a pattern: *swirl a little cream into the soup.*
▶ **noun** a quantity of something moving in a twisting or spiralling pattern: *swirls of dust swept across the floor.* ■ a twisting or spiralling movement or pattern: *she emerged with a swirl of skirts | swirls of colour.*
– DERIVATIVES **swirly adjective** (**swirlier, swirliest**).
– ORIGIN late Middle English (originally Scots in the sense 'whirlpool'): perhaps of Low German or Dutch origin; compare with Dutch *zwirrelen* 'to whirl'.

swish ▶ **verb 1** [no obj., with adverbial of direction] move with a hissing or rushing sound: *a car swished by.* ■ [with obj.] cause to move with a hissing or rushing sound: *a girl came in, swishing her long skirts.* ■ aim a swinging blow at something: *he* **swished at** *a bramble with a piece of stick.*
2 [with obj.] Basketball sink (a shot) without the ball touching the backboard or rim.
▶ **noun 1** a hissing or rustling sound: *he could hear the swish of a distant car.* ■ a rapid swinging movement: *the cow gave a swish of its tail.*
2 Basketball, informal a shot that goes through the basket without touching the backboard or rim.
3 N. Amer. informal, derogatory an effeminate male homosexual.
▶ **adjective** Brit. informal impressively smart and fashionable: *dinner at a swish hotel.*
– ORIGIN mid 18th cent.: imitative.

swishy ▶ **adjective** (**swishier, swishiest**) **1** making a swishing sound or movement.
2 N. Amer. informal effeminate.

Swiss ▶ **adjective** relating to Switzerland or its people.
▶ **noun** (pl. **same**) a native or inhabitant of Switzerland, or a person of Swiss descent.
– ORIGIN early 16th cent.: from French *Suisse*, from Middle High German *Swīz* 'Switzerland'.

Swiss army knife (also **Swiss army penknife**) ▶ **noun** (trademark in the UK) a penknife incorporating several blades and other tools such as scissors and screwdrivers.

Swiss bank account ▶ **noun** an account held at a bank in Switzerland, identified by a number rather than a name in order to preserve the client's anonymity and security.

Swiss chard ▶ **noun** see **CHARD**.

Swiss cheese ▶ **noun** [mass noun] cheese from Switzerland, typically containing large holes.

Swiss cheese plant ▶ **noun** a large monstera with perforated leaves (supposedly resembling the holes in a Swiss cheese), popularly grown as a houseplant while young, and with creamy arum-like spathes followed by pineapple-flavoured fruit when mature. ● *Monstera deliciosa*, family Araceae.

Swiss Confederation the confederation of cantons forming Switzerland.

Swiss darning ▶ **noun** [mass noun] a technique in which coloured stitches are sewn on to knitted garments to make patterns or motifs that seem to have been knitted.

Swiss guard ▶ **noun** [often treated as pl.] Swiss mercenaries employed as a special guard, formerly by sovereigns of France, now only at the Vatican.

S

Swiss roll ▶ **noun** Brit. a cylindrical cake with a spiral cross section, made from a flat sponge cake spread with a filling such as jam and rolled up.

switch ▶ **noun 1** a device for making and breaking the connection in an electric circuit: *the guard hit a switch and the gate swung open.* ■ Computing a program variable which activates or deactivates a certain function of a program. ■ Computing a device which forwards data packets to an appropriate part of the network.
2 an act of changing to or adopting one thing in place of another: *his friends were surprised at his switch from newspaper owner to farmer.*
3 a slender, flexible shoot cut from a tree.
4 N. Amer. a set of points on a railway track.
5 a tress of false or detached hair tied at one end, used in hairdressing to supplement natural hair.
▶ **verb** [with obj.] **1** change the position, direction, or focus of: *the company switched the boats to other routes.* ■ adopt (something different) in place of something else; change: *she's managed to switch careers | [no obj.] she worked as a librarian and then switched to journalism.* ■ substitute (two items) for each other; exchange: *after ten minutes, listener and speaker switch roles.*
2 archaic beat or flick with or as if with a switch.
– PHRASAL VERBS **switch off** informal cease to pay attention: *as he waffles on, I switch off.* **switch something off** (or **on**) turn an electrical device off (or on): *she switched on the kettle.*
– DERIVATIVES **switchable adjective**.
– ORIGIN late 16th cent. (denoting a thin tapering riding whip): probably from Low German.

switchback ▶ **noun 1** Brit. a road, path, or railway with alternate sharp ascents and descents. ■ a roller coaster.
2 N. Amer. a 180° bend in a road or path, especially one leading up the side of a mountain.

switchblade ▶ **noun** chiefly N. Amer. another term for **FLICK KNIFE**.

switchboard ▶ **noun 1** an installation for the manual control of telephone connections in an office, hotel, or other large building.
2 an apparatus for varying connections between electric circuits in other applications.

switched-on ▶ **adjective** Brit. informal aware of what is going on or what is up to date: *your shortcomings will be apparent to a switched-on youngster.*

switcher ▶ **noun 1** US a shunting engine.
2 a piece of electronic equipment used to select or combine different video and audio signals.

switcheroo /ˌswɪtʃəˈruː/ ▶ **noun** N. Amer. informal a change, reversal, or exchange, especially a surprising or deceptive one.
– ORIGIN 1930s: from the noun **SWITCH** + *-eroo* in the sense 'unexpected'.

switchgear ▶ **noun** [mass noun] **1** switching equipment used in the transmission of electricity.
2 the switches or electrical controls in a motor vehicle.

switchgrass ▶ **noun** [mass noun] a tall North American panic grass which forms large clumps. ● *Panicum virgatum*, family Gramineae.

switch-hitter ▶ **noun 1** Baseball an ambidextrous batter.
2 N. Amer. informal a bisexual person.
– DERIVATIVES **switch-hitting adjective**.

switchover ▶ **noun** an instance of changing from one system, method, policy, etc. to another: *the switchover from analogue to digital TV.*

switch selling ▶ **noun** [mass noun] a sales technique whereby cheap or non-existent goods are placed on offer on favourable terms to entice the consumer into buying similar but more expensive items.

switchyard ▶ **noun** US **1** the part of a railway yard taken up by points, in which trains are made up.
2 an enclosed area of a power system containing the switchgear.

swither /ˈswɪðə/ Scottish ▶ **verb** [no obj.] be uncertain as to which course of action to choose: *Leonard swithered as to whether he should enter the arts or commerce.*
▶ **noun** [in sing.] a state of uncertainty.
– ORIGIN early 16th cent.: of unknown origin.

Swithin, St (also **Swithun**) (d.862), English ecclesiastic. He was bishop of Winchester from 852. The tradition that if it rains on St Swithin's day it will do so for the next forty days may have its origin in the heavy rain said to have occurred when his relics were to be transferred to a shrine in Winchester cathedral. Feast day, 15 July.

Switzerland a mountainous, landlocked country in central Europe; pop. 7,604,500 (est. 2009); official languages, French, German, Italian, and Romansh; capital, Berne. French name **SUISSE**, German name **SCHWEIZ**, Italian name **SVIZZERA**; also called by its Latin name **HELVETIA**.

> Switzerland emerged as an independent country in the 14th and 15th centuries, when the states or cantons formed a confederation to defeat first their Habsburg overlords and then their Burgundian neighbours. After a period of French domination (1798–1815) the Swiss Confederation's neutrality was guaranteed by the other European powers. Neutral in both world wars, Switzerland has emerged as an international financial centre and as the headquarters of several international organizations such as the Red Cross.

swive /swʌɪv/ ▶ **verb** [with obj.] archaic or humorous have sexual intercourse with.
– ORIGIN Middle English: apparently from the Old English verb *swīfan* 'move (along a course), sweep'.

swivel ▶ **noun** a coupling between two parts enabling one to revolve without turning the other.
▶ **verb** (**swivels, swivelling, swivelled**; US **swivels, swiveling, swiveled**) [often with adverbial] turn around a point or axis or on a swivel: [no obj.] *he swivelled in the chair* | [with obj.] *she swivelled her eyes round.*
– ORIGIN Middle English, from the base of Old English *swīfan* 'to move (along a course), sweep'.

swivel chair ▶ **noun** a chair with a seat able to be turned on its base to face in any direction.

swivet /ˈswɪvɪt/ ▶ **noun** [in sing.] US a fluster or panic: *the incomprehensible did not throw him into a swivet.*
– ORIGIN late 19th cent.: of unknown origin.

swizz (also **swiz**) ▶ **noun** [usu. in sing.] Brit. informal a thing that is disappointing or represents a mild swindle: *what a swizz!*
– ORIGIN early 20th cent.: abbreviation of **SWIZZLE²**.

swizzle¹ ▶ **noun** a mixed alcoholic drink, especially a frothy one of rum or gin and bitters.
▶ **verb** [with obj.] stir (a drink) with a swizzle stick.
– ORIGIN early 19th cent.: of unknown origin.

swizzle² ▶ **noun** Brit. informal another term for **SWIZZ**.
– ORIGIN early 20th cent.: probably an alteration of **SWINDLE**.

swizzle stick ▶ **noun** a stick used for frothing up still drinks or taking the fizz out of sparkling ones.

SWM ▶ **abbreviation** single white male (used in personal advertisements).

swollen past participle of **SWELL**.

swoon ▶ **verb** [no obj.] **1** literary faint, especially from extreme emotion: *Frankie's mother swooned and had to be helped to the headmaster's office.*
2 be overcome with admiration, adoration, or other strong emotion: *women* **swoon over** *his manly, unaffected ways.*
▶ **noun** literary an occurrence of fainting: *he found his wife in a swoon.*
– ORIGIN Middle English: the verb from obsolete *swown* 'fainting', the noun from *aswoon* 'in a faint', both from Old English *geswōgen* 'overcome'.

swoony ▶ **adjective** informal experiencing or inducing a state of rapture or other strong emotion: *he gave me a big swoony kiss on the mouth.*

swoop ▶ **verb** [no obj., with adverbial of direction] (especially of a bird) move rapidly downwards through the air: *the barn owl can* **swoop down on** *a mouse in total darkness | the aircraft swooped in to land.* ■ carry out a sudden attack, especially in order to make a capture or arrest: *armed police* **swooped on** *a flat after a tip-off.* ■ [with obj.] informal seize with a sweeping motion: *she* **swooped up** *the hen in her arms.*
▶ **noun** a swooping or snatching movement or action: *four members were arrested following a swoop by detectives on their homes.*
– PHRASES **at** (or **in**) **one fell swoop** see **FELL⁴**.
– ORIGIN mid 16th cent. (in the sense 'sweep along in a stately manner'): perhaps a dialect variant of Old English *swāpan* (see **SWEEP**). The early sense of the noun was 'a blow, stroke'.

swoosh /swuːʃ, swʊʃ/ ▶ **noun 1** the sound produced by a sudden rush of air or liquid: *the swoosh of surf.*
2 an emblem or design representing a flash or stripe of colour: *white running shoes with the Nike swoosh.*
▶ **verb** [no obj., with adverbial of direction] move with a rushing sound: *cars swooshed by on the street below.*
– ORIGIN mid 19th cent.: imitative.

swop ▶ **verb & noun** variant spelling of **SWAP**.

sword ▶ **noun** a weapon with a long metal blade and a hilt with a hand guard, used for thrusting or striking and now typically worn as part of ceremonial dress. ■ (**the sword**) literary military power, violence, or destruction: *not many perished by the sword.* ■ (**swords**) one of the suits in a tarot pack.
– PHRASES **beat** (or **turn**) **swords into ploughshares** devote resources to peaceful rather than warlike ends. [with biblical allusion to Is. 2:4 and Mic. 4:3.] **fall on one's sword** assume responsibility or blame on behalf of other people, especially by resigning from a position: *he heroically fell on his sword, insisting that it was his decision.* **he who lives by the sword dies by the sword** proverb those who commit violent acts must expect to suffer violence themselves. **put to the sword** kill, especially in war. **the sword of justice** judicial authority.
– DERIVATIVES **sword-like adjective**.
– ORIGIN Old English *sw(e)ord*, of Germanic origin; related to Dutch *zwaard* and German *Schwert*.

sword and sorcery ▶ **noun** [mass noun] a genre of fiction characterized by heroic adventures and elements of fantasy.

sword-bearer ▸ noun an official who carries a sword for a sovereign or other dignitary on formal occasions.

swordbill (also **sword-billed hummingbird**) ▸ noun a mainly green hummingbird with a very long bill, found in northern South America. ● *Ensifera ensifera*, family Trochilidae.

sword dance ▸ noun a dance in which the performers brandish swords or step around swords laid on the ground, originally as a tribal preparation for war or as a victory celebration.

sword fern ▸ noun a fern with long, slender fronds. ● Genera *Polystichum* and *Nephrolepis*, family Dryopteridaceae: several species, including the North American *P. munitum* and the tropical *N. exaltata*.

swordfish ▸ noun (pl. **same** or **swordfishes**) a large edible marine fish with a streamlined body and a long flattened sword-like snout, related to the billfishes and popular as a game fish. ● *Xiphias gladius*, the only member of the family Xiphiidae.

sword knot ▸ noun a ribbon or tassel attached to a sword hilt, originally for securing it to the wrist.

sword lily ▸ noun a gladiolus.

sword of Damocles /ˈdaməkliːz/ ▸ noun see **Damocles**.

sword of state ▸ noun the sword carried in front of a sovereign on state occasions.

swordplay ▸ noun [mass noun] the activity or skill of fencing with swords or foils. ■ repartee; skilful debate: *this intellectual swordplay went on for several minutes.*

swordsman ▸ noun (pl. **swordsmen**) a man who fights with a sword (typically with his level of skill specified): *an expert swordsman.*
– DERIVATIVES **swordsmanship** noun.

swordstick ▸ noun a hollow walking stick containing a blade that can be used as a sword.

sword swallower ▸ noun a person who passes (or pretends to pass) a sword blade down their throat and gullet as entertainment.

swordtail ▸ noun a live-bearing freshwater fish of Central America, popular in aquaria. The lower edge of the tail is elongated and brightly marked in the male. ● *Xiphophorus helleri*, family Poeciliidae.

swore past of **swear**.

sworn past participle of **swear**. ▸ adjective **1** (of testimony or evidence) given under oath: *he made a sworn statement.*
2 determined to remain in the role or condition specified: *they were sworn enemies.*

swot Brit. informal ▸ verb (**swots, swotting, swotted**) [no obj.] study assiduously: *kids swotting for GCSEs.* ■ (**swot up on**) study (a subject) intensively, especially in preparation for something: *swot up on the country's driving laws before you go* | [with obj.] (**swot something up**) *I've always been interested in old furniture and I've swotted it up a bit.*
▸ noun derogatory a person who studies very hard.
– DERIVATIVES **swotty** adjective (**swottier, swottiest**).
– ORIGIN mid 19th cent.: dialect variant of **sweat**.

SWOT analysis ▸ noun a study undertaken by an organization to identify its internal strengths and weaknesses, as well as its external opportunities and threats.
– ORIGIN 1990s: *SWOT*, acronym from *strengths, weaknesses, opportunities, threats.*

swum past participle of **swim**.

swung past and past participle of **swing**.

swung dash ▸ noun a dash (~) in the form of a reverse *s* on its side.

swy /swʌɪ/ ▸ noun Austral./NZ another term for the game of **two-up**.
– ORIGIN 1940s: from German *zwei* 'two'.

SY ▸ abbreviation steam yacht: *the SY Morning.*

-sy ▸ suffix forming diminutive nouns and adjectives such as *folksy, mopsy*, also pet names such as *Patsy*.
– ORIGIN variant of **-y²**.

sybarite /ˈsɪbərʌɪt/ ▸ noun a person who is self-indulgent in their fondness for sensuous luxury.
– DERIVATIVES **sybaritism** noun.
– ORIGIN mid 16th cent. (originally denoting an inhabitant of Sybaris, an ancient Greek city in southern Italy, noted for luxury): via Latin from Greek *Subaritēs*.

sybaritic /ˌsɪbəˈrɪtɪk/ ▸ adjective fond of sensuous luxury or pleasure; self-indulgent: *their opulent and sybaritic lifestyle.*
– DERIVATIVES **sybaritically** adverb.

sycamine /ˈsɪkəmɪn, -ʌɪn/ ▸ noun (in biblical use) the black mulberry tree (see Luke 17:6; in modern versions translated as 'mulberry tree').
– ORIGIN early 16th cent.: via Latin from Greek *sukaminos* 'mulberry tree', from Hebrew *šiqmāh* 'sycamore', assimilated to Greek *sukon* 'fig'.

sycamore ▸ noun **1** a large Eurasian maple with winged fruits, native to central and southern Europe. It is planted as a fast-growing ornamental but tends to displace native trees. ● *Acer pseudoplatanus*, family Aceraceae.
2 N. Amer. the buttonwood tree.
3 (also **sycomore** or **sycomore fig**) (in biblical use) a fig tree that grows in the Middle East. ● *Ficus sycomorus*, family Moraceae.
– ORIGIN Middle English: from Old French *sic(h)amor*, via Latin from Greek *sukomoros*, from *sukon* 'fig' + *moron* 'mulberry'.

syce /sʌɪs/ (also **sice**) ▸ noun (especially in India) a person who takes care of horses; a groom.
– ORIGIN from Persian and Urdu *sā'is*, from Arabic.

syconium /sʌɪˈkəʊnɪəm/ ▸ noun (pl. **syconia** /-nɪə/) Botany a fleshy hollow receptacle that develops into a multiple fruit, as in the fig.
– ORIGIN mid 19th cent.: modern Latin, from Greek *sukon* 'fig'.

sycophant /ˈsɪkəfant/ ▸ noun a person who acts obsequiously towards someone important in order to gain advantage.
– DERIVATIVES **sycophancy** noun.
– ORIGIN mid 16th cent. (denoting an informer): from French *sycophante*, or via Latin from Greek *sukophantēs* 'informer', from *sukon* 'fig' + *phainein* 'to show', perhaps with reference to making the insulting gesture of the 'fig' (sticking the thumb between two fingers) to informers.

sycophantic ▸ adjective behaving or done in an obsequious way in order to gain advantage: *a sycophantic interview.*
– DERIVATIVES **sycophantically** adverb.

sycosis /sʌɪˈkəʊsɪs/ ▸ noun [mass noun] inflammation of the hair follicles in the bearded part of a man's face, caused by bacterial infection.
– ORIGIN late 16th cent. (originally denoting any fig-shaped skin ulcer): modern Latin, from Greek *sukōsis*, from *sukon* 'fig'.

Sydenham /ˈsɪd(ə)nəm/, Thomas (*c.*1624–89), English physician, known as 'the English Hippocrates'. He emphasized the healing power of nature, made a study of epidemics, and explained the nature of the type of chorea that is named after him.

Sydenham's chorea ▸ noun [mass noun] a form of chorea chiefly affecting children, associated with rheumatic fever. Formerly called **St Vitus's dance**.

Sydney the capital of New South Wales in SE Australia; pop. 4,399,722 (2008). It was the first British settlement in Australia and is the country's largest city and chief port. It has a fine natural harbour, crossed by the Sydney Harbour Bridge (opened 1932), and a striking opera house (opened 1973).

syenite /ˈsʌɪənʌɪt/ ▸ noun [mass noun] Geology a coarse-grained grey igneous rock composed mainly of alkali feldspar and ferromagnesian minerals such as hornblende.
– DERIVATIVES **syenitic** adjective.
– ORIGIN late 18th cent.: from French *syénite*, from Latin *Syenites (lapis)* '(stone) of *Syene*' (from Greek *Suēnē* **Aswan** in Egypt).

Syktyvkar /ˌsɪktɪfˈkɑː/ a city in NW Russia, capital of the autonomous republic of Komi; pop. 231,000 (est. 2008).

syl- ▸ prefix variant spelling of **syn-** assimilated before *l* (as in *syllogism*).

Sylheti /sɪlˈhɛtɪ/ ▸ noun (pl. **same** or **Sylhetis**) **1** a native or inhabitant of the region around Sylhet, a city in north-eastern Bangladesh.
2 the dialect of Bengali spoken in this region.
▸ adjective relating to the Sylheti or their language.

syllabary /ˈsɪləb(ə)ri/ ▸ noun (pl. **syllabaries**) a set of written characters representing syllables and (in some languages or stages of writing) serving the purpose of an alphabet.
– ORIGIN mid 19th cent.: from modern Latin *syllabarium*, from Latin *syllaba* (see **syllable**).

syllabi plural form of **syllabus**.

syllabic /sɪˈlabɪk/ ▸ adjective relating to or based on syllables: *a system of syllabic symbols.* ■ Prosody (of verse or metre) based on the number of syllables in a line. ■ (of a consonant, especially a nasal or other continuant) constituting a whole syllable, such as the *m* in *Mbabane* or the *l* in *bottle*. ■ articulated in syllables: *syllabic singing.*
▸ noun a written character that represents a syllable: *Inuit syllabics.*
– DERIVATIVES **syllabically** adverb, **syllabicity** noun.
– ORIGIN early 18th cent.: from French *syllabique* or late Latin *syllabicus*, from Greek *sullabikos*, from *sullabē* 'syllable'.

syllabification /sɪˌlabɪfɪˈkeɪʃ(ə)n/ (also **syllabication**) ▸ noun [mass noun] the division of words into syllables, either in speech or in writing.
– DERIVATIVES **syllabify** verb (**syllabifies, syllabifying, syllabified**).

syllabize (also **syllabise**) ▸ verb [with obj.] divide into or articulate by syllables.
– ORIGIN late 16th cent.: via medieval Latin from Greek *sullabizein*, from *sullabē* 'syllable'.

syllable /ˈsɪləb(ə)l/ ▸ noun a unit of pronunciation having one vowel sound, with or without surrounding consonants, forming the whole or a part of a word; for example, there are two syllables in *water* and three in *inferno*. ■ a character or characters representing a syllable. ■ [usu. with negative] the least amount of speech or writing; the least mention of something: *I'd never have breathed a syllable if he'd kept quiet.*
▸ verb [with obj.] pronounce (a word or phrase) clearly, syllable by syllable.
– PHRASES **in words of one syllable** using very simple language; expressed plainly.
– DERIVATIVES **syllabled** adjective [usu. in combination] *many-syllabled words.*
– ORIGIN late Middle English: from an Anglo-Norman French alteration of Old French *sillabe*, via Latin from Greek *sullabē*, from *sun-* 'together' + *lambanein* 'take'.

syllable-timed ▸ adjective (of a language) characterized by a rhythm in which syllables occur at roughly equivalent time intervals, irrespective of the stress placed on them. French is a syllable-timed language. Contrasted with **stress-timed**.

syllabub /ˈsɪləbʌb/ ▸ noun a whipped cream dessert, typically flavoured with white wine or sherry.
– ORIGIN mid 16th cent.: of unknown origin.

syllabus /ˈsɪləbəs/ ▸ noun (pl. **syllabuses** or **syllabi** /-bʌɪ/) **1** the subjects in a course of study or teaching: *there isn't time to cover the syllabus* | *the history syllabus.*
2 (in the Roman Catholic Church) a summary of points decided by papal decree regarding heretical doctrines or practices.
– ORIGIN mid 17th cent. (in the sense 'concise table of headings of a discourse'): modern Latin, originally a misreading of Latin *sittybas*, accusative plural of *sittyba*, from Greek *sittuba* 'title slip, label'.

syllepsis /sɪˈlɛpsɪs/ ▸ noun (pl. **syllepses** /-siːz/) a figure of speech in which a word is applied to two others of which it grammatically suits only one (e.g. *neither they nor it is working*). ■ another term for **zeugma**.
– DERIVATIVES **sylleptic** adjective.
– ORIGIN late Middle English: via late Latin from Greek *sullēpsis* 'taking together'.

syllogism /ˈsɪləˌdʒɪz(ə)m/ ▸ noun an instance of a form of reasoning in which a conclusion is drawn from two given or assumed propositions (premises); a common or middle term is present in the two premises but not in the conclusion, which may be invalid (e.g. *all dogs are animals; all animals have four legs; therefore all dogs have four legs*). ■ [mass noun] deductive reasoning as distinct from induction.
– DERIVATIVES **syllogistic** adjective, **syllogistically** adverb.
– ORIGIN late Middle English: via Old French or Latin from Greek *sullogismos*, from *sullogizesthai*, from *sun-* 'with' + *logizesthai* 'to reason' (from *logos* 'reasoning').

syllogize /ˈsɪlədʒʌɪz/ (also **syllogise**) ▸ verb [no obj.] use syllogisms. ■ [with obj.] put (facts or an argument) in the form of syllogism.
– ORIGIN late Middle English: via Old French or late Latin from Greek *sullogizesthai* (see **syllogism**).

sylph /sɪlf/ ▸ noun **1** an imaginary spirit of the air. ■ a slender woman or girl.

S

2 a mainly dark green and blue hummingbird, the male of which has a long forked tail. ● Genus *Aglaiocercus* (and *Neolesbia*), family Trochilidae: three species.
– ORIGIN mid 17th cent.: from modern Latin *sylphes, sylphi* and the German plural *Sylphen*, perhaps based on Latin *sylvestris* 'of the woods' + *nympha* 'nymph'.

sylphlike ▶ adjective (of a woman or girl) slender and graceful: *his arm curled around her sylphlike waist.*

sylvan (also **silvan**) ▶ adjective chiefly literary consisting of or associated with woods; wooded: *a sylvan glade.* ■ pleasantly rural or pastoral: *vistas of sylvan charm.*
– ORIGIN mid 16th cent. (as a noun denoting an inhabitant of the woods): from French *sylvain* or Latin *Silvanus* 'woodland deity', from *silva* 'a wood'.

Sylvaner /sɪlˈvɑːnə/ ▶ noun [mass noun] a variety of wine grape first developed in German-speaking districts, the dominant form being a white grape. ■ a white wine made from the Sylvaner grape.
– ORIGIN German.

sylvatic /sɪlˈvatɪk/ ▶ adjective Veterinary Medicine relating to or denoting certain diseases when contracted by wild animals, and the pathogens causing them: *an epidemic of sylvatic plague among prairie dogs.*
– ORIGIN 1930s: from Latin *silvaticus*, from *silva* 'wood'.

Sylvian fissure /ˈsɪlvɪən/ (also **fissure of Sylvius**) ▶ noun Anatomy a large diagonal fissure on the lateral surface of the brain which separates off the temporal lobe.
– ORIGIN mid 19th cent.: named after François de la Boë *Sylvius* (1614–72), Flemish anatomist.

sylvine /ˈsɪlviːn/ ▶ noun another term for SYLVITE.

sylvinite /ˈsɪlvɪnʌɪt/ ▶ noun [mass noun] a mixture of the minerals sylvite and halite, mined as a source of potash.
– ORIGIN late 19th cent.: from SYLVINE + -ITE[1].

sylvite /ˈsɪlvʌɪt/ ▶ noun [mass noun] a colourless or white mineral consisting of potassium chloride, occurring typically as cubic crystals.
– ORIGIN mid 19th cent.: from modern Latin (*sal digestivus*) *Sylvii*, the old name of this salt, + -ITE[1].

sym- ▶ prefix variant spelling of SYN- assimilated before *b, m, p* (as in *symbiosis, symmetry, symphysis*).

symbiont /ˈsɪmbɪɒnt, -bʌɪ-/ ▶ noun an organism living in symbiosis with another.
– ORIGIN late 19th cent.: formed irregularly from Greek *sumbiōn* 'living together', present participle of *sumbioun* (see SYMBIOSIS).

symbiosis /ˌsɪmbɪˈəʊsɪs, -bʌɪ-/ ▶ noun (pl. **symbioses** /-siːz/) [mass noun] Biology interaction between two different organisms living in close physical association, typically to the advantage of both. Compare with ANTIBIOSIS. ■ [count noun] a mutually beneficial relationship between different people or groups: *a perfect mother and daughter symbiosis.*
– DERIVATIVES **symbiotic** /-ˈɒtɪk/ adjective, **symbiotically** adverb.
– ORIGIN late 19th cent.: modern Latin, from Greek *sumbiōsis* 'a living together', from *sumbioun* 'live together', from *sumbios* 'companion'.

symbol ▶ noun **1** a mark or character used as a conventional representation of an object, function, or process, e.g. the letter or letters standing for a chemical element or a character in musical notation. ■ a shape or sign used to represent something such as an organization, e.g. a red cross or a Star of David.
2 a thing that represents or stands for something else, especially a material object representing something abstract: *the limousine was another symbol of his wealth and authority.*
▶ verb (**symbols, symbolling, symbolled**; US **symbols, symboling, symboled**) [with obj.] archaic symbolize.
– ORIGIN late Middle English (denoting the Apostles' Creed): from Latin *symbolum* 'symbol, Creed (as the mark of a Christian)', from Greek *sumbolon* 'mark, token', from *sun-* 'with' + *ballein* 'to throw'.

S

symbolic ▶ adjective **1** serving as a symbol: *a repeating design* ***symbolic of*** *eternity.* ■ significant purely in terms of what is being represented or implied: *the release of the dissident was an important symbolic gesture.*
2 involving the use of symbols or symbolism: *Klimt's symbolic painting of 1900–7.*
– DERIVATIVES **symbolical** adjective, **symbolically** adverb.
– ORIGIN mid 17th cent.: from French *symbolique* or late Latin *symbolicus*, from Greek *sumbolikos*. The adjective *symbolical* dates from the early 17th cent.

symbolic interactionism ▶ noun [mass noun] Sociology the view of social behaviour that emphasizes linguistic or gestural communication and its subjective understanding, especially the role of language in the formation of the child as a social being.

symbolic logic ▶ noun [mass noun] the use of symbols to denote propositions, terms, and relations in order to assist reasoning.

symbolism ▶ noun [mass noun] **1** the use of symbols to represent ideas or qualities: *he has always believed in the importance of symbolism in garden art.* ■ symbolic meaning attributed to natural objects or facts: *the old-fashioned symbolism of flowers.*
2 (also **Symbolism**) an artistic and poetic movement or style using symbolic images and indirect suggestion to express mystical ideas, emotions, and states of mind. It originated in late 19th-century France and Belgium, with important figures including Mallarmé, Maeterlinck, Verlaine, Rimbaud, and Redon.
– DERIVATIVES **symbolist** noun & adjective.

symbolize (also **symbolise**) ▶ verb [with obj.] be a symbol of: *the ceremonial dagger symbolizes justice.* ■ represent by means of symbols: *a tendency to symbolize the father as the sun.*
– DERIVATIVES **symbolization** noun.

symbology ▶ noun [mass noun] the study or use of symbols. ■ symbols collectively: *the use of religious symbology.*

symmetrical ▶ adjective made up of exactly similar parts facing each other or around an axis; showing symmetry.
– DERIVATIVES **symmetric** adjective, **symmetrically** adverb.

symmetry /ˈsɪmɪtri/ ▶ noun (pl. **symmetries**) [mass noun] the quality of being made up of exactly similar parts facing each other or around an axis: *this series has a line of symmetry through its centre | a crystal structure with hexagonal symmetry.* ■ correct or pleasing proportion of the parts of a thing: *the overall symmetry makes the poem pleasant to the ear.* ■ similarity or exact correspondence between different things: *the political* ***symmetry between*** *the two debates* | [count noun] *history sometimes exhibits weird symmetries between events.* ■ [count noun] Physics & Mathematics a law or operation where a physical property or process has an equivalence in two or more directions.
– DERIVATIVES **symmetrize** (also **symmetrise**) verb.
– ORIGIN mid 16th cent. (denoting proportion): from French *symétrie* or Latin *symmetria*, from Greek, from *sun-* 'with' + *metron* 'measure'.

symmetry breaking ▶ noun [mass noun] Physics the absence or reduction of manifest symmetry in a situation despite its presence in the laws of nature underlying it.

sympathectomy /ˌsɪmpəˈθɛktəmi/ ▶ noun [mass noun] the surgical cutting of a sympathetic nerve or removal of a ganglion to relieve a condition affected by its stimulation.

sympathetic ▶ adjective **1** feeling, showing, or expressing sympathy: *she was* ***sympathetic towards*** *staff with family problems | he spoke in a sympathetic tone.*
2 showing approval of or favour towards an idea or action: *he was* ***sympathetic to*** *evolutionary ideas.*
3 (of a person) attracting the liking of others: *Hubbell is a more sympathetic character.* ■ (of a structure) designed in a sensitive or appropriate way: *buildings that were* ***sympathetic to*** *their surroundings.*
4 relating to or denoting the part of the autonomic nervous system consisting of nerves arising from ganglia near the middle part of the spinal cord, supplying the internal organs, blood vessels, and glands, and balancing the action of the parasympathetic nerves.
5 relating to, producing, or denoting an effect which arises in response to a similar action elsewhere.
– DERIVATIVES **sympathetically** adverb.
– ORIGIN mid 17th cent. (in the sense 'relating to an affinity or paranormal influence', as in SYMPATHETIC MAGIC): from SYMPATHY, on the pattern of *pathetic*.

sympathetic magic ▶ noun [mass noun] primitive or magical ritual using objects or actions resembling or symbolically associated with the event or person over which influence is sought.

sympathetic string ▶ noun each of a group of additional wire strings fitted to certain stringed instruments to give extra resonance.

sympathique /ˌsãpaˈtiːk/ ▶ adjective (of a person) agreeably in tune with another's personality or mood: *he is sympathique to women.* ■ (of a place) pleasantly and comfortably appropriate to one's tastes or inclinations: *the most important quality of a restaurant is a sympathique atmosphere.*
– ORIGIN French.

sympathize (also **sympathise**) ▶ verb [no obj.] **1** feel or express sympathy: *it is easy to understand and* ***sympathize with*** *his predicament.*
2 agree with a sentiment, opinion, or ideology: *they* ***sympathize with*** *critiques of traditional theory.*
– ORIGIN late 16th cent. (in the sense 'suffer with another person'): from French *sympathiser*, from *sympathie* 'sympathy, friendly understanding' (see SYMPATHY).

sympathizer (also **sympathiser**) ▶ noun a person who agrees with or supports a sentiment, opinion, or ideology: *a Nazi sympathizer.*

sympatholytic /ˌsɪmpəθə(ʊ)ˈlɪtɪk/ Medicine ▶ adjective (of a drug) antagonistic to or inhibiting the transmission of nerve impulses in the sympathetic nervous system.
▶ noun a drug having a sympatholytic effect, often used in the treatment of high blood pressure.

sympathomimetic /ˌsɪmpəθəʊmɪˈmɛtɪk, -mʌɪ-/ Medicine ▶ adjective (of a drug) producing physiological effects characteristic of the sympathetic nervous system by promoting the stimulation of sympathetic nerves.
▶ noun a drug having a sympathomimetic effect, often used in nasal decongestants.

sympathy ▶ noun (pl. **sympathies**) [mass noun] **1** feelings of pity and sorrow for someone else's misfortune: *they had great* ***sympathy for*** *the flood victims.* ■ (**one's sympathies**) formal expression of such feelings; condolences: *all Tony's friends joined in sending their sympathies to his widow Jean.*
2 understanding between people; common feeling: *the special sympathy between the two boys was obvious to all.* ■ (**sympathies**) support in the form of shared feelings or opinions: *his sympathies lay with his constituents.* ■ agreement with or approval of an opinion or aim; a favourable attitude: *I have some* ***sympathy for*** *this view.* ■ (**in sympathy**) relating harmoniously to something else; in keeping: *repairs had to be* ***in sympathy with*** *the original structure.*
3 the state or fact of responding in a way similar or corresponding to an action elsewhere: *the magnetic field oscillates* ***in sympathy.***
– ORIGIN late 16th cent. (in sense 3): via Latin from Greek *sumpatheia*, from *sumpathēs*, from *sun-* 'with' + *pathos* 'feeling'.

> **USAGE** On the difference between **sympathy** and **empathy**, see **USAGE** at **EMPATHY**.

sympatric /sɪmˈpatrɪk/ ▶ adjective (of animals or plant species or populations) occurring within the same or overlapping geographical areas. Compare with ALLOPATRIC. ■ (of speciation) taking place without geographical separation.
– DERIVATIVES **sympatry** noun.
– ORIGIN early 20th cent.: from SYM- 'with, together' + Greek *patra* 'fatherland' + -IC.

sympetalous /sɪmˈpɛt(ə)ləs/ ▶ adjective Botany (of a flower or corolla) having the petals united along their margins to form a tubular shape.
– DERIVATIVES **sympetaly** noun.

symphonic ▶ adjective (of music) relating to or having the form or character of a symphony: *Franck's Symphonic Variations.* ■ relating to or written for a symphony orchestra: *symphonic and chamber music.*
– DERIVATIVES **symphonically** adverb.

symphonic poem ▶ noun another term for TONE POEM.

symphonist ▶ noun a composer of symphonies.

symphony ▶ noun (pl. **symphonies**) an elaborate musical composition for full orchestra, typically in four movements, at least one of which is traditionally in sonata form. ■ chiefly historical an orchestral interlude in a large-scale vocal work. ■ chiefly N. Amer. (especially in names of orchestras) short for SYMPHONY ORCHESTRA: *the Boston Symphony.* ■ something regarded as a composition of different elements: *autumn is* ***a symphony of*** *texture and pattern.*
– ORIGIN Middle English (denoting any of various instruments such as the dulcimer or the virginal): from Old French *symphonie*, via Latin from Greek *sumphōnia*, from *sumphōnos* 'harmonious', from *sun-* 'together' + *phōnē* 'sound'.

symphony orchestra ▶ noun a large classical orchestra, including string, wind, brass, and percussion instruments.

Symphyla /sɪmˈfʌɪlə/ ▶ **plural noun** Zoology a small class of myriapod invertebrates which resemble the centipedes. They are small eyeless animals with one pair of legs per segment, typically living in soil and leaf mould.
– ORIGIN modern Latin (plural), from **SYM-** 'together' + Greek *phulē*, *phulon* 'tribe'.

symphysis /ˈsɪmfɪsɪs/ ▶ **noun** (pl. **symphyses** /-siːz/) Anatomy & Zoology **1** [mass noun] the process of growing together.
2 a place where two bones are closely joined, either forming an immovable joint (as between the pubic bones in the centre of the pelvis) or completely fused (as at the midline of the lower jaw).
– DERIVATIVES **symphyseal** /-ˈfɪzɪəl/ adjective, **symphysial** /-ˈfɪzɪəl/ adjective.
– ORIGIN late 16th cent. (in sense 2): modern Latin, from Greek *sumphusis*, from *sun-* 'together' + *phusis* 'growth'.

symplasm /ˈsɪmplaz(ə)m/ ▶ **noun** Botany a symplast, especially the cytoplasm of which it is composed.
– DERIVATIVES **symplasmic** adjective.

symplast /ˈsɪmplast, -plɑːst/ ▶ **noun** Botany a continuous network of interconnected plant cell protoplasts.
– DERIVATIVES **symplastic** adjective.
– ORIGIN 1930s: from German *Symplast*.

sympodium /sɪmˈpəʊdɪəm/ ▶ **noun** (pl. **sympodia** /-dɪə/) Botany the apparent main axis or stem of a plant, made up of successive secondary axes due to the death of each season's terminal bud, as in the vine.
– DERIVATIVES **sympodial** adjective.
– ORIGIN mid 19th cent.: modern Latin, from Greek *syn-* 'together' + *pous, pod-* 'foot'.

symposiast /sɪmˈpəʊzɪast/ ▶ **noun** a participant in a symposium.

symposium /sɪmˈpəʊzɪəm/ ▶ **noun** (pl. **symposia** /-zɪə/ or **symposiums**) **1** a conference or meeting to discuss a particular subject. ■ a collection of essays or papers on a particular subject by a number of contributors.
2 a drinking party or convivial discussion, especially as held in ancient Greece after a banquet (and notable as the title of a work by Plato).
– ORIGIN late 16th cent. (denoting a drinking party): via Latin from Greek *sumposion*, from *sumpotēs* 'fellow drinker', from *sun-* 'together' + *potēs* 'drinker'.

symptom ▶ **noun** a physical or mental feature which is regarded as indicating a condition of disease, particularly such a feature that is apparent to the patient: *dental problems may be a symptom of other illness*. Compare with **SIGN** (sense 1 of the noun). ■ an indication of the existence of something, especially of an undesirable situation: *the government was plagued by leaks—a symptom of divisions and poor morale*.
– DERIVATIVES **symptomless** adjective.
– ORIGIN late Middle English *synthoma*, from medieval Latin, based on Greek *sumptōma* 'chance, symptom', from *sumpiptein* 'happen'; later influenced by French *symptome*.

symptomatic ▶ **adjective 1** serving as a symptom or sign, especially of something undesirable: *these difficulties are **symptomatic of** fundamental problems*.
2 exhibiting or involving medical symptoms: *patients with symptomatic coeliac disease | symptomatic patients*.
– DERIVATIVES **symptomatically** adverb.

symptomatology /ˌsɪm(p)tə(ʊ)məˈtɒlədʒi/ (also **symptomology** /ˌsɪm(p)tə(ʊ)ˈmɒlədʒi/) ▶ **noun** [mass noun] the set of symptoms characteristic of a medical condition or exhibited by a patient.

symptomize (also **symptomise**) ▶ **verb** [with obj.] chiefly N. Amer. be a symptom or sign of: *hypothermia is symptomized by confusion, slurred speech, and stiff muscles*.

sympto-thermal method /ˌsɪmptə(ʊ)ˈθəːm(ə)l/ ▶ **noun** a contraceptive method based on the monitoring of a woman's body temperature and of physical symptoms related to ovulation, enabling awareness of the time of the month at which sexual intercourse is most likely to lead to pregnancy.

syn- ▶ **prefix** acting or considered together; united: *synchrony | syncarpous*.
– ORIGIN from Greek *sun* 'with'.

synaesthesia /ˌsɪnɪsˈθiːzɪə/ (US **synesthesia**) ▶ **noun** [mass noun] Physiology & Psychology the production of a sense impression relating to one sense or part of the body by stimulation of another sense or part of the body.
– DERIVATIVES **synaesthete** /sɪnˈiːsθiːt, -ˈɛs-/ noun, **synaesthetic** adjective.
– ORIGIN late 19th cent.: modern Latin, from **SYN-** 'with', on the pattern of *anaesthesia*.

synagogue /ˈsɪnəgɒg/ ▶ **noun** the building where a Jewish assembly or congregation meets for religious observance and instruction. ■ such a Jewish assembly or congregation.
– DERIVATIVES **synagogal** adjective.
– ORIGIN Middle English: via Old French and late Latin from Greek *sunagōgē* 'meeting', from *sun-* 'together' + *agein* 'bring'.

synapomorphy /sɪˈnapə(ʊ)ˌmɔːfi/ ▶ **noun** (pl. **synapomorphies**) [mass noun] Biology the possession by two organisms of a characteristic (not necessarily the same in each) that is derived from one characteristic in an organism from which they both evolved. ■ [count noun] a characteristic derived in this way.
– ORIGIN 1960s: from **SYN-** 'together' + **APO-** 'away from' + Greek *morphē* 'form'.

synapse /ˈsʌɪnaps, ˈsɪn-/ ▶ **noun** a junction between two nerve cells, consisting of a minute gap across which impulses pass by diffusion of a neurotransmitter.
– ORIGIN late 19th cent.: from Greek *sunapsis*, from *sun-* 'together' + *hapsis* 'joining', from *haptein* 'to join'.

synapsid /sʌɪˈnapsɪd, sɪ-/ ▶ **noun** a fossil reptile of a Permian and Triassic group, the members of which show increasingly mammalian characteristics and include the ancestors of mammals. Also called **MAMMAL-LIKE REPTILE**. ● Subclass Synapsida; includes the pelycosaurs and the therapsids.
– ORIGIN early 20th cent.: from modern Latin *Synapsida*, from Greek *sun-* 'together' + *apsis, apsid-* 'arch'.

synapsis /sɪˈnapsɪs/ ▶ **noun** [mass noun] Biology the fusion of chromosome pairs at the start of meiosis.
– ORIGIN late 19th cent.: modern Latin, from Greek *sunapsis* 'connection, junction'.

synaptic /sɪˈnaptɪk, sʌɪ-/ ▶ **adjective** Anatomy relating to a synapse or synapses between nerve cells: *the synaptic membrane*.
– DERIVATIVES **synaptically** adverb.

synaptonemal complex /sɪˌnaptə(ʊ)ˈniːm(ə)l, sʌɪ-/ ▶ **noun** Biology a ladder-like series of parallel threads visible in electron microscopy adjacent to and coaxial with pairing chromosomes in meiosis.
– ORIGIN 1950s: from *synapto-* (combining form of **SYNAPSIS**) + Greek *nēma* 'thread' + **-AL**.

synarchy /ˈsɪnɑːki/ ▶ **noun** [mass noun] joint rule or government by two or more individuals or parties.
– DERIVATIVES **synarchist** noun.
– ORIGIN mid 18th cent.: from Greek *sunarkhia*, from *sunarkhein* 'rule jointly'.

synarthrosis /ˌsɪnɑːˈθrəʊsɪs/ ▶ **noun** (pl. **synarthroses** /-siːz/) Anatomy an immovably fixed joint between bones connected by fibrous tissue (for example, the sutures of the skull).
– ORIGIN late 16th cent.: from modern Latin, from Greek *sunarthrōsis*, from *sun-* 'together' + *arthrōsis* 'jointing' (from *arthron* 'joint').

synastry /sɪˈnastri/ ▶ **noun** [mass noun] Astrology comparison between the horoscopes of two or more people in order to determine their likely compatibility and relationship.
– ORIGIN mid 17th cent.: via late Latin from Greek *sunastria*, from *sun-* 'together' + *astēr, astr-* 'star'.

sync (also **synch**) informal ▶ **noun** [mass noun] synchronization: *images flash on to your screen **in sync** with the music*.
▶ **verb** [with obj.] synchronize: *the flash needs to be synced to your camera*.
– PHRASES **in** (or **out of**) **sync** working well (or badly) together; in (or out of) agreement: *her eyes and her brain seemed to be seriously out of sync*.
– ORIGIN 1920s: abbreviation.

syncarpous /sɪnˈkɑːpəs/ ▶ **adjective** Botany (of a flower, fruit, or ovary) having the carpels united. Often contrasted with **APOCARPOUS**.
– ORIGIN mid 19th cent.: from **SYN-** 'together' + Greek *karpos* 'fruit' + **-OUS**.

synchondrosis /ˌsɪŋkɒnˈdrəʊsɪs/ ▶ **noun** (pl. **synchondroses** /-siːz/) Anatomy an almost immovable joint between bones bound by a layer of cartilage, as in the spinal vertebrae.
– ORIGIN late 16th cent.: from modern Latin, from Greek *sunkhondrōsis*, from *sun-* 'together' + *khondros* 'cartilage'.

synchro /ˈsɪŋkrəʊ/ ▶ **noun 1** short for **SYNCHROMESH**.
2 a synchronizing device or facility.
3 short for **SYNCHRONIZED SWIMMING**.

synchro- ▶ **combining form** synchronous: *synchrotron*.

synchrocyclotron /ˌsɪŋkrə(ʊ)ˈsʌɪklə(ʊ)trɒn/ ▶ **noun** Physics a cyclotron able to achieve higher energies by decreasing the frequency of the accelerating electric field as the particles increase in energy and mass.

synchromesh ▶ **noun** [mass noun] a system of gear changing, especially in motor vehicles, in which the driving and driven gearwheels are made to revolve at the same speed during engagement by means of a set of friction clutches, thereby easing the change.
– ORIGIN 1920s: contraction of *synchronized mesh*.

synchronic /sɪŋˈkrɒnɪk/ ▶ **adjective** concerned with something, especially a language, as it exists at one point in time: *synchronic linguistics*. Often contrasted with **DIACHRONIC**.
– DERIVATIVES **synchronically** adverb.
– ORIGIN 1920s: from late Latin *synchronus* (see **SYNCHRONOUS**) + **-IC**.

synchronicity /ˌsɪŋkrəˈnɪsɪti/ ▶ **noun** [mass noun] **1** the simultaneous occurrence of events which appear significantly related but have no discernible causal connection: *such synchronicity is quite staggering*.
2 another term for **SYNCHRONY** (sense 1).
– ORIGIN 1950s: coined (in sense 1) by C. G. Jung.

synchronism /ˈsɪŋkrənɪz(ə)m/ ▶ **noun** another term for **SYNCHRONY**.
– DERIVATIVES **synchronistic** adjective, **synchronistically** adverb.
– ORIGIN late 16th cent.: from Greek *sunkhronismos*, from *sunkhronos* (see **SYNCHRONOUS**).

synchronize /ˈsɪŋkrənʌɪz/ (also **synchronise**) ▶ **verb** [with obj.] cause to occur or operate at the same time or rate: *soldiers used watches to synchronize movements*. ■ [no obj.] occur at the same time or rate: *their breathing slowly synchronized*. ■ adjust (a clock or watch) to show the same time as another: *It is now 05.48. Synchronize watches*. ■ [no obj.] agree with something else: *their version failed to synchronize with the police view*.
– DERIVATIVES **synchronization** noun, **synchronizer** noun.

synchronized swimming ▶ **noun** [mass noun] a sport in which members of a team of swimmers perform coordinated or identical movements in time to music.
– DERIVATIVES **synchronized swimmer** noun.

synchronous /ˈsɪŋkrənəs/ ▶ **adjective 1** existing or occurring at the same time: *glaciations were approximately synchronous in both hemispheres*.
2 Astronomy making or denoting an orbit around the earth or another celestial body in which one revolution is completed in the period taken for the body to rotate about its axis.
– DERIVATIVES **synchronously** adverb.
– ORIGIN mid 17th cent.: from late Latin *synchronus* (from Greek *sunkhronos*, from *sun-* 'together' + *khronos* 'time') + **-OUS**.

synchronous motor ▶ **noun** an electric motor having a speed exactly proportional to the current frequency.

synchrony /ˈsɪŋkrəni/ ▶ **noun** [mass noun] **1** simultaneous action, development, or occurrence. ■ the state of operating or developing according to the same time scale as something else: *some individuals do not remain in synchrony with the twenty-four-hour day*.
2 synchronic treatment or study: *the structuralist distinction between synchrony and diachrony*.
– ORIGIN mid 19th cent.: from Greek *sunkhronos* (see **SYNCHRONOUS**).

synchrotron /ˈsɪŋkrə(ʊ)trɒn/ ▶ **noun** Physics a cyclotron in which the magnetic field strength increases with the energy of the particles to keep their orbital radius constant.

synchrotron radiation ▶ **noun** [mass noun] Physics polarized radiation emitted by a charged particle spinning in a magnetic field.

syncline /ˈsɪŋklʌɪn/ ▶ **noun** Geology a trough or fold of stratified rock in which the strata slope upwards from the axis. Compare with **ANTICLINE**.
– DERIVATIVES **synclinal** adjective.
– ORIGIN late 19th cent.: from **SYN-** 'together' + Greek *klinein* 'to lean', on the pattern of *incline*.

syncopate /ˈsɪŋkəpeɪt/ ▶ **verb** [with obj.] **1** (usu. as adj. **syncopated**) displace the beats or accents in (music or a rhythm) so that strong beats become weak and vice versa: *syncopated dance music*.
2 shorten (a word) by dropping sounds or letters in the middle, as in *symbology* for *symbolology*, or *Gloster* for *Gloucester*.

S

– DERIVATIVES **syncopation** noun.
– ORIGIN early 17th cent.: from late Latin *syncopat-* 'affected with syncope', from the verb *syncopare* 'to swoon' (see **SYNCOPE**).

syncope /ˈsɪŋkəpi/ ▸ **noun** [mass noun] **1** Medicine temporary loss of consciousness caused by a fall in blood pressure.
2 Grammar the omission of sounds or letters from within a word, for example when *library* is pronounced /ˈlʌɪbri/.
– DERIVATIVES **syncopal** adjective.
– ORIGIN late Middle English: via late Latin from Greek *sunkopē*, from *sun-* 'together' + *koptein* 'strike, cut off'.

syncretism /ˈsɪŋkrɪtɪz(ə)m/ ▸ **noun** [mass noun] **1** the amalgamation or attempted amalgamation of different religions, cultures, or schools of thought.
2 Linguistics the merging of different inflectional varieties of a word during the development of a language.
– DERIVATIVES **syncretic** adjective, **syncretist** noun & adjective, **syncretistic** adjective.
– ORIGIN early 17th cent.: from modern Latin *syncretismus*, from Greek *sunkrētismos*, from *sunkrētizein* 'unite against a third party', from *sun-* 'together' + *krēs* 'Cretan' (originally with reference to ancient Cretan communities).

syncretize (also **syncretise**) ▸ **verb** [with obj.] attempt to amalgamate or reconcile (differing things, especially religious beliefs, cultural elements, or schools of thought).
– DERIVATIVES **syncretization** noun.

syncytium /sɪnˈsɪtɪəm/ ▸ **noun** (pl. **syncytia** /-tɪə/) Biology a single cell or cytoplasmic mass containing several nuclei, formed by fusion of cells or by division of nuclei. ■ Embryology material of this kind forming the outermost layer of the trophoblast.
– DERIVATIVES **syncytial** adjective.
– ORIGIN late 19th cent.: from **SYN-** 'together' + **-CYTE** 'cell' + **-IUM**.

syndactyly /sɪnˈdaktɪli/ ▸ **noun** [mass noun] Medicine & Zoology the condition of having some or all of the fingers or toes wholly or partly united, either naturally (as in web-footed animals) or as a malformation.
– ORIGIN mid 19th cent.: from **SYN-** 'united' + Greek *daktulos* 'finger' + **-Y³**.

syndesmosis /ˌsɪndɛzˈməʊsɪs/ ▸ **noun** (pl. **syndesmoses** /-siːz/) Anatomy an immovable joint in which bones are joined by connective tissue (e.g. between the fibula and tibia at the ankle).
– ORIGIN late 16th cent.: modern Latin, from Greek *sundesmos* 'binding, fastening'.

syndetic /sɪnˈdɛtɪk/ ▸ **adjective** Grammar of or using conjunctions.
– ORIGIN early 17th cent.: from Greek *sundetikos*, from *sundein* 'bind together'.

syndic ▸ **noun 1** a government official in various countries.
2 (in the UK) a business agent of certain universities and corporations, especially a member of a senate committee at Cambridge University.
– DERIVATIVES **syndical** adjective.
– ORIGIN early 17th cent.: from French, via late Latin from Greek *sundikos*, from *sun-* 'together' + *dikē* 'justice'.

syndicalism ▸ **noun** [mass noun] historical a movement for transferring the ownership and control of the means of production and distribution to workers' unions. Influenced by Proudhon and by the French social philosopher Georges Sorel (1847–1922), syndicalism developed in French trade unions during the late 19th century and was at its most vigorous between 1900 and 1914, particularly in France, Italy, Spain, and the US.
– DERIVATIVES **syndicalist** noun & adjective.
– ORIGIN early 20th cent.: from French *syndicalisme*, from *syndical*, from *syndic* 'a delegate' (see **SYNDIC**).

syndicate ▸ **noun** /ˈsɪndɪkət/ **1** a group of individuals or organizations combined to promote a common interest: *large-scale buyouts involving a syndicate of financial institutions | a crime syndicate.* ■ an association or agency supplying material simultaneously to a number of newspapers or periodicals.
2 a committee of syndics.
▸ **verb** /ˈsɪndɪkeɪt/ [with obj.] control or manage by a syndicate. ■ publish or broadcast (material) simultaneously in a number of newspapers, television stations, etc.: *her cartoon strip is syndicated in 1,400 newspapers worldwide.* ■ sell (a horse) to a syndicate: *the stallion was syndicated for a record $5.4 million.*
– DERIVATIVES **syndication** noun.
– ORIGIN early 17th cent. (denoting a committee of syndics): from French *syndicat*, from medieval Latin *syndicatus*, from late Latin *syndicus* 'delegate of a corporation' (see **SYNDIC**). Current verb senses date from the late 19th cent.

syndiotactic /ˌsɪndʌɪə(ʊ)ˈtaktɪk/ ▸ **adjective** Chemistry (of a polymer or polymeric structure) in which the repeating units have alternating stereochemical configurations.
– ORIGIN 1950s: from Greek *sunduo* 'two together' + *taktos* 'arranged' + **-IC**.

syndrome ▸ **noun** a group of symptoms which consistently occur together, or a condition characterized by a set of associated symptoms: *a rare syndrome in which the production of white blood cells is damaged.* ■ a characteristic combination of opinions, emotions, or behaviour: *the 'Not In My Back Yard' syndrome.*
– DERIVATIVES **syndromic** adjective.
– ORIGIN mid 16th cent.: modern Latin, from Greek *sundromē*, from *sun-* 'together' + *dramein* 'to run'.

syne /sʌɪn/ ▸ **adverb** Scottish ago. See also **AULD LANG SYNE, LANG SYNE**.
– ORIGIN Middle English: contraction of dialect *sithen* 'ever since'.

synecdoche /sɪˈnɛkdəki/ ▸ **noun** a figure of speech in which a part is made to represent the whole or vice versa, as in *England lost by six wickets* (meaning ' the English cricket team').
– DERIVATIVES **synecdochic** adjective, **synecdochical** adjective, **synecdochically** adverb.
– ORIGIN late Middle English: via Latin from Greek *sunekdokhē*, from *sun-* 'together' + *ekdekhesthai* 'take up'.

synecology /ˌsɪnɪˈkɒlədʒi/ ▸ **noun** [mass noun] the ecological study of whole plant or animal communities. Contrasted with **AUTECOLOGY**.
– DERIVATIVES **synecological** /-ˌiːkəˈlɒdʒɪk(ə)l, -ˌɛk-/ adjective.
– ORIGIN early 20th cent.: from **SYN-** 'together' + **ECOLOGY**.

synectics /sɪˈnɛktɪks/ ▸ **plural noun** [treated as sing.] trademark (in the US) a problem-solving technique which seeks to promote creative thinking, typically among small groups of people of diverse expertise.
– ORIGIN 1960s: from late Latin *synecticus* (based on Greek *sunekhein* 'hold together'), on the pattern of *dialectics*.

syneresis /sɪˈnɪərɪsɪs/ ▸ **noun** (pl. **synereses** /-siːz/) [mass noun] **1** the contraction of two vowels into a diphthong or single vowel.
2 Chemistry the contraction of a gel accompanied by the separating out of liquid.
– ORIGIN late 16th cent.: via late Latin from Greek *sunairesis*, based on *sun-* 'together' + *hairein* 'take'.

synergist ▸ **noun** a substance, organ, or other agent that participates in an effect of synergy.
– DERIVATIVES **synergistic** adjective, **synergistically** adverb.

synergy /ˈsɪnədʒi/ (also **synergism**) ▸ **noun** [mass noun] the interaction or cooperation of two or more organizations, substances, or other agents to produce a combined effect greater than the sum of their separate effects: *the synergy between artist and record company.*
– DERIVATIVES **synergetic** adjective, **synergic** adjective.
– ORIGIN mid 19th cent.: from Greek *sunergos* 'working together', from *sun-* 'together' + *ergon* 'work'.

synesthesia ▸ **noun** US spelling of **SYNAESTHESIA**.

synfuel /ˈsɪnfjʊəl, sɪnˈfjuːəl/ ▸ **noun** [mass noun] fuel made from coal, oil shale, etc. as a substitute for a petroleum product.

syngamy /ˈsɪŋgəmi/ ▸ **noun** [mass noun] Biology the fusion of two cells, or of their nuclei, in reproduction.
– ORIGIN early 20th cent.: from **SYN-** 'with' + Greek *gamos* 'marriage'.

syngas ▸ **noun** short for **SYNTHESIS GAS**.

Synge /sɪŋ/, J. M. (1871–1909), Irish dramatist; full name *Edmund John Millington Synge*. He is best known for *The Playboy of the Western World* (1907), which caused riots at the Abbey Theatre, Dublin, because of its explicit language and its implication that Irish peasants would condone a brutal murder.

syngeneic /ˌsɪndʒɪˈniːɪk, ˌsɪndʒɪˈneɪɪk/ ▸ **adjective** Medicine & Biology (of organisms or cells) genetically similar or identical and hence immunologically compatible, especially so closely related that transplantation does not provoke an immune response.
– ORIGIN 1960s: from **SYN-** 'together' + Greek *genea* 'race, stock' + **-IC**.

syngenetic /ˌsɪndʒɪˈnɛtɪk/ ▸ **adjective** Geology relating to or denoting a mineral deposit or formation produced at the same time as the enclosing or surrounding rock.

synod /ˈsɪnəd, -ɒd/ ▸ **noun 1** an assembly of the clergy and sometimes also the laity in a diocese or other division of a particular Church.
2 a Presbyterian ecclesiastical court above the presbyteries and subject to the General Assembly.
– ORIGIN late Middle English: via late Latin from Greek *sunodos* 'meeting', from *sun-* 'together' + *hodos* 'way'.

synodic /sɪˈnɒdɪk/ ▸ **adjective** Astronomy relating to or involving the conjunction of stars, planets, or other celestial objects.
– ORIGIN mid 17th cent.: via late Latin from Greek *sunodikos*, from *sunodos* (see **SYNOD**).

synodical ▸ **adjective 1** Christian Church relating to or constituted as a synod: *synodical government.*
2 Astronomy another term for **SYNODIC**.
– DERIVATIVES **synodal** adjective (sense 1).

synodic month ▸ **noun** Astronomy another term for **LUNAR MONTH**.

synodic period ▸ **noun** Astronomy the time between successive conjunctions of a planet with the sun.

synonym /ˈsɪnənɪm/ ▸ **noun** a word or phrase that means exactly or nearly the same as another word or phrase in the same language, for example *shut* is a synonym of *close*. ■ a person or thing so closely associated with a particular quality or idea that the mention of their name calls it to mind: *the Victorian age is a synonym for sexual puritanism.* ■ Biology a taxonomic name which has the same application as another, especially one which has been superseded and is no longer valid.
– DERIVATIVES **synonymic** adjective, **synonymity** noun.
– ORIGIN late Middle English: via Latin from Greek *sunōnumon*, neuter (used as a noun) of the adjective *sunōnumos*, from *sun-* 'with' + *onoma* 'name'.

synonymous /sɪˈnɒnɪməs/ ▸ **adjective 1** (of a word or phrase) having the same meaning as another word or phrase in the same language.
2 closely associated with or suggestive of something: *his deeds had made his name **synonymous with** victory.*
– DERIVATIVES **synonymously** adverb.

synonymy /sɪˈnɒnɪmi/ ▸ **noun** [mass noun] the state of being synonymous.
– ORIGIN mid 16th cent.: via late Latin from Greek *sunōnumia*, from *sunōnumos* (see **SYNONYM**).

synopsis /sɪˈnɒpsɪs/ ▸ **noun** (pl. **synopses** /-siːz/) a brief summary or general survey of something: *a synopsis of the insurance cover provided is set out below.* ■ an outline of the plot of a play, film, or book.
– DERIVATIVES **synopsize** (also **synopsise**) verb.
– ORIGIN early 17th cent.: via late Latin from Greek, from *sun-* 'together' + *opsis* 'seeing'.

synoptic ▸ **adjective 1** of or forming a general summary or synopsis: *a synoptic outline of the contents.* ■ taking or involving a comprehensive mental view: *a synoptic model of higher education.*
2 relating to the Synoptic Gospels.
▸ **noun** (**Synoptics**) the Synoptic Gospels.
– DERIVATIVES **synoptical** adjective, **synoptically** adverb.
– ORIGIN early 17th cent.: from Greek *sunoptikos*, from *sunopsis* (see **SYNOPSIS**).

Synoptic Gospels ▸ **plural noun** the Gospels of Matthew, Mark, and Luke, which describe events from a similar point of view, as contrasted with that of John.

synoptist ▸ **noun** the writer of a Synoptic Gospel.

synostosis /ˌsɪnɒˈstəʊsɪs/ ▸ **noun** (pl. **synostoses** /-siːz/) [mass noun] Physiology & Medicine the union or fusion of adjacent bones by the growth of bony substance, either as a normal process during growth or as the result of ankylosis.
– ORIGIN mid 19th cent.: from **SYN-** 'together' + Greek *osteon* 'bone' + **-OSIS**.

synovial /sʌɪˈnəʊvɪəl, sɪ-/ ▸ **adjective** Anatomy relating to or denoting a type of joint which is surrounded by a thick flexible membrane forming a sac into which is secreted a viscous fluid that lubricates the joint.
– ORIGIN mid 18th cent.: from modern Latin *synovia*, probably formed arbitrarily by Paracelsus.

synovitis /ˌsʌɪnə(ʊ)ˈvʌɪtɪs, ˌsɪn-/ ▸ **noun** [mass noun] Medicine inflammation of a synovial membrane.

synsacrum /sɪnˈseɪkrəm, sɪnˈsakrəm/ ▸ **noun** (pl. **synsacra** /-krə/ or **synsacrums**) Zoology an elongated

S

composite sacrum containing a number of fused vertebrae, present in birds and some extinct reptiles.

syntactic /sɪnˈtaktɪk/ ▶ **adjective** of or according to syntax: *syntactic analysis*.
– DERIVATIVES **syntactical** adjective, **syntactically** adverb.
– ORIGIN early 19th cent.: from Greek *suntaktikos*, from *suntassein* 'arrange together' (see **SYNTAX**).

syntagm /ˈsɪntam/ (also **syntagma** /sɪnˈtagmə/) ▶ **noun** (pl. **syntagms**, **syntagmas**, or **syntagmata** /-mətə/) a linguistic unit consisting of a set of linguistic forms (phonemes, words, or phrases) that are in a sequential relationship to one another. Often contrasted with **PARADIGM**. ■ the relationship between any two syntagms.
– ORIGIN mid 17th cent.: via late Latin from Greek *suntagma*, from *suntassein* 'arrange together'.

syntagmatic /ˌsɪntagˈmatɪk/ ▶ **adjective** of or denoting the relationship between two or more linguistic units used sequentially to make well-formed structures. Contrasted with **PARADIGMATIC**.
– DERIVATIVES **syntagmatically** adverb, **syntagmatics** plural noun.

syntax /ˈsɪntaks/ ▶ **noun** [mass noun] **1** the arrangement of words and phrases to create well-formed sentences in a language: *the syntax of English*. ■ a set of rules for or an analysis of this: *generative syntax*. ■ the branch of linguistics that deals with this.
2 the structure of statements in a computer language.
– ORIGIN late 16th cent.: from French *syntaxe*, or via late Latin from Greek *suntaxis*, from *sun-* 'together' + *tassein* 'arrange'.

syntenic /sɪnˈtɛnɪk/ ▶ **adjective** (of genes) occurring on the same chromosome: *syntenic sequences*.
– DERIVATIVES **synteny** noun.
– ORIGIN 1970s: from **SYN-** 'together' + Greek *tainia* 'band, ribbon' + **-IC**.

synth ▶ **noun** informal short for **SYNTHESIZER**.
– DERIVATIVES **synthy** adjective.

synthase /ˈsɪnθeɪz/ ▶ **noun** [often with modifier] Biochemistry an enzyme which catalyses the linking together of two molecules, especially without the direct involvement of ATP: *nitric oxide synthases*. Compare with **LIGASE**.

synthesis /ˈsɪnθɪsɪs/ ▶ **noun** (pl. **syntheses** /-siːz/) [mass noun] **1** the combination of components or elements to form a connected whole: *the synthesis of intellect and emotion in his work* | [count noun] *the ideology represented a synthesis of certain ideas*. Often contrasted with **ANALYSIS**. ■ Grammar the process of making compound and derivative words. ■ Linguistics the tendency in a language to use inflected forms rather than word order to express grammatical structure.
2 the production of chemical compounds by reaction from simpler materials: *the synthesis of methanol from carbon monoxide and hydrogen*.
3 (in Hegelian philosophy) the final stage in the process of dialectical reasoning, in which a new idea resolves the conflict between thesis and antithesis.
– DERIVATIVES **synthesist** noun.
– ORIGIN early 17th cent.: via Latin from Greek *sunthesis*, from *suntithenai* 'place together'.

synthesis gas ▶ **noun** [mass noun] a mixture of carbon monoxide and hydrogen produced industrially, especially from coal, and used as a feedstock in making synthetic chemicals.

synthesize /ˈsɪnθɪsʌɪz/ (also **synthetize**, **synthesise**) ▶ **verb 1** [with obj.] make (something) by synthesis, especially chemically: *the element was first synthesized by Russian chemists in 1964*. ■ combine (a number of things) into a coherent whole.
2 produce (sound) electronically: *trigger chips that synthesize speech* | (as adj **synthesized**) *synthesized chords*.

synthesizer (also **synthesiser**) ▶ **noun** an electronic musical instrument, typically operated by a keyboard, producing a wide variety of sounds by generating and combining signals of different frequencies.

synthespian /sɪnˈθɛspɪən/ ▶ **noun** (trademark in the US) a computer-generated actor, either in a wholly animated film or one that appears to interact with human actors.

synthetic /sɪnˈθɛtɪk/ ▶ **adjective 1** (of a substance) made by chemical synthesis, especially to imitate a natural product: *synthetic rubber*. ■ (of an emotion or action) not genuine; insincere: *their tears are a bit synthetic*.
2 Logic (of a proposition) having truth or falsity determinable by recourse to experience. Compare with **ANALYTIC**.
3 Linguistics (of a language) characterized by the use of inflections rather than word order to express grammatical structure. Contrasted with **ANALYTIC** and **AGGLUTINATIVE**.
▶ **noun** (usu. **synthetics**) a synthetic material or chemical, especially a textile fibre.
DERIVATIVES **synthetical** adjective, **synthetically** adverb.
– ORIGIN late 17th cent.: from French *synthétique* or modern Latin *syntheticus*, from Greek *sunthetikos*, based on *suntithenai* 'place together'.

synthetic resin ▶ **noun** see **RESIN** (sense 2 of the noun).

synthon /ˈsɪnθɒn/ ▶ **noun** Chemistry a constituent part of a molecule to be synthesized which is regarded as the basis of a synthetic procedure.
– ORIGIN 1960s: from **SYNTHESIS** + **-ON**.

synth-pop ▶ **noun** [mass noun] a type of pop music featuring heavy use of synthesizers and other electronic instruments, originating in the early 1980s.

syntonic /sɪnˈtɒnɪk/ ▶ **adjective** Psychology (of a person) responsive to and in harmony with their environment so that affect is appropriate to the given situation: *culturally syntonic*. ■ [in combination] (of a psychiatric condition or psychological process) consistent with other aspects of an individual's personality and belief system: *this phobia was ego-syntonic*. ■ dated relating to or denoting the lively and responsive type of temperament formerly considered liable to manic-depressive psychosis.
– ORIGIN late 19th cent.: from German *Syntonie* 'state of being syntonic' + **-IC**.

syntype ▶ **noun** Botany & Zoology each of a set of type specimens of equal status, upon which the description and name of a new species is based. Compare with **HOLOTYPE**.

syphilis ▶ **noun** [mass noun] a chronic bacterial disease that is contracted chiefly by infection during sexual intercourse, but also congenitally by infection of a developing fetus. ● This is caused by the spirochaete *Treponema pallidum*. The infection progresses in four successive stages: **primary syphilis**, characterized by a chancre in the part infected; **secondary syphilis**, affecting chiefly the skin, lymph nodes, and mucous membranes; **tertiary syphilis**, involving the spread of tumour-like lesions (gummas) throughout the body, frequently damaging the cardiovascular and central nervous systems; **quaternary syphilis** neurosyphilis.
– DERIVATIVES **syphilitic** adjective & noun.
– ORIGIN early 18th cent.: modern Latin, from *Syphilis, sive Morbus Gallicus*, the title of a Latin poem (1530), from the name of the character *Syphilus*, the supposed first sufferer of the disease.

syphon ▶ **noun & verb** variant spelling of **SIPHON**.

SYR ▶ **abbreviation** Syria (international vehicle registration).

Syracuse 1 /ˈsʌɪrəˌkjuːz/ a port on the east coast of Sicily; pop. 124,083 (2008). It became a flourishing centre of Greek culture, especially in the 5th and 4th centuries BC under the rule of Dionysius I and II. It was taken by the Romans at the end of the 3rd century BC. Italian name **SIRACUSA**.
2 /ˈsɪrəˌkjuːz/ a city in New York State, to the south-east of Lake Ontario; pop. 138,068 (est. 2008). The site of salt springs, it was an important centre of salt production during the 19th century.

Syrah /ˈsiːrə/ ▶ **noun** another term for **SHIRAZ²**.

Syr-Darya /ˌsɪrdarʲˈja/ Russian name for **SIRDARYO**.

syrette /sɪˈrɛt/ ▶ **noun** Medicine, trademark a disposable injection unit comprising a collapsible tube with an attached hypodermic needle and a single dose of a drug, commonly morphine.
– ORIGIN 1940s: from **SYRINGE** + **-ETTE**.

Syria /ˈsɪrɪə/ a country in the Middle East with a coastline on the eastern Mediterranean Sea; pop. 21,763,000 (est. 2009); official language, Arabic; capital, Damascus.

> Syria was the site of various early civilizations, notably that of the Phoenicians. Falling successively within the empires of Persia, Macedon, and Rome, it became a centre of Islamic power and civilization from the 7th century and a province of the Ottoman Empire in 1516. After the Turkish defeat in the First World War Syria was mandated to France, becoming independent with the ejection of Vichy troops by the Allies in 1941. From 1958 to 1961 Syria was united with Egypt as the United Arab Republic.

– DERIVATIVES **Syrian** adjective & noun.

Syriac /ˈsɪrɪak/ ▶ **noun** [mass noun] the language of ancient Syria, a western dialect of Aramaic in which many important early Christian texts are preserved, and which is still used by Syrian Christians as a liturgical language.
▶ **adjective** relating to Syriac.

syringa /sɪˈrɪŋgə/ ▶ **noun 1** a plant of the genus *Syringa* (family Oleaceae), especially (in gardening) the lilac.
2 informal a mock orange shrub.
– ORIGIN modern Latin, from Greek *surinx*, *suring-* 'tube' (with reference to the use of its stems as pipe stems).

syringe /sɪˈrɪn(d)ʒ, ˈsɪ-/ ▶ **noun** a tube with a nozzle and piston or bulb for sucking in and ejecting liquid in a thin stream, used for cleaning wounds or body cavities, or fitted with a hollow needle for injecting or withdrawing fluids. ■ any similar device used in gardening or cooking.
▶ **verb** (**syringes**, **syringing**, **syringed**) [with obj.] clean (the ear, a wound, etc.) by spraying liquid from a syringe: *I had my ears syringed*. ■ spray liquid over (plants) with a syringe: *syringe the leaves frequently during warm weather*.
– ORIGIN late Middle English: from medieval Latin *syringa*, from *syrinx* (see **SYRINX**).

syringomyelia /sɪˌrɪŋgə(ʊ)mʌɪˈiːlɪə/ ▶ **noun** [mass noun] Medicine a chronic progressive disease in which longitudinal cavities form in the cervical region of the spinal cord. This characteristically results in wasting of the muscles in the hands and a loss of sensation.
– ORIGIN late 19th cent.: modern Latin, from Greek *surinx*, *suring-* 'tube, channel' + *muelos* 'marrow'.

syrinx /ˈsɪrɪŋks/ ▶ **noun** (pl. **syrinxes**) **1** a set of pan pipes.
2 Ornithology the lower larynx or voice organ in birds, situated at or near the junction of the trachea and bronchi and well developed in songbirds.
– DERIVATIVES **syringeal** /sɪˈrɪn(d)ʒɪəl/ adjective.
– ORIGIN early 17th cent.: via Latin from Greek *surinx* 'pipe, channel'.

Syro- /ˈsʌɪrəʊ/ ▶ **combining form** Syrian; Syrian and ...: *Syro-Palestinian*. ■ relating to Syria.

syrphid /ˈsəːfɪd/ ▶ **noun** Entomology a fly of the hoverfly family (Syrphidae).
– ORIGIN late 19th cent.: from modern Latin *Syrphidae* (plural), from the genus name *Syrphus*, from Greek *surphos* 'gnat'.

syrtaki /səːˈtaki/ (also **sirtaki**) ▶ **noun** (pl. **syrtakis**) a Greek folk dance in which dancers form a line or chain.
– ORIGIN modern Greek, from Greek *surtos* 'drawn, led' + the diminutive suffix *-aki*.

syrup (US also **sirup**) ▶ **noun 1** [mass noun] a thick, sweet liquid made by dissolving sugar in boiling water, often used for preserving fruit. ■ a thick, sweet liquid containing medicine or used as a drink: *cough syrup*. ■ a thick, sticky liquid obtained from sugar cane as part of the processing of sugar. ■ excessive sweetness or sentimentality of style or manner: *Mr Gurney's poems are almost all of them syrup*.
2 Brit. informal a wig. [from rhyming slang *syrup of figs*.]
– ORIGIN late Middle English: from Old French *sirop* or medieval Latin *siropus*, from Arabic *šarāb* 'beverage'; compare with **SHERBET** and **SHRUB²**.

syrup of figs ▶ **noun** [mass noun] a laxative syrup made from dried figs, typically with senna and carminatives.

syrupy (US also **sirupy**) ▶ **adjective** having the consistency or sweetness of syrup: *syrupy puddings*. ■ excessively sentimental: *a particularly syrupy moment from a corny film*.

sysadmin /sɪsˈadmɪn/ ▶ **noun** Computing, informal a system administrator.

sysop /ˈsɪsɒp/ ▶ **noun** Computing, informal a system operator.

system ▶ **noun 1** a set of things working together as parts of a mechanism or an interconnecting network; a complex whole: *the state railway system* | *fluid is pushed through a system of pipes or channels*. ■ Physiology a set of organs in the body with a common structure or function: *the digestive system*. ■ the human or animal body as a whole: *you need to get the cholesterol out of your system*. ■ Computing a group of related hardware units or programs or both, especially when dedicated to a single application. ■ Geology (in chronostratigraphy) a major range of strata that corresponds to a period in time, subdivided into series. ■ Astronomy a group of celestial objects connected by

their mutual attractive forces, especially moving in orbits about a centre: *the system of bright stars known as the Gould Belt.* ■ short for CRYSTAL SYSTEM.
2 a set of principles or procedures according to which something is done; an organized scheme or method: *a multiparty system of government* | *the public-school system.* ■ a set of rules used in measurement or classification: *the metric system.* ■ [mass noun] organized planning or behaviour; orderliness: *there was no system at all in the company.* ■ a method of choosing one's procedure in gambling.
3 (**the system**) the prevailing political or social order, especially when regarded as oppressive and intransigent: *don't try bucking the system.*
4 Music a set of staves in a musical score joined by a brace.
– PHRASES **get something out of one's system** informal get rid of a preoccupation or anxiety: *yelling is an ace way of getting stress out of your system.*
– DERIVATIVES **systemless** adjective.
– ORIGIN early 17th cent.: from French *système* or late Latin *systema*, from Greek *sustēma*, from *sun-* 'with' + *histanai* 'set up'.

systematic ▶ adjective done or acting according to a fixed plan or system; methodical: *a systematic search of the whole city.*
– DERIVATIVES **systematically** adverb, **systematist** /ˈsɪstəmətɪst/ noun.
– ORIGIN early 18th cent.: from French *systématique*, via late Latin from late Greek *sustēmatikos*, from *sustēma* (see SYSTEM).

systematic desensitization (also **systematic desensitisation**) ▶ noun [mass noun] Psychiatry a treatment for phobias in which the patient is exposed to progressively more anxiety-provoking stimuli and taught relaxation techniques.

systematic error ▶ noun Statistics an error having a non-zero mean, so that its effect is not reduced when observations are averaged.

systematic name ▶ noun a standardized name, especially for a chemical element or compound, a biological taxon, or a star or other astronomical object.

systematics ▶ plural noun [treated as sing.] the branch of biology that deals with classification and nomenclature; taxonomy.

systematic theology ▶ noun [mass noun] a form of theology in which the aim is to arrange religious truths in a self-consistent whole.
– DERIVATIVES **systematic theologian** noun.

systematize /ˈsɪstəməˌtʌɪz/ (also **systematise**) ▶ verb [with obj.] arrange according to an organized system; make systematic: *Galen set about systematizing medical thought* | (as adj. **systematized**) *systematized reading schemes.*
– DERIVATIVES **systematization** noun, **systematizer** noun.

systemic /sɪˈstɛmɪk, -ˈstiːm-/ ▶ adjective **1** relating to a system, especially as opposed to a particular part: *the disease is localized rather than systemic.*
2 Physiology denoting the part of the circulatory system concerned with the transport of oxygen to and carbon dioxide from the body in general, especially as distinct from the pulmonary part concerned with the transport of oxygen from and carbon dioxide to the lungs.
3 (of an insecticide, fungicide, or similar substance) entering the plant via the roots or shoots and passing through the tissues.
– DERIVATIVES **systemically** adverb.
– ORIGIN early 19th cent.: formed irregularly from SYSTEM + -IC.

systemic grammar (also **systemic linguistics**) ▶ noun [mass noun] Linguistics a method of analysis based on the conception of language as a network of systems determining the options from which speakers choose in accordance with their communicative goals.

system integrator (also **systems integrator**) ▶ noun see INTEGRATOR.

systemize (also **systemise**) ▶ verb another term for SYSTEMATIZE.
– DERIVATIVES **systemization** noun, **systemizer** noun.

system operator (also **system administrator**) ▶ noun a person who manages the operation of a computer system or particular electronic communication service.

systems analyst ▶ noun a person who analyses a complex process or operation in order to improve its efficiency, especially by applying a computer system.
– DERIVATIVES **systems analysis** noun.

systole /ˈsɪstəli/ ▶ noun Physiology the phase of the heartbeat when the heart muscle contracts and pumps blood from the chambers into the arteries. Often contrasted with DIASTOLE.
– DERIVATIVES **systolic** /-ˈstɒlɪk/ adjective.
– ORIGIN late 16th cent.: via late Latin from Greek *sustolē*, from *sustellein* 'to contract'.

syzygy /ˈsɪzɪdʒi/ ▶ noun (pl. **syzygies**) **1** Astronomy a conjunction or opposition, especially of the moon with the sun.
2 a pair of connected or corresponding things.
– ORIGIN early 17th cent.: via late Latin from Greek *suzugia*, from *suzugos* 'yoked, paired', from *sun-* 'with, together' + the stem of *zeugnunai* 'to yoke'.

Szczecin /ˈʃtʃɛtʃɪn/ a city in NW Poland, a port on the Oder River near the border with Germany; pop. 408,583 (2007). German name **Stettin**.

Szechuan /sɛˈtʃwɑːn/ (also **Szechwan**) variant of SICHUAN.

Szeged /ˈsɛgɛd/ a city in southern Hungary, a port on the River Tisza near the border with Serbia; pop. 169,030 (2009).

Szent-Györgyi /sɛntˈdʒɔːdʒi/, Albert von (1893–1986), American biochemist, born in Hungary. He discovered ascorbic acid, later identified with vitamin C.

Szilard /ˈsɪlɑːd/, Leo (1898–1964), Hungarian-born American physicist and molecular biologist. He fled from Nazi Germany to the US, where he became a central figure in the Manhattan Project to develop the atom bomb.

T^{1} (also **t**) ▶ noun (pl. **Ts** or **T's**) **1** the twentieth letter of the alphabet. ■ denoting the next after S in a set of items, categories, etc.
2 (**T**) (also **tee**) a shape like that of a capital T: [in combination] *make a T-shaped wound in the rootstock and insert the cut bud.*
– PHRASES **cross the T** historical (of a naval force) cross in front of an enemy force approximately at right angles, securing a tactical advantage for the firing of guns. **to a T** informal exactly; to perfection: *I baked it to a T, and of course it was delicious.*

T^{2} ▶ abbreviation [in combination] ■ (in units of measurement) tera- (10^{12}): *12 Tbytes of data storage.* ■ tesla. ■ Thailand (international vehicle registration). ■ (in names of sports clubs) Town: *Mansfield T.*
▶ symbol ■ temperature. ■ Chemistry the hydrogen isotope tritium.

t ▶ abbreviation imperial or metric ton(s).
▶ symbol (*t*) Statistics a number characterizing the distribution of a sample taken from a population with a normal distribution (see **STUDENT'S T-TEST**).

't ▶ contraction the word 'it', attached to the end of a verb, especially in the transcription of regional spoken use: *I'll never do't again.*

-t^{1} ▶ suffix equivalent to **-ED**^{2} (as in *crept, sent, spoilt*).

-t^{2} ▶ suffix equivalent to **-EST**^{2} (as in *shalt*).

TA ▶ abbreviation (in the UK) Territorial Army.

Ta ▶ symbol the chemical element tantalum.

ta ▶ exclamation Brit. informal thank you.
– ORIGIN late 18th cent.: a child's word.

t/a ▶ abbreviation trading as: *Mark Watson, t/a Wolsingham Motor Company.*

taal ▶ noun variant of **TALA**^{1}.

TAB ▶ abbreviation ■ Austral./NZ Totalizator Agency Board. ■ typhoid–paratyphoid A and B vaccine.

tab^{1} ▶ noun **1** a small flap or strip of material attached to or projecting from something, used to hold, fasten, or manipulate it, or for identification and information. ■ Military, Brit. a marking on the collar distinguishing an officer of high rank or (formerly) a staff officer. ■ North American term for **RING PULL**.
2 Computing a second or further document or page that can be opened on a spreadsheet or Internet browser.
3 informal, chiefly N. Amer. a restaurant bill. ■ a tally of items ordered in a bar or restaurant: *Bobby had told the barman to put everything on the tab.*
4 (**tabs**) short for **TABLEAU CURTAINS**.
5 Aeronautics a part of a control surface, typically hinged, that modifies the action or response of the surface.
6 N. English informal a cigarette.
▶ verb (**tabs, tabbing, tabbed**) [with obj.] mark or identify with a projecting piece of material: *he opened the book at a page tabbed by a cloth bookmark.* ■ chiefly N. Amer. identify as being of a specified type or suitable for a specified position: *he was tabbed by the President as the next Republican National Committee chairman.*
– PHRASES **keep tabs** (or **a tab**) **on** informal monitor the activities or development of; keep under observation: *they liked to keep tabs on their former employees.* **pick up the tab** informal pay for something: *my company will pick up the tab for all moving expenses.*
– DERIVATIVES **tabbed** adjective.
– ORIGIN late Middle English: perhaps related to **TAG**^{1}.

tab^{2} ▶ noun a facility in a word-processing program, or a device on a keyboard, for advancing to a sequence of set positions in tabular work: [as modifier] *the tab key.*
▶ verb (**tabs, tabbing, tabbed**) **1** [no obj.] use the tab key on a computer or typewriter keyboard: *the user can tab to the phrase and press Enter.*
2 [with obj.] short for **TABULATE**.
– ORIGIN early 20th cent.: short for **TABULATOR**.

tab^{3} ▶ noun informal a tablet, especially one containing an illicit drug.
– ORIGIN 1960s: abbreviation.

tab^{4} ▶ noun N. Amer. informal a tabloid newspaper.

tabac /ta'bak/, French /taba/ ▶ noun (pl. pronunc. **same**) (in French-speaking countries) a tobacconist's shop.
– ORIGIN French, literally *tobacco*.

tabanca /ta'baŋka/ ▶ noun [mass noun] W. Indian a painful feeling of unrequited love, typically for a former lover and causing unbalanced or violent behaviour.
– ORIGIN probably from Kikongo *tabaka* 'buy up or sell out completely'.

tabard /'tabəd, -ɑːd/ ▶ noun a sleeveless jerkin consisting only of front and back pieces with a hole for the head. ■ a herald's official coat emblazoned with the arms of the sovereign.
– ORIGIN Middle English: from Old French *tabart*, of unknown origin.

tabaret /'tabərɪt/ ▶ noun [mass noun] an upholstery fabric of alternate satin and watered silk stripes.
– ORIGIN late 18th cent.: probably from **TABBY**.

Tabasco^{1} /tə'baskəʊ/ a state of SE Mexico, on the Gulf of Mexico; capital, Villahermosa.

Tabasco^{2} /tə'baskəʊ/ (also **Tabasco sauce**) ▶ noun [mass noun] trademark a pungent sauce made from the fruit of a capsicum pepper. ● The plant is *Capsicum frutescens* (or *C. annuum*), family Solanaceae.
– ORIGIN late 19th cent.: named after the state of *Tabasco* (see **TABASCO**^{1}).

tabbouleh /tə'buːleɪ, 'tabuːleɪ/ ▶ noun [mass noun] an Arab salad of cracked wheat mixed with finely chopped ingredients such as tomatoes, onions, and parsley.
– ORIGIN from Arabic *tabbūla*.

tabby ▶ noun (pl. **tabbies**) **1** (also **tabby cat**) a grey or brownish cat mottled or streaked with dark stripes.
2 [mass noun] a fabric with a watered pattern, typically silk.
3 [mass noun] a plain weave.
4 [mass noun] a type of concrete made of lime, shells, gravel, and stones, which dries very hard. [early 19th cent. (originally *tabby work*): perhaps a different word, or from a resemblance in colour to that of a tabby cat.]
5 a small moth with dark wavy markings on the forewings. ● Genus *Aglossa* (family Pyralidae), often found in barns and warehouses, and genus *Epizeuxis* (family Noctuidae).
▶ adjective (of a cat) grey or brownish in colour and streaked with dark stripes.
– ORIGIN late 16th cent. (denoting a kind of silk taffeta, originally striped, later with a watered finish: see sense 2 of the noun): from French *tabis*, based on Arabic *al-'Attābiyya*, the name of the quarter of Baghdad where tabby was manufactured.

tabernacle /'tabəˌnak(ə)l/ ▶ noun **1** (in biblical use) a fixed or movable dwelling, typically of light construction. ■ a tent used as a sanctuary for the Ark of the Covenant by the Israelites during the Exodus and until the building of the Temple.
2 a meeting place for worship used by Nonconformists or Mormons.
3 an ornamented receptacle or cabinet in which a pyx containing the reserved sacrament may be placed in Catholic churches, usually on or above an altar. ■ archaic a canopied niche or recess in the wall of a church.
4 a partly open socket or double post on a sailing boat's deck into which a mast is fixed, with a pivot near the top so that the mast can be lowered to pass under bridges.
– DERIVATIVES **tabernacled** adjective.
– ORIGIN Middle English: via French from Latin *tabernaculum* 'tent', diminutive of *taberna* 'hut, tavern'.

tabernacle clock ▶ noun a small clock having a metal case in the form of a tower.

tabes /'teɪbiːz/ ▶ noun [mass noun] Medicine emaciation. See also **TABES DORSALIS**.
– DERIVATIVES **tabetic** /tə'bɛtɪk/ adjective.
– ORIGIN late 16th cent.: from Latin, literally 'wasting away'.

tabescent /tə'bɛs(ə)nt/ ▶ adjective rare wasting away.
– ORIGIN late 19th cent.: from Latin *tabescent-* 'beginning to waste away', from the verb *tabescere*, from *tabere* 'waste away'.

tabes dorsalis /dɔː'seɪlɪs/ ▶ noun another term for **LOCOMOTOR ATAXIA**.
– ORIGIN modern Latin, literally 'wasting of the back'.

tabi /'tɑːbi/ ▶ noun (pl. **same**) a thick-soled Japanese ankle sock with a separate section for the big toe.
– ORIGIN Japanese.

tabla /'tablə, 'tʌblə/ ▶ noun a pair of small hand drums used in Indian music, one of which is slightly larger than the other and is played using pressure from the heel of the hand to vary the pitch.
– ORIGIN from Persian and Urdu *tablah*, Hindi *tablā*, from Arabic *tabl* 'drum'.

tablature /'tablətʃə/ ▶ noun [mass noun] a form of musical notation indicating fingering rather than the pitch of notes, written on lines corresponding to, for example, the strings of a guitar or the holes on a flute.
– ORIGIN late 16th cent.: from French, probably from Italian *tavolatura*, from *tavolare* 'set to music'.

table ▶ noun **1** a piece of furniture with a flat top and one or more legs, providing a level surface for eating, writing, or working at. ■ [in sing.] food provided in a restaurant or household: *he was reputed to have the finest French table of the time.* ■ a group seated at table for a meal: *the whole table was in gales of laughter.* ■ (**the table**) a meeting place or forum for formal discussions held to settle an issue or dispute: *the negotiating table.* ■ [in sing.] Bridge the dummy hand (which is exposed on the table).
2 a set of facts or figures systematically displayed, especially in columns. ■ a list of rivals or competitors showing their positions relative to one another; a league table. ■ (**tables**) multiplication tables: *children at the school have spelling tests and learn their tables.* ■ Computing a collection of data stored in memory as a series of records, each defined by a unique key stored with it.
3 Architecture a flat, typically rectangular, vertical surface; a panel. ■ a slab of wood or stone bearing an inscription. ■ a flat surface of a gem. ■ a cut gem

with two flat faces. ■ each half or quarter of a folding board for backgammon.
4 Architecture a horizontal moulding, especially a cornice.
▶ **verb** [with obj.] **1** Brit. present formally for discussion or consideration at a meeting: *more than 200 amendments to the bill have already been tabled.*
2 chiefly US postpone consideration of: *I'd like the issue to be tabled for the next few months.*
3 Sailing strengthen (a sail) by making a hem at the edge.
– PHRASES **bring something to the table** see BRING. **lay something on the table 1** make something known so that it can be freely discussed. **2** chiefly US postpone something indefinitely. **on the table** offered for discussion: *our offer remains on the table.* **turn the tables** reverse one's position relative to someone else, especially by turning a position of disadvantage into one of advantage. **under the table 1** informal very drunk: *by 3.30 everybody was under the table.* **2** another term for UNDER THE COUNTER (see COUNTER[1]).
– DERIVATIVES **tableful** noun (pl. **tablefuls**).
– ORIGIN Old English *tabule* 'flat slab, inscribed tablet', from Latin *tabula* 'plank, tablet, list', reinforced in Middle English by Old French *table*.

tableau /ˈtabləʊ/ ▶ **noun** (pl. **tableaux** /-ləʊz/) a group of models or motionless figures representing a scene from a story or from history; a tableau vivant.
– ORIGIN late 17th cent. (in the sense 'picture', figuratively 'picturesque description'): from French, literally 'picture', diminutive of *table* (see TABLE).

tableau curtains ▶ **plural noun** (in the theatre) a pair of curtains drawn open by diagonal cords fixed to the lower inner corners.

tableau vivant /ˌtabləʊ ˈviːvɒ̃/, French /tablo vivɑ̃/ ▶ **noun** (pl. **tableaux vivants** pronunc. **same**) a silent and motionless group of people arranged to represent a scene or incident.
– ORIGIN French, literally 'living picture'.

tablecloth ▶ **noun** a cloth spread over a table, especially during meals.

table d'hôte /ˌtɑːbl(ə) ˈdəʊt/, French /tabl dot/ ▶ **noun** a restaurant meal offered at a fixed price and with few if any choices.
– ORIGIN early 17th cent.: French, literally 'host's table'. The term originally denoted a table in a hotel or restaurant where all guests ate together, hence a meal served there at a stated time and for a fixed price.

table lamp ▶ **noun** a small lamp designed to stand on a table.

tableland ▶ **noun** a broad, high level region; a plateau.

table licence ▶ **noun** Brit. a licence permitting a restaurateur or hotelier to serve alcoholic drinks only with meals.

table linen ▶ **noun** [mass noun] fabric items used at mealtimes, such as tablecloths and napkins, collectively.

table manners ▶ **plural noun** behaviour that is conventionally required while eating at table.

table mat ▶ **noun** Brit. a small mat used for protecting the surface of a table from hot dishes.

tablemate ▶ **noun** a person's companion at a meal.

Table Mountain a flat-topped mountain near the south-west tip of South Africa, overlooking Cape Town and Table Bay, rising to a height of 1,087 m (3,563 ft).

T

table napkin ▶ **noun** see NAPKIN.

table salt ▶ **noun** [mass noun] salt suitable for sprinkling on food at meals.

table skittles ▶ **noun** see SKITTLE (sense 1 of the noun).

tablespoon ▶ **noun** a large spoon for serving food. ■ (abbrev.: **tbsp** or **tbs**) the amount held by a tablespoon, in the UK considered to be 15 millilitres when used as a measurement in cookery.
– DERIVATIVES **tablespoonful** noun (pl. **tablespoonfuls**).

tablet ▶ **noun 1** a flat slab of stone, clay, or wood, used especially for an inscription. ■ Architecture another term for TABLE (sense 3 of the noun).
2 chiefly Brit. a small disc or cylinder of a compressed solid substance, typically a measured amount of a medicine or drug. ■ Brit. a small block or bar of soap.
3 N. Amer. a writing pad. ■ (also **tablet PC**) trademark a small portable computer that accepts input directly on to its screen rather than via than a keyboard or mouse.
4 a kind of token giving authority for a train to proceed over a single-track line.
5 [mass noun] Scottish a traditional sweet made from sugar, condensed milk, and butter.
– ORIGIN Middle English: from Old French *tablete*, from a diminutive of Latin *tabula* (see TABLE).

table talk ▶ **noun** [mass noun] informal conversation carried on at meals.

table tennis ▶ **noun** [mass noun] an indoor game based on tennis, played with small bats and a ball bounced on a table divided by a net.

tabletop ▶ **noun** the horizontal top part of a table. ■ [as modifier] small or portable enough to be placed or used on a table: *a tabletop copier.*

tabletop sale ▶ **noun** Brit. an occasion when participants sell unwanted possessions from tables, especially one where at least some of the proceeds go to charity.

table-turning ▶ **noun** [mass noun] a process or phenomenon in which a table is turned or moved supposedly by spiritual agency acting through a group of people who have placed their hands on its surface.

tableware ▶ **noun** [mass noun] crockery, cutlery, and glassware used for serving and eating meals at a table.

table wine ▶ **noun** [mass noun] wine of moderate quality considered suitable for drinking with a meal.

tablier /ˈtablɪeɪ/ ▶ **noun** historical a part of a woman's dress resembling an apron.
– ORIGIN mid 19th cent.: from French, based on Latin *tabula* (see TABLE).

tabloid ▶ **noun** a newspaper having pages half the size of those of the average broadsheet, typically popular in style and dominated by sensational stories. ■ [as modifier] chiefly N. Amer. lurid and sensational: *a tabloid TV show.*
– DERIVATIVES **tabloidization** noun (also **tabloidisation**).
– ORIGIN late 19th cent.: from TABLET + -OID. Originally the proprietary name of a medicine sold in tablets, the term came to denote any small medicinal tablet; the current sense reflects the notion of 'concentrated, easily assimilable'.

taboo /təˈbuː/ ▶ **noun** (pl. **taboos**) a social or religious custom prohibiting or forbidding discussion of a particular practice or forbidding association with a particular person, place, or thing. ■ a practice that is prohibited or restricted in this way: *speaking about sex is a taboo in his country.*
▶ **adjective** prohibited or restricted by social custom: *sex was a taboo subject.* ■ designated as sacred and prohibited: *the burial ground was seen as a taboo place.*
▶ **verb** (**taboos, tabooing, tabooed**) [with obj.] place under a taboo: *traditional societies taboo female handling of food during this period.*
– ORIGIN late 18th cent.: from Tongan *tabu* 'set apart, forbidden'; introduced into English by Captain Cook.

tabor /ˈteɪbə/ ▶ **noun** historical a small drum, especially one used simultaneously by the player of a simple pipe.
– ORIGIN Middle English: from Old French *tabour* 'drum'; perhaps related to Persian *tabīra* 'drum'. Compare with TAMBOUR.

tabouret /ˈtabərɛt, -reɪ/ (US also **taboret**) ▶ **noun** a low stool or small table.
– ORIGIN mid 17th cent.: from French, 'stool', diminutive of *tabour* 'drum' (see TABOR).

Tabriz /taˈbriːz/ a city in NW Iran; pop. 1,398,060 (2006). It lies at about 1,367 m (4,485 ft) above sea level at the centre of a volcanic region and has been subject to frequent destructive earthquakes.

Tabriz rug ▶ **noun** a rug made in Tabriz, the older styles of which typically have a rich decorative medallion pattern.

tabu /təˈbuː/ ▶ **noun** (pl. **tabus**) & **adjective** variant form of TABOO in archaic or anthropological use.

tabular /ˈtabjʊlə/ ▶ **adjective 1** (of data) consisting of or presented in columns or tables: *a tabular presentation of running costs.*
2 broad and flat like the top of a table: *a huge tabular iceberg.* ■ (of a crystal) relatively broad and thin, with two well-developed parallel faces.
– ORIGIN mid 17th cent. (in sense 2): from Latin *tabularis*, from *tabula* (see TABLE).

tabula rasa /ˌtabjʊlə ˈrɑːzə/ ▶ **noun** (pl. **tabulae rasae** /ˌtabjʊliː ˈrɑːziː/) an absence of preconceived ideas or predetermined goals; a clean slate: *the team did not have complete freedom and a tabula rasa from which to work.* ■ the human mind, especially at birth, viewed as having no innate ideas.
– ORIGIN Latin, literally 'scraped tablet', denoting a tablet with the writing erased.

tabulate /ˈtabjʊleɪt/ ▶ **verb** [with obj.] arrange (data) in tabular form: (as adj. **tabulated**) *tabulated results.*
– DERIVATIVES **tabulation** noun.
– ORIGIN early 17th cent. (originally Scots in the sense 'enter on a roll'): in modern use from TABLE + -ATE[3].

tabulator ▶ **noun** a person or thing that arranges data in tabular form. ■ a facility in a word-processing program, or a device on a keyboard, for advancing to a sequence of set positions in tabular work.

tabun /ˈtɑːbʊn/ ▶ **noun** [mass noun] an organophosphorus nerve gas, developed in Germany during the Second World War.
– ORIGIN German, of unknown origin.

tacamahac /ˈtakəməˌhak/ ▶ **noun** another term for BALSAM POPLAR.
– ORIGIN late 16th cent. (originally denoting the aromatic resin of *Bursera simaruba*: see ELEMI): from obsolete Spanish *tacamahaca*, from Aztec *tecomahiyac*.

tacan /ˈtak(ə)n/ ▶ **noun** [mass noun] an electronic ultra-high-frequency navigational aid system for aircraft, which measures bearing and distance from a ground beacon.
– ORIGIN 1950s: from *tac(tical) a(ir) n(avigation)*.

tac-au-tac /ˈtakəʊˌtak/ ▶ **noun** Fencing a parry combined with a riposte.
– ORIGIN early 20th cent.: French, literally 'clash for clash', from imitative *tac*.

tacet /ˈtasɪt, ˈteɪ-/ ▶ **adverb & adjective** Music (as a direction) indicating that a voice or instrument is silent.
– ORIGIN Latin, literally 'is silent', from *tacere* 'be silent'.

tach /tak/ ▶ **noun** N. Amer. informal short for TACHOMETER.

tache ▶ **noun** variant spelling of TASH.

tachi /ˈtatʃi/ ▶ **noun** historical a long, single-edged samurai sword with a slightly curved blade, worn slung from the belt.
– ORIGIN Japanese.

Taching /tɑːˈtʃɪŋ/ variant of DAQING.

tachism /ˈtaʃɪz(ə)m/ (also **tachisme**) ▶ **noun** [mass noun] a style of painting adopted by some French artists from the 1940s, involving the use of dabs or splotches of colour, similar in aims to abstract expressionism.
– ORIGIN 1950s: from French *tachisme*, from *tache* 'a stain'.

tachistoscope /taˈkɪstəˌskəʊp/ ▶ **noun** an instrument used for exposing objects to the eye for a very brief measured period of time.
– DERIVATIVES **tachistoscopic** adjective, **tachistoscopically** adverb.
– ORIGIN late 19th cent.: from Greek *takhistos* 'swiftest' + -SCOPE.

tacho /ˈtakəʊ/ ▶ **noun** (pl. **tachos**) Brit. informal short for TACHOGRAPH or TACHOMETER.

tacho- ▶ **combining form** relating to speed: *tachograph.*
– ORIGIN from Greek *takhos* 'speed'.

tachograph ▶ **noun** a tachometer providing a record of engine speed over a period, especially in a commercial road vehicle.

tachometer /taˈkɒmɪtə/ ▶ **noun** an instrument which measures the working speed of an engine (especially in a road vehicle), typically in revolutions per minute.

tachy- ▶ **combining form** rapid: *tachycardia.*
– ORIGIN from Greek *takhus* 'swift'.

tachycardia /ˌtakɪˈkɑːdɪə/ ▶ **noun** [mass noun] an abnormally rapid heart rate.
– ORIGIN late 19th cent.: from TACHY- 'swift' + Greek *kardia* 'heart'.

tachygraphy /taˈkɪgrəfi/ ▶ **noun** [mass noun] stenography or shorthand, especially that of ancient or medieval scribes.

tachykinin /ˌtakɪˈkʌɪnɪn/ ▶ **noun** Biochemistry any of a class of substances formed in bodily tissue in response to injury and having a rapid stimulant effect on smooth muscle.

tachymeter /taˈkɪmɪtə/ ▶ **noun 1** a theodolite for the rapid measurement of distances in surveying.
2 a facility on a watch for measuring speed.
– DERIVATIVES **tachymetric** adjective.

tachyon /ˈtakɪɒn/ ▶ **noun** Physics a hypothetical particle that travels faster than light.
– ORIGIN 1960s: from **TACHY-** 'swift' + **-ON**.

tachyphylaxis /ˌtakɪfɪˈlaksɪs/ ▶ **noun** [mass noun] Medicine rapidly diminishing response to successive doses of a drug, rendering it less effective. The effect is common with drugs acting on the nervous system.

tachypnoea /ˌtakɪpˈniːə/ (US **tachypnea**) ▶ **noun** [mass noun] Medicine abnormally rapid breathing.
– ORIGIN late 19th cent.: from **TACHY-** 'swift' + Greek *pnoē* 'breathing'.

tacit /ˈtasɪt/ ▶ **adjective** understood or implied without being stated: *your silence may be taken to mean tacit agreement.*
– DERIVATIVES **tacitly** adverb.
– ORIGIN early 17th cent. (in the sense 'wordless, noiseless'): from Latin *tacitus*, past participle of *tacere* 'be silent'.

taciturn /ˈtasɪtəːn/ ▶ **adjective** (of a person) reserved or uncommunicative in speech; saying little.
– DERIVATIVES **taciturnity** noun, **taciturnly** adverb.
– ORIGIN late 18th cent.: from Latin *taciturnus*, from *tacitus* (see **TACIT**).

Tacitus /ˈtasɪtəs/ (c.56–c.120 AD), Roman historian; full name *Publius*, or *Gaius, Cornelius Tacitus*. His *Annals* (covering the years 14–68) and *Histories* (69–96) are major works on the history of the Roman Empire.

tack¹ ▶ **noun 1** a small, sharp broad-headed nail. ■ N. Amer. a drawing pin.
2 a long stitch used to fasten fabrics together temporarily, prior to permanent sewing.
3 a method of dealing with a situation or problem; a course of action or policy: *as she could not stop him going she tried another tack and insisted on going with him.*
4 Sailing an act of changing course by turning a boat's head into and through the wind, so as to bring the wind on the opposite side. ■ a boat's course relative to the direction of the wind: *the brig bowled past **on the opposite tack**.* ■ a distance sailed between such changes of course.
5 Sailing a rope for securing the corner of certain sails. ■ the corner to which a rope is fastened.
6 [mass noun] the quality of being sticky: *cooking the sugar to caramel gives tack to the texture.*
▶ **verb 1** [with obj. and adverbial] fasten or fix in place with tacks: *he used the tool to **tack down** sheets of fibreboard.*
2 [with obj. and adverbial] fasten (pieces of cloth) together temporarily with long stitches. ■ (**tack something on**) add or append something to something already existing.
3 [no obj.] Sailing change course by turning a boat's head into and through the wind. Compare with **WEAR²**. [from the practice of shifting ropes (see sense 5 of the noun of noun) to change direction.] ■ [with obj.] alter the course of (a boat) by tacking. ■ [with adverbial of direction] make a series of changes of course while sailing: *she spent the entire night tacking back and forth.*
– PHRASES **on the port** (or **starboard**) **tack** Sailing with the wind coming from the port (or starboard) side of the boat.
– DERIVATIVES **tacker** noun.
– ORIGIN Middle English (in the general sense 'something that fastens one thing to another'): probably related to Old French *tache* 'clasp, large nail'.

tack² ▶ **noun** [mass noun] equipment used in horse riding, including the saddle and bridle.
– ORIGIN late 18th cent. (originally dialect in the general sense 'apparatus, equipment'): contraction of **TACKLE**. The current sense dates from the 1920s.

tack³ ▶ **noun** [mass noun] informal cheap, shoddy, or tasteless material.
– ORIGIN 1980s: back-formation from **TACKY²**.

tack coat ▶ **noun** (in road-making) a thin coating of tar or asphalt applied before a road is laid to form an adhesive bond.

tackie /ˈtaki/ (also **takkie**) ▶ **noun** (pl. **tackies** or **takkies**) S. African informal **1** a rubber-soled canvas sports shoe.
2 a tyre.
– PHRASES **a piece of old tackie** an easy task.
– ORIGIN perhaps from **TACKY¹**, with reference to the adhesion of the rubber, or **TACKY²**, with reference to their cheapness.

tackle ▶ **noun 1** [mass noun] the equipment required for a task or sport: *fishing tackle.* ■ (also **wedding tackle**) Brit. vulgar slang a man's genitals.
2 a mechanism consisting of ropes, pulley blocks, hooks, or other things for lifting heavy objects. ■ the running rigging and pulleys used to work a boat's sails.
3 Soccer & Hockey an act of playing the ball, or attempting to do so, when it is in the possession of an opponent. ■ American Football & Rugby an act of seizing and attempting to stop a player in possession of the ball.
4 American Football a player who lines up next to the end along the line of scrimmage.
▶ **verb** [with obj.] **1** make determined efforts to deal with (a problem or difficult task): *police have launched an initiative to tackle rising crime.* ■ initiate discussion with (someone) about a disputed or sensitive issue: *a young man tackled him over why the council had spent money on a swimming pool.*
2 Soccer & Hockey try to take the ball from (an opponent) by intercepting them. ■ American Football & Rugby try to stop the forward progress of (the ball carrier) by seizing them and knocking them to the ground.
– DERIVATIVES **tackler** noun.
– ORIGIN Middle English (denoting equipment for a specific task): probably from Middle Low German *takel*, from *taken* 'lay hold of'. Early senses of the verb (late Middle English) described the provision and handling of a ship's equipment.

tackle block ▶ **noun** a pulley over which a rope runs.

tackle fall ▶ **noun** a rope for applying force to the blocks of a tackle.

tack room ▶ **noun** a room in a stable building where saddles, bridles, and other equipment are kept.

tacky¹ ▶ **adjective** (**tackier**, **tackiest**) (of glue, paint, or other substances) not fully dry and retaining a slightly sticky feel: *the paint was still tacky.*
– DERIVATIVES **tackiness** noun.

tacky² ▶ **adjective** (**tackier**, **tackiest**) informal showing poor taste and quality: *even in her faintly tacky costumes, she won our hearts.*
– DERIVATIVES **tackily** adverb, **tackiness** noun.
– ORIGIN early 19th cent.: of unknown origin. Early use was as a noun denoting a horse of little value, later applied to a poor white in some Southern states of the US, hence 'shabby, cheap, in bad taste' (mid 19th cent.).

taco /ˈtakəʊ, ˈtɑːkəʊ/ ▶ **noun** (pl. **tacos**) a Mexican dish consisting of a folded or rolled tortilla filled with various mixtures, such as seasoned mince, chicken, or beans.
– ORIGIN Mexican Spanish, from Spanish, literally 'plug, wad'.

taco chip ▶ **noun** a fried fragment of a taco, flavoured with chilli and spices and eaten as a snack.

taconite /ˈtakənʌɪt/ ▶ **noun** [mass noun] a low-grade iron ore consisting largely of chert, occurring chiefly around Lake Superior in North America.
– ORIGIN early 20th cent.: from the name of the *Taconic* Range of mountains, US, + **-ITE¹**.

tacrine /ˈtakriːn/ ▶ **noun** [mass noun] Medicine a synthetic drug used in Alzheimer's disease to inhibit the breakdown of acetylcholine by cholinesterase and thereby enhance neurological function. ● An acridine derivative; chem. formula: $C_{13}H_{15}N_2Cl$.
– ORIGIN 1960s: from *t(etra-)* + *acr(id)ine*.

tact ▶ **noun** [mass noun] skill and sensitivity in dealing with others or with difficult issues: *the inspector broke the news to me with tact and consideration.*
– ORIGIN mid 17th cent. (denoting the sense of touch): via French from Latin *tactus* 'touch, sense of touch', from *tangere* 'to touch'.

Tactel /ˈtaktɛl/ ▶ **noun** [mass noun] trademark a polyamide fabric or fibre with a soft, silky feel.

tactful ▶ **adjective** having or showing skill and sensitivity in dealing with others or with difficult issues: *they need a tactful word of advice.*
– DERIVATIVES **tactfully** adverb, **tactfulness** noun.

tactic ▶ **noun** an action or strategy carefully planned to achieve a specific end. ■ (**tactics**) [also treated as sing.] the art of disposing armed forces in order of battle and of organizing operations, especially during contact with an enemy. Often contrasted with **STRATEGY**.
– DERIVATIVES **tactician** noun.
– ORIGIN mid 18th cent.: from modern Latin *tactica*, from Greek *taktikē (tekhnē)* '(art) of tactics', feminine of *taktikos*, from *taktos* 'ordered, arranged', from the base of *tassein* 'arrange'.

tactical ▶ **adjective 1** relating to or constituting actions carefully planned to gain a specific military end: *as a tactical officer in the field he had no equal.* ■ (of bombing or weapons) done or for use in immediate support of military or naval operations. Often contrasted with **STRATEGIC**.
2 showing adroit planning; aiming at an end beyond the immediate action: *in a tactical retreat, she moved into a hotel with her daughters.*
3 Brit. (of voting) aimed at preventing the strongest candidate from winning by supporting the next strongest, without regard to one's true political allegiance.
– DERIVATIVES **tactically** adverb.
– ORIGIN late 16th cent. (in the sense 'relating to military or naval tactics'): from Greek *taktikos* (see **TACTIC**) + **-AL**.

tacticity /takˈtɪsɪti/ ▶ **noun** [mass noun] Chemistry the stereochemical arrangement of the units in the main chain of a polymer.

tactile ▶ **adjective** of or connected with the sense of touch: *vocal and visual signals become less important as tactile signals intensify.* ■ perceptible by touch or apparently so; tangible. ■ designed to be perceived by touch: *tactile exhibitions help blind people enjoy the magic of sculpture.* ■ (of a person) given to touching others, especially as an unselfconscious expression of sympathy or affection.
– DERIVATIVES **tactility** noun.
– ORIGIN early 17th cent. (in the sense 'perceptible by touch, tangible'): from Latin *tactilis*, from *tangere* 'to touch'.

tactless ▶ **adjective** having or showing a lack of skill and sensitivity in dealing with others or with difficult issues: *a tactless remark.*
– DERIVATIVES **tactlessly** adverb, **tactlessness** noun.

tactual ▶ **adjective** another term for **TACTILE**.

tactus /ˈtaktəs/ ▶ **noun** Music a principal accent or rhythmic unit, especially in 15th- and 16th- century music.
– ORIGIN Latin.

tad informal ▶ **adverb** (**a tad**) to a small extent; somewhat: *Mark looked a tad embarrassed.*
▶ **noun** [in sing.] a small amount of something: *crumpets sweetened with **a tad of** honey.*
– ORIGIN late 19th cent. (denoting a small child): origin uncertain, perhaps from **TADPOLE**. The current usage dates from the 1940s.

ta-da /təˈdɑː/ (also **ta-dah**) ▶ **exclamation** an imitation of a fanfare (typically used to indicate an impressive entrance or a dramatic announcement).
– ORIGIN 1970s: imitative.

tadger ▶ **noun** variant spelling of **TODGER**.

Tadjik ▶ **noun & adjective** variant spelling of **TAJIK**.

Tadmur /ˈtadmʊə/ (also **Tadmor** /-mɔː/) another name for **PALMYRA**.

tadpole ▶ **noun** the tailed aquatic larva of an amphibian (frog, toad, newt, or salamander), breathing through gills and lacking legs until the later stages of its development.
– ORIGIN late 15th cent.: from Old English *tāda* 'toad' + **POLL** (probably because the tadpole seems to consist of a large head and a tail in its early development stage).

Tadzhik ▶ **noun & adjective** variant spelling of **TAJIK**.

Tadzhikistan variant spelling of **TAJIKISTAN**.

tae-bo /ˈtʌɪbəʊ/ ▶ **noun** [mass noun] trademark an exercise system combining elements of aerobics and kickboxing.
– ORIGIN 1990s: from Korean *tae* 'leg' + *bo*, short for **BOXING** (see **BOX²**).

taedium vitae /ˌtiːdiəm ˈviːtʌɪ, ˈvʌɪtiː/ ▶ **noun** [mass noun] a state of extreme ennui; weariness of life.
– ORIGIN Latin.

Taegu /taˈguː/ a city in SE South Korea; pop. 2,512,600 (est. 2008). Nearby is the Haeinsa temple, established in AD 802, which contains 80,000 Buddhist printing blocks dating from the 13th century.

Taejon /taˈdʒɒn/ a city in central South Korea; pop. 1,495,000 (est. 2008).

tae kwon do /ˌtʌɪ kwɒn ˈdəʊ/ ▶ **noun** [mass noun] a modern Korean martial art similar to karate.
– ORIGIN Korean, literally 'art of hand and foot fighting', from *tae* 'kick' + *kwon* 'fist' + *do* 'art, method'.

tael /teɪl/ ▶ **noun** a weight used in China and East Asia, originally of varying amount but later fixed at about 38 grams (1⅓ oz.). ■ a former Chinese monetary unit based on the value of a tael of standard silver.
– ORIGIN from Malay *tahil* 'weight'.

taenia /ˈtiːnɪə/ (US **tenia**) ▶ **noun** (pl. **taeniae** /-nɪiː/ or **taenias**) **1** Anatomy a flat ribbon-like structure in the

T

body. ■ **(taeniae coli** /ˈkəʊlʌɪ/) the smooth longitudinal muscles of the colon.
2 Architecture a fillet between a Doric architrave and frieze.
3 (in ancient Greece) a band or ribbon worn round a person's head.
– ORIGIN mid 16th cent. (in sense 2): via Latin from Greek *tainia* 'band, ribbon'.

taeniodont /ˈtiːnɪə(ʊ)dɒnt/ ▶ **noun** a primitive fossil herbivorous mammal from the Palaeocene and Eocene of North America, with deep powerful jaws and short stout limbs. ● Suborder Taeniodonta, order Cimolesta.
– ORIGIN 1930s: from modern Latin *Taeniodontia* (order name), from Greek *tainia* 'band, ribbon' + *odous, odont-* 'tooth'.

taffeta /ˈtafɪtə/ ▶ **noun** [mass noun] a fine lustrous silk or similar synthetic fabric with a crisp texture.
– ORIGIN late Middle English (originally denoting a plain-weave silk): from Old French *taffetas* or medieval Latin *taffata*, based on Persian *tāftan* 'to shine'.

taffrail ▶ **noun** a rail round a ship's stern.
– ORIGIN early 19th cent.: alteration (by association with RAIL[1]), of obsolete *tafferel* 'panel', used to denote the flat part of a ship's stern above the transom, from Dutch *tafereel*.

Taffy (also **Taff**) ▶ **noun** (pl. **Taffies**) Brit. informal, often offensive a Welshman.
– ORIGIN mid 17th cent.: representing a supposed Welsh pronunciation of the given name *Davy* or *David* (Welsh *Dafydd*).

taffy ▶ **noun** (pl. **taffies**) [mass noun] **1** N. Amer. a sweet similar to toffee, made from brown sugar or treacle, boiled with butter and pulled until glossy.
2 US informal insincere flattery.
– ORIGIN early 19th cent.: earlier form of TOFFEE, ultimate origin unknown.

tafia /ˈtafɪə/ ▶ **noun** [mass noun] W. Indian a drink similar to rum, distilled from molasses or waste from the production of brown sugar.
– ORIGIN via French from West Indian creole, alteration of RATAFIA.

Taft /taft/, William Howard (1857–1930), American Republican statesman, 27th President of the US 1909–13. His presidency is remembered for its dollar diplomacy and tariff laws.

tag[1] ▶ **noun 1** a label attached to someone or something for the purpose of identification or to give other information. ■ an electronic device that can be attached to someone or something for monitoring purposes, e.g. to track offenders under house arrest or to deter shoplifters. ■ a nickname or description popularly given to someone or something: *he lived up to his tag as the team's saviour.* ■ informal a nickname or other identifying mark written as the signature of a graffiti artist: *scrawled felt-tip tags on city walls.* ■ Computing a character or set of characters appended to a piece of text or data in order to identify or categorize it. ■ US the licence plate of a motor vehicle.
2 a small piece or part that is attached to a main body. ■ a ragged lock of wool on a sheep. ■ the tip of an animal's tail when it is distinctively coloured. ■ a loose or spare end of something; a leftover. ■ a metal or plastic point at the end of a shoelace that stiffens it, making it easier to insert through an eyelet.
3 a frequently repeated quotation or stock phrase. ■ Theatre a closing speech addressed to the audience. ■ a refrain or musical phrase in a song or piece of music. ■ Grammar a short phrase or clause added to an already complete sentence, as in *I like it, I do.*
▶ **verb (tags, tagging, tagged)** [with obj.] **1** attach a label to: *mothers suspected that their babies had been wrongly tagged during an alarm at the hospital.* ■ attach an electronic tag to: (as noun **tagging**) *the tagging of remand prisoners.* ■ [with obj. and adverbial or complement] give a specified name or description to: *he left because he didn't want to be tagged as a soap star.* ■ informal (of a graffiti artist) write one's nickname or mark on (a surface): *metal hoardings tagged with hip-hop graffiti.* ■ Computing add a character or set of characters to (a piece of text or data) in order to identify or categorize it. ■ Biology & Chemistry label (something) with a radioactive isotope, fluorescent dye, or other marker.
2 [with obj. and adverbial] add to something, especially as an afterthought or with no real connection: *she meant to tag her question* **on** *at the end of her remarks.* ■ [no obj., with adverbial] follow or accompany someone, especially without invitation: *that'll teach you not to tag along where you're not wanted.* ■ [with obj.] Brit. informal follow closely: *we were tagged—that car was following us.*
3 shear away ragged locks of wool from (sheep).
– ORIGIN late Middle English (denoting a narrow hanging section of a decoratively slashed garment): of unknown origin; compare with DAG. The verb dates from the early 17th cent.

tag[2] ▶ **noun** [mass noun] a children's game in which one chases the rest, and anyone who is caught then becomes the pursuer. ■ Baseball the action of tagging a runner.
▶ **verb (tags, tagging, tagged)** [with obj.] touch (someone being chased) in a game of tag. ■ Baseball put (a runner) out by touching with the ball or with the hand holding the ball.
– ORIGIN mid 18th cent.: perhaps a variant of TIG.

Tagalog /təˈgɑːlɒg/ ▶ **noun 1** a member of a people originally of central Luzon in the Philippine Islands.
2 [mass noun] the Austronesian language of the Tagalogs, with over 17 million speakers. Its vocabulary has been much influenced by Spanish and English, and to some extent by Chinese and Arabic, and it is the basis of a standardized national language of the Philippines (Filipino).
▶ **adjective** relating to the Tagalogs or their language.
– ORIGIN the name in Tagalog, from *tagá* 'native' + *ilog* 'river'.

Tagamet /ˈtagəmɛt/ ▶ **noun** trademark for CIMETIDINE.
– ORIGIN 1970s: an arbitrary formation.

Taganrog /ˌtagənˈrɒg/ an industrial port in SW Russia, on the Gulf of Taganrog, an inlet of the Sea of Azov; pop. 260,700 (est. 2008). It was founded in 1698 by Peter the Great as a fortress and naval base.

tagati /təˈgɑːti/ ▶ **noun** (pl. **same**) (among some South African peoples) an evil witch or wizard. ■ [mass noun] witchcraft.
▶ **verb** [no obj.] (among some South African peoples) practise witchcraft. ■ [with obj.] bewitch (someone).
– ORIGIN from Xhosa and Zulu *umthakathi* 'wizard'.

tag cloud ▶ **noun** a visual depiction of the word content of a website, or of user-generated tags attached to online content, typically using colour and font size to represent the prominence or frequency of the words or tags depicted.

tag day ▶ **noun** N. Amer. dated a flag day.

tag end ▶ **noun** chiefly N. Amer. the last remaining part of something: *the tag end of the season.*

tagetes /təˈdʒiːtiːz/ ▶ **noun** a plant of the genus *Tagetes* in the daisy family, especially (in gardening) an African or French marigold.
– ORIGIN modern Latin, from Latin *Tages*, the name of an Etruscan god.

tagger ▶ **noun 1** a person who writes graffiti using their nickname or identifying mark.
2 Computing a piece of software that adds identifying or classifying tags to pieces of text or data.

tagine /təˈʒiːn, təˈdʒiːn/ (also **tajine**) ▶ **noun** a North African stew of spiced meat and vegetables prepared by slow cooking in a shallow earthenware cooking dish with a tall, conical lid. ■ the dish used for cooking tagines.
– ORIGIN from Moroccan Arabic *ṭažin* from Arabic *ṭājin* 'frying pan'.

tagliatelle /ˌtaljəˈtɛleɪ, -li/ ▶ **plural noun** pasta in narrow ribbons.
– ORIGIN Italian, from *tagliare* 'to cut'.

tag line ▶ **noun** N. Amer. informal a catchphrase or slogan, especially as used in advertising, or the punchline of a joke.

tagma /ˈtagmə/ ▶ **noun** (pl. **tagmata** /-mətə/) Zoology (in the bodies of arthropods and some other segmented animals) a morphologically distinct region, typically comprising several adjoining segments, such as the head, thorax, and abdomen of insects.
– ORIGIN early 20th cent.: from Greek, literally 'something arranged', from *tassein* 'set in order'.

tagmeme /ˈtagmiːm/ ▶ **noun** Linguistics (in tagmemics) a slot in a syntactic frame which may be filled by any member of a set of appropriate linguistic items.
– ORIGIN 1930s: from Greek *tagma* 'arrangement' + -EME.

tagmemics /tagˈmiːmɪks/ ▶ **plural noun** [treated as sing.] Linguistics a mode of linguistic analysis based on identifying the function of each grammatical position in the sentence or phrase and the class of words by which it can be filled.
– DERIVATIVES **tagmemic** adjective.

Tagore /təˈgɔː/, Rabindranath (1861–1941), Indian writer and philosopher. His poetry pioneered the use of colloquial Bengali, and his own translations established his reputation in the West. Nobel Prize for Literature (1913).

tag question ▶ **noun** Grammar a question converted from a statement by an appended interrogative formula, e.g. *it's nice out, isn't it?*

tag sale ▶ **noun** US a sale of miscellaneous secondhand items.

tag team ▶ **noun** a pair of wrestlers who fight as a team, taking the ring alternately. One team member cannot enter the ring until the other tags or touches hands with them on leaving. ■ informal, chiefly N. Amer. a pair of people working together.

tagua nut /ˈtagwə/ ▶ **noun** another term for IVORY NUT.
– ORIGIN mid 19th cent.: *tagua*, via Spanish from Quechua *tawa*.

Tagus /ˈteɪgəs/ a river in SW Europe, the longest river of the Iberian peninsula, which rises in the mountains of eastern Spain and flows over 1,000 km (625 miles) generally westwards into Portugal, where it turns south-westwards, emptying into the Atlantic near Lisbon. Spanish name TAJO, Portuguese name TEJO.

tag wrestling ▶ **noun** [mass noun] a form of wrestling involving tag teams.

tahini /tɑːˈhiːni/ (also **tahina** /tɑːˈhiːnə/) ▶ **noun** [mass noun] a Middle Eastern paste or spread made from ground sesame seeds.
– ORIGIN from modern Greek *takhini*, based on Arabic *ṭaḥana* 'to crush'.

Tahiti /təˈhiːti/ an island in the central South Pacific, one of the Society Islands, forming part of French Polynesia; pop. 178,173 (2007); capital, Papeete. One of the largest islands in the South Pacific, it was claimed for France in 1768 and declared a French colony in 1880.

Tahitian /tɑːˈhiːʃ(ə)n, -ˈhiːtɪən/ ▶ **noun 1** a native or inhabitant of Tahiti, or a person of Tahitian descent.
2 [mass noun] the language of Tahiti, a Polynesian language with about 125,000 speakers.
▶ **adjective** relating to Tahiti, its people, or their language.

tahr /tɑː/ ▶ **noun** a goat-like mammal inhabiting cliffs and mountain slopes in Oman, southern India, and the Himalayas. ● Genus *Hemitragus*, family Bovidae: three species.
– ORIGIN mid 19th cent.: a local word in Nepal.

tahsil /tɑːˈsiːl/ ▶ **noun** variant of TEHSIL.

Tai /tʌɪ/ ▶ **adjective** relating to or denoting a family of tonal SE Asian languages, including Thai and Lao, of uncertain affinity to other language groups (sometimes being linked with the Sino-Tibetan family).

tai /tʌɪ/ ▶ **noun** (pl. **same**) a deep red-brown Pacific sea bream, eaten as a delicacy in Japan. ● *Pagrus major*, family Sparidae.
– ORIGIN early 17th cent.: from Japanese.

Tai'an /tʌɪˈɑːn/ a city in NE China, in Shandong province; pop. 698,200 (est. 2006).

t'ai chi ch'uan /ˌtʌɪ tʃiː ˈtʃwɑːn/ (also **t'ai chi** /ˌtʌɪ ˈtʃiː/) ▶ **noun** [mass noun] **1** a Chinese martial art and system of callisthenics, consisting of sequences of very slow controlled movements.
2 (in Chinese philosophy) the ultimate source and limit of reality, from which spring yin and yang and all of creation.
– ORIGIN Chinese, literally 'great ultimate boxing', from *tài* 'extreme' + *jí* 'limit' + *quán* 'fist, boxing'.

Taichung /tʌɪˈtʃʊŋ/ a city in west central Taiwan; pop. 1,055,900 (est. 2007).

Ta'if /ˈtɑːɪf/ a city in western Saudi Arabia, situated to the south-east of Mecca in the Asir Mountains; pop. 521,300 (est. 2004). It is the unofficial seat of government of Saudi Arabia during the summer.

Taig /teɪg/ ▶ **noun** offensive (in Northern Ireland) a Protestant name for a Catholic.
– ORIGIN 1970s: variant of *Teague*, anglicized spelling of the Irish name *Tadhg*, used since the mid 17th cent. as a nickname for an Irishman.

taiga /ˈtʌɪgə/ ▶ **noun** [mass noun] (often **the taiga**) the swampy coniferous forest of high northern latitudes, especially that between the tundra and steppes of Siberia.
– ORIGIN late 19th cent.: from Russian *taĭga*, from Mongolian.

taiko /ˈtʌɪkəʊ/ ▶ **noun** (pl. **same** or **taikos**) a Japanese barrel-shaped drum.
– ORIGIN late 19th cent.: Japanese.

taikonaut /ˈtʌɪkənɔːt/ ▶ **noun** a Chinese astronaut.

T

– ORIGIN blend of Chinese *taikong* 'outer space' and ASTRONAUT.

tail[1] ▶ noun **1** the hindmost part of an animal, especially when prolonged beyond the rest of the body, such as the flexible extension of the backbone in a vertebrate, the feathers at the hind end of a bird, or a terminal appendage in an insect. ■ a slender backward prolongation of each hindwing in some butterflies.
2 a thing resembling an animal's tail in its shape or position, typically extending downwards or outwards at the end of something: *the tail of a capital Q.* ■ the rear part of an aeroplane, with the tailplane and rudder. ■ the lower or hanging part of a garment, especially the back of a shirt or coat. ■ (**tails**) informal a tailcoat, or a man's formal evening suit with such a coat: *the men looked debonair in white tie and tails.* ■ the luminous trail of particles following a comet. ■ the lower end of a pool or stream. ■ the exposed end of a slate or tile in a roof. ■ Mathematics an extremity of a curve approaching the horizontal axis of a graph, especially that of a frequency distribution.
3 the end of a long train or line of people or vehicles: *a catering truck at the tail of the convoy.* ■ the final, more distant, or weaker part of something: *the tail of a hurricane.* ■ Cricket the end of the batting order, with the weakest batsmen.
4 informal a person secretly following another to observe their movements.
5 informal, chiefly N. Amer. a person's buttocks. ■ vulgar slang a woman's genitals. ■ [mass noun] informal women collectively regarded in sexual terms: *my wife thinks going out with you guys will keep me from chasing tail.*
6 (**tails**) the side of a coin without the image of a head on it (used when tossing a coin to determine a winner).
▶ verb [with obj.] **1** informal follow and observe (someone) closely, especially in secret: *a flock of paparazzi had tailed them all over London.* ■ [no obj., with adverbial of direction] follow: *they went to their favourite cafe—Owen and Sally tailed along.*
2 [no obj., with adverbial of direction] N. Amer. (of an object in flight) drift or curve in a particular direction: *the next pitch tailed in on me at the last second.*
3 remove the stalks or ends of (fruit or vegetables) in preparation for cooking.
4 pull on the end of (a rope) after it has been wrapped round the drum of a winch a few times, in order to prevent slipping when the winch rotates.
5 archaic join (one thing) to another.
– PHRASES **chase one's (own) tail** informal rush around ineffectually. **on someone's tail** following someone closely: *a police car stayed on his tail for half a mile.* **the tail of one's eye** dated the outer corner of one's eye. **the tail wags the dog** the less important or subsidiary factor, person, or thing dominates a situation; the usual roles are reversed: *the financing system is becoming the tail that wags the dog.* **with one's tail between one's legs** informal in a state of dejection or humiliation. **with one's tail up** informal in a confident or cheerful mood.
– PHRASAL VERBS **tail back** Brit. (of traffic) become congested and form a tailback: *traffic tailed back fourteen miles after a chemical spillage.* **tail something in** (or **into**) insert the end of a beam, stone, or brick into (a wall). **tail off** (or **away**) gradually diminish in amount, strength, or intensity: *the economic boom was beginning to tail off.*
– DERIVATIVES **tailed** adjective [in combination] *a white-tailed deer*, **tailless** adjective.
– ORIGIN Old English *tæg(e)l*, from a Germanic base meaning 'hair, hairy tail'; related to Middle Low German *tagel* 'twisted whip, rope's end'. The early sense of the verb (early 16th cent.) was 'fasten to the back of something'.

tail[2] ▶ noun [mass noun] Law, chiefly historical limitation of ownership, especially of an estate or title limited to a person and their direct descendants: *the land was held in tail general.* See also FEE TAIL.
– ORIGIN Middle English (denoting a tallage): from Old French *taille* 'notch, tax', from *taillier* 'to cut', based on Latin *talea* 'twig, cutting'.

tailback ▶ noun **1** Brit. a long queue of stationary or slow-moving traffic extending back from a busy junction or similar obstruction on the road.
2 American Football the offensive back stationed furthest from the line of scrimmage.

tailboard ▶ noun Brit. a tailgate.

tail bone ▶ noun less technical term for COCCYX.

tail boom ▶ noun a main spar of several making up the longitudinal framework carrying the tail of an aeroplane when not supported by the fuselage.

tailcoat ▶ noun a man's formal morning or evening coat, with a long skirt divided at the back into tails and cut away in front.

tail comb ▶ noun a comb with a tapering tail or handle used in styling to lift, divide, or curl the hair.

tail covert ▶ noun (in a bird's tail) each of the smaller feathers covering the bases of the main feathers.

taildragger ▶ noun an aeroplane whose undercarriage includes a tailwheel or tail skid rather than a nose wheel.

tail end ▶ noun the last or hindmost part of something: *we joined the tail end of a queue.* ■ Cricket the end of the batting order; the tail.
– DERIVATIVES **tail-ender** noun (Cricket).

tail-end Charlie ▶ noun informal a person or thing that brings up the rear in a group or formation. ■ a member of the crew of a military aircraft who operates a gun from a compartment at the rear.

tail feather ▶ noun a strong flight feather of a bird's tail.

tail fin ▶ noun **1** Zoology a fin at the posterior extremity of a fish's body, typically continuous with the tail. Also called CAUDAL FIN.
2 Aeronautics a projecting vertical surface on the tail of an aircraft, providing stability and typically housing the rudder.
3 an upswept projection on each rear corner of a car, popular in the 1950s.

tail gas ▶ noun [mass noun] gas produced in a refinery and not required for further processing.

tailgate ▶ noun a hinged flap at the back of a truck which may be lowered or removed when loading or unloading the vehicle. ■ the door at the back of an estate or hatchback car. ■ [as modifier] N. Amer. relating to or denoting an informal meal served from the back of a parked vehicle: *a tailgate picnic.* ■ [as modifier] denoting a style of jazz trombone playing characterized by improvisation in the manner of the early New Orleans musicians.
▶ verb [with obj.] informal drive too closely behind (another vehicle): *he started tailgating the motorist in front.*
– DERIVATIVES **tailgater** noun.

tailing ▶ noun **1** (**tailings**) the residue of something, especially ore. ■ [mass noun] grain or flour of inferior quality.
2 [mass noun] the action of cutting the stalks or ends off fruit or vegetables: *the green beans only needed topping and tailing.*
3 the part of a beam or projecting brick or stone embedded in a wall.

taille /tɑːj/, French /taj/ ▶ noun (pl. pronunc. **same**) **1** (in France before 1789) a tax levied on the common people by the king or an overlord.
2 Music, historical the register of a tenor or similar voice, or an instrument of this register.
3 [mass noun] the juice produced from a second pressing of the grapes during winemaking. ■ low-quality wine made from a second pressing of the grapes.
– ORIGIN French, from Old French: see TAIL[2].

Tailleferre /tʌɪˈfɛː/, French /tajfɛʀ/, Germaine (1892–1983), French composer and pianist. A member of Les Six, she composed concertos for unusual combinations of instruments.

tailleur /tɑːˈjəː/ ▶ noun (pl. pronunc. **same**) dated or formal a woman's tailor-made suit.
– ORIGIN French.

tail light (also **tail lamp**) ▶ noun a red light at the rear of a motor vehicle, train, or bicycle.

tail male ▶ noun [mass noun] Law, historical the limitation of the succession of property or title to male descendants.

tail-off ▶ noun [in sing.] a decline or gradual reduction in something: *a tail-off in customers.*

tailor ▶ noun **1** a person whose occupation is making fitted clothes such as suits, trousers, and jackets to fit individual customers.
2 (also **tailorfish**) another term for BLUEFISH.
▶ verb [with obj.] **1** (of a tailor) make (clothes) to fit individual customers: *he was wearing a sports coat which had obviously been tailored in London.*
2 make or adapt for a particular purpose or person: *arrangements can be* ***tailored to*** *meet individual requirements.*
– ORIGIN Middle English: from Anglo-Norman French *taillour*, literally 'cutter', based on late Latin *taliare* 'to cut'. The verb dates from the mid 17th cent.

tailorbird ▶ noun a small southern Asian warbler that makes a row of holes in one or two large leaves and stitches them together with cottony fibres or silk to form a container for the nest. ● Genus *Orthotomus*, family Sylviidae: several species.

tailored ▶ adjective (of clothes) smart, fitted, and well cut: *a tailored charcoal-grey suit.*

tailoring ▶ noun [mass noun] the activity or trade of a tailor. ■ the style or cut of a garment or garments.

tailor-made ▶ adjective **1** (of clothes) made by a tailor for a particular customer: *tailor-made suits.*
2 made, adapted, or suited for a particular purpose or person: *he was* ***tailor-made for*** *the job.*
▶ noun a garment that has been specially made for a particular customer: *a lady in a red tailor-made.*

tailor's chalk ▶ noun [mass noun] hard chalk or soapstone used in tailoring and dressmaking for marking fabric.

tailor's twist ▶ noun [mass noun] strong thread used by tailors.

tailpiece ▶ noun **1** a part added to the end of a story or piece of writing. ■ a small decorative design at the foot of a page or the end of a chapter or book.
2 the piece at the base of a violin or other stringed instrument to which the strings are attached.

tailpipe ▶ noun chiefly N. Amer. the rear section of the exhaust pipe of a motor vehicle.

tailplane ▶ noun Brit. a horizontal aerofoil at the tail of an aircraft.

tail race ▶ noun a fast-flowing stretch of a river or stream below a dam or watermill.

tail rhyme ▶ noun Prosody a rhyme involving couplets, triplets, or stanzas, each with a tag or additional short line.

tail rotor ▶ noun Aeronautics an auxiliary rotor at the tail of a helicopter designed to counterbalance the torque of the main rotor.

tail skid ▶ noun a support for the tail of an aircraft when on the ground.

tail slide ▶ noun a backward movement of an aircraft from a vertical stalled position.

tailspin ▶ noun a spin by an aircraft. ■ a state of rapidly increasing chaos or panic: *the rise in interest rates sent the stock market into a tailspin.*
▶ verb (**tailspins**, **tailspinning**; past and past participle **tailspun**) [no obj.] become increasingly chaotic and out of control: *an economy tailspinning into chaos.*

tailstock ▶ noun the adjustable part of a lathe holding the fixed spindle.

tail-walk ▶ verb [no obj., usu. with adverbial of direction] (of a fish) move over the surface of water by propulsion with the tail.
– DERIVATIVES **tail-walking** noun.

tailwater ▶ noun [mass noun] the water in a mill race below the wheel, or in a canal below a lock.

tailwheel ▶ noun a wheel supporting the tail of an aircraft while on the ground.

tailwind ▶ noun a wind blowing in the direction of travel of a vehicle or aircraft; a wind blowing from behind.

taimen /ˈtʌɪmən/ ▶ noun (pl. **same**) a food fish that is closely related to the huchen, widespread in Siberia and eastern Asia. ● *Hucho taimen*, family Salmonidae.
– ORIGIN from Russian.

Taimyr Peninsula /tʌɪˈmɪə/ (also **Taymyr**) a vast, almost uninhabited peninsula on the north coast of central Russia, extending into the Arctic Ocean and separating the Kara Sea from the Laptev Sea. Its northern tip is the northernmost point of Asia.

Tainan /tʌɪˈnɑːn/ a city on the SW coast of Taiwan; pop. 764,700 (est. 2007). Settled from mainland China in 1590, it is one of the oldest cities on the island and was its capital from 1684 until 1885, when it was replaced by Taipei. Its original name was Taiwan, the name later given to the whole island.

Taino /ˈtʌɪnəʊ/ ▶ noun (pl. **same** or **Tainos**) **1** a member of an extinct Arawak people formerly inhabiting the Greater Antilles and the Bahamas.
2 [mass noun] an extinct Caribbean language of the Arawakan group.
▶ adjective relating to or denoting this people or their language.
– ORIGIN from Taino *taino* 'noble, lord'.

taint ▶ noun a trace of a bad or undesirable substance or quality: *the lingering taint of creosote | the taint of corruption which adhered to the government.* ■ something with a contaminating influence or effect: *the taint that threatens to stain most of the company's other partners.*

T

▸ **verb** [with obj.] contaminate or pollute (something): *the air was tainted by fumes from the cars.* ■ affect with a bad or undesirable quality: *his administration was tainted by scandal.* ■ [no obj.] archaic (of food or water) become contaminated or polluted.
– DERIVATIVES **taintless adjective** (literary).
– ORIGIN Middle English (as a verb in the sense 'convict, prove guilty'): partly from Old French *teint* 'tinged', based on Latin *tingere* 'to dye, tinge'; partly a shortening of **ATTAINT**.

taipan¹ /ˈtʌɪpan/ ▸ **noun** a foreigner who is head of a business in China.
– ORIGIN mid 19th cent.: from Chinese (Cantonese dialect) *daaihbāan*.

taipan² /ˈtʌɪpan/ ▸ **noun** a large brown highly venomous Australian snake. ● Genus *Oxyuranus*, family Elapidae: two species, in particular *O. scutellatus*.
– ORIGIN 1930s: from Wik Munkan (an extinct Aboriginal language of North Queensland) *dhayban*.

Taipei /tʌɪˈpeɪ/ the capital of Taiwan; pop. 2,629,300 (est. 2007). It developed as an industrial city in the 19th century, and became the capital in 1885.

Taiping Rebellion /tʌɪˈpɪŋ/ a sustained uprising against the Qing dynasty in China 1850–64.

The rebellion was led by Hong Xiuquan (1814–64), who had founded a religious group inspired by elements of Christian theology and proposing egalitarian social policies. His large army captured Nanjing in 1853 but was eventually defeated at Shanghai at the hands of an army trained by the British general Charles Gordon.

– ORIGIN *Taiping* from Chinese *T'ai-p'ing-wang* 'Prince of great peace', a title given to Hong Xiuquan.

Taiwan /tʌɪˈwɑːn/ an island country off the SE coast of China; pop. 22,974,300 (est. 2009); official language, Mandarin Chinese; capital, Taipei. Official name **CHINA, REPUBLIC OF**. Former name **FORMOSA**.

In 1949, towards the end of the war with the Communist regime of mainland China, Chiang Kai-shek withdrew to the island with 500,000 nationalist Kuomintang troops. Taiwan became the headquarters of the Kuomintang, which held power continuously until defeated in presidential elections in 2000. Since the 1950s Taiwan has undergone steady economic growth, especially in its export industries.

– DERIVATIVES **Taiwanese** /ˌtʌɪwəˈniːz/ **adjective & noun**.

Taiyuan /ˌtʌɪjʊˈɑːn/ a city in northern China, capital of Shanxi province; pop. 2,162,000 (est. 2006).

Tai Yue Shan /ˌtʌɪ jʊeɪ ˈʃan/ Chinese name for **LANTAU**.

Ta'iz /taˈɪz/ a city in SW Yemen; pop. 467,000 (est. 2004). It was the administrative capital of Yemen from 1948 to 1962.

Taizé /ˈteɪzeɪ/ ▸ **noun** [mass noun] [usu. as modifier] the style of Christian worship practised by the ecumenical Taizé community in France, characterized by the repetitive singing of simple harmonized tunes, often in various languages, interspersed with readings, prayers, and periods of silence.
– ORIGIN the name of a village in Burgundy, France, where the community was founded in 1949.

taj /tɑːdʒ/ ▸ **noun 1** a tall conical cap worn by a dervish.
2 historical a crown worn by an Indian prince of high rank.
– ORIGIN mid 19th cent.: from Persian *tāj* 'crown'.

T

Tajik /tɑːˈdʒiːk/ (also **Tadjik** or **Tadzhik**) ▸ **noun 1** a member of a mainly Muslim people inhabiting Tajikistan and parts of neighbouring countries. ■ a native or inhabitant of the republic of Tajikistan.
2 [mass noun] (also **Tajiki** /tɑːˈdʒiːki/) the language of the Tajiks, a member of the Iranian branch of the Indo-European family.
▸ **adjective** relating to Tajikistan, the Tajiks, or their language.
– ORIGIN from Persian *tājik* 'a Persian, someone who is neither an Arab nor a Turk'.

Tajikistan /təˌdʒiːkɪˈstɑːn, -ˈstan/ (also **Tadzhikistan**) a mountainous republic in central Asia, north of Afghanistan; pop. 7,349,100 (est. 2009); languages, Tajik (official), Russian; capital, Dushanbe.

The region was conquered by the Mongols in the 13th century and absorbed into the Russian empire during the 1880s and 1890s. From 1929 Tajikistan formed a constituent republic of the Soviet Union; it became an independent republic within the Commonwealth of Independent States in 1991.

tajine ▸ **noun** variant spelling of **TAGINE**.

Taj Mahal /ˌtɑːʒ məˈhɑːl, ˌtɑːdʒ/ a mausoleum at Agra in northern India built by the Mogul emperor Shah Jahan (1592–1666) in memory of his favourite wife, completed *c.*1649. Set in formal gardens, the domed building in white marble is reflected in a pool flanked by cypresses.
– ORIGIN perhaps a corruption of Persian *Mumtaz Mahal*, from *mumtāz* 'chosen one' (the title of the wife of Shah Jahan) and **MAHAL**.

Tajo /ˈtaxəʊ/ Spanish name for **TAGUS**.

taka /ˈtɑːkɑː/ ▸ **noun** (pl. **same**) the basic monetary unit of Bangladesh, equal to 100 poisha.
– ORIGIN from Bengali *ṭākā*.

takaful /ˈtɑːkəfuːl/ ▸ **noun** [mass noun] Islam a type of insurance system devised to comply with the sharia laws, in which money is pooled and invested.
– ORIGIN Arabic, literally 'mutual obligation'.

takahe /ˈtɑːkəhi/ ▸ **noun** a large, rare flightless rail with bluish-black and olive-green plumage and a large red bill, found in mountain grassland in New Zealand. ● *Porphyrio mantelli*, family Rallidae.
– ORIGIN mid 19th cent.: from Maori.

take ▸ **verb** (past **took**; past participle **taken**) [with obj.] **1** lay hold of (something) with one's hands; reach for and hold: *he leaned forward to take her hand.* ■ capture or gain possession of by force or military means: *twenty of their ships were sunk or taken | the French took Ghent.* ■ (in bridge, whist, and similar card games) win (a trick). ■ Chess capture (an opposing piece or pawn). ■ Cricket dismiss a batsman from (his wicket). ■ dispossess someone of (something); steal or illicitly remove: *someone must have sneaked in here and taken it.* ■ occupy (a place or position): *we found that all the seats were taken.* ■ rent (a house). ■ agree to buy (an item): *I'll take the one on the end.* ■ (**be taken**) humorous (of a person) already be married or in an emotional relationship. ■ [in imperative] use or have ready to use: *take half the marzipan and roll out.* ■ [usu. in imperative] use as an instance or example in support of an argument: *let's take Napoleon, for instance.* ■ Brit. regularly buy or subscribe to (a particular newspaper or periodical). ■ ascertain by measurement or observation: *the nurse takes my blood pressure.* ■ write down: *he was taking notes.* ■ make (a photograph) with a camera. ■ (especially of illness) suddenly strike or afflict (someone): *mum's been taken bad.* ■ have sexual intercourse with.
2 [with obj. and adverbial of direction] remove (someone or something) from a particular place: *he took an envelope from his inside pocket | the police took him away.* ■ subtract: ***take** two **from** ten | add the numbers together and **take away** five.*
3 [with obj. and usu. with adverbial] carry or bring with one; convey: *he took along a portfolio of his drawings | the drive takes you through some wonderful scenery |* [with two objs] *I took him a letter.* ■ accompany or guide (someone) to a specified place: *I'll take you to your room.* ■ bring into a specified state: *the invasion took Europe to the brink of war.* ■ use as a route or a means of transport: *take the A43 towards Bicester | we took the night train to Scotland.*
4 accept or receive (someone or something): *she was advised to take any job offered | they don't take children.* ■ understand or accept as valid: *I take your point.* ■ acquire or assume (a position, state, or form): *teaching methods will take various forms | he took office in September.* ■ receive (a specified amount of money) as payment or earnings: *on its first day of trading the shop took 1.6 million roubles.* ■ achieve or attain (a victory or result): *John Martin took the men's title.* ■ act on (an opportunity): *he took his chance to get out while the house was quiet.* ■ experience or be affected by: *the lad took a savage beating.* ■ [with obj. and adverbial] react to or regard (news or an event) in a specified way: *she took the news well | everything you say, he takes it the wrong way.* ■ [with obj. and adverbial] deal with (a physical obstacle or course) in a specified way: *he takes the corners with no concern for his own safety.* ■ regard or view in a specified way: *he somehow **took** it **as** a personal insult |* [with obj. and infinitive] *I fell over what I took to be a heavy branch.* ■ (**be taken by/with**) be attracted or charmed by: *Billie was very taken with him.* ■ submit to, tolerate, or endure: *they refused to take it any more | some people found her hard to take.* ■ (**take it**) [with clause] assume: *I take it that someone is coming to meet you.*
5 consume as food, drink, medicine, or drugs: *take an aspirin and lie down.*
6 make, undertake, or perform (an action or task): *Lucy took a deep breath | the key decisions are still to be taken.* ■ conduct (a ceremony or gathering). ■ be taught or examined in (a subject): *some degrees require a student to take a secondary subject.* ■ Brit. obtain (an academic degree) after fulfilling the required conditions: *she took a degree in business studies.*
7 require or use up (a specified amount of time): *the jury took an hour and a half to find McPherson guilty |* [with two objs] *it takes me about a quarter of an hour to walk to work.* ■ (of a task or situation) need or call for (a particular person or thing): *it will take an electronics expert to dismantle it.* ■ hold; accommodate: *an exclusive island hideaway that takes just twenty guests.* ■ wear or require (a particular size of garment or type of complementary article): *he only takes size 5 boots.*
8 [no obj.] (of a plant or seed) take root or begin to grow; germinate: *the fuchsia cuttings had taken and were looking good.* ■ (of an added substance) become successfully established.
9 Grammar have or require as part of the appropriate construction: *verbs which take both the infinitive and the finite clause as their object.*
▸ **noun 1** a scene or sequence of sound or vision photographed or recorded continuously at one time: *he completed a particularly difficult scene in two takes.* ■ a particular version of or approach to something: *his own whimsical **take on** life.*
2 an amount of something gained or acquired from one source or in one session: *the take from commodity taxation.* ■ chiefly US the money received at a cinema or theatre for seats.
3 Printing an amount of copy set up at one time or by one compositor.
– PHRASES **be on the take** informal take bribes. **be taken ill** become ill suddenly. **have what it takes** informal have the necessary qualities for success. **take advantage of** (or **take advice** etc.) see **ADVANTAGE**, **ADVICE**, etc. **take something as read** see **READ**. **take five** informal, chiefly N. Amer. have a short break. **take a lot of** (or **some**) —— be difficult to do or effect in the specified way: *he might take some convincing.* **take someone in hand** undertake to control or reform someone. **take something in hand** start doing or dealing with a task. **take ill** (US **sick**) informal become ill, especially suddenly. **take something ill** archaic resent something done or said. **take it from me** I can assure you: *take it from me, kid—I've been there, done it, seen it all.* **take it on one** (or **oneself**) **to do something** decide to do something without asking for permission or advice. **take it or leave it** [usu. in imperative] said to express that the offer one has made is not negotiable and that one is indifferent to another's reaction to it: *that's the deal—take it or leave it.* **take it out of 1** exhaust the strength of (someone): *parties and tours can take it out of you, especially if you are over 65.* **2** Brit. take reprisals against. **take someone out of themselves** make a person forget their worries. **take that!** exclaimed when hitting someone or taking decisive action against them. **take one's time** not hurry.
– PHRASAL VERBS **take after** resemble (a parent or ancestor): *the rest of us take after our mother.* **take against** Brit. begin to dislike (someone), often for no strong or obvious reason: *from the moment he arrived, they took against this talented loudmouth.* **take something apart** dismantle something. ■ (**take someone/thing apart**) informal attack, criticize, or defeat someone or something in a vigorous or forceful way. **take something away** Brit. buy food at a cafe or restaurant for eating elsewhere: *he ordered a lamb madras to take away.* **take away from** detract from: *that shouldn't take away from the achievement of the French.* **take someone back** strongly remind someone of a past time: *if 'Disco Inferno' doesn't take you back, the bell-bottom pants will.* **take something back 1** retract a statement: *I take back nothing of what I said.* **2** return unsatisfactory goods to a shop. ■ (of a shop) accept such goods. **3** Printing transfer text to the previous line. **take something down 1** write down spoken words: *I took down the address.* **2** dismantle and remove a structure: *the old Norman church was taken down in 1819.* **take from** another way of saying **TAKE AWAY FROM**. **take someone in 1** accommodate someone as a lodger or because they are homeless or in difficulties. **2** cheat, fool, or deceive someone: *she tried to pass this off as an amusing story, but nobody was taken in.* **take something in 1** undertake work at home. **2** make a garment tighter by altering its seams. ■ Sailing furl a sail. **3** include or encompass something: *the sweep of his arm took in most of Main Street.* ■ fully understand or absorb something heard or seen: *she took in the scene at a glance.* **4** visit or attend a place or event in a casual way or on the way to another: *he'd maybe take in a movie, or just relax.*

take off 1 (of an aircraft or bird) become airborne. ■ (of an enterprise) become successful or popular: *the newly launched electronic newspaper has really taken off.* **2** (also **take oneself off**) depart hastily: *the officer took off after his men.* **take someone off** informal mimic someone humorously. **take something off 1** remove clothing from one's or another's body: *she took off her cardigan.* **2** deduct part of an amount. **3** choose to have a period away from work: *I took the next day off.* **take on** Brit. informal become very upset, especially needlessly: *don't take on so—no need to upset yourself.* **take someone on 1** engage an employee. **2** be willing or ready to meet an adversary or opponent: *a group of villagers has taken on the planners.* **take something on 1** undertake a task or responsibility, especially a difficult one: *whoever takes on the trout farm will have their work cut out.* **2** acquire a particular meaning or quality: *the subject has taken on a new significance in the past year.* **take someone out 1** escort someone to a social event or place of entertainment: *I took her out to dinner the following night.* **2** Bridge respond to a bid or double by one's partner by bidding a different suit. **take someone/thing out** informal kill, destroy, or disable someone or something. **take something out 1** obtain an official document or service: *you can take out a loan for a specific purchase.* ■ get a licence or summons issued. **2** chiefly US another way of saying TAKE SOMETHING AWAY. **take something out on** relieve frustration or anger by attacking or mistreating (a person or thing not responsible for such feelings). **take something over 1** (also **take over**) assume control of something: *British troops had taken over the German trenches.* ■ (of a company) buy out another. ■ become responsible for a task in succession to another: *he will take over as chief executive in April.* **2** Printing transfer text to the next line. **take to 1** begin or fall into the habit of: *he took to hiding some secret supplies in his desk.* **2** form a liking for: *Mrs Brady never took to Moran.* ■ develop an ability for (something), especially quickly or easily: *I took to pole-vaulting right away.* **3** go to (a place) to escape danger or an enemy: *they took to the hills.* **take someone up** adopt someone as a protégé. **take something up 1** become interested or engaged in a pursuit: *she took up tennis at the age of 11.* ■ begin to hold or fulfil a position or post: *he left to take up an appointment as a missionary.* ■ accept an offer or challenge. **2** occupy time, space, or attention: *I don't want to take up any more of your time.* **3** pursue a matter later or further: *he'll have to **take it up with** the bishop.* ■ (also **take up**) resume speaking after an interruption: *I took up where I had left off.* **4** shorten a garment by turning up the hem. **take someone up on 1** challenge or question a speaker on (a particular point): *the interviewer did not take him up on his quotation.* **2** accept (an offer or challenge) from someone: *I'd like to take you up on that offer.* **take up with** begin to associate with (someone), especially in a way disapproved of by the speaker: *he's taken up with a divorced woman, I understand.*
– DERIVATIVES **takable** (also **takeable**) adjective.
– ORIGIN late Old English *tacan* 'get (especially by force), capture', from Old Norse *taka* 'grasp, lay hold of', of unknown ultimate origin.

takeaway ▶ noun **1** Brit. a restaurant or shop selling cooked food to be eaten elsewhere: *a fast-food takeaway* | [as modifier] *a takeaway pizza.* ■ a meal or dish bought from a shop or restaurant to be eaten elsewhere.
2 Golf another term for BACKSWING.

takedown chiefly N. Amer. ▶ noun **1** a wrestling manoeuvre in which an opponent is swiftly brought to the mat from a standing position.
2 informal a police raid or arrest.
3 [as modifier] denoting a firearm with the capacity to have the barrel and magazine detached from the stock.

take-home pay ▶ noun [mass noun] the pay received by an employee after the deduction of tax and insurance.

take-off ▶ noun **1** an instance of becoming airborne: *a perfect take-off* | [mass noun] *the plane accelerated down the runway for take-off.*
2 informal an act of mimicking someone or something: *the film is a take-off of Star Wars.*

takeout ▶ noun **1** N. Amer. a takeaway.
2 Bridge a bid (in a different suit) made in response to a bid or double by one's partner.

take-out double ▶ noun Bridge a double which, by convention, requires one's partner to bid, used to convey information rather than to score penalty points. Often contrasted with BUSINESS DOUBLE.

takeover ▶ noun an act of assuming control of something, especially the buying out of one company by another.

taker ▶ noun **1** [in combination] a person who takes a specified thing: *a drug-taker* | *a risk-taker.*
2 a person who takes a bet or accepts an offer or challenge: *there were plenty of takers when I offered a small wager.*

take-up ▶ noun [mass noun] chiefly Brit. **1** the acceptance of something offered: *education is aiding the take-up of birth control.*
2 Stock Exchange the action of paying in full for securities originally bought on margin.

takht /tɑːkt/ ▶ noun (in Eastern countries) a sofa or long bench, or a bed.
– ORIGIN from Persian *takt.*

takin /ˈtɑːkɪn/ ▶ noun a large, heavily built goat-antelope found in steep, dense woodlands of the eastern Himalayas. ● *Budorcas taxicolor*, family Bovidae.
– ORIGIN mid 19th cent.: a local word.

taking ▶ noun **1** [mass noun] the action or process of taking something: *the taking of life.*
2 (**takings**) the amount of money earned by a business from the sale of goods or services: *the big test for the shop's new look is whether it'll boost takings.*
▶ adjective dated (of a person) captivating in manner; charming: *he was not a very taking person, she felt.*
– PHRASES **for the taking** ready or available for someone to take advantage of: *the fourth game was Wright's for the taking.*
– DERIVATIVES **takingly** adverb.

Taki-Taki /ˈtɑːkɪˌtɑːki/ ▶ noun [mass noun] an English-based creole language of Suriname. Also called SRANAN.
– ORIGIN an alteration of TALKEE-TALKEE.

takkie ▶ noun variant spelling of TACKIE.

Taklimakan Desert /ˌtakləməˈkɑːn/ (also **Takla Makan**) a desert in the Xinjiang autonomous region of NW China, lying between the Kunlun Shan and Tien Shan mountains and forming the greater part of the Tarim Basin.

Takoradi /ˌtɑːkəˈrɑːdi/ a seaport in western Ghana, on the Gulf of Guinea; pop. 308,300 (est. 2009). It is part of the joint urban area of Sekondi-Takoradi and is one of the major seaports of West Africa.

tal /tɑːl/ ▶ noun Indian a lake.
– ORIGIN from Sanskrit *tāl* 'pond, tank'.

tala¹ /ˈtɑːlə/ (also **taal** /ˈtɑːl/) ▶ noun a traditional rhythmic pattern in classical Indian music.
– ORIGIN from Sanskrit *tāla* 'handclapping, musical time'.

tala² /ˈtɑːlə/ ▶ noun (pl. **same** or **talas**) the basic monetary unit of Samoa, equal to 100 sene.
– ORIGIN from Samoan *tālā.*

Talaing /təˈlʌɪŋ/ ▶ noun (pl. **same** or **Talaings**) & adjective another term for MON.
– ORIGIN the name in Burmese.

talapoin /ˈtaləpɔɪn/ ▶ noun **1** a Buddhist monk or priest.
2 a small West African monkey that lives in large groups near watercourses and in swamp forest. ● *Miopithecus talapoin*, family Cercopithecidae.
– ORIGIN late 16th cent.: from Portuguese *talapão*, from Mon *tala pói*, literally 'lord of merit', used as a respectful title for a Buddhist monk.

talaq /taˈlɑːk/ ▶ noun [mass noun] (in Islamic law) divorce effected by the husband's enunciation of the word 'talaq', this constituting a formal repudiation of his wife. Compare with KHULA.
– ORIGIN from Arabic *ṭalaq*, from *ṭalaqa* 'repudiate'.

talaria /təˈlɛːrɪə/ ▶ plural noun (in Roman mythology) winged sandals as worn by certain gods and goddesses, especially Mercury.
– ORIGIN Latin, neuter plural of *talaris*, from *talus* 'ankle'.

Talbot /ˈtɔːlbət, ˈtɒl-/, (William Henry) Fox (1800–77), English pioneer of photography. He produced the first photograph on paper in 1835. Five years later he discovered a process for producing a negative from which multiple positive prints could be made, though the independently developed daguerreotype proved to be superior.

talbot /ˈtɔːlbət, ˈtɒl-/ ▶ noun a dog of an extinct light-coloured breed of hound with large ears and heavy jaws.
– ORIGIN late Middle English: probably from the family name *Talbot*; the term was also used to denote the representation of such a dog in the badge and supporters of the Talbot family, earls of Shrewsbury.

talc ▶ noun [mass noun] **1** talcum powder.
2 a white, grey, or pale green soft mineral with a greasy feel, occurring as translucent masses or laminae and consisting of hydrated magnesium silicate.
▶ verb (**talcs**, **talcing**, **talced**) [with obj.] powder or treat (something) with talc.
– DERIVATIVES **talcose** adjective (Geology), **talcy** adjective.
– ORIGIN late 16th cent. (denoting the mineral): from medieval Latin *talcum* (see TALCUM).

talcum (also **talcum powder**) ▶ noun [mass noun] a cosmetic or toilet preparation consisting of the mineral talc in powdered form, typically perfumed.
▶ verb (**talcums**, **talcuming**, **talcumed**) [with obj.] powder (something) with talcum.
– ORIGIN mid 16th cent.: from medieval Latin, from Arabic *ṭalq*, from Persian.

tale ▶ noun **1** a fictitious or true narrative or story, especially one that is imaginatively recounted. ■ a lie.
2 archaic a number or total: *an exact tale of the dead bodies.*
– PHRASES **a tale of a tub** archaic an apocryphal story. **tell tales** gossip about or reveal another person's secrets or wrongdoings.
– ORIGIN Old English *talu* 'telling, something told', of Germanic origin; related to Dutch *taal* 'speech' and German *Zahl* 'number', also to TELL¹. Sense 2 is probably from Old Norse.

Taleban variant spelling of TALIBAN.

talebearer ▶ noun dated a person who maliciously gossips or reveals secrets.
– DERIVATIVES **talebearing** noun & adjective.

taleggio /taˈlɛdʒɪəʊ/ ▶ noun [mass noun] a type of soft Italian cheese made from cow's milk.
– ORIGIN named after the *Taleggio* valley in Lombardy.

talent ▶ noun **1** [mass noun] natural aptitude or skill: *he possesses more talent than any other player* | [count noun] *she displayed **a talent for** garden design.* ■ people possessing natural aptitude or skill: *I signed all the talent in Rome* | [count noun] *Simon is a talent to watch.* ■ Brit. informal people regarded as sexually attractive or as prospective sexual partners: *most Saturday nights I have this urge to go on the hunt for new talent.*
2 a former weight and unit of currency, used especially by the ancient Romans and Greeks.
– DERIVATIVES **talentless** adjective.
– ORIGIN Old English *talente, talentan* (as a unit of weight), from Latin *talenta*, plural of *talentum* 'weight, sum of money', from Greek *talanton*. Sense 1 is a figurative use with biblical allusion to the parable of the talents (Matt. 25:14–30).

talented ▶ adjective having a natural aptitude or skill for something: *a talented young musician.*

talent scout ▶ noun a person whose job is to search for talented performers who can be employed or promoted, especially in sport and entertainment.

talent spotter ▶ noun Brit. a talent scout.
– DERIVATIVES **talent-spot** verb.

tales /ˈteɪliːz/ ▶ noun Law a writ for summoning substitute jurors when the original jury has become deficient in number.
– ORIGIN from Latin *tales (de circumstantibus)* 'such (of the bystanders)', the first words of the writ.

talesman /ˈteɪliːzmən, ˈteɪlz-/ ▶ noun (pl. **talesmen**) Law a person summoned by a tales.

tale teller ▶ noun a person who tells stories. ■ a person who spreads gossip or reveals secrets.
– DERIVATIVES **tale-telling** noun.

tali plural form of TALUS¹.

Talib /ˈtalɪb/ ▶ noun a member of the Taliban.

Taliban /ˈtalɪban/ (also **Taleban**) a fundamentalist Muslim movement whose militia took control of much of Afghanistan from early 1995, and in 1996 took Kabul and set up an Islamic state. The Taliban were overthrown by US-led forces and Afghan groups in 2001 following the events of September 11.
– DERIVATIVES **Talibanization** (also **Talibanisation**) noun, **Talibanize** (also **Talibanise**) verb.
– ORIGIN from Persian *ṭālibān*, pl. of *ṭālib* 'student, seeker of knowledge', from Arabic (so named because the movement reputedly began amongst Afghani students exiled in Pakistan).

Taliesin /ˌtalɪˈɛsɪn/ (*fl.* 550), Welsh bard, perhaps a mythic figure. He is first mentioned in written accounts of the late 7th century, and a large body of prophetic poems included in the Mabinogion have been ascribed to him.

talik /ˈtalɪk/ ▶ **noun** Geology an area of unfrozen ground surrounded by permafrost.
– ORIGIN 1940s: from Russian, from *tayat'* 'melt'.

talipes /ˈtalɪpiːz/ ▶ **noun** Medicine technical term for **CLUB FOOT**.
– ORIGIN mid 19th cent.: modern Latin, from Latin *talus* 'ankle' + *pes* 'foot'.

talipot /ˈtalɪpɒt/ ▶ **noun** a tall Indian palm with very large fan-shaped leaves and a flower that can reach 8 m tall. The leaves are used as sunshades and for thatching, and to make the material on which Buddhist sacred books are written. ● *Corypha umbraculifera*, family Palmae.
– ORIGIN late 17th cent.: from Malayalam *tālipat*, from Sanskrit *tālīpatra*, from *tālī* 'palm' + *patra* 'leaf'.

talisman /ˈtalɪzmən/ ▶ **noun** (pl. **talismans**) an object, typically an inscribed ring or stone, that is thought to have magic powers and to bring good luck.
– DERIVATIVES **talismanic** /-ˈmanɪk/ **adjective**.
– ORIGIN mid 17th cent.: based on Arabic *ṭilsam*, apparently from an alteration of late Greek *telesma* 'completion, religious rite', from *telein* 'complete, perform a rite', from *telos* 'result, end'.

talk ▶ **verb** [no obj.] **1** speak in order to give information or express ideas or feelings; converse or communicate by spoken words: *the two men talked* | *we'd sit and* ***talk about*** *jazz* | *it was no use* ***talking to*** *Anthony* | [with obj.] *you're talking rubbish*. ■ have the power of speech: *he can talk as well as you or I can*. ■ discuss personal or intimate feelings: *we need to talk, Maggie*. ■ [with obj. and adverbial] persuade or cause (someone) to do something by talking: *don't try to talk me into acting as a go-between*. ■ [with obj.] (**be talking**) informal used to emphasize the seriousness, importance, or extent of the thing one is discussing: *we're talking big money*. ■ reveal secret or confidential information. ■ gossip: *you'll have the whole school talking*.
2 have formal dealings or discussions; negotiate: *they won't* ***talk to*** *the regime that killed their families*.
3 [with obj.] use (a particular language) in speech: *we were talking German*.
▶ **noun 1** [mass noun] communication by spoken words; conversation or discussion: *there was a slight but noticeable lull in the talk*. ■ [count noun] a period of conversation or discussion, especially a relatively serious one: *my mother had a talk with Louis*. ■ rumour, gossip, or speculation: *there is* ***talk of*** *an armistice*. ■ empty promises or boasting: *he's all talk*. ■ (**the talk of**) a current subject of widespread gossip or speculation in (a particular place): *within days I was* ***the talk of the town***.
2 (**talks**) formal discussions or negotiations over a period: *peace talks*.
3 an informal address or lecture.
– PHRASES **you can't** (or **can**) **talk** (US **you shouldn't** or **should talk**) informal used to convey that a criticism made applies equally well to the person who has made it: *'He'd chase anything in a skirt!' 'You can't talk!'* **know what one is talking about** be expert or authoritative on a particular subject. **look** (or **hark**) **who's talking** another way of saying **YOU CAN'T TALK**. **talk a blue streak** see **BLUE**[1]. **talk about ——!** informal used to emphasize that something is an extreme or striking example of a particular situation, state, or experience: *talk about hangovers!* **talk big** informal talk boastfully or overconfidently. **talk dirty** see **DIRTY**. **talk the hind leg off a donkey** Brit. informal talk incessantly. **talk nineteen to the dozen** see **DOZEN**. **talk of the devil** see **DEVIL**. **talk sense into** persuade (someone) to behave more sensibly. **talk shop** see **SHOP**. **talk through one's hat** (or Brit. **arse** or **backside** or US **ass**) informal talk foolishly, wildly, or ignorantly. **talk the talk** informal speak fluently or convincingly about something or in a way intended to please or impress others: *we may not look like true rock jocks yet, but we talk the talk*. **talk turkey** see **TURKEY**.
– PHRASAL VERBS **talk at** address (someone) in a hectoring or self-important way without listening to their replies: *he never talked at you*. **talk back** reply defiantly or insolently. **talk down to** speak patronizingly or condescendingly to. **talk something out** Brit. (in Parliament) block the course of a bill by prolonging discussion to the time of adjournment. **talk someone out of** persuade someone not to do (something unwise). **talk someone round** (or US **around**) bring someone to a particular point of view by talking. **talk someone through** enable someone to perform (a task) by giving them continuous instruction. **talk something over** (or **through**) discuss something thoroughly. **talk to** reprimand or scold (someone): *someone will have to talk to Lily*. **talk someone/thing up** (or **down**) discuss someone or something in a way that makes them seem more (or less) interesting or attractive.
– DERIVATIVES **talker** **noun**.
– ORIGIN Middle English: frequentative verb from the Germanic base of **TALE** or **TELL**[1].

talkathon ▶ **noun** informal a prolonged discussion or debate.
– ORIGIN 1930s (originally US, denoting a debate artificially prolonged to prevent the progress of a bill): blend of **TALK** and **MARATHON**.

talkative ▶ **adjective** fond of or given to talking: *the talkative driver hadn't stopped chatting*.
– DERIVATIVES **talkatively** **adverb**, **talkativeness** **noun**.

talkback ▶ **noun 1** a system of two-way communication by loudspeaker.
2 another term for **PHONE-IN**.

talkboard ▶ **noun** an Internet message board or chat room.

talkee-talkee /ˈtɔːkɪˌtɔːki/ ▶ **noun** [mass noun] dated an English-based creole or pidgin language, particularly in the Caribbean region. See also **TAKI-TAKI**.
– ORIGIN from **TALK**.

talkfest ▶ **noun** informal, chiefly N. Amer. a session of lengthy discussion or conversation, especially a television chat show or debate.

talkie ▶ **noun** informal a film with a soundtrack, as distinct from a silent film.
– ORIGIN early 20th cent. (originally US in the phrase *the talkies*): from **TALK**, on the pattern of *movie*.

talking ▶ **adjective** [attrib.] engaging in speech. ■ (of an animal or object) able to make sounds similar to those of speech: *the world's greatest talking bird*. ■ silently expressive: *he did have talking eyes*.
▶ **noun** [mass noun] the action of talking; speech or discussion: *I'll do the talking—you just back me up*.
– PHRASES **talking of ——** chiefly Brit. while we are on the subject of —— (said when one is reminded of something by the present topic of conversation): *talking of cards, you'd better take a couple of my business cards*.

talking blues ▶ **plural noun** [mass noun] a style of blues music in which the lyrics are more or less spoken rather than sung.

talking book ▶ **noun** a recorded reading of a book, originally designed for use by blind people.

talking drum ▶ **noun** one of a set of West African drums, each having a different pitch, which are beaten to transmit a tonal language.

talking film (also **talking picture**) ▶ **noun** a film with a soundtrack, as distinct from a silent film.

talking head ▶ **noun** informal a presenter or reporter on television who addresses the camera and is viewed in close-up.

talking point ▶ **noun** a topic that invites discussion or argument.

talking shop (also **talk shop**) ▶ **noun** Brit. a place or group regarded as a centre for unproductive talk rather than action.

talking-to ▶ **noun** [in sing.] informal a sharp reprimand in which someone is told that they have done wrong.

talk radio ▶ **noun** [mass noun] a type of radio broadcast in which the presenter talks about topical issues and encourages listeners to phone in to give their opinions.

talk show ▶ **noun** a chat show, especially one in which listeners, viewers, or the studio audience are invited to participate in the discussion.

talk time ▶ **noun** [mass noun] the time during which a mobile telephone is in use to handle calls, especially as a measure of the duration of the telephone's battery.

tall ▶ **adjective** of great or more than average height, especially (with reference to an object) relative to width: *a tall, broad-shouldered man* | *a tall glass of iced tea*. ■ (after a measurement and in questions) measuring a specified distance from top to bottom: *he was over six feet tall* | *how tall are you?*
– PHRASES **a tall order** an unreasonable or difficult demand. **a tall story** (or **tale**) an account that is fanciful and difficult to believe. **walk** (or **stand**) **tall** be proud and confident: *stop wishing that you were somehow different—start to walk tall!*
– DERIVATIVES **tallish** **adjective**, **tallness** **noun**.
– ORIGIN late Middle English: probably from Old English *getæl* 'swift, prompt'. Early senses also included 'fine, handsome' and 'bold, strong, good at fighting'.

tallage /ˈtalɪdʒ/ ▶ **noun** historical a form of arbitrary taxation levied by kings on the towns and lands of the Crown, abolished in the 14th century. ■ a tax levied on feudal dependants by their superiors.
– ORIGIN Middle English: from Old French *taillage*, from *tailler* 'to cut' (see **TAIL**[2]).

Tallahassee /ˌtaləˈhasi/ the state capital of Florida; pop. 171,922 (est. 2008).

tallboy ▶ **noun** Brit. a tall chest of drawers, typically one mounted on legs and in two sections, one standing on the other. Compare with **HIGHBOY**.

Talleyrand /ˈtalɪrand/, French /talɛʀɑ̃/, Charles Maurice de (1754–1838), French statesman; full surname *Talleyrand-Périgord*. Involved in the coup that brought Napoleon to power, he became head of the new government after the fall of Napoleon (1814) and was later instrumental in the overthrow of Charles X and the accession of Louis Philippe (1830).

tall hat ▶ **noun** another term for **TOP HAT**.

Tallinn /ˈtalɪn/ the capital of Estonia, a port on the Gulf of Finland; pop. 397,000 (est. 2007).

Tallis /ˈtalɪs/, Thomas (*c.*1505–85), English composer. Organist of the Chapel Royal jointly with William Byrd, he served under Henry VIII, Edward VI, Mary, and Elizabeth I. His works include the forty-part motet *Spem in Alium*.

tallith /ˈtalɪθ/ ▶ **noun** a fringed shawl traditionally worn by Jewish men at prayer.
– ORIGIN from Rabbinical Hebrew *ṭallīt*, from biblical Hebrew *ṭillel* 'to cover'.

tallow ▶ **noun** [mass noun] a hard fatty substance made from rendered animal fat, used (especially formerly) in making candles and soap.
▶ **verb** [with obj.] archaic smear (something, especially the bottom of a boat) with tallow.
– DERIVATIVES **tallowy** **adjective**.
– ORIGIN Middle English: perhaps from Middle Low German; related to Dutch *talk* and German *Talg*.

tallow tree ▶ **noun** a tree with fatty seeds from which vegetable tallow or other oils are extracted. ● Several species and families, in particular the **Chinese** (or **vegetable**) **tallow tree** (*Sapium sebiferum*, family Euphorbiaceae), native to eastern Asia.

tallow-wood ▶ **noun** a large Australian eucalyptus which yields very hard, greasy timber. ● *Eucalyptus microcorys*, family Myrtaceae.

tall poppy syndrome ▶ **noun** [mass noun] informal a perceived tendency to discredit or disparage those who have achieved notable wealth or prominence in public life.

tall ship ▶ **noun** a sailing ship with a high mast or masts.

tall timber ▶ **noun** [mass noun] N. Amer. dense and uninhabited forest. ■ (also **tall timbers**) informal a remote or unknown place.

tally ▶ **noun** (pl. **tallies**) **1** a current score or amount: *that takes his tally to 10 goals in 10 games*. ■ a record of a score or amount: *I* ***kept a tally of*** *David's debt on a note above my desk*. ■ a particular number taken as a group or unit to facilitate counting. ■ a mark registering a tally. ■ an account kept by means of a tally.
2 (also **tally stick**) historical a piece of wood scored across with notches for the items of an account and then split into halves, each party keeping one.
3 archaic a counterpart or duplicate of something.
4 a label giving information about a plant or tree.
▶ **verb** (**tallies**, **tallying**, **tallied**) **1** [no obj.] agree or correspond: *their signatures should* ***tally with*** *their names on the register* | *their books never tallied*.
2 [with obj.] calculate the total number of: *the votes were being tallied with abacuses*.
– ORIGIN late Middle English (denoting a notched tally stick): from Anglo-Norman French *tallie*, from Latin *talea* 'twig, cutting'. Compare with **TAIL**[2].

tally-ho ▶ **exclamation** a huntsman's cry to the hounds on sighting a fox.
▶ **noun** (pl. **tally-hos**) **1** a cry of 'tally-ho'.
2 historical a fast horse-drawn coach.
▶ **verb** (**tally-hoes**, **tally-hoing**, **tally-hoed**) [no obj.] utter a cry of 'tally-ho'.
– ORIGIN late 18th cent.: apparently an alteration of French *taïaut*, of unknown origin.

tallyman ▶ **noun** (pl. **tallymen**) **1** Brit. a person who sells goods on credit, especially from door to door.
2 a person who keeps a score or record of something.

T

tally system ▸ noun Brit. a system of selling goods on short-term credit or an instalment plan.

Talmud /ˈtalmʊd, -məd/ ▸ noun (**the Talmud**) the body of Jewish civil and ceremonial law and legend comprising the Mishnah and the Gemara. There are two versions of the Talmud: the Babylonian Talmud (which dates from the 5th century AD but includes earlier material) and the earlier Palestinian or Jerusalem Talmud.
DERIVATIVES **Talmudic** adjective, **Talmudical** adjective, **Talmudist** noun.
– ORIGIN from late Hebrew *talmūḏ* 'instruction', from Hebrew *lāmaḏ* 'learn'.

Talmud Torah ▸ noun [mass noun] Judaism the field of study that deals with the Jewish law. ■ [count noun] a communal school where children are instructed in Judaism.

talon ▸ noun **1** a claw, especially one belonging to a bird of prey.
2 the part of a bolt against which the key presses to slide it in a lock.
3 (in various card games) the cards that have not yet been dealt.
4 a printed form attached to a bearer bond that enables the holder to apply for a new sheet of coupons when the existing coupons have been used up.
5 an ogee moulding.
– DERIVATIVES **taloned** adjective.
– ORIGIN late Middle English (denoting any heel-like part or object): from Old French, literally 'heel', from Latin *talus* 'ankle bone, heel'.

taluk /ˈtɑːlʊk/ (also **taluka** /ˈtɑːlʊkɑː/) ▸ noun (in South Asia) an administrative district for taxation purposes, typically comprising a number of villages.
– ORIGIN via Persian and Urdu from Arabic *ta'allaqa* 'be connected'.

talus[1] /ˈteɪləs/ ▸ noun (pl. **tali** /-lʌɪ/) Anatomy the large bone in the ankle, which articulates with the tibia of the leg and the calcaneus and navicular bone of the foot. Also called **ASTRAGALUS**.
– ORIGIN late 16th cent.: from Latin, literally 'ankle, heel'.

talus[2] /ˈteɪləs/ ▸ noun (pl. **taluses**) [mass noun] a sloping mass of rock fragments at the foot of a cliff. ■ [count noun] the sloping side of an earthwork, or of a wall that tapers to the top.
– ORIGIN mid 17th cent.: from French, of unknown origin.

talwar /tʌlˈwɑː/ (also **tulwar**) ▸ noun Indian a sword, especially a type of sabre.
– ORIGIN early 19th cent.: Hindi *talvār* from Sanskrit *taravāri*.

TAM ▸ abbreviation television audience measurement.

tam ▸ noun a tam-o'-shanter. ■ a tall woollen hat worn by Rastafarians.
– ORIGIN late 19th cent.: abbreviation.

tamagotchi /ˌtaməˈgɒtʃi/ ▸ noun trademark an electronic toy displaying a digital image of a creature, which has to be looked after and responded to by the 'owner' as if it were a pet.
– ORIGIN Japanese.

tamale /təˈmɑːleɪ, -ˈmɑːli/ ▸ noun a Mexican dish of seasoned meat and maize flour steamed or baked in maize husks.
– ORIGIN from Mexican Spanish *tamal*, plural *tamales*, from Nahuatl *tamalli*.

tamandua /təˈmand(j)ʊə, ˌtam(ə)nˈduːə/ ▸ noun a small nocturnal arboreal anteater with a naked prehensile tail, native to tropical America. ● Genus *Tamandua*, family Myrmecophagidae: two species.
– ORIGIN early 17th cent.: via Portuguese from Tupi *tamanduá*, from *taly* 'ant' + *monduar* 'hunter'.

Tamang /taˈmaŋ/ ▸ noun (pl. **same** or **Tamangs**) **1** a member of a Buddhist people inhabiting mountainous parts of Nepal and Sikkim.
2 [mass noun] the Tibeto-Burman language of the Tamang.
▸ adjective relating to the Tamang or their language.
– ORIGIN Nepali, from *rtamaṅ* 'owner of many horses'.

Tamar /ˈteɪmɑː/ a river in SW England which rises in NW Devon and flows 98 km (60 miles) generally southwards, forming the boundary between Devon and Cornwall and emptying into the English Channel through Plymouth Sound.

tamarack /ˈtaməræk/ ▸ noun a slender North American larch. ● *Larix laricina*, family Pinaceae.
– ORIGIN early 19th cent.: from Canadian French *tamarac*, probably of Algonquian origin.

tamarau /ˈtaməraʊ/ ▸ noun a small brownish-black buffalo similar to the anoa, found only on Mindoro in the Philippines. ● *Bubalus mindorensis*, family Bovidae.
– ORIGIN late 19th cent.: from Tagalog.

tamari /təˈmɑːri/ (also **tamari sauce**) ▸ noun [mass noun] a variety of rich, naturally fermented soy sauce.
– ORIGIN Japanese.

tamarillo /ˌtaməˈrɪləʊ/ ▸ noun (pl. **tamarillos**) a tropical South American plant of the nightshade family, which bears edible egg-shaped red fruits. Also called **TREE TOMATO**. ● *Cyphomandra betaceae*, family Solanaceae.
■ the fruit of the tamarillo.
– ORIGIN 1960s (originally NZ): an invented name, perhaps suggested by Spanish *tomatillo*, diminutive of *tomate* 'tomato'.

tamarin /ˈtam(ə)rɪn/ ▸ noun a small forest-dwelling South American monkey of the marmoset family, typically brightly coloured and with tufts and crests of hair around the face and neck. ● Genera *Saguinus* and *Leontopithecus*, family Callitrichidae (or Callithricidae): several species.
– ORIGIN late 18th cent.: from French, from Galibi.

tamarind /ˈtam(ə)rɪnd/ ▸ noun **1** [mass noun] sticky brown acidic pulp from the pod of a tree of the pea family, widely used as a flavouring in Asian cookery.
■ [count noun] the pod from which tamarind pulp is extracted.
2 the tropical African tree which yields tamarind pods, cultivated throughout the tropics and also grown as an ornamental and shade tree. ● *Tamarindus indica*, family Leguminosae.
– ORIGIN late Middle English: from medieval Latin *tamarindus*, from Arabic *tamr hindī* 'Indian date'.

tamarisk /ˈtam(ə)rɪsk/ ▸ noun an Old World shrub or small tree with tiny scale-like leaves borne on slender branches, giving it a feathery appearance.
● Genus *Tamarix*, family Tamaricaceae: many species, including the **French tamarisk** (*T. gallica*), a common coastal shrub of SW Europe.
– ORIGIN late Middle English: from late Latin *tamariscus*, variant of Latin *tamarix*, of unknown origin.

tamasha /təˈmɑːʃə/ ▸ noun Indian a grand show, performance, or celebration, especially one involving dance. ■ a fuss or commotion: *there was a huge tamasha when she wrote to say she'd be in Karachi for a few hours.*
– ORIGIN via Persian and Urdu from Arabic *tamāšā* 'walk about together'.

Tamashek /ˈtaməʃɛk/ ▸ noun [mass noun] the dialect of Berber spoken by the Tuareg, sometimes regarded as a separate language.
– ORIGIN the name in Berber.

Tamaulipas /ˌtamaʊˈliːpas/ a state of NE Mexico with a coastline on the Gulf of Mexico; capital, Ciudad Victoria.

tambala /tamˈbɑːlə/ ▸ noun (pl. **same** or **tambalas**) a monetary unit of Malawi, equal to one hundredth of a kwacha.
– ORIGIN from Nyanja, literally 'cockerel'.

tambotie /tamˈbʊti, -ˈbuːti, -ˈbʊəti/ ▸ noun S. African an African tree of the spurge family, with scented timber and caustic sap. ● *Spirostachys africana*, family Euphorbiaceae.
– ORIGIN mid 19th cent.: from Xhosa *um-Thombothi*, literally 'poison tree'.

tambour /ˈtambʊə/ ▸ noun **1** historical a small drum.
2 a circular frame for holding fabric taut while it is being embroidered.
3 Architecture a wall of circular plan, such as one supporting a dome or surrounded by a colonnade. ■ each of a sequence of cylindrical stones forming the shaft of a column.
4 a lobby enclosed by a ceiling and folding doors to prevent draughts, typically within a church porch.
■ [usu. as modifier] a sliding flexible shutter or door on a piece of furniture: *a tambour door.*
5 a sloping buttress or projection in a real tennis or fives court.
▸ verb [with obj.] (often as adj. **tamboured**) decorate or embroider on a tambour: *a tamboured waistcoat.*
– ORIGIN late 15th cent.: from French *tambour* 'drum'; perhaps related to Persian *tabīra* 'drum'. Compare with **TABOR**.

tamboura /tamˈbʊərə/ (also **tambura**) ▸ noun **1** a long-necked lute or mandolin of Balkan countries.
2 another term for **TANPURA**.
– ORIGIN late 16th cent. (denoting a type of long-necked lute): from Arabic *ṭanbūr* or Persian *tunbūra*, both from Persian *dunbara*, literally 'lamb's tail'.

tambourin /ˈtambərɪn/ ▸ noun a long, narrow drum used in Provence. ■ a dance accompanied by the tambourin.
– ORIGIN French, diminutive of *tambour* (see **TAMBOUR**).

tambourine /ˌtambəˈriːn/ ▸ noun a percussion instrument resembling a shallow drum with metal discs in slots around the edge, played by being shaken or hit with the hand.
– DERIVATIVES **tambourinist** noun.
– ORIGIN late 16th cent.: from French *tambourin* (see **TAMBOURIN**).

Tambov /tamˈbɒf/ an industrial city in SW Russia; pop. 279,800 (est. 2008).

tambura ▸ noun variant spelling of **TAMBOURA**.

tamburitza /tamˈbʊrɪtsə/ ▸ noun a kind of long-necked mandolin played in Croatia and neighbouring countries.
– ORIGIN Croatian, diminutive of *tambura* **TAMBOURA**.

tame ▸ adjective **1** (of an animal) not dangerous or frightened of people; domesticated: *the fish are so tame you have to push them away.* ■ informal (of a person) willing to cooperate.
2 derogatory not exciting, adventurous, or controversial: *network TV on Saturday night is a pretty tame affair.*
3 N. Amer. (of a plant) produced by cultivation. ■ (of land) cultivated.
▸ verb [with obj.] domesticate (an animal). ■ make less powerful and easier to control: *the battle to tame inflation.*
– DERIVATIVES **tameable** (also **tamable**) adjective, **tamely** adverb, **tameness** noun, **tamer** noun [in combination] *a lion-tamer.*
– ORIGIN Old English *tam* (adjective), *temmian* (verb), of Germanic origin; related to Dutch *tam* and German *zahm*, from an Indo-European root shared by Latin *domare* and Greek *daman* 'tame, subdue'.

Tamerlane /ˈtaməleɪn/ (also **Tamburlaine** /ˈtambə-/) (1336–1405), Mongol ruler of Samarkand 1369–1405; Tartar name *Timur Lenk* ('lame Timur'). Leading a force of Mongols and Turks, he conquered Persia, northern India, and Syria and established his capital at Samarkand. He was the ancestor of the Mogul dynasty in India.

Tamil /ˈtamɪl/ ▸ noun **1** a member of a people inhabiting parts of South India and Sri Lanka.
2 [mass noun] the Dravidian language of the Tamils, at least 2,000 years old, spoken by about 68 million people.
▸ adjective relating to the Tamils or their language.
– DERIVATIVES **Tamilian** adjective & noun.
– ORIGIN the name in Tamil.

Tamil Nadu /ˈnɑːduː/ a state in the extreme south-east of the Indian peninsula, on the Coromandel Coast, with a largely Tamil-speaking, Hindu population; capital, Chennai (Madras). Tamil Nadu was formerly an ancient kingdom comprising a much larger area, stretching northwards to Orissa and including the Lakshadweep Islands and part of the Malabar Coast. Former name (until 1968) **MADRAS**.

Tamil Tigers a Sri Lankan guerrilla organization founded in 1972 that seeks the establishment of an independent state (Eelam) in the north-east of the country for the Tamil community. They waged an armed campaign until defeated by the Sri Lankan army in 2009. Also called **LIBERATION TIGERS OF TAMIL EELAM**.

Tamla Motown /ˈtamlə/ ▸ noun trade name for **MOTOWN** (sense 1).

Tammany /ˈtaməni/ (also **Tammany Hall**) (in the US) a powerful organization within the Democratic Party that was widely associated with corruption. Founded as a fraternal and benevolent society in 1789, it came to dominate political life in New York City in the 19th and early 20th centuries, before being reduced in power by Franklin D. Roosevelt in the early 1930s. ■ (as noun **a Tammany**) a corrupt political organization or group.
– DERIVATIVES **Tammanyite** noun.
– ORIGIN named after an American Indian chief of the late 17th cent., said to have welcomed William Penn, and regarded as 'patron saint' of Pennsylvania and other northern colonies.

Tammerfors /ˌtamərˈfɔrs/ Swedish name for **TAMPERE**.

Tammuz[1] /ˈtamʊz/ a Mesopotamian god, lover of Ishtar and similar in some respects to the Greek Adonis. He became the personification of the seasonal death and rebirth of crops.

Tammuz[2] variant spelling of **THAMMUZ**.

T

tam-o'-shanter /ˌtaməˈʃantə/ ▶ **noun** a round woollen or cloth cap of Scottish origin, with a bobble in the centre.
– ORIGIN mid 19th cent.: named after the hero of Burns's poem *Tam o' Shanter* (1790).

tamoxifen /təˈmɒksɪfɛn/ ▶ **noun** [mass noun] Medicine a synthetic drug used to treat breast cancer and infertility in women. It acts as an oestrogen antagonist.
– ORIGIN 1970s: an arbitrary formation based on TRANS-, AMINE, OXY-², PHENOL, elements of the drug's chemical name.

tamp ▶ **verb** [with obj.] pack (a blast hole) full of clay or sand to concentrate the force of the explosion: *when the hole was tamped to the top, gunpowder was inserted.* ■ [with obj. and adverbial of direction] ram or pack (a substance) down or into something firmly: *he **tamped down** the tobacco with his thumb.*
– ORIGIN early 19th cent.: probably a back-formation from *tampin* (interpreted as 'tamping'), variant of TAMPION.

Tampa /ˈtampə/ a port and resort on the west coast of Florida; pop. 340,882 (est. 2008).

Tampax (also **tampax**) ▶ **noun** (pl. **same**) trademark a sanitary tampon.
– ORIGIN 1930s: an arbitrary formation from TAMPON.

tamper ▶ **verb** [no obj.] (**tamper with**) interfere with (something) in order to cause damage or make unauthorized alterations: *someone tampered with the brakes of my car.*
▶ **noun** a machine or tool for tamping down earth or ballast.
– DERIVATIVES **tamperer** noun.
– ORIGIN mid 16th cent. (in the sense 'busy oneself to a particular end, machinate'): alteration of the verb TEMPER.

Tampere /ˈtampəreɪ/ a city in SW Finland; pop. 209,690 (2009). Swedish name TAMMERFORS.

tamper-evident ▶ **adjective** (of packaging) designed to reveal any interference with the contents.

tamper-proof ▶ **adjective** made so that it cannot be interfered with or changed.

Tampico /tamˈpiːkəʊ/ one of Mexico's principal seaports, on the Gulf of Mexico; pop. 303,635 (2005).

tampion /ˈtampɪən/ (also **tompion**) ▶ **noun 1** a wooden stopper for the muzzle of a gun.
2 a plug for the top of an organ pipe.
– ORIGIN late Middle English: from French *tampon* 'tampon'.

tampon ▶ **noun 1** a plug of soft material inserted into the vagina to absorb menstrual blood.
2 Medicine a plug of material used to stop a wound or block an opening in the body and absorb blood or secretions.
▶ **verb** (**tampons**, **tamponing**, **tamponed**) [with obj.] plug with a tampon.
– ORIGIN mid 19th cent.: from French, nasalized variant of *tapon* 'plug, stopper', ultimately of Germanic origin and related to TAP¹.

tamponade /ˌtampəˈneɪd/ ▶ **noun** [mass noun] Medicine **1** (in full **cardiac tamponade**) compression of the heart by an accumulation of fluid in the pericardial sac.
2 the surgical use of a plug of absorbent material.

tam-tam ▶ **noun** a large metal gong.
– ORIGIN mid 19th cent.: perhaps from Hindi *ṭam-ṭam* (see TOM-TOM).

T

Tamworth¹ /ˈtamwəːθ, -wəθ/ a town in central England, in Staffordshire; pop. 74,800 (est. 2009).

Tamworth² /ˈtamwəθ/ ▶ **noun** a pig of a long-bodied, typically red or brown breed.

Tamworth Manifesto (in English history) an election speech by Sir Robert Peel in 1834 in his Tamworth constituency, in which he accepted the changes instituted by the Reform Act and expressed his belief in moderate political reform. The manifesto is widely held to signal the emergence of the Conservative Party from the old loose grouping of Tory interests.

tan¹ ▶ **noun 1** [mass noun] a yellowish-brown colour: [as modifier] *she dressed in tan cords.*
2 a golden-brown shade of skin developed by pale-skinned people after exposure to the sun: *Jenna managed to get an even golden tan.*
3 (also **tanbark**) [mass noun] bark of oak or other trees, bruised and used as a source of tannin for converting hides into leather. ■ (also **spent tan**) tan from which the tannin has been extracted, used for covering the ground for walking, riding, children's play, etc., and in gardening.
▶ **verb** (**tans**, **tanning**, **tanned**) [with obj.] **1** (usu. as adj. **tanned**) (of the sun) cause (a pale-skinned person) to become brown or browner: *he looked tanned and fit.* ■ [no obj.] (of a pale-skinned person) become brown or browner after exposure to the sun: *you'll tan very quickly in the pure air.*
2 convert (animal skin) into leather by soaking in a liquid containing tannic acid, or by the use of other chemicals.
3 informal, dated beat (someone) repeatedly as a punishment.
▶ **adjective** N. Amer. (of a pale-skinned person) having golden-brown skin after exposure to the sun: *she looks tall, tan, and healthy.*
– DERIVATIVES **tannish** adjective.
– ORIGIN late Old English *tannian* 'convert into leather', probably from medieval Latin *tannare*, perhaps of Celtic origin; reinforced in Middle English by Old French *tanner*. Early use of the noun (late Middle English) was in sense 3 of the noun.

tan² ▶ **abbreviation** tangent.

Tana, Lake /ˈtɑːnə/ a lake in northern Ethiopia, the source of the Blue Nile.

tanager /ˈtanədʒə/ ▶ **noun** a small American songbird of the bunting family, the male of which typically has brightly coloured plumage. ● Family Emberizidae (subfamily Thraupinae): many genera, in particular *Tangara*, and numerous species.
– ORIGIN early 17th cent. (originally as *tangara*): from Tupi *tangará*, later refashioned on the pattern of the modern Latin genus name *Tanagra*.

Tanagra /ˈtanəgrə/ an ancient Greek city in Boeotia, site of a battle in 457 BC during the Peloponnesian War. It has given its name to a type of terracotta figurine, often of a young woman, made there and elsewhere mainly in the 4th and 3rd centuries BC.

Tánaiste /ˈtɔːnɪʃtə/, Irish /ˈtaːnəsʲtʲə/ ▶ **noun** the deputy Prime Minister of the Republic of Ireland.
– ORIGIN Irish *tánaiste*, literally 'second in excellence'.

Tananarive /ˌtananəˈriːv/ former name (until 1975) for ANTANANARIVO.

tanbark /ˈtanbɑːk/ ▶ **noun** see TAN¹ (sense 3 of the noun).

tandem ▶ **noun** a bicycle with seats and pedals for two riders, one behind the other. ■ a carriage driven by two animals harnessed one in front of the other. ■ a group of two people or machines working together.
▶ **adverb** with two or more horses harnessed one behind another: *I rode tandem to Paris.* ■ alongside each other; together.
▶ **adjective** having two things arranged one in front of the other: *a tandem trailer.*
– PHRASES **in tandem** alongside each other. ■ one behind another.
– ORIGIN late 18th cent.: humorously from Latin, literally 'at length'.

tandoor /ˈtandʊə, tanˈdʊə, ˈtandɔː, tanˈdɔː/ ▶ **noun** a clay oven of a type used originally in northern India and Pakistan.
– ORIGIN from Urdu *tandūr*, from Persian *tanūr*, based on Arabic *tannūr* 'oven'.

tandoori /tanˈdʊəri/ ▶ **adjective** denoting or relating to a style of Indian cooking based on the use of a tandoor: *tandoori chicken.*
▶ **noun** [mass noun] tandoori food or cooking.
– ORIGIN from Urdu and Persian *tandūrī*, from *tandūr* (see TANDOOR).

Tang /taŋ/ a dynasty ruling China 618–*c.*906, a period noted for territorial conquest and great wealth and regarded as the golden age of Chinese poetry and art.

tang¹ ▶ **noun 1** [in sing.] a strong taste, flavour, or smell: *the clean salty tang of the sea.* ■ a characteristic quality: *his words came out with a distinct tang of broad Lancashire.*
2 the projection on the blade of a tool such as a knife, by which the blade is held firmly in the handle.
– ORIGIN Middle English (denoting a snake's tongue, formerly believed to be a stinging organ; also denoting the sting of an insect): from Old Norse *tangi* 'point, tang of a knife'.

tang² ▶ **verb** [no obj.] make a loud ringing or clanging sound: *the bronze bell tangs.*
– ORIGIN mid 16th cent.: imitative.

tang³ ▶ **noun** a surgeonfish which occurs around reefs and rocky areas, where it browses on algae. ● Genus *Acanthurus*, family Acanthuridae: several species, in particular the **blue tang** (*A. coeruleus*) of the western Atlantic, and the **convict tang** (*A. triostegus*) of the Indo-Pacific.
– ORIGIN mid 18th cent.: from TANG¹.

Tanga /ˈtaŋgə/ one of the principal ports of Tanzania, situated in the north-east of the country on the Indian Ocean; pop. 240,000 (est. 2009).

tanga /ˈtaŋgə/ (also **tanga briefs**) ▶ **noun** Brit. a pair of briefs consisting of small panels connected by strings at the sides.
– ORIGIN early 20th cent. (denoting a loincloth worn by indigenous peoples in tropical America): from Portuguese, ultimately of Bantu origin. The current sense dates from the 1970s.

Tanganyika /ˌtaŋgəˈniːkə, -ˈnjiːkə/ see TANZANIA.

Tanganyika, Lake a lake in East Africa, in the Great Rift Valley. The deepest lake in Africa and the longest freshwater lake in the world, it forms most of the border of the Democratic Republic of the Congo (Zaire) with Tanzania and Burundi.

tangata whenua /ˌtaŋatə ˈfɛnʊə/ ▶ **plural noun** used to describe the Maori people of a particular locality, or as a whole as the original inhabitants of New Zealand.
– ORIGIN Maori, literally 'people of the land'.

tangelo /ˈtan(d)ʒələʊ/ ▶ **noun** (pl. **tangelos**) a hybrid of the tangerine and grapefruit.
– ORIGIN early 20th cent.: blend of TANGERINE and POMELO.

tangent /ˈtan(d)ʒ(ə)nt/ ▶ **noun 1** a straight line or plane that touches a curve or curved surface at a point, but if extended does not cross it at that point.
2 a completely different line of thought or action: *Loretta's mind **went off at a tangent**.*
3 Mathematics the trigonometric function that is equal to the ratio of the sides (other than the hypotenuse) opposite and adjacent to an angle in a right-angled triangle.
▶ **adjective** (of a line or plane) touching, but not intersecting, a curve or curved surface.
– DERIVATIVES **tangency** noun.
– ORIGIN late 16th cent. (in sense 3 of the noun and as an adjective): from Latin *tangent-* 'touching', from the verb *tangere*.

tangential /tanˈdʒɛnʃ(ə)l/ ▶ **adjective 1** relating to or along a tangent: *a tangential line.*
2 diverging from a previous course or line; erratic: *tangential thoughts.* ■ hardly touching a matter; peripheral: *the reforms were **tangential to** efforts to maintain a basic standard of life.*
– DERIVATIVES **tangentially** adverb.

tangerine ▶ **noun 1** a small citrus fruit with a loose skin, especially one of a variety with deep orange-red skin. ■ [mass noun] a deep orange-red colour.
2 the citrus tree which bears the tangerine. ● *Citrus reticulata*, family Rutaceae.
– ORIGIN mid 19th cent.: from *Tanger* (former name of TANGIER) + -INE¹. The fruit, exported from Tangier, was originally called the *tangerine orange*.

tangi /ˈtaŋi/ ▶ **noun** (pl. **tangis**) a ceremonial Maori funeral or wake.
– ORIGIN Maori.

tangible /ˈtan(d)ʒɪb(ə)l/ ▶ **adjective** perceptible by touch: *the atmosphere of neglect and abandonment was **almost tangible**.* ■ clear and definite; real: *the emphasis is now on tangible results.*
▶ **noun** (usu. **tangibles**) a thing that is perceptible by touch.
– DERIVATIVES **tangibility** noun, **tangibleness** noun, **tangibly** adverb.
– ORIGIN late 16th cent.: from French, or from late Latin *tangibilis*, from *tangere* 'to touch'.

Tangier /tanˈdʒɪə/ (also **Tangiers**) a seaport on the northern coast of Morocco, on the Strait of Gibraltar commanding the western entrance to the Mediterranean; pop. 762,583 (2004). Portuguese from the end of the 15th century, Tangier was ruled by the sultan of Morocco 1684–1904, when it came under international control; it passed to the newly independent monarchy of Morocco in 1956.

tangle¹ ▶ **verb 1** [with obj.] twist together into a confused mass: *the broom somehow got **tangled up** in my long skirt.* ■ make (something) complicated or confused: *a ploy to tangle matters even further.*
2 [no obj.] (**tangle with**) informal become involved in a conflict or fight with: *they usually come a cropper when they tangle with the heavy mobs.*
▶ **noun 1** a confused mass of something twisted together: *a tangle of golden hair.* ■ a confused or complicated state; a muddle.
2 informal a fight, argument, or disagreement.
– DERIVATIVES **tangly** adjective (**tanglier**, **tangliest**).

– ORIGIN Middle English (in the sense 'entangle, catch in a tangle'): probably of Scandinavian origin and related to Swedish dialect *taggla* 'disarrange'.

tangle[2] ▶ noun [mass noun] any of a number of brown seaweeds, especially oarweed.
– ORIGIN mid 16th cent.: probably from Norwegian *tongul*.

tangled ▶ adjective twisted together untidily; matted: *his hair was a tangled mess*. ■ complicated and confused; chaotic: *a tangled tale*.
– PHRASES **a tangled web** a complex, difficult, and confusing situation or thing. [from 'O what a tangled web we weave, When first we practise to deceive' (Scott's *Marmion*).]

tanglefoot ▶ noun [mass noun] N. Amer. material applied to a tree trunk as a grease band, especially to prevent infestation by insects.

tango[1] ▶ noun (pl. **tangos**) **1** a ballroom dance originating in Buenos Aires, characterized by marked rhythms and postures and abrupt pauses. ■ a piece of music written for or in the style of the tango, typically in a slow, dotted duple rhythm.
2 a code word representing the letter T, used in radio communication.
▶ verb (**tangoes, tangoing, tangoed**) [no obj.] dance the tango.
– PHRASES **it takes two to tango** informal both parties involved in a situation or argument are equally responsible for it.
– ORIGIN late 19th cent.: from Latin American Spanish, perhaps of African origin.

tango[2] ▶ noun [mass noun] Brit. informal, dated an orange-yellow colour.
– ORIGIN early 20th cent.: abbreviation of TANGERINE, influenced by TANGO[1].

tangram /ˈtaŋgram/ ▶ noun a Chinese geometrical puzzle consisting of a square cut into seven pieces which can be arranged to make various other shapes.
– ORIGIN mid 19th cent.: of unknown origin.

Tangshan /taŋˈʃan/ an industrial city in Hebei province, NE China; pop. 1,658,200 (est. 2006). The city had to be rebuilt after a devastating earthquake in 1976.

Tangut /ˈtaŋguːt/ ▶ noun (pl. **same** or **Tanguts**) **1** a member of a Tibetan people who established a kingdom in NW China and western Inner Mongolia from the late 10th to the mid 13th centuries.
2 [mass noun] the extinct language of the Tangut.
▶ adjective relating to the Tangut or their language.
– ORIGIN apparently from Mongolian, from Chinese *Dǎng Xiàng*.

tangy ▶ adjective (**tangier, tangiest**) having a strong, piquant flavour or smell: *a tangy salad*.
– DERIVATIVES **tanginess** noun.

tanh /tanˈeɪtʃ, tanʃ, θan/ ▶ abbreviation Mathematics hyperbolic tangent.

tania ▶ noun variant spelling of TANNIA.

tanist /ˈtanɪst/ ▶ noun the heir apparent to a Celtic chief, typically the most vigorous adult of his kin, elected during the chief's lifetime.
– DERIVATIVES **tanistry** noun.
– ORIGIN mid 16th cent.: from Irish, Scottish Gaelic *tánaiste*, literally 'second in excellence'.

taniwha /ˈtanɪwɑː, ˈtanɪfa/ ▶ noun (pl. **same** or **taniwhas**) a water monster of Maori legend.
– ORIGIN Maori.

Tanjungkarang /ˌtandʒʊŋkəˈraŋ/ see BANDAR LAMPUNG.

tank ▶ noun **1** a large receptacle or storage chamber, especially for liquid or gas. ■ the container holding the fuel supply in a motor vehicle. ■ a receptacle with transparent sides in which to keep fish; an aquarium. ■ Indian & Austral./NZ a reservoir.
2 a heavy armoured fighting vehicle carrying guns and moving on a continuous articulated metal track.
3 short for TANK ENGINE.
4 N. Amer. informal a cell in a police station or jail.
5 short for TANK TOP.
▶ verb **1** [no obj.] fill the tank of a vehicle with fuel: *the cars stopped to tank up*. ■ (**be/get tanked up**) Brit. informal drink heavily; become drunk: *they get tanked up before the game*.
2 [no obj.] US informal fail completely, especially at great financial cost. ■ [with obj.] N. Amer. informal (in sport) deliberately lose or fail to finish (a match).
3 [with obj.] informal, chiefly Scottish defeat heavily: *Rangers tanked the local side 8–0*.
– DERIVATIVES **tankful** noun (pl. **tankfuls**), **tankless** adjective.
– ORIGIN early 17th cent.: perhaps from Gujarati *tānkū* or Marathi *tānkē* 'underground cistern', from Sanskrit *taḍāga* 'pond', probably influenced by Portuguese *tangue* 'pond', from Latin *stagnum*. The military vehicle took its name from the use of *tank* as a secret code word during manufacture in 1915.

tanka[1] /ˈtaŋkə/ ▶ noun (pl. **same** or **tankas**) a Japanese poem in five lines and thirty-one syllables, giving a complete picture of an event or mood.
– ORIGIN Japanese, from *tan* 'short' + *ka* 'song'.

tanka[2] /ˈtɑːŋka/ ▶ noun (pl. **tankas**) a Tibetan religious painting on a scroll, hung as a banner in temples and carried in processions.
– ORIGIN from Tibetan *t'áṅ-ka* 'image, painting'.

tankage ▶ noun [mass noun] **1** the storage capacity of a tank. ■ the storage of something in a tank.
2 a fertilizer or animal feed obtained from the residue from tanks in which animal carcasses have been rendered.

tankard ▶ noun a tall beer mug, typically made of silver or pewter, with a handle and sometimes a hinged lid. ■ the contents of or an amount held by a tankard: *I've downed **a tankard of** ale*.
– ORIGIN Middle English (denoting a large tub for carrying liquid): perhaps related to Dutch *tanckaert*.

tank engine ▶ noun a steam locomotive carrying fuel and water receptacles in its own frame, not in a tender.

tanker ▶ noun a ship, road vehicle, or aircraft for carrying liquids, especially mineral oils, in bulk.
▶ verb [with obj.] transport (a liquid) in a tanker.

tank farm ▶ noun an area of oil or gas storage tanks.

tank-farming ▶ noun [mass noun] the practice of growing plants in tanks of water without soil.

tankini ▶ noun a women's two-piece swimsuit combining a top half styled like a tank top with a bikini bottom.

tank killer ▶ noun an aircraft, vehicle, or missile that is effective against tanks.

tank top ▶ noun a close-fitting sleeveless top typically worn over a shirt or blouse.

tank town ▶ noun N. Amer. informal a small unimportant town (originally a town at which trains stopped to take on water).

tanner[1] ▶ noun **1** a person who is employed to tan animal hides.
2 a lotion or cream designed to promote the development of a suntan or produce a similar skin colour artificially.

tanner[2] ▶ noun Brit. informal, historical a sixpence.
– ORIGIN early 19th cent.: of unknown origin.

tannery ▶ noun (pl. **tanneries**) a place where animal hides are tanned; the workshop of a tanner.

Tannhäuser /ˈtanˌhɔɪzə/, German /ˈtanˌhɔyzɐ/ (c.1200–c.1270), German poet. In reality a Minnesinger whose works included lyrics and love poetry, he became a legendary figure as a knight who visited Venus's grotto and spent seven years in debauchery, then repented and sought absolution from the Pope.

tannia /ˈtanɪə/ (also **tania**) ▶ noun a tall Caribbean plant of the arum family, cultivated in the tropics for its edible pear-shaped tubers and large arrow-shaped leaves. Also called MALANGA. ● *Xanthosoma sagittifolium*, family Araceae.
■ a tuber of the tannia. ■ [mass noun] the leaves or tubers of the tannia eaten as food.
– ORIGIN mid 18th cent.: from Carib *taya*, Tupi *taña*.

tannic ▶ adjective relating to or resembling tannin: *a dry wine with a slightly tannic aftertaste*.
– ORIGIN mid 19th cent.: from French *tannique*, from *tanin* (see TANNIN).

tannic acid ▶ noun another term for TANNIN.
– DERIVATIVES **tannate** noun.

tannie /ˈtani/ ▶ noun (pl. **tannies**) S. African a woman who is older than the speaker (often used as a respectful and affectionate title or form of address).
– ORIGIN Afrikaans, literally 'auntie', familiar form of *tante* (see TANTE).

tannin ▶ noun [mass noun] a yellowish or brownish bitter-tasting organic substance present in some galls, barks, and other plant tissues, consisting of derivatives of gallic acid.
– ORIGIN early 19th cent.: from French *tanin*, from *tan* 'tanbark' (ultimately related to TAN[1]) + -IN[1].

tannoy Brit. ▶ noun trademark a type of public address system.
▶ verb [with obj.] transmit or announce over a tannoy: *the news was tannoyed one afternoon*.
– ORIGIN 1920s: contraction of *tantalum alloy*, which is used as a rectifier in the system.

Tannu-Tuva /ˌtanuːˈtuːvə/ former name for TUVA.

Tanoan /təˈnəʊən/ ▶ noun [mass noun] a small language family comprising a number of Pueblo Indian languages.
▶ adjective relating to the Tanoan language family.
– ORIGIN from Spanish *Tano* + -AN.

tanpura /tʌnˈpuːrə/ ▶ noun a large four-stringed lute used in Indian music as a drone accompaniment.
– ORIGIN mid 19th cent.: variant of TAMBOURA.

Tansen /ˈtansɛn/ (c.1500–89), Indian musician and singer. A leading exponent of northern Indian classical music, he became an honoured member of the court of Akbar the Great.

tansu /ˈtansuː/ ▶ noun (pl. **same**) a Japanese chest of drawers or cabinet.
– ORIGIN Japanese.

tansy /ˈtanzi/ ▶ noun a plant of the daisy family with yellow flat-topped button-like flower heads and aromatic leaves, formerly used in cookery and medicine.
● Genus *Tanacetum*, family Compositae: several species, in particular the common Eurasian *T. vulgare*.
– ORIGIN Middle English: from Old French *tanesie*, probably from medieval Latin *athanasia* 'immortality', from Greek.

tantalite /ˈtantəlʌɪt/ ▶ noun [mass noun] a rare, dense black mineral consisting of a mixed oxide of iron and tantalum, of which it is the principal source.
– ORIGIN early 19th cent.: from TANTALUM + -ITE[1].

tantalize (also **tantalise**) ▶ verb [with obj.] torment or tease (someone) with the sight or promise of something that is unobtainable: *such ambitious questions have long tantalized the world's best thinkers*. ■ excite the senses or desires of (someone): *she still tantalized him* | (as adj. **tantalizing**) *the tantalizing fragrance of fried bacon*.
– DERIVATIVES **tantalization** noun, **tantalizer** noun, **tantalizingly** adverb.
– ORIGIN late 16th cent.: from TANTALUS + -IZE.

tantalum /ˈtantələm/ ▶ noun [mass noun] the chemical element of atomic number 73, a hard silver-grey metal of the transition series. (Symbol: **Ta**)
– ORIGIN early 19th cent.: from TANTALUS, with reference to its frustrating insolubility in acids.

Tantalus /ˈtantələs/ Greek Mythology a Lydian king, son of Zeus and father of Pelops. For his crimes (which included killing Pelops) he was punished by being provided with fruit and water which receded when he reached for them. His name is the origin of the word *tantalize*.

tantalus ▶ noun Brit. a stand in which spirit decanters may be locked up though still visible.

tantamount ▶ adjective (**tantamount to**) equivalent in seriousness to; virtually the same as: *the resignations were tantamount to an admission of guilt*.
– ORIGIN mid 17th cent.: from the earlier verb *tantamount* 'amount to as much', from Italian *tanto montare*.

tante /tɑ̃ːt, tɑːnt, ˈtantə/ ▶ noun (especially among those of French, German, or Afrikaans origin) a mature or elderly woman who is related or well known to the speaker (often used as a respectful form of address).
– ORIGIN French, Dutch *tante*, German *Tante* 'aunt'.

tantivy /tanˈtɪvi/ archaic ▶ noun (pl. **tantivies**) a rapid gallop or ride.
▶ exclamation used as a hunting cry.
– ORIGIN mid 17th cent.: probably imitative of the sound of galloping.

tant mieux /tɒ̃ ˈmjəː/, French /tɑ̃ mjø/ ▶ exclamation so much the better.
– ORIGIN French.

tanto[1] /ˈtantəʊ/ ▶ noun (pl. **tantos**) a Japanese short sword or dagger.
– ORIGIN Japanese.

tanto[2] /ˈtantəʊ/ ▶ adverb [usu. with negative] Music (as a direction) too much: [postpositive] [as submodifier] *allegro non tanto*.
– ORIGIN Italian.

tant pis /tɒ̃ ˈpiː/, French /tɑ̃ pi/ ▶ exclamation so much the worse; the situation is regrettable but now beyond retrieval.
– ORIGIN French.

tantra /ˈtantrə, ˈtʌntrə/ ▶ noun a Hindu or Buddhist mystical or magical text, dating from the 7th century

T

or earlier. ■ [mass noun] adherence to the doctrines or principles of the tantras, involving mantras, meditation, yoga, and ritual.
– DERIVATIVES **tantric** adjective, **tantrism** noun.
– ORIGIN Sanskrit, literally 'loom, groundwork, doctrine', from *tan* 'stretch'.

tantrum ▶ noun an uncontrolled outburst of anger and frustration, typically in a young child.
– ORIGIN early 18th cent.: of unknown origin.

Tanzania /ˌtanzəˈnɪə/ a country in East Africa with a coastline on the Indian Ocean; pop. 41,048,500 (est. 2009); official languages, Swahili and English; capital, Dodoma.

> Tanzania consists of a mainland area (the former Tanganyika) and the island of Zanzibar. A German colony (German East Africa) from the late 19th century, Tanganyika became a British mandate after the First World War and a trust territory, administered by Britain, after the Second, before becoming independent within the Commonwealth in 1961. It was named Tanzania after its union with Zanzibar in 1964.

– DERIVATIVES **Tanzanian** adjective & noun.

tanzanite /ˈtanzənʌɪt/ ▶ noun [mass noun] a blue or violet gem variety of zoisite, containing vanadium.
– ORIGIN 1960s: from TANZANIA + -ITE[1].

Tao /taʊ, ˈtɑːəʊ/ ▶ noun (in Chinese philosophy) the absolute principle underlying the universe, combining within itself the principles of yin and yang and signifying the way, or code of behaviour, that is in harmony with the natural order. The interpretation of Tao in the Tao-te-Ching developed into the philosophical religion of Taoism.
– ORIGIN Chinese, literally '(right) way'.

Taoiseach /ˈtiːʃəx/, Irish /ˈtiːʃəx/ ▶ noun the Prime Minister of the Republic of Ireland.
– ORIGIN Irish, literally 'chief, leader'.

Taoism /ˈtaʊɪz(ə)m, ˈtɑːəʊ-/ ▶ noun [mass noun] a Chinese philosophy based on the writings of Lao-tzu, advocating humility and religious piety.

> The central concept and goal is the Tao, and its most important text is the Tao-te-Ching. Taoism has both a philosophical and a religious aspect. Philosophical Taoism emphasizes inner contemplation and mystical union with nature; wisdom, learning, and purposive action should be abandoned in favour of simplicity and **wu-wei** (non-action, or letting things take their natural course). The religious aspect of Taoism developed later, c.3rd century AD, incorporating certain Buddhist features and developing a monastic system.

– DERIVATIVES **Taoist** /-ɪst/ noun & adjective, **Taoistic** /-ˈɪstɪk/ adjective.

taonga /tɑːˈɒŋə/ ▶ noun (pl. **same**) (in Maori culture) an object or natural resource which is highly prized.
– ORIGIN Maori.

Taormina /ˌtɑːɔːˈmiːnə/ a resort town on the east coast of Sicily; pop. 11,096 (2008). It was founded by Greek colonists in the 4th century BC.

Tao-te-Ching /ˌtaʊtiːˈtʃɪŋ/ ▶ noun the central Taoist text, ascribed to Lao-tzu, the traditional founder of Taoism. Apparently written as a guide for rulers, it defined the Tao, or way, and established the philosophical basis of Taoism.
– ORIGIN Chinese, literally 'the Book of the Way and its Power'.

tap[1] ▶ noun **1** a device by which a flow of liquid or gas from a pipe or container can be controlled. ■ (also **tapping**) Brit. an electrical connection made to some point between the end terminals of a transformer coil or other component.
2 a device connected to a telephone for listening secretly to someone's conversations. ■ an act of listening secretly to someone's telephone conversation.
3 an instrument for cutting a threaded hole in a material.
4 Brit. a taproom.
▶ verb (**taps**, **tapping**, **tapped**) [with obj.] **1** draw liquid through the tap or spout of (a cask, barrel, or other container). ■ draw (liquid) from a cask, barrel, or other container. ■ draw sap from (a tree) by cutting into it.
2 exploit or draw a supply from (a resource): *clients from industry seeking to tap Edinburgh's resources of expertise* | [no obj.] *these magazines have **tapped into** a target market of consumers.* ■ informal obtain money or information from (someone): *he considered whom he could **tap for** information.*
3 connect a device to (a telephone) so that conversation can be listened to secretly: *the telephones were tapped by the state security police.*
4 cut a thread in (something) to accept a screw.
– PHRASES **on tap** ready to be poured from a tap. ■ informal freely available whenever needed. ■ N. Amer. informal on schedule to occur.
– DERIVATIVES **tappable** adjective.
– ORIGIN Old English *tæppa* 'peg for the vent-hole of a cask', *tæppian* 'provide (a cask) with a stopper', of Germanic origin; related to Dutch *tap* and *German Zapfen* (nouns).

tap[2] ▶ verb (**taps**, **tapping**, **tapped**) [with obj.] **1** strike with a quick light blow or blows: *one of my staff tapped me on the shoulder.* ■ strike (something) against something else with a quick light blow or blows: *Gloria was tapping her feet in time to the music.* ■ (**tap something out**) produce (a rhythm) with a series of quick light blows on a surface. ■ write or enter (something) using a keyboard or keypad.
2 (**tap someone up**) Brit. informal approach (a sports player) illegally with a view to signing them to another club while they are still under contract with their current one.
3 US informal designate or select (someone) for a task or honour, especially membership of an organization or committee.
▶ noun **1** a quick light blow, or the sound of such a blow.
2 [mass noun] tap dancing. ■ [count noun] a piece of metal attached to the toe and heel of a tap dancer's shoe to make a tapping sound.
3 (**taps**) [treated as sing. or pl.] US a bugle call for lights to be put out in army quarters. [so named because the signal was originally sounded on a drum.] ■ a bugle call sounded at a military funeral. ■ Brit. (in the Guide movement) a closing song sung at an evening camp fire or at the end of a meeting.
– DERIVATIVES **tapper** noun.
– ORIGIN Middle English: from Old French *taper*, or of imitative origin; compare with CLAP[1] and RAP[1].

tapa /ˈtɑːpə/ ▶ noun [mass noun] the bark of the paper mulberry tree. ■ (also **tapa cloth**) cloth made from tapa, used in the Pacific islands.
– ORIGIN early 19th cent.: of Polynesian origin.

tapas /ˈtapas/ ▶ plural noun small Spanish savoury dishes, typically served with drinks at a bar.
– ORIGIN Spanish *tapa*, literally 'cover, lid' (because the dishes were given free with the drink, served on a dish balanced on, therefore 'covering', the glass).

tap changer ▶ noun an apparatus for changing the connection to an electrical transformer from one tap to another, so as to vary the turns ratio and hence control the output voltage under a varying load.

tap dance ▶ noun a dance performed wearing shoes fitted with metal taps, characterized by rhythmical tapping of the toes and heels.
▶ verb (**tap-dance**) [no obj.] perform a tap dance.
– DERIVATIVES **tap dancer** noun, **tap-dancing** noun.

tape ▶ noun [mass noun] **1** a narrow strip of material, typically used to hold or fasten something: *a reel of tape* | [count noun] *a dirty apron fastened with thin tapes.* ■ (also **adhesive tape** or Brit. **sticky tape**) a strip of paper or plastic coated with adhesive and sold in a roll, used to stick things together. ■ [count noun] a strip of material stretched across the finishing line of a race, to be broken or dislodged by the winner. ■ a strip of material used to mark off an area or form a notional barrier. ■ [count noun] a tape measure.
2 [often with modifier] long, narrow flexible material with magnetic properties, used for recording sound, pictures, or computer data: *they put four songs **on tape**.* ■ [count noun] a cassette or reel containing magnetic tape for recording. ■ [count noun] a recording on a cassette or reel.
▶ verb [with obj.] **1** record (sound or pictures) on audio or video tape: *it is not known who taped the conversation.*
2 fasten or attach (something) with adhesive tape. ■ (**tape something off**) seal or mark off an area or thing with tape.
– PHRASES **have** (or **get**) **someone/thing taped** Brit. informal understand a person or thing fully.
– ORIGIN Old English *tæppa*, *tæppe*; perhaps related to Middle Low German *teppen* 'pluck, tear'.

tape deck ▶ noun a piece of equipment for playing audio tapes, especially as part of a stereo system.

tape echo ▶ noun a facility which allows the repeat of a sound to be delayed by adjusting the time lapse between the recording and playback heads of a tape recorder.

tape-grass ▶ noun [mass noun] a submerged aquatic plant of the frogbit family, with narrow grass-like leaves. Also called RIBBON-GRASS and (in North America) EELGRASS. ● Genus *Vallisneria*, family Hydrocharitaceae: several species.

tape hiss ▶ noun [mass noun] extraneous high-frequency background noise during the playing of a tape recording.

tape machine ▶ noun **1** a tape recorder.
2 a machine for receiving and recording telegraph messages on paper tape.

tape measure ▶ noun a length of tape or thin flexible metal, marked at graded intervals for measuring.

tapenade /ˈtapənɑːd/ ▶ noun [mass noun] a Provençal savoury paste or dip, made from black olives, capers, and anchovies.
– ORIGIN French, from Provençal.

taper ▶ verb diminish or reduce in thickness towards one end: [no obj.] *the tail tapers to a rounded tip* | [with obj.] *David asked my dressmaker to taper his trousers* | (as adj. **tapering**) *the five tapering fingers of her hand.* ■ [no obj.] (**taper off**) gradually lessen: *the impact of the dollar's depreciation started to taper off.*
▶ noun **1** a slender candle. ■ a wick coated with wax, used for conveying a flame.
2 a gradual narrowing: *the strong taper of her back* | [mass noun] *a small degree of taper.*
– ORIGIN Old English (denoting any wax candle), dissimilated form (by alteration of *p-* to *t-*) of Latin *papyrus* (see PAPYRUS), the pith of which was used for candle wicks.

tape recorder ▶ noun an apparatus for recording sounds on magnetic tape and afterwards reproducing them.
– DERIVATIVES **tape-record** verb, **tape recording** noun.

taper pin ▶ noun a short round metal rod having a small degree of taper which enables it to act as a stop or wedge when driven into a hole.

tape streamer ▶ noun Computing a device for writing data very quickly on to magnetic tape, used typically for making backups of large amounts of data.

tapestry ▶ noun (pl. **tapestries**) a piece of thick textile fabric with pictures or designs formed by weaving coloured weft threads or by embroidering on canvas, used as a wall hanging or soft furnishing. ■ used in reference to an intricate or complex sequence of events: *the loopiness of the Commons adds to life's rich tapestry.*
– DERIVATIVES **tapestried** adjective.
– ORIGIN late Middle English: from Old French *tapisserie*, from *tapissier* 'tapestry worker' or *tapisser* 'to carpet', from *tapis* 'carpet, tapis'.

tapetum /təˈpiːtəm/ ▶ noun Zoology a reflective layer of the choroid in the eyes of many animals, causing them to shine in the dark.
– ORIGIN early 18th cent.: from late Latin, from Latin *tapete* 'carpet'.

tapeworm ▶ noun a parasitic flatworm, the adult of which lives in the intestines. It has a long ribbon-like body with many segments that can become independent, and a small head bearing hooks and suckers. ● Class Cestoda, phylum Platyhelminthes.

taphonomy /taˈfɒnəmi/ ▶ noun [mass noun] the branch of palaeontology that deals with the processes of fossilization.
– DERIVATIVES **taphonomic** adjective, **taphonomist** noun.
– ORIGIN 1940s: from Greek *taphos* 'grave' + -NOMY.

tap-in ▶ noun chiefly Soccer & Basketball a relatively gentle close-range kick or tap that scores a goal.

tapioca /ˌtapɪˈəʊkə/ ▶ noun [mass noun] a starchy substance in the form of hard white grains, obtained from cassava and used in cookery for puddings and other dishes.
– ORIGIN early 18th cent.: from Tupi-Guarani *tipioca*, from *tipi* 'dregs' + *og*, *ok* 'squeeze out'.

tapir /ˈteɪpə, -ɪə/ ▶ noun a nocturnal hoofed mammal with a stout body, sturdy limbs, and a short flexible proboscis, native to the forests of tropical America and Malaysia. ● Family Tapiridae and genus *Tapirus*: four species, including the black and white **Malayan tapir** (*T. indicus*).
– ORIGIN late 18th cent.: via Spanish and Portuguese from Tupi *tapyra*.

tapis /ˈtapiː/ ▶ noun (pl. **same**) archaic a tapestry or richly decorated cloth, used as a hanging or a covering.
– ORIGIN French, from Old French *tapiz*, via late Latin from Greek *tapētion*, diminutive of *tapēs* 'tapestry'.

tapotement /təˈpəʊtm(ə)nt/ ▶ noun [mass noun] rapid and repeated striking of the body as a technique in massage.
– ORIGIN late 19th cent.: French, from *tapoter* 'to tap'.

tappa /ˈtɒpʌ/ ▶ **noun** Indian a short folk song of northern Indian origin.
– ORIGIN from Hindi *ṭappā*.

tap pants ▶ **plural noun** N. Amer. a pair of brief lingerie shorts, usually worn with a camisole top.

tap penalty ▶ **noun** Rugby a penalty taken by kicking the ball lightly to a teammate.

tappet /ˈtapɪt/ ▶ **noun** a moving part in a machine which transmits motion in a straight line between a cam and another part.
– ORIGIN mid 18th cent.: apparently an irregular diminutive of TAP².

tapping ▶ **noun** another term for TAP¹ (sense 1 of the noun).

taproom ▶ **noun** a room in which alcoholic drinks, especially beer, are available on tap; a bar in a pub or hotel.

taproot ▶ **noun** a straight tapering root growing vertically downwards and forming the centre from which subsidiary rootlets spring.

tap shoe ▶ **noun** a shoe with a specially hardened sole or attached metal plates at toe and heel to make a tapping sound in tap dancing.

tapster ▶ **noun** archaic a person who draws and serves alcoholic drinks at a bar.
– ORIGIN Old English *tæppestre*, denoting a woman serving ale (see TAP¹, -STER).

tapu /ˈtɑːpuː/ ▶ **adjective** NZ forbidden; taboo.
– ORIGIN Maori.

tap water ▶ **noun** water from a piped supply.

taquerla /ˌtɑːkəˈriːə/ ▶ **noun** chiefly US a Mexican restaurant specializing in tacos.
– ORIGIN Mexican Spanish.

tar¹ ▶ **noun** [mass noun] a dark, thick flammable liquid distilled from wood or coal, consisting of a mixture of hydrocarbons, resins, alcohols, and other compounds. It is used in road-making and for coating and preserving timber. ■ a substance resembling tar, formed by burning tobacco or other material: [in combination] *low-tar cigarettes*.
▶ **verb** (**tars**, **tarring**, **tarred**) [with obj.] (usu. as adj. **tarred**) cover (something) with tar: *a newly tarred road*.
– PHRASES **beat** (or **whale**) **the tar out of** N. Amer. informal beat or thrash severely. **tar and feather** smear with tar and then cover with feathers as a punishment. **tar people with the same brush** consider certain people to have the same faults.
– ORIGIN Old English *teru*, *teoru*, of Germanic origin; related to Dutch *teer*, German *Teer*, and perhaps ultimately to TREE.

tar² ▶ **noun** informal, dated a sailor.
– ORIGIN mid 17th cent.: perhaps an abbreviation of TARPAULIN, also used as a nickname for a sailor at this time.

Tara /ˈtɑːrə/ a hill in County Meath in the Republic of Ireland, site in early times of the residence of the high kings of Ireland and still marked by ancient earthworks.

ta-ra /təˈrɑː/ ▶ **exclamation** informal, chiefly N. English goodbye.
– ORIGIN 1950s: variant of TA-TA.

Tarabulus al-Gharb /təˌrɑːbələs alˈɡɑːb/ Arabic name for TRIPOLI (sense 1).

Tarabulus ash-Sham /aʃˈʃam/ Arabic name for TRIPOLI (sense 2).

taradiddle /ˈtarəˌdɪd(ə)l/ (also **tarradiddle**) ▶ **noun** informal, chiefly Brit. a petty lie. ■ [mass noun] pretentious nonsense.
– ORIGIN late 18th cent.: perhaps related to DIDDLE.

tarakihi /ˌtarəˈkiːhi, ˌtarəˈkiː/ ▶ **noun** a silver marine fish with a black band behind the head, related to the morwong and caught for food off the coasts of New Zealand. ● *Cheilodactylus macropterus*, family Cheilodactylidae.
– ORIGIN late 19th cent.: from Maori.

taramasalata /ˌtarəməsəˈlɑːtə/ (also **tarama** /ˈtarəmə/) ▶ **noun** [mass noun] a pinkish paste or dip made from the roe of certain fish, mixed with olive oil and seasoning.
– ORIGIN from modern Greek *taramas* 'roe' (from Turkish *tarama*, denoting a preparation of soft roe or red caviar) + *salata* 'salad'.

Taranaki /ˌtarəˈnaki/ official name for Mount Egmont (see EGMONT, MOUNT).

tarantass /ˌtar(ə)nˈtas/ ▶ **noun** a four-wheeled horse-drawn Russian carriage without springs, mounted on a long flexible wooden chassis.
– ORIGIN from Russian *tarantas*.

tarantella /ˌtar(ə)nˈtɛlə/ (also **tarantelle** /-ˈtɛl/) ▶ **noun** a rapid whirling dance originating in southern Italy. ■ a piece of music written in fast 6/8 time in the style of the tarantella.
– ORIGIN late 18th cent.: Italian, from the name of the seaport TARANTO. The dance was thought to be a cure for tarantism, the victim dancing the tarantella until exhausted. See also TARANTULA.

tarantism /ˈtar(ə)nˌtɪz(ə)m/ ▶ **noun** [mass noun] a psychological illness characterized by an extreme impulse to dance, prevalent in southern Italy from the 15th to the 17th century, and widely believed at the time to be caused by the bite of a tarantula.
– ORIGIN mid 17th cent.: from Italian *tarantismo*, from the name of the seaport TARANTO, after which the tarantula is also named. Compare with TARANTELLA.

Taranto /təˈrantəʊ/, Italian /taˈrantəo/ a seaport and naval base in Apulia, SE Italy; pop. 194,021 (2008). Founded by the Greeks in the 8th century BC, it came under Roman rule in 272 BC.

tarantula /təˈrantjʊlə/ ▶ **noun 1** a very large hairy spider found chiefly in tropical and subtropical America, some kinds of which are able to catch small lizards, frogs, and birds. Also called BIRD-EATING SPIDER. ● Family Theraphosidae, suborder Mygalomorphae.
2 a large black wolf spider of southern Europe, whose bite was formerly believed to cause tarantism. ● *Lycosa tarentula*, family Lycosidae.
– ORIGIN mid 16th cent.: from medieval Latin, from Old Italian *tarantola* 'tarantula', from the name of the seaport TARANTO. Compare with TARANTELLA and TARANTISM.

tarata /təˈrɑːtə/ ▶ **noun** New Zealand term for LEMONWOOD.
– ORIGIN Maori.

Tarawa /ˈtarəwə, təˈrɑːwə/ an atoll in the South Pacific, one of the Gilbert Islands; pop. 45,989 (2005). It is the location of Bairiki, the capital of Kiribati.

tar baby ▶ **noun** informal a difficult problem which is only aggravated by attempts to solve it.
– ORIGIN with allusion to the doll smeared with tar as a trap for Brer Rabbit, in J. C. Harris's *Uncle Remus*.

tarboosh /tɑːˈbuːʃ/ ▶ **noun** a man's cap similar to a fez, typically of red felt with a tassel at the top.
– ORIGIN early 18th cent.: from Egyptian Arabic *ṭarbūš*, based on Persian *sarpūš*, from *sar* 'head' + *pūš* 'cover'.

tarbrush ▶ **noun** (**the tarbrush**) offensive black or Indian ancestry.

Tardenoisian /ˌtɑːdɪˈnɔɪzɪən/ ▶ **adjective** relating to or denoting a late Mesolithic culture of west and central Europe, especially France, dated to about 8,000–6,000 years ago. ■ (as noun **the Tardenoisian**) the Tardenoisian culture or period.
– ORIGIN 1920s: from French *Tardenoisien*, from the name of *Fère-en-Tardenois* in NE France, where objects from this culture were found.

Tardigrada /ˌtɑːdɪˈɡreɪdə/ ▶ **plural noun** Zoology a small phylum that comprises the water bears.
– ORIGIN modern Latin (plural), from Latin *tardigradus*, from *tardus* 'slow' + *gradi* 'to walk'.

tardigrade /ˈtɑːdɪɡreɪd/ ▶ **noun** Zoology a minute animal of the phylum Tardigrada; a water bear.

tardiness ▶ **noun** [mass noun] the quality or fact of being late; lateness: *forgive my tardiness, I had some very important business to attend to*.

Tardis /ˈtɑːdɪs/ ▶ **noun 1** a time machine.
2 a building or container that is larger inside than it appears to be from outside.
– ORIGIN the name (said to be an acronym of *time and relative dimensions in space*) of a time machine which had the exterior of a police telephone box in the British TV science-fiction series *Doctor Who*, first broadcast in 1963.

tardive dyskinesia /ˌtɑːdɪv ˌdɪskɪˈniːzɪə/ ▶ **noun** [mass noun] Medicine a neurological disorder characterized by involuntary movements of the face and jaw.
– ORIGIN 1960s: *tardive* from French *tardif*, *tardive* (see TARDY).

tardy ▶ **adjective** (**tardier**, **tardiest**) delaying or delayed beyond the right or expected time; late: *please forgive this tardy reply*. ■ slow in action or response; sluggish.
– DERIVATIVES **tardily** adverb.
– ORIGIN mid 16th cent.: from French *tardif*, *-ive*, from Latin *tardus* 'slow'.

tare¹ /tɛː/ ▶ **noun 1** a vetch, especially the common vetch.
2 (**tares**) (in biblical use) an injurious weed resembling corn when young (Matt. 13:24–30).
– ORIGIN Middle English: of unknown origin.

tare² /tɛː/ ▶ **noun** an allowance made for the weight of the packaging in order to determine the net weight of goods. ■ the weight of a motor vehicle, railway carriage, or aircraft without its fuel or load.
– ORIGIN late Middle English: from French, literally 'deficiency, tare', from medieval Latin *tara*, based on Arabic *ṭaraḥa* 'reject, deduct'.

tare and tret ▶ **noun** [mass noun] historical the arithmetical rule used for calculating the net weight of goods by subtracting the tare and the tret from the gross weight.

targa /ˈtɑːɡə/ ▶ **noun** [usu. as modifier] trademark a type of convertible sports car with a hood or panel that can be removed, leaving a central roll bar for passenger safety: *a targa roof*.
– ORIGIN Italian, literally 'shield', given as a name to a model of Porsche with a detachable hood (1965), probably suggested by the *Targa Florio* ('Florio Shield'), a motor time trial held annually in Sicily.

targe /tɑːdʒ/ ▶ **noun** archaic term for TARGET (sense 2 of the noun).
– ORIGIN Old English *targa*, *targe*, of Germanic origin; reinforced in Middle English by Old French *targe*.

target ▶ **noun 1** a person, object, or place selected as the aim of an attack. ■ a mark or point at which one fires or aims, especially a round or rectangular board marked with concentric circles used in archery or shooting. ■ an objective or result towards which efforts are directed: *the car met its sales target in record time*. ■ a person or thing against whom criticism or abuse is directed: *they were the target for a wave of abuse from the press*. ■ Phonetics an idealization of the articulation of a speech sound, with reference to which actual utterances can be described.
2 historical a small round shield or buckler.
▶ **verb** (**targets**, **targeting**, **targeted**) [with obj.] select as an object of attention or attack: *two men were targeted by the attackers*. ■ aim or direct (something): *warheads were **targeted on** a European city*.
– PHRASES **on** (or **off**) **target** hitting (or missing) the thing aimed at: *McGrath was on target with a header*. ■ proceeding or improving at a rate good enough (or not good enough) to achieve an objective: *the new police station is on target for a June opening*.
– DERIVATIVES **targetable** adjective.
– ORIGIN late Middle English (in sense 2 of the noun): diminutive of TARGE. The verb dates from the early 17th cent.

target cell ▶ **noun 1** Physiology a cell which bears receptors for a hormone, drug, or other signalling molecule, or is the focus of contact by a virus, phagocyte, nerve fibre, etc.
2 Medicine an abnormal form of red blood cell which appears as a dark ring surrounding a dark central spot, typical of certain kinds of anaemia.

target language ▶ **noun** the language into which a text, document, or speech is translated. ■ a foreign language which a person intends to learn.

target man ▶ **noun** Soccer & Hockey a forward in a central position to whom other players direct long passes.

target organ ▶ **noun** Physiology & Medicine a specific organ on which a hormone, drug, or other substance acts.

Targum /ˈtɑːɡəm/ ▶ **noun** an ancient Aramaic paraphrase or interpretation of the Hebrew Bible, of a type made from about the 1st century AD when Hebrew was ceasing to be a spoken language.
– ORIGIN from Aramaic *targūm* 'interpretation'.

Tar Heel State informal name for NORTH CAROLINA.

tariff ▶ **noun** a tax or duty to be paid on a particular class of imports or exports. ■ a list of import or export tariffs. ■ a table of the fixed charges made by a business, especially in a hotel or restaurant. ■ Law a scale of sentences and damages for crimes and injuries of different severities.
▶ **verb** [with obj.] fix the price of (something) according to a tariff: *these services are tariffed by volume*.
– ORIGIN late 16th cent. (also denoting an arithmetical table): via French from Italian *tariffa*, based on Arabic *'arrafa* 'notify'.

Tarim /tɑːˈriːm/ a river of NW China, in Xinjiang autonomous region. It rises as the Yarkand in the

T

Kunlun Shan mountains and flows for over 2,000 km (1,250 miles) generally eastwards through the dry Tarim Basin, petering out in the Lop Nor depression. For much of its course the river is unformed, following no clearly defined bed and subject to much evaporation.

tariqa /taˈriːkə/ (also **tariqat** /taˈriːkət/) ▶ **noun** [mass noun] the Sufi doctrine or path of spiritual learning. ■ [count noun] a Sufi missionary.
– ORIGIN from Arabic *ṭarīqa* 'manner, way, creed'.

tarka dal /ˌtɑːkə ˈdɑːl/ (also **tarka dhal**) ▶ **noun** [mass noun] (in Indian cookery) a dish of creamy lentils cooked with onion, garlic, and spices.
– ORIGIN Hindi *tarka dāl*, from *taṛaknā* 'to season' + *dāl* (see DAL[1]).

Tarkovsky /tɑːˈkɒfski/, Andrei (Arsenevich) (1932–86), Russian film director. Featuring a poetic and impressionistic style, his films include *Solaris* (1972) and *The Sacrifice* (1986).

tarlatan /ˈtɑːlət(ə)n/ ▶ **noun** [mass noun] a thin, open-weave muslin fabric, used for stiffening ball dresses.
– ORIGIN early 18th cent.: from French *tarlatane*, probably of Indian origin.

tarmac ▶ **noun** [mass noun] (trademark in the UK) material used for surfacing roads or other outdoor areas, consisting of broken stone mixed with tar. ■ (**the tarmac**) a runway or other area surfaced with tarmac or a similar material.
▶ **verb** (**tarmacs, tarmacking, tarmacked**) [with obj.] surface (a road or other outdoor area) with tarmac or a similar material: (as adj. **tarmacked**) *there are no tarmacked roads.*
– ORIGIN early 20th cent.: abbreviation of TARMACADAM.

tarmacadam /ˌtɑːməˈkadəm/ ▶ **noun** another term for TARMAC.
– DERIVATIVES **tarmacadamed** adjective.
– ORIGIN late 19th cent.: from TAR[1] + MACADAM.

Tarn /tɑːn/, French /taʀn/ a river of southern France, which rises in the Cévennes and flows 380 km (235 miles) generally south-westwards through deep gorges before meeting the Garonne north-west of Toulouse.

tarn ▶ **noun** a small mountain lake.
– ORIGIN Middle English (originally northern English dialect): from Old Norse *tjǫrn*.

tarnation ▶ **noun & exclamation** chiefly N. Amer. used as a euphemism for 'damnation'.
– ORIGIN late 18th cent.: alteration.

tarnish ▶ **verb** lose or cause to lose lustre, especially as a result of exposure to air or moisture: [no obj.] *silver tarnishes too easily* | [with obj.] *lemon juice would tarnish the gilded metal.* ■ make or become less valuable or respected: [with obj.] *his regime had not been tarnished by human rights abuses.*
▶ **noun** [mass noun] dullness of colour; loss of brightness. ■ a film or stain formed on an exposed surface of a mineral or metal. ■ damage or harm done to something.
– ORIGIN late Middle English (as a verb): from French *terniss-*, lengthened stem of *ternir*, from *terne* 'dark, dull'.

Tarnów /ˈtɑːnʊf/ an industrial city in southern Poland; pop. 116,527 (2007).

taro /ˈtɑːrəʊ, ˈtarəʊ/ ▶ **noun** [mass noun] a tropical Asian plant of the arum family which has edible starchy corms and edible fleshy leaves, especially a variety with a large central corm grown as a staple in the Pacific. Also called DASHEEN, COCOYAM. Compare with EDDO. ● *Colocasia esculenta* var. *esculenta*, family Araceae. ■ the corm of the taro.
– ORIGIN mid 18th cent.: of Polynesian origin.

tar oil ▶ **noun** [mass noun] a volatile oil obtained by distilling tar, sometimes used as an insecticide.

tarot /ˈtarəʊ/ ▶ **noun** [mass noun] (**the Tarot**) playing cards, traditionally a pack of 78 with five suits, used for fortune-telling and (especially in Europe) in certain games. The suits are typically swords, cups, coins (or pentacles), batons (or wands), and a permanent suit of trumps. ■ a card game played with tarot cards. ■ [count noun] a card from a pack of tarot cards.
– ORIGIN late 16th cent.: from French, from Italian *tarocchi*, of unknown origin.

tarp ▶ **noun** N. Amer. informal a tarpaulin sheet or cover.
– ORIGIN early 20th cent.: abbreviation.

tarpan /ˈtɑːpan/ ▶ **noun** a greyish wild horse that was formerly common in eastern Europe and western Asia, hunted to extinction by 1919. ● *Equus caballus gomelini*, family Equidae.
– ORIGIN Kyrgyz.

tarpaper ▶ **noun** [mass noun] N. Amer. paper impregnated with tar, used as a building material.
– DERIVATIVES **tarpapered** adjective.

tarpaulin /tɑːˈpɔːlɪn/ ▶ **noun 1** [mass noun] heavy-duty waterproof cloth, originally of tarred canvas. ■ [count noun] a sheet or covering of tarpaulin.
2 historical a sailor's tarred or oilskin hat. ■ archaic a sailor.
– ORIGIN early 17th cent.: probably from TAR[1] + PALL[1] + -ING[1].

Tarpeia /tɑːˈpiːə/ one of the Vestal Virgins, the daughter of a commander of the Capitol in ancient Rome. According to legend she betrayed the citadel to the Sabines in return for whatever they wore on their arms, hoping to receive their golden bracelets; however, the Sabines killed her by throwing their shields on to her.

Tarpeian Rock /tɑːˈpiːən/ a cliff in ancient Rome, at the south-western corner of the Capitoline Hill, over which murderers and traitors were hurled.

tar pit ▶ **noun** a hollow in which natural tar accumulates by seepage.

tarpon /ˈtɑːpɒn/ ▶ **noun** a large tropical marine fish of herring-like appearance. ● Two species in the family Megalopidae: *Tarpon atlanticus*, a prized Atlantic game fish, and *Megalops cyprinoides* of the Indo-Pacific.
– ORIGIN late 17th cent.: probably from Dutch *tarpoen*, perhaps from a Central American language.

Tarquinius /tɑːˈkwɪnɪəs/ the name of two semi-legendary Etruscan kings of ancient Rome; anglicized name *Tarquin*: ■ **Tarquinius Priscus**, reigned *c.*616–*c.*578 BC; full name *Lucius Tarquinius Priscus*. According to tradition he was murdered by the sons of the previous king. ■ **Tarquinius Superbus**, reigned *c.*534–*c.*510 BC; full name *Lucius Tarquinius Superbus*; known as **Tarquin the Proud**. According to tradition he was the son or grandson of Tarquinius Priscus. Noted for his cruelty, he was expelled from the city and the Republic was founded. He repeatedly, but unsuccessfully, attacked Rome, assisted by Lars Porsenna.

tarradiddle ▶ **noun** variant spelling of TARADIDDLE.

tarragon /ˈtarəɡ(ə)n/ ▶ **noun** [mass noun] a perennial plant of the daisy family, with narrow aromatic leaves that are used as a culinary herb. ● *Artemisia dracunculus*, family Compositae.
– ORIGIN mid 16th cent.: representing medieval Latin *tragonia* and *tarchon*, perhaps from an Arabic alteration of Greek *drakōn* 'dragon' (by association with *drakontion* 'dragon arum').

Tarragona wine /ˌtarəˈɡəʊnə/ ▶ **noun** [mass noun] a sweet fortified red or white wine produced in the Tarragona region of Spain.

tarras /təˈras/ ▶ **noun** variant spelling of TRASS.

Tarrasa /təˈrasə/, Spanish /taˈrasa/ (also **Terrassa**) an industrial city in Catalonia, NE Spain; pop. 206,245 (2008).

tarry[1] /ˈtɑːri/ ▶ **adjective** (**tarrier, tarriest**) like or covered with tar: *a length of tarry rope.*

tarry[2] /ˈtari/ ▶ **verb** (**tarries, tarrying, tarried**) [no obj.] archaic or literary stay longer than intended; delay leaving a place: *she could tarry a bit and not get home until four.*
– ORIGIN Middle English: of unknown origin.

tarsal /ˈtɑːs(ə)l/ Anatomy & Zoology ▶ **adjective** relating to the tarsus: *the tarsal claws of beetles.*
▶ **noun** a bone of the tarsus.
– ORIGIN early 19th cent.: from TARSUS + -AL.

tar sand ▶ **noun** (often **tar sands**) Geology a deposit of sand impregnated with bitumen.

tarsi plural form of TARSUS.

tarsier /ˈtɑːsɪə/ ▶ **noun** a small insectivorous, tree-dwelling, nocturnal primate with very large eyes, a long tufted tail, and very long hindlimbs, native to the islands of SE Asia. ● Family Tarsiidae and genus *Tarsius*, suborder Prosimii: four species.
– ORIGIN late 18th cent.: from French, from *tarse* 'tarsus', with reference to the animal's long tarsal bones.

tarsometatarsus /ˌtɑːsəʊmɛtəˈtɑːsəs/ ▶ **noun** (pl. **tarsometatarsi** /-sʌɪ, -siː/) Zoology a long bone in the lower leg of birds and some reptiles, formed by fusion of tarsal and metatarsal structures.
– DERIVATIVES **tarsometatarsal** adjective.

Tarsus /ˈtɑːsəs/ an ancient city in southern Turkey, the capital of Cilicia and the birthplace of St Paul. It is now a market town.

tarsus /ˈtɑːsəs/ ▶ **noun** (pl. **tarsi** /-sʌɪ, -siː/) Anatomy **1** a group of small bones between the main part of the hindlimb and the metatarsus in terrestrial vertebrates. The seven bones of the human tarsus form the ankle and upper part of the foot. They are the talus, calcaneus, navicular, and cuboid, and the three cuneiform bones. ■ Zoology the shank or tarsometatarsus of the leg of a bird or reptile. ■ Zoology the foot or fifth joint of the leg of an insect or other arthropod, typically consisting of several small segments and ending in a claw.
2 a thin sheet of fibrous connective tissue which supports the edge of each eyelid.
– ORIGIN late Middle English: modern Latin, from Greek *tarsos* 'flat of the foot, the eyelid'.

tart[1] ▶ **noun** an open pastry case containing a sweet or savoury filling: *an apple tart.*
– DERIVATIVES **tartlet** noun.
– ORIGIN late Middle English (denoting a savoury pie): from Old French *tarte* or medieval Latin *tarta*, of unknown origin.

tart[2] informal ▶ **noun** derogatory a prostitute or a promiscuous woman.
▶ **verb** chiefly Brit. **1** [with obj.] (**tart oneself up**) dress or make oneself up in order to look attractive. ■ (**tart something up**) improve the appearance of something, typically in a way regarded as flashy or superficial: *the page layouts have been tarted up with cartoons.*
2 [with obj.] (**tart about** (or **around**)) (especially of a girl or woman) behave in a provocative or flamboyant way: *she tarted around the room in one of Georgie's dresses.*
– ORIGIN mid 19th cent.: probably an abbreviation of SWEETHEART.

tart[3] ▶ **adjective** sharp or acid in taste: *a tart apple.* ■ (of a remark or tone of voice) cutting, bitter, or sarcastic: *a tart reply.*
– DERIVATIVES **tartly** adverb, **tartness** noun.
– ORIGIN Old English *teart* 'harsh, severe', of unknown origin.

tartan[1] ▶ **noun** a woollen cloth woven in one of several patterns of coloured checks and intersecting lines, especially of a design associated with a particular Scottish clan.
▶ **adjective** used allusively in reference to Scotland or the Scots: *the financing proposals for the Scottish parliament amounted to a tartan tax.*
– ORIGIN late 15th cent. (originally Scots): perhaps from Old French *tertaine*, denoting a kind of cloth; compare with *tartarin*, a rich fabric formerly imported from the east through Tartary.

tartan[2] ▶ **noun** historical a lateen-rigged, single-masted ship used in the Mediterranean.
– ORIGIN early 17th cent.: from French *tartane*, from Italian *tartana*, perhaps from Arabic *ṭarīda*.

Tartar /ˈtɑːtə/ ▶ **noun** a member of the combined forces of central Asian peoples, including Mongols and Turks, who under the leadership of Genghis Khan conquered much of Asia and eastern Europe in the early 13th century, and under Tamerlane (14th century) established an empire with its capital at Samarkand. See also TATAR. ■ (**tartar**) a harsh, fierce, or intractable person.
– DERIVATIVES **Tartarian** /-ˈtɛːrɪən/ adjective.
– ORIGIN from Old French *Tartare* or medieval Latin *Tartarus*, alteration (influenced by TARTARUS) of TATAR.

tartar /ˈtɑːtə/ ▶ **noun** [mass noun] a hard calcified deposit that forms on the teeth and contributes to their decay. ■ a deposit of impure potassium hydrogen tartrate formed during the fermentation of wine.
– DERIVATIVES **tartaric** adjective.
– ORIGIN late Middle English: via medieval Latin from medieval Greek *tartaron*, of unknown origin.

tartare /tɑːˈtɑː/ ▶ **adjective** [postpositive] (of fish) served raw, typically seasoned and shaped into small cakes. See also STEAK TARTARE.
– ORIGIN French, literally 'Tartar'.

tartar emetic ▶ **noun** [mass noun] a toxic compound used in treating protozoal disease in animals, as a mordant in dyeing, and formerly as an emetic. ● Alternative name: **potassium antimony tartrate**; chem. formula: $K(SbO)C_4H_4O_6$.

tartare sauce (also **tartar sauce**) ▶ **noun** [mass noun] a cold sauce, typically eaten with fish, consisting of mayonnaise mixed with chopped onions, gherkins, and capers.

tartaric acid ▶ **noun** [mass noun] Chemistry a crystalline organic acid which is present especially in unripe grapes and is used in baking powders and

T

as a food additive. ● A dibasic acid; chem. formula: $COOH(CHOH)_2COOH$.

Tartarus /ˈtɑːtərəs/ Greek Mythology **1** a primeval god, offspring of Chaos.
2 a part of the underworld where the wicked suffered punishment for their misdeeds, especially those such as Ixion and Tantalus who had committed some outrage against the gods.
– DERIVATIVES **Tartarean** /-ˈtɛːrɪən/ adjective.

Tartary /ˈtɑːtəri/ a historical region of Asia and eastern Europe, especially the high plateau of central Asia and its NW slopes, which formed part of the Tartar empire in the Middle Ages.

tarte Tatin /ˌtɑːt taˈtã/ ▶ **noun** a type of upside-down apple tart consisting of pastry baked over slices of fruit arranged in caramelized sugar, served fruit side up after cooking.
– ORIGIN French, from *tarte* 'tart' + *Tatin*, the surname of the sisters said to have created the dish.

tartrate /ˈtɑːtreɪt/ ▶ **noun** Chemistry a salt or ester of tartaric acid.
– ORIGIN late 18th cent.: from French, from *tartre* 'tartar' + **-ATE**^{1}.

tartrazine /ˈtɑːtrəziːn/ ▶ **noun** [mass noun] Chemistry a brilliant yellow synthetic dye derived from tartaric acid and used to colour food, drugs, and cosmetics.
– ORIGIN late 19th cent.: from French *tartre* 'tartar' + **AZO-** + **-INE**^{4}.

Tartuffe /tɑːˈtʊːf/ ▶ **noun** literary or humorous a religious hypocrite, or a hypocritical pretender to excellence of any kind.
– DERIVATIVES **Tartufferie** (also **Tartuffery**) **noun**.
– ORIGIN from the name of the principal character (a religious hypocrite) in Molière's *Tartuffe* (1664).

tartufo /tɑːˈtuːfəʊ/ ▶ **noun** (pl. **tartufos**) **1** an edible fungus, especially the white truffle.
2 an Italian dessert, containing chocolate, of a creamy mousse-like consistency.
– ORIGIN Italian, literally 'truffle'.

tarty ▶ **adjective** (**tartier**, **tartiest**) informal (of a woman) dressed in a sexually provocative manner that is considered to be in bad taste. ■ (of clothes) contributing to a sexually provocative appearance.
– DERIVATIVES **tartily adverb**, **tartiness noun**.

tarweed ▶ **noun** [mass noun] any of a number of American plants of the daisy family with sticky leaves and heavy scent. ● *Madia, Grindelia, Hemizonia*, and related genera, family Compositae.

tarwhine /ˈtɑːwʌɪn/ ▶ **noun** (pl. **same**) a yellowish sea bream of warm shallow inshore waters, which is an important food and game fish in the Indo-Pacific. ● *Rhabdosargus globiceps*, family Sparidae.
– ORIGIN late 19th cent.: from Dharuk *darawayn* 'a fish'.

Tarzan a fictitious character created by Edgar Rice Burroughs. Tarzan (Lord Greystoke by birth) is orphaned in West Africa in his infancy and reared by apes in the jungle. ■ (as noun **a Tarzan**) a man of great agility and powerful physique.

Tas. ▶ **abbreviation** chiefly Austral. Tasmania.

tasca /ˈtaska/ ▶ **noun** (in Spain and Portugal) a tavern or bar, especially one serving food.
– ORIGIN Spanish and Portuguese.

taser /ˈteɪzə/ ▶ **noun** US trademark a weapon firing barbs attached by wires to batteries, causing temporary paralysis.
▶ **verb** (also **tase**) fire a taser at (someone) in order to incapacitate them temporarily.
– ORIGIN 1970s: from the initial letters of *Tom Swift's electric rifle* (a fictitious weapon), on the pattern of *laser*.

tash (also **tache**) ▶ **noun** informal a moustache.
– ORIGIN late 19th cent.: shortened form.

Tashi Lama /ˈtaʃɪ ˌlɑːmə/ ▶ **noun** another name for **PANCHEN LAMA**.

Tashkent /taʃˈkɛnt/ the capital of Uzbekistan, in the far north-east of the country in the western foothills of the Tien Shan mountains: pop. 2,192,700 (est. 2009). One of the oldest cities in central Asia, Tashkent was an important centre on the trade route between Europe and the Orient. It became part of the Mongol empire in the 13th century, was captured by the Russians in 1865, and replaced Samarkand as capital of Uzbekistan in 1930.

task ▶ **noun** a piece of work to be done or undertaken: *a new manager was given the task of developing the club's talent*.
▶ **verb** [with obj.] assign a task to: *NATO troops are tasked with separating the warring parties*. ■ make great demands on (someone's resources or abilities): *it tasked his diplomatic skill to effect his departure in safety*.
– PHRASES **take someone to task** reprimand or criticize someone severely for a fault or mistake.
– ORIGIN Middle English: from an Old Northern French variant of Old French *tasche*, from medieval Latin *tasca*, alteration of *taxa*, from Latin *taxare* 'censure, charge' (see **TAX**). An early sense of the verb was 'impose a tax on'.

task force (also **task group**) ▶ **noun** an armed force organized for a special operation. ■ a unit specially organized for a task: *the government has set up a task force to survey mental health services*.

taskmaster ▶ **noun** (fem. **taskmistress** /-mɪstrɪs/) a person who imposes a harsh or onerous workload on someone: *he was a hard taskmaster*.

Tasman /ˈtazmən/, Abel (Janszoon) (1603–*c*.1659), Dutch navigator. Sent in 1642 by the Governor General of the Dutch East Indies, Anthony van Diemen (1593–1645), to explore Australian waters, he reached Tasmania (which he named Van Diemen's Land) and New Zealand, and in 1643 arrived at Tonga and Fiji.

Tasmania /tazˈmeɪnɪə/ a state of Australia consisting of the mountainous island of Tasmania itself and several smaller islands; pop. 497,529 (2008); capital, Hobart. It was known as Van Diemen's Land until 1855.
– DERIVATIVES **Tasmanian adjective & noun**.

Tasmanian devil ▶ **noun** a heavily built marsupial with a large head, powerful jaws, and mainly black fur, found only in Tasmania. It is slow-moving and aggressive, feeding mainly on carrion. ● *Sarcophilus harrisii*, family Dasyuridae.

Tasmanian wolf (also **Tasmanian tiger**) ▶ **noun** another term for **THYLACINE**.

Tasman Sea an arm of the South Pacific lying between Australia and New Zealand.

Tass /tas/ the official news agency of the former Soviet Union, renamed ITAR-Tass in 1992.
– ORIGIN Russian acronym, from *Telegrafnoe agentstvo Sovetskogo Soyuza* 'Telegraphic Agency of the Soviet Union'.

tass ▶ **noun** Scottish archaic a cup or small goblet. ■ a small draught of an alcoholic drink.
– ORIGIN late 15th cent.: from Old French *tasse* 'cup', via Arabic from Persian *tašt* 'bowl'.

tassa drum /ˈtasə/ ▶ **noun** W. Indian a large one-sided Indian goatskin drum, typically hung from the neck and played with two sticks.
– ORIGIN *tassa* from Hindi.

tassel^1 ▶ **noun** a tuft of loosely hanging threads or cords knotted at one end and attached for decoration to soft furnishings, clothing, or other items. ■ the tufted head of some plants, especially a flower head with prominent stamens at the top of a maize stalk.
▶ **verb** (**tassels**, **tasselling**, **tasselled**; US **tassels**, **tasseling**, **tasseled**) **1** [with obj.] (usu. as adj. **tasselled**) provide with a tassel or tassels: *tasselled curtains*.
2 [no obj.] N. Amer. (of maize or other plants) form tassels.
– ORIGIN Middle English (also denoting a clasp for a cloak): from Old French *tassel* 'clasp', of unknown origin.

tassel^2 (also **torsel**) ▶ **noun** a small piece of stone or wood supporting the end of a beam or joist.
– ORIGIN mid 17th cent.: from obsolete French, from Latin *taxillus* 'small die'.

tassie ▶ **noun** Scottish archaic a small cup.
– ORIGIN late 18th cent.: from **TASS** + **-IE**.

Tasso /ˈtasəʊ/, Torquato (1544–95), Italian poet, known for his epic poem *Gerusalemme liberata* (1581).

taste ▶ **noun 1** the sensation of flavour perceived in the mouth and throat on contact with a substance: *the wine had a fruity taste*. ■ [mass noun] the faculty of perceiving taste: *birds do not have a highly developed sense of taste*. ■ a small portion of food or drink taken as a sample: *try a taste of cheese*. ■ a brief experience of something, conveying its basic character: *it was his first taste of serious action*.
2 a person's liking for particular flavours: *this pudding is too sweet for my taste*. ■ a person's tendency to like or be interested in something: *he found the aggressive competitiveness of the profession was not to his taste | have you lost your taste for fancy restaurants?*
3 [mass noun] the ability to discern what is of good quality or of a high aesthetic standard: *she has frightful taste in literature*. ■ conformity or failure to conform with generally held views concerning what is offensive or acceptable: *that's a joke in very bad taste*.
▶ **verb** [with obj.] **1** perceive or experience the flavour of: *she had never tasted ice cream before*. ■ [no obj.] have a specified flavour: *the coffee tasted of acorns* | [with complement] *the spinach tastes delicious*. ■ sample the flavour of (food or drink) by taking it into the mouth: *the waiter poured some wine for him to taste*. ■ eat or drink a small portion of.
2 have experience of: *the team has not yet tasted victory at home*.
– PHRASES **a bad** (or **bitter** or **nasty**) **taste in the** (or US **someone's**) **mouth** informal a strong feeling of distress or disgust following an experience. **taste blood** see **BLOOD**. **to taste** according to personal liking: *add salt and pepper to taste*.
– ORIGIN Middle English (also in the sense 'touch'): from Old French *tast* (noun), *taster* (verb) 'touch, try, taste', perhaps based on a blend of Latin *tangere* 'to touch' and *gustare* 'to taste'.

taste bud ▶ **noun** (usu. **taste buds**) any of the clusters of bulbous nerve endings on the tongue and in the lining of the mouth which provide the sense of taste.

tasteful ▶ **adjective** showing good aesthetic judgement or appropriate behaviour: *a tasteful lounge bar*.
– DERIVATIVES **tastefully adverb**, **tastefulness noun**.

tasteless ▶ **adjective 1** lacking flavour.
2 considered to be lacking in aesthetic judgement or to constitute inappropriate behaviour: *a tasteless joke*.
– DERIVATIVES **tastelessly adverb**, **tastelessness noun**.

tastemaker ▶ **noun** a person who decides or influences what is or will become fashionable.

taster ▶ **noun 1** a person employed to test food or drink for quality by tasting it: *a tea taster*. ■ a small cup used by a person tasting wine. ■ an instrument for extracting a small sample from within a cheese.
2 Brit. a small quantity or brief experience of something, intended as a sample: *the song is a taster for the band's new LP*.
– ORIGIN late Middle English: in early use from Anglo-Norman French *tastour*, from Old French *taster* 'to taste'; later from **TASTE** + **-ER**^{1}.

tastevin /ˈtastəvã, ˌtastəˈvã/, French /tastəvɛ̃/ ▶ **noun** (pl. pronunc. **same**) a small, shallow silver cup for tasting wines, of a type used in France.
– ORIGIN French, literally 'wine taster'.

tasting ▶ **noun** a gathering at which people sample, compare, and evaluate different wines, or other drinks or food.

tasting menu ▶ **noun** a type of meal offered in certain restaurants, consisting of sample portions of many different dishes served in several courses for a set price.

tasty ▶ **adjective** (**tastier**, **tastiest**) (of food) having a pleasant, distinct flavour: *a tasty snack*. ■ informal, chiefly Brit. attractive; very appealing: *a tasty deal at the building society*. ■ Brit. informal very good; impressive: *he's a bit tasty with a football*.
– DERIVATIVES **tastily adverb**, **tastiness noun**.

tat^1 ▶ **noun** [mass noun] Brit. informal tasteless or shoddy clothes, jewellery, or ornaments: *the place was decorated with all manner of gaudy tat*.
– ORIGIN mid 19th cent. (in the senses 'rag' and 'person in rags'): probably a back-formation from **TATTY**.

tat^2 ▶ **verb** (**tats**, **tatting**, **tatted**) [with obj.] make (a decorative mat or edging) by tying knots in thread and using a small shuttle to form lace.
– ORIGIN late 19th cent.: back-formation from **TATTING**.

tat^3 ▶ **noun** (in phrase **tit for tat**) see **TIT**^{3}.

tat^4 ▶ **noun** informal a tattoo.

ta-ta /taˈtɑː/ ▶ **exclamation** Brit. informal goodbye.
– ORIGIN early 19th cent.: of unknown origin; compare with earlier *da-da*.

tataki /təˈtaki/ ▶ **noun** [mass noun] (in Japanese cookery) a dish consisting of meat or fish steak, served either raw or lightly seared.
– ORIGIN Japanese, literally 'pounded, minced'.

tatami /təˈtɑːmi/ (also **tatami mat**) ▶ **noun** (pl. **same** or **tatamis**) a rush-covered straw mat forming a traditional Japanese floor covering.
– ORIGIN Japanese.

Tatar /ˈtɑːtə/ ▶ **noun 1** a member of a Turkic people living in Tatarstan and various other parts of Russia

T

and Ukraine. They are the descendants of the Tartars who ruled central Asia in the 14th century.
2 [mass noun] the Turkic language of the Tatars, with about 6 million speakers.
▸ adjective relating to the Tatars or their language.
– ORIGIN the Turkic name of a Tartar tribe.

Tatarstan /ˌtɑːtəˈstɑːn, -ˈstan/ an autonomous republic in European Russia, in the valley of the River Volga; pop. 3,755,800 (est. 2009); capital, Kazan.

Tate, Nahum (1652–1715), Irish dramatist and poet, resident in London from the 1670s. He was appointed Poet Laureate in 1692.

Tate Gallery a national museum of art at Millbank, London, founded in 1897 by the sugar manufacturer Sir Henry Tate (1819–99) to house his collection of modern British paintings, as a nucleus for a permanent national collection of modern art. It was renamed Tate Britain in 2000, when the new Tate Modern gallery opened.

tater /ˈteɪtə/ (Brit. also **tatie** /-ti/) ▸ noun informal a potato.
– ORIGIN mid 18th cent.: alteration.

Tathagata /təˈtɑːgətə, təˈθɑːgətə/ ▸ noun an honorific title of a Buddha, especially the Buddha Gautama, or a person who has attained perfection by following Buddhist principles.
– ORIGIN from Pali *Tathāgata*, from *tathā* 'in that manner' + *gata* 'gone'.

tathata /ˌtatəˈtɑː, ˌtaθəˈtɑː/ ▸ noun [mass noun] Buddhism the ultimate nature of all things, as expressed in phenomena but inexpressible in language. Compare with SUNYATA.
– ORIGIN Pali, literally 'true state of things'.

Tati /ˈtati/, Jacques (1908–82), French film director and actor; born *Jacques Tatischeff*. He introduced the comically inept character Monsieur Hulot in *Monsieur Hulot's Holiday* (1953), seen again in films including the Oscar-winning *Mon oncle* (1958).

Tatra Mountains /ˈtɑːtrə, ˈtatrə/ (also **the Tatras**) a range of mountains in eastern Europe on the Polish–Slovak border, the highest range in the Carpathians, rising to 2,655 m (8,710 ft) at Mount Gerlachovsky.

tatsoi /tatˈsɔɪ/ ▸ noun a kind of Chinese cabbage with glossy dark green leaves. ● *Brassica rapa* var. *rosularis*, family Cruciferae.
– ORIGIN Chinese *daat-choi*, from *daat-* 'sink, fall flat' + *choi* 'vegetable'.

tatterdemalion /ˌtatədɪˈmeɪljən/ ▸ adjective tattered or dilapidated.
▸ noun a person in tattered clothing.
– ORIGIN early 17th cent.: from TATTERS or TATTERED: ending unexplained.

tattered ▸ adjective old and torn; in poor condition: *an old woman in tattered clothes* | figurative *the tattered remnants of my pride.*
– ORIGIN Middle English (in the sense 'dressed in decoratively slashed or jagged clothing'): apparently originally from the noun *tatter* 'scrap of cloth' + -ED[1]; later treated as a past participle.

tatters ▸ plural noun irregularly torn pieces of cloth, paper, or other material.
– PHRASES **in tatters** torn in many places; in shreds: *wallpaper hung in tatters.* ■ destroyed; ruined: *the ceasefire was in tatters within hours.*
– DERIVATIVES **tattery** adjective.
– ORIGIN late Middle English (also in the singular meaning 'scrap of cloth'): from Old Norse *tǫtrar* 'rags'.

T

tattersall /ˈtatəs(ə)l, -sɔːl/ (also **tattersall check**) ▸ noun a woollen fabric with a pattern of coloured checks and intersecting lines, resembling a tartan.
– ORIGIN late 19th cent.: named after TATTERSALLS, by association with the traditional design of horse blankets.

Tattersalls /ˈtatəsɔːlz/ an English firm of horse auctioneers founded in 1776 by the horseman Richard Tattersall (1724–95).

tattie ▸ noun informal, chiefly Scottish a potato.
– ORIGIN late 18th cent.: alteration.

tatting ▸ noun [mass noun] a kind of knotted lace made by hand with a small shuttle, used chiefly for trimming. ■ the process of making knotted lace with a small shuttle.
– ORIGIN mid 19th cent.: of unknown origin.

tattle ▸ noun [mass noun] gossip; idle talk.
▸ verb [no obj.] gossip idly. ■ chiefly N. Amer. report another's wrongdoing; tell tales.
– ORIGIN late 15th cent. (in the sense 'falter, stammer', also 'make meaningless sounds', referring to a small child): from Middle Flemish *tatelen*, *tateren*, of imitative origin.

tattler ▸ noun **1** a person who engages in gossip or who tells tales.
2 a migratory sandpiper with mainly grey plumage, breeding in NW Canada or eastern Siberia. ● Genus *Heteroscelus*, family Scolopacidae: two species, in particular the **wandering tattler** (*H. incanus*) of Canada.

tattletale US ▸ noun a person, especially a child, who reveals secrets or informs on others; a telltale.
▸ verb [no obj.] reveal someone's secrets; tell tales.

tattoo[1] ▸ noun (pl. **tattoos**) an evening drum or bugle signal recalling soldiers to their quarters. ■ Brit. an entertainment consisting of music, marching, and the performance of displays and exercises by military personnel. ■ a rhythmic tapping or drumming.
– ORIGIN mid 17th cent. (originally as *tap-too*) from Dutch *taptoe!*, literally 'close the tap (of the cask)!'

tattoo[2] ▸ verb (**tattoos, tattooing, tattooed**) [with obj.] mark (a part of the body) with an indelible design by inserting pigment into punctures in the skin: *his cheek was tattooed with a winged fist.* ■ make (an indelible design) on a part of the body by inserting pigment into punctures in the skin: *he has a heart tattooed on his left hand.*
▸ noun (pl. **tattoos**) a design made by tattooing.
– DERIVATIVES **tattooer** noun, **tattooist** noun.
– ORIGIN mid 18th cent.: from Tahitian, Tongan, and Samoan *ta-tau* or Marquesan *ta-tu*.

tatty ▸ adjective (**tattier, tattiest**) informal worn and shabby; in poor condition: *tatty upholstered furniture.* ■ of poor quality: *the generally tatty output of the current Celtic revival.*
– DERIVATIVES **tattily** adverb, **tattiness** noun.
– ORIGIN early 16th cent. (originally Scots, in the sense 'tangled, matted, shaggy'): apparently ultimately related to Old English *tættec* 'rag', of Germanic origin; compare with TATTERED.

tau /tɔː, taʊ/ ▸ noun the nineteenth letter of the Greek alphabet (Τ, τ), transliterated as 't'. ■ (**Tau**) [followed by Latin genitive] Astronomy the nineteenth star in a constellation: *Tau Ceti.* ■ (in full **tau particle** or **tau lepton**) Physics an unstable subatomic particle of the lepton class, with a charge of −1 and a mass roughly 3,500 times that of the electron.
– ORIGIN Greek.

tau cross ▸ noun a T-shaped cross.

taught past and past participle of TEACH.

tau neutrino ▸ noun Physics a neutrino of the type associated with the tau particle.

taunt ▸ noun a remark made in order to anger, wound, or provoke someone.
▸ verb [with obj.] provoke or challenge (someone) with insulting remarks: *pupils began taunting her about her weight* | (as adj. **taunting**) *taunting comments.* ■ reproach (someone) with something in a contemptuous way: *she had taunted him with going to another man.*
– DERIVATIVES **taunter** noun, **tauntingly** adverb.
– ORIGIN early 16th cent.: from French *tant pour tant* 'like for like, tit for tat', from *tant* 'so much', from Latin *tantum*, neuter of *tantus*. An early use of the verb was 'exchange banter'.

Taunton /ˈtɔːntən/ the county town of Somerset, in SW England; pop. 61,000 (est. 2009).

tau particle ▸ noun see TAU.

taupe /təʊp/ ▸ noun [mass noun] grey with a tinge of brown: [as modifier] *a taupe overcoat.*
– ORIGIN early 20th cent.: from French, literally 'mole, moleskin', from Latin *talpa*.

Taupo, Lake /ˈtaʊpəʊ/ the largest lake of New Zealand, in the centre of the North Island. The town of Taupo is situated on its northern shore. Maori name **Taupomoana**.

Tauranga /taʊˈraŋə/ a port on the Bay of Plenty in the North Island of New Zealand; pop. 103,632 (2006).

taurine[1] /ˈtɔːriːn/ ▸ noun [mass noun] Biochemistry an amino acid containing sulphur and important in the metabolism of fats. ● Chem. formula: $NH_2CH_2CH_2SO_3H$.
– ORIGIN mid 19th cent.: from Greek *tauros* 'bull' (because it was originally obtained from ox bile) + -INE[4].

taurine[2] /ˈtɔːrʌɪn/ ▸ adjective of or like a bull. ■ relating to bullfighting: *taurine skill.*
– ORIGIN early 17th cent.: from Latin *taurinus*, from *taurus* 'bull'.

taurocholate /tɔːˈrɒkəleɪt/ ▸ noun Chemistry a salt or ester of taurocholic acid.

taurocholic acid /ˌtɔːrə(ʊ)ˈkɒlɪk/ ▸ noun [mass noun] Biochemistry an acid formed by the combination of taurine with cholic acid, occurring in bile.
– ORIGIN mid 19th cent.: from Greek *tauros* 'bull' + *kholē* 'bile' + -IC.

tauromachy /tɔːˈrɒməki/ ▸ noun (pl. **tauromachies**) [mass noun] rare bullfighting. ■ [count noun] a bullfight.
– ORIGIN mid 19th cent.: from Greek *tauromakhia*, from *tauros* 'bull' + *makhē* 'battle'.

Taurus /ˈtɔːrəs/ **1** Astronomy a constellation (the Bull), said to represent a bull that was tamed by Jason. Its many bright stars include Aldebaran (the bull's eye), and it contains the star clusters of the Hyades and the Pleiades, and the Crab Nebula.
2 Astrology the second sign of the zodiac, which the sun enters on about 21 April. ■ (**a Taurus**) a person born when the sun is in the sign of Taurus.
– DERIVATIVES **Taurean** /ˈtɔːrɪən, tɔːˈriːən/ noun & adjective (sense 2).
– ORIGIN Latin.

Taurus Mountains a range of mountains in southern Turkey, parallel to the Mediterranean coast. Rising to 3,734 m (12,250 ft) at Mount Aladaë, the range forms the southern edge of the Anatolian plateau.

taut ▸ adjective stretched or pulled tight; not slack: *the fabric stays taut without adhesive.* ■ (especially of muscles or nerves) tense; not relaxed. ■ (of writing, music, etc.) concise and controlled: *a taut text of only a hundred and twenty pages.* ■ (of a ship) having a disciplined and efficient crew.
– DERIVATIVES **tauten** verb, **tautly** adverb, **tautness** noun.
– ORIGIN Middle English *tought* 'distended', perhaps originally a variant of TOUGH.

tauto- /ˈtɔːtəʊ/ ▸ combining form same: *tautology.*
– ORIGIN from Greek *tauto*, contraction of *to auto* 'the same'.

tautog /tɔːˈtɒg/ ▸ noun a greyish-olive edible wrasse (fish) which occurs off the Atlantic coast of North America. ● *Tautoga onitis*, family Labridae.
– ORIGIN mid 17th cent.: from Narragansett *tautauog*, plural of *taut*.

tautology /tɔːˈtɒlədʒi/ ▸ noun (pl. **tautologies**) [mass noun] the saying of the same thing twice over in different words, generally considered to be a fault of style (e.g. *they arrived one after the other in succession*). ■ [count noun] a phrase or expression in which the same thing is said twice in different words. ■ Logic a statement that is true by necessity or by virtue of its logical form.
– DERIVATIVES **tautological** /-təˈlɒdʒɪk(ə)l/ adjective, **tautologically** adverb, **tautologist** noun, **tautologize** (also **tautologise**) verb, **tautologous** adjective.
– ORIGIN mid 16th cent.: via late Latin from Greek, from *tautologos* 'repeating what has been said', from *tauto-* 'same' + *-logos* (see -LOGY).

tautomer /ˈtɔːtəmə/ ▸ noun Chemistry each of two or more isomers of a compound which exist together in equilibrium, and are readily interchanged by migration of an atom or group within the molecule.
– DERIVATIVES **tautomeric** /-ˈmɛrɪk/ adjective, **tautomerism** /-tɔːˈtɒmərɪz(ə)m/ noun.
– ORIGIN early 20th cent.: blend of TAUTO- 'same' and ISOMER.

tautonym /ˈtɔːtə(ʊ)nɪm/ ▸ noun Botany & Zoology a scientific name in which the same word is used for both genus and species, for example *Vulpes vulpes* (the red fox).

Tavel /taˈvɛl/ ▸ noun [mass noun] a fine rosé wine produced at Tavel in the south of France.

Tavener, Sir John (Kenneth) (b.1944), English composer. His music is primarily religious and has been influenced by his conversion to the Russian Orthodox Church.

tavern ▸ noun chiefly archaic or N. Amer. an inn or public house.
– ORIGIN Middle English: from Old French *taverne*, from Latin *taberna* 'hut, tavern'. Compare with TABERNACLE.

taverna /təˈvɑːnə/ ▸ noun a small Greek restaurant or cafe.
– ORIGIN modern Greek, from Latin *taberna* (see TAVERN).

Taverner, John (*c.*1490–1545), English composer, an influential writer of early polyphonic church music.

taw[1] /tɔː/ ▸ verb [with obj.] make (hide) into leather without the use of tannin, especially by soaking it in a solution of alum and salt.
– DERIVATIVES **tawer** noun.

– ORIGIN Old English *tawian* 'prepare raw material for use or further processing', of Germanic origin; related to TOOL.

taw² /tɔː/ ▸ noun a large marble. ▪ [mass noun] a game of marbles. ▪ a line from which players throw marbles.
– ORIGIN early 18th cent.: of unknown origin.

tawa¹ /ˈtɑːwə, ˈtaʊə/ ▸ noun a tall New Zealand forest tree of the laurel family, which bears damson-like fruit. ● *Beilschmiedia tawa*, family Lauraceae.
– ORIGIN mid 19th cent.: from Maori.

tawa² /ˈtɑːwə/ ▸ noun a circular griddle used in South Asia, especially for cooking chapattis.
– ORIGIN from Hindi and Punjabi *tavā*.

tawdry ▸ adjective (**tawdrier**, **tawdriest**) showy but cheap and of poor quality: *tawdry jewellery*. ▪ sordid or unpleasant: *the tawdry business of politics*.
▸ noun [mass noun] archaic cheap and gaudy finery.
– DERIVATIVES **tawdrily** adverb, **tawdriness** noun.
– ORIGIN early 17th cent.: short for *tawdry lace*, a fine silk lace or ribbon worn as a necklace in the 16th–17th cents, contraction of *St Audrey's lace*: *Audrey* was a later form of *Etheldrida* (died 679), patron saint of Ely where tawdry laces, along with cheap imitations and other cheap finery, were traditionally sold at a fair.

tawny ▸ adjective (**tawnier**, **tawniest**) of an orange-brown or yellowish-brown colour: *tawny eyes*.
▸ noun [mass noun] an orange-brown or yellowish-brown colour: *pine needles turning from tawny to amber*.
– DERIVATIVES **tawniness** noun.
– ORIGIN Middle English: from Old French *tane*, from *tan* 'tanbark'; related to TAN¹.

tawny eagle ▸ noun a uniformly brown eagle found in Asia and Africa. ● *Aquila rapax*, family Accipitridae.

tawny owl ▸ noun **1** a common Eurasian owl with either reddish-brown or grey plumage and a familiar quavering hoot. ● *Strix aluco*, family Strigidae.
2 (**Tawny Owl**) informal (in the UK) the assistant adult leader of a pack of Brownie Guides, officially termed *Assistant Brownie Guider* since 1968.

tawny port ▸ noun [mass noun] a port wine made from a blend of several vintages matured in wood.

tawse /tɔːz/ (also **taws**) ▸ noun Scottish a thong with a slit end, formerly used in schools for punishing children.
– ORIGIN early 16th cent. (denoting a whip for driving a spinning top): apparently the plural of obsolete *taw* 'tawed leather', from TAW¹.

tax ▸ noun **1** a compulsory contribution to state revenue, levied by the government on workers' income and business profits, or added to the cost of some goods, services, and transactions.
2 [in sing.] a strain or heavy demand: ***a heavy tax on** the reader's attention*.
▸ verb [with obj.] **1** impose a tax on (someone or something): *the income will be **taxed at** the top rate*. ▪ pay tax on (something, especially a vehicle).
2 make heavy demands on (someone's powers or resources): *she knew that the ordeal to come must tax all her strength*.
3 confront (someone) with a fault or wrongdoing: *why are you **taxing** me **with** these preposterous allegations?*
4 Law examine and assess (the costs of a case).
– DERIVATIVES **taxable** adjective, **taxer** noun.
– ORIGIN Middle English (also in the sense 'estimate or determine the amount of a penalty or damages', surviving in sense 4 of the verb): from Old French *taxer*, from Latin *taxare* 'to censure, charge, compute', perhaps from Greek *tassein* 'fix'.

taxa plural form of TAXON.

tax allowance ▸ noun a sum to be deducted from gross income in the calculation of taxable income.

tax and spend ▸ noun [mass noun] [often as modifier] a political policy of increasing taxes in order to fund an increase in government spending: *an old-fashioned, left-of-centre tax-and-spend party*.

taxation ▸ noun [mass noun] the levying of tax. ▪ money paid as tax.
– ORIGIN Middle English (in the sense 'the assessment of a penalty or damages'; compare with TAX): via Old French from Latin *taxatio(n-)*, from *taxare* 'to censure, charge'.

tax avoidance ▸ noun [mass noun] the arrangement of one's financial affairs to minimize tax liability within the law. Compare with TAX EVASION.

tax bracket ▸ noun a range of incomes taxed at a given rate.

tax break ▸ noun informal a tax concession or advantage allowed by government.

tax code ▸ noun a code number representing the tax-free part of an employee's income, assigned by tax authorities for use by employers in calculating the tax to be deducted under the PAYE system.

tax credit ▸ noun a sum that can be offset against a tax liability.

tax-deductible ▸ adjective able to be deducted from taxable income or the amount of tax to be paid.

tax disc ▸ noun Brit. a circular label displayed on the windscreen of a motor vehicle, certifying payment of road tax.

tax evasion ▸ noun [mass noun] the illegal non-payment or underpayment of tax. Compare with TAX AVOIDANCE.

tax exile ▸ noun a person with a high income or considerable wealth who chooses to live in a country or area with low rates of tax.

tax-free ▸ adjective & adverb (of goods, income, etc.) exempt from tax: [as adj.] *a tax-free lump sum* | [as adv.] *your return is paid to you tax-free*.

tax haven ▸ noun a country or independent area where taxes are levied at a low rate.

taxi ▸ noun (pl. **taxis**) a motor vehicle licensed to transport passengers in return for payment of a fare and typically fitted with a taximeter. ▪ a boat or other means of transportation used in the same way as a taxi. ▪ (in South Africa) a light vehicle, especially a minibus, transporting passengers along a fixed route for a set fare but not operating to a timetable.
▸ verb (**taxis**, **taxiing**, **taxied**) [no obj., with adverbial of direction] **1** (of an aircraft) move slowly along the ground before take-off or after landing: *the plane taxies up to a waiting limousine*. ▪ [with obj.] (of a pilot) cause (an aircraft) to taxi.
2 take a taxi as a means of transport: *I would taxi home and sleep till eight*.
– ORIGIN early 20th cent.: abbreviation of *taxicab* or *taximeter cab* (see TAXIMETER).

taxicab ▸ noun a taxi.

taxi dancer ▸ noun chiefly N. Amer. a professional dance partner.

taxidermist /ˌtaksɪˈdəːmɪst/ ▸ noun a person who practises taxidermy.

taxidermy /ˈtaksɪˌdəːmi/ ▸ noun [mass noun] the art of preparing, stuffing, and mounting the skins of animals with lifelike effect.
– DERIVATIVES **taxidermal** adjective, **taxidermic** adjective, **taxidermically** adverb.
– ORIGIN early 19th cent.: from Greek *taxis* 'arrangement' + *derma* 'skin'.

taximeter ▸ noun a device used in taxis that automatically records the distance travelled and the fare payable.
– ORIGIN late 19th cent.: from French *taximètre*, from *taxe* 'tariff', from the verb *taxer* 'to tax' + *-mètre* '(instrument) measuring'.

taxing ▸ adjective physically or mentally demanding: *they find the work too taxing*.

tax inspector ▸ noun Brit. another term for INSPECTOR OF TAXES.

taxi rank (N. Amer. **taxi stand**) ▸ noun a place where taxis park while waiting to be hired.

taxis /ˈtaksɪs/ ▸ noun (pl. **taxes** /ˈtaksiːz/) **1** [mass noun] Surgery the restoration of displaced bones or organs by manual pressure alone.
2 Biology a motion or orientation of a cell, organism, or part in response to an external stimulus. Compare with KINESIS.
3 [mass noun] Linguistics the systematic arrangement of linguistic units (phonemes, morphemes, words, phrases, or clauses) in linear sequence.
– ORIGIN mid 18th cent. (in sense 1): from Greek, literally 'arrangement', from *tassein* 'arrange'. Sense 2 dates from the late 19th cent.

taxi squad ▸ noun American Football a group of players taking part in practices and available as reserves for the team.

taxiway ▸ noun a route along which an aircraft can taxi when moving to or from a runway.

tax loss ▸ noun Economics a loss that can be offset against taxable profit earned elsewhere or in a different period.

taxman ▸ noun (pl. **taxmen**) informal an inspector or collector of taxes. ▪ (**the taxman**) the government department that collects tax: *he denies conspiracy to cheat the taxman*.

taxol /ˈtaksɒl/ ▸ noun [mass noun] Medicine, trademark a compound, originally obtained from the bark of the Pacific yew tree, which has been found to inhibit the growth of certain cancers.
– ORIGIN 1970s: from Latin *taxus* 'yew' + -OL.

taxon /ˈtaksɒn/ ▸ noun (pl. **taxa** /ˈtaksə/) Biology a taxonomic group of any rank, such as a species, family, or class.
– ORIGIN 1920s: back-formation from TAXONOMY.

taxonomy /takˈsɒnəmi/ ▸ noun [mass noun] chiefly Biology the branch of science concerned with classification, especially of organisms; systematics. ▪ the classification of something, especially organisms: *the taxonomy of these fossils*. ▪ [count noun] a scheme of classification: *a **taxonomy** of smells*.
– DERIVATIVES **taxonomic** /-səˈnɒmɪk/ adjective, **taxonomical** adjective, **taxonomically** adverb, **taxonomist** noun.
– ORIGIN early 19th cent.: coined in French from Greek *taxis* 'arrangement' + *-nomia* 'distribution'.

taxpayer ▸ noun a person who pays taxes.
– DERIVATIVES **taxpaying** adjective.

tax point ▸ noun the date on which value added tax becomes chargeable on a transaction.

tax return ▸ noun a form on which a taxpayer makes an annual statement of income and personal circumstances, used by the tax authorities to assess liability for tax.

tax shelter ▸ noun a financial arrangement made to avoid or minimize taxes.

tax year ▸ noun a year as reckoned for taxation (in Britain reckoned from 6 April).

Tay the longest river in Scotland, flowing 192 km (120 miles) eastwards through Loch Tay, entering the North Sea through the Firth of Tay.

Tay, Firth of the estuary of the River Tay, on the North Sea coast of Scotland. It is spanned by the longest railway bridge in Britain, a structure opened in 1888 that has 85 spans and a total length of 3,553 m (11,653 feet); its predecessor collapsed in a gale in 1879 while a passenger train was crossing it.

tayberry ▸ noun (pl. **tayberries**) a dark red soft fruit produced by crossing a blackberry and a raspberry.
– ORIGIN named after the River TAY in Scotland, near where it was introduced in 1977.

Taylor¹, Dame Elizabeth (b.1932), American actress, born in England. Notable films include *National Velvet* (made when she was still a child in 1944), *Cleopatra* (1963), and *Who's Afraid of Virginia Woolf?* (1966), for which she won an Oscar. She has been married eight times, including twice to the actor Richard Burton.

Taylor², Jeremy (1613–67), English Anglican churchman and writer. Chaplain to Charles I during the English Civil War, he is now remembered chiefly for his devotional writings.

Taylor³, Zachary (1784–1850), American Whig statesman, 12th President of the US 1849–50. He became a national hero after his victories in the war with Mexico (1846–8).

Taylorism ▸ noun [mass noun] the principles or practice of scientific management and work efficiency as practised in a system known as the Taylor System.
– DERIVATIVES **Taylorist** noun & adjective.
– ORIGIN mid 19th cent.: from the name of Frederick W. *Taylor* (1856–1915), the American engineer who expounded the system, + -ISM.

Taylor's series ▸ noun Mathematics an infinite sum giving the value of a function $f(z)$ in the neighbourhood of a point a in terms of the derivatives of the function evaluated at a.
– ORIGIN early 19th cent.: named after Brook *Taylor* (1685–1731), English mathematician.

Taymyr Peninsula variant spelling of TAIMYR PENINSULA.

tayra /ˈtʌɪrə/ ▸ noun a large, agile tree-dwelling animal of the weasel family, with a short dark coat, native to Central and South America. ● *Eira barbara*, family Mustelidae.
– ORIGIN mid 19th cent.: from Tupi *taira*.

Tay–Sachs disease /teɪˈsaks/ ▸ noun [mass noun] an inherited metabolic disorder in which certain lipids accumulate in the brain, causing spasticity and death in childhood.
– ORIGIN early 20th cent.: from the names of Warren *Tay* (1843–1927), English ophthalmologist, and

T

Bernard *Sachs* (1858–1944), American neurologist, who described it in 1881 and 1887 respectively.

Tayside a former local government region in eastern Scotland, dissolved in 1996.

tazza /ˈtɑːtsə/ ▸ **noun** a shallow ornamental wine cup mounted on a foot.
– ORIGIN early 19th cent.: from Italian, from Arabic *ṭasa* 'bowl' (see TASS).

TB ▸ **abbreviation** ■ terabyte(s). ■ tubercle bacillus; tuberculosis.

Tb ▸ **abbreviation** terabyte(s).
▸ **symbol** the chemical element terbium.

TBA ▸ **abbreviation** to be announced (or arranged).

T-back ▸ **noun** a high-cut undergarment or swimming costume having only a thin strip of material passing between the buttocks. ■ a style of back on a bra or bikini top in which the shoulder straps meet before joining the horizontal strap below the shoulder blades.

T-bar ▸ **noun 1** a beam or bar shaped like the letter T. ■ (also **T-bar lift**) a type of ski lift in the form of a series of inverted T-shaped bars for towing two skiers at a time uphill. ■ [often as modifier] a T-shaped fastening on a shoe or sandal: *a pair of T-bar sandals*.
2 the horizontal line of the letter *T*.

TBC ▸ **abbreviation** to be confirmed.

Tbilisi /ˌtəbɪˈliːsi/ the capital of Georgia; pop. 1,100,000 (est. 2007). Former name (1845–1936) **TIFLIS**.

T-bill ▸ **noun** informal short for **TREASURY BILL**.

T-bone ▸ **noun** (also **T-bone steak**) a large choice piece of loin steak containing a T-shaped bone.
▸ **verb** [with obj.] N. Amer. informal crash head-on into the side of (another vehicle).

tbsp (also **tbs**) ▸ **abbreviation** (pl. **same** or **tbsps**) tablespoonful.

Tc ▸ **symbol** the chemical element technetium.

TCCB ▸ **abbreviation** (in the UK until 1997) Test and County Cricket Board.

TCD ▸ **abbreviation** Trinity College, Dublin.

TCDD ▸ **abbreviation** tetrachlorodibenzoparadioxin (see **DIOXIN**).

T-cell ▸ **noun** another term for **T-LYMPHOCYTE**.

tch /tʃ/ ▸ **exclamation** used to express irritation, annoyance, or impatience.

tchagra /ˈtʃagrə/ ▸ **noun** an African shrike (bird) that feeds mainly on the ground, typically having a brown back and black eyestripe. ● Genus *Tchagra*, family Laniidae: several species.
– ORIGIN modern Latin, perhaps imitative.

Tchaikovsky /ˌtʃʌɪˈkɒfski/, Pyotr (Ilich) (1840–93), Russian composer. Notable works include the ballets *Swan Lake* (1877) and *The Nutcracker* (1892), the First Piano Concerto (1875), the opera *Eugene Onegin* (1879), the overture *1812* (1880), and his sixth symphony, the 'Pathétique' (1893).

tchotchke /ˈtʃɒtʃkə/ (also **tsatske**) ▸ **noun** informal
1 N. Amer. a small object that is decorative rather than strictly functional; a trinket.
2 US a pretty girl or woman.
– ORIGIN 1960s: Yiddish.

TCM ▸ **abbreviation** traditional Chinese medicine.

T

TCP ▸ **noun** [mass noun] Brit. trademark a disinfectant and germicidal solution containing various phenols and sodium salicylate.
– ORIGIN 1930s: abbreviation of *trichlorophenyl*, part of the chemical name of one of the ingredients.

TCP/IP ▸ **abbreviation** Computing, trademark transmission control protocol/Internet protocol, used to govern the connection of computer systems to the Internet.

TD ▸ **abbreviation** ■ (in the Republic of Ireland) Teachta Dála, Member of the Dáil: *Tom Meaney TD*. ■ technical drawing. ■ (in the UK) Territorial (Officer's) Decoration. ■ American Football touchdown.

Te ▸ **symbol** the chemical element tellurium.

te (N. Amer. **ti**) ▸ **noun** (in tonic sol-fa) the seventh note of a major scale. ■ the note B in the fixed-doh system.
– ORIGIN mid 19th cent.: alteration of **SI**, adopted to avoid having two notes (*soh* and *si*) beginning with the same letter (see **SOLMIZATION**).

tea ▸ **noun** [mass noun] **1** a hot drink made by infusing the dried crushed leaves of the tea plant in boiling water. ■ the dried leaves used to make tea. ■ [usu. with modifier] a drink made from the infused leaves, fruits, or flowers of plants other than tea: *herbal tea* | [count noun] *fruit teas*. ■ W. Indian any hot drink, for example, coffee or cocoa.
2 (also **tea plant**) the evergreen shrub or small tree which produces tea leaves, native to southern and eastern Asia and grown as a major cash crop. ● *Camellia sinensis*, family Theaceae.
3 chiefly Brit. a light afternoon meal consisting typically of tea to drink, sandwiches, and cakes. ■ Brit. a cooked evening meal. See also **HIGH TEA**. ■ W. Indian breakfast, typically consisting of a hot drink and bread.
▸ **verb** (**teas, teaing, teaed** or **tea'd**) [no obj., with adverbial] archaic drink tea or take afternoon tea: *I teaed with Professor Herron*.
– PHRASES **not for all the tea in China** informal there is nothing at all that could induce one to do something. **tea and sympathy** informal kind and attentive behaviour towards someone who is upset or in trouble.
– ORIGIN mid 17th cent.: probably via Malay from Chinese (Min dialect) *te*; related to Mandarin *chá*. Compare with **CHAR**[3].

teabag ▸ **noun** a small porous sachet containing tea leaves or powdered tea, on to which boiling water is poured in order to make a drink of tea.

tea ball ▸ **noun** a hollow ball of perforated metal to hold tea leaves, over which boiling water is poured in order to make a drink of tea.

tea bread ▸ **noun** [mass noun] a type of cake, baked in the shape of a loaf, containing dried fruit that has been soaked in tea before baking.

tea break ▸ **noun** Brit. a short rest period during the working day, in which people typically drink a cup of tea or coffee.

teacake ▸ **noun** Brit. a light yeast-based sweet bun with dried fruit, typically served toasted and buttered.

tea ceremony ▸ **noun** an elaborate Japanese ritual of serving and drinking tea, as an expression of Zen Buddhist philosophy.

teach ▸ **verb** (past and past participle **taught**) **1** [with obj. and infinitive or clause] impart knowledge to or instruct (someone) as to how to do something: *she taught him to read* | *he taught me how to ride a bike*. ■ [with obj.] give information about or instruction in (a subject or skill): *he came one day each week to teach painting* | [with two objs] *she teaches me French*. ■ [no obj.] work as a teacher: *she teaches at the local high school*.
2 [with obj. and clause] cause (someone) to learn or understand something by example or experience: *she'd been taught that it paid to be passive* | *my upbringing taught me never to be disrespectful to elders*. ■ [with obj.] encourage someone to accept (something) as a fact or principle: *the philosophy teaches self-control*. ■ informal make (someone) less inclined to do something: *'I'll teach you to forget my tea,' he said, and gave me six with his cane*.
▸ **noun** informal a teacher.
– PHRASES **teach someone a lesson** see **LESSON**. **teach school** US be a schoolteacher.
– ORIGIN Old English *tǣcan* 'show, present, point out', of Germanic origin; related to **TOKEN**, from an Indo-European root shared by Greek *deiknunai* 'show', *deigma* 'sample'.

> **USAGE** The verbs **teach** and **learn** do not have the same meaning and should not be used interchangeably: see **USAGE** at **LEARN**.

teachable ▸ **adjective 1** (of a person) able to learn by being taught.
2 (of a subject) able to be taught.
– DERIVATIVES **teachability** noun, **teachableness** noun.

teacher ▸ **noun** a person who teaches, especially in a school.
– DERIVATIVES **teacherly** adjective.

teacherage /ˈtiːtʃərɪdʒ/ ▸ **noun** N. Amer. a house or lodgings provided for a teacher by a school.

tea chest ▸ **noun** Brit. a light metal-lined wooden box in which tea is transported.

teach-in ▸ **noun** informal an informal lecture and discussion or series of lectures on a subject of public interest.

teaching ▸ **noun 1** [mass noun] the occupation, profession, or work of a teacher.
2 (**teachings**) ideas or principles taught by an authority: *the teachings of the Koran*.

teaching fellow ▸ **noun** a postgraduate student who carries out teaching or laboratory duties in return for accommodation, tuition, or expenses.

teaching hospital ▸ **noun** a hospital that is affiliated to a medical school, in which medical students receive practical training.

teaching machine ▸ **noun** a machine or computer that gives instruction to a pupil according to a program, reacting to their responses.

Teachta Dála /ˌtjɒxtə ˈdɔːlə/, Irish /ˌtʲaxtə ˈdɑːlə/ (abbrev.: **TD**) ▸ **noun** (pl. **Teachtai** /-ti/) (in the Republic of Ireland) a member of the Dáil or lower house of Parliament.
– ORIGIN Irish.

tea cloth ▸ **noun** a tea towel.

tea cosy ▸ **noun** a thick or padded cover placed over a teapot to keep the tea hot.

teacup ▸ **noun** a cup from which tea is drunk. ■ an amount held by a teacup, about 150 ml.
– DERIVATIVES **teacupful** noun (pl. **teacupfuls**).

tea dance ▸ **noun** an occasion consisting of afternoon tea with dancing, originating in 19th-century society.

tea garden ▸ **noun 1** a garden in which tea and other refreshments are served to the public.
2 a tea plantation.

tea gown ▸ **noun** a long, loose-fitting dress, typically made of fine fabric and lace-trimmed, worn at afternoon tea and popular in the late 19th and early 20th centuries.

teahead ▸ **noun** US informal, dated a habitual user of cannabis.

teahouse ▸ **noun** a place serving tea and other refreshments.

teak ▸ **noun 1** [mass noun] hard durable timber used in shipbuilding and for making furniture.
2 the large deciduous tree native to India and SE Asia which yields teak. ● *Tectona grandis*, family Verbenaceae.
– ORIGIN late 17th cent.: from Portuguese *teca*, from Tamil and Malayalam *tēkku*.

tea kettle ▸ **noun** a metal container with a lid, spout, and handle, used for boiling water.

teal ▸ **noun** (pl. **same** or **teals**) a small freshwater duck, typically with a greenish band on the wing that is most prominent in flight. ● Genus *Anas*, family Anatidae: several species, in particular the common Eurasian and Canadian (**green-winged**) **teal** (*A. crecca*).
■ (also **teal blue**) [mass noun] a dark greenish-blue colour.
– ORIGIN Middle English: of unknown origin; related to Dutch *teling*.

tea lady ▸ **noun** Brit. a woman employed to make and serve tea in a workplace.

tea leaf ▸ **noun 1** (**tea leaves**) dried leaves of tea, especially after infusion in tea-making or as dregs.
2 Brit. rhyming slang a thief.

tea light ▸ **noun** a small, squat candle in a metal case, used for decoration or within a stand to keep food or drink warm.

team ▸ **noun** [treated as sing. or pl.] a group of players forming one side in a competitive game or sport.
■ two or more people working together: *a team of researchers*. ■ two or more animals, especially horses, in harness together to pull a vehicle.
▸ **verb 1** [no obj.] (**team up**) come together as a team to achieve a common goal: *he teamed up with the band to produce the disc*.
2 [with obj.] (usu. **team something with**) match or coordinate a garment with (another): *a pinstripe suit teamed with a crisp white shirt*.
3 [with obj.] harness (animals, especially horses) together to pull a vehicle: *the horses are teamed in pairs*.
– DERIVATIVES **teamer** noun [usu. in combination] *I was a third-teamer most of my life*.
– ORIGIN Old English *tēam* 'team of draught animals', of Germanic origin; related to German *Zaum* 'bridle', also to **TEEM**[1] and **TOW**[1], from an Indo-European root shared by Latin *ducere* 'to lead'.

teammate ▸ **noun** a fellow member of a team.

team ministry ▸ **noun** a group of clergy of incumbent status who minister jointly to several parishes under the leadership of a rector or vicar.

team player ▸ **noun** a person who plays or works well as a member of a team.

team spirit ▸ **noun** [mass noun] feelings of camaraderie among the members of a group, enabling them to cooperate and work well together.

teamster ▸ noun **1** N. Amer. a lorry driver. ▪ a member of the Teamsters Union, including lorry drivers, chauffeurs, and warehouse workers.
2 a driver of a team of animals.

team-teaching ▸ noun [mass noun] coordinated teaching by a team of teachers working together.

teamwork ▸ noun [mass noun] the combined action of a group, especially when effective and efficient.

tea oil ▸ noun [mass noun] an oil resembling olive oil obtained from the seeds of the sasanqua and related plants, used chiefly in China and Japan.

tea party ▸ noun a social gathering in the afternoon at which tea, cakes, and other light refreshments are served.

tea plant ▸ noun another term for TEA (sense 2 of the noun).

tea planter ▸ noun a proprietor or cultivator of a tea plantation.

teapot ▸ noun a pot with a handle, spout, and lid, in which tea is brewed and from which it is poured.

teapoy /ˈtiːpɔɪ/ ▸ noun a small three-legged table or stand, especially one that holds a tea caddy.
– ORIGIN early 19th cent.: from Hindi *tī-* 'three' + Urdu and Persian *pāī* 'foot', the sense and spelling influenced by TEA.

tear¹ /tɛː/ ▸ verb (past **tore**; past participle **torn**) **1** [with obj. and adverbial] pull (something) apart or to pieces with force: *I tore up the letter* | figurative *a nation torn asunder by political pressures.* ▪ remove by pulling forcefully: *he tore up the floorboards.* ▪ [with obj.] make a hole or split in (something) by pulling it or piercing it with a sharp implement: *she was always tearing her clothes.* ▪ make (a hole or split) in something by force: *the blast tore a hole in the wall.* ▪ [no obj.] come apart; rip: *the material wouldn't tear.* ▪ [with obj.] damage (a muscle or ligament) by overstretching it: *he tore a ligament playing squash.*
2 [no obj., with adverbial of direction] informal move very quickly in a reckless or excited manner: *she tore along the footpath on her bike.*
3 (**be torn**) be in a state of uncertainty between two conflicting options or parties: *he was torn between his duty and his better instincts.*
▸ noun a hole or split in something caused by it having been pulled apart forcefully.
– PHRASES **tear one's hair out** informal feel extreme desperation. **tear someone off a strip** (or **tear a strip off someone**) Brit. informal rebuke someone angrily. **that's torn it** Brit. informal used to express dismay when something unfortunate has happened to disrupt one's plans.
– PHRASAL VERBS **tear someone/thing apart** **1** destroy something, especially good relations between people: *a bloody civil war had torn the country apart.* **2** upset someone greatly: *stop crying—it's tearing me apart.* **3** criticize someone or something harshly. **tear oneself away** [often with negative] leave despite a strong desire to stay: *she couldn't tear herself away from the view.* **tear someone/thing down** **1** demolish something, especially a building. **2** US informal criticize or punish someone severely. **tear into 1** attack verbally: *she tore into him: 'Don't you realize what you've done to me?'* **2** make an energetic or enthusiastic start on: *a jazz trio are tearing into the tune with gusto.*
– DERIVATIVES **tearer** noun.
– ORIGIN Old English *teran*, of Germanic origin; related to Dutch *teren* and German *zehren*, from an Indo-European root shared by Greek *derein* 'flay'. The noun dates from the early 17th cent.

tear² /tɪə/ ▸ noun a drop of clear salty liquid secreted from glands in a person's eye when they cry or when the eye is irritated.
▸ verb [no obj.] US (of the eye) produce tears: *the freezing wind made her eyes tear.*
– PHRASES **in tears** crying: *he was so hurt by her attitude he was nearly in tears.* **without tears** (of a subject) presented so as to be learned or achieved easily: *tennis without tears.* [first used in the titles of books by F. L. Mortimer, such as *Reading without Tears* (1857) and *Latin without Tears* (1877).]
– DERIVATIVES **tear-like** adjective, **teary** adjective (**tearier**, **teariest**).
– ORIGIN Old English *tēar*, of Germanic origin; related to German *Zähre*, from an Indo-European root shared by Old Latin *dacruma* (Latin *lacrima*) and Greek *dakru*.

tearaway ▸ noun Brit. a person who behaves in a wild or reckless manner.

teardown ▸ noun US informal an act of completely dismantling something: *an engine teardown.* ▪ an act of demolishing a building and building a new one on the same plot: *every teardown has an impact on the look and feel of a community.* ▪ a building bought solely for this purpose: *a $2 million teardown.*

teardrop ▸ noun a single tear. ▪ [as modifier] shaped like a single tear: *a wardrobe with brass teardrop handles.*

tear duct ▸ noun a passage through which tears pass from the lachrymal glands to the eye or from the eye to the nose.

tearful ▸ adjective crying or inclined to cry: *a tearful infant* | *Stephen felt tearful.* ▪ causing tears; sad or emotional: *a tearful farewell.*
– DERIVATIVES **tearfully** adverb, **tearfulness** noun.

tear gas ▸ noun [mass noun] gas that causes severe irritation to the eyes, chiefly used in riot control to force crowds to disperse.
▸ verb (**tear-gas**) [with obj.] attack with tear gas: *he and his crew were tear-gassed.*

tearing ▸ adjective [attrib.] violent; extreme: *he did seem to be in a tearing hurry* | *the tearing wind.*

tear-jerker ▸ noun informal a sentimental story, film, or song, calculated to evoke sadness or sympathy.
– DERIVATIVES **tear-jerking** noun & adjective.

tearless ▸ adjective not crying: *Mary watched in tearless silence as the coffin was lowered.*
– DERIVATIVES **tearlessly** adverb, **tearlessness** noun.

tear-off ▸ adjective denoting something that is removed by being torn off, typically along a perforated line: *please complete the tear-off slip.*

tea room ▸ noun **1** a small restaurant or cafe where tea and other light refreshments are served.
2 S. African dated a shop selling sweets, cigarettes, newspapers, and perishable goods.
3 N. Amer. informal a public toilet used as a meeting place by homosexuals.

tea rose ▸ noun a garden rose with flowers that are typically pale yellow with a pink tinge and have a delicate scent said to resemble that of tea. ● Cultivars of the Chinese hybrid *Rosa × odorata*.

tear sheet ▸ noun a page that can be or has been removed from a newspaper, magazine, or book for use separately.

tear-stained ▸ adjective wet with tears: *I looked at the man's tear-stained face.*

tease ▸ verb [with obj.] **1** make fun of or attempt to provoke (a person or animal) in a playful way: *I used to tease her about being so house-proud* | [no obj.] *she was just teasing* | (as adj. **teasing**) *teasing comments.* ▪ tempt (someone) sexually with no intention of satisfying the desire aroused.
2 [with obj. and adverbial of direction] gently pull or comb (tangled wool, hair, etc.) into separate strands: *she was teasing out the curls into her usual hairstyle.* ▪ (**tease something out**) find something out from a mass of irrelevant information: *a historian who tries to tease out the truth.* ▪ chiefly N. Amer. backcomb (hair) in order to make it appear fuller. ▪ archaic comb (the surface of woven cloth) to raise a nap.
▸ noun **1** informal a person who makes fun of someone playfully or unkindly. ▪ a person who tempts someone sexually with no intention of satisfying the desire aroused.
2 [in sing.] an act of teasing someone: *she couldn't resist a gentle tease.*
– DERIVATIVES **teasingly** adverb.
– ORIGIN Old English *tǣsan* (in sense 2 of the verb), of West Germanic origin; related to Dutch *teezen* and German dialect *zeisen*, also to TEASEL. Sense 1 is a development of the earlier and more serious 'irritate by annoying actions' (early 17th cent.), a figurative use of the word's original sense.

teasel (also **teazle** or **teazel**) ▸ noun a tall prickly Eurasian plant with spiny purple flower heads. ● Genus *Dipsacus*, family Dipsacaceae: several species, including **fuller's teasel**.
▪ a large dried head from a teasel, or a device serving as a substitute for one of these, used in the textile industry to raise a nap on woven cloth.
▸ verb [with obj.] (often as noun **teaseling**) chiefly archaic raise a nap on (cloth) with or as if with teasels.
– ORIGIN Old English *tǣsl, tǣsel*, of West Germanic origin; related to TEASE.

teaser ▸ noun **1** informal a tricky question or task.
2 a person who makes fun of or provokes others in a playful or unkind way. ▪ a person who tempts someone sexually with no intention of satisfying the desire aroused. ▪ an inferior stallion or ram used to excite mares or ewes before they are served by the stud animal.
3 a short introductory advertisement for a product that stimulates interest by remaining cryptic.
4 Fishing a lure or bait trailed behind a boat to attract fish.

tea set ▸ noun a set of crockery for serving tea.

tea shop ▸ noun another term for TEA ROOM (sense 1).

Teasmade ▸ noun trademark an automatic tea-maker.

teaspoon ▸ noun a small spoon used typically for adding sugar to and stirring hot drinks or for eating some foods. ▪ (abbrev.: **tsp**) the amount held by a teaspoon, in the UK considered to be 5 millilitres when used as a measurement in cookery.
– DERIVATIVES **teaspoonful** noun (pl. **teaspoonfuls**).

tea strainer ▸ noun a small device incorporating a fine mesh for straining tea.

teat ▸ noun a nipple of the mammary gland of a female mammal, from which the milk is sucked by the young. ▪ Brit. a thing resembling a teat or nipple, especially a perforated plastic bulb by which an infant or young animal can suck milk from a bottle.
– ORIGIN Middle English (superseding earlier TIT²): from Old French *tete*, probably of Germanic origin.

teatime ▸ noun chiefly Brit. the time in the afternoon when tea is traditionally served.

tea towel ▸ noun chiefly Brit. a cloth for drying washed crockery, cutlery, and glasses.

tea tray ▸ noun a tray from which tea is served.

tea tree ▸ noun **1** (also **ti tree**) an Australasian flowering shrub or small tree whose leaves are sometimes used for tea. Some species yield an oil valued for its antiseptic properties. ● Genera *Leptospermum* and *Melaleuca*, family Myrtaceae: several species, in particular *Melaleuca alternifolia*, whose leaves yield an essential oil.
2 (also **Duke of Argyll's tea tree**) an ornamental boxthorn native to the Mediterranean. ● *Lycium barbarum*, family Solanaceae.

teazle (also **teazel**) ▸ noun variant spelling of TEASEL.

Tebet /ˈtɛbɛt/ (also **Tevet**) ▸ noun (in the Jewish calendar) the fourth month of the civil and tenth of the religious year, usually coinciding with parts of December and January.
– ORIGIN from Hebrew *ṭēḇēṯ*.

tec ▸ noun informal, dated a detective.
– ORIGIN late 19th cent.: abbreviation.

tech (also **tec**) ▸ noun informal **1** Brit. a technical college.
2 [mass noun] technology. See also HIGH-TECH, LOW-TECH. ▪ [count noun] a technician.
– ORIGIN early 20th cent. (originally US): abbreviation.

techie /ˈtɛki/ (also **techy**) ▸ noun (pl. **techies**) informal a person who is expert in or enthusiastic about technology, especially computing.
– ORIGIN 1960s: from TECH + -IE. First recorded as a US slang term for a technical college student, the word was later used as British service slang, denoting a technician. The current sense dates from the 1980s.

technetium /tɛkˈniːʃɪəm/ ▸ noun [mass noun] the chemical element of atomic number 43, a radioactive metal. Technetium was the first element to be created artificially, in 1937, by bombarding molybdenum with deuterons. (Symbol: **Tc**)
– ORIGIN 1940s: modern Latin, from Greek *tekhnētos* 'artificial', from *tekhnasthai* 'make by art', from *tekhnē* 'art'.

technic ▸ noun **1** chiefly N. Amer. technique.
2 (**technics**) [treated as sing. or pl.] technical terms, details, and methods; technology.
– DERIVATIVES **technicist** noun.
– ORIGIN early 17th cent. (as an adjective in the sense 'to do with art or an art'): from Latin *technicus*, from Greek *tekhnikos*, from *tekhnē* 'art'. The noun dates from the 19th cent.

technical ▸ adjective **1** relating to a particular subject, art, or craft, or its techniques: *technical terms.* ▪ (especially of a book or article) requiring special knowledge to be understood: *a technical report.*
2 involving or concerned with applied and industrial sciences: *an important technical achievement.*
3 resulting from mechanical failure: *a technical fault.*
4 according to a strict application or interpretation of the law or rules: *the arrest was a technical violation of the treaty.*
▸ noun chiefly N. Amer. a small truck with a machine gun mounted on the back. ▪ a gunman who rides in such a truck.

T

technical area ▶ noun Soccer a designated area around a team's dugout, from where a coach or manager may give instructions to players on the field.

technical college ▶ noun a college of further education providing courses in a range of practical subjects, such as information technology, applied sciences, engineering, agriculture, and secretarial skills.

technical drawing ▶ noun [mass noun] the practice or skill of delineating objects in a precise way using certain techniques of draughtsmanship, as employed in architecture or engineering. ■ [count noun] a drawing produced in such a way.

technical foul ▶ noun Basketball a foul which does not involve contact between opponents.

technicality ▶ noun (pl. **technicalities**) a point of law or a small detail of a set of rules, as contrasted with the intent or purpose of the rules: *their convictions were overturned on a technicality.* ■ (**technicalities**) the specific details or terms belonging to a particular field: *he has great expertise in the technicalities of the game.* ■ [mass noun] the state of being technical; the use of technical terms or methods: *the extreme technicality of the proposed constitution.*

technical knockout ▶ noun Boxing the ending of a fight by the referee on the grounds of a contestant's inability to continue, the opponent being declared the winner.

technically ▶ adverb **1** [usu. sentence adverb] according to the facts or exact meaning of something; strictly: *technically, a nut is a single-seeded fruit.*
2 with reference to the technique displayed: *a technically brilliant boxing contest.*
3 involving or regarding the technology available: *technically advanced tools.*

technical sergeant ▶ noun a rank of non-commissioned officer in the US air force, above staff sergeant and below master sergeant.

technical support ▶ noun [mass noun] Computing a service provided by a hardware or software company which provides registered users with help and advice about their products.

technician ▶ noun a person employed to look after technical equipment or do practical work in a laboratory. ■ an expert in the practical application of a science. ■ a person skilled in the technique of an art or craft.

Technicolor ▶ noun [mass noun] [often as modifier] trademark ■ (**technicolor**) (Brit. also **technicolour**) informal vivid colour: [as modifier] *a technicolor bruise.*
– DERIVATIVES **technicolored** adjective.
– ORIGIN early 20th cent.: blend of TECHNICAL and COLOR.

technicolor yawn ▶ noun informal, humorous an act of vomiting.

technikon /ˈtɛknɪkɒn/ ▶ noun (in South Africa) an institution offering technical and vocational education at tertiary level.
– ORIGIN Greek, noun use of the neuter of *tekhnikos* 'relating to skills'.

technique ▶ noun a way of carrying out a particular task, especially the execution or performance of an artistic work or a scientific procedure. ■ [mass noun] skill or ability in a particular field: *he has excellent technique* | [in sing.] *an established athlete with a very good technique.* ■ a skilful or efficient way of doing or achieving something: *tape recording is a good technique for evaluating our own communications.*
– ORIGIN early 19th cent.: from French, from Latin *technicus* (see TECHNIC).

T

techno ▶ noun [mass noun] a style of fast, heavy electronic dance music, typically with few or no vocals.
– ORIGIN 1980s: abbreviation of TECHNOLOGICAL.

techno- ▶ combining form relating to technology or its use: *technophobe.*
– ORIGIN from Greek *tekhnē* 'art, craft'.

technobabble ▶ noun [mass noun] informal incomprehensible technical jargon.

technocracy /tɛkˈnɒkrəsi/ ▶ noun (pl. **technocracies**) [mass noun] the government or control of society or industry by an elite of technical experts. ■ [count noun] an instance or application of technocracy. ■ [count noun] an elite of technical experts.
– ORIGIN early 20th cent.: from Greek *tekhnē* 'art, craft' + -CRACY.

technocrat ▶ noun an exponent or advocate of technocracy. ■ a member of a technically skilled elite.
– DERIVATIVES **technocratic** adjective, **technocratically** adverb.

technofear ▶ noun [mass noun] informal fear of using technological equipment, especially computers.

technological ▶ adjective relating to or using technology: *the quickening pace of technological change.*
– DERIVATIVES **technologically** adverb.

technology ▶ noun (pl. **technologies**) [mass noun] the application of scientific knowledge for practical purposes, especially in industry: *advances in computer technology* | [count noun] *recycling technologies.* ■ machinery and equipment developed from scientific knowledge. ■ the branch of knowledge dealing with engineering or applied sciences.
– DERIVATIVES **technologist** noun.
– ORIGIN early 17th cent.: from Greek *tekhnologia* 'systematic treatment', from *tekhnē* 'art, craft' + *-logia* (see -LOGY).

technology park ▶ noun a science park.

technology transfer ▶ noun [mass noun] the transfer of new technology from the originator to a secondary user, especially from developed to developing countries in an attempt to boost their economies.

technophile ▶ noun a person who is enthusiastic about new technology.
– DERIVATIVES **technophilia** noun, **technophilic** adjective.

technophobe ▶ noun a person who fears, dislikes, or avoids new technology.
– DERIVATIVES **technophobia** noun, **technophobic** adjective.

technopreneur /ˌtɛknəʊprəˈnəː, ˈtɛknəʊprənəː/ ▶ noun (especially in South and SE Asia) a person who sets up a business concerned with computers or similar technology.
– ORIGIN 1990s: blend of TECHNO- and ENTREPRENEUR.

technospeak ▶ noun another term for TECHNOBABBLE.

technostress ▶ noun [mass noun] informal stress or psychosomatic illness caused by working with computer technology on a daily basis.

technostructure ▶ noun [treated as sing. or pl.] a group of technologists or technical experts having considerable control over the workings of industry or government.
– ORIGIN 1960s: coined by J. K. Galbraith.

techy ▶ noun variant spelling of TECHIE.

tectonic /tɛkˈtɒnɪk/ ▶ adjective **1** Geology relating to the structure of the earth's crust and the large-scale processes which take place within it. ■ (of a change or development) very significant or considerable: *the last decade has witnessed a tectonic shift in world affairs.*
2 relating to building or construction.
– DERIVATIVES **tectonically** adverb.
– ORIGIN mid 17th cent. (in sense 2): via late Latin from Greek *tektonikos*, from *tektōn* 'carpenter, builder'.

tectonics ▶ plural noun [treated as sing. or pl.] Geology large-scale processes affecting the structure of the earth's crust.

tectonophysics /tɛkˌtɒnə(ʊ)ˈfɪzɪks/ ▶ plural noun [treated as sing.] the branch of geophysics that deals with the forces that cause movement and deformation in the earth's crust.
– ORIGIN 1950s: from TECTONICS + PHYSICS.

tectonostratigraphic /tɛkˌtɒnə(ʊ)ˌstratɪˈgrafɪk/ ▶ adjective Geology relating to the correlation of rock formations with each other in terms of their connection with a tectonic event.
– ORIGIN 1970s: from TECTONICS + *stratigraphic* (see STRATIGRAPHY).

tectorial /tɛkˈtɔːrɪəl/ ▶ adjective Anatomy forming a covering. ■ denoting the membrane covering the organ of Corti in the inner ear.
– ORIGIN late 19th cent.: from Latin *tectorium* 'covering, a cover' (from *tegere* 'to cover') + -AL.

tectrices /ˈtɛktrɪsiːz, tɛkˈtrʌɪsiːz/ ▶ plural noun (sing. **tectrix** /-trɪks/) Ornithology the coverts of a bird.
– ORIGIN late 19th cent.: modern Latin, from Latin *tect-* 'covered', from the verb *tegere*.

tectum /ˈtɛktəm/ ▶ noun Anatomy the uppermost part of the midbrain, lying to the rear of the cerebral aqueduct. ■ (in full **optic tectum**) a rounded swelling (colliculus) forming part of this and containing cells involved in the visual system.
– ORIGIN early 20th cent.: from Latin, literally 'roof'.

Ted ▶ noun Brit. informal a Teddy boy.
– ORIGIN 1950s: abbreviation.

ted ▶ verb (**teds, tedding, tedded**) [with obj.] (often as noun **tedding**) turn over and spread out (grass, hay, or straw) to dry or for bedding.
– DERIVATIVES **tedder** noun.
– ORIGIN Middle English: from Old Norse *tethja* 'spread manure' (past tense *tadda*), related to *tad* 'dung'.

teddy ▶ noun (pl. **teddies**) **1** (also **teddy bear**) a soft toy bear.
2 a woman's all-in-one undergarment.
– ORIGIN early 20th cent.: from *Teddy*, pet form of the given name *Theodore*: in sense 1 alluding to *Theodore* ROOSEVELT[3], an enthusiastic bear-hunter.

Teddy boy ▶ noun Brit. (in the 1950s) a young man of a subculture characterized by a style of dress based on Edwardian fashion (typically with drainpipe trousers, bootlace tie, and hair slicked up in a quiff) and a liking for rock-and-roll music.
– ORIGIN from *Teddy*, pet form of the given name *Edward* (with reference to Edward VII's reign).

Te Deum /tiː ˈdiːəm, teɪ ˈdeɪəm/ ▶ noun a hymn beginning *Te Deum laudamus*, 'We praise Thee, O God', sung at matins or on special occasions such as a thanksgiving. ■ an expression of thanksgiving or exultation.
– ORIGIN Latin.

tedious ▶ adjective too long, slow, or dull; tiresome or monotonous: *a tedious journey.*
– DERIVATIVES **tediously** adverb, **tediousness** noun.
– ORIGIN late Middle English: from Old French *tedieus* or late Latin *taediosus*, from Latin *taedium* (see TEDIUM).

tedium ▶ noun [mass noun] the state or quality of being tedious: *the tedium of car journeys.*
– ORIGIN mid 17th cent.: from Latin *taedium*, from *taedere* 'be weary of'.

tee[1] ▶ noun see T[1] (sense 2).

tee[2] ▶ noun **1** a cleared space on a golf course, from which the ball is struck at the beginning of play for each hole. ■ a small peg with a concave head which can be placed in the ground to support a golf ball before it is struck from a tee. [late 17th cent. (originally Scots, as *teaz*): of unknown origin.]
2 a mark aimed at in bowls, quoits, curling, and other similar games. [late 18th cent. (originally Scots): perhaps the same word as TEE[1].]
▶ verb (**tees, teeing, teed**) [no obj.] Golf place the ball on a tee ready to make the first stroke of the round or hole. ■ [with obj.] place (something) in position, especially to be struck: *a wary man tees up the rest of the coconuts.*
– PHRASAL VERBS **tee off** begin a round or hole of golf by playing the ball from a tee. ■ informal make a start on something: *in November, the Society teed off with their inaugural meeting.* **tee someone off** N. Amer. informal make someone angry or annoyed: *Tommy was really teed off at Ernie.* [probably a euphemistic alteration of PEED OFF (see PEE).]

tee[3] ▶ noun informal a T-shirt.

tee-hee ▶ noun a giggle or titter, especially a derisive one: [as exclamation] *They won't mind what I get up to. Tee-hee!*
▶ verb (**tee-hees, tee-heeing, tee-heed**) [no obj.] titter or giggle, especially derisively.
– ORIGIN Middle English (as a verb): imitative.

teem[1] ▶ verb [no obj.] (**teem with**) be full of or swarming with: *every garden is teeming with wildlife* | (as adj. **teeming**) *she walked briskly through the teeming streets.*
– ORIGIN Old English *tēman, tīeman*, of Germanic origin; related to TEAM. The original senses included 'give birth to', also 'be or become pregnant', giving rise to 'be full of' in the late 16th cent.

teem[2] ▶ verb [no obj.] (of water, especially rain) pour down; fall heavily: *with the rain **teeming down** at the manor, Italy seemed a long way off.*
– ORIGIN Middle English: from Old Norse *tœma* 'to empty', from *tómr* 'empty'. The original sense was 'to empty', specifically 'to drain liquid from, pour liquid out'; the current sense (originally dialect) dates from the early 19th cent.

teen informal ▶ adjective [attrib.] relating to teenagers: *a teen idol.*
▶ noun a teenager.
– ORIGIN early 19th cent. (as a noun): abbreviation. The adjective dates from the 1940s.

-teen ▶ suffix forming the names of numerals from 13 to 19: *fourteen* | *eighteen.*
– ORIGIN Old English, inflected form of TEN.

teenage ▶ **adjective** [attrib.] denoting a person between 13 and 19 years old: *a teenage girl*. ■ relating to or characteristic of teenagers: *teenage magazines*.
– DERIVATIVES **teenaged** adjective.

teenager ▶ **noun** a person aged between 13 and 19 years.

WORD TRENDS See **YOUTH**.

teens ▶ **plural noun** the years of a person's age from 13 to 19: *they were both in their late teens*.
– ORIGIN late 17th cent.: plural of *teen*, independent usage of **-TEEN**.

teensy /ˈtiːnzi, -si/ ▶ **adjective** (**teensier**, **teensiest**) informal tiny: *a teensy bit of custard powder*.
– ORIGIN late 19th cent. (originally US dialect): probably an extension of **TEENY**.

teeny ▶ **adjective** (**teenier**, **teeniest**) informal tiny: *a teeny bit of criticism*.
– ORIGIN early 19th cent.: variant of **TINY**.

teenybopper ▶ **noun** informal a young teenager, typically a girl, who keenly follows the latest fashions in clothes and pop music.
– DERIVATIVES **teenybop** adjective.

teeny-weeny (also **teensy-weensy**) ▶ **adjective** informal very tiny: *doesn't he have a teeny-weeny twinge of conscience?*

teepee ▶ **noun** variant spelling of **TEPEE**.

Tees /tiːz/ a river of NE England which rises in Cumbria and flows 128 km (80 miles) generally southeastwards to the North Sea at Middlesbrough.

tee shirt ▶ **noun** variant spelling of **T-SHIRT**.

Teesside an industrial region in NE England around the lower Tees valley, including Middlesbrough.

teeter ▶ **verb** [no obj., usu. with adverbial] move or balance unsteadily; sway back and forth: *she teetered after him in her high-heeled sandals*. ■ (often **teeter between**) be unable to decide between different courses; waver: *she teetered between tears and anger*.
– PHRASES **teeter on the brink** (or **edge**) be very close to a difficult or dangerous situation.
– ORIGIN mid 19th cent.: variant of dialect *titter*, from Old Norse *titra* 'shake, shiver'.

teeter-totter N. Amer. or dialect ▶ **noun** a see-saw.
▶ **verb** [no obj.] teeter; waver.
– ORIGIN late 19th cent.: reduplication of **TEETER** or **TOTTER**[1].

teeth plural form of **TOOTH**.

teethe ▶ **verb** [no obj.] grow or cut milk teeth: (as noun **teething**) *it soothes the discomfort of teething*.
– ORIGIN late Middle English: from **TEETH**.

teething ring ▶ **noun** a small ring for an infant to bite on while teething.

teething troubles (also **teething problems**) ▶ **plural noun** short-term problems that occur in the early stages of a new project.

teetotal ▶ **adjective** choosing or characterized by abstinence from alcohol: *a teetotal lifestyle*.
– DERIVATIVES **teetotalism** noun.
– ORIGIN mid 19th cent.: emphatic extension of **TOTAL**, apparently first used by Richard Turner, a worker from Preston, in a speech (1833) urging total abstinence from all alcohol, rather than mere abstinence from spirits, advocated by some early temperance reformers.

teetotaller (US **teetotaler**) ▶ **noun** a person who never drinks alcohol.

teetotum /tiːˈtəʊtəm/ ▶ **noun** a small spinning top spun with the fingers, especially one with four sides lettered to determine whether the spinner has won or lost.
– ORIGIN early 18th cent. (as *T totum*): from *T* (representing *totum*, inscribed on the side of the toy) + Latin *totum* 'the whole' (stake). The letters on the sides (representing Latin words) were *T* (= *totum*), *A* (= *auferre* 'take away'), *D* (= *deponere* 'put down'), and *N* (= *nihil* 'nothing').

teevee ▶ **noun** non-standard spelling of **TV**.

teff /tɛf/ ▶ **noun** [mass noun] an African cereal which is cultivated almost exclusively in Ethiopia, used mainly to make flour. ● *Eragrostis tef*, family Gramineae.
– ORIGIN late 18th cent.: from Amharic *ṭēf*.

tefillin /tiːˈfɪliːn/ ▶ **plural noun** collective term for Jewish phylacteries.
– ORIGIN from Aramaic *tĕpillīn* 'prayers'.

TEFL /ˈtɛf(ə)l/ ▶ **abbreviation** teaching of English as a foreign language.

Teflon /ˈtɛflɒn/ ▶ **noun 1** trademark a tough synthetic resin made by polymerizing tetrafluoroethylene, chiefly used to coat non-stick cooking utensils and to make seals and bearings. Also called **POLYTETRAFLUOROETHYLENE**.
2 [as modifier] denoting someone whose reputation remains undamaged in spite of scandal or misjudgement: *acquittal earned him the nickname 'the Teflon Don'*.
– ORIGIN 1940s: from **TETRA-** 'four' + **FLUORO-** + *-on* on the pattern of words such as *nylon* and *rayon*.

teg ▶ **noun** a sheep in its second year.
– ORIGIN early 16th cent. (as a contemptuous term for a woman; later applied specifically to a ewe in her second year): perhaps related to Swedish *tacka* 'ewe'.

tegmen /ˈtɛgmɛn/ ▶ **noun** (pl. **tegmina**) Biology a covering structure or roof of an organ, in particular: ■ Entomology a sclerotized forewing serving to cover the hindwing in grasshoppers and related insects. ■ Botany the delicate inner protective layer of a seed. ■ (also **tegmen tympani**) Anatomy a plate of thin bone forming the roof of the middle ear, a part of the temporal bone.
– ORIGIN early 19th cent.: from Latin, 'covering', from *tegere* 'to cover'.

tegmentum /tɛgˈmɛntəm/ ▶ **noun** (pl. **tegmenta** /-ə/) Anatomy a region of grey matter on either side of the cerebral aqueduct in the midbrain.
– DERIVATIVES **tegmental** adjective.
– ORIGIN mid 19th cent.: from Latin, variant of *tegumentum* 'tegument'.

tegu /ˈtɛguː/ ▶ **noun** (pl. **same** or **tegus**) a large stocky lizard that has dark skin with pale cross-bands of small spots, native to the tropical forests of South America. ● Genus *Tupinambis*, family Teiidae: several species, in particular the **common tegu** (*T. teguixin*).
– ORIGIN 1950s: abbreviation of *teguexin*, from Aztec *tecoixin* 'lizard'.

Tegucigalpa /tɛˌguːsɪˈgalpə/ capital of Honduras; pop. 967,200 (est. 2008).

tegula /ˈtɛgjʊlə/ ▶ **noun** (pl. **tegulae** /-liː/) Entomology a small scale-like sclerite covering the base of the forewing in many insects.
– ORIGIN early 19th cent.: from Latin, literally 'tile', from *tegere* 'to cover'.

tegument /ˈtɛgjʊm(ə)nt/ ▶ **noun** chiefly Zoology the integument of an organism, especially a parasitic flatworm.
– DERIVATIVES **tegumental** adjective, **tegumentary** adjective.
– ORIGIN late Middle English (in the general sense 'a covering or coating'): from Latin *tegumentum*, from *tegere* 'to cover'.

Tehran /tɛːˈrɑːn/ (also **Teheran**) the capital of Iran, situated in the foothills of the Elburz Mountains; pop. 7,088,287 (2006). It replaced Isfahan as capital of Persia in 1788.

tehsil /tʌˈsiːl/ (also **tahsil**) ▶ **noun** an administrative area in parts of India.
– ORIGIN from Persian and Urdu *taḥsīl*, from Arabic, 'collection, levying of taxes'.

teichoic acid /tʌɪˈkəʊɪk/ ▶ **noun** [mass noun] Biochemistry a compound present in the walls of Gram-positive bacteria. It is a polymer of ribitol or glycerol phosphate.
– ORIGIN 1950s: *teichoic* from Greek *teikhos* 'wall' + **-IC**.

Teilhard de Chardin /ˌteɪɑː də ˈʃɑːdã/, French /tejaʀ də ʃaʀdɛ̃/, Pierre (1881–1955), French Jesuit philosopher and palaeontologist. He is best known for his theory, blending science and Christianity, that man is evolving mentally and socially towards a perfect spiritual state. The Roman Catholic Church declared his views were unorthodox and his major works (e.g. *The Phenomenon of Man*, 1955) were published posthumously.

tein /ˈteɪɪn/ ▶ **noun** (pl. **same** or **teins**) a monetary unit of Kazakhstan, equal to one hundredth of a tenge.
– ORIGIN Kazakh.

tej /tɛdʒ/ ▶ **noun** [mass noun] a kind of honey wine or mead, the national drink of Ethiopia.
– ORIGIN probably Amharic.

Tejano /tɛˈhɑːnəʊ/ ▶ **noun** (pl. **Tejanos**) a Mexican-American inhabitant of southern Texas. ■ [mass noun] a style of folk or popular music with elements from Mexican-Spanish vocal traditions and Czech and German dance tunes and rhythms, traditionally played by small groups featuring accordion and guitar.
– ORIGIN American Spanish, alteration of *Texano* 'Texan'.

Tejo /ˈtəʒu/ Portuguese name for **TAGUS**.

tekke /ˈtɛkeɪ/ ▶ **noun** (pl. **tekkes**) a monastery of dervishes, especially in Ottoman Turkey.
– ORIGIN Turkish.

tektite /ˈtɛktʌɪt/ ▶ **noun** Geology a small black glassy object found in numbers over certain areas of the earth's surface, believed to have been formed as molten debris in meteorite impacts and scattered widely through the air.
– ORIGIN early 20th cent.: coined in German from Greek *tēktos* 'molten' (from *tēkein* 'melt') + **-ITE**[1].

tel. ▶ **abbreviation** telephone.

telamon /ˈtɛləmən, -məʊn/ ▶ **noun** (pl. **telamones** /-ˈməʊniːz/) Architecture a male figure used as a pillar to support an entablature or other structure.
– ORIGIN early 17th cent.: via Latin from Greek *telamōnes*, plural of *Telamōn*, the name of a mythical hero.

telangiectasia /tɛˌlandʒɪɛkˈteɪzɪə/ (also **telangiectasis** /tɛˌlandʒɪˈɛktəsɪs/) ▶ **noun** [mass noun] Medicine a condition characterized by dilatation of the capillaries causing them to appear as small red or purple clusters, often spidery in appearance, on the skin or the surface of an organ.
– DERIVATIVES **telangiectatic** adjective.
– ORIGIN mid 19th cent.: modern Latin, from Greek *telos* 'end' + *angeion* 'vessel' + *ektasis* 'dilatation'.

Tel Aviv /ˌtɛl əˈviːv/ (also **Tel Aviv-Jaffa**) a city on the Mediterranean coast of Israel; pop. 392,500 (est. 2008) (with Jaffa). It was founded as a suburb of Jaffa by Russian Jewish immigrants in 1909 and named Tel Aviv a year later.

telco ▶ **noun** (pl. **telcos**) a telecommunications company.
– ORIGIN 1970s: abbreviation.

Tele /ˈtɛli/ ▶ **noun** trademark a Fender Telecaster electric guitar.

tele ▶ **noun** non-standard spelling of **TELLY**.

tele- /ˈtɛli/ ▶ **combining form 1** to or at a distance: *telekinesis*. ■ used in names of instruments used when operating over long distances: *telemeter*.
2 relating to television: *telecine*.
3 done by means of the telephone: *telemarketing*.
– ORIGIN from Greek *tēle-* 'far off'. Sense 2, sense 3 are abbreviations.

tele-ad ▶ **noun** an advertisement placed in a newspaper or magazine by telephone.

telebanking ▶ **noun** another term for **TELEPHONE BANKING**.

telecast ▶ **noun** a television broadcast.
▶ **verb** (past and past participle **telecast**) [with obj.] transmit by television: *the programme will be telecast simultaneously to nearly 150 cities*.
– DERIVATIVES **telecaster** noun.

telecentre ▶ **noun** another term for **TELECOTTAGE**.

telecine /ˈtɛlɪˌsɪni/ ▶ **noun** [mass noun] the broadcasting of cinema film on television. ■ equipment used in telecine broadcasting.

telecommunication ▶ **noun** [mass noun] communication over a distance by cable, telegraph, telephone, or broadcasting. ■ (**telecommunications**) [treated as sing.] the branch of technology concerned with telecommunication. ■ [count noun] formal a message sent by telecommunication.
– ORIGIN 1930s: from French *télécommunication*, from *télé-* 'at a distance' + *communication* 'communication'.

telecommute ▶ **verb** [no obj.] (usu. as noun **telecommuting**) work from home, making use of the Internet, email, and the telephone.
– DERIVATIVES **telecommuter** noun.

telecoms (also **telecomms**) ▶ **plural noun** [treated as sing.] telecommunications: *businesses such as telecoms or public relations* | [as modifier] (also **telecom**) *telecom companies*.

telecon ▶ **noun** informal a teleconference.

teleconference ▶ **noun** a conference with participants in different locations linked by telecommunication devices.
– DERIVATIVES **teleconferencing** noun.

teleconnection ▶ **noun** a causal connection or correlation between meteorological or other environmental phenomena which occur a long distance apart.

teleconverter ▶ **noun** Photography a camera lens designed to be fitted in front of a standard lens to increase its effective focal length.

telecottage ▸ noun a room or building, especially in a rural area, filled with computer equipment for the shared use of people living in the area.

teledu /ˈtɛlɪduː/ ▸ noun a stink badger having brownish-black fur with a white stripe along the top of the head and back, native to Sumatra, Java, and Borneo. ● *Mydaus javanensis*, family Mustelidae.
– ORIGIN early 19th cent.: from Javanese.

tele-evangelist ▸ noun variant of TELEVANGELIST.

telefacsimile ▸ noun another term for FAX[1].

telefax trademark ▸ noun [mass noun] the transmission of documents by fax. ■ [count noun] a document sent by fax. ■ [count noun] a fax machine.
▸ verb [with obj.] (usu. as adj. **telefaxed**) send (a message) by fax: *telefaxed bills of lading.*
– ORIGIN 1940s: abbreviation of TELEFACSIMILE.

teleferic /ˌtɛlɪˈfɛrɪk/ ▸ noun variant spelling of TÉLÉPHÉRIQUE.

telefilm ▸ noun a film made for or broadcast on television.

telegenic /ˌtɛlɪˈdʒɛnɪk/ ▸ adjective having an appearance or manner that is appealing on television: *his telegenic charm appears to be his major asset.*
– ORIGIN 1930s (originally US): from TELE- 'television' + -GENIC 'well suited to', on the pattern of *photogenic*.

telegram ▸ noun a message sent by telegraph and then delivered in written or printed form, used in the UK only for international messages since 1981.
– ORIGIN mid 19th cent.: from TELE- 'at a distance' + -GRAM[1], on the pattern of *telegraph*.

telegraph ▸ noun **1** [mass noun] a system for transmitting messages from a distance along a wire, especially one creating signals by making and breaking an electrical connection: *news came from the outside world by telegraph.* ■ [count noun] a device for transmitting messages by telegraph.
2 (also **telegraph board**) a board displaying scores or other information at a sports match or race meeting.
▸ verb [with obj.] send (someone) a message by telegraph: *I must go and telegraph Mama.* ■ send (a message) by telegraph: *she would rush off to telegraph news to her magazine.* ■ convey (an intentional or unconscious message), especially with facial expression or body language.
– DERIVATIVES **telegrapher** /ˈtɛlɪˌɡrɑːfə, tɪˈlɛɡrəfə/ noun.
– ORIGIN early 18th cent.: from French *télégraphe*, from *télé-* 'at a distance' + *-graphe* (see -GRAPH).

telegraphese ▸ noun [mass noun] informal the terse, abbreviated style of language used in telegrams.

telegraphic ▸ adjective **1** of or by a telegraph or telegram: *the telegraphic transfer of the funds.*
2 (especially of speech) omitting inessential words; concise.
– DERIVATIVES **telegraphically** adverb.

telegraphic address ▸ noun chiefly historical an abbreviated or other registered address for use in telegrams.

telegraphist ▸ noun a person skilled or employed in telegraphy.

telegraph key ▸ noun a button which is pressed to produce a signal when transmitting Morse code.

telegraph plant ▸ noun a tropical Asian plant of the pea family, whose leaves have a spontaneous jerking motion. It is sometimes grown as a curiosity under glass. ● *Codariocalyx motorius* (formerly *Desmodium gyrans*), family Leguminosae.

T

telegraph pole ▸ noun a tall pole used to carry telegraph or telephone wires above the ground.

telegraphy ▸ noun [mass noun] the science or practice of using or constructing communication systems for the transmission or reproduction of information.

Telegu /ˈtɛlɪɡuː/ ▸ noun variant spelling of TELUGU.

telekinesis /ˌtɛlɪkʌɪˈniːsɪs, -kɪˈniːsɪs/ ▸ noun [mass noun] the supposed ability to move objects at a distance by mental power or other non-physical means.
– DERIVATIVES **telekinetic** adjective.
– ORIGIN late 19th cent.: from TELE- 'at a distance' + Greek *kinēsis* 'motion' (from *kinein* 'to move').

Telemachus /tɪˈlɛməkəs/ Greek Mythology the son of Odysseus and Penelope.

Telemann /ˈteɪləman/, German /ˈteːlaman/, Georg Philipp (1681–1767), German composer and organist. His prolific output includes six hundred overtures, forty-four Passions, and forty operas.

telemark Skiing ▸ noun (also **telemark turn**) a turn, performed on skis to which only the toe of each boot is fixed, with the outer ski advanced and the knee bent: [as modifier] *telemark skiing.*
▸ verb [no obj., with adverbial] perform a telemark turn while skiing: *they went telemarking silently through the trees.*
– ORIGIN early 20th cent.: named after *Telemark*, a district in Norway, where it originated.

telemarketing ▸ noun [mass noun] the marketing of goods or services by means of telephone calls, typically unsolicited, to potential customers.
– DERIVATIVES **telemarketer** noun.

telematics ▸ plural noun [treated as sing.] the branch of information technology which deals with the long-distance transmission of computerized information.
– DERIVATIVES **telematic** adjective.
– ORIGIN 1970s: blend of TELECOMMUNICATION and INFORMATICS.

telemedicine ▸ noun [mass noun] the remote diagnosis and treatment of patients by means of telecommunications technology.

telemessage ▸ noun trademark a message sent by telephone or telex and delivered in written form, which replaced the telegram for inland messages in the UK in 1981.

telemeter /ˈtɛlɪmiːtə, tɪˈlɛmɪtə/ ▸ noun an apparatus for recording the readings of an instrument and transmitting them by radio.
▸ verb [with obj.] transmit (readings) to a distant receiving set or station.
– DERIVATIVES **telemetric** adjective, **telemetry** noun.

telemovie ▸ noun chiefly Austral. a feature film produced for distribution by a television channel.

telencephalon /ˌtɛlɛnˈsɛf(ə)lɒn, -ˈkɛf-, ˌtiːlɛnˈsɛf(ə)lɒn, -ˈkɛf-/ ▸ noun Anatomy the most highly developed and anterior part of the forebrain, consisting chiefly of the cerebral hemispheres. Compare with DIENCEPHALON.
– ORIGIN late 19th cent.: from TELE- + ENCEPHALON.

telenovela /ˈtɛlnəʊˌvɛlə/ ▸ noun (in Latin America) a television soap opera.
– ORIGIN Spanish.

teleological argument ▸ noun Philosophy the argument for the existence of God from the evidence of order, and hence design, in nature. Compare with COSMOLOGICAL ARGUMENT and ONTOLOGICAL ARGUMENT.

teleology /ˌtɛlɪˈɒlədʒi, ˌtiːl-/ ▸ noun (pl. **teleologies**) [mass noun] Philosophy the explanation of phenomena by the purpose they serve rather than by postulated causes. ■ Theology the doctrine of design and purpose in the material world.
– DERIVATIVES **teleologic** adjective, **teleological** adjective, **teleologically** adverb, **teleologism** noun, **teleologist** noun.
– ORIGIN mid 18th cent. (denoting the branch of philosophy that deals with ends or final causes): from modern Latin *teleologia*, from Greek *telos* 'end' + *-logia* (see -LOGY).

teleoperation ▸ noun [mass noun] the electronic remote control of machines.
– DERIVATIVES **teleoperate** verb, **teleoperator** noun.

teleost /ˈtɛlɪɒst, ˈtiːl-/ ▸ noun Zoology a fish of a large group that comprises all ray-finned fishes apart from the primitive bichirs, sturgeons, paddlefishes, freshwater garfishes, and bowfins. ● Division (or infraclass) Teleostei, subclass Actinopterygii: many orders.
– ORIGIN mid 19th cent.: from Greek *teleos* 'complete' + *osteon* 'bone'.

telepath /ˈtɛlɪpaθ/ ▸ noun a person with the ability to use telepathy.
– ORIGIN late 19th cent. (as a verb, meaning 'to use telepathy'): back-formation from TELEPATHY.

telepathic ▸ adjective supposedly capable of transmitting thoughts to other people and of knowing their thoughts; psychic: *a team of telepathic superheroes who can read each other's thoughts.* ■ relating to or characteristic of telepathy: *suppose that telepathic communication between human minds occurs.*
– DERIVATIVES **telepathically** adverb.

telepathy ▸ noun [mass noun] the supposed communication of thoughts or ideas by means other than the known senses.
– DERIVATIVES **telepathist** noun.

téléphérique /ˌtɛlɪfɛˈriːk/, French /telefeʁik/ (also **teleferic**) ▸ noun a cableway. ■ a mountain cable car.
– ORIGIN French.

telephone ▸ noun [mass noun] a system for transmitting voices over a distance using wire or radio, by converting acoustic vibrations to electrical signals: [as modifier] *a telephone call.* ■ [count noun] an instrument used as part of a telephone system, typically a single unit including a handset with a transmitting microphone and a set of numbered buttons by which a connection can be made to another such instrument.
▸ verb [with obj.] contact (someone) using the telephone: *he telephoned his wife at 9.30.* ■ [no obj.] make a telephone call: *she telephoned for help.* ■ send (a message) by telephone: *Barbara had telephoned the news.*
– PHRASES **on the telephone 1** using the telephone. **2** Brit. connected to a telephone system.
– DERIVATIVES **telephonic** adjective, **telephonically** adverb.

telephone banking ▸ noun [mass noun] a method of banking in which the customer conducts transactions by telephone.

telephone book ▸ noun a telephone directory.

telephone box ▸ noun Brit. a public booth or enclosure housing a payphone.

telephone directory ▸ noun a book listing the names, addresses, and telephone numbers of the people in a particular area.

telephone exchange ▸ noun a set of equipment that connects telephone lines during a call.

telephone kiosk ▸ noun see KIOSK.

telephone number ▸ noun a number assigned to a particular telephone and used in making connections to it. ■ (usu. **telephone numbers**) informal a number with many digits (used especially to represent a large sum of money): *we're talking telephone numbers in terms of sales.*

telephone operator ▸ noun chiefly US a person who works at the switchboard of a telephone exchange.

telephone tag ▸ noun [mass noun] informal a situation in which two people trying to communicate by telephone continually miss each other.

telephonist ▸ noun Brit. an operator of a switchboard.

telephony /tɪˈlɛf(ə)ni/ ▸ noun [mass noun] the working or use of telephones.

telephoto (also **telephoto lens**) ▸ noun (pl. **telephotos**) a lens with a longer focal length than standard, giving a narrow field of view and a magnified image.

teleplay /ˈtɛlɪpleɪ/ ▸ noun **1** a play written or adapted for television.
2 a screenplay for a television drama.

teleport ▸ verb (especially in science fiction) transport or be transported across space and distance instantly.
▸ noun **1** a centre providing interconnections between different forms of telecommunications, especially one which links satellites to ground-based communications. [1980s: originally the name of such a centre in New York.]
2 an act of teleporting.
– DERIVATIVES **teleportation** noun.
– ORIGIN 1950s: back-formation from *teleportation* (1930s), from TELE- 'at a distance' + a shortened form of TRANSPORTATION.

telepresence ▸ noun [mass noun] the use of virtual reality technology, especially for remote control of machinery or for apparent participation in distant events. ■ a sensation of being elsewhere, created by virtual reality technology.

teleprinter ▸ noun Brit. a device for transmitting telegraph messages as they are keyed, and for printing messages received.

teleprompter ▸ noun North American term for AUTOCUE.

telerecord ▸ verb [with obj.] record (a television programme) during transmission.

telerecording ▸ noun a recording of a television programme made while it is being transmitted.

telesales ▸ plural noun chiefly Brit. the selling of goods or services over the telephone.

telescope ▸ noun an optical instrument designed to make distant objects appear nearer, containing an arrangement of lenses, or of curved mirrors and lenses, by which rays of light are collected and focused and the resulting image magnified. ■ short for RADIO TELESCOPE.
▸ verb (with reference to an object made of concentric tubular parts) slide or cause to slide into itself, so that it becomes smaller. ■ [with obj.] crush (a vehicle) by the force of an impact. ■ [with obj.] condense or conflate so as to occupy less space or time: *a large portion of the past had to be telescoped and summarized for her.*

– ORIGIN mid 17th cent.: from Italian *telescopio* or modern Latin *telescopium*, from *tele-* 'at a distance' + *-scopium* (see -SCOPE).

telescopic ▸ adjective **1** relating to or made with a telescope. ▪ capable of viewing and magnifying distant objects. ▪ Astronomy visible through a telescope. **2** having or consisting of concentric tubular sections designed to slide into one another: *a telescopic umbrella*.
– DERIVATIVES **telescopically** adverb.

telescopic sight ▸ noun a small telescope used for sighting, typically mounted on a rifle.

Telescopium /ˌtɛlɪˈskəʊpɪəm/ Astronomy an inconspicuous southern constellation (the Telescope), south of Sagittarius.
– ORIGIN modern Latin.

teleshopping ▸ noun [mass noun] the ordering of goods by customers using a telephone or direct computer link.

teletex ▸ noun [mass noun] trademark an enhanced version of telex.
– ORIGIN 1970s: probably a blend of TELEX and TEXT.

teletext ▸ noun [mass noun] a news and information service in the form of text and graphics, transmitted using the spare capacity of existing television channels to televisions with appropriate receivers.

telethon ▸ noun a very long television programme, typically one broadcast to raise money for a charity.
– ORIGIN 1940s (originally US): from TELE- 'at a distance' + *-thon* on the pattern of *marathon*.

teletype ▸ noun trademark a kind of teleprinter. ▪ a message received and printed by a teleprinter.
▸ verb [with obj. and usu. with adverbial of direction] send (a message) by means of a teleprinter.

teletypewriter ▸ noun chiefly US a teleprinter.

televangelist (also **tele-evangelist**) ▸ noun chiefly N. Amer. an evangelical preacher who appears regularly on television to promote beliefs and appeal for funds.
– DERIVATIVES **televangelical** adjective, **televangelism** noun.

televiewer ▸ noun a person who watches television.
– DERIVATIVES **televiewing** noun & adjective.

televise ▸ verb [with obj.] (usu. as adj. **televised**) record for or transmit by television: *a live televised debate between the party leaders*.
– DERIVATIVES **televisable** adjective.
– ORIGIN 1920s: back-formation from TELEVISION.

television ▸ noun **1** [mass noun] a system for converting visual images (with sound) into electrical signals, transmitting them by radio or other means, and displaying them electronically on a screen. ▪ the activity, profession, or medium of broadcasting on television: *she has a job in television* | [as modifier] *television news*. ▪ television programmes: *Dan was sitting on the settee watching television* | *Norman was on television yesterday*.
2 (also **television set**) a device with a screen for receiving television signals.
– ORIGIN early 20th cent.: from TELE- 'at a distance' + VISION.

television tube ▸ noun another term for PICTURE TUBE.

televisual ▸ adjective relating to or suitable for television: *the world of televisual images*.
– DERIVATIVES **televisually** adverb.

telework ▸ verb [no obj.] (usu. as noun **teleworking**) another term for TELECOMMUTE.
▸ noun [mass noun] the practice of working from home, making use of the Internet, email, and the telephone.
– DERIVATIVES **teleworker** noun.

telex ▸ noun [mass noun] an international system of telegraphy with printed messages transmitted and received by teleprinters using the public telecommunications network. ▪ [count noun] a device used for telex. ▪ [count noun] a message sent by telex.
▸ verb [with obj.] communicate with (someone) by telex. ▪ send (a message) by telex.
– ORIGIN 1930s: blend of TELEPRINTER and EXCHANGE.

Telford[1] a town in Shropshire, west central England, to the east of Shrewsbury; pop. 161,700 (est. 2007). Named after Thomas Telford, it was designated a new town in 1963.

Telford[2], Thomas (1757–1834), Scottish civil engineer. He built hundreds of miles of roads, more than a thousand bridges (including the Menai suspension bridge 1819–26), and a number of canals, including the Caledonian Canal across Scotland (opened 1822).

telic /ˈtɛlɪk/ ▸ adjective (of an action or attitude) directed or tending to a definite end. ▪ Linguistics (of a verb, conjunction, or clause) expressing purpose.
– DERIVATIVES **telicity** noun.
– ORIGIN mid 19th cent.: from Greek *telikos* 'final', from *telos* 'end'.

Tell, William, a legendary hero of the liberation of Switzerland from Austrian oppression. He was required to hit with an arrow an apple placed on the head of his son, which he did successfully. The events are placed in the 14th century, but there is no evidence for a historical person of this name, and similar legends are of widespread occurrence.

tell[1] ▸ verb (past and past participle **told**) **1** [reporting verb] communicate information to someone in spoken or written words: [with obj. and clause] *I told her you were coming* | [with obj. and direct speech] *'We have nothing in common,' she told him* | [with obj.] *he's telling the truth* | [with two objs] *we must be told the facts*. ▪ [with obj. and infinitive] order or advise someone to do something: *tell him to go away*. ▪ [with obj.] relate (a story). ▪ [with obj.] reveal (information) to someone in a non-verbal way: *the figures tell a different story* | [with two objs] *the smile on her face told him everything*. ▪ [no obj.] divulge confidential or private information: *promise you won't tell*. ▪ [no obj.] (**tell on**) informal inform someone of the misdemeanours of: *friends don't tell on each other*.
2 [with clause] decide or determine correctly or with certainty: *you can tell they're in love* | *I couldn't tell if he believed me*. ▪ [with obj. and adverbial] perceive (the difference between one person or thing and another): *I can't tell the difference between margarine and butter*.
3 [no obj.] (of an experience or period of time) have a noticeable, typically harmful, effect on someone: *the strain of supporting the family was beginning to **tell on him***. ▪ (of a particular factor) play a part in the success or otherwise of someone or something: *lack of fitness **told against** him on his first run of the season*.
4 archaic count (the members of a group): *the shepherd had told all his sheep*.
▸ noun (especially in poker) an unconscious action that is thought to betray an attempted deception.
– PHRASES **as far as one can tell** judging from the available information. **I tell you** (or **I can tell you**) used to emphasize a statement: *that took me by surprise, I can tell you!* **I** (or **I'll**) **tell you what** used to introduce a suggestion: *I tell you what, why don't we meet for lunch tomorrow?* **I told you** (**so**) used to point out that one's warnings, although ignored, have been proved to be well founded. **tell one's beads** see BEAD. **tell someone's fortune** see FORTUNE. **tell it like it is** informal describe the true facts of a situation no matter how unpleasant they may be. **tell its own tale** (or **story**) be significant or revealing, without any further explanation being necessary: *the worried expression on Helen's face told its own tale*. **tell me about it** informal used as an ironic acknowledgement of one's familiarity with an unpleasant situation or experience described by someone else. **tell me another** informal used as an expression of incredulity. **tell something a mile off** see MILE. **tell that to the marines** see MARINE. **tell the time** (or N. Amer. **tell time**) be able to ascertain the time from reading the face of a clock or watch. **tell someone where to get off** (or **where they get off**) informal angrily dismiss or rebuke someone. **tell someone where to put** (or **what to do with**) **something** informal angrily reject something: *I told him what he could do with his diamond*. **that would be telling** informal used to convey that one is not prepared to divulge confidential information. **there is no telling** used to convey the impossibility of knowing what has happened or will happen: *there's no telling how she will react*. **to tell** (**you**) **the truth** used as a preface to a confession or admission of something: *to tell you the truth, he gave me the creeps*. **you're telling me** informal used to emphasize that one is already well aware of or in complete agreement with something.
– PHRASAL VERBS **tell someone off 1** informal reprimand or scold someone: *my parents told me off for coming home late*. **2** archaic assign a member of a group to a particular task: *there used to be a chap told off every day to fetch us beer*.
– DERIVATIVES **tellable** adjective.
– ORIGIN Old English *tellan* 'relate, count, estimate', of Germanic origin; related to German *zählen* 'reckon, count', *erzählen* 'recount, relate', also to TALE.

tell[2] ▸ noun Archaeology (in the Middle East) an artificial mound formed by the accumulated remains of ancient settlements.
– ORIGIN mid 19th cent.: from Arabic *tall* 'hillock'.

Tell el-Amarna /ˌtɛl ɛl əˈmɑːnə/ the site of the ruins of the ancient Egyptian capital Akhetaten, on the east bank of the Nile.

Teller /ˈtɛlə/, Edward (1908–2003), Hungarian-born American physicist. After moving to the US he worked on the first atomic reactor and the first atom bombs. Work under his guidance led to the detonation of the first hydrogen bomb in 1952.

teller ▸ noun **1** chiefly N. Amer. a person employed to deal with customers' transactions in a bank. ▪ N. Amer. a cashpoint machine. ▪ historical (in the UK) each of the four officers of the Exchequer responsible for the receipt and payment of moneys.
2 a person who tells something: *a foul-mouthed teller of lies*.
3 a person appointed to count votes, especially in a parliament.

tellin /ˈtɛlɪn/ ▸ noun a marine bivalve mollusc which lives buried in the sand siphoning detritus from the surface around its burrow. ● Family Tellinidae: *Tellina* and other genera.
– ORIGIN early 18th cent.: from Greek *tellinē*, denoting a kind of shellfish.

telling ▸ adjective having a striking or revealing effect; significant: *a telling argument against this theory*.
– DERIVATIVES **tellingly** adverb.

telling-off ▸ noun (pl. **tellings-off**) Brit. informal a reprimand.

telltale ▸ adjective [attrib.] revealing, indicating, or betraying something: *the telltale bulge of a concealed weapon*.
▸ noun **1** Brit. a person, especially a child, who reports others' wrongdoings or reveals their secrets.
2 a device or object that automatically gives a visual indication of the state or presence of something.

tellurate /ˈtɛljʊreɪt/ ▸ noun Chemistry a salt or ester of telluric acid.

tellurian /tɛˈljʊərɪən/ formal or literary ▸ adjective of or inhabiting the earth.
▸ noun an inhabitant of the earth.
– ORIGIN mid 19th cent.: from Latin *tellus, tellur-* 'earth' + -IAN.

telluric /tɛˈljʊərɪk/ ▸ adjective of the earth as a planet. ▪ of the soil.
– ORIGIN mid 19th cent.: from Latin *tellus, tellur-* 'earth' + -IC.

telluric acid ▸ noun [mass noun] Chemistry a crystalline acid made by oxidizing tellurium dioxide. ● Chem. formula: $Te(OH)_6$.

tellurite /ˈtɛljʊrʌɪt/ ▸ noun Chemistry a salt of the anion TeO_3^{2-}.

tellurium /tɛˈljʊərɪəm/ ▸ noun [mass noun] the chemical element of atomic number 52, a brittle, shiny, silvery-white semimetal resembling selenium and occurring mainly in small amounts in metallic sulphide ores. (Symbol: **Te**)
– DERIVATIVES **telluride** /ˈtɛljʊrʌɪd/ noun.
– ORIGIN early 19th cent.: modern Latin, from Latin *tellus, tellur-* 'earth', probably named in contrast to URANIUM.

telly ▸ noun (pl. **tellies**) Brit. informal term for TELEVISION.

telnet Computing ▸ noun [mass noun] a network protocol that allows a user on one computer to log in to another computer that is part of the same network. ▪ [count noun] a program that establishes a connection from one computer to another by means of telnet. ▪ [count noun] a link established using a telnet program.
▸ verb (**telnets, telnetting, telnetted**) [no obj.] informal log into a remote computer using a telnet program.
– ORIGIN 1970s: blend of TELECOMMUNICATION and NETWORK.

telogen /ˈtɛlə(ʊ)dʒ(ə)n, ˈtiːl-/ ▸ noun [mass noun] Physiology the resting phase of a hair follicle. Often contrasted with ANAGEN.
– ORIGIN 1920s: from Greek *telos* 'end' + -GEN.

telolecithal /ˌtiːlə(ʊ)ˈlɛsɪθ(ə)l, ˌtɛl-/ ▸ adjective Zoology (of an egg or egg cell) having a large yolk situated at or near one end.
– ORIGIN late 19th cent.: from Greek *telos* 'end' + *lekithos* 'egg yolk' + -AL.

telomerase ▸ noun Genetics the enzyme in a eukaryote that repairs the telomeres of the chromosomes so that they do not become progressively shorter during successive rounds of chromosome replication.

T

telomere /ˈtiːlə(ʊ)mɪə, ˈtɛl-/ ▸ **noun** Genetics a compound structure at the end of a chromosome.
– DERIVATIVES **telomeric** adjective.
– ORIGIN 1940s: from Greek *telos* 'end' + *meros* 'part'.

telophase /ˈtiːlə(ʊ)feɪz, ˈtɛl-/ ▸ **noun** [mass noun] Biology the final phase of cell division, between anaphase and interphase, in which the chromatids or chromosomes move to opposite ends of the cell and two nuclei are formed.
– ORIGIN late 19th cent.: from Greek *telos* 'end' + PHASE.

telos /ˈtɛlɒs/ ▸ **noun** (pl. **teloi** /-lɔɪ/) chiefly Philosophy or literary an ultimate object or aim.
– ORIGIN Greek, literally 'end'.

telson /ˈtɛls(ə)n/ ▸ **noun** Zoology the last segment in the abdomen, or a terminal appendage to it, in crustaceans, chelicerates, and embryonic insects.
– ORIGIN mid 19th cent.: from Greek, literally 'limit'.

Telstar the first of the active communications satellites (i.e. both receiving and retransmitting signals, not merely reflecting signals from the earth). It was launched by the US in 1962 and used in the transmission of television broadcasting and telephone communication.

Telugu /ˈtɛləguː/ (also **Telegu**) ▸ **noun** (pl. **same** or **Telugus**) **1** a member of a people forming the majority population of the south Indian state of Andhra Pradesh.
2 [mass noun] the Dravidian language of the Telugu, with about 72 million speakers.
▸ **adjective** relating to the Telugu or their language.
– ORIGIN from the name in Telugu, *teluṅgu*.

temazepam /təˈmeɪzɪpam, -ˈmazɪ-/ ▸ **noun** [mass noun] Medicine a compound of the benzodiazepine class used as a tranquillizer and short-acting hypnotic. ● A tricyclic compound; chem. formula: $C_{16}H_{13}ClN_2O_2$.
– ORIGIN 1970s: from *tem-* (of unknown origin) + AZO- + *epline* (suffix denoting an unsaturated seven-membered ring containing nitrogen) + AMIDE.

temblor /tɛmˈblɔː/ ▸ **noun** US an earthquake.
– ORIGIN late 19th cent.: from American Spanish.

Tembu ▸ **noun & adjective** variant spelling of THEMBU.

temenos /ˈtɛmənɒs/ ▸ **noun** (pl. **temenoi** /-nɔɪ/) Archaeology a piece of ground surrounding or adjacent to a temple; a sacred enclosure or precinct.
– ORIGIN early 19th cent.: from Greek, from the stem of *temnein* 'cut off'.

temerarious /ˌtɛməˈrɛːrɪəs/ ▸ **adjective** literary reckless; rash.
– ORIGIN mid 16th cent.: from Latin *temerarius* (from *temere* 'rashly') + -OUS.

temerity /tɪˈmɛrɪti/ ▸ **noun** [mass noun] excessive confidence or boldness; audacity: *no one had the temerity to question his conclusions.*
– ORIGIN late Middle English: from Latin *temeritas*, from *temere* 'rashly'.

Temesvár /ˈtɛmɛʃˌvɑːr/ Hungarian name for TIMIŞOARA.

Temne /ˈtɛmni/ ▸ **noun** (pl. **same** or **Temnes**) **1** a member of a people of Sierra Leone.
2 [mass noun] the Niger–Congo language of the Temne, the main language of Sierra Leone, with about 1 million speakers.
▸ **adjective** relating to the Temne or their language.
– ORIGIN the name in Temne.

T

temnospondyl /ˌtɛmnə(ʊ)ˈspɒndɪl/ ▸ **noun** a fossil amphibian of a large group that was dominant from the Carboniferous to the Triassic. ● Order (or grade) Temnospondyli: many families.
– ORIGIN early 20th cent.: from modern Latin *Temnospondyli* (plural), from Greek *temnein* 'to cut' + *spondulos* 'vertebra'.

temp¹ informal ▸ **noun** a temporary employee, typically an office worker who finds employment through an agency.
▸ **verb** [no obj.] work as a temporary employee.
– ORIGIN 1930s (originally US): abbreviation.

temp² ▸ **abbreviation** temperature.

temp. ▸ **abbreviation** in or from the time of: *a Roman aqueduct temp. Augustus.*
– ORIGIN from Latin *tempore*, ablative of *tempus* 'time'.

tempeh /ˈtɛmpeɪ/ ▸ **noun** [mass noun] an Indonesian dish made by deep-frying fermented soya beans.
– ORIGIN from Indonesian *tempe*.

temper ▸ **noun** **1** [in sing.] a person's state of mind seen in terms of their being angry or calm: *he rushed out in a very bad temper.* ■ a tendency to become angry easily: *I know my temper gets the better of me at times.* ■ an angry state of mind: *Drew had walked out in a temper* | [mass noun] *I only said it in a fit of temper.*
2 [mass noun] the degree of hardness and elasticity in steel or other metal.
▸ **verb** [with obj.] **1** improve the hardness and elasticity of (steel or other metal) by reheating and then cooling it. ■ improve the consistency or resiliency of (a substance) by heating it or adding particular substances to it.
2 act as a neutralizing or counterbalancing force to (something): *their idealism is tempered with realism.*
3 tune (a piano or other instrument) so as to adjust the note intervals correctly.
– PHRASES **keep** (or **lose**) **one's temper** retain (or fail to retain) composure when angry. **out of temper** in an irritable mood.
– ORIGIN Old English *temprian* 'bring something into the required condition by mixing it with something else', from Latin *temperare* 'mingle, restrain'. Sense development was probably influenced by Old French *temprer* 'to temper, moderate'. The noun originally denoted a proportionate mixture of elements or qualities, also the combination of the four bodily humours, believed in medieval times to be the basis of temperament, hence sense 1 of the noun (late Middle English). Compare with TEMPERAMENT.

tempera /ˈtɛmp(ə)rə/ ▸ **noun** [mass noun] a method of painting with pigments dispersed in an emulsion miscible with water, typically egg yolk. The method was used in Europe for fine painting, mainly on wood panels, from the 12th or early 13th century until the 15th, when it began to give way to oils. ■ emulsion used in tempera painting.
– ORIGIN mid 19th cent.: from Italian, in the phrase *pingere a tempera* 'paint in distemper'.

temperament ▸ **noun** **1** a person's or animal's nature, especially as it permanently affects their behaviour: *she had an artistic temperament.* ■ [mass noun] the tendency to behave angrily or emotionally: *he had begun to show signs of temperament.*
2 [mass noun] the adjustment of intervals in tuning a piano or other musical instrument so as to fit the scale for use in different keys; in **equal temperament**, the octave consists of twelve equal semitones.
– ORIGIN late Middle English: from Latin *temperamentum* 'correct mixture', from *temperare* 'mingle'. In early use the word was synonymous with the noun TEMPER.

temperamental ▸ **adjective** **1** (of a person) liable to unreasonable changes of mood.
2 relating to a person's temperament: *they were firm friends in spite of temperamental differences.*
– DERIVATIVES **temperamentally** adverb.

temperance ▸ **noun** [mass noun] abstinence from alcoholic drink: [as modifier] *the temperance movement.*
– ORIGIN Middle English: from Anglo-Norman French *temperaunce*, from Latin *temperantia* 'moderation', from *temperare* 'restrain'.

temperate ▸ **adjective** **1** relating to or denoting a region or climate characterized by mild temperatures.
2 showing moderation or self-restraint: *Charles was temperate in his consumption of both food and drink.*
– DERIVATIVES **temperately** adverb, **temperateness** noun.
– ORIGIN late Middle English (in the sense 'not affected by passion or emotion'): from Latin *temperatus* 'mingled, restrained', from the verb *temperare*.

temperate zone ▸ **noun** each of the two belts of latitude between the torrid zone and the northern and southern frigid zones.

temperature ▸ **noun** the degree or intensity of heat present in a substance or object, especially as expressed according to a comparative scale and shown by a thermometer or perceived by touch. ■ the degree of internal heat of a person's body: *I'll take her temperature.* ■ informal a body temperature above the normal: *he was running a temperature.* ■ the degree of excitement or tension in a discussion or confrontation: *the temperature of the debate was lower than before.*
– ORIGIN late Middle English: from French *température* or Latin *temperatura*, from *temperare* 'restrain'. The word originally denoted the state of being tempered or mixed, later becoming synonymous with TEMPERAMENT. The modern sense dates from the late 17th cent.

temperature coefficient ▸ **noun** Physics a coefficient expressing the relation between a change in a physical property and the change in temperature that causes it.

temperature–humidity index ▸ **noun** a quantity expressing the discomfort felt as a result of the combined effects of the temperature and humidity of the air.

temperature inversion ▸ **noun** see INVERSION (sense 2).

-tempered ▸ **combining form** having a specified temper or disposition: *ill-tempered.*
– DERIVATIVES **-temperedly** combining form in corresponding adverbs, **-temperedness** combining form in corresponding nouns.

tempest ▸ **noun** a violent windy storm.
– PHRASES **a tempest in a teapot** North American term for A STORM IN A TEACUP (see STORM).
– ORIGIN Middle English: from Old French *tempeste*, from Latin *tempestas* 'season, weather, storm', from *tempus* 'time, season'.

tempestuous /tɛmˈpɛstjʊəs/ ▸ **adjective** **1** characterized by strong and turbulent or conflicting emotion: *he had a reckless and tempestuous streak.*
2 very stormy: *a tempestuous wind.*
– DERIVATIVES **tempestuously** adverb, **tempestuousness** noun.
– ORIGIN late Middle English: from late Latin *tempestuosus*, from Latin *tempestas* (see TEMPEST).

tempi plural form of TEMPO¹.

Templar /ˈtɛmplə/ ▸ **noun** historical a member of the Knights Templar.
– ORIGIN Middle English: from Old French *templier*, from medieval Latin *templarius*, from Latin *templum* (see TEMPLE¹).

template /ˈtɛmpleɪt, -plɪt/ ▸ **noun** **1** a shaped piece of rigid material used as a pattern for processes such as cutting out, shaping, or drilling. ■ something that serves as a model for others to copy: *the plant was to serve as the template for change throughout the company.* ■ Computing a preset format for a document or file. ■ Biochemistry a nucleic acid molecule that acts as a pattern for the sequence of assembly of a protein, nucleic acid, or other large molecule.
2 a timber or plate used to distribute the weight in a wall or under a support.
– ORIGIN late 17th cent. (as *templet*): probably from TEMPLE³ + -ET¹. The change in the ending in the 19th cent. was due to association with PLATE.

Temple, Shirley (b.1928), American child star; latterly *Shirley Temple Black*. In the 1930s she appeared in a succession of films, such as *Rebecca of Sunnybrook Farm* (1938). She later became active in Republican politics and represented the US at the United Nations and as an ambassador.

temple¹ ▸ **noun** **1** a building devoted to the worship of a god or gods. ■ (**the Temple**) either of two successive religious buildings of the Jews in Jerusalem. The first (957–586 BC) was built by Solomon and destroyed by Nebuchadnezzar; it contained the Ark of the Covenant. The second (515 BC–AD 70) was enlarged by Herod the Great from 20 BC and destroyed by the Romans during a Jewish revolt; all that remains is the Wailing Wall. ■ N. Amer. a synagogue. ■ a place of Christian public worship, especially a Protestant church in France. ■ a thing regarded as holy or likened to a temple, especially a person's body. [with biblical allusion to 1 Corinthians 6:19.] ■ a place devoted to or seen as the centre of a particular activity or interest: *a temple of science.*
2 (**the Temple**) a group of buildings in Fleet Street, London, which stand on land formerly occupied by the headquarters of the Knights Templar. Located there are the Inner and Outer Temple, two of the Inns of Court.
– ORIGIN Old English *templ*, *tempel*, reinforced in Middle English by Old French *temple*, both from Latin *templum* 'open or consecrated space'.

temple² ▸ **noun** the flat part of either side of the head between the forehead and the ear.
– ORIGIN Middle English: from Old French, from an alteration of Latin *tempora*, plural of *tempus* 'temple of the head'.

temple³ ▸ **noun** a device in a loom for keeping the cloth stretched.
– ORIGIN late Middle English: from Old French, perhaps ultimately the same word as TEMPLE².

temple block ▸ **noun** a percussion instrument consisting of a hollow block of wood which is struck with a stick.

tempo¹ ▸ **noun** (pl. **tempos** or **tempi** /-piː/) **1** Music the speed at which a passage of music is or should be played.

2 the rate or speed of motion or activity; pace: *the tempo of life dictated by a heavy workload.*
– ORIGIN mid 17th cent. (as a fencing term denoting the timing of an attack): from Italian, from Latin *tempus* 'time'.

tempo² ▶ noun (pl. **tempos**) trademark (in South Asia) a light three-wheeled delivery van.
– ORIGIN an invented word.

temporal¹ /ˈtɛmp(ə)r(ə)l/ ▶ adjective **1** relating to worldly as opposed to spiritual affairs; secular.
2 relating to time. ■ Grammar relating to or denoting time or tense.
– DERIVATIVES **temporally** adverb.
– ORIGIN Middle English: from Old French *temporel* or Latin *temporalis*, from *tempus, tempor-* 'time'.

temporal² /ˈtɛmpər(ə)l/ ▶ adjective Anatomy of or situated in the temples of the head.
– ORIGIN late Middle English: from late Latin *temporalis*, from *tempora* 'the temples' (see TEMPLE²).

temporal bone ▶ noun Anatomy either of a pair of bones which form part of the side of the skull on each side and enclose the middle and inner ear.

temporalis /ˌtɛmpəˈreɪlɪs/ ▶ noun Anatomy a fan-shaped muscle which runs from the side of the skull to the back of the lower jaw and is involved in closing the mouth and chewing.
– ORIGIN late 17th cent.: from late Latin.

temporality ▶ noun (pl. **temporalities**) **1** [mass noun] the state of existing within or having some relationship with time.
2 (usu. **temporalities**) a secular possession, especially the properties and revenues of a religious body or a member of the clergy.
– ORIGIN late Middle English (denoting temporal matters or secular authority): from late Latin *temporalitas*, from *temporalis* (see TEMPORAL¹).

temporal lobe ▶ noun each of the paired lobes of the brain lying beneath the temples, including areas concerned with the understanding of speech.

temporal power ▶ noun [mass noun] the power of a bishop or cleric, especially the Pope, in secular matters.

temporarily ▶ adverb for a limited period of time; not permanently: *symptoms may disappear temporarily | a temporarily vacant department store.*

temporary ▶ adjective lasting for only a limited period of time; not permanent: *a temporary job.*
▶ noun (pl. **temporaries**) a person employed on a temporary basis, typically an office worker who finds employment through an agency. See also TEMP¹.
– DERIVATIVES **temporariness** noun.
– ORIGIN mid 16th cent.: from Latin *temporarius*, from *tempus, tempor-* 'time'.

temporary hardness ▶ noun [mass noun] the presence in water of mineral salts (chiefly calcium bicarbonate) that are removed by boiling.

temporize (also **temporise**) ▶ verb [no obj.] avoid making a decision or committing oneself in order to gain time: *the opportunity was missed because the queen still temporized.*
– DERIVATIVES **temporization** noun, **temporizer** noun.
– ORIGIN late 16th cent.: from French *temporiser* 'bide one's time', from medieval Latin *temporizare* 'to delay', from Latin *tempus, tempor-* 'time'.

temporomandibular joint /ˌtɛmpərəʊmanˈdɪbjʊlə/ ▶ noun Anatomy the hinge joint between the temporal bone and the lower jaw.

tempo rubato ▶ noun fuller term for RUBATO.

Tempranillo /ˌtɛmprəˈniːjəʊ, -ˈniːljəʊ/ ▶ noun [mass noun] a variety of wine grape grown in Spain, used to make Rioja wine. ■ a red wine made from the Tempranillo grape.
– ORIGIN named after a village in northern Spain.

temps levé /ˌtɑ̃ ləˈveɪ/ ▶ noun (pl. **temps levés** pronunc. **same**) Ballet a movement like a small hop in which there is no transfer of weight from one foot to the other.
– ORIGIN French, literally 'raised time'.

tempt ▶ verb [with obj.] entice or try to entice (someone) to do something that they find attractive but know to be wrong or unwise: *there'll always be someone tempted by the rich pickings of poaching* | [with obj. and infinitive] *jobs which involve entertaining may tempt you to drink more than you intend.* ■ (**be tempted to do something**) have an urge or inclination to do something: *I was tempted to look at my watch, but didn't dare.* ■ persuade (someone) to do something: *he was tempted out of retirement to save the team from relegation.* ■ archaic risk provoking (a deity or abstract force), usually with undesirable consequences.
– PHRASES **tempt fate** (or **providence**) do something that is risky or dangerous.
– DERIVATIVES **temptability** noun.
– ORIGIN Middle English: from Old French *tempter* 'to test', from Latin *temptare* 'handle, test, try'.

temptation ▶ noun the desire to do something, especially something wrong or unwise: *he resisted the temptation to call Celia at the office* | [mass noun] *we almost gave in to temptation.* ■ a thing that attracts or tempts someone: *the temptations of life in London.* ■ (**the Temptation**) the tempting of Jesus by the Devil (see Matt. 4).
– ORIGIN Middle English: from Old French *temptacion*, from Latin *temptatio(n-)*, from *temptare* 'handle, test, try'.

tempter ▶ noun a person or thing that tempts. ■ (**the Tempter**) the Devil.
– ORIGIN late Middle English: from Old French *tempteur*, from ecclesiastical Latin *temptator*, from Latin *temptare* 'to handle, test, try'.

tempting ▶ adjective appealing to or attracting someone, even if wrong or unwise: *a tempting financial offer* | [with infinitive] *it is often tempting to bring about change rapidly.*
– DERIVATIVES **temptingly** adverb.

temptress ▶ noun a woman who tempts someone to do something, typically a sexually attractive woman who sets out to allure or seduce someone.

tempura /ˈtɛmpʊrə/ ▶ noun [mass noun] a Japanese dish of fish, shellfish, or vegetables, fried in batter.
– ORIGIN Japanese, probably from Portuguese *tempêro* 'seasoning'.

ten ▶ cardinal number equivalent to the product of five and two; one more than nine; 10: *the last ten years | the house comfortably sleeps ten | a ten-foot shrub.* (Roman numeral: **x**, **X**) ■ a group or unit of ten people or things: *count in tens.* ■ ten years old: *the boy was no more than ten.* ■ ten o'clock: *at about ten at night I got a call.* ■ a size of garment or other merchandise denoted by ten. ■ a ten-pound note or ten-dollar bill: *he took the money in tens.* ■ a playing card with ten pips.
– PHRASES **be ten a penny** see PENNY. **ten out of ten** Brit. a perfect mark. ■ used to indicate that someone has done something well: *you have to give her ten out of ten for persistence.* **ten to one** very probably: *ten to one you'll never find out who did this.*
– ORIGIN Old English *tēn, tien*, of Germanic origin; related to Dutch *tien* and German *zehn*, from an Indo-European root shared by Sanskrit *daśa*, Greek *deka*, and Latin *decem*.

ten. ▶ abbreviation Music tenuto.

tenable ▶ adjective **1** able to be maintained or defended against attack or objection: *such a simplistic approach is no longer tenable.*
2 (of an office, position, scholarship, etc.) able to be held or used: *a scholarship of £200 per annum tenable for three years.*
– DERIVATIVES **tenability** noun.
– ORIGIN late 16th cent.: from French, from *tenir* 'to hold', from Latin *tenere*.

tenace /ˈtɛnəs/ ▶ noun (in bridge, whist, and similar card games) a pair of cards in one hand which rank immediately above and below a card held by an opponent, e.g. the ace and queen in a suit of which an opponent holds the king.
– ORIGIN mid 17th cent.: from French, from Spanish *tenaza*, literally 'pincers'.

tenacious /tɪˈneɪʃəs/ ▶ adjective tending to keep a firm hold of something; clinging or adhering closely: *a tenacious grip.* ■ not readily relinquishing a position, principle, or course of action; determined: *this tenacious defence of local liberties | you're tenacious and you get at the truth.* ■ persisting in existence; not easily dispelled: *a tenacious local legend.*
– DERIVATIVES **tenaciously** adverb, **tenaciousness** noun.
– ORIGIN early 17th cent.: from Latin *tenax, tenac-* (from *tenere* 'to hold') + -IOUS.

tenacity /tɪˈnasɪti/ ▶ noun [mass noun] the quality or fact of being able to grip something firmly; grip: *the sheer tenacity of the limpet.* ■ the quality or fact of being very determined; determination: *you have to admire the tenacity of these two guys.* ■ the quality or fact of continuing to exist; persistence: *the tenacity of certain myths within the historical record.*

tenaculum /tɪˈnakjʊləm/ ▶ noun (pl. **tenacula** /-lə/) a sharp hook used by a surgeon for picking up small pieces of tissue such as the ends of arteries.
– ORIGIN late 17th cent.: from Latin, literally 'holder, holding instrument', from *tenere* 'to hold'.

tenancy ▶ noun (pl. **tenancies**) [mass noun] possession of land or property as a tenant: *Holding took over the tenancy of the farm.*

tenancy in common ▶ noun Law a shared tenancy in which each holder has a distinct, separately transferable interest.

tenant ▶ noun a person who occupies land or property rented from a landlord. ■ Law a person in possession of real property by any right or title.
▶ verb [with obj.] occupy (property) as a tenant: *the house was tenanted by his cousin.*
– DERIVATIVES **tenantable** adjective (formal), **tenantless** adjective.
– ORIGIN Middle English: from Old French, literally 'holding', present participle of *tenir*, from Latin *tenere*.

tenant at will ▶ noun (pl. **tenants at will**) Law a tenant that can be evicted without notice.

tenant farmer ▶ noun a person who farms rented land.

tenantry ▶ noun **1** [treated as sing. or pl.] the tenants of an estate.
2 [mass noun] tenancy.

Tencel /ˈtɛnsɛl/ ▶ noun [mass noun] trademark a cellulosic fibre obtained from wood pulp using recyclable solvents. ■ a fabric made from Tencel.
– ORIGIN 1960s (proprietary name of various yarns and fabrics): an invented word.

tench ▶ noun (pl. **same**) a European freshwater fish of the carp family, popular with anglers and widely introduced elsewhere. ● *Tinca tinca*, family Cyprinidae.
– ORIGIN Middle English: from Old French *tenche*, from late Latin *tinca*.

Ten Commandments (in the Bible) the divine rules of conduct given by God to Moses on Mount Sinai, according to Exod. 20:1–17.

> The commandments are generally enumerated as: have no other gods; do not make or worship idols; do not take the name of the Lord in vain; keep the sabbath holy; honour one's father and mother; do not kill; do not commit adultery; do not steal; do not give false evidence; do not covet another's property or wife.

tend¹ ▶ verb [no obj., with infinitive] regularly or frequently behave in a particular way or have a certain characteristic: *written language tends to be formal | her hair tended to come loose.* ■ [no obj.] (**tend to/towards**) be liable to possess or display (a particular characteristic): *Walter tended towards corpulence.* ■ [no obj., with adverbial] go or move in a particular direction: *fire is hot and tends upwards.* ■ [no obj.] (**tend to**) Mathematics (of a variable) approach a given quantity as a limit: *the orbit tends to infinity.*
– ORIGIN Middle English (in the sense 'move or be inclined to move in a certain direction'): from Old French *tendre* 'stretch, tend', from Latin *tendere*.

tend² ▶ verb [with obj.] care for or look after; give one's attention to: *Varela tended plants on the roof* | [no obj.] *ambulance crews were tending to the injured.* ■ US direct or manage; work in: *I've been tending bar at the airport lounge.* ■ archaic wait on as an attendant or servant.
– DERIVATIVES **tendance** noun (archaic).
– ORIGIN Middle English: shortening of ATTEND.

tendency ▶ noun (pl. **tendencies**) [often with infinitive] an inclination towards a particular characteristic or type of behaviour: *for students, there is a tendency to socialize in the evenings | criminal tendencies.* ■ a group within a larger political party or movement.
– ORIGIN early 17th cent.: from medieval Latin *tendentia*, from *tendere* 'to stretch' (see TEND¹).

tendentious /tɛnˈdɛnʃəs/ ▶ adjective expressing or intending to promote a particular cause or point of view, especially a controversial one: *a tendentious reading of history.*
– DERIVATIVES **tendentiously** adverb, **tendentiousness** noun.
– ORIGIN early 20th cent.: suggested by German *tendenziös*.

tender¹ ▶ adjective (**tenderer, tenderest**) **1** showing gentleness, kindness, and affection: *he was being so kind and tender | she covered his face with tender kisses.* ■ (**tender of**) archaic solicitous of: *be tender of a lady's reputation.*

T

2 (of a part of the body) sensitive to pain: *the pale, tender skin of her forearm.* ■ (of a plant) easily injured by severe weather and therefore needing protection. ■ requiring tact or careful handling: *the issue of conscription was a particularly tender one.*
3 (of food) easy to cut or chew; not tough: *tender green beans.*
4 young, inexperienced, or vulnerable: *he started sailing at the tender age of ten.*
5 Nautical (of a ship) leaning or readily inclined to roll in response to the wind.
– PHRASES **tender mercies** used ironically to refer to attention or treatment not in the best interests of its recipients: *they abandoned their children to the tender mercies of the social services.*
– DERIVATIVES **tenderly** adverb.
– ORIGIN Middle English: from Old French *tendre*, from Latin *tener* 'tender, delicate'.

tender² ▶ verb [with obj.] offer or present (something) formally: *he tendered his resignation as leader.* ■ offer (money) as payment: *she tendered her fare.* ■ [no obj.] make a formal written offer to carry out work, supply goods, or buy land, shares, or another asset for a stated fixed price: *firms of interior decorators have been tendering for the work.* ■ make such an offer giving (a stated fixed price): *what price should we tender for a contract?* ■ (**tender something out**) seek offers to carry out work at a stated fixed price.
▶ noun an offer to carry out work, supply goods, or buy land, shares, or another asset at a stated fixed price.
– PHRASES **put something out to tender** seek offers to carry out work or supply goods at a stated fixed price.
– DERIVATIVES **tenderer** noun.
– ORIGIN mid 16th cent. (as a legal term meaning 'formally offer a plea or evidence, or money to discharge a debt', also as a noun denoting such an offer): from Old French *tendre*, from Latin *tendere* 'to stretch, hold forth' (see TEND¹).

tender³ ▶ noun 1 [with modifier] a vehicle used by a fire service for carrying specified supplies or equipment or fulfilling a specified role. ■ a vehicle used in mobile operations by a public service or the armed forces.
2 a dinghy or other boat used to ferry people and supplies to and from a ship.
3 a trailing vehicle closely coupled to a steam locomotive to carry fuel and water.
4 [usu. in combination or with modifier] a person who looks after someone else or a machine or place: *Alexei signalled to one of the engine tenders.*
– ORIGIN late Middle English (in the sense 'attendant, nurse'): from TEND² or shortening of *attender* (see ATTEND).

tenderfoot ▶ noun (pl. **tenderfoots** or **tenderfeet**)
1 chiefly N. Amer. a newcomer or novice, especially a person unaccustomed to hardship.
2 dated a new member of the Scout or Guide movement who has passed the enrolment tests.

tender-hearted ▶ adjective having a kind, gentle, or sentimental nature.
– DERIVATIVES **tender-heartedness** noun.

tenderize (also **tenderise**) ▶ verb make (meat) more tender by beating or slow cooking.

tenderizer (also **tenderiser**) ▶ noun a thing used to make meat tender, in particular: ■ a substance such as papain which is rubbed on to meat or used as a marinade to soften the fibres. ■ a small hammer with teeth on the head, used to beat meat.

T

tenderloin ▶ noun 1 [mass noun] the tenderest part of a loin of beef, pork, etc., taken from under the short ribs in the hindquarters. ■ US the undercut of a sirloin.
2 N. Amer. informal a district of a city where vice and corruption are prominent. [late 19th cent.: originally a term applied to a district of New York, seen as a 'choice' assignment by police because of the bribes offered to them to turn a blind eye.]

tender-minded ▶ adjective easily affected emotionally by other people's distress or by criticism.
– DERIVATIVES **tender-mindedness** noun.

tenderness ▶ noun [mass noun] 1 gentleness and kindness; kindliness: *he picked her up in his arms with great tenderness.* ■ feelings of deep affection; devotion: *tenderness for the opposite sex.*
2 sensitivity to pain; soreness: *abdominal tenderness.*
3 the quality of being easy to cut or chew; succulence: *steak braised to perfect tenderness in a red-wine-and-brandy sauce.*

tendinitis /ˌtɛndɪˈnʌɪtəs/ (also **tendonitis** /ˌtɛndə-/) ▶ noun [mass noun] inflammation of a tendon, most commonly from overuse but also from infection or rheumatic disease.

tendon /ˈtɛndən/ ▶ noun a flexible but inelastic cord of strong fibrous collagen tissue attaching a muscle to a bone. ■ the hamstring of a quadruped.
– DERIVATIVES **tendinous** adjective.
– ORIGIN late Middle English: from French or medieval Latin *tendo(n-)*, translating Greek *tenōn* 'sinew', from *teinein* 'to stretch'.

tendon organ ▶ noun Anatomy a sensory receptor within a tendon that responds to tension and relays impulses to the central nervous system.

tendresse /tɒ̃ˈdrɛs/ (also **tendre** /ˈtɒ̃dr(ə)/) ▶ noun [in sing.] a feeling of fondness or love: *the local grande dame for whom George had a tendresse.*
– ORIGIN French.

tendril ▶ noun a slender thread-like appendage of a climbing plant, often growing in a spiral form, which stretches out and twines round any suitable support. ■ something resembling a plant tendril, especially a slender curl or ringlet of hair.
– ORIGIN mid 16th cent.: probably a diminutive of Old French *tendron* 'young shoot', from Latin *tener* 'tender'.

tendu /tɒ̃ˈd(j)uː/ ▶ adjective [postpositive] Ballet (of a position) stretched out or held tautly: *battement tendu.*
– ORIGIN French.

tendu leaf /teɪnˈduː/ ▶ noun [mass noun] the leaves of an Asian ebony tree, gathered in India as a cheap tobacco substitute. ● *Diospyros melanoxylon*, family Ebenaceae.
– ORIGIN Hindi *tendu*.

Tenebrae /ˈtɛnɪbriː, -breɪ/ ▶ plural noun (in the Roman Catholic Church) matins and lauds for the last three days of Holy Week, at which candles are successively extinguished. Several composers have set parts of the office to music.
– ORIGIN Latin, literally 'darkness'.

tenebrionid /tɪˌnɛbrɪˈɒnɪd/ ▶ noun Entomology a beetle of a family (Tenebrionidae) that comprises the darkling beetles.
– ORIGIN 1920s: from modern Latin *Tenebrionidae* (plural), from *tenebrio* 'night spirit'.

tenebrism /ˈtɛnəbrɪz(ə)m/ ▶ noun [mass noun] a style of painting developed by Caravaggio and other 17th-century Spanish and Italian artists, characterized by predominantly dark tones and shadows with dramatically contrasting effects of light.
– DERIVATIVES **tenebrist** noun.
– ORIGIN from Italian *tenebroso* 'dark' + -ISM.

tenebrous /ˈtɛnɪbrəs/ ▶ adjective literary dark; shadowy or obscure.
– ORIGIN late Middle English: via Old French from Latin *tenebrosus*, from *tenebrae* 'darkness'.

tenement /ˈtɛnəm(ə)nt/ ▶ noun 1 (especially in Scotland or the US) a room or a set of rooms forming a separate residence within a house or block of flats. ■ (also **tenement house**) a house divided into and let as separate residences.
2 a piece of land held by an owner. ■ Law any kind of permanent property, e.g. lands or rents, held from a superior.
– ORIGIN Middle English (in the sense 'tenure, property held by tenure'): via Old French from medieval Latin *tenementum*, from *tenere* 'to hold'.

Tenerife /ˌtɛnəˈriːf/, Spanish /teneˈrife/ a volcanic island in the Atlantic, the largest of the Canary Islands; pop. 866,033 (2008); capital, Santa Cruz.

tenesi /ˈtɛnɛsi/ ▶ noun (pl. **same**) a monetary unit of Turkmenistan, equal to one hundredth of a manat.
– ORIGIN Turkmen.

tenesmus /tɪˈnɛzməs/ ▶ noun [mass noun] Medicine a continual or recurrent inclination to evacuate the bowels, caused by disorder of the rectum or other illness.
– ORIGIN early 16th cent.: via medieval Latin from Greek *teinesmos* 'straining', from *teinein* 'stretch, strain'.

tenet /ˈtɛnɪt, ˈtiːnɛt/ ▶ noun a principle or belief, especially one of the main principles of a religion or philosophy: *the tenets of classical liberalism.*
– ORIGIN late 16th cent. (superseding earlier *tenent*): from Latin, literally 'he holds', from the verb *tenere.*

tenfold ▶ adjective ten times as great or as numerous: *a tenfold increase in the use of insecticides.* ■ having ten parts or elements.
▶ adverb by ten times; to ten times the number or amount: *production increased tenfold.*

ten-gallon hat ▶ noun a large broad-brimmed hat, traditionally worn by cowboys.

tenge /ˈtɛŋɡeɪ/ ▶ noun (pl. **same** or **tenges**) the basic monetary unit of Kazakhstan, equal to 100 teins.
– ORIGIN Kazakh and Turkmen, literally 'coin, rouble'.

Teng Hsiao-p'ing /ˌtɛŋ ʃaʊˈpɪŋ/ variant of DENG XIAOPING.

tenia ▶ noun US spelling of TAENIA.

Teniers /ˈtɛnɪəz/, David (1610–90), Flemish painter; known as **David Teniers the Younger**. From 1651 he was court painter to successive regents of the Netherlands.

Ten Lost Tribes of Israel see LOST TRIBES.

ten-minute rule ▶ noun a rule of the House of Commons allowing brief discussion of a motion to introduce a bill, each speech being limited to ten minutes.

Tenn. ▶ abbreviation Tennessee.

Tennant Creek /ˈtɛnənt/ a mining town between Alice Springs and Darwin in Northern Territory, Australia; pop. 2,916 (2008).

tennantite /ˈtɛnəntʌɪt/ ▶ noun [mass noun] a grey-black mineral consisting of a sulphide of copper, iron, and arsenic. It is an important ore of copper.
– ORIGIN mid 19th cent.: from the name of Smithson *Tennant* (1761–1815), English chemist, + -ITE¹.

tenné /ˈtɛni/ Heraldry ▶ noun [mass noun] orange-brown, as a stain used in blazoning.
▶ adjective [usu. postpositive] of the colour of tenné.
– ORIGIN mid 16th cent.: obsolete French, variant of Old French *tane* (see TAWNY).

tenner ▶ noun Brit. informal a ten-pound note.

Tennessee /ˌtɛnəˈsiː/ 1 a river in the south-eastern US, flowing some 1,400 km (875 miles) in a great loop, generally westwards through Tennessee and Alabama, then northwards to re-enter Tennessee, joining the Ohio River in western Kentucky.
2 a state in the central south-eastern US; pop. 6,214,888 (est. 2008); capital, Nashville. Ceded by Britain to the US in 1783, it became the 16th state in 1796.
– DERIVATIVES **Tennesseean** noun & adjective.

Tennessee Valley Authority (abbrev.: **TVA**) an independent federal government agency in the US, created in 1933 as part of the New Deal proposals. Responsible for the development of the whole Tennessee River basin, it provides one of the world's greatest irrigation and hydroelectric power systems.

Tennessee Walking Horse ▶ noun a powerful riding horse of a breed with a characteristic fast walking pace.

Tenniel /ˈtɛnɪəl/, Sir John (1820–1914), English illustrator and cartoonist. He illustrated Lewis Carroll's *Alice's Adventures in Wonderland* (1865) and *Through the Looking Glass* (1871).

tennies ▶ plural noun N. Amer. informal tennis shoes.

tennis ▶ noun [mass noun] a game in which two or four players strike a ball with rackets over a net stretched across a court. The usual form (originally called **lawn tennis**) is played with a felt-covered hollow rubber ball on a grass, clay, or artificial surface. See also REAL TENNIS.
– ORIGIN late Middle English *tenetz*, *tenes* 'real tennis', apparently from Old French *tenez* 'take, receive' (called by the server to an opponent), imperative of *tenir*.

tennis court ▶ noun a rectangular area marked with lines on which tennis is played.

tennis elbow ▶ noun [mass noun] inflammation of the tendons of the elbow (epicondylitis) caused by overuse of the muscles of the forearm.

tennis shoe ▶ noun a light canvas or leather soft-soled shoe suitable for tennis or casual wear.

Tenno /ˈtɛnəʊ/ ▶ noun (pl. **Tennos**) the Emperor of Japan.
– ORIGIN Japanese.

Tennyson /ˈtɛnɪs(ə)n/, Alfred, 1st Baron Tennyson of Aldworth and Freshwater (1809–92), English poet, Poet Laureate from 1850. His reputation was established by *In Memoriam* (1850), a long poem concerned with immortality, change, and evolution. Other notable works: 'The Charge of the Light Brigade' (1854) and *Idylls of the King* (1859).

Tennysonian /ˌtɛnɪˈsəʊnɪən/ ▶ adjective relating to or in the style of Tennyson.
▶ noun an admirer or student of Tennyson or his work.

Tenochtitlán /tɛˌnɒtʃtɪˈtlɑːn/ the ancient capital of the Aztec empire, founded *c.*1320. In 1521 the Spanish conquistador Cortés destroyed it and established Mexico City on its site.

tenon ▸ **noun** a projecting piece of wood made for insertion into a mortise in another piece.
▸ **verb** [with obj.] join by means of a tenon: *the rail was tenoned into oak stiles.* ■ cut as a tenon.
– DERIVATIVES **tenoner** noun.
– ORIGIN late Middle English: from French, from *tenir* 'to hold', from Latin *tenere.*

tenon saw ▸ **noun** a small saw with a strong brass or steel back for precise work.

tenor[1] ▸ **noun 1** a singing voice between baritone and alto or countertenor, the highest of the ordinary adult male range. ■ a singer with a tenor voice. ■ a part written for a tenor voice.
2 [usu. as modifier] an instrument, especially a saxophone, trombone, tuba, or viol, of the second or third lowest pitch in its family: *a tenor sax.* ■ (in full **tenor bell**) the largest and deepest bell of a ring or set.
– DERIVATIVES **tenorist** noun.
– ORIGIN late Middle English: via Old French from medieval Latin, based on *tenere* 'to hold'; so named because the tenor part was allotted (and therefore 'held') the melody.

tenor[2] ▸ **noun 1** [in sing.] the general meaning, sense, or content of something: *the general tenor of the debate.* ■ a settled or prevailing character or direction, especially the course of a person's life or habits: *the even tenor of life in the kitchen was disrupted the following day.*
2 Law the actual wording of a document.
3 Finance the time that must elapse before a bill of exchange or promissory note becomes due for payment.
– ORIGIN Middle English: from Old French *tenour,* from Latin *tenor* 'course, substance, import of a law', from *tenere* 'to hold'.

tenor clef ▸ **noun** Music a clef placing middle C on the second-highest line of the stave, used chiefly for cello and bassoon music.

tenorino /ˌtɛnəˈriːnəʊ/ ▸ **noun** (pl. **tenorini** /-ˈriːni/) a high tenor.
– ORIGIN Italian, diminutive of *tenore* 'tenor'.

tenorist ▸ **noun** a person who plays a tenor instrument, especially the tenor saxophone.

tenosynovitis /ˌtɛnəʊˌsʌɪnə(ʊ)ˈvʌɪtɪs/ ▸ **noun** [mass noun] Medicine inflammation and swelling of a tendon, typically in the wrist, often caused by repetitive movements such as typing.
– ORIGIN late 19th cent.: from Greek *tenōn* 'tendon' + SYNOVITIS.

tenotomy /təˈnɒtəmi/ ▸ **noun** [mass noun] the surgical cutting of a tendon, especially as a remedy for club foot.
– ORIGIN mid 19th cent.: coined in French from Greek *tenōn* 'tendon' + *-tomia* (see -TOMY).

tenpin ▸ **noun** a skittle used in tenpin bowling. ■ (**tenpins**) [treated as sing.] N. Amer. tenpin bowling.

tenpin bowling ▸ **noun** [mass noun] a game in which ten skittles are set up at the end of a track (typically one of several in a large automated alley) and bowled down with hard rubber or plastic balls.

tenpounder ▸ **noun** a large silvery-blue herring-like fish of tropical seas, which is popular as a game fish. Also called LADYFISH. ● *Elops saurus* (or *machnata*), family Elopidae.

tenrec /ˈtɛnrɛk/ ▸ **noun** a small insectivorous mammal native to Madagascar, different kinds of which resemble hedgehogs, shrews, or small otters. ● Several genera in the family Tenrecidae: many species.
– ORIGIN late 18th cent.: from French *tanrec,* from Malagasy *tàndraka.*

TENS ▸ **abbreviation** transcutaneous electrical nerve stimulation, a technique intended to provide pain relief by applying electrodes to the skin to block impulses in underlying nerves.

tense[1] ▸ **adjective 1** (especially of a muscle) stretched tight or rigid. ■ Phonetics (of a speech sound, especially a vowel) pronounced with the vocal muscles stretched tight. The opposite of LAX.
2 unable to relax because of nervousness, anxiety, or stimulation: *he was tense with excitement.* ■ causing or characterized by anxiety and nervousness: *they waited in tense silence | relations between the two neighbouring states were tense.*
▸ **verb** [no obj.] become tense, typically through anxiety or nervousness: *her body tensed up.* ■ [with obj.] make (a muscle or one's body) tight or rigid: *carefully stretch and then tense your muscles.*
– DERIVATIVES **tensely** adverb, **tenseness** noun, **tensity** noun (rare).
– ORIGIN late 17th cent.: from Latin *tensus* 'stretched', from the verb *tendere.*

tense[2] ▸ **noun** Grammar a set of forms taken by a verb to indicate the time (and sometimes also the continuance or completeness) of the action in relation to the time of the utterance: *the past tense.*
– DERIVATIVES **tenseless** adjective.
– ORIGIN Middle English (in the general sense 'time'): from Old French *tens,* from Latin *tempus* 'time'.

tensegrity /tɛnˈsɛgrɪti/ ▸ **noun** [mass noun] Architecture the characteristic property of a stable three-dimensional structure consisting of members under tension that are contiguous and members under compression that are not.
– ORIGIN 1950s: from *tensional integrity.*

tensile /ˈtɛnsʌɪl/ ▸ **adjective 1** relating to tension: *a tensile force.*
2 capable of being drawn out or stretched: *a tensile steel rod.*
– DERIVATIVES **tensility** noun.
– ORIGIN early 17th cent. (in sense 2): from medieval Latin *tensilis,* from Latin *tendere* 'to stretch'.

tensile strength ▸ **noun** the resistance of a material to breaking under tension. Compare with COMPRESSIVE STRENGTH.

tension ▸ **noun** [mass noun] **1** the state of being stretched tight: *the parachute keeps the cable under tension as it drops.* ■ the state of having the muscles stretched tight, especially as causing strain or discomfort: *the elimination of neck tension can relieve headaches.* ■ a strained state or condition resulting from forces acting in opposition to each other. ■ the degree of tightness of stitches in knitting and machine sewing. ■ electromotive force.
2 mental or emotional strain: *a mind which is affected by stress or tension cannot think as clearly.* ■ a strained political or social state or relationship: *the coup followed months of tension between the military and the government* | [count noun] *racial tensions.* ■ a relationship between ideas or qualities with conflicting demands or implications: *the basic tension between freedom and control.*
▸ **verb** [with obj.] apply a force to (something) which tends to stretch it.
– DERIVATIVES **tensional** adjective, **tensioner** noun, **tensionless** adjective.
– ORIGIN mid 16th cent. (as a medical term denoting a condition or feeling of being physically stretched or strained): from French, or from Latin *tensio(n-),* from *tendere* 'stretch'.

tensive ▸ **adjective** causing or expressing tension.

tenson /ˈtɛns(ə)n/ (also **tenzon**) ▸ **noun** historical a contest in verse-making between troubadours. ■ a piece of verse composed for such a contest.
– ORIGIN mid 19th cent.: from French *tenson* (related to Provençal *tenso*), based on Latin *tendere* 'to stretch'.

tensor /ˈtɛnsə, -sɔː/ ▸ **noun 1** Mathematics a mathematical object analogous to but more general than a vector, represented by an array of components that are functions of the coordinates of a space.
2 Anatomy a muscle that tightens or stretches a part of the body.
– DERIVATIVES **tensorial** adjective.
– ORIGIN early 18th cent.: modern Latin, from Latin *tendere* 'to stretch'.

tent[1] ▸ **noun** a portable shelter made of cloth, supported by one or more poles and stretched tight by cords or loops attached to pegs driven into the ground. ■ Medicine short for OXYGEN TENT.
▸ **verb 1** [with obj.] cover with or as if with a tent: *the garden had been completely tented over for supper.* ■ (as adj. **tented**) composed of or provided with tents: *they were living in large tented camps.* ■ arrange in a tent-like shape: *Tim tented his fingers.*
2 [no obj.] (especially of travelling circus people) live in a tent.
– ORIGIN Middle English: from Old French *tente,* based on Latin *tent-* 'stretched', from the verb *tendere.* The verb dates from the mid 16th cent.

tent[2] ▸ **noun** [mass noun] a deep red sweet wine chiefly from Spain, used especially as sacramental wine.
– ORIGIN late Middle English: from Spanish *tinto* 'deep-coloured', from Latin *tinctus* 'dyed, stained', from the verb *tingere.*

tent[3] ▸ **noun** Surgery a piece of absorbent material inserted into an opening to keep it open, or especially to widen it gradually as the material absorbs moisture.
– ORIGIN late Middle English (also denoting a surgical probe): from Old French *tente,* from *tenter* 'to probe', from Latin *temptare* 'handle, test, try'.

tentacle ▸ **noun** a slender, flexible limb or appendage in an animal, especially around the mouth of an invertebrate, used for grasping or moving about, or bearing sense organs. ■ (in a plant) a tendril or a sensitive glandular hair. ■ something resembling a tentacle in shape or flexibility: *trailing tentacles of vapour.* ■ (usu. **tentacles**) an insidious spread of influence and control: *the Party's tentacles reached into every nook and cranny of people's lives.*
– DERIVATIVES **tentacled** adjective [also in combination], **tentacular** adjective, **tentaculate** adjective.
– ORIGIN mid 18th cent.: anglicized from modern Latin *tentaculum,* from Latin *tentare, temptare* 'to feel, try'.

tentage ▸ **noun** [mass noun] tents collectively.

tentative ▸ **adjective** not certain or fixed; provisional: *a tentative conclusion.* ■ done without confidence; hesitant: *he eventually tried a few tentative steps round his hospital room.*
– DERIVATIVES **tentatively** adverb, **tentativeness** noun.
– ORIGIN late 16th cent.: from medieval Latin *tentativus,* from *tentare,* variant of *temptare* 'handle, try'.

tent caterpillar ▸ **noun** a chiefly American moth caterpillar that lives in groups inside communal silken webs in a tree, which it often defoliates. ● Several species in the family Lasiocampidae, especially *Malacosoma americana,* related to the lackey.

tent city ▸ **noun** a large collection of tents, typically one forming temporary or makeshift accommodation for refugees or homeless people.

tent dress ▸ **noun** a full, loose-fitting dress that is narrow at the shoulders and very wide at the hem, having no waistline or darts.

tenter[1] ▸ **noun** a framework on which fabric can be held taut for drying or other treatment during manufacture.
– ORIGIN Middle English: from medieval Latin *tentorium,* from *tent-* 'stretched', from the verb *tendere.*

tenter[2] ▸ **noun** archaic a person in charge of something, especially of machinery in a factory.
– ORIGIN early 19th cent.: from Scots and northern English dialect *tent* 'pay attention', apparently from Middle English *attent* 'heed'.

tenterhook ▸ **noun** historical a hook used to fasten cloth on a drying frame or tenter.
– PHRASES **on tenterhooks** in a state of suspense or agitation because of uncertainty about a future event.

tenth ▸ **ordinal number 1** constituting number ten in a sequence; 10th: *the tenth century | the tenth of September | the tenth-floor locker room.* ■ Music an interval or chord spanning an octave and a third in the diatonic scale, or a note separated from another by this interval.
2 each of ten equal parts into which something is or may be divided: *a tenth of a litre.*
– DERIVATIVES **tenthly** adverb.

tenth-rate ▸ **adjective** informal of extremely poor quality: *rough strip joints and tenth-rate clubs.*

tentorium /tɛnˈtɔːrɪəm/ ▸ **noun** (pl. **tentoria** /-rɪə/) **1** Anatomy a fold of the dura mater forming a partition between the cerebrum and cerebellum.
2 Entomology an internal skeletal framework in the head of an insect.
– ORIGIN early 19th cent.: from Latin, literally 'tent'.

tent peg ▸ **noun** see PEG (sense 1 of the noun).

tent pole ▸ **noun 1** a pole supporting a tent.
2 [usu. as modifier] informal, chiefly US a film that is expected to be very successful and so able to fund a range of related products or films: *this year's big tent-pole movie.*

tent stitch ▸ **noun** [mass noun] a series of parallel diagonal stitches.

tenuity /tɪˈnjuːɪti/ ▸ **noun** [mass noun] lack of solidity or substance; thinness.
– ORIGIN late Middle English: from Latin *tenuitas,* from *tenuis* 'thin'.

tenuous ▸ **adjective** very weak or slight: *the tenuous link between interest rates and investment.* ■ very slender or fine; insubstantial: *a tenuous cloud.*
– DERIVATIVES **tenuously** adverb, **tenuousness** noun.
– ORIGIN late 16th cent.: formed irregularly from Latin *tenuis* 'thin' + -OUS.

tenure /ˈtɛnjə/ ▸ **noun** [mass noun] **1** the conditions under which land or buildings are held or occupied.
2 the holding of an office: *his tenure of the premiership would be threatened.* ■ [count noun] a period for which an office is held.
3 (also **security of tenure**) guaranteed permanent employment, especially as a teacher or lecturer, after a probationary period.
▸ **verb** [with obj.] give (someone) a permanent post, especially as a teacher or lecturer: *I had recently been tenured and then promoted to full professor.* ■ (as adj. **tenured**) having or denoting a permanent academic post: *a tenured academic appointment.*
– PHRASES **security of tenure 1** the right of a tenant of property to occupy it after the lease expires (unless a court should order otherwise). **2** see **TENURE** (sense 3 of the noun) above.
– ORIGIN late Middle English: from Old French, from *tenir* 'to hold', from Latin *tenere*.

tenure track ▸ **noun** [usu. as modifier] chiefly N. Amer. an employment structure whereby the holder of a post, typically an academic one, is guaranteed consideration for eventual tenure: *a tenure-track position.*

tenurial ▸ **adjective** relating to the tenure of land.
– DERIVATIVES **tenurially** adverb.
– ORIGIN late 19th cent.: from medieval Latin *tenura* 'tenure' + **-AL**.

tenuto /təˈnuːtəʊ/ Music ▸ **adverb & adjective** (of a note) held for its full time value or slightly more.
▸ **noun** (pl. **tenutos** or **tenuti**) a note or chord performed in this way.
– ORIGIN Italian, literally 'held', past participle of *tenere*.

ten-week stock ▸ **noun** a stock of a fast-maturing variety which can be made to bloom ten weeks after sowing, widely grown as a bedding plant. ● *Matthiola incana* var. 'Annua', family Cruciferae.

Tenzing Norgay /ˌtɛnsɪŋ ˈnɔːɡeɪ/ (1914–86), Sherpa mountaineer. In 1953, as members of the British expedition, he and Sir Edmund Hillary were the first to reach the summit of Mount Everest.

tenzon /ˈtɛnz(ə)n/ ▸ **noun** variant spelling of **TENSON**.

teocalli /ˌtiːəˈkali/ ▸ **noun** (pl. **teocallis**) a temple of the Aztecs or other Mexican peoples, typically standing on a truncated pyramid.
– ORIGIN American Spanish, from Nahuatl *teo:kalli*, from *teo:tl* 'god' + *kalli* 'house'.

Teochew /ˌtiːəʊˈtʃjuː/ ▸ **noun** (pl. **same**) **1** a member of a people of the Guangdong province of SE China.
2 [mass noun] the dialect spoken by the Teochew.
▸ **adjective** relating to the Teochew or their dialect.
– ORIGIN Chinese dialect form of the name of the city *Chaozhou*.

teosinte /ˌtiːəʊˈsɪnteɪ/ ▸ **noun** [mass noun] a Mexican grass which is grown as fodder and is considered to be one of the parent plants of modern maize. ● *Zea mays* subsp. *mexicana*, family Gramineae.
– ORIGIN late 19th cent.: from French *téosinté*, from Nahuatl *teocintli*, apparently from *teo:tl* 'god' + *cintli* 'dried ear of maize'.

Teotihuacán /teɪˌəʊtɪwəˈkɑːn/ the largest city of pre-Columbian America, situated about 40 km (25 miles) north-east of Mexico City. Built *c.*300 BC, it reached its zenith *c.*300–600 AD, when it was the centre of an influential culture which spread throughout Meso-America. It was sacked by the invading Toltecs *c.*900.

tepache /tɛˈpatʃeɪ/ ▸ **noun** [mass noun] a Mexican drink, typically made with pineapple, water, and brown sugar and partially fermented.
– ORIGIN Mexican Spanish.

tepal /ˈtɛp(ə)l, ˈtiːp(ə)l/ ▸ **noun** Botany a segment of the outer whorl in a flower that has no differentiation between petals and sepals.
– ORIGIN mid 19th cent.: from French *tépale*, blend of *pétale* 'petal' and *sépal* 'sepal'.

tepary bean /ˈtɛpəri/ ▸ **noun** a bean plant native to the south-western US, cultivated in Mexico and Arizona for its drought-resistant qualities. ● *Phaseolus acutifolius*, family Leguminosae.
– ORIGIN early 20th cent.: of unknown origin.

tepee /ˈtiːpiː/ (also **teepee** or **tipi**) ▸ **noun** a conical tent made of skins, cloth, or canvas on a frame of poles, used by American Indians of the Plains and Great Lakes regions.
– ORIGIN mid 18th cent.: from Sioux *tīpi* 'dwelling'.

tephra /ˈtɛfrə/ ▸ **noun** [mass noun] Geology rock fragments and particles ejected by a volcanic eruption.
– ORIGIN 1940s: from Greek, literally 'ash, ashes'.

tephrochronology /ˌtɛfrə(ʊ)krəˈnɒlədʒi/ ▸ **noun** [mass noun] Geology the dating of volcanic eruptions and other events by studying layers of tephra.
– DERIVATIVES **tephrochronological** adjective.

Tepic /tɛˈpiːk/ a city in western Mexico, capital of the state of Nayarit; pop. 265,800 (2000).

tepid ▸ **adjective** (especially of a liquid) only slightly warm; lukewarm. ■ showing little enthusiasm: *the applause was tepid.*
– DERIVATIVES **tepidity** noun, **tepidly** adverb, **tepidness** noun.
– ORIGIN late Middle English: from Latin *tepidus*, from *tepere* 'be warm'.

tepidarium /ˌtɛpɪˈdɛːrɪəm/ ▸ **noun** (pl. **tepidaria** /-rɪə/) a warm room in an ancient Roman bath.
– ORIGIN Latin.

teppanyaki /ˌtɛpanˈjaki/ ▸ **noun** [mass noun] a Japanese dish of meat, fish, or both, fried with vegetables on a hot steel plate forming the centre of the table.
– ORIGIN Japanese, from *teppan* 'steel plate' + *yaki* 'to fry'.

tequila /tɪˈkiːlə/ ▸ **noun** [mass noun] a Mexican alcoholic spirit made from an agave.
– ORIGIN Mexican Spanish, named after the town of *Tequila* in Mexico, where the drink was first made.

tequila slammer ▸ **noun** see **SLAMMER** (sense 3).

tequila sunrise ▸ **noun** a cocktail containing tequila, orange juice, and grenadine.

ter- ▸ **combining form** three; having three: *tercentenary*.
– ORIGIN from Latin *ter* 'thrice'.

tera- /ˈtɛrə/ ▸ **combining form** used in units of measurement: **1** denoting a factor of 10^{12}: *terawatt*.
2 Computing denoting a factor of 2^{40}.
– ORIGIN from Greek *teras* 'monster'.

terabyte (abbrev.: **Tb** or **TB**) ▸ **noun** Computing a unit of information equal to one million million (10^{12}) or (strictly) 2^{40} bytes.

teraflop ▸ **noun** Computing a unit of computing speed equal to one million million (10^{12}) floating-point operations per second.

terai /təˈrʌɪ/ (also **terai hat**) ▸ **noun 1** a wide-brimmed felt hat, typically with a double crown, worn chiefly by travellers in subtropical regions.
2 a belt of marshy jungle lying between the lower foothills of the Himalayas and the plains.
– ORIGIN late 19th cent.: from Hindi *tarāī* 'marshy lowlands'.

teraphim /ˈtɛrəfɪm/ ▸ **plural noun** [also treated as sing.] small images or cult objects used as domestic deities or oracles by ancient Semitic peoples.
– ORIGIN late Middle English: via late Latin from Greek *theraphin*, from Hebrew *tĕrāpīm*.

terato- ▸ **combining form** relating to monsters or abnormal forms: *teratology*.
– ORIGIN from Greek *teras*, *terat-* 'monster'.

teratocarcinoma /ˌtɛrətəʊkɑːsɪˈnəʊmə/ ▸ **noun** (pl. **teratocarcinomata** or **teratocarcinomas**) Medicine a form of malignant teratoma occurring especially in the testis.

teratogen /tɛˈratədʒ(ə)n, ˈtɛrətədʒ(ə)n/ ▸ **noun** an agent or factor which causes malformation of an embryo.
– DERIVATIVES **teratogenic** adjective, **teratogenicity** noun.

teratogenesis /ˌtɛrətə(ʊ)ˈdʒɛnɪsɪs/ ▸ **noun** [mass noun] the process by which congenital malformations are produced in an embryo or fetus.

teratology /ˌtɛrəˈtɒlədʒi/ ▸ **noun** [mass noun] **1** Medicine & Biology the scientific study of congenital abnormalities and abnormal formations.
2 mythology relating to fantastic creatures and monsters.
– DERIVATIVES **teratological** /-təˈlɒdʒɪk(ə)l/ adjective, **teratologist** noun.

teratoma /ˌtɛrəˈtəʊmə/ ▸ **noun** (pl. **teratomas** or **teratomata** /-mətə/) Medicine a tumour composed of tissues not normally present at the site (the site being typically in the gonads).

terawatt /ˈtɛrəwɒt/ ▸ **noun** a unit of power equal to 10^{12} watts or a million megawatts.

terbium /ˈtəːbɪəm/ ▸ **noun** [mass noun] the chemical element of atomic number 65, a silvery-white metal of the lanthanide series. (Symbol: **Tb**)
– ORIGIN mid 19th cent.: modern Latin, from *Ytterby*, the name of a village in Sweden where it was discovered. Compare with **ERBIUM** and **YTTERBIUM**.

terbutaline /təːˈbjuːtəliːn/ ▸ **noun** [mass noun] Medicine a synthetic compound with bronchodilator properties, used especially in the treatment of asthma. ● Chem. formula: $C_{12}H_{19}NO_3$.
– ORIGIN 1960s: from **TER-** + **BUTYL** (elements of the systematic name), on the pattern of words such as *isoprenaline*.

terce /təːs/ ▸ **noun** a service forming part of the Divine Office of the Western Christian Church, traditionally said (or chanted) at the third hour of the day (i.e. 9 a.m.).
– ORIGIN late Middle English: from Old French, from Latin *tertia*, feminine of *tertius* 'third'. Compare with **TIERCE**.

tercel /ˈtəːs(ə)l/ (also **tiercel**) ▸ **noun** Falconry the male of a hawk, especially a peregrine or a goshawk. Compare with **FALCON**.
– ORIGIN Middle English: from Old French, based on Latin *tertius* 'third', perhaps from the belief that the third egg of a clutch produced a male.

tercentenary ▸ **noun** (pl. **tercentenaries**) the three-hundredth anniversary of a significant event.
▸ **adjective** relating to a three-hundredth anniversary: *his tercentenary year.*

tercentennial ▸ **adjective & noun** another term for **TERCENTENARY**.

tercet /ˈtəːsɪt/ ▸ **noun** Prosody a set or group of three lines of verse rhyming together or connected by rhyme with an adjacent triplet.
– ORIGIN late 16th cent.: from French, from Italian *terzetto*, diminutive of *terzo* 'third', from Latin *tertius*.

terebinth /ˈtɛrəbɪnθ/ ▸ **noun** a small southern European tree which was formerly a source of turpentine and galls for use in tanning. ● *Pistacia terebinthus*, family Anacardiaceae.
– ORIGIN late Middle English: from Old French *therebinte*, or via Latin from Greek *terebinthos*.

terebratulid /ˌtɛrɪˈbratjʊlɪd/ ▸ **noun** Zoology a brachiopod of a mainly fossil order that originated in the Devonian, having a short pedicle and a calcareous loop supporting the tentacles. ● Order Terebratulida, class Articulata: many families.
– ORIGIN 1970s: from modern Latin *Terebratulida*, based on Latin *terebrare* 'to bore'.

teredo /təˈriːdəʊ/ ▸ **noun** Zoology (pl. **teredos**) a worm-like marine bivalve mollusc with reduced shells which it uses to drill into wood. It can cause substantial damage to wooden structures and (formerly) ships. Also called **SHIPWORM**. ● Genus *Teredo*, family Teredinidae: several species, in particular *T. navalis*.
– ORIGIN late Middle English: via Latin from Greek *terēdōn*; related to *teirein* 'rub hard, wear away'.

Terence (*c.*190–159 BC), Roman comic dramatist; Latin name *Publius Terentius Afer*. His six surviving comedies are based on the Greek New Comedy; they are marked by more realism and a greater consistency of plot than the works of Plautus.

Terengganu /ˌtɛrɛŋˈɡɑːnuː/ variant of **TRENGGANU**.

Te Reo /tɛ ˈreɪəʊ/ ▸ **noun** [mass noun] NZ the Maori language.
– ORIGIN from Maori *te* 'the' and *reo* 'language, dialect'.

terephthalate /ˌtɛrɛfˈθaleɪt/ ▸ **noun** Chemistry a salt or ester of terephthalic acid.

terephthalic acid /ˌtɛrɛfˈθalɪk/ ▸ **noun** [mass noun] Chemistry a crystalline organic acid used in making polyester resins and other polymers. ● The *para*-isomer of phthalic acid; chem. formula: $C_6H_4(COOH)_2$.
– ORIGIN mid 19th cent.: blend of *terebic* 'of or from turpentine' (from **TEREBINTH**) and **PHTHALIC ACID**.

teres /ˈtɛriːz/ ▸ **noun** Anatomy either of two muscles passing below the shoulder joint from the scapula to the upper part of the humerus, one (**teres major**) drawing the arm towards the body and rotating it inwards, the other (**teres minor**) rotating it outwards.
– ORIGIN early 18th cent.: modern Latin, from Latin, literally 'rounded'.

Teresa, Mother /təˈreɪzə, -ˈriːzə/ (also **Theresa**) (1910–97), Roman Catholic nun and missionary; born *Agnes Gonxha Bojaxhiu* in what is now Macedonia of Albanian parentage. She became an Indian citizen in 1948. She founded the Order of Missionaries of Charity, which became noted for its work among the poor in Calcutta (Kolkata) and now operates in many parts of the world. Nobel Peace Prize (1979).

Teresa of Ávila, St /ˈavɪlə/ (1515–82), Spanish Carmelite nun and mystic. She instituted the 'discalced' reform movement with St John of the Cross. Her writings include *The Way of Perfection* (1583) and *The Interior Castle* (1588). Feast day, 15 October.

Teresa of Lisieux, St /liːˈzjəː/ (also **Thérèse**) (1873–97), French Carmelite nun; born *Marie-Françoise Thérèse Martin*. In her autobiography *L'Histoire d'une âme* (1898) she taught that sanctity can be attained through continual renunciation in small matters, and not only through extreme self-mortification. Feast day, 3 October.

Tereshkova /ˌtɛrɪʃˈkəʊvə/, Valentina (Vladimirovna) (b.1937), Russian cosmonaut. In June 1963 she became the first woman in space.

Teresina /ˌtɛrɛˈziːnə/ a river port in NE Brazil, on the Parnaíba River, capital of the state of Piauí; pop. 779,939 (2007).

terete /təˈriːt/ ▶ **adjective** chiefly Botany cylindrical or slightly tapering, and without substantial furrows or ridges.
– ORIGIN early 17th cent.: from Latin *teres, teret-* 'rounded off'.

tergal /ˈtəːg(ə)l/ ▶ **adjective** Zoology relating to the terga of an arthropod.
– ORIGIN mid 19th cent.: from Latin *tergum* 'back' + **-AL**.

tergite /ˈtəːgʌɪt/ ▶ **noun** Entomology (in an insect) a sclerotized plate forming the tergum of a segment. Compare with **STERNITE**.
– ORIGIN late 19th cent.: from **TERGUM** + **-ITE**[1].

tergiversate /ˈtəːdʒɪvəˌseɪt, -ˈvəːseɪt/ ▶ **verb** [no obj.]
1 make conflicting or evasive statements; equivocate: *the more she tergiversated, the greater grew the ardency of the reporters for an interview.*
2 change one's loyalties; abandon a belief or principle.
– DERIVATIVES **tergiversation** noun, **tergiversator** noun.
– ORIGIN mid 17th cent.: from Latin *tergiversat-* 'with one's back turned', from the verb *tergiversari*, from *tergum* 'back' + *vertere* 'to turn'.

tergum /ˈtəːgəm/ ▶ **noun** (pl. **terga**) Zoology a thickened dorsal plate on each segment of the body of an arthropod.
– ORIGIN early 19th cent.: from Latin, literally 'back'.

-teria ▶ **suffix** denoting self-service establishments: *washeteria*.
– ORIGIN on the pattern of *(cafe)teria*.

teriyaki /ˌtɛrɪˈjɑːki/ ▶ **noun** [mass noun] a Japanese dish consisting of fish or meat marinated in soy sauce and grilled. ■ (also **teriyaki sauce**) a mixture of soy sauce, sake, ginger, and other flavourings, used in Japanese cookery as a marinade or glaze for fish or meat dishes.
– ORIGIN Japanese.

term ▶ **noun 1** a word or phrase used to describe a thing or to express a concept, especially in a particular kind of language or branch of study: *the musical term 'leitmotiv'* | *a term of abuse.* ■ (**terms**) language used on a particular occasion; a way of expressing oneself: *a protest in the strongest possible terms.* ■ Logic a word or words that may be the subject or predicate of a proposition.
2 a fixed or limited period for which something, for example office, imprisonment, or investment, lasts or is intended to last: *the President is elected for a single four-year term.* ■ (also **term day**) (especially in Scotland) a fixed day of the year appointed for the making of payments, the start or end of tenancies, etc. ■ (also **full term**) [mass noun] the completion of a normal length of pregnancy: *the pregnancy went to full term.* ■ (Brit. also **term of years** or US **term for years**) Law a tenancy of a fixed period. ■ archaic the duration of a person's life. ■ archaic a boundary or limit, especially of time.
3 each of the periods in the year, alternating with holiday or vacation, during which instruction is given in a school, college, or university, or during which a law court holds sessions: *the summer term* | *term starts tomorrow.*
4 (**terms**) conditions under which an action may be undertaken or agreement reached; stipulated or agreed requirements: *their solicitors had agreed terms* | *he could only be dealt with **on his own terms**.* ■ conditions with regard to payment for something; stated charges: *loans on favourable terms.* ■ agreed conditions under which a war or other dispute is brought to an end: *a deal in Bosnia that could force the Serbs to **come to terms**.*
5 Mathematics each of the quantities in a ratio, series, or mathematical expression.
6 Architecture another term for **TERMINUS**.
▶ **verb** [with obj. and usu. with complement] give a descriptive name to; call by a specified term: *he has been termed the father of modern theology.*
– PHRASES **come to terms with** come to accept (a new and painful or difficult event or situation); reconcile oneself to: *she had come to terms with the tragedies in her life.* **in terms of** (or **in —— terms**) with regard to the particular aspect or subject specified: *replacing the printers is difficult to justify in terms of cost.* **the long/short/medium term** used to refer to a time that is a specified way into the future: *these ventures are unlikely to yield much return in the short term.* **on terms** in a state of friendship or equality. ■ (in sport) level in score or on points. **on —— terms** in a specified relation or on a specified footing: *we are all on friendly terms.* **terms of reference** see **REFERENCE**.
– ORIGIN Middle English (denoting a limit in space or time, or (in the plural) limiting conditions): from Old French *terme*, from Latin *terminus* 'end, boundary, limit'.

termagant /ˈtəːməg(ə)nt/ ▶ **noun 1** a harsh-tempered or overbearing woman.
2 (**Termagant**) historical an imaginary deity of violent and turbulent character, often appearing in morality plays.
– ORIGIN Middle English (in sense 2): via Old French from Italian *Trivagante*, taken to be from Latin *tri-* 'three' + *vagant-* 'wandering', and to refer to the moon 'wandering' between heaven, earth, and hell under the three names *Selene, Artemis*, and *Persephone*.

term for years ▶ **noun** see **TERM** (sense 2 of the noun).

terminable ▶ **adjective 1** able to be terminated.
2 coming to an end after a certain time.

terminal ▶ **adjective 1** [attrib.] forming or situated at the end or extremity of something: *a terminal date* | *the terminal tip of the probe.* ■ of or forming a transport terminal: *the terminal building.* ■ Zoology situated at, forming, or denoting the end of a part or series of parts furthest from the centre of the body. ■ Botany (of a flower, inflorescence, etc.) borne at the end of a stem or branch. Often contrasted with **AXILLARY**.
2 (of a disease) predicted to lead to death, especially slowly; incurable: *terminal cancer.* ■ [attrib.] suffering from or relating to a terminal disease: *a hospice for terminal cases.* ■ [attrib.] (of a condition) forming the last stage of a terminal disease. ■ informal extreme and usually beyond cure or alteration (used for emphasis): *an industry in terminal decline* | *you're making a terminal ass of yourself.*
3 done or occurring each school, college, university, or law term: *terminal examinations.*
▶ **noun 1** the end of a railway or other transport route, or a station at such a point. ■ a departure and arrival building for air passengers at an airport. ■ an installation where oil or gas is stored at the end of a pipeline or at a port.
2 a point of connection for closing an electric circuit.
3 a device at which a user enters data or commands for a computer system and which displays the received output.
4 (also **terminal figure**) another term for **TERMINUS** (sense 3).
5 Brit. a patient suffering from a terminal illness.
– DERIVATIVES **terminally** adverb [as submodifier] *a terminally ill woman.*
– ORIGIN early 19th cent.: from Latin *terminalis*, from *terminus* 'end, boundary'.

terminal moraine ▶ **noun** Geology a moraine deposited at the point of furthest advance of a glacier or ice sheet.

terminal velocity ▶ **noun** Physics the constant speed that a freely falling object eventually reaches when the resistance of the medium through which it is falling prevents further acceleration.

terminate ▶ **verb 1** [with obj.] bring to an end: *he was advised to terminate the contract.* ■ end (a pregnancy) before term by artificial means. ■ [no obj.] (of a train, bus, or boat service) end its journey: *the train will terminate at Stratford.* ■ chiefly N. Amer. end the employment of (someone); dismiss: *Adamson's putting pressure on me to terminate you.* ■ euphemistic, chiefly N. Amer. murder (someone): *he was terminated by persons unknown.*
2 [no obj.] (**terminate in**) (of a thing) have its end at (a specified place) or of (a specified form): *the chain terminated in an iron ball covered with spikes.* ■ [with obj.] archaic form the physical end or extremity of (an area).
– PHRASES **terminate someone with extreme prejudice** euphemistic, chiefly US murder someone.
– ORIGIN late 16th cent. (in the sense 'direct an action towards a specified end'): from Latin *terminat-* 'limited, ended', from the verb *terminare*, from *terminus* 'end, boundary'.

termination ▶ **noun 1** [mass noun] the action of terminating something or the fact of being terminated: *the termination of a contract.* ■ [count noun] an induced abortion. ■ [count noun] chiefly N. Amer. an act of dismissing someone from employment. ■ [count noun] chiefly N. Amer. an assassination.
2 a word's final syllable or letters or letter, especially when constituting an element in inflection or derivation.
3 [with adj.] archaic an ending or result of a specified kind: *a good result and a happy termination.*
– ORIGIN late Middle English (in the sense 'determination, decision'): from Old French, or from Latin *terminatio(n-)*, from *terminare* 'to limit, end'.

terminator ▶ **noun 1** a person or thing that terminates something. ■ Biochemistry a sequence of polynucleotides that causes transcription to end and the newly synthesized nucleic acid to be released from the template molecule.
2 Astronomy the dividing line between the light and dark part of a planetary body.

terminator gene ▶ **noun** a gene in a genetically modified crop plant that stops the plant from setting fertile seed, thus preventing the farmer from saving seed for the next season.

terminer ▶ **noun** see **OYER AND TERMINER**.

termini plural form of **TERMINUS**.

terminological inexactitude ▶ **noun** a lie (used as a humorous euphemism).
– ORIGIN first used by Winston Churchill in a Commons speech in 1906.

terminology ▶ **noun** (pl. **terminologies**) [mass noun] the body of terms used with a particular technical application in a subject of study, theory, profession, etc.: *the terminology of semiotics* | [count noun] *specialized terminologies for higher education.*
– DERIVATIVES **terminological** adjective, **terminologically** adverb.
– ORIGIN early 19th cent.: from German *Terminologie*, from medieval Latin *terminus* 'term'.

terminus ▶ **noun** (pl. **termini** or **terminuses**) **1** chiefly Brit. the end of a railway or other transport route, or a station at such a point; a terminal. ■ an oil or gas terminal.
2 a final point in space or time; an end or extremity: *the exhibition's terminus is 1962.* ■ Biochemistry the end of a polypeptide or polynucleotide chain or similar long molecule.
3 Architecture a figure of a human bust or an animal ending in a square pillar from which it appears to spring, originally used as a boundary marker in ancient Rome.
– ORIGIN mid 16th cent. (in the sense 'final point in space or time'): from Latin, 'end, limit, boundary'.

terminus ad quem /ˌtəːmɪnəs ad ˈkwɛm/ ▶ **noun** the point at which something ends or finishes. ■ an aim or goal.
– ORIGIN Latin, literally 'end to which'.

terminus ante quem /ˌantɪ ˈkwɛm/ ▶ **noun** the latest possible date for something.
– ORIGIN Latin, literally 'end before which'.

terminus a quo /ɑː ˈkwəʊ/ ▶ **noun** the earliest possible date for something. ■ a starting point or initial impulse.
– ORIGIN Latin, literally 'end from which'.

terminus post quem /pəʊst ˈkwɛm/ ▶ **noun** the earliest possible date for something.
– ORIGIN Latin, literally 'end after which'.

termitarium /ˌtəːmʌɪˈtɛːrɪəm/ ▶ **noun** (pl. **termitaria**) a colony of termites, typically within a tall mound of cemented earth.
– ORIGIN mid 19th cent.: modern Latin, from Latin *termes, termit-* 'termite'.

termitary /ˈtəːmɪtəri/ ▶ **noun** (pl. **termitaries**) another term for **TERMITARIUM**.

termite /ˈtəːmʌɪt/ ▶ **noun** a small, pale soft-bodied insect that lives in large colonies with several different castes, typically within a mound of cemented earth. Many kinds feed on wood and can be highly destructive to trees and timber. Also called **WHITE ANT**.
● Order Isoptera: several families.
– ORIGIN late 18th cent.: from late Latin *termes, termit-* 'woodworm', alteration of Latin *tarmes*, perhaps by association with *terere* 'to rub'.

T

termly ▸ adjective & adverb Brit. happening or done once in each school, college, university, or law term: [as adj.] *termly examinations* | [as adv.] *the committee meets termly.*

term of years ▸ noun see TERM (sense 2 of the noun).

term paper ▸ noun N. Amer. a student's lengthy essay on a subject drawn from the work done during a school or college term.

terms of trade ▸ plural noun Economics the ratio of an index of a country's export prices to an index of its import prices.

tern¹ /təːn/ ▸ noun a seabird related to the gulls, typically smaller and more slender, with long pointed wings and a forked tail. ● Family Sternidae (or Laridae): several genera, in particular *Sterna*, and many species.
– ORIGIN late 17th cent.: of Scandinavian origin; related to Danish *terne* and Swedish *tärna*, both from Old Norse *therna*.

tern² /təːn/ ▸ noun rare a set of three, especially three lottery numbers that when drawn together win a large prize.
– ORIGIN late Middle English: apparently from French *terne*, from Latin *terni* 'three at once, three each', from *ter* 'thrice'.

ternary /ˈtəːnəri/ ▸ adjective composed of three parts. ■ Mathematics using three as a base.
– ORIGIN late Middle English: from Latin *ternarius*, from *terni* 'three at once'.

ternary form ▸ noun [mass noun] Music the form of a movement in which the first subject is repeated after an interposed second subject in a related key.

ternate /ˈtəːneɪt/ ▸ adjective Botany arranged in threes, especially (of a compound leaf) having three leaflets.
– ORIGIN mid 18th cent.: from modern Latin *ternatus*, from medieval Latin *ternare* 'make threefold', from *terni* 'three at once'.

terne /təːn/ ▸ noun (also **terne metal**) [mass noun] a lead alloy containing about 20 per cent tin and often some antimony. ■ (also **terne plate**) thin sheet iron or steel coated with terne.
– ORIGIN mid 19th cent. (denoting terne plate): probably from French *terne* 'dull, tarnished'.

ternlet ▸ noun (in Australia, New Zealand, and India) a small tern. ● Family Sternidae (or Laridae): several species, in particular the **grey ternlet** (*Procelsterna cerulea*) (alternative name: **blue-grey noddy**).

terotechnology /ˌtɛrə(ʊ)tɛkˈnɒlədʒi, ˌtɪərə(ʊ)-/ ▸ noun [mass noun] Brit. the branch of technology and engineering concerned with the installation and maintenance of equipment.
– ORIGIN 1970s: from Greek *tērein* 'take care of' + TECHNOLOGY.

terpene /ˈtəːpiːn/ ▸ noun Chemistry any of a large group of volatile unsaturated hydrocarbons found in the essential oils of plants, especially conifers and citrus trees. They are based on a cyclic molecule having the formula $C_{10}H_{16}$.
– ORIGIN late 19th cent.: from German *Terpentin* 'turpentine' + -ENE.

terpenoid /ˈtəːpɪnɔɪd/ ▸ noun Chemistry any of a large class of organic compounds including terpenes, diterpenes, and sesquiterpenes. They have unsaturated molecules composed of linked isoprene units, generally having the formula $(C_5H_8)n$.

terpolymer /təːˈpɒlɪmə/ ▸ noun Chemistry a polymer synthesized from three different monomers.

T

Terpsichore /təːpˈsɪkəri/ Greek & Roman Mythology the Muse of lyric poetry and dance.
– ORIGIN Greek, literally 'delighting in dancing'.

terpsichorean /ˌtəːpsɪkəˈriːən/ formal or humorous ▸ adjective relating to dancing.
▸ noun a dancer.
– ORIGIN early 19th cent.: from TERPSICHORE (used in the 18th cent. to denote a female dancer or the art of dance) + -AN.

terra /ˈtɛrə/ ▸ noun **1** [usu. with modifier] land or territory.
2 (also **Terra**) (in science fiction) the planet earth.
– ORIGIN Latin, literally 'earth'.

terra alba /tɛrə ˈalbə/ ▸ noun [mass noun] pulverized gypsum, especially as an ingredient of medicines.
– ORIGIN Latin, literally 'white earth'.

terrace ▸ noun **1** a level paved area next to a building; a patio.
2 each of a series of flat areas made on a slope, used for cultivation. ■ (usu. **terraces**) Brit. a flight of wide, shallow steps providing standing room for spectators in a stadium, especially a soccer ground. ■ Geology a natural horizontal shelf-like formation, such as a raised beach.
3 Brit. a row of houses built in one block in a uniform style. ■ an individual house in a terrace.
▸ verb [with obj.] make or form (sloping land) into a number of level flat areas resembling a series of steps.
– ORIGIN early 16th cent. (denoting an open gallery, later a platform or balcony in a theatre): from Old French, literally 'rubble, platform', based on Latin *terra* 'earth'.

terraced ▸ adjective **1** Brit. (of a house) forming part of a terrace.
2 (of land) having been formed into terraces.

terraced roof ▸ noun a flat roof, especially the roof of an Indian or Eastern house that is used as a cool resting area.

terracing ▸ noun [mass noun] **1** terraced ground.
2 Brit. wide, shallow steps used to provide standing room for spectators in a stadium.

terracotta /ˌtɛrəˈkɒtə/ ▸ noun [mass noun] a type of fired clay, typically of a brownish-red colour and unglazed, used as an ornamental building material and in modelling. ■ [count noun] a statuette or other object made of terracotta. ■ a strong brownish-red or brownish-orange colour.
– ORIGIN early 18th cent.: from Italian *terra cotta* 'baked earth', from Latin *terra cocta*.

terra firma /ˈfəːmə/ ▸ noun [mass noun] dry land; the ground as distinct from the sea or air.
– ORIGIN early 17th cent. (denoting the territories on the Italian mainland which were subject to the state of Venice): from Latin, literally 'firm land'.

terraform ▸ verb [with obj.] (especially in science fiction) transform (a planet) so as to resemble the earth, especially so that it can support human life.
– DERIVATIVES **terraformer** noun.
– ORIGIN 1940s: from Latin *terra* 'earth' + the verb FORM.

terrain /tɛˈreɪn/ ▸ noun [mass noun] a stretch of land, especially with regard to its physical features: *they were delayed by rough terrain.*
– ORIGIN early 18th cent. (denoting part of the training ground in a riding school): from French, from a popular Latin variant of Latin *terrenum*, neuter of *terrenus* (see TERRENE).

terra incognita /ɪnˈkɒgnɪtə, ˌɪnkɒgˈniːtə/ ▸ noun [mass noun] unknown or unexplored territory.
– ORIGIN Latin, 'unknown land'.

terrain park ▸ noun a specially designed outdoor area for snowboarding, containing a variety of ramps, jumps, etc.

terramare /ˌtɛrəˈmɑːri, -ˈmɛːri/ ▸ noun [mass noun] an ammoniacal earthy deposit found in mounds in prehistoric lake dwellings or settlements, especially in Italy. ■ a dwelling or settlement characterized by the presence of terramare.
– ORIGIN mid 19th cent.: from French, from Italian dialect *terramara*, from Italian *terra* 'earth' + *marna* 'marl'.

Terramycin /ˌtɛrəˈmʌɪsɪn/ ▸ noun trademark for OXYTETRACYCLINE.
– ORIGIN 1950s: from Latin *terra* 'earth' + -MYCIN.

terrane /tɛˈreɪn/ ▸ noun Geology a fault-bounded area or region with a distinctive stratigraphy, structure, and geological history.
– ORIGIN early 19th cent: from popular Latin *terranum*. Compare with TERRAIN.

terrapin ▸ noun **1** a freshwater turtle, especially one of the smaller kinds of the Old World. Called TURTLE in North America. ● Emydidae and other families, order Chelonia: several genera and species, in particular the **European pond terrapin**.
2 (also **diamondback terrapin**) US a small edible turtle with lozenge-shaped markings on its shell, found in coastal marshes of the eastern US. ● *Malaclemys terrapin*, family Emydidae.
3 (**Terrapin**) Brit. trademark a type of prefabricated one-storey building for temporary use.
– ORIGIN early 17th cent. (denoting the diamondback terrapin): of Algonquian origin.

terraqueous /tɛˈreɪkwɪəs/ ▸ adjective consisting or formed of land and water.
– ORIGIN mid 17th cent.: from Latin *terra* 'land' + AQUEOUS.

terrarium /tɛˈrɛːrɪəm/ ▸ noun (pl. **terrariums** or **terraria** /-rɪə/) a vivarium for smaller land animals, especially reptiles, amphibians, or terrestrial invertebrates, typically in the form of a glass-fronted case. ■ a sealed transparent globe or similar container in which plants are grown.
– ORIGIN late 19th cent.: modern Latin, from Latin *terra* 'earth', on the pattern of *aquarium*.

terra rossa /ˈrɒsə/ ▸ noun [mass noun] a reddish soil occurring on limestone in Mediterranean climates.
– ORIGIN late 19th cent.: Italian, literally 'red earth'.

terra sigillata /ˌsɪdʒɪˈleɪtə/ ▸ noun [mass noun] **1** astringent clay from Lemnos or Samos, formerly used as a medicine.
2 another term for SAMIAN WARE.
– ORIGIN late Middle English: from medieval Latin, literally 'sealed earth'.

Terrassa variant spelling of TARRASA.

terrasse /tɛras/ ▸ noun (pl. pronunc. **same**) (in France) a flat, paved area outside a cafe where people sit to take refreshments.
– ORIGIN French, literally 'terrace'.

terrazzo /tɛˈratsəʊ/ ▸ noun [mass noun] flooring material consisting of chips of marble or granite set in concrete and polished to give a smooth surface.
– ORIGIN early 20th cent.: Italian, literally 'terrace', based on Latin *terra* 'earth'.

Terre Haute /ˌtɛrə ˈhəʊt/ a city in western Indiana, on the Wabash River, near the border with Illinois; pop. 60,007 (est. 2008).

terrene /tɛˈriːn/ ▸ adjective archaic of or like earth. ■ occurring on or inhabiting dry land. ■ of the world; secular rather than spiritual.
– ORIGIN Middle English: from Anglo-Norman French, from Latin *terrenus*, from *terra* 'earth'.

terreplein /ˈtɛːpleɪn/ ▸ noun chiefly historical a level space where a battery of guns is mounted.
– ORIGIN late 16th cent. (denoting a sloping bank behind a rampart): from French *terre-plein*, from Italian *terrapieno* 'filled with earth'.

terrestrial /təˈrɛstrɪəl/ ▸ adjective **1** on or relating to the earth: *increased ultraviolet radiation may disrupt terrestrial ecosystems.* ■ denoting television broadcast using equipment situated on the ground rather than by satellite: *a fifth terrestrial channel.* ■ Astronomy (of a planet) similar in size or composition to the earth, especially being one of the four inner planets. ■ archaic relating to the earth as opposed to heaven.
2 of or on dry land: *a submarine eruption will be much more explosive than its terrestrial counterpart.* ■ (of an animal) living on or in the ground; not aquatic, arboreal, or aerial. ■ (of a plant) growing on land or in the soil; not aquatic or epiphytic.
▸ noun an inhabitant of the earth.
– DERIVATIVES **terrestrially** adverb.
– ORIGIN late Middle English (in the sense 'temporal, worldly, mundane'): from Latin *terrestris* (from *terra* 'earth') + -AL.

terrestrial globe ▸ noun a spherical representation of the earth with a map on the surface.

terrestrial magnetism ▸ noun [mass noun] the magnetic properties of the earth as a whole.

terrestrial telescope ▸ noun a telescope used for observing terrestrial objects, which gives an image that is not inverted.

terret /ˈtɛrɪt/ ▸ noun each of the loops or rings on a horse's harness pad for the driving reins to pass through.
– ORIGIN late 15th cent. (denoting either of two rings by which a leash is attached to a hawk's jesses): from Old French *touret*, diminutive of *tour* 'a turn'.

terre verte /tɛː ˈvɛːt/ ▸ noun [mass noun] a greyish-green pigment made from a kind of clay (glauconite) and used especially for watercolours and tempera. Also called GREEN EARTH.
– ORIGIN mid 17th cent.: French, literally 'green earth'.

terribilità /ˌtɛrɪbɪlɪˈtɑː/ ▸ noun [mass noun] awesomeness or emotional intensity of conception and execution in an artist or work of art, originally as a quality attributed to Michelangelo by his contemporaries.
– ORIGIN Italian.

terrible ▸ adjective **1** extremely bad or serious: *a terrible crime* | *the terrible conditions in which the ordinary people lived.* ■ extremely unpleasant or disagreeable: *the weather was terrible.* very unskilful: *despite passing my driving test first time, I'm a terrible driver* | *I was terrible at basketball.* ■ [attrib.] informal used to emphasize the extent of something unpleasant or bad: *what a terrible mess.* ■ very unwell or troubled: *I was sick all night and felt terrible for two days.*
2 causing or likely to cause terror; sinister: *the stranger gave a terrible smile.*

– PHRASES **terrible twos** informal a period in a child's social development (typically around the age of two years) which is associated with very defiant or unruly behaviour.
– DERIVATIVES **terribleness** noun.
– ORIGIN late Middle English (in the sense 'causing terror'): via French from Latin *terribilis*, from *terrere* 'frighten'.

terribly ▸ adverb **1** [as submodifier] very; extremely: *I'm terribly sorry* | *it was all terribly frustrating.* ■ very much: *your father misses you terribly.*
2 very badly or unpleasantly: *he came into the kitchen, swearing terribly.*

terricolous /tɛˈrɪkələs/ ▸ adjective Zoology (of an animal such as an earthworm) living on the ground or in the soil. ■ Botany (of a plant, especially a lichen) growing on soil or on the ground.
– ORIGIN mid 19th cent.: from Latin *terricola* 'earth dweller' (from *terra* 'earth' + *colere* 'inhabit') + **-ous**.

terrier[1] /ˈtɛrɪə/ ▸ noun **1** a small dog of a breed originally used for turning out foxes and other burrowing animals from their earths. ■ used in similes to emphasize tenacity or eagerness: *she would fight like a terrier for every penny.*
2 (**Terrier**) Brit. informal a member of the Territorial Army.
– ORIGIN late Middle English: from Old French (*chien*) *terrier* 'earth (dog)', from medieval Latin *terrarius*, from Latin *terra* 'earth'.

terrier[2] /ˈtɛrɪə/ ▸ noun historical a register of the lands belonging to a landowner, originally including a list of tenants, their holdings, and the rents paid, later consisting of a description of the acreage and boundaries of the property. ■ an inventory of property or goods.
– ORIGIN late 15th cent.: from Old French *terrier*, from medieval Latin *terrarius* (*liber*) '(book) of land', from Latin *terra* 'earth'.

terrific ▸ adjective **1** of great size, amount, or intensity: *there was a terrific bang.* ■ informal extremely good; excellent: *it's been such a terrific day* | *you look terrific.*
2 archaic causing terror.
– DERIVATIVES **terrifically** adverb [as submodifier] *she's been terrifically busy lately.*
– ORIGIN mid 17th cent. (in sense 2): from Latin *terrificus*, from *terrere* 'frighten'.

terrify ▸ verb (**terrifies**, **terrifying**, **terrified**) [with obj.] cause to feel extreme fear: *the thought terrifies me.* (as adj. **terrified**) *he is terrified of spiders* | [with clause] *she was terrified he would drop her* | (as adj. **terrifying**) *the terrifying events of the past few weeks.*
– DERIVATIVES **terrifier** noun, **terrifyingly** adverb [as submodifier] *the bombs are terrifyingly accurate.*
– ORIGIN late 16th cent.: from Latin *terrificare*, from *terrificus* 'frightening' (see **TERRIFIC**).

terrigenous /tɛˈrɪdʒɪnəs/ ▸ adjective Geology (of a marine deposit) made of material eroded from the land.
– ORIGIN late 17th cent. (in the sense 'produced from the earth, earth-born'): from Latin *terrigenus* (from *terra* 'earth' + *-genus* 'born') + **-ous**.

terrine /təˈriːn/ ▸ noun a meat, fish, or vegetable mixture that has been cooked or otherwise prepared in advance and allowed to cool or set in its container, typically served in slices. ■ a container used for a terrine, typically of an oblong shape and made of earthenware.
– ORIGIN early 18th cent. (denoting a tureen): from French, literally 'large earthenware pot', from *terrin* 'earthen'. Compare with **TUREEN**.

territorial ▸ adjective **1** relating to the ownership of an area of land or sea: *territorial disputes.* ■ Zoology (of an animal or species) defending a territory: *these sharks are aggressively territorial.* ■ relating to an animal's territory: *the gerbils' territorial behaviour.*
2 relating to a particular territory, district, or locality: *a bizarre territorial rite.* ■ (usu. **Territorial**) relating to a Territory, especially in the US or Canada.
▸ noun (**Territorial**) (in the UK) a member of the Territorial Army.
– DERIVATIVES **territoriality** noun, **territorially** adverb.
– ORIGIN early 17th cent.: from late Latin *territorialis*, from Latin *territorium* (see **TERRITORY**).

Territorial Army (in the UK) a volunteer force locally organized to provide a reserve of trained and disciplined manpower for use in an emergency.

territorial imperative ▸ noun Zoology & Psychology the need to claim and defend a territory.

territorial waters ▸ plural noun the waters under the jurisdiction of a state, especially the part of the sea within a stated distance of the shore (traditionally three miles from low-water mark).

territory ▸ noun (pl. **territories**) **1** an area of land under the jurisdiction of a ruler or state: *the government was prepared to give up the nuclear weapons on its territory* | [mass noun] *sorties into enemy territory.* ■ Zoology an area defended by an animal or group of animals against others of the same sex or species. ■ an area defended by a team or player in a game or sport. ■ an area in which one has certain rights or for which one has responsibility with regard to a particular type of activity: *don't go committing murders on my territory.* ■ [mass noun] [with adj. or noun modifier] land with a specified characteristic: *woodland territory.*
2 (**Territory**) (especially in the US, Canada, or Australia) an organized division of a country that is not yet admitted to the full rights of a state.
3 [mass noun] an area of knowledge, activity, or experience: *the contentious territory of clinical standards* | *the way she felt now—she was in unknown territory.*
– PHRASES **go** (or **come**) **with the territory** be an unavoidable result of a particular situation.
– ORIGIN late Middle English: from Latin *territorium*, from *terra* 'land'. The word originally denoted the district surrounding and under the jurisdiction of a town or city, specifically a Roman or provincial city.

terroir /tɛrˈwɑː/, French /tɛrwar/ ▸ noun the complete natural environment in which a particular wine is produced, including factors such as the soil, topography, and climate. ■ (also **goût de terroir** /ˌguː də/, French /gu də/) the characteristic taste and flavour imparted to a wine by the environment in which it is produced.
– ORIGIN French, 'land', from medieval Latin *terratorium*.

terror ▸ noun **1** [mass noun] extreme fear: *people fled in terror* | [in sing.] *she had a terror of darkness.* ■ the use of extreme fear to intimidate people: *weapons of terror.* ■ [often as modifier] terrorism: *a terror suspect* | *a terror attack.* ■ [in sing.] a person or thing that causes extreme fear: *his delivery is **the terror of** even world-class batsmen.* ■ (**the Terror**) the period of the French Revolution between mid 1793 and July 1794 when the ruling Jacobin faction, dominated by Robespierre, ruthlessly executed anyone considered a threat to their regime. Also called **REIGN OF TERROR**.
2 (also **holy terror**) informal a person, especially a child, that causes trouble or annoyance.
– PHRASES **have** (or **hold**) **no terrors for someone** not frighten or worry someone.
– ORIGIN late Middle English: from Old French *terrour*, from Latin *terror*, from *terrere* 'frighten'.

> **WORD TRENDS** When George W. Bush declared a 'War on Terror' in September 2001 he was employing a new, and highly charged, synonym for terrorism. Before 2001 **terror** was a fairly uncommon word in the Oxford English Corpus, but it has since shown a steady rise in use, with the majority of examples being used synonymously with **terrorism**. It is now commonly seen as a modifier, with *attack*, *bombing*, *suspect*, and *plot* all common collocates. However, the use of **terror** has dropped off since a peak in 2007. In March 2009 the US Defense Department officially changed the name of its operations from 'Global War on Terror' to 'Overseas Contingency Operation'.

terrorism ▸ noun [mass noun] the unofficial or unauthorized use of violence and intimidation in the pursuit of political aims.

terrorist ▸ noun a person who uses terrorism in the pursuit of political aims.
– DERIVATIVES **terroristic** adjective, **terroristically** adverb.
– ORIGIN late 18th cent.: from French *terroriste*, from Latin *terror* (see **TERROR**). The word was originally applied to supporters of the Jacobins in the French Revolution, who advocated repression and violence in pursuit of the principles of democracy and equality.

terrorize (also **terrorise**) ▸ verb [with obj.] create and maintain a state of extreme fear and distress in (someone); fill with terror: *the union said staff would not be terrorized into ending their strike.*
– DERIVATIVES **terrorization** noun, **terrorizer** noun.

terror-stricken (also **terror-struck**) ▸ adjective feeling or expressing extreme fear.

Terry, Dame (Alice) Ellen (1847–1928), English actress. She played in many of Henry Irving's Shakespearean productions, and George Bernard Shaw created a number of roles for her.

terry ▸ noun (pl. **terries**) [mass noun] a fabric with raised uncut loops of thread covering both surfaces, used especially for towels.
– ORIGIN late 18th cent.: of unknown origin.

terse ▸ adjective (**terser**, **tersest**) sparing in the use of words; abrupt: *a terse statement.*
– DERIVATIVES **tersely** adverb, **terseness** noun.
– ORIGIN early 17th cent.: from Latin *tersus* 'wiped, polished', from the verb *tergere*. The original sense was 'polished, trim, spruce', (relating to language) 'polished, polite', hence 'concise and to the point' (late 18th cent.).

tertian /ˈtəːʃ(ə)n/ ▸ adjective Medicine denoting a form of malaria causing a fever that recurs every second day: *tertian fever.* ● The common benign tertian malaria (or tertian ague) is caused by infection with *Plasmodium vivax* or *P. ovale*, and malignant tertian malaria is caused by *P. falciparum*. Compare with **QUARTAN**.
– ORIGIN late Middle English (*fever*) *terciane*, from Latin (*febris*) *tertiana*, from *tertius* 'third' (the fever recurring every third day by inclusive reckoning).

tertiary /ˈtəːʃ(ə)ri/ ▸ adjective **1** third in order or level: *the tertiary stage of the disease.* ■ chiefly Brit. relating to or denoting education at a level beyond that provided by schools, especially that provided by a college or university. ■ relating to or denoting the medical treatment provided at a specialist institution.
2 (**Tertiary**) Geology relating to or denoting the first period of the Cenozoic era, between the Cretaceous and Quaternary periods, and comprising the Palaeogene and Neogene sub-periods.
3 Chemistry (of an organic compound) having its functional group located on a carbon atom which is itself bonded to three other carbon atoms. ■ (chiefly of amines) derived from ammonia by replacement of three hydrogen atoms by organic groups.
▸ noun **1** (**the Tertiary**) Geology the Tertiary period or the system of rocks deposited during it.

> The Tertiary lasted from about 65 to 1.6 million years ago. The mammals diversified following the demise of the dinosaurs and became dominant, as did the flowering plants.

2 a lay associate of certain Christian monastic organizations: *a Franciscan tertiary.*
– ORIGIN mid 16th cent. (in sense 2 of the noun): from Latin *tertiarius* 'of the third part or rank', from *tertius* 'third'.

tertiary industry ▸ noun [mass noun] Economics the part of a country's economy concerned with the provision of services.

tertiary sector ▸ noun the sector of an economy concerned with or relating to tertiary industry.

tertiary structure ▸ noun Biochemistry the overall three-dimensional structure resulting from folding and covalent cross-linking of a protein or polynucleotide molecule.

tertium quid /ˌtəːʃɪəm ˈkwɪd, ˌtəːtɪəm/ ▸ noun a third thing that is indefinite and undefined but is related to two definite or known things.
– ORIGIN early 18th cent.: from late Latin, translation of Greek *triton ti* 'some third thing'.

Tertullian /təːˈtʌlɪən/ (*c*.160–*c*.240), early Christian theologian; Latin name *Quintus Septimius Florens Tertullianus*. His writings include Christian apologetics and attacks on pagan idolatry and Gnosticism.

tervalent /təːˈveɪl(ə)nt/ ▸ adjective Chemistry another term for **TRIVALENT**.

Terylene ▸ noun [mass noun] Brit. trademark an artificial textile fibre made from a polyester, used to make light, crease-resistant clothing, bed linen, and sails.
– ORIGIN 1940s: formed by inversion of (*polyeth*) *ylene ter*(*ephthalate*).

terza rima /ˌtɛːtsə ˈriːmə/ ▸ noun Prosody an arrangement of triplets, especially in iambic pentameter, that rhyme *aba bcb cdc* etc., as in Dante's *Divine Comedy*.
– ORIGIN Italian, literally 'third rhyme'.

terzetto /tɛːtˈsɛtəʊ, təːt-/ ▸ noun (pl. **terzettos** or **terzetti** /-ti/) Music a vocal or instrumental trio.
– ORIGIN Italian (see **TERCET**).

TESL ▸ abbreviation teaching of English as a second language.

Tesla /ˈtɛslə/, Nikola (1856–1943), American electrical engineer and inventor, born in what is now Croatia of Serbian descent. He developed the first alternating-current induction motor, as well as several forms of oscillators, the Tesla coil, and a wireless guidance system for ships.

T

tesla /ˈtɛslə, ˈtɛzlə/ (abbrev.: **T**) ▸ **noun** Physics the SI unit of magnetic flux density.
– ORIGIN 1960s: named after N. TESLA.

Tesla coil ▸ **noun** a form of induction coil for producing high-frequency alternating currents.

TESOL /ˈtɛsɒl/ ▸ **abbreviation** teaching of English to speakers of other languages.

TESSA (also **Tessa**) ▸ **noun** (in the UK) a tax-exempt special savings account allowing savers to invest a certain amount in a bank or building society with no tax to pay on the interest, provided that the capital remains in the account for five years (replaced in 1999 by the ISA).
– ORIGIN acronym.

tessellate /ˈtɛsəleɪt/ (US also **tesselate**) ▸ **verb** [with obj.] **1** (often as adj. **tessellated**) decorate (a floor or pavement) with mosaics.
2 cover (a plane surface) by repeated use of a single shape, without gaps or overlapping.
– ORIGIN late 17th cent. (as *tessellated*): from late Latin *tessellat-*, from the verb *tessellare*, from *tessella*, diminutive of *tessera* (see TESSERA).

tessellation /ˌtɛsəˈleɪʃ(ə)n/ (US also **tesselation**) ▸ **noun** [mass noun] the process or art of tessellating a surface, or the state of being tessellated. ▪ [count noun] an arrangement of shapes closely fitted together, especially of polygons in a repeated pattern without gaps or overlapping.

tessera /ˈtɛs(ə)rə/ ▸ **noun** (pl. **tesserae** /-riː/) a small block of stone, tile, glass, or other material used in the construction of a mosaic. ▪ (in ancient Greece and Rome) a small tablet of wood or bone used as a token.
– ORIGIN mid 17th cent.: via Latin from Greek, neuter of *tesseres*, variant of *tessares* 'four'.

Tessin French /tɛsɛ̃/, German /tɛˈsiːn/ French and German name for TICINO.

tessitura /ˌtɛsɪˈtjʊərə/ ▸ **noun** Music the range within which most notes of a vocal part fall.
– ORIGIN Italian, literally 'texture', from Latin *textura* (see TEXTURE).

test[1] ▸ **noun 1** a procedure intended to establish the quality, performance, or reliability of something, especially before it is taken into widespread use: *both countries carried out nuclear tests in May* | [mass noun] *four fax modems are* ***on test****.* ▪ a short written or spoken examination of a person's proficiency or knowledge: *a spelling test.* ▪ an event or situation that reveals the strength or quality of someone or something by putting them under strain: *this is the first serious test of the peace agreement.* ▪ an examination of part of the body or a body fluid for medical purposes, especially by means of a chemical or mechanical procedure rather than simple inspection: *a test for HIV* | *eye tests.* ▪ Chemistry a procedure employed to identify a substance or to reveal the presence or absence of a constituent within a substance. ▪ the result of a medical examination or analytical procedure: *a positive test for protein.* ▪ a means of establishing whether an action, item, or situation is an instance of a specified quality, especially one held to be undesirable: *a statutory test of obscenity.*
2 (**Test**) short for TEST MATCH.
3 Metallurgy a movable hearth in a reverberating furnace, used for separating gold or silver from lead.
▸ **verb** [with obj.] take measures to check the quality, performance, or reliability of (something), especially before putting it into widespread use or practice: *this range has not been tested on animals* | *several trial runs were carried out to test the special brakes.* ▪ give (someone) a short written or oral examination of their proficiency or knowledge: *all children are tested at eleven.* ▪ judge or measure (someone's proficiency or knowledge) by means of a test: *the exam will test accuracy and neatness.* ▪ reveal the strengths or capabilities of (someone or something) by putting them under strain: *such behaviour would severely test any marriage.* ▪ carry out a medical test on (a person, a part of the body, or a body fluid): *he's been tested for drugs.* ▪ [no obj., with complement] produce a specified result in a medical test, especially a drugs test or AIDS test: *he* ***tested positive*** *for steroids during the race.* ▪ Chemistry examine (a substance) by means of a reagent. ▪ touch or taste (something) to check that it is acceptable before proceeding further: *she tested the water with the tip of her elbow.*
– PHRASES **put someone/thing to the test** find out how useful, strong, or effective someone or something is. **stand the test of time** last or remain popular for a long time. **test the water** judge people's feelings or opinions before taking further action.
– DERIVATIVES **testability** noun, **testable** adjective, **testee** noun.
– ORIGIN late Middle English (denoting a cupel used to treat gold or silver alloys or ore): via Old French from Latin *testu, testum* 'earthen pot', variant of *testa* 'jug, shell'. Compare with TEST[2]. The verb dates from the early 17th cent.

test[2] ▸ **noun** Zoology the shell or integument of some invertebrates and protozoans, especially the chalky shell of a foraminiferan or the tough outer layer of a tunicate.
– ORIGIN mid 19th cent.: from Latin *testa* 'tile, jug, shell'. Compare with TEST[1].

testa ▸ **noun** (pl. **testae** /-tiː/) Botany the protective outer covering of a seed; the seed coat.
– ORIGIN late 18th cent.: from Latin, literally 'tile, shell'.

testaceous /tɛˈsteɪʃəs/ ▸ **adjective** chiefly Entomology of a dull brick-red colour.
– ORIGIN mid 17th cent.: from Latin *testaceus* (from *testa* 'tile') + **-OUS**.

Test Act ▸ **noun 1** (in the UK) an act in force between 1673 and 1828 that made an oath of allegiance to the Church of England and the supremacy of the monarch as its head and repudiation of the doctrine of transubstantiation a condition of eligibility for public office.
2 (in the UK) an act of 1871 relaxing restrictions on university entrance for candidates who were not members of the Church of England.

testament ▸ **noun 1** a person's will, especially the part relating to personal property.
2 something that serves as a sign or evidence of a specified fact, event, or quality: *growing attendance figures are a* ***testament to*** *the event's popularity.*
3 (in biblical use) a covenant or dispensation. ▪ (**Testament**) a division of the Bible. See also OLD TESTAMENT, NEW TESTAMENT. ▪ (**Testament**) a copy of the New Testament.
– ORIGIN Middle English: from Latin *testamentum* 'a will' (from *testari* 'testify'), in Christian Latin also translating Greek *diathēkē* 'covenant'.

testamentary ▸ **adjective** relating to or bequeathed or appointed through a will.
– ORIGIN late Middle English: from Latin *testamentarius*, from *testamentum* 'a will', from *testari* 'testify'.

testate /ˈtɛsteɪt/ ▸ **adjective** [predic.] having made a valid will before one dies.
▸ **noun** a person who has died leaving a valid will.
– ORIGIN late Middle English (as a noun): from Latin *testatus* 'testified, witnessed', past participle of *testari*, from *testis* 'a witness'.

testation ▸ **noun** [mass noun] Law the disposal of property by will.

testator /tɛˈsteɪtə/ ▸ **noun** Law a person who has made a will or given a legacy.
– ORIGIN Middle English: from Anglo-Norman French *testatour*, from Latin *testator*, from the verb *testari* 'testify'.

testatrix /tɛˈsteɪtrɪks/ ▸ **noun** (pl. **testatrices** /-trɪsiːz/ or **testatrixes**) Law a woman who has made a will or given a legacy.
– ORIGIN late 16th cent.: from late Latin, feminine of *testator* (see TESTATOR).

Test Ban Treaty an international agreement not to test nuclear weapons in the atmosphere, in space, or under water, signed in 1963 by the US, the UK, and the USSR, and later by more than 100 governments.

test bed ▸ **noun** a piece of equipment used for testing new machinery, especially aircraft engines.

test card ▸ **noun** Brit. a still television picture transmitted outside normal programme hours and designed for use in judging the quality and position of the image.

test case ▸ **noun** Law a case that sets a precedent for other cases involving the same question of law.

test drive ▸ **noun** an act of driving a motor vehicle that one is considering buying, in order to determine its qualities.
▸ **verb** (**test-drive**) [with obj.] drive (a motor vehicle) to determine its qualities with a view to buying it.

tester[1] ▸ **noun 1** a person who tests something, especially a new product. ▪ a person who tests another's proficiency. ▪ a device that tests the functioning of something: *a mains tester.*
2 a sample of a product provided so that customers can try it before buying it.

tester[2] ▸ **noun** a canopy over a four-poster bed.
– ORIGIN late Middle English: from medieval Latin *testerium, testrum*, from a Romance word meaning 'head', based on Latin *testa* 'tile'.

testes plural form of TESTIS.

test flight ▸ **noun** a flight during which the performance of an aircraft or its equipment is tested.
– DERIVATIVES **test-fly** verb (**test-flies, test-flying, test-flew, test-flown**).

testicle ▸ **noun** either of the two oval organs that produce sperm in men and other male mammals, enclosed in the scrotum behind the penis. Also called TESTIS.
– DERIVATIVES **testicular** adjective.
– ORIGIN late Middle English: from Latin *testiculus*, diminutive of *testis* 'a witness' (i.e. to virility).

testicular feminization ▸ **noun** [mass noun] a condition produced in genetically male people by the failure of tissue to respond to male sex hormones, resulting in normal female anatomy but with testes in place of ovaries.

testiculate /tɛˈstɪkjʊlət/ ▸ **adjective** Botany (especially of the twin tubers of some orchids) shaped like a pair of testicles.
– ORIGIN mid 18th cent.: from late Latin *testiculatus*, from *testiculus* (see TESTICLE).

testify ▸ **verb** (**testifies, testifying, testified**) [no obj.] give evidence as a witness in a law court: *he testified against his own commander* | [with clause] *two guards testified that he was one of the assailants.* ▪ serve as evidence or proof that something exists or is the case: *the bleak lines* ***testify to*** *inner torment.*
– DERIVATIVES **testifier** noun.
– ORIGIN late Middle English: from Latin *testificari*, from *testis* 'a witness'.

testimonial /ˌtɛstɪˈməʊnɪəl/ ▸ **noun 1** a formal statement testifying to someone's character and qualifications. ▪ a public tribute to someone and to their achievements.
2 (in sport) a game or event held in honour of a player, who typically receives part of the income generated: [as modifier] *a testimonial match.*
– ORIGIN late Middle English: from Old French *testimonial* 'testifying, serving as evidence', from late Latin *testimonialis*, from Latin *testimonium* (see TESTIMONY).

testimony ▸ **noun** (pl. **testimonies**) a formal written or spoken statement, especially one given in a court of law. ▪ [mass noun] evidence or proof of something: *his blackened finger was* ***testimony to*** *the fact that he had played in pain.* ▪ a public recounting of a religious conversion or experience. ▪ archaic a solemn protest or declaration.
– ORIGIN Middle English: from Latin *testimonium*, from *testis* 'a witness'.

testing ▸ **adjective** revealing a person's capabilities by putting them under strain; challenging: *it's been quite a testing time for all of us.*

testing ground ▸ **noun** an area or field of activity used for the testing of a product or an idea, especially a military site used for the testing of weapons.

testis /ˈtɛstɪs/ ▸ **noun** (pl. **testes** /-tiːz/) Anatomy & Zoology an organ which produces spermatozoa (male reproductive cells). Compare with TESTICLE.
– ORIGIN early 18th cent.: from Latin, literally 'a witness' (i.e. to virility). Compare with TESTICLE.

Test match ▸ **noun** an international cricket or rugby match, typically one of a series, played between teams representing two different countries: *the Test match between Pakistan and the West Indies.*

test meal ▸ **noun** Medicine a portion of food of specified quantity and composition, eaten to stimulate digestive secretions which can then be analysed.

testosterone /tɛˈstɒstərəʊn/ ▸ **noun** [mass noun] a steroid hormone that stimulates development of male secondary sexual characteristics, produced mainly in the testes, but also in the ovaries and adrenal cortex.
– ORIGIN 1930s: from TESTIS + *sterone* (blend of STEROL and KETONE).

test paper ▸ **noun 1** a paper set to test the knowledge of a student, especially in preparation for an examination.
2 Chemistry a paper impregnated with an indicator which changes colour under known conditions, used especially to test for acidity.

test piece ▸ **noun** a piece of music set to be performed by contestants in a competition.

T

test pilot ▸ noun a pilot who flies an aircraft to test its performance.

test pit ▸ noun a small preliminary excavation made to gain an idea of the contents or stratigraphy of an archaeological site.

test rig ▸ noun an apparatus used for assessing the performance of a piece of mechanical or electrical equipment.

test strip ▸ noun a strip of material used in testing, especially (in photography) a strip of sensitized material, sections of which are exposed for varying lengths of time to assess its response.

test tube ▸ noun a thin glass tube closed at one end, used to hold small amounts of material for laboratory testing or experiments. ■ [as modifier] denoting things produced or processes performed in a laboratory: *new forms of test-tube life.*

test-tube baby ▸ noun informal a baby conceived by in vitro fertilization.

Testudines /tɛˈstjuːdɪniːz/ ▸ plural noun Zoology an order of reptiles which comprises the turtles, terrapins, and tortoises. They are distinguished by having a shell of bony plates covered with horny scales, and many kinds are aquatic. Also called **CHELONIA**.
– ORIGIN modern Latin (plural), based on Latin *testa* 'shell'.

testudo /tɛˈstjuːdəʊ, -ˈstuː-/ ▸ noun (pl. **testudos** or **testudines** /-dɪniːz/) (in ancient Rome) a wheeled screen with an arched roof, used to protect besieging troops. ■ a protective screen formed by a body of troops holding their shields above their heads in such a way that the shields overlap.
– ORIGIN late Middle English: from Latin, literally 'tortoise', from *testa* 'tile, shell'.

testy ▸ adjective (**testier**, **testiest**) easily irritated; impatient and somewhat bad-tempered.
– DERIVATIVES **testily** adverb, **testiness** noun.
– ORIGIN late Middle English (in the sense 'headstrong, impetuous'): from Anglo-Norman French *testif*, from Old French *teste* 'head', from Latin *testa* 'shell'.

tetanic /tɪˈtanɪk/ ▸ adjective relating to or characteristic of tetanus, especially in connection with tonic muscle spasm.
– ORIGIN early 18th cent.: via Latin from Greek *tetanikos*, from *tetanos* (see **TETANUS**).

tetanus ▸ noun [mass noun] **1** a bacterial disease marked by rigidity and spasms of the voluntary muscles. See also **TRISMUS**. ● This disease is caused by the bacterium *Clostridium tetani*; Gram-positive anaerobic rods.
2 Physiology the prolonged contraction of a muscle caused by rapidly repeated stimuli.
– ORIGIN late Middle English: from Latin, from Greek *tetanos* 'muscular spasm', from *teinein* 'to stretch'.

tetany /ˈtɛt(ə)ni/ ▸ noun [mass noun] a condition marked by intermittent muscular spasms, caused by malfunction of the parathyroid glands and a consequent deficiency of calcium.
– ORIGIN late 19th cent.: from French *tétanie*, from Latin *tetanus* (see **TETANUS**).

tetchy ▸ adjective (**tetchier**, **tetchiest**) irritable and bad-tempered.
– DERIVATIVES **tetchily** adverb, **tetchiness** noun.
– ORIGIN late 16th cent.: probably from a variant of Scots *tache* 'blotch, fault', from Old French *teche*.

tête-à-tête /ˌtɛtaˈtɛt, ˌteɪtɑːˈteɪt/ ▸ noun (pl. **tête-à-têtes** pronunc. **same**) **1** a private conversation between two people.
2 an S-shaped sofa on which two people can sit face to face.
▸ adjective & adverb involving or happening between two people in private: [as adj.] *a tête-à-tête meal* | [as adv.] *his business was conducted tête-à-tête.*
– ORIGIN late 17th cent.: French, literally 'head-to-head'.

tête-bêche /ˌtɛtˈbɛʃ/, French /tɛtbɛʃ/ ▸ adjective (of a postage stamp) printed upside down or sideways relative to another.
– ORIGIN French, from *tête* 'head' and *bêche*, contraction of obsolete *béchevet* 'double bedhead'.

tête de cuvée /ˌtɛt də kjuːˈveɪ, ˌteɪt/, French /tɛt də kyve/ ▸ noun (pl. **têtes de cuvées** pronunc. **same**) a wine produced from the first pressing of the grapes, generally considered superior in quality. ■ a vineyard producing the best wine in the locality of a village.
– ORIGIN French, literally 'head of the vatful'.

tether ▸ verb [with obj.] tie (an animal) with a rope or chain so as to restrict its movement: *the horse had been tethered to a post.*
▸ noun a rope or chain with which an animal is tied to restrict its movement.
– PHRASES **the end of one's tether** see **END**.
– ORIGIN late Middle English: from Old Norse *tjóthr*, from a Germanic base meaning 'fasten'.

Tethys /ˈtɛθɪs/ **1** Greek Mythology a goddess of the sea, daughter of Uranus (Heaven) and Gaia (Earth).
2 Astronomy a satellite of Saturn, the ninth closest to the planet and probably composed mainly of ice, discovered by Cassini in 1684 (diameter 1,050 km).
3 Geology an ocean formerly separating the supercontinents of Gondwana and Laurasia, the forerunner of the present-day Mediterranean.

Tet Offensive (in the Vietnam War) an offensive launched in January–February 1968 by the Vietcong and the North Vietnamese army. Timed to coincide with the first day of the Tet (Vietnamese New Year), it was a surprise attack on South Vietnamese cities, notably Saigon. Although repulsed after initial successes, the attack shook US confidence and hastened the withdrawal of its forces.

Teton /ˈtiːtɒn, -t(ə)n/ (also **Teton Sioux**) ▸ noun another term for **LAKOTA**.
– ORIGIN the name in Dakota, literally 'dwellers on the prairie'.

Tétouan /teɪˈtwɑːn/ a city in northern Morocco; pop. 613,506 (2004).

tetra /ˈtɛtrə/ ▸ noun a small tropical freshwater fish that is typically brightly coloured. Native to Africa and America, many tetras are popular in aquaria. ● Numerous genera and species in the family Characidae, including the **neon tetra**.
– ORIGIN mid 20th cent.: abbreviation of modern Latin *Tetragonopterus* (former genus name), literally 'tetragonal finned'.

tetra- (also **tetr-** before a vowel) ▸ combining form **1** four; having four: *tetramerous* | *tetragram* | *tetrode*.
2 Chemistry (in names of compounds) containing four atoms or groups of a specified kind: *tetracycline*.
– ORIGIN from Greek, from *tettares* 'four'.

tetrachloroethylene /ˌtɛtrəˌklɔːrəʊˈɛθɪliːn, -ˌklɒrəʊ-/ ▸ noun another term for **PERCHLOROETHYLENE**.

tetrachord ▸ noun Music a scale of four notes, the interval between the first and last being a perfect fourth. ■ historical an instrument with four strings.

tetracyclic /ˌtɛtrəˈsʌɪklɪk, -ˈsɪk-/ ▸ adjective Chemistry (of a compound) having a molecular structure of four fused hydrocarbon rings.

tetracycline /ˌtɛtrəˈsʌɪkliːn/ ▸ noun Medicine any of a large group of antibiotics with a molecular structure containing four rings. ● These antibiotics are often obtained from bacteria of the genus **Streptomyces**.
– ORIGIN 1950s: from **TETRA-** + **CYCLIC** + **-INE**[4].

tetrad /ˈtɛtrad/ ▸ noun technical a group or set of four.
– ORIGIN mid 17th cent.: from Greek *tetras*, *tetrad-* 'four, a group of four'.

tetradactyl /ˌtɛtrəˈdaktɪl/ ▸ adjective Zoology (of a vertebrate limb) having four toes or fingers.
– DERIVATIVES **tetradactyly** noun.

tetraethyl lead /ˌtɛtrəˈiːθʌɪl/ ▸ noun [mass noun] Chemistry a toxic colourless oily liquid made synthetically and used as an anti-knock agent in leaded petrol. ● Chem. formula: $Pb(C_2H_5)_4$.

tetrafluoroethylene /ˌtɛtrəˌflʊərəʊˈɛθɪliːn, -ˌflɔː-/ ▸ noun [mass noun] Chemistry a dense colourless gas which is polymerized to make plastics such as polytetrafluoroethylene. ● Chem. formula: $F_2C{=}CF_2$.

tetragonal /tɪˈtrag(ə)n(ə)l/ ▸ adjective of or denoting a crystal system or three-dimensional geometrical arrangement having three axes at right angles, two of them equal.
– ORIGIN late 16th cent.: via late Latin from Greek *tetragōnon* (neuter of *tetragōnos* 'four-angled') + **-AL**.

tetragram ▸ noun a word consisting of four letters or characters.

Tetragrammaton /ˌtɛtrəˈgramətɒn/ ▸ noun the Hebrew name of God transliterated in four letters as *YHWH* or *JHVH* and articulated as *Yahweh* or *Jehovah*.
– ORIGIN Greek, neuter of *tetragrammatos* 'having four letters', from *tetra-* 'four' + *gramma*, *grammat-* 'letter'.

tetrahedrite /ˌtɛtrəˈhiːdrʌɪt, -ˈhɛdrʌɪt/ ▸ noun [mass noun] a grey mineral consisting of a sulphide of antimony, iron, and copper, typically occurring as tetrahedral crystals.

tetrahedron /ˌtɛtrəˈhiːdrən, -ˈhɛd-/ ▸ noun (pl. **tetrahedra** /-drə/ or **tetrahedrons**) a solid having four plane triangular faces; a triangular pyramid.
– DERIVATIVES **tetrahedral** adjective.
– ORIGIN late 16th cent.: from late Greek *tetraedron*, neuter (used as a noun) of *tetraedros* 'four-sided'.

tetrahydrocannabinol /ˌtɛtrəˌhʌɪdrə(ʊ)ˈkanəbɪnɒl, -kəˈnab-/ ▸ noun [mass noun] Chemistry a crystalline compound that is the main active ingredient of cannabis. ● Chem. formula: $C_{21}H_{30}O_2$.

tetrahydrofuran /ˌtɛtrəˌhʌɪdrəʊˈfjʊəran/ ▸ noun [mass noun] Chemistry a colourless liquid used chiefly as a solvent for plastics and as an intermediate in organic syntheses. ● A heterocyclic compound; chem. formula: C_4H_8O.

tetralogy /tɪˈtralədʒi/ ▸ noun (pl. **tetralogies**) **1** a group of four related literary or operatic works. ■ a series of four ancient Greek dramas, three tragic and one a comedy featuring a chorus of satyrs, originally presented together.
2 Medicine a set of four related symptoms or abnormalities frequently occurring together.

tetralogy of Fallot /ˈfaləʊ/ ▸ noun Medicine a congenital heart condition involving four abnormalities occurring together, including a defective septum between the ventricles and narrowing of the pulmonary artery, and accompanied by cyanosis.
– ORIGIN 1920s: named after Etienne L. A. *Fallot* (1850–1911), French physician.

tetramer /ˈtɛtrəmə/ ▸ noun Chemistry a polymer comprising four monomer units.
– DERIVATIVES **tetrameric** adjective.

tetramerous /tɪˈtram(ə)rəs/ ▸ adjective Botany & Zoology having parts arranged in groups of four. ■ consisting of four joints or parts.

tetrameter /tɪˈtramɪtə/ ▸ noun Prosody a verse of four measures.
– ORIGIN early 17th cent.: from late Latin *tetrametrus*, from Greek *tetrametros*, from *tetra-* 'four' + *metron* 'measure'.

Tetra Pak (also **tetrapack**) ▸ noun trademark a type of plasticized cardboard carton for milk and other drinks, folded from a single sheet into a box shape.

tetraplegia /ˌtɛtrəˈpliːdʒə/ ▸ noun another term for **QUADRIPLEGIA**.
– DERIVATIVES **tetraplegic** adjective & noun.
– ORIGIN early 20th cent.: from **TETRA-** 'four' + **PARAPLEGIA**.

tetraploid /ˈtɛtrəplɔɪd/ Biology ▸ adjective (of a cell or nucleus) containing four homologous sets of chromosomes. ■ (of an organism or species) composed of tetraploid cells.
▸ noun an organism, variety, or species composed of or featuring tetraploid cells.
– DERIVATIVES **tetraploidy** noun.

tetrapod ▸ noun Zoology a four-footed animal, especially a member of a group which includes all vertebrates higher than fishes. ● Superclass Tetrapoda: the amphibians, reptiles, birds, and mammals.
■ an object or structure with four feet, legs, or supports.
– ORIGIN early 19th cent.: from modern Latin *tetrapodus*, from Greek *tetrapous*, *tetrapod-* 'four-footed', from *tetra-* 'four' + *pous* 'foot'.

tetrapterous /tɪˈtrapt(ə)rəs/ ▸ adjective Entomology (of an insect) having two pairs of wings.
– ORIGIN early 19th cent.: from modern Latin *tetrapterus* (from Greek *tetrapteros*, from *tetra-* 'four' + *pteron* 'wing') + **-OUS**.

tetrarch /ˈtɛtrɑːk/ ▸ noun (in the Roman Empire) the governor of one of four divisions of a country or province. ■ each of four joint rulers. ■ archaic a subordinate ruler.
– DERIVATIVES **tetrarchy** noun (pl. **tetrarchies**).
– ORIGIN Old English, from late Latin *tetrarcha*, from Latin *tetrarches*, from Greek *tetrarkhēs*, from *tetra-* 'four' + *arkhein* 'to rule'.

tetraspore ▸ noun Botany a spore occurring in groups of four, in particular (in a red alga) each of four spores produced together, two of which produce male plants and two female.

tetrastich /ˈtɛtrəstɪk/ ▸ noun Prosody a group of four lines of verse.
– ORIGIN late 16th cent.: via Latin from Greek *tetrastikhon* 'having four rows', from *tetra-* 'four' + *stikhon* 'row, line of verse'.

tetrastyle Architecture ▸ noun a building or part of a building, especially a portico, that has four pillars.

T

▸ **adjective** (of a building or part of a building) having four pillars.
– ORIGIN early 18th cent.: via Latin from Greek *tetrastulos*, from *tetra-* 'four' + *stulos* 'column'.

tetrasyllable ▸ **noun** a word of four syllables.
– DERIVATIVES **tetrasyllabic** adjective.

tetrathlon /tɛˈtraθlɒn, -lən/ ▸ **noun** a sporting contest in which each participant competes in four events, typically riding, shooting, swimming, and running.
– ORIGIN 1950s: from TETRA- 'four' + Greek *athlon* 'contest', on the pattern of *pentathlon*.

tetratomic ▸ **adjective** Chemistry consisting of four atoms.

tetravalent /ˌtɛtrəˈveɪl(ə)nt/ ▸ **adjective** Chemistry having a valency of four.

tetrazole /ˈtɛtrəzəʊl/ ▸ **noun** [mass noun] Chemistry an acidic crystalline compound whose molecule is a five-membered ring of one carbon and four nitrogen atoms. • Chem. formula: CH_2N_4.
– ORIGIN late 19th cent.: from TETRA- 'four' + AZO- + -OLE.

tetrazolium /ˌtɛtrəˈzəʊlɪəm/ ▸ **noun** [as modifier] Chemistry a cation derived from tetrazole or one of its derivatives, especially the triphenyl derivative. ■ (also **nitroblue tetrazolium**) [mass noun] a yellow dye used as a test for viability in biological material.

tetri ▸ **noun** (pl. **same** or **tetris**) a monetary unit of Georgia, equal to one-hundredth of a lari.
– ORIGIN Georgian.

tetrode /ˈtɛtrəʊd/ ▸ **noun** a thermionic valve having four electrodes.
– ORIGIN early 20th cent.: from TETRA- 'four' + Greek *hodos* 'way'.

tetrodotoxin /ˌtɛtrədə(ʊ)ˈtɒksɪn/ ▸ **noun** [mass noun] a poisonous compound present in the ovaries of certain pufferfishes. It is a powerful neurotoxin.
– ORIGIN early 20th cent.: from modern Latin *Tetrodon* (former genus name, from Greek *tetra-* 'four-fold' + *odous, odont-* 'tooth') + TOXIN.

tetrose /ˈtɛtrəʊz, -s/ ▸ **noun** Chemistry any of a group of monosaccharide sugars whose molecules contain four carbon atoms.

tetroxide /tɛˈtrɒksʌɪd/ ▸ **noun** Chemistry an oxide containing four atoms of oxygen in its molecule or empirical formula.

tetter ▸ **noun** chiefly archaic a skin disease in humans or animals causing itchy or pustular patches, such as eczema or ringworm.
– ORIGIN Old English *teter*, of Germanic origin; from an Indo-European root shared by Sanskrit *dadru* 'skin disease'.

Teuton /ˈtjuːt(ə)n/ ▸ **noun** a member of a people who lived in Jutland in the 4th century BC and fought the Romans in France in the 2nd century BC. ■ often derogatory a German.
– ORIGIN from Latin *Teutones, Teutoni* (plural), from an Indo-European root meaning 'people' or 'country'.

Teutonic /tjuːˈtɒnɪk/ ▸ **adjective 1** relating to the Teutons. ■ often derogatory displaying the characteristics popularly attributed to Germans: *making preparations with Teutonic thoroughness*.
2 archaic denoting the Germanic branch of the Indo-European language family.
▸ **noun** [mass noun] archaic the language of the Teutons.
– DERIVATIVES **Teutonicism** noun.

Teutonic Knights a military and religious order of German knights, priests, and lay brothers, originally enrolled *c.*1191 as the Teutonic Knights of St Mary of Jerusalem.

> They became a great sovereign power through conquests made in campaigns against Germany's non-Christian neighbours, such as Prussia and Livonia from 1225. Abolished by Napoleon in 1809, the order was re-established in Vienna as an honorary ecclesiastical institution in 1834 and maintains a titular existence.

Tevere /ˈtevere/ Italian name for TIBER.

Tevet /ˈtɛvɛt/ ▸ **noun** variant spelling of TEBET.

Tewa /ˈteɪwə/ ▸ **noun** (pl. **same** or **Tewas**) **1** a member of a Pueblo Indian people of the Rio Grande area in the south-western US.
2 [mass noun] the Tanoan language of the Tewa, with fewer than 3,000 speakers. Compare with TIWA.
▸ **adjective** relating to the Tewa or their language.
– ORIGIN from Tewa *téwa* 'moccasins'.

Tex. ▸ **abbreviation** Texas.

Texas a state in the southern US, on the border with Mexico, with a coastline on the Gulf of Mexico; pop. 24,326,974 (est. 2008); capital, Austin. The area formed part of Mexico until 1836, when it declared independence and became a republic. It became the 28th state of the US in 1845.
– DERIVATIVES **Texan** adjective & noun.

Texas Hold 'Em ▸ **noun** [mass noun] a form of poker in which each player is dealt two cards face down and combines these with any of five community cards to make the best available five-card hand.

Texas leaguer ▸ **noun** Baseball, dated a fly ball that falls to the ground between the infield and the outfield and results in a base hit.

Texas Ranger ▸ **noun** a member of the Texas State police force (formerly, of certain locally mustered regiments during the Mexican War).

Texel /ˈtɛks(ə)l/ ▸ **noun** a sheep of a hardy, hornless breed with a heavy fleece, originally developed on the Dutch island of Texel.

Tex-Mex ▸ **adjective** (especially of cooking and music) having a blend of Mexican and southern American features originally characteristic of the border regions of Texas and Mexico.
▸ **noun** [mass noun] **1** Tex-Mex music or cookery.
2 a variety of Mexican Spanish spoken in Texas.
– ORIGIN 1940s: blend of *Texan* and *Mexican*.

text ▸ **noun 1** a book or other written or printed work, regarded in terms of its content rather than its physical form: *a text which explores pain and grief*. ■ a piece of written or printed material regarded as conveying the authentic or primary form of a particular work: *in some passages it is difficult to establish the original text*. ■ [mass noun] written or printed words, typically forming a connected piece of work: *stylistic features of journalistic text*. ■ [mass noun] Computing data in the form of words or alphabetic characters.
2 [in sing.] the main body of a book or other piece of writing, as distinct from other material such as notes, appendices, and illustrations: *the pictures are clear and relate well to the text*. ■ a script or libretto.
3 a written work chosen or set as a subject of study: *too much concentration on set texts can turn pupils against reading*. ■ a textbook. ■ a passage from the Bible or other religious work, especially when used as the subject of a sermon. ■ a subject or theme for a discussion or exposition: *he took as his text the fact that Australia is paradise*.
4 a text message: *just give us a call or send us a text*.
5 (also **text-hand**) [mass noun] fine, large handwriting, used especially for manuscripts.
▸ **verb** [with obj.] send (someone) a text message: *if she was going to go she would have texted us* | (as noun **texting**) *his father banned him from texting and confiscated the phone*.
– DERIVATIVES **texter** noun, **textless** adjective.
– ORIGIN late Middle English: from Old Northern French *texte*, from Latin *textus* 'tissue, literary style' (in medieval Latin, 'Gospel'), from *text-* 'woven', from the verb *texere*.

textbook ▸ **noun** a book used as a standard work for the study of a particular subject.
▸ **adjective** [attrib.] conforming or corresponding to an established standard or type: *he had the presence of mind to carry out a textbook emergency descent*.
– DERIVATIVES **textbookish** adjective.

text editor ▸ **noun** Computing a system or program that allows a user to edit text.

textile ▸ **noun 1** a type of cloth or woven fabric: *a fascinating range of pottery, jewellery, and textiles*. ■ (**textiles**) the branch of industry involved in the manufacture of cloth.
2 informal (among nudists) a non-nudist, especially on a beach.
▸ **adjective 1** [attrib.] relating to fabric or weaving: *the textile industry*.
2 informal used by nudists in reference to non-nudists.
– ORIGIN early 17th cent.: from Latin *textilis*, from *text-* 'woven', from the verb *texere*.

text message ▸ **noun** an electronic communication sent and received by mobile phone.
– DERIVATIVES **text messaging** noun.

textphone ▸ **noun** a telephone developed for use by people who are deaf or hard of hearing, having a small screen and a keyboard on which a message may be typed to be received by another textphone.

text processing ▸ **noun** [mass noun] Computing the manipulation of text, especially the transformation of text from one format to another.

textual ▸ **adjective** relating to a text or texts: *textual analysis*.
– DERIVATIVES **textually** adverb.
– ORIGIN late Middle English: from medieval Latin *textualis*, from Latin *textus* (see TEXT).

textual criticism ▸ **noun** [mass noun] the process of attempting to ascertain the original wording of a text.

textualist ▸ **noun** a person who adheres strictly to a text, especially that of the scriptures.
– DERIVATIVES **textualism** noun.

textuality ▸ **noun 1** the quality or use of language characteristic of written works as opposed to spoken usage.
2 strict adherence to a text; textualism.

texture ▸ **noun** [mass noun] the feel, appearance, or consistency of a surface or a substance: *skin texture and tone* | *the cheese is firm in texture* | [count noun] *the different colours and textures of bark*. ■ the character or appearance of a textile fabric as determined by the arrangement and thickness of its threads: *a dark shirt of rough texture*. ■ Art the tactile quality of the surface of a work of art. ■ the quality created by the combination of the different elements in a work of music or literature: *a closely knit symphonic texture*.
▸ **verb** [with obj.] (usu. as adj. **textured**) give (a surface) a rough or raised texture: *wallcoverings which create a textured finish*.
– DERIVATIVES **textural** adjective, **texturally** adverb, **textureless** adjective.
– ORIGIN late Middle English (denoting a woven fabric or something resembling this): from Latin *textura* 'weaving', from *text-* 'woven', from the verb *texere*.

textured vegetable protein ▸ **noun** [mass noun] a type of protein obtained from soya beans and made to resemble minced meat.

texture mapping ▸ **noun** [mass noun] Computing the application of patterns or images to three-dimensional graphics to enhance the realism of their surfaces.

texturing ▸ **noun** [mass noun] the representation or use of texture, especially in music, fine art, and interior design.

texturize (also **texturise**) ▸ **verb** [with obj.] impart a particular texture to (a product, especially a fabric or foodstuff) in order to make it more attractive.

text wrap ▸ **noun** [mass noun] (in word processing) a facility allowing text to surround embedded features such as pictures.

T-formation ▸ **noun** American Football a T-shaped offensive formation of players.

TFT ▸ **abbreviation** Electronics thin-film transistor, denoting a technology used to make flat colour display screens, especially for portable computers.

TG ▸ **abbreviation** ■ Togo (international vehicle registration). ■ transformational grammar or transformational-generative grammar.

TGIF ▸ **abbreviation** informal thank God (or goodness) it's Friday.

T-group ▸ **noun** Psychology a group of people undergoing therapy or training in which they observe and seek to improve their own interpersonal relationships or communication skills.
– ORIGIN 1950s: *T* for *training*.

TGV ▸ **noun** a French high-speed electric passenger train.
– ORIGIN abbreviation of French *train à grande vitesse*.

Th ▸ **symbol** the chemical element thorium.

Th. ▸ **abbreviation** Thursday.

-th[1] (also **-eth**) ▸ **suffix** forming ordinal and fractional numbers from *four* onwards: *fifth* | *sixty-sixth*.
– ORIGIN Old English *(o)tha, -(o)the*.

-th[2] ▸ **suffix** forming nouns: **1** (from verbs) denoting an action or process: *birth* | *growth*.
2 (from adjectives) denoting a state: *filth* | *health* | *width*.
– ORIGIN Old English *-thu, -tho, -th*.

-th[3] ▸ **suffix** variant spelling of -ETH[2] (as in *doth*).

Thackeray /ˈθakəri/, William Makepeace (1811–63), British novelist, born in India. He established his reputation with *Vanity Fair* (1847–8), a satire of the upper middle class of early 19th-century society.

Thaddaeus /ˈθadɪəs/ an apostle named in St Matthew's Gospel, traditionally identified with St Jude.

Thai /tʌɪ/ ▸ **adjective** relating to Thailand, its people, or their language.
▸ **noun** (pl. **same** or **Thais**) **1** a native or inhabitant of Thailand. ■ a member of the largest ethnic group in Thailand. ■ a person of Thai descent.

2 [mass noun] the official language of Thailand, spoken by over 20 million people, mainly in central Thailand. It belongs to the Tai language group.
– ORIGIN Thai, literally 'free'.

Thai boxing ▶ **noun** [mass noun] a traditional Thai martial art in which the fists, elbows, knees, and bare feet may all be used to deliver blows.
– DERIVATIVES **Thai boxer noun.**

Thailand a kingdom in SE Asia; pop. 65,998,400 (est. 2009); official language, Thai; capital, Bangkok. Former name (until 1939) **SIAM**.

> A powerful Thai kingdom emerged in the 14th century. In the 19th century it lost territory in the east to France and in the south to Britain. Thailand was occupied by the Japanese in the Second World War; it supported the US in the Vietnam War, later experiencing a large influx of refugees from Cambodia, Laos, and Vietnam. Absolute monarchy was abolished in 1932, the king remaining head of state.

Thailand, Gulf of an inlet of the South China Sea between the Malay Peninsula to the west and Thailand and Cambodia to the east. It was formerly known as the Gulf of Siam.

Thai stick ▶ **noun** strong cannabis in leaf form, twisted into a small, tightly packed cylinder ready for smoking.

thakur /ˈtɑːkʊr, ˈtɑːkʊə/ ▶ **noun** Indian a respectful title for a nobleman and landowner.
– ORIGIN from Hindi *ṭhākur* 'lord', from Sanskrit *ṭhakkura* 'chief, lord'.

thalamus /ˈθaləməs/ ▶ **noun** (pl. **thalami** /-mʌɪ, -miː/) Anatomy either of two masses of grey matter lying between the cerebral hemispheres on either side of the third ventricle, relaying sensory information and acting as a centre for pain perception.
– DERIVATIVES **thalamic** /θəˈlamɪk, ˈθaləmɪk/ **adjective.**
– ORIGIN late 17th cent. (denoting the part of the brain at which a nerve originates): via Latin from Greek *thalamos*.

thalassaemia /ˌθaləˈsiːmɪə/ (US **thalassemia**) ▶ **noun** [mass noun] Medicine any of a group of hereditary haemolytic diseases caused by faulty haemoglobin synthesis, widespread in Mediterranean, African, and Asian countries.
– ORIGIN 1930s: from Greek *thalassa* 'sea' (because the diseases were first known around the Mediterranean) + **-AEMIA**.

thalassic /θəˈlasɪk/ ▶ **adjective** literary or technical relating to the sea.
– ORIGIN mid 19th cent.: from French *thalassique*, from Greek *thalassa* 'sea'.

thalassotherapy /θəˌlasəʊˈθɛrəpi/ ▶ **noun** [mass noun] the use of seawater in cosmetic and health treatment.
– ORIGIN late 19th cent.: from Greek *thalassa* 'sea' + **THERAPY**.

thale cress /θeɪl/ ▶ **noun** a small white-flowered plant of north temperate regions, widely used in genetics experiments due to its small number of chromosomes and short life cycle. ● *Arabidopsis thaliana*, family Cruciferae.
– ORIGIN late 18th cent.: named after Johann *Thal* (1542–83), German physician.

thaler /ˈtɑːlə/ ▶ **noun** historical a German silver coin.
– ORIGIN German, earlier form of *Taler* (see **DOLLAR**).

Thales /ˈθeɪliːz/ (*c.*624–*c.*545 BC), Greek philosopher, mathematician, and astronomer, living at Miletus. Judged by Aristotle to be the founder of physical science, he is also credited with discovering the principles of geometry. He proposed that water was the primary substance from which all things were derived.

thali /ˈtɑːli/ ▶ **noun** (pl. **thalis**) a set meal at an Indian restaurant. ■ a metal plate on which Indian food is served.
– ORIGIN from Hindi *thālī*, from Sanskrit *sthālī*.

Thalia /ˈθeɪlɪə, θəˈlʌɪə, ˈtɑːlɪə/ **1** Greek & Roman Mythology the Muse of comedy.
2 Greek Mythology one of the Graces.
– ORIGIN Greek, literally 'rich, plentiful'.

thalidomide /θəˈlɪdəmʌɪd/ ▶ **noun** [mass noun] a drug formerly used as a sedative, but withdrawn in the UK in the early 1960s after it was found to cause congenital malformation or absence of limbs in children whose mothers took the drug during early pregnancy.
– ORIGIN 1950s: from *(ph)thal(ic acid)* + *(im)ido* + *(i)mide*.

thalli plural form of **THALLUS**.

thallium /ˈθalɪəm/ ▶ **noun** [mass noun] the chemical element of atomic number 81, a soft silvery-white metal which occurs naturally in small amounts in iron pyrites, sphalerite, and other ores. Its compounds are very poisonous. (Symbol: **Tl**)
– ORIGIN mid 19th cent.: modern Latin, from Greek *thallos* 'green shoot', because of the green line in its spectrum.

thallophyte /ˈθalə(ʊ)fʌɪt/ ▶ **noun** Botany a plant that consists of a thallus.
– ORIGIN mid 19th cent.: from modern Latin *Thallophyta* (former taxon), from Greek *thallos* (see **THALLUS**) + **-PHYTE**.

thallus /ˈθaləs/ ▶ **noun** (pl. **thalli** /-lʌɪ, -liː/) Botany a plant body that is not differentiated into stem and leaves and lacks true roots and a vascular system. Thalli are typical of algae, fungi, lichens, and some liverworts.
– DERIVATIVES **thalloid adjective.**
– ORIGIN early 19th cent.: from Greek *thallos* 'green shoot', from *thallein* 'to bloom'.

thalweg /ˈtɑːlvɛg, ˈθɑːlwɛg/ ▶ **noun** Geology a line connecting the lowest points of successive cross-sections along the course of a valley or river.
– ORIGIN mid 19th cent.: from German, from obsolete *Thal* 'valley, dale' + *Weg* 'way'.

Thames /tɛmz/ a river of southern England, flowing 338 km (210 miles) eastwards from the Cotswolds in Gloucestershire through London to the North Sea. ■ a shipping forecast area covering the southernmost part of the North Sea, roughly as far north as the latitude of northern Norfolk.

thamin /θəˈmɪn/ ▶ **noun** a reddish-brown deer which lives in low-lying marshy areas of SE Asia. ● *Cervus eldi*, family Cervidae.
– ORIGIN late 19th cent.: from Burmese.

Thammuz /ˈtamʊz/ (also **Tammuz**) ▶ **noun** (in the Jewish calendar) the tenth month of the civil and fourth of the religious year, usually coinciding with parts of June and July.
– ORIGIN from Hebrew *tammūz*.

than ▶ **conjunction & preposition 1** introducing the second element in a comparison: [as prep.] *he was much smaller than his son* | *Jack doesn't know any more than I do.*
2 used in expressions introducing an exception or contrast: [as prep.] *he claims not to own anything* ***other than*** *his home* | [as conjunction] *they observe* ***rather than*** *act.*
3 [conjunction] used in expressions indicating one thing happening immediately after another: ***scarcely*** *was the work completed* ***than*** *it was abandoned.*
– ORIGIN Old English *than(ne)*, *thon(ne)*, *thænne*, originally the same word as **THEN**.

> **USAGE** Traditional grammar holds that personal pronouns following **than** should be in the subjective rather than the objective case: *he is smaller* ***than she*** rather than *he is smaller* ***than her***. This is based on an analysis of **than** by which **than** is a conjunction and the personal pronoun ('she') is standing in for a full clause: *he is smaller* ***than she is***. However, it is arguable that **than** in this context is not a conjunction but a preposition, similar grammatically to words like **with**, **between**, or **for**. In this case the personal pronoun is objective: *he is smaller* ***than her*** is standard in just the same way as, for example, *I work* ***with her*** is standard (not *I work* ***with she***). Whatever the grammatical analysis, the evidence confirms that sentences like *he is smaller* ***than she*** are uncommon in modern English and only ever found in formal contexts. Uses such as *he is smaller* ***than her***, on the other hand, are almost universally accepted. For more explanation see **USAGE** at **PERSONAL PRONOUN** and **BETWEEN**.

thana /ˈθɑːnɑː/ ▶ **noun** Indian a police station.
– ORIGIN from Hindi *thānā*, from Sanskrit *sthāna* 'place, station'.

thanage /ˈθeɪnɪdʒ/ ▶ **noun** [mass noun] historical the tenure, land, and rank granted to a thane.
– ORIGIN late Middle English: from Anglo-Norman French (see **THANE**, **-AGE**).

thanatology /ˌθanəˈtɒlədʒi/ ▶ **noun** [mass noun] the scientific study of death and the practices associated with it, including the study of the needs of the terminally ill and their families.
– DERIVATIVES **thanatological adjective, thanatologist noun.**
– ORIGIN mid 19th cent.: from Greek *thanatos* 'death' + **-LOGY**.

Thanatos /ˈθanətɒs/ ▶ **noun** [mass noun] (in Freudian theory) the death instinct. Often contrasted with **EROS**.
– ORIGIN from Greek *thanatos* 'death'.

thane /θeɪn/ ▶ **noun** historical (in Anglo-Saxon England) a man who held land granted by the king or by a military nobleman, ranking between an ordinary freeman and a hereditary noble. ■ (in Scotland) a man, often the chief of a clan, who held land from a Scottish king and ranked with an earl's son.
– DERIVATIVES **thanedom noun.**
– ORIGIN Old English *theg(e)n* 'servant, soldier', of Germanic origin; related to German *Degen* 'warrior', from an Indo-European root shared by Greek *teknon* 'child', *tokeus* 'parent'.

thang ▶ **noun** informal non-standard spelling of **THING** representing Southern US pronunciation, and typically used to denote a feeling or tendency: *yet another dimension of this Canadian groove thang.*

thank ▶ **verb** [with obj.] express gratitude to (someone), especially by saying 'Thank you': *Mac* ***thanked*** *her* ***for*** *the meal and left.* ■ used ironically to assign blame or responsibility for something: *you have only yourself to thank for the plight you are in.*
– PHRASES **I will thank you to do something** used to make a request conveying reproach or annoyance: *I'll thank you not to interrupt me again.* **thank goodness** (or **God** or **heavens**) used as an expression of relief: *thank goodness no one was badly injured.* **thank one's lucky stars** feel grateful for one's good fortune.
– ORIGIN Old English *thancian*, of Germanic origin; related to Dutch and German *danken*; compare with **THANKS**.

thankful ▶ **adjective** pleased and relieved: [with clause] *they were thankful that the war was finally over* | [with infinitive] *I was very thankful to be alive.* ■ expressing gratitude and relief: *an earnest and thankful prayer.*
– DERIVATIVES **thankfulness noun.**
– ORIGIN Old English *thancful* (see **THANK**, **-FUL**).

thankfully ▶ **adverb** in a thankful manner: *she thankfully accepted the armchair she was offered.* ■ [sentence adverb] used to express pleasure or relief at a fortunate outcome: *thankfully, everything went smoothly.*
– ORIGIN Old English *thancfullīce* (see **THANKFUL**, **-LY²**).

> **USAGE** **Thankfully** has been used for centuries to mean 'in a thankful manner', as in *she accepted the offer* ***thankfully***. Since the 1960s it has also been used as a sentence adverb to mean 'fortunately', as in ***thankfully***, *we didn't have to wait*. Although this use has not attracted the same amount of attention as **hopefully**, it has been criticized for the same reasons. It is, however, far commoner now than the traditional use, accounting for more than 80 per cent of citations for **thankfully** in the Oxford English Corpus. For further explanation, see **USAGE** at **HOPEFULLY**.

thankless ▶ **adjective** (of a job or task) difficult or unpleasant and not likely to be satisfying or to be appreciated by others. ■ (of a person) not expressing or feeling gratitude.
– DERIVATIVES **thanklessly adverb, thanklessness noun.**

thank-offering ▶ **noun** an offering made as an act of thanksgiving.

thanks ▶ **plural noun** an expression of gratitude: *festivals were held to* ***give thanks for*** *the harvest* | *a letter of thanks.* ■ another way of saying **THANK YOU**: *thanks for being so helpful* | *many thanks.*
– PHRASES **no thanks to** used to convey that someone has failed to contribute to, or has hindered, a successful outcome: *we've won, but no thanks to you.* **thanks a million** informal thank you very much. **thanks to** as a result of; due to: *it's thanks to you that he's in this mess.*
– ORIGIN Old English *thancas*, plural of *thanc* '(kindly) thought, gratitude', of Germanic origin; related to Dutch *dank* and German *Dank*, also to **THINK**.

thanksgiving ▶ **noun** [mass noun] **1** the expression of gratitude, especially to God: *he offered prayers* ***in thanksgiving for*** *his safe arrival* | [count noun] *he described the service as a thanksgiving.*
2 (**Thanksgiving** or **Thanksgiving Day**) (in North America) an annual national holiday marked by religious observances and a traditional meal. The holiday commemorates a harvest festival celebrated by the Pilgrim Fathers in 1621, and is held in the US on the fourth Thursday in November. A similar holiday is held in Canada, usually on the second Monday in October.

thank you ▶ **exclamation** a polite expression used when acknowledging a gift, service, or compliment, or accepting or refusing an offer: ***thank you for*** *your letter* | *no thank you, I'll give it a miss.*

T

▶ **noun** an instance or means of expressing thanks: *Lucy planned a party as a thank you to hospital staff* | [as modifier] *thank-you letters.*

Thar Desert /tɑː/ a desert region to the east of the River Indus, lying in the Rajasthan and Gujarat states of NW India and the Punjab and Sind regions of SE Pakistan. Also called **Great Indian Desert**.

that ▶ **pronoun** (pl. **those**) **1** used to identify a specific person or thing observed or heard by the speaker: *that's his wife over there* | *hello, is that Ben?* ■ referring to the more distant of two things near to the speaker (the other, if specified, being identified by 'this'): *this is stronger than that.*
2 referring to a specific thing previously mentioned, known, or understood: *that's a good idea* | *what are we going to do about that?*
3 [often with clause] used in singling out someone or something and ascribing a distinctive feature to them: *it is part of human nature to be attracted to **that which** is aesthetically pleasing* | *his appearance was **that of** someone used to sleeping on the streets.*
4 informal, chiefly Brit. expressing strong agreement with a description just given: *'He's a fussy man.' 'He is that.'*
5 (pl. **that**) [relative pronoun] used to introduce a defining clause, especially one essential to identification: ■ instead of 'which', 'who', or 'whom': *the woman that owns the place.* ■ instead of 'when' after an expression of time: *the year that Anna was born.*
▶ **determiner** (pl. **those**) **1** used to identify a specific person or thing observed or heard by the speaker: *look at that chap there* | *how much are those brushes?* ■ referring to the more distant of two things near to the speaker (the other, if specified, being identified by 'this').
2 referring to a specific thing previously mentioned, known, or understood: *he lived in Mysore at that time* | *seven people died in that incident.*
3 [usu. with clause] used in singling out someone or something and ascribing a distinctive feature to them: *I have always envied those people who make their own bread.*
4 referring to a specific person or thing assumed as understood or familiar to the person being addressed: *where is that son of yours?* | *I let him spend all that money on me* | *Dad got that hunted look.*
▶ **adverb** [as submodifier] to such a degree; so: *I wouldn't go that far.* ■ used with a gesture to indicate size: *it was that big, perhaps even bigger.* ■ informal very: *I couldn't get out of the house fast enough, I was that embarrassed!*
▶ **conjunction 1** introducing a subordinate clause expressing a statement or hypothesis: *she said that she was satisfied* | *it is possible that we have misunderstood.* ■ expressing a reason or cause: *he seemed pleased that I wanted to continue.* ■ expressing a result: *she was **so** tired **that** she couldn't think.* ■ [usu. with modal] expressing a purpose, hope, or intention: *we pray that the coming year may be a year of peace* | *I eat that I may live.*
2 [usu. with modal] literary expressing a wish or regret: *oh that he could be restored to health.*
– PHRASES **and all that** (or **and that**) informal and that sort of thing; and so on: *other people depend on them for food and clothing and all that.* **be all that** see **all**. **at that** see **at¹**. **like that 1** of that nature or in that manner: *we need more people like that* | *don't talk like that.* **2** informal with no preparation or introduction; instantly or effortlessly: *he can't just leave like that.* **not all that —— not very ——**: *it wasn't all that long ago.* **that is** (or **that is to say**) a formula introducing or following an explanation or further clarification of a preceding word or words: *androcentric—that is to say, male-dominated—concepts* | *He was a long-haired kid with freckles. Last time I saw him, that is.* **that said** even so (introducing a concessive statement): *It's just a gimmick. That said, I'd love to do it.* **that's it** see **it¹**. **that's that** there is nothing more to do or say about the matter. **—— that was** as the specified person or thing was formerly known: *General Dunstaple had married Miss Hughes that was.* **that will do** no more is needed or desirable.
– ORIGIN Old English *thæt*, nominative and accusative singular neuter of *se* 'the', of Germanic origin; related to Dutch *dat* and German *das*.

> **USAGE 1** The word **that** can be omitted in standard English where it introduces a subordinate clause, as in *she said (**that**) she was satisfied*. It can also be dropped in a relative clause where the subject of the subordinate clause is not the same as the subject of the main clause, as in *the book (**that**) I've just written* ('the book' and 'I' are two different subjects). Where the subject of the subordinate clause and the main clause are the same, use of the word **that** is obligatory, as in *the woman **that** owns the place* ('the woman' is the subject of both clauses).
> **2** It is sometimes argued that, in relative clauses, **that** should be used for non-human references, while **who** should be used for human references: *a house **that** overlooks the park but the woman **who** lives next door.* In practice, while it is true to say that **who** is restricted to human references, the function of **that** is flexible. It has been used for human and non-human references since at least the 11th century, and is invaluable where both a person and a thing is being referred to, as in *a person or thing that is believed to bring bad luck.*
> **3** Is there any difference between the use of **that** and **which** in sentences such as *any book **that** gets children reading is worth having*, and *any book **which** gets children reading is worth having?* The general rule in British English is that, in **restrictive relative clauses**, where the relative clause serves to define or restrict the reference to the particular one described, **which** can replace **that**. However, in non-restrictive relative clauses, where the relative clause serves only to give additional information, **that** cannot be used: *this book, **which** is set in the last century, is very popular with teenagers* but not *this book, **that** is set in the last century, is very popular with teenagers.* In US English **which** is generally used only for non-restrictive relative clauses.

thataway ▶ **adverb** informal, chiefly US **1** in that direction: *he went thataway!*
2 in that way; like that.

thatch ▶ **noun** [mass noun] a roof covering of straw, reeds, palm leaves, or a similar material. ■ straw or a similar material used for covering a roof. ■ [in sing.] informal a person's hair, especially when thick or unruly: *a young man **with a thatch of** untidy blond hair.* ■ a matted layer of dead stalks, moss, and other material in a lawn.
▶ **verb** [with obj.] cover (a roof or a building) with straw or a similar material: (as adj. **thatched**) *thatched cottages.*
– DERIVATIVES **thatcher** noun.
– ORIGIN Old English *theccan* 'cover', of Germanic origin; related to Dutch *dekken* and German *decken*.

Thatcher, Margaret (Hilda), Baroness Thatcher of Kesteven (b.1925), British Conservative stateswoman, Prime Minister 1979–90. She was the country's first woman Prime Minister, and became the longest-serving British Prime Minister of the 20th century. Her period in office was marked by an emphasis on monetarist policies, privatization of nationalized industries, and trade union legislation. She became known for her determination and her emphasis on individual responsibility and enterprise.
– DERIVATIVES **Thatcherism** noun, **Thatcherite** noun & adjective.

thaumatin /ˈθɔːmətɪn/ ▶ **noun** [mass noun] a sweet-tasting protein isolated from a West African fruit, used as a sweetener in food.
– ORIGIN 1970s: *thaumat-* from modern Latin *Thaumatococcus daniellii* (name of the plant from which the fruit is obtained), from Greek *thauma, thaumat-* 'marvel' + **-in¹**.

thaumatrope /ˈθɔːmətrəʊp/ ▶ **noun** a scientific toy devised in the 19th century, consisting of a disc with a different picture on each of its two sides, these appearing to combine into one image when the disc is rapidly rotated. ■ another term for **zoetrope**.
– ORIGIN early 19th cent.: from Greek *thauma* 'marvel' + *-tropos* '-turning'.

thaumaturge /ˈθɔːmətəːdʒ/ ▶ **noun** a worker of wonders and performer of miracles; a magician.
– DERIVATIVES **thaumaturgic** adjective, **thaumaturgical** adjective, **thaumaturgy** noun.
– ORIGIN early 18th cent. (as *thaumaturg*): via medieval Latin from Greek *thaumatourgos*, from *thauma* 'marvel' + *-ergos* '-working'.

thaw ▶ **verb** [no obj.] (of ice, snow, or another frozen substance, such as food) become liquid or soft as a result of warming up: *the river thawed and barges of food began to reach the capital* | (as noun **thawing**) *catastrophic summer floods caused by thawing.* ■ (**it thaws, it is thawing**, etc.) the weather becomes warmer and causes snow and ice to melt. ■ [with obj.] make (something) warm enough to become liquid or soft: *European exporters simply thawed their beef before unloading.* ■ (of a part of the body) become warm enough to stop feeling numb: *Riven began to feel his ears and toes **thaw out**.* ■ make or become friendlier or more cordial: [no obj.] *she **thawed out** sufficiently to allow a smile to appear.*
▶ **noun** a period of warmer weather that thaws ice and snow: *the thaw came yesterday afternoon.* ■ an increase in friendliness or cordiality: *a thaw in relations between the USA and the USSR.*
– ORIGIN Old English *thawian* (verb), of West Germanic origin; related to Dutch *dooien*. The noun (first recorded in Middle English) developed its figurative use in the mid 19th cent.

THC ▶ **abbreviation** tetrahydrocannabinol.

the [called the definite article] ▶ **determiner 1** denoting one or more people or things already mentioned or assumed to be common knowledge: *what's the matter?* | *call the doctor* | *the phone rang.* Compare with **a¹**. ■ used to refer to a person, place, or thing that is unique: *the Queen* | *the Mona Lisa* | *the Nile.* ■ informal or archaic denoting a disease or affliction: *I've got the flu.* ■ (with a unit of time) the present; the current: *dish of the day* | *man of the moment.* ■ informal used instead of a possessive to refer to someone with whom the speaker or person addressed is associated: *I'm meeting the boss* | *how's the family?* ■ used with a surname to refer to a family or married couple: *the Johnsons were not wealthy.* ■ used before the surname of the chief of a Scottish or Irish clan: *the O'Donoghue.*
2 used to point forward to a following qualifying or defining clause or phrase: *the fuss that he made of her* | *the top of a bus* | *I have done the best I could.* ■ (chiefly with rulers and family members with the same name) used after a name to qualify it: *George the Sixth* | *Edward the Confessor* | *Jack the Ripper.*
3 used to make a generalized reference to something rather than identifying a particular instance: *he taught himself to play the violin* | *I worry about the future.* ■ used with a singular noun to indicate that it represents a whole species or class: *they placed the African elephant on their endangered list.* ■ used with an adjective to refer to those people who are of the type described: *the unemployed.* ■ used with an adjective to refer to something of the class or quality described: *they are trying to accomplish the impossible.* ■ used with the name of a unit to state a rate: *they can do 120 miles **to the** gallon* | *35p **in the** pound.*
4 enough of (a particular thing): *he hoped to publish monthly, if only he could find the money.*
5 (pronounced stressing 'the') used to indicate that someone or something is the best known or most important of that name or type: *he was **the** hot young piano prospect in jazz.*
6 used adverbially with comparatives to indicate how one amount or degree of something varies in relation to another: ***the more** she thought about it, **the more** devastating it became.* ■ (usu. **all the ——**) used to emphasize the amount or degree to which something is affected: *commodities made all the more desirable by their rarity.*
– ORIGIN Old English *se, sēo, thæt*, ultimately superseded by forms from Northumbrian and North Mercian *thē*, of Germanic origin; related to Dutch *de, dat*, and German *der, die, das*.

theanthropic /ˌθiːanˈθrɒpɪk/ ▶ **adjective** embodying deity in a human form; both divine and human.
– ORIGIN mid 17th cent.: from ecclesiastical Greek *theanthrōpos* 'god-man' (from *theos* 'god' + *anthrōpos* 'human being') + **-ic**.

thearchy /ˈθiːɑːki/ ▶ **noun** (pl. **thearchies**) [mass noun] archaic rule by a god or gods.
– ORIGIN mid 17th cent.: from ecclesiastical Greek *thearkhia* 'godhead', from *theos* 'god' + *arkhein* 'to rule'.

theatre (US **theater**) ▶ **noun 1** a building or outdoor area in which plays and other dramatic performances are given. ■ [mass noun] (often **the theatre**) the activity or profession of acting in, producing, directing, or writing plays: *what made you want to go into the theatre?* ■ [mass noun] a play or other activity or presentation considered in terms of its dramatic quality: *this is intense, moving, and inspiring theatre.* ■ chiefly N. Amer. & W. Indian a cinema.
2 (also **lecture theatre**) a room or hall for lectures with seats in tiers. ■ Brit. an operating theatre.
3 the area in which something happens: *a new **theatre of war** has been opened up.* ■ [as modifier] denoting weapons intermediate between tactical and strategic: *he was working on theatre defence missiles.*
– ORIGIN late Middle English: from Old French, or from Latin *theatrum*, from Greek *theatron*, from *theasthai* 'behold'.

theatre-going ▶ **adjective** going frequently to the theatre.
– DERIVATIVES **theatregoer** noun.

theatre-in-the-round ▶ **noun** [mass noun] a form of theatrical presentation in which the audience is seated in a circle around the stage or on at least three of its sides.

theatreland ▶ **noun** [mass noun] informal the district of a city in which most theatres are situated.

Theatre of the Absurd ▶ **noun** (**the Theatre of the Absurd**) drama using the abandonment of conventional dramatic form to portray the futility of human struggle in a senseless world. Major exponents include Samuel Beckett, Eugène Ionesco, and Harold Pinter.

theatric /θɪˈatrɪk/ ▶ **adjective** theatrical.
▶ **noun** (**theatrics**) dramatic performances; theatricals. ■ overdramatic behaviour.

theatrical ▶ **adjective** relating to acting, actors, or the theatre: *theatrical productions*. ■ exaggerated and excessively dramatic: *Henry looked over his shoulder with theatrical caution*.
▶ **noun 1** (**theatricals**) dramatic performances: *I was persuaded to act in some amateur theatricals*. ■ overdramatic behaviour: *their love affair ended without theatricals*.
2 a professional actor or actress: *a boarding house that catered for theatricals*.
– DERIVATIVES **theatricalism** noun, **theatricality** noun, **theatricalization** (also **theatricalisation**) noun, **theatricalize** (also **theatricalise**) verb, **theatrically** adverb.
– ORIGIN mid 16th cent.: via late Latin from Greek *theatrikos* (from *theatron* 'theatre') + -AL.

thebe /ˈθeɪbeɪ/ ▶ **noun** (pl. **same**) a monetary unit of Botswana, equal to one hundredth of a pula.
– ORIGIN Setswana, literally 'shield'.

Thebes /θiːbz/ **1** the Greek name for an ancient city of Upper Egypt, whose ruins are situated on the Nile about 675 km (420 miles) south of Cairo. It was the capital of ancient Egypt under the 18th dynasty (*c*.1550–1290 BC) and is the site of the major temples of Luxor and Karnak.
2 a city in Greece, in Boeotia, north-west of Athens. Thebes became a major military power in Greece following the defeat of the Spartans at the battle of Leuctra in 371 BC. It was destroyed by Alexander the Great in 336 BC. Greek name THÍVAI.
– DERIVATIVES **Theban** adjective & noun.

theca /ˈθiːkə/ ▶ **noun** (pl. **thecae** /-siː/) a receptacle, sheath, or cell enclosing an organ, part, or structure, in particular: ■ Anatomy the loose sheath enclosing the spinal cord. ■ Zoology a cup-like or tubular structure containing a coral polyp. ■ Botany either of the lobes of an anther, each containing two pollen sacs. ■ (also **theca folliculi** /fəˈlɪkjʊlʌɪ/) Anatomy the outer layer of cells of a Graafian follicle.
– DERIVATIVES **thecate** adjective.
– ORIGIN early 17th cent.: via Latin from Greek *thēkē* 'case'.

thecodont /ˈθiːkə(ʊ)dɒnt/ ▶ **noun** a fossil quadrupedal or partly bipedal reptile of the Triassic period, having teeth fixed in sockets in the jaw. Thecodonts are ancestral to the dinosaurs and other archosaurs.
● Order Thecodontia, subdivision Archosauria.
– ORIGIN mid 19th cent.: from modern Latin *Thecodontia*, from Greek *thēkē* 'case' + *odous*, *odont-* 'tooth'.

thé dansant /ˌteɪ dɒ̃ˈsɒ̃/, French /te dɑ̃sɑ̃/ ▶ **noun** (pl. **thés dansants** pronunc. **same**) French term for TEA DANCE.

thee ▶ **pronoun** [second person singular] archaic or dialect form of YOU, as the singular object of a verb or preposition: *we beseech thee O lord*. Compare with THOU[1].
– ORIGIN Old English *thē*, accusative and dative case of *thū* 'thou'.

> **USAGE** The word **thee** is still used in some traditional dialects (e.g. in northern England) and among certain religious groups, but in standard English it is restricted to archaic contexts. For more details on **thee** and **thou**, see USAGE at THOU[1].

theft ▶ **noun** [mass noun] the action or crime of stealing: *he was convicted of theft* | [count noun] *the latest theft happened at a garage*.
– ORIGIN Old English *thīefth*, *thēofth*, of Germanic origin; related to THIEF.

thegn /θeɪn/ ▶ **noun** historical an English thane.
– ORIGIN mid 19th cent.: modern representation of Old English *theg(e)n*, adopted to distinguish the Old English use of THANE from the Scots use made familiar by Shakespeare.

theine /ˈθiːiːn, ˈθiːɪn/ ▶ **noun** [mass noun] caffeine, especially when it occurs in tea.
– ORIGIN mid 19th cent.: from modern Latin *Thea* (former genus name of the tea plant, from Dutch *thee*) + -INE[4].

their ▶ **possessive determiner 1** belonging to or associated with the people or things previously mentioned or easily identified: *parents keen to help their children*. ■ belonging to or associated with a person of unspecified sex: *she heard someone blow their nose loudly*.
2 (**Their**) used in titles: *a double portrait of Their Majesties*.
– ORIGIN Middle English: from Old Norse *their(r) a* 'of them', genitive plural of the demonstrative *sá*; related to THEM and THEY.

> **USAGE 1** Do not confuse **their** and **there**: **their** is a possessive determiner, used for example in *they all tried to hide their faces and said nothing*, while **there** is an adverb of place or position, as in *I took a trip up there last week*, and is used in phrases such as **there is/are**: *we are aware there are problems*.
> **2** On the use of **their** in the singular to mean 'his or her', see USAGE at THEY.

theirs ▶ **possessive pronoun** used to refer to a thing or things belonging to or associated with two or more people or things previously mentioned: *they think everything is theirs* | *a favourite game* **of theirs**.
– ORIGIN Middle English: from THEIR + -'S[1].

> **USAGE** There is no need for an apostrophe: the spelling should be **theirs** not **their's**.

theirselves ▶ **pronoun** [third person plural] dialect form of THEMSELVES.

theism /ˈθiːɪz(ə)m/ ▶ **noun** [mass noun] belief in the existence of a god or gods, specifically of a creator who intervenes in the universe. Compare with DEISM.
– DERIVATIVES **theist** noun, **theistic** /-ˈɪstɪk/ adjective.
– ORIGIN late 17th cent.: from Greek *theos* 'god' + -ISM.

thekedar /ˈtɛkedɑːr/ (also **thikadar** /ˈtɛkʌdɑːr/)
▶ **noun** Indian a person who undertakes to provide labour or materials to do a job; a contractor.
– ORIGIN Hindi.

them ▶ **pronoun** [third person plural] **1** used as the object of a verb or preposition to refer to two or more people or things previously mentioned or easily identified: *I bathed the kids and read them stories* | *rows of doors, most* **of them** *locked*. Compare with THEY. ■ used after the verb 'to be' and after 'than' or 'as': *you reckon that's them?* | *we're better than them*. ■ [singular] referring to a person of unspecified sex: *how well do you have to know someone before you call them a friend?*
2 archaic themselves: *they bethought them of a new expedient*.
▶ **determiner** informal or dialect those: *look at them eyes*.
– ORIGIN Middle English: from Old Norse *theim* 'to those, to them', dative plural of *sá*; related to THEIR and THEY.

> **USAGE** On the use of **them** in the singular to mean 'him or her', see USAGE at THEY.

thematic ▶ **adjective 1** having or relating to subjects or a particular subject: *the book is organized into nine thematic chapters*. ■ relating to the collecting of postage stamps with designs connected with the same subject. ■ Music relating to or containing melodic subjects: *the concerto relies on the frequent repetition of thematic fragments*.
2 Linguistics relating to or denoting the theme of a sentence. ■ relating to the theme of an inflected word. ■ (of a vowel) connecting the theme of a word to its inflections. ■ (of a word) having a vowel connecting its theme to its inflections.
▶ **noun 1** (**thematics**) [treated as sing. or pl.] a body of topics for study or discussion.
2 a postage stamp forming part of a set with designs connected with the same subject.
– DERIVATIVES **thematically** adverb.
– ORIGIN late 17th cent.: from Greek *thematikos*, from *thema* (see THEME).

Thematic Apperception Test ▶ **noun** Psychology a projective test designed to reveal a person's social drives or needs by their interpretation of a series of pictures of emotionally ambiguous situations.

thematic catalogue ▶ **noun** Music a catalogue giving the opening themes of works as well as their names and other details.

thematic role ▶ **noun** (in Chomskyan linguistics) any of a set of semantic roles that a noun phrase may have in relation to a verb, for example agent, patient, location, source, or goal. Also called THETA ROLE.

thematize (also **thematise**) ▶ **verb** [with obj.] present or select (a subject) as a theme. ■ Linguistics place (a word or phrase) at the start of a sentence in order to focus attention on it.
– DERIVATIVES **thematization** noun.

Thembu /ˈtɛmbuː/ (also **Tembu**) ▶ **noun** (pl. **same** or **Thembus**) a member of a Xhosa-speaking people originating in present-day KwaZulu-Natal and now living in the Transkei.
▶ **adjective** relating to the Thembu.
– ORIGIN from Xhosa *umThembu*.

theme ▶ **noun 1** the subject of a talk, piece of writing, exhibition, etc.; a topic: *the theme of the sermon was reverence*. ■ US an essay written by a school pupil on a particular subject.
2 an idea that recurs in or pervades a work of art or literature: *love and honour are the pivotal themes of the Hornblower books*. ■ Music a prominent or frequently recurring melody or group of notes in a composition. ■ [usu. as modifier] a piece of music that frequently recurs in or accompanies the beginning and end of a film, play, or musical: *a theme song*.
3 [usu. as modifier] a setting given to a restaurant, pub, or leisure venue, intended to evoke a particular country, historical period, culture, etc.: *an Irish theme pub*.
4 Linguistics the first major constituent of a clause, indicating the subject matter, typically being the subject but optionally other constituents, as in '*smitten* he is not'. Contrasted with RHEME. ■ the stem of a noun or verb; the part to which inflections are added, especially one composed of the root and an added vowel.
5 historical any of the twenty-nine provinces in the Byzantine empire.
▶ **verb** [with obj.] give a particular theme or setting to (a leisure venue, event, etc.): *the amusement park will be themed as a Caribbean pirate stronghold* | (as adj. **themed**) *a themed party*.
– ORIGIN Middle English: via Old French from Latin *thema*, from Greek, literally 'proposition'; related to *tithenai* 'to set or place'.

theme park ▶ **noun** an amusement park with a unifying setting or idea.

Themis /ˈθɛmɪs/ Greek Mythology a goddess, daughter of Uranus (Heaven) and Gaia (Earth). In Homer she was the personification of order and justice, who convened the assembly of the gods.

Themistocles /θɪˈmɪstəˌkliːz/ (*c*.528–462 BC), Athenian statesman. He helped build up the Athenian fleet, and defeated the Persian fleet at Salamis in 480.

themself ▶ **pronoun** [third person singular] used instead of 'himself' or 'herself' to refer to a person of unspecified sex: *the casual observer might easily think themself back in 1945*.

> **USAGE** The standard reflexive form corresponding to **they** and **them** is **themselves**, as in *they can do it themselves*. The singular form **themself**, first recorded in the 14th century, has re-emerged in recent years corresponding to the singular gender-neutral use of **they**, as in *this is the first step in helping someone to help* **themself**. The form is not widely accepted in standard English, however. For more details, see USAGE at THEY.

themselves ▶ **pronoun** [third person plural] **1** [reflexive] used as the object of a verb or preposition to refer to a group of people or things previously mentioned as the subject of the clause: *countries unable to look after themselves*.
2 [emphatic] used to emphasize a particular group of people or things mentioned: *excellent at organizing others, they may well be disorganized themselves*.
3 [singular] used instead of 'himself' or 'herself' to refer to a person of unspecified sex: *anyone who fancies themselves as a racing driver*.
– PHRASES (**not**) **be themselves** see BE ONESELF, NOT BE ONESELF at BE. **by themselves** see BY ONESELF at BY.

> **USAGE** On the use of **themselves** in the singular to mean 'himself or herself', see USAGE at THEY.

then ▶ **adverb 1** at that time; at the time in question: *I was living in Cairo then* | [after prep.] *Phoebe by then was exhausted* | [as adj.] *he accepted a peerage from the then Prime Minister, Edward Heath*.
2 after that; next; afterwards: *she won the first and then the second game*. ■ also; in addition: *I'm paid a generous salary, and then there's the money I've made at the races*.
3 in that case; therefore: *if you do what I tell you, then there's nothing to worry about* | *well, that's okay then*. ■ used at the end of a sentence to emphasize an inference being drawn: *so you're still here then*. ■ used to finish off a conversation: *see you in an hour then*.

T

– PHRASES **but then (again)** after all; on the other hand (introducing a contrasting comment): *it couldn't help, but then again, it probably couldn't hurt.* **then and there** immediately.
– ORIGIN Old English *thænne, thanne, thonne*, of Germanic origin; related to Dutch *dan* and German *dann*, also to THAT and THE.

thenar /ˈθiːnə/ ▸ **adjective** Anatomy relating to the rounded fleshy part of the hand at the base of the thumb (the ball of the thumb).
– ORIGIN mid 17th cent.: from Greek, literally 'palm of the hand, sole of the foot'.

thenardite /θɛˈnɑːdʌɪt/ ▸ **noun** [mass noun] a white to brownish translucent crystalline mineral occurring in evaporated salt lakes, consisting of anhydrous sodium sulphate.
– ORIGIN mid 19th cent.: from the name of Baron Louis-Jacques *Thénard* (1777–1857), French chemist, + -ITE[1].

thence (also **from thence**) ▸ **adverb** formal from a place or source previously mentioned: *they intended to cycle on into France and thence home via Belgium.* ■ as a consequence: *studying maps to assess past latitudes and thence an indication of climate.*
– ORIGIN Middle English *thennes*, from earlier *thenne* (from Old English *thanon*, of West Germanic origin) + -S[3] (later respelled *-ce* to denote the unvoiced sound).

> **USAGE** The use of **thence** is similar to **whence** in that **thence** and **from thence** are both used to mean 'from a place or source previously mentioned'. See also USAGE at WHENCE.

thenceforth (also **from thenceforth**) ▸ **adverb** archaic or literary from that time, place, or point onward: *thenceforth he made his life in England.*

thenceforward ▸ **adverb** another term for THENCEFORTH.

theo- ▸ **combining form** relating to God or deities: *theocentric | theocracy.*
– ORIGIN from Greek *theos* 'god'.

theobromine /ˌθɪə(ʊ)ˈbrəʊmɪn, -miːn/ ▸ **noun** [mass noun] Chemistry a bitter, volatile compound obtained from cacao seeds. It is an alkaloid resembling caffeine in its physiological effects. ● Chem. formula: $C_7H_8N_4O_2$.
– ORIGIN mid 19th cent.: from modern Latin *Theobroma* (genus name, from Greek *theos* 'god' and *brōma* 'food') + -INE[4].

theocentric /ˌθɪə(ʊ)ˈsɛntrɪk/ ▸ **adjective** having God as a central focus: *a theocentric civilization.*

theocracy /θɪˈɒkrəsi/ ▸ **noun** (pl. **theocracies**) a system of government in which priests rule in the name of God or a god. ■ **(the Theocracy)** the commonwealth of Israel from the time of Moses until the election of Saul as king.
– DERIVATIVES **theocrat** noun, **theocratic** adjective, **theocratically** adverb.
– ORIGIN early 17th cent.: from Greek *theokratia* (see THEO-, -CRACY).

Theocritus /θɪˈɒkrɪtəs/ (*c*.310–*c*.250 BC), Greek poet, born in Sicily. He is chiefly known for his *Idylls*, hexameter poems presenting the lives of imaginary shepherds which were the model for Virgil's *Eclogues*.

theodicy /θɪˈɒdɪsi/ ▸ **noun** (pl. **theodicies**) [mass noun] the vindication of divine providence in view of the existence of evil.
– ORIGIN late 18th cent.: from French *Théodicée*, the title of a work by Leibniz, from Greek *theos* 'god' + *dikē* 'justice'.

T

theodolite /θɪˈɒdəlʌɪt/ ▸ **noun** a surveying instrument with a rotating telescope for measuring horizontal and vertical angles.
– ORIGIN late 16th cent. (originally denoting an instrument for measuring horizontal angles): from modern Latin *theodelitus*, of unknown origin.

Theodora /θɪəˈdɔːrə/ (*c*.500–48), Byzantine empress, wife of Justinian. As Justinian's closest adviser, she exercised a considerable influence on political affairs and the theological questions of the time.

Theodoric /θɪˈɒdərɪk/ (*c*.454–526), king of the Ostrogoths 471–526; known as **Theodoric the Great**. At its greatest extent his empire included Italy, Sicily, Dalmatia, and parts of Germany.

Theodosius I /θɪəˈdəʊsɪəs/ (*c*.346–95), Roman emperor 379–95; full name *Flavius Theodosius*; known as **Theodosius the Great**. Proclaimed joint emperor by the Emperor Gratian in 379, he took control of the Eastern Empire and ended the war with the Visigoths. A pious Christian, in 391 he banned all forms of pagan worship.

theogony /θɪˈɒgəni/ ▸ **noun** (pl. **theogonies**) the genealogy of a group or system of gods.
– ORIGIN early 17th cent.: from Greek *theogonia*, from *theos* 'god' + Greek *-gonia* '-begetting'.

theologian /θɪəˈləʊdʒɪən, -dʒ(ə)n/ ▸ **noun** a person who engages or is an expert in theology.
– ORIGIN late 15th cent.: from French *théologien*, from *théologie* or Latin *theologia* (see THEOLOGY).

theological /θɪəˈlɒdʒɪk(ə)l/ ▸ **adjective** relating to the study of the nature of God and religious belief.
– DERIVATIVES **theologically** adverb.
– ORIGIN late Middle English (in the sense 'relating to the word of God or the Bible'): from medieval Latin *theologicalis*, from late Latin *theologicus*, from Greek *theologikos*, from *theologia* (see THEOLOGY).

theological virtues ▸ **plural noun** the three virtues of faith, hope, and charity. Often contrasted with NATURAL VIRTUES.

theologize (also **theologise**) ▸ **verb 1** [no obj.] engage in theological reasoning or speculation.
2 [with obj.] treat (a person or subject) in theological terms.

theology /θɪˈɒlədʒi/ ▸ **noun** (pl. **theologies**) [mass noun] the study of the nature of God and religious belief. ■ religious beliefs and theory when systematically developed: *in Christian theology, God comes to be conceived as Father and Son* | [count noun] *a willingness to tolerate new theologies.*
– DERIVATIVES **theologist** noun.
– ORIGIN late Middle English (originally applying only to Christianity): from French *théologie*, from Latin *theologia*, from Greek, from *theos* 'god' + *-logia* (see -LOGY).

theomachy /θɪˈɒməki/ ▸ **noun** (pl. **theomachies**) a war or struggle against God or among or against the gods.
– ORIGIN late 16th cent. (denoting fighting against God): from Greek *theomakhia*, from *theos* 'god' + *-makhia* 'fighting'.

theophany /θɪˈɒf(ə)ni/ ▸ **noun** (pl. **theophanies**) a visible manifestation to humankind of God or a god.
– ORIGIN Old English, via ecclesiastical Latin from Greek *theophaneia*, from *theos* 'god' + *phainein* 'to show'.

theophoric /θɪəˈfɒrɪk/ (also **theophorous**) ▸ **adjective** bearing the name of a god.

Theophrastus /θɪəˈfrastəs/ (*c*.370–*c*.287 BC), Greek philosopher and scientist, the pupil and successor of Aristotle. The most influential of his works was *Characters*, a collection of sketches of psychological types.

theophylline /θɪəˈfɪliːn, -lɪn/ ▸ **noun** [mass noun] Chemistry a bitter crystalline compound present in small quantities in tea leaves, isomeric with theobromine.
– ORIGIN late 19th cent.: from modern Latin *Thea* (former genus name of the tea plant, from Dutch *thee*) + Greek *phullon* 'leaf' + -INE[4].

theorbo /θɪˈɔːbəʊ/ ▸ **noun** (pl. **theorbos**) a large lute with the neck extended to carry several long bass strings, used for accompaniment in 17th and early 18th century music.
– ORIGIN early 17th cent.: from Italian *tiorba*, of unknown origin.

theorem /ˈθɪərəm/ ▸ **noun** Physics & Mathematics a general proposition not self-evident but proved by a chain of reasoning; a truth established by means of accepted truths. ■ a rule in algebra or other branches of mathematics expressed by symbols or formulae.
– ORIGIN mid 16th cent.: from French *théorème*, or via late Latin from Greek *theōrēma* 'speculation, proposition', from *theōrein* 'look at', from *theōros* 'spectator'.

theoretic /θɪəˈrɛtɪk/ ▸ **adjective** another term for THEORETICAL.
– ORIGIN early 17th cent. (in the sense 'conjectural'): via late Latin from Greek *theōrētikos*, from *theōrētos* 'that may be seen', from *theōrein* (see THEOREM).

theoretical ▸ **adjective** concerned with or involving the theory of a subject or area of study rather than its practical application: *a theoretical physicist* | *the training is practical rather than theoretical.* ■ based on or calculated through theory rather than experience or practice: *the theoretical value of their work.*
– DERIVATIVES **theoretically** adverb [sentence adverb] *theoretically we might expect this to be true.*

theoretician /ˌθɪərɪˈtɪʃ(ə)n/ ▸ **noun** a person who forms, develops, or studies the theoretical framework of a subject.

theorist ▸ **noun** a person concerned with the theoretical aspects of a subject; a theoretician.

theorize (also **theorise**) ▸ **verb** [no obj.] form a theory or theories about something: *he theorized that the atolls marked the sites of vanished volcanoes* | (as noun **theorizing**) *they are more interested in obtaining results than in political theorizing.* ■ [with obj.] create a theoretical premise or framework for: *women should be doing feminism rather than theorizing it.*
– DERIVATIVES **theorization** noun, **theorizer** noun.

theory ▸ **noun** (pl. **theories**) a supposition or a system of ideas intended to explain something, especially one based on general principles independent of the thing to be explained: *Darwin's theory of evolution.* ■ a set of principles on which the practice of an activity is based: *a theory of education* | [mass noun] *music theory.* ■ an idea used to account for a situation or justify a course of action: *my theory would be that the place has been seriously mismanaged.* ■ Mathematics a collection of propositions to illustrate the principles of a subject.
– PHRASES **in theory** used in describing what is supposed to happen or be possible, usually with the implication that it does not in fact happen: *in theory, things can only get better; in practice, they may well become a lot worse.*
– ORIGIN late 16th cent. (denoting a mental scheme of something to be done): via late Latin from Greek *theōria* 'contemplation, speculation', from *theōros* 'spectator'.

theory-laden ▸ **adjective** denoting a term, concept, or statement which has meaning only as part of some theory, so that its use implies the acceptance of that theory.

theory of games ▸ **noun** another term for GAME THEORY.

theosophy /θɪˈɒsəfi/ ▸ **noun** [mass noun] any of a number of philosophies maintaining that a knowledge of God may be achieved through spiritual ecstasy, direct intuition, or special individual relations, especially the movement founded in 1875 as the Theosophical Society by Helena Blavatsky and Henry Steel Olcott (1832–1907).
– DERIVATIVES **theosopher** noun, **theosophic** adjective, **theosophical** adjective, **theosophically** adverb, **theosophist** noun.
– ORIGIN mid 17th cent.: from medieval Latin *theosophia*, from late Greek, from *theosophos* 'wise concerning God', from *theos* 'god' + *sophos* 'wise'.

Theotokos /θɪˈɒtəkɒs/ ▸ **noun** **(the Theotokos)** Mother of God (used in the Eastern Orthodox Church as a title of the Virgin Mary).
– ORIGIN from ecclesiastical Greek, from *theos* 'god' + *-tokos* 'bringing forth'.

Thera /ˈθɪərə/ a Greek island in the southern Cyclades. The island suffered a violent volcanic eruption in about 1500 BC; remains of an ancient Minoan civilization have been discovered beneath the pumice and volcanic debris. Also called SANTORINI. Greek name THÍRA.

therapeutic /ˌθɛrəˈpjuːtɪk/ ▸ **adjective** relating to the healing of disease: *diagnostic and therapeutic facilities.* ■ administered or applied for reasons of health: *a therapeutic shampoo.* ■ having a good effect on the body or mind; contributing to a sense of well-being: *a therapeutic silence.*
▸ **noun 1** **(therapeutics)** the branch of medicine concerned with the treatment of disease and the action of remedial agents.
2 a treatment, therapy, or drug: *current therapeutics for asthma.*
– DERIVATIVES **therapeutical** adjective, **therapeutically** adverb.
– ORIGIN mid 17th cent.: via modern Latin from Greek *therapeutikos*, from *therapeuein* 'minister to, treat medically'.

therapeutic alliance ▸ **noun** [in sing.] the relationship between a psychologist or psychotherapist and a patient, regarded as important for the outcome of psychological therapy.

therapist ▸ **noun** a person skilled in a particular kind of therapy: *a certified massage therapist.* ■ a person who treats psychological problems; a psychotherapist: *cost is one factor keeping them from the therapist's couch.*

therapize (also **therapise**) ▶ **verb** [with obj.] subject to psychological therapy: *you certainly don't need to therapize or fix each other.*

therapsid /θɛˈrapsɪd/ ▶ **noun** a fossil reptile of a Permian and Triassic order, the members of which are related to the ancestors of mammals. ● Order Therapsida, subclass Synapsida: many families and numerous genera, including the cynodonts.
– ORIGIN early 20th cent.: from modern Latin *Therapsida*, from Greek *thēr* 'beast' + *hapsis, hapsid-* 'arch' (referring to the structure of the skull).

therapy ▶ **noun** (pl. **therapies**) [mass noun] treatment intended to relieve or heal a disorder: *a course of antibiotic therapy* | [count noun] *cancer therapies.* ■ the treatment of mental or psychological disorders by psychological means: *he is currently **in therapy*** | [as modifier] *therapy sessions.*
– ORIGIN mid 19th cent.: from modern Latin *therapia*, from Greek *therapeia* 'healing', from *therapeuein* 'minister to, treat medically'.

Theravada /ˌθɛrəˈvɑːdə/ (also **Theravada Buddhism**) ▶ **noun** [mass noun] the more conservative of the two major traditions of Buddhism (the other being Mahayana), which developed from Hinayana Buddhism. It is practised mainly in Sri Lanka, Burma (Myanmar), Thailand, Cambodia, and Laos.
– ORIGIN from Pali *theravāda*, literally 'doctrine of the elders', from *thera* 'elder, old' + *vāda* 'speech, doctrine'.

there ▶ **adverb 1** in, at, or to that place or position: *we went to Paris and stayed there ten days* | [with infinitive] *at the end of the day we are there to make money* | [after prep.] *I'm not going in there—it's freezing.* ■ used when gesturing to indicate the place intended: *there on the right.* ■ at that point (in speech, performance, writing, etc.): *'I'm quite—.' There she stopped.* ■ in that respect; on that issue: *I don't agree with you there.*
2 used in attracting someone's attention or calling attention to someone or something: *hello there!* | *there goes the phone.*
3 (usu. **there is/are**) used to indicate the fact or existence of something: *there's a restaurant round the corner* | *there comes a point where you give up.*
▶ **exclamation 1** used to focus attention on something: *there, I told you she wouldn't mind!*
2 used to comfort someone: ***there, there**, you must take all of this philosophically.*
– PHRASES **been there, done that** informal used to express past experience of or overfamiliarity with something. **be there for someone** be available to provide support or comfort for someone. **have been there before** informal know all about a situation from experience. **here and there** see HERE. **so there** informal used to express one's defiance: *you can't share, so there!* **there and then** immediately. **there goes ——** used to express the destruction or failure of something: *there goes my career.* **there it is** that is the situation: *pretty ridiculous, I know, but there it is.* **there or thereabouts** in or very near a particular place or position. ■ approximately. **there you are** (or **go**) informal **1** this is what you wanted: *there you are—that'll be £3.80 please.* **2** used to express confirmation, triumph, or resignation: *there you are! I told you the problem was a political one* | *sometimes it is embarrassing, but there you go.* **there you go again** used to criticize someone for behaving in a way that is typical of them. **there you have it** used to draw attention to a fact or to emphasize the simplicity of a process or action: *simply turn the handle three times and there you have it.*
– ORIGIN Old English *thær, thēr* of Germanic origin; related to Dutch *daar* and German *da*, also to THAT and THE.

thereabouts (also **thereabout**) ▶ **adverb** near that place: *the land is dry in places thereabouts.* ■ used to indicate that a date or figure is approximate: *the notes were written in 1860 or thereabouts.*

thereafter ▶ **adverb** formal after that time: *thereafter their fortunes suffered a steep decline.*

thereanent /ˌðɛːrəˈnɛnt/ ▶ **adverb** Scottish concerning that matter: *optimistic views thereanent.*

thereat ▶ **adverb** archaic or formal **1** at that place.
2 on account of or after that.

thereby ▶ **adverb** by that means; as a result of that: *students perform in hospitals, thereby gaining a deeper awareness of the therapeutic power of music.*
– PHRASES **thereby hangs a tale** used to indicate that there is more to say about something.

therefor ▶ **adverb** archaic for that object or purpose.

therefore ▶ **adverb** for that reason; consequently: *he was injured and therefore unable to play.*

therefrom ▶ **adverb** archaic or formal from that or that place.

therein ▶ **adverb** archaic or formal in that place, document, or respect.

thereinafter ▶ **adverb** archaic or formal in a later part of that document.

thereinbefore ▶ **adverb** archaic or formal in an earlier part of that document.

thereinto ▶ **adverb** archaic or formal into that place.

theremin /ˈθɛrəmɪn/ ▶ **noun** an electronic musical instrument in which the tone is generated by two high-frequency oscillators and the pitch controlled by the movement of the performer's hand towards and away from the circuit.
– ORIGIN early 20th cent.: named after Lev *Theremin* (1896–1993), its Russian inventor.

thereof ▶ **adverb** formal of the thing just mentioned; of that: *the member state or a part thereof.*

thereon ▶ **adverb** formal on or following from the thing just mentioned: *the order of the court and the taxation consequent thereon.*

thereout ▶ **adverb** archaic out of that; from that source.

there's ▶ **contraction 1** there is: *there's nothing there.* ■ informal, chiefly Brit. used to make a request or express approval in a patronizing manner: *make a cup of tea, there's a good girl.*
2 there has: *there's been a break-in at the shop*

Theresa, Mother see TERESA, MOTHER.

Thérèse of Lisieux, St /tɛˈrɛz/, French /teʀɛz/ variant spelling of TERESA OF LISIEUX, ST.

therethrough ▶ **adverb** archaic through or by reason of that; thereby.

thereto ▶ **adverb** archaic or formal to that or that place: *the third party assents thereto.*

theretofore ▶ **adverb** archaic or formal before that time.

thereunder ▶ **adverb** archaic or formal in accordance with the thing mentioned: *the act and the regulations made thereunder.*

thereunto ▶ **adverb** archaic or formal to that: *his agent thereunto lawfully authorized in writing or by will.*

thereupon ▶ **adverb** formal immediately or shortly after that: *he thereupon returned to Moscow.*

therewith ▶ **adverb** archaic or formal **1** with or in the thing mentioned: *documents lodged therewith.*
2 soon or immediately after that; forthwith: *therewith he rose.*

therewithal ▶ **adverb** archaic together with that; besides: *he was to make a voyage and his fortune therewithal.*

Theria /ˈθɪərɪə/ ▶ **plural noun** Zoology a major group of mammals that comprises the marsupials and placentals. Compare with PROTOTHERIA. ● Subclass Theria, class Mammalia.
– ORIGIN modern Latin (plural), from Greek *thēria* 'wild animals'.

theriac /ˈθɪərɪak/ ▶ **noun** [mass noun] archaic an ointment or other medicinal compound used as an antidote to snake venom or other poison.
– ORIGIN late Middle English: from Latin *theriaca* (see TREACLE).

therian Zoology ▶ **noun** a mammal of the major group Theria, which comprises the marsupials and placentals.
▶ **adjective** relating to or denoting therians.

therianthropic /ˌθɪərɪanˈθrɒpɪk/ ▶ **adjective** (especially of a deity) combining the form of an animal with that of a man.
– ORIGIN late 19th cent.: from Greek *thērion* 'wild animal' + *anthrōpos* 'human being' + -IC.

theriomorphic /ˌθɪərɪə(ʊ)ˈmɔːfɪk/ ▶ **adjective** (especially of a deity) having an animal form.
– ORIGIN late 19th cent.: from Greek *thērion* 'wild beast' + -MORPH + -IC.

therm ▶ **noun** a unit of heat, especially as the former statutory unit of gas supplied in the UK equivalent to 100,000 British thermal units or 1.055×10^8 joules.
– ORIGIN 1920s: from Greek *thermē* 'heat'.

thermae /ˈθəːmiː/ ▶ **plural noun** (in ancient Greece and Rome) hot baths used for public bathing.
– ORIGIN Latin, from Greek *thermai* 'hot baths', from *thermē* 'heat'.

thermal ▶ **adjective** relating to heat. ■ another term for GEOTHERMAL. ■ (of a garment) made of a fabric that provides exceptional insulation to keep the body warm: *thermal underwear.*
▶ **noun 1** an upward current of warm air, used by gliders, balloonists, and birds to gain height.
2 (usu. **thermals**) a thermal garment, especially underwear.
– DERIVATIVES **thermally** adverb.
– ORIGIN mid 18th cent. (in the sense 'relating to hot springs'): from French, from Greek *thermē* 'heat'.

thermal capacity ▶ **noun** the number of heat units needed to raise the temperature of a body by one degree.

thermal diffusivity ▶ **noun** the thermal conductivity of a substance divided by the product of its density and its specific heat capacity.

thermal efficiency ▶ **noun** the efficiency of a heat engine measured by the ratio of the work done by it to the heat supplied to it.

thermal imaging ▶ **noun** [mass noun] the technique of using the heat given off by an object to produce an image of it or to locate it.

thermal inversion ▶ **noun** see INVERSION (sense 2).

thermalize (also **thermalise**) ▶ **verb** attain or cause to attain thermal equilibrium with the environment.
– DERIVATIVES **thermalization** noun.

thermal neutron ▶ **noun** a neutron in thermal equilibrium with its surroundings.

thermal noise ▶ **noun** [mass noun] Electronics electrical fluctuations arising from the random thermal motion of electrons.

thermal paper ▶ **noun** [mass noun] heat-sensitive paper used in thermal printers.

thermal printer ▶ **noun** a printer in which fine heated pins form characters on heat-sensitive paper.

thermal reactor ▶ **noun** a nuclear reactor using thermal neutrons.

thermal shock ▶ **noun** [mass noun] a sudden temperature fluctuation causing stress in an object or substance.

thermal spring ▶ **noun** a spring of naturally hot water.

thermal unit ▶ **noun** a unit of measurement for heat.

thermic ▶ **adjective** relating to heat.
– ORIGIN mid 19th cent.: from Greek *thermē* 'heat' + -IC.

thermic lance ▶ **noun** a steel pipe packed with steel wool through which a jet of oxygen or other gas may be passed to generate a very hot cutting flame.

Thermidor /ˈθəːmɪdɔː/, French /tɛʀmidɔʀ/ ▶ **noun** the eleventh month of the French Republican calendar (1793–1805), originally running from 19 July to 17 August.
– DERIVATIVES **Thermidorian** adjective.
– ORIGIN French, from Greek *thermē* 'heat' + *dōron* 'gift'.

thermion /ˈθəːmɪɒn/ ▶ **noun** an ion or electron emitted by a substance at high temperature.
– ORIGIN early 20th cent.: from THERMO- 'of heat' + ION.

thermionic ▶ **adjective** relating to electrons emitted from a substance at very high temperature.

thermionic emission ▶ **noun** the emission of electrons from a heated source.

thermionics ▶ **plural noun** [treated as sing.] the branch of science and technology concerned with thermionic emission.

thermionic valve (US **thermionic tube**) ▶ **noun** Electronics a device giving a flow of thermionic electrons in one direction, used especially in the rectification of a current and in radio reception.

thermistor /θəːˈmɪstə/ ▶ **noun** an electrical resistor whose resistance is greatly reduced by heating, used for measurement and control.
– ORIGIN 1940s: contraction of *thermal resistor*.

thermite /ˈθəːmʌɪt/ (also **thermit** /-mɪt/) ▶ **noun** [mass noun] a mixture of finely powdered aluminium and iron oxide that produces a very high temperature on combustion, used in welding and for incendiary bombs.
– ORIGIN early 20th cent.: coined in German from THERMO- 'of heat' + -ITE[1].

thermo- ▶ **combining form** relating to heat: *thermodynamics* | *thermoelectric.*
– ORIGIN from Greek *thermos* 'hot', *thermē* 'heat'.

thermobaric /ˌθəːməʊˈbarɪk/ ▶ **adjective** denoting or relating to a very large fuel–air bomb which ignites into a fireball when detonated, creating a powerful wave of pressure that sucks out oxygen from any confined spaces nearby.
– ORIGIN 1990s: from THERMO- + Greek *barus* 'heavy'.

thermochemistry ▶ noun [mass noun] the branch of chemistry concerned with the quantities of heat evolved or absorbed during chemical reactions.
– DERIVATIVES **thermochemical** adjective.

thermochromic /ˌθəːmə(ʊ)ˈkrəʊmɪk/ ▶ adjective (of a substance) undergoing a reversible change of colour when heated or cooled.

thermocline /ˈθəːmə(ʊ)klʌɪn/ ▶ noun an abrupt temperature gradient in a body of water such as a lake, marked by a layer above and below which the water is at different temperatures.

thermocouple ▶ noun a thermoelectric device for measuring temperature, consisting of two wires of different metals connected at two points, a voltage being developed between the two junctions in proportion to the temperature difference.

thermodynamics ▶ plural noun [treated as sing.] the branch of physical science that deals with the relations between heat and other forms of energy (such as mechanical, electrical, or chemical energy), and, by extension, of the relationships between all forms of energy.

> The **first law of thermodynamics** states the equivalence of heat and work and reaffirms the principle of conservation of energy. The **second law** states that heat does not of itself pass from a cooler to a hotter body. Another, equivalent, formulation of the second law is that the entropy of a closed system can only increase. The **third law** (also called Nernst's heat theorem) states that it is impossible to reduce the temperature of a system to absolute zero in a finite number of operations.

– DERIVATIVES **thermodynamic** adjective, **thermodynamical** adjective, **thermodynamically** adverb, **thermodynamicist** noun.

thermo-elastic ▶ adjective relating to elasticity in connection with heat.

thermoelectric ▶ adjective producing electricity by a difference of temperatures.
– DERIVATIVES **thermoelectrically** adverb, **thermoelectricity** noun.

thermoforming ▶ noun the process of heating a thermoplastic material and shaping it in a mould.
– DERIVATIVES **thermoformer** noun.

thermogenesis /ˌθəːmə(ʊ)ˈdʒɛnɪsɪs/ ▶ noun [mass noun] the production of heat, especially in a human or animal body.
– DERIVATIVES **thermogenic** adjective.

thermogram ▶ noun a record made by a thermograph.

thermograph ▶ noun an instrument that produces a trace or image representing a record of the varying temperature or infrared radiation over an area or during a period of time.

thermography ▶ noun [mass noun] **1** the use of thermograms to study heat distribution in structures or regions, for example in detecting tumours.
2 a printing technique in which a wet ink image is fused by heat or infrared radiation with a resinous powder to produce a raised impression.
– DERIVATIVES **thermographic** adjective.

thermohaline circulation /ˌθəːmə(ʊ)ˈheɪlʌɪn, -ˈheɪliːn/ ▶ noun [mass noun] Oceanography the movement of seawater in a pattern of flow dependent on variations in temperature, which give rise to changes in salt content and hence in density.

T

thermokarst /ˈθəːmə(ʊ)kɑːst/ ▶ noun [mass noun] Geology a form of periglacial topography resembling karst, with hollows produced by the selective melting of permafrost.

thermolabile /ˌθəːmə(ʊ)ˈleɪbʌɪl, -bɪl/ ▶ adjective chiefly Biochemistry (of a substance) readily destroyed or deactivated by heat.

thermoluminescence ▶ noun [mass noun] the property of some materials which have accumulated energy over a long period of becoming luminescent when pretreated and subjected to high temperatures, used as a means of dating ancient ceramics and other artefacts.
– DERIVATIVES **thermoluminescent** adjective.

thermolysis /θəˈmɒlɪsɪs/ ▶ noun [mass noun] Chemistry the breakdown of molecules by the action of heat.
– DERIVATIVES **thermolytic** adjective.

thermometer ▶ noun an instrument for measuring and indicating temperature, typically one consisting of a narrow, hermetically sealed glass tube marked with graduations and having at one end a bulb containing mercury or alcohol which extends along the tube as it expands.
– DERIVATIVES **thermometric** adjective, **thermometrical** adjective, **thermometry** noun.
– ORIGIN mid 17th cent.: from French *thermomètre* or modern Latin *thermometrum*, from **THERMO-** 'of heat' + *-metrum* 'measure'.

thermonuclear ▶ adjective relating to or using nuclear reactions that occur only at very high temperatures. ■ relating to or involving weapons in which explosive force is produced by thermonuclear reactions.

thermophile /ˈθəːmə(ʊ)fʌɪl/ ▶ noun Microbiology a bacterium or other microorganism that grows best at higher than normal temperatures.
– DERIVATIVES **thermophilic** adjective.

thermopile /ˈθəːmə(ʊ)pʌɪl/ ▶ noun a set of thermocouples arranged for measuring small quantities of radiant heat.

thermoplastic Chemistry ▶ adjective denoting substances (especially synthetic resins) that become plastic on heating and harden on cooling, and are able to repeat these processes. Often contrasted with **THERMOSETTING**.
▶ noun (usu. **thermoplastics**) a thermoplastic substance.

Thermopylae /θəˈmɒpɪliː/ a pass between the mountains and the sea in Greece, about 200 km (120 miles) north-west of Athens, originally narrow but now much widened by the recession of the sea. In 480 BC it was the scene of a defensive action by an outnumbered Greek force of 6,000 men against the invading Persians under Xerxes I. Among the defenders were 300 Spartans, all of whom, including their king Leonidas, were killed.

thermoregulate ▶ verb [no obj.] regulate temperature, especially one's own body temperature.
– DERIVATIVES **thermoregulation** noun, **thermoregulatory** adjective.

thermos (also **thermos flask**, US also **thermos bottle**) ▶ noun trademark a vacuum flask.
– ORIGIN early 20th cent.: from Greek, literally 'hot'.

thermosetting ▶ adjective Chemistry denoting substances (especially synthetic resins) which set permanently when heated. Often contrasted with **THERMOPLASTIC**.
– DERIVATIVES **thermoset** adjective & noun.

thermosphere ▶ noun the region of the atmosphere above the mesosphere and below the height at which the atmosphere ceases to have the properties of a continuous medium. The thermosphere is characterized throughout by an increase in temperature with height.

thermostable ▶ adjective chiefly Biochemistry (of a substance) not readily destroyed or deactivated by heat.

thermostat /ˈθəːməstat/ ▶ noun a device that automatically regulates temperature, or that activates a device when the temperature reaches a certain point.
– DERIVATIVES **thermostatic** adjective, **thermostatically** adverb.

thermotaxis /ˌθəːmə(ʊ)ˈtaksɪs/ ▶ noun [mass noun] Biology movement of an organism towards or away from a source of heat.

thermotropism /ˌθəːmə(ʊ)ˈtrəʊpɪz(ə)m/ ▶ noun [mass noun] Biology the turning or bending of a plant or other organism in response to a directional source of heat.
– DERIVATIVES **thermotropic** adjective.

theropod /ˈθɪərə(ʊ)pɒd/ ▶ noun a carnivorous dinosaur of a group whose members were typically bipedal and ranged from small and delicately built to very large. ● Suborder Theropoda, order Saurischia; includes the carnosaurs, ornithomimosaurs, coelurosaurs, and dromaeosaurids.
– ORIGIN 1930s: from Greek *thēr* 'beast' + *pous, pod-* 'foot'.

thesaurus /θɪˈsɔːrəs/ ▶ noun (pl. **thesauri** /-rʌɪ/ or **thesauruses**) a book that lists words in groups of synonyms and related concepts. ■ archaic a dictionary or encyclopedia.
– ORIGIN late 16th cent.: via Latin from Greek *thēsauros* 'storehouse, treasure'. The original sense 'dictionary or encyclopedia' was narrowed to the current meaning by the publication of Roget's *Thesaurus of English Words and Phrases* (1852).

these plural form of **THIS**.

Theseus /ˈθiːsɪəs/ Greek Mythology the legendary hero of Athens, son of Poseidon (or, in another account, of Aegeus, king of Athens) and husband of Phaedra. He slew the Cretan Minotaur with the help of Ariadne.

thesis /ˈθiːsɪs/ ▶ noun (pl. **theses** /-siːz/) **1** a statement or theory that is put forward as a premise to be maintained or proved: *his central thesis is that psychological life is not part of the material world*. ■ (in Hegelian philosophy) a proposition forming the first stage in the process of dialectical reasoning. Compare with **ANTITHESIS**, **SYNTHESIS**.
2 a long essay or dissertation involving personal research, written by a candidate for a university degree: *a doctoral thesis*.
3 /ˈθiːsɪs, ˈθɛsɪs/ Prosody an unstressed syllable or part of a metrical foot in Greek or Latin verse. Often contrasted with **ARSIS**.
– ORIGIN late Middle English (in sense 3): via late Latin from Greek, literally 'placing, a proposition', from the root of *tithenai* 'to place'.

thesp ▶ abbreviation informal thespian.

thespian /ˈθɛspɪən/ formal or humorous ▶ adjective relating to drama and the theatre: *thespian talents*.
▶ noun an actor or actress.
– ORIGIN late 17th cent.: from the name **THESPIS** + **-IAN**.

Thespis /ˈθɛspɪs/ (6th century BC), Greek dramatic poet, regarded as the founder of Greek tragedy.

Thess. ▶ abbreviation Epistle to the Thessalonians (in biblical references).

Thessalonians, Epistle to the /ˌθɛsəˈləʊnɪənz/ either of two books of the New Testament, letters of St Paul, to the new Church at Thessalonica.

Thessalonica /ˌθɛsəˈlɒnɪkə, -ləˈnʌɪkə/ Latin name for **THESSALONÍKI**.

Thessaloníki /ˌθɛsələˈniːki/ a seaport in NE Greece, the second-largest city in Greece and capital of the Greek region of Macedonia; pop. 348,900 (est. 2009). Former name **SALONICA**; Latin name **THESSALONICA**.

Thessaly /ˈθɛsəli/ a region of NE Greece. Greek name **Thessalía** /ˌθɛsaˈlia/.
– DERIVATIVES **Thessalian** /θɛˈseɪlɪən/ adjective & noun.

theta /ˈθiːtə/ ▶ noun the eighth letter of the Greek alphabet (Θ, θ), transliterated as 'th'. ■ (**Theta**) [followed by Latin genitive] Astronomy the eighth star in a constellation: *Theta Draconis*. ■ [as modifier] Chemistry denoting a temperature at which a polymer solution behaves ideally as regards its osmotic pressure.
▶ symbol ■ (θ) temperature (especially in degrees Celsius). ■ (θ) a plane angle. ■ (θ) a polar coordinate. Often coupled with φ (phi).
– ORIGIN Greek.

theta rhythm ▶ noun [mass noun] Physiology electrical activity observed in the brain under certain conditions, consisting of oscillations (**theta waves**) with a frequency of 4 to 7 hertz.

theta role ▶ noun another term for **THEMATIC ROLE**.

Thetis /ˈθɛtɪs/ Greek Mythology a sea nymph, mother of Achilles.

theurgy /ˈθiːəːdʒi/ ▶ noun [mass noun] the operation or effect of a supernatural or divine agency in human affairs. ■ a system of white magic practised by the early Neoplatonists.
– DERIVATIVES **theurgic** adjective, **theurgical** adjective, **theurgist** noun.
– ORIGIN mid 16th cent.: via late Latin from Greek *theourgia* 'sorcery', from *theos* 'god' + *-ergos* 'working'.

thew /θjuː/ ▶ noun [mass noun] literary muscular strength. ■ (**thews**) muscles and tendons perceived as generating strength.
– DERIVATIVES **thewed** adjective, **thewy** adjective.
– ORIGIN Old English *thēaw* 'usage, custom', (plural) 'manner of behaving', of unknown origin. The sense 'good bodily proportions, muscular development' arose in Middle English.

they ▶ pronoun [third person plural] **1** used to refer to two or more people or things previously mentioned or easily identified: *the two men could get life sentences if they are convicted*. ■ people in general: *the rest, as they say, is history*. ■ informal people in authority regarded collectively: *they cut my water off*.
2 [singular] used to refer to a person of unspecified sex: *ask a friend if they could help*.
– ORIGIN Middle English: from Old Norse *their*, nominative plural masculine of *sá*; related to **THEM** and **THEIR**, also to **THAT** and **THE**.

> **USAGE** The word **they** (with its counterparts **them**, **their**, and **themselves**) as a singular pronoun to refer to a person of unspecified sex has been used since at least the 16th century. In the late 20th century, as the traditional use of **he** to refer to a person of either sex came under scrutiny on the grounds of sexism, this use of **they** became more common. It is now generally accepted in contexts where it follows an indefinite pronoun such as **anyone**, **no one**, **someone**, or **a person**, as in ***anyone** can join if **they** are a resident* and ***each** to **their** own*. In other contexts,

coming after singular nouns, the use of **they** is now common, though less widely accepted, especially in formal contexts. Sentences such as *ask a **friend** if **they** could help* are still criticized for being ungrammatical. Nevertheless, in view of the growing acceptance of **they** and its obvious practical advantages, **they** is used in this dictionary in many cases where **he** would have been used formerly. See also **USAGE** at **HE** and **SHE**.

they'd ▸ **contraction** they had. ■ they would.

they'll ▸ **contraction** they shall; they will.

they're ▸ **contraction** they are.

they've ▸ **contraction** they have.

THI ▸ **abbreviation** temperature–humidity index.

thiabendazole /ˌθʌɪəˈbɛndəzəʊl/ ▸ **noun** [mass noun] Medicine a synthetic compound with anthelmintic properties, derived from thiazole and used chiefly to treat infestation with intestinal nematodes.
– ORIGIN 1960s: from elements from **THIAZOLE** + **BENZENE** + **IMIDAZOLE**.

thiamine /ˈθʌɪəmiːn, -mɪn/ (also **thiamin**) ▸ **noun** [mass noun] Biochemistry a vitamin of the B complex, found in unrefined cereals, beans, and liver, a deficiency of which causes beriberi. It is a sulphur-containing derivative of thiazole and pyrimidine. Also called **VITAMIN** B_1.

thiazide /ˈθʌɪəzʌɪd/ ▸ **noun** Medicine any of a class of sulphur-containing drugs that increase the excretion of sodium and chloride and are used as diuretics and to assist in lowering the blood pressure.
– ORIGIN 1950s: from elements of **THIO-** + **AZINE** + **OXIDE**.

thiazine /ˈθʌɪəziːn/ ▸ **noun** any of a class of dyes whose molecules contain a ring of one nitrogen, one sulphur, and four carbon atoms.
– ORIGIN late 19th cent.: from **THIO-** + **AZINE**.

thiazole /θʌɪˈeɪzəʊl/ ▸ **noun** [mass noun] Chemistry a foul-smelling synthetic liquid whose molecule is a ring of one nitrogen, one sulphur, and three carbon atoms. ● Chem. formula: C_3H_3NS.

thick ▸ **adjective 1** with opposite sides or surfaces that are far or relatively far apart: *thick slices of bread* | *thick metal cables* | *the walls are 5 feet thick.* ■ (of a garment or other knitted or woven item) made of heavy material: *a thick sweater.* ■ (of writing or printing) consisting of broad lines: *a headline in thick black type.*
2 made up of a large number of things or people close together: *his hair was long and thick* | *the road winds through thick forest.* ■ (**thick with**) densely filled or covered with: *the ground was thick with yellow leaves* | figurative *the air was thick with tension.* ■ (of the air or atmosphere, or a substance in the air) opaque, dense, or heavy: *a motorway pile-up in thick fog* | *a thick cloud of smoke.* ■ (of a person's head) having a dull pain or heavy feeling, especially as a result of a hangover or illness.
3 (of a liquid or a semi-liquid substance) relatively firm in consistency; not flowing freely: *thick mud.*
4 informal of low intelligence; stupid: *he's a bit thick.*
5 (of a voice) not clear or distinct; hoarse or husky. ■ (of an accent) very marked and difficult to understand.
6 [predic.] informal having a very close, friendly relationship: *he's very thick with the new master.*
▸ **noun** (**the thick**) the most active or crowded part of something: *we were in the thick of the battle.*
▸ **adverb** in or with deep, dense, or heavy mass: *bread spread thick with butter.*
– PHRASES **be thick on the ground** see **GROUND**[1]. **a bit thick** Brit. informal unfair or unreasonable. **give someone** (or **get**) **a thick ear** Brit. informal punish someone (or be punished) with a blow on the ear or head. **have a thick skin** see **SKIN**. **thick and fast** rapidly and in great numbers. **(as) thick as a brick** another way of saying **THICK AS TWO PLANKS** below. **(as) thick as thieves** informal (of two or more people) very close or friendly. **(as) thick as two (short) planks** (or **as a plank**) Brit. informal very stupid. **the thick end of something** Brit. informal the greater part of something: *he was borrowing the thick end of £750 every week.* **through thick and thin** under all circumstances, no matter how difficult: *they stuck together through thick and thin.*
– DERIVATIVES **thickish** adjective, **thickly** adverb [as submodifier] *thickly carpeted corridors.*
– ORIGIN Old English *thicce*, of Germanic origin; related to Dutch *dik* and German *dick*.

thicken ▸ **verb** make or become thick or thicker: [with obj.] *thicken the sauce with flour* | [no obj.] *the fog had thickened.*
– PHRASES **the plot thickens** used when a situation is becoming more and more complicated and puzzling.

thickener ▸ **noun** a substance added to a liquid to make it firmer, especially in cooking. ■ Chemistry an apparatus for the sedimentation of solids from suspension in a liquid.

thickening ▸ **noun** [mass noun] **1** the process or result of becoming broader, deeper, or denser. ■ [count noun] a broader, deeper, or denser area of animal or plant tissue.
2 another term for **THICKENER**.
▸ **adjective** becoming broader, deeper, or denser: *a hazardous journey through thickening fog.*

thicket ▸ **noun** a dense group of bushes or trees.
– ORIGIN Old English *thiccet* (see **THICK**, **-ET**[1]).

thick-film ▸ **adjective** (of a process or device) using or involving a relatively thick solid or liquid film. ■ Electronics denoting a miniature circuit or device based on a metal film.

thickhead ▸ **noun 1** informal a stupid person.
2 another term for **WHISTLER** (sense 2).

thickheaded ▸ **adjective** informal unintelligent; stupid: *what a thickheaded business decision!*
– DERIVATIVES **thickheadedness** noun.

thick-knee ▸ **noun** another term for **STONE CURLEW**.

thickness ▸ **noun 1** [mass noun] the distance through an object, as distinct from width or height: *the gateway is several feet in thickness* | [count noun] *paving slabs can be obtained in varying thicknesses.* ■ [count noun] a layer of a specified material: *the framework has to support two thicknesses of plasterboard.* ■ [in sing.] a broad or deep part of a specified thing: *the beams were set into the thickness of the wall.*
2 [mass noun] the state or quality of being thick: *he gave his eyes time to adjust to the thickness of the fog* | *the shampoo dramatically increases the thickness of your hair.*
▸ **verb** [with obj.] plane or cut (wood) to a desired breadth or depth.
– DERIVATIVES **thicknesser** noun.
– ORIGIN Old English *thicness* (see **THICK**, **-NESS**).

thicko ▸ **noun** (pl. **thickos**) informal an unintelligent person.

thickset ▸ **adjective** (of a person or animal) heavily or solidly built; stocky.

thick-skinned ▸ **adjective** insensitive to criticism or insults: *I suppose you have to be pretty thick-skinned to be an MP.*

thick-skulled (also **thick-witted**) ▸ **adjective** dull and stupid.

thief ▸ **noun** (pl. **thieves**) a person who steals another person's property, especially by stealth and without using force or threat of violence.
– ORIGIN Old English *thīof*, *thēof*, of Germanic origin; related to Dutch *dief* and German *Dieb*, also to **THEFT**.

thieve ▸ **verb** [no obj.] be a thief; steal something: *they began thieving again* | [with obj.] *the students have been thieving my favourite art books.*
– ORIGIN Old English *thēofian*, from *thēof* 'thief'. Transitive uses began in the late 17th cent.

thievery ▸ **noun** [mass noun] the action of stealing another person's property.

thieves plural form of **THIEF**.

thieving ▸ **adjective** [attrib.] keen to steal; thievish: *securing the zip on my backpack against thieving fingers* | *get lost, you thieving swine.*
▸ **noun** [mass noun] the action of stealing; theft: *he supplemented his income with petty thieving.*

thievish ▸ **adjective** relating to or given to stealing.
DERIVATIVES **thievishly** adverb.

thigh ▸ **noun** the part of the human leg between the hip and the knee. ■ the corresponding part in other animals.
– DERIVATIVES **thighed** adjective [in combination] *a big-thighed man.*
– ORIGIN Old English *thēh*, *thēoh*, *thīoh*, of Germanic origin; related to Dutch *dij*.

thigh bone ▸ **noun** the femur.

thigh-high ▸ **adjective & adverb** reaching as high as a person's thigh: [as adj.] *black thigh-high boots* | [as adv.] *skirts are sexily split thigh-high.*

thigh-slapper ▸ **noun** informal a joke or anecdote considered to be exceptionally funny.
– DERIVATIVES **thigh-slapping** adjective.

thigmotaxis /ˌθɪgməˈtaksɪs/ ▸ **noun** [mass noun] Biology the motion or orientation of an organism in response to a touch stimulus.
– DERIVATIVES **thigmotactic** adjective.
– ORIGIN early 20th cent.: from Greek *thigma* 'touch' + **TAXIS**.

thigmotropism /ˌθɪgmə(ʊ)ˈtrəʊpɪz(ə)m/ ▸ **noun** [mass noun] Biology the turning or bending of a plant or other organism in response to a touch stimulus.
– DERIVATIVES **thigmotropic** adjective.
– ORIGIN early 20th cent.: from Greek *thigma* 'touch' + **TROPISM**.

thill ▸ **noun** historical a shaft, especially one of a pair, used to attach a cart or carriage to the animal drawing it.
– ORIGIN Middle English: of unknown origin.

thiller ▸ **noun** historical a horse pulling a cart or carriage between shafts.

thimble ▸ **noun 1** a small metal or plastic cap with a closed end, worn to protect the finger and push the needle in sewing.
2 a short metal tube or ferrule.
3 Nautical a metal ring, concave on the outside, around which a loop of rope is spliced.
– ORIGIN Old English *thȳmel* 'fingerstall' (see **THUMB**, **-LE**[1]).

thimbleberry ▸ **noun** (pl. **thimbleberries**) a North American blackberry or raspberry with thimble-shaped fruit. ● Genus *Rubus*, family Rosaceae: several species, including *R. odoratus*, which has large, fragrant flowers and unpalatable fruit.

thimbleful ▸ **noun** (pl. **thimblefuls**) a small quantity of liquid, especially alcohol: *a thimbleful of brandy.*

thimblerig ▸ **noun** [mass noun] a game involving sleight of hand, in which three inverted thimbles or cups are moved about, contestants having to spot which is the one with a pea or other object underneath.
– DERIVATIVES **thimblerigger** noun.
– ORIGIN early 19th cent.: from **THIMBLE** + **RIG**[2] in the sense 'trick, dodge'.

Thimphu /ˈtɪmpuː, ˈθɪm-/ (also **Thimbu** /ˈtɪmbuː, ˈθɪm-/) the capital of Bhutan, in the Himalayas at an altitude of 2,450 m (8,000 ft); pop. 98,676 (2005).

thin ▸ **adjective** (**thinner**, **thinnest**) **1** with opposite surfaces or sides that are close or relatively close together: *thin slices of bread* | *a thin line of paint.* ■ (of a garment or other knitted or woven item) made of light material. ■ (of a garment or fabric) having become less thick as a result of wear. ■ (of writing or printing) consisting of narrow lines: *tall, thin lettering.*
2 having little, or too little, flesh or fat on the body: *a thin, gawky adolescent.*
3 having few parts or members relative to the area covered or filled; sparse: *a depressingly thin crowd* | *his hair was going thin.* ■ (of the air or a substance in the air) not dense: *the thin cold air of the mountains.* ■ Climbing denoting a route on which the holds are small or scarce.
4 (of a liquid substance) not containing much solid; flowing freely: *thin soup.*
5 lacking substance or quality; weak or inadequate: *the evidence is rather thin.* ■ (of a sound) faint and high-pitched: *a thin, reedy little voice.* ■ (of a smile) weak and forced.
▸ **adverb** with little thickness or depth: *cut the ham as thin as possible* | [in combination] *a thin-sliced loaf.*
▸ **verb** (**thins**, **thinning**, **thinned**) **1** make or become less dense, crowded, or numerous: [with obj.] *the remorseless fire of archers thinned their ranks* | [no obj.] *the trees began to thin out* | (as adj. **thinning**) *thinning hair.* ■ [with obj.] remove some plants from (a row or area) to allow the others more room to grow: *thin out the rows of peas.* ■ make or become more watery in consistency: [with obj.] *if the soup is too thick, add a little water to thin it down* | [no obj.] *the blood thins.*
2 make or become smaller in thickness: [with obj.] *their effect in thinning the ozone layer is probably slowing the global warming trend.*
3 [with obj.] Golf hit (a ball) above its centre.
– PHRASES **have a thin time** Brit. informal have an unpleasant period or experience. **on thin ice** see **ICE**. **thin air** used to refer to the state of being invisible or non-existent: *she just vanished into thin air.* **the thin blue line** informal used to refer to the police, typically in the context of maintaining order during unrest. **thin end of the wedge** see **WEDGE**[1]. **thin on the ground** see **GROUND**[1]. **thin on top** informal balding.
– DERIVATIVES **thinly** adverb, **thinness** noun, **thinnish** adjective.
– ORIGIN Old English *thynne*, of Germanic origin; related to Dutch *dun* and German *dünn*, from an Indo-European root shared by Latin *tenuis*.

-thin ▸ combining form denoting a specified degree of thinness: *gossamer-thin | wafer-thin*.

thine ▸ possessive pronoun archaic form of **YOURS**; the thing or things belonging to or associated with thee: *his spirit will take courage from thine*.
▸ possessive determiner form of **THY** used before a vowel: *inquire into thine own heart*.
– ORIGIN Old English *thīn*, of Germanic origin; related to German *dein*, also to **THOU**[1].

> **USAGE** The use of **thine** is still found in some traditional dialects but elsewhere it is restricted to archaic contexts. See also **USAGE** at **THOU**[1].

thin-film ▸ adjective (of a process or device) using or involving a very thin solid or liquid film. ■ Electronics denoting a miniature circuit or device consisting of a thin layer of metal or semiconductor on a ceramic or glass substrate.

thing ▸ noun **1** an object that one need not, cannot, or does not wish to give a specific name to: *look at that metal rail thing over there | there are lots of things I'd like to buy*. ■ (**things**) personal belongings or clothing: *she began to unpack her things*. ■ (with adj. or noun modifier **things**) equipment, utensils, or other objects used for a particular purpose: *they cleared away the lunch things*. ■ [with negative] (**a thing**) anything (used for emphasis): *she couldn't find a thing to wear*. ■ used to express one's disapproval of or contempt for something: *you won't find me smoking those filthy things*. ■ [with postpositive adj.] (**things**) all that can be described in the specified way: *his love for all things English*. ■ used euphemistically to refer to a man's penis.
2 an inanimate material object as distinct from a living sentient being: *I'm not a thing, not a work of art to be cherished*. ■ [with adj.] a living creature or plant: *the sea is the primal source of all living things on earth*. ■ [with adj.] used to express one's feelings of pity, affection, approval, or contempt for a person or animal: *have a nice weekend in the country, you lucky thing! | the lamb was a puny little thing*.
3 an action, event, thought, or utterance: *she said the first thing that came into her head | the only thing I could do well was cook*. ■ (**things**) circumstances or matters that are unspecified: *things haven't gone entirely to plan | how are things with you?* ■ an abstract entity, quality, or concept: *mourning and depression are not the same thing | they had one thing in common—they were men of action*. ■ an example or type of something: *the game is the latest thing in family fun*. ■ [with adj. or noun modifier] informal a situation or activity of a specified type or quality: *your being here is just a friendship thing, OK?*
4 (**the thing**) informal what is needed or required: *you need a tonic—and here's just the thing*. ■ what is socially acceptable or fashionable: *it wouldn't be quite the thing to go to a royal garden party in wellies*.
5 (**one's thing**) informal one's special interest or inclination: *reading isn't my thing*.
6 (**the thing**) informal used to introduce or emphasize an important point: *the thing is, I am going to sell this house*.
– PHRASES **be all things to all men** (or **people**) please everyone, typically by fitting in with their needs or expectations. ■ be able to be interpreted or used differently by different people. **be on to a good thing** informal have found a job or other situation that is pleasant, profitable, or easy. **be hearing** (or **seeing**) **things** imagine that one can hear (or see) something that is not in fact there. **a close** (or **near**) **thing** a narrow avoidance of something unpleasant. **do one's own thing** informal follow one's own interests or inclinations regardless of others. **do the —— thing** informal, chiefly N. Amer. engage in the kind of behaviour typically associated with someone or something: *a film in which he does the bad-guy thing*. **do things to** informal have a powerful emotional effect on. **for one thing** used to introduce one of two or more possible reasons for something, the remainder of which may or may not be stated: *Why hadn't he arranged to see her at the house? For one thing, it would have been warmer*. **have a thing about** informal have an obsessive interest in or dislike of: *she had a thing about men who wore glasses*. **—— is one thing, —— is another** used to indicate that the second item mentioned is much more important than the first, and cannot be compared to it: *physical attraction was one thing, love was quite another*. **make a** (**big**) **thing of** (or **about**) informal make (something) seem more important than it actually is: *Meadows made a big thing of paying the bill*. **of all things** out of all conceivable possibilities (used to express surprise): *What had he been thinking about? A kitten, of all things!* (**just**) **one of those things** informal used to indicate that one wishes to pass over an unfortunate experience by regarding it as unavoidable or to be accepted. **one thing leads to another** used to suggest that the exact sequence of events is too obvious to need recounting. **there is only one thing for it** there is only one possible course of action. (**now**) **there's a thing** informal used as an expression of surprise. **a thing of the past** a thing that no longer happens or exists: *house-price booms were seen as a thing of the past*. **a thing or two** informal used to refer to useful information that can be imparted or learned: *Teddy taught me a thing or two about wine*. **things that go bump in the night** informal, humorous unexplained and frightening noises at night, regarded as being caused by ghosts.
– ORIGIN Old English, of Germanic origin; related to German *Ding*. Early senses included 'meeting' and 'matter, concern' as well as 'inanimate object'.

thingamabob /ˈθɪŋəməbɒb/ (also **thingumabob**, **thingamajig**, or **thingumajig** /ˈθɪŋəmədʒɪg/) ▸ noun another term for **THINGUMMY**.

thingummy /ˈθɪŋəmi/ (also **thingamy**) ▸ noun (pl. **thingummies**) informal a person or thing whose name one has forgotten, does not know, or does not wish to mention: *one of those thingummies for keeping all the fire tools together*.
– ORIGIN late 18th cent.: from **THING** + a meaningless suffix.

thingy ▸ noun (pl. **thingies**) another term for **THINGUMMY**.

think ▸ verb (past and past participle **thought**) **1** [with clause] have a particular belief or idea: *she thought that nothing would be the same again* | (**be thought**) *it's thought he may have collapsed from shock* | [with infinitive] *up to 300 people were thought to have died*. ■ used in questions to express anger or surprise: *what do you think you're doing?* ■ (**I think**) used in speech to reduce the force of a statement, or to politely suggest or refuse something: *I thought we could go out for a meal*.
2 [no obj.] direct one's mind towards someone or something; use one's mind actively to form connected ideas: *he was thinking about Colin | Jack thought for a moment* | [with obj.] *any writer who so rarely produces a book is not thinking deep thoughts*. ■ have a particular mental attitude or approach: *he thought like a general* | [with complement] *one should always think positive*. ■ (**think of/about**) take into consideration when deciding on a possible action: *you can live how you like, but there's the children to think about*. ■ (**think of**) call to mind: *lemon thyme is a natural pair with any chicken dish you can think of*. ■ (**think of/about**) consider the possibility or advantages of (a course of action): *he was thinking of becoming a zoologist*. ■ (**think to do something**) have sufficient foresight or awareness to do something: *I hadn't thought to warn Rachel about him*. ■ imagine or expect (an actual or possible situation): *think of being paid a salary to hunt big game!* | [with clause] *I never thought we'd raise so much money*. ■ (**think oneself into**) imagine what it would be like to be in (a position or role): *she tried to think herself into the part of Peter's fiancée*.
3 [no obj.] (**think of**) have a specified opinion of: *she did not think highly of modern art | what would John think of her? | I think of him as a friend*.
▸ noun [in sing.] informal an act of thinking: *I went for a walk to have a think*.
– PHRASES **have** (**got**) **another think coming** informal used to express the speaker's disagreement with or unwillingness to do something suggested by someone else: *if they think I'm going to do physical jerks, they've got another think coming*. **think again** reconsider something. **think aloud** express one's thoughts as soon as they occur. **think better of** decide not to do (something) after reconsideration. **think big** see **BIG**. **think fit** see **FIT**[1]. **think for oneself** have an independent mind or attitude. **think nothing of** consider (an activity others regard as unusual, wrong, or difficult) as straightforward or normal: *ordinarily, our elected representatives would think nothing of spending another $20 billion*. **think nothing of it** see **NOTHING**. **think on one's feet** see **FOOT**. **think twice** consider a course of action carefully before embarking on it. **think the world of** see **WORLD**.
– PHRASAL VERBS **think back** recall a past event or time: *I keep thinking back to school*. **think on** dialect & N. Amer. think of or about. **think something out** (or **through**) consider something in all its aspects before taking action: *the plan had not been properly thought out*. **think something over** consider something carefully. **think something up** informal use one's ingenuity to devise something.
– ORIGIN Old English *thencan*, of Germanic origin; related to Dutch and German *denken*.

thinkable ▸ adjective able to be thought of or imagined; conceivable: *something that was barely thinkable just 70 years ago*.

thinker ▸ noun a person who thinks deeply and seriously. ■ a person with highly developed intellectual powers, especially one whose profession involves intellectual activity: *a leading scientific thinker*.

thinking ▸ noun [mass noun] the process of considering or reasoning about something: *the selectors have some thinking to do before the match*. ■ a person's ideas or opinions: *his thinking is reflected in his later autobiography*. ■ (**thinkings**) archaic thoughts; meditations.
▸ adjective [attrib.] using thought or rational judgement; intelligent: *he seemed a thinking man*.
– PHRASES **good** (or **nice**) **thinking** used as an expression of approval for an ingenious plan or observation. **put on one's thinking cap** informal meditate on a problem.

thinko ▸ noun (pl. **thinkos**) informal a mistake in one's thought processes; a mental lapse or failure to reason correctly.
– ORIGIN 1990s: formed on the pattern of **TYPO**.

think piece ▸ noun an article in a newspaper, magazine, or journal presenting personal opinions, analysis, or discussion, rather than bare facts.

think tank ▸ noun a body of experts providing advice and ideas on specific political or economic problems.
– DERIVATIVES **think-tanker** noun.

thin-layer chromatography ▸ noun [mass noun] Chemistry chromatography in which compounds are separated on a thin layer of adsorbent material, typically a coating of silica gel on a glass plate or plastic sheet.

thinner ▸ noun [mass noun] (also **thinners**) a volatile solvent used to make paint or other solutions less viscous.

thinnings ▸ plural noun seedlings, trees, or fruit which have been removed to improve the growth of those remaining.

thin section ▸ noun a thin, flat piece of material prepared for examination with a microscope, in particular a piece of rock about 0.03 mm thick, or, for electron microscopy, a piece of tissue about 30 nm thick.
▸ verb (**thin-section**) [with obj.] prepare (something) for examination with a microscope by taking a thin section.

thin-skinned ▸ adjective sensitive to criticism or insults: *he isn't the only successful politician to be cliquey and thin-skinned*.

thio- ▸ combining form Chemistry denoting replacement of oxygen by sulphur in a compound: *thiosulphate*.
– ORIGIN from Greek *theion* 'sulphur'.

thiocyanate /ˌθʌɪə(ʊ)ˈsʌɪəneɪt/ ▸ noun Chemistry a salt containing the anion SCN^-.

thiol /ˈθʌɪɒl/ ▸ noun Chemistry an organic compound containing the group –SH, i.e. a sulphur-containing analogue of an alcohol.

thiomersal /ˌθʌɪə(ʊ)ˈməːs(ə)l/ ▸ noun [mass noun] a compound able to inhibit the growth of bacteria and other microorganisms, used as a medical disinfectant and preservative for biological products. ● Chem. formula: $C_9H_9O_2SHgNa$.
ORIGIN 1950s; from **THIO-** + *mer(cury)* + *sal(icylate)*.

thionyl /ˈθʌɪənʌɪl, -nɪl/ ▸ noun [as modifier] Chemistry of or denoting the divalent radical =SO.
– ORIGIN 1857: so named by H. Schiff (see **SCHIFF BASE**).

thiopental ▸ noun North American term for **THIOPENTONE**.

thiopentone /ˌθʌɪə(ʊ)ˈpɛntəʊn/ ▸ noun [mass noun] Medicine a sulphur-containing barbiturate drug used as a general anaesthetic and hypnotic, and (reputedly) as a truth drug.
– ORIGIN 1940s: from **THIO-** + a contraction of **PENTOBARBITONE**.

thioridazine /ˌθʌɪə(ʊ)rɪˈdeɪziːn/ ▸ noun [mass noun] Medicine a synthetic compound derived from phenothiazine, used as a tranquillizer, chiefly in the treatment of mental illness.
– ORIGIN 1950s: from **THIO-** + *(pipe)rid(ine)* + **AZINE**.

T

thiosulphate (US **thiosulfate**) ▸ **noun** Chemistry a salt containing the anion $S_2O_3^{2-}$, i.e. a sulphate with one oxygen atom replaced by sulphur.

thiourea /ˌθʌɪə(ʊ)jʊˈriːə/ ▸ **noun** [mass noun] Chemistry a synthetic crystalline compound used in photography and the manufacture of synthetic resins. ● The sulphur analogue of urea; chem. formula: $SC(NH_2)_2$.

Thíra /ˈθiːra/ Greek name for **THERA**.

thiram /ˈθʌɪram/ ▸ **noun** [mass noun] Chemistry a synthetic sulphur-containing compound used as a fungicide and seed protectant. ● Chem. formula: $(CH_3)_2NCSS_2SCN(CH_3)_2$.
– ORIGIN 1950s: from **THIO-**, *(u)r(ea)*, and *am(ine)*, elements of the systematic name.

third ▸ **ordinal number 1** constituting number three in a sequence; 3rd: *the third century | the third of October | Edward the Third.* ■ the third finisher or position in a race or competition: *Hill finished third.* ■ the third in a sequence of a vehicle's gears: *he took the corner in third.* ■ Baseball third base. ■ chiefly Brit. the third form of a school or college. ■ thirdly (used to introduce a third point or reason): *second, they are lightly regulated; and third, they do business with non-resident clients.* ■ Brit. a place in the third grade in an examination, especially that for a degree.
2 each of three equal parts into which something is or may be divided: *a third of a mile.*
3 Music an interval spanning three consecutive notes in a diatonic scale, e.g. C to E (**major third**, equal to two tones) or A to C (**minor third**, equal to a tone and a semitone). ■ the note which is higher by a third than the tonic of a diatonic scale or root of a chord.
– PHRASES **third time lucky** (or US **third time is the charm**) used to express the hope that, after twice failing to accomplish something, one may succeed in the third attempt.
– ORIGIN Old English *thridda*, of Germanic origin; related to Dutch *derde* and German *dritte*, also to **THREE**. The spelling *thrid* was dominant until the 16th cent. (but *thirdda* is recorded in Northumbrian dialect as early as the 10th cent.).

third age ▸ **noun** (**the third age**) Brit. the period in life of active retirement, following middle age.
– DERIVATIVES **third ager** noun.

third class ▸ **noun** [in sing.] a group of people or things considered together as third best. ■ Brit. a university degree or examination result in the third-highest classification. ■ [mass noun] US a cheap class of mail for the handling of advertising and other printed material that weighs less than 16 ounces and is unsealed. ■ [mass noun] chiefly historical the cheapest and least comfortable accommodation in a train or ship.
▸ **adjective & adverb** of the third-best quality or of lower status: [as adj.] *many indigenous groups are still viewed as third-class citizens.* ■ [as adj.] Brit. relating to the third-highest division in a university examination: *he left university with a third-class degree.* ■ US relating to a cheap class of mail including advertising and other printed material weighing less than 16 ounces: [as adj.] *third-class mail.* ■ chiefly historical relating to the cheapest and least comfortable accommodation in a train or ship: [as adj.] *a suffocating third-class compartment* | [as adv.] *I travelled third class across Europe.*

third country ▸ **noun** a Third World country.

third cousin ▸ **noun** see **COUSIN**.

third-degree ▸ **adjective** [attrib.] **1** denoting burns of the most severe kind, affecting tissue below the skin.
2 N. Amer. Law denoting the least serious category of a crime, especially murder.
▸ **noun** (**the third degree**) long and harsh questioning, especially by police, to obtain information or a confession.

third estate ▸ **noun** [treated as sing. or pl.] the common people as part of a country's political system. [the first two estates were formerly represented by the clergy, and the barons and knights; later the Lords spiritual and the Lords temporal.] ■ (**the Third Estate**) the French bourgeoisie and working class before the Revolution. [translating French *le tiers état*.]

third eye ▸ **noun 1** Hinduism & Buddhism the 'eye of insight' in the forehead of an image of a deity, especially the god Shiva. ■ the faculty of intuitive insight or prescience.
2 informal term for **PINEAL EYE**.

third eyelid ▸ **noun** informal term for **NICTITATING MEMBRANE**.

third force ▸ **noun** a political group or party acting as a check on conflict between two extreme or opposing groups.

third-generation ▸ **adjective** of a more advanced stage of technology than a second-generation model or system. ■ denoting a broadband digital telephone technology that uses packet switching, supporting Internet connection and multimedia services for both mobile and landline phones.

third-hand ▸ **adjective 1** (of goods) having had two previous owners: *a third-hand dinner suit.*
2 (of information) acquired from or via several intermediate sources and consequently not authoritative or reliable: *the accounts are third-hand, told years after the event.*
▸ **adverb** from or via several intermediate sources: *I heard about the case third-hand.*

Third International see **INTERNATIONAL** (sense 2 of the noun).

third-level ▸ **adjective** chiefly Irish relating to or denoting education at a college or university.

thirdly ▸ **adverb** in the third place (used to introduce a third point or reason).

third man ▸ **noun** Cricket a fielding position near the boundary behind the slips. ■ a fielder at this position.

third market ▸ **noun** Finance used to refer to trading in listed stock outside the stock exchange.

third party ▸ **noun** a person or group besides the two primarily involved in a situation, especially a dispute.
▸ **adjective** [attrib.] relating to a person or group besides the two primarily involved in a situation: *third-party suppliers.* ■ Brit. (of insurance) covering damage or injury suffered by a person other than the insured.

third person ▸ **noun 1** a third party.
2 see **PERSON** (sense 2). ■ (**the third person**) a type of narrative in which the story is related by an omniscient narrator, using third-person forms.

third position ▸ **noun 1** Ballet a posture in which the turned-out feet are placed one in front of the other, so that the heel of the front foot fits into the hollow of the instep of the back foot. ■ a position of the arms in which one is held curved in front of the body and the other curved to the side, both at waist level.
2 Music a position of the left hand on the fingerboard of a stringed instrument nearer to the bridge than the second position, enabling a higher set of notes to be played.

Third Programme one of the three national radio networks of the BBC from 1946 until 1967, when it was replaced by Radio 3.

third rail ▸ **noun 1** an additional rail supplying electric current, used in some electric railway systems.
2 US informal a subject considered by politicians to be too controversial to discuss.

third-rate ▸ **adjective** of inferior or very poor quality.
– DERIVATIVES **third-rater** noun.

third reading ▸ **noun** a third presentation of a bill to a legislative assembly, in the UK to debate committee reports and in the US to consider it for the last time.

Third Reich the Nazi regime, 1933–45.

Third Republic the republican regime in France between the fall of Napoleon III (1870) and the German occupation of 1940.

third sector ▸ **noun** the part of an economy or society comprising non-governmental and non-profit-making organizations or associations, including charities, voluntary and community groups, cooperatives, etc.

third ventricle ▸ **noun** Anatomy the central cavity of the brain, lying between the thalamus and hypothalamus of the two cerebral hemispheres.

third way ▸ **noun** any option regarded as an alternative to two extremes, especially a political agenda which is centrist and consensus-based rather than left- or right-wing.

Third World ▸ **noun** (usu. **the Third World**) the developing countries of Asia, Africa, and Latin America.
– ORIGIN first applied in the 1950s by French commentators who used *tiers monde* to distinguish the developing countries from the capitalist and Communist blocs.

thirst ▸ **noun** [mass noun] a feeling of needing or wanting to drink something: *they quenched their thirst with spring water.* ■ lack of the liquid needed to sustain life: *tens of thousands died of thirst and starvation.* ■ (usu. **thirst for**) a strong desire for something: *his thirst for knowledge was mainly academic.*
▸ **verb** [no obj.] **1** (usu. **thirst for/after**) have a strong desire for something: *an opponent thirsting for revenge.*
2 archaic feel a need to drink something.
– ORIGIN Old English *thurst* (noun), *thyrstan* (verb), of Germanic origin; related to Dutch *dorst*, *dorsten* and German *Durst*, *dürsten*.

thirstland ▸ **noun** S. African a large arid area.

thirsty ▸ **adjective** (**thirstier**, **thirstiest**) **1** feeling a need to drink: *the Guides were hot and thirsty.* ■ (of land or plants) in need of water; dry or parched. ■ (of an engine, plant, or crop) consuming a lot of fuel or water. ■ [attrib.] informal (of activity, weather, or a time) causing thirst: *modelling is **thirsty work**.*
2 having or showing a strong desire for something: *Joe was as **thirsty for** scandal as anyone else.*
– DERIVATIVES **thirstily** adverb, **thirstiness** noun.

thirteen ▸ **cardinal number** equivalent to the sum of six and seven; one more than twelve, or seven less than twenty; 13: *thirteen miles away | a rise of 13 per cent | thirteen of the bishops voted against the motion.* (Roman numeral: **xiii** or **XIII**) ■ a size of garment or other merchandise denoted by thirteen. ■ thirteen years old: *two boys aged eleven and thirteen.*
– DERIVATIVES **thirteenth** ordinal number.
– ORIGIN Old English *thrēotiene* (see **THREE**, **-TEEN**). The spelling with initial *thi-* is recorded in late Middle English.

Thirteen Colonies the British colonies that ratified the Declaration of Independence in 1776 and thereby became founding states of the US. The colonies were Virginia, Massachusetts, Maryland, Connecticut, Rhode Island, North Carolina, South Carolina, New York, New Jersey, Delaware, New Hampshire, Pennsylvania, and Georgia.

thirteenth cheque ▸ **noun** S. African an annual pay bonus, equal to one month's salary and paid at the end of the year.

thirty ▸ **cardinal number** (pl. **thirties**) the number equivalent to the product of three and ten; ten less than forty; 30: *thirty or forty years ago | thirty were hurt | thirty of her school friends.* (Roman numeral: **xxx** or **XXX**) ■ (**thirties**) the numbers from thirty to thirty-nine, especially the years of a century or of a person's life: *a woman in her thirties | she was a famous actress in the thirties.* ■ thirty years old: *I've got a long way to go before I'm thirty.* ■ thirty miles an hour: *doing about thirty.* ■ a size of garment or other merchandise denoted by thirty.
– DERIVATIVES **thirtieth** ordinal number, **thirtyfold** adjective & adverb.
– ORIGIN Old English *thrītig* (see **THREE**, **-TY²**). The spelling with initial *thi-* is recorded in literature in the 15th cent., and has been the prevalent form since the 16th cent.

thirty-eight ▸ **noun** a revolver of .38 calibre.

Thirty-nine Articles ▸ **plural noun** a series of points of doctrine historically accepted as representing the teaching of the Church of England.

thirty-second note ▸ **noun** Music, chiefly N. Amer. a demisemiquaver.

thirty-two-mo ▸ **noun** (pl. **thirty-two-mos**) a size of book page that results from folding each printed sheet into thirty-two leaves (sixty-four pages). ■ a book of thirty-two-mo size.

thirty-year rule ▸ **noun** a rule that public records may be open to inspection after a lapse of thirty years.

Thirty Years War a European war of 1618–48 which broke out between the Catholic Holy Roman emperor and some of his German Protestant states and developed into a struggle for continental hegemony with France, Sweden, Spain, and the Holy Roman Empire as the major protagonists. It was ended by the Treaty of Westphalia.

Thiruvananthapuram /tɪruːˌwʌntəˈpʊərəm/ the capital of the state of Kerala, a port on the SW coast of India; pop. 822,400 (est. 2009). Also called **TRIVANDRUM**.

this ▸ **pronoun** (pl. **these**) **1** used to identify a specific person or thing close at hand or being indicated or experienced: *is this your bag? | he soon knew that this was not the place for him.* ■ used to introduce someone or something: *this is the captain speaking | listen to this.* ■ referring to the nearer of two things close to the speaker (the other, if specified, being identified by 'that'): *this is different from that.*
2 referring to a specific thing just mentioned: *the company was transformed and Ward had played a vital role in bringing this about.*

▶ **determiner** (pl. **these**) **1** used to identify a specific person or thing close at hand or being indicated or experienced: *don't listen to this guy | these croissants are delicious.* ■ referring to the nearer of two things close to the speaker (the other, if specified, being identified by 'that'): *this one or that one?*
2 referring to a specific thing just mentioned: *there was a court case resulting from this incident.*
3 used with periods of time related to the present: *I thought you were busy all this week | how are you this morning?* ■ referring to a period of time that has just passed: *I haven't left my bed these three days.*
4 informal used in speech to draw attention to someone or something: *I turned round and there was this big mummy standing next to us! | I've slept in this here bed for forty years.*
▶ **adverb** [as submodifier] to the degree or extent indicated: *they can't handle a job this big | he's not used to this much attention.*
– PHRASES **this and that** (or **this, that, and the other**) informal various unspecified things: *they stayed up chatting about this and that.*
– ORIGIN Old English, neuter of *thes*, of West Germanic origin; related to **THAT** and **THE**.

Thisbe /'θɪzbi/ Roman Mythology a Babylonian girl, lover of Pyramus.

thistle /'θɪs(ə)l/ ▶ **noun 1** a widely distributed herbaceous plant of the daisy family, which typically has a prickly stem and leaves and rounded heads of purple flowers. ● *Carlina*, *Carduus*, and other genera, family Compositae.
2 a plant of the thistle type as the Scottish national emblem. ● This is usually identified as the **cotton thistle** (*Onopordum acanthium*).
– DERIVATIVES **thistly** adjective.
– ORIGIN Old English *thistel*, of Germanic origin; related to Dutch *distel* and German *Distel*.

Thistle, Order of the see **ORDER OF THE THISTLE**.

thistledown /'θɪs(ə)ldaʊn/ ▶ **noun** [mass noun] light fluffy down which is attached to thistle seeds, enabling them to be blown about in the wind.

this-worldly ▶ **adjective** relating to or concerned with the physical or material world, as opposed to a spiritual one: *his distrust of this-worldly pleasures.*

thither /'ðɪðə/ ▶ **adverb** archaic or literary to or towards that place: *no trickery had been necessary to attract him thither.*
– ORIGIN Old English *thider*, alteration (by association with **HITHER**) of *thæder*, of Germanic origin; related to **THAT** and **THE**.

Thívai /'θiːvɛ/ Greek name for **THEBES** (sense 2).

thixotropy /θɪk'sɒtrəpi/ ▶ **noun** [mass noun] Chemistry the property of becoming less viscous when subjected to an applied stress, shown for example by some gels which become temporarily fluid when shaken or stirred.
– DERIVATIVES **thixotropic** adjective.
– ORIGIN 1920s: from Greek *thixis* 'touching' + *tropē* 'turning'.

tho' (also **tho**) ▶ **conjunction & adverb** informal spelling of **THOUGH**.

thole[1] /θəʊl/ (also **thole pin**) ▶ **noun** a pin, typically one of a pair, fitted to the gunwale of a rowing boat and on which an oar pivots.
– ORIGIN Old English, of Germanic origin; related to Dutch *dol*.

T

thole[2] /θəʊl/ ▶ **verb** [with obj.] Scottish or archaic endure (something) without complaint or resistance; tolerate.
– ORIGIN Old English *tholian*, of Germanic origin.

tholeiite /'θəʊlɪʌɪt/ ▶ **noun** [mass noun] Geology a basaltic rock containing augite and a calcium-poor pyroxene (pigeonite or hypersthene), and with a higher silica content than an alkali basalt.
– DERIVATIVES **tholeiitic** /,θəʊlɪ'ɪtɪk/ adjective.
– ORIGIN mid 19th cent.: from *Tholei*, the name of a village (now *Tholey*) in the Saarland, Germany, + **-ITE[1]**.

tholos /'θɒlɒs/ ▶ **noun** (pl. **tholoi** /-lɔɪ/) Archaeology a dome-shaped tomb of ancient Greek origin, especially one dating from the Mycenaean period.
– ORIGIN Greek.

Thomas[1], Dylan (Marlais) (1914–53), Welsh poet. In 1953 he narrated on radio *Under Milk Wood*, a portrait of a small Welsh town, interspersing poetic alliterative prose with songs and ballads. Other notable works: *Portrait of the Artist as a Young Dog* (prose, 1940).

Thomas[2], (Philip) Edward (1878–1917), English poet. His work offers a sympathetic but unidealized depiction of rural English life, adapting colloquial speech rhythms to poetic metre.

Thomas, St an Apostle; known as **Doubting Thomas**. He earned his nickname by saying that he would not believe that Christ had risen again until he had seen and touched his wounds (John 20:24–9). Feast day, 21 December.

Thomas à Kempis /ə 'kɛmpɪs/ (*c.*1380–1471), German theologian; born *Thomas Hemerken*. He is the probable author of *On the Imitation of Christ* (*c.*1415–24), a manual of spiritual devotion.

Thomas Aquinas, St, see **AQUINAS, ST THOMAS**.

Thomas More, St see **MORE[1]**.

Thomism /'təʊmɪz(ə)m/ ▶ **noun** [mass noun] the theology of Thomas Aquinas or of his followers.
– DERIVATIVES **Thomist** noun & adjective, **Thomistic** adjective.

Thompson, Francis (1859–1907), English poet. His best-known work, such as 'The Hound of Heaven' (1893), uses powerful imagery to convey intense religious experience.

Thomson[1], James (1700–48), Scottish poet. The words of the song 'Rule, Britannia' (1740) have been attributed to him.

Thomson[2], James (1834–82), Scottish poet, chiefly remembered for the poem 'The City of Dreadful Night' (1874).

Thomson[3], Sir Joseph John (1856–1940), English atomic physicist. He discovered the electron, deducing its existence as a particle smaller than the atom from his experiments. Thomson received the 1906 Nobel Prize for Physics for his researches into the electrical conductivity of gases. His son **Sir George Paget Thomson** (1892–1975) shared the 1937 Nobel Prize for Physics for his discovery of electron diffraction by crystals.

Thomson[4], Roy Herbert, 1st Baron Thomson of Fleet (1894–1976), Canadian-born British newspaper proprietor and media entrepreneur. He settled in Edinburgh in 1952, buying the *Scotsman*, and later the *Sunday Times* (1959) and *The Times* (1966).

Thomson[5], Sir William, see **KELVIN**.

Thomson's gazelle ▶ **noun** a light brown gazelle with a dark band along the flanks, living in large herds on the open plains of East Africa. ● *Gazella thomsonii*, family Bovidae.
– ORIGIN late 19th cent.: named after Joseph *Thomson* (1858–94), Scottish explorer.

thong ▶ **noun 1** a narrow strip of leather or other material, used especially as a fastening or as the lash of a whip.
2 a skimpy bathing garment or pair of knickers like a G-string.
3 N. Amer. & Austral. a light sandal or flip-flop.
▶ **verb** [with obj.] archaic flog or lash with a whip.
– DERIVATIVES **thonged** adjective, **thongy** adjective.
– ORIGIN Old English *thwang*, *thwong*, of Germanic origin; related to German *Zwang* 'compulsion'. Compare with **WHANG**.

Thor /θɔː/ Scandinavian Mythology the god of thunder, the weather, agriculture, and the home, the son of Odin and Freya (Frigga). Thursday is named after him.

thoracic /θɔː'rasɪk/ ▶ **adjective** Anatomy & Zoology relating to the thorax.

thoracic duct ▶ **noun** Anatomy the main vessel of the lymphatic system, passing upwards in front of the spine and draining into the left innominate vein near the base of the neck.

thoracic vertebra ▶ **noun** Anatomy each of the twelve bones of the backbone to which the ribs are attached.

thoracolumbar /,θɔːrəkəʊ'lʌmbə/ ▶ **adjective** Anatomy relating to the thoracic and lumbar regions of the spine. ■ denoting the sympathetic nervous system.

thoracotomy /,θɔːrə'kɒtəmi/ ▶ **noun** [mass noun] surgical incision into the chest wall.
– ORIGIN late 19th cent.: from Greek *thōrax*, *thōrāc-* 'chest' + **-TOMY**.

thorax /'θɔːraks/ ▶ **noun** (pl. **thoraces** /'θɔːrəsiːz/ or **thoraxes**) Anatomy & Zoology the part of the body of a mammal between the neck and the abdomen, including the cavity enclosed by the ribs, breastbone, and dorsal vertebrae, and containing the chief organs of circulation and respiration; the chest. ■ Zoology the corresponding part of a bird, reptile, amphibian, or fish. ■ Entomology the middle section of the body of an insect, between the head and the abdomen, bearing the legs and wings.
– ORIGIN late Middle English: via Latin from Greek *thōrax*.

Thorazine /'θɔːrəziːn/ ▶ **noun** trademark for **CHLORPROMAZINE**.
– ORIGIN 1950s: formed from elements of the systematic name.

Thoreau /'θɔːrəʊ/, Henry David (1817–62), American essayist and poet, and a key figure in Transcendentalism. He is best known for his book *Walden, or Life in the Woods* (1854), an account of a two-year experiment in self-sufficiency.

thoria /'θɔːrɪə/ ▶ **noun** [mass noun] Chemistry thorium dioxide, a white refractory solid used in making gas mantles and other materials for high-temperature applications. ● Chem. formula: ThO_2.
– ORIGIN mid 19th cent.: from **THORIUM**, on the pattern of words such as *alumina* and *magnesia*.

thorium /'θɔːrɪəm/ ▶ **noun** [mass noun] the chemical element of atomic number 90, a white radioactive metal of the actinide series. (Symbol: **Th**)
– ORIGIN mid 19th cent.: named after the god **THOR**.

Thorn /tɔːɛn/ German name for **TORUŃ**.

thorn ▶ **noun 1** a stiff, sharp-pointed woody projection on the stem or other part of a plant. ■ a source of discomfort, annoyance, or difficulty; an irritation or obstacle: *the issue has become a thorn in renewing the peace talks.*
2 (also **thorn bush** or **thorn tree**) a thorny bush, shrub, or tree, especially a hawthorn.
3 an Old English and Icelandic runic letter, þ or Þ, representing the dental fricatives /ð/ and /θ/. It was eventually superseded by the digraph *th*. Compare with **ETH**. [so named from the word of which it was the first letter.]
4 a yellowish-brown woodland moth which rests with the wings raised over the back, with twig-like caterpillars. ● *Ennomos* and other genera, family Geometridae.
– PHRASES **there is no rose without a thorn** proverb every apparently desirable situation has its share of trouble or difficulty. **a thorn in someone's side** (or **flesh**) a source of continual annoyance or trouble: *the pastor has long been a thorn in the side of the regime.*
– DERIVATIVES **thorned** adjective, **thornless** adjective, **thornlike** adjective, **thornproof** adjective.
– ORIGIN Old English, of Germanic origin; related to Dutch *doorn* and German *Dorn*.

thorn apple ▶ **noun** a poisonous datura with large trumpet-shaped white flowers and toothed leaves, which has become a weed of waste ground in many countries. Also called **JIMSON WEED** in North America. ● *Datura stramonium*, family Solanaceae.
■ the prickly fruit of the thorn apple, which resembles that of a horse chestnut.

thornback (also **thornback ray**) ▶ **noun** a ray of shallow inshore waters which has spines on the back and tail, in particular: ● a prickly-skinned European ray which is often eaten as 'skate' (*Raja clavata*, family Rajidae). ● *a ray which lives in the warm waters of the Pacific (Platyrhinoidis triseriata*, family Platyrhinidae).

thornbill ▶ **noun 1** a small Australian warbler with drab plumage and a pointed bill. ● Genus *Acanthiza*, family Acanthizidae: several species.
2 a tropical American hummingbird with a short, sharply pointed bill. ● Family Trochilidae: three genera, in particular *Chalcostigma*, and several species.

thorntail ▶ **noun** a tropical American hummingbird with bright green plumage and projecting outer tail feathers. ● Genus *Popelairia*, family Trochilidae: four species.

thornveld /'θɔːnvɛlt/ ▶ **noun** [mass noun] S. African land on which the vegetation consists mainly of thorny trees and bushes.
– ORIGIN from **THORN** + Afrikaans *veld* (see **VELD**).

thorny ▶ **adjective** (**thornier**, **thorniest**) **1** having many thorns or thorn bushes.
2 causing distress, difficulty, or trouble: *a thorny problem for our team to solve.*
– DERIVATIVES **thornily** adverb, **thorniness** noun.

thorny devil ▶ **noun** another term for **MOLOCH**.

thorny-headed worm ▶ **noun** a parasitic worm with a thornlike proboscis for attachment to the gut of vertebrates. Also called **SPINY-HEADED WORM**. ● Phylum Acanthocephala.

thorny oyster ▶ **noun** a bivalve mollusc of warm seas, the pinkish-brown shell of which is heavily ribbed and bears blunt or flattened spines. ● Family Spondylidae: *Spondylus* and other genera.

thorough /ˈθʌrə/ ▶ **adjective** complete with regard to every detail; not superficial or partial: *planners need a thorough understanding of the subject.* ■ performed or written with great care and completeness: *officers have made a thorough examination of the wreckage.* ■ taking pains to do something carefully and completely: *the British authorities are very thorough.* ■ [attrib.] Brit. absolute (used to emphasize the degree of something, typically something unwelcome or unpleasant): *the child is being a thorough nuisance.*
– DERIVATIVES **thoroughness** noun.
– ORIGIN Old English *thuruh*, alteration of *thurh* 'through'. Original use was as an adverb and preposition, in senses of *through*. The adjective dates from the late 15th cent., when it also had the sense 'that goes or extends through something', surviving in *thoroughfare*.

thorough bass ▶ **noun** Music basso continuo (see CONTINUO).

thoroughbred ▶ **adjective** (of a horse) of pure breed, especially of a breed originating from English mares and Arab stallions and widely used as racehorses. ■ informal of outstanding quality: *this thoroughbred car affords the luxury of three spoilers.*
▶ **noun** a horse of a thoroughbred breed. ■ informal an outstanding or first-class person or thing: *this is a real thoroughbred of a record.*

thoroughfare ▶ **noun** a road or path forming a route between two places. ■ a main road in a town.

thoroughgoing ▶ **adjective** involving or attending to every detail or aspect of something: *a thoroughgoing reform of the whole economy.* ■ [attrib.] exemplifying a specified characteristic fully; absolute: *a thoroughgoing chocoholic.*

thoroughly /ˈθʌrəli/ ▶ **adverb 1** in a thorough manner: *he searched the house thoroughly.*
2 very much; greatly: *I thoroughly enjoyed the day* | [as submodifier] *she was soon thoroughly bored.*

thorough-paced ▶ **adjective** archaic (of a horse) trained to all paces. ■ highly skilled or trained. ■ complete; thoroughgoing.

thoroughpin ▶ **noun** a swelling of the tendon sheath above the hock of a horse, which may be pressed from inside to outside and vice versa.

thorow-wax /ˈθʌrəwaks/ ▶ **noun** a European plant of the parsley family with yellowish-green flowers, formerly a widespread weed of cornfields. ● Genus *Bupleurum*, family Umbelliferae: two species, including *B. rotundifolium*, which is extinct in the wild in Britain.
– ORIGIN mid 16th cent.: from THOROUGH 'through' + WAX² (because the stem appears to grow through the leaves).

thorp (also **thorpe**) ▶ **noun** [in place names] a village or hamlet: *Althorpe.*
– ORIGIN Old English *thorp*, *throp*, of Germanic origin; related to Dutch *dorp* and German *Dorf*.

Thorpe, Ian (James) (b.1982), Australian swimmer. He won three gold medals in the 2000 Olympics, and two further golds at the 2004 Olympics.

Thorshavn variant spelling of TÓRSHAVN.

Thorvaldsen /ˈtɔːvals(ə)n/ (also **Thorwaldsen**), Bertel (*c.*1770–1844), Danish neoclassical sculptor. Major works include a statue of Jason in Rome (1803) and the tomb of Pius VII (1824–31).

Thos ▶ **abbreviation** Thomas.

those plural form of THAT.

Thoth /θəʊθ, təʊt/ Egyptian Mythology a moon god, the god of wisdom, justice, and writing, patron of the sciences, and messenger of the sun god Ra.

thou¹ ▶ **pronoun** [second person singular] archaic or dialect form of YOU, as the singular subject of a verb: *thou art fair, O my beloved.* Compare with THEE.
– ORIGIN Old English *thu*, of Germanic origin; related to German *du*, from an Indo-European root shared by Latin *tu*.

> **USAGE** In modern English, the personal pronoun **you** (together with the possessives **your** and **yours**) covers a number of uses: it is both singular and plural, both objective and subjective, and both formal and familiar. This has not always been the case. In Old English and Middle English some of these different functions of **you** were supplied by different words. Thus, **thou** was at one time the singular subjective case (*thou art a beast*), while **thee** was the singular objective case (*he cares not for thee*). In addition, the form **thy** (modern equivalent **your**) was the singular possessive determiner and **thine** (modern equivalent **yours**) the singular possessive pronoun, both corresponding to **thee**. The forms **you** and **ye**, on the other hand, were at one time reserved for plural uses. By the 19th century these forms were universal in standard English for both singular and plural, polite and familiar. In present-day use **thou, thee, thy,** and **thine** survive in some traditional dialects but otherwise are found only in archaic contexts.

thou² ▶ **noun** (pl. **same** or **thous**) informal a thousand. ■ one thousandth of an inch.
– ORIGIN mid 19th cent.: abbreviation.

though ▶ **conjunction** despite the fact that; although: *though they were speaking in undertones, Percival could hear them.* ■ [with modal] even if (introducing a possibility): *you will be informed of its progress, slow though that may be.* ■ however; but (introducing something opposed to or qualifying what has just been said): *her first name was Rose, though no one called her that.*
▶ **adverb** however (indicating that a factor qualifies or imposes restrictions on what was said previously): *I was hunting for work. Jobs were scarce though.*
– ORIGIN Old English *thēah*, of Germanic origin; related to Dutch and German *doch*; superseded in Middle English by forms from Old Norse *thó*, *thau*.

> **USAGE** On the differences in use between **though** and **although**, see USAGE at ALTHOUGH.

thought¹ ▶ **noun 1** an idea or opinion produced by thinking, or occurring suddenly in the mind: *Maggie had a sudden thought* | *I asked him if he had any thoughts on how it had happened* | *Mrs Oliver's first thought was to get help.* ■ (**one's thoughts**) one's mind or attention: *he's very much **in our thoughts** and prayers.* ■ an act of considering or remembering someone or something: *she hadn't **given a thought to** Max for some time.* ■ (usu. **thought of**) an intention, hope, or idea of doing or receiving something: *he had given up **all thoughts of** making London his home.* ■ [as adv.] (**a thought**) dated to a small extent; somewhat: *those of us who work at home may find our hands a thought freer.*
2 [mass noun] the action or process of thinking: *Sophie sat deep in thought.* ■ careful consideration or attention: *I haven't given it much thought.* ■ concern for another's well-being or convenience: *he is carrying on the life of a single man, with **no thought for** me.*
3 [mass noun] the formation of opinions, especially as a philosophy or system of ideas, or the opinions so formed: *the freedom of thought and action* | *the traditions of Western thought.*
– PHRASES **don't give it another thought** informal used to tell someone not to worry when they have apologized for something. **it's the thought that counts** informal used to indicate that it is the kindness behind an act that matters, however imperfect or insignificant the act may be. **a second thought** [with negative] more than the slightest consideration: *the admiral dismissed the rumour **without a second thought**.* **take thought** dated reflect or consider. **that's a thought!** informal used to express approval of a comment or suggestion.
– ORIGIN Old English *thōht*, of Germanic origin; related to Dutch *gedachte*, also to THINK.

thought² past and past participle of THINK.

thought control ▶ **noun** [mass noun] the attempt to restrict ideas and impose opinions through censorship and the control of curricula in schools.

thoughtcrime ▶ **noun** an instance of unorthodox or controversial thinking, considered as a criminal offence or as socially unacceptable.
– ORIGIN 1949: from George Orwell's *Nineteen Eighty-Four*.

thought disorder ▶ **noun** [mass noun] Psychiatry a disorder of cognitive organization, characteristic of psychotic mental illness, in which thoughts and conversation appear illogical and lacking in sequence and may be delusional or bizarre in content.

thought experiment ▶ **noun** a mental assessment of the implications of a hypothesis.

thought form ▶ **noun** a combination of presuppositions, imagery, and vocabulary current at a particular time or place and forming the context for thinking on a subject.

thoughtful ▶ **adjective 1** absorbed in or involving thought: *brows drawn together in thoughtful consideration.* ■ showing careful consideration or attention: *her work is thoughtful and provocative.*
2 showing consideration for the needs of other people: *he was attentive and thoughtful* | *how very **thoughtful of** you!*
– DERIVATIVES **thoughtfully** adverb, **thoughtfulness** noun.

thoughtless ▶ **adjective 1** (of a person or their behaviour) not showing consideration for the needs of other people: *it was **thoughtless of** her to have rushed out and not said where she would be going.*
2 without consideration of the possible consequences: *to think a few minutes of thoughtless pleasure could end in this.*
– DERIVATIVES **thoughtlessly** adverb, **thoughtlessness** noun.

thought pattern ▶ **noun** a habit of thinking in a particular way, using particular assumptions. ■ another term for THOUGHT FORM.

thought police ▶ **noun** [treated as pl.] a group of people who aim or are seen as aiming to suppress ideas that deviate from the way of thinking that they believe to be correct.

thought-provoking ▶ **adjective** stimulating careful consideration or attention: *thought-provoking questions.*

thought-reader ▶ **noun** a person who can supposedly discern what someone else is thinking.
– DERIVATIVES **thought-reading** noun.

thought reform ▶ **noun** [mass noun] the systematic alteration of a person's mode of thinking, especially (in Communist China) a process of individual political indoctrination.

thought transference ▶ **noun** another term for TELEPATHY.

thought wave ▶ **noun** a supposed pattern of energy by which it is claimed that thoughts are transferred from one person to another.

thousand ▶ **cardinal number** (pl. **thousands** or (with numeral or quantifying word) **same**) (**a/one thousand**) the number equivalent to the product of a hundred and ten; 1,000: *a thousand metres* | *two thousand acres* | *thousands have been killed.* (Roman numeral: **m, M**) ■ (**thousands**) the numbers from one thousand to 9,999: *the cost of repairs could be in the thousands.* ■ (usu. **thousands**) informal an unspecified large number: *you'll meet thousands of girls before you find the one you like* | *I have imagined it a thousand times.*
– DERIVATIVES **thousandfold** adjective & adverb, **thousandth** ordinal number.
– ORIGIN Old English *thūsend*, of Germanic origin; related to Dutch *duizend* and German *Tausend*.

Thousand and One Nights another name for ARABIAN NIGHTS.

Thousand Island dressing ▶ **noun** [mass noun] a dressing for salad or seafood consisting of mayonnaise with ketchup and chopped gherkins.

Thousand Islands 1 a group of about 1,500 islands in a widening of the St Lawrence River in North America, just below Kingston. Some of the islands belong to Canada and some to the US.
2 a group of about 100 small islands off the north coast of Java, forming part of Indonesia. Indonesian name PULAU SERIBU.

Thrace /θreɪs/ an ancient country lying west of the Black Sea and north of the Aegean. It is now divided between Turkey, Bulgaria, and Greece.
– DERIVATIVES **Thracian** /ˈθreɪʃ(ə)n/ adjective & noun.

Thrale /θreɪl/, Mrs Hester Lynch (1741–1821), English writer; latterly *Hester Lynch Piozzi*. She was a close friend of Dr Johnson, who lived with her and her husband for several years.

thrall /θrɔːl/ ▶ **noun 1** [mass noun] literary the state of being in someone's power, or of having great power over someone: *she was **in thrall to** her abusive husband.*
2 archaic a slave, servant, or captive.
– DERIVATIVES **thraldom** (also **thralldom**) noun.
– ORIGIN Old English *thrǣl* 'slave', from Old Norse *þræll*.

thrash ▶ **verb** [with obj.] **1** beat (a person or animal) repeatedly and violently with a stick or whip: *she thrashed him across the head and shoulders.* ■ hit (something) hard and repeatedly: *the wind screeched and the mast thrashed the deck.*
2 [no obj.] move in a violent and convulsive way: *he lay on the ground **thrashing around** in pain* | [with obj.] *she thrashed her arms, attempting to swim.* ■ (**thrash around**) struggle in a desperate or unfocused way to do something: *two months of thrashing around on my own have produced nothing.* ■ [no obj., with adverbial of direction] informal move in a fast or uncontrolled way:

T

I wrench the steering wheel back and thrash on up the hill.
3 informal defeat heavily in a contest or match: *I thrashed Pete at cards* | [with obj. and complement] *Newcastle were thrashed 8–1 by the Czech team.*
▸ **noun 1** [usu. in sing.] a violent or noisy movement of beating or thrashing: *the thrash of the waves.* ■ informal a fast and exciting motor race or other sporting event.
2 Brit. informal a party, especially a loud or lavish one.
3 a short, fast, loud piece or passage of rock music. ■ (also **thrash metal**) [mass noun] a style of fast, loud, harsh-sounding rock music, combining elements of punk and heavy metal.
– PHRASAL VERBS **thrash something out** discuss something frankly and thoroughly, especially to reach a decision: *it is essential that conflicting views are heard and thrashed out.*
– ORIGIN Old English, variant of **THRESH** (an early sense). Current senses of the noun date from the mid 19th cent.

thrasher[1] ▸ **noun 1** a person or thing that thrashes.
2 archaic spelling of **THRESHER** (sense 1).

thrasher[2] ▸ **noun** a thrush-like American songbird of the mockingbird family, with mainly brown or grey plumage, a long tail, and a downcurved bill. ● Family Mimidae: five genera, in particular *Toxostoma*, and several species.
– ORIGIN early 19th cent.: perhaps from English dialect *thrusher, thresher* 'thrush'.

thrashing ▸ **noun 1** an act of physically beating someone; a beating: *a* ***sound thrashing*** *might teach the individual to refrain from complaining.*
2 a heavy defeat of a sporting opponent: *the thrashings administered by Celtic to Aberdeen.*

thrawn /θrɔːn/ ▸ **adjective** Scottish **1** twisted; crooked: *a slightly thrawn neck.*
2 perverse; ill-tempered: *mother's looking a bit thrawn this morning.*
– ORIGIN late Middle English: Scots form of *thrown* (see **THROW**), in the obsolete sense 'twisted, wrung'.

thread ▸ **noun 1** a long, thin strand of cotton, nylon, or other fibres used in sewing or weaving. ■ [mass noun] cotton, nylon, or other fibres spun into long, thin strands and used for sewing. ■ literary a long, thin line or piece of something: *the Thames was a thread of silver below them.*
2 a theme or characteristic running throughout a situation or piece of writing: *a major thread running through the book is the primacy of form over substance.* ■ a group of linked messages posted on an Internet forum that share a common subject or theme. ■ Computing a programming structure or process formed by linking a number of separate elements or subroutines, especially each of the tasks executed concurrently in multithreading.
3 (also **screw thread**) a helical ridge on the outside of a screw, bolt, etc. or on the inside of a cylindrical hole, to allow two parts to be screwed together.
4 (**threads**) informal, chiefly N. Amer. clothes.
▸ **verb** [with obj.] **1** pass a thread through the eye of (a needle) or through the needle and guides of (a sewing machine). ■ [with obj. and adverbial of direction] pass (a long, thin object or piece of material) through something and into the required position for use: *he threaded the rope through a pulley.* ■ [no obj., with adverbial of direction] move carefully or skilfully in and out of obstacles: *she* ***threaded her way*** *through the tables.* ■ interweave or intersperse as if with threads: *his hair had become ill-kempt and* ***threaded with*** *grey.* ■ put (beads or other small objects) on a thread, chain, etc.: *Constance sat threading beads.*
2 (usu. as adj. **threaded**) cut a screw thread in or on (a hole, screw, or other object).
– PHRASES **hang by a thread** be in a highly precarious state. **lose the** (or **one's**) **thread** be unable to follow what someone is saying or remember what one is going to say next.
– DERIVATIVES **thread-like** adjective.
– ORIGIN Old English *thrǣd* (noun), of Germanic origin; related to Dutch *draad* and German *Draht*, also to the verb **THROW**. The verb dates from late Middle English.

threadbare ▸ **adjective** (of cloth, clothing, or soft furnishings) becoming thin and tattered with age: *tatty rooms with threadbare carpets.* ■ (of a person, building, or room) poor or shabby in appearance. ■ (of an argument, excuse, idea, etc.) used so often that it is no longer effective: *the song was a tissue of threadbare clichés.*

threader ▸ **noun 1** a device for passing a thread through the needle and guides of a sewing machine. ■ a factory worker who attaches spools of yarn to a loom.
2 a device for cutting a spiral ridge on the outside of a screw or the inside of a hole.

threadfin ▸ **noun** a tropical marine fish that has long streamers or rays arising from its pectoral fins, locally important as a food fish. ● Family Polynemidae: several genera and species.

threading ▸ **noun** [mass noun] a method of hair removal in which unwanted hairs are plucked out by using a twisted cotton thread.

thread mark ▸ **noun** a mark in the form of a thin line made in banknote paper with highly coloured silk fibres to prevent photographic counterfeiting.

Threadneedle Street a street in the City of London containing the premises of the Bank of England.
– ORIGIN *Threadneedle* from *three-needle*, possibly from a tavern with the arms of the City of London Guild of Needlemakers.

thread vein ▸ **noun** a very slender vein, especially one on the face that is visible through the skin.

threadworm ▸ **noun** a very slender parasitic nematode worm, especially a pinworm.

thready ▸ **adjective** (**threadier**, **threadiest**) **1** relating to or resembling a thread.
2 (of a sound, especially the voice) scarcely audible: *he managed a thready whisper.* ■ Medicine (of a person's pulse) scarcely perceptible.

threat ▸ **noun 1** a statement of an intention to inflict pain, injury, damage, or other hostile action on someone in retribution for something done or not done: *members of her family have received* ***death threats****.* ■ Law a menace of bodily harm, such as may restrain a person's freedom of action.
2 a person or thing likely to cause damage or danger: *hurricane damage poses a major* ***threat to*** *many coastal communities.* ■ [in sing.] the possibility of trouble, danger, or ruin: *the company faces the threat of liquidation proceedings* | [mass noun] *thousands of rail freight jobs came* ***under threat****.*
– ORIGIN Old English *thrēat* 'oppression', of Germanic origin; related to Dutch *verdrieten* 'grieve', German *verdriessen* 'irritate'.

threaten ▸ **verb** [with obj.] **1** state one's intention to take hostile action against (someone) in retribution for something done or not done: *how dare you threaten me?* | *the men* ***threatened*** *staff* ***with*** *a handgun* | [with direct speech] *'I might sue for damages,' he threatened.* ■ state one's intention to do (something undesirable) in retribution: *the trade unions threatened a general strike* | [with infinitive] *she forced a scene and Toby threatened to leave.*
2 cause (someone or something) to be vulnerable or at risk; endanger: *a broken finger threatened his career* | *one of four London hospitals* ***threatened with*** *closure.* ■ [with infinitive] seem likely to produce an unpleasant or unwelcome result: *the dispute threatened to spread to other cities* | [with obj.] *the air was raw and threatened rain.* ■ [no obj.] (of something undesirable) seem likely to occur: *unless war threatened, national politics remained the focus of attention.*
– DERIVATIVES **threatener** noun.
– ORIGIN Old English *thrēatnian* 'urge or induce, especially by using threats', from *thrēat* (see **THREAT**).

threatening ▸ **adjective** having a hostile or deliberately frightening quality or manner: *her mother had received a threatening letter.* ■ Law (of behaviour) showing an intention to cause bodily harm. ■ causing someone to feel vulnerable or at risk: *she was a type he found threatening.* ■ (of weather conditions) indicating that bad weather is likely: *black threatening clouds.*
– DERIVATIVES **threateningly** adverb.

three ▸ **cardinal number** equivalent to the sum of one and two; one more than two; 3: *her three children* | *a crew of three* | *a three-bedroom house* | *all three of them are buried there.* (Roman numeral: **iii** or **III**) ■ a group or unit of three people or things: *students clustered in twos or threes.* ■ three years old: *she is only three.* ■ three o'clock: *I'll come at three.* ■ a size of garment or other merchandise denoted by three. ■ a playing card or domino with three pips.
– PHRASES **three parts** three out of four equal parts; three quarters.
– ORIGIN Old English *thrīe* (masculine), *thrīo, thrēo* (feminine), of Germanic origin; related to Dutch *drie* and German *drei*, from an Indo-European root shared by Latin *tres* and Greek *treis*.

three-card monte ▸ **noun** see **MONTE**.

three-card trick ▸ **noun** [mass noun] a game, traditionally associated with confidence tricksters, in which bets are made on which is the queen among three cards lying face downwards.

three cheers ▸ **plural noun** see **CHEER**.

three-colour process ▸ **noun** Photography a means of reproducing natural colours by combining photographic images in the three primary colours.

three-cornered ▸ **adjective** triangular. ■ (especially of a contest) between three people or groups.

three-dimensional ▸ **adjective** having or appearing to have length, breadth, and depth: *a three-dimensional object.* ■ (of a literary or dramatic work) sufficiently full in characterization and representation of events to be believable.
– DERIVATIVES **three-dimensionality** noun, **three-dimensionally** adverb.

threefold ▸ **adjective** three times as great or as numerous: *a threefold increase in the number of stolen cars.* ■ having three parts or elements: *the differences are threefold.*
▸ **adverb** by three times; to three times the number or amount: *the aftershocks intensify threefold each time.*

Three Graces see **GRACE**.

three-legged race ▸ **noun** a race run by pairs of people, one member of each pair having their left leg tied to the right leg of the other.

three-line whip ▸ **noun** (in the UK) a written notice, underlined three times to denote urgency, to members of a political party to attend a parliamentary vote.

Three Mile Island an island in the Susquehanna River near Harrisburg, Pennsylvania, site of a nuclear power station. In 1979 an accident caused damage to the reactor core, provoking strong reactions against the nuclear industry in the US.

three-peat N. Amer. informal ▸ **verb** [no obj.] win a particular sporting championship three times, especially consecutively.
▸ **noun** [in sing.] a third win of a particular sporting championship, especially the third of three consecutive wins.
– ORIGIN 1980s: from **THREE** + a shortened form of **REPEAT**.

threepence /ˈθrɛp(ə)ns, ˈθrʊ-, ˈθrʌ-/ ▸ **noun** Brit. the sum of three pence, especially before decimalization (1971).

threepenny /ˈθrɛp(ə)ni, ˈθrʊ-, ˈθrʌ-/ ▸ **adjective** [attrib.] Brit. costing or worth three pence, especially before decimalization (1971).

threepenny bit ▸ **noun** Brit. historical a coin worth three old pence ($1^1/_4$ p).

three-phase ▸ **adjective** (of an electric generator, motor, or other device) designed to supply or use simultaneously three separate alternating currents of the same voltage, but with phases differing by a third of a period.

three-piece ▸ **adjective** [attrib.] consisting of three separate and complementary items, in particular: ■ (of a set of furniture) consisting of a sofa and two armchairs. ■ (of a set of clothes) consisting of trousers or a skirt with a waistcoat and jacket.
▸ **noun** a set of three separate and complementary items. ■ a group consisting of three musicians.

three-ply ▸ **adjective** (of material or yarn) having three layers or strands.
▸ **noun** [mass noun] **1** yarn made of three strands.
2 plywood made by gluing together three layers with the grain in different directions.

three-point landing ▸ **noun** a landing of an aircraft on the two main wheels and the tailwheel or skid simultaneously.

three-point turn ▸ **noun** a method of turning a vehicle round in a narrow space by moving forwards, backwards, and forwards again in a sequence of arcs.

three-pronged ▸ **adjective** having three projecting, pointed parts: *a three-pronged hook.* ■ (especially of an attack or operation) having three separate parts.

three-quarter ▸ **adjective** [attrib.] consisting of three quarters of something in terms of size, length, time, etc.: *a three-quarter-length cashmere coat.* ■ (of a view or depiction of a person's face) at an angle between full face and profile.
▸ **noun 1** Rugby each of four players in a team positioned across the field behind the half backs.
2 a point in time forty-five minutes after any full hour of the clock: *the cathedral clock was chiming the three-quarter.*

T

▸ adverb to a size or extent of three quarters: *three-quarter-grown rabbits.*

three quarters ▸ plural noun three of the four equal parts into which something may be divided: ***three quarters of** an hour.*
▸ adverb to the extent of three quarters: *Vermont is more than three quarters woodland.*

threequel ▸ noun the third film, book, etc. in a series; a second sequel.
– ORIGIN 1980s: from THREE + SEQUEL.

three-ring circus ▸ noun N. Amer. informal a disorganized or frenetic scene or spectacle: *his attempt at a dignified resignation turned into a three-ring circus.*

threescore ▸ cardinal number literary sixty.

threesome ▸ noun a group of three people engaged in the same activity. ▪ a game or activity for three people.

three-star ▸ adjective (especially of accommodation or service) given three stars in a grading system in which this denotes a high class or quality, being one grade below four-star. ▪ having or denoting the third-highest military rank, distinguished in the US armed forces by three stars on the shoulder piece of the uniform.

three strikes ▸ noun [mass noun] [usu. as modifier] US legislation which makes an offender's third felony punishable by life imprisonment or other severe sentence.
– ORIGIN 1990s: from the phrase *three strikes and you're out* (with allusion to baseball).

three-way ▸ adjective involving three directions, processes, or participants: *a three-way race for the presidency | a three-way switch.*

three-wheeler ▸ noun a vehicle with three wheels.

Three Wise Men another name for the MAGI.

threnody /ˈθrɛnədi/ ▸ noun (pl. **threnodies**) a lament.
– DERIVATIVES **threnodial** adjective, **threnodic** adjective.
– ORIGIN mid 17th cent.: from Greek *thrēnōidia*, from *thrēnos* 'wailing' + *ōidē* 'song'.

threonine /ˈθriːəniːn/ ▸ noun [mass noun] Biochemistry a hydrophilic amino acid which is a constituent of most proteins. It is an essential nutrient in the diet of vertebrates. ● Chem. formula: $CH_3CH(OH)CH(NH_2)COOH$.
– ORIGIN 1930s: from *threose* (the name of a tetrose sugar) + -INE[4].

thresh /θrɛʃ/ ▸ verb **1** [with obj.] separate grain from (corn or other crops), typically with a flail or by the action of a revolving mechanism: *machinery that can reap and thresh corn in the same process* | (as noun **threshing**) *farm workers started the afternoon's threshing.*
2 [no obj.] move violently; thrash: *a creature threshing in a net* | [with obj.] *it threshes its wings frantically overhead.*
– ORIGIN Old English *therscan*, later *threscan*, of Germanic origin; related to Dutch *dorsen* and German *dreschen*. Compare with THRASH.

thresher /ˈθrɛʃə/ ▸ noun **1** a person or machine that separates grain from corn or other crops by beating.
2 (also **thresher shark**) a surface-living shark with a long upper lobe to the tail. Threshers often hunt in pairs, lashing the water with their tails to herd fish into a tightly packed shoal. ● *Alopias vulpinus*, family Alopidae.

threshing floor ▸ noun a hard, level surface on which corn or other grain is threshed with a flail.

threshing machine ▸ noun a power-driven machine for separating the grain from corn or other crops.

threshold /ˈθrɛʃəʊld, ˈθrɛʃ,həʊld/ ▸ noun **1** a strip of wood or stone forming the bottom of a doorway and crossed in entering a house or room. ▪ [in sing.] a point of entry or beginning: *she was **on the threshold of** a dazzling career.* ▪ the beginning of an airport runway on which an aircraft is attempting to land.
2 the magnitude or intensity that must be exceeded for a certain reaction, phenomenon, result, or condition to occur or be manifested. ▪ the maximum level of radiation or a concentration of a substance considered to be acceptable or safe. ▪ the level at which one starts to feel or react to something: *he has a low boredom threshold.* ▪ a level, rate, or amount at which something comes into effect: *the inheritance tax threshold.*
– ORIGIN Old English *therscold, threscold*; related to German dialect *Drischaufel*; the first element is related to THRESH (in a Germanic sense 'tread'), but the origin of the second element is unknown.

threw past of THROW.

thrice /θrʌɪs/ ▸ adverb chiefly formal or literary three times: *a dose of 25 mg thrice daily.* ▪ [as submodifier] extremely; very: *I was thrice blessed.*
– ORIGIN Middle English *thries*, from earlier *thrie* (from Old English *thrīga*, related to THREE) + -S[3] (later respelled -*ce* to denote the unvoiced sound); compare with ONCE.

thrift ▸ noun [mass noun] **1** the quality of using money and other resources carefully and not wastefully: *the values of thrift and self-reliance.* ▪ [count noun] US another term for SAVINGS AND LOAN.
2 a European plant which forms low-growing tufts of slender leaves with rounded pink flower heads, growing chiefly on sea cliffs and mountains. Also called SEA PINK. ● *Armeria maritima*, family Plumbaginaceae.
– ORIGIN Middle English (in the sense 'prosperity, acquired wealth, success'): from Old Norse, from *thrífa* 'grasp, get hold of'. Compare with THRIVE.

thriftless ▸ adjective (of a person or their behaviour) spending money in an extravagant and wasteful way.
– DERIVATIVES **thriftlessly** adverb, **thriftlessness** noun.

thrift shop (also **thrift store**) ▸ noun N. Amer. a shop selling second-hand clothes and household goods, typically to raise funds for a Church or charity.

thrifty ▸ adjective (**thriftier, thriftiest**) **1** using money and other resources carefully and not wastefully: *he had been brought up to be thrifty and careful.*
2 chiefly archaic or dialect (of livestock or plants) strong and healthy. ▪ archaic prosperous.
– DERIVATIVES **thriftily** adverb, **thriftiness** noun.

thrill ▸ noun **1** a sudden feeling of excitement and pleasure: *the thrill of jumping out of an aeroplane.* ▪ an experience that produces a sudden feeling of excitement and pleasure: *to ride a winner is always a thrill.* ▪ a wave or nervous tremor of emotion or sensation: *a thrill of excitement ran through her.*
2 Medicine a vibratory movement or resonance heard through a stethoscope. ▪ archaic a throb or pulsation.
▸ verb **1** [with obj.] cause (someone) to have a sudden feeling of excitement and pleasure: *his kiss thrilled and excited her | they were **thrilled with** the results | I'm **thrilled to bits.*** ▪ [no obj.] experience such feeling: ***thrill to** the magic of the world's greatest guitarist.*
2 [no obj., with adverbial] (of an emotion or sensation) pass with a nervous tremor: *the shock of alarm **thrilled through** her.* ▪ [no obj.] literary quiver or throb.
– PHRASES **the thrill of the chase** pleasure and excitement derived from seeking something desired, especially a sexual partner. **thrills and spills** excitement and exhilaration, especially when derived from dangerous sports or entertainments.
– ORIGIN Middle English (as a verb in the sense 'pierce or penetrate'): alteration of dialect *thirl* 'pierce'.

thriller ▸ noun a novel, play, or film with an exciting plot, typically involving crime or espionage. ▪ a very exciting contest or experience: *a seven-goal thriller.*

thrilling ▸ adjective causing excitement and pleasure; exhilarating: *a thrilling adventure | it's very thrilling to be here and to congratulate the team on another splendid success.*
– DERIVATIVES **thrillingly** adverb.

thrips /θrɪps/ (also **thrip**) ▸ noun (pl. **same**) a minute black winged insect which sucks plant sap and can be a serious pest of ornamental and food plants when present in large numbers. Thrips swarm on warm still summer days and cause irritation by crawling on the skin. Also called THUNDERBUG, THUNDERFLY.
● Order Thysanoptera: many species, including the **pea thrips** (*Kakothrips robustus*), which can cause considerable losses to pea crops.
– ORIGIN late 18th cent.: via Latin from Greek, literally 'woodworm'.

thrive ▸ verb (**thrives, thriving**, past **throve** or **thrived**; past participle **thriven** or **thrived**) [no obj.] (of a child, animal, or plant) grow or develop well or vigorously: *the new baby thrived.* ▪ prosper; flourish: *education groups **thrive on** organization.*
– ORIGIN Middle English (originally in the sense 'grow, increase'): from Old Norse *thrífask*, reflexive of *thrífa* 'grasp, get hold of'. Compare with THRIFT.

thriving ▸ adjective prosperous and growing; flourishing: *the thriving business George has built up.*

thro' ▸ preposition, adverb, & adjective literary or informal spelling of THROUGH.

throat ▸ noun the passage which leads from the back of the mouth of a person or animal. ▪ the front part of a person's or animal's neck: *a gold pendant gleamed at her throat.* ▪ literary a voice of a person or a songbird: *from a hundred throats came the cry 'Vive l'Empereur!'* ▪ a thing compared to a throat, especially a narrow passage, entrance, or exit. ▪ Sailing the forward upper corner of a quadrilateral fore-and-aft sail.
– PHRASES **be at each other's throats** (of people or organizations) quarrel or fight persistently. **force** (or **ram** or **shove**) **something down someone's throat** force ideas or material on a person's attention by repeatedly putting them forward. **grab** (or **take**) **someone by the throat** put one's hands around someone's throat, typically in an attempt to throttle them. ▪ (**grab something by the throat**) seize control of something: *Scotland took the game by the throat.* ▪ attract someone's undivided attention: *the film grabs you by the throat and refuses to let go.*
– DERIVATIVES **throated** adjective [in combination] *a full-throated baritone.*
– ORIGIN Old English *throte, throtu*, of Germanic origin; related to German *Drossel*. Compare with THROTTLE.

throatlatch (also **throatlash**) ▸ noun a strap passing under a horse's throat to help keep the bridle in position.

throat microphone ▸ noun a microphone attached to a speaker's throat and actuated by the larynx.

throatwort ▸ noun a tall Eurasian bellflower that is reputed to cure sore throats. ● Genus *Campanula*, family Campanulaceae: several species, in particular *C. trachelium* and *C. latifolia*.

throaty ▸ adjective (**throatier, throatiest**) (of a voice or other sound) deep and husky: *rich, throaty laughter.*
– DERIVATIVES **throatily** adverb, **throatiness** noun.

throb ▸ verb (**throbs, throbbing, throbbed**) [no obj.] beat or sound with a strong, regular rhythm; pulsate steadily: *the war drums throbbed* | figurative *the crowded streets **throbbed with** life.* ▪ feel pain in a series of regular beats: *her foot **throbbed with** pain* | (as adj. **throbbing**) *a throbbing headache.*
▸ noun [usu. in sing.] a strong, regular beat or sound; a steady pulsation: *the throb of the ship's engines.* ▪ a feeling of pain in a series of regular beats.
– ORIGIN late Middle English: probably imitative.

throes /θrəʊz/ ▸ plural noun intense or violent pain and struggle, especially accompanying birth, death, or great change: *he convulsed in his **death throes**.*
– PHRASES **in the throes of** in the middle of doing or dealing with something very difficult or painful: *a friend was in the throes of a divorce.*
– ORIGIN Middle English *throwe* (singular); perhaps related to Old English *thrēa, thrawu* 'calamity', influenced by *thrōwian* 'suffer'.

thrombectomy /θrɒmˈbɛktəmi/ ▸ noun [mass noun] surgical removal of a thrombus from a blood vessel.

thrombi plural form of THROMBUS.

thrombin /ˈθrɒmbɪn/ ▸ noun [mass noun] Biochemistry an enzyme in blood plasma which causes the clotting of blood by converting fibrinogen to fibrin.
– ORIGIN late 19th cent.: from Greek *thrombos* 'blood clot' + -IN[1].

thrombo- ▸ combining form relating to the clotting of blood: *thromboembolism.*
– ORIGIN from Greek *thrombos* 'blood clot'.

thrombocyte /ˈθrɒmbə(ʊ)sʌɪt/ ▸ noun another term for PLATELET.

thrombocythaemia /ˌθrɒmbə(ʊ)sʌɪtˈhiːmɪə/ ▸ noun [mass noun] Medicine abnormal proliferation of the cells that produce blood platelets, leading to an excess of platelets in the blood and increasing risk either of thrombosis or of bleeding.

thrombocytopenia /ˌθrɒmbə(ʊ)ˌsʌɪtə(ʊ)ˈpiːnɪə/ ▸ noun [mass noun] Medicine deficiency of platelets in the blood. This causes bleeding into the tissues, bruising, and slow blood clotting after injury.
– ORIGIN 1920s: from THROMBOCYTE + Greek *penia* 'poverty'.

thromboembolism /ˌθrɒmbəʊˈɛmbəlɪz(ə)m/ ▸ noun Medicine obstruction of a blood vessel by a blood clot that has become dislodged from another site in the circulation.
– DERIVATIVES **thromboembolic** adjective.

thrombogenic /ˌθrɒmbə(ʊ)ˈdʒɛnɪk/ ▸ adjective Medicine (of a substance or condition) producing coagulation of the blood, especially as predisposing to thrombosis.
– DERIVATIVES **thrombogenicity** noun.

T

thrombolysis /θrɒmˈbɒlɪsɪs/ ▸ **noun** [mass noun] Medicine the dissolution of a blood clot, especially as induced artificially by infusion of an enzyme into the blood.
– DERIVATIVES **thrombolytic** adjective.

thrombophilia /ˌθrɒmbə(ʊ)ˈfɪlɪə/ ▸ **noun** [mass noun] Medicine an abnormal tendency to develop blood clots.

thrombophlebitis /ˌθrɒmbəʊflɪˈbʌɪtɪs/ ▸ **noun** [mass noun] Medicine inflammation of the wall of a vein with associated thrombosis, often occurring in the legs during pregnancy.

thromboplastin /ˌθrɒmbə(ʊ)ˈplastɪn/ ▸ **noun** [mass noun] Biochemistry an enzyme released from damaged cells, especially platelets, which converts prothrombin to thrombin during the early stages of blood coagulation.

thrombose /θrɒmˈbəʊz, -s/ ▸ **verb** affect with or be affected by thrombosis.
– ORIGIN late 19th cent.: back-formation from THROMBOSIS.

thrombosis /θrɒmˈbəʊsɪs/ ▸ **noun** (pl. **thromboses** /-siːz/) [mass noun] local coagulation or clotting of the blood in a part of the circulatory system: *increased risk of thrombosis* | [count noun] *a coronary thrombosis*.
– DERIVATIVES **thrombotic** adjective.
– ORIGIN early 18th cent.: modern Latin, from Greek *thrombōsis* 'curdling', from *thrombos* 'blood clot'.

thromboxane /θrɒmˈbɒkseɪn/ ▸ **noun** [mass noun] Biochemistry a hormone of the prostacyclin type released from blood platelets, which induces platelet aggregation and arterial constriction.

thrombus /ˈθrɒmbəs/ ▸ **noun** (pl. **thrombi** /-bʌɪ/) a blood clot formed in situ within the vascular system of the body and impeding blood flow.
– ORIGIN mid 19th cent.: modern Latin, from Greek *thrombos* 'lump, blood clot'.

throne ▸ **noun** a ceremonial chair for a sovereign, bishop, or similar figure. ▪ (**the throne**) used to signify sovereign power: *the heir to the throne*. ▪ humorous a toilet. ▪ (**thrones**) (in traditional Christian angelology) the third-highest order of the ninefold celestial hierarchy.
▸ **verb** [with obj.] literary place (someone) on a throne: *the king was throned on a rock*.
– ORIGIN Middle English: from Old French *trone*, via Latin from Greek *thronos* 'elevated seat'.

throng ▸ **noun** a large, densely packed crowd of people or animals: *he pushed his way through the throng* | *a throng of birds*.
▸ **verb** [with obj.] (of a crowd) fill or be present in (a place or area): *a crowd thronged the station* | *the pavements are thronged with people*. ▪ [no obj., with adverbial of direction] flock or be present in great numbers: *tourists thronged to the picturesque village*.
– ORIGIN Old English (*ge*)*thrang* 'crowd, tumult', of Germanic origin. The early sense of the verb (Middle English) was 'press violently, force one's way'.

throstle /ˈθrɒs(ə)l/ ▸ **noun** 1 Brit. old-fashioned term for SONG THRUSH.
2 (also **throstle frame**) historical a machine for continuously spinning wool or cotton.
– ORIGIN Old English, of Germanic origin, from an Indo-European root shared by Latin *turdus* 'thrush'. Sense 2 dates from the early 19th cent. and was apparently named from the humming sound of the machine.

throttle ▸ **noun** 1 a device controlling the flow of fuel or power to an engine: *the engines were at full throttle*.
2 archaic a person's throat, gullet, or windpipe.
▸ **verb** [with obj.] 1 attack or kill (someone) by choking or strangling them: *she was sorely tempted to throttle him* | figurative *the revolution has throttled the free exchange of information and opinion*.
2 control (an engine or vehicle) with a throttle. ▪ [no obj.] (**throttle back** or **down**) reduce the power of an engine or vehicle by use of the throttle.
– ORIGIN late Middle English (as a verb): perhaps a frequentative, from THROAT; the noun (dating from the mid 16th cent. in sense 2) is perhaps a diminutive of THROAT, but the history of the word is not clear.

T

through ▸ **preposition & adverb** 1 moving in one side and out of the other side of (an opening, channel, or location): [as prep.] *stepping boldly through the doorway* | [as adv.] *as soon as we opened the gate they came streaming through*. ▪ so as to make a hole or opening in (a physical object): [as prep.] *the lorry smashed through a brick wall* | [as adv.] *a cucumber, slit, but not right through*. ▪ moving around or from one side to the other within (a crowd or group): [as prep.] *making my way through the guests*. ▪ so as to be perceived from the other side of (an intervening obstacle): [as prep.] *the sun was streaming in through the window* | [as adv.] *the glass in the front door where the moonlight streamed through*. ▪ [prep.] expressing the position or location of something beyond or at the far end of (an opening or an obstacle): *the approach to the church is through a gate*. ▪ expressing the extent of turning from one orientation to another: [as prep.] *each joint can move through an angle within fixed limits*.
2 continuing in time towards completion of (a process or period): [as prep.] *the goal came midway through the second half* | [as adv.] *to struggle through until pay day*. ▪ so as to complete (a particular stage or trial) successfully: [as prep.] *she had come through her sternest test* | [as adv.] *I will struggle through alone rather than ask for help*. ▪ from beginning to end of (an experience or activity, typically a tedious or stressful one): [as prep.] *we sat through some very boring speeches* | *she's been through a bad time* | [as adv.] *Karl will see you through, Ingrid*.
3 so as to inspect all or part of (a collection, inventory, or publication): [as prep.] *flipping through the pages of a notebook* | [as adv.] *she read the letter through carefully*.
4 [prep.] N. Amer. up to and including (a particular point in an ordered sequence): *they will be in London from March 24 through May 7*.
5 [prep.] by means of (a process or intermediate stage): *dioxins get into mothers' milk through contaminated food*. ▪ by means of (an intermediary or agent): *seeking justice through the proper channels*.
6 [adverb] so as to be connected by telephone: *he put a call through to the Naturalists' Trust Office*.
▸ **adjective** 1 [attrib.] (with reference to public transport) continuing or valid to the final destination: *a through train from London*. ▪ (of traffic) passing from one side of a place to another in the course of a longer journey: *precincts from which through traffic would be excluded*. ▪ (of a road) open at both ends, allowing free passage from one end to the other: *the village lies on a busy through road*.
2 [attrib.] (of a room) running the whole length of a building.
3 [predic.] (of a team or competitor) having successfully passed to the next stage of a competition: *Swindon Town are through to the third round*.
4 [predic.] informal having no prospect of any future relationship, dealings, or success: *she told him she was through with him* | *you and I are through*.
– PHRASES **through and through** in every aspect; thoroughly or completely: *Harriet was a political animal through and through*.
– ORIGIN Old English *thurh* (preposition and adverb), of Germanic origin; related to Dutch *door* and German *durch*. The spelling change to *thr-* appears *c.*1300, becoming standard from Caxton onwards.

through ball ▸ **noun** Soccer a forward pass which goes through the opposing team's defence.

through-composed ▸ **adjective** another term for DURCHKOMPONIERT.

throughfall ▸ **noun** [mass noun] the part of rainfall or other precipitation which falls to the forest floor from the canopy.

throughflow ▸ **noun** [mass noun] the flowing of liquid or air through something.

through-hole ▸ **adjective** (of an electronic component) having leads which are designed to go through holes to the other side of a circuit board for soldering. Often contrasted with SURFACE-MOUNT.

throughother Scottish & Irish ▸ **adverb** mingled through one another: *their life together had been woven throughother*.
▸ **adjective** (of a person) disordered; confused.

throughout ▸ **preposition & adverb** in every part of (a place or object): [as prep.] *it had repercussions throughout Europe* | [as adv.] *the house is in good order throughout*. ▪ from beginning to end of (an event or period of time): [as prep.] *the Church of which she was a faithful member throughout her life* | [as adv.] *both MPs retained a smiling dignity throughout*.

through pass ▸ **noun** another term for THROUGH BALL.

throughput ▸ **noun** the amount of material or items passing through a system or process.

through-ticketing ▸ **noun** [mass noun] a system whereby a traveller passing through a number of different transport networks can purchase one ticket for the complete journey.

throughway (also **thruway**) ▸ **noun** N. Amer. a major road or motorway.

throve past of THRIVE.

throw ▸ **verb** (**throws, throwing**; past **threw**; past participle **thrown**) 1 [with obj. and usu. with adverbial] propel (something) with force through the air by a movement of the arm and hand: *I threw a brick through the window*. ▪ [with obj. and adverbial or complement] push or force (someone or something) violently and suddenly into a particular physical position or state: *the pilot and one passenger were thrown clear and survived* | *the door was thrown open and a uniformed guard entered the room*. ▪ put in place or erect quickly: *the stewards had thrown a cordon across the fairway*. ▪ move (a part of the body) quickly or suddenly in a particular direction: *she threw her head back and laughed*. ▪ project or cast (light or shadow) in a particular direction: *a chandelier threw its bright light over the walls*. ▪ deliver (a punch). ▪ direct a particular kind of look or facial expression: *she threw a withering glance at him*. ▪ project (one's voice) so that it appears to come from someone or something else, as in ventriloquism. ▪ (**throw something off/on**) put on or take off (a garment) hastily: *I tumbled out of bed, threw on my tracksuit, and joined the others*. ▪ move (a switch or lever) so as to operate a device. ▪ roll (dice). ▪ obtain (a specified number) by rolling dice. ▪ informal lose (a race or contest) intentionally, especially in return for a bribe. ▪ Cricket bowl (the ball) with an unlawful bent arm action. ▪ (of a horse) lose (a shoe).
2 [with obj. and adverbial] send suddenly into a particular state or condition: *he threw all her emotions into turmoil* | *the bond market was thrown into confusion*. ▪ put (someone) in a particular place or state in a rough, abrupt, or summary fashion: *these guys should be thrown in jail*. ▪ [with obj.] disconcert; confuse: *she frowned, thrown by this apparent change of tack*.
3 [with obj.] send (one's opponent) to the ground in wrestling, judo, or similar activity. ▪ (of a horse) unseat (its rider).
4 [with obj.] form (ceramic ware) on a potter's wheel: *further on a potter was throwing pots*. ▪ turn (wood or other material) on a lathe. ▪ twist (silk or other fabrics) into thread or yarn.
5 [with obj.] have (a fit or tantrum).
6 [with obj.] give or hold (a party).
7 [with obj.] (of an animal) give birth to (young, especially of a specified kind): *sometimes a completely black calf is thrown*.
▸ **noun** 1 an act of throwing something: *Holding's throw hit the stumps*. ▪ an act of throwing one's opponent in wrestling, judo, or a similar sport: *a shoulder throw*. ▪ Cricket an illegitimate delivery considered to have been thrown rather than properly bowled. ▪ short for THROW OF THE DICE below.
2 a light cover for furniture.
3 (**a throw**) informal used to indicate how much a single item, turn, or attempt costs: *he was offering to draw on-the-spot portraits at £25 a throw*.
4 Geology the extent of vertical displacement in a fault.
5 a machine or device by or on which an object is turned while being shaped.
6 [usu. in sing.] the action or motion of a slide valve or of a crank, eccentric wheel, or cam. ▪ the distance moved by the pointer of an instrument.
– PHRASES **throw away the key** used to suggest that someone who has been put in prison should or will never be released: *the judge should lock up these robbers and throw away the key*. **throw dust in someone's eyes** seek to mislead or deceive someone by misrepresentation or distraction. **throw good money after bad** incur further loss in a hopeless attempt to recoup a previous loss. **throw one's hand in** withdraw from a card game, especially poker, because one has a poor hand. ▪ withdraw from a contest or activity; give up. **throw in the towel** (or **sponge**) (of boxers or their seconds) throw a towel (or sponge) into the ring as a token of defeat. ▪ abandon a struggle; admit defeat. **throw of the dice** a risky attempt to do or achieve something: *a struggling actor giving it a last throw of the dice as he stages a self-financed production of Hamlet*. **throw oneself on** (or **upon**) **someone's mercy** abjectly ask someone for help, forgiveness, or leniency. **throw up one's hands** raise both hands in the air as an indication of one's exasperation.
– PHRASAL VERBS **be thrown back on** be forced to rely on (something) because there is no alternative: *we are once again thrown back on the resources of our imagination*. **throw oneself at** appear too eager to become the sexual partner of. **throw something away 1** discard something as useless or unwanted. ▪ discard a playing card in a game. ▪ waste or fail to make use of an opportunity or advantage: *I've thrown away my chances in life*. **2** (of an actor) deliver a line

with deliberate underemphasis for increased dramatic effect. **throw something down** informal (especially of a DJ, rapper, or similar artiste) play or perform a piece of music: *the DJ was throwing down some sweet tunes.* **throw something in 1** include something free with a purchase: *they cut the price by £100 and threw in the add-on TV adaptor.* **2** make a remark casually as an interjection: *he threw in a sensible remark about funding.* **3** Soccer & Rugby return the ball to play by means of a throw-in. **throw oneself into** start to do (something) with enthusiasm and vigour: *Evelyn threw herself into her work.* **throw off** Hunting begin hunting. **throw something off 1** rid oneself of something: *he was struggling to throw off a viral-hepatitis problem.* **2** write or utter in an offhand manner: *Thomas threw off the question lightly.* **throw oneself on** (or **upon**) attack someone vigorously: *they threw themselves on the enemy.* **throw something open** make something accessible: *the market was* **thrown open to** *any supplier to compete for contracts.* ■ invite general discussion of or participation in a subject or a debate or other event: *the debate will be* **thrown open to** *the audience.* **throw someone out 1** expel someone unceremoniously from a place, organization, or activity. **2** confuse or distract someone from the matter in hand: *do keep quiet or you'll throw me out in my calculations.* **3** Cricket & Baseball put out an opponent by throwing the ball to the wicket or a base. **throw something out 1** discard something as unwanted. **2** (of a court, legislature, or other body) dismiss or reject something brought before it: *the charges were thrown out by the magistrate.* **3** put forward a suggestion tentatively: *a suggestion that Dunne threw out caught many a reader's fancy.* **4** cause numbers or calculations to become inaccurate: *an undisclosed stock option throws out all your figures.* **5** emit or radiate something: *a big range fire that threw out heat like a furnace.* **6** (of a plant) rapidly develop a side shoot, bud, etc. **throw someone over** abandon or reject someone as a lover. **throw people together** bring people into contact, especially by chance. **throw something together** make or produce something hastily, without careful planning or arrangement: *the meal was quickly thrown together at news of Rose's arrival.* **throw up** informal vomit. **throw something up 1** abandon or give up something, especially one's job: *why has he thrown up a promising career in politics?* **2** informal vomit something one has eaten or drunk. **3** produce something and bring it to notice: *he saw the prayers of the Church as a living and fruitful tradition which threw up new ideas.*

– DERIVATIVES **throwable** adjective, **thrower** noun.

– ORIGIN Old English *thrāwan* 'to twist, turn', of West Germanic origin; related to Dutch *draaien* and German *drehen*, from an Indo-European root shared by Latin *terere* 'to rub', Greek *teirein* 'wear out'. Sense 1 of the verb, expressing propulsion and sudden action, dates from Middle English.

throwaway ▶ **adjective 1** denoting or relating to products that are intended to be discarded after being used once or a few times: *a throwaway camera | we live in a throwaway society.*
2 (of a remark) expressed in a casual or understated way: *some people overreacted to a few throwaway lines.*
▶ **noun** a thing intended to be discarded after brief use.

throwback ▶ **noun** a reversion to an earlier ancestral characteristic: *the eyes could be an ancestral throwback.* ■ a person or thing having the characteristics of a former time: *a lot of his work is* **a throwback to** *the fifties.*

throwdown ▶ **noun** informal a performance by or competition between DJs, rappers, or similar artistes: *a funky hip-hop throwdown.*

throw-in ▶ **noun** Soccer & Rugby an act of throwing the ball from the sideline to restart play after the ball has gone into touch.

throw-off ▶ **noun** the release of the hounds at the start of a hunt.

throw-over ▶ **adjective** denoting a bedspread or other large piece of cloth used as a loose-fitting decorative cover for a piece of furniture.

throw rug ▶ **noun** another term for SCATTER RUG.

throwster ▶ **noun** a person who twists silk fibres into thread.

thru ▶ **preposition, adverb, & adjective** chiefly N. Amer. informal spelling of THROUGH.

thrum[1] ▶ **verb** (**thrums, thrumming, thrummed**) [no obj.] make a continuous rhythmic humming sound: *the boat's huge engines thrummed in his ears.* ■ [with obj.] strum (the strings of a musical instrument) in a rhythmic way.
▶ **noun** [usu. in sing.] a continuous rhythmic humming sound: *the steady thrum of rain on the windows.*
– ORIGIN late 16th cent. (as a verb): imitative.

thrum[2] ▶ **noun** (in weaving) an unwoven end of a warp thread, or a fringe of such ends, left in the loom when the finished cloth is cut away. ■ any short loose thread.
▶ **verb** (**thrums, thrumming, thrummed**) [with obj.] cover or adorn (cloth or clothing) with ends of thread.
– ORIGIN Old English *thrum* (only in *tungethrum* 'ligament of the tongue'): of Germanic origin; related to Dutch *dreum* 'thrum' and German *Trumm* 'end piece'. The current sense dates from Middle English.

thrush[1] ▶ **noun** a small or medium-sized songbird, typically having a brown back, spotted breast, and loud song. ● Family Turdidae (the **thrush family**): many genera, in particular *Turdus*, and numerous species. The thrush family also includes the chats, robins, blackbirds, nightingales, redstarts, and wheatears.
– ORIGIN Old English *thrysce*, of Germanic origin; related to THROSTLE.

thrush[2] ▶ **noun** [mass noun] **1** infection of the mouth and throat by a yeast-like fungus, causing whitish patches. Also called CANDIDIASIS. ● The fungus belongs to the genus *Candida*, subdivision Deuteromycotina, in particular *C. albicans*.
■ infection of the genitals with the same fungus.
2 a chronic condition affecting the frog of a horse's foot, causing the accumulation of a dark, foul-smelling substance. Also called CANKER.
– ORIGIN mid 17th cent.: origin uncertain; sense 1 possibly related to Swedish *torsk* and Danish *troske*; sense 2 perhaps from dialect *frush* in the same sense, perhaps from Old French *fourchette* 'frog of a horse's hoof'.

thrush nightingale ▶ **noun** a songbird that is closely related to the nightingale and which replaces it in eastern Europe, the Baltic, and western Asia. Also called SPROSSER. ● *Luscinia luscinia*, family Turdidae.

thrust ▶ **verb** (**thrusts, thrusting**; past and past participle **thrust**) [with obj. and adverbial of direction] push suddenly or violently in a specified direction: *she thrust her hands into her pockets* | figurative *Howard was thrust into the limelight* | [no obj.] *he* **thrust at** *his opponent with his sword.* ■ [no obj., with adverbial of direction] move or advance forcibly: *she thrust through the bramble canes | he tried to* **thrust his way** *past her.* ■ [no obj., with adverbial of direction] extend so as to project conspicuously: *beside the boathouse a jetty thrust out into the water.* ■ (**thrust something on/upon**) force (someone) to accept or deal with something: *he felt that fame had been thrust upon him.*
▶ **noun 1** a sudden or violent lunge with a pointed weapon or a bodily part: *he drove the blade upwards with one powerful thrust.* ■ a forceful attack or effort: *executives led a new thrust in business development.* ■ [in sing.] the principal purpose or theme of a course of action or line of reasoning: *anti-Americanism became* **the main thrust of** *their policy.*
2 [mass noun] the propulsive force of a jet or rocket engine. ■ the lateral pressure exerted by an arch or other support in a building.
3 (also **thrust fault**) Geology a reverse fault of low angle, with older strata displaced horizontally over newer.
– ORIGIN Middle English (as a verb): from Old Norse *thrýsta*; perhaps related to Latin *trudere* 'to thrust'. The noun is first recorded (early 16th cent.) in the sense 'act of pressing'.

thrust bearing ▶ **noun** a bearing designed to take a load in the direction of the axis of a shaft, especially one transmitting the thrust of a propeller shaft to the hull of a ship.

thrust block ▶ **noun** a casting or frame carrying or containing the bearings on which the collars of a propeller shaft press.

thruster ▶ **noun** a person or thing that thrusts. ■ a small rocket engine on a spacecraft, used to make alterations in its flight path or altitude. ■ a secondary jet or propeller on a ship or offshore rig, used for accurate manoeuvring and maintenance of position. ■ a surfboard or sailboard capable of increased speed and manoeuvrability.

thrusting ▶ **adjective 1** aggressively ambitious: *thrusting entrepreneurs.*
2 (of an object or part of the body) projecting in a conspicuous way: *a thrusting jaw.*

thrust reverser ▶ **noun** Aeronautics a device for reversing the flow of gas from a jet engine so as to produce a retarding backward force.

thrust slice ▶ **noun** Geology a relatively thin, broad mass of rock situated between two approximately parallel thrust faults.

thrust stage ▶ **noun** a stage that extends into the auditorium so that the audience is seated around three sides.

thrutch ▶ **noun** N. English a narrow gorge or ravine.
▶ **verb** [no obj., with adverbial of direction] chiefly Climbing push, press, or squeeze into a space.
– ORIGIN Old English (as a verb), of West Germanic origin.

thruway ▶ **noun** N. Amer. informal spelling of THROUGHWAY.

Thucydides /θjuːˈsɪdɪdiːz/ (*c.*455–*c.*400 BC), Greek historian. He is remembered for his *History of the Peloponnesian War*, which analyses the origins and course of the war; he fought in the conflict on the Athenian side.

thud ▶ **noun** a dull, heavy sound, such as that made by an object falling to the ground: *he hit the floor with a terrific thud.*
▶ **verb** (**thuds, thudding, thudded**) [no obj.] move, fall, or strike something with a dull, heavy sound: *the bullets thudded into the dusty ground* | (as noun **thudding**) *he heard the hollow thudding of hooves.* ■ (as adj. **thudding**) used to emphasize the clumsiness or awkwardness of something: *great thudding conversation-stoppers.*
– DERIVATIVES **thuddingly** adverb.
– ORIGIN late Middle English (originally Scots): probably from Old English *thyddan* 'to thrust, push'; related to *thoden* 'violent wind'. The noun is recorded first denoting a sudden blast or gust of wind, later the sound of a thunderclap, whence a dull, heavy sound. The verb dates from the early 16th cent.

thug ▶ **noun 1** a violent person, especially a criminal: *he was attacked by a gang of thugs.*
2 (**Thug**) historical a member of an organization of robbers and assassins in India. Devotees of the goddess Kali, the Thugs waylaid and strangled their victims, usually travellers, in a ritually prescribed manner. They were suppressed by the British in the 1830s.
– DERIVATIVES **thuggery** noun, **thuggish** adjective, **thuggishly** adverb, **thuggishness** noun, **thuggism** noun.
– ORIGIN early 19th cent. (in sense 2): from Hindi *ṭhag* 'swindler, thief', based on Sanskrit *sthagati* 'he covers or conceals'. Sense 1 arose in the mid 19th cent.

thuggee /θʌˈgiː/ ▶ **noun** [mass noun] historical the robbery and murder practised by the Thugs in accordance with their ritual.
– ORIGIN from Hindi *ṭhagī*, from *ṭhag* (see THUG).

thuja /ˈθ(j)uːjə/ (also **thuya**) ▶ **noun** an evergreen coniferous tree of a genus that includes the western red cedar. Also called ARBOR VITAE. ● Genus *Thuja*, family Cupressaceae.
– ORIGIN modern Latin (genus name), from Greek *thuia*, denoting an African tree formerly included in the genus.

Thule 1 /ˈθjuːli/ a country described by the ancient Greek explorer Pytheas (*c.*310 BC) as being six days' sail north of Britain, most plausibly identified with Norway. It was regarded by the ancients as the northernmost part of the world.
2 /θuːl, θjuːl/ an Eskimo culture widely distributed from Alaska to Greenland *c.*500–1400 AD.
3 /ˈtuːli/ a settlement on the NW coast of Greenland, founded in 1910 by the Danish explorer Knud Rasmussen (1879–1933).

thulium /ˈθ(j)uːlɪəm/ ▶ **noun** [mass noun] the chemical element of atomic number 69, a soft silvery-white metal of the lanthanide series. (Symbol: **Tm**)
– ORIGIN late 19th cent.: modern Latin, from Latin *Thule* (see THULE (sense 1)), from Greek *Thoulē*, of unknown origin.

thumb ▶ **noun** the short, thick first digit of the human hand, set lower and apart from the other four and opposable to them. ■ the digit of primates or other mammals that corresponds to the human thumb. ■ the part of a glove that covers the thumb.
▶ **verb** [with obj.] **1** press, move, or touch (something) with one's thumb: *as soon as she thumbed the button, the door slid open.* ■ [no obj.] use one's thumb to indicate something: *he thumbed towards the men behind him.*

T

2 turn over (pages) with or as if with one's thumb: *I've thumbed my address book and found quite a range of smaller hotels* | [no obj.] *he was* ***thumbing through*** *USA Today for the umpteenth time.* ■ wear or soil (a book's pages) by repeated handling: *his dictionaries were thumbed and ink-stained.*
3 request or obtain (a free ride in a passing vehicle) by signalling with one's thumb: *three cars passed me and I tried to* ***thumb a lift*** | *he was thumbing his way across France.*
– PHRASES **be all thumbs** another way of saying BE ALL FINGERS AND THUMBS (see FINGER). **thumb one's nose at** informal show disdain or contempt for. **thumbs up** (or **down**) informal an indication of satisfaction or approval (or of rejection or failure): *plans to build a house on the site have been given the thumbs down by the Department of the Environment.* [with reference to the signal of approval or disapproval used by spectators at a Roman amphitheatre; the sense has been reversed, as the Romans used 'thumbs down' to signify that a beaten gladiator had performed well and should be spared, and 'thumbs up' to call for his death.] **under someone's thumb** completely under someone's influence or control.
– DERIVATIVES **thumbed** adjective, **thumbless** adjective.
– ORIGIN Old English *thūma*, of West Germanic origin; related to Dutch *duim* and German *Daumen*, from an Indo-European root shared by Latin *tumere* 'to swell'. The verb dates from the late 16th cent., first in the sense 'play (a musical instrument) with the thumbs'.

thumb index ▶ noun a set of lettered grooves cut down the side of a book, especially a diary, address book, or dictionary, for easy reference.
– DERIVATIVES **thumb-indexed** adjective.

thumbnail ▶ noun 1 the nail of the thumb.
2 [usu. as modifier] a very small or concise description, representation, or summary: *a thumbnail sketch.*
■ Computing a small picture of an image or page layout.

thumb nut ▶ noun another term for WING NUT.

thumb piano ▶ noun any of various musical instruments, mainly of African origin, made from strips of metal fastened to a resonator and played by plucking with the fingers and thumbs. Also called KALIMBA, MBIRA, or SANSA.

thumbprint ▶ noun an impression or mark made on a surface by the inner part of the top joint of the thumb, especially as used for identifying individuals from the unique pattern of whorls and lines.
■ a distinctive identifying characteristic: *it has an individuality and thumbprint of its own.*

thumbscrew ▶ noun 1 (usu. **thumbscrews**) an instrument of torture for crushing the thumbs.
2 a screw with a protruding winged or flattened head for turning with the thumb and forefinger.

thumb stick ▶ noun 1 a tall walking stick with a forked thumb rest at the top.
2 a basic control lever for audio and televisual equipment.

thumbsucker ▶ noun US informal, often derogatory a serious piece of journalism which concentrates on the background and interpretation of events rather than on the news or action.

thumbtack ▶ noun North American term for DRAWING PIN.

thumbwheel ▶ noun a control device for electrical or mechanical equipment in the form of a wheel operated with the thumb.

T

Thummim /ˈθʌmɪm/ ▶ noun see URIM AND THUMMIM.

thump ▶ verb [with obj.] 1 hit or strike heavily, especially with the fist or a blunt implement: *Holman thumped the desk with his hand* | [no obj.] *she thumped on the cottage door.* ■ [with adverbial of direction] move forcefully or with a heavy deadened sound: [with obj.] *she picked up the kettle then thumped it down again* | [no obj.] *Philip thumped down on the settee.* ■ [no obj.] (of a person's heart or pulse) beat or pulsate strongly, typically because of fear or excitement.
■ (**thump something out**) play a tune enthusiastically but heavy-handedly.
2 informal defeat heavily: [with obj. and complement] *Bristol thumped Rugby 35–13.*
▶ noun a dull, heavy blow with a person's fist or a blunt implement: *I felt a thump on my back.* ■ a heavy deadened sound: *his wife put down her iron with a thump* | [mass noun] *through the wall came the thump of rock music.* ■ a strong heartbeat, especially one caused by fear or excitement.
– DERIVATIVES **thumper** noun.
– ORIGIN mid 16th cent.: imitative.

thumping ▶ adjective [attrib.] Brit. informal of an impressive size, extent, or amount: *a thumping 64 per cent majority* | [as submodifier] *a thumping great lie.*
– DERIVATIVES **thumpingly** adverb.

thumri /ˈtʊmriː/ ▶ noun (pl. **thumris**) [mass noun] (in Hindustani classical music) a light romantic form.
■ [count noun] a romantic song.
– ORIGIN from Hindi *ṭhumrī*.

thunder ▶ noun [mass noun] a loud rumbling or crashing noise heard after a lightning flash due to the expansion of rapidly heated air. ■ a loud, deep resounding noise: *you can hear the thunder of the falls in the distance.* ■ used to refer to an angry facial expression or tone of voice: *'I am Brother Joachim,' he announced in a voice like thunder.* ■ [as exclamation] dated used to express emphasis, anger, or incredulity: *none of this did the remotest good, but, by thunder, it kept the union activists feeling good.*
▶ verb [no obj.] 1 (**it thunders, it is thundering**, etc.) thunder sounds: *it began to thunder.* ■ make a loud, deep resounding noise: *the motorcycle thundered into life* | *the train thundered through the night.* ■ [with obj. and adverbial of direction] strike powerfully: *Briggs thundered home a 30-yard free kick.*
2 speak loudly and forcefully or angrily, especially to denounce or criticize: *he* ***thundered against*** *the evils of the age* | [with direct speech] *'Sit down!' thundered Morse with immense authority.*
– DERIVATIVES **thunderer** noun, **thundery** adjective.
– ORIGIN Old English *thunor* (noun), *thunrian* (verb), of Germanic origin; related to Dutch *donder* and German *Donner* (noun), from an Indo-European root shared by Latin *tonare* 'to thunder'.

Thunder Bay a city on an inlet of Lake Superior in SW Ontario; pop. 109,140 (2006). It is one of Canada's major ports.

thunderbird ▶ noun 1 a mythical bird thought by some North American Indians to bring thunder.
2 Austral. either of two thickheads (birds) which become noisy before and during thunderstorms.
● The golden whistler (*Pachycephala pectoralis*) and the rufous whistler (*P. rufiventris*), family Pachycephalidae.

thunderbolt ▶ noun literary a flash of lightning with a simultaneous crash of thunder. ■ a supposed bolt or shaft believed to be the destructive agent in a lightning flash, especially as an attribute of a god such as Jupiter or Thor. ■ used to refer to a very sudden or unexpected event or item of news, especially of an unpleasant nature: *the full force of what she had been told hit her like a thunderbolt.* ■ informal a very fast and powerful shot, throw, or stroke.

thunderbox ▶ noun Brit. informal a primitive or makeshift toilet.

thunderbug ▶ noun another term for THRIPS.

thunderclap ▶ noun a crash of thunder. ■ used in similes to refer to something startling or unexpected: *the door opened like a thunderclap.*

thundercloud ▶ noun a cumulus cloud with a towering or spreading top, charged with electricity and producing thunder and lightning.

thunderflash ▶ noun a noisy but harmless pyrotechnic device used especially in military exercises.

thunderfly ▶ noun (pl. **thunderflies**) another term for THRIPS.

thunderhead ▶ noun a rounded, projecting head of a cumulus cloud, which portends a thunderstorm.

thundering ▶ adjective 1 [attrib.] making a resounding, loud, deep noise: *thundering waterfalls.*
2 informal extremely great, severe, or impressive: *a thundering bore* | [as submodifier] *a thundering good read.*
– DERIVATIVES **thunderingly** adverb [as submodifier] *it was so thunderingly dull.*

thunderous ▶ adjective 1 relating to or resembling thunder: *a thunderous grey cloud.* ■ very loud: *thunderous applause.* ■ very powerful or intense: *no goalkeeper cares to face his thunderous shots.*
2 (of a person's expression or behaviour) very angry or menacing: *Robin's thunderous mood hadn't lightened.*
– DERIVATIVES **thunderously** adverb, **thunderousness** noun.

thundershower ▶ noun chiefly US a shower of rain accompanied by thunder and lightning.

thunderstorm ▶ noun a storm with thunder and lightning and typically also heavy rain or hail.

thunderstruck ▶ adjective extremely surprised or shocked: *they were thunderstruck by this revelation.*

thunder thighs ▶ plural noun informal a woman's large or fat thighs.

thunk[1] ▶ noun & verb informal term for THUD.

thunk[2] informal or humorous past and past participle of THINK.

Thur. ▶ abbreviation Thursday.

Thurber /ˈθəːbə/, James (Grover) (1894–1961), American humorist and cartoonist. His collections of essays, stories, and sketches include *My World—And Welcome to It* (1942), which contains the story 'The Secret Life of Walter Mitty'.

thurible /ˈθjʊərɪb(ə)l/ ▶ noun a censer.
– ORIGIN late Middle English: from Old French, or from Latin *thuribulum*, from *thus, thur-* 'incense' (see THURIFER).

thurifer /ˈθjʊərɪfə/ ▶ noun an acolyte carrying a censer in a religious ceremony.
– ORIGIN mid 19th cent.: from late Latin, from Latin *thus, thur-* 'incense' (from Greek *thuos* 'sacrifice') + *-fer* '-bearing'.

Thuringia /ˌθjʊəˈrɪndʒɪə/ a densely forested state of central Germany; capital, Erfurt. German name **Thüringen** /ˈtyːrɪŋən/.

Thurs. ▶ abbreviation Thursday.

Thursday ▶ noun the day of the week before Friday and following Wednesday: *the committee met* ***on Thursday*** | *the music programme for Thursdays in April* | [as modifier] *Thursday morning.*
▶ adverb chiefly N. Amer. on Thursday: *he called her up Thursday.* ■ (**Thursdays**) on Thursdays; each Thursday.
– ORIGIN Old English *Thu(n)resdæg* 'day of thunder', translation of late Latin *Jovis dies* 'day of Jupiter' (god associated with thunder): compare with Dutch *donderdag* and German *Donnerstag.*

Thurso /ˈθəːsəʊ/ a fishing port on the northern coast of Scotland, in Highland council area, the northernmost town on the mainland of Britain; pop. 7,300 (est. 2009).

thus ▶ adverb literary or formal 1 as a result or consequence of this; therefore: *Burke knocked out Byrne, thus becoming champion.*
2 in the manner now being indicated or exemplified; in this way: *she rang up Susan, and while she was thus engaged Chignell summoned the doctor.*
3 [as submodifier] to this point; so: *the Ryder Cup is the highlight of Torrance's career* ***thus far.***
– ORIGIN Old English, of unknown origin.

thusly ▶ adverb informal another term for THUS (sense 2): *the review was conducted thusly.*

thuya ▶ noun variant spelling of THUJA.

thwack ▶ verb [with obj.] strike forcefully with a sharp blow: *she thwacked the back of their knees with a cane.*
▶ noun a sharp blow: *he hit it with a hefty thwack.*
– ORIGIN late Middle English: imitative.

thwaite /θweɪt/ ▶ noun [in place names] a piece of wild land cleared or reclaimed for cultivation: *Bassenthwaite.*
– ORIGIN Middle English: from Old Norse *thveit, thveiti* 'paddock', literally 'cut piece'.

thwart /θwɔːt/ ▶ verb [with obj.] prevent (someone) from accomplishing something: *he never did anything to thwart his father* | *he was* ***thwarted in*** *his desire to punish Uncle Fred.* ■ oppose (a plan, attempt, or ambition) successfully: *the government had been able to thwart all attempts by opposition leaders to form new parties.*
▶ noun a structural crosspiece forming a seat for a rower in a boat.
▶ preposition & adverb archaic or literary from one side to another side of; across: [as prep.] *a pink-tinged cloud spread thwart the shore.*
– ORIGIN Middle English *thwerte*, from the adjective *thwert* 'perverse, obstinate, adverse', from Old Norse *thvert*, neuter of *thverr* 'transverse', from an Indo-European root shared by Latin *torquere* 'to twist'.

thy (also **thine** before a vowel) ▶ possessive determiner archaic or dialect form of YOUR: *honour thy father and thy mother.*
– ORIGIN Middle English *thi* (originally before words beginning with any consonant except *h*), reduced from *thin*, from Old English *thīn* (see THINE).

> **USAGE** The use of **thy** is still found in some traditional dialects but elsewhere it is restricted to archaic contexts. See also USAGE at THOU[1].

Thyestes /θʌɪˈɛstiːz/ Greek Mythology the brother of Atreus and father of Aegisthus.
– DERIVATIVES **Thyestean** /-ˈɛstɪən/ adjective.

thylacine /ˈθʌɪləsiːn, -sʌɪn, -sɪn/ ▸ **noun** a doglike carnivorous marsupial with stripes across the rump, found only in Tasmania. There have been no confirmed sightings since one was captured in 1933, and it is probably now extinct. Also called **TASMANIAN WOLF**. ● *Thylacinus cynocephalus*, family Thylacinidae.
– ORIGIN mid 19th cent.: from modern Latin *Thylacinus* (genus name), from Greek *thulakos* 'pouch'.

thylakoid /ˈθʌɪləkɔɪd/ ▸ **noun** Botany each of a number of flattened sacs inside a chloroplast, bounded by pigmented membranes on which the light reactions of photosynthesis take place, and arranged in stacks or grana.
– ORIGIN 1960s: from German *Thylakoid*, from Greek *thulakoidēs* 'pouch-like', from *thulakos* 'pouch'.

thyme /tʌɪm/ ▸ **noun** [mass noun] a low-growing aromatic plant of the mint family. The small leaves are used as a culinary herb and the plant yields a medicinal oil. ● Genus *Thymus*, family Labiatae: many species, in particular **common** (or **garden**) **thyme** (*T. vulgaris*).
– DERIVATIVES **thymy** adjective.
– ORIGIN Middle English: from Old French *thym*, via Latin from Greek *thumon*, from *thuein* 'burn, sacrifice'.

thymectomy /θʌɪˈmɛktəmi/ ▸ **noun** (pl. **thymectomies**) surgical removal of the thymus gland.

thymi plural form of **THYMUS**.

thymic /ˈθʌɪmɪk/ ▸ **adjective** Physiology relating to the thymus gland or its functions.

thymidine /ˈθʌɪmɪdiːn/ ▸ **noun** [mass noun] Biochemistry a crystalline nucleoside present in DNA, consisting of thymine linked to deoxyribose.
– ORIGIN early 20th cent.: from **THYMINE** + **-IDE** + **-INE**[4].

thymine /ˈθʌɪmiːn/ ▸ **noun** [mass noun] Biochemistry a compound which is one of the four constituent bases of nucleic acids. A pyrimidine derivative, it is paired with adenine in double-stranded DNA. ● Alternative name; **5-methyluracil**; chem. formula: $C_5H_6N_2O_2$.
– ORIGIN late 19th cent.: from **THYMUS** + **-INE**[4].

thymocyte /ˈθʌɪmə(ʊ)sʌɪt/ ▸ **noun** Physiology a lymphocyte within the thymus gland.
– ORIGIN 1920s: from **THYMUS** + **-CYTE**.

thymol /ˈθʌɪmɒl/ ▸ **noun** [mass noun] Chemistry a white crystalline compound present in oil of thyme and used as a flavouring and preservative. ● Alternative name: **2-isopropyl-5-methylphenol**; chem. formula: $C_{10}H_{13}OH$.
– ORIGIN mid 19th cent.: from Greek *thumon* 'thyme' + **-OL**.

thymoma /θʌɪˈməʊmə/ ▸ **noun** (pl. **thymomas** or **thymomata** /-mətə/) Medicine a rare, usually benign tumour arising from thymus tissue and sometimes associated with myasthenia gravis.
– ORIGIN early 20th cent.: from **THYMUS** + **-OMA**.

thymus /ˈθʌɪməs/ (also **thymus gland**) ▸ **noun** (pl. **thymi** /-mʌɪ/) a lymphoid organ situated in the neck of vertebrates which produces T-lymphocytes for the immune system. The human thymus becomes much smaller at the approach of puberty.
– ORIGIN late 16th cent. (denoting a growth or tumour resembling a bud): from Greek *thumos* 'excrescence like a thyme bud, thymus gland'.

thyristor /θʌɪˈrɪstə/ ▸ **noun** Electronics a four-layered semiconductor rectifier in which the flow of current between two electrodes is triggered by a signal at a third electrode.
– ORIGIN 1950s: blend of *thyratron*, denoting a kind of thermionic valve (from Greek *thura* 'gate') and **TRANSISTOR**.

thyro- ▸ **combining form** representing **THYROID**.

thyroglobulin /ˌθʌɪrə(ʊ)ˈɡlɒbjʊlɪn/ ▸ **noun** [mass noun] Biochemistry a protein present in the thyroid gland, from which thyroid hormones are synthesized.

thyroid /ˈθʌɪrɔɪd/ ▸ **noun 1** (also **thyroid gland**) a large ductless gland in the neck which secretes hormones regulating growth and development through the rate of metabolism. ■ [mass noun] an extract prepared from the thyroid gland of animals and used in treating deficiency of thyroid hormones.
2 (also **thyroid cartilage**) a large cartilage of the larynx, a projection of which forms the Adam's apple in humans.
– ORIGIN early 18th cent. (as an adjective): from Greek (*khondros*) *thureoeidēs* 'shield-shaped (cartilage)', from *thureos* 'oblong shield'.

thyroid-stimulating hormone ▸ **noun** another term for **THYROTROPIN**.

thyrotoxicosis /ˌθʌɪrəʊˌtɒksɪˈkəʊsɪs/ ▸ **noun** another term for **HYPERTHYROIDISM**.

thyrotropin /ˌθʌɪrə(ʊ)ˈtrəʊpɪn/ (also **thyrotrophin** /-ˈtrəʊfɪn/) ▸ **noun** [mass noun] Biochemistry a hormone secreted by the pituitary gland which regulates the production of thyroid hormones.

thyrotropin-releasing hormone (also **thyrotropin-releasing factor**) ▸ **noun** [mass noun] Biochemistry a hormone secreted by the hypothalamus which stimulates release of thyrotropin.

thyroxine /θʌɪˈrɒksiːn, -sɪn/ ▸ **noun** [mass noun] Biochemistry the main hormone produced by the thyroid gland, acting to increase metabolic rate and so regulating growth and development. ● An iodine-containing amino acid; chem. formula: $C_{15}H_{11}NO_4I_4$.
– ORIGIN early 20th cent.: from **THYROID** + **OX-** 'oxygen' + *in* from **INDOLE** (because of an early misunderstanding of its chemical structure), altered by substitution of **-INE**[4].

thyrsus /ˈθəːsəs/ ▸ **noun** (pl. **thyrsi** /-sʌɪ, -siː/) (in ancient Greece and Rome) a staff or spear tipped with an ornament like a pine cone, carried by Bacchus and his followers.
– ORIGIN Latin, from Greek *thursos* 'plant stalk, Bacchic staff'.

Thysanoptera /ˌθʌɪsəˈnɒpt(ə)rə/ ▸ **plural noun** Entomology an order of insects that comprises the thrips. ■ (**thysanoptera**) insects of this order; thrips.
– DERIVATIVES **thysanopteran** noun & adjective.
– ORIGIN modern Latin (plural), from Greek *thusanos* 'tassel' + *pteron* 'wing'.

Thysanura /ˌθʌɪsəˈn(j)ʊərə/ ▸ **plural noun** Entomology an order of insects that comprises the true, or three-pronged, bristletails. ■ (**thysanura**) insects of this order; bristletails.
– DERIVATIVES **thysanuran** noun & adjective.
– ORIGIN modern Latin (plural), from Greek *thusanos* 'tassel' + *oura* 'tail'.

thyself ▸ **pronoun** [second person singular] archaic or dialect form of **YOURSELF**, corresponding to the subject thou: *thou shalt love thy neighbour as thyself.*

Ti ▸ **symbol** the chemical element titanium.

ti ▸ **noun** North American form of **TE**.

TIA ▸ **abbreviation** Medicine transient ischaemic attack, particularly affecting the brain of a person susceptible to strokes.

Tia Maria /ˌtiːə məˈriːə/ ▸ **noun** [mass noun] trademark a coffee-flavoured liqueur based on rum, made originally in the Caribbean.
– ORIGIN from Spanish *Tía María*, literally 'Aunt Mary'.

Tiamat /ˈtɪamat, tɪˈɑːmat/ Babylonian Mythology a monstrous she-dragon who was the mother of the first Babylonian gods. She was slain by Marduk.

tian /tjɑ̃/ ▸ **noun** (pl. pronunc. **same**) a dish of sliced vegetables cooked in olive oil and then layered in a dish and baked au gratin. ■ a large oval earthenware cooking pot traditionally used in Provence.
– ORIGIN Provençal, based on Greek *tēganon* 'frying pan'.

Tiananmen Square /ˈtjɛnənmən/ a square in the centre of Beijing adjacent to the Forbidden City, the largest public open space in the world.
– ORIGIN Chinese, literally 'square of heavenly peace'.

Tianjin /tjɛnˈdʒɪn/ (also **Tientsin**) a port in NE China, in Hebei province; pop. 5,332,100 (est. 2006).

Tian Shan variant spelling of **TIEN SHAN**.

tiara /tɪˈɑːrə/ ▸ **noun 1** a jewelled ornamental band worn on the front of a woman's hair.
2 a high diadem encircled with three crowns and worn by a pope. ■ historical a turban worn by ancient Persian kings.
– ORIGIN mid 16th cent. (denoting the Persian royal headdress): via Latin from Greek, partly via Italian. Sense 1 dates from the early 18th cent.

tiare /tiːˈɑːreɪ/ ▸ **noun** (pl. **same**) (in Tahiti) a gardenia of a variety bearing fragrant white flowers.
– ORIGIN late 19th cent.: special use of French *tiare* 'tiara'.

tiarella /tɪəˈrɛlə/ ▸ **noun** a small chiefly North American plant of the saxifrage family. ● Genus *Tiarella*, family Saxifragaceae, especially *T. cordifolia*.
– ORIGIN modern Latin, from Latin *tiara* 'turban, tiara' + the diminutive suffix *-ella*.

Tiber /ˈtʌɪbə/ a river of central Italy, upon which Rome stands. It rises in the Tuscan Apennines and flows 405 km (252 miles) generally south-westwards, entering the Tyrrhenian Sea at Ostia. Italian name **TEVERE**.

Tiberias, Lake /tʌɪˈbɪərɪəs/ another name for the Sea of Galilee (see **GALILEE, SEA OF**).

Tiberius /tʌɪˈbɪərɪəs/ (42 BC–AD 37), Roman emperor AD 14–37; full name *Tiberius Julius Caesar Augustus*. The adopted successor of his stepfather and father-in-law Augustus, he became increasingly tyrannical and his reign was marked by a growing number of treason trials and executions.

Tibesti Mountains /tɪˈbɛsti/ a mountain range in north central Africa, in the Sahara in northern Chad and southern Libya. It rises to 3,415 m (11,201 ft) at Emi Koussi, the highest point in the Sahara.

Tibet /tɪˈbɛt/ a mountainous country in Asia on the northern side of the Himalayas, since 1965 forming an autonomous region in the west of China; pop. 2,840,000 (est. 2007); official languages, Tibetan and Chinese; capital, Lhasa. Chinese name **XIZANG**.

> Most of Tibet forms a high plateau with an average elevation of over 4,000 m (12,500 ft). Ruled by Buddhist lamas since the 7th century, it was conquered by the Mongols in the 13th century and the Manchus in the 18th. China extended its authority over Tibet in 1951 but gained full control only after crushing a revolt in 1959, during which the country's spiritual leader, the Dalai Lama, escaped to India; he remains in exile and sporadic unrest has continued.

Tibetan ▸ **noun 1** a native of Tibet or a person of Tibetan descent.
2 [mass noun] the Sino-Tibetan language of Tibet, spoken by about 4 million people in Tibet and in neighbouring areas of China, India, and Nepal.
▸ **adjective** relating to Tibet, its people, or its language.

Tibetan antelope ▸ **noun** another term for **CHIRU**.

Tibetan Buddhism ▸ **noun** [mass noun] the religion of Tibet, a form of Mahayana Buddhism. It was formed in the 8th century AD from a combination of Buddhism and the indigenous Tibetan religion. The head of the religion is the Dalai Lama.

Tibetan mastiff ▸ **noun** an animal of a breed of large black-and-tan dog with a thick coat and drop ears.

Tibetan spaniel ▸ **noun** an animal of a breed of small white, brown, or black dog with a silky coat of medium length.

Tibetan terrier ▸ **noun** an animal of a breed of grey, black, cream, or particoloured terrier with a thick shaggy coat.

Tibeto-Burman ▸ **adjective** relating to or denoting a division of the Sino-Tibetan language family that includes Tibetan, Burmese, and a number of other languages spoken in mountainous regions of central southern Asia.

tibia /ˈtɪbɪə/ ▸ **noun** (pl. **tibiae** /-bɪiː/ or **tibias**) Anatomy the inner and typically larger of the two bones between the knee and the ankle (or the equivalent joints in other terrestrial vertebrates), parallel with the fibula. ■ Zoology the tibiotarsus of a bird. ■ Entomology the fourth segment of the leg of an insect, between the femur and the tarsus.
– DERIVATIVES **tibial** adjective.
– ORIGIN late Middle English: from Latin, 'shin bone'.

tibialis /ˌtɪbɪˈeɪlɪs/ ▸ **noun** Anatomy any of several muscles and tendons in the calf of the leg concerned with movements of the foot.
– ORIGIN late 19th cent.: from Latin, 'relating to the shin bone'.

T

tibiotarsus /ˌtɪbɪə(ʊ)ˈtɑːsəs/ ▸ **noun** (pl. **tibiotarsi** /-sʌɪ, -siː/) Zoology the bone in a bird's leg corresponding to the tibia, fused at the lower end with some bones of the tarsus.
– ORIGIN late 19th cent.: blend of **TIBIA** and **TARSUS**.

Tibullus /tɪˈbʌləs/, Albius (*c.*50–19 BC), Roman poet. He is known for his elegiac love poetry and for his celebration of peaceful rural life.

tic ▸ **noun** a habitual spasmodic contraction of the muscles, most often in the face.
– ORIGIN early 19th cent.: from French, from Italian *ticchio*.

tic douloureux /tɪk ˌduːləˈruː, -ˈrəː/ ▸ **noun** another term for **TRIGEMINAL NEURALGIA**.
– ORIGIN early 19th cent.: French, literally 'painful tic'.

tich /tɪtʃ/ ▸ **noun** variant spelling of **TITCH**.

Tichborne claimant /ˈtɪtʃbɔːn/ see **ORTON**[1].

Ticino /tiˈtʃiːnəʊ/, Italian /tiˈtsinəʊ/ a predominantly Italian-speaking canton in southern Switzerland, on the Italian border; capital, Bellinzona. It joined the

Swiss Confederation in 1803. French and German name **Tessin**.

tick[1] ▶ **noun 1** Brit. a mark (✓) used to indicate that an item in a list or text is correct or has been chosen, checked, or dealt with.
2 a regular short, sharp sound, especially that made every second by a clock or watch. ■ Brit. informal a moment: *I shan't be a tick | I'll be with you in a tick.*
3 Stock Exchange the smallest recognized amount by which a price of a security or future may fluctuate.
▶ **verb** [with obj.] **1** chiefly Brit. mark (an item) with a tick, typically to show that it has been chosen, checked, approved, or dealt with: *just tick the appropriate box below.*
2 [no obj.] (of a clock or other mechanical device) make regular short, sharp sounds: *I could hear the clock ticking.* ■ (**tick away/by/past**) (of time) pass: *the minutes were ticking away till the actor's appearance.* ■ proceed or progress: *her book was ticking along nicely.*
– PHRASES **tick all the (right) boxes** Brit. informal fulfil all the necessary requirements: *the new album should tick all the right boxes for their many fans.* **what makes someone tick** informal what motivates someone: *people are curious to know what makes British men tick.*
– PHRASAL VERBS **tick someone off 1** Brit. informal reprimand or rebuke someone: *he was ticked off by Angela |* (as noun **ticking off**) *he got a ticking off from the magistrate.* **2** N. Amer. informal make someone annoyed or angry: (as adj. **ticked off**) *Jefferson was a little ticked off, but he'll come around.* **tick something off** chiefly Brit. **1** mark an item in a list with a tick to show that it has been dealt with: *I ticked several items off my 'to do' list.* **2** list items one by one in one's mind or during a speech: *he ticked the points off on his fingers.* **tick over** (of an engine) run slowly in neutral. ■ work or function at a basic or minimum level: *they are keeping things ticking over until their father returns.*
– ORIGIN Middle English (as a verb in the sense 'pat, touch'): probably of Germanic origin and related to Dutch *tik* (noun), *tikken* (verb) 'pat, touch'. The noun was recorded in late Middle English as 'a light tap'; current senses date from the late 17th cent.

tick[2] ▶ **noun 1** a parasitic arachnid which attaches itself to the skin of a terrestrial vertebrate from which it sucks blood, leaving the host when sated. Some species transmit diseases, including tularaemia and Lyme disease. ● Suborder Ixodida, order Acari (or order and subclass).
■ informal a parasitic louse fly, especially the sheep ked.
2 Brit. informal a worthless or contemptible person.
– PHRASES **full** (or **tight**) **as a tick** informal replete after eating (or very drunk).
– ORIGIN Old English *ticia*, of Germanic origin; related to Dutch *teek* and German *Zecke*.

tick[3] ▶ **noun** (in phrase **on tick**) Brit. informal on credit.
– ORIGIN mid 17th cent.: apparently short for **ticket** in the phrase *on the ticket*, referring to an IOU or promise to pay.

tick[4] ▶ **noun** a fabric case stuffed with feathers or other material to form a mattress or pillow. ■ short for **ticking**.
– ORIGIN late Middle English: probably Middle Low German, Middle Dutch *tēke*, or Middle Dutch *tīke*, via West Germanic from Latin *theca* 'case', from Greek *thēkē*.

T

tick bean ▶ **noun** a field bean of a variety with small rounded seeds, used for feeding to pigeons.
– ORIGIN mid 18th cent.: so named from the resemblance of the seeds to dog ticks.

tick-bird ▶ **noun 1** another term for **oxpecker**.
2 South African term for **cattle egret**.

ticker ▶ **noun 1** informal a watch. ■ a person's heart.
2 N. Amer. a telegraphic or electronic machine that prints out data on a strip of paper, especially stock market information or news reports. ■ another term for **news ticker**.

ticker tape ▶ **noun** a paper strip on which messages are recorded in a telegraphic tape machine. ■ [as modifier] denoting a parade or other celebratory event in which ticker tape or similar material is thrown from windows.

ticket ▶ **noun 1** a piece of paper or card that gives the holder a certain right, especially to enter a place, travel by public transport, or participate in an event: *admission is by ticket only.* ■ a receipt for goods that have been received. ■ (**ticket to/out of**) a method of getting into or out of (a specified state or situation): *drugs are seen as the only ticket out of poverty | companies that appeared to have a **one-way ticket to** profitability.*
2 a certificate or warrant, in particular: ■ an official notice of a traffic offence. ■ a certificate of qualification as a ship's master, pilot, or other crew member. ■ Brit. a certificate of discharge from the army.
3 a label attached to a retail product, giving its price, size, and other details.
4 [in sing.] chiefly N. Amer. a list of candidates put forward by a party in an election: *his presence on the Republican ticket.* ■ a set of principles or policies supported by a party in an election: *he stood for office on a strong right-wing, no-nonsense ticket.*
5 (**the ticket**) informal the desirable or correct thing: *a wet spring would be **just the ticket** for the garden.*
6 [with adj.] Scottish & US informal a person of a specified kind: *I think you're all a bunch of sick tickets.*
▶ **verb** (**tickets, ticketing, ticketed**) [with obj.] **1** issue (someone) with an official notice of a traffic offence: *park illegally and you are likely to be ticketed.*
2 (**be ticketed**) (of a passenger) be issued with a travel ticket: *passengers can now get electronically ticketed |* (as adj. **ticketed**) *ticketed passengers.* ■ N. Amer. be destined for a specified state or position: *they were sure that Downing was ticketed for greatness.*
3 (**be ticketed**) (of a retail product) be marked with a label giving its price, size, and other details.
– PHRASES **be tickets** S. African informal be the end: *if that man talks to the police, it's tickets for him.* **have tickets on oneself** Austral./NZ informal be excessively proud of oneself. **punch one's ticket** US informal deliberately undertake particular assignments that are likely to lead to promotion at work. ■ (in sport) ensure one's progress to a further contest or tournament: *in scoring 13 points, they punched their ticket to the Super Bowl in Jacksonville.* **write one's (own) ticket** N. Amer. informal dictate one's own terms.
– DERIVATIVES **ticketless** adjective.
– ORIGIN early 16th cent. (in the general senses 'short written note' and 'a licence or permit'): shortening of obsolete French *étiquet*, from Old French *estiquet(te)*, from *estiquier* 'to fix', from Middle Dutch *steken*. Compare with **etiquette**.

ticket office ▶ **noun** an office or kiosk where tickets are sold.

ticket of leave ▶ **noun** Brit. historical a document granting certain concessions, especially leave, to a prisoner or convict who had served part of their time.

ticket tout ▶ **noun** see **tout**[1] (sense 1 of the noun).

tickety-boo ▶ **adjective** [predic.] Brit. informal, dated in good order; fine: *everything is tickety-boo.*
– ORIGIN 1930s: perhaps from Hindi *ṭhīk hai* 'all right'.

tickey /ˈtɪkiː/ ▶ **noun** (pl. **tickeys**) S. African informal a small silver threepenny piece, withdrawn from circulation in 1961.
– ORIGIN of unknown origin.

tickey box ▶ **noun** S. African informal a public telephone.

tickey-draai /ˈtɪkiːˌdrʌɪ/ ▶ **noun** (pl. **tickey-draais**) S. African a dance involving a fast movement in which couples link hands and spin round on the spot. ■ [mass noun] the music played to accompany a tickey-draai dance.
– ORIGIN partly translating Afrikaans *tiekiedraai*, from *tiekie* **tickey** + *draai* 'a turn' (because of the spinning movement).

tick fever ▶ **noun** [mass noun] any bacterial or rickettsial fever transmitted by the bite of a tick.

ticking ▶ **noun** [mass noun] a strong, durable material, typically striped, used to cover mattresses.
– ORIGIN mid 17th cent.: from **tick**[4] + **-ing**[1].

tickle ▶ **verb** [with obj.] **1** lightly touch or prod (a person or a part of the body) in a way that causes mild discomfort or itching and often laughter: *I tickled him under the ears.* ■ [no obj.] (of a part of the body) have a sensation of mild irritation or discomfort: *his throat had stopped tickling.* ■ catch (a trout) by lightly rubbing it so that it moves backwards into the hand.
2 appeal to (someone's taste, curiosity, etc.): *here are a couple of anecdotes that might **tickle your fancy**.* ■ cause (someone) amusement or pleasure: *he is tickled by the idea.*
▶ **noun** [in sing.] an act of tickling someone: *Dad gave my chin a little tickle.* ■ a sensation like that of being lightly touched or prodded: *I had a tickle between my shoulder blades.*
– PHRASES **be tickled pink** (or **to death**) informal be extremely amused or pleased. **tickle the ivories** informal play the piano.
– ORIGIN Middle English (in the sense 'be delighted or thrilled'): perhaps a frequentative of **tick**[1], or an alteration of Scots and dialect *kittle* 'to tickle' (compare with **kittle**).

tickler ▶ **noun 1** a thing that tickles.
2 N. Amer. a memorandum.

ticklish ▶ **adjective 1** (of a person) sensitive to being tickled: *I'm ticklish on the feet.* ■ (of a cough) characterized by persistent irritation in the throat.
2 (of a situation or problem) difficult or tricky and requiring careful handling: *her skill in evading ticklish questions.* ■ (of a person) easily upset.
– DERIVATIVES **ticklishly** adverb, **ticklishness** noun.

tickly ▶ **adjective** (**ticklier, tickliest**) another term for **ticklish**.

tickover ▶ **noun** [mass noun] the lowest number of revolutions per minute that an engine will run at without stalling.

tickseed ▶ **noun** chiefly N. Amer. another term for **coreopsis**.
– ORIGIN mid 16th cent.: so named because of the resemblance of the seed to a parasitic tick.

tick-tack-toe ▶ **noun** variant spelling of **tic-tac-toe**.

tick-tock ▶ **noun** [in sing.] the sound of a large clock ticking.
▶ **verb** [no obj.] make a ticking sound.
– ORIGIN mid 19th cent.: imitative; compare with **tick**[1].

ticky-tacky N. Amer. informal ▶ **noun** [mass noun] inferior or cheap material, especially as used in suburban building.
▶ **adjective** made of inferior material; cheap or in poor taste: *ticky-tacky little houses.*
– ORIGIN 1960s: probably a reduplication of **tacky**[2].

tic-tac (also **tick-tack**) ▶ **noun** [mass noun] (in the UK) a kind of manual semaphore used by racecourse bookmakers to exchange information.
– ORIGIN mid 16th cent. (denoting a repeated ticking sound): imitative; compare with **tick-tock**. The current usage (originally slang) dates from the late 19th cent.

tic-tac-toe (also **tick-tack-toe**) ▶ **noun** North American term for **noughts and crosses**.
– ORIGIN 1960s: imitative; from *tick-tack*, used earlier to denote games in which the pieces made clicking sounds.

tidal ▶ **adjective** relating to or affected by tides: *the river here is not tidal | strong tidal currents.*
– DERIVATIVES **tidally** adverb.

tidal basin ▶ **noun** a basin for boats which is accessible or navigable only at high tide.

tidal bore ▶ **noun** a large wave or bore caused by the constriction of the spring tide as it enters a long, narrow, shallow inlet.

tidal wave ▶ **noun** an exceptionally large ocean wave, especially one caused by an underwater earthquake or volcanic eruption. ■ a widespread or overwhelming manifestation of an emotion or phenomenon: ***a tidal wave of** crime.*

tidbit ▶ **noun** US spelling of **titbit**.

tiddledywink ▶ **noun** US spelling of **tiddlywink**.

tiddler ▶ **noun** Brit. informal a small fish, especially a stickleback or minnow. ■ a young or unusually small person or thing.
– ORIGIN late 19th cent.: perhaps related to **tiddly**[2] or *tittlebat*, a childish form of *stickleback*.

tiddly[1] ▶ **adjective** (**tiddlier, tiddliest**) Brit. informal slightly drunk: *we were all a little bit tiddly.*
– ORIGIN mid 19th cent. (as a noun denoting an alcoholic drink, particularly of spirits): perhaps from slang *tiddlywink*, denoting an unlicensed public house. The current sense dates from the early 20th cent.

tiddly[2] ▶ **adjective** (**tiddlier, tiddliest**) Brit. informal little; tiny: ***a tiddly little** pool.*
– ORIGIN mid 19th cent.: variant of colloquial *tiddy*, of unknown origin.

tiddlywink (US **tiddledywink**) ▶ **noun 1** (**tiddlywinks**) [treated as sing.] a game in which small plastic counters are flicked into a central receptacle by being pressed on the edge with a larger counter.
2 a counter used in the game of tiddlywinks.
– ORIGIN mid 19th cent.: of unknown origin; perhaps related to **tiddly**[1]. The word originally denoted an unlicensed public house, also a game of dominoes.

tiddy oggy /ˈtɪdi ˌɒgi/ ▶ **noun** Brit. dialect or Nautical slang a Cornish pasty.

– ORIGIN probably from West Country dialect *tiddy* 'potato' and Cornish *hogen* 'pastry'.

tide ▸ **noun** the alternate rising and falling of the sea, usually twice in each lunar day at a particular place, due to the attraction of the moon and sun: *the changing patterns of the tides* | [mass noun] *they were driven on by wind and tide.* ▪ the water as affected by the tide: *the rising tide covered the wharf.* ▪ a powerful surge of feeling or trend of events: *he drifted into sleep on a tide of euphoria* | *we must reverse the growing tide of racism sweeping Europe.*
▸ **verb** [no obj., with adverbial of direction] archaic drift with or as if with the tide. ▪ (of a ship) work in or out of harbour with the help of the tide.
– PHRASAL VERBS **tide someone over** help someone through a difficult period, especially with financial assistance: *she needed a small loan to tide her over.*
– DERIVATIVES **tideless** adjective.
– ORIGIN Old English *tīd* 'time, period, era', of Germanic origin; related to Dutch *tijd* and German *Zeit*, also to TIME. The sense relating to the sea dates from late Middle English.

-tide ▸ **combining form** literary denoting a specified time or season: *springtide.* ▪ denoting a festival of the Christian Church: *Shrovetide.*

tideland ▸ **noun** [mass noun] (also **tidelands**) N. Amer. land that is submerged at high tide.

tideline ▸ **noun** a line left or reached by the sea on a shore at the highest point of a tide.

tidemark ▸ **noun** a mark left or reached by the sea on a shore at the highest point of a tide. ▪ Brit. informal a grimy mark left on a surface, especially around the inside of a bath or washbasin, at the level reached by water.

tide mill ▸ **noun** a mill with a waterwheel driven by the tide.

tide rip ▸ **noun** an area of rough water typically caused by opposing tides or by a rapid current passing over an uneven bottom.

tide table ▸ **noun** a table indicating the times of high and low tides at a particular place.

tidewaiter ▸ **noun** historical a customs officer who boarded ships on their arrival to enforce the customs regulations.

tidewater ▸ **noun** [mass noun] water brought or affected by tides. ▪ N. Amer. an area that is affected by tides, especially eastern Virginia: [as modifier] *tidewater country.*

tideway ▸ **noun** a channel in which a tide runs, especially the tidal part of a river.

tidings ▸ **plural noun** literary news; information: *the bearer of glad tidings.*
– ORIGIN late Old English *tīdung* 'announcement, piece of news', probably from Old Norse *títhindi* 'news of events', from *títhr* 'occurring'.

tidy ▸ **adjective** (**tidier**, **tidiest**) **1** arranged neatly and in order: *his scrupulously tidy apartment* | figurative *the lives they lead don't fit into tidy patterns.* ▪ inclined to keep things or one's appearance neat and in order: *she was a tidy little girl.* ▪ neat and controlled: *he wrote down her replies in a small, tidy hand.*
2 [attrib.] informal (of an amount, especially of money) considerable: *the book will bring in a tidy sum.* ▪ used as a general term of approval: *City have the backbone of a tidy side.*
▸ **noun** (pl. **tidies**) **1** (also **tidy-up**) [in sing.] Brit. an act or spell of tidying something.
2 [usu. with modifier] a receptacle for holding small objects or waste scraps: *a desk tidy.*
3 chiefly US a detachable ornamental cover for a chair back.
▸ **verb** (**tidies**, **tidying**, **tidied**) [with obj.] bring order to; arrange neatly: *the boys have finally tidied their bedroom* | figurative *the Bill is intended to* **tidy up** *the law on this matter* | [no obj.] *I'll just go and* **tidy up**. ▪ (**tidy something away**) put something away for the sake of neatness: *I was tidying away papers in my office.*
– DERIVATIVES **tidily** adverb, **tidiness** noun.
– ORIGIN Middle English: from the noun TIDE + -Y[1]. The original meaning was 'timely, opportune'; it later had various senses expressing approval, usually of a person, including 'attractive', 'healthy', and 'skilful'; the sense 'orderly, neat' dates from the early 18th cent.

tie ▸ **verb** (**ties**, **tying**, **tied**) **1** [with obj. and usu. with adverbial] attach or fasten with string or similar cord: *Gabriel tied up his horse* | *they tied Max to a chair* | *her long hair was tied back in a bow.* ▪ fasten (something) by means of its strings or by forming the ends into a knot or bow: *Lewis tied on his apron.* ▪ form (a string, ribbon, or lace) into a knot or bow. ▪ form (a knot or bow) in a ribbon, lace, etc.: *tie a knot in one end of the cotton.* ▪ [no obj.] be fastened with a knot or bow: *a sarong which ties at the waist.*
2 [with obj.] restrict or limit (someone) to a particular situation or place: *she didn't want to be like her mother,* **tied to** *a feckless man* | *she didn't want to be* **tied down** *by a full-time job.*
3 [with obj.] connect; link: *self-respect is closely* **tied up with** *the esteem in which one is held by one's fellows.* ▪ hold together by a crosspiece or tie: *ceiling joists are used to tie the rafter feet.* ▪ Music unite (written notes) by a tie. ▪ Music perform (two notes) as one unbroken note.
4 [no obj.] achieve the same score or ranking as another competitor or team: *Norman needed a par to* **tie with** *Nicklaus* | [with obj.] *Muir tied the score at 5–5.*
▸ **noun** (pl. **ties**) **1** a piece of string, cord, or similar used for fastening or tying something: *he tightened the tie of his robe.* ▪ US a shoe tied with a lace.
2 a rod or beam holding parts of a structure together. ▪ N. Amer. short for CROSS TIE. ▪ Music a curved line above or below two notes of the same pitch indicating that they are to be played for the combined duration of their time values.
3 (usu. **ties**) a thing that unites or links people: *it is important that we keep family ties strong.* ▪ a thing that restricts someone's freedom of action: *some cities and merchants were freed from feudal ties.*
4 a strip of material worn round the collar and tied in a knot at the front with the ends hanging down, typically forming part of a man's smart or formal outfit.
5 a result in a game or other competitive situation in which two or more competitors or teams have the same score or ranking; a draw: *there was a tie for first place.* ▪ Cricket a game in which the scores are level and both sides have completed their innings, as distinct from a draw (a game left incomplete through lack of time).
6 Brit. a sports match between two or more players or teams in which the winners proceed to the next round of the competition.
– PHRASES **tie someone hand and foot** see HAND. **tie someone (up) in knots** see KNOT[1]. **tie the knot** see KNOT[1]. **tie one on** N. Amer. informal get drunk.
– PHRASAL VERBS **tie something in** (or **tie in**) cause something to fit or harmonize with something else (or fit or harmonize with something): *her husband is able to* **tie in** *his shifts* **with** *hers at the hospital* | *she may have developed ideas which don't necessarily* **tie in with** *mine.* **tie into** N. Amer. informal attack or get to work on vigorously: *tie into breakfast now and let's get a move on.* **tie someone up** bind someone so that they cannot move or escape: *robbers tied her up and ransacked her home.* ▪ informal occupy someone to the exclusion of any other activity: *she would be tied up at the meeting all day.* **tie something up 1** moor a boat. **2** invest or reserve capital so that it is not immediately available for use: *money tied up in accounts must be left to grow.* **3** bring something to a satisfactory conclusion; settle: *he said he had a business deal to tie up.*
– DERIVATIVES **tieless** adjective.
– ORIGIN Old English *tīgan* (verb), *tēah* (noun), of Germanic origin.

tie-back ▸ **noun** a decorative strip of fabric or cord, typically used for holding an open curtain back from the window.

tie beam ▸ **noun** a horizontal beam connecting two rafters in a roof or roof truss.

tiebreaker (also **tiebreak**) ▸ **noun** a means of deciding a winner from competitors who have tied, in particular (in tennis) a special game to decide the winner of a set when the score is six games all.

tie clip ▸ **noun** an ornamental clip for holding a tie in place.

tied ▸ **adjective 1** fastened or attached with string or similar cord: *a neatly tied package.* ▪ Music (of two or more notes) united by a tie and performed as one unbroken note.
2 (of a game or contest) with both or more competitors or teams achieving the same score: *the first tied match in the league* | *a tied vote.*
3 Brit. restricted or limited in some way, in particular: ▪ (of a house) occupied subject to the tenant's working for its owner: *agricultural workers living in tied accommodation.* ▪ (of a pub) owned by a brewery and bound to supply the products produced or specified by that brewery. ▪ (of aid or an international loan) given subject to the condition that it should be spent on goods or services from the donor or lender.

tie-down ▸ **noun** a device to which something may be attached or secured with rope, cord, or similar.

tie-dye ▸ **verb** [with obj.] produce patterns in (a garment or piece of cloth) by tying parts of it to shield it from the dye.
▸ **noun** a tie-dyed garment or piece of fabric.

tief /tiːf/ W. Indian ▸ **verb** [with obj.] steal (something).
▸ **noun** a thief.
– ORIGIN representing a pronunciation of THIEF.

tie-in ▸ **noun** a connection or association: *there's a tie-in to another case I'm working on.* ▪ a book, film, or other product produced to take advantage of a related work in another medium: [as modifier] *a tie-in book.* ▪ [as modifier] chiefly N. Amer. denoting sales made conditional on the purchase of an additional item or items from the same supplier.

tie line ▸ **noun** a transmission line connecting parts of a system, especially a telephone line connecting two private branch exchanges.

tienda /tɪˈɛndə/ ▸ **noun** (in the south-western US) a shop, especially a general store.
– ORIGIN mid 19th cent.: Spanish.

Tien Shan /tjɛn ˈʃan/ (also **Tian Shan**) a range of mountains lying to the north of the Tarim Basin in the Xinjiang autonomous region and eastern Kyrgyzstan. Extending for about 2,500 km (1,500 miles), it rises to 7,439 m (24,406 ft) at Pik Pobedy.

tiento /ˈtjɛntəʊ/ ▸ **noun** (pl. **tientos**) (in 16th- and 17th-century Spanish music) a contrapuntal piece resembling a ricercar, originally for strings and later for organ.
– ORIGIN Spanish, literally 'touch, feel'.

Tientsin /tjɛnˈtʃɪn/ variant of TIANJIN.

tiepin ▸ **noun** an ornamental pin for holding a tie in place.

Tiepolo /tɪˈɛpələʊ/, Giovanni Battista (1696–1770), Italian painter. He painted numerous rococo frescoes and altarpieces including the *Antony and Cleopatra* frescoes in the Palazzo Labia, Venice (*c.*1750), and the decoration of the residence of the Prince-Bishop at Würzburg (1751–3).

tier ▸ **noun** each in a series of rows or levels of a structure placed one above the other: *a tier of seats* | [in combination] *the room was full of three-tier metal bunks.* ▪ each of a number of successively overlapping ruffles or flounces on a garment. ▪ a level or grade within the hierarchy of an organization or system: *companies have taken out a tier of management to save money.*
– DERIVATIVES **tiered** adjective.
– ORIGIN late 15th cent.: from French *tire* 'sequence, order', from *tirer* 'elongate, draw'.

tierce /tɪəs/ ▸ **noun 1** another term for TERCE.
2 Music an organ stop sounding two octaves and a major third above the pitch of the diapason.
3 (in piquet) a sequence of three cards of the same suit.
4 Fencing the third of eight parrying positions.
5 a former measure of wine equal to one third of a pipe, usually equivalent to 35 gallons (about 156 litres). ▪ archaic a cask containing a certain quantity of provisions, the amount varying with the goods.
– ORIGIN late Middle English: variant of TERCE.

tierced /tɪəst/ (also **tiercé** /ˈtjəːseɪ/) ▸ **adjective** Heraldry divided into three equal parts of different tinctures.
– ORIGIN early 18th cent.: originally as *tiercé* 'divided into three parts', French past participle of *tiercer*.

tiercel /ˈtɪəs(ə)l/ ▸ **noun** variant spelling of TERCEL.

tie rod ▸ **noun** a rod acting as a tie in a building or other structure, or in the steering gear of a motor vehicle.

Tierra del Fuego /tɪˌɛːrə dɛl ˈfweɪgəʊ/ an island at the southern extremity of South America, separated from the mainland by the Strait of Magellan. Discovered by Ferdinand Magellan in 1520, it is now divided between Argentina and Chile.
– ORIGIN Spanish, literally 'land of fire'.

tie-up ▸ **noun 1** a link or connection, especially one between commercial companies: *marketing tie-ups.* ▪ US a telecommunications link or network.
2 US a building where cattle are tied up for the night. ▪ a place for mooring a boat.
3 US a traffic hold-up.

TIFF ▸ **noun** Computing a format for image files: [as modifier] *a TIFF image.*
– ORIGIN 1990s: acronym from *tagged image file format.*

T

tiff ▶ **noun** informal a petty quarrel, especially one between friends or lovers: *Joanna had a tiff with her boyfriend*.
– ORIGIN early 18th cent. (denoting a slight outburst of temper): probably of dialect origin.

Tiffany /ˈtɪf(ə)ni/, Louis Comfort (1848–1933), American glass-maker and interior decorator. A leading exponent of American art nouveau, he established an interior decorating firm in New York which produced stained glass, vases, lamps, and mosaic.

tiffany /ˈtɪf(ə)ni/ ▶ **noun** [mass noun] thin gauze muslin.
– ORIGIN early 17th cent.: from Old French *tifanie*, via ecclesiastical Latin from Greek *theophaneia* 'epiphany'. The word is usually taken to be short for *Epiphany silk* or *muslin*, i.e., that worn on Twelfth Night, but may be a humorous allusion to *epiphany* in the sense 'manifestation' (because tiffany is semi-transparent).

tiffin ▶ **noun** [mass noun] dated or Indian a snack or light meal.
– ORIGIN early 19th cent.: apparently from dialect *tiffing* 'sipping', of unknown origin.

tiffin carrier ▶ **noun** chiefly Indian a set of shallow metal food containers which sit on top of each other inside a hinged metal frame fastened by a clasp.

Tiflis /tɪfˈliːs/ official Russian name (1845–1936) for **TBILISI**.

tig ▶ **noun & verb** chiefly Brit. another term for **TAG**[2].
– ORIGIN early 18th cent.: perhaps a variant of the verb **TICK**[1].

tiger ▶ **noun 1** a very large solitary cat with a yellow-brown coat striped with black, native to the forests of Asia but becoming increasingly rare. ● *Panthera tigris*, family Felidae.
■ used to refer to someone fierce, determined, or ambitious: *despite his wound, he still fought like a tiger | one of the sport's young tigers*. ■ (also **tiger economy**) a dynamic economy of one of the smaller East Asian countries, especially that of Singapore, Taiwan, or South Korea. ■ informal, chiefly Austral./NZ a person with an insatiable appetite for something: *I'm a tiger for a bargain*.
2 used in names of tiger moths and striped butterflies, e.g. **scarlet tiger**, **plain tiger**.
3 (**Tigers**) another term for **TAMIL TIGERS**.
– PHRASES **have a tiger by the tail** (also **be riding a tiger**) have embarked on a course of action which proves unexpectedly difficult but which cannot easily or safely be abandoned.
– ORIGIN Middle English: from Old French *tigre*, from Latin *tigris*, from Greek.

Tiger balm ▶ **noun** [mass noun] trademark a mentholated ointment widely used in Eastern medicine for a variety of conditions.

tiger beetle ▶ **noun** a fast-running predatory beetle which has spotted or striped wing cases and flies in sunshine. The larvae live in tunnels from which they snatch passing insect prey. ● Family Cicindelidae: *Cicindela* and other genera.

tiger cat ▶ **noun** a small forest cat that has a light brown coat with dark stripes and blotches, native to Central and South America. ● *Felis tigrina*, family Felidae.
■ any moderate-sized striped cat, such as the ocelot, serval, or margay. ■ Australian term for **QUOLL**.

tiger economy ▶ **noun** see **TIGER** (sense 1).

tiger fish ▶ **noun** any of a number of aggressive predatory fish, in particular: ● a large African characin, popular with anglers (*Hydrocynus vittatus*, family Characidae). ● an edible fish of the Indo-Pacific (*Therapon jarbua*, family Theraponidae).

T

tigerish ▶ **adjective** resembling or likened to a tiger, especially in being fierce and determined: *she was in tigerish mood*.
– DERIVATIVES **tigerishly** adverb.

tiger lily ▶ **noun** a tall Asian lily which has orange flowers spotted with black or purple. ● *Lilium lancifolium* (or *tigrinum*), family Liliaceae.

tiger maple ▶ **noun** [mass noun] N. Amer. the timber of an American maple which contains contrasting light and dark lines.

tiger moth ▶ **noun** a stout moth which has boldly spotted and streaked wings and a hairy caterpillar (woolly bear). ● *Arctia* and other genera, family Arctiidae: many species. See **GARDEN TIGER**.

tiger nut ▶ **noun** the small dried edible tuber of a kind of sedge. ● The sedge is *Cyperus esculentus*, family Cyperaceae.

tiger prawn (also **tiger shrimp**) ▶ **noun** a large edible prawn marked with dark bands, found in the Indian and Pacific oceans. ● Genus *Penaeus*, class Malacostraca: several species, in particular the widely farmed *P. monodon*.

tiger's eye (also **tiger eye**) ▶ **noun** [mass noun] a semi-precious yellowish-brown variety of quartz with a silky or chatoyant lustre, formed by replacement of crocidolite.

tiger shark ▶ **noun** an aggressive shark of warm seas, with dark vertical stripes on the body. ● *Galeocerdo cuvieri*, family Carcharhinidae.

tiger snake ▶ **noun 1** a deadly Australian snake, typically marked with brown and yellow bands. ● Genus *Notechis*, family Elapidae: two species.
2 a very slender harmless nocturnal snake found in Africa. ● Genus *Telescopus*, family Colubridae: several species.

tiger team ▶ **noun** a team of specialists in a particular field brought together to work on specific tasks.

tigerwood ▶ **noun** [mass noun] striped or streaked wood used for cabinetmaking.

tiger worm ▶ **noun** another term for **BRANDLING**.

Tiggerish ▶ **adjective** Brit. very lively, energetic, and cheerful: *his Tiggerish enthusiasm*.
– ORIGIN from *Tigger*, a tiger in A. A. Milne's *Winnie-the-Pooh*, characterized by his vitality.

tight ▶ **adjective 1** fixed, fastened, or closed firmly; hard to move, undo, or open: *she twisted her handkerchief into a tight knot | I prised the tight lid off with my knife*. ■ (of clothes or shoes) close-fitting, especially uncomfortably so: *the dress was too tight for her | a tight-fitting top*. ■ (of a grip) very firm: *she released her tight hold on the dog* | figurative *presidential advisers **keep a tight grip on** domestic policy*. ■ (of a ship, building, or object) well sealed against something such as water or air: [in combination] *a light-tight container*.
2 (of a rope, fabric, or surface) stretched so as to leave no slack; not loose: *the drawcord pulls tight*.
■ (of part of the body) feeling painful and constricted as a result of anxiety or illness: *there was a tight feeling in his gut*. ■ (of appearance or manner) tense, irritated, or angry: *she gave him a tight smile*.
■ (of a rule or form of control) strictly imposed: *security was tight at yesterday's ceremony*. ■ (of a written work or form) concise, condensed, or well structured: *a tight argument*. ■ (of an organization or group of people) disciplined or well coordinated: *the vocalists are strong and the band is tight*.
3 (of an area or space) having or allowing little room for manoeuvre: *a tight parking spot | it was a tight squeeze in the tiny vestibule*. ■ (of a bend, turn, or angle) changing direction sharply; having a short radius. ■ (of money or time) limited or restricted: *David was out of work and money was tight | an ability to work to tight deadlines*.
4 (of a formation or group) closely or densely packed together: *he levered the bishop out from a tight knot of clerical wives*. ■ (of a community or other group of people) having close relations; tight-knit.
5 (of a game or contest) with evenly matched competitors; very close: *he won in a tight finish*.
6 Brit. informal not willing to spend or give much money; mean.
7 [predic.] informal drunk: *he got tight on brandy*.
▶ **adverb** very firmly, closely, or tensely: *he went downstairs, holding tight to the bannisters*.
– PHRASES **run a tight ship** be very strict in managing an organization or operation. **a tight corner** (or **spot** or **place**) a difficult situation: *her talent for talking her way out of tight corners*.
– DERIVATIVES **tightly** adverb, **tightness** noun.
– ORIGIN Middle English (in the sense 'healthy, vigorous', later 'firm, solid'): probably an alteration of *thight* 'firm, solid', later 'close-packed, dense', of Germanic origin; related to German *dicht* 'dense, close'.

tight-ass ▶ **noun** N. Amer. informal an inhibited, repressed, or excessively conventional person.
– DERIVATIVES **tight-assed** adjective.

tighten ▶ **verb** make or become tight or tighter: [with obj.] *he **tightened up** the clips | central government has tightened control over local authority spending* | [no obj.] *his arms tightened around her*.

tight end ▶ **noun** American Football an offensive end who lines up close to the tackle.

tight-fisted ▶ **adjective** informal not willing to spend or give much money; miserly.

tight head ▶ **noun** Rugby the prop forward supporting the hooker on the opposite side of the scrum from the loose head.

tight junction ▶ **noun** Biology a specialized connection of two adjacent animal cell membranes such that the space usually lying between them is absent.

tight-knit (also **tightly knit**) ▶ **adjective** (of a group of people) bound together by strong relationships and common interests: *tight-knit mining communities*.

tight-lipped ▶ **adjective** with the lips firmly closed, especially as a sign of suppressed emotion or determined reticence: *she stayed tight-lipped and shook her head*.

tight money ▶ **noun** [mass noun] Finance money or finance that is available only at high rates of interest.

tightrope ▶ **noun** a rope or wire stretched tightly high above the ground, on which acrobats perform feats of balancing: [as modifier] *a tightrope walker* | figurative *he continues to **walk a tightrope** between success and failure*.
▶ **verb** [no obj.] walk or perform on a tightrope.

tights ▶ **plural noun** a woman's close-fitting garment made of nylon or other knitted yarn, covering the legs, hips, and bottom. ■ a similar garment worn by a dancer or acrobat.

tightwad ▶ **noun** N. Amer. informal a mean or miserly person.

Tiglath-pileser /ˌtɪglaθpʌɪˈliːzə/ the name of three kings of Assyria, notably: ■ **Tiglath-pileser I**, reigned *c.*1115–*c.*1077 BC. He extended Assyrian territory, taking Cappadocia, reaching Syria, and defeating the king of Babylonia. ■ **Tiglath-pileser III**, reigned *c.*745–727 BC. He brought the Assyrian empire to the height of its power, subduing large parts of Syria and Palestine, and conquered Babylonia.

tignon /ˈtiːjɒn/ ▶ **noun** a piece of cloth worn as a turban headdress by Creole women from Louisiana.
– ORIGIN Louisana French, from French *tigne*, dialect variant of *teigne* 'moth'.

tigon /ˈtʌɪg(ə)n/ (also **tiglon** /ˈtʌɪglɒn, ˈtɪg-/) ▶ **noun** the hybrid offspring of a male tiger and a lioness.
– ORIGIN 1920s: portmanteau word from **TIGER** and **LION**.

Tigray /ˈtiːgreɪ/ (also **Tigre**) a province of Ethiopia, in the north of the country, bordering Eritrea; capital, Mekele. An ancient kingdom, Tigray was annexed as a province of Ethiopia in 1855. It engaged in a bitter guerrilla war against the government of Ethiopia 1975–91, during which time the region suffered badly from drought and famine.
– DERIVATIVES **Tigrayan** (also **Tigrean**) **adjective & noun**.

Tigre[1] variant spelling of **TIGRAY**.

Tigre[2] /ˈtiːgreɪ/ ▶ **noun** [mass noun] a Semitic language spoken in Eritrea and adjoining parts of Sudan. It is not the language of Tigray, which is Tigrinya.
– ORIGIN the name in Tigre.

tigress ▶ **noun** a female tiger. ■ a fierce or passionate woman.

Tigrinya /tɪˈgriːnjə/ ▶ **noun** [mass noun] a Semitic language spoken in Tigray, with about 4 million speakers. Compare with **TIGRE**[2].
– ORIGIN the name in Tigrinya.

Tigris /ˈtʌɪgrɪs/ a river in SW Asia, the more easterly of the two rivers of ancient Mesopotamia. It rises in the mountains of eastern Turkey and flows 1,850 km (1,150 miles) south-eastwards through Iraq, passing through Baghdad, to join the Euphrates, forming the Shatt al-Arab, which flows into the Persian Gulf.

Tigua ▶ **noun & adjective** variant spelling of **TIWA**.

Tihwa /tiːˈhwɑː/ former name (until 1954) for **URUMQI**.

Tijuana /tɪˈ(h)wɑːnə/ a town in NW Mexico, situated just south of the US frontier; pop. 1,286,187 (2005).

tika /ˈtiːkɑː/ ▶ **noun** another term for **TILAK**.
– ORIGIN from Hindi *ṭīkā*, from Punjabi *ṭikkā*.

Tikal /tɪˈkɑːl/ an ancient Mayan city in the tropical Petén region of northern Guatemala, with great plazas, pyramids, and palaces. It flourished AD 300–800.

tike ▶ **noun** variant spelling of **TYKE**.

tiki /ˈtɪki/ ▶ **noun** (pl. **tikis**) **1** NZ a large wooden or small greenstone image of a human figure.
2 [as modifier] denoting something that is imitative of objects or customs associated with the tropical islands of the South Pacific: *a tiki bar | tiki huts*.
– ORIGIN Maori, literally 'image'. Sense 2 represents an independent development, which first became widespread in the mid 20th century in the US tourist industry.

tikia /ˈtɪkɪɑː/ ▶ **noun** an Indian fried cake of spiced meat or mashed potato.
– ORIGIN from Hindi *ṭikiā*.

tiki torch ▶ **noun** an outdoor light that burns gas or oil and is attached to the end of a long pole fixed into the ground.

tikka /ˈtɪkə, ˈtiːkə/ ▶ **noun** [mass noun] [usu. with modifier] an Indian dish of small pieces of meat or vegetables marinated in a spice mixture: *lamb tikka*.
– ORIGIN from Punjabi *ṭikkā*.

tilak /ˈtɪlʌk/ ▶ **noun** a mark worn by a Hindu on the forehead to indicate caste, status, or sect, or as an ornament.
– ORIGIN from Sanskrit *tilaka*.

tilapia /tɪˈleɪpɪə, -ˈlap-/ ▶ **noun** an African freshwater cichlid fish that has been widely introduced to many areas for food, such as St Peter's fish. ● *Tilapia* and related genera, family Cichlidae: several species.
– ORIGIN modern Latin, of unknown origin.

Tilburg /ˈtɪlbəːɡ/ an industrial city in the southern Netherlands, in the province of North Brabant; pop. 202,091 (2008).

Tilbury /ˈtɪlb(ə)ri/ the principal container port of London and SE England, on the north bank of the River Thames.

tilbury /ˈtɪlb(ə)ri/ ▶ **noun** (pl. **tilburies**) historical a light open two-wheeled carriage.
– ORIGIN early 19th cent.: named after its inventor.

tilde /ˈtɪldə/ ▶ **noun** an accent (˜) placed over Spanish *n* when pronounced *ny* (as in *señor*) or Portuguese *a* or *o* when nasalized (as in *São Paulo*), or over a vowel in phonetic transcription, indicating nasalization. ■ a symbol similar to a tilde used in mathematics and logic to indicate negation, inversion, etc.
– ORIGIN mid 19th cent.: from Spanish, based on Latin *titulus* (see TITLE).

tile /tʌɪl/ ▶ **noun** a thin rectangular slab of baked clay or other material, used in overlapping rows for covering roofs. ■ a thin square slab of glazed pottery or other material for covering floors, walls, or other surfaces. ■ a thin, flat piece used in Scrabble, mah-jong, and certain other games. ■ Mathematics a plane shape used in tiling.
▶ **verb** [with obj.] cover with tiles: *the lobby was tiled in blue*. ■ Computing arrange (two or more windows) on a computer screen so that they do not overlap.
– PHRASES **on the tiles** informal, chiefly Brit. having a lively night out: *it won't be the first time he's spent a night on the tiles*.
– ORIGIN Old English *tigele*, from Latin *tegula*, from an Indo-European root meaning 'cover'.

tilefish ▶ **noun** (pl. **same** or **tilefishes**) a long, slender bottom-dwelling fish of warm seas. ● Several species in the family Malacanthidae (or Branchiostegidae), in particular the large and edible *Lopholatilus chamaeleonticeps* of the Atlantic coast of North America.

tiler ▶ **noun 1** a person who lays tiles: *a roof tiler*.
2 the doorkeeper of a Freemasons' lodge, who prevents outsiders from entering.

tiling ▶ **noun** [mass noun] **1** a surface covered by tiles: *an area of plain tiling*.
2 Mathematics a way of arranging identical plane shapes so that they completely cover an area without overlapping.

till[1] ▶ **preposition & conjunction** less formal way of saying UNTIL.
– ORIGIN Old English *til*, of Germanic origin; related to Old Norse *til* 'to', also ultimately to TILL[3].

> **USAGE** In most contexts till and until have the same meaning and are interchangeable. The main difference is that **till** is generally considered to be the more informal of the two, and occurs less frequently than **until** in writing. **Until** also tends to be the natural choice at the beginning of a sentence: *until very recently, there was still a chance of rescuing the situation*.
> Interestingly, while it is commonly assumed that **till** is an abbreviated form of until (the spellings **'till** and **'til** reflect this), **till** is in fact the earlier form. **Until** appears to have been formed by the addition of Old Norse *und* 'as far as' several hundred years after the date of the first records for **till**.

till[2] ▶ **noun** a cash register or drawer for money in a shop, bank, or restaurant.
– PHRASES **have** (or **with**) **one's fingers** (or **hand**) **in the till** used in reference to theft from one's place of work: *he was caught with his hand in the till and sacked*.
– ORIGIN late Middle English (in the general sense 'drawer or compartment for valuables'): of unknown origin.

till[3] ▶ **verb** [with obj.] prepare and cultivate (land) for crops: *no land was being tilled or crops sown*.
– DERIVATIVES **tillable** adjective.
– ORIGIN Old English *tilian* 'strive for, obtain by effort', of Germanic origin; related to Dutch *telen* 'produce, cultivate' and German *zielen* 'aim, strive', also ultimately to TILL[1]. The current sense dates from Middle English.

till[4] ▶ **noun** [mass noun] Geology boulder clay or other sediment deposited by melting glaciers or ice sheets.
– ORIGIN late 17th cent. (originally Scots, denoting shale): of unknown origin.

tillage /ˈtɪlɪdʒ/ ▶ **noun** [mass noun] the preparation of land for growing crops. ■ land under cultivation: *forty acres of tillage*.

tiller[1] ▶ **noun** a horizontal bar fitted to the head of a boat's rudder post and used for steering.
– ORIGIN late Middle English: from Anglo-Norman French *telier* 'weaver's beam, stock of a crossbow', from medieval Latin *telarium*, from Latin *tela* 'web'.

tiller[2] ▶ **noun** a lateral shoot from the base of the stem of a plant, especially in a grass or cereal.
▶ **verb** [no obj.] (usu. as noun **tillering**) (of a plant) develop tillers.
– ORIGIN mid 17th cent. (denoting a sapling arising from the stool of a felled tree): apparently based on Old English *telga* 'bough', of Germanic origin.

tiller[3] ▶ **noun** an implement or machine for breaking up soil; a plough or cultivator.

tilleul /tɪˈjəːl/ ▶ **noun** a lime or linden tree. ■ [mass noun] a tea made from an infusion of the flowers of the lime or linden tree, originally used as a remedy for headache.
– ORIGIN mid 16th cent.: from French, from a diminutive form of Latin *tilia* 'linden'.

tilley lamp /ˈtɪli/ (also **tilly lamp**) ▶ **noun** trademark a portable oil or paraffin lamp in which air pressure is used to supply the burner with fuel.
– ORIGIN 1930s: from the name of the manufacturers.

Tillich /ˈtɪlɪk/, Paul (Johannes) (1886–1965), German-born American theologian and philosopher. He proposed a form of Christian existentialism. Notable works: *Systematic Theology* (1951–63).

tillite /ˈtɪlʌɪt/ ▶ **noun** [mass noun] Geology sedimentary rock composed of compacted glacial till.

Tilsit /ˈtɪlsɪt/ ▶ **noun** [mass noun] a semi-hard mild cheese.
– ORIGIN named after the town in East Prussia (now Sovetsk, Russia) where it was first produced.

tilt ▶ **verb 1** move or cause to move into a sloping position: [no obj.] *the floor tilted slightly* | [with obj.] *he tilted his head to one side*. ■ change or cause to change in favour of one person or thing as opposed to another: [no obj.] *the balance of industrial power tilted towards the workers*. ■ [with obj.] move (a camera) in a vertical plane.
2 [no obj.] (**tilt at**) historical (in jousting) thrust at with a lance or other weapon: *he tilts at his prey* | figurative *the lonely hero tilting at the system*. ■ (**tilt with**) archaic engage in a contest with: *I resolved never to tilt with a French lady in compliment*.
▶ **noun 1** a sloping position or movement: *the tilt of her head*. ■ an upwards or downwards pivoting movement of a camera: *pans and tilts*. ■ an inclination or bias: *the paper's tilt towards the United States*.
2 historical a combat for exercise or sport between two men on horseback with lances; a joust. ■ (**tilt at**) an attempt at winning (something) or defeating (someone): *a tilt at the European Cup*.
3 Canadian a small hut in a forest.
– PHRASES **(at) full tilt** with maximum energy or force; at top speed. **tilt at windmills** attack imaginary enemies or evils. [with allusion to Cervantes' story of Don Quixote tilting at windmills, believing they were giants.]
– DERIVATIVES **tilter** noun.
– ORIGIN late Middle English (in the sense 'fall or cause to fall, topple'): perhaps related to Old English *tealt* 'unsteady', or perhaps of Scandinavian origin and related to Norwegian *tylten* 'unsteady' and Swedish *tulta* 'totter'.

tilth ▶ **noun** [mass noun] cultivation of land; tillage. ■ [in sing.] the condition of tilled soil, especially in respect to suitability for sowing seeds: *he could determine whether the soil was of the right tilth*. ■ prepared surface soil.
– ORIGIN Old English *tilth*, *tilthe*, from *tilian* (see TILL[3]).

tilt hammer ▶ **noun** a heavy pivoted hammer used in forging, raised mechanically and allowed to drop on the metal being worked.

tilt yard ▶ **noun** historical a place where jousts took place.

Tim. ▶ **abbreviation** Timothy (especially in biblical references).

Timaru /ˈtɪməru:/ a port on the east coast of the South Island, New Zealand; pop. 26,900 (est. 2006).

timbal /ˈtɪmb(ə)l/ ▶ **noun** archaic a kettledrum.
– ORIGIN late 17th cent.: from French *timbale*, alteration (influenced by *cymbale* 'cymbal') of obsolete *tamballe*, from Spanish *atabal*, from Arabic *aṭ-ṭabl* 'the drum'.

timbale /tamˈbɑːl/ ▶ **noun 1** a dish of finely minced meat or fish cooked with other ingredients in a pastry shell or in a mould.
2 (**timbales**) paired cylindrical drums played with sticks in Latin American dance music.
– ORIGIN French, 'drum' (in sense 1 with reference to the shape of the prepared dish; in sense 2 short for *timbales cubains* or *timbales creoles* 'Cuban' or 'creole drums').

timber ▶ **noun** [mass noun] **1** wood prepared for use in building and carpentry: *the exploitation of forests for timber* | [as modifier] *a small timber building*. ■ trees grown for use in building or carpentry: *contracts to cut timber*. ■ [count noun] (usu. **timbers**) a wooden beam or board used in building a house or ship. ■ [as exclamation] used to warn that a tree is about to fall after being cut: *we cried 'Timber!' as our tree fell*.
2 [usu. with adj.] US informal personal qualities or character: *she is frequently hailed as presidential timber*.
– ORIGIN Old English in the sense 'a building', also 'building material', of Germanic origin; related to German *Zimmer* 'room', from an Indo-European root meaning 'build'.

timbered ▶ **adjective 1** (of a building) made wholly or partly of timber: *black-and-white timbered buildings*. ■ (of the walls or other surface of a room) covered with wooden panels: *the timbered banqueting hall*.
2 having many trees; wooded.

timber-frame ▶ **adjective** denoting a house or other structure having a wooden frame.
▶ **noun** [mass noun] pre-prepared sections of wood used for building a house.
– DERIVATIVES **timber-framed** adjective **timber-framing** noun.

timber-getter ▶ **noun** Austral. a lumberjack.

timber hitch ▶ **noun** a knot used in attaching a rope to a log or spar.

timbering ▶ **noun** [mass noun] wood as a building material, or finished work built from wood.

timberland ▶ **noun** [mass noun] (also **timberlands**) N. Amer. land covered with forest suitable or managed for timber.

timberline ▶ **noun** chiefly N. Amer. another term for TREELINE.

timberman ▶ **noun** (pl. **timbermen**) **1** a person who works with timber.
2 a greyish-brown longhorn beetle with extremely long antennae, occurring in the old pine forests of northern Europe. The wood-boring larvae live chiefly in fallen or felled trees. ● *Acanthocinus aedilis*, family Cerambycidae.

timber wolf ▶ **noun** a wolf of a large variety found mainly in northern North America, with grey brindled fur. Also called GREY WOLF.

T

timbre /ˈtambə/ ▶ **noun** the character or quality of a musical sound or voice as distinct from its pitch and intensity: *trumpet mutes with different timbres* | [mass noun] *a voice high in pitch but rich in timbre*. ■ [mass noun] the distinctive quality or character of someone or something: *you must demonstrate your moral timbre as a human being*.
– ORIGIN mid 19th cent.: from French, from medieval Greek *timbanon*, from Greek *tumpanon* 'drum'.

timbrel /ˈtɪmbr(ə)l/ ▶ **noun** archaic a tambourine or similar instrument.
– ORIGIN early 16th cent.: perhaps a diminutive of obsolete *timbre*, in the same sense, from Old French (see TIMBRE).

Timbuktu /ˌtɪmbʌkˈtuː/ (also **Timbuctoo**) a town in northern Mali; pop. 35,600 (est. 2009). It was formerly a major trading centre for gold and salt on the trans-Saharan trade routes, reaching the height of its prosperity in the 16th century but falling into decline after its capture by the Moroccans in 1591. French name TOMBOUCTOU. ■ used in reference to a remote or extremely distant place: *from here to Timbuktu*.

time ▸ noun **1** [mass noun] the indefinite continued progress of existence and events in the past, present, and future regarded as a whole: *travel through space and time | one of the greatest wits of all time*. ■ the progress of this as affecting people and things: *things were getting better as time passed*. ■ time or an amount of time as reckoned by a conventional standard: *it's eight o'clock New York Time*. ■ (**Time** or **Father Time**) the personification of time, typically as an old man with a scythe and hourglass.
2 a point of time as measured in hours and minutes past midnight or noon: *the time is 9.30*. ■ a moment or definite portion of time allotted, used, or suitable for a purpose: *the scheduled departure time | shall we fix a time for the meeting?* ■ (often **time for/to do something**) the favourable or appropriate time to do something: *it was time to go | it's time for bed*. ■ (**a time**) an indefinite period: *travelling always distorts one's feelings for a time*. ■ (also **times**) a portion of time in history or characterized by particular events or circumstances: *Victorian times | at the time of Galileo | the park is beautiful at this time of year*. ■ (also **times**) the conditions of life during a particular period: *times have changed*. ■ (**the Times**) used in names of newspapers: *the Oxford Times*. ■ (**one's time**) one's lifetime: *I've known a lot of women in my time*. ■ (**one's time**) the successful, fortunate, or influential part of a person's life or career: *in my time that was unheard of*. ■ (**one's time**) the appropriate or expected time for something, in particular childbirth or death: *he seemed old before his time*. ■ an apprenticeship: *engineering officers traditionally **served their time** as fitters in the yards*. ■ dated a period of menstruation or pregnancy. ■ [mass noun] the normal rate of pay for time spent working: *if called out at the weekend they are **paid time and a half***. ■ the length of time taken to run a race or complete an event or journey: *his time for the mile was 3:49.31*. ■ Brit. the moment at which the opening hours of a pub end: *the landlord **called time***. ■ short for FULL TIME:: *he scored the third five minutes from time*. ■ Baseball & American Football a moment at which play stops temporarily within a game: *the umpire **called time***.
3 [mass noun] time as allotted, available, or used: *we need more time | it would be a waste of time*. ■ informal a prison sentence: *he was **doing time for** fraud*.
4 an instance of something happening or being done; an occasion: *this is the first time I have got into debt | the nurse came in four times a day*. ■ an event, occasion, or period experienced in a particular way: *she was **having a rough time of it***.
5 (**times**) (following a number) expressing multiplication: *eleven times four is forty-four*.
6 [mass noun] the rhythmic pattern of a piece of music, as expressed by a time signature: *tunes **in waltz time***. ■ the tempo at which a piece of music is played or marked to be played.
▸ verb **1** [with obj. and adverbial or infinitive] plan, schedule, or arrange when (something) should happen or be done: *the first track race is timed for 11.15 | the bomb had been timed to go off an hour later*. ■ perform (an action) at a particular moment: *Williams timed his pass perfectly from about thirty yards*.
2 [with obj.] measure the time taken by (a process or activity, or a person doing it): *we were timed and given certificates according to our speed* | [with clause] *I timed how long it took to empty that tanker*.
3 [with obj.] (**time something out**) Computing (of a computer or a program) cancel an operation automatically because a predefined interval of time has passed without a certain event happening. ■ (**time out**) (of an operation) be cancelled in this way.
– PHRASES **about time** used to convey that something now happening or about to happen should have happened earlier: *it's about time I came clean and admitted it*. **against time** with utmost speed, so as to finish by a specified time: *he was working against time*. **ahead of time** earlier than expected or required. **ahead of one's time** having ideas too enlightened or advanced to be accepted by one's contemporaries. **all the time** constantly or very frequently: *the airfield was in use all the time*. **at one time** in or during a known but unspecified past period: ***she was a nurse at one time***. **at the same time 1** simultaneously; at once. **2** nevertheless (used to introduce a fact that should be taken into account): *I can't really explain it, but at the same time I'm not convinced*. **at a time** separately in the specified groups or numbers: *he took the stairs two at a time*. **at times** sometimes; on occasions. **before time** before the due or expected time. **behind time** late. **behind the times** not aware of or using the latest ideas or techniques; out of date. **for the time being** for the present; until some other arrangement is made. **give someone the time of day** [usu. with negative] be pleasantly polite or friendly to someone: *I wouldn't give him the time of day if I could help it*. **half the time** as often as not. **have no time for** be unable or unwilling to spend time on: *he had no time for anything except essays and projects*. ■ dislike or disapprove of: *he's got no time for airheads*. **have the time 1** be able to spend the time needed to do something: *she didn't have the time to look very closely*. **2** know from having a watch what time it is. **in (less than) no time** very quickly or very soon: *the video has sold 30,000 copies in no time*. **in one's own time 1** (also **in one's own good time**) at a time and a rate decided by oneself. **2** (US **on one's own time**) outside working hours; without being paid. **in time 1** not late; punctual: *I came back **in time for** Molly's party*. **2** eventually: *there is the danger that he might, in time, not be able to withstand temptation*. **3** in accordance with the appropriate musical rhythm or tempo. **keep good** (or **bad**) **time 1** (of a clock or watch) record time accurately (or inaccurately). **2** (of a person) be habitually punctual (or not punctual). **keep time** play or rhythmically accompany music in time. **lose no time** do a specified thing as soon as possible: *the administration **lost no time in** trying to regain the initiative*. **not before time** used to convey that something now happening or about to happen should have happened earlier. **no time** a very short interval or period: *the renovations were done **in no time***. **on time** punctual; punctually: *the train was on time | we paid our bills on time*. **out of time** at the wrong time or period: *I felt that I was born out of time*. **pass the time of day** exchange greetings or casual remarks. **time after time** (also **time and again** or **time and time again**) on very many occasions; repeatedly. **time and tide wait for no man** proverb if you don't make use of a favourable opportunity, you may never get the same chance again. **time immemorial** a time in the past that was so long ago that people have no knowledge or memory of it: *markets had been held there **from time immemorial***. **time is money** proverb time is a valuable resource, therefore it's better to do things as quickly as possible. **the time of one's life** a period or occasion of exceptional enjoyment. **time out of mind** another way of saying TIME IMMEMORIAL. **time was** there was a time when: *time was, each street had its own specialized trade*. **(only) time will tell** the truth or correctness of something will (only) be established at some time in the future.
– ORIGIN Old English *tīma*, of Germanic origin; related to TIDE, which it superseded in temporal senses. The earliest of the current verb senses (dating from late Middle English) is 'do (something) at a particular moment'.

time-and-motion study ▸ noun a procedure in which the efficiency of an industrial or other operation is evaluated.

time ball ▸ noun a timepiece consisting of a sphere which at a certain moment each day is allowed to fall down a vertical rod.

time base ▸ noun Electronics a signal for uniformly and repeatedly deflecting the electron beam of a cathode ray tube. ■ a line on the display produced in this way and serving as a time axis.

time bomb ▸ noun a bomb designed to explode at a preset time. ■ a developing and problematic situation which will eventually become dangerous if not addressed: *the demographic time bomb*.

time capsule ▸ noun a container storing a selection of objects chosen as being typical of the present time, buried for discovery in the future.

time clock ▸ noun **1** a clock with a device for recording employees' times of arrival and departure.
2 a switch mechanism activated at preset times by a built-in clock.

time code ▸ noun a coded signal on videotape or film giving information about such things as frame number, time of recording, or exposure.

time constant ▸ noun Physics a time which represents the speed with which a particular system can respond to change, typically equal to the time taken for a specified parameter to vary by a factor of $1 - 1/e$ (approximately 0.6321).

time-consuming ▸ adjective taking a lot of or too much time: *an extremely time-consuming process*.

time deposit ▸ noun a deposit in a bank account that cannot be withdrawn before a set date or for which notice of withdrawal is required.

time difference ▸ noun **1** the difference in standard time between places in different time zones.
2 the difference in the time at which two things happen or in how long they last.

time division multiplex ▸ noun [mass noun] Telecommunications a technique for transmitting two or more signals over the same telephone line, radio channel, or other medium. Each signal is sent as a series of pulses or packets, which are interleaved with those of the other signal or signals and transmitted as a continuous stream. Compare with FREQUENCY DIVISION MULTIPLEX.

time domain ▸ noun Physics time considered as an independent variable in the analysis or measurement of time-dependent phenomena.

time domain reflectometer ▸ noun see REFLECTOMETER.

time exposure ▸ noun the exposure of photographic film for longer than the maximum normal shutter setting.

time frame ▸ noun a specified period of time in which something occurs or is planned to take place: *the work had to be done in a time frame of fourteen working days*.

time fuse ▸ noun a fuse calculated to burn for or explode a bomb, shell, or explosive charge at a specified time.

time-honoured ▸ adjective (of a custom or tradition) respected or valued because it has existed for a long time.

timekeeper ▸ noun **1** a person who measures or records the amount of time taken, especially in a sports competition.
2 [usu. with adj.] a person regarded as being punctual or not punctual: *we were good timekeepers*. ■ a watch or clock regarded as recording time accurately or inaccurately: *these watches are accurate timekeepers*. ■ archaic a clock.
– DERIVATIVES **timekeeping** noun.

time lag ▸ noun see LAG[1] (sense 1 of the noun).

time-lapse ▸ adjective denoting the photographic technique of taking a sequence of frames at set intervals to record changes that take place slowly over time. When the frames are shown at normal speed the action seems much faster.

timeless ▸ adjective not affected by the passage of time or changes in fashion: *antiques add to the timeless atmosphere of the dining room*.
– DERIVATIVES **timelessly** adverb, **timelessness** noun.

time limit ▸ noun a limit of time within which something must be done.
– DERIVATIVES **time-limited** adjective.

timeline ▸ noun a graphical representation of a period of time, on which important events are marked.

time lock ▸ noun a lock fitted with a device that prevents it from being unlocked until a set time. ■ a device built into a computer program to stop it operating after a certain time.
▸ verb (**time-lock**) [with obj.] secure (a door or other locking mechanism) with a time lock.

timely ▸ adjective (**timelier**, **timeliest**) done or occurring at a favourable or useful time; opportune: *a timely warning*.
– DERIVATIVES **timeliness** noun.

time machine ▸ noun (in science fiction) a machine capable of transporting a person backwards or forwards in time.

time off ▸ noun [mass noun] time for rest or recreation away from one's usual work or studies: *we're too busy to take time off*.

time-of-flight ▸ adjective Physics relating to or denoting techniques and apparatus that depend on the time taken by subatomic particles to traverse a set distance.

timeous /'tʌɪməs/ ▸ adjective chiefly Scottish in good time; sufficiently early: *ensure timeous completion and posting of applications*.
– DERIVATIVES **timeously** adverb.

time out ▸ noun **1** [mass noun] time for rest or recreation away from one's usual work or studies: *she is **taking time out** from her hectic tour*. ■ a brief period of time during which a misbehaving child is put on their own so that they can regain control over their emotions.
2 (**timeout**) a brief break in play in a game or sport: *he called for a timeout from the game*.

T

3 (**timeout**) Computing a cancellation or cessation that automatically occurs when a predefined interval of time has passed without a certain event occurring.

timepass ▶ noun [mass noun] Indian the action or fact of passing the time, typically in an aimless or unproductive way: *college has become a euphemism for three years of timepass.*

timepiece ▶ noun an instrument, such as a clock or watch, for measuring time.

timer ▶ noun **1** an automatic mechanism for activating a device at a preset time: *a video timer.* ■ a person or device that measures or records the amount of time taken by a process or activity.
2 [in combination] used to indicate how many times someone has done something: *for most first-timers the success rate is 45 per cent.*

time-release ▶ adjective denoting something, especially a drug preparation, that releases an active substance gradually.

time-resolved ▶ adjective Physics & Chemistry relating to or denoting a spectroscopic technique in which a spectrum is obtained at a series of time intervals after excitation of the sample.

time reversal ▶ noun Physics a transformation in which the passage of time, and so all velocities, are represented as reversed.

times ▶ verb (**timeses, timesing, timesed**) [with obj.] informal multiply (a number): *you times the six by four to get twenty-four.*
– ORIGIN late 20th cent.: use as a verb of *times* expressing multiplication (dating from late Middle English): see TIME (sense 5 of the noun).

timescale ▶ noun the time allowed for or taken by a process or sequence of events: *climatic changes on a timescale of tens of thousands of years.*

time series ▶ noun Statistics a series of values of a quantity obtained at successive times, often with equal intervals between them.

time-served ▶ adjective Brit. having completed a period of apprenticeship or training: *all the carpet-fitters are time-served experts.*

time-server ▶ noun **1** a person who makes very little effort at work because they are waiting to leave or retire.
2 a person who changes their views to suit the prevailing circumstances or fashion.
3 (**time server**) Computing a server that distributes synchronized time information to all members of a network.
– DERIVATIVES **time-serving** adjective.

timeshare ▶ noun [mass noun] the arrangement whereby several joint owners have the right to use a property as a holiday home under a time-sharing scheme: *a growing interest in timeshare.* ■ [count noun] a timeshare property.

time-sharing ▶ noun [mass noun] **1** the use of a property as a holiday home at specified times by several joint owners.
2 the operation of a computer system by several users for different operations at the same time.

time sheet ▶ noun a piece of paper for recording the number of hours worked.

time-shift ▶ verb **1** [no obj.] move from one period in time to another.
2 [with obj.] record (a television programme) for later viewing.
▶ noun (**time shift**) a movement from one period in time to another, especially in a play or film.

time signal ▶ noun an audible signal indicating the exact time of day, especially one broadcast by radio at certain times.

time signature ▶ noun Music an indication of rhythm following a clef, generally expressed as a fraction with the denominator defining the beat as a division of a semibreve and the numerator giving the number of beats in each bar.

time slice ▶ noun a short interval of time during which a computer or its central processor deals uninterruptedly with one user or program, before switching to another.

time span ▶ noun a period of time between fixed points or marked by the continuation of a particular process: *the time span of one human life.*

times table ▶ noun informal term for MULTIPLICATION TABLE.

time switch ▶ noun a switch automatically activated at a preset time.

timetable ▶ noun a chart showing the departure and arrival times of trains, buses, or aircraft. ■ a plan of times at which events are scheduled to take place, especially towards a particular end: *the acceleration of the timetable for monetary union.* ■ Brit. a chart showing how the weekly time of a school or college is allotted to classes.
▶ verb [with obj.] schedule (something) to take place at a particular time: *German lessons were timetabled on Wednesday and Friday.*

time travel ▶ noun [mass noun] (in science fiction) travel through time into the past or the future.
– DERIVATIVES **time traveller** noun.

time trial ▶ noun **1** (in various sports) a test of a competitor's individual speed over a set distance, especially a cycling race in which competitors are separately timed.
2 an exercise designed to test the time needed for a task or activity.

time warp ▶ noun (especially in science fiction) an imaginary distortion of space in relation to time whereby people or objects of one period can be moved to another.

time-wasting ▶ noun [mass noun] the action of wasting time. ■ the tactic of slowing down play towards the end of a match to prevent the opposition scoring.
– DERIVATIVES **time-waster** noun.

time-worn ▶ adjective damaged or made less interesting or attractive as a result of age or much use: *the time-worn faces of the veterans | a time-worn aphorism.*

time zone ▶ noun see ZONE (sense 1 of the noun).

timid ▶ adjective (**timider, timidest**) showing a lack of courage or confidence; easily frightened: *I was too timid to ask for what I wanted.*
– DERIVATIVES **timidity** noun, **timidly** adverb, **timidness** noun.
– ORIGIN mid 16th cent.: from Latin *timidus*, from *timere* 'to fear'.

timing ▶ noun [mass noun] the choice, judgement, or control of when something should be done: *one of the secrets of cricket is good timing.* ■ [count noun] a particular point or period of time when something happens. ■ (in an internal-combustion engine) the times when the valves open and close, and the time of the ignition spark, in relation to the movement of the piston in the cylinder.

Timişoara /ˌtɪmɪˈʃwɑːrə/ an industrial city in western Romania; pop. 303,796 (2006). Formerly part of Hungary, the city has substantial Hungarian and German-speaking populations. Hungarian name TEMESVÁR.

timocracy /tɪˈmɒkrəsi/ ▶ noun (pl. **timocracies**) chiefly Philosophy **1** a form of government in which possession of property is required in order to hold office.
2 a form of government in which rulers are motivated by ambition or love of honour.
– DERIVATIVES **timocratic** adjective.
– ORIGIN late 15th cent.: from Old French *timocracie*, via medieval Latin from Greek *timokratia*, from *timē* 'honour, worth' + *-kratia* 'power'. Sense 1 reflects Aristotle's usage, sense 2 Plato's.

timolol /ˈtɪməlɒl/ ▶ noun [mass noun] Medicine a synthetic compound which acts as a beta blocker and is used to treat hypertension, migraine, and glaucoma. ● Chem. formula: $C_{13}H_{24}N_4O_3$.
– ORIGIN 1970s: from *tim-* (of unknown origin) + *(propran)olol.*

Timor /ˈtiːmɔː/ the largest of the Lesser Sunda Islands, in the southern Malay Archipelago.

> The island was formerly divided into Dutch West Timor and Portuguese East Timor. In 1950 West Timor was absorbed into the newly formed Republic of Indonesia. In 1975 East Timor declared itself independent but was invaded and occupied by Indonesia. It became an independent country in 2002 (see EAST TIMOR).

– DERIVATIVES **Timorese** /ˌtiːmɔːˈriːz/ adjective & noun.

Timor deer ▶ noun another term for RUSA.

Timor Leste /tiːˌmɔː ˈleʃteɪ/ official name of EAST TIMOR.

timorous ▶ adjective showing or suffering from nervousness or a lack of confidence: *a timorous voice.*
– DERIVATIVES **timorously** adverb, **timorousness** noun.
– ORIGIN late Middle English (in the sense 'feeling fear'): from Old French *temoreus*, from medieval Latin *timorosus*, from Latin *timor* 'fear', from *timere* 'to fear'.

Timor pony ▶ noun a small stocky pony of a breed originally from Timor, widely used on ranches in Australia.

Timor Sea an arm of the Indian Ocean between Timor and NW Australia.

timothy (also **timothy grass**) ▶ noun [mass noun] a Eurasian grass which is widely grown for grazing and hay. It is naturalized in North America, where many cultivars have been developed. ● *Phleum pratense*, family Gramineae.
– ORIGIN mid 18th cent.: named after *Timothy* Hanson, the American farmer who introduced it to Carolina from New York (*c.*1720).

Timothy, Epistle to either of two books of the New Testament, epistles of St Paul addressed to St Timothy.

Timothy, St (1st century AD), convert and disciple of St Paul. Traditionally he was the first bishop of Ephesus and was martyred in the reign of the Roman emperor Nerva. Feast day, January 22 or 26.

timpani /ˈtɪmpəni/ (also **tympani**) ▶ plural noun kettledrums, especially when played by one musician in an orchestra.
– DERIVATIVES **timpanist** noun.
– ORIGIN late 19th cent.: from Italian, plural of *timpano* 'kettledrum', from Latin *tympanum* 'drum' (see TYMPANUM).

Timur /tiːˈmʊə/ Tartar name of TAMERLANE.

tin ▶ noun **1** [mass noun] a silvery-white metal, the chemical element of atomic number 50. (Symbol: **Sn**) ■ short for TINPLATE. ■ Brit. informal, dated money.

> Tin is quite a rare element, occurring chiefly in the mineral cassiterite. Pure crystalline tin exists in two allotropic modifications, the metallic form (**white tin**), and a semimetallic form (**grey tin**). It is used in various alloys, notably bronze, and for electroplating iron or steel sheets to make tinplate.

2 an airtight container made of tinplate or aluminium: *Albert got out the biscuit tin.* ■ Brit. an airtight sealed container for preserving food, made of tinplate or aluminium; a can: *she had opened a tin of beans.* ■ the contents of a tin: *how many tins of paint would it take?* ■ Brit. an open metal container for baking food: *grease a 450g loaf tin.* ■ Brit. a rectangular loaf of bread baked in such a tin.
▶ verb (**tins, tinning, tinned**) [with obj.] cover with a thin layer of tin: *the copper pans are tinned inside.*
– PHRASES **have a tin ear** informal be tone-deaf. **put the tin lid on** another way of saying PUT THE LID ON IT (see LID).
– ORIGIN Old English, of Germanic origin; related to Dutch *tin* and German *Zinn.*

tinamou /ˈtɪnəmuː/ ▶ noun a ground-dwelling tropical American bird that looks somewhat like a grouse but is related to the ratites. ● Family Tinamidae: several genera and many species.
– ORIGIN late 18th cent.: via French from Galibi *tinamu.*

Tinbergen[1] /ˈtɪnbəːɡ(ə)n/, Jan (1903–94), Dutch economist. He shared the first Nobel Prize for Economics (1969) with Ragnar Frisch for his pioneering work on econometrics. He was the brother of the zoologist Nikolaas Tinbergen.

Tinbergen[2] /ˈtɪnbəːɡ(ə)n/, Nikolaas (1907–88), Dutch zoologist. From his studies he found that much animal behaviour is innate and stereotyped, and he introduced the concept of displacement activity. Tinbergen shared a Nobel Prize in 1973 with Karl von Frisch and Konrad Lorenz. He was the brother of the economist Jan Tinbergen.

tin can ▶ noun a can for preserving food.

tinctorial /tɪŋ(k)ˈtɔːrɪəl/ ▶ adjective technical relating to dyeing, colouring, or staining properties.
– ORIGIN mid 17th cent.: from Latin *tinctorius* (from *tinctor* 'dyer', from *tingere* 'to dye or colour') + -AL.

tincture /ˈtɪŋ(k)tʃə/ ▶ noun **1** a medicine made by dissolving a drug in alcohol: *the remedies can be administered in form of tinctures* | [mass noun] *a bottle containing tincture of iodine.* ■ Brit. informal an alcoholic drink.
2 a slight trace of something: *she could not keep a tincture of bitterness out of her voice.*
3 Heraldry any of the conventional colours (including the metals and stains, and often the furs) used in coats of arms.
▶ verb (**be tinctured**) be tinged or imbued with a slight amount of: *Arthur's affability was tinctured with faint sarcasm.*

T

– ORIGIN late Middle English (denoting a dye or pigment): from Latin *tinctura* 'dyeing', from *tingere* 'to dye or colour'. Sense 2 of the noun (early 17th cent.) comes from the obsolete sense 'imparted quality', likened to a tint imparted by a dye.

tinder ▶ noun [mass noun] dry, flammable material, such as wood or paper, used for lighting a fire.
– DERIVATIVES **tindery** adjective.
– ORIGIN Old English *tynder*, *tyndre*, of Germanic origin; related to Dutch *tonder* and German *Zunder*.

tinderbox ▶ noun **1** a thing that is readily ignited: *dry winds and no rain have turned parts of the state into a tinderbox* | figurative *the estate was a tinderbox where riots could explode at any moment*.
2 historical a box containing tinder, flint, a steel, and other items for kindling fires.

tinder-dry ▶ adjective (of vegetation) extremely dry and flammable.

tinder fungus ▶ noun a bracket fungus with a hard hoof-like upper surface, growing chiefly on birch and beech. Also called HOOF FUNGUS. ● *Fomes fomentarius*, family Polyporaceae, class Hymenomycetes.

tine /tʌɪn/ ▶ noun a prong or sharp point, such as that on a fork or antler.
– DERIVATIVES **tined** adjective [in combination] *a three-tined fork*.
– ORIGIN Old English *tind*, of Germanic origin; related to German *Zinne* 'pinnacle'.

tinea /ˈtɪnɪə/ ▶ noun technical term for RINGWORM.
– ORIGIN late Middle English: from Latin, 'worm'.

tinfoil ▶ noun [mass noun] foil made of aluminium or a similar grey metal, used especially for covering or wrapping food.

ting ▶ noun a sharp, clear ringing sound, such as that made when a glass is struck by a metal object.
▶ verb [no obj.] emit a ting.
– ORIGIN late Middle English (as a verb): imitative. The noun dates from the early 17th cent.

tinge ▶ verb (**tinges**, **tinging** or **tingeing**, **tinged**) [with obj.] colour slightly: *a mass of white blossom **tinged with** pink* | [with obj. and complement] *towards the sun the sky was tinged crimson*. ■ permeate or imbue slightly with a feeling or quality: *this visit will be **tinged with** sadness*.
▶ noun a trace of a colour: *there was a faint pink tinge to the sky*. ■ a slight trace of a feeling or quality.
– ORIGIN late 15th cent.: from Latin *tingere* 'to dip or colour'. The noun dates from the mid 18th cent.

tin glaze ▶ noun a glaze made white and opaque by the addition of tin oxide.
– DERIVATIVES **tin-glazed** adjective.

tingle[1] ▶ verb experience or cause to experience a slight prickling or stinging sensation: [no obj.] *she was tingling with excitement* | [with obj.] *a standing ovation that tingled your spine*.
▶ noun a slight prickling or stinging sensation: *a tingle of anticipation*.
– ORIGIN late Middle English: perhaps a variant of TINKLE. The original notion was perhaps 'ring in response to a loud noise', but the term was very early applied to the result of hearing something shocking.

tingle[2] ▶ noun an S-shaped metal clip used to support heavy panes of glass or slates on a roof.
– ORIGIN Middle English (denoting a small tack): related to Middle High German *zingel* 'small tack or hook', probably from a Germanic base meaning 'fasten'. The current sense dates from the late 19th cent.

T

tingly ▶ adjective (**tinglier**, **tingliest**) causing or experiencing a slight prickling or stinging sensation: *a tingly sense of excitement*.

tin god ▶ noun a person, especially a minor official, who is pompous and self-important. ■ an object of unjustified veneration or respect.

tin hat ▶ noun Brit. informal a soldier's steel helmet.

tinhorn ▶ noun N. Amer. informal a person who pretends to have money, influence, or ability.

tinker ▶ noun **1** (especially in former times) a person who makes a living by travelling from place to place mending pans and other metal utensils. ■ Brit., chiefly derogatory a Gypsy or other person living in an itinerant community.
2 Brit. informal a mischievous child.
3 an act of attempting to repair something.
▶ verb [no obj.] attempt to repair or improve something in a casual or desultory way: *he spent hours tinkering with the car*.
– PHRASES **not give a tinker's curse** (or **cuss** or **damn**) informal not care at all.
– DERIVATIVES **tinkerer** noun.
– ORIGIN Middle English (first recorded in Anglo-Latin as a surname): of unknown origin.

tinkerbird ▶ noun a small African barbet with a monotonous metallic call like a hammer striking an anvil, repeated for long periods. ● Genus *Pogonulus*, family Capitonidae: several species. Alternative name: **tinker barbet**.

tinkle ▶ verb **1** make or cause to make a light, clear ringing sound: [no obj.] *cool water tinkled in the stone fountains* | [with obj.] *the maid tinkled a bell*.
2 [no obj.] Brit. informal urinate.
▶ noun **1** a light, clear ringing sound: *the distant tinkle of a cow bell*. ■ Brit. informal a telephone call: *I'll **give them a tinkle***.
2 Brit. informal an act of urinating.
– DERIVATIVES **tinkly** adjective (**tinklier**, **tinkliest**).
– ORIGIN late Middle English (also in the sense 'tingle'): frequentative of obsolete *tink* 'to chink or clink', of imitative origin.

tinktinkie /tɪŋkˈtɪŋki/ ▶ noun (pl. **tinktinkies**) South African term for CISTICOLA.
– ORIGIN Afrikaans, imitative of its call.

Tin Lizzie ▶ noun N. Amer. informal, dated a car, especially a very early Ford.
– ORIGIN early 20th cent.: *Lizzie*, a pet form of the given name *Elizabeth*.

tinned ▶ adjective **1** Brit. (of food) preserved in a can: *tinned fruit*.
2 covered or coated in tin or a tin alloy.

tinner ▶ noun a tin miner or tinsmith.

tinning ▶ noun [mass noun] **1** the action of covering or coating something with tin.
2 tin mining.

tinnitus /ˈtɪnɪtəs/ ▶ noun [mass noun] Medicine ringing or buzzing in the ears.
– ORIGIN mid 19th cent.: from Latin, from *tinnire* 'to ring, tinkle', of imitative origin.

tinny ▶ adjective (**tinnier**, **tinniest**) **1** having a displeasingly thin, metallic sound: *tinny music played in the background*. ■ made of thin or poor-quality metal: *a tinny little car*. ■ having an unpleasantly metallic taste: *canned artichokes taste somewhat tinny*.
2 Austral./NZ informal lucky. [early 20th cent.: from *tin* 'luck' (literally 'money, cash'.]
▶ noun (also **tinnie**) (pl. **tinnies**) Austral./NZ informal **1** a can of beer.
2 a small boat with an aluminium hull.
– DERIVATIVES **tinnily** adverb, **tinniness** noun.

tin opener ▶ noun Brit. a tool for opening tins of food.

Tin Pan Alley the name given to a district in New York (28th Street, between 5th Avenue and Broadway) where many songwriters, arrangers, and music publishers were formerly based. ■ [as noun] [usu. as modifier] the world of composers and publishers of popular music.

tinplate ▶ noun [mass noun] sheet steel or iron coated with tin.
▶ verb [with obj.] (often as adj. **tinplated**) coat (an object) with tin.

tinpot ▶ adjective [attrib.] Brit. informal (especially of a country or its leader) having or showing poor leadership or organization: *a tinpot dictator*.

tinsel ▶ noun [mass noun] a form of decoration consisting of thin strips of shiny metal foil attached to a long piece of thread. ■ showy or superficial attractiveness or glamour: *his taste for the tinsel of the art world*.
– DERIVATIVES **tinselled** (US **tinseled**) adjective, **tinselly** adjective.
– ORIGIN late Middle English (denoting fabric either interwoven with metallic thread or spangled): from Old French *estincele* 'spark', or *estinceler* 'to sparkle', based on Latin *scintilla* 'a spark'.

Tinseltown ▶ noun [mass noun] derogatory Hollywood, or the superficially glamorous world it represents.

tinsmith ▶ noun a person who makes or repairs articles of tin or tinplate.

tin snips ▶ plural noun a pair of clippers for cutting sheet metal.

tin soldier ▶ noun a toy soldier made of metal.

tinstone ▶ noun another term for CASSITERITE.

tint ▶ noun **1** a shade or variety of a colour: *the sky was taking on an apricot tint*. ■ Printing an area of faint even colour printed as a half-tone, used for highlighting overprinted text. ■ a set of parallel engraved lines to give uniform shading. ■ a trace of something: *a tint of glamour*.
2 an artificial dye for colouring the hair. ■ an application of hair dye: *peering into the mirror to see if any white hair showed after her last tint*.
▶ verb [with obj.] colour (something) slightly; tinge: *her skin was tinted with delicate colour* | (as adj. **tinted**) *a black car with tinted windows*. ■ dye (someone's hair) with a tint.
– DERIVATIVES **tinter** noun.
– ORIGIN early 18th cent.: alteration (perhaps influenced by Italian *tinta*) of obsolete *tinct* 'to colour, tint', from Latin *tinctus* 'dyeing', from *tingere* 'to dye or colour'.

Tintagel /tɪnˈtadʒəl/ a village on the coast of northern Cornwall. Nearby are the ruins of Tintagel Castle, the legendary birthplace of King Arthur.

tintinnabulation /ˌtɪntɪnabjʊˈleɪʃ(ə)n/ ▶ noun a ringing or tinkling sound.
– ORIGIN mid 19th cent.: from Latin *tintinnabulum* 'tinkling bell' (from *tintinnare*, reduplication of *tinnire* 'to ring, tinkle') + -ATION.

tinto /ˈtɪntəʊ/ ▶ noun (pl. **tintos**) [mass noun] Spanish or Portuguese red wine.
– ORIGIN Spanish, literally 'tinted, dark-coloured'.

Tintoretto /ˌtɪntəˈrɛtəʊ/ (1518–94), Italian painter; born *Jacopo Robusti*. His work, chiefly dealing with religious themes, was typified by a mannerist style, including unusual viewpoints and chiaroscuro effects.

tintype ▶ noun historical a photograph taken as a positive on a thin tin plate.

tinware ▶ noun [mass noun] kitchen utensils or other articles made of tin or tinplate.

tin whistle ▶ noun a small flute-like instrument made from a thin metal tube, with six finger holes of varying size on top and no thumb holes.

tiny ▶ adjective (**tinier**, **tiniest**) very small: *a tiny hummingbird*.
▶ noun (pl. **tinies**) informal a very young child.
– DERIVATIVES **tinily** adverb, **tininess** noun.
– ORIGIN late 16th cent.: extension of obsolete *tine*, 'small, diminutive', of unknown origin.

-tion ▶ suffix forming nouns of action, condition, etc. such as *completion*, *relation*.
– ORIGIN from Latin participial stems ending in *-t* + -ION.

tip[1] ▶ noun the pointed or rounded end or extremity of something slender or tapering: *George pressed the tips of his fingers together* | *the northern tip of Scotland*. ■ a small piece or part fitted to the end of an object: *the rubber tip of the walking stick*.
▶ verb (**tips**, **tipping**, **tipped**) [with obj.] **1** (usu. as adj. **tipped**) attach to or cover the end or extremity of: *mountains tipped with snow* | [in combination] *steel-tipped spears*. ■ colour (something) at its end or edge: *velvety red petals tipped with white*.
2 (**tip a page in**) (in bookbinding) paste a single page, typically an illustration, to the neighbouring page of a book by a thin line of paste down its inner margin.
– PHRASES **on the tip of one's tongue** almost but not quite brought to mind or spoken: *his name's on the tip of my tongue!* **the tip of the iceberg** see ICEBERG.
– ORIGIN late Middle English: from Old Norse *typpi* (noun), *typpa* (verb), *typptr* 'tipped'; related to TOP[1].

tip[2] ▶ verb (**tips**, **tipping**, **tipped**) **1** overbalance so as to fall or turn over: [no obj.] *the hay caught fire when the candle **tipped over*** | [with obj.] *a youth sprinted past, **tipping over** her glass*. ■ be or cause to be in a sloping position with one end or side higher than the other: [with obj. and adverbial] *I tipped my seat back, preparing myself for sleep* | [no obj., with adverbial] *the car had tipped to one side*.
2 [with obj. and adverbial of direction] cause (the contents of a container) to be emptied out by holding it at an angle: *Sarah tipped the washing-up water down the sink*. ■ [no obj.] (**it tips down, it is tipping down**, etc.) Brit. rain heavily.
3 [with obj.] strike or touch lightly: *I tipped his hoof with the handle of a knife*. ■ [with obj. and adverbial of direction] cause (an object) to move somewhere by striking or touching it lightly: *his twenty-yard shot was tipped over the bar by Nixon*.
4 [no obj.] (**tip off**) Basketball put the ball in play by throwing it up between two opponents.
▶ noun **1** Brit. a place where rubbish is left. ■ informal a dirty or untidy place: *your room's an absolute tip!*
2 Baseball a pitched ball that is slightly deflected by the batter.
– PHRASES **tip one's hand** N. Amer. informal reveal one's intentions inadvertently. **tip one's hat** (or **cap**)

raise or touch one's hat or cap as a way of greeting or acknowledging someone. **tip** (or **turn**) **the scales** (or **balance**) be the deciding factor; make the critical difference: *her current form tips the scales in her favour*. **tip** (or **turn**) **the scales at** have a weight of (a specified amount): *the phone tips the scales at only 150 g*.
– ORIGIN late Middle English: perhaps of Scandinavian origin, influenced later by TIP[1] in the sense 'touch with a tip or point'. Current senses of the noun date from the mid 19th cent.

tip[3] ▸ **noun 1** a sum of money given to someone as a reward for a service.
2 a small but useful piece of practical advice. ■ a prediction or piece of expert information about the likely winner of a race or contest: *Barry had a* **hot tip**.
▸ **verb** (**tips, tipping, tipped**) [with obj.] **1** give (someone) a sum of money as a reward for a service: [with two objs] *I tipped her five dollars* | [no obj.] *that sort never tip*.
2 Brit. predict as likely to win or achieve something: *Christine was widely* **tipped to** *get the job*.
3 (**tip someone off**) informal give someone information in a discreet or confidential way: *they were arrested after police were tipped off by local residents*.
– PHRASES **tip someone the wink** Brit. informal give someone private information.
– ORIGIN early 17th cent. (in the sense 'give, hand, pass'): probably from TIP[1].

tip-and-run ▸ **noun** [mass noun] an informal way of playing cricket in which the batsman must run after every hit. ■ [as modifier] (of a military raid) executed swiftly and followed by immediate withdrawal.

tipcat ▸ **noun** [mass noun] chiefly historical a game in which a piece of wood tapered at both ends is struck at one end with a stick so as to spring up and is then knocked away by the same player. ■ [count noun] a tapered piece of wood of this kind.

tipi ▸ **noun** variant spelling of TEPEE.

tip-in ▸ **noun** Basketball a score made by tipping a rebound into the basket.

tip-off ▸ **noun** informal a piece of information given in a discreet or confidential way.

tipper ▸ **noun 1** (also **tipper truck** or **lorry**) a truck having a rear platform which can be raised at its front end, thus enabling a load to be discharged.
2 [usu. with adj.] a person who leaves a specified size of tip: *he's a big tipper*.
3 a person who dumps waste, especially illegally.

Tipperary /ˌtɪpəˈrɛːri/ a county in the centre of the Republic of Ireland, in the province of Munster; county town, Clonmel.

tippet ▸ **noun** a woman's long fur scarf or shawl worn around the neck and shoulders. ■ a similar ceremonial garment worn especially by the clergy. ■ historical a long, narrow strip of cloth forming part of or attached to a hood or sleeve.
– ORIGIN Middle English: probably from an Anglo-Norman derivative of the noun TIP[1].

Tippett /ˈtɪpɪt/, Sir Michael (Kemp) (1905–98), English composer. He established his reputation with the oratorio *A Child of Our Time* (1941), which drew on jazz, madrigals, and spirituals besides classical sources. Other works include five operas, four symphonies, and several song cycles.

Tippex (also **Tipp-Ex**) Brit. trademark ▸ **noun** [mass noun] a type of correction fluid.
▸ **verb** [with obj.] delete with correction fluid.
– ORIGIN 1960s: from German, from *tippen* 'to type' and Latin *ex* 'out'.

tipping point ▸ **noun** the point at which a series of small changes or incidents becomes significant enough to cause a larger, more important change.

tipple ▸ **verb** [no obj.] **1** drink alcohol, especially habitually: *those who liked to tipple and gamble*.
2 (**it tipples down, it is tippling down**, etc.) Brit. informal rain heavily: *it was tippling down with rain*.
▸ **noun** informal an alcoholic drink.
– ORIGIN late 15th cent. (in the sense 'sell (alcoholic drink) by retail'): back-formation from TIPPLER[1].

tippler[1] ▸ **noun** a habitual drinker of alcohol.
– ORIGIN late Middle English (denoting a retailer of alcoholic liquor): of unknown origin.

tippler[2] ▸ **noun** a revolving frame or cage in which a truck is inverted to discharge its load.
– ORIGIN early 19th cent.: from dialect *tipple* 'tumble over' + -ER[1].

tippy ▸ **adjective** (**tippier, tippiest**) N. Amer. inclined to tilt or overturn; unsteady: *they crossed the water in tippy canoes*.

tippy-toe ▸ **verb** [no obj., with adverbial of direction] informal, chiefly US walk on the tips of one's toes; tiptoe: *he tippy-toed around the house*.
– PHRASES **on tippy-toe** (or **tippy-toes**) on tiptoe: *Kurt was mincing around on tippy-toes*.
– ORIGIN late 19th cent.: alteration of TIPTOE.

tipstaff ▸ **noun** a sheriff's officer; a bailiff.
– ORIGIN mid 16th cent. (first denoting a metal-tipped staff): contraction of *tipped staff* (carried by a bailiff).

tipster ▸ **noun** a person who gives tips, especially about the likely winner of a race or contest.

tipsy ▸ **adjective** (**tipsier, tipsiest**) slightly drunk: *tipsy revellers*.
– DERIVATIVES **tipsily** adverb, **tipsiness** noun.
– ORIGIN late 16th cent.: from the verb TIP[2] + -SY.

tipsy cake ▸ **noun** Brit. a sponge cake saturated with wine or spirits, typically served with custard.

tip-tilted ▸ **adjective** (especially of a person's nose) turned up at the tip.

tiptoe ▸ **verb** (**tiptoes, tiptoeing, tiptoed**) [no obj., with adverbial of direction] walk quietly and carefully with one's heels raised and one's weight on the balls of the feet: *Liz tiptoed out of the room*. ■ (**tiptoe round/around**) carefully avoid discussing or dealing with (a difficult or sensitive subject): *he admits he has never been one to tiptoe around controversial issues*.
– PHRASES **on tiptoe** (or **tiptoes**) (N. Amer. also **on one's tiptoes**) with one's heels raised and one's weight on the balls of the feet, especially in order to move quietly or make oneself taller: *Jane stood on tiptoe to kiss him*.

tip-top ▸ **adjective** of the very best class or quality; excellent: *an athlete in tip-top condition*.
▸ **noun 1** the highest part or point of excellence.
2 N. Amer. a line guide on a fishing rod.

tip-up ▸ **adjective** denoting a seat in a theatre or other public place that is designed to tilt up vertically when unoccupied so as to let people pass easily. ■ denoting a rear platform of a truck or lorry that may be raised up, enabling a load to be discharged.
▸ **noun** N. Amer. a device used in ice-fishing in which a wire attached to the rod is tripped, raising a signal flag, when a fish takes the bait.

tirade /tʌɪˈreɪd, tɪ-/ ▸ **noun** a long, angry speech of criticism or accusation: *a tirade of abuse*.
– ORIGIN early 19th cent.: from French, literally 'long speech', from Italian *tirata* 'volley', from *tirare* 'to pull'.

tirailleur /ˌtɪrʌɪˈjəː/ ▸ **noun** chiefly historical a sharpshooter.
– ORIGIN late 18th cent. (originally denoting a skirmisher employed in the wars of the French Revolution): French, from *tirailler* 'shoot independently', from *tirer* 'shoot, draw'.

tiramisu /ˌtɪrəmɪˈsuː/ ▸ **noun** [mass noun] an Italian dessert consisting of layers of sponge cake soaked in coffee and brandy or liqueur with powdered chocolate and mascarpone cheese.
– ORIGIN Italian, from the phrase *tira mi sù* 'pick me up'.

Tirana /tɪˈrɑːnə/ (also **Tiranë**) the capital of Albania, on the Ishm River in central Albania; pop. 407,000 (est. 2009). Founded by the Turks in the 17th century, it became capital of Albania in 1920.

tire[1] ▸ **verb 1** feel or cause to feel in need of rest or sleep: [no obj.] *soon the ascent grew steeper and he began to tire* | [with obj.] *the journey had tired her* | *the training* **tired** *us* **out**.
2 [no obj.] (**tire of**) lose interest in; become bored with: *she will stay with him until he tires of her*. ■ [with obj.] exhaust the patience or interest of; bore.
– ORIGIN Old English *tēorian* 'fail, come to an end', also 'become physically exhausted', of unknown origin.

tire[2] ▸ **noun** US spelling of TYRE.

tired ▸ **adjective 1** in need of sleep or rest; weary: *Fisher rubbed his tired eyes* | *she was* **tired out** *now that the strain was over*. ■ (of a thing) no longer fresh or in good condition: *a few boxes of tired vegetables*.
2 (**tired of**) bored or impatient with: *I have to look after these animals when you get tired of them*.
3 (especially of a statement or idea) boring or uninteresting because overfamiliar: *tired clichés like the 'information revolution'*.
– PHRASES **tired and emotional** humorous used euphemistically to indicate that someone is drunk.
– DERIVATIVES **tiredly** adverb.

tiredness ▸ **noun** [mass noun] the state of wishing for sleep or rest; weariness: *tiredness overcame her and she fell into a deep slumber* | *depression and tiredness caused by overwork*.

Tiree /tʌɪˈriː/ an island in the Inner Hebrides, to the west of the isles of Mull and Coll.

tire iron ▸ **noun** N. Amer. a steel lever for removing tyres from wheel rims.

tireless ▸ **adjective** having or showing great effort or energy: *a tireless campaigner*.
– DERIVATIVES **tirelessly** adverb, **tirelessness** noun.

Tiresias /tʌɪˈriːsɪəs/ Greek Mythology a blind Theban prophet, so wise that even his ghost had its wits and was not a mere phantom. Legends account variously for his wisdom and blindness; some stories hold also that he spent seven years as a woman.

tiresome ▸ **adjective** causing one to feel bored or annoyed: *weeding is a tiresome but essential job*.
– DERIVATIVES **tiresomely** adverb [as submodifier] *a tiresomely predictable attitude*, **tiresomeness** noun.

Tîrgu Mureş /ˌtɪəguː ˈmʊəreʃ/ a city in central Romania, on the River Mureş; pop. 146,448 (2006).

Tirich Mir /ˌtɪrɪtʃ ˈmɪə/ the highest peak in the Hindu Kush, in NW Pakistan, rising to 7,690 m (25,230 ft).

tiring ▸ **adjective** causing one to need rest or sleep; fatiguing: *it had been a tiring day*.

Tir-na-nog /ˌtɪənanˈəʊg/, Irish /ˌtʲir nə ˈnəʊg/ Irish Mythology a land of perpetual youth, the Irish equivalent of Elysium.
– ORIGIN Irish, literally 'land of the young'.

tiro ▸ **noun** variant spelling of TYRO.

Tirol /tiˈrəʊːl/ German name for TYROL.

tirtha /ˈtɪəθə/ (also **tirth** /ˈtɪəθ/) ▸ **noun** a Hindu place of pilgrimage, especially one by a river or lake.
– ORIGIN Hindi *tīrtha*.

Tiruchirapalli /ˌtɪrʊtʃɪˈrɑːpəli/ a city in Tamil Nadu, southern India; pop. 813,400 (est. 2009). Also called TRICHINOPOLY.

'tis chiefly literary ▸ **contraction** it is.

Tisa /ˈtiːsa/ Serbian name for TISZA.

tisane /tɪˈzan/ ▸ **noun** a herb tea.
– ORIGIN 1930s: from French.

Tishri /ˈtɪʃriː/ (also **Tisri** /ˈtɪzriː/) ▸ **noun** (in the Jewish calendar) the first month of the civil and seventh of the religious year, usually coinciding with parts of September and October.
– ORIGIN from Hebrew *tišrī*.

Tisiphone /tɪˈsɪfəni/ Greek Mythology one of the Furies.
– ORIGIN Greek, literally 'the avenger of blood'.

tissue /ˈtɪʃuː, ˈtɪsjuː/ ▸ **noun** [mass noun] **1** any of the distinct types of material of which animals or plants are made, consisting of specialized cells and their products: *inflammation is a reaction of living tissue to infection or injury* | (**tissues**) *the organs and tissues of the body*.
2 tissue paper. ■ [count noun] a disposable piece of absorbent paper, used especially as a handkerchief or for cleaning the skin. ■ rich or fine material of a delicate or gauzy texture: [as modifier] *the blue and silver tissue sari*.
3 [in sing.] an intricate structure or network made from a number of connected items: *such scandalous stories are* **a tissue of lies**.
– DERIVATIVES **tissuey** adjective.
– ORIGIN late Middle English: from Old French *tissu* 'woven', past participle of *tistre*, from Latin *texere* 'to weave'. The word originally denoted a rich material, often interwoven with gold or silver threads, later (mid 16th cent.) any woven fabric, hence the notion of 'intricacy'.

tissue culture ▸ **noun** [mass noun] Biology & Medicine the growth in an artificial medium of cells derived from living tissue. ■ [count noun] a cell culture of this kind.

tissue fluid ▸ **noun** [mass noun] Physiology extracellular fluid which bathes the cells of most tissues, arriving via blood capillaries and being removed via the lymphatic vessels.

tissue paper ▸ **noun** [mass noun] thin, soft paper, typically used for wrapping or protecting fragile or delicate articles.

tissue type ▸ **noun** a class of tissues which are immunologically compatible with one another.
▸ **verb** (**tissue-type**) [with obj.] determine the tissue type of. ■ (as noun **tissue-typing**) the assessment of the

T

immunological compatibility of tissue from separate sources, particularly prior to organ transplantation.

Tisza /ˈtiːsə/ a river in SE Europe, the longest tributary of the Danube, which rises in the Carpathian Mountains of western Ukraine and flows 960 km (600 miles) westwards into Hungary, then southwards, joining the Danube in Serbia north-west of Belgrade. Serbian name **Tisa**.

tit[1] ▶ **noun** a small songbird that searches acrobatically for insects among foliage and branches. Also called **titmouse** or (in North America) **chickadee**. ● Family Paridae: three genera, especially *Parus*, and numerous species. See **blue tit**, **great tit**.
■ used in names of similar or related birds, e.g. **penduline tit**, **New Zealand tit**.
– ORIGIN mid 16th cent.: probably of Scandinavian origin and related to Icelandic *titlingur* 'sparrow'; compare with **titling**[2] and **titmouse**. Earlier senses were 'small horse' and 'girl'; the current sense dates from the early 18th cent.

tit[2] ▶ **noun 1** vulgar slang a woman's breast. ■ Brit. informal a foolish or ineffectual person.
2 military slang a button that is pushed to fire a gun or release a bomb.
– PHRASES **get on someone's tits** Brit. vulgar slang irritate someone intensely. **tits and ass** (or chiefly Brit. **tits and bums**) vulgar slang, chiefly N. Amer. used in reference to the use of crudely sexual images of women.
– ORIGIN Old English *tit* 'teat, nipple', of Germanic origin; related to Dutch *tit* and German *Zitze*. The vulgar slang use was originally US and dates from the early 20th cent.

tit[3] ▶ **noun** (in phrase **tit for tat**) the infliction of an injury or insult in return for one that one has suffered: [as modifier] *the conflict staggered on with tit-for-tat assassinations*.
– ORIGIN mid 16th cent.: variant of obsolete *tip for tap*.

Tit. ▶ **abbreviation** Titus (in biblical references).

Titan /ˈtʌɪt(ə)n/ **1** Greek Mythology any of the older gods who preceded the Olympians and were the children of Uranus (Heaven) and Gaia (Earth). Led by Cronus, they overthrew Uranus; Cronus' son, Zeus, then rebelled against his father and eventually defeated the Titans. ■ (as noun **a titan**) a person or thing of very great strength, intellect, or importance: *a titan of American industry*.
2 Astronomy the largest satellite of Saturn (diameter 5,150 km), the fifteenth closest to the planet, discovered by C. Huygens in 1655. It is unique in having a hazy atmosphere of nitrogen, methane, and oily hydrocarbons.

titanate /ˈtʌɪtəneɪt/ ▶ **noun** Chemistry a salt in which the anion contains both titanium and oxygen, in particular one of the anion TiO_3^{2-}.
– ORIGIN mid 19th cent.: from **titanium** + **-ate**[1].

Titaness /ˈtʌɪtənɪs, -ˈnɛs/ ▶ **noun** a female Titan.

Titania /tɪˈtɑːnɪə, -ˈteɪnɪə/ Astronomy the largest satellite of Uranus (diameter 1,600 km), the fourteenth closest to the planet and having an icy surface, discovered by W. Herschel in 1787.
– ORIGIN the name of the queen of the fairies in Shakespeare's *A Midsummer Night's Dream*.

Titanic a British passenger liner, the largest ship in the world when she was built and supposedly unsinkable, that struck an iceberg in the North Atlantic on her maiden voyage in April 1912 and sank with the loss of 1,490 lives.

titanic[1] ▶ **adjective** of exceptional strength, size, or power: *a series of titanic explosions*.
– DERIVATIVES **titanically** adverb.
– ORIGIN mid 17th cent. (in the sense 'relating to the sun'): from Greek *titanikos*, from *Titan* (see **Titan**).

titanic[2] ▶ **adjective** Chemistry of titanium with a valency of four; of titanium(IV). Compare with **titanous**.
– ORIGIN early 19th cent.: from **titanium** + **-ic**.

titaniferous /ˌtʌɪtəˈnɪf(ə)rəs/ ▶ **adjective** (of rocks and minerals) containing or yielding titanium.

titanite /ˈtʌɪtənʌɪt/ ▶ **noun** another term for **sphene**.
– ORIGIN late 18th cent.: from **titanium** + **-ite**[1].

titanium /tʌɪˈteɪnɪəm, tɪ-/ ▶ **noun** [mass noun] the chemical element of atomic number 22, a hard silver-grey metal of the transition series, used in strong, light, corrosion-resistant alloys. (Symbol: **Ti**)
– ORIGIN late 18th cent.: from **Titan**, on the pattern of *uranium*.

titanium dioxide (also **titanium oxide**) ▶ **noun** [mass noun] a white unreactive solid which occurs naturally as the mineral rutile and is used extensively as a white pigment. ● Chem. formula: TiO_2.

titanium white ▶ **noun** [mass noun] a white pigment consisting chiefly or wholly of titanium dioxide.

titanous /tʌɪˈtanəs/ ▶ **adjective** Chemistry of titanium with a lower valency, usually three. Compare with **titanic**[2].
– ORIGIN mid 19th cent.: from **titanium**, on the pattern of words such as *ferrous*.

titbit (N. Amer. **tidbit**) ▶ **noun** a small piece of tasty food. ■ a small and particularly interesting item of gossip or information.
– ORIGIN mid 17th cent. (as *tyd bit*, *tid-bit*): from dialect *tid* 'tender' (of unknown origin) + **bit**[1].

titch (also **tich**) ▶ **noun** Brit. informal a small person.
– ORIGIN 1930s: from *Little Tich*, stage name of Harry Relph (1868–1928), an English music-hall comedian of small stature. He was given the nickname because he resembled Arthur Orton, the Tichborne claimant (see **Orton**[1]).

titchy ▶ **adjective** (**titchier**, **titchiest**) Brit. informal very small: *a titchy theatre*.

titer ▶ **noun** US spelling of **titre**.

titfer ▶ **noun** Brit. informal a hat.
– ORIGIN 1930s: abbreviation of rhyming slang *tit for tat*.

tithe /tʌɪð/ ▶ **noun** one tenth of annual produce or earnings, formerly taken as a tax for the support of the Church and clergy. ■ (in certain religious denominations) a tenth of an individual's income pledged to the Church. ■ [in sing.] archaic a tenth of a specified thing: *he hadn't said **a tithe of** the prayers he knew*.
▶ **verb** [with obj.] pay or give as a tithe: *he tithes 10 per cent of his income to the Church*. ■ historical subject to a tax of one tenth of income or produce.
– DERIVATIVES **tithable** adjective.
– ORIGIN Old English *tēotha* (adjective in the ordinal sense 'tenth', used in a specialized sense as a noun), *tēothian* (verb).

tithe barn ▶ **noun** a barn built to hold tithes paid in kind.

tithing /ˈtʌɪðɪŋ/ ▶ **noun 1** [mass noun] the practice of taking or paying a tithe.
2 historical (in England) a group of ten householders who lived close together and were collectively responsible for each other's behaviour. ■ a rural division, originally regarded as a tenth of a hundred.
– ORIGIN Old English *tēothung* (see **tithe**, **-ing**[1]).

Tithonus /tɪˈθəʊnəs/ Greek Mythology a Trojan prince with whom the goddess Aurora fell in love. She asked Zeus to make him immortal but omitted to ask for eternal youth, and he became very old and decrepit although he talked perpetually. Tithonus prayed her to remove him from this world and she changed him into a grasshopper, which chirps ceaselessly.

titi[1] /ˈtiːtiː/ (also **titi monkey**) ▶ **noun** (pl. **titis**) a small forest-dwelling monkey of South America. ● Genus *Callicebus*, family Cebidae: several species.
– ORIGIN mid 18th cent.: from Aymara.

titi[2] /ˈtʌɪtʌɪ, ˈtiːtiː/ ▶ **noun** (pl. **titis**) another term for **leatherwood** (sense 1).
– ORIGIN early 19th cent.: perhaps of American Indian origin.

Titian[1] /ˈtɪʃ(ə)n/ (*c.*1488–1576), Italian painter; Italian name *Tiziano Vecellio*. The most important painter of the Venetian school, he experimented with vivid colours and often broke conventions of composition. He painted many sensual mythological works, including *Bacchus and Ariadne* (*c.*1518–23).

Titian[2] /ˈtɪʃ(ə)n/ ▶ **adjective** (of hair) bright golden auburn: *a mass of Titian curls*.
– ORIGIN early 19th cent.: from **Titian**[1], by association with the bright auburn hair portrayed in many of his works.

Titicaca, Lake /ˌtɪtɪˈkɑːkɑː/ a lake in the Andes, on the border between Peru and Bolivia. At an altitude of 3,809 m (12,497 ft), it is the highest large lake in the world.

titihoya /ˌtɪtɪˈhɔɪə/ ▶ **noun** an African plover related to the lapwing, with a distinctive plaintive cry.
● *Vanellus melanopterus*, family Charadridae. Alternative name: **black-winged plover**.
– ORIGIN 1940s: from Zulu, of imitative origin.

titillate /ˈtɪtɪleɪt/ ▶ **verb** [with obj.] arouse (someone) to interest or mild excitement, especially through sexually suggestive images or words: *the press are paid to titillate the public*. ■ archaic lightly touch; tickle.
– DERIVATIVES **titillation** noun.
– ORIGIN early 17th cent. (earlier (Middle English) as *titillation*): from Latin *titillat-* 'tickled', from the verb *titillare*.

titillating ▶ **adjective** arousing mild sexual excitement or interest; salacious: *she let slip titillating details about her clients*.
– DERIVATIVES **titillatingly** adverb.

titivate /ˈtɪtɪveɪt/ ▶ **verb** [with obj.] make minor enhancements to: *she slapped on her warpaint and titivated her hair*. ■ (**titivate oneself**) make oneself look smart.
– DERIVATIVES **titivation** noun.
– ORIGIN early 19th cent. (in early use, also as *tidivate*): perhaps from **tidy**, on the pattern of *cultivate*.

> **USAGE** The verbs **titillate** and **titivate** sound alike but do not have the same meaning. **Titillate**, a far commoner word, means 'stimulate or excite', as in *the press are paid to titillate the public*. **Titivate**, on the other hand, means 'adorn or smarten up', as in *she **titivated** her hair*.

titlark ▶ **noun** dialect a pipit, especially the meadow pipit.

title ▶ **noun 1** the name of a book, composition, or other artistic work: *the author and title of the book*. ■ a caption or credit in a film or broadcast. ■ a book, magazine, or newspaper considered as a publication: *the company publishes 400 titles a year*.
2 a name that describes someone's position or job: *Leese assumed the title of director general*. ■ a word such as *Lord* or *Dame* that is used before someone's name, or a form that is used instead of someone's name, to indicate high social or official rank: *he will inherit the title of Duke of Marlborough*. ■ a word such as *Mrs* or *Dr* that is used before someone's name to indicate their profession or marital status. ■ a descriptive or distinctive name that is earned or chosen: *the restaurant deserved the title of Best Restaurant of the Year*.
3 the position of being the champion of a major sports competition: *Davis won the world title for the first time in 1981*.
4 [mass noun] Law a right or claim to the ownership of property or to a rank or throne: *a grocery family had **title to** the property* | [count noun] *the buyer acquires a good title to the goods*.
5 (in church use) a fixed sphere of work and source of income as a condition for ordination. ■ a parish church in Rome under a cardinal.
▶ **verb** [with obj. and complement] give a name to (a book, composition, or other work): *a report titled The Lost Land*.
– ORIGIN Old English *titul*, reinforced by Old French *title*, both from Latin *titulus* 'inscription, title'. The word originally denoted a placard or inscription placed on an object, giving information about it, hence a descriptive heading in a book or other composition.

title bar ▶ **noun** Computing a horizontal bar at the top of a window, bearing the name of the program and typically the name of the currently active document.

titled ▶ **adjective** (of a person) having a title indicating high social or official rank.

title deed ▶ **noun** a legal deed or document constituting evidence of a right, especially to ownership of property.

title-holder ▶ **noun** a person who is the current champion of a major sports competition.

title music ▶ **noun** [mass noun] music played during the credits at the beginning or end of a television programme or film.

title page ▶ **noun** a page at the beginning of a book giving its title and the names of the author and publisher.

title role ▶ **noun** the part in a play or film from which the work's title is taken.

titling[1] /ˈtʌɪtlɪŋ/ ▶ **noun** [mass noun] **1** titles, captions, or subtitles added to something such as a book cover or video.
2 Printing type consisting only of capital letters and figures which are the full height of the type size.

titling[2] /ˈtɪtlɪŋ/ ▶ **noun** Scottish & N. English the meadow pipit.
– ORIGIN mid 16th cent.: from **tit**[1] + **-ling**.

titmouse ▶ **noun** (pl. **titmice**) another term for **tit**[1].
– ORIGIN Middle English: from **tit**[1] + obsolete *mose* 'titmouse'. The change in the ending in the 16th cent. was due to association with **mouse**, probably because of the bird's size and quick movements.

T

Tito /ˈtiːtəʊ/ (1892–1980), Yugoslav Marshal and statesman, Prime Minister 1945–53 and President 1953–80; born *Josip Broz*. He organized a Communist resistance movement against the German invasion of Yugoslavia (1941). He became head of the new government at the end of the war, establishing Yugoslavia as a non-aligned Communist state with a federal constitution.
– DERIVATIVES **Titoism** noun, **Titoist** noun & adjective.

Titograd /ˈtiːtəʊgrad/ former name (1946–93) for **PODGORICA**.

titrate /tʌɪˈtreɪt, tɪ-/ ▶ verb [with obj.] Chemistry ascertain the amount of a constituent in (a solution) by measuring the volume of a known concentration of reagent required to complete a reaction with it, typically using an indicator. ■ Medicine continuously measure and adjust the balance of (a physiological function or drug dosage).
– DERIVATIVES **titratable** adjective, **titration** noun.
– ORIGIN late 19th cent.: from French *titrer* (from *titre* in the sense 'fineness of alloyed gold or silver') + **-ATE**[3].

titre /ˈtʌɪtə, ˈtiːtə/ (US **titer**) ▶ noun Chemistry the concentration of a solution as determined by titration. ■ the minimum volume of a solution needed to reach the end point in a titration. ■ Medicine the concentration of an antibody, as determined by finding the highest dilution at which it is still able to cause agglutination of the antigen.
– ORIGIN mid 19th cent.: from French, from *titrer* (see **TITRATE**).

ti tree ▶ noun variant spelling of **TEA TREE** (sense 1).

titter ▶ verb [no obj.] give a short, half-suppressed laugh; giggle: *her stutter caused the children to titter*.
▶ noun a short, half-suppressed laugh.
– DERIVATIVES **tittering** adjective, **titteringly** adverb.
– ORIGIN early 17th cent.: imitative.

tittivate ▶ verb archaic spelling of **TITIVATE**.

tittle ▶ noun [in sing.] a tiny amount or part of something: *the rules have* **not** *been altered* **one jot or tittle** *since*.
– ORIGIN late Middle English: from Latin *titulus* (see **TITLE**), in medieval Latin 'small stroke, accent'; the phrase *jot or tittle* is from Matt. 5:18.

tittle-tattle ▶ noun [mass noun] idle talk; gossip.
▶ verb [no obj.] engage in such talk.
– ORIGIN early 16th cent.: reduplication of **TATTLE**.

tittup /ˈtɪtəp/ ▶ verb (**tittups, tittuping, tittuped**, or **tittups, tittupping, tittupped**) [no obj., with adverbial of direction] chiefly Brit. move with jerky or exaggerated movements: *Nicky came tittupping along in a rakish mood*.
– ORIGIN late 17th cent. (as a noun): perhaps imitative of hoof-beats.

titty (also **tittie**) ▶ noun (pl. **titties**) chiefly N. Amer. another term for **TIT**[2].

titubation /ˌtɪtjʊˈbeɪʃ(ə)n/ ▶ noun [mass noun] Medicine nodding movement of the head or body, especially as caused by a nervous disorder.
– ORIGIN mid 17th cent.: from Latin *titubatio(n-)*, from *titubare* 'to totter'.

titular /ˈtɪtjʊlə/ ▶ adjective **1** holding or constituting a purely formal position or title without any real authority: *the queen is titular head of the Church of England | a titular post*. ■ (of a cleric) nominally appointed to serve a diocese, abbey, or other foundation no longer in existence, and typically in fact having authority in another capacity.
2 relating to or denoted by a title: *the work's titular song*.
3 denoting any of the parish churches in Rome to which cardinals are formally appointed.
– ORIGIN late 16th cent. (in the sense 'existing only in name'): from French *titulaire* or modern Latin *titularis*, from *titulus* (see **TITLE**).

titularly ▶ adverb in name or in name only: *he was titularly a chief petty officer*.

Titus /ˈtʌɪtəs/ (AD 39–81), Roman emperor 79–81, son of Vespasian; full name *Titus Vespasianus Augustus*; born *Titus Flavius Vespasianus*. In 70 he ended a revolt in Judaea with the conquest of Jerusalem.

Titus, Epistle to a book of the New Testament, an epistle of St Paul addressed to St Titus.

Titus, St (1st century AD), Greek churchman. A convert and helper of St Paul, he was traditionally the first bishop of Crete. Feast day (in the Eastern Church) 23 August; (in the Western Church) 6 February.

Tiv /tɪv/ ▶ noun (pl. **same** or **Tivs**) **1** a member of a people of SE Nigeria.
2 [mass noun] the Benue-Congo language of the Tiv, with about 1.5 million speakers.
▶ adjective relating to the Tiv or their language.
– ORIGIN the name in Tiv.

Tiwa /ˈtiːwə/ (also **Tigua**) ▶ noun (pl. **same** or **Tiwas**) **1** a member of a Pueblo Indian people living mainly in the region of Taos, New Mexico.
2 [mass noun] the Tanoan language of the Tiwa, with fewer than 5,000 speakers. Compare with **TEWA**.
▶ adjective relating to the Tiwa or their language.
– ORIGIN the name in Tiwa.

tiyin /tiːˈjɪn/ ▶ noun (pl. **same** or **tiyins**) a monetary unit of Kyrgyzstan and Uzbekistan, equal to one hundredth of a som.
– ORIGIN Kyrgyz.

tizzy (also **tizz**) ▶ noun (pl. **tizzies**) [in sing.] informal a state of nervous excitement or agitation: *he got into a tizzy and was talking absolute tosh*.
– ORIGIN 1930s (originally US): of unknown origin.

T-junction ▶ noun Brit. a junction in the shape of a 'T', in particular a road junction at which one road joins another at right angles without crossing it.

TKO ▶ abbreviation Boxing technical knockout.

Tl ▶ symbol the chemical element thallium.

Tlaxcala /tlɑːsˈkɑːlə/ a state of east central Mexico. ■ its capital city; pop. 15,777 (2005).

TLC ▶ abbreviation informal tender loving care.

Tlemcen /tlɛmˈsɛn/ a city in NW Algeria; pop. 122,300 (est. 2009). In the 13th–15th centuries it was the capital of a Berber dynasty.

Tlingit /ˈklɪŋkɪt, ˈklɪŋgɪt, ˈtlɪŋ-/ ▶ noun (pl. **same** or **Tlingits**) **1** a member of an American Indian people of the coasts and islands of SE Alaska.
2 [mass noun] the language of the Tlingit, which has about 2,000 surviving speakers.
▶ adjective relating to the Tlingit or their language.
– ORIGIN the name in Tlingit.

T-lymphocyte ▶ noun Physiology a lymphocyte of a type produced or processed by the thymus gland and actively participating in the immune response. Also called **T-CELL**. Compare with **B-LYMPHOCYTE**.
– ORIGIN 1970s: from *T* for *thymus*.

TM ▶ abbreviation (trademark in the US) Transcendental Meditation.

Tm ▶ symbol the chemical element thulium.

tmesis /ˈtmiːsɪs/ ▶ noun (pl. **tmeses** /-siːz/) [mass noun] the separation of parts of a compound word by an intervening word or words, used mainly in informal speech for emphasis (e.g. *can't find it any-blooming-where*).
– ORIGIN mid 16th cent.: from Greek *tmēsis* 'cutting', from *temnein* 'to cut'.

TMT ▶ abbreviation technology, media, and telecom (or telecommunications).

TMV ▶ abbreviation tobacco mosaic virus.

TN ▶ abbreviation ■ Tennessee (in official postal use). ■ Tunisia (international vehicle registration).

tn ▶ abbreviation ■ US ton(s). ■ town.

TNC ▶ abbreviation transnational corporation.

TNT ▶ noun [mass noun] a high explosive formed from toluene by substitution of three hydrogen atoms with nitro groups. It is relatively insensitive to shock and can be conveniently melted. ● Alternative name: **trinitrotoluene**; chem. formula: $C_7H_5(NO_2)_3$.

to ▶ preposition **1** expressing motion in the direction of (a particular location): *walking down to the shops | my first visit to Africa*. ■ expressing location, typically in relation to a specified point of reference: *forty miles to the south of the site | place the cursor to the left of the first word*. ■ expressing a point reached at the end of a range or after a period of time: *a drop in profits from £105 m to around £75 m | from 1938 to 1945*. ■ chiefly Brit. (in telling the time) before (the hour specified): *it's five to ten*.
2 approaching or reaching (a particular condition): *Christopher's expression changed from amazement to joy | she was close to tears*. ■ expressing the result of a process or action: *smashed to smithereens*. ■ governing a phrase expressing someone's reaction to something: *to her astonishment, he smiled*.
3 identifying the person or thing affected by or receiving something: *you were terribly unkind to her | they donated £400 to the hospice*.
4 identifying a particular relationship between one person and another: *he is married to his cousin Emma | he's economic adviser to the president*. ■ used in various phrases to indicate how something is related to something else (often followed by a noun without a determiner): *made to order | a prelude to disaster*. ■ indicating a rate of return on something, for example the distance travelled in exchange for fuel used: *my car only does ten miles to the gallon*. ■ (**to the**) Mathematics indicating the power (exponent) to which a number is raised: *ten to the minus thirty-three*.
5 indicating that two things are attached or linked: *he had left his dog tied to a drainpipe | they are inextricably linked to this island*.
6 concerning or likely to concern (something): *a threat to world peace | a reference to Psalm 22:18*.
7 used to introduce the second element in a comparison: *the club's nothing to what it once was*.
8 placed before a debit entry in accounting.
▶ infinitive marker **1** used with the base form of a verb to indicate that the verb is in the infinitive, in particular: ■ expressing purpose or intention: *I set out to buy food | I am* **going to** *tell you a story*. ■ expressing an outcome or result: *she was left to die | I managed to escape*. ■ expressing a cause: *I'm sorry to hear that*. ■ indicating a desired or advisable action: *I'd love to go to France this summer | the leaflet explains how to start a course*. ■ indicating a proposition that is known, believed, or reported about a specified person or thing: *a house that people believed to be haunted*. ■ (**about to**) forming a future tense with reference to the immediate future: *he was about to sing*. ■ after a noun, indicating its function or purpose: *a chair to sit on | something to eat*. ■ after a phrase containing an ordinal number: *the first person to arrive*.
2 used without a verb following when the missing verb is clearly understood: *he asked her to come but she said she didn't want to*.
▶ adverb so as to be closed or nearly closed: *he pulled the door to behind him*.
– ORIGIN Old English *tō* (adverb and preposition), of West Germanic origin; related to Dutch *toe* and German *zu*.

toad ▶ noun **1** a tailless amphibian with a short stout body and short legs, typically having dry warty skin that can exude poison. ● Several families in the order Anura, in particular Bufonidae, which includes the **European common toad** (*Bufo bufo*).
2 a contemptible or detestable person (used as a general term of abuse): *you're an arrogant little toad*.
– DERIVATIVES **toadish** adjective.
– ORIGIN Old English *tādde, tāda*, abbreviation of *tadige*, of unknown origin.

toad-eater ▶ noun archaic a toady.

toadfish ▶ noun (pl. **same** or **toadfishes**) any of a number of fishes with a wide flattened head: ● a chiefly bottom-dwelling large-mouthed fish of warm seas that can produce loud grunts (family Batrachoididae: several genera). ● Australian term for **PUFFERFISH**.

toadflax ▶ noun a Eurasian plant of the figwort family, typically having yellow or purplish flowers which resemble snapdragons and slender leaves. ● *Linaria* and related genera, family Scrophulariaceae: several species, in particular the common **yellow toadflax** (*L. vulgaris*) and **ivy-leaved toadflax** (*Cymbalaria muralis*).

toad-in-the-hole ▶ noun [mass noun] Brit. a dish consisting of sausages baked in batter.

toadlet ▶ noun **1** a small kind of toad. ● Several genera, including *Pseudophryne* of Australia (family Myobatrachidae), and *Pelophryne* of SE Asia (family Bufonidae).
2 a tiny toad that has recently developed from a tadpole.

toadstone ▶ noun a gem, fossil tooth, or other stone formerly supposed to have been formed in the body of a toad, and credited with therapeutic or protective properties.

toadstool ▶ noun the spore-bearing fruiting body of a fungus, typically in the form of a rounded cap on a stalk, especially one that is believed to be inedible or poisonous. See also **MUSHROOM**.
– ORIGIN late Middle English: a fanciful name.

toady ▶ noun (pl. **toadies**) **1** a person who behaves obsequiously to someone important.
2 Australian term for **PUFFERFISH**.
▶ verb (**toadies, toadying, toadied**) [no obj.] act in an obsequious way: *she imagined him* **toadying to** *his rich clients*.
– DERIVATIVES **toadyish** adjective, **toadyism** noun.
– ORIGIN early 19th cent.: said to be a contraction of *toad-eater*, a charlatan's assistant who ate toads; toads were regarded as poisonous, and the assistant's

survival was thought to be due to the efficacy of the charlatan's remedy.

to and fro ▶ adverb in a constant movement backwards and forwards or from side to side: *she cradled him, rocking him to and fro.*
▶ verb [no obj.] (**be toing and froing**) move constantly backwards and forwards: *the ducks were toing and froing* | (as noun **toing and froing**) *it does cost a lot, all this toing and froing up to London.* ■ repeatedly discuss or think about something without making any progress.
▶ noun [in sing.] constant movement backwards and forwards: *Wilkie watched the to and fro of their dancing.*

toast[1] ▶ noun **1** [mass noun] sliced bread browned on both sides by exposure to radiant heat, such as a grill or fire.
2 a call to a gathering of people to raise their glasses and drink together in honour of a person or thing, or an instance of drinking in this way: *he raised his glass in a toast to his son.* ■ [in sing.] a person or thing that is very popular or held in high regard by a particular group of people: *he found himself* **the toast of** *the baseball world.*
▶ verb [with obj.] **1** cook or brown (food, especially bread or cheese) by exposure to a grill, fire, or other source of radiant heat: *he sat by the fire and toasted a piece of bread* | (as adj. **toasted**) *a toasted cheese sandwich.* ■ [no obj.] (of food) cook or become brown by exposure to radiant heat: *place under a hot grill until the nuts have toasted.* ■ warm (oneself or part of one's body) in front of a fire or other source or heat.
2 drink to the health or in honour of (someone or something) by raising one's glass together with others: *happy families toasting each other's health* | figurative *he is toasted by the trade as the outstanding dealer in children's books.*
– PHRASES **be toast** informal be or be likely to become finished, defunct, or dead: *one mistake and you're toast.* **have someone on toast** Brit. informal be in a position to deal with someone as one wishes.
– ORIGIN late Middle English (as a verb in the sense 'burn as the sun does, parch'): from Old French *toster* 'roast', from Latin *torrere* 'parch'. The practice of drinking a toast (sense 2 of the noun) goes back to the late 17th cent., and originated in naming a lady whose health the company was requested to drink, the idea being that the lady's name flavoured the drink like the pieces of spiced toast that were formerly placed in drinks such as wine.

toast[2] ▶ verb [no obj.] (usu. as noun **toasting**) (of a DJ) accompany a reggae backing track or music with improvised rhythmic speech.
– ORIGIN 1970s: perhaps the same word as TOAST[1].

toaster ▶ noun **1** an electrical device for making toast.
2 a DJ who accompanies reggae with improvised rhythmic speech.

toastie ▶ noun Brit. informal a toasted sandwich or snack.

toasting fork ▶ noun a long-handled fork for making toast in front of a fire.

toastmaster (or **toastmistress**) ▶ noun an official responsible for proposing toasts, introducing speakers, and making other formal announcements at a large social event.

toast rack ▶ noun a rack for holding slices of toast at table. ■ informal a tram or bus with full-width seats and open sides.

T

toasty ▶ adjective (**toastier, toastiest**) of or resembling toast. ■ informal comfortably warm: *a roaring fire may make a home seem toasty.*

Tob. ▶ abbreviation (in biblical references) Tobit (Apocrypha).

tobacco ▶ noun (pl. **tobaccos**) **1** [mass noun] a preparation of the nicotine-rich leaves of an American plant, which are cured by a process of drying and fermentation for smoking or chewing.
2 (also **tobacco plant**) the plant of the nightshade family which yields tobacco, native to tropical America. It is widely cultivated in warm regions, especially in the US and China. ● *Nicotiana tabacum*, family Solanaceae.
■ an ornamental plant related to tobacco. See NICOTIANA.
– ORIGIN mid 16th cent.: from Spanish *tabaco*; said to be from a Carib word denoting a tobacco pipe or from a Taino word for a primitive cigar, but perhaps from Arabic.

tobacco beetle ▶ noun another term for CIGARETTE BEETLE.

tobacco mosaic virus ▶ noun a virus that causes mosaic disease in tobacco, much used in biochemical research.

tobacconist ▶ noun chiefly Brit. a shopkeeper who sells cigarettes, tobacco, and other items used by smokers.

tobacco pipe ▶ noun another term for PIPE (sense 2 of the noun).

Tobago see TRINIDAD AND TOBAGO.

Tobit /ˈtəʊbɪt/ a pious Israelite living during the Babylonian Captivity, described in the Apocrypha. ■ a book of the Apocrypha telling the story of Tobit.

toboggan ▶ noun a long, light, narrow vehicle, typically on runners, used for sliding downhill over snow or ice.
▶ verb [no obj.] (usu. as noun **tobogganing**) ride on a toboggan: *he thought he would enjoy the tobogganing.*
– DERIVATIVES **tobogganer** noun, **tobogganist** noun.
– ORIGIN early 19th cent.: from Canadian French *tabaganne*, from Micmac *topăgan* 'sled'.

tobramycin /ˌtɒbrəˈmʌɪsɪn/ ▶ noun [mass noun] Medicine a bacterial antibiotic used chiefly to treat pseudomonas infections. ● The drug is obtained from the bacterium *Streptomyces tenebrarius*.
– ORIGIN 1970s: from *to-* (of unknown origin) + Latin (*tene*)*bra*(*rius*) 'belonging to darkness' (part of the name of the bacterium) + -MYCIN.

Tobruk /təˈbrʊk/ a port on the Mediterranean coast of NE Libya; pop. 134,600 (est. 2009). It was the scene of fierce fighting during the North African campaign in the Second World War. Arabic name TUBRUQ.

toby ▶ noun (pl. **tobies**) **1** another term for MOORISH IDOL.
2 South African term for PUFFERFISH.

Toby jug ▶ noun chiefly Brit. a beer jug or mug in the form of a stout old man wearing a three-cornered hat.
– ORIGIN mid 19th cent.: pet form of the given name *Tobias*, and said to come from an 18th-cent. poem about *Toby Philpot* (with a pun on *fill pot*), a soldier who liked to drink.

TOC ▶ abbreviation (in the UK) train operating company.

Tocantins /ˌtəʊkənˈtiːns/ **1** a river of South America, which rises in central Brazil and flows 2,640 km (1,640 miles) northwards, joining the Pará to enter the Atlantic through a large estuary at Belém.
2 a state of central Brazil; capital, Palmas.

toccata /təˈkɑːtə/ ▶ noun a musical composition for a keyboard instrument designed to exhibit the performer's touch and technique.
– ORIGIN early 18th cent.: from Italian, feminine past participle of *toccare* 'to touch'.

Toc H /tɒk ˈeɪtʃ/ (in the UK) a society, originally of ex-service personnel, founded after the First World War for promoting Christian fellowship and social service.
– ORIGIN from *toc* (former telegraphy code for *T*) and *H*, from the initials of *Talbot House*, a soldier's club established in Belgium in 1915.

Tocharian /təˈkɛːrɪən, -ˈkɑːrɪən/ ▶ noun **1** a member of a central Asian people who inhabited the Tarim Basin in the 1st millennium AD.
2 [mass noun] either of two extinct languages (**Tocharian A** and **Tocharian B**) spoken by the Tocharians, the most easterly of known ancient Indo-European languages, surviving in a few documents and inscriptions and showing curious affinities to Celtic and Italic languages.
▶ adjective relating to the Tocharians or their languages.
– ORIGIN from French *tocharien*, via Latin from Greek *Tokharoi*, the name of a Scythian tribe (almost certainly unrelated to the Tocharians).

tochus /ˈtəʊxəs, ˈtɒxəs/ ▶ noun informal, chiefly N. Amer. a person's buttocks or anus.
– ORIGIN early 20th cent.: from Yiddish *tokhes*, from Hebrew *tahạtẖ* 'beneath'.

toco /ˈtəʊkə/ (also **toco toucan**) ▶ noun (pl. **tocos**) the largest and most familiar South American toucan, with mainly black plumage, a white throat and breast, and a massive black-tipped orange bill. ● *Ramphastos toco*, family Ramphastidae.
– ORIGIN late 18th cent.: via Portuguese from Tupi; compare with TOUCAN.

tocopherol /tɒˈkɒfərɒl/ ▶ noun Biochemistry any of several closely related compounds, found in wheatgerm oil, egg yolk, and leafy vegetables, which collectively constitute vitamin E. They are fat-soluble alcohols with antioxidant properties, important in the stabilization of cell membranes.
– ORIGIN 1930s: from Greek *tokos* 'offspring' + *pherein* 'to bear' + -OL.

tocsin /ˈtɒksɪn/ ▶ noun archaic an alarm bell or signal.
– ORIGIN late 16th cent.: from Old French *toquassen*, from Provençal *tocasenh*, from *tocar* 'to touch' + *senh* 'signal bell'.

tod ▶ noun (in phrase **on one's tod**) Brit. informal on one's own: *I'm going to do something, not just sit here on my tod.*
– ORIGIN 1930s: from rhyming slang *Tod Sloan*, the name of an American jockey (1873–1933).

today ▶ adverb on or in the course of this present day: *she's thirty today* | *he will appear in court today.* ■ at the present period of time; nowadays: *millions of people in Britain today cannot afford adequate housing.*
▶ noun this present day: *today is a rest day* | *today's match against United.* ■ the present period of time: *the powerful computers of today* | *today's society.*
– PHRASES **today week** Brit. a week from today.
– ORIGIN Old English *tō dæg* 'on (this) day'. Compare with TOMORROW and TONIGHT.

Todd, Sweeney, a barber who murdered his customers, the central character of a play by George Dibdin Pitt (1799–1855) and of later plays.

toddle ▶ verb [no obj. and with adverbial of direction] (of a young child) move with short unsteady steps while learning to walk: *William toddled curiously towards the TV crew.* ■ informal walk or go somewhere in a casual or leisurely way: *they would go for a drink and then toddle off home.*
▶ noun [in sing.] a young child's unsteady walk.
– ORIGIN late 16th cent.: of unknown origin.

toddler ▶ noun a young child who is just beginning to walk.
– DERIVATIVES **toddlerhood** noun.

toddy ▶ noun (pl. **toddies**) [mass noun] **1** a drink made of spirits with hot water, sugar, and sometimes spices.
2 the naturally alcoholic sap of some kinds of palm, used as a beverage in tropical countries.
– ORIGIN early 17th cent. (in sense 2): from Marathi *tāḍī*, Hindi *tāṛī*, from Sanskrit *tāḍī* 'palmyra'.

toddy cat ▶ noun the common palm civet of Asia, which is noted for its habit of stealing toddy from the bamboo tubes placed to collect it from palm trunks.

todger (also **tadger**) ▶ noun Brit. informal a man's penis.
– ORIGIN 1950s: of unknown origin.

to-do ▶ noun [in sing.] informal a commotion or fuss: *he made a great to-do about fetching a cup.*
– ORIGIN late 16th cent.: from *to do* as in *much to do*, originally meaning 'much needing to be done' but later interpreted as the adjective *much* and a noun; compare with ADO.

tody /ˈtəʊdi/ ▶ noun (pl. **todies**) a small insectivorous Caribbean bird related to the motmots, with a large head, long bill, bright green upper parts, and a red throat. ● Family Todidae and genus *Todus*: five species.
– ORIGIN late 18th cent.: from French *todier*, from Latin *todus*, the name of a small bird.

toe ▶ noun **1** any of the five digits at the end of the human foot: *he cut his big toe on a sharp stone.* ■ any of the digits of the foot of a quadruped or bird. ■ the part of an item of footwear that covers a person's toes.
2 the lower end, tip, or point of something, in particular: ■ the tip of the head of a golf club, furthest from the shaft. ■ the base of a cliff, slope, or embankment. ■ a flattish portion at the foot of an otherwise steep curve on a graph. ■ a section of a rhizome or similar fleshy root from which a new plant may be propagated.
▶ verb (**toes, toeing, toed**) **1** [with obj. and usu. with adverbial] push, touch, or kick with one's toe: *he toed off his shoes and flexed his feet.* ■ Golf strike (the ball) with the toe of the club.
2 [no obj.] (**toe in/out**) walk with the toes pointed in (or out). ■ (of a pair of wheels) converge (or diverge) slightly at the front: *on a turn, the inner wheel toes out more.*
– PHRASES **make someone's toes curl** informal bring about an extreme reaction of embarrassment or delight in someone. **on one's toes** ready for any eventuality; alert: *he carries out random spot checks to keep everyone on their toes.* **toe the line** accept the authority, policies, or principles of a particular group, especially unwillingly. [from the literal sense 'stand with the tips of the toes exactly touching a line'.] **toe to toe** (of two people) standing directly in

front of one another, especially in order to fight or argue. **turn up one's toes** informal die.
– DERIVATIVES **toed** adjective [in combination] *steel-toed boots*, **toeless** adjective.
– ORIGIN Old English *tā*, of Germanic origin; related to Dutch *tee* and German *Zeh, Zehe*. Current senses of the verb date from the mid 19th cent.

> **USAGE** The phrase **toe the line**, derived from an earlier sense 'stand with one's toes touching a line, as for a contest', is sometimes misunderstood and written as **tow the line**. In the Oxford English Corpus around 15 per cent of the citations for the phrase are for the erroneous form.

toea /ˈtəʊeɪə/ ▶ noun (pl. **same**) a monetary unit of Papua New Guinea, equal to one hundredth of a kina.
– ORIGIN Motu, literally 'cone-shaped shell'.

toe box ▶ noun a piece of stiffened material between the lining and the toecap of a shoe.

toecap ▶ noun a piece of steel or leather constituting or fitted over the front part of a boot or shoe as protection or reinforcement.

toe clip ▶ noun a clip on a bicycle pedal to prevent the foot from slipping.

toe-curling ▶ adjective informal very embarrassing or excessively sentimental: *a toe-curling ballad*.
– DERIVATIVES **toe-curlingly** adverb.

toehold ▶ noun a small place where a person's foot can be lodged to support them, especially while climbing. ■ a relatively insignificant position from which further progress may be made: *the initiative is helping companies to gain a toehold in the Gulf*.

toe-in /ˈtəʊɪn/ ▶ noun [mass noun] a slight forward convergence of a pair of wheels so that they are closer together in front than behind.

toe loop ▶ noun Skating a jump, initiated with the help of the supporting foot, in which the skater makes a full turn in the air, taking off from and landing on the outside edge of the same foot.

toenail ▶ noun **1** the nail at the tip of each toe.
2 a nail driven obliquely through a piece of wood to secure it.
▶ verb [with obj.] fasten (a piece of wood) in this way.

toe-out /ˈtəʊaʊt/ ▶ noun [mass noun] a slight forward divergence of a pair of wheels so that they are closer together behind than in front.

toerag ▶ noun Brit. informal a contemptible or worthless person.
– ORIGIN mid 19th cent.: originally denoting a rag wrapped round the foot as a sock or, by extension, the wearer (such as a vagrant).

toe-tapping ▶ adjective informal (of music) making one want to tap one's feet; lively.

toey ▶ adjective [predic.] Austral./NZ informal on edge; ill at ease: *voters being toey about foreign investment*.

toff Brit. informal ▶ noun derogatory a rich or upper-class person.
▶ verb (**be toffed up**) dated be smartly dressed: *he was all toffed up in officer's broadcloth*.
– ORIGIN mid 19th cent.: perhaps an alteration of **TUFT**, used to denote a gold tassel worn on the cap by titled undergraduates at Oxford and Cambridge.

toffee ▶ noun [mass noun] **1** a kind of firm or hard sweet which softens when sucked or chewed, made by boiling together sugar and butter, often with other ingredients or flavourings added. ■ [count noun] a small shaped piece of toffee.
2 Brit. informal, dated nonsense; rubbish: *his wife swallowed this load of old toffee*.
– PHRASES **not be able to do something for toffee** Brit. informal be totally incompetent at doing something: *Jill said I couldn't sing for toffee*.
– ORIGIN early 19th cent.: alteration of **TAFFY**.

toffee apple ▶ noun Brit. an apple coated with a thin layer of toffee and fixed on a stick.

toffee-nosed ▶ adjective Brit. informal pretentiously superior; snobbish: *toffee-nosed creeps who think they're the same as royalty*.
– DERIVATIVES **toffee nose** noun.

Tofranil /ˈtɒfrənɪl/ ▶ noun trademark for **IMIPRAMINE**.
– ORIGIN 1950s: of unknown origin.

toft ▶ noun Brit. historical a homestead.
– ORIGIN Old English, from Old Norse *topt*.

tofu /ˈtəʊfuː/ ▶ noun [mass noun] a soft white substance made from mashed soya beans, used chiefly in Asian and vegetarian cookery.
– ORIGIN from Japanese *tōfu*, from Chinese *dòufu*, from *dòu* 'beans' + *fŭ* 'rot, turn sour'.

tog[1] informal ▶ noun (**togs**) clothes: *running togs*. ■ Austral./NZ & Irish a swimming costume.
▶ verb (**be/get togged up/out**) be or get dressed for a particular occasion or activity: *we got togged up in our glad rags*.
– ORIGIN early 18th cent. (as a slang term for a coat or outer garment): apparently an abbreviation of obsolete criminals' slang *togeman(s)* 'a light cloak', from French *toge* or Latin *toga* (see **TOGA**).

tog[2] ▶ noun Brit. a unit of thermal resistance used to express the insulating properties of clothes and quilts.
– ORIGIN 1940s: from **TOG[1]**, on the pattern of an earlier unit called the *clo* (first element of *clothes*).

toga /ˈtəʊgə/ ▶ noun a loose flowing outer garment worn by the citizens of ancient Rome, made of a single piece of cloth and covering the whole body apart from the right arm.
– ORIGIN Latin; related to *tegere* 'to cover'.

together ▶ adverb **1** with or in proximity to another person or people: *together they climbed the dark stairs | they stood together in the kitchen*. ■ so as to touch or combine: *she held her hands together as if she was praying | mix together the soya sauce and sesame oil*. ■ in combination; collectively: *taken together, these measures would significantly improve people's chances of surviving a coach crash*.
2 into companionship or close association: *the experience has brought us together*. ■ (of a couple) married or in a sexual relationship: *they split up after ten years together*. ■ so as to be in agreement: *he won the confidence of the government and the rebels, but could not bring the two sides together*.
3 at the same time: *they both spoke together*.
4 without interruption; continuously: *she sits for hours together in the lotus position*.
▶ adjective informal self-confident, level-headed, or well organized: *she looks a very together young woman*.
– PHRASES **together with** as well as; along with: *their meal arrived, together with a carafe of red wine*.
– ORIGIN Old English *tōgædere*, based on the preposition **TO** + a West Germanic word related to **GATHER**. The adjective dates from the 1960s.

togetherness ▶ noun [mass noun] the state of being close to another person or other people: *the sense of family togetherness was strong and excluded neighbours*.

Toggenburg /ˈtɒgənbəːg/ ▶ noun a goat of a hornless light brown breed developed in the region of Toggenburg, a valley in the region of St Gallen, Switzerland.

toggery ▶ noun [mass noun] informal, humorous clothes.

toggle ▶ noun **1** a short rod of wood or plastic sewn to one side of a coat or other garment, pushed through a hole or loop on the other side and twisted so as to act as a fastener. ■ a pin or other crosspiece put through the eye of a rope or a link of a chain to keep it in place. ■ (also **toggle bolt**) a kind of wall fastener for use on open-backed plasterboard, having a part that springs open or turns through 90° after it is inserted so as to prevent withdrawal. ■ a movable pivoted crosspiece acting as a barb on a harpoon.
2 (also **toggle switch** or **toggle key**) Computing a key or command that is operated the same way but with opposite effect on successive occasions.
▶ verb **1** [no obj., with adverbial] Computing switch from one effect, feature, or state to another by using a toggle.
2 [with obj.] provide or fasten with a toggle or toggles.
– ORIGIN mid 18th cent. (originally in nautical use): of unknown origin.

toggle switch ▶ noun **1** an electric switch operated by means of a projecting lever that is moved up and down.
2 Computing another term for **TOGGLE**.

Togliatti /tɒˈljati/ an industrial city and river port in SW Russia, on the River Volga; pop. 705,500 (est. 2008). It was founded in 1738 but relocated in the mid 1950s to make way for the Kuibyshev reservoir. Former name (until 1964) **STAVROPOL**; Russian name **TOLYATTI**.
– ORIGIN renamed in 1964 after Palmiro *Togliatti* (1893–1964), leader of the Italian Communist Party.

Togo /ˈtəʊgəʊ/ a country in West Africa with a short coastline on the Gulf of Guinea; pop. 6,031,800 (est. 2009); languages, French (official), West African languages; capital, Lomé. Official name **Togolese Republic**.

> The region formerly known as Togoland lay between the military powers of Ashanti and Dahomey and became a centre of the slave trade. It was annexed by Germany in 1884 and divided between France and Britain after the First World War. The western, British section joined Ghana on the latter's independence (1957). The remainder, administered by France under a UN mandate after the Second World War, became an independent republic with the name Togo in 1960.

– DERIVATIVES **Togolese** /ˌtəʊgəˈliːz/ adjective & noun.

togt /tɒxt/ ▶ adjective [attrib.] S. African (of a labourer or their work) hired or paid for by the day; casual.
– ORIGIN Afrikaans, from Dutch *tocht* 'expedition, journey'.

Tohoku /təʊˈhəʊkuː/ a region of Japan, on the island of Honshu; capital, Sendai.

tohubohu /ˌtəʊhuːˈbəʊhuː/ ▶ noun N. Amer. informal a state of chaos; utter confusion: *a fearful tohubohu*.
– ORIGIN from Hebrew *tōhū wa-ḇōhū* 'emptiness and desolation', translated in Gen. 1:2 (Bible of 1611) as 'without form and void'.

toil ▶ verb [no obj.] work extremely hard or incessantly: *we toiled away* | [with infinitive] *Richard toiled to build his editorial team*. ■ [with adverbial of direction] move slowly and with difficulty: *she began to toil up the cliff path*.
▶ noun [mass noun] exhausting physical labour: *a life of toil*.
– DERIVATIVES **toiler** noun.
– ORIGIN Middle English (in the senses 'contend verbally' and 'strife'): from Anglo-Norman French *toiler* 'strive, dispute', *toil* 'confusion', from Latin *tudiculare* 'stir about', from *tudicula* 'machine for crushing olives', related to *tundere* 'crush'.

toile /twɑːl/ ▶ noun **1** an early version of a finished garment made up in cheap material so that the design can be tested and perfected.
2 [mass noun] a translucent linen or cotton fabric, used for making clothes. ■ short for **TOILE DE JOUY**.
– ORIGIN late Middle English (denoting cloth or canvas for painting on): from French *toile* 'cloth, web', from Latin *tela* 'web'.

toile de Jouy /də ʒwiː/ ▶ noun [mass noun] a type of printed calico with a characteristic floral, figure, or landscape design on a light background.
– ORIGIN originally made at *Jouy*-en-Josas, near Paris.

toilet ▶ noun **1** a large bowl for urinating or defecating into, typically plumbed into a sewage system and with a flushing mechanism; a lavatory: *Liz heard the toilet flush*. ■ a room, building, or cubicle containing a toilet or toilets.
2 [in sing.] the process of washing oneself, dressing, and attending to one's appearance: *her toilet completed, she finally went back downstairs*. ■ [as modifier] denoting articles used in this process: *a bathroom cabinet stocked with toilet articles*. ■ the cleansing of part of a person's body as a medical procedure.
▶ verb (**toilets, toileting, toileted**) [with obj.] (usu. as noun **toileting**) assist or supervise (someone, especially an infant or invalid) in using a toilet.
– PHRASES **go down the toilet** informal be completely lost or wasted; fail utterly: *they didn't want to see their investment go down the toilet*.
– ORIGIN mid 16th cent.: from French *toilette* 'cloth, wrapper', diminutive of *toile* (see **TOILE**). The word originally denoted a cloth used as a wrapper for clothes; then (in the 17th cent.) a cloth cover for a dressing table, the articles used in dressing, and the process of dressing, later also of washing oneself (sense 2 of the noun). In the 19th cent. the word came to denote a dressing room, and, in the US, one with washing facilities; hence, a lavatory (early 20th cent.).

toilet bag ▶ noun Brit. a waterproof bag for holding toothpaste, soap, and other bathroom items when travelling.

toilet paper ▶ noun [mass noun] paper in sheets or on a roll for wiping oneself clean after urination or defecation.

toiletries ▶ plural noun articles used in washing and taking care of one's body, such as soap, shampoo, and toothpaste.

toilet roll ▶ noun Brit. a roll of toilet paper.

toilet set ▶ noun a set of items used in arranging the hair, including a hairbrush, comb, and mirror. ■ a set of items formerly used in washing and cleaning oneself, including a wash bowl, jug, and chamber pot.

toilet soap ▶ noun soap for washing oneself.

toilet table ▶ noun old-fashioned term for **DRESSING TABLE**.

toilette /twɑːˈlɛt/ ▶ noun [in sing.] dated the process of washing oneself, dressing, and attending to one's

appearance: *Emily got up to begin her morning toilette.*
– ORIGIN late 17th cent.: French (see TOILET).

toilet tissue ▶ noun another term for TOILET PAPER.

toilet-train ▶ verb [with obj.] teach (a young child) to use the toilet: *she was toilet-trained by the age of one.*

toilet water ▶ noun a dilute form of perfume. Also called EAU DE TOILETTE.

toils ▶ plural noun literary used in reference to a situation regarded as a trap: *Henry had become caught in the toils of his own deviousness.*
– ORIGIN early 16th cent. (denoting a net into which a hunted quarry is driven): plural of *toil*, from Old French *toile* 'net, trap' (see TOILE).

toilsome ▶ adjective archaic or literary involving hard or tedious work: *toilsome chores.*
– DERIVATIVES **toilsomely** adverb.

toilworn ▶ adjective literary exhausted by punishing physical labour: *a toilworn old woman.*

Tojo /ˈtəʊdʒəʊ/, Hideki (1884–1948), Japanese military leader and statesman, Prime Minister 1941–4. He initiated the Japanese attack on Pearl Harbor and by 1944 he had assumed virtual control of all political and military decision-making. After Japan's surrender he was tried and hanged as a war criminal.

tokamak /ˈtəʊkəmak/ ▶ noun Physics a toroidal apparatus for producing controlled fusion reactions in hot plasma.
– ORIGIN 1960s: Russian, from *toroidal'naya kamera s magnitnym polem* 'toroidal chamber with magnetic field'.

Tokay /təʊˈkeɪ/ ▶ noun [mass noun] a sweet aromatic wine, originally made near Tokaj in Hungary.

tokay /təʊˈkeɪ/ (also **tokay gecko**) ▶ noun a large grey SE Asian gecko with orange and blue spots, having a loud call that resembles its name. ● *Gekko gecko*, family Gekkonidae.
– ORIGIN mid 18th cent.: from Malay dialect *toke'*, from Javanese *tekèk*, imitative of its call.

toke informal ▶ noun a pull on a cigarette or pipe, typically one containing cannabis.
▶ verb [no obj.] smoke cannabis or tobacco: *he muses while toking on a cigarette* | [with obj.] *we toke some grass.*
– DERIVATIVES **toker** noun.
– ORIGIN 1950s: of unknown origin.

Tokelau /ˌtəʊkəˈlaːuː/ a group of three islands in the western Pacific, between Kiribati and Samoa, forming an overseas territory of New Zealand; pop. 1,466 (2006).

token ▶ noun **1** a thing serving as a visible or tangible representation of a fact, quality, feeling, etc.: *mistletoe was cut from an oak tree as a token of good fortune* | *I wanted to offer you a small token of my appreciation.* ■ archaic a badge or favour worn to indicate allegiance to a particular person or party. ■ archaic a word or object conferring authority on or serving to authenticate the speaker or holder. ■ a staff or other object given to a train driver on a single-track railway as authority to proceed over a given section of line.
2 a voucher that can be exchanged for goods or services, typically one given as a gift or forming part of a promotional offer: *a record token.* ■ a metal or plastic disc used to operate a machine or in exchange for particular goods or services: *a milk token.*
3 an individual occurrence of a symbol or string, in particular: ■ Linguistics an individual occurrence of a linguistic unit in speech or writing. Contrasted with TYPE. ■ Computing the smallest meaningful unit of information in a sequence of data for a compiler.
4 Computing a sequence of bits passed continuously between nodes in a fixed order and enabling a node to transmit information.
▶ adjective done for the sake of appearances or as a symbolic gesture: *cases like these often bring just token fines from magistrates.* ■ [attrib.] chosen by way of tokenism as a representative of a particular minority or under-represented group: *she took offence at being called the token woman on the force.*
– PHRASES **by the same** (or **that** or **this**) **token** in the same way or for the same reason: *there was little evidence to substantiate the gossip and, by the same token, there was little to disprove it.* **in token of** as a sign or symbol of: *adults exchanging drinks around a pub bar in token of temporary friendship.*
– DERIVATIVES **tokenize** (also **tokenise**) verb (sense 3 of the noun).
– ORIGIN Old English *tāc(e)n*, of Germanic origin; related to Dutch *teken* and German *Zeichen*, also to TEACH.

tokenism ▶ noun [mass noun] the practice of making only a perfunctory or symbolic effort to do a particular thing, especially by recruiting a small number of people from under-represented groups in order to give the appearance of sexual or racial equality within a workforce.
– DERIVATIVES **tokenistic** adjective.

token money ▶ noun [mass noun] money where the face value of notes or coins is unrelated to the value of the material of which they are composed.

token ring ▶ noun Computing a local area network in which a node can only transmit when in possession of a sequence of bits (the token), which is passed to each node in turn.

tokkin /tɒˈkɪn/ (also **tokkin fund**) ▶ noun (pl. **same** or **tokkins**) (in Japan) a type of short-term corporate investment fund managed by a trust bank, providing a reduction of tax liability and other financial advantages.
– ORIGIN Japanese, acronym from *Tokutei Kinsen Shintaku*, literally 'specifically oriented money in trust'.

tokoloshe /ˈtɒkɒlɒʃ/ ▶ noun S. African (in African folklore) a mischievous and lascivious hairy water sprite.
– ORIGIN Sesotho, Xhosa, and Zulu.

tokonoma /ˌtɒkəʊˈnəʊmə/ ▶ noun (in a Japanese house) a recess or alcove, typically a few inches above floor level, for displaying flowers, pictures, and ornaments.
– ORIGIN Japanese.

Tok Pisin /tɒk ˈpɪsɪn/ ▶ noun [mass noun] an English-based creole used as a commercial and administrative language by over 2 million people in Papua New Guinea. Also called NEO-MELANESIAN.
– ORIGIN the name in Tok Pisin, literally 'pidgin talk'.

tok-tokkie /tɒkˈtɒki/ ▶ noun (pl. **tok-tokkies**) S. African **1** [mass noun] a children's game that involves tricking a victim, especially by knocking on a door and running away before it is answered.
2 a dark rounded African beetle which strikes its abdomen on the ground, making a rapid tapping sound to attract a mate. ● *Dichtha* and other genera, family Tenebrionidae.
– ORIGIN early 20th cent. (in sense 2): Afrikaans, from Dutch *tokken* 'to tap', of imitative origin.

Tokugawa /ˌtɒkuˈgaːwə/ the last shogunate in Japan (1603–1867), founded by Tokugawa Ieyasu (1543–1616). The shogunate was followed by the restoration of imperial power under Meiji Tenno.

Tokyo /ˈtəʊkɪəʊ/ the capital of Japan; pop. 12,758,000 (est. 2007). Formerly called Edo, it was the centre of the military government under the shoguns (1603–1867). It was renamed Tokyo in 1868, when it replaced Kyoto as the imperial capital.

tolar /ˈtɒlaː/ ▶ noun the former basic monetary unit of Slovenia, equal to 100 stotins.
– ORIGIN Slovene; compare with THALER.

tolbooth ▶ noun variant spelling of TOLLBOOTH.

Tolbukhin /tɒlˈbuːkɪn/ former name (1949–91) for DOBRICH.

tolbutamide /tɒlˈbjuːtəmʌɪd/ ▶ noun [mass noun] Medicine a synthetic compound used to lower blood sugar levels in the treatment of diabetes. ● Alternative name: **1-butyl-3-tosylurea**; chem. formula: $C_{12}H_{18}N_2O_3S$.
– ORIGIN 1950s: from *tol(uene)* + *but(yl)* + AMIDE.

told past and past participle of TELL[1].

tole /təʊl/ (also **tôle** /toːl/) ▶ noun [mass noun] painted, enamelled, or lacquered tin plate used to make decorative domestic objects.
– DERIVATIVES **toleware** noun.
– ORIGIN 1940s: French *tôle*, 'sheet iron', from dialect *taule* 'table', from Latin *tabula* 'flat board'.

Toledo 1 /təˈleɪdəʊ/ a city in central Spain on the River Tagus, capital of Castilla-La Mancha region; pop. 80,810 (2008). It was a pre-eminent city and cultural centre of Castile. Toledan steel and sword blades have been famous since the first century BC.
2 /təˈliːdəʊ/ an industrial city and port on Lake Erie, in NW Ohio; pop. 293,201 (est. 2008).
– DERIVATIVES **Toledan** adjective & noun.

tolerable ▶ adjective able to be endured: *a stimulant to make life more tolerable.* ■ fairly good; mediocre: *he was fond of music and had a tolerable voice.*
– DERIVATIVES **tolerability** noun, **tolerably** adverb [as submodifier] *the welfare state works tolerably well.*
– ORIGIN late Middle English: via Old French from Latin *tolerabilis*, from *tolerare* (see TOLERATE).

tolerance ▶ noun **1** [mass noun] the ability or willingness to tolerate the existence of opinions or behaviour that one dislikes or disagrees with: *the tolerance of corruption* | *an advocate of religious tolerance.*
2 the capacity to endure continued subjection to something such as a drug or environmental conditions without adverse reaction: *the desert camel shows the greatest tolerance to dehydration* | [count noun] *various species of diatoms display different tolerances to acid.* ■ diminution in the body's response to a drug after continued use.
3 an allowable amount of variation of a specified quantity, especially in the dimensions of a machine or part: *250 parts in his cars were made to tolerances of one thousandth of an inch.*
– ORIGIN late Middle English (denoting the action of bearing hardship, or the ability to bear pain and hardship): via Old French from Latin *tolerantia*, from *tolerare* (see TOLERATE).

tolerance dose ▶ noun a dose of something toxic, in particular of nuclear radiation, believed to be the maximum that can be taken without harm.

tolerant ▶ adjective **1** showing willingness to allow the existence of opinions or behaviour that one does not necessarily agree with: *we must be tolerant of others* | *a more tolerant attitude towards other religions.*
2 (of a plant, animal, or machine) able to endure specified conditions or treatment: *rye is reasonably tolerant of drought* | [in combination] *fault-tolerant computer systems.*
– DERIVATIVES **tolerantly** adverb TOLERANT (sense 1).
– ORIGIN late 18th cent.: from French *tolérant*, present participle of *tolérer*, from Latin *tolerare* (see TOLERATE). Compare with earlier INTOLERANT.

tolerate ▶ verb [with obj.] **1** allow the existence, occurrence, or practice of (something that one dislikes or disagrees with) without interference: *a regime unwilling to tolerate dissent.* ■ accept or endure (someone or something unpleasant or disliked) with forbearance: *how was it that she could tolerate such noise?*
2 be capable of continued subjection to (a drug, toxin, or environmental condition) without adverse reaction: *lichens grow in conditions that no other plants tolerate.*
– DERIVATIVES **tolerator** noun.
– ORIGIN early 16th cent. (in the sense 'endure pain'): from Latin *tolerat-* 'endured', from the verb *tolerare*.

toleration ▶ noun [mass noun] the practice of tolerating something, in particular differences of opinion or behaviour: *the king demanded greater religious toleration.*
– ORIGIN late 15th cent. (denoting the granting of permission by authority): from French *tolération*, from Latin *toleratio(n-)*, from *tolerare* (see TOLERATE).

Toleration Act an act of 1689 granting freedom of worship to dissenters (excluding Roman Catholics and Unitarians) on certain conditions. Its real purpose was to unite all Protestants under William III against the deposed Roman Catholic James II.

Tolkien /ˈtɒlkiːn/, J. R. R. (1892–1973), British novelist and literary scholar, born in South Africa; full name *John Ronald Reuel Tolkien*. He is famous for the fantasy adventures *The Hobbit* (1937) and *The Lord of the Rings* (1954–5), set in Middle Earth.

toll[1] /təʊl/ ▶ noun **1** a charge payable to use a bridge or road: *motorway tolls* | [as modifier] *a toll bridge.* ■ N. Amer. a charge for a long-distance telephone call.
2 [in sing.] the number of deaths or casualties arising from a natural disaster, conflict, accident, etc.: *the toll of dead and injured mounted.* ■ the adverse effect of something: *the environmental toll of the policy has been high.*
▶ verb [with obj.] (usu. as noun **tolling**) charge a toll for the use of (a bridge or road): *the report advocates motorway tolling.*
– PHRASES **take its toll** (or **take a heavy toll**) have an adverse effect: *years of pumping iron have taken their toll on his body.*
– ORIGIN Old English (denoting a charge, tax, or duty), from medieval Latin *toloneum*, alteration of late Latin *teloneum*, from Greek *telōnion* 'toll house', from *telos* 'tax'. Sense 2 of the noun (late 19th cent.) arose from the notion of paying a toll or tribute in human lives (to an adversary or to death).

toll[2] /təʊl/ ▶ verb (with reference to a bell) sound or cause to sound with a slow, uniform succession of strokes, as a signal or announcement: [no obj.] *the*

T

cathedral bells began to toll for evening service | [with obj.] *the priest began tolling the bell.* ▪ [with obj.] (of a bell) announce or mark (the time, a service, or a person's death): *the bell of St Mary's began to toll the curfew.*
▸ **noun** [in sing.] a single ring of a bell.
– ORIGIN late Middle English: probably a special use of dialect *toll* 'drag, pull'.

tollbooth (also **tolbooth**) ▸ **noun 1** a roadside kiosk where drivers or pedestrians must pay to use a bridge or road.
2 Scottish archaic a town hall. ▪ a town jail.

toll bridge ▸ **noun** a bridge where drivers or pedestrians must pay to cross.

toll gate ▸ **noun** a barrier across a road where drivers or pedestrians must pay to go further.

toll house ▸ **noun** a small house by a toll gate or toll bridge where money is collected from road users.

tollhouse cookie ▸ **noun** US a sweet biscuit made with flour, brown sugar, chocolate chips, and sometimes chopped nuts.
– ORIGIN named after the *Toll House* in Whitman, Massachusetts, source of the original recipe.

toll plaza ▸ **noun** US a row of tollbooths on a toll road.

Tollund Man /ˈtɒlənd/ the well-preserved corpse of an Iron Age man (*c.*500 BC–AD 400) found in 1950 in a peat bog in central Jutland, Denmark. Around the neck was a plaited leather noose, indicating that Tollund Man had met his death by hanging.
– ORIGIN named after *Tollund* Fen, where it was found.

tollway ▸ **noun** US a highway for the use of which a charge is made.

Tolpuddle martyrs /ˈtɒlpʌd(ə)l/ six farm labourers from the village of Tolpuddle in Dorset who attempted to form a trade union and were sentenced in 1834 to seven years' transportation on a charge of administering unlawful oaths. Their harsh sentences caused widespread protests, and two years later they were pardoned and repatriated from Australia.

Tolstoy /ˈtɒlstɔɪ/, Count Leo (1828–1910), Russian writer; Russian name *Lev Nikolaevich Tolstoi*. He is best known for the novels *War and Peace* (1863–9), an epic tale of the Napoleonic invasion, and *Anna Karenina* (1873–7).

Toltec /ˈtɒltɛk/ ▸ **noun** a member of an American Indian people that flourished in Mexico before the Aztecs.
▸ **adjective** relating to the Toltecs.
– ORIGIN via Spanish from Nahuatl *toltecatl*, literally 'a person from *Tula*' (see **TULA**).

tolu /təˈluː, ˈtəʊluː/ (also **tolu balsam**) ▸ **noun** [mass noun] a fragrant brown balsam obtained from a South American tree, used in perfumery and medicine.
● This balsam is obtained mainly from *Myroxylon balsamum*, family Leguminosae.
– ORIGIN late 17th cent.: named after *Santiago de Tolú* in Colombia, from where it was exported.

Toluca /təˈluːkə/ a city in central Mexico, capital of the state of Mexico; pop. 467,712 (2005). It lies at the foot of the extinct volcano Nevado de Toluca, at an altitude of 2,680 m (8,793 ft). Full name **Toluca de Lerdo** /dɛɪ ˈlɛːdəʊ/.

toluene /ˈtɒljʊiːn/ ▸ **noun** [mass noun] Chemistry a colourless liquid hydrocarbon present in coal tar and petroleum and used as a solvent and in organic synthesis.
● Alternative name: **methylbenzene**; chem. formula: $C_6H_5CH_3$.
– ORIGIN late 19th cent.: from **TOLU** + **-ENE**.

toluidine blue /tɒˈljuːɪdiːn, tɒˈljuː-/ ▸ **noun** [mass noun] a synthetic blue dye used chiefly as a stain in biology.
● A thiazine dye; chem. formula: $C_{15}H_{16}ClN_3S$.
– ORIGIN late 19th cent.: *toluidine* from **TOLUENE** + **-IDE** + **-INE**[4].

Tolyatti /taˈlʲjattʲi/ Russian name for **TOGLIATTI**.

tom[1] ▸ **noun 1** the male of various animals, especially a domestic cat.
2 Brit. informal a female prostitute. [early 20th cent.: from criminals' slang.]
3 (**Tom**) US informal short for **UNCLE TOM**.
▸ **verb** (**toms, tomming, tommed**) [no obj.] informal **1** (**be tomming**) Brit. work as a prostitute.
2 US (of a black person) behave in an excessively obedient or servile way.
– ORIGIN late Middle English (denoting an ordinary man, surviving in *tomfool, tomboy*, and the phrase *Tom, Dick, and Harry*): abbreviation of the given name *Thomas*. Sense 1 of the noun dates from the mid 18th cent.

tom[2] ▸ **noun** (usu. **toms**) informal short for **TOMATO**.

tomahawk /ˈtɒməhɔːk/ ▸ **noun** a light axe used as a tool or weapon by American Indians. ▪ Austral./NZ a hatchet.
▸ **verb** [with obj.] strike or cut with or as if with a tomahawk.
– ORIGIN early 17th cent.: from a Virginia Algonquian language.

tomalley /ˈtɒmali/ ▸ **noun** N. Amer. the digestive gland of a lobster, which turns green when cooked, and is considered a delicacy.
– ORIGIN mid 17th cent.: from French *taumalin*, from Carib *taumali*.

Tom and Jerry ▸ **noun** (pl. **Tom and Jerries**) US a kind of hot spiced rum cocktail, made with eggs.
– ORIGIN early 19th cent. (also as a verb in the sense 'drink and behave riotously'): with allusion to the chief characters in Pierce Egan's *Life in London* (1821).

tomatillo /ˌtɒməˈtɪləʊ, -ˈtiːjəʊ, -ˈtiːljəʊ/ ▸ **noun** (pl. **tomatillos**) **1** an edible purple or yellow fruit which is chiefly used for sauces and preserves.
2 the Mexican plant, related to the Cape gooseberry, which bears the tomatillo. ● *Physalis philadelphica*, family Solanaceae.
– ORIGIN early 20th cent.: from Spanish, diminutive of *tomate* 'tomato'.

tomatine /ˈtɒmətiːn/ (also **tomatin** /ˈtɒmətɪn/) ▸ **noun** [mass noun] Chemistry a compound of the steroid glycoside class, present in the stems and leaves of the tomato and related plants.
– ORIGIN 1940s: from **TOMATO** + **-INE**[4].

tomato ▸ **noun** (pl. **tomatoes**) **1** a glossy red, or occasionally yellow, pulpy edible fruit which is eaten as a vegetable or in salad. ▪ [mass noun] the bright red colour of a ripe tomato.
2 the South American plant of the nightshade family which produces the tomato. It is widely grown as a cash crop and many varieties have been developed.
● *Lycopersicon esculentum*, family Solanaceae.
– DERIVATIVES **tomatoey** adjective.
– ORIGIN early 17th cent.: from French, Spanish, or Portuguese *tomate*, from Nahuatl *tomatl*.

tomb ▸ **noun** a large vault, typically an underground one, for burying the dead. ▪ an enclosure for a corpse cut in the earth or in rock. ▪ a monument to the memory of a dead person, erected over their burial place. ▪ (**the tomb**) literary death: *none escape the tomb.*
– ORIGIN Middle English: from Old French *tombe*, from late Latin *tumba*, from Greek *tumbos*.

Tombaugh /ˈtɒmbɔː/, Clyde William (1906–97), American astronomer. His chief discovery was that of Pluto on 13 March 1930, which he made from the Lowell Observatory in Arizona. Tombaugh subsequently discovered numerous asteroids.

tombola /tɒmˈbəʊlə/ ▸ **noun** Brit. a game in which people pick tickets out of a revolving drum and certain tickets win immediate prizes, typically played at a fete or fair.
– ORIGIN late 19th cent.: from French or Italian, from Italian *tombolare* 'turn a somersault'.

tombolo /ˈtɒmbələʊ/ ▸ **noun** (pl. **tombolos**) a bar of sand or shingle joining an island to the mainland.
– ORIGIN late 19th cent.: from Italian, literally 'sand dune'.

Tombouctou /tɔ̃buktu/ French name for **TIMBUKTU**.

tomboy ▸ **noun** a girl who enjoys rough, noisy activities traditionally associated with boys.
– DERIVATIVES **tomboyish** adjective, **tomboyishly** adverb, **tomboyishness** noun.

tombstone ▸ **noun 1** a large, flat inscribed stone standing or laid over a grave.
2 (also **tombstone advertisement**) an advertisement listing the underwriters or firms associated with a new issue of shares, bonds, warrants, etc.
▸ **verb** [no obj.] (usu. as noun **tombstoning**) informal jump into the sea from a cliff or other high point.
– DERIVATIVES **tombstoner** noun.

tomcat ▸ **noun** a male domestic cat.

tomcod ▸ **noun** (pl. **same** or **tomcods**) a small edible greenish-brown North American fish of the cod family, popular with anglers. ● Genus *Microgadus*, family Gadidae: *M. proximus* of the Pacific coasts, and *M. tomcod* of the Atlantic coasts and fresh water.

Tom Collins ▸ **noun** a cocktail made from gin mixed with soda, sugar, and lemon or lime juice.
– ORIGIN sometimes said to have been named after a 19th-cent. London bartender.

Tom, Dick, and Harry (also **Tom, Dick, or Harry**) ▸ **noun** used to refer to ordinary people in general: *he didn't want every Tom, Dick, and Harry knowing their business.*

tome ▸ **noun** chiefly humorous a book, especially a large, heavy, scholarly one: *a weighty tome.*
– ORIGIN early 16th cent. (denoting one volume of a larger work): from French, via Latin from Greek *tomos* 'section, roll of papyrus, volume'; related to *temnein* 'to cut'.

-tome ▸ **combining form 1** denoting an instrument for cutting: *microtome.*
2 denoting a section or segment: *myotome.*
– ORIGIN Sense 1 from Greek *-tomon* (neuter) 'that cuts'; sense 2 from Greek *tomē* 'a cutting', both from *temnein* 'to cut'.

tomentum /təˈmɛntəm/ ▸ **noun** (pl. **tomenta** /-tə/) Botany a layer of matted woolly down on the surface of a plant.
– DERIVATIVES **tomentose** /təˈmɛntəʊs, ˈtəʊ-/ adjective.
– ORIGIN late 17th cent.: from Latin, literally 'cushion stuffing'.

tomfool ▸ **noun** dated a foolish person: [as modifier] *she was destined to take part in some tomfool caper.*

tomfoolery ▸ **noun** [mass noun] foolish or silly behaviour: *the tomfoolery of MPs at question time.*

Tomis /ˈtəʊmɪs/ ancient name for **CONSTANŢA**.

tomme /tɒm/ ▸ **noun** (pl. pronunc. **same**) [mass noun] a cheese made in Savoy.
– ORIGIN French.

Tommy ▸ **noun** (pl. **Tommies**) informal **1** a British private soldier. [pet form of the given name *Thomas*; from a use of the name *Thomas Atkins* in specimens of completed official forms in the British army during the 19th cent.]
2 a Thomson's gazelle.

tommy bar ▸ **noun** a short bar used to turn a box spanner.

tommy gun ▸ **noun** informal a type of sub-machine gun.
– ORIGIN 1920s: contraction of *Thompson gun*, named by its designer after John T. *Thompson* (1860–1940), the American army officer who conceived the idea for it.

tommyrot ▸ **noun** [mass noun] informal, dated nonsense; rubbish: *did you ever hear such awful tommyrot?*

tommy ruff (also **tommy rough**) ▸ **noun** see **RUFF**[2] (sense 1).

tomogram /ˈtəʊmə(ʊ)gram, ˈtɒm-/ ▸ **noun** a record obtained by tomography.

tomography /təˈmɒgrəfi/ ▸ **noun** [mass noun] a technique for displaying a representation of a cross section through a human body or other solid object using X-rays or ultrasound.
– DERIVATIVES **tomographic** adjective, **tomographically** adverb.
– ORIGIN 1930s: from Greek *tomos* 'slice, section' + **-GRAPHY**.

tomorrow ▸ **adverb** on the day after today: *the show opens tomorrow.* ▪ in the future, especially the near future: *fickle buyers who may be gone tomorrow.*
▸ **noun** the day after today: *tomorrow is going to be a special day.* ▪ the future, especially the near future: *today's engineers are tomorrow's buyers.*
– PHRASES **as if there was** (or **as though there were**) **no tomorrow** with no regard for the future consequences: *I ate as if there was no tomorrow.* **tomorrow morning** (or **afternoon** etc.) in the morning (or afternoon etc.) of tomorrow. **tomorrow is another day** said after a bad experience to express one's belief that the future will be better. **tomorrow week** Brit. a week from tomorrow.
– ORIGIN Middle English (as two words): from the preposition **TO** + **MORROW**. Compare with **TODAY** and **TONIGHT**.

Tompion /ˈtɒmpɪən/, Thomas (*c.*1639–1713), English clock- and watchmaker. He made one of the first balance-spring watches and made two large pendulum clocks for the Royal Greenwich Observatory.

tompion /ˈtɒmpɪən/ ▸ **noun** variant spelling of **TAMPION**.

Tomsk /tɒmsk/ an industrial city in southern Siberian Russia, a port on the River Tom; pop. 496,500 (est. 2008).

Tom Thumb ▸ **noun 1** [usu. as modifier] a dwarf variety of a cultivated flower or vegetable: *Tom Thumb lettuce.*
2 a small wild flower, especially bird's-foot trefoil.

T

– ORIGIN late 19th cent.: from the name of the hero of a children's story, a ploughman's son who was only as tall as his father's thumb.

tomtit ▶ noun a popular name for any of a number of small active songbirds: ● Brit. the blue tit. ● NZ the black-and-white New Zealand tit (*Petroica macrocephala*, family Eopsaltridae). ● Austral. the yellow-tailed thornbill (*Acanthiza chrysorrhoa*, family Acanthizidae).

tom-tom ▶ noun a medium-sized cylindrical drum, of which one to three may be used in a drum kit. ■ a drum beaten with the hands, associated with North American Indian, African, or Eastern cultures.
▶ verb [with obj.] chiefly Indian proclaim or boast about: *the government tom-tommed a 40 per cent turnout of the state's electorate*.
– ORIGIN late 17th cent.: from Hindi *ṭam ṭam*, Telugu *ṭamaṭama*, of imitative origin.

-tomy ▶ combining form cutting, especially as part of a surgical process: *episiotomy*.
– ORIGIN from Greek *-tomia* 'cutting', from *temnein* 'to cut'.

ton¹ /tʌn/ (abbrev.: **t**, also US **tn**) ▶ noun **1** (also **long ton**) a unit of weight equal to 2,240 lb avoirdupois (1016.05 kg). ■ (also **short ton**) chiefly N. Amer. a unit of weight equal to 2,000 lb avoirdupois (907.19 kg). ■ short for METRIC TON. ■ (also **displacement ton**) a unit of measurement of a ship's weight representing the weight of water it displaces with the load line just immersed, equal to 2,240 lb or 35 cu. ft (0.99 cubic metres). ■ (also **freight ton**) a unit of weight or volume of sea cargo, equal to a metric ton (1,000 kg) or 40 cu. ft.
2 (also **gross ton**) a unit of gross internal capacity, equal to 100 cu. ft (2.83 cubic metres). ■ (also **net** or **register ton**) an equivalent unit of net internal capacity. ■ a measure of capacity for various materials, especially 40 cu. ft of timber. ■ a unit of refrigerating power able to freeze 2,000 lb of water at 0°C in 24 hours.
3 (usu. **a ton of/tons of**) informal a large number or amount: *all of a sudden I had tons of friends*.
4 Brit. informal a hundred, in particular a speed of 100 mph, a score of 100 or more, or a sum of £100: *he scored 102 not out, his third ton of the tour*.
▶ adverb (**tons**) Brit. informal much; a lot: *I feel tons better*.
– PHRASES **like a ton of bricks** see BRICK.
– ORIGIN Middle English: variant of TUN, both spellings being used for the container and the weight. The senses were differentiated in the late 17th cent.

ton² /tɔ̃/ ▶ noun [mass noun] fashionable style or distinction: *riches and fame were no guarantee of a ticket—one had to have ton*. ■ (**the ton**) [treated as sing. or pl.] fashionable society.
– ORIGIN French, from Latin *tonus* (see TONE).

tonal /ˈtəʊn(ə)l/ ▶ adjective relating to the tone of music, colour, or writing: *his ear for tonal colour* | *the poem's tonal lapses*. ■ relating to music written using conventional keys and harmony. ■ Phonetics (of a language) expressing semantic differences by varying the intonation given to words or syllables of a similar sound.
– DERIVATIVES **tonally** adverb.
– ORIGIN late 18th cent. (designating church music in plainsong mode): from medieval Latin *tonalis*, from Latin *tonus* (see TONE).

tonalite /ˈtɒn(ə)lʌɪt/ ▶ noun [mass noun] Geology a coarse-grained plutonic rock consisting chiefly of sodic plagioclase, quartz, and hornblende or other mafic minerals.
– DERIVATIVES **tonalitic** adjective.
– ORIGIN late 19th cent.: from *Tonale* Pass, northern Italy, + -ITE¹.

tonality ▶ noun (pl. **tonalities**) [mass noun] **1** the character of a piece of music as determined by the key in which it is played or the relations between the notes of a scale or key. ■ [count noun] the harmonic effect of being in a particular key: *the first bar would seem set to create a tonality of C major*. ■ the use of conventional keys and harmony as the basis of musical composition.
2 the colour scheme or range of tones used in a picture.

tondo /ˈtɒndəʊ/ ▶ noun (pl. **tondi** /-di/) a circular painting or relief.
– ORIGIN late 19th cent.: from Italian, literally 'round object', from *rotondo* 'round', from Latin *rotundus*.

Tone /təʊn/, (Theobald) Wolfe (1763–98), Irish nationalist. In 1794 he induced a French invasion of Ireland to overthrow English rule, which failed. Tone was captured by the British during the Irish insurrection in 1798 and committed suicide in prison.

tone ▶ noun **1** a musical or vocal sound with reference to its pitch, quality, and strength: *they were speaking in hushed tones* | *the piano tone appears lacking in warmth*. ■ a modulation of the voice expressing a particular feeling or mood: *a firm tone of voice*. ■ a musical note or other sound used as a signal on a telephone or answering machine.
2 the general character or attitude of a place, piece of writing, situation, etc.: *trust her to lower the tone of the conversation* | *there was a general tone of ill-concealed glee in the reporting*. ■ [mass noun] informal an atmosphere of respectability or class: *they don't feel he gives the place tone*.
3 (also **whole tone**) a basic interval in classical Western music, equal to two semitones and separating, for example, the first and second notes of an ordinary scale (such as C and D, or E and F sharp); a major second.
4 the particular quality of brightness, deepness, or hue of a shade of a colour: *stained glass in vivid tones of red and blue* | [mass noun] *an attractive colour which is even in tone and texture*. ■ [mass noun] the general effect of colour or of light and shade in a picture. ■ a slight degree of difference in the intensity of a colour.
5 Phonetics (in some languages, such as Chinese) a particular pitch pattern on a syllable used to make semantic distinctions. ■ (in some languages, such as English) intonation on a word or phrase used to add functional meaning.
6 (also **muscle tone**) [mass noun] the normal level of firmness or slight contraction in a resting muscle. ■ Physiology the normal level of activity in a nerve fibre.
▶ verb [with obj.] **1** give greater strength or firmness to (the body or a muscle): *exercise tones up the muscles*. ■ [no obj.] (**tone up**) (of a muscle or other bodily part) became stronger or firmer.
2 [no obj.] (**tone with**) harmonize with (something) in terms of colour: *the rich orange colour of the wood tones beautifully with the yellow roses*.
3 Photography give (a monochrome picture) an altered colour in finishing by means of a chemical solution.
– PHRASAL VERBS **tone something down** make something less harsh in sound or colour. ■ make something less extreme or intense: *she saw the need to tone down her protests*.
– DERIVATIVES **toned** adjective [in combination] *the fresh-toned singing*.
– ORIGIN Middle English: from Old French *ton*, from Latin *tonus*, from Greek *tonos* 'tension, tone', from *teinein* 'to stretch'.

tone arm ▶ noun the movable arm supporting the pickup of a record player.

toneburst ▶ noun an audio signal used in testing the transient response of audio components.

tone cluster ▶ noun another term for NOTE CLUSTER.

tone colour ▶ noun Music another term for TIMBRE.

tone-deaf ▶ adjective (of a person) unable to perceive differences of musical pitch accurately.
– DERIVATIVES **tone-deafness** noun.

tone dialling ▶ noun [mass noun] a method of telephone dialling in which each digit is represented by a particular combination of tones.

tone group ▶ noun Phonetics a group of words forming a distinctive unit in an utterance, containing a nucleus and optionally one or more other syllables before and after the nucleus.

tone language ▶ noun Linguistics a language in which variations in pitch distinguish different words.

toneless ▶ adjective (of a voice or musical sound) lacking expression or interest: *he began to sing in a toneless voice*.
– DERIVATIVES **tonelessly** adverb.

toneme /ˈtəʊniːm/ ▶ noun Phonetics a phoneme distinguished from another only by its tone.
– ORIGIN 1920s: from TONE, on the pattern of *phoneme*.

tone-on-tone ▶ adjective (of a fabric or design) dyed with or using different shades of the same colour.

tonepad ▶ noun a device generating specific tones to control a device at the other end of a telephone line, where the caller's phone does not generate such tones itself.

tone poem ▶ noun a piece of orchestral music, typically in one movement, on a descriptive or rhapsodic theme.

toner ▶ noun **1** an astringent liquid applied to the skin to reduce oiliness and improve its condition.
2 a device or exercise for making a specified part of the body firmer and stronger: *a tummy toner*.
3 a black or coloured powder used in xerographic copying processes. ■ [usu. with adj. or noun modifier] a chemical bath for changing the colour or shade of a photographic print, especially as specified: *sepia or blue toners*.

tone row ▶ noun a particular sequence of the twelve notes of the chromatic scale used as a basis for twelve-note (serial) music.

tone unit ▶ noun another term for TONE GROUP.

tong¹ ▶ noun (in the US) a Chinese association or secret society, frequently associated with organized crime.
– ORIGIN late 19th cent.: from Chinese (Cantonese dialect) *t'ǒng*, literally 'meeting place'.

tong² ▶ verb [with obj.] **1** curl (hair) using tongs.
2 collect (oysters) using oyster tongs.

Tonga¹ /ˈtɒŋə, ˈtɒŋgə/ a country in the South Pacific consisting of an island group south-east of Fiji; pop. 120,900 (est. 2009); official languages, Tongan and English; capital, Nuku'alofa. Also called the FRIENDLY ISLANDS.

> The kingdom of Tonga consists of about 170 volcanic and coral islands, of which thirty-six are inhabited. Visited by the Dutch in the early 17th century, Tonga became a British protectorate in 1900 and an independent Commonwealth state in 1970. It has been a constitutional monarchy since 1875.

Tonga² /ˈtɒŋgə/ ▶ noun (pl. **same** or **Tongas**) **1** a member of any of three peoples of southern Africa, living mainly in Zambia, Malawi, and Mozambique respectively.
2 [mass noun] any of the three different Bantu languages spoken by the Tonga.
▶ adjective relating to the Tonga or their languages.

tonga /ˈtɒŋgə/ ▶ noun a light horse-drawn two-wheeled vehicle used in India.
– ORIGIN from Hindi *tāṅgā*.

Tongan /ˈtɒŋən, ˈtɒŋg(ə)n/ ▶ adjective relating to Tonga or its people or language.
▶ noun **1** a native or inhabitant of Tonga.
2 [mass noun] the Polynesian language spoken in Tonga.

Tongariro, Mount /ˌtɒŋəˈrɪərəʊ/ a mountain in the North Island of New Zealand. It rises to a height of 1,968 m (6,457 ft) and is held sacred by the Maoris.

tongs ▶ plural noun (also **a pair of tongs**) **1** an instrument with two movable arms that are joined at one end, used for picking up and holding things: *sugar tongs*.
2 short for CURLING TONGS.
– ORIGIN Old English *tang(e)* (singular), of Germanic origin; related to Dutch *tang* and German *Zange*.

Tongshan /tɒŋˈʃan/ former name (1912–45) for XUZHOU.

tongue ▶ noun **1** the fleshy muscular organ in the mouth of a mammal, used for tasting, licking, swallowing, and (in humans) articulating speech. ■ the equivalent organ in other vertebrates, sometimes used (in snakes) as a scent organ or (in chameleons) for catching food. ■ an analogous organ in insects, formed from some of the mouthparts and used in feeding. ■ [mass noun] the tongue of an ox or lamb as food.
2 [in sing.] used in reference to a person's style or manner of speaking: *he was a redoubtable debater with a caustic tongue*. ■ [count noun] a particular language: *the girls were singing in their native tongue*.
3 a thing resembling or likened to a tongue, in particular: ■ a long, low promontory of land. ■ a jet of flame: *a tongue of flame flashed from the gun*. ■ a strip of leather or fabric under the laces in a shoe, attached only at the front end. ■ the free-swinging metal piece inside a bell which is made to strike the bell to produce the sound. ■ the pin of a buckle. ■ a projecting strip on a wooden board fitting into a groove on another. ■ the vibrating reed of a musical instrument or organ pipe.
▶ verb (**tongues, tonguing, tongued**) [with obj.] **1** Music sound (a note) distinctly on a wind instrument by interrupting the air flow with the tongue.
2 lick or caress with the tongue: *the other horse tongued every part of the colt's mane*.
– PHRASES **find** (or **lose**) **one's tongue** be able (or unable) to express oneself after a shock. **get one's tongue round** pronounce (words): *she found it very difficult to get her tongue round the unfamiliar words*. **the gift of tongues** the power of speaking

T

in unknown languages, regarded as one of the gifts of the Holy Spirit (Acts 2). **give tongue** (of hounds) bark, especially on finding a scent. ■ express one's feelings or opinions freely. **keep a civil tongue in one's head** speak politely. **(with) tongue in cheek** speaking or writing in an ironic or insincere way. **someone's tongue is hanging out** someone is very eager for something: *I'm going to have a whisky—my tongue's hanging out*.
– DERIVATIVES **tongueless** adjective.
– ORIGIN Old English *tunge*, of Germanic origin; related to Dutch *tong*, German *Zunge*, and Latin *lingua*.

tongue and groove ▸ noun [mass noun] wooden planking in which adjacent boards are joined by means of interlocking ridges and hollows down their sides.
– DERIVATIVES **tongued-and-grooved** adjective.

tongued ▸ adjective **1** [in combination] having a specified kind of tongue: *the blue-tongued lizard*.
2 (in carpentry) constructed using a tongue.
3 (of a note) played by tonguing.

tonguefish ▸ noun (pl. **same** or **tonguefishes**) a small teardrop-shaped flatfish of warm seas, which is an important food fish in some areas. ● Family Cynoglossidae: *Symphurus* and other genera; numerous species.

tongue-in-cheek ▸ adjective & adverb in an ironic or insincere way: [as adj.] *her delightful tongue in cheek humour* | [as adv.] *'I swear there's a female conspiracy against men!' he complained, tongue-in-cheek*.

tongue-lashing ▸ noun [in sing.] a loud or severe scolding: *the incensed boss gave him a tongue-lashing*.

tongue tie ▸ noun a malformation which restricts the movement of the tongue and causes a speech impediment.

tongue-tied ▸ adjective **1** too shy or embarrassed to speak: *Barbara was tongue-tied in the presence of her parents*.
2 having a malformation restricting the movement of the tongue.

tongue-twister ▸ noun a sequence of words or sounds, typically of an alliterative kind, that are difficult to pronounce quickly and correctly, as for example *Peter Piper picked a peck of pickled pepper*.
– DERIVATIVES **tongue-twisting** adjective.

tongue worm ▸ noun a flattened worm-like parasite which infests vertebrates, especially reptiles, having a sucking mouth with hooks for attachment to the lining of the respiratory tract. ● Subphylum Pentastomida, phylum Arthropoda; sometimes regarded as a class of crustacean.

tonic ▸ noun **1** a medicinal substance taken to give a feeling of vigour or well-being. ■ something with an invigorating effect: *being needed is a tonic for someone at my age*.
2 short for TONIC WATER.
3 Music the first note in a scale which, in conventional harmony, provides the keynote of a piece of music.
▸ adjective **1** giving a feeling of vigour or well-being; invigorating: *a tonic body shampoo*.
2 Music relating to or denoting the first degree of a scale.
3 Phonetics denoting or relating to the syllable within a tone group that has greatest prominence, because it carries the main change of pitch.
4 relating to or restoring normal tone to muscles or other organs. ■ Physiology relating to, denoting, or producing continuous muscular contraction.
– DERIVATIVES **tonically** adverb.
– ORIGIN mid 17th cent.: from French *tonique*, from Greek *tonikos* 'of or for stretching', from *tonos* (see TONE).

tonic–clonic /ˌtɒnɪ(k)ˈklɒnɪk/ ▸ adjective Medicine of or characterized by successive phases of tonic and clonic spasm (as in *grand mal* epilepsy).

tonicity /tə(ʊ)ˈnɪsɪti/ ▸ noun [mass noun] **1** muscle tone.
2 Linguistics the pattern of tones or stress in speech.
3 Biology the state of a solution in respect of osmotic pressure: *the tonicity of the fluid*.

tonic sol-fa ▸ noun [mass noun] a system of naming the notes of the scale (usually **doh**, **ray**, **me**, **fah**, **soh**, **lah**, **te**) used especially to teach singing, with doh as the keynote of all major keys and lah as the keynote of all minor keys. See SOLMIZATION.

tonic water ▸ noun [mass noun] a carbonated soft drink with a bitter flavour, used as a mixer with gin or other spirits (originally used as a stimulant of appetite and digestion).

tonify /ˈtəʊnɪfʌɪ/ ▸ verb (**tonifies**, **tonifying**, **tonified**) [with obj.] impart tone to (the body or a part of it). ■ (of acupuncture or herbal medicine) increase the available energy of (a bodily part or system).
– DERIVATIVES **tonification** noun.

tonight ▸ adverb on the present or approaching evening or night: *are you doing anything tonight?*
▸ noun the evening or night of the present day: *tonight is a night to remember*.
– ORIGIN Old English *tō niht*, from the preposition TO + NIGHT. Compare with TODAY and TOMORROW.

tonk ▸ verb [with obj.] informal hit hard. ■ defeat heavily; trounce: *Villa were tonked by local rivals Birmingham City*.
– ORIGIN early 20th cent.: imitative of the sound of a powerful blow reaching its target.

tonka bean /ˈtɒŋkə/ ▸ noun the black seed of a South American tree, which has a vanilla-like fragrance. The dried beans are cured in rum or other alcohol and then used in perfumery and for scenting and flavouring tobacco, ice cream, and other products. ● The tree is *Dipteryx odorata*, family Leguminosae.
– ORIGIN late 18th cent.: *tonka*, a local word in Guyana.

Tonkin /tɒnˈkɪn/ a mountainous region of northern Vietnam, centred on the delta of the Red River.

Tonkin, Gulf of an arm of the South China Sea, bounded by the coasts of southern China and northern Vietnam. Its chief port is Haiphong. An incident there in 1964 led to increased US military involvement in the area prior to the Vietnam War.

Tonlé Sap /ˌtɒnleɪ ˈsap/ a lake in central Cambodia, linked to the Mekong River by the Tonlé Sap River.

ton-mile ▸ noun one ton of goods carried one mile, as a unit of traffic.

tonnage ▸ noun [mass noun] weight in tons, especially of cargo or freight: *road convoys carry more tonnage*. ■ the size or carrying capacity of a ship measured in tons. ■ shipping considered in terms of total carrying capacity: *the European Community's total tonnage*.
– ORIGIN early 17th cent. (denoting a charge per ton on cargo): from TON[1] + -AGE.

tonne /tʌn/ ▸ noun another term for METRIC TON.
– ORIGIN late 19th cent.: from French; compare with TON[1].

tonneau /ˈtɒnəʊ/ ▸ noun **1** the part of a car, typically an open car, occupied by the back seats. ■ short for TONNEAU COVER.
2 a unit of capacity for French wine, especially Bordeaux, usually equal to 900 litres or 198 gallons.
– ORIGIN late 18th cent. (in sense 2): French, literally 'cask, tun'.

tonneau cover ▸ noun a protective cover for the seats in an open car or cabin cruiser when they are not in use.

tonometer /tə(ʊ)ˈnɒmɪtə/ ▸ noun **1** a tuning fork or other instrument for measuring the pitch of musical tones.
2 an instrument for measuring the pressure in a part of the body, such as the eyeball (to test for glaucoma) or a blood vessel.
– ORIGIN early 18th cent.: from Greek *tonos* (see TONE) + -METER.

tonoplast /ˈtəʊnə(ʊ)plast, -plɑːst/ ▸ noun Botany a membrane which bounds the chief vacuole of a plant cell.
– ORIGIN late 19th cent.: from Greek *tonos* 'tension, tone' + *plastos* 'formed'.

tonsil ▸ noun either of two small masses of lymphoid tissue in the throat, one on each side of the root of the tongue.
– DERIVATIVES **tonsillar** adjective.
– ORIGIN late 16th cent.: from French *tonsilles* or Latin *tonsillae* (plural).

tonsillectomy /ˌtɒnsɪˈlɛktəmi/ ▸ noun (pl. **tonsillectomies**) a surgical operation to remove the tonsils.

tonsillitis ▸ noun [mass noun] inflammation of the tonsils.

tonsorial /tɒnˈsɔːrɪəl/ ▸ adjective formal or humorous relating to hairdressing: *she'd had her customary go at me over tonsorial neglect*.
– DERIVATIVES **tonsorially** adverb.
– ORIGIN early 19th cent.: from Latin *tonsorius* (from *tonsor* 'barber', from *tondere* 'shear, clip') + -AL.

tonsure /ˈtɒnsjə, ˈtɒnʃə/ ▸ noun a part of a monk's or priest's head left bare on top by shaving off the hair. ■ [in sing.] an act of shaving the top of a monk's or priest's head as a preparation for entering a religious order.
▸ verb [with obj.] (often as adj. **tonsured**) give a tonsure to.
– ORIGIN late Middle English: from Old French, or from Latin *tonsura*, from *tondere* 'shear, clip'.

tontine /tɒnˈtiːn, ˈtɒn-/ ▸ noun an annuity shared by subscribers to a loan or common fund, the shares increasing as subscribers die until the last survivor enjoys the whole income. ■ a scheme for life assurance in which the beneficiaries are those who survive and maintain a policy to the end of a given period.
– ORIGIN mid 18th cent.: from French, named after Lorenzo Tonti (1630–95), a Neapolitan banker who started such a scheme to raise government loans in France (*c.*1653).

Tonton Macoute /ˌtɒntɒn məˈkuːt/ ▸ noun (pl. **Tontons Macoutes** pronunc. **same**) a member of a notoriously brutal militia formed by President François Duvalier of Haiti, active from 1961 to 1986.
– ORIGIN Haitian French, apparently with reference to an ogre of folk tales.

ton-up ▸ adjective [attrib.] Brit. informal **1** (of a person) fond of travelling at high speed.
2 achieving a score of 100 or more.

tonus /ˈtəʊnəs/ ▸ noun [mass noun] the constant low-level activity of a body tissue, especially muscle tone.
– ORIGIN late 19th cent.: from Latin, from Greek *tonos* 'tension'.

Tony ▸ noun (pl. **Tonys**) (in the US) any of a number of awards given annually for outstanding achievement in the theatre in various categories.
– ORIGIN from the nickname of Antoinette Perry (1888-1946), American actress and director.

tony ▸ adjective (**tonier**, **toniest**) N. Amer. informal fashionable among wealthy or stylish people: *a tony restaurant*.
– ORIGIN late 19th cent.: from the noun TONE + -Y[1].

too ▸ adverb **1** [as submodifier] to a higher degree than is desirable, permissible, or possible; excessively: *he was driving too fast* | *he wore suits that seemed a size too small for him*. ■ informal very: *you're too kind*.
2 in addition; also: *is he coming too?* ■ moreover (used when adding a further point): *she is a grown woman, and a strong one too*.
– PHRASES **all too ——** used to emphasize that something is the case to an extreme or unwelcome extent: *failures are all too common*. **none too ——** far from; not very: *her sight's none too good*. **only too** see ONLY. **too bad** see BAD. **too besides** W. Indian moreover; also: *'You not listening, and too besides you don't have to shout at the damn bird so!'* **too far** see FAR. **too much** see MUCH. **too right** see RIGHT.
– ORIGIN Old English, stressed form of TO, spelled *too* from the 16th cent.

toodle-oo (also **toodle-pip**) ▸ exclamation informal, dated goodbye: *we'll see you later, toodle-oo!*
– ORIGIN early 20th cent.: perhaps an alteration of French *à tout à l'heure* 'see you soon'.

took past of TAKE.

tool ▸ noun **1** a device or implement, especially one held in the hand, used to carry out a particular function: *gardening tools*. ■ a thing used to help perform a job: *computers are an essential tool* | *the ability to write clearly is **a tool of the trade***. ■ a person used or exploited by another: *the beautiful Estella is Miss Havisham's tool*. ■ Computing a piece of software that carries out a particular function, typically creating or modifying another program.
2 a distinct design in the tooling of a book. ■ a small stamp or roller used to make a tooled design.
3 vulgar slang a man's penis.
▸ verb **1** [with obj.] impress a design on (leather, especially a leather book cover): *volumes bound in green leather and tooled in gold*.
2 equip or be equipped with tools for industrial production: [with obj.] *the factory must be tooled to produce the models* | [no obj.] *they were tooling up for production*. ■ (**tool up** or **be tooled up**) Brit. informal be or become armed, especially for criminal activity.
3 [no obj., with adverbial of direction] informal, chiefly N. Amer. drive or ride in a casual or leisurely manner: *tooling around town in a pink Rolls-Royce*.
4 [with obj.] dress (stone) with a chisel.
– DERIVATIVES **tooler** noun.
– ORIGIN Old English *tōl*, from a Germanic base meaning 'prepare'; compare with TAW[1]. The verb dates from the early 19th cent.

toolbar ▸ noun Computing (in a program with a graphical user interface) a strip of icons used to perform certain functions.

toolbox ▸ noun a box or container for keeping tools in. ■ Computing a set of software tools. ■ Computing the

T

set of programs or functions accessible from a single menu.

tooling ▶ noun [mass noun] **1** assorted tools, especially ones required for a mechanized process. ■ the process of making or working something with tools.
2 the ornamentation of a leather book cover with designs impressed by heated tools.

tool kit ▶ noun a set of tools, especially one kept in a bag or box and used for a particular purpose. ■ another term for TOOLSET.

toolmaker ▶ noun a maker of tools, especially a person who makes and maintains tools for use in a manufacturing process.
– DERIVATIVES **toolmaking** noun.

tool post ▶ noun the post of a machine tool which holds a cutting tool steady.

tool pusher ▶ noun a person who directs the drilling on an oil rig.

toolset ▶ noun Computing a set of software tools.

tool steel ▶ noun [mass noun] hard steel of a quality used for making cutting tools.

tooltip ▶ noun Computing a message which appears when a cursor is positioned over an icon, image, hyperlink, or other element in a graphical user interface.

toon ▶ noun informal a cartoon film. ■ a character in a cartoon film.
– ORIGIN 1930s: shortening of CARTOON.

toot ▶ noun **1** a short, sharp sound made by a horn, trumpet, or similar instrument.
2 informal a snort of a drug, especially cocaine. ■ [mass noun] cocaine.
3 N. Amer. informal a spell of drinking and lively enjoyment; a spree: *a sales manager **on a toot**.*
▶ verb [with obj.] **1** sound (a horn or similar) with a short, sharp sound: *an impatient motorist tooted a horn.* ■ [no obj.] make a toot: *a car **tooted at** us.*
2 informal snort (cocaine).
– DERIVATIVES **tooter** noun.
– ORIGIN early 16th cent.: probably from Middle Low German *tūten*, but possibly an independent imitative formation.

tooth ▶ noun (pl. **teeth**) **1** each of a set of hard, bony enamel-coated structures in the jaws of most vertebrates, used for biting and chewing. ■ a similar hard, pointed structure in invertebrate animals, typically functioning in the mechanical breakdown of food. ■ (**teeth**) genuine power or effectiveness of an organization or in a law or agreement: *the Charter would be fine if it had teeth and could be enforced.* ■ (**teeth**) used in curses or exclamations: *Hell's teeth!*
2 a projecting part on a tool or other instrument, especially one of a series that function or engage together, such as a cog on a gearwheel or a point on a saw. ■ a projecting part on an animal or plant, especially one of a jagged or dentate row on the margin of a leaf or shell.
3 [in sing.] an appetite or liking for a particular thing: *what a tooth for fruit a monkey has!*
4 [mass noun] roughness given to a surface to allow colour or glue to adhere.
– PHRASES **fight tooth and nail** fight very fiercely. **get** (or **sink**) **one's teeth into** work energetically and productively on (a task): *the course gives students something to get their teeth into.* **in the teeth of** directly against (the wind). ■ in spite of (opposition or difficulty): *the firm has expanded its building contracting division in the teeth of recession.* **set someone's teeth on edge** see EDGE.
– DERIVATIVES **toothed** adjective, **tooth-like** adjective.
– ORIGIN Old English *tōth* (plural *tēth*), of Germanic origin; related to Dutch *tand* and German *Zahn*, from an Indo-European root shared by Latin *dent-*, Greek *odont-*.

toothache ▶ noun [mass noun] pain in a tooth or teeth.

toothbrush ▶ noun a small brush with a long handle, used for cleaning the teeth.

toothbrush moustache ▶ noun a short bristly moustache trimmed to a rectangular shape.

toothcarp ▶ noun (pl. **same**) a small fish that resembles the carp but possesses small teeth, occurring mainly in fresh water in America. Many toothcarp are popular in aquaria. ● Order Cyprinodontiformes: several families, in particular Cyprinodontidae (or Fundulidae) (the egg-laying killifishes and topminnows), and Poeciliidae (the livebearers).

toothcomb ▶ noun Brit. used with reference to a very thorough search or analysis of something: *Cropper will have **been through** the manuscript **with a toothcomb** | the boys have **been over** the area **with a fine toothcomb**.*

> **USAGE** There is no such thing as a **toothcomb**. The forms **toothcomb** and **fine toothcomb** arose from a misreading of the compound noun **fine-tooth comb**, a comb with closely spaced teeth. However, in modern use all the forms are accepted in standard English.

toothed whale ▶ noun a predatory whale having teeth rather than baleen plates. Toothed whales include sperm whales, killer whales, beaked whales, narwhals, dolphins, and porpoises. ● Suborder Odontoceti, order Cetacea: six families and numerous species.

tooth fairy ▶ noun a fairy said to take children's milk teeth after they fall out and leave a coin under the child's pillow.

toothfish (also **Patagonian toothfish**) ▶ noun a large deep-sea fish of the southern Atlantic and Pacific oceans, prized as food and now endangered. ● *Dissostichus eleginoides*, family Nototheniidae.

toothing ▶ noun [mass noun] **1** the teeth on a saw.
2 projecting bricks or stones left at the end of a wall to allow its continuation.

toothless ▶ adjective having no teeth, typically through old age: *a toothless old man.* ■ lacking genuine force or effectiveness: *laws that are well intentioned but toothless.*
– DERIVATIVES **toothlessly** adverb, **toothlessness** noun.

toothpaste ▶ noun [mass noun] a thick, soft, moist substance used on a brush for cleaning one's teeth.

toothpick ▶ noun a short pointed piece of wood or plastic used for removing bits of food lodged between the teeth.

tooth powder ▶ noun [mass noun] powder used for cleaning the teeth.

tooth shell ▶ noun another term for TUSK SHELL.

toothsome ▶ adjective (of food) temptingly tasty: *a toothsome morsel.* ■ informal (of a person) good-looking; attractive.
– DERIVATIVES **toothsomely** adverb, **toothsomeness** noun.

toothwort ▶ noun a Eurasian plant which is parasitic on the roots of hazel and beech, with a thick rhizome bearing rows of tooth-like scales. ● *Lathraea squamaria*, family Scrophulariaceae (or Orobanchaceae).

toothy ▶ adjective (**toothier**, **toothiest**) having or showing large, numerous, or prominent teeth: *a toothy smile.*
– DERIVATIVES **toothily** adverb.

tootin' ▶ adjective N. Amer. informal used for emphasis: *he said he was damned tootin' he was right.*

tootle ▶ verb **1** [no obj.] casually make a series of sounds on a horn, trumpet, or similar instrument: *he tootled on the horn.* ■ [with obj.] play (an instrument) or make (a sound or tune) in such a way: *the video games tootled their tunes.*
2 [no obj., with adverbial of direction] informal go or travel in a leisurely way: *they were **tootling along** the coast road.*
▶ noun [usu. in sing.] **1** an act or sound of casual playing on an instrument such as a horn or trumpet.
2 informal a leisurely journey.
– ORIGIN early 19th cent.: frequentative of TOOT.

too-too ▶ adverb & adjective informal, dated used affectedly to convey that one finds something excessively annoying or fatiguing: [as adv.] *it had become too-too tiring* | [as adj.] *it is all just too-too.*
– ORIGIN late 19th cent.: reduplication of TOO.

tootsie (also **tootsy**) ▶ noun (pl. **tootsies**) informal **1** a person's foot.
2 a young woman, especially one perceived as being sexually available.
– ORIGIN mid 19th cent.: humorous diminutive of FOOT.

toot sweet ▶ adverb informal immediately: *hop down here toot sweet and let's have a look at it.*
– ORIGIN early 20th cent.: anglicized form of French *tout de suite*.

Toowoomba /təˈwʊmbə/ a town in Queensland, Australia, to the west of Brisbane; pop. 114,479 (2008). It was formerly known as The Swamps.

top[1] ▶ noun **1** [usu. in sing.] the highest or uppermost point, part, or surface of something: *Doreen stood at the top of the stairs | fill the cup almost to the top* | [in combination] *the springy turf of the clifftop.* ■ (usu. **tops**) the leaves, stems, and shoots of a plant, especially those of a vegetable grown for its root. ■ chiefly Brit. the uppermost creamy layer of milk.
2 a thing or part placed on, fitted to, or covering the upper part of something, in particular: ■ a garment covering the upper part of the body and worn with a skirt, trousers, or shorts. ■ a lid, cover, or cap: *beer-bottle tops.* ■ (in a sailing ship) a platform around the head of each of the lower masts, serving to extend the topmast rigging.
3 (**the top**) the highest or most important rank, level, or position: *her talent will take her right to the top | the people **at the top** must be competent.* ■ the utmost degree or the highest level: *she shouted at the top of her voice.* ■ (**tops**) informal a person or thing regarded as particularly good: *professionally you're the tops.* ■ Brit. the highest gear of a motor vehicle. ■ [mass noun] the high-frequency component of reproduced sound.
4 chiefly Brit. the end of something that is furthest from the speaker or a point of reference: *the bus shelter at the top of the road.*
5 short for TOPSPIN.
6 (usu. **tops**) a bundle of long wool fibres prepared for spinning.
7 [mass noun] Physics one of six flavours of quark.
▶ adjective [attrib.] **1** highest in position, rank, or degree: *the top button of his shirt | a top executive.*
2 chiefly Brit. furthest away from the speaker or a point of reference: *the top end of Fulham Road.*
▶ verb (**tops, topping, topped**) [with obj.] **1** exceed (an amount, level, or number); be more than: *losses are expected to top £100 m this year.* ■ be at the highest place or rank in (a list, poll, or league): *her debut album topped the charts for five weeks.* ■ be taller than: *he topped her by several inches.* ■ surpass (a person or previous achievement); outdo: *he was baffled as to how he could top his past work.* ■ appear as the chief performer or attraction at: *Hopper topped a great night of boxing.*
2 provide with a top or topping: *toast topped with baked beans.* ■ complete (an outfit) with an upper garment, hat, or item of jewellery: *a white dress topped by a dark cardigan.* ■ remove the top of (a vegetable or fruit) in preparation for cooking.
3 reach the top of (a hill or other elevation): *they topped a rise and began a slow descent.*
4 Brit. informal kill: *I wasn't sorry when he topped himself.*
5 Golf mishit (the ball or a stroke) by hitting above the centre of the ball.
▶ adverb (**tops**) informal at the most: *some civil servant earning twenty-eight thousand a year, tops.*
– PHRASES **be at the top of one's game** informal be performing as well as one can: *this film is the work of a director at the top of his game.* **from top to bottom** completely; thoroughly: *we searched the place from top to bottom.* **from top to toe** all over: *she seemed to glow from top to toe.* **from the top** informal from the beginning: *they rehearsed Act One from the top.* **get on top of** be too much for (someone) to bear or cope with. **off the top of one's head** see HEAD. **on top 1** on the highest point or uppermost surface. ■ on the upper part of the head: *Graeme's going a bit thin on top.* ■ so as to cover; over: *she put on a grey raincoat on top.* **2** in a leading or the dominant position: *United were on top for most of the first half.* **3** in addition: *the price was £75, with VAT on top.* **on top of 1** on the highest point or uppermost surface of: *a town perched on top of a hill.* ■ so as to cover; over. **2** in command or control of: *he couldn't **get on top of** his work.* **3** in addition to: *on top of everything else he's a brilliant linguist.* **4** in close proximity to: *we all lived on top of each other.* **on top of the world** informal happy and elated. **over the top 1** informal, chiefly Brit. to an excessive or exaggerated degree: *her reactions had been a bit over the top.* **2** chiefly historical over the parapet of a trench and into battle. **top and tail** Brit. **1** remove the top and bottom of (a fruit or vegetable) while preparing it as food. **2** wash the face and bottom of (a baby or small child). **top dollar** informal a very high price: *I pay top dollar for my materials.* **top of the morning** Irish used as a friendly morning greeting. **the top of the tree** the highest level of a profession or career. **top ten** (or **twenty** etc.) the first ten (or twenty etc.) records in the pop music charts. **to top it all** as a culminating, typically unpleasant, event or action in a series. **up top** see UP.
– PHRASAL VERBS **top something off 1** finish something in a memorable or notable way: *the festive celebration was topped off with the awarding of prizes.* **2** US informal fill up a partly full tank with fuel. **top out** reach an upper limit: *collectors whose budgets tend to top out at about $50,000.* **top something out** put the highest structural feature on a building, typically as a ceremony to mark the building's completion. **top someone up** informal refill a partly

full glass or cup for someone. **top something up** chiefly Brit. add to a number or amount to bring it up to a certain level: *a 0.5 per cent bonus is offered to top up savings rates.* ■ add additional credit to a pay-as-you-go mobile phone account. ■ fill up a glass or other partly full container.
– DERIVATIVES **topped** adjective [in combination] *a glass-topped table.*
– ORIGIN late Old English *topp* (noun), of Germanic origin; related to Dutch *top* 'summit, crest'.

top² ▶ noun **1** (also **spinning top**) a conical, spherical, or pear-shaped toy that with a quick or vigorous twist may be set to spin.
2 used in names of top shells, e.g. **strawberry top**.
– ORIGIN late Old English, of unknown origin.

topaz ▶ noun **1** a precious stone, typically colourless, yellow, or pale blue, consisting of an aluminium silicate that contains fluorine. ■ [mass noun] a dark yellow colour.
2 a large tropical American hummingbird with a yellowish throat and a long tail. ● Genus *Topaza*, family Trochilidae: two species.
– ORIGIN Middle English (denoting a yellow sapphire): from Old French *topace*, via Latin from Greek *topazos*.

topazolite /tə(ʊ)ˈpazəlʌɪt/ ▶ noun [mass noun] a variety of andradite (garnet) that is yellowish green.
– ORIGIN early 19th cent.: from TOPAZ + -LITE.

top boot ▶ noun chiefly historical a high boot with a broad band of a different material or colour at the top.

top brass ▶ noun see BRASS.

topcoat ▶ noun **1** an overcoat.
2 an outer coat of paint.

top copy ▶ noun the original typed or handwritten copy of a letter or document of which carbon copies have been made.

top dead centre ▶ noun the furthest point of a piston's travel, at which it changes from an upward to a downward stroke.

top dog ▶ noun informal a person who is successful or dominant in their field: *he was a top dog in the City.*

top-down ▶ adjective **1** denoting a system of government or management in which actions and policies are initiated at the highest level; hierarchical.
2 proceeding from the general to the particular: *a top-down approach to research.* ■ Computing working from the top or root of a tree-like system towards the branches.

top drawer informal ▶ noun (**the top drawer**) high social position or class: *George and Madge were not out of the top drawer.*
▶ adjective (**top-drawer**) of the highest quality or social class: *a top-drawer performance.*

top dressing ▶ noun an application of manure or fertilizer to the surface layer of soil or a lawn.
– DERIVATIVES **top-dress** verb.

tope¹ ▶ verb [no obj.] archaic or literary drink alcohol to excess, especially on a regular basis.
– DERIVATIVES **toper** noun.
– ORIGIN mid 17th cent.: perhaps an alteration of obsolete *top* 'overbalance'; perhaps from Dutch *top-pen* 'slant or tilt a ship's yard'.

tope² ▶ noun (in South Asia) a grove or plantation of trees, especially mango trees.
– ORIGIN from Telugu *tōpu* or Tamil *tōppu*.

tope³ ▶ noun another term for STUPA.
– ORIGIN from Punjabi *thūp*, *thop* 'barrow, mound', apparently related to Sanskrit *stūpa*.

tope⁴ ▶ noun a small greyish slender bodied shark, occurring chiefly in inshore waters. ● Genus *Galeorhinus*, family Carcharhinidae: the East Atlantic *G. galeus*, favoured by British sea anglers, and the commercially important *G. australis* of Australia.
– ORIGIN late 17th cent.: perhaps of Cornish origin.

top edge Cricket ▶ noun a shot hit into the air off the upper edge of a bat held sideways.
▶ verb (**top-edge**) [with obj.] hit (the ball) in this way; hit a ball delivered by (a bowler) in this way.

topee ▶ noun variant spelling of TOPI¹.

Topeka /təˈpiːkə/ the state capital of Kansas; pop. 123,446 (est. 2008).

top-end ▶ adjective (of a product) at the top of a range; high quality or sophisticated: *top-end, high-quality video equipment.*

top fermentation ▶ noun [mass noun] the process by which ale-type beers are fermented, proceeding for a relatively short period at high temperature with the yeast rising to the top.

top flight ▶ noun (**the top flight**) the highest rank or level.
▶ adjective [attrib.] of the highest rank or level: *a top-flight batsman.*

top fruit ▶ noun [mass noun] Brit. fruit grown on trees rather than bushes.

topgallant /tɒpˈgal(ə)nt, təˈgal-/ ▶ noun (also **topgallant mast**) the section of a square-rigged sailing ship's mast immediately above the topmast. ■ (also **topgallant sail**) a sail set on a topgallant mast.

top hamper ▶ noun [mass noun] Sailing sails, rigging, or other things above decks creating top-heavy weight or wind-resistant surfaces.

top hat ▶ noun a man's formal hat with a high cylindrical crown.

top-heavy ▶ adjective **1** disproportionately heavy at the top so as to be in danger of toppling.
2 (of an organization) having a disproportionately large number of senior administrative staff.
– DERIVATIVES **top-heavily** adverb, **top-heaviness** noun.

Tophet /ˈtəʊfɪt/ ▶ noun a term for hell.
– ORIGIN late Middle English: from Hebrew *tōpet*, the name of a place in the Valley of Hinnom near Jerusalem used for idolatrous worship, including the sacrifice of children (see Jer. 19:6), and later for burning refuse.

top-hole ▶ adjective Brit. informal, dated or humorous excellent; first-rate: *this CD is a top-hole purchase.*

tophus /ˈtəʊfəs/ ▶ noun (pl. **tophi** /-fʌɪ/) Medicine a deposit of crystalline uric acid and other substances at the surface of joints or in skin or cartilage, typically as a feature of gout.
– ORIGIN early 17th cent.: from Latin, denoting loose porous stones of various kinds.

topi¹ /ˈtəʊpi/ (also **topee**) ▶ noun (pl. **topis** or **topees**) short for SOLA TOPI. ■ Indian a hat or cap.
– ORIGIN from Hindi *topī* 'hat'.

topi² /ˈtəʊpi/ ▶ noun (pl. **same** or **topis**) a large African antelope related to the hartebeests, with a pattern of bold black patches on a reddish coat, and thick ridged horns. ● *Damaliscus lunatus*, family Bovidae, in particular the race *D. l. topi* of East Africa. Compare with TSESSEBI.
– ORIGIN late 19th cent.: from Mende.

topiary /ˈtəʊpɪəri/ ▶ noun (pl. **topiaries**) [mass noun] the art or practice of clipping shrubs or trees into ornamental shapes. ■ shrubs or trees clipped into ornamental shapes: *a cottage surrounded by topiary and flowers.*
– DERIVATIVES **topiarist** noun.
– ORIGIN late 16th cent.: from French *topiaire*, from Latin *topiarius* 'ornamental gardener', from *topia opera* 'fancy gardening', from a diminutive of Greek *topos* 'place'.

topic ▶ noun a matter dealt with in a text, discourse, or conversation; a subject: *her favourite topic of conversation is her partner.* ■ Linguistics that part of a sentence about which something is said, typically the first major constituent.
– ORIGIN late 15th cent. (originally denoting a set or book of general rules or ideas): from Latin *topica*, from Greek *ta topika*, literally 'matters concerning commonplaces' (the title of a treatise by Aristotle), from *topos* 'a place'.

topical ▶ adjective **1** (of a subject) of immediate relevance, interest, or importance owing to its relation to current events: *a popular topical affairs programme.* ■ relating to a particular subject; classified according to subject: *foreign or topical stamps.*
2 chiefly Medicine relating or applied directly to a part of the body.
– DERIVATIVES **topicality** noun, **topically** adverb.
– ORIGIN late 16th cent.: from Greek *topikos* + -AL. Early use was as a term in logic and rhetoric describing a rule or argument as 'applicable in most but not all cases'.

topicalize (also **topicalise**) ▶ verb [with obj.] Linguistics cause (a subject, word, or phrase) to be the topic of a sentence or discourse, typically by placing it first.
– DERIVATIVES **topicalization** noun.

topic sentence ▶ noun a sentence that expresses the main idea of the paragraph in which it occurs.

Topkapi Palace /tɒpˈkɑːpi/ the former seraglio or residence in Istanbul of the sultans of the Ottoman Empire, last occupied by Mahmut II (1808–39) and now a museum.

topknot ▶ noun a knot of hair arranged on the top of the head. ■ a decorative knot or bow of ribbon worn on the top of the head, popular in the 18th century. ■ (in an animal or bird) a tuft or crest of hair or feathers.

topless ▶ adjective (of a woman) having the breasts uncovered: *a topless dancer.*
– DERIVATIVES **toplessness** noun.

top-level ▶ adjective of the highest level of importance or prestige: *top-level talks.*

top light ▶ noun **1** a small pane above a main window, which typically opens outwards and upwards.
2 a skylight.

top-line ▶ adjective [attrib.] of the highest quality or ranking: *a top-line act.*

toplofty ▶ adjective US informal haughty and arrogant.

topman ▶ noun (pl. **topmen**) chiefly historical **1** a sawyer working the upper handle of a pit saw; a top-sawyer.
2 a sailor on duty in a sailing ship's tops.

topmast /ˈtɒpmɑːst, -məst/ ▶ noun the second section of a square-rigged sailing ship's mast, immediately above the lower mast.

topminnow ▶ noun an American killifish, often seen at the water surface. ● *Fundulus* and other genera in the families Cyprinodontidae (or Fundulidae) (many species), and Poeciliidae (one or two species).

topmost ▶ adjective highest in physical position; highest: *we watched a squirrel negotiate the topmost branches of a nearby tree.* ■ highest in status or importance; foremost: *the rider's safety must be the topmost priority.*

top-notch ▶ adjective informal of the highest quality; excellent: *a top-notch hotel.*
– DERIVATIVES **top-notcher** noun.

top note ▶ noun **1** the highest or a very high note in a piece of music or a singer's vocal range.
2 a dominant scent in a perfume.

topo /ˈtɒpəʊ/ ▶ noun (pl. **topos**) informal, chiefly N. Amer. a topographic map. ■ Climbing a diagram of a mountain with details of routes to the top marked on it.
– ORIGIN 1970s: abbreviation of *topographic* (see TOPOGRAPHICAL).

topographical /ˌtɒpəˈgrafɪkəl/ ▶ adjective **1** relating to the arrangement or accurate representation of the physical features of an area: *the topographical features of the river valley.* ■ (of a work of art or an artist) dealing with or depicting landscapes or other areas in a realistic and detailed manner.
2 Anatomy & Biology relating to or representing the physical distribution of parts or features on the surface of or within an organ or organism.
– DERIVATIVES **topographic** adjective, **topographically** adverb.

topography /təˈpɒgrəfi/ ▶ noun (pl. **topographies**) [mass noun] **1** the arrangement of the natural and artificial physical features of an area: *the topography of the island.* ■ [count noun] a detailed description or representation on a map of the physical features of an area.
2 Anatomy & Biology the distribution of parts or features on the surface of or within an organ or organism.
– DERIVATIVES **topographer** noun.
– ORIGIN late Middle English: via late Latin from Greek *topographia*, from *topos* 'place' + *-graphia* (see -GRAPHY).

topoi plural form of TOPOS.

topoisomer /ˌtɒpəʊˈʌɪsəmə/ ▶ noun Biochemistry a topologically distinct isomer, especially of DNA.

topoisomerase /ˌtɒpəʊʌɪˈsɒməreɪz/ ▶ noun Biochemistry an enzyme which alters the supercoiled form of a DNA molecule.
– ORIGIN 1970s: from Greek *topos* 'place' + ISOMER + -ASE.

topological space ▶ noun Mathematics a space which has an associated family of subsets that constitute a topology. The relationships between members of the space are mathematically analogous to those between points in ordinary two- and three-dimensional space.

topology /təˈpɒlədʒi/ ▶ noun (pl. **topologies**) **1** [mass noun] Mathematics the study of geometrical properties and spatial relations unaffected by the continuous change of shape or size of figures. ■ [count noun] a family of open subsets of an abstract space such that the union and the intersection of any two of them are members of the family, and which includes the space itself and the empty set.
2 the way in which constituent parts are interrelated or arranged: *the topology of a computer network.*
– DERIVATIVES **topological** adjective, **topologically** adverb, **topologist** noun.

T

– ORIGIN late 19th cent.: via German from Greek *topos* 'place' + -LOGY.

toponym /ˈtɒpənɪm/ ▸ noun a place name, especially one derived from a topographical feature.
– ORIGIN 1930s: from Greek *topos* 'place' + -ONYM.

toponymy /təˈpɒnɪmi/ ▸ noun [mass noun] the study of place names.
– DERIVATIVES **toponymic** adjective.
– ORIGIN late 19th cent.: from Greek *topos* 'place' + *onuma* 'name'.

topos /ˈtɒpɒs/ ▸ noun (pl. **topoi** /ˈtɒpɔɪ/) a traditional theme or formula in literature.
– ORIGIN 1940s: from Greek, literally 'place'.

topper ▸ noun **1** a machine that cuts the tops of weeds.
2 US a hard protective lightweight cover or shell mounted on the back or bed of a pickup truck. ■ a type of camper van mounted on a truck bed.
3 informal a top hat.
4 Brit. informal, dated an exceptionally good person or thing.

toppie¹ /ˈtɒpi/ ▸ noun (pl. **toppies**) an African bulbul (songbird) with a black or dark brown head and crest. ● Genus *Pycnonotus*, family Pycnonotidae: several species.
– ORIGIN late 19th cent.: from TOPKNOT.

toppie² /ˈtɒpi/ ▸ noun (pl. **toppies**) S. African informal a middle-aged or elderly man.
– ORIGIN 1960s: perhaps from Zulu *thopi* 'growing sparsely' (describing thinning hair), or from Hindi *ṭopī* 'hat'.

topping ▸ adjective Brit. informal, dated excellent: *that really is a topping dress.*
▸ noun a layer of food poured or spread over a base of a different type of food to add flavour.

topping lift ▸ noun a rope or cable on a sailing boat that supports the weight of a boom or yard and can be used to lift it.

topple ▸ verb overbalance or cause to overbalance and fall: [no obj., with adverbial of direction] *she toppled over when I touched her* | [with obj.] *the push almost toppled him to the ground.* ■ [with obj.] remove (a government or person in authority) from power; overthrow: *disagreement had threatened to topple the government.*
– ORIGIN mid 16th cent. (in the sense 'tumble about'): frequentative of TOP¹.

top rope Climbing ▸ noun a rope lowered from above to the lead climber in a group, typically to give assistance at a difficult part of a climb.
▸ verb (**top-rope**) [with obj.] climb (a route or part of one) using a top rope.

topsail /ˈtɒpseɪl, -s(ə)l/ ▸ noun a sail set on a ship's topmast. ■ a fore-and-aft sail set above the gaff.

top-sawyer ▸ noun chiefly historical a sawyer holding the upper handle of a pit saw and standing in the upper position above the saw pit. ■ archaic a distinguished person.

top-score ▸ verb [no obj.] (of a sports player) score the most goals, runs, or points in a particular competition, match, etc.: *Taylor top-scored with 66 not out.*
– DERIVATIVES **top scorer** noun.

top secret ▸ adjective of the highest secrecy; highly confidential: *the experiments were top secret.*

top-shelf ▸ adjective **1** Brit. (of a magazine) pornographic.
2 chiefly N. Amer. of a high quality; excellent: *some top-shelf cars are shipped overseas.*

T

top shell ▸ noun a marine mollusc which has a low conical shell with a pearly interior, widespread in tropical and temperate seas. ● Family Trochidae, class Gastropoda.

topside ▸ noun **1** [mass noun] Brit. the outer side of a round of beef: *roast topside.*
2 (often **topsides**) the upper part of a ship's side, above the waterline.
▸ adverb on or towards the upper decks of a ship: *we stayed topside.*

Top-Sider ▸ noun US trademark a casual shoe, typically made of leather or canvas with a rubber sole, designed to be worn on boats.

top-slice ▸ verb [with obj.] take (part of a budget or fund) and allocate it to finance a specific project, service, etc.

top-slicing ▸ noun [mass noun] a method of assessing tax chargeable on a lump sum by averaging the sum out over the years it has accrued and charging accordingly.

topsoil ▸ noun [mass noun] the top layer of soil.

topspin ▸ noun [mass noun] a fast forward spinning motion imparted to a ball when throwing or hitting it, often resulting in a curved path or a strong forward motion on rebounding.
– DERIVATIVES **topspinner** noun.

topstitch ▸ verb [no obj.] make a row of continuous stitches on the top or right side of a garment or other article as a decorative feature.

topsy-turvy ▸ adjective & adverb upside down: [as adv.] *the fairground ride turned riders topsy-turvy.* ■ in a state of confusion: [as adj.] *the topsy-turvy months of the invasion.*
▸ noun [in sing.] a state of utter confusion.
– DERIVATIVES **topsy-turvily** adverb, **topsy-turviness** noun.
– ORIGIN early 16th cent.: a jingle apparently based on TOP¹ and obsolete *terve* 'overturn'.

top table ▸ noun the table at which the chief guests are placed at a formal dinner.

top-tier ▸ adjective of the highest level or quality: *a top-tier medical school.*

top-up ▸ noun Brit. an additional or extra amount or payment that restores something to the level that is required: *they will miss out on hundreds of pounds worth of pension top-ups* | [as modifier] *top-up fees for university students.* ■ a quantity of a drink that refills a partly full glass or cup: *he headed back to the bar for a top-up.*

topwater ▸ adjective Fishing, N. Amer. (of a bait) floating on or near the top of the water.

top weight ▸ noun the heaviest weight carried by a horse in a race.

toque /təʊk/ ▸ noun a woman's small hat, typically having a narrow, closely turned-up brim. ■ historical a small cap or bonnet resembling a toque worn by a man or woman. ■ a tall white hat with a full pouched crown, worn by chefs.
– ORIGIN early 16th cent.: from French, of unknown origin.

tor /tɔː/ ▸ noun a hill or rocky peak: [in place names] *Glastonbury Tor.*
– ORIGIN Old English *torr*, perhaps of Celtic origin and related to Welsh *tor* 'belly' and Scottish Gaelic *tòrr* 'bulging hill'.

Torah /ˈtɔːrɑː, tɔːˈrɑː/ ▸ noun (usu. **the Torah**) (in Judaism) the law of God as revealed to Moses and recorded in the first five books of the Hebrew scriptures (the Pentateuch).
– ORIGIN from Hebrew *tōrāh* 'instruction, doctrine, law', from *yārāh* 'show, direct, instruct'.

Torbay a borough in Devon, SW England; pop. 138,800 (est. 2009). It was formed in 1968 from the amalgamation of the seaside resorts Torquay, Paignton, and Brixham.

torc /tɔːk/ (also **torque**) ▸ noun historical a neck ornament consisting of a band of twisted metal, worn especially by the ancient Gauls and Britons.
– ORIGIN mid 19th cent.: from French *torque*, from Latin *torques* (see TORCH).

torch ▸ noun **1** Brit. a portable battery-powered electric lamp. ■ chiefly historical a portable means of illumination such as a piece of wood or cloth soaked in tallow and ignited, sometimes carried ceremonially. ■ [in sing.] used to refer to a valuable quality, principle, or cause, which needs to be protected and maintained: *mountain warlords carried the torch of Greek independence.*
2 chiefly N. Amer. a blowlamp.
3 US informal an arsonist.
▸ verb [with obj.] informal set fire to: *the shops had been looted and torched.*
– PHRASES **carry a torch for** suffer from unrequited love for. **put to the torch** (or **put a torch to**) destroy by burning.
– ORIGIN Middle English: from Old French *torche*, from Latin *torqua*, variant of *torques* 'necklace, wreath', from *torquere* 'to twist'. The current verb sense was originally US slang and dates from the 1930s.

torchbearer ▸ noun a person who carries a ceremonial torch. ■ a person who leads or inspires others in working towards a valued goal: *some of the original feminist torchbearers.*

torchère /tɔːˈʃɛː/ ▸ noun a tall ornamental flat-topped stand, traditionally used as a stand for a candlestick.
– ORIGIN early 20th cent.: French, from *torche* (see TORCH).

torchlight ▸ noun [mass noun] the light of a torch or torches.
– DERIVATIVES **torchlit** adjective.

torchon /ˈtɔːʃ(ə)n/ (also **torchon lace**) ▸ noun [mass noun] coarse bobbin lace with geometrical designs.
– ORIGIN mid 19th cent.: from French, literally 'duster, dishcloth', from *torcher* 'to wipe'.

torch song ▸ noun a sad or sentimental love song, typically about unrequited love.
– DERIVATIVES **torch singer** noun.

tore¹ past of TEAR¹.

tore² /tɔː/ ▸ noun archaic term for TORUS.
– ORIGIN mid 17th cent.: from French.

toreador /ˈtɒrɪədɔː, ˌtɒrɪəˈdɔː/ ▸ noun a bullfighter, especially one on horseback.
– ORIGIN Spanish, from *torear* 'fight bulls', from *toro* 'bull'.

toreador pants ▸ plural noun chiefly N. Amer. women's tight-fitting calf-length trousers.

torero /tɒˈrɛːrəʊ/ ▸ noun (pl. **toreros**) a bullfighter, especially one on foot.
– ORIGIN Spanish, from *toro* 'bull' (see TOREADOR).

toreutics /təˈruːtɪks/ ▸ plural noun [treated as sing.] the art of making designs in relief or intaglio, especially by chasing, carving, and embossing in metal.
– DERIVATIVES **toreutic** adjective.
– ORIGIN mid 19th cent.: from Greek *toreutikos*, from *toreuein* 'to work in relief'.

torgoch /ˈtɔːgɒx/ ▸ noun (in Wales) an Arctic charr (fish).
– ORIGIN early 17th cent.: Welsh, from *tor* 'belly' + *coch* 'red'.

tori plural form of TORUS.

toric /ˈtɒrɪk, ˈtɔːrɪk/ ▸ adjective Geometry having the form of a torus or part of a torus. ■ (of a contact lens) having two different curves instead of one, used to correct both astigmatism and short- or long-sightedness.

torii /ˈtɔːriː/ ▸ noun (pl. **same**) the gateway of a Shinto shrine, with two uprights and two crosspieces.
– ORIGIN Japanese, from *tori* 'bird' + *i* 'sit, perch'.

Torino /təʊˈriːnəʊ/ Italian name for TURIN.

torment ▸ noun [mass noun] severe physical or mental suffering: *their deaths have left both families in torment.* ■ [count noun] a cause of severe suffering: *the journey must have been a torment for them.*
▸ verb [with obj.] cause to experience severe mental or physical suffering: *he was tormented by jealousy.* ■ annoy or provoke in an unkind way: *every day I have kids tormenting me because they know I live alone.*
– DERIVATIVES **tormented** adjective, **tormentedly** adverb, **tormenting** adjective, **tormentingly** adverb, **tormentor** noun.
– ORIGIN Middle English (as both noun and verb referring to the infliction or suffering of torture): Old French *torment* (noun), *tormenter* (verb), from Latin *tormentum* 'instrument of torture', from *torquere* 'to twist'.

tormentil /ˈtɔːm(ə)ntɪl/ ▸ noun a low-growing Eurasian plant with bright yellow flowers. The root is used in herbal medicine to treat diarrhoea. ● *Potentilla erecta*, family Rosaceae.
– ORIGIN late Middle English: from French *tormentille*, from medieval Latin *tormentilla*, of unknown origin.

torn past participle of TEAR¹.

tornado /tɔːˈneɪdəʊ/ ▸ noun (pl. **tornadoes** or **tornados**) a mobile, destructive vortex of violently rotating winds having the appearance of a funnel-shaped cloud and advancing beneath a large storm system. ■ a person or thing characterized by violent or devastating action or emotion: *teenagers caught up in a tornado of sexual confusion.*
– DERIVATIVES **tornadic** /-ˈnadɪk/ adjective.
– ORIGIN mid 16th cent. (denoting a violent thunderstorm of the tropical Atlantic Ocean): perhaps an alteration of Spanish *tronada* 'thunderstorm' (from *tronar* 'to thunder') by association with Spanish *tornar* 'to turn'.

Tornio /ˈtɔːnɪəʊ/ a river which rises in NE Sweden and flows 566 km (356 miles) generally southwards, forming the border between Sweden and Finland before emptying into the Gulf of Bothnia. Swedish name **Torne Älv** /ˌtɔːrnə ˈɛlv/.

toro /ˈtɔːrəʊ/ ▸ noun [mass noun] (in Japanese cookery) tuna meat from the belly of the fish, pale pink and rich in fat and used in sushi and sashimi.
– ORIGIN Japanese, probably short for *torori to* 'melting in the mouth'.

toroid /ˈtɒrɔɪd, ˈtɔː-/ ▶ **noun** Geometry a figure of toroidal shape.

toroidal /tɒˈrɔɪd(ə)l, tɔː-/ ▶ **adjective** Geometry of or resembling a torus.
– DERIVATIVES **toroidally** adverb.

Toronto the capital of Ontario and the largest city in Canada, situated on the north shore of Lake Ontario; pop. 2,503,281 (2006).
– ORIGIN originally named York but renamed *Toronto* in 1834, from a Huron word meaning 'meeting place'.

torpedo ▶ **noun** (pl. **torpedoes**) **1** a cigar-shaped self-propelled underwater missile designed to be fired from a ship or submarine or dropped into the water from an aircraft and to explode on reaching a target. ■ US a firework that explodes on impact with a hard surface.
2 US a railway fog signal.
3 (also **torpedo ray**) an electric ray.
▶ **verb** (**torpedoes, torpedoing, torpedoed**) [with obj.] attack or sink (a ship) with a torpedo or torpedoes. ■ destroy or ruin (a plan or project): *fighting between the militias torpedoed peace talks.*
– DERIVATIVES **torpedo-like** adjective.
– ORIGIN early 16th cent. (in sense 3 of the noun): from Latin, literally 'stiffness, numbness', by extension 'electric ray' (which gives a shock causing numbness), from *torpere* 'be numb or sluggish'. Sense 1 of the noun dates from the late 18th cent. and first described a timed explosive device for detonation under water.

torpedo boat ▶ **noun** a small, fast, light warship armed with torpedoes.

torpedo net ▶ **noun** historical a net made of steel wire, hung in the water round an anchored ship to intercept torpedoes.

torpedo tube ▶ **noun** a tube in a submarine or other ship from which torpedoes are fired by the use of compressed air or an explosive charge.

torpefy /ˈtɔːpɪfʌɪ/ ▶ **verb** (**torpefies, torpefying, torpefied**) [with obj.] formal make (someone or something) numb, paralysed, or lifeless.
– ORIGIN early 19th cent.: from Latin *torpefacere*, from *torpere* 'be numb or sluggish'.

torpid ▶ **adjective** mentally or physically inactive; lethargic: *we sat around in a torpid state.* ■ (of an animal) dormant, especially during hibernation.
– DERIVATIVES **torpidity** noun, **torpidly** adverb.
– ORIGIN late Middle English: from Latin *torpidus*, from *torpere* 'be numb or sluggish'.

torpor /ˈtɔːpə/ ▶ **noun** [mass noun] a state of physical or mental inactivity; lethargy: *they veered between apathetic torpor and hysterical fanaticism.*
– ORIGIN late Middle English: from Latin, from *torpere* 'be numb or sluggish'.

Torquay a resort town in SW England, in Devon, administratively part of Torbay since 1968; pop. 67,400 (est. 2009).

torque /tɔːk/ ▶ **noun 1** [mass noun] Mechanics a force that tends to cause rotation.
2 variant spelling of TORC.
▶ **verb** [with obj.] apply torque or a twisting force to (an object): *he gently torqued the hip joint.*
– DERIVATIVES **torquey** adjective (**torquier, torquiest**).
– ORIGIN late 19th cent.: from Latin *torquere* 'to twist'.

torque converter ▶ **noun** a device that transmits or multiplies torque generated by an engine.

Torquemada /ˌtɔːkrˈmɑːdə/, Spanish /təorkeˈmaða/, Tomás de (*c.*1420–98), Spanish cleric and Grand Inquisitor. A Dominican monk, he became confessor to Ferdinand and Isabella, whom he persuaded to institute the Inquisition in 1478. He was also the prime mover behind the expulsion of the Jews from Spain in and after 1492.

torque wrench ▶ **noun** a tool for setting and adjusting the tightness of nuts and bolts to a desired value.

torr /tɔː/ ▶ **noun** (pl. **same**) a unit of pressure equivalent to 1 mm of mercury in a barometer and equal to 133.32 pascals.
– ORIGIN 1940s: named after E. TORRICELLI.

Torrens system /ˈtɒr(ə)nz/ ▶ **noun** Law a system of land title registration, adopted originally in Australia and later in some states of the US and Malaysia.
– ORIGIN mid 19th cent.: named after Sir Robert *Torrens* (1814–84), third Premier of South Australia.

torrent ▶ **noun** a strong and fast-moving stream of water or other liquid: *rain poured down in torrents | after the rains, the stream becomes a raging torrent.* ■ (**a torrent of/torrents of**) an overwhelming outpouring of (something, typically words): *she was subjected to a torrent of abuse.*
– ORIGIN late 16th cent.: from French, from Italian *torrente*, from Latin *torrent-* 'boiling, roaring', from *torrere* 'parch, scorch'.

torrential ▶ **adjective** (of rain) falling rapidly and in copious quantities: *a torrential downpour.* ■ (of water) flowing rapidly and with force.
– DERIVATIVES **torrentially** adverb.

Torres Strait /ˈtɒrɪs/ a channel separating the northern tip of Queensland, Australia, from the island of New Guinea and linking the Arafura Sea and the Coral Sea.
– ORIGIN named after the Spanish explorer Luis V. de *Torres*, the first European to sail along the south coast of New Guinea (1606).

Torricelli /ˌtɒrɪˈtʃɛli/, Evangelista (1608–47), Italian mathematician and physicist. He invented the mercury barometer, with which he demonstrated that the atmosphere exerts a pressure sufficient to support a column of mercury in an inverted closed tube.

Torricellian vacuum /ˌtɔːrɪˈtʃɛlɪən, -ˈsɛlɪən/ ▶ **noun** a vacuum formed above the column of mercury in a mercury barometer.

torrid ▶ **adjective 1** very hot and dry: *the torrid heat of the afternoon.* ■ full of passion arising from sexual love: *a torrid love affair.*
2 Brit. full of difficulty: *he'd been given a pretty torrid time by the nation's voters.*
3 N. Amer. (especially in financial contexts) characterized by intense activity; hard to contain or stop: *the world's most torrid economies.*
– DERIVATIVES **torridity** noun, **torridly** adverb.
– ORIGIN late 16th cent.: from French *torride* or Latin *torridus*, from *torrere* 'parch, scorch'.

Torridonian /ˌtɒrɪˈdəʊnɪən/ ▶ **adjective** Geology relating to or denoting the later stage of the Proterozoic aeon in NW Scotland, from about 1100 to 600 million years ago. ■ (as noun **the Torridonian**) the Torridonian period, or the system of rocks deposited during it.
– ORIGIN late 19th cent.: from the name of Loch *Torridon*, in NW Scotland, + -IAN.

torrid zone ▶ **noun** the hot central belt of the earth bounded by the tropics of Cancer and Capricorn.

torsade /tɔːˈseɪd/ ▶ **noun** a decorative twisted braid, ribbon, or other strand used as trimming. ■ an artificial plait of hair.
– ORIGIN late 19th cent.: from French, from Latin *tors-* 'twisted', from *torquere* 'to twist'.

torsade de pointes /tɔːˌsɑːd də ˈpwãt/ ▶ **noun** [mass noun] Medicine a form of tachycardia in which the electrical pulse in the heart undergoes a cyclical variation in strength, giving a characteristic electrocardiogram resembling a twisted fringe of spikes.
– ORIGIN 1960s: French, literally 'twist of spikes'.

torse /tɔːs/ ▶ **noun** Heraldry a wreath.
– ORIGIN late 16th cent.: from obsolete French, from Latin *torta*, feminine past participle of *torquere* 'twist'.

torsel /ˈtɔːs(ə)l/ ▶ **noun** another term for TASSEL².

Tórshavn /ˈtɔːshaʊn/ (also **Thorshavn**) the capital of the Faroe Islands, a port on the island of Strømø; pop. 12,400 (est. 2007).

torsion /ˈtɔːʃ(ə)n/ ▶ **noun** [mass noun] the action of twisting or the state of being twisted, especially of one end of an object relative to the other. ■ the twisting of the cut end of an artery after surgery to impede bleeding. ■ Mathematics the extent to which a curve departs from being planar. ■ Zoology (in a gastropod mollusc) the spontaneous twisting of the visceral hump through 180° during larval development.
– DERIVATIVES **torsional** adjective, **torsionally** adverb.
– ORIGIN late Middle English (as a medical term denoting colic or in the sense 'twisting' (especially of a loop of the intestine)): via Old French from late Latin *torsio(n-)*, variant of *tortio(n-)* 'twisting, torture', from Latin *torquere* 'to twist'.

torsion balance ▶ **noun** an instrument for measuring very weak forces by their effect upon a system of fine twisted wire.

torsion bar (also **torsion beam**) ▶ **noun** a bar forming part of a vehicle suspension, twisting in response to the motion of the wheels and absorbing their vertical movement.

torsion pendulum ▶ **noun** a pendulum that rotates rather than swings.

torsk /tɔːsk/ ▶ **noun** a North Atlantic fish of the cod family, occurring in deep water and of some commercial importance. Also called CUSK. ● *Brosme brosme*, family Gadidae.
– ORIGIN early 18th cent.: from Norwegian, from Old Norse *thorskr*; probably related to *thurr* 'dry'.

torso ▶ **noun** (pl. **torsos** or US also **torsi**) the trunk of the human body. ■ the trunk of a statue without, or considered independently of, the head and limbs. ■ an unfinished or mutilated thing, especially a work of art or literature.
– ORIGIN late 18th cent.: from Italian, literally 'stalk, stump', from Latin *thyrsus* (see THYRSUS).

tort ▶ **noun** Law a wrongful act or an infringement of a right (other than under contract) leading to legal liability.
– ORIGIN Middle English (in the general sense 'wrong, injury'): from Old French, from medieval Latin *tortum* 'wrong, injustice', neuter past participle of Latin *torquere* 'to twist'.

torte /ˈtɔːtə/ ▶ **noun** (pl. **torten** /ˈtɔːt(ə)n/ or **tortes**) a sweet cake or tart.
– ORIGIN from German *Torte*, via Italian from late Latin *torta* 'round loaf, cake'. Compare with TORTILLA.

tortelli /tɔːˈtɛli/ ▶ **plural noun** small pasta parcels stuffed with a cheese or vegetable mixture.
– ORIGIN Italian, plural of *tortello* 'small cake, fritter'.

tortellini /ˌtɔːtəˈliːni/ ▶ **noun** tortelli which have been rolled and formed into small rings.
– ORIGIN Italian, plural of *tortellino*, diminutive of *tortello* 'small cake, fritter'.

tortfeasor /ˈtɔːtfiːzə/ ▶ **noun** Law a person who commits a tort.
– ORIGIN mid 17th cent.: from Old French *tort-fesor*, from *tort* 'wrong' and *fesor* 'doer'.

torticollis /ˌtɔːtɪˈkɒlɪs/ ▶ **noun** [mass noun] Medicine a condition in which the head becomes persistently turned to one side, often associated with painful muscle spasms. Also called WRYNECK.
– ORIGIN early 19th cent.: modern Latin, from Latin *tortus* 'crooked, twisted' + *collum* 'neck'.

tortilla /tɔːˈtiːjə/ ▶ **noun 1** (in Mexican cookery) a thin, flat maize pancake, eaten hot or cold, typically with a savoury filling.
2 (in Spanish cookery) an omelette.
– ORIGIN Spanish, diminutive of *torta* 'cake'.

tortious /ˈtɔːʃəs/ ▶ **adjective** Law constituting a tort; wrongful.
– DERIVATIVES **tortiously** adverb.
– ORIGIN late Middle English: from Anglo-Norman French *torcious*, from the stem of *torcion* 'extortion, violence', from late Latin *tortio(n-)* (see TORSION). The original sense was 'injurious'.

tortoise /ˈtɔːtəs, -tɔɪz/ ▶ **noun 1** a slow-moving typically herbivorous land reptile of warm climates, enclosed in a scaly or leathery domed shell into which it can retract its head and thick legs. Called TURTLE in North America. ● Family Testudinidae: numerous genera and species, including the **European tortoise** (*Testudo graeca*).
■ Austral. a freshwater turtle.
2 another term for TESTUDO.
– DERIVATIVES **tortoise-like** adjective & adverb.
– ORIGIN late Middle English *tortu*, *tortuce*: from Old French *tortue* and Spanish *tortuga*, both from medieval Latin *tortuca*, of uncertain origin. The current spelling dates from the mid 16th cent.

tortoiseshell ▶ **noun 1** [mass noun] the semi-transparent mottled yellow and brown shell of certain turtles, typically used to make jewellery or ornaments. ■ a synthetic substance made to imitate tortoiseshell.
2 short for TORTOISESHELL CAT.
3 short for TORTOISESHELL BUTTERFLY.

tortoiseshell butterfly ▶ **noun** a butterfly with mottled orange, yellow, and black markings, and wavy wing margins. ● Genera *Aglais* and *Nymphalis*, subfamily Nymphalinae, family Nymphalidae: several species, including the common Eurasian **small tortoiseshell** (*A. urticae*).

tortoiseshell cat ▶ **noun** a domestic cat with markings resembling tortoiseshell.

Tortola /tɔːˈtəʊlə/ the principal island of the British Virgin Islands in the Caribbean. Its chief town, Road Town, is the capital of the British Virgin Islands.
– ORIGIN Spanish, literally 'turtle dove'.

tortrix /ˈtɔːtrɪks/ (also **tortrix moth**) ▶ **noun** (pl. **tortrices** /-trɪsiːz/) a small moth with typically green caterpillars that live inside rolled leaves and can be a serious pest of fruit and other trees. ● Family

T

Tortricidae: many species, including *Pammene rhediella*, whose larvae damage apple and plum trees.
– DERIVATIVES **tortricid** noun & adjective.
– ORIGIN late 18th cent.: modern Latin, feminine of Latin *tortor* 'twister', from *torquere* 'to twist'.

tortuous /ˈtɔːtʃʊəs, -juəs/ ▶ **adjective** full of twists and turns: *the route is remote and tortuous.* ■ excessively lengthy and complex: *a tortuous argument.*
– DERIVATIVES **tortuosity** noun (pl. **tortuosities**), **tortuously** adverb, **tortuousness** noun.
– ORIGIN late Middle English: via Old French from Latin *tortuosus*, from *tortus* 'twisting, a twist', from Latin *torquere* 'to twist'.

> **USAGE** The two words **tortuous** and **torturous** have different core meanings. **Tortuous** means 'full of twists and turns', as in *a **tortuous** route*. **Torturous** means 'involving or causing torture', as in *a **torturous** five days of fitness training*. In extended senses, however, **tortuous** is used to mean 'excessively lengthy and complex' and hence may become indistinguishable from **torturous**: something which is **tortuous** is often also **torturous**, as in *a **tortuous** piece of bureaucratic language; their way had been **tortuous** and very difficult*. The overlap in sense has led to **tortuous** being sometimes used interchangeably with **torturous**, as in *he would at last draw in a **tortuous** gasp of air*.

torture ▶ **noun** [mass noun] the action or practice of inflicting severe pain on someone as a punishment or in order to force them to do or say something. ■ great physical or mental suffering: *the torture I've gone through because of loving you so.* ■ a cause of great physical or mental suffering: *dances were absolute torture because I was so small.*
▶ **verb** [with obj.] inflict severe pain on: *most of the victims had been brutally tortured.* ■ cause great mental suffering to: *he was tortured by grief.*
– DERIVATIVES **torturer** noun.
– ORIGIN late Middle English (in the sense 'distortion, twisting', or a physical disorder characterized by this): via French from late Latin *tortura* 'twisting, torment', from Latin *torquere* 'to twist'.

torturous ▶ **adjective** characterized by, involving, or causing pain or suffering: *a torturous five days of fitness training.*
– DERIVATIVES **torturously** adverb.
– ORIGIN late 15th cent.: from Anglo-Norman French, from *torture* 'torture'.

> **USAGE** On the difference between **torturous** and **tortuous**, see **USAGE** at **TORTUOUS**.

torula /ˈtɒrʊlə, -(j)ʊlə/ ▶ **noun** (pl. **torulae** /-liː/)
1 (also **torula yeast**) a yeast which is cultured for use in medicine and as a food additive, especially as a source of vitamins and protein. ● *Candida utilis*, subdivision Deuteromycotina.
2 a yeast-like fungus composed of chains of rounded cells, several kinds growing on dead vegetation and some causing infections. ● Genus *Torula* (or formerly this genus), subdivision Deuteromycotina: several species, in particular *T. herbarum*, which grows on dead grasses.
– ORIGIN modern Latin (genus name), diminutive of Latin *torus* 'swelling, bolster'.

torulosis /ˌtɒruːˈləʊsɪs, ˌtɒr(j)ʊ-/ ▶ **noun** another term for **CRYPTOCOCCOSIS**.

Toruń /ˈtɒrʊn/ an industrial city in northern Poland, on the River Vistula; pop. 206,765 (2007). German name **THORN**.

torus /ˈtɔːrəs/ ▶ **noun** (pl. **tori** /-rʌɪ/ or **toruses**) **1** Geometry a surface or solid formed by rotating a closed curve, especially a circle, about a line which lies in the same plane but does not intersect it (e.g. like a ring doughnut). ■ a ring-shaped object, especially a large ring-shaped chamber used in physical research.
2 Architecture a large convex moulding, typically semicircular in cross section, especially as the lowest part of the base of a column.
3 Anatomy a ridge of bone or muscle: *the maxillary torus.*
4 Botany the receptacle of a flower.
– ORIGIN mid 16th cent. (in sense 2): from Latin, literally 'swelling, bolster, round moulding'. The other senses date from the 19th cent.

Tory ▶ **noun** (pl. **Tories**) **1** (in the UK) a member or supporter of the Conservative Party. ■ a member of the English political party opposing the exclusion of James II from the succession. It remained the name for members of the English, later British, parliamentary party supporting the established religious and political order until the emergence of the Conservative Party in the 1830s. Compare with **WHIG** (sense 1).
2 US a colonist who supported the British side during the War of American Independence.
▶ **adjective** relating to the British Conservative Party or its supporters: *the Tory party | Tory voters.*
– DERIVATIVES **Toryism** noun.
– ORIGIN mid 17th cent.: probably from Irish *toraidhe* 'outlaw, highwayman', from *tóir* 'pursue'. The word was used of Irish peasants dispossessed by English settlers and living as robbers, and extended to other marauders especially in the Scottish Highlands. It was then adopted *c.*1679 as an abusive nickname for supporters of the Catholic James II.

tosa /ˈtəʊsə/ ▶ **noun** a dog of a breed of mastiff originally kept for dogfighting.
– ORIGIN 1940s: from *Tosa*, the name of a former province in Japan.

Toscana Italian /təɔˈskana/ Italian name for **TUSCANY**.

Toscanini /ˌtɒskəˈniːni/, Arturo (1867–1957), Italian conductor. He was musical director at La Scala in Milan (1898–1903; 1906–8) before becoming a conductor at the Metropolitan Opera, New York (1908–21).

tosh[1] ▶ **noun** [mass noun] Brit. informal rubbish; nonsense: *it's sentimental tosh.*
– ORIGIN late 19th cent.: of unknown origin.

tosh[2] ▶ **noun** Brit. informal used as a casual form of address, especially to an unknown person.
– ORIGIN 1950s: of unknown origin.

Tosk /tɒsk/ ▶ **noun** (pl. **same** or **Tosks**) **1** a member of one of the main ethnic groups of Albania, living mainly in the south of the country.
2 [mass noun] the dialect of Albanian spoken by the Tosk, with about 4 million speakers, forming the basis for standard Albanian. Compare with **GHEG**.
▶ **adjective** relating to the Tosk or their dialect.
– ORIGIN from Albanian *Toskë*.

toss ▶ **verb 1** [with obj. and adverbial of direction] throw (something) somewhere lightly or casually: *Suzy tossed her bag on to the sofa* | [with two objs] *she tossed me a box of matches.* ■ [with obj.] (of a horse) throw (a rider) off its back. ■ [with obj.] throw (a coin) into the air in order to make a decision between two alternatives, based on which side of the coin faces uppermost when it lands: *we could just toss a coin* | [no obj.] ***he tossed up** between courgettes and tomatoes and courgettes won.* ■ [with obj.] settle a matter with (someone) by tossing a coin: *I'll **toss you for** it.*
2 move or cause to move from side to side or back and forth: [no obj.] *the trees tossed in the wind* | [with obj.] *the yachts were tossed around like toys in the harbour* | (as adj., in combination **-tossed**) *a storm-tossed sea.* ■ [with obj.] jerk (one's head or hair) sharply backwards. ■ [with obj.] shake or turn (food) in a liquid, so as to coat it lightly: *toss the pasta in the sauce.*
3 [with obj.] N. Amer. informal search (a place).
▶ **noun** an act or instance of tossing something: *a defiant toss of her head | the toss of a coin.* ■ (**the toss**) the action of tossing a coin as a method of deciding which team has the right to make a particular decision at the beginning of a game: *Somerset won the toss and chose to bat.*
– PHRASES **give** (or **care**) **a toss** [usu. with negative] Brit. informal care at all: *I don't give a toss what you think.* **take a toss** fall off a horse. **toss one's cookies** N. Amer. informal vomit. **tossing the caber** see **CABER**. **toss a pancake** turn a pancake by flipping it into the air so that it lands in the pan on its opposite side.
– PHRASAL VERBS **toss something off** produce something rapidly or without thought or effort: *some of the best letters are tossed off in a burst of inspiration.* ■ drink something rapidly or all at once. **toss someone/oneself off** (or **toss off**) Brit. vulgar slang masturbate.
– ORIGIN early 16th cent.: of unknown origin.

tosser ▶ **noun 1** [usu. in combination] a person or thing that tosses something: *a contest to find the best pancake-tosser.*
2 Brit. vulgar slang a person who masturbates (used as a general term of abuse).

tosspot ▶ **noun** informal a habitual drinker (also used as a general term of abuse).

toss-up ▶ **noun** informal the tossing of a coin to make a decision between two alternatives. ■ a situation in which any of two or more outcomes or options is equally possible or equally attractive: *in the end it was a toss-up between the mussels, the crispy prawn parcels, and the smoked trout.*

tostada /tɒˈstɑːdə/ (also **tostado** /tɒˈstɑːdəʊ/) ▶ **noun** (pl. **tostadas** or **tostados**) a Mexican deep-fried maize flour pancake topped with a seasoned mixture of beans, mincemeat, and vegetables.
– ORIGIN Spanish, literally 'toasted', past participle of *tostar*.

tostone /tɒˈstəʊneɪ/ ▶ **noun** a Mexican dish of fried plantain, typically served with a dip.
– ORIGIN Spanish.

tosyl /ˈtəʊsʌɪl, -sɪl/ ▶ **noun** [as modifier] Chemistry of or denoting the toluene-4-sulphonyl radical $-SO_2C_6H_4CH_3$, used in organic synthesis.
– ORIGIN 1930s: from German, from *to(luol)* and *s(ulphon)yl*.

tosylate /ˈtəʊsʌɪleɪt, -sɪleɪt/ ▶ **noun** Chemistry an ester containing a tosyl group.

tot[1] ▶ **noun 1** a very young child.
2 chiefly Brit. a small amount of a strong alcoholic drink such as whisky or brandy: ***a tot of** brandy.*
– ORIGIN early 18th cent. (originally dialect): of unknown origin.

tot[2] ▶ **verb** (**tots, totting, totted**) [with obj.] chiefly Brit. (**tot something up**) add up numbers or amounts. ■ accumulate something over a period of time: *he totted up 180 League appearances.*
– ORIGIN mid 18th cent.: from archaic *tot* 'set of figures to be added up', abbreviation of **TOTAL** or of Latin *totum* 'the whole'.

tot[3] ▶ **verb** (**tots, totting, totted**) [no obj.] (usu. as noun **totting**) Brit. informal salvage saleable items from dustbins or rubbish heaps.
– ORIGIN late 19th cent.: from slang *tot* 'bone', of unknown origin.

total ▶ **adjective 1** [attrib.] comprising the whole number or amount: *a total cost of £4,000.*
2 complete; absolute: *it is a matter of total indifference to me | a total stranger.*
▶ **noun** the whole number or amount of something: *he scored a total of thirty-three points* | ***in total**, 200 people were interviewed.*
▶ **verb** (**totals, totalling, totalled**; US **totals, totaling, totaled**) **1** [with obj.] amount in number to: *they were left with debts totalling £6,260.* ■ add up the full number or amount of: *the scores were totalled.*
2 [with obj.] informal, chiefly N. Amer. damage (something, typically a vehicle) beyond repair; wreck. ■ kill or severely injure (someone).
– ORIGIN late Middle English: via Old French from medieval Latin *totalis*, from *totum* 'the whole', neuter of Latin *totus* 'whole, entire'. The verb, at first in the sense 'add up', dates from the late 16th cent.

total allergy syndrome ▶ **noun** [mass noun] a condition involving a wide range of symptoms thought to be caused by sensitivity to the chemical substances encountered in the modern environment. Its medical characterization is controversial.

total depravity ▶ **noun** [mass noun] Christian Theology the Calvinist doctrine that human nature is thoroughly corrupt and sinful as a result of the Fall.

total eclipse ▶ **noun** an eclipse in which the whole of the disc of the sun or moon is obscured.

total harmonic distortion ▶ **noun** [mass noun] the distortion produced by an amplifier, as measured in terms of the harmonics of the sinusoidal components of the signal that it introduces.

total heat ▶ **noun** another term for **ENTHALPY**.

total internal reflection ▶ **noun** [mass noun] Physics the complete reflection of a light ray reaching an interface with a less dense medium when the angle of incidence exceeds the critical angle.

totalitarian /ˌtəʊtalɪˈtɛːrɪən, tə(ʊ)ˌtalɪ-/ ▶ **adjective** relating to a system of government that is centralized and dictatorial and requires complete subservience to the state: *a totalitarian regime.*
▶ **noun** a person advocating a totalitarian system of government.
– DERIVATIVES **totalitarianism** noun.

totality ▶ **noun** (pl. **totalities**) the whole of something: *the totality of their current policies.* ■ Astronomy the moment or duration of total obscuration of the sun or moon during an eclipse.
– PHRASES **in its totality** as a whole: *a deeper exploration of life in its totality.*

totalizator (also **totalisator**) ▶ **noun** a device showing the number and amount of bets staked on a race, to facilitate the division of the total among those backing the winner. ■ another term for **TOTE**.

totalize (also **totalise**) ▶ **verb** [with obj.] (usu. as adj. **totalizing**) combine into a total.
– DERIVATIVES **totalization** noun.

totalizer (also **totaliser**) ▶ **noun** another term for **TOTALIZATOR**.

Napoleon (wishing to restore slavery) took over the island and Toussaint died in prison in France.

tout¹ /taʊt/ ▸ **verb 1** [with obj.] attempt to sell (something), typically by a direct or persistent approach: *Sanjay was touting his wares* | [no obj.] *shop managers would stand in the street **touting for** business.* ▪ attempt to persuade people of the merits of: *she was touted as a potential Prime Minister.* ▪ Brit. sell (a ticket) for an event at a price higher than the official one.
2 [no obj.] N. Amer. offer racing tips for a share of any resulting winnings. ▪ [with obj.] chiefly Brit. spy out the movements and condition of (a racehorse in training) in order to gain information to be used when betting.
▸ **noun 1** (also **ticket tout**) Brit. a person who buys up tickets for an event to resell them at a profit. ▪ a person soliciting custom or business, typically in a direct or persistent manner.
2 N. Amer. a person who offers racing tips for a share of any resulting winnings.
3 N. Irish & Scottish informal an informer.
– DERIVATIVES **touter** noun.
– ORIGIN Middle English *tute* 'look out', of Germanic origin; related to Dutch *tuit* 'spout, nozzle'. Later senses were 'watch, spy on' (late 17th cent.) and 'solicit custom' (mid 18th cent.). The noun was first recorded (early 18th cent.) in the slang use 'thieves' lookout'.

tout² /tuː/, French /tu/ ▸ **determiner** (often **le tout**) used before the name of a city to refer to its high society or people of importance: *le tout Washington adored him.*
– ORIGIN French, suggested by *le tout Paris* 'all (of) Paris', used to refer to Parisian high society.

tout court /tuː ˈkʊə/, French /tu kuʀ/ ▸ **adverb** with no addition or qualification; simply: *he saw religion as an illusion, tout court.*
– ORIGIN French, literally 'very short'.

tout de suite /ˌtuː də ˈswiːt/, French /tu d(ə) sɥit/ ▸ **adverb** immediately; at once: *she left tout de suite.*
– ORIGIN French, literally 'quite in sequence'.

tovarish /tɒˈvɑːrɪʃ/ (also **tovarich**) ▸ **noun** (in the former Soviet Union) a comrade (often used as a form of address).
– ORIGIN from Russian *tovarishch*, from Turkic.

TOW ▸ **abbreviation** tube-launched, optically guided, wire-guided (missile).

tow¹ ▸ **verb** [with obj.] (of a motor vehicle or boat) pull (another vehicle or boat) along with a rope, chain, or tow bar. ▪ (of a person) pull along behind one: *she saw Florian towing Nicky along by the hand.*
▸ **noun** [in sing.] an act of towing a vehicle or boat. ▪ a rope or line used to tow a vehicle or boat.
– PHRASES **in tow 1** (also **on tow**) being towed by another vehicle or boat. **2** accompanying or following someone: *trying to shop with three children in tow is no joke.*
– DERIVATIVES **towable** adjective.
– ORIGIN Old English *togian* 'draw, drag', of Germanic origin; related to TUG. The noun dates from the early 17th cent.

> **USAGE** The phrase is **toe the line**, not **tow the line**: see **USAGE** at **TOE**.

tow² ▸ **noun** [mass noun] the coarse and broken part of flax or hemp prepared for spinning. ▪ [count noun] a bundle of untwisted natural or man-made fibres.
– DERIVATIVES **towy** adjective.
– ORIGIN Old English (recorded in *towcræft* 'spinning'), of Germanic origin.

towage ▸ **noun** [mass noun] **1** [usu. as modifier] the action or process of towing a vehicle or boat.
2 a charge for towing a boat.

towai /ˈtəʊwʌɪ/ ▸ **noun** a large New Zealand timber tree related to the kamahi. ● *Weinmannia silvicola*, family Cunoniaceae.
– ORIGIN mid 19th cent.: from Maori.

toward ▸ **preposition** /təˈwɔːd, twɔːd, tɔːd/ variant of TOWARDS.
▸ **adjective** /ˈtəʊəd/ [predic.] archaic going on; in progress: *is something new toward?*
– ORIGIN Old English *tōweard* (see TO, -WARD).

towards /təˈwɔːdz, twɔːdz, ˈtɔːdz/ (chiefly N. Amer. also **toward**) ▸ **preposition 1** in the direction of: *they drove towards the German frontier.* ▪ getting closer to achieving (a goal): *moves towards EU political and monetary union.* ▪ close or closer to (a particular time): *towards the end of April.*
2 expressing the relation between behaviour or an attitude and the person or thing at which it is directed or with which it is concerned: *he was warm and tender towards her* | *our attitude towards death.*
3 contributing to the cost of: *the council provided a grant towards the cost of new buses.*
– ORIGIN Old English *tōweardes* (see TO, -WARD).

tow bar ▸ **noun** a bar fitted to the back of a vehicle, used in towing a trailer or caravan.

tow-coloured ▸ **adjective** (of hair) very light blonde.

towel ▸ **noun 1** a piece of thick absorbent cloth or paper used for drying oneself or wiping things dry.
2 Brit. a sanitary towel.
▸ **verb** (**towels**, **towelling**, **towelled**; US **towels**, **toweling**, **toweled**) [with obj.] **1** wipe or dry with a towel: [with obj. and complement] *she **towelled** her hair **dry**.*
2 informal, chiefly Austral./NZ thrash or beat (someone).
– ORIGIN Middle English: from Old French *toaille*, of Germanic origin. Sense 2 of the verb dates from the early 18th cent.; sense 1 from the mid 19th cent.

towelette /taʊəˈlɛt/ ▸ **noun** a small moistened paper or cloth towel in a sealed package, used for cleansing.

towelhead ▸ **noun** informal, offensive a person who wears a turban or keffiyeh (often used as a term of abuse for a Muslim or Arab).

towel horse ▸ **noun** a free-standing frame on which to hang towels.

towelling (US **toweling**) ▸ **noun** [mass noun] thick absorbent cloth, typically cotton with uncut loops, used for towels and robes.

tower ▸ **noun** a tall narrow building, either free-standing or forming part of a building such as a church or castle. ▪ [with modifier] a tall structure that houses machinery, operators, etc.: *a control tower.* ▪ [with modifier] a tall structure used as a receptacle or for storage: *a CD tower.* ▪ a tall pile or mass of something: ***a titanic tower of garbage.*** ▪ (**the Tower**) see TOWER OF LONDON.
▸ **verb** [no obj.] **1** rise to or reach a great height: *he seemed to **tower over** everyone else.*
2 (of a bird) soar up to a great height, especially (of a falcon) so as to be able to swoop down on the quarry.
– PHRASES **tower of strength** see STRENGTH.
– DERIVATIVES **towered** adjective (chiefly literary), **towery** adjective (literary).
– ORIGIN Old English *torr*, reinforced in Middle English by Old French *tour*, from Latin *turris*, from Greek.

tower block ▸ **noun** Brit. a tall modern building containing numerous floors of offices or flats.

Tower Bridge a bridge across the Thames in London, famous for its twin towers and for the two bascules of which the roadway consists, able to be lifted to allow the passage of large ships. It was completed in 1894.

towering ▸ **adjective 1** extremely tall, especially in comparison with the surroundings: *Hari looked up at the towering buildings.*
2 of great importance or influence: *a majestic, towering album.* ▪ of great intensity: *his towering anger.*

Tower of Babel /ˈbeɪb(ə)l/ (in the Bible) a tower built in an attempt to reach heaven, which God frustrated by making its builders speak different languages so that they could not understand one another (Genesis 11:1–9).
– ORIGIN *Babel* from Hebrew *Bāḇel* 'Babylon', from Akkadian *bāb ili* 'gate of god'.

Tower of London (also **the Tower**) a fortress by the Thames just east of the City of London. The oldest part, the White Tower, was begun in 1078. It was later used as a state prison, and is now open to the public as a repository of ancient armour and weapons, and of the Crown Jewels.

tower of silence ▸ **noun** a tall open-topped structure on which Parsees traditionally place and leave exposed the body of someone who has died.

tow-headed ▸ **adjective** having tow-coloured or untidy hair.

towhee /ˈtəʊ(h)iː, ˈtaʊ-/ ▸ **noun** a North American songbird of the bunting family, typically with brownish plumage but sometimes black and rufous.
● Genus *Pipilo* (and *Chlorurus*), family Emberizidae (subfamily Emberizinae): several species.
– ORIGIN mid 18th cent.: imitative of the call of *Pipilo erythrophthalmus*.

towing path ▸ **noun** another term for TOWPATH.

towing rope ▸ **noun** another term for TOW ROPE.

towline ▸ **noun** another term for TOW ROPE.

town ▸ **noun 1** a built-up area with a name, defined boundaries, and local government, that is larger than a village and generally smaller than a city. ▪ the particular town under consideration, especially one's own town: *Churchill **was in town**.* ▪ Brit. dated the chief city or town of a region: *he **has moved to town**.* ▪ [mass noun] the permanent residents of a university town: *a rift between the city's **town and gown**.* Often contrasted with GOWN.
2 the central part of a neighbourhood, with its business or shopping area: *Rachel left to drive back **into town**.*
3 [mass noun] densely populated areas, especially as contrasted with the country or suburbs: *the cultural differences between town and country.*
4 N. Amer. another term for TOWNSHIP (sense 3).
– PHRASES **go to town** informal do something thoroughly, enthusiastically, or extravagantly: *I thought I'd **go to town** on the redecoration.* **on the town** informal enjoying the nightlife of a city or town: *a lot of guys out for **a night on the town**.*
– DERIVATIVES **townish** adjective, **townlet** noun, **townward** adjective & adverb, **townwards** adverb.
– ORIGIN Old English *tūn* 'enclosed piece of land, homestead, village', of Germanic origin; related to Dutch *tuin* 'garden' and German *Zaun* 'fence'.

town car ▸ **noun** US a limousine.

town clerk ▸ **noun 1** N. Amer. a public official in charge of the records of a town.
2 (in the UK, until 1974) the secretary and legal adviser of a town corporation.

town council ▸ **noun** (especially in the UK) the elected governing body in a municipality.
– DERIVATIVES **town councillor** noun.

town crier ▸ **noun** historical a person employed to make public announcements in the streets or marketplace of a town.

townee ▸ **noun** variant spelling of TOWNIE.

tow net ▸ **noun** Biology a dragnet that is towed behind a boat to collect specimens.

town gas ▸ **noun** Brit. old-fashioned term for COAL GAS.

town hall ▸ **noun** a building used for the administration of local government.

town house ▸ **noun 1** a tall, narrow traditional terraced house, generally having three or more floors. ▪ a modern two- or three-storey house built as one of a group of similar houses.
2 a house in a town or city belonging to someone who has another property in the country.
3 archaic a town hall.

townie ▸ **noun** informal, chiefly derogatory a person who lives in a town, especially as distinct from one who lives in the country. ▪ a person who is a local resident in a university town, rather than a student. ▪ Brit. a loutish or aggressive young person: *a gang of townies cornered one of his friends near the Museum Gardens.*

townland ▸ **noun** (especially in Ireland) a small territorial division of land.

town major ▸ **noun** historical the chief executive officer in a garrison town or fortress.

town mayor ▸ **noun** Brit. the chairperson of a town council.

town meeting ▸ **noun** US a meeting of the voters of a town for the transaction of public business.

town planning ▸ **noun** [mass noun] the planning and control of the construction, growth, and development of a town or other urban area.
– DERIVATIVES **town planner** noun.

townscape ▸ **noun** the visual appearance of a town or urban area; an urban landscape: *the building's contribution to the townscape* | *an industrial townscape.* ▪ a picture of a town.

townsfolk ▸ **plural noun** another term for TOWNSPEOPLE.

township ▸ **noun 1** (in South Africa) a suburb or city of predominantly black occupation, formerly officially designated for black occupation by apartheid legislation.
2 S. African a new area being developed for residential or industrial use by speculators.
3 N. Amer. a division of a county with some corporate powers. ▪ a district six miles square.
4 Brit. historical a manor or parish as a territorial division. ▪ a small town or village forming part of a large parish.
5 Austral./NZ a small town.
– ORIGIN Old English *tūnscipe* 'the inhabitants of a village' (see TOWN, -SHIP).

T

townsite ▶ **noun** N. Amer. a tract of land set apart by legal authority to be occupied by a town and usually surveyed and laid out with streets.

townsman (or **townswoman**) ▶ **noun** (pl. **townsmen** or **townswomen**) a resident of a particular town or city (often used to contrast with a visitor or a person living in the country).

townspeople (also **townsfolk**) ▶ **plural noun** the people living in a particular town or city.

Townsville an industrial port and resort on the coast of Queensland, NE Australia; pop. 175,542 (2008).

Townswomen's Guild (in the UK) a branch of a network of women's organizations, first set up in 1929, that functions as an urban counterpart of the Women's Institute.

towpath (also **towing path**) ▶ **noun** a path beside a river or canal, originally used as a pathway for horses towing barges.

towplane ▶ **noun** an aircraft that tows gliders.

tow rope (also **towing rope**) ▶ **noun** a rope, cable, or other line used in towing.

toxaemia /tɒk'siːmɪə/ (US **toxemia**) ▶ **noun** [mass noun] blood poisoning by toxins from a local bacterial infection. ■ (also **toxaemia of pregnancy**) another term for **PRE-ECLAMPSIA**.
– DERIVATIVES **toxaemic** adjective.
– ORIGIN mid 19th cent.: from **TOXI-** + **-AEMIA**.

toxaphene /'tɒksəfiːn/ ▶ **noun** [mass noun] a synthetic amber waxy solid with an odour of chlorine and camphor, used as an insecticide. It is a chlorinated terpene.
– ORIGIN 1940s: from **TOXIN** + (*cam*)*phene*, a related terpene.

toxi- ▶ **combining form** representing **TOXIC** or **TOXIN**.

toxic /'tɒksɪk/ ▶ **adjective 1** poisonous: *the dumping of toxic waste* | *alcohol is toxic to the ovaries*. ■ relating to or caused by poison: *toxic hazards* | *toxic liver injury*. ■ very bad, unpleasant, or harmful: *a toxic relationship*.
2 Finance denoting or relating to debt which has a high risk of default: *toxic debts*. ■ denoting securities which are based on toxic debt and for which there is not a healthy or functioning market: *the financial system has become clogged with toxic assets*.
▶ **noun** (**toxics**) poisonous substances.
– DERIVATIVES **toxically** adverb, **toxicity** noun.
– ORIGIN mid 17th cent.: from medieval Latin *toxicus* 'poisoned', from Latin *toxicum* 'poison', from Greek *toxikon* (*pharmakon*) '(poison for) arrows', from *toxon* 'bow'.

WORD TRENDS The financial sense of **toxic** describes debts which are unlikely to be repaid and assets suddenly found to be worthless: *banks will be pressured to come clean on the amount of toxic debt they hold* | *no one wants to buy any of these toxic assets*. **Toxic** has been used metaphorically to describe something very bad or harmful since the late 20th century (*the scandal could be politically toxic*), and the specific financial sense is first recorded around 1990. Before that, though, risky stocks and bonds were referred to as *toxic waste*—they are dangerous to (financial) health and very difficult to dispose of.

toxicant /'tɒksɪk(ə)nt/ ▶ **noun** a toxic substance introduced into the environment, e.g. a pesticide.
– ORIGIN late 19th cent.: variant of **INTOXICANT**, differentiated in sense.

T

toxico- ▶ **combining form** equivalent to **TOXI-**.
– ORIGIN from Greek *toxicon* 'poison'.

toxicology /ˌtɒksɪ'kɒlədʒi/ ▶ **noun** [mass noun] the branch of science concerned with the nature, effects, and detection of poisons.
– DERIVATIVES **toxicological** adjective, **toxicologically** adverb, **toxicologist** noun.

toxic shock syndrome (abbrev.: **TSS**) ▶ **noun** [mass noun] acute septicaemia in women, typically caused by bacterial infection from a retained tampon or IUD.

toxigenic /ˌtɒksɪ'dʒɛnɪk/ ▶ **adjective** (especially of a bacterium) producing a toxin or toxic effect.
– DERIVATIVES **toxigenicity** noun.

toxin /'tɒksɪn/ ▶ **noun** a poison of plant or animal origin, especially one produced by or derived from microorganisms and acting as an antigen in the body.
– ORIGIN late 19th cent.: from **TOXIC** + **-IN**[1].

toxo- ▶ **combining form** equivalent to **TOXI-**.

toxocara /ˌtɒksə'kɑːrə/ ▶ **noun** a parasitic nematode worm, especially a common worm of dogs or cats which is transmissible to humans. ● Genus *Toxocara*, class Phasmida, in particular *T. canis* (in dogs) and *T. cati* (in cats).
– ORIGIN modern Latin, from **TOXO-** (see **TOXI-**) + Greek *kara* 'head'.

toxocariasis /ˌtɒksəʊkə'rʌɪəsɪs/ ▶ **noun** [mass noun] infection of a human with the larvae of toxocara worms, causing illness and a risk of blindness from cyst formation in the eye.

toxoid ▶ **noun** Medicine a chemically modified toxin from a pathogenic microorganism, which is no longer toxic but is still antigenic and can be used as a vaccine.

toxophilite /tɒk'sɒfɪlʌɪt/ rare ▶ **noun** a student or lover of archery.
▶ **adjective** relating to archers and archery.
– DERIVATIVES **toxophily** noun.
– ORIGIN late 18th cent.: from *Toxophilus* (a name invented by Roger Ascham, used as the title of his treatise on archery (1545), from Greek *toxon* 'bow' + *-philos* 'loving') + **-ITE**[1].

toxoplasma /ˌtɒksə(ʊ)'plazmə/ ▶ **noun** a parasitic spore-forming protozoan that can sometimes cause disease in humans. ● Genus *Toxoplasma*, phylum Sporozoa, in particular *T. gondii*.

toxoplasmosis /ˌtɒksəʊplaz'məʊsɪs/ ▶ **noun** [mass noun] a disease caused by toxoplasmas, transmitted chiefly through undercooked meat, soil, or in cat faeces. Symptoms of infection generally pass unremarked in adults, but can be dangerous to unborn children.

toy ▶ **noun 1** an object for a child to play with, typically a model or miniature replica of something: [as modifier] *a toy car*. ■ an object, especially a gadget or machine, regarded as providing amusement for an adult: *in 1914 the car was still a rich man's toy*. ■ a person treated by another as a source of pleasure or amusement rather than with due seriousness: *a man needed a friend, an ally, not an idol or a toy*.
2 [as modifier] denoting a diminutive breed or variety of dog: *a toy poodle*.
▶ **verb** [no obj.] (**toy with**) **1** consider (an idea or proposal) casually or indecisively: *I was toying with the idea of writing a book*. ■ treat (someone or their feelings) in a superficially amorous way.
2 move or handle (an object) absent-mindedly or nervously: *Alan toyed with his glasses*. ■ eat or drink (something) in an unenthusiastic way.
– PHRASES **throw one's toys out of the pram** Brit. informal behave in a childish and petulant way; have a tantrum: *Lorenzo threw his toys out of the pram after being sent off*.
– DERIVATIVES **toylike** adjective.
– ORIGIN late Middle English: of unknown origin. The word originally denoted a funny story or remark, later an antic or trick, or a frivolous entertainment. The verb dates from the early 16th cent.

toy boy ▶ **noun** Brit. informal a male lover who is much younger than his partner.

toyi-toyi /'tɔɪtɔɪ/ S. African ▶ **noun** (pl. **toyi-toyis**) a dance step characterized by high-stepping movements, typically performed at protest gatherings or marches.
▶ **verb** (**toyi-toyis**, **toyi-toying** or **toyi-toyiing**, **toyi-toyied**) [no obj.] perform such a dance.
– ORIGIN Ndebele and Shona; probably introduced into South Africa by ANC exiles returning from military training in Zimbabwe.

toymaker ▶ **noun** a maker or manufacturer of toys.

Toynbee[1] /'tɔɪnbi:/, Arnold (1852–83), English economist and social reformer. He taught both undergraduates and workers' adult education classes in Oxford and worked with the poor in London's East End. He is best known for his pioneering work *The Industrial Revolution* (1884).

Toynbee[2] /'tɔɪnbi:/, Arnold (Joseph) (1889–1975), English historian. He is best known for his twelve-volume *Study of History* (1934–61), in which he traced the pattern of growth, maturity, and decay of different civilizations.

toyon /'tɔɪɒn/ ▶ **noun** an evergreen Californian shrub of the rose family, the fruiting branches of which are used for Christmas decorations. ● *Heteromeles arbutifolia*, family Rosaceae.
– ORIGIN mid 19th cent.: from Mexican Spanish *tollón*.

toyshop ▶ **noun** a shop which sells toys.

toytown ▶ **adjective** [attrib.] resembling a quaint or miniature replica of something: *below you, far away, was a single toytown rooftop*. ■ having no real value, substance, or merit: *toytown tunes, daft haircuts, and even dafter trousers*.

Tpr ▶ **abbreviation** Trooper.

TQM ▶ **abbreviation** Total Quality Management.

TR ▶ **abbreviation** Turkey (international vehicle registration).

trabeation /ˌtreɪbɪ'eɪʃ(ə)n/ ▶ **noun** [mass noun] the use of beams in architectural construction, rather than arches or vaulting.
– DERIVATIVES **trabeated** /'treɪbɪeɪtɪd/ adjective.
– ORIGIN mid 16th cent. (denoting a horizontal beam): formed irregularly from Latin *trabs*, *trab-* 'beam, timber' + **-ATION**.

trabecula /trə'bɛkjʊlə/ ▶ **noun** (pl. **trabeculae** /-liː/)
1 Anatomy each of a series or group of partitions formed by bands or columns of connective tissue, especially a plate of the calcareous tissue forming cancellous bone.
2 Botany any of a number of rod-like structures in plants, e.g. a strand of sterile tissue dividing the cavity in a sporangium.
– DERIVATIVES **trabecular** adjective.
– ORIGIN mid 19th cent.: from Latin, diminutive of *trabs* 'beam, timber'.

Trâblous /trɑː'bluːs/ Arabic name for **TRIPOLI** (sense 2).

Trabzon /'trabz(ə)n/ a port on the Black Sea in northern Turkey; pop. 228,800 (est. 2007). In 1204, after the sack of Constantinople by the Crusaders, an offshoot of the Byzantine Empire was founded with Trabzon as its capital, which was annexed to the Ottoman Empire in 1461. Also called **TREBIZOND**.

tracasserie /trə'kas(ə)ri/ ▶ **noun** (usu. **tracasseries**) archaic a fuss; a petty quarrel.
– ORIGIN French, from *tracasser* 'to bustle or fuss'.

trace[1] ▶ **verb** [with obj.] **1** find or discover by investigation: *police are trying to trace a white van seen in the area*. ■ find or describe the origin or development of: *Bob's book traces his flying career with the RAF*.
2 follow or mark the course or position of (something) with one's eye, mind, or finger: *through the binoculars, I traced the path I had taken the night before*. ■ take (a particular path or route): *a tear traced a lonely path down her cheek*.
3 copy (a drawing, map, or design) by drawing over its lines on a superimposed piece of transparent paper. ■ draw (a pattern or line), especially with one's finger or toe.
4 give an outline of: *the article **traces out** some of the connections between education, qualifications, and the labour market*.
▶ **noun 1** a mark, object, or other indication of the existence or passing of something: *remove all traces of the old adhesive* | [mass noun] *the aircraft disappeared without trace*. ■ a line or pattern displayed by an instrument to show the existence or nature of something which is being recorded or measured. ■ a physical change in the brain presumed to be caused by a process of learning or memory.
2 a very small quantity, especially one too small to be accurately measured: *his body contained traces of amphetamines* | [as modifier] *trace quantities of PCBs*. ■ a barely discernible indication of something: *just a trace of a smile*.
3 a procedure to investigate the source of something, such as the place from which a telephone call was made: *we've got a trace on the call*.
4 N. Amer. & W. Indian a path or track.
5 a line which represents the projection of a curve or surface on a plane or the intersection of a curve or surface with a plane.
6 Mathematics the sum of the elements in the principal diagonal of a square matrix.
– DERIVATIVES **traceability** noun, **traceable** adjective, **traceless** adjective.
– ORIGIN Middle English (first recorded as a noun in the sense 'path that someone or something takes'): from Old French *trace* (noun), *tracier* (verb), based on Latin *tractus* (see **TRACT**[1]).

trace[2] ▶ **noun** each of the two side straps, chains, or ropes by which a horse is attached to a vehicle that it is pulling.
– PHRASES **kick over the traces** Brit. become insubordinate or reckless.
– ORIGIN Middle English (denoting a pair of traces): from Old French *trais*, plural of *trait* (see **TRAIT**).

trace element ▶ **noun** a chemical element present only in minute amounts in a particular sample or environment. ■ a chemical element required only in minute amounts by living organisms for normal growth.

trace fossil ▶ **noun** Geology a fossil of a footprint, trail, burrow, or other trace of an animal rather than of the animal itself.

trace-horse ▶ **noun** historical a horse put in traces to pull a vehicle.

tracer ▶ **noun** a person or thing that traces something or by which something may be traced, in particular: ■ a bullet or shell whose course is made visible in flight by a trail of flames or smoke, used to assist in aiming. ■ a substance introduced into a biological organism or other system so that its subsequent distribution may be readily followed from its colour, radioactivity, or other distinctive property. ■ a device which transmits a signal and so can be located when attached to a moving vehicle or other object.

tracery ▶ **noun** (pl. **traceries**) [mass noun] Architecture ornamental stone openwork, typically in the upper part of a Gothic window. ■ [count noun] a delicate branching pattern: *a tracery of red veins.*
– DERIVATIVES **traceried** **adjective.**

trachea /trəˈkiːə, ˈtreɪkɪə/ ▶ **noun** (pl. **tracheae** /-ˈkiːiː/ or **tracheas**) Anatomy a large membranous tube reinforced by rings of cartilage, extending from the larynx to the bronchial tubes and conveying air to and from the lungs; the windpipe. ■ Entomology each of a number of fine chitinous tubes in the body of an insect, conveying air direct to the tissues. ■ Botany a duct or vessel in a plant.
– DERIVATIVES **tracheal** /ˈtreɪkɪəl/ **adjective**, **tracheate** /ˈtreɪkɪeɪt/ **adjective.**
– ORIGIN late Middle English: from medieval Latin, from late Latin *trachia*, from Greek *trakheia* (*artēria*) 'rough (artery)', from *trakhus* 'rough'.

tracheid /ˈtreɪkɪɪd/ ▶ **noun** Botany a type of water-conducting cell in the xylem which lacks perforations in the cell wall.
– ORIGIN late 19th cent.: from German *Tracheide*, from medieval Latin *trachea* (see **TRACHEA**).

tracheitis /ˌtreɪkɪˈʌɪtɪs/ ▶ **noun** [mass noun] Medicine inflammation of the trachea, usually secondary to a nose or throat infection.

tracheo- /trəˈkiːəʊ, ˈtrakɪəʊ, ˈtreɪkɪəʊ/ ▶ **combining form** relating to the trachea: *tracheotomy.*

tracheotomy /ˌtrakɪˈɒtəmi/ (also **tracheostomy** /-ˈɒstəmi/) ▶ **noun** (pl. **tracheotomies**) Medicine an incision in the windpipe made to relieve an obstruction to breathing.

tracheotomy tube ▶ **noun** a breathing tube inserted into a tracheotomy.

trachoma /trəˈkəʊmə/ ▶ **noun** [mass noun] a contagious bacterial infection of the eye, causing inflamed granulation on the inner surface of the lids. ● The disease is caused by the chlamydial organism *Chlamydia trichomatis.*
– DERIVATIVES **trachomatous** /-ˈkəʊmətəs, -ˈkɒmətəs/ **adjective.**
– ORIGIN late 17th cent.: from Greek *trakhōma* 'roughness', from *trakhus* 'rough'.

trachyte /ˈtreɪkʌɪt, ˈtrakʌɪt/ ▶ **noun** [mass noun] Geology a grey fine-grained volcanic rock consisting largely of alkali feldspar.
– ORIGIN early 19th cent. (denoting a volcanic rock with a rough or gritty surface): from Greek *trakhus* 'rough' or *trakhutēs* 'roughness'.

trachytic /trəˈkɪtɪk/ ▶ **adjective** Geology relating to or denoting a rock texture (characteristic of trachyte) in which crystals show parallel alignment due to liquid flow.

tracing ▶ **noun 1** a copy of a drawing, map, or design made by tracing.
2 a faint or delicate mark or pattern: *tracings of apple blossoms against the deep greens of pines.* ■ [mass noun] the action of marking out a figure on the ice when skating. ■ a line or pattern corresponding to something which is being recorded or measured; a trace.

tracing paper ▶ **noun** [mass noun] transparent paper used for tracing maps, drawings, or designs.

track¹ ▶ **noun 1** a rough path or road, typically one beaten by use rather than constructed: *follow the track to the farm.*
2 a prepared course or circuit for athletes, horses, motor vehicles, bicycles, or dogs to race on: *a Formula One Grand Prix track.* ■ [mass noun] the sport of running on a track.
3 (usu. **tracks**) a mark or line of marks left by a person, animal, or vehicle in passing: *he followed the tracks made by the cars in the snow.* ■ the course or route followed by someone or something (used especially in talking about their pursuit by others): *I didn't want them on my track.* ■ a course of action or line of thought: *in terms of social arrangements, you are not too far off the track.*
4 a continuous line of rails on a railway. ■ a metal or plastic strip or rail along which a curtain or spotlight may be moved. ■ Sailing a strip on the mast, boom, or floor of a yacht along which a slide attached to a sail can be moved, used to adjust the position of the sail.
5 a recording of one song or piece of music: *the CD contains early Elvis Presley tracks.* [originally denoting a groove on a gramophone record.] ■ a lengthwise strip of magnetic tape containing one sequence of signals. ■ the soundtrack of a film or video.
6 a continuous articulated metal band around the wheels of a heavy vehicle such as a tank, intended to facilitate movement over rough or soft ground. ■ Electronics a continuous line of copper or other conductive material on a printed circuit board, used to connect parts of a circuit.
7 the transverse distance between a vehicle's wheels.
8 US term for **STREAM** (sense 4 of the noun).
▶ **verb** [with obj.] **1** follow the trail or movements of (someone or something), typically in order to find them or note their course: *secondary radars that track the aircraft in flight | he tracked Anna to her room.* ■ note the progress or course of: *City have been tracking the striker since the summer.* ■ [no obj., with adverbial of direction] follow a particular course: *the storm was tracking across the ground at 30 mph.* ■ (of a stylus) follow (a groove in a record). ■ [no obj., with adverbial of direction] (of a film or television camera) move in relation to the subject being filmed: *the camera eventually tracked away.* [with reference to early filming when a camera was mobile by means of a track.]
2 [no obj.] (of wheels) run so that the back ones are exactly in the track of the front ones.
3 [no obj.] Electronics (of a tunable circuit or component) vary in frequency in the same way as another circuit or component, so that the frequency difference between them remains constant.
– PHRASES **in one's tracks** informal where one or something is at that moment; suddenly: *Turner immediately* ***stopped dead in his tracks.*** **keep** (or **lose**) **track of** keep (or fail to keep) fully aware of or informed about: *she had lost all track of time and had fallen asleep.* **make tracks** (**for**) informal leave (for a place). **off the beaten track** see **BEATEN**. **on the right** (or **wrong**) **track** following a course that is likely to result in success (or failure): *we are on the right track for continued growth.* **on track** following a course that is likely to achieve what is required: *formulas for keeping the economy on track.* **the wrong side of the tracks** informal a poor or less prestigious part of town. [with reference to the railway tracks of American towns, once serving as a line of demarcation between rich and poor quarters.]
– PHRASAL VERBS **track someone/thing down** find someone or something after a thorough or difficult search: *it took seventeen years to track down the wreck of the ship.* **track something up** N. Amer. leave a trail of dirty footprints on a surface. **track something in** leave a trail of dirt, debris, or snow from one's feet: *the road salt I'd tracked in from the street.*
– ORIGIN late 15th cent. (in the sense 'trail, marks left behind'): the noun from Old French *trac*, perhaps from Low German or Dutch *trek* 'draught, drawing'; the verb (current senses dating from the mid 16th cent.) from French *traquer* or directly from the noun.

track² ▶ **verb** [with obj. and adverbial of direction] tow (a canoe) along a waterway from the bank.
– ORIGIN early 18th cent.: apparently from Dutch *trekken* 'to draw, pull, or travel'. The change in the vowel was due to association with **TRACK¹**.

trackage ▶ **noun** [mass noun] N. Amer. the tracks or lines of a railway system collectively.

trackball (also **tracker ball**) ▶ **noun** a small ball that is set in a holder and can be rotated by hand to move a cursor on a computer screen.

trackbed ▶ **noun** the foundation structure on which railway tracks are laid.

track circuit ▶ **noun** an electric circuit made in a section of railway track as an aid to signalling, and able to be short-circuited by the presence of a train.

tracker ▶ **noun 1** a person who tracks someone or something by following their trail. ■ a device that follows and records the movements of someone or something: *electronic trackers are now showing ornithologists where the birds go.*
2 Finance an investment fund which aims to follow in value a stock market index or group of indexes. ■ a mortgage or savings product whose interest rate aims to follow a particular public interest rate.
3 Music a connecting rod in the mechanism of an organ.

tracker dog ▶ **noun** a dog trained to pick up and follow a scent.

track events ▶ **plural noun** athletic events that take place on a running track. Compare with **FIELD EVENTS**.

trackie ▶ **noun** [usu. as modifier] Brit. informal a tracksuit: *trackie bottoms.* ■ (**trackies**) tracksuit trousers.

tracking ▶ **noun** [mass noun] **1** Electronics the maintenance of a constant difference in frequency between two or more connected circuits or components. ■ the formation of a conducting path for an electric current over the surface of an insulating material.
2 the alignment of the wheels of a vehicle.
3 US the streaming of school pupils.

tracking station ▶ **noun** a place from which the movements of missiles, aircraft, or satellites are tracked by radar or radio.

tracklayer ▶ **noun 1** a tractor or other vehicle equipped with continuous tracks.
2 N. Amer. another term for **TRACKMAN**.

tracklement ▶ **noun** Brit. a savoury jelly, served with meat.
– ORIGIN 1950s: of unknown origin.

trackless ▶ **adjective 1** (of land) having no paths or tracks on it: *leading travellers into trackless wastelands.* ■ literary not leaving a track or trace.
2 (of a vehicle or component) not running on a track or tracks.

trackman ▶ **noun** (pl. **trackmen**) a person employed in laying and maintaining railway track.

trackpants ▶ **plural noun** informal tracksuit trousers.

track record ▶ **noun** the best recorded performance in a particular athletics event at a particular track. ■ the past achievements or performance of a person, organization, or product: *he has an excellent track record as an author.*

track rod ▶ **noun** a rod that connects the two front wheels of a motor vehicle and transmits the steering action from the steering column to the wheels.

track shoe ▶ **noun** a running shoe.

trackside ▶ **noun** the area adjacent to a railway track or a sports track.
▶ **adjective & adverb** by the side of a railway track or sports track: [as adj.] *a trackside bookmaker* | [as adv.] *rail fans will enjoy sitting trackside.*

tracksuit ▶ **noun** a loose, warm set of clothes consisting of a sweatshirt and trousers with an elasticated or drawstring waist, worn when exercising or as casual wear.

trackway ▶ **noun** a path formed by the repeated treading of people or animals. ■ an ancient roadway.

trackwork ▶ **noun** [mass noun] railway track and associated equipment. ■ work involved in constructing or maintaining railway track.

tract¹ ▶ **noun 1** an area of land, typically a large one: *large tracts of natural forest.* ■ an indefinitely large extent of something: *it took courage to privatize vast tracts of nationalized industry.*
2 a major passage in the body, large bundle of nerve fibres, or other continuous elongated anatomical structure or region: *the digestive tract.*
– ORIGIN late Middle English (in the sense 'duration or course of time'): from Latin *tractus* 'drawing, draught', from *trahere* 'draw, pull'.

tract² ▶ **noun** a short treatise in pamphlet form, typically on a religious subject.
– ORIGIN late Middle English (denoting a written work treating a particular topic), apparently an abbreviation of Latin *tractatus* (see **TRACTATE**). The current sense dates from the early 19th cent.

tract³ ▶ **noun** (in the Roman Catholic Church) an anthem of Scriptural verses formerly replacing the alleluia in certain penitential and requiem Masses.
– ORIGIN late Middle English: from medieval Latin *tractus* (*cantus*) 'drawn-out (song)', past participle of Latin *trahere* 'draw'.

tractable ▶ **adjective** (of a person) easy to control or influence: *she has always been tractable and obedient, even as a child.* ■ (of a situation or problem) easy to deal with: *trying to make the mathematical tractable.*
– DERIVATIVES **tractability** **noun**, **tractably** **adverb.**
– ORIGIN early 16th cent.: from Latin *tractabilis*, from *tractare* 'to handle' (see **TRACTATE**).

T

Tractarianism /trakˈtɛːrɪənɪz(ə)m/ ▸ **noun** [mass noun] another name for **OXFORD MOVEMENT**.
– DERIVATIVES **Tractarian** adjective & noun.
– ORIGIN mid 19th cent.: from *Tracts for the Times*, the title of a series of pamphlets started by J. H. Newman and published in Oxford 1833–41, which set out the doctrines on which the movement was based.

tractate /ˈtrakteɪt/ ▸ **noun** formal a treatise.
– ORIGIN late 15th cent.: from Latin *tractatus*, from *tractare* 'to handle', frequentative of *trahere* 'draw'.

tract house (also **tract home**) ▸ **noun** N. Amer. a house forming part of a housing estate.

traction ▸ **noun** [mass noun] **1** the action of drawing or pulling something over a surface, especially a road or track: *a primitive vehicle used in animal traction*. ■ motive power provided for such movement, especially on a railway: *the changeover to diesel and electric traction*. ■ locomotives collectively.
2 the grip of a tyre on a road or a wheel on a rail: *his car hit a patch of ice and lost traction*.
3 the extent to which an idea, product, etc. gains popularity or acceptance: *analysts predicted that the technology would rapidly* ***gain traction*** *in the corporate mobile market*.
4 Medicine the application of a sustained pull on a limb or muscle, especially in order to maintain the position of a fractured bone or to correct a deformity: *his leg is* ***in traction***.
– ORIGIN late Middle English (denoting contraction, such as that of a muscle): from French, or from medieval Latin *tractio(n-)*, from Latin *trahere* 'draw, pull'. Current senses date from the early 19th cent.

> **WORD TRENDS** Fast cars and successful businesses seem to go together, so it's appropriate that the world of commerce has borrowed expressions from the road. **Traction** still has its literal senses of 'the action of pulling something' and 'the grip of a tyre on the road', with *traction control* the most common compound in the Oxford English Corpus. The new figurative sense, which refers to the popularity and success of a product or service, is steadily rising in use, however, with the commonest accompanying verbs being *gain*, *get*, and *lose*: *they are losing traction in foreign markets | his product has gained national traction*. The sense can now also express progress in any sphere or the extent to which an idea has been accepted by the general public: *polls in key states showed he wasn't gaining traction | deranged conspiracy theories which are circulating through the media and have now gained serious traction*.

traction engine ▸ **noun** a steam or diesel-powered road vehicle used (especially formerly) for pulling very heavy loads.

tractive /ˈtraktɪv/ ▸ **adjective** relating to or denoting the power exerted in pulling, especially by a vehicle or other machine.

tractor ▸ **noun** a powerful motor vehicle with large rear wheels, used chiefly on farms for hauling equipment and trailers.
– ORIGIN late 18th cent. (in the general sense 'someone or something that pulls'): from Latin, from *tract-* 'pulled', from the verb *trahere*.

tractor beam ▸ **noun** (in science fiction) a hypothetical beam of energy that can be used to move objects such as spaceships or hold them stationary.

tractor trailer ▸ **noun** N. Amer. an articulated lorry.

tractotomy /trakˈtɒtəmi/ ▸ **noun** [mass noun] the surgical severing of nerve tracts especially in the medulla of the brain, typically to relieve intractable pain or mental illness, or in research.

tractrix /ˈtraktrɪks/ ▸ **noun** (pl. **tractrices** /-trɪsiːz/) Geometry a curve whose tangents all intercept the *x*-axis at the same distance from the point of contact, being the involute of a catenary. ■ one of a class of curves similarly traced by one end of a rigid rod, whose other end moves along a fixed line or curve.
– ORIGIN early 18th cent.: modern Latin, feminine of late Latin *tractor* 'that which pulls' (see **TRACTOR**).

Tracy, Spencer (1900–67), American actor, particularly known for his screen partnership with Katharine Hepburn, with whom he co-starred in films such as *Guess Who's Coming to Dinner?* (1967).

trad informal ▸ **adjective** (especially of music) traditional: *trad jazz*.
▸ **noun** [mass noun] traditional jazz or folk music.
– ORIGIN 1950s: abbreviation.

trade ▸ **noun 1** [mass noun] the action of buying and selling goods and services: *a move to ban all* ***trade in*** *ivory | a significant increase in foreign trade*. ■ [count noun] N. Amer. (in sport) a transfer: *players can demand a trade after five years of service*.
2 a job requiring manual skills and special training: *the fundamentals of the construction trade* | [mass noun] *he's a carpenter by trade*.
3 (**the trade**) [treated as sing. or pl.] the people engaged in a particular area of business: *in the trade this sort of computer is called 'a client-based system'*. ■ Brit. people licensed to sell alcoholic drink. ■ [mass noun] dated, chiefly derogatory the practice of making one's living in business, as opposed to in a profession or from unearned income: *the aristocratic classes were contemptuous of those* ***in trade***.
4 (usu. **trades**) a trade wind: *the north-east trades*.
▸ **verb 1** [no obj.] buy and sell goods and services: *middlemen* ***trading in*** *luxury goods*. ■ [with obj.] buy or sell (a particular item or product): *she has traded millions of dollars' worth of metals*. ■ (especially of shares or currency) be bought and sold at a specified price: *the dollar was trading where it was in January*.
2 [with obj.] exchange (something) for something else, typically as a commercial transaction: *they* ***trade*** *mud-shark livers* ***for*** *fish oil*. ■ give and receive (something, typically insults or blows): *they traded a few punches*. ■ N. Amer. transfer (a player) to another team.
– PHRASES **trade places** US change places.
– PHRASAL VERBS **trade down** (or **up**) sell something in order to buy something similar but less (or more) expensive. **trade something in** exchange a used article in part payment for another: *she* ***traded in*** *her Ford* ***for*** *a Land Rover*. **trade something off** exchange something of value, especially as part of a compromise: *the government* ***traded off*** *economic advantages* ***for*** *political gains*. **trade on** take advantage of (something), especially in an unfair way: *the government is trading on fears of inflation*.
– DERIVATIVES **tradable** (or **tradeable**) adjective.
– ORIGIN late Middle English (as a noun): from Middle Low German, literally 'track', of West Germanic origin; related to **TREAD**. Early senses included 'course, way of life', which gave rise in the 16th cent. to 'habitual practice of an occupation', 'skilled handicraft'. The current verb senses date from the late 16th cent.

Trade Board ▸ **noun** Brit. historical a statutory body with members from workers and management, set up to settle disputes and regulate conditions of employment in certain industries.

trade book ▸ **noun** a book published by a commercial publisher and intended for general readership.

trade cycle ▸ **noun** another term for **BUSINESS CYCLE**.

trade deficit ▸ **noun** the amount by which the cost of a country's imports exceeds the value of its exports.

trade discount ▸ **noun** a discount on the retail price of something allowed or agreed between traders or to a retailer by a wholesaler.

trade dispute ▸ **noun** a dispute among workers or between employers and workers that is connected with the terms or conditions of employment.

traded option ▸ **noun** an option on a stock exchange or futures exchange which can itself be bought and sold.

trade edition ▸ **noun** an edition of a book intended for general sale rather than for book clubs or specialist suppliers.

trade gap ▸ **noun** another term for **TRADE DEFICIT**.

trade-in ▸ **noun** [usu. as modifier] a used article accepted by a retailer in part payment for another.

trade journal ▸ **noun** a periodical containing news and items of interest concerning a particular trade.

trade-last ▸ **noun** US dated a compliment from a third person that is relayed to the person complimented in exchange for a similarly relayed compliment.

trademark ▸ **noun** a symbol, word, or words legally registered or established by use as representing a company or product. ■ a distinctive characteristic or object: *the murder had all the trademarks of a Mafia hit*.
▸ **verb** [with obj.] (usu. as adj. **trademarked**) provide with a trademark: *they are counterfeiting trademarked goods*. ■ identify (a habit, quality, or way of life) as typical of someone: *his trademarked grandiose style*.

trade name ▸ **noun 1** a name that has the status of a trademark.
2 a name by which something is known in a particular trade or profession.

trade-off ▸ **noun** a balance achieved between two desirable but incompatible features; a compromise: *a trade-off between objectivity and relevance*.

trade paper ▸ **noun** another term for **TRADE JOURNAL**.

trade plates ▸ **plural noun** Brit. temporary number plates used by car dealers or manufacturers on unlicensed cars.

trade price ▸ **noun** the price paid for goods by a retailer to a manufacturer or wholesaler.

trader ▸ **noun** a person who buys and sells goods, currency, or shares. ■ a merchant ship.

Tradescant /ˈtradɪskant/, John (1570–1638), English botanist and horticulturalist. He was the earliest known collector of plants and other natural history specimens, and took part in collecting trips to western Europe, Russia, and North Africa. His son **John** (1608–62) added many plants to his father's collection, which was eventually bequeathed to Elias Ashmole.

tradescantia /ˌtradɪˈskantɪə/ ▸ **noun** an American plant with triangular three-petalled flowers, especially a tender kind widely grown as a houseplant for its trailing, typically variegated, foliage. Compare with **SPIDERWORT**. ● Genus *Tradescantia*, family Commelinaceae.
– ORIGIN modern Latin, named in honour of John **TRADESCANT**.

trade secret ▸ **noun** a secret device or technique used by a company in manufacturing its products.

tradesman (also **tradesperson**) ▸ **noun** (pl. **tradesmen** or **tradespeople**) a person engaged in trading or a trade, typically on a relatively small scale.

Trades Union Congress (abbrev.: **TUC**) (in the UK) the official representative body of British trade unions, founded in 1868 and meeting annually.

trade surplus ▸ **noun** the amount by which the value of a country's exports exceeds the cost of its imports.

trade union (Brit. also **trades union**) ▸ **noun** an organized association of workers in a trade, group of trades, or profession, formed to protect and further their rights and interests.

trade unionist (Brit. also **trades unionist**) ▸ **noun** a member of a trade union or an advocate of trade unionism.
– DERIVATIVES **trade unionism** noun.

trade-up ▸ **noun** a sale of an article in order to buy something similar but more expensive and of higher quality.

trade war ▸ **noun** a situation in which countries try to damage each other's trade, typically by the imposition of tariffs or quota restrictions.

trade-weighted ▸ **adjective** (especially of exchange rates) weighted according to the importance of the trade with the various countries involved.

trade wind ▸ **noun** a wind blowing steadily towards the equator from the north-east in the northern hemisphere or the south-east in the southern hemisphere, especially at sea. Two belts of trade winds encircle the earth, blowing from the tropical high-pressure belts to the low-pressure zone at the equator.
– ORIGIN mid 17th cent.: from the phrase *blow trade* 'blow steadily in the same direction'. Because of the importance of these winds to navigation, 18th-cent. etymologists were led erroneously to connect the word *trade* with 'commerce'.

trading ▸ **noun** [mass noun] the action or activity of buying and selling goods and services.

trading card ▸ **noun** each of a set of picture cards, typically featuring popular cartoon characters, that are collected and traded, especially by children.

trading estate ▸ **noun** Brit. a specially designed industrial and commercial area.

trading floor ▸ **noun** an area within an exchange or a bank or securities house where dealers trade in shares or other securities.

trading post ▸ **noun** a store or small settlement established for trading, typically in a remote place.

trading stamp ▸ **noun** a stamp given by some stores to a customer according to the amount spent, and exchangeable in the appropriate number for various articles.

tradition ▸ **noun 1** [mass noun] the transmission of customs or beliefs from generation to generation, or the fact of being passed on in this way: *members of different castes have* ***by tradition*** *been associated with specific occupations*. ■ [count noun] a long-established custom or belief that has been passed on from one generation to another: *Japan's unique cultural traditions*. ■ [in sing.] an artistic or literary method or style established by an artist, writer, or movement, and

subsequently followed by others: *visionary works in the tradition of William Blake.*
2 Theology a doctrine believed to have divine authority though not in the scriptures, in particular: ■ [mass noun] (in Christianity) doctrine not explicit in the Bible but held to derive from the oral teaching of Christ and the Apostles. ■ (in Judaism) an ordinance of the oral law not in the Torah but held to have been given by God to Moses. ■ (in Islam) a saying or act ascribed to the Prophet but not recorded in the Koran. See **HADITH**.
– DERIVATIVES **traditionary** adjective, **traditionist** noun, **traditionless** adjective.
– ORIGIN late Middle English: from Old French *tradicion*, or from Latin *traditio(n-)*, from *tradere* 'deliver, betray', from *trans-* 'across' + *dare* 'give'.

traditional ▶ adjective existing in or as part of a tradition; long-established: *the traditional festivities of the Church year.* ■ produced, done, or used in accordance with tradition: *a traditional fish soup.* ■ habitually done, used, or found: *the traditional drinks in the clubhouse.* ■ (of a person or group) adhering to tradition, or to a particular tradition: *traditional Elgarians.* ■ (of jazz) in the style of the early 20th century.
– DERIVATIVES **traditionally** adverb.

traditionalism ▶ noun [mass noun] the upholding or maintenance of tradition, especially so as to resist change. ■ chiefly historical the theory that all moral and religious truth comes from divine revelation passed on by tradition, human reason being incapable of attaining it.
– DERIVATIVES **traditionalist** noun & adjective, **traditionalistic** adjective.

traduce /trəˈdjuːs/ ▶ verb [with obj.] speak badly of or tell lies about (someone) so as to damage their reputation.
– DERIVATIVES **traducement** noun, **traducer** noun.
– ORIGIN mid 16th cent. (in the sense 'transport, transmit'): from Latin *traducere* 'lead in front of others, expose to ridicule', from *trans-* 'over, across' + *ducere* 'to lead'.

Trafalgar, Battle of /trəˈfalgə/ a decisive naval battle fought on 21 October 1805 off the cape of Trafalgar on the south coast of Spain during the Napoleonic Wars. The British fleet under Horatio Nelson defeated the combined fleets of France and Spain, which were attempting to clear the way for Napoleon's projected invasion of Britain.

Trafalgar Square a square in central London, planned by John Nash and built between the 1820s and 1840s. It is dominated by Nelson's Column, a memorial to Lord Nelson.

traffic ▶ noun [mass noun] **1** vehicles moving on a public highway: *a stream of heavy traffic.* ■ the movement of ships, trains, aircraft, or pedestrians: *Europe's air traffic.* ■ the transportation of goods or passengers: *the increased use of railways for goods traffic.*
2 the messages or signals transmitted through a communications system: *data traffic between remote workstations.*
3 the action of dealing or trading in something illegal: *the traffic in stolen cattle.*
4 archaic dealings or communication between people.
▶ verb (**traffics, trafficking, trafficked**) [no obj.] deal or trade in something illegal: *the government will vigorously pursue individuals who traffic in drugs.*
– DERIVATIVES **trafficker** noun, **trafficless** adjective.
– ORIGIN early 16th cent. (denoting commercial transportation of merchandise or passengers): from French *traffique*, Spanish *tráfico*, or Italian *traffico*, of unknown origin. Sense 1 dates from the early 19th cent.

trafficator /ˈtrafɪkeɪtə/ ▶ noun Brit. an obsolete kind of signalling device on the side of a motor vehicle, having the form of a small illuminated pointer which could be extended to indicate a change of direction.
– ORIGIN 1930s: blend of **TRAFFIC** and **INDICATOR**.

traffic calming ▶ noun [mass noun] the deliberate slowing of traffic in residential areas, by building road humps or other obstructions.
– ORIGIN 1980s: translation of German *Verkehrsberuhigung*.

traffic circle ▶ noun North American term for **ROUNDABOUT** (sense 1 of the noun).

traffic island ▶ noun a small raised area in the middle of a road which provides a safe place for pedestrians to stand and marks a division between two opposing streams of traffic.

traffic jam ▶ noun a line or lines of stationary or very slow-moving traffic, caused by roadworks, an accident, or heavy congestion.

traffic lights (also **traffic light** or **traffic signal**) ▶ plural noun a set of automatically operated coloured lights, typically red, amber, and green, for controlling traffic at road junctions, pedestrian crossings, and roundabouts.

traffic pattern ▶ noun chiefly N. Amer. a pattern in the air above an airport of permitted lanes for aircraft to follow after take-off or prior to landing.

traffic sign ▶ noun a sign conveying information, an instruction, or a warning to drivers.

traffic warden ▶ noun Brit. a uniformed official employed to locate and report on infringements of parking regulations.

tragacanth /ˈtragəkanθ/ (also **gum tragacanth**) ▶ noun [mass noun] a white or reddish plant gum, used in the food, textile, and pharmaceutical industries.
● This gum is obtained from plants of the genus *Astragalus*, family Leguminosae, in particular the Eurasian *A. gummifer*.
– ORIGIN late 16th cent.: from French *tragacante*, via Latin from Greek *tragakantha* 'goat's thorn', from *tragos* 'goat' (because it is browsed by goats) + *akantha* 'thorn' (referring to the shrub's spines).

tragedian /trəˈdʒiːdɪən/ ▶ noun an actor who specializes in tragic roles. ■ a writer of tragedies.
– ORIGIN late Middle English (denoting a writer of tragedies): from Old French *tragediane*, from *tragedie* (see **TRAGEDY**).

tragedienne /trəˌdʒiːdɪˈɛn/ ▶ noun an actress who specializes in tragic roles.
– ORIGIN mid 19th cent.: from French *tragédienne*, feminine of *tragédien*.

tragedy ▶ noun (pl. **tragedies**) **1** an event causing great suffering, destruction, and distress, such as a serious accident, crime, or natural catastrophe: *a tragedy that killed 95 people* | [mass noun] *his life had been plagued by tragedy.*
2 a play dealing with tragic events and having an unhappy ending, especially one concerning the downfall of the main character. ■ [mass noun] the dramatic genre represented by tragedies: *Greek tragedy.* Compare with **COMEDY**.
– ORIGIN late Middle English: from Old French *tragedie*, via Latin from Greek *tragōidia*, apparently from *tragos* 'goat' (the reason remains unexplained) + *ōidē* 'song, ode'. Compare with **TRAGIC**.

Trager /ˈtreɪdʒə/ ▶ noun [mass noun] trademark a type of low-impact massage therapy, used especially in treating neuromuscular disorders.
– ORIGIN 1980s: from the name of Milton *Trager* (1908–97), the American doctor who invented the technique.

traghetto /traˈgɛtəʊ/ ▶ noun (pl. **traghetti** /traˈgɛti/) (in Venice) a landing place or jetty for gondolas. ■ a gondola ferry.
– ORIGIN Italian.

tragic ▶ adjective causing or characterized by extreme distress or sorrow: *the shooting was a tragic accident.* ■ suffering extreme distress or sorrow: *the tragic parents reached the end of their tether.* ■ relating to tragedy in a literary work.
– DERIVATIVES **tragical** adjective, **tragically** adverb.
– ORIGIN mid 16th cent.: from French *tragique*, via Latin from Greek *tragikos*, from *tragos* 'goat', but associated with *tragōidia* (see **TRAGEDY**).

tragic flaw ▶ noun less technical term for **HAMARTIA**.

tragic irony ▶ noun see **IRONY**[1].

tragicomedy /ˌtradʒɪˈkɒmɪdi/ ▶ noun (pl. **tragicomedies**) a play or novel containing elements of both comedy and tragedy. ■ [mass noun] tragicomedies as a genre.
– DERIVATIVES **tragicomic** adjective, **tragicomically** adverb.
– ORIGIN late 16th cent.: from French *tragicomédie* or Italian *tragicomedia*, based on Latin *tragicocomoedia*, from *tragicus* (see **TRAGIC**) + *comoedia* (see **COMEDY**).

tragopan /ˈtragəpan/ ▶ noun an Asian pheasant of highland forests, the male of which has brightly coloured plumage used in courtship. ● Genus *Tragopan*, family Phasianidae: five species.
– ORIGIN modern Latin, from Greek, the name of a horned bird, from *tragos* 'goat' + the name *Pan* (see **PAN**).

tragus /ˈtreɪgəs/ ▶ noun (pl. **tragi** /ˈtreɪgʌɪ, ˈtreɪdʒʌɪ/) Anatomy & Zoology a prominence on the inner side of the external ear, in front of and partly closing the passage to the organs of hearing.
– ORIGIN late 17th cent.: from late Latin, via Latin from Greek *tragos* 'goat' (with reference to the characteristic tuft of hair that is often present, likened to a goat's beard).

Traherne /trəˈhəːn/, Thomas (1637–74), English religious writer and metaphysical poet. His major prose work *Centuries* (1699) was rediscovered in 1896 and republished as *Centuries of Meditation* (1908). It consists of brief meditations showing his joy in creation and in divine love and is noted for its description of his childhood.

trahison des clercs /ˌtrɑːɪzɒ̃ deɪ ˈklɛː/, French /tʀaizɔ̃ de klɛʀ/ ▶ noun literary a betrayal of intellectual, artistic, or moral standards by writers, academics, or artists.
– ORIGIN French, literally 'treason of the scholars', the title of a book by Julien Benda (1927).

trail ▶ noun **1** a mark or a series of signs or objects left behind by the passage of someone or something: *a trail of blood on the grass* | *the torrential rain left a trail of devastation.* ■ a track, scent, or other indication used in following someone or hunting an animal: *police followed his trail to Dorset.*
2 a long thin part or line stretching behind or hanging down from something: *smoke trails* | *we drove down in a trail of tourist cars.*
3 a beaten path through the countryside. ■ a route followed for a particular purpose: *the hotel is well off the tourist trail.* ■ (also **ski trail**) N. Amer. a downhill ski run or cross-country ski route.
4 a trailer for a film or broadcast.
5 the rear end of a gun carriage, resting or sliding on the ground when the gun is unlimbered.
▶ verb **1** [with adverbial] draw or be drawn along behind someone or something: [with obj.] *Alex trailed a hand through the clear water* | [no obj.] *her robe trailed along the ground.* ■ [no obj.] (typically of a plant) grow or hang over the edge of something or along the ground: *the roses grew wild, their stems trailing over the banks.*
2 [no obj., with adverbial of direction] walk or move slowly or wearily: *he baulked at the idea of trailing around the shops.* ■ (of the voice or a speaker) fade gradually before stopping: *her voice **trailed away**.*
3 [with obj.] follow (a person or animal) by using marks or scent left behind: *Sam suspected they were trailing him.*
4 [no obj.] be losing to an opponent in a game or contest: [with complement] *the defending champions were trailing 10—5 at half-time.*
5 [with obj.] give advance publicity to (a film, broadcast, or proposal): *the bank's plans have been extensively trailed.*
6 [with obj.] apply (slip) through a nozzle or spout to decorate ceramic ware.
– PHRASES **at the trail** Military with a rifle hanging balanced in one hand and (in Britain) parallel to the ground. **trail arms** Military let a rifle hang balanced in one hand and (in Britain) parallel to the ground. **trail one's coat** deliberately provoke a quarrel or fight.
– ORIGIN Middle English (as a verb): from Old French *traillier* 'to tow', or Middle Low German *treilen* 'haul a boat', based on Latin *tragula* 'dragnet', from *trahere* 'to pull'. Compare with **TRAWL**. The noun originally denoted the train of a robe, later generalized to denote something trailing.

trail bike ▶ noun a light motorcycle for use on rough terrain.

trailblazer ▶ noun a person who makes a new track through wild country. ■ a person who is the first to do something; an innovator: *he was a trailblazer for many ideas that are now standard fare.*
– DERIVATIVES **trailblazing** noun & adjective.

trail boss ▶ noun US a foreman in charge of a cattle drive.

trailer ▶ noun **1** an unpowered vehicle towed by another, in particular: ■ the rear section of an articulated lorry. ■ an open cart. ■ a platform for transporting a boat. ■ N. Amer. a caravan.
2 a series of extracts from a film or broadcast, used for advance publicity.
3 a thing that trails, especially a trailing plant.
▶ verb [with obj.] **1** give advance publicity to (a film, broadcast, or proposal) by releasing extracts or selected details.
2 transport (something) by trailer.

trailer park ▶ noun N. Amer. a caravan site. ■ [as modifier] US lacking refinement, taste, or quality; coarse: *her trailer-park bleached perm.*

T

trailer trash ▶ noun [mass noun] US informal, derogatory poor, lower-class white people, typified as living in mobile homes.

trailer truck ▶ noun US an articulated lorry.

trailing arbutus ▶ noun a creeping North American plant of the heather family, with leathery evergreen leaves and clusters of pink or white flowers. Also called MAYFLOWER. ● *Epigaea repens*, family Ericaceae.

trailing edge ▶ noun 1 the rear edge of a moving body, especially an aircraft wing or propeller blade. 2 Electronics the part of a pulse in which the amplitude diminishes.

trailing wheel ▶ noun a wheel on a railway locomotive or other vehicle that is not given direct motive power.

trail mix ▶ noun [mass noun] a mixture of dried fruit and nuts eaten as a snack food, originally by walkers and campers.

train ▶ verb [with obj.] 1 teach (a person or animal) a particular skill or type of behaviour through sustained practice and instruction: *the scheme trains people for promotion* | [with obj. and infinitive] *the dogs are trained to sniff out illegal stowaways*. ■ [no obj.] be taught through sustained practice and instruction: *he trained as a plumber*. ■ (usu. as adj. **trained**) develop and improve (a mental or physical faculty) through instruction or practice: *an alert mind and trained eye give astute evaluations*.
2 [no obj.] undertake a course of exercise and diet in order to reach or maintain peak physical fitness in preparation for a specific sport or event: *she trains three times a week*. ■ [with obj.] prepare (a person or animal) in this way: *the horse was trained in Paris*. ■ (**train down**) reduce one's weight through diet and exercise in order to be fit for a particular event: *he trained down to heavyweight*.
3 (**train something on/at**) point or aim something, typically a gun or camera, at: *the detective trained his gun on the side door*.
4 cause (a plant) to grow in a particular direction or into a required shape: *they trained crimson ramblers over their houses*.
5 [no obj., with adverbial of direction] dated go by train: *Charles trained to London with Emma*.
6 archaic entice (someone).
▶ noun 1 a series of connected railway carriages or wagons moved by a locomotive or by integral motors: *a freight train* | *the journey took two hours* **by train**. ■ a series of gears or other connected parts in machinery.
2 a number of vehicles or pack animals moving in a line: *a camel train*. ■ a retinue of attendants accompanying an important person.
3 a series of connected events or thoughts: *the train of events leading to Pascoe's death* | *I failed to follow his train of thought*.
4 a long piece of material attached to the back of a formal dress or robe that trails along the ground.
5 a trail of gunpowder for firing an explosive charge.
– PHRASES **in train** (of arrangements) in progress: *an investigation is in train*. **in the train of** following behind. ■ as a consequence of: *unemployment brings great difficulties in its train*.
– DERIVATIVES **trainability** noun, **trainable** adjective.
– ORIGIN Middle English (as a noun in the sense 'delay'): from Old French *train* (masculine), *traine* (feminine), from *trahiner* (verb), from Latin *trahere* 'pull, draw'. Early noun senses were 'trailing part of a robe' and 'retinue'; the latter gave rise to 'line of travelling people or vehicles', later 'a connected series of things'. The early verb sense 'cause a plant to grow in a desired shape' was the basis of the sense 'instruct'.

T

trainband ▶ noun historical a division of civilian soldiers in London and other areas, in particular in the Stuart period.

train-bearer ▶ noun a person whose job is to hold up the train of a dress or robe.

trainee ▶ noun a person undergoing training for a particular job or profession.
– DERIVATIVES **traineeship** noun.

trainer ▶ noun 1 a person who trains people or animals. ■ informal an aircraft or simulator used to train pilots.
2 Brit. a soft sports shoe suitable for casual wear.

training ▶ noun [mass noun] the action of teaching a person or animal a particular skill or type of behaviour: *in-service training for staff*. ■ the action of undertaking a course of exercise and diet in preparation for a sporting event: *you'll have to go into strict training*.
– PHRASES **in** (or **out of**) **training** undergoing (or no longer undergoing) physical training for a sporting event. ■ physically fit (or unfit) as a result of the amount of training one has undertaken.

training college ▶ noun (in the UK) a college where people, typically prospective teachers, are trained.

training ship ▶ noun a ship on which people are taught how to sail and related skills.

training shoe ▶ noun another term for TRAINER (sense 2).

training wheels ▶ plural noun N. Amer. a pair of small supporting wheels fitted on either side of the rear wheel of a child's bicycle.

trainload ▶ noun a number of people or a quantity of a commodity transported by train.

trainman ▶ noun (pl. **trainmen**) a railway employee who works on trains.

train mile ▶ noun one mile travelled by one train, as a unit of traffic.

train oil ▶ noun [mass noun] chiefly historical oil obtained from the blubber of a whale (and formerly of other sea creatures), especially the right whale.
– ORIGIN mid 16th cent.: from obsolete *train* 'train oil', from Middle Low German *trän*, Middle Dutch *traen*, literally 'tear' (because it was extracted in droplets).

train set ▶ noun 1 a set of railway wagons or carriages, often with a locomotive, coupled together for a particular service.
2 Brit. a set of trains, tracks, and other items making up a child's model railway.

train shed ▶ noun a large structure providing a shelter over the tracks and platforms of a railway station.

trainsick ▶ adjective affected with nausea by the motion of a train.

trainspotter ▶ noun Brit. a person who collects train or locomotive numbers as a hobby. ■ often derogatory a person who obsessively studies the minutiae of any minority interest or specialized hobby.
– DERIVATIVES **trainspotting** noun.

train wreck ▶ noun informal a chaotic or disastrous situation that holds a ghoulish fascination for observers: *his train wreck of a private life guaranteed front-page treatment*.

traipse /treɪps/ ▶ verb [no obj., with adverbial of direction] walk or move wearily or reluctantly: *students had to traipse all over London to attend lectures*. ■ walk about casually or needlessly: *there's people traipsing in and out all the time*.
▶ noun 1 [in sing.] a tedious or tiring journey on foot.
2 archaic a slovenly woman.
– ORIGIN late 16th cent. (as a verb): of unknown origin. The noun is first recorded in sense 2 of the noun in the late 17th cent.

trait /treɪt, treɪ/ ▶ noun a distinguishing quality or characteristic, typically one belonging to a person: *the traditionally British trait of self-denigration*. ■ a genetically determined characteristic.
– ORIGIN mid 16th cent.: from French, from Latin *tractus* 'drawing, draught' (see TRACT[1]). An early sense was 'stroke of the pen or pencil in a picture', giving rise to the sense 'a particular feature of mind or character' (mid 18th cent.).

traiteur /trɛˈtəː/, French /tʀɛtœʀ/ ▶ noun (in France or French-speaking countries) a delicatessen.
– ORIGIN French, from *traiter* 'to treat'.

traitor ▶ noun a person who betrays someone or something, such as a friend, cause, or principle: *he was a traitor to his own class*.
– PHRASES **turn traitor** betray a group or person.
– ORIGIN Middle English: from Old French *traitour*, from Latin *traditor*, from *tradere* 'hand over'.

traitorous ▶ adjective relating to or characteristic of a traitor; treacherous: *when his traitorous actions were discovered, he was imprisoned*.
– DERIVATIVES **traitorously** adverb.

Trajan /ˈtreɪdʒ(ə)n/ (*c*.53–117 AD), Roman emperor 98–117; Latin name *Marcus Ulpius Traianus*. His reign is noted for the many public works undertaken and for the Dacian wars (101–6), which ended in the annexation of Dacia as a province.

trajectory /trəˈdʒɛkt(ə)ri, ˈtradʒɪkt(ə)ri/ ▶ noun (pl. **trajectories**) 1 the path followed by a projectile flying or an object moving under the action of given forces: *the missile's trajectory was preset* | figurative *the rapid upward trajectory of Rich's career*.
2 Geometry a curve or surface cutting a family of curves or surfaces at a constant angle.
– ORIGIN late 17th cent.: from modern Latin *trajectoria* (feminine), from Latin *traject-* 'thrown across', from the verb *traicere*, from *trans-* 'across' + *jacere* 'to throw'.

Trakehner /traˈkeɪnə/ ▶ noun 1 a saddle horse of a light breed first developed at the Trakehnen stud near Kaliningrad in Russia.
2 a type of fence used in horse trials, which consists of a ditch spanned by centre rails.
– ORIGIN early 20th cent.: from German.

tra la ▶ exclamation chiefly ironic expressing joy or gaiety: *off to his life, kids, and wife, tra la*.
– ORIGIN early 19th cent.: imitative of a fanfare or of the refrain of a song.

Tralee /trəˈliː/ the county town of Kerry, a port on the SW coast of the Republic of Ireland; pop. 20,288 (2006).

tram (also **tramcar**) ▶ noun 1 Brit. a passenger vehicle powered by electricity conveyed by overhead cables, and running on rails laid in a public road.
2 historical a low four-wheeled cart or barrow used in coal mines.
– ORIGIN early 16th cent. (denoting a shaft of a barrow; also in sense 2): from Middle Low German and Middle Dutch *trame* 'beam, barrow shaft'. In the early 19th cent. the word denoted the parallel wheel tracks used in a mine, on which the public tramway was modelled; hence sense 1 (late 19th cent.).

Traminer /trəˈmiːnə/ ▶ noun [mass noun] a variety of white wine grape grown chiefly in Germany and Alsace. ■ a white wine with a perfumed bouquet made from the Traminer grape.
– ORIGIN named after the Italian village *Termeno*.

tramline /ˈtramlʌɪn/ ▶ noun (usu. **tramlines**) a railway track for a tramcar. ■ (**tramlines**) a pair of parallel lines, especially at the sides of a tennis court (enclosing the extra width used in doubles play) or at the sides or back of a badminton court. ■ an inflexible principle or course of action: *when choosing a job, do pupils simply follow academic tramlines?*

trammel /ˈtram(ə)l/ ▶ noun 1 (**trammels**) literary restrictions or impediments to freedom of action: *we will forge our own future, free from the trammels of materialism*.
2 (also **trammel net**) a three-layered dragnet, designed so that a fish entering through one of the large-meshed outer sections will push part of the finer-meshed central section through the large meshes on the further side, forming a pocket in which the fish is trapped.
3 an instrument consisting of a board with two grooves intersecting at right angles, in which the two ends of a beam compass can slide to draw an ellipse. [early 18th cent.: so named because the motion of the beam is 'restricted' by the grooves.] ■ a beam compass.
4 US a hook in a fireplace for a kettle.
▶ verb (**trammels**, **trammelling**, **trammelled**; US **trammels**, **trammeling**, **trammeled**) [with obj.] deprive of freedom of action: *those less trammelled by convention than himself*.
– ORIGIN late Middle English (in sense 2 of the noun): from Old French *tramail*, from a medieval Latin variant of *trimaculum*, perhaps from Latin *tri-* 'three' + *macula* 'mesh'.

tramontana /ˌtrampnˈtɑːnə/ ▶ noun a cold north wind blowing in Italy or the adjoining regions of the Adriatic and Mediterranean.
– ORIGIN Italian, 'north wind, Pole Star' (see TRAMONTANE).

tramontane /trəˈmpnteɪn/ ▶ adjective rare relating to or living on the other side of mountains, especially the Alps as seen from Italy.
▶ noun 1 another term for TRAMONTANA.
2 archaic a person who lives on the other side of mountains (used especially by Italians to refer to people beyond the Alps).
– ORIGIN Middle English (as a noun denoting the Pole Star): from Italian *tramontana* 'Pole Star, north wind', *tramontani* 'people living beyond the Alps', from Latin *transmontanus* 'beyond the mountains', from *trans-* 'across' + *mons, mont-* 'mountain'.

tramp ▶ verb [no obj., with adverbial of direction] walk heavily or noisily: *he tramped about the room*. ■ walk over a long distance wearily or reluctantly: *he had tramped all over the city*. ■ [with obj.] tread or stamp on: *one of the few wines still tramped by foot*.
▶ noun 1 a person who travels from place to place on foot in search of work or as a vagrant or beggar.
2 [in sing.] the sound of heavy steps: *the tramp of marching feet*.
3 [in sing.] a long walk, typically a tiring one: *she was freshly returned from a tramp round Norwich*.

4 [usu. as modifier] a cargo vessel that carries goods between many different ports rather than sailing a fixed route: *a tramp steamer*.
5 informal, chiefly N. Amer. a promiscuous woman.
6 a metal plate protecting the sole of a boot used for digging. ■ the top of the blade of a spade.
– DERIVATIVES **tramper** noun, **trampish** adjective, **trampy** adjective.
– ORIGIN late Middle English (as a verb): probably of Low German origin. The noun dates from the mid 17th cent.

trample ▶ verb [with obj.] tread on and crush: *the fence had been trampled down* | [no obj.] *her dog* **trampled on** *his tulips*. ■ [no obj.] (**trample on/upon/over**) treat with contempt: *a lay statesman ought not to trample upon the opinions of his Church advisers*.
▶ noun literary an act or the sound of trampling.
– DERIVATIVES **trampler** noun.
– ORIGIN late Middle English (in the sense 'tread heavily'): frequentative of TRAMP.

trampoline /ˈtrampəliːn/ ▶ noun a strong fabric sheet connected by springs to a frame, used as a springboard and landing area in doing acrobatic or gymnastic exercises. See also REBOUNDER (sense 1).
▶ verb [no obj.] (usu. as noun **trampolining**) do acrobatic or gymnastic exercises on a trampoline as a recreation or sport: *his hobby is trampolining*. ■ [no obj., with adverbial of direction] leap or rebound from something with a springy base: *she trampolined across the bed*.
– DERIVATIVES **trampolinist** noun.
– ORIGIN late 18th cent.: from Italian *trampolino*, from *trampoli* 'stilts'.

tram road ▶ noun historical a road with wooden, stone, or metal tracks for wheels, used by wagons in mining districts.

tramway ▶ noun 1 Brit. a set of rails which forms the route for a tram. ■ a tram system.
2 historical another term for TRAM ROAD.

trance /trɑːns/ ▶ noun a half-conscious state characterized by an absence of response to external stimuli, typically as induced by hypnosis or entered by a medium: *she put him into a light trance*. ■ a state of abstraction: *the kind of trance he went into whenever illness was discussed*. ■ (also **trance music**) [mass noun] a type of electronic dance music characterized by hypnotic rhythms and sounds.
▶ verb [with obj.] literary put into a trance: *she's been tranced and may need waking*.
– DERIVATIVES **trance-like** adjective.
– ORIGIN Middle English (originally as a verb in the sense 'be in a trance'): from Old French *transir* 'depart, fall into trance', from Latin *transire* 'go across'.

tranche /trɑːnʃ/ ▶ noun a portion of something, especially money: *they released the first* **tranche** *of the loan*.
– ORIGIN late 15th cent.: from Old French, literally 'slice'.

tranexamic acid /ˌtranɛkˈsamɪk/ ▶ noun [mass noun] Medicine a synthetic compound derived from cyclohexane which inhibits the breakdown of fibrin in blood clots and is used to treat haemorrhage. ● Chem. formula: $NH_2CH_2C_6H_{10}COOH$.
– ORIGIN 1960s: from elements of the systematic name, *trans-4-aminomethylcyclohexanecarboxylic acid*.

trank ▶ noun informal term for TRANQUILLIZER.
– DERIVATIVES **tranked** adjective.

tranny (also **trannie**) ▶ noun (pl. **trannies**) informal
1 chiefly Brit. a transistor radio.
2 a photographic transparency.
3 N. Amer. the transmission in a motor vehicle.
4 (usu. **trannie**) a transvestite.
– ORIGIN 1960s: abbreviation.

tranquil ▶ adjective free from disturbance; calm: *her tranquil gaze* | *the sea was tranquil*.
– DERIVATIVES **tranquilly** adverb.
– ORIGIN late Middle English: from French *tranquille* or Latin *tranquillus*.

tranquillity (also **tranquility**) ▶ noun [mass noun] the quality or state of being tranquil; calm: *passing cars are the only noise that disturbs the tranquillity of rural life*.

tranquillize (also **tranquillise**; US **tranquilize**) ▶ verb [with obj.] (usu. as adj. **tranquillizing**) (of a drug) have a calming or sedative effect on. ■ administer a tranquillizer to (a person or animal). ■ literary make tranquil: *joys that tranquillize the mind*.

tranquillizer (also **tranquilliser**; US also **tranquilizer**) ▶ noun a medicinal drug taken to reduce tension or anxiety.

trans ▶ adjective Chemistry denoting or relating to a molecular structure in which two particular atoms or groups lie on opposite sides of a given plane in the molecule, in particular denoting an isomer in which substituents at opposite ends of a carbon–carbon double bond are also on opposite sides of the bond: *the trans isomer of stilbene*. Compare with CIS.
– ORIGIN independent usage of TRANS-.

trans- /trans, trɑːns, -nz/ ▶ prefix 1 across; beyond: *transcontinental* | *transgress*. ■ on or to the other side of: *transatlantic* | *transalpine*. Often contrasted with CIS-.
2 through: *transonic*. ■ into another state or place: *transform* | *translate*. ■ surpassing; transcending: *transfinite*.
3 Chemistry (usu. *trans-*) denoting molecules with trans arrangements of substituents: *trans-1,2-dichloroethene*. ■ Genetics denoting alleles on different chromosomes.
– ORIGIN from Latin *trans* 'across'.

transact ▶ verb [with obj.] conduct or carry out (business).
– DERIVATIVES **transactor** noun.
– ORIGIN late 16th cent.: from Latin *transact-* 'driven through', from the verb *transigere*, from *trans-* 'through' + *agere* 'do, lead'.

transaction ▶ noun 1 an instance of buying or selling something: *in an ordinary commercial transaction a delivery date is essential*. ■ [mass noun] the action of conducting business. ■ an exchange or interaction between people: *intellectual transactions in the classroom*.
2 (**transactions**) published reports of proceedings at the meetings of a learned society.
3 an input message to a computer system dealt with as a single unit of work.
– DERIVATIVES **transactional** adjective, **transactionally** adverb.
– ORIGIN late Middle English (as a term in Roman Law): from late Latin *transactio(n-)*, from *transigere* 'drive through' (see TRANSACT).

transactional analysis ▶ noun [mass noun] a system of popular psychology based on the idea that one's behaviour and social relationships reflect an interchange between parental (critical and nurturing), adult (rational), and childlike (intuitive and dependent) aspects of personality established early in life.

transactivation ▶ noun [mass noun] Biochemistry activation of a gene at one locus by the presence of a particular gene at another locus, typically following infection by a virus.

transalpine ▶ adjective related to or situated in the area beyond the Alps, in particular as viewed from Italy. See also GAUL[1]. ■ crossing the Alps: *transalpine road freight*.
– ORIGIN late 16th cent.: from Latin *transalpinus*, from *trans-* 'across' + *alpinus* (see ALPINE).

transaminase /tranˈzamɪneɪz, trɑːn-, -ˈsa-/ ▶ noun Biochemistry an enzyme which catalyses a particular transamination reaction.

transamination /ˌtransamɪˈneɪʃ(ə)n, ˌtrɑːns-, -nz-/ ▶ noun [mass noun] Biochemistry the transfer of an amino group from one molecule to another, especially from an amino acid to a keto acid.

transatlantic ▶ adjective crossing the Atlantic: *a transatlantic flight*. ■ concerning countries on both sides of the Atlantic, typically Britain and the US: *the transatlantic relationship*. ■ relating to or situated on the other side of the Atlantic; American (from a British point of view); British or European (from an American point of view).

transaxle ▶ noun an integral driving axle and differential gear in a motor vehicle.

transborder ▶ adjective crossing or extending across a border between two countries: *transborder trade* | *transborder regions*.

Transcaucasia /ˌtranzkɔːˈkeɪʒə, ˌtrɑːnz-, -ˈkeɪzɪə/ a region lying to the south of the Caucasus mountains, between the Black Sea and the Caspian, and comprising the present-day republics of Georgia, Armenia, and Azerbaijan. It was created a republic of the Soviet Union in 1922 as the Transcaucasian Soviet Federated Socialist Republic, but was broken up into its constituent republics in 1936.
– DERIVATIVES **Transcaucasian** adjective.

transceiver ▶ noun a device that can both transmit and receive communications, in particular a combined radio transmitter and receiver.
– ORIGIN 1930s: blend of TRANSMITTER and RECEIVER.

transcend ▶ verb [with obj.] be or go beyond the range or limits of (a field of activity or conceptual sphere): *this was an issue transcending party politics*. ■ surpass (a person or achievement).
– ORIGIN Middle English: from Old French *transcendre* or Latin *transcendere*, from *trans-* 'across' + *scandere* 'climb'.

transcendence (also **transcendency**) ▶ noun [mass noun] existence or experience beyond the normal or physical level: *the possibility of spiritual transcendence in the modern world*.

transcendent ▶ adjective 1 beyond or above the range of normal or physical human experience: *the search for a transcendent level of knowledge*. ■ surpassing the ordinary; exceptional: *her transcendent beauty*. ■ (of God) existing apart from and not subject to the limitations of the material universe. Often contrasted with IMMANENT.
2 (in scholastic philosophy) higher than or not included in any of Aristotle's ten categories. ■ (in Kantian philosophy) not realizable in experience.
– DERIVATIVES **transcendently** adverb.
– ORIGIN late Middle English: from Latin *transcendent-* 'climbing over', from the verb *transcendere* (see TRANSCEND).

transcendental ▶ adjective 1 relating to a spiritual realm: *the transcendental importance of each person's soul*. ■ relating to or denoting Transcendentalism.
2 (in Kantian philosophy) presupposed in and necessary to experience; a priori.
3 Mathematics (of a number, e.g. *e* or π) real but not a root of an algebraic equation with rational coefficients. ■ (of a function) not capable of being produced by the algebraical operations of addition, multiplication, and involution, or the inverse operations.
– DERIVATIVES **transcendentalize** (also **transcendentalise**) verb, **transcendentally** adverb.
– ORIGIN early 17th cent.: from medieval Latin *transcendentalis* (see TRANSCENDENT).

transcendentalism ▶ noun [mass noun] 1 (**Transcendentalism**) an idealistic philosophical and social movement which developed in New England around 1836 in reaction to rationalism. Influenced by romanticism, Platonism, and Kantian philosophy, it taught that divinity pervades all nature and humanity, and its members held progressive views on feminism and communal living. Ralph Waldo Emerson and Henry David Thoreau were central figures.
2 a system developed by Immanuel Kant, based on the idea that, in order to understand the nature of reality, one must first examine and analyse the reasoning process which governs the nature of experience.
– DERIVATIVES **transcendentalist** noun & adjective.

Transcendental Meditation (abbrev.: **TM**) ▶ noun [mass noun] (trademark in the US) a technique for detaching oneself from anxiety and promoting harmony and self-realization by meditation, repetition of a mantra, and other yogic practices, promulgated by an international organization founded by the Indian guru Maharishi Mahesh Yogi (*c*.1911–2008).

transcode ▶ verb [with obj.] convert (language or information) from one form of coded representation to another.

transconductance ▶ noun Electronics the ratio of the change in current at the output terminal to the change in the voltage at the input terminal of an active device.

transconjugant /ˌtransˈkɒndʒʊɡənt, ˌtrɑːns, -nz/ ▶ noun Biology a bacterial cell which has received genetic material by conjugation with another bacterium.

transcontinental ▶ adjective (especially of a railway line) crossing a continent. ■ extending across or relating to two or more continents: *a transcontinental radio audience*.
▶ noun Canadian a transcontinental railway or train.
– DERIVATIVES **transcontinentally** adverb.

transcortical /ˌtransˈkɔːtɪk(ə)l, ˌtrɑːns, -nz/ ▶ adjective Physiology relating to nerve pathways which cross the cerebral cortex of the brain.

transcribe ▶ verb [with obj.] 1 put (thoughts, speech, or data) into written or printed form: *each interview was taped and transcribed*. ■ transliterate (foreign characters) or write or type out (shorthand, notes, or

T

other abbreviated forms) into ordinary characters or full sentences.
2 arrange (a piece of music) for a different instrument, voice, or group of these: *his largest early work was transcribed for organ.*
3 Biochemistry synthesize (RNA) using a template of existing DNA (or vice versa), so that the genetic information is copied.
– DERIVATIVES **transcriber** noun.
– ORIGIN mid 16th cent. (in the sense 'make a copy in writing'): from Latin *transcribere*, from *trans-* 'across' + *scribere* 'write'.

transcript ▶ noun **1** a written or printed version of material originally presented in another medium.
2 Biochemistry a length of RNA or DNA that has been transcribed respectively from a DNA or RNA template.
3 an official record of a student's work, showing courses taken and grades achieved.
– DERIVATIVES **transcriptive** adjective.
– ORIGIN Middle English: from Old French *transcrit*, from Latin *transcriptum*, neuter past participle of *transcribere* (see TRANSCRIBE). The spelling change in the 15th cent. was due to association with the Latin.

transcriptase /tran'skrɪpteɪz, trɑːn-/ ▶ noun [mass noun] Biochemistry an enzyme which catalyses the formation of RNA from a DNA template during transcription, or (**reverse transcriptase**) the formation of DNA from an RNA template in reverse transcription.

transcription ▶ noun **1** a written or printed version of something; a transcript. ■ [mass noun] the action or process of transcribing something: *the funding covers transcription of nearly illegible photocopies.* ■ a form in which a speech sound or a foreign character is represented.
2 an arrangement of a piece of music for a different instrument, voice, or group of these: *a transcription for voice and lute.*
3 [mass noun] Biochemistry the process of transcribing RNA, with existing DNA serving as a template, or vice versa.
– DERIVATIVES **transcriptional** adjective, **transcriptionally** adverb, **transcriptionist** noun (N. Amer.).
– ORIGIN late 16th cent.: from French, or from Latin *transcriptio(n-)*, from the verb *transcribere* (see TRANSCRIBE).

transcriptome ▶ noun Biochemistry the sum total of all the messenger RNA molecules expressed from the genes of an organism.

transcultural ▶ adjective relating to or involving more than one culture; cross-cultural: *the increasingly transcultural relationships among writers in the twentieth century.*

transcutaneous /ˌtranzkjuˈteɪnɪəs, ˌtrɑːnz-, -ns-/ ▶ adjective existing, applied, or measured across the depth of the skin.

transdermal /ˌtranz'dəːməl, trɑːnz, -ns-/ ▶ adjective relating to or denoting the application of a medicine or drug through the skin, typically by using an adhesive patch, so that it is absorbed slowly into the body.

transducer /tranz'djuːsə, trɑːnz-, -ns-/ ▶ noun a device that converts variations in a physical quantity, such as pressure or brightness, into an electrical signal, or vice versa.
– DERIVATIVES **transduce** verb, **transduction** noun.
– ORIGIN 1920s: from Latin *transducere* 'lead across' (from *trans-* 'across' + *ducere* 'lead') + -ER¹.

T

transect technical ▶ verb [with obj.] cut across or make a transverse section in.
▶ noun a straight line or narrow section through an object or natural feature or across the earth's surface, along which observations are made or measurements taken.
– DERIVATIVES **transection** noun.
– ORIGIN mid 17th cent. (as a verb): from TRANS- 'through' + Latin *sect-* 'divided by cutting' (from the verb *secare*).

transept /'transɛpt, 'trɑːn-/ ▶ noun (in a cross-shaped church) either of the two parts forming the arms of the cross shape, projecting at right angles from the nave: *the north transept.*
– DERIVATIVES **transeptal** adjective.
– ORIGIN mid 16th cent.: from modern Latin *transeptum* (see TRANS-, SEPTUM).

transexual ▶ adjective & noun variant spelling of TRANSSEXUAL.

trans-fat ▶ noun another term for TRANS-FATTY ACID.

trans-fatty acid ▶ noun an unsaturated fatty acid with a trans arrangement of the carbon atoms adjacent to its double bonds. Such acids occur especially in margarines and cooking oils as a result of the hydrogenation process.

transfect /tranz'fɛkt, trɑːnz-, -ns-/ ▶ verb [with obj.] Microbiology infect (a cell) with free nucleic acid. ■ introduce (genetic material) in this way.
– DERIVATIVES **transfectant** noun, **transfection** noun.
– ORIGIN 1960s: from TRANS- 'across' + INFECT, or a blend of TRANSFER and INFECT.

transfer ▶ verb (**transfers, transferring, transferred**) **1** move from one place to another: [with obj.] *he intends to transfer the fund's assets to the Treasury* | [no obj.] *I went to sleep on the couch before transferring to my bedroom later in the night.* ■ move to another department, occupation, etc.: [no obj.] *she transferred to the Physics Department* | [with obj.] *employees have been transferred to the installation team.* ■ (in football and other sports) move to another team: [no obj.] *he transferred to the Brooklyn Dodgers* | [with obj.] *he was transferred to Arsenal for £750,000.* ■ [with obj.] redirect (a telephone call) to a new line or extension. ■ [with obj.] copy (a drawing or design) from one surface to another. ■ [with obj.] copy (data, music, etc.) from one medium or device to another: *the new product lets users transfer data from palmtop to desktop with a click of the mouse.*
2 [no obj.] change to another place, route, or means of transport during a journey: *passengers have to transfer at Heathrow for onward international flights.*
3 [with obj.] make over the possession of (property, a right, or a responsibility) to another.
4 [with obj.] (usu. as adj. **transferred**) change (the sense of a word or phrase) by extension or metaphor: *a transferred use of the Old English noun.*
▶ noun **1** an act of moving something or someone to another place, organization, team, etc.: *a transfer of wealth to the EU's poorer nations* | *she asked her boss for a transfer to the city* | [mass noun] *a patient had died after transfer from the County Hospital to St Peter's.* ■ a conveyance of property, especially stocks and shares, from one person to another. ■ [mass noun] the action of copying data from one medium or device to another.
2 Brit. a small coloured picture or design on paper, which can be transferred to another surface by being pressed or heated: *T-shirts with iron-on transfers.*
3 an act of changing to another place, route, or means of transport during a journey: *bus transfers between the airport and the city centre cost about £11.* ■ N. Amer. a ticket allowing a passenger to change from one public transport vehicle to another as part of a single journey.
– DERIVATIVES **transferee** noun, **transferor** noun (chiefly Law), **transferrer** noun.
– ORIGIN late Middle English (as a verb): from French *transférer* or Latin *transferre*, from *trans-* 'across' + *ferre* 'to bear'. The earliest use of the noun (late 17th cent.) was as a legal term in the sense 'conveyance of property'.

transferable /trans'fəːrəb(ə)l, 'transf(ə)r-, trɑː-, -nz-/ ▶ adjective (especially of financial assets, liabilities, or legal rights) able to be transferred or made over to the possession of another person.
– DERIVATIVES **transferability** noun.

transferase /'transf(ə)reɪz, 'trɑːns-, -nz-/ ▶ noun Biochemistry an enzyme which catalyses the transfer of a particular group from one molecule to another.

transference /'transf(ə)r(ə)ns, 'trɑːns-, -nz-/ ▶ noun [mass noun] the action of transferring something or the process of being transferred: *education involves the transference of knowledge.* ■ Psychoanalysis the redirection to a substitute, usually a therapist, of emotions that were originally felt in childhood (in a phase of analysis called **transference neurosis**).

transfer factor ▶ noun Biology a substance released by antigen-sensitized lymphocytes and capable of transferring the response of delayed hypersensitivity to a non-sensitized cell or individual into which it is introduced.

transfer fee ▶ noun Brit. a fee paid by one soccer or rugby club to another for the transfer of a player.

transfer function ▶ noun Electronics a mathematical function relating the output or response of a system such as a filter circuit to the input or stimulus.

transfer list Brit. ▶ noun a soccer or rugby club's list of players available for transfer.
▶ verb (**transfer-list**) [with obj.] make (a player) available for transfer.

transfer orbit ▶ noun a trajectory by which a spacecraft can pass from one orbit to another at a higher altitude, especially a geostationary orbit.

transfer payment ▶ noun Economics a payment made or income received in which no goods or services are being paid for, such as a benefit payment or subsidy.

transferral ▶ noun [mass noun] the action of transferring someone or something: *the transferral of ownership in the form of a takeover.*

transferrin /trans'fɛrɪn, trɑːns-, -nz-/ ▶ noun [mass noun] Biochemistry a protein of the beta globulin group which binds and transports iron in blood serum.
– ORIGIN 1940s: from TRANS- 'across' + Latin *ferrum* 'iron' + -IN¹.

transfer RNA ▶ noun [mass noun] Biochemistry RNA consisting of folded molecules which transport amino acids from the cytoplasm of a cell to a ribosome.

transferware ▶ noun [mass noun] pottery decorated with transfers.

transfiguration ▶ noun a complete change of form or appearance into a more beautiful or spiritual state: *in this light the junk undergoes a transfiguration; it shines.* ■ (**the Transfiguration**) Christ's appearance in radiant glory to three of his disciples (Matthew 17:2 and Mark 9:2–3). ■ the Church festival commemorating Christ's transfiguration, held on 6 August.
– ORIGIN late Middle English (with biblical reference): from Old French, or from Latin *transfiguratio(n-)*, from the verb *transfigurare* (see TRANSFIGURE).

transfigure ▶ verb [with obj.] transform into something more beautiful or elevated: *the world is made luminous and is transfigured.*
– ORIGIN Middle English: from Old French *transfigurer* or Latin *transfigurare*, from *trans-* 'across' + *figura* 'figure'.

transfinite ▶ adjective Mathematics relating to or denoting a number corresponding to an infinite set in the way that a natural number denotes or counts members of a finite set.

transfix ▶ verb [with obj.] **1** cause (someone) to become motionless with horror, wonder, or astonishment: *he was transfixed by the pain in her face* | *she stared at him, transfixed.*
2 pierce with a sharp implement or weapon: *a field mouse is transfixed by the curved talons of an owl.*
– DERIVATIVES **transfixion** noun.
– ORIGIN late 16th cent. (in sense 2): from Latin *transfix-* 'pierced through', from the verb *transfigere*, from *trans-* 'across' + *figere* 'fix, fasten'.

transform ▶ verb [with obj.] **1** make a marked change in the form, nature, or appearance of: *lasers have transformed cardiac surgery* | *he wanted to transform himself into a successful businessman.* ■ [no obj.] undergo a marked change. ■ change the voltage of (an electric current).
2 Mathematics change (a mathematical entity) by transformation.
▶ noun Mathematics & Linguistics the product of a transformation. ■ a rule for making a transformation.
– DERIVATIVES **transformable** adjective, **transformative** adjective.
– ORIGIN Middle English (as a verb): from Old French *transformer* or Latin *transformare* (see TRANS-, FORM).

transformation ▶ noun **1** a marked change in form, nature, or appearance: *British society underwent a radical transformation.* ■ (also **transformation scene**) a sudden dramatic change of scenery on stage. ■ a metamorphosis during the life cycle of an animal. ■ Physics the induced or spontaneous change of one element into another by a nuclear process.
2 Mathematics & Logic a process by which one figure, expression, or function is converted into another one of similar value.
3 Linguistics a process by which an element in the underlying logical deep structure of a sentence is converted to an element in the surface structure.
4 [mass noun] Biology the genetic alteration of a cell by introduction of extraneous DNA, especially by a plasmid. ■ the heritable modification of a cell from its normal state to a malignant state.
– ORIGIN late Middle English: from Old French, or from late Latin *transformatio(n-)*, from the verb *transformare* (see TRANSFORM).

transformational ▶ adjective relating to or involving transformation or transformations. ■ relating to transformational grammar.
– DERIVATIVES **transformationally** adverb.

transformational grammar ▶ noun [mass noun] Linguistics a type of grammar which describes a language in terms of transformations applied to an underlying logical deep structure in order to generate the surface structure of sentences which can actually occur. See also GENERATIVE GRAMMAR.

transformer ▸ noun **1** an apparatus for reducing or increasing the voltage of an alternating current. **2** a person or thing that transforms something.

transform fault ▸ noun Geology a strike-slip fault occurring at the boundary between two plates of the earth's crust.

transfuse ▸ verb [with obj.] **1** Medicine transfer (blood or its components) from one person or animal to another. ■ inject (liquid) into a blood vessel to replace lost fluid. **2** cause (something or someone) to be permeated or infused by something: *we became transfused by a radiance of joy.*
– ORIGIN late Middle English (in the sense 'cause to pass from one person to another'): from Latin *transfus-* 'poured from one container to another', from the verb *transfundere*, from *trans-* 'across' + *fundere* 'pour'.

transfusion /trans'fjuːʒ(ə)n, trɑːns-, -nz-/ ▸ noun an act of transfusing donated blood, blood products, or other fluid into the circulatory system of a person or animal.

transgender (also **transgendered**) ▸ adjective another term for TRANSSEXUAL.

transgenderism ▸ noun [mass noun] a state or condition in which a person's identity does not conform unambiguously to conventional ideas of male or female gender.
– DERIVATIVES **transgenderist** noun & adjective.

transgenic /tranz'dʒɛnɪk, trɑːnz-, -ns-/ ▸ adjective Biology relating to or denoting an organism that contains genetic material into which DNA from an unrelated organism has been artificially introduced.
– DERIVATIVES **transgene** noun.
– ORIGIN 1980s: from TRANS- 'across' + GENE + -IC.

transgenics ▸ plural noun [usu. treated as sing.] the branch of biology concerned with transgenic organisms.

transglobal ▸ adjective (of an expedition, enterprise, search, or network) moving or extending across or round the world.

transgress ▸ verb [with obj.] **1** go beyond the limits of (what is morally, socially, or legally acceptable): *she had transgressed an unwritten social law.* **2** Geology (of the sea) spread over (an area of land).
– DERIVATIVES **transgressor** noun.
– ORIGIN late 15th cent. (earlier (late Middle English) as *transgression*): from Old French *transgresser* or Latin *transgress-* 'stepped across', from the verb *transgredi*, from *trans-* 'across' + *gradi* 'go'.

transgression ▸ noun an act that goes against a law, rule, or code of conduct; an offence: *I'll be keeping an eye out for further transgressions* | [mass noun] *her transgression of genteel etiquette.*

transgressive ▸ adjective **1** involving a violation of moral or social boundaries: *her experiences of transgressive love with both sexes.* ■ relating to art or literature in which orthodox moral, social, and artistic boundaries are challenged by the representation of unconventional behaviour and the use of experimental forms. **2** Geology (of a stratum) overlapping others unconformably, especially as a result of marine transgression.

tranship ▸ verb variant spelling of TRANS-SHIP.

transhistorical ▸ adjective transcending historical boundaries; eternal: *femininity may not be a transhistorical absolute.*

transhumance /tranz'hjuːməns, trɑːnz-, -ns-/ ▸ noun [mass noun] the action or practice of moving livestock from one grazing ground to another in a seasonal cycle, typically to lowlands in winter and highlands in summer.
– DERIVATIVES **transhumant** adjective.
– ORIGIN early 20th cent.: from French, from the verb *transhumer*, based on Latin *trans-* 'across' + *humus* 'ground'.

transhumanism ▸ noun [mass noun] the belief or theory that the human race can evolve beyond its current physical and mental limitations, especially by means of science and technology.
– DERIVATIVES **transhumanist** adjective & noun.

transience /'tranzɪəns/ (also **transiency**) ▸ noun [mass noun] the state or fact of lasting only for a short time; transitoriness: *the transience of life and happiness.*

transient /'tranzɪənt/ ▸ adjective lasting only for a short time; impermanent: *a transient cold spell.* ■ staying or working in a place for a short time only: *the transient nature of the labour force in catering.*
▸ noun **1** a person who is staying or working in a place for a short time only. **2** a momentary variation in current, voltage, or frequency.
– DERIVATIVES **transiently** adverb.
– ORIGIN late 16th cent.: from Latin *transient-* 'going across', from the verb *transire*, from *trans-* 'across' + *ire* 'go'.

transilluminate ▸ verb [with obj.] pass strong light through (an organ or part of the body) in order to detect disease or abnormality.
– DERIVATIVES **transillumination** noun.

transire /tran'zʌɪə, trɑː-, -s-, -ʌɪri/ ▸ noun (in the UK) a customs document on which the cargo loaded on to a ship is listed, issued to prove that the goods listed on it have come from a home port rather than an overseas one.
– ORIGIN late 16th cent.: from Latin *transire* 'go across'.

transistor ▸ noun a semiconductor device with three connections, capable of amplification in addition to rectification. ■ (also **transistor radio**) a portable radio using circuits containing transistors rather than valves.
– ORIGIN 1940s: from TRANSCONDUCTANCE, on the pattern of words such as *varistor*.

transistorize (also **transistorise**) ▸ verb [with obj.] (usu. as adj. **transistorized**) design or make with transistors rather than valves: *a transistorized tape recorder.*

transit ▸ noun [mass noun] **1** the carrying of people or things from one place to another: *a painting was damaged **in transit**.* ■ N. Amer. the conveyance of passengers on public transport. **2** the action of passing through or across a place: *Guatemala is to have freedom of transit across Belize.* ■ Astronomy the passage of an inferior planet across the face of the sun, or of a moon or its shadow across the face of a planet. ■ Astronomy the apparent passage of a celestial body across the meridian of a place. ■ Astrology the passage of a celestial body through a specified sign, house, or area of a chart.
▸ verb (**transits, transiting, transited**) [with obj.] pass across or through (an area): *the new large ships will be too big to transit the Panama Canal.* ■ Astronomy (of a planet or other celestial body) pass across (the face of another body, or a meridian). ■ Astrology (of a celestial body) pass across (a specified sign, house, or area of a chart).
– ORIGIN late Middle English (denoting passage from one place to another): from Latin *transitus*, from *transire* 'go across'.

transit camp ▸ noun a camp for the temporary accommodation of people, e.g. refugees or soldiers, who are travelling through a country or region.

transit circle (also **transit instrument**) ▸ noun another term for MERIDIAN CIRCLE.

transition ▸ noun [mass noun] the process or a period of changing from one state or condition to another: *students **in transition** from one programme to another* | [count noun] *a transition to multiparty democracy.* ■ [count noun] Music a momentary modulation from one key to another. ■ [count noun] Physics a change of an atom, nucleus, electron, etc. from one quantum state to another, with emission or absorption of radiation.
▸ verb chiefly N. Amer. undergo or cause to undergo a process or period of transition: [no obj.] *he transitioned into filmmaking easily.*
– DERIVATIVES **transitionary** adjective.
– ORIGIN mid 16th cent.: from French, or from Latin *transitio(n-)*, from *transire* 'go across'.

transitional ▸ adjective relating to or characteristic of a process or period of transition: *a transitional government was appointed.* ■ (**Transitional**) Architecture of or denoting the last stage of Romanesque style, in which Gothic elements begin to appear.
– DERIVATIVES **transitionally** adverb.

transition curve ▸ noun a curve of constantly changing radius, used to connect a circular arc to a straight line or to an arc of different curvature.

transition metal (also **transition element**) ▸ noun Chemistry any of the set of metallic elements occupying a central block (Groups IVB–VIII, IB, and IIB, or 4–12) in the periodic table, e.g. iron, manganese, chromium, and copper. Chemically they show variable valency and a strong tendency to form coordination compounds, and many of their compounds are coloured.

transition point ▸ noun Chemistry the set of conditions of temperature and pressure at which different phases of the same substance can be in equilibrium.

transition series ▸ noun Chemistry the set of transition metals.

transition temperature ▸ noun Physics the temperature at which a substance acquires or loses a distinctive property, in particular superconductivity.

transitive /'transɪtɪv, 'trɑːns-, -nz-/ ▸ adjective **1** Grammar (of a verb or a sense or use of a verb) able to take a direct object (expressed or implied), e.g. *saw* in *he saw the donkey*. The opposite of INTRANSITIVE. **2** Logic & Mathematics (of a relation) such that, if it applies between successive members of a sequence, it must also apply between any two members taken in order. For instance, if A is larger than B, and B is larger than C, then A is larger than C.
– DERIVATIVES **transitively** adverb, **transitiveness** noun, **transitivity** noun.
– ORIGIN mid 16th cent. (in the sense 'transitory'): from late Latin *transitivus*, from *transit-* 'gone across' (see TRANSIT).

transit lounge ▸ noun a lounge at an airport for passengers waiting between flights.

transitory /'transɪt(ə)ri, 'trɑːns-, -nz-/ ▸ adjective not permanent: *transitory periods of medieval greatness.*
– DERIVATIVES **transitorily** adverb, **transitoriness** noun.
– ORIGIN late Middle English: from Old French *transitoire*, from Christian Latin *transitorius*, from *transit-* 'gone across' (see TRANSIT).

transit visa ▸ noun a visa allowing its holder to pass through a country only, not to stay there.

Transjordan former name (until 1949) of the region east of the River Jordan now forming the main part of the kingdom of Jordan.
– DERIVATIVES **Transjordanian** adjective.

Transkei /tran'skʌɪ/ a former homeland established in South Africa for the Xhosa people, now part of the province of Eastern Cape.

transketolase /tranz'kiːtəleɪz, trɑːnz, -ns-/ ▸ noun [mass noun] Biochemistry an enzyme which catalyses the transfer of an alcohol group between sugar molecules.

translate /trans'leɪt, trɑːns-, -nz-/ ▸ verb [with obj.] **1** express the sense of (words or text) in another language: *several of his books were **translated into** English.* ■ [no obj.] be expressed or be capable of being expressed in another language: *shiatsu literally translates as 'finger pressure'.* **2** (**translate something into/translate into**) convert something or be converted into (another form or medium): [with obj.] *few of Shakespeare's other works have been translated into ballets* | [no obj.] *twenty years of critical success which rarely translated into public acclaim.* ■ [with obj.] Biology convert (a sequence of nucleotides in messenger RNA) to an amino-acid sequence in a protein or polypeptide during synthesis. **3** move from one place or condition to another: *she had been translated from familiar surroundings to a foreign court.* ■ formal move (a bishop or, in Scotland, a minister) to another see or pastoral charge. ■ formal remove (a saint's relics) to another place. ■ literary convey (someone who is not dead) to heaven. **4** Physics cause (a body) to move so that all its parts travel in the same direction, without rotation or change of shape. ■ Mathematics transform (a geometrical figure) in an analogous way.
– DERIVATIVES **translatability** noun, **translatable** adjective.
– ORIGIN Middle English: from Latin *translat-* 'carried across', past participle of *transferre* (see TRANSFER).

translation ▸ noun [mass noun] **1** the process of translating words or text from one language into another: *the translation of the Bible into English.* ■ [count noun] a written or spoken rendering of the meaning of a word or text in another language: *a Spanish translation of Calvin's great work.* **2** the conversion of something from one form or medium into another: *the translation of research findings into clinical practice.* ■ Biology the process by which a sequence of nucleotide triplets in a messenger RNA molecule gives rise to a specific sequence of amino acids during synthesis of a polypeptide or protein. **3** formal or technical the process of moving something from one place to another: *the translation of the relics of St Thomas of Canterbury.* ■ Mathematics movement of a body from one point of space to another such that every point of the body moves in the same

T

direction and over the same distance, without any rotation, reflection, or change in size.
– DERIVATIVES **translational** adjective, **translationally** adverb.
– ORIGIN Middle English: from Old French, or from Latin *translatio(n-)*, from *translat-* 'carried across' (see TRANSLATE).

translation table ▶ noun Computing a table of stored information used in translating one code into another.

translator ▶ noun **1** a person who translates from one language into another, especially as a profession. ■ a computer program that translates from one programming language into another.
2 a television relay transmitter.

transliterate ▶ verb [with obj.] write or print (a letter or word) using the closest corresponding letters of a different alphabet or language: *names from one language are often transliterated into another.*
– DERIVATIVES **transliteration** noun, **transliterator** noun.
– ORIGIN mid 19th cent.: from TRANS- 'across' + Latin *littera* 'letter' + -ATE³.

translocate ▶ verb [with obj.] chiefly technical move from one place to another: *translocating rhinos to other reserves* | [no obj.] *the cell bodies translocate into the other side of the brain.* ■ [with obj.] Physiology & Biochemistry transport (a dissolved substance) within an organism, especially in the phloem of a plant, or actively across a cell membrane. ■ [with obj.] Genetics move (a portion of a chromosome) to a new position on the same or another chromosome.
– DERIVATIVES **translocation** noun.

translucent /trans'luːs(ə)nt, trɑːns-, -nz-/ ▶ adjective (of a substance) allowing light, but not detailed shapes, to pass through; semi-transparent: *her beautiful translucent skin.*
– DERIVATIVES **translucence** noun, **translucency** noun, **translucently** adverb.
– ORIGIN late 16th cent. (in the Latin sense): from Latin *translucent-* 'shining through', from the verb *translucere*, from *trans-* 'through' + *lucere* 'to shine'.

translunar /tranz'luːnə, trɑːnz-, -ns-/ ▶ adjective relating to or denoting the trajectory of a spacecraft travelling between the earth and the moon.

transmarine /ˌtranzmə'riːn, ˌtrɑːnz-, -ns-/ ▶ adjective dated situated or originating on the other side of the sea: *an alien, or a transmarine stranger.* ■ of or involving crossing the sea: *some birds make long transmarine migrations.*
– ORIGIN late 16th cent.: from Latin *transmarinus*, from *trans-* 'across' + *marinus* 'marine, of the sea'.

transmembrane /ˌtranz'mɛmbreɪn, trɑːnz-, -ns-/ ▶ adjective Biology existing or occurring across a cell membrane: *transmembrane conductance.*

transmigrant ▶ noun a person passing through a country or region in the course of emigrating to another region.
– ORIGIN early 17th cent.: from Latin *transmigrant-* 'migrating across', from the verb *transmigrare* (see TRANSMIGRATE).

transmigrate ▶ verb [no obj.] **1** (of the soul) pass into a different body after death.
2 rare migrate.
– DERIVATIVES **transmigration** noun, **transmigratory** adjective.
– ORIGIN late Middle English (as an adjective in the sense 'transferred'): from Latin *transmigrat-* 'removed from one place to another', from the verb *transmigrare* (see TRANS-, MIGRATE).

transmission ▶ noun **1** [mass noun] the action or process of transmitting something or the state of being transmitted: *the transmission of the HIV virus.* ■ [count noun] a programme or signal that is broadcast or sent out: *television transmissions.*
2 the mechanism by which power is transmitted from an engine to the axle in a motor vehicle.
– ORIGIN early 17th cent.: from Latin *transmissio(n-)* (see TRANS-, MISSION).

transmission electron microscope ▶ noun a form of electron microscope in which an image is derived from electrons which have passed through the specimen, in particular one in which the whole image is formed at once rather than by scanning.

transmission line ▶ noun a conductor or conductors designed to carry electricity or an electrical signal over large distances with minimum losses and distortion.

transmissivity /ˌtranzmɪ'sɪvɪti, ˌtrɑːnz-, -ns-/ ▶ noun (pl. **transmissivities**) the degree to which a medium allows something, in particular electromagnetic radiation, to pass through it.

transmit ▶ verb (**transmits, transmitting, transmitted**) [with obj.] **1** cause (something) to pass on from one person or place to another: *knowledge is transmitted from teacher to pupil* | (as adj. **transmitted**) *sexually transmitted diseases.* ■ communicate or be a medium for (an idea or emotion): *the theatrical gift of being able to transmit emotion.*
2 broadcast or send out (an electrical signal or a radio or television programme): *the programme was transmitted on 7 October.*
3 allow (heat, light, sound, electricity, or other energy) to pass through a medium: *the three bones transmit sound waves to the inner ear.*
– DERIVATIVES **transmissibility** noun (chiefly Medicine), **transmissible** adjective (chiefly Medicine), **transmissive** adjective, **transmittable** adjective, **transmittal** noun.
– ORIGIN late Middle English: from Latin *transmittere*, from *trans-* 'across' + *mittere* 'send'.

transmittance ▶ noun Physics the ratio of the light energy falling on a body to that transmitted through it.

transmitter ▶ noun a set of equipment used to generate and transmit electromagnetic waves carrying messages or signals, especially those of radio or television. ■ a person or thing that transmits something: *reggae has established itself as the principal transmitter of the Jamaican language.* ■ short for NEUROTRANSMITTER.

transmogrify /tranz'mɒgrɪfʌɪ, trɑːnz-, -ns-/ ▶ verb (**transmogrifies, transmogrifying, transmogrified**) [with obj.] chiefly humorous transform in a surprising or magical manner: *his home was **transmogrified into** a hippy crash pad.*
– DERIVATIVES **transmogrification** noun.
– ORIGIN mid 17th cent.: of unknown origin.

transmontane /tranz'mɒnteɪn, trɑːnz-, -mɒn'teɪn, -ns-/ ▶ adjective another term for TRAMONTANE.

transmural /tranz'mjʊər(ə)l, trɑːnz-, -ns-/ ▶ adjective Medicine existing or occurring across the entire wall of an organ or blood vessel.

transmutation /tranzmjuː'teɪʃ(ə)n, trɑːnz-, -ns-/ ▶ noun [mass noun] the action of changing or the state of being changed into another form: *the transmutation of the political economy of the post-war years was complete* | [count noun] *grotesque transmutations.* ■ Physics the changing of one element into another by radioactive decay, nuclear bombardment, or similar processes. ■ Biology, chiefly historical the conversion or transformation of one species into another. ■ the supposed alchemical process of changing base metals into gold.
– DERIVATIVES **transmutational** adjective.

transmute /tranz'mjuːt, trɑːnz-, -ns-/ ▶ verb change in form, nature, or substance: [with obj.] *the raw material of his experience was **transmuted into** stories* | [no obj.] *the discovery that elements can transmute by radioactivity.* ■ [with obj.] subject (base metals) to alchemical transmutation: *the quest to **transmute** lead **into** gold.*
– DERIVATIVES **transmutability** noun, **transmutable** adjective, **transmutative** adjective, **transmuter** noun.
– ORIGIN late Middle English: from Latin *transmutare*, from *trans-* 'across' + *mutare* 'to change'.

transnational ▶ adjective extending or operating across national boundaries: *transnational advertising agencies.*
▶ noun a multinational company.
– DERIVATIVES **transnationalism** noun, **transnationally** adverb.

transoceanic ▶ adjective crossing an ocean: *the transoceanic cable system.* ■ coming from or situated beyond an ocean: *there is a higher rate for letters intended for transoceanic countries.*

transom /'trans(ə)m/ ▶ noun the flat surface forming the stern of a boat. ■ a horizontal beam reinforcing the stern of a boat. ■ a strengthening crossbar, in particular one set above a window or door. Compare with MULLION. ■ US term for TRANSOM WINDOW.
– PHRASES **over the transom** N. Amer. informal offered or sent without prior agreement; unsolicited: *the editors receive about ten manuscripts a week over the transom.*
– DERIVATIVES **transomed** adjective.
– ORIGIN late Middle English (earlier as *traversayn*): from Old French *traversin*, from the verb *traverser* 'to cross' (see TRAVERSE).

transom window ▶ noun a window set above the transom of a door or larger window; a fanlight.

transonic /tran'sɒnɪk, trɑːn-/ (also **trans-sonic**) ▶ adjective denoting or relating to speeds close to that of sound.
– ORIGIN 1940s: from TRANS- 'through, across' + SONIC, on the pattern of words such as *supersonic.*

trans-Pacific ▶ adjective crossing the Pacific: *trans-Pacific routes to India.* ■ relating to an area beyond the Pacific: *a journal influenced by trans-Pacific pomposity.*

transparence ▶ noun rare term for TRANSPARENCY (sense 1).

transparency ▶ noun (pl. **transparencies**) **1** [mass noun] the condition of being transparent: *the transparency of ice.*
2 a positive transparent photograph printed on transparent plastic or glass, able to be viewed using a slide projector.
– ORIGIN late 16th cent. (as a general term denoting a transparent object): from medieval Latin *transparentia*, from *transparent-* 'shining through' (see TRANSPARENT).

transparent /tran'spar(ə)nt, trɑːn-, -'spɛː-/ ▶ adjective **1** (of a material or article) allowing light to pass through so that objects behind can be distinctly seen: *transparent blue water* | *fine transparent fabrics.*
2 easy to perceive or detect: *the residents will see through any transparent attempt to buy their votes* | *the meaning of the poem is by no means transparent.* ■ having thoughts or feelings that are easily perceived; open: *you'd be no good at poker—you're too transparent.* ■ (of an organization or its activities) open to public scrutiny: *if you had transparent government procurement, corruption would go away.*
3 Computing (of a process or interface) functioning without the user being aware of its presence.
4 Physics transmitting heat or other radiation without distortion.
– DERIVATIVES **transparently** adverb [as submodifier] *a transparently feeble argument.*
– ORIGIN late Middle English: from Old French, from medieval Latin *transparent-* 'shining through', from Latin *transparere*, from *trans-* 'through' + *parere* 'appear'.

transpersonal ▶ adjective denoting or relating to states or areas of consciousness beyond the limits of personal identity: *the book covers shamanism and transpersonal psychology.*

transpicuous /tran'spɪkjʊəs, trɑːn-/ ▶ adjective rare transparent. ■ easily understood, lucid.
– ORIGIN mid 17th cent.: from modern Latin *transpicuus* (from Latin *transpicere* 'look through') + -OUS.

transpierce ▶ verb [with obj.] literary pierce through (someone or something).

transpiration stream ▶ noun Botany the flow of water through a plant, from the roots to the leaves, via the xylem vessels.

transpire ▶ verb [no obj.] **1** [with clause] (usu. **it transpires**) (of a secret or something unknown) come to be known; be revealed: ***it transpired that** millions of dollars of debt had been hidden in a complex web of transactions.* ■ prove to be the case: *as it transpired, he was right.* ■ occur; happen: *I'm going to find out exactly what transpired.*
2 Botany (of a plant or leaf) give off water vapour through the stomata.
– DERIVATIVES **transpiration** noun (sense 2).
– ORIGIN late Middle English (in the sense 'emit as vapour through the surface'): from French *transpirer* or medieval Latin *transpirare*, from Latin *trans-* 'through' + *spirare* 'breathe'. Sense 1 (mid 18th cent.) is a figurative use comparable with 'leak out'.

USAGE The standard general sense of **transpire** is 'come to be known' (as in ***it transpired that** millions of dollars of debt had been hidden in a complex web of transactions*). From this, a looser sense has developed, meaning 'happen or occur' (*I'm going to find out exactly what **transpired***). This looser sense, first recorded in US English towards the end of the 18th century, is criticized for being jargon, an unnecessarily long word used where **occur** and **happen** would do just as well. The newer sense is very common, however, accounting for around half of the citations for **transpire** in the Oxford English Corpus.

transplant ▶ verb /trans'plɑːnt, trɑːns-, -nz-/ [with obj.] **1** move or transfer (someone or something) to another place or situation: *it was proposed to transplant the club to the vacant site* | (as adj. **transplanted**) *she's a transplanted New Yorker.* ■ replant (a plant) in another place.

2 take (living tissue or an organ) and implant it in another part of the body or in another body.
▶ **noun** /ˈtranspla:nt, ˈtra:ns-, -nz-/ **1** an operation in which an organ or tissue is transplanted: *a heart transplant* | [mass noun] *kidneys available for transplant.* ■ an organ or tissue which is transplanted.
2 a person or thing that has been moved to a new place or situation.
– DERIVATIVES **transplantable** /-ˈpla:ntəb(ə)l/ **adjective**, **transplantation** /-ˈteɪʃ(ə)n/ **noun**, **transplanter** /-ˈpla:ntə/ **noun**.
– ORIGIN late Middle English (as a verb describing the repositioning of a plant): from late Latin *transplantare*, from Latin *trans-* 'across' + *plantare* 'to plant'. The noun, first in sense 2, dates from the mid 18th cent.

transponder /tranˈspɒndə, tra:n-/ ▶ **noun** a device for receiving a radio signal and automatically transmitting a different signal.
– ORIGIN 1940s: blend of **TRANSMIT** and **RESPOND**, + **-ER**[1].

transpontine /transˈpɒntʌɪn, tra:ns-, -nz-/ ▶ **adjective** dated on or from the other side of an ocean, in particular the Atlantic as viewed from Britain; American: *she approached the task with typical transpontine enthusiasm.*
– ORIGIN late 19th cent.: from **TRANS-** 'across' + Latin *pontus* 'sea' + **-INE**[1].

transport ▶ **verb** [with obj.] **1** take or carry (people or goods) from one place to another by means of a vehicle, aircraft, or ship: *the bulk of freight traffic was transported by lorry.* ■ historical send (a convict) to a penal colony. ■ cause (someone) to feel that they are in another place or time: *the book transported her to new worlds.*
2 overwhelm (someone) with a strong emotion, especially joy: *she was* ***transported with*** *pleasure.*
▶ **noun 1** [mass noun] a system or means of conveying people or goods from place to place: *many possess their own forms of transport* | *air transport.* ■ the action of transporting something or the state of being transported: *the transport of crude oil.* ■ [count noun] a large vehicle, ship, or aircraft used to carry troops or stores. ■ [count noun] historical a convict who was transported to a penal colony.
2 (usu. **transports**) an overwhelmingly strong emotion: *art can send people into* ***transports of*** *delight.*
– ORIGIN late Middle English: from Old French *transporter* or Latin *transportare*, from *trans-* 'across' + *portare* 'carry'.

transportable ▶ **adjective 1** able to be carried or moved: *the first transportable phones.*
2 historical (of an offender or an offence) punishable by transportation.
– DERIVATIVES **transportability** **noun**.

transportation ▶ **noun** [mass noun] **1** the action of transporting someone or something or the process of being transported: *the era of global mass transportation.* ■ chiefly N. Amer. a system or means of transporting people or goods: *transportation on the site includes a monorail.*
2 historical the action or practice of transporting convicts to a penal colony.

transport cafe ▶ **noun** Brit. a roadside cafe for drivers of haulage vehicles.

transporter ▶ **noun** a person or thing that transports something, in particular: ■ a large vehicle used to carry heavy objects, e.g. cars. ■ (in science fiction) a device that conveys people or things instantaneously from one place to another.

transpose ▶ **verb** [with obj.] **1** cause (two or more things) to exchange places: *the situation might have been the same if the parties in opposition and government had been transposed.*
2 transfer to a different place or context: *an evacuation order transposed the school from Kent to Shropshire* | *the themes are transposed from the sphere of love to that of work.* ■ write or play (music) in a different key from the original: *the basses are* ***transposed down*** *an octave.* ■ Mathematics transfer (a term), with its sign changed, to the other side of an equation. ■ translate into another language: *a sequence of French tales transposed into English.*
▶ **noun** Mathematics a matrix obtained from a given matrix by interchanging each row and the corresponding column.
– DERIVATIVES **transposable** **adjective**, **transposer** **noun**.
– ORIGIN late Middle English (also in the sense 'transform, convert'): from Old French *transposer*, from *trans-* 'across' + *poser* 'to place'.

transposing instrument ▶ **noun** an orchestral instrument for which parts are written in a different key from that in which they sound, e.g. the clarinet and many brass instruments.

transposition ▶ **noun** [mass noun] the action of transposing something: *transposition of word order* | [count noun] *a transposition of an old story into a contemporary context.* ■ [count noun] a thing that has been produced by transposing something: *many acclaimed novels and plays have been little more than modern transpositions of classic myth.*
– DERIVATIVES **transpositional** **adjective**.
– ORIGIN mid 16th cent.: from late Latin *transpositio(n-)* (see **TRANS-**, **POSITION**).

transposon /transˈpəʊzɒn, tra:ns-, -nz-/ ▶ **noun** Genetics a chromosomal segment that can undergo transposition, especially a segment of bacterial DNA that can be translocated as a whole between chromosomal, phage, and plasmid DNA in the absence of a complementary sequence in the host DNA. Also called **JUMPING GENE**.
– ORIGIN 1970s: from **TRANSPOSITION** + **-ON**.

transputer /transˈpju:tə, tra:ns-, -nz-/ ▶ **noun** a microprocessor with integral memory designed for parallel processing.
– ORIGIN 1970s: blend of **TRANSISTOR** and **COMPUTER**.

transracial ▶ **adjective** across or crossing racial boundaries.

transsexual /transˈsɛkʃʊəl, tra:ns-, -nz-, -sjʊəl/ (also **transexual**) ▶ **noun** a person who emotionally and psychologically feels that they belong to the opposite sex. ■ a person who has undergone treatment in order to acquire the physical characteristics of the opposite sex.
▶ **adjective** relating to a transsexual person.
– DERIVATIVES **transsexualism** **noun**, **transsexuality** **noun**.

trans-ship (also **tranship**) ▶ **verb** (**trans-ships**, **trans-shipping**, **trans-shipped**) [with obj.] transfer (cargo) from one ship or other form of transport to another.
– DERIVATIVES **trans-shipment** **noun**.

Trans-Siberian Railway a railway running from Moscow east around Lake Baikal to Vladivostok on the Sea of Japan, a distance of 9,311 km (5,786 miles). Begun in 1891 and virtually completed by 1904, it opened up Siberia and advanced Russian interest in eastern Asia.

trans-sonic ▶ **adjective** variant spelling of **TRANSONIC**.

trans-synaptic ▶ **adjective** Physiology occurring or existing across a nerve synapse.

transubstantiate /ˌtransəbˈstanʃɪeɪt, ˌtra:n-, -sɪ-/ ▶ **verb** [with obj.] Christian Theology convert (the substance of the Eucharistic elements) into the body and blood of Christ. ■ literary change the form or substance of (something) into something different.
– ORIGIN late Middle English: from medieval Latin *transubstantiat-* 'changed in substance', from the verb *transubstantiare*, from Latin *trans-* 'across' + *substantia* 'substance'.

transubstantiation ▶ **noun** [mass noun] Christian Theology the conversion of the substance of the Eucharistic elements into the body and blood of Christ at consecration, only the appearances of bread and wine still remaining.

transude /tranˈsju:d, tra:n-/ ▶ **verb** archaic (with reference to a fluid) discharge or be discharged gradually through pores in a membrane, especially within the body.
– DERIVATIVES **transudate** **noun**, **transudation** **noun**.
– ORIGIN mid 17th cent.: from French *transsuder* (in Old French *tressuer*), from Latin *trans-* 'across' + Latin *sudare* 'to sweat'.

transuranic /ˌtransjʊˈranɪk, ˌtra:ns-, -nz-/ ▶ **adjective** Chemistry (of an element) having a higher atomic number than uranium (92).

transurethral /ˌtranzjʊˈri:θrəl, ˌtra:nz-/ ▶ **adjective** (of a medical procedure) performed via the urethra.

Transvaal /tranzˈva:l, tra:nz-, -ns-/ (also **the Transvaal**) a former province in north-eastern South Africa, lying north of the Vaal River.

Home to Bantu-speaking peoples, it was first settled by Boers c.1840 after the Great Trek, becoming the core of the Boer republic in 1857. Resistance to Britain's annexation of Transvaal in 1877 led to the Boer Wars, after which the Transvaal became a Crown Colony. It became a founding province of the Union of South Africa in 1910. In 1994 it was divided into the provinces of Northern Province (now called Limpopo), Mpumalanga, Gauteng, and the eastern part of North West.

Transvaal daisy ▶ **noun** a South African gerbera, grown for its large brightly coloured daisy-like flowers. ● *Gerbera jamesonii*, family Compositae.

transvalue ▶ **verb** (**transvalues**, **transvaluing**, **transvalued**) [with obj.] represent (something, typically an idea, custom, or quality) in a different way, causing it to be revalued: *survival strategies are aesthetically* ***transvalued into*** *weapons of attack.*
– DERIVATIVES **transvaluation** **noun**.

transversal /tranzˈvə:s(ə)l, tra:nz-, -ns-/ Geometry ▶ **adjective** (of a line) cutting a system of lines.
▶ **noun** a transversal line.
– DERIVATIVES **transversality** **noun**, **transversally** **adverb**.
– ORIGIN late Middle English (as a synonym of **TRANSVERSE**): from medieval Latin *transversalis*, from Latin *transversus* 'lying across'.

transverse /tranzˈvə:s, tra:nz-, -ns-/ ▶ **adjective** situated or extending across something: *a transverse beam supports the dashboard.*
– DERIVATIVES **transversely** **adverb**.
– ORIGIN late Middle English: from Latin *transversus* 'turned across', past participle of *transvertere*, from *trans-* 'across' + *vertere* 'to turn'.

transverse colon ▶ **noun** Anatomy the middle part of the large intestine, passing across the abdomen from right to left below the stomach.

transverse flute ▶ **noun** a flute which is held horizontally when played.

transverse magnet ▶ **noun** a magnet with poles at the sides and not the ends.

transverse wave ▶ **noun** Physics a wave in which the medium vibrates at right angles to the direction of its propagation.

transvestite ▶ **noun** a person, typically a man, who derives pleasure from dressing in clothes appropriate to the opposite sex.
– DERIVATIVES **transvestism** **noun**, **transvestitism** **noun**.
– ORIGIN 1920s: from German *Transvestit*, from Latin *trans-* 'across' + *vestire* 'clothe'.

Transylvania /ˌtransɪlˈveɪnɪə/ a large tableland region of NW Romania, separated from the rest of the country by the Carpathian Mountains and the Transylvanian Alps. Part of Hungary until it became a principality of the Ottoman Empire in the 16th century, it was returned to Hungary at the end of the 17th century and was incorporated into Romania in 1918.
– DERIVATIVES **Transylvanian** **adjective**.
– ORIGIN based on Latin *trans* 'across, beyond' + *silva* 'forest'.

trap[1] ▶ **noun 1** a device or enclosure designed to catch and retain animals, typically by allowing entry but not exit or by catching hold of a part of the body. ■ the compartment from which a greyhound is released at the start of a race.
2 a situation in which people lie in wait to make a surprise attack: *police deliberately herded 400 demonstrators into a trap and then attacked and arrested them.* ■ a trick by which someone is misled into acting contrary to their interests or intentions: *by keeping quiet I was* ***walking into a trap.*** ■ an unpleasant situation from which it is hard to escape: *they* ***fell into the trap of*** *relying too little on equity finance.*
3 [with modifier] a container or device used to collect something, or a place where something collects: *one fuel filter and water trap are sufficient on the fuel system.* ■ a curve in the waste pipe from a bath, basin, or toilet that is always full of liquid and prevents gases from coming up the pipe into the building. ■ a bunker or other hollow on a golf course.
4 a light, two-wheeled carriage pulled by a horse or pony.
5 a device for hurling an object such as a clay pigeon into the air to be shot at. ■ historical (in the game of trapball) the shoe-shaped device that is hit with a bat to send the ball into the air.
6 short for **TRAPDOOR**.
7 informal a person's mouth (used in expressions to do with speaking): *keep your trap shut!*
8 (**traps**) informal (among jazz musicians) drums or percussion instruments.
▶ **verb** (**traps**, **trapping**, **trapped**) [with obj.] **1** catch (an animal) in a trap. ■ prevent (someone) from escaping from a place: *twenty workers were trapped by flames.* ■ have (something, typically a part of the body) held tightly by something so that it cannot

T

be freed: *he had trapped his finger in a spring-loaded hinge.* ■ Soccer bring (the ball) under control with the foot or other part of the body on receiving it.
2 trick or deceive (someone) into doing something contrary to their interests or intentions: *I hoped to trap him into an admission.*
– DERIVATIVES **trap-like** adjective.
– ORIGIN Old English *træppe* (in *coltetræppe* 'Christ's thorn'); related to Middle Dutch *trappe* and medieval Latin *trappa*, of uncertain origin. The verb dates from late Middle English.

trap² ▸ verb (**traps, trapping, trapped**) [with obj.] (usu. as adj. **trapped**) archaic put trappings on (a horse).
– ORIGIN late Middle English: from the obsolete noun *trap* 'trappings', from Old French *drap* 'drape'.

trap³ (also **traprock**) ▸ noun [mass noun] N. Amer. basalt or a similar dark, fine-grained igneous rock.
– ORIGIN late 18th cent.: from Swedish *trapp*, from *trappa* 'stair' (because of the often stair-like appearance of its outcroppings).

trapball ▸ noun [mass noun] historical a game in which the player uses a bat to hit a trap (see TRAP¹ (sense 5 of the noun)) to send a ball into the air and then hits the ball itself.

trap crop ▸ noun a crop planted to attract insect pests from another crop, especially one in which the pests fail to survive or reproduce.

trapdoor ▸ noun a hinged or removable panel in a floor, ceiling, or roof. ■ a feature or defect of a computer system which allows surreptitious unauthorized access to data.

trapdoor spider ▸ noun a spider which lives in a burrow with a hinged cover like a trapdoor. ● Family Ctenizidae, suborder Mygalomorphae. ■ Austral. a funnel-web spider.

trapes ▸ verb & noun archaic spelling of TRAIPSE.

trapeze ▸ noun **1** (also **flying trapeze**) a horizontal bar hanging by two ropes and free to swing, used by acrobats in a circus.
2 Sailing a harness attached by a cable to a dinghy's mast, enabling a sailor to balance the boat by leaning backwards far out over the windward side.
– ORIGIN mid 19th cent.: from French *trapèze*, from late Latin *trapezium* (see TRAPEZIUM).

Trapezium /trə'piːzɪəm/ (**the Trapezium**) Astronomy the multiple star Theta Orionis, which lies within the Great Nebula of Orion and illuminates it. Four stars are visible in a small telescope and two more with a larger telescope.

trapezium /trə'piːzɪəm/ ▸ noun (pl. **trapezia** /-zɪə/ or **trapeziums**) **1** Geometry, Brit. a quadrilateral with one pair of sides parallel. ■ N. Amer. a quadrilateral with no sides parallel. Compare with TRAPEZOID.
2 (also **os trapezium**) Anatomy a carpal bone below the base of the thumb.
– ORIGIN late 16th cent.: via late Latin from Greek *trapezion*, from *trapeza* 'table'. The term has been used in anatomy since the mid 19th cent.

trapezium rule ▸ noun Mathematics a method of estimating the area under a curve by dividing it into a series of strips, each of which is approximately a trapezium.

trapezius /trə'piːzɪəs/ (also **trapezius muscle**) ▸ noun (pl. **trapezii** /-zɪʌɪ/) Anatomy either of a pair of large triangular muscles extending over the back of the neck and shoulders and moving the head and shoulder blade.
– ORIGIN early 18th cent.: from modern Latin, from Greek *trapezion* 'trapezium' (because of the shape formed by the muscles).

trapezohedron /ˌtrapɪzə(ʊ)'hiːdrən, -'hɛd-/ ▸ noun (pl. **trapezohedra** /-drə/ or **trapezohedrons**) a solid figure whose faces are trapeziums or trapezoids.
– DERIVATIVES **trapezohedral** adjective.
– ORIGIN early 19th cent.: from TRAPEZIUM + -HEDRON, on the pattern of words such as *polyhedron*.

trapezoid /'trapɪzɔɪd, trə'piːzɔɪd/ ▸ noun **1** Geometry, Brit. a quadrilateral with no sides parallel. ■ N. Amer. a quadrilateral with one pair of sides parallel. Compare with TRAPEZIUM.
2 (also **trapezoid bone**) Anatomy a small carpal bone in the base of the hand, articulating with the metacarpal of the index finger.
– DERIVATIVES **trapezoidal** adjective.
– ORIGIN early 18th cent.: from modern Latin *trapezoides*, from late Greek *trapezoeidēs*, from *trapeza* 'table' (see TRAPEZIUM).

trapline ▸ noun N. Amer. a series of game traps.

trapper ▸ noun a person who traps wild animals, especially for their fur.

trappings ▸ plural noun **1** the outward signs, features, or objects associated with a particular situation, role, or job: *I had the trappings of success.*
2 a horse's ornamental harness.
– ORIGIN late Middle English: derivative of TRAP².

Trappist ▸ adjective relating to or denoting a branch of the Cistercian order of monks founded in 1664 and noted for an austere rule that includes remaining silent for much of the time.
▸ noun a member of the Trappist order.
– ORIGIN early 19th cent.: from French *trappiste*, from *La Trappe* in Normandy.

traprock ▸ noun see TRAP³.

traps ▸ plural noun informal personal belongings; baggage: *I was ready to pack my traps and leave.*
– ORIGIN early 19th cent.: perhaps a contraction of TRAPPINGS.

trap shooting ▸ noun [mass noun] the sport of shooting at clay pigeons released from a spring trap.
– DERIVATIVES **trap shooter** noun.

trash ▸ noun [mass noun] **1** chiefly N. Amer. waste material; refuse. ■ cultural items, ideas, or objects of poor quality: *if they read at all, they read trash.*
2 N. Amer. a person or people regarded as being of very low social standing: *clubs patronized by rock trash.*
3 (also **cane trash**) W. Indian the leaves, tops, and crushed stems of sugar cane, used as fuel.
▸ verb [with obj.] **1** informal, chiefly N. Amer. damage or destroy: *my apartment's been totally trashed.* ■ Computing kill (a file or process) or wipe (a disk).
2 informal, chiefly N. Amer. criticize severely: *trade associations trashed the legislation as deficient.*
3 (as adj. **trashed**) informal intoxicated with alcohol or drugs: *there was booze, but nobody really got trashed.*
4 strip (sugar canes) of their outer leaves to ripen them faster.
– ORIGIN late Middle English: of unknown origin. The verb is first recorded (mid 18th cent.) in sense 4 of the verb; the other senses have arisen in the 20th cent.

trash can ▸ noun N. Amer. a dustbin.

trash talk US informal ▸ noun [mass noun] insulting or boastful speech intended to demoralize, intimidate, or humiliate someone, especially a sporting opponent.
▸ verb [no obj.] (**trash-talk**) use insulting or boastful speech for such a purpose.
– DERIVATIVES **trash talker** noun.

trashy ▸ adjective (**trashier, trashiest**) (especially of items of popular culture) of poor quality: *trashy novels and formulaic movies.*
– DERIVATIVES **trashily** adverb, **trashiness** noun.

Trás-os-Montes /ˌtraʒuːʃ'mɒnteʃ/ a mountainous region of NE Portugal, north of the Douro River.
– ORIGIN Portuguese, literally 'beyond the mountains'.

trass (also **tarras**) ▸ noun [mass noun] a light-coloured variety of volcanic ash resembling pozzolana, used in making water-resistant cement.
– ORIGIN late 18th cent.: from Dutch *tras*, German *Trass*, based on Latin *terra* 'earth'.

trattoria /ˌtratə'riːə/ ▸ noun an Italian restaurant.
– ORIGIN Italian.

trauma /'trɔːmə, 'traʊmə/ ▸ noun (pl. **traumas** or **traumata** /-mətə/) **1** a deeply distressing or disturbing experience: *they were reluctant to talk about the traumas of the revolution.* ■ [mass noun] emotional shock following a stressful event or a physical injury, which may lead to long-term neurosis.
2 [mass noun] Medicine physical injury.
– ORIGIN late 17th cent.: from Greek, literally 'wound'.

traumatic ▸ adjective **1** deeply disturbing or distressing: *she was going through a traumatic divorce.* ■ relating to or causing psychological trauma.
2 Medicine relating to or denoting physical injury.
– DERIVATIVES **traumatically** adverb.
– ORIGIN mid 19th cent.: via late Latin from Greek *traumatikos*, from *trauma* (see TRAUMA).

traumatism ▸ noun chiefly technical a traumatic effect or condition.

traumatize (also **traumatise**) ▸ verb [with obj.] subject to lasting shock as a result of a disturbing experience or physical injury: *the children were traumatized by separation from their families.* ■ Medicine cause physical injury to.
– DERIVATIVES **traumatization** noun.

travail /'traveɪl/ literary ▸ noun [mass noun] (also **travails**) painful or laborious effort: *advice for those who wish to save great sorrow and travail.* ■ labour pains: *a woman in travail.*
▸ verb [no obj.] engage in painful or laborious effort. ■ (of a woman) be in labour.
– ORIGIN Middle English: via Old French from medieval Latin *trepalium* 'instrument of torture', from Latin *tres* 'three' + *palus* 'stake'.

travel ▸ verb (**travels, travelling, travelled**; US **travels, traveling, traveled**) **1** [no obj., with adverbial] make a journey, typically of some length: *the vessel had been travelling from Libya to Ireland* | *we travelled thousands of miles.* ■ [with obj.] journey along (a road) or through (a region): *he travelled the world with the army.* ■ withstand a journey without illness or impairment: *he usually travels well, but he did get a bit upset on a very rough crossing.* ■ be successful away from the place of origin: *accordion music travels well.*
2 [no obj.] (of an object or radiation) move, typically in a constant or predictable way: *light travels faster than sound.* ■ (usu. as adj. **travelling**) go or be moved from place to place: *a travelling exhibition.* ■ informal (of a vehicle) move quickly.
▸ noun [mass noun] **1** the action of travelling: *my job involves a lot of travel.* ■ [count noun] (**travels**) journeys, especially abroad: *perhaps you'll write a book about your travels.* ■ [as modifier] (of a device) sufficiently compact for use on a journey: *a travel iron.*
2 the range, rate, or mode of motion of a part of a machine: *two proximity switches detect when the valve has reached the end of its travel.*
– ORIGIN Middle English: a variant of TRAVAIL, and originally in the same sense.

travel agency (also **travel bureau**) ▸ noun an agency that makes the necessary arrangements for travellers.
– DERIVATIVES **travel agent** noun.

travelator /'travəleɪtə/ (also **travolator**) ▸ noun a moving walkway, typically at an airport.
– ORIGIN 1950s: from TRAVEL, suggested by ESCALATOR.

travel card ▸ noun a prepaid card allowing unlimited travel on buses or trains for a specified period of time: *a one-day travel card.*

travelled /'trav(ə)ld/ ▸ adjective [with submodifier or in combination] **1** having travelled to many places: *he was widely travelled.*
2 used by people travelling: *a less well-travelled route.*

traveller (US also **traveler**) ▸ noun a person who is travelling or who often travels. ■ (usu. **Traveller**) Brit. a Gypsy or other nomadic person. ■ (also **New Age traveller**) Brit. a person who holds New Age values and leads an itinerant and unconventional lifestyle.

traveller's cheque ▸ noun a cheque for a fixed amount that may be cashed or used in payment abroad after endorsement by the holder's signature.

traveller's joy ▸ noun a tall scrambling clematis with small fragrant flowers and tufts of grey hairs around the seeds. Native to Eurasia and North Africa, it grows chiefly on calcareous soils. Also called OLD MAN'S BEARD. ● *Clematis vitalba*, family Ranunculaceae.

traveller's tale ▸ noun a story about the unusual characteristics or customs of a foreign country, regarded as typically exaggerated or untrue.

travelling ▸ adjective (of a device) sufficiently compact for use on a journey: *a travelling clock.*

travelling crane ▸ noun a crane able to move on rails, especially along an overhead support.

travelling people ▸ plural noun people whose lifestyle is nomadic, for example Gypsies (a term typically used by such people of themselves).

travelling salesman ▸ noun a representative of a firm who visits shops and other businesses to show samples and gain orders.

travelling salesman problem ▸ noun a mathematical problem in which one has to find which is the shortest route which passes through each of a set of points once and only once.

travelling scholarship ▸ noun a scholarship given to enable the holder to travel for the purpose of study or research.

travelling wave ▸ noun Physics a wave in which the positions of maximum and minimum amplitude travel through the medium.

travelogue ▸ noun a film, book, or illustrated lecture about the places visited by or experiences of a traveller.

– ORIGIN early 20th cent.: from **TRAVEL**, on the pattern of *monologue*.

travel-sick ▶ **adjective** suffering from nausea caused by the motion of a moving vehicle, boat, or aircraft.
– DERIVATIVES **travel-sickness noun.**

travers /ˈtravəs/ (also **traverse**) ▶ **noun** a movement performed in dressage, in which the horse moves parallel to the side of the arena, with its shoulders carried closer to the wall than its hindquarters and its body curved towards the centre.
– ORIGIN French, from *pied de travers* 'foot askew'.

traverse /ˈtravəs, trəˈvəːs/ ▶ **verb** [with obj.] **1** travel across or through: *he traversed the forest.* ■ extend across or through: *a moving catwalk that traversed a vast cavernous space.* ■ [no obj., with adverbial of direction] cross a rock face by means of a series of sideways movements from one practicable line of ascent or descent to another. ■ ski diagonally across (a slope), losing only a little height. ■ consider the whole extent of (a subject).
2 [with obj. and adverbial of direction] move back and forth or sideways: *a probe is traversed along the tunnel.* ■ turn (a large gun or other device on a pivot) to face a different direction.
3 Law deny (an allegation) in pleading. ■ archaic oppose or thwart (a plan).
▶ **noun 1** an act of traversing something. ■ a rock face where traversing is necessary: *a narrow traverse made lethal by snow and ice.* ■ a movement following a diagonal course made by a skier descending a slope. ■ a zigzag course taken by a ship because winds or currents prevent it from sailing directly towards its destination.
2 a part of a structure that extends or is fixed across something. ■ a gallery extending from side to side of a church or other building.
3 a mechanism enabling a large gun to be turned to face a different direction. ■ [mass noun] the sideways movement of a part in a machine.
4 a single line of survey, usually plotted from compass bearings and chained or paced distances between angular points. ■ an area surveyed in this way.
5 Military a pair of right-angled bends incorporated in a trench to avoid enfilading fire.
6 variant spelling of **TRAVERS**.
– DERIVATIVES **traversable** adjective, **traversal** noun.
– ORIGIN Middle English (in sense 3 of the verb): from Old French *traverser*, from late Latin *traversare*; the noun is from Old French *travers* (masculine), *traverse* (feminine), partly based on *traverser*.

traverser /trəˈvəːsə/ ▶ **noun** a sideways-moving platform for transferring a railway vehicle from one set of rails to another parallel set.

travertine /ˈtravətɪn/ ▶ **noun** [mass noun] white or light-coloured calcareous rock deposited from mineral springs, used in building.
– ORIGIN late 18th cent.: from Italian *travertino*, *tivertino*, from Latin *tiburtinus* 'of Tibur' (now Tivoli, a district near Rome).

travesty /ˈtravɪsti/ ▶ **noun** (pl. **travesties**) a false, absurd, or distorted representation of something: *the absurdly lenient sentence is **a travesty of** justice.*
▶ **verb** (**travesties, travestying, travestied**) [with obj.] represent in a false, absurd, or distorted way: *Michael has betrayed the family by travestying them in his plays.*
– ORIGIN mid 17th cent. (as an adjective in the sense 'dressed to appear ridiculous'): from French *travesti* 'disguised', past participle of *travestir*, from Italian *travestire*, from *trans-* 'across' + *vestire* 'clothe'.

travois /trəˈvɔɪ/ ▶ **noun** (pl. **same** /-ˈvɔɪz/) a type of sledge formerly used by North American Indians to carry goods, consisting of two joined poles pulled by a horse.
– ORIGIN mid 19th cent.: alteration of synonymous *travail*, from French.

travolator ▶ **noun** variant spelling of **TRAVELATOR**.

trawl ▶ **verb** [no obj.] **1** fish with a trawl net or seine: *the boats **trawled for** flounder* | (as noun **trawling**) *restrictions on trawling.* ■ [with obj.] catch with a trawl or seine. ■ [with obj.] drag or trail (something) through water: *she trawled a toe to test the temperature.*
2 search thoroughly: *the Home Office **trawled through** twenty-five-year-old confidential files* | [with obj.] *he trawled his memory and remembered locking the door.*
▶ **noun 1** an act of fishing with a trawl net or seine. ■ (also **trawl net**) a large wide-mouthed fishing net dragged by a boat along the bottom of the sea or a lake.
2 a thorough search: *a constant **trawl for** information.*
3 (also **trawl line**) N. Amer. a long sea-fishing line along which are tied buoys supporting baited hooks on short lines.
– ORIGIN mid 16th cent. (as a verb): probably from Middle Dutch *traghelen* 'to drag' (related to *traghel* 'dragnet'), perhaps from Latin *tragula* 'dragnet'.

trawler ▶ **noun** a fishing boat used for trawling.
– DERIVATIVES **trawlerman** noun (pl. **trawlermen**).

tray ▶ **noun** a flat, shallow container with a raised rim, typically used for carrying food and drink, or for holding small items or loose material.
– DERIVATIVES **trayful** noun (pl. **trayfuls**).
– ORIGIN late Old English *trīg*, from the Germanic base of **TREE**; the primary sense may have been 'wooden container'.

trayf /treɪf/ ▶ **adjective** another term for **TREFA**.

TRC ▶ **abbreviation** (in South Africa) Truth and Reconciliation Commission, a body set up by the government in 1995 to investigate violations of human rights committed under apartheid.

treacherous ▶ **adjective 1** guilty of or involving betrayal or deception: *a treacherous Gestapo agent* | *memory is particularly treacherous.*
2 (of ground, water, conditions, etc.) presenting hidden or unpredictable dangers: *a holidaymaker was swept away by treacherous currents.*
– DERIVATIVES **treacherously** adverb, **treacherousness** noun.
– ORIGIN Middle English (in sense 1): from Old French *trecherous*, from *trecheor* 'a cheat', from *trechier* 'to cheat'.

treachery ▶ **noun** (pl. **treacheries**) [mass noun] betrayal of trust: *many died because of his treachery* | [count noun] *his distaste for plots and treacheries.* ■ the quality of being deceptive: *the treachery of language.*
– ORIGIN Middle English: from Old French *trecherie*, from *trechier* 'to cheat'.

treacle ▶ **noun** [mass noun] Brit. a thick, sticky dark syrup made from partly refined sugar; molasses. ■ golden syrup.
– ORIGIN Middle English (originally denoting an antidote against venom): from Old French *triacle*, via Latin from Greek *thēriakē* 'antidote against venom', feminine of *thēriakos* (adjective), from *thērion* 'wild beast'. Current senses date from the late 17th cent.

treacly ▶ **adjective** (**treaclier, treacliest**) **1** resembling treacle in consistency, taste, or appearance: *a treacly black fuel.*
2 excessively sentimental: *treacly melodramas.*

tread ▶ **verb** (past **trod**; past participle **trodden** or **trod**) [no obj., with adverbial] walk in a specified way: *Rosa trod as lightly as she could* | figurative *the government had to **tread carefully** so as not to offend the judiciary.* ■ (**tread on**) chiefly Brit. set one's foot down on top of. ■ [with obj.] walk on or along: *shoppers will soon be treading the floors of the new shopping mall.* ■ [with obj. and adverbial] press down or crush with the feet: *food had been **trodden into** the carpet.*
▶ **noun 1** [in sing.] a person's manner of walking or the sound made as they walk: *I heard the heavy tread of Dad's boots.*
2 (also **tread board**) the top surface of a step or stair.
3 the thick moulded part of a vehicle tyre that grips the road. ■ the part of a wheel that touches the ground or a rail. ■ the upper surface of a railway track, in contact with the wheels.
4 the part of the sole of a shoe that rests on the ground.
– PHRASES **tread the boards** (or **stage**) see **BOARD**. **tread on air** see **AIR**. **tread** (or chiefly N. Amer. **step**) **on someone's toes** offend someone by encroaching on their area of responsibility. **tread water** maintain an upright position in deep water by moving the feet with a walking movement and the hands with a downward circular motion. ■ fail to make progress: *men who are treading water in their careers.*
– DERIVATIVES **treader** noun.
– ORIGIN Old English *tredan* (as a verb), of West Germanic origin; related to Dutch *treden* and German *treten*.

treadle /ˈtrɛd(ə)l/ ▶ **noun** a lever worked by the foot and imparting motion to a machine.
▶ **verb** [with obj.] operate (a machine) with a treadle.
– ORIGIN Old English *tredel* 'stair, step' (see **TREAD**).

treadmill ▶ **noun** a large wheel turned by the weight of people or animals treading on steps fitted into its inner surface, formerly used to drive machinery. ■ a device used for exercise, consisting of a continuous moving belt on which to walk or run. ■ a job or situation that is tiring or boring and from which it is hard to escape: *the soulless treadmill of urban existence.*

treadwheel ▶ **noun** another term for **TREADMILL**.

treason ▶ **noun** (also **high treason**) [mass noun] the crime of betraying one's country, especially by attempting to kill or overthrow the sovereign or government: *they were convicted of treason.* ■ the action of betraying someone or something: *doubt is the ultimate treason against faith.* ■ (**petty treason**) historical the crime of murdering someone to whom the murderer owed allegiance, such as a master or husband.
– DERIVATIVES **treasonous** adjective.
– ORIGIN Middle English: from Anglo-Norman French *treisoun*, from Latin *traditio(n-)* 'handing over', from the verb *tradere*.

> **USAGE** Formerly, there were two types of crime to which the term **treason** was applied: **petty treason**, the crime of murdering one's master, and **high treason**, the crime of betraying one's country. The crime of **petty treason** was abolished in 1828 and in modern use **high treason** is often simply called **treason**.

treasonable ▶ **adjective** (of an offence or offender) punishable as treason or as committing treason: *there was no evidence of treasonable activity.*
– DERIVATIVES **treasonably** adverb.

treasure ▶ **noun** [mass noun] a quantity of precious metals, gems, or other valuable objects. ■ [count noun] a very valuable object: *she set out to look at the art treasures.* ■ [count noun] informal a much loved or highly valued person: *the housekeeper is a real treasure—I don't know what he would do without her.*
▶ **verb** [with obj.] keep carefully (a valuable or valued item). ■ value highly: *the island is treasured by walkers and conservationists* | (as adj. **treasured**) *his library was his most treasured possession.*
– ORIGIN Middle English: from Old French *tresor*, based on Greek *thēsauros* (see **THESAURUS**).

treasure hunt ▶ **noun** a game in which players search for hidden objects by following a trail of clues.

treasurer ▶ **noun** a person appointed to administer or manage the financial assets and liabilities of a society, company, local authority, or other body. ■ Austral. the minister of finance. ■ (also **Lord Treasurer** or **Lord High Treasurer**) Brit. historical the head of the Exchequer.
– DERIVATIVES **treasurership** noun.
– ORIGIN Middle English: from Old French *tresorier*, from *tresor* (see **TREASURE**), influenced by late Latin *thesaurarius*.

Treasure State informal name for **MONTANA**.

treasure trove ▶ **noun** [mass noun] English Law (abolished in 1996) valuables of unknown ownership that are found hidden and declared the property of the Crown. ■ [count noun] a collection or store of valuable or delightful things: *your book is a treasure trove of delights.*
– ORIGIN late Middle English: from Anglo-Norman French *tresor trové*, literally 'found treasure'.

treasury ▶ **noun** (pl. **treasuries**) **1** the funds or revenue of a state, institution, or society: *the landowners' estates and assets were seized for the imperial treasury.* ■ (**Treasury**) (in some countries) the government department responsible for budgeting for and controlling public expenditure, management of the national debt, and the overall management of the economy.
2 a place or building where treasure is stored. ■ a store or collection of valuable or delightful things: *the old town is a treasury of ancient monuments.*
– ORIGIN Middle English: from Old French *tresorie* (see **TREASURE**).

Treasury bench ▶ **noun** (in the UK) the front bench in the House of Commons occupied by the Prime Minister, the Chancellor of the Exchequer, and other members of the government.

Treasury bill ▶ **noun** a short-dated UK or US government security, yielding no interest but issued at a discount on its redemption price.

Treasury bond ▶ **noun** an interest-bearing bond issued by the US Treasury.

Treasury note ▶ **noun 1** an intermediate-term interest-bearing bond issued by the US Treasury.
2 (in the UK) a currency note issued by the Treasury in 1914, valid until 1928.

treat ▶ **verb** [with obj.] **1** behave towards or deal with in a certain way: *she had been brutally treated* | *he*

treated her with grave courtesy. ■ (**treat something as**) regard something as being of a specified nature with implications for one's actions concerning it: *the names are being treated as classified information.* ■ present or discuss (a subject): *the issue is more fully treated in chapter five.*
2 give medical care or attention to; try to heal or cure: *the two were **treated for** cuts and bruises.*
3 apply a process or a substance to (something) to protect or preserve it or to give it particular properties: *the lawns were **treated with** weedkiller every year.*
4 (**treat someone to**) provide someone with (food, drink, or entertainment) at one's own expense: *he treated her to a slap-up lunch.* ■ give someone (something) as a favour: *he treated her to one of his smiles.* ■ (**treat oneself**) do or have something that gives one great pleasure: *treat yourself—you can diet tomorrow.*
5 [no obj.] negotiate terms with someone, especially an opponent: *propagandists claimed that he was treating with the enemy.*
▶ **noun** an event or item that is out of the ordinary and gives great pleasure: *he wanted to take her to the pictures as a treat.* ■ (**one's treat**) an act of treating someone to something: *'My treat,' he insisted, reaching for the bill.* ■ N. Amer. a sweet, biscuit, or other item of sweet food.
– PHRASES **—— a treat** Brit. informal do something specified very well or satisfactorily: *their tactics worked a treat.* ■ (**look a treat**) look attractive: *I don't know whether she can act, but she looks a treat.* **treat something lightly** regard something as unimportant: *this is a serious matter and he can't treat it lightly.*
– DERIVATIVES **treatable** adjective, **treater** noun.
– ORIGIN Middle English (in the senses 'negotiate' and 'discuss a subject'): from Old French *traitier*, from Latin *tractare* 'handle', frequentative of *trahere* 'draw, pull'. The current noun sense dates from the mid 17th cent.

treatise /ˈtriːtɪs, -ɪz/ ▶ **noun** a written work dealing formally and systematically with a subject: *his treatise on Scottish political theory.*
– ORIGIN late Middle English: from Anglo-Norman French *tretis*, from Old French *traitier* (see **TREAT**).

treatment ▶ **noun** [mass noun] **1** the manner in which someone behaves towards or deals with someone or something: *the directive required equal treatment for men and women in social security schemes.* ■ the presentation or discussion of a subject: *comparison with earlier artists is useful in analysis of the treatment of women in her painting.* ■ (**the full treatment**) informal used to indicate that something is done enthusiastically, vigorously, or to an extreme degree: *a bit of soft-shoe shuffle got the full treatment.*
2 medical care given to a patient for an illness or injury: *I'm receiving **treatment for** an injured shoulder* | [count noun] *anti-cancer treatments.* ■ [count noun] a session of beauty or health care: *they now offer the latest in beauty and body treatments.*
3 the use of a chemical, physical, or biological agent to preserve or give particular properties to something: *the treatment of hazardous waste is particularly expensive.*

treaty ▶ **noun** (pl. **treaties**) a formally concluded and ratified agreement between states.
– ORIGIN late Middle English: from Old French *traite*, from Latin *tractatus* 'treatise' (see **TRACTATE**).

T

treaty Indian ▶ **noun** chiefly Canadian a North American Indian whose people have signed a treaty with the government.

Treaty of Rome, Treaty of Versailles, etc. see **ROME, TREATY OF; VERSAILLES, TREATY OF,** etc.

treaty port ▶ **noun** historical a port bound by treaty to be open to foreign trade, especially in 19th and early 20th-century China and Japan.

Trebbiano /ˌtrɛbɪˈɑːnəʊ/ ▶ **noun** [mass noun] a variety of wine grape widely cultivated in Italy and elsewhere. ■ a wine made from the Trebbiano grape.
– ORIGIN Italian, from the name of the River *Trebbia*, in northern central Italy.

Trebizond /ˈtrɛbɪzɒnd/ another name for **TRABZON**.

treble[1] ▶ **adjective** [attrib.] consisting of three parts; threefold: *the fish were caught with large treble hooks.* ■ multiplied or occurring three times: *she turned back to make a double and treble check.* ■ (of a number) occurring three times in succession: *call Kate on 0500 403 treble zero.*
▶ **predeterminer** three times as much or as many: *the tip was at least treble what she would normally have given.*
▶ **noun 1** Brit. three sporting victories or championships in the same season, event, etc.: *the victory completed a treble for the horse's trainer.*
2 Darts a hit on the narrow ring enclosed by the two middle circles of a dartboard, scoring treble.
3 Brit. a system of betting in which the winnings and stake from the first bet are transferred to a second and then (if successful) to a third.
4 a threefold quantity or thing, in particular: ■ (in showjumping) a fence consisting of three elements. ■ a crochet stitch made with three loops of wool on the hook at a time. ■ a drink of spirits of three times the standard measure.
▶ **pronoun** a number or amount which is three times as large as a contrasting or usual number or amount: *by paying treble, he had a double room to himself.*
▶ **verb** make or become three times as large or numerous: [with obj.] *rents were doubled and probably trebled* | [no obj.] *his salary has trebled in a couple of years.*
– ORIGIN Middle English: via Old French from Latin *triplus* (see **TRIPLE**).

treble[2] ▶ **noun 1** a high-pitched voice, especially a boy's singing voice. ■ a boy (or girl) with a high-pitched singing voice. ■ a part written for a high voice or an instrument of a high pitch.
2 [as modifier] denoting a relatively high-pitched member of a family of similar instruments: *a treble viol.* ■ (also **treble bell**) the smallest and highest-pitched bell of a ring or set.
3 [mass noun] the high-frequency output of a radio, or audio system, corresponding to the treble in music.
– ORIGIN late Middle English: from **TREBLE[1]**, because it was the highest part in a three-part contrapuntal composition.

treble chance ▶ **noun** [mass noun] Brit. a form of football pool in which different numbers of points are awarded for a draw, an away win, and a home win.

treble clef ▶ **noun** a clef placing G above middle C on the second-lowest line of the stave.

Treblinka /trɛˈblɪŋkə/ a Nazi concentration camp in Poland in the Second World War, where a great many of the Jews of the Warsaw ghetto were murdered.

trebly ▶ **adjective** (**treblier, trebliest**) (of sound, especially recorded music) having too much treble; tinny.
▶ **adverb** [as submodifier] three times as much: *to Katherine, the house was trebly impressive.*

trebuchet /ˈtrɛbjʊʃɛt, -bəʃɛt/ ▶ **noun** a machine used in medieval siege warfare for hurling large stones or other missiles.
– ORIGIN Middle English: from Old French, from *trebucher* 'overthrow'.

trecento /treɪˈtʃɛntəʊ/ ▶ **noun** (**the trecento**) the 14th century as a period of Italian art, architecture, or literature.
– ORIGIN Italian, literally '300', shortened from *milletrecento* '1300', used with reference to the years 1300–99.

tree ▶ **noun 1** a woody perennial plant, typically having a single stem or trunk growing to a considerable height and bearing lateral branches at some distance from the ground. ■ (in general use) any bush, shrub, or herbaceous plant with a tall erect stem, e.g. a banana plant.
2 a wooden structure or part of a structure. ■ archaic or literary the cross on which Christ was crucified. ■ archaic a gibbet.
3 a thing that has a branching structure resembling that of a tree. ■ (also **tree diagram**) a diagram with a structure of branching connecting lines, representing different processes and relationships.
▶ **verb** (**trees, treeing, treed**) [with obj.] **1** N. Amer. force (a hunted animal) to take refuge in a tree. ■ informal, chiefly US force (someone) into a difficult situation.
2 (as adj. **treed**) (of an area) planted with trees: *sparsely treed grasslands.*
– PHRASES **out of one's tree** informal completely stupid; mad. **up a tree** informal, chiefly N. Amer. in a difficult situation without escape; cornered.
– DERIVATIVES **treeless** adjective, **treelessness** noun, **tree-like** adjective.
– ORIGIN Old English *trēow, trēo*: from a Germanic variant of an Indo-European root shared by Greek *doru* 'wood, spear', *drus* 'oak'.

tree calf ▶ **noun** [mass noun] calfskin stained with a tree-like design and used in bookbinding.

treecreeper ▶ **noun** a small songbird with drab plumage and a downcurved bill, which creeps about on the trunks of trees to search for insects. Compare with **CREEPER** (sense 2). ● a Eurasian and North American bird (*Certhia*, family Certhiidae, in particular the common *C. familiaris*). ● an Australasian bird (family Climacteridae and genus *Climacteris*).

tree diagram ▶ **noun** see **TREE** (sense 3 of the noun).

tree duck ▶ **noun** another term for **WHISTLING DUCK**.

tree fern ▶ **noun** a large palm-like fern with a trunk-like stem bearing a crown of large fronds, sometimes reaching a height of 24 m and occurring chiefly in the tropics, particularly the southern hemisphere.
● Cyatheaceae and related families, class Filicopsida: seven genera, in particular *Cyathea* and *Dicksonia*.

tree frog ▶ **noun** an arboreal frog that has long toes with adhesive disks and is typically small and brightly coloured. ● Families Hylidae (of Eurasia, America, and Australia) and Rhacophoridae (of Africa and Asia): numerous species, including the common **green tree frog** (*Hyla arborea*) of southern Europe.

tree heath ▶ **noun** a white-flowered shrub or tree of the heather family, with woody nodules that are used to make briar pipes. It is native to southern Europe and parts of Africa. Also called **BRIAR[2]**. ● *Erica arborea*, family Ericaceae.

treehopper ▶ **noun** a tree-dwelling jumping bug that lives chiefly in the tropics. A tall backward-curving projection of the thorax gives the bug a thornlike appearance for camouflage. ● Family Membracidae, suborder Homoptera: many species, including the bright green **buffalo treehopper** (*Stictocephalus bisonia*) of North America.

tree house ▶ **noun** a structure built in the branches of a tree for children to play in.

tree-hugger ▶ **noun** informal, chiefly derogatory an environmental campaigner (used in reference to the practice of embracing a tree in an attempt to prevent it from being felled).
– DERIVATIVES **tree-hugging** noun.

tree kangaroo ▶ **noun** an agile tree-climbing kangaroo with a long furred tail, and fore- and hindlimbs that are of almost equal length, found in the rainforests of Queensland and New Guinea. ● Genus *Dendrolagus*, family Macropodidae: six species.

treeline ▶ **noun** (on a mountain) the line or altitude above which no trees grow. ■ (in high northern (or southern) latitudes) the line north (or south) of which no trees grow.

tree lupin ▶ **noun** a shrubby yellow-flowered Californian lupin, widely planted to reclaim sandy land.
● *Lupinus arboreus*, family Leguminosae.

tree mallow ▶ **noun** a tall woody-stemmed European mallow of coastal regions. ● *Lavatera arborea*, family Malvaceae.

treen ▶ **noun** [treated as pl.] small domestic wooden objects, especially antiques.
▶ **adjective** chiefly archaic wooden: *a treen snuffbox.*
– ORIGIN Old English *trēowen* 'wooden' (see **TREE, -EN[2]**).

treenail (also **trenail** or US **trunnel**) ▶ **noun** a hard wooden pin used for fastening timbers together.

tree of heaven ▶ **noun** a tall, fast-growing Chinese tree, widely cultivated as an ornamental and shade tree. ● *Ailanthus altissima*, family Simaroubaceae.

tree of knowledge (also **tree of knowledge of good and evil**) ▶ **noun** (in the Bible) the tree in the Garden of Eden bearing the forbidden fruit which Adam and Eve disobediently ate (Gen. 2:9, 3).

tree of life ▶ **noun 1** (**Tree of Life**) (in the Bible) the tree in the Garden of Eden bearing fruit which gave eternal life (Gen. 3:22–24). ■ (in the Kabbalah) a diagram in the form of a tree bearing spheres which represent the sephiroth.
2 the thuja or arbor vitae.

tree pie ▶ **noun** a long-tailed tree-dwelling Asian crow, with blackish or brown and grey plumage.
● Family Corvidae: three genera, in particular *Dendrocitta*, and several species.
– ORIGIN late 19th cent.: *pie* from **PIE[2]**.

tree pipit ▶ **noun** a widespread Old World pipit which inhabits open country with scattered trees.
● *Anthus trivialis*, family Motacillidae.

tree ring ▶ **noun** each of a number of concentric rings in the cross section of a tree trunk, representing a single year's growth.

tree shrew ▶ **noun** a small squirrel-like insectivorous mammal with a pointed snout, native to SE Asia, especially Borneo. ● Family Tupaiidae and order Scandentia: several genera, in particular *Tupaia*; tree shrews were formerly placed with either the insectivores or the primates.

tree snake ▶ **noun** a harmless arboreal snake, typically very slender and able to mimic a twig. ● Several genera in the family Colubridae, e.g. *Dendrelaphis* and *Ahaetulla* (of Asia), and *Leptophis* and *Oxybelis* (of America).

tree sparrow ▶ noun **1** a Eurasian sparrow with a chocolate brown cap in both sexes, inhabiting agricultural land. ● *Passer montanus*, family Passeridae (or Ploceidae).
2 a migratory sparrow-like songbird of the bunting family, breeding on the edge of the North American tundra. ● *Spizella arborea*, family Emberizidae (subfamily Emberizidae).

tree squirrel ▶ noun an arboreal squirrel that is typically active in daylight and does not hibernate. ● *Sciurus* and other genera, family Sciuridae: numerous species.

tree structure ▶ noun Computing a structure in which there are successive branchings or subdivisions.

tree surgeon ▶ noun a person who prunes and treats old or damaged trees in order to preserve them.
– DERIVATIVES **tree surgery** noun.

tree toad ▶ noun another term for TREE FROG.

tree tomato ▶ noun another term for TAMARILLO.

treetop ▶ noun (usu. **treetops**) the uppermost part of a tree.

tree trunk ▶ noun the main woody stem of a tree, from which its branches grow.

treeware ▶ noun [mass noun] informal paper-based printed material, typically as contrasted with media that store or convey information electronically.

trefa /ˈtreɪfə/ (also **trifa** or **trayf**) ▶ adjective (of food) not satisfying the requirements of Jewish law.
– ORIGIN mid 19th cent.: from Hebrew *ṭĕrēpāh* 'the flesh of an animal torn or mauled', from *ṭārap* 'rend'.

trefid /ˈtrɛfɪd/ ▶ adjective variant spelling of TRIFID (sense 2).

trefoil /ˈtrɛfɔɪl, ˈtriːfɔɪl/ ▶ noun a small European plant of the pea family, with yellow flowers and three-lobed clover-like leaves. ● Genera *Trifolium* and *Lotus*, family Leguminosae: several species, in particular the **bird's-foot trefoil**.
■ a similar or related plant with three-lobed leaves.
■ an ornamental design of three rounded lobes like a clover leaf, used typically in architectural tracery. ■ a thing having three parts; a set of three: *a trefoil of parachutes lowers the shuttle's used rockets to Earth.*
– DERIVATIVES **trefoiled** adjective.
– ORIGIN Middle English: from Anglo-Norman French *trifoil*, from Latin *trifolium*, from *tri-* 'three' + *folium* 'leaf'.

trehalose /ˈtriːhələʊs, trɪˈhɑːləʊs, -z/ ▶ noun [mass noun] Chemistry a sugar of the disaccharide class produced by some fungi, yeasts, and similar organisms.
– ORIGIN mid 19th cent.: from *trehala* (from Turkish, denoting a sweet substance derived from insect cocoons) + -OSE².

trek ▶ noun **1** a long arduous journey, especially one made on foot: *a trek to the South Pole.* ■ (**the Trek**) S. African see GREAT TREK. ■ S. African a leg or stage of a journey.
2 [mass noun] S. African informal a person's possessions: *I was at the new flat waiting for my trek to arrive.*
3 S. African a haul of fish caught using a trek net.
▶ verb (**treks, trekking, trekked**) **1** [no obj., with adverbial of direction] go on a long arduous journey, typically on foot: *we trekked through the jungle.* ■ S. African travel constantly from place to place: *my plan is to trek about seeing the world.* ■ historical, chiefly S. African migrate or journey with one's belongings by ox wagon. ■ [no obj., usu. in imperative] S. African (of an ox) draw a vehicle or pull a load.
2 [no obj.] S. African fish using a trek net.
– DERIVATIVES **trekker** noun.
– ORIGIN mid 19th cent.: from South African Dutch *trek* (noun), *trekken* (verb) 'pull, travel'.

Trekkie (also **Trekker**) ▶ noun (pl. **Trekkies**) informal a fan of the US science-fiction television programme *Star Trek*.

trek net ▶ noun S. African a large fishing net, weighted at one end and fitted with floats on the other so that it hangs vertically in the water, usually dropped from a boat and hauled in from the shore.

trellis ▶ noun a framework of light wooden or metal bars used as a support for fruit trees or creepers, typically fastened against a wall.
▶ verb (**trellises, trellising, trellised**) [with obj.] (usu. as adj. **trellised**) provide with or enclose in a trellis: *a trellised archway.* ■ support (a climbing plant) with a trellis.
– ORIGIN late Middle English (denoting any latticed screen): from Old French *trelis*, from Latin *trilix* 'three-ply', from *tri-* 'three' + *licium* 'warp thread'. Current senses date from the early 16th cent.

trelliswork ▶ noun [mass noun] interlacing strips of wood or metal forming a trellis or lattice.

Trematoda /ˌtrɛməˈtəʊdə/ ▶ plural noun Zoology a class of flatworms that comprises those flukes that are internal parasites. The monogenean flukes are sometimes also placed in this class. See FLUKE² (sense 1).
– ORIGIN modern Latin (plural), from Greek *trēmatōdēs* 'perforated', from *trēma* 'hole'.

trematode /ˈtrɛmətəʊd/ ▶ noun Zoology a parasitic flatworm of the class Trematoda.

tremble ▶ verb [no obj.] shake involuntarily, typically as a result of anxiety, excitement, or frailty: *Isobel was trembling with excitement.* ■ be in a state of extreme apprehension: [with infinitive] *I **tremble to think that** we could ever return to conditions like these.* ■ shake or quiver slightly: *the earth trembled beneath their feet.*
▶ noun **1** a trembling feeling, movement, or sound: *there was a slight tremble in his voice.*
2 (**the trembles**) informal a physical or emotional condition marked by trembling. ■ another term for MILK SICKNESS.
– PHRASES **all of a tremble** informal extremely agitated or excited.
– DERIVATIVES **trembling** adjective, **tremblingly** adverb.
– ORIGIN Middle English (as a verb): from Old French *trembler*, from medieval Latin *tremulare*, from Latin *tremulus* (see TREMULOUS).

trembler ▶ noun **1** Brit. an automatic vibrator for making and breaking an electric circuit, typically used as a fuse for an explosive device sensitive to physical disturbance.
2 a songbird related to the thrashers, found in the Lesser Antilles and named from its habit of violent shaking. ● Genera *Cinclocerthia* and *Ramphocinclus*, family Mimidae: three species.
3 informal an earthquake.

trembling poplar ▶ noun the European aspen.

tremblor /ˈtrɛmblɔː/ ▶ noun US an earth tremor.
– ORIGIN early 20th cent.: alteration of Spanish *temblor* 'shudder', influenced by TREMBLER.

trembly ▶ adjective (**tremblier, trembliest**) informal shaking or quivering involuntarily: *her eyes were tearful, her hands trembly | she gave a queer trembly laugh.*

tremendous ▶ adjective **1** very great in amount, scale, or intensity: *Penny put in a tremendous amount of time | there was a tremendous explosion.* ■ informal extremely good or impressive; excellent: *the crew did a tremendous job.*
2 archaic inspiring awe or dread.
– DERIVATIVES **tremendously** adverb, **tremendousness** noun.
– ORIGIN mid 17th cent.: from Latin *tremendus* (gerundive of *tremere* 'tremble') + -OUS.

tremolando /ˌtrɛməˈlandəʊ/ Music ▶ noun (pl. **tremolandi**) another term for TREMOLO.
▶ adverb & adjective (especially as a direction) with tremolo.
– ORIGIN Italian, literally 'trembling'.

tremolite /ˈtrɛm(ə)lʌɪt/ ▶ noun [mass noun] a white to grey amphibole mineral which occurs widely in igneous rocks and is characteristic of metamorphosed dolomitic limestones.
– ORIGIN late 18th cent.: from *Tremola* Valley, Switzerland, + -ITE¹.

tremolo ▶ noun (pl. **tremolos**) Music a wavering effect in a musical tone, produced either by rapid reiteration of a note, by rapid repeated slight variation in the pitch of a note, or by sounding two notes of slightly different pitches to produce prominent overtones. Compare with VIBRATO. ■ a mechanism in an organ producing a tremolo effect. ■ (also **tremolo arm**) a lever on an electric guitar, used to produce a tremolo effect.
– ORIGIN mid 18th cent.: from Italian.

tremor ▶ noun **1** an involuntary quivering movement: *a disorder that causes tremors and muscle rigidity.* ■ a tremble or quiver in a person's voice. ■ a sudden feeling of fear or excitement: *a tremor of unease.*
2 (also **earth tremor**) a slight earthquake.
▶ verb [no obj.] undergo a tremor or tremors: *a muscle in my jaw tremored uncontrollably.*
– ORIGIN early 17th cent.: from Latin *tremor*, from *tremere* 'to tremble'.

tremulous /ˈtrɛmjʊləs/ ▶ adjective shaking or quivering slightly: *Barbara's voice was tremulous.* ■ timid; nervous: *he gave a tremulous smile.*
– DERIVATIVES **tremulously** adverb, **tremulousness** noun.
– ORIGIN early 17th cent.: from Latin *tremulus* (from *tremere* 'tremble') + -OUS.

trenail ▶ noun variant spelling of TREENAIL.

trench ▶ noun **1** a long, narrow ditch. ■ a long, narrow ditch dug by troops to provide a place of shelter from enemy fire. ■ (**trenches**) a connected system of such ditches forming an army's line. ■ (**the trenches**) the battlefields of northern France and Belgium in the First World War: *the slaughter in the trenches created a new cynicism.*
2 (also **ocean trench**) a long, narrow, deep depression in the ocean bed, typically one running parallel to a plate boundary and marking a subduction zone.
3 a trench coat.
▶ verb **1** [with obj.] dig a trench or trenches in (the ground): *she trenched the terrace to a depth of 6 feet.* ■ turn over the earth of (a field or garden) by digging a succession of adjoining ditches.
2 [no obj.] (**trench on/upon**) archaic border closely on; encroach on: *this would surely trench very far on the dignity and liberty of citizens.*
– ORIGIN late Middle English (in the senses 'track cut through a wood' and 'sever by cutting'): from Old French *trenche* (noun), *trenchier* (verb), based on Latin *truncare* (see TRUNCATE).

trenchant /ˈtrɛn(t)ʃ(ə)nt/ ▶ adjective **1** vigorous or incisive in expression or style: *the White Paper makes trenchant criticisms of health authorities.*
2 archaic or literary (of a weapon or tool) having a sharp edge: *a trenchant blade.*
– DERIVATIVES **trenchancy** noun (sense 1), **trenchantly** adverb (sense 1).
– ORIGIN Middle English (in sense 2): from Old French, literally 'cutting', present participle of *trenchier* (see TRENCH).

Trenchard /ˈtrɛnʃəd/, Hugh Montague, 1st Viscount of Wolfeton (1873–1956), British Marshal of the RAF. As chief of staff (1918) then First Marshal (1927) of the RAF he developed the force as a major element in the British armed services.

trench coat ▶ noun a loose belted, double-breasted raincoat in a military style. ■ a lined or padded waterproof coat worn by soldiers.

trench digging ▶ noun another term for DOUBLE DIGGING.

trencher¹ ▶ noun **1** historical a wooden plate or platter for food. ■ a thick slice of bread used as a plate or platter.
2 old-fashioned term for MORTAR BOARD (sense 1).
– ORIGIN Middle English: from Anglo-Norman French *trenchour*, from Old French *trenchier* 'to cut' (see TRENCH).

trencher² ▶ noun a machine or attachment used in digging trenches.

trencherman ▶ noun (pl. **trenchermen**) [usu. with adj.] humorous a person who eats in a specified manner, typically heartily: *a doughty trencherman who gives the Simpson's beef trolley a good run for its money.*

trench fever ▶ noun [mass noun] a highly contagious rickettsial disease transmitted by lice, that infested soldiers in the trenches in the First World War.

trench foot ▶ noun [mass noun] a painful condition of the feet caused by long immersion in cold water or mud and marked by blackening and death of surface tissue.

trench mortar ▶ noun a light simple mortar designed to propel a bomb into enemy trenches.

trench mouth ▶ noun [mass noun] ulcerative gingivitis.

trench warfare ▶ noun [mass noun] a type of combat in which opposing troops fight from trenches facing each other.

trend ▶ noun **1** a general direction in which something is developing or changing: *an upward trend in sales and profit margins.*
2 a fashion: *the latest trends in modern dance.*
▶ verb [no obj., with adverbial of direction] (especially of a geographical feature) bend or turn away in a specified direction: *the Richelieu River trending southward to Lake Champlain.* ■ change or develop in a general direction: *unemployment has been trending upwards.*
– ORIGIN Old English *trendan* 'revolve, rotate', of Germanic origin; compare with TRUNDLE. The verb sense 'turn in a specified direction' dates from the late 16th cent, and gave rise to the figurative use 'develop in a

T

general direction' in the mid 19th cent., a development paralleled in the noun.

Trendelenburg position /trɛn'dɛlənbəːg/ ▸ **noun** a position, used for pelvic surgery and to treat shock, in which a patient lies face upwards on a tilted table or bed with the pelvis higher than the head.
– ORIGIN late 19th cent.: named after Friedrich *Trendelenburg* (1844–1924), German surgeon.

trendify ▸ **verb** (**trendifies, trendifying, trendified**) [with obj.] informal, chiefly derogatory make very fashionable or up to date in style or influence: *the cafe has been trendified to look like a wine bar*.

trend line ▸ **noun** a line indicating the general course or tendency of something, e.g. a geographical feature or a set of points on a graph.

trendoid ▸ **noun** informal a person who follows fashion blindly or excessively.

trendsetter ▸ **noun** a person who leads the way in fashion or ideas.
– DERIVATIVES **trendsetting** adjective.

trendspotter ▸ **noun** a person who identifies or predicts new trends in fashion, culture, etc.
– DERIVATIVES **trendspotting** noun.

trendy informal ▸ **adjective** (**trendier, trendiest**) very fashionable or up to date: *I enjoyed being able to go out and buy trendy clothes*.
▸ **noun** (pl. **trendies**) a person who is very fashionable or up to date.
– DERIVATIVES **trendily** adverb, **trendiness** noun.

Trengganu /trɛŋ'gɑːnuː/ (also **Terengganu**) a state of Malaysia, on the east coast of the Malay Peninsula; capital, Kuala Trengganu.

Trent the chief river of central England, which rises in Staffordshire and flows 275 km (170 miles) generally north-eastwards, uniting with the River Ouse 25 km (15 miles) west of Hull to form the Humber estuary.

Trent, Council of an ecumenical council of the Roman Catholic Church, held in three sessions between 1545 and 1563 in Trento in Italy. Prompted by the opposition of the Reformation, the council clarified and redefined the Church's doctrine, abolished many ecclesiastical abuses, and strengthened the authority of the papacy. These measures provided the Church with a solid foundation for the Counter-Reformation.

trente et quarante /ˌtrɒt eɪ ka'rɒt/, French /trɑ̃t e kaʀɑ̃t/ ▸ **noun** [mass noun] a gambling game in which cards are turned up on a table marked with red and black diamonds.
– ORIGIN French, literally 'thirty and forty', these being winning and losing numbers respectively in the game.

Trentino-Alto Adige /trɛnˌtiːnəʊ ˌaltəʊ 'adɪdʒeɪ/ a region of NE Italy, comprising Bolzano-Bozen and Trento provinces. Situated on the border with Austria, it includes the Dolomites.

Trento /'trɛntəʊ/ a city on the Adige River in northern Italy; pop. 114,236 (2008).

Trenton /'trɛntən/ the state capital of New Jersey; pop. 82,883 (est. 2008).

trepan /trɪ'pan/ ▸ **noun 1** chiefly historical a trephine (hole saw) used by surgeons for perforating the skull. **2** a borer for sinking shafts.
▸ **verb** (**trepans, trepanning, trepanned**) [with obj.] perforate (a person's skull) with a trepan.
– DERIVATIVES **trepanation** /ˌtrɛpə'neɪʃ(ə)n/ noun.
– ORIGIN late Middle English: the noun via medieval Latin from Greek *trupanon*, from *trupan* 'to bore', from *trupē* 'hole'; the verb from Old French *trepaner*.

trepang /trɪ'paŋ/ ▸ **noun** another term for BÊCHE-DE-MER (sense 1).
– ORIGIN late 18th cent.: from Malay *teripang*.

trephine /trɪ'fʌɪn, -'fiːn/ ▸ **noun** a hole saw used in surgery to remove a circle of tissue or bone.
▸ **verb** [with obj.] operate on with a trephine.
– DERIVATIVES **trephination** /ˌtrɛfɪ'neɪʃ(ə)n/ noun.
– ORIGIN early 17th cent.: from Latin *tres fines* 'three ends', apparently influenced by TREPAN.

trepidation ▸ **noun** [mass noun] **1** a feeling of fear or anxiety about something that may happen: *the men set off in fear and trepidation*. **2** archaic trembling movements or motion.
– ORIGIN late 15th cent.: from Latin *trepidatio(n-)*, from *trepidare* 'be agitated, tremble', from *trepidus* 'alarmed'.

trepidatious ▸ **adjective** informal apprehensive or nervous; filled with trepidation: *if you're trepidatious about foreign travel, start with an English-speaking country*.
– DERIVATIVES **trepidatiously** adverb.

treponeme /'trɛpəniːm/ (also **treponema** /-ə/) ▸ **noun** a spirochaete bacterium that is parasitic or pathogenic in humans and warm-blooded animals, including the causal agents of syphilis and yaws.
● Genus *Treponema*, order Spirochaetales; Gram-negative.
– DERIVATIVES **treponemal** adjective.
– ORIGIN early 20th cent.: from modern Latin *Treponema*, from Greek *trepein* 'to turn' + *nēma* 'thread'.

trespass ▸ **verb** [no obj.] **1** enter someone's land or property without permission: *there is no excuse for trespassing on railway property*. ■ (**trespass on**) make unfair claims on or take advantage of (something): *she really must not trespass on his hospitality*. **2** (**trespass against**) archaic or literary commit an offence against (a person or a set of rules): *a man who had trespassed against Judaic law*.
▸ **noun 1** [mass noun] Law entry to a person's land or property without permission: *the defendants were guilty of trespass* | [count noun] *a mass trespass on the moor*. **2** archaic or literary a sin or offence: *the worst trespass against the goddess Venus is to see her naked and asleep*.
– ORIGIN Middle English (in sense 2 of the verb): from Old French *trespasser* 'pass over, trespass', *trespas* 'passing across', from medieval Latin *transpassare* (see TRANS-, PASS[1]).

trespasser ▸ **noun** a person entering someone's land or property without permission: *a trespasser on his land*.

tress ▸ **noun** (usu. **tresses**) a long lock of a woman's hair: *her golden tresses tumbled about her face*.
▸ **verb** [with obj.] archaic arrange (a person's hair) into long locks.
– DERIVATIVES **tressed** adjective [usu. in combination] *a blonde-tressed sex symbol*.
– ORIGIN Middle English: from Old French *tresse*, perhaps based on Greek *trikha* 'threefold'.

tressure /'trɛʃə, 'trɛs(j)ʊə/ ▸ **noun** Heraldry a thin border inset from the edge of a shield, narrower than an orle and usually borne double. ■ an ornamental enclosure containing a figure or distinctive device, formerly found on various gold and silver coins.
– ORIGIN Middle English (denoting a ribbon or band for the hair): from Old French *tressour* (see TRESS).

trestle ▸ **noun** a framework consisting of a horizontal beam supported by two pairs of sloping legs, used in pairs to support a flat surface such as a table top. ■ short for TRESTLE TABLE. ■ (also **trestlework**) an open braced framework used to support an elevated structure such as a bridge. ■ (also **trestletree**) each of a pair of horizontal pieces on a sailing ship's lower mast supporting the topmast.
– ORIGIN Middle English: from Old French *trestel*, based on Latin *transtrum* 'beam'.

trestle table ▸ **noun** a table consisting of a board or boards laid on trestles.

tret /trɛt/ ▸ **noun** [mass noun] historical an allowance of extra weight made to purchasers of certain goods to compensate for waste during transportation.
– ORIGIN late 15th cent: from an Old French variant of *trait* 'draught' (see TRAIT).

tretinoin /trə'tɪnəʊɪn/ ▸ **noun** [mass noun] Medicine a preparation of retinoic acid, applied to the skin to treat acne and other disorders.
– ORIGIN 1970s: from *t-* of unknown origin + RETINOIC ACID + -IN[1].

Tretyakov Gallery /'trɛtjəkɒf/ an art gallery in Moscow, one of the largest in the world. It houses exhibits ranging from early Russian art to contemporary work, and has a huge collection of icons.
– ORIGIN named after P. M. *Tretyakov* (1832–98), who founded it in 1856.

trevally /trɪ'vali/ ▸ **noun** (pl. **trevallies**) a marine sporting fish of the Indo-Pacific. ● *Caranx* and other genera, family Carangidae: several species.
– ORIGIN late 19th cent.: probably an alteration of *cavally* 'horse mackerel', from Spanish *caballo* 'horse'.

Trèves /trɛv/ French name for TRIER.

Trevino /trə'viːnəʊ/, Lee (Buck) (b.1939), American golfer; known as **Supermex**. In 1971 he became the first man to win all three Open championships (Canadian, US, and British) in the same year.

Trevira /trə'vɪərə/ ▸ **noun** [mass noun] trademark a polyester fibre, used chiefly to make clothes and soft furnishings.
– ORIGIN 1950s: of unknown origin.

Trevithick /trə'vɪθɪk/, Richard (1771–1833), English engineer. His chief contribution was in the use of high-pressure steam to drive a double-acting engine. Trevithick built the world's first railway locomotive (1804) and many stationary engines.

trews /truːz/ ▸ **plural noun** chiefly Brit. trousers. ■ close-fitting tartan trousers worn by certain Scottish regiments.
– ORIGIN mid 16th cent.: from Irish *triús*, Scottish Gaelic *triubhas* (singular); compare with TROUSERS.

trey /treɪ/ ▸ **noun** (pl. **treys**) **1** a playing card or dice with three spots. **2** US (in basketball) a shot scoring three points.
– ORIGIN late Middle English: from Old French *trei* 'three', from Latin *tres*.

TRH ▸ **abbreviation** ■ Their Royal Highnesses. ■ Biochemistry thyrotropin-releasing hormone.

tri- /trʌɪ/ ▸ **combining form** three; having three: *triathlon*. ■ Chemistry (in names of compounds) containing three atoms or groups of a specified kind: *trichloroethane*.
– ORIGIN from Latin and Greek, from Latin *tres*, Greek *treis* 'three'.

triable /'trʌɪəb(ə)l/ ▸ **adjective** Law (of an offence) liable to a judicial trial. ■ (of a case or issue) able to be investigated and decided judicially.
– ORIGIN late Middle English: from Anglo-Norman French, from Old French *trier* 'sift' (see TRY).

triac /'trʌɪak/ ▸ **noun** Electronics a three-electrode semiconductor device that will conduct in either direction when triggered by a positive or negative signal at the gate electrode.
– ORIGIN 1960s: from TRIODE + AC (short for *alternating current*).

triacetate /trʌɪ'asɪteɪt/ (also **cellulose triacetate**) ▸ **noun** [mass noun] a form of cellulose acetate containing three acetate groups per glucose monomer, used as a basis for man-made fibres.

triad /'trʌɪad/ ▸ **noun 1** a group or set of three related people or things: *the triad of medication, diet, and exercise are necessary in diabetes care*. ■ a chord of three musical notes, consisting of a given note with the third and fifth above it. ■ a Welsh form of literary composition with an arrangement of subjects or statements in groups of three. **2** (also **Triad**) a secret society originating in China, typically involved in organized crime. ■ a member of such a society.
– DERIVATIVES **triadic** adjective (sense 1).
– ORIGIN mid 16th cent.: from French *triade*, or via late Latin from Greek *trias, triad-*, from *treis* 'three'. Sense 2 is a translation of Chinese *San Ho Hui*, literally 'three unite society', i.e. 'triple union society', said to mean 'the union of Heaven, Earth, and Man'.

triage /'triːɑːʒ/ ▸ **noun** [mass noun] (in medical use) the assignment of degrees of urgency to wounds or illnesses to decide the order of treatment of a large number of patients or casualties. ■ the process of determining the most important people or things from amongst a large number that require attention: *a system of educational triage that allows a few students to get help while the needs of others are neglected*.
▸ **verb** [with obj.] decide the order of treatment of (patients or casualties): *victims were triaged by paramedics before being transported to hospitals*.
– ORIGIN early 18th cent. (in the sense 'the action of sorting items according to quality'): from French, from *trier* 'separate out'. The current sense dates from the 1930s, from the military system of assessing the wounded on the battlefield.

trial ▸ **noun 1** a formal examination of evidence by a judge, typically before a jury, in order to decide guilt in a case of criminal or civil proceedings: *the newspaper accounts of the trial* | [mass noun] *the editor was summoned to* ***stand trial*** *for libel*. **2** a test of the performance, qualities, or suitability of someone or something: *clinical trials must establish whether the new hip replacements are working*. ■ a sports match to test the ability of players eligible for selection to a team. ■ a test of individual ability on a motorcycle over rough ground or on a road. ■ (**trials**) an event in which horses, dogs, or other animals compete or perform: *horse trials*. **3** a person, experience, or situation that tests a person's endurance or forbearance: *the trials and tribulations of married life*.
▸ **verb** (**trials, trialling, trialled**; US **trials, trialing, trialed**) **1** [with obj.] test (something, especially a new product) to assess its suitability or performance: *teachers all over the UK are trialling the materials*.

T

2 [no obj.] (of a horse, dog, or other animal) compete in trials: *the pup trialled on Saturday.*
– PHRASES **on trial 1** being tried in a court of law. **2** being tested for performance or suitability: *water metering has been on trial in England and Wales.* **trial and error** the process of experimenting with various methods of doing something until one finds the most successful.
– ORIGIN late Middle English (as a noun): from Anglo-Norman French, or from medieval Latin *triallum*. The verb dates from the 1980s.

trial balance ▶ **noun** a statement of all debits and credits in a double-entry account book, with any disagreement indicating an error.

trial balloon ▶ **noun** a tentative measure taken or statement made to see how a new policy will be received.
– ORIGIN 1930s: from translation of French *ballon d'essai*.

trial court ▶ **noun** chiefly N. Amer. a court of law where cases are tried in the first place, as opposed to an appeal court.

trialist (Brit. also **triallist**) ▶ **noun** a person who participates in a sports trial or motorcycle trial. ■ a person who takes part in a clinical or market test of a new product.

trial lawyer ▶ **noun** N. Amer. a lawyer who practises in a trial court, especially one who represents plaintiffs in tort suits.

trialogue ▶ **noun** a dialogue between three people.
– ORIGIN mid 16th cent.: formed irregularly from **TRI-** 'three' + **DIALOGUE** (the prefix *di-* misinterpreted as 'two').

trial run ▶ **noun** a preliminary test of how a new system or product works.

triangle ▶ **noun 1** a plane figure with three straight sides and three angles: *an equilateral triangle.* ■ a thing shaped like a triangle: *a small triangle of grass.* ■ a musical instrument consisting of a steel rod bent into a triangle and sounded by being struck with a small steel rod. ■ a frame used to position the pool balls in snooker and pool. ■ N. Amer. a drawing instrument in the form of a right-angled triangle. ■ (**triangles**) historical a frame of three halberds joined at the top to which a soldier was bound for flogging.
2 (also **eternal triangle**) an emotional relationship involving a couple and a third person with whom one of them is also involved.
3 a small brownish Eurasian moth of oak and beech woods. ● *Heterogenea asella*, family Limacodidae.
– ORIGIN late Middle English: from Old French *triangle* or Latin *triangulum*, neuter of *triangulus* 'three-cornered' (see **TRI-**, **ANGLE**[1]).

triangle of forces ▶ **noun** Physics a triangle whose sides represent in magnitude and direction three forces in equilibrium.

triangular ▶ **adjective** shaped like a triangle; having three sides and three corners: *dainty triangular sandwiches.* ■ involving three people or parties: *a triangular cricket competition.* ■ (of a pyramid) having a three-sided base.
– DERIVATIVES **triangularity** noun, **triangularly** adverb.
– ORIGIN mid 16th cent.: from late Latin *triangularis*, from Latin *triangulum* (see **TRIANGLE**).

triangular number ▶ **noun** any of the series of numbers (1, 3, 6, 10, 15, etc.) obtained by continued summation of the natural numbers 1, 2, 3, 4, 5, etc.

triangular trade ▶ **noun** [mass noun] a multilateral system of trading in which a country pays for its imports from one country by its exports to another.

triangulate ▶ **verb** /trʌɪˈaŋɡjʊleɪt/ **1** [with obj.] divide (an area) into triangles for surveying purposes. ■ measure and map (an area) by the use of triangles with a known base length and base angles. ■ determine (a height, distance, or location) in this way.
2 [with obj.] form into a triangle or triangles.
3 [no obj.] chiefly US (in politics) position oneself in such a way as to appeal to or appease both left-wing and right-wing standpoints: *will the president decide to triangulate?*
– ORIGIN mid 19th cent.: from Latin *triangulum* 'triangle' (see **TRIANGLE**) + **-ATE**[3].

triangulation ▶ **noun** [mass noun] **1** (in surveying) the tracing and measurement of a series or network of triangles in order to determine the distances and relative positions of points spread over an area, especially by measuring the length of one side of each triangle and deducing its angles and the length of the other two sides by observation from this baseline.
2 formation of or division into triangles.
3 chiefly US (in politics) the action or process of positioning oneself in such a way as to appeal to or appease both left-wing and right-wing standpoints.

triangulation point ▶ **noun** another term for **TRIG POINT**.

Triangulum /trʌɪˈaŋɡjʊləm/ Astronomy a small northern constellation (the Triangle), between Andromeda and Aries.
– ORIGIN Latin.

Triangulum Australe /ɒˈstrɑːliː/ Astronomy a small southern constellation (the Southern Triangle), lying in the Milky Way near the south celestial pole.
– ORIGIN Latin.

Trianon /ˈtriːənɒn/, French /tʀiɑ̃nɔ̃/ either of two small palaces in the great park at Versailles in France. The larger was built by Louis XIV in 1687; the smaller, built by Louis XV 1762–8, was used first by his mistress Madame du Barry (1743–93) and afterwards by Marie Antoinette.

Triassic /trʌɪˈasɪk/ ▶ **adjective** Geology relating to or denoting the earliest period of the Mesozoic era, between the Permian and Jurassic periods. See also **PERMO–TRIASSIC**. ■ (as noun **the Triassic** or **the Trias**) the Triassic period or the system of rocks deposited during it.

> The Triassic lasted from about 245 to 208 million years ago. Many new organisms appeared following the mass extinctions of the end of the Palaeozoic era, including the earliest dinosaurs and ammonites and the first primitive mammals.

– ORIGIN mid 19th cent.: from late Latin *trias* (see **TRIAD**), because the strata are divisible into three groups, + **-IC**.

triathlon /trʌɪˈaθlɒn, -lən/ ▶ **noun** an athletic contest consisting of three different events, typically swimming, cycling, and long-distance running.
– DERIVATIVES **triathlete** noun.
– ORIGIN 1970s: from **TRI-** 'three', on the pattern of *decathlon*.

triatomic /ˌtrʌɪəˈtɒmɪk/ ▶ **adjective** Chemistry consisting of three atoms.

triaxial /trʌɪˈaksɪəl/ ▶ **adjective** having or relating to three axes, especially in mechanical or astronomical contexts.

tri-axle ▶ **noun** a trailer or articulated lorry with three axles.

triazine /ˈtrʌɪəziːn, trʌɪˈaziːn, -zɪn/ ▶ **noun** Chemistry any of a group of compounds whose molecules contain an unsaturated ring of three carbon and three nitrogen atoms.

triazole /ˈtrʌɪəzəʊl, trʌɪˈazəʊl/ ▶ **noun** Chemistry any compound whose molecule contains a ring of three nitrogen and two carbon atoms, in particular each of five isomeric compounds containing such a ring with two double bonds. ● Chem. formula: $C_2H_3N_3$.

tribade /ˈtrɪbəd/ ▶ **noun** rare a lesbian.
– ORIGIN early 17th cent.: from French, or via Latin from Greek *tribas*, from *tribein* 'to rub'.

tribadism /ˈtrɪbədɪz(ə)m/ ▶ **noun** [mass noun] a lesbian practice in which one partner lies on top of the other and simulates the movements of the male in heterosexual intercourse.
– ORIGIN early 19th cent.: from **TRIBADE**.

tribal ▶ **adjective** of or characteristic of a tribe or tribes: *tribal people in Malaysia.* ■ chiefly derogatory characterized by or reflecting strong group loyalty: *people don't want political parties stuck in rigid tribal boundaries.*
▶ **noun** (**tribals**) members of tribal communities, especially in South Asia.
– DERIVATIVES **tribally** adverb.

tribalism ▶ **noun** [mass noun] the state or fact of being organized in a tribe or tribes. ■ chiefly derogatory the behaviour and attitudes that stem from strong loyalty to one's own tribe or social group: *a society motivated by cultural tribalism.*
– DERIVATIVES **tribalist** noun (chiefly derogatory), **tribalistic** adjective (chiefly derogatory).

tri-band ▶ **adjective** (of a mobile phone) having three frequencies, enabling it to be used in different regions (typically Europe and the US).

tribasic /trʌɪˈbeɪsɪk/ ▶ **adjective** Chemistry (of an acid) having three replaceable hydrogen atoms.

tribe ▶ **noun 1** a social division in a traditional society consisting of families or communities linked by social, economic, religious, or blood ties, with a common culture and dialect, typically having a recognized leader: *indigenous Indian tribes.* ■ (in ancient Rome) each of several political divisions, originally three, later thirty, ultimately thirty-five. ■ derogatory a distinctive or close-knit group: *she made a stand against the social codes of her English middle-class tribe | an outburst against the whole tribe of theoreticians.* ■ informal a large number of people: *tribes of children playing under the watchful eyes of nurses.*
2 Biology a taxonomic category that ranks above genus and below family or subfamily, usually ending in *-ini* (in zoology) or *-eae* (in botany).
– ORIGIN Middle English: from Old French *tribu* or Latin *tribus* (singular and plural); perhaps related to *tri-* 'three' and referring to the three divisions of the early people of Rome.

> **USAGE** In historical contexts the word **tribe** is broadly accepted (*the area was inhabited by Slavic* ***tribes***), but in contemporary contexts it is problematic when used to refer to a community living within a traditional society. It is strongly associated with past attitudes of white colonialists towards so-called primitive or uncivilized peoples living in remote undeveloped places. For this reason it is generally preferable to use alternative terms such as **community** or **people**.

tribesman (or **tribeswoman**) ▶ **noun** (pl. **tribesmen** or **tribeswomen**) a person belonging to a tribe in a traditional society or group.

Tribes of Israel the twelve divisions of ancient Israel, traditionally descended from the twelve sons of Jacob. Ten of the tribes (Asher, Dan, Gad, Issachar, Levi, Manasseh, Naphtali, Reuben, Simeon, and Zebulun, known as the **Lost Tribes**) were deported to captivity in Assyria *c.*720 BC, leaving only the tribes of Judah and Benjamin. Also called **TWELVE TRIBES OF ISRAEL**.

tribespeople ▶ **plural noun** people belonging to a tribe in a traditional society or group.

triblet /ˈtrɪblɪt/ ▶ **noun** a cylindrical rod used for forging nuts, rings, tubes, and other rounded metallic objects.
– ORIGIN early 17th cent.: from French *triboulet*, of unknown origin.

tribo- /ˈtrʌɪbəʊ, ˈtrɪbəʊ/ ▶ **combining form** relating to friction: *triboelectricity*.
– ORIGIN from Greek *tribos* 'rubbing'.

tribology /trʌɪˈbɒlədʒi/ ▶ **noun** [mass noun] the study of friction, wear, lubrication, and the design of bearings; the science of interacting surfaces in relative motion.
– DERIVATIVES **tribological** adjective, **tribologist** noun.

triboluminescence ▶ **noun** [mass noun] the emission of light from a substance caused by rubbing, scratching, or similar frictional contact.
– DERIVATIVES **triboluminescent** adjective.

tribometer /trʌɪˈbɒmɪtə/ ▶ **noun** an instrument for measuring friction in sliding.

tribrach /ˈtrʌɪbrak, ˈtrɪ-/ ▶ **noun** Prosody a metrical foot of three short or unstressed syllables.
– DERIVATIVES **tribrachic** /-ˈbrakɪk/ adjective.
– ORIGIN late 16th cent.: via Latin from Greek *tribrakhus*, from *tri-* 'three' + *brakhus* 'short'.

tribulation /ˌtrɪbjʊˈleɪʃ(ə)n/ ▶ **noun** (usu. **tribulations**) a cause of great trouble or suffering: *the tribulations of being a megastar.* ■ [mass noun] a state of great trouble or suffering: *his time of tribulation was just beginning.*
– ORIGIN Middle English: via Old French from ecclesiastical Latin *tribulatio(n-)*, from Latin *tribulare* 'press, oppress', from *tribulum* 'threshing board (constructed of sharp points)', based on *terere* 'rub'.

tribunal /trʌɪˈbjuːn(ə)l, trɪ-/ ▶ **noun 1** Brit. a body established to settle certain types of dispute: *an industrial tribunal ruled that he was unfairly dismissed.*
2 a court of justice: *an international war crimes tribunal.* ■ a seat or bench for a judge or judges.
– ORIGIN late Middle English (denoting a seat for judges): from Old French, or from Latin *tribunal* 'raised platform provided for magistrate's seats', from *tribunus* (see **TRIBUNE**[1]). Sense 1 dates from the early 20th cent.

tribune[1] ▶ **noun** (also **tribune of the people**) an official in ancient Rome chosen by the plebeians to protect their interests. ■ (also **military tribune**) a Roman legionary officer. ■ a popular leader; a champion of people's rights.
– DERIVATIVES **tribunate** noun, **tribuneship** noun.

– ORIGIN late Middle English: from Latin *tribunus*, literally 'head of a tribe', from *tribus* 'tribe'.

tribune[2] ▶ **noun 1** an apse in a basilica.
2 a dais or rostrum, especially in a church. ■ a raised area or gallery with seats, especially in a church.
– ORIGIN mid 17th cent. (denoting the principal room in an Italian mansion): via French from Italian, from medieval Latin *tribuna*, alteration of Latin *tribunal* (see TRIBUNAL).

Tribune Group a left-wing group within the British Labour Party consisting of supporters of the views put forward in the weekly journal *Tribune*.

tributary /'trɪbjʊt(ə)ri/ ▶ **noun** (pl. **tributaries**) **1** a river or stream flowing into a larger river or lake: *the Illinois River, a tributary of the Mississippi.*
2 historical a person or state that pays tribute to another state or ruler: *tributaries of the Ottoman Empire.*
– ORIGIN late Middle English (in sense 2): from Latin *tributarius*, from *tributum* (see TRIBUTE). Sense 1 dates from the early 19th cent.

tribute ▶ **noun 1** an act, statement, or gift that is intended to show gratitude, respect, or admiration: *the video is a tribute to the musicals of the 40s* | [mass noun] *a symposium organized to **pay tribute to** Darwin.* ■ [in sing.] something resulting from a particular quality or feature and indicating its worth: *his victory in the championship was **a tribute to** his persistence.* ■ [as modifier] denoting or relating to a group or musician that performs the music of a more famous one and typically imitates them in appearance and style of performance: *an Abba tribute band* | *a tribute show.*
2 [mass noun] historical payment made periodically by one state or ruler to another, especially as a sign of dependence: *the king had at his disposal plunder and tribute amassed through warfare.*
3 historical a proportion of ore or its equivalent, paid to a miner for his work, or to the owner or lessor of a mine.
– ORIGIN late Middle English (in sense 2): from Latin *tributum*, neuter past participle (used as a noun) of *tribuere* 'assign' (originally 'divide between tribes'), from *tribus* 'tribe'.

tricar /'trʌɪkɑː/ ▶ **noun** Brit. dated a three-wheeled car.

tricarboxylic acid cycle /trʌɪˌkɑːbɒk'sɪlɪk/ ▶ **noun** another term for KREBS CYCLE.

tricast /'trʌɪkɑːst/ ▶ **noun** Brit. a bet in which the person betting forecasts the first three horses in a race in the correct order.
– ORIGIN 1970s: from TRI- 'three' + the noun FORECAST.

trice /trʌɪs/ ▶ **noun** (in phrase **in a trice**) in a moment; very quickly.
– ORIGIN late Middle English *trice* 'a tug', figuratively 'an instant', from Middle Dutch *trisen* 'pull sharply', related to *trīse* 'pulley'.

Tricel /'trʌɪsɛl/ ▶ **noun** [mass noun] trademark a textile fibre made from cellulose triacetate.
– ORIGIN 1950s: blend of TRIACETATE + CELLULOSE.

tricentenary ▶ **noun** (pl. **tricentenaries**) another term for TERCENTENARY.

tricentennial ▶ **adjective & noun** another term for TERCENTENARY.

triceps /'trʌɪsɛps/ ▶ **noun** (pl. **same**) Anatomy any of several muscles having three points of attachment at one end, particularly (also **triceps brachii** /'breɪkɪʌɪ/) the large muscle at the back of the upper arm.
– ORIGIN late 16th cent.: from Latin, literally 'three-headed', from *tri-* 'three' + *-ceps* (from *caput* 'head').

triceratops /trʌɪ'sɛrətɒps/ ▶ **noun** a large quadrupedal herbivorous dinosaur living at the end of the Cretaceous period, having a massive head with two large horns, a smaller horn on the beaked snout, and a bony frill above the neck. ● Genus *Triceratops*, infraorder Ceratopsia, order Ornithischia.
– ORIGIN modern Latin, from Greek *trikeratos* 'three-horned' + *ōps* 'face'.

trichiasis /ˌtrɪkɪ'eɪsɪs, trɪ'kʌɪəsɪs/ ▶ **noun** [mass noun] Medicine ingrowth or introversion of the eyelashes.
– ORIGIN mid 17th cent.: via late Latin from Greek *trikhiasis*, from *trikhian* 'be hairy'.

trichina /'trɪkɪnə, trɪ'kʌɪnə/ ▶ **noun** (pl. **trichinae** /-niː/) a parasitic nematode worm of humans and other mammals, the adults of which live in the small intestine. The larvae form hard cysts in the muscles, where they remain until eaten by the next host. ● Genus *Trichinella*, class Aphasmida (or Adenophorea).
– ORIGIN mid 19th cent.: from modern Latin (former genus name), from Greek *trikhinos* 'of hair'.

Trichinopoly /ˌtrɪtʃɪ'nɒpəli/ another name for TIRUCHIRAPALLI.

trichinosis /ˌtrɪkɪ'nəʊsɪs/ ▶ **noun** [mass noun] a disease caused by trichinae, typically from infected meat, characterized by digestive disturbance, fever, and muscular rigidity. ● This disease is typically caused by *Trichinella spiralis*.

trichloroacetate /ˌtrʌɪklɔːrəʊ'asɪteɪt/ ▶ **noun** Chemistry a salt or ester of trichloroacetic acid.

trichloroacetic acid /trʌɪˌklɔːrəʊə'siːtɪk, -ˌklɒrəʊ-/ (also **trichloracetic acid** /-ˌklɔːrə'siːtɪk, -ˌklɒr-/) ▶ **noun** [mass noun] Chemistry a toxic deliquescent crystalline solid used as a solvent, analgesic, and anaesthetic. ● Chem. formula: CCl_3COOH.

trichloroethane /ˌtrʌɪklɔːrəʊ'iːθeɪn, -klɒr-/ ▶ **noun** [mass noun] Chemistry a colourless non-flammable volatile liquid, used as a solvent and cleaner. ● Alternative name: **1,1,1-trichloroethane**; chem. formula: CCl_3CH_3.

trichloroethylene /ˌtrʌɪklɔːrəʊ'ɛθɪliːn, -klɒr-/ ▶ **noun** [mass noun] Chemistry a colourless volatile liquid used as a solvent and formerly as an anaesthetic. ● Chem. formula: $CCl_2{=}CHCl$.

trichlorophenol /ˌtrʌɪklɔːrə(ʊ)'fiːnɒl, -klɒr-/ ▶ **noun** [mass noun] Chemistry a synthetic crystalline compound used as an insecticide and preservative and in the synthesis of pesticides. ● Chem. formula: $C_6H_2Cl_3(OH)$; six isomers.

tricho- /'trɪkəʊ, 'trʌɪkəʊ/ ▶ **combining form** relating to hair: *trichology*.
– ORIGIN from Greek *thrix*, *trikhos* 'hair'.

trichocyst /'trɪkə(ʊ)sɪst, 'trʌɪ-/ ▶ **noun** Biology any of numerous minute rod-like structures, each containing a protrusible filament, found near the surface of ciliates and dinoflagellates.

trichology /trɪ'kɒlədʒi/ ▶ **noun** [mass noun] the branch of medical and cosmetic study and practice concerned with the hair and scalp.
– DERIVATIVES **trichological adjective**, **trichologist noun**.

trichome /'trʌɪkəʊm, 'trɪ-/ ▶ **noun** Botany a small hair or other outgrowth from the epidermis of a plant, typically unicellular and glandular.
– ORIGIN late 19th cent.: from Greek *trikhōma*, from *trikhoun* 'cover with hair'.

trichomonad /ˌtrɪkə(ʊ)'mɒnad/ ▶ **noun** Zoology & Medicine a parasitic protozoan with four to six flagella and an undulating membrane, infesting the urogenital or digestive system. ● Order Trichomonadida, phylum Parabasilia, kingdom Protista.
– DERIVATIVES **trichomonal adjective**.
– ORIGIN mid 19th cent.: from modern Latin *Trichomonadida* (plural), from Greek *thrix*, *trikh-* 'hair' + *monas*, *monad-* 'unit'.

trichomoniasis /ˌtrɪkə(ʊ)mə'nʌɪəsɪs/ ▶ **noun** [mass noun] Medicine an infection caused by parasitic trichomonads, chiefly affecting the urinary tract, vagina, or digestive system. ● Genus *Trichomonas*, in particular *T. vaginalis* (in the reproductive tract) and *T. hominis* (in the large intestine).

Trichoptera /trʌɪ'kɒpt(ə)rə/ ▶ **plural noun** Entomology an order of insects that comprises the caddis flies. ■ (**trichoptera**) insects of this order.
– ORIGIN modern Latin (plural), from TRICHO- 'hair' + *pteron* 'wing'.

trichopteran Entomology ▶ **noun** an insect of the order Trichoptera; a caddis fly.
▶ **adjective** relating to or denoting trichopterans.

trichotomy /trʌɪ'kɒtəmi, trɪ-/ ▶ **noun** (pl. **trichotomies**) a division into three categories: *the pragmatics–semantics–syntax trichotomy.*
– DERIVATIVES **trichotomous adjective**.
– ORIGIN 17th cent.: from Greek *trikha* 'threefold' from *treis* 'three', on the pattern of *dichotomy*.

trichroic /trʌɪ'krəʊɪk/ ▶ **adjective** Crystallography (of a crystal) appearing with different colours when viewed along the three crystallographic directions.
– DERIVATIVES **trichroism** /'trʌɪkrəʊɪz(ə)m/ **noun**.
– ORIGIN late 19th cent.: from Greek *trikhroos* (from *tri-* 'three' + *khrōs* 'colour') + -IC.

trichromatic /ˌtrʌɪkrə'matɪk/ ▶ **adjective** having or using three colours. ■ having normal colour vision, which is sensitive to all three primary colours.

trichrome /'trʌɪkrəʊm/ ▶ **adjective** Biology denoting a stain or method of histological staining in which different tissues are stained, each in one of three different colours.
– ORIGIN early 20th cent.: from TRI- 'three' + Greek *khrōma* 'colour'.

trick ▶ **noun 1** a cunning act or scheme intended to deceive or outwit someone: *he's a double-dealer capable of any mean trick.* ■ a mischievous practical joke: *she thought Elaine was **playing some trick on** her.* ■ an illusion: *I thought I saw a flicker of emotion, but it was probably **a trick of the light**.*
2 a skilful act performed for entertainment or amusement: *he did conjuring tricks for his daughters.* ■ a clever or particular way of doing something: *the trick is to put one ski forward and kneel.*
3 a peculiar or characteristic habit or mannerism: *she had a trick of clipping off certain words and phrases.*
4 (in bridge, whist, and similar card games) a sequence of cards forming a single round of play. One card is laid down by each player, the highest card being the winner.
5 informal a prostitute's client.
6 a sailor's turn at the helm, usually lasting for two or four hours.
▶ **verb** [with obj.] **1** cunningly deceive or outwit: *many people have been tricked by villains with false identity cards.* ■ (**trick someone into**) use deception to make someone do (something): *he tricked her into parting with the money.* ■ (**trick someone out of**) use deception to deprive someone of (something): *two men tricked a pensioner out of several hundred pounds.*
2 Heraldry sketch (a coat of arms) in outline, with the colours indicated by letters or signs.
▶ **adjective** [attrib.] **1** intended or used to deceive or mystify, or to create an illusion: *a trick question.*
2 N. Amer. liable to fail; defective: *a trick knee.*
– PHRASES **do the trick** informal achieve the required result. **every trick in the book** informal every available method of achieving what one wants. **how's tricks?** informal used as a friendly greeting: *'How's tricks in your neck of the woods?'* **not miss a trick** see MISS[1]. **the oldest trick in the book** a ruse so hackneyed that it should no longer deceive anyone. **tricks of the trade** special ingenious techniques used in a profession or craft, especially those that are little known by outsiders. **turn a trick** informal (of a prostitute) have a session with a client. **up to one's (old) tricks** informal misbehaving in a characteristic way.
– PHRASAL VERBS **trick someone/thing out** (or **up**) dress or decorate someone or something in an elaborate or showy way: *a Marine **tricked out** in World War II kit and weaponry.*
– DERIVATIVES **tricker noun**, **trickish adjective** (dated).
– ORIGIN late Middle English (as a noun): from an Old French dialect variant of *triche*, from *trichier* 'deceive', of unknown origin. Current senses of the verb date from the mid 16th cent.

trick cyclist ▶ **noun** Brit. humorous a psychiatrist.

trickery ▶ **noun** (pl. **trickeries**) [mass noun] the practice of deception: *the dealer resorted to trickery.*

trickle ▶ **verb** [no obj., with adverbial of direction] (of a liquid) flow in a small stream: *a solitary tear trickled down her cheek.* ■ [with obj. and adverbial of direction] cause (a liquid) to flow in a small stream: *Philip trickled a line of sauce on his fish fingers.* ■ come or go slowly or gradually: *the first members of the congregation began to trickle in.*
▶ **noun** a small flow of liquid: *a trickle of blood.* ■ a small group or number of people or things moving slowly: *the traffic had dwindled to a trickle.*
– PHRASAL VERBS **trickle down** (of wealth) gradually benefit the poorest as a result of the increasing wealth of the richest.
– ORIGIN Middle English (as a verb): imitative.

trickle charger ▶ **noun** an electrical charger for batteries that works at a steady slow rate from the mains.

trickle-down ▶ **noun** [usu. as modifier] the theory that the poorest in society gradually benefit as a result of the increasing wealth of the richest: *the trickle-down effect.*

trickle irrigation ▶ **noun** [mass noun] the supply of a controlled restricted flow of water to a number of points in a cultivated area.

trick or treat ▶ **noun** a children's custom of calling at houses at Halloween with the threat of pranks if they are not given a small gift (often used as a greeting by children doing this).
▶ **verb** [no obj.] (**trick-or-treat**) take part in the custom of trick or treat: *kids are going to go trick-or-treating tomorrow night.*
– DERIVATIVES **trick-or-treater noun**.

trickster ▶ **noun** a person who cheats or deceives people.

tricksy ▶ adjective (**tricksier**, **tricksiest**) playful or mischievous. ■ ingenious, intricate, or complicated: *a tricksy little device.*
– DERIVATIVES **tricksily** adverb, **tricksiness** noun.

tricky ▶ adjective (**trickier**, **trickiest**) **1** (of a task, problem, etc.) requiring care and skill because difficult or awkward: *applying eyeliner can be a tricky business | the radio is tricky to operate.*
2 deceitful or crafty: *I wouldn't trust her—she's tricky.*
– DERIVATIVES **trickily** adverb, **trickiness** noun.

triclad /ˈtrʌɪklad/ ▶ noun Zoology a free-living flatworm of an order characterized by having a gut with three branches, including the planarians. ● Order Tricladida, class Turbellaria.
– ORIGIN late 19th cent.: from modern Latin *Tricladida*, from TRI- 'three' + Greek *klados* 'branch'.

triclinic /trʌɪˈklɪnɪk/ ▶ adjective of or denoting a crystal system or three-dimensional geometrical arrangement having three unequal oblique axes.
– ORIGIN mid 19th cent.: from Greek TRI- 'three' + *-clinic*, on the pattern of *monoclinic*.

triclinium /trʌɪˈklɪnɪəm, trɪ-, -ˈklʌɪn-/ ▶ noun (pl. **triclinia** /-nɪə/) a dining table with couches along three sides, used in ancient Rome. ■ a room containing such a table.
– ORIGIN Latin, from Greek *triklinion*, from *tri-* 'three' + *klinē* 'couch'.

tricolour /ˈtrɪkələ, ˈtrʌɪkʌlə/ (US **tricolor**) ▶ noun a flag with three bands or blocks of different colours, especially the French national flag with equal upright bands of blue, white, and red.
▶ adjective (also **tricoloured**) having three colours.
– ORIGIN late 18th cent.: from French *tricolore*, from late Latin *tricolor* (see TRI-, COLOUR).

tricorne /ˈtrʌɪkɔːn/ (also **tricorn**) ▶ adjective (of a hat) having a brim turned up on three sides.
▶ noun a tricorne hat.
– ORIGIN mid 19th cent.: from French *tricorne* or Latin *tricornis*, from *tri-* 'three' + *cornu* 'horn'.

tricot /ˈtrɪkəʊ, ˈtriː-/ ▶ noun [mass noun] a fine knitted fabric made of a natural or man-made fibre.
– ORIGIN late 18th cent.: from French, literally 'knitting', from *tricoter* 'to knit', of unknown origin.

tricoteuse /ˌtrɪkəˈtəːz/, French /tʀikɔtøz/ ▶ noun (pl. pronunc. **same**) one of a number of women who sat and knitted while attending public executions during the French Revolution.
– ORIGIN French, from *tricoter* 'to knit'.

tric-trac ▶ noun [mass noun] historical a form of backgammon.
– ORIGIN late 17th cent.: from French, from the clicking sound made by the game pieces.

tricuspid /trʌɪˈkʌspɪd/ ▶ adjective **1** denoting a tooth with three cusps or points.
2 denoting or relating to a valve formed of three triangular segments, particularly that between the right atrium and ventricle of the heart: *tricuspid atresia.*
– ORIGIN late 17th cent.: from TRI- 'three' + Latin *cuspis, cuspid-* 'cusp'.

tricycle ▶ noun a vehicle similar to a bicycle, but having three wheels, two at the back and one at the front. ■ a three-wheeled motor vehicle for a disabled driver.
▶ verb [no obj.] (often as noun **tricycling**) ride on a tricycle.
– DERIVATIVES **tricyclist** noun.

tricyclic /trʌɪˈsʌɪklɪk/ ▶ adjective Chemistry (of a compound) having three rings of atoms in its molecule.
▶ noun (usu. **tricyclics**) Medicine any of a class of antidepressant drugs having molecules with three fused rings.
– ORIGIN late 19th cent.: from TRI- 'three' + Greek *kuklos* 'circle' + -IC.

tridactyl /trʌɪˈdaktɪl/ ▶ adjective Zoology (of a vertebrate limb) having three toes or fingers.
– ORIGIN early 19th cent.: from TRI- 'three' + Greek *daktulos* 'finger'.

trident ▶ noun **1** a three-pronged spear, especially as an attribute of Poseidon (Neptune) or Britannia.
2 (**Trident**) a US design of submarine-launched long-range ballistic missile.
– ORIGIN late Middle English: from Latin *trident-*, from *tri-* 'three' + *dens, dent-* 'tooth'.

Tridentine /trɪˈdɛntʌɪn, trʌɪ-/ ▶ adjective relating to the Council of Trent, especially as the basis of Roman Catholic doctrine.
– ORIGIN from medieval Latin *Tridentinus*, from *Tridentum* 'Trent'.

Tridentine mass ▶ noun the Latin Eucharistic liturgy used by the Roman Catholic Church from 1570 to 1964.

triduum /ˈtrɪdjʊəm, ˈtrʌɪ-/ ▶ noun [in sing.] (especially in the Roman Catholic Church) a period of three days' observance, specifically Maundy Thursday, Good Friday, and Holy Saturday.
– ORIGIN Latin, from *tri-* 'three' + *dies* 'day'.

tridymite /ˈtrɪdɪmʌɪt/ ▶ noun [mass noun] a high-temperature form of quartz found as thin hexagonal crystals in some igneous rocks and stony meteorites.
– ORIGIN mid 19th cent.: from German *Tridymit*, from Greek *tridumos* 'threefold', from *tri-* 'three' + *-dumos* (as in *didumos* 'twin'), because of its occurrence in groups of three crystals.

tried past and past participle of TRY.
– PHRASES **tried and tested** (or **tried and trusted** or N. Amer. **tried and true**) denoting something that has proven in the past to be effective or reliable: *a tried-and-tested recipe.*

triene /ˈtrʌɪiːn/ ▶ noun Chemistry an unsaturated hydrocarbon containing three double bonds between carbon atoms.

triennial /trʌɪˈɛnɪəl/ ▶ adjective recurring every three years: *the triennial meeting of the Association.* ■ lasting for or relating to a period of three years.
▶ noun a visitation of an Anglican diocese by its bishop every three years.
– DERIVATIVES **triennially** adverb.
– ORIGIN mid 16th cent.: from late Latin *triennis* (from Latin *tri-* 'three' + *annus* 'year') + -AL.

triennium /trʌɪˈɛnɪəm/ ▶ noun (pl. **triennia** /-nɪə/ or **trienniums**) a specified period of three years.
– ORIGIN mid 19th cent.: from Latin, from *tri-* 'three' + *annum* 'year'.

Trier /trɪə/ a city on the River Mosel in Rhineland-Palatinate, western Germany; pop. 103,500 (est. 2006). French name **TRÈVES** Established by a Germanic tribe, the Treveri, *c.*400 BC, Trier is one of the oldest cities in Europe. It was a powerful archbishopric from 815 until the 18th century, but fell into decline after the French occupation in 1797.

trier ▶ noun **1** a person who always makes an effort, however unsuccessful they may be: *Kelly was described by her teachers as a real trier.*
2 a person or body responsible for investigating and deciding a case judicially: *the jury is the trier of fact.*

Trieste /trɪˈɛst/ a city in NE Italy, the largest port on the Adriatic and capital of Friuli-Venezia Giulia region; pop. 205,341 (2008). Formerly held by Austria (1382–1918), Trieste was annexed by Italy after the First World War. The Free Territory of Trieste was created after the Second World War but returned to Italy in 1954.

trifa /ˈtrʌɪfə/ ▶ adjective another term for TREFA.

trifacial nerve /trʌɪˈfeɪʃ(ə)l/ ▶ noun another term for TRIGEMINAL NERVE.

trifecta /trʌɪˈfɛktə/ ▶ noun N. Amer. & Austral./NZ a bet in which the person betting forecasts the first three finishers in a race in the correct order. ■ [in sing.] a run of three wins or grand events: *he will attempt a trifecta of the long jump, triple jump, and 110-meter high hurdles.*
– ORIGIN 1970s: from TRI- 'three' + PERFECTA.

triffid ▶ noun (in science fiction) a member of a race of predatory plants which are capable of growing to a gigantic size and are possessed of locomotive ability and a poisonous sting.
– ORIGIN coined by John Wyndham in *Day of the Triffids* (1951).

trifid /ˈtrʌɪfɪd/ ▶ adjective **1** chiefly Biology partly or wholly split into three divisions or lobes.
2 (also **trefid**) (of an antique spoon) with three notches splitting the end of the handle.
– ORIGIN mid 18th cent.: from Latin *trifidus*, from *tri-* 'three' + *fid-* 'split, divided' (from the verb *findere*).

trifle ▶ noun **1** a thing of little value or importance: *we needn't trouble the headmaster over such trifles.* ■ [in sing.] a small amount of something: *the thousand yen he'd paid seemed the merest trifle.*
2 Brit. a cold dessert of sponge cake and fruit covered with layers of custard, jelly, and cream.
▶ verb [no obj.] **1** (**trifle with**) treat without seriousness or respect: *he is **not a man to be trifled with** | men who trifle with women's affections.*
2 archaic talk or act frivolously: *we will not trifle—life is too short.* ■ [with obj.] (**trifle something away**) waste something, especially time, frivolously.
– PHRASES **a trifle** a little; somewhat: *his methods are a trifle eccentric.*
– DERIVATIVES **trifler** noun.
– ORIGIN Middle English (also denoting an idle story told to deceive or amuse): from Old French *trufle*, by-form of *trufe* 'deceit', of unknown origin. The verb derives from Old French *truffler* 'mock, deceive'.

trifling ▶ adjective unimportant or trivial: *a trifling sum.*
– DERIVATIVES **triflingly** adverb.

trifluoperazine /ˌtrʌɪfluːə(ʊ)ˈpɛrəziːn/ ▶ noun [mass noun] Medicine an antipsychotic and sedative drug related to phenothiazine.
– ORIGIN 1950s: from TRI- + *fluo(rine)* + *(pi)perazine*.

trifocal ▶ adjective (of a pair of glasses) having lenses with three parts with different focal lengths.
▶ noun (**trifocals**) a pair of glasses with trifocal lenses.

trifold /ˈtrʌɪfəʊld/ ▶ adjective triple; threefold: *a trifold partnership between government, employers, and students.*

trifoliate /trʌɪˈfəʊlɪət/ ▶ adjective (of a compound leaf) having three leaflets: *dark green trifoliate leaves.* ■ (of a plant) having trifoliate leaves. ■ (of an object or design) having the form of a trifoliate leaf: *a bronze trifoliate key handle.*

triforium /trʌɪˈfɔːrɪəm/ ▶ noun (pl. **triforia** /-rɪə/) a gallery or arcade above the arches of the nave, choir, and transepts of a church.
– ORIGIN early 18th cent.: from Anglo-Latin, of unknown origin.

triform ▶ adjective technical composed of three parts: *strawberries nestling among their triform leaves.*

trifurcate ▶ verb /ˈtrʌɪfəkeɪt/ [no obj.] divide into three branches or forks.
▶ adjective /trʌɪˈfəːkət/ divided into three branches or forks.
– DERIVATIVES **trifurcation** noun.
– ORIGIN mid 19th cent.: from Latin *trifurcus* 'three-forked' (from *tri-* 'three' + *furca* 'fork') + -ATE[2].

trig[1] ▶ noun [mass noun] informal trigonometry.
– ORIGIN late 19th cent.: abbreviation.

trig[2] US or archaic ▶ adjective neat and smart in appearance: *two trig little boys, each in a gray flannel suit.*
▶ verb (**trigs**, **trigging**, **trigged**) [with obj.] make neat and smart in appearance: *he has rigged her and trigged her with paint and spar.*
– ORIGIN Middle English (in the sense 'faithful, trusty'): from Old Norse *tryggr*; related to TRUE. The current verb sense dates from the late 17th cent.

trigamous /ˈtrɪgəməs/ ▶ adjective having three wives or husbands at the same time.
– DERIVATIVES **trigamist** noun, **trigamy** noun.
– ORIGIN mid 19th cent.: from Greek *trigamos* (from *tri-* 'three' + *gamos* 'marriage') + **-OUS**. The nouns *trigamist* and *trigamy* date from the mid 17th cent.

trigeminal nerve /trʌɪˈdʒɛmɪn(ə)l/ ▶ noun Anatomy each of the fifth and largest pair of cranial nerves, supplying the front part of the head and dividing into the ophthalmic, maxillary, and mandibular nerves.

trigeminal neuralgia ▶ noun [mass noun] Medicine neuralgia involving one or more of the branches of the trigeminal nerves, and often causing severe pain.

trigeminus /trʌɪˈdʒɛmɪnəs/ ▶ noun (pl. **trigemini** /-nʌɪ/) Anatomy each of the trigeminal nerves.
– ORIGIN late 19th cent.: from Latin, literally 'three born at the same birth', extended to mean 'threefold'.

trigger ▶ noun a small device that releases a spring or catch and so sets off a mechanism, especially in order to fire a gun: *he pulled the trigger of the shotgun.* ■ an event that is the cause of a particular action, process, or situation: *the trigger for the strike was the closure of a mine.*
▶ verb [with obj.] cause (a device) to function: *burglars fled empty-handed after triggering the alarm.* ■ (also **trigger something off**) cause (an event or situation) to happen or exist: *an allergy can be triggered by stress or overwork.*
– PHRASES **quick on the trigger** quick to respond.
– DERIVATIVES **triggered** adjective.
– ORIGIN early 17th cent.: from dialect *tricker*, from Dutch *trekker*, from *trekken* 'to pull'.

trigger finger ▶ noun **1** the forefinger of the right hand, as that with which the trigger of a gun is typically pulled.
2 [mass noun] Medicine a defect in a tendon causing a finger to jerk or snap straight when the hand is extended.

triggerfish ▶ noun (pl. **same** or **triggerfishes**) a marine fish occurring chiefly in tropical inshore

T

waters. It has a large stout dorsal spine which can be erected and locked into place, allowing the fish to wedge itself into crevices. ● Family Balistidae: numerous genera and species.

trigger hair ▶ noun **1** Zoology (in a coelenterate) a filament at the mouth of a nematocyst which triggers the emission of the stinging hair when touched.
2 Botany a bristle on the leaf of a Venus flytrap which triggers the closure of the leaf around an insect.

trigger-happy ▶ adjective ready to react violently, especially by shooting, on the slightest provocation: *territory controlled by trigger-happy bandits.*

trigger point ▶ noun **1** a particular circumstance which causes an event: *the army's refusal to withdraw from the territory was the trigger point for military action.*
2 Physiology & Medicine a sensitive area of the body, stimulation or irritation of which causes a specific effect in another part, especially a tender area in a muscle which causes generalized musculoskeletal pain when overstimulated.

Triglav /ˈtriːglaf/ a mountain in the Julian Alps, NW Slovenia, near the Italian border. Rising to 2,863 m (9,392 ft), it is the highest peak in the mountains east of the Adriatic.

triglyceride /trʌɪˈglɪsərʌɪd/ ▶ noun Chemistry an ester formed from glycerol and three fatty acid groups. Triglycerides are the main constituents of natural fats and oils.

triglyph /ˈtrʌɪglɪf/ ▶ noun Architecture a tablet in a Doric frieze with three vertical grooves alternating with metopes.
– ORIGIN mid 16th cent.: via Latin from Greek *trigluphos*, from *tri-* 'three' + *gluphē* 'carving'.

trigon /ˈtrʌɪgɒn/ ▶ noun archaic term for **TRIANGLE**. ■ an ancient triangular lyre or harp. ■ a triangular cutting region formed by three cusps on an upper molar tooth.
– ORIGIN early 17th cent. (in the sense 'triangle'): via Latin from Greek *trigōnon*, neuter of *trigōnos* 'three-cornered'.

trigonal /ˈtrɪg(ə)n(ə)l/ ▶ adjective triangular: *square or trigonal double-sided inserts.* ■ chiefly Biology triangular in cross section: *large trigonal shells.* ■ of or denoting a crystal system or three-dimensional geometrical arrangement having three equal axes separated by equal angles that are not right angles.
– DERIVATIVES **trigonally** adverb.
– ORIGIN late 16th cent.: from medieval Latin *trigonalis*, from Latin *trigonum* (see **TRIGON**).

trigone /trɪˈgəʊn, ˈtrʌɪ-/ ▶ noun Anatomy a triangular region or tissue, particularly the area at the base of the urinary bladder, between the openings of the ureters and urethra.
– ORIGIN mid 19th cent.: from French, from Latin *trigonum* 'triangle'.

trigonometry /ˌtrɪgəˈnɒmɪtri/ ▶ noun [mass noun] the branch of mathematics dealing with the relations of the sides and angles of triangles and with the relevant functions of any angles.
– DERIVATIVES **trigonometric** /-nəˈmɛtrɪk/ adjective, **trigonometrical** adjective.
– ORIGIN early 17th cent.: from modern Latin *trigonometria* (see **TRIGON**, **-METRY**).

trig point ▶ noun Brit. a reference point on high ground used in surveying, typically marked by a small pillar.
– ORIGIN mid 19th cent.: abbreviation of *trigonometrical point*.

trigram /ˈtrʌɪgram/ ▶ noun **1** another term for **TRIGRAPH**.
2 each of the eight figures formed of three parallel lines, each either whole or broken, combined to form the sixty-four hexagrams of the *I Ching*.

trigraph /ˈtrʌɪgrɑːf/ ▶ noun a group of three letters representing one sound, for example German *sch-*.

trihedral /trʌɪˈhiːdr(ə)l, -ˈhɛdr(ə)l/ ▶ adjective (of a solid figure or body) having three sides or faces (in addition to the base or ends); triangular in cross section.
▶ noun a trihedral figure.
– ORIGIN late 18th cent.: from Greek *tri-* 'three' + *hedra* 'base' + **-AL**.

trihedron /trʌɪˈhiːdrən, -ˈhɛdrən/ ▶ noun (pl. **trihedra** /-drə/ or **trihedrons**) a solid figure having three sides or faces (in addition to the base or ends).
– ORIGIN early 19th cent.: from **TRI-** 'three' + **-HEDRON**, on the pattern of words such as *polyhedron*.

trihydric /trʌɪˈhʌɪdrɪk/ ▶ adjective Chemistry (of an alcohol) containing three hydroxyl groups.
– ORIGIN mid 19th cent.: from **TRI-** 'three' + **HYDROGEN** + **-IC**.

triiodomethane /trʌɪˌʌɪədə(ʊ)ˈmiːθeɪn/ ▶ noun another term for **IODOFORM**.

triiodothyronine /trʌɪˌʌɪədə(ʊ)ˈθʌɪrəniːn/ ▶ noun [mass noun] Biochemistry a thyroid hormone similar to thyroxine but having greater potency.

trike informal ▶ noun **1** a tricycle.
2 a kind of ultralight aircraft.
▶ verb [no obj.] ride on a tricycle.
– ORIGIN late 19th cent.: abbreviation.

trilateral ▶ adjective **1** shared by or involving three parties: *trilateral negotiations.*
2 Geometry of or having three sides.
▶ noun a triangle.

trilby ▶ noun (pl. **trilbies**) chiefly Brit. a soft felt hat with a narrow brim and indented crown.
– DERIVATIVES **trilbied** adjective.
– ORIGIN late 19th cent.: from the name of the heroine in G. du Maurier's novel *Trilby* (1894), in the stage version of which such a hat was worn.

trilinear ▶ adjective Mathematics of or having three lines.

trilingual ▶ adjective speaking three languages fluently. ■ (of a text or an activity) written or conducted in three languages: *CNN have begun offering a trilingual entertainment service.*
– DERIVATIVES **trilingualism** noun.
– ORIGIN mid 19th cent.: from **TRI-** 'three' + Latin *lingua* 'tongue' + **-AL**.

trilithon /trʌɪˈlɪθ(ə)n/ (also **trilith** /ˈtrʌɪlɪθ/) ▶ noun Archaeology a megalithic structure consisting of two upright stones and a third across the top as a lintel.
– ORIGIN mid 18th cent.: from Greek, from *tri-* 'three' + *lithos* 'stone'.

trill ▶ noun a quavering or vibratory sound, especially a rapid alternation of sung or played notes: *the caged bird launched into a piercing trill.* ■ the pronunciation of a consonant, especially *r*, with rapid vibration of the tongue against the hard or soft palate or the uvula.
▶ verb [no obj.] produce a quavering or warbling sound: *a skylark was trilling overhead* | [with direct speech] *'Coming sir,' they both trilled* | [with obj.] *trilling a love ballad, she led him to her chair.* ■ [with obj.] pronounce (a consonant) by rapid vibration of the tongue against the hard or soft palate or the uvula.
– ORIGIN mid 17th cent.: from Italian *trillo* (noun), *trillare* (verb).

triller ▶ noun an Australasian and SE Asian songbird of the cuckoo-shrike family, with mainly black and white plumage. ● Family Campephagidae: two genera, in particular *Lalage*, and several species.

trillion ▶ cardinal number (pl. **trillions** or (with numeral or quantifying word) **same**) a million million (1,000,000,000,000 or 10^{12}). ■ (**trillions**) informal a very large number or amount: *the yammering of trillions of voices.* ■ Brit. dated a million million million (1,000,000,000,000,000,000 or 10^{18}).
– DERIVATIVES **trillionth** ordinal number.
– ORIGIN late 17th cent.: from French, from *million*, by substitution of the prefix *tri-* 'three' for the initial letters.

trillium /ˈtrɪlɪəm/ ▶ noun (pl. **trilliums**) a plant with a solitary three-petalled flower above a whorl of three leaves, native to North America and Asia. ● Genus *Trillium*, family Liliaceae (or Trilliaceae).
– ORIGIN modern Latin, apparently an alteration of Swedish *trilling* 'triplet'.

trilobite /ˈtrʌɪlə(ʊ)bʌɪt, ˈtrɪ-/ ▶ noun a fossil marine arthropod that occurred abundantly during the Palaeozoic era, with a carapace over the forepart, and a segmented hind part divided longitudinally into three lobes. ● Subphylum Trilobita, phylum Arthropoda: numerous classes and orders.
– ORIGIN mid 19th cent.: from modern Latin *Trilobites*, from Greek *tri-* 'three' + *lobos* 'lobe'.

trilogy ▶ noun (pl. **trilogies**) a group of three related novels, plays, films, etc. ■ (in ancient Greece) a series of three tragedies performed one after the other. ■ a group of three related things: *a trilogy of cases reflected this development.*

Trim a town in Meath, in the Republic of Ireland, situated to the north-west of Dublin; pop. 7,700 (est. 2009).

trim ▶ verb (**trims**, **trimming**, **trimmed**) [with obj.] **1** make (something) neat or of the required size or form by cutting away irregular or unwanted parts: *trim the grass using a sharp mower.* ■ [with obj. and adverbial] cut off (irregular or unwanted parts): *he was trimming the fat off some pork chops.* ■ reduce the size, amount, number, or cost of: *Congress had to decide which current defence programmes should be trimmed.* ■ [no obj.] (**trim down**) (of a person) lose weight; become slimmer: *he trimmed down from twenty-two stone to a mere eighteen.* ■ firm up or lose weight from (a part of one's body): *the machine is ideal for trimming the waist, hips, and thighs.*
2 decorate (something), typically with contrasting items or pieces of material: *a pair of black leather gloves trimmed with fake fur.*
3 adjust (a sail) to take advantage of the wind. ■ adjust the balance of (a ship or aircraft) by rearranging its cargo or by means of its trim tabs. ■ keep or adjust the degree to which (an aircraft) can be maintained at a constant altitude without any control forces being present. ■ [no obj.] adapt one's views to the prevailing political trends for personal advancement.
4 informal, dated get the better of (someone), typically by cheating them out of money.
5 informal, dated rebuke (someone) angrily.
▶ noun [mass noun] **1** additional decoration, typically along the edges of something and in contrasting colour or material: *a red blazer with gold trim* | [count noun] *the buildings were off-white with a blue trim.* ■ decorative additions to a vehicle, typically the upholstery or interior lining of a car.
2 [count noun] an act of cutting something in order to neaten it: *his hair needs a trim.* ■ a short piece of film cut out during the final editing stage.
3 the state of being in good order or condition: *no one had been there for months—everything was out of trim.*
4 the degree to which an aircraft can be maintained at a constant altitude without any control forces being present.
5 the way in which a ship floats in the water, especially in relation to the fore-and-aft line.
▶ adjective (**trimmer**, **trimmest**) neat and smart in appearance; in good order: *she kept her husband's clothes neat and trim* | *a trim little villa.* ■ slim and fit: *she has a trim, athletic figure.*
– PHRASES **in trim** slim and fit. ■ Nautical in good order. **trim one's sails (to the wind)** make changes to suit one's new circumstances.
– DERIVATIVES **trimly** adverb, **trimness** noun.
– ORIGIN Old English *trymman*, *trymian* 'make firm, arrange', of which the adjective appears to be a derivative. The word's history is obscure; current verb senses date from the early 16th cent. when usage became frequent and served many purposes: this is possibly explained by spoken or dialect use in the Middle English period not recorded in extant literature.

trimaran /ˈtrʌɪməran/ ▶ noun a yacht with three hulls in parallel.
– ORIGIN 1940s: from **TRI-** + **CATAMARAN**.

trimer /ˈtrʌɪmə/ ▶ noun Chemistry a polymer comprising three monomer units.
– DERIVATIVES **trimeric** adjective.

trimerous /ˈtrɪm(ə)rəs, ˈtrʌɪ-/ ▶ adjective Botany & Zoology having parts arranged in groups of three. ■ consisting of three joints or parts.

trimester /trʌɪˈmɛstə/ ▶ noun a period of three months, especially as a division of the duration of pregnancy. ■ N. Amer. each of the three terms in an academic year.
– ORIGIN early 19th cent.: from French *trimestre*, from Latin *trimestris*, from *tri-* 'three' + *mensis* 'month'.

trimeter /ˈtrɪmɪtə, ˈtrʌɪ-/ ▶ noun Prosody a line of verse consisting of three metrical feet.
– DERIVATIVES **trimetric** adjective, **trimetrical** adjective.
– ORIGIN mid 16th cent.: via Latin from Greek *trimetros*, from *tri-* 'three' + *metron* 'measure'.

trimethoprim /trʌɪˈmɛθə(ʊ)prɪm/ ▶ noun [mass noun] Medicine a synthetic antibiotic used to treat malaria and respiratory and urinary infections (usually in conjunction with a sulphonamide).
– ORIGIN 1960s: from *trimeth(yl)* + *o(xy-)* + *p(y)rim(idine)*.

trimix /ˈtrʌɪmɪks/ ▶ noun [mass noun] a breathing mixture for deep-sea divers, composed of nitrogen, helium, and oxygen.

trimmer ▶ noun **1** an implement used for cutting and neatening something: *a hedge trimmer.*
2 a person who adapts their views to the prevailing political trends for personal advancement.

T

3 a person who decorates something: *window trimmers*.
4 (also **trimmer joist**) Architecture a crosspiece fixed between full-length joists (and often across the end of truncated joists) to form part of the frame of an opening in a floor or roof.
5 a person responsible for trimming the sails of a yacht. ▪ a person employed to arrange cargo or fuel in a ship's hold.
6 a small capacitor or other component used to tune a circuit such as a radio set.
7 Austral./NZ informal an excellent or outstanding person or thing.

trimming ▶ noun (usu. **trimmings**) 1 small pieces trimmed off something: *hedge trimmings*.
2 decoration, especially for clothing: *a white romper suit with pink trimmings* | [mass noun] *a party dress with lace trimming*. ▪ (**the trimmings**) informal the traditional accompaniments to something, especially a meal: *roast turkey **with all the trimmings***.

Trimontium /trʌɪˈmɒntɪəm/ Roman name for **Plovdiv**.

trimpot ▶ noun a small potentiometer used to make small adjustments to the value of resistance or voltage in an electronic circuit.

trim tab (also **trimming tab**) ▶ noun 1 Aeronautics an adjustable tab or aerofoil attached to a control surface, used to trim an aircraft in flight.
2 Nautical an adjustable flap fitted to the trailing edge of a rudder or keel, used to adjust steering, or fitted horizontally as one of a pair on the stern and used to trim a boat at speed.

Trimurti /trɪˈmʊrti, trɪˈmʊəti/ Hinduism the trinity of Brahma, Vishnu, and Shiva.
– ORIGIN from Sanskrit *tri* 'three' + *mūrti* 'form'.

Trincomalee /ˌtrɪŋkəməˈliː/ the principal port of Sri Lanka, on the east coast; pop. 51,600 (est. 2007). It was the chief British naval base in SE Asia during the Second World War after the fall of Singapore.

trine /trʌɪn/ Astrology ▶ noun an aspect of 120° (one third of a circle): *Venus **in trine to** Mars* | [as modifier] *a trine aspect*. See also **grand trine**.
▶ verb [with obj.] (of a planet) be in a trine aspect with (another planet or position): *Jupiter trines Pluto all month*.
– ORIGIN late Middle English (in the sense 'made up of three parts'): from Old French *trin(e)*, from Latin *trinus* 'threefold', from *tres* 'three'.

Trini /ˈtrɪni/ ▶ noun (pl. **Trinis**) W. Indian a Trinidadian.

Trinidad and Tobago /ˈtrɪnɪdad, təˈbeɪgəʊ/ a country in the Caribbean consisting of two islands off the NE coast of Venezuela; pop. 1,230,000 (est. 2009); languages, English (official), Creoles; capital, Port-of-Spain (on Trinidad).

> Much the larger of the two islands is Trinidad, with Tobago to the north-east. Trinidad, inhabited by Arawaks, was visited by Columbus in 1498 and settled by the Spanish; Tobago, occupied by Caribs, was colonized by the French and later the British in the 18th century. Trinidad became British during the Napoleonic Wars and was formally amalgamated with Tobago as a Crown Colony in 1888. Trinidad and Tobago became an independent member state of the Commonwealth in 1962 and finally a republic in 1976.

– DERIVATIVES **Trinidadian** /ˌtrɪnɪˈdeɪdɪən, -ˈdadɪən/ adjective & noun, **Tobagonian** /ˌtəʊbəˈgəʊnɪən/ adjective & noun.

Trinitarian /ˌtrɪnɪˈtɛːrɪən/ ▶ adjective relating to belief in the doctrine of the Trinity.
▶ noun a person who believes in the doctrine of the Trinity.
– DERIVATIVES **Trinitarianism** noun.

trinitrotoluene /trʌɪˌnʌɪtrəʊˈtɒljʊiːn/ ▶ noun see **TNT**.

trinity ▶ noun (pl. **trinities**) (**the Trinity** or **the Holy Trinity**) the three persons of the Christian Godhead; Father, Son, and Holy Spirit. ▪ a group of three people or things: *the wine was the first of a trinity of three excellent vintages*. ▪ [mass noun] the state of being three: *God is said to be trinity in unity*.
– ORIGIN Middle English: from Old French *trinite*, from Latin *trinitas* 'triad', from *trinus* 'threefold' (see **trine**).

Trinity Brethren ▶ plural noun the members of Trinity House.

Trinity House an association founded in 1514 responsible for the licensing of ships' pilots and the construction and maintenance of buoys and lighthouses around the coasts of England and Wales.

Trinity Sunday ▶ noun the next Sunday after Pentecost, observed in the Western Christian Church as a feast in honour of the Holy Trinity.

Trinity term ▶ noun Brit. (in some universities) the term beginning after Easter.

trinket ▶ noun a small ornament or item of jewellery that is of little value.
– DERIVATIVES **trinketry** noun.
– ORIGIN mid 16th cent.: of unknown origin.

trinomial /trʌɪˈnəʊmɪəl/ ▶ adjective 1 (of an algebraic expression) consisting of three terms.
2 Biology (of a taxonomic name) consisting of three terms where the first is the name of the genus, the second that of the species, and the third that of the subspecies or variety.
▶ noun 1 an algebraic expression of three terms.
2 Biology a trinomial taxonomic name.
– ORIGIN late 17th cent.: from **tri-** 'three', on the pattern of *binomial*.

trio ▶ noun (pl. **trios**) a set or group of three people or things: *the hotel was run by a trio of brothers*. ▪ a group of three musicians: *a jazz trio*. ▪ a composition written for three musicians: *Chopin's G minor Trio*. ▪ the central, typically contrastive, section of a minuet, scherzo, or march. ▪ (in piquet) a set of three aces, kings, queens, jacks, or tens held in one hand.
– ORIGIN early 18th cent.: from Italian, from Latin *tres* 'three', on the pattern of *duo*.

triode /ˈtrʌɪəʊd/ ▶ noun a thermionic valve having three electrodes. ▪ a semiconductor rectifier having three connections.
– ORIGIN early 20th cent.: from **tri-** 'three' + **electrode**.

triolet /ˈtriːə(ʊ)lɛt, ˈtrʌɪəlɛt/ ▶ noun a poem of eight lines, typically of eight syllables each, rhyming *abaaabab* and so structured that the first line recurs as the fourth and seventh and the second as the eighth.
– ORIGIN mid 17th cent.: from French.

triose /ˈtrʌɪəʊz, -s/ ▶ noun Chemistry any of a group of monosaccharide sugars whose molecules contain three carbon atoms.

trio sonata ▶ noun a baroque composition written in three parts, two upper parts and one bass, and usually performed with a keyboard continuo.

trioxide ▶ noun Chemistry an oxide containing three atoms of oxygen in its molecule or empirical formula.

trip ▶ verb (**trips, tripping, tripped**) 1 [no obj.] catch one's foot on something and stumble or fall: *he **tripped over** his cat* | *she **tripped up** during the penultimate lap*. ▪ [with obj.] cause to stumble and fall: *she shot out her foot to **trip him up***. ▪ (**trip up**) make a mistake: *taxpayers often trip up by not declaring taxable income*. ▪ [with obj.] (**trip someone up**) detect or expose someone in a mistake or inconsistency: *the man was determined to trip him up on his economics*.
2 [no obj., with adverbial] walk, run, or dance with quick light steps: *they tripped up the terrace steps*. ▪ (of words) flow lightly and easily: *a name which **trips off the tongue***.
3 [with obj.] activate (a mechanism), especially by contact with a switch, catch, or other electrical device: *somebody tripped the alarm*. ▪ [no obj.] (of part of an electric circuit) disconnect automatically as a safety measure: *the plugs will trip as soon as any change in current is detected*.
4 [with obj.] Nautical release and raise (an anchor) from the seabed by means of a cable. ▪ turn (a yard or other object) from a horizontal to a vertical position for lowering.
5 [no obj.] informal experience hallucinations induced by taking a psychedelic drug, especially LSD: *a couple of boys were tripping*.
6 [no obj., with adverbial of direction] go on a short journey: *when tripping through the Yukon take some time to explore our museums*.
▶ noun 1 a journey or excursion, especially for pleasure: *Sammy's gone on a school trip* | *a trip to America*. ▪ the distance from start to finish of a race: *the dog clocked a tremendous 27.47 secs for the 450 metres trip*.
2 a stumble or fall due to catching one's foot on something. ▪ archaic a mistake: *an occasional trip in the performance*.
3 informal a hallucinatory experience caused by taking a psychedelic drug, especially LSD: *acid trips*. ▪ an exciting or stimulating experience: *it was quite a trip talking to you*. ▪ a self-indulgent attitude or activity: *I'm not sure if she really liked me or if I was just part of her power trip*.
4 a device that activates or disconnects a mechanism, circuit, etc.
5 archaic a light, lively movement of a person's feet: *yonder comes Dalinda; I know her by her trip*.
– PHRASES **trip the light fantastic** humorous dance, in particular engage in ballroom dancing. [from 'Trip it as you go On the light fantastic toe' (Milton's *L'Allegro*).]
– ORIGIN Middle English: from Old French *triper*, from Middle Dutch *trippen* 'to skip, hop'.

tripartite /trʌɪˈpɑːtʌɪt/ ▶ adjective 1 shared by or involving three parties: *a tripartite coalition government*.
2 consisting of three parts: *a tripartite classification*.
– DERIVATIVES **tripartition** noun.
– ORIGIN late Middle English: from Latin *tripartitus*, from *tri-* 'three' + *partitus* 'divided' (past participle of *partiri*).

trip computer ▶ noun an electronic odometer, typically with extra capabilities such as the ability to calculate fuel consumption.

tripe ▶ noun [mass noun] 1 the first or second stomach of a cow or other ruminant used as food.
2 informal nonsense; rubbish: *you do talk tripe sometimes*.
– ORIGIN Middle English: from Old French, of unknown origin.

tripeptide /trʌɪˈpɛptʌɪd/ ▶ noun Biochemistry any of a group of peptides containing three amino-acid residues in the molecule.

trip hammer ▶ noun a large, heavy pivoted hammer used in forging, raised by a cam or lever and allowed to drop on the metal being worked.

trip hop ▶ noun [mass noun] a style of dance music, usually slow in tempo, that combines elements of hip hop and dub reggae with softer, more ambient sounds.

triphthong /ˈtrɪfθɒŋ, ˈtrɪpθɒŋ/ ▶ noun a union of three vowels (letters or sounds) pronounced in one syllable (as in *fire*). Contrasted with **diphthong**, **monophthong**. ▪ three written vowel characters representing the sound of a single vowel (as in *beau*).
– ORIGIN mid 16th cent.: from French *triphtongue*, from *tri-* 'three', on the pattern of *diphthong*.

Tripitaka /trɪˈpɪtəkə/ ▶ noun (**the Tripitaka**) the sacred canon of Theravada Buddhism, written in the Pali language.
– ORIGIN from Sanskrit *tripiṭaka*, literally 'the three baskets or collections'.

triplane ▶ noun an early type of aeroplane with three pairs of wings, one above the other.

triple ▶ adjective [attrib.] consisting of or involving three items or people: *a triple murder* | *triple somersaults*. ▪ having three times the usual size, quality, or strength: *a triple dark rum*.
▶ predeterminer three times as much or as many: *the copper energy cells had triple the efficiency of silicon cells*.
▶ noun 1 a thing that is three times as large as usual or is made up of three standard units or items: *two whiskies—triples, please*.
2 (**triples**) a sporting contest in which each side has three players.
3 (**triples**) Bell-ringing a system of change-ringing using seven bells, with three pairs changing places each time.
4 Baseball a hit which enables the batter to reach third base.
▶ verb [no obj.] become three times as much or as many: *grain prices were expected to triple*. ▪ [with obj.] multiply by three: *the party more than tripled its share of the vote*.
– DERIVATIVES **triply** adverb.
– ORIGIN Middle English (as an adjective and adverb): from Old French, or from Latin *triplus*, from Greek *triplous*.

triple A ▶ noun 1 [usu. as modifier] Finance the highest grading available from credit rating agencies.
2 the highest competitive level of achievement in baseball.

triple acrostic ▶ noun an acrostic in which the first, middle, and last letters of each line form hidden words.

Triple Alliance ▶ noun a union or association between three powers or states, in particular that made in 1668 between England, the Netherlands, and Sweden against France, and that in 1882 between Germany, Austria–Hungary, and Italy against France and Russia.

T

triple bond ▸ noun Chemistry a chemical bond in which three pairs of electrons are shared between two atoms.

triple crown ▸ noun **1** (**Triple Crown**) an award or honour for winning a group of three important events in a sport, in particular (in rugby union) victory by one of the four British home countries over all the other three in the same season.
2 the papal tiara.

Triple Entente an early 20th-century alliance between Great Britain, France, and Russia. Originally a series of loose agreements, the Triple Entente began to assume the nature of a more formal alliance as the prospect of war with the Central Powers became more likely, and formed the basis of the Allied powers in the First World War.

triple harp ▸ noun a large harp without pedals, and with three rows of strings, the middle row providing sharps and flats. Also called WELSH HARP.

triple jump ▸ noun **1** (**the triple jump**) an athletic event in which competitors attempt to jump as far as possible by performing a hop, a step, and a jump from a running start.
2 Skating a jump in which the skater makes three full turns while in the air.
▸ verb (**triple-jump**) [no obj.] (of an athlete) perform a triple jump.
– DERIVATIVES **triple jumper** noun.

triple play ▸ noun Baseball a defensive play in which three runners are put out.

triple point ▸ noun Chemistry the temperature and pressure at which the solid, liquid, and vapour phases of a pure substance can coexist in equilibrium.

triple rhyme ▸ noun a rhyme involving three syllables.

triple sec /ˌtrɪp(ə)l ˈsɛk/ ▸ noun [mass noun] a colourless orange-flavoured liqueur.
– ORIGIN late 19th cent.: *sec*, French, 'dry'.

triplet ▸ noun **1** (usu. **triplets**) one of three children or animals born at the same birth.
2 a set or succession of three similar things. ■ Music a group of three equal notes to be performed in the time of two or four. ■ a set of three rhyming lines of verse.
3 Physics & Chemistry an atomic or molecular state characterized by two unpaired electrons with parallel spins. ■ a group of three associated lines close together in a spectrum or electrophoretic gel.
– ORIGIN mid 17th cent.: from TRIPLE, on the pattern of *doublet*.

triplet code ▸ noun Biology the standard version of the genetic code, in which a sequence of three nucleotides on a DNA or RNA molecule codes for a specific amino acid in protein synthesis.

triple time ▸ noun [mass noun] musical time with three beats to the bar.

triple tonguing ▸ noun [mass noun] Music a technique in which alternate movements of the tongue are made (typically as in sounding *ttk*) to facilitate rapid playing of a wind instrument.

triplex /ˈtrɪplɛks/ ▸ noun **1** (**Triplex**) [mass noun] Brit. trademark toughened or laminated safety glass, used especially for car windows.
2 N. Amer. a building divided into three self-contained residences. ■ a flat on three floors.
3 Biochemistry a triple-stranded polynucleotide molecule.
▸ adjective having three parts. ■ Biochemistry consisting of three polynucleotide strands linked side by side.
▸ verb (**be triplexed**) (of electrical equipment or systems) be provided or fitted in triplicate so as to ensure reliability.
– ORIGIN early 17th cent. (as an adjective in the sense 'threefold'): from Latin, 'threefold', from *tri-* 'three' + *plicare* 'to fold'. Current specific senses date from the 1920s.

triplicate ▸ adjective /ˈtrɪplɪkət/ [attrib.] existing in three copies or examples: *triplicate measurements*.
▸ noun /ˈtrɪplɪkət/ archaic a thing which is part of a set of three copies or corresponding parts: *the triplicate of a letter to the Governor*.
▸ verb /ˈtrɪplɪkeɪt/ [with obj.] make three copies of; multiply by three.
– PHRASES **in triplicate** three times in exactly the same way: *the procedure was repeated in triplicate*. ■ existing as a set of three exact copies: *this form is in triplicate and must be handed to all employees*.
– DERIVATIVES **triplication** /-ˈkeɪʃ(ə)n/ noun.
– ORIGIN late Middle English: from Latin *triplicat-* 'made three', from the verb *triplicare*, from *triplex*, *triplic-* 'threefold' (see TRIPLEX). The verb dates from the early 17th cent.

triplicity /trɪˈplɪsɪti/ ▸ noun (pl. **triplicities**) rare a group of three people or things. ■ [mass noun] archaic the state of being triple.
– ORIGIN late Middle English (as a term in astrology): from late Latin *triplicitas*, from Latin *triplex*, *triplic-* 'threefold' (see TRIPLEX).

triploblastic /ˌtrɪplə(ʊ)ˈblastɪk/ ▸ adjective Zoology having a body derived from three embryonic cell layers (ectoderm, mesoderm, and endoderm), as in all multicellular animals except sponges and coelenterates.
– ORIGIN late 19th cent.: from Greek *triploos* 'threefold' + -BLAST + -IC.

triploid /ˈtrɪplɔɪd/ Genetics ▸ adjective (of a cell or nucleus) containing three homologous sets of chromosomes. ■ (of an organism or species) composed of triploid cells.
▸ noun a triploid organism, variety, or species.
– DERIVATIVES **triploidy** noun.

tripmeter ▸ noun a vehicle instrument that can be set to record the distance of individual journeys.

tripod /ˈtrʌɪpɒd/ ▸ noun **1** a three-legged stand for supporting a camera or other apparatus.
2 archaic a stool, table, or cauldron resting on three legs. ■ historical the bronze altar at Delphi on which a priestess sat to utter oracles.
– DERIVATIVES **tripodal** /ˈtrɪpəd(ə)l/ adjective.
– ORIGIN early 17th cent.: via Latin from Greek *tripod-*, *tripous*, from *tri-* 'three' + *pod-*, *pous* 'foot'.

Tripoli /ˈtrɪpəli/ **1** the capital and chief port of Libya, on the Mediterranean coast in the north-west of the country; pop. 1,065,400 (est. 2006). Founded by Phoenicians in the 7th century BC, its ancient name was Oea. Arabic name TARABULUS AL-GHARB (literally 'western Tripoli').
2 a port in NW Lebanon; pop. 190,800 (est. 2009). It was founded *c.*700 BC and was the capital of the Phoenician triple federation formed by the city-states Sidon, Tyre, and Arvad. Today it is a major port and commercial centre of Lebanon. Arabic names TARABULUS ASH-SHAM (literally 'eastern Tripoli'), TRÂBLOUS.

tripoli /ˈtrɪpəli/ ▸ noun another term for ROTTENSTONE.
– ORIGIN early 17th cent.: from French, from TRIPOLI.

Tripolitania /ˌtrɪpəlɪˈteɪnɪə, trɪˌpɒlɪ-/ a coastal region surrounding Tripoli in North Africa, in what is now NE Libya.
– DERIVATIVES **Tripolitanian** adjective & noun.
– ORIGIN based on Latin *tripolis* 'three cities', referring to the Phoenician cities Oea (now Tripoli), Leptis Magna, and Sabratha, established there in the 7th cent. BC.

tripos /ˈtrʌɪpɒs/ ▸ noun [in sing.] the final honours examination for a BA degree at Cambridge University.
– ORIGIN late 16th cent.: alteration of Latin *tripus* 'tripod', with reference to the stool on which a designated graduate (known as the 'Tripos') sat to deliver a satirical speech at the degree ceremony. A sheet of humorous verses (at one time composed by the Tripos) was published on this occasion until the late 19th cent., on the back of which the list of successful candidates for the honours degree in mathematics was originally printed; hence the current sense.

trippant /ˈtrɪp(ə)nt/ ▸ adjective [usu. postpositive] Heraldry (of a stag or deer) represented as walking. Compare with PASSANT.
– ORIGIN mid 17th cent.: from Old French, literally 'walking or springing lightly', present participle of *triper*.

tripper ▸ noun Brit. informal a person who goes on a pleasure trip or excursion.

tripple S. African ▸ noun [in sing.] a horse's gait in which both left and then both right legs move together.
▸ verb [no obj.] (of a horse) move at the pace of a tripple.
– ORIGIN late 19th cent.: from Dutch *trippelen*, from *trippen* 'to skip, trip'.

trippy ▸ adjective (**trippier**, **trippiest**) informal resembling or inducing the hallucinatory effect produced by taking a psychedelic drug: *trippy house music*.

triptych /ˈtrɪptɪk/ ▸ noun a picture or relief carving on three panels, typically hinged together vertically and used as an altarpiece. ■ a set of three associated artistic, literary, or musical works intended to be appreciated together.
– ORIGIN mid 18th cent. (denoting a set of three writing tablets hinged or tied together): from TRI- 'three', on the pattern of *diptych*.

Tripura /ˈtrɪpʊərə/ a small state in the far north-east of India, on the eastern border of Bangladesh; capital, Agartala. An ancient Hindu kingdom, Tripura acceded to India after independence in 1947, and achieved full status as a state in 1972.

tripwire ▸ noun a wire stretched close to the ground, working a trap, explosion, or alarm when disturbed and serving to detect or prevent people or animals entering an area. ■ a comparatively weak military force employed as a first line of defence, engagement with which will trigger the intervention of stronger forces.

triquetra /trʌɪˈkwɛtrə, -ˈkwiːtrə/ ▸ noun (pl. **triquetrae** /-triː/) a symmetrical triangular ornament of three interlaced arcs used on metalwork and stone crosses.
– ORIGIN late 16th cent. (originally denoting a triangle): from Latin, feminine of *triquetrus* 'three-cornered'.

triquetral (also **triquetral bone**) ▸ noun Anatomy a carpal bone on the outside of the wrist, articulating with the lunate, hamate, and pisiform bones.
– ORIGIN mid 17th cent.: from Latin *triquetrus* 'three-cornered' + -AL.

trireme /ˈtrʌɪriːm/ ▸ noun an ancient Greek or Roman war galley with three banks of oars. The rowers are believed to have sat in threes on angled benches, rather than in three superimposed banks.
– ORIGIN from Latin *triremis*, from *tri-* 'three' + *remus* 'oar'.

tris[1] /trɪs/ (also **tris buffer**) ▸ noun [mass noun] a flammable compound which forms a corrosive solution in water and is used as a buffer and emulsifying agent. ● Alternative name: **trishydroxymethylaminomethane**; chem. formula: $(HOCH_2)_3CNH_2$.
– ORIGIN 1950s: from *tris-*, the prefix of the systematic name.

tris[2] /trɪs/ ▸ noun [mass noun] an organophosphorus compound, used as a flame retardant. ● Alternative name: **tris-2,3-dibromopropylphosphate**; chem. formula: $(Br_2C_3H_5)_3PO_4$.
– ORIGIN 1970s: from *tris-*, the prefix of the systematic name.

trisaccharide /trʌɪˈsakərʌɪd/ ▸ noun Chemistry any of the class of sugars whose molecules contain three monosaccharide molecules.

Trisagion /trɪˈsagɪən, -ˈseɪgɪən/ ▸ noun a hymn, especially in the Orthodox Church, with a triple invocation of God as holy.
– ORIGIN late Middle English: from Greek, neuter of *trisagios*, from *tris* 'three times' + *hagios* 'holy'.

trisect /trʌɪˈsɛkt/ ▸ verb [with obj.] divide (something) into three parts, typically three equal parts.
– DERIVATIVES **trisection** noun, **trisector** noun.
– ORIGIN late 17th cent.: from TRI- 'three' + Latin *sect-* 'divided, cut' (from the verb *secare*).

trishaw /ˈtrʌɪʃɔː/ ▸ noun a light three-wheeled vehicle with pedals used in East Asia.
– ORIGIN 1940s: from TRI- 'three' + RICKSHAW.

triskaidekaphobia /ˌtrɪskʌɪdɛkəˈfəʊbɪə/ ▸ noun [mass noun] extreme superstition regarding the number thirteen.
– ORIGIN early 20th cent.: from Greek *treiskaideka* 'thirteen' + -PHOBIA.

triskelion /trɪˈskɛlɪən/ ▸ noun a Celtic symbol consisting of three legs or lines radiating from a centre.
– ORIGIN mid 19th cent.: from TRI- 'three' + Greek *skelos* 'leg'.

trismus /ˈtrɪzməs/ ▸ noun [mass noun] Medicine spasm of the jaw muscles, causing the mouth to remain tightly closed, typically as a symptom of tetanus. Also called LOCKJAW.
– ORIGIN late 17th cent.: from modern Latin, from Greek *trismos* 'a scream, grinding'.

trisomy /ˈtrɪsəmi/ ▸ noun Medicine a condition in which an extra copy of a chromosome is present in the cell nuclei, causing developmental abnormalities.
– ORIGIN 1930s: from TRI- 'three' + -SOME[3].

trisomy-21 ▸ noun [mass noun] Medicine the most common form of Down's syndrome, caused by an extra copy of chromosome number 21.

Tristan /ˈtrɪstən/ variant spelling of TRISTRAM.

Tristan da Cunha /ˌtrɪstən də ˈkuːnə/ the largest of a small group of volcanic islands in the South Atlantic, 2,112 km (1,320 miles) south-west of the British colony of St Helena, of which it is a dependency; pop. 300 (est. 2006). It was discovered in 1506 by the Portuguese admiral Tristão da Cunha and annexed to Britain in 1816.

tristesse /trɪˈstɛs/ ▶ **noun** [mass noun] literary a state of melancholy sadness.
– ORIGIN French.

Tristram /ˈtrɪstrəm/ (also **Tristan**) (in medieval legend) a knight who was the lover of Iseult.

trisyllable /trʌɪˈsɪləb(ə)l/ ▶ **noun** a word or metrical foot of three syllables.
– DERIVATIVES **trisyllabic** adjective.

tritagonist /trʌɪˈtag(ə)nɪst, trɪ-/ ▶ **noun** the person who is third in importance, after the protagonist and deuteragonist, in an ancient Greek drama.
– ORIGIN late 19th cent.: from Greek *tritagōnistēs*, from *tritos* 'third' + *agōnistēs* 'actor'.

tritanopia /ˌtrɪtəˈnəʊpɪə/ ▶ **noun** [mass noun] a rare form of colour blindness resulting from insensitivity to blue light, causing confusion of greens and blues. Compare with PROTANOPIA.
– ORIGIN early 20th cent.: from TRITO- 'third' (referring to blue as the third colour in the spectrum) + AN-[1] 'without' + -OPIA.

trite ▶ **adjective** (of a remark or idea) lacking originality or freshness; dull on account of overuse: *this point may now seem obvious and trite.*
– DERIVATIVES **tritely** adverb, **triteness** noun.
– ORIGIN mid 16th cent.: from Latin *tritus*, past participle of *terere* 'to rub'.

triterpene /trʌɪˈtəːpiːn/ ▶ **noun** Chemistry any of a group of terpenes found in plant gums and resins, having unsaturated molecules based on a unit with the formula $C_{30}H_{48}$.
– DERIVATIVES **triterpenoid** adjective & noun.

tritheism /ˈtrʌɪˌθiːɪz(ə)m/ ▶ **noun** [mass noun] (in Christian theology) the doctrine of or belief in the three persons of the Trinity as three distinct gods.

tritiated /ˈtrɪtɪeɪtɪd/ ▶ **adjective** Chemistry (of a compound) in which the ordinary isotope of hydrogen has been replaced with tritium.

triticale /ˌtrɪtɪˈkeɪli/ ▶ **noun** [mass noun] a hybrid cereal produced by crossing wheat and rye, grown as a fodder crop.
– ORIGIN 1950s: modern Latin, from a blend of the genus names *Triticum* 'wheat' and *Secale* 'rye'.

tritium /ˈtrɪtɪəm/ ▶ **noun** [mass noun] Chemistry a radioactive isotope of hydrogen with a mass approximately three times that of the usual isotope. (Symbol: **T**)

> Discovered in 1934, tritium has two neutrons as well as a proton in the nucleus. It occurs in minute traces in nature and can be made artificially from lithium or deuterium in nuclear reactors; it is used as a fuel in thermonuclear bombs.

– ORIGIN 1930s: from modern Latin, from Greek *tritos* 'third'.

trito- /ˈtrɪtəʊ, ˈtrʌɪtəʊ/ ▶ **combining form** third: *tritocerebrum.*
– ORIGIN from Greek *tritos* 'third'.

tritocerebrum /ˌtrɪtə(ʊ)ˈsɛrɪbrəm/ ▶ **noun** (pl. **tritocerebra** /-brə/) Entomology the third and hindmost segment of an insect's brain.

Triton /ˈtrʌɪt(ə)n/ **1** Greek Mythology a minor sea god usually represented as a man with a fish's tail and carrying a trident and shell-trumpet.
2 Astronomy the largest satellite of Neptune, the seventh closest to the planet and having a retrograde orbit and a thin nitrogen atmosphere, discovered in 1846 (diameter 2,700 km).

triton[1] ▶ **noun** a large mollusc which has a tall spiral shell with a large aperture, living in tropical and subtropical seas. ● Genus *Charonia*, family Cymatiidae, class Gastropoda, in particular *C. tritonis*, which is used as a trumpet shell.
– ORIGIN late 18th cent.: from TRITON.

triton[2] ▶ **noun** a nucleus of a tritium atom, consisting of a proton and two neutrons.
– ORIGIN 1940s: from TRITIUM + -ON.

tritone ▶ **noun** Music an interval of three whole tones (an augmented fourth), as between C and F sharp.

triturate /ˈtrɪtjʊreɪt/ ▶ **verb** [with obj.] technical grind to a fine powder. ■ chew or grind (food) thoroughly.
– DERIVATIVES **trituration** noun **triturator** noun.
– ORIGIN mid 18th cent.: from Latin *triturat-* '(of corn) threshed', from *tritura* 'rubbing' (from the verb *terere*).

triumph ▶ **noun 1** a great victory or achievement: *a garden built to celebrate Napoleon's many triumphs.* ■ [mass noun] the state of being victorious or successful: *the king returned home **in triumph**.* ■ [mass noun] joy or satisfaction resulting from a success or victory: *'Here it is!' Helen's voice rose **in triumph**.* ■ a highly successful example of something: *the marriage had been **a triumph of** togetherness.*
2 the processional entry of a victorious general into ancient Rome.
▶ **verb** [no obj.] **1** achieve a victory; be successful: *they had no chance of **triumphing over** the Nationalists.* ■ rejoice or exult at a victory or success: *she stopped **triumphing over** Mrs Ward's failure.*
2 (of a Roman general) ride into ancient Rome after a victory.
– ORIGIN late Middle English: from Old French *triumphe* (noun), from Latin *triump(h)us*, probably from Greek *thriambos* 'hymn to Bacchus'. Current senses of the verb date from the early 16th cent.

triumphal ▶ **adjective** made, carried out, or used in celebration of a great victory or achievement: *a vast triumphal arch | a triumphal procession.*
– DERIVATIVES **triumphally** adverb.
– ORIGIN late Middle English: from Old French *triumphal* or Latin *triumphalis*, from *triump(h)us* (see TRIUMPH).

triumphalism ▶ **noun** [mass noun] excessive exultation over one's success or achievements (used especially in a political context): *an air of triumphalism reigns in his administration.*
– DERIVATIVES **triumphalist** adjective & noun.

triumphant ▶ **adjective** having won a battle or contest; victorious: *two of their triumphant Cup team* | [postpositive] *a comic fairy tale about innocence triumphant.* ■ feeling or expressing jubilation after a victory or achievement: *he couldn't suppress a triumphant smile.*
– DERIVATIVES **triumphantly** adverb.
– ORIGIN late Middle English (in the sense 'victorious'): from Old French, or from Latin *triumphant-* 'celebrating a triumph', from the verb *triumphare* (see TRIUMPH).

triumvir /trʌɪˈʌmvə, ˈtrʌɪəmvə/ ▶ **noun** (pl. **triumvirs** or **triumviri** /-rʌɪ/) (in ancient Rome) each of three public officers jointly responsible for overseeing any of the administrative departments.
– DERIVATIVES **triumviral** adjective.
– ORIGIN Latin, originally as *triumviri* (plural), back-formation from *trium virorum* 'of three men', genitive of *tres viri*.

triumvirate /trʌɪˈʌmvɪrət/ ▶ **noun 1** (in ancient Rome) a group of three men holding power, in particular (**the First Triumvirate**) the unofficial coalition of Julius Caesar, Pompey, and Crassus in 60 BC and (**the Second Triumvirate**) a coalition formed by Antony, Lepidus, and Octavian in 43 BC. ■ a group of three powerful or notable people or things: *a triumvirate of three executive vice-presidents.*
2 the office of triumvir in ancient Rome.
– ORIGIN late 16th cent.: from Latin *triumviratus*, from *triumvir* (see TRIUMVIR).

triune /ˈtrʌɪjuːn/ ▶ **adjective** consisting of three in one (used especially with reference to the Trinity): *the triune Godhead.*
– DERIVATIVES **triunity** noun (pl. **triunities**).
– ORIGIN early 17th cent.: from TRI- 'three' + Latin *unus* 'one'.

trivalent /trʌɪˈveɪl(ə)nt/ ▶ **adjective** Chemistry having a valency of three.

Trivandrum /trɪˈvandrəm/ another name for THIRUVANANTHAPURAM.

trivet ▶ **noun** an iron tripod placed over a fire for a cooking pot or kettle to stand on. ■ an iron bracket designed to hook on to bars of a grate for a similar purpose. ■ a stand or support with three or more legs.
– PHRASES **(as) right as a trivet** Brit. informal perfectly all right; in good health.
– ORIGIN late Middle English: apparently from Latin *tripes, triped-* 'three-legged', from *tri-* 'three' + *pes, ped-* 'foot'.

trivia ▶ **plural noun** details, considerations, or pieces of information of little importance or value: *we fill our days with meaningless trivia.*
– ORIGIN early 20th cent.: from modern Latin, plural of *trivium* 'place where three roads meet', influenced in sense by TRIVIAL.

trivial ▶ **adjective 1** of little value or importance: *huge fines were imposed for trivial offences | trivial details.* ■ (of a person) concerned only with petty things.
2 Mathematics denoting a subgroup that either contains only the identity element or is identical with the given group.
– DERIVATIVES **trivially** adverb.
– ORIGIN late Middle English (in the sense 'belonging to the trivium'): from medieval Latin *trivialis*, from Latin *trivium* (see TRIVIUM).

triviality ▶ **noun** (pl. **trivialities**) [mass noun] lack of seriousness or importance; insignificance: *the mediocrity and triviality of current popular culture.* ■ [count noun] an insignificant detail; a trifle: *an over-concentration on trivialities.*

trivialize (also **trivialise**) ▶ **verb** [with obj.] make (something) seem less important, significant, or complex than it really is: *the problem was either trivialized or ignored by teachers.*
– DERIVATIVES **trivialization** noun.

trivial name ▶ **noun** chiefly Chemistry a name that is in general use although not part of systematic nomenclature: *its common trivial name is citric acid.* ■ chiefly Zoology another term for SPECIFIC EPITHET.

trivium /ˈtrɪvɪəm/ ▶ **noun** historical an introductory course at a medieval university involving the study of grammar, rhetoric, and logic. Compare with QUADRIVIUM.
– ORIGIN early 19th cent.: from Latin, literally 'place where three roads meet', from *tri-* 'three' + *via* 'road'.

-trix ▶ **suffix** (pl. **-trices** /trɪˈsiːz, ˈtrʌɪsiːz/ or **-trixes**) (chiefly in legal terms) forming feminine agent nouns corresponding to masculine nouns ending in *-tor* (such as *executrix* corresponding to *executor*).
– ORIGIN from Latin.

> **USAGE** The suffix **trix** has been used since the 15th century to form feminine agent nouns corresponding to masculine forms ending in **-tor**. Although a wide variety of forms have been coined, few of them have ever had wide currency. In modern use the suffix is found chiefly in legal terms such as **executrix, administratrix,** and **testatrix.**

tRNA ▶ **abbreviation** Biology transfer RNA.

Troad /ˈtrəʊad/ an ancient region of NW Asia Minor, of which ancient Troy was the chief city.

Trobriand Islands /ˈtrəʊbrɪənd/ a small group of islands in the SW Pacific, in Papua New Guinea, situated off the south-eastern tip of the island of New Guinea.

trocar /ˈtrəʊkɑː/ ▶ **noun** a surgical instrument with a three-sided cutting point enclosed in a tube, used for withdrawing fluid from a body cavity.
– ORIGIN early 18th cent.: from French *trocart, trois-quarts*, from *trois* 'three' + *carre* 'side, face of an instrument'.

trochaic /trə(ʊ)ˈkeɪɪk/ Prosody ▶ **adjective** consisting of or featuring trochees.
▶ **noun** (usu. **trochaics**) a type of verse that consists of or features trochees.
– ORIGIN late 16th cent.: via Latin from Greek *trokhaikos*, from *trokhaios* (see TROCHEE).

trochal disc /ˈtrəʊk(ə)l/ ▶ **noun** Zoology (in a rotifer) a ring of cilia that is used in feeding and (in most kinds) swimming.
– ORIGIN mid 19th cent.: *trochal* from Greek *trokhos* 'wheel' + -AL.

trochanter /trəˈkantə/ ▶ **noun 1** Anatomy any of a number of bony protuberances by which muscles are attached to the upper part of the thigh bone.
2 Entomology the small second segment of the leg of an insect, between the coxa and the femur.
– ORIGIN early 17th cent.: from French, from Greek *trokhantēr*, from *trekhein* 'to run'.

trochee /ˈtrəʊkiː/ ▶ **noun** Prosody a foot consisting of one long or stressed syllable followed by one short or unstressed syllable.
– ORIGIN late 16th cent.: via Latin from Greek *trokhaios (pous)* 'running (foot)', from *trekhein* 'to run'.

trochlea /ˈtrɒklɪə/ ▶ **noun** (pl. **trochleae** /-lɪiː/) Anatomy a structure resembling or acting like a pulley, such as the groove at the lower end of the humerus forming part of the elbow joint.
– DERIVATIVES **trochlear** adjective.
– ORIGIN late 17th cent.: Latin, 'pulley'; compare with Greek *trokhilia* 'sheave of a pulley'.

trochlear nerve ▶ **noun** Anatomy each of the fourth pair of cranial nerves, supplying the superior oblique muscle of the eyeball.

trochoid /ˈtrəʊkɔɪd/ ▶ **adjective 1** Anatomy denoting a joint in which one element rotates on its own axis (e.g. the atlas vertebra).
2 Geometry denoting a curve traced by a point on a radius of a circle rotating along a straight line or another circle (a cycloid, epicycloid, or hypocycloid).

T

3 Zoology having or denoting a form of mollusc shell which is conical with a flat base, like a top shell.
▶ **noun 1** a trochoid curve.
2 a trochoid joint.
– DERIVATIVES **trochoidal** adjective.
– ORIGIN early 18th cent.: from Greek *trokhoeidēs* 'wheel-like', from *trokhos* 'wheel'.

trochophore /ˈtrəʊkə(ʊ)fɔː, ˈtrɒk-/ ▶ **noun** Zoology the planktonic larva of certain invertebrates, including some molluscs and polychaete worms, having a roughly spherical body, a band of cilia, and a spinning motion.
– ORIGIN late 19th cent.: from Greek *trokhos* 'wheel' + **-PHORE**.

Trockenbeerenauslese /ˈtrɒk(ə)n,bɛːr(ə) n,aʊslɛːzə/, German /ˈtrɔknbeːrən,aʊsleːzə/ ▶ **noun** [mass noun] a sweet German white wine made from selected individual grapes picked later than the general harvest and affected by noble rot.
– ORIGIN German, from *trocken* 'dry' + **BEERENAUSLESE**.

troctolite /ˈtrɒktə(ʊ)lʌɪt/ ▶ **noun** [mass noun] Geology gabbro made up mainly of olivine and calcic plagioclase, often having a spotted appearance likened to a trout's back.
– ORIGIN late 19th cent.: from German *Troklotit*, from Greek *trōktēs*, a marine fish (taken to be 'trout').

trod past and past participle of **TREAD**.

trodden past participle of **TREAD**.

trog[1] ▶ **noun** Brit. informal a person regarded as contemptible or socially inferior.
– ORIGIN 1950s: abbreviation of **TROGLODYTE**.

trog[2] ▶ **verb** (**trogs, trogging, trogged**) [no obj., with adverbial of direction] Brit. informal walk heavily or laboriously; trudge: *I left him trogging off to the tube station*.
– ORIGIN 1980s: perhaps a blend of **TRUDGE** or **TREK** and **SLOG**.

troglodyte /ˈtrɒɡlədʌɪt/ ▶ **noun** (especially in prehistoric times) a person who lived in a cave. ■ a hermit. ■ a person who is regarded as being deliberately ignorant or old-fashioned.
– DERIVATIVES **troglodytic** /-ˈdɪtɪk/ adjective, **troglodytism** noun.
– ORIGIN late 15th cent.: via Latin from Greek *trōglodutēs*, alteration of the name of an Ethiopian people, influenced by *trōglē* 'hole'.

trogon /ˈtrəʊɡɒn/ ▶ **noun** a bird of tropical American forests, with a long tail and brilliantly coloured plumage. ● Family Trogonidae: several genera, in particular *Trogon*, and many species; the quetzals also belong to this family.
– ORIGIN late 18th cent.: from modern Latin, from Greek *trōgōn*, from *trōgein* 'gnaw'.

troika /ˈtrɔɪkə/ ▶ **noun 1** a Russian vehicle pulled by a team of three horses abreast. ■ a team of three horses for a troika.
2 a group of three people working together, especially in an administrative or managerial capacity.
– ORIGIN Russian, from *troe* 'set of three'.

troilism /ˈtrɔɪlɪz(ə)m/ ▶ **noun** [mass noun] sexual activity involving three participants.
– ORIGIN 1950s: perhaps based on French *trois* 'three'.

Troilus /ˈtrɔɪləs/ Greek Mythology a Trojan prince, the son of Priam and Hecuba, killed by Achilles. In medieval legends of the Trojan war he is portrayed as the forsaken lover of Cressida.

Trojan ▶ **adjective** relating to ancient Troy in Asia Minor: *Trojan legends*.
▶ **noun 1** a native or inhabitant of ancient Troy.
2 Computing a Trojan Horse program.
– PHRASES **work like a Trojan** (or **Trojans**) work extremely hard.
– ORIGIN Middle English: from Latin *Troianus*, from *Troia* 'Troy'.

Trojan asteroid ▶ **noun** an asteroid belonging to one of two groups which orbit the sun at the same distance as Jupiter, at the Lagrangian points roughly 60 degrees ahead of it and behind it.
– ORIGIN early 20th cent.: so named because the first asteroids discovered were named after heroes of the Trojan War.

Trojan Horse ▶ **noun** (in Greek mythology) a hollow wooden statue of a horse in which the Greeks are said to have concealed themselves in order to enter Troy. ■ a person or thing intended to undermine or secretly overthrow an enemy or opponent: *the rebels may use this peace accord as a Trojan horse to try and take over*. ■ Computing a program designed to breach the security of a computer system while ostensibly performing some innocuous function.

Trojan War the legendary ten-year siege of Troy by a coalition of Greeks, described in Homer's *Iliad*.

> The Greeks were attempting to recover Helen, wife of Menelaus, who had been abducted by the Trojan prince Paris. The war ended with the capture of the city by a trick: the Greeks ostensibly ended the siege but left behind a group of men concealed in a hollow wooden horse so large that the city walls had to be breached for it to be drawn inside.

troll[1] /trəʊl, trɒl/ ▶ **noun** (in folklore) an ugly cave-dwelling creature depicted as either a giant or a dwarf.
– ORIGIN from Old Norse and Swedish *troll*, Danish *trold*; adopted into English in the mid 19th cent.

troll[2] /trəʊl, trɒl/ ▶ **verb** [no obj.] **1** fish by trailing a baited line along behind a boat: *we **trolled for** mackerel*. ■ search for something: *a group of companies trolling for partnership opportunities* | [with obj.] *I spent tonight trolling the Internet for expensive lighting gear*. ■ [with obj.] informal send or submit (a provocative email or posting) with the intention of inciting an angry response.
2 [with adverbial of direction] chiefly Brit. walk in a leisurely way; stroll: *we all trolled into town*.
3 [with obj.] sing (something) in a happy and carefree way: *he trolled a note or two*.
▶ **noun** a line or bait used in trolling for fish. ■ informal a provocative email or posting intended to incite an angry response. ■ informal a person who sends such an email or submits such a posting.
– DERIVATIVES **troller** noun.
– ORIGIN late Middle English (in the sense 'stroll, roll'): origin uncertain; compare with Old French *troller* 'wander here and there (in search of game)' and Middle High German *trollen* 'stroll'.

trolley ▶ **noun** (pl. **trolleys**) **1** Brit. a large metal basket or frame on wheels, used for transporting heavy or large items, such as supermarket purchases or luggage at an airport or railway station. ■ a small table on wheels or castors, typically used to convey food and drink. ■ a hospital bed on wheels for transporting patients.
2 (also **trolley wheel**) a wheel attached to a pole, used for collecting current from an overhead electric wire to drive a tram.
3 short for **TROLLEYBUS** or **TROLLEY CAR**.
– PHRASES **off one's trolley** informal mad; insane.
– ORIGIN early 19th cent.: of dialect origin, perhaps from **TROLL**[2].

trolleybus ▶ **noun** Brit. a bus powered by electricity obtained from overhead wires by means of a pole.

trolley car ▶ **noun** US a tram powered by electricity obtained from an overhead cable by means of a trolley wheel.

trolley dolly ▶ **noun** Brit. informal an air stewardess.

trolleys (also **trollies**) ▶ **plural noun** Brit. informal underpants or knickers.
– ORIGIN late 19th cent. (originally dialect): of uncertain origin.

trollius /ˈtrɒlɪəs/ ▶ **noun** (pl. **same**) a plant of a genus that comprises the globeflowers. ● Genus *Trollius*, family Ranunculaceae.
– ORIGIN modern Latin, apparently representing German *Trollblume* 'globeflower', from the stem of *trollen* 'to roll' (because of the globular flowers).

trollop ▶ **noun** dated or humorous a sexually disreputable or promiscuous woman.
– ORIGIN early 17th cent.: perhaps related to **TRULL**.

Trollope /ˈtrɒləp/, Anthony (1815–82), English novelist. He is best known for the six 'Barsetshire' novels, including *Barchester Towers* (1857), and for the six political 'Palliser' novels. He also worked for the General Post Office 1834–67 and introduced the pillar box to Britain.

trombone ▶ **noun** a large brass wind instrument with straight tubing in three sections, ending in a bell over the player's left shoulder, different fundamental notes being made using a forward-pointing extendable slide. ■ an organ stop with the quality of a trombone.
– DERIVATIVES **trombonist** noun.
– ORIGIN early 18th cent.: from French or Italian, from Italian *tromba* 'trumpet'.

trommel /ˈtrɒm(ə)l/ ▶ **noun** Mining a rotating cylindrical sieve or screen used for washing and sorting pieces of ore or coal.
– ORIGIN late 19th cent.: from German, literally 'drum'.

tromp ▶ **verb** [no obj., with adverbial of direction] N. Amer. informal walk heavily; trudge: *she tromped across the yard*. ■ (**tromp on**) tread or stamp on: *Larry took a step forward and tromped on his wrist*.
– ORIGIN late 19th cent: alteration of **TRAMP**.

trompe l'œil /trɒmp ˈlɔɪ/, French /trɔ̃p lœj/ ▶ **noun** (pl. **trompe l'œils** pronunc. **same**) [mass noun] visual illusion in art, especially as used to trick the eye into perceiving a painted detail as a three-dimensional object. ■ [count noun] a painting or design intended to create a visual illusion.
– ORIGIN French, literally 'deceives the eye'.

Tromsø /ˈtrɒmsəː/ the principal city of Arctic Norway, situated on an island just west of the mainland; pop. 53,622 (2007).

-tron ▶ **suffix** Physics **1** denoting a subatomic particle: *positron*.
2 denoting a particle accelerator: *cyclotron*.
3 denoting a thermionic valve: *ignitron*.
– ORIGIN from *(elec)tron*.

trona /ˈtrəʊnə/ ▶ **noun** [mass noun] a grey mineral which occurs as an evaporite in salt deposits and consists of a hydrated carbonate and bicarbonate of sodium.
– ORIGIN late 18th cent.: from Swedish, from Arabic *naṭrūn* (see **NATRON**).

tronc /trɒŋk/ ▶ **noun** (in a hotel or restaurant) a common fund into which tips and service charges are paid for distribution to the staff.
– ORIGIN 1920s: from French, literally 'collecting box'.

Trondheim /ˈtrɒndhʌɪm/ a town and major regional centre on the coast of west central Norway; pop. 152,845 (2007). It was the capital of Norway during the Viking period.

Troon /truːn/ a town on the west coast of Scotland, in South Ayrshire; pop. 14,100 (est. 2009). It is noted for its championship golf course.

troop ▶ **noun 1** (**troops**) soldiers or armed forces: *UN peacekeeping troops* | (as modifier **troop**) *troop cuts*.
2 a cavalry unit commanded by a captain. ■ a unit of artillery and armoured formation. ■ a group of three or more Scout patrols.
3 a group of people or animals of a particular kind: *a **troop of** musicians*.
▶ **verb** [no obj., with adverbial of direction] (of a group of people) come or go together or in large numbers: *the girls **trooped in** for dinner*. ■ (of a lone person) walk at a slow or steady pace: *Caroline trooped wearily home from work*.
– PHRASES **troop the colour** Brit. perform the ceremony of parading a regiment's flag along ranks of soldiers.
– ORIGIN mid 16th cent.: from French *troupe*, back-formation from *troupeau*, diminutive of medieval Latin *troppus* 'flock', probably of Germanic origin.

troop carrier ▶ **noun** a large aircraft or armoured vehicle or ship designed for transporting troops.

trooper ▶ **noun 1** a private soldier in a cavalry or armoured unit. ■ a cavalry horse. ■ chiefly Brit. a troopship.
2 chiefly US a mounted police officer. ■ US a state police officer.
– PHRASES **swear like a trooper** swear a great deal.

troopie ▶ **noun** (pl. **troopies**) S. African informal a soldier, especially a national serviceman.

troopship ▶ **noun** a ship designed or used for transporting troops.

tropaeolum /trə(ʊ)ˈpiːələm/ ▶ **noun** (pl. **tropaeolums**) a Central and South American trailing or climbing plant of a genus that includes the nasturtium and the canary creeper. ● Genus *Tropaeolum*, family Tropaeolaceae.
– ORIGIN modern Latin, from Latin *tropaeum* 'trophy', because of the resemblance of the flower and leaf to a helmet and shield.

trope /trəʊp/ ▶ **noun** a figurative or metaphorical use of a word or expression. ■ a significant or recurrent theme; a motif: *she uses the Eucharist as a pictorial trope*.
– ORIGIN mid 16th cent.: via Latin from Greek *tropos* 'turn, way, trope', from *trepein* 'to turn'.

trophallaxis /ˌtrɒfəˈlaksɪs/ ▶ **noun** [mass noun] Entomology the mutual exchange of regurgitated liquids between adult social insects or between them and their larvae.
– ORIGIN early 20th cent.: from **TROPHO-** 'nourishment' + Greek *allaxis* 'exchange'.

trophectoderm /trɒˈfɛktə(ʊ)dəːm, trəʊ-/ ▶ **noun** another term for **TROPHOBLAST**.

trophic /ˈtrəʊfɪk, ˈtrɒfɪk/ ▶ **adjective 1** Ecology relating to feeding and nutrition.
2 (also **tropic**) Physiology (of a hormone or its effect) stimulating the activity of another endocrine gland.

– ORIGIN late 19th cent.: from Greek *trophikos*, from *trophē* 'nourishment', from *trephein* 'nourish'.

-trophic ▶ combining form **1** relating to nutrition: *oligotrophic*.
2 relating to maintenance or regulation of a bodily organ or function, especially by a hormone: *gonadotrophic*.
– DERIVATIVES **-trophism** combining form in corresponding nouns., **-trophy** combining form in corresponding nouns.
– ORIGIN from Greek *trophikos*, from *trophē* 'nourishment'.

trophic level ▶ noun Ecology each of several hierarchical levels in an ecosystem, consisting of organisms sharing the same function in the food chain and the same nutritional relationship to the primary sources of energy.

tropho- ▶ combining form relating to nourishment: *trophoblast*.
– ORIGIN from Greek *trophē* 'nourishment'.

trophoblast /ˈtrɒfə(ʊ)blast, ˈtrəʊf-/ ▶ noun Embryology a layer of tissue on the outside of a mammalian blastula, supplying the embryo with nourishment and later forming the major part of the placenta.
– DERIVATIVES **trophoblastic** adjective.

trophozoite /ˌtrɒfə(ʊ)ˈzəʊʌɪt, ˌtrəʊfə(ʊ)-/ ▶ noun Zoology & Medicine a growing stage in the life cycle of some sporozoan parasites, when they are absorbing nutrients from the host.

trophy ▶ noun (pl. **trophies**) **1** a cup or other decorative object awarded as a prize for a victory or success. ■ a souvenir of an achievement, especially a part of an animal taken when hunting.
2 (in ancient Greece or Rome) the weapons of a defeated army set up as a memorial of victory.
– ORIGIN late 15th cent. (in sense 2): from French *trophée*, via Latin from Greek *tropaion*, from *tropē* 'a rout', from *trepein* 'to turn'.

trophy wife ▶ noun informal, derogatory a young, attractive wife regarded as a status symbol for an older man.

tropic[1] /ˈtrɒpɪk/ ▶ noun the parallel of latitude 23°26′ north (**tropic of Cancer**) or south (**tropic of Capricorn**) of the equator. ■ Astronomy each of two corresponding circles on the celestial sphere where the sun appears to turn after reaching its greatest declination, marking the northern and southern limits of the ecliptic. ■ (**the tropics**) the region between the tropics of Cancer and Capricorn.
▶ adjective another term for TROPICAL (sense 1).
– ORIGIN late Middle English (denoting the point on the ecliptic reached by the sun at the solstice): via Latin from Greek *tropikos*, from *tropē* 'turning', from *trepein* 'to turn'.

tropic[2] /ˈtrəʊpɪk/ ▶ adjective **1** Biology relating to, consisting of, or exhibiting tropism.
2 Physiology variant spelling of TROPHIC.

-tropic ▶ combining form **1** turning towards: *heliotropic*.
2 affecting: *psychotropic*.
3 (especially in names of hormones) equivalent to -TROPHIC.
– ORIGIN from Greek *tropē* 'turn, turning'.

tropical ▶ adjective **1** of, typical of, or peculiar to the tropics: *tropical countries | a tropical rainforest*. ■ very hot and humid: *some plants thrived in last year's tropical summer heat*.
2 archaic of or involving a trope; figurative.
– DERIVATIVES **tropically** adverb.

tropical sprue ▶ noun see SPRUE[2].

tropical storm (also **tropical cyclone**) ▶ noun a localized, very intense low-pressure wind system, forming over tropical oceans and with winds of hurricane force.

tropical year ▶ noun see YEAR (sense 1).

tropicbird ▶ noun a tropical seabird with mainly white plumage and very long central tail feathers.
● Family Phaethontidae and genus *Phaethon*: three species.

tropic of Cancer ▶ noun see TROPIC[1].

tropic of Capricorn ▶ noun see TROPIC[1].

tropism /ˈtrəʊpɪz(ə)m, ˈtrɒp-/ ▶ noun [mass noun] Biology the turning of all or part of an organism in a particular direction in response to an external stimulus.
– ORIGIN late 19th cent.: from Greek *tropos* 'turning' (from *trepein* 'to turn') + -ISM.

tropology /trəˈpɒlədʒi/ ▶ noun [mass noun] the figurative use of language. ■ Christian Theology the figurative interpretation of the scriptures as a source of moral guidance.
– DERIVATIVES **tropological** adjective.
– ORIGIN late Middle English: via late Latin from Greek *tropologia*, from *tropos* (see TROPE).

tropolone /ˈtrɒpələʊn/ ▶ noun [mass noun] Chemistry an organic compound present in various plants, with a molecule based on a seven-membered carbon ring.
● Chem. formula: $C_7H_6O_2$.
– ORIGIN 1940s: from *tropilidine* (a liquid hydrocarbon) + -OL + -ONE.

tropomyosin /ˌtrəʊpə(ʊ)ˈmʌɪəsɪn/ ▶ noun [mass noun] Biochemistry a protein involved in muscle contraction. It is related to myosin and occurs together with troponin in the thin filaments of muscle tissue.
– ORIGIN 1940s: from Greek *tropos* 'turning' + MYOSIN.

troponin /ˈtrəʊpə(ʊ)nɪn/ ▶ noun [mass noun] Biochemistry a globular protein complex involved in muscle contraction. It occurs with tropomyosin in the thin filaments of muscle tissue.
– ORIGIN 1960s: from TROPOMYOSIN + *-n-* + -IN[1].

tropopause /ˈtrɒpə(ʊ)pɔːz, ˈtrəʊp-/ ▶ noun the interface between the troposphere and the stratosphere.
– ORIGIN early 20th cent.: from Greek *tropos* 'turning' + PAUSE.

troposphere /ˈtrɒpə(ʊ)sfɪə, ˈtrəʊp-/ ▶ noun the lowest region of the atmosphere, extending from the earth's surface to a height of about 6–10 km (the lower boundary of the stratosphere).
– DERIVATIVES **tropospheric** adjective.
– ORIGIN early 20th cent.: from Greek *tropos* 'turning' + SPHERE.

troppo[1] /ˈtrɒpəʊ/ ▶ adverb [usu. with negative] Music (in directions) too much; excessively: *allegro ma non troppo*.
– ORIGIN Italian.

troppo[2] /ˈtrɒpəʊ/ ▶ adjective Austral./NZ informal mentally disturbed, supposedly as a result of spending too much time in a tropical climate: *have you gone troppo?*
– ORIGIN 1940s: from TROPIC[1] + -O.

Trossachs /ˈtrɒsəks/ (**the Trossachs**) a picturesque wooded valley in central Scotland, between Loch Achray and the lower end of Loch Katrine.

Trot ▶ noun informal, chiefly derogatory a Trotskyist or supporter of extreme left-wing views.
– ORIGIN 1960s: abbreviation.

trot ▶ verb (**trots, trotting, trotted**) **1** (with reference to a horse or other quadruped) proceed or cause to proceed at a pace faster than a walk, lifting each diagonal pair of legs alternately: [no obj.] *the horses trotted slowly through the night* | [with obj.] *he trotted his horse forward*.
2 [no obj., with adverbial of direction] (of a person) run at a moderate pace with short steps: *the child trotted across to her obediently*. ■ informal go or walk briskly: *I may trot round to Portobello market for vegetables*.
▶ noun **1** a trotting pace: *our horses slowed to a trot*. ■ an act or period of trotting: *you might like an early morning trot round the crew deck*. ■ (**the trots**) Austral./NZ informal trotting races: *she was taking me to the trots*.
2 (**the trots**) informal diarrhoea.
3 [with adj.] Austral./NZ informal a period of luck of a specified kind: *Simpson believes his bad trot is about to end*.
– PHRASES **on the trot** informal **1** Brit. in succession: *they lost seven matches on the trot*. **2** continually busy: *I've been on the trot all day*.
– PHRASAL VERBS **trot something out** informal produce the same information or account that has been produced many times before: *everyone trots out the old excuse*.
– ORIGIN Middle English: from Old French *trot* (noun), *troter* (verb), from medieval Latin *trottare*, of Germanic origin.

troth /trəʊθ, trɒθ/ ▶ noun [mass noun] **1** archaic or formal faith or loyalty when pledged in a solemn agreement or undertaking: *a token of troth*.
2 archaic truth.
– PHRASES **pledge** (or **plight**) **one's troth** make a solemn pledge of commitment or loyalty, especially in marriage.
– ORIGIN Middle English: variant of TRUTH.

tro-tro /ˈtrəʊtrəʊ/ ▶ noun (pl. **tro-tros**) (in Ghana) a converted lorry or van used as a public conveyance.
– ORIGIN probably from Akan *tro* 'threepence', with reference to the fare.

Trotsky /ˈtrɒtski/, Leon (1879–1940), Russian revolutionary; born *Lev Davidovich Bronshtein*. He helped to organize the October Revolution with Lenin, and built up the Red Army. He was expelled from the Communist Party by Stalin in 1927 and exiled in 1929. He settled in Mexico in 1937, where he was later murdered by a Stalinist assassin.

Trotskyism ▶ noun [mass noun] the political or economic principles of Leon Trotsky, especially the theory that socialism should be established throughout the world by continuing revolution. Trotskyism has generally included elements of anarchism and syndicalism, but the term has come to be used indiscriminately to describe a great many forms of radical socialism.
– DERIVATIVES **Trotskyist** noun & adjective, **Trotskyite** noun & adjective (derogatory).

trotter ▶ noun **1** a pig's foot used as food. ■ humorous a human foot.
2 a horse bred or trained for the sport of trotting.

trotting ▶ noun [mass noun] racing for trotting horses pulling a two-wheeled vehicle (a sulky) and driver. Also called HARNESS RACING.

troubadour /ˈtruːbədɔː/ ▶ noun a French medieval lyric poet composing and singing in Provençal in the 11th to 13th centuries, especially on the theme of courtly love. ■ a poet who writes verse to music.
– ORIGIN French, from Provençal *trobador*, from *trobar* 'find, invent, compose in verse'.

trouble ▶ noun [mass noun] **1** difficulty or problems: *I had trouble finding somewhere to park | friends should support each other when they are **in trouble** | the government's policies **ran into trouble*** | [count noun] *our troubles are just beginning*. ■ the malfunction of something such as a machine or a part of the body: *their helicopter developed engine trouble*. ■ effort or exertion made to do something, especially when inconvenient: *I wouldn't want to put you to any trouble | he's **gone to a lot of trouble** to help you*. ■ a cause of worry or inconvenience: *the kid had **been no trouble** up to now*. ■ a particular aspect of something regarded as unsatisfactory or as a source of difficulty: *that's **the trouble with** capitalism*. ■ a situation in which one is liable to incur punishment or blame: *he's **been in trouble with** the police*. ■ informal, dated used to refer to the condition of a pregnant unmarried woman: *she's not the first girl who's **got herself into trouble***.
2 public unrest or disorder: *there was crowd trouble before and during the match*. ■ (**the Troubles**) any of various periods of civil war or unrest in Ireland, especially in 1919–23 and (in Northern Ireland) since 1968.
▶ verb [with obj.] cause distress or anxiety to: *he was not troubled by doubts*. ■ [no obj.] (**trouble about/over/with**) be distressed or anxious about: *she was too concerned with her own feelings to trouble about Clare's*. ■ cause (someone) pain: *my legs started to trouble me*. ■ cause (someone) inconvenience (typically used as a polite way of asking someone to do something): *sorry to trouble you | could I **trouble** you **for** a receipt?* ■ [no obj., with infinitive] make the effort required to do something: *oh, don't trouble to answer*.
– PHRASES **ask for trouble** informal act in a way that is likely to incur problems or difficulties: *hitching a lift is asking for trouble*. **look for trouble** informal behave in a way that is likely to provoke an argument or fight: *youths take a cocktail of drink and drugs before going out to look for trouble*. **trouble and strife** Brit. rhyming slang wife. **a trouble shared is a trouble halved** proverb talking to someone else about one's problems helps to alleviate them.
– DERIVATIVES **troubler** noun.
– ORIGIN Middle English: from Old French *truble* (noun), *trubler* (verb), based on Latin *turbidus* (see TURBID).

troubled ▶ adjective beset by problems or difficulties: *his troubled private life*. ■ showing distress or anxiety: *his troubled face*.
– PHRASES **troubled waters** a difficult situation or time.

troublemaker ▶ noun a person who habitually causes difficulty or problems, especially by inciting others to defy those in authority.
– DERIVATIVES **troublemaking** noun & adjective.

troubleshoot ▶ verb [no obj.] (usu. as noun **troubleshooting**) analyse and solve serious problems for a company or other organization. ■ trace and correct faults in a mechanical or electronic system.
– DERIVATIVES **troubleshooter** noun.

troublesome ▶ adjective causing difficulty or annoyance: *schools are removing troublesome pupils*.
– DERIVATIVES **troublesomely** adverb, **troublesomeness** noun.

trouble spot ▶ **noun** a place where difficulties regularly occur, especially a country or area where there is a continuous cycle of violence.

troubling ▶ **adjective** causing distress or anxiety: *this is a troubling development for the prime minister* | *the lack of attention to security is equally troubling.*
– DERIVATIVES **troublingly adverb.**

troublous ▶ **adjective** archaic or literary full of difficulty or agitation: *those were troublous times.*
– ORIGIN late Middle English: from Old French *troubleus*, from *truble* (see **TROUBLE**).

trough ▶ **noun 1** a long, narrow open container for animals to eat or drink out of: *a water trough.* ■ a container of a similar shape used for a purpose such as growing plants.
2 a channel used to convey a liquid. ■ a long hollow in the earth's surface: *a vast glacial trough.* ■ a hollow between two wave crests in the sea.
3 an elongated region of low barometric pressure.
4 a point of low activity or achievement: *seasonal* ***peaks and troughs*** *in the demand for goods and services.* ■ Mathematics a region around the minimum on a curve of variation of a quantity.
▶ **verb** [no obj.] informal eat greedily.
– ORIGIN Old English *trog*, of Germanic origin; related to Dutch *trog* and German *Trog*, also to **TREE**.

trough shell ▶ **noun** a burrowing marine bivalve mollusc with a thin smooth shell. ● Family Mactridae: *Spisula* and other genera.

trounce ▶ **verb** [with obj.] defeat heavily in a contest: *Essex trounced Cambridgeshire 5–1 in the final.* ■ rebuke or punish severely: *insider dealing has been roundly trounced.*
– ORIGIN mid 16th cent. (also in the sense 'afflict'): of unknown origin.

troupe ▶ **noun** a group of dancers, actors, or other entertainers who tour to different venues.
– ORIGIN early 19th cent.: from French, literally 'troop'.

trouper ▶ **noun** an actor or other entertainer, typically one with long experience. ■ a reliable and uncomplaining person: ***a real trouper,*** *Ma concealed her troubles.*

troupial /ˈtruːpɪəl/ ▶ **noun** a gregarious songbird of the American oriole family, typically having orange and black plumage and yellow eyes. ● Genus *Icterus*, family Icteridae: several species, in particular the tropical American *Icterus icterus*.
– ORIGIN early 19th cent.: from French *troupiale*, alteration of American Spanish *turpial*, of unknown origin.

trouser ▶ **noun** [as modifier] relating to trousers: *his trouser pocket* | *a trouser press.* ■ a trouser leg: *his trouser was torn.*
▶ **verb** [with obj.] Brit. informal receive or take (something, especially money) for oneself; pocket: *they claimed that he had trousered a £2 million advance.*

trouser clip ▶ **noun** another term for **BICYCLE CLIP**.

trousers (also **a pair of trousers**) ▶ **plural noun** an outer garment covering the body from the waist to the ankles, with a separate part for each leg.
– PHRASES **catch someone with their trousers down** see **CATCH SOMEONE WITH THEIR PANTS DOWN** at **PANTS**. **wear the trousers** informal be the dominant partner in a relationship.
– DERIVATIVES **trousered adjective.**
– ORIGIN early 17th cent.: from archaic *trouse* (singular) from Irish *triús* and Scottish Gaelic *triubhas* (see **TREWS**), on the pattern of *drawers*.

trouser suit ▶ **noun** Brit. a pair of trousers and a matching jacket worn by women.

trousseau /ˈtruːsəʊ/ ▶ **noun** (pl. **trousseaux** or **trousseaus** /-səʊz/) the clothes, linen, and other belongings collected by a bride for her marriage.
– ORIGIN mid 19th cent.: from French, diminutive of *trousse* 'bundle' (a sense also found in Middle English).

trout ▶ **noun** (pl. **same** or **trouts**) a chiefly freshwater fish of the salmon family, found in both Eurasia and North America and highly valued for food and game. ● Genera *Salmo* (several species of true trouts, including the European **brown trout**), *Onchorhyncus* (several species including the **rainbow trout**), and *Salvelinus* (several North American species), family Salmonidae. See also **LAKE TROUT**, **SEA TROUT**.
– PHRASES **old trout** informal an annoying or bad-tempered old woman.
– ORIGIN late Old English *truht*, from late Latin *tructa*, based on Greek *trōgein* 'gnaw'.

trouting ▶ **noun** [mass noun] the activity of fishing for trout, either for food or as a sport.

trout lily ▶ **noun** a North American dog's-tooth violet with yellow flowers, so called from its mottled leaves. ● *Erythronium americanum*, family Liliaceae.

trouvaille /ˈtruːvʌɪ/ ▶ **noun** a lucky find: *one of numerous trouvailles to be gleaned from his book.*
– ORIGIN French, from *trouver* 'find'.

trouvère /truːˈvɛː/ ▶ **noun** a medieval epic poet in northern France in the 11th–14th centuries.
– ORIGIN from Old French *trovere*, from *trover* 'to find'; compare with **TROUBADOUR**.

trove ▶ **noun** a store of valuable or delightful things: *the cellar contained a trove of rare wines.*
– ORIGIN late 19th cent.: from **TREASURE TROVE**.

trover ▶ **noun** [mass noun] Law common-law action to recover the value of personal property that has been wrongfully disposed of by another person.
– ORIGIN late 16th cent.: from an Anglo-Norman French noun use of Old French *trover* 'to find'.

trow /trəʊ/ ▶ **verb** [no obj., with clause] archaic think or believe: *why, this is strange, I trow!*
– ORIGIN Old English *trūwian*, *trēowian* 'to trust'; related to **TRUCE**.

Trowbridge /ˈtrəʊbrɪdʒ/ a town in SW England, the county town of Wiltshire; pop. 39,800 (est. 2009).

trowel ▶ **noun 1** a small handheld tool with a flat, pointed blade, used to apply and spread mortar or plaster.
2 a small handheld tool with a curved scoop for lifting plants or earth.
▶ **verb** (**trowels, trowelling, trowelled**; US **trowels, troweling, troweled**) [with obj.] apply or spread with or as if with a trowel: *trowel in enough soil to form a dome* | *Kerrie trowelled jam on to her toast.*
– ORIGIN Middle English (as a noun): from Old French *truele*, from medieval Latin *truella*, alteration of Latin *trulla* 'scoop', diminutive of *trua* 'skimmer'.

Troy (in Homeric legend) the city of King Priam, besieged for ten years by the Greeks during the Trojan War. It was regarded as having been a purely legendary city until Heinrich Schliemann identified the mound of Hissarlik on the NE Aegean coast of Turkey as the site of Troy. The city was apparently sacked and destroyed by fire in the mid 13th century BC, a period coinciding with the Mycenaean civilization of Greece. Also called **ILIUM**.

troy (in full **troy weight**) ▶ **noun** a system of weights used mainly for precious metals and gems, with a pound of 12 ounces or 5,760 grains. Compare with **AVOIRDUPOIS**.
– ORIGIN late Middle English: from a weight used at the fair of *Troyes* (see **TROYES[1]**).

Troyes[1] /trwʌ/, French /tʀwa/ a town in northern France, on the River Seine; pop. 63,044 (2006). It was capital of the former province of Champagne.

Troyes[2], Chrétien de, see **CHRÉTIEN DE TROYES**.

truancy ▶ **noun** [mass noun] the action of staying away from school without good reason; absenteeism: *fines to tackle truancy.*

truant ▶ **noun** a pupil who stays away from school without leave or explanation.
▶ **adjective** (of a pupil) being a truant: *truant children.* ■ wandering; straying: *her truant husband.*
▶ **verb** [no obj.] another way of saying **PLAY TRUANT** below.
– PHRASES **play truant** chiefly Brit. (of a pupil) stay away from school without leave or explanation.
– ORIGIN Middle English (denoting a person begging through choice rather than necessity): from Old French, probably ultimately of Celtic origin; compare with Welsh *truan*, Scottish Gaelic *truaghan* 'wretched'.

truce ▶ **noun** an agreement between enemies or opponents to stop fighting or arguing for a certain time: *the guerrillas called a three-day truce.*
– ORIGIN Middle English *trewes*, *trues* (plural), from Old English *trēowa*, plural of *trēow* 'belief, trust', of Germanic origin; related to Dutch *trouw* and German *Treue*, also to **TRUE**.

Trucial States /ˈtruːʃ(ə)l/ former name (until 1971) for **UNITED ARAB EMIRATES**.

truck[1] ▶ **noun 1** a wheeled vehicle, in particular: ■ a large road vehicle, used for carrying goods, materials, or troops; a lorry. ■ Brit. a railway vehicle for carrying freight, especially a small open one. ■ a low flat-topped trolley used for moving heavy items.
2 a railway bogie. ■ each of two axle units on a skateboard, to which the wheels are attached.
3 a wooden disc at the top of a ship's mast or flagstaff, with holes for halyards to slide through.
▶ **verb** [with obj. and adverbial of direction] chiefly N. Amer. convey by truck: *the food was trucked to St Petersburg* | (as noun **trucking**) *industries such as trucking.* ■ [no obj.] drive a truck. ■ [no obj., with adverbial of direction] informal go or proceed in a casual or leisurely way: *my mate walked confidently behind them and trucked on through!*
– ORIGIN Middle English (denoting a solid wooden wheel): perhaps short for **TRUCKLE[1]** in the sense 'wheel, pulley'. The sense 'wheeled vehicle' dates from the late 18th cent.

truck[2] ▶ **noun** [mass noun] **1** archaic barter. ■ chiefly historical the payment of workers in kind or with vouchers rather than money.
2 chiefly archaic small wares. ■ informal odds and ends.
3 N. Amer. market-garden produce, especially vegetables: [as modifier] *a truck garden.*
▶ **verb** [with obj.] archaic barter or exchange.
– PHRASES **have** (or **want**) **no truck with** avoid or wish to avoid dealings or being associated with: *we have no truck with that style of gutter journalism.*
– ORIGIN Middle English (as a verb): probably from Old French, of unknown origin; compare with medieval Latin *trocare*.

Truck Acts (in the UK) a series of Acts directed, from 1830 onwards, against the system whereby workers received their wages in the form of vouchers for goods redeemable only at a special shop (often run by the employer). The Acts required wages to be paid in cash.

trucker ▶ **noun** a long-distance lorry driver.

truckie ▶ **noun** Austral./NZ informal term for **TRUCKER**.

truckle[1] ▶ **noun** a small barrel-shaped cheese, especially Cheddar.
– ORIGIN late Middle English (denoting a wheel or pulley): from Anglo-Norman French *trocle*, from Latin *trochlea* 'sheaf of a pulley'. The current sense dates from the early 19th cent. and was originally dialect.

truckle[2] ▶ **verb** [no obj.] submit or behave obsequiously: *she despised her husband, who* ***truckled to*** *her.*
– DERIVATIVES **truckler noun.**
– ORIGIN mid 17th cent.: figuratively, from **TRUCKLE BED**; an earlier use of the verb was in the sense *sleep in a truckle bed.*

truckle bed ▶ **noun** chiefly Brit. a low bed on wheels that can be stored under a larger bed.
– ORIGIN late Middle English: from **TRUCKLE[1]** in the sense 'wheel' + **BED**.

truckload ▶ **noun** a quantity of goods that can be transported in a truck: ***a truckload of*** *chemicals.* ■ (**a truckload/truckloads of**) informal a large quantity or number of something: *the government had ploughed* ***truckloads of*** *money into this land.*
– PHRASES **by the truckload** informal in large quantities or numbers: *he had charm by the truckload.*

truck stop ▶ **noun** North American term for **TRANSPORT CAFE**.

truculent /ˈtrʌkjʊl(ə)nt/ ▶ **adjective** eager or quick to argue or fight; aggressively defiant: *the truculent attitude of farmers to cheaper imports.*
– DERIVATIVES **truculence noun, truculently adverb.**
– ORIGIN mid 16th cent.: from Latin *truculentus*, from *trux*, *truc-* 'fierce'.

Trudeau /ˈtruːdəʊ, truːˈdəʊ/, Pierre (Elliott) (1919–2000), Canadian Liberal statesman, Prime Minister of Canada 1968–79 and 1980–4. Noted for his commitment to federalism, Trudeau made both English and French official languages of the Canadian government (1969), and presided over the transfer of residual constitutional powers from Britain to Canada in 1982.

trudge ▶ **verb** [no obj., with adverbial of direction] walk slowly and with heavy steps, typically because of exhaustion or harsh conditions: *I trudged up the stairs* | *she trudged through blinding snow.*
▶ **noun** a difficult or laborious walk: *he began the long trudge back to Stokenchurch Street.*
– ORIGIN mid 16th cent. (as a verb): of unknown origin.

trudgen /ˈtrʌdʒ(ə)n/ ▶ **noun** a swimming stroke like the crawl with a scissors movement of the legs.
– ORIGIN late 19th cent.: named after John *Trudgen* (1852–1902), English swimmer.

true ▶ **adjective** (**truer, truest**) **1** in accordance with fact or reality: *a true story* | *of course it's true* | *that is not true of the people I am talking about.* ■ [attrib.] rightly or strictly so called; genuine: *people are still*

willing to pay for true craftsmanship | we believe in true love. ■ [attrib.] real or actual: *he has guessed my true intentions.* ■ said when conceding a point: *true, the house faced north, but you got used to that.*
2 accurate or exact: *it was a true depiction.* ■ (of a note) exactly in tune. ■ (of a compass bearing) measured relative to true north: *steer 085 degrees true.* ■ correctly positioned, balanced, or aligned; upright or level.
3 loyal or faithful: *he was a true friend.* ■ (**true to**) accurately conforming to (a standard or expectation); faithful to: *this entirely new production remains true to the essence of Lorca's play.*
4 chiefly archaic honest: *we appeal to all good men and true to rally to us.*
▸ **adverb 1** chiefly literary truly: *Hobson spoke truer than he knew.*
2 accurately or without variation.
▸ **verb** (**trues, truing** or **trueing, trued**) [with obj.] bring (an object, wheel, or other construction) into the exact shape or position required.
– PHRASES **come true** actually happen or become the case: *dreams can come true.* **out of true** (or **the true**) not in the correct or exact shape or alignment: *take care not to pull the frame out of true.* **many a true word is spoken in jest** proverb a humorous remark not intended to be taken seriously may turn out to be accurate after all. **true as Bob** (or **God**) S. African informal absolutely true: *true as Bob, I nearly went right through the windscreen.* [*Bob* represents a euphemistic substitution of *God*, the idiom translating obsolete Afrikaans *so waar as God.*] **true to form** (or **type**) being or behaving as expected: *true to type, they took it well.* **true to life** accurately representing real events or objects.
– DERIVATIVES **trueness** noun.
– ORIGIN Old English *trēowe, trȳwe* 'steadfast, loyal'; related to Dutch *getrouw*, German *treu*, also to TRUCE.

true bill ▸ **noun** US Law a bill of indictment found by a grand jury to be supported by sufficient evidence to justify prosecution.

true-blue ▸ **adjective 1** Brit. staunchly loyal to the Conservative Party. ■ N. Amer. extremely loyal or orthodox: *I'm a dyed-in-the-wool, true-blue patriot.*
2 real; genuine: *the tournament was won by a team of true-blue amateurs.*
▸ **noun** (**true blue**) Brit. a staunchly loyal supporter of the Conservative Party.

true-born ▸ **adjective** [attrib.] of a specified kind by birth; genuine: *a true-born criminal.*

true bug ▸ **noun** see BUG (sense 3 of the noun).

true-hearted ▸ **adjective** literary loyal or faithful: *a true-hearted paladin.*

true horizon ▸ **noun** Astronomy see HORIZON (sense 1).

true leaf ▸ **noun** Botany a foliage leaf of a plant, as opposed to a seed leaf or cotyledon.

true-love knot (also **true-lover's knot**) ▸ **noun** a kind of knot with interlacing bows on each side, symbolizing the bonds of love.

Trueman, Fred (1931–2006), English cricketer; full name *Frederick Sewards Trueman*. A fast bowler for Yorkshire and England, he became the first bowler to take 300 test wickets (1964).

true north ▸ **noun** north according to the earth's axis, not magnetic north.

true rib ▸ **noun** a rib which is attached directly to the breastbone. Compare with FLOATING RIB.

Truffaut /ˈtruːfəʊ/, French /tʀyfo/, François (1932–84), French film director. His first feature film, *Les Quatre cents coups* (1959), established him as a leading director of the *nouvelle vague*. Other films include *Jules et Jim* (1961) and *The Last Metro* (1980).

truffle ▸ **noun 1** a strong-smelling underground fungus that resembles an irregular, rough-skinned potato, growing chiefly in broadleaved woodland on calcareous soils. It is considered a culinary delicacy and found, especially in France, with the aid of trained dogs or pigs. ● Family Tuberaceae, subdivision Ascomycotina: *Tuber* and other genera.
2 a soft sweet made of a chocolate mixture, typically flavoured with rum and covered with cocoa.
– ORIGIN late 16th cent.: probably via Dutch from obsolete French *truffle*, perhaps based on Latin *tubera*, plural of *tuber* 'hump, swelling'. Sense 2 dates from the 1920s.

truffled ▸ **adjective** (of food) cooked, garnished, or stuffed with truffles: *a truffled turkey.*

truffling ▸ **noun** [mass noun] the activity of hunting or rooting for truffles.

trug (also **trug basket**) ▸ **noun** Brit. a shallow oblong basket made of strips of wood, traditionally used for carrying garden flowers and produce.
– ORIGIN late Middle English (denoting a basin): perhaps a dialect variant of TROUGH.

truism ▸ **noun** a statement that is obviously true and says nothing new or interesting: *the truism that you get what you pay for.* ■ Logic a proposition that states nothing beyond what is implied by any of its terms.
– DERIVATIVES **truistic** /-ˈɪstɪk/ adjective.

Trujillo /truːˈhiːjəʊ, -ˈhiːljəʊ/ a city on the coast of NW Peru; pop. 682,800 (est. 2007).

Truk Islands /trʌk/ former name for CHUUK ISLANDS.

trull /trʌl/ ▸ **noun** archaic a prostitute.
– ORIGIN early 16th cent.: from German *Trulle*.

truly ▸ **adverb 1** in a truthful way: *he speaks truly.* ■ used to emphasize emotional sincerity or seriousness: *it is truly a privilege to be here* | [as submodifier] *I'm truly sorry, but I can't join you today.*
2 to the fullest degree; genuinely or properly: *management does not truly understand about the residents.* ■ [as submodifier] absolutely or completely (used for emphasis): *a truly dreadful song.*
3 in actual fact or without doubt; really: *this is truly a miracle.*
4 archaic loyally or faithfully: *why cannot all masters be served truly?*
– PHRASES **yours truly** used as a formula for ending a letter. ■ humorous used to refer to oneself: *the demos will be organized by yours truly.*
– ORIGIN Old English *treowlīce* 'faithfully' (see TRUE, -LY[2]).

Truman, Harry S. (1884–1972), American Democratic statesman, 33rd President of the US 1945–53. He authorized the use of the atom bomb against Hiroshima and Nagasaki, introduced the Marshall Plan of emergency aid in 1948 to war-shattered European countries, and involved the US in the Korean War.

Truman Doctrine the principle that the US should give support to countries or peoples threatened by Soviet forces or Communist insurrection. First expressed in 1947 by US President Truman in a speech to Congress seeking aid for Greece and Turkey, the doctrine was seen by the Communists as an open declaration of the Cold War.

trumeau /truːˈməʊ/ ▸ **noun** (pl. **trumeaux** /-ˈməʊz/) a section of wall or a pillar between two openings, especially a pillar dividing a large doorway in a church.
– ORIGIN late 19th cent.: from French, literally 'calf of the leg'.

trump[1] ▸ **noun** (in bridge, whist, and similar card games) a playing card of the suit chosen to rank above the others, which can win a trick where a card of a different suit has been led. ■ (**trumps**) the suit having this rank in a particular hand: *the ace of trumps.* ■ (in a tarot pack) any of a special suit of 22 cards depicting symbolic and typical figures and scenes. ■ (also **trump card**) a valuable resource that may be used, especially as a surprise, in order to gain an advantage: *in this month General Haig decided to play his trump card: the tank.* ■ informal, dated a helpful or admirable person.
▸ **verb** [with obj.] (in bridge, whist, and similar card games) play a trump on (a card of another suit). ■ surpass (something) by saying or doing something better: *if the fetus is human life, that trumps any argument about the freedom of the mother.*
– PHRASES **come** (or **turn**) **up trumps** informal, chiefly Brit. (of a person or situation) have a better performance or outcome than expected: *Conrad came up trumps again, finishing fourth in the 800 metres.* ■ be especially generous or helpful: *Mother had been absent throughout, but Aunt Edie had come up trumps.*
– PHRASAL VERBS **trump something up** invent a false accusation or excuse: *they've trumped up charges against her.*
– ORIGIN early 16th cent.: alteration of TRIUMPH, once used in card games in the same sense.

trump[2] ▸ **noun** archaic a trumpet or a trumpet blast.
▸ **verb** [no obj.] informal break wind audibly.
– ORIGIN Middle English: from Old French *trompe*, of Germanic origin; probably imitative.

trumpery archaic ▸ **noun** (pl. **trumperies**) [mass noun] attractive articles of little value or use. ■ practices or beliefs that are superficially or visually appealing but have little real value or worth.
▸ **adjective** showy but worthless: *trumpery jewellery.* ■ delusive or shallow: *that trumpery hope which lets us dupe ourselves.*
– ORIGIN late Middle English (denoting trickery): from Old French *tromperie*, from *tromper* 'deceive'.

trumpet ▸ **noun 1** a brass musical instrument with a flared bell and a bright, penetrating tone. The modern instrument has the tubing looped to form a straight-sided coil, with three valves. ■ an organ reed stop with a quality resembling that of a trumpet. ■ a sound resembling that of a trumpet, especially the loud cry of an elephant. ■ something shaped like a trumpet, especially the tubular corona of a daffodil flower.
2 (**trumpets**) a North American pitcher plant. ● Genus *Sarracenia*, family Sarraceniaceae: several species, in particular **yellow trumpets** (*S. flava*).
▸ **verb** (**trumpets, trumpeting, trumpeted**) **1** [no obj.] play a trumpet: (as adj. **trumpeting**) *figures of two trumpeting angels.* ■ make a loud, penetrating sound resembling that of a trumpet: *wild elephants trumpeting in the bush.*
2 [with obj.] proclaim widely or loudly: *the press trumpeted another defeat for the government.*
– PHRASES **blow one's (own) trumpet** chiefly Brit. talk boastfully about one's achievements: *he refused to blow his own trumpet and blushingly declined to speak.*
– ORIGIN Middle English: from Old French *trompette*, diminutive of *trompe* (see TRUMP[2]). The verb dates from the mid 16th cent.

trumpet creeper ▸ **noun** another term for TRUMPET VINE.

trumpeter ▸ **noun 1** a person who plays a trumpet. ■ a cavalry or artillery soldier who gives signals with a trumpet.
2 a large gregarious ground-dwelling bird of tropical South American forests, with mainly black plumage and loud trumpeting and booming calls. ● Family Psophiidae and genus *Psophia*: three species.
3 a pigeon of a domestic breed that makes a trumpet-like sound.
4 an edible marine fish with a spiny dorsal fin, found chiefly in cool Australasian waters and said to make a grunting or trumpeting sound when taken out of the water. ● Family Latridae: several genera and species, including the **Tasmanian trumpeter** (*Latris lineata*), prized as food.

trumpeter swan ▸ **noun** a large migratory swan with a black and yellow bill and a honking call, breeding in northern North America. ● *Cygnus buccinator*, family Anatidae.

trumpetfish ▸ **noun** (pl. **same** or **trumpetfishes**) an elongated marine fish with a long, narrow snout, resembling a pipefish. It lives around reefs and rocks in tropical waters and typically hangs in a semi-vertical position. ● Family Aulostomidae and genus *Aulostomus*: several species.

trumpet major ▸ **noun** the chief trumpeter of a cavalry regiment, typically a principal musician in a regimental band.

trumpet shell ▸ **noun** the shell of a large marine mollusc which can be blown to produce a loud note. ● Several species in the class Gastropoda, in particular the triton (*Charonia tritonis*, family Cymatiidae).

trumpet vine (also **trumpet creeper**) ▸ **noun** a climbing shrub with orange or red trumpet-shaped flowers, cultivated as an ornamental. ● Genus *Campsis*, family Bignoniaceae: the North American *C. radicans* and the Chinese *C. grandiflora*.

truncal ▸ **adjective** Medicine of or affecting the trunk of the body, or of a nerve.

truncate ▸ **verb** /trʌŋˈkeɪt, ˈtrʌŋ-/ [with obj.] **1** (often as adj. **truncated**) shorten (something) by cutting off the top or the end: *a truncated cone shape | discussion was truncated by the arrival of tea.*
2 Crystallography replace (an edge or an angle) by a plane, typically so as to make equal angles with the adjacent faces.
▸ **adjective** /ˈtrʌŋkeɪt/ Botany & Zoology (of a leaf, feather, or other part) ending abruptly as if cut off across the base or tip.
– DERIVATIVES **truncation** noun.
– ORIGIN late 15th cent. (earlier (Middle English) as *truncation*): from Latin *truncat-* 'maimed', from the verb *truncare*.

truncheon /ˈtrʌn(t)ʃ(ə)n/ ▸ **noun** chiefly Brit. a short, thick stick carried as a weapon by a police officer. ■ a staff or baton acting as a symbol of authority, especially that used by the Earl Marshal.
– ORIGIN Middle English (denoting a piece broken off (especially from a spear), also a cudgel): from Old French *tronchon* 'stump', based on Latin *truncus* 'trunk'.

T

trundle ▸ verb (with reference to a wheeled vehicle or its occupants) move or cause to move slowly and heavily: [no obj., with adverbial of direction] *ten vintage cars trundled past* | [with obj. and adverbial of direction] *we trundled a wheelbarrow down to the river and collected driftwood.* ■ [no obj., with adverbial of direction] (of a person) move heavily and slowly: *she heard him coughing as he trundled out.*
▸ noun [in sing.] an act of moving slowly or heavily.
– ORIGIN mid 16th cent. (denoting a small wheel or roller): a parallel formation to obsolete or dialect *trendle, trindle* 'revolve'; related to TREND.

trundle bed ▸ noun chiefly N. Amer. a truckle bed.

trunk ▸ noun **1** the main woody stem of a tree as distinct from its branches and roots. ■ the main part of an artery, nerve, or other anatomical structure from which smaller branches arise. ■ an enclosed shaft or conduit for cables or ventilation.
2 a person's or animal's body apart from the limbs and head.
3 the elongated, prehensile nose of an elephant.
4 a large box with a hinged lid for storing or transporting clothes and other articles.
5 N. Amer. the boot of a car.
– DERIVATIVES **trunkful** noun (pl. **trunkfuls**), **trunkless** adjective.
– ORIGIN late Middle English: from Old French *tronc*, from Latin *truncus*.

trunk call ▸ noun dated, chiefly Brit. a long-distance telephone call made within the same country.

trunkfish ▸ noun (pl. **same** or **trunkfishes**) another term for BOXFISH.

trunking ▸ noun [mass noun] **1** a system of shafts or conduits for cables or ventilation.
2 the use or arrangement of trunk lines.

trunk line ▸ noun a main line of a railway, telephone system, or other network.

trunk road ▸ noun Brit. an important main road used for long-distance travel.

trunks ▸ plural noun men's shorts, worn especially for swimming or boxing.
– ORIGIN late 19th cent. (originally US): from an earlier theatrical use denoting short breeches of thin material worn over tights.

trunnel /ˈtrʌn(ə)l/ ▸ noun US variant spelling of TREENAIL.

trunnion /ˈtrʌnjən/ ▸ noun a pin or pivot forming one of a pair on which something is supported. ■ a supporting cylindrical projection on each side of a cannon or mortar.
– ORIGIN early 17th cent.: from French *trognon* 'core, tree trunk', of unknown origin.

Truro /ˈtrʊərəʊ/ the county town of Cornwall in SW England; pop. 23,700 (est. 2009).

truss ▸ noun **1** a framework, typically consisting of rafters, posts, and struts, supporting a roof, bridge, or other structure: *roof trusses.* ■ a large projection of stone or timber, typically one supporting a cornice.
2 a surgical appliance worn to support a hernia, typically a padded belt.
3 Brit., chiefly historical a bundle of old hay (56 lb), new hay (60 lb), or straw (36 lb).
4 a compact cluster of flowers or fruit growing on one stalk.
5 Sailing a heavy metal ring securing the lower yards to a mast.
▸ verb [with obj.] **1** tie up the wings and legs of (a chicken or other bird) before cooking. ■ tie up (someone) with their arms at their sides: *I found him trussed up in his cupboard.* ■ (usu. **be trussed up in**) dress (someone) in elaborate or uncomfortable clothing: *he was trussed up in a heavily padded suit, complete with face mask and protective gloves.*
2 (usu. as adj. **trussed**) support (a roof, bridge, or other structure) with a truss or trusses.
– DERIVATIVES **trusser** noun.
– ORIGIN Middle English (in the sense 'bundle'): from Old French *trusse* (noun), *trusser* 'pack up, bind in', based on late Latin *tors-* 'twisted', from the verb *torquere*. Sense 1 of the noun dates from the mid 17th cent.

trust ▸ noun [mass noun] **1** firm belief in the reliability, truth, or ability of someone or something: *relations have to be built on trust* | *they have been able to win the trust of the others.* ■ acceptance of the truth of a statement without evidence or investigation: *I used only primary sources, taking nothing on trust.* ■ the state of being responsible for someone or something: *a man in a position of trust.* ■ [count noun] literary a person or duty for which one has responsibility: *rulership is a trust from God.*
2 [count noun] Law an arrangement whereby a person (a trustee) holds property as its nominal owner for the good of one or more beneficiaries: *a trust was set up* | [mass noun] *the property is to be* ***held in trust*** *for his son.* ■ a body of trustees. ■ an organization or company managed by trustees: *a charitable trust* | [in names] *the National Trust.*
3 [count noun] US dated a large company that has or attempts to gain monopolistic control of a market.
4 W. Indian or archaic commercial credit: *my master lived on trust at an alehouse.*
5 [count noun] archaic a hope or expectation: *all the great trusts of womanhood.*
▸ verb [with obj.] **1** believe in the reliability, truth, or ability of: *I should never have trusted her* | [with obj. and infinitive] *he can be trusted to carry out an impartial investigation* | (as adj. **trusted**) *a trusted adviser.* ■ (**trust someone with**) allow someone to have, use, or look after (someone or something of importance or value) with confidence: *I'd trust you with my life.* ■ (**trust someone/thing to**) commit someone or something to the safekeeping of: *they don't like to trust their money to anyone outside the family.* ■ [with clause] have confidence; hope (used as a polite formula in conversation): *I trust that you have enjoyed this book.* ■ [no obj.] have faith or confidence: *she trusted in the powers of justice.* ■ [no obj.] (**trust to**) place reliance on (luck, fate, or chance): *I hurtled down the path, trusting to luck that I wouldn't put a foot wrong.*
2 archaic allow credit to (a customer).
– PHRASES **not trust someone as far as one can throw them** informal not trust or hardly trust a particular person at all. **trust someone to ——** it is characteristic or predictable for someone to act in the specified way: *trust Sam to have all the inside information.*
– DERIVATIVES **trustable** adjective, **truster** noun.
– ORIGIN Middle English: from Old Norse *traust*, from *traustr* 'strong'; the verb from Old Norse *treysta*, assimilated to the noun.

Trustafarian /trʌstəˈfɛːrɪən/ ▸ noun Brit. informal a rich young person who adopts an ethnic lifestyle and lives in a non-affluent urban area.
– ORIGIN 1990s: blend of TRUST FUND and RASTAFARIAN.

trustbuster ▸ noun informal, chiefly US a person or agency employed to enforce antitrust legislation.

trust company ▸ noun a company formed to act as a trustee or to deal with trusts.

trust corporation ▸ noun English Law a corporation empowered to act as a trustee, provided that it is a registered company which satisfies certain conditions.

trust deed ▸ noun Law a deed of conveyance creating and setting out the conditions of a trust.

trustee ▸ noun **1** Law an individual person or member of a board given control or powers of administration of property in trust with a legal obligation to administer it solely for the purposes specified.
2 a state made responsible for the government of an area by the United Nations.
– DERIVATIVES **trusteeship** noun.

trustee in bankruptcy ▸ noun Law a person taking administrative responsibility for the financial affairs of a bankrupt and the distribution of assets to creditors.

trustful ▸ adjective having or marked by a total belief in the reliability, truth, or ability of someone: *a trustful acceptance of authority.*
– DERIVATIVES **trustfully** adverb, **trustfulness** noun.

trust fund ▸ noun a fund consisting of assets belonging to a trust, held by the trustees for the beneficiaries.

trusting ▸ adjective showing or tending to have a belief in a person's honesty or sincerity; not suspicious: *it is foolish to be too* ***trusting of*** *other people* | *a shy and trusting child.*
– DERIVATIVES **trustingly** adverb, **trustingness** noun.

trust territory ▸ noun a territory under the trusteeship of the United Nations or of a state designated by them.

trustworthy ▸ adjective able to be relied on as honest or truthful: *leave a spare key with a trustworthy neighbour.*
– DERIVATIVES **trustworthily** adverb, **trustworthiness** noun.

trusty ▸ adjective (**trustier, trustiest**) [attrib.] archaic or humorous having served for a long time and regarded as reliable or faithful: *my trusty old Morris Minor* | *their trusty steeds.*
▸ noun (pl. **trusties**) a prisoner who is given special privileges or responsibilities in return for good behaviour.
– DERIVATIVES **trustily** adverb, **trustiness** noun.

Truth, Sojourner (*c.*1797–1883), American evangelist and reformer; previously *Isabella Van Wagener*. Born into slavery, she was sold to an Isaac Van Wagener, who released her in 1827. She became a zealous evangelist, preaching in favour of black rights and women's suffrage.

truth ▸ noun (pl. **truths** /truːðz, truːθs/) [mass noun] the quality or state of being true: *he had to accept the truth of her accusation.* ■ (also **the truth**) that which is true or in accordance with fact or reality: *tell me the truth* | *she found out the truth about him.* ■ [count noun] a fact or belief that is accepted as true: *the emergence of scientific truths* | *the fundamental truths about mankind.*
– PHRASES **in truth** really; in fact: *in truth, she was more than a little unhappy.* **to tell the truth** (or **truth to tell** or **if truth be told**) to be frank (used especially when making an admission): *I think, if truth be told, we were all a little afraid of him.* **the truth, the whole truth, and nothing but the truth** used to emphasize the absolute veracity of a statement. [part of a statement sworn by witnesses in court.]
– ORIGIN Old English *trīewth, trēowth* 'faithfulness, constancy' (see TRUE, -TH²).

truth condition ▸ noun Logic the condition under which a given proposition is true. ■ a statement of this condition, sometimes taken to be the meaning of the proposition.

truth drug ▸ noun a drug supposedly able to induce a state in which a person answers questions truthfully.

truthful ▸ adjective telling or expressing the truth; honest: *I want a truthful answer.* ■ (of artistic or literary representation) characterized by accuracy or realism; true to life: *astonishingly truthful acting.*
– DERIVATIVES **truthfully** adverb.

truthfulness ▸ noun [mass noun] the fact of being true; truth: *we have had to judge the truthfulness of the evidence.* ■ the fact of being realistic or true to life; realism: *the truthfulness of her playing of an ageing American spinster.*

truth function ▸ noun Logic a function whose truth value is dependent on the truth value of its arguments.

truthiness ▸ noun [mass noun] informal the quality of seeming or being felt to be true, even if not necessarily true.
– ORIGIN early 19th cent. (in the sense 'truthfulness'): coined in the modern sense by the US humorist Stephen Colbert.

truth table ▸ noun Logic a diagram in rows and columns showing how the truth or falsity of a proposition varies with that of its components.

truth value ▸ noun Logic the attribute assigned to a proposition in respect of its truth or falsehood, which in classical logic has only two possible values (true or false).

try ▸ verb (**tries, trying, tried**) **1** [no obj.] make an attempt or effort to do something: [with infinitive] *he tried to regain his breath* | *I started to* ***try and*** *untangle the mystery* | *I decided to try writing fiction* | [with obj.] *three times he tried the manoeuvre and three times he failed.* ■ [with obj.] (also **try something out**) use, test, or do (something new or different) in order to see if it is suitable, effective, or pleasant: *everyone wanted to know if I'd tried jellied eel* | *these methods are* ***tried and tested.*** ■ (**try for**) attempt to achieve or attain: *they decided to try for another baby.* ■ (**try out for**) N. Amer. compete or audition for (a post or place on a team): *she tried out for the team.* ■ [with obj.] attempt to contact: *I've tried the apartment, but the number is engaged.* ■ [with obj.] push or pull (a door or window) to determine whether it is locked: *I tried the doors, but they were locked.* ■ [with obj.] make severe demands on (a person or a quality, typically patience): *Mary tried everyone's patience to the limit.*
2 [with obj.] subject (someone) to trial: *he was arrested and tried for the murder.* ■ investigate and decide (a case or issue) in a formal trial: *the case is to be tried by a jury in the Crown Court.*
3 [with obj.] smooth (roughly planed wood) with a plane to give an accurately flat surface.
4 [with obj.] extract (oil or fat) by heating: *some of the fat may be tried out and used.*
▸ noun (pl. **tries**) **1** an effort to accomplish something; an attempt: *he got his membership card on his third try.* ■ an act of trying something new or different to

T

see if it is suitable, effective, or pleasant: *she agreed that they should give the idea a try.* **2** Rugby an act of touching the ball down behind the opposing goal line, scoring points and entitling the scoring side to a kick at goal. ■ American Football an attempt to score an extra point after a touchdown.
– PHRASES **I** (or **he** etc.) **will try anything once** used to indicate willingness to do or experience something new. **try conclusions with** see CONCLUSION. **try something (on) for size** assess whether something is suitable: *he was trying the role for size.* **try for white** S. African (under the apartheid system) attempt to pass oneself off as a white person by assimilating oneself into a white community. **try one's hand at** attempt to do (something) for the first time, typically in order to find out if one is good at it: *a chance to try your hand at the ancient art of drystone walling.* **try it on** Brit. informal attempt to deceive or seduce someone: *he was trying it on with my wife.* ■ deliberately test someone's patience to see how much one can get away with. **try one's luck** see LUCK. **try me** used to suggest that one may be willing to do something unexpected or unlikely: *'You won't use a gun up here.' 'Try me.'*
– PHRASAL VERBS **try something on** put on an item of clothing to see if it fits or suits one.
– ORIGIN Middle English: from Old French *trier* 'sift', of unknown origin. Sense 1 of the noun dates from the early 17th cent.

> **USAGE** Is there any difference between **try to** plus infinitive and **try and** plus infinitive in sentences such as *we should **try to** (or **try and**) help them?* In practice there is little discernible difference in meaning, although there is a difference in formality, with **try to** being regarded as more formal than **try and**. The construction **try and** is grammatically odd, however, in that it cannot be inflected for tense (e.g. sentences like *she **tried and** fix it* or *they are **trying and** renew their visa* are not acceptable, while their equivalents *she **tried to** fix it* or *they are **trying to** renew their visa* undoubtedly are). For this reason **try and** is best regarded as a fixed idiom used only in its infinitive and imperative form. See also USAGE at AND.

trying ▶ adjective difficult or annoying; hard to endure: *it had been a very trying day.*
– DERIVATIVES **tryingly** adverb.

trying plane ▶ noun a long, heavy plane used in smoothing the edges of roughly planed wood.

try-on ▶ noun [in sing.] Brit. informal an attempt to fool or deceive someone.

try-out ▶ noun a test of the potential of someone or something, especially in the context of entertainment or sport.

trypan blue ▶ noun [mass noun] a diazo dye used as a biological stain due to its absorption by macrophages of the reticuloendothelial system.
– ORIGIN early 20th cent.: *trypan* from TRYPANOSOME.

trypanosome /ˈtrɪp(ə)nəsəʊm, trɪˈpanə-/ ▶ noun Medicine & Zoology a single-celled parasitic protozoan with a trailing flagellum, infesting the blood. ● Genus *Trypanosoma*, phylum Kinetoplastida, kingdom Protista.
– ORIGIN early 20th cent.: from Greek *trupanon* 'borer' + -SOME[3].

trypanosomiasis /ˌtrɪp(ə)nə(ʊ)sə(ʊ)ˈmʌɪəsɪs, trɪˌpanə(ʊ)-/ ▶ noun [mass noun] Medicine any tropical disease caused by trypanosomes and typically transmitted by biting insects, especially sleeping sickness and Chagas' disease.

trypsin /ˈtrɪpsɪn/ ▶ noun [mass noun] a digestive enzyme which breaks down proteins in the small intestine, secreted by the pancreas as trypsinogen.
– DERIVATIVES **tryptic** adjective.
– ORIGIN late 19th cent.: from Greek *tripsis* 'friction', from *tribein* 'to rub' (because it was first obtained by rubbing down the pancreas with glycerine), + -IN[1].

trypsinogen /trɪpˈsɪnədʒ(ə)n/ ▶ noun [mass noun] Biochemistry an inactive substance secreted by the pancreas, from which the digestive enzyme trypsin is formed in the duodenum.

tryptamine /ˈtrɪptəmiːn/ ▶ noun [mass noun] Biochemistry a compound, of which serotonin is a derivative, produced from tryptophan by decarboxylation. ● A heterocyclic amine; chem. formula: $C_8H_6NCH_2CH_2NH$.

tryptophan /ˈtrɪptəfan/ ▶ noun [mass noun] Biochemistry an amino acid which is a constituent of most proteins. It is an essential nutrient in the diet of vertebrates. ● An indole derivative; chem. formula: $C_8H_6NCH_2CH(NH_2)COOH$.
– ORIGIN late 19th cent.: from *tryptic* 'relating to trypsin' + Greek *phainein* 'appear'.

trysail /ˈtrʌɪs(ə)l/ ▶ noun a small strong fore-and-aft sail set on the mainmast or other mast of a sailing vessel in heavy weather.

try square ▶ noun an implement used to check and mark right angles in constructional work.

tryst /trɪst/ literary ▶ noun a private romantic rendezvous between lovers: *a moonlight tryst.*
▶ verb [no obj.] keep a private, romantic rendezvous with a lover: (as noun **trysting**) *a trysting place.*
– DERIVATIVES **tryster** noun.
– ORIGIN late Middle English (originally Scots): variant of obsolete *trist* 'an appointed place in hunting', from French *triste* or medieval Latin *trista*.

tsaddik /ˈtsadɪk/ (also **tzaddik**, **zaddik**) ▶ noun (pl. **tsaddikim** /-kɪm/, **tsaddiks**) Judaism a Hasidic spiritual leader or guide.
– ORIGIN Hebrew *ṣaddīq* 'just, righteous'.

tsamma /ˈtsamə/ (also **tsamma melon**) ▶ noun S. African a watermelon, especially one growing wild in the desert.
– ORIGIN from Nama *tsamas* 'watermelon'.

Tsao-chuang /tʃaʊˈtʃwaŋ/ variant of ZAOZHUANG.

tsar /zɑː, tsɑː/ (also **czar** or **tzar**) ▶ noun **1** an emperor of Russia before 1917: [as title] *Tsar Nicholas II.* ■ a South Slav ruler in former times, especially one reigning over Serbia in the 14th century.
2 (often **czar**) [usu. with adj. or noun modifier] a person appointed by government to advise on and coordinate policy in a particular area: *the former British drugs czar.*
– DERIVATIVES **tsardom** noun, **tsarism** noun, **tsarist** noun & adjective.
– ORIGIN from Russian *tsar'*, representing Latin *Caesar*.

> **WORD TRENDS** There seem to be so many **tsars** or **czars** involved in politics these days, you could be forgiven for thinking that the government had been overrun by Russian autocrats. In the US the word has been used since the 1930s to describe an official appointed to coordinate policy in a particular area, and it is now familiar in British English. A modifiying word usually specifies the **czar's** area of responsibility: *drug* is the commonest, followed by terms such as *health*, *border*, *security*, and *counterterrorism*. Many people are uncomfortable with the power and influence of these modern **czars**, a feeling that can't be helped by the choice of a name traditionally associated with authoritarian rule. See also OLIGARCH.

tsarevich /ˈzɑːrɪvɪtʃ, ˈtsɑː-, -ˈrjeɪ-/ (also **czarevich**, **tzarevich**) ▶ noun historical the eldest son of an emperor of Russia.
– ORIGIN Russian, literally 'son of a tsar'.

tsarina /zɑːˈriːnə, tsɑː-/ (also **czarina** or **tzarina**) ▶ noun an empress of Russia before 1917.
– ORIGIN via Italian and Spanish from German *Czarin*, *Zarin*, feminine of *Czar*, *Zar*.

Tsaritsyn /tsɑːˈriːtsɪn/ former name (until 1925) for VOLGOGRAD.

tsatske /ˈtsɒtskə/ ▶ noun variant spelling of TCHOTCHKE.

Tsavo National Park /ˈtsɑːvəʊ/ an extensive national park in SE Kenya, established in 1948.

Tselinograd /(t)seˈlɪnə(ʊ),grad/ former name for AKMOLA.

tsessebi /tseˈseɪbi/ (also **tsessebe** or **sassaby**) ▶ noun a topi (antelope) of a race found mainly in southern Africa. ● *Damaliscus lunatus lunatus*, family Bovidae. Alternative name: **bastard hartebeest**.
– ORIGIN mid 19th cent.: from Setswana.

tsetse /ˈtsɛtsi, ˈtɛtsi/ (also **tsetse fly**) ▶ noun an African bloodsucking fly which bites humans and other mammals, transmitting sleeping sickness and nagana. ● Genus *Glossina*, family Tabanidae.
– ORIGIN mid 19th cent.: from Setswana.

TSgt ▶ abbreviation Technical Sergeant.

TSH ▶ abbreviation thyroid-stimulating hormone.

T-shirt (also **tee shirt**) ▶ noun a short-sleeved casual top, generally made of cotton, having the shape of a T when spread out flat.

tsimmes /ˈtsɪməs/ (also **tzimmes** or **tzimmis**) ▶ noun (pl. **same**) a Jewish stew of sweetened vegetables or vegetables and fruit, sometimes with meat. ■ a fuss or muddle: *why are you making such a tsimmes?*
– ORIGIN Yiddish.

Tsimshian /ˈtʃɪmʃɪən/ ▶ noun (pl. **same**) **1** a member of an American Indian people of the northern Pacific coast.
2 [mass noun] the Penutian language of the Tsimshian, now with few speakers.
▶ adjective relating to the Tsimshian or their language.
– ORIGIN from Tsimshian *ĉamsián*, literally 'inside the Skeena River'.

Tsinan /tsiːˈnan/ variant of JINAN.

Tsinghai variant of QINGHAI.

Tskhinvali /tskɪnˈvɑːli/ the capital of South Ossetia.

tsk tsk /t(ə)sk t(ə)sk/ ▶ exclamation expressing disapproval or annoyance: *you of all people, Goldie—tsk, tsk.*
▶ verb (**tsk-tsk**) [no obj.] make such an exclamation.
– ORIGIN 1940s: imitative.

Tsonga /ˈtsɒŋgə/ ▶ noun (pl. **same** or **Tsongas**) **1** a member of a people living in the Limpopo province of South Africa, southern Mozambique, and southern Zimbabwe. Also called SHANGAAN.
2 [mass noun] the Bantu language of the Tsonga, which has about 3 million speakers.
▶ adjective relating to the Tsonga or their language.
– ORIGIN a local name, from either Tsonga or Zulu.

tsores variant spelling of TSURIS.

tsotsi /ˈtsɒtsi/ ▶ noun (pl. **tsotsis**) S. African a young black urban criminal. ■ historical a young black gangster belonging to a group prominent in the 1940s and 1950s, affecting a special language and flashy dress.
– ORIGIN said to be a Sotho corruption of ZOOT SUIT.

tsp ▶ abbreviation (pl. **same** or **tsps**) teaspoonful.

T-square ▶ noun a T-shaped instrument for drawing or testing right angles.

TSR ▶ abbreviation Computing terminate and stay resident, denoting a type of program that remains in the memory of a computer after it has finished running and which can be quickly reactivated.

TSS ▶ abbreviation toxic shock syndrome.

tsuba /ˈtsuːbɑː/ ▶ noun (pl. **same** or **tsubas**) a Japanese sword guard, typically elaborately decorated and made of iron or leather.
– ORIGIN Japanese.

tsubo /ˈtsuːbəʊ/ ▶ noun (pl. **same** or **tsubos**) **1** a Japanese unit of area equal to approximately 3.31 sq. metres (3.95 sq. yards).
2 (in complementary medicine) a point on the face or body to which pressure or other stimulation is applied during treatment.
– ORIGIN Japanese.

tsukemono /ˌtsuːkɪˈməʊnəʊ/ ▶ noun (pl. **tsukemonos**) a Japanese side dish of pickled vegetables, usually served with rice.
– ORIGIN Japanese, from *tsukeru* 'pickle' + *mono* 'thing'.

tsunami /tsuːˈnɑːmi/ ▶ noun (pl. **same** or **tsunamis**) a long, high sea wave caused by an earthquake or other disturbance.
– ORIGIN late 19th cent.: from Japanese, from *tsu* 'harbour' + *nami* 'wave'.

tsuris /ˈtsʊrɪs/ (also **tsores** /ˈtsɒrəs/) ▶ noun [mass noun] N. Amer. informal problems or difficulties; trouble: *the NBA has its share of tsuris these days.*
– ORIGIN early 20th cent.: Yiddish, plural of *tsore* 'trouble, woe', from Hebrew *ṣārāh*.

Tsushima /tsuːˈʃiːmə/ a Japanese island in the Korea Strait, between South Korea and Japan. In 1905 it was the scene of a defeat for the Russian navy during the Russo-Japanese War.

tsutsugamushi disease /ˌtsuːtsuːgəˈmʊʃi/ ▶ noun another term for SCRUB TYPHUS.
– ORIGIN early 20th cent.: *tsutsugamushi*, from the Japanese name of the mite which transmits the disease.

Tswana /ˈtswɑːnə/ ▶ noun (pl. **same**, **Tswanas**, or **Batswana**) **1** a member of a southern African people living in Botswana, South Africa, and neighbouring areas.
2 [mass noun] the language of the Tswana, also called Setswana.
▶ adjective relating to the Tswana or their language.
– ORIGIN stem of Setswana *moTswana*, plural *baTswana*.

TT ▶ abbreviation ■ teetotal. ■ teetotaller. ■ Tourist Trophy. ■ tuberculin-tested.

TTL ▶ noun [mass noun] Electronics a widely used technology for making integrated circuits. [abbreviation of *transistor transistor logic*.]
▶ adjective Photography (of a camera focusing system) through-the-lens.

T-top ▶ noun N. Amer. a car roof with removable panels. ■ a car with removable panels in its roof.

T

TTS ▶ abbreviation text-to-speech, a form of speech synthesis used to create a spoken version of the text in an electronic document.

TTYL ▶ abbreviation informal talk to you later: *Anyway, gotta run now! TTYL.*

TU ▶ abbreviation Trade Union.

Tu. ▶ abbreviation Tuesday.

Tuamotu Archipelago /ˌtuːəˈməʊtuː/ a group of about eighty coral islands forming part of French Polynesia, in the South Pacific; pop. 18,317 (2007). It is the largest group of coral atolls in the world.

tuan /ˈtjuːən/ ▶ noun another term for PHASCOGALE.
– ORIGIN mid 19th cent.: an Aboriginal word.

Tuareg /ˈtwɑːrɛg/ ▶ noun (pl. **same** or **Tuaregs**) a member of a Berber people of the western and central Sahara, living mainly in Algeria, Mali, Niger, and western Libya, traditionally as nomadic pastoralists.
▶ adjective relating to the Tuareg.
– ORIGIN the name in Berber.

tuatara /ˌtuːəˈtɑːrə/ ▶ noun a nocturnal burrowing lizard-like reptile with a crest of soft spines along its back, now confined to some small islands off New Zealand. ● Order Rhynchocephalia and genus *Sphenodon*: two species, in particular *S. punctatum*. All other members of the order became extinct during the Mesozoic era.
– ORIGIN late 19th cent.: from Maori, from *tua* 'on the back' + *tara* 'spine'.

Tuatha Dé Danann /ˌtʊəhə deɪ ˈdanən/ ▶ plural noun Irish Mythology the members of an ancient race said to have inhabited Ireland before the historical Irish. Formerly believed to have been a real people, they are credited with the possession of magical powers and great wisdom.
– ORIGIN Irish, literally 'people of the goddess Danann'.

tub ▶ noun **1** a wide, open, deep, typically round container with a flat bottom used for holding liquids, growing plants, etc.: *a rainwater tub.* ■ a small plastic or cardboard container in which food is bought or stored: *a margarine tub.* ■ the contents of a tub or the amount it can contain: *she ate **a tub of** yogurt.* ■ a washtub. ■ informal, chiefly N. Amer. a bath: *a soak in the tub.* ■ Mining a container for conveying ore, coal, etc.
2 informal, derogatory a short, broad boat that handles awkwardly.
▶ verb (**tubs**, **tubbing**, **tubbed**) [with obj.] **1** (usu. as adj. **tubbed**) plant in a tub: *tubbed fruit trees.*
2 dated wash or bathe in or as in a tub or bath. ■ [no obj.] Brit. informal have a bath.
– DERIVATIVES **tubful** noun (pl. **tubfuls**).
– ORIGIN Middle English: probably of Low German or Dutch origin; compare with Middle Low German, Middle Dutch *tubbe*.

tuba ▶ noun a large brass wind instrument of bass pitch, with three to six valves and a broad bell typically facing upwards. ■ a powerful reed stop on an organ with the quality of a tuba.
– ORIGIN mid 19th cent.: via Italian from Latin, 'trumpet'.

tubal ▶ adjective relating to or occurring in a tube, especially the fallopian tubes.

tubal ligation ▶ noun a surgical procedure for female sterilization which involves severing and tying the fallopian tubes.

tubal pregnancy ▶ noun Medicine an ectopic pregnancy in which the fetus develops in a fallopian tube.

T

tubby ▶ adjective (**tubbier**, **tubbiest**) **1** informal short and rather fat: *a small, tubby man.*
2 (of a sound) lacking resonance; dull (as that of a tub when struck).
– DERIVATIVES **tubbiness** noun.

tub chair ▶ noun a chair with solid arms continuous with a semicircular back.

tube ▶ noun **1** a long, hollow cylinder of metal, plastic, glass, etc. for holding or transporting something, chiefly liquids or gases: *a plastic tube is connected to the tap and the beer is ready to be pulled.* ■ the inner tube of a bicycle tyre. ■ [mass noun] material in a tubular form; tubing: *the firm manufactures steel tube for a wide variety of applications.*
2 a thing in the form of or resembling a tube, in particular: ■ a flexible metal or plastic container sealed at one end and having a screw cap at the other, for holding a semi-liquid substance ready for use: *a tube of toothpaste.* ■ a rigid cylindrical container: *a tube of Smarties.* ■ Austral. informal a can of beer: *a tube of lager.* ■ [usu. with adj. or noun modifier] Anatomy, Zoology, & Botany a hollow cylindrical organ or structure in an animal body or in a plant (e.g. a Eustachian tube, a sieve tube). ■ (**tubes**) informal a woman's fallopian tubes: *women with blocked tubes.* ■ a woman's close-fitting garment, typically without darts or other tailoring and made from a single piece of stretch fabric: [as modifier] *a tube skirt.* ■ (in surfing) the hollow curve under the crest of a breaking wave. ■ informal a cigarette.
3 (**the Tube**) Brit. trademark the underground railway system in London: *a cross-London trek on the Tube.* ■ a train running on the Tube: *I caught the tube home.*
4 a sealed container, typically of glass and either evacuated or filled with gas, containing two electrodes between which an electric current can be made to flow. ■ a cathode ray tube, especially in a television set. ■ (**the tube**) N. Amer. informal television: *watching the tube in a country bar.* ■ N. Amer. a thermionic valve.
▶ verb [with obj.] **1** (usu. as adj. **tubed**) provide with a tube or tubes: [in combination] *a giant eight-tubed hookah.*
2 informal fit (a person or animal) with a tube to assist breathing, especially after a laryngotomy.
3 [with adverbial] convey in a tube.
4 (**tube it**) Brit. informal travel on the Tube: *we tubed it back to Queensway* | [no obj.] *I tubed to St Pancras.*
– PHRASES **go down the tube** (or **tubes**) informal be completely lost or wasted; fail utterly: *the country is going slowly and surely down the tubes.*
– DERIVATIVES **tubeless** adjective, **tube-like** adjective.
– ORIGIN mid 17th cent.: from French *tube* or Latin *tubus*.

tubectomy ▶ noun (pl. **tubectomies**) another term for SALPINGECTOMY.

tube foot ▶ noun (usu. **tube feet**) Zoology (in an echinoderm) each of a large number of small flexible hollow appendages protruding through the ambulacra, used either for locomotion or for collecting food and operated by hydraulic pressure within the water-vascular system.

tube-nosed bat ▶ noun an Old World bat with tubular nostrils: ● a fruit bat found chiefly in New Guinea and Sulawesi (genus *Nyctimene*, family Pteropodidae). ● an insectivorous Asian bat (genus *Murina*, family Vespertilionidae).

tuber ▶ noun **1** a much thickened underground part of a stem or rhizome, e.g. in the potato, serving as a food reserve and bearing buds from which new plants arise. ■ a tuberous root, e.g. of the dahlia.
2 Anatomy a rounded swelling or protuberant part.
– ORIGIN mid 17th cent.: from Latin, literally 'hump, swelling'.

tuber cinereum /ˌtjuːbə sɪˈnɪərɪəm/ ▶ noun (pl. **tuber cinereums**) Anatomy the part of the hypothalamus to which the pituitary gland is attached.
– ORIGIN Latin *cinereum*, neuter of *cinereus* 'ash-coloured'.

tubercle /ˈtjuːbək(ə)l/ ▶ noun **1** Anatomy, Zoology, & Botany a small rounded projection or protuberance, especially on a bone or on the surface of an animal or plant.
2 Medicine a small nodular lesion in the lungs or other tissues, characteristic of tuberculosis.
– DERIVATIVES **tuberculate** /-ˈbəːkjʊlət/ adjective (sense 1).
– ORIGIN late 16th cent.: from Latin *tuberculum*, diminutive of *tuber* (see TUBER).

tubercle bacillus ▶ noun a bacterium that causes tuberculosis.

tubercular /tjʊˈbəːkjʊlə/ ▶ adjective Medicine relating to or affected with tuberculosis: *a tubercular kidney.* ■ Biology & Medicine having or covered with tubercles.
▶ noun a person with tuberculosis.

tuberculation /tjʊˌbəːkjʊˈleɪʃ(ə)n/ ▶ noun [mass noun] chiefly Biology the formation or presence of tubercles, especially of a specified type.
– ORIGIN mid 19th cent.: from Latin *tuberculum* (see TUBERCLE) + -ATION.

tuberculin /tjʊˈbəːkjʊlɪn/ ▶ noun [mass noun] a sterile protein extract from cultures of tubercle bacillus, used in a test by hypodermic injection for infection with or immunity to tuberculosis, and also formerly in the treatment of the disease.
– ORIGIN late 19th cent.: from Latin *tuberculum* (see TUBERCLE) + -IN[1].

tuberculin-tested ▶ adjective (of milk) certified as free from tuberculosis.

tuberculoid /tjʊˈbəːkjʊlɔɪd/ ▶ adjective Medicine resembling tuberculosis or its symptoms. ■ relating to or denoting the milder of the two principal forms of leprosy, marked by few, well-defined lesions similar to those of tuberculosis, often with loss of feeling in the affected areas. Compare with LEPROMATOUS.

tuberculosis /tjʊˌbəːkjʊˈləʊsɪs/ (abbrev.: **TB**) ▶ noun [mass noun] an infectious bacterial disease characterized by the growth of nodules (tubercles) in the tissues, especially the lungs. ● The disease is caused by the bacterium *Mycobacterium tuberculosis* or (especially in animals) a related species; Gram-positive acid-fast rods.

> The most common form, **pulmonary tuberculosis** (formerly known as 'consumption'), is caused by inhalation of the bacteria. It was widespread in 19th-century Europe, and still causes millions of deaths each year in developing countries. The disease can affect other parts of the body, notably the bones and joints and the central nervous system. Its spread is countered by vaccination and by the pasteurization of milk to prevent transmission from cattle. It was once considered incurable, but early X-ray diagnosis permits its arrest by drugs and surgery.

– ORIGIN mid 19th cent.: modern Latin, from Latin *tuberculum* (see TUBERCLE) + -OSIS.

tuberculous /tjʊˈbəːkjʊləs/ ▶ adjective another term for TUBERCULAR.

tuberose /ˈtjuːbərəʊz/ ▶ noun a Mexican plant with heavily scented white waxy flowers and a bulb-like base. Unknown in the wild, it was formerly cultivated as a flavouring for chocolate; the flower oil is used in perfumery. ● *Polianthes tuberosa*, family Agavaceae.
▶ adjective variant spelling of TUBEROUS.
– ORIGIN mid 17th cent.: the noun from Latin *tuberosa*, feminine of *tuberosus* 'with protuberances'; the adjective from Latin *tuberosus*.

tuberous /ˈtjuːb(ə)rəs/ (also **tuberose** /ˈtjuːb(ə)rəʊs/) ▶ adjective **1** Botany of the nature of a tuber. See TUBEROUS ROOT. ■ (of a plant) having tubers or a tuberous root.
2 Medicine characterized by or affected by rounded swellings: *tuberous sclerosis.*
– DERIVATIVES **tuberosity** /-ˈrɒsɪti/ noun.
– ORIGIN mid 17th cent.: from French *tubéreux* or Latin *tuberosus*, from *tuber* (see TUBER).

tuberous root ▶ noun a thick and fleshy root like a tuber but without buds, as in the dahlia.

tube top ▶ noun North American term for BOOB TUBE.

tube well ▶ noun a well consisting of an iron pipe with a solid steel point and lateral perforations near the end, which is driven into the earth until a water-bearing stratum is reached, when a suction pump is applied to the upper end.

tube worm ▶ noun a marine bristle worm, especially a fan worm, which lives in a tube made from sand particles or in a calcareous tube that it secretes. ● Families Serpulidae and Sabellidae, phylum Polychaeta. ■ a pogonophoran or vestimentiferan worm.

tubicolous /tjuːˈbɪkələs/ ▶ adjective Zoology (of a marine worm) living in a tube.

tubifex /ˈtjuːbɪfɛks/ ▶ noun a small red annelid worm that lives in fresh water, partly buried in the mud. Also called BLOODWORM. ● Genus *Tubifex*, family Tubificidae, class Oligochaeta.
– ORIGIN modern Latin, from Latin *tubus* 'tube' + *-fex* from *facere* 'make'.

tubiform ▶ adjective technical having the shape of a tube; tube-shaped.

tubing ▶ noun [mass noun] **1** a length or lengths of metal, plastic, glass, etc., in tubular form: *use the plastic tubing to siphon the beer into the bottles.*
2 N. Amer. the leisure activity of riding on water or snow on a large inflated inner tube.

tubocurarine /ˌtjuːbə(ʊ)ˈkjʊərəriːn/ ▶ noun [mass noun] Medicine a compound of the alkaloid class obtained from curare and used to produce relaxation of voluntary muscles before surgery and in tetanus, encephalitis, and poliomyelitis.
– ORIGIN late 19th cent.: from Latin *tubus* 'tube' + CURARE + -INE[4].

Tubruq /tʊˈbruːk/ Arabic name for TOBRUK.

tub-thumping informal, derogatory ▶ adjective [attrib.] expressing opinions in a loud or aggressive manner: *a tub-thumping speech.*
▶ noun [mass noun] the expression of opinions in a loud or aggressive way.
– DERIVATIVES **tub-thumper** noun.

Tubuai Islands /tuːbˈwɑːi/ a group of volcanic islands in the South Pacific, forming part of French Polynesia; chief town, Mataura (on the island of Tubuai); pop. 6,669 (2007). Also called the AUSTRAL ISLANDS.

tubular ▶ adjective **1** long, round, and hollow like a tube: *tubular flowers of deep crimson.* ■ made from a tube or tubes: *tubular steel chairs.* ■ Surfing (of a wave) hollow and well curved.
2 Medicine of or involving tubules or other tube-shaped structures.
▶ noun **1** short for TUBULAR TYRE.
2 (**tubulars**) oil-drilling equipment made from tubes.
– ORIGIN late 17th cent.: from Latin *tubulus* 'small tube' + -AR[1].

tubular bells ▶ plural noun an orchestral instrument consisting of a row of vertically suspended metal tubes struck with a mallet.

tubular tyre ▶ noun a completely enclosed tyre cemented on to the wheel rim, used on racing bicycles.

tubule /ˈtjuːbjuːl/ ▶ noun a minute tube, especially as an anatomical structure: *kidney tubules.*
– ORIGIN late 17th cent.: from Latin *tubulus*, diminutive of *tubus* 'tube'.

Tubulidentata /ˌtjuːbjʊlɪdɛnˈtɑːtə, -ˈteɪtə/ ▶ plural noun Zoology an order of mammals which comprises only the aardvark.
– ORIGIN modern Latin (plural), from TUBULE + Greek *odous, odont-* 'tooth'.

tubulin /ˈtjuːbjʊlɪn/ ▶ noun [mass noun] Biochemistry a protein that is the main constituent of the microtubules of living cells.
– ORIGIN 1960s: from TUBULE + -IN[1].

TUC ▶ abbreviation (in the UK) Trades Union Congress.

Tucana /tʊˈkɑːnə/ Astronomy a southern constellation (the Toucan), south of Grus and Phoenix. It contains the Small Magellanic Cloud.
– ORIGIN modern Latin.

tuck ▶ verb **1** [with obj. and usu. with adverbial of place] push, fold, or turn (the edges or ends of something, especially a garment or bedclothes) so as to hide or secure them: *he tucked his shirt into his trousers.* ■ (**tuck someone in/up**) make someone, especially a child, comfortable in bed by pulling the edges of the bedclothes firmly under the mattress: *Emily was only too willing to be tucked up in bed by nine.* ■ draw (something, especially part of one's body) together into a small space: *she tucked her legs under her.* ■ put or keep (something) in a specified place so as to be hidden, secure, comfortable, or tidy: *the Colonel walked towards her, his gun tucked under his arm | savers are turning to unit trusts as the best place to tuck away their money.*
2 [with obj.] make a flattened, stitched fold in (a garment or material), typically so as to shorten or tighten it, or for decoration.
▶ noun **1** a flattened, stitched fold in a garment or material, typically one of several parallel folds put in to improve the fit or for decoration: *a dress with tucks along the bodice.* ■ [usu. with modifier] informal a surgical operation to reduce surplus flesh or fat: *a tummy tuck.*
2 [mass noun] Brit. informal food eaten by children at school as a snack: [as modifier] *a tuck shop.*
3 (also **tuck position**) (in diving, gymnastics, downhill skiing, etc.) a position with the knees bent and held close to the chest, often with the hands clasped round the shins.
– PHRASAL VERBS **tuck something away 1** store something in a secure place: *employees can tuck away a percentage of their pretax salary.* ■ (**be tucked away**) be located in an inconspicuous or concealed place: *the police station was tucked away in a square behind the main street.* **2** eat a lot of food: *Sammy managed to tuck away everything his father couldn't eat.* **tuck in** (or **into**) informal eat food heartily: *I tucked into the bacon and eggs.*
– ORIGIN Old English *tūcian* 'to punish, ill-treat': of West Germanic origin; related to TUG. Influenced in Middle English by Middle Dutch *tucken* 'pull sharply'.

tuckahoe /ˈtʌkəhəʊ/ ▶ noun [mass noun] a root or other underground plant part formerly eaten by North American Indians, in particular: ● the starchy rhizome of an arum that grows chiefly in marshland (*Peltandra virginica*, family Araceae). ● the underground sclerotium of a bracket fungus (*Poria cocos*, class Hymenomycetes).
– ORIGIN early 17th cent.: from Virginia Algonquian *tockawhoughe*.

tucker ▶ noun **1** [mass noun] Austral./NZ informal food. [early 19th cent.: derivative of British English slang *tuck* 'consume food or drink'.]
2 historical a piece of lace or linen worn in or around the top of a bodice or as an insert at the front of a low-cut dress. See also ONE'S BEST BIB AND TUCKER at BIB[1].
▶ verb [with obj.] (usu. **be tuckered out**) N. Amer. informal exhaust; wear out.

tucket ▶ noun archaic a flourish on a trumpet.
– ORIGIN late 16th cent.: from obsolete *tuck* 'beat a drum', from Old Northern French *toquer*, from the base of TOUCH.

tuck-in ▶ noun Brit. informal, dated a large meal.

tucking ▶ noun [mass noun] a series of stitched tucks in a garment.

tuck-point ▶ verb [with obj.] point (brickwork) with coloured mortar so as to have a narrow groove which is filled with fine white lime putty allowed to project slightly.

tuck position ▶ noun see TUCK (sense 3 of the noun).

tuco-tuco /ˈtuːkəʊˌtuːkəʊ/ ▶ noun (pl. **tuco-tucos**) a burrowing rat-like rodent native to South America. ● Family Ctenomyidae and genus *Ctenomys*: numerous species.
– ORIGIN mid 19th cent.: imitative of the call of some species.

Tucson /ˈtuːsɒn/ a city in SE Arizona; pop. 541,811 (est. 2008).

tucuxi /tʊˈkuːhi/ ▶ noun (pl. **same**) a small stout-bodied dolphin with a grey back and pinkish underparts, living along the coasts and rivers from Panama to Brazil and in the Amazon. ● *Sotalia fluviatilis*, family Delphinidae.

'tude ▶ noun N. Amer. informal short for ATTITUDE: *the song bristles with lotsa 'tude.*

-tude ▶ suffix forming abstract nouns such as *beatitude, solitude.*
– ORIGIN from French *-tude*, from Latin *-tudo*.

Tudeh /ˈtuːdeɪ/ (also **Tudeh Party**) the Communist Party of Iran.
– ORIGIN Persian, literally 'mass'.

Tudor[1] ▶ adjective relating to the English royal dynasty which held the throne from the accession of Henry VII in 1485 until the death of Elizabeth I in 1603. ■ denoting or relating to the prevalent architectural style of the Tudor period, characterized especially by half-timbering.
▶ noun a member of the Tudor dynasty.

Tudor[2], Henry, Henry VII of England (see HENRY[1]).

Tudor[3], Mary, Mary I of England (see MARY[2]).

Tudorbethan /ˌtjuːdəˈbiːθ(ə)n/ ▶ adjective (of a contemporary house or architectural design) imitative of Tudor and Elizabethan styles.
– ORIGIN 1930s: blend of TUDOR[1] and ELIZABETHAN.

Tudor rose ▶ noun a conventionalized, typically five-lobed figure of a rose used in architectural and other decoration in the Tudor period, in particular a combination of the red and white roses of Lancaster or York adopted as a badge by Henry VII.

Tues. (also **Tue.**) ▶ abbreviation Tuesday.

Tuesday ▶ noun the day of the week before Wednesday and following Monday: *come to dinner on Tuesday | the following Tuesday* | [as modifier] *Tuesday afternoons.*
▶ adverb chiefly N. Amer. on Tuesday: *they're all leaving Tuesday.* ■ (**Tuesdays**) on Tuesdays; each Tuesday: *she works late Tuesdays.*
– ORIGIN Old English *Tīwesdæg*, named after the Germanic god *Tīw* (associated with Mars); translation of Latin *dies Marti* 'day of Mars'; compare with Swedish *tisdag*.

tufa /ˈt(j)uːfə/ ▶ noun [mass noun] a porous rock composed of calcium carbonate and formed by precipitation from water, e.g. around mineral springs. ■ another term for TUFF.
– DERIVATIVES **tufaceous** /-ˈfeɪʃəs/ adjective.
– ORIGIN late 18th cent.: from Italian, variant of *tufo* (see TUFF).

tuff /tʌf/ ▶ noun [mass noun] a light, porous rock formed by consolidation of volcanic ash.
– DERIVATIVES **tuffaceous** /-ˈfeɪʃəs/ adjective.
– ORIGIN mid 16th cent.: via French from Italian *tufo*, from late Latin *tofus*, Latin *tophus* (see TOPHUS).

tuffet ▶ noun **1** a tuft or clump of something: *grass tuffets.*
2 a footstool or low seat.
– ORIGIN mid 16th cent.: alteration of TUFT.

tuft ▶ noun a bunch or collection of threads, grass, hair, etc., held or growing together at the base: *scrubby tufts of grass.* ■ Anatomy & Zoology a bunch of small blood vessels, respiratory tentacles, or other small anatomical structures.
▶ verb [with obj.] **1** provide with a tuft or tufts.
2 Needlework strengthen (upholstery) by passing a cluster of threads through the material, so making depressions at regular intervals.
– DERIVATIVES **tufty** adjective (**tuftier, tuftiest**).
– ORIGIN late Middle English: probably from Old French *tofe*, of unknown origin. The final *-t* is typical of phonetic confusion between *-ʃ* and *-ft* at the end of words; compare with GRAFT[1].

tufted ▶ adjective having or growing in a tuft or tufts: *tufted grass.*

tufted duck ▶ noun a Eurasian freshwater diving duck with a drooping crest, the male having mainly black and white plumage. ● *Aythya fuligula*, family Anatidae.

tuft hunter ▶ noun informal a sycophantic or obsequious person.
– ORIGIN mid 18th cent.: originally used with reference to the 'tufts' or gold tassels formerly worn by titled Oxbridge undergraduates.

Tu Fu /tuː ˈfuː/ (also **Du Fu**) (AD 712–70), Chinese poet. He is noted for his bitter satirical poems attacking social injustice and corruption at court.

tug ▶ verb (**tugs, tugging, tugged**) [with obj.] pull (something) hard or suddenly: *she tugged off her boots* | [no obj.] *he tugged at Tom's coat sleeve.* ■ tow (a ship) by means of a tugboat.
▶ noun **1** a hard or sudden pull: *another tug and it came loose* | figurative *an overwhelming tug of attraction.*
2 (also **tugboat**) a small, powerful boat used for towing larger boats and ships, especially in harbour. ■ an aircraft towing a glider.
3 a loop from a horse's saddle which supports a shaft or trace.
– PHRASES **tug of love** Brit. informal a dispute over the custody of a child.
– DERIVATIVES **tugger** noun.
– ORIGIN Middle English: from the base of TOW[1]. The noun is first recorded (late Middle English) in sense 3 of the noun.

tug of war ▶ noun a contest in which two teams pull at opposite ends of a rope until one drags the other over a central line. ■ a situation in which two evenly matched people or factions are striving to keep or obtain the same thing: *a tug of war between builders and environmentalists.*

tugrik /ˈtuːgriːk/ ▶ noun (pl. **same** or **tugriks**) the basic monetary unit of Mongolia, equal to 100 mongos.
– ORIGIN Mongolian.

tui /ˈtuːi/ ▶ noun a large New Zealand honeyeater with glossy blackish plumage and two white tufts at the throat. Also called PARSON-BIRD. ● *Prosthemadura novaeseelandiae*, family Meliphagidae.
– ORIGIN mid 19th cent.: from Maori.

tuile /twiːl/ ▶ noun (pl. pronunc. **same**) a thin curved biscuit, typically made with almonds.
– ORIGIN French, literally 'tile'.

Tuileries /ˈtwiːləri/, French /tɥilʀi/ (also **Tuileries Gardens**) formal gardens next to the Louvre in Paris. The gardens are all that remain of the Tuileries Palace, a royal residence begun in 1564 and burnt down in 1871 during the Commune of Paris.
– ORIGIN French, literally 'Tile-works': the palace was built on the site of an ancient tile-works.

Tuinal /ˈt(j)uːɪnal, -nəl/ ▶ noun [mass noun] Medicine, trademark a sedative and sleep-inducing drug consisting of a combination of two barbiturates.

tuition ▶ noun [mass noun] teaching or instruction, especially of individual pupils or small groups: *private tuition in French* | [as modifier] *tuition fees.* ■ N. Amer. a sum of money charged for teaching by a college or university: *I'm not paying next year's tuition.*
– DERIVATIVES **tuitional** adjective.
– ORIGIN late Middle English (in the sense 'custody, care'): via Old French from Latin *tuitio(n-)*, from *tueri* 'to watch, guard'. Current senses date from the late 16th cent.

tuk-tuk /ˈtʊktʊk/ ▶ noun (in Thailand) a three-wheeled motorized vehicle used as a taxi.
– ORIGIN imitative.

Tula /ˈtuːlə/ **1** an industrial city in European Russia, to the south of Moscow; pop. 500,000 (est. 2008).
2 the ancient capital city of the Toltecs, generally identified with a site near the town of Tula in Hidalgo State, central Mexico.

tularaemia /ˌt(j)uːləˈriːmɪə/ (US **tularemia**) ▶ noun [mass noun] a severe infectious bacterial disease of

T

animals transmissible to humans, characterized by ulcers at the site of infection, fever, and loss of weight. Compare with RABBIT FEVER. ● This disease is caused by the bacterium *Pasteurella tularense*; Gram-negative rods or cocci.
– ORIGIN 1920s: modern Latin, from *Tulare*, the county in California where it was first observed.

tule /ˈtuːli/ ▶ **noun** a clubrush that is abundant in marshy areas of California. ● *Scirpus acutus* and *S. validus*, family Cyperaceae.
– ORIGIN mid 19th cent.: via Spanish from Nahuatl *tullin*.

tulip ▶ **noun** a bulbous spring-flowering plant of the lily family, with boldly coloured cup-shaped flowers. ● Genus *Tulipa*, family Liliaceae: numerous complex hybrids.
– ORIGIN late 16th cent.: from French *tulipe*, via Turkish from Persian *dulband* 'turban', from the shape of the expanded flower.

tulip shell ▶ **noun** a predatory marine mollusc with a sculptured spiral shell resembling that of a whelk. ● Family Fasciolariidae, class Gastropoda, in particular *Fasciolaria tulipa*, which is common in the Caribbean.

tulip tree ▶ **noun 1** a deciduous North American tree which has large distinctively lobed leaves and insignificant tulip-like flowers. ● *Liriodendron tulipifera*, family Magnoliaceae.
2 informal term for MAGNOLIA (in the plant sense).

tulipwood ▶ **noun 1** an Australian tree of rainforest and scrub, with heavy black and yellow timber that is used mainly for cabinetmaking. ● *Harpullia pendula*, family Sapindaceae.
2 [mass noun] the pale timber of the tulip tree.

Tull /tʌl/, Jethro (1674–1741), English agriculturalist. In 1701 he invented the seed drill, a machine which could sow seeds in accurately spaced rows at a controlled rate, reducing the need for farm labourers.

Tullamore /ˌtʊləˈmɔː/ the county town of Offaly, in the Republic of Ireland; pop. 10,900 (2006).

tulle /t(j)uːl/ ▶ **noun** [mass noun] a soft, fine silk, cotton, or nylon material like net, used for making veils and dresses.
– ORIGIN early 19th cent.: from *Tulle*, a town in SW France, where it was first made.

tullibee /ˈtʌlɪbiː/ ▶ **noun** (pl. **same** or **tullibees**) a lake cisco (fish) of a deep-bodied race living in the Great Lakes of Canada. ● *Coregonus artedii tullibee*, family Salmonidae.
– ORIGIN late 18th cent.: from Canadian French *toulibi*, ultimately from Ojibwa.

tulp /təːlp/ ▶ **noun** an African plant of the iris family, which is grown for its showy flowers but is toxic to livestock. ● Genera *Homeria* and *Moraea*, family Iridaceae: several species, including the **blue tulp** (*M. polystachya*).
– ORIGIN mid 19th cent.: from Afrikaans, from Dutch.

Tulsa /ˈtʌlsə/ a port on the Arkansas River in NE Oklahoma; pop. 385,635 (est. 2008).

tulsi /ˈtʊlsiː/ ▶ **noun** [mass noun] a kind of basil which is cultivated by Hindus as a sacred plant. ● *Ocimum sanctum*, family Labiatae.
– ORIGIN from Hindi *tulsī*.

Tulsidas /ˈtʊlsɪdɑːs/ (*c.*1543–1623), Indian poet. A leading Hindu devotional poet, he is chiefly remembered for the *Ramcaritmanas* (*c.*1574–7), a work consisting of seven cantos based on the Sanskrit epic the Ramayana.

T

tum ▶ **noun** informal a person's stomach or abdomen.
– ORIGIN mid 19th cent.: abbreviation of TUMMY.

tumbaga /tʊmˈbɑːɡə/ ▶ **noun** [mass noun] an alloy of gold and copper commonly used in pre-Columbian South and Central America.
– ORIGIN 1930s: from Spanish, from Malay *tembaga* 'copper, brass'.

tumble ▶ **verb 1** [no obj., with adverbial] fall suddenly, clumsily, or headlong: *she pitched forward, tumbling down the remaining stairs.* ■ move or rush in a headlong or uncontrolled way: *police and dogs tumbled from the vehicle.* ■ [with obj.] rumple; disarrange: (as adj. **tumbled**) *his tumbled bedclothes.*
2 [no obj.] perform acrobatic feats, typically handsprings and somersaults in the air. ■ (of a breed of pigeon) repeatedly turn over backwards in flight.
3 fall rapidly in amount or value: *property prices tumbled.*
4 [with obj.] dry (washing) in a tumble dryer.
5 [no obj.] (**tumble to**) informal understand the meaning or hidden implication of (a situation): *she'll ring again as soon as she tumbles to what she's done.*
6 [with obj.] informal have sexual intercourse with.
7 [with obj.] clean (castings, gemstones, etc.) in a tumbling barrel.
▶ **noun 1** a sudden or headlong fall: *I took a tumble in the nettles.* ■ an untidy or confused arrangement or state: *her hair was a tumble of untamed curls.*
2 a handspring, somersault in the air, or other acrobatic feat.
3 a rapid fall in amount or value: *a tumble in share prices.*
4 informal an act of sexual intercourse.
5 US informal a friendly sign of recognition, acknowledgement, or interest: *not a soul gave him a tumble.*
– ORIGIN Middle English (as a verb, also in the sense 'dance with contortions'): from Middle Low German *tummelen*; compare with Old English *tumbian* 'to dance'. The sense was probably influenced by Old French *tomber* 'to fall'. The noun, first in the sense 'tangled mass', dates from the mid 17th cent.

tumblebug ▶ **noun** N. Amer. a dung beetle that rolls balls of dung along the ground.

tumbledown ▶ **adjective** (of a building or other structure) falling or fallen into ruin; dilapidated.

tumble dryer ▶ **noun** Brit. a machine that dries washed clothes by spinning them in hot air inside a rotating drum.
– DERIVATIVES **tumble-dry** verb.

tumblehome ▶ **noun** [mass noun] the inward slope of the upper part of a boat's sides.

tumbler ▶ **noun 1** a drinking glass with straight sides and no handle or stem. [formerly having a rounded bottom so as not to stand upright.]
2 an acrobat, especially one who performs somersaults. ■ a pigeon of a breed that repeatedly turns over backwards in flight.
3 (also **tumbler dryer**) a tumble dryer.
4 a pivoted piece in a lock that holds the bolt until lifted by a key. ■ a notched pivoted plate in a gunlock.
5 an electrical switch worked by pushing a small sprung lever.
6 another term for TUMBLING BARREL.
– DERIVATIVES **tumblerful** noun (pl. **tumblerfuls**).

tumbleweed ▶ **noun** [mass noun] N. Amer. & Austral./NZ a plant of arid regions which breaks off near the ground in late summer, forming light globular masses which are tumbled about by the wind. ● Genera *Salsola* (family Chenopodiaceae) and *Amaranthus* (family Amaranthaceae).

tumbling barrel ▶ **noun** a revolving device containing an abrasive substance, in which castings, gemstones, or other hard objects can be cleaned by friction.

tumbling bay ▶ **noun** historical an outfall from a river, reservoir, or canal, or the pool into which this flows.

tumbril /ˈtʌmbr(ə)l, -brɪl/ (also **tumbrel**) ▶ **noun** historical an open cart that tilted backwards to empty out its load, in particular one used to convey condemned prisoners to the guillotine during the French Revolution. ■ a two-wheeled covered cart which carried tools or ammunition for an army.
– ORIGIN Middle English (originally denoting a type of cucking-stool): from Old French *tomberel*, from *tomber* 'to fall'.

tumefy /ˈtjuːmɪfʌɪ/ ▶ **verb** (**tumefies**, **tumefying**, **tumefied**) [no obj.] become swollen.
– DERIVATIVES **tumefaction** noun.
– ORIGIN late 16th cent. (earlier (Middle English) as *tumefaction*): from French *tuméfier*, from Latin *tumefacere*, from *tumere* 'to swell'.

tumescent /tjʊˈmɛs(ə)nt/ ▶ **adjective** swollen or becoming swollen, especially as a response to sexual arousal.
– DERIVATIVES **tumescence** noun, **tumescently** adverb.
– ORIGIN mid 19th cent.: from Latin *tumescent*- 'beginning to swell', from the verb *tumescere*, from *tumere* 'to swell'.

tumid /ˈtjuːmɪd/ ▶ **adjective 1** (especially of a part of the body) swollen: *a tumid belly.*
2 (especially of language or literary style) pompous or bombastic: *tumid oratory.*
– ORIGIN mid 16th cent.: from Latin *tumidus*, from *tumere* 'to swell'.

tummler /ˈtʊmlə/ ▶ **noun** US a professional comedian or entertainer, especially one whose function is to encourage an audience, guests at a resort, etc. to participate in the entertainments or activities.
– ORIGIN 1960s: Yiddish, from German *tummeln* 'to stir'.

tummy ▶ **noun** (pl. **tummies**) informal a person's stomach or abdomen: [as modifier] *a tummy upset.*
– ORIGIN mid 19th cent.: child's pronunciation of STOMACH.

tummy button ▶ **noun** informal a person's navel.

tummy tuck ▶ **noun** informal a surgical operation to remove excess flesh from the abdomen, for cosmetic purposes.

tumorigenesis /ˌtjuːmərɪˈdʒɛnɪsɪs/ ▶ **noun** [mass noun] the production or formation of a tumour or tumours.

tumorigenic /ˌtjuːmərɪˈdʒɛnɪk/ ▶ **adjective** capable of forming or tending to form tumours.
– DERIVATIVES **tumorigenicity** noun.

tumour (US **tumor**) ▶ **noun** a swelling of a part of the body, generally without inflammation, caused by an abnormal growth of tissue, whether benign or malignant. ■ archaic a swelling of any kind.
– DERIVATIVES **tumorous** adjective.
– ORIGIN late Middle English: from Latin *tumor*, from *tumere* 'to swell'.

tump /tʌmp/ ▶ **noun** [often in place names] chiefly dialect **1** a small rounded hill or mound; a tumulus.
2 a clump of trees, shrubs, or grass.
– ORIGIN late 16th cent.: of unknown origin.

tumpline /ˈtʌmplʌɪn/ ▶ **noun** N. Amer. a sling for carrying a load on the back, with a strap which passes round the forehead. ■ a strap used as a part of a tumpline.
– ORIGIN late 18th cent.: based on Algonquian (*mat*)*tump* + the noun LINE[1].

tumult ▶ **noun** a loud, confused noise, especially one caused by a large mass of people: *a tumult of shouting and screaming broke out.* ■ [mass noun] a state of confusion or disorder: *the whole neighbourhood was in a state of fear and tumult | his personal tumult ended when he began writing songs.*
– ORIGIN late Middle English: from Old French *tumulte* or Latin *tumultus*.

tumultuous /tjʊˈmʌltjʊəs/ ▶ **adjective** making an uproar or loud, confused noise: *tumultuous applause.* ■ excited, confused, or disorderly: *a tumultuous crowd | a tumultuous personal life.*
– DERIVATIVES **tumultuously** adverb, **tumultuousness** noun.
– ORIGIN mid 16th cent.: from Old French *tumultuous* or Latin *tumultuosus*, from *tumultus* (see TUMULT).

tumulus /ˈtjuːmjʊləs/ ▶ **noun** (pl. **tumuli** /-lʌɪ, -liː/) an ancient burial mound; a barrow.
– ORIGIN late Middle English: from Latin; related to *tumere* 'swell'.

tun ▶ **noun 1** a large beer or wine cask. ■ a brewer's fermenting vat.
2 an imperial measure of capacity, equal to 4 hogsheads.
3 (also **tun shell**) a large marine mollusc which has a rounded barrel-like shell with broad spirals. ● Family Tonnidae, class Gastropoda.
▶ **verb** (**tuns**, **tunning**, **tunned**) [with obj.] archaic store (wine or other alcoholic drinks) in a tun.
– ORIGIN Old English *tunne*, from medieval Latin *tunna*, probably of Gaulish origin.

tuna[1] ▶ **noun** (pl. **same** or **tunas**) a large and active predatory schooling fish of warm seas, extensively fished commercially and popular as a game fish. See also TUNNY. ● *Thunnus* and other genera, family Scombridae: several species, including the albacore, bigeye, bluefin, skipjack, and yellowfin.
– ORIGIN late 19th cent.: from American Spanish, from Spanish *atún* 'tunny'.

tuna[2] ▶ **noun** N. Amer. **1** the edible fruit of a prickly pear cactus.
2 a prickly pear cactus, widely cultivated in Mexico for its edible fruit. ● Genus *Opuntia*, family Cactaceae: many species, in particular *O. tuna* of Central America and the Caribbean.
– ORIGIN mid 16th cent.: via Spanish from Taino.

Tunbridge Wells a spa town in Kent, SE England; pop. 59,400 (est. 2009). Founded in the 1630s after the discovery of iron-rich springs, the town was patronized by royalty throughout the 17th and 18th centuries. Official name ROYAL TUNBRIDGE WELLS.

tundish /ˈtʌndɪʃ/ ▶ **noun** Brit. a broad open container or large funnel with one or more holes at the bottom, used especially in plumbing or metal-founding.
– ORIGIN from TUN + DISH.

tundra /ˈtʌndrə/ ▶ **noun** a vast, flat, treeless Arctic region of Europe, Asia, and North America in which the subsoil is permanently frozen.
– ORIGIN late 16th cent.: from Lappish.

tundra swan ▸ **noun** an Arctic-breeding migratory swan with a yellow and black bill, often known by the names of its constituent races (Bewick's swan and whistling swan). ● *Cygnus columbianus*, family Anatidae.

tune ▸ **noun** a melody, especially one which characterizes a certain piece of music: *she left the theatre humming a cheerful tune.*
▸ **verb** [with obj.] **1** adjust (a musical instrument) to the correct or uniform pitch: *he tuned the harp for me* | [no obj.] *we could hear the band* ***tuning up***.
2 adjust (a receiver circuit such as a radio or television) to the frequency of the required signal: *the radio was* ***tuned to*** *the BBC.* ■ [no obj.] (**tune in**) watch or listen to a television or radio broadcast. ■ (**tune something out**) exclude a sound or transmission of a particular frequency.
3 adjust (an engine) or balance (mechanical parts) so that a vehicle runs smoothly and efficiently.
4 adjust or adapt (something) to a particular purpose or situation: *the animals are finely* ***tuned to*** *life in the desert.*
5 [with two objs] S. African informal tell (something) to (someone): *he starts tuning you stories about his youth.* [transferred use of *tune* 'adjust, put right'.]
– PHRASES **call the tune** see CALL. **change one's tune** see CHANGE. **in** (or **out of**) **tune** with correct (or incorrect) pitch or intonation. ■ (of a motor engine or other machine) properly (or poorly) adjusted. ■ in (or not in) agreement or harmony: *he was out of tune with conventional belief.* **there's many a good tune played on an old fiddle** proverb someone's abilities do not depend on their being young. **to the tune of** informal amounting to or involving (a specified considerable sum): *he was in debt to the tune of forty thousand pounds.*
– PHRASAL VERBS **be tuned in** informal be sensitive to or able to understand something: *it's important to* ***be tuned in to*** *your child's needs.* **tune into** become sensitive to: *you must tune into the needs of loved ones.* **tune out** informal stop listening or paying attention: *if you're in a boring lecture you can tune out.*
– DERIVATIVES **tunable** (also **tuneable**) **adjective**.
– ORIGIN late Middle English: unexplained alteration of TONE. The verb is first recorded (late 15th cent.) in the sense 'celebrate in music, sing'.

tuneage /ˈtʃuːnədʒ/ ▸ **noun** [mass noun] informal (especially in music journalism) music: *more quality tuneage from Nottingham's finest.*

tuneful ▸ **adjective** having a pleasing tune; melodious: *a musical full of tuneful songs.*
– DERIVATIVES **tunefully adverb**, **tunefulness noun**.

tuneless ▸ **adjective** not pleasing to listen to; unmelodious: *tuneless whistling.*
– DERIVATIVES **tunelessly adverb**, **tunelessness noun**.

tuner ▸ **noun** a person who tunes musical instruments, especially pianos. ■ an electronic device for tuning a guitar or other instrument. ■ an electronic device for varying the frequency to which a radio or television is tuned. ■ a separate unit for detecting and preamplifying a programme signal and supplying it to an audio amplifier. ■ a person who tunes car engines or other machines.

tunesmith ▸ **noun** informal a composer of popular music or songs.

tune-up ▸ **noun** an act of tuning something up: *take your car in for a tune-up if it's an older model.* ■ chiefly US a sporting event that serves as a practice for a subsequent event: *a tune-up for the college's fall league.*

tung oil ▸ **noun** [mass noun] an oil used as a drying agent in inks, paints, and varnishes. ● This oil is obtained from the seeds of trees of the genus *Aleurites*, family Euphorbiaceae.
– ORIGIN late 19th cent.: *tung*, from Chinese.

tungstate /ˈtʌŋsteɪt/ ▸ **noun** Chemistry a salt in which the anion contains both tungsten and oxygen, especially one of the anion WO_4^{2-}.
– ORIGIN early 19th cent.: from TUNGSTEN + -ATE[1].

tungsten /ˈtʌŋst(ə)n/ ▸ **noun** [mass noun] the chemical element of atomic number 74, a hard steel-grey metal of the transition series. It has a very high melting point (3410°C) and is used to make electric light filaments. (Symbol: **W**)
– ORIGIN late 18th cent.: from Swedish, from *tung* 'heavy' + *sten* 'stone'.

tungsten carbide ▸ **noun** [mass noun] a very hard grey compound made by reaction of tungsten and carbon at high temperatures, used in making engineering dies, cutting and drilling tools, etc. ● Chem. formula: WC; some forms also contain W_2C.

tungstite /ˈtʌŋstʌɪt/ ▸ **noun** [mass noun] a yellow mineral consisting of hydrated tungsten oxide, typically occurring as a powdery coating on tungsten ores.
– ORIGIN mid 19th cent.: from TUNGSTEN + -ITE[1].

Tungus /ˈtʊŋʊs, tʊŋˈguːs/ ▸ **noun** (pl. **same**) a member of the northern Evenki people of Siberia. ■ older term for EVENKI (the language).
– ORIGIN the name in Yakut.

Tungusic /tʊŋˈguːsɪk/ ▸ **adjective** relating to or denoting a small family of Altaic languages of Siberia and northern China.
▸ **noun** the Tungusic family of languages.

Tunguska /tʊŋˈguːskə/ two rivers in Siberian Russia, the **Lower Tunguska** and **Stony Tunguska**, flowing westwards into the Yenisei River through the forested, sparsely populated Tunguska Basin. The area was the scene in 1908 of a devastating explosion believed to have been due to the disintegration in the atmosphere of a meteorite or small comet.

tunic ▸ **noun** **1** a loose garment, typically sleeveless and reaching to the knees, as worn in ancient Greece and Rome. ■ a loose, thigh-length garment, worn typically by women over a skirt or trousers. ■ a gymslip.
2 a close-fitting short coat as part of a uniform, especially a police or military uniform.
3 Biology & Anatomy an integument or membrane enclosing or lining an organ or part. ■ Botany any of the concentric layers of a plant bulb, e.g. an onion. ■ Zoology the rubbery outer coat of a sea squirt.
– ORIGIN Old English, from Old French *tunique* or Latin *tunica*.

tunica /ˈtjuːnɪkə/ ▸ **noun** (pl. **tunicae** /-kiː/) **1** Anatomy a membranous sheath enveloping or lining an organ.
2 Botany the outer layer or layers of cells in an apical meristem, which contribute to surface growth.
– ORIGIN late 17th cent.: from Latin, literally 'tunic'.

tunicate /ˈtjuːnɪkət, -keɪt/ ▸ **noun** Zoology a marine invertebrate of a group which includes the sea squirts and salps. They have a rubbery or hard outer coat and two siphons to draw water into and out of the body. ● Subphylum Urochordata: three classes.
▸ **adjective** (also **tunicated**) Botany (of a plant bulb, e.g. an onion) having concentric layers.
– ORIGIN mid 18th cent.: from Latin *tunicatus*, past participle of *tunicare* 'clothe with a tunic', from *tunica* (see TUNICA).

tunicle /ˈtjuːnɪk(ə)l/ ▸ **noun** a short liturgical vestment which is traditionally worn over the alb by a subdeacon at celebrations of the Mass.
– ORIGIN late Middle English: from Old French *tunicle* or Latin *tunicula*, diminutive of *tunica* (see TUNICA).

tuning ▸ **noun** [mass noun] the action or process of tuning something. ■ the extent to which a musical instrument, performance, or ensemble is in tune: *at times the tuning is uncertain, and the solos often lack conviction.* ■ a particular key or set of pitches to which an instrument, especially one with strings, is tuned: *E-flat tuning.* ■ the facility on a radio allowing for the reception of different stations, frequencies, or wavelengths. ■ Electronics the variation of the resonant frequency of an oscillatory circuit.

tuning fork ▸ **noun** a two-pronged steel device used by musicians, which vibrates when struck to give a note of specific pitch.

tuning peg ▸ **noun** any of the pegs in the neck of a stringed musical instrument around which the strings are wound, and which are turned to adjust their tension and so tune the instrument.

Tunis /ˈtjuːnɪs/ the capital of Tunisia, a port on the Mediterranean coast of North Africa; pop. 745,000 (est. 2007).

Tunisia /tjuːˈnɪzɪə/ a country in North Africa; pop. 10,486,300 (est. 2009); official language, Arabic; capital, Tunis.

> Tunisia has a Mediterranean coastline and extends south into the Sahara Desert. Phoenician coastal settlements developed into the commercial empire of Carthage (near modern Tunis). The area was conquered by the Arabs in the 7th century and became part of the Ottoman Empire in the 16th century; a French protectorate was established in 1886. The rise of nationalism led to independence and the establishment of a republic in 1956–7.

– DERIVATIVES **Tunisian adjective & noun**.

tunnel ▸ **noun** **1** an artificial underground passage, especially one built through a hill or under a building, road, or river. ■ an underground passage dug by a burrowing animal. ■ a passage in a sports stadium by which players enter or leave the field.
2 short for WIND TUNNEL.
3 a long, half-cylindrical enclosure used to protect plants, made of clear plastic stretched over hoops.
▸ **verb** (**tunnels**, **tunnelling**, **tunnelled**; US **tunnels**, **tunneling**, **tunneled**) **1** [no obj., with adverbial of direction] dig or force a passage underground or through something: *he tunnelled under the fence* | (**tunnel one's way**) *the insect tunnels its way out of the plant.*
2 [no obj.] Physics (of a particle) pass through a potential barrier.
– PHRASES **light at the end of the tunnel** see LIGHT[1].
– DERIVATIVES **tunneller noun**.
– ORIGIN late Middle English (in the senses 'tunnel-shaped net' and 'flue of a chimney'): from Old French *tonel*, diminutive of *tonne* 'cask'. Sense 1 of the noun dates from the mid 18th cent.

tunnel diode ▸ **noun** Electronics a two-terminal semiconductor diode using tunnelling electrons to perform high-speed switching operations.

tunnel kiln ▸ **noun** an industrial kiln in which ceramic items being fired are carried on trucks along a continuously heated passage.

tunnel of love ▸ **noun** a fairground amusement for couples involving a train- or boat-ride through a darkened tunnel.

tunnel vision ▸ **noun** [mass noun] defective sight in which objects cannot be properly seen if not close to the centre of the field of view. ■ informal the tendency to focus exclusively on a single or limited objective or view.

tunny (also **tunny fish**) ▸ **noun** (pl. **same** or **tunnies**) a tuna, especially the bluefin.
– ORIGIN mid 16th cent.: from French *thon*, via Latin from Greek *thunnos*.

tun shell ▸ **noun** see TUN (sense 3 of the noun).

tup /tʌp/ ▸ **noun** chiefly Brit. a ram.
▸ **verb** (**tups**, **tupping**, **tupped**) [with obj.] **1** (often as noun **tupping**) chiefly Brit. (of a ram) copulate with (a ewe). ■ vulgar slang (of a man) have sexual intercourse with (a woman).
2 N. English informal headbutt (someone) in a fight.
– ORIGIN Middle English: of unknown origin.

Tupamaro /ˌtuːpəˈmɑːrəʊ/ ▸ **noun** (pl. **Tupamaros**) a member of a Marxist urban guerrilla organization in Uruguay that was active mainly in the late 1960s and early 1970s.
– ORIGIN 1960s: from *Tupac Amarú*, the name of an 18th-cent. Inca leader.

Tupelo /ˈt(j)uːpələʊ/ a city in NE Mississippi; pop. 36,233 (est. 2008).

tupelo /ˈt(j)uːpɪləʊ/ ▸ **noun** (pl. **tupelos**) a North American or Asian tree of damp and swampy habitats, which yields useful timber. ● Genus *Nyssa*, family Nyssaceae: several species, in particular *N. sylvatica* (also called PEPPERIDGE).
– ORIGIN mid 18th cent.: from Creek, from *ito* 'tree' + *opilwa* 'swamp'.

Tupi /ˈtuːpi/ ▸ **noun** (pl. **same** or **Tupis**) **1** a member of a group of American Indian peoples living in scattered areas throughout the Amazon valley.
2 [mass noun] any of the languages of the Tupi, which constitute a branch of the Tupi-Guarani language family.
▸ **adjective** relating to the Tupi or their languages.
– DERIVATIVES **Tupian adjective**.
– ORIGIN a local name.

Tupi-Guarani ▸ **noun** [mass noun] a South American Indian language family whose principal members are Guarani and the Tupian languages.
▸ **adjective** relating to or denoting these languages.

tupik /ˈtuːpɪk/ ▸ **noun** a hut or tent made of animal skins used by Inuits in the Canadian Arctic as a summer dwelling.
– ORIGIN from Inuit *tupiq*.

tuple /ˈtjuːp(ə)l/ ▸ **noun** Computing a data structure consisting of multiple parts. ■ (in a relational database) an ordered set of data constituting a record.
– ORIGIN from -TUPLE.

-tuple /ˈtjuːp(ə)l/ ▸ **combining form** chiefly Mathematics forming nouns and adjectives with a preceding algebraic symbol with the sense '(an entity or set) consisting of as many parts or elements as indicated by the symbol, such as *n-tuple*.
– ORIGIN from the ending of QUINTUPLE, OCTUPLE, etc.

Tupolev /ˈtuːpəlɛf/, Andrei (Nikolaievich) (1888–1972), Russian aeronautical engineer. He produced Russia's first jet bomber (1946) and jet passenger plane. With his son **Alexei** (1925–2001) he designed the world's first supersonic airliner, whose maiden

T

flight in December 1968 preceded that of Concorde by two months; it was, however, never commercially viable.

tuppence ▶ noun Brit. variant spelling of TWOPENCE.

tuppenny ▶ adjective Brit. variant spelling of TWOPENNY.

Tupperware /ˈtʌpəwɛː/ ▶ noun [mass noun] trademark a range of plastic containers used for storing food.
– ORIGIN 1950s: from *Tupper*, the name of the American manufacturer, + WARE[1].

tupuna /ˈtʊpʊnə, ˈtuːpʊnə/ ▶ noun (pl. **same** or **tupunas**) NZ a grandparent or ancestor.
– ORIGIN mid 19th cent.: from Maori.

tuque /tuːk/ ▶ noun Canadian a close-fitting knitted stocking cap.
– ORIGIN Canadian French form of TOQUE.

tur /tʊə/ ▶ noun a wild goat native to the Caucasian mountains. ● Genus *Capra*, family Bovidae: two species, *C. caucasica* and *C. cylindricornis*.
– ORIGIN late 19th cent.: from Russian.

turaco /ˈtʊərəkəʊ/ (also **touraco**) ▶ noun (pl. **turacos**) a fruit-eating African bird with brightly coloured plumage, a prominent crest, and a long tail. Also called LOERIE or LOURIE in South Africa. ● Family Musophagidae (the **turaco family**): three genera, especially *Musophaga* and *Tauraco*, and several species. The turaco family also includes the go-away birds and plantain-eaters.
– ORIGIN mid 18th cent.: from French *touraco*, from a West African word.

Turanian /tjʊˈreɪnɪən/ ▶ adjective dated relating to or denoting the languages of central Asia, particularly those of the Uralic and Altaic families, or the peoples that speak them.
– ORIGIN late 18th cent.: from Persian *Tūrān*, the region beyond the Oxus, + -IAN.

turban ▶ noun **1** a man's headdress, consisting of a long length of cotton or silk wound round a cap or the head, worn especially by Muslims and Sikhs.
2 (also **turban shell**) a marine mollusc with a sculptured spiral shell and a distinctive operculum which is smooth on the inside and sculptured and typically patterned on the outside. ● Family Turbinidae, class Gastropoda: *Turbo* and other genera.
– DERIVATIVES **turbaned** (also **turbanned**) adjective.
– ORIGIN mid 16th cent.: via French from Turkish *tülbent*, from Persian *dulband*. Compare with TULIP.

turbary /ˈtəːb(ə)ri/ ▶ noun (in full **common of turbary**) (pl. **turbaries**) [mass noun] Brit. the legal right to cut turf or peat for fuel on common ground or on another person's ground. ■ [count noun] a place where turf or peat is dug or cut under such a right.
– ORIGIN late Middle English: from Anglo-Norman French *turberie*, from Old French *tourbe* 'turf'.

Turbellaria /ˌtəːbɪˈlɛːrɪə/ ▶ plural noun Zoology a class of typically free-living flatworms which have a ciliated surface and a simple branched gut with a single opening.
– DERIVATIVES **turbellarian** adjective & noun.
– ORIGIN modern Latin (plural), from Latin *turbella* 'bustle, stir', diminutive of *turba* 'crowd'.

turbid /ˈtəːbɪd/ ▶ adjective (of a liquid) cloudy, opaque, or thick with suspended matter: *the turbid estuary*. ■ confused or obscure in meaning or effect: *a turbid piece of cinéma vérité*.
– DERIVATIVES **turbidity** noun, **turbidly** adverb, **turbidness** noun.
– ORIGIN late Middle English (in the figurative sense): from Latin *turbidus*, from *turba* 'a crowd, a disturbance'.

T

turbidimeter /ˌtəːbɪˈdɪmɪtə/ ▶ noun an instrument for measuring the turbidity of a liquid suspension, usually as a means of determining the surface area of the suspended particles.
– DERIVATIVES **turbidimetric** adjective, **turbidimetry** noun.

turbidite /ˈtəːbɪdʌɪt/ ▶ noun Geology a sediment or rock deposited by a turbidity current.
– DERIVATIVES **turbiditic** adjective.
– ORIGIN 1950s: from *turbidity* (see TURBID) + -ITE[1].

turbidity current ▶ noun an underwater current flowing swiftly downslope owing to the weight of sediment it carries.

turbinal /ˈtəːbɪn(ə)l/ ▶ noun (usu. **turbinals**) Anatomy & Zoology each of three thin curved shelves of bone in the sides of the nasal cavity in humans and other warm-blooded vertebrates, covered in mucous membrane.
– ORIGIN late 16th cent. (as an adjective in the sense 'top-shaped'): from Latin *turbo*, *turbin-* 'spinning top' + -AL.

turbinate /ˈtəːbɪnət/ ▶ adjective chiefly Zoology (especially of a shell) shaped like a spinning top or inverted cone. ■ Anatomy relating to or denoting the turbinals.
▶ noun (also **turbinate bone**) Anatomy another term for TURBINAL.
– ORIGIN mid 17th cent.: from Latin *turbinatus*, from *turbo*, *turbin-* (see TURBINE).

turbine /ˈtəːbʌɪn, -ɪn/ ▶ noun a machine for producing continuous power in which a wheel or rotor, typically fitted with vanes, is made to revolve by a fast-moving flow of water, steam, gas, air, or other fluid.
– ORIGIN mid 19th cent.: from French, from Latin *turbo*, *turbin-* 'spinning top, whirl'.

turbit /ˈtəːbɪt/ ▶ noun a stoutly built pigeon of a domestic breed with a neck frill and short beak.
– ORIGIN late 17th cent.: apparently from Latin *turbo* 'spinning top', from its shape.

turbo /ˈtəːbəʊ/ ▶ noun (pl. **turbos**) short for TURBOCHARGER. ■ a motor vehicle equipped with a turbocharger.

turbo- ▶ combining form having or driven by a turbine: *turboshaft*.
– ORIGIN from TURBINE.

turboboost ▶ noun [mass noun] the increase in speed or power produced by turbocharging a car's engine or, specifically, when the turbocharger becomes activated.

turbocharge ▶ verb [with obj.] (often as adj. **turbocharged**) equip (an engine or vehicle) with a turbocharger: *a turbocharged coupé*. ■ make more powerful, fast, or exciting: *turbocharged business growth*.

turbocharger ▶ noun a supercharger driven by a turbine powered by the engine's exhaust gases.

turbo diesel ▶ noun a turbocharged diesel engine. ■ a vehicle equipped with a turbocharged diesel engine.

turbofan ▶ noun a jet engine in which a turbine-driven fan provides additional thrust. ■ an aircraft powered by a turbofan.

turbogenerator ▶ noun a large electricity generator driven by a steam turbine.

turbojet ▶ noun a jet engine in which the jet gases also operate a turbine-driven compressor for compressing the air drawn into the engine. ■ an aircraft powered by a turbojet.

turboprop ▶ noun a jet engine in which a turbine is used to drive a propeller. ■ an aircraft powered by a turboprop.

turboshaft ▶ noun a gas turbine engine in which the turbine drives a shaft other than a propeller shaft.

turbosupercharger ▶ noun another term for TURBOCHARGER.

turbot ▶ noun (pl. **same** or **turbots**) a European flatfish of inshore waters, which has large bony tubercles on the body and is prized as food. ● *Scophthalmus maximus*, family Scophthalmidae (or Bothidae). ■ used in names of similar flatfishes, e.g. **black turbot**.
– ORIGIN Middle English: from Old French, of Scandinavian origin.

turbulence ▶ noun [mass noun] violent or unsteady movement of air or water, or of some other fluid: *the plane shuddered as it entered some turbulence*. ■ a state of conflict or confusion: *political turbulence*.
– ORIGIN late Middle English: from Old French, or from late Latin *turbulentia*, from *turbulentus* 'full of commotion' (see TURBULENT).

turbulent /ˈtəːbjʊl(ə)nt/ ▶ adjective characterized by conflict, disorder, or confusion; not stable or calm: *the country's turbulent history* | *her turbulent emotions*. ■ (of air or water) moving unsteadily or violently: *the turbulent sea*. ■ technical relating to or denoting flow of a fluid in which the velocity at any point fluctuates irregularly and there is continual mixing rather than a steady or laminar flow pattern.
– DERIVATIVES **turbulently** adverb.
– ORIGIN late Middle English: from Latin *turbulentus* 'full of commotion', from *turba* 'crowd'.

Turco /ˈtəːkəʊ/ ▶ noun (pl. **Turcos**) historical an Algerian soldier in the French army.
– ORIGIN mid 19th cent.: from Spanish, Portuguese, and Italian, literally 'Turk'.

Turco- (also **Turko-**) ▶ combining form Turkish; Turkish and ...: *Turco-Tartar*. ■ relating to Turkey.

Turcoman ▶ noun variant spelling of TURKOMAN.

turd ▶ noun vulgar slang **1** a lump of excrement.
2 a person regarded as obnoxious or contemptible.
– ORIGIN Old English *tord*, of Germanic origin.

turducken /təːˈdʌkən/ ▶ noun [mass noun] chiefly US a roast dish consisting of a boned chicken inside a boned duck which is then placed inside a partially boned turkey.
– ORIGIN 1980s: blend of TURKEY and DUCK[1] and CHICKEN.

tureen /tjʊˈriːn, tə-/ ▶ noun a deep covered dish from which soup is served.
– ORIGIN mid 18th cent.: alteration of earlier *terrine*, from French *terrine* (see TERRINE), feminine of Old French *terrin* 'earthen', based on Latin *terra* 'earth'.

turf ▶ noun (pl. **turfs** or **turves**) [mass noun] **1** grass and the surface layer of earth held together by its roots: *they walked across the springy turf*. ■ [count noun] a piece of turf cut from the ground. ■ peat used for fuel.
2 (**the turf**) horse racing or racecourses generally: *he spent his money gambling on the turf*.
3 informal an area or sphere of activity regarded as someone's personal territory: *he did not like poachers on his turf*.
▶ verb **1** [with obj. and adverbial] informal, chiefly Brit. force (someone) to leave somewhere: *they were turfed off the bus*.
2 [with obj.] (often as adj. **turfed**) cover (a patch of ground) with turf: *a turfed lawn*.
– ORIGIN Old English, of Germanic origin; related to Dutch *turf* and German *Torf*, from an Indo-European root shared by Sanskrit *darbha* 'tuft of grass'.

turf accountant ▶ noun Brit. formal a bookmaker.

Turfan Depression /ˈtʊəfan, tʊəˈfan/ (also **Turpan**) a low-lying area in Xinjiang, western China, descending to 154 m (505 ft) below sea level, with an area of 50,000 sq. km (20,000 sq. miles). It is China's lowest point below sea level.

turfman ▶ noun (pl. **turfmen**) chiefly US a devotee of horse racing, especially one who owns or trains horses.

turf war (also **turf battle**) ▶ noun informal an acrimonious dispute between rival groups over territory or a particular sphere of influence.

turfy ▶ adjective (**turfier**, **turfiest**) covered with or consisting of turf; grassy: *a turfy plain*. ■ of or like peat; peaty: *the damp, turfy odour of a meadow*.

Turgenev /təːˈgeɪnjɛf, tʊəˈgenjɛf/, Ivan (Sergeevich) (1818–83), Russian novelist, dramatist, and short-story writer. His novels, such as *Fathers and Sons* (1862), examine individual lives to illuminate the social, political, and philosophical issues of his day.

turgescent /təːˈdʒɛs(ə)nt/ ▶ adjective chiefly technical becoming or seeming swollen or distended.
– DERIVATIVES **turgescence** noun.
– ORIGIN early 18th cent.: from Latin *turgescent-* 'beginning to swell', from the verb *turgescere*, from *turgere* 'to swell'.

turgid /ˈtəːdʒɪd/ ▶ adjective **1** swollen and distended or congested: *a turgid and fast-moving river*.
2 (of language or style) tediously pompous or bombastic: *some turgid verses on the death of Prince Albert*.
– DERIVATIVES **turgidity** noun, **turgidly** adverb.
– ORIGIN early 17th cent.: from Latin *turgidus*, from *turgere* 'to swell'.

turgor /ˈtəːgə/ ▶ noun [mass noun] chiefly Botany the state of turgidity and resulting rigidity of cells or tissues, typically due to the absorption of fluid.
– ORIGIN late 19th cent.: from late Latin, from *turgere* 'to swell'.

Turin /tjʊˈrɪn/ a city in NW Italy on the River Po, capital of Piedmont region; pop. 908,825 (2008). Turin was the capital of the kingdom of Sardinia from 1720 and became the first capital of a unified Italy (1861–4). Italian name **TORINO**.

Turing /ˈtjʊərɪŋ/, Alan Mathison (1912–54), English mathematician. He developed the concept of a theoretical computing machine, a key step in the development of the first computer, and carried out important code-breaking work in the Second World War. He also investigated artificial intelligence.

Turing machine ▶ noun a mathematical model of a hypothetical computing machine which can use a predefined set of rules to determine a result from a set of input variables.

Turing test ▶ noun a test for intelligence in a computer, requiring that a human being should be unable to distinguish the machine from another human being by using the replies to questions put to both.

Turin Shroud a relic, preserved at Turin since 1578, venerated as the winding sheet in which Christ's body was wrapped for burial. It bears the imprint of the front and back of a human body as well as markings that correspond to the traditional stigmata. Scientific tests carried out in 1988 dated the shroud to the 13th–14th centuries.

turion /ˈt(j)ʊərɪən/ ▸ noun Botany (in some aquatic plants) a wintering bud which becomes detached and remains dormant at the bottom of the water.
– ORIGIN early 18th cent.: from French, from Latin *turio(n-)* 'a shoot'.

turista /t(j)ʊˈrɪstə/ ▸ noun informal, chiefly US **1** a tourist.
2 [mass noun] diarrhoea as suffered by holidaymakers when visiting certain foreign countries.
– ORIGIN Spanish.

Turk ▸ noun **1** a native or inhabitant of Turkey, or a person of Turkish descent.
2 historical a member of any of the ancient central Asian peoples who spoke Turkic languages, including the Seljuks and Ottomans.
3 archaic a member of the ruling Muslim population of the Ottoman Empire.
– ORIGIN late Middle English: via Old French from Turkish *türk*.

Turkana /təːˈkɑːnə/ ▸ noun (pl. **same**) **1** a member of an East African people living between Lake Turkana and the Nile.
2 [mass noun] the Nilotic language of the Turkana, spoken by about 250,000 people.
▸ adjective relating to the Turkana or their language.
– ORIGIN a local name.

Turkana, Lake a salt lake in NW Kenya, with no outlet. It was visited in 1888 by the Hungarian explorer Count Teleki (1845–1916), who named it Lake Rudolf after the Crown Prince of Austria. It was given its present name in 1979.

Turkestan /ˌtəːkɪˈstɑːn, -ˈstan/ (also **Turkistan**) a region of central Asia between the Caspian Sea and the Gobi Desert, inhabited mainly by Turkic peoples. It is divided by the Pamir and Tien Shan mountains into eastern Turkestan, now the Xinjiang autonomous region of China, and western Turkestan, which comprises present-day Turkmenistan, Kazakhstan, Uzbekistan, Tajikistan, and Kyrgyzstan.

Turkey a country comprising the whole of the Anatolian peninsula in western Asia, with a small enclave in SE Europe to the west of Istanbul; pop. 76,805,500 (est. 2009); official language, Turkish; capital, Ankara.

> Turkey was the centre of the Ottoman Empire, established in the late Middle Ages and largely maintained until its collapse at the end of the First World War, in which Turkey supported the Central Powers. The nationalist leader Kemal Atatürk established the modern republic of Turkey in the 1920s. Turkey was neutral in the Second World War but is a member of NATO.

turkey ▸ noun (pl. **turkeys**) **1** a large mainly domesticated game bird native to North America, having a bald head and (in the male) red wattles. It is a popular food on festive occasions such as Christmas and (in the US) Thanksgiving. ● *Meleagris gallopavo*, family Meleagridae (or Phasianidae).
■ [mass noun] the flesh of the turkey as food.
2 informal, chiefly N. Amer. something that is extremely or completely unsuccessful, especially a play or film.
■ a stupid or inept person.
– PHRASES **like turkeys voting for Christmas** informal used to suggest that a particular action or decision is hopelessly self-defeating. **talk turkey** N. Amer. informal discuss something frankly and straightforwardly.
– ORIGIN mid 16th cent.: short for **TURKEY COCK** or *turkeyhen*, originally applied to the guinea fowl (which was imported through Turkey), and then erroneously to the American bird.

turkey buzzard ▸ noun North American term for **TURKEY VULTURE**.

turkey cock ▸ noun a male turkey. ■ a pompous or self-important person.

turkey oak ▸ noun a southern European oak with a domed spreading crown and acorn cups with long outward-pointing scales. ● *Quercus cerris*, family Fagaceae.

Turkey red ▸ noun [mass noun] a scarlet textile dye obtained from madder or alizarin. ■ cotton cloth dyed with Turkey red, popular in the 19th century.

turkey shoot ▸ noun informal, chiefly N. Amer. a situation, typically in a war, in which the aggressor has an overwhelming advantage.

turkey trot ▸ noun a kind of ballroom dance to ragtime music which originated in the US and was popular in the early 20th century.

turkey vulture ▸ noun a common American vulture with black plumage and a bare red head. ● *Cathartes aura*, family Cathartidae.

Turkic /ˈtəːkɪk/ ▸ adjective relating to or denoting a large group of closely related Altaic languages of western and central Asia, including Turkish, Azerbaijani, Kazakh, Kyrgyz, Uighur, Uzbek, and Tatar.
▸ noun [mass noun] the Turkic languages collectively.
– ORIGIN mid 19th cent.: from **TURK** + **-IC**.

Turkish ▸ adjective relating to Turkey or to the Turks or their language. ■ historical relating to or associated with the Ottoman Empire.
▸ noun [mass noun] the official language of Turkey, a Turkic language spoken by about 50 million people. It was written in the Arabic script until 1928, when the Roman alphabet was adopted.

Turkish bath ▸ noun a cleansing or relaxing treatment that involves a period of time spent sitting in a room filled with very hot air or steam, generally followed by washing and massage. ■ a building or room where a Turkish bath is available.

Turkish carpet (also **Turkish rug**) ▸ noun a rug woven in Turkey in a traditional fashion, typically with a bold coloured design and thick wool pile, or made elsewhere in this style.

Turkish coffee ▸ noun [mass noun] very strong black coffee served with the fine grounds in it.

Turkish delight ▸ noun [mass noun] a gelatinous sweet traditionally made of syrup and cornflour, dusted with icing sugar.

Turkish slipper ▸ noun a soft heelless slipper with a turned-up toe.

Turkish towel ▸ noun a towel made of cotton terry towelling.

Turkish Van (in full **Turkish Van cat**) ▸ noun a cat of a long-haired breed, with a white body, auburn markings on the head and tail, and light orange eyes.
– ORIGIN 1960s: named after the town of *Van*, Turkey.

Turkistan variant spelling of **TURKESTAN**.

Turkmen /ˈtəːkmən/ ▸ noun (pl. **same** or **Turkmens**)
1 a member of a group of Turkic peoples inhabiting the region east of the Caspian Sea and south of the Aral Sea, now comprising Turkmenistan and parts of Iran and Afghanistan.
2 [mass noun] the Turkic language of the Turkmen, having about 3 million speakers.
▸ adjective relating to the Turkmen, their language, or the region which they inhabit.
– ORIGIN from Persian *turkmān*, from Turkish *türkmen*; also influenced by Russian *turkmen*.

Turkmenistan /təːkˌmɛnɪˈstɑːn, -ˈstan/ a republic in central Asia, lying between the Caspian Sea and Afghanistan; pop. 4,884,900 (est. 2009); languages, Turkoman (official), Russian; capital, Ashgabat. Also called **Turkmenia** /-ˈmiːnɪə/.

> Turkmenistan is dominated by the Karakum Desert, which occupies about 90 per cent of the country. Previously part of Turkestan, from 1924 it formed a separate constituent republic of the Soviet Union; Turkmenistan became an independent republic within the Commonwealth of Independent States in 1991.

Turko- ▸ combining form variant spelling of **TURCO-**.

Turkoman /ˈtəːkə(ʊ)mən/ (also **Turcoman**) ▸ noun (pl. **Turkomans**) **1** another term for **TURKMEN**.
2 (also **Turkoman carpet** or **rug**) a kind of large, soft, richly coloured rug made by the Turkmens.
– ORIGIN early 17th cent.: from medieval Latin *Turcomannus*, French *turcoman*, from Persian *turkmān* (see **TURKMEN**).

Turks and Caicos Islands /ˈkeɪkɒs/ a British overseas territory in the Caribbean, comprising two island groups between Haiti and the Bahamas; pop. 22,900 (est. 2009); capital, Cockburn Town (on the island of Grand Turk).

Turk's cap ▸ noun any of a number of plants which have parts that are said to resemble a turban or similar headdress, in particular: ● (also **Turk's cap lily**) the martagon lily. ● (also **Turk's cap cactus**) a barrel-shaped Caribbean cactus (*Melocactus communis*, family Cactaceae).

Turk's head ▸ noun an ornamental knot resembling a turban in shape, made in the end of a rope to form a stopper.

Turku /ˈtʊəkuː/ an industrial port in SW Finland; pop. 175,279 (2009). It was the capital of Finland until 1812. Swedish name **ÅBO**.

turlough /ˈtʊələʊx/ ▸ noun (in Ireland) a low-lying area on limestone which becomes flooded in wet weather through the welling up of groundwater from the rock.
– ORIGIN late 17th cent.: from Irish *turloch*, from *tur* 'dry' + *loch* 'lake'.

turmeric /ˈtəːmərɪk/ ▸ noun [mass noun] **1** a bright yellow aromatic powder obtained from the rhizome of a plant of the ginger family, used for flavouring and colouring in Asian cookery and formerly as a fabric dye.
2 the Asian plant from which turmeric is obtained. ● *Curcuma longa*, family Zingiberaceae.
– ORIGIN late Middle English (earlier as *tarmaret*): perhaps from French *terre mérite* and modern Latin *terra merita*, literally 'deserving earth', or perhaps an alteration of an oriental word.

turmoil ▸ noun [mass noun] a state of great disturbance, confusion, or uncertainty: *the country was in turmoil* | *he endured years of inner turmoil*.
– ORIGIN early 16th cent.: of unknown origin.

turn ▸ verb **1** move or cause to move in a circular direction wholly or partly around an axis or point: [no obj.] *the big wheel was turning* | [with obj.] *I turned the key in the door and crept in*. ■ [with obj.] perform (a somersault or cartwheel). ■ [with obj.] twist or sprain (an ankle).
2 [with obj. and adverbial] move (something) so that it is in a different position in relation to its surroundings or its previous position: *we waited in suspense for him to turn the cards over*. ■ [no obj.] change the position of one's body so that one is facing in a different direction: *Charlie turned and looked at his friend*. ■ move (something) so as to be aimed or pointed in a particular direction: *she turned her head towards me* | *the government has now turned its attention to primary schools*. ■ change or cause to change direction: [no obj., with adverbial of direction] *we turned round and headed back to the house*. ■ [no obj.] (of the tide) change from flood to ebb or vice versa. ■ [with obj.] move (a page) over so that it is flat against the previous or next page: *she turned a page noisily* | [no obj.] *turn to page five for the answer*. ■ fold or unfold (fabric or a piece of a garment) in the specified way: *he turned up the collar of his coat*. ■ [with obj.] (usu. as adj. **turned**) Printing set or print (a type or letter) upside down. ■ [with obj.] pass round (the flank or defensive lines of an army) so as to attack it from the side or rear. ■ [with obj.] archaic bend back (the edge of a blade) so as to make it blunt.
3 change or cause to change in nature, state, form, or colour; become or make: [no obj., with complement or adverbial] *she turned pale* | [with obj. and complement or adverbial] *cover potatoes with sacking to keep the light from turning them green* | *most of the sugars are turned into alcohol*. ■ [with obj. and complement or adverbial] send or put into a specified place or condition: *the dogs were turned loose on the crowd*. ■ [with obj.] pass the age or time of: *I've just turned forty*. ■ [no obj.] (of leaves) change colour in the autumn. ■ (with reference to the stomach) make or become nauseated: [with obj.] *the smell was bad enough to turn the strongest stomach*. ■ (with reference to milk) make or become sour.
4 [no obj.] (**turn to**) start doing or becoming involved with: *in 1939 he turned to films in earnest*. ■ go on to consider next: *we can now turn to another aspect of the problem*. ■ go to for help or information: *who can she turn to?* ■ have recourse to (something, especially something harmful): *he turned to drink and drugs for solace*.
5 [with obj.] shape (something) on a lathe: *the faceplate is turned rather than cast*. ■ give a graceful or elegant form to: (as adj., with submodifier **turned**) *a production full of so many finely turned words*.
6 [with obj.] make (a profit).
▸ noun **1** an act of moving something in a circular direction around an axis or point: *a safety lock requiring four turns of the key*. ■ a bend or curve in a road, path, river, etc.: *the twists and turns in the passageways*. ■ [mass noun] Cricket deviation in the direction of the ball when bouncing off the pitch. ■ one round in a coil of rope or other material.
2 a change of direction when moving: *they made a left turn and picked up speed*. ■ a development or change in a situation: *the latest turn of events* | *life has taken a turn for the better*. ■ a time when one period of time ends and another begins: *the turn of the century*. ■ a place where a road meets or branches off another; a turning. ■ a change of the tide from ebb to flow or vice versa. ■ (**the turn**) the beginning of the second nine holes of a round of golf: *he made the turn in one under par*.

T

3 an opportunity or obligation to do something that comes successively to each of a number of people: *it was his turn to speak.* ■ a short performance, especially one of a number given by different performers in succession: *a comic turn.* ■ a performer giving such a performance.
4 a short walk or ride: *why don't you take a turn around the garden?*
5 informal a shock: *you gave us quite a turn!* ■ a brief feeling or experience of illness: *he has these funny turns.*
6 the difference between the buying and selling price of stocks or other financial products. ■ a profit made from the difference between the buying and selling price of stocks or other financial products.
7 Music a melodic ornament consisting of the principal note with those above and below it.
– PHRASES **at every turn** on every occasion; continually: *her name seemed to come up at every turn.* **by turns** one after the other; alternately: *he was by turns amused and mildly annoyed by her.* **do someone a good** (or **bad**) **turn** do something that is helpful (or unhelpful) for someone. **in turn** in succession; one after the other: *everyone took it in turn to attack my work.* ■ (also **in one's/its turn**) used to convey that an action, process, or situation is the result of a previous one: *he would shout until she, in her turn, lost her temper.* **not know which way** (or **where**) **to turn** not know what to do. **not turn a hair** see HAIR. **one good turn deserves another** proverb if someone does you a favour, you should take the chance to repay it. **on the turn** at a turning point; in a state of change: *my luck is on the turn.* ■ (of certain foods or liquids) going off: *the smell of meat on the turn.* **out of turn** at a time when it is not one's turn. **speak** (or **talk**) **out of turn** speak in a tactless way. **take turns** (or Brit. **take it in turns**) (of two or more people) do something alternately or in succession. **to a turn** to exactly the right degree (used especially in relation to cooking): *beefburgers done to a turn.* **turn and turn about** chiefly Brit. one after another; in succession: *the two men were working in rotation, turn and turn about.* **turn one's back on** see BACK. **turn the** (or **a**) **corner** pass the critical point and start to improve: *the industry has turned the corner and things are looking up.* **turn a deaf ear** see DEAF. **turn one's hand to something** see HAND. **turn one's head** see HEAD. **turn heads** see HEAD. **turn an honest penny** see HONEST. **turn in one's grave** see GRAVE[1]. **turn of mind** a particular way of thinking: *people with a practical turn of mind.* **turn of speed** the ability to go fast when necessary. **turn on one's heel** see HEEL[1]. **turn the other cheek** see CHEEK. **turn over a new leaf** start to act or behave in a better or more responsible way. **turn something over in one's mind** think about something thoroughly. **turn round and do** (or **say**) **something** informal used to convey that someone's actions or words are perceived as unexpected or unwelcome: *then she just turned round and said she wasn't coming after all.* **turn the scales** see SCALE[2]. **turn the tables** see TABLE. **turn tail** informal turn round and run away. **turn the tide** reverse the trend of events. **turn something to** (**good**) **account** see ACCOUNT. **turn a trick** see TRICK. **turn turtle** see TURTLE. **turn up one's nose at** see NOSE.
– PHRASAL VERBS **turn about** move so as to face in the opposite direction: *Alice turned about and walked down the corridor.* **turn against** (or **turn someone against**) become (or cause someone to become) hostile towards: *public opinion turned against him.* **turn something around** chiefly N. Amer. see TURN SOMETHING ROUND. **turn someone away** refuse to allow someone to enter or pass through a place. **turn back** (or **turn someone/thing back**) go (or cause someone or something to go) back in the direction in which they have come: *they turned back before reaching the church | police turned back hundreds of cars.* **turn someone down** reject an offer or application made by someone: *the RAF turned him down on medical grounds.* **turn something down 1** reject something offered or proposed: *his novel was turned down by publisher after publisher.* **2** adjust a control on an electrical device to reduce the volume, heat, etc. **turn in** informal go to bed in the evening. **turn someone in** hand someone over to the authorities. **turn something in** give something to someone in authority: *I've turned in my resignation.* ■ produce or achieve a particular score or a performance of a specified quality. **turn into** become (a particular kind of thing or person); be transformed into: *the slight drizzle turned into a downpour | that dream turned into a nightmare | in the next instant he turned into a tiny mouse.* **turn someone/thing into** cause to become (a particular kind of thing or person); transform into: *the town was turned into a thriving seaside destination | every single good children's book has been turned into a feature-length cartoon.* **turn off** leave one road in order to join another. **turn someone off** informal cause someone to feel bored, disgusted, or sexually repelled. **turn something off** stop the operation or flow of something by means of a tap, switch, or button: *remember to turn off the gas.* ■ adjust a tap or switch in order to stop the operation or flow of something. **turn on 1** suddenly attack physically or verbally: *he turned on her with cold savagery.* **2** have as the main topic or point of interest: *for most businessmen, the central questions will turn on taxation.* **turn someone on** informal excite or stimulate the interest of someone, especially sexually. **turn something on** start the flow or operation of something by means of a tap, switch, or button: *she turned on the TV.* ■ adjust a tap or switch in order to start the operation or flow of something. **turn someone on to** informal cause someone to become interested or involved in (something, especially drugs): *he turned her on to heroin.* **turn out 1** prove to be the case: *the job turned out to be beyond his rather limited abilities.* **2** go somewhere in order to attend a meeting, vote, play in a game, etc.: *over 75 per cent of the electorate turned out to vote.* **turn someone out 1** eject or expel someone from a place. **2** Military call a guard from the guardroom. **3** (**be turned out**) be dressed in the manner specified: *she was smartly turned out and as well groomed as always.* **turn something out 1** extinguish a light. **2** produce something: *the plant takes 53 hours to turn out each car.* **3** empty something, especially one's pockets. ■ Brit. clean out a drawer, room, etc. by taking out and reorganizing its contents. **4** tip prepared food from a mould or other container. **turn over** (of an engine) start or continue to run properly. **turn someone over to** deliver someone to the care or custody of (an authority): *they turned him over to the police.* **turn something over 1** cause an engine to run. **2** transfer control or management of something to someone else: *a plan to turn the pub over to a new manager.* **3** change the function or use of something: *the works was turned over to the production of aircraft parts.* **4** informal rob a place. **5** (of a business) have a turnover of a specified amount: *last year the company turned over £12 million.* **turn something round** (or **around**) **1** prepare a ship or aircraft for its return journey. **2** reverse the previously poor performance of an organization and make it successful. **turn up 1** be found, especially by chance, after being lost: *all the missing documents had turned up.* **2** put in an appearance; arrive: *half the guests failed to turn up.* **turn something up 1** increase the volume or strength of sound, heat, etc. by turning a knob or switch on a device. **2** reveal or discover something: *New Yorkers confidently expect the inquiry to turn up nothing.* **3** shorten a garment by raising the hem.
– ORIGIN Old English *tyrnan, turnian* (verb), from Latin *tornare*, from *tornus* 'lathe', from Greek *tornos* 'lathe, circular movement'; probably reinforced in Middle English by Old French *turner*. The noun (Middle English) is partly from Anglo-Norman French *tourn*, partly from the verb.

turnabout ▶ noun a sudden and complete change or reversal of policy, opinion, or of a situation: *the move was a significant turnabout for the company.*

turnaround (also **turnround**) ▶ noun **1** an abrupt or unexpected change, especially one that results in a more favourable situation: *it was a remarkable turnaround in his fortunes.*
2 the process of completing or the time needed to complete a task, especially one involving receiving something, processing it, and sending it out again: *a seven-day turnaround.* ■ the process of or time taken for unloading and reloading a ship, aircraft, or vehicle.
3 N. Amer. a space for vehicles to turn round in, especially one at the end of a driveway.

turnback ▶ noun a part of a garment that is folded back: [as modifier] *the jacket has turnback cuffs.*

turnbuckle ▶ noun a coupling with internal screw threads used to connect two rods, lengths of boat's rigging, etc. lengthwise or to regulate their length or tension.

turncoat ▶ noun a person who deserts one party or cause in order to join an opposing one.

turncock ▶ noun historical a waterworks official responsible for turning on water at the mains.

turndown ▶ noun **1** a rejection or refusal.
2 a decline in something; a downturn.
▶ adjective (of a collar) turned down.

Turner, J. M. W. (1775–1851), English painter; full name *Joseph Mallord William Turner*. He made his name with landscapes and stormy seascapes, becoming increasingly concerned with depicting the power of light by the use of primary colours, often arranged in a swirling vortex. Notable works: *Rain, Steam, Speed* (1844); *The Fighting Téméraire* (1838).

turner ▶ noun **1** a person who is skilled in turning wood on a lathe.
2 an implement that can be used to turn or flip something over: *a pancake turner.*
– ORIGIN Middle English: from Old French *torneor*, from late Latin *tornator*, from the verb *tornare* (see TURN).

Turner's syndrome ▶ noun [mass noun] Medicine a genetic defect in which affected women have only one X chromosome, causing developmental abnormalities and infertility.
– ORIGIN named after Henry Hubert *Turner* (1892–1970), the American physician who described it.

turnery ▶ noun [mass noun] the action or skill of making objects on a lathe. ■ objects made on a lathe.

turning ▶ noun **1** a place where a road branches off from another: *take the first turning on the right.*
2 [mass noun] the action or skill of using a lathe.
■ (**turnings**) shavings of wood resulting from turning wood on a lathe.

turning circle ▶ noun the smallest circle in which a vehicle or vessel can turn without reversing.

turning point ▶ noun a time at which a decisive change in a situation occurs, especially one with beneficial results: *this could be the turning point in Nigel's career.*

turnip ▶ noun **1** a round root with white or cream flesh which is eaten as a vegetable and also has edible leaves. ■ a similar or related root, especially a swede.
2 the European plant of the cabbage family which produces the turnip. ● *Brassica rapa*, family Cruciferae: 'rapifera' group.
3 informal, dated a large, thick, old-fashioned watch.
– DERIVATIVES **turnipy** adjective.
– ORIGIN mid 16th cent.: first element of unknown origin + NEEP.

turnip tops (US **turnip greens**) ▶ plural noun the leaves of a turnip eaten as a vegetable.

turnkey ▶ noun (pl. **turnkeys**) archaic a jailer.
▶ adjective of or involving the provision of a complete product or service that is ready for immediate use: *turnkey systems for telecommunications customers.*

turn-off ▶ noun **1** a junction at which a road branches off from a main road: *Adam missed the turn-off to the village.*
2 [usu. in sing.] informal a person or thing that causes someone to feel bored, disgusted, or sexually repelled: *he smelled of carbolic soap, a dreadful turn-off.*

turn-on ▶ noun [usu. in sing.] informal a person or thing that causes someone to feel excited or sexually aroused: *tight jeans are a real turn-on.*

turnout ▶ noun **1** [usu. in sing.] the number of people attending or taking part in an event, especially the number of people voting in an election.
2 N. Amer. a road turning. ■ a point at which a railway track diverges; a set of points. ■ a widened place in a road for cars to pass each other or park temporarily.
3 a carriage or other horse-drawn vehicle with its horse or horses.
4 [in sing.] the way in which a person or thing is equipped or dressed: *his turnout was exceedingly elegant.*
5 [mass noun] Ballet the ability to rotate the legs outward in the hip socket.

turnover ▶ noun **1** the amount of money taken by a business in a particular period: *a turnover approaching £4 million.*
2 the rate at which employees leave a workforce and are replaced. ■ the rate at which goods are sold and replaced in a shop.
3 a small pie made by folding a piece of pastry over on itself to enclose a sweet filling: *an apple turnover.*
4 N. Amer. (in a game) a loss of possession of the ball to the opposing team.

turnpike ▶ noun **1** historical a toll gate. ■ (also **turnpike road**) a road on which a toll was collected at a toll gate. ■ US a motorway on which a toll is charged.
2 historical a spiked barrier fixed in or across a road or passage as a defence against sudden attack.

T

turnround ▶ noun Brit. another term for TURNAROUND.

turn signal ▶ noun N. Amer. an indicator on a vehicle.

turnsole ▶ noun a Mediterranean plant of the spurge family, whose flowers are said to turn with the sun. ● *Chrozophora tinctoria* (family Euphorbiaceae), from which a blue or purple dye was formerly obtained.
– ORIGIN late Middle English: from Old French *tournesole*, based on Latin *tornare* (see TURN) + *sol* 'sun'.

turnspit ▶ noun historical a servant (or a small dog running on a treadmill) whose job was to turn a spit on which meat was roasting.

turns ratio ▶ noun the ratio of the number of turns on the primary coil of an electrical transformer to the number on the secondary, or vice versa.

turnstile ▶ noun a mechanical gate consisting of revolving horizontal arms fixed to a vertical post, allowing only one person at a time to pass through.

turnstone ▶ noun a small short-billed wading bird of the sandpiper family that turns over stones to feed on small animals beneath them. ● Genus *Arenaria*, family Scolopacidae: two species, in particular the (**ruddy**) **turnstone** (*A. interpres*), breeding in northern Eurasia and northern Canada.

turntable ▶ noun a circular revolving plate supporting a record as it is played. ■ a circular revolving platform for turning a railway locomotive or other vehicle.

turntable ladder ▶ noun Brit. a power operated extending and revolving ladder mounted on a fire engine.

turntablist ▶ noun a DJ who is an expert in sampling, scratching, and similar techniques.
– DERIVATIVES **turntablism** noun.

turn-up ▶ noun Brit. **1** (usu. **turn-ups**) the end of a trouser leg folded upwards on the outside.
2 [in sing.] informal an unusual or unexpected event or occurrence; a surprise: *fancy you being in New York too—what **a turn-up for the books**.*

Turpan Depression variant of TURFAN DEPRESSION.

turpentine /ˈtəːp(ə)ntʌɪn/ ▶ noun **1** (also **oil of turpentine**) [mass noun] a volatile pungent oil distilled from gum turpentine or pine wood, used in mixing paints and varnishes and in liniment. ■ (also **crude turpentine** or **gum turpentine**) an oleoresin secreted by certain trees, especially pines, and distilled to make rosin and oil of turpentine.
2 (also **turpentine tree**) any of a number of trees which yield turpentine or a similar resin, in particular: ● a coniferous tree of the pine family (*Larix, Pinus*, and other genera, family Pinaceae). ● the terebinth.
▶ verb [with obj.] apply turpentine to.
– ORIGIN Middle English: from Old French *ter(e) bentine*, from Latin *ter(e)binthina (resina)* '(resin) of the turpentine tree', from *terebinthus* (see TEREBINTH).

Turpin, Dick (1706–39), English highwayman. He was a cattle and deer thief in Essex before entering into partnership with Tom King, a notorious highwayman. Turpin was hanged at York for horse-stealing.

turpitude /ˈtəːpɪtjuːd/ ▶ noun [mass noun] formal depraved or wicked behaviour or character: *acts of moral turpitude*.
– ORIGIN late 15th cent.: from French, or from Latin *turpitudo*, from *turpis* 'disgraceful, base'.

turps ▶ noun [mass noun] informal turpentine.
– ORIGIN early 19th cent.: abbreviation.

turquoise /ˈtəːkwɔɪz, -kwɑːz/ ▶ noun [mass noun] **1** a semi-precious stone, typically opaque and of a greenish-blue or sky-blue colour, consisting of a hydrated phosphate of copper and aluminium.
2 a greenish-blue colour: [as modifier] *the turquoise waters of the bay*.
– ORIGIN late Middle English: from Old French *turqueise* 'Turkish (stone)'.

turret ▶ noun a small tower on top of a larger tower or at the corner of a building or wall, typically of a castle. ■ a low armoured tower, typically one that revolves, for a gun and gunners in a ship, aircraft, fort, or tank. ■ a rotating holder for tools, especially on a lathe.
– DERIVATIVES **turreted** adjective.
– ORIGIN Middle English: from Old French *tourete*, diminutive of *tour* 'tower'.

turret lathe ▶ noun another term for CAPSTAN LATHE.

turret shell ▶ noun a mollusc with a long, slender, pointed spiral shell, typically brightly coloured and living in tropical seas. ● Family Turitellidae, class Gastropoda: *Turitella* and other genera.

turron /tʊˈrɒn/ ▶ noun [mass noun] a kind of Spanish confectionery resembling nougat, made from almonds and honey.
– ORIGIN from Spanish *turrón*.

turtle ▶ noun **1** (also **sea turtle**) a large marine reptile with a bony or leathery shell and flippers, coming ashore annually on sandy beaches to lay eggs. ● Families Cheloniidae (seven species) and Dermochelyidae (the leatherback).
■ [mass noun] the flesh of a sea turtle, especially the green turtle, used chiefly for soup.
2 a freshwater reptile related to the sea turtles and tortoises, typically having a flattened shell. Called TERRAPIN in South Africa and India and TORTOISE in Australia. ● Order Chelonia: several families, in particular Emydidae and Kinosternidae.
■ N. Amer. any reptile of this order, including the terrapins and tortoises.
3 a directional cursor in a computer graphics system which can be instructed to move around a screen.
– PHRASES **turn turtle** (chiefly of a boat) turn upside down.
– ORIGIN mid 16th cent.: apparently an alteration of French *tortue* (see TORTOISE).

turtle dove ▶ noun a small Old World dove with a soft purring call, noted for the apparent affection shown for its mate. ● Genus *Streptopelia*, family Columbidae: several species, in particular the migratory European and North African *S. turtur*, with a reddish-brown back and pinkish breast.
– ORIGIN Middle English: *turtle* from Old English *turtla, turtle* 'turtle dove' (from Latin *turtur*, of imitative origin).

turtle-grass ▶ noun [mass noun] a submerged marine flowering plant found in the Caribbean, with long grass-like leaves. ● *Thalassia testudinum*, family Hydrocharitaceae.

turtlehead ▶ noun a North American plant which produces spikes of pink or white flowers which are said to resemble the head of a turtle. ● Genus *Chelone*, family Scrophulariaceae.

turtleneck ▶ noun Brit. a high, round, close-fitting neck on a knitted garment. ■ a sweater with a neck of this type. ■ North American term for POLO NECK.

turtleshell ▶ noun another term for TORTOISESHELL.

turves plural form of TURF.

Tuscan /ˈtʌsk(ə)n/ ▶ adjective **1** relating to Tuscany, its inhabitants, or the form of Italian spoken there, which is a standard variety widely taught to foreign learners.
2 relating to or denoting a classical order of architecture resembling the Doric but lacking all ornamentation.
▶ noun **1** a native or inhabitant of Tuscany.
2 [mass noun] the form of Italian spoken in Tuscany.
3 [mass noun] the Tuscan order of architecture.
– ORIGIN late Middle English (as a noun denoting an Etruscan): via French from Latin *Tuscanus*, from *Tuscus* 'an Etruscan'.

Tuscany /ˈtʌskəni/ a region of west central Italy, on the Ligurian Sea; capital, Florence. Italian name TOSCANA.

Tuscarora /ˌtʌskəˈrɔːrə/ ▶ noun (pl. **same** or **Tuscaroras**) **1** an American Indian people forming part of the Iroquois confederacy, originally inhabiting the Carolinas and later New York State.
2 [mass noun] the extinct Iroquoian language of the Tuscarora.
▶ adjective relating to the Tuscarora or their language.
– ORIGIN the name in Iroquois.

tush[1] /tʌʃ/ ▶ exclamation archaic or humorous expressing disapproval, impatience, or dismissal: *tush, these are trifles and mere old wives' tales*.
– ORIGIN natural utterance: first recorded in late Middle English.

tush[2] /tʌʃ/ ▶ noun a long pointed tooth, in particular a canine tooth of a male horse. ■ a stunted tusk of some Indian elephants.
– ORIGIN Old English *tusc* (see TUSK).

tush[3] /tʊʃ/ (also **tushy**) ▶ noun (pl. **tushes** or **tushies**) informal, chiefly N. Amer. a person's buttocks.
– ORIGIN 1960s (as *tushy*): from Yiddish *tokhes*, from Hebrew *taḥat* 'beneath'.

tusk ▶ noun a long pointed tooth, especially one which protrudes from the closed mouth, as in the elephant, walrus, or wild boar. ■ a long, tapering object or projection resembling a tusk.
– DERIVATIVES **tusked** adjective, **tusky** adjective (literary).
– ORIGIN Old English *tux*, variant of *tusc* (see TUSH[2]).

tusker ▶ noun an elephant or wild boar with well-developed tusks.

tusk shell ▶ noun a burrowing mollusc with a slender tusk-shaped shell, which is open at both ends and typically white, and a three-lobed foot. ● Class Scaphopoda, in particular the genus *Dentalium*.

tussah /ˈtʌsə/ ▶ noun variant form of TUSSORE.

Tussaud /təˈsɔːd/, French /tysəo/, Madame (1761–1850), French founder of Madame Tussaud's waxworks, resident in Britain from 1802; née *Marie Grosholtz*. She took death masks in wax of prominent victims of the French Revolution and later toured Britain with her wax models. In 1835 she founded a permanent waxworks exhibition in Baker Street, London.

tussie-mussie /ˈtʌsɪmʌsi/ ▶ noun (pl. **tussie-mussies**) archaic a small bunch of flowers or aromatic herbs.
– ORIGIN late Middle English: of unknown origin.

tussive /ˈtʌsɪv/ ▶ adjective Medicine relating to coughing.
– ORIGIN mid 19th cent.: from Latin *tussis* 'a cough' + -IVE.

tussle ▶ noun a vigorous struggle or scuffle, typically in order to obtain or achieve something: *there was a tussle for the ball*.
▶ verb [no obj.] engage in a vigorous struggle or scuffle: *the demonstrators tussled with police*.
– ORIGIN late Middle English (as a verb, originally Scots and northern English): perhaps a diminutive of dialect *touse* 'handle roughly' (see TOUSLE).

tussock /ˈtʌsək/ ▶ noun a small area of grass that is thicker or longer than the grass growing around it.
– DERIVATIVES **tussocky** adjective.
– ORIGIN mid 16th cent.: perhaps an alteration of dialect *tusk* 'tuft', of unknown origin.

tussock grass ▶ noun a grass which grows in tussocks. ● Genera *Poa, Nassella*, or *Deschampsia*, family Gramineae: several species, in particular *D. cespitosa*, a coarse fodder grass of the northern hemisphere.

Tussock moth ▶ noun a woodland moth whose adults and brightly coloured caterpillars both bear tufts of irritant hairs. The caterpillars can be a pest of trees, damaging fruit and stripping leaves. ● Family Lymantriidae: many genera.

tussore /ˈtʌsɔː, ˈtʌsə/ (also **tussah**) ▶ noun (also **tussore silk**) [mass noun] coarse silk from the larvae of the tussore moth and related species.
– ORIGIN late 16th cent.: from Hindi *tasar*, from Sanskrit *tasara* 'shuttle'.

tussore moth ▶ noun a silk moth that is sometimes kept in India and China, with caterpillars (**tussore silkworms**) that yield a strong but coarse brown silk. ● *Antheraea mylitta*, family Saturniidae.

tut ▶ exclamation, noun, & verb short for TUT-TUT.

Tutankhamen /ˌtuːt(ə)nˈkɑːm(ə)n/ (also **Tutankhamun** /-kɑːˈmuːn/) (died *c.*1352 BC), Egyptian pharaoh of the 18th dynasty, reigned *c.*1361–*c.*1352 BC. His tomb, containing a wealth of rich and varied contents, was discovered virtually intact by the English archaeologist Howard Carter in 1922.

tutee /tjuːˈtiː/ ▶ noun a student or pupil of a tutor.

tutelage /ˈtjuːtɪlɪdʒ/ ▶ noun [mass noun] protection of or authority over someone or something; guardianship: *the organizations remained under firm government tutelage*. ■ instruction; tuition: *he felt privileged to be **under the tutelage of** an experienced actor*.
– ORIGIN early 17th cent.: from Latin *tutela* 'keeping', (from *tut-* 'watched', from the verb *tueri*) + -AGE.

tutelary /ˈtjuːtɪləri/ (also **tutelar** /-tɪlə/) ▶ adjective serving as a protector, guardian, or patron: *the tutelary spirits of these regions*. ■ relating to protection or a guardian: *the state maintained a tutelary relation with the security police*.
– ORIGIN early 17th cent.: from Latin *tutelarius*, from *tutela* 'keeping' (see TUTELAGE).

Tuthmosis III /tʌθˈməʊsɪs/ (died *c.*1450 BC), son of Tuthmosis II, Egyptian pharaoh of the 18th dynasty *c.*1504–*c.*1450. His reign was marked by extensive building; the monuments he erected included Cleopatra's Needles (*c.*1475).

tutor ▶ noun a private teacher, typically one who teaches a single pupil or a very small group. ■ chiefly Brit. a university or college teacher responsible for the teaching and supervision of assigned students. ■ US an assistant lecturer in a college or university. ■ Brit. a book of instruction in a particular subject.

T

▶ verb [with obj.] act as a tutor to (a single pupil or a very small group): *his children were privately tutored.* ■ [no obj.] work as a tutor.
– DERIVATIVES **tutorage** noun, **tutorship** noun.
– ORIGIN late Middle English: from Old French *tutour* or Latin *tutor*, from *tueri* 'to watch, guard'.

tutorial ▶ adjective relating to a tutor or a tutor's tuition: *tutorial sessions | a tutorial college.*
▶ noun a period of tuition given by a university or college tutor to an individual or very small group. ■ an account or explanation of a subject, printed or on a computer screen, intended for private study.
– ORIGIN early 18th cent.: from Latin *tutorius* (see TUTOR) + -AL.

tutsan /ˈtʌts(ə)n/ ▶ noun a Eurasian St John's wort with large aromatic leaves and a berry-like fruit, formerly used medicinally. ● *Hypericum androsaemum*, family Guttiferae.
– ORIGIN late Middle English: from Anglo-Norman French *tutsaine* 'all wholesome'.

Tutsi /ˈtʊtsi/ ▶ noun (pl. **same** or **Tutsis**) a member of a people forming a minority of the population of Rwanda and Burundi but who formerly dominated the Hutu majority. Historical antagonism between the peoples led in 1994 to large-scale ethnic violence, especially in Rwanda.
▶ adjective relating to the Tutsi.
– ORIGIN a local name. See also WATUSI.

tutti /ˈtʊti/ Music ▶ adverb & adjective (especially as a direction) with all voices or instruments together.
▶ noun (pl. **tuttis**) a passage to be performed in this way.
– ORIGIN Italian, plural of *tutto* 'all', from Latin *totus*.

tutti-frutti /ˌtuːtɪˈfruːti/ ▶ noun (pl. **tutti-fruttis**) [mass noun] a type of ice cream containing or flavoured with mixed fruits and sometimes nuts.
– ORIGIN Italian, literally 'all fruits'.

tut-tut (also **tut**) ▶ exclamation expressing disapproval or annoyance: *tut-tut, Robin, you disappoint me.*
▶ noun an exclamation of disapproval or annoyance: *tut-tuts of disapproval.*
▶ verb (**tut-tuts, tut-tutting, tut-tutted**) [no obj.] make such an exclamation: *Aunt Mary tut-tutted at all the goings-on.*
– ORIGIN natural utterance (representing a reduplicated clicking sound made by the tongue against the teeth): first recorded in English in the early 16th cent.

Tutu /ˈtuːtuː/, Desmond (Mpilo) (b.1931), South African clergyman. As General Secretary of the South African Council of Churches (1979–84) he became a leading voice in the struggle against apartheid. He was Archbishop of Cape Town 1986–96. Nobel Peace Prize (1984).

tutu¹ /ˈtuːtuː/ ▶ noun a female ballet dancer's costume consisting of a bodice and an attached skirt incorporating numerous layers of fabric, this being either short and stiff and projecting horizontally from the waist (the **classical tutu**) or long, soft, and bell-shaped (the **romantic tutu**).
– ORIGIN early 20th cent.: from French, child's alteration of *cucu*, informal diminutive of *cul* 'buttocks'.

tutu² /ˈtuːtuː/ ▶ noun a New Zealand shrub which bears poisonous purplish-black berries. ● *Coriaria arborea*, family Coriariaceae.
– ORIGIN mid 19th cent.: from Maori.

T

Tuva /ˈtuːvə/ an autonomous republic in south central Russia, on the border with Mongolia; pop. 310,600 (est. 2009); capital, Kyzyl. Former name TANNU-TUVA.

Tuvalu /tuːˈvɑːluː/ a country in the SW Pacific consisting of a group of nine main islands, formerly called the Ellice Islands; pop. 12,400 (est. 2009); official languages, English and Tuvaluan (local Austronesian language); capital, Funafuti. The islands formed part of the British colony of the Gilbert and Ellice Islands but separated from the Gilberts after a referendum in 1975. Tuvalu became independent within the Commonwealth in 1978.
– DERIVATIVES **Tuvaluan** /ˌtuːvəˈluːən, tuːˈvɑːlʊən/ adjective & noun.

tu-whit tu-whoo ▶ noun used to represent the cry of the tawny owl.
– ORIGIN late 16th cent.: imitative.

tux ▶ noun informal, chiefly N. Amer. a tuxedo.

tuxedo /tʌkˈsiːdəʊ/ ▶ noun (pl. **tuxedos** or **tuxedoes**) chiefly N. Amer. a man's dinner jacket. ■ a suit of formal evening clothes including a tuxedo.
– DERIVATIVES **tuxedoed** adjective.
– ORIGIN late 19th cent.: from *Tuxedo* Park, the site of a country club in New York, where it was first worn.

Tuxtla Gutiérrez /ˌtʊstlə ˌɡuːtɪˈɛːrɛz/ a city in SE Mexico, capital of the state of Chiapas; pop. 490,455 (2005).

tuyère /twiːˈjɛː, tuː-/ ▶ noun a nozzle through which air is forced into a smelter, furnace, or forge.
– ORIGIN late 18th cent.: French, from *tuyau* 'pipe'.

Tuzla /ˈtʊzlə/ a town in NE Bosnia; pop. 83,800 (est. 2008). The town, a Muslim enclave, suffered damage and heavy casualties when besieged by Bosnian Serb forces between 1992 and 1994.

TV ▶ abbreviation ■ television (the system or a set): *anything good on TV tonight?* ■ transvestite.

TVA ▶ abbreviation (in the US) Tennessee Valley Authority.

TV dinner ▶ noun a prepared pre-packed meal that only requires heating before it is ready to eat.

TVEI ▶ abbreviation (in the UK) Technical and Vocational Educational Initiative, a national scheme encouraging students to gain practical experience of technology and industry, often through work placement.

Tver /tvɛː/ an industrial port in European Russia, on the River Volga north-west of Moscow; pop. 402,700 (est. 2009). It was known as Kalinin, in honour of President Kalinin, from 1931 until 1991.

TVP ▶ abbreviation trademark textured vegetable protein.

Twa /twɑː/ ▶ noun (pl. **same, Twas,** or **Batwa** /ˈbatwɑː/) a member of a Pygmy people inhabiting parts of Burundi, Rwanda, and the Democratic Republic of the Congo (Zaire).
▶ adjective relating to the Twa.
– ORIGIN a local word meaning 'foreigner, outsider'.

twaddle informal ▶ noun [mass noun] trivial or foolish speech or writing; nonsense: *he dismissed the novel as self-indulgent twaddle.*
▶ verb [no obj.] archaic talk or write in a trivial or foolish way: *what is that old fellow twaddling about?*
– DERIVATIVES **twaddler** noun.
– ORIGIN late 18th cent.: alteration of earlier *twattle*, of unknown origin.

Twain, Mark (1835–1910), American novelist and humorist; pseudonym of *Samuel Langhorne Clemens*. His best-known novels, *The Adventures of Tom Sawyer* (1876) and *The Adventures of Huckleberry Finn* (1885), give a vivid evocation of Mississippi frontier life.

twain ▶ cardinal number archaic term for TWO: *he split the spar in twain.*
– PHRASES **never the twain shall meet** used to suggest that two things are too different to exist alongside each other: *families were either 'church' or 'chapel' and never the twain shall meet.* [from Rudyard Kipling's 'Oh, East is East, and West is West, and never the twain shall meet' (*Barrack-room Ballads*, 1892).]
– ORIGIN Old English *twegen*, masculine of *twā* (see TWO).

twaite shad /tweɪt/ ▶ noun a European shad (fish) with a deep blue back, silvery sides, and some spotting. ● *Alosa fallax*, family Clupeidae.
– ORIGIN early 17th cent. (as *twaite*): of unknown origin.

twang ▶ noun **1** a strong ringing sound such as that made by the plucked string of a musical instrument or a released bowstring.
2 a nasal or other distinctive manner of pronunciation or intonation characteristic of the speech of an individual, area, or country: *an American twang.*
▶ verb **1** make or cause to make a twang: [no obj.] *a spring twanged beneath him* | [with obj.] *some old men were twanging banjos.*
2 [with obj.] utter (something) with a nasal twang: *the announcer was twanging out all the details.*
– DERIVATIVES **twangy** adjective (**twangier, twangiest**).
– ORIGIN mid 16th cent.: imitative.

'twas archaic or literary ▶ contraction it was.

twat /twɒt, twat/ ▶ noun **1** vulgar slang a woman's genitals. **2** ■ a person regarded as stupid or obnoxious.
▶ verb [with obj.] Brit. informal hit or punch (someone).
– ORIGIN mid 17th cent.: of unknown origin.

twayblade ▶ noun an orchid with a slender spike of greenish or brownish flowers and a single pair of broad leaves near the base. ● Genus *Listera*, family Orchidaceae: several species, including the Eurasian **common twayblade** (*L. ovata*).
– ORIGIN late 16th cent.: from *tway* (variant of TWAIN) + BLADE, translating Latin *bifolium*.

tweak ▶ verb [with obj.] **1** twist or pull (something) sharply: *he tweaked the boy's ear.*
2 informal improve (a mechanism or system) by making fine adjustments to it: *engineers tweak the car's operating systems during the race.*
▶ noun **1** a sharp twist or pull.
2 informal a fine adjustment to a mechanism or system.
– DERIVATIVES **tweaker** noun.
– ORIGIN early 17th cent.: probably an alteration of dialect *twick* 'pull sharply'; related to TWITCH.

twee ▶ adjective (**tweer, tweest**) Brit. excessively or affectedly quaint, pretty, or sentimental: *although the film's a bit twee, it's watchable.*
– DERIVATIVES **tweely** adverb, **tweeness** noun.
– ORIGIN early 20th cent.: representing a child's pronunciation of SWEET.

Tweed a river which rises in the Southern Uplands of Scotland and flows generally eastwards, crossing into NE England and entering the North Sea at Berwick-upon-Tweed. For part of its lower course it forms the border between Scotland and England.

tweed ▶ noun [mass noun] a rough-surfaced woollen cloth, typically of mixed flecked colours, originally produced in Scotland: [as modifier] *a tweed sports jacket.* ■ (**tweeds**) clothes made of tweed: *boisterous Englishwomen in tweeds.*
– ORIGIN mid 19th cent.: originally a misreading of *tweel*, Scots form of TWILL, influenced by association with the River *Tweed*.

Tweedledum and Tweedledee ▶ noun a pair of people or things that are virtually indistinguishable.
– ORIGIN originally names applied to the composers Bononcini (1670–1747) and Handel, in a 1725 satire by John Byrom (1692–1763); they were later used for two identical characters in Lewis Carroll's *Through the Looking Glass*.

tweedy ▶ adjective (**tweedier, tweediest**) (of a garment) made of tweed cloth: *a tweedy suit.* ■ informal habitually wearing tweed clothes: *a stout, tweedy woman.* ■ informal of a robust traditional or rural character (by association with the country gentry who traditionally wear tweeds): *a tweedy gathering of the Cheshire young farmers.*
– DERIVATIVES **tweedily** adverb, **tweediness** noun.

Tween ▶ noun trademark any of a class of compounds used especially as emulsifiers and surfactants. They are derivatives of fatty acid esters of sorbitan.
– ORIGIN 1940s: of unknown origin.

tween (also **tweenie**) ▶ noun short for TWEENAGER.

'tween archaic or literary ▶ contraction between.

tweenager ▶ noun informal a child between the ages of about 10 and 14.

'tween decks ▶ plural noun Nautical the space between the decks of a ship, especially that between the continuous inside decks below the main or upper deck.

tweener ▶ noun US informal a person or thing considered to be in between two other recognized categories or types: *we're a couple of tweeners, born after baby boomers and before generation Xers.* ■ another term for TWEENAGER.

tweeny ▶ noun (pl. **tweenies**) archaic, informal a maid who assisted two other members of a domestic staff.
– ORIGIN late 19th cent.: from *between-maid*, a servant assisting two others.

tweet ▶ noun **1** the chirp of a small or young bird: *the gentle tweet of a bird can be heard.*
2 a posting made on the social networking service Twitter: *he started posting tweets via his mobile phone to let his parents know he was safe.*
▶ verb [no obj.] **1** make a chirping noise: *the birds were tweeting in the branches.*
2 make a posting on the social networking service Twitter: *it's easy to tweet all the time.*
– ORIGIN mid 19th cent.: imitative.

WORD TRENDS Once invoking nothing beyond the sound of birds gently chirping, **tweet** is a striking example of the Internet's influence on language trends. Since the social networking service Twitter was set up in 2006, 'tweeting' (posting short messages, known as **tweets**, on the Web) has become so popular that the frequency of the noun **tweet** in the Oxford English Corpus has risen tenfold. The millions of people using Twitter may take themselves and their tweets very seriously, but the site's name suggests otherwise: the Corpus shows that the majority of uses of **twitter** in the sense 'talk rapidly and at length' imply foolishness or triviality: *two posh English girls twitter incessantly | twittering on about the good old days.*

tweeter ▶ noun a loudspeaker designed to reproduce high frequencies.

tweetup ▶ noun a meeting or other gathering organized by means of posts on the social networking service Twitter.
– ORIGIN early 21st cent.: from TWEET + UP, on the pattern of MEETUP.

tweeze (also **tweezer**) ▶ verb [with obj.] pluck, grasp, or pull with or as if with tweezers: *the brows were tweezed to an almost invisible line.*
– ORIGIN 1930s: back-formation from *tweezer* (see TWEEZERS).

tweezers ▶ plural noun (also **a pair of tweezers**) a small instrument like a pair of pincers for plucking out hairs and picking up small objects.
– ORIGIN mid 17th cent.: extended form of obsolete *tweeze* 'case of surgical instruments', shortening of *etweese*, anglicized plural of ETUI.

twelfth /twɛlfθ/ ▶ ordinal number **1** constituting number twelve in a sequence; 12th: *the twelfth of November | his twelfth birthday | the twelfth in a series of essays.* ■ Music an interval or chord spanning an octave and a fifth in the diatonic scale, or a note separated from another by this interval. ■ (**the Twelfth** or **the Glorious Twelfth**) (in the UK) 12 August, the day on which the grouse-shooting season begins. ■ (**the Twelfth**) 12 July, celebrated by upholders of Protestant supremacy in Ireland as the anniversary of William III's victory over James II at the Battle of the Boyne.
2 (**a twelfth/one twelfth**) each of twelve equal parts into which something is or may be divided.
– DERIVATIVES **twelfthly** adverb, **twelvefold** adjective & adverb.

Twelfth Day ▶ noun archaic term for TWELFTH NIGHT.

twelfth man ▶ noun Cricket a player nominated to act as a reserve in a game, typically carrying out duties such as fielding as a substitute, taking out drinks, etc.

Twelfth Night ▶ noun 6 January, the feast of the Epiphany. ■ strictly, the evening of 5 January, the eve of the Epiphany and formerly the twelfth and last day of Christmas festivities.

twelve ▶ cardinal number equivalent to the product of three and four; two more than ten; 12: *he walked twelve miles | there are just twelve of us in all | a twelve-string guitar.* (Roman numeral: **xii** or **XII**) ■ a group or unit of twelve people or things. ■ twelve years old: *a small blonde girl of about twelve.* ■ twelve o'clock: *it's half past twelve.* ■ a size of garment or other merchandise denoted by twelve. ■ (**the Twelve**) the twelve Apostles. ■ (**12**) Brit. (of a film) classified as suitable for people of 12 years and over.
– ORIGIN Old English *twelf(e)*, from the base of TWO + a second element (probably expressing the sense 'left over'); of Germanic origin and related to Dutch *twaalf* and German *zwölf*. Compare with ELEVEN.

twelve-bar ▶ adjective denoting or relating to a musical structure based around a sequence lasting twelve bars and typically consisting of three chords, the basic unit of much blues and rock-and-roll music.

twelve-bore ▶ noun Brit. a shotgun with a bore corresponding to the diameter of a round bullet of which twelve constitute a pound in weight.

twelve-gauge ▶ noun North American term for TWELVE-BORE.

twelvemo ▶ noun another term for DUODECIMO.

twelvemonth ▶ noun archaic a year.

twelve-note (also **twelve-tone**) ▶ adjective denoting a system of musical composition using the twelve chromatic notes of the octave on an equal basis without dependence on a key system. Developed by Arnold Schoenberg, the technique is central to serialism and involves the transposition and inversion of a fixed sequence of pitches.

twelve-step ▶ adjective [attrib.] denoting or relating to a process of recovery from an addiction by following a twelve-stage programme, especially one devised or similar to that devised by Alcoholics Anonymous.
▶ verb [no obj.] (often as noun **twelve-stepping**) undergo a twelve-step programme.
– DERIVATIVES **twelve-stepper** noun.

Twelve Tables a set of laws drawn up in ancient Rome in 451 and 450 BC, embodying the most important rules of Roman law.

Twelve Tribes of Israel see TRIBES OF ISRAEL.

Twentieth Century Fox a US film production company formed in 1935 by the merger of the Fox Company with Twentieth Century. Under production head Darryl F. Zanuck the company pioneered widescreen film techniques.

twenty ▶ cardinal number (pl. **twenties**) the number equivalent to the product of two and ten; ten less than thirty; 20: *twenty or thirty years ago | twenty of us stood and waited | a twenty-foot aerial.* (Roman numeral: **xx** or **XX**) ■ (**twenties**) the numbers from twenty to twenty-nine, especially the years of a century or of a person's life: *he's in his late twenties.* ■ twenty years old: *he's about twenty.* ■ twenty miles an hour. ■ a size of garment or other merchandise denoted by twenty.
– DERIVATIVES **twentieth** ordinal number, **twentyfold** adjective & adverb.
– ORIGIN Old English *twentig*, from the base of TWO + -TY².

twenty-four-hour clock (also **24-hour clock**) ▶ noun a method of measuring the time based on the full twenty-four hours of the day, rather than dividing it into two units of twelve hours.

twenty-one ▶ noun [mass noun] the card game blackjack or pontoon.

Twenty-Six Counties the counties of the Republic of Ireland. Compare with SIX COUNTIES.

twenty-twenty (also **20/20**) ▶ adjective denoting vision of normal sharpness.
– ORIGIN the Snellen fraction for normal visual acuity (see SNELLEN TEST).

Twenty20 ▶ noun [mass noun] a type of cricket match in which each team has a single innings consisting of a maximum of twenty overs.

'twere archaic or literary ▶ contraction it were.

twerp (also **twirp**) ▶ noun informal a silly or annoying person.
– ORIGIN late 19th cent.: of unknown origin.

Twi /twiː, tʃwiː/ ▶ noun (pl. **same** or **Twis**) **1** a member of an Akan-speaking people of Ghana.
2 another term for AKAN (the language).
▶ adjective relating to the Twi or their language.
– ORIGIN the name in Akan.

twibill /ˈtwʌɪbɪl/ ▶ noun archaic a double-bladed battleaxe.
– ORIGIN Old English *twibile* 'axe with two cutting edges', from *twi-* 'double' + BILL³.

twice ▶ adverb two times; on two occasions: *the earl married twice | the tablets should be taken twice a day.* ■ double in degree or quantity: *I'm twice your age | an engine **twice as** big **as** the original.*
– PHRASES **be twice the man/woman** (**that someone is**) be much better or stronger (than someone): *how dare you criticize him, he's twice the man that you are!* **once bitten, twice shy** see BITE. **think twice** see THINK.
– ORIGIN late Old English *twiges*, from the base of TWO + -S³ (later respelled *-ce* to denote the unvoiced sound); compare with ONCE.

twice-born ▶ adjective having undergone a renewal of faith or life, in particular: ■ (of a Hindu) belonging to one of the three highest castes, especially as an initiated Brahmin. ■ (of a Christian) born-again.

twiddle ▶ verb [with obj.] twist, move, or fiddle with (something), typically in a purposeless or nervous way: *she twiddled the dials on the radio* | [no obj.] *he began twiddling with the curtain cord.* ■ [no obj.] archaic turn or move in a twirling way.
▶ noun an act of twisting or fiddling with something: *one twiddle of a button.* ■ a twisted or curled mark or design: *twiddles and twirls.* ■ a rapid or intricate series of musical notes: *gay little twiddles from the clarinet.*
– PHRASES **twiddle one's thumbs** rotate one's thumbs round each other with the fingers linked together. ■ be bored or idle because one has nothing to do.
– DERIVATIVES **twiddler** noun, **twiddly** adjective (**twiddlier**, **twiddliest**).
– ORIGIN mid 16th cent. (in the sense 'trifle'): apparently imitative, combining the notion *twirl* or *twist* with that of trifling action expressed by *fiddle*.

twig¹ ▶ noun **1** a slender woody shoot growing from a branch or stem of a tree or shrub.
2 Anatomy a small branch of a blood vessel or nerve.
– DERIVATIVES **twigged** adjective, **twiggy** adjective.
– ORIGIN Old English *twigge*, of Germanic origin; related to Dutch *twijg* and German *Zweig*, also to TWAIN and TWO.

twig² ▶ verb (**twigs**, **twigging**, **twigged**) [no obj.] Brit. informal understand or realize something: *it was amazing that Graham hadn't twigged before.* ■ [with obj.] archaic perceive; observe: *nine days now since my eyes have twigged any terra firma.*
– ORIGIN mid 18th cent.: of unknown origin.

twig furniture ▶ noun [mass noun] N. Amer. a rustic style of furniture in which the natural state of the wood is retained as an aesthetic feature.

twilight /ˈtwʌɪlʌɪt/ ▶ noun **1** [mass noun] the soft glowing light from the sky when the sun is below the horizon, caused by the reflection of the sun's rays from the atmosphere. ■ the period of the evening during which this takes place, between daylight and darkness: *a pleasant walk **in the** woods **at twilight.***
2 [in sing.] a period or state of obscurity, ambiguity, or gradual decline: *he was **in the twilight of** his career* | [as modifier] ***a twilight world** of secrecy.*
– ORIGIN late Middle English: from Old English *twi-* 'two' (used in an obscure sense in this compound) + LIGHT¹.

twilight home ▶ noun a residential home for elderly people.

twilight of the gods Scandinavian & Germanic Mythology the destruction of the gods and the world in a final conflict with the powers of evil. Also called GÖTTERDÄMMERUNG, RAGNARÖK.
– ORIGIN translating Icelandic *ragna rökr* (see RAGNARÖK).

twilight sleep ▶ noun [mass noun] Medicine a state of partial narcosis or stupor without total loss of consciousness, in particular a state induced by an injection of morphine and scopolamine, formerly popular for use during childbirth.

twilight zone ▶ noun **1** a situation or conceptual area that is characterized by being undefined, intermediate, or mysterious: *the twilight zone between the middle and working classes.*
2 an urban area in a state of dilapidation or economic decline.
3 the lowest level of the ocean to which light can penetrate.

twilit (also **twilighted**) ▶ adjective dimly illuminated by or as if by twilight: *the deserted twilit street.* ■ relating to or denoting the period of twilight: *twilit hours.*
– ORIGIN mid 19th cent.: past participle of the literary verb *twilight*.

twill ▶ noun [mass noun] a fabric so woven as to have a surface of diagonal parallel ridges.
▶ verb [with obj.] (usu. as adj. **twilled**) weave (fabric) so as to have a surface of diagonal parallel ridges: *twilled cotton.*
– ORIGIN Middle English: from a Scots and northern English variant of obsolete *twilly*, from Old English *twi-* 'two', suggested by Latin *bilix* 'two-threaded'.

'twill archaic or literary ▶ contraction it will.

twin ▶ noun **1** one of two children or animals born at the same birth. ■ a person or thing that is exactly like another: *there was a bruise on his cheek, **a twin to** the one on mine.* ■ (**the Twins**) the zodiacal sign or constellation Gemini.
2 something containing or consisting of two matching or corresponding parts, in particular: ■ a twin-bedded room. ■ a twin-engined aircraft. ■ a twinned crystal.
▶ adjective [attrib.] forming, or being one of, a pair born at one birth: *she gave birth to twin boys | her twin sister.* ■ forming a matching, complementary, or closely connected pair: *the twin problems of economic failure and social disintegration.* ■ Botany growing in pairs: *twin seed leaves.* ■ (of a bedroom) containing two single beds. ■ (of a crystal) twinned.
▶ verb (**twins**, **twinning**, **twinned**) [with obj.] Brit. link (a town or district) with another in a different country or cause (two towns or districts) to be linked, for the purposes of friendship and cultural exchange: *the Russian city of Kostroma **is twinned with** Durham.* ■ link; combine: *the company twinned its core business of brewing with that of distilling.*
– ORIGIN late Old English *twinn* 'double', from *twi-* 'two'; related to Old Norse *tvinnr*. Current verb senses date from late Middle English.

twin bed ▶ noun one of a pair of matching single beds, particularly in a hotel or guest room intended for two people.
– DERIVATIVES **twin-bedded** adjective.

twin-cam ▶ adjective denoting an engine having two camshafts.

twin city ▶ noun either of two neighbouring cities lying close together. ■ (**the Twin Cities**) N. Amer. Minneapolis and St Paul in Minnesota. ■ a city which has been twinned with another.

twine ▶ noun [mass noun] strong thread or string consisting of two or more strands of hemp or cotton twisted together.

T

▸ **verb** wind or cause to wind round something: [no obj.] *the plant will twine round its support* | [with obj.] *she **twined** her arms **round** his neck.* ■ [with obj.] interlace: *a spray of jasmine was twined in her hair.*
– DERIVATIVES **twiner** noun.
– ORIGIN Old English *twīn* 'thread, linen', from the Germanic base of *twi-* 'two'; related to Dutch *twijn*.

twin-engined ▸ **adjective** (chiefly of an aircraft) having two engines.

twinflower ▸ **noun** a slender evergreen trailing plant with pairs of very small trumpet-shaped pink flowers in the leaf axils, native to coniferous woodland in northern latitudes. ● *Linnaea borealis*, family Caprifoliaceae.

twinge ▸ **noun** a sudden, sharp localized pain: *he felt a twinge in his knee.* ■ a brief experience of an emotion, typically an unpleasant one: *Kate felt a twinge of guilt.*
▸ **verb** (**twinges**, **twingeing** or **twinging**, **twinged**) [no obj.] (of a part of the body) suffer a sudden, sharp localized pain: *stop the exercises if the tummy twinges.*
– ORIGIN Old English *twengan* 'pinch, wring', of Germanic origin. The noun dates from the mid 16th cent.

twin-jet ▸ **adjective** (of an aircraft) having two jet engines.
▸ **noun** (**twin jet**) a twin-jet aircraft.

twinkie ▸ **noun** (pl. **twinkies**) US **1** trademark a small finger-shaped sponge cake with a synthetic cream filling.
2 informal, derogatory a homosexual or effeminate man.
– ORIGIN 1970s: probably related to TWINKLE.

twinkle ▸ **verb 1** [no obj.] (of a star or light, or a shiny object) shine with a gleam that changes constantly from bright to faint: *the lights twinkled in the distance.* ■ (of a person's eyes) sparkle, especially with amusement. ■ smile so that one's eyes sparkle: *'Aha!' he said, **twinkling at** her.*
2 [no obj., with adverbial] (of a person's feet) move lightly and rapidly: *his sandalled feet twinkled over the ground.*
▸ **noun** a sparkle or gleam in a person's eyes. ■ a light which appears continually to grow brighter and fainter: *the distant twinkle of the lights.*
– DERIVATIVES **twinkler** noun, **twinkly** adjective (**twinklier**, **twinkliest**).
– ORIGIN Old English *twinclian* (verb), of Germanic origin.

twinkle-toed ▸ **adjective** informal nimble and quick on one's feet: *a twinkle-toed midfielder.*
– DERIVATIVES **twinkletoes** noun.

twinkling ▸ **adjective** shining with a gleam that changes from bright to faint: *twinkling harbour lights.* ■ (of a person's eyes) sparkling, especially with amusement: *twinkling eyes, happy smiles.*
– PHRASES **in a twinkling** (or **the twinkling of an eye**) in an instant; very quickly: *I'll have supper ready in a twinkling.*

twin-lens ▸ **adjective** (of a camera) having two identical sets of lenses, either for taking stereoscopic pictures, or with one forming an image for viewing and the other an image to be photographed (**twin-lens reflex**).

twinned ▸ **adjective** (of a crystal) that is a composite consisting of two (or sometimes more) parts which are reversed in orientation with respect to each other (typically by reflection in a particular plane).

twinning ▸ **noun** [mass noun] the bearing of twins: *the study showed an increased level of twinning in cattle.* ■ the occurrence or formation of twinned crystals.

twin paradox ▸ **noun** Physics the apparent paradox arising from relativity theory that if one of a pair of twins makes a long journey at near the speed of light and then returns, he or she will have aged less than the twin who remains behind.

twin-screw ▸ **adjective** (of a ship) having two propellers on separate shafts with opposite twists.

twinset ▸ **noun** chiefly Brit. a woman's matching cardigan and jumper.

twinspot ▸ **noun** an African waxbill with white-spotted black underparts, the male typically having a reddish face and breast. ● *Hypargos* and related genera, family Estrildidae: several species.

twin town ▸ **noun** Brit. a town which has established official or social links with another, typically in a different country.

twin-tub ▸ **adjective** (of a washing machine) having two separate top-loading drums, one for washing and the other for spin-drying.
▸ **noun** a twin-tub washing machine.

twirl ▸ **verb** [no obj.] spin quickly and lightly round, especially repeatedly: *she twirled in delight to show off her new dress.* ■ [with obj.] cause to rotate: *she twirled her fork in the pasta.*
▸ **noun** an act of spinning: *Kate did a twirl in front of the mirror.* ■ a spiralling or swirling shape, especially a flourish made with a pen.
– DERIVATIVES **twirler** noun, **twirly** adjective (**twirlier**, **twirliest**).
– ORIGIN late 16th cent.: probably an alteration (by association with WHIRL) of *tirl*, a variant of archaic *trill* 'twiddle, spin'.

twirp ▸ **noun** variant spelling of TWERP.

twist ▸ **verb** [with obj.] **1** form into a bent, curling, or distorted shape: *a strip of metal is twisted to form a hollow tube* | *her pretty features twisted into a fearsome expression.* ■ [with obj. and adverbial] form (something) into a particular shape by taking hold of one or both ends and turning them: *she twisted her handkerchief into a knot.* ■ [with obj. and adverbial] turn or bend into a specified position or in a specified direction: *he grabbed the man and twisted his arm behind his back.* ■ (**twist something off**) remove something by pulling and rotating it: *beetroot can be stored once the leaves have been twisted off.* ■ [no obj.] move one's body so that the shoulders and hips are facing in different directions: *she twisted in her seat to look at the buildings.* ■ [no obj., with adverbial] move in a wriggling or writhing fashion: *he **twisted himself** free.* ■ injure (a joint) by wrenching it: *he twisted his ankle trying to avoid his opponent's lunge.* ■ distort or misrepresent the meaning of (words): *he twisted my words to make it seem that I'd claimed she was a drug addict.*
2 cause to rotate around a stationary point; turn: *she twisted her ring round and round on her finger.* ■ [with obj. and adverbial] wind around or through something: *she twisted a lock of hair around her finger.* ■ move or cause to move around each other; interlace: [with obj.] *she twisted her hands together nervously* | *the machine twists together strands to make a double yarn.* ■ make (something) by interlacing or winding strands together. ■ [no obj.] take or have a winding course: *the railway lines twist and turn round the hills.*
3 [no obj.] dance the twist.
4 Brit. informal cheat; defraud.
5 [no obj.] (in pontoon) request, deal, or be dealt a card face upwards.
▸ **noun 1** an act of twisting something around a stationary point: *the taps needed a single twist to turn them on.* ■ an act of turning one's body or part of one's body: *with a sudden twist, she got away from him.* ■ (**the twist**) a dance with a twisting movement of the body, popular in the 1960s. ■ [mass noun] the extent of twisting of a rod or other object. ■ [mass noun] force producing twisting; torque. ■ [mass noun] forward motion combined with rotation about an axis. ■ the rifling in the bore of a gun: *barrels with a 1:24 inch twist.*
2 a thing with a spiral shape: *a barley sugar twist.* ■ Brit. a paper packet with twisted ends. ■ a small quantity of tobacco, sugar, salt, or a similar substance, wrapped in such a packet. ■ a curled piece of lemon peel used to flavour a drink.
3 a distorted shape: *he had a cruel twist to his mouth.* ■ an unusual feature of a person's personality, typically an unhealthy one. ■ Brit. informal a swindle.
4 a point at which something turns or bends: *the car negotiated the twists and turns of the mountain road.* ■ an unexpected development of events: *it was soon time for the next **twist of fate** in his extraordinary career.* ■ a new treatment or outlook; a variation: *she takes conventional subjects and gives them a twist.*
5 [mass noun] a fine strong thread consisting of twisted strands of cotton or silk.
6 Brit. a drink consisting of two ingredients mixed together.
7 a carpet with a tightly curled pile.
– PHRASES **round the twist** Brit. informal out of one's mind; crazy: *the games she plays **drive me round the twist**.* **twist someone's arm** informal pressurize someone into doing something that they are reluctant to do. **twist in the wind** be left in a state of suspense or uncertainty. **twist someone around one's little finger** see LITTLE FINGER. **twists and turns** complicated dealings or circumstances: *the twists and turns of her political career.*
– ORIGIN Old English (as a noun), of Germanic origin; probably from the base of TWIN and TWINE. Current verb senses date from late Middle English.

twist drill ▸ **noun** a drill with a twisted body like that of an auger.

twisted ▸ **adjective 1** forced out of its natural or proper shape; crumpled: *the crash left a trail of twisted metal across the carriageway.* ■ (of a joint) injured by wrenching; sprained: *suffering a twisted ankle, he was carried from the field.*
2 (of a personality or a way of thinking) unpleasantly or unhealthily abnormal; warped: *a man with a twisted mind.*

twisted pair ▸ **noun** Electronics a cable consisting of two wires twisted round each other, used especially for telephone or computer applications.

twister ▸ **noun 1** Brit. informal a swindler; a dishonest person.
2 N. Amer. a tornado.

twist-grip ▸ **noun** a control operated manually by twisting, especially one serving as a handgrip for operating the throttle on a motorcycle or for changing gear on a bicycle.

twist-lock ▸ **noun** a locking device for securing freight containers to the trailers on which they are transported.

twistor /ˈtwɪstə/ ▸ **noun** Physics a complex variable used in some descriptions of space–time.

twist tie ▸ **noun** a small piece of plastic-covered wire, to be twisted around the neck of a plastic bag as a closure.

twisty ▸ **adjective** (**twistier**, **twistiest**) not arranged or moving in a straight line; winding: *a twisty country road.*

twit[1] ▸ **noun** informal, chiefly Brit. a silly or foolish person.
– DERIVATIVES **twittish** adjective.
– ORIGIN 1930s (earlier dialect, in the sense 'tale-bearer'): perhaps from TWIT[2].

twit[2] ▸ **verb** (**twits**, **twitting**, **twitted**) [with obj.] informal tease or taunt (someone), especially in a good-humoured way.
– ORIGIN Old English *ætwītan* 'reproach with', from *æt* 'at' + *wītan* 'to blame'.

twitch ▸ **verb 1** give or cause to give a short, sudden jerking or convulsive movement: [no obj.] *her lips twitched and her eyelids fluttered* | [with obj.] *the dog twitched his ears.* ■ [with obj. and adverbial] cause to move in a specified direction by giving a sharp pull: *he twitched a cigarette out of a packet.*
2 [with obj.] use a twitch to subdue (a horse).
▸ **noun 1** a short, sudden jerking or convulsive movement: *his mouth gave a slight twitch.* ■ a sudden pull or jerk: *he gave a twitch at his moustache.* ■ a sudden sharp sensation; a pang: *he felt a **twitch of** annoyance.*
2 a small noose attached to a stick, which may be twisted around the upper lip or the ear of a horse to subdue it during veterinary procedures.
– ORIGIN Middle English: of Germanic origin; related to Old English *twiccian* 'to pluck, pull sharply'.

twitcher ▸ **noun 1** a person or thing that twitches.
2 Brit. informal a birdwatcher whose main aim is to collect sightings of rare birds.

twitch grass ▸ **noun** [mass noun] couch grass.
– ORIGIN late 16th cent.: *twitch*, alteration of QUITCH.

twitchy ▸ **adjective** (**twitchier**, **twitchiest**) **1** informal nervous; anxious: *she felt twitchy about the man hovering in the background.*
2 given to twitching: *a mouse with a twitchy nose.*

twite /twʌɪt/ ▸ **noun** a Eurasian moorland finch related to the linnet, having streaky brown plumage with a pink rump. ● *Acanthis flavirostris*, family Fringillidae.
– ORIGIN mid 16th cent.: imitative of its call.

twitten /ˈtwɪt(ə)n/ ▸ **noun** Brit. dialect a narrow path or passage between two walls or hedges.
– ORIGIN early 19th cent.: perhaps related to Low German *twiete* 'alley, lane'.

twitter ▸ **verb** [no obj.] **1** (of a bird) give a call consisting of repeated light tremulous sounds. ■ talk in a light, high-pitched voice: *old ladies in the congregation twittered.* ■ talk rapidly and at length in a trivial way: *he **twittered on** about buying a new workshop* | [with direct speech] *'What a great crowd', Perry twittered.*
2 make a posting on the social networking site Twitter: *many active bloggers are twittering more and more these days.*
▸ **noun** a series of short, high-pitched calls or sounds: *his words were cut off by a faint electronic twitter.*

■ [mass noun] idle or ignorant talk: *drawing-room twitter.*
– PHRASES **in** (or **of**) **a twitter** informal in a state of agitation or excitement.
– DERIVATIVES **twitterer** noun, **twittery** adjective.
– ORIGIN late Middle English (as a verb): imitative.

WORD TRENDS See **TWEET**.

'twixt ▶ contraction betwixt.

twizzle informal or dialect ▶ verb spin or cause to spin around.
▶ noun a twisting or spinning movement.
– ORIGIN late 18th cent.: probably imitative, influenced by **TWIST**.

two ▶ cardinal number equivalent to the sum of one and one; one less than three; 2: *two years ago | a romantic weekend for two in Paris | two of Amy's friends.* (Roman numeral: **ii** or **II**) ■ a group or unit of two people or things: *they would straggle home in ones and twos.* ■ two years old: *he is only two.* ■ two o'clock: *the pub closed at two.* ■ a size of garment or other merchandise denoted by two. ■ a playing card or domino with two pips.
– PHRASES **a —— or two** (or **two or three ——**) a small but unspecified number: *a minute or two had passed.* **be two a penny** see **PENNY**. **in two** in or into two halves or pieces: *he tore the piece of paper in two.* **in two shakes** (**of a lamb's tail**) see **SHAKE**. **it takes two to tango** see **TANGO**[1]. **put two and two together** draw an obvious conclusion from what is known or evident. ■ (**put two and two together and make five**) draw a plausible but incorrect conclusion from what is known or evident. **that makes two of us** informal one is in the same position or holds the same opinion as the previous speaker: *'I haven't a clue!' 'That makes two of us.'* **two by two** (or **two and two**) side by side in pairs. **two can play at that game** informal used to assert that one is equally capable of copying another's strategy, to their disadvantage. **two cents** (or **two cents' worth**) N. Amer. informal an unsolicited opinion: *Mom got her two cents in.* **two's company, three's a crowd** two people, especially lovers, should be left alone together. **two heads are better than one** proverb it's helpful to have the advice or opinion of a second person.
– ORIGIN Old English *twā* (feminine and neuter) of Germanic origin; related to Dutch *twee* and German *zwei*, from an Indo-European root shared by Latin and Greek *duo*. Compare with **TWAIN**.

two-bit ▶ adjective [attrib.] N. Amer. informal insignificant, cheap, or worthless: *some two-bit town.*

two-by-four ▶ noun **1** a length of wood with a rectangular cross section nominally two inches by four inches.
2 [usu. as modifier] W. Indian & US a small or insignificant thing, typically a building: *they lived in a two-by-four shack of one bedroom.*

twoc /twɒk/ ▶ verb (**twocs, twoccing, twocced**) [with obj.] Brit. informal steal (a car): *people are fed up with having their cars twocced.*
– ORIGIN 1990s (originally police slang): acronym from *taken without owner's consent.*

two-cycle ▶ adjective another term for **TWO-STROKE**.

two-dimensional ▶ adjective having or appearing to have length and breadth but no depth. ■ lacking depth or substance; superficial: *a nether world of two-dimensional heroes and villains.*
– DERIVATIVES **two-dimensionality** noun, **two-dimensionally** adverb.

two-edged ▶ adjective double-edged.

two-faced ▶ adjective insincere and deceitful.

twofer /ˈtuːfə/ ▶ noun N. Amer. informal an item or offer that comprises two items but is sold for the price of one.
– ORIGIN early 20th cent. (originally denoting a cigar sold at two for a quarter of a cent): representing a pronunciation of *two for* in 'two for the price of one'.

two fingers ▶ plural noun [often treated as sing.] Brit. another term for **V-SIGN** (sense 1).

two-fisted ▶ adjective N. Amer. informal tough, aggressive, or vigorous: *a two-fisted drinking man.*

twofold ▶ adjective twice as great or as numerous: *a twofold increase in the risk.* ■ having two parts or elements: *the twofold demands of the business and motherhood.*
▶ adverb so as to double; to twice the number or amount: *use increased more than twofold from 1979 to 1989.*

two-handed ▶ adjective & adverb having, using, or requiring the use of two hands.
– DERIVATIVES **two-handedly** adverb.

two-hander ▶ noun a play for two actors.

two-horse ▶ adjective (of a race or other contest) in which only two of the competitors or participants are likely winners.

twoness ▶ noun [mass noun] the fact or state of being two; duality.

twonk ▶ noun Brit. informal a stupid or foolish person.
– ORIGIN 1980s: perhaps a blend of **TWIT**[1] or **TWAT** and **PLONKER**.

twopence /ˈtʌp(ə)ns/ (also **tuppence**) ▶ noun Brit. the sum of two pence, especially before decimalization (1971). ■ [with negative] informal a trivial sum; anything at all: *he didn't care twopence for her.*

twopenn'orth /tuːˈpɛnəθ/ ▶ noun an amount of something that is worth or costs twopence. ■ a paltry or insignificant amount.
– PHRASES **add** (or **put in**) **one's twopenn'orth** informal contribute one's opinion.

twopenny /ˈtʌp(ə)ni/ (also **tuppenny**) ▶ adjective [attrib.] Brit. costing or worth two pence, especially before decimalization (1971).

twopenny-halfpenny ▶ adjective Brit. informal not worthy of consideration or respect; worthless or unimportant: *a twopenny-halfpenny dictator.*

two-phase ▶ adjective (of an electric generator, motor, or other device) designed to supply or use simultaneously two separate alternating currents of the same voltage, but with phases differing by half a period.

two-piece ▶ adjective denoting something consisting of two matching items: *a two-piece suit.*
▶ noun a thing consisting of two matching parts, especially a suit.

two-ply ▶ adjective (of a material or yarn) consisting of two layers or strands.
▶ noun [mass noun] **1** yarn consisting of two strands.
2 plywood made by gluing together two layers with the grain in different directions.

two-seater ▶ noun a vehicle or piece of furniture with seating for two people.

two shot ▶ noun a cinema or television shot of two people together.

two-sided ▶ adjective having two sides: *a colourful two-sided leaflet.* ■ having two aspects: *the two-sided nature of the debate.*

twosome ▶ noun a pair of people considered together. ■ a game or dance for or involving two people.

two-spirited ▶ adjective Canadian (of a member of the First Nations) gay, lesbian, transsexual, or transgender.

two-star ▶ adjective given two stars in a grading system in which this denotes a low middle standard, being the next above one-star: *a two-star award in the Michelin guide.* ■ having or denoting the fourth-highest military rank, distinguished in the US armed forces by two stars on the shoulder piece of the uniform.

two-state ▶ adjective capable of existing in either of two states or conditions.

two-step ▶ noun **1** a round dance with a sliding step in march or polka time.
2 [mass noun] another term for **GARAGE** (sense 3 of the noun).

two-stroke ▶ adjective denoting an internal-combustion engine having its power cycle completed in one up-and-down movement of the piston. ■ denoting a vehicle having a two-stroke engine.
▶ noun a two-stroke engine or vehicle.

two-tailed ▶ adjective Statistics (of a test) testing for deviation from the null hypothesis in both directions.

two-tailed pasha ▶ noun see **PASHA**.

two-time ▶ verb [with obj.] informal deceive or be unfaithful to (a lover or spouse).
– DERIVATIVES **two-timer** noun.

two-tone ▶ adjective **1** having two different shades or colours: *a two-tone jacket.*
2 emitting or consisting of two different sounds, typically alternately and at intervals: *a two-tone horn.*
– DERIVATIVES **two-toned** adjective.

'twould archaic ▶ contraction it would.

two-up ▶ noun (in Australia and New Zealand) a gambling game in which two coins are tossed in the air and bets are laid as to whether both will fall heads or tails uppermost.

two-up two-down ▶ noun Brit. informal a house with two reception rooms downstairs and two bedrooms upstairs.

two-way ▶ adjective allowing or involving movement or communication in opposite directions: *a two-way radio | make the interview a two-way process.* ■ (of a switch) permitting a current to be switched on or off from either of two points.
– PHRASES **two-way street** a situation or relationship involving mutual or reciprocal action or obligation: *trust is a two-way street.*

two-way mirror ▶ noun a panel of glass that can be seen through from one side and is a mirror on the other.

two-wheeler ▶ noun a bicycle or motorcycle.

TX ▶ abbreviation Texas (in official postal use).

tx ▶ abbreviation informal thanks; thank you.

-ty[1] ▶ suffix forming nouns denoting quality or condition such as *beauty, royalty.*
– ORIGIN via Old French from Latin *-tas, -tat-.*

-ty[2] ▶ suffix denoting specified groups of ten: *forty | ninety.*
– ORIGIN Old English *-tig.*

Tyburn /ˈtʌɪbəːn/ a place in London, near Marble Arch, where public hangings were held *c.*1300–1783.
– ORIGIN named after a tributary of the Thames, which flows in an underground culvert nearby.

tychism /ˈtʌɪkɪz(ə)m/ ▶ noun [mass noun] Philosophy the doctrine that account must be taken of the element of chance in reasoning or explanation of the universe.
– ORIGIN late 19th cent.: from Greek *tukhē* 'chance' + **-ISM**.

Tycho Brahe see **BRAHE**.

tycoon /tʌɪˈkuːn/ ▶ noun **1** a wealthy, powerful person in business or industry: *a newspaper tycoon.*
2 a title applied by foreigners to the shogun of Japan in power between 1857 and 1868.
– ORIGIN mid 19th cent.: from Japanese *taikun* 'great lord'.

Tyddewi /tɪˈðewi/ Welsh name for **ST DAVID'S**.

tying present participle of **TIE**.

tying-up ▶ noun another term for **AZOTURIA** in horses.

tyke (also **tike**) ▶ noun **1** informal a small child, especially a cheeky or mischievous one: *is the little tyke up to his tricks again?* ■ [usu. as modifier] Canadian an initiation level of sports competition for young children: *tyke hockey.*
2 dated, chiefly Brit. an unpleasant or coarse man.
3 a dog, especially a mongrel.
4 (also **Yorkshire tyke**) Brit. informal a person from Yorkshire.
5 Austral./NZ informal, derogatory a Roman Catholic. [early 20th cent.: alteration of **TAIG**.]
– ORIGIN late Middle English (sense 2, sense 3): from Old Norse *tík* 'bitch'.

Tylenol /ˈtʌɪlənɒl/ ▶ noun chiefly N. Amer. trademark for **PARACETAMOL**.

Tyler[1], John (1790–1862), American Whig statesman, 10th President of the US 1841–5.

Tyler[2], Wat (d.1381), English leader of the Peasants' Revolt of 1381. He captured Canterbury and went on to take London and secure Richard II's concession to the rebels' demands, which included the lifting of the newly imposed poll tax. He was killed by royal supporters.

tylopod /ˈtʌɪlə(ʊ)pɒd/ ▶ noun Zoology an even-toed ungulate mammal of a group that comprises the camels, llamas, and their extinct relatives. They are distinguished by bearing their weight on the sole-pads of the feet rather than on the hoofs, and they do not chew the cud. ● Suborder Tylopoda, order Artiodactyla: family Camelidae.
– ORIGIN late 19th cent.: from modern Latin *Tylopoda*, from Greek *tulos* 'knob' or *tulē* 'callus, cushion' + *pous, pod-* 'foot'.

tympan /ˈtɪmpən/ ▶ noun **1** (in letterpress printing) a layer of packing, typically of paper, placed between the platen and the paper to be printed to equalize the pressure over the whole forme.
2 Architecture another term for **TYMPANUM**.
– ORIGIN late 16th cent. (in sense 1): from French *tympan* or Latin *tympanum* (see **TYMPANUM**). Sense 2 dates from the early 18th cent.

tympana plural form of TYMPANUM.

tympani ▶ plural noun variant spelling of TIMPANI.

tympanic /tɪmˈpanɪk/ ▶ adjective **1** Anatomy relating to or having a tympanum.
2 resembling or acting like a drumhead.

tympanic bone ▶ noun Zoology a small bone supporting the tympanic membrane in some vertebrates.

tympanic membrane ▶ noun a membrane forming part of the organ of hearing, which vibrates in response to sound waves. In humans and other higher vertebrates it forms the eardrum, between the outer and middle ear.

tympanites /ˌtɪmpəˈnʌɪtiːz/ ▶ noun [mass noun] Medicine swelling of the abdomen with air or gas.
– DERIVATIVES **tympanitic** adjective.
– ORIGIN late Middle English: via late Latin from Greek *tumpanitēs*, from *tumpanon* (see TYMPANUM).

tympanum /ˈtɪmpənəm/ ▶ noun (pl. **tympanums** or **tympana** /-nə/) **1** Anatomy & Zoology the tympanic membrane or eardrum. ■ Entomology a membrane covering the hearing organ on the leg or body of some insects, sometimes adapted (as in cicadas) for producing sound.
2 Architecture a vertical recessed triangular space forming the centre of a pediment, typically decorated. ■ a similar space over a door between the lintel and the arch.
3 archaic a drum.
– ORIGIN early 17th cent.: via Latin from Greek *tumpanon* 'drum', based on *tuptein* 'to strike'.

tympany /ˈtɪmpəni/ ▶ noun another term for TYMPANITES (used especially in veterinary medicine).
– ORIGIN early 16th cent.: from Greek *tumpanias*, from *tumpanon* (see TYMPANUM).

Tyndale /ˈtɪnd(ə)l/, William (*c.*1494–1536), English translator and Protestant martyr. Faced with ecclesiastical opposition to his project for translating the Bible into English, Tyndale left England in 1524. His translations of the Bible later formed the basis of the Authorized Version. He was burnt at the stake as a heretic in Antwerp.

Tyndall /ˈtɪnd(ə)l/, John (1820–93), Irish physicist. He is best known for his work on heat but he also worked on the transmission of sound and the scattering of light by suspended particles.

Tyne a river in NE England, formed by the confluence of two headstreams, the North Tyne, which rises in the Cheviot Hills, and the South Tyne, which rises in the northern Pennines. It flows generally eastwards, entering the North Sea at Tynemouth. ■ a shipping forecast area covering English coastal waters roughly from Flamborough Head in the south to Berwick in the north.

Tyne and Wear /wɪə/ a former metropolitan county of NE England.

Tyneside an industrial conurbation on the banks of the River Tyne, in NE England, stretching from Newcastle upon Tyne to the coast.
– DERIVATIVES **Tynesider** noun.

Tynwald /ˈtɪnw(ə)ld/ the parliament of the Isle of Man. It meets annually and consists of the governor (representing the sovereign) and council acting as the upper house, and an elected assembly called the House of Keys.
– ORIGIN from Old Norse *thing-vǫllr* 'place of assembly', from *thing* 'assembly' + *vǫllr* 'field'.

T

type ▶ noun **1** a category of people or things having common characteristics: *this type of heather grows better in a drier habitat* | *blood types*. ■ [with adj. or noun modifier] informal a person of a specified character or nature: *two sporty types in tracksuits*. ■ **(one's type)** informal the sort of person one likes or finds attractive: *she's not really my type*.
2 a person or thing exemplifying the ideal or defining characteristics of something: *she characterized his witty sayings as the type of modern wisdom*. ■ an object, conception, or work of art serving as a model for subsequent artists. ■ a symbol of someone or something: *the dolphin is a conventional type of Christ*. ■ Theology a person or event in the Old Testament taken as a foreshadowing of someone or something in the New Testament. ■ Botany & Zoology an organism or taxon chosen as having the essential characteristics of its group. ■ short for TYPE SPECIMEN.
3 [mass noun] characters or letters that are printed or shown on a screen: *bold type*. ■ [count noun] a piece of metal with a raised letter or character on its upper surface, for use in letterpress printing. ■ such pieces collectively.
4 a design on either side of a medal or coin.
5 Linguistics an abstract category or class of linguistic item or unit, as distinct from actual occurrences in speech or writing. Contrasted with TOKEN.
▶ verb [with obj.] **1** write (something) on a typewriter or computer by pressing the keys: *he typed out the second draft* | [no obj.] *I'm learning to type*.
2 Medicine determine the type to which (a person or their blood or tissue) belongs: *the kidney was typed*.
– PHRASES **in type** Printing composed and ready for printing.
– DERIVATIVES **typal** adjective.
– ORIGIN late 15th cent. (in the sense 'symbol, emblem'): from French, or from Latin *typus*, from Greek *tupos* 'impression, figure, type', from *tuptein* 'to strike'. The use in printing dates from the early 18th cent.; the general sense 'category with common characteristics' arose in the mid 19th cent.

-type ▶ suffix (forming adjectives) resembling or having the characteristics of a specified thing: *the dish-type radio telescope* | *a champagne-type fizzy wine*.

Type A ▶ noun a personality type characterized by ambition, impatience, and competitiveness, and thought to be susceptible to stress and heart disease.

type approval ▶ noun [mass noun] official confirmation from a government or other body that a manufactured item meets required specifications.

Type B ▶ noun a personality type characterized as easy-going and thought to have low susceptibility to stress.

typecast ▶ verb (past and past participle **typecast**) [with obj.] assign (an actor or actress) repeatedly to the same type of role, as a result of the appropriateness of their appearance or previous success in such roles: *he tends to be typecast as the caring, intelligent male*. ■ represent or regard (a person or their role) as fitting a particular stereotype: *people are not as likely to be typecast by their accents as they once were*.

typeface ▶ noun Printing a particular design of type.

type founder ▶ noun Printing a designer and maker of metal type.
– DERIVATIVES **type foundry** noun.

type locality ▶ noun **1** Botany & Zoology the place in which a type specimen was found.
2 Geology a place where deposits regarded as defining the characteristics of a particular geological formation or period occur.

type metal ▶ noun [mass noun] Printing an alloy of lead, tin, and antimony, used for casting type.

typescript ▶ noun a typed copy of a text.

typeset ▶ verb (**typesets**, **typesetting**; past and past participle **typeset**) [with obj.] arrange the type or process the data for (text that is to be printed).
– DERIVATIVES **typesetter** noun, **typesetting** noun.

type site ▶ noun **1** Archaeology a site where objects or materials regarded as defining the characteristics of a particular period were found.
2 another term for TYPE LOCALITY (sense 1).

type species ▶ noun Botany & Zoology the species on which a genus is based and with which the genus name remains associated during any taxonomic revision.

type specimen ▶ noun Botany & Zoology the specimen, or each of a set of specimens, on which the description and name of a new species is based. See also HOLOTYPE, SYNTYPE.

typewriter ▶ noun an electric, electronic, or manual machine with keys for producing print-like characters one at a time on paper inserted round a roller.
– DERIVATIVES **typewriting** noun, **typewritten** adjective.

typhlitis /tɪˈflʌɪtɪs/ ▶ noun [mass noun] Medicine inflammation of the caecum.
– ORIGIN mid 19th cent.: modern Latin, from Greek *tuphlon* 'caecum or blind gut' (from *tuphlos* 'blind') + -ITIS.

typhoid ▶ noun (also **typhoid fever**) [mass noun] an infectious bacterial fever with an eruption of red spots on the chest and abdomen and severe intestinal irritation. ● Typhoid is caused by the bacterium *Salmonella typhi*: Gram-negative rods.
– DERIVATIVES **typhoidal** adjective.
– ORIGIN early 19th cent.: from TYPHUS + -OID.

Typhoid Mary ▶ noun (pl. **Typhoid Marys**) informal a transmitter of undesirable opinions or attitudes.
– ORIGIN the nickname of *Mary* Mallon (died 1938), an Irish-born cook who transmitted typhoid fever in the US.

typhoon /tʌɪˈfuːn/ ▶ noun a tropical storm in the region of the Indian or western Pacific oceans.
– DERIVATIVES **typhonic** adjective.
– ORIGIN late 16th cent.: partly via Portuguese from Arabic *ṭūfān* (perhaps from Greek *tuphōn* 'whirlwind'); reinforced by Chinese dialect *tai fung* 'big wind'.

typhus /ˈtʌɪfəs/ ▶ noun [mass noun] an infectious disease caused by rickettsiae, characterized by a purple rash, headaches, fever, and usually delirium, and historically a cause of high mortality during wars and famines. There are several forms, transmitted by vectors such as lice, ticks, mites, and rat fleas. Also called SPOTTED FEVER.
– ORIGIN mid 17th cent.: modern Latin, from Greek *tuphos* 'smoke, stupor', from *tuphein* 'to smoke'.

typical ▶ adjective **1** having the distinctive qualities of a particular type of person or thing: *a typical day* | *a typical example of 1930s art deco* | *typical symptoms*. ■ characteristic of a particular person or thing: *he brushed the incident aside with typical good humour* | *how* **typical of** *Iris to think of such a detail*. ■ informal showing the characteristics expected of or popularly associated with a particular person or thing: *'Typical woman!' John said disapprovingly*.
2 representative as a symbol; symbolic: *the pit is* **typical of** *hell*.
– DERIVATIVES **typicality** /-ˈkalɪti/ noun, **typically** adverb [sentence adverb] *typically, she showed no alarm* | [as submodifier] *a typically British stiff upper lip*.
– ORIGIN early 17th cent.: from medieval Latin *typicalis*, via Latin from Greek *tupikos*, from *tupos* (see TYPE).

typify ▶ verb (**typifies**, **typifying**, **typified**) [with obj.] **1** be characteristic or a representative example of: *tough, low-lying vegetation typifies this arctic area*.
2 represent; symbolize: *the sun typified the Greeks, and the moon the Persians*.
– DERIVATIVES **typification** noun.
– ORIGIN mid 17th cent.: from Latin *typus* (see TYPE) + -FY.

typing ▶ noun [mass noun] the action or skill of writing something by means of a typewriter or computer: *they learned shorthand and typing* | [as modifier] *typing errors*. ■ writing produced by typing: *five pages of typing*.

typist ▶ noun a person who is skilled in typing, especially one who is employed for this purpose.

typo /ˈtʌɪpəʊ/ ▶ noun (pl. **typos**) informal a typographical error.
– ORIGIN early 19th cent.: abbreviation.

typography /tʌɪˈpɒgrəfi/ ▶ noun [mass noun] the style and appearance of printed matter. ■ the art or procedure of arranging type or processing data and printing from it.
– DERIVATIVES **typographer** noun, **typographic** adjective, **typographical** adjective, **typographically** adverb.
– ORIGIN early 17th cent.: from French *typographie* or modern Latin *typographia* (see TYPE, -GRAPHY).

typology ▶ noun (pl. **typologies**) **1** a classification according to general type, especially in archaeology, psychology, or the social sciences: *a typology of Saxon cremation vessels*. ■ [mass noun] study or analysis using a classification according to a general type.
2 [mass noun] the study and interpretation of types and symbols, originally especially in the Bible.
– DERIVATIVES **typological** /-əˈlɒdʒɪk(ə)l/ adjective, **typologist** noun.
– ORIGIN mid 19th cent. (in sense 2): from Greek *tupos* 'type' + -LOGY.

Tyr /tɪə/ Scandinavian Mythology the god of battle, identified with Mars, after whom Tuesday is named.

tyramine /ˈtʌɪrəmiːn/ ▶ noun [mass noun] Biochemistry a compound which occurs naturally in cheese and other foods and can cause dangerously high blood pressure in people taking a monoamine oxidase inhibitor. ● An amine related to tyrosine; chem. formula: $C_6H_4(OH)CH_2CH_2NH_2$.
– ORIGIN early 20th cent.: from *tyr(osine)* + AMINE.

tyrannical /tɪˈranɪk(ə)l, tʌɪ-/ ▶ adjective exercising power in a cruel or arbitrary way: *a tyrannical government*. ■ characteristic of tyranny; oppressive and controlling: *a momentary quieting of her tyrannical appetite*.
– DERIVATIVES **tyrannically** adverb.
– ORIGIN mid 16th cent.: from Old French *tyrannique*, via Latin from Greek *turannikos*, from *turannos* (see TYRANT).

tyrannicide /tɪˈranɪsʌɪd, tʌɪ-/ ▶ **noun** [mass noun] the killing of a tyrant. ■ [count noun] the killer of a tyrant.
– ORIGIN mid 17th cent.: from French, from Latin *tyrannicida* 'killer of a tyrant', *tyrannicidium* 'killing of a tyrant' (see TYRANT, -CIDE).

tyrannize /ˈtɪrənʌɪz/ (also **tyrannise**) ▶ **verb** [with obj.] rule or treat (someone) despotically or cruelly: *she tyrannized her family* | [no obj.] *he tyrannizes over the servants*.
– ORIGIN late 15th cent.: from French *tyranniser*, from *tyran* 'tyrant'.

tyrannosaur /tɪˈranəsɔː, tʌɪ-/ (also **tyrannosaurus** /tɪˌranəˈsɔːrəs/) ▶ **noun** a very large bipedal carnivorous dinosaur of the late Cretaceous period, with powerful jaws and small claw-like front legs. ● Family Tyrannosauridae, infraorder Carnosauria, suborder Theropoda: several species, in particular *Tyrannosaurus rex*.
– ORIGIN modern Latin, from Greek *turannos* 'tyrant' + *sauros* 'lizard', on the pattern of *dinosaur*.

tyrannulet /tʌɪˈranjʊlɪt/ ▶ **noun** a small tropical American bird of the tyrant flycatcher family, typically with drab greyish or greenish plumage. ● Family Tyrannidae: several genera and many species.
– ORIGIN diminutive based on modern Latin *Tyrannus* (genus name), from Greek *turannos* 'tyrant'.

tyranny ▶ **noun** (pl. **tyrannies**) [mass noun] cruel and oppressive government or rule: *refugees fleeing tyranny and oppression*. ■ [count noun] a state under cruel and oppressive government. ■ cruel, unreasonable, or arbitrary use of power or control: *the tyranny of her stepmother* | figurative *the tyranny of the nine-to-five day*. ■ (especially in ancient Greece) rule by one who has absolute power without legal right.
– DERIVATIVES **tyrannous** adjective, **tyrannously** adverb.
– ORIGIN late Middle English: from Old French *tyrannie*, from late Latin *tyrannia*, from Latin *turannus* (see TYRANT).

tyrant /ˈtʌɪr(ə)nt/ ▶ **noun** **1** a cruel and oppressive ruler: *the tyrant was deposed by popular demonstrations*. ■ a person exercising power or control in a cruel, unreasonable, or arbitrary way: *her father was a tyrant and a bully*. ■ (especially in ancient Greece) a ruler who seized absolute power without legal right.
2 a tyrant flycatcher.
– ORIGIN Middle English: from Old French, via Latin from Greek *turannos*.

tyrant flycatcher ▶ **noun** a New World perching bird that resembles the Old World flycatchers in behaviour, typically with brightly coloured plumage. ● Family Tyrannidae: many genera and numerous species.
– ORIGIN mid 18th cent.: so named because of its aggressive behaviour towards other birds approaching its nest.

Tyre /ˈtʌɪə/ a port on the Mediterranean in southern Lebanon; pop. 41,800 (est. 2009). Founded in the 2nd millennium BC as a colony of Sidon, it was for centuries a Phoenician port and trading centre.
– DERIVATIVES **Tyrian** adjective & noun.

tyre (US **tire**) ▶ **noun** a rubber covering, typically inflated or surrounding an inflated inner tube, placed round a wheel to form a soft contact with the road. ■ a strengthening band of metal fitted around the rim of a wheel, especially of a railway vehicle.
– DERIVATIVES **tyred** adjective [in combination] *a rubber-tyred vehicle*.
– ORIGIN late 15th cent. (denoting the curved pieces of iron plate with which carriage wheels were formerly shod): perhaps a variant of archaic *tire*, shortening of ATTIRE (because the tyre was the 'clothing' of the wheel).

tyre gauge ▶ **noun** a portable pressure gauge for measuring the air pressure in a tyre.

Tyrian purple ▶ **noun** see PURPLE.

tyro /ˈtʌɪrəʊ/ (also **tiro**) ▶ **noun** (pl. **tyros**) a beginner or novice.
– ORIGIN late Middle English: from Latin *tiro*, medieval Latin *tyro* 'recruit'.

Tyrode's solution /ˈtʌɪrəʊdz/ (also **Tyrode's**) ▶ **noun** [mass noun] Biology & Medicine a type of physiological saline solution.
– ORIGIN 1920s: named after Maurice V. *Tyrode* (1878–1930), American pharmacologist.

Tyrol /tɪˈrəʊl/ an Alpine state of western Austria; capital, Innsbruck. The southern part was ceded to Italy after the First World War. German name **TIROL**.
– DERIVATIVES **Tyrolean** /ˌtɪrəˈliːən/ adjective & noun, **Tyrolese** adjective & noun.

Tyrolean finish ▶ **noun** a rough-textured plaster finish for an exterior wall.

Tyrone /tɪˈrəʊn/ one of the Six Counties of Northern Ireland, formerly an administrative area; chief town, Omagh.

tyrosinase /ˈtʌɪrəsɪneɪz, tʌɪˈrɒs-/ ▶ **noun** [mass noun] Biochemistry a copper-containing enzyme which catalyses the formation of quinones from phenols and polyphenols (e.g. melanin from tyrosine).
– ORIGIN late 19th cent.: from TYROSINE + -ASE.

tyrosine /ˈtʌɪrəsiːn/ ▶ **noun** [mass noun] Biochemistry a hydrophilic amino acid which is a constituent of most proteins and is important in the synthesis of some hormones. ● Chem. formula: $C_6H_4(OH)CH_2CH(NH_2)COOH$.
– ORIGIN mid 19th cent.: formed irregularly from Greek *turos* 'cheese' + -INE[4].

Tyrrhene /ˈtɪriːn/ ▶ **adjective & noun** archaic term for ETRUSCAN.
– ORIGIN late Middle English: from Latin *Tyrrhenus* 'Etruscan'.

Tyrrhenian /tɪˈriːnɪən/ ▶ **adjective** **1** relating to or denoting the Tyrrhenian Sea or the surrounding region.
2 archaic Etruscan.
▶ **noun** archaic an Etruscan.

Tyrrhenian Sea a part of the Mediterranean Sea between mainland Italy and the islands of Sicily and Sardinia.

Tyson /ˈtʌɪs(ə)n/, Mike (b.1966), American boxer; full name *Michael Gerald Tyson*. He became undisputed world heavyweight champion in 1987, winning the WBA, WBC, and IBF titles. He was imprisoned in 1992 for rape; after his release in 1995 he reclaimed the WBC and WBA titles in the following year.

tystie /ˈtʌɪsti, ˈtiːsti/ ▶ **noun** (pl. **tysties**) chiefly Scottish another term for BLACK GUILLEMOT.
– ORIGIN late 18th cent.: of Norse origin.

Tyumen /tjuːˈmɛn/ a city in west Siberian Russia, in the eastern foothills of the Ural Mountains; pop. 560,000 (est. 2008). Founded in 1586, it is regarded as the oldest city in Siberia.

tyuyamunite /ˌtjuːjəˈmuːnʌɪt/ ▶ **noun** [mass noun] a yellowish earthy mineral which is an ore of uranium. It consists of a hydrated vanadate of calcium and uranium.
– ORIGIN early 20th cent.: from *Tyuya Muyun*, the name of a Kyrgyz village, + -ITE[1].

tzaddik ▶ **noun** variant spelling of TSADDIK.

tzar ▶ **noun** variant spelling of TSAR.

Tzara /ˈzɑːrə/, Tristan (1896–1963), Romanian-born French poet; born *Samuel Rosenstock*. He was one of the founders of the Dada movement and wrote its manifestos. His poetry, with its continuous flow of unconnected images, helped form the basis for surrealism.

tzarevich ▶ **noun** variant spelling of TSAREVICH.

tzarina ▶ **noun** variant spelling of TSARINA.

tzatziki /tsatˈsiːki/ ▶ **noun** [mass noun] a Greek side dish of yogurt with cucumber, garlic, and often mint.
– ORIGIN modern Greek.

tzedakah /tsɛˈdɒka/ ▶ **noun** [mass noun] (among Jewish people) charitable giving, typically seen as a moral obligation.
– ORIGIN from Hebrew *ṣĕḏāqāh* 'righteousness'.

Tzeltal /tsɛlˈtɑːl, ˈtsɛltɑːl/; /s-/ ▶ **noun** (pl. **same** or **Tzeltals**) **1** a member of an American Indian people inhabiting parts of southern Mexico.
2 [mass noun] the Mayan language of the Tzeltal.
▶ **adjective** relating to the Tzeltal or their language.
– ORIGIN Spanish name of one of the three regions of the Mexican state of *Chiapas*, of uncertain origin.

tzigane /tsɪˈgɑːn/ ▶ **noun** (pl. **same** or **tziganes**) a Hungarian Gypsy.
– ORIGIN mid 18th cent.: from French, from Hungarian *c(z)igány*.

tzimmes (also **tzimmis**) ▶ **noun** variant spelling of TSIMMES.

T-zone ▶ **noun** the central part of a person's face, including the forehead, nose, and chin, especially as having oilier skin than the rest of the face.
– ORIGIN *T* designating the shape of the area defined.

Tzotzil /ˈtsəʊtsɪl, tsəʊtˈsɪl, s-/ ▶ **noun** (pl. **same** or **Tzotzils**) **1** a member of an American Indian people inhabiting parts of southern Mexico.
2 [mass noun] the Mayan language of the Tzotzil.
▶ **adjective** relating to the Tzotzil or their language.
– ORIGIN the name in Tzotzil.

Tzu-po /tsuːˈpəʊ/ variant of ZIBO.

T

U[1] /juː/ (also **u**) ▶ **noun** (pl. **Us** or **U's**) **1** the twenty-first letter of the alphabet. ■ denoting the next after T in a set of items, categories, etc.
2 (**U**) a shape like that of a capital U, especially a cross section: [in combination] *U-shaped glaciated valleys.*

U[2] /juː/ ▶ **abbreviation** ■ (in names of sports clubs) United: *Oxford U.* ■ Brit. universal (denoting films classified as suitable without restriction). ■ Uruguay (international vehicle registration).
▶ **symbol** the chemical element uranium.

U[3] /juː/ ▶ **adjective** Brit. informal (of language or social behaviour) characteristic of or appropriate to the upper social classes: *U manners.*
– ORIGIN abbreviation of UPPER CLASS; coined in 1954 by Alan S. C. Ross, professor of linguistics, the term was popularized by its use in Nancy Mitford's *Noblesse Oblige* (1956).

U[4] /uː/ ▶ **noun** a Burmese title of respect before a man's name, equivalent to Mr: *U Thien San.*

u ▶ **abbreviation** Physics denoting quantum states or wave functions which change sign on inversion through the origin. The opposite of G. [from German *ungerade* 'odd'.]
▶ **symbol** [in combination] (in units of measurement) micro- (10^{-6}). [substituted for MU.]

UAE ▶ **abbreviation** United Arab Emirates.

uakari /wəˈkɑːri/ ▶ **noun** (pl. **uakaris**) a short-tailed monkey with a long, coarse coat and a bare red, white, or black face, found in the Amazon rainforest.
● Genus *Cacajao*, family Cebidae: two or three species.
– ORIGIN mid 19th cent.: from Tupi.

UB40 ▶ **noun** (formerly in the UK) a card issued to a person registered as unemployed.

ubac /ˈjuːbak/ ▶ **noun** Geography a mountain slope which receives little sunshine, especially one facing north. Compare with ADRET.
– ORIGIN 1930s: from French, apparently from Latin *opacus* 'shady'.

Ubaid /uːˈbeɪd/ ▶ **adjective** Archaeology relating to or denoting a pre-urban culture in Mesopotamia, dated to the 5th millennium BC. ■ (as noun **the Ubaid**) the Ubaid culture or period.
– ORIGIN from the name of the tell Al *'Ubaid* near Ur in the Euphrates valley.

Ubanghi Shari /juːˌbaŋɡɪ ˈʃɑːri/ former name (until 1958) for CENTRAL AFRICAN REPUBLIC.

U-bend ▶ **noun** a section of a pipe, in particular of a waste pipe, shaped like a U.

uber- /ˈuːbə/ (also **über-** /ˈyːbə/) ▶ **combining form** denoting an outstanding or supreme example of a particular kind of person or thing: *she's a self-proclaimed uberbitch | an audience composed largely of ubergeeks.* ■ to a great or extreme degree: *an uber-cool bar.*
– ORIGIN German *über* 'over', after ÜBERMENSCH.

Übermensch /ˈuːbəˌmɛnʃ/ ▶ **noun** the ideal superior man of the future who could rise above conventional Christian morality to create and impose his own values, originally described by Nietzsche in *Thus Spake Zarathustra* (1883–5). Also called SUPERMAN and OVERMAN.
– ORIGIN German, literally 'superhuman person'.

ubiety /juːˈbʌɪɪti/ ▶ **noun** [mass noun] literary the condition of being in a definite place.
– ORIGIN late 17th cent.: from medieval Latin *ubietas*, from Latin *ubi* 'where'.

-ubility ▶ **suffix** forming nouns from or corresponding to adjectives ending in *-uble* (such as *solubility* from *soluble*).

ubiquinone /juːˈbɪkwɪnəʊn/ ▶ **noun** Biochemistry any of a class of compounds which occur in all living cells and which act as electron-transfer agents in cell respiration. They are substituted quinones.
– ORIGIN 1950s: blend of UBIQUITOUS and QUINONE.

ubiquitarian /juːˌbɪkwɪˈtɛːrɪən/ Christian Theology ▶ **noun** a person, typically a Lutheran, who believes that Christ is present everywhere at all times.
▶ **adjective** relating to or believing in such a doctrine.
– ORIGIN mid 17th cent.: from modern Latin *ubiquitarius* (from Latin *ubique* 'everywhere') + -AN.

ubiquitin /juːˈbɪkwɪtɪn/ ▶ **noun** [mass noun] Biochemistry a compound found in living cells which plays a role in the degradation of defective and superfluous proteins. It is a single-chain polypeptide.
– ORIGIN 1970s: from UBIQUITOUS + -IN[1].

ubiquitous /juːˈbɪkwɪtəs/ ▶ **adjective** present, appearing, or found everywhere: *his ubiquitous influence was felt by all the family | cowboy hats are ubiquitous among the male singers.*
– DERIVATIVES **ubiquitously** adverb, **ubiquitousness** noun, **ubiquity** noun.
– ORIGIN mid 19th cent.: from modern Latin *ubiquitas* (from Latin *ubique* 'everywhere', from *ubi* 'where') + -OUS.

-uble ▶ **suffix** (forming adjectives) able to: *voluble.* ■ able to be: *soluble.* Compare with -ABLE.
– ORIGIN from French, from Latin *-ubilis.*

-ubly ▶ **suffix** forming adverbs corresponding to adjectives ending in *-uble* (such as *volubly* corresponding to *voluble*).

U-boat ▶ **noun** a German submarine used in the First or Second World War.
– ORIGIN from German *U-Boot*, abbreviation of *Unterseeboot* 'undersea boat'.

UBR ▶ **abbreviation** uniform business rate (a tax on business property in England and Wales).

ubuntu /ʊˈbʊntʊ/ ▶ **noun** [mass noun] S. African a quality that includes the essential human virtues; compassion and humanity.
– ORIGIN Xhosa and Zulu.

UC ▶ **abbreviation** University College.

u.c. ▶ **abbreviation** upper case.

UCAS /ˈjuːkas/ ▶ **abbreviation** (in the UK) Universities and Colleges Admissions Service (created by the amalgamation of UCCA and PCAS in the 1993–4 academic year).

UCCA /ˈʌkə/ ▶ **abbreviation** (in the UK) Universities Central Council on Admissions (incorporated into UCAS in the 1993–4 academic year).

Uccello /uːˈtʃɛləʊ/, Paolo (*c.*1397–1475), Italian painter; born *Paolo di Dono.* His paintings are associated with the early use of perspective and include *The Rout of San Romano* (*c.*1454–7) and *A Hunt in a Forest* (after 1460), one of the earliest known paintings on canvas.

UDA ▶ **abbreviation** Ulster Defence Association (a Loyalist paramilitary organization).

udal /ˈjuːd(ə)l/ ▶ **noun** [mass noun] Law a kind of freehold tenure based on uninterrupted possession, formerly practised in northern Europe and still in use in Orkney and Shetland.
– ORIGIN late 15th cent.: from Old Norse *othal* 'property held by inheritance', of Germanic origin.

UDC ▶ **abbreviation** ■ (in the UK) Urban Development Corporation. ■ historical (in the UK) Urban District Council.

udder ▶ **noun** the mammary gland of female cattle, sheep, goats, horses, and related ungulates, hanging near the hind legs as a bag-like organ with two or more teats.
– DERIVATIVES **uddered** adjective [in combination].
– ORIGIN Old English *ūder*, of West Germanic origin; related to Dutch *uier* and German *Euter.*

UDI ▶ **abbreviation** unilateral declaration of independence.

Udmurt /ˈʊdmʊət/ ▶ **noun 1** a member of a people of central Russia, living mainly in Udmurtia.
2 [mass noun] the Finno-Ugric language of the Udmurts, with about 500,000 speakers. Formerly called VOTYAK.
▶ **adjective** relating to or denoting the Udmurts or their language.

Udmurtia /ʊdˈmʊətɪə/ an autonomous republic in central Russia; pop. 1,527,800 (est. 2009); capital, Izhevsk. Also called **Udmurt Republic** /ˈʊdmʊət/.

udon /ˈuːdɒn/ ▶ **noun** [mass noun] (in Japanese cookery) wheat pasta made in thick strips.
– ORIGIN Japanese.

UDR ▶ **abbreviation** Ulster Defence Regiment (a former reserve unit of the British army based in Northern Ireland).

udyog /ˈʊdjɔːg/ ▶ **noun** Indian a company, especially one involved in manufacturing.
– ORIGIN from Hindi.

UEFA /juːˈiːfə, -ˈeɪfə/ ▶ **abbreviation** Union of European Football Associations, the governing body of soccer in Europe.

U-ey /ˈjuːi/ ▶ **noun** (pl. **U-eys**) informal a U-turn.

Ufa /uːˈfɑː/ the capital of Bashkiria, in the Ural Mountains; pop. 1,021,500 (est. 2008).

Uffizi /ʊˈfiːtsi/ an art gallery and museum in Florence, housing one of Europe's finest art collections.

UFO ▶ **noun** (pl. **UFOs**) a mysterious object seen in the sky for which it is claimed no orthodox scientific explanation can be found, often supposed to be a vehicle carrying extraterrestrials.
– ORIGIN 1950s: acronym from *unidentified flying object.*

ufology /juːˈfɒlədʒi/ ▶ **noun** [mass noun] the study of UFOs.
– DERIVATIVES **ufological** adjective, **ufologist** noun.

ugali /uːˈgɑːli/ ▶ **noun** [mass noun] a type of maize porridge eaten in east and central Africa.
– ORIGIN Kiswahili.

Uganda /juːˈgandə/ a landlocked country in East Africa; pop. 32,369,600 (est. 2009); languages, English (official), Swahili, and others; capital, Kampala.

Ethnically and culturally diverse, Uganda became a British protectorate in 1894 and an independent Commonwealth state in 1962. The country was ruled 1971–9 by the brutal dictator Idi Amin, who came to power after an army coup. His overthrow, with Tanzanian military support, was followed by several years of conflict, partly resolved in 1986 by the formation of a government under President Yoweri Museveni.

– DERIVATIVES **Ugandan** adjective & noun.

Ugarit /ʊ'gɑːrɪt, 'juːgərɪt/ an ancient port and Bronze Age trading city in northern Syria, founded in Neolithic times and destroyed by the Sea Peoples in about the 12th century BC. Its people spoke a Semitic language written in a distinctive cuneiform alphabet.
– DERIVATIVES **Ugaritic** /ˌjuːgə'rɪtɪk/ adjective & noun.

Ugg boot (also **Ugh boot**) ▸ noun trademark a type of soft sheepskin boot.
– ORIGIN 1960s: perhaps named after *Ugh*, a series of cartoon characters, or an abbreviation of UGLY.

ugh ▸ exclamation informal used to express disgust or horror: *ugh—what's this disgusting object?*
– ORIGIN mid 18th cent.: imitative.

Ugli fruit /'ʌgli/ ▸ noun (pl. **same**) trademark a mottled green and yellow citrus fruit which is a hybrid of a grapefruit and a tangerine. ● This fruit is obtained from the tree *Citrus × tangelo*, family Rutaceae.
– ORIGIN 1930s: *ugli*, alteration of UGLY.

ugly ▸ adjective (**uglier**, **ugliest**) **1** unpleasant or repulsive, especially in appearance: *she thought she was ugly and fat* | *the ugly sound of a fire alarm.*
2 involving or likely to involve violence or other unpleasantness: *the mood in the room turned ugly.*
■ unpleasantly suggestive; causing disquiet: *ugly rumours persisted that there had been a cover-up.*
■ morally repugnant: *racism and its most ugly manifestations, racial attacks and harassment.*
– DERIVATIVES **uglification** noun, **uglify** verb (**uglifies**, **uglifying**, **uglified**), **uglily** adverb, **ugliness** noun.
– ORIGIN Middle English: from Old Norse *uggligr* 'to be dreaded', from *ugga* 'to dread'.

ugly American ▸ noun informal an American who behaves offensively when abroad.

ugly duckling ▸ noun a person who turns out to be beautiful or talented against all expectations.
– ORIGIN from the title of one of Hans Christian Andersen's fairy tales, in which the 'ugly duckling' becomes a swan.

Ugrian /'uːgrɪən, 'juː-/ ▸ adjective another term for UGRIC.

Ugric /'uːgrɪk, 'juː-/ ▸ adjective relating to or denoting a branch of the Finno-Ugric language family including only Hungarian and the Ob-Ugric languages.
– ORIGIN from Russian *ugry* (the name of a people dwelling east of the Urals) + -IC.

uh ▸ exclamation **1** used to express hesitation: *I was just, uh, passing by.*
2 used in questions to invite agreement or further comment or to express a lack of understanding: *You want to get there pretty bad, uh?*
– ORIGIN 1960s: imitative.

UHF ▸ abbreviation ultra-high frequency.

uh-huh ▸ exclamation used to express assent or as a non-committal response to a question or remark: *'Do you understand?' 'Uh-huh.'*
– ORIGIN 1920s: imitative.

uhlan /'uːlɑːn, 'juː-, ʊ'lɑːn/ ▸ noun historical a cavalryman armed with a lance as a member of various European armies.
– ORIGIN mid 18th cent.: via French and German from Polish *(h)ulan*, from Turkish *oğlan* 'youth, servant'.

uh-oh ▸ exclamation an expression of alarm, dismay, or realization of a difficulty: *Uh-oh! Take cover!*

UHT ▸ abbreviation Brit. ultra heat treated (a process used to extend the shelf life of milk).

uh-uh ▸ exclamation used to express a negative response to a question or remark.
– ORIGIN 1920s: imitative.

Uighur /'wiːgə/ (also **Uigur**, **Uygur**) ▸ noun **1** a member of a Turkic people of NW China, particularly the Xinjiang region, and adjoining areas.
2 [mass noun] the Turkic language of the Uighurs, which has about 7 million speakers.
▸ adjective relating to the Uighurs or their language.
– ORIGIN the name in Uighur.

uillean pipes /'ɪlɪn, 'ɪlən/ ▸ plural noun Irish bagpipes played held on the knee using bellows worked by the elbow, and having three extra pipes on which chords can be played.
– ORIGIN early 20th cent.: from Irish *píob uilleann*, literally 'pipe of the elbow'.

uintathere /juː'ɪntəθɪə/ ▸ noun an early fossil hoofed mammal of the Eocene epoch, with a heavy rhinoceros-like body and a grotesque head with several bony horn-like swellings and long canine teeth. ● Family Uintatheriidae, order Dinocerata, including *Uintatherium*.
– ORIGIN late 19th cent.: from modern Latin *Uintatherium*, from *Uinta(h)*, the name of a mountain range in Utah, US (where remains were found), + Greek *thērion* 'wild beast'.

Uist /'juːɪst/ two islands in the Outer Hebrides, **North Uist** and **South Uist**, lying to the south of Lewis and Harris and separated from each other by the island of Benbecula.

uitlander /'eɪtlandə, 'ɔɪt-/ ▸ noun S. African a foreigner or outsider.
– ORIGIN Afrikaans, from Dutch *uit* 'out' + *land* 'land'.

ujamaa /ˌʊdʒa'mɑː/ ▸ noun [mass noun] (in Tanzania) a socialist system of village cooperatives based on equality of opportunity and self-help, established in the 1960s.
– ORIGIN Kiswahili, literally 'brotherhood', from *jamaa* 'family', from Arabic *jamā'a* 'community'.

Ujiyamada /ˌuːdʒiːjə'mɑːdə/ former name (until 1956) for ISE.

Ujjain /'uːdʒʌɪn/ a city in west central India, in Madhya Pradesh; pop. 483,300 (est. 2009).

Ujung Pandang /uːˌdʒʊŋ pan'daŋ/ the chief seaport of the island of Sulawesi in Indonesia; pop. 1,168,300 (est. 2005). Former name (until 1973) MAKASSAR.

UK ▸ abbreviation United Kingdom.

UKAEA ▸ abbreviation United Kingdom Atomic Energy Authority.

ukase /juː'keɪz/ ▸ noun (in tsarist Russia) a decree with the force of law. ■ an arbitrary or peremptory command.
– ORIGIN from Russian *ukaz* 'ordinance, edict', from *ukazat'* 'show, decree'.

uke ▸ noun informal short for UKULELE.

ukelele ▸ noun variant spelling of UKULELE.

UKIP /'juːkɪp/ ▸ abbreviation (in the UK) United Kingdom Independence Party.

ukiyo-e /uːˌkiːjəʊ'eɪ/ ▸ noun [mass noun] a school of Japanese art depicting subjects from everyday life, dominant in the 17th–19th centuries.
– ORIGIN Japanese, from *ukiyo* 'fleeting world' + *e* 'picture'.

Ukraine /juː'kreɪn/ a country in eastern Europe, to the north of the Black Sea; pop. 45,700,400 (est. 2009); languages, Ukrainian and Russian; capital, Kiev.

Ukraine was united with Russia, with the capital at Kiev, in the 9th century. After a period of division between Poland, Russia, and the Ottoman Empire it was reunited with Russia in 1785. Briefly independent following the 1917 revolution, it became one of the original constituent republics (and the third largest) of the USSR. In 1991, on the break-up of the Soviet Union, Ukraine became an independent republic.

– ORIGIN from obsolete Russian *ukraina* 'frontier regions', from *u* 'at' + *kraĭ* 'edge'.

Ukrainian ▸ noun **1** a native or inhabitant of Ukraine, or a person of Ukrainian descent.
2 [mass noun] the Eastern Slavic language of Ukraine, which has about 60 million speakers worldwide.
▸ adjective relating to Ukraine, its people, or their language.

ukulele /ˌjuːkə'leɪli/ (also **ukelele**) ▸ noun a small four-stringed guitar of Hawaiian origin.
– ORIGIN late 19th cent.: from Hawaiian, literally 'jumping flea'.

Ulala /ˌuːlɑː'lɑː/ former name (until 1932) for GORNO-ALTAISK.

ulama ▸ noun variant spelling of ULEMA.

Ulan Bator /ˌuːlɑːn 'bɑːtə/ (also **Ulaanbaatar**) the capital of Mongolia; pop. 922,100 (est. 2009). Former name (until 1924) URGA.

Ulanova /uː'lɑːnəvə/, Galina (Sergeevna) (1910–98), Russian ballet dancer. She gave notable interpretations of *Swan Lake* and *Giselle* and created the role of Juliet in Prokofiev's *Romeo and Juliet*.

Ulan-Ude /uːˌlɑːnuː'deɪ/ an industrial city in southern Siberian Russia, capital of the republic of Buryatia; pop. 340,800 (est. 2008). Former name (until 1934) VERKHNEUDINSK.

-ular ▸ suffix forming adjectives, sometimes corresponding to nouns ending in *-ule* (such as *pustular* corresponding to *pustule*), but often without diminutive force (as in *angular*, *granular*).
– DERIVATIVES **-ularity** suffix forming corresponding nouns.
– ORIGIN from Latin *-ularis*.

ulcer /'ʌlsə/ ▸ noun an open sore on an external or internal surface of the body, caused by a break in the skin or mucous membrane which fails to heal. Ulcers range from small, painful sores in the mouth to bedsores and serious lesions of the stomach or intestine.
■ a moral blemish or corrupting influence: *he's a conman with an incurable ulcer called gambling.*
– DERIVATIVES **ulcered** adjective
– ORIGIN late Middle English: from Latin *ulcus*, *ulcer-*.

ulcerate ▸ verb [no obj.] develop into or become affected by an ulcer.
– DERIVATIVES **ulceration** noun, **ulcerative** adjective.
– ORIGIN late Middle English: from Latin *ulcerat-* 'made ulcerous', from the verb *ulcerare*.

ulcerous /'ʌlsərəs/ ▸ adjective having or constituting an ulcer: *the parasites created ulcerous sores.*

-ule ▸ suffix forming diminutive nouns such as *capsule*, *pustule*.
– ORIGIN from Latin *-ulus*, *-ula*, *-ulum*.

Uleåborg /ˌuːleəʊ'bɒrj/ Swedish name for OULU.

ulema /'ʊləmə, 'uːlɪmə, ˌuːlə'mɑː/ (also **ulama**) ▸ noun [treated as sing. or pl.] a body of Muslim scholars who are recognized as having specialist knowledge of Islamic sacred law and theology. ■ a member of such a body.
– ORIGIN from Arabic *'ulamā'*, plural of *'ālim* 'learned', from *'alima* 'know'.

-ulent ▸ suffix (forming adjectives) abounding in; full of: *fraudulent* | *purulent*. Compare with -LENT.
– DERIVATIVES **-ulence** suffix forming corresponding nouns.
– ORIGIN from Latin *-ulentus*.

ulexite /'juːlɛksʌɪt/ ▸ noun [mass noun] a mineral occurring on alkali flats as rounded masses of small white crystals. It is a hydrated borate of sodium and calcium.
– ORIGIN mid 19th cent.: from George L. *Ulex* (died 1883), German chemist, + -ITE[1].

Ulfilas /'ʊlfɪlas/ (also **Wulfila**) (*c.*311–*c.*381), bishop and translator. Believed to be of Cappadocian descent, he became bishop of the Visigoths in 341. His translation of the Bible from Greek into Gothic (of which fragments survive) is the earliest known translation of the Bible into a Germanic language. Ulfilas is traditionally held to have invented the Gothic alphabet, based on Latin and Greek characters.

Ulhasnagar /ˌuːlhəs'nʌgə/ a city in western India, in the state of Maharashtra; pop. 563,800 (est. 2009).

ullage /'ʌlɪdʒ/ ▸ noun [mass noun] the amount by which a container falls short of being full. ■ loss of liquid, by evaporation or leakage.
– ORIGIN late Middle English: from Anglo-Norman French *ulliage*, from Old French *euillier* 'fill up', based on Latin *oculus* 'eye' (with reference to a container's bunghole).

ullage rocket ▸ noun an auxiliary rocket engine used in weightless conditions to provide sufficient acceleration to maintain the flow of liquid propellant from the tank.

Ulm /ʊlm/ an industrial city on the Danube in Baden-Württemberg, southern Germany; pop. 120,900 (est. 2006). Its Gothic cathedral has the highest church tower in the world.

ulmo /'ʌlməʊ/ ▸ noun (pl. **ulmos**) a Chilean eucryphia tree which is sometimes cultivated as an ornamental. ● *Eucryphia cordifolia*, family Eucryphiaceae.
– ORIGIN Spanish.

ulna /'ʌlnə/ ▸ noun (pl. **ulnae** /-niː/ or **ulnas**) the thinner and longer of the two bones in the human forearm, on the side opposite to the thumb. Compare with RADIUS (sense 2 of the noun). ■ the corresponding bone in a quadruped's foreleg or a bird's wing.
– DERIVATIVES **ulnar** adjective.
– ORIGIN late Middle English (denoting the humerus): from Latin; related to ELL[1].

U-lock ▸ noun another term for D-LOCK.

-ulous ▸ suffix forming adjectives such as *incredulous*, *garrulous*.
– ORIGIN from Latin *-ulosus*, *-ulus*.

Ulpian /'ʌlpɪən/ (died *c.*228), Roman jurist, born in Phoenicia; Latin name *Domitius Ulpianus*. His numerous legal writings provided one of the chief sources for Justinian's *Digest* of 533.

Ulsan /uːl'sɑːn/ an industrial port on the south coast of South Korea; pop. 1,126,900 (est. 2008).

Ulster a former province of Ireland, in the north of the island. The nine counties of Ulster are now divided between Northern Ireland (Antrim, Down,

U

Armagh, Londonderry, Tyrone, and Fermanagh) and the Republic of Ireland (Cavan, Donegal, and Monaghan). ■ (in general use) Northern Ireland.
– DERIVATIVES **Ulsterman** noun (pl. **Ulstermen**), **Ulsterwoman** noun (pl. **Ulsterwomen**).

ulster ▶ noun a man's long, loose overcoat of rough cloth, typically with a belt at the back.
– ORIGIN late 19th cent.: from ULSTER, where it was originally sold.

Ulster Democratic Unionist Party an extreme Loyalist political party in Northern Ireland, co-founded by Ian Paisley in 1972.

Ulster Unionist Council (abbrev.: **UUC**) a political party in Northern Ireland seeking to maintain the union with Britain. Founded in 1905, the UUC is regarded as being more moderate than the Ulster Democratic Unionist Party.

ult. ▶ abbreviation ■ ultimate. ■ ultimo.

ulterior ▶ adjective existing beyond what is obvious or admitted; intentionally hidden: *could there be an **ulterior motive** behind his request?* ■ beyond what is immediate or present; coming in the future.
– DERIVATIVES **ulteriorly** adverb.
– ORIGIN mid 17th cent.: from Latin, literally 'further, more distant'.

ultimate ▶ adjective **1** being or happening at the end of a process; final: *their ultimate aim was to force his resignation.* ■ basic or fundamental: *the ultimate constituents of anything that exists are atoms.* ■ Physics denoting the maximum possible strength or resistance beyond which an object breaks.
2 being the best or most extreme example of its kind: *the ultimate accolade.*
▶ noun **1** (**the ultimate**) the best achievable or imaginable of its kind: ***the ultimate in** decorative luxury.*
2 a final or fundamental fact or principle.
– DERIVATIVES **ultimacy** noun (pl. **ultimacies**).
– ORIGIN mid 17th cent.: from late Latin *ultimatus*, past participle of *ultimare* 'come to an end'.

ultimately ▶ adverb finally; in the end: *the largest firms may ultimately become unstoppable.* ■ at the most basic level: *ultimately he has only himself to blame.*

ultima Thule ▶ noun a distant unknown region; the extreme limit of travel and discovery.
– ORIGIN Latin, literally 'furthest Thule' (see THULE).

ultimatum ▶ noun (pl. **ultimatums** or **ultimata** /-tə/) a final demand or statement of terms, the rejection of which will result in retaliation or a breakdown in relations: ***their employers issued an ultimatum** demanding an immediate return to work.*
– ORIGIN mid 18th cent.: from Latin, neuter past participle of *ultimare* 'come to an end'.

ultimo /ˈʌltɪməʊ/ (abbrev.: **ult.** or **ulto**) ▶ adjective [postpositive] dated of last month: *the 3rd ultimo.*
– ORIGIN from Latin *ultimo mense* 'in the last month'.

ultimobranchial /ˌʌltɪmə(ʊ)ˈbraŋkɪəl/ ▶ adjective Zoology relating to or denoting a gland in the neck which in many lower vertebrates regulates the calcium level in the body.

ultisol /ˈʌltɪsɒl/ ▶ noun Soil Science a highly weathered leached red or reddish-yellow acid soil with a clay-rich B horizon, occurring in warm, humid climates.
– ORIGIN 1960s: from ULTIMATE + Latin *solum* 'soil'.

ultra ▶ noun informal an extremist: *ultras in the animal rights movement.*
– ORIGIN early 19th cent.: an independent usage of ULTRA-, originally as an abbreviation of French *ultraroyaliste*.

ultra- ▶ prefix **1** to an extreme degree; very: *ultramicroscopic.*
2 beyond; on the other side of: *ultramontane.* Often contrasted with CIS-.
– ORIGIN from Latin *ultra* 'beyond'.

ultrabasic ▶ adjective Geology relating to or denoting igneous rocks having a silica content less than 45 per cent by weight.

ultracentrifuge ▶ noun a very fast centrifuge used to precipitate large biological molecules from solution or separate them by their different rates of sedimentation.
▶ verb [with obj.] subject to the action of an ultracentrifuge.
– DERIVATIVES **ultracentrifugal** adjective, **ultracentrifugation** noun.

ultracold ▶ adjective Physics (of a neutron) having an energy of the order of 10^{-7} eV or less.

ultradian /ʌlˈtreɪdɪən/ ▶ adjective Physiology (of a rhythm or cycle) having a period of recurrence shorter than a day but longer than an hour. Compare with INFRADIAN.
– ORIGIN 1960s: from ULTRA- 'beyond' (being of greater frequency than circadian) + -IAN.

ultrafiltration ▶ noun [mass noun] filtration using a medium fine enough to retain colloidal particles, viruses, or large molecules.

ultra-high frequency (abbrev.: **UHF**) ▶ noun a radio frequency in the range 300 to 3,000 MHz.

ultraist ▶ noun a holder of extreme opinions.
– DERIVATIVES **ultraism** noun.

ultralight ▶ adjective extremely lightweight.
▶ noun chiefly N. Amer. another term for MICROLIGHT.

ultramafic /ˌʌltrəˈmafɪk/ ▶ adjective Geology relating to or denoting igneous rocks composed chiefly of mafic minerals.

ultramarine ▶ noun [mass noun] a brilliant deep blue pigment originally obtained from lapis lazuli. ■ an imitation of such a pigment, made from powdered fired clay, sodium carbonate, sulphur, and resin. ■ a brilliant deep blue colour.
– ORIGIN late 16th cent.: from medieval Latin *ultramarinus* 'beyond the sea'; the name of the pigment is from obsolete Italian *(azzurro) oltramarino*, literally '(azure) from overseas'.

ultramicroscope ▶ noun an optical microscope used to detect particles smaller than the wavelength of light by illuminating them at an angle and observing the light scattered by the Tyndall effect against a dark background.

ultramicroscopic ▶ adjective too small to be seen by an ordinary optical microscope. ■ relating to an ultramicroscope.

ultra-modern ▶ adjective extremely modern; advanced: *this computer is a high-performance ultra-modern machine.*

ultramontane /ˌʌltrəˈmɒnteɪn/ ▶ adjective **1** advocating supreme papal authority in matters of faith and discipline. Compare with GALLICAN.
2 situated on the other side of the Alps from the point of view of the speaker.
▶ noun a person advocating supreme papal authority.
– DERIVATIVES **ultramontanism** noun.
– ORIGIN late 16th cent. (denoting a representative of the Roman Catholic Church north of the Alps): from medieval Latin *ultramontanus*, from Latin *ultra* 'beyond' + *mons, mont-* 'mountain'.

ultramundane /ˌʌltrəˈmʌndeɪn/ ▶ adjective literary existing outside the known world, the solar system, or the universe.
– ORIGIN mid 17th cent.: from late Latin *ultramundanus*, from *ultra* 'beyond' + *mundanus* (from *mundus* 'world').

ultraportable ▶ noun a type of laptop computer that is very slim and lightweight.

ultrasaurus /ˈʌltrəsɔːrəs/ ▶ noun a late Jurassic dinosaur related to brachiosaurus, known from only a few bones but probably the tallest ever animal, and possibly the heaviest at up to 130 tons. ● Genus *Ultrasaurus*, infraorder Sauropoda, order Saurischia.
– ORIGIN modern Latin, from Latin *ultra* 'beyond' + Greek *sauros* 'lizard'.

ultrashort ▶ adjective (of radio waves) having a wavelength significantly shorter than that of the usual short waves, in particular shorter than 10 metres (i.e. of a VHF frequency above 30 MHz).

ultrasonic ▶ adjective of or involving sound waves with a frequency above the upper limit of human hearing.
– DERIVATIVES **ultrasonically** adverb.

ultrasonics ▶ plural noun [treated as sing.] the science and application of ultrasonic waves. ■ [treated as sing. or pl.] ultrasonic waves; ultrasound.

ultrasonography /ˌʌltrəsəˈnɒgrəfi/ ▶ noun [mass noun] Medicine a technique using echoes of ultrasound pulses to delineate objects or areas of different density in the body.
– DERIVATIVES **ultrasonographic** adjective.

ultrasound ▶ noun [mass noun] sound or other vibrations having an ultrasonic frequency, particularly as used in medical imaging. ■ [count noun] an ultrasound scan, especially one of a pregnant woman to examine the fetus.

ultrastructure ▶ noun Biology fine structure, especially within a cell, that can be seen only with the high magnification obtainable with an electron microscope.

ultraviolet Physics ▶ adjective (of electromagnetic radiation) having a wavelength shorter than that of the violet end of the visible spectrum but longer than that of X-rays. ■ (of equipment or techniques) using or concerned with ultraviolet radiation: *an ultraviolet telescope.*
▶ noun [mass noun] the ultraviolet part of the spectrum; ultraviolet radiation.

> Ultraviolet radiation spans wavelengths from about 10 nm to 400 nm, and is an important component of sunlight, although the ozone layer prevents much of it from reaching the earth's surface. While ultraviolet is necessary for the production of vitamin D_2 in the skin, it is now known that excessive exposure can be harmful, causing skin cancer and genetic mutation.

ultra vires /ˌʌltrə ˈvʌɪriːz, ˌʊltrɑː ˈviːreɪz/ ▶ adjective & adverb Law beyond one's legal power or authority: [as adj.] *jurisdictional errors render the decision ultra vires.*
– ORIGIN Latin, literally 'beyond the powers'.

ulu /ˈuːluː/ ▶ noun (pl. **ulus**) an Eskimo woman's short-handled knife with a broad crescent-shaped blade.
– ORIGIN Inuit.

ululate /ˈjuːljʊleɪt, ˈʌl-/ ▶ verb [no obj.] howl or wail as an expression of strong emotion, typically grief: *women were ululating as the body was laid out.*
– DERIVATIVES **ululant** adjective, **ululation** noun.
– ORIGIN early 17th cent.: from Latin *ululat-* 'howled, shrieked', from the verb *ululare*, of imitative origin.

Ulundi /ʊˈlʊndi/ a town in KwaZulu-Natal, South Africa, formerly capital of Zululand and KwaZulu.

Uluru /ʊˈlʊəruː/ official name for AYERS ROCK.

Ulyanov /uːlˈjɑːnɒf/, Vladimir Ilich, see LENIN.

Ulyanovsk /uːlˈjɑːnəfsk/ former name (1924–92) for SIMBIRSK.

Ulysses /ˈjuːlɪsiːz/ **1** Roman Mythology Roman name for ODYSSEUS.
2 a space probe of the European Space Agency, launched in 1990 to investigate the polar regions of the sun.

um ▶ exclamation expressing hesitation or a pause in speech: *anyway, um, where was I?*
– ORIGIN natural utterance: first recorded in English in the early 17th cent.

-um ▶ suffix variant spelling of -IUM (sense 2).

umami /uːˈmɑːmi/ ▶ noun [mass noun] a category of taste in food (besides sweet, sour, salt, and bitter), corresponding to the flavour of glutamates, especially monosodium glutamate.
– ORIGIN Japanese, literally 'deliciousness'.

U-matic ▶ noun [mass noun] trademark a system for recording and playing audiovisual material and videos, mainly restricted to professional use.
– ORIGIN 1970s: *U* from the shape of the path followed by the tape around the drum and heads of the machine + *-matic* from AUTOMATIC.

Umayyad /ʊˈmʌɪjad/ (also **Omayyad**) ▶ noun a member of a Muslim dynasty that ruled the Islamic world from AD 660 (or 661) to 750 and Moorish Spain 756–1031. The dynasty claimed descent from Umayya, a distant relative of Muhammad.
▶ adjective relating to the Umayyad dynasty.

Umayyad Mosque a mosque in Damascus, Syria, built AD 705–15 on the site of a church dedicated to St John the Baptist.

Umbanda /ʊmˈbandə/ ▶ noun [mass noun] a Brazilian folk religion combining elements of macumba, Roman Catholicism, and South American Indian practices.
– ORIGIN Portuguese.

umbel /ˈʌmb(ə)l/ ▶ noun Botany a flower cluster in which stalks of nearly equal length spring from a common centre and form a flat or curved surface, characteristic of the parsley family.
– DERIVATIVES **umbellate** adjective.
– ORIGIN late 16th cent.: from obsolete French *umbelle* or Latin *umbella* 'sunshade', diminutive of *umbra* (see UMBRA).

umbellifer /ʌmˈbɛlɪfə/ ▶ noun Botany a plant of the parsley family, having its flowers arranged in umbels. ● Family Umbelliferae: numerous genera and species.
– DERIVATIVES **umbelliferous** adjective.
– ORIGIN early 18th cent.: from obsolete French *umbellifère*, from Latin *umbella* 'parasol' + *-fer* 'bearing'.

umber /ˈʌmbə/ ▶ noun **1** [mass noun] a natural pigment resembling but darker than ochre, normally dark yellowish-brown in colour (**raw umber**) or dark brown when roasted (**burnt umber**). ■ either of the colours of umber.

U

2 a brownish moth with colouring that resembles tree bark. ● Several species in the family Geometridae.
– ORIGIN mid 16th cent.: from French *(terre d') ombre* or Italian *(terra di) ombra*, literally '(earth of) shadow', from Latin *umbra* 'shadow' or *Umbra* (feminine) 'Umbrian'.

umbilical /ʌmˈbɪlɪk(ə)l, ˌʌmbɪˈlʌɪk(ə)l/ ▶ **adjective** relating to or affecting the navel or umbilical cord: *the umbilical artery.* ■ extremely close; inseparable: *the umbilical link between commerce and international rugby.* ■ (of a pipe or cable) connecting someone or something to a source of essential supplies.
▶ **noun** short for **UMBILICAL CORD**.
– DERIVATIVES **umbilically** adverb.
– ORIGIN mid 16th cent.: from French *ombilical*, or based on Latin *umbilicus* (see **UMBILICUS**).

umbilical cord ▶ **noun** a flexible cord-like structure containing blood vessels and attaching a human or other mammalian fetus to the placenta during gestation. ■ a flexible cable, pipe, or other line carrying essential services or supplies.

umbilicate /ʌmˈbɪlɪkət/ ▶ **adjective** Botany & Zoology (especially of the cap of a fungus) having a central depression. ■ (of a shell) having an umbilicus.

umbilicus /ʌmˈbɪlɪkəs, ˌʌmbɪˈlʌɪkəs/ ▶ **noun** (pl. **umbilici** /-sʌɪ/ or **umbilicuses**) **1** Anatomy the navel.
2 Zoology a depression or hole at the centre of the shell whorls of some gastropod molluscs and many ammonites. ■ a hole at each end of the hollow shaft of a feather.
– ORIGIN late 17th cent.: from Latin: related to Greek *omphalos*, also to **NAVEL**.

umbles ▶ **plural noun** variant spelling of **NUMBLES**. See also **EAT HUMBLE PIE**.

umbo /ˈʌmbəʊ/ ▶ **noun** (pl. **umbones** /-ˈbəʊniːz/ or **umbos**) **1** historical the central boss of a shield.
2 Biology a rounded knob or protuberance. ■ Zoology the highest point of each valve of a bivalve shell. ■ Botany a central swelling on the cap of a mushroom or toadstool.
– DERIVATIVES **umbonal** adjective (chiefly Zoology), **umbonate** adjective (chiefly Botany).
– ORIGIN early 18th cent.: from Latin, 'shield boss'.

umbra /ˈʌmbrə/ ▶ **noun** (pl. **umbras** or **umbrae** /-briː/) **1** the fully shaded inner region of a shadow cast by an opaque object, especially the area on the earth or moon experiencing the total phase of an eclipse. Compare with **PENUMBRA**. ■ Astronomy the dark central part of a sunspot.
2 [mass noun] literary shadow or darkness.
– DERIVATIVES **umbral** adjective.
– ORIGIN late 16th cent. (denoting a phantom or ghost): from Latin, literally 'shade'.

umbrage /ˈʌmbrɪdʒ/ ▶ **noun** [mass noun] **1** offence or annoyance: *she **took umbrage at** his remarks.*
2 archaic shade or shadow, especially as cast by trees.
– DERIVATIVES **umbrageous** adjective.
– ORIGIN late Middle English (in sense 2): from Old French, from Latin *umbra* 'shadow'. An early sense was 'shadowy outline', giving rise to 'ground for suspicion', whence the current notion of 'offence'.

umbrella ▶ **noun 1** a device consisting of a circular canopy of cloth on a folding metal frame supported by a central rod, used as protection against rain.
2 a protecting force or influence: *Europe sought a measure of independence from the US defence umbrella.* ■ a screen of fighter aircraft or anti-aircraft artillery.
3 [usu. as modifier] a thing that includes or contains many different elements or parts: *the umbrella body for more than 100 training organizations.*
4 Zoology the gelatinous disc of a jellyfish, which it contracts and expands to move through the water.
– DERIVATIVES **umbrellaed** adjective, **umbrella-like** adjective.
– ORIGIN early 17th cent.: from Italian *ombrella*, diminutive of *ombra* 'shade', from Latin *umbra* (see **UMBRA**).

umbrellabird ▶ **noun** a large tropical American cotinga with black plumage, a radiating crest, and typically long wattles. ● Genus *Cephalopterus*, family Cotingidae: three species.

umbrella fund ▶ **noun** an offshore investment fund which invests only in other investment funds.

umbrella pine ▶ **noun 1** another term for **STONE PINE**.
2 a tall Japanese evergreen conifer related to the redwoods, with leaves growing in umbrella-like whorls. ● *Sciadopitys verticillata*, family Taxodiaceae.

umbrella plant ▶ **noun** a tropical Old World sedge which has stiff green stems, each terminating in a whorl of arching green leaf-like bracts. It is commonly grown as a houseplant. ● *Cyperus involucratus*, family Cyperaceae.

umbrella tree ▶ **noun** either of two small trees or shrubs with leaves or leaflets arranged in umbrella-like whorls: ● an Australian plant which is grown elsewhere as a houseplant (*Schefflera actinophylla*, family Araliaceae). ● a North American magnolia (*Magnolia tripetala*, family Magnoliaceae).

Umbria /ˈʌmbrɪə/ a region of central Italy, in the valley of the Tiber; capital, Perugia.

Umbrian ▶ **adjective** relating to Umbria, its people, or their languages.
▶ **noun 1** a native or inhabitant of Umbria, especially in pre-Roman times.
2 [mass noun] an extinct Italic language of central Italy, related to Oscan and surviving in inscriptions mainly of the 2nd and 1st centuries BC.

Umbrian School a Renaissance school of Italian painting, to which Raphael and Perugino belonged.

Umbriel /ˈʌmbrɪəl/ Astronomy a satellite of Uranus, the thirteenth closest to the planet, discovered in 1851 (diameter 1,190 km).
– ORIGIN named after a sprite in *The Rape of the Lock* by Alexander Pope.

umbriferous /ʌmˈbrɪf(ə)rəs/ ▶ **adjective** literary providing shade.
– ORIGIN early 17th cent.: from Latin *umbrifer* (from *umbra* 'shade' + *-fer* 'bearing') + **-OUS**.

Umbundu see **MBUNDU**.

Umeå /ˈuːməˌɔː/ a city in NE Sweden, on an inlet of the Gulf of Bothnia; pop. 112,728 (2008).

umfaan /ʊmˈfɑːn, ʌm-/ ▶ **noun** S. African (among Xhosa-speaking people) a young man who has gone through initiation but is not yet married. ■ (among Zulu-speaking people) a boy. ■ offensive a black male domestic servant.
– ORIGIN from Zulu and Xhosa *umfana*.

umfundisi /ʊmˈfʊndɪsi, ˌʊmfʊnˈdiːzi/ ▶ **noun** (pl. **bafundisi** or **same**) S. African (among speakers of Xhosa and Zulu) a teacher, priest, or missionary.
– ORIGIN early 19th cent.: from Xhosa and Zulu.

umiak /ˈuːmɪak/ ▶ **noun** an Eskimo open boat made of wood and skin, traditionally rowed by women.
– ORIGIN from Inuit *umiaq*.

umlaut /ˈʊmlaʊt/ Linguistics ▶ **noun** a mark (¨) used over a vowel, especially in German, to indicate a different vowel quality. ■ [mass noun] the process in Germanic languages by which the quality of a vowel was altered in certain phonetic contexts, resulting for example in the differences between modern German *Mann* and *Männer*.
▶ **verb** [with obj.] modify (a form or sound) by using an umlaut.
– ORIGIN mid 19th cent.: from German *Umlaut*, from *um* 'about' + *Laut* 'sound'.

umma /ˈʊmə/ (also **ummah**) ▶ **noun** the whole community of Muslims bound together by ties of religion.
– ORIGIN Arabic, literally 'people, community'.

Umm al-Qaiwain /ˌʊm alkʌɪˈwʌɪn/ one of the seven member states of the United Arab Emirates; pop. 69,900 (est. 2009).

ump ▶ **noun** informal, chiefly N. Amer. an umpire.
– ORIGIN early 20th cent.: abbreviation.

umph ▶ **noun** variant spelling of **OOMPH**.

umpire ▶ **noun** (in some sports) an official who watches a game or match closely to enforce the rules and arbitrate on matters arising from the play. ■ a person chosen to arbitrate between contending parties.
▶ **verb** [no obj.] act as an umpire in a game or match: *he could be seen regularly umpiring for the club* | [with obj.] *he umpired the World Cup final.*
– ORIGIN late Middle English (originally as *noumpere*) (denoting an arbitrator): from Old French *nonper* 'not equal'. The *n* was lost by wrong division of *a noumpere*; compare with **ADDER**¹.

umpteen ▶ **cardinal number** informal indefinitely many; a lot of: *you need umpteen pieces of identification to cash a cheque* | *umpteen of them arrived at once.*
– DERIVATIVES **umpteenth** ordinal number.
– ORIGIN early 20th cent.: humorous formation based on **-TEEN**.

umrah /ˈʊmrɑː/ ▶ **noun** the non-mandatory lesser pilgrimage made by Muslims to Mecca, which may be performed at any time of the year. Compare with **HAJJ**.
– ORIGIN Arabic *ʿumra*.

Umtali /ʊmˈtɑːli/ former name (until 1982) for **MUTARE**.

UMTS ▶ **abbreviation** Universal Mobile Telephone System.

umu /ˈʊmʊ/ ▶ **noun** a Maori oven consisting of a hollow in the earth in which food is cooked on heated stones.
– ORIGIN Maori.

Umwelt /ˈʊmvɛlt/ ▶ **noun** (pl. **Umwelten** /-t(ə)n/) (in ethology) the world as it is experienced by a particular organism.
– ORIGIN German, literally 'environment'.

UN ▶ **abbreviation** United Nations.

'un informal ▶ **contraction** one: *a good 'un* | *a wild 'un.*

un-¹ ▶ **prefix 1** (added to adjectives, participles, and their derivatives) denoting the absence of a quality or state; not: *unabashed* | *unacademic* | *unrepeatable.* ■ the reverse of (usually with an implication of approval or disapproval, or with another special connotation): *unselfish* | *unprepossessing* | *unworldly.*
2 (added to nouns) a lack of: *unrest* | *untruth.*
– ORIGIN Old English, of Germanic origin; from an Indo-European root shared by Latin *in-* and Greek *a-*.

> **USAGE** The prefixes **un-** and **non-** both mean 'not', but there is often a distinction in terms of emphasis. **un-** tends to be stronger and less neutral than **non-**: consider the differences between **unacademic** and **non-academic**, for example (*his language was refreshingly unacademic; a non-academic life suits him*).

un-² ▶ **prefix** added to verbs: **1** denoting the reversal or cancellation of an action or state: *untie* | *unsettle.*
2 denoting deprivation, separation, or reduction to a lesser state: *unmask* | *unman.* ■ denoting release: *unburden* | *unhand.*
– ORIGIN Old English *un-*, *on-*, of Germanic origin; related to Dutch *ont-* and German *ent-*.

UNA ▶ **abbreviation** United Nations Association.

unabashed ▶ **adjective** not embarrassed, disconcerted, or ashamed: *he was unabashed by the furore his words provoked.*
– DERIVATIVES **unabashedly** adverb.

unabated ▶ **adjective** without any reduction in intensity or strength: *the storm was raging unabated.*
– DERIVATIVES **unabatedly** adverb.

unable ▶ **adjective** [with infinitive] lacking the skill, means, or opportunity to do something: *she was unable to conceal her surprise.*

unabridged ▶ **adjective** (of a text) not cut or shortened; complete: *an unabridged edition.*

unabsorbed ▶ **adjective** not taken in or soaked up; not absorbed: *unabsorbed nutrients.*

unacademic ▶ **adjective** not adopting or characteristic of a scholarly approach or language: *his language was refreshingly unacademic.* ■ (of a person) not suited or drawn to academic study.

unaccented ▶ **adjective** having no accent, stress, or emphasis: *his English is fluent and unaccented.*

unacceptable ▶ **adjective** not satisfactory or allowable: *unacceptable behaviour.*
– DERIVATIVES **unacceptability** noun, **unacceptably** adverb.

unaccommodating ▶ **adjective** not fitting in with the wishes or demands of others; unhelpful.

unaccompanied ▶ **adjective 1** having no companion or escort: *no unaccompanied children allowed.*
2 taking place without something specified taking place at the same time: *the political change was unaccompanied by social change.*
3 (of a piece of music) sung or played without instrumental accompaniment.

unaccomplished ▶ **adjective 1** showing little skill.
2 not accomplished or carried out.

unaccountable ▶ **adjective 1** unable to be explained: *a strange and unaccountable fact.* ■ (of a person or their behaviour) unpredictable and strange.
2 (of a person, organization, or institution) not required or expected to justify actions or decisions; not responsible for results or consequences.
– DERIVATIVES **unaccountability** noun, **unaccountably** adverb.

unaccounted ▶ **adjective** (**unaccounted for**) not included in (an account or calculation) through being lost or disregarded: *a substantial amount of money is unaccounted for.*

unaccredited ▶ **adjective** not recognized as having attained an acceptable standard.

unaccustomed ▶ **adjective** not familiar or usual; out of the ordinary: *they finished their supper with unaccustomed speed.* ■ (**unaccustomed to**) not familiar with or used to: *the visitors were unaccustomed to country roads.*
– DERIVATIVES **unaccustomedly** adverb.

U

unachievable ▶ adjective (of an aim or objective) too difficult to be achieved: *an unachievable political goal.*

unacknowledged ▶ adjective **1** existing or having taken place but not accepted, recognized, or admitted to: *her unacknowledged feelings.*
2 (of a person or their work) deserving but not receiving praise or recognition.

una corda /ˌuːnə ˈkɔːdə/ Music ▶ adverb & adjective (especially as a direction) using the soft pedal on a piano.
▶ noun a device in a piano that shifts the mechanism slightly to one side when the soft pedal is depressed, so that the hammers do not strike all of the strings when sounding each note and the tone is therefore quieter.
– ORIGIN Italian, literally 'one string'.

unacquainted ▶ adjective (of two or more people) not having met before; not knowing each other.
■ (**unacquainted with**) having no experience of or familiarity with: *I regret that I am unacquainted with the place.*

unadaptable ▶ adjective not adaptable.

unadapted ▶ adjective not adapted.

unaddressed ▶ adjective **1** not considered or dealt with: *wider questions remain unaddressed.*
2 (of a letter or other item sent in the post) having no address written or printed on it.

unadjacent ▶ adjective not adjacent.

unadjusted ▶ adjective (especially of figures or statistics) not adjusted or refined: *the unadjusted jobless total increased last month.*

unadopted ▶ adjective Brit. (of a road) not taken over for maintenance by a local authority.

unadorned ▶ adjective not adorned; plain.

unadulterated ▶ adjective **1** (especially of food or drink) having no inferior added substances; pure: *unadulterated whole-milk yogurt.*
2 not mixed or diluted with any different or extra elements; complete and absolute: *pure, unadulterated jealousy.*

unadventurous ▶ adjective not offering, involving, or eager for new or stimulating things: *he was the unadventurous type | an unadventurous menu.*
– DERIVATIVES **unadventurously** adverb.

unadvertised ▶ adjective existing or taking place without being made public.

unadvisable ▶ adjective another term for **INADVISABLE**.

unadvisedly ▶ adverb in an unwise or rash manner: *they enter into nothing lightly or unadvisedly.*

unaesthetic ▶ adjective not visually pleasing; unattractive. ■ not motivated by aesthetic principles.

unaffected ▶ adjective **1** feeling or showing no effects or changes: *the walks are suitable only for people who are unaffected by vertigo.*
2 without artificiality or insincerity: *her effortless, unaffected charm.*
– DERIVATIVES **unaffectedly** adverb, **unaffectedness** noun.

unaffectionate ▶ adjective feeling, showing, or having no fondness or tenderness.

unaffiliated ▶ adjective not officially attached to or connected with an organization or group.

unaffordable ▶ adjective too expensive to be afforded by the average person: *medical care has become unaffordable.*

U

unafraid ▶ adjective [predic.] feeling no fear or anxiety: *she was calm and unafraid.*

unaggressive ▶ adjective tending not to attack without provocation; not hostile or violent.

unaided ▶ adjective needing or having no assistance; without help: *she can no longer walk unaided.*

unaired ▶ adjective **1** not exposed to the open air for ventilation.
2 not previously broadcast: *the original unaired pilot episode.*

unalienable ▶ adjective another term for **INALIENABLE**.

unaligned ▶ adjective **1** not placed or arranged in a straight line, in parallel, or in correct relative positions.
2 not allied with or giving support to a particular organization or cause.

unalike ▶ adjective [predic.] (of two or more subjects) differing from each other; not similar: *they are unalike in personality.*

unalive ▶ adjective lacking in vitality; not living or lively.

unalleviated ▶ adjective not alleviated; relentless: *a time of unalleviated misery.*

unallied ▶ adjective not allied; having no allies.

unallocated ▶ adjective (of resources or duties) not yet allocated: *£2.8 m of contingency funds remained unallocated.*

unallowable ▶ adjective not allowable.

unalloyed ▶ adjective **1** (of metal) not alloyed; pure: *unalloyed copper.*
2 (chiefly of emotions) complete and unreserved: *unalloyed delight.*

unalterable ▶ adjective not able to be changed.
– DERIVATIVES **unalterably** adverb.

unaltered ▶ adjective remaining the same; unchanged: *many buildings survive unaltered.*

unamazed ▶ adjective not amazed.

unambiguous ▶ adjective not open to more than one interpretation: *instructions should be unambiguous.*
– DERIVATIVES **unambiguity** noun, **unambiguously** adverb.

unambitious ▶ adjective not motivated or driven by a strong desire or determination to succeed. ■ (of a plan or piece of work) not involving anything new, exciting, or demanding.
– DERIVATIVES **unambitiously** adverb.

unambivalent ▶ adjective having or showing no mixed feelings or contradictory ideas.
– DERIVATIVES **unambivalently** adverb.

unamended ▶ adjective not amended.

un-American ▶ adjective not in accordance with American characteristics: *such un-American concepts as subsidized medicine and free education.* ■ US, chiefly historical contrary to the interests of the US and therefore treasonable.
– DERIVATIVES **un-Americanism** noun.

Unami /uːˈnɒmi/ ▶ noun see **DELAWARE²** (sense 2 of the noun).
– ORIGIN the name in Unami.

unamiable ▶ adjective not having a friendly manner; not pleasant.

unamplified ▶ adjective not amplified.

unamused ▶ adjective not responding in a positive way to something intended to be amusing; feeling somewhat annoyed or disapproving: *she was unamused by some of the things written about her.*

unanalysable (US **unanalyzable**) ▶ adjective not able to be explained or interpreted through methodical examination: *unanalysable recorded data.*

unanalysed (US **unanalyzed**) ▶ adjective not revealed, explained, or interpreted through methodical examination.

unanchored ▶ adjective not anchored or securely fixed.

unaneled /ˌʌnəˈniːld/ ▶ adjective archaic having died without receiving extreme unction; not anointed.

Unani /juːˈnɑːni/ ▶ noun [mass noun] [usu. as modifier] a system of medicine practised in parts of India, thought to be derived via medieval Muslim physicians from Byzantine Greece.
– ORIGIN from Arabic *Yūnānī* 'Greek'.

unanimity /juːnəˈnɪmɪti/ ▶ noun [mass noun] agreement by all people involved; consensus: *there is almost complete unanimity on this issue.*

unanimous /juːˈnanɪməs/ ▶ adjective [mass noun] (of two or more people) fully in agreement: *the doctors were unanimous in their diagnoses.* ■ (of an opinion, decision, or vote) held or carried by everyone involved.
– ORIGIN early 17th cent.: from Latin *unanimus* (from *unus* 'one' + *animus* 'mind') + **-ous**.

unanimously /juːˈnanɪməsli/ ▶ adverb without opposition; with the agreement of all people involved: *a committee of MPs has unanimously agreed to back his bill.*

unannounced ▶ adjective not made known; not publicized. ■ without previous notice or arrangement and therefore unexpected: *he arrived unannounced.*

unanswerable ▶ adjective unable to be answered: *unanswerable questions concerning our own mortality.* ■ unable to be disclaimed or proved wrong: *the case for abolishing the fee is unanswerable.*
– DERIVATIVES **unanswerably** adverb.

unanswered ▶ adjective not answered or responded to: *unanswered letters.*

unanticipated ▶ adjective not expected or predicted.

unapologetic ▶ adjective not acknowledging or expressing regret: *he remained unapologetic about his decision.*
– DERIVATIVES **unapologetically** adverb.

unapparent ▶ adjective not visible or in evidence.

unappealable ▶ adjective Law (of a case or ruling) not subject to being referred to a higher court for review.

unappealing ▶ adjective not inviting or attractive: *the company faces some unappealing choices.*
– DERIVATIVES **unappealingly** adverb.

unappeasable ▶ adjective not able to be pacified, placated, or satisfied.

unappeased ▶ adjective not pacified, placated, or satisfied.

unappetizing (also **unappetising**) ▶ adjective not inviting or attractive; unwholesome.
– DERIVATIVES **unappetizingly** adverb.

unapplied ▶ adjective not applied.

unappreciated ▶ adjective not fully understood, recognized, or valued: *she had been brought up in a family where she felt unappreciated and undervalued.*

unappreciative ▶ adjective not fully understanding, recognizing, or valuing something: *they were unappreciative of country problems.*

unapprehended ▶ adjective **1** not perceived or understood.
2 not arrested for a crime.

unapproachable ▶ adjective **1** not welcoming or friendly: *he seems stuffy and unapproachable.*
2 archaic (of a place) remote and inaccessible.
– DERIVATIVES **unapproachability** noun, **unapproachably** adverb.

unappropriated ▶ adjective not taken, allocated, or assigned: *vacant and unappropriated land.*

unapproved ▶ adjective not officially accepted or sanctioned: *they deposit waste on unapproved sites.*

unapt ▶ adjective not appropriate or suitable in the circumstances: *it is not an unapt word.*
– DERIVATIVES **unaptly** adverb, **unaptness** noun.

unarguable ▶ adjective not open to disagreement; indisputable: *unarguable proof of conspiracy.*
– DERIVATIVES **unarguably** adverb.

unarm ▶ verb [with obj.] deprive or free (someone) of arms or armour.

unarmed ▶ adjective not equipped with or carrying weapons: *he was shooting unarmed civilians.*

unarmed combat ▶ noun [mass noun] a mode of combat in which weapons are not used.

unarticulated ▶ adjective not mentioned or coherently expressed: *previously unarticulated anger.*

unartistic ▶ adjective not artistic or concerned with art.

unary /ˈjuːnəri/ ▶ adjective (especially of a mathematical operation) consisting of or involving a single component or element.

unascertained ▶ adjective not confirmed or ascertained; unknown.
– DERIVATIVES **unascertainable** adjective.

unashamed ▶ adjective expressed or acting openly and without guilt or embarrassment: *an unashamed emotionalism.*
– DERIVATIVES **unashamedly** adverb, **unashamedness** noun.

unasked ▶ adjective **1** (of a question) not asked.
2 (often **unasked for**) not sought or requested: *unasked-for advice | the memories he had poured unasked into her head.*

unaspirated ▶ adjective Phonetics (of a sound) not aspirated.

unassailable ▶ adjective unable to be attacked, questioned, or defeated: *an unassailable lead.*
– DERIVATIVES **unassailability** noun, **unassailably** adverb.

unassertive ▶ adjective (of a person) not having or showing a confident and forceful personality.
– DERIVATIVES **unassertively** adverb, **unassertiveness** noun.

unassigned ▶ adjective not allocated or set aside for a specific purpose.
– DERIVATIVES **unassignable** adjective.

unassimilated ▶ adjective (especially of a people, an idea, or a culture) not absorbed or integrated into a wider society or culture.

– DERIVATIVES **unassimilable** adjective.

unassisted ▸ adjective not helped by anyone or anything: *medically unassisted births* | *I could never find the place unassisted.*

unassociated ▸ adjective not connected or associated: *the issue is being raised by thousands of unassociated individuals.*

unassuaged ▸ adjective not soothed or relieved: *her unassuaged grief.*
– DERIVATIVES **unassuageable** adjective.

unassuming ▸ adjective not pretentious or arrogant; modest: *he was an unassuming and kindly man.*
– DERIVATIVES **unassumingly** adverb, **unassumingness** noun.

unatoned ▸ adjective not atoned for.

unattached ▸ adjective **1** not working for or belonging to a particular body or organization: *local people* ***unattached to*** *any organization.*
2 not married or having an established partner; single.

unattainable ▸ adjective not able to be reached or achieved: *an unattainable goal.*
– DERIVATIVES **unattainableness** noun, **unattainably** adverb.

unattempted ▸ adjective not previously attempted or embarked upon; untried.

unattended ▸ adjective **1** not noticed or dealt with: *her behaviour went unnoticed and* ***unattended to.***
2 not supervised or looked after: *it is not acceptable for parents to leave children unattended at that age* | *an unattended vehicle.*

unattested ▸ adjective not attested or recorded.

unattractive ▸ adjective not pleasing or appealing to look at. ■ having no inviting or beneficial features: *if the revised bid is unattractive, it may not be accepted.*
– DERIVATIVES **unattractively** adverb, **unattractiveness** noun.

unattributed ▸ adjective (of a quotation, story, or work of art) not ascribed to any source; of unknown or unpublished provenance.
– DERIVATIVES **unattributable** adjective, **unattributably** adverb.

unaudited ▸ adjective (of financial accounts) not having been officially examined.

unauthentic ▸ adjective not made or done in a way that reflects tradition or faithfully resembles an original.

unauthenticated ▸ adjective not proven or validated: *an unauthenticated report.*

unauthorized (also **unauthorised**) ▸ adjective not having official permission or approval: *unauthorized access to the computer system.*

unavailable ▸ adjective **1** not able to be used or obtained; not at someone's disposal: *material which is* ***unavailable to*** *the researcher.*
2 (of a person) not free to do something; otherwise occupied: *the men were* ***unavailable for*** *work.*
– DERIVATIVES **unavailability** noun.

unavailing ▸ adjective achieving little or nothing; ineffective: *their efforts were unavailing.*
– DERIVATIVES **unavailingly** adverb.

unavenged ▸ adjective (of a person, injury, or wrong) not avenged: *these murders should not be allowed to go unavenged.*

unavoidable ▸ adjective not able to be avoided, prevented, or ignored; inevitable: *the natural and unavoidable consequences of growing old.*
– DERIVATIVES **unavoidability** noun, **unavoidably** adverb.

unavowed ▸ adjective not openly or publicly declared; unstated: *an underlying, unavowed hostility.*

unawakened ▸ adjective not aware of or roused to particular sensations or feelings.

unaware ▸ adjective having no knowledge of a situation or fact: *they were* ***unaware of*** *his absence.*
▸ adverb variant of UNAWARES.
– DERIVATIVES **unawareness** noun.

unawares (also **unaware**) ▸ adverb without being aware of a situation: *the photographer had* ***caught*** *her* ***unawares.***
– ORIGIN mid 16th cent.: from UNAWARE + -S[3].

unawed ▸ adjective not filled with awe.

unbacked ▸ adjective **1** having no financial, material, or moral support. ■ (of a horse) having no backers in a race.
2 having no backing layer: *unbacked hessian.*

unbaked ▸ adjective not baked.

unbalance ▸ verb [with obj.] **1** make (someone or something) unsteady so that they tip or fall.
2 upset or disturb the equilibrium of (a situation or person's state of mind): *this sharing can often unbalance even the closest of relationships.*
▸ noun a lack of symmetry, balance, or stability.

unbalanced ▸ adjective **1** (of a person) emotionally or mentally disturbed.
2 not giving accurate, fair, or equal coverage to all aspects; partial: *this may give an unbalanced impression of the competition.*

unban ▸ verb (**unbans, unbanning, unbanned**) [with obj.] remove a ban on (a person, group, or activity).

unbaptized (also **unbaptised**) ▸ adjective not having been baptized.

unbar ▸ verb (**unbars, unbarring, unbarred**) [with obj.] remove the bars from (a gate or door); unlock.

unbearable ▸ adjective not able to be endured or tolerated: *the heat was getting unbearable.*
– DERIVATIVES **unbearableness** noun, **unbearably** adverb [as submodifier] *it was unbearably hot.*

unbeatable ▸ adjective not able to be defeated or bettered in a contest or commercial market: *the team is unbeatable* | *bikes at unbeatable prices.* ■ extremely good; outstanding: *views from the patio are unbeatable.*
– DERIVATIVES **unbeatably** adverb.

unbeaten ▸ adjective not defeated or surpassed: *they were the only side to remain unbeaten.*

unbeautiful ▸ adjective without beauty.
– DERIVATIVES **unbeautifully** adverb.

unbecoming ▸ adjective **1** (especially of clothing or a colour) not flattering: *a stout lady in an unbecoming striped sundress.*
2 (of behaviour) not fitting or appropriate; unseemly: *it was unbecoming for a university to do anything so crass as advertising its wares.*
– DERIVATIVES **unbecomingly** adverb, **unbecomingness** noun.

unbefitting ▸ adjective not appropriate; unsuitable: *unbefitting conduct.*
– DERIVATIVES **unbefittingly** adverb, **unbefittingness** noun.

unbegotten ▸ adjective archaic not brought into existence by the process of reproduction.

unbeholden ▸ adjective formal owing no one any duty or thanks; free of any obligation.

unbeknown (also **unbeknownst**) ▸ adjective (**unbeknown to**) without the knowledge of (someone): *unbeknown to me, she made some enquiries.*
– ORIGIN mid 17th cent.: from UN-[1] 'not' + archaic *beknown* 'known'.

unbelief ▸ noun [mass noun] lack of religious belief; an absence of faith.

unbelievable ▸ adjective **1** not able to be believed; unlikely to be true: *unbelievable or not, it happened.*
2 so great or extreme as to be difficult to believe; extraordinary: *your audacity is unbelievable.*
– DERIVATIVES **unbelievability** noun, **unbelievably** adverb [as submodifier] *he worked unbelievably long hours.*

unbeliever ▸ noun someone who has no religious beliefs, or who does not follow a particular religion.

unbelieving ▸ adjective not believing someone or something; incredulous: *Drew could only stand there, wide-eyed and unbelieving.* ■ having no religious beliefs, or not following a particular religion: *they were to preach to the unbelieving people.*
– DERIVATIVES **unbelievingly** adverb.

unbeloved ▸ adjective not loved: *he plays Anne's unbeloved room-mate.* ■ (**unbeloved by/of**) not popular with (a specified set of people): *he died unmourned and unbeloved of his people.*

unbelt ▸ verb [with obj.] remove or undo the belt of (a garment): *he unbelted his kimono.*

unbelted ▸ adjective **1** (of a garment) without a belt.
2 not wearing a belt, in particular a vehicle seat belt.

unbend ▸ verb (past and past participle **unbent**) **1** make or become straight from a bent or twisted form or position: [with obj.] *I had trouble unbending my cramped knees* | [no obj.] *he unbent from the cockpit.* ■ [no obj.] become less reserved, formal, or strict: *you could be fun too, you know, if you'd only unbend a little.*
2 [with obj.] Sailing unfasten (sails) from yards and stays. ■ untie or cast loose (a rope or cable).

unbending ▸ adjective reserved, formal, or strict in one's behaviour or attitudes; austere and inflexible.
– DERIVATIVES **unbendingly** adverb.

unbiased ▸ adjective showing no prejudice for or against something; impartial.

unbiblical ▸ adjective not found in, authorized by, or based on the Bible.

unbiddable ▸ adjective not easily controlled; unruly or disobedient.

unbidden ▸ adjective without having been commanded or invited: *unbidden guests.* ■ (especially of a thought or feeling) arising without conscious effort: *unbidden tears came to his eyes.*

unbind ▸ verb (past and past participle **unbound**) [with obj.] release from bonds or restraints.

unbirthday ▸ noun humorous any day except one's birthday: [as modifier] *an unbirthday present.*
– ORIGIN 1871: coined by Lewis Carroll in *Through the Looking Glass.*

unbleached ▸ adjective (especially of paper or cloth) not made whiter or lighter by a chemical process: *unbleached cotton.*

unblemished ▸ adjective not damaged or marked in any way.

unblended ▸ adjective not mixed with other types of the same substance: *unblended whisky.*

unblessed (also **unblest**) ▸ adjective not blessed: *to us, unblessed with our own children, he was almost a son.*

unblind ▸ verb [with obj.] conduct (a test or experiment) in such a way that it is no longer blind.

unblinking ▸ adjective (of a person or their eyes) not blinking. ■ (of an assessment or account) direct, thorough, and honest: *the film is an unblinking look at the porn trade.*
– DERIVATIVES **unblinkingly** adverb.

unblock ▸ verb [with obj.] **1** remove an obstruction from (something, especially a pipe or drain).
2 restore access to or the use of (email or a website or mobile phone): *crooks are using software to unblock the phones so they can be resold.*
3 Bridge play in such a way that (a long suit) becomes established.
– DERIVATIVES **unblocker** noun.

unblown ▸ adjective informal (of a vehicle or its engine) not provided with a turbocharger.

unblushing ▸ adjective not feeling or showing embarrassment or shame.
– DERIVATIVES **unblushingly** adverb.

unbolt ▸ verb [with obj.] open (a door or window) by drawing back a bolt.

unbolted ▸ adjective **1** (of a door or window) not bolted.
2 (of flour, powder, etc.) not sifted.

unbonnet ▸ verb (**unbonnets, unbonneting, unbonneted**) [no obj.] archaic remove one's hat, especially as a mark of respect.

unbookish ▸ adjective not particularly interested in reading and studying.

unborn ▸ adjective (of a baby) not yet born.

unbosom ▸ verb [with obj.] archaic disclose (one's thoughts or secrets): *she* ***unbosomed herself*** *to a trusty female friend.*

unbothered ▸ adjective lacking concern about something: *she was unbothered by the mess in the sink.*

unbound[1] ▸ adjective not bound or tied up: *her hair was unbound* | figurative *they were unbound by convention.* ■ (of printed sheets) not bound together. ■ (of a bound book) not provided with a proper or permanent cover. ■ Chemistry & Physics not held by a chemical bond, gravity, or other physical force: *unbound electrons.*

U

unbound[2] past and past participle of UNBIND.

unbounded ▸ adjective having or appearing to have no limits: *the possibilities are unbounded.*
– DERIVATIVES **unboundedly** adverb, **unboundedness** noun.

unbowed ▸ adjective not having submitted to pressure or demands: *they are unbowed by centuries of colonial rule.*

unbrace ▸ verb [with obj.] remove a support from.

unbraid ▸ verb [with obj.] untie (a braid).

unbranched ▸ adjective chiefly technical not having or divided into branches.

unbranded ▸ adjective **1** (of a product) not bearing a brand name: *unbranded computer systems.*

2 (of livestock) not branded with the owner's mark.

unbreachable ▸ adjective not able to be breached or overcome: *a virtually unbreachable position.*

unbreakable ▸ adjective not liable to break or able to be broken easily: *the flask is guaranteed unbreakable | an unbreakable code.*

unbreathable ▸ adjective (of air) not fit or pleasant to breathe.

unbribable ▸ adjective (of a person) not susceptible to bribery.

unbridgeable ▸ adjective (of a gap or difference) not able to be bridged or made less significant: *a seemingly unbridgeable cultural abyss.*

unbridled ▸ adjective uncontrolled; unconstrained: *a moment of unbridled ambition | unbridled lust.*

unbroken ▸ adjective 1 not broken, fractured, or damaged: *an unbroken glass.*
2 not interrupted or disturbed; continuous: *a night of sleep unbroken by nightmares.* ▪ (of a record) not surpassed: *a 13-year unbroken record of increasing profits.*
3 (of a horse) not tamed or accustomed to being ridden.
4 (of land) not cultivated.
– DERIVATIVES **unbrokenly** adverb, **unbrokenness** noun.

unbruised ▸ adjective not bruised.

unbuckle ▸ verb [with obj.] unfasten the buckle of (something, especially a belt or shoe).

unbuild ▸ verb (past and past participle **unbuilt**) 1 [with obj.] demolish or destroy (something, especially a building).
2 (as adj. **unbuilt**) not yet built or built on: *the houses remain unbuilt.*

unbundle ▸ verb [with obj.] 1 market or charge for (items or services) separately rather than as part of a package.
2 split (a company or conglomerate) into its constituent businesses, especially prior to selling them off.

unburden ▸ verb [with obj.] relieve (someone) of a burden. ▪ relieve (someone) of something that is causing them anxiety or distress: *the need to unburden yourself to someone who will listen.*

unburdened ▸ adjective not burdened or encumbered: *they are unburdened by expectations of success.*

unburied ▸ adjective (especially of a dead body) not buried.

unburnt (also **unburned**) ▸ adjective not damaged or destroyed by fire. ▪ (especially of bricks) not exposed to heat in a kiln.

unbury ▸ verb (**unburies, unburying, unburied**) [with obj.] remove (something) from under the ground.

unbusinesslike ▸ adjective not businesslike.

unbutton ▸ verb 1 [with obj.] unfasten the buttons of (a garment).
2 [no obj.] informal relax and become less inhibited: *unbutton a little, Molly.*

uncaged ▸ adjective released from or not confined in a cage.

uncalled ▸ adjective 1 not summoned or invited.
2 (**uncalled for**) (especially of a person's behaviour) undesirable and unnecessary: *uncalled-for remarks.*

uncandid ▸ adjective not candid or frank.

uncanny ▸ adjective (**uncannier, uncanniest**) strange or mysterious, especially in an unsettling way: *an uncanny feeling that she was being watched.*
– DERIVATIVES **uncannily** adverb, **uncanniness** noun.
– ORIGIN late 16th cent. (originally Scots in the sense 'relating to the occult, malicious'): from UN-[1] 'not' + CANNY.

U

uncanonical ▸ adjective 1 not conforming to or ordered by canon law.
2 not belonging to a literary or other canon.
– DERIVATIVES **uncanonically** adverb.

uncap ▸ verb (**uncaps, uncapping, uncapped**) [with obj.] 1 remove the lid or cover from.
2 remove a limit or restriction on (a price, rate, or amount).

uncapped ▸ adjective chiefly Brit. (of a player) never having been chosen as a member of a particular sports team, especially a national one.

uncared ▸ adjective (**uncared for**) not looked after properly: *it was sad to see the old place uncared for and neglected.*

uncaring ▸ adjective 1 not displaying sympathy or concern for others: *an uncaring father.*
2 not feeling interest in or attaching importance to something: *she had always been uncaring of her appearance.*
– DERIVATIVES **uncaringly** adverb.

uncarpeted ▸ adjective (of a floor) not covered with a carpet.

uncase ▸ verb [with obj.] remove from a cover or case.

uncashed ▸ adjective (of a cheque or money order) not yet cashed.

uncastrated ▸ adjective (of a male animal) not castrated.

uncatalogued (US **uncataloged**) ▸ adjective (of a book, document, etc.) not yet catalogued.

uncatchable ▸ adjective not able to be caught, in particular (of an athlete or sports team) not able or likely to be equalled or bettered.

uncaught ▸ adjective not caught.

unceasing ▸ adjective not coming to an end; continuous: *the unceasing efforts of the staff.*
– DERIVATIVES **unceasingly** adverb.

uncelebrated ▸ adjective not publicly acclaimed: *an uncelebrated but indispensable role.*

uncensored ▸ adjective not censored.

unceremonious ▸ adjective having or showing a lack of courtesy; rough or abrupt: *he was known for his strong views and unceremonious manners.*
– DERIVATIVES **unceremoniously** adverb, **unceremoniousness** noun.

uncertain ▸ adjective not able to be relied on; not known or definite: *an uncertain future.* ▪ (of a person) not completely confident or sure of something: *I was uncertain how to proceed.*
– PHRASES **in no uncertain terms** clearly and forcefully: *she has already refused me, in no uncertain terms.*
– DERIVATIVES **uncertainly** adverb.

uncertainty ▸ noun (pl. **uncertainties**) [mass noun] the state of being uncertain: *times of uncertainty and danger.* ▪ [count noun] (usu. **uncertainties**) something that is uncertain or that causes one to feel uncertain: *financial uncertainties.*

uncertainty principle ▸ noun Physics the principle that the momentum and position of a particle cannot both be precisely determined at the same time.

uncertified ▸ adjective not officially recognized as having a certain status or meeting certain standards: *uncertified accountants.* ▪ not attested or confirmed in a formal statement.

unchain ▸ verb [with obj.] remove the chains fastening or securing (someone or something).

unchallengeable ▸ adjective not able to be disputed, opposed, or defeated: *the unchallengeable truth of these basic facts.*
– DERIVATIVES **unchallengeably** adverb.

unchallenged ▸ adjective 1 not disputed or questioned: *the report's findings did not go unchallenged.* ▪ not called on to prove one's identity or allegiance: *they walked unchallenged into a hospital and stole a baby.*
2 (especially of a person in power) not opposed or defeated: *a position of unchallenged supremacy.*

unchallenging ▸ adjective 1 (of a task or situation) not testing one's abilities: *my job was unchallenging.*
2 not threatening someone's position: *his voice was gentle and unchallenging.*

unchancy ▸ adjective (**unchancier, unchanciest**) chiefly Scottish unlucky, inauspicious, or dangerous.

unchangeable ▸ adjective not liable to variation or able to be altered: *personality characteristics are virtually unchangeable.*
– DERIVATIVES **unchangeability** noun, **unchangeableness** noun, **unchangeably** adverb.

unchanged ▸ adjective not changed; unaltered: *an unchanged side for tonight's home game.*

unchanging ▸ adjective not changing; remaining the same: *the party stood for unchanging principles.*
– DERIVATIVES **unchangingly** adverb.

unchaperoned ▸ adjective unaccompanied or unsupervised.

uncharacteristic ▸ adjective not typical of a particular person or thing: *an uncharacteristic display of temper.*
– DERIVATIVES **uncharacteristically** adverb.

uncharged ▸ adjective 1 not having an electric charge.
2 not accused of an offence under the law: *she was released uncharged.*
3 not charged to a particular account: *an uncharged fixed cost.*

uncharismatic ▸ adjective lacking the charm and attractiveness that can inspire enthusiasm in others.

uncharitable ▸ adjective (of a person's behaviour or attitude towards others) unkind; unsympathetic: *this uncharitable remark possibly arose out of jealousy.*
– DERIVATIVES **uncharitableness** noun, **uncharitably** adverb.

uncharted ▸ adjective (of an area of land or sea) not mapped or surveyed: *the plane landed on a previously uncharted islet* | figurative *the present study is a foray into uncharted territory.*

> **USAGE** Uncharted means 'not yet mapped or surveyed'. Especially in the phrase **uncharted territory**, it is confused with **unchartered**, a far less common word that means 'not having a charter or written constitution'. **Unchartered territory** constitutes around 10 per cent of the total citations for the phrase in the Oxford English Corpus.

unchartered ▸ adjective not having a charter or written constitution.

unchaste ▸ adjective relating to or engaging in sexual activity, especially of an illicit or extramarital nature: *unchaste desires.*
– DERIVATIVES **unchastely** adverb, **unchastity** noun.

unchastened ▸ adjective (of a person) not restrained or subdued: *he was unchastened and ready for fresh mischief.*

unchecked ▸ adjective 1 (especially of something undesirable) not controlled or restrained: *prices rose unchecked, hitting the poor worst of all.*
2 not examined or checked.

unchivalrous ▸ adjective (of a man or his behaviour) discourteous, especially towards women.
– DERIVATIVES **unchivalrously** adverb.

unchosen ▸ adjective not chosen.

unchristian ▸ adjective not professing Christianity or its teachings. ▪ informal unkind, unfair, or morally wrong.
– DERIVATIVES **unchristianly** adjective & adverb.

unchurch ▸ verb [with obj.] officially exclude (someone) from participation in the Christian sacraments; excommunicate. ▪ deprive (a building) of its status as a church.

unchurched ▸ adjective not belonging to or connected with a Church.

uncial /ˈʌnsɪəl, -ʃ(ə)l/ ▸ adjective 1 of or written in a majuscule script with rounded unjoined letters which is found in European manuscripts of the 4th–8th centuries and from which modern capital letters are derived.
2 rare relating to an inch or an ounce.
▸ noun an uncial letter or script. ▪ a manuscript in uncial script.
– ORIGIN mid 17th cent.: from Latin *uncialis*, from *uncia* 'inch'. Sense 1 of the adjective is in the late Latin sense of *unciales litterae* 'uncial letters', the original application of which is unclear.

unciform /ˈʌnsɪfɔːm/ ▸ adjective another term for UNCINATE. ▪ dated denoting the hamate bone of the wrist.

uncinariasis /ˌʌnsɪnəˈrʌɪəsɪs/ ▸ noun another term for ANCYLOSTOMIASIS.
– ORIGIN early 20th cent.: from modern Latin *Uncinaria* (the name of a genus of hookworms) + -IASIS.

uncinate /ˈʌnsɪnət, -eɪt/ ▸ adjective chiefly Anatomy having a hooked shape.
– ORIGIN mid 18th cent.: from Latin *uncinatus*, from *uncinus* 'hook'.

uncirculated ▸ adjective (especially of a note or coin) that has not been in circulation.

uncircumcised ▸ adjective (of a boy or man) not circumcised. ▪ archaic irreligious or heathen.
– DERIVATIVES **uncircumcision** noun.

uncivil ▸ adjective discourteous; impolite.
– DERIVATIVES **uncivilly** adverb.

uncivilized (also **uncivilised**) ▸ adjective (of a place or people) not socially, culturally, or morally advanced. ▪ impolite; bad-mannered.

unclad ▸ adjective 1 unclothed; naked.
2 not provided with cladding: *unclad girders.*

unclaimed ▸ adjective not demanded or requested as being something one has a right to: *unclaimed benefits.*

unclamp ▸ verb [with obj.] remove the clamp from.

unclasp ▶ verb [with obj.] unfasten (something fastened with a clasp or similar device): *they unclasped their seat belts.* ■ release the grip of: *I unclasped her fingers from my hair.*

unclassifiable ▶ adjective not able to be assigned to a particular class or category.

unclassified ▶ adjective **1** not arranged in or assigned to classes or categories: *many texts remain unclassified or uncatalogued.* ■ Brit. (of a road) not classified according to the overall system of road numbering. ■ Brit. denoting a university degree without honours. ■ Brit. (of a grade in an examination) denoting a fail.
2 (of information or documents) not designated as secret.

uncle ▶ noun the brother of one's father or mother or the husband of one's aunt. ■ informal an unrelated older male friend, especially of a child. ■ archaic, informal a pawnbroker.
– PHRASES **cry** (or **say** or **yell**) **uncle** N. Amer. informal surrender or admit defeat. **Uncle Tom Cobley** (or **Cobleigh**) **and all** Brit. informal used to denote a long list of people. [with allusion to the ballad *Widdicombe Fair* in G. Bantock's *One Hundred Songs of England*.]
– ORIGIN Middle English: from Old French *oncle*, from late Latin *aunculus*, alteration of Latin *avunculus* 'maternal uncle' (see AVUNCULAR).

-uncle ▶ suffix forming chiefly diminutive nouns: *carbuncle | peduncle.*
– ORIGIN from Old French *-oncle*, *-uncle*, or from Latin *-unculus*, a special form of *-ulus*.

unclean ▶ adjective **1** dirty: *the firm was fined for operating in unclean premises.*
2 morally wrong: *unclean thoughts.* ■ (of food) regarded in a particular religion as impure and unfit to be eaten: *both religions regard pork as unclean.* ■ (in biblical use) ritually impure; (of a spirit) evil.
– DERIVATIVES **uncleanness** noun.
– ORIGIN Old English *unclǣne* (see UN-[1], CLEAN).

uncleanliness ▶ noun [mass noun] the state of being dirty: *general uncleanliness in schools.*

uncleanly ▶ adjective archaic term for UNCLEAN.

unclear ▶ adjective not easy to see, hear, or understand: *the motive for this killing is unclear.* ■ not obvious or definite; ambiguous: *their future remains unclear.* ■ having or feeling doubt or confusion: *users are still unclear about what middleware does.*
– DERIVATIVES **unclearly** adverb, **unclearness** noun.

uncleared ▶ adjective **1** (of land) not cleared of vegetation before cultivation.
2 (of a cheque) not having passed through a clearing house and been paid into the payee's account.

unclench ▶ verb [with obj.] release (a clenched part of the body): *slowly she unclenched her fist.* ■ [no obj.] relax from a clenched state.

Uncle Sam a personification of the federal government or citizens of the US.
– ORIGIN early 19th cent.: said (from the time of the first recorded instances) to have arisen as an expansion of the letters US.

Uncle Tom ▶ noun derogatory, chiefly N. Amer. a black man considered to be excessively obedient or servile to whites.
– ORIGIN 1920s: from the name of the hero of H. B. Stowe's *Uncle Tom's Cabin* (1852).

unclimbed ▶ adjective (of a mountain or rock face) not previously climbed: *the unclimbed south ridge.*
– DERIVATIVES **unclimbable** adjective.

unclip ▶ verb (**unclips**, **unclipping**, **unclipped**) [with obj.] release from being fastened or held with a clip.

uncloak ▶ verb [with obj.] literary uncover; reveal.

unclog ▶ verb (**unclogs**, **unclogging**, **unclogged**) [with obj.] remove accumulated matter from (a drain or other channel).

unclose ▶ verb [with obj.] rare open.

unclosed ▶ adjective not closed.

unclothe ▶ verb [with obj.] remove the clothes from (oneself or someone else).

unclothed ▶ adjective not wearing clothes; naked: *her unclothed body.*

unclouded ▶ adjective **1** (of the sky) not dark or overcast: *you wake up to sunshine and unclouded skies.*
2 not troubled or spoiled by anything: *six months of unclouded happiness.*

uncluttered ▶ adjective not having or impeded by too many objects, details, or elements: *the rooms were plain and uncluttered.*

unco /ˈʌŋkə/ Scottish ▶ adjective unusual or remarkable.
▶ adverb [as submodifier] remarkably; very: *it's got an unco fine taste.*
▶ noun (pl. **uncos**) a stranger. ■ (**uncos**) news.
– PHRASES **the unco guid** /ɡɪd/ chiefly derogatory strictly religious people.
– ORIGIN late Middle English (in the sense 'unknown, strange'): alteration of UNCOUTH.

uncoated ▶ adjective not covered with a coating of a particular substance.

uncoil ▶ verb straighten or cause to straighten from a coiled or curled position: [no obj.] *the rope uncoiled like a snake* | [with obj.] *she uncoiled her feather boa.*

uncollected ▶ adjective not collected or claimed: *the reward remained uncollected.*

uncolonized (also **uncolonised**) ▶ adjective (of a place) not yet colonized.

uncoloured (US **uncolored**) ▶ adjective **1** having no colour; neutral in colour.
2 not influenced, especially in a negative way: *explanations which are uncoloured by the observer's feelings.*

uncombed ▶ adjective (of a person's hair) not combed: *his hair was matted and uncombed.*

uncomely ▶ adjective archaic or humorous (especially of a woman) not attractive: *she was nineteen and not uncomely.* ■ archaic not agreeable or suitable.

uncomfortable ▶ adjective causing or feeling slight pain or physical discomfort: *his hard, uncomfortable bed.* ■ causing or feeling unease or awkwardness: *he began to feel uncomfortable at the man's hard stare | an uncomfortable silence.*
– DERIVATIVES **uncomfortableness** noun, **uncomfortably** adverb [as submodifier] *the house was dark and uncomfortably cold.*

uncomfy ▶ adjective informal not comfortable.

uncomment ▶ verb [with obj.] Computing change (a piece of text within a program) from being a comment to be part of the program that is run by the computer.

uncommercial ▶ adjective not making, intended to make, or allowing a profit.

uncommercialized (also **uncommercialised**) ▶ adjective not having profit as a primary aim.

uncommitted ▶ adjective not committed to a cause, activity, etc.: *uncommitted voters.* ■ (of resources) not pledged or set aside for future use: *there is very little uncommitted money to fund new policies.*

uncommon ▶ adjective out of the ordinary; unusual: *prostate cancer is not uncommon in men over 60 | an uncommon name.* ■ [attrib.] remarkably great (used for emphasis): *an uncommon amount of noise.*
▶ adverb [as submodifier] archaic remarkably: *he was uncommon afraid.*

uncommonly ▶ adverb [usu. as submodifier] exceptionally; very: *he is an uncommonly good talker.*

uncommunicative ▶ adjective unwilling to talk or impart information.
– DERIVATIVES **uncommunicatively** adverb, **uncommunicativeness** noun.

uncompanionable /ʌnkəmˈpanjənəb(ə)l/ ▶ adjective not friendly and sociable.

uncompassionate ▶ adjective not showing compassion or sympathy for other people.

uncompensated ▶ adjective (of a person or expense) not compensated or reimbursed. ■ (of an action) not compensated for: *uncompensated exploitation of the Third World.*

uncompetitive ▶ adjective not competitive: *that would destroy jobs and make industry uncompetitive.* ■ characterized by a desire to avoid fair competition: *uncompetitive practices.*
– DERIVATIVES **uncompetitively** adverb, **uncompetitiveness** noun.

uncomplaining ▶ adjective not complaining; resigned: *she was uncomplaining, accepting of her lot.*
– DERIVATIVES **uncomplainingly** adverb.

uncompleted ▶ adjective not completed.

uncomplexed ▶ adjective Chemistry (of an atom or molecule) not combined in a complex.

uncomplicated ▶ adjective simple or straightforward: *he was an extraordinarily uncomplicated man.*
– DERIVATIVES **uncomplicatedly** adverb, **uncomplicatedness** noun.

uncomplimentary ▶ adjective not complimentary; negative or insulting: *uncomplimentary remarks.*

uncompounded ▶ adjective not mixed. ■ (of a word) not made up of two or more existing words.

uncomprehending ▶ adjective showing or having an inability to comprehend something: *an uncomprehending silence.*
– DERIVATIVES **uncomprehendingly** adverb.

uncompressed ▶ adjective (of data) not compressed.

uncompromising ▶ adjective showing an unwillingness to make concessions to others, especially by changing one's ways or opinions. ■ harsh or relentless: *the uncompromising ugliness of her home.*
– DERIVATIVES **uncompromisingly** adverb, **uncompromisingness** noun.

unconcealed ▶ adjective (especially of an emotion) not concealed; obvious: *Sophia looked around her with unconcealed curiosity.*

unconcern ▶ noun [mass noun] a lack of worry or interest, especially when surprising or callous.

unconcerned ▶ adjective showing a lack of worry or interest, especially when this is surprising or callous: *Scott seemed unconcerned by his companion's problem.*
– DERIVATIVES **unconcernedly** adverb.

unconcluded ▶ adjective not yet brought to a conclusion: *unconcluded agreements.*

unconditional ▶ adjective not subject to any conditions: *unconditional surrender.*
– DERIVATIVES **unconditionality** noun, **unconditionally** adverb.

unconditioned ▶ adjective **1** not subject to conditions or to an antecedent condition; unconditional.
2 relating to or denoting instinctive reflexes or other behaviour not formed or influenced by conditioning or learning: *an unconditioned response.*
3 not subjected to a conditioning process: *waste in its raw, unconditioned form.*

unconfessed ▶ adjective not acknowledged: *the hope that remains unconfessed.* ■ (of a sin) not confessed to a priest.

unconfident ▶ adjective not confident; hesitant.
– DERIVATIVES **unconfidently** adverb.

unconfined ▶ adjective not confined to a limited space: *sows should be unconfined at farrowing.* ■ (of joy or excitement) very great: *joy was unconfined.*

unconfirmed ▶ adjective not confirmed as to truth or validity: *an unconfirmed report of shots being fired.*

unconformable ▶ adjective Geology (of rock strata in contact) marking a discontinuity in the geological record, and typically not having the same direction of stratification.
– DERIVATIVES **unconformably** adverb.

unconformity ▶ noun Geology a surface of contact between two groups of unconformable strata. ■ [mass noun] the condition of being unconformable.

uncongenial ▶ adjective (of a person) not friendly or pleasant to be with: *uncongenial dining companions.* ■ unsuitable and therefore unlikely to promote success or well-being: *the religious climate proved **uncongenial to** such ideas.*

unconnected ▶ adjective **1** not joined together or to something else: *the earth wire was left unconnected.*
2 not associated or linked in a sequence: *two unconnected events | the question was **unconnected to** anything they had been discussing.*
– DERIVATIVES **unconnectedly** adverb, **unconnectedness** noun.

unconquerable ▶ adjective (especially of a place, people, or emotion) not conquerable: *an unconquerable pride.*
– DERIVATIVES **unconquerably** adverb.

unconquered ▶ adjective not conquered.

unconscionable /ʌnˈkɒnʃ(ə)nəb(ə)l/ ▶ adjective not right or reasonable: *the unconscionable conduct of his son.* ■ unreasonably excessive: *shareholders have had to wait an unconscionable time for the facts to be established.*
– DERIVATIVES **unconscionably** adverb.
– ORIGIN mid 16th cent.: from UN-[1] 'not' + obsolete *conscionable*, from CONSCIENCE (interpreted as a plural) + -ABLE.

unconscious ▶ adjective **1** not awake and aware of and responding to one's environment: [as complement] *the boy was beaten unconscious.*
2 done or existing without one realizing: *he would wipe back his hair in an unconscious gesture of annoyance.* ■ (**unconscious of**) unaware of: *'What is it?' he said again, unconscious of the repetition.*
▶ noun (**the unconscious**) the part of the mind which is inaccessible to the conscious mind but which affects behaviour and emotions.
– DERIVATIVES **unconsciously** adverb.

U

unconsciousness ▸ **noun** [mass noun] the state of being unconscious: *someone gave me a crack across the head and I slipped into unconsciousness.* ■ the state of being uninformed or unaware: *part of her beauty was her unconsciousness of it.*

unconsecrated ▸ **adjective** not consecrated.

unconsenting ▸ **adjective** not consenting.

unconsidered ▸ **adjective 1** disregarded and unappreciated: *a snapper-up of unconsidered trifles.*
2 (of a statement or action) not thought about in advance, and therefore rash or harsh.

unconsolable ▸ **adjective** inconsolable.
– DERIVATIVES **unconsolably adverb.**

unconsolidated ▸ **adjective** not consolidated: *unconsolidated gravel and sand.*

unconstitutional ▸ **adjective** not in accordance with the political constitution or with procedural rules.
– DERIVATIVES **unconstitutionality noun, unconstitutionally adverb.**

unconstrained ▸ **adjective** not restricted or limited: *unconstrained growth.*
– DERIVATIVES **unconstrainedly adverb.**

unconstricted ▸ **adjective** not constricted.

unconstructed ▸ **adjective** chiefly N. Amer. (of a garment) unstructured.

unconsulted ▸ **adjective** not consulted for information or an opinion.

unconsumed ▸ **adjective** (especially of food or fuel) not consumed.

unconsummated ▸ **adjective** (of a marriage or other relationship) not having been consummated.

uncontainable ▸ **adjective** (especially of an emotion) very strong: *his uncontainable enthusiasm.*

uncontaminated ▸ **adjective** not contaminated: *uncontaminated air and food.*

uncontentious ▸ **adjective** not causing or likely to cause an argument: *an uncontentious view.*

uncontested ▸ **adjective** not contested: *these claims have not gone uncontested.*
– DERIVATIVES **uncontestedly adverb.**

uncontradicted ▸ **adjective** (of a statement) not contradicted.

uncontrived ▸ **adjective** not appearing artificial: *the whole effect was uncontrived.*

uncontrollable ▸ **adjective** not controllable: *her brother had an uncontrollable temper.*
– DERIVATIVES **uncontrollableness noun, uncontrollably adverb.**

uncontrolled ▸ **adjective** not controlled.
– DERIVATIVES **uncontrolledly adverb.**

uncontroversial ▸ **adjective** not controversial.
– DERIVATIVES **uncontroversially adverb.**

uncontroverted ▸ **adjective** of which the truth or validity is not disputed.

unconventional ▸ **adjective** not based on or conforming to what is generally done or believed: *his unconventional approach to life.*
– DERIVATIVES **unconventionality noun, unconventionally adverb.**

unconverted ▸ **adjective 1** (of a building) not adapted to a different use.
2 not having adopted a different religion, belief, or practice: *unconverted pagans.*
3 Rugby (of a try) not followed by a successful kick at goal.

unconvinced ▸ **adjective** not certain that something is true or can be relied on or trusted: *Parisians remain unconvinced that the project will be approved.*

unconvincing ▸ **adjective** failing to make someone believe that something is true or valid: *she felt the lie was unconvincing.* ■ failing to impress: *a slightly bizarre and unconvincing fusion of musical forces.*
– DERIVATIVES **unconvincingly adverb.**

uncooked ▸ **adjective** not cooked; raw.

uncool ▸ **adjective** informal not fashionable or impressive: *an uncool haircut.*

uncooperative ▸ **adjective** unwilling to help others or do what they ask.
– DERIVATIVES **uncooperatively adverb.**

uncoordinated ▸ **adjective 1** badly organized: *expensive mistakes resulting from uncoordinated manufacturing strategies.*
2 (of a person or their movements) clumsy.

uncopiable ▸ **adjective** impossible to copy or reproduce.

U

uncork ▸ **verb** [with obj.] **1** pull the cork out of (a bottle or other container).
2 N. Amer. informal (in a game or sport) deliver (a kick, throw, or punch): *Stulce uncorked the best throw of his career.*

uncorrected ▸ **adjective** not corrected.

uncorrelated ▸ **adjective** not correlated; lacking a mutual relationship or connection.

uncorroborated ▸ **adjective** not confirmed or supported by other evidence or information: *the unreliability of uncorroborated confessions.*

uncorrupted ▸ **adjective** not corrupted: *Lucinda is uncorrupted by nefarious influences.*

uncountable ▸ **adjective** too many to be counted (usually in hyperbolic use): *she'd spent uncountable nights in this very bed.*
– DERIVATIVES **uncountability noun, uncountably adverb.**

uncountable noun (also **uncount noun**) ▸ **noun** another term for **MASS NOUN.**

uncounted ▸ **adjective** not counted. ■ very numerous: *uncounted millions of dollars.*

uncouple ▸ **verb** [with obj.] disconnect (something, especially a railway vehicle that has been coupled to another). ■ [no obj.] become disconnected.

uncourtly ▸ **adjective** not courteous or refined.

uncouth ▸ **adjective 1** lacking good manners, refinement, or grace: *he is unwashed, uncouth, and drunk most of the time.* ■ (of art or language) lacking sophistication or delicacy.
2 archaic (of a place) wild, remote, or spartan.
– DERIVATIVES **uncouthly adverb, uncouthness noun.**
– ORIGIN Old English *uncūth* 'unknown', from **UN-**[1] 'not' + *cūth* (past participle of *cunnan* 'know, be able').

uncovenanted ▸ **adjective** not bound by or in accordance with a covenant or agreement. ■ not promised by or based on a covenant, especially a covenant with God.

uncover ▸ **verb** [with obj.] **1** remove a cover or covering from: *he uncovered the face of the dead man.* ■ [no obj.] archaic remove one's hat, especially as a mark of respect.
2 discover (something previously secret or unknown): *further evidence has been uncovered.*

uncovered ▸ **adjective** not covered: *uncovered stone floors.*

uncrate ▸ **verb** [with obj.] remove (something) from a crate.

uncrease ▸ **verb** [with obj.] remove the creases from.

uncreased ▸ **adjective** not creased: *uncreased paper.*

uncreate ▸ **verb** [with obj.] literary destroy.

uncreated ▸ **adjective** not yet created, or existing without having been created.

uncreative ▸ **adjective** not having or involving imagination or original ideas.

uncredited ▸ **adjective** (of a person or their work) not publicly acknowledged as having contributed to something, especially a publication or broadcast.

uncritical ▸ **adjective 1** not expressing criticism or using one's critical faculties: *an uncritical acceptance of the results.*
2 not in accordance with the principles of critical analysis: *uncritical reasoning.*
– DERIVATIVES **uncritically adverb.**

uncropped ▸ **adjective** not cropped.

uncross ▸ **verb** [with obj.] move (something) back from a crossed position: *the reporter uncrossed his legs.*

uncrossed ▸ **adjective 1** (of a person's legs or arms) not folded across each other.
2 Brit. (of a cheque) not crossed.

uncrowded ▸ **adjective** not filled with a large number of people: *miles of uncrowded beaches.*

uncrown ▸ **verb** [with obj.] deprive (a monarch) of their ruling position.

uncrowned ▸ **adjective** not formally crowned as a monarch.

uncrumple ▸ **verb** [with obj.] remove the crumples from; straighten.

uncrushable ▸ **adjective** (of a fabric) resistant to creasing.

uncrushed ▸ **adjective** not crushed.

UNCSTD ▸ **abbreviation** United Nations Conference on Science and Technology for Development.

UNCTAD /ˈʌŋ(k)tad/ ▸ **abbreviation** United Nations Conference on Trade and Development.

unction /ˈʌŋ(k)ʃ(ə)n/ ▸ **noun** [mass noun] **1** formal the action of anointing someone with oil or ointment as a religious rite or as a symbol of investiture as a monarch. ■ short for **EXTREME UNCTION.**
2 archaic treatment with a medicinal oil or ointment. ■ [count noun] an ointment: *mercury in the form of unctions.*
3 a fervent manner of expression apparently arising from deep emotion, especially when assumed: *the headlines gloated with the kind of effusive unction only the English press can muster.*
– ORIGIN late Middle English: from Latin *unctio(n-)*, from *unguere* 'anoint'. Sense 3 arises from the link between religious fervour and 'anointing' with the Holy Spirit.

unctuous /ˈʌŋ(k)tjʊəs/ ▸ **adjective 1** excessively flattering or ingratiating; oily: *he seemed anxious to please but not in an unctuous way.*
2 (chiefly of minerals) having a greasy or soapy feel.
– DERIVATIVES **unctuously adverb, unctuousness noun.**
– ORIGIN late Middle English (in the sense 'greasy'): from medieval Latin *unctuosus*, from Latin *unctus* 'anointing', from *unguere* 'anoint'.

unculled ▸ **adjective** (of an animal) not culled.

uncultivable ▸ **adjective** impossible to cultivate.

uncultivated ▸ **adjective 1** (of land) not used for growing crops.
2 (of a person) not highly educated.

uncultured ▸ **adjective** not characterized by good taste, manners, or education: *to my uncultured palate most of the wines were good.*

uncurbed ▸ **adjective** not restrained or kept in check: *their activities continue to be largely uncurbed.*

uncured ▸ **adjective 1** (of a person) not restored to health.
2 (of meat, fish, tobacco, or animal skins) not preserved by salting, drying, or smoking.

uncurl ▸ **verb** straighten or cause to straighten from a curled position: [no obj.] *in spring the new leaves uncurl* | [with obj.] *the doctor uncurled his fingers.*

uncurtained ▸ **adjective** (of a window) not provided with a curtain or curtains.

uncut ▸ **adjective 1** not cut: *her hair was left uncut.* ■ (of a stone, especially a diamond) not shaped by cutting. ■ chiefly historical (of a book) with the edges of its pages not slit open or trimmed off. ■ (of fabric) having its pile loops intact.
2 (of a text, film, or performance) complete; unabridged.
3 (of alcohol or a drug) not diluted or adulterated: *large amounts of uncut heroin.*

undamaged ▸ **adjective** not harmed or damaged: *buildings undamaged during the war.*

undated ▸ **adjective** not provided or marked with a date: *most of his letters are undated.*

undaunted ▸ **adjective** not intimidated or discouraged by difficulty, danger, or disappointment: *they were undaunted by the huge amount of work needed.*
– DERIVATIVES **undauntedly adverb, undauntedness noun.**

undead ▸ **adjective** (of a fictional being, especially a vampire) technically dead but still animate.

undecagon /ʌnˈdɛkəg(ə)n/ ▸ **noun** another term for **HENDECAGON.**
– ORIGIN early 18th cent.: formed irregularly from Latin *undecim* 'eleven', on the pattern of *decagon.*

undeceive ▸ **verb** [with obj.] tell (someone) that an idea or belief is mistaken: *they took her for a nun and Mary said nothing to undeceive them.*

undecidable ▸ **adjective** not able to be firmly established or refuted. ■ Logic (of a proposition or theorem) not able to be proved or disproved.
– DERIVATIVES **undecidability noun.**

undecided ▸ **adjective** (of a person) not having made a decision: *the jury remained undecided.* ■ not settled or resolved: *the match was still undecided.*
▸ **noun** a person who has not decided how they are going to vote in an election.
– DERIVATIVES **undecidedly adverb.**

undecipherable ▸ **adjective** (of speech or writing) not able to be read or understood.
– DERIVATIVES **undeciphered adjective.**

undeclared ▸ **adjective 1** not publicly announced, admitted, or acknowledged: *undeclared war.*
2 (of taxable income or dutiable goods) not declared.

undecorated ▸ adjective **1** not adorned or decorated: *the walls were completely undecorated.*
2 (of a member of the armed forces) not honoured with an award.

undee /ˈʌndeɪ/ ▸ adjective variant spelling of UNDY.

undefeated ▸ adjective not defeated, especially in a battle or other contest: *the undefeated champion.*

undefended ▸ adjective not defended: *undefended frontiers | legal aid for undefended divorces.*

undefiled ▸ adjective not defiled; pure.

undefined ▸ adjective not clear or defined: *undefined areas of jurisdiction | he felt an undefined longing.*
– DERIVATIVES **undefinable** adjective, **undefinably** adverb.

undelete ▸ verb [with obj.] Computing cancel the deletion of (text or a file).

undelivered ▸ adjective not delivered: *undelivered letters.*

undemanding ▸ adjective (especially of a task) not demanding: *undemanding clerical jobs.*

undemocratic ▸ adjective not relating or according to democratic principles: *an undemocratic regime.*
– DERIVATIVES **undemocratically** adverb.

undemonstrated ▸ adjective not shown to exist or be true.

undemonstrative ▸ adjective (of a person) not tending to express feelings, especially of affection, openly: *the English are an undemonstrative lot.*
– DERIVATIVES **undemonstratively** adverb, **undemonstrativeness** noun.

undeniable ▸ adjective unable to be denied or disputed: *it is an undeniable fact that some dogs are easier to train than others.*
– DERIVATIVES **undeniably** adverb [sentence adverb] *the topic is undeniably an important one.*

undenied ▸ adjective not denied.

undenominational ▸ adjective not attached to any religious denomination.

undented ▸ adjective (of a surface) not marked with a dent.

undependable ▸ adjective not trustworthy and reliable: *evidence is scarce and often undependable.*

under ▸ preposition **1** extending or directly below: *vast stores of gas under the North Sea | the streams that ran under the melting glaciers.* ■ below (something covering or protecting): *under several feet of water | a hot plate under an insulated lid.*
2 at a lower level than: *the room under his study.* ■ behind (a physical surface): *it was written on the new canvas under a gluey coating.* ■ behind or hidden behind (an appearance): *he had a deep sense of fun under his quiet exterior.* ■ lower in grade or rank than: *under him in the hierarchy.*
3 lower than (a specified amount, rate, norm, or age): *they averaged just under 2.8 per cent.*
4 controlled, managed, or governed by: *the province is now under martial law | I was under his spell.* ■ during the rule of: *the coinage standard was reformed under Elizabeth I.* ■ as a reaction to or undergoing the pressure of (something): *the sofa creaked under his weight | certain institutions may be under threat.* ■ as provided for by the rules of; in accordance with: *flowers supplied under contract by a local florist.* ■ used to express grouping or classification: *file it under 'lost' | published under his own name.* ■ Computing within the environment of (a particular operating system): *the program runs under DOS.*
5 undergoing (a process): *under construction.* ■ in a state of: *children living under difficult circumstances.* ■ planted with: *fields under wheat.*
▸ adverb **1** extending or directly below something: *weaving the body through the crossbars, over and under, over and under.*
2 under water: *he was floating for some time but suddenly went under.* ■ affected by an anaesthetic; unconscious: *the operation was quick; she was only under for 15 minutes.*
– DERIVATIVES **undermost** adjective.
– ORIGIN Old English, of Germanic origin; related to Dutch *onder* and German *unter.*

under- ▸ prefix **1** below; beneath: *underclothes | undercover.* ■ lower in status; subordinate: *undersecretary.*
2 insufficiently; incompletely: *undernourished.*

underachieve ▸ verb [no obj.] do less well than expected, especially in schoolwork.
– DERIVATIVES **underachievement** noun, **underachiever** noun.

underact ▸ verb [no obj.] act a part in a play or film in an overly restrained or unemotional way.

underactive ▸ adjective insufficiently active: *a health problem such as an underactive thyroid.*

underage ▸ adjective (of a person) too young to engage legally in a particular activity, especially drinking alcohol or having sex. ■ [attrib.] (of an activity) engaged in by people who are under age: *underage drinking.*

underappreciate ▸ verb [with obj.] (usu. as adj. **underappreciated**) fail to value sufficiently highly: *one of the jazz world's most underappreciated artists.*
– DERIVATIVES **underappreciation** noun.

underarm ▸ adjective & adverb (of a throw or stroke in sport) made with the arm or hand below shoulder level: [as adj.] *a good-length underarm serve* | [as adv.] *bowling underarm.*
▸ noun a person's armpit: [as modifier] *use an underarm deodorant.*

underbelly ▸ noun (pl. **underbellies**) the soft underside or abdomen of an animal. ■ an area vulnerable to attack: *these multinationals have a soft underbelly.* ■ a hidden unpleasant or criminal part of society.

underbid ▸ verb (**underbids, underbidding**; past and past participle **underbid**) [with obj.] **1** (in an auction or competitive tendering) make a lower bid than (someone).
2 Bridge make a lower bid on (one's hand) than its strength warrants.
▸ noun a bid that is lower than another or than is justified.
– DERIVATIVES **underbidder** noun.

underbite ▸ noun (in non-technical use) the projection of the lower teeth beyond the upper.

underbody ▸ noun (pl. **underbodies**) the underside of a road vehicle, ship, or animal's body.

underboss ▸ noun informal a boss's deputy, especially in the Mafia or another criminal organization.

underbred ▸ adjective dated bad-mannered; rude.

underbridge ▸ noun a bridge spanning an opening under a railway or road.

underbrush ▸ noun [mass noun] N. Amer. shrubs and small trees forming the undergrowth in a forest.

undercapitalize (also **undercapitalise**) ▸ verb [with obj.] provide (a company) with insufficient capital to achieve desired results.
– DERIVATIVES **undercapitalization** noun.

undercard ▸ noun the list of less important bouts on the same bill as a main boxing match.

undercarriage ▸ noun a wheeled structure beneath an aircraft, typically retracted when not in use, which supports the aircraft on the ground. ■ the supporting frame under the body of a vehicle.

undercart ▸ noun Brit. dated the undercarriage of an aircraft.

undercast ▸ verb (past and past participle **undercast**) [with obj.] allocate the parts in (a play or film) to insufficiently skilled actors.

undercharge ▸ verb [with obj.] **1** charge (someone) a price or amount that is too low.
2 give less than the proper charge to (an electric battery).
▸ noun a charge that is insufficient.

underclass ▸ noun the lowest social stratum in a country or community, consisting of the poor and unemployed.

undercliff ▸ noun a terrace or lower cliff formed by a landslip.

undercling Climbing ▸ noun a handhold which faces down the rock face.
▸ verb [no obj.] climb using such handholds.

underclothes ▸ plural noun clothes worn under others, typically next to the skin.
– DERIVATIVES **underclothing** noun.

undercoat ▸ noun **1** a layer of paint applied after the primer and before the topcoat.
2 an animal's underfur or down.
▸ verb [with obj.] apply an undercoat of paint to.

underconsumption ▸ noun [mass noun] Economics the purchase of goods and services at a level lower than that of their supply.

undercook ▸ verb [with obj.] (usu. as adj. **undercooked**) cook (something) insufficiently: *undercooked meats.*

undercool ▸ verb another term for SUPERCOOL.

undercount ▸ verb [with obj.] enumerate (something, especially a sector of a population in a census) at a lower figure than the actual figure.
▸ noun a count or figure that is inaccurately low. ■ the amount by which such a count or figure falls short of the actual figure.

undercover ▸ adjective involving secret work within a community or organization, especially for the purposes of police investigation or espionage: *an undercover police operation* | [as adv.] *he worked undercover in Northern Ireland.*

undercrackers ▸ plural noun Brit. informal men's underpants.

undercroft ▸ noun the crypt of a church.
– ORIGIN late Middle English: from UNDER- + the rare term *croft* 'crypt', from Middle Dutch *crofte* 'cave', from Latin *crypta.*

undercurrent ▸ noun **1** a current of water below the surface and moving in a different direction from any surface current.
2 an underlying feeling or influence, especially one that is contrary to the prevailing atmosphere and is not expressed openly: *racial undercurrents.*

undercut ▸ verb (**undercuts, undercutting**; past and past participle **undercut**) [with obj.] **1** offer goods or services at a lower price than (a competitor): *these industries have been undercut by more efficient foreign producers.*
2 cut or wear away the part below or under (something, especially a cliff). ■ cut away material to leave (a carved design) in relief.
3 weaken; undermine: *the chairman denied his authority was being undercut.*
4 Tennis strike (a ball) with backspin so that it bounces high on landing.
▸ noun **1** a space formed by the removal or absence of material from the lower part of something. ■ N. Amer. a notch cut in a tree trunk to guide its fall when felled.
2 Brit. the underside of a sirloin of beef.

underdamp ▸ verb [with obj.] Physics damp (a system) incompletely, so as to allow a few oscillations after a single disturbance.

underdetermine ▸ verb [with obj.] account for (a theory or phenomenon) with less than the amount of evidence needed for proof or certainty.
– DERIVATIVES **underdetermination** noun.

underdeveloped ▸ adjective **1** not fully developed: *underdeveloped kidneys | the community services are underfunded and underdeveloped.* ■ (of a country or region) not advanced economically.
2 (of a photographic film) not developed sufficiently to give a normal image.
– DERIVATIVES **underdevelopment** noun.

underdog ▸ noun a competitor thought to have little chance of winning a fight or contest. ■ a person who has little status in society.

underdone ▸ adjective (of food) insufficiently cooked.

underdrawing ▸ noun [mass noun] sketched lines made by a painter as a preliminary guide, and subsequently covered with paint. ■ [count noun] such a preliminary sketch.

underdress ▸ verb [no obj.] (also **be underdressed**) dress too plainly or too informally: *without a pinstripe you'd be underdressed.*

undereducated ▸ adjective poorly educated.

underemphasize (also **underemphasise**) ▸ verb [with obj.] place insufficient emphasis on: *history is underemphasized in the curriculum.*
– DERIVATIVES **underemphasis** noun.

underemployed ▸ adjective (of a person) not having enough paid work or not doing work that makes full use of their skills and abilities.
– DERIVATIVES **underemployment** noun.

under-equipped ▸ adjective not having all the necessary equipment or resources: *many hospitals and clinics were understaffed and under-equipped.*

underestimate ▸ verb [with obj.] estimate (something) to be smaller or less important than it really is: *the government has grossly underestimated the extent of the problem.* ■ regard (someone) as less capable than they really are: *he had underestimated the new President.*
▸ noun an estimate that is too low.
– DERIVATIVES **underestimation** noun.

underexpose ▸ verb [with obj.] Photography expose (film or an image) for too short a time.
– DERIVATIVES **underexposure** noun.

underfed ▸ adjective insufficiently fed or nourished.

underfelt ▸ noun [mass noun] Brit. felt laid under a carpet to add thickness and reduce wear.

U

underfinanced ▶ adjective not having or receiving sufficient funding: *underfinanced inner-city schools.*

under-fives ▶ plural noun chiefly Brit. children who are less than five years old, especially those who are not in full-time education.

underfloor ▶ adjective (especially of a heating system) situated or operating beneath the floor.

underflow ▶ noun **1** an undercurrent. ■ a horizontal flow of water through the ground, especially beneath a riverbed.
2 [mass noun] Computing the generation of a number that is too small to be represented in the device meant to store it.

underfoot ▶ adverb under one's feet; on the ground: *it was very muddy underfoot* | figurative *genuine rights were being trodden underfoot.* ■ constantly present and in one's way: *the last thing my mother wanted was a child underfoot.*
▶ adjective [attrib.] relating to the state of the ground, especially in a horse race: *the underfoot conditions were good.*

underframe ▶ noun the supporting frame or substructure of something, in particular a vehicle or piece of furniture.

underfund ▶ verb [with obj.] provide with insufficient funding.
– DERIVATIVES **underfunding** noun.

underfur ▶ noun [mass noun] an inner layer of short, fine fur or down underlying an animal's outer fur, providing warmth and waterproofing.

undergarment ▶ noun an article of underclothing.

undergird ▶ verb [with obj.] secure or fasten from the underside, especially by a rope or chain passed underneath. ■ formal provide support or a firm basis for.

underglaze ▶ noun a colour or design applied to pottery before it is glazed.

undergo ▶ verb (**undergoes**, **undergoing**; past **underwent**; past participle **undergone**) [with obj.] experience or be subjected to (something, typically something unpleasant or arduous): *he underwent a life-saving brain operation.*
– ORIGIN Old English *undergān* 'undermine' (see **UNDER-**, **GO[1]**).

undergrad ▶ noun informal an undergraduate.

undergraduate ▶ noun a university student who has not yet taken a first degree.

underground ▶ adverb beneath the surface of the ground: *miners working underground.* ■ in or into secrecy or hiding, especially as a result of carrying out subversive political activities: *many were forced to go underground by the government.*
▶ adjective situated beneath the surface of the ground: *an underground car park.* ■ relating to or denoting the secret activities of people working to subvert an established order: *Czech underground literature.* ■ relating to or denoting a group or movement seeking to explore alternative forms of lifestyle or artistic expression; radical and experimental: *the New York underground art scene.*
▶ noun **1** (often **the Underground**) Brit. an underground railway, especially the one in London: *travel chaos on the Underground.*
2 a group or movement organized secretly to work against an existing regime. ■ a group or movement seeking to explore alternative forms of lifestyle or artistic expression: *the late sixties underground.*
▶ verb [with obj.] lay (cables) below ground level.

underground economy ▶ noun North American term for **BLACK ECONOMY**.

U

Underground Railroad (in the US) a secret network for helping slaves escape from the South to the North and Canada in the years before the American Civil War.

undergrowth ▶ noun [mass noun] Brit. a dense growth of shrubs and other plants, especially under trees in woodland.

underhand ▶ adjective **1** acting or done in a secret or dishonest way: *underhand dealings.*
2 another term for **UNDERARM**: *underhand bowling* | [as adv.] *I served underhand.* ■ with the palm of the hand upward or outward: *an underhand grip.*
– ORIGIN Old English in the sense 'in or into subjection, under control' (see **UNDER-**, **HAND**).

underhanded ▶ adjective another term for **UNDERHAND**: *underhanded practices.*
– DERIVATIVES **underhandedly** adverb.

underhung ▶ adjective another term for **UNDERSHOT** (sense 2).

underinsured ▶ adjective (of a person) having inadequate insurance cover.
– DERIVATIVES **underinsurance** noun.

underinvest ▶ verb [no obj.] fail to invest sufficient money or resources in a project or enterprise: *we persistently underinvest in historic buildings.*
– DERIVATIVES **underinvestment** noun.

underlay[1] ▶ verb (past and past participle **underlaid**) [with obj.] place something under (something else), especially to support or raise it.
▶ noun [mass noun] **1** something placed under or behind something else, especially material laid under a carpet for protection or support.
2 Music the manner in which the words are fitted to the notes of a piece of vocal music.
– ORIGIN Old English *underlecgan* (see **UNDER-**, **LAY[1]**).

underlay[2] past tense of **UNDERLIE**.

underlease ▶ noun & verb another term for **SUBLEASE**.

underlet ▶ verb (**underlets**, **underletting**; past and past participle **underlet**) another term for **SUBLEASE**.

underlever ▶ noun a lever behind the trigger guard on a rifle.

underlie ▶ verb (**underlies**, **underlying**; past **underlay**; past participle **underlain**) [with obj.] **1** (especially of a layer of rock or soil) lie or be situated under (something).
2 be the cause or basis of (something): *the fundamental issue which underlies the conflict* | (as adj. **underlying**) *the underlying causes of poverty and drug addiction.*
– ORIGIN Old English *underlicgan* 'be subject or subordinate to' (see **UNDER-**, **LIE[1]**).

underlife ▶ noun (pl. **underlives**) a way of living with which the general public do not normally come into contact.

underline ▶ verb [with obj.] draw a line under (a word or phrase) to give emphasis or indicate special type. ■ emphasize (something): *the improvement in retail sales was underlined by these figures.*
▶ noun **1** a line drawn under a word or phrase, especially for emphasis.
2 the line of the lower part of an animal's body.

underlinen ▶ noun [mass noun] archaic underclothes, especially those made of linen.

underling ▶ noun chiefly derogatory a person lower in status or rank.

underlip ▶ noun the lower lip of a person or animal.

underlit ▶ adjective having insufficient light or lighting; dim.

underlying present participle of **UNDERLIE**.

underman ▶ verb (**undermans**, **undermanning**, **undermanned**) [with obj.] fail to provide with enough workers or crew: *the public prosecutor's offices are hopelessly undermanned.*

undermanager ▶ noun a manager who is subordinate to another manager.

undermentioned ▶ adjective Brit. mentioned at a later place in a book or document.

undermine ▶ verb [with obj.] **1** erode the base or foundation of (a rock formation). ■ dig or excavate beneath (a building or fortification) so as to make it collapse.
2 lessen the effectiveness, power, or ability of, especially gradually or insidiously: *this could undermine years of hard work.*
– DERIVATIVES **underminer** noun.
– ORIGIN Middle English: from **UNDER-** + the verb **MINE[2]**, probably suggested by Middle Dutch *ondermineren.*

underneath ▶ preposition & adverb **1** situated directly below (something else): [as prep.] *our bedroom's right underneath theirs* | *four names written underneath each other* | [as adv.] *his eyes were red-rimmed with black bags underneath* | [as adj.] *on longer hair, the underneath layers can be permed to give extra body.*
2 so as to be concealed by (something else): [as prep.] *money changed hands underneath the table* | figurative *underneath his aloof air, Nicky was a warm and open young man* | [as adv.] *paint was peeling off in flakes to reveal greyish plaster underneath.* ■ partly or wholly concealed by (a garment): [as prep.] *she could easily see the broadness of his shoulders underneath a tailored white sports shirt* | [as adv.] *undoing her jacket to reveal nothing but a bra underneath.*
▶ noun [in sing.] the part or side of something facing towards the ground; the underside.
– ORIGIN Old English *underneothan*; compare with **BENEATH**.

undernourished ▶ adjective having insufficient food or other substances for good health and condition: *undernourished children.*
– DERIVATIVES **undernourishment** noun.

underoccupancy ▶ noun [mass noun] Brit. (with reference to holiday or hospital accommodation) the state of not being occupied to the expected or advertised capacity.

underpaid past and past participle of **UNDERPAY**.

underpainting ▶ noun [mass noun] paint subsequently overlaid with another layer or with a finishing coat.

underpants ▶ plural noun an undergarment, especially for men or boys, covering the lower part of the body and having two holes for the legs.

underpart ▶ noun a lower part of something. ■ (**underparts**) the underside of an animal's body, especially when of a specified colour or pattern.

underpass ▶ noun a road or pedestrian tunnel passing under a road or railway.

underpay ▶ verb (past and past participle **underpaid**) [with obj.] pay too little to (someone). ■ pay less than is due for (something): (as adj. **underpaid**) *late or underpaid tax.*
– DERIVATIVES **underpayment** noun.

underperform ▶ verb [no obj.] perform less well than expected. ■ [with obj.] increase in value less than: *the shares have underperformed the market.*
– DERIVATIVES **underperformance** noun.

underpin ▶ verb (**underpins**, **underpinning**, **underpinned**) [with obj.] **1** support (a building or other structure) from below by laying a solid foundation below ground level or by substituting stronger for weaker materials.
2 support, justify, or form the basis for: *the theme of honour underpinning the two books.*

underpinning ▶ noun **1** a solid foundation laid below ground level to support or strengthen a building.
2 a set of ideas, motives, or devices which justify or form the basis for something: *the theoretical underpinning for free-market economics.*

underplant ▶ verb [with obj.] plant or cultivate the ground around (a tall plant) with smaller plants: *the roses are underplanted with pink and white bulbs.*

underplay ▶ verb [with obj.] **1** perform (something) in a restrained way: *the violins underplayed the romantic element in the music.*
2 represent (something) as being less important than it really is: *I do not wish to underplay the tragedies that have occurred.*

underplot ▶ noun a subordinate plot in a play, novel, or similar work.

underpopulated ▶ adjective having an insufficient or very small population.
– DERIVATIVES **underpopulation** noun.

underpowered ▶ adjective lacking sufficient mechanical, electrical, or other power.

underprepared ▶ adjective not having prepared sufficiently to carry out a task.

underprice ▶ verb [with obj.] sell or offer at too low a price: *water shares were underpriced.* ■ sell or offer something at a lower price than (the competition): *Wal-Mart has underpriced its traditional competitors.*

underprivileged ▶ adjective (of a person) not enjoying the same standard of living or rights as the majority of people in a society.

underproduce ▶ verb [with obj.] **1** produce less of (a commodity) than is wanted or needed.
2 (often as adj. **underproduced**) record or produce (a song or film) in such a basic way that it appears rough or unfinished.
– DERIVATIVES **underproduction** noun.

underproof ▶ adjective containing less alcohol than proof spirit does.

underprop ▶ verb (**underprops**, **underpropping**, **underpropped**) [with obj.] archaic support, especially with a prop.

underqualified ▶ adjective insufficiently qualified for a particular job.

underquote ▶ verb [with obj.] give too low an estimated cost for (a commodity or service).

underrate ▶ verb [with obj.] (often as adj. **underrated**) underestimate the extent, value, or importance of (someone or something): *a very underrated film.*

under-read ▶ verb (past and past participle **under-read**) [no obj.] (of a gauge or dial) show a reading lower than the true one.

under-record ▸ verb [with obj.] record (a number or amount) as being lower than it really is. ▪ record (data or information) insufficiently or inadequately: *such conditions had been markedly under-recorded in medical inspection.*

under-rehearsed ▸ adjective (of a performance or performer) insufficiently rehearsed.

under-report ▸ verb [with obj.] fail to report (something, especially news or data) fully.

under-represent ▸ verb [with obj.] provide with insufficient or inadequate representation: *women are under-represented at high levels.*
– DERIVATIVES **under-representation** noun.

under-resourced ▸ adjective provided with insufficient resources: *under-resourced schools.*
– DERIVATIVES **under-resourcing** noun.

undersaturated ▸ adjective technical falling short of being saturated with a particular constituent.
– DERIVATIVES **undersaturation** noun.

underscore ▸ noun a line drawn under a word or phrase for emphasis. ▪ (on a computer or typewriter keyboard) a short horizontal line _ on the baseline.
▸ verb [with obj.] underline (something). ▪ emphasize: *the company underscored the progress made with fuel cells.*

undersea ▸ adjective situated, occurring, or done below the sea or the surface of the sea.

underseal chiefly Brit. ▸ verb [with obj.] coat (the under part of a motor vehicle) with waterproof material as protection against rust.
▸ noun [mass noun] waterproof coating used as protection against rust.

undersecretary ▸ noun (pl. **undersecretaries**) a subordinate official, in particular (in the UK) a junior minister or senior civil servant, or (in the US) the principal assistant to a member of the cabinet.

undersell ▸ verb (past and past participle **undersold**) [with obj.] sell something at a lower price than (a competitor). ▪ promote or value (something) insufficiently.

underserved ▸ adjective inadequately provided with a service or facility: *a medically underserved community.*

undersexed ▸ adjective having unusually weak sexual desires.

undersheriff ▸ noun a deputy sheriff.

undershirt ▸ noun chiefly N. Amer. an undergarment worn under a shirt; a vest.

undershoot ▸ verb (past and past participle **undershot**) [with obj.] **1** (of an aircraft) land short of (the runway).
2 fall short of (a point or target): *the figure undershot the government's original estimate.*
▸ noun an act of undershooting.

undershorts ▸ plural noun chiefly N. Amer. underpants.

undershot past and past participle of UNDERSHOOT.
▸ adjective **1** (of a waterwheel) turned by water flowing under it.
2 denoting or having a lower jaw which projects beyond the upper jaw.

undershrub ▸ noun another term for SUBSHRUB.

underside ▸ noun the bottom or lower side or surface of something: *the butterfly's wings have a mottled brown pattern on the underside.* ▪ the less favourable aspect of something: *the sordid underside of the glamorous 1980s.*

undersigned formal ▸ noun (**the undersigned**) the signatory or co-signatories to the document in question: *we, the undersigned, wish to protest at the current activities of the company.*
▸ adjective having appended one's signature to the document in question.

undersized (also **undersize**) ▸ adjective of less than the usual size.

underskirt ▸ noun a skirt worn under another; a petticoat.

underslung ▸ adjective suspended from the underside of something: *helicopters hover to lift underslung loads.* ▪ (of a vehicle chassis) hanging lower than the axles.

undersoil ▸ noun [mass noun] subsoil.

undersold past and past participle of UNDERSELL.

undersow ▸ verb (past participle **undersown**) [with obj.] sow (a later-growing crop) on land already seeded with another crop.

underspend ▸ verb (past and past participle **underspent**) [no obj.] spend too little. ▪ [with obj.] spend less than (a specified or allocated amount): *schools have underspent their training budgets.*
▸ noun [in sing.] an act of underspending: *areas in the year's budget where there has been an underspend.*

understaffed ▸ adjective having too few members of staff to operate effectively: *the department is understaffed and overworked.*
– DERIVATIVES **understaffing** noun.

understairs ▸ adjective in the space below a staircase: *an understairs storage cupboard.*

understand ▸ verb (past and past participle **understood**) [with obj.] **1** perceive the intended meaning of (words, a language, or a speaker): *he didn't understand a word I said | he could usually **make himself understood*** | [with clause] *she understood what he was saying.* ▪ perceive the significance, explanation, or cause of: *she didn't really understand the situation* | [with clause] *he couldn't understand why we burst out laughing.*
2 interpret or view (something) in a particular way: *as the term is usually understood, legislation refers to regulations and directives.* ▪ [with clause] infer something from information received (often used as a polite formula in conversation): *I understand you're at art school* | [with obj.] *as I understood it, she was flying back to the States tomorrow.* ▪ regard (a missing word, phrase, or idea) as present: *'present company excepted' is always understood when sweeping generalizations are being made.* ▪ [with clause] assume to be the case; take for granted: *he liked to play the field, that was understood.*
3 be sympathetically or knowledgeably aware of the character or nature of: *Picasso understood colour* | [with clause] *I understand how you feel.*
– DERIVATIVES **understander** noun.
– ORIGIN Old English *understandan* (see UNDER-, STAND).

understandable ▸ adjective able to be understood: *though his accent was strange, the words were perfectly understandable.* ▪ to be expected; natural, reasonable, or forgivable: *such fears are understandable | it is understandable that mistakes occur sometimes.*
– DERIVATIVES **understandability** noun, **understandably** adverb [sentence adverb] *understandably, Richard did not believe me.*

understanding ▸ noun [mass noun] **1** the ability to understand something; comprehension: *foreign visitors with little understanding of English.* ▪ the power of abstract thought; intellect: *a child of sufficient intelligence and understanding.* ▪ an individual's perception or judgement of a situation: *my understanding was that he would find a new supplier.*
2 sympathetic awareness or tolerance: *he wrote with understanding and affection of the people of Dent.*
3 [count noun] an informal or unspoken agreement or arrangement: *he and I have an understanding | he had only been allowed to come **on the understanding that** he would be on his best behaviour.*
▸ adjective **1** sympathetically aware of other people's feelings; tolerant and forgiving.
2 archaic having insight or good judgement.
– DERIVATIVES **understandingly** adverb.

understate ▸ verb [with obj.] describe or represent (something) as being smaller or less good or important than it really is: *the press have understated the extent of the problem.*

understated ▸ adjective presented or expressed in a subtle and effective way: *understated elegance.*
– DERIVATIVES **understatedly** adverb.

understatement ▸ noun [mass noun] the presentation of something as being smaller or less good or important than it really is: *a master of English understatement* | [count noun] *to say I am delighted is an understatement.*

understeer ▸ verb [no obj.] (of a motor vehicle) have a tendency to turn less sharply than is intended: *the turbo understeers on very fast bends.*
▸ noun [mass noun] the tendency of a vehicle to turn less sharply than intended.

understocked ▸ adjective having insufficient stock of goods, farm animals, etc.

understood past and past participle of UNDERSTAND.

understorey ▸ noun (pl. **understoreys**) Ecology a layer of vegetation beneath the main canopy of a forest.

understrapper ▸ noun informal, dated an assistant or junior official.

understudy ▸ noun (pl. **understudies**) (in the theatre) a person who learns another's role in order to be able to act at short notice in their absence.
▸ verb (**understudies**, **understudying**, **understudied**) [with obj.] study (a role or actor) as an understudy: *he had to understudy Prospero.*

undersubscribed ▸ adjective (of a course or event) having more places available than applications. ▪ (of a share issue) having fewer applications for shares than there are shares available.

undersurface ▸ noun the lower or under surface of something.

underswell ▸ noun an undercurrent.

undertake ▸ verb (past **undertook**; past participle **undertaken**) [with obj.] commit oneself to and begin (an enterprise or responsibility); take on: *a firm of builders undertook the construction work.* ▪ [usu. with infinitive] promise to do a particular thing: *the firm undertook to keep price increases to a minimum.* ▪ [with clause] guarantee or affirm something; give as a formal pledge: *a lorry driver implicitly undertakes that he is reasonably skilled as a driver.*

undertaker ▸ noun a person whose business is preparing dead bodies for burial or cremation and making arrangements for funerals.

undertaking ▸ noun **1** a formal pledge or promise to do something: *I give an undertaking that we shall proceed with the legislation.* ▪ [mass noun] the action of undertaking to do something: *the knowing undertaking of an obligation.*
2 a task that is taken on; an enterprise: *a mammoth undertaking that involved digging into the side of a cliff face.* ▪ a company or business: *national transport undertakings.*
3 [mass noun] the business of managing funerals.

undertenant ▸ noun a subtenant.
– DERIVATIVES **undertenancy** noun (pl. **undertenancies**).

underthings ▸ plural noun underclothes.

underthrust Geology ▸ verb (past and past participle **underthrust**) [with obj.] force (a crustal plate or other body of rock) beneath another formation. ▪ be forced underneath (another formation).
▸ noun an instance of such forced movement.

undertip ▸ verb (**undertips**, **undertipping**, **undertipped**) [with obj.] give (someone) an excessively small tip: *I was so mad I undertipped the waiter at the sushi bar.*

undertone ▸ noun a subdued or muted tone of sound or colour: *they were talking in undertones.* ▪ an underlying quality or feeling: *the sexual undertones of most advertising.*

undertook past participle of UNDERTAKE.

undertow ▸ noun another term for UNDERCURRENT.

undertrained ▸ adjective (of a person) with insufficient training for a job, sport, etc.

undertrial ▸ noun Indian informal a person who is on trial in a court of law.

undertrick ▸ noun Bridge a trick by which the declarer falls short of their contract.

underuse ▸ verb /ʌndəˈjuːz/ [with obj.] (usu. as adj. **underused**) use (something) below the optimum level: *massive acreages of underused land.*
▸ noun /ʌndəˈjuːs/ [mass noun] insufficient use: *underuse of existing services.*

underutilize (also **underutilise**) ▸ verb [with obj.] underuse (something).
– DERIVATIVES **underutilization** noun.

undervalue ▸ verb (**undervalues**, **undervaluing**, **undervalued**) [with obj.] (often as adj. **undervalued**) rate (something) insufficiently highly; fail to appreciate: *the skills of the housewife remain undervalued in society.* ▪ underestimate the financial value of (something): *the company's assets were undervalued in its balance sheet.*
▸ noun a price below the real value.
– DERIVATIVES **undervaluation** noun.

undervest ▸ noun a vest worn as an undergarment.

undervote ▸ noun US a ballot paper or vote that is not counted because of unclear marking by the voter.

underwater ▸ adjective & adverb situated, occurring, or done beneath the surface of the water: *there are underwater volcanoes in the region* | [as adv.] *the seal spent a lot of time underwater.*

under way (also **underway**) ▸ adverb **1** having started and in progress; being done or carried out: *recruitment is well under way.*
2 (of a boat) moving through the water: *no time was lost in getting under way.*
– ORIGIN mid 18th cent. (as a nautical term): from Dutch *onderweg.*

underwear ▸ noun [mass noun] clothing worn under other clothes, typically next to the skin.

U

underweight ▸ adjective **1** below a weight considered normal or desirable: *he was thirty pounds underweight.*
2 Finance having less investment in a particular area than is considered desirable: *the company is still underweight in Japan.*
▸ verb [with obj.] apply too little weight to: *we feared the hot-air balloon had been underweighted.*
▸ noun [mass noun] insufficient weight.

underwent past of UNDERGO.

underwhelm ▸ verb [with obj.] humorous fail to impress or make a positive impact on (someone); disappoint: *American voters seem underwhelmed by the choices for president.*
– ORIGIN 1950s: suggested by OVERWHELM.

underwing ▸ noun **1** the hindwing of an insect, especially when it is normally hidden by a forewing.
2 the underside of a bird's wing.
3 (also **underwing moth**) [usu. with modifier] a moth with drab forewings and brightly coloured hindwings, typically yellow with a black terminal band.
● Several genera in the family Noctuidae.

underwire ▸ noun a semicircular wire support stitched under each cup of a bra.
– DERIVATIVES **underwired** adjective.

underwood ▸ noun [mass noun] small trees and shrubs growing beneath taller timber trees.

underwork ▸ verb [with obj.] impose too little work on (someone).

underworld ▸ noun **1** the world of criminals or of organized crime.
2 the mythical abode of the dead, imagined as being under the earth.

underwrite ▸ verb (past **underwrote**; past participle **underwritten**) [with obj.] **1** sign and accept liability under (an insurance policy), thus guaranteeing payment in case loss or damage occurs. ■ accept (a liability or risk) in this way.
2 (of a bank or other financial institution) engage to buy all the unsold shares in (an issue of new shares). ■ undertake to finance or otherwise support or guarantee (something): *they were willing to underwrite, in part, the construction of a ship.*
3 archaic write (something) below something else, especially other written matter.
– DERIVATIVES **underwriter** noun.

undescended ▸ adjective Medicine (of a testicle) remaining in the abdomen instead of descending normally into the scrotum.

undeserved ▸ adjective not warranted, merited, or earned: *an undeserved term of imprisonment.*
– DERIVATIVES **undeservedly** adverb.

undeserving ▸ adjective not deserving or worthy of something positive, especially help or praise.
– DERIVATIVES **undeservingly** adverb.

undesigned ▸ adjective unintended.

undesirable ▸ adjective not wanted or desirable because harmful, objectionable, or unpleasant: *the drug's undesirable side effects.*
▸ noun a person considered to be objectionable in some way.
– DERIVATIVES **undesirability** noun, **undesirableness** noun, **undesirably** adverb.

undesired ▸ adjective (especially of an act or consequence) not wanted or desired.

undesirous ▸ adjective [predic.] formal not wanting or wishing something: *the prince was* **undesirous of** *seeing the Lady Anne.*

undetectable ▸ adjective not able to be detected.
– DERIVATIVES **undetectability** noun, **undetectably** adverb.

U

undetected ▸ adjective not detected or discovered: *the thieves escaped undetected.*

undetermined ▸ adjective not authoritatively decided or settled: *the acquisition will result in an as yet undetermined number of lay-offs.* ■ not known: *the bus was travelling with an undetermined number of passengers when it crashed.*

undeterred ▸ adjective persevering with something despite setbacks: *he was undeterred by these disasters.*

undetonated ▸ adjective (of a bomb or other explosive weapon) not having been detonated.

undeveloped ▸ adjective not having been developed: *undeveloped coal reserves.* ■ not having developed: *undeveloped buds and shoots.*

undeviating ▸ adjective showing no deviation; constant and steady: *the undeviating loyalty of his wife.*
– DERIVATIVES **undeviatingly** adverb.

undiagnosed ▸ adjective not diagnosed or having been subject to diagnosis.

undid past of UNDO.

undies ▸ plural noun informal articles of underwear, especially those of a woman or girl.
– ORIGIN early 20th cent.: abbreviation.

undifferenced ▸ adjective Heraldry (of arms) not made distinct by a mark of difference.

undifferentiated ▸ adjective not different or differentiated.

undigested ▸ adjective (of food) not digested. ■ (of information, facts, or ideas) not having been properly assessed, considered, or understood.

undignified ▸ adjective appearing foolish and unseemly; lacking in dignity: *an undignified exit.*

undiluted ▸ adjective (of a liquid) not diluted. ■ not moderated or weakened in any way: *a sudden surge of pure, undiluted happiness.*

undiminished ▸ adjective not diminished, reduced, or lessened: *his enthusiasm for the game remains undiminished.*

undimmed ▸ adjective not dimmed.

undine /ˈʌndiːn/ ▸ noun a female spirit or nymph imagined as inhabiting water.
– ORIGIN early 19th cent.: from modern Latin *undina* (a word invented by Paracelsus), from Latin *unda* 'a wave'.

undiplomatic ▸ adjective being or appearing insensitive and tactless.
– DERIVATIVES **undiplomatically** adverb.

undirected ▸ adjective lacking direction; without a particular aim, purpose, or target: *she was full of ineffectual undirected anger.*

undiscerning ▸ adjective lacking judgement, insight, or taste: *an undiscerning audience.*

undischarged ▸ adjective not discharged: *an undischarged bankrupt | an undischarged gun.*

undisciplined ▸ adjective lacking in discipline; uncontrolled in behaviour or manner.

undisclosed ▸ adjective not revealed or made known publicly: *the precise terms of the agreement remained undisclosed.*

undiscoverable ▸ adjective not able to be discovered.

undiscovered ▸ adjective not discovered: *the novel had lain undiscovered for years among his papers.*

undiscriminating ▸ adjective not having or showing good judgement or taste.

undiscussed ▸ adjective not discussed.

undisguised ▸ adjective (of a feeling) not disguised or concealed; open: *she looked at him with undisguised contempt.*
– DERIVATIVES **undisguisedly** adverb.

undismayed ▸ adjective not dismayed or discouraged by a setback.

undisputed ▸ adjective not disputed or called in question; accepted.

undissociated ▸ adjective Chemistry (of a molecule) not dissociated into oppositely charged ions.

undissolved ▸ adjective not dissolved.

undistinguishable ▸ adjective indistinguishable.

undistinguished ▸ adjective lacking distinction; unexceptional: *an undistinguished career.*

undistorted ▸ adjective not distorted: *it may be difficult to provide undistorted information.*

undistracted ▸ adjective able to concentrate fully on something; not distracted: *she was undistracted by the flashing cameras.*

undistributed ▸ adjective not distributed.

undistributed middle ▸ noun Logic a fallacy arising from the failure of the middle term of a syllogism to refer to all the members of a class in at least one premise.

undisturbed ▸ adjective not disturbed: *a quiet weekend of undisturbed tranquillity | the tombs had lain undisturbed for 2,500 years.*

undivided ▸ adjective **1** not divided, separated, or broken into parts.
2 devoted completely to one object: *I can now give you my undivided attention.*

undo ▸ verb (**undoes**, **undoing**; past **undid**; past participle **undone**) [with obj.] **1** unfasten, untie, or loosen (something): *the knot was difficult to undo.*
2 cancel or reverse the effects or results of (a previous action or measure): *there wasn't any way Evelyn could undo the damage.* ■ cancel (the last command executed by a computer).
3 formal cause the downfall or ruin of: *Iago's hatred of women undoes him.*
▸ noun Computing a feature of a computer program that allows a user to cancel or reverse the last command executed.
– ORIGIN Old English *undōn* (see UN-², DO¹).

undock ▸ verb [with obj.] **1** separate (a spacecraft) from another in space.
2 take (a ship) out of a dock.

undocumented ▸ adjective **1** not recorded in or proved by documents.
2 N. Amer. not having the appropriate legal document or licence: *undocumented immigrants.*

undoing ▸ noun [in sing.] a person's ruin or downfall: *he knew of his ex-partner's role in his undoing.* ■ the cause of a person's ruin or downfall: *that complacency was to be their undoing.*

undomesticated ▸ adjective not domesticated: *I never cook for him and I am totally undomesticated.*

undone ▸ adjective **1** not tied or fastened: *the top few buttons of his shirt were undone.*
2 not done or finished: *he had left his homework undone.*
3 formal or humorous (of a person) ruined by a disastrous or devastating setback or reverse: *I am undone!*

undoubtable ▸ adjective rare not able to be doubted; indubitable.
– DERIVATIVES **undoubtably** adverb.

undoubted ▸ adjective not questioned or doubted by anyone: *her undoubted ability.*

undoubtedly ▸ adverb without doubt; certainly: *they are undoubtedly guilty.*

UNDP ▸ abbreviation United Nations Development Programme.

undrained ▸ adjective not emptied of water; not drained: *undrained marshes.*

undramatic ▸ adjective lacking the qualities expected in drama: *an undramatic libretto.* ■ unexciting: *research tends to be undramatic and unglamorous.*

undraped ▸ adjective not covered with cloth or drapery. ■ (especially of a model or subject in art) naked.

undrawn ▸ adjective **1** (of curtains) not drawn across the window; open.
2 (of money) not drawn from a bank account.

undreamed /ʌnˈdriːmd, -ˈdrɛmt/ (Brit. also **undreamt** /ʌnˈdrɛmt/) ▸ adjective (**undreamed of**) not thought to be possible (used to express pleasant surprise at the amount, extent, or level of something): *she is now enjoying undreamed-of success.*

undress ▸ verb [no obj.] take off one's clothes: *she undressed and climbed into bed | I went into the bathroom to* **get undressed**. ■ [with obj.] take the clothes off (someone else).
▸ noun [mass noun] **1** the state of being naked or only partially clothed: *women in various states of undress.*
2 Military ordinary clothing or uniform, as opposed to that worn on ceremonial occasions. Compare with FULL DRESS.

undressed ▸ adjective **1** wearing no clothes; naked: *he was undressed and ready for bed.*
2 not treated, processed, or prepared for use: *undressed deerskin | a rough, undressed stone slab.*
3 (of food) not having a dressing: *an undressed salad.*

undrinkable ▸ adjective not fit to be drunk because of impurity or poor quality.

UNDRO ▸ abbreviation United Nations Disaster Relief Office.

undue ▸ adjective unwarranted or inappropriate because excessive or disproportionate: *this figure did not give rise to undue concern.*

undue influence ▸ noun [mass noun] Law influence by which a person is induced to act otherwise than by their own free will or without adequate attention to the consequences.

undulant /ˈʌndjʊl(ə)nt/ ▸ adjective having a rising and falling motion or appearance like that of waves; undulating.
– ORIGIN mid 19th cent.: from Latin *undulant-* 'moving like a wave', from the verb *undulare*.

undulant fever ▸ noun [mass noun] brucellosis in humans.
– ORIGIN late 19th cent.: so named because of the intermittent fever associated with the disease.

undulate ▸ verb /ˈʌndjʊleɪt/ [no obj.] move with a smooth wave-like motion: *her body undulated to the thumping rhythm of the music.* ■ (usu. as adj.

undulating) have a wavy form or outline: *delightful views over undulating countryside.*
▸ **adjective** /ˈʌndjʊlət/ Botany & Zoology (especially of a leaf) having a wavy surface or edge.
– DERIVATIVES **undulation** noun, **undulatory** adjective.
– ORIGIN mid 17th cent.: from late Latin *undulatus*, from Latin *unda* 'a wave'.

unduly ▸ adverb to an unwarranted degree; inordinately: *there is no need to be unduly alarmed.*

undutiful ▸ adjective not respectful or obedient.
– DERIVATIVES **undutifully** adverb, **undutifulness** noun.

undy /ˈʌndi/ (also **undee**) ▸ adjective [usu. postpositive] Heraldry another term for **WAVY**.

undyed ▸ adjective (especially of fabric) not dyed; of its natural colour.

undying ▸ adjective (especially of an emotion) lasting forever: *promises of undying love.*
– DERIVATIVES **undyingly** adverb.

unearned ▸ adjective not earned or deserved: *unearned privileges.* ■ Baseball (of a run) resulting from an error by the fielding side.

unearned income ▸ noun [mass noun] income derived from private means rather than from work.

unearned increment ▸ noun an increase in the value of land or property without labour or expenditure on the part of the owner.

unearth ▸ verb [with obj.] **1** find (something) in the ground by digging. ■ discover (something hidden, lost, or kept secret) by investigation or searching: *they have done all they can to unearth the truth.*
2 drive (an animal, especially a fox) out of a hole or burrow.

unearthly ▸ adjective (**unearthlier**, **unearthliest**)
1 unnatural or mysterious, especially in a disturbing way: *unearthly quiet.*
2 informal unreasonably early or inconvenient: *a job which involves getting up at an unearthly hour.*
– DERIVATIVES **unearthliness** noun.

unease ▸ noun [mass noun] anxiety or discontent: *public unease about defence policy.*

uneasy ▸ adjective (**uneasier**, **uneasiest**) **1** causing or feeling anxiety; troubled or uncomfortable: *she felt guilty now and a little uneasy | an uneasy silence.*
2 (of a situation or relationship) not settled; liable to change: *she lived in a state of uneasy truce with her strict father.*
– DERIVATIVES **uneasily** adverb, **uneasiness** noun.

uneatable ▸ adjective not fit to be eaten: *we all complained about the uneatable breakfast.*

uneaten ▸ adjective not eaten: *salad lying uneaten on the plate.*

uneconomic ▸ adjective unprofitable: *the closure of uneconomic pits.* ■ constituting an inefficient use of money or other resources: *it may be uneconomic to repair some goods.*

uneconomical ▸ adjective wasteful of money or other resources; not economical: *the old buses eventually become uneconomical to run.*
– DERIVATIVES **uneconomically** adverb.

unedifying ▸ adjective (especially of an event taking place in public) distasteful; unpleasant: *the unedifying sight of the two leaders screeching conflicting proposals.*
– DERIVATIVES **unedifyingly** adverb.

unedited ▸ adjective (of material for publication or broadcasting) not edited.

uneducated ▸ adjective having or showing a poor level of education.
– DERIVATIVES **uneducable** adjective.

unelectable ▸ adjective (of a candidate or party) very likely to be defeated at an election.

unelected ▸ adjective (of an official) not elected: *unelected bureaucrats.*

unembarrassed ▸ adjective not feeling or showing embarrassment.

unembellished ▸ adjective not embellished or decorated: *the unembellished truth.*

unemotional ▸ adjective not having or showing strong feelings: *a flat, unemotional voice.*
– DERIVATIVES **unemotionally** adverb.

unemphatic ▸ adjective (especially of tone or a gesture) not emphatic: *an unemphatic 'yes'.*
– DERIVATIVES **unemphatically** adverb.

unemployable ▸ adjective (of a person) not able or likely to get paid employment because of a lack of skills or qualifications.
▸ noun an unemployable person.
– DERIVATIVES **unemployability** noun.

unemployed ▸ adjective (of a person) without a paid job but available to work: *I was unemployed for three months* | (as plural noun **the unemployed**) *a training programme for the long-term unemployed.* ■ (of a thing) not in use.

unemployment ▸ noun [mass noun] the state of being unemployed. ■ the number or proportion of unemployed people: *a time of high unemployment.*

unemployment benefit (also US **unemployment compensation**) ▸ noun [mass noun] payment made by the state or, in the US, a trade union, to an unemployed person.

unenclosed ▸ adjective (especially of land) not enclosed: *the unenclosed uplands of Wales.*

unencrypted ▸ adjective Computing (of information or data) not converted into a code that would prevent unauthorized access.

unencumbered ▸ adjective not having any burden or impediment: *he needed to travel light and unencumbered.* ■ free of debt or other financial liability.

unending ▸ adjective having or seeming to have no end: *the charity rescues children from unending poverty.* ■ countless or continual: *unending demands.*
– DERIVATIVES **unendingly** adverb, **unendingness** noun.

unendowed ▸ adjective not endowed, especially by donated funds.

unendurable ▸ adjective not able to be tolerated or endured: *cries of unendurable suffering.*
– DERIVATIVES **unendurably** adverb.

unenforceable ▸ adjective (especially of an obligation or law) impossible to enforce.

unengaged ▸ adjective not occupied or engaged.

un-English ▸ adjective not considered characteristic of English people or the English language.

unenjoyable ▸ adjective (of an activity or occasion) not giving pleasure.

unenlightened ▸ adjective not having or showing an enlightened outlook: *unenlightened thinking.*
– DERIVATIVES **unenlightening** adjective, **unenlightenment** noun.

unenriched ▸ adjective (especially of uranium) not enriched.

unentangle ▸ verb another term for **DISENTANGLE**.

unenterprising ▸ adjective not having or showing initiative or entrepreneurial ability.

unenthusiastic ▸ adjective not having or showing enthusiasm: *an unenthusiastic response.*
– DERIVATIVES **unenthusiastically** adverb.

unenviable ▸ adjective difficult, undesirable, or unpleasant: *an unenviable reputation for drunkenness.*
– DERIVATIVES **unenviably** adverb.

unenvied ▸ adjective not regarded with envy.

UNEP ▸ abbreviation United Nations Environment Programme.

unequal ▸ adjective **1** not equal in quantity, size, or value: *two rooms of unequal size | unequal odds.* ■ not fair, evenly balanced, or having equal advantage: *an unequal distribution of power.*
2 (**unequal to**) lacking the ability or resources to cope with: *she felt unequal to the task before her.*
▸ noun a person or thing regarded as unequal to another in status or level.
– DERIVATIVES **unequalize** (also **unequalise**) verb, **unequally** adverb.

unequalled (US **unequaled**) ▸ adjective superior to all others in performance or extent: *a range of facilities unequalled in London | trout of unequalled quality.*

unequipped ▸ adjective [predic.] not equipped with the necessary items or skills: *kids unequipped to deal with the situation.*

unequivocal ▸ adjective leaving no doubt; unambiguous: *an unequivocal answer | he was unequivocal in condemning the violence.*
– DERIVATIVES **unequivocally** adverb, **unequivocalness** noun.

unerring ▸ adjective always right or accurate: *an unerring sense of direction.*
– DERIVATIVES **unerringly** adverb.

unescapable ▸ adjective unable to be avoided or denied.

UNESCO /juːˈnɛskəʊ/ (also **Unesco**) an agency of the United Nations set up in 1945 to promote the exchange of information, ideas, and culture.
– ORIGIN acronym from *United Nations Educational, Scientific, and Cultural Organization.*

unescorted ▸ adjective not escorted: *children unescorted by an adult.*

unessential ▸ adjective & noun another term for **INESSENTIAL**.

unestablished ▸ adjective **1** not established.
2 not forming part of the permanent staff: *an unestablished professor of anatomy.*

unethical ▸ adjective not morally correct: *it is unethical to torment any creature for entertainment.*
– DERIVATIVES **unethically** adverb.

unevangelical ▸ adjective not evangelical.

uneven ▸ adjective **1** not level or smooth: *the floors are cracked and uneven.*
2 not regular, consistent, or equal: *the uneven distribution of resources.* ■ (of a contest) not equally balanced: *Fran struggled briefly but soon gave up the uneven match.*
– DERIVATIVES **unevenly** adverb, **unevenness** noun.
– ORIGIN Old English *unefen* 'not corresponding exactly' (see **UN-[1]**, **EVEN[1]**).

uneven bars ▸ plural noun North American term for **ASYMMETRIC BARS**.

uneventful ▸ adjective not marked by interesting or exciting events.
– DERIVATIVES **uneventfully** adverb, **uneventfulness** noun.

unevolved ▸ adjective in a primitive or early stage of development: *relatively unevolved stars.*

unexamined ▸ adjective not investigated or examined: *widely held but largely unexamined preconceptions.*

unexampled ▸ adjective formal having no precedent or parallel: *a regime which brought such unexampled disaster on its people.*

unexceptionable ▸ adjective not open to objection, but not particularly new or exciting: *the unexceptionable belief that society should be governed by law.*
– DERIVATIVES **unexceptionably** adverb.

unexceptional ▸ adjective not out of the ordinary; usual: *an unexceptional movie.*
– DERIVATIVES **unexceptionally** adverb.

unexcitable ▸ adjective (of a person) not easily excited.

unexciting ▸ adjective not exciting; dull.

unexecuted ▸ adjective not executed, carried out, or put into effect: *unexecuted schemes for redeveloping the main buildings.*

unexercised ▸ adjective **1** not made use of or put into practice: *unexercised stock options.*
2 (of a person) not taking exercise; unfit.

unexhausted ▸ adjective (especially of resources or reserves) not exhausted.

unexpected ▸ adjective not expected or regarded as likely to happen: *his death was totally unexpected* | (as noun **the unexpected**) *he seemed to have a knack for saying the unexpected.*
– DERIVATIVES **unexpectedly** adverb [as submodifier] *an unexpectedly high price,* **unexpectedness** noun.

unexpired ▸ adjective (of an agreement or period of time) not yet having come to an end: *the unexpired portion of the lease.*

unexplainable ▸ adjective unable to be explained or accounted for: *he was subject to unexplainable rages.*
– DERIVATIVES **unexplainably** adverb.

unexplained ▸ adjective not described or made clear; unknown: *the reason for her summons was as yet unexplained.* ■ not accounted for or attributable to an identified cause: *cot death is still an unexplained phenomenon.*

unexploded ▸ adjective (of a bomb or other explosive device) not having exploded.

unexploited ▸ adjective (of resources) not used to maximum benefit: *unexploited reserves of natural gas.*

unexplored ▸ adjective (of a country or area) not investigated or mapped. ■ not evaluated or discussed in detail: *the research focuses on an unexplored theme in European history.*

U

unexposed ▸ adjective **1** covered or protected; not vulnerable. ■ (of photographic film) not subjected to light.
2 [predic.] not introduced to or acquainted with something: *a person **unexposed to** spiritualist traditions.*
3 not made public; concealed: *no secrets were left unexposed.*

unexpressed ▸ adjective **1** (of a thought or feeling) not communicated or made known: *he thought it best to leave his doubts unexpressed.*
2 Genetics (of a gene) not appearing in a phenotype.

unexpressive ▸ adjective showing no expression; emotionless: *his big brown eyes were dull and unexpressive.*

unexpurgated ▸ adjective (of a text) complete and containing all the original material; uncensored.

unfaceable ▸ adjective (of a situation or circumstance) not able to be confronted or dealt with.

unfading ▸ adjective not losing brightness, vitality, or strength.

unfailing ▸ adjective without error or fault: *his unfailing memory for names.* ■ reliable or constant: *his mother had always been an unfailing source of reassurance.*
– DERIVATIVES **unfailingly** adverb.

unfair ▸ adjective not based on or behaving according to the principles of equality and justice: *at times like these the legal system appears inhuman and unfair | it would be unfair to blame her for the situation.* ■ not following the rules of a game or sport: *he was sent off for unfair play.*
– DERIVATIVES **unfairly** adverb, **unfairness** noun.
– ORIGIN Old English *unfæger* 'not beautiful' (see **UN-**[1], **FAIR**[1]).

unfaithful ▸ adjective not faithful, in particular: ■ engaging in sexual relations with a person other than one's regular partner in contravention of a previous promise or understanding: *you haven't **been unfaithful to** him, have you? | her unfaithful husband.* ■ disloyal, treacherous, or insincere: *she felt that to sell the house would be **unfaithful to** her parents' memory.*
– DERIVATIVES **unfaithfully** adverb, **unfaithfulness** noun.

unfaltering ▸ adjective not faltering; steady; resolute: *her unfaltering energy and determination.*
– DERIVATIVES **unfalteringly** adverb.

unfamiliar ▸ adjective **1** not known or recognized: *he felt a stranger among the crowd of unfamiliar faces | his voice was **unfamiliar to** her.* ■ unusual or uncharacteristic: *the yellow taxicab was an unfamiliar sight on these roads.*
2 (**unfamiliar with**) not having knowledge or experience of: *he seems unfamiliar with recent research on this topic.*
– DERIVATIVES **unfamiliarity** noun.

unfancied ▸ adjective (of a sports team or racehorse) not considered likely to win.

unfashionable ▸ adjective not fashionable or popular at a particular time: *they lived in an unfashionable part of London.*
– DERIVATIVES **unfashionableness** noun, **unfashionably** adverb.

unfashioned ▸ adjective chiefly literary not made into a specific shape; formless.

unfasten ▸ verb [with obj.] open the fastening of; undo (something): *Allie stands before the mirror unfastening her earrings.* ■ [no obj.] become loose or undone.

U

unfathered ▸ adjective dated having no known or acknowledged father; illegitimate. ■ chiefly literary of unknown or obscure origin: *unfathered rumours.*

unfatherly ▸ adjective not having or showing the affectionate or protective characteristics associated with a father.

unfathomable ▸ adjective **1** incapable of being fully explored or understood: *her grey eyes were dark with some unfathomable emotion.*
2 (of water or a natural feature) impossible to measure the extent of.
– DERIVATIVES **unfathomableness** noun, **unfathomably** adverb.

unfathomed ▸ adjective **1** not fully explored or understood.
2 (of water) of unascertained depth.

unfavourable (US **unfavorable**) ▸ adjective
1 expressing or showing a lack of approval or support: *single mothers are often the target of unfavourable press attention.*
2 likely to lead to an adverse outcome: *unfavourable economic conditions.*
– DERIVATIVES **unfavourableness** noun, **unfavourably** adverb.

unfazed ▸ adjective informal not disconcerted or perturbed: *the protestors were unfazed by the prospect of arrest.*

unfeasible ▸ adjective inconvenient or impractical: *childcare is expensive, making the return to work unfeasible for many women.*
– DERIVATIVES **unfeasibility** noun, **unfeasibly** adverb.

unfed ▸ adjective not having been fed.

unfeeling ▸ adjective **1** unsympathetic, harsh, or callous.
2 lacking physical sensation or sensitivity.
– DERIVATIVES **unfeelingly** adverb, **unfeelingness** noun.
– ORIGIN late Old English *unfēlende* 'insensible' (see **UN-**[1], **FEELING**).

unfeigned ▸ adjective genuine; sincere: *a broad smile of unfeigned delight.*
– DERIVATIVES **unfeignedly** adverb.

unfelt ▸ adjective not felt or experienced.

unfeminine ▸ adjective not having or showing qualities traditionally associated with women.
– DERIVATIVES **unfemininity** noun.

unfenced ▸ adjective not provided with fences.

unfermented ▸ adjective not fermented.

unfertile ▸ adjective not fertile; infertile.

unfertilized (also **unfertilised**) ▸ adjective not fertilized: *an unfertilized egg | unfertilized land.*

unfetter ▸ verb [with obj.] release from restraint or inhibition.

unfettered ▸ adjective not confined or restricted: *his imagination is unfettered by the laws of logic.*

unfilial ▸ adjective not having or showing the qualities associated with a son or daughter.

unfilled ▸ adjective not filled: *there are a number of unfilled posts in this area of nursing.*

unfilmable ▸ adjective (especially of a novel) not able to be adapted into a film.

unfiltered ▸ adjective **1** not filtered: *unfiltered tap water.*
2 (of a cigarette) not provided with a filter.

unfinished ▸ adjective **1** not finished or concluded; incomplete: *her last novel is unfinished.*
2 (of an object) not having been given an attractive surface appearance as the final stage of manufacture.

unfired ▸ adjective **1** (of clay or pottery) not fired.
2 (of a gun) not discharged.

unfit ▸ adjective **1** (of a thing) not of the necessary quality or standard to meet a particular purpose: *the land is **unfit for** food crops.* ■ (of a person) not having the requisite qualities or skills to undertake something competently: *she is unfit to have care and control of her children.*
2 (of a person) not in good physical condition, typically as a result of failure to take regular exercise.
▸ verb (**unfits, unfitting, unfitted**) [with obj.] archaic make (something or someone) unsuitable; disqualify.
– DERIVATIVES **unfitly** adverb, **unfitness** noun.

unfitted ▸ adjective **1** [predic.] (of a person) not fitted or suited for a particular task or vocation: *she was **unfitted for** marriage.*
2 (of furniture) not fitted.

unfitting ▸ adjective not fitting or suitable; unbecoming: *certain occupations were held unfitting for baptized believers.*
– DERIVATIVES **unfittingly** adverb.

unfixable ▸ adjective not able to be repaired or put right: *I do not think the problem is unfixable.*

unfixed ▸ adjective not fixed, in particular: ■ not fixed in a definite place or position; unfastened; loose: *the green cloth cover had become unfixed in a dozen places.* ■ uncertain or variable: *a being of unfixed gender.*
– DERIVATIVES **unfix** verb.

unflagging ▸ adjective tireless; persistent: *his apparently unflagging enthusiasm impressed her.*
– DERIVATIVES **unflaggingly** adverb.

unflappable ▸ adjective informal having or showing calmness in a crisis.
– DERIVATIVES **unflappability** noun, **unflappably** adverb.

unflashy ▸ adjective not seeking attention through being ostentatiously impressive; restrained or tasteful: *a solid, unflashy performance.*

unflattering ▸ adjective not flattering: *the reviews of the book were very unflattering | an unflattering portrait.*
– DERIVATIVES **unflatteringly** adverb.

unflavoured (US **unflavored**) ▸ adjective (of food or drink) not containing additional flavourings.

unfledged ▸ adjective (of a bird) not yet fledged. ■ (of a person) inexperienced; youthful.

unfleshed ▸ adjective chiefly literary not covered with flesh.

unflinching ▸ adjective not showing fear or hesitation in the face of danger or difficulty: *he has shown unflinching determination throughout the campaign.*
– DERIVATIVES **unflinchingly** adverb.

unflustered ▸ adjective not agitated; calm and self-controlled: *she seemed surprisingly unflustered by the delay.*

unfocused (also **unfocussed**) ▸ adjective **1** (of a person's eyes or gaze) not focusing on a particular person or thing. ■ (of an optical device) not adjusted to focus. ■ (of a lens) not making incident light rays meet at a single point. ■ (of an object of vision) not in focus; indistinct.
2 (of feelings or plans) without a specific aim or direction: *his voice quavered with an unfocused rage.*

unfold ▸ verb **1** open or spread out from a folded position: [with obj.] *he unfolded the map and laid it out on the table* | [no obj.] *the white flowers were just starting to unfold.*
2 [no obj.] (of events or information) gradually develop or be revealed: *there was a fascinating scene unfolding before me.* ■ [with obj.] reveal or disclose (thoughts or information): *Eva **unfolded** her secret exploits **to** Mattie.*
– DERIVATIVES **unfoldment** noun (US).
– ORIGIN Old English *unfealdan* (see **UN-**[2], **FOLD**[1]).

unforced ▸ adjective not produced by effort; natural: *an unforced cheerfulness.* ■ not compelled or constrained: *his retirement was an unforced departure.*
– DERIVATIVES **unforcedly** adverb.

unfordable ▸ adjective (of a watercourse) not able to be forded.

unforeseeable ▸ adjective not able to be anticipated or predicted: *too many unforeseeable political consequences could arise from such a decision.*

unforeseen ▸ adjective not anticipated or predicted.

unforested ▸ adjective (of land) not covered with forest.

unforetold ▸ adjective literary not foretold; unpredicted.

unforgettable ▸ adjective impossible to forget; very memorable: *that unforgettable first kiss.*
– DERIVATIVES **unforgettably** adverb.

unforgivable ▸ adjective so bad as to be unable to be forgiven or excused: *losing your temper with him was unforgivable.*
– DERIVATIVES **unforgivably** adverb.

unforgiven ▸ adjective not forgiven: *the catalogue of unforgiven wrongs simply grows and grows.*

unforgiving ▸ adjective not willing to forgive or excuse people's faults or wrongdoings: *he was always a proud and unforgiving man.* ■ (of a place or situation) harsh or hostile: *the moor can be a wild and unforgiving place in bad weather.*
DERIVATIVES **unforgivingly** adverb, **unforgivingness** noun.

unforgotten ▸ adjective not forgotten.

unformatted ▸ adjective Computing (of a document, storage medium, etc.) not formatted.

unformed ▸ adjective without a definite form or shape: *she packed the unformed butter into the mould.* ■ not having developed or been developed fully: *he had an ambitious, albeit unformed, idea for a novel | unformed youths.*

unformulated ▸ adjective not formulated: *the unformulated rules of society.*

unforthcoming ▸ adjective **1** (of a person) not willing to divulge information: *the sergeant seemed unforthcoming, so he enquired at the gate.*
2 (of something required) not ready or made available when wanted or needed: *with money unforthcoming from the company, the project has had to be delayed.*

unfortified ▶ adjective **1** not fortified against attack: *there seems to have been an unfortified village on the site.*
2 (of wine) without added spirits.

unfortunate ▶ adjective **1** having or marked by bad fortune; unlucky: *there'd been an unfortunate accident.* ■ not indicating a good chance of success; inauspicious: *the delay at the airport was an unfortunate start to our holiday.*
2 regrettable or inappropriate: *his unfortunate remark silenced the gathering.*
▶ noun **1** a person who suffers bad fortune.
2 archaic a person who is considered immoral or lacking in religious faith or instruction, especially a prostitute.

unfortunately ▶ adverb [sentence adverb] it is unfortunate that: *unfortunately, we do not have the time to interview every applicant.*

unfounded ▶ adjective having no foundation or basis in fact: *her fear that she had cancer was unfounded.*
– DERIVATIVES **unfoundedly** adverb.

UNFPA ▶ abbreviation United Nations Fund for Population Activities.

unframed ▶ adjective (especially of a picture) not having a frame.

unfree ▶ adjective deprived or devoid of liberty.
– DERIVATIVES **unfreedom** noun.

unfreeze ▶ verb (past **unfroze**; past participle **unfrozen**) **1** thaw or cause to thaw.
2 [with obj.] remove restrictions on the use or transfer of (an asset).

unfrequented ▶ adjective (of a place) visited only rarely: *a region with only a few unfrequented tracks.*

unfriend ▶ verb [with obj.] informal remove (someone) from a list of friends or contacts on a social networking site: *she broke up with her boyfriend, but she hasn't unfriended him.*

unfriended ▶ adjective literary without friends: *murder left innocent people bereft and unfriended.*

unfriendly ▶ adjective (**unfriendlier**, **unfriendliest**) not friendly: *she shot him an unfriendly glance.*
– DERIVATIVES **unfriendliness** noun.

unfrock ▶ verb another term for DEFROCK.

unfroze past of UNFREEZE.

unfrozen[1] past participle of UNFREEZE.

unfrozen[2] ▶ adjective not or no longer frozen: *larvae remain unfrozen under the ice.*

unfruitful ▶ adjective **1** not producing good or helpful results; unproductive: *the meeting was unfruitful.*
2 not producing fruit or crops; unfertile.
– DERIVATIVES **unfruitfully** adverb, **unfruitfulness** noun.

unfulfilled ▶ adjective not carried out or brought to completion: *it was his unfulfilled ambition to write.* ■ not having fully utilized or exploited one's abilities or character.
– DERIVATIVES **unfulfillable** adjective, **unfulfilling** adjective.

unfunded ▶ adjective not funded, in particular: ■ not receiving public funds: *a new education bill remained unfunded.* ■ (of a debt) repayable on demand rather than having been converted into a more or less permanent debt at fixed interest. ■ denoting or relating to a pension scheme without a pension fund, the current beneficiaries being paid by a former employer from revenue or contributions by present employees.

unfunny ▶ adjective (**unfunnier**, **unfunniest**) (of something intended to be funny) not amusing: *a hideously unfunny spoof film.*
– DERIVATIVES **unfunnily** adverb, **unfunniness** noun.

unfurl ▶ verb make or become spread out from a rolled or folded state, especially in order to be open to the wind: [with obj.] *a man was unfurling a sail* | [no obj.] *the flags unfurl.*

unfurnished ▶ adjective **1** (especially of a house or flat available for rent) without furniture: *an unfurnished apartment.*
2 archaic not supplied: *he is* ***unfurnished with*** *the ideas of justice.*

unfused ▶ adjective not fused or joined.

unfussy ▶ adjective not fussy: *a simple unfussy design.*
– DERIVATIVES **unfussily** adverb.

ungainly ▶ adjective (of a person or movement) awkward; clumsy: *an ungainly walk.*
– DERIVATIVES **ungainliness** noun.
– ORIGIN mid 17th cent.: from UN-[1] 'not' + obsolete *gainly* 'graceful', based on Old Norse *gegn* 'straight'.

ungainsayable /ˌʌnɡeɪnˈseɪəb(ə)l/ ▶ adjective formal undeniable; irrefutable.

ungallant ▶ adjective not gallant.
– DERIVATIVES **ungallantly** adverb.

ungeared ▶ adjective **1** (of a vehicle) not having gears or gearing.
2 (of a company or its balance sheet) having or showing no debt.

ungenerous ▶ adjective not generous; mean.
– DERIVATIVES **ungenerously** adverb.

ungenial ▶ adjective not genial.

ungentle ▶ adjective not gentle: *an ungentle grip.*
– DERIVATIVES **ungentleness** noun, **ungently** adverb.

ungentlemanly ▶ adjective not appropriate to or behaving like a gentleman: *an ungentlemanly lack of sportsmanship.*
– DERIVATIVES **ungentlemanliness** noun.

unget-at-able ▶ adjective informal inaccessible.

ungifted ▶ adjective not having any exceptional talents.

ungird ▶ verb [with obj.] archaic release or take off by undoing a belt or girth.

ungiving ▶ adjective **1** (of a person) cold or stubborn towards other people.
2 (of a substance or material) not pliable; stiff.

unglamorous ▶ adjective lacking glamour and excitement: *an unglamorous family car.*

unglazed ▶ adjective not glazed: *unglazed porcelain.*

ungloved ▶ adjective not wearing a glove or gloves.

unglued ▶ adjective not or no longer stuck.
– PHRASES **come unglued** informal **1** (of plans or an enterprise) end in failure. **2** (of a person) become confused or upset.

ungodly ▶ adjective (**ungodlier**, **ungodliest**) **1** irreligious or immoral: *ungodly lives of lust and pleasure.*
2 informal unreasonably early or inconvenient: *I've been troubled by telephone calls at ungodly hours.*
– DERIVATIVES **ungodliness** noun.

ungovernable ▶ adjective impossible to control or govern.
– DERIVATIVES **ungovernability** noun, **ungovernably** adverb.

ungraceful ▶ adjective lacking grace; clumsy.
– DERIVATIVES **ungracefully** adverb, **ungracefulness** noun.

ungracious ▶ adjective **1** not polite or friendly: *after Anna's kindness I wouldn't want to seem ungracious.*
2 not graceful or elegant.
– DERIVATIVES **ungraciously** adverb, **ungraciousness** noun.

ungraded ▶ adjective not graded.

ungrammatical ▶ adjective not conforming to grammatical rules: *ungrammatical sentences.*
– DERIVATIVES **ungrammaticality** noun (pl. **ungrammaticalities**), **ungrammatically** adverb, **ungrammaticalness** noun.

ungraspable ▶ adjective impossible to comprehend or understand.

ungrateful ▶ adjective not feeling or showing gratitude: *she's so ungrateful for everything we do.*
– DERIVATIVES **ungratefully** adverb, **ungratefulness** noun.

ungreased ▶ adjective not greased.

ungreen ▶ adjective harmful to the environment: *an ungreen commercial development.* ■ (of a person) not supporting protection of the environment.

ungroomed ▶ adjective not neat and tidy in appearance.

unground ▶ adjective not reduced to fine particles by grinding.

ungrounded ▶ adjective **1** having no basis or justification; unfounded: *ungrounded fears.*
2 not electrically earthed.
3 (**ungrounded in**) not properly instructed or proficient in (a subject or activity).

ungroup ▶ verb [with obj.] Computing separate (items) from a group formed within a word-processing or graphics package.

ungrudging ▶ adjective not grudging: *he showed her ungrudging courtesy and kindness.*
– DERIVATIVES **ungrudgingly** adverb.

ungual /ˈʌŋɡw(ə)l/ ▶ adjective Zoology & Medicine relating to or affecting a nail, hoof, or claw.
– ORIGIN mid 19th cent.: from Latin *unguis* 'nail' + -AL.

unguard ▶ verb [with obj.] (in bridge and whist) expose (a high card) to a risk of defeat by discarding low cards in the same suit.

unguarded ▶ adjective **1** without protection or a guard: *the museum was unguarded at night.*
2 not well considered; careless: *an unguarded remark.*
– DERIVATIVES **unguardedly** adverb, **unguardedness** noun.

unguent /ˈʌŋɡwənt/ ▶ noun a soft greasy or viscous substance used as ointment or for lubrication.
– ORIGIN late Middle English: from Latin *unguentum*, from *unguere* 'anoint'.

unguessable ▶ adjective impossible to guess or imagine: *a manor of an unguessable antiquity.*

unguiculate /ʌŋˈɡwɪkjʊlət/ ▶ adjective **1** Zoology having one or more nails or claws.
2 Botany (of a petal) having a narrow stalk-like base.
– ORIGIN early 19th cent.: from modern Latin *unguiculatus*, from Latin *unguiculus* 'fingernail, toenail', diminutive of *unguis* 'nail'.

unguided ▶ adjective not guided in a particular path or direction. ■ (of a missile) not directed by remote control or internal equipment.

unguis /ˈʌŋɡwɪs/ ▶ noun (pl. **ungues** /-wiːz/) Zoology a nail, claw, or fang.
– ORIGIN early 18th cent.: from Latin.

ungulate /ˈʌŋɡjʊlət, -leɪt/ ▶ noun Zoology a hoofed mammal. ● Former order Ungulata, now divided into two unrelated orders (see ARTIODACTYLA and PERISSODACTYLA).
– ORIGIN early 19th cent.: from late Latin *ungulatus*, from Latin *ungula* 'hoof'.

unguled /ˈʌŋɡjuːld/ ▶ adjective Heraldry (of an animal) having hoofs of a specified different tincture.

unhallowed ▶ adjective not formally consecrated: *unhallowed ground.* ■ unholy; wicked: *unhallowed retribution.*

unhampered ▶ adjective not impeded or encumbered: *a press unhampered by government censorship.*

unhand ▶ verb [with obj.] [usu. in imperative] archaic or humorous release (someone) from one's grasp: *'Unhand me, sir!' she cried.*

unhandled ▶ adjective not handled, in particular (of an animal) not tamed.

unhandsome ▶ adjective [often with negative] not handsome: *Bobby was not unhandsome in his uniform.*

unhandy ▶ adjective **1** not easy to handle or manage; awkward.
2 not skilful in using the hands.
– DERIVATIVES **unhandiness** noun.

unhang ▶ verb (past and past participle **unhung**) [with obj.] rare take down from a hanging position.

unhappen ▶ verb [no obj.] (of an occurrence) become as though never having happened; be reversed: *things had happened that could never unhappen.*

unhappily ▶ adverb in an unhappy manner. ■ [sentence adverb] unfortunately: *unhappily, such days do not come too often.*

unhappiness ▶ noun [mass noun] the feeling of not being happy; sadness: *I've seen too much unhappiness caused by broken marriages.* ■ the feeling of not being satisfied or pleased with a situation: *residents expressed their unhappiness at the council's decision.*

unhappy ▶ adjective (**unhappier**, **unhappiest**) **1** not happy: *an unhappy marriage.* ■ (**unhappy at**/**about**/**with**) not satisfied or pleased with (a situation): *many were unhappy about the scale of the cuts.*
2 unfortunate: *an unhappy coincidence.*

unharmed ▶ adjective not harmed; uninjured: *all the hostages were released unharmed.*

unharmful ▶ adjective not harmful.

unharmonious ▶ adjective not harmonious.

unharness ▶ verb [with obj.] remove a harness from (a horse or other animal).

unhasp ▶ verb [with obj.] archaic unfasten.

unhatched ▶ adjective (of an egg or young bird) not yet hatched.

UNHCR an agency of the United Nations set up in 1951 to aid, protect, and monitor refugees.
– ORIGIN abbreviation of *United Nations High Commissioner for Refugees.*

unhealed ▶ adjective not yet healed.

unhealthful ▶ adjective harmful to health.
– DERIVATIVES **unhealthfulness** noun.

unhealthy ▶ adjective (**unhealthier**, **unhealthiest**) harmful to health: *an unhealthy diet.* ■ not having

or showing good health: *his skin looked pale and unhealthy.* ■ (of a person's attitude or behaviour) not sensible or well balanced: *an unhealthy obsession with fast cars.*
– DERIVATIVES **unhealthily** adverb, **unhealthiness** noun.

unheard ▶ adjective **1** not heard or listened to: *my protests went unheard.*
2 (**unheard of**) not previously known of or done: *it was unheard of for a boy to miss church* | *wines from unheard-of villages.*

unheated ▶ adjective not heated.

unhedged ▶ adjective **1** not bounded by a hedge.
2 (of an investment or investor) not protected against loss by balancing or compensating contracts or transactions.

unheeded ▶ adjective heard or noticed but disregarded: *my protest went unheeded.*

unheedful ▶ adjective not noticing or paying attention: *I charged down the stairs, **unheedful of** the missing bannister.*

unheeding ▶ adjective not paying attention: *Mary, unheeding, watched the television.*

unheimlich /ʊnˈhʌɪmlɪx/ ▶ adjective uncanny; weird.
– ORIGIN German.

unhelpful ▶ adjective not helpful: *several complained that the staff were unhelpful.*
– DERIVATIVES **unhelpfully** adverb, **unhelpfulness** noun.

unhemmed ▶ adjective (of a garment or piece of fabric) not having a hem: *unhemmed jeans.*

unheralded ▶ adjective not previously announced, expected, or acclaimed.

unheroic ▶ adjective not heroic: *an unheroic death.*
– DERIVATIVES **unheroically** adverb.

unhesitating ▶ adjective without doubt or hesitation; immediate: *unequivocal and unhesitating condemnation.*
– DERIVATIVES **unhesitatingly** adverb.

unhindered ▶ adjective not hindered or obstructed.

unhinge ▶ verb (**unhinges**, **unhinging**, **unhinged**) [with obj.] **1** make (someone) mentally unbalanced: *the loneliness had nearly unhinged him.* ■ deprive of stability; throw into disorder.
2 take (a door) off its hinges.

unhinged ▶ adjective mentally unbalanced; deranged: *the violent acts of unhinged minds.*

unhip ▶ adjective (**unhipper**, **unhippest**) informal unaware of current fashions or trends.

unhistoric ▶ adjective not historic or historical.

unhistorical ▶ adjective not in accordance with history or with historical analysis.
– DERIVATIVES **unhistorically** adverb.

unhitch ▶ verb [with obj.] unhook or unfasten (something tethered to or caught on something else).

unholster ▶ verb [with obj.] remove (a gun) from a holster.

unholy ▶ adjective (**unholier**, **unholiest**) sinful; wicked. ■ unnatural and potentially harmful: *an **unholy alliance** between the medical profession and the pharmaceutical industry.* ■ informal used to emphasize how bad something is; dreadful: *she was making an unholy racket.*
– DERIVATIVES **unholiness** noun.
– ORIGIN Old English *unhālig* (see **UN-**[1], **HOLY**).

unhonoured ▶ adjective not given public praise or respect.

unhood ▶ verb [with obj.] remove the hood from (an animal or person).

unhook ▶ verb [with obj.] unfasten or detach (something that is held or caught by a hook).

unhoped ▶ adjective (**unhoped for**) exceeding hope or expectation: *an unhoped-for piece of good luck.*

unhorse ▶ verb [with obj.] drag or cause to fall from a horse.

unhoused ▶ adjective having no accommodation or shelter: *the poor remain unhoused.*

unhouseled /ʌnˈhaʊz(ə)ld/ ▶ adjective archaic not having received the Eucharist.
– ORIGIN mid 16th cent.: from **UN-**[1] 'not' + the past participle of obsolete *housel* 'offer the Eucharist to', from *housel* 'Eucharist'.

unhuman ▶ adjective not resembling or having the qualities of a human being.

unhung[1] ▶ adjective (especially of a picture) not hanging or hung.

unhung[2] past and past participle of **UNHANG**.

unhurried ▶ adjective moving, acting, or taking place without haste or urgency.
– DERIVATIVES **unhurriedly** adverb.

unhurt ▶ adjective not hurt or harmed.

unhusk ▶ verb [with obj.] remove a husk or shell from (a seed or fruit): (as adj. **unhusked**) *unhusked rice.*

unhygienic ▶ adjective not clean or sanitary: *damp, unhygienic accommodation.*
– DERIVATIVES **unhygienically** adverb.

unhyphenated ▶ adjective (of a word or phrase) not written with a hyphen.

uni ▶ noun (pl. **unis**) informal university.
– ORIGIN late 19th cent.: abbreviation.

uni- ▶ combining form one; having or consisting of one: *unicellular* | *unicycle.*
– ORIGIN from Latin *unus* 'one'.

Uniate /ˈjuːnɪeɪt/ (also **Uniat**) ▶ adjective denoting or relating to any community of Christians in eastern Europe or the Near East that acknowledges papal supremacy but retains its own liturgy.
▶ noun a member of such a community.
– ORIGIN mid 19th cent.: from Russian *uniat*, from *uniya*, from Latin *unio* (see **UNION**).

uniaxial /juːnɪˈaksɪəl/ ▶ adjective having or relating to a single axis. ■ (of crystals) having one optic axis, as in the hexagonal, trigonal, and tetragonal systems.
– DERIVATIVES **uniaxially** adverb.

unibody ▶ noun (pl. **unibodies**) a single moulded unit forming both the bodywork and chassis of a vehicle.

unicameral /juːnɪˈkam(ə)r(ə)l/ ▶ adjective (of a legislative body) having a single legislative chamber.
– ORIGIN mid 19th cent.: from **UNI-** 'one' + Latin *camera* 'chamber' + **-AL**.

UNICEF /ˈjuːnɪsɛf/ an agency of the United Nations established in 1946 to help governments (especially in developing countries) improve the health and education of children and their mothers.
– ORIGIN acronym from *United Nations Children's* (originally *International Children's Emergency*) *Fund.*

unicellular ▶ adjective Biology (of protozoans, certain algae, spores, etc.) consisting of a single cell. ■ (of an evolutionary or developmental stage) characterized by the formation or presence of a single cell or cells.

unicity /juːˈnɪsɪti/ ▶ noun [mass noun] rare the fact of being or consisting of one, or of being united as a whole. ■ the fact or quality of being unique.

Unicode ▶ noun [mass noun] Computing an international encoding standard for use with different languages and scripts, by which each letter, digit, or symbol is assigned a unique numeric value that applies across different platforms and programs.

unicolour (also **unicoloured**) (US **unicolor** or **unicolored**) ▶ adjective of one colour.

unicom ▶ noun a radio communications system of a type used at small airports.

unicorn ▶ noun **1** a mythical animal typically represented as a horse with a single straight horn projecting from its forehead. ■ a heraldic representation of a unicorn, with a twisted horn, a deer's feet, a goat's beard, and a lion's tail.
2 historical a carriage drawn by three horses, two abreast and one leader. ■ a team of three horses arranged in such a way.
– ORIGIN Middle English: via Old French from Latin *unicornis*, from *uni-* 'single' + *cornu* 'horn', translating Greek *monokerōs*.

unicorn fish ▶ noun any of a number of fishes with a horn-like projection on the head: ● an Indo-Pacific surgeonfish (genus *Naso*, family Acanthuridae). ● a crestfish with a dorsal fin that extends forward from the head (*Lophotes fiskii*, family Lophotidae).

unicorn root ▶ noun [mass noun] US any of a number of plants in the lily family, especially those with roots having medicinal uses, in particular: ● the blazing star (*Chamaelirium luteum*). ● colic root.

unicum /ˈjuːnɪkəm/ ▶ noun (pl. **unica**) rare a unique example or specimen.
– ORIGIN late 19th cent.: from Latin, neuter of *unicus* 'unique'.

unicursal /juːnɪˈkəːs(ə)l/ ▶ adjective Mathematics relating to or denoting a curve or surface which is closed and can be drawn or swept out in a single movement.
– ORIGIN mid 19th cent.: from **UNI-** 'one' + Latin *cursus* 'course' + **-AL**.

unicuspid ▶ adjective having one cusp or point.
▶ noun a tooth with a single cusp, especially a canine tooth.

unicycle ▶ noun a cycle with a single wheel, typically used by acrobats.
– DERIVATIVES **unicyclist** noun.

unidea'd ▶ adjective archaic having no ideas.

unideal ▶ adjective not satisfying one's perception of what is perfect: *we have all had unideal parents.*

unidealized (also **unidealised**) ▶ adjective not regarded or represented as better than in reality; true to life: *he painted unidealized views of country life.*

unidentifiable ▶ adjective unable to be identified: *an unidentifiable accent.*

unidentified ▶ adjective not recognized or identified: *a picture of an unidentified motorcyclist.*

unidimensional ▶ adjective having one dimension: *a unidimensional model.*

unidiomatic ▶ adjective not using or containing expressions natural to a native speaker of a language.

unidirectional ▶ adjective moving or operating in a single direction.
– DERIVATIVES **unidirectionality** noun, **unidirectionally** adverb.

UNIDO /juːˈniːdəʊ/ ▶ abbreviation United Nations Industrial Development Organization.

uniface ▶ adjective (of a coin or medallion) having one side blank or unfinished.

unifactorial ▶ adjective (of an inherited characteristic or disorder) dependent on a single gene.

unification ▶ noun [mass noun] the process of being united or made into a whole.
– DERIVATIVES **unificatory** adjective.

Unification Church an evangelistic religious and political organization founded in 1954 in Korea by Sun Myung Moon. Also called **HOLY SPIRIT ASSOCIATION FOR THE UNIFICATION OF WORLD CHRISTIANITY**.

unified field theory ▶ noun Physics a theory that describes two or more of the four interactions (electromagnetic, gravitational, weak, and strong) previously described by separate theories.

uniflow ▶ adjective involving flow in one direction (used especially with reference to the flow of steam or gases through the cylinder in a steam or internal-combustion engine): *a uniflow engine.*

uniform ▶ adjective **1** remaining the same in all cases and at all times; unchanging in form or character: *blocks of stone of uniform size.* ■ of a similar form or character to another or others: *a uniform package of amenities at a choice of hotels.*
2 denoting a garment forming part of a person's uniform: *black uniform jackets.*
▶ noun **1** the distinctive clothing worn by members of the same organization or body or by children attending certain schools: *airline pilots in dark blue uniforms* | [mass noun] *an officer in uniform.* ■ informal, chiefly N. Amer. a police officer wearing a uniform: *uniforms were already on the scene.*
2 a code word representing the letter U, used in radio communication.
▶ verb [with obj.] make uniform.
– DERIVATIVES **uniformly** adverb.
– ORIGIN mid 16th cent. (as an adjective): from French *uniforme* or Latin *uniformis* (see **UNI-**, **FORM**). Sense 1 of the noun dates from the mid 18th cent.

uniformed ▶ adjective wearing a uniform: *uniformed police officers.*

uniformitarianism ▶ noun [mass noun] Geology the theory that changes in the earth's crust during geological history have resulted from the action of continuous and uniform processes. Often contrasted with **CATASTROPHISM**.
– DERIVATIVES **uniformitarian** adjective & noun.

uniformity ▶ noun (pl. **uniformities**) [mass noun] the quality or state of being uniform: *an attempt to impose administrative and cultural uniformity.*
– ORIGIN late Middle English: from Old French *uniformite* or late Latin *uniformitas*, from Latin *uniformis* (see **UNIFORM**).

Uniformity, Act of (in British history) any of four acts (especially that of 1662) establishing the foundations of the English Protestant Church and securing uniformity in public worship and use of a particular Book of Common Prayer.

unify /ˈjuːnɪfʌɪ/ ▶ verb (**unifies**, **unifying**, **unified**) make or become united, uniform, or whole: [with obj.] *the government hoped to centralize and unify the nation* | [no obj.] *opposition groups struggling to unify*

around the goal of replacing the regime | (as adj. **unified**) *a unified system of national education.*
– DERIVATIVES **unifier** noun.
– ORIGIN early 16th cent.: from French *unifier* or late Latin *unificare* 'make into a whole'.

unijunction ▸ noun Electronics a negative resistance device consisting of a rectifying p–n junction in the middle of a length of semiconducting material that has an ohmic contact at each end, used as a switching element.

unilateral ▸ adjective **1** (of an action or decision) performed by or affecting only one person, group, or country involved in a situation, without the agreement of another or the others: *unilateral nuclear disarmament.*
2 relating to or affecting only one side of an organ, the body, or another structure.
– DERIVATIVES **unilaterally** adverb.

Unilateral Declaration of Independence (abbrev.: **UDI**) the declaration of independence from the United Kingdom made by Rhodesia under Ian Smith in 1965. See ZIMBABWE.

unilateralism ▸ noun [mass noun] the process of acting, reaching a decision, or espousing a principle unilaterally. ■ the pursuit of or belief in unilateral nuclear disarmament: *the party's commitment to unilateralism.*
– DERIVATIVES **unilateralist** noun & adjective.

unilingual ▸ adjective conducted in, concerned with, or speaking only one language.
– DERIVATIVES **unilingualism** noun, **unilingually** adverb.

unilluminated ▸ adjective not illuminated.

unillustrated ▸ adjective having no illustrations.

unilocular /juːnɪˈlɒkjʊlə/ ▸ adjective Botany & Zoology having, consisting of, or characterized by only one loculus or cavity; single-chambered.

unimaginable ▸ adjective difficult or impossible to imagine or comprehend: *lives of almost unimaginable deprivation.*
– DERIVATIVES **unimaginably** adverb.

unimaginative ▸ adjective not readily using or demonstrating the use of the imagination; stolid and somewhat dull.
– DERIVATIVES **unimaginatively** adverb, **unimaginativeness** noun.

unimagined ▸ adjective not having been imagined or thought of as possible: *a previously unimagined degree of economic and social freedom.*

unimodal ▸ adjective having or involving one mode. ■ (of a statistical distribution) having one maximum.

unimodular ▸ adjective Mathematics having a determinant of ±1.

unimolecular ▸ adjective Chemistry consisting of or involving a single molecule.

unimpaired ▸ adjective not weakened or damaged: *unimpaired mobility.*

unimpassioned ▸ adjective having or showing no emotion or intensity: *a flat, unimpassioned voice.*

unimpeachable ▸ adjective not able to be doubted, questioned, or criticized; entirely trustworthy: *an unimpeachable witness.*
– DERIVATIVES **unimpeachably** adverb.

unimpeded ▸ adjective not obstructed or hindered: *an unimpeded view across the headland.*
– DERIVATIVES **unimpededly** adverb.

unimportance ▸ noun [mass noun] the state or fact of lacking in importance or significance: *the relative unimportance of wider kin ties in British culture.*

unimportant ▸ adjective lacking in importance or significance: *trivial and unimportant details.*

unimposing ▸ adjective not imposing or impressive in appearance.
– DERIVATIVES **unimposingly** adverb.

unimpressed ▸ adjective feeling no admiration, interest, or respect.

unimpressionable ▸ adjective (of a person) not easily influenced.

unimpressive ▸ adjective evoking no admiration or respect; not striking.
– DERIVATIVES **unimpressively** adverb, **unimpressiveness** noun.

unimproved ▸ adjective not made better. ■ (of land) not cleared or cultivated.

unincorporated ▸ adjective **1** (of a company or other organization) not formed into a legal corporation: *an unincorporated business.*
2 not included as part of a whole. ■ N. Amer. (of territory) not designated as belonging to a particular country, town, or area.

uninfected ▸ adjective not harbouring a disease-causing organism. ■ Computing not affected with a virus.

uninflamed ▸ adjective (of a part of the body) not affected by inflammation: *an uninflamed appendix.*

uninflected ▸ adjective **1** Grammar (of a word or a language) not undergoing changes to express particular grammatical functions or attributes: *English is largely uninflected.*
2 not varying in intonation or pitch: *her voice was flat and uninflected.*

uninfluenced ▸ adjective not influenced or affected: *styles of dress relatively uninfluenced by popular fashion.*

uninfluential ▸ adjective having little or no influence.

uninformative ▸ adjective not providing particularly useful or interesting information.

uninformed ▸ adjective not having or showing awareness or understanding of the facts: *uninformed criticism of conservation projects.*

uninhabitable ▸ adjective (of a place) unsuitable for living in.

uninhabited ▸ adjective (of a place) without inhabitants: *small uninhabited islands.*

uninhibited ▸ adjective expressing one's feelings or thoughts unselfconsciously and without restraint: *fits of uninhibited laughter.*
– DERIVATIVES **uninhibitedly** adverb, **uninhibitedness** noun.

uninitiated ▸ adjective without special knowledge or experience: (as plural noun **the uninitiated**) *the discussion wasn't easy to follow for the uninitiated.*

uninjured ▸ adjective (of a person or part of the body) not harmed or damaged.

uninspired ▸ adjective **1** lacking in imagination or originality: *he writes repetitive and uninspired poetry.*
2 (of a person) not filled with excitement: *they were uninspired by the Nationalist Party.*

uninspiring ▸ adjective not producing excitement or interest: *an uninspiring game that United scarcely deserved to win.*
– DERIVATIVES **uninspiringly** adverb.

uninstall (also **uninstal**) ▸ verb (**uninstalls** or **uninstals**, **uninstalling**, **uninstalled**) [with obj.] remove (an application or file) from a computer.
– DERIVATIVES **uninstaller** noun.

uninstructed ▸ adjective (of a person) not taught or having learned a subject or skill. ■ (of behaviour) not acquired by teaching; natural or spontaneous: *her own instinctive, uninstructed response.*

uninsulated ▸ adjective not insulated.

uninsurable ▸ adjective not eligible for insurance cover: *some risky activities are uninsurable at any price.*

uninsured ▸ adjective not covered by insurance: *an uninsured driver.*

unintelligent ▸ adjective having or showing a low level of intelligence: *a good-natured but unintelligent boy.*
– DERIVATIVES **unintelligence** noun, **unintelligently** adverb.

unintelligible ▸ adjective impossible to understand: *dolphin sounds are unintelligible to humans.*
– DERIVATIVES **unintelligibility** noun, **unintelligibly** adverb.

unintended ▸ adjective not planned or meant: *the unintended consequences of people's actions.*

unintentional ▸ adjective not done on purpose: *the translation added a layer of unintentional comedy.*
– DERIVATIVES **unintentionally** adverb.

uninterested ▸ adjective not interested in or concerned about something or someone: *I was totally uninterested in boys | an uninterested voice.*
– DERIVATIVES **uninterestedly** adverb.

> **USAGE** On the meaning and use of **uninterested** and **disinterested**, see **USAGE** at **DISINTERESTED**.

uninteresting ▸ adjective not arousing curiosity or interest: *the scenery is dull and uninteresting.*
– DERIVATIVES **uninterestingly** adverb, **uninterestingness** noun.

uninterpretable ▸ adjective impossible to explain or understand in terms of meaning or significance.

uninterrupted ▸ adjective without a break in continuity: *an uninterrupted flow of traffic.* ■ (of a view) unobstructed.
– DERIVATIVES **uninterruptedly** adverb.

uninterruptible ▸ adjective not able to be broken in continuity: *an uninterruptible power supply.*

uninucleate ▸ adjective Biology having a single nucleus.

uninventive ▸ adjective not showing creativity or original thought: *the oils were sensitively painted but uninventive in design.*
– DERIVATIVES **uninventively** adverb, **uninventiveness** noun.

uninvestigated ▸ adjective not systematically investigated: *uninvestigated deaths in custody.*

uninvited ▸ adjective (of a person) arriving somewhere or acting without having been asked: *their privacy was disrupted by a series of uninvited guests.* ■ (of a thought or act) involuntary or unwarranted: *strange uninvited thoughts crossed her mind.*
– DERIVATIVES **uninvitedly** adverb.

uninviting ▸ adjective (especially of a place or prospect) not attractive: *the house was dark and uninviting.*
– DERIVATIVES **uninvitingly** adverb.

uninvolved ▸ adjective not connected or concerned with someone or something, especially on an emotional level.

uninvolving ▸ adjective failing to engage someone's interest or attention; dull: *a pointless and uninvolving storyline.*

union ▸ noun **1** [mass noun] the action of joining together or the fact of being joined together, especially in a political context: *he was opposed to closer political or economic union with Europe* | [count noun] *a currency union between the two countries.* ■ (**the Union**) historical the uniting of the English and Scottish crowns in 1603, of the English and Scottish parliaments in 1707, or of the parliaments of Great Britain and Ireland in 1801. ■ a state of harmony or agreement: *they live in perfect union.* ■ [count noun] a marriage: *their union had not been blessed with children.*
2 a society or association formed by people with a common interest or purpose: [in names] *the Mothers' Union.* ■ a trade union: [in names] *the National Farmers' Union.* ■ Brit. an association of independent Churches, especially Congregational or Baptist, for purposes of cooperation.
3 (**the Union**) a political unit consisting of a number of states or provinces with the same central government, in particular: ■ the United States, especially from its founding by the original thirteen states in 1787–90 to the secession of the Confederate states in 1860–1. ■ (also **the Federal Union**) the northern states of the United States which opposed the seceding Confederate states in the American Civil War. ■ South Africa, especially before it became a republic in 1961.
4 Mathematics the set that comprises all the elements (and no others) contained in any of two or more given sets. ■ [mass noun] the operation of forming such a set.
5 a joint or coupling for pipes.
6 Brit. historical a number of parishes consolidated for the purposes of administering the Poor Laws.
7 (in South Asia) a local administrative unit comprising several rural villages.
8 a part of a flag with an emblem symbolizing national union, typically occupying the upper corner next to the staff.
9 [mass noun] a fabric made of two or more different yarns, typically cotton and linen or silk.
– ORIGIN late Middle English: from Old French, or from ecclesiastical Latin *unio(n-)* 'unity', from Latin *unus* 'one'.

Union, Act of (in British history) either of the parliamentary acts by which the countries of the United Kingdom were brought together as a political whole. By the first Act of Union (1707) Scotland was joined with England to form Great Britain. The second Act of Union (1801) established the United Kingdom of Great Britain and Ireland. Wales had been incorporated with England in 1536.

union catalogue ▸ noun a list of the combined holdings of several libraries.

Union flag ▸ noun another term for UNION JACK (sense 1).

unionist ▸ noun **1** a member of a trade union.
2 (**Unionist**) a person, especially a member of a Northern Ireland political party, who is in favour of

the union of Northern Ireland with Great Britain. ■ historical a member of a British political party formed in 1886 which supported maintenance of the parliamentary union between Great Britain and Ireland. ■ an opponent of secession during the American Civil War of 1861–5.
– DERIVATIVES **unionism** noun, **unionistic** adjective.

unionize (also **unionise**) ▸ verb become or cause to become members of a trade union.
– DERIVATIVES **unionization** noun.

unionized (also **unionised**) ▸ adjective (of workers or their workplace) belonging to, or having workers belonging to, a trade union: *unionized factories*.

Union Jack ▸ noun **1** the national flag of the United Kingdom, formed by combining the red and white crosses of St George, St Andrew, and St Patrick and retaining the blue ground of the flag of St Andrew. Also called **UNION FLAG**. [originally a small British union flag flown as the jack of a ship.]
2 (**union jack**) (in the US) a small flag consisting of the union from the national flag, flown at the bows of vessels in harbour.

Union of Myanmar official name for **BURMA**.

Union of Soviet Socialist Republics (abbrev.: **USSR**) full name of **SOVIET UNION**.

union shop ▸ noun a place of work where all employees must belong to a trade union or join one within an agreed time. Compare with **CLOSED SHOP**.

union suit ▸ noun N. Amer. dated a single undergarment covering the body and legs, worn by men and boys.

Union Territory any of several territories of India which are administered by the central government.

uniparous /juːˈnɪp(ə)rəs/ ▸ adjective chiefly Zoology producing a single offspring at a birth.
– ORIGIN mid 17th cent.: from modern Latin *uniparus* (from Latin *uni-* 'one' + *-parus* 'bearing') + **-OUS**.

uniped /ˈjuːnɪpɛd/ ▸ noun rare a person or animal having only one foot or leg.
– ORIGIN early 19th cent.: from **UNI-** 'one' + *pes, ped-* 'foot'.

unipersonal ▸ adjective rare comprising or existing as one person only.

uniplanar ▸ adjective lying in one plane.

unipod /ˈjuːnɪpɒd/ ▸ noun a one-legged support for a camera.
– ORIGIN 1930s: from **UNI-** 'one', suggested by **TRIPOD**.

unipolar ▸ adjective **1** having or relating to a single pole or kind of polarity: *a unipolar magnetic charge*. ■ Electronics (of a transistor or other device) using charge carriers of a single polarity.
2 (of psychiatric illness) characterized by either depressive or manic episodes but not both.
3 (of a nerve cell) having only one axon or process.
– DERIVATIVES **unipolarity** /-ˈlarɪti/ noun.

unipotent /ˌjuːnɪˈpəʊt(ə)nt/ ▸ adjective
1 Mathematics (of a subgroup) having only one idempotent element.
2 Biology (of an immature or stem cell) capable of giving rise to only one cell type.

unique ▸ adjective being the only one of its kind; unlike anything else: *the situation was unique in British politics | original and unique designs*. ■ (**unique to**) belonging or connected to (one particular person, place, or thing): *a style of architecture that is unique to Portugal*. ■ particularly remarkable, special, or unusual: *a unique opportunity to see the spectacular Bolshoi Ballet*.
▸ noun archaic a unique person or thing.
– DERIVATIVES **uniquely** adverb, **uniqueness** noun.
– ORIGIN early 17th cent.: from French, from Latin *unicus*, from *unus* 'one'.

U

> **USAGE** There is a set of adjectives—including **unique**, **complete**, **equal**, **infinite**, and **perfect**—whose core meaning embraces a mathematically absolute concept and which therefore, according to a traditional argument, cannot be modified by adverbs such as **really**, **quite**, or **very**. For example, since the core meaning of **unique** (from Latin 'one') is 'being only one of its kind', it is logically impossible, the argument goes, to submodify it: it either is 'unique' or it is not, and there are no in-between stages. In practice the situation in the language is more complex than this. Words like **unique** have a core sense but they often also have a secondary, less precise sense: in this case, the meaning 'very remarkable or unusual', as in *a **really unique** opportunity*. In its secondary sense, **unique** does not relate to an absolute concept, and so the use of submodifying adverbs is grammatically acceptable.

unironed ▸ adjective (of clothes or other fabric articles) not smoothed with an iron.

unironic ▸ adjective not ironic.
– DERIVATIVES **unironically** adverb.

uniserial ▸ adjective Botany & Zoology arranged in or consisting of one series or row.

unisex ▸ adjective (especially of clothing or hairstyles) designed to be suitable for both sexes.
▸ noun [mass noun] a style in which men and women look and dress in a similar way.

unisexual ▸ adjective (of an organism) either male or female; not hermaphrodite. ■ Botany (of a flower) having either stamens or pistils but not both.
– DERIVATIVES **unisexuality** noun, **unisexually** adverb.

un-Islamic ▸ adjective contrary to the tenets of Islam.

UNISON /ˈjuːnɪs(ə)n/ (in the UK) a trade union formed in 1993 and representing employees in the health service and public sector.

unison /ˈjuːnɪs(ə)n/ ▸ noun [mass noun] **1** simultaneous performance or utterance of action or speech: *'Yes, sir,' said the girls **in unison***.
2 Music coincidence in pitch of sounds or notes: *the flutes play in unison with the violas*. ■ [count noun] a combination of notes, voices, or instruments at the same pitch or (especially when singing) in octaves: *good unisons are formed by flutes, oboes, and clarinets*.
▸ adjective performed in unison.
– ORIGIN late Middle English (in sense 2 of the noun): from Old French, or from late Latin *unisonus*, from Latin *uni-* 'one' + *sonus* 'sound'.

unison string ▸ noun a string in a piano or other instrument tuned to the same pitch (or to a pitch an octave higher) as another string and meant to be sounded with it.

unissued ▸ adjective (especially of shares) not yet issued.

unit ▸ noun **1** an individual thing or person regarded as single and complete but which can also form an individual component of a larger or more complex whole: *large areas of land made up of smaller units | the sentence as a unit of grammar | the family unit*. ■ a self-contained section in a building or group of buildings: *one- and two-bedroom units*. ■ a department of an institution with a specific function: *the intensive-care unit*. ■ a subdivision of a larger military grouping: *he returned to Germany with his unit*. ■ a self-contained part of an educational course: *students take three compulsory core units*. ■ a single manufactured item: [as modifier] *unit cost*. ■ Brit. the smallest measure of investment in a unit trust.
2 a device that has a specified function, especially one forming part of a complex mechanism: *the gearbox and transmission unit*. ■ a piece of furniture or equipment for fitting with others like it or made of complementary parts: *a sink unit*. ■ US a police car: *he eased into his unit and flicked the siren on*.
3 a quantity chosen as a standard in terms of which other quantities may be expressed: *a unit of measurement | fifty units of electricity*.
4 the number one. ■ (**units**) the digit before the decimal point in decimal notation, representing an integer less than ten.
– ORIGIN late 16th cent. (as a mathematical term): from Latin *unus*, probably suggested by **DIGIT**.

UNITA /juːˈniːtə/ an Angolan nationalist movement founded in 1966 by Jonas Savimbi (1934–2002) to fight Portuguese rule. After independence was achieved in 1975 UNITA continued to fight against the ruling Marxist MPLA; a ceasefire was agreed in 2002.
– ORIGIN acronym from Portuguese *União Nacional para a Independencia Total de Angola*.

UNITAR /juːˈniːtɑː/ ▸ abbreviation United Nations Institute for Training and Research.

unitard /ˈjuːnɪtɑːd/ ▸ noun a tight-fitting one-piece garment of stretchable fabric which covers the body from the neck to the knees or feet.
– ORIGIN 1960s: from **UNI-** 'single' + **LEOTARD**.

Unitarian /ˌjuːnɪˈtɛːrɪən/ Christian Theology ▸ noun a person who asserts the unity of God and rejects the doctrine of the Trinity. ■ a member of a Church or religious body maintaining this belief and typically rejecting formal dogma in favour of a rationalist and inclusivist approach to belief.
▸ adjective relating to the Unitarians.
– DERIVATIVES **Unitarianism** noun.
– ORIGIN late 17th cent.: from modern Latin *unitarius* (from Latin *unitas* 'unity') + **-AN**.

unitarist /ˈjuːnɪt(ə)rɪst/ ▸ noun an advocate of a unitary system of government.

unitary /ˈjuːnɪt(ə)ri/ ▸ adjective **1** forming a single or uniform entity: *a sort of unitary wholeness*. ■ relating to a system of government or organization in which the powers of the constituent parts are vested in a central body: *a unitary rather than a federal state*.
2 relating to a unit or units.
– DERIVATIVES **unitarily** adverb, **unitarity** /-ˈtarɪti/ noun.

unitary authority (also **unitary council**) ▸ noun (chiefly in the UK) an administrative division of local government established in place of, or as an alternative to, a two-tier system of local councils.

unit cell ▸ noun Crystallography the smallest group of atoms which has the overall symmetry of a crystal, and from which the entire lattice can be built up by repetition in three dimensions.

unite ▸ verb come or bring together for a common purpose or action: [no obj.] *he called on the party to unite* | [with obj.] *they are united by their love of cars*. ■ come or bring together to form a whole: [no obj.] *the two Germanys officially united* | [with obj.] *his work unites theory and practice*. ■ [with obj.] archaic join in marriage: *Lady Midlothian united herself to a man of bad character*.
– DERIVATIVES **unitive** adjective.
– ORIGIN late Middle English: from Latin *unit-* 'joined together', from the verb *unire*, from *unus* 'one'.

united ▸ adjective joined together politically, for a common purpose, or by common feelings: *women acting together in a united way*. ■ Brit. used in names of soccer and other sports teams formed by amalgamation: *Oxford United*.
– DERIVATIVES **unitedly** adverb.

United Arab Emirates (abbrev.: **UAE**) an independent state on the south coast of the Persian Gulf, west of the Gulf of Oman; pop. 4,798,500 (est. 2009); official language, Arabic; capital, Abu Dhabi. The United Arab Emirates was formed in 1971 by the federation of the independent sheikhdoms formerly called the Trucial States: Abu Dhabi, Ajman, Dubai, Fujairah, Ras al-Khaimah (joined early 1972), Sharjah, and Umm al-Qaiwain.

United Arab Republic (abbrev.: **UAR**) a former political union established by Egypt and Syria in 1958. It was seen as the first step towards the creation of a pan-Arab union in the Middle East, but only Yemen entered into loose association with it (1958–66) and Syria withdrew in 1961. Egypt retained the name United Arab Republic until 1971.

United Artists a US film production company founded in 1919 by Charlie Chaplin, Douglas Fairbanks, Mary Pickford, and D. W. Griffith.

United Free Church a Presbyterian Church in Scotland formed in 1900 by the union of the Free Church of Scotland with the United Presbyterian Church. In 1929 the majority of its congregation joined the established Church of Scotland.

United Kingdom (abbrev.: **UK**) a country of western Europe consisting of England, Wales, Scotland, and Northern Ireland; pop. 61,113,200 (est. 2009); capital, London. Full name **United Kingdom of Great Britain and Northern Ireland**.

> England (which had incorporated Wales in the 16th century) and Scotland have had the same monarch since 1603, when James VI of Scotland succeeded to the English crown as James I; the kingdoms were formally united by the Act of Union in 1707. An Act of Parliament joined Great Britain and Ireland in 1801, but the Irish Free State (later the Republic of Ireland) broke away in 1921. The UK became a member of the EC (now the EU) in 1973.

United Nations (abbrev.: **UN**) an international organization of countries set up in 1945, in succession to the League of Nations, to promote international peace, security, and cooperation.

> Its members, originally the countries that fought against the Axis Powers in the Second World War, now number almost 200 and include most sovereign states of the world. Administration is by a secretariat headed by the Secretary General. The chief deliberative body is the General Assembly, in which each member state has one vote; recommendations are passed but are not binding on members, and in general have had little effect on world politics. The Security Council bears the primary responsibility for the maintenance of peace and security, and may call on members to take action, chiefly peacekeeping action, to enforce its decisions. The UN's headquarters are in New York.

United Presbyterian Church a Presbyterian Church in Scotland formed in 1847. In 1900 it joined with the Free Church of Scotland to form the United Free Church.

United Provinces historical **1** the seven provinces united in 1579 and forming the basis of the republic of the Netherlands.
2 an Indian administrative division formed by the union of Agra and Oudh and called Uttar Pradesh since 1950.

United Provinces of Central America a former federal republic in Central America, formed in 1823 to unite the states of Guatemala, El Salvador, Honduras, Nicaragua, and Costa Rica, all newly independent from Spain. The federation collapsed in 1838.

United Reformed Church a Church formed in 1972 by the union of the Congregational Church in England and Wales with the Presbyterian Church in England. Most of the Churches of Christ in the UK joined the union in 1981.

> **USAGE** The correct term is **United Reformed Church**, although it is sometimes called **United Reform Church** in general use.

United States (abbrev.: **US** or **USA**) a country occupying most of the southern half of North America and including also Alaska and the Hawaiian Islands; pop. 304,059,724 (est. 2008), capital, Washington DC. Full name **United States of America**.

> The US is a federal republic comprising fifty states and the Federal District of Columbia. It originated in the American War of Independence, the successful rebellion of the British colonies on the east coast in 1775–83. The original thirteen states which formed the Union drew up a federal constitution in 1787, and George Washington was elected the first President in 1789. In the 19th century the territory of the US was extended across the continent through the westward spread of pioneers and settlers (at the expense of the American Indian peoples), and acquisitions such as that of Texas and California from Mexico in the 1840s. After a long period of isolation in foreign affairs the US participated on the Allied side in both world wars, and came out of the Cold War as the world's leading military and economic power.

unitholder ▶ **noun** chiefly Brit. a person with an investment in a unit trust.

unitize (also **unitise**) ▶ **verb** [with obj.] form into a unit; unite into a whole. ■ (usu. as adj. **unitized**) package (cargo) into unit loads: *a unitized load.* ■ convert (an investment trust) into a unit trust.

unit-linked ▶ **adjective** Brit. denoting or relating to a life assurance policy or other investment in which the premiums or payments are invested in a unit trust.

unit matrix ▶ **noun** another term for **IDENTITY MATRIX**.

unit membrane ▶ **noun** Biology a lipoprotein membrane which encloses many cells and cell organelles and is composed of two electron-dense layers enclosing a less dense layer.

unit train ▶ **noun** N. Amer. a train transporting a single commodity.

unit trust ▶ **noun** Brit. a trust formed to manage a portfolio of stock exchange securities, in which small investors can buy units.

unit vector ▶ **noun** Mathematics a vector which has a magnitude of one.

unity ▶ **noun** (pl. **unities**) [mass noun] **1** the state of being united or joined as a whole: *European unity | ways of preserving family unity.* ■ the state of forming a complete and harmonious whole, especially in an artistic context: *the repeated phrase gives the piece unity and cohesion.* ■ [count noun] a thing forming a complex whole: *they speak of the three parts as a unity.*
2 Mathematics the number one.
3 [count noun] each of the three dramatic principles requiring limitation of the supposed time of a drama to that occupied in acting it or to a single day (**unity of time**), use of one scene throughout (**unity of place**), and concentration on the development of a single plot (**unity of action**).
– ORIGIN Middle English: from Old French *unite*, from Latin *unitas*, from *unus* 'one'.

Univ. ▶ **abbreviation** University.

univalent ▶ **adjective 1** /juːˈnɪvəl(ə)nt/ Biology (of a chromosome) remaining unpaired during meiosis.
2 /juːnɪˈveɪl(ə)nt/ Chemistry another term for **MONOVALENT**.
▶ **noun** /juːˈnɪvəl(ə)nt/ Biology a univalent chromosome.

univalve Zoology ▶ **adjective** having one valve or shell.
▶ **noun** another term for **GASTROPOD**.

univariate /juːnɪˈvɛːrɪət/ ▶ **adjective** Statistics involving one variate or variable quantity.

Universal a US film production company formed in 1912.

universal ▶ **adjective** relating to or done by all people or things in the world or in a particular group; applicable to all cases: *universal adult suffrage | the incidents caused universal concern.* ■ Logic denoting a proposition in which something is asserted of all of a class. Contrasted with **PARTICULAR**. ■ Linguistics denoting or relating to a grammatical rule, set of rules, or other linguistic feature that is found in all languages. ■ (of a tool or machine) adjustable to or appropriate for all requirements.
▶ **noun** a thing having universal effect, currency, or application, in particular: ■ Logic a universal proposition. ■ Philosophy a term or concept of general application. ■ Philosophy a nature or essence signified by a general term. ■ Linguistics a universal grammatical rule or linguistic feature.
– DERIVATIVES **universality** noun.
– ORIGIN late Middle English: from Old French, or from Latin *universalis*, from *universus* (see **UNIVERSE**).

universal compass ▶ **noun** a pair of compasses with legs that may be extended for large circles.

universal donor ▶ **noun** a person of blood group O, who can in theory donate blood to recipients of any ABO blood group.

universal indicator ▶ **noun** [mass noun] Chemistry a mixture of dyes that changes colour gradually over a range of pH and is used (especially as indicator paper) in testing for acids and alkalis.

universalist ▶ **noun 1** Christian Theology a person who believes that all humankind will eventually be saved.
2 a person advocating loyalty to and concern for others without regard to national or other allegiances.
▶ **adjective 1** Christian Theology relating to universalists.
2 universal in scope or character.
– DERIVATIVES **universalism** noun, **universalistic** adjective.

universalize (also **universalise**) ▶ **verb** [with obj.] give a universal character or application to (something, especially something abstract): *theories that universalize experience.* ■ bring into universal use; make available for all: *attempts to universalize basic education.*
– DERIVATIVES **universalizability** noun, **universalization** noun.

universal joint (also **universal coupling**) ▶ **noun** a coupling or joint which can transmit rotary power by a shaft at any selected angle.

universally ▶ **adverb** by everyone; in every case: *progress is not always universally welcomed.*

Universal Postal Union (abbrev.: **UPU**) an agency of the United Nations that regulates international postal affairs.

Universal Product Code ▶ **noun** more formal term for **BARCODE**.

universal quantifier ▶ **noun** Logic a formal expression used in asserting that a stated general proposition is true of all the members of the delineated universe or class.

universal recipient ▶ **noun** a person of blood group AB, who can in theory receive donated blood of any ABO blood group.

universal set ▶ **noun** Mathematics & Logic the set containing all objects or elements and of which all other sets are subsets.

universal suffrage ▶ **noun** [mass noun] the right of almost all adults to vote in political elections.

Universal Time (also **Universal Time Coordinated**) another term for **GREENWICH MEAN TIME**.

universe ▶ **noun 1** (**the universe**) all existing matter and space considered as a whole; the cosmos. The universe is believed to be at least 10 billion light years in diameter and contains a vast number of galaxies; it has been expanding since its creation in the Big Bang about 13 billion years ago.
2 a particular sphere of activity or experience: *the front parlour was the hub of her universe.*
3 (Logic also **universe of discourse**) another term for **UNIVERSAL SET**.
– ORIGIN late Middle English: from Old French *univers* or Latin *universum*, neuter of *universus* 'combined into one, whole', from *uni-* 'one' + *versus* 'turned' (past participle of *vertere*).

university ▶ **noun** (pl. **universities**) a high-level educational institution in which students study for degrees and academic research is done: *I went to university at the Sorbonne | his daughter is at university.*
– PHRASES **the university of life** the experience of life regarded as a means of instruction.
– ORIGIN Middle English: from Old French *universite*, from Latin *universitas* 'the whole', in late Latin 'society, guild', from *universus* (see **UNIVERSE**).

University of the Third Age ▶ **noun** an organization providing courses of education for retired or elderly people.

univocal /juːnɪˈvəʊk(ə)l, juːˈnɪvək(ə)l/ ▶ **adjective** Philosophy & Linguistics (of a word or term) having only one possible meaning; unambiguous: *a univocal set of instructions.*
– DERIVATIVES **univocality** noun, **univocally** adverb.

Unix /ˈjuːnɪks/ ▶ **noun** [mass noun] Computing, trademark an operating system analogous to DOS and Windows, supporting multiple concurrent users.
– ORIGIN 1970s: from **UNI-** 'one' + a respelling of **-ICS**, on the pattern of an earlier less compact system called *Multics*.

unjoin ▶ **verb** [with obj.] archaic detach; separate.

unjoined ▶ **adjective** not joined together.

unjoint ▶ **verb** [with obj.] rare separate or dislocate the joints of.

unjointed ▶ **adjective** lacking a joint or joints; consisting of a single piece: *a flat, unjointed surface.*

unjust ▶ **adjective** not based on or behaving according to what is morally right and fair: *resistance to unjust laws.*
– DERIVATIVES **unjustly** adverb, **unjustness** noun.

unjustifiable ▶ **adjective** not able to be shown to be right or reasonable: *an unjustifiable restriction on their freedom.*
– DERIVATIVES **unjustifiably** adverb [sentence adverb] *they seemed, unjustifiably, to be taking things out on the students.*

unjustified ▶ **adjective 1** not shown to be right or reasonable: *unjustified price increases.*
2 Printing (of printed text) not justified.

unkempt /ʌnˈkɛm(p)t/ ▶ **adjective** (especially of a person) having an untidy or dishevelled appearance: *they were unwashed and unkempt.*
– DERIVATIVES **unkemptness** noun.
– ORIGIN late Middle English: from **UN-**[1] 'not' + *kempt* 'combed' (past participle of archaic *kemb*, related to **COMB**).

unkept ▶ **adjective 1** (of a commitment or undertaking) not honoured or fulfilled: *unkept appointments and broken promises.*
2 not tidy or cared for.

unkillable ▶ **adjective** not able to be killed.

unkind ▶ **adjective** inconsiderate and harsh to others: *you were terribly unkind to her | he was the butt of some unkind jokes | it was unkind of her to criticize.*
– DERIVATIVES **unkindly** adverb.

unkindness ▶ **noun** [mass noun] inconsiderate and harsh behaviour: *she had had enough of her father's unkindness.*

unking ▶ **verb** [with obj.] archaic remove (a monarch) from power.

unkink ▶ **verb** straighten or become straight.

unknit ▶ **verb** (**unknits**, **unknitting**, **unknitted**) [with obj.] separate (things that are joined, knotted, or interlocked).

unknot ▶ **verb** (**unknots**, **unknotting**, **unknotted**)
1 [with obj.] release or untie the knot or knots in: *he swiftly unknotted his tie.*
2 [no obj.] (of a muscle) relax after being tense and hard: *his shoulders unknotted.*

unknowable ▶ **adjective** not able to be known: *the total cost is unknowable.*
– DERIVATIVES **unknowability** noun.

unknowing ▶ **adjective** not knowing or aware: *the lions moved stealthily towards their unknowing victims.*
▶ **noun** [mass noun] literary lack of awareness or knowledge.
– DERIVATIVES **unknowingly** adverb, **unknowingness** noun.

unknown ▶ **adjective** not known or familiar: *exploration into unknown territory | his whereabouts are unknown to his family.* ■ (of a performer or artist) not well known or famous.
▶ **noun** an unknown person or thing: *she is a relative unknown.* ■ (**the unknown**) that which is unknown: *our fear of the unknown.* ■ Mathematics an unknown

U

quantity or variable: *find the unknown in the following equations.*
– PHRASES **unknown to** without the knowledge of.
– DERIVATIVES **unknownness** noun.

unknown quantity ▶ noun a person or thing whose nature, value, or significance cannot be determined or is not yet known.

Unknown Soldier (also **Unknown Warrior**) ▶ noun an unidentified representative member of a country's armed forces killed in war, given burial with special honours in a national memorial.

unlabelled (US **unlabeled**) ▶ adjective without a label; not labelled: *bottles of unlabelled white wine.*

unlaboured (US **unlabored**) ▶ adjective done with ease or fluency: *flexibility and unlaboured movement.*

unlace ▶ verb [with obj.] undo the laces of (a shoe or garment).

unlade /ʌnˈleɪd/ ▶ verb [with obj.] archaic unload (a ship or cargo).

unladen ▶ adjective not carrying a load: *unladen, the boat heeled to starboard.*

unladen weight ▶ noun the weight of a vehicle when not loaded with goods.

unladylike ▶ adjective not appropriate for or typical of a well-bred, decorous woman: *Sharon gave an unladylike snort | he thought it was unladylike for his daughter to work on a farm.*

unlaid[1] ▶ adjective not laid: *the table was still unlaid.*

unlaid[2] past and past participle of **UNLAY**.

unlamented ▶ adjective (of a person who has died or something that has gone or finished) not mourned or regretted.

unlash ▶ verb [with obj.] unfasten (something tied in place with a cord or rope): *he unlashed the dinghy.*

unlatch ▶ verb [with obj.] unfasten the latch of (a door or gate).

unlawful ▶ adjective not conforming to, permitted by, or recognized by law or rules: *the use of unlawful violence | they claimed the ban was unlawful.*
– DERIVATIVES **unlawfully** adverb, **unlawfulness** noun.

> **USAGE** On the difference between **unlawful** and **illegal**, see **USAGE** at **ILLEGAL**.

unlawful assembly ▶ noun English Law, historical a meeting of three or more people likely to cause a breach of the peace or to endanger the public.

unlay ▶ verb (past and past participle **unlaid**) [with obj.] Nautical untwist (a rope) into separate strands.
– ORIGIN early 18th cent.: from **UN-**[2] (expressing reversal) + **LAY**[1].

unleaded ▶ adjective **1** (especially of petrol) without added lead.
2 not covered, weighted, or framed with lead.
3 Printing (of type) with no space or leads added between lines.
▶ noun [mass noun] petrol without added lead.

unlearn ▶ verb (past and past participle **unlearned** or chiefly Brit. **unlearnt**) [with obj.] discard (something learned, especially a bad habit or false or outdated information) from one's memory: *teachers are being asked to unlearn rigid rules for labelling and placing children.*

unlearned[1] /ʌnˈləːnd, -ˈləːnɪd/ ▶ adjective (of a person) not well educated.

unlearned[2] /ʌnˈləːnd/ (also **unlearnt** /-ˈləːnt/) ▶ adjective not having been learned: *she found herself on the stage, lines unlearned.* ■ not needing to be learned; innate: *an unlearned behaviour pattern.*

unleash ▶ verb [with obj.] release (a dog) from a leash: *they dig up badger setts and unleash terriers into them.* ■ cause (a strong or violent force) to be released or become unrestrained: *the failure of the talks could unleash more fighting | his comment unleashed a storm of protest in India.*

unleavened ▶ adjective (of bread) made without yeast or other raising agent.

unless ▶ conjunction except if (used to introduce the case in which a statement being made is not true or valid): *unless you have a photographic memory, repetition is vital | manuscripts cannot be returned unless accompanied by a self-addressed envelope.*
– ORIGIN late Middle English: from **ON** or **IN** (assimilated through lack of stress to **UN-**[1]) + **LESS**.

unlet ▶ adjective not let or rented out.

unlettered ▶ adjective (of a person) poorly educated or illiterate.

unliberated ▶ adjective (of a person or their behaviour) not liberated: *she never minded housework—Jenny said she was appallingly unliberated.*

unlicensed (also **unlicenced**) ▶ adjective not having an official licence: *unlicensed weapons.* ■ chiefly Brit. (of premises) not having a licence for the sale of alcohol: *unlicensed restaurants.*

unlighted ▶ adjective unlit.

unlike ▶ preposition different from; not similar to: *a large house not unlike Mr Shah's | they were unlike anything ever seen before.* ■ in contrast to; differently from: *unlike Elena he was not superstitious.* ■ uncharacteristic of (someone): *he sounded irritable, which was unlike him.*
▶ adjective dissimilar or different from each other: *they seemed utterly unlike, despite being twins.* ■ (**unlike to/from**) archaic not like; different from: *he was very unlike to any other man.*
– DERIVATIVES **unlikeness** noun.
– ORIGIN Middle English: perhaps originally an alteration of Old Norse *úlíkr*; compare with Old English *ungelīc* 'not of the same kind, not comparable'.

> **USAGE** The use of **unlike** as a conjunction, as in *she was behaving **unlike** she'd ever behaved before*, is not considered standard English. It can be avoided by using **as** with a negative instead: *she was behaving **as** she'd never behaved before.*

unlikeable (also chiefly US **unlikable**) ▶ adjective (especially of a person) not likeable: *a thoroughly unlikeable bully.*

unlikely ▶ adjective (**unlikelier**, **unlikeliest**) not likely to happen, be done, or be true; improbable: *an unlikely explanation | it is unlikely that they will ever be used | [with infinitive] prices are unlikely to change.*
– DERIVATIVES **unlikelihood** noun, **unlikeliness** noun.

unlimber ▶ verb [with obj.] detach (a gun) from its limber so that it can be used. ■ chiefly US unpack or unfasten (something) ready for use: *we had to unlimber some of the gear.*

unlimited ▶ adjective **1** not limited or restricted in terms of number, quantity, or extent: *offshore reserves of gas and oil are not unlimited.* ■ Mathematics (of a problem) having an infinite number of solutions.
2 (of a company) not limited.
– DERIVATIVES **unlimitedly** adverb, **unlimitedness** noun.

unlined[1] ▶ adjective not marked or covered with lines: *her face was still unlined | unlined paper.*

unlined[2] ▶ adjective (of a container or garment) without a lining: *unlined curtains.*

unlink ▶ verb **1** [with obj.] detach; separate: *she unlinked her arm to pull back her coat sleeve.*
2 (as adj. **unlinked**) not linked or connected; separate: *three previously unlinked murders.*

unliquidated ▶ adjective (of a debt) not cleared or paid off.

unlisted ▶ adjective not included on a list. ■ denoting or relating to a company whose shares are not listed on a stock exchange. ■ chiefly N. Amer. another term for **EX-DIRECTORY**. ■ Brit. (of a building) not having listed status.

unlistenable ▶ adjective (especially of music) impossible or unbearable to listen to.

unlit ▶ adjective **1** not provided with lighting: *an unlit staircase.*
2 not having been set light to: *his unlit pipe.*

unlivable ▶ adjective not able to be lived in; uninhabitable: *humanity had made the world unlivable.*

unlived ▶ adjective (**unlived in**) not appearing to be used or inhabited; not homely or comfortable.

unliving ▶ adjective not living.

unload ▶ verb [with obj.] **1** remove goods from (a vehicle, ship, container, etc.): *she hadn't finished unloading the car.* ■ remove (goods) from a vehicle, ship, container, etc.: *men were unloading sacks of olives from a tractor.* ■ informal get rid of (something unwanted): *he had **unloaded** his depreciating stock **on** his unsuspecting wife.* ■ give expression to (oppressive thoughts or feelings): *the meeting had been a chance for her to unload some of her feelings about her son.*
2 remove (ammunition) from a gun or (film) from a camera.
– DERIVATIVES **unloader** noun.

unlock ▶ verb [with obj.] undo the lock of (something) using a key: *he unlocked the door to his room.* ■ make (something previously inaccessible or unexploited) available for use: *the campaign has helped us unlock rich reserves of talent among our employees.*

unlocked ▶ adjective not locked: *unlocked doors.*

unlooked ▶ adjective (**unlooked for**) unexpected; unforeseen: *in his family he found unlooked-for happiness.*

unloose ▶ verb [with obj.] undo; let free: *he rushed across to unloose the dog.*

unloosen ▶ verb another term for **UNLOOSE**.

unlovable (also **unloveable**) ▶ adjective not lovable: *a very unlovable child.*
– DERIVATIVES **unlovability** noun.

unloved ▶ adjective not loved.

unlovely ▶ adjective not attractive; ugly.
– DERIVATIVES **unloveliness** noun.

unloving ▶ adjective not loving: *an unloving father.*
– DERIVATIVES **unlovingly** adverb, **unlovingness** noun.

unlucky ▶ adjective (**unluckier**, **unluckiest**) having, bringing, or resulting from bad luck: *an unlucky defeat | [with infinitive] the visitors were unlucky to have a goal disallowed.*
– DERIVATIVES **unluckily** adverb, **unluckiness** noun.

unmade ▶ adjective **1** (of a bed) not having the bedclothes arranged tidily ready for sleeping in.
2 Brit. (of a road) without a hard, smooth surface.

unmaidenly ▶ adjective not befitting or characteristic of a young, sexually inexperienced woman.

unmake ▶ verb (past and past participle **unmade**) [with obj.] reverse or undo the making of; annul: *Parliament can make and unmake any law.*

unman ▶ verb (**unmans**, **unmanning**, **unmanned**) [with obj.] literary deprive of qualities traditionally associated with men, such as self-control or courage: *sitting in the dock awaiting a sentence will unman the stoutest heart.*

unmanageable ▶ adjective difficult or impossible to manage, manipulate, or control: *his behaviour was becoming unmanageable at home.*
– DERIVATIVES **unmanageableness** noun, **unmanageably** adverb.

unmanaged ▶ adjective **1** not controlled or regulated: *a critique of unmanaged capitalism.*
2 (of land) left wild; in a natural state.

unmanly ▶ adjective not manly: *unmanly behaviour.*
– DERIVATIVES **unmanliness** noun.

unmanned ▶ adjective not having or needing a crew or staff: *an unmanned level crossing.*

unmannered ▶ adjective not affected or artificial in style.

unmannerly ▶ adjective not having or showing good manners: *uncouth, unmannerly fellows.*
– DERIVATIVES **unmannerliness** noun.

unmapped ▶ adjective (of an area or feature) not represented on a geographical map. ■ unexplored: *unmapped corners of Africa.* ■ Biology (of a gene or chromosome) not yet mapped.

unmarked ▶ adjective **1** not marked or bearing identifying markings: *an unmarked police car | his skin was unmarked.* ■ Linguistics (of a word or other linguistic unit) having a more general meaning or use than a corresponding marked term: *'duck' is unmarked, whereas 'drake' is marked.*
2 not noticed: *it's a pleasure to reward them for work which might otherwise go unmarked.*
3 Brit. (of a player in a team game) not marked by a player from the opposing team: *Eyres was left unmarked and duly scored from eight yards.*

unmarketable ▶ adjective not marketable.

unmarred ▶ adjective not marred.

unmarried ▶ adjective not married; single.

unmask ▶ verb [with obj.] expose the true character of or hidden truth about: *the trial unmasked him as a complete charlatan.*
– DERIVATIVES **unmasker** noun.

unmasked ▶ adjective not wearing a mask: *an unmasked gunman.*

unmatchable ▶ adjective incapable of being matched, equalled, or rivalled.
– DERIVATIVES **unmatchably** adverb.

unmatched ▶ adjective not matched or equalled: *he has a talent unmatched by any other politician.*

unmatured ▶ adjective not yet matured: *unmatured cheese.*

unmeaning ▶ adjective having no meaning or significance; meaningless: *a sweet, unmeaning smile.*
– DERIVATIVES **unmeaningly** adverb.

U

unmeant ▶ adjective not meant or intended: *an unmeant threat.*

unmeasurable ▶ adjective not able to be measured objectively: *the unmeasurable qualities of a scientist.*
– DERIVATIVES **unmeasurably** adverb.

unmeasured ▶ adjective **1** not having been measured: *unmeasured risk factors.*
2 chiefly literary immense; limitless: *he is regarded by his congregation with unmeasured adoration.*

unmediated ▶ adjective without anyone or anything intervening or acting as an intermediate; direct.

unmelodious ▶ adjective not melodious; discordant: *an unmelodious chorus of horns.*
– DERIVATIVES **unmelodiously** adverb.

unmelted ▶ adjective not melted: *unmelted snow.*

unmemorable ▶ adjective not memorable.
– DERIVATIVES **unmemorably** adverb.

unmentionable ▶ adjective too embarrassing, offensive, or shocking to be spoken about: *the unmentionable subject of incontinence.*
▶ noun (usu. **unmentionables**) chiefly humorous a person or thing that is too shocking or embarrassing to be mentioned by name: *wearing nothing but fig leaves over their unmentionables.*
– DERIVATIVES **unmentionability** noun, **unmentionableness** noun, **unmentionably** adverb.

unmentioned ▶ adjective not mentioned: *a monument unmentioned in all the architectural guides.*

unmerchantable ▶ adjective not suitable for purchase or sale.

unmerciful ▶ adjective cruel or harsh; showing no mercy.
– DERIVATIVES **unmercifully** adverb, **unmercifulness** noun.

unmerited ▶ adjective not deserved or merited: *an unmerited insult.*

unmet ▶ adjective (of a requirement) not achieved or fulfilled: *an unmet need.*

unmetalled ▶ adjective Brit. (of a road) not having a hard surface of road metal.

unmetered ▶ adjective not measured by means of a meter.

unmethodical ▶ adjective not orderly and systematic.
– DERIVATIVES **unmethodically** adverb.

unmetrical ▶ adjective not composed in or using metre: *an unmetrical poet.*

unmilitary ▶ adjective not typical of, suitable for, or connected with the military.

unmindful ▶ adjective not conscious or aware: *Danielle seemed **unmindful of** her parents' plight.*
– DERIVATIVES **unmindfully** adverb, **unmindfulness** noun.

unmissable ▶ adjective **1** so good that it should not be missed: *the special effects make this an unmissable treat.*
2 so clear or obvious that it cannot be missed.

unmistakable (also **unmistakeable**) ▶ adjective not able to be mistaken for anything else; very distinctive: *the unmistakable sound of his laughter.*
– DERIVATIVES **unmistakability** noun **unmistakably** adverb.

unmistaken ▶ adjective not mistaken; correct.

unmitigated ▶ adjective absolute; unqualified: *the tour had been an unmitigated disaster.*
– DERIVATIVES **unmitigatedly** adverb.

unmixed ▶ adjective not mixed: *bold unmixed colours.*

unmixed blessing ▶ noun [usu. with negative] a situation having advantages and no disadvantages: *motherhood is not an unmixed blessing.*

unmoderated ▶ adjective (of an Internet message board or chat room) not monitored for inappropriate or offensive content.

unmodernized (also **unmodernised**) ▶ adjective (especially of a building) not modernized; retaining the original features.

unmodified ▶ adjective not modified.

unmodulated ▶ adjective not modulated.

unmolested ▶ adjective not pestered or molested; left in peace: *they allowed him to pass unmolested.*

unmonitored ▶ noun not monitored or kept under observation: *unmonitored patients | unmonitored Internet access.*

unmoor ▶ verb [with obj.] release the moorings of (a vessel).

unmoral ▶ adjective not influenced by or concerned with morality. Compare with IMMORAL.
– DERIVATIVES **unmorality** noun.

unmothered ▶ adjective deprived of or without a mother or maternal care.

unmotherly ▶ adjective not having or showing the affectionate feelings associated with a mother.

unmotivated ▶ adjective **1** not having interest in or enthusiasm for something, especially work or study.
2 without a reason or motive: *an unmotivated attack.*

unmounted ▶ adjective not mounted.

unmourned ▶ adjective not mourned: *he would die alone and unmourned.*

unmoved ▶ adjective not affected by emotion or excitement: *he was clearly unmoved by her outburst.* ■ not changed in one's purpose or intention: *her opponents were unmoved and plan to return to court.*
– DERIVATIVES **unmovable** (also **unmoveable**) adjective.

unmoving ▶ adjective **1** not moving; still: *Claudia sat unmoving behind her desk.*
2 not stirring any emotion.

unmown ▶ adjective not mown: *unmown grass.*

unmuffle ▶ verb [with obj.] free from something that muffles or conceals.

unmurmuring ▶ adjective literary not complaining.
– DERIVATIVES **unmurmuringly** adverb.

unmusical ▶ adjective **1** not pleasing to the ear.
2 unskilled in or indifferent to music.
– DERIVATIVES **unmusically** adverb, **unmusicalness** noun.

unmutilated ▶ adjective not mutilated.

unmuzzle ▶ verb [with obj.] remove a muzzle from (an animal). ■ allow (a person or the press) to express their views freely and without censorship.

unmuzzled ▶ adjective (of an animal) not wearing a muzzle.

unnameable (also **unnamable**) ▶ adjective not able to be named, especially because too bad or horrific: *his mind was blank with an unnameable fear.*

unnamed ▶ adjective not named.

unnatural ▶ adjective **1** contrary to the ordinary course of nature; abnormal: *death by unnatural causes.* ■ (of feelings or behaviour) contrary to what is seen as normal, conventional, or acceptable: *wanting to help other people is not unnatural.*
2 not existing in nature; artificial: *the artificial turf looks an unnatural green.* ■ affected or stilted: *the formal tone of the programmes caused them to sound stilted and unnatural.*
– DERIVATIVES **unnaturally** adverb, **unnaturalness** noun.

unnavigable ▶ adjective (of a waterway or sea) not able to be sailed on by ships or boats.

unnecessary ▶ adjective not needed: *some people feel that holiday insurance is unnecessary.* ■ more than is needed; excessive: *good construction is essential to avoid unnecessary waste.*
▶ plural noun (**unnecessaries**) unnecessary things.
– DERIVATIVES **unnecessarily** adverb, **unnecessariness** noun.

unneeded ▶ adjective not needed: *the disposal of unneeded assets.*

unneighbourly ▶ adjective not neighbourly.
– DERIVATIVES **unneighbourliness** noun.

unnerve ▶ verb [with obj.] make (someone) lose courage or confidence: (as adj. **unnerving**) *an unnerving experience.*
– DERIVATIVES **unnervingly** adverb.

unnoticeable ▶ adjective not easily observed or noticed: *the reverberation will be so slight as to be unnoticeable.*
– DERIVATIVES **unnoticeably** adverb.

unnoticed ▶ adjective not noticed: *a deliberate kick that went unnoticed by the referee.*

unnumbered ▶ adjective **1** not marked with or assigned a number.
2 not counted, typically because very great.

UNO ▶ abbreviation United Nations Organization.

unoaked ▶ adjective (of wine) not matured in an oak container.

unobjectionable ▶ adjective not objectionable; acceptable: *the bail conditions were unobjectionable as far as he was concerned.*
– DERIVATIVES **unobjectionably** adverb.

unobliging ▶ adjective not helpful or cooperative.

unobscured ▶ adjective not obscured.

unobservable ▶ adjective not able to be observed.

unobservant ▶ adjective not observant.
– DERIVATIVES **unobservantly** adverb.

unobserved ▶ adjective not observed: *their courtship has not gone unobserved by Giles.*

unobstructed ▶ adjective not obstructed: *an unobstructed view of the traffic lights.*

unobtainable ▶ adjective not able to be obtained.

unobtrusive ▶ adjective not conspicuous or attracting attention: *the service was unobtrusive and efficient.*
– DERIVATIVES **unobtrusively** adverb, **unobtrusiveness** noun.

unoccupied ▶ adjective **1** (of a building, seat, etc.) not being occupied or used: *the house has been unoccupied for some time.* ■ (of a country or area) not occupied by an enemy: *unoccupied France.*
2 (of a person) not busy or active.

unoffended ▶ adjective not having taken offence.

unoffending ▶ adjective not causing offence; harmless.

unofficial ▶ adjective not officially authorized or confirmed: *unofficial reports said that dozens of people were injured.* ■ Brit. denoting strike action not called or endorsed by the union to which the strikers belong.
– DERIVATIVES **unofficially** adverb.

unoiled ▶ adjective not oiled: *unoiled hinges.*

unopened ▶ adjective not opened: *unopened mail.*

unopposed ▶ adjective not opposed; unchallenged: *she was elected unopposed as leader.*

unordained ▶ adjective not having been ordained as a priest or minister.

unordered ▶ adjective **1** not put in order; disorderly.
2 (of goods or services) not ordered.

unordinary ▶ adjective not ordinary; unusual.

unorganized (also **unorganised**) ▶ adjective not organized: *unorganized data.* ■ not represented by or formed into a trade union: *unorganized white-collar workers.*

unoriginal ▶ adjective lacking originality; derivative: *an uninteresting and unoriginal essay.*
– DERIVATIVES **unoriginality** noun, **unoriginally** adverb.

unornamental ▶ adjective not ornamental; plain.

unornamented ▶ adjective not having any decoration.

unorthodox ▶ adjective contrary to what is usual, traditional, or accepted; not orthodox: *he frequently upset other scholars with his unorthodox views.*
– DERIVATIVES **unorthodoxly** adverb, **unorthodoxy** noun.

unostentatious ▶ adjective not ostentatious: *he was generous in a quiet, unostentatious way.*
– DERIVATIVES **unostentatiously** adverb, **unostentatiousness** noun.

unowned ▶ adjective **1** not having an owner.
2 not admitted to; unacknowledged.

unoxidized (also **unoxidised**) ▶ adjective not oxidized.

unpack ▶ verb [with obj.] open and remove the contents of (a suitcase, bag, or package): *she unpacked her bags and put everything away* | [no obj.] *I haven't unpacked yet.* ■ remove (something) from a suitcase, bag, or package: *we unpacked the sandwiches.* ■ analyse (something) into its component elements: *let us unpack this question.* ■ Computing convert (data) from a compressed form to a usable form.
– DERIVATIVES **unpacker** noun.

unpackaged ▶ adjective **1** (of goods) not enclosed in a package.
2 (of a holiday) not organized as an inclusive package.

unpadded ▶ adjective not padded.

unpaged ▶ adjective (of a book) not having the pages numbered.

unpaid ▶ adjective **1** (of a debt) not yet discharged by payment: *unpaid bills.*
2 (of work or a period of leave) undertaken without payment: *unpaid labour in the home.* ■ (of a person) not receiving payment for work done.

unpainted ▶ adjective not painted.

unpaired ▶ adjective **1** not arranged in pairs.
2 not forming one of a pair.

U

unpalatable ▸ adjective not pleasant to taste. ■ difficult to put up with or accept: *the unpalatable fact that many of the world's people are starving.*
– DERIVATIVES **unpalatability** noun, **unpalatably** adverb.

unparalleled ▸ adjective having no parallel or equal; exceptional: *the sudden rise in unemployment is unparalleled in the post-war period.*

unpardonable ▸ adjective (of a fault or offence) too severe to be pardoned; unforgivable: *an unpardonable sin.*
– DERIVATIVES **unpardonably** adverb.

unparliamentary ▸ adjective (especially of language) contrary to the rules or procedures of parliament: *an unparliamentary expression.*

unpasteurized (also **unpasteurised**) ▸ adjective not pasteurized: *unpasteurized milk.*

unpatched ▸ adjective (especially of a computer routine or programme) not provided with a patch.

unpatented ▸ adjective not patented: *an unpatented invention.*

unpatriotic ▸ adjective not patriotic.
– DERIVATIVES **unpatriotically** adverb.

unpatronizing (also **unpatronising**) ▸ adjective not showing condescension.
– DERIVATIVES **unpatronizingly** adverb.

unpaved ▸ adjective not paved: *unpaved streets.*

unpeeled ▸ adjective not peeled: *an unpeeled orange.*

unpeg ▸ verb (**unpegs, unpegging, unpegged**)
1 [with obj.] unfasten by the removal of pegs: *she hastily unpegged her washing.*
2 cease to maintain a fixed relationship between (a currency) and another currency.

unpeopled ▸ adjective empty of people: *the eerily unpeopled streets.*

unperceived ▸ adjective not perceived; unobserved: *the full significance of this **went unperceived**.*

unperceptive ▸ adjective not perceptive.
– DERIVATIVES **unperceptively** adverb.

unperfected ▸ adjective not perfected: *an unperfected sketch.*

unperforated ▸ adjective not perforated.

unperformed ▸ adjective not having been performed: *an unperformed play.*

unperfumed ▸ adjective not perfumed.

unperson ▸ noun (pl. **unpersons**) a person whose name or existence is denied or ignored, especially because of a political misdemeanour.

unpersuadable ▸ adjective not able to be persuaded; obstinate.

unpersuaded ▸ adjective not persuaded; unconvinced.

unpersuasive ▸ adjective not persuasive.
– DERIVATIVES **unpersuasively** adverb.

unperturbed ▸ adjective not perturbed or concerned: *Kenneth seems unperturbed by the news.*
– DERIVATIVES **unperturbedly** adverb.

unphilosophical ▸ adjective not following philosophical principles or method.
– DERIVATIVES **unphilosophic** adjective (rare), **unphilosophically** adverb.

unphysical ▸ adjective not in accordance with the laws or principles of physics; not corresponding to a physically possible situation.

unphysiological ▸ adjective not in accordance with normal physiological conditions.
– DERIVATIVES **unphysiologic** adjective, **unphysiologically** adverb.

U

unpick ▸ verb [with obj.] undo the sewing of: *I unpicked the seams of his trousers.* ■ carefully analyse the different elements of (something), especially in order to find faults.

unpicked ▸ adjective 1 (of a flower, fruit, or vegetable) not picked: *unpicked tomatoes.*
2 not selected.

unpicturesque ▸ adjective not picturesque.

unpin ▸ verb (**unpins, unpinning, unpinned**) [with obj.] unfasten or detach by removing a pin or pins. ■ Chess release (a pinned piece or pawn), e.g. by moving away the piece it is shielding.

unpitied ▸ adjective not pitied.

unpitying ▸ adjective not feeling or showing pity.
– DERIVATIVES **unpityingly** adverb.

unplaceable ▸ adjective not able to be placed or classified: *an unplaceable accent.*

unplaced ▸ adjective not having or assigned to a specific place. ■ chiefly Horse Racing not one of the first three to finish in a race or competition.

unplanned ▸ adjective not planned: *an unplanned pregnancy.*

unplanted ▸ adjective (of land) uncultivated.

unplausible ▸ adjective not plausible.

unplayable ▸ adjective 1 unable to be played: *he thinks the ball is unplayable | an unplayable guitar solo.*
2 (of a sports pitch) too poor to play on.
– DERIVATIVES **unplayably** adverb.

unplayed ▸ adjective not played.

unpleasant ▸ adjective causing discomfort, unhappiness, or revulsion; disagreeable: *an unpleasant smell | the symptoms are extremely unpleasant.* ■ (of a person or their manner) unfriendly and inconsiderate; rude: *when drunk, he could become very unpleasant.*
– DERIVATIVES **unpleasantly** adverb.

unpleasantness ▸ noun [mass noun] the state or quality of being unpleasant. ■ bad feeling or quarrelling between people.

unpleasantry ▸ noun (pl. **unpleasantries**)
1 (**unpleasantries**) disagreeable matters or comments: *why dwell on niggling little unpleasantries at a time like this?*
2 [mass noun] dated quarrelling or other disagreeable behaviour: *a little unpleasantry with the authorities.*

unpleasing ▸ adjective not giving satisfaction, especially of an aesthetic kind: *the sound was not unpleasing.*
– DERIVATIVES **unpleasingly** adverb.

unpleasure ▸ noun [mass noun] Psychoanalysis the sense of inner pain, discomfort, or anxiety which results from the blocking of an instinctual impulse by the ego.

unploughed (US **unplowed**) ▸ adjective 1 (of an area of land) not having been ploughed.
2 N. Amer. (of a road) not cleared of snow by a snowplough.

unplucked ▸ adjective not plucked: *unplucked eyebrows.*

unplug ▸ verb (**unplugs, unplugging, unplugged**) [with obj.] 1 disconnect (an electrical device) by removing its plug from a socket: *she unplugged the fridge.*
2 remove an obstacle or blockage from: *a procedure to unplug blocked arteries.*

unplugged ▸ adjective trademark (of pop or rock music) performed or recorded with acoustic rather than electrically amplified instruments.

unplumbed ▸ adjective 1 not fully explored or understood: *one-dimensional performances that leave the play's psychological depths unplumbed.*
2 (of a building or room) not having water and drainage pipes installed and connected.
– DERIVATIVES **unplumbable** adjective.

unpoetic ▸ adjective not having a style of expression characteristic of poetry.
– DERIVATIVES **unpoetical** adjective, **unpoetically** adverb.

unpointed ▸ adjective 1 not having a sharpened or tapered tip.
2 (of a Semitic language) written without dots or small strokes to indicate vowels or distinguish consonants.
3 (of brickwork, a brick structure, or tiling) having joints that are not filled in or repaired.

unpolished ▸ adjective not having a polished surface: *his shoes were unpolished.* ■ unrefined in style or behaviour: *his work is unpolished and sometimes incoherent.*

unpolitic ▸ adjective rare term for IMPOLITIC.

unpolitical ▸ adjective not concerned with politics: *large numbers of otherwise unpolitical people responded to the war.*

unpolled ▸ adjective 1 (of a voter) not having voted, or registered to vote, at an election.
2 (of a person) not included in an opinion poll.

unpolluted ▸ adjective not contaminated with noxious or poisonous substances.

unpopular ▸ adjective not liked or popular: *unpopular measures | Luke was **unpopular with** most of the teachers.*
– DERIVATIVES **unpopularity** noun.

unpopulated ▸ adjective 1 (of a place) having no inhabitants: *three missiles landed in unpopulated areas.*
2 Electronics (of a printed circuit board) having no components fitted.

unposed ▸ adjective (of a photograph) not having an artificially posed subject.

unpossessed ▸ adjective not possessed or owned: *a skill unpossessed by outsiders.* ■ (**unpossessed of**) not having (an ability, quality, or characteristic): *the money men are unpossessed of the social graces.*

unpowered ▸ adjective having no fuel-burning source of power for propulsion.

unpractical ▸ adjective another term for IMPRACTICAL (sense 1).
– DERIVATIVES **unpracticality** noun.

unpractised (US **unpracticed**) ▸ adjective not trained or experienced: *to the unpractised eye, the result might appear a hotchpotch.* ■ not often done before; not rehearsed or practised: *an unpractised improvisation.*

unprecedented /ʌnˈprɛsɪdɛntɪd/ ▸ adjective never done or known before: *the government took the unprecedented step of releasing confidential correspondence.*
– DERIVATIVES **unprecedentedly** adverb.

unpredictable ▸ adjective not able to be predicted; changeable: *the unpredictable weather of the Scottish islands.*
– DERIVATIVES **unpredictability** noun, **unpredictably** adverb.

unpredicted ▸ adjective (of an event or result) unforeseen: *the unpredicted change of weather.*

unprejudiced ▸ adjective not having or showing a dislike or distrust based on fixed or preconceived ideas.

unpremeditated ▸ adjective (of an act, remark, or state) not thought out or planned beforehand: *it was a totally unpremeditated attack.*
– DERIVATIVES **unpremeditatedly** adverb.

unprepared ▸ adjective 1 not ready or able to deal with something: *she was totally **unprepared for** what happened next | the transformation caught them unprepared.* ■ [with infinitive] not willing to do something: *they were unprepared to accept what was proposed.*
2 not made ready for use: *paintings on unprepared canvas.*
– DERIVATIVES **unpreparedness** noun.

unprepossessing ▸ adjective not attractive or appealing to the eye.

unprescribed ▸ adjective (of a medicine) not prescribed or recommended by a medical practitioner.

unpresentable ▸ adjective not clean, smart, or decent enough to be seen in public.

unpressed ▸ adjective 1 (of clothing) unironed.
2 not shaped or obtained by pressing or pressure: *soft, unpressed, cheeses.*

unpressurized (also **unpressurised**) ▸ adjective (of a gas or its container) not having raised pressure that is produced or maintained artificially. ■ (of an aircraft cabin) not having normal atmospheric pressure maintained at a high altitude.

unpresuming ▸ adjective modest; unassuming: *a quiet, unpresuming man.*

unpretending ▸ adjective archaic not pretentious or false: *unpretending sympathy.*

unpretentious ▸ adjective not attempting to impress others with an appearance of greater importance, talent, or culture than is actually possessed. ■ (of a place) pleasantly simple and functional; modest.
– DERIVATIVES **unpretentiously** adverb, **unpretentiousness** noun.

unpreventable ▸ adjective not able to be prevented or avoided: *until now this devastating disease has been unpreventable.*

unpriced ▸ adjective having no marked or stated price.

unprimed ▸ adjective not made ready for use or action. ■ (of wood, canvas, or metal) not covered with primer or undercoat.

unprincipled ▸ adjective (of a person or their behaviour) not acting in accordance with moral principles: *an unprincipled womanizer.*

unprintable ▸ adjective (of words, comments, or thoughts) too offensive or shocking to be published: *Peter's first reply was unprintable.*
– DERIVATIVES **unprintably** adverb.

unprinted ▸ adjective (of a book or piece of writing) not published: *unprinted law reports.*

unprivileged ▶ adjective not having special rights, advantages, or immunities.

unproblematic ▶ adjective not constituting or presenting a problem or difficulty: *none of these approaches is unproblematic.*
– DERIVATIVES **unproblematical** adjective, **unproblematically** adverb.

unprocessed ▶ adjective not processed: *fresh, unprocessed food.*

unproclaimed ▶ adjective not announced officially or publicly.

unproductive ▶ adjective not producing or able to produce large amounts of goods, crops, or other commodities: *unproductive land must be reforested.* ■ (of an activity or period) not achieving much; not very useful: *unproductive meetings.*
– DERIVATIVES **unproductively** adverb, **unproductiveness** noun.

unprofessional ▶ adjective below or contrary to the standards expected in a particular profession: *a report on unprofessional conduct.*
– DERIVATIVES **unprofessionalism** noun, **unprofessionally** adverb.

unprofitable ▶ adjective (of a business or activity) not yielding profit or financial gain: *the mines became increasingly unprofitable.* ■ (of an activity) not beneficial or useful: *there has been much unprofitable speculation.*
– DERIVATIVES **unprofitability** noun, **unprofitably** adverb.

unprogressive ▶ adjective not favouring or implementing social reform or new, typically liberal, ideas.

unpromising ▶ adjective not giving hope of future success or good results: *the boy's natural intellect had survived in unpromising circumstances.*
– DERIVATIVES **unpromisingly** adverb.

unprompted ▶ adjective said, done, or acting without being encouraged or assisted: *unprompted remarks.*

unpronounceable ▶ adjective (of a word or name) too difficult to say.
– DERIVATIVES **unpronounceably** adverb.

unpropitious ▶ adjective (of a circumstance) not giving or indicating a good chance of success; unfavourable.
– DERIVATIVES **unpropitiously** adverb.

unprosperous ▶ adjective not enjoying or bringing financial success.

unprotected ▶ adjective **1** not protected or kept safe from harm or injury: *health-care workers remained **unprotected against** hepatitis B infection.* ■ (of a machine or mechanism) not fitted with safety guards. ■ Computing (of data or a memory location) able to be accessed or used without restriction.
2 (of sexual intercourse) performed without a condom.

unprotesting ▶ adjective not objecting to what someone has said or done.
– DERIVATIVES **unprotestingly** adverb.

unproud ▶ adjective not having a high opinion of one's worth or accomplishments.

unprovable ▶ adjective unable to be demonstrated by evidence or argument as true or existing: *the hypothesis is not merely unprovable, but false.*
– DERIVATIVES **unprovability** noun.

unproven /ʌnˈpruːv(ə)n, -ˈprəʊ-/ (also **unproved** /-ˈpruːvd/) ▶ adjective not demonstrated by evidence or argument as true or existing: *long-standing but unproven allegations | the risks are unproven.* ■ (of a new method, system, or treatment) not tried and tested.

unprovided ▶ adjective not provided, supplied, or equipped with something: *she was almost entirely **unprovided with** funds.* ■ (**unprovided for**) (of a dependant) not supplied with sufficient money to cover the cost of living: *he left a widow and children totally unprovided for.*

unprovoked ▶ adjective carried out, occurring, or acting without direct provocation: *an unprovoked attack on an innocent man.*

unpruned ▶ adjective not pruned.

unpublicized (also **unpublicised**) ▶ adjective not made widely known.

unpublished ▶ adjective (of a piece of writing or music) not issued in print for public sale or consumption. ■ (of an author) having no writings issued in print.
– DERIVATIVES **unpublishable** adjective.

unpunctual ▶ adjective not happening or doing something at the agreed or proper time.
– DERIVATIVES **unpunctuality** noun.

unpunctuated ▶ adjective (of text) not containing punctuation marks. ■ not interrupted or marked by something occurring at intervals: *we seldom had a conversation unpunctuated by laughter.*

unpunishable ▶ adjective not able to be punished.

unpunished ▶ adjective (of an offence or offender) not receiving any punishment or penalty: *I can't allow such a mistake to **go unpunished**.*

unpurified ▶ adjective not made pure: *unpurified water.*

unputdownable ▶ adjective informal (of a book) so engrossing that one cannot stop reading it.

unqualified ▶ adjective **1** (of a person) not officially recognized as a practitioner of a particular profession or activity through having satisfied the relevant conditions or requirements. ■ [usu. with infinitive] not competent or sufficiently knowledgeable to do something: *I am singularly unqualified to write about football.*
2 without reservation or limitation; total: *the experiment was not an unqualified success.*
– DERIVATIVES **unqualifiedly** adverb.

unquantifiable ▶ adjective impossible to express or measure in terms of quantity.

unquantified ▶ adjective not expressed or measured in terms of quantity: *we now have abundant, if unquantified, evidence.*

unquenchable ▶ adjective not able to be quenched: *his enthusiasm was unquenchable.*
– DERIVATIVES **unquenchably** adverb.

unquenched ▶ adjective not quenched.

unquestionable ▶ adjective not able to be disputed or doubted: *his musicianship is unquestionable.*
– DERIVATIVES **unquestionability** noun, **unquestionably** adverb [sentence adverb] *unquestionably, the loss of his father was a grievous blow.*

unquestioned ▶ adjective not disputed or doubted; certain: *his loyalty to John is unquestioned.* ■ not examined or enquired into: *an unquestioned assumption.*

unquestioning ▶ adjective accepting something without dissent or doubt: *an unquestioning acceptance of the traditional curriculum.*
– DERIVATIVES **unquestioningly** adverb.

unquiet ▶ adjective unable to be still; restless: *poor Amy's unquiet spirit.* ■ uneasy; anxious: *an unquiet mind.*
– DERIVATIVES **unquietly** adverb, **unquietness** noun.

unquotable ▶ adjective not able to be quoted.

unquote ▶ verb see **QUOTE** —— **UNQUOTE** at **QUOTE**.

unquoted ▶ adjective not quoted or listed on a stock exchange.

unranked ▶ adjective not having achieved or been given a rank or ranking: *the team have two matches against unranked opponents.*

unrated ▶ adjective not having received a rating or assessment. ■ US (of a film) not allocated an official classification due to its level of sexually explicit material. ■ informal not highly regarded.

unravel ▶ verb (**unravels**, **unravelling**, **unravelled**; US **unravels**, **unraveling**, **unraveled**) [with obj.] **1** undo (twisted, knitted, or woven threads). ■ [no obj.] (of such threads) become undone: *part of the crew neck had unravelled | figurative his painstaking diplomacy of the last eight months could quickly unravel.*
2 investigate and solve or explain (something complicated or puzzling): *they were attempting to unravel the cause of death.*

unreachable ▶ adjective unable to be reached or contacted.
– DERIVATIVES **unreachably** adverb.

unreached ▶ adjective not yet reached, especially by people seeking to convert others to Christianity.

unreactive ▶ adjective having little tendency to react chemically.

unread ▶ adjective **1** (of a book or document) not read.
2 archaic (of a person) not well read.

unreadable ▶ adjective **1** not clear enough to read; illegible. ■ too dull or difficult to be worth reading: *a heavy, unreadable novel.*
2 (of data or a storage medium or device) not capable of being processed or interpreted by a computer or other electronic device.
– DERIVATIVES **unreadability** noun, **unreadably** adverb.

unready ▶ adjective not prepared for a situation or activity: *she was young and unready for motherhood.* ■ archaic slow to act; hesitant.
– DERIVATIVES **unreadiness** noun.

unreal ▶ adjective **1** imaginary or illusory: *in the half-light the tiny cottages seemed unreal.* ■ informal, chiefly N. Amer. incredible; amazing.
2 unrealistic: *many people have unreal expectations of marriage.*
– DERIVATIVES **unreality** noun, **unreally** adverb.

unrealism ▶ noun [mass noun] lack of realism.

unrealistic ▶ adjective not realistic: *it was unrealistic to expect changes to be made overnight.*
– DERIVATIVES **unrealistically** adverb.

unrealizable (also **unrealisable**) ▶ adjective not able to be achieved or made to happen: *the summit might generate unrealizable public expectations.*

unrealized (also **unrealised**) ▶ adjective **1** not achieved or created: *an unrealized dream.*
2 not converted into money: *unrealized property assets.*

unreason ▶ noun [mass noun] inability to act or think reasonably.
– ORIGIN Middle English (in the senses 'unreasonable intention' and 'impropriety'): from **UN-**[1] 'lack of' + **REASON**.

unreasonable ▶ adjective not guided by or based on good sense: *she knew she was being unreasonable, but she resented his domesticity.* ■ beyond the limits of acceptability or fairness: *an unreasonable request.*
– DERIVATIVES **unreasonableness** noun, **unreasonably** adverb.

unreasoned ▶ adjective not based on good sense or logic: *an unreasoned reaction to the idea.*

unreasoning ▶ adjective not guided by or based on good sense; illogical: *unreasoning panic.*
– DERIVATIVES **unreasoningly** adverb.

unreceptive ▶ adjective not receptive, especially to new suggestions or ideas.

unreciprocated ▶ adjective not reciprocated: *his feelings for her were unreciprocated.*

unreckoned ▶ adjective not calculated or taken into account.

unreclaimed ▶ adjective (especially of land) not reclaimed.

unrecognizable (also **unrecognisable**) ▶ adjective not able to be recognized or identified from previous encounters.
– DERIVATIVES **unrecognizably** adverb.

unrecognized (also **unrecognised**) ▶ adjective **1** not identified from previous encounters or knowledge.
2 not acknowledged as valuable or valid.

unrecompensed ▶ adjective not rewarded or made amends for.

unreconciled ▶ adjective not reconciled: *unreconciled conflict.*

unreconstructed ▶ adjective **1** not reconciled or converted to the current political theory or movement: *he's an unreconstructed Thatcherite.*
2 not rebuilt.

unrecorded ▶ adjective not recorded.
– DERIVATIVES **unrecordable** adjective.

unrecoverable ▶ adjective not able to be recovered or corrected.

unrectified ▶ adjective not corrected or amended.

unredeemable ▶ adjective not able to be redeemed: *an unredeemable defect.*

unredeemed ▶ adjective not redeemed.

unredressed ▶ adjective not corrected or compensated for: *unredressed grievances and protests.*

unreel ▶ verb [with obj.] unwind: *the fibre optic cable must be unreeled before installation.* ■ [no obj.] (of a film) wind from one reel to another during projection.

unreeve ▶ verb (**unreeves**, **unreeving**, past **unrove**) [with obj.] Nautical withdraw (a rope) from a securing ring or block.

unrefined ▶ adjective **1** not processed to remove impurities or unwanted elements: *unrefined sugar.*
2 (of a person or their behaviour) not elegant or cultured.

unreflecting ▶ adjective **1** not engaging in reflection or thought: *an unreflecting hedonist.*
2 not reflecting light.

U

– DERIVATIVES **unreflectingly** adverb, **unreflective** adjective.

unreformed ▸ adjective not changed or improved.

unregarded ▸ adjective not respected or considered; ignored: *her sarcasm went unregarded.*

unregenerate /ˌʌnrɪˈdʒɛn(ə)rət/ ▸ adjective not reforming or showing repentance; obstinately wrong or bad.
– DERIVATIVES **unregeneracy** noun, **unregenerately** adverb.

unregistered ▸ adjective not officially recognized and recorded: *unregistered births.*

unregulated ▸ adjective not controlled or supervised by regulations or laws.

unrehearsed ▸ adjective not practised before a performance: *spontaneous and unrehearsed music.*

unrelated ▸ adjective not related or linked: *unrelated facts | households containing two or more unrelated people.*
– DERIVATIVES **unrelatedness** noun.

unrelaxed ▸ adjective tense.

unreleased ▸ adjective (especially of a film or recording) not released.

unrelenting ▸ adjective not yielding in strength, severity, or determination: *the heat was unrelenting.* ■ not giving way to kindness or compassion: *unrelenting opponents.*
– DERIVATIVES **unrelentingly** adverb, **unrelentingness** noun.

unreliable ▸ adjective not able to be relied upon: *he's lazy and unreliable | unreliable information.*
– DERIVATIVES **unreliability** noun, **unreliably** adverb.

unrelieved ▸ adjective **1** lacking variation or change; monotonous: *flowing gowns of unrelieved black.* **2** not provided with relief; not aided or assisted.
– DERIVATIVES **unrelievedly** adverb.

unreligious ▸ adjective indifferent or hostile to religion. ■ not connected with religion.

unremarkable ▸ adjective not particularly interesting or surprising: *his early childhood was unremarkable | an unremarkable house.*
– DERIVATIVES **unremarkably** adverb.

unremarked ▸ adjective not mentioned or remarked upon; unnoticed: *she let his bitterness* **go unremarked.**

unremembered ▸ adjective not remembered; forgotten.

unremitting ▸ adjective never relaxing or slackening; incessant: *unremitting drizzle.*
– DERIVATIVES **unremittingly** adverb, **unremittingness** noun.

unremorseful ▸ adjective lacking feelings of regret or guilt.
– DERIVATIVES **unremorsefully** adverb.

unremovable ▸ adjective not able to be removed.

unremunerative ▸ adjective bringing little or no profit or income: *unremunerative research work.*

unrenewable ▸ adjective not able to be renewed: *unrenewable fossil fuels.*
– DERIVATIVES **unrenewed** adjective.

unrepealed ▸ adjective not repealed.

unrepeatable ▸ adjective **1** not able to be done or made again: *an extraordinary and unrepeatable event.* **2** too offensive or shocking to be said again.
– DERIVATIVES **unrepeatability** noun.

unrepentant ▸ adjective showing no regret for one's wrongdoings.
– DERIVATIVES **unrepentantly** adverb.

unreported ▸ adjective not reported: *many human rights abuses* **went unreported.**

unrepresentative ▸ adjective not typical of a class, group, or body of opinion: *an unrepresentative minority.*
– DERIVATIVES **unrepresentativeness** noun.

unrepresented ▸ adjective not represented.

unrequested ▸ adjective not asked for.

unrequited ▸ adjective (of a feeling, especially love) not returned.
– DERIVATIVES **unrequitedly** adverb, **unrequitedness** noun.

unreserve ▸ noun [mass noun] archaic lack of reserve; frankness.

unreserved ▸ adjective **1** without reservations; complete: *he has had their unreserved support.* **2** frank and open: *a tall, unreserved young man.* **3** not set apart for a particular purpose or booked in advance: *unreserved grandstand seats.*
– DERIVATIVES **unreservedly** adverb, **unreservedness** noun.

unresisted ▸ adjective not resisted.

unresisting ▸ adjective not showing, producing, or putting up any resistance.
– DERIVATIVES **unresistingly** adverb.

unresolvable ▸ adjective not able to be resolved.

unresolved ▸ adjective (of a problem, question, or dispute) not resolved: *a number of issues remain unresolved.* ■ archaic (of a person) uncertain of what to think or do.

unresponsive ▸ adjective not responsive: *these symptoms may be* **unresponsive to** *conventional treatment.*
– DERIVATIVES **unresponsively** adverb, **unresponsiveness** noun.

unrest ▸ noun [mass noun] a state of dissatisfaction, disturbance, and agitation, typically involving public demonstrations or disorder: *years of industrial unrest.* ■ a feeling of disturbance and dissatisfaction in a person: *the frenzy and unrest of her own life.*

unrested ▸ adjective (of a person) not refreshed by rest: *she woke feeling unrested.*

unrestful ▸ adjective not restful.

unresting ▸ adjective ceaselessly active.
– DERIVATIVES **unrestingly** adverb.

unrestored ▸ adjective not repaired or renovated: *an unrestored farmhouse.*

unrestrained ▸ adjective not restrained or restricted: *a display of unrestrained delight.*
– DERIVATIVES **unrestrainedly** adverb, **unrestrainedness** noun.

unrestricted ▸ adjective not limited or restricted: *unrestricted access to both military bases.*
– DERIVATIVES **unrestrictedly** adverb.

unreturned ▸ adjective not reciprocated or responded to: *the pain of unreturned love.*

unrevealed ▸ adjective not revealed; secret: *some feelings can run so deep that they are better left unrevealed.*
– DERIVATIVES **unrevealing** adjective.

unreversed ▸ adjective not reversed.

unrevised ▸ adjective not revised; in an original form: *the manuscript was unrevised when he died.*

unrevoked ▸ adjective not revoked or annulled; still in force.

unrewarded ▸ adjective not rewarded: *he gave untiring and unrewarded service.*

unrewarding ▸ adjective not rewarding or satisfying: *it was dull, unrewarding work.*

unrhymed ▸ adjective without rhymes; not rhymed.

unridden ▸ adjective not ridden or never having been ridden.

unriddle ▸ verb [with obj.] rare solve; explain.

unrideable (also **unridable**) ▸ adjective not able to be ridden.

unrig ▸ verb (**unrigs, unrigging, unrigged**) [with obj.] remove the rigging from (a ship). ■ archaic or dialect undress (someone).

unrighteous ▸ adjective formal not righteous; wicked.
– DERIVATIVES **unrighteously** adverb, **unrighteousness** noun.
– ORIGIN Old English *unrihtwīs* (see **UN-**[1], **RIGHTEOUS**).

unrip ▸ verb (**unrips, unripping, unripped**) [with obj.] rare open by ripping: *he carefully unripped one of the seams.*

unripe ▸ adjective not ripe: *unripe fruit.*
– DERIVATIVES **unripeness** noun.

unrisen ▸ adjective not having risen: *the unrisen sun.*

unrivalled (US **unrivaled**) ▸ adjective better than everyone or everything of the same type: *the paper's coverage of foreign news is unrivalled.*

unrivet ▸ verb (**unrivets, unriveting, unriveted**) [with obj.] rare undo, unfasten, or detach by the removal of rivets.

unroadworthy ▸ adjective (of a vehicle) not roadworthy.

unrobe ▸ verb less common term for **DISROBE**.

unroll ▸ verb open or cause to open out from a rolled-up state: [no obj.] *the blanket unrolled as he tugged it* | [with obj.] *two carpets had been unrolled.*

unromantic ▸ adjective not romantic.
– DERIVATIVES **unromantically** adverb.

unroof ▸ verb [with obj.] remove the roof of.

unroofed ▸ adjective not having a roof.

unroot ▸ verb uproot (something).

unrope ▸ verb [no obj.] Climbing detach oneself from a rope.

unrounded ▸ adjective not rounded. ■ Phonetics (of a vowel) pronounced with the lips not rounded.

unrove past of **UNREEVE**.

unroyal ▸ adjective not royal.
– DERIVATIVES **unroyally** adverb.

unruffled ▸ adjective not disordered or disarranged: *the unruffled waters of the lake.* ■ (of a person or their manner) not agitated or disturbed; calm: *Robbie seemed unruffled by her words.*

unruled ▸ adjective **1** literary not ruled, governed, or under control: *men with passions unruled.* **2** (of paper) not having ruled lines.

unruly ▸ adjective (**unrulier, unruliest**) disorderly and disruptive and not amenable to discipline or control: *a group of unruly children* | figurative *Kate tried to control her unruly emotions.*
– DERIVATIVES **unruliness** noun.
– ORIGIN late Middle English: from **UN-**[1] 'not' + archaic *ruly* 'amenable to discipline or order' (from **RULE**).

UNRWA ▸ abbreviation United Nations Relief and Works Agency.

unsaddle ▸ verb [with obj.] remove the saddle from (a horse). ■ dislodge (a rider) from a saddle.

unsafe ▸ adjective **1** not safe; dangerous: *drinking water in some areas may be unsafe.* **2** Law (of a verdict or conviction) not based on reliable evidence and likely to constitute a miscarriage of justice.
– DERIVATIVES **unsafely** adverb, **unsafeness** noun.

unsafe sex ▸ noun [mass noun] sexual activity in which precautions are not taken to reduce the risk of spreading sexually transmitted diseases, especially AIDS.

unsaid[1] past and past participle of **UNSAY**.

unsaid[2] ▸ adjective not said or uttered: *the rest of the remark he* **left unsaid.**

unsalaried ▸ adjective not being paid or involving the payment of a salary: *an unsalaried post.*

unsaleable (also **unsalable**) ▸ adjective not able to be sold: *the house proved unsaleable.*
– DERIVATIVES **unsaleability** noun.

unsalted ▸ adjective not salted: *unsalted butter.*

unsanctified ▸ adjective not sanctified.

unsanctioned ▸ adjective not sanctioned.

unsanitary ▸ adjective not sanitary: *the unsanitary conditions in the orphanage.*

unsatisfactory ▸ adjective **1** not satisfactory; not good enough: *years of living in unsatisfactory rented accommodation.* **2** Law another term for **UNSAFE**.
– DERIVATIVES **unsatisfactorily** adverb, **unsatisfactoriness** noun.

unsatisfied ▸ adjective not satisfied: *the compromise left all sides unsatisfied.*

unsatisfying ▸ adjective not satisfying: *an unsatisfying relationship.*
– DERIVATIVES **unsatisfyingly** adverb.

unsaturated ▸ adjective Chemistry (of organic molecules) having carbon–carbon double or triple bonds and therefore not containing the greatest possible number of hydrogen atoms.
– DERIVATIVES **unsaturation** noun.

unsaved ▸ adjective not saved, in particular (in Christian use) not having had one's soul saved from damnation.

unsavoury (US **unsavory**) ▸ adjective disagreeable to taste, smell, or look at. ■ disagreeable and unpleasant because morally disreputable: *an unsavoury reputation.*
– DERIVATIVES **unsavourily** adverb, **unsavouriness** noun.

unsay ▸ verb (**unsays, unsaying**; past and past participle **unsaid**) [with obj.] withdraw or retract (a statement).

unsayable ▸ adjective not able to be said, especially because considered too controversial or offensive to mention.

unscalable (also **unscaleable**) ▸ adjective not able to be scaled or climbed: *a prison with unscalable walls.*

unscaled ▸ adjective (of a mountain) not yet climbed: *they had climbed a hitherto unscaled peak.*

unscarred ▸ adjective not scarred or damaged: *he did not escape unscarred.*

U

unscathed ▸ adjective without suffering any injury, damage, or harm: *I came through all those perils unscathed.*

unscented ▸ adjective not scented: *unscented soap.*

unscheduled ▸ adjective not scheduled: *his plane made an unscheduled stop.*

unscholarly ▸ adjective not showing the learning and attention to detail characteristic of a scholar.

unschooled ▸ adjective not educated or trained: *she was unschooled in the niceties of royal behaviour.* ■ natural; spontaneous: *he reacts with intense, unschooled emotion.*

unscientific ▸ adjective **1** not in accordance with scientific principles or methodology: *our whole approach is hopelessly unscientific.* **2** lacking knowledge of or interest in science.
– DERIVATIVES **unscientifically** adverb.

unscramble ▸ verb [with obj.] restore (something that has been scrambled) to an intelligible, readable, or viewable state.
– DERIVATIVES **unscrambler** noun.

unscreened ▸ adjective **1** not subjected to testing or investigation by screening: *transfusion with unscreened blood.* ■ not filtered or sorted using a screen.
2 (of a film or programme) not shown or broadcast: *copies of the unscreened episodes.*
3 not provided with or hidden by a screen.

unscrew ▸ verb (with reference to a lid or other object held in place by a spiral thread) unfasten or be unfastened by twisting: [with obj.] *Will unscrewed the cap from a metal flask* | [no obj.] *the spout usually unscrews or lifts off easily.* ■ [with obj.] detach, open, or slacken (something) by removing or loosening the screws holding it in place: *he unscrewed the number plates from his old Renault.*

unscripted ▸ adjective said or delivered without a prepared script; impromptu.

unscriptural ▸ adjective not in accordance with the Bible: *sacraments deemed unscriptural by Luther.*

unscrupulous ▸ adjective having or showing no moral principles; not honest or fair.
– DERIVATIVES **unscrupulously** adverb, **unscrupulousness** noun.

unseal ▸ verb [with obj.] remove or break the seal of: *she slowly unsealed the envelope.*

unsealed ▸ adjective **1** not sealed: *unsealed envelopes.*
2 chiefly Austral./NZ (of a road) not surfaced with bitumen or a similar substance.

unsearchable ▸ adjective literary unable to be clearly understood; inscrutable.
– DERIVATIVES **unsearchableness** noun.

unsearched ▸ adjective not searched or examined: *more than half of the grounds were still unsearched.*

unseasonable ▸ adjective **1** (of weather) unusual for the time of year: *an unseasonable warm spell.*
2 untimely; inopportune.
– DERIVATIVES **unseasonableness** noun, **unseasonably** adverb.

unseasonal ▸ adjective (especially of weather) unusual or inappropriate for the time of year: *temperatures rose to an unseasonal 12°C.*

unseasoned ▸ adjective **1** (of food) not flavoured with salt, pepper, or other spices.
2 (of timber) not treated or matured. ■ (of a person) inexperienced.

unseat ▸ verb [with obj.] cause (someone) to fall from a horse or bicycle. ■ remove (a government or person in authority) from power.

unseaworthy ▸ adjective (of a boat or ship) not in a good enough condition to sail on the sea.
– DERIVATIVES **unseaworthiness** noun.

unsecured ▸ adjective **1** (of a loan) made without an asset given as security. ■ (of a creditor) having made such a loan.
2 not made secure or safe.

unseeable ▸ adjective not able to be seen; invisible.

unseeded ▸ adjective **1** (of a competitor or team in a sports tournament) not seeded.
2 (of a grape) not having seeds.

unseeing ▸ adjective with one's eyes open but without noticing or seeing anything.
– DERIVATIVES **unseeingly** adverb.

unseemly ▸ adjective (**unseemlier**, **unseemliest**) (of behaviour or actions) not proper or appropriate: *an unseemly squabble.*
– DERIVATIVES **unseemliness** noun.

unseen ▸ adjective not seen or noticed: *it seemed she might escape unseen.* ■ not foreseen or predicted: *unseen problems.* ■ chiefly Brit. (of a passage for translation in a test or examination) not previously read or prepared.
▸ noun Brit. an unseen passage for translation.

unsegmented ▸ adjective chiefly Zoology not divided into segments.

unsegregated ▸ adjective not segregated or set apart from the rest or from others.

unselect ▸ verb [with obj.] cancel the selection of.

unselected ▸ adjective not selected.

unselective ▸ adjective not selective.

unselfconscious ▸ adjective not suffering from or exhibiting self-consciousness; not shy or embarrassed.
– DERIVATIVES **unselfconsciously** adverb, **unselfconsciousness** noun.

unselfish ▸ adjective willing to put the needs or wishes of others before one's own: *unselfish devotion.*
– DERIVATIVES **unselfishly** adverb, **unselfishness** noun.

unsellable ▸ adjective not able to be sold, or very difficult to sell: *many of the houses are unsellable.*

unsensational ▸ adjective not sensational or seeking to provoke interest or excitement at the expense of accuracy.
– DERIVATIVES **unsensationally** adverb.

unsentimental ▸ adjective not displaying or influenced by sentimental feelings.
– DERIVATIVES **unsentimentally** adverb.

unseparated ▸ adjective not separated or divided: *five heads of garlic, three unseparated and two separated into cloves.*

unserious ▸ adjective not serious; light-hearted.

unserved ▸ adjective **1** not attended to or catered for.
2 Law (of a writ or summons) not officially delivered to a person.
3 (of a female animal) not mated with a male.

unserviceable ▸ adjective not in working order or fulfilling its function adequately; unfit for use.
– DERIVATIVES **unserviceability** noun.

unset ▸ adjective (of a jewel) not yet placed in a setting; unmounted: *ten unset sapphires.*

unsettle ▸ verb [with obj.] cause to feel anxious or uneasy; disturb: *the crisis has unsettled financial markets* | *an unsettling conversation.*
– DERIVATIVES **unsettlement** noun, **unsettlingly** adverb.

unsettled ▸ adjective **1** lacking order or stability: *an unsettled childhood.* ■ worried and uneasy: *she felt edgy and unsettled.* ■ liable to change; unpredictable: *a spell of unsettled weather.*
2 not yet resolved: *one question remains unsettled.* ■ (of a bill) not yet paid.
3 (of an area) having no settlers or inhabitants.
– DERIVATIVES **unsettledness** noun.

unsewn ▸ adjective not sewn: *a piece of unsewn fabric.*

unsewn binding ▸ noun Brit. another term for PERFECT BINDING.

unsex ▸ verb [with obj.] deprive of gender, sexuality, or the characteristic attributes or qualities of one or other sex.

unsexy ▸ adjective (**unsexier**, **unsexiest**) not sexually attractive or exciting.

unshackle ▸ verb [with obj.] release from shackles, chains, or other physical restraints: *the slaves were unshackled and brought out.* ■ liberate; set free: *more homebuyers want to unshackle themselves from their mortgages early.*

unshackled ▸ adjective not chained or shackled: *he had handcuffs on his wrists but his feet were unshackled.*

unshaded ▸ adjective **1** (of a light bulb or lamp) not having a shade or cover. ■ not screened from direct light.
2 (of an area of a diagram) not shaded with pencil lines or a block of colour.

unshadowed ▸ adjective not covered or darkened by a shadow or shadows.

unshakeable (also **unshakable**) ▸ adjective (of a belief, feeling, or opinion) strongly felt and unable to be changed: *my unshakeable faith in the goodness of mankind.* ■ unable to be disputed or questioned: *an unshakeable alibi.*
– DERIVATIVES **unshakeability** noun, **unshakeably** adverb.

unshaken ▸ adjective not disturbed from a firm position or state; steadfast and unwavering: *their trust in him remained unshaken.*

unshaped ▸ adjective having a vague, ill-formed, or unfinished shape.

unshapely ▸ adjective not shapely.

unshared ▸ adjective not shared with or by another or others.

unsharp ▸ adjective Photography (of a picture or image) not well defined.
– DERIVATIVES **unsharpness** noun.

unshaved ▸ adjective unshaven.

unshaven ▸ adjective not having recently shaved or been shaved.

unsheathe ▸ verb [with obj.] draw or pull out (a knife, sword, or similar weapon) from its sheath or covering: *Alexei unsheathed the dagger.*

unsheathed ▸ adjective not placed in or protected by a sheath or covering: *all unsheathed wires must be enclosed in a non-combustible housing.*

unshed ▸ adjective (of tears) welling in a person's eyes but not falling on their cheeks.

unshelled ▸ adjective not extracted from its shell: *unshelled peanuts.*

unsheltered ▸ adjective not sheltered or protected: *a square sandstone building unsheltered by any trees.*

unshielded ▸ adjective not protected or shielded.

unship ▸ verb (**unships**, **unshipping**, **unshipped**)
1 [with obj.] chiefly Nautical remove (an oar, mast, or other object) from its fixed or regular position: *they unshipped the oars.*
2 unload (a cargo) from a ship or boat.

unshockable ▸ adjective impossible to shock, horrify, or disgust: *most doctors are fairly unshockable.*
– DERIVATIVES **unshockability** noun.

unshod ▸ adjective not wearing shoes.

unshorn ▸ adjective not cut or shorn.

unshowy ▸ adjective not showy in appearance or style; restrained or understated.

unshrinkable ▸ adjective (especially of fabric) not liable to shrink.

unshrinking ▸ adjective unhesitating; fearless.
– DERIVATIVES **unshrinkingly** adverb.

unshriven ▸ adjective not shriven.

unsighted ▸ adjective **1** lacking the power of sight: *blind or unsighted people.* ■ (especially in sport) prevented from having a clear view of something: *the umpires had been unsighted and had not seen the ball.*
2 not seen: *a distant unsighted object.*

unsightly ▸ adjective unpleasant to look at; ugly: *an unsightly rubbish tip.*
– DERIVATIVES **unsightliness** noun.

unsigned ▸ adjective **1** not identified or authorized by a person's signature: *an unsigned cheque.* ■ (of a musician or sports player) not having signed a contract of employment.
2 Mathematics & Computing not having a plus or minus sign, or a bit representing this.

unsinkable ▸ adjective (of a ship or boat) unable to be sunk: *the supposedly unsinkable ship hit an iceberg.*
– DERIVATIVES **unsinkability** noun.

unsisterly ▸ adjective not showing the support and affection which is thought to be characteristic of a sister.

unsized ▸ adjective (of fabric, paper, or a wall) not treated with size.

unskilful (also chiefly US **unskillful**) ▸ adjective not having or showing skill.
– DERIVATIVES **unskilfully** adverb, **unskilfulness** noun.

unskilled ▸ adjective not having or requiring special skill or training: *unskilled manual workers.*

unskimmed ▸ adjective (of milk) not skimmed.

unslakeable (also **unslakable**) ▸ adjective not able to be quenched or satisfied: *her unslakeable desire.*

unsleeping ▸ adjective not or never sleeping: *much of that night she lay unsleeping.*
– DERIVATIVES **unsleepingly** adverb.

unsliced ▸ adjective (especially of a commercially produced loaf of bread) not having been cut into slices.

unsling ▸ verb (**unslings**, **unslinging**; past and past participle **unslung**) [with obj.] remove (something) from the place where it has been slung or suspended.

U

unsmiling ▸ adjective (of a person or their manner or expression) serious or unfriendly; not smiling.
– DERIVATIVES **unsmilingly** adverb, **unsmilingness** noun.

unsmoked ▸ adjective **1** (of meat or fish) not cured by exposure to smoke: *smoked and unsmoked bacon.* **2** (of tobacco or a cigarette) not having been smoked.

unsnap ▸ verb (**unsnaps, unsnapping, unsnapped**) [with obj.] unfasten or open with a brisk movement and a sharp sound: *he put the case on the table and unsnapped the clasps.*

unsnarl ▸ verb [with obj.] disentangle.

unsociable ▸ adjective not enjoying or making an effort to behave sociably in the company of others: *Terry was grumpy and unsociable.* ▪ not conducive to friendly social relations: *watching TV is a fairly unsociable activity.*
– DERIVATIVES **unsociability** noun, **unsociableness** noun, **unsociably** adverb.

> **USAGE** There is some overlap in the use of the adjectives **unsociable, unsocial,** and **antisocial,** but they also have distinct core meanings. Generally speaking, **unsociable** means 'not enjoying the company of others', as in *Terry was grumpy and* ***unsociable.*** **Antisocial** means 'contrary to the laws and customs of a society', as in *aggressive and* ***antisocial*** *behaviour.* **Unsocial** is usually only used to describe hours 'falling outside the normal working day', as in *employees were expected to work* ***unsocial*** *hours.*

unsocial ▸ adjective **1** Brit. (of the hours of work of a job) falling outside the normal working day and thus socially inconvenient.
2 causing annoyance and disapproval in others; antisocial: *the unsocial behaviour of young teenagers.*
3 not seeking the company of others.
– DERIVATIVES **unsocially** adverb.

unsoiled ▸ adjective not stained or dirty.

unsold ▸ adjective (of an item) not sold.

unsolder ▸ verb [with obj.] undo the soldering of.

unsoldierly ▸ adjective inappropriate to or not befitting a soldier: *he was accused of unsoldierly conduct.*

unsolicited ▸ adjective not asked for; given or done voluntarily: *unsolicited junk mail.*
– DERIVATIVES **unsolicitedly** adverb.

unsolvable ▸ adjective not able to be solved.
– DERIVATIVES **unsolvability** noun.

unsolved ▸ adjective not solved: *an unsolved mystery.*

unsophisticated ▸ adjective **1** lacking refined worldly knowledge or tastes: *an unsophisticated young man.*
2 not complicated or highly developed; basic: *unsophisticated computer software.*
– DERIVATIVES **unsophisticatedly** adverb, **unsophistication** noun.

unsorted ▸ adjective not sorted or arranged: *a mass of unsorted papers.*

unsought ▸ adjective not searched for, requested, or desired.

unsound ▸ adjective **1** not safe or robust; in poor condition: *the tower is structurally unsound.* ▪ not healthy or well: *Dorinda was mentally unsound.*
2 not based on sound or reliable evidence or reasoning: *this line of argument is unsound.* ▪ not acceptable: *activities deemed to be environmentally unsound.* ▪ (of a person) not holding acceptable views.
– PHRASES **of unsound mind** insane.
– DERIVATIVES **unsoundly** adverb, **unsoundness** noun.

U

unsounded[1] ▸ adjective not uttered, pronounced, or made to sound.

unsounded[2] ▸ adjective unfathomed.

unsourced ▸ adjective (of information) not having or attributed to a known source or origin: *an unsourced story in an Italian newspaper.*

unsoured ▸ adjective not soured: *unsoured milk.*

unsown ▸ adjective not having been sown.

unsparing ▸ adjective **1** merciless; severe: *he is unsparing in his criticism of the arms trade.*
2 given freely and generously: *she had won her mother's unsparing approval.*
– DERIVATIVES **unsparingly** adverb, **unsparingness** noun.

unspeakable ▸ adjective not able to be expressed in words: *I felt an unspeakable tenderness towards her.* ▪ too bad or horrific to express in words.
– DERIVATIVES **unspeakableness** noun, **unspeakably** adverb [as submodifier] *he was unspeakably cruel.*

unspeaking ▸ adjective not speaking; silent.

unspecialized (also **unspecialised**) ▸ adjective not specialized.

unspecific ▸ adjective not specific; vague: *he was unspecific about his relationship with Marian.*

unspecified ▸ adjective not stated clearly or exactly: *an unspecified number of people.*

unspectacular ▸ adjective not spectacular; unremarkable: *she had been an unspectacular student.*
– DERIVATIVES **unspectacularly** adverb.

unspent ▸ adjective not spent: *unspent receipts from the sale of council houses.* ▪ not exhausted or used up: *he shook with unspent rage.*

unspilled (also **unspilt**) ▸ adjective not spilt.

unspiritual ▸ adjective not spiritual; worldly: *the clergymen were deplorably unspiritual.*
– DERIVATIVES **unspirituality** noun.

unspoilt (also **unspoiled**) ▸ adjective not spoilt, in particular (of a place) not marred by development: *unspoilt countryside.*

unspoken ▸ adjective not expressed in speech; tacit: *an unspoken assumption.*

unsponsored ▸ adjective not supported or promoted by a sponsor.

unspool ▸ verb unwind or cause to unwind from or as if from a spool: [with obj.] *he unspooled the tape from the casing.*

unsporting ▸ adjective not fair, generous, or sportsmanlike: *the unsporting behaviour of some of the crowd.*
– DERIVATIVES **unsportingly** adverb.

unsportsmanlike ▸ adjective unsporting.

unspotted ▸ adjective not marked with spots.

unsprayed ▸ adjective not having been sprayed, especially with pesticides or other chemicals.

unsprung ▸ adjective not provided with springs.

unstable ▸ adjective (**unstabler, unstablest**) likely to give way; not stable: *the unstable cliff tops.* ▪ likely to change or fail; not firmly established: *an unstable government.* ▪ prone to psychiatric problems or sudden changes of mood: *he was mentally unstable.*
– DERIVATIVES **unstableness** noun, **unstably** adverb.

unstable equilibrium ▸ noun Physics a state of equilibrium in which a small disturbance will produce a large change.

unstaffed ▸ adjective not provided with staff.

unstageable ▸ adjective (of a play) impossible or very difficult to present to an audience.

unstained ▸ adjective not stained.

unstamped ▸ adjective **1** not marked by stamping. **2** not having a postage stamp affixed.

unstapled ▸ adjective (of sheets of paper) not stapled together.

unstarched ▸ adjective (especially of fabric or clothing) not starched.

unstated ▸ adjective not stated or declared: *a series of unstated assumptions.*

unstatesmanlike ▸ adjective not suitable for or befitting a statesman.

unstayed ▸ adjective (especially of a mast) not provided with stays; unsupported.

unsteady ▸ adjective (**unsteadier, unsteadiest**) liable to fall or shake; not steady in position: *he was very unsteady on his feet | Nathan pushed the mug into her unsteady hand.* ▪ not regular in pitch or rhythm: *his deep voice was unsteady.*
– DERIVATIVES **unsteadily** adverb, **unsteadiness** noun.

unstep ▸ verb (**unsteps, unstepping, unstepped**) [with obj.] Nautical detach (a mast) from its step.

unsterile ▸ adjective chiefly Medicine not sterile or sterilized: *unsterile needles.*

unsterilized (also **unsterilised**) ▸ adjective (especially of medical instruments) not sterilized.

unstick ▸ verb (**unsticks, unsticking**; past and past participle **unstuck**) **1** [with obj.] cause to become no longer stuck together.
2 [no obj.] Brit. informal (of an aircraft) take off. ▪ [with obj.] cause (an aircraft) to take off.
▸ noun [in sing.] Brit. informal the moment at which an aircraft takes off.
– PHRASES **come** (or **get**) **unstuck** become separated or unfastened. ▪ informal fail completely: *all their clever ideas came unstuck.*

unstimulated ▸ adjective not having been stimulated: *sci-fi fans will remain unstimulated by the film.*

unstinted ▸ adjective given without restraint; liberal: *they received unstinted praise.*
– DERIVATIVES **unstintedly** adverb.

unstinting ▸ adjective given or giving without restraint; unsparing: *he was unstinting in his praise.*
– DERIVATIVES **unstintingly** adverb.

unstirred ▸ adjective not moved, agitated, or stirred.

unstitch ▸ verb [with obj.] undo the stitches of.

unstop ▸ verb (**unstops, unstopping, unstopped**) [with obj.] free (something) from obstruction. ▪ remove the stopper from (a bottle or other container).

unstoppable ▸ adjective impossible to stop or prevent: *an unstoppable left-foot volley.*
– DERIVATIVES **unstoppability** noun, **unstoppably** adverb.

unstopper ▸ verb [with obj.] remove the stopper from (a bottle or other container): *he unstoppered the jar.*

unstrained ▸ adjective **1** not forced or produced by effort: *a lovely, warm unstrained smile.*
2 not subjected to straining or stretching.

unstrap ▸ verb (**unstraps, unstrapping, unstrapped**) [with obj.] undo the strap or straps of: *she unstrapped the harness.* ▪ release (someone or something) by undoing straps: *they unstrapped themselves.*

unstreamed ▸ adjective Brit. (of schoolchildren, a class, or a school) not arranged in streams.

unstressed ▸ adjective **1** Phonetics (of a syllable) not pronounced with stress.
2 not subjected to stress: *a well-balanced, unstressed person.*

unstring ▸ verb (**unstrings, unstringing**; past and past participle **unstrung**) [with obj.] **1** remove from a string: *unstringing the beads from the rosary.*
2 remove or relax the string or strings of (a bow or musical instrument).
3 unnerve; upset: *the small mishap unstrung her completely.*

unstructured ▸ adjective **1** without formal organization or structure: *an unstructured interview.*
2 (of a garment) made with little or no interfacing or other material which would give definition to its shape.

unstuck past and past participle of UNSTICK.

unstudied ▸ adjective not laboured or artificial; natural: *she had an unstudied grace in every step.*

unstuffed ▸ adjective not containing stuffing.

unstuffy ▸ adjective (**unstuffier, unstuffiest**) **1** not old-fashioned or formal in manner or behaviour: *she was unstuffy and always approachable.*
2 having fresh air or ventilation.

unstylish ▸ adjective not elegant or stylish.

unsubdued ▸ adjective not restrained or subdued.

unsubjugated ▸ adjective not subjugated.

unsubscribe ▸ verb [no obj.] cancel a subscription to an electronic mailing list or online service.

unsubstantial ▸ adjective having little or no solidity, reality, or factual basis.
– DERIVATIVES **unsubstantiality** noun, **unsubstantially** adverb.

unsubstantiated ▸ adjective not supported or proven by evidence: *unsubstantiated claims.*

unsubtle ▸ adjective not subtle; obvious; clumsy: *a grindingly unsubtle joke.*
– DERIVATIVES **unsubtly** adverb.

unsuccess ▸ noun [mass noun] lack of success: *I had done two shows with spectacular unsuccess.*

unsuccessful ▸ adjective not successful: *an unsuccessful attempt to enter Parliament.*
– DERIVATIVES **unsuccessfully** adverb, **unsuccessfulness** noun.

unsugared ▸ adjective not sweetened with sugar.

unsuitable ▸ adjective not fitting or appropriate: *the display is unsuitable for young children.*
– DERIVATIVES **unsuitability** noun, **unsuitableness** noun, **unsuitably** adverb.

unsuited ▸ adjective not right or appropriate: *he was totally unsuited for the job.*

unsullied ▸ adjective not spoiled or made impure: *an unsullied reputation.*

unsummoned ▸ adjective not summoned: *these visions appeared, unsummoned.*

unsung ▸ adjective not celebrated or praised: *Harvey is one of the unsung heroes of the industrial revolution.*

unsupervised ▸ adjective not done or acting under supervision: *unsupervised visits | a safe garden where children may play unsupervised.*

unsupportable ▸ adjective another term for INSUPPORTABLE.
– DERIVATIVES **unsupportably** adverb.

unsupported ▸ adjective **1** not supported physically: *a toddler who can stand unsupported.*
2 not given financial or other assistance. ■ Computing (of a program, language, or device) not having assistance for the user available from a manufacturer or system manager.
3 not borne out by evidence or facts: *the assumption was unsupported by evidence.*

unsupportive ▸ adjective not providing encouragement or emotional help.

unsure ▸ adjective not feeling, showing, or done with confidence and certainty: *she was feeling nervous, **unsure of herself** |* [with clause] *she was unsure how to reply.* ■ (of a fact) not fixed or certain: *the date is unsure.*
– DERIVATIVES **unsurely** adverb, **unsureness** noun.

unsurfaced ▸ adjective (of a road or path) not provided with a durable upper layer.

unsurmountable ▸ adjective not able to be overcome; insurmountable.

unsurpassable ▸ adjective not able to be exceeded in quality or degree.
– DERIVATIVES **unsurpassably** adverb.

unsurpassed ▸ adjective better or greater than any other: *the quality of workmanship is unsurpassed.*

unsurprised ▸ adjective not feeling or showing surprise at something unexpected: *he replied in a flat and unsurprised voice.*

unsurprising ▸ adjective not unexpected and so not causing surprise: *the outcome of this sombre film is unsurprising.*
– DERIVATIVES **unsurprisingly** adverb [sentence adverb] *unsurprisingly, recession is the theme of most reports.*

unsusceptible ▸ adjective **1** not likely or liable to be influenced or harmed by a particular thing: *infants are relatively **unsusceptible to** infections.*
2 (**unsusceptible of**) not capable or admitting of: *their meaning is unsusceptible of analysis.*

unsuspected ▸ adjective **1** not known or thought to exist or be present; not imagined possible: *the actor displays an unsuspected talent for comedy.*
2 (of a person) not regarded with suspicion.
– DERIVATIVES **unsuspectedly** adverb.

unsuspecting ▸ adjective (of a person or animal) not aware of the presence of danger; feeling no suspicion: *anti-personnel mines lie in wait for their unsuspecting victims.*
– DERIVATIVES **unsuspectingly** adverb, **unsuspectingness** noun.

unsuspicious ▸ adjective not having or showing suspicion.
– DERIVATIVES **unsuspiciously** adverb.

unsustainable ▸ adjective **1** not able to be maintained at the current rate or level: *macroeconomic instability led to an unsustainable boom.* ■ Ecology upsetting the ecological balance by depleting natural resources: *unsustainable fishing practices.*
2 not able to be upheld or defended: *both remarks are unsustainable.*
– DERIVATIVES **unsustainably** adverb.

unsustained ▸ adjective not prolonged for an extended period or without interruption.

unswathe ▸ verb [with obj.] literary unwrap (someone or something) from several layers of fabric.

unswayed ▸ adjective (of a person) not influenced or affected: *investors are unswayed by suggestions that the numbers are overblown.*

unsweetened ▸ adjective (of food or drink) without sugar or a similar substance having been added: *unsweetened grapefruit juice.*

unswept ▸ adjective (of an area) not swept clean of dirt or litter.

unswerving ▸ adjective not changing or becoming weaker; steady or constant: *unswerving loyalty.*
– DERIVATIVES **unswervingly** adverb.

unsworn ▸ adjective Law (of testimony or evidence) not given under oath.

unsymmetrical ▸ adjective another term for ASYMMETRICAL.
– DERIVATIVES **unsymmetrically** adverb.

unsympathetic ▸ adjective **1** not feeling, showing, or expressing sympathy: *I'm not being unsympathetic, but I can't see why you put up with him.*
2 not showing approval or favour towards an idea or action: *they were initially **unsympathetic towards** the cause of Irish freedom.*
3 (of a person) not friendly or cooperative; unlikeable: *a totally unsympathetic character.*
– DERIVATIVES **unsympathetically** adverb.

unsystematic ▸ adjective not done or acting according to a fixed plan or system; unmethodical.
– DERIVATIVES **unsystematically** adverb.

untack[1] ▸ verb [with obj.] detach (something) by the removal of tacks.

untack[2] ▸ verb [with obj.] remove the saddle and bridle from (a horse).

untainted ▸ adjective not contaminated, polluted, or tainted: *the island remains virtually **untainted by** commercialism.*

untaken ▸ adjective **1** not taken by force; not captured.
2 not carried out or put into effect: *hard decisions have been left untaken.*

untalented ▸ adjective (of a person) not having a natural aptitude or skill.

untameable (also **untamable**) ▸ adjective (of an animal) not capable of being domesticated. ■ not capable of being controlled: *her untameable mop of thick black hair.*

untamed ▸ adjective not domesticated or otherwise controlled.

untangle ▸ verb [with obj.] free from a tangled or twisted state: *fishermen untangled their nets.* ■ make (something complicated or confusing) easier to understand or deal with.

untanned ▸ adjective **1** (of a person or their skin) not tanned by exposure to the sun.
2 (of animal skin) not converted into leather by tanning: *untanned hides.*

untapped ▸ adjective (of a resource) not yet exploited or used: *the vast untapped potential of individual women and men.*

untarnished ▸ adjective (of metal or metalware) not having lost its lustre. ■ not spoiled or damaged: *his ministers enjoyed an untarnished reputation.*

untasted ▸ adjective (of food or drink) not sampled or tested for flavour.

untaught ▸ adjective not having been taught or educated: *she is totally untaught and will not listen.* ■ not acquired by teaching; natural or spontaneous: *by untaught instinct they know that scent means food.*

untaxed ▸ adjective not taxed or subject to taxation.

unteach ▸ verb (past and past participle **untaught**) [with obj.] cause (someone) to forget something learned previously. ■ remove (something previously known or taught) from a person's mind.

unteachable ▸ adjective (of a pupil or skill) unable to be taught.

untechnical ▸ adjective not having or requiring technical knowledge.

untempered ▸ adjective **1** not moderated or lessened by anything: *the products of a technological mastery untempered by political imagination.*
2 (of a material) not brought to the proper hardness or consistency.

untenable ▸ adjective (especially of a position or view) not able to be maintained or defended against attack or objection: *this argument is clearly untenable.*
– DERIVATIVES **untenability** noun, **untenably** adverb.

untended ▸ adjective not cared for or looked after; neglected: *untended gravestones.*

untenured ▸ adjective (of a teacher or lecturer) not having a permanent post. ■ (of an academic post) not permanent.

Untermensch /ˈʊntəmɛn(t)ʃ/, German /ˈʊntɐmɛnʃ/ ▸ noun (pl. **Untermenschen** /-mɛn(t)ʃ(ə)n/, German /-mɛnʃn/) a person considered racially or socially inferior.
– ORIGIN German, literally 'underperson'.

untested ▸ adjective (of an idea, product, or person) not subjected to examination, experiment, or experience; unproven: *analyses based on dubious and untested assumptions.*
– DERIVATIVES **untestable** adjective.

untether ▸ verb [with obj.] release or free from a tether: *I reached the horses and untethered them.*

unthanked ▸ adjective without receiving thanks: *the women's kind gesture did not go unthanked.*

unthankful ▸ adjective not feeling or showing pleasure, relief, or gratitude.
– DERIVATIVES **unthankfully** adverb, **unthankfulness** noun.

unthaw ▸ verb **1** N. Amer. melt or thaw: [with obj.] *the warm weather helped unthaw the rail lines.*
2 (as adj. **unthawed**) still frozen: *you can cook prawns from frozen by plunging them, unthawed, into boiling water.*

> **USAGE** Logically, the verb **unthaw** should mean 'freeze', but in North America it means exactly the same as **thaw** (as in *the warm weather helped unthaw the rail lines*); because of the risk of confusion it is not part of standard usage. **Unthawed** as an adjective always means 'still frozen', but it is best avoided because many contexts may be ambiguous, such as *use frozen (unthawed) blueberries*.

untheorized (also **untheorised**) ▸ adjective not given a theoretical premise or framework.

unthinkable ▸ adjective (of a situation or event) too unlikely or undesirable to be considered a possibility: *it was unthinkable that John could be dead* | (as noun **the unthinkable**) *the unthinkable happened—I spoke up.*
– DERIVATIVES **unthinkability** noun, **unthinkably** adverb [as submodifier] *a land of unthinkably vast spaces.*

unthinking ▸ adjective expressed, done, or acting without proper consideration of the consequences: *she was at pains to correct unthinking prejudices.*
– DERIVATIVES **unthinkingly** adverb, **unthinkingness** noun.

unthought ▸ adjective **1** (**unthought of**) not imagined or dreamed of: *the old develop interests unthought of in earlier years.*
2 not formed by the process of thinking.

unthread ▸ verb [with obj.] take (a thread) out of a needle. ■ remove (an object) from a thread, chain, etc.: *Meredith was unthreading his monocle from its ribbon.*

unthreatening ▸ adjective not having a hostile or frightening quality or manner: *the nymphet image renders women safe, unthreatening, and biddable.*
– DERIVATIVES **unthreatened** adjective.

unthrifty ▸ adjective **1** not using money and other resources carefully; wasteful.
2 chiefly archaic or dialect (of livestock or plants) not strong and healthy.
– DERIVATIVES **unthriftiness** noun.

unthrone ▸ verb archaic term for DETHRONE.

untidy ▸ adjective (**untidier**, **untidiest**) not arranged neatly and in order: *the place was dreadfully untidy.* ■ not inclined to keep one's possessions or appearance neat and in order.
– DERIVATIVES **untidily** adverb, **untidiness** noun.

untie ▸ verb (**unties**, **untying**, **untied**) [with obj.] undo or unfasten (something that is tied or tied up): *she knelt to untie her laces | Morton untied the parcel.*
– ORIGIN Old English *untīgan* (see UN-[2], TIE).

untied ▸ adjective **1** not fastened or knotted.
2 (of an international loan or aid) not given subject to the condition that it should be used for purchases from the donor country.

until ▸ preposition & conjunction up to (the point in time or the event mentioned): [as prep.] *the kidnappers have given us until October 11th to deliver the documents | he held the office until his death* | [as conjunction] *you don't know what you can achieve until you try.*
– ORIGIN Middle English: from Old Norse *und* 'as far as' + TILL[1] (the sense thus duplicated).

> **USAGE** On the differences between **until** and **till**, see **USAGE** at TILL[1].

untilled ▸ adjective (of land) not prepared and cultivated for crops.

untimely ▸ adjective (**untimelier**, **untimeliest**) (of an event or act) happening or done at an unsuitable time: *Dave's untimely return.* ■ (of a death or end) happening too soon or sooner than normal: *his untimely death in military action.*
▸ adverb archaic at a time that is unsuitable or premature: *the moment was very untimely chosen.*
– DERIVATIVES **untimeliness** noun.

U

untinged ▸ adjective (**untinged by/with**) not in the slightest affected by: *a cold-blooded killing untinged by any remorse on your part.*

untiring ▸ adjective (of a person or their actions) continuing at the same rate without loss of vigour: *his untiring efforts in commissioning ecological reports.*
– DERIVATIVES **untiringly** adverb.

untitled ▸ adjective **1** (of a book, composition, or other artistic work) having no name.
2 (of a person) not having a title indicating high social or official rank: *lesser untitled officials.*

unto ▸ preposition **1** archaic term for TO: *do unto others as you would have them do unto you | I say unto you, be gone.*
2 archaic term for UNTIL: *marriage was forever—unto death.*
– ORIGIN Middle English: from UNTIL, with TO replacing TILL[1] (in its northern dialect meaning 'to').

untold ▸ adjective **1** [attrib.] too much or too many to be counted or measured: *thieves caused untold damage.*
2 (of a story or event) not narrated or recounted: *no event, however boring, is left untold.*
– ORIGIN Old English *unteald* 'not counted' (see UN-[1], TOLD).

untoned ▸ adjective **1** (of a person's body) lacking in tone or muscular definition.
2 (especially of music) lacking in variation of tone or subtlety.

untouchable ▸ adjective **1** not able or allowed to be touched or affected: *drug barons who were legally untouchable.* ■ unable to be matched or rivalled: *when the band retreat to ambience and minimalism, they are untouchable.*
2 of or belonging to the lowest-caste Hindu group or the people outside the caste system.
▸ noun a member of the lowest-caste Hindu group or a person outside the caste system, contact with whom is traditionally held to defile members of higher castes.
– DERIVATIVES **untouchability** noun.

> **USAGE** In senses relating to the traditional Hindu caste system, the term **untouchable** and the social restrictions accompanying it were declared illegal in the constitution of India in 1949 and of Pakistan in 1953. The official term today is **scheduled caste.**

untouched ▸ adjective **1** not handled, used, or tasted: *Annabel pushed aside her untouched plate.* ■ (of a subject) not treated in writing or speech; not discussed: *no detail is left untouched.*
2 not affected, changed, or damaged in any way: *Prague was relatively untouched by the war.*

untouristed ▸ adjective (of a place) rarely visited by tourists: *a charming, untouristed village.*

untoward ▸ adjective unexpected and inappropriate or inconvenient: *both tried to behave as if nothing untoward had happened | untoward remarks.*
– DERIVATIVES **untowardly** adverb, **untowardness** noun.

untraceable ▸ adjective unable to be found, discovered, or traced: *many use false addresses and are untraceable.*
– DERIVATIVES **untraceably** adverb.

untraced ▸ adjective not found or discovered by investigation: *patients with untraced records.*

untracked ▸ adjective (of land) without a path or tracks: *a vast untracked wilderness.*
– PHRASES **get untracked** US (especially in sporting contexts) get into one's stride or find good form.

untraditional ▸ adjective not existing in or as part of a tradition; not customary or long-established.

untrained ▸ adjective not having been trained in a particular skill: *self-styled doctors **untrained in** diagnosis | **to the untrained eye**, the two products look remarkably similar.*
– DERIVATIVES **untrainable** adjective.

untrammelled (US also **untrammeled**) ▸ adjective not deprived of freedom of action or expression; not restricted or hampered: *a mind untrammelled by convention.*

untransferable ▸ adjective not able to be transferred to another place, occupation, or person.

untransformed ▸ adjective not having been transformed in form, appearance, or character.

untranslatable /ˌʌntransˈleɪtəb(ə)l, ˌʌntrɑːns-, -z-/ ▸ adjective (of a word, phrase, or text) not able to have its sense expressed in another language: *an untranslatable German pun.*
– DERIVATIVES **untranslatability** noun.

untranslated ▸ adjective **1** (of words or text) not having their sense expressed in another language: *a nine-volume work, as yet untranslated from the Icelandic.*
2 (of a sequence of nucleotides in messenger RNA) not converted to the amino acid sequence of a protein or polypeptide during synthesis.

untravelled (US also **untraveled**) ▸ adjective (of a person) not having travelled much. ■ (of a road or region) not journeyed along or through: *an unknown and untravelled wilderness.*

untreatable ▸ adjective (of a patient, disease, or other condition) for whom or which no medical care is available or possible.

untreated ▸ adjective **1** (of a patient, disease, or other condition) not given medical care: *untreated cholera can kill up to half of those infected.*
2 not preserved, improved, or altered by the use of a chemical, physical, or biological agent: *untreated sewage is pumped directly into the sea.*

untrendy ▸ adjective informal not very fashionable or up to date: *his untrendy long hair.*

untried ▸ adjective **1** not yet tested to discover quality or reliability; inexperienced: *he chose two untried actors for leading roles.*
2 Law (of an accused person) not yet subjected to a trial in court.

untrimmed ▸ adjective not having been trimmed.

untrodden ▸ adjective (of a surface) not having been walked on: *untrodden snow.*

untroubled ▸ adjective not feeling, showing, or affected by anxiety or problems: *a man untroubled by a guilty conscience | an untroubled gaze.*

untrue ▸ adjective **1** not in accordance with fact or reality; false or incorrect: *these suggestions are totally untrue | a malicious and untrue story.*
2 not faithful or loyal.
3 incorrectly positioned or balanced; not upright or level.
– DERIVATIVES **untruly** adverb.
– ORIGIN Old English *untrēowe* 'unfaithful' (see UN-[1], TRUE).

untrussed ▸ adjective (of a chicken or other bird prepared for eating) having had its wings and legs unfastened before cooking: *an untrussed chicken.*

untrusting ▸ adjective not tending to believe in other people's honesty or sincerity; suspicious.

untrustworthy ▸ adjective not able to be relied on as honest or truthful.
– DERIVATIVES **untrustworthiness** noun.

untruth ▸ noun (pl. **untruths**) a lie or false statement (often used euphemistically): *they go off and tell untruths about organizations for which they worked.* ■ [mass noun] the quality of being false.
– ORIGIN Old English *untrēowth* 'unfaithfulness' (see UN-[1], TRUTH).

untruthful ▸ adjective saying or consisting of something that is false or incorrect: *companies issuing untruthful recruitment brochures.*
– DERIVATIVES **untruthfully** adverb, **untruthfulness** noun.

untuck ▸ verb [with obj.] free the edges or ends of (something) from being hidden or held in place.

untucked ▸ adjective with the edges or ends hanging loose; not tucked in: *an untucked shirt.*

untunable ▸ adjective (of a piano or other musical instrument) unable to be tuned.

untuned ▸ adjective not tuned or properly adjusted.

untuneful ▸ adjective not having a pleasing melody; unmusical: *an untuneful hymn.*

unturned ▸ adjective not turned: *unturned soil.*

untutored ▸ adjective not formally taught or trained: *the species are all much the same **to the untutored eye**.*

untwine ▸ verb make or become unwound or untwisted: [with obj.] *Robyn untwined her fingers.*

untwist ▸ verb open or cause to open from a twisted position: [with obj.] *he untwisted the wire and straightened it out.*

untying present participle of UNTIE.

untypical ▸ adjective not having the distinctive qualities of a particular type of person or thing; uncharacteristic: *he considers the film untypical of college movies.*
– DERIVATIVES **untypically** adverb.

unusable ▸ adjective not fit to be used: *the steps were overgrown and unusable.*

unused ▸ adjective **1** not being, or never having been, used: *any unused equipment will be welcomed back.*
2 (**unused to**) not familiar with or accustomed to: *unused to spicy food, she took a long mouthful of water.*

unusual ▸ adjective not habitually or commonly occurring or done: *the government has taken the unusual step of calling home its ambassador | it was unusual for Dennis to be late.* ■ remarkable or interesting because different from or better than others: *a man of unusual talent.*
– DERIVATIVES **unusually** adverb [sentence adverb] ***unusually for** a city hotel, it is set around a lovely garden* | [as submodifier] *he made an unusually large number of mistakes*, **unusualness** noun.

unutterable ▸ adjective too great or awful to describe: *moments of unutterable grief | I felt an unutterable fool.*
– DERIVATIVES **unutterably** adverb [as submodifier] *Juliet felt unutterably weary.*

unuttered ▸ adjective (of words or thoughts) not spoken or expressed.

unvaccinated ▸ adjective not inoculated with a vaccine to provide immunity against a disease.

unvalidated ▸ adjective not validated or proven to be accurate or true.

unvalued ▸ adjective **1** not considered to be important or beneficial: *he felt unvalued.*
2 archaic not valued or appraised with regard to monetary worth.

unvanquished ▸ adjective (of an opponent or obstacle) not conquered or overcome.

unvaried ▸ adjective not involving change: *a plain, unvaried diet.*

unvarnished ▸ adjective **1** not covered with varnish.
2 (of a statement or manner) plain and straightforward: *please tell me the unvarnished truth.*

unvarying ▸ adjective not changing; constant or uniform: *the unvarying routine of parsonage life.*
– DERIVATIVES **unvaryingly** adverb [as submodifier] *they found her to be unvaryingly polite*, **unvaryingness** noun.

unveil ▸ verb [with obj.] remove a veil or covering from, in particular uncover (a new monument or work of art) as part of a public ceremony: *the Princess unveiled a plaque* | (as noun **unveiling**) *the unveiling of the memorial.* ■ show or announce publicly for the first time: *the Home Secretary has unveiled plans to crack down on crime.*

unvented ▸ adjective without a vent or outlet.

unventilated ▸ adjective (of a room or space) not provided with fresh air.

unverifiable ▸ adjective not able to be verified: *an unverifiable hypothesis.*

unverified ▸ adjective not having been verified.

unversed ▸ adjective not experienced, skilled, or knowledgeable: *he was **unversed in** Washington ways.*

unviable ▸ adjective not capable of working successfully; not feasible: *the commission found the plan to be financially unviable.*
– DERIVATIVES **unviability** noun.

unviolated ▸ adjective not violated or desecrated.

unvisited ▸ adjective (of a place) having had no people visit it: *Antarctica remained unvisited until the late 18th century.*

unvitiated /ʌnˈvɪʃɪeɪtɪd/ ▸ adjective archaic pure and uncorrupted.

unvoiced ▸ adjective **1** not expressed in words; unuttered: *a person's unvoiced thoughts.*
2 Phonetics (of a speech sound) uttered without vibration of the vocal cords.

unwaged ▸ adjective Brit. (of a person) out of work or doing unpaid work: *unwaged adults claiming income support.* ■ (of work) unpaid.

unwaisted ▸ adjective (of a dress) not having a structured waistline; loose-fitting.

unwalled ▸ adjective (of a place) without enclosing or defensive walls.

unwanted ▸ adjective not or no longer desired: *affairs can lead to unwanted pregnancies | she felt unwanted.*

unwarlike ▸ adjective not disposed towards war or hostilities.

unwarmed ▸ adjective not made warm: *the mist was still unwarmed by the sun.*

unwarned ▸ adjective (of a person) not warned in advance about something.

unwarrantable ▸ adjective not able to be authorized or sanctioned; unjustifiable: *an unwarrantable intrusion into personal matters.*
– DERIVATIVES **unwarrantably** adverb.

unwarranted ▸ adjective not justified or authorized: *I am sure your fears are unwarranted.*
– DERIVATIVES **unwarrantedly** adverb.

unwary ▸ adjective not cautious of possible dangers or problems: *accidents can happen to the unwary traveller* | (as plural noun **the unwary**) *hidden traps for the unwary.*
– DERIVATIVES **unwarily** adverb, **unwariness** noun.

unwashed ▸ adjective not having been washed.
– PHRASES **the (great) unwashed** derogatory the mass or multitude of ordinary people.

unwatchable ▸ adjective (of a film or television programme) too poor, tedious, or disturbing to be viewed.

unwatched ▸ adjective not looked at or observed.

unwatchful ▸ adjective not alert or vigilant.

unwatered ▸ adjective not supplied or sprinkled with water.

unwavering ▸ adjective not wavering; steady or resolute: *she fixed him with an unwavering stare.*
– DERIVATIVES **unwaveringly** adverb.

unweaned ▸ adjective (of an infant or other young mammal) not accustomed to food other than its mother's milk.

unwearable ▸ adjective (of a garment) not fit to be worn.

unwearied ▸ adjective not tired or becoming tired.
– DERIVATIVES **unweariedly** adverb.

unweary ▸ adjective not tired or weary.

unwearying ▸ adjective never tiring or slackening.
– DERIVATIVES **unwearyingly** adverb.

unwed (also **unwedded**) ▸ adjective not married: *an unwed teenage mother.*

unweeded ▸ adjective not cleared of weeds.

unweighed ▸ adjective (of goods) not weighed.

unweight ▸ verb [with obj.] momentarily stop pressing heavily on (a ski or skateboard) in order to make a turn more easily.
– ORIGIN 1930s: back-formation from **UNWEIGHTED**.

unweighted ▸ adjective **1** without a weight attached.
2 Statistics (of a figure or sample) not adjusted or biased to reflect importance or value.

unwelcome ▸ adjective (of a guest or new arrival) not gladly received: *guards kept out unwelcome visitors.* ■ not wanted: *unwelcome attentions from men.*
– DERIVATIVES **unwelcomely** adverb, **unwelcomeness** noun.

unwelcoming ▸ adjective having an inhospitable or uninviting quality: *Jean crept into her cold and unwelcoming bed.* ■ (of a person or their expression) not friendly towards a guest or new arrival.

unwell ▸ adjective ill: *he was admitted to hospital for tests after feeling unwell.*

unwept ▸ adjective chiefly literary (of a person) not mourned or lamented.

unwetted ▸ adjective not wetted.

unwhipped ▸ adjective Brit. (of an MP or vote) not subject to a party whip.

unwholesome ▸ adjective not characterized by or conducive to health or moral well-being: *the use of the living room as sleeping quarters led to unwholesome crowding.*
– DERIVATIVES **unwholesomely** adverb, **unwholesomeness** noun.

unwieldy ▸ adjective (**unwieldier**, **unwieldiest**) (of an object) difficult to move because of its size, shape, or weight: *huge, unwieldy arc lamps.* ■ (of a system) too large or disorganized to function efficiently.
– DERIVATIVES **unwieldily** adverb, **unwieldiness** noun.
– ORIGIN late Middle English (in the sense 'lacking strength, infirm'): from **UN-**[1] 'not' + **WIELDY** (in the obsolete sense 'active').

unwilling ▸ adjective [often with infinitive] not ready, eager, or prepared to do something: *he was unwilling to take on that responsibility* | *unwilling conscripts.*
– DERIVATIVES **unwillingly** adverb.
– ORIGIN Old English *unwillende* (see **UN-**[1], **WILLING**).

unwillingness ▸ noun [mass noun] the quality or state of being unwilling to do something; reluctance: *he deplored the Government's unwillingness to provide adequate funds.*

unwind ▸ verb (past and past participle **unwound**)
1 undo or be undone after winding or being wound: [with obj.] *Ella unwound the long woollen scarf from her neck* | [no obj.] *the net unwinds from the reel.*
2 [no obj.] relax after a period of work or tension: *the Grand Hotel is a superb place to unwind.*

unwinking ▸ adjective (of a person's eyes or gaze, or a light) steady; unwavering: *the lights shone unwinking in the still air* | *unwinking blue eyes.*

unwinnable ▸ adjective not able to be won: *an immoral and unwinnable war.*

unwired ▸ adjective not wired.

unwisdom ▸ noun [mass noun] folly; lack of wisdom: *it stresses the unwisdom of fathers leaving their children.*
– ORIGIN Old English *unwīsdōm* (see **UN-**[1], **WISDOM**).

unwise ▸ adjective (of a person or action) not wise or sensible; foolish: *it is unwise to rely on hearsay evidence* | *unwise policy decisions.*
– DERIVATIVES **unwisely** adverb [sentence adverb] *unwisely, she repeated the remark to her mother.*
– ORIGIN Old English *unwīs* (see **UN-**[1], **WISE**[1]).

unwished ▸ adjective not wanted or desired.

unwithered ▸ adjective not withered.

unwitnessed ▸ adjective (especially of an event) not witnessed.

unwitting ▸ adjective **1** (of a person) not aware of the full facts: *an unwitting accomplice.*
2 not done on purpose; unintentional: *we are anxious to rectify the unwitting mistakes made in the past.*
– DERIVATIVES **unwittingly** adverb, **unwittingness** noun.
– ORIGIN Old English *unwitende* 'not knowing or realizing' (see **UN-**[1], **WIT**[2]).

unwomanly ▸ adjective not having or showing qualities traditionally associated with women: *initiative of any overt sort was considered unwomanly.*
– DERIVATIVES **unwomanliness** noun.

unwonted /ʌnˈwəʊntɪd/ ▸ adjective [attrib.] unaccustomed or unusual: *there was an unwonted gaiety in her manner.*
– DERIVATIVES **unwontedly** adverb [as submodifier] *she was unwontedly shy and subdued.*

unwooded ▸ adjective **1** not having many trees.
2 (of a wine) not stored in a wooden cask.

unworkable ▸ adjective **1** not able to function or be carried out successfully; impractical: *an unworkable scheme.*
2 (of a material) not able to be worked: *the alloy becomes brittle and almost unworkable.*
– DERIVATIVES **unworkability** noun, **unworkably** adverb.

unworked ▸ adjective not cultivated, mined, or carved: *unworked fields* | *unworked flint nodules.*

unworkmanlike ▸ adjective badly done or made.

unworldly ▸ adjective **1** (of a person) having little awareness of the practicalities of life; unmotivated by material considerations: *a pedantic, unworldly boffin.*
2 not seeming to belong to this planet; strange: *an almost unworldly stillness.*
– DERIVATIVES **unworldliness** noun.

unworn ▸ adjective **1** not damaged or shabby-looking as a result of much use: *the tyres appear unworn, even after many fast miles* | *unworn carpeting.*
2 (of a garment) never worn.

unworried ▸ adjective not anxious or uneasy: *foreign investors are largely unworried by the government's fall.*

unworthy ▸ adjective (**unworthier**, **unworthiest**) not deserving respect or attention: *he was unworthy of trust and unfit to hold office.* ■ (of an action) not acceptable, especially from someone with a good reputation or social position: *such a suggestion is unworthy of the Honourable Gentleman.* ■ having little merit: *many pieces are unworthy and ungrammatical.*
– DERIVATIVES **unworthily** adverb, **unworthiness** noun.

unwound[1] ▸ adjective (of a clock or watch) not wound or wound up.

unwound[2] past and past participle of **UNWIND**.

unwounded ▸ adjective not hurt or injured.

unwoven ▸ adjective (of fabric) not woven.

unwrap ▸ verb (**unwraps**, **unwrapping**, **unwrapped**) [with obj.] remove the wrapping from (a package): *I began to unwrap my presents.*

unwrinkled ▸ adjective (especially of fabric or the skin) free from wrinkles.

unwritable ▸ adjective not able to be written.

unwritten ▸ adjective **1** not recorded in writing: *documenting unwritten languages.*
2 (especially of a law) resting originally on custom or judicial decision rather than on statute: *an unwritten constitution.* ■ (of a convention) understood and generally accepted, although not formally established: *the unwritten rules of social life.*

unwrought ▸ adjective (of metals or other materials) not worked into a finished condition.

unyielding ▸ adjective (of a mass or structure) not giving way to pressure; hard or solid: *the Atlantic hurled its waves at the unyielding rocks.* ■ (of a person or their behaviour) unlikely to be swayed; resolute: *his unyielding faith.*
– DERIVATIVES **unyieldingly** adverb, **unyieldingness** noun.

unyoke ▸ verb [with obj.] release (a pair of animals) from a yoke.

unzip ▸ verb (**unzips**, **unzipping**, **unzipped**) [with obj.]
1 unfasten the zip fastener of.
2 Computing decompress (a compressed file).

up ▸ adverb **1** towards a higher place or position: *he jumped up* | *two of the men hoisted her up* | *the curtain went up.* ■ upstairs: *she made her way up to bed.* ■ (of the sun) visible after daybreak: *the sun was already up when they set off.* ■ expressing movement towards or position in the north: *he's driving up to Inverness to see the old man.* ■ to or at a place perceived as higher: *I'm going for a walk up to the shops.* ■ [as exclamation] used as a command to a soldier or an animal to stand up and be ready to move or attack: *up, boys, and at 'em.* ■ (of food that has been eaten) regurgitated from the stomach: *I was ill and vomited up everything.*
2 at or to a higher level of intensity, volume, or activity: *she turned the volume up* | *liven up the graphics* | *US environmental groups had been stepping up their attack on GATT.* ■ at or to a higher price, value, or rank: *sales are up 22.8 per cent at $50.2 m* | *unemployment is up.* ■ winning or at an advantage by a specified margin: *United were 3–1 up at half time* | *we came away £300 up on the evening.*
3 to the place where someone is: *Dot didn't hear Mrs Parvis come creeping up behind her.*
4 towards or in the capital or a major city: *give me a ring when you're up in London.* ■ Brit. at or to a university, especially Oxford or Cambridge: *they were up at Cambridge about the same time.*
5 into the desired or a proper condition: *the government agreed to set up a committee of inquiry.* ■ so as to be finished or closed: *I've got a bit of paperwork to finish up* | *he zipped up the holdall.*
6 into a happy mood: *I don't think anything's going to cheer me up.*
7 out of bed: *Miranda hardly ever got up for breakfast.*
8 displayed on a noticeboard or other publicly visible site: *sticking up posters to advertise concerts.*
9 (of sailing) against the current or the wind. ■ (of a ship's helm) moved round to windward so that the rudder is to leeward.
10 Baseball at bat: *every time up, he had a different stance.*
▸ preposition **1** from a lower to a higher point of (something): *she climbed up a flight of steps.* ■ to a higher part of (a river or stream), away from the sea: *a cruise up the Rhine.*
2 along or further along (a street or road): *he lived up the road* | *walking up the street.*
3 informal at or to (a place): *we're going up the Palais.*
▸ adjective **1** [attrib.] directed or moving towards a higher place or position: *the up escalator.* ■ relating to or denoting trains travelling towards the major point on a route: *the first up train.*
2 [predic.] at an end: *his contract was up in three weeks* | *time's up.*
3 [predic.] (of a road) being repaired.
4 [predic.] (of a computer system) functioning properly: *the system is now up.*
5 [predic.] in a cheerful mood; ebullient: *the mood here is resolutely up.*
6 (of a jockey) in the saddle.
7 Physics denoting a flavour of quark having a charge of $+^{2}/_{3}$. Protons and neutrons are thought to be composed of combinations of up and down quarks.

U

▶ noun informal a period of good fortune: *you can't have ups all the time in football.*
▶ verb (**ups, upping, upped**) **1** [no obj.] (**up and do something**) informal do something unexpectedly: *she upped and left him.*
2 [with obj.] increase (a level or amount): *capacity will be upped by 70 per cent next year.*
3 [with obj.] lift (something) up: *everybody was cheering and upping their glasses.* ■ [no obj.] (**up with**) W. Indian & US informal raise or pick up (something): *this woman ups with a stone.*
– PHRASES **be up on** be well informed about: *they are well up on current environmental trends.* **it is all up with** informal it is the end or there is no hope for. **on the up and up** informal **1** Brit. becoming more successful. **2** chiefly N. Amer. honest or sincere. **something is up** informal something unusual or undesirable is happening. **up against** close to or in contact with: *crowds pressed up against the barricades.* ■ informal confronted with: *I began to think of what teachers are up against today.* ■ (**up against it**) informal in a difficult situation: *they play better when they're up against it.* **up and about** no longer in bed (after sleep or an illness). **up and doing** active; busy: *a normal young chap wants to be up and doing.* **up and down 1** to and fro: *pacing up and down in front of her desk.* ■ [as prep.] to and fro along: *strolling up and down the corridor.* **2** in various places throughout: *in clubs up and down the country.* **3** informal in varying states or moods; changeable: *my relationship with her was up and down.* **up and running** (especially of a computer system) in operation; functioning: *the new computer is up and running.* **up the ante** see **ANTE**. **up before** appearing for a hearing in the presence of: *we'll have to come up before a magistrate.* **up for 1** available for: *the house next door is up for sale.* **2** being considered for: *he had been up for promotion.* **3** due for: *his contract is up for renewal in June.* **4** informal ready to take part in (a particular activity): *Nigel was really up for it, as always.* **up hill and down dale** all over the place: *he led me up hill and down dale till my feet were dropping off.* **up one's street** (or N. Amer. **alley**) informal well suited to one's tastes, interests, or abilities: *this job would be right up your street.* **ups and downs** a mixture of both good and bad experiences. **up sticks** see **STICK¹**. **up to 1** as far as: *I could reach just up to his waist.* ■ (also **up until**) until: *up to now I hadn't had a relationship.* **2** indicating a maximum amount: *the process is expected to take up to two years.* **3** [with negative or in questions] good enough for: *I was not up to her standards.* ■ capable of or fit for: *he is simply not up to the job.* **4** the responsibility or choice of (someone): *it was up to them to gauge the problem.* **5** informal occupied or busy with: *what's he been up to?* **up top** Brit. informal by way of intelligence: *a man with nothing much up top.* **up with ——** an exclamation expressing support for a stated person or thing. **up yours** vulgar slang an exclamation expressing contemptuous defiance or rejection of someone. **what's up?** informal **1** what is going on? **2** what is the matter?: *what's up with you?*
– ORIGIN Old English *up(p)*, *uppe*, of Germanic origin; related to Dutch *op* and German *auf*.

up- ▶ prefix **1** (added to verbs and their derivatives) upwards: *upturned* | *upthrow.* ■ to a more recent time: *update.*
2 (added to nouns) denoting motion up: *upriver* | *uphill.*
3 (added to nouns) higher: *upland* | *upstroke.* ■ increased: *up-tempo.*

up-anchor ▶ verb [no obj.] (of a ship) weigh anchor.

up-and-coming ▶ adjective (of a person beginning a particular activity or occupation) making good progress and likely to become successful: *up-and-coming young players.*
– DERIVATIVES **up-and-comer** noun.

up-and-over ▶ adjective (of a door, typically one to a garage) opened by being raised and pushed back into a horizontal position.

up-and-under ▶ noun Rugby a high kick that allows time for fellow team members to reach the point where the ball will come down.

Upanishad /uːˈpanɪʃad/ ▶ noun each of a series of Hindu sacred treatises written in Sanskrit *c.*800–200 BC, expounding the Vedas in predominantly mystical and monistic terms.
– ORIGIN from Sanskrit, literally 'sitting near (i.e. at the feet of a master)', from *upa* 'near' + *ni-ṣad* 'sit down'.

upas /ˈjuːpəs/ (also **upas tree**) ▶ noun a tropical Asian tree, the milky sap of which has been used as arrow poison and for ritual purposes. ● *Antiaris toxicaria*, family Moraceae.
■ (in folklore) a Javanese tree alleged to poison its surroundings and said to be fatal to approach.
– ORIGIN late 18th cent.: from Malay (*pohun*) *upas* 'poison'.

upbeat ▶ noun (in music) an unaccented beat preceding an accented beat.
▶ adjective informal cheerful; optimistic: *he was upbeat about the company's future.*

upbraid ▶ verb [with obj.] find fault with (someone); scold: *he was upbraided for his slovenly appearance.*
– ORIGIN late Old English *upbrēdan* 'allege (something) as a basis for censure', based on **BRAID** in the obsolete sense 'brandish'. The current sense dates from Middle English.

upbringing ▶ noun the treatment and instruction received by a child from its parents throughout its childhood: *she had had a Christian upbringing* | *he was a countryman by upbringing.*
– ORIGIN late 15th cent.: from obsolete *upbring* 'to rear' (see **UP-**, **BRING**).

upbuild ▶ verb (past and past participle **upbuilt**) [with obj.] chiefly literary construct or develop (something).

up card ▶ noun chiefly US a playing card turned face up on the table, especially the top card of the waste heap in rummy.

upcase ▶ verb [with obj.] change (a lower-case letter) to an upper-case one.

upcast ▶ noun (also **upcast shaft**) a shaft through which air leaves a mine.
▶ verb (past and past participle **upcast**) [with obj.] cast (something) upward: (as adj. **upcast**) *upcast light.*

upchuck N. Amer. informal ▶ verb vomit: [with obj.] *I almost upchucked my toasted marshmallows.*
▶ noun [mass noun] matter vomited from the stomach.

upcoast ▶ adverb & adjective further up the coast.

upcoming ▶ adjective about to happen; forthcoming: *the upcoming election.*

upcountry ▶ adverb & adjective in or towards the interior of a country; inland: [as adv.] *she comes from somewhere up-country* | [as adj.] *a little up-country town.*

update ▶ verb /ʌpˈdeɪt/ [with obj.] make (something) more modern or up to date: *security measures are continually updated and improved* | (as adj. **updated**) *an updated list of subscribers.* ■ give (someone) the latest information about something: *the reporter promised to keep the viewers updated.*
▶ noun /ˈʌpdeɪt/ an act of updating something or someone or an updated version of something: *an update on recently published crime figures.*
– DERIVATIVES **updatable** adjective.

Updike /ˈʌpdʌɪk/, John (Hoyer) (1932–2009), American novelist, poet, and short-story writer. He is noted for his quartet of novels *Rabbit, Run* (1960), *Rabbit Redux* (1971), *Rabbit is Rich* (Pulitzer Prize, 1981), and *Rabbit at Rest* (Pulitzer Prize, 1990).

updo /ˈʌpduː/ ▶ noun (pl. **updos**) informal a women's hairstyle in which the hair is swept up and secured on top or at the back of the head.

updoming /ˈʌpdəʊmɪŋ/ ▶ noun [mass noun] Geology the upward deformation of a rock mass into a dome shape.

updraught (US **updraft**) ▶ noun an upward current or draught of air.

upend ▶ verb [with obj.] set or turn (something) on its end or upside down: *she upended a can of soup over the portions* | (as adj. **upended**) *an upended box.* ■ [no obj.] (of a swimming duck or other waterbird) submerge the head and foreparts in order to feed, so that the tail is raised in the air.

upfield ▶ adverb **1** (in sport) in or to a position nearer to the opponents' end of a field.
2 Physics in a direction corresponding to increasing field strength.

upflung ▶ adjective chiefly literary (especially of limbs) flung upwards, especially in a gesture of helplessness or alarm.

upfold ▶ noun Geology an anticline.

upfront informal ▶ adverb (usu. **up front**) **1** at the front; in front: *he can play up front or in defence.*
2 (of a payment) in advance.
▶ adjective **1** bold, honest, and frank: *he'd been upfront about his intentions.*
2 [attrib.] (of a payment) made in advance.
3 chiefly N. Amer. at the front or the most prominent position: *a literary weekly with an upfront section modelled on the New Yorker.*

upful ▶ adjective W. Indian (especially of music) cheerful and positive.

upgrade ▶ verb [with obj.] raise (something) to a higher standard, in particular improve (equipment or machinery) by adding or replacing components: (as adj. **upgraded**) *upgraded computers.* ■ raise (an employee) to a higher grade or rank.
▶ noun an act of upgrading something. ■ an improved or more modern version of something, especially a piece of computing equipment.
– PHRASES **on the upgrade** improving; progressing.
– DERIVATIVES **upgradeability** (also **upgradability**) noun, **upgradeable** (also **upgradable**) adjective, **upgrader** noun.

upgrowth ▶ noun [mass noun] the process or result of growing upwards. ■ [count noun] an upward growth.

uphaul ▶ noun a rope used for hauling up a boat's sail or centreboard.

upheaval ▶ noun **1** a violent or sudden change or disruption to something: *major upheavals in the financial markets* | [mass noun] *times of political upheaval.*
2 an upward displacement of part of the earth's crust.

upheave ▶ verb [with obj.] literary heave or lift up (something, especially part of the earth's surface): *the area was first upheaved from the primeval ocean.*

Up-Helly-Aa /ˌʌphɛlɪˈɑː/ (also **Up-Helly-A'**) ▶ noun an annual festival held at Lerwick in the Shetland Islands, celebrated as the revival of a traditional midwinter fire festival.
– ORIGIN variant of Scots *Uphaliday*, denoting Epiphany as the end of the Christmas holiday.

uphill ▶ adverb towards the top of a hill or slope: *follow the track uphill.*
▶ adjective sloping upwards: *the journey is slightly uphill.* ■ requiring great effort; difficult: *an uphill struggle to gain worldwide recognition.*
▶ noun an upward slope.

uphold ▶ verb (past and past participle **upheld**) [with obj.] confirm or support (something which has been questioned): *the court upheld his claim for damages.* ■ maintain (a custom or practice): *they uphold a tradition of not causing distress to living creatures.*
– DERIVATIVES **upholder** noun.

upholster /ʌpˈhəʊlstə, -ˈhɒl-/ ▶ verb [with obj.] provide (furniture) with a soft, padded covering: *the chairs were upholstered in red velvet* | (as adj. **upholstered**) *an upholstered stool.* ■ cover the walls or furniture in (a room) with textiles.
– ORIGIN mid 19th cent.: back-formation from **UPHOLSTERER**.

upholsterer ▶ noun a person who upholsters furniture, especially professionally.
– ORIGIN early 17th cent.: from the obsolete noun *upholster* (from **UPHOLD** in the obsolete sense 'keep in repair') + **-STER**.

upholstery ▶ noun [mass noun] soft, padded textile covering that is fixed to furniture such as armchairs and sofas. ■ the art or practice of fitting such a covering.

upkeep ▶ noun [mass noun] the process of keeping something in good condition: *we will be responsible for the upkeep of the access road.* ■ financial or material support of a person or animal: *payments for the children's upkeep.*

upland ▶ noun [mass noun] (also **uplands**) an area of high or hilly land: *conservation of areas of upland.*

upland cotton ▶ noun [mass noun] cotton of a type grown in the US, which typically yields medium- and short-stapled forms of cotton. ● *Gossypium hirsutum* var. *latifolium*, family Malvaceae.

uplift ▶ verb [with obj.] **1** (usu. as adj. **uplifted**) lift (something) up; raise: *her uplifted face.* ■ Scottish pick up or take away: *we will be only too pleased to uplift any items you wish us to sell for you.* ■ (**be uplifted**) (of an island, mountain, etc.) be created by an upward movement of the earth's surface.
2 (often as adj. **uplifted**) elevate (someone) morally or spiritually: *people leave my shows feeling uplifted.*
▶ noun **1** an act of uplifting something. ■ Geology an upward movement of part of the earth's surface. ■ [mass noun] [often as modifier] support from a garment, especially for a woman's bust: *an uplift bra.*
2 a morally or spiritually elevating influence: *their love will prove an enormous uplift.*
– DERIVATIVES **uplifter** noun, **upliftment** noun.

U

uplifting ▸ adjective morally or spiritually elevating; inspiring happiness or hope: *an uplifting tune.*
– DERIVATIVES **upliftingly** adverb.

uplighter (also **uplight**) ▸ noun a light placed or designed to throw illumination upwards.
– DERIVATIVES **uplighting** noun.

uplink ▸ noun a communications link to a satellite.
▸ verb [with obj.] provide (someone) with or send (something) by such a link: *I can uplink fax transmissions to a satellite.*

upload Computing ▸ verb [with obj.] transfer (data) to a larger computer system.
▸ noun [mass noun] the action or process of uploading data.

upmarket ▸ adjective & adverb chiefly Brit. towards or relating to the more expensive or affluent sector of the market: [as adj.] *an upmarket housing estate* | [as adv.] *they used their newly acquired cash to move upmarket.*

upmost ▸ adjective another term for UPPERMOST.

upon ▸ preposition more formal term for ON, especially in abstract senses: *it was based upon two principles* | *a school's dependence upon parental support.*
– ORIGIN Middle English: from UP + ON, suggested by Old Norse *upp á.*

> **USAGE** The preposition **upon** has the same core meaning as the preposition **on**. However, in modern English **upon** tends to be restricted to more formal contexts or to established phrases and idioms, as in *once* **upon** *a time* and *row* **upon** *row of seats.*

upper[1] ▸ adjective **1** situated above another part: *his upper arm* | *the upper atmosphere.* ■ higher in position or status: *the upper end of the social scale.*
2 situated on higher ground. ■ situated to the north: [in place names] *Upper California.*
3 Geology & Archaeology denoting a younger (and hence usually shallower) part of a stratigraphic division or archaeological deposit or the period in which it was formed or deposited: *the Upper Palaeolithic age.*
▸ noun the part of a boot or shoe above the sole.
– PHRASES **have** (or **gain**) **the upper hand** have or gain advantage or control over someone or something. **on one's uppers** informal extremely short of money. **the upper crust** informal the upper classes.
– ORIGIN Middle English: from the adjective UP + -ER[2].

upper[2] ▸ noun (usu. **uppers**) informal a stimulating drug, especially amphetamine.
– ORIGIN 1960s: from the verb UP + -ER[1].

Upper Austria a state of NW Austria; capital, Linz. German name **OBERÖSTERREICH**.

Upper Canada the mainly English-speaking region of Canada north of the Great Lakes and west of the Ottawa River, in what is now southern Ontario.

upper case ▸ noun [mass noun] capital letters as opposed to small letters (lower case): *the keywords must be in upper case* | [as modifier] *upper-case letters.*
– ORIGIN referring originally to two type cases positioned on an angled stand, the case containing the capital letters being higher and further away from the compositor.

upper chamber ▸ noun another term for UPPER HOUSE.

upper circle ▸ noun the tier of seats in a theatre above the dress circle.

upper class ▸ noun [treated as sing. or pl.] the social group that has the highest status in society, especially the aristocracy.
▸ adjective relating to or characteristic of the upper class: *upper-class accents.*

upperclassman ▸ noun (pl. **upperclassmen**) US a junior or senior in high school or college.

uppercut ▸ noun **1** a punch delivered with an upwards motion and the arm bent.
2 Baseball an upward batting stroke, typically resulting in a fly ball.
▸ verb (**uppercuts**, **uppercutting**; past and past participle **uppercut**) [with obj.] hit with an uppercut.

upper house ▸ noun the higher house in a bicameral parliament or similar legislature. ■ (**the Upper House**) (in the UK) the House of Lords.

upper middle class ▸ noun [treated as sing. or pl.] the social group between the upper and the middle class made up of well-paid professionals, managers, and their families.
▸ adjective (**upper-middle-class**) relating to the upper middle class.

uppermost ▸ adjective (also **upmost**) highest in place, rank, or importance: *the uppermost windows* | *her father was uppermost in her mind.*
▸ adverb at or to the highest or most important position: *investors put environmental concerns uppermost on their list.*

upper regions ▸ plural noun archaic or literary the sky or heaven.

upper school ▸ noun (in the UK) a secondary school for children aged from about fourteen upwards, generally following on from a middle school. ■ the section of a school which comprises or caters for the older pupils.

Upper Volta former name (until 1984) for BURKINA FASO.

upper works ▸ plural noun the parts of a ship that are above the water when it is fully laden.

uppish ▸ adjective informal arrogantly self-assertive.
– DERIVATIVES **uppishly** adverb, **uppishness** noun.

uppity ▸ adjective informal self-important; arrogant: *an uppity MP and his lady wife.*
– ORIGIN late 19th cent.: a fanciful formation from UP.

Uppsala /ˈʊpsɑːlə/ a city in eastern Sweden; pop. 190,668 (2008). Its university, founded in 1477, is the oldest in northern Europe.

upraise ▸ verb [with obj.] raise (something) to a higher level: (as adj. **upraised**) *an upraised arm.*

uprate ▸ verb [with obj.] **1** increase the value of (a payment or benefit): *income support will be uprated.*
2 improve the performance of; upgrade: *the gas plants are to be expanded and uprated.*

upright ▸ adjective **1** (of a person) sitting or standing with the back straight. ■ placed in a vertical position: *upright stone slabs.* ■ denoting a device designed to be used in a vertical position: *an upright vacuum cleaner.* ■ (of a piano) having vertical strings. ■ denoting a chair with a straight back and typically no arms.
2 greater in height than breadth: *an upright freezer.*
3 strictly honourable or honest: *an upright member of the community.*
▸ adverb in or into an upright position: *she was sitting upright in bed.*
▸ noun **1** a post or rod fixed vertically, especially as a structural support: *the stone uprights of the parapet.*
2 an upright piano.
– DERIVATIVES **uprightly** adverb.
– ORIGIN Old English *upriht*, of Germanic origin; related to Dutch *oprecht* and German *aufrecht* (see UP, RIGHT).

uprightness ▸ noun [mass noun] **1** the state of being in a vertical position.
2 the condition or quality of being honourable or honest; rectitude: *there is a general lack of uprightness in these postmodern times.*

uprise ▸ verb (past **uprose**; past participle **uprisen**) [no obj.] archaic or literary rise to a standing or elevated position: *bright and red uprose the morning sun.*

uprising ▸ noun an act of resistance or rebellion; a revolt: *an armed uprising.*

upriver ▸ adverb & adjective towards or situated at a point nearer the source of a river: [as adv.] *the salmon heads upriver to spawn* | [as adj.] *they headed for the upriver side.*

uproar ▸ noun a loud and impassioned noise or disturbance: *the room was in an uproar* | [mass noun] *the assembly dissolved in uproar.* ■ a public expression of protest or outrage: *it caused an uproar in the press.*
– ORIGIN early 16th cent.: from Middle Dutch *uproer*, from *op* 'up' + *roer* 'confusion', associated with ROAR.

uproarious ▸ adjective characterized by or provoking loud noise or uproar: *an uproarious party.* ■ provoking loud laughter; very funny.
– DERIVATIVES **uproariously** adverb, **uproariousness** noun.

uproot ▸ verb [with obj.] **1** pull (something, especially a tree or plant) out of the ground. ■ remove or destroy completely; eradicate: *a revolution is necessary to uproot the social order.*
2 move (someone) from their home or a familiar location: *my father travelled constantly and uprooted his family several times.*
– DERIVATIVES **uprooter** noun.

uprose past of UPRISE.

uprush ▸ noun a sudden upward surge or flow, especially of a feeling: *an uprush of joy.*

UPS ▸ abbreviation uninterruptible power supply.

ups-a-daisy ▸ exclamation variant spelling of UPSY-DAISY.

upscale ▸ adjective & adverb N. Amer. upmarket.

upsell ▸ verb [no obj.] persuade a customer to buy something additional or more expensive.

upset ▸ verb /ʌpˈsɛt/ (**upsets**, **upsetting**; past and past participle **upset**) [with obj.] **1** make (someone) unhappy, disappointed, or worried: *the accusation upset her* | (as adj. **upsetting**) *a painful and upsetting divorce.*
2 knock (something) over: *he upset a tureen of soup.*
3 cause disorder in; disrupt: *the dam will upset the ecological balance.* ■ disturb the digestion of (a person's stomach).
4 (often as noun **upsetting**) shorten and thicken the end or edge of (a metal bar, wheel rim, or other object), especially by hammering or pressure when heated.
▸ noun /ˈʌpsɛt/ **1** an unexpected result or situation: *the greatest upset in boxing history.*
2 [mass noun] the state of being unhappy, disappointed, or worried: *a legal dispute will cause worry and upset.*
3 a disturbance of a person's digestive system: *a stomach upset.*
▸ adjective **1** /ʌpˈsɛt/ unhappy, disappointed, or worried: *she looked pale and upset.*
2 /ˈʌpsɛt/ (of a person's stomach) having disturbed digestion, especially because of something eaten.
– DERIVATIVES **upsetter** noun, **upsettingly** adverb.

upset price ▸ noun the lowest acceptable selling price for a property in an auction; a reserve price.

upshift ▸ verb **1** [no obj.] change to a higher gear in a motor vehicle.
2 [with obj.] increase: *stricter driving laws that upshifted the penalties for drunk-driving.*
▸ noun **1** a change to a higher gear.
2 an increase in something.

upshot ▸ noun [in sing.] the final or eventual outcome or conclusion of a discussion, action, or series of events: *the upshot of the meeting was that he was on the next plane to New York.*

upside ▸ noun [in sing.] **1** the more positive aspect of a situation: *being self-employed has its upside.*
2 an upward movement of share prices.
▸ preposition N. Amer. informal against; on: *if her mother saw her drinkin' that stuff she'd slap her upside her head.*

upside down ▸ adverb & adjective with the upper part where the lower part should be; in an inverted position: [as adv.] *the car rolled and landed upside down* | [as adj.] *an upside-down canoe.* ■ in or into total disorder or confusion: [as adv.] *burglars have* **turned** *our house* **upside down.**
– ORIGIN Middle English: originally *up so down*, perhaps in the sense 'up as if down'.

upside-down cake ▸ noun a sponge cake that is baked over a layer of fruit in syrup and inverted for serving.

upside-down catfish ▸ noun a small freshwater catfish that habitually swims upside down so as to browse on algae on the undersides of floating leaves. Native to central Congo, it is popular in aquaria.
● *Synodontis nigriventris*, family Mochokidae.

upsides ▸ adverb (especially in horse racing) alongside; on a level: *the horse came upsides.* ■ (**upsides with**) archaic even or equal with.
– ORIGIN early 18th cent.: from UPSIDE in the sense 'upper part' + the adverbial suffix *-s*.

upsilon /ʌpˈsʌɪlən, juːp-, ˈʊpsɪlɒn, ˈjuːp-/ ▸ noun the twentieth letter of the Greek alphabet (Υ, υ), transliterated as 'u' or (chiefly in English words derived through Latin) as 'y'. ■ (**Upsilon**) [followed by Latin genitive] Astronomy the twentieth star in a constellation: *Upsilon Scorpii.* ■ (also **upsilon particle**) Physics a meson thought to contain a *b* quark bound to its antiparticle, produced in particle accelerators.
– ORIGIN Greek, literally 'slender U', from *psilos* 'slender', referring to the need to distinguish upsilon from the diphthong *oi*: in late Greek the two had the same pronunciation.

upsize ▸ verb [with obj.] increase the size, extent, or complexity of: *they are considering upsizing their information systems.* ■ [no obj.] undergo an increase in size, extent, or complexity: *the economy kept on upsizing.*

upskill ▸ verb [with obj.] teach (an employee) additional skills: *this is an opportunity to upskill staff and expand their capabilities.* ■ [no obj.] (of an employee) learn additional skills: *they will provide grants of up to 75% for staff who decide to upskill.*

upslope ▸ noun an upward slope.

U

▸ adverb & adjective at or towards a higher point on a slope.

upstage ▸ adverb & adjective **1** at or towards the back of a theatre stage: [as adv.] *Hamlet turns to face upstage* | [as adj.] *an upstage exit.*
2 [as adj.] informal, dated superior; aloof.
▸ verb **1** [with obj.] divert attention from (someone) towards oneself: *they were totally upstaged by their co-star in the film.*
2 (of an actor) move towards the back of a stage to make (another actor) face away from the audience.

upstairs ▸ adverb on or to an upper floor of a building: *I tiptoed upstairs.*
▸ adjective (also **upstair**) [attrib.] situated on an upper floor: *an upstairs bedroom.*
▸ noun an upper floor: *she was cleaning the upstairs.*
– PHRASES **Him** (or **the man**) **upstairs** a humorous name for God: *I bowed my head and thanked Him upstairs for my family.*

upstand ▸ noun an upright structure or object. ■ a turned-up edge of a flat surface or sheeting, especially in a roof space where it meets the wall.

upstanding ▸ adjective **1** honest; respectable: *an upstanding member of the community.*
2 standing up; erect: *upstanding feathered plumes.* ■ (of an animal) strong and healthy.

upstart ▸ noun **1** derogatory a person who has risen suddenly in rank or importance, especially one who behaves arrogantly: *the upstarts who dare to challenge the legitimacy of his rule.*
2 a series of movements on the parallel or asymmetric bars, by which a gymnast swings to a position in which their body is supported by their arms above the bar, especially at the start of a routine.

upstate US ▸ adjective & adverb of, in, or to a part of a state remote from its large cities, especially the northern part: [as adj.] *upstate New York.*
▸ noun such an area: *visiting farmers from upstate.*
– DERIVATIVES **upstater** noun.

upstream ▸ adverb & adjective **1** moving or situated in the opposite direction from that in which a stream or river flows; nearer to the source: [as adv.] *a lone motor cruiser rumbled upstream* | [as adj.] *the upstream stretch of the Nene.*
2 Biology situated in or towards the part of a sequence of genetic material where transcription takes place earlier than at a given point.
3 at a stage in the process of gas or oil extraction and production before the raw material is ready for refining.

upstroke ▸ noun a stroke made upwards: *the upstroke of the whale's tail.*

upsurge ▸ noun an upward surge in the strength or quantity of something; an increase: *an upsurge in vandalism and violent crime.*

upswell ▸ noun an increase or upsurge.

upswept ▸ adjective curved, sloping, or directed upwards: *an upswept moustache.* ■ (of the hair) brushed or held upwards and off the face: *an elegant upswept style.*

upswing ▸ noun an increase in strength or quantity; an upward trend: *an upswing in economic activity.*

upsy-daisy (also **ups-a-daisy**, **oops-a-daisy**) ▸ exclamation expressing encouragement to a child who has fallen or is being lifted.
– ORIGIN mid 19th cent.: alteration of earlier *up-a-daisy*; compare with **LACKADAISICAL**.

uptake ▸ noun [mass noun] the action of taking up or making use of something that is available: *the uptake of free school meals.* ■ the taking in or absorption of a substance by a living organism or bodily organ: *the uptake of glucose into the muscles.*
– PHRASES **be quick** (or **slow**) **on the uptake** informal be quick (or slow) to understand something.

U

uptalk ▸ noun [mass noun] a manner of speaking in which declarative sentences are uttered with rising intonation at the end, as if they were questions.

uptempo ▸ adjective & adverb Music played with a fast or increased tempo: [as adj.] *uptempo guitar work.*

upthrow Geology ▸ verb [with obj.] (usu. as adj. **upthrown**) displace (a rock formation) upwards.
▸ noun an upward displacement of rock strata.

upthrust ▸ noun Physics the upward force that a liquid or gas exerts on a body floating in it. ■ Geology another term for **UPLIFT**.
▸ verb [with obj.] (usu. as adj. **upthrust**) thrust (something) upwards: *Turco's upthrust beard.*

uptick ▸ noun N. Amer. a small increase.

uptight ▸ adjective informal anxious or angry in a tense and overly controlled way: *he is so uptight about everything.*

uptime ▸ noun [mass noun] time during which a machine, especially a computer, is in operation.

up to date ▸ adjective incorporating the latest developments and trends: *a modern, up-to-date hospital.* ■ incorporating or aware of the latest information.

up to the minute ▸ adjective incorporating the very latest information or developments: *it is fitted with up-to-the-minute security devices.*

uptown chiefly N. Amer. ▸ adjective of, in, or characteristic of the residential area of a town or city. ■ of or characteristic of an affluent area or people: *I don't pay uptown prices.*
▸ adverb in or into such an area.
▸ noun the uptown area of a town or city.
– DERIVATIVES **uptowner** noun.

uptrend ▸ noun an upward tendency, especially a rise in economic value.

upturn ▸ noun an improvement or upward trend, especially in economic conditions or someone's fortunes: *an upturn in the economy.*
▸ verb [with obj.] (usu. as adj. **upturned**) turn (something) upwards or upside down: *a sea of upturned faces.*

UPU ▸ abbreviation Universal Postal Union.

uPVC ▸ abbreviation unplasticized polyvinyl chloride, a rigid, chemically resistant form of PVC used for pipework, window frames, and other structures.

upward ▸ adverb (also **upwards**) towards a higher place, point, or level: *she peered upward at the sky.*
▸ adjective moving, pointing, or leading to a higher place, point, or level: *an upward trend in sales.*
– PHRASES **upwards** (or **upward**) **of** more than.
– ORIGIN Old English *upweard(es)* (see **UP**, **-WARD**).

upwardly ▸ adverb in an upward direction.
– PHRASES **upwardly mobile** see **MOBILE**.

upwarp Geology ▸ noun a broad elevated area of the earth's surface.
▸ verb (**be upwarped**) (of part of the earth's surface) be elevated to form an upwarp.

upwelling ▸ noun an instance or amount of seawater, magma, or other liquid rising up.
▸ adjective (especially of emotion) building up or gathering strength: *upwelling grief.*

upwind /ʌpˈwɪnd/ ▸ adverb & adjective against the direction of the wind: [as adv.] *you learn how to sail upwind* | [as adj.] *the upwind wing tip.*

UR ▸ abbreviation informal you are or your.

Ur /əː, ʊə/ an ancient Sumerian city formerly on the Euphrates, in southern Iraq. It was one of the oldest cities of Mesopotamia, dating from the 4th millennium BC, and reached its zenith in the late 3rd millennium BC.

ur- /əː, ʊə/ ▸ combining form primitive, original, or earliest: *urtext.* ■ denoting someone or something regarded as embodying the basic or intrinsic qualities of a particular class or type: *ur-thespians Patrick Stewart and Ian McKellen.*
– ORIGIN from German.

uracil /ˈjʊərəsɪl/ ▸ noun [mass noun] Biochemistry a compound found in living tissue as a constituent base of RNA. In DNA it is replaced by thymine. ● A pyrimidine derivative; chem. formula: $C_4H_4N_2O_2$.
– ORIGIN late 19th cent.: from *ur(ea)* + *ac(etic)* + **-IL**.

uraemia /jʊˈriːmɪə/ (US **uremia**) ▸ noun [mass noun] Medicine a raised level in the blood of urea and other nitrogenous waste compounds that are normally eliminated by the kidneys.
– DERIVATIVES **uraemic** adjective.
– ORIGIN mid 19th cent.: modern Latin, from Greek *ouron* 'urine' + *haima* 'blood'.

uraeus /jʊˈriːəs/ ▸ noun (pl. **uraei** /jʊˈriːʌɪ/) a representation of a sacred serpent as an emblem of supreme power, worn on the headdresses of ancient Egyptian deities and sovereigns.
– ORIGIN mid 19th cent.: modern Latin, from Greek *ouraios*, representing the Egyptian word for 'cobra'.

Ural-Altaic ▸ adjective relating to or denoting a hypothetical language group formerly proposed to include both the Uralic and the Altaic languages.

Uralic /jʊˈralɪk/ ▸ adjective **1** relating to or denoting a family of languages spoken from northern Scandinavia to western Siberia, comprising the Finno-Ugric and Samoyedic groups.
2 relating to the Ural Mountains or the surrounding areas.
▸ noun [mass noun] the Uralic languages collectively.

Ural Mountains /ˈjʊərəl/ (also **the Urals**) a mountain range in Russia, extending 1,600 km (1,000 miles) from the Arctic Ocean to the Aral Sea in Kazakhstan, and rising to 1,894 m (6,214 ft) at Mount Narodnaya. It forms part of the conventional boundary between Europe and Asia.

Urania /jʊˈreɪnɪə/ Greek & Roman Mythology the Muse of astronomy.
– ORIGIN Greek, literally 'heavenly woman'.

Uranian[1] /jʊˈreɪnɪən/ ▸ adjective relating to the planet Uranus.
▸ noun (in science fiction) an imagined inhabitant of Uranus.

Uranian[2] /jʊˈreɪnɪən/ literary ▸ adjective **1** relating to heaven; celestial.
2 homosexual. [late 19th cent.: with allusion to a reference to Aphrodite in Plato's *Symposium*.]
▸ noun a homosexual.
– ORIGIN early 17th cent.: from **URANIA** + **-AN**.

uraninite /jʊˈranɪnʌɪt/ ▸ noun [mass noun] a black, grey, or brown mineral which consists mainly of uranium dioxide and is the chief ore of uranium.
– ORIGIN late 19th cent.: from **URANO-**[2] + **-ITE**[1].

uranium /jʊˈreɪnɪəm/ ▸ noun [mass noun] the chemical element of atomic number 92, a dense grey radioactive metal used as a fuel in nuclear reactors. (Symbol: **U**)

> Uranium is a chemically reactive metal belonging to the actinide series. Becquerel discovered radioactivity in uranium in 1896, and its capacity to undergo fission led to its use as a source of energy, though the fissile isotope, uranium-235, has to be separated from the more common uranium-238 before it can be used in nuclear weapons. The atom bomb exploded over Hiroshima in 1945 contained uranium-235.

– ORIGIN late 18th cent.: modern Latin, from **URANUS**: compare with **TELLURIUM**.

urano-[1] /ˈjʊər(ə)nəʊ/ ▸ combining form relating to the heavens: *uranography.*
– ORIGIN from Greek *ouranos* 'heavens, sky'.

urano-[2] /ˈjʊər(ə)nəʊ/ ▸ combining form representing **URANIUM**.

uranography /ˌjʊərəˈnɒgrəfi/ ▸ noun [mass noun] archaic the branch of astronomy concerned with describing and mapping the stars.

Uranus /ˈjʊərənəs, jʊˈreɪnəs/ **1** Greek Mythology a personification of heaven or the sky, the most ancient of the Greek gods and first ruler of the universe. He was overthrown and castrated by his son Cronus.
2 Astronomy a distant planet of the solar system, seventh in order from the sun, discovered by William Herschel in 1781.

> Uranus orbits between Jupiter and Neptune at an average distance of 2,870 million km from the sun. It has an equatorial diameter of 51,120 km, and is one of the gas giants. The planet is bluish-green in colour, having an upper atmosphere consisting almost entirely of hydrogen and helium. There are at least seventeen satellites, the largest of which are Oberon and Titania, and a faint ring system.

uranyl /ˈjʊər(ə)nʌɪl, ˈjʊər(ə)nɪl/ ▸ noun [as modifier] Chemistry the cation UO_2^{2+}, present in some compounds of uranium: *uranyl acetate.*
– ORIGIN mid 19th cent.: from **URANIUM** + **-YL**.

Urartian /ʊˈrɑːtɪən/ ▸ adjective relating to the ancient kingdom of Urartu in eastern Anatolia (*c.*1500–585 BC).
▸ noun **1** a native or inhabitant of ancient Urartu.
2 [mass noun] the language of Urartu, related to Hurrian.

urate /ˈjʊəreɪt/ ▸ noun Chemistry a salt or ester of uric acid.

urban ▸ adjective **1** in, relating to, or characteristic of a town or city: *the urban population.*
2 (also **urban contemporary**) denoting or relating to popular dance music of black origin: *hip-hop's traditionally urban vibe.*
– DERIVATIVES **urbanism** noun, **urbanist** noun.
– ORIGIN early 17th cent.: from Latin *urbanus*, from *urbs, urb-* 'city'.

urban district ▸ noun Brit. historical a group of urban communities governed by an elected council.

urbane /əːˈbeɪn/ ▸ adjective (of a person, especially a man) courteous and refined in manner.
– DERIVATIVES **urbanely** adverb.
– ORIGIN mid 16th cent. (in the sense 'urban'): from French *urbain* or Latin *urbanus* (see **URBAN**).

urbanite ▶ **noun** informal a person who lives in a town or city.

urbanity ▶ **noun** [mass noun] **1** courteousness and refinement of manner.
2 urban life.
– ORIGIN mid 16th cent.: from French *urbanité* or Latin *urbanitas*, from *urbanus* 'belonging to the city' (see **URBAN**).

urbanize (also **urbanise**) ▶ **verb** make or become urban in character: [with obj.] *once an agrarian society, the island has recently been urbanized* | (as adj. **urbanized**) *urbanized areas*.
– DERIVATIVES **urbanization** noun.

urban myth (also N. Amer. **urban legend**) ▶ **noun** a humorous or horrific story or piece of information circulated as though true, especially one purporting to involve someone vaguely related or known to the teller.

urban renewal ▶ **noun** [mass noun] the redevelopment of areas within a large city, typically involving the clearance of slums.

urbs /ə:bz/ ▶ **noun** chiefly literary the city, especially as a symbol of harsh or busy modern life.
– ORIGIN Latin.

URC ▶ **abbreviation** United Reformed Church.

urchin /ˈə:tʃɪn/ ▶ **noun** **1** a young child who is poorly or raggedly dressed.
2 dialect a hedgehog.
3 short for **SEA URCHIN**.
– ORIGIN Middle English *hirchon*, *urchon* 'hedgehog', from Old Northern French *herichon*, based on Latin *hericius* 'hedgehog'.

Urdu /ˈʊədu:, ˈə:du:/ ▶ **noun** [mass noun] an Indic language closely related to Hindi but written in the Persian script and having many loanwords from Persian and Arabic. It is the official language of Pakistan, and is also widely used in India and elsewhere, with about 50 million speakers worldwide.
– ORIGIN from Persian (*zabān-i-*)*urdū* '(language of the) camp' (because it developed as a lingua franca after the Muslim invasions between the occupying armies and the local people of the region around Delhi), *urdū* being from Turkic *ordu* (see **HORDE**).

-ure ▶ **suffix** forming nouns: **1** denoting an action, process, or result: *censure* | *closure* | *scripture*.
2 denoting an office or function: *judicature*.
3 denoting a collective: *legislature*.
– ORIGIN from Old French *-ure*, from Latin *-ura*.

urea /jʊˈri:ə, ˈjʊərɪə/ ▶ **noun** [mass noun] Biochemistry a colourless crystalline compound which is the main nitrogenous breakdown product of protein metabolism in mammals and is excreted in urine. ● Chem. formula: $CO(NH_2)_2$.
– ORIGIN early 19th cent.: modern Latin, from French *urée*, from Greek *ouron* 'urine'.

ureaplasma /jʊərɪəˈplazmə/ ▶ **noun** a small bacterium related to the mycoplasmas, characterized by the ability to metabolize urea. ● Genus *Ureaplasma*, order Mycoplasmatales.

ureide /ˈjʊərɪʌɪd/ ▶ **noun** Chemistry any of a group of compounds which are acyl derivatives of urea.

uremia ▶ **noun** US spelling of **URAEMIA**.

ureter /jʊˈri:tə, ˈjʊərɪtə/ ▶ **noun** Anatomy & Zoology the duct by which urine passes from the kidney to the bladder or cloaca.
– DERIVATIVES **ureteral** adjective, **ureteric** /jʊərɪˈtɛrɪk/ adjective.
– ORIGIN late 16th cent.: from French *uretère* or modern Latin *ureter*, from Greek *ourētēr*, from *ourein* 'urinate'.

urethane /ˈjʊərɪθeɪn, jʊˈrɛθeɪn/ ▶ **noun** [mass noun] Chemistry a synthetic crystalline compound used in making pesticides and fungicides, and formerly as an anaesthetic. ● Alternative name: **ethyl carbamate**; chem. formula: $CO(NH_2)OC_2H_5$.
■ short for **POLYURETHANE**.
– ORIGIN mid 19th cent.: from French *uréthane* (see **UREA**, **ETHANE**).

urethra /jʊˈri:θrə/ ▶ **noun** Anatomy & Zoology the duct by which urine is conveyed out of the body from the bladder, and which in male vertebrates also conveys semen.
– DERIVATIVES **urethral** adjective.
– ORIGIN mid 17th cent.: from late Latin, from Greek *ourēthra*, from *ourein* 'urinate'.

urethritis /jʊri:ˈθrʌɪtɪs/ ▶ **noun** [mass noun] Medicine inflammation of the urethra.

Urga /ˈʊəgə/ former name (until 1924) for **ULAN BATOR**.

urge ▶ **verb** [with obj. and usu. infinitive] try earnestly or persistently to persuade (someone) to do something: *he urged her to come and stay with us* | [with direct speech] *'Do try to relax,' she urged*. ■ recommend (something) strongly: *I urge caution in interpreting these results* | [with clause] *they are urging that more treatment facilities be provided*. ■ [with obj. and adverbial] encourage (a person or animal) to move more quickly or in a particular direction: *drawing up outside the house, he urged her inside*. ■ (**urge someone on**) encourage someone to continue or succeed: *he could hear her voice urging him on*.
▶ **noun** [often with infinitive] a strong desire or impulse: *he felt the urge to giggle* | *sexual urges*.
– ORIGIN mid 16th cent.: from Latin *urgere* 'press, drive'.

urgency ▶ **noun** [mass noun] **1** importance requiring swift action: *the discovery of the ozone hole gave urgency to the issue of CFCs*.
2 an earnest and persistent quality; insistence: *Emilia heard the urgency in his voice*.

urgent ▶ **adjective** **1** requiring immediate action or attention: *an urgent demand for more state funding*.
2 (of an action or event) done or arranged in response to an urgent situation: *she needs urgent treatment*. ■ (of a person or their manner) earnest and persistent: *an urgent whisper*.
– DERIVATIVES **urgently** adverb.
– ORIGIN late 15th cent.: from Old French, from Latin *urgent-* 'pressing, driving', from the verb *urgere* (see **URGE**).

urger /ˈə:dʒə/ ▶ **noun** Austral. informal a person who gives tips at a race meeting. ■ a person who takes advantage of others; a racketeer.

urging ▶ **noun** [mass noun] the action of urging someone to do something: *she bought a new one at Gregory's urging* | [count noun] *the urgings of the crowd made him look around*. ■ (**urgings**) urges: *I have had maternal urgings*.

-uria ▶ **combining form** in nouns denoting that a substance is present in the urine, especially in excess: *glycosuria*.
– ORIGIN modern Latin, from Greek *-ouria*, from *ouron* 'urine'.

Uriah /jʊˈrʌɪə/ (in the Bible) a Hittite officer in David's army, whom David, desiring his wife Bathsheba, caused to be killed in battle (2 Sam. 11).

urial /ˈʊərɪəl/ ▶ **noun** (pl. **same**) a wild sheep with long legs and relatively small horns, native to central Asia. ● *Ovis vignei*, family Bovidae.
– ORIGIN mid 19th cent.: from Punjabi *ūrial*.

uric /ˈjʊərɪk/ ▶ **adjective** relating to urine.
– ORIGIN late 18th cent.: from French *urique* (see **URINE**).

uric acid ▶ **noun** [mass noun] Biochemistry an almost insoluble compound which is a breakdown product of nitrogenous metabolism. It is the main excretory product in birds, reptiles, and insects. ● A bicyclic acid derived from purine; chem. formula: $C_5H_4N_4O_3$.

uridine /ˈjʊərɪdi:n/ ▶ **noun** [mass noun] Biochemistry a compound formed by partial hydrolysis of RNA. It is a nucleoside containing uracil linked to ribose.
– ORIGIN early 20th cent.: from *ur*(*acil*) + **-IDE** + **-INE**[4].

Urim and Thummim ▶ **plural noun** historical two objects of a now unknown nature, possibly used for divination, worn on the breastplate of a Jewish high priest.
– ORIGIN from Hebrew.

urinal /jʊˈrʌɪn(ə)l, ˈjʊərɪn(ə)l/ ▶ **noun** a bowl or other receptacle, typically attached to a wall in a public toilet, into which men may urinate.
– ORIGIN Middle English (denoting a glass container for the medical inspection of urine): via Old French from Latin *urinal*, from *urina* (see **URINE**).

urinalysis /jʊərɪˈnalɪsɪs/ ▶ **noun** (pl. **urinalyses** /-si:z/) [mass noun] Medicine analysis of urine by physical, chemical, and microscopical means to test for the presence of disease, drugs, etc.

urinary ▶ **adjective** relating to urine. ■ relating to or denoting the system of organs, structures, and ducts by which urine is produced and discharged, in mammals comprising the kidneys, ureters, bladder, and urethra.

urinary tract ▶ **noun** Anatomy the series of channels by which the urine passes from the renal pelvis out of the body.

urinate ▶ **verb** [no obj.] discharge urine; pass water.
– DERIVATIVES **urination** noun.
– ORIGIN late 16th cent.: from medieval Latin *urinat-* 'urinated', from the verb *urinare*.

urine /ˈjʊərɪn, -rʌɪn/ ▶ **noun** [mass noun] a watery, typically yellowish fluid stored in the bladder and discharged through the urethra. It is one of the body's chief means of eliminating excess water and salt, and also contains nitrogen compounds such as urea and other waste substances removed from the blood by the kidneys.
– ORIGIN Middle English: via Old French from Latin *urina*.

uriniferous tubule /jʊərɪˈnɪf(ə)rəs/ ▶ **noun** another term for **KIDNEY TUBULE**.

URL ▶ **abbreviation** uniform (or universal) resource locator, the address of a World Wide Web page.

urn ▶ **noun** **1** a tall, rounded vase with a stem and base, especially one used for storing the ashes of a cremated person. ■ an ornamental sculpture shaped like an urn.
2 a large metal container with a tap, in which tea or coffee is made and kept hot, or water for making such drinks is boiled: *a tea urn*.
▶ **verb** [with obj.] archaic place in an urn.
– ORIGIN late Middle English: from Latin *urna*; related to *urceus* 'pitcher'.

urnfield Archaeology ▶ **noun** a prehistoric cemetery of the European late Bronze Age and early Iron Age, in which cremated remains were placed in pottery vessels (cinerary urns) and buried.
▶ **adjective** (often **Urnfield**) relating to or denoting a people or culture characterized by burial in an urnfield. The **Urnfield complex** is equated with the Hallstatt culture and is dated to *c.*1200–800 BC.

uro-[1] ▶ **combining form** relating to urine or the urinary organs: *urogenital*.
– ORIGIN from Greek *ouron* 'urine'.

uro-[2] ▶ **combining form** Zoology relating to a tail or the caudal region: *urodele*.
– ORIGIN from Greek *oura* 'tail'.

uroboros /jʊərə(ʊ)ˈbɒrəs/ (also **ouroboros**) ▶ **noun** a circular symbol depicting a snake, or less commonly a dragon, swallowing its tail, as an emblem of wholeness or infinity.
– DERIVATIVES **uroboric** adjective.
– ORIGIN 1940s: from Greek (*drakōn*) *ouroboros* '(snake) devouring its tail'.

Urochordata /jʊərə(ʊ)kɔ:ˈdeɪtə/ ▶ **plural noun** Zoology a group of chordate animals that comprises the tunicates. ● Subphylum Urochordata, phylum Chordata.
– ORIGIN modern Latin (plural), from **URO-**[2] 'tail' + **CHORDATA**.

urochordate Zoology ▶ **noun** a marine invertebrate of the group Urochordata, which comprises the tunicates.
▶ **adjective** relating to or denoting urochordates.

Urodela /jʊərə(ʊ)ˈdi:lə/ ▶ **plural noun** Zoology an order of amphibians that comprises the newts and salamanders, which retain the tail as adults. Also called **CAUDATA**.
– ORIGIN modern Latin (plural), from **URO-**[2] 'tail' + Greek *dēlos* 'evident'.

urodele /ˈjʊərə(ʊ)di:l/ ▶ **noun** Zoology an amphibian of the order Urodela; a newt or salamander.

urodynamics ▶ **plural noun** [treated as sing.] Medicine the diagnostic study of pressure in the bladder, in treating incontinence.
– DERIVATIVES **urodynamic** adjective.

urogenital ▶ **adjective** relating to or denoting both the urinary and genital organs.

urography /jʊˈrɒgrəfi/ ▶ **noun** another term for **PYELOGRAPHY**.
– DERIVATIVES **urogram** noun.

urokinase /jʊərə(ʊ)ˈkʌɪneɪz/ ▶ **noun** [mass noun] Biochemistry an enzyme produced in the kidneys which promotes the conversion of plasminogen to plasmin and can be used to dissolve blood clots.

urolagnia /jʊərə(ʊ)ˈlagnɪə/ ▶ **noun** [mass noun] a tendency to derive sexual pleasure from the sight or thought of urination. Also called **UROPHILIA**.
– ORIGIN early 20th cent.: from **URO-**[1] 'of urine' + Greek *lagneia* 'lust'.

urolithiasis /jʊərə(ʊ)lɪˈθʌɪəsɪs/ ▶ **noun** [mass noun] Medicine the formation of stony concretions in the bladder or urinary tract.

urology /jʊˈrɒlədʒi/ ▶ **noun** [mass noun] the branch of medicine and physiology concerned with the function and disorders of the urinary system.
– DERIVATIVES **urologic** adjective, **urological** adjective, **urologist** noun.

U

uronic acid /jʊˈrɒnɪk/ ▸ **noun** Biochemistry any of a class of compounds which are derived from sugars by oxidizing a $-CH_2OH$ group to an acid group ($-COOH$).
– ORIGIN 1920s: *uronic* from **URO-**[1] 'urine' + **-IC**, with the insertion of *-n-*.

urophilia /ˌjʊərə(ʊ)ˈfɪlɪə/ ▸ **noun** another term for **UROLAGNIA**.

uropod /ˈjʊərə(ʊ)pɒd/ ▸ **noun** Zoology the sixth and last pair of abdominal appendages of lobsters and related crustaceans, forming part of the tail fan.
– ORIGIN late 19th cent.: from **URO-**[2] 'tail' + Greek *pous, pod-* 'foot'.

uropygium /ˌjʊərə(ʊ)ˈpɪdʒɪəm/ ▸ **noun** Zoology the rump of a bird, supporting the tail feathers.
– DERIVATIVES **uropygial adjective**.
– ORIGIN late 18th cent.: via medieval Latin from Greek *ouropugion*.

uroscopy /jʊˈrɒskəpi/ ▸ **noun** [mass noun] Medicine, historical the diagnostic examination of urine by simple inspection.

urostyle /ˈjʊərə(ʊ)stʌɪl/ ▸ **noun** Zoology a long bone formed from fused vertebrae at the base of the vertebral column in some lower vertebrates, especially frogs and toads.

Ursa Major /ˌəːsə ˈmeɪdʒə/ Astronomy one of the largest and most prominent northern constellations (the Great Bear). The seven brightest stars form a familiar formation variously called the Plough, Big Dipper, or Charles's Wain, and include the Pointers.
– ORIGIN Latin, from the story in Greek mythology that the nymph Callisto was turned into a bear and placed as a constellation in the heavens by Zeus.

Ursa Minor /əːsə ˈmʌɪnə/ Astronomy a northern constellation (the Little Bear), which contains the north celestial pole and the pole star Polaris. The brightest stars form a shape that is also known as the Little Dipper.
– ORIGIN Latin.

ursine /ˈəːsʌɪn, -ɪn/ ▸ **adjective** relating to or resembling bears.
– ORIGIN mid 16th cent.: from Latin *ursinus*, from *ursus* 'bear'.

Ursula, St /ˈəːsjʊlə/ a legendary British saint and martyr, said to have been put to death with 11,000 virgins after being captured by Huns near Cologne while on a pilgrimage.

Ursuline /ˈəːsjʊlʌɪn, -lɪn/ ▸ **noun** a nun of an order founded by St Angela Merici (1470–1540) at Brescia in 1535 for nursing the sick and teaching girls.
▸ **adjective** relating to the Ursulines.
– ORIGIN from St *Ursula*, the founder's patron saint (see **URSULA, ST**), + **-INE**[1].

urtext /ˈuːətɛkst/ ▸ **noun** (pl. **urtexte** /-tə/ or **urtexts**) an original or the earliest version of a text, to which later versions can be compared.

urticaria /ˌəːtɪˈkɛːrɪə/ ▸ **noun** [mass noun] Medicine a rash of round, red weals on the skin which itch intensely, sometimes with dangerous swelling, caused by an allergic reaction, typically to specific foods. Also called **NETTLERASH** or **HIVES**.
– ORIGIN late 18th cent.: modern Latin, from Latin *urtica* 'nettle', from *urere* 'to burn'.

urticate /ˈəːtɪkeɪt/ ▸ **verb** [no obj.] cause a stinging or prickling sensation like that given by a nettle: (as adj. **urticating**) *the urticating hairs*.
– DERIVATIVES **urtication noun**.
– ORIGIN mid 19th cent. (earlier (mid 17th cent.) as *urtication*): from medieval Latin *urticat-* 'stung', from the verb *urticare*, from Latin *urtica* (see **URTICARIA**).

U

Uruguay /ˈjʊərəgwʌɪ/, Spanish /uruˈɣwaj/ a country on the Atlantic coast of South America south of Brazil; pop. 3,494,400 (est. 2009); official language, Spanish; capital, Montevideo.

> Uruguay was liberated from Spanish colonial rule in 1825, and in the early 20th century was moulded into South America's first welfare state. Civil unrest beginning in the 1960s, and particularly fighting against the Marxist Tupamaro guerrillas, led to a period of military rule, but civilian government was restored in 1985.

– DERIVATIVES **Uruguayan adjective & noun**.

Uruk /ˈʊrʊk/ an ancient city in southern Mesopotamia, to the north-west of Ur. One of the greatest cities of Sumer, it was built in the 5th millennium BC and is associated with the legendary hero Gilgamesh. Arabic name **WARKA**; biblical name **ERECH**.

Urumqi /ʊˈrʊmtʃi/ (also **Urumchi**) the capital of Xinjiang autonomous region in NW China; pop. 1,504,300 (est. 2006). Former name (until 1954) **TIHWA**.

urus /ˈjʊərəs/ ▸ **noun** another term for **AUROCHS**.
– ORIGIN early 17th cent.: from Latin, from Greek *ouros*.

urushiol /ʊˈruːʃɪɒl/ ▸ **noun** [mass noun] Biochemistry an oily liquid which is the main constituent of Japanese lacquer and is responsible for the irritant properties of poison ivy and other plants. It consists of a mixture of catechol derivatives.
– ORIGIN early 20th cent.: from Japanese *urushi* 'Japanese lacquer' + **-OL**.

US ▸ **abbreviation** ■ Brit. undersecretary. ■ United States. ■ Brit. informal unserviceable; useless.

us ▸ **pronoun** [first person plural] **1** used by a speaker to refer to himself or herself and one or more other people as the object of a verb or preposition: *let us know* | *we asked him to come with us* | *both of us*. Compare with **WE**. ■ used after the verb 'to be' and after 'than' or 'as': *it's us or them* | *they are richer than us*. ■ N. Amer. informal to or for ourselves: *we got us some good hunting*.
2 informal me: *give us a kiss*.
– PHRASES **one of us** a person recognized as an accepted member of a particular group, typically one that is exclusive in some way. **us and them** (or **them and us**) expressing a sense of division within a group of people: *negotiations were hampered by an 'us and them' attitude between management and unions*.
– ORIGIN Old English *ūs*, accusative and dative of **WE**, of Germanic origin; related to Dutch *ons* and German *uns*.

> **USAGE** Is it correct to say *they are richer than* **us**, or is it better to say *they are richer than* **we (are)**? See **USAGE** at **PERSONAL PRONOUN** and **THAN**.

USA ▸ **abbreviation** ■ United States of America. ■ United States Army.

usable (also **useable**) ▸ **adjective** able or fit to be used: *usable information*.
– DERIVATIVES **usability noun**.

USAF ▸ **abbreviation** United States Air Force.

usage ▸ **noun** [mass noun] the action of using something or the fact of being used: *a survey of water usage* | *the usage of equipment*. ■ the way in which a word or phrase is normally and correctly used. ■ habitual or customary practice, especially as creating a right, obligation, or standard.
– ORIGIN Middle English (in the sense 'customary practice'): from Old French, from *us* 'a use' (see **USE**).

usance /ˈjuːz(ə)ns/ ▸ **noun** [mass noun] archaic **1** another term for **USAGE**.
2 the time allowed for the payment of foreign bills of exchange, according to law or commercial practice.
– ORIGIN late Middle English: from Old French, from the base of the verb *user* 'to use'.

USB ▸ **abbreviation** Computing universal serial bus, a standardized technology for attaching peripheral devices to a computer.

USB flash drive (also **USB stick**) ▸ **noun** Computing a small external flash drive that can be used with any computer that has a USB port.

USD ▸ **abbreviation** United States dollar(s).

USDA ▸ **abbreviation** United States Department of Agriculture.

use ▸ **verb** /juːz/ [with obj.] **1** take, hold, or deploy (something) as a means of accomplishing or achieving something; employ: *she used her key to open the front door* | *the poem uses simple language*. ■ [with obj. and adverbial] treat (someone) in a particular way: *use your troops well and they will not let you down*. ■ exploit (a person or situation) for one's own advantage: *I couldn't help feeling that she was using me*. ■ apply (a name or title) to oneself: *she still used her maiden name professionally*.
2 take or consume (an amount) from a limited supply: *we have used all the available funds*. ■ take (an illegal drug).
3 /juːst/ [in past, with infinitive] **(used to)** describing an action or situation that was done repeatedly or existed for a period in the past: *this road used to be a dirt track* | *I used to give him lifts home*.
4 /juːst/ **(be/get used to)** be or become familiar with (someone or something) through experience: *she was used to getting what she wanted* | *he's weird, but you just have to get used to him*.
5 (one could use) informal one would like or benefit from: *I could use another cup of coffee*.
▸ **noun** /juːs/ [mass noun] **1** the action of using something or the state of being used for a purpose: *hypermodern trains are now in use* | *theatre owners were charging too much for the use of their venues*. ■ the ability or power to exercise or manipulate one's mind or body: *the horse lost the use of his hind legs*. ■ [count noun] a purpose for or way in which something can be used: *the herb has various culinary uses*.
2 the value or advantage of something: *it was no use trying to persuade her* | *what's the use of crying?* ■ Law, historical the benefit or profit of lands, especially lands that are in the possession of another who holds them solely for the beneficiary.
3 the habitual consumption of a drug.
4 the characteristic ritual and liturgy of a Christian Church or diocese.
– PHRASES **have its (or one's) uses** informal be useful in certain respects. **have no use for** informal dislike or be impatient with. **make use of** use for a purpose. ■ benefit from: *they were educated enough to make use of further training*. **use and wont** formal established custom. **use someone's name** cite someone as an authority or reference.
– PHRASAL VERBS **use something up** consume or expend the whole of something: *the money was soon used up*. ■ **(be used up)** informal (of a person) be exhausted or emotionally drained: *she was tired and used up*.
– ORIGIN Middle English: the noun from Old French *us*, from Latin *usus*, from *uti* 'to use'; the verb from Old French *user*, based on Latin *uti*.

> **USAGE 1** The construction **used to** is standard, but difficulties arise with the formation of negatives and questions. Traditionally, **used to** behaves as a modal verb, so that questions and negatives are formed without the auxiliary verb **do**, as in *it* **used not to** *be like that* and **used** *she* **to** *come here?* In modern English this question form is now regarded as very formal or old-fashioned and the use with **do** is broadly accepted as standard, as in **did** *she* **use to** *come here?* Negative constructions with **do**, on the other hand (as in *it* **didn't use to** *be like that*), though common, are informal and are not generally accepted.
> **2** There is sometimes confusion over whether to use the form **used to** or **use to**, which has arisen largely because the pronunciation is the same in both cases. Except in negatives and questions, the correct form is **used to**: *we* **used to** *go to the cinema all the time*, not *we* **use to** *go to the cinema all the time*. However, in negatives and questions using the auxiliary verb **do**, the correct form is **use to**, because the form of the verb required is the infinitive: *I* **didn't use to** *like mushrooms*, not *I* **didn't used to** *like mushrooms*.

useable ▸ **adjective** variant spelling of **USABLE**.

use-by date ▸ **noun** chiefly Brit. a date marked on a perishable product, especially a foodstuff, indicating the recommended date by which it should be used or consumed.

used /juːzd/ ▸ **adjective 1** having already been used: *scrawling on the back of a used envelope*.
2 second-hand: *a used car*.

useful ▸ **adjective** able to be used for a practical purpose or in several ways: *aspirins are useful for headaches*. ■ Brit. informal very able or competent in a particular area: *a useful pace bowler*.
– PHRASES **make oneself useful** do something that is of some value or benefit to someone: *make yourself useful—get Jenny a drink*.
– DERIVATIVES **usefully adverb**.

useful load ▸ **noun** the load carried by an aircraft in addition to its own weight.

usefulness ▸ **noun** [mass noun] the quality or fact of being useful: *faults that affect the book's usefulness*.

useless ▸ **adjective** not fulfilling or not expected to achieve the intended purpose or desired outcome: *a piece of useless knowledge* | *we tried to pacify him but it was useless*. ■ informal having no ability or skill in a specified activity or area: *he was useless at football*.
– DERIVATIVES **uselessly adverb**, **uselessness noun**.

Usenet ▸ **noun** an early non-centralized computer network for the discussion of particular topics and the sharing of files via newsgroups.

user ▸ **noun 1** a person who uses or operates something. ■ a person who takes illegal drugs; an addict.
2 a person who exploits others: *he was a gifted user of other people*.
3 [mass noun] Law the continued use or enjoyment of a right.

user-definable ▸ **adjective** Computing having a function or meaning that can be specified and varied by a user.

user-friendly ▶ adjective (**user-friendlier, user-friendliest**) (of a machine or system) easy to use or understand: *the search software is user-friendly.*
– DERIVATIVES **user-friendliness** noun.

user-hostile ▶ adjective (of a machine or system) difficult to use or understand.

user interface ▶ noun Computing the means by which the user and a computer system interact, in particular the use of input devices and software.

username ▶ noun an identification used by a person with access to a computer, network, or online service.

user-oriented ▶ adjective (of a machine or system) designed with the user's convenience given priority.

ushabti /ʊˈʃabti/ ▶ noun (pl. **ushabtis**) variant form of SHABTI.

usher ▶ noun **1** a person who shows people to their seats, especially in a cinema or theatre or at a wedding. ■ Brit. a person employed to walk before a person of high rank on special occasions.
2 an official in a law court whose duties include swearing in jurors and witnesses and keeping order.
3 archaic an assistant teacher.
▶ verb [with obj. and adverbial of direction] **1** show or guide (someone) somewhere: *a waiter ushered me to a table.*
2 (**usher something in**) cause or mark the start of something new: *the railways ushered in an era of cheap mass travel.*
– ORIGIN late Middle English (denoting a doorkeeper): from Anglo-Norman French *usser*, from medieval Latin *ustiarius*, from Latin *ostiarius*, from *ostium* 'door'.

usherette ▶ noun a woman who shows people to their seats in a cinema or theatre.

Ushuaia /uːˈswʌɪə/ a port in Argentina, in Tierra del Fuego; pop. 74,400 (est. 2009). It is the southernmost town in the world.

Üsküdar /ˌuːskʊˈdɑː/ a suburb of Istanbul, on the eastern side of the Bosporus where it joins the Sea of Marmara; pop. 643,800 (est. 2009). Former name SCUTARI.

USM ▶ abbreviation Unlisted Securities Market.

USN ▶ abbreviation United States Navy.

usnic acid /ˈʌznɪk/ ▶ noun [mass noun] Biochemistry a yellow crystalline compound which is present in many lichens and is used as an antibiotic. ● A tricyclic phenol; chem. formula: $C_{18}H_{16}O_7$.
– ORIGIN mid 19th cent.: *usnic* from medieval Latin *usnea* (from Arabic *ushnah* 'moss') + -IC.

Usonian /juːˈsəʊnɪən/ ▶ adjective relating to the United States: *the Usonian city.* ■ relating to or denoting the style of buildings designed in the 1930s by Frank Lloyd Wright, characterized by inexpensive construction and flat roofs.
▶ noun a native or inhabitant of the United States. ■ a house built in the 1930s by Frank Lloyd Wright.

USP ▶ abbreviation (pl. **USPs**) unique selling point.

Uspallata Pass /ˌuːspəˈjɑːtə/ a pass over the Andes near Santiago, in southern South America.

usquebaugh /ˈʌskwɪbɔː/ ▶ noun [mass noun] chiefly Irish & Scottish whisky.
– ORIGIN late 16th cent.: from Irish and Scottish Gaelic *uisge beatha* 'water of life'; compare with WHISKY.

USS ▶ abbreviation United States Ship, used in the names of ships in the US navy: *USS Saratoga.*

USSR ▶ abbreviation historical Union of Soviet Socialist Republics.

Ust-Abakanskoe /ˌuːstabəˈkɑːnskəʊjɛ/ former name (until 1931) for ABAKAN.

ustad /ʊsˈtɑːd/ ▶ noun Indian an expert or highly skilled person, especially a musician.
– ORIGIN from Urdu *ustād*.

Ustashe /uːˈstɑːʃi/ (also **Ustashas** or **Ustashi**) ▶ plural noun [treated as sing. or pl.] the members of a Croatian extreme nationalist movement that engaged in terrorist activity before the Second World War and ruled Croatia with Nazi support after Yugoslavia was invaded and divided by the Germans in 1941.
– ORIGIN Croatian *Ustaše* 'rebels'.

Ustinov /uːˈstiːnɒf/ former name (1984–7) for IZHEVSK.

usual ▶ adjective habitually or typically occurring or done; customary: *he carried out his usual evening routine | their room was a shambles **as usual**.*
▶ noun the thing which is typically done or present: *the band was a bit sick of playing all the usuals.* ■ (**the/one's usual**) informal the drink one habitually prefers.
– DERIVATIVES **usualness** noun.
– ORIGIN late Middle English: from Old French, or from late Latin *usualis*, from Latin *usus* 'a use' (see USE).

usually ▶ adverb under normal conditions; generally: *he usually arrives home about one o'clock | heat-resistant paints are usually black or aluminium-coloured.*

usucaption /ˌjuːzjʊˈkapʃ(ə)n/ (also **usucapion** /ˌjuːzjʊˈkeɪpɪən/) ▶ noun [mass noun] Roman Law, chiefly historical the acquisition of a title or right to property by uninterrupted and undisputed possession for a prescribed term.
– ORIGIN mid 17th cent.: from medieval Latin *usucaptio(n-)*, from *usucapere* 'acquire by prescription', from *usu* 'by use' + *capere* 'take'.

usufruct /ˈjuːzjʊfrʌkt/ ▶ noun [mass noun] Roman Law the right to enjoy the use and advantages of another's property short of the destruction or waste of its substance.
– DERIVATIVES **usufructuary** adjective & noun.
– ORIGIN early 17th cent.: from medieval Latin *usufructus*, from Latin *usus (et) fructus* 'use (and) enjoyment', from *usus* 'a use' + *fructus* 'fruit'.

Usumbura /ˌuːz(ə)mˈbʊərə/ former name (until 1962) for BUJUMBURA.

usurer /ˈjuːʒ(ə)rə/ ▶ noun a person who lends money at unreasonably high rates of interest.
– ORIGIN Middle English: from Anglo-Norman French, from Old French *usure*, from Latin *usura* (see USURY).

usurious /juːˈʒʊərɪəs, juːˈzj-/ ▶ adjective relating to or characterized by usury; extortionate: *they lend money at usurious rates.*
– DERIVATIVES **usuriously** adverb.

usurp /jʊˈzəːp, jʊˈsəːp/ ▶ verb [with obj.] take (a position of power or importance) illegally or by force: *Richard usurped the throne.* ■ take the place of (someone in a position of power) illegally; supplant: *the Hanoverian dynasty had usurped the Stuarts.* ■ [no obj.] (**usurp on/upon**) archaic encroach or infringe upon (someone's rights): *the Church had usurped upon the domain of the state.*
– DERIVATIVES **usurpation** /ˌjuːzəˈpeɪʃ(ə)n, ˌjuːs-/ noun, **usurper** noun.
– ORIGIN Middle English (in the sense 'appropriate a right wrongfully'): from Old French *usurper*, from Latin *usurpare* 'seize for use'.

usury /ˈjuːʒ(ə)ri/ ▶ noun [mass noun] the action or practice of lending money at unreasonably high rates of interest. ■ archaic interest at unreasonably high rates.
– ORIGIN Middle English: from Anglo-Norman French *usurie*, or from medieval Latin *usuria*, from Latin *usura*, from *usus* 'a use' (see USE).

UT ▶ abbreviation ■ Universal Time. ■ Utah (in official postal use).

Utah /ˈjuːtɔː, -tɑː/ a state in the western US; pop. 2,736,424 (est. 2008); capital, Salt Lake City. The region became part of Mexico in 1821 and was ceded to the US in 1848, becoming the 45th state of the US in 1896.
– DERIVATIVES **Utahan** /juːˈtɔːən, -ˈtɑːən/ adjective & noun.

utahraptor /ˈjuːtɔːˌraptə, ˈjuːtə-/ ▶ noun a large dromaeosaurid dinosaur, the remains of which were discovered in Utah in 1992. It was twice the size of deinonychus. ● Genus *Utahraptor*, family Dromaeosauridae, suborder Theropoda.
– ORIGIN modern Latin, from UTAH + RAPTOR.

Utamaro /ˌuːtəˈmɑːrəʊ/, Kitagawa (1753–1806), Japanese painter and printmaker; born *Kitagawa Nebsuyoshi*. A leading exponent of the ukiyo-e school, he was noted for his sensual depictions of women.

UTC ▶ abbreviation Universal Time Coordinated. Also expanded as COORDINATED UNIVERSAL TIME.

Utd ▶ abbreviation United (in names of soccer teams): *Scunthorpe Utd.*

Ute /juːt/ ▶ noun (pl. **same** or **Utes**) **1** a member of an American Indian people living chiefly in Colorado, Utah, and New Mexico.
2 [mass noun] the Uto-Aztecan language of the Ute, now with few speakers.
▶ adjective relating to the Ute or their language.
– ORIGIN from Spanish *Yuta*; compare with PAIUTE.

ute /juːt/ ▶ noun Austral./NZ informal a utility vehicle; a pickup.
– ORIGIN 1940s: abbreviation.

utensil ▶ noun a tool, container, or other article, especially for household use: *kitchen utensils.*
– ORIGIN late Middle English (denoting domestic implements or vessels collectively): from Old French *utensile*, from medieval Latin, neuter of Latin *utensilis* 'usable', from *uti* 'to use' (see USE).

uteri plural form of UTERUS.

uterine /ˈjuːtərɪn, -ʌɪn/ ▶ adjective relating to the uterus or womb: *uterine contractions.* ■ [attrib.] born of the same mother but not having the same father: *a uterine sister.*
– ORIGIN late Middle English: from UTERUS + -INE[1], or, in the sense 'born of the same mother', from late Latin *uterinus*.

uterus ▶ noun (pl. **uteri** /-rʌɪ/ or **uteruses**) the womb (as a bodily organ, especially in medical and technical contexts).
– ORIGIN Latin.

Uther Pendragon /ˌjuːθə pɛnˈdrag(ə)n/ (in Arthurian legend) king of the Britons and father of Arthur.

utile[1] /ˈjuːtʌɪl/ ▶ adjective rare advantageous.
– ORIGIN late 15th cent.: via Old French from Latin *utilis*, from *uti* 'to use'.

utile[2] /ˈjuːtɪli/ ▶ noun a large tropical African hardwood tree with timber that is widely used as a substitute for mahogany. ● *Entandrophragma utile*, family Meliaceae.
– ORIGIN 1950s: modern Latin, specific epithet (see above).

utilitarian /jʊˌtɪlɪˈtɛːrɪən/ ▶ adjective **1** designed to be useful or practical rather than attractive.
2 Philosophy relating to or adhering to the doctrine of utilitarianism: *a utilitarian theorist.*
▶ noun Philosophy an adherent of utilitarianism.

utilitarianism ▶ noun [mass noun] the doctrine that actions are right if they are useful or for the benefit of a majority. ■ the doctrine that an action is right in so far as it promotes happiness, and that the greatest happiness of the greatest number should be the guiding principle of conduct.

> The most famous exponents of utilitarianism were Jeremy Bentham and J. S. Mill. It has been criticized for focusing on the consequences rather than the motive or intrinsic nature of an action, for the difficulty of adequately comparing the happiness of different individuals, and for failing to account for the value placed on concepts such as justice and equality.

utility ▶ noun (pl. **utilities**) **1** [mass noun] the state of being useful, profitable, or beneficial. ■ (in game theory or economics) a measure of that which is sought to be maximized in any situation involving a choice.
2 a public utility.
3 Computing a utility program.
4 Austral./NZ a utility vehicle.
▶ adjective [attrib.] **1** useful, especially through being able to perform several functions: *a utility truck.* ■ denoting a player capable of playing in several different positions in a sport.
2 functional rather than attractive: *utility clothing.*
– ORIGIN late Middle English: from Old French *utilite*, from Latin *utilitas*, from *utilis* 'useful'.

utility function ▶ noun Economics a mathematical function which ranks alternatives according to their utility to an individual.

utility knife ▶ noun a knife with a small sharp blade, often retractable, designed to cut wood, cardboard, and other materials.

utility pole ▶ noun North American term for TELEGRAPH POLE.

utility program ▶ noun Computing a program for carrying out a routine function.

utility room ▶ noun a room equipped with appliances for washing and other domestic work.

utility vehicle (also **utility truck**) ▶ noun a truck with low sides designed for carrying small loads.

utilize (also **utilise**) ▶ verb [with obj.] make practical and effective use of: *vitamin C helps your body utilize the iron present in your diet.*
– DERIVATIVES **utilizable** adjective, **utilization** noun, **utilizer** noun.
– ORIGIN early 19th cent.: from French *utiliser*, from Italian *utilizzare*, from *utile* (see UTILE[1]).

-ution ▶ suffix (forming nouns) equivalent to -ATION (as in *solution*).
– ORIGIN via French from Latin *-utio(n-)*.

utmost ▶ adjective [attrib.] most extreme; greatest: *a matter of the utmost importance.*

U

▸ noun (**the utmost**) the greatest or most extreme extent or amount: *a plot that stretches credulity to the utmost.*
– PHRASES **do one's utmost** do the most that one is able: *Dan was doing his utmost to be helpful.*
– ORIGIN Old English *ūt(e)mest* 'outermost' (see **OUT**, **-MOST**).

Uto-Aztecan /ˌjuːtəʊˈaztɛk(ə)n/ ▸ noun [mass noun] a language family of Central America and western North America including Nahuatl (the language of the Aztecs), Shoshone, and Paiute.
▸ adjective relating to or denoting this language family.

Utopia /juːˈtəʊpɪə/ ▸ noun an imagined place or state of things in which everything is perfect. The word was first used in the book *Utopia* (1516) by Sir Thomas More. The opposite of **DYSTOPIA**.
– ORIGIN based on Greek *ou* 'not' + *topos* 'place'.

utopian ▸ adjective modelled on or aiming for a state in which everything is perfect; idealistic.
▸ noun an idealistic reformer.
– DERIVATIVES **utopianism** noun.

utopian socialism ▸ noun [mass noun] socialism achieved by the moral persuasion of capitalists to surrender the means of production peacefully to the people. It was advocated by Johann Fichte and Robert Owen among others.

Utrecht /juːˈtrɛxt/ a city in the central Netherlands, capital of a province of the same name; pop. 294,737 (2008).

Utrecht, Peace of a series of treaties (1713–14) ending the War of the Spanish Succession. The disputed throne of Spain was given to the French Philip V, but the union of the French and Spanish thrones was forbidden. The House of Hanover succeeded to the British throne and the former Spanish territories in Italy were ceded to the Habsburgs.

Utrecht velvet ▸ noun [mass noun] a strong, thick plush velvet, used in upholstery.

utricle /ˈjuːtrɪk(ə)l/ ▸ noun a small cell, sac, or bladder-like protuberance in an animal or plant. ▪ (also **utriculus** /juːˈtrɪkjʊləs/) the larger of the two fluid-filled cavities forming part of the labyrinth of the inner ear (the other being the sacculus). It contains hair cells and otoliths which send signals to the brain concerning the orientation of the head.
– DERIVATIVES **utricular** /juːˈtrɪkjʊlə/ adjective.
– ORIGIN mid 18th cent.: from French *utricule* or Latin *utriculus*, diminutive of *uter* 'leather bag'.

Utrillo /juːˈtrɪləʊ/, French /ytʀijo/, Maurice (1883–1955), French painter, chiefly known for his depictions of Paris street scenes.

Utsire /ʊtˈsɪərə/ a small island off the coast of southern Norway to the north-west of Stavanger. The shipping forecast area **North Utsire** covers Norwegian coastal waters immediately to the north of the island, while **South Utsire** covers the area to the south, as far as the mouth of the Skagerrak.

uttapam /ˈʊtəpʌm/ ▸ noun Indian a thick pancake made from rice flour to which onions, tomatoes, chillies, and other vegetables are added during cooking.
– ORIGIN from Tamil.

Uttarakhand /ˈʊtərəˌkʌnd/ a state in northern India, formed in 2000 from the northern part of Uttar Pradesh; capital, Dehra Dun. Former name (until 2007) **Uttaranchal** /ˈʊtərəntʃəl/.

Uttar Pradesh /ˌʊtə prəˈdɛʃ/ a state in northern India, bordering on Tibet and Nepal; capital, Lucknow. It was formed in 1950 from the United Provinces of Agra and Oudh.

utter[1] ▸ adjective [attrib.] complete; absolute: *Charlotte stared at her in utter amazement.*
– ORIGIN Old English *ūtera*, *ūttra* 'outer', comparative of *ūt* 'out'; compare with **OUTER**.

utter[2] ▸ verb [with obj.] **1** make (a sound) with one's voice: *he uttered an exasperated snort.* ▪ say (something) aloud: *they are busily scribbling down every word she utters.*
2 Law put (forged money) into circulation.
– DERIVATIVES **utterable** adjective, **utterer** noun.
– ORIGIN late Middle English: from Middle Dutch *ūteren* 'speak, make known, give currency to coins'.

utterance ▸ noun a spoken word, statement, or vocal sound. ▪ [mass noun] the action of saying or expressing something aloud: *the simple utterance of a few platitudes.* ▪ Linguistics an uninterrupted chain of spoken or written language.

utterly ▸ adverb [usu. as submodifier] completely and without qualification; absolutely: *he looked utterly ridiculous.*

uttermost ▸ adjective & noun another term for **UTMOST**.

U-turn ▸ noun the turning of a vehicle in a U-shaped course so as to face in the opposite direction. ▪ a change of plan, especially a reversal of political policy: *another U-turn by the government.*

UUC ▸ abbreviation Ulster Unionist Council.

UV ▸ abbreviation ultraviolet.

UVA ▸ abbreviation ultraviolet radiation of relatively long wavelengths.

uvarovite /uːˈvarə(ʊ)vʌɪt/ ▸ noun [mass noun] an emerald green variety of garnet, containing chromium.
– ORIGIN mid 19th cent.: from the name of Count Sergei S. *Uvarov* (1785–1855), Russian statesman, + **-ITE**[1].

UVB ▸ abbreviation ultraviolet radiation of relatively short wavelengths.

UVC ▸ abbreviation ultraviolet radiation of very short wavelengths, which does not penetrate the earth's ozone layer.

uvea /ˈjuːvɪə/ ▸ noun the pigmented layer of the eye, lying beneath the sclera and cornea, and comprising the iris, choroid, and ciliary body.
– DERIVATIVES **uveal** adjective.
– ORIGIN late Middle English (denoting the choroid layer of the eye): from medieval Latin, from Latin *uva* 'grape'.

uveitis /ˌjuːvɪˈʌɪtɪs/ ▸ noun [mass noun] Medicine inflammation of the uvea.

uvula /ˈjuːvjʊlə/ ▸ noun (pl. **uvulae** /-liː/ or **uvulas**) Anatomy (also **palatine uvula**) a fleshy extension at the back of the soft palate which hangs above the throat. ▪ a similar fleshy, hanging structure in any organ of the body, particularly one at the opening of the bladder.
– ORIGIN late Middle English: from late Latin, diminutive of Latin *uva* 'grape'.

uvular /ˈjuːvjʊlə/ ▸ adjective **1** Phonetics (of a sound) articulated with the back of the tongue and the uvula, as *r* in French and *q* in Arabic.
2 Anatomy relating to the uvula.
▸ noun Phonetics a uvular consonant.

UWB ▸ abbreviation ultra wideband, a radio communications technology for the transmission of signals over a very broad range of frequencies, typically using very low-energy pulses with a duration of a nanosecond or less.

uxorial /ʌkˈsɔːrɪəl/ ▸ adjective relating to a wife.
– ORIGIN early 19th cent.: from Latin *uxor* 'wife' + **-IAL**.

uxoricide /ʌkˈsɔːrɪsʌɪd/ ▸ noun [mass noun] the killing of one's wife. ▪ [count noun] a man who kills his wife.
– ORIGIN mid 19th cent.: from Latin *uxor* 'wife' + **-CIDE**.

uxorilocal /ˌʌksɒrɪˈləʊk(ə)l/ ▸ adjective another term for **MATRILOCAL**.
– ORIGIN 1930s: from Latin *uxorius* 'of a wife' (from *uxor* 'wife') + **LOCAL**.

uxorious /ʌkˈsɔːrɪəs/ ▸ adjective having or showing a great or excessive fondness for one's wife.
– DERIVATIVES **uxoriously** adverb, **uxoriousness** noun.
– ORIGIN late 16th cent.: from Latin *uxoriosus*, from *uxor* 'wife'.

Uygur ▸ noun & adjective variant spelling of **UIGHUR**.

Uzbek /ˈʊzbɛk, ˈʌz-/ ▸ noun **1** a member of a Turkic people living mainly in the republic of Uzbekistan and also in Turkmenistan, Tajikistan, Kazakhstan, and Afghanistan. ▪ a native or inhabitant of Uzbekistan.
2 [mass noun] the Turkic language of Uzbekistan, having some 16 million speakers.
▸ adjective relating to Uzbekistan, the Uzbeks, or their language.
– ORIGIN the name in Uzbek.

Uzbekistan /ʊzˌbɛkɪˈstɑːn, ʌz-, -ˈstan/ an independent republic in central Asia, lying south and south-east of the Aral Sea; pop. 27,606,000 (est. 2009); official language, Uzbek; capital, Tashkent.

> Uzbekistan was formerly a constituent republic of the USSR (established in 1924). It became independent within the Commonwealth of Independent States on the break-up of the Soviet Union in 1991.

Uzi /ˈuːzi/ ▸ noun a type of sub-machine gun of Israeli design.
– ORIGIN 1950s: from *Uziel* Gal (1923–2002), the Israeli army officer who designed it.

U

Vv

V¹ (also **v**) ▸ **noun** (pl. **Vs** or **V's**) **1** the twenty-second letter of the alphabet. ▪ denoting the next after U in a set of items, categories, etc.
2 (also **vee**) a shape like that of a letter V: [in combination] *deep, V-shaped valleys.* ▪ [as modifier] denoting an internal-combustion engine with a number of cylinders arranged in two rows at an angle to each other in a V-shape: *a V-engine.*
3 the Roman numeral for five.

V² ▸ **abbreviation** ▪ Vatican City (international vehicle registration). ▪ volt(s).
▸ **symbol** ▪ the chemical element vanadium. ▪ voltage or potential difference: $V = IR$. ▪ (in mathematical formulae) volume: $pV = nRT$.

v (also **v.**) ▸ **abbreviation** ▪ Grammar verb. ▪ (in textual references) verse. ▪ verso. ▪ versus. ▪ very. ▪ (in textual references) *vide.*
▸ **symbol** velocity.

V. & A. ▸ **abbreviation** Victoria and Albert Museum.

V-1 ▸ **noun** a small flying bomb powered by a simple jet engine, used by the Germans in the Second World War. Also called DOODLEBUG.
– ORIGIN abbreviation of German *Vergeltungswaffe* 'reprisal weapon'.

V-2 ▸ **noun** a rocket-powered flying bomb which was the first ballistic missile, used by the Germans in the Second World War.
– ORIGIN see **V-1**.

VA ▸ **abbreviation** ▪ (in the UK) Order of Victoria and Albert. ▪ (in the US) Veterans' Administration. ▪ Vicar Apostolic. ▪ Vice Admiral. ▪ Virginia (in official postal use).

Va ▸ **abbreviation** Virginia.

Vaal /vɑːl/ a river of South Africa, the chief tributary of the Orange River, rising in the Drakensberg Mountains and flowing 1,200 km (750 miles) southwestwards to the Orange River near Douglas, in Northern Cape. For much of its length it forms the border between North West and Free State.

Vaasa /ˈvɑːsə/ a port in western Finland, on the Gulf of Bothnia; pop. 58,607 (2009). Swedish name **VASA**.

vac ▸ **noun** Brit. **1** informal term for VACATION.
2 informal term for VACUUM CLEANER.

vacancy ▸ **noun** (pl. **vacancies**) **1** an unoccupied position or job: *a vacancy for a shorthand typist.* ▪ an available room in a hotel or other establishment providing accommodation.
2 [mass noun] empty space: *Cathy stared into vacancy, seeing nothing.*
3 [mass noun] lack of intelligence or understanding: *vacancy, vanity, and inane deception.*

vacant ▸ **adjective 1** (of a place) not occupied; empty: *40 per cent of the offices are still vacant.* ▪ (of a position or employment) not filled: *the President resigned and the post was left vacant.*
2 having or showing no intelligence or interest: *a vacant stare.*
– DERIVATIVES **vacantly** adverb.
– ORIGIN Middle English: from Old French, or from Latin *vacant-* 'remaining empty', from the verb *vacare.*

vacant possession ▸ **noun** [mass noun] Brit. the right of a purchaser to exclusive use of a property on completion of the sale, any previous occupant having moved out.

vacate /verˈkeɪt, vəˈkeɪt/ ▸ **verb** [with obj.] **1** leave (a place that one previously occupied): *rooms must be vacated by noon on the last day of your holiday.* ▪ give up (a position or employment): *he vacated his office as Director.*
2 Law cancel or annul (a judgement, contract, or charge).
– ORIGIN mid 17th cent. (as a legal term, also in the sense 'make ineffective'): from Latin *vacat-* 'left empty', from the verb *vacare.*

vacation ▸ **noun 1** a fixed holiday period between terms in universities and law courts. ▪ N. Amer. a holiday: *he took a vacation in the south of France | people come here on vacation.*
2 [mass noun] the action of leaving something one previously occupied: *his marriage was the reason for the vacation of his fellowship.*
▸ **verb** [no obj.] N. Amer. take a holiday: *I was vacationing in Europe with my family.*
– DERIVATIVES **vacationer** noun (N. Amer.).
– ORIGIN late Middle English: from Old French, or from Latin *vacatio(n-)*, from *vacare* 'be unoccupied' (see VACATE).

vacationland ▸ **noun** N. Amer. an area providing attractions for holidaymakers.

vaccinate /ˈvaksɪneɪt/ ▸ **verb** [with obj.] treat with a vaccine to produce immunity against a disease; inoculate: *all the children were vaccinated against tuberculosis.*
– DERIVATIVES **vaccination** noun, **vaccinator** noun.

vaccine /ˈvaksiːn, -ɪn/ ▸ **noun** Medicine an antigenic substance prepared from the causative agent of a disease or a synthetic substitute, used to provide immunity against one or several diseases: *there is no vaccine against HIV infection.* ▪ Computing a program designed to detect computer viruses and inactivate them.
– ORIGIN late 18th cent.: from Latin *vaccinus*, from *vacca* 'cow' (because of the early use of the cowpox virus against smallpox).

vaccinia /vakˈsɪnɪə/ ▸ **noun** [mass noun] Medicine cowpox, or the virus which causes it.
– ORIGIN early 19th cent.: modern Latin, from Latin *vaccinus* (see VACCINE).

vaccinology /vaksɪˈnɒlədʒi/ ▸ **noun** [mass noun] the branch of medicine concerned with the development of vaccines.
– DERIVATIVES **vaccinologist** noun.

Vacherin /ˈvaʃ(ə)rã/ ▸ **noun** [mass noun] a type of soft French or Swiss cheese made from cow's milk.
– ORIGIN French, from earlier *vachelin*, from *vache* 'cow'.

vacillate /ˈvasɪleɪt/ ▸ **verb** [no obj.] waver between different opinions or actions; be indecisive: *I vacillated between teaching and journalism.*
– DERIVATIVES **vacillator** noun.
– ORIGIN late 16th cent. (in the sense 'sway unsteadily'): from Latin *vacillat-* 'swayed', from the verb *vacillare.*

vacillating /ˈvasɪleɪtɪŋ/ ▸ **adjective** wavering between different opinions or actions; irresolute: *he was accused of vacillating leadership.*

vacillation /vasɪˈleɪʃ(ə)n/ ▸ **noun** [mass noun] the inability to decide between different opinions or actions; indecision: *the First Minister's vacillation over the affair.*

vacua plural form of VACUUM.

vacuity /vəˈkjuːɪti/ ▸ **noun** [mass noun] **1** lack of thought or intelligence; empty-headedness: *he denounced what he considered the frivolity or vacuity of much contemporary painting.*
2 empty space; emptiness.

vacuole /ˈvakjʊəʊl/ ▸ **noun** Biology a space or vesicle within the cytoplasm of a cell, enclosed by a membrane and typically containing fluid. ▪ a small cavity or space in tissue, especially in nervous tissue as the result of disease.
– DERIVATIVES **vacuolar** /ˈvakjʊələ/ adjective, **vacuolation** noun.
– ORIGIN mid 19th cent.: from French, diminutive of Latin *vacuus* 'empty'.

vacuous /ˈvakjʊəs/ ▸ **adjective 1** having or showing a lack of thought or intelligence; mindless: *a vacuous smile | vacuous slogans.*
2 archaic empty.
– DERIVATIVES **vacuously** adverb, **vacuousness** noun.
– ORIGIN mid 17th cent. (in the sense 'empty of matter'): from Latin *vacuus* 'empty' + -OUS.

vacuum /ˈvakjʊəm/ ▸ **noun** (pl. **vacuums** or **vacua** /-jʊə/) **1** a space entirely devoid of matter. ▪ a space or container from which the air has been completely or partly removed. ▪ [usu. in sing.] a gap left by the loss, death, or departure of someone or something significant: *the political vacuum left by the death of the Emperor.*
2 (pl. **vacuums**) a vacuum cleaner.
▸ **verb** [with obj.] clean with a vacuum cleaner: *the room needs to be vacuumed.*
– PHRASES **in a vacuum** (of an activity or a problem to be considered) isolated from the normal context in which it can best be understood or assessed.
– ORIGIN mid 16th cent.: modern Latin, neuter of Latin *vacuus* 'empty'.

vacuum brake ▸ **noun** a railway vehicle brake operated by changes in pressure in a continuous pipe which is generally kept exhausted of air by a pump and controls similar brakes throughout the train.

vacuum cleaner ▸ **noun** an electrical apparatus that by means of suction collects dust and small particles from floors and other surfaces.
– DERIVATIVES **vacuum-clean** verb.

vacuum distillation ▸ **noun** [mass noun] Chemistry distillation of a liquid under reduced pressure, enabling it to boil at a lower temperature than normal.

vacuum extraction ▸ **noun** [mass noun] the application of reduced pressure to extract something, particularly to assist childbirth or as a method of abortion, or as a technique for removing components of a chemical mixture.

vacuum extractor ▸ **noun** a cup-shaped appliance for performing vacuum extraction in childbirth. Also called VENTOUSE.

vacuum flask ▸ **noun** chiefly Brit. a container that keeps a substance hot or cold by means of a double wall enclosing a vacuum.

vacuum gauge ▸ **noun** a gauge for testing pressure after the production of a vacuum.

vacuum-pack ▸ **verb** [with obj.] seal (a product) in a pack or wrapping after any air has been removed so that the pack or wrapping is tight and firm: (as adj. **vacuum-packed**) *vacuum-packed cheese.*
▸ **noun** (**vacuum pack**) a pack of this kind.

vacuum pump ▶ noun a pump used for creating a vacuum.

vacuum tube ▶ noun a sealed glass tube containing a near-vacuum which allows the free passage of electric current.

VAD ▶ abbreviation historical Voluntary Aid Detachment, a British organization of first-aid workers and nurses.

vada /ˈvɑːdə/ (also **wada**) ▶ noun an Indian dish consisting of a ball made from ground pulses and deep-fried.
– ORIGIN Hindi *vaḍā*.

vade mecum /ˌvɑːdi ˈmeɪkəm, ˌveɪdi ˈmiːkəm/ ▶ noun a handbook or guide that is kept constantly at hand for consultation.
– ORIGIN early 17th cent.: modern Latin, literally 'go with me'.

Vadodara /vəˈdəʊdərə/ a city in the state of Gujarat, western India; pop. 1,513,800 (est. 2009). The capital of the former state of Baroda, the city was known as Baroda until 1976.

vadose /ˈveɪdəʊs/ ▶ adjective Geology relating to or denoting underground water above the water table. Compare with **PHREATIC**.
– ORIGIN late 19th cent.: from Latin *vadosus*, from *vadum* 'shallow expanse of water'.

Vaduz /vaˈdʊts/ the capital of Liechtenstein; pop. 5,000 (est. 2007).

vagabond ▶ noun a person who wanders from place to place without a home or job. ■ informal, dated a dishonest or unprincipled person.
▶ adjective [attrib.] having no settled home.
▶ verb [no obj.] archaic wander about as or like a vagabond.
– DERIVATIVES **vagabondage** noun.
– ORIGIN Middle English (originally denoting a criminal): from Old French, or from Latin *vagabundus*, from *vagari* 'wander'.

vagal ▶ adjective relating to the vagus nerve.

vagarious /vəˈɡɛːrɪəs/ ▶ adjective rare erratic and unpredictable in behaviour or direction.
– ORIGIN late 18th cent. (in the sense 'changing, inconstant'): from **VAGARY** + **-OUS**.

vagary /ˈveɪɡ(ə)ri/ ▶ noun (pl. **vagaries**) (usu. **vagaries**) an unexpected and inexplicable change in a situation or in someone's behaviour: *the vagaries of the weather*.
– ORIGIN late 16th cent. (also as a verb in the sense 'roam'): from Latin *vagari* 'wander'.

vagi plural form of **VAGUS**.

vagina /vəˈdʒʌɪnə/ ▶ noun (pl. **vaginas** or **vaginae** /-niː/) **1** the muscular tube leading from the external genitals to the cervix of the uterus in women and most female mammals.
2 Botany & Zoology any sheath-like structure, especially a sheath formed round a stem by the base of a leaf.
– DERIVATIVES **vaginal** adjective, **vaginally** adverb.
– ORIGIN late 17th cent.: from Latin, literally 'sheath, scabbard'.

vagina dentata /dɛnˈtɑːtə/ ▶ noun the motif of a vagina with teeth, occurring in folklore and fantasy and said to symbolize male fears of castration or the dangers of sexual intercourse.
– ORIGIN early 20th cent.: *dentata*, feminine of Latin *dentatus* 'having teeth'.

vaginal plug ▶ noun Zoology a secretion which blocks the vagina of some rodents and insectivores after mating.

vaginismus /ˌvadʒɪˈnɪzməs/ ▶ noun [mass noun] painful spasmodic contraction of the vagina in response to physical contact or pressure, especially during sexual intercourse.
– ORIGIN mid 19th cent.: modern Latin, from Latin *vagina* (see **VAGINA**).

V

vaginitis /ˌvadʒɪˈnʌɪtɪs/ ▶ noun [mass noun] inflammation of the vagina.

vaginoplasty /vəˈdʒʌɪnə(ʊ)plasti/ ▶ noun [mass noun] Medicine plastic surgery performed to create a vagina.
– ORIGIN late 19th cent.: from **VAGINA** + **-PLASTY**.

vaginosis /ˌvadʒɪˈnəʊsɪs/ ▶ noun [mass noun] a bacterial infection of the vagina causing a smelly white discharge.

vagotomy /veɪˈɡɒtəmi/ ▶ noun (pl. **vagotomies**) [mass noun] a surgical operation in which one or more branches of the vagus nerve are cut, typically to reduce the rate of gastric secretion (e.g. in treating peptic ulcers).
– DERIVATIVES **vagotomized** (also **vagotomised**) adjective.

vagrancy /ˈveɪɡr(ə)nsi/ ▶ noun [mass noun] the state of living as a vagrant; homelessness: *a descent into vagrancy and drug abuse*.

vagrant /ˈveɪɡr(ə)nt/ ▶ noun a person without a settled home or regular work who wanders from place to place and lives by begging. ■ archaic a wanderer. ■ Ornithology a bird that has strayed or been blown from its usual range or migratory route. Also called **ACCIDENTAL**.
▶ adjective [attrib.] relating to or living the life of a vagrant: *vagrant beggars*. ■ moving from place to place; wandering: *vagrant whales*. ■ literary moving or behaving unpredictably; inconstant: *the vagrant heart of my mother*.
– DERIVATIVES **vagrantly** adverb.
– ORIGIN late Middle English: from Anglo-Norman French *vagarant* 'wandering about', from the verb *vagrer*.

vague ▶ adjective of uncertain, indefinite, or unclear character or meaning: *many patients suffer vague symptoms*. ■ thinking or communicating in an unfocused or imprecise way: *he had been very vague about his activities*.
– DERIVATIVES **vagueness** noun, **vaguish** adjective.
– ORIGIN mid 16th cent.: from French, or from Latin *vagus* 'wandering, uncertain'.

vaguely ▶ adverb **1** in a way that is uncertain, indefinite or unclear; roughly: *he vaguely remembered talking to her once*. ■ in a way that is unfocused or lacks attention; absent-mindedly: *he nodded vaguely*.
2 [as submodifier] slightly: *he looked vaguely familiar*.

vagus /ˈveɪɡəs/ ▶ noun (pl. **vagi** /-dʒʌɪ, -ɡʌɪ/) (also **vagus nerve**) Anatomy each of the tenth pair of cranial nerves, supplying the heart, lungs, upper digestive tract, and other organs of the chest and abdomen.
– ORIGIN mid 19th cent.: from Latin (see **VAGUE**).

vaidya /vɛːdjə/ (also **vaid** /vɛːd/) ▶ noun a practitioner of Ayurvedic medicine.
– ORIGIN from Hindi *vaidyă*.

vail /veɪl/ ▶ verb [with obj.] archaic take off or lower (one's hat or crown) as a token of respect or submission. ■ [no obj.] take off one's hat or otherwise show respect or submission to someone.
– ORIGIN Middle English (originally in the sense 'lower (one's eyes, weapon, banner, etc.) as a sign of submission'): shortening of obsolete *avale*, from Old French *avaler* 'to lower', from *a val* 'down' (literally 'in the valley').

vain ▶ adjective **1** having or showing an excessively high opinion of one's appearance, abilities, or worth: *their flattery made him vain | a vain woman with a streak of snobbery*.
2 [attrib.] producing no result; useless: *a vain attempt to tidy up the room | the vain hope of finding work*. ■ having no likelihood of fulfilment; empty: *a vain boast*.
– PHRASES **in vain** without success or a result: *they waited in vain for a response*. **take someone's name in vain** use someone's name in a way that shows a lack of respect.
– DERIVATIVES **vainly** adverb.
– ORIGIN Middle English (in the sense 'devoid of real worth'): via Old French from Latin *vanus* 'empty, without substance'.

vainglory ▶ noun [mass noun] literary inordinate pride in oneself or one's achievements; excessive vanity.
– DERIVATIVES **vainglorious** adjective, **vaingloriously** adverb, **vaingloriousness** noun.
– ORIGIN Middle English: suggested by Old French *vaine gloire*, Latin *vana gloria*.

vair /vɛː/ ▶ noun [mass noun] **1** fur obtained from a variety of red squirrel, used in the 13th and 14th centuries as a trimming or lining for garments.
2 Heraldry fur represented by interlocking rows of shield-shaped or bell-shaped figures which are typically alternately blue and white, as a tincture.
– ORIGIN Middle English: via Old French from Latin *varius* (see **VARIOUS**).

vairy /ˈvɛːri/ ▶ adjective Heraldry of a pattern resembling vair but usually in other colours.

Vaishnava /ˈvʌɪʃnəvə/ ▶ noun a member of one of the main branches of modern Hinduism, devoted to the worship of the god Vishnu as the supreme being. Compare with **SAIVA**.
– ORIGIN from Sanskrit *vaiṣṇava*.

Vaisya /ˈvʌɪsjə, -ʃjə/ (also **Vaishya**) ▶ noun a member of the third of the four Hindu castes, comprising the merchants and farmers.
– ORIGIN from Sanskrit *vaiśya* 'peasant, labourer'.

vajra /ˈvʌdʒrə/ ▶ noun (in Buddhism and Hinduism) a thunderbolt or mythical weapon, especially one wielded by the god Indra.
– ORIGIN Sanskrit.

Vajrayana /ˌvadʒrəˈjɑːnə/ ▶ noun [mass noun] the Tantric tradition of Buddhism, especially when regarded as distinct from the Mahayana tradition from which it developed.
– ORIGIN Sanskrit *vajrayāna*, from *vajra* 'thunderbolt' (the god Indra's symbolic vehicle) and *yāna* 'path, journey'.

vakil /vəˈkiːl/ (also **vakeel**) ▶ noun Indian **1** a lawyer or solicitor.
2 an agent or representative.
– ORIGIN from Persian and Urdu *wakīl*, Turkish *vakīl*, from Arabic *wakīl*.

valance /ˈval(ə)ns/ (also **valence**) ▶ noun a length of decorative drapery attached to the canopy or frame of a bed in order to screen the structure or the space beneath it. ■ a sheet with a deep pleated or gathered border that is designed to hang down over the mattress and sides of a bed. ■ chiefly N. Amer. a length of decorative drapery hung above a window to screen the curtain fittings. ■ a protective panel screening the wheels of a vehicle.
– DERIVATIVES **valanced** adjective.
– ORIGIN late Middle English: perhaps Anglo-Norman French, from a shortened form of Old French *avaler* 'descend' (see **VAIL**).

vale[1] /veɪl/ ▶ noun a valley (used in place names or as a poetic term): *the Vale of Glamorgan*.
– PHRASES **vale of tears** literary the world regarded as a scene of trouble or sorrow.
– ORIGIN Middle English: from Old French *val*, from Latin *vallis, valles*.

vale[2] /ˈvɑːleɪ/ archaic ▶ exclamation farewell.
▶ noun a written or spoken farewell.
– ORIGIN Latin, literally 'be well!, be strong!', imperative of *valere*.

valediction /ˌvalɪˈdɪkʃ(ə)n/ ▶ noun [mass noun] the action of saying farewell: *he lifted his hand and spread his palm in valediction*. ■ [count noun] a statement or address made at or as a farewell: *his official memorial valediction*.
– ORIGIN mid 17th cent.: based on Latin *vale* 'goodbye' + *dicere* 'to say', on the pattern of *benediction*.

valedictorian /ˌvalɪdɪkˈtɔːrɪən/ ▶ noun (in North America) a student who delivers the valedictory at a graduation ceremony.

valedictory /ˌvalɪˈdɪkt(ə)ri/ ▶ adjective serving as a farewell: *a valedictory wave*.
▶ noun (pl. **valedictories**) a farewell address.

valence[1] /ˈveɪl(ə)ns/ ▶ noun Chemistry & Linguistics another term for **VALENCY**. ■ [as modifier] relating to or denoting electrons involved in or available for chemical bond formation: *molecules with unpaired valence electrons*.

valence[2] ▶ noun variant spelling of **VALANCE**.

Valencia /vəˈlɛnsɪə/, Spanish /baˈlenθja, -sja/ **1** an autonomous region of eastern Spain, on the Mediterranean coast. It was formerly a Moorish kingdom (1021–1238). ■ the capital of Valencia, a port on the Mediterranean coast; pop. 807,200 (2008).
2 a city in northern Venezuela; pop. 1,408,400 (est. 2009).

Valenciennes /ˌvalɒ̃ˈsjɛn/ ▶ noun [mass noun] a type of bobbin lace.
– ORIGIN named after a town in NE France, where it was made in the 17th and 18th cents.

valency /ˈveɪl(ə)nsi/ ▶ noun (pl. **valencies**) Chemistry, chiefly Brit. the combining power of an element, especially as measured by the number of hydrogen atoms it can displace or combine with: *carbon always has a valency of 4*. Compare with **VALENCE**[1]. ■ Linguistics the number of grammatical elements with which a particular word, especially a verb, combines in a sentence.
– ORIGIN early 17th cent.: from late Latin *valentia* 'power, competence', from *valere* 'be well or strong'.

valentine ▶ noun a card sent, often anonymously, on St Valentine's Day, 14 February, to a person one loves or is attracted to. ■ a person to whom one sends such a card or whom one asks to be one's sweetheart.
– ORIGIN late Middle English (denoting a person chosen (sometimes by lot) as a sweetheart or special friend): from Old French *Valentin*, from Latin *Valentinus*.

Valentine, St either of two early Italian saints (who may have been the same person) traditionally commemorated on 14 February: a Roman priest martyred *c.*269 and a bishop of Terni martyred at Rome.

St Valentine is traditionally regarded as the patron of lovers.

Valentino /ˌvalənˈtiːnəʊ/, Rudolph (1895–1926), Italian-born American actor; born *Rodolfo Guglielmi di Valentina d'Antonguolla*. He played the romantic hero in silent films such as *The Sheikh* (1921).

Valera, Eamon de, see **DE VALERA**.

Valerian /vəˈlɪərɪən/ (d.260), Roman emperor 253–60; Latin name *Publius Licinius Valerianus*. He renewed the persecution of the Christians initiated by Decius.

valerian /vəˈlɪərɪən/ ▸ **noun** a Eurasian plant which typically bears clusters of small pink or white flowers. ● Family Valerianaceae: several species, in particular **common valerian** (*Valeriana officinalis*), a valued medicinal herb, and the Mediterranean **red valerian** (*Centranthus ruber*), grown for its spurred flowers which attract butterflies.
■ [mass noun] a drug obtained from the root of common valerian, used as a sedative and antispasmodic.
– ORIGIN late Middle English: from Old French *valeriane*, from medieval Latin *valeriana* (*herba*), apparently the feminine of *Valerianus* 'of Valerius' (a personal name).

valeric acid /vəˈlɛrɪk, -ˈlɪərɪk/ ▸ **noun** Chemistry another term for **PENTANOIC ACID**.
– DERIVATIVES **valerate** noun.
– ORIGIN mid 19th cent.: *valeric* from **VALERIAN** + **-IC**.

Valéry /ˌvalɛˈriː/, French /valeʀi/, (Ambroise) Paul (Toussaint Jules) (1871–1945), French poet, essayist, and critic. His poetry, influenced by symbolist poets such as Mallarmé, includes *La Jeune parque* (1917) and 'Le Cimetière marin' (1922).

valet /ˈvalɪt, ˈvaleɪ/ ▸ **noun 1** a man's personal male attendant, who is responsible for his clothes and appearance. ■ a hotel employee who attends to the clothes of guests.
2 N. Amer. a person employed to clean or park cars.
▸ **verb** (**valets, valeting, valeted**) [with obj.] **1** act as a valet to (a particular man). ■ [no obj.] work as a valet.
2 clean (a car), especially on the inside.
– ORIGIN late 15th cent. (denoting a footman acting as an attendant to a horseman): from French; related to **VASSAL**.

valeta ▸ **noun** variant spelling of **VELETA**.

valetudinarian /ˌvalɪtjuːdɪˈnɛːrɪən/ ▸ **noun** a person who is unduly anxious about their health. ■ a person suffering from poor health.
▸ **adjective** showing undue concern about one's health. ■ suffering from poor health.
– ORIGIN early 18th cent.: from Latin *valetudinarius* 'in ill health' (from *valetudo* 'health', from *valere* 'be well') + **-AN**.

valetudinary /ˌvalɪˈtjuːdɪn(ə)ri/ ▸ **adjective & noun** (pl. **valetudinaries**) another term for **VALETUDINARIAN**.

valgus /ˈvalgəs/ ▸ **noun** [mass noun] Medicine a deformity involving oblique displacement of part of a limb away from the midline. The opposite of **VARUS**.
– ORIGIN early 19th cent.: from Latin, literally 'knock-kneed'.

Valhalla /valˈhalə/ Scandinavian Mythology a palace in which heroes killed in battle were believed to feast with Odin for eternity.
– ORIGIN modern Latin, from Old Norse *Valhǫll*, from *valr* 'the slain' + *hǫll* 'hall'.

valiant ▸ **adjective** possessing or showing courage or determination: *she made a valiant effort to hold her anger in check | a valiant warrior.*
– DERIVATIVES **valiantly** adverb.
– ORIGIN Middle English (also in the sense 'robust, well-built'): from Old French *vailant*, based on Latin *valere* 'be strong'.

valid ▸ **adjective** (of an argument or point) having a sound basis in logic or fact; reasonable or cogent: *a valid criticism.* ■ legally binding due to having been executed in compliance with the law: *a valid contract.* ■ legally or officially acceptable: *the visas are valid for thirty days | a valid password.*
– DERIVATIVES **validly** adverb.
– ORIGIN late 16th cent.: from French *valide* or Latin *validus* 'strong', from *valere* 'be strong'.

validate ▸ **verb** [with obj.] check or prove the validity or accuracy of: *all analytical methods should be validated in respect of accuracy.* ■ demonstrate or support the truth or value of: *acclaim was seen as a means of validating one's existence.* ■ make or declare legally valid.
– DERIVATIVES **validation** noun.
– ORIGIN mid 17th cent. (in the sense 'make legally valid'): from medieval Latin *validat-* 'made legally valid', from the verb *validare*, from Latin *validus* (see **VALID**).

validity ▸ **noun** [mass noun] the quality of being logically or factually sound; soundness or cogency: *one might question the validity of our data.* ■ the state of being legally or officially binding or acceptable: *return travel must be within the validity of the ticket.*

valine /ˈveɪliːn/ ▸ **noun** [mass noun] Biochemistry an amino acid which is a constituent of most proteins. It is an essential nutrient in the diet of vertebrates. ● Chem. formula: $(CH_3)_2CHCH(NH_2)COOH$.
– ORIGIN early 20th cent.: from *val(eric acid)* + **-INE**[4].

valise /vəˈliːz/ ▸ **noun** a small travelling bag or suitcase.
– ORIGIN early 17th cent.: from French, from Italian *valigia*; compare with medieval Latin *valesia*, of unknown origin.

Valium /ˈvalɪəm/ ▸ **noun** trademark for **DIAZEPAM**.
– ORIGIN 1960s: of unknown origin.

Valkyrie /valˈkɪəri, ˈvalkɪri/ ▸ **noun** Scandinavian Mythology each of Odin's twelve handmaids who conducted the slain warriors of their choice from the battlefield to Valhalla.
– ORIGIN from Old Norse *Valkyrja*, literally 'chooser of the slain', from *valr* 'the slain' + *kyrja* 'chooser'.

Valladolid /ˌvalədəˈliːd/, Spanish /bajaðoˈlið/ **1** a city in northern Spain, capital of Castilla-León region; pop. 318,461 (2008). It was the principal residence of the kings of Castile in the 15th century.
2 former name (until 1828) for **MORELIA**.

vallecula /vaˈlɛkjʊlə/ ▸ **noun** (pl. **valleculae** /-liː/) Anatomy & Botany a groove or furrow.
– DERIVATIVES **vallecular** adjective.
– ORIGIN mid 19th cent.: from a late Latin variant of Latin *vallicula*, diminutive of Latin *vallis* 'valley'.

Valle d'Aosta /ˌvaleɪ dɑːˈɒstə/ an Alpine region in the north-western corner of Italy; capital, Aosta.

Valletta /vəˈlɛtə/ the capital and chief port of Malta; pop. 6,300 (est. 2006); urban harbour area pop. 199,000 (est. 2007).
– ORIGIN named after Jean de *Valette*, Grand Master of the Knights of St John, who built the town after the victory over the Turks in 1565.

valley ▸ **noun** (pl. **valleys**) **1** a low area of land between hills or mountains, typically with a river or stream flowing through it.
2 Architecture an internal angle formed by the intersecting planes of a roof, or by the slope of a roof and a wall.
– ORIGIN Middle English: from Old French *valee*, based on Latin *vallis*, *valles*; compare with **VALE**[1].

valley fever (also **San Joaquin valley fever**) ▸ **noun** [mass noun] N. Amer. informal term for **COCCIDIOIDOMYCOSIS**.

Valley Forge the site on the Schuylkill River in Pennsylvania, about 32 km (20 miles) to the north-west of Philadelphia, where George Washington's Continental Army spent the winter of 1777–8 in conditions of extreme hardship.

Valley Girl ▸ **noun** US informal a fashionable and affluent teenage girl from the San Fernando valley in southern California.

Valley of the Kings a valley near ancient Thebes (present-day Luxor) in Egypt where the pharaohs of the New Kingdom (*c.*1550–1070 BC) were buried.

vallum /ˈvaləm/ ▸ **noun** (in ancient Rome) a defensive wall, rampart, or stockade.
– ORIGIN Latin, collective from *vallus* 'stake, palisade'.

Valois[1] /ˈvalwɑː/ **1** a medieval duchy of northern France, home of the Valois dynasty.
2 the French royal house from the accession of Philip VI in 1328 to the death of Henry III (1589).

Valois[2], Dame Ninette de, see **DE VALOIS**.

Valona /vaˈlɒnə/ Italian name for **VLORË**.

valonia /vəˈləʊnɪə/ ▸ **noun** (also **valonia oak**) an evergreen oak tree native to southern Europe and western Asia. See also **ALEPPO GALL**. ● *Quercus macrolepis*, family Fagaceae.
■ the acorn cups of the valonia, which yield a black dye and are used in tanning.
– ORIGIN early 18th cent.: from Italian *vallonia*, based on Greek *balanos* 'acorn'.

valor ▸ **noun** US spelling of **VALOUR**.

valorize /ˈvalərʌɪz/ (also **valorise**) ▸ **verb** [with obj.] give or ascribe value or validity to: *the culture valorizes the individual.* ■ raise or fix the price or value of (a commodity or currency) by artificial means, especially by government action.
– DERIVATIVES **valorization** noun.
– ORIGIN 1920s: back-formation from *valorization* (from French *valorisation*, from *valeur* 'value').

valour (US **valor**) ▸ **noun** [mass noun] great courage in the face of danger, especially in battle: *the medals are awarded for acts of valour.*
– DERIVATIVES **valorous** adjective.
– ORIGIN Middle English (denoting worth derived from personal qualities or rank): via Old French from late Latin *valor*, from *valere* 'be strong'.

Valparaíso /ˌvalpəˈrʌɪzəʊ/, Spanish /balparaˈisəo/ the principal port of Chile, in the centre of the country, near the capital Santiago; pop. 275,000 (est. 2006).

Valpolicella /ˌvalpɒlɪˈtʃɛlə/ ▸ **noun** [mass noun] red Italian wine made in the Val Policella district.

valproate /ˈvalprəʊeɪt/ ▸ **noun** Chemistry a salt or ester of valproic acid.

valproic acid /valˈprəʊɪk/ ▸ **noun** [mass noun] Chemistry a synthetic crystalline compound with anticonvulsant properties, used (generally as salts) in the treatment of epilepsy. ● Alternative name: **2-propylpentanoic acid**; chem. formula: $C_7H_{15}COOH$.
– ORIGIN 1970s: *valproic* from *valeric* (see **VALERIC ACID**) + *pro(pyl)* + **-IC**.

Valsalva manoeuvre /valˈsalvə/ ▸ **noun** Medicine the action of attempting to exhale with the nostrils and mouth, or the glottis, closed. This increases pressure in the middle ear and the chest, as when bracing to lift heavy objects, and is used as a means of equalizing pressure in the ears.
– ORIGIN late 19th cent.: named after Antonio M. *Valsalva* (1666–1723), Italian anatomist.

valse /vals, vɔːls/ ▸ **noun** (pl. pronunc. **same**) French term for **WALTZ** (especially as used in the titles of pieces of music).
– ORIGIN late 18th cent.: via French from German *Walzer*.

valuable ▸ **adjective** worth a great deal of money: *a valuable antique.* ■ extremely useful or important: *my time is valuable.*
▸ **noun** (usu. **valuables**) a thing that is of great worth, especially a small item of personal property: *put all your valuables in the hotel safe.*
– DERIVATIVES **valuably** adverb.

valuable consideration ▸ **noun** [mass noun] Law legal consideration having some economic value, which is necessary for a contract to be enforceable.

valuation ▸ **noun** an estimation of the worth of something, especially one carried out by a professional valuer: *it is wise to obtain an independent valuation.* ■ the monetary worth of something, especially as estimated by a valuer.
– DERIVATIVES **valuate** verb (chiefly N. Amer.).

valuator ▸ **noun** archaic a person who makes valuations; a valuer.

value ▸ **noun 1** [mass noun] the regard that something is held to deserve; the importance, worth, or usefulness of something: *your support is of great value.* ■ the material or monetary worth of something: *prints seldom rise in value* | [count noun] *equipment is included up to a total value of £500.* ■ the worth of something compared to the price paid or asked for it: *at £12.50 the book is **good value*** | [count noun] N. Amer. *the wine represents **a good value** for $17.95.*
2 (**values**) principles or standards of behaviour; one's judgement of what is important in life: *they internalize their parents' rules and values.*
3 the numerical amount denoted by an algebraic term; a magnitude, quantity, or number: *the mean value of x.*
4 Music the relative duration of the sound signified by a note.
5 Linguistics the meaning of a word or other linguistic unit. ■ the quality or tone of a spoken sound; the sound represented by a letter.
6 the relative degree of lightness or darkness of a particular colour: *the artist has used adjacent colour values as the landscape recedes.*
▸ **verb** (**values, valuing, valued**) [with obj.] **1** estimate the monetary worth of: *his estate was valued at £45,000.*
2 consider (someone or something) to be important or beneficial; have a high opinion of: *she had come to value her privacy.*
– PHRASES **value for money** Brit. used in reference to something that is well worth the money spent on it: *this camera is really good value for money.*
– ORIGIN Middle English: from Old French, feminine past participle of *valoir* 'be worth', from Latin *valere*.

value added ▶ noun [mass noun] Economics **1** the amount by which the value of an article is increased at each stage of its production, exclusive of initial costs. **2** the addition of features to a basic line or model for which the buyer is prepared to pay extra: [as modifier] *value-added digital technology*. ■ [as modifier] (of a company) offering specialized or extended services in a commercial area.

value added tax (abbrev.: **VAT**) ▶ noun [mass noun] a tax on the amount by which the value of an article has been increased at each stage of its production or distribution.

value analysis ▶ noun [mass noun] the systematic and critical assessment by an organization of every feature of a product to ensure that its cost is no greater than is necessary to carry out its functions.

value chain ▶ noun the process or activities by which a company adds value to an article, including production, marketing, and the provision of after-sales service.

valued ▶ adjective considered to be important or beneficial; cherished: *a valued friend*.

value engineering ▶ noun [mass noun] the modification of designs and systems according to value analysis.

value-free ▶ adjective free from criteria imposed by subjective values or standards; purely objective: *real science could and should be value-free*.

value judgement ▶ noun an assessment of something as good or bad in terms of one's standards or priorities.

value-laden ▶ adjective presupposing the acceptance of a particular set of values: *governments' judgements are value-laden*.

valueless ▶ adjective having no value; worthless: *cherished but valueless heirlooms*.
– DERIVATIVES **valuelessness** noun.

value-neutral ▶ adjective not presupposing the acceptance of any particular values.

value proposition ▶ noun (in marketing) an innovation, service, or feature intended to make a company or product attractive to customers.

valuer ▶ noun Brit. a person whose job is to estimate the value of something that is to be purchased.

value received ▶ noun [mass noun] Finance used on a bill of exchange to indicate that the bill is a means of paying for goods or services to the value of the bill.

valuta /vəˈljuːtə, -ˈluː-/ ▶ noun [mass noun] the value of one currency with respect to its exchange rate with another. ■ foreign currency: *these internal flights supply valuta to the cash-starved confederation*.
– ORIGIN late 19th cent.: from Italian, literally 'value'.

valvate /ˈvalveɪt/ ▶ adjective Botany (of sepals or other parts) having adjacent edges abutting rather than overlapping. Compare with **IMBRICATE**.
– ORIGIN early 19th cent.: from Latin *valvatus* 'having folding doors', from *valva* 'valve'.

valve ▶ noun **1** a device for controlling the passage of fluid through a pipe or duct, especially an automatic device allowing movement in one direction only. ■ Brit. short for **THERMIONIC VALVE**. ■ Music a cylindrical mechanism in a brass instrument which, when depressed or turned, admits air into different sections of tubing and so extends the range of available notes. ■ Anatomy & Zoology a membranous fold in a hollow organ or tubular structure, such as a blood vessel or the digestive tract, which maintains the flow of the contents in one direction by closing in response to any pressure from reverse flow.
2 Zoology each of the halves of the hinged shell of a bivalve mollusc or brachiopod, or of the parts of the compound shell of a barnacle. ■ Botany each of the halves or sections into which a dry fruit (especially a pod or capsule) dehisces.
– DERIVATIVES **valved** adjective [in combination] *a branchiopod has a two-valved outer covering*, **valveless** adjective.
– ORIGIN late Middle English (denoting a leaf of a folding or double door): from Latin *valva*.

V

valve gear ▶ noun the mechanism that controls the opening and closing of the cylinder valves in a steam engine or internal-combustion engine.

valve head ▶ noun the part of a vertically opening valve that is lifted off the valve aperture to open the valve.

valvular ▶ adjective relating to, having, or acting as a valve or valves: *valvular heart disease | three pairs of valvular apertures*.
– ORIGIN late 18th cent.: from modern Latin *valvula* (diminutive of Latin *valva* 'leaf of a door') + **-AR**[1].

valvulitis /ˌvalvjʊˈlʌɪtɪs/ ▶ noun [mass noun] Medicine inflammation of the valves of the heart.

vambrace /ˈvambreɪs/ ▶ noun historical a piece of armour for the arm, especially the forearm.
– ORIGIN Middle English: from an Anglo-Norman French shortening of Old French *avantbras*, from *avant* 'before' + *bras* 'arm'. Compare with **VAMPLATE**.

vamoose /vəˈmuːs/ ▶ verb [no obj.] informal depart hurriedly: *we'd better vamoose before we're caught*.
– ORIGIN mid 19th cent.: from Spanish *vamos* 'let us go'.

vamp[1] ▶ noun **1** the upper front part of a boot or shoe.
2 (in jazz and popular music) a short, simple introductory passage, usually repeated several times until otherwise instructed.
▶ verb **1** [with obj.] (**vamp something up**) informal repair or improve something: *the production values have been vamped up*.
2 [no obj.] repeat a short, simple passage of music: *the band was vamping gently behind his busy lead guitar*.
3 [with obj.] attach a new upper to (a boot or shoe).
– ORIGIN Middle English (denoting the foot of a stocking): shortening of Old French *avantpie*, from *avant* 'before' + *pie* 'foot'. The musical sense of the verb developed from the general sense 'improvise'.

vamp[2] informal ▶ noun a woman who uses sexual attraction to exploit men.
▶ verb [with obj.] blatantly set out to attract (a man): *she had not vamped him like some wicked Jezebel*.
– DERIVATIVES **vampish** adjective, **vampishly** adverb, **vampishness** noun, **vampy** adjective (**vampier**, **vampiest**).
– ORIGIN early 20th cent.: abbreviation of **VAMPIRE**.

vampire /ˈvampʌɪə/ ▶ noun **1** a corpse supposed, in European folklore, to leave its grave at night to drink the blood of the living by biting their necks with long pointed canine teeth. ■ a person who preys ruthlessly on others: *the protectionist vampires in the Congress*.
2 (also **vampire bat**) a small bat that feeds on the blood of mammals or birds using its two sharp incisor teeth and anticoagulant saliva, found mainly in tropical America. See also **FALSE VAMPIRE**. ● Family Desmodontidae (or Phyllostomidae): three species, in particular the **common vampire** (*Desmodus rotundus*).
3 (also **vampire trap**) Theatre a small spring trapdoor used for sudden disappearances from a stage.
– DERIVATIVES **vampiric** /-ˈpɪrɪk/ adjective.
– ORIGIN mid 18th cent.: from French, from Hungarian *vampir*, perhaps from Turkish *uber* 'witch'.

vampirism /ˈvampʌɪərɪz(ə)m/ ▶ noun [mass noun] the action or practices of a vampire.

vamplate /ˈvampleɪt/ ▶ noun historical a circular plate on a spear or lance designed to protect the hand.
– ORIGIN Middle English: from Anglo-Norman French *vauntplate*, from *avant* 'before' + *plate* 'thin plate'. Compare with **VAMBRACE**.

van[1] ▶ noun a covered motor vehicle, typically without side windows, used for transporting goods or people. ■ Brit. an enclosed railway vehicle for conveying luggage, mail, etc. ■ Brit. a caravan.
– ORIGIN early 19th cent.: shortening of **CARAVAN**.

van[2] ▶ noun (**the van**) the foremost part of a group of people moving or preparing to move forwards, especially the foremost division of an advancing military force: ***in the van*** *were the foremost chiefs and some of the warriors astride horses*. ■ the forefront: *he was* ***in the van*** *of the movement to encourage the cultivation of wild flowers*.
– ORIGIN early 17th cent.: abbreviation of **VANGUARD**.

van[3] ▶ noun **1** archaic a winnowing fan.
2 archaic or literary a bird's wing.
– ORIGIN late Middle English: dialect variant of **FAN**[1], probably reinforced by Old French *van* or Latin *vannus*.

van[4] ▶ noun Brit. Tennis informal term for **ADVANTAGE**.
– ORIGIN 1920s: abbreviation.

Van, Lake /van/ a large salt lake in the mountains of eastern Turkey.

vanadate /ˈvanədeɪt/ ▶ noun Chemistry a salt in which the anion contains both vanadium and oxygen, especially one of the anion VO_4^{3-}.
– ORIGIN mid 19th cent.: from **VANADIUM** + **-ATE**[1].

vanadinite /vəˈnadɪnʌɪt/ ▶ noun [mass noun] a rare reddish-brown mineral consisting of a vanadate and chloride of lead, typically occurring as an oxidation product of lead ores.
– ORIGIN mid 19th cent.: from **VANADIUM** + **-ITE**[1].

vanadium /vəˈneɪdɪəm/ ▶ noun [mass noun] the chemical element of atomic number 23, a hard grey metal of the transition series, used to make alloy steels. (Symbol: **V**)
– ORIGIN mid 19th cent.: modern Latin, from Old Norse *Vanadis* (a name of the Scandinavian goddess Freya).

Van Allen /van ˈalən/, James Alfred (1914–2006), American physicist. He used balloons and rockets to study cosmic radiation in the upper atmosphere, showing that specific zones of high radiation were the result of charged particles from the solar wind being trapped in two belts around the earth.

Van Allen belt ▶ noun each of two regions of intense radiation partly surrounding the earth at heights of several thousand kilometres.

vanaspati /vəˈnʌspəˌtiː/ ▶ noun [mass noun] a type of thick vegetable oil used in India.
– ORIGIN from Sanskrit *vanas-pati*, literally 'lord of the wood, lord of plants'.

Vanbrugh /ˈvanbrə/, Sir John (1664–1726), English architect and dramatist. His comedies include *The Relapse* (1696) and *The Provok'd Wife* (1697). Among his architectural works are Castle Howard in Yorkshire (1702) and Blenheim Palace in Oxfordshire (1705), both produced in collaboration with Nicholas Hawksmoor.

Van Buren /van ˈbjʊərən/, Martin (1782–1862), American Democratic statesman, 8th President of the US 1837–41.

vancomycin /ˌvaŋkəˈmʌɪsɪn/ ▶ noun [mass noun] Medicine a bacterial antibiotic used against resistant strains of streptococcus and staphylococcus. ● This antibiotic is obtained from the bacterium *Streptomyces orientalis*.
– ORIGIN 1950s: from *vanco-* (of unknown origin) + **-MYCIN**.

Vancouver[1] /vanˈkuːvə/ a city and port in British Columbia, SW Canada, situated on the mainland opposite Vancouver Island; pop. 578,041 (2006). It is the largest city in western Canada and its chief Pacific port.

Vancouver[2] /vanˈkuːvə/, George (1757–98), English navigator. He led an exploration of the coasts of Australia, New Zealand, and Hawaii (1791–2), and later charted much of the west coast of North America between southern Alaska and California.

Vancouver Island a large island off the Pacific coast of Canada, in SW British Columbia. Its capital, Victoria, is the capital of British Columbia. It became a British Crown Colony in 1849, later uniting with British Columbia to join the Dominion of Canada.

Vanda /ˈvanda/ Swedish name for **VANTAA**.

vandal ▶ noun **1** a person who deliberately destroys or damages public or private property: *the rear window of the car was smashed by vandals*.
2 (**Vandal**) a member of a Germanic people that ravaged Gaul, Spain, Rome (455), and North Africa in the 4th–5th centuries.
– ORIGIN from Latin *Vandalus*, of Germanic origin. Sense 1 dates from the mid 17th cent.

vandalism ▶ noun [mass noun] action involving deliberate destruction of or damage to public or private property.
– DERIVATIVES **vandalistic** adjective, **vandalistically** adverb.

vandalize (also **vandalise**) ▶ verb [with obj.] deliberately destroy or damage (public or private property): *stations have been vandalized beyond recognition*.

Van de Graaff generator /ˌvan də ˈɡrɑːf/ ▶ noun Physics a machine devised to generate electrostatic charge by means of a vertical endless belt collecting charge from a voltage source and transferring it to a large insulated metal dome, where a high voltage is produced.
– ORIGIN 1930s: named after Robert Jemison *van de Graaff* (1901–67), American physicist.

Vanderbijlpark /ˈvandəbʌɪlˌpɑːk/ a city in South Africa, in the province of Gauteng, south of Johannesburg; pop. 220,100 (est. 2009). It is a centre for the production of steel.

Vanderbilt /ˈvandəbɪlt/, Cornelius (1794–1877), American businessman and philanthropist. He amassed a fortune from shipping and railroads, and made an endowment to found Vanderbilt University in Nashville, Tennessee (1873).

Van der Hum /ˌvan də ˈhʌm/ ▶ noun [mass noun] a South African brandy-based liqueur made with naartjies (mandarin oranges).
– ORIGIN perhaps from a personal name.

van der Waals forces /ˌvan də ˈwɑːlz, ˈvɑːlz/ ▸ **plural noun** Chemistry weak, short-range electrostatic attractive forces between uncharged molecules, arising from the interaction of permanent or transient electric dipole moments.
– ORIGIN late 19th cent.: named after Johannes *van der Waals* (1837–1923), Dutch physicist.

van de Velde /ˌvan də ˈvɛldə/ the name of a family of Dutch painters: ▪ **Willem** (1611–93); known as **Willem van de Velde the Elder**. He painted marine subjects and was official artist to the Dutch fleet. He also worked for Charles II. ▪ **Willem** (1633–1707), son of Willem the Elder; known as **Willem van de Velde the Younger**. He was also a notable marine artist who painted for Charles II. ▪ **Adriaen** (1636–72); son of Willem the Elder. He painted landscapes, portraits, and biblical and genre scenes.

Van Diemen's Land /van ˈdiːmənz/ former name (until 1855) for **TASMANIA**.

Van Dyck /van ˈdʌɪk/ (also **Vandyke**), Sir Anthony (1599–1641), Flemish painter. He is famous for his portraits of members of the English court, which determined the course of portraiture in England for more than 200 years.

Vandyke /vanˈdʌɪk/ (also **vandyke**) ▸ **noun 1** a broad lace or linen collar with an edge deeply cut into large points (in imitation of a style frequently depicted in portraits by Sir Anthony Van Dyck), fashionable in the 18th century. ▪ each of a number of large deep-cut points on the border or fringe of a garment or piece of material.
2 (also **Vandyke beard**) a neat, pointed beard.
▸ **adjective** [attrib.] denoting a style of garment or decorative design associated with the portraits of Van Dyck: *a Vandyke handkerchief*.

Vandyke brown ▸ **noun** [mass noun] a deep rich brown.

vane ▸ **noun** a broad blade attached to a rotating axis or wheel which pushes or is pushed by wind or water and forms part of a machine or device such as a windmill, propeller, or turbine. ▪ short for **WEATHERVANE**. ▪ the flat part on either side of the shaft of a feather. ▪ a broad, flat projecting surface designed to guide the motion of a projectile, such as a feather on an arrow or a fin on a torpedo.
– DERIVATIVES **vaned** adjective [usu. in combination] *a three-vaned windmill*.
– ORIGIN late Middle English: dialect variant of obsolete *fane* 'banner', of Germanic origin.

Vänern /ˈveɪnən/ a lake in SW Sweden, the largest lake in Sweden and the third largest in Europe.

vanessid /vəˈnɛsɪd/ ▸ **noun** Entomology a butterfly of a group that includes many of the better-known kinds found in temperate regions. Compare with **NYMPHALID**. ● Subfamily Nymphalinae, family Nymphalidae (formerly the family Vanessidae).
– ORIGIN early 20th cent.: from modern Latin *Vanessidae*, from *Vanessa* (female given name adopted as a genus name).

Van Eyck /van ˈʌɪk/, Jan (*c.*1370–1441), Flemish painter. He made innovative use of oils, bringing greater flexibility, richer and denser colour, and a wider range from light to dark. Notable works: *The Adoration of the Lamb* (known as the Ghent Altarpiece, 1432) in the church of St Bavon in Ghent and *The Arnolfini Marriage* (1434).

vang /vaŋ/ ▸ **noun** Sailing each of two guy ropes running from the end of a gaff to the deck. ▪ (also **boom vang**) a fitting used to pull a boat's boom down and help control the shape of the sail.
– ORIGIN mid 18th cent.: variant of obsolete *fang*, denoting a gripping device, from Old Norse *fang* 'grasp', of Germanic origin.

vanga /ˈvaŋgə/ (also **vanga shrike**) ▸ **noun** a shrike-like songbird found in Madagascar. ● Family Vangidae: several genera and species.
– ORIGIN mid 19th cent.: modern Latin (genus name), from Latin, literally 'mattock' (because of the shape of the bill).

Van Gogh /van ˈgɒx, ˈgɒf/, Vincent (Willem) (1853–90), Dutch painter. He is best known for his post-Impressionist work, influenced by contact with Impressionist painting and Japanese woodcuts after he moved to Paris in 1886. His most famous pictures include several studies of sunflowers. Suffering from severe depression, he cut off part of his own ear and eventually committed suicide.

vanguard ▸ **noun** a group of people leading the way in new developments or ideas: *the experimental spirit of the modernist vanguard*. ▪ a position at the forefront of new developments or ideas: *the prototype was in the vanguard of technical development*. ▪ the foremost part of an advancing army or naval force.
– ORIGIN late Middle English (denoting the foremost part of an army): shortening of Old French *avan(t) garde*, from *avant* 'before' + *garde* 'guard'.

vanilla ▸ **noun 1** [mass noun] a substance obtained from vanilla pods or produced artificially and used to flavour foods or to impart a fragrant scent to cosmetic preparations: [as modifier] *vanilla ice cream*. ▪ ice cream flavoured with vanilla: *four scoops of vanilla with hot fudge sauce*. ▪ [as modifier] of the creamy colour of vanilla ice cream: *a vanilla dress*.
2 a tropical climbing orchid which has fragrant flowers and long pod-like fruit. ● Genus *Vanilla*, family Orchidaceae: many species, in particular *V. planifolia*, the chief commercial source of vanilla pods.
▪ (also **vanilla pod**) the fruit of the vanilla plant which is cured and then either used in cookery or processed to extract an essence which is used for flavour and fragrance.
▸ **adjective** (also **plain vanilla**) informal having no special or extra features; ordinary: *it will be able to do tricks that plain vanilla CD-ROMs can't*.
– ORIGIN mid 17th cent.: from Spanish *vainilla* 'pod', diminutive of *vaina* 'sheath, pod', from Latin *vagina* 'sheath'. The spelling change was due to association with French *vanille*.

vanillin ▸ **noun** [mass noun] Chemistry a fragrant compound which is the essential constituent of vanilla. ● Alternative name: **3-methoxy-4-hydroxybenzaldehyde**; chem. formula: $CH_3OC_6H_3(OH)CHO$.
– ORIGIN mid 19th cent.; from **VANILLA** + **-IN**[1].

vanish ▸ **verb** [no obj.] **1** disappear suddenly and completely: *Moira vanished without trace*. ▪ gradually cease to exist: *the environment is under threat—hedgerows and woodlands are vanishing*.
2 Mathematics become zero.
– ORIGIN Middle English: shortening of Old French *e(s)vaniss-*, lengthened stem of *e(s)vanir*, from Latin *evanescere* 'die away'.

vanishing cream ▸ **noun** [mass noun] dated a cream or ointment that leaves no visible trace when rubbed into the skin.

vanishingly ▸ **adverb** [as submodifier] in such a manner or to such a degree as almost to become invisible, non-existent, or negligible: *an event of **vanishingly small** probability*.

vanishing point ▸ **noun 1** the point at which receding parallel lines viewed in perspective appear to converge.
2 [in sing.] the point at which something that has been decreasing disappears altogether: *rates of interest dwindled to vanishing point*.

vanitas /ˈvanɪtɑːs/ ▸ **noun** a still-life painting of a 17th-century Dutch genre containing symbols of death or change as a reminder of their inevitability.
– ORIGIN Latin, literally 'vanity'.

Vanitory unit /ˈvanɪt(ə)ri/ ▸ **noun** trademark a vanity unit.
– ORIGIN 1950s: *Vanitory* from **VANITY**, on the pattern of *lavatory*.

vanity ▸ **noun** (pl. **vanities**) **1** [mass noun] excessive pride in or admiration of one's own appearance or achievements: *it flattered his vanity to think I was in love with him* | [count noun] *the vanities and ambitions of politicians*. ▪ [as modifier] denoting a person or company publishing works at the author's expense: *a vanity press*.
2 [mass noun] the quality of being worthless or futile: *the vanity of human wishes*.
3 N. Amer. a dressing table.
– ORIGIN Middle English: from Old French *vanite*, from Latin *vanitas*, from *vanus* 'empty' (see **VAIN**).

vanity case ▸ **noun** a small case fitted with a mirror and compartments for make-up.

Vanity Fair the world regarded as a place of frivolity and idle amusement (originally with reference to Bunyan's *Pilgrim's Progress*).

vanity mirror ▸ **noun** a small mirror used for applying make-up, especially one fitted in a motor vehicle.

vanity plate ▸ **noun** N. Amer. a vehicle licence plate bearing a distinctive or personalized combination of letters, numbers, or both.

vanity sizing ▸ **noun** [mass noun] the practice of assigning smaller sizes to articles of manufactured clothing than is really the case, in order to encourage sales.

vanity table ▸ **noun** a dressing table.

vanity unit ▸ **noun** a unit consisting of a washbasin set into a flat top with cupboards beneath.

van Leyden, Lucas, see **LUCAS VAN LEYDEN**.

vanquish /ˈvaŋkwɪʃ/ ▸ **verb** [with obj.] literary defeat thoroughly: *he successfully vanquished his rival*.
– DERIVATIVES **vanquishable** adjective, **vanquisher** noun.
– ORIGIN Middle English: from Old French *vencus*, *venquis* (past participle and past tense of *veintre*), *vainquiss-* (lengthened stem of *vainquir*), from Latin *vincere* 'conquer'.

Vantaa /ˈvantɑː/ a city in southern Finland; pop. 196,934 (2009). Swedish name **VANDA**.

vantage /ˈvɑːntɪdʒ/ (also **vantage point**) ▸ **noun** a place or position affording a good view of something: *from my vantage point I could see into the front garden* | figurative *the past is continuously reinterpreted from the vantage point of the present*.
– ORIGIN Middle English: from Anglo-Norman French, shortening of Old French *avantage* 'advantage'.

Vanuatu /ˌvanuːˈɑːtuː/ a country consisting of a group of islands in the SW Pacific; pop. 218,500 (est. 2009); official languages, Bislama, English, and French; capital, Vila. The islands were administered jointly by Britain and France as the condominium of the New Hebrides. Vanuatu became an independent republic within the Commonwealth in 1980.
– DERIVATIVES **Vanuatuan** adjective & noun.

vapid /ˈvapɪd/ ▸ **adjective** offering nothing that is stimulating or challenging; bland: *tuneful but vapid musical comedies*.
– DERIVATIVES **vapidity** noun, **vapidly** adverb.
– ORIGIN mid 17th cent. (used originally in description of drinks as 'lacking in flavour'): from Latin *vapidus*.

vapor ▸ **noun** US spelling of **VAPOUR**.

vaporetto /ˌvapəˈrɛtəʊ/ ▸ **noun** (pl. **vaporetti** /-ti/ or **vaporettos**) (in Venice) a canal boat (originally a steamboat, now a motor boat) used for public transport.
– ORIGIN Italian, diminutive of *vapore* 'steam', from Latin *vapor*.

vaporize (also **vaporise**) ▸ **verb** convert or be converted into vapour: [with obj.] *there is a large current which is sufficient to vaporize carbon* | [no obj.] *cold gasoline does not vaporize readily*.
– DERIVATIVES **vaporizable** adjective, **vaporization** noun.

vaporizer (also **vaporiser**) ▸ **noun** a device that generates a particular substance in the form of vapour, especially for medicinal inhalation.

vapour (US **vapor**) ▸ **noun 1** [mass noun] a substance diffused or suspended in the air, especially one normally liquid or solid: *dense clouds of smoke and toxic vapour* | [count noun] *petrol vapours*. ▪ [count noun] Physics a gaseous substance that is below its critical temperature, and can therefore be liquefied by pressure alone. Compare with **GAS**.
2 (**the vapours**) dated a sudden feeling of faintness or nervousness or a state of depression.
▸ **verb** [no obj.] talk in a vacuous, boasting, or pompous way: *he was vapouring on about the days of his youth*.
– DERIVATIVES **vaporous** adjective, **vapoury** adjective.
– ORIGIN late Middle English: from Old French, or from Latin *vapor* 'steam, heat'. The current verb sense dates from the early 17th cent.

vapour density ▸ **noun** Chemistry the density of a particular gas or vapour relative to that of hydrogen at the same pressure and temperature.

vapourer (also **vapourer moth**) ▸ **noun** a day-flying tussock moth, the female of which is wingless and lays eggs on the cocoon from which she emerged. ● Genus *Orgyia*, family Lymantriidae: several species, in particular *O. antiqua*, which is often seen in towns.

vapour lock ▸ **noun** an interruption in the flow of a liquid through a fuel line or other pipe as a result of vaporization of the liquid.

vapour pressure ▸ **noun** Chemistry the pressure of a vapour in contact with its liquid or solid form.

vapour trail ▸ **noun** a trail of condensed water from an aircraft or rocket at high altitude, seen as a white streak against the sky.

vapourware (US **vaporware**) ▸ **noun** [mass noun] Computing, informal software or hardware that has been advertised but is not yet available to buy, either because it is only a concept or because it is still being written or designed.

vaquero /vəˈkɛːrəʊ/ ▸ **noun** (pl. **vaqueros**) (in Spanish-speaking parts of the US) a cowboy; a cattle driver.
– ORIGIN Spanish, from *vaca* 'cow'.

VAR ▶ abbreviation ■ value-added reseller, a company that adds extra features to products it has bought before selling them on. ■ value at risk, a method of quantifying the risk of holding a financial asset.

var. ▶ abbreviation variety.

varactor /vəˈraktə/ ▶ noun a semiconductor diode with a capacitance dependent on the applied voltage.
– ORIGIN 1950s: from elements of *variable reactor*.

Varanasi /vəˈrɑːnəsi/ a city on the Ganges, in Uttar Pradesh, northern India; pop. 1,200,600 (est. 2009). It is a holy city and a place of pilgrimage for Hindus, who undergo ritual purification in the Ganges. Former name BENARES.

Varangian /vəˈrandʒɪən/ ▶ noun a member of the bands of Scandinavian voyagers who travelled by land and up rivers into Russia in the 9th and 10th centuries AD, establishing the Rurik dynasty and gaining great influence in the Byzantine Empire.
– ORIGIN from medieval Latin *Varangus* (a name ultimately from Old Norse, probably based on *vár* 'pledge') + -IAN.

Varangian guard the bodyguard of the later Byzantine emperors, comprising Varangians and later also Anglo-Saxons.

vardo /ˈvɑːdəʊ/ (also **varda** /ˈvɑːdə/) ▶ noun (pl. **vardos** or **vardas**) a Gypsy caravan.
– ORIGIN early 19th cent.: from Romany.

varec /ˈvarɛk/ ▶ noun [mass noun] seaweed, especially kelp.
– ORIGIN late 17th cent.: from French *varec(h)*, from Old Norse; related to WRECK.

Varese /vəˈreɪzeɪ, -zi/ a town in Lombardy, northern Italy; pop. 81,990 (2008).

Varèse /vaˈrɛz/, Edgard (1883–1965), French-born American composer. His music explored dissonance, unusual orchestration, and (from the 1950s) tape-recording and electronic instruments.

Vargas Llosa /ˌvɑːgəs ˈljəʊsə, ˈjəʊsə/, (Jorge) Mario (Pedro) (b.1936), Peruvian novelist, dramatist, and essayist. Novels include *Aunt Julia and the Scriptwriter* (1977) and *The War of the End of the World* (1982).

vari- /ˈvɛːri/ ▶ combining form various: *variform*.
– ORIGIN from Latin *varius*.

variable ▶ adjective **1** not consistent or having a fixed pattern; liable to change: *the quality of hospital food is highly variable | awards can be for variable amounts*. ■ (of a wind) tending to change direction. ■ Mathematics (of a quantity) able to assume different numerical values. ■ Botany & Zoology (of a species) liable to deviate from the typical colour or form, or to occur in different colours or forms.
2 able to be changed or adapted: *the drill has variable speed*. ■ (of a gear) designed to give varying ratios or speeds.
▶ noun an element, feature, or factor that is liable to vary or change: *there are too many variables involved to make any meaningful predictions*. ■ Mathematics a quantity which during a calculation is assumed to vary or be capable of varying in value. ■ Computing a data item that may take on more than one value during the runtime of a program. ■ Astronomy short for VARIABLE STAR. ■ (**variables**) the region of light, variable winds to the north of the NE trade winds or (in the southern hemisphere) between the SE trade winds and the westerlies.
– DERIVATIVES **variability** noun, **variableness** noun, **variably** adverb.
– ORIGIN late Middle English: via Old French from Latin *variabilis*, from *variare* (see VARY).

variable cost ▶ noun a cost that varies with the level of output.

variable-geometry ▶ adjective denoting a swing-wing aircraft.

variable star ▶ noun Astronomy a star whose brightness changes, either irregularly or regularly.

variance ▶ noun **1** [mass noun] the fact or quality of being different, divergent, or inconsistent: *her light tone was at variance with her sudden trembling*. ■ the state or fact of disagreeing or quarrelling: *they were at variance with all their previous allies*. ■ [count noun] chiefly Law a discrepancy between two statements or documents. ■ Statistics a quantity equal to the square of the standard deviation.
2 US Law an official dispensation from a rule or regulation, typically a building regulation.
– ORIGIN Middle English: via Old French from Latin *variantia* 'difference', from the verb *variare* (see VARY).

variant ▶ noun a form or version of something that differs in some respect from other forms of the same thing or from a standard: *clinically distinct variants of malaria* | [as modifier] *a variant spelling*.
– ORIGIN late Middle English (as an adjective in the sense 'tending to vary'): from Old French, literally 'varying', present participle of *varier* (see VARY). The noun dates from the mid 19th cent.

variate /ˈvɛːrɪət/ ▶ noun Statistics a quantity having a numerical value for each member of a group, especially one whose values occur according to a frequency distribution.
– ORIGIN late 19th cent.: from Latin *variatus* 'diversified', past participle of *variare* (see VARY).

variation ▶ noun **1** a change or slight difference in condition, amount, or level, typically within certain limits: *regional variations in house prices* | [mass noun] *the figures showed marked variation from year to year*. ■ Astronomy a deviation of a celestial body from its mean orbit or motion. ■ Mathematics a change in the value of a function due to small changes in the values of its argument or arguments. ■ (also **magnetic variation**) the angular difference between true north and magnetic north at a particular place. ■ [mass noun] Biology the occurrence of an organism in more than one distinct colour or form.
2 a different or distinct form or version of something: *hurling is an Irish variation of hockey*. ■ Music a version of a theme, modified in melody, rhythm, harmony, or ornamentation, so as to present it in a new but still recognizable form: *Elgar's Enigma Variations*. ■ Ballet a solo dance as part of a performance.
– DERIVATIVES **variational** adjective.
– ORIGIN late Middle English (denoting variance or conflict): from Old French, or from Latin *variatio(n-)*, from the verb *variare* (see VARY).

variationist ▶ noun a person who studies variations in usage among different speakers of the same language.

variceal /ˌvarɪˈsiːəl/ ▶ adjective Zoology & Medicine relating to or involving a varix.
– ORIGIN 1960s: from Latin *varix*, *varic-*, on the pattern of words such as *corneal* and *laryngeal*.

varicella /ˌvarɪˈsɛlə/ ▶ noun [mass noun] Medicine technical term for CHICKENPOX. ■ (also **varicella zoster**) a herpesvirus that causes chickenpox and shingles; herpes zoster.
– ORIGIN late 18th cent.: modern Latin, irregular diminutive of VARIOLA.

varices plural form of VARIX.

varicocele /ˈvarɪkə(ʊ)ˌsiːl/ ▶ noun Medicine a mass of varicose veins in the spermatic cord.
– ORIGIN mid 18th cent.: from Latin *varix*, *varic-* 'dilated vein' + -CELE.

varicoloured /ˈvɛːrɪˌkʌləd/ (US **varicolored**) ▶ adjective consisting of several different colours.
– ORIGIN mid 17th cent.: from VARI- + COLOURED.

varicose /ˈvarɪkəʊs, -kəs, -z/ ▶ adjective [attrib.] (of a vein, especially in the leg) swollen, twisted, and lengthened, as a result of poor circulation.
– DERIVATIVES **varicosed** adjective, **varicosity** noun.
– ORIGIN late Middle English: from Latin *varicosus*, from *varix* (see VARIX).

varied ▶ adjective incorporating a number of different types or elements; showing variation or variety: *the phenomena were very varied | a long and varied career*.
– DERIVATIVES **variedly** adverb.

variegated /ˈvɛːrɪgeɪtɪd, ˈvɛːrɪə-/ ▶ adjective exhibiting different colours, especially as irregular patches or streaks: *variegated yellow bricks*. ■ Botany (of a plant or foliage) having or consisting of leaves that are edged or patterned in a second colour, especially white as well as green. ■ marked by variety: *his variegated and amusing observations*.
– DERIVATIVES **variegate** verb, **variegation** /-ˈgeɪʃ(ə)n/ noun.
– ORIGIN mid 17th cent.: from Latin *variegat-* 'made varied' (from the verb *variegare*, from *varius* 'diverse') + -ED².

varietal /vəˈrʌɪət(ə)l/ ▶ adjective **1** (of a wine or grape) made from or belonging to a single specified variety of grape.
2 chiefly Botany & Zoology relating to, characteristic of, or forming a variety: *varietal names*.
▶ noun a varietal wine or grape.
– DERIVATIVES **varietally** adverb.

varietist /vəˈrʌɪətɪst/ ▶ noun dated a person who enjoys sexual variety.

variety ▶ noun (pl. **varieties**) **1** [mass noun] the quality or state of being different or diverse; the absence of uniformity or monotony: *it's the variety that makes my job so enjoyable*. ■ (**a variety of**) a number or range of things of the same general class that are distinct in character or quality: *the centre offers a variety of leisure activities*. ■ [count noun] a thing which differs in some way from others of the same general class or sort; a type: *fifty varieties of fresh and frozen pasta*. ■ a form of television or theatre entertainment consisting of a series of different types of act, such as singing, dancing, and comedy: [as modifier] *a variety show*.
2 Biology a taxonomic category that ranks below subspecies (where present) or species, its members differing from others of the same subspecies or species in minor but permanent or heritable characteristics. Varieties are more often recognized in botany, in which they are designated in the style *Apium graveolens* (var. *dulce*). ■ a cultivated form of a plant. See CULTIVAR.
– PHRASES **variety is the spice of life** proverb new and exciting experiences make life more interesting.
– ORIGIN late 15th cent.: from French *variété* or Latin *varietas*, from *varius* (see VARIOUS).

variety meats ▶ plural noun N. Amer. offal.

variety store ▶ noun N. Amer. a small shop selling a wide range of inexpensive items.

varifocal /ˌvɛːrɪˈfəʊk(ə)l/ ▶ adjective denoting a lens that allows an infinite number of focusing distances for near, intermediate, and far vision.
▶ noun (**varifocals**) varifocal glasses.

variform /ˈvɛːrɪfɔːm/ ▶ adjective (of a group of things) differing from one another in form: *variform languages*. ■ (of a single thing or a mass) consisting of a variety of forms or things: *a variform education*.
– ORIGIN mid 17th cent.: from VARI- + -FORM.

varimax /ˈvɛːrɪmaks/ ▶ noun [mass noun] Statistics a method of factor analysis in which uncorrelated factors are sought by a rotation that maximizes the variance of the factor loadings.
– ORIGIN 1950s: blend of VARIANCE and MAXIMUM.

variola /vəˈrʌɪələ/ ▶ noun Medicine technical term for SMALLPOX.
– DERIVATIVES **variolous** adjective (archaic).
– ORIGIN late 18th cent.: from medieval Latin, literally 'pustule, pock', from Latin *varius* 'diverse'.

varioloid /ˈvɛːrɪəlɔɪd/ Medicine ▶ adjective resembling smallpox.
▶ noun [mass noun] a mild form of smallpox affecting people who have already had the disease or have been vaccinated against it.

variometer /ˌvɛːrɪˈɒmɪtə/ ▶ noun **1** a device for indicating an aircraft's rate of climb or descent.
2 an inductor whose total inductance can be varied by altering the relative position of two coaxial coils connected in series, or by permeability tuning, and so usable to tune an electric circuit.
3 an instrument for measuring variations in the intensity of the earth's magnetic field.

variorum /ˌvɛːrɪˈɔːrəm/ ▶ adjective (of an edition of an author's works) having notes by various editors or commentators. ■ including variant readings from manuscripts or earlier editions.
▶ noun (pl. **variorums**) a variorum edition.
– ORIGIN early 18th cent.: genitive plural of *varius* 'diverse', from Latin *editio cum notis variorum* 'edition with notes by various (commentators)'.

various ▶ adjective different from one another; of different kinds or sorts: *dresses of various colours | his grievances were many and various*. ■ having or showing different properties or qualities: *their environments are locally various*.
▶ determiner & pronoun more than one; individual and separate: *various people arrived late* | [as pronoun] *various of her friends had called*.
– DERIVATIVES **variousness** noun.
– ORIGIN late Middle English: from Latin *varius* 'changing, diverse' + -OUS.

> **USAGE** In standard English the word **various** is normally used as an adjective and determiner. It is sometimes also used as a pronoun followed by **of**, as in ***various of** her friends had called*. Although this pronoun use is similar to that of words such as **several** and **many** (e.g. ***several of** her friends had called*), it is sometimes regarded as incorrect.

variously ▶ adverb in several or different ways: *his early successes can be variously accounted for*.

Variscan /vəˈrɪsk(ə)n/ ▶ adjective Geology another term for HERCYNIAN.

– ORIGIN early 20th cent.: from Latin *Varisci* (the name of a Germanic tribe) + -AN.

varistor /vɛːˈrɪstə, və-/ ▶ noun a semiconductor diode with resistance dependent on the applied voltage.
– ORIGIN 1930s: contraction of *varying resistor*.

varix /ˈvɛːrɪks/ ▶ noun (pl. **varices** /ˈvarɪsiːz/) **1** Medicine a varicose vein.
2 Zoology each of the ridges on the shell of a gastropod mollusc, marking a former position of the aperture.
– ORIGIN late Middle English: from Latin.

varlet /ˈvɑːlɪt/ ▶ noun **1** historical a man or boy acting as an attendant or servant.
2 archaic a dishonest or unprincipled man.
– ORIGIN late Middle English: from Old French, variant of *valet* 'attendant' (see VALET). The sense 'rogue' dates from the mid 16th cent.

varmint /ˈvɑːmɪnt/ ▶ noun N. Amer. informal or dialect a troublesome wild animal. ■ a troublesome and mischievous person, especially a child.
– ORIGIN mid 16th cent.: alteration of VERMIN.

Varna /ˈvɑːnə/ a port and resort in eastern Bulgaria, on the western shores of the Black Sea; pop. 318,313 (2008).

varna /ˈvɑːnə/ ▶ noun each of the four Hindu castes, Brahman, Kshatriya, Vaisya, and Sudra.
– ORIGIN Sanskrit, literally 'colour, class'.

varnish ▶ noun [mass noun] resin dissolved in a liquid for applying on wood, metal, or other materials to form a hard, clear, shiny surface when dry. ■ short for NAIL VARNISH. ■ [in sing.] literary an external or superficially attractive appearance of a specific quality: *an outward varnish of civilization.*
▶ verb [with obj.] apply varnish to: *we stripped the floor and varnished it* | [with obj. and complement] *her toenails were varnished red.*
– DERIVATIVES **varnisher** noun.
– ORIGIN Middle English: from Old French *vernis*, from medieval Latin *veronix* 'fragrant resin, sandarac' or medieval Greek *berenikē*, probably from *Berenice*, a town in Cyrenaica.

Varro /ˈvarəʊ/, Marcus Terentius (116–27 BC), Roman scholar and satirist. His works covered many subjects, including philosophy, agriculture, the Latin language, and education.

varroa /ˈvarəʊə/ (also **varroa mite**) ▶ noun a microscopic mite which is a debilitating parasite of the honeybee, causing loss of honey production. ● *Varroa jacobsoni*, order (or subclass) Acari.
– ORIGIN 1970s: modern Latin, from VARRO (with reference to his work on bee-keeping) + -A[1].

varsity ▶ noun (pl. **varsities**) Brit. dated, S. African, or NZ university: *he had his hair cut when he got back from varsity.* ■ [as modifier] Brit. (especially of a sporting event or team) of or relating to a university, especially Oxford or Cambridge: *a varsity match.* ■ chiefly N. Amer. a sports team representing a university or college.
– ORIGIN mid 17th cent.: shortening of UNIVERSITY, reflecting an archaic pronunciation.

Varuna /ˈvʌrʊnə/ Hinduism one of the gods in the Rig Veda. Originally the sovereign lord of the universe and guardian of cosmic law, he is known in later Hinduism as god of the waters.

varus /ˈvɛːrəs/ ▶ noun [mass noun] Medicine a deformity involving oblique displacement of part of a limb towards the midline. The opposite of VALGUS.
– ORIGIN early 19th cent.: from Latin, literally 'bent'.

varve /vɑːv/ ▶ noun Geology a pair of thin layers of clay and silt of contrasting colour and texture which represent the deposit of a single year (summer and winter) in a lake. Such layers can be measured to determine the chronology of glacial sediments.
– DERIVATIVES **varved** adjective.
– ORIGIN early 20th cent.: from Swedish *varv* 'layer'.

vary ▶ verb (**varies**, **varying**, **varied**) [no obj.] differ in size, amount, degree, or nature from something else of the same general class: *the properties vary in price* | (as adj. **varying**) *varying degrees of success.* ■ change from one condition, form, or state to another: *your skin's moisture content varies according to climatic conditions.* ■ [with obj.] introduce modifications or changes into (something) so as to make it different or less uniform: *he tried to vary his diet.*
– DERIVATIVES **varyingly** adverb.
– ORIGIN Middle English: from Old French *varier* or Latin *variare*, from *varius* 'diverse'.

vas /vas/ ▶ noun (pl. **vasa** /ˈveɪsə/) Anatomy a vessel or duct.
– DERIVATIVES **vasal** /ˈveɪs(ə)l/ adjective.
– ORIGIN late 16th cent.: from Latin, literally 'vessel'.

Vasa /ˈvɑːsa/ Swedish name for VAASA.

Vasarely /ˌvasəˈrɛli/, Viktor (1908–97), Hungarian-born French painter. A pioneer of op art, he was best known for a style of geometric abstraction that used repeated geometric forms and interacting colours to create visual disorientation.

Vasari /vəˈsɑːri/, Giorgio (1511–74), Italian painter, architect, and biographer. His *Lives of the Most Excellent Painters, Sculptors, and Architects* (1550, enlarged 1568) laid the basis for later study of art history in the West.

vasbyt /ˈfasbeɪt/ ▶ verb [no obj.] S. African be stoical: *I am expected to vasbyt and bite back my tears.*
– ORIGIN Afrikaans, literally 'bite hard'.

Vasco da Gama /ˈvaskəʊ/ see DA GAMA.

vascular /ˈvaskjʊlə/ ▶ adjective Anatomy, Zoology, & Medicine relating to, affecting, or consisting of a vessel or vessels, especially those which carry blood: *vascular disease* | *the vascular system.* ■ Botany relating to or denoting the plant tissues (xylem and phloem) which conduct water, sap, and nutrients in flowering plants, ferns, and their relatives.
– DERIVATIVES **vascularity** /-ˈlarɪti/ noun.
– ORIGIN late 17th cent.: from modern Latin *vascularis*, from Latin *vasculum* (see VASCULUM).

vascular bundle ▶ noun Botany a strand of conducting vessels in the stem or leaves of a plant, typically with phloem on the outside and xylem on the inside.

vascular cryptogam ▶ noun Botany a plant of the division Pteridophyta, i.e. a fern, horsetail, or clubmoss.

vascular cylinder ▶ noun another term for STELE (sense 1).

vascularize (also **vascularise**) ▶ verb [with obj.] Biology & Anatomy provide (a tissue or structure) with vessels, especially blood vessels; make vascular: (as adj. **vascularized**) *vascularized pelvic fins.*
– DERIVATIVES **vascularization** noun.

vascular plant ▶ noun Botany a plant that is characterized by the presence of conducting tissue. ● Subkingdom Tracheophyta: divisions Pteridophyta (ferns, horsetails, and clubmosses) and Spermatophyta (cycads, conifers, and flowering plants).

vasculature /ˈvaskjʊlətʃə/ ▶ noun Anatomy the vascular system of a part of the body and its arrangement: *diseases affecting the pulmonary vasculature.*

vasculitis /ˌvaskjʊˈlʌɪtɪs/ ▶ noun (pl. **vasculitides** /-ˈlʌɪtɪdiːz/) [mass noun] Medicine inflammation of a blood vessel or blood vessels.
– DERIVATIVES **vasculitic** /-ˈlɪtɪk/ adjective.

vasculum /ˈvaskjʊləm/ ▶ noun (pl. **vascula** /-lə/) a container used by botanists when collecting plants, typically in the form of a flattened cylindrical metal case with a lengthwise opening, carried by a shoulder strap.
– ORIGIN late 18th cent.: from Latin, diminutive of *vas* 'vessel'.

vas deferens /ˈdɛfərɛnz/ ▶ noun (pl. **vasa deferentia** /ˌdɛfəˈrɛnʃɪə/) Anatomy the duct which conveys sperm from the testicle to the urethra.
– ORIGIN late 16th cent.: from VAS + Latin *deferens* 'carrying away', present participle of *deferre*.

vase ▶ noun a decorative container without handles, typically made of glass or china and used as an ornament or for displaying cut flowers.
– DERIVATIVES **vaseful** noun (pl. **vasefuls**).
– ORIGIN late Middle English: from French, from Latin *vas* 'vessel'.

vasectomy /vəˈsɛktəmi/ ▶ noun (pl. **vasectomies**) the surgical cutting and sealing of part of each vas deferens, typically as a means of sterilization.
– DERIVATIVES **vasectomize** (also **vasectomise**) verb.

vaseline /ˈvasɪliːn/ ▶ noun [mass noun] trademark a type of petroleum jelly used as an ointment and lubricant.
▶ verb [with obj.] cover or smear with vaseline.
– ORIGIN late 19th cent.: formed irregularly from German *Wasser* + Greek *elaion* 'oil' + -INE[4].

vase shell ▶ noun a predatory mollusc of warm seas, with a heavy ribbed shell that has blunt spines and is typically pale with chestnut markings. ● Genus *Vasum*, family Vasidae, class Gastropoda.

vaso- /ˈveɪzəʊ/ ▶ combining form relating to a vessel or vessels, especially blood vessels: *vasoconstriction.*
– ORIGIN from Latin *vas* 'vessel'.

vasoactive ▶ adjective Physiology affecting the diameter of blood vessels (and hence blood pressure).

vasoconstriction ▶ noun [mass noun] the constriction of blood vessels, which increases blood pressure.
– DERIVATIVES **vasoconstrictive** adjective, **vasoconstrictor** noun.

vasodilation (also **vasodilatation** /-ˌdʌɪleɪˈteɪʃ(ə)n/) ▶ noun the dilatation of blood vessels, which decreases blood pressure.
– DERIVATIVES **vasodilator** noun, **vasodilatory** adjective.

vasomotor ▶ adjective [attrib.] causing or relating to the constriction or dilatation of blood vessels. ■ denoting a region in the medulla of the brain (the **vasomotor centre**) which regulates blood pressure by controlling reflex alterations in the heart rate and the diameter of the blood vessels, in response to stimuli from receptors in the circulatory system or from other parts of the brain.

vasopressin /ˌveɪzəʊˈprɛsɪn/ ▶ noun [mass noun] Biochemistry a pituitary hormone which acts to promote the retention of water by the kidneys and increase blood pressure.
– ORIGIN 1920s: blend of VASOPRESSOR and -IN[1].

vasopressor /veɪzəʊˈprɛsə/ ▶ noun Medicine a drug or other agent which causes the constriction of blood vessels.
– ORIGIN 1920s: from VASO- + PRESSOR.

vasospasm /ˈveɪzəʊˌspaz(ə)m/ ▶ noun [mass noun] sudden constriction of a blood vessel, reducing its diameter and flow rate.
– DERIVATIVES **vasospastic** adjective.

vasovagal /ˌveɪzəʊˈveɪg(ə)l/ ▶ adjective [attrib.] Medicine relating to or denoting a temporary fall in blood pressure, with pallor, fainting, sweating, and nausea, caused by overactivity of the vagus nerve, especially as a result of stress.

vassal /ˈvas(ə)l/ ▶ noun historical a holder of land by feudal tenure on conditions of homage and allegiance. ■ a person or country in a subordinate position to another: [as modifier] *a vassal state of the Ottoman Empire.*
– DERIVATIVES **vassalage** noun.
– ORIGIN late Middle English: via Old French from medieval Latin *vassallus* 'retainer', of Celtic origin; compare with VAVASOUR.

vast ▶ adjective of very great extent or quantity; immense: *a vast plain full of orchards.*
▶ noun archaic an immense space.
– DERIVATIVES **vastly** adverb, **vastness** noun.
– ORIGIN late Middle English: from Latin *vastus* 'void, immense'.

vastation /vaˈsteɪʃ(ə)n/ ▶ noun [mass noun] archaic or literary **1** the purification of someone or something by the destruction of evil qualities or elements; spiritual purgation.
2 devastation.
– ORIGIN mid 16th cent.: from Latin *vastatio(n-)*, from *vastare* 'lay waste'.

Västerås /ˌvɛstəˈrəʊs/ a port on Lake Mälaren in eastern Sweden; pop. 134,684 (2008).

VAT ▶ abbreviation value added tax.

vat ▶ noun **1** a large tank or tub used to hold liquid, especially in industry: ***a vat of hot tar.***
2 (also **vat dye**) a water-insoluble dye, such as indigo, that is applied to a fabric in a reducing bath which converts it to a soluble form, the colour being obtained on subsequent oxidation in the fabric fibres.
▶ verb (**vats**, **vatting**, **vatted**) [with obj.] place or treat in a vat.
– DERIVATIVES **vatful** noun (pl. **vatfuls**).
– ORIGIN Middle English: southern and western dialect variant of obsolete *fat* 'container', of Germanic origin; related to Dutch *vat* and German *Fass*.

vatic /ˈvatɪk/ ▶ adjective literary describing or predicting what will happen in the future.
– ORIGIN early 17th cent.: from Latin *vates* 'prophet' + -IC.

Vatican noun (usu. **the Vatican**) the palace and official residence of the Pope in Rome. ■ [treated as sing. or pl.] the administrative centre of the Roman Catholic Church.
– ORIGIN mid 16th cent.: from French, or from Latin *Vaticanus*, the name of a hill in Rome.

Vatican City an independent papal state in the city of Rome, the seat of government of the Roman Catholic Church; pop. 800 (est. 2009). It covers an area of 44 hectares (109 acres) around St Peter's Basilica and the palace of the Vatican. Having been suspended after the incorporation of the former Papal States into Italy in 1870, the temporal power of the Pope was restored by the Lateran Treaty of 1929.

V

Vatican Council noun each of two general councils of the Roman Catholic Church, held in 1869–70 and 1962–5. The first (**Vatican I**) proclaimed the infallibility of the Pope when speaking *ex cathedra*; the second (**Vatican II**) made numerous reforms, abandoning the universal Latin liturgy and acknowledging ecumenism.

vaticinate /vaˈtɪsɪneɪt/ ▶ verb [no obj.] rare foretell the future.
– DERIVATIVES **vaticinal** adjective, **vaticination** noun, **vaticinator** noun, **vaticinatory** adjective.
– ORIGIN early 17th cent.: from Latin *vaticinat-* 'prophesied', from the verb *vaticinari*, from *vates* 'prophet'.

VATman ▶ noun (pl. **VATmen**) Brit. informal a customs and excise officer who deals with VAT.

Vättern /ˈvɛt(ə)n/ a large lake in southern Sweden.

vatu /ˈvatuː/ ▶ noun (pl. **same**) the basic monetary unit of Vanuatu, equal to 100 centimes.
– ORIGIN Bislama.

Vaud /vəʊ/ a canton on the shores of Lake Geneva in western Switzerland; capital, Lausanne. German name **WAADT**.

vaudeville /ˈvɔːdəvɪl, ˈvəʊd-/ ▶ noun [mass noun] a type of entertainment popular chiefly in the US in the early 20th century, featuring a mixture of speciality acts such as burlesque comedy and song and dance. ■ [count noun] a light or comic stage play with interspersed songs. ■ [count noun] archaic a satirical or topical song with a refrain.
– DERIVATIVES **vaudevillian** adjective & noun.
– ORIGIN mid 18th cent.: from French, earlier *vau de ville* (or *vire*), said to be a name given originally to songs composed by Olivier Basselin, a 15th-cent. fuller born in *Vau de Vire* in Normandy.

Vaudois[1] /ˈvəʊdwɑː/ ▶ adjective relating to Vaud, its people, or their dialect of French.
▶ noun (pl. **same**) **1** a native of Vaud.
2 [mass noun] the French dialect spoken in Vaud.
– ORIGIN French.

Vaudois[2] /ˈvəʊdwɑː/ ▶ noun (pl. **same**) historical a member of the Waldenses religious sect.
▶ adjective relating to the Waldenses.
– ORIGIN mid 16th cent.: French, representing medieval Latin *Valdensis* (see **WALDENSES**).

Vaughan[1] /vɔːn/, Henry (1621–95), Welsh religious writer and metaphysical poet.

Vaughan[2] /vɔːn/, Sarah (Lois) (1924–90), American jazz singer and pianist. She was notable for her vocal range, her use of vibrato, and her improvisational skills.

Vaughan Williams, Ralph (1872–1958), English composer. His strongly melodic music frequently reflects his interest in Tudor composers and English folk songs. Notable works: *Fantasia on a Theme by Thomas Tallis* (1910), *A London Symphony* (1914), and the Mass in G minor (1922).

vault[1] /vɔːlt/ ▶ noun **1** a roof in the form of an arch or a series of arches, typical of churches and other large, formal buildings. ■ literary a thing resembling an arched roof, especially the sky: *the vault of heaven*. ■ Anatomy the arched roof of a cavity, especially that of the skull: *the cranial vault*.
2 a large room or chamber used for storage, especially an underground one. ■ a secure room in a bank in which valuables are stored. ■ a chamber beneath a church or in a graveyard used for burials.
▶ verb [with obj.] (usu. as adj. **vaulted**) provide (a building or room) with an arched roof or roofs: *a vaulted arcade*. ■ construct (a roof) in the form of a vault: *an unusual brick vaulted ceiling*.
– ORIGIN Middle English: from Old French *voute*, based on Latin *volvere* 'to roll'.

V

vault[2] /vɔːlt/ ▶ verb [no obj., with adverbial of direction] leap or spring while supporting or propelling oneself with one or both hands or with the help of a pole: *he vaulted over the gate*. ■ [with obj.] jump over (an obstacle) in such a way: *Ryker vaulted the barrier*.
▶ noun an act of vaulting.
– DERIVATIVES **vaulter** noun.
– ORIGIN mid 16th cent.: from Old French *volter* 'to turn (a horse), gambol', based on Latin *volvere* 'to roll'.

vaulting ▶ noun [mass noun] ornamental work in a vaulted roof or ceiling.

vaulting horse ▶ noun a padded wooden block used for vaulting over by gymnasts and athletes.

vaunt /vɔːnt/ ▶ verb [with obj.] (usu. as adj. **vaunted**) boast about or praise (something), especially excessively: *the much vaunted information superhighway*.
▶ noun archaic a boast.
– DERIVATIVES **vaunter** noun, **vaunting** adjective, **vauntingly** adverb.
– ORIGIN late Middle English: the noun a shortening of obsolete *avaunt* 'boasting, a boast'; the verb (originally in the sense 'use boastful language') from Old French *vanter*, from late Latin *vantare*, based on Latin *vanus* 'vain, empty'.

vavasory /ˈvavəs(ə)ri/ ▶ noun (pl. **vavasories**) historical the estate of a vavasour.
– ORIGIN early 17th cent.: from Old French *vavasorie* or medieval Latin *vavasoria* (see **VAVASOUR**).

vavasour /ˈvavəsʊə/ ▶ noun historical a vassal owing allegiance to a great lord and having other vassals under him.
– ORIGIN Middle English: from Old French *vavas(s)our*, from medieval Latin *vavassor*, perhaps from *vassus vassorum* 'vassal of vassals'.

va-va-voom ▶ noun [mass noun] informal the quality of being exciting, vigorous, or sexually attractive: *she's lost none of her va-va-voom since giving birth to her daughter*.
▶ adjective sexually attractive: *her va-va-voom figure*.
– ORIGIN 1950s (originally US): representing the sound of a car engine being revved.

Vavilov /ˈvavɪlɒf/, Nikolai (Ivanovich) (1887–*c.*1943), Soviet plant geneticist. He amassed a considerable collection of new plants, utilizing their genetic resources for crop improvement.

VC ▶ abbreviation ■ Vice Chairman. ■ Vice Chancellor. ■ Vice Consul. ■ Victoria Cross.

V-chip ▶ noun a computer chip installed in a television receiver that can be programmed by the user to block or scramble material containing a special code in its signal indicating that it is deemed violent or sexually explicit.

vCJD ▶ abbreviation new variant Creutzfeld–Jakob disease.

VCR ▶ noun (pl. **VCRs**) a videocassette recorder.

VD ▶ abbreviation venereal disease.

VDT ▶ abbreviation N. Amer. visual display terminal.

VDU ▶ abbreviation Brit. visual display unit.

've ▶ abbreviation informal have (usually after the pronouns I, you, we, and they): *we've tried our best*.

veal ▶ noun [mass noun] the flesh of a young calf, used as food.
– ORIGIN Middle English: from Anglo-Norman French *ve(e)l*, from Latin *vitellus*, diminutive of *vitulus* 'calf'.

veal crate ▶ noun a partitioned area with restricted light and space in which a calf is reared for slaughter so as to ensure the whiteness of the meat.

Veblen /ˈvɛblən/, Thorstein (Bunde) (1857–1929), American economist and social scientist. His works include the critique of capitalism *The Theory of the Leisure Class* (1899) and *The Theory of Business Enterprise* (1904).

vector /ˈvɛktə/ ▶ noun **1** Mathematics & Physics a quantity having direction as well as magnitude, especially as determining the position of one point in space relative to another. ■ a matrix with one row or one column. ■ [as modifier] Computing denoting a type of graphical representation using lines to construct the outlines of objects.
2 an organism, typically a biting insect or tick, that transmits a disease or parasite from one animal or plant to another. ■ Genetics a bacteriophage or plasmid which transfers genetic material into a cell, or from one bacterium to another.
3 a course to be taken by an aircraft.
▶ verb [with obj. and adverbial of direction] direct (an aircraft in flight) to a desired point.
– DERIVATIVES **vectorial** /-ˈtɔːrɪəl/ adjective, **vectorially** adverb, **vectorization** (also **vectorisation**) noun (sense 1 of the noun), **vectorize** (also **vectorise**) verb (sense 1 of the noun).
– ORIGIN mid 19th cent.: from Latin, literally 'carrier', from *vehere* 'convey'.

vector field ▶ noun Mathematics a function of a space whose value at each point is a vector quantity.

vector processor ▶ noun Computing a processor that is able to process sequences of data with a single instruction.

vector product ▶ noun Mathematics the product of two real vectors in three dimensions which is itself a vector at right angles to both the original vectors. Its magnitude is the product of the magnitudes of the original vectors and the sine of the angle between their directions. Also called **CROSS PRODUCT**. ● Written as **a** × **b**.

vector space ▶ noun Mathematics a space consisting of vectors, together with the associative and commutative operation of addition of vectors, and the associative and distributive operation of multiplication of vectors by scalars.

VED ▶ abbreviation vehicle excise duty.

Veda /ˈveɪdə, ˈviːdə/ ▶ noun any of the four collections forming the earliest body of Indian scripture, consisting of the Rig Veda, Sama Veda, Yajur Veda, and Atharva Veda, which codified the ideas and practices of Vedic religion and laid down the basis of classical Hinduism. They were probably composed between 1500 and 700 BC, and contain hymns, philosophy, and guidance on ritual.
– ORIGIN Sanskrit, literally '(sacred) knowledge'.

vedalia beetle /vɪˈdeɪlɪə/ ▶ noun an Australian ladybird which has been introduced into California and elsewhere to control scale insects. ● *Rodolia cardinalis*, family Coccinellidae.
– ORIGIN late 19th cent.: modern Latin *Vedalia* (former genus name), of unknown origin.

Vedanta /vɪˈdɑːntə, -ˈda-, vɛ-/ ▶ noun [mass noun] a Hindu philosophy based on the doctrine of the Upanishads, especially in its monistic form.
– DERIVATIVES **Vedantic** adjective, **Vedantist** noun.
– ORIGIN from Sanskrit *vedānta*, from *veda* (see **VEDA**) + *anta* 'end'.

VE day ▶ noun the day (8 May) marking the Allied victory in Europe in 1945.
– ORIGIN *VE*, abbreviation of *Victory in Europe*.

Vedda /ˈvɛdə/ ▶ noun (pl. **same** or **Veddas**) a member of an aboriginal people inhabiting the forests of Sri Lanka.
– ORIGIN from Sinhalese *vaddā* 'hunter'.

vedette /vɪˈdɛt/ ▶ noun **1** historical a mounted sentry positioned beyond an army's outposts to observe the movements of the enemy.
2 a leading star of stage, screen, or television.
– ORIGIN late 17th cent.: from French, literally 'scout', from an alteration of southern Italian *veletta*, perhaps based on Spanish *velar* 'keep watch'.

Vedic /ˈveɪdɪk, ˈviː-/ ▶ adjective relating to the Veda or Vedas.
▶ noun [mass noun] the language of the Vedas, an early form of Sanskrit.
– ORIGIN from French *védique* or German *vedisch* (see **VEDA**).

Vedic religion ▶ noun [mass noun] the ancient religion of the Aryan peoples who entered NW India from Persia *c.*2000–1200 BC. It was the precursor of Hinduism, and its beliefs and practices are contained in the Vedas.

> Its characteristics included ritual sacrifice to many gods, especially Indra, Varuna, and Agni; social classes (varnas) that formed the basis of the caste system; and the emergence of the priesthood which dominated orthodox Brahmanism from c.900 BC. Transition to classical Hinduism began in about the 5th century BC.

vee ▶ noun a thing shaped like the letter V: *a vee of geese goes over*.

veejay ▶ noun informal a person who introduces and plays music videos on television.
– ORIGIN 1980s: representing a pronunciation of *VJ*, short for *video jockey*, on the pattern of *deejay*.

veena /ˈviːnə/ (also **vina**) ▶ noun an Indian stringed instrument, with four main and three auxiliary strings. The southern type has a lute-like body; the older northern type has a tubular body and a gourd fitted to each end as a resonator.
– ORIGIN Sanskrit *vīṇā*.

veep ▶ noun N. Amer. informal a vice-president.
– ORIGIN 1940s: from the initials *VP*.

veer[1] ▶ verb [no obj., with adverbial of direction] change direction suddenly: *an oil tanker that had veered off course*. ■ suddenly change an opinion, subject, type of behaviour, etc.: *the conversation eventually veered away from theatrical things*. ■ (of the wind) change direction clockwise around the points of the compass: *the wind veered a point*. The opposite of **BACK**.
▶ noun **1** a sudden change of direction.
2 American Football an offensive play using a modified T-formation with a split backfield, which allows the quarterback the option of passing to the fullback, pitching to a running back, or running with the ball.
– ORIGIN late 16th cent.: from French *virer*, perhaps from an alteration of Latin *gyrare* (see **GYRATE**).

veer² ▶ verb [with obj.] Nautical, dated slacken or let out (a rope or cable) in a controlled way.
– ORIGIN late Middle English: from Middle Dutch *vieren*.

veery /ˈvɪəri/ ▶ noun (pl. **veeries**) a North American woodland thrush with a brown back and speckled breast. ● *Catharus fuscescens*, family Turdidae.
– ORIGIN mid 19th cent.: perhaps imitative.

veg¹ /vɛdʒ/ ▶ noun (pl. **same**) Brit. informal a vegetable or vegetables: *meat and two veg*.
– ORIGIN late 19th cent.: abbreviation.

veg² /vɛdʒ/ ▶ verb (**vegges, vegging, vegged**) [no obj.] informal relax to the point of complete inertia: *they were vegging out in front of the TV*.
– ORIGIN 1920s: abbreviation of VEGETATE.

Vega¹ /ˈveɪɡə/, Spanish /ˈbeɣa/, Lope de (1562–1635), Spanish dramatist and poet; full name *Lope Felix de Vega Carpio*. He is regarded as the founder of Spanish drama.

Vega² /ˈviːɡə/ Astronomy the fifth-brightest star in the sky, and the brightest in the constellation Lyra, overhead in summer to observers in the northern hemisphere.
– ORIGIN via Spanish or medieval Latin from Arabic, literally 'the falling vulture'.

vega /ˈveɪɡə/ ▶ noun (in Spain and Spanish America) a large grassy plain or valley.
– ORIGIN Spanish and Catalan.

vegan ▶ noun a person who does not eat or use animal products: [as modifier] *a vegan diet*.
– DERIVATIVES **veganism** noun.
– ORIGIN 1940s: from VEGETARIAN + -AN.

Vegeburger ▶ noun trademark for VEGGIE BURGER.

Vegemite /ˈvɛdʒɪmʌɪt/ ▶ noun [mass noun] Austral./NZ trademark a type of savoury spread made from concentrated yeast extract.
– ORIGIN 1920s: from VEGETABLE, on the pattern of MARMITE.

vegetable /ˈvɛdʒtəb(ə)l, ˈvɛdʒɪtə-/ ▶ noun **1** a plant or part of a plant used as food, such as a cabbage, potato, turnip, or bean.
2 informal, offensive a person who is incapable of normal mental or physical activity, especially through brain damage. ■ informal a person with a dull or inactive life: *I thought I'd sort of flop back and be a vegetable for a bit*.
▶ adjective [attrib.] relating to vegetables as food: *a vegetable garden | vegetable soup*. ■ relating to plants or plant life, especially as distinct from animal life or mineral substances: *decaying vegetable matter*.
– ORIGIN late Middle English (in the sense 'growing as a plant'): from Old French, or from late Latin *vegetabilis* 'animating', from Latin *vegetare* (see VEGETATE). The noun dates from the late 16th cent.

vegetable ivory ▶ noun [mass noun] a hard white material obtained from the endosperm of the ivory nut.

vegetable marrow ▶ noun see MARROW¹ (sense 1).

vegetable oil ▶ noun [mass noun] an oil derived from plants, e.g. rapeseed oil, olive oil, sunflower oil.

vegetable oyster ▶ noun [mass noun] the edible root of salsify, the taste of which is said to resemble that of oysters.

vegetable sheep ▶ noun a New Zealand plant of the daisy family, which has greyish hairy leaves and forms hummocks which look like sheep from a distance. ● *Raoulia eximia*, family Compositae.

vegetable spaghetti ▶ noun [mass noun] Brit. an edible squash of a variety with slightly stringy flesh which when cooked has a texture and appearance like that of spaghetti.

vegetable sponge ▶ noun another term for LOOFAH.

vegetal /ˈvɛdʒɪt(ə)l/ ▶ adjective **1** formal relating to plants: *a vegetal aroma*.
2 [attrib.] Embryology relating to that pole of the ovum or embryo that contains the less active cytoplasm, and frequently most of the yolk, in the early stages of development: *vegetal cells | the vegetal region*.
– ORIGIN late Middle English: from medieval Latin *vegetalis*, from Latin *vegetare* 'animate'. Sense 2 dates from the early 20th cent.

vegetarian ▶ noun a person who does not eat meat or fish, and sometimes other animal products, especially for moral, religious, or health reasons.
▶ adjective relating to vegetarians or vegetarianism: *a vegetarian restaurant*.
– DERIVATIVES **vegetarianism** noun.
– ORIGIN mid 19th cent.: formed irregularly from VEGETABLE + -ARIAN.

vegetate ▶ verb [no obj.] **1** live or spend a period of time in a dull, inactive, unchallenging way: *if she left him alone, he'd sit in front of the television and vegetate*.
2 dated (of a plant or seed) grow; sprout. ■ [with obj.] cause plants to grow in or cover (a place).
– ORIGIN early 17th cent.: from Latin *vegetat-* 'enlivened', from the verb *vegetare*, from *vegetus* 'active', from *vegere* 'be active'.

vegetated ▶ adjective covered with vegetation or plant life: *densely vegetated wetlands*.

vegetation ▶ noun [mass noun] **1** plants considered collectively, especially those found in a particular area or habitat: *the chalk cliffs are mainly sheer with little vegetation*.
2 the action or process of vegetating.
– DERIVATIVES **vegetational** adjective.
– ORIGIN mid 16th cent. (in sense 2): from medieval Latin *vegetatio(n-)* 'power of growth', from the verb *vegetare* (see VEGETATE).

vegetative /ˈvɛdʒɪtətɪv, -teɪtɪv/ ▶ adjective **1** Biology relating to or denoting reproduction or propagation achieved by asexual means, either naturally (budding, rhizomes, runners, bulbs, etc.) or artificially (grafting, layering, or taking cuttings): *vegetative spores | a vegetative replicating phase*. ■ relating to or concerned with growth rather than sexual reproduction: *environmental factors trigger the switch from vegetative to floral development*.
2 relating to vegetation or plant life: *diverse vegetative types*.
3 Medicine (of a person) alive but comatose and without apparent brain activity or responsiveness. See PERSISTENT VEGETATIVE STATE.
– DERIVATIVES **vegetatively** adverb.
– ORIGIN late Middle English (in sense 2): from Old French *vegetatif, -ive* or medieval Latin *vegetativus* (see VEGETATE).

vegetative cell ▶ noun Botany & Microbiology a cell of a bacterium or unicellular alga that is actively growing rather than forming spores.

veggie (also **vegie**) ▶ noun & adjective informal **1** chiefly Brit. another term for VEGETARIAN.
2 another term for VEGETABLE.
– ORIGIN 1970s: abbreviation.

veggie burger (also trademark **Vegeburger**) ▶ noun a savoury cake resembling a hamburger but made with vegetable protein, soya, etc., instead of meat.

vehemence /ˈviːɪm(ə)ns/ ▶ noun [mass noun] great forcefulness or intensity of feeling or expression: *the vehemence of his reaction*.

vehement /ˈviːɪm(ə)nt/ ▶ adjective showing strong feeling; forceful, passionate, or intense: *her voice was low but vehement | vehement criticism*.
– DERIVATIVES **vehemently** adverb.
– ORIGIN late Middle English (describing pain or temperature, in the sense 'intense, high in degree'): from French *véhément* or Latin *vehement-* 'impetuous, violent', perhaps from an unrecorded adjective meaning 'deprived of mind', influenced by *vehere* 'carry'.

vehicle ▶ noun **1** a thing used for transporting people or goods, especially on land, such as a car, lorry, or cart.
2 a thing used to express, embody, or fulfil something: *I use paint as a* **vehicle for** *my ideas*. ■ a substance that facilitates the use of a drug, pigment, or other material mixed with it.
3 a film, television programme, song, etc. that is intended to display the leading performer to the best advantage: *a vehicle for a star who was one of Hollywood's hottest properties*.
4 a privately controlled company through which an individual or organization conducts a particular kind of business, especially investment.
– DERIVATIVES **vehicular** /vɪˈhɪkjʊlə/ adjective (sense 1).
– ORIGIN early 17th cent.: from French *véhicule* or Latin *vehiculum*, from *vehere* 'carry'.

veil ▶ noun **1** a piece of fine material worn by women to protect or conceal the face: *a white bridal veil*. ■ a piece of fabric forming part of a nun's headdress, resting on the head and shoulders. ■ a thing that conceals, disguises, or obscures something: *shrouded in an eerie veil of mist*. ■ (in Jewish antiquity) the piece of precious cloth separating the sanctuary from the body of the Temple or the Tabernacle.
2 Botany a membrane which is attached to the immature fruiting body of some toadstools and ruptures in the course of development, either (**universal veil**) enclosing the whole fruiting body or (**partial veil**) joining the edges of the cap to the stalk.
▶ verb [with obj.] cover with or as if with a veil: *she veiled her face*. ■ (usu. as adj. **veiled**) partially conceal, disguise, or obscure: *a thinly veiled threat*.
– PHRASES **beyond the veil** in a mysterious or hidden place or state, especially the unknown state of life after death. **draw a veil over** avoid discussing or calling attention to (something embarrassing or unpleasant). **take the veil** become a nun.
– DERIVATIVES **veilless** adjective.
– ORIGIN Middle English: from Anglo-Norman French *veil(e)*, from Latin *vela*, plural of *velum* (see VELUM).

veiling ▶ noun [mass noun] a light gauzy fabric used for veils.

vein ▶ noun **1** any of the tubes forming part of the blood circulation system of the body, carrying mainly oxygen-depleted blood towards the heart. Compare with ARTERY. ■ (in general use) a blood vessel: *he felt the adrenalin course through his veins*. ■ (in plants) a slender rib running through a leaf or bract, typically dividing or branching, and containing a vascular bundle. ■ (in insects) a hardened branching rib that forms part of the supporting framework of a wing, consisting of an extension of the tracheal system; a nervure.
2 a fracture in rock containing a deposit of minerals or ore and typically having an extensive course underground. ■ a streak or stripe of a different colour in wood, marble, cheese, etc. ■ a source of a specified quality: *he managed to tap into the thick vein of discontent to his own advantage*.
3 [in sing.] a distinctive quality, style, or tendency: *he closes his article in a somewhat humorous vein*.
– DERIVATIVES **veinless** adjective, **veinlet** noun, **veinlike** adjective, **veiny** adjective (**veinier, veiniest**).
– ORIGIN Middle English: from Old French *veine*, from Latin *vena*. The earliest senses were 'blood vessel' and 'small natural underground channel of water'.

veined ▶ adjective marked with or as if with veins: [in combination] *a blue-veined cheese*.

veining ▶ noun [mass noun] a pattern of lines, streaks, or veins: *the marble's characteristic surface veining*.

veinous ▶ adjective having prominent or noticeable veins. Compare with VENOUS.

veinstone ▶ noun another term for GANGUE.

veitchberry /ˈviːtʃb(ə)ri, -bɛri/ ▶ noun (pl. **veitchberries**) a bushy plant that is a hybrid of a raspberry and a blackberry, first produced in 1925. ● *Rubus inermis* × *idaeus*, family Rosaceae.
■ the edible fruit of the veitchberry, which resembles a mulberry.
– ORIGIN 1920s: from *Veitch*, the surname of a family of nurserymen, + BERRY.

Vela /ˈviːlə/ Astronomy a southern constellation (the Sails), lying partly in the Milky Way between Carina and Pyxis and originally part of Argo.
– ORIGIN Latin, plural of *velum* 'sail'.

vela plural form of VELUM.

velamen /vɪˈleɪmən/ ▶ noun (pl. **velamina** /-mɪnə/) Botany an outer layer of empty cells in the aerial roots of epiphytic orchids and aroids.
– ORIGIN late 19th cent.: from Latin, from *velare* 'to cover'.

velar /ˈviːlə/ ▶ adjective **1** relating to a veil or velum.
2 Phonetics (of a speech sound) pronounced with the back of the tongue near the soft palate, as in *k* and *g* in English.
▶ noun a velar sound.
– ORIGIN early 18th cent.: from Latin *velaris*, from *velum* (see VELUM).

velaric airstream /vɪˈlarɪk/ ▶ noun Phonetics the creation of an ingressive airstream in the mouth by use of tongue contact with the velum, used to make clicks. Contrasted with PULMONIC AIRSTREAM.

V

velarium /vɪˈlɛːrɪəm/ ▶ noun (pl. **velaria** /-rɪə/) a large awning used in ancient Rome to shelter an amphitheatre from the weather. ■ an inner ceiling used to improve acoustics in a theatre.
– ORIGIN Latin.

velarization /ˌviːlərʌɪˈzeɪʃ(ə)n/ (also **velarisation**) ▶ noun [mass noun] Phonetics a secondary articulation involving movement of the back of the tongue towards the velum.

Velázquez /vɪˈlaskwɪz/, Spanish /beˈlaskeθ, -kes/, Diego Rodríguez de Silva y (1599–1660), Spanish painter, court painter to Philip IV. His portraits humanized the formal Spanish tradition of idealized figures. Notable works: *Pope Innocent X* (1650), *The Toilet of*

Venus (known as The Rokeby Venus, *c.*1651), and *Las Meninas* (*c.*1656).

Velázquez de Cuéllar /deɪ ˈkweɪjɑː, ˈkweɪljɑː/, Spanish /de ˈkwejar/, Diego (*c.*1465–1524), Spanish conquistador. After sailing with Columbus to the New World in 1493, he began the conquest of Cuba in 1511; he later initiated expeditions to conquer Mexico.

Velcro /ˈvɛlkrəʊ/ ▶ **noun** [mass noun] trademark a fastener for clothes or other items, consisting of two strips of thin plastic sheet, one covered with tiny loops and the other with tiny flexible hooks, which adhere when pressed together and can be separated when pulled apart deliberately.
▶ **verb** [with obj. and adverbial] fasten, join, or fix with Velcro.
– DERIVATIVES **Velcroed** **adjective**.
– ORIGIN 1960s: from French *velours croché* 'hooked velvet'.

veld /vɛlt/ (also **veldt**) ▶ **noun** [mass noun] open, uncultivated country or grassland in southern Africa. It is conventionally divided by altitude into highveld, middleveld, and lowveld.
– ORIGIN Afrikaans, from Dutch, literally 'field'.

Velde, van de[1], Henri, see **VAN DE VELDE**[2].

Velde, van de[2], Willem and sons, see **VAN DE VELDE**[1].

veldskoen /ˈfɛltskʊn, ˈfɛls-/ (S. African also **velskoen** /ˈfɛlskʊn/) ▶ **noun** a strong suede or leather shoe or boot. ■ S. African used as a symbol of conservative or reactionary attitudes: [as modifier] *he is a veldskoen bitter-ender*.
– ORIGIN Afrikaans, from Dutch *veld* 'field' or *vel* 'skin, hide' + *schoen* 'shoe'.

veleta /vəˈliːtə/ (also **valeta**) ▶ **noun** a ballroom dance in triple time, faster than a waltz and with partners side by side.
– ORIGIN early 20th cent.: from Spanish, literally 'weathervane'.

veliger /ˈviːlɪdʒə/ ▶ **noun** Zoology the final larval stage of certain molluscs, having two ciliated flaps for swimming and feeding.
– ORIGIN late 19th cent.: from **VELUM** + Latin *-ger* 'bearing'.

velleity /vɛˈliːɪti/ ▶ **noun** (pl. **velleities**) formal a wish or inclination not strong enough to lead to action: *the notion intrigued me, but remained a velleity*.
– ORIGIN early 17th cent.: from medieval Latin *velleitas*, from Latin *velle* 'to wish'.

Velleius Paterculus /vɛˌleɪəs pəˈtəːkjʊləs/ (*c.*19 BC–*c.*30 AD), Roman historian and soldier. His *Roman History*, covering the period from the early history of Rome to AD 30, is notable for its eulogistic depiction of Tiberius.

vellum /ˈvɛləm/ ▶ **noun** [mass noun] fine parchment made originally from the skin of a calf.
– ORIGIN late Middle English: from Old French *velin*, from *veel* (see **VEAL**).

velocimeter /ˌvɛlə(ʊ)ˈsɪmɪtə/ ▶ **noun** an instrument for measuring velocity.
– DERIVATIVES **velocimetry** **noun**.
– ORIGIN mid 19th cent.: from Latin *velox, veloc-* 'swift' + **-METER**.

velocipede /vɪˈlɒsɪpiːd/ ▶ **noun** historical an early form of bicycle propelled by working pedals on cranks fitted to the front axle. ■ US a child's tricycle.
– DERIVATIVES **velocipedist** **noun**.
– ORIGIN early 19th cent.: from French *vélocipède*, from Latin *velox, veloc-* 'swift' + *pes, ped-* 'foot'.

velociraptor /vɪˌlɒsɪˈraptə/ ▶ **noun** a small dromaeosaurid dinosaur of the late Cretaceous period. ● Genus *Velociraptor*, family Dromaeosauridae, suborder Theropoda.
– ORIGIN modern Latin, from Latin *velox, veloc-* 'swift' + **RAPTOR**.

V

velocity /vɪˈlɒsɪti/ ▶ **noun** (pl. **velocities**) the speed of something in a given direction: *the velocities of the emitted particles*. ■ (in general use) speed: *the tank shot backwards at an incredible velocity*. ■ (also **velocity of circulation**) Economics the rate at which money changes hands within an economy.
– ORIGIN late Middle English: from French *vélocité* or Latin *velocitas*, from *velox, veloc-* 'swift'.

velocity profile ▶ **noun** Physics the variation in velocity along a line at right angles to the general direction of flow.

velodrome /ˈvɛlədrəʊm/ ▶ **noun** a cycle-racing track, typically with steeply banked curves. ■ a stadium containing a banked cycle-racing track.
– ORIGIN late 19th cent.: from French *vélodrome*, from *vélo* 'bicycle' + *-drome* (see **-DROME**).

velour /vəˈlʊə/ (also **velours**) ▶ **noun** [mass noun] a plush woven fabric resembling velvet, used for soft furnishings, casual clothing,and hats. ■ [count noun] dated a hat made of velour.
– ORIGIN early 18th cent.: from French *velours* 'velvet', from Old French *velour*, from Latin *villosus* 'hairy', from *villus* (see **VELVET**).

velouté /vəˈluːteɪ/ ▶ **noun** [mass noun] a white sauce made from a roux of butter and flour with chicken, veal, or pork stock.
– ORIGIN French, literally 'velvety'.

velum /ˈviːləm/ ▶ **noun** (pl. **vela** /-lə/) a membrane or membranous structure, typically covering another structure or partly obscuring an opening, in particular: ■ Anatomy the soft palate. ■ Zoology a membrane, typically bordering a cavity, especially in certain molluscs, medusae, and other invertebrates. ■ Botany the veil of a toadstool.
– ORIGIN mid 18th cent.: from Latin, literally 'sail, curtain, covering, veil'.

velvet ▶ **noun** [mass noun] a closely woven fabric of silk, cotton, or nylon, that has a thick short pile on one side. ■ soft downy skin that covers a deer's antler while it is growing.
– PHRASES **on velvet** informal, dated in an advantageous or prosperous position.
– DERIVATIVES **velveted** **adjective**, **velvety** **adjective**.
– ORIGIN Middle English: from Old French *veluotte*, from *velu* 'velvety', from medieval Latin *villutus*, from Latin *villus* 'tuft, down'.

velvet ant ▶ **noun** an ant-like velvety-bodied insect that is related to the wasps. The female is wingless and the larvae parasitize the young of bees and wasps in the nest. ● Family Mutillidae, superfamily Scolioidea: numerous species, including the European *Mutilla europaea*.

velvet bean ▶ **noun** see **MUCUNA**.

velveteen ▶ **noun** [mass noun] a cotton fabric with a pile resembling velvet. ■ (**velveteens**) dated trousers made of velveteen.

velvetleaf ▶ **noun** [mass noun] a Eurasian plant of the mallow family, with large heart-shaped velvety leaves and yellow flowers. It is naturalized in North America, where it has become a serious weed of farmland. ● *Abutilon theophrasti*, family Malvaceae.

velvet revolution ▶ **noun** a non-violent political revolution, especially the relatively smooth change from Communism to a Western-style democracy in Czechoslovakia at the end of 1989.
– ORIGIN translating Czech *sametová revoluce*.

velvet worm ▶ **noun** an onychophoran.

Ven. ▶ **abbreviation** Venerable (as the title of an archdeacon): *the Ven. William Davies*.

vena cava /ˌviːnə ˈkeɪvə/ ▶ **noun** (pl. **venae cavae** /ˌviːniː ˈkeɪviː/) a large vein carrying deoxygenated blood into the heart. There are two in humans, the **inferior vena cava** (carrying blood from the lower body) and the **superior vena cava** (carrying blood from the head, arms, and upper body).
– ORIGIN late 16th cent.: from Latin, literally 'hollow vein'.

venal /ˈviːn(ə)l/ ▶ **adjective** showing or motivated by susceptibility to bribery; corrupt: *local customs officers are notoriously venal | their generosity had been at least partly venal*.
– DERIVATIVES **venality** **noun**, **venally** **adverb**.
– ORIGIN mid 17th cent. (in the sense 'available for purchase', referring to merchandise or a favour): from Latin *venalis*, from *venum* 'thing for sale'.

> **USAGE** On the difference between **venal** and **venial**, see **USAGE** at **VENIAL**.

venation /vɪˈneɪʃ(ə)n/ ▶ **noun** [mass noun] Biology the arrangement of veins in a leaf or in an insect's wing. ■ the system of venous blood vessels in an animal.
– DERIVATIVES **venational** **adjective**.
– ORIGIN mid 17th cent.: from Latin *vena* 'vein' + **-ATION**.

vend ▶ **verb** [with obj.] offer (small items) for sale, either from a stall or from a slot machine: *there was a man vending sticky cakes and ices*. ■ Law or formal sell (something).
– DERIVATIVES **vendible** **adjective**.
– ORIGIN early 17th cent. (in the sense 'be sold'): from French *vendre* or Latin *vendere* 'sell', from *venum* 'something for sale' + a variant of *dare* 'give'.

Venda[1] /ˈvɛndə/ a former homeland established in South Africa for the Venda people, now part of Limpopo.

Venda[2] /ˈvɛndə/ ▶ **noun** (pl. **same** or **Vendas**) **1** a member of a people traditionally living in Limpopo province and southern Zimbabwe.
2 [mass noun] the Bantu language of the Venda, which has about 800,000 speakers in South Africa.
▶ **adjective** relating to the Venda or their language.
– ORIGIN the stem of Venda *Muvenda* (in sense 1 of the noun), *Tshivenda* (in sense 2 of the noun).

vendace /ˈvɛndɪs/ ▶ **noun** an edible whitefish found in lakes in northern Europe. In Britain it is now confined to two lakes in the English Lake District. ● *Coregonus albula*, family Salmonidae.
– ORIGIN mid 18th cent.: from obsolete French *vendese*, from a base related to Welsh *gwyn* 'white'.

vendange /vɒ̃ˈdɒ̃ʒ/, French /vɑ̃dɑ̃ʒ/ ▶ **noun** (pl. pronunc. **same**) (in France) the grape harvest.
– ORIGIN French.

Vendemiaire /vɛnˌdɛmɪˈɛː/ (also **Vendémiaire** French /vɑ̃demjɛʀ/) ▶ **noun** the first month of the French Republican calendar (1793–1805), originally running from 22 September to 21 October.
– ORIGIN French, from Latin *vindemia* 'vintage'.

vender ▶ **noun** US variant spelling of **VENDOR**.

vendetta /vɛnˈdɛtə/ ▶ **noun** a blood feud in which the family of a murdered person seeks vengeance on the murderer or the murderer's family. ■ a prolonged bitter quarrel with or campaign against someone: *he has accused the British media of pursuing a vendetta against him*.
– ORIGIN mid 19th cent.: from Italian, from Latin *vindicta* 'vengeance'.

vendeuse /vɒ̃ˈdəːz/, French /vɑ̃døz/ ▶ **noun** a saleswoman, especially one in a fashionable dress shop.
– ORIGIN French.

vending machine ▶ **noun** a machine that dispenses small articles such as food, drinks, or cigarettes when a coin or token is inserted.

vendor (US also **vender**) ▶ **noun** a person or company offering something for sale, especially a trader in the street: *an Italian ice-cream vendor*. ■ also /ˈvɛndɔː/ Law the seller in a sale, especially of property.
– ORIGIN late 16th cent.: from Anglo-Norman French *vendour* (see **VEND**).

vendor placing ▶ **noun** [mass noun] Finance a type of placing used as a method of financing a takeover in which the purchasing company issues its own shares as payment to the company being bought, with the prearranged agreement that these shares are then placed with investors in exchange for cash.

vendue /vɛnˈdjuː/ ▶ **noun** US & W. Indian a public auction.
– ORIGIN late 17th cent.: via Dutch from French dialect *vendue* 'sale', from *vendre* 'sell'.

veneer /vɪˈnɪə/ ▶ **noun** **1** a thin decorative covering of fine wood applied to a coarser wood or other material: *a fine-grained veneer* | [mass noun] *the ceiling was of maple veneer*. ■ a layer of wood used to make plywood. ■ [in sing.] an attractive appearance that covers or disguises someone or something's true nature or feelings: *her veneer of composure cracked a little*.
2 (also **veneer crown**) Dentistry a crown in which the restoration is placed over the prepared surface of a natural crown.
▶ **verb** [with obj.] (usu. as adj. **veneered**) cover (something) with a decorative layer of fine wood. ■ cover or disguise (someone or something's true nature) with an attractive appearance.
– ORIGIN early 18th cent. (earlier as *fineer*): from German *furni(e)ren*, from Old French *fournir* 'furnish'.

veneering ▶ **noun** [mass noun] material used as a veneer.

venepuncture /ˈvɛnɪˌpʌŋ(k)tʃə, ˈviːnɪ-/ (chiefly N. Amer. also **venipuncture**) ▶ **noun** [mass noun] the puncture of a vein as part of a medical procedure, typically to withdraw a blood sample or for an intravenous injection.
– ORIGIN 1920s: from Latin *vena* 'vein' + **PUNCTURE**.

venerable ▶ **adjective** accorded a great deal of respect, especially because of age, wisdom, or character: *a venerable statesman*. ■ (in the Anglican Church) a title given to an archdeacon. ■ (in the Roman Catholic Church) a title given to a deceased person who has attained a certain degree of sanctity but has not been fully beatified or canonized.
– DERIVATIVES **venerability** **noun**, **venerably** **adverb**.
– ORIGIN late Middle English: from Old French, or from Latin *venerabilis*, from the verb *venerari* (see **VENERATE**).

venerate /ˈvɛnəreɪt/ ▸ **verb** [with obj.] regard with great respect; revere: *Philip of Beverley was venerated as a saint.*
– DERIVATIVES **venerator** noun.
– ORIGIN early 17th cent. (earlier (Middle English) as *veneration*): from Latin *venerat-* 'adored, revered', from the verb *venerari*.

veneration /vɛnəˈreɪʃ(ə)n/ ▸ **noun** [mass noun] great respect; reverence: *the traditional veneration of saints.*

venereal /vɪˈnɪərɪəl/ ▸ **adjective** relating to sexual desire or sexual intercourse. ■ relating to venereal disease.
– DERIVATIVES **venereally** adverb.
– ORIGIN late Middle English: from Latin *venereus* (from *venus, vener-* 'sexual love') + -AL.

venereal disease ▸ **noun** a disease typically contracted by sexual intercourse with a person already infected; a sexually transmitted disease.

venereology /vɪˌnɪərɪˈɒlədʒi/ ▸ **noun** [mass noun] the branch of medicine concerned with venereal diseases.
– DERIVATIVES **venereologist** noun.

venery¹ /ˈvɛn(ə)ri/ ▸ **noun** [mass noun] archaic sexual indulgence.
– ORIGIN late Middle English: from medieval Latin *veneria*, from *venus, vener-* 'sexual love'.

venery² /ˈvɛn(ə)ri/ ▸ **noun** [mass noun] archaic hunting.
– ORIGIN Middle English: from Old French *venerie*, from *vener* 'to hunt', from Latin *venari*.

venesection /ˌvɛnɪˈsɛkʃ(ə)n, ˈvɛnɪ-/ ▸ **noun** another term for PHLEBOTOMY.
– ORIGIN mid 17th cent.: from medieval Latin *venae sectio(n-)* 'cutting of a vein'.

Venetia /vɪˈniːʃə/ a region of NE Italy; capital, Venice. Italian name **Veneto** /ˈvɛnetəʊ/.
– ORIGIN named after the *Veneti*, the pre-Roman inhabitants of the region.

Venetian ▸ **adjective** relating to Venice or its people.
▸ **noun 1** a native or citizen of Venice.
2 (**venetians**) venetian blinds.
– ORIGIN late Middle English: from Old French *Venicien*, assimilated to medieval Latin *Venetianus*, from Latin *Venetia* 'Venice'.

venetian blind ▸ **noun** a window blind consisting of horizontal slats which can be pivoted to control the amount of light that passes through it.

Venetian glass ▸ **noun** another term for MURANO GLASS.

Venetian red ▸ **noun** [mass noun] a reddish-brown pigment consisting of ferric oxide. ■ a strong reddish-brown colour.

Venetian window ▸ **noun** a window with three separate openings, the central one being arched and taller than the others; a Palladian window.

Venezia /veˈnettsja/ Italian name for VENICE.

Venezuela /ˌvɛnɪˈzweɪlə/, Spanish /beneˈswela, -θwela/ a republic on the north coast of South America, with a coastline on the Caribbean Sea; pop. 26,814,800 (est. 2009); official language, Spanish; capital, Caracas. Official name **Bolivarian Republic of Venezuela**.

> Colonized by the Spanish in the 16th century, Venezuela won its independence in 1821 after a ten-year struggle, but did not finally emerge as a separate nation until its secession from federation with Colombia (1830). It is a major oil-exporting country, with the industry based on the area around Lake Maracaibo in the north-west.

– DERIVATIVES **Venezuelan** adjective & noun.
– ORIGIN Spanish, literally 'little Venice', named by early explorers when they saw native houses built on stilts over water.

vengeance /ˈvɛn(d)ʒ(ə)ns/ ▸ **noun** [mass noun] punishment inflicted or retribution exacted for an injury or wrong: *voters are ready to wreak vengeance on all politicians.*
– PHRASES **with a vengeance** used to emphasize the degree to which something occurs or is true: *her headache was back with a vengeance.*
– ORIGIN Middle English: from Old French, from *venger* 'avenge'.

vengeful ▸ **adjective** seeking to harm someone in return for a perceived injury: *a vengeful ex-con.*
– DERIVATIVES **vengefully** adverb, **vengefulness** noun.
– ORIGIN late 16th cent.: from obsolete *venge* 'avenge' (see VENGEANCE), on the pattern of *revengeful*.

venial /ˈviːnɪəl/ ▸ **adjective** Christian Theology denoting a sin that is not regarded as depriving the soul of divine grace. Often contrasted with MORTAL. ■ (of a fault or offence) slight and pardonable.
– DERIVATIVES **veniality** /-ˈalɪti/ noun, **venially** adverb.
– ORIGIN Middle English: via Old French from late Latin *venialis*, from *venia* 'forgiveness'.

> **USAGE** Venal and venial are sometimes confused. **Venal** means 'susceptible to bribery, corrupt', as in *local customs officers are notoriously venal*, whereas **venial** is used to refer to a sin or offence that is excusable or pardonable, as opposed to a *mortal* sin.

Venice /ˈvɛnɪs/ a city in NE Italy, capital of Venetia region; pop. 270,098 (2008). Italian name **VENEZIA**.

> Situated on a lagoon of the Adriatic, Venice is built on numerous islands that are separated by canals and linked by bridges. It was a powerful republic in the Middle Ages and from the 13th to the 16th centuries a leading sea power, controlling trade to the eastern Mediterranean. After the Napoleonic Wars Venice was placed under Austrian rule and was incorporated into a unified Italy in 1866.

venipuncture ▸ **noun** chiefly N. Amer. variant spelling of VENEPUNCTURE.

venison /ˈvɛnɪs(ə)n, ˈvɛnɪz(ə)n/ ▸ **noun** [mass noun] meat from a deer.
– ORIGIN Middle English: from Old French *veneso(u)n*, from Latin *venatio(n-)* 'hunting', from *venari* 'to hunt'.

Venite /vɪˈnʌɪti, vɪˈniːti, -teɪ/ ▸ **noun** Psalm 95 used as a canticle in Christian liturgy, chiefly at matins.
– ORIGIN Latin, literally 'come ye', the first word of the psalm.

Venn diagram ▸ **noun** a diagram representing mathematical or logical sets pictorially as circles or closed curves within an enclosing rectangle (the universal set), common elements of the sets being represented by intersections of the circles.
– ORIGIN early 20th cent.: named after John Venn (1834–1923), English logician.

vennel /ˈvɛn(ə)l/ ▸ **noun** chiefly Scottish a narrow lane or passage between buildings; an alley.
– ORIGIN late Middle English: from Old French *venele*, from medieval Latin *venella*, diminutive of Latin *vena* 'vein'.

venogram /ˈviːnə(ʊ)gram/ ▸ **noun** Medicine an image produced by venography.

venography /vɪˈnɒgrəfi/ ▸ **noun** [mass noun] Medicine radiography of a vein after injection of a radiopaque fluid.
– DERIVATIVES **venographic** /ˌviːnə(ʊ)ˈgrafɪk/ adjective, **venographically** adverb.
– ORIGIN 1930s: from Latin *vena* 'vein' + -GRAPHY.

venom ▸ **noun** [mass noun] poisonous fluid secreted by animals such as snakes and scorpions and typically injected into prey or aggressors by biting or stinging. ■ extreme malice and bitterness shown in someone's attitudes, speech, or actions: *his voice was full of venom.*
– DERIVATIVES **venomed** adjective.
– ORIGIN Middle English: from Old French *venim*, variant of *venin*, from an alteration of Latin *venenum* 'poison'.

venomous /ˈvɛnəməs/ ▸ **adjective** (of animals, especially snakes, or their parts) secreting venom; capable of injecting venom by means of a bite or sting. ■ (of a person or their behaviour) full of malice or spite: *she replied with a venomous glance.*
– DERIVATIVES **venomously** adverb.
– ORIGIN Middle English: from Old French *venimeux*, from *venim* (see VENOM).

venous /ˈviːnəs/ ▸ **adjective** relating to a vein or the veins.
– DERIVATIVES **venously** adverb.
– ORIGIN early 17th cent.: from Latin *venosus* 'having many veins', from *vena* 'vein'.

vent¹ ▸ **noun 1** an opening that allows air, gas, or liquid to pass out of or into a confined space. ■ the opening of a volcano, through which lava and other materials are emitted. ■ chiefly Scottish a flue of a chimney. ■ historical the touch hole of a gun. ■ the anus, especially one in a lower animal such as a fish that serves for both excretion and reproduction.
2 [mass noun] the release or expression of a strong emotion, energy, etc.: *children give vent to their anger in various ways.*
▸ **verb** [with obj.] **1** give free expression to (a strong emotion): *we vent our spleen on drug barons.*
2 provide with an outlet for air, gas, or liquid: *tumble-dryers must be vented to the outside.* ■ discharge or expel (air, gas, or liquid) through an outlet: *the plant was isolated and the gas vented.* ■ permit air to enter (a beer cask).
– DERIVATIVES **vented** adjective, **ventless** adjective.
– ORIGIN late Middle English: partly from French *vent* 'wind', from Latin *ventus*, reinforced by French *évent*, from *éventer* 'expose to air', based on Latin *ventus* 'wind'.

vent² ▸ **noun** an opening or slit in a garment, especially in the lower part of the seam at the back of a coat.
– ORIGIN late Middle English: alteration of dialect *fent*, from Old French *fente* 'slit', based on Latin *findere* 'cleave'.

venter ▸ **noun** Zoology the underside or abdomen of an animal.
– ORIGIN early 18th cent.: from Latin, literally 'belly'.

venti /ˈvɛnti/ ▸ **noun** [usu. as modifier] US trademark a serving of a drink of coffee measuring 20 US fluid ounces.
– ORIGIN 1990s: Italian, literally 'twenty'.

ventiduct /ˈvɛntɪdʌkt/ ▸ **noun** Architecture a duct passing through a wall for ventilation.
– ORIGIN early 17th cent.: from Latin *ventus* 'wind' + *ductus* 'duct'.

ventifact /ˈvɛntɪfakt/ ▸ **noun** Geology a stone shaped by the erosive action of wind-blown sand.
– ORIGIN early 20th cent.: from Latin *ventus* 'wind' + *factum*, neuter past participle of *facere* 'make'.

ventil /ˈvɛntɪl/ ▸ **noun** Music **1** a valve in a wind instrument.
2 a shutter for regulating the airflow in an organ.
– ORIGIN late 19th cent.: from German, from Italian *ventile*, from medieval Latin *ventile* 'sluice', from Latin *ventus* 'wind'.

ventilate ▸ **verb** [with obj.] **1** cause air to enter and circulate freely in (a room, building, etc.): *ventilate the greenhouse well* | (as adj., in combination **-ventilated**) *gas heaters should only ever be used in well-ventilated rooms.*
2 discuss or examine (an opinion, issue, or complaint) in public: *he used the club to ventilate an ongoing complaint.*
3 Medicine subject to artificial respiration. ■ archaic oxygenate (the blood).
4 informal kill (someone) by shooting: *I pull out a gun and ventilate her dinner companion.*
– ORIGIN late Middle English (in the sense 'winnow, scatter'): from Latin *ventilat-* 'blown, winnowed', from the verb *ventilare*, from *ventus* 'wind'. Sense 1 dates from the mid 18th cent.

ventilation ▸ **noun** [mass noun] **1** the provision of fresh air to a room, building, etc. ■ Medicine the supply of air to the lungs, especially by artificial means.
2 public discussion or examination of an opinion, issue, or complaint.
– ORIGIN late Middle English (in the sense 'current of air'): from Old French, or from Latin *ventilatio(n-)*, from the verb *ventilare* (see VENTILATE). Sense 1 dates from the mid 17th cent.

ventilator ▸ **noun 1** an appliance or aperture for ventilating a room or other space.
2 Medicine an appliance for artificial respiration; a respirator.

ventilatory /ˈvɛntɪləˌt(ə)ri/ ▸ **adjective** Physiology relating to or serving for the provision of air to the lungs or respiratory system.

Ventolin /ˈvɛntəlɪn/ ▸ **noun** trademark for SALBUTAMOL.
– ORIGIN 1960s: perhaps from VENTILATE + -OL + -IN¹.

Ventose /vɒ̃ˈtəʊz/ (also **Ventôse** French /vɑ̃toz/) ▸ **noun** the sixth month of the French Republican calendar (1793–1805), originally running from 19 February to 20 March.
– ORIGIN French *Ventôse*, from Latin *ventosus* 'windy', from *ventus* 'wind'.

ventouse /ˈvɛntuːs/ ▸ **noun** Medicine a cup-shaped suction device applied to the baby's head in childbirth, to assist the birth.
– ORIGIN 1960s: from French, literally 'cupping-glass', based on Latin *ventus* 'wind'.

ventral ▸ **adjective** Anatomy, Zoology, & Botany on or relating to the underside of an animal or plant; abdominal: *a ventral nerve cord* | *the ventral part of the head.* Compare with DORSAL.
– DERIVATIVES **ventrally** adverb.
– ORIGIN late Middle English: from Latin *venter, ventr-* 'belly' + -AL.

ventral fin ▸ **noun 1** Zoology another term for PELVIC FIN. ■ an unpaired fin on the underside of certain fishes.
2 a single vertical fin under the fuselage or tail of an aircraft.

V

ventre à terre /ˌvɒ̃tr(ə) ɑː ˈtɛː/, French /vɑ̃tʀ a tɛʀ/ ▶ **adverb** at full speed (used especially of a horse's movement or its representation in painting).
– ORIGIN French, literally '(with) belly to the ground'.

ventricle /ˈvɛntrɪk(ə)l/ ▶ **noun** Anatomy a hollow part or cavity in an organ, in particular: ■ each of the two main chambers of the heart, left and right. ■ each of the four connected fluid-filled cavities in the centre of the brain.
– DERIVATIVES **ventricular** /-ˈtrɪkjʊlə/ **adjective**.
– ORIGIN late Middle English: from Latin *ventriculus*, diminutive of *venter* 'belly'.

ventriculography /vɛnˌtrɪkjʊˈlɒgrəfi/ ▶ **noun** [mass noun] Medicine radiography of the ventricles of the brain with the cerebral fluid replaced by air (pneumoencephalography) or radiopaque material or labelled with a radionuclide.

ventriloquist /vɛnˈtrɪləkwɪst/ ▶ **noun** a person, especially an entertainer, who can make their voice appear to come from somewhere else, typically a dummy of a person or animal.
– DERIVATIVES **ventriloquial** /ˌvɛntrɪˈləʊkwɪəl/ **adjective**, **ventriloquism** **noun**, **ventriloquize** (also **ventriloquise**) **verb**, **ventriloquy** **noun**.
– ORIGIN mid 17th cent.: from modern Latin *ventriloquium* (from Latin *venter* 'belly' + *loqui* 'speak') + -IST.

ventrolateral /ˌvɛntrə(ʊ)ˈlatər(ə)l/ ▶ **adjective** Biology situated towards the junction of the ventral and lateral sides.
– DERIVATIVES **ventrolaterally** **adverb**.

ventromedial /ˌvɛntrə(ʊ)ˈmiːdɪəl/ ▶ **adjective** Biology situated towards the middle of the ventral side.
– DERIVATIVES **ventromedially** **adverb**.

venture ▶ **noun** a risky or daring journey or undertaking: *pioneering ventures into little-known waters.* ■ a business enterprise, typically one that involves risk: *a joint venture between two aircraft manufacturers.*
▶ **verb 1** [no obj., with adverbial] undertake a risky or daring journey or course of action: *she **ventured out** into the blizzard.* ■ [with obj.] expose to the risk of loss: *agents for other people's money, they do not venture their own capital.*
2 [no obj., with infinitive] dare to do or say something that may be considered audacious (often used as a polite expression of hesitation or apology): *may I venture to add a few comments?* | [with obj.] *he ventured the opinion that Putt was insane.*
– PHRASES **at a venture** archaic trusting to chance rather than to previous consideration or preparation. **nothing ventured, nothing gained** proverb you can't expect to achieve anything if you never take any risks.
– ORIGIN late Middle English (in the sense 'adventure', also 'risk the loss of'): shortening of ADVENTURE.

venture capital ▶ **noun** [mass noun] capital invested in a project in which there is a substantial element of risk, typically a new or expanding business.
– DERIVATIVES **venture capitalist** **noun**.

venturer ▶ **noun** archaic a person who undertakes or shares in a trading venture.

Venture Scout ▶ **noun** a member of the Scout Association aged between 16 and 20.

venturesome ▶ **adjective** willing to take risks or embark on difficult or unusual courses of action.
– DERIVATIVES **venturesomely** **adverb**, **venturesomeness** **noun**.

Venturi /vɛnˈtjʊəri/, Robert (Charles) (b.1925), American architect, pioneer of postmodernist architecture. Among his buildings are the Humanities Classroom Building of the State University of New York (1973) and the Sainsbury Wing of the National Gallery in London (1991).

V

venturi /vɛnˈtjʊəri/ ▶ **noun** (pl. **venturis**) a short piece of narrow tube between wider sections for measuring flow rate or exerting suction.
– ORIGIN late 19th cent.: named after Giovanni B. *Venturi* (1746–1822), Italian physicist.

venue /ˈvɛnjuː/ ▶ **noun** the place where something happens, especially an organized event such as a concert, conference, or sports competition: *the club is the city's main venue for live music.* ■ Law the jurisdiction within which a criminal or civil case may or must be heard.
– ORIGIN late 16th cent. (denoting a thrust or bout in fencing; also in the Law sense): from Old French, literally 'a coming', feminine past participle of *venir* 'come' from Latin *venire*.

venule /ˈvɛnjuːl/ ▶ **noun** Anatomy a very small vein, especially one collecting blood from the capillaries.
– ORIGIN mid 19th cent.: from Latin *venula*, diminutive of *vena* 'vein'.

Venus 1 Roman Mythology a goddess, worshipped as the goddess of love in classical Rome though apparently a spirit of kitchen gardens in earlier times. Greek equivalent APHRODITE. ■ (as noun **a Venus**) literary a beautiful woman.
2 Astronomy the second planet from the sun in the solar system, the brightest celestial object after the sun and moon and frequently appearing in the twilight sky as the evening or morning star.

> Venus orbits between Mercury and the earth at an average distance of 108 million km from the sun. It is almost equal in size to the earth, with a diameter of 12,104 km, and shows phases similar to the moon. The planet is completely covered by clouds consisting chiefly of sulphuric acid droplets, and no surface detail can be seen by telescope. There is a dense atmosphere of carbon dioxide, which traps the heat of the sun by the greenhouse effect to produce a surface temperature of 460°C. The planet has no natural satellite.

3 (also **venus**, **Venus shell**, or (chiefly US) **Venus clam**) a burrowing marine bivalve mollusc with clearly defined growth lines on the shell. ● *Venus*, *Venerupis*, and other genera, family Veneridae.
– DERIVATIVES **Venusian** /vɪˈnjuːzɪən/ **adjective & noun**.

Venusberg /ˈviːnəsbəːg/ ▶ **noun** (in German legend) the court of Venus.
– ORIGIN German, literally 'mountain of Venus'.

Venus de Milo /də ˈmʌɪləʊ, ˈmiːləʊ/ a classical sculpture of Aphrodite dated to *c.*100 BC. It was discovered on the Greek island of Melos in 1820 and is now in the Louvre in Paris.
– ORIGIN French, 'Venus of Melos'.

Venus flytrap (also **Venus's flytrap**) ▶ **noun** a small carnivorous bog plant with hinged leaves that spring shut on and digest insects which land on them. Native to the south-eastern US, it is also kept as an indoor plant. ● *Dionaea muscipula*, family Droseraceae.

Venus's comb ▶ **noun** another term for SHEPHERD'S NEEDLE.

Venus's flower basket ▶ **noun** a slender upright glass sponge with a filmy lattice-like skeleton. ● Genus *Euplectella*, class Hexactinellida.

Venus's girdle ▶ **noun** a large, almost transparent comb jelly with a flattened ribbon-like body, living chiefly in warmer seas. ● Genus *Cestum*, phylum Ctenophora.

Venus's looking glass ▶ **noun** a blue-flowered plant of the bellflower family, whose shiny brown seeds inside their open capsule supposedly resemble looking glasses. ● Two species in the family Campanulaceae: *Legousia hybrida* of Europe, and *Triodanis perfoliata* of North America.

vera causa /ˌvɛːrə ˈkaʊzə/ ▶ **noun** (pl. **verae causae** /ˌvɛːriː ˈkaʊziː/) chiefly historical (in Newtonian philosophy) the true cause of a natural phenomenon, by an agency whose existence is independently evidenced.
– ORIGIN Latin, literally 'real cause'.

veracious /vəˈreɪʃəs/ ▶ **adjective** formal speaking or representing the truth: *a veracious account.*
– DERIVATIVES **veraciously** **adverb**, **veraciousness** **noun**.
– ORIGIN late 17th cent.: from Latin *verax*, *verac-* (from *verus* 'true') + -IOUS.

veracity /vəˈrasɪti/ ▶ **noun** [mass noun] conformity to facts; accuracy: *officials expressed doubts concerning the veracity of the story.* ■ habitual truthfulness: *voters should be concerned about his veracity and character.*
– ORIGIN early 17th cent.: from French *véracité* or medieval Latin *veracitas*, from *verax* 'speaking truly' (see VERACIOUS).

Veracruz /ˌvɪərəˈkruːz/, Spanish /beraˈkrus, -kruθ/ **1** a state of east central Mexico, with a long coastline on the Gulf of Mexico; capital, Jalapa Enriquez.
2 a city and port of Mexico, in Veracruz state, on the Gulf of Mexico; pop. 444,438 (2005).

veranda (also **verandah**) ▶ **noun** a roofed platform along the outside of a house, level with the ground floor. ■ Austral./NZ a roof over the pavement in front of a shop.
– DERIVATIVES **verandaed** **adjective**.
– ORIGIN early 18th cent.: from Hindi *varaṇḍā*, from Portuguese *varanda* 'railing, balustrade'.

verapamil /vəˈrapəmɪl/ ▶ **noun** [mass noun] Medicine a synthetic compound which acts as a calcium antagonist and is used to treat angina pectoris and cardiac arrhythmias.
– ORIGIN 1960s: from *v(al)er(onitr)il(e)* (from VALERIC ACID + NITRILE), with the insertion of *-apam-* (of unknown origin).

veratrine /ˈvɛrətriːn, -ɪn/ ▶ **noun** [mass noun] Chemistry a poisonous substance consisting of a mixture of alkaloids which occurs in the seeds of sabadilla and related plants.
– ORIGIN early 19th cent.: from French *vératrine*, from Latin *veratrum* 'hellebore'.

veratrum /vəˈreɪtrəm/ ▶ **noun** (pl. **veratrums**) a plant of a genus that includes the false helleborines. ● Genus *Veratrum*, family Liliaceae.
– ORIGIN modern Latin, from Latin, literally 'hellebore'.

verb ▶ **noun** Grammar a word used to describe an action, state, or occurrence, and forming the main part of the predicate of a sentence, such as *hear*, *become*, *happen*.
– DERIVATIVES **verbless** **adjective**.
– ORIGIN late Middle English: from Old French *verbe* or Latin *verbum* 'word, verb'.

verbal ▶ **adjective 1** relating to or in the form of words: *the root of the problem is visual rather than verbal* | *verbal abuse.* ■ spoken rather than written; oral: *a verbal agreement.* ■ tending to talk a lot: *he's very verbal.*
2 Grammar relating to or derived from a verb: *a verbal adjective.*
▶ **noun 1** Grammar a word or words functioning as a verb. ■ a verbal noun.
2 [mass noun] (also **verbals**) Brit. informal abuse; insults: *just a bit of air-wave verbals.*
3 (**verbals**) informal the lyrics of a song or the dialogue of a film.
4 (usu. **verbals**) Brit. informal a verbal statement containing a damaging admission alleged to have been made to the police, and offered as evidence by the prosecution.
▶ **verb** (**verbals**, **verballing**, **verballed**) [with obj.] Brit. informal attribute a damaging statement to (a suspect), especially dishonestly.
– DERIVATIVES **verbally** **adverb**.
– ORIGIN late 15th cent. (describing a person who deals with words rather than things): from French, or from late Latin *verbalis*, from *verbum* 'word' (see VERB).

> **USAGE** It is sometimes said that the true sense of the adjective **verbal** is 'of or concerned with words', whether spoken or written (as in *verbal abuse*), and that it should not be used to mean 'spoken rather than written' (as in *a verbal agreement*). For this sense, it is said that the adjective **oral** should be used instead. In practice, however, **verbal** is well established in this sense and, in certain idiomatic phrases (such as *a verbal agreement*), cannot be simply replaced by **oral**.

verbal diarrhoea ▶ **noun** [mass noun] informal the quality or habit of talking too much.

verbalism ▶ **noun** [mass noun] concentration on forms of expression rather than content. ■ [count noun] a verbal expression. ■ excessive or empty use of language.
– DERIVATIVES **verbalistic** **adjective**.

verbalize (also **verbalise**) ▶ **verb** [with obj.] **1** express (ideas or feelings) in words, especially by speaking out loud: *they are unable to verbalize their real feelings.*
2 [no obj.] speak, especially at length and with little real content: *the dangers of verbalizing about art.*
3 make (a word, especially a noun) into a verb.
– DERIVATIVES **verbalizable** **adjective**, **verbalization** **noun**, **verbalizer** **noun**.

verbal noun ▶ **noun** Grammar a noun formed as an inflection of a verb and partly sharing its constructions, such as *smoking* in *smoking is forbidden*. See -ING[1].

verbascum /vəːˈbaskəm/ ▶ **noun** (pl. **verbascums**) a plant of a genus that comprises the mulleins. ● Genus *Verbascum*, family Scrophulariaceae.
– ORIGIN modern Latin, from Latin, literally 'mullein'.

verbatim /vəːˈbeɪtɪm/ ▶ **adverb & adjective** in exactly the same words as were used originally: [as adv.] *subjects were instructed to recall the passage verbatim* | *a verbatim account.*
– ORIGIN late 15th cent.: from medieval Latin, from Latin *verbum* 'word'. Compare with LITERATIM.

verbena /vəːˈbiːnə/ ▶ **noun** a chiefly American herbaceous plant which bears heads of bright showy flowers, widely cultivated as a garden ornamental.

● Genus *Verbena*, family Verbenaceae: many species, in particular a group of complex cultivars (*V.* × *hybrida*).
– ORIGIN modern Latin, from Latin, literally 'sacred bough', in medieval Latin 'vervain'.

verbiage /ˈvəːbɪɪdʒ/ ▶ **noun** [mass noun] excessively lengthy or technical speech or writing.
– ORIGIN early 18th cent.: from French, from obsolete *verbeier* 'to chatter', from *verbe* 'word' (see **VERB**).

verbose /vəːˈbəʊs/ ▶ **adjective** using or expressed in more words than are needed: *much academic language is obscure and verbose.*
– DERIVATIVES **verbosely adverb**.
– ORIGIN late 17th cent.: from Latin *verbosus*, from *verbum* 'word'.

verbosity /vəˈbɒsɪti/ ▶ **noun** [mass noun] the fact or quality of using more words than needed; wordiness: *a critic with a reputation for verbosity.*

verboten /vəːˈbəʊt(ə)n/, German /fɛɐˈboːtn/ ▶ **adjective** forbidden, especially by an authority.
– ORIGIN German.

verb phrase ▶ **noun** Grammar **1** a verb with another word or words indicating tense, mood, or person.
2 a phrasal verb.

verdant /ˈvəːd(ə)nt/ ▶ **adjective** (of countryside) green with grass or other rich vegetation: *verdant valleys.* ■ of the bright green colour of lush grass.
– DERIVATIVES **verdancy noun**, **verdantly adverb**.
– ORIGIN late 16th cent.: perhaps from Old French *verdeant*, present participle of *verdoier* 'be green', based on Latin *viridis* 'green'.

verd-antique /ˌvəːdanˈtiːk/ ▶ **noun** [mass noun] a green ornamental marble consisting of serpentine with calcite and dolomite. ■ verdigris on ancient bronze or copper. ■ a green form of porphyry.
– ORIGIN mid 18th cent.: from obsolete French, literally 'antique green'.

Verdelho /vəːˈdɛljuː, -ljəʊ/ ▶ **noun** (pl. **Verdelhos**) a white grape originally grown in Madeira, now also in Portugal, Sicily, Australia, and South Africa. ■ [mass noun] a medium Madeira made from the Verdelho grape.
– ORIGIN Portuguese.

verderer /ˈvəːd(ə)rə/ ▶ **noun** Brit. a judicial officer of a royal forest.
– ORIGIN mid 16th cent.: from Anglo-Norman French, based on Latin *viridis* 'green'.

Verdi /ˈvɛːdi/, Italian /ˈverdi/, Giuseppe (Fortunino Francesco) (1813–1901), Italian composer. His many operas, such as *La Traviata* (1853), *Aida* (1871), and *Otello* (1887), emphasize the dramatic element, treating personal stories on a heroic scale and often against backgrounds that reflect his political interests. Verdi is also famous for his *Requiem* (1874).

Verdicchio /vɛːˈdiːkɪəʊ/ ▶ **noun** [mass noun] a variety of white wine grape grown in the Marche region of Italy. ■ a dry white wine made from the Verdicchio grape.
– ORIGIN Italian.

verdict ▶ **noun** a decision on an issue of fact in a civil or criminal case or an inquest: *the jury returned a verdict of not guilty.* ■ an opinion or judgement: *this seems a fair verdict on the tabloids.*
– ORIGIN Middle English: from Anglo-Norman French *verdit*, from Old French *veir* 'true' (from Latin *verus*) + *dit* (from Latin *dictum* 'saying').

verdigris /ˈvəːdɪgriː, -griːs/ ▶ **noun** [mass noun] a bright bluish-green encrustation or patina formed on copper or brass by atmospheric oxidation, consisting of basic copper carbonate.
– ORIGIN Middle English: from Old French *verte gres*, earlier *vert de Grece* 'green of Greece'.

verdigris agaric ▶ **noun** a toadstool with a slimy blue-green cap and dark brown gills, found in both Eurasia and North America. ● *Stropharia aeruginosa*, family Strophariaceae, class Hymenomycetes.

verdin /ˈvəːdɪn/ ▶ **noun** a small songbird with a grey body and yellowish head, found in the semi-deserts of south-western North America. ● *Auriparus flaviceps*, family Remizidae.
– ORIGIN late 19th cent.: from French, literally 'yellowhammer'.

verditer /ˈvəːdɪtə/ ▶ **noun** [mass noun] a light blue or bluish-green pigment, typically prepared by adding chalk or whiting to a solution of copper nitrate, used in making crayons and as a watercolour.
▶ **adjective** of a light blue or bluish-green colour.
– ORIGIN early 16th cent.: from Old French *verd de terre*, literally 'earth green'.

Verdun, Battle of /vəːˈdʌn/, French /vɛʀdœ̃/ a long and severe battle in 1916, during the First World War, at the fortified town of Verdun in NE France.

verdure /ˈvəːdjə, -jʊə/ ▶ **noun** [mass noun] lush green vegetation. ■ literary the fresh green colour of lush vegetation.
– DERIVATIVES **verdured adjective**, **verdurous adjective**.
– ORIGIN late Middle English: via French from Old French *verd* 'green', from Latin *viridis*.

Vereeniging /fəˈriːnɪkɪŋ, fəˈreɪnɪxɪŋ/ a city in South Africa, in the province of Gauteng; pop. 474,000 (est. 2009).

verge¹ ▶ **noun 1** an edge or border: *they came down to the verge of the lake.* ■ Brit. a grass edging such as that by the side of a road or path. ■ Architecture an edge of tiles projecting over a gable.
2 an extreme limit beyond which something specified will happen: *I was on the verge of tears.*
▶ **verb** [no obj.] (**verge on**) be very close or similar to: *despair verging on the suicidal.*
– ORIGIN late Middle English: via Old French from Latin *virga* 'rod'. The current verb sense dates from the late 18th cent.

verge² ▶ **noun** a wand or rod carried before a bishop or dean as an emblem of office.
– ORIGIN late Middle English: from Latin *virga* 'rod'.

verge³ ▶ **verb** [no obj., with adverbial of direction] incline in a certain direction or towards a particular state: *his style verged into the art nouveau school.*
– ORIGIN early 17th cent. (in the sense 'descend to the horizon'): from Latin *vergere* 'to bend, incline'.

vergence ▶ **noun** [mass noun] **1** Physiology the simultaneous movement of the pupils of the eyes towards or away from one another during focusing.
2 Geology the direction in which a fold is inclined or overturned: *a zone of opposing fold vergence.*
– ORIGIN 1980s: common element of **CONVERGENCE** and **DIVERGENCE**.

verger ▶ **noun 1** an official in a church who acts as a caretaker and attendant.
2 an officer who carries a rod before a bishop or dean as a symbol of office.
– ORIGIN Middle English (in sense 2): from Anglo-Norman French (see **VERGE²**).

Vergil variant spelling of **VIRGIL**.
– DERIVATIVES **Vergilian adjective**.

verglas /ˈvɛːglɑː/ ▶ **noun** [mass noun] a thin coating of ice or frozen rain on an exposed surface.
– ORIGIN early 19th cent.: French, from *verre* 'glass' + *glas* (now *glace*) 'ice'.

veridical /vɪˈrɪdɪk(ə)l/ ▶ **adjective** formal truthful. ■ coinciding with reality: *such memories are not necessarily veridical.*
– DERIVATIVES **veridicality noun**, **veridically adverb**.
– ORIGIN mid 17th cent.: from Latin *veridicus* (from *verus* 'true' + *dicere* 'say') + **-AL**.

veriest ▶ **adjective** [attrib.] (**the veriest**) archaic used to emphasize the degree to which a description applies to someone or something: *everyone but the veriest greenhorn knows by now.*
– ORIGIN early 16th cent.: superlative of **VERY**.

verification ▶ **noun** [mass noun] the process of establishing the truth, accuracy, or validity of something: *the verification of official documents.* ■ [often as modifier] Philosophy the establishment by empirical means of the validity of a proposition. ■ the process of ensuring that procedures laid down in weapons limitation agreements are followed.
– ORIGIN early 16th cent.: from Old French or from medieval Latin *verificatio(n-)*, from the verb *verificare* (see **VERIFY**).

verification principle ▶ **noun** Philosophy the characteristic doctrine of logical positivism, that a statement which cannot be verified is strictly meaningless.

verify /ˈvɛrɪfʌɪ/ ▶ **verb** (**verifies**, **verifying**, **verified**) [with obj.] make sure or demonstrate that (something) is true, accurate, or justified: *his conclusions have been verified by later experiments* | [with clause] *'Can you verify that the guns are licensed?'* ■ Law swear to or support (a statement) by affidavit.
– DERIVATIVES **verifiable adjective**, **verifiably adverb**, **verifier noun**.
– ORIGIN Middle English (as a legal term): from Old French *verifier*, from medieval Latin *verificare*, from *verus* 'true'.

verily ▶ **adverb** archaic truly; certainly: [sentence adverb] *verily these men are mad.*
– ORIGIN Middle English: from **VERY** + **-LY²**, suggested by Old French *verrai(e)ment*.

verisimilitude /ˌvɛrɪsɪˈmɪlɪtjuːd/ ▶ **noun** [mass noun] the appearance of being true or real: *the detail gives the novel some verisimilitude.*
– DERIVATIVES **verisimilar adjective**.
– ORIGIN early 17th cent.: from Latin *verisimilitudo*, from *verisimilis* 'probable', from *veri* (genitive of *verus* 'true') + *similis* 'like'.

verismo /vɛˈrɪzməʊ/ ▶ **noun** [mass noun] realism in the arts, especially late 19th-century Italian opera. ■ this genre of opera, as composed principally by Puccini, Mascagni, and Leoncavallo.
– ORIGIN Italian.

veristic /vɪəˈrɪstɪk/ ▶ **adjective** (of art or literature) extremely or strictly naturalistic.
– DERIVATIVES **verism noun**, **verist noun & adjective**.
– ORIGIN late 19th cent.: from Latin *verum* (neuter) 'true' or Italian *vero* 'true' + **-IST** + **-IC**.

veritable ▶ **adjective** [attrib.] used for emphasis, often to qualify a metaphor: *the early 1970s witnessed a veritable price explosion.*
– DERIVATIVES **veritably adverb**.
– ORIGIN late Middle English: from Old French, from *verite* 'truth' (see **VERITY**). Early senses included 'true' and 'speaking the truth', later 'genuine, actual'.

vérité /ˈvɛrɪteɪ/, French /veʀite/ ▶ **noun** [mass noun] a genre of film, television, and radio programmes emphasizing realism and naturalism.
– ORIGIN French, literally 'truth'.

verity ▶ **noun** (pl. **verities**) a true principle or belief, especially one of fundamental importance: *the eternal verities.* ■ [mass noun] truth: *irrefutable, objective verity.*
– ORIGIN late Middle English: from Old French *verite*, from Latin *veritas*, from *verus* 'true'.

verjuice /ˈvəːdʒuːs/ ▶ **noun** [mass noun] a sour juice obtained from crab apples, unripe grapes, or other fruit, used in cooking and formerly in medicine.
– ORIGIN Middle English: from Old French *vertjus*, from *vert* 'green' + *jus* 'juice'.

Verkhneudinsk /ˌvɛːxnjɛˈuːdɪnsk/ former name (until 1934) for **ULAN-UDE**.

verkrampte /fɛːˈkramptə/ (also **verkramp** /fɛːˈkramp/) S. African ▶ **adjective** conservative or reactionary, especially as regards apartheid.
▶ **noun** a person holding bigoted and reactionary views.
– ORIGIN Afrikaans, literally 'narrow, cramped'.

Verlaine /vɛːˈlɛn/, French /vɛʀlɛn/, Paul (1844–96), French symbolist poet. Notable collections of poetry include *Poèmes saturniens* (1867), *Fêtes galantes* (1869), and *Romances sans paroles* (1874).

verligte /fɛːˈlɪxtə/ (also **verlig**) S. African ▶ **adjective** progressive or enlightened, especially as regards apartheid.
▶ **noun** a person holding progressive and enlightened views.
– ORIGIN Afrikaans, literally 'enlightened'.

Vermeer /vəːˈmɪə/, Jan (1632–75), Dutch painter. He chiefly painted domestic genre scenes, for example *The Kitchen-Maid* (*c.*1658). His work is distinguished by its balanced composition and treatment of light.

vermeil /ˈvəːmeɪl/, /-mɪl/ ▶ **noun** [mass noun] [often as modifier] **1** gilded silver or bronze.
2 literary vermilion.
– ORIGIN late Middle English (in sense 2): from Old French (see **VERMILION**).

vermi- ▶ **combining form** relating to a worm or worms, especially parasitic ones: *vermiform.*
– ORIGIN from Latin *vermis* 'worm'.

vermian /ˈvəːmɪən/ ▶ **adjective 1** literary relating to or resembling a worm; worm-like.
2 Anatomy relating to the vermis of the brain.
– ORIGIN late 19th cent.: from Latin *vermis* 'worm' + **-IAN**.

V

vermicelli /ˌvəːmɪˈtʃɛli, ˌvɛːm-, -ˈsɛli/ ▶ **plural noun**
1 pasta in the form of long slender threads.
2 Brit. shreds of chocolate used to decorate cakes or other sweet foods.
– ORIGIN Italian, plural of *vermicello*, diminutive of *verme* 'worm', from Latin *vermis*.

vermicide /ˈvəːmɪsʌɪd/ ▶ **noun** a substance that is poisonous to worms.

vermicomposting /ˈvəːmɪkɒmpɒstɪŋ/ ▶ **noun** [mass noun] the use of earthworms to convert organic waste into fertilizer.
– DERIVATIVES **vermicomposter noun**.

vermicular /vəˈmɪkjʊlə/ ▶ **adjective 1** like a worm in form or movement; vermiform.

2 denoting or caused by intestinal worms.
– ORIGIN late 17th cent.: from medieval Latin *vermicularis*, from Latin *vermiculus*, diminutive of *vermis* 'worm'.

vermiculate /vəˈmɪkjʊlət/ ▸ adjective 1 another term for VERMICULAR.
2 another term for VERMICULATED.
– ORIGIN early 17th cent.: from Latin *vermiculatus*, past participle of *vermiculari* 'be full of worms' (see VERMICULAR).

vermiculated ▸ adjective 1 (especially of the plumage of a bird) marked with sinuous or wavy lines.
2 archaic worm-eaten.

vermiculation ▸ noun a marking made by, or resembling the track of, a worm. ■ [mass noun] Architecture wavy lines cut into the surface of stone, used for decoration.
– ORIGIN early 17th cent.: from Latin *vermiculatio(n-)*, from the verb *vermiculari* (see VERMICULATE).

vermiculite /vəˈmɪkjʊlʌɪt/ ▸ noun [mass noun] a yellow or brown mineral found as an alteration product of mica and other minerals, used for insulation or as a moisture-retentive medium for growing plants.
– ORIGIN early 19th cent.: from Latin *vermiculari* 'be full of worms' (because on expansion due to heat, it shoots out forms resembling small worms) + -ITE[1].

vermiculture /ˈvəːmɪkʌltʃə/ ▸ noun [mass noun] the cultivation of earthworms, especially in order to use them to convert organic waste into fertilizer.

vermiform ▸ adjective chiefly Zoology or Anatomy resembling or having the form of a worm.

vermiform appendix ▸ noun technical term for APPENDIX (sense 1).

vermifuge /ˈvəːmɪfjuːdʒ/ ▸ noun Medicine an anthelmintic medicine.

vermilion /vəˈmɪljən/ ▸ noun [mass noun] a brilliant red pigment made from mercury sulphide (cinnabar). ■ a brilliant red colour: *a lateral stripe of vermilion* | [as modifier] *vermilion streaks of sunset*.
– ORIGIN Middle English: from Old French *vermeillon*, from *vermeil*, from Latin *vermiculus*, diminutive of *vermis* 'worm'.

vermin ▸ noun [treated as pl.] wild mammals and birds which are believed to be harmful to crops, farm animals, or game, or which carry disease, e.g. foxes, rodents, and insect pests. ■ parasitic worms or insects. ■ people perceived as despicable and as causing problems for the rest of society: *the vermin who ransacked her house*.
– DERIVATIVES **verminous** adjective.
– ORIGIN Middle English (originally denoting animals such as reptiles and snakes): from Old French, based on Latin *vermis* 'worm'.

verminate ▸ verb [no obj.] (usu. as adj. **verminating**) archaic breed or become infested with vermin.
– ORIGIN late 17th cent.: from Latin *verminat-* 'full of worms', from the verb *verminare*, from *vermis* 'worm'.

vermis /ˈvəːmɪs/ ▸ noun Anatomy the rounded and elongated central part of the cerebellum, between the two hemispheres.
– ORIGIN late 19th cent.: from Latin, literally 'worm'.

Vermont /vəˈmɒnt/ a state in the north-eastern US, on the border with Canada; pop. 621,270 (est. 2008); capital, Montpelier. Explored and settled by the French during the 17th and 18th centuries, it became an independent republic in 1777 and the 14th state of the US in 1791.
– DERIVATIVES **Vermonter** noun.

vermouth /ˈvəːməθ, vəˈmuːθ/ ▸ noun [mass noun] a red or white wine flavoured with aromatic herbs, chiefly made in France and Italy and drunk mixed with gin.
– ORIGIN from French *vermout*, from German *Wermut* 'wormwood'.

Vernaccia /vəˈnatʃə/ ▸ noun [mass noun] a variety of wine grape grown in the San Gimignano area of Italy and in Sardinia. ■ a dry white wine made from the Vernaccia grape.
– ORIGIN Italian.

vernacular /vəˈnakjʊlə/ ▸ noun 1 (usu. **the vernacular**) the language or dialect spoken by the ordinary people of a country or region: *he wrote in the vernacular to reach a larger audience*. ■ [with adj. or noun modifier] informal the terminology used by people belonging to a specified group or engaging in a specialized activity: [mass noun] *gardening vernacular*.
2 [mass noun] architecture concerned with domestic and functional rather than public or monumental buildings: *buildings in which Gothic merged into farmhouse vernacular*.
▸ adjective 1 (of language) spoken as one's mother tongue; not learned or imposed as a second language. ■ (of speech or written works) using the mother tongue of a country or region: *vernacular literature*.
2 (of architecture) concerned with domestic and functional rather than public buildings.
– DERIVATIVES **vernacularism** noun, **vernacularity** noun, **vernacularize** (also **vernacularise**) verb, **vernacularly** adverb.
– ORIGIN early 17th cent.: from Latin *vernaculus* 'domestic, native' (from *verna* 'home-born slave') + -AR[1].

vernal /ˈvəːn(ə)l/ ▸ adjective of, in, or appropriate to spring: *the vernal freshness of the land*.
– ORIGIN mid 16th cent.: from Latin *vernalis*, from *vernus* 'of the spring', from *ver* 'spring'.

vernal equinox ▸ noun Astronomy another term for SPRING EQUINOX. ■ another term for FIRST POINT OF ARIES (see ARIES).

vernal grass (also **sweet vernal grass**) ▸ noun [mass noun] a sweet-scented Eurasian grass which is sometimes grown as a meadow or hay grass. ● *Anthoxanthum odoratum*, family Gramineae.

vernalization (also **vernalisation**) ▸ noun [mass noun] the cooling of seed during germination in order to accelerate flowering when it is planted.
– DERIVATIVES **vernalize** (also **vernalise**) verb.
– ORIGIN 1930s: translation of Russian *yarovizatsiya*.

vernation /vəːˈneɪʃ(ə)n/ ▸ noun [mass noun] Botany the arrangement of bud scales or young leaves in a leaf bud before it opens. Compare with AESTIVATION.
– ORIGIN late 18th cent.: from modern Latin *vernatio(n-)*, from Latin *vernare* 'to grow (as in the spring)', from *vernus* (see VERNAL).

Verne /vəːn/, Jules (1828–1905), French novelist. One of the first writers of science fiction, he often anticipated later scientific and technological developments, as in *Twenty Thousand Leagues under the Sea* (1870). Other novels include *Around the World in Eighty Days* (1873).

Verner's Law /ˈvɛːnəz, ˈvəːnəz/ ▸ noun Linguistics the observation that voiceless fricatives in Germanic predicted by Grimm's Law became voiced if the preceding syllable in the corresponding Indo-European word was unstressed.
– ORIGIN late 19th cent.: named after Karl A. *Verner* (1846–96), Danish philologist.

vernicle /ˈvəːnɪk(ə)l/ ▸ noun another term for VERONICA (sense 2).
– ORIGIN Middle English: from Old French, alteration of *vernique*, from medieval Latin *veronica*.

vernier /ˈvəːnɪə/ ▸ noun a small movable graduated scale for obtaining fractional parts of subdivisions on a fixed main scale of a barometer, sextant, or other measuring instrument.
– ORIGIN mid 18th cent.: named after Pierre *Vernier* (1580–1637), French mathematician.

vernier engine ▸ noun a thruster on a spacecraft.
– ORIGIN 1950s: named after P. *Vernier* (see VERNIER).

vernissage /ˌvɛːnɪˈsɑːʒ/ ▸ noun (pl. pronunc. **same**) a private view of paintings before public exhibition.
– ORIGIN French, literally 'varnishing', originally referring to the day prior to an exhibition when artists were allowed to retouch and varnish hung work.

vernix /ˈvəːnɪks/ (in full **vernix caseosa** /ˌkeɪsɪˈəʊsə/) ▸ noun [mass noun] a greasy deposit covering the skin of a baby at birth.
– ORIGIN late 16th cent.: from medieval Latin, variant of *veronix* 'fragrant resin' (see VARNISH).

Verny /ˈvɛːni/ former name (until 1921) for ALMATY.

Vero board /ˈvɛrəʊ, ˈvɪərəʊ/ ▸ noun Brit. trademark a type of board used to make electronic circuits, where some of the electrical connections are formed by strips of copper on the underside of the board.

Verona /vəˈrəʊnə/ a city on the River Adige, in NE Italy; pop. 265,368 (2008).

veronal /ˈvɛrən(ə)l/ ▸ noun another term for BARBITONE.
– ORIGIN early 20th cent.: from German, from VERONA + -AL.

Veronese /ˌvɛrəˈneɪzeɪ, -zi/, Paolo (*c.*1528–88), Italian painter; born *Paolo Caliari*. He is particularly known for his richly coloured feast scenes (for example *The Marriage at Cana*, 1562) and for his frescoes in the Doges' Palace in Venice.

veronica ▸ noun 1 a herbaceous plant of north temperate regions, typically with upright stems bearing narrow pointed leaves and spikes of blue or purple flowers. ● Genus *Veronica*, family Scrophulariaceae: many species, including the speedwells.
2 a cloth supposedly impressed with an image of Christ's face.
3 the movement of a matador's cape away from a charging bull.
– ORIGIN early 16th cent.: from medieval Latin, from the given name *Veronica*. Sense 2, sense 3 are with reference to St Veronica (see VERONICA, ST); sense 3 is said to be by association of the attitude of the matador with the depiction of St Veronica holding out a cloth to Christ.

Veronica, St /vəˈrɒnɪkə/ a woman of Jerusalem who offered her head cloth to Christ on the way to Calvary, to wipe the blood and sweat from his face. The cloth is said to have retained the image of his features.

veronique /ˌvɛrəˈniːk/ ▸ adjective [postpositive] denoting a dish, typically of fish or chicken, prepared or garnished with grapes.
– ORIGIN from the French given name *Véronique*.

Verrazano-Narrows Bridge /ˌvɛrəˈzɑːnəʊ/ a suspension bridge across New York harbour between Brooklyn and Staten Island, the longest in the world when it was completed in 1964.
– ORIGIN named after Giovanni da *Verrazano* (1485–1528), Italian explorer.

verre églomisé /vɛː ˌeɪglɒmiːˈzeɪ/, French /vɛʀ eglɔmize/ ▸ noun [mass noun] glass decorated on the back with engraved gold or silver leaf or paint.
– ORIGIN early 20th cent.: French, from *verre* 'glass' + *églomisé*, from *Glomy*, the name of an 18th-cent. Parisian picture-framer.

verruca /vəˈruːkə/ ▸ noun (pl. **verrucae** /-kiː, -siː/ or **verrucas**) a contagious and usually painful wart on the sole of the foot; a plantar wart. ■ (in medical use) a wart of any kind.
– DERIVATIVES **verrucose** /ˈvɛrʊkəʊz, vəˈruː-/ adjective, **verrucous** /ˈvɛrʊkəs, vəˈruː-/ adjective.
– ORIGIN late Middle English: from Latin.

Versace /vəːˈsɑːtʃeɪ, -tʃi/, Italian /verˈsatʃe/, Gianni (1946–97), Italian fashion designer.

Versailles /vɛːˈsʌɪ/ a palace built for Louis XIV near the town of Versailles, south-west of Paris. It was built around a château belonging to Louis XIII, which was transformed by additions in the grand French classical style.

Versailles, Treaty of 1 a treaty which terminated the War of American Independence in 1783.
2 a treaty signed in 1919 which brought a formal end to the First World War.

> The treaty redivided the territory of the defeated Central Powers, restricted Germany's armed forces, and established the League of Nations. It left Germany resentful about what it considered a vindictive settlement while not sufficiently restricting its ability eventually to rearm and seek forcible redress.

versal /ˈvəːs(ə)l/ ▸ adjective relating to a style of ornate capital letter used to start a verse, paragraph, etc., in a manuscript, typically built up by inking between pen strokes and with long, rather flat serifs.
▸ noun a versal letter.
– ORIGIN late 19th cent.: from Latin *vers-* 'turned' + -AL, influenced by VERSE.

versant /ˈvəːs(ə)nt/ ▸ noun a region of land sloping in one general direction.
– ORIGIN mid 19th cent.: from French, present participle (used as a noun) of *verser* 'tilt over', from Latin *versare*.

versatile ▸ adjective 1 able to adapt or be adapted to many different functions or activities: *a versatile sewing machine* | *he was versatile enough to play on either wing*.
2 archaic changeable; inconstant.
– DERIVATIVES **versatilely** adverb, **versatility** noun.
– ORIGIN early 17th cent. (in the sense 'inconstant, fluctuating'): from French, or from Latin *versatilis*, from *versat-* 'turned about, revolved', from the verb *versare*, frequentative of *vertere* 'to turn'.

vers de société /ˌvɛː də səʊsɪɛːˈteɪ, sɒ-/, French /vɛʀ də sɔsjete/ ▸ noun [mass noun] verse dealing with topics provided by polite society in a light, witty style.
– ORIGIN French, literally 'verse of society'.

verse ▸ noun [mass noun] writing arranged with a metrical rhythm, typically having a rhyme: *a lament in verse* | [as modifier] *verse drama*. ■ [count noun] a group of lines that form a unit in a poem or song; a stanza: *the second verse*. ■ [count noun] each of the short numbered divisions of a chapter in the Bible or other scripture.

V

■ [count noun] a versicle. ■ [count noun] archaic a line of poetry. ■ [count noun] a passage in an anthem for a soloist or a small group of voices.
▶ **verb** [no obj.] archaic speak in or compose verse; versify.
– ORIGIN Old English *fers*, from Latin *versus* 'a turn of the plough, a furrow, a line of writing', from *vertere* 'to turn'; reinforced in Middle English by Old French *vers*, from Latin *versus*.

versed ▶ **adjective** (**versed in**) experienced or skilled in; knowledgeable about: *a solicitor **well versed** in employment law.*
– ORIGIN early 17th cent.: from French *versé* or Latin *versatus*, past participle of *versari* 'be engaged in'.

versed sine ▶ **noun 1** Mathematics unity minus cosine. **2** Architecture the rise of an arch of a bridge.

verset /ˈvəːsɪt/ ▶ **noun** Music a short prelude or interlude for organ.
– ORIGIN Middle English (denoting a versicle): from Old French, diminutive of *vers* 'verse'.

versicle /ˈvəːsɪk(ə)l/ ▶ **noun** (usu. **versicles**) a short sentence said or sung by the minister in a church service, to which the congregation gives a response.
– ORIGIN Middle English: from Old French *versicule* or Latin *versiculus*, diminutive of *versus* (see **VERSE**).

versicoloured /ˈvəːsɪˌkʌləd/ (US **versicolored**) ▶ **adjective** archaic **1** changing from one colour to another in different lights.
2 variegated.
– ORIGIN early 18th cent.: from Latin *versicolor* (from *versus* 'turned' + *color* 'colour') + **-ED²**.

versify ▶ **verb** (**versifies**, **versifying**, **versified**) [with obj.] turn into or express in verse: *it was never suggested that Wordsworth should simply versify Coleridge's ideas* | (as noun **versifying**) *a talent for versifying.*
– DERIVATIVES **versification** noun, **versifier** noun.
– ORIGIN late Middle English: from Old French *versifier*, from Latin *versificare*, from *versus* (see **VERSE**).

versin /ˈvəːsɪn, -sʌɪn/ (also **versine**) ▶ **noun** Mathematics another term for **VERSED SINE**.
– ORIGIN early 19th cent.: abbreviation.

version ▶ **noun 1** a particular form of something differing in certain respects from an earlier form or other forms of the same type of thing: *a revised version of the paper was produced for a later meeting* | *they make yachts in both standard and master versions.* ■ a particular edition or translation of a book or other work: *the English version will be published next year.* ■ [usu. with modifier] an adaptation of a novel, piece of music, etc. into another medium or style: *a film version of a wonderfully funny cult novel.* ■ a particular release of a piece of computer software.
2 an account of a matter from a particular person's point of view: *he told her his version of events.*
3 [mass noun] Medicine the manual turning of a fetus in the womb to make delivery easier.
▶ **verb** [with obj.] create a new version of: (as adj. **versioned**) *versioned software.*
– DERIVATIVES **versional** adjective.
– ORIGIN late Middle English (in the sense 'translation'): from French, or from medieval Latin *versio(n-)*, from Latin *vertere* 'to turn'.

vers libre /veː ˈliːbr(ə)/, French /vɛʀ libʀ/ ▶ **noun** another term for **FREE VERSE**.
– ORIGIN French, literally 'free verse'.

verso /ˈvəːsəʊ/ ▶ **noun** (pl. **versos**) **1** a left-hand page of an open book, or the back of a loose document. Contrasted with **RECTO**.
2 the reverse of something such as a coin or painting.
– ORIGIN mid 19th cent.: from Latin *verso* (*folio*) 'on the turned (leaf)'.

verst /vəːst/ ▶ **noun** a Russian measure of length, about 1.1 km (0.66 mile).
– ORIGIN from Russian *versta*.

Verstehen /fɛːˈʃteɪən/, German /fɛɐ̯ˈʃteːən/ ▶ **noun** [mass noun] Sociology empathic understanding of human behaviour.
– ORIGIN German, literally 'understanding'.

versus (abbrev.: **v**, **v.**, or **vs**) ▶ **preposition** against (especially in sporting and legal use): *England versus Australia.* ■ as opposed to; in contrast to: *weighing up the pros and cons of organic versus inorganic produce.*
– ORIGIN late Middle English: from a medieval Latin use of Latin *versus* 'towards'.

vert¹ /vəːt/ ▶ **noun** [mass noun] green, as a heraldic tincture: [postpositive] *three piles vert.*
– ORIGIN late Middle English (as an adjective): via Old French from Latin *viridis* 'green'.

vert² /vəːt/ ▶ **noun** a vertical or very steeply sloping part of a ramp, used by skateboarders, snowboarders, skiers, etc. to perform jumps and other manoeuvres.
– ORIGIN 1970s: abbreviation of **VERTICAL**.

vertebra /ˈvəːtɪbrə/ ▶ **noun** (pl. **vertebrae** /-breɪ, -briː/) each of the series of small bones forming the backbone, having several projections for articulation and muscle attachment, and a hole through which the spinal cord passes.

> In the human spine (or vertebral column) there are seven cervical vertebrae (in the neck), twelve thoracic vertebrae (to which the ribs are attached), and five lumbar vertebrae (in the lower back). In addition, five fused vertebrae form the sacrum, and four the coccyx.

– DERIVATIVES **vertebral** adjective.
– ORIGIN early 17th cent.: from Latin, from *vertere* 'to turn'.

vertebral column ▶ **noun** another term for **SPINAL COLUMN**.

vertebrate /ˈvəːtɪbrət/ ▶ **noun** an animal of a large group distinguished by the possession of a backbone or spinal column, including mammals, birds, reptiles, amphibians, and fishes. Compare with **INVERTEBRATE**. ● Subphylum Vertebrata, phylum Chordata: seven classes.
▶ **adjective** relating to the vertebrates.
– ORIGIN early 19th cent.: from Latin *vertebratus* 'jointed', from *vertebra* (see **VERTEBRA**).

vertex /ˈvəːtɛks/ ▶ **noun** (pl. **vertices** /-tɪsiːz/ or **vertexes**) **1** the highest point; the top or apex. ■ Anatomy the crown of the head.
2 Geometry each angular point of a polygon, polyhedron, or other figure. ■ a meeting point of two lines that form an angle. ■ the point at which an axis meets a curve or surface.
– ORIGIN late Middle English: from Latin, 'whirlpool, crown of a head, vertex', from *vertere* 'to turn'.

vertical ▶ **adjective 1** at right angles to a horizontal plane; in a direction, or having an alignment, such that the top is directly above the bottom: *the vertical axis* | *keep your back vertical.*
2 involving different levels or stages of a hierarchy or process. ■ involving all the stages from the production to the sale of a class of goods. ■ (especially of the transmission of disease or genetic traits) passed from one generation to the next.
3 Anatomy relating to the crown of the head.
4 archaic denoting a point at the zenith or the highest point of something.
▶ **noun 1** (usu. **the vertical**) a vertical line or plane: *the columns incline several degrees away from the vertical.*
2 an upright structure: *we remodelled the opening with a simple lintel and unadorned verticals.*
3 the distance between the highest and lowest points of a ski area: *the resort claims a vertical of 2,100 metres.*
– DERIVATIVES **verticality** noun, **verticalize** (also **verticalise**) verb, **vertically** adverb.
– ORIGIN mid 16th cent. (in the sense 'directly overhead'): from French, or from late Latin *verticalis*, from *vertex* (see **VERTEX**).

vertical angles ▶ **plural noun** Mathematics each of the pairs of opposite angles made by two intersecting lines.

vertical fin ▶ **noun** Zoology any of the unpaired fins in the midline of a fish's body, i.e. a dorsal, anal, or caudal fin.

vertical integration ▶ **noun** [mass noun] the combination in one firm of two or more stages of production normally operated by separate firms.

vertical market ▶ **noun** a market comprising all the potential purchasers in a particular occupation or industry.

vertical stabilizer ▶ **noun** US the tail fin of an aircraft.

vertical thinking ▶ **noun** [mass noun] chiefly Brit. the solving of problems using conventional logical processes. Contrasted with **LATERAL THINKING**.

verticillium /ˌvəːtɪˈsɪlɪəm/ ▶ **noun** a fungus of a genus which includes a number that cause wilt in plants. ● Genus *Verticillium*, subdivision Deuteromycotina, in particular *V. albo-atrum* and *V. dahliae*.
■ [mass noun] wilt caused by verticillium.
– ORIGIN modern Latin, from Latin *verticillus* 'whorl of a spindle'.

vertiginous /vəːˈtɪdʒɪnəs/ ▶ **adjective** extremely high or steep: *vertiginous drops to the valleys below.* ■ relating to or affected by vertigo.
– DERIVATIVES **vertiginously** adverb.
– ORIGIN early 17th cent.: from Latin *vertiginosus*, from *vertigo* 'whirling about' (see **VERTIGO**).

vertigo /ˈvəːtɪɡəʊ/ ▶ **noun** [mass noun] a sensation of whirling and loss of balance, associated particularly with looking down from a great height, or caused by disease affecting the inner ear or the vestibular nerve; giddiness.
– ORIGIN late Middle English: from Latin, 'whirling', from *vertere* 'to turn'.

vertisol /ˈvəːtɪsɒl/ ▶ **noun** Soil Science a clayey soil with little organic matter which occurs in regions having distinct wet and dry seasons.
– ORIGIN 1960s: from **VERTICAL** + Latin *solum* 'soil'.

vertu ▶ **noun** variant spelling of **VIRTU**.

Verulamium /ˌvɛrʊˈleɪmɪəm/ Roman name for **ST ALBANS**.

vervain /ˈvəːveɪn/ ▶ **noun** [mass noun] a widely distributed herbaceous plant with small blue, white, or purple flowers and a long history of use as a magical and medicinal herb. ● *Verbena officinalis*, family Verbenaceae.
– ORIGIN late Middle English: from Old French *verveine*, from Latin *verbena* (see **VERBENA**).

verve ▶ **noun** [mass noun] vigour and spirit or enthusiasm: *Kollo sings with supreme verve and flexibility.*
– ORIGIN late 17th cent. (denoting special talent in writing): from French, 'vigour', earlier 'form of expression', from Latin *verba* 'words'.

vervet /ˈvəːvɪt/ (also **vervet monkey**) ▶ **noun** a common African guenon with greenish-brown upper parts and a black face. Compare with **GREEN MONKEY**, **GRIVET**. ● *Cercopithecus aethiops*, family Cercopithecidae, in particular the race *C. a. pygerythrus* of southern and eastern Africa.
– ORIGIN late 19th cent.: from French, of unknown origin.

Verviers /ˈvɛːvɪeɪ/, French /vɛʀvje/ a manufacturing town in eastern Belgium; pop 54,519 (2008).

Verwoerd /fə(r)ˈvʊət/, Hendrik (Frensch) (1901–66), South African statesman, Prime Minister 1958–66. As Minister of Bantu Affairs (1950–8) he developed the segregation policy of apartheid. As Premier he banned the ANC and the Pan-Africanist Congress in 1960, following the Sharpeville massacre. He withdrew South Africa from the Commonwealth and declared it a republic in 1961.
– DERIVATIVES **Verwoerdian** /fə(r)ˈvʊədɪən/ adjective.

very ▶ **adverb** used for emphasis: ■ in a high degree: *a very large amount* | *the river rose very quickly* | *very much so.* ■ (with superlative or **own**) used to emphasize that the following description applies without qualification: *the very best quality* | *his very own car.*
▶ **adjective 1** actual; precise (used to emphasize the exact identity of someone or something): *those were his very words* | *he might be phoning her at this very moment.* ■ archaic real; genuine: *the very God of Heaven.*
2 emphasizing an extreme point in time or space: *from the very beginning of the book* | *at the very back of the skull.*
3 with no addition of anything else; mere: *the very thought of drink made him feel sick.*
– PHRASES **not very 1** in a low degree: *'Bad news?' 'Not very.'* **2** far from being: *I'm not very impressed.* **the very idea!** see **IDEA**. **the very same** see **SAME**. **very good** (or **well**) an expression of consent.
– ORIGIN Middle English (as an adjective in the sense 'real, genuine'): from Old French *verai*, based on Latin *verus* 'true'.

Very light /ˈvɛri, ˈvɪəri/ ▶ **noun** a flare fired into the air from a pistol for signalling or for temporary illumination.
– ORIGIN early 20th cent.: named after Edward W. *Very* (1847–1910), American naval officer.

Very pistol /ˈvɛri, ˈvɪəri/ ▶ **noun** a handheld gun used for firing a Very light.

Very Reverend ▶ **noun** a title given to a dean in the Anglican Church: *the Very Reverend James Wilkins.*

VESA ▶ **abbreviation** Video Electronics Standards Association, a US-based organization that defines formats for displays and buses used in computers.

Vesak /ˈvɛsak/ (also **Wesak** or **Visākha**) ▶ **noun** [mass noun] the most important Buddhist festival, taking place at the full moon when the sun is in the zodiacal sign of Taurus, and commemorating the birth, enlightenment, and death of the Buddha. ■ the month in which the festival of Vesak occurs.
– ORIGIN Sinhalese *vesak*, via Pali from Sanskrit *vaiśākha*, denoting the month April–May.

Vesalius /vɪˈseɪlɪəs/, Andreas (1514–64), Flemish anatomist, the founder of modern anatomy. His

V

major work, *De Humani Corporis Fabrica* (1543), contained accurate descriptions of human anatomy, but owed much of its great historical impact to the woodcuts of his dissections.

vesical /ˈvɛsɪk(ə)l, ˈviː-/ ▶ **adjective** Anatomy & Medicine relating to or affecting the urinary bladder: *vesical function | the vesical artery.*
– ORIGIN late 18th cent.: from Latin *vesica* 'bladder' + **-AL**.

vesicant /ˈvɛsɪkənt, ˈviː-/ technical ▶ **adjective** tending to cause blistering.
▶ **noun** an agent that causes blistering.
– ORIGIN late Middle English: from late Latin *vesicant-* 'forming pustules', from the verb *vesicare*, from *vesica* 'bladder'.

vesica piscis /ˌvɛsɪkə ˈpɪskɪs, ˈviː-/ ▶ **noun** (pl. **vesicae piscis** /ˈvɛsɪkiː, ˈviː-/) a pointed oval figure used as an architectural feature and as an aureole enclosing figures such as Christ or the Virgin Mary in medieval art. Also called **MANDORLA**.
– ORIGIN Latin, literally 'fish's bladder'.

vesicate /ˈvɛsɪkeɪt, ˈviː-/ ▶ **verb** chiefly Medicine blister or cause to blister.
– ORIGIN mid 17th cent.: from late Latin *vesicat-* 'having pustules', from *vesica* 'bladder'.

vesicle /ˈvɛsɪk(ə)l, ˈviː-/ ▶ **noun 1** Anatomy & Zoology a small fluid-filled bladder, sac, cyst, or vacuole within the body. ■ Medicine a small blister full of clear fluid.
2 Botany an air-filled swelling in a plant, especially a seaweed.
3 Geology a small cavity in volcanic rock, produced by gas bubbles.
– DERIVATIVES **vesicular** adjective, **vesiculated** adjective, **vesiculation** noun.
– ORIGIN late 16th cent.: from French *vésicule* or Latin *vesicula*, diminutive of *vesica* 'bladder'.

vesicoureteric reflux /ˌvɛsɪkəʊjʊərɪˈtɛrɪk, ˈviː-/ ▶ **noun** [mass noun] Medicine flow of urine from the bladder back into the ureters, arising from defective valves and causing a high risk of kidney infection.
– ORIGIN 1960s: *vesicoureteric* from Latin *vesica* 'bladder' + *ureteric* (see **URETER**).

Vespa ▶ **noun** trademark an Italian make of motor scooter.
– ORIGIN 1950s: Italian, literally 'wasp'.

Vespasian /vɛˈspeɪʒ(ə)n/ (AD 9–79), Roman emperor 69–79 and founder of the Flavian dynasty; Latin name *Titus Flavius Vespasianus*. He was acclaimed emperor by the legions in Egypt during the civil wars following the death of Nero and gained control of Italy after the defeat of Vitellius. His reign saw the restoration of financial and military order and the initiation of a public building programme.

vesper ▶ **noun 1** [usu. as modifier] evening prayer; vespers: *vesper service.*
2 archaic evening. ■ (**Vesper**) literary Venus as the evening star.
– ORIGIN late Middle English: from Latin *vesper* 'evening (star)'.

vespers ▶ **noun** a service of evening prayer in the Divine Office of the Western Christian Church (sometimes said earlier in the day). ■ a service of evening prayer in other churches.
– ORIGIN late 15th cent.: from Old French *vespres* 'evensong', from Latin *vesperas* (accusative plural), on the pattern of *matutinas* 'matins'.

vesper sparrow ▶ **noun** a small North American songbird related to the buntings, having streaked brown plumage and known for its evening song.
● *Pooecetes gramineus*, family Emberizidae (subfamily Emberizidae).

vespertilionid /ˌvɛspəˈtɪlɪˈɒnɪd/ ▶ **noun** Zoology a bat of a large family (Vespertilionidae) that includes most of the typical insectivorous bats of northern temperate regions.
– ORIGIN late 19th cent.: from modern Latin *Vespertilionidae* (plural), from Latin *vespertilio* 'bat'.

vespertine /ˈvɛspətʌɪn, -tɪn/ ▶ **adjective** technical or literary relating to, occurring, or active in the evening.
– ORIGIN late Middle English: from Latin *vespertinus*, from *vesper* 'evening'.

Vespucci /vɛˈspuːtʃi/, Amerigo (1451–1512), Italian merchant and explorer. He travelled to the New World, reaching the coast of Venezuela on his first voyage (1499–1500) and exploring the Brazilian coastline in 1501–2. The Latin form of his first name is believed to have given rise to the name of America.

vessel ▶ **noun 1** a ship or large boat.
2 a hollow container, especially one used to hold liquid, such as a bowl or cask. ■ (chiefly in biblical use) a person regarded as having or embodying a particular quality: *giving honour unto the wife, as unto the weaker vessel.*
3 Anatomy & Zoology a duct or canal holding or conveying blood or other fluid. See also **BLOOD VESSEL**.
■ Botany any of the tubular structures in the vascular system of a plant, serving to conduct water and mineral nutrients from the root.
– ORIGIN Middle English: from Anglo-Norman French *vessel(e)*, from late Latin *vascellum*, diminutive of *vas* 'vessel'.

vest ▶ **noun 1** Brit. an undergarment worn on the upper part of the body, typically having no sleeves.
2 a garment worn on the upper part of the body for a particular purpose: *a running vest | a bulletproof vest.*
3 US & Austral. a waistcoat or sleeveless jacket.
▶ **verb 1** [with obj.] (usu. **be vested in**) confer or bestow (power, authority, property, etc.) on someone: *executive power is vested in the President.* ■ (usu. **be vested with**) give (someone) the legal right to power, property, etc.: *the local planning authorities are vested with powers to regulate land use and development.* ■ [no obj.] (**vest in**) (of power, property, etc.) come into the possession of: *the bankrupt's property vests in his trustee.*
2 [no obj.] (of a chorister or member of the clergy) put on vestments. ■ [with obj.] literary dress (someone): *the Speaker vested him with a rich purple robe.*
– ORIGIN late Middle English (as a verb): from Old French *vestu* 'clothed', past participle of *vestir*, from Latin *vestire*; the noun (early 17th cent., denoting a loose outer garment) from French *veste*, via Italian from Latin *vestis* 'garment'.

Vesta 1 Roman Mythology the goddess of the hearth and household. Her temple in Rome contained no image but a fire which was kept constantly burning and was tended by the Vestal Virgins.
2 Astronomy asteroid 4, discovered in 1807. It is the brightest asteroid and the third largest (diameter 501 km), and appears to consist of basaltic rock.

vesta ▶ **noun** chiefly historical a short wooden or wax match.
– ORIGIN mid 19th cent.: from the name of the goddess **VESTA**.

vestal ▶ **adjective** relating to the Roman goddess Vesta: *a vestal temple.* ■ literary chaste; pure.
▶ **noun** a Vestal Virgin. ■ literary a chaste woman, especially a nun.

Vestal Virgin ▶ **noun** (in ancient Rome) a virgin consecrated to Vesta and vowed to chastity, sharing the charge of maintaining the sacred fire burning on the goddess's altar.

vested interest ▶ **noun 1** a personal stake or involvement in an undertaking or situation, especially one with an expectation of financial or other gain: *banks have **a vested interest in** the growth of their customers.* ■ a person or group having such a personal stake or involvement: *the problem is that the authorities are a vested interest.*
2 Law an interest (usually in land or money held in trust) recognized as belonging to a particular person.

vestee ▶ **noun** N. Amer. another term for **VEST** (sense 3 of the noun).

Vesterålen /ˈvɛstəˌrɔːlən/ a group of islands of Norway, north of the Arctic Circle.

vestiary /ˈvɛstɪəri/ ▶ **adjective** literary relating to clothes or dress.
▶ **noun** (pl. **vestiaries**) a room or building in a monastery or other large establishment in which clothes are kept.
– ORIGIN Middle English (denoting a vestry): from Old French *vestiarie*, from Latin *vestiarium* (see **VESTRY**).

vestibular /vɛˈstɪbjʊlə/ ▶ **adjective** chiefly Anatomy relating to a vestibule, particularly that of the inner ear, or more generally to the sense of balance.

vestibule /ˈvɛstɪbjuːl/ ▶ **noun 1** an antechamber, hall, or lobby next to the outer door of a building. ■ an enclosed entrance compartment in a railway carriage.
2 Anatomy a chamber or channel opening into another, in particular: ■ the central cavity of the labyrinth of the inner ear. ■ the part of the mouth outside the teeth. ■ the space in the vulva into which both the urethra and vagina open.
– DERIVATIVES **vestibuled** adjective.
– ORIGIN early 17th cent. (denoting the space in front of the main entrance of a classical Roman or Greek building): from French, or from Latin *vestibulum* 'entrance court'.

vestibulocochlear nerve /vɛˌstɪbjʊləʊˈkɒklɪə/ ▶ **noun** Anatomy each of the eighth pair of cranial nerves, conveying sensory impulses from the organs of hearing and balance in the inner ear to the brain. The vestibulocochlear nerve on each side branches into the **vestibular nerve** and the **cochlear nerve**.

vestibulo-ocular reflex /vɛˌstɪbjʊləʊˈɒkjʊlə/ ▶ **noun** the reflex by which the direction of the eyes remains constant when the head is moved.

vestige /ˈvɛstɪdʒ/ ▶ **noun 1** a trace or remnant of something that is disappearing or no longer exists: *the last vestiges of colonialism.* ■ [usu. with negative] the smallest amount: *he waited patiently, but without a vestige of sympathy.*
2 Biology a part or organ of an organism which has become reduced or functionless in the course of evolution.
– ORIGIN late Middle English: from French, from Latin *vestigium* 'footprint'.

vestigial /vɛˈstɪdʒɪəl, -dʒ(ə)l/ ▶ **adjective 1** forming a very small remnant of something that was once greater or more noticeable: *he felt a vestigial flicker of anger from last night.*
2 Biology (of an organ or part of the body) degenerate, rudimentary, or atrophied, having become functionless in the course of evolution: *the vestigial wings of kiwis are entirely hidden.*
– DERIVATIVES **vestigially** adverb.

vestimentary /ˌvɛstɪˈmɛnt(ə)ri/ ▶ **adjective** formal relating to clothing or dress: *a vestimentary code.*
– ORIGIN early 19th cent.: from Latin *vestimentum* 'clothing' + **-ARY**[1].

vestimentiferan /ˌvɛstɪmɛnˈtɪfərən/ ▶ **noun** Zoology a very large marine worm which lives in upright tubes near hydrothermal vents, subsisting on the products of chemoautotrophic bacteria. ● Order Vestimentifera, phylum Pogonophora; sometimes regarded as a separate phylum.
– ORIGIN 1980s: from modern Latin *Vestimentifera* (from Latin *vestimentum* 'clothing' + *-fer* 'bearing') + **-AN**.

vestiture /ˈvɛstɪtjə, -tʃə/ ▶ **noun** [mass noun] archaic clothing.
– ORIGIN mid 19th cent.: based on Latin *vestire* 'clothe'.

Vestmannaeyjar /ˌvɛstmanəˈeɪjaːr/ Icelandic name for **WESTMANN ISLANDS**.

vestment ▶ **noun** (usu. **vestments**) a chasuble or other robe worn by the clergy or choristers during services. ■ archaic a garment, especially a ceremonial or official robe.
– ORIGIN Middle English: from Old French *vestiment*, from Latin *vestimentum*, from *vestire* 'clothe' (see **VEST**).

vest-pocket ▶ **adjective** [attrib.] N. Amer. (especially of a reference book) small enough to fit into a pocket: *a series of popular vest-pocket dictionaries.* ■ very small in size or scale: *a vest-pocket park.*

vestry ▶ **noun** (pl. **vestries**) a room or building attached to a church, used as an office and for changing into ceremonial vestments. ■ a meeting of parishioners, originally in a vestry, for the conduct of parochial business.
– ORIGIN late Middle English: probably from an Anglo-Norman French alteration of Old French *vestiarie*, from Latin *vestiarium*.

vestryman ▶ **noun** (pl. **vestrymen**) a member of a parochial vestry.

vesture ▶ **noun** [mass noun] literary clothing; dress: *a man garbed in ancient vesture.*
– ORIGIN Middle English: from Old French, based on Latin *vestire* 'clothe'.

vesuvianite /vɪˈsuːvɪənʌɪt/ ▶ **noun** another term for **IDOCRASE**.
– ORIGIN late 19th cent.: from **VESUVIUS** + **-AN** + **-ITE**[1].

Vesuvius /vɪˈsuːvɪəs/ an active volcano near Naples, in southern Italy, 1,277 m (4,190 ft) high. A violent eruption in AD 79 buried the towns of Pompeii and Herculaneum.

vet[1] ▶ **noun** chiefly Brit. a veterinary surgeon.
▶ **verb** (**vets, vetting, vetted**) [with obj.] make a careful and critical examination of (something): *proposals for vetting large takeover bids.* ■ Brit. investigate (someone) thoroughly, especially in order to ensure that they are suitable for a job requiring secrecy, loyalty, or trustworthiness: *each applicant will be vetted by police* | (as noun **vetting**) *the vetting of people who work with children.*
– ORIGIN mid 19th cent: abbreviation of **VETERINARY** or **VETERINARIAN**.

V

vet² ▶ noun N. Amer. informal a veteran.
– ORIGIN mid 19th cent.: abbreviation.

vetch ▶ noun a widely distributed scrambling herbaceous plant of the pea family, which is cultivated as a silage or fodder crop. See also TARE¹. ● Genus *Vicia*, family Leguminosae: several species, in particular the European **common vetch** (*V. sativa*).
– ORIGIN Middle English: from Anglo-Norman French *veche*, from Latin *vicia*.

vetchling ▶ noun a widely distributed scrambling plant related to the vetches, typically having fewer leaflets. ● Genus *Lathyrus*, family Leguminosae.

veteran ▶ noun a person who has had long experience in a particular field: *a veteran of two world wars* | [as modifier] *a veteran left-wing MP*. ■ an ex-member of the armed forces: *a Vietnam veteran*.
– ORIGIN early 16th cent.: from French *vétéran* or Latin *veteranus*, from *vetus* 'old'.

veteran car ▶ noun Brit. an old style or model of car, specifically one made before 1919 or (strictly) before 1905. Compare with VINTAGE CAR.

Veterans Day ▶ noun (in the US) a public holiday held on the anniversary of the end of the First World War (11 November) to honour US veterans and victims of all wars. It replaced Armistice Day in 1954.

veterinarian /ˌvɛt(ə)rɪˈnɛːrɪən/ ▶ noun North American term for VETERINARY SURGEON.

veterinary /ˈvɛt(ə)rɪn(ə)ri, ˈvɛt(ə)nri/ ▶ adjective relating to the diseases, injuries, and treatment of farm and domestic animals: *a veterinary nurse*.
▶ noun (pl. **veterinaries**) dated a veterinary surgeon.
– ORIGIN late 18th cent.: from Latin *veterinarius*, from *veterinae* 'cattle'.

veterinary surgeon ▶ noun Brit. a person qualified to treat diseased or injured animals.

vetiver /ˈvɛtɪvə/ (also **vetivert**) ▶ noun [mass noun] a fragrant extract or essential oil obtained from the root of an Indian grass, used in perfumery and aromatherapy. ● The grass is *Vetiveria zizanioides*, family Gramineae.
– ORIGIN mid 19th cent.: from French *vétiver*, from Tamil *veṭṭivēr*, from *vēr* 'root'.

vetkoek /ˈfɛtkʊk/ ▶ noun (pl. **same**, **vetkoeks**, or **vetkoeke**) S. African a small, unsweetened cake of deep-fried dough.
– ORIGIN Afrikaans, from *vet* 'fat' + *koek* 'cake'.

veto /ˈviːtəʊ/ ▶ noun (pl. **vetoes**) a constitutional right to reject a decision or proposal made by a lawmaking body: *neither state was given a veto over amendments to the Act* | [mass noun] *the royal power of veto*. ■ a rejection by right of veto. ■ any ban or prohibition: *his veto on our drinking after the meal was annoying*.
▶ verb (**vetoes**, **vetoing**, **vetoed**) [with obj.] exercise a veto against (a decision or proposal): *the president vetoed the bill*. ■ refuse to accept or allow: *I vetoed the idea of a holiday*.
– DERIVATIVES **vetoer** noun.
– ORIGIN early 17th cent.: from Latin, literally 'I forbid', used by Roman tribunes of the people when opposing measures of the Senate.

vex ▶ verb [with obj.] make (someone) feel annoyed, frustrated, or worried, especially with trivial matters: *the memory of the conversation still vexed him* | (as adj. **vexing**) *the most vexing questions for policymakers*. ■ [no obj.] W. Indian be annoyed, irritated, or unhappy. ■ archaic cause distress to: *thou shalt not vex a stranger*.
▶ adjective chiefly W. Indian angry; annoyed: *I ain't vex with you*.
– DERIVATIVES **vexer** noun, **vexingly** adverb.
– ORIGIN late Middle English: from Old French *vexer*, from Latin *vexare* 'shake, disturb'.

vexation ▶ noun [mass noun] the state of being annoyed, frustrated, or worried: *Jenna bit her lip in vexation*. ■ [count noun] a cause of annoyance, frustration, or worry: *the vexations of life under canvas*.
– ORIGIN late Middle English: from Old French, or from Latin *vexatio(n-)*, from *vexare* (see VEX).

vexatious ▶ adjective causing or tending to cause annoyance, frustration, or worry: *the vexatious questions posed by software copyrights*. ■ Law denoting an action or the bringer of an action that is brought without sufficient grounds for winning, purely to cause annoyance to the defendant.
– DERIVATIVES **vexatiously** adverb, **vexatiousness** noun.

vexed ▶ adjective **1** [attrib.] (of a problem or issue) difficult and much debated; problematic: *the vexed question of how much money the government is going to spend*.
2 annoyed, frustrated, or worried: *I'm very vexed with you!*
– DERIVATIVES **vexedly** adverb.

vexillology /ˌvɛksɪˈlɒlədʒi/ ▶ noun [mass noun] the study of flags.
– DERIVATIVES **vexillological** adjective, **vexillologist** noun.
– ORIGIN 1950s: from Latin *vexillum* 'flag' + -LOGY.

vexillum /vɛkˈsɪləm/ ▶ noun (pl. **vexilla** /-lə/) **1** (in ancient Rome) a military standard or banner, especially one of a maniple. ■ a body of troops under a vexillum. ■ a flag attached to a bishop's staff. ■ a processional banner or cross.
2 Botany the standard of a papilionaceous flower.
3 Ornithology the vane of a feather.
– ORIGIN Latin, from *vehere* 'carry'.

VF ▶ abbreviation Medicine ventricular fibrillation.

VFR ▶ abbreviation visual flight rules, used to regulate the flying and navigating of an aircraft under conditions of good visibility.

VG ▶ abbreviation ■ very good. ■ Vicar General.

VGA ▶ abbreviation videographics array, a standard for defining colour display screens for computers.

vgc ▶ abbreviation very good condition (used in advertisements).

VHF ▶ abbreviation very high frequency (denoting radio waves of a frequency of *c*.30–300 MHz and a wavelength of *c*.1–10 metres).

VHS ▶ abbreviation trademark video home system, denoting the video system and tape used by domestic video recorders and some camcorders.

VI ▶ abbreviation Virgin Islands.

via ▶ preposition travelling through (a place) en route to a destination: *they came to Europe via Turkey*. ■ by way of; through: *most people buy a home with a mortgage via a building society*. ■ by means of: *a file sent via electronic mail*.
– ORIGIN late 18th cent.: from Latin, ablative of *via* 'way, road'.

Via Appia /ˌviːə ˈapɪə, ˌvʌɪə/ Latin name for APPIAN WAY.

viable /ˈvʌɪəb(ə)l/ ▶ adjective capable of working successfully; feasible: *the proposed investment was economically viable*. ■ Botany (of a seed or spore) able to germinate. ■ Biology (of a plant, animal, or cell) capable of surviving or living successfully, especially under particular environmental conditions. ■ Medicine (of a fetus or unborn child) able to live after birth.
– DERIVATIVES **viability** noun, **viably** adverb.
– ORIGIN early 19th cent.: from French, from *vie* 'life', from Latin *vita*.

Via Crucis /ˈkruːtʃɪs/ ▶ noun another term for THE WAY OF THE CROSS (see WAY). ■ a lengthy and distressing or painful procedure: *we embarked on a Via Crucis of tired comic formulae*.
– ORIGIN Latin.

via dolorosa /ˌdɒləˈrəʊzə/ ▶ noun (**the Via Dolorosa**) the route believed to have been taken by Christ through Jerusalem to Calvary. ■ a distressing or painful journey or process: *he commenced a via dolorosa to the coast*.
– ORIGIN Latin, literally 'painful path'.

viaduct ▶ noun a long bridge-like structure, typically a series of arches, carrying a road or railway across a valley or other low ground.
– ORIGIN early 19th cent.: from Latin *via* 'way', on the pattern of *aqueduct*.

via ferrata /fəˈruːtə/ ▶ noun a mountain route equipped with fixed ladders, cables, and bridges in order to be accessible to climbers and walkers.
– ORIGIN Italian: literally 'iron road'.

Viagra /vʌɪˈagrə/ ▶ noun [mass noun] trademark the drug sildenafil, used to enhance male potency.
– ORIGIN 1990s: probably suggested by words such as *virile* and *virility*.

vial /ˈvʌɪəl/ ▶ noun a small container, typically cylindrical and made of glass, used especially for holding liquid medicines.
– ORIGIN Middle English: alteration of PHIAL.

via media /ˈmiːdɪə, viːə ˈmɛdɪə/ ▶ noun formal a middle way or compromise between extremes: *the settlement has sometimes been described as a via media between Catholicism and Protestantism*.
– ORIGIN Latin.

viand /ˈvʌɪənd/ ▶ noun (usu. **viands**) archaic an item of food: *an unlimited assortment of viands*.
– ORIGIN late Middle English: from Old French *viande* 'food', from an alteration of Latin *vivenda*, neuter plural gerundive of *vivere* 'to live'.

via negativa /viːə nɛgəˈtiːvə/ ▶ noun a philosophical approach to theology which asserts that no finite concepts or attributes can be adequately used of God, but only negative terms.
– ORIGIN Latin, literally 'negative path'.

viatical settlement /vʌɪˈatɪk(ə)l/ ▶ noun an arrangement whereby a person with a terminal illness sells their life insurance policy to a third party for less than its mature value, in order to benefit from the proceeds while alive. See also DEATH FUTURES.
– ORIGIN 1990s: *viatical* from Latin *viaticus* 'relating to a journey or departing' + -AL.

viaticum /vʌɪˈatɪkəm/ ▶ noun (pl. **viatica** /-kə/) **1** the Eucharist as given to a person near or in danger of death.
2 archaic a supply of provisions or an official allowance of money for a journey.
– ORIGIN mid 16th cent.: from Latin, neuter of *viaticus*, from *via* 'road'.

vibe informal ▶ noun **1** (usu. **vibes**) a person's emotional state or the atmosphere of a place as communicated to and felt by others: *we've been picking up some* ***bad vibes on that guy***. [1960s: abbreviation of *vibrations*.]
2 (**vibes**) another term for VIBRAPHONE.
▶ verb **1** [no obj.] enjoy oneself by listening to or dancing to popular music: *another classic CD for you to vibe with*. ■ get on; have a good relationship: *we vibe so well with each other*.
2 [with obj.] transmit or give out (a feeling or atmosphere): *he vibed pure hate in my direction*.

vibist /ˈvʌɪbɪst/ ▶ noun a musician who plays the vibraphone.

vibraculum /vʌɪˈbrakjʊləm, vɪ-/ ▶ noun (pl. **vibracula** /-lə/) Zoology (in some bryozoans) any of a number of modified zooids that bear a long whip-like seta, serving to prevent other organisms from settling on the colony. Compare with AVICULARIUM.
– ORIGIN mid 19th cent.: modern Latin, from Latin *vibrare* (see VIBRATE).

vibrant ▶ adjective **1** full of energy and life: *a vibrant cosmopolitan city*. ■ (of colour) bright and striking: *a huge room decorated in vibrant blues and greens*. ■ (of sound) strong or resonating: *his vibrant voice*.
2 quivering; pulsating: *Rose was* ***vibrant with*** *anger*.
– DERIVATIVES **vibrancy** noun, **vibrantly** adverb.
– ORIGIN early 17th cent. (in the sense 'moving rapidly, vibrating'): from Latin *vibrant-* 'shaking to and fro', from the verb *vibrare* (see VIBRATE).

vibraphone /ˈvʌɪbrəfəʊn/ ▶ noun a musical percussion instrument with a double row of tuned metal bars, each above a tubular resonator containing a motor-driven rotating vane, giving a vibrato effect.
– DERIVATIVES **vibraphonist** noun.
– ORIGIN 1920s: from VIBRATO + -PHONE.

vibrate ▶ verb **1** move continuously and rapidly to and fro: [no obj.] *the cabin started to vibrate* | [with obj.] *the bumblebee vibrated its wings for a few seconds*. ■ [no obj.] (**vibrate with**) quiver with (a quality or emotion): *his voice vibrated with terror*. ■ [no obj.] (of a sound) resonate; continue to be heard: *a low rumbling sound that began to vibrate through the car*.
2 [no obj.] (of a pendulum) swing to and fro.
– ORIGIN late Middle English (in the sense 'give out light or sound as if by vibration'): from Latin *vibrat-* 'moved to and fro', from the verb *vibrare*.

vibratile /ˈvʌɪbrətʌɪl/ ▶ adjective Biology (of cilia, flagella, or other small appendages) capable of or characterized by oscillatory motion.
– ORIGIN early 19th cent.: alteration of VIBRATORY, on the pattern of words such as *pulsatile*.

vibration ▶ noun **1** an instance of vibrating: *powerful vibrations from an earthquake* | [mass noun] *the big-capacity engine generated less vibration*. ■ Physics an oscillation of the parts of a fluid or an elastic solid whose equilibrium has been disturbed or of an electromagnetic wave.
2 (**vibrations**) informal a person's emotional state, the atmosphere of a place, or the associations of an object, as communicated to and felt by others.
– DERIVATIVES **vibrational** adjective.
– ORIGIN mid 17th cent.: from Latin *vibratio(n-)*, from the verb *vibrare* (see VIBRATE).

vibration white finger ▶ noun [mass noun] Raynaud's disease caused by prolonged use of vibrating hand tools or machinery.

vibrato /vɪˈbrɑːtəʊ/ ▶ noun (pl. **vibratos**) Music a rapid, slight variation in pitch in singing or playing some

V

musical instruments, producing a stronger or richer tone. Compare with **TREMOLO**.
– ORIGIN mid 19th cent.: Italian, past participle of *vibrare* 'vibrate'.

vibrator ▶ **noun 1** a device used for massage or sexual stimulation.
2 a device for compacting concrete before it has set.
3 Music a reed in a reed organ.

vibratory /ˈvʌɪbrət(ə)ri, vʌɪˈbreɪt(ə)ri/ ▶ **adjective** relating to or causing vibration.

vibrio /ˈvɪbrɪəʊ, ˈvʌɪ-/ ▶ **noun** (pl. **vibrios**) Medicine a water-borne bacterium of a group that includes some pathogenic kinds that cause cholera, gastroenteritis, and septicaemia. ● *Vibrio* and related genera; motile Gram-negative bacteria occurring as curved flagellated rods.
– ORIGIN modern Latin, from Latin *vibrare* 'vibrate'.

vibrissae /vʌɪˈbrɪsiː/ ▶ **plural noun** Zoology long stiff hairs growing around the mouth or elsewhere on the face of many mammals, used as organs of touch; whiskers. ■ Ornithology coarse bristle-like feathers growing around the gape of certain insectivorous birds that catch insects in flight.
– ORIGIN late 17th cent.: from Latin, literally 'nostril hairs'.

vibrotactile /ˌvʌɪbrə(ʊ)ˈtakθʌɪl/ ▶ **adjective** relating to the perception of vibration through touch.

viburnum /vʌɪˈbəːnəm/ ▶ **noun** (pl. **viburnums**) a shrub or small tree of temperate and warm regions, typically bearing flat or rounded clusters of small white flowers. ● Genus *Viburnum*, family Caprifoliaceae: many species and ornamental hybrids, including the guelder rose and wayfaring tree.
– ORIGIN modern Latin, from Latin, 'wayfaring tree'.

Vic. ▶ **abbreviation** Victoria.

vicar ▶ **noun** (in the Church of England) an incumbent of a parish where tithes formerly passed to a chapter or religious house or layman. Compare with **RECTOR** (sense 1). ■ (in other Anglican Churches) a member of the clergy deputizing for another. ■ (in the Roman Catholic Church) a representative or deputy of a bishop. ■ (in the US Episcopal Church) a clergyman in charge of a chapel. ■ a cleric or choir member appointed to sing certain parts of a cathedral service.
– DERIVATIVES **vicarship** noun.
– ORIGIN Middle English: via Anglo-Norman French from Old French *vicaire*, from Latin *vicarius* 'substitute', from *vic-* 'change, turn, place' (compare with **VICE**[3]).

vicarage ▶ **noun** the residence of a vicar. ■ historical the benefice or living of a vicar.

vicar apostolic ▶ **noun 1** a Roman Catholic missionary.
2 a titular bishop.

vicar general ▶ **noun** (pl. **vicars general**) an Anglican official serving as a deputy or assistant to a bishop or archbishop. ■ (in the Roman Catholic Church) a bishop's representative in matters of jurisdiction or administration.

vicarial /vɪˈkɛːrɪəl, vʌɪ-/ ▶ **adjective** archaic relating to or serving as a vicar.

vicariance /vɪˈkɛːrɪəns, vʌɪ-/ ▶ **noun** [mass noun] Biology the geographical separation of a population, typically by a physical barrier such as a mountain range or river, resulting in a pair of closely related species.
– ORIGIN 1950s: from Latin *vicarius* 'substitute' + **-ANCE**.

vicariate /vɪˈkɛːrɪət, vʌɪ-/ ▶ **noun** the office or authority of a vicar. ■ a church or parish ministered to by a vicar.

vicarious /vɪˈkɛːrɪəs, vʌɪ-/ ▶ **adjective 1** experienced in the imagination through the feelings or actions of another person: *this catalogue brings vicarious pleasure in luxury living.*
2 acting or done for another: *a vicarious atonement.*
– DERIVATIVES **vicariously** adverb, **vicariousness** noun.
– ORIGIN mid 17th cent.: from Latin *vicarius* 'substitute' (see **VICAR**) + **-OUS**.

Vicar of Christ ▶ **noun** (in the Roman Catholic Church) a title of the Pope.

vice[1] /vʌɪs/ ▶ **noun** [mass noun] immoral or wicked behaviour. ■ criminal activities involving prostitution, pornography, or drugs. ■ [count noun] an immoral or wicked personal characteristic. ■ [count noun] a weakness of character or behaviour; a bad habit: *cigars happen to be my father's vice.* ■ (also **stable vice**) [count noun] a bad or neurotic habit of stabled horses, typically arising as a result of boredom.
– DERIVATIVES **viceless** adjective.
– ORIGIN Middle English: via Old French from Latin *vitium*.

vice[2] /vʌɪs/ (US **vise**) ▶ **noun** a metal tool with movable jaws which are used to hold an object firmly in place while work is done on it, typically attached to a workbench.
– DERIVATIVES **vice-like** adjective.
– ORIGIN Middle English (denoting a screw or winch): from Old French *vis*, from Latin *vitis* 'vine'.

vice[3] /ˈvʌɪsi/ ▶ **preposition** as a substitute for: *the letter was drafted by David Hunt, vice Bevin who was ill.*
– ORIGIN Latin, ablative of *vic-* 'change'.

vice[4] /vʌɪs/ ▶ **noun** informal short for **VICE-PRESIDENT**, **VICE ADMIRAL**, etc.

vice- ▶ **combining form** next in rank to, and typically denoting capacity to deputize for: *vice admiral* | *vice-president.*
– ORIGIN from Latin *vice* 'in place of' (compare with **VICE**[3]).

vice admiral ▶ **noun** a high rank of naval officer, above rear admiral and below admiral.

vice anglais /vis ɑ̃glɛ/ ▶ **noun** [in sing.] humorous a vice considered characteristic of the English, especially the use of corporal punishment for the purpose of sexual stimulation.
– ORIGIN French, literally 'English vice'.

vice chamberlain ▶ **noun** a deputy chamberlain, especially (in the UK) the deputy of the Lord Chamberlain.

vice chancellor ▶ **noun** a deputy chancellor, especially one of a British university who discharges most of its administrative duties.

vicegerent /vʌɪsˈdʒɪər(ə)nt, -ˈdʒɛ-/ ▶ **noun** formal a person exercising delegated power on behalf of a sovereign or ruler. ■ a person regarded as an earthly representative of God or a god, especially the Pope.
– DERIVATIVES **vicegerency** noun (pl. **vicegerencies**).
– ORIGIN mid 16th cent.: from medieval Latin *vicegerent-* '(person) holding office', from Latin *vic-* 'office, place, turn' + *gerere* 'carry on, hold'.

Vicente /vɪˈsɛnti/, Gil (*c.*1465–*c.*1536), Portuguese dramatist and poet. He is regarded as Portugal's most important dramatist; many of his works were written to commemorate national or court events and include religious dramas, farces, pastoral plays, and satirical comedies.

Vicenza /vɪˈtʃɛntsə/ a city in NE Italy; pop. 115,012 (2008).

vice-president ▶ **noun** an official or executive ranking below and deputizing for a president.
– DERIVATIVES **vice-presidency** noun (pl. **vice-presidencies**), **vice-presidential** adjective.

viceregal ▶ **adjective** relating to a viceroy.

vicereine /ˈvʌɪsreɪn/ ▶ **noun** the wife of a viceroy. ■ a female viceroy.
– ORIGIN early 19th cent.: from French, from *vice-* 'in place of' + *reine* 'queen'.

vice ring ▶ **noun** a group of criminals involved in organizing illegal prostitution.

viceroy /ˈvʌɪsrɔɪ/ ▶ **noun** a ruler exercising authority in a colony on behalf of a sovereign.
– DERIVATIVES **viceroyal** adjective, **viceroyship** noun.
– ORIGIN early 16th cent.: from archaic French, from *vice-* 'in place of' + *roi* 'king'.

viceroyalty (also **Viceroyalty**) ▶ **noun** (pl. **viceroyalties**) the office, position, or authority of a viceroy. ■ a territory governed by a viceroy.

vice squad ▶ **noun** a department or division of a police force that enforces laws against prostitution, drug abuse, illegal gambling, etc.

vice versa /ˌvʌɪs ˈvəːsə, vʌɪsə/ ▶ **adverb** with the main items in the preceding statement the other way round: *cruise from Cairo to Aswan or vice versa.*
– ORIGIN early 17th cent.: from Latin, literally 'in-turned position'.

Vichy /ˈviːʃi/ a town in south central France; pop. 26,555 (2006). A noted spa town, it is the source of an effervescent mineral water.

> During the Second World War the town was the headquarters of the regime that was set up after the German occupation of northern France, to administer unoccupied France and the colonies. Never recognized by the Allies, the regime functioned as a puppet government for the Nazis.

vichyssoise /ˌviːʃiːˈswɑːz/ ▶ **noun** [mass noun] a soup made with potatoes, leeks, and cream and typically served chilled.
– ORIGIN French (feminine) 'of *Vichy*' (see **VICHY**).

vicinage /ˈvɪsɪnɪdʒ/ ▶ **noun** chiefly US another term for **VICINITY**.
– ORIGIN Middle English: from Old French *vis(e)nage*, from an alteration of Latin *vicinus* 'neighbour'.

vicinal /ˈvɪsɪn(ə)l, vɪˈsʌɪn(ə)l/ ▶ **adjective 1** rare neighbouring; adjacent. ■ Chemistry relating to or denoting substituents attached to adjacent atoms in a ring or chain.
2 (of a railway or road) serving a neighbourhood; local.
– ORIGIN early 17th cent.: from French, or from Latin *vicinalis*, from *vicinus* 'neighbour'.

vicinity ▶ **noun** (pl. **vicinities**) the area near or surrounding a particular place: *the number of people living in the immediate vicinity was small.* ■ [mass noun] archaic proximity in space or relationship: *the abundance and vicinity of country seats.*
– ORIGIN mid 16th cent. (in the sense 'proximity'): from Latin *vicinitas*, from *vicinus* 'neighbour'.

vicious ▶ **adjective 1** deliberately cruel or violent: *a vicious assault.* ■ (of an animal) wild and dangerous to people. ■ serious or dangerous: *a vicious flu bug.*
2 literary immoral: *every soul on earth, virtuous or vicious, shall perish.*
3 archaic (of language or a line of reasoning) imperfect; defective.
– DERIVATIVES **viciously** adverb, **viciousness** noun.
– ORIGIN Middle English (in the sense 'characterized by immorality'): from Old French *vicious* or Latin *vitiosus*, from *vitium* 'vice'.

vicious circle (also **vicious cycle**) ▶ **noun** a sequence of reciprocal cause and effect in which two or more elements intensify and aggravate each other, leading inexorably to a worsening of the situation.

vicissitude /vɪˈsɪsɪtjuːd, vʌɪ-/ ▶ **noun 1** (usu. **vicissitudes**) a change of circumstances or fortune, typically one that is unwelcome or unpleasant: *her husband's sharp vicissitudes of fortune.*
2 [mass noun] literary alternation between opposite or contrasting things: *the vicissitude of the seasons.*
– DERIVATIVES **vicissitudinous** /-ˈtjuːdɪnəs/ adjective.
– ORIGIN early 17th cent. (in the sense 'alternation'): from French, or from Latin *vicissitudo*, from *vicissim* 'by turns', from *vic-* 'turn, change'.

Vicksburg /ˈvɪksbəːg/ a city on the Mississippi River, in western Mississippi; pop. 24,974 (est. 2008). In 1863, during the American Civil War, it was successfully besieged by Union forces. It was the last Confederate-held outpost on the river and its loss effectively split the secessionist states in half.

Vico /ˈviːkəʊ/, Giambattista (1668–1744), Italian philosopher. In *Scienza Nuova* (1725) he asserted that civilizations are subject to recurring cycles of barbarism, heroism, and reason, accompanied by corresponding cultural, linguistic, and political modes. His historicist approach influenced later philosophers such as Marx.

vicomte /ˈviːkɔ̃t, ˈviːkɒmt/, French /vikɔ̃t/ ▶ **noun** (pl. pronunc. **same**) a French nobleman corresponding in rank to a British or Irish viscount.
– ORIGIN French.

vicomtesse /ˌvikɔ̃ˈtɛs, ˌviːkɒnˈtɛs/, French /vikɒmtɛs/ ▶ **noun** (pl. pronunc. **same**) a French noblewoman corresponding in rank to a British or Irish viscountess.
– ORIGIN French.

victim ▶ **noun** a person harmed, injured, or killed as a result of a crime, accident, or other event or action: *victims of domestic violence* | *earthquake victims.* ■ a person who is tricked or duped: *the victim of a hoax.* ■ a person who has come to feel helpless and passive in the face of misfortune or ill-treatment: *I saw myself as a victim* | [as modifier] *a victim mentality.* ■ a living creature killed as a religious sacrifice.
– PHRASES **fall victim to** be hurt, killed, damaged, or destroyed by: *he fell victim to a fatal blood infection.*
– DERIVATIVES **victimhood** noun.
– ORIGIN late 15th cent. (denoting a creature killed as a religious sacrifice): from Latin *victima*.

victimize (also **victimise**) ▶ **verb** [with obj.] single (someone) out for cruel or unjust treatment: *they are victimized by racism or discriminatory barriers.*
– DERIVATIVES **victimization** noun, **victimizer** noun.

victimless ▶ **adjective** (of a crime) in which there is no injured party.

victimology ▶ **noun** (pl. **victimologies**) [mass noun]
1 the study of the victims of crime and the psychological effects of their experience.
2 a mental attitude which tends to indulge and perpetuate the feeling of being a victim.

victim support ▶ **noun** [mass noun] the provision of advice and counselling to victims of crime.

victor ▶ **noun 1** a person who defeats an enemy or opponent in a battle, game, or other competition.
2 a code word representing the letter V, used in radio communication.
– ORIGIN Middle English: from Anglo-Norman French *victo(u)r* or Latin *victor*, from *vincere* 'conquer'.

Victor Emmanuel II (1820–78), ruler of the kingdom of Sardinia 1849–61 and first king of united Italy 1861–78. He hastened the drive towards Italian unification by appointing Cavour as Premier of Piedmont in 1852. After being crowned king of Italy he added Venetia to the kingdom in 1866 and Rome in 1870.

Victor Emmanuel III (1869–1947), last king of Italy 1900–46. He invited Mussolini to form a government in 1922 and lost all political power. After the loss of Sicily to the Allies (1943), he acted to dismiss Mussolini and conclude an armistice.

Victoria[1] /vɪkˈtɔːrɪə/ **1** a state of SE Australia; pop. 5,313,823 (2008); capital, Melbourne. Originally a district of New South Wales, it became a separate colony in 1851 and was federated with the other states of Australia in 1901.
2 a port at the southern tip of Vancouver Island, capital of British Columbia; pop. 78,057 (2006).
3 the capital of the Seychelles, a port on the island of Mahé; pop. 26,000 (est. 2007).
4 the administrative centre of Hong Kong; pop. 981,700 (est. 2006).

Victoria[2] /vɪkˈtɔːrɪə/ (1819–1901), queen of Great Britain and Ireland 1837–1901 and empress of India 1876–1901. She succeeded to the throne on the death of her uncle, William IV, and married her cousin Prince Albert in 1840. She took an active interest in the policies of her ministers, but largely retired from public life after Prince Albert's death in 1861. Her reign was the longest in British history.

Victoria[3] /vɪkˈtɔːrɪə/, Spanish /bikˈtəorja/, Tomás Luis de (1548–1611), Spanish composer. His music, all of it religious, resembles that of Palestrina in its contrapuntal nature; it includes motets, masses, and hymns.

victoria /vɪkˈtɔːrɪə/ ▶ **noun** historical a light four-wheeled horse-drawn carriage with a collapsible hood, seats for two passengers, and an elevated driver's seat in front.
– ORIGIN late 19th cent.: named after Queen *Victoria* (see **VICTORIA**[2]).

Victoria, Lake the largest lake in Africa, with shores in Uganda, Tanzania, and Kenya, and drained by the Nile. Also called **VICTORIA NYANZA**.

Victoria and Albert Museum (abbrev.: **V & A**) a national museum of fine and applied art in South Kensington, London, created in 1852 and having collections principally of pictures, textiles, ceramics, and furniture.

Victoria Cross (abbrev.: **VC**) ▶ **noun** a decoration awarded for conspicuous bravery in the Commonwealth armed services, instituted by Queen Victoria in 1856.

Victoria Day ▶ **noun** (in Canada) the Monday preceding May 24, observed as a national holiday to commemorate the birthday of Queen Victoria.

Victoria de Durango full name for **DURANGO**.

Victoria Falls a spectacular waterfall 109 m (355 ft) high, located on the River Zambezi, on the Zimbabwe–Zambia border. Its native name is Mosi-oa-tunya, 'the smoke that thunders'.

Victoria Island an island in the Canadian Arctic, in the Northwest Territories.

Victoria lily ▶ **noun** a tropical South American water lily which has gigantic floating leaves with raised sides. ● Genus *Victoria*, family Nymphaeaceae: two species.

Victorian ▶ **adjective** relating to the reign of Queen Victoria: *a Victorian house.* ■ relating to the attitudes and values of society during Queen Victoria's reign, regarded as characterized especially by prudishness and a high moral tone.
▶ **noun** a person who lived during the Victorian period.
– DERIVATIVES **Victorianism** noun.

Victoriana ▶ **plural noun** articles, especially collectors' items, from the Victorian period.

Victoria Nile the upper part of the White Nile, between Lake Victoria and Lake Albert.

Victoria Nyanza /nɪˈanzə/ another name for Lake Victoria (see **VICTORIA, LAKE**).

Victoria Peak a mountain on Hong Kong Island, rising to 554 m (1,818 ft).

Victoria plum ▶ **noun** Brit. a plum of a large red dessert variety.

Victoria sandwich (also **Victoria sponge**) ▶ **noun** Brit. a cake consisting of two layers of sponge made with additional fat and filled with jam.

victorious ▶ **adjective** having won a victory; triumphant: *a victorious army* | *the team defied the odds and emerged victorious.* ■ of or characterized by victory: *he'd participated in the victorious campaigns of the Franco-Prussian War.*
– DERIVATIVES **victoriously** adverb.
– ORIGIN late Middle English: from Anglo-Norman French *victorious*, from Latin *victoriosus*, from *victoria* (see **VICTORY**).

victor ludorum /luːˈdɔːrəm/ ▶ **noun** Brit. a boy or man who is the overall champion in a sports competition, especially at a school or college.
– ORIGIN Latin, literally 'victor of the games'.

Victory the flagship of Lord Nelson at the Battle of Trafalgar, launched in 1765. It has been restored, and is now on display in dry dock at Portsmouth.

victory ▶ **noun** (pl. **victories**) an act of defeating an enemy or opponent in a battle, game, or other competition: *an election victory* | [mass noun] *they won their heat and went on to victory in the final* | [as modifier] *a victory celebration.*
– ORIGIN Middle English: from Anglo-Norman French *victorie*, from Latin *victoria*.

victory bond ▶ **noun** a bond issued by a government during or immediately after a major war.

victory roll ▶ **noun** a roll performed by an aircraft as a sign of triumph, typically after a successful mission.

victory sign ▶ **noun** a signal of triumph or celebration made by holding up the hand with the palm outwards and the first two fingers spread apart to represent the letter V.

victrix /ˈvɪktrɪks/ ▶ **noun** (pl. **victrices** /-trɪsiːz/) rare a female victor or champion.
– ORIGIN Latin, feminine of *victor* (see **VICTOR**).

victrix ludorum ▶ **noun** Brit. a girl or woman who is the overall champion in a sports competition, especially at a school or college.
– ORIGIN Latin, feminine of **VICTOR LUDORUM**.

Victrola /vɪkˈtrəʊlə/ ▶ **noun** trademark a kind of gramophone used particularly in the 1920s and 1930s.
– ORIGIN early 20th cent.: from the name of the *Victor* Talking Machine Company + *-ola* (as in *pianola*).

victual /ˈvɪt(ə)l/ dated ▶ **noun** (**victuals**) food or provisions.
▶ **verb** (**victuals, victualling, victualled** ; US **victuals, victualing, victualed**) [with obj.] provide with food or other stores: *the ship wasn't even properly victualled.*
■ [no obj.] archaic obtain or lay in food or other stores: *a voyage of such length, that no ship could victual for.*
■ [no obj.] archaic eat: *victual with me next Saturday.*
– ORIGIN Middle English: from Old French *vitaille*, from late Latin *victualia*, neuter plural of Latin *victualis*, from *victus* 'food'; related to *vivere* 'to live'. The pronunciation still represents the early spelling *vittel*; later spelling has been influenced by the Latin form.

victualler /ˈvɪt(ə)lə/ (US **victualer**) ▶ **noun 1** (also **licensed victualler**) Brit. a person who is licensed to sell alcohol.
2 dated a person providing or selling food or other provisions. ■ a ship providing supplies for troops or other ships.
– ORIGIN late Middle English: from Old French *vitaill(i)er*, from *vitaille* (see **VICTUAL**).

vicuña /vɪˈkjuːnjə, -kuː-, vɪˈkuːnə/ ▶ **noun** a wild relative of the llama, inhabiting mountainous regions of South America and valued for its fine silky wool.
● *Vicugna vicugna*, family Camelidae.
■ [mass noun] cloth made from the wool of the vicuña or an imitation of it.
– ORIGIN early 17th cent.: from Spanish, from Quechua.

vicus /ˈvʌɪkəs, ˈviːkəs/ ▶ **noun** (pl. **vici** /ˈvʌɪkiː, ˈviːkiː/) the smallest unit of ancient Roman municipal administration, consisting of a village or part of a town. ■ a medieval European township.
– ORIGIN Latin, literally 'group of dwellings'.

Vic-Wells Ballet a ballet company set up by Ninette de Valois, based first at the Old Vic and from 1931 established at Sadler's Wells Theatre. The company later became the Sadler's Wells Ballet which in turn became part of the newly formed Royal Ballet.

vid ▶ **noun** informal short for **VIDEO**.

Vidal /vɪˈdɑːl/, Gore (b.1925), American novelist, dramatist, and essayist; born *Eugene Luther Vidal.* His novels, many of them satirical comedies, include *Williwaw* (1946) and *Myra Breckenridge* (1968).

vide /ˈvɪdeɪ, ˈviː-, ˈvʌɪdi/ ▶ **verb** [with obj., in imperative] see; consult (used as an instruction in a text to refer the reader to a specified passage, book, author, etc., for further information): *vide the comments cited in Schlosser.*
– ORIGIN Latin, 'see!', imperative of *videre*.

videlicet /vɪˈdɛlɪsɛt, vʌɪ-, -kɛt/ ▶ **adverb** more formal term for **VIZ.**
– ORIGIN Latin, from *videre* 'to see' + *licet* 'it is permissible'.

video ▶ **noun** (pl. **videos**) **1** [mass noun] the system of recording, reproducing, or broadcasting moving visual images on or from videotape.
2 a film or other piece of material recorded on videotape. ■ a video cassette: *a blank video* | [mass noun] *the film will soon be released **on video**.* ■ a short film made by a pop or rock group to accompany a song when broadcast on television. ■ Brit. a video recorder.
▶ **verb** (**videoes, videoing, videoed**) [with obj.] chiefly Brit.
1 make a video recording of (something broadcast on television).
2 film with a video camera: *he videoed our wedding.*
– ORIGIN 1930s: from Latin *videre* 'to see', on the pattern of *audio.*

video amplifier ▶ **noun** a device designed to amplify the wide range of frequencies present in video signals and deliver the signal to the picture tube of a television set.

video camera ▶ **noun** a camera for recording images on videotape or for transmitting them to a monitor screen.

video card ▶ **noun** Computing a printed circuit board controlling output to a display screen.

videocassette ▶ **noun** a cassette of videotape.

videoconference ▶ **noun** a conference in which participants in different locations are able to communicate with each other in sound and vision.
– DERIVATIVES **videoconferencing** noun.

video diary ▶ **noun** a record on videotape of a notable period of someone's life, or of a particular event, made using a camcorder.

videodisc ▶ **noun** a CD-ROM or other disc used to store visual images.

video frequency ▶ **noun** a frequency in the range used for video signals in television.

video game ▶ **noun** a game played by electronically manipulating images produced by a computer program on a television screen or display.

videographics ▶ **plural noun** visual images produced using computer technology. ■ [treated as sing.] the manipulation of video images using a computer.

videography ▶ **noun** [mass noun] the process or art of making video films.
– DERIVATIVES **videographer** noun.

video jockey ▶ **noun** a person who introduces and plays music videos on television.

video link ▶ **noun** an electronic facility that enables audiovisual communication between people in different locations.

video nasty ▶ **noun** Brit. informal a film on video that contains scenes that are considered to be gratuitously and offensively violent or pornographic.

video on demand ▶ **noun** [mass noun] a system in which viewers choose their own filmed entertainment, by means of a PC or interactive TV system, from a wide available selection.

videophone ▶ **noun** a telephone device transmitting and receiving a visual image as well as sound.

video piracy ▶ **noun** [mass noun] the unauthorized and illegal production and sale of copies of commercial video films.

video recorder ▶ **noun** a device which, when linked to a television set, can be used to record programmes and play videotapes.
– DERIVATIVES **video recording** noun.

videotape ▶ **noun** [mass noun] magnetic tape for recording and reproducing visual images and sound. ■ [count noun] a videocassette.
▶ **verb** another term for **VIDEO**: *his arrest was videotaped.*

V

videotelephony ▶ noun [mass noun] the transmission of video signals along telephone wires.

videotex (also **videotext**) ▶ noun [mass noun] trademark an electronic information system such as teletext or viewdata.
– ORIGIN 1970s: from **VIDEO** + **TEXT**.

videshi /vɪˈdɛʃi/ ▶ adjective Indian not Indian; foreign. ■ (especially of manufactured goods) made in a country other than India.
– ORIGIN from Hindi.

vidicon ▶ noun Electronics a small television camera tube in which the image is formed on a transparent electrode coated with photoconductive material, the current from which varies as it is scanned by a beam of low-speed electrons.
– ORIGIN 1950s: from the initial elements of **VIDEO** and *iconoscope* (an early television camera tube).

vidiot /ˈvɪdɪət/ ▶ noun N. Amer. informal a habitual, undiscriminating watcher of television or videotapes.
– ORIGIN 1960s: blend of **VIDEO** and **IDIOT**.

vie /vʌɪ/ ▶ verb (**vies, vying, vied**) [no obj.] compete eagerly with someone in order to do or achieve something: *the athletes were* ***vying for*** *a place in the British team.*
– ORIGIN mid 16th cent.: probably a shortening of obsolete *envy*, via Old French from Latin *invitare* 'challenge'.

vielle /vɪˈɛl/ ▶ noun a hurdy-gurdy.
– ORIGIN mid 18th cent.: from French, from Old French *viele* (see **VIOL**).

Vienna /vɪˈɛnə/ the capital of Austria, situated in the north-east of the country on the River Danube; pop. 1,661,206 (2006). From 1278 to 1918 it was the seat of the Habsburgs. It has long been a centre of the arts, especially music; Mozart, Beethoven, and the Strauss family were among the great composers who lived and worked there. German name **WIEN**.
– DERIVATIVES **Viennese** /vɪəˈniːz/ adjective & noun.

Vienna, Congress of an international conference held 1814–15 to agree the settlement of Europe after the Napoleonic Wars. The guiding principle of the settlement was the restoration and strengthening of hereditary and sometimes despotic rulers; the result was a political stability that lasted for three or four decades.

Vienna Circle a group of empiricist philosophers, scientists, and mathematicians active in Vienna from the 1920s until 1938, including Rudolf Carnap and Kurt Gödel. Their work laid the foundations of logical positivism.

Vienna sausage ▶ noun a small frankfurter made of pork, beef, or veal.

Vienna Secession ▶ noun see **SEZESSION**.

Viennese coffee ▶ noun [mass noun] a blend of coffee flavoured with fig extract.

Viennese waltz ▶ noun a waltz characterized by a slight anticipation of the second beat of the bar and having a romantic quality.

Vientiane /ˌvjɛnˈtjɑːn/ the capital and chief port of Laos, on the Mekong River; pop. 231,700 (est. 2009).

Vierwaldstättersee /ˌfiːɐˈvaltˌʃtɛtɐˌzeː/ German name for Lake Lucerne (see **LUCERNE, LAKE**).

Vietcong /vjɛtˈkɒŋ/ ▶ noun (pl. **same**) the Communist guerrilla movement in Vietnam which fought the South Vietnamese government forces 1954–75 with the support of the North Vietnamese army and opposed the South Vietnam and US forces in the Vietnam War. ■ a member of the Vietcong.
– ORIGIN Vietnamese, literally 'Vietnamese Communist'.

Vietminh /vjɛtˈmɪn/ ▶ noun (pl. **same**) a member of a Communist-dominated nationalist movement, formed in 1941, that fought for Vietnamese independence from French rule. Members of the Vietminh later joined with the Vietcong.
– ORIGIN from Vietnamese *Viet-Nam Dôc-Lâp Dông-Minh* 'Vietnamese Independence League'.

Vietnam /vjɛtˈnam/ a country in SE Asia, with a coastline on the South China Sea; pop. 88,576,800 (est. 2009); official language, Vietnamese; capital, Hanoi.

> Traditionally dominated by China, Vietnam came under French influence between 1862 and 1954. After the Second World War the Vietminh defeated the French, who then withdrew. Vietnam was partitioned along the 17th parallel between Communist North Vietnam (capital, Hanoi) and non-Communist South Vietnam (capital, Saigon). The Vietnam War between the North and the US-backed South ended in the victory of the North in 1975 and the reunification of the country under a Communist regime in the following year.

– ORIGIN from Vietnamese *Viet*, the name of the inhabitants, + *nam* 'south'.

Vietnamese ▶ adjective relating to Vietnam, its people, or their language.
▶ noun (pl. **same**) **1** a native or inhabitant of Vietnam, or a person of Vietnamese descent.
2 [mass noun] the language of Vietnam, spoken by about 60 million people. It probably belongs to the Mon-Khmer group, although much of its vocabulary is derived from Chinese.

Vietnamese pot-bellied pig ▶ noun see **POT-BELLIED PIG**.

Vietnamization (also **Vietnamisation**) ▶ noun [mass noun] (in the Vietnam War) the US policy of withdrawing its troops and transferring the responsibility and direction of the war effort to the government of South Vietnam.

Vietnam War a war between Communist North Vietnam and US-backed South Vietnam.

> Since the partition of Vietnam in 1954 the Communist North had attempted to unite the country as a Communist state, fuelling US concern over the possible spread of Communism in SE Asia. After two US destroyers were reportedly fired on in the Gulf of Tonkin in 1964, a US army was sent to Vietnam, supported by contingents from South Korea, Australia, New Zealand, and Thailand, while American aircraft bombed North Vietnamese forces and areas of Cambodia. The Tet Offensive of 1968 damaged US confidence and US forces began to be withdrawn, finally leaving in 1973. The North Vietnamese captured the southern capital Saigon to end the war in 1975.

vieux jeu /vjəː ˈʒəː/, French /vjø ʒø/ ▶ adjective old-fashioned; hackneyed: *a joke that was vieux jeu even in my day.*
– ORIGIN French, literally 'old game'.

view ▶ noun **1** [mass noun] the ability to see something or to be seen from a particular place: *the end of the tunnel came into view* | [count noun] *they stood on the bar to get a better view.* ■ [count noun] an inspection of things for sale by prospective purchasers, especially of works of art at an exhibition.
2 a sight or prospect, typically of attractive natural scenery, that can be taken in by the eye from a particular place: *a fine view of the castle.* ■ a work of art depicting a sight of natural scenery. ■ [count noun] the visual appearance or an image of something when looked at in a particular way: *an aerial view of the military earthworks.*
3 a particular way of considering or regarding something; an attitude or opinion: *strong political views.*
▶ verb **1** [with obj.] look at or inspect: *the public can view the famous hall with its unique staircase.* ■ inspect (a house or other property) with the intention of possibly buying or renting it. ■ watch (something) on television. ■ Hunting see (a fox) break cover.
2 [with obj. and adverbial] regard in a particular light or with a particular attitude: *farmers are viewing the rise in rabbit numbers with concern.*
– PHRASES **in full view** clearly visible. **in view 1** visible: *the youth was keeping him in view.* **2** as one's aim or in one's mind: *the operation they* ***had in view.*** **in view of** because or as a result of. **on view** being shown or exhibited to the public. ■ easily visible: *it is advisable not to leave handbags on view.* **with a view to** with the hope, aim, or intention of.
– DERIVATIVES **viewable** adjective, **viewless** adjective.
– ORIGIN Middle English: from Anglo-Norman French *vieue*, feminine past participle of *veoir* 'see', from Latin *videre*. The verb dates from the early 16th cent.

viewdata ▶ noun [mass noun] a news and information service in which computer data is sent by a telephone link and displayed on a monitor.

viewer ▶ noun **1** a person who looks at or inspects something. ■ a person watching television or a film.
2 a device for looking at film transparencies or similar photographic images.

viewership ▶ noun [treated as sing. or pl.] the audience for a particular television programme or channel.

viewfinder ▶ noun a device on a camera showing the field of view of the lens, used in framing and focusing the picture.

viewgraph ▶ noun a graph or other data produced as a transparency for projection on to a screen or for transmission during a teleconference.

view halloo ▶ noun a shout given by a hunter on seeing a fox break cover.

viewing ▶ noun [mass noun] the action of inspecting or looking at something: *the owner may allow viewing by appointment.* ■ the action of watching something on television: *the film is quite unsuitable for family viewing.* ■ [count noun] an opportunity to see something, especially works of art.

viewpoint ▶ noun **1** a position giving a good view.
2 a person's opinion or point of view: *I do try to put over our viewpoint* | *from a purely aesthetic viewpoint, I must say that I dislike the design.*

viewport ▶ noun **1** a window in a spacecraft or in the conning tower of an oil rig.
2 Computing a framed area on a display screen for viewing information.

viewscreen ▶ noun the screen on a television, computer, or similar device on which images and data are displayed.

VIFF (also **viff**) Aeronautics, informal ▶ noun [mass noun] a technique used by a vertical take-off aircraft to change direction abruptly by altering the direction of thrust of the aircraft's jet engines.
▶ verb [no obj.] (of a vertical take-off aircraft) change direction in such a way.
– ORIGIN 1970s: acronym from *vectoring in forward flight.*

vig ▶ noun short for **VIGORISH**.

viga /ˈviːɡə/ ▶ noun US a rough-hewn roof timber or rafter, especially in an adobe building.
– ORIGIN Spanish.

Vigée-Lebrun /ˌviːʒeɪləˈbrəːn/, French /viʒeləbrœ̃/, (Marie Louise) Élisabeth (1755–1842), French painter. She is known for her portraits of women and children, especially Marie Antoinette and Lady Hamilton.

vigesimal /vɪˈdʒɛsɪm(ə)l, vʌɪ-/ ▶ adjective rare relating to or based on the number twenty.
– ORIGIN mid 17th cent.: from Latin *vigesimus* (from *viginti* 'twenty') + **-AL**.

vigil /ˈvɪdʒɪl/ ▶ noun **1** a period of keeping awake during the time usually spent asleep, especially to keep watch or pray: *my birdwatching vigils lasted for hours* | *as he lay in a coma the family* ***kept vigil.*** ■ a stationary, peaceful demonstration in support of a particular cause, typically without speeches.
2 (in the Christian Church) the eve of a festival or holy day as an occasion of religious observance. ■ (**vigils**) nocturnal devotions.
– ORIGIN Middle English (in sense 2): via Old French from Latin *vigilia*, from *vigil* 'awake'.

vigilance ▶ noun [mass noun] the action or state of keeping careful watch for possible danger or difficulties: *security duties that demand long hours of vigilance.*
– ORIGIN late 16th cent.: from French, or from Latin *vigilantia*, from *vigilare* 'keep awake', from *vigil* (see **VIGIL**).

vigilance committee ▶ noun US a group of vigilantes.

vigilant ▶ adjective keeping careful watch for possible danger or difficulties: *the burglar was spotted by vigilant neighbours.*
– DERIVATIVES **vigilantly** adverb.
– ORIGIN late 15th cent.: from Latin *vigilant-* 'keeping awake', from the verb *vigilare*, from *vigil* (see **VIGIL**).

vigilante /ˌvɪdʒɪˈlanti/ ▶ noun a member of a self-appointed group of citizens who undertake law enforcement in their community without legal authority, typically because the legal agencies are thought to be inadequate.
– DERIVATIVES **vigilantism** noun.
– ORIGIN mid 19th cent.: from Spanish, literally 'vigilant'.

vigneron /ˈviːnjərɒ̃/, French /viɲ(ə)rɔ̃/ ▶ noun a person who cultivates grapes for winemaking.
– ORIGIN French, from *vigne* 'vine'.

vignette /viːˈnjɛt, vɪ-/ ▶ noun **1** a brief evocative description, account, or episode: *a classic vignette of embassy life.*
2 a small illustration or portrait photograph which fades into its background without a definite border.
3 a small ornamental design filling a space in a book or carving, typically based on foliage.
▶ verb [with obj.] portray (someone) in the style of a vignette. ■ produce (a photograph) in the style of a vignette by softening or shading away the edges of the subject.
– DERIVATIVES **vignettist** noun.
– ORIGIN late Middle English (in sense 3 of the noun; also as an architectural term denoting a carved representation of a vine): from French, diminutive of *vigne* 'vine'.

Vignola /vɪˈnjəʊlə/, Giacomo Barozzi da (1507–73), Italian architect. His designs were mannerist in style and include the Palazzo Farnese near Viterbo (1559–73) and the church of Il Gesù in Rome (begun 1568).

Vigny /ˈviːnji/, Alfred Victor, Comte de (1797–1863), French poet, novelist, and dramatist. His poetry reveals his faith in 'man's unconquerable mind'. Other works include the play *Chatterton* (1835).

Vigo[1] /ˈviːgəʊ/ a port on the Atlantic in Galicia, NW Spain; pop. 295,703 (2008).

Vigo[2] /ˈviːgəʊ/, Jean (1905–34), French film director. His experimental films, which combine lyrical, surrealist, and realist elements, include *Zéro de conduite* (1933) and *L'Atalante* (1934).

vigor ▸ **noun** US spelling of **VIGOUR**.

vigorish ▸ **noun** US informal **1** [in sing.] an excessive rate of interest on a loan, typically one from an illegal moneylender.
2 [mass noun] the percentage deducted from a gambler's winnings by the organizers of a game.
– ORIGIN early 20th cent.: probably from Yiddish, from Russian *vyigrysh* 'gain, winnings'.

vigoro /ˈvɪg(ə)rəʊ/ ▸ **noun** [mass noun] an Australian team ball game combining elements of cricket and baseball, traditionally played by women.
– ORIGIN 1930s: apparently from **VIGOROUS**.

vigorous ▸ **adjective** strong, healthy, and full of energy: *a tall, vigorous, and muscular man.* ■ characterized by or involving physical strength, effort, or energy: *vigorous aerobic exercise.* ■ (of language) forceful: *a vigorous denial.*
– DERIVATIVES **vigorousness** noun.
– ORIGIN Middle English: via Old French from medieval Latin *vigorosus*, from Latin *vigor* (see **VIGOUR**).

vigorously ▸ **adverb** in a way that involves physical strength, effort, or energy; strenuously: *she shook her head vigorously.* ■ forcefully: *he vigorously denied the allegation.*

vigour (US **vigor**) ▸ **noun** [mass noun] physical strength and good health. ■ effort, energy, and enthusiasm: *they set about the new task with vigour.*
– ORIGIN Middle English: from Old French, from Latin *vigor*, from *vigere* 'be lively'.

vihara /vɪˈhɑːrə/ ▸ **noun** a Buddhist temple or monastery.
– ORIGIN Sanskrit.

vihuela /vɪˈ(h)weɪlə/ ▸ **noun** a type of early Spanish stringed musical instrument, in particular **vihuela de mano** /deɪ ˈmanəʊ/ a type of guitar and **vihuela de arco** /deɪ ˈɑːkəʊ/ a type of viol.
– ORIGIN mid 19th cent.: Spanish.

Vijayawada /ˌvɪdʒʌɪəˈwɑːdə/ a city on the Krishna River in Andhra Pradesh, SE India; pop. 971,700 (est. 2009).

Viking[1] /ˈvʌɪkɪŋ/ ▸ **noun** any of the Scandinavian seafaring pirates and traders who raided and settled in many parts of NW Europe in the 8th–11th centuries.
– ORIGIN from Old Norse *víkingr*, from *vík* 'creek' or Old English *wīc* 'camp, dwelling place'.

Viking[2] /ˈvʌɪkɪŋ/ a shipping forecast area covering the open sea between southern Norway and the Shetland Islands.

Viking[3] /ˈvʌɪkɪŋ/ either of two American space probes sent to Mars in 1975, each of which consisted of a lander that conducted experiments on the surface and an orbiter.

Vila /ˈviːlə/ (also **Port Vila**) the capital of Vanuatu, on the SW coast of the island of Efate; pop. 40,000 (est. 2007).

vilayet /vɪˈlɑːjɛt/ ▸ **noun** (in Turkey, and formerly in the Ottoman Empire) a major administrative district or province with its own governor.
– ORIGIN Turkish, from Arabic *wilāya(t)* 'government, administrative district'.

vile ▸ **adjective** extremely unpleasant: *he has a vile temper | vile smells.* ■ morally bad; wicked: *as vile a rogue as ever lived.* ■ archaic of little worth or value.
– DERIVATIVES **vilely** adverb, **vileness** noun.
– ORIGIN Middle English: via Old French from Latin *vilis* 'of low value'.

vilification /ˌvɪlɪfɪˈkeɪʃ(ə)n/ ▸ **noun** [mass noun] abusively disparaging speech or writing: *the vilification of minority groupings.*

vilify /ˈvɪlɪfʌɪ/ ▸ **verb** (**vilifies**, **vilifying**, **vilified**) [with obj.] speak or write about in an abusively disparaging manner: *he has been vilified in the press.*
– DERIVATIVES **vilifier** noun.
– ORIGIN late Middle English (in the sense 'lower in value'): from late Latin *vilificare*, from Latin *vilis* 'of low value' (see **VILE**).

vill ▸ **noun** (in medieval England) the smallest administrative unit under the feudal system, consisting of a number of houses and their adjacent lands, roughly corresponding to the modern parish.
– ORIGIN early 17th cent.: from Anglo-Norman French, from Latin *villa* 'country house'.

Villa /ˈviːjə, ˈviːljə/, Pancho (1878–1923), Mexican revolutionary; born *Doroteo Arango*. After playing a prominent role in the revolution of 1910–11 he overthrew the dictatorial regime of General Victoriano Huerta in 1914 together with Venustiano Carranza, but then rebelled against Carranza's regime with Emiliano Zapata.

villa ▸ **noun 1** (especially in continental Europe) a large and luxurious country house in its own grounds. ■ Brit. a detached or semi-detached house in a residential district, typically one that is Victorian or Edwardian in style. ■ Brit. a rented holiday home abroad.
2 a large country house of Roman times, having an estate and consisting of farm and residential buildings arranged around a courtyard.
– ORIGIN early 17th cent.: from Italian, from Latin.

Villafranchian /ˌvɪləˈfraŋkɪən/ ▸ **adjective** relating to or denoting an age (or stage) in Europe crossing the boundary of the Upper Pliocene and Lower Pleistocene, lasting from about 3 to 1 million years ago. ■ (as noun **the Villafranchian**) the Villafranchian age or stage, or the system of deposits laid down during it.
– ORIGIN late 19th cent.: from French *villafranchien*, from *Villafranca* d'Asti, the village in northern Italy near which exposures of this period occur.

village ▸ **noun 1** a group of houses and associated buildings, larger than a hamlet and smaller than a town, situated in a rural area. ■ a self-contained district or community within a town or city, regarded as having features characteristic of village life: *the Olympic village.* ■ US a small municipality with limited corporate powers.
2 Austral./NZ a select suburban shopping centre.
– DERIVATIVES **villager** noun, **villagey** adjective.
– ORIGIN late Middle English: from Old French, from Latin *villa* 'country house'.

village idiot ▸ **noun** chiefly humorous a person of very low intelligence resident in a village.

villagization /ˌvɪlɪdʒʌɪˈzeɪʃ(ə)n/ (also **villagisation**) ▸ **noun** [mass noun] (in Africa and Asia) the concentration of the population in villages as opposed to scattered settlements. ■ the transfer of land to the communal control of villagers.

Villahermosa /ˌviːjəɛːˈməʊsə/, Spanish /bijaerˈmosa/ a city in SE Mexico, capital of the state of Tabasco; pop. 335,778 (2005). Full name **Villahermosa de San Juan Bautista** /deɪ san ˌhwɑːn baʊˈtiːstə/, Spanish /ðe saŋ xwan bauˈtista/.

villain /ˈvɪlən/ ▸ **noun 1** (fem. **villainess**) (in a film, novel, or play) a character whose evil actions or motives are important to the plot: *a pantomime villain | I have played more good guys than villains.* ■ Brit. informal a criminal: *some people have been tricked by villains with false identity cards.* ■ the person or thing responsible for specified problems, harm, or damage: *the industrialized nations are the real environmental villains.*
2 archaic variant spelling of **VILLEIN**.
– PHRASES **the villain of the piece** Brit. the person or thing responsible for all of the trouble or harm in a particular situation: *TV tends to be cast as the villain of the piece | Holdsworth was the villain of the piece when he missed an open goal.*
– ORIGIN Middle English (in the sense 'a rustic, boor'): from Old French *vilein*, based on Latin *villa* (see **VILLA**).

villainous ▸ **adjective 1** relating to, constituting, or guilty of wicked or criminal behaviour: *a villainous plot.*
2 informal extremely bad or unpleasant: *a villainous smell.*
– DERIVATIVES **villainously** adverb, **villainousness** noun.

villainy ▸ **noun** (pl. **villainies**) [mass noun] wicked or criminal behaviour: *the villainy of professional racketeers* | [count noun] *minor villainies.*
– ORIGIN Middle English: from Old French *vilenie*, from *vilein* (see **VILLAIN**).

Villa-Lobos /ˌvɪləˈləʊbɒs/, Heitor (1887–1959), Brazilian composer. He used folk music in many of his instrumental compositions, notably the nine *Bachianas brasileiras* (1930–45).

villancico /ˌviːjanˈsiːkəʊ/ ▸ **noun** (pl. **villancicos** /-əʊz/) a form of Spanish and Portuguese song with short stanzas and a refrain, originally a folk song, later used in sacred music, and now especially as a Christmas carol.
– ORIGIN Spanish, diminutive of *villano* 'peasant'.

villanella /ˌvɪləˈnɛlə/ ▸ **noun** (pl. **villanelle** /ˌvɪləˈnɛleɪ/ or **villanellas**) a form of Italian part-song originating in Naples in the 16th century, in rustic style with a vigorous rhythm.
– ORIGIN Italian, feminine of *villanello* 'rural', diminutive of *villano* 'peasant'.

villanelle /ˌvɪləˈnɛl/ ▸ **noun** a pastoral or lyrical poem of nineteen lines, with only two rhymes throughout, and some lines repeated.
– ORIGIN late 19th cent.: from French, from Italian *villanella* (see **VILLANELLA**).

-ville ▸ **combining form** informal used in fictitious place names with reference to a particular quality: *dullsville.*
– ORIGIN from French *ville* 'town', used in many US town names.

villein /ˈvɪlən, -eɪn/ ▸ **noun** (in medieval England) a feudal tenant entirely subject to a lord or manor to whom he paid dues and services in return for land.
– ORIGIN Middle English: variant of **VILLAIN**.

villeinage /ˈvɪlənɪdʒ, -leɪn-/ ▸ **noun** [mass noun] historical the tenure or status of a villein in the feudal system.

villi plural form of **VILLUS**.

Villon /ˈviːjɒ̃/, French /vijɔ̃/, François (*fl.c.*1460), French poet; born *François de Montcorbier* or *François des Loges*. He is best known for *Le Lais* or *Le Petit testament* (1456) and the longer, more serious *Le Grand testament* (1461).

villous /ˈvɪləs/ ▸ **adjective** Anatomy (of a structure, especially the epithelium) covered with villi. ■ Medicine (of a condition) affecting the villi: *villous atrophy.* ■ Botany shaggy.

villus /ˈvɪləs/ ▸ **noun** (pl. **villi** /-lʌɪ, -liː/) Anatomy any of numerous minute elongated projections set closely together on a surface, in particular: ■ a finger-like projection of the lining of the small intestine. ■ a fold of the chorion.
– DERIVATIVES **villiform** adjective, **villose** adjective.
– ORIGIN early 18th cent.: from Latin, literally 'shaggy hair'.

Vilnius /ˈvɪlnɪəs/ the capital of Lithuania; pop. 558,165 (2009).

vim ▸ **noun** [mass noun] informal energy; enthusiasm: *in his youth he was full of vim and vigour.*
– ORIGIN mid 19th cent. (originally US): perhaps from Latin, accusative of *vis* 'energy'.

Vimy Ridge, Battle of /ˈviːmi/ an Allied attack on the German position of Vimy Ridge, near Arras, during the First World War. One of the key points on the Western Front, it had long resisted assaults, but on 9 April 1917 it was taken by Canadian troops in fifteen minutes, at the cost of heavy casualties.

VIN ▸ **abbreviation** vehicle identification number.

vin /vã/ ▸ **noun** (pl. pronunc. **same**) [mass noun] [usu. with modifier] French wine: *vin rouge.*
– ORIGIN French, literally 'wine'.

vina ▸ **noun** variant spelling of **VEENA**.

vinaceous /vʌɪˈneɪʃəs/ ▸ **adjective** chiefly technical of the colour of red wine.
– ORIGIN late 17th cent.: from Latin *vinaceus* (from *vinum* 'wine') + **-OUS**.

vinaigrette /ˌvɪnɪˈgrɛt, ˌvɪneɪ-/ ▸ **noun 1** [mass noun] salad dressing of oil, wine vinegar, and seasoning.
2 historical a small ornamental bottle for holding smelling salts.
– ORIGIN French, diminutive of *vinaigre* 'vinegar'.

vinblastine /vɪnˈblastiːn/ ▸ **noun** [mass noun] Medicine a cytotoxic compound of the alkaloid class obtained from the Madagascar periwinkle and used to treat Hodgkin's disease and other cancers of the lymphatic system.
– ORIGIN 1960s: from modern Latin *Vinca* (see **VINCA**) + (*leuco*)*blast* (a cell from which a leucocyte develops) + **-INE**[4].

vinca /ˈvɪŋkə/ ▸ **noun** another term for **PERIWINKLE**[1].
– ORIGIN 1930s: from modern Latin *Vinca* (genus name), from late Latin *pervinca* (see **PERIWINKLE**[1]).

Vincent de Paul, St (1581–1660), French priest. He devoted his life to work among the poor and the sick and established institutions to continue his

V

work, including the Daughters of Charity (Sisters of Charity of St Vincent de Paul) (1633). Feast day, 19 July.

Vincentian /vɪnˈsɛnʃ(ə)n/ ▶ **noun** another name for LAZARIST.

Vinci, Leonardo da, see LEONARDO DA VINCI.

vincible /ˈvɪnsɪb(ə)l/ ▶ **adjective** literary (of an opponent or obstacle) able to be overcome or conquered.
– DERIVATIVES **vincibility** noun.
– ORIGIN mid 16th cent.: from Latin *vincibilis*, from *vincere* 'to overcome'.

vincristine /vɪnˈkrɪstiːn/ ▶ **noun** [mass noun] Medicine a cytotoxic compound of the alkaloid class obtained from the Madagascar periwinkle and used to treat acute leukaemia and other cancers.
– ORIGIN 1960s: from modern Latin *Vinca* (see VINCA) + a second element perhaps based on CRISTA + -INE[4].

vinculum /ˈvɪŋkjʊləm/ ▶ **noun** (pl. **vincula** /-lə/)
1 Anatomy a connecting band of tissue, such as that attaching a flexor tendon to the bone of a finger or toe.
2 Mathematics a horizontal line drawn over a group of terms in a mathematical expression to indicate that they are to be operated on as a single entity by the preceding or following operator.
– ORIGIN mid 17th cent. (in the sense 'bond, tie'): from Latin, literally 'bond', from *vincire* 'bind'. The term has been used in anatomy since the mid 19th cent.

vindaloo /ˌvɪndəˈluː/ ▶ **noun** [mass noun] (pl. **vindaloos**) a very hot and spicy curry.
– ORIGIN probably from Portuguese *vin d'alho* 'wine and garlic (sauce)', from *vinho* 'wine' + *alho* 'garlic'.

vin de garde /ˌvã də ˈɡɑːd/ ▶ **noun** (pl. **vins de garde**) [mass noun] wine which will significantly improve in quality if left to mature.
– ORIGIN French, literally 'wine for keeping'.

vin de paille /ˌvã də ˈpɑːj/ ▶ **noun** (pl. **vins de paille**) [mass noun] a rich dessert wine made chiefly in the Jura region from grapes dried or partly dried in the sun on straw mats or wire frames.
– ORIGIN French, literally 'straw wine'.

vin de pays /ˌvã də peˈiː/ (also **vin du pays** /ˌvã d(j)uː peˈiː/) ▶ **noun** (pl. **vins de pays** /ˌvã də peˈiː/) [mass noun] French wine produced in a particular area and meeting certain standards of quality, superior to vin de table.
– ORIGIN French, literally 'wine of the region'.

vin de table /ˌvã də ˈtɑːbl(ə)/ ▶ **noun** (pl. **vins de table**) [mass noun] French table wine of reasonable quality, suitable for accompanying a meal.
– ORIGIN French, literally 'table wine'.

vin d'honneur /vã dɒˈnəː/ ▶ **noun** (pl. **vins d'honneur**) [mass noun] wine formally offered in honour of a special guest.
– ORIGIN French, literally 'wine of honour'.

vindicate /ˈvɪndɪkeɪt/ ▶ **verb** [with obj.] clear (someone) of blame or suspicion: *hospital staff were vindicated by the inquest verdict*. ■ show or prove to be right, reasonable, or justified: *more sober views were vindicated by events*.
– DERIVATIVES **vindication** noun, **vindicator** noun, **vindicatory** adjective.
– ORIGIN mid 16th cent. (in the sense 'deliver, rescue'): from Latin *vindicat-* 'claimed, avenged', from the verb *vindicare*, from *vindex*, *vindic-* 'claimant, avenger'.

vindicative /ˈvɪndɪˌkətɪv/ ▶ **adjective** archaic **1** another term for VINDICTIVE.
2 serving to vindicate someone or something.

vindictive /vɪnˈdɪktɪv/ ▶ **adjective** having or showing a strong or unreasoning desire for revenge: *the criticism was both vindictive and personalized*.
– DERIVATIVES **vindictively** adverb, **vindictiveness** noun.
– ORIGIN early 17th cent.: from Latin *vindicta* 'vengeance' + -IVE.

vine ▶ **noun** **1** a climbing or trailing woody-stemmed plant related to the grapevine. ● *Vitis* and other genera, family Vitaceae.
■ used in names of climbing or trailing plants of other families, e.g. **Russian vine**. ■ the slender stem of a trailing or climbing plant.
2 (**vines**) US informal clothes: *the hip got their vines at Wolmuth's on Market Street*.
– DERIVATIVES **viny** adjective.
– ORIGIN Middle English: from Old French, from Latin *vinea* 'vineyard, vine', from *vinum* 'wine'.

vine dresser ▶ **noun** a person who prunes, trains, and cultivates vines.

vinegar ▶ **noun** [mass noun] a sour-tasting liquid containing acetic acid, obtained by fermenting dilute alcoholic liquids, typically wine, cider, or beer, and used as a condiment or for pickling. ■ sourness or peevishness of behaviour, character, or speech: *her aggrieved tone held a touch of vinegar*.
– DERIVATIVES **vinegarish** adjective, **vinegary** adjective.
– ORIGIN Middle English: from Old French *vyn egre*, based on Latin *vinum* 'wine' + *acer* 'sour'.

vinery ▶ **noun** (pl. **vineries**) a greenhouse for grapevines. ■ a vineyard.

vineyard ▶ **noun** a plantation of grapevines, typically producing grapes used in winemaking.

vingt-et-un /ˌvãterˈəːn/, French /vɛ̃teœ̃/ ▶ **noun** [mass noun] the card game pontoon or blackjack.
– ORIGIN French, literally 'twenty-one'.

vinho verde /ˌviːnəʊ ˈvɛːdi/ ▶ **noun** (pl. **vinhos verdes**) [mass noun] a young Portuguese wine, not allowed to mature.
– ORIGIN Portuguese, literally 'green wine'.

vini- ▶ **combining form** relating to wine: *viniculture*.
– ORIGIN from Latin *vinum* 'wine'.

viniculture /ˈvɪnɪˌkʌltʃə/ ▶ **noun** [mass noun] the cultivation of grapevines for winemaking.
– DERIVATIVES **vinicultural** adjective, **viniculturist** noun.
– ORIGIN late 19th cent.: from Latin *vinum* 'wine' + CULTURE, on the pattern of words such as *agriculture*.

vinification /ˌvɪnɪfɪˈkeɪʃ(ə)n/ ▶ **noun** [mass noun] the conversion of grape juice or other vegetable extract into wine by fermentation.
– DERIVATIVES **vinify** verb (**vinifies**, **vinifying**, **vinified**).

vining /ˈvʌɪnɪŋ/ ▶ **noun** [mass noun] the separation of leguminous crops from their vines and pods.
▶ **adjective** [attrib.] (of a plant) growing as a vine with climbing or trailing woody stems.

vin jaune /vã ˈʒəʊn/ ▶ **noun** (pl. **vins jaunes**) [mass noun] a strong yellowish white wine made in the Jura region of eastern France from the Sauvignon grape.
– ORIGIN French, literally 'yellow wine'.

Vinland the region of the NE coast of North America which was visited in the 11th century by Norsemen led by Leif Ericsson. It was so named from the report that grapevines were found growing there. The exact location is uncertain.

Vinnytsya /ˈviːnɪtsjə/ a city in central Ukraine; pop. 367,800 (est. 2009). Russian name **Vinnitsa** /ˈviːnɪtsə/.

vino /ˈviːnəʊ/ ▶ **noun** (pl. **vinos**) [mass noun] informal wine, typically that which is cheap or of inferior quality.
– ORIGIN Spanish and Italian, 'wine'.

vino da tavola /da ˈtɑːvɒla/ ▶ **noun** [mass noun] Italian wine of reasonable quality, suitable for drinking with a meal.
– ORIGIN Italian, literally 'table wine'.

vin ordinaire /vã ˌɔːdɪˈnɛː/ ▶ **noun** (pl. **vins ordinaires**) [mass noun] cheap table wine for everyday use.
– ORIGIN French, literally 'ordinary wine'.

vinous /ˈvʌɪnəs/ ▶ **adjective** resembling, associated with, or fond of wine: *a vinous smell*. ■ literary resembling red wine in colour.
– DERIVATIVES **vinosity** noun, **vinously** adverb.
– ORIGIN late Middle English: from Latin *vinum* 'wine' + -OUS.

Vinson Massif /ˌvɪns(ə)n maˈsiːf/ the highest mountain range in Antarctica, in Ellsworth Land, rising to 5,140 m (16,863 ft).

vint /vɪnt/ ▶ **verb** [with obj.] produce (wine or another alcoholic drink).
– ORIGIN mid 19th cent.: back-formation from VINTAGE.

vintage ▶ **noun** **1** the year or place in which wine, especially wine of high quality, was produced: *1982 is one of the best vintages of the century*. ■ a wine of high quality made from the crop of a single identified district in a good year. ■ [mass noun] literary wine. ■ the harvesting of grapes for winemaking. ■ the grapes or wine produced in a particular season.
2 the time that something of quality was produced: *rifles of various sizes and vintages*.
▶ **adjective** **1** relating to or denoting wine of high quality: *vintage claret*.
2 denoting something from the past of high quality, especially something representing the best of its kind: *a vintage Sherlock Holmes adventure*.
– ORIGIN late Middle English: alteration (influenced by VINTNER) of earlier *vendage*, from Old French *vendange*, from Latin *vindemia* (from *vinum* 'wine' + *demere* 'remove').

vintage car ▶ **noun** Brit. an old style or model of car, specifically one made between 1919 and 1930. Compare with VETERAN CAR.

vintage port ▶ **noun** [mass noun] port of special quality, all of one year, which is bottled early and aged in the bottle.

vintager ▶ **noun** a person who harvests grapes.

vintner /ˈvɪntnə/ ▶ **noun** a wine merchant.
– ORIGIN late Middle English: via Anglo-Latin from Old French *vinetier*, from medieval Latin *vinetarius*, from Latin *vinetum* 'vineyard', from *vinum* 'wine'.

vinyasa /vɪnˈjɑːsə/ ▶ **noun** [mass noun] movement between poses in yoga, typically accompanied by regulated breathing. ■ a method of yoga in which these movements form a flowing sequence in coordination with the breath.
– ORIGIN Sanskrit *vinyāsa* 'movement, position (of limbs)'.

vinyl /ˈvʌɪn(ə)l/ ▶ **noun** **1** [mass noun] synthetic resin or plastic consisting of polyvinyl chloride or a related polymer, used for wallpapers and other covering materials and for gramophone records. ■ vinyl used as the standard material for records: *fans had to wait almost a year before the song eventually appeared on vinyl*.
2 also /ˈvʌɪnʌɪl, -nɪl/ [as modifier] Chemistry of or denoting the unsaturated hydrocarbon radical $-CH=CH_2$, derived from ethylene by removal of a hydrogen atom: *a vinyl group*.
– ORIGIN mid 19th cent.: from Latin *vinum* 'wine' + -YL.

vinyl acetate ▶ **noun** [mass noun] Chemistry a colourless liquid ester used in the production of polyvinyl acetate and other commercially important polymers.
● Chem. formula: $CH_2CHOCOCH_3$.

vinyl chloride ▶ **noun** [mass noun] Chemistry a colourless toxic gas used in the production of polyvinyl chloride and other commercially important polymers. ● Chem. formula: CH_2CHCl.

Viognier /viˈɒnjeɪ/ ▶ **noun** a white wine grape grown chiefly in the northern Rhône area of France. ■ a white wine made from the Viognier grape.

viol /ˈvʌɪəl/ ▶ **noun** a musical instrument of the Renaissance and baroque periods, typically six-stringed, held vertically and played with a bow.
– ORIGIN late 15th cent. (originally denoting a violin-like instrument): from Old French *viele*, from Provençal *viola*; probably related to FIDDLE.

viola[1] /vɪˈəʊlə/ ▶ **noun** an instrument of the violin family, larger than the violin and tuned a fifth lower.
– ORIGIN early 18th cent.: from Italian and Spanish; compare with VIOL.

viola[2] /ˈvʌɪələ/ ▶ **noun** a plant of a genus that includes the pansies and violets. ● Genus *Viola*, family Violaceae: many species.
– ORIGIN modern Latin, from Latin, literally 'violet'.

violaceous /ˌvʌɪəˈleɪʃəs/ ▶ **adjective** **1** chiefly technical of a violet colour.
2 Botany relating to or denoting plants of the violet family (Violaceae).
– ORIGIN mid 17th cent.: from Latin *violaceus* (from *viola* 'violet') + -OUS.

viola da braccio /vɪˌəʊlə da ˈbrɑːtʃɪəʊ/ ▶ **noun** an early musical instrument of the violin family (as distinct from a viol), specifically one corresponding to the modern viola.
– ORIGIN Italian, literally 'viol for the arm'.

viola da gamba /ˈɡambə/ (also **viol da gamba**) ▶ **noun** a viol, specifically a bass viol (corresponding to the modern cello).
– ORIGIN Italian, literally 'viol for the leg'.

viola d'amore /daˈmɔːreɪ/ ▶ **noun** a sweet-toned 18th-century musical instrument similar to a viola, but with six or seven strings, and additional sympathetic strings below the fingerboard.
– ORIGIN Italian, literally 'viol of love'.

violate ▶ **verb** [with obj.] **1** break or fail to comply with (a rule or formal agreement): *they violated the terms of a ceasefire*. ■ fail to respect (someone's peace, privacy, or rights): *they denied that human rights were being violated*.
2 treat (something sacred) with irreverence or disrespect: *he was accused of violating a tomb*.
3 rape or sexually assault (someone).
– DERIVATIVES **violator** noun, **violable** adjective.
– ORIGIN late Middle English: from Latin *violat-* 'treated violently', from the verb *violare*.

violation ▸ **noun** [mass noun] the action of violating someone or something: *the aircraft were in violation of UN resolutions* | [count noun] *flagrant violations of normal democratic procedure.*

violence ▸ **noun** [mass noun] **1** behaviour involving physical force intended to hurt, damage, or kill someone or something: *violence erupted in protest marches* | *the fear of physical violence.* ■ Law the unlawful exercise of physical force or intimidation by the exhibition of such force.
2 strength of emotion or of a destructive natural force: *the violence of her own feelings.*
– PHRASES **do violence to** damage or adversely affect.
– ORIGIN Middle English: via Old French from Latin *violentia*, from *violent-* 'vehement, violent' (see **VIOLENT**).

violent ▸ **adjective 1** using or involving physical force intended to hurt, damage, or kill someone or something: *a violent confrontation with riot police.* ■ Law involving an unlawful exercise or exhibition of force.
2 (especially of an emotion or a destructive natural force) very strong or powerful: *violent dislike* | *the violent eruption killed 1,700 people.* ■ (of a colour) vivid.
– DERIVATIVES **violently** adverb.
– ORIGIN Middle English (in the sense 'having a marked or powerful effect'): via Old French from Latin *violent-* 'vehement, violent'.

violent storm ▸ **noun** a wind of force 11 on the Beaufort scale (56–63 knots or 103–117 kph).

violet ▸ **noun 1** a herbaceous plant of temperate regions, typically having purple, blue, or white five-petalled flowers, one petal of which forms a landing pad for pollinating insects. ● Genus *Viola*, family Violaceae (the **violet family**): many species, including the **dog violet** and **sweet violet**. See also **VIOLA**[2].
■ used in names of similar-flowered plants of other families, e.g. **African violet**.
2 [mass noun] a bluish-purple colour seen at the end of the spectrum opposite red.
▸ **adjective** of a bluish-purple colour.
– ORIGIN Middle English: from Old French *violette*, diminutive of *viole*, from Latin *viola* 'violet'.

violet-ear ▸ **noun** a tropical American hummingbird with green or brown plumage and a glittering purple patch behind each eye. ● Genus *Colibri*, family Trochilidae: four species.

violet snail (also **violet sea snail**) ▸ **noun** a small marine snail which drifts on the surface of the sea attached to a raft of bubbles. The shell is typically purple-violet and the animal emits a violet fluid when attacked. ● Family Janthinidae, class Gastropoda.

violin ▸ **noun** a stringed musical instrument of treble pitch, played with a horsehair bow. The classical European violin was developed in the 16th century. It has four strings and a body of characteristic rounded shape, narrowed at the middle and with two f-shaped soundholes.
– DERIVATIVES **violinist** noun.
– ORIGIN late 16th cent.: from Italian *violino*, diminutive of *viola* (see **VIOLA**[1]).

violist ▸ **noun 1** /vɪˈəʊlɪst/ a viola player.
2 /ˈvʌɪəlɪst/ a viol player.

viologen /vʌɪˈəʊlədʒ(ə)n/ ▸ **noun** Chemistry any of a series of synthetic compounds related to the weedkiller paraquat, used as redox indicators. They contain heteroaromatic cations of the general formula $(C_5H_4NR)_2^{2+}$.
– ORIGIN 1930s: from **VIOLET** (because of the purple colour when electrochemically reduced) + **-GEN**.

violoncello /ˌvʌɪələnˈtʃeləʊ, ˌviːə-/ ▸ **noun** (pl. **violoncellos**) formal term for **CELLO**.
– DERIVATIVES **violoncellist** noun.
– ORIGIN early 18th cent.: Italian, diminutive of *violone* (see **VIOLONE**).

violone /vɪəˈləʊneɪ, -ni/ ▸ **noun** an early form of double bass, especially a large bass viol.
– ORIGIN Italian, augmentative of *viola* (see **VIOLA**[1]).

VIP[1] ▸ **noun** (pl. **VIPs**) a very important person.

VIP[2] ▸ **abbreviation** Biochemistry vasoactive intestinal polypeptide (or peptide), a substance which acts as a neurotransmitter, especially in the brain and gastrointestinal tract.

vipassana /vɪˈpasənə/ ▸ **noun** [mass noun] (in Theravada Buddhism) meditation involving concentration on the body or its sensations, or the insight which this provides.
– ORIGIN Pali, literally 'inward vision'.

viper /ˈvʌɪpə/ ▸ **noun** a venomous snake with large hinged fangs, typically having a broad head and stout body, with dark patterns on a lighter background.
● Family Viperidae: numerous genera and species. See also **PIT VIPER, ADDER**[1].
■ a spiteful or treacherous person.
– PHRASES **viper in one's bosom** a person whom one has supported but now behaves treacherously towards one.
– DERIVATIVES **viperine** /-rʌɪn/ adjective, **viperish** adjective, **viperous** adjective.
– ORIGIN early 16th cent.: from French *vipère* or Latin *vipera*, from *vivus* 'alive' + *parere* 'bring forth'.

viperfish ▸ **noun** (pl. **same** or **viperfishes**) a small, elongated deep-sea fish that has large jaws with long protruding fangs. ● Family Chauliodontidae: several genera and species.

viper's bugloss ▸ **noun** a bristly Eurasian plant of the borage family, with pink buds which open to blue flowers. It was formerly used in the treatment of snake bites. ● *Echium vulgare*, family Boraginaceae.

viper's grass ▸ **noun** [mass noun] scorzonera, the juice of which was formerly believed to be a remedy for snake bites.

viraemia /vʌɪˈriːmɪə/ (also **viremia**) ▸ **noun** [mass noun] Medicine the presence of viruses in the blood.
– DERIVATIVES **viraemic** adjective.
– ORIGIN 1940s: from **VIRUS** + **-AEMIA**.

virago /vɪˈrɑːgəʊ, -ˈreɪgəʊ/ ▸ **noun** (pl. **viragos** or **viragoes**) a domineering, violent, or bad-tempered woman. ■ archaic a woman of masculine strength or spirit; a female warrior.
– ORIGIN Old English (used only as the name given by Adam to Eve, following the Vulgate), from Latin 'heroic woman, female warrior', from *vir* 'man'. The current sense dates from late Middle English.

viral /ˈvʌɪr(ə)l/ ▸ **adjective 1** of the nature of, caused by, or relating to a virus or viruses.
2 relating to or involving the rapid spread of information about a product or service by viral marketing techniques: *a viral video ad.*
▸ **noun** an image, video, advertisement, etc. that is circulated rapidly on the Internet: *the rise of virals in online marketing.*
– DERIVATIVES **virally** adverb.

> **WORD TRENDS** Most people are now happy to spread **viral** infections to their friends, family, and work colleagues. They do so not by sneezing on them but by forwarding emails, images, or videos that have amused or intrigued them. The influence of this word-of-mouth publicity on brand awareness and sales is enormous, and one of the commonest compounds of **viral** is *viral marketing*. There are now entire companies, known as *viral agencies*, devoted to creating potential *viral hits* for businesses. See also **MEME**.

viral load ▸ **noun** Medicine a measure of the number of viral particles present in an organism or environment, especially the number of HIV viruses in the bloodstream.

viral marketing ▸ **noun** [mass noun] a marketing technique whereby information about a company's goods or services is passed electronically from one Internet user to another.

Virchow /ˈvəːkaʊ/, German /ˈfɪrço/, Rudolf Karl (1821–1902), German physician and pathologist, founder of cellular pathology. He argued that the cell was the basis of life and that diseases were reflected in specific cellular abnormalities. Virchow also stressed the importance of environmental factors in disease.

virelay /ˈvɪrəleɪ/ ▸ **noun** a short lyric poem of a type originating in France in the 14th century, consisting of short lines arranged in stanzas with only two rhymes, the end rhyme of one stanza being the chief one of the next.
– ORIGIN late Middle English: from Old French *virelai*.

virement /ˈvʌɪəm(ə)nt, ˈvɪəmɒ̃/ ▸ **noun** [mass noun] Brit. Finance the process of transferring items from one financial account to another.
– ORIGIN early 20th cent.: from French, from *virer* 'to turn'.

viremia ▸ **noun** variant spelling of **VIRAEMIA**.

vireo /ˈvɪrɪəʊ/ ▸ **noun** (pl. **vireos**) a small American songbird, typically having a green or grey back and yellow or white underparts. ● Family Vireonidae (the **vireo family**): two genera, especially *Vireo*, and several species. The vireo family also includes the greenlets and pepper-shrikes.
– ORIGIN mid 19th cent.: from Latin, perhaps denoting a greenfinch.

virescent /vɪˈrɛs(ə)nt/ ▸ **adjective** literary greenish.
– ORIGIN early 19th cent.: from Latin *virescent-* 'turning green', inceptive of *virere* 'be green'.

virga /ˈvəːgə/ ▸ **noun** (pl. **virgae** /ˈvəːgiː/) Meteorology a mass of streaks of rain appearing to hang under a cloud and evaporating before reaching the ground.
– ORIGIN 1940s: from Latin, literally 'rod, stripe'.

virgate /ˈvəːgət/ ▸ **noun** Brit. historical a varying measure of land, typically 30 acres.
– ORIGIN mid 17th cent.: from Latin *virgatus*, from *virga* 'rod'.

virger ▸ **noun** chiefly archaic variant spelling of **VERGER**.

Virgil /ˈvəːdʒɪl/ (also **Vergil**) (70–19 BC), Roman poet; Latin name *Publius Vergilius Maro*. He wrote three major works: the *Eclogues*, ten pastoral poems, blending traditional themes of Greek bucolic poetry with contemporary political and literary themes; the *Georgics*, a didactic poem on farming; and the *Aeneid* (see **AENEID**).
– DERIVATIVES **Virgilian** adjective.

virgin ▸ **noun 1** a person, typically a woman, who has never had sexual intercourse. ■ **(the Virgin)** the mother of Jesus; the Virgin Mary. ■ **(the Virgin)** the zodiacal sign or constellation Virgo.
2 a person who is naive, innocent, or inexperienced in a particular context: *he's a political virgin.*
3 Entomology a female insect that produces eggs without being fertilized.
▸ **adjective 1** [attrib.] being, relating to, or appropriate for a virgin: *his virgin bride.*
2 not yet used, exploited, or processed: *acres of virgin forests.* ■ (of clay) not yet fired. ■ (of wool) not yet, or only once, spun or woven. ■ (of olive oil) obtained from the first pressing of olives. ■ (of metal) made from ore by smelting.
– ORIGIN Middle English: from Old French *virgine*, from Latin *virgo, virgin-*.

virginal ▸ **adjective** being, relating to, or appropriate for a virgin: *virginal shyness.*
▸ **noun** (usu. **virginals**) an early spinet with the strings parallel to the keyboard, typically rectangular, and popular in 16th and 17th century houses.
– DERIVATIVES **virginalist** noun, **virginally** adverb.
– ORIGIN late Middle English: from Old French, or from Latin *virginalis*, from *virgo* 'young woman'. The musical instrument is perhaps so called because it was usually played by young women.

virgin birth ▸ **noun 1 (the Virgin Birth)** the doctrine of Christ's birth from a mother, Mary, who was a virgin.
2 [mass noun] Zoology parthenogenesis.

virgin comb ▸ **noun** a honeycomb that has been used only once for honey and never for storing eggs.

virgin honey ▸ **noun** [mass noun] honey taken from a virgin comb, or drained from the comb without heat or pressure.

Virginia[1] a state of the eastern US, on the Atlantic coast; pop. 7,769,089 (est. 2008); capital, Richmond. It was the site of the first permanent European settlement in North America in 1607, and was named in honour of Elizabeth I, the 'Virgin Queen'. It was one of the original thirteen states of the Union (1788).
– DERIVATIVES **Virginian** noun & adjective.

Virginia[2] ▸ **noun** [mass noun] a type of tobacco grown and manufactured in Virginia.

Virginia Beach a city and resort on the Atlantic coast of SE Virginia; pop. 433,746 (est. 2008).

Virginia bluebell ▸ **noun** a North American woodland plant of the borage family, bearing blue trumpet-shaped flowers. ● *Mertensia virginica*, family Boraginaceae.

Virginia creeper ▸ **noun** a North American vine which is chiefly cultivated for its red autumn foliage.
● Genus *Parthenocissus*, family Vitaceae: several species, in particular *P. quinquefolia*.

Virginia opossum ▸ **noun** a cat-sized opossum with a greyish body and a white face, widespread throughout North and Central America. ● *Didelphis virginiana*, family Didelphidae.

Virginia reel ▸ **noun** a lively North American country dance performed by a number of couples facing each other in parallel lines.

Virginia stock (also **Virginian stock**) ▸ **noun** a low-growing sweetly scented Mediterranean plant with white, pink, or lilac flowers. ● *Malcolmia maritima*, family Cruciferae.

Virgin Islands a group of Caribbean islands at the eastern extremity of the Greater Antilles, divided between British and US administration.

The islands were settled, mainly in the 17th century, by British and Danish sugar planters, who introduced African slaves. The British Virgin Islands consists of about forty islands in the north-east of the group, and are a British overseas territory; pop. 24,500 (est. 2009); capital, Road Town (on Tortola). The remaining islands (about fifty) make up the US unincorporated territory of the Virgin Islands; pop. 109,800 (est. 2009); capital, Charlotte Amalie (on St Thomas).

virginity ▶ **noun** [mass noun] the state of never having had sexual intercourse: *I lost my virginity.* ■ the state of being naive, innocent, or inexperienced in a particular context: *the lawsuit will be remembered as the moment the computer industry lost its political virginity.*
– ORIGIN Middle English: from Old French *virginite*, from Latin *virginitas*, from *virgo* (see VIRGIN).

Virgin Mary the mother of Jesus (see MARY[1]).

virgin queen ▶ **noun 1** an unfertilized queen bee.
2 (**the Virgin Queen**) Queen Elizabeth I of England, who died unmarried.

virgin's bower ▶ **noun** a North American clematis. ● *Clematis virginiana*, family Ranunculaceae.

Virgo /ˈvəːɡəʊ/ **1** Astronomy a large constellation (the Virgin), said to represent a maiden or goddess associated with the harvest. It contains several bright stars, the brightest of which is Spica, and a dense cluster of galaxies.
2 Astrology the sixth sign of the zodiac, which the sun enters about 23 August. ■ (**a Virgo**) (pl. **Virgos**) a person born when the sun is in this sign.
– DERIVATIVES **Virgoan** noun & adjective (sense 2).
– ORIGIN Latin.

virgo intacta /ˌvəːɡəʊ ɪnˈtaktə/ ▶ **noun** chiefly Law a girl or woman who has never had sexual intercourse, originally a virgin whose hymen is intact.
– ORIGIN Latin, literally 'untouched virgin'.

virgule /ˈvəːɡjuːl/ ▶ **noun** another term for SLASH (sense 2 of the noun).
– ORIGIN mid 19th cent.: from French, literally 'comma', from Latin *virgula*, diminutive of *virga* 'rod'.

viridescent /ˌvɪrɪˈdɛs(ə)nt/ ▶ **adjective** literary greenish or becoming green: *viridescent vegetation.*
– DERIVATIVES **viridescence** noun.
– ORIGIN mid 19th cent.: from late Latin *viridescent-* 'becoming green', from the verb *viridescere*, from Latin *viridis* 'green'.

viridian /vɪˈrɪdɪən/ ▶ **noun** [mass noun] a bluish-green pigment consisting of hydrated chromium hydroxide. ■ the bluish-green colour of this pigment.
– ORIGIN late 19th cent.: from Latin *viridis* 'green' (from *virere* 'be green') + -IAN.

virile ▶ **adjective** (of a man) having strength, energy, and a strong sex drive. ■ having or characterized by strength and energy: *a strong, virile performance of the Mass.*
– ORIGIN late 15th cent. (in the sense 'characteristic of a man'): from French *viril* or Latin *virilis*, from *vir* 'man'.

virilism /ˈvɪrɪlɪz(ə)m/ ▶ **noun** [mass noun] Medicine the condition which results from virilization.

virility ▶ **noun** [mass noun] (in a man) the quality of having strength, energy, and a strong sex drive; manliness: *great importance is placed on a man's virility.*

virilization /ˌvɪrɪlʌɪˈzeɪʃ(ə)n/ (also **virilisation**) ▶ **noun** [mass noun] Medicine the development of male physical characteristics (such as muscle bulk, body hair, and deep voice) in a female or precociously in a boy, typically as a result of excess androgen production.

virilocal /ˌvɪrɪˈləʊk(ə)l/ ▶ **adjective** another term for PATRILOCAL.
– ORIGIN 1940s: from Latin *virilis* 'of a man' + LOCAL.

V

virino /vɪˈriːnəʊ/ ▶ **noun** (pl. **virinos**) Microbiology a hypothetical infectious particle postulated as the cause of scrapie, BSE, and CJD, consisting of non-coding nucleic acid in a protective coat made from host cell proteins. Compare with PRION[2].
– ORIGIN 1970s: from VIRUS + the diminutive suffix *-ino*.

virion /ˈvɪrɪɒn/ ▶ **noun** Microbiology the complete, infective form of a virus outside a host cell, with a core of RNA and a capsid.
– ORIGIN 1950s: from VIRUS + -ON.

viroid /ˈvʌɪrɔɪd/ ▶ **noun** Microbiology an infectious entity affecting plants, smaller than a virus and consisting only of nucleic acid without a protein coat.

virology /vʌɪˈrɒlədʒi/ ▶ **noun** [mass noun] the branch of science that deals with the study of viruses.
– DERIVATIVES **virological** adjective, **virologically** adverb, **virologist** noun.

viropexis /ˌvʌɪrə(ʊ)ˈpɛksɪs/ ▶ **noun** [mass noun] Microbiology the process by which a virus particle becomes attached to a cell wall and incorporated into the cell by phagocytosis.
– ORIGIN 1940s: from VIRUS + Greek *pēxis* 'fixing'.

virtu /vəːˈt(j)uː/ (also **vertu**) ▶ **noun** [mass noun] **1** knowledge of or expertise in the fine arts. ■ curios or objets d'art collectively.
2 literary the good qualities inherent in a person or thing.
– PHRASES **article** (or **object**) **of virtu** an article that is interesting because of its antiquity, beauty, quality of workmanship, etc.
– ORIGIN early 18th cent.: from Italian *virtù* 'virtue'; the variant *vertu* is an alteration, as if from French.

virtual /ˈvəːtjʊəl/ ▶ **adjective 1** almost or nearly as described, but not completely or according to strict definition: *the virtual absence of border controls.*
2 Computing not physically existing as such but made by software to appear to do so: *virtual images.* See also VIRTUAL REALITY. ■ carried out, accessed, or stored by means of a computer, especially over a network: *a virtual library | virtual learning.*
3 Optics relating to the points at which rays would meet if produced backwards.
4 Mechanics relating to or denoting infinitesimal displacements of a point in a system.
5 Physics denoting particles or interactions with extremely short lifetimes and (owing to the uncertainty principle) indefinitely great energies, postulated as intermediates in some processes.
– DERIVATIVES **virtuality** /-jʊˈalɪti/ noun.
– ORIGIN late Middle English (also in the sense 'possessing certain virtues'): from medieval Latin *virtualis*, from Latin *virtus* 'virtue', suggested by late Latin *virtuosus*.

virtual image ▶ **noun** Optics an optical image formed from the apparent divergence of light rays from a point, as opposed to an image formed from their actual divergence.

virtualize (also **virtualise**) ▶ **verb** [with obj.] convert (something) to a computer-generated simulation of reality. ■ create a virtual version of (a computing resource or facility).
– DERIVATIVES **virtualization** noun, **virtualizer** noun.

virtually ▶ **adverb 1** [as submodifier] nearly; almost: *the disease destroyed virtually all the vineyards in Orange County | the college became virtually bankrupt.*
2 by means of virtual reality techniques. ■ by means of a computer; computationally.

virtual memory (also **virtual storage**) ▶ **noun** [mass noun] Computing memory that appears to exist as main storage although most of it is supported by data held in secondary storage, transfer between the two being made automatically as required.

virtual reality ▶ **noun** [mass noun] the computer-generated simulation of a three-dimensional image or environment that can be interacted with in a seemingly real or physical way by a person using special electronic equipment, such as a helmet with a screen inside or gloves fitted with sensors.

virtue /ˈvəːtjuː, -tʃuː/ ▶ **noun 1** [mass noun] behaviour showing high moral standards: *paragons of virtue.* ■ [count noun] a quality considered morally good or desirable in a person: *patience is a virtue.* ■ [count noun] a good or useful quality of a thing: *Mike was extolling the virtues of the car | [mass noun] there's no virtue in suffering in silence.* ■ [mass noun] archaic virginity or chastity, especially of a woman.
2 (**virtues**) (in traditional Christian angelology) the seventh-highest order of the ninefold celestial hierarchy.
– PHRASES **by** (or **in**) **virtue of** because or as a result of. **make a virtue of** derive benefit or advantage from submitting to (an unwelcome obligation or unavoidable circumstance).
– DERIVATIVES **virtueless** adjective.
– ORIGIN Middle English: from Old French *vertu*, from Latin *virtus* 'valour, merit, moral perfection', from *vir* 'man'.

virtuosity /ˌvəːtʃʊˈɒsɪti/ ▶ **noun** [mass noun] great skill in music or another artistic pursuit: *a performance of considerable virtuosity.*

virtuoso /ˌvəːtjʊˈəʊzəʊ, -səʊ/ ▶ **noun** (pl. **virtuosi** /-si/ or **virtuosos**) **1** a person highly skilled in music or another artistic pursuit: *a celebrated clarinet virtuoso | [as modifier] virtuoso guitar playing.*
2 a person with a special knowledge of or interest in works of art or curios.
– DERIVATIVES **virtuosic** adjective.
– ORIGIN early 17th cent.: from Italian, literally 'learned, skilful', from late Latin *virtuosus* (see VIRTUOUS).

virtuous ▶ **adjective** having or showing high moral standards: *she considered herself very virtuous because she neither drank nor smoked.* ■ archaic (especially of a woman) chaste.
– DERIVATIVES **virtuously** adverb, **virtuousness** noun.
– ORIGIN Middle English: from Old French *vertuous*, from late Latin *virtuosus*, from *virtus* 'virtue'.

virtuous circle ▶ **noun** a recurring cycle of events, the result of each one being to increase the beneficial effect of the next.

virulent /ˈvɪrʊl(ə)nt, ˈvɪrjʊ-/ ▶ **adjective 1** (of a disease or poison) extremely severe or harmful in its effects. ■ (of a pathogen, especially a virus) highly infective.
2 bitterly hostile: *a virulent attack on liberalism.*
– DERIVATIVES **virulence** noun, **virulently** adverb.
– ORIGIN late Middle English (originally describing a poisoned wound): from Latin *virulentus*, from *virus* 'poison' (see VIRUS).

virus /ˈvʌɪrəs/ ▶ **noun 1** an infective agent that typically consists of a nucleic acid molecule in a protein coat, is too small to be seen by light microscopy, and is able to multiply only within the living cells of a host: *the hepatitis B virus | [as modifier] a virus infection.* ■ an infection or disease caused by a virus. ■ a harmful or corrupting influence: *the virus of cruelty that is latent in all human beings.*
2 (also **computer virus**) a piece of code which is capable of copying itself and typically has a detrimental effect, such as corrupting the system or destroying data.
– ORIGIN late Middle English (denoting the venom of a snake): from Latin, literally 'slimy liquid, poison'. The earlier medical sense, superseded by the current use as a result of improved scientific understanding, was 'a substance produced in the body as the result of disease, especially one capable of infecting others'.

Vis. ▶ **abbreviation** Viscount.

visa /ˈviːzə/ ▶ **noun** an endorsement on a passport indicating that the holder is allowed to enter, leave, or stay for a specified period of time in a country.
– ORIGIN mid 19th cent.: via French from Latin *visa*, past participle (neuter plural) of *videre* 'to see'.

visage /ˈvɪzɪdʒ/ ▶ **noun** literary a person's face, with reference to the form or proportions of the features: *an elegant, angular visage.* ■ a person's facial expression: *there was something hidden behind his visage of cheerfulness.*
– DERIVATIVES **visaged** adjective [in combination] *a stern-visaged old man.*
– ORIGIN Middle English: via Old French from Latin *visus* 'sight', from *videre* 'to see'.

visagiste /ˌviːzɑːˈʒiːst/ ▶ **noun** a make-up artist.
– ORIGIN French.

Visākha /vɪˈsɑːkə/ ▶ **noun** variant spelling of VESAK.

Visakhapatnam /vɪˌsɑːkəˈpʌtnəm/ a port on the coast of Andhra Pradesh, in SE India; pop. 1,058,200 (est. 2009).

vis-à-vis /ˌviːzɑːˈviː/, French /vizavi/ ▶ **preposition** in relation to; with regard to: *many agencies now have a unit to deal with women's needs vis-à-vis employment.* ■ as compared with; as opposed to: *the advantage for US exports is the value of the dollar vis-à-vis other currencies.*
▶ **adverb** archaic in a position facing a specified or implied subject: *he was there vis à vis with Miss Arundel.*
▶ **noun** (pl. **same**) **1** a person or group occupying a corresponding position to that of another in a different sphere; a counterpart: *his admiration for the US armed services extends to their vis-à-vis, the Russian military.*
2 a face-to-face meeting: *the dreaded vis-à-vis with his boss.*
– ORIGIN mid 18th cent.: French, literally 'face to face', from Old French *vis* 'face'.

Visby /ˈvɪzbi/, Swedish /ˈviːsbyː/ a port on the west coast of the Swedish island of Gotland, of which it is the capital; pop. 21,400 (est. 2002).

Visc. ▶ **abbreviation** Viscount.

viscacha /vɪˈskatʃə/ ▶ **noun** a large South American burrowing rodent of the chinchilla family, sometimes hunted for its fur and flesh. ● Genera *Lagidium* and *Lagostomus*, family Chinchillidae: four species.

– ORIGIN early 17th cent.: via Spanish from Quechua (*h*)*uiscacha*.

viscera /ˈvɪs(ə)rə/ ▶ **plural noun** (sing. **viscus**) the internal organs in the main cavities of the body, especially those in the abdomen, e.g. the intestines.
– ORIGIN mid 17th cent.: from Latin, plural of *viscus* (see **VISCUS**).

visceral ▶ **adjective 1** relating to the viscera: *the visceral nervous system*.
2 relating to deep inward feelings rather than to the intellect: *the voters' visceral fear of change*.
– DERIVATIVES **viscerally** adverb.

viscerotropic /ˌvɪs(ə)rə(ʊ)ˈtrəʊpɪk, -ˈtrɒpɪk/ ▶ **adjective** (of a microorganism) tending to attack or affect the viscera.

viscid /ˈvɪsɪd/ ▶ **adjective** having a glutinous or sticky consistency: *the viscid mucus lining of the intestine*.
– DERIVATIVES **viscidity** noun.
– ORIGIN mid 17th cent.: from late Latin *viscidus*, from Latin *viscum* 'birdlime'.

viscoelasticity /ˌvɪskəʊɛlaˈstɪsɪti, -iːla-, -ɪla-/ ▶ **noun** [mass noun] Physics the property of a substance of exhibiting both elastic and viscous behaviour, the application of stress causing temporary deformation if the stress is quickly removed but permanent deformation if it is maintained.
– DERIVATIVES **viscoelastic** adjective.

viscometer /vɪsˈkɒmɪtə/ ▶ **noun** an instrument for measuring the viscosity of liquids.
– DERIVATIVES **viscometric** adjective, **viscometrically** adverb, **viscometry** noun.
– ORIGIN late 19th cent.: from late Latin *viscosus* 'viscous' + **-METER**.

Visconti /vɪsˈkɒnti/, Luchino (1906–76), Italian film and theatre director; full name *Don Luchino Visconti, Conte di Modrone*. His first film, *Obsession* (1942), was regarded as the forerunner of neo-realism. Other films include *The Leopard* (1963) and *Death in Venice* (1971).

viscose /ˈvɪskəʊz, -kəʊs/ ▶ **noun** [mass noun] a viscous orange-brown solution obtained by treating cellulose with sodium hydroxide and carbon disulphide, used as the basis of manufacturing rayon fibre and transparent cellulose film. ■ rayon fabric or fibre made from viscose.
– ORIGIN late 19th cent.: from late Latin *viscosus*, from Latin *viscus* 'birdlime'.

viscosimeter /vɪskəˈsɪmɪtə/ ▶ **noun** another term for **VISCOMETER**.

viscosity /vɪˈskɒsɪti/ ▶ **noun** (pl. **viscosities**) [mass noun] the state of being thick, sticky, and semi-fluid in consistency, due to internal friction. ■ [count noun] a quantity expressing the magnitude of internal friction in a fluid, as measured by the force per unit area resisting uniform flow.
– ORIGIN late Middle English: from Old French *viscosite* or medieval Latin *viscositas*, from late Latin *viscosus* (see **VISCOUS**).

viscount /ˈvʌɪkaʊnt/ ▶ **noun** a British nobleman ranking above a baron and below an earl.
– DERIVATIVES **viscountcy** noun.
– ORIGIN late Middle English: from Old French *visconte*, from medieval Latin *vicecomes*, *vicecomit-* (see **VICE-**, **COUNT²**).

viscountess /ˈvʌɪkaʊntɪs/ ▶ **noun** the wife or widow of a viscount. ■ a woman holding the rank of viscount in her own right.

viscounty ▶ **noun** (pl. **viscounties**) the land under the authority of a particular viscount.

viscous /ˈvɪskəs/ ▶ **adjective** having a thick, sticky consistency between solid and liquid; having a high viscosity: *viscous lava*.
– DERIVATIVES **viscously** adverb, **viscousness** noun.
– ORIGIN late Middle English: from Anglo-Norman French *viscous* or late Latin *viscosus*, from Latin *viscum* 'birdlime'.

viscus /ˈvɪskəs/ singular form of **VISCERA**.
– ORIGIN Latin.

vise ▶ **noun** US spelling of **VICE²**.

Vishnu /ˈvɪʃnuː/ Hinduism a god, originally a minor Vedic god, now regarded by his worshippers as the supreme deity and saviour, by others as the preserver of the cosmos in a triad with Brahma and Shiva. Vishnu is considered by Hindus to have had nine earthly incarnations or avatars, including Rama, Krishna, and the historical Buddha; the tenth avatar will herald the end of the world.
– DERIVATIVES **Vishnuism** noun, **Vishnuite** noun & adjective.
– ORIGIN from Sanskrit *Viṣṇu*.

visibility ▶ **noun** [mass noun] the state of being able to see or be seen: *a reduction in police presence and visibility on the streets*. ■ the distance one can see as determined by light and weather conditions: *visibility was down to 15 yards*. ■ the degree to which something has attracted general attention; prominence: *the issue began to lose its visibility*.
– ORIGIN late Middle English: from French *visibilite* or late Latin *visibilitas*, from Latin *visibilis* (see **VISIBLE**).

visible ▶ **adjective 1** able to be seen: *the church spire is visible from miles away*. ■ Physics (of light) within the range of wavelengths to which the eye is sensitive. ■ able to be perceived or noticed easily: *a visible improvement*. ■ in a position of public prominence: *a highly visible member of the royal entourage*.
2 relating to imports or exports of tangible commodities: *the visible trade gap*.
▶ **noun** (**visibles**) visible imports or exports.
– DERIVATIVES **visibly** adverb [as submodifier] *he was visibly uncomfortable*.
– ORIGIN Middle English: from Old French, or from Latin *visibilis*, from *videre* 'to see'.

Visigoth /ˈvɪzɪɡɒθ/ ▶ **noun** a member of the branch of the Goths who invaded the Roman Empire between the 3rd and 5th centuries AD and ruled much of Spain until overthrown by the Moors in 711.
– DERIVATIVES **Visigothic** adjective.
– ORIGIN from late Latin *Visigothus*, the first element possibly meaning 'west' (compare with **OSTROGOTH**).

vision ▶ **noun 1** [mass noun] the faculty or state of being able to see: *she had defective vision*. ■ the images seen on a television screen.
2 [mass noun] the ability to think about or plan the future with imagination or wisdom: *the organization had lost its vision and direction*. ■ [count noun] a mental image of what the future will or could be like: *a utopian vision of society*.
3 an experience of seeing someone or something in a dream or trance, or as a supernatural apparition: *the idea came to him in a vision*. ■ (often **visions**) a vivid mental image, especially a fanciful one of the future: *he* ***had visions of*** *becoming the Elton John of his time*.
4 a person or sight of unusual beauty: *madame was a vision in black velvet*.
▶ **verb** [with obj.] rare imagine.
– DERIVATIVES **visional** adjective, **visionless** adjective.
– ORIGIN Middle English (denoting a supernatural apparition): via Old French from Latin *visio(n-)*, from *videre* 'to see'.

visionary ▶ **adjective 1** thinking about or planning the future with imagination or wisdom: *a visionary leader*. ■ archaic (of a scheme or idea) not practical.
2 relating to or having the ability to see visions in a dream or trance, or as a supernatural apparition: *visionary dreams*. ■ archaic existing only in a vision or in the imagination.
▶ **noun** (pl. **visionaries**) a person with original ideas about what the future will or could be like.

visioning ▶ **noun** [mass noun] **1** the action of developing a plan, goal, or vision for the future: *they all agree on the importance of goal-setting and visioning*.
2 the action or fact of seeing visions.

vision quest ▶ **noun** an attempt to achieve a vision of a future guardian spirit, traditionally undertaken at puberty by boys of the Plains Indian peoples, typically through fasting or self-torture.

visit ▶ **verb** (**visits**, **visiting**, **visited**) [with obj.] **1** go to see and spend time with (someone) socially: *I came to visit my grandmother* | [no obj.] N. Amer. *he went out to* ***visit with*** *his pals*. ■ stay temporarily with (someone) or at (a place) as a guest or tourist: *they would like to visit Oxford* | [no obj.] *I don't live here—I'm only visiting*. ■ [no obj.] N. Amer. informal chat: *there was nothing to do but* ***visit with*** *one another*.
2 go to see (someone or something) for a specific purpose, such as to give or receive professional advice: *inspectors visit all the hotels*. ■ (as adj. **visiting**) (of an academic) working for a fixed period of time at another institution: *a visiting professor*. ■ access and view (a website or web page): *high entertainment value is one good reason to visit the site's ultra-cool home page*. ■ (chiefly in biblical use) (of God) come to (a person or place) in order to bring comfort or salvation.
3 inflict (something harmful or unpleasant) on someone: *the mockery* ***visited upon*** *him by his schoolmates*. ■ (of something harmful or unpleasant) afflict (someone): *they were* ***visited with*** *epidemics of a strange disease*. ■ archaic punish (a person or wrongful act): *offences were visited with the loss of eyes or ears*.
▶ **noun** an act of going to see a person or place as a guest, tourist, etc.: *I'll* ***pay him a visit*** *soon* | *a visit to the doctor*. ■ a temporary stay with a person or at a place. ■ N. Amer. informal a chat.
– DERIVATIVES **visitable** adjective.
– ORIGIN Middle English: from Old French *visiter* or Latin *visitare* 'go to see', frequentative of *visare* 'to view', from *videre* 'to see'.

visitant ▶ **noun 1** literary a supernatural being or agency; an apparition.
2 archaic a visitor or guest.
3 Ornithology a visitor.
▶ **adjective** archaic or literary paying a visit: *the housekeeper was abrupt with the poor visitant niece*.
– ORIGIN late 16th cent.: from French, or from Latin *visitant-* 'going to see', from the verb *visitare* (see **VISIT**).

visitation ▶ **noun 1** the appearance of a divine or supernatural being.
2 an official visit of inspection, especially one by a bishop to a church in his diocese. ■ a pastoral or charitable visit, especially to the sick or poor. ■ informal an unwelcome or unduly protracted social visit.
3 [mass noun] US Law a divorced person's right to spend time with their children in the custody of a former spouse.
4 US a gathering with the family of a deceased person before the funeral.
5 a disaster or difficulty regarded as a divine punishment: *a visitation of the plague*.
6 (**the Visitation**) the visit of the Virgin Mary to Elizabeth related in Luke 1:39–56. ■ the festival commemorating this on 31 May (formerly 2 July).
– ORIGIN Middle English: from Old French, or from late Latin *visitatio(n-)*, from the verb *visitare* (see **VISIT**).

visitatorial /ˌvɪzɪtəˈtɔːrɪəl/ ▶ **adjective** another term for **VISITORIAL**.

visiting card ▶ **noun** Brit. a card bearing a person's name and address, sent or left in lieu of a formal social or business visit.

visiting fireman ▶ **noun** N. Amer. informal a visitor to a city or organization who is given an official welcome and especially cordial treatment.

visiting hours ▶ **plural noun** a designated time when visitors may come to see a person in a hospital or other institution.

visitor ▶ **noun** a person visiting someone or somewhere, especially socially or as a tourist: *she's a frequent visitor to London* | *I'm expecting visitors later this evening*. ■ (usu. **visitors**) a member of a sports team on tour or playing away from home. ■ Brit. a person with the right or duty of occasionally inspecting and reporting on a college or other academic institution. ■ Ornithology a migratory bird present in a locality for only part of the year.
– ORIGIN late Middle English: from Anglo-Norman French *visitour*, from Old French *visiter* (see **VISIT**).

visitorial ▶ **adjective** relating to an official visitor or visit of inspection: *visitorial jurisdiction*.

visitors' book ▶ **noun** chiefly Brit. a book in which visitors to a public building write their names and addresses, and sometimes remarks.

Visking /ˈvɪskɪŋ/ (also **Visking tubing**) ▶ **noun** [mass noun] trademark a type of seamless cellulose tubing used as a membrane in dialysis and as an edible casing for sausages.
– ORIGIN 1930s: named after the *Visking* Corporation of Chicago, US.

vis medicatrix naturae /vɪs mɛdɪˌkeɪtrɪks ˈnatʃərʌɪ/ ▶ **noun** [mass noun] the body's natural ability to heal itself.
– ORIGIN Latin, 'the healing power of nature'.

visna /ˈviznə/ ▶ **noun** [mass noun] Veterinary Medicine a fatal disease of sheep in which there is progressive demyelination of neurons in the brain and spinal cord, caused by the maedi virus.
– ORIGIN 1950s: from Old Norse, 'to wither'.

visor /ˈvʌɪzə/ (also **vizor**) ▶ **noun 1** a movable part of a helmet that can be pulled down to cover the face. ■ a screen for protecting the eyes from unwanted light, especially one at the top of a vehicle windscreen. ■ N. Amer. a stiff peak at the front of a cap.
2 historical a mask.
– DERIVATIVES **visored** adjective.
– ORIGIN Middle English: from Anglo-Norman French *viser*, from Old French *vis* 'face', from Latin *visus* (see **VISAGE**).

Visqueen /ˈvɪskwiːn/ ▶ **noun** [mass noun] trademark durable polyethylene sheeting, used in various building applications and in the manufacture of waterproof household articles.
– ORIGIN 1940s: from **VISKING**, with humorous alteration of *-king* to *-queen*.

vista ▶ **noun** a pleasing view: *sweeping lawns and landscaped vistas*. ■ a long, narrow view as between rows of trees or buildings, especially one closed by a building or other structure. ■ a mental view of a succession of remembered or anticipated events: *vistas of freedom seemed to open ahead of him*.
– ORIGIN mid 17th cent.: from Italian, literally 'view', from *visto* 'seen', past participle of *vedere* 'see', from Latin *videre*.

vista dome ▶ **noun** N. Amer. an observation compartment in the roof of a railway carriage.

Vistavision ▶ **noun** [mass noun] US trademark a form of widescreen cinematography employing standard 35 mm film in such a way as to give a larger projected image using ordinary methods of projection.

Vistula /ˈvɪstjʊlə/ a river in Poland which rises in the Carpathian Mountains and flows 940 km (592 miles) generally northwards, through Cracow and Warsaw, to the Baltic near Gdańsk. Polish name **WISŁA**.

visual /ˈvɪʒjʊəl, -zj-/ ▶ **adjective** relating to seeing or sight: *visual perception*.
▶ **noun** (usu. **visuals**) a picture, piece of film, or display used to illustrate or accompany something.
– DERIVATIVES **visuality** noun, **visually** adverb.
– ORIGIN late Middle English (originally describing a beam imagined to proceed from the eye and make vision possible): from late Latin *visualis*, from Latin *visus* 'sight', from *videre* 'to see'. The current noun sense dates from the 1950s.

visual agnosia ▶ **noun** [mass noun] Medicine a condition in which a person can see but cannot recognize or interpret visual information, due to a disorder in the parietal lobes.

visual aid ▶ **noun 1** (usu. **visual aids**) an item of illustrative matter, such as a film, slide, or model, designed to supplement written or spoken information so that it can be understood more easily.
2 a device used to improve vision, such as a magnifying glass or glasses.

visual angle ▶ **noun** Optics the angle formed at the eye by rays from the extremities of an object viewed.

visual binary ▶ **noun** Astronomy a binary star of which the components are sufficiently far apart to be resolved by an optical telescope.

visual cortex ▶ **noun** Anatomy the part of the cerebral cortex that receives and processes sensory nerve impulses from the eyes.

visual display unit (abbrev.: **VDU**) ▶ **noun** chiefly Brit. a device for displaying input signals as characters on a screen.

visual field ▶ **noun** another term for **FIELD OF VISION**.

visualize (also **visualise**) ▶ **verb** [with obj.] **1** form a mental image of; imagine: *it is not easy to visualize the future*.
2 make (something) visible to the eye: *the DNA was visualized by staining with ethidium bromide*.
– DERIVATIVES **visualizable** adjective, **visualization** noun, **visualizer** noun.

visually impaired ▶ **adjective** partially or completely blind.

visual purple ▶ **noun** [mass noun] a purplish-red light-sensitive pigment present in the retinas of humans and many other animal groups.

visual ray ▶ **noun** Optics an imaginary line representing the path of light from an object to the eye.

V

visuomotor /ˈvɪʒjʊə(ʊ),məʊtə, -zj-/ ▶ **adjective** [attrib.] relating to or denoting the coordination of movement and visual perception by the brain.

visuospatial /ˌvɪʒjʊəʊˈspeɪʃ(ə)l, -zj-/ ▶ **adjective** [attrib.] Psychology relating to or denoting the visual perception of the spatial relationships of objects.

vita /ˈviːtə/ ▶ **noun** US a curriculum vitae.
– ORIGIN Latin, literally 'life'.

vital ▶ **adjective 1** absolutely necessary; essential: *secrecy is of vital importance | it is vital that the system is regularly maintained*. ■ indispensable to the continuance of life: *the vital organs*.
2 full of energy; lively: *a beautiful, vital girl*.
3 archaic fatal: *the wound is vital*.
▶ **noun** (**vitals**) the body's important internal organs.
– DERIVATIVES **vitally** adverb [as submodifier] *eating sensibly is vitally important for health*.
– ORIGIN late Middle English (describing the animating principle of living beings, also in sense 2 of the adjective): via Old French from Latin *vitalis*, from *vita* 'life'. The sense 'essential' dates from the early 17th cent.

vital capacity ▶ **noun** the greatest volume of air that can be expelled from the lungs after taking the deepest possible breath.

vital force ▶ **noun** [mass noun] the energy or spirit which animates living creatures; the soul. ■ Philosophy (in some theories, particularly that of Bergson) a hypothetical force, independent of physical and chemical forces, regarded as being the causative factor in the evolution and development of living organisms. [translating French *élan vital*.]

vitalism ▶ **noun** [mass noun] the theory that the origin and phenomena of life are dependent on a force or principle distinct from purely chemical or physical forces.
– DERIVATIVES **vitalist** noun & adjective, **vitalistic** adjective.
– ORIGIN early 19th cent.: from French *vitalisme*, or from **VITAL** + **-ISM**.

vitality ▶ **noun** [mass noun] the state of being strong and active; energy: *changes that will give renewed vitality to our democracy*. ■ the power giving continuance of life, present in all living things: *the vitality of seeds*.
– ORIGIN late 16th cent.: from Latin *vitalitas*, from *vitalis* (see **VITAL**).

vitalize /ˈvʌɪt(ə)lʌɪz/ (also **vitalise**) ▶ **verb** [with obj.] give strength and energy to: *yoga calms and vitalizes body and mind*.
– DERIVATIVES **vitalization** noun.

vital signs ▶ **plural noun** clinical measurements, specifically pulse rate, temperature, respiration rate, and blood pressure, that indicate the state of a patient's essential body functions.

vital statistics ▶ **plural noun 1** quantitative data concerning the population, such as the number of births, marriages, and deaths.
2 Brit. informal the measurements of a woman's bust, waist, and hips.

vitamin /ˈvɪtəmɪn, ˈvʌɪt-/ ▶ **noun** any of a group of organic compounds which are essential for normal growth and nutrition and are required in small quantities in the diet because they cannot be synthesized by the body.
– ORIGIN early 20th cent.: from Latin *vita* 'life' + **AMINE**, because vitamins were originally thought to contain an amino acid.

vitamin A ▶ **noun** another term for **RETINOL**.

vitamin B ▶ **noun** [mass noun] any of a group of substances (the **vitamin B complex**) which are essential for the working of certain enzymes in the body and, although not chemically related, are generally found together in the same foods. They include thiamine (**vitamin B_1**), riboflavin (**vitamin B_2**), pyridoxine (**vitamin B_6**), and cyanocobalamin (**vitamin B_{12}**).

vitamin C ▶ **noun** another term for **ASCORBIC ACID**.

vitamin D ▶ **noun** [mass noun] any of a group of vitamins found in liver and fish oils, essential for the absorption of calcium and the prevention of rickets in children and osteomalacia in adults. They include calciferol (**vitamin D_2**) and cholecalciferol (**vitamin D_3**).

vitamin E ▶ **noun** another term for **TOCOPHEROL**.

vitamin H ▶ **noun** chiefly US another term for **BIOTIN**.

vitaminize (also **vitaminise**) ▶ **verb** [with obj.] add vitamins to (food): (as adj. **vitaminized**) *vitaminized biscuits*.

vitamin K ▶ **noun** [mass noun] any of a group of vitamins found mainly in green leaves and essential for the blood-clotting process. They include phylloquinone (**vitamin K_1**) and menaquinone (**vitamin K_2**).

vitamin M ▶ **noun** chiefly US another term for **FOLIC ACID**.

vitamin P ▶ **noun** [mass noun] chiefly US the bioflavonoids, regarded collectively as a vitamin.

Vitebsk /ˈvʲitʲipsk/ Russian name for **VITSEBSK**.

vitelli plural form of **VITELLUS**.

vitellin /vɪˈtɛlɪn, vʌɪ-/ ▶ **noun** [mass noun] Biochemistry the chief protein constituent of egg yolk.
– ORIGIN mid 19th cent.: from **VITELLUS** + **-IN**[1].

vitelline /vɪˈtɛlʌɪn, vʌɪ-, -lɪn/ ▶ **adjective** Zoology & Embryology relating to the yolk (or yolk sac) of an egg or embryo, or to yolk-producing organs.
– ORIGIN late Middle English (in the sense 'coloured like egg yolk'): from medieval Latin *vitellinus*, from *vitellus* (see **VITELLUS**).

vitelline membrane ▶ **noun** Embryology a transparent membrane surrounding and secreted by the fertilized ovum, preventing the entry of further spermatozoa.

Vitellius /vɪˈtɛlɪəs/, Aulus (15–69), Roman emperor. He was acclaimed emperor in January 69 by the legions in Germany during the civil wars that followed the death of Nero. He defeated Otho but was killed by the supporters of Vespasian.

vitellogenin /vɪˌtɛlə(ʊ)ˈdʒɛnɪn, ˌvɪt(ə)ləʊˈdʒɛnɪn/ ▶ **noun** Biochemistry a protein present in the blood, from which the substance of egg yolk is derived.
– ORIGIN 1960s: from **VITELLUS** + **-GEN** + **-IN**[1].

vitello tonnato /vɪˈtɛləʊ tɒˈnɑːtəʊ/ ▶ **noun** [mass noun] an Italian dish consisting of roast or poached veal served cold in a tuna and anchovy mayonnaise.
– ORIGIN Italian, from *vitello* 'veal' + *tonno* 'tuna'.

vitellus /vɪˈtɛləs, vʌɪ-/ ▶ **noun** [mass noun] Embryology the yolk of an egg or ovum.
– ORIGIN early 18th cent.: from Latin, literally 'yolk'.

vitiate /ˈvɪʃɪeɪt/ ▶ **verb** [with obj.] formal spoil or impair the quality or efficiency of: *development programmes have been vitiated by the rise in population*. ■ destroy or impair the legal validity of.
– DERIVATIVES **vitiation** noun.
– ORIGIN mid 16th cent.: from Latin *vitiat-* 'impaired', from the verb *vitiare*, from *vitium* (see **VICE**[1]).

viticulture /ˈvɪtɪˌkʌltʃə/ ▶ **noun** [mass noun] the cultivation of grapevines. ■ the study of grape cultivation.
– DERIVATIVES **viticultural** adjective, **viticulturist** noun.
– ORIGIN late 19th cent.: from Latin *vitis* 'vine' + **CULTURE**, on the pattern of words such as *agriculture*.

Viti Levu /ˌviːtiː ˈlɛvuː/ the largest of the Fiji islands. Its chief settlement is Suva.

vitiligo /ˌvɪtɪˈlʌɪgəʊ/ ▶ **noun** [mass noun] Medicine a condition in which the pigment is lost from areas of the skin, causing whitish patches, often with no clear cause. Also called **LEUCODERMA**.
– ORIGIN late 16th cent.: from Latin, literally 'tetter'.

Vitoria /vɪˈtɔːrɪə/, Spanish /biˈtəorja/ a city in NE Spain, capital of the Basque Provinces; pop. 232,477 (2008). In 1813 Wellington defeated a French force there, and thus freed Spain from French domination.

Vitória /vɪˈtɔːrɪə/ a port in eastern Brazil, capital of the state of Espírito Santo; pop. 314,042 (2007).

vitrectomy /vɪˈtrɛktəmi/ ▶ **noun** [mass noun] the surgical operation of removing the vitreous humour from the eyeball.

vitreous /ˈvɪtrɪəs/ ▶ **adjective** like glass in appearance or physical properties. ■ (of a substance) derived from or containing glass: *vitreous china*.
– ORIGIN late Middle English: from Latin *vitreus* (from *vitrum* 'glass') + **-OUS**.

vitreous humour ▶ **noun** [mass noun] the transparent jelly-like tissue filling the eyeball behind the lens. Compare with **AQUEOUS HUMOUR**.

vitrescent /vɪˈtrɛs(ə)nt/ ▶ **adjective** rare capable of or susceptible to being turned into glass.
– ORIGIN mid 18th cent.: from Latin *vitrum* 'glass' + **-ESCENT**.

vitriform /ˈvɪtrɪfɔːm/ ▶ **adjective** having the form or appearance of glass.

vitrify /ˈvɪtrɪfʌɪ/ ▶ **verb** (**vitrifies**, **vitrifying**, **vitrified**) [with obj.] convert (something) into glass or a glass-like substance, typically by exposure to heat.
– DERIVATIVES **vitrifaction** /-ˈfakʃ(ə)n/ noun, **vitrification** /-fɪˈkeɪʃ(ə)n/ noun.
– ORIGIN late Middle English: from French *vitrifier* or based on Latin *vitrum* 'glass'.

vitrine /ˈvɪtriːn/ ▶ **noun** a glass display case.
– ORIGIN French, from *vitre* 'glass pane'.

vitriol /ˈvɪtrɪəl/ ▶ **noun** [mass noun] **1** bitter criticism or malice: *her mother's sudden gush of fury and vitriol*.
2 archaic or literary sulphuric acid. ■ in names of metallic sulphates, e.g. **blue vitriol** (copper sulphate) and **green vitriol** (ferrous sulphate).
– ORIGIN late Middle English (denoting the sulphate of various metals): from Old French, or from medieval Latin *vitriolum*, from Latin *vitrum* 'glass'.

vitriolic /ˌvɪtrɪˈɒlɪk/ ▶ **adjective** filled with bitter criticism or malice: *vitriolic attacks on the politicians | vitriolic outbursts*.
– DERIVATIVES **vitriolically** adverb.

Vitruvius /vɪˈtruːvɪəs/ (*fl.* 1st century BC), Roman architect and military engineer; full name *Marcus Vitruvius Pollio*. He wrote a comprehensive ten-volume treatise on architecture which includes matters such as acoustics and water supply as well as the more obvious aspects of architectural design, decoration, and building.

Vitsebsk /ˈviːtsjɛbsk/ a city in NE Belarus; pop. 347,500 (est. 2009). Russian name **Vitebsk**.

vitta /ˈvɪtə/ ▶ **noun** (pl. **vittae** /ˈvɪtiː/) Zoology a band or stripe of colour.
– ORIGIN early 19th cent.: from Latin, literally 'band, chaplet'.

vittle ▶ **noun** archaic variant spelling of **victual**.

vituperate /vɪˈtjuːpəreɪt, vʌɪ-/ ▶ **verb** [with obj.] archaic blame or insult (someone) in strong or violent language.
– DERIVATIVES **vituperator** noun.
– ORIGIN mid 16th cent.: from Latin *vituperat-* 'censured, disparaged' (see **vituperation**).

vituperation /vɪˌtʃuːpəˈreɪʃ(ə)n, vʌɪ-/ ▶ **noun** [mass noun] bitter and abusive language: *no one else attracted such vituperation from him*.
– ORIGIN Middle English: from Old French or Latin, from Latin *vituperat-* 'censured, disparaged', from the verb *vituperare*, from *vitium* 'fault' + *parare* 'prepare'.

vituperative /vɪˈtjuːp(ə)rətɪv, vʌɪ-/ ▶ **adjective** bitter and abusive: *a vituperative outburst*.

Vitus, St /ˈvʌɪtəs/ (died *c*.300), Christian martyr. He was the patron of those who suffered from epilepsy and certain nervous disorders, including St Vitus's dance (Sydenham's chorea). Feast day, 15 June.

viva¹ /ˈvʌɪvə/ Brit. ▶ **noun** short for **viva voce**.
▶ **verb** (**vivas, vivaing, vivaed** /-vəd/ or **viva'd**) [with obj.] subject (someone) to an oral examination.

viva² /ˈviːvə/ ▶ **exclamation** long live! (used to express acclaim or support for a specified person or thing): *'Viva Mexico!'*.
▶ **noun** a cry of this as a salute or cheer.
– ORIGIN Italian.

vivace /vɪˈvɑːtʃeɪ/ Music ▶ **adverb & adjective** (especially as a direction) in a lively and brisk manner.
▶ **noun** a passage or movement marked to be performed in a lively and brisk manner.
– ORIGIN Italian, 'brisk, lively', from Latin *vivax, vivac-*.

vivacious /vɪˈveɪʃəs, vʌɪ-/ ▶ **adjective** (especially of a woman) attractively lively and animated.
– DERIVATIVES **vivaciously** adverb, **vivaciousness** noun.
– ORIGIN mid 17th cent.: from Latin *vivax, vivac-* 'lively, vigorous' (from *vivere* 'to live') + **-ious**.

vivacity /vɪˈvasɪti/ ▶ **noun** [mass noun] (especially in a woman) the quality of being attractively lively and animated: *he was struck by her vivacity, humour and charm*.

Vivaldi /vɪˈvaldi/, Antonio (Lucio) (1678–1741), Italian composer and violinist, one of the most important baroque composers. His feeling for texture and melody is evident in his numerous compositions such as *The Four Seasons* (concerto, 1725).

vivarium /vʌɪˈvɛːrɪəm, vɪ-/ ▶ **noun** (pl. **vivaria** /-rɪə/) an enclosure, container, or structure adapted or prepared for keeping animals under semi-natural conditions for observation or study or as pets; an aquarium or terrarium.
– ORIGIN early 17th cent.: from Latin, literally 'warren, fish pond', from *vivus* 'living', from *vivere* 'to live'.

vivat /ˈvʌɪvat, ˈviː-/ ▶ **exclamation & noun** Latin term for **viva²**.

viva voce /ˌvʌɪvə ˈvəʊtʃeɪ, ˈvəʊtʃi/ ▶ **adjective** (especially of an examination) oral rather than written.
▶ **adverb** orally rather than in writing.
▶ **noun** Brit. an oral examination, typically for an academic qualification.
– ORIGIN mid 16th cent.: from medieval Latin, literally 'with the living voice'.

Vivekananda /ˌviveɪkɑːˈnʌndə/, Swami (1863–1902), Indian spiritual leader and reformer; born *Narendranath Datta*. He spread the teachings of the Indian mystic Ramakrishna and introduced Vedantic philosophy to the US and Europe.

vive la difference /ˌviːv lɑː ˌdɪfəˈrɒns/ ▶ **exclamation** chiefly humorous an expression of approval of difference, especially that between the sexes.
– ORIGIN from French *vive la différence*, literally 'long live the difference'.

viverrid /vɪˈvɛrɪd, vʌɪ-/ ▶ **noun** Zoology a mammal of the civet family (Viverridae).
– ORIGIN early 20th cent.: from modern Latin *Viverridae*, from Latin *viverra* 'ferret'.

vivers /ˈvʌɪvəz/ ▶ **plural noun** Scottish, chiefly literary food; provisions.
– ORIGIN mid 16th cent.: from French *vivres*, from *vivre* 'to live', from Latin *vivere*.

vivianite /ˈvɪvɪənʌɪt/ ▶ **noun** [mass noun] a mineral consisting of a phosphate of iron which occurs as a secondary mineral in ore deposits. It is colourless when fresh but becomes blue or green with oxidization.
– ORIGIN early 19th cent.: named after John H. *Vivian* (1785–1855), British mineralogist, + **-ite¹**.

vivid ▶ **adjective 1** producing powerful feelings or strong, clear images in the mind: *memories of that evening were still vivid* | *a vivid description*.
2 (of a colour) intensely deep or bright: *the rhododendron bush provides a vivid splash of mauve*.
3 archaic (of a person or animal) lively and vigorous.
– DERIVATIVES **vividly** adverb, **vividness** noun.
– ORIGIN mid 17th cent.: from Latin *vividus*, from *vivere* 'to live'.

vivify /ˈvɪvɪfʌɪ/ ▶ **verb** (**vivifies, vivifying, vivified**) [with obj.] make more lively or interesting; enliven: *outings vivify learning for children*.
– DERIVATIVES **vivification** /-fɪˈkeɪʃ(ə)n/ noun.
– ORIGIN late Middle English: from French *vivifier*, from late Latin *vivificare*, from Latin *vivus* 'living', from *vivere* 'to live'.

viviparous /vɪˈvɪp(ə)rəs, vʌɪ-/ ▶ **adjective 1** Zoology (of an animal) bringing forth live young which have developed inside the body of the parent. Compare with **oviparous** and **ovoviviparous**.
2 Botany (of a plant) reproducing from buds which form plantlets while still attached to the parent plant, or from seeds which germinate within the fruit.
– DERIVATIVES **viviparity** /ˌvɪvɪˈparɪti/ noun, **viviparously** adverb.
– ORIGIN mid 17th cent.: from Latin *viviparus* (from *vivus* 'alive' + *-parus* 'bearing') + **-ous**.

viviparous lizard ▶ **noun** a small brownish-grey Eurasian lizard which gives birth to live young which have hatched from eggs inside the female. ● *Lacerta vivipara*, family Lacertidae. Alternative name: **common lizard**.

vivisect /ˈvɪvɪsɛkt, ˌvɪvɪˈsɛkt/ ▶ **verb** [with obj.] (used only by opponents of the practice) perform vivisection on (an animal).
– DERIVATIVES **vivisector** noun.
– ORIGIN mid 19th cent.: back-formation from **vivisection**.

vivisection ▶ **noun** [mass noun] the practice of performing operations on live animals for the purpose of experimentation or scientific research (used only by opponents of such work). ■ ruthlessly sharp and detailed criticism or analysis: *the vivisection of America's seamy underbelly*.
– DERIVATIVES **vivisectionist** noun & adjective.
– ORIGIN early 18th cent.: from Latin *vivus* 'living', on the pattern of *dissection*.

vixen ▶ **noun** a female fox. ■ informal a spirited or quarrelsome woman.
– DERIVATIVES **vixenish** adjective.
– ORIGIN late Middle English *fixen*, perhaps from the Old English adjective *fyxen* 'of a fox'. The *v-* is from the form of the word in southern English dialect.

Viyella /vʌɪˈɛlə/ ▶ **noun** [mass noun] trademark a fabric made from a twilled mixture of cotton and wool.
– ORIGIN late 19th cent.: from *Via Gellia*, a valley in Derbyshire where it was first made.

viz. ▶ **adverb** chiefly Brit. namely; in other words (used to introduce a gloss or explanation): *the first music-reproducing media, viz. the music box and the player piano*.
– ORIGIN abbreviation of **videlicet**, *z* being a medieval Latin symbol for *-et*.

vizard /ˈvɪzəd/ ▶ **noun** archaic a mask or disguise.
– ORIGIN mid 16th cent.: alteration of **visor**.

vizier /vɪˈzɪə, ˈvɪzɪə/ ▶ **noun** historical a high official in some Muslim countries, especially in Turkey under Ottoman rule.
– ORIGIN mid 16th cent.: via Turkish from Arabic *wazīr* 'caliph's chief counsellor'.

vizor ▶ **noun** variant spelling of **visor**.

vizsla /ˈvɪʒlə/ ▶ **noun** a dog of a breed of golden-brown pointer with large drooping ears.
– ORIGIN 1940s: from the name of a town in Hungary.

VJ ▶ **abbreviation** video jockey.

VJ day ▶ **noun** the day (15 August) in 1945 on which Japan ceased fighting in the Second World War, or the day (2 September) when Japan formally surrendered.
– ORIGIN *VJ*, abbreviation of *Victory over Japan*.

Vlach /vlak/ ▶ **noun** a member of the indigenous population of Romania and Moldova, claiming descent from the inhabitants of the Roman province of Dacia.
– ORIGIN from a Slavic word meaning 'foreigner', from a Germanic word related to Old English *Wælisc* (see **Welsh**). Compare with **Wallachia**.

Vladikavkaz /ˌvladɪkafˈkɑːs/ a city in SW Russia, capital of the autonomous republic of North Ossetia; pop. 312,800 (est. 2008). Former names **Ordzhonikidze** (1931–44 and 1954–93) and **Dzaudzhikau** (1944–54).

Vladimir /ˈvladɪˌmɪə, vləˈdiːmɪə/ a city in European Russia, east of Moscow; pop. 339,500 (est. 2008).

Vladimir I (956–1015), grand prince of Kiev 980–1015; known as **Vladimir the Great**; canonized as **St Vladimir**. His marriage to a sister of the Byzantine emperor Basil II resulted in his conversion to Christianity and in Christianity in Russia developing in close association with the Orthodox Church. Feast day, 15 July.

Vladivostok /ˌvladɪˈvɒstɒk/ a city in the extreme south-east of Russia, on the coast of the Sea of Japan, capital of Primorsky; pop. 578,800 (est. 2008). It is the chief port of Russia's Pacific coast.

Vlaminck /vlaˈmaŋk/, French /vlamɛ̃k/, Maurice de (1876–1958), French painter and writer. With Derain and Matisse he became a leading exponent of Fauvism, though later his colour became more subdued.

vlast /vlast/ ▶ **noun** (pl. **vlasti** /-ti/) [mass noun] (in countries of the former Soviet Union) political power.
■ (**the vlasti**) the government or the establishment.
– ORIGIN Russian.

vlei /fleɪ, vlʌɪ/ ▶ **noun** S. African a shallow natural pool of water. ■ [mass noun] low-lying, marshy ground, covered with water during the rainy season.
– ORIGIN Afrikaans, from Dutch *vallei* 'valley'.

vlei rat ▶ **noun** see **swamp rat**.

VLF ▶ **abbreviation** very low frequency (denoting radio waves of frequency 3–30 kHz and wavelength 10–100 km).

Vlissingen /ˈvlɪsɪŋə(n)/ Dutch name for **Flushing**.

Vlorë /ˈvlɔːrə/ a port in SW Albania, on the Adriatic coast; pop. 95,200 (est. 2009). Also called **Vlona** /ˈvləʊnə/. Italian name **Valona**.

VLSI ▶ **abbreviation** Electronics very large-scale integration, the process of integrating hundreds of thousands of components on a single silicon chip.

Vltava /ˈvəltəvə/ a river of the Czech Republic, which rises in the Bohemian Forest on the German–Czech border and flows 435 km (270 miles) generally northwards, passing through Prague before joining the Elbe north of the city. German name **Moldau**.

VN ▶ **abbreviation** Vietnam (international vehicle registration).

V-neck ▶ **noun** a neckline having straight sides meeting at a point to form a V-shape. ■ a garment with a V-shaped neckline.
– DERIVATIVES **V-necked** adjective.

VO ▶ **abbreviation** (in the UK) Royal Victorian Order.

VO2 max ▶ **noun** the maximum or optimum rate at which the heart, lungs, and muscles can effectively use oxygen during exercise, used as a way of measuring a person's individual aerobic capacity.
– ORIGIN from *volume*, O_2 (the chemical formula for oxygen), and *maximum*.

vobla /ˈvɒblə/ ▶ **noun** [mass noun] dried and smoked roach eaten in Russia as a delicacy.
– ORIGIN Russian.

vocable /ˈvəʊkəb(ə)l/ ▶ **noun** a word, especially with reference to form rather than meaning.
– ORIGIN late Middle English (denoting a name): from French, or from Latin *vocabulum*, from *vocare* 'call'.

vocabulary ▶ **noun** (pl. **vocabularies**) **1** the body of words used in a particular language. ■ a part of such a body of words used on a particular occasion or in a particular sphere: *the vocabulary of law* | [mass noun] *you will want to learn vocabulary that is used frequently*. ■ the body of words known to an individual person: *he had a wide vocabulary*. ■ a list of difficult or unfamiliar words with an explanation of their meanings, accompanying a piece of specialist or foreign-language text.
2 a range of artistic or stylistic forms, techniques, or movements: *dance companies have their own vocabularies of movement*.
– ORIGIN mid 16th cent. (denoting a list of words with definitions or translations): from medieval Latin *vocabularius*, from Latin *vocabulum* (see **vocable**).

vocal ▶ **adjective 1** relating to the human voice: *non-linguistic vocal effects like laughs and sobs.* ■ Anatomy used in the production of speech sounds: *the vocal apparatus.*
2 (of music) consisting of or incorporating singing.
3 expressing opinions or feelings freely or loudly: *he was vocal in condemning the action.*
▶ **noun** (often **vocals**) a part of a piece of music that is sung. ■ a musical performance involving singing.
– DERIVATIVES **vocality** noun, **vocally** adverb.
– ORIGIN late Middle English: from Latin *vocalis*, from *vox, voc-* (see VOICE). Current senses of the noun date from the 1920s.

vocal cords (also **vocal folds**) ▶ **plural noun** folds of membranous tissue which project inwards from the sides of the larynx to form a slit across the glottis in the throat, and whose edges vibrate in the airstream to produce the voice.

vocalese /ˌvəʊkəˈliːz/ ▶ **noun** [mass noun] a style of singing in which singers put words to jazz tunes, especially to previously improvised instrumental solos.

vocalic /və(ʊ)ˈkalɪk/ ▶ **adjective** Phonetics relating to or consisting of a vowel or vowels.

vocalise /ˌvəʊkəˈliːz, ˈvəʊkəliːz/ ▶ **noun** Music a singing exercise using individual syllables or vowel sounds to develop flexibility and control of pitch and tone. ■ a vocal passage consisting of a melody without words: *the second movement is in the spirit of a vocalise.*
▶ **verb** variant spelling of VOCALIZE.

vocalism ▶ **noun 1** [mass noun] the use of the voice or vocal organs in speech. ■ the skill or art of exercising the voice in singing.
2 Phonetics a vowel sound or articulation. ■ a system of vowels used in a given language.

vocalist ▶ **noun** a singer, typically one who regularly performs with a jazz or pop group.

vocalize /ˈvəʊk(ə)lʌɪz/ (also **vocalise**) ▶ **verb** [with obj.] **1** utter (a sound or word): *the child vocalizes a number of distinct sounds* | [no obj.] *a warbler vocalized from a reed bed.* ■ express in words: *Gillie could scarcely vocalize her responses.* ■ [no obj.] Music sing with several notes to one vowel.
2 Phonetics change (a consonant) to a semivowel or vowel.
3 write (a language such as Hebrew) with vowel points.
– DERIVATIVES **vocalization** noun, **vocalizer** noun.

vocal sac ▶ **noun** Zoology (in many male frogs) a loose fold of skin on each side of the mouth, which can be inflated to produce sound.

vocal score ▶ **noun** a musical score showing the voice parts in full, but with the accompaniment reduced or omitted.

vocation /və(ʊ)ˈkeɪʃ(ə)n/ ▶ **noun** a strong feeling of suitability for a particular career or occupation: *not all of us have a vocation to be nurses or doctors.* ■ a person's employment or main occupation, especially regarded as worthy and requiring dedication: *her vocation as a poet.* ■ a trade or profession.
– ORIGIN late Middle English: from Old French, or from Latin *vocatio(n-)*, from *vocare* 'to call'.

vocational ▶ **adjective** relating to an occupation or employment: *vocational training.* ■ (of education or training) directed at a particular occupation and its skills.
– DERIVATIVES **vocationalism** noun, **vocationalize** (also **vocationalise**) verb, **vocationally** adverb.

vocative /ˈvɒkətɪv/ Grammar ▶ **adjective** relating to or denoting a case of nouns, pronouns, and adjectives in Latin and other languages, used in addressing or invoking a person or thing.
▶ **noun** a word in the vocative case. ■ (**the vocative**) the vocative case.
– ORIGIN late Middle English: from Old French *vocatif, -ive* or Latin *vocativus*, from *vocare* 'to call'.

vociferate /və(ʊ)ˈsɪfəreɪt/ ▶ **verb** [no obj.] shout, complain, or argue loudly or vehemently: *he then began to vociferate loudly* | [with obj.] *he entered, vociferating curses.*
– DERIVATIVES **vociferation** noun.
– ORIGIN late 16th cent.: from Latin *vociferat-* 'exclaimed', from the verb *vociferari*, from *vox* 'voice' + *ferre* 'carry'.

vociferous ▶ **adjective** expressing or characterized by vehement opinions: *he was a vociferous opponent of the takeover.*
– DERIVATIVES **vociferously** adverb, **vociferousness** noun.

V

vocoder /vəʊˈkəʊdə/ ▶ **noun** a synthesizer that produces sounds from an analysis of speech input.
– ORIGIN 1930s: from VOICE + CODE + -ER[1].

VOD ▶ **abbreviation** video on demand.

vodka /ˈvɒdkə/ ▶ **noun** [mass noun] an alcoholic spirit of Russian origin made by distillation of rye, wheat, or potatoes.
– ORIGIN Russian, diminutive of *voda* 'water'.

vodun /ˈvəʊduːn/ ▶ **noun** another term for VOODOO.
– ORIGIN Fon, 'fetish'.

voe /vəʊ/ ▶ **noun** a small bay or creek in Orkney or Shetland.
– ORIGIN late 17th cent.: from Norwegian *våg*, from Old Norse *vágr*.

voetsak /ˈfʊtsak/ (also **voetsek**) ▶ **verb** [no obj., usu. in imperative] S. African informal, often offensive go away: *voetsak out of here!* | [as exclamation] *150,000 rand for a Mercedes? Voetsak!*
– ORIGIN South African Dutch, contraction of Dutch *voort seg ik!* 'away, say I!'.

voetstoots /ˈfʊtˌstʊəts/ ▶ **adverb & adjective** S. African
1 Law (of a sale or purchase) without guarantee or warranty; at the buyer's risk.
2 without reservation or qualification: [as adv.] *I'm not entirely in favour of school uniforms voetstoots.*
– ORIGIN Afrikaans, from the Dutch phrase *met de voet te stoten* 'to push with the foot'.

vogue ▶ **noun** the prevailing fashion or style at a particular time: *the vogue is to make realistic films.* ■ [mass noun] general acceptance or favour; popularity: *crochet garments are **in vogue** this season.*
▶ **adjective** [attrib.] popular; fashionable: *'citizenship' was to be the government's vogue word.*
▶ **verb** (**vogues, vogueing** or **voguing, vogued**) [no obj.] dance to music in such a way as to imitate the characteristic poses struck by a model on a catwalk. [1980s: from the name of the fashion magazine *Vogue*.]
– DERIVATIVES **voguish** adjective.
– ORIGIN late 16th cent. (in *the vogue*, denoting the foremost place in popular estimation): from French, from Italian *voga* 'rowing, fashion', from *vogare* 'row, go well'.

voice ▶ **noun 1** the sound produced in a person's larynx and uttered through the mouth, as speech or song: *Meg raised her voice* | [mass noun] *a worried tone of voice.* ■ the ability to speak or sing: *she'd lost her voice.* ■ (**usu. voices**) the supposed utterance of a guiding spirit. ■ the distinctive tone or style of a literary work or author: *she had strained and falsified her literary voice.*
2 a particular opinion or attitude expressed: *a dissenting voice.* ■ an agency by which a point of view is expressed or represented: *once the proud voice of middle-class conservatism, the paper had fallen on hard times.* ■ [in sing.] the right to express an opinion: *the new electoral system gives minority parties a voice.*
3 Music the range of pitch or type of tone with which a person sings, such as soprano or tenor. ■ a vocal part in a composition. ■ a constituent part in a fugue. ■ each of the notes or sounds able to be produced simultaneously by a musical instrument (especially an electronic one) or a computer. ■ (in an electronic musical instrument) each of a number of preset or programmable tones.
4 [mass noun] Phonetics sound uttered with resonance of the vocal cords (used in the pronunciation of vowels and certain consonants).
5 Grammar a form or set of forms of a verb showing the relation of the subject to the action: *the passive voice.*
▶ **verb** [with obj.] **1** express in words: *get teachers to voice their opinions on important subjects.*
2 (usu. as adj. **voiced**) Phonetics utter (a speech sound) with resonance of the vocal cords (e.g. *b, d, g, v, z*).
3 Music regulate the tone quality of (organ pipes).
– PHRASES **give voice to** allow (a particular emotion or opinion) to be expressed. **in voice** in proper vocal condition for singing or speaking: *the soprano is in marvellous voice.* **with one voice** in complete agreement; unanimously.
– DERIVATIVES **voiced** adjective [in combination] *deep-voiced*, **voicer** noun (sense 3 of the verb).
– ORIGIN Middle English: from Old French *vois*, from Latin *vox, voc-*.

voice box ▶ **noun** the larynx.

voice channel ▶ **noun** Telecommunications a channel with a bandwidth sufficiently great to accommodate speech.

voice coil ▶ **noun** Telecommunications a coil that drives the cone of a loudspeaker according to the signal current flowing in it. ■ a similar coil with the converse function in a moving-coil microphone.

voiceless ▶ **adjective 1** not able to speak or express opinions: *millions of Americans feel voiceless and powerless to bring positive change to the political system.* ■ not expressed: *the air was charged with voiceless currents of thought.*
2 Phonetics (of a speech sound) uttered without resonance of the vocal cords (e.g. *f, k, p, s, t*).
– DERIVATIVES **voicelessly** adverb, **voicelessness** noun.

voicemail ▶ **noun** [mass noun] a centralized electronic system which can store messages from telephone callers.

Voice of America an official US radio station founded in 1942, operated by the Board for International Broadcasting, that broadcasts around the world in English and other languages.

voice-over ▶ **noun** a piece of narration in a film or broadcast, not accompanied by an image of the speaker.
▶ **verb** [with obj.] narrate (spoken material) for a film or broadcast as a voice-over.

voiceprint ▶ **noun** a visual record of speech, analysed with respect to frequency, duration, and amplitude.
– ORIGIN 1960s: from the noun VOICE, on the pattern of *fingerprint*.

voice recognition ▶ **noun** [mass noun] computer analysis of the human voice, especially for the purposes of interpreting words and phrases or identifying an individual voice.

voice vote ▶ **noun** a vote taken by noting the relative strength and volume of calls of *aye* and *no*.

void /vɔɪd/ ▶ **adjective 1** not valid or legally binding: *the contract was void.* ■ (of speech or action) ineffectual; useless: *all the stratagems you've worked out are rendered void.*
2 completely empty: *void spaces surround the tanks.* ■ (**void of**) free from; lacking: *what were once the masterpieces of literature are now void of meaning.* ■ formal (of an office or position) vacant.
3 [predic.] (in bridge and whist) having been dealt no cards in a particular suit.
▶ **noun 1** a completely empty space: *the black void of space.* ■ an unfilled space in a wall, building, or other structure. ■ an emptiness caused by the loss of something: *his loss leaves a void in the community.*
2 (in bridge and whist) a suit in which a player is dealt no cards.
▶ **verb** [with obj.] **1** chiefly N. Amer. declare that (something) is not valid or legally binding: *the Supreme court voided the statute.*
2 discharge or drain away (water, gases, etc.). ■ chiefly Medicine excrete (waste matter). ■ (usu. as adj. **voided**) empty or evacuate (a container or space).
3 (as adj. **voided**) Heraldry (of a bearing) having the central area cut away so as to show the field.
– DERIVATIVES **voidable** adjective, **voidness** noun.
– ORIGIN Middle English (in the sense 'unoccupied'): from a dialect variant of Old French *vuide*; related to Latin *vacare* 'vacate'; the verb partly a shortening of AVOID, reinforced by Old French *voider*.

voidance ▶ **noun 1** [mass noun] the action of voiding or the state of being voided: *the voidance of exhaust gases.*
2 chiefly Law an annulment of a contract.
3 Christian Church a vacancy in a benefice.
– ORIGIN late Middle English: from Old French, from the verb *voider* (see VOID).

void deck ▶ **noun** SE Asian the ground floor of a block of flats, which is left vacant and typically used for communal activities.

voila /vwʌˈlɑː/ ▶ **exclamation** there it is; there you are: *'Voila!' she said, producing a pair of strappy white sandals.*
– ORIGIN French *voilà*.

voile /vɔɪl, vwɑːl/ ▶ **noun** [mass noun] a thin, semi-transparent fabric of cotton, wool, or silk.
– ORIGIN late 19th cent.: French, literally 'veil'.

VoIP ▶ **abbreviation** voice over Internet protocol, a technology for making telephone calls over the Internet in which speech sounds are converted into binary data.

voir dire /ˌvwɑː ˈdɪə/ (also **voire dire**) ▶ **noun** Law a preliminary examination of a witness or the jury pool by a judge or counsel.
– ORIGIN Law French, from Old French *voir* 'true' + *dire* 'say'.

voix celeste /ˌvwʌ səˈlɛst/ ▶ **noun** French term for VOX ANGELICA.
– ORIGIN late 19th cent.: French *voix céleste*, literally 'heavenly voice'.

Vojvodina /vɔɪ'vɒdɪnə/ a mainly Hungarian-speaking province of northern Serbia, on the Hungarian border; capital, Novi Sad.

vol. ▶ **abbreviation** volume.

Volans /'vəʊlənz/ Astronomy an inconspicuous southern constellation (the Flying Fish), between Carina and the south celestial pole.
– ORIGIN Latin, from the former name *Piscis Volans*.

volant /'vəʊlənt/ ▶ **adjective** Zoology (of an animal) able to fly or glide: *newly volant young*. ■ relating to or characterized by flight. ■ [usu. postpositive] Heraldry represented as flying: *a falcon volant*. ■ literary moving rapidly or lightly: *her sails caught a volant wind*.
– ORIGIN mid 16th cent. (as a military term in the sense 'capable of rapid movement'): from French, literally 'flying', present participle of *voler*, from Latin *volare* 'to fly'.

Volapük /'vɒlə,p(j)u:k/ ▶ **noun** [mass noun] an artificial language devised in 1879 for universal use by a German cleric, Johann M. Schleyer, and based on extremely modified forms of words from English and Romance languages, with complex inflections.
– ORIGIN from *vol* representing English *world* + *-a-* (as a connective) + *pük* representing English *speak* or *speech*.

volar /'vəʊlə/ ▶ **adjective** Anatomy relating to the palm of the hand or the sole of the foot.
– ORIGIN early 19th cent.: from Latin *vola* 'hollow of the hand or foot' + **-AR**[1].

volatile /'vɒlətʌɪl/ ▶ **adjective 1** (of a substance) easily evaporated at normal temperatures.
2 liable to change rapidly and unpredictably, especially for the worse: *the political situation was becoming more volatile*. ■ (of a person) liable to display rapid changes of emotion.
3 (of a computer's memory) retaining data only as long as there is a power supply connected.
▶ **noun** (usu. **volatiles**) a volatile substance.
– DERIVATIVES **volatility noun**.
– ORIGIN Middle English (in the sense 'creature that flies', also, as a collective, 'birds'): from Old French *volatil* or Latin *volatilis*, from *volare* 'to fly'.

volatile oil ▶ **noun** another term for **ESSENTIAL OIL**.

volatilize /və'latɪlʌɪz, 'vɒlətɪlʌɪz/ (also **volatilise**) ▶ **verb** (with reference to a substance) make or become volatile.
– DERIVATIVES **volatilization noun**.

vol-au-vent /'vɒlə(ʊ)vɒ̃/ ▶ **noun** a small round case of puff pastry filled with a savoury mixture, typically of meat or fish in a richly flavoured sauce.
– ORIGIN French, literally 'flight in the wind'.

volcanic ▶ **adjective** relating to or produced by a volcano or volcanoes. ■ (of a feeling or emotion) bursting out or liable to burst out violently: *the kind of volcanic passion she'd felt last night*.
– DERIVATIVES **volcanically adverb**.
– ORIGIN late 18th cent.: from French *volcanique*, from *volcan* (see **VOLCANO**).

volcanic bomb ▶ **noun** see **BOMB** (sense 2 of the noun).

volcanic glass ▶ **noun** another term for **OBSIDIAN**.

volcanicity ▶ **noun** another term for **VOLCANISM**.

volcaniclastic /vɒl,kanɪ'klastɪk/ ▶ **adjective** Geology relating to or denoting a clastic rock which contains volcanic material.

volcanic neck ▶ **noun** see **NECK** (sense 2 of the noun).

volcanism /'vɒlkənɪz(ə)m/ (also **vulcanism**) ▶ **noun** [mass noun] Geology volcanic activity or phenomena.

volcano ▶ **noun** (pl. **volcanoes** or **volcanos**) a mountain or hill, typically conical, having a crater or vent through which lava, rock fragments, hot vapour, and gas are or have been erupted from the earth's crust. ■ a state or situation which is liable to erupt into anger or violence: *Clare had been building up a silent volcano of resentment*.
– ORIGIN early 17th cent.: from Italian, from Latin *Volcanus* 'Vulcan'.

volcanology /,vɒlkə'nɒlədʒi/ (also **vulcanology**) ▶ **noun** [mass noun] the scientific study of volcanoes.
– DERIVATIVES **volcanological adjective**, **volcanologist noun**.

vole ▶ **noun** a small, typically burrowing, mouse-like rodent with a rounded muzzle, found in both Eurasia and North America. ● Subfamily Microtinae (or Arvicolinae), family Muridae: several genera, in particular *Microtus*, and numerous species.
– ORIGIN early 19th cent. (originally *vole-mouse*): from Norwegian *voll(mus)* 'field (mouse)'.

volet /'vɒleɪ/ ▶ **noun** a panel or wing of a triptych (picture or carving on three panels).
– ORIGIN mid 19th cent.: from French, literally 'shutter', from *voler* 'to fly'.

Volga /'vɒlgə/ the longest river in Europe, which rises in NW Russia and flows 3,688 km (2,292 miles) generally eastwards to Kazan, where it turns southeastwards to the Caspian Sea. It has been dammed at several points to provide hydroelectric power, and is navigable for most of its length.

Volgograd /'vɒlgəgrad/ an industrial city in SW Russia, situated at the junction of the Don and Volga Rivers; pop. 983,900 (est. 2008). Former names **TSARITSYN** (until 1925) and **STALINGRAD** (1925–61).

volition /və'lɪʃ(ə)n/ ▶ **noun** [mass noun] the faculty or power of using one's will: *without conscious volition she backed into her office*.
– PHRASES **of** (or **by** or **on**) **one's own volition** voluntarily: *they choose to leave early of their own volition*.
– DERIVATIVES **volitional adjective**, **volitionally adverb**, **volitive adjective** (formal or technical).
– ORIGIN early 17th cent. (denoting a decision or choice made after deliberation): from French, or from medieval Latin *volitio(n-)*, from *volo* 'I wish'.

volk /fɒlk/ ▶ **noun** (pl. **volke**) **1** S. African a nation or people, in particular the Afrikaner people.
2 the German people (with reference to Nazi ideology).
ORIGIN Dutch and Afrikaans.

Völkerwanderung /'fə:lkə,vɑ:ndərʊŋ/, German /'fœlkɐ,vandərʊŋ/ ▶ **noun** a migration of peoples, especially that of Germanic and Slavic peoples into Europe from the 2nd to the 11th centuries.
– ORIGIN German, from *Völker* 'nations' + *Wanderung* 'migration'.

völkisch /'fə:lkɪʃ/, German /'fœlkɪʃ/ (also **volkisch** /'fɒlkɪʃ/) ▶ **adjective** (of a person or ideology) populist or nationalist, and typically racist: *völkisch ideas and traditions*.
– ORIGIN German.

volley ▶ **noun** (pl. **volleys**) **1** a number of bullets, arrows, or other projectiles discharged at one time: *the infantry let off a couple of volleys*. ■ a series of utterances directed at someone in quick succession: *he unleashed a volley of angry questions*.
2 (in sport, especially tennis or soccer) a strike or kick of the ball made before it touches the ground.
▶ **verb** (**volleys**, **volleying**, **volleyed**) [with obj.] **1** (in sport, especially tennis or soccer) strike or kick (the ball) before it touches the ground: *she volleyed the ball home* | [no obj.] *he took his chance well, volleying into the top corner from 25 yards*.
2 utter or discharge in quick succession: *the dog was volleying joyful barks*.
– DERIVATIVES **volleyer noun**.
– ORIGIN late 16th cent.: from French *volée*, based on Latin *volare* 'to fly'.

volleyball ▶ **noun** [mass noun] a game for two teams, usually of six players, in which a large ball is hit by hand over a high net, the aim being to score points by making the ball reach the ground on the opponent's side of the court. ■ [count noun] the inflated ball used in volleyball.

Vologda /'vɒləgdə/ a city in northern Russia; pop. 286,100 (est. 2008).

Volos /'vɒlɒs/ a port on an inlet of the Aegean Sea, in Thessaly, eastern Greece; pop. 82,000 (est. 2009). Greek name **Vólos** /'vɔlɔs/.

volplane /'vɒlpleɪn/ Aeronautics ▶ **noun** a controlled dive or downward flight at a steep angle, especially by an aeroplane with the engine shut off.
▶ **verb** [no obj., with adverbial of direction] (of an aeroplane) make a steep controlled dive or downward flight.
– ORIGIN early 20th cent.: from French *vol plané*, literally 'glided flight'.

vols ▶ **abbreviation** volumes.

Volscian /'vɒlʃ(ə)n/ ▶ **noun** a member of an ancient Italic people who fought the Romans in Latium in the 5th and 4th centuries BC until absorbed into Rome after their final defeat in 304 BC.
▶ **adjective** relating to the Volscians.
– ORIGIN from Latin *Volsci* (the name of the people) + **-AN**.

Volstead Act /'vɒlstɛd/ a law which enforced alcohol prohibition in the US 1920–33.
– ORIGIN named after Andrew J. *Volstead* (1860–1947), American legislator.

volt[1] /vəʊlt, vɒlt/ (abbrev.: **V**) ▶ **noun** the SI unit of electromotive force, the difference of potential that would carry one ampere of current against one ohm resistance.
– ORIGIN late 19th cent.: named after A. *Volta* (see **VOLTA**[2]).

volt[2] /vɒlt, vəʊlt/ ▶ **noun** variant spelling of **VOLTE**.
▶ **verb** [no obj.] Fencing make a quick movement to avoid a thrust.
– ORIGIN late 17th cent.: from French *volter* (see **VOLTE**).

Volta[1] /'vɒltə/ a river of West Africa, which is formed in central Ghana and flows into the Gulf of Guinea near the border with Togo. At Akosombo in SE Ghana the river has been dammed, creating Lake Volta, one of the world's largest man-made lakes.

Volta[2] /'vɒltə/, Alessandro Giuseppe Antonio Anastasio, Count (1745–1827), Italian physicist. Volta is best known for the voltaic pile or electrochemical battery (1800), the first device to produce a continuous electric current.

voltage ▶ **noun** Physics an electromotive force or potential difference expressed in volts.

voltage clamp Physiology ▶ **noun** a constant electrical potential applied to a cell membrane, typically in order to measure ionic currents.
▶ **verb** (**voltage-clamp**) [with obj.] apply a voltage clamp to (a membrane, cell, etc.).

voltage divider ▶ **noun** a series of resistors or capacitors which can be tapped at any intermediate point to produce a specific fraction of the voltage applied between its ends.

Voltaic ▶ **adjective & noun** another term for **GUR**.

voltaic /vɒl'teɪɪk/ ▶ **adjective** relating to electricity produced by chemical action in a primary battery; galvanic.
– ORIGIN early 19th cent.: from the name of A. *Volta* (see **VOLTA**[2]) + **-IC**.

Voltaire /vɒl'tɛ:/, French /vɔltɛʀ/ (1694–1778), French writer, dramatist, and poet; pseudonym of *François-Marie Arouet*. He was a leading figure of the Enlightenment, and frequently came into conflict with the Establishment as a result of his radical views and satirical writings. Notable works: *Lettres philosophiques* (1734) and the satire *Candide* (1759).

volte /vɒlt, vəʊlt/ (also **volt**) ▶ **noun 1** Fencing a sudden quick jump or other movement to escape a thrust, especially a swinging round of the rear leg to turn the body sideways.
2 a movement performed in dressage and classical riding, in which a horse describes a circle of 6 yards diameter.
– ORIGIN late 17th cent. (as a fencing term): from French, from Italian *volta* 'a turn', from *volgere* 'to turn'. Sense 2 dates from the early 18th cent.

volte-face /vɒlt'fas, -'fɑ:s/ ▶ **noun 1** an act of turning round so as to face in the opposite direction.
2 an abrupt and complete reversal of attitude, opinion, or position: *a remarkable volte-face on taxes*.
– ORIGIN early 19th cent.: from French, from Italian *voltafaccia*, based on Latin *volvere* 'to roll' + *facies* 'appearance, face'.

voltmeter ▶ **noun** an instrument for measuring electric potential in volts.

volubility /,vɒljʊ'bɪlɪti/ ▶ **noun** [mass noun] the quality of talking fluently, readily, or incessantly; talkativeness: *her legendary volubility deserted her*.

voluble /'vɒljʊb(ə)l/ ▶ **adjective** (of a person) talking fluently, readily, or incessantly: *she was as voluble as her husband was silent*. ■ (of speech) characterized by fluency and readiness of utterance: *an excited and voluble discussion*.
– DERIVATIVES **volubly adverb**.
– ORIGIN Middle English (in senses 'rotating about an axis' and 'having a tendency to change'): from French, or from Latin *volubilis*, from *volvere* 'to roll'. The modern meanings arose in the late 16th cent.

volume ▶ **noun 1** a book forming part of a work or series. ■ a single book or a bound collection of printed sheets. ■ a consecutive sequence of issues of a periodical. ■ historical a scroll of parchment or papyrus containing written matter.
2 [mass noun] the amount of space that a substance or object occupies, or that is enclosed within a container: *the sewer could not cope with the volume of rainwater*. ■ an amount or quantity of something, especially when great: *changes in the volume of consumer spending* | [count noun] *the volumes of data handled are vast*. ■ fullness or expansive thickness of something, especially of a person's hair.
3 [mass noun] quantity or power of sound; degree of loudness: *he turned the volume up on the radio*.

V

– DERIVATIVES **volumed** adjective [usu. in combination] *a four-volumed boxed set.*
– ORIGIN late Middle English (originally denoting a roll of parchment containing written matter): from Old French *volum(e)*, from Latin *volumen, volumin-* 'a roll', from *volvere* 'to roll'. An obsolete meaning 'size or extent (of a book)' gave rise to sense 2.

volumetric /ˌvɒljʊˈmɛtrɪk/ ▸ adjective relating to the measurement of volume. ■ (of chemical analysis) based on measuring the volumes of reagents, especially by titration.
– DERIVATIVES **volumetrically** adverb.
– ORIGIN mid 19th cent.: from VOLUME + METRIC[1].

volumetric efficiency ▸ noun the ratio of the volume of fluid actually displaced by a piston or plunger to its swept volume.

voluminous /vəˈljuːmɪnəs/ ▸ adjective **1** (of clothes) very loose or full; having much fabric: *a voluminous purple cloak.* ■ (of a piece of furniture) large and accommodating: *he sank into a voluminous armchair.*
2 (of writing) very lengthy and detailed: *we all scribbled down voluminous notes.* ■ (of a writer) producing many books.
– DERIVATIVES **voluminously** adverb, **voluminousness** noun.
– ORIGIN early 17th cent.: partly from late Latin *voluminosus* 'having many coils', partly from Latin *volumen, volumin-* (see VOLUME).

volumize (also **volumise**) ▸ verb [with obj.] (of a product or styling technique) give body to (hair).
– DERIVATIVES **volumizer** noun.

voluntarily ▸ adverb of one's own free will: *he voluntarily attended a police station.*

voluntarism ▸ noun [mass noun] **1** the principle of relying on voluntary action (used especially with reference to the involvement of voluntary organizations in social welfare). ■ historical (especially in the 19th century) the principle that the Church or schools should be independent of the state and supported by voluntary contributions.
2 Philosophy the doctrine that the will is a fundamental or dominant factor in the individual or the universe.
– DERIVATIVES **voluntarist** noun & adjective, **voluntaristic** adjective.
– ORIGIN mid 19th cent.: formed irregularly from VOLUNTARY.

voluntary ▸ adjective **1** done, given, or acting of one's own free will: *we are funded by voluntary contributions.* ■ Physiology under the conscious control of the brain.
2 working, done, or maintained without payment: *a voluntary helper.* ■ Law (of a conveyance or disposition) made without return in money or other consideration.
▸ noun (pl. **voluntaries**) **1** an organ solo played before, during, or after a church service. ■ historical a piece of music performed extempore, especially as a prelude to other music, or composed in a free style.
2 (in a competition) a special performance left to the performer's choice.
– DERIVATIVES **voluntariness** noun.
– ORIGIN late Middle English: from Old French *volontaire* or Latin *voluntarius*, from *voluntas* 'will'.

voluntary-aided ▸ adjective (in the UK) denoting a voluntary school that is funded mainly by the local authority.

voluntary-controlled ▸ adjective (in the UK) denoting a voluntary school that is fully funded by the local authority.

voluntaryism /ˈvɒlənt(ə)rɪˌɪz(ə)m/ ▸ noun less common term for VOLUNTARISM (sense 1).

voluntary school ▸ noun (in the UK) a school which, though not established by the local education authority, is funded mainly or entirely by it, and which typically encourages a particular set of religious beliefs.

V

Voluntary Service Overseas (abbrev.: **VSO**) a British charitable organization founded in 1958 to promote voluntary work in developing countries.

voluntary simplicity ▸ noun [mass noun] a philosophy or way of life that rejects materialism in favour of human and spiritual values, and is characterized by minimal consumption, environmental responsibility, and community cooperation.

volunteer ▸ noun **1** a person who freely offers to take part in an enterprise or undertake a task. ■ a person who freely enrols for military service rather than being conscripted, especially a member of a force formed by voluntary enrolment and distinct from the regular army. ■ a plant that has not been deliberately planted.
2 a person who works for an organization without being paid. ■ Law a person to whom a voluntary conveyance or disposition is made.
▸ verb **1** [no obj.] freely offer to do something: *140 employees volunteered for redundancy* | [with infinitive] *I rashly volunteered to be a contestant.* ■ [with obj.] offer (help) freely: *he volunteered his services as a driver for the convoy.* ■ [reporting verb] say or suggest something without being asked: [with obj.] *it never paid to volunteer information* | [with direct speech] *'Her name's Louise,' Christina volunteered.* ■ [with obj.] commit (someone) to a particular undertaking, typically without consulting them: *he was volunteered for parachute training by friends.*
2 [no obj.] work for an organization without being paid.
– ORIGIN late 16th cent. (as a noun, with military reference): from French *volontaire* 'voluntary'. The change in the ending was due to association with -EER.

volunteerism ▸ noun [mass noun] chiefly N. Amer. the use or involvement of volunteer labour, especially in community services.

Volunteer State informal name for TENNESSEE.

volupté /ˌvɒlʊpˈteɪ/, French /vɔlypte/ ▸ noun [mass noun] literary the quality of being voluptuous or sensual.
– ORIGIN French.

voluptuary /vəˈlʌptjʊəri/ ▸ noun (pl. **voluptuaries**) a person devoted to luxury and sensual pleasure.
▸ adjective concerned with or characterized by luxury and sensual pleasure.
– ORIGIN early 17th cent.: from Latin *volupt(u)arius*, from *voluptas* 'pleasure'.

voluptuous /vəˈlʌptjʊəs/ ▸ adjective (of a woman) curvaceous and sexually attractive. ■ relating to or characterized by luxury or sensual pleasure: *long curtains in voluptuous crimson velvet.*
– DERIVATIVES **voluptuously** adverb, **voluptuousness** noun.
– ORIGIN late Middle English: from Old French *voluptueux* or Latin *voluptuosus*, from *voluptas* 'pleasure'.

volute /vəˈl(j)uːt/ ▸ noun **1** Architecture a spiral scroll characteristic of Ionic capitals and also used in Corinthian and composite capitals.
2 a deep-water marine mollusc with a thick colourful spiral shell which is prized by collectors. ● Family Volutidae, class Gastropoda: *Voluta* and other genera.
▸ adjective forming a spiral curve or curves.
– DERIVATIVES **voluted** adjective.
– ORIGIN mid 16th cent.: from French, or from Latin *voluta*, feminine past participle of *volvere* 'to roll'.

volution ▸ noun **1** literary a rolling or revolving motion.
2 a single turn of a spiral or coil.
– ORIGIN late 15th cent.; from late Latin *volutio(n-)*, from Latin *volut-* 'rolled', from the verb *volvere*.

volva /ˈvɒlvə/ ▸ noun Botany (in certain fungi) a veil which encloses the fruiting body, often persisting after rupture as a sheath at the base of the stalk.
– ORIGIN mid 18th cent.: modern Latin, from Latin *volvere* 'to roll, wrap round'.

volvox /ˈvɒlvɒks/ ▸ noun Biology a green single-celled aquatic organism which forms minute free-swimming spherical colonies. ● Genus *Volvox*, division Chlorophyta (or phylum Chlorophyta, kingdom Protista).
– ORIGIN modern Latin, from Latin *volvere* 'to roll'.

volvulus /ˈvɒlvjʊləs/ ▸ noun (pl. **volvuli** /ˈvɒlvjʊlʌɪ, -liː/ or **volvuluses**) Medicine an obstruction caused by twisting of the stomach or intestine.
– ORIGIN late 17th cent.: modern or medieval Latin, from Latin *volvere* 'to roll'.

Volzhsky /ˈvɒlʒski/ an industrial city in SW Russia, on the Volga; pop. 306,400 (est. 2008).

vomer /ˈvəʊmə/ ▸ noun Anatomy the small, thin bone separating the left and right nasal cavities in humans and most vertebrates.
– ORIGIN early 18th cent.: from Latin, literally 'ploughshare' (because of the shape).

vomit ▸ verb (**vomits, vomiting, vomited**) [no obj.] eject matter from the stomach through the mouth: *the sickly stench made him want to vomit* | *she used to vomit up her food.* ■ [with obj.] emit (something) in an uncontrolled stream or flow: *the machine vomited fold after fold of paper.*
▸ noun **1** [mass noun] matter vomited from the stomach.
2 archaic an emetic.
– DERIVATIVES **vomiter** noun.
– ORIGIN late Middle English: from Old French *vomite* (noun) or Latin *vomitus*, from *vomere* 'to vomit'.

vomitorium /ˌvɒmɪˈtɔːrɪəm/ ▸ noun (pl. **vomitoria** /-rɪə/) **1** each of a series of entrance or exit passages in an ancient Roman amphitheatre or theatre.
2 a place in which, according to popular misconception, the ancient Romans are supposed to have vomited during feasts to make room for more food.
– ORIGIN Latin.

vomitory /ˈvɒmɪt(ə)ri/ ▸ adjective rare relating to or inducing vomiting.
▸ noun (pl. **vomitories**) another term for VOMITORIUM (sense 1).
– ORIGIN early 17th cent.: from Latin *vomitorius*, based on *vomere* 'to vomit', partly as an anglicization of Latin *vomitorium* (see VOMITORIUM).

vomitous ▸ adjective chiefly N. Amer. nauseating.

vomitus /ˈvɒmɪtəs/ ▸ noun [mass noun] chiefly Medicine matter that has been vomited.
– ORIGIN early 20th cent.: from Latin.

von Braun see BRAUN[3].

Vonnegut /ˈvɒnɪɡət/, Kurt (1922–2007), American novelist and short-story writer. His works blend elements of realism, science fiction, fantasy, and satire, and include *Slaughterhouse-Five* (1969).

von Neumann see NEUMANN.

von Recklinghausen's disease /ˈrɛklɪŋˌhaʊz(ə)nz/ ▸ noun [mass noun] **1** a hereditary disease in which numerous benign tumours develop in various parts of the body, especially the skin and the fibrous sheaths of the nerves. It is a form of neurofibromatosis.
2 a disease in which the bones are weakened as a result of excessive secretion of the parathyroid hormone, leading to bowing and fracture of long bones and sometimes deformities of the chest and spine. Also called OSTEITIS FIBROSA CYSTICA.
– ORIGIN early 20th cent.: named after Friedrich *von Recklinghausen* (1833–1910), German pathologist.

von Sternberg /ˈstəːnbəːɡ/, Josef (1894–1969), Austrian-born American film director. His best-known film *Der Blaue Engel* (1930; *The Blue Angel*) made Marlene Dietrich an international star.

von Willebrand's disease /ˈwɪləbrand/ ▸ noun [mass noun] Medicine an inherited disorder characterized by a tendency to bleed, caused by deficiency or abnormality of a plasma coagulation factor (**von Willebrand factor**).
– ORIGIN 1940s: named after Erik A. *von Willebrand* (1870–1949), Finnish physician.

voodoo ▸ noun [mass noun] a black religious cult practised in the Caribbean and the southern US, combining elements of Roman Catholic ritual with traditional African magical and religious rites, and characterized by sorcery and spirit possession. ■ [count noun] a person skilled in voodoo.
▸ verb (**voodoos, voodooing, voodooed**) [with obj.] affect (someone) by the practice of voodoo.
– DERIVATIVES **voodooism** noun, **voodooist** noun.
– ORIGIN early 19th cent.: from Louisiana French, from Kwa *vodũ*.

Voortrekker /ˈfʊəˌtrɛkə/ ▸ noun S. African **1** historical a member of one of the groups of Dutch-speaking people who migrated by wagon from the Cape Colony into the interior from 1836 onwards, in order to live beyond the borders of British rule.
2 a member of an Afrikaner youth movement similar to the Boy Scouts and Girl Guides.
– ORIGIN Afrikaans, from Dutch *voor* 'fore' + *trekken* 'to travel'.

VOR ▸ abbreviation VHF omnirange, denoting a type of navigation system using a series of radio beacons.

voracious /vəˈreɪʃəs/ ▸ adjective wanting or devouring great quantities of food: *a voracious appetite.* ■ engaging in an activity with great eagerness or enthusiasm: *she's a voracious reader.*
– DERIVATIVES **voraciously** adverb, **voraciousness** noun, **voracity** noun.
– ORIGIN mid 17th cent.: from Latin *vorax, vorac-* (from *vorare* 'devour') + -IOUS.

Vorarlberg /ˈfɔːˌrɑːlbəːɡ/, German /ˈfoːɐ̯ˌarlbɛrk/ an Alpine state of western Austria; capital, Bregenz.

Voronezh /vəˈrɒnɛʒ/ a city in Russia, south of Moscow; pop. 839,900 (est. 2008).

Voroshilovgrad /ˌvɒrəˈʃiːləfɡrad/ former name (1935–58 and 1970–91) for LUHANSK.
– ORIGIN named in honour of Marshal Kliment *Voroshilov* (1881–1969), Soviet military and political leader.

-vorous /v(ə)rəs/ ▸ combining form feeding on a specified food: *carnivorous* | *herbivorous.*

– DERIVATIVES **-vora** /v(ə)rə/ **combining form** in corresponding names of groups., **-vore** /vɔː/ **combining form** in corresponding names of individuals within such groups.
– ORIGIN from Latin *-vorus* (from *vorare* 'devour') + **-OUS**.

Vorstellung /ˈfɔː,ʃtɛlʊŋ/, German /ˈfoːɐ̯,ʃtɛlʊŋ/ ▸ **noun** (pl. **Vorstellungen** /-,ʃtɛlʊŋ(ə)n/) Philosophy a mental image or idea produced by prior perception of an object, as in memory or imagination, rather than by actual perception.
– ORIGIN German.

vortal /ˈvɔːt(ə)l/ ▸ **noun** an Internet site that provides a directory of links to information related to a particular industry.
– ORIGIN 1990s: blend of **VERTICAL** (as in *vertical industry*, an industry specializing in a narrow range of goods and services), and **PORTAL**[1].

vortex /ˈvɔːtɛks/ ▸ **noun** (pl. **vortexes** or **vortices** /-tɪsiːz/) a whirling mass of fluid or air, especially a whirlpool or whirlwind: *we were caught in a vortex of water* | figurative *a swirling vortex of emotions*.
– DERIVATIVES **vortical** adjective, **vortically** adverb, **vorticity** /vɔːˈtɪsɪti/ noun, **vorticular** /vɔːˈtɪkjʊlə/ adjective.
– ORIGIN mid 17th cent.: from Latin *vortex*, *vortic-*, literally 'eddy', variant of **VERTEX**.

vorticella /,vɔːtɪˈsɛlə/ ▸ **noun** Zoology a sedentary, single-celled aquatic animal with a contractile stalk and a bell-shaped body bearing a ring of cilia. ● Genus *Vorticella*, phylum Ciliophora, kingdom Protista.
– ORIGIN late 18th cent.: modern Latin, diminutive of Latin *vortex*, *vortic-* 'eddy'.

Vorticist /ˈvɔːtɪsɪst/ ▸ **noun** a member of a British artistic movement of 1914–15 influenced by cubism and futurism and favouring machine-like forms.
– DERIVATIVES **Vorticism** noun.
– ORIGIN from Latin *vortex*, *vortic-* 'eddy' + **-IST**.

Vosges /vəʊʒ/ a mountain system of eastern France, in Alsace near the border with Germany.

Vostok /ˈvɒstɒk/ a series of six manned Soviet orbiting spacecraft, the first of which, launched in April 1961, carried the first man in space (Yuri Gagarin).

vostro account /ˈvɒstrəʊ/ ▸ **noun** a bank account held by a foreign bank with a UK bank, usually in sterling.
– ORIGIN *vostro* from Italian, 'your, yours'.

votary /ˈvəʊt(ə)ri/ ▸ **noun** (pl. **votaries**) a person, such as a monk or nun, who has made vows of dedication to religious service. ■ a devoted follower, adherent, or advocate of someone or something: *he was a votary of John Keats*.
– DERIVATIVES **votarist** noun.
– ORIGIN mid 16th cent.: from Latin *vot-* 'vowed' (from the verb *vovere*) + **-ARY**[1].

vote ▸ **noun** a formal indication of a choice between two or more candidates or courses of action, expressed typically through a ballot or a show of hands. ■ an act of expressing such an indication of choice: *they are ready to* **put it to a vote**. ■ (**the vote**) the choice expressed collectively by a body of electors or by a specified group: *the nationalist vote in Northern Ireland*. ■ (**the vote**) the right to register a choice in an election.
▸ **verb** [no obj.] give or register a vote: *they voted against the resolution* | [with complement] *I voted Labour*. ■ [with obj. and adverbial or complement] cause (someone) to gain or lose a particular post or honour by means of a vote: *incompetent judges are voted out of office*. ■ [with clause] informal used to express a wish to follow a particular course of action: *I vote we have one more game*. ■ [with obj.] (of a legislature) grant or confer by vote: *Parliament has voted the money for the proposed expenditure*. ■ [with obj.] (**vote something down**) reject (something) by means of a vote.
– PHRASES **vote of confidence** a vote showing that a majority continues to support the policy of a leader or governing body. **vote of no confidence** (or **vote of censure**) a vote showing that a majority does not support the policy of a leader or governing body. **vote with one's feet** informal indicate an opinion by being present or absent.
– DERIVATIVES **voteless** adjective.
– ORIGIN late Middle English: from Latin *votum* 'a vow, wish', from *vovere* 'to vow'. The verb dates from the mid 16th cent.

vote bank ▸ **noun** (in South Asia) a group of people who can be relied upon to vote together in support of the same party.

voter ▸ **noun** a person who votes or has the right to vote at an election.

voting booth ▸ **noun** US term for **POLLING BOOTH**.

voting machine ▸ **noun** (especially in the US) a machine for the automatic registering of votes.

votive ▸ **adjective** offered or consecrated in fulfilment of a vow: *votive offerings*.
▸ **noun** an object offered in fulfilment of a vow, such as a candle used as a vigil light.
– ORIGIN late 16th cent.: from Latin *votivus*, from *votum* (see **VOTE**). The original sense was 'expressing a desire', preserved in **VOTIVE MASS**.

votive Mass ▸ **noun** (in the Roman Catholic Church) a Mass celebrated for a special purpose or occasion.

Votyak /ˈvɒtjak/ ▸ **noun** former term for **UDMURT** (the language).

vouch ▸ **verb** [no obj.] (**vouch for**) assert or confirm as a result of one's own experience the truth or accuracy of (something): *the explosive used is of my own formulation, and I can vouch for its efficiency*. ■ confirm the identity or good character of (someone): *he was refused entrance until someone could vouch for him*.
– ORIGIN Middle English (as a legal term in the sense 'summon a person to court to prove title to property'): from Old French *voucher* 'summon', based on Latin *vocare* 'to call'.

voucher /ˈvaʊtʃə/ ▸ **noun** a small printed piece of paper that entitles the holder to a discount, or that may be exchanged for goods or services. ■ chiefly Brit. a receipt.
– ORIGIN early 17th cent.: from **VOUCH**.

vouchsafe ▸ **verb** [with two objs] give or grant (something) to (someone) in a gracious or condescending manner: *it is a blessing vouchsafed him by heaven*. ■ [with obj.] reveal or disclose (information): *you'd never vouchsafed that interesting titbit before*.
– ORIGIN Middle English: originally as the phrase *vouch* something *safe* on someone, i.e. 'warrant the secure conferment of (something on someone)'.

voulu /vuːˈluː/, French /vuly/ ▸ **adjective** literary lacking in spontaneity; contrived.
– ORIGIN French, literally 'wanted, wished', past participle of *vouloir*.

voussoir /ˈvuːswɑː/ ▸ **noun** Architecture a wedge-shaped or tapered stone used to construct an arch.
– ORIGIN early 18th cent: via French from popular Latin *volsorium*, based on Latin *volvere* 'to roll'. The word, borrowed from Old French, was also used for a time in late Middle English.

Vouvray /ˈvuːvreɪ/, French /vuvʀɛ/ ▸ **noun** [mass noun] dry white wine, either still or sparkling, produced in the Vouvray district of the Loire Valley.
– ORIGIN French.

vow ▸ **noun** a solemn promise. ■ (**vows**) a set of solemn promises committing one to a prescribed role, calling, or course of action, typically to marriage or a monastic career: *the vows of celibacy*.
▸ **verb 1** [reporting verb] solemnly promise to do a specified thing: [with infinitive] *the rebels vowed to continue fighting* | [with clause] *I vowed that my family would never go hungry* | [with direct speech] *'never again!' he vowed*.
2 [with obj.] archaic dedicate to someone or something, especially a deity: *I* **vowed myself to** *this enterprise*.
– ORIGIN Middle English: from Old French *vou*, from Latin *votum* (see **VOTE**); the verb is from Old French *vouer*.

vowel ▸ **noun** a speech sound which is produced by comparatively open configuration of the vocal tract, with vibration of the vocal cords but without audible friction, and which is a unit of the sound system of a language that forms the nucleus of a syllable. Contrasted with **CONSONANT**. ■ a letter representing a vowel sound, such as *a*, *e*, *i*, *o*, *u*.
– DERIVATIVES **vowelled** (US **voweled**) adjective, **vowelless** adjective, **vowelly** adjective.
– ORIGIN Middle English: from Old French *vouel*, from Latin *vocalis* (*littera*) 'vocal (letter)'.

vowel gradation ▸ **noun** another term for **ABLAUT**.

vowel harmony ▸ **noun** [mass noun] the phenomenon in some languages, e.g. Turkish, for all the vowels in a word to be members of the same subclass, for example all front vowels or all back vowels.

vowel height ▸ **noun** [mass noun] Phonetics the degree to which the tongue is raised or lowered in the articulation of a particular vowel.

vowelize (also **vowelise**) ▸ **verb** [with obj.] supply (something such as a Hebrew or shorthand text) with vowel points or signs representing vowels.

vowel mutation ▸ **noun** see **MUTATION** (sense 3).

vowel point ▸ **noun** each of a set of marks indicating vowels in writing phonetically explicit text in Semitic languages such as Hebrew and Arabic.

vowel shift ▸ **noun** a phonetic change in a vowel or vowels. ■ (**the Great Vowel Shift**) a series of changes between medieval and modern English affecting the long vowels of the standard language.

vox /vɒks/ ▸ **noun** (especially in music journalism) vocals; voice: *his matinee-idol vox*.
– DERIVATIVES **-voxed** adjective.
– ORIGIN 1980s: shortened from *vocals*, probably after Latin *vox* 'voice'.

vox angelica /,vɒks anˈdʒɛlɪkə/ ▸ **noun** a soft stop on an organ or harmonium which is tuned slightly sharp to produce a tremolo effect.
– ORIGIN mid 19th cent.: from late Latin, literally 'angelic voice'.

voxel /ˈvɒksɛl/ ▸ **noun** (in computer-based modelling or graphic simulation) each of an array of elements of volume that constitute a notional three-dimensional space, especially each of an array of discrete elements into which a representation of a three-dimensional object is divided.
– ORIGIN 1970s: from the initial letters of **VOLUME** and **ELEMENT**, with the insertion of *-x-* for ease of pronunciation.

vox humana /hjuːˈmɑːnə/ ▸ **noun** an organ stop with a tone supposedly resembling the human voice.
– ORIGIN early 18th cent.: from Latin, literally 'human voice'.

vox pop ▸ **noun** [mass noun] Brit. informal popular opinion as represented by informal comments from members of the public, especially when broadcast or published: *paragraphs of vox pop*.
– ORIGIN 1960s: abbreviation of **VOX POPULI**.

vox populi /ˈpɒpjʊliː, -lʌɪ/ ▸ **noun** [mass noun] the opinions or beliefs of the majority.
– ORIGIN mid 16th cent.: from Latin, literally 'the people's voice'.

voyage ▸ **noun** a long journey involving travel by sea or in space: *his voyage to America* | figurative *writing a biography is* **a voyage of discovery**.
▸ **verb** [no obj., with adverbial of direction] go on a voyage: *he spent part of his life voyaging along the South African coast*. ■ [with obj.] archaic sail over or along (a sea or river).
– DERIVATIVES **voyager** noun.
– ORIGIN Middle English (as a noun denoting a journey): from Old French *voiage*, from Latin *viaticum* 'provisions for a journey' (in late Latin 'journey').

Voyager either of two American space probes launched in 1977 to investigate the outer planets. Voyager 1 encountered Jupiter and Saturn, while Voyager 2 reached Jupiter, Saturn, Uranus, and finally Neptune (1989).

voyageur /,vwʌjəˈʒəː, ,vɔɪə-/ ▸ **noun** historical (in Canada) a boatman employed by the fur companies to transport goods and passengers to and from the trading posts on the lakes and rivers.
– ORIGIN French, literally 'voyager', from *voyager* 'to travel'.

voyeur /vwʌˈjəː, vɔɪ-/ ▸ **noun** a person who gains sexual pleasure from watching others when they are naked or engaged in sexual activity. ■ a person who enjoys seeing the pain or distress of others.
– DERIVATIVES **voyeurism** noun, **voyeuristic** adjective, **voyeuristically** adverb.
– ORIGIN early 20th cent.: from French, from *voir* 'see'.

VP ▸ **abbreviation** Vice-President.

VPL ▸ **abbreviation** informal visible panty line, especially as revealed by tight trousers or skirts.

VPN ▸ **abbreviation** Computing virtual private network, an arrangement whereby a secure, apparently private network is achieved using encryption over a public network, typically the Internet.

VR ▸ **abbreviation** ■ Queen Victoria. [abbreviation of Latin *Victoria Regina*.] ■ variant reading. ■ virtual reality.

VRAM ▸ **noun** a type of RAM used in computer display cards.
– ORIGIN 1990s: abbreviation of *video RAM*.

VRML ▸ **abbreviation** Computing virtual reality modelling language.

vroom informal ▸ **verb** [no obj.] (of a vehicle or its engine) make a roaring sound when travelling or running at high speed. ■ [with obj.] cause (a vehicle's engine) to make a roaring sound.
▸ **noun** the roaring sound of an engine or motor vehicle.

▶ **exclamation** used to convey the idea of speed or acceleration: *press the ignition button and vroom!*
– ORIGIN 1960s: imitative.

vrou /frəʊ/ (also **vrouw**) ▶ **noun** chiefly S. African a woman or wife.
– ORIGIN Afrikaans, from Dutch *vrouw*.

VS ▶ **abbreviation** Veterinary Surgeon.

vs ▶ **abbreviation** versus.

V-sign ▶ **noun 1** Brit. a sign resembling the letter V made with the first two fingers pointing up and the back of the hand facing outwards, used as a gesture of abuse or contempt.
2 a similar sign made with the palm of the hand facing outwards, used as a symbol or gesture of victory.

V-six (also **V-6**) ▶ **noun** a motor vehicle with a six cylinder V-engine.

VSO ▶ **abbreviation** Voluntary Service Overseas.

VSOP ▶ **abbreviation** Very Special Old Pale, a kind of brandy.

VT ▶ **abbreviation** Vermont (in official postal use).

Vt ▶ **abbreviation** Vermont.

VTO ▶ **abbreviation** vertical take-off.

VTOL ▶ **abbreviation** vertical take-off and landing.

VTR ▶ **abbreviation** videotape recorder.

vug /vʌg/ ▶ **noun** Geology a cavity in rock, lined with mineral crystals.
– DERIVATIVES **vuggy adjective**.
– ORIGIN early 19th cent.: from Cornish *vooga*.

Vuillard /ˈvwiːɑː/, French /vwijaʀ/, (Jean) Édouard (1868–1940), French painter and graphic artist. A member of the Nabi Group, he produced decorative panels, murals, paintings, and lithographs, particularly of domestic interiors and portraits.

Vulcan Roman Mythology the god of fire. Greek equivalent **HEPHAESTUS**.

Vulcanian /vʌlˈkeɪnɪən/ ▶ **adjective** Geology relating to or denoting a type of volcanic eruption marked by periodic explosive events.
– ORIGIN early 20th cent.: from *Vulcano*, the name of a volcano in the Lipari Islands, Italy, + **-IAN**.

vulcanism /ˈvʌlkənɪz(ə)m/ ▶ **noun** variant spelling of **VOLCANISM**.

vulcanite /ˈvʌlkənʌɪt/ ▶ **noun** [mass noun] hard, black vulcanized rubber.
– ORIGIN mid 19th cent.: from **VULCAN** + **-ITE**[1].

vulcanize /ˈvʌlkənʌɪz/ (also **vulcanise**) ▶ **verb** [with obj.] harden (rubber or rubber-like material) by treating it with sulphur at a high temperature.
– DERIVATIVES **vulcanizable adjective**, **vulcanization noun**, **vulcanizer noun**.
– ORIGIN early 19th cent. (in the sense 'throw into a fire'): from **VULCAN** + **-IZE**.

vulcanology ▶ **noun** variant spelling of **VOLCANOLOGY**.

vulgar ▶ **adjective 1** lacking sophistication or good taste: *a vulgar check suit*.
2 making explicit and offensive reference to sex or bodily functions; coarse and rude: *a vulgar joke*.
3 dated characteristic of or belonging to ordinary people.
– DERIVATIVES **vulgarly adverb**.
– ORIGIN late Middle English: from Latin *vulgaris*, from *vulgus* 'common people'. The original senses were 'used in ordinary calculations' (surviving in **VULGAR FRACTION**) and 'in ordinary use, used by the people' (surviving in **VULGAR TONGUE**).

vulgar fraction ▶ **noun** Brit. a fraction expressed by numerator and denominator, not decimally.

vulgarian /vʌlˈgɛːrɪən/ ▶ **noun** an unrefined person, especially one with newly acquired power or wealth.

vulgarism ▶ **noun** a word or expression that is considered inelegant, especially one that makes explicit and offensive reference to sex or bodily functions.
■ archaic an instance of rude or offensive behaviour.

vulgarity ▶ **noun** (pl. **vulgarities**) [mass noun] the state or quality of being vulgar: *he was seen as the embodiment of the vulgarity of the 1980s*. ■ [count noun] a vulgar remark or act: *his letters were full of vulgarities*.

vulgarize (also **vulgarise**) ▶ **verb** [with obj.] make less refined: *her voice, vulgarized by its accent, was full of caressing tones*. ■ make less subtle or complex: (as adj. **vulgarized**) *a vulgarized version of the argument*.
– DERIVATIVES **vulgarization noun**.

vulgar Latin ▶ **noun** [mass noun] informal Latin of classical times.

vulgar tongue ▶ **noun** (**the vulgar tongue**) dated the national or vernacular language of a people (used typically to contrast such a language with Latin).

Vulgate /ˈvʌlgeɪt, -gət/ ▶ **noun 1** the principal Latin version of the Bible, prepared mainly by St Jerome in the late 4th century, and (as revised in 1592) adopted as the official text for the Roman Catholic Church.
2 (**vulgate**) [in sing.] common or colloquial speech.
– ORIGIN from Latin *vulgata* (*editio*(*n*-)) '(edition) prepared for the public', feminine past participle of *vulgare*, from *vulgus* 'common people'.

vuln /vʌln/ ▶ **verb** [with obj.] Heraldry wound.
– ORIGIN late 16th cent.: formed irregularly from Latin *vulnerare* 'to wound'.

vulnerable ▶ **adjective** exposed to the possibility of being attacked or harmed, either physically or emotionally: *we were in a vulnerable position | small fish are vulnerable to predators*. ■ Bridge (of a partnership) liable to higher penalties, either by convention or through having won one game towards a rubber.
– DERIVATIVES **vulnerability noun** (pl. **vulnerabilities**), **vulnerably adverb**.
– ORIGIN early 17th cent.: from late Latin *vulnerabilis*, from Latin *vulnerare* 'to wound', from *vulnus* 'wound'.

vulnerary /ˈvʌln(ə)rəri/ archaic ▶ **adjective** (of a drug, plant, etc.) of use in the healing of wounds.
▶ **noun** (pl. **vulneraries**) a medicine used in the healing of wounds.
– ORIGIN late 16th cent.: from Latin *vulnerarius*, from *vulnus* 'wound'.

Vulpecula /vʌlˈpɛkjʊlə/ Astronomy an inconspicuous northern constellation (the Fox), lying in the Milky Way between Cygnus and Aquila.
– ORIGIN Latin, diminutive of *vulpes* 'fox'.

vulpine /ˈvʌlpʌɪn/ ▶ **adjective** relating to a fox or foxes. ■ crafty; cunning: *Karl gave a vulpine smile*.
– ORIGIN early 17th cent.: from Latin *vulpinus*, from *vulpes* 'fox'.

vulture /ˈvʌltʃə/ ▶ **noun 1** a large bird of prey with the head and neck more or less bare of feathers, feeding chiefly on carrion and reputed to gather with others in anticipation of the death of a sick or injured animal or person. ● Order Accipitriformes: the **Old World vultures** (family Accipitridae, especially *Gyps* and *Aegypius*) and the **New World vultures** (with the condors in the family Cathartidae).
2 a contemptible person who preys on or exploits others.
– DERIVATIVES **vulturine** /-rʌɪn/ **adjective**, **vulturish adjective**, **vulturous adjective**.
– ORIGIN late Middle English: from Anglo-Norman French *vultur*, from Latin *vulturius*.

vulture fund ▶ **noun** Finance a fund which invests in companies or properties which are performing poorly and may therefore be undervalued.

vulva /ˈvʌlvə/ ▶ **noun** Anatomy the female external genitals. ■ Zoology the external opening of the vagina or reproductive tract in a female mammal or nematode.
– DERIVATIVES **vulval adjective**, **vulvar adjective**.
– ORIGIN late Middle English: from Latin, literally 'womb'.

vulvitis /vʌlˈvʌɪtɪs/ ▶ **noun** [mass noun] Medicine inflammation of the vulva.

vuvuzela /vuːvəˈzɛlə/ ▶ **noun** (trademark in the UK) a long horn blown by fans at soccer matches in South Africa.
– ORIGIN perhaps from Zulu.

vv. ▶ **abbreviation** ■ verses. ■ volumes.

Vyatka /ˈvjɑːtkə/ an industrial town in north central European Russia, on the Vyatka River; pop. 464,500 (est. 2008). Former name (1934–92) **KIROV**.

vygie /ˈfeɪxi/ ▶ **noun** (pl. **vygies**) S. African another term for **MESEMBRYANTHEMUM**.
– ORIGIN 1920s: from Afrikaans, from Dutch *vyg* 'fig' + the diminutive suffix *-ie*.

vying present participle of **VIE**.

Ww

W[1] (also **w**) ▸ **noun** (pl. **Ws** or **W's**) **1** the twenty-third letter of the alphabet. ■ denoting the next after V in a set of items, categories, etc.
2 a shape like that of a letter W: [in combination] *the W-shaped northern constellation of Cassiopeia.*

W[2] ▸ **abbreviation** ■ (in tables of sports results) games won. ■ watt(s). ■ West or Western: *104° W | W Europe.* ■ Cricket (on scorecards) wicket(s). ■ women's (clothes size).
▸ **symbol** the chemical element tungsten. [from modern Latin *wolframium*.]

w ▸ **abbreviation** ■ weight. ■ Cricket (on scorecards) wide(s). ■ with.

WA ▸ **abbreviation** ■ Washington (State) (in official postal use). ■ Western Australia.

Wa /wɑː/ ▸ **noun** (pl. **same** or **Was**) **1** a member of a hill people living on the borders of China and Burma (Myanmar).
2 [mass noun] the language of the Wa, belonging to the Mon-Khmer family.
▸ **adjective** relating to or denoting the Wa or their language.

Waadt /vaːt/ German name for **Vaud**.

Waaf /waf/ ▸ **noun** (in the UK) a member of the Women's Auxiliary Air Force (1939–48, subsequently reorganized as part of the Women's Royal Air Force).
– ORIGIN acronym.

Waal /vɑːl/ a river of the south central Netherlands. The most southerly of two major distributaries of the Rhine, it flows for 84 km (52 miles) from the point where the Rhine forks, just west of the border with Germany, to the estuary of the Meuse (Maas) on the North Sea.

wabbit /ˈwabɪt/ ▸ **adjective** [predic.] Scottish exhausted or slightly unwell: *I'm feeling a bit wabbit.*
– ORIGIN late 19th cent.: of unknown origin.

wabi /ˈwabi/ ▸ **noun** [mass noun] (in Japanese art) a quality of austere and serene beauty expressing a mood of spiritual solitude recognized in Zen Buddhist philosophy.
– ORIGIN Japanese, literally 'solitude'.

waboom /ˈvɑːbʊəm/ ▸ **noun** S. African a protea with large pale yellow flowers and reddish timber. ● *Protea nitida*, family Proteaceae.
– ORIGIN from South African Dutch *wagenboom*, literally 'wagon tree', so named by colonists who found the wood suitable for making wheel rims.

WAC ▸ **abbreviation** (in the US) Women's Army Corps.

wack[1] ▸ **noun** Brit. informal used as a familiar term of address, chiefly in Liverpool.
– ORIGIN 1960s: of unknown origin.

wack[2] informal, chiefly US ▸ **noun 1** a crazy or eccentric person.
2 [mass noun] worthless or stupid ideas or talk; rubbish: *this track is a load of wack.*
▸ **adjective** bad; inferior: *a wack radio station.*
– ORIGIN 1930s: probably a back-formation from **wacky**.

wacke /ˈwakə/ ▸ **noun** [mass noun] Geology a sandstone of which the mud matrix in which the grains are embedded amounts to between 15 and 75 per cent of the mass.
– ORIGIN early 19th cent.: from German, from Middle High German *wacke* 'large stone', Old High German *wacko* 'pebble'.

wacked ▸ **adjective** variant spelling of **whacked**.

wacko (also **whacko**) informal, chiefly N. Amer. ▸ **adjective** mad; insane: *his wacko conspiracy theories.*
▸ **noun** (pl. **wackos** or **wackoes**) a crazy person.
– ORIGIN 1970s: from **wacky** + **-o**.

wacky (also **whacky**) ▸ **adjective** (**wackier**, **wackiest**; **whackier**, **whackiest**) informal funny or amusing in a slightly odd or peculiar way: *a wacky chase movie.*
– DERIVATIVES **wackily** adverb, **wackiness** noun.
– ORIGIN mid 19th cent. (originally dialect): from the noun **whack** + **-y**[1].

wacky baccy ▸ **noun** [mass noun] Brit. informal cannabis.

wad /wɒd/ ▸ **noun 1** a mass or lump of a soft material, used for padding, stuffing, or wiping: *a wad of lint-free rag.* ■ a portion of tobacco or another narcotic when used for chewing. ■ chiefly historical a disc of felt or another material used to keep powder or shot in place in a gun barrel.
2 a bundle or roll of paper or banknotes: *she held up a wad of greenbacks.* ■ informal a large amount of something, especially money: *she was working on TV and had wads of money.*
3 Brit. informal a bun, cake, sandwich, or other piece of food.
▸ **verb** (**wads**, **wadding**, **wadded**) [with obj.] (usu. as adj. **wadded**) **1** compress (a soft material) into a lump or mass: *a knob of wadded lint.*
2 line or stuff (a garment or piece of furniture) with wadding: *a wadded jacket.* ■ stop up (an aperture) with a lump of soft material: *he had something wadded behind his teeth.*
– ORIGIN mid 16th cent. (denoting wadding): perhaps related to Dutch *watten*, French *ouate* 'padding, cotton wool'.

wada ▸ **noun** variant spelling of **vada**.

wadcutter ▸ **noun** chiefly US a bullet designed to cut a neat hole in a paper range target.

wadding ▸ **noun** [mass noun] soft, thick material used to line garments or pack fragile items, especially cotton wool formed into a fleecy layer. ■ material from which wads for guns are made.

waddle ▸ **verb** [no obj., with adverbial of direction] walk with short steps and a clumsy swaying motion: *three geese waddled across the road.*
▸ **noun** [in sing.] a waddling gait: *I walk with a waddle.*
– DERIVATIVES **waddler** noun.
– ORIGIN late 16th cent.: perhaps a frequentative of **wade**.

waddy /ˈwɒdi/ ▸ **noun** (pl. **waddies**) an Australian Aboriginal's war club. ■ Austral./NZ a club or stick, especially a walking stick.
– ORIGIN from Dharuk *wadi* 'tree, stick, club'.

Wade[1], George (1673–1748), English soldier. He was responsible for the construction of a network of roads and bridges in the Scottish Highlands to facilitate government control of the Jacobite clans after the 1715 uprising.

Wade[2], (Sarah) Virginia (b.1945), English tennis player. She won many singles titles, including the US Open (1968), the Italian championship (1971), the Australian Open (1972), and Wimbledon (1977).

wade ▸ **verb** [no obj., with adverbial] **1** walk with effort through water or another liquid or viscous substance: *he waded out to the boat.* ■ [with obj.] walk through (something filled with water): *I waded ditches instead of finding easier crossing places.* ■ (**wade through**) read laboriously through (a long piece of writing).
2 (**wade into**) informal intervene in (something) or attack (someone) vigorously or forcefully: *Seb waded into the melee and started to beat off the boys.* ■ (**wade in**) informal make a vigorous attack or intervention: *Nicola waded in and grabbed the baby.*
▸ **noun** [in sing.] an act of wading.
– DERIVATIVES **wadable** (also **wadeable**) adjective.
– ORIGIN Old English *wadan* 'move onward', also 'penetrate', from a Germanic word meaning 'go (through)', from an Indo-European root shared by Latin *vadere* 'go'.

Wade–Giles ▸ **noun** a system of romanized spelling for transliterating Chinese, devised by the British diplomat Sir Thomas Francis Wade (1818–95), professor of Chinese at Cambridge, and modified by his successor Herbert Allen Giles (1845–1935). It has been largely superseded by Pinyin.

wader ▸ **noun 1** a person or animal, especially a bird, that wades, in particular: ■ chiefly Brit. a wading bird of the order Charadriiformes, which comprises the sandpipers, plovers, and related birds. Also called **shorebird**, especially in North America. ■ chiefly N. Amer. a wading bird of the order Ciconiiformes, which comprises the herons, storks, and ibises.
2 (**waders**) high waterproof boots, or a waterproof garment for the legs and body, used especially by anglers when fishing.

wadi /ˈwɑːdi, ˈwɒdi/ ▸ **noun** (pl. **wadis**) (in certain Arabic-speaking countries) a valley, ravine, or channel that is dry except in the rainy season.
– ORIGIN early 17th cent.: from Arabic *wādī*.

Wadi Halfa /ˌwɒdi ˈhalfə, ˌwɑːdɪ/ a town in northern Sudan, on the border with Egypt. It is situated on the Nile at the southern end of Lake Nasser and is the terminus of the railway from Khartoum.

wading bird ▸ **noun** a waterbird, especially one with long legs, that habitually wades; a wader.

wading pool ▸ **noun** North American term for **paddling pool**.

WAF ▸ **abbreviation** (in the US) Women in the Air Force.
▸ **noun** a member of the WAF.

wafer ▸ **noun 1** a thin, light, crisp biscuit, especially one of a kind eaten with ice cream.
2 a thin piece of something: *wafers of smoked salmon.* ■ a thin disc of unleavened bread used in the Eucharist. ■ Electronics a very thin slice of a semiconductor crystal used as the substrate for solid-state circuitry. ■ (also **wafer seal**) a disc of red paper stuck on a legal document as a seal. ■ historical a small disc of dried paste used for fastening letters or holding papers together.
▸ **verb** [with obj.] archaic fasten or seal (a letter or document) with a wafer.
– DERIVATIVES **wafery** adjective.
– ORIGIN late Middle English: from an Anglo-Norman French variant of Old French *gaufre* (see **goffer**), from Middle Low German *wāfel* 'waffle'; compare with **waffle**[2].

wafer-thin ▸ **adjective & adverb** very thin or thinly: [as adj.] *plates of wafer-thin metal* | [as adv.] *slicing meat wafer-thin.*

Waffen SS /ˈvaf(ə)n/ ▶ **noun** the combat units of the SS in Nazi Germany during the Second World War.
– ORIGIN German *Waffen* 'armed'.

waffle[1] informal ▶ **verb** [no obj.] **1** Brit. speak or write at length in a vague or trivial manner: *he waffled on about his problems*.
2 N. Amer. fail to make up one's mind: *Joseph had been waffling over where to go*.
▶ **noun 1** [mass noun] Brit. lengthy but vague or trivial talk or writing.
2 [in sing.] US a failure to make up one's mind: *his waffle on abortion*.
– DERIVATIVES **waffler** noun, **waffly** adjective (**wafflier**, **waffliest**).
– ORIGIN late 17th cent. (originally in the sense 'yap, yelp'): frequentative of dialect *waff* 'yelp', of imitative origin.

waffle[2] ▶ **noun** a small crisp batter cake, baked in a waffle iron and eaten hot with butter or syrup.
▶ **adjective** denoting a style of fine honeycomb weaving or a fabric woven to give a honeycomb effect.
– ORIGIN mid 18th cent.: from Dutch *wafel*; compare with **WAFER** and **GOFFER**.

waffle iron ▶ **noun** a utensil, typically consisting of two shallow metal pans hinged together, used for baking waffles.

waft /wɒft, wɑːft/ ▶ **verb** (with reference to a scent, sound, etc.) pass or cause to pass gently through the air: [no obj., with adverbial of direction] *the smell of stale fat wafted out from the cafe* | [with obj. and adverbial of direction] *each breeze would waft pollen round the house*. ■ [no obj., with adverbial of direction] move with a gliding motion: *models wafted down the catwalk in filmy organza skirts*.
▶ **noun 1** a gentle movement of air. ■ a scent carried in the air.
2 (also **weft**) Nautical, historical a knotted ensign, garment, etc. displayed by a ship as a signal. [perhaps related to Scots and northern *waff* 'a signal, waving of something in the hand', a variant of **WAVE**.]
– ORIGIN early 16th cent. (in the sense 'escort a ship'): back-formation from obsolete *wafter* (used only by opponents of the practice) 'armed convoy vessel', from Low German, Dutch *wachter*, from *wachten* 'to guard'. A sense 'convey by water' gave rise to the current use of the verb.

WAG[1] ▶ **noun** informal a wife or girlfriend of a sports player.
– ORIGIN early 21st cent.: from the acronym *WAGs* 'wives and girlfriends'.

WAG[2] ▶ **abbreviation** Gambia (international vehicle registration).
– ORIGIN from *West Africa Gambia*.

wag[1] ▶ **verb** (**wags**, **wagging**, **wagged**) (especially with reference to an animal's tail) move or cause to move rapidly to and fro: [no obj.] *his tail began to wag* | [with obj.] *the dog went out, wagging its tail*. ■ [with obj.] move (an upwards-pointing finger) from side to side to signify disapproval: *she wagged a finger at Elinor*.
▶ **noun** a single rapid movement from side to side: *a chirpy wag of the head*.
– PHRASES **how the world wags** dated how affairs are going or being conducted. **the tail wags the dog** see **TAIL**[1]. **tongues wag** used to convey that people are gossiping about someone or something: *this is a small island and tongues are beginning to wag*.
– ORIGIN Middle English (as a verb): from the Germanic base of Old English *wagian* 'to sway'.

wag[2] ▶ **noun** dated a person who makes jokes.
▶ **verb** (**wags**, **wagging**, **wagged**) [with obj.] Austral./NZ informal play truant from (school).
– ORIGIN mid 16th cent. (denoting a young man or mischievous boy, also used as a term of endearment to an infant): probably from obsolete *waghalter* 'person likely to be hanged' (see **WAG**[1], **HALTER**). The verb dates from the late 20th cent.

wage ▶ **noun** (also **wages**) a fixed regular payment earned for work or services, typically paid on a daily or weekly basis. Compare with **SALARY**. ■ (**wages**) Economics the part of total production that is the return to labour as earned income as distinct from the remuneration received by capital as unearned income. ■ the result or effect of doing something considered wrong or unwise: *disasters are the wages of sin*.
▶ **verb** [with obj.] carry on (a war or campaign): *it is necessary to destroy their capacity to wage war*.
– ORIGIN Middle English: from Anglo-Norman French and Old Northern French, of Germanic origin; related to **GAGE**[1] and **WED**.

waged ▶ **adjective** having or relating to regular paid employment: *a larger class of waged workers*.

wage drift ▶ **noun** [mass noun] the tendency for the average level of wages actually paid to rise above wage rates through increases in overtime and other factors.

wager ▶ **noun & verb** more formal term for **BET**.
– ORIGIN Middle English (also in the sense 'solemn pledge'): from Anglo-Norman French *wageure*, from *wager* 'to wage'.

wager of battle ▶ **noun** historical a form of trial by which someone's guilt or innocence was decided by personal combat between the parties or their champions.

wager of law ▶ **noun** historical a form of trial in which the defendant was required to produce witnesses who would swear to his or her innocence.

wages council ▶ **noun** (in the UK) one of a number of statutory bodies, now abolished, consisting of workers' and employers' representatives responsible for determining wages in particular industries.

wage slave ▶ **noun** informal a person who is wholly dependent on income from employment, typically employment of an arduous or menial nature.
– DERIVATIVES **wage slavery** noun.

Wagga Wagga /ˌwɒɡə ˈwɒɡə/ a town on the Murrumbidgee River, in New South Wales, SE Australia; pop. 61,656 (2008).

waggery ▶ **noun** (pl. **waggeries**) [mass noun] dated waggish behaviour or remarks; jocularity. ■ [count noun] archaic a waggish action or remark.

waggish ▶ **adjective** dated humorous in a playful, mischievous, or facetious manner: *a waggish riposte*.
– DERIVATIVES **waggishly** adverb, **waggishness** noun.

waggle ▶ **verb** move or cause to move with short quick movements from side to side or up and down: [no obj.] *his arm waggled* | [with obj.] *Mary waggled a glass at them*. ■ [with obj.] swing (a golf club) loosely to and fro over the ball before playing a shot.
▶ **noun** an act of waggling.
– ORIGIN late 16th cent.: frequentative of **WAG**[1].

waggle dance ▶ **noun** a waggling movement performed by a honeybee at the hive or nest, to indicate to other bees the direction and distance of a source of food.

waggler ▶ **noun** Fishing a type of long float designed to be especially sensitive to movement of the bait, chiefly used in semi-still water.

waggly ▶ **adjective** (**wagglier**, **waggliest**) moving with quick short movements from side to side or up and down: *a waggly tail*.

wag-'n-bietjie /ˈvaxəˌbɪki/ ▶ **noun** S. African any of a number of shrubs bearing strong curved thorns, in particular: ● a plant related to asparagus (genus *Asparagus*, family Liliaceae, in particular *A. capensis*). ● a wait-a-bit.
– ORIGIN late 18th cent.: from Afrikaans, literally 'wait a bit'.

Wagner /ˈvɑːɡnə/, (Wilhelm) Richard (1813–83), German composer. He developed an operatic genre which he called music drama, synthesizing music, drama, verse, legend, and spectacle. Notable works: *The Flying Dutchman* (opera, 1841), *Der Ring des Nibelungen* (a cycle of four operas, 1847–74), *Tristan and Isolde* (music drama, 1859), and the *Siegfried Idyll* (1870).
– DERIVATIVES **Wagnerian** adjective & noun.

Wagner tuba ▶ **noun** a brass instrument of baritone pitch with an oval shape and upward-pointing bell, combining features of the tuba and the French horn and first used in Wagner's *Der Ring des Nibelungen*.

wagon (Brit. also **waggon**) ▶ **noun 1** a vehicle used for transporting goods or another specified purpose: *a timber wagon* | *a breakdown wagon*. ■ a four-wheeled trailer for agricultural use. ■ Brit. a railway freight vehicle; a truck. ■ a light horse-drawn vehicle, especially a covered one used by early settlers in North America and elsewhere. ■ chiefly N. Amer. a wheeled cart or hut used as a food stall. ■ a vehicle like a caravan used by Gypsies or circus performers. ■ informal short for **STATION WAGON**.
2 Irish informal an unpleasant or disliked woman.
– PHRASES **on** (or **off**) **the wagon** informal abstaining (or not abstaining) from drinking alcohol: *Monty was supposed to be on the wagon*.
– ORIGIN late 15th cent.: from Dutch *wagen*; related to **WAIN**.

wagoner (Brit. also **waggoner**) ▶ **noun** the driver of a horse-drawn wagon.
– ORIGIN mid 16th cent.: from Dutch *wagenaar*, from *wagen* (see **WAGON**).

wagonette (Brit. also **waggonette**) ▶ **noun** a four-wheeled horse-drawn pleasure vehicle, typically open, with facing side seats and one or two seats arranged crosswise in front.

wagon-lit /ˌvaɡɒ̃ˈliː/ ▶ **noun** (pl. **wagons-lits** pronunc. **same**) a sleeping car on a continental railway.
– ORIGIN French, from *wagon* 'railway coach' + *lit* 'bed'.

wagonload ▶ **noun** an amount of something that can be carried in one wagon: *a wagonload of food*.

wagon-roof (also **wagon-vault**) ▶ **noun** another term for **BARREL VAULT**.

wagon train ▶ **noun** historical a convoy or train of covered horse-drawn wagons, as used by pioneers or settlers in North America.

wagtail ▶ **noun** a slender Eurasian and African songbird with a long tail that is frequently wagged up and down, typically living by water. ● Family Motacillidae: two genera, in particular *Motacilla*, and several species.

Wagyu /ˈwɑːɡjuː/ ▶ **noun** [mass noun] [often as modifier] a breed of Japanese cattle. ■ the tender beef obtained from such cattle, typically containing a high percentage of unsaturated fat.
– ORIGIN Japanese, from *wa* 'Japanese' + *gyu* 'cattle, beef'.

wah ▶ **exclamation** Indian used typically to express admiration: *wah, you look handsome enough to gladden my mother's heart!*
– ORIGIN from Hindi *vāh*.

wahey /wəˈheɪ/ ▶ **exclamation** used to express delight, pleasure, or exhilaration.
– ORIGIN 1970s: imitative.

Wahhabi /wəˈhɑːbi/ (also **Wahabi**) ▶ **noun** (pl. **Wahhabis**) a member of a strictly orthodox Sunni Muslim sect founded by Muhammad ibn Abd al-Wahhab (1703–92). It advocates a return to the early Islam of the Koran and Sunna, rejecting later innovations; the sect is still the predominant religious force in Saudi Arabia.
– DERIVATIVES **Wahhabism** noun, **Wahhabist** noun.

wahine /wɑːˈhiːni/ ▶ **noun** NZ a Maori woman or wife.
– ORIGIN Maori.

wahoo[1] /wɑːˈhuː/ (also **wahoo elm**) ▶ **noun** a North American elm which yields useful timber. ● *Ulmus alata*, family Ulmaceae.
– ORIGIN late 18th cent.: perhaps from Creek *ahá-hwa* 'walnut'.

wahoo[2] /wɑːˈhuː/ ▶ **noun** a North American spindle tree. ● Genus *Euonymus*, family Celastraceae: two species.
– ORIGIN mid 19th cent.: from Dakota, literally 'arrow wood'.

wahoo[3] /wɑːˈhuː/ ▶ **noun** a large predatory tropical marine fish of the mackerel family, prized as a game fish. ● *Acanthocybium solandri*, family Scombridae.
– ORIGIN early 20th cent.: of unknown origin.

wahoo[4] /wɑːˈhuː/ ▶ **exclamation** N. Amer. another word for **YAHOO**[2].
– ORIGIN 1940s: probably a natural exclamation.

wah-wah (also **wa-wa**) ▶ **noun** [mass noun] a musical effect achieved on brass instruments by alternately applying and removing a mute and on an electric guitar by controlling the output from the amplifier with a pedal. ■ [count noun] a pedal for producing a wah-wah effect on an electric guitar.
– ORIGIN 1920s: imitative.

waiata /ˈwʌɪətə/ ▶ **noun** a Maori song.
– ORIGIN Maori.

waif ▶ **noun** a homeless, neglected, or abandoned person, especially a child: *she is foster-mother to various waifs and strays*. ■ a person who appears thin or poorly nourished. ■ an abandoned pet animal.
– DERIVATIVES **waifish** adjective, **waiflike** adjective.
– ORIGIN late Middle English: from an Anglo-Norman French variant of Old Northern French *gaif*, probably of Scandinavian origin. Early use was often in *waif and stray*, as a legal term denoting a piece of property found and, if unclaimed, falling to the lord of the manor.

Waikato /wʌɪˈkɑːtəʊ/ the longest river of New Zealand, which flows 434 km (270 miles) generally north-westwards from Lake Taupo, at the centre of the North Island, to the Tasman Sea.

Waikiki /ˈwʌɪkɪˌkiː/ a beach resort, a suburb of Honolulu, on the island of Oahu in Hawaii.

W

wail ▶ noun a prolonged high-pitched cry of pain, grief, or anger: *Christopher let out a wail.* ■ a prolonged high-pitched sound: *the wail of an air-raid siren.*
▶ verb [no obj.] utter a wail: *Tina ran off wailing* | [with direct speech] *'But why?' she wailed.* ■ make a prolonged high-pitched sound: *the wind wailed and buffeted the timber structure* | (as adj. **wailing**) *wailing sirens.* ■ [with obj.] literary manifest or feel deep sorrow for; lament: *she wailed her wretched life.*
– DERIVATIVES **wailer** noun, **wailful** adjective (literary), **wailingly** adverb.
– ORIGIN Middle English: from Old Norse; related to WOE.

Wailing Wall a high wall in Jerusalem said to stand on the site of Herod's temple, where Jews traditionally pray and lament on Fridays.

wain ▶ noun archaic a wagon or cart. ■ (**the Wain**) short for CHARLES'S WAIN.
– ORIGIN Old English *wæg(e)n*, of Germanic origin; related to Dutch *wagen* and German *Wagen*, also to WAY and WEIGH[1].

wainscot /ˈweɪnskət, -kɒt/ ▶ noun **1** [in sing.] an area of wooden panelling on the lower part of the walls of a room. ■ [mass noun] Brit. historical imported oak of fine quality, used mainly to make panelling.
2 a drab yellowish to brown-coloured European moth. ● *Mythimna* and other genera, family Noctuidae: several species.
▶ verb (**wainscots, wainscoting, wainscoted** or **wainscots, wainscotting, wainscotted**) [with obj.] line (a room or wall) with wooden panelling.
– ORIGIN Middle English: from Middle Low German *wagenschot*, apparently from *wagen* 'wagon' + *schot*, probably meaning 'partition'. Sense 2 of the noun dates from the early 19th cent.

wainscoting (also **wainscotting**) ▶ noun [mass noun] wooden panelling that lines the lower part of the walls of a room. ■ material used to make wainscoting.

wainwright ▶ noun historical a wagon-builder.

WAIS ▶ abbreviation Computing wide area information service, designed to provide access to information across a computer network.

waist ▶ noun **1** the part of the human body below the ribs and above the hips, often narrower than the areas above and below. ■ the circumference of a person's waist: *her waist has reduced from 35 to 28 inches.* ■ the part of a garment around or covering the waist. ■ the point at which a garment is shaped so as to narrow between the ribcage and the hips: *a jacket with a high waist.*
2 a narrow part in the middle of something, such as a violin or hourglass. ■ the middle part of a ship, between the forecastle and the quarterdeck.
3 US a blouse or bodice.
– DERIVATIVES **waisted** adjective [in combination] *high-waisted*, **waistless** adjective.
– ORIGIN late Middle English: apparently representing an Old English word from the Germanic root of WAX[2].

waistband ▶ noun a strip of cloth forming the waist of a garment such as a skirt or a pair of trousers.

waist cloth ▶ noun a loincloth.

waistcoat ▶ noun Brit. a close-fitting waist-length garment, typically having no sleeves or collar and buttoning down the front, worn especially by men over a shirt and under a jacket.

waist-deep ▶ adjective & adverb of or at a depth to reach the waist: [as adj.] *the waist-deep snow* | [as adv.] *the anglers were standing waist-deep in frigid water.*

waist-high ▶ adjective & adverb of or at a height to reach the waist: [as adj.] *a ruin surrounded by waist-high grass* | [as adv.] *weeds grew waist-high.*

waistline ▶ noun **1** the measurement around a person's body at the waist: *eliminating inches from the waistline.* ■ the shaping and position of the waist of a garment.
2 an imaginary line around a car or other vehicle at the level of the bottom of the windows.

wait ▶ verb [no obj.] **1** stay where one is or delay action until a particular time or event: *he did not wait for a reply* | *we're waiting for Allan to get back* | *Vera did not wait on a Home Office ruling* | [with infinitive] *Ben stood on the street corner waiting to cross* | [with obj.] *I had to wait my turn to play.* ■ (**wait for** or **on**) stay where one is or delay action until (someone) arrives or is ready: *he sits on the corner waiting for Mary* | *she was waiting on her boyfriend.* ■ be left until a later time before being dealt with: *we shall need a statement later, but that will have to wait.* ■ [with obj.] informal defer (a meal) until a person's arrival: *I told my parents not to wait supper.*
2 remain in readiness for a purpose: *he found the train waiting on the platform.* ■ (of a vehicle) be parked for a short time at the side of a road.
3 (**cannot wait**) used to indicate that one is eagerly impatient to do something or for something to happen: *I can't wait to tell Nick what happened.*
4 act as a waiter or waitress, serving food and drink: *a local man was employed to **wait on** them at table* | [with obj.] *we had to wait tables in the mess hall.*
▶ noun **1** [in sing.] a period of waiting: *we had a long wait.*
2 (**waits**) archaic street singers of Christmas carols. ■ historical official bands of musicians maintained by a city or town.
– PHRASES **in wait** watching for an enemy or potential victim and preparing to attack them: *he decided to **lie in wait for** the thief.* **wait and see** wait to find out what will happen before doing something: *we will have to wait and see what happens.* **you wait** used to convey a threat or promise: *you wait until your Dad gets in!*
– PHRASAL VERBS **wait on** (or **upon**) **1** act as an attendant to: *a maid was appointed to wait on her.* ■ archaic pay a respectful visit to. **2** await the convenience of: *to see the full series, we will have to wait on the BBC.* ■ Austral./NZ & N. English informal refrain from doing something until something else happens: *wait on, I've an important message for you.* **wait up 1** not go to bed until someone arrives or something happens. **2** N. Amer. go more slowly or stop until someone catches up.
– ORIGIN Middle English: from Old Northern French *waitier*, of Germanic origin; related to WAKE[1]. Early senses included 'lie in wait (for)', 'observe carefully', and 'be watchful'.

wait-a-bit (also **wait-a-bit thorn**) ▶ noun chiefly S. African an African bush with hooked thorns that catch the clothing, in particular an acacia.
– ORIGIN translating Afrikaans WAG-'N-BIETJIE.

Waitangi, Treaty of /wʌɪˈtaŋi/ a treaty signed in 1840 at the settlement of Waitangi in New Zealand, which formed the basis of the British annexation of New Zealand. Subsequent contraventions of the treaty by the British led to the New Zealand Wars.

Waitangi Day ▶ noun the anniversary of the signing of the Treaty of Waitangi, celebrated as a public holiday in New Zealand on 6 February since 1960.

waiter ▶ noun **1** a man whose job is to serve customers at their tables in a restaurant.
2 a person who waits for a time, event, or opportunity.
3 a small tray; a salver.

waiting ▶ noun [mass noun] **1** the action of staying where one is or delaying action until a particular time or event.
2 the action or occupation of working as a waiter or waitress.
3 official attendance at court. See also LADY-IN-WAITING.

waiting game ▶ noun a tactic in which one refrains from action for a time in order to act more effectively at a later date or stage: *policemen were last night **playing a waiting game** outside the cottage.*

waiting list ▶ noun a list of people waiting for something, such as housing or admission to a hospital or school.

waiting room ▶ noun a room provided for the use of people who are waiting to be seen by a doctor or dentist or who are waiting in a station for a bus or train.

wait list N. Amer. ▶ noun a waiting list.
▶ verb (**wait-list**) [with obj.] put (someone) on a waiting list.

waitperson ▶ noun (pl. **waitpersons**) chiefly N. Amer. a waiter or waitress (used as a neutral alternative).

waitress ▶ noun a woman whose job is to serve customers at their tables in a restaurant.

waitressing ▶ noun [mass noun] the action or occupation of working as a waitress.

waitron ▶ noun US a waiter or waitress (used as a neutral alternative).

waitstaff ▶ noun [treated as sing. or pl.] N. Amer. waiters and waitresses collectively.

wait state ▶ noun the condition of computer software or hardware being unable to process further instructions while waiting for some event such as the completion of a data transfer.

waive ▶ verb [with obj.] refrain from insisting on or using (a right or claim): *he will waive all rights to the money.* ■ refrain from demanding compliance with (a rule or fee): *her tuition fees would be waived.*
– ORIGIN Middle English (originally as a legal term relating to removal of the protection of the law): from an Anglo-Norman French variant of Old French *gaiver* 'allow to become a waif, abandon'.

> **USAGE** Waive is sometimes confused with **wave**. **Waive** means 'refrain from insisting on or demanding', as in *he will waive all rights to the money or her fees would be waived*, whereas the much more common word **wave** means 'move to and fro'. A **waiver** is a document recording that a right or claim has been waived, whereas to **waver** is to move in a quivering way or be undecided between two alternatives.

waiver ▶ noun an act or instance of waiving a right or claim. ■ a document recording the waiving of a right or claim.

Wajda /ˈvʌɪdə/, Andrzej (b.1926), Polish film director. Notable films: *Ashes and Diamonds* (1958), *Man of Iron* (1981), and *Danton* (1983).

waka /ˈwɒkə/ ▶ noun NZ a traditional Maori canoe.
– ORIGIN Maori.

Wakamba /waˈkambə/ plural form of KAMBA.

wakame /ˈwakameɪ/ ▶ noun [mass noun] an edible brown seaweed used, typically in dried form, in Chinese and Japanese cookery. ● *Undaria pinnitafida*, class Phaeophyceae.
– ORIGIN Japanese.

Wakashan /waˈkaʃ(ə)n/ ▶ adjective relating to or denoting a small family of almost extinct American Indian languages of the northern Pacific coast, including Kwakiutl and Nootka.
▶ noun [mass noun] the Wakashan family of languages.
– ORIGIN from Nootka *waukash* 'good' (said to have been applied to the people by Captain Cook) + -AN.

wake[1] ▶ verb (past **woke** or US, dialect, or archaic **waked**; past participle **woken** or US, dialect, or archaic **waked**)
1 emerge or cause to emerge from sleep; stop sleeping: [no obj.] *she **woke up** feeling better* | [with obj.] *I woke him gently.* ■ [no obj.] (**wake up to**) become alert to or aware of: *he needs to wake up to reality.* ■ [with obj.] cause to stir or come to life: *his voice wakes desire in others.*
2 [with obj.] Irish or N. Amer. dialect hold a vigil beside (someone who has died): *we waked Jim last night.*
▶ noun **1** a watch or vigil held beside the body of someone who has died, sometimes accompanied by ritual observances. ■ (especially in Ireland) a party held after a funeral.
2 (**wakes**) [treated as sing.] an annual festival and holiday held in some parts of northern England, originally one held in a rural parish on the feast day of the patron saint of the church. [probably from Old Norse *vaka*.]
– PHRASES **wake up and smell the coffee** [usu. in imperative] informal, chiefly N. Amer. become aware of the realities of a situation, however unpleasant.
– DERIVATIVES **waker** noun.
– ORIGIN Old English (recorded only in the past tense *wōc*), also partly from the weak verb *wacian* 'remain awake, hold a vigil', of Germanic origin; related to Dutch *waken* and German *wachen*; compare with WATCH.

wake[2] ▶ noun a trail of disturbed water or air left by the passage of a ship or aircraft.
– PHRASES **in the wake of** following (someone or something), especially as a consequence: *the committee was set up **in the wake of** the inquiry.*
– ORIGIN late 15th cent. (denoting a track made by a person or thing): probably via Middle Low German from Old Norse *vǫk*, *vaka* 'hole or opening in ice'.

wakeboarding ▶ noun [mass noun] the sport of riding on a short, wide board resembling a surfboard and performing acrobatic manoeuvres while being towed behind a motor boat.
– DERIVATIVES **wakeboard** noun, **wakeboarder** noun.
– ORIGIN 1990s: from WAKE[2], on the pattern of *surfboarding*.

Wakefield a town in West Yorkshire, northern England; pop. 74,800 (est. 2009).

wakeful ▶ adjective (of a person) unable or not needing to sleep: *he had been wakeful all night.* ■ (of a period of time) passed with little or no sleep: *wakeful nights.*
– DERIVATIVES **wakefully** adverb, **wakefulness** noun.

waken ▶ verb another term for WAKE[1] (sense 1 of the verb).
– ORIGIN Old English *wæcnan* 'be aroused', of Germanic origin; related to WAKE[1].

W

wake-robin ▶ noun **1** Brit. another term for CUCKOO PINT. **2** N. Amer. another term for TRILLIUM.

wake-up ▶ noun [in sing.] an instance of a person waking up or being woken up.
– PHRASES **be a wake-up** Austral./NZ informal be fully alert or aware: *I'm a wake-up to you.*

wake-up call ▶ noun a telephone call made at a prearranged time in order to wake someone up. ■ a thing that alerts people to an unsatisfactory situation and prompts them to remedy it: *today's statistics will be a wake-up call for the administration.*

wakey-wakey ▶ exclamation Brit. informal used to rouse or wake someone.
– ORIGIN 1940s: reduplicated extension of the verb WAKE[1].

Wakhan Salient /wəˈkɑːn/ a narrow corridor of land, 300 km in length, in the north-eastern corner of Afghanistan.

waking ▶ noun [mass noun] the state of being awake: *he hangs between sleeping and waking.*

waking dream ▶ noun an involuntary dream occurring while a person is awake.

wakizashi /ˌwakɪˈzaʃi/ ▶ noun (pl. **same**) a Japanese sword shorter than a katana.
– ORIGIN Japanese, from *waki* 'side' + *sasu* 'wear at one's side'.

WAL ▶ abbreviation Sierra Leone (international vehicle registration).
– ORIGIN from *West Africa Leone*.

Walachia variant spelling of WALLACHIA.

Waldenses /wɒlˈdɛnsiːz/ ▶ plural noun a puritan religious sect based originally in southern France, now chiefly in Italy and America, founded *c.*1170 by Peter Valdes (d.1205), a merchant of Lyons.
– DERIVATIVES **Waldensian** adjective & noun.

Waldheim /ˈvaldhʌɪm/, German /ˈvalthaɪm/, Kurt (1918–2007), Austrian diplomat and statesman, President 1986–92. He was Secretary General of the United Nations 1972–81. During the presidential election campaign of 1986 he denied allegations that as an army intelligence officer he had had direct knowledge of Nazi atrocities during the Second World War.

waldo /ˈwɔːldəʊ/ ▶ noun (pl. **waldos**) a remote-controlled device for handling or manipulating objects.
– ORIGIN 1940s: named after *Waldo* F. Jones, a fictional inventor described by Robert Heinlein in a science-fiction story.

Waldorf salad /ˈwɔːldɔːf/ ▶ noun a salad made from apples, walnuts, celery, and mayonnaise.
– ORIGIN named after the *Waldorf*-Astoria Hotel in New York, where it was first served.

waldrapp /ˈwɔːldrap/ ▶ noun an ibis with a bare red head and mainly dark metallic green plumage, now breeding only in Morocco. ● *Geronticus eremita*, family Threskiornithidae. Alternative names: **hermit ibis**, **bald ibis**.
– ORIGIN 1920s: from German, from *Wald* 'forest' + *Rapp*, variant of *Rabe* 'raven'.

Waldsterben /ˈvaltˌʃtɛːb(ə)n/, German /ˈvaltˌʃtɛrbn/ ▶ noun [mass noun] disease and death in forest trees in central Europe as a result of atmospheric pollution.
– ORIGIN 1980s: from German, from *Wald* 'forest' + *Sterben* 'death'.

wale ▶ noun **1** a ridge on a textured woven fabric such as corduroy.
2 Nautical a horizontal wooden strip fitted as strengthening to a boat's side.
3 a horizontal band around a woven basket.
– ORIGIN late Old English *walu* 'stripe, weal'.

wale knot (also **wall knot**) ▶ noun a knot made at the end of a rope by intertwining the strands.

Waler /ˈweɪlə/ ▶ noun **1** a horse of a typically light breed from Australia, especially from New South Wales.
2 informal a native or inhabitant of Australia, especially New South Wales.

Wales a principality of Great Britain and the United Kingdom, to the west of central England; pop. 2,993,000 (est. 2008); capital, Cardiff. Welsh name CYMRU.

> The Celtic inhabitants of Wales successfully maintained independence against the Anglo-Saxons who settled in England following the withdrawal of the Romans. Norman colonization from England began in the 12th century, and their control over the country was assured by Edward I's conquest (1277–84). Edward began the custom of making the English sovereign's eldest son Prince of Wales. Wales was formally brought into the English legal and parliamentary system by Henry VIII (1536), but has retained a distinct cultural identity. In 1997 a referendum narrowly approved proposals for a Welsh assembly, which was inaugurated in 1999.

Wales, Prince of see PRINCE OF WALES; CHARLES, PRINCE.

Wałęsa /vaˈwɛnsə/, Lech (b.1943), Polish trade unionist and statesman, President 1990–5. The founder of Solidarity (1980), he was imprisoned 1981–2 after the movement was banned. After Solidarity's landslide victory in the 1989 elections he became President. Nobel Peace Prize (1983).

wali /ˈwɑːliː/ ▶ noun the governor of a province in an Arab country.
– ORIGIN from Arabic *(al-)wālī*.

walk ▶ verb **1** [no obj., usu. with adverbial] move at a regular pace by lifting and setting down each foot in turn, never having both feet off the ground at once: *I walked across the lawn* | *she turned and walked a few paces.* ■ go on foot for recreation and exercise: *you can walk in 21,000 acres of moorland.* ■ [with obj.] travel over (a route or area) on foot: *the police department has encouraged officers to walk the beat.* ■ used to suggest that someone has achieved a state or position easily or undeservedly: *no one has the right to **walk straight into** a well-paid job for life.* ■ move in a similar way to walking, but using one's hands or a support such as stilts: *he could walk on his hands carrying a plate on one foot.* ■ (of a quadruped) proceed with the slowest gait, always having at least two feet on the ground at once. ■ [with obj.] ride (a horse) at the slowest pace: *he walked his horse towards her.*
2 [with obj. and adverbial of direction] guide, accompany, or escort (someone) on foot: *he walked her home to her door* | figurative *a meeting to walk parents through the complaint process.* ■ [with obj.] take (a dog) out for exercise: *she spotted a man walking his retriever.* ■ [with obj.] train and look after (a hound puppy).
3 [no obj.] informal (of a thing) go missing or be stolen: *customers have to leave a deposit to ensure the beer glasses don't walk.*
4 [no obj.] N. Amer. informal abandon or suddenly withdraw from a job or commitment: *he was in place as the male lead but walked at the eleventh hour.* ■ be released from suspicion or from a charge: *had any of the others come clean during the trial, he might have walked.*
5 [no obj.] (of a ghost) be visible; appear: *the ghosts of Bannockburn walked abroad.*
6 [no obj.] Cricket (of a batsman) leave the field without waiting to be given out by the umpire.
7 [no obj.] Baseball reach first base automatically after not hitting at four balls pitched outside the strike zone. ■ [with obj.] allow or enable (a batter) to do this.
8 [no obj.] archaic live or behave in a particular way: *walk humbly with your God.*
▶ noun **1** an act of travelling or an outing on foot: *he was too restless to sleep, so he went out for a walk.* ■ [in sing.] used to indicate the time that it will take to reach a place on foot or the distance to be travelled: *the library is within five minutes' walk.*
2 a route recommended or marked out for recreational walking. ■ a path: *the street lamps illuminated the riverside walk.*
3 [in sing.] an unhurried rate of movement on foot: *they crossed the field at a leisurely walk.* ■ the slowest gait of an animal. ■ a person's manner of walking: *the spring was back in his walk.*
4 Brit. a part of a forest under one keeper. ■ the place where a gamecock is kept.
5 Brit. a farm where a hound puppy is trained.
6 Baseball an instance of reaching first base automatically after not hitting at four balls pitched outside the strike zone.
– PHRASES **walk before one can run** grasp the basic skills before attempting something more difficult. **walking encyclopedia** (also **walking dictionary**) informal a person who has an impressive knowledge of facts or words. **walk the boards** see BOARD. **a walk in the park** informal something that is very easy to accomplish: *as any director will tell you, doing Shakespeare isn't a walk in the park.* **walk it** informal achieve a victory easily. **walk Matilda** see MATILDA[2]. **walk someone off their feet** walk with someone until they are exhausted. **walk of life** a person's occupation or position within society: *the courses attracted people from all walks of life.* **walk on air** see AIR. **walk on eggshells** be extremely cautious about one's words or actions. **walk the plank** see PLANK. **walk the streets 1** walk freely in a town or city. **2** work as a prostitute. **walk the walk** (also **walk the talk**) informal, chiefly N. Amer. suit one's actions to one's words. **walk the wards** dated gain experience as a clinical medical student. **win in a walk** N. Amer. win without effort or competition.
– PHRASAL VERBS **walk (all) over** informal treat in an inconsiderate or exploitative manner: *don't let the cops walk all over you.* ■ defeat easily. **walk away** casually or irresponsibly withdraw from a situation in which one is involved or for which one is responsible: *they can **walk away from** the deal and leave the other person stranded.* **walk away with** informal another way of saying WALK OFF WITH. **walk in on** come upon (a person or situation) suddenly or unexpectedly: *he was clearly not expecting her to walk in on him just then.* **walk into** informal become involved in through ignorance or carelessness: *I had walked into a situation from which there was no escape.* **walk off with** informal **1** steal. **2** win: *the group walked off with a silver medal.* **walk something off** take a walk in order to undo the effects of a heavy meal. **walk out 1** depart or leave suddenly or angrily. ■ go on strike. ■ abandon someone or something towards which one has responsibilities: *he **walked out on** his wife.* **2** Brit. informal, dated go for walks in courtship: *you were **walking out with** Tom.* **walk over 1** informal another way of saying WALK OVER. **2** Horse Racing traverse (a racecourse) without needing to hurry, because one has no opponents or only inferior ones. **walk up!** Brit. used by a showman as an invitation to enter a circus or other show.
– DERIVATIVES **walkable** adjective.
– ORIGIN Old English *wealcan* 'roll, toss', also 'wander', of Germanic origin. The sense 'move about', and specifically 'go about on foot', arose in Middle English.

walkabout ▶ noun **1** chiefly Brit. an informal stroll among a crowd conducted by an important visitor. **2** Austral. a journey (originally on foot) undertaken by an Australian Aboriginal in order to live in the traditional manner.
– PHRASES **go walkabout 1** wander around from place to place in a protracted or leisurely way. **2** (of an Australian Aboriginal) journey into the bush in order to live in the traditional manner.

walkathon ▶ noun informal a long-distance walk organized as a fundraising event.
– ORIGIN 1930s: from WALK, on the pattern of *marathon*.

Walker[1], Alice (Malsenior) (b.1944), American writer and critic. Notable novels: *The Color Purple* (Pulitzer Prize, 1982) and *Possessing the Secret of Joy* (1992).

Walker[2], John (b.1952), New Zealand athlete. He was the first athlete to run a mile in less than 3 minutes 50 seconds (1975).

walker ▶ noun **1** a person who walks, especially for exercise or enjoyment.
2 short for BABY WALKER. ■ N. Amer. a walking frame.

Walker Cup a golf tournament held every two years and played between teams of male amateurs from the US and from Great Britain and Ireland, first held in 1922. The tournament was instituted by George Herbert Walker, a former President of the US Golf Association.

walkies ▶ noun informal a period of exercising a dog.
– PHRASES **go walkies** go missing, especially as a result of theft: *the insurers have drawn up a list of cars most likely to go walkies.*

walkie-talkie ▶ noun a portable two-way radio.

walk-in ▶ adjective **1** (especially of a storage area) large enough to walk into: *a walk-in cupboard.*
2 (of a service) available for customers or clients without the need for an appointment: *a walk-in clinic.*

walking bass ▶ noun Music a bass part in $^4/_4$ time in which a note is played on each beat of the bar and which typically moves up and down the scale in small steps.

walking fern ▶ noun a North American fern with long slender tapering fronds that form new plantlets where the tips touch the ground, typically growing on limestone. ● *Asplenium* (or *Camptosorus*) *rhizophyllus*, family Aspleniaceae.

walking frame ▶ noun Brit. a frame used by disabled or infirm people for support while walking, typically made of metal tubing with rubber feet.

walking leaf ▶ noun another term for WALKING FERN.

walking leg ▶ noun Zoology (in certain arthropods, especially crustaceans) a limb used for walking.

walking papers ▸ plural noun N. Amer. informal notice of dismissal from a job: *the reporter has been given his walking papers.*

walking shoe ▸ noun a sturdy, practical shoe, suitable for regular or extensive walking.

walking stick ▸ noun **1** a stick with a curved handle used for support when walking.
2 (also **walking-stick insect**) North American term for STICK INSECT.

walking tour ▸ noun a sightseeing tour made on foot.

walking wounded ▸ plural noun (usu. **the walking wounded**) people who have been injured in a battle or major accident but who are still able to walk.

Walkman ▸ noun (pl. **Walkmans** or **Walkmen**) trademark a type of personal stereo.

walk-on ▸ adjective denoting or having a small non-speaking part in a play or film.
▸ noun **1** a person who plays a walk-on part.
2 N. Amer. a sports player with no regular status in a team.

walkout ▸ noun a sudden angry departure, especially as a protest or strike.

walkover ▸ noun an easy victory: *they won in a 12–2 walkover.*

walk-through ▸ noun **1** a tour or demonstration of an area or task: *a floor-by-floor walk-through of the library.* ▪ a software model of a building or other object in which the user can simulate walking around. ▪ a rough rehearsal of a play, film, or other performance, without an audience or cameras. ▪ Computing a product review of software carried out before release. ▪ (in computer gaming) a document giving advice on how to complete a game.
2 an undemanding task or role.
▸ adjective (of a building or other structure) permitting access from either end: *a walk-through gallery.*

walk-up ▸ noun N. Amer. a building allowing access to the upper floors by stairs only. ▪ a room or flat in a walk-up building.

walkway ▸ noun a passage or path for walking along, especially a raised passageway connecting different sections of a building or a wide path in a park or garden.

wall ▸ noun **1** a continuous vertical brick or stone structure that encloses or divides an area of land: *a garden wall.* ▪ an upright side of a building or room: *opulent rooms with tapestries on the walls.* ▪ any high vertical surface, especially one that is imposing in scale: *the eastern wall of the valley* | figurative *flash floods sent a six-foot wall of water through the village.* ▪ (**the Wall**) short for BERLIN WALL.
2 a thing regarded as a protective or restrictive barrier: *police investigating the murders met a wall of silence from witnesses.* ▪ Soccer a line of defenders forming a barrier against a free kick taken near the penalty area.
3 Anatomy & Zoology the membranous outer layer or lining of an organ or cavity: *the wall of the stomach.*
4 Mining the rock enclosing a lode or seam.
5 another term for WALL BROWN.
▸ verb [with obj.] enclose (an area) within walls, especially for protection or privacy: *parts of the city's East End had been walled off with concrete barricades* | (as adj. **walled**) *a walled garden.* ▪ (**wall something up**) block or seal a place by building a wall around or across it: *one doorway has been walled up.* ▪ (**wall someone/thing in/up**) confine or imprison someone or something in a restricted or sealed place: *the grey tenements walled in the space completely.*
– PHRASES **between you and me and the wall** see BEDPOST. **drive someone up the wall** informal make someone very irritated or angry. **go to the wall** informal **1** (of a business) go out of business; fail. **2** support someone or something, no matter what the cost to oneself: *the tendency for poets to go to the wall for their beliefs.* **go up the wall** informal become very angry in reaction to something: *this causes the dog to go up the wall and bark his head off.* **hit the wall** (of an athlete) experience a sudden loss of energy in a long race. **off the wall** N. Amer. informal **1** eccentric or unconventional. **2** angry: *the president was off the wall about the article.* **walls have ears** proverb be careful what you say as people may be eavesdropping. **wall-to-wall** (of a carpet) fitted to cover an entire floor. ▪ informal very numerous or extensive: *wall-to-wall media coverage.*
– DERIVATIVES **wall-less** adjective.
– ORIGIN Old English, from Latin *vallum* 'rampart', from *vallus* 'stake'.

wallaby ▸ noun (pl. **wallabies**) an Australasian marsupial that is similar to, but smaller than, a kangaroo. ● Family Macropodidae: several genera and numerous species. ▪ (**the Wallabies**) informal the Australian international rugby union team.
– PHRASES **on the wallaby (track)** Austral./NZ informal, dated (of a person) unemployed and having no fixed address.
– ORIGIN early 19th cent.: from Dharuk *walabi* or *waliba.*

Wallace[1], Alfred Russel (1823–1913), English naturalist and a founder of zoogeography. He independently formulated a theory of the origin of species very similar to that of Charles Darwin.

Wallace[2], (Richard Horatio) Edgar (1875–1932), English novelist, screenwriter, and dramatist, noted for his crime novels.

Wallace[3], Sir William (*c.*1270–1305), Scottish national hero. He was a leader of Scottish resistance to Edward I, defeating the English army at Stirling in 1297. After Edward's second invasion of Scotland in 1298 Wallace was defeated and subsequently executed.

Wallacea /wɒˈleɪsɪə/ Zoology a zoogeographical area constituting a transition zone between the Oriental and Australian regions, east of Wallace's line. It is generally held to comprise Sulawesi and other islands between the two continental shelves.
– DERIVATIVES **Wallacean** adjective.
– ORIGIN 1920s: from the name of A. R. *Wallace* (see WALLACE[1]).

Wallace's line Zoology a hypothetical line, proposed by Alfred Russel Wallace, marking the boundary between the Oriental and Australian zoogeographical regions. Wallace's line is now placed along the continental shelf of SE Asia. To the west of the line Asian mammals predominate, while to the east of it the fauna is dominated by marsupials.

Wallachia /wɒˈleɪkɪə/ (also **Walachia**) a former principality of SE Europe, between the Danube and the Transylvanian Alps. In 1861 it was united with Moldavia to form Romania.
– DERIVATIVES **Wallachian** adjective & noun.
– ORIGIN based on a variant of VLACH.

wallah /ˈwɒlə/ ▸ noun [in combination or with modifier] Indian or informal a person concerned or involved with a specified thing or business: *a rickshaw-wallah.* ▪ a native or inhabitant of a specified place: *Bombay wallahs.*
– ORIGIN from the Hindi suffix *-vālā* 'doer' (commonly interpreted in the sense 'fellow'), from Sanskrit *pālaka* 'keeper'.

wallaroo /ˌwɒləˈruː/ ▸ noun a large stocky kangaroo found in hilly country in Australia. ● Genus *Macropus,* family Macropodidae: two species, in particular the **common wallaroo** (*M. robustus*).
– ORIGIN early 19th cent.: from Dharuk *walaru.*

Wallasey /ˈwɒləsi/ a town in NW England on the Wirral Peninsula; pop. 58,400 (est. 2009).

wall bar ▸ noun (usu. **wall bars**) Brit. one of a set of parallel horizontal bars attached to the wall of a gymnasium, on which exercises are performed.

wallboard ▸ noun [mass noun] chiefly N. Amer. a type of board made from wood pulp, plaster, or other material, used for covering walls and ceilings. ▪ [count noun] a piece of wallboard.

wall brown ▸ noun a brown Eurasian butterfly with orange markings on the wings, which breeds on grasses. ● *Lasiommata megera,* subfamily Satyrinae, family Nymphalidae.

wallchart ▸ noun a chart or poster for display on a wall as a teaching aid or source of information.

wallcovering ▸ noun [mass noun] material such as wallpaper or textured fabric used as a decorative covering for interior walls.

wallcreeper ▸ noun a Eurasian songbird related to the nuthatches, having mainly grey plumage with broad bright red wings, and living among rocks in mountainous country. ● *Tichodroma muraria,* family Sittidae (or Tichodromadidae).

wall cress ▸ noun another term for ARABIS.

walled garden ▸ noun a garden enclosed by high walls. ▪ Computing & Telecommunications a restricted range of information to which subscribers to a particular service are limited.

Wallenberg /ˈvɑːlənbəːɡ/, Raoul (1912–?), Swedish diplomat. In 1944 in Budapest he helped many thousands of Jews to escape death by issuing them with Swedish passports. In 1945 he was arrested by Soviet forces and imprisoned in Moscow. Although the Soviet authorities stated that Wallenberg had died in prison in 1947, his fate remains uncertain.

Waller /ˈwɒlə/, Fats (1904–43), American jazz pianist, songwriter, bandleader, and singer; born *Thomas Wright Waller.* He was the foremost exponent of the New York 'stride school' of piano playing.

wallet ▸ noun a pocket-sized flat folding case for holding money and plastic cards. ▪ archaic a bag for holding provisions, especially when travelling, typically used by pedlars and pilgrims.
– ORIGIN late Middle English (denoting a bag for provisions): probably via Anglo-Norman French from a Germanic word related to WELL[2]. The current sense (originally US) dates from the mid 19th cent.

wall eye ▸ noun **1** an eye with a streaked or opaque white iris. ▪ an eye squinting outwards.
2 (**walleye**) a North American pikeperch with large, opaque silvery eyes. It is a commercially valuable food fish and a popular sporting fish. ● *Stizostedion vitreum,* family Percidae.
– DERIVATIVES **wall-eyed** adjective.
– ORIGIN early 16th cent.: back-formation from earlier *wall-eyed,* from Old Norse *vagleygr;* related to Icelandic *vagl* 'film over the eye'.

wallflower ▸ noun **1** a southern European plant with fragrant yellow, orange-red, dark red, or brown flowers that bloom in early spring. ● *Cheiranthus cheiri,* family Cruciferae.
2 informal a shy or excluded person at a dance or party, especially a girl without a partner.

wall game (also **Eton wall game**) ▸ noun (in the UK) an early form of football played traditionally at Eton College, in which, in a series of scrimmages, players attempt to take the ball past the opposing team while keeping the ball against a wall.

wall hanging ▸ noun a large decorative piece of fabric or other material hung on the wall of a room.

wall-hung ▸ adjective another term for WALL-MOUNTED.

walling ▸ noun [mass noun] **1** a length of wall: *the castle's high perimeter walling.* ▪ the material from which a wall is built.
2 the action of building a wall.

Wallis, Sir Barnes Neville (1887–1979), English inventor. His designs include the bouncing bomb used against the Ruhr dams in Germany in the Second World War.

Wallis and Futuna Islands /fəˈtjuːnə/ an overseas territory of France comprising two groups of islands to the west of Samoa in the central Pacific; pop. 15,300 (est. 2009); capital, Mata-Utu.

wall knot ▸ noun another term for WALE KNOT.

wall lizard ▸ noun a small brownish-grey Eurasian lizard which typically has black and white bars on the tail, frequently seen on walls and rocks. ● Genus *Podarcis,* family Lacertidae: several species, in particular *P. muralis.*

wall-mounted ▸ adjective fixed to a wall.

Wall of Death ▸ noun a fairground sideshow in which a motorcyclist uses gravitational force to ride around the inside walls of a vertical cylinder.

Walloon /wɒˈluːn/ ▸ noun **1** a member of a people who speak a French dialect and live in southern and eastern Belgium and neighbouring parts of France. Compare with FLEMING[3].
2 [mass noun] the French dialect spoken by the Walloons.
▸ adjective of or concerning the Walloons or their language.
– ORIGIN from French *Wallon,* from medieval Latin *Wallo(n-),* from the same Germanic origin as WELSH.

wallop informal ▸ verb (**wallops, walloping, walloped**) [with obj.] strike or hit very hard: *they walloped the back of his head with a stick* | figurative *they were tired of getting walloped with income taxes.* ▪ heavily defeat (an opponent).
▸ noun **1** a heavy blow or punch. ▪ [in sing.] chiefly N. Amer. a powerful effect: *the script packs a wallop.*
2 [mass noun] Brit. alcoholic drink, especially beer.
– ORIGIN Middle English (as a noun denoting a horse's gallop): from Old Northern French *walop* (noun), *waloper* (verb), perhaps from a Germanic phrase meaning 'run well', from the bases of WELL[1] and LEAP. Compare with GALLOP. From 'gallop' the senses 'bubbling noise of a boiling liquid' and then 'sound of a clumsy movement' arose, leading to the current senses.

walloper ▸ noun informal **1** a person or thing that wallops someone or something.

W

2 N. English a strikingly large person or thing. ■ a blatant lie.
3 Austral. a policeman.

walloping informal ▸ **noun** a beating: *she gave him a good walloping.*
▸ **adjective** [attrib.] large and powerful: *a walloping shock.*

wallow ▸ **verb** [no obj.] **1** (chiefly of large mammals) roll about or lie in mud or water, especially to keep cool or avoid biting insects: *there were watering places where buffalo liked to wallow.* ■ (of a boat or aircraft) roll from side to side: *a ship* ***wallowing in*** *stormy seas.*
2 (**wallow in**) (of a person) indulge in an unrestrained way in (something that one finds pleasurable): *I was wallowing in the luxury of the hotel* | *he had been wallowing in self-pity.*
▸ **noun 1** an act of wallowing: *a* ***wallow in*** *nostalgia.*
2 a depression containing mud or shallow water, formed by the wallowing of large mammals.
– DERIVATIVES **wallower** noun.
– ORIGIN Old English *walwian* 'to roll about', of Germanic origin, from an Indo-European root shared by Latin *volvere* 'to roll'.

wall painting ▸ **noun** a painting made directly on a wall, such as a fresco or mural.

wallpaper ▸ **noun** [mass noun] paper that is pasted in vertical strips over the walls of a room to provide a decorative surface. ■ something, especially music, that provides a bland or unvaried background: *soothing sonic wallpaper.* ■ an optional background pattern or picture on a computer screen.
▸ **verb** [with obj.] apply wallpaper to (a wall or room).

wall pass ▸ **noun** Soccer a short pass to a teammate who immediately returns it; a one-two.

wall pepper ▸ **noun** the yellow stonecrop (plant).

wall plate ▸ **noun** a timber laid horizontally in or on a wall as a support for a girder, rafter, or joist.

wall plug ▸ **noun** a fibre or plastic dowel inserted into a drilled hole to provide a gripping base for a screw.

wall pocket ▸ **noun** a receptacle for small household items, designed to hang on a wall. ■ a vase having one flat side, designed to be hung on a wall.

wall rock ▸ **noun** Geology the rock adjacent to or enclosing a vein, hydrothermal ore deposit, fault, or other geological feature.

wall rocket ▸ **noun** a yellow-flowered European plant which resembles mustard and emits a foul smell when crushed. ● *Diplotaxis muralis*, family Cruciferae.

wall rue ▸ **noun** a small delicate spleenwort (fern) which resembles rue, growing on walls and rocks in both Europe and North America and sensitive to atmospheric pollution. ● *Asplenium ruta-muraria*, family Aspleniaceae.

Wall Street a street at the south end of Manhattan, where the New York Stock Exchange and other leading American financial institutions are located. ■ used allusively to refer to the American money market or financial interests.
– ORIGIN named after a wooden stockade which was built in 1653 around the original Dutch settlement of New Amsterdam.

Wall Street Crash the collapse of prices on the New York Stock Exchange in October 1929, a major factor in the early stages of the Depression.

wall tent ▸ **noun** N. Amer. a tent with nearly perpendicular sides; a frame tent.

wallwasher ▸ **noun** a lighting fixture designed to illuminate a wall evenly without lighting the floor.

wally ▸ **noun** (pl. **wallies**) Brit. informal a silly or inept person.
– ORIGIN 1960s: perhaps a shortened form of the given name *Walter*. There are many theories of the origin: one story tells of a *Wally* who became separated from companions at a 1960s pop festival; the name, announced many times over a loudspeaker, was taken up as a chant by the crowd.

W

walnut ▸ **noun 1** the large wrinkled edible seed of a deciduous tree, consisting of two halves contained within a hard shell which is enclosed in a green fruit.
2 (also **walnut tree**) the tall tree which produces walnuts, with compound leaves and valuable ornamental timber that is used chiefly in cabinetmaking and gun stocks. ● Genus *Juglans*, family Juglandaceae: several species, including the **common** (or **English**) **walnut** (*J. regia*).
– ORIGIN late Old English *walh-hnutu*, from a Germanic compound meaning 'foreign nut'.

Walpole[1] /ˈwɔːlpəʊl/, Horace, 4th Earl of Orford (1717–97), English writer and Whig politician, son of Sir Robert Walpole. He wrote *The Castle of Otranto* (1764), one of the first Gothic novels.

Walpole[2] /ˈwɔːlpəʊl/, Sir Hugh (Seymour) (1884–1941), British novelist, born in New Zealand. He is best known for *The Herries Chronicle* (1930–3), a historical sequence set in the Lake District.

Walpole[3] /ˈwɔːlpəʊl/, Sir Robert, 1st Earl of Orford (1676–1745), British Whig statesman, First Lord of the Treasury and Chancellor of the Exchequer 1715–17 and 1721–42, father of Horace Walpole. Walpole is generally regarded as the first British Prime Minister, having presided over the cabinet for George I and George II.

Walpurgisnacht /valˈpʊrgɪsnaxt/ ▸ **noun** German for **WALPURGIS NIGHT**.

Walpurgis night /valˈpʊəgɪs/ ▸ **noun** (in German folklore) the night of April 30 (May Day's eve), when witches meet on the Brocken mountain and hold revels with the Devil.
– ORIGIN named after St *Walburga*, an English nun who in the 8th cent. helped to convert the Germans to Christianity; her feast day coincided with an ancient pagan festival whose rites were intended to give protection from witchcraft.

Walras' law /ˈvalrɑːs/ ▸ **noun** Economics a law stating that the total value of goods and money supplied equals that of goods and money demanded.
– ORIGIN 1940s: named after M. E. Léon *Walras* (1834–1910), French economist.

walrus ▸ **noun** a large gregarious marine mammal related to the eared seals, having two large downward-pointing tusks and found in the Arctic Ocean. ● *Odobenus rosmarus*, the only member of the family Odobenidae.
– ORIGIN early 18th cent.: probably from Dutch *walrus*, perhaps by an inversion of elements (influenced by *walvis* 'whale fish') of Old Norse *hrosshvalr* 'horse whale'.

walrus moustache ▸ **noun** a long, thick, drooping moustache.

Walsall /ˈwɔːlsɔːl, ˈwɒl-/ an industrial town in the west Midlands; pop. 172,100 (est. 2009).

Walsingham /ˈwɔːlsɪŋəm, ˈwɒl-/, Sir Francis (*c.*1530–90), English politician. As Secretary of State to Queen Elizabeth I he developed a spy network that gathered information about Catholic plots against Elizabeth I.

Walter Mitty ▸ **noun** [often as modifier] a person who fantasizes about a life much more exciting and glamorous than their own: *my client is very much a Walter Mitty character.*
– ORIGIN the hero of the story *The Secret Life of Walter Mitty* (by James Thurber, 1939), who indulged in extravagant daydreams of his own triumphs.

Walton[1] /ˈwɔːlt(ə)n, ˈwɒl-/, Ernest Thomas Sinton (1903–95), Irish physicist. In 1932 he succeeded, with Sir John Cockcroft, in splitting the atom. Nobel Prize for Physics (1951, shared with Cockcroft).

Walton[2] /ˈwɔːlt(ə)n, ˈwɒl-/, Izaak (1593–1683), English writer. He is chiefly known for *The Compleat Angler* (1653; largely rewritten, 1655) which combines practical information on fishing with folklore, interspersed with pastoral songs and ballads.

Walton[3] /ˈwɔːlt(ə)n, ˈwɒl-/, Sir William (Turner) (1902–83), English composer. Notable works: *Façade* (1921–3, a setting of poems by Edith Sitwell for recitation), the oratorio *Belshazzar's Feast* (1930–1), and film scores for three Shakespeare plays and the film *The Battle of Britain* (1969).

waltz /wɔːl(t)s, wɒl-/ ▸ **noun** a dance in triple time performed by a couple, who turn rhythmically round and round as they progress around the dance floor. ■ a piece of music written for or in the style of a waltz.
▸ **verb** [no obj.] **1** dance a waltz. ■ [with obj. and adverbial of direction] guide (someone) in or as if in a waltz: *he waltzed her round the table.*
2 [with adverbial of direction] act casually, confidently, or inconsiderately: *you can't waltz in here and bark orders at me.* ■ achieve something without difficulty: *the car has waltzed through test after test* | *it is the third time that he has* ***waltzed off with*** *the award.*
– PHRASES **waltz Matilda** see **MATILDA**[2].
– ORIGIN late 18th cent.: from German *Walzer*, from *walzen* 'revolve'.

waltzer ▸ **noun** a person who dances the waltz. ■ a fairground ride in which cars spin round as they are carried round an undulating track.

Walvis Bay /ˈwɔːlvɪs/ a port in Namibia; pop. 55,000 (est. 2009). It was administratively an exclave of the former Cape Province, South Africa until it was transferred to Namibia in 1994.

wambenger /ˈwɒmbɛŋə/ ▸ **noun** another term for **PHASCOGALE**.
– ORIGIN perhaps from Nyungar.

Wampanoag /ˌwɑːmpəˈnəʊag/ ▸ **noun** (pl. **same** or **Wampanoags**) a member of a confederacy of American Indian peoples of SE Massachusetts.
▸ **adjective** relating to or denoting the Wampanoag.
– ORIGIN Narragansett, literally 'easterners'.

wampum /ˈwɒmpəm/ ▸ **noun** [mass noun] historical small cylindrical beads made by North American Indians from shells, strung together and worn as decoration or used as money.
– ORIGIN from Algonquian *wampumpeag*, from *wap* 'white' + *umpe* 'string' + the plural suffix *-ag*.

WAN ▸ **abbreviation** ■ Computing wide area network. ■ Nigeria (international vehicle registration). [from *West Africa Nigeria*.]

wan /wɒn/ ▸ **adjective** (of a person's complexion or appearance) pale and giving the impression of illness or exhaustion: *she was looking wan and bleary-eyed.* ■ (of light) pale; weak: *the wan dawn light.* ■ (of a smile) lacking enthusiasm or energy. ■ literary (of the sea) without lustre; dark and gloomy.
– DERIVATIVES **wanly** adverb, **wanness** /ˈwɒnnɪs/ noun.
– ORIGIN Old English *wann* 'dark, black', of unknown origin.

wananchi /wəˈnantʃi/ ▸ **noun** [mass noun] (in East Africa) the ordinary people; the public.
– ORIGIN Kiswahili, plural of *mwananchi* 'inhabitant, citizen'.

wand ▸ **noun 1** a long, thin stick or rod, in particular: ■ a rod thought to have magic properties, used in casting spells or performing conjuring tricks: *the fairy godmother waves her magic wand and grants the heroine's wishes.* ■ a staff or rod held as a symbol of office. ■ informal a conductor's baton. ■ a small stick with a brush at one end used to apply mascara.
2 a handheld electronic device which can be passed over a barcode to read the encoded data. ■ a device emitting a laser beam, used especially to create a pointer on a projected image or text. ■ each of a pair of handheld lights used by a person on the ground to guide a taxiing aircraft at night.
3 (**wands**) one of the suits in some tarot packs, corresponding to batons in others.
– ORIGIN Middle English: from Old Norse *vǫndr*, probably of Germanic origin and related to **WEND** and **WIND**[2].

wander ▸ **verb** [no obj.] **1** [with adverbial of direction] walk or move in a leisurely or aimless way: *I wandered through the narrow streets.* ■ [with obj.] travel aimlessly through or over (an area): *he found her wandering the streets.* ■ (of a road or river) meander.
2 move slowly away from a fixed point or place: *please don't* ***wander off*** *again* | figurative *his attention had wandered.*
3 be unfaithful to one's regular sexual partner.
▸ **noun** an act or instance of wandering: *she'd go on wanders like that in her nightgown.*
– ORIGIN Old English *wandrian*, of West Germanic origin; related to **WEND** and **WIND**[2].

wanderer ▸ **noun** a person who travels aimlessly; a traveller: *he is a longtime seaman, a rootless wanderer.*

wandering ▸ **adjective** travelling aimlessly from place to place; itinerant: *a wandering preacher.*

wandering albatross ▸ **noun** a very large albatross of southern oceans, having white plumage with black wings and a wingspan of up to 3.3 m. ● *Diomedea exulans*, family Diomedeidae.

wandering Jew ▸ **noun 1** a legendary man said to have been condemned by Christ to wander the earth until the Second Coming. ■ a person who never settles down.
2 a tender trailing tradescantia, typically having striped leaves which are suffused with purple. ● Genus *Tradescantia*, family Commelinaceae: *T. albiflora* and *T. pendula* (formerly *Zebrina pendula*).

wanderings ▸ **plural noun** leisurely or aimless travels; journeys from place to place: *his wanderings in the Derbyshire dales laid the foundations for his lifelong love of landscape.*

wandering sailor ▸ **noun** either of two creeping plants: ● creeping jenny. ● ivy-leaved toadflax. See **TOADFLAX**.

Wanderjahr /ˈvandəjɑː/ ▶ **noun** (pl. **Wanderjahre** /-rə/) chiefly N. Amer. a year spent travelling abroad, typically immediately before or after a university or college course.
– ORIGIN late 19th cent.: German, literally 'wander year'.

wanderlust ▶ **noun** [mass noun] a strong desire to travel: *a man consumed by wanderlust.*
– ORIGIN early 20th cent.: from German *Wanderlust*.

wanderoo /ˌwɒndəˈruː/ ▶ **noun** (in Sri Lanka) a leaf monkey or langur. ● Genus *Presbytis*, family Cercopithecidae: the purple-faced leaf monkey (*P. vetulus*), or the hanuman (*P. entellus*).
– ORIGIN late 17th cent.: from Sinhalese *wanderu* 'monkey'.

Wandervogel /ˈvandəˌfəʊɡəl/, German /ˈvandɐˌfoːɡl/ ▶ **noun** (pl. **Wandervögel** /-føːɡəl/, German /-føːɡl/) a member of a German youth organization founded at the end of the 19th century for the promotion of outdoor activities and folk culture.
– ORIGIN German, literally 'bird of passage'.

wane[1] ▶ **verb** [no obj.] **1** (of the moon) have a progressively smaller part of its visible surface illuminated, so that it appears to decrease in size.
2 (of a state or feeling) decrease in vigour or extent; become weaker: *confidence in the dollar waned.*
– PHRASES **on the wane** becoming weaker or less extensive: *the epidemic was on the wane.*
– ORIGIN Old English *wanian* 'lessen', of Germanic origin; related to Latin *vanus* 'vain'.

wane[2] ▶ **noun** the amount by which a plank or log is bevelled or falls short of a squared shape.
– DERIVATIVES **waney** adjective.
– ORIGIN mid 17th cent.: from WANE[1].

Wanganui /ˌwɒŋəˈnuːi/ a port in New Zealand, on the west coast of the North Island; pop. 39,000 (est. 2006).

wangle informal ▶ **verb** [with obj.] obtain (something) by using persuasion or clever manipulation: *I wangled an invitation to her flat | I think we should be able to* **wangle it** *so that you can start tomorrow.*
▶ **noun** an act or an instance of obtaining something in such a way.
– DERIVATIVES **wangler** noun.
– ORIGIN late 19th cent. (first recorded as printers' slang): of unknown origin; perhaps based on the verb WAGGLE.

wank Brit. vulgar slang ▶ **verb** [no obj.] (also **wank off**) (typically of a man) masturbate.
▶ **noun** an act of masturbating.
– ORIGIN 1940s: of unknown origin.

Wankel engine /ˈwaŋk(ə)l, ˈvaŋ-/ ▶ **noun** a rotary internal-combustion engine in which a curvilinear, triangular, eccentrically pivoted piston rotates in an elliptical chamber, forming three combustion spaces that vary in volume as it turns.
– ORIGIN 1960s: named after Felix *Wankel* (1902–88), German engineer.

wanker ▶ **noun** Brit. vulgar slang a contemptible person (used as a generalized term of abuse).

Wankie /ˈwɑːŋki/ former name (until 1982) for HWANGE.

wanky ▶ **adjective** Brit. vulgar slang contemptible, worthless, or stupid.

wanna informal ▶ **contraction** want to; want a.

wannabe /ˈwɒnəbi/ ▶ **noun** informal, derogatory a person who tries to be like someone else or to fit in with a particular group of people: *a star-struck wannabe.*
– ORIGIN 1980s: representing a pronunciation of *want to be*.

want ▶ **verb 1** [with obj.] have a desire to possess or do (something); wish for: *I want an apple* | [with infinitive] *we want to go to the beach* | [with obj. and infinitive] *she wanted me to leave* | [no obj.] *I'll give you a lift into town if you want.* ■ wish to speak to (someone): *Tony wants me in the studio.* ■ **(be wanted)** (of a suspected criminal) be sought by the police for questioning: *he is wanted by the police in connection with an arms theft.* ■ desire (someone) sexually: *I've wanted you since the first moment I saw you.* ■ [no obj.] **(want in/into/out)** informal, chiefly N. Amer. desire to be in or out of a particular place or situation: *if anyone wants out, there's the door.*
2 [with infinitive] informal should or need to do something: *you don't want to believe everything you hear.* ■ [with present participle] chiefly Brit. (of a thing) require to be attended to in a specified way: *the wheel wants greasing.*
3 [no obj.] literary lack something desirable or essential: *you shall* **want for nothing** *while you are with me.* ■ [with obj.] archaic (chiefly used in expressions of time) lack or be short of (a specified amount or thing): *it wanted twenty minutes to midnight.*
▶ **noun 1** [mass noun] a lack or deficiency of something: *Victorian houses which are* **in want of** *repair | for* **want of** *a better location we ate our picnic in the cemetery.* ■ the state of being poor and in need of essentials; poverty: *freedom from want.*
2 a desire for something: *the expression of our wants and desires.*
– DERIVATIVES **wanter** noun.
– ORIGIN Middle English: the noun from Old Norse *vant*, neuter of *vanr* 'lacking'; the verb from Old Norse *vanta* 'be lacking'. The original notion of 'lack' was early extended to 'need' and from this developed the sense 'desire'.

want ad ▶ **noun** N. Amer. informal a classified advertisement in a newspaper or magazine; a small ad.

wanting ▶ **adjective** [predic.] lacking in a required or necessary quality: *they weren't wanting in confidence | the English batting technique has been* **found wanting**. ■ not existing; absent: *mandibles are wanting in many of these insects.* ■ informal deficient in intelligence.

wanton ▶ **adjective 1** (of a cruel or violent action) deliberate and unprovoked: *sheer wanton vandalism.*
2 (especially of a woman) sexually immodest or promiscuous.
3 literary growing profusely; luxuriant: *where wanton ivy twines.* ■ lively; playful: *a wanton fawn.*
▶ **noun** archaic a sexually immodest or promiscuous woman.
▶ **verb** [no obj.] archaic or literary **1** play; frolic.
2 behave in a sexually immodest or promiscuous way.
– DERIVATIVES **wantonly** adverb, **wantonness** noun.
– ORIGIN Middle English *wantowen* 'rebellious, lacking discipline', from *wan-* 'badly' + Old English *togen* 'trained' (related to TEAM and TOW[1]).

WAP ▶ **abbreviation** Wireless Application Protocol, a set of protocols enabling mobile phones and other radio devices to be connected to the Internet.

wapentake /ˈwɒp(ə)nteɪk, ˈwap-/ ▶ **noun** historical (in the UK) a subdivision of certain northern and midland English counties, corresponding to a hundred in other counties.
– ORIGIN late Old English *wǣpen(ge)tæc*, from Old Norse *vápnatak*, from *vápn* 'weapon' + *taka* 'take', perhaps with reference to voting in an assembly by a show of weapons.

wapiti /ˈwɒpɪti/ ▶ **noun** (pl. **wapitis**) a red deer of a large race native to North America. Also called ELK in North America. ● *Cervus elaphus canadensis*, family Cervidae; it is sometimes treated as a separate species (*C. canadensis*).
– ORIGIN early 19th cent.: from Shawnee, literally 'white rump'.

waqf /vʌkf/ ▶ **noun** (pl. **same**) an endowment made by a Muslim to a religious, educational, or charitable cause.
– ORIGIN from Arabic, literally 'stoppage, immobilization (of ownership of property)', from *waqafa* 'come to a standstill'.

war ▶ **noun** [mass noun] a state of armed conflict between different countries or different groups within a country: *Japan* **declared war on** *Germany | the two countries were* **at war** *for the next eight years* | [count noun] *I fought in two wars.* ■ a state of competition or hostility between different people or groups: *she was* **at war with** *her parents* | [count noun] *a price war among tour operators.* ■ a sustained campaign against an undesirable situation or activity: *the authorities are* **waging war against** *smuggling* | [count noun] *a* **war on** *drugs.*
▶ **verb (wars, warring, warred)** [no obj.] engage in a war: *small states warred against each another* | figurative *conflicting emotions warred within her.*
– PHRASES **go to war** declare, begin, or see active service in a war. **go to the wars** archaic serve as a soldier. **be in the wars** informal be (or have been) injured: *Roebuck continues to be in the wars and suffered a broken jaw.* **war clouds** used to refer to a threatening situation of instability in international relations: *the war clouds were looming.* **war of attrition** a prolonged period of conflict during which each side seeks to gradually wear down the other by a series of small-scale actions. **war of nerves** see NERVE. **war of words** a prolonged, often acrimonious, debate. **war to end all wars** a war, especially the First World War, regarded as making subsequent wars unnecessary.
– ORIGIN late Old English *werre*, from an Anglo-Norman French variant of Old French *guerre*, from a Germanic base shared by WORSE.

waragi /ˈwaraɡi/ ▶ **noun** [mass noun] (in Uganda) a strong alcoholic drink made from bananas or cassava.
– ORIGIN from Kiswahili *wargi*.

war artist ▶ **noun** an artist employed to draw or paint events and situations arising during a war.

waratah /ˈwɔːrətɑː, ˌwɒrəˈtɑː/ ▶ **noun** an Australian shrub which bears slender leathery leaves and clusters of crimson flowers. ● Genus *Telopea*, family Proteaceae: several species, in particular *T. speciosissima*, which is the emblem of New South Wales.
– ORIGIN late 18th cent.: from Dharuk *warata*.

war baby ▶ **noun** a child born in wartime, especially one fathered by a serviceman.

Warbeck /ˈwɔːbɛk/, Perkin (1474–99), Flemish claimant to the English throne. In an attempt to overthrow Henry VII, he claimed to be one of the Princes in the Tower. After attempting to begin a revolt he was captured and imprisoned in the Tower of London in 1497 and later executed.

warbird ▶ **noun** a vintage military aircraft.

warble[1] ▶ **verb** [no obj.] (of a bird) sing softly and with a succession of constantly changing notes: *larks were warbling in the trees.* ■ (of a person) sing in a trilling or quavering voice: *he warbled in an implausible soprano.*
▶ **noun** a warbling sound or utterance.
– ORIGIN late Middle English (as a noun in the sense 'melody'): from Old Northern French *werble* (noun), *werbler* (verb), of Germanic origin; related to WHIRL.

warble[2] ▶ **noun** a swelling or abscess beneath the skin on the back of cattle, horses, and other mammals, caused by the presence of the larva of a warble fly. ■ the larva of the warble fly.
– ORIGIN late Middle English: of uncertain origin.

warble fly ▶ **noun** a large fly which lays its eggs on the legs of mammals such as cattle and horses. The larvae migrate internally to the host's back, where they form a small lump with a breathing hole, dropping to the ground later when fully grown. ● Genus *Hypoderma*, family Oestridae: several species, including the widespread *H. bovis*.

warbler ▶ **noun 1** any of a number of small insectivorous songbirds that typically have a warbling song: ● an Old World bird of the family Sylviidae, which includes the blackcap, whitethroat, and chiffchaff. ● (also **wood warbler**) N. Amer. a New World bird of the family Parulidae. ● Austral./NZ an Australasian bird of the family Acanthizidae.
2 informal a person who sings in a trilling or quavering voice.

warbonnet ▶ **noun** an elongated slender fish of the North Pacific that has branched tentacles above the eye, over the back of the head, and at the front of the long dorsal fin. ● Genus *Chirolophis*, family Stichaeidae: several species.

war bonnet ▶ **noun** see BONNET (sense 1).

war bride ▶ **noun** a woman who marries a man whom she met while he was on active service.

Warburg[1] /ˈwɔːbəːɡ/, German /ˈvaːɐbʊrk/, Aby (Moritz) (1866–1929), German art historian. From 1905 he built up a library in Hamburg, dedicated to preserving the classical heritage of Western culture. In 1933 it was transferred to England and housed in the Warburg Institute (part of the University of London).

Warburg[2] /ˈwɔːbəːɡ/, German /ˈvaːɐbʊrk/, Otto Heinrich (1883–1970), German biochemist. He pioneered the use of the techniques of chemistry for biochemical investigations, especially for his work on intracellular respiration. Nobel Prize for Physiology or Medicine (1931); he was prevented by the Nazi regime from accepting a second one in 1944 because of his Jewish ancestry.

warby /ˈwɔːbi/ ▶ **adjective** Austral. informal shabby or decrepit: *a warby, unshaven young man.*
– ORIGIN 1920s: probably from *warb* 'larva of the warble fly' + -Y[1].

war chest ▶ **noun** a reserve of funds used for fighting a war. ■ a sum of money used for conducting a campaign or business: *the party's election war chest.*

war correspondent ▶ **noun** a journalist who reports from a scene of war.

war crime ▶ **noun** an act carried out during the conduct of a war that violates accepted international rules of war.
– DERIVATIVES **war criminal** noun.

W

war cry ▶ noun a call made to rally soldiers for battle or to gather together participants in a campaign.

Ward, Mrs Humphry (1851–1920), English writer and anti-suffrage campaigner, niece of Matthew Arnold; née *Mary Augusta Arnold*. She is best known for several novels dealing with social and religious themes, especially *Robert Elsmere* (1888). An active opponent of the women's suffrage movement, she became the first president of the Anti-Suffrage League in 1908.

ward ▶ noun **1** a separate room in a hospital, typically one allocated to a particular type of patient: *a children's ward*.
2 an administrative division of a city or borough that typically elects and is represented by a councillor or councillors.
3 a child or young person under the care and control of a guardian appointed by their parents or a court. ■ [mass noun] archaic the state of being in the care of a guardian: *the ward and care of the Crown*.
4 (usu. **wards**) any of the internal ridges or bars in a lock which prevent the turning of any key which does not have grooves of corresponding form or size. ■ the corresponding grooves in the bit of a key.
5 [mass noun] archaic the action of keeping a lookout for danger: *I saw them keeping ward at one of those huge gates*.
6 historical an area of ground enclosed by the encircling walls of a fortress or castle.
▶ verb [with obj.] **1** admit (a patient) to a hospital ward.
2 archaic guard; protect: *it was his duty to ward the king*.
– PHRASES **ward of court** a child or young person for whom a guardian has been appointed by the Court of Chancery or who has become directly subject to the authority of that court.
– PHRASAL VERBS **ward someone/thing off** prevent someone or something from harming or affecting one: *she put up a hand as if to ward him off*.
– DERIVATIVES **wardship** noun.
– ORIGIN Old English *weard* (in sense 5 of the noun, also 'body of guards'), *weardian* 'keep safe, guard', of Germanic origin; reinforced in Middle English by Old Northern French *warde* (noun), *warder* (verb) 'guard'.

-ward (also **-wards**) ▶ suffix added to nouns of place or destination and to adverbs of direction: **1** (usu. **-wards**) (forming adverbs) towards the specified place or direction: *eastwards* | *homewards*.
2 (usu. **-ward**) (forming adjectives) turned or tending towards: *onward* | *upward*.
– ORIGIN Old English *-weard*, from a Germanic base meaning 'turn'.

war dance ▶ noun a ceremonial dance performed before a battle or to celebrate victory.

warden ▶ noun a person responsible for the supervision of a particular place or activity or for enforcing the regulations associated with it: *the warden of a nature reserve* | *an air-raid warden*. ■ Brit. the head of certain schools, colleges, or other institutions. ■ a prison officer. ■ chiefly N. Amer. a prison governor.
– DERIVATIVES **wardenship** noun.
– ORIGIN Middle English (originally denoting a guardian or protector): from Anglo-Norman French and Old Northern French *wardein*, variant of Old French *guarden* 'guardian'.

warder ▶ noun chiefly Brit. a guard in a prison.
– ORIGIN late Middle English (denoting a watchman or sentinel): from Anglo-Norman French *wardere*, from Old Northern French *warder* 'to guard'. The current sense dates from the mid 19th cent.

ward heeler ▶ noun US informal, chiefly derogatory a person who assists in a political campaign by canvassing votes for a party and performing menial tasks for its leaders.

Wardour Street /ˈwɔːdə/ ▶ noun used allusively to refer to the British film industry.
– ORIGIN the name of a street in central London, now the site of the central offices of the British film industry.

W

wardress ▶ noun chiefly Brit. a female prison guard.

wardrobe ▶ noun a large, tall cupboard in which clothes may be hung or stored. ■ a person's entire collection of clothes: *her wardrobe is extensive*. ■ the costume department or costumes of a theatre or film company: [as modifier] *a wardrobe assistant*. ■ a department of a royal or noble household in charge of clothing.
– ORIGIN Middle English (in the sense 'private chamber'): from Old Northern French *warderobe*, variant of Old French *garderobe* (see GARDEROBE).

wardrobe malfunction ▶ noun informal an instance of a person accidentally exposing an intimate part of their body as a result of an article of clothing slipping out of position.

wardrobe mistress (or **wardrobe master**) ▶ noun a woman (or man) in charge of the making and organization of the costumes in a theatrical company.

wardrobe trunk ▶ noun chiefly N. Amer. a trunk fitted with rails and shelves for use as a travelling wardrobe.

wardroom ▶ noun a commissioned officers' mess on board a warship.

ward round ▶ noun visits paid by a doctor in a hospital to each of the patients in their care or in a particular ward or wards.

war drum ▶ noun a drum beaten as a summons or an accompaniment to battle.

-wards ▶ suffix variant spelling of **-WARD**.

ware[1] /wɛː/ ▶ noun [mass noun] [usu. with adj. or noun modifier] pottery, typically that of a specified type: *blue-and-white majolica ware* | (**wares**) *Minoan potters produced an astonishing variety of wares*. ■ manufactured articles of a specified type: *crystal ware* | *aluminium ware*. ■ (**wares**) articles offered for sale: *traders in the street markets displayed their wares*.
– ORIGIN Old English *waru* 'commodities', of Germanic origin, perhaps the same word as Scots *ware* 'cautiousness', and having the primary sense 'object of care'; related to **WARE**[3].

ware[2] /wɛː/ (also **'ware**) ▶ exclamation used as a warning cry, typically during a hunt.
– ORIGIN Old English *warian* 'be on one's guard', from a Germanic base meaning 'observe, take care'.

ware[3] /wɛː/ ▶ adjective [predic.] archaic aware: *thou speak'st wiser than thou art ware of*.
– ORIGIN Old English *wær*, from the Germanic base of **WARE**[2].

-ware ▶ combining form **1** denoting articles made of ceramic or used in cooking and serving food: *tableware* | *bakeware*.
2 denoting a kind of software: *groupware*.

warehou /ˈwɒrəˌhaʊ/ ▶ noun (pl. **same**) NZ a marine fish of coastal Australasian waters. See **SEA BREAM**.
– ORIGIN mid 19th cent.: from Maori.

warehouse /ˈwɛːhaʊs/ ▶ noun a large building where raw materials or manufactured goods may be stored prior to their distribution for sale. ■ a large wholesale or retail store: *a discount warehouse*.
▶ verb also /ˈwɛːhaʊz/ [with obj.] **1** store (goods) in a warehouse. ■ place (imported goods) in a bonded warehouse pending the payment of import duty.
2 N. Amer. informal place (a prisoner or a psychiatric patient) in a large, impersonal institution in which their problems are not satisfactorily addressed.

warehouse club ▶ noun an organization which operates from a large out-of-town store and sells goods in bulk at discounted prices to business and private customers who must first become club members.

warehouseman ▶ noun (pl. **warehousemen**) a person who is employed in, manages, or owns a warehouse.

warehouse party ▶ noun a large public party with dancing held in a warehouse or similar building, typically organized without official permission.

warehousing ▶ noun [mass noun] **1** the action or process of storing goods in a warehouse. ■ warehouses collectively.
2 Stock Exchange the building up of a holding of shares in a company by buying numerous small lots of shares in the names of nominees, in order to make a takeover bid while remaining anonymous.

war establishment ▶ noun the level of equipment and manning laid down for a military unit in wartime.

warez /wɛːz/ ▶ plural noun Computing, informal software that has been illegally copied and made available.
– ORIGIN 1990s: respelling of *wares*.

warfare ▶ noun [mass noun] engagement in or the activities involved in war or conflict: *guerrilla warfare*.

warfarin /ˈwɔːfərɪn/ ▶ noun [mass noun] a water-soluble compound with anticoagulant properties, used as a rat poison and in the treatment of thrombosis.
● A coumarin derivative; chem. formula: $C_{19}H_{16}O_4$.
– ORIGIN 1950s: from the initial letters of *Wisconsin Alumni Research Foundation* + *-arin* on the pattern of *coumarin*.

warfighter ▶ noun US a soldier in combat.

war game ▶ noun a military exercise carried out to test or improve tactical expertise. ■ a simulated military conflict carried out as a game, leisure activity, or exercise in personal development.
▶ verb [with obj.] (**war-game**) N. Amer. engage in (a campaign or course of action) using the strategies of a war game: *there seemed to be no point war-gaming an election 15 months away*.
– DERIVATIVES **war-gamer** noun, **war-gaming** noun.

war grave ▶ noun a grave of a member of the armed forces who has died on active service, especially one in a special cemetery that serves as a monument.

warhead ▶ noun the explosive head of a missile, torpedo, or similar weapon.

Warhol /ˈwɔːhəʊl/, Andy (*c.*1928–87), American painter, graphic artist, and film-maker; born *Andrew Warhola*. A major exponent of pop art, he achieved fame for a series of silk-screen prints and acrylic paintings of familiar objects (such as Campbell's soup tins) and famous people (such as Marilyn Monroe), treated with objectivity and precision.
– DERIVATIVES **Warholian** adjective.

warhorse ▶ noun (in historical contexts) a powerful horse ridden in a battle. ■ informal a soldier, politician, or sports player who has fought many campaigns or contests.

warily ▶ adverb cautiously; carefully: *they walk warily down the street, terrified of being caught*. ■ in a way that shows a lack of trust; suspiciously: *she looked at him warily*.

wariness ▶ noun [mass noun] caution about possible dangers or problems: *her mother's wariness of computers*. ■ lack of trust; suspicion: *they had all regarded her with wariness*.

Warka /wəˈkɑː/ Arabic name for **URUK**.

Warks. ▶ abbreviation Warwickshire.

warlike ▶ adjective disposed towards or threatening war; hostile: *a warlike clan*. ■ (of plans, preparations, or munitions) directed towards or prepared for war.

war loan ▶ noun [mass noun] stock issued by the British government to raise funds at a time of war.

warlock ▶ noun a man who practises witchcraft; a sorcerer.
– ORIGIN Old English *wǣrloga* 'traitor, scoundrel, monster', also 'the Devil', from *wǣr* 'covenant' + an element related to *lēogan* 'belie, deny'. From its application to the Devil, the word was transferred in Middle English to a person in league with the Devil, and hence a sorcerer. It was chiefly Scots until given wider currency by Sir Walter Scott.

warlord ▶ noun a military commander, especially an aggressive regional commander with individual autonomy.

Warlpiri /ˈwɔːlpəri/ ▶ noun [mass noun] an Australian Aboriginal language of Northern Territory, with about 2,800 speakers.

warm ▶ adjective **1** of or at a fairly or comfortably high temperature: *a warm September evening* | [as complement] *I walked quickly to keep warm*. ■ (of clothes or coverings) made of a material that helps the body to retain heat: *a warm winter coat*. ■ (of a soil) quick to absorb heat or retaining heat.
2 having or showing enthusiasm, affection, or kindness: *they exchanged warm, friendly smiles* | *a warm welcome*. ■ archaic characterized by lively or heated disagreement: *a warm debate arose*. ■ archaic sexually explicit or titillating.
3 (of a colour) containing red, yellow, or orange tones: *her fair colouring suited soft, warm shades*.
4 (of a scent or trail) fresh; strong. ■ [predic.] informal (especially in children's games) close to discovering something or guessing the correct answer: *we're getting warmer, sir*.
▶ verb make or become warm: [with obj.] *I stamped my feet to warm them up* | figurative *the film warmed our hearts* | [no obj.] *it's a bit chilly in here, but it'll soon warm up*. ■ [with obj.] informal spank (someone's buttocks).
▶ noun **1** (**the warm**) a warm place or area: *stay in the warm, I've made up the fire for you*. ■ [in sing.] an act of warming something or oneself: *he had a cup of tea and a warm by the kitchen range*.
2 short for **BRITISH WARM**.
– PHRASES **warm fuzzy** (or **warm and fuzzy**) informal, chiefly US used to refer to a sentimentally emotional response or something designed to evoke such a response: *babies require a lot of attention, not just momentary warm fuzzies*. (**as**) **warm as toast** pleasantly warm.

– PHRASAL VERBS **warm down** recover from strenuous physical exertion by doing gentle stretches and exercises. **warm to/towards** (or N. Amer. **warm up to/towards**) begin to like (someone). ▪ become more interested in or enthusiastic about (something): *she was warming to her theme.* **warm up** prepare for physical exertion or a performance by exercising or practising gently beforehand: *the band were warming up.* ▪ (of an engine or electrical appliance) reach a temperature high enough to allow it to operate efficiently. ▪ become livelier or more animated: *after several more rounds, things began to warm up in the bar.* **warm something up** (or US **over**) **1** reheat previously cooked food. **2** entertain an audience so as to make them more receptive to the main act. **3** (as adj. **warmed-up**) (of an idea or product) not new or original.
– DERIVATIVES **warmer** noun [usu. in combination] *a towel-warmer*, **warmish** adjective, **warmly** adverb, **warmness** noun.
– ORIGIN Old English *wearm* (adjective), *werman*, *wearmian* (verb), of Germanic origin; related to Dutch and German *warm*, from an Indo-European root shared by Latin *formus* 'warm' and Greek *thermos* 'hot'.

war machine ▸ noun **1** the military resources of a country organized for waging war.
2 an instrument or weapon of war.

warmblood ▸ noun a horse of a breed that is a cross between an Arab or similar breed and another breed of the draught or pony type.

warm-blooded ▸ adjective **1** relating to or denoting animals (chiefly mammals and birds) which maintain a constant body temperature, typically above that of the surroundings, by metabolic means; homeothermic.
2 ardent; passionate.
– DERIVATIVES **warm-bloodedness** noun.

warm-down ▸ noun a series of gentle exercises designed to relax the body after strenuous physical exertion.

war memorial ▸ noun a monument commemorating those killed in a war.

warm front ▸ noun Meteorology the boundary of an advancing mass of warm air, in particular the leading edge of the warm sector of a low-pressure system.

warm-hearted ▸ adjective sympathetic and kind: *a warm-hearted, affectionate girl.*
– DERIVATIVES **warm-heartedly** adverb, **warm-heartedness** noun.

warming pan ▸ noun historical a wide, flat brass pan on a long handle, filled with hot coals and used for warming a bed.

warmonger /ˈwɔːmʌŋɡə/ ▸ noun a person who encourages or advocates aggression or warfare towards other nations or groups.
– DERIVATIVES **warmongering** noun & adjective.

warmth ▸ noun [mass noun] **1** the quality, state, or sensation of being warm; moderate heat: *the warmth of the sun on her skin.*
2 enthusiasm, affection, or kindness: *she smiled with real warmth.* ▪ intensity of emotion: *'Of course not,' he snapped, with a warmth that he regretted.*

warm-up ▸ noun a period or act of preparation for a match, performance, or exercise session, involving gentle exercise or practice. ▪ (**warm-ups**) N. Amer. a garment worn during light exercise or training; a tracksuit. ▪ a period before a stage performance in which the audience is entertained in order to make it more receptive to the main act.

warm work ▸ noun [mass noun] **1** physical action that makes one warm through exertion.
2 archaic dangerous conflict.

warn ▸ verb [reporting verb] inform someone in advance of a possible danger, problem, or other unpleasant situation: [with obj.] *his father had warned him of what might happen* | [with direct speech] *'He's going to humiliate you,' John warned* | [no obj.] *traffic signals warned of fog* | [with clause] *the union warned that its members were going on strike.* ▪ [with obj.] give someone cautionary advice about their actions or conduct: *he warned the chancellor* ***against*** *raising taxes* | [with obj. and infinitive] *police warned people not to keep large amounts of cash in their homes* | [no obj.] *they warned* ***against*** *false optimism.*
– PHRASES **warn someone off the course** Horse Racing prohibit someone who has broken the laws of the Jockey Club from riding or running horses at meetings under the Jockey Club's jurisdiction.
– PHRASAL VERBS **warn someone off** order someone to keep away from (somewhere) or refrain from doing (something): *he has been warned off booze.*
– DERIVATIVES **warner** noun.
– ORIGIN Old English *war(e)nian*, *wearnian*, from a West Germanic base meaning 'be cautious'; compare with WARE[3].

Warne, Shane (Keith) (b.1969), Australian cricketer. He holds the record for Australian bowlers in taking over 600 test wickets.

Warner Brothers a US film production company founded in 1923 by the brothers Harry, Jack, Sam, and Albert Warner.

warning ▸ noun a statement or event that warns of something or that serves as a cautionary example: *police issued a warning about fake £20 notes* | *his sad death should be a warning to everyone* | [as modifier] *a red warning light.* ▪ [mass noun] cautionary advice: *a word of warning—don't park illegally.* ▪ [mass noun] advance notice of something: *she had only had four days' warning before leaving Berlin* | *without any warning, the army opened fire.*
– DERIVATIVES **warningly** adverb.
– ORIGIN Old English *war(e)nung* (see WARN, -ING[1]).

warning coloration ▸ noun [mass noun] Zoology conspicuous colouring that warns a predator that an animal is unpalatable or poisonous.

warning track ▸ noun Baseball a strip around the outside of the outfield which warns approaching fielders of the proximity of a wall.

warning triangle ▸ noun a triangular red frame, made of reflective material, carried by motorists to be set up on the road as a danger signal in case of a breakdown or other hazard.

War of 1812 a conflict between the US and the UK (1812–14), prompted by restrictions on US trade resulting from the British blockade of French and allied ports during the Napoleonic Wars, and by British and Canadian support for American Indians trying to resist westward expansion. It was ended by a treaty which restored all conquered territories to their owners before outbreak of war.

War of American Independence see AMERICAN INDEPENDENCE, WAR OF.

War Office a former department of the British government that was in charge of the army (incorporated into the Ministry of Defence in 1964).

War of Jenkins's Ear see JENKINS'S EAR, WAR OF.

warp ▸ verb **1** make or become bent or twisted out of shape, typically as a result of the effects of heat or damp: [with obj.] *moisture had warped the box* | [no obj.] *wood has a tendency to warp.* ▪ [with obj.] make abnormal or strange; distort: *your judgement has been warped by your obvious dislike of him* | (as adj. **warped**) *a warped sense of humour.*
2 (with reference to a ship) move or be moved along by hauling on a rope attached to a stationary object ashore: [with obj. and adverbial of direction] *crew and passengers helped warp the vessels through the shallow section.*
3 [with obj.] (in weaving) arrange (yarn) so as to form the warp of a piece of cloth.
4 [with obj.] cover (land) with a deposit of alluvial soil by natural or artificial flooding.
▸ noun **1** a twist or distortion in the shape of something: *the head of the racket had a curious warp.* ▪ [as modifier] relating to or denoting (fictional or hypothetical) space travel by means of distorting space–time: *warp speed.* ▪ an abnormality or perversion in a person's character.
2 [in sing.] (in weaving) the threads on a loom over and under which other threads (the weft) are passed to make cloth: *the warp and weft are the basic constituents of all textiles* | figurative *rugby is woven into the warp and weft of South African society.*
3 a rope attached at one end to a fixed point and used for moving or mooring a ship.
4 [mass noun] archaic alluvial sediment; silt.
– DERIVATIVES **warpage** noun (sense 1 of the verb), **warper** noun.
– ORIGIN Old English *weorpan* (verb), *wearp* (noun), of Germanic origin; related to Dutch *werpen* and German *werfen* 'to throw'. Early verb senses included 'throw' and 'hit with a missile'; the sense 'bend' dates from late Middle English. The noun was originally a term in weaving (see sense 2 of the noun).

warpaint ▸ noun [mass noun] a pigment or paint traditionally used in some societies, especially those of North American Indians, to decorate the face and body before battle. ▪ informal elaborate or excessively applied make-up.

warpath ▸ noun (in phrase **on the warpath**) angry and ready or eager for confrontation: *her outraged husband was on the warpath.*
– ORIGIN with reference to American Indians heading towards a battle with an enemy.

war pension ▸ noun a pension paid to someone who is disabled or bereaved by war.

warplane ▸ noun an aeroplane designed and equipped to engage in air combat or to drop bombs.

war poet ▸ noun a poet writing at the time of and on the subject of war, especially one on military service during the First World War.

warp speed ▸ noun informal an extremely high speed: *these exciting developments are moving ahead at warp speed.*
– ORIGIN 1970s: popularized by the US television series *Star Trek* (originally referring to a faster-than-light speed attained by a spaceship travelling in a space warp).

warragal ▸ noun & adjective variant spelling of WARRIGAL.

warrant ▸ noun **1** a document issued by a legal or government official authorizing the police or another body to make an arrest, search premises, or carry out some other action relating to the administration of justice: *magistrates issued a warrant for his arrest* | *an extradition warrant.* ▪ a document that entitles the holder to receive goods, money, or services: *we'll issue you with a travel warrant.* ▪ Finance a negotiable security allowing the holder to buy shares at a specified price at or before a future date.
2 [mass noun] [usu. with negative] justification or authority for an action, belief, or feeling: *there is* ***no warrant*** *for this assumption.*
3 an official certificate of appointment issued to an officer of lower rank than a commissioned officer.
▸ verb [with obj.] **1** justify or necessitate (a course of action): *the employees feel that industrial action is warranted.*
2 officially affirm or guarantee: *the vendor warrants the accuracy of the report.*
– PHRASES **I** (or **I'll**) **warrant (you)** dated used to express the speaker's certainty about something: *I'll warrant you'll thank me for it in years to come.*
– ORIGIN Middle English (in the senses 'protector' and 'safeguard', also, as a verb, 'keep safe from danger'): from variants of Old French *guarant* (noun), *guarantir* (verb), of Germanic origin; compare with GUARANTEE.

warrantable ▸ adjective (of an action or statement) able to be authorized or sanctioned; justifiable: *a warrantable assertion.*
– DERIVATIVES **warrantableness** noun, **warrantably** adverb.

warrant card ▸ noun a document of authorization and identification carried by a police officer.

warrantee ▸ noun Law a person to whom a warranty is given.

warrantless ▸ adjective chiefly N. Amer. carried out without legal or official authorization: *warrantless searches and wiretaps.*

warrant officer ▸ noun a rank of officer in the army, RAF, or US navy, below the commissioned officers and above the NCOs.

warrantor /ˈwɒrəntə/ ▸ noun a person or company that provides a warranty.

warranty ▸ noun (pl. **warranties**) **1** a written guarantee, issued to the purchaser of an article by its manufacturer, promising to repair or replace it if necessary within a specified period of time: *the car comes with a three-year warranty* | [mass noun] *as your machine is under warranty, I suggest getting it checked.* ▪ (in an insurance contract) an engagement by the insured party that certain statements are true or that certain conditions shall be fulfilled, the breach of which will invalidate the policy.
2 [mass noun] [usu. with negative] archaic justification or grounds for an action or belief: *you have no warranty for such an audacious doctrine.*
– ORIGIN Middle English: from Anglo-Norman French *warantie*, variant of *garantie* (see GUARANTY). Early use was as a legal term denoting a covenant annexed to a conveyance of property, in which the vendor affirmed the security of the title.

Warren[1], Earl (1891–1974), American judge. As Chief Justice of the Supreme Court (1953–69) he did much to improve civil liberties and is also remembered for heading the Warren Commission (1964) into the assassination of President Kennedy.

W

Warren², Robert Penn (1905–89), American poet, novelist, and critic. An advocate of New Criticism, he was the first person to win Pulitzer Prizes in both fiction and poetry categories and in 1986 he was made the first American Poet Laureate.

warren ▶ noun (also **rabbit warren**) a network of interconnecting rabbit burrows. ■ a densely populated or labyrinthine building or district: *a warren of narrow gas-lit streets*. ■ Brit. historical an enclosed piece of land set aside for breeding game, especially rabbits.
– ORIGIN late Middle English: from an Anglo-Norman French and Old Northern French variant of Old French *garenne* 'game park', of Gaulish origin.

warrener ▶ noun Brit. historical a gamekeeper. ■ a keeper of a rabbit warren.
– ORIGIN late Middle English: from Anglo-Norman French *warener*, from *warenne* 'game park'.

warrigal /ˈwɒrɪg(ə)l/ (also **warragal**) Austral. ▶ noun
1 a dingo dog.
2 a wild or untamed horse.
3 another term for MYALL (sense 2).
▶ adjective (of a plant) not cultivated: *warrigal melons*. ■ untamed; undisciplined: *half a dozen warrigal knockabout men, proper tearaway types*.
– ORIGIN from Dharuk *warrigal* 'wild dingo'.

warring /ˈwɔːrɪŋ/ ▶ adjective [attrib.] (of two or more people or groups) in conflict with each other: *warring factions | a warring couple*.

Warrington /ˈwɒrɪŋtən/ an industrial town on the River Mersey in Cheshire, NW England; pop. 79,900 (est. 2009).

warrior ▶ noun (especially in former times) a brave or experienced soldier or fighter.
– ORIGIN Middle English: from Old Northern French *werreior*, variant of Old French *guerreior*, from *guerreier* 'make war', from *guerre* 'war'.

Warsaw /ˈwɔːsɔː/ the capital of Poland, on the River Vistula; pop. 1,704,717 (2007). The city suffered severe damage and the loss of 700,000 lives during the Second World War and was almost completely rebuilt. Polish name **Warszawa** /varˈʃava/.

Warsaw Pact a treaty of mutual defence and military aid signed at Warsaw on 14 May 1955 by Communist states of Europe under Soviet influence, in response to the admission of West Germany to NATO. The Pact was dissolved in 1991.

warship ▶ noun a ship equipped with weapons and designed to take part in warfare at sea.

Wars of Religion another term for FRENCH WARS OF RELIGION.

Wars of the Roses the 15th-century English civil wars between the Houses of York and Lancaster, represented by white and red roses respectively, during the reigns of Henry VI, Edward IV, and Richard III. The struggle was largely ended in 1485 by the defeat and death of the Yorkist king Richard III at the Battle of Bosworth and the accession of the Lancastrian Henry Tudor (Henry VII), who united the two houses by marrying Elizabeth, daughter of Edward IV.

wart ▶ noun a small, hard, benign growth on the skin, caused by a virus. ■ any rounded excrescence on the skin of an animal or the surface of a plant. ■ an undesirable or disfiguring feature: *few products are without their warts*. ■ informal an obnoxious or objectionable person.
– PHRASES **warts and all** informal including features or qualities that are not appealing or attractive: *Philip must learn to accept me, warts and all*.
– DERIVATIVES **warty** adjective (**wartier**, **wartiest**).
– ORIGIN Old English *wearte*, of Germanic origin; related to Dutch *wrat* and German *Warze*.

wart-biter ▶ noun a large mottled green or brown bush cricket that inhabits coarse grassland in Europe. ● *Decticus verrucivorous*, family Tettigoniidae.
– ORIGIN mid 19th cent.: so named from the reputed former use in Sweden of such crickets to bite off warts.

W

wart disease ▶ noun [mass noun] a fungal disease of potatoes which produces warty outgrowths on the tubers. ● The fungus is *Synchytrium endobioticum*, subdivision Mastigomycotina.

warthog ▶ noun an African wild pig with a large head, warty lumps on the face, and curved tusks. ● *Phacochoerus aethiopicus*, family Suidae.

wartime ▶ noun [mass noun] a period during which a war is taking place.

war-torn ▶ adjective (of a place) racked or devastated by war: *a war-torn republic*.

wart snake ▶ noun a large aquatic fish-eating snake with coarse-textured scales which give it a file-like appearance, native to SE Asia and Australia. Also called FILE SNAKE. ● Family Achrochordidae and genus *Achrochordus*: three species, e.g. the **Asian wart snake** (*A. arafurae*).

warty newt ▶ noun another term for CRESTED NEWT.

war-weary ▶ adjective exhausted and dispirited by war or conflict: *an increasingly war-weary population*.
– DERIVATIVES **war-weariness** noun.

Warwick¹ /ˈwɒrɪk/ the county town of Warwickshire, in central England, on the River Avon; pop. 24,800 (est. 2009).

Warwick² /ˈwɒrɪk/, Richard Neville, Earl of (1428–71), English statesman; known as **Warwick the Kingmaker**. During the Wars of the Roses he fought first on the Yorkist side, helping Edward IV to gain the throne (1461), and then on the Lancastrian side, briefly restoring Henry VI to the throne (1470). Warwick was killed at the battle of Barnet.

Warwickshire a county of central England; county town, Warwick.

war widow ▶ noun a woman whose husband has been killed in war.

wary ▶ adjective (**warier**, **wariest**) feeling or showing caution about possible dangers or problems: *dogs which have been mistreated often remain very **wary of** strangers | a wary look*.
– ORIGIN late 15th cent.: from WARE³ + -Y¹.

war zone ▶ noun a region in which a war is being fought.

was first and third person singular past of BE.

wasabi /wəˈsɑːbi/ ▶ noun [mass noun] a Japanese plant with a thick green root which tastes like strong horseradish and is used in cookery, especially in powder or paste form as an accompaniment to raw fish. ● *Eutrema wasabi*, family Cruciferae.
– ORIGIN early 20th cent.: from Japanese.

wash ▶ verb **1** [with obj.] clean with water and, typically, soap or detergent: *Auntie Lou had washed all their clothes | he **washed down** the woodwork in the kitchen*. ■ [no obj.] clean oneself with soap and water. ■ (with reference to a stain or dirt) remove or be removed by cleaning with water and detergent: [with obj. and adverbial] *they have to keep washing the mould off the walls* | figurative *all that hate can't wash away the guilt* | [no obj., with adverbial] *the dirt on his clothes would easily wash out*. ■ [no obj., with adverbial] (of fabric, a garment, or dye) withstand cleaning to a specified degree without shrinking or fading: *a linen-mix yarn which washes well*. ■ [no obj.] do one's laundry: *I need someone to cook and wash for me*. ■ literary wet or moisten (something) thoroughly: *you are beautiful with your face washed with rain*.
2 [with obj. and adverbial of direction] (of flowing water) carry (someone or something) in a particular direction: *floods washed away the bridges*. ■ [no obj., with adverbial of direction] be carried by flowing water: *an oil slick washed up on the beaches*. ■ [no obj., with adverbial of direction] (especially of waves) sweep or splash in a particular direction: *the sea began to wash along the decks*. ■ [with obj.] (of a river, sea, or lake) flow through or lap against (a country, coast, etc.): *offshore islands washed by warm blue seas*. ■ [with obj.] sift metallic particles from (earth or gravel) by running water through it.
3 [with obj.] brush with a thin coat of dilute paint or ink: *the walls were washed with shades of umber*. ■ (**wash something with**) coat inferior metal with (a film of gold or silver from a solution).
4 [no obj., with negative] informal seem convincing or genuine: *charm won't wash with this crew*.
▶ noun **1** [usu. in sing.] an act of washing something or an instance of being washed: *her hair needs a wash*. ■ a quantity of clothes needing to be or just having been washed: *she hung out her Tuesday wash*.
2 [in sing.] the water or air disturbed by a moving boat or aircraft: *the wash of a smart motor boat*. ■ the breaking of waves on a shore: *the wash of waves on the pebbled beach*.
3 (**the Wash**) an inlet of the North Sea on the east coast of England between Norfolk and Lincolnshire.
4 [mass noun] a medicinal or cleansing solution applied to the skin: *citrus-scented body wash*.
5 a layer of paint or metal spread thinly on a surface: *the walls were covered with a pale lemon wash*.
6 [mass noun] silt or gravel carried by a stream or river and deposited as sediment. ■ [count noun] a sandbank exposed only at low tide.
7 [mass noun] kitchen slops and other food waste fed to pigs.
8 [mass noun] malt fermenting in preparation for distillation.
9 [in sing.] N. Amer. informal a situation or result that is of no benefit to either of two opposing sides.
– PHRASES **come out in the wash** informal be resolved eventually with no lasting harm: *he's not happy but he assures me **it'll all come out in the wash***. **in the wash** (of clothes, bed linen, or similar) put aside for washing or in the process of being washed. **wash one's dirty linen** (or **laundry**) **in public** informal discuss one's personal affairs in public. **wash one's hands** go to the toilet (used euphemistically). **wash one's hands of** disclaim responsibility for: *the social services washed their hands of his daughter*. [originally with biblical allusion to Matt. 27:24.] **wash one's mouth out** (**with soap and water**) [often as imperative] stop swearing.
– PHRASAL VERBS **wash something down** accompany or follow food with a drink: *bacon and eggs **washed down with** a cup of tea*. **wash out** (or **wash someone out**) N. Amer. be excluded (or exclude someone) from a course or position after a failure to meet the required standards: *a lot of them had washed out of pilot training*. **wash something out 1** cause an event to be postponed or cancelled because of rain: *their match against Australia was washed out*. **2** (of a flood or downpour) make a breach in a road. **wash up 1** (also **wash something up**) chiefly Brit. clean crockery and cutlery after use. **2** N. Amer. clean one's hands and face. **wash over** (of a feeling) affect (someone) suddenly: *a deep feeling of sadness washed over her*. ■ occur all around without greatly affecting (someone): *she allowed the babble of conversation to wash over her*.
– ORIGIN Old English *wæscan* (verb), of Germanic origin; related to Dutch *wassen*, German *waschen*, also to WATER.

Wash. ▶ abbreviation Washington.

washable ▶ adjective (especially of fabric or clothes) able to be washed without shrinkage or other damage: *washable curtains*.
– DERIVATIVES **washability** noun.

wash-and-wear ▶ adjective (of a garment or fabric) easily washed, drying quickly, and not needing to be ironed.

washbag ▶ noun Brit. a toilet bag.

washbasin ▶ noun a basin, typically fixed to a wall or on a pedestal, used for washing one's hands and face.

washboard ▶ noun **1** a board made of ridged wood or a sheet of corrugated zinc, used when washing clothes as a surface against which to scrub them. ■ a similar board played as a percussion instrument by scraping. ■ [as modifier] denoting a man's stomach that is lean and has well-defined muscles. ■ [mass noun] N. Amer. a ridged, uneven road surface.
2 a board fixed along the side of a boat to prevent water from spilling in over the edge.
▶ verb [with obj.] (usu. as adj. **washboarded**) chiefly N. Amer. cause ridges to develop in (a road or road surface): *a road left washboarded by winter frost*.

wash bottle ▶ noun Chemistry a bottle, typically plastic, with a nozzle for directing a stream of liquid on to something. ■ a bottle containing liquid through which gases are passed for purification.

washbowl ▶ noun a washbasin.

washcloth ▶ noun N. Amer. a facecloth.

washday ▶ noun a day on which a household's clothes, bed linen, etc. are washed, especially when the same day each week.

washdown ▶ noun an act of washing someone or something thoroughly. ■ [as modifier] denoting a toilet having a flushing system in which the pan is automatically washed clean.

wash drawing ▶ noun a picture or sketch made by laying on washes of watercolour, typically in monochrome, over a pen or pencil drawing.

washed out ▶ adjective faded by or as if by sunlight or repeated washing: *washed-out jeans*. ■ (of a person) pale and tired.

washed-up ▶ adjective **1** deposited by the tide on a shore: *washed-up jellyfish*.
2 informal no longer effective or successful: *a washed-up actress*.

washer ▶ noun **1** [usu. with modifier] a person or device that washes something: *a glass washer*. ■ a washing machine.

2 a small flat metal, rubber, or plastic ring fixed between two joining surfaces or between a nut and a bolt to spread the pressure or act as a spacer or seal.
3 Austral. a facecloth.

washer-dryer ▸ **noun** a washing machine with an inbuilt tumble dryer.

washerman ▸ **noun** (pl. **washermen**) (especially in South Asia) a man whose occupation is washing clothes.

washer-up ▸ **noun** (pl. **washers-up**) Brit. a person whose job or task it is to wash the dishes and other utensils in a kitchen.

washerwoman ▸ **noun** (pl. **washerwomen**) a woman whose occupation is washing clothes.

washery ▸ **noun** (pl. **washeries**) (in the mining industry) a place where coal is washed.

washeteria ▸ **noun** another term for **LAUNDERETTE**.
– ORIGIN 1950s: from **WASH**, on the pattern of *cafeteria*.

wash-hand basin ▸ **noun** another term for **WASHBASIN**.

wash-hand stand ▸ **noun** another term for **WASHSTAND**.

wash house ▸ **noun** an outhouse or room in which clothes are washed.

washing ▸ **noun** [mass noun] the action of washing oneself or laundering clothes, bed linen, etc. ■ a quantity of clothes, bed linen, etc. that is to be washed or has just been washed: *she took her washing around to the launderette*.

washing line ▸ **noun** Brit. a clothes line.

washing machine ▸ **noun** a machine for washing clothes, bed linen, etc.

washing powder ▸ **noun** [mass noun] Brit. detergent in the form of a powder for washing clothes, bed linen, etc.

washing soda ▸ **noun** [mass noun] sodium carbonate, used dissolved in water for washing and cleaning.

Washington[1] **1** a state of the north-western US, on the Pacific coast; pop. 6,549,224 (est. 2008); capital, Olympia. It became the 42nd state in 1889.
2 the capital of the US; pop. 591,833 (est. 2008). It is coextensive with the District of Columbia, a federal district on the Potomac River with boundaries on the states of Virginia and Maryland. Founded in 1790, during the presidency of George Washington, it was planned and built as a capital city. Full name **Washington DC**.
3 an industrial town in NE England, designated as a new town in 1964; pop. 51,700 (est. 2009).
– DERIVATIVES **Washingtonian** noun & adjective.

Washington[2], Booker T. (1856–1915), American educationist; full name *Booker Taliaferro Washington*. A leading commentator for black Americans, Washington established the Tuskegee Institute in Alabama (1881). His support for segregation and his emphasis on black people's vocational skills attracted criticism from other black leaders.

Washington[3], George (1732–99), American general and statesman, 1st President of the US 1789–97. Washington helped win the War of Independence by keeping his army together through the winter at Valley Forge and winning a decisive battle at Yorktown (1781). He chaired the convention at Philadelphia (1787) that drew up the American Constitution and subsequently served two terms as President, following a policy of neutrality in international affairs.

washing-up ▸ **noun** [mass noun] Brit. the process of washing used crockery, cutlery, and other kitchen utensils: *they've finished the washing-up*. ■ crockery, cutlery, and other kitchen utensils that are to be washed: *the sink is full of washing-up*.

washland ▸ **noun** [mass noun] land that is periodically flooded by a river or stream.

wash leather ▸ **noun** [mass noun] dated chamois or a similar leather.

washout ▸ **noun 1** informal an event that is spoiled by constant or heavy rain. ■ a disappointing failure: *the film was branded a colossal washout*.
2 a breach in a road or railway track caused by flooding. ■ Geology a channel cut into a sedimentary deposit by rushing water and filled with younger material.
3 Medicine the removal of material or a substance from the body or a part of it, especially by washing with a fluid.

washrag ▸ **noun** US a facecloth.

washroom ▸ **noun** N. Amer. a room with washing and toilet facilities.

washstand ▸ **noun** a piece of furniture formerly used to hold a jug, bowl, or basin for the purpose of washing one's hands and face.

washtub ▸ **noun** a large metal tub used for washing clothes and linen.

wash-up ▸ **noun 1** an act of washing. ■ Brit. informal a person employed to wash dishes in the kitchen of a restaurant or hotel.
2 informal a debriefing session or follow-up discussion.

washy ▸ **adjective** (**washier**, **washiest**) **1** archaic (of food or drink) too watery: *washy potatoes*. ■ lacking in strength or vigour; insipid: *a weak and washy production*.
2 (of a colour) having a faded look.
– DERIVATIVES **washiness** noun.

wasn't ▸ contraction was not.

Wasp (also **WASP**) ▸ **noun** N. Amer. an upper- or middle-class American white Protestant, considered to be a member of the most powerful group in society.
– DERIVATIVES **Waspish** adjective, **Waspy** adjective (**Waspier**, **Waspiest**).
– ORIGIN 1960s: acronym from *white Anglo-Saxon Protestant*.

wasp ▸ **noun 1** a social winged insect which has a narrow waist and a sting and is typically yellow with black stripes. It constructs a paper nest from wood pulp and raises the larvae on a diet of insects. ● Family Vespidae, superfamily Vespoidea, order Hymenoptera: several genera, in particular *Vespula* and *Polistes*.
2 a solitary winged insect with a narrow waist, mostly distantly related to the social wasps and including many parasitic kinds. ● Several superfamilies in the sections Aculeata (digger, mason, and potter wasps) and Parasitica (parasitic wasps and gall wasps), order Hymenoptera.
– DERIVATIVES **wasp-like** adjective.
– ORIGIN Old English *wæfs*, *wæps*, *wæsp*, of West Germanic origin, from an Indo-European root shared by Latin *vespa*; perhaps related to **WEAVE**[1] (from the web-like form of its nest).

wasp beetle ▸ **noun** a black and yellow longhorn beetle that mimics the appearance and behaviour of a wasp. ● *Clytus arietis*, family Cerambycidae.

waspie ▸ **noun** (pl. **waspies**) a woman's corset or belt designed to accentuate a slender waist.
– ORIGIN 1950s: diminutive of *wasp* from **WASP WAIST**.

waspish ▸ **adjective** readily expressing anger or irritation: *he had a waspish tongue*.
– DERIVATIVES **waspishly** adverb, **waspishness** noun.

wasp waist ▸ **noun** a very narrow or tightly corseted waist.
– DERIVATIVES **wasp-waisted** adjective.

wassail /ˈwɒseɪl, ˈwɒs(ə)l, ˈwa-/ archaic ▸ **noun** [mass noun] spiced ale or mulled wine drunk during celebrations for Twelfth Night and Christmas Eve. ■ lively and noisy festivities involving the drinking of plentiful amounts of alcohol; revelry.
▸ **verb** [no obj.] **1** drink plentiful amounts of alcohol and enjoy oneself with others in a noisy, lively way. ■ [with obj.] historical (in SW England) drink to (fruit trees, typically apple trees) in a custom intended to ensure a fruitful crop.
2 go from house to house at Christmas singing carols: *here we go a-wassailing*.
– ORIGIN Middle English *wæs hæil* 'be in (good) health!': from Old Norse *ves heill* (compare with **HAIL**[2]). The drinking formula *wassail* (and the reply *drinkhail* 'drink good health') were probably introduced by Danish-speaking inhabitants of England, and then spread, so that by the 12th cent. the usage was considered by the Normans to be characteristic of Englishmen.

wassail bowl (also **wassail cup**) ▸ **noun** a large bowl in which wassail was made and from which it was dispensed for the drinking of toasts.

Wassermann test /ˈvɑːsəmən/ ▸ **noun** Medicine a diagnostic test for syphilis using a specific antibody reaction (the **Wassermann reaction**) of the patient's blood serum.
– ORIGIN early 20th cent.: named after August P. *Wassermann* (1866–1925), German pathologist.

wast /wɒst, wəst/ archaic or dialect second person singular past of **BE**.

wastage ▸ **noun** [mass noun] **1** the action or process of losing or destroying something by using it carelessly or extravagantly: *the wastage of natural resources*. ■ the amount of something that is wasted: *wastage was cut by 50 per cent*.
2 (also **natural wastage**) Brit. the reduction in the size of a workforce as a result of voluntary resignation or retirement rather than enforced redundancy. ■ the number of people leaving a job or further educational establishment before they have completed their training or education.
3 the weakening or deterioration of a part of the body, typically as a result of illness or lack of use: *the wastage of muscle tissue*.

waste ▸ **verb 1** [with obj.] use or expend carelessly, extravagantly, or to no purpose: *we can't afford to waste electricity* | *I don't use the car, so why should I* ***waste*** *precious money* ***on*** *it?* ■ expend on an unappreciative recipient: *her small talk* ***was wasted on*** *this guest*. ■ fail to make full or good use of: *we're wasted in this job*. ■ deliberately dispose of (surplus stock).
2 [no obj.] (of a person or a part of the body) become progressively weaker and more emaciated: *she was dying of AIDS, visibly* ***wasting away*** | (as adj. **wasting**) *a wasting disease*. ■ [with obj.] archaic make progressively weaker and more emaciated.
3 [with obj.] N. Amer. informal kill or severely injure (someone).
4 [with obj.] literary devastate or ruin (a place): *he seized their cattle and wasted their country*.
5 [no obj.] literary (of time) pass away: *the years were wasting*.
▸ **adjective 1** (of a material, substance, or by-product) eliminated or discarded as no longer useful or required after the completion of a process: *ensure that waste materials are disposed of responsibly* | *plants produce oxygen as a waste product*.
2 (of an area of land, typically an urban one) not used, cultivated, or built on: *a patch of waste ground*.
▸ **noun 1** an act or instance of using or expending something carelessly, extravagantly, or to no purpose: *it's a waste of time trying to argue with him* | [mass noun] *they had learned to avoid waste*. ■ [mass noun] archaic the gradual loss or diminution of something: *he was pale and weak from waste of blood*.
2 [mass noun] (also **wastes**) unwanted or unusable material, substances, or by-products: *nuclear waste* | *hazardous industrial wastes*.
3 (usu. **wastes**) a large area of barren, typically uninhabited land: *the icy wastes of the Antarctic*.
4 [mass noun] Law damage to an estate caused by an act or by neglect, especially by a life tenant.
– PHRASES **go to waste** be unused or expended to no purpose. **lay waste to** (or **lay something (to) waste**) completely destroy: *a land laid waste by war*. **waste one's breath** see **BREATH**. **waste of space** informal a person regarded as useless or incompetent. **waste not, want not** proverb if you use a commodity or resource carefully and without extravagance you will never be in need. **waste words** see **WORD**.
– DERIVATIVES **wasteless** adjective.
– ORIGIN Middle English: from Old Northern French *wast(e)* (noun), *waster* (verb), based on Latin *vastus* 'unoccupied, uncultivated'.

wastebasket ▸ **noun** N. Amer. a waste-paper basket.

waste bin ▸ **noun** a dustbin or rubbish bin.

wasted ▸ **adjective 1** used or expended carelessly or to no purpose: *wasted fuel* | *a wasted opportunity*. ■ (of an action) not producing the desired result: *I'm sorry you've had a wasted journey*.
2 (of a person or a part of the body) weak or emaciated: *her wasted arm*.
3 informal under the influence of alcohol or illegal drugs: *he looked kind of wasted*.

waste-disposal unit (also **waste disposer**) ▸ **noun** Brit. an electrically operated device fitted to the waste pipe of a kitchen sink for grinding up food waste.

wasteful ▸ **adjective** (of a person, action, or process) using or expending something of value carelessly, extravagantly, or to no purpose: *wasteful energy consumption*.
– DERIVATIVES **wastefully** adverb, **wastefulness** noun.

wastegate ▸ **noun** a device in a turbocharger which regulates the pressure at which exhaust gases pass to the turbine by opening or closing a vent to the exterior.

wasteland ▸ **noun** [mass noun] an unused area of land that has become barren or overgrown. ■ (also **wastelands**) a bleak and unused or neglected urban or industrial area: *the restoration of industrial wasteland* | [count noun] figurative *the mid 70s are now seen as something of a cultural wasteland*.

waste-paper basket ▸ **noun** chiefly Brit. a receptacle for small quantities of rubbish.

W

waste pipe ▸ noun a pipe carrying waste water, such as that from a sink, bath, or shower, to a drain.

waster ▸ noun **1** a wasteful person or thing: *you are a great waster of time.* ■ informal a person who does little or nothing of value.
2 a discarded piece of defective pottery.

wastrel /ˈweɪstr(ə)l/ ▸ noun **1** literary a wasteful or good-for-nothing person.
2 archaic a waif; a neglected child.
– ORIGIN late 16th cent. (denoting a strip of waste land): from the verb WASTE + -REL.

wat /wɑt/ ▸ noun (in Thailand, Cambodia, and Laos) a Buddhist monastery or temple.
– ORIGIN Thai, from Sanskrit *vāṭa* 'enclosure'.

watch ▸ verb **1** [with obj.] look at or observe attentively over a period of time: *Lucy watched him go* | [no obj.] *as she watched, two women came into the garden* | [with clause] *everyone stopped to watch what was going on.* ■ keep under careful, protective, or secret observation: *there aren't enough staff to watch him properly* | *he told me my telephones were tapped and that I was being watched.* ■ [no obj.] (**watch over**) observe and guard in a protective way: *I guess I can rest a while, with you here to watch over me.* ■ follow closely or maintain an interest in: *the girls watched the development of this relationship with incredulity.*
2 [with obj.] exercise care, caution, or restraint about: *most women watch their diet during pregnancy* | [with clause] *you should watch what you say!* ■ [no obj.] (**watch for**) look out or be on the alert for: *in spring and summer, watch for kingfishers* | ***watch out for** broken glass.* ■ [no obj.] [usu. in imperative] (usu. **watch out**) be careful: *credit-card fraud is on the increase, so watch out.* ■ (**watch it/yourself**) [usu. in imperative] informal be careful (used as a warning or threat): *if anyone finds out, you're dead meat, so watch it.*
3 [no obj.] archaic remain awake for the purpose of religious observance: *she watched whole nights in the church.*
▸ noun **1** a small timepiece worn typically on a strap on one's wrist.
2 [usu. in sing.] an act or instance of carefully observing someone or something over a period of time: *the security forces have been **keeping a close watch on** our activities.* ■ a period during which a person is stationed to look out for danger or trouble, typically at night: *Murray took the last watch before dawn.* ■ a fixed period of duty on a ship, usually lasting four hours. ■ (also **starboard** or **port watch**) the officers and crew on duty during a watch. ■ a shift worked by firefighters or police officers. ■ (**the watch**) historical a watchman or group of watchmen who patrolled and guarded the streets of a town before the introduction of the police force.
3 [in sing. with adj.] informal a film or programme considered in terms of its appeal to the public: *this movie's an engrossing watch.*
– PHRASES **be on the watch** be on the alert for something, especially a possible danger. **keep watch** stay on the lookout for danger or trouble. **watch one's** (or **someone's**) **back** protect oneself (or someone else) against danger from an unexpected quarter. **watch one's mouth** see MOUTH. **the watches of the night** literary the hours of night, portrayed as a time when one cannot sleep. **watch the pennies** see PENNY. **watch one's step** see STEP. **watch this space** see SPACE. **watch the time** ensure that one is aware of the time in order to avoid being late. **watch the world go by** spend time observing other people going about their business.
– ORIGIN Old English *wæcce* 'watchfulness', *wæccende* 'remaining awake'; related to WAKE[1]. The sense 'small timepiece' probably developed by way of a sense 'alarm device attached to a clock'.

watcha ▸ exclamation variant spelling of WOTCHA[2].

watchable ▸ adjective (of a film or television programme) moderately enjoyable to watch.
– DERIVATIVES **watchability** noun.

watch cap ▸ noun a close-fitting knitted cap of a kind worn by members of the US Navy in cold weather.

watch case ▸ noun a metal case enclosing the works of a watch.

watch chain ▸ noun a metal chain securing a pocket watch.

Watch Committee ▸ noun historical (in the UK) the committee of a county borough council dealing with policing and public lighting.

watchdog ▸ noun a dog kept to guard private property. ■ a person or group that monitors the practices of companies providing a particular service or utility: *the consumer watchdog for transport in London.*
▸ verb (**watchdogs, watchdogging, watchdogged**) [with obj.] monitor (a person, activity, or situation): *how can we watchdog our investments?*

watcher ▸ noun a person who observes something attentively or regularly: [in combination] *a badger-watcher.*

watchfire ▸ noun a fire maintained during the night as a signal or for the use of someone who is on watch.

watchful ▸ adjective watching someone or something closely; alert and vigilant: *they attended dances under **the watchful eye of** their father.* ■ archaic wakeful; sleepless.
– DERIVATIVES **watchfully** adverb, **watchfulness** noun.

watch glass ▸ noun Brit. a glass disc covering the dial of a watch. ■ a concave glass disc used in a laboratory to hold material for use in experiments.

watching brief ▸ noun Law, Brit. a brief held by a barrister to follow a case on behalf of a client who is not directly involved. ■ an interest in a proceeding in which one is not directly or immediately concerned.

watchkeeper ▸ noun a person who keeps watch or acts as a lookout, especially on board a ship.

watch list ▸ noun a list of individuals, groups, or items that require close surveillance, typically for legal or political reasons.

watchmaker ▸ noun a person who makes and repairs watches and clocks.
– DERIVATIVES **watchmaking** noun.

watchman ▸ noun (pl. **watchmen**) a man employed to look after an empty building, especially at night. ■ historical a member of a body of people employed to keep watch in a town at night.

watchnight ▸ noun a religious service held on New Year's Eve or Christmas Eve.

watch spring ▸ noun a mainspring in a watch.

watchtower ▸ noun a tower built to create an elevated observation point.

watchword ▸ noun a word or phrase expressing a person's or group's core aim or belief: *on all educational fronts, innovation was the watchword.* ■ archaic a military password.

water ▸ noun [mass noun] **1** a colourless, transparent, odourless, liquid which forms the seas, lakes, rivers, and rain and is the basis of the fluids of living organisms. ■ one of the four elements in ancient and medieval philosophy and in astrology (considered essential to the nature of the signs Cancer, Scorpio, and Pisces): [as modifier] *a water sign.* ■ (usu. **the waters**) the water of a mineral spring as used medicinally for bathing in or drinking: *you can take the waters at the Pump Room.* ■ [with modifier] a solution of a specified substance in water: *ammonia water.*

> Water is a compound of oxygen and hydrogen (chem. formula: H_2O) with highly distinctive physical and chemical properties: it is able to dissolve many other substances; its solid form (ice) is *less* dense than the liquid form; its boiling point, viscosity, and surface tension are unusually high for its molecular weight, and it is partially dissociated into hydrogen and hydroxyl ions.

2 (**the water**) a stretch or area of water, such as a river, sea, or lake: *the lawns ran down to the water's edge.* ■ the surface of an area of water: *she ducked under the water.* ■ [as modifier] found in, on, or near areas of water: *a water plant.* ■ (**waters**) the water of a particular sea, river, or lake: *the waters of Hudson Bay* | figurative *the government are taking us into unknown waters with these changes in the legislation.* ■ (**waters**) an area of sea regarded as under the jurisdiction of a particular country: *Japanese coastal waters.*
3 urine: *drinking alcohol will make you need to **pass water** more often.*
4 (**waters**) the amniotic fluid surrounding a fetus in the womb, especially as discharged in a flow shortly before birth: *I think my waters have broken.*
5 the quality of transparency and brilliance shown by a diamond or other gem.
6 Finance capital stock which represents a book value greater than the true assets of a company.
▸ verb **1** [with obj.] pour or sprinkle water over (a plant or area) in order to encourage plant growth: *I went out to water the geraniums.* ■ give a drink of water to (an animal): *they stopped to water the horses.* ■ take a fresh supply of water on board (a ship or steam train).
2 [no obj.] (of a person's eyes) fill with tears: *Rory blinked, his eyes watering.* ■ (of a person's mouth) produce saliva, typically in response to the sight or smell of appetizing food: *the smell of frying bacon made Hilary's mouth water.*
3 [with obj.] dilute or adulterate (a drink, typically an alcoholic one) with water: *staff at the club had been **watering down** the drinks.* ■ (**water something down**) make a statement or proposal less forceful or controversial by changing or leaving out certain details: *the army's report of its investigation was considerably watered down.*
4 (of a river) flow through (an area of land): *the valley is watered by the River Dee.*
5 Finance increase (a company's debt, or nominal capital) by the issue of new shares without a corresponding addition to assets.
– PHRASES **by water** using a ship or boat for travel or transport: *at the end of the lake was a small kiosk, accessible only by water.* **cast one's bread upon the waters** see BREAD. **like water** in great quantities: *George was spending money like water.* **make water** (of a ship or boat) take in water through a leak. **of the first water** (of a diamond or pearl) of the greatest brilliance and transparency. ■ used to refer to a person or thing that is unsurpassed of their kind, typically in an undesirable way: *she was a bore of the first water.* **under water** submerged; flooded. **the water of life** whisky. **water off a duck's back** see DUCK[1]. **water on the brain** informal hydrocephalus. **water under the bridge** (or N. Amer. **water over the dam**) used to refer to events that are in the past and consequently no longer to be regarded as important.
– DERIVATIVES **waterer** noun, **waterless** adjective.
– ORIGIN Old English *wæter* (noun), *wæterian* (verb), of Germanic origin; related to Dutch *water*, German *Wasser*, from an Indo-European root shared by Russian *voda* (compare with VODKA), also by Latin *unda* 'wave' and Greek *hudōr* 'water'.

water bag ▸ noun a bag made of leather, canvas, or other material, used for carrying water.

water bailiff ▸ noun Brit. **1** an official who enforces fishing laws.
2 historical a customs officer at a port.

water-based ▸ adjective **1** (of a substance or solution) using or having water as a medium or main ingredient: *a water-based paint.*
2 (of a sporting activity) carried out on water.

water bath ▸ noun Chemistry a container of water heated to a given temperature, used for heating substances placed in smaller containers.

water bear ▸ noun a minute animal with a short plump body and four pairs of stubby legs, living in water or in the film of water on plants such as mosses. ● Phylum Tardigrada.

Water Bearer (**the Water Bearer**) the zodiacal sign or constellation Aquarius.

waterbed ▸ noun a bed with a water-filled rubber or plastic mattress.

water beetle ▸ noun any of a large number of beetles that live in fresh water. ● Several families, in particular Dytiscidae (the predatory diving beetles) and Hydrophilidae (scavenging beetles).

waterbird ▸ noun a bird that frequents water, especially one that habitually wades or swims in fresh water.

water birth ▸ noun a birth in which the mother spends the final stages of labour in a birthing pool, with delivery taking place either in or out of the water.

water biscuit ▸ noun a thin, crisp unsweetened biscuit made from flour and water.

water blinks ▸ noun see BLINKS.

waterblommetjie /ˈvɑːtə(r),blɒmək i/ ▸ noun (pl. **waterblommetjies**) South African term for WATER HAWTHORN.
– ORIGIN 1950s: Afrikaans, literally 'little water flower'.

water bloom ▸ noun another term for ALGAL BLOOM.

waterboarding ▸ noun [mass noun] an interrogation technique simulating the experience of drowning, in which a person is strapped head downwards on a sloping board with the mouth and nose covered, while large quantities of water are poured over the face.

water boatman ▸ noun **1** a predatory aquatic bug that swims on its back using its long back legs as oars. It is able to capture large prey such as tadpoles and fish. Also called BACKSWIMMER. ● Family Notonectidae, suborder Heteroptera: *Notonecta* and other genera.
2 an aquatic bug which spends much of its time on the bottom, using its front legs to sieve food from

the water and its hair-fringed rear legs for swimming. ● Family Corixidae, suborder Heteroptera: *Corixa*, *Sigara*, and other genera.

waterbody ▶ noun (pl. **waterbodies**) a body of water forming a physiographical feature, for example a sea or a reservoir.

water bomber ▶ noun an aircraft used for extinguishing forest fires by dropping water.

waterborne ▶ adjective conveyed by, travelling on, or involving travel or transport on water: *troops were deployed by waterborne craft.* ■ (of a disease) communicated or propagated by contaminated water.

waterbrash ▶ noun [mass noun] a sudden flow of saliva associated with indigestion.
– ORIGIN early 19th cent.: from WATER + dialect *brash* 'eruption of fluid from the stomach'.

waterbuck ▶ noun a large African antelope occurring near rivers and lakes in the savannah. ● *Kobus ellipsiprymnus*, family Bovidae.

water buffalo ▶ noun a large black domesticated buffalo with heavy swept-back horns, used as a beast of burden throughout the tropics. ● Genus *Bubalus*, family Bovidae: the domesticated *B. bubalis*, descended from the wild *B. arnee*, which is confined to remote parts of India and SE Asia.

water butt ▶ noun a large barrel used for catching and storing rainwater.

water calla ▶ noun another term for BOG ARUM.

water cannon ▶ noun a device that ejects a powerful jet of water, typically used to disperse a crowd.

Water Carrier (**the Water Carrier**) the zodiacal sign or constellation Aquarius.

water chestnut ▶ noun **1** (also **Chinese water chestnut**) the crisp, white-fleshed tuber of a tropical sedge, used in oriental cookery.
2 the sedge which yields the water chestnut, which is cultivated in flooded fields in SE Asia. ● *Eleocharis tuberosa*, family Cyperaceae.
3 (also **water caltrop**) an aquatic plant with small white flowers, producing an edible rounded seed with two large projecting horns. ● *Trapa natans*, family Trapaceae.

water clock ▶ noun historical a clock that used the flow of water to measure time.

water closet ▶ noun dated a flush toilet. ■ a room containing a flush toilet.

watercock ▶ noun a brown and grey aquatic Asian rail, the male of which develops black plumage and a red frontal shield in the breeding season. ● *Gallicrex cinerea*, family Rallidae.

watercolour (US **watercolor**) ▶ noun [mass noun] (also **watercolours**) artists' paint made with a water-soluble binder such as gum arabic, and thinned with water rather than oil, giving a transparent colour. ■ [count noun] a picture painted with watercolours. ■ the art of painting with watercolours, especially using a technique of producing paler colours by diluting rather than by adding white.
– DERIVATIVES **watercolourist** noun.

water cooler ▶ noun a dispenser of cooled drinking water, typically used in places of work. ■ informal used to refer to the type of informal conversation among office workers that takes place around a water cooler: *the subtleties of film noir haven't exactly been a hot topic around the water cooler* | [as modifier] *water-cooler chat.*

watercourse ▶ noun a brook, stream, or artificially constructed water channel. ■ the bed along which a watercourse flows.

watercraft ▶ noun (pl. **same**) **1** a boat or other vessel that travels on water.
2 [mass noun] skill in sailing and other activities which take place on water.

watercress ▶ noun [mass noun] a Eurasian cress which grows in running water and whose pungent leaves are used in salad. ● *Rorippa nasturtium-aquaticum*, family Cruciferae.

water cricket ▶ noun a predatory water bug that runs on the surface film of water, related to the pond skater but with shorter legs. ● Family Veliidae, suborder Heteroptera: several genera, in particular *Velia*.

water crowfoot ▶ noun see CROWFOOT.

water cure ▶ noun chiefly historical a session of treatment by hydropathy.

water cycle ▶ noun the cycle of processes by which water circulates between the earth's oceans, atmosphere, and land, involving precipitation as rain and snow, drainage in streams and rivers, and return to the atmosphere by evaporation and transpiration.

water deer (also **Chinese water deer**) ▶ noun a small deer without antlers, the male having a pair of tusk-like canine teeth, native to China and Korea. ● *Hydropotes inermis*, family Cervidae.

water diviner ▶ noun Brit. a person who searches for underground water by using a dowsing rod.

waterdog ▶ noun an aquatic North American salamander which is a smaller relative of the mud puppy, typically living in flowing water. ● Genus *Necturus*, family Proteidae: several species.

water dropwort ▶ noun a widely distributed poisonous plant of the parsley family, which grows in wet habitats. ● Genus *Oenanthe*, family Umbelliferae: several species, in particular *O. crocata* of Europe.

water drum ▶ noun **1** a West African instrument played by striking a bowl or gourd floating upside down in a pail of water.
2 an American Indian drum partly filled with water to adjust the pitch and timbre.

watered silk ▶ noun [mass noun] silk that has been treated in such a way as to give it a wavy, lustrous finish.

waterfall ▶ noun a cascade of water falling from a height, formed when a river or stream flows over a precipice or steep incline.

water feature ▶ noun a pond or fountain in a garden.

water fern ▶ noun **1** a small aquatic or semiaquatic fern which is either free-floating or anchored by the roots, found chiefly in tropical and warm countries. ● Families Azollaceae, Marsileaceae and Salviniaceae: many species, in particular the minute floating *Azolla filiculoides* of tropical America, which has been naturalized elsewhere.
2 an Australian fern with large coarse fronds, typically growing in marshy areas and rainforests. ● Genus *Blechnum*, family Blechnaceae: several species.

water flea ▶ noun another term for DAPHNIA.

Waterford a county in the south-east of the Republic of Ireland, in the province of Munster; main administrative centre, Dungarvan. ■ the county town of Waterford, a port on an inlet of St George's Channel; pop. 45,748 (2006).

Waterford glass ▶ noun [mass noun] fine clear, colourless flint glassware first manufactured in Waterford in the 18th and 19th centuries.

waterfowl ▶ plural noun ducks, geese, or other large aquatic birds, especially when regarded as game.

waterfowling ▶ noun [mass noun] the practice or activity of hunting waterfowl.
– DERIVATIVES **waterfowler** noun.

waterfront ▶ noun a part of a town that borders the sea or a lake or river.

water garden ▶ noun a garden with pools or a stream, for growing aquatic plants.

water gas ▶ noun [mass noun] a fuel gas consisting mainly of carbon monoxide and hydrogen, made by passing steam over incandescent coke.

Watergate a US political scandal in which an attempt to bug the national headquarters of the Democratic Party (in the Watergate building in Washington DC) led to the resignation of President Nixon (1974).

watergate ▶ noun a gate of a town or castle opening on to a lake, river, or sea.

water glass ▶ noun **1** [mass noun] a solution of sodium or potassium silicate which solidifies on exposure to air, used for preserving eggs and hardening artificial stone.
2 a tube with a glass bottom, for observing beneath the surface of water.

water gun ▶ noun N. Amer. a water pistol.

water hammer ▶ noun [mass noun] a knocking noise in a water pipe that occurs when a tap is turned off briskly.

water hawthorn ▶ noun [mass noun] an ornamental water plant with long oval floating leaves and erect aromatic flower spikes, native to the South African province of Western Cape where the flower spikes are used in cooking. ● *Aponogeton distachyus*, family Aponogetonaceae.

water hemlock ▶ noun a highly poisonous European plant of the parsley family, which grows in ditches and marshy ground. Also called COWBANE. ● *Cicuta virosa*, family Umbelliferae.

waterhen ▶ noun an aquatic rail, especially a moorhen or related bird. ● Genera *Gallinula* and *Amaurornis*, family Rallidae.

waterhole ▶ noun a depression in which water collects, especially one that is regularly drunk from by animals.

Waterhouse, Alfred (1830–1905), English architect. His designs include the Manchester Assize courts (1859) and Town Hall (1869–77), and the Natural History Museum in London (1873–81).

water hyacinth ▶ noun [mass noun] a free-floating tropical American water plant which has been introduced elsewhere as an ornamental and in some warmer regions has become a serious weed of waterways. ● *Eichhornia crassipes*, family Pontederiaceae.

water ice ▶ noun a dessert consisting of frozen fruit juice or flavoured water and sugar.

watering can ▶ noun a portable water container with a long spout and a detachable perforated cap, used for watering plants.

watering hole ▶ noun a waterhole from which animals regularly drink. ■ informal a pub or bar.

watering place ▶ noun a watering hole. ■ a spa or seaside resort.

water injection ▶ noun [mass noun] (in the oil industry) the forcing of water into a reservoir formation, in particular as a technique of secondary recovery.

water jacket ▶ noun a casing containing water placed around something to protect it from extremes of temperature.
– DERIVATIVES **water-jacketed** adjective.

water jump ▶ noun an obstacle in a jumping competition or steeplechase, where a horse must jump over or into water.

water knot ▶ noun a kind of knot used to join two fishing lines.

waterleaf ▶ noun a North American woodland plant with bell-shaped flowers and leaves that appear to be stained with water. ● Genus *Hydrophyllum*, family Hydrophyllaceae.

water lettuce ▶ noun [mass noun] a tropical aquatic plant of the arum family which forms a floating rosette of leaves. ● *Pistia stratiotes*, family Araceae.

water level ▶ noun the height reached by the water in a reservoir, river, storage tank, or similar.

water lily ▶ noun an ornamental aquatic plant with large round floating leaves and large, typically cup-shaped, floating flowers. ● Family Nymphaeaceae: several genera and many species, including the Eurasian **white water lily** (*Nymphaea alba*, with numerous cultivars), and the widely distributed **yellow water lily** or brandy-bottle (*Nuphar luteum*).

waterline ▶ noun **1** the level normally reached by the water on the side of a ship. ■ the level reached by the sea or a river visible as a line on a rock face, beach, or riverbank. ■ any of various structural lines of a ship, parallel with the surface of the water, representing the contour of the hull at various heights above the keel.
2 a linear watermark in paper.

waterlogged ▶ adjective saturated with or full of water: *parts of the racecourse were waterlogged.*
– ORIGIN mid 18th cent.: past participle of the verb *waterlog* 'make (a ship) unmanageable by flooding', from WATER + the verb LOG[1].

Waterloo, Battle of /ˌwɔːtəˈluː/ a battle fought on 18 June 1815 near the village of Waterloo (in what is now Belgium), in which Napoleon's army was defeated by the British (under the Duke of Wellington) and Prussians. The allied pursuit caused Napoleon's army to disintegrate entirely, ending his bid to return to power. ■ (as noun **a Waterloo**) a decisive defeat or failure: *the coach rued the absence of his top player as his team met their Waterloo.*

water main ▶ noun the main pipe in a water supply system.

waterman ▶ noun (pl. **watermen**) a boatman. ■ an oarsman who has attained a particular level of knowledge or skill.

watermark ▶ noun a faint design made in some paper during manufacture that is visible when held against the light and typically identifies the maker.
▶ verb [with obj.] mark (paper) with a watermark.

water mass ▶ noun a large body of seawater that is distinguishable by its characteristic temperature and salinity range.

water meadow ▶ noun a meadow that is periodically flooded by a stream or river.

W

water measurer ▶ **noun** a long, thin aquatic bug which walks slowly on the surface film of water and spears small prey with its beak. ● Genus *Hydrometra*, family Hydrometridae, suborder Heteroptera: several species.

watermelon ▶ **noun 1** the large melon-like fruit of a plant of the gourd family, with smooth green skin, red pulp, and watery juice.
2 the African plant which yields watermelons. ● *Citrullus lanatus*, family Cucurbitaceae.

water milfoil ▶ **noun** see MILFOIL (sense 2).

watermill ▶ **noun** a mill worked by a waterwheel.

water moccasin ▶ **noun** another term for COTTONMOUTH.

water nymph ▶ **noun** (in folklore and classical mythology) a nymph inhabiting or presiding over water, especially a naiad or nereid.

water of crystallization ▶ **noun** [mass noun] Chemistry water molecules forming an essential part of the crystal structure of some compounds.

water opossum ▶ **noun** another term for YAPOK.

water ouzel ▶ **noun** dialect term for DIPPER (sense 1).

water parsnip ▶ **noun** a tall plant of the parsley family which lives in or near water. ● *Sium latifolium* and *Berula erecta*, family Umbelliferae.

water pepper ▶ **noun** a widely distributed plant of the dock family which grows in wet ground, with peppery-tasting leaves and sap which is a skin irritant. ● Genus *Polygonum*, family Polygonaceae: several species, in particular *P. hydropiper*.

water pipe ▶ **noun 1** a pipe for conveying water.
2 a pipe for smoking tobacco, cannabis, etc., that draws the smoke through water to cool it.

water pipit ▶ **noun** a dark-coloured European pipit that frequents waterside habitats. ● *Anthus spinoletta*, family Motacillidae; formerly thought to be conspecific with the rock pipit.

water pistol ▶ **noun** a toy pistol that shoots a jet of water.

waterplane ▶ **noun** the horizontal plane which passes through a floating ship on a level with the waterline.

water plantain ▶ **noun** an aquatic or marshland plant of north temperate regions, with leaves that resemble those of plantains and a tall stem bearing numerous pink flowers. ● Genus *Alisma*, family Alismataceae.

water polo ▶ **noun** [mass noun] a seven-a-side game played by swimmers in a pool, with a ball like a football that is thrown into the opponents' net. The game developed in Britain from about 1870.

water power ▶ **noun** [mass noun] power that is derived from the weight or motion of water, used as a force to drive machinery.
– DERIVATIVES **water-powered** adjective.

waterproof ▶ **adjective** impervious to water: *a waterproof hat*. ■ not liable to be washed away by water: *waterproof ink*.
▶ **noun** Brit. a garment, especially a coat, that keeps out water.
▶ **verb** [with obj.] make impervious to water.
– DERIVATIVES **waterproofer** noun, **waterproofness** noun.

water purslane ▶ **noun** a creeping Eurasian plant of damp places and bare ground. ● *Lythrum portula*, family Lythraceae.

water rail ▶ **noun** a secretive Eurasian marshbird with dark grey and brown plumage, making loud grunts and squeals in the breeding season. ● *Rallus aquaticus*, family Rallidae.

water rat ▶ **noun** a large semiaquatic rat-like rodent. ● Several genera in the family Muridae, in particular *Hydromys* of Australasia.
■ Brit. another term for WATER VOLE.

W

water rate ▶ **noun** (usu. **water rates**) a charge made for the use of a public water supply.

water-repellent ▶ **adjective** not easily penetrated by water, especially as a result of being treated for such a purpose with a surface coating.

water-resistant ▶ **adjective** able to resist the penetration of water to some degree but not entirely.
– DERIVATIVES **water-resistance** noun.

Waters, Muddy (1915–83), American blues singer and guitarist; born *McKinley Morganfield*. Waters impressed new rhythm-and-blues bands such as the Rolling Stones, who took their name from his 1950 song.

waterscape ▶ **noun** a landscape in which an expanse of water is a dominant feature.

water scorpion ▶ **noun** a mainly tropical predatory water bug with grasping forelegs, breathing from the surface via a bristle-like 'tail'. ● Family Nepidae, suborder Heteroptera: several genera and species, including the European *Nepa cinerea*.

watershed ▶ **noun 1** an area or ridge of land that separates waters flowing to different rivers, basins, or seas. ■ an area or region drained by a river, river system, or other body of water.
2 an event or period marking a turning point in a situation: *these works were a watershed in the history of music*. ■ Brit. the time after which programmes that are regarded as unsuitable for children are broadcast on television.
– ORIGIN early 19th cent.: from WATER + *shed* in the sense 'ridge of high ground' (related to SHED²), suggested by German *Wasserscheide*.

water shoot ▶ **noun** a vigorous but unproductive shoot from the trunk, main branch, or root of a tree.

water shrew ▶ **noun** a large semiaquatic shrew that preys on aquatic invertebrates. ● Four genera, family Soricidae: several species, in particular the **Eurasian water shrew** (*Neomys fodiens*) and the **American water shrew** (*Sorex palustris*).

waterside ▶ **noun** the edge of or area adjoining a sea, lake, or river.

watersider ▶ **noun** Austral./NZ a person employed to load and unload a ship's cargo.

waterski ▶ **noun** (pl. **waterskis**) each of a pair of skis enabling the wearer to skim the surface of the water when towed by a motor boat.
▶ **verb** (**waterskis**, **waterskiing**, **waterskied**) [no obj.] skim the surface of water on waterskis.
– DERIVATIVES **waterskier** noun.

water slide ▶ **noun** a slide into a swimming pool, typically flowing with water and incorporating a number of twists and turns.

water snake ▶ **noun** a harmless snake which is a powerful swimmer and spends part of its time in fresh water hunting for prey. Water snakes are found in Africa, Asia, and America. ● *Natrix* and other genera, family Colubridae: several species.

water softener ▶ **noun** a device or substance that softens hard water by removing certain minerals.

water soldier ▶ **noun** an aquatic European plant with slender spiny-toothed leaves in submerged rosettes that rise to the surface at flowering time. ● *Stratiotes aloides*, family Hydrocharitaceae.

water-soluble ▶ **adjective** able to be dissolved in water: *the paint is water-soluble | water-soluble vitamins*.

water spider ▶ **noun** a semiaquatic spider. ● Several species, including the European *Argyroneta aquatica* (family Argyronetidae), which lives in an underwater dome of silk filled with air. See also RAFT SPIDER.

water splash ▶ **noun** Brit. a water-filled dip in a road.

water sports ▶ **plural noun 1** sports that are carried out on water, such as waterskiing and windsurfing.
2 informal sexual activity involving urination.

waterspout ▶ **noun** a rotating column of water and spray formed by a whirlwind occurring over the sea or other body of water.

water starwort ▶ **noun** a widely distributed slender-leaved plant which grows in water or on mud and is sometimes used in aquaria. ● Genus *Callitriche*, family Callitrichaceae.

water stick insect ▶ **noun** a very long, slender European water bug related to the water scorpion, which waits motionless in vegetation for prey to pass. ● *Ranatra linearis*, family Nepidae, suborder Heteroptera.

water stone ▶ **noun** a whetstone used with water rather than oil.

water strider ▶ **noun** North American term for POND SKATER and WATER CRICKET.

water table ▶ **noun** the level below which the ground is saturated with water.

water taxi ▶ **noun** a small motor boat for transporting paying passengers on rivers, canals, etc.

waterthrush ▶ **noun** a thrush-like North American warbler related to the ovenbird, found near woodland streams and swamps. ● Genus *Seiurus*, family Parulidae: two species.

watertight ▶ **adjective 1** closely sealed, fastened, or fitted so that no water enters or passes through: *a watertight compartment*.
2 (of an argument or account) unable to be disputed or questioned: *their alibis are watertight*.

water torture ▶ **noun** [mass noun] a form of torture in which the victim is exposed to the incessant dripping of water on the head or to the sound of dripping.

water tower ▶ **noun** a tower supporting an elevated water tank, whose height creates the pressure required to distribute the water through a piped system.

water-tube boiler ▶ **noun** a form of boiler in which steam is generated by circulating water through tubes exposed to the source of heat (as opposed to the more usual arrangement in which tubes carry hot gases through the water).

water-vascular system ▶ **noun** Zoology (in an echinoderm) a network of water vessels in the body, the tube feet being operated by hydraulic pressure within the vessels.

water violet ▶ **noun** an aquatic plant of the primrose family, with lilac flowers and finely divided submerged leaves. ● *Hottonia palustris*, family Primulaceae.

water vole ▶ **noun** a large semiaquatic vole which excavates burrows in the banks of rivers. ● Genera *Arvicola* and *Microtus*, family Muridae: three species, in particular the **European water vole** (*A. terrestris*) and the **American water vole** (*M. richardsoni*).

waterway ▶ **noun 1** a river, canal, or other route for travel by water.
2 a channel at the outer edge of a deck of a boat that allows water to run off.

waterweed ▶ **noun** [mass noun] **1** any aquatic plant with inconspicuous flowers.
2 a submerged aquatic American plant which is grown in ornamental ponds. ● Genus *Elodea*, family Hydrocharitaceae: several species, in particular Canadian pondweed.

waterwheel ▶ **noun** a large wheel driven by flowing water, used to work machinery or to raise water to a higher level.

water wings ▶ **plural noun** inflated floats that may be fixed to the arms of someone learning to swim to give increased buoyancy.

water witch (also **water-witcher**) ▶ **noun** US a water diviner.
– DERIVATIVES **water-witching** noun.

waterworks ▶ **plural noun 1** [treated as sing.] an establishment for managing a water supply.
2 informal used to refer to the shedding of tears: *she is an expert at **turning on the waterworks** to manipulate others*. ■ Brit. used as a humorous euphemism for the urinary system.

watery ▶ **adjective** consisting of, containing, or resembling water: *a watery fluid*. ■ (of a person's eyes) full of tears. ■ thin or tasteless as a result of containing too much water: *watery coffee*. ■ pale or weak, as if diluted by water: *watery sunshine*.
– DERIVATIVES **wateriness** noun.
– ORIGIN Old English *wæterig* (see WATER, -Y¹).

Watford a town in Hertfordshire, SE England; pop. 121,300 (est. 2009).
– PHRASES **north of Watford** informal used to refer to any part of England that is north of London, typically considered as remote or out of touch with the latest news and developments: *all you metropolitan folk who think it's just darkness and barbarism north of Watford, think again*.

Watling Street a Roman road (now largely underlying modern roads) running north-westwards across England, from Richborough in Kent through London and St Albans to Wroxeter in Shropshire.

Watson¹, James Dewey (b.1928), American biologist. Together with Francis Crick he proposed a model for the structure of the DNA molecule. He shared the Nobel Prize for Physiology or Medicine with Crick and Maurice Wilkins in 1962.

Watson², John Broadus (1878–1958), American psychologist, founder of the school of behaviourism. He held that the role of the psychologist was to discern, through observation and experimentation, the innate behaviour and acquired behaviour in an individual.

Watsu /ˈwɒtsuː/ ▶ **noun** [mass noun] trademark a form of shiatsu massage that takes place in water.
– ORIGIN 1980s: blend of WATER and SHIATSU.

Watt, James (1736–1819), Scottish engineer. Among his many innovations he greatly improved the efficiency of the Newcomen steam engine, which was then adopted for a variety of purposes. He also introduced the term *horsepower*.

watt (abbrev.: **W**) ▸ noun the SI unit of power, equivalent to one joule per second, corresponding to the rate of consumption of energy in an electric circuit where the potential difference is one volt and the current one ampere.
– ORIGIN late 19th cent.: named after James **WATT**.

wattage ▸ noun an amount of electrical power expressed in watts. ■ the operating power of a lamp or other electrical appliance expressed in watts.

Watteau /ˈwɒtəʊ/, Jean Antoine (1684–1721), French painter, of Flemish descent. An initiator of the rococo style, he is also known for his invention of the *fête galante*.

watt-hour ▸ noun a measure of electrical energy equivalent to a power consumption of one watt for one hour.

wattle¹ /ˈwɒt(ə)l/ ▸ noun **1** [mass noun] a material for making fences, walls, etc., consisting of rods or stakes interlaced with twigs or branches. ■ [count noun] dialect a wicker hurdle.
2 chiefly Austral. an acacia. ● Genus *Acacia*, family Leguminosae: many species, including the **golden wattle**.
▸ verb [with obj.] make, enclose, or fill up with wattle.
– ORIGIN Old English *watul*, of unknown origin.

wattle² /ˈwɒt(ə)l/ ▸ noun a coloured fleshy lobe hanging from the head or neck of the turkey and some other birds.
– DERIVATIVES **wattled** adjective.
– ORIGIN early 16th cent.: of unknown origin.

wattle and daub ▸ noun [mass noun] a material formerly or traditionally used in building walls, consisting of a network of interwoven sticks and twigs covered with mud or clay.

wattlebird ▸ noun **1** the largest of the honeyeaters found in Australia, with a wattle hanging from each cheek. ● Genus *Anthochaera* (and *Melidectes*), family Meliphagidae: four species.
2 a songbird of a New Zealand family distinguished by wattles hanging from the base of the bill. ● Family Callaeidae: the saddleback and the kokako, together with the extinct huia.

wattle-eye ▸ noun a small African flycatcher with a coloured patch of bare skin around or above the eye, typically having black and white plumage. ● Genus *Platysteira*, family Platysteiridae (or Monarchidae): several species.

wattmeter ▸ noun a meter for measuring electric power in watts.

Watts¹, George Frederick (1817–1904), English painter and sculptor. He is best known for his portraits of public figures, including Gladstone, Tennyson, and J. S. Mill. He was married to the actress Ellen Terry from 1864 to 1877.

Watts², Isaac (1674–1748), English hymn writer and poet, remembered for hymns such as 'O God, Our Help in Ages Past' (1719).

Watusi /wəˈtuːsi/ (also **Watutsi** /wəˈtʊtsi/) ▸ noun **1** [treated as pl.] the Tutsi people collectively (now dated in English use).
2 an energetic dance popular in the 1960s.
▸ verb (**Watusies**, **Watusiing**, **Watusied**) [no obj.] dance the Watusi.
– ORIGIN a local name, from the plural prefix *wa-* + **TUTSI**.

Waugh /wɔː/, Evelyn (Arthur St John) (1903–66), English novelist. His work was profoundly influenced by his conversion to Roman Catholicism in 1930. Notable works: *Decline and Fall* (1928); *Brideshead Revisited* (1945).

waul /wɔːl/ ▸ verb [no obj.] give a loud plaintive cry like that of a cat.
– ORIGIN early 16th cent.: imitative.

wave ▸ verb **1** [no obj.] move one's hand to and fro in greeting or as a signal: *he waved to me from the train.* ■ [with obj.] move (one's hand or arm, or something held in one's hand) to and fro: *he waved a sheaf of papers in the air.* ■ [with obj.] convey (a greeting or other message) by waving one's hand or something held in it: *we waved our farewells* | [with two objs] *she waved him goodbye.* ■ [with obj. and adverbial of direction] instruct (someone) to move in a particular direction by moving one's hand: *he waved her back.*
2 [no obj.] move to and fro with a swaying motion while remaining fixed to one point: *the flag waved in the wind.*
3 [with obj.] style (hair) so that it curls slightly: *her hair had been carefully waved for the evening.* ■ [no obj.] (of hair) grow with a slight curl: (as adj. **waving**) *thick, waving grey hair sprouted back from his forehead.*
▸ noun **1** a long body of water curling into an arched form and breaking on the shore: *he was swept out to sea by a freak wave.* ■ a ridge of water between two depressions in open water: *gulls and cormorants bobbed on the waves.* ■ a shape regarded as resembling a breaking wave: *a wave of treetops stretched to the horizon.* ■ (**the waves**) literary the sea.
2 a sudden occurrence of or increase in a phenomenon, feeling, or emotion: *a wave of strikes had paralysed the government* | *fear came over me in waves.*
3 a gesture or signal made by moving one's hand to and fro: *he gave a little wave and walked off.*
4 a slightly curling lock of hair: *his hair was drying in unruly waves.* ■ [in sing.] a tendency to curl in a person's hair: *her hair has a slight natural wave.*
5 Physics a periodic disturbance of the particles of a substance which may be propagated without net movement of the particles, such as in the passage of undulating motion, heat, or sound. See also **STANDING WAVE** and **TRAVELLING WAVE**. ■ a single curve in the course of this motion. ■ a similar variation of an electromagnetic field in the propagation of light or other radiation through a medium or vacuum.
– PHRASES **make waves** informal create a significant impression: *he has already made waves as a sculptor.* ■ cause trouble: *I don't want to risk her welfare by making waves.*
– PHRASAL VERBS **wave something aside** dismiss something as unnecessary or irrelevant: *he waved the objection aside and carried on.* **wave someone/thing down** use one's hand to give a signal to stop to a driver or vehicle.
– DERIVATIVES **waveless** adjective, **wave-like** adjective.
– ORIGIN Old English *wafian* (verb), from the Germanic base of **WAVER**; the noun by alteration (influenced by the verb) of Middle English *wawe* '(sea) wave'.

> **USAGE** On confusion between wave and waive, see **USAGE** at **WAIVE**.

waveband ▸ noun a range of wavelengths falling between two given limits, used in radio transmission.

wave equation ▸ noun Mathematics a differential equation expressing the properties of motion in waves.

wave farm ▸ noun an area of the sea where machinery is installed to harness the energy produced by waves in order to generate electricity.

waveform ▸ noun Physics a curve showing the shape of a wave at a given time.

wavefront ▸ noun Physics a surface containing points affected in the same way by a wave at a given time.

wave function ▸ noun Physics a function that satisfies a wave equation and describes the properties of a wave.

waveguide ▸ noun a metal tube or other device confining and conveying microwaves.

wavelength /ˈweɪvlɛŋθ, -lɛŋkθ/ ▸ noun **1** Physics the distance between successive crests of a wave, especially points in a sound wave or electromagnetic wave. (Symbol: λ) ■ this distance as a distinctive feature of radio waves from a transmitter.
2 a person's ideas and way of thinking, especially as it affects their ability to communicate with others: *when we met we hit it off immediately—we're* ***on the same wavelength****.*

wavelet ▸ noun a small wave of water; a ripple.

wave machine ▸ noun a machine that creates waves in the water in a swimming pool.

wave mechanics ▸ plural noun [treated as sing.] Physics a method of analysis of the behaviour of atomic phenomena with particles represented by wave equations.

wave number ▸ noun Physics the number of waves in a unit distance.

wave packet ▸ noun Physics a group of superposed waves which together form a travelling localized disturbance, especially one described by Schrödinger's equation and regarded as representing a particle.

wave power ▸ noun [mass noun] power obtained by harnessing the energy produced by waves at sea.

waver ▸ verb [no obj.] **1** move in a quivering way; flicker: *the flame wavered in the draught.*
2 become weaker; falter: *his love for her had never wavered* | (as adj. **wavering**) *she gave a wavering smile.* ■ be undecided between two opinions or courses of action: *she never* ***wavered from*** *her intention.*
– DERIVATIVES **waverer** noun, **waveringly** adverb, **wavery** adjective.
– ORIGIN Middle English: from Old Norse *vafra* 'flicker', of Germanic origin. Compare with **WAVE**.

WAVES ▸ plural noun the women's section of the US Naval Reserve, established in 1942, or, since 1948, of the US Navy.
– ORIGIN acronym from *Women Appointed* (later *Accepted*) *for Volunteer Emergency Service*.

wavetable ▸ noun Computing a file or memory device containing data that represents a sound such as a piece of music.

wave theory ▸ noun Physics, historical the theory that light is propagated through the ether by a wave motion imparted to the ether by the molecular vibrations of the radiant body.

wave train ▸ noun a group of waves of equal or similar wavelengths travelling in the same direction.

WAV file /weɪv/ (also **wave file**) ▸ noun Computing a format for storing uncompressed audio files.
– ORIGIN 1990s: shortened from *waveform audio format*.

wavicle /ˈweɪvɪk(ə)l/ ▸ noun Physics an entity having characteristic properties of both waves and particles.
– ORIGIN 1920s: blend of **WAVE** and **PARTICLE**.

wavy ▸ adjective (**wavier**, **waviest**) having or consisting of a series of undulating and wave-like curves: *she had long, wavy hair.* ■ [usu. postpositive] Heraldry divided or edged with a line formed of alternating shallow curves.
– DERIVATIVES **waviness** noun.

wa-wa ▸ noun variant spelling of **WAH-WAH**.

wax¹ ▸ noun [mass noun] **1** a sticky yellowish mouldable substance secreted by honeybees as the material of a honeycomb; beeswax. ■ a white translucent material obtained by bleaching and purifying beeswax and used for such purposes as making candles, modelling, and as a basis of polishes. ■ a similar viscous substance, typically a lipid or hydrocarbon. ■ earwax.
2 informal used in reference to records: *he didn't get* ***on wax*** *until 1959.*
▸ verb [with obj.] **1** cover or treat (something) with wax or a similar substance, typically to polish or protect it: *I washed and waxed the floor.* ■ remove unwanted hair from (a part of the body) by applying wax and then peeling off the wax and hairs together.
2 informal make a recording of: *he waxed a series of tracks that emphasized his lead guitar work* | (as noun **waxing**) *the latest waxing by the Grams.*
– DERIVATIVES **waxer** noun.
– ORIGIN Old English *wæx*, *weax*, of Germanic origin; related to Dutch *was* and German *Wachs*. The verb dates from late Middle English.

wax² ▸ verb [no obj.] **1** (of the moon between new and full) have a progressively larger part of its visible surface illuminated, increasing its apparent size. ■ literary become larger or stronger: *his anger waxed.*
2 [with complement] begin to speak or write about something in the specified manner: *they* ***waxed lyrical*** *about the old days.*
– PHRASES **wax and wane** undergo alternate increases and decreases: *green sentiment has waxed and waned.*
– ORIGIN Old English *weaxan*, of Germanic origin; related to Dutch *wassen* and German *wachsen*, from an Indo-European root shared by Greek *auxanein* and Latin *augere* 'to increase'.

wax³ ▸ noun [usu. in sing.] Brit. informal, dated a fit of anger: *she is* ***in a wax*** *about the delay to the wedding.*
– ORIGIN mid 19th cent.: origin uncertain; perhaps from phrases such as *wax angry*.

wax bean ▸ noun another term for **WAXPOD**.

waxberry ▸ noun (pl. **waxberries**) a shrub with berries that have a waxy coating, in particular a bayberry.

waxbill ▸ noun a small finch-like Old World songbird, typically brightly coloured and with a red bill that resembles sealing wax in colour. ● Family Estrildidae (the **waxbill family**): about three genera, especially *Estrilda*, and several species. The waxbill family also includes the avadavats, mannikins, cordon-bleu, Java sparrow, zebra finch, etc., many being popular as cage birds.

waxcloth ▸ noun [mass noun] cloth that is impregnated with oil for covering floors and tables; oilcloth.

waxed jacket ▸ noun an outdoor jacket made of a fabric that has been impregnated with wax to make it waterproof.

waxed paper ▸ noun [mass noun] paper that has been impregnated with wax to make it waterproof or greaseproof, used especially in cooking and the wrapping of foodstuffs.

waxen ▶ adjective **1** having a smooth, pale, translucent surface or appearance like that of wax: *a canopy of waxen, creamy blooms.*
2 archaic or literary made of wax: *a waxen effigy.*

wax flower ▶ noun a plant bearing flowers with a waxy appearance: ● an Australian shrub with white or pink flowers (genus *Eriostemon*, family *Rutaceae*). ● a hoya.

waxhead ▶ noun Austral. informal a surfer.

wax light ▶ noun historical a taper or candle made from wax.

wax moth ▶ noun a brownish moth which lays its eggs in beehives. The caterpillars cover the combs with silken tunnels and feed on beeswax. ● Genera *Galleria* and *Achroea*, family Pyralidae: several species, in particular *G. mellonella*.

wax myrtle ▶ noun another term for **BAYBERRY**.

wax painting ▶ noun another term for **ENCAUSTIC**.

wax palm ▶ noun either of two South American palm trees from which wax is obtained: ● an Andean palm with a stem coated in a mixture of resin and wax (*Ceroxylon alpinum*, family Palmae). ● a carnauba.

wax resist ▶ noun [mass noun] a process similar to batik used in pottery and printing.

wax tree (also **Japanese wax tree**) ▶ noun an East Asian tree with white berries that produce a wax which is used as a substitute for beeswax. ● *Rhus succedanea*, family Anacardiaceae.

waxwing ▶ noun a crested Eurasian and American songbird with mainly pinkish-brown plumage, having small tips like red sealing wax to some wing feathers. ● Genus *Bombycilla*, family Bombycillidae: three species, in particular the (**Bohemian**) **waxwing** (*B. garrulus*).

waxwork ▶ noun a lifelike dummy modelled in wax. ■ (**waxworks**) [treated as sing.] chiefly Brit. an exhibition of wax dummies.

waxy[1] ▶ adjective (**waxier, waxiest**) resembling wax in consistency or appearance: *waxy potatoes.*
– DERIVATIVES **waxily** adverb, **waxiness** noun.

waxy[2] ▶ adjective (**waxier, waxiest**) Brit. informal, dated angry; bad-tempered.

way /weɪ/ ▶ noun **1** a method, style, or manner of doing something; an optional or alternative form of action: *I hated their way of cooking potatoes* | *there are two ways of approaching this problem.* ■ (**one's way**) one's characteristic or habitual manner of behaviour or expression: *it was not his way to wait passively for things to happen.* ■ (**ways**) the customary behaviour or practices of a group: *my years of acclimatization to British ways.* ■ the typical manner in which something happens or in which someone or something behaves: *he was showing off, as is the way with adolescent boys.* ■ a particular aspect of something; a respect: *I have changed in every way.* ■ [with adj.] a specified condition or state: *the family was in a poor way.*
2 a road, track, or path for travelling along: [in place names] *No. 3, Church Way.* ■ a course of travel or route taken in order to reach a place: *can you tell me the way to Leicester Square?* ■ a specified direction of travel or movement: *we just missed another car coming the other way.* ■ a means of entry or exit from somewhere, such as a door or gate: *I nipped out the back way.* ■ (also N. Amer. informal **ways**) a distance travelled or to be travelled; the distance from one place to another: *they still had a long way ahead of them* | figurative *the area's wine industry still has some way to go to full maturity.* ■ a period between one point in time and another: *September was a long way off.* ■ travel or motion along a particular route; the route along which someone or something would travel if unobstructed: *Christine tried to follow but Martin blocked her way* | *that table's in the way* | *get out of my way!* ■ (**one's way**) used with a verb and adverbial phrase to intensify the force of an action or to denote movement or progress: *I shouldered my way to the bar.* ■ [with modifier or possessive] informal a particular area or locality: *the family's main estate over Maidenhead way.*
3 (**ways**) parts into which something divides or is divided: *the national vote split three ways.*
4 formal or Scottish a person's occupation or line of business.
5 [mass noun] forward motion or momentum of a ship or boat through water: *the dinghy lost way and drifted towards the shore.*
6 (**ways**) a sloping structure down which a new ship is launched.
▶ adverb informal at or to a considerable distance or extent; far (used before an adverb or preposition for emphasis): *his understanding of what constitutes good writing is way off target* | *my grandchildren are way ahead of others their age.* ■ [as submodifier] chiefly N. Amer. much: *I was cycling way too fast.* ■ [usu. as submodifier] US extremely; really (used for emphasis): *the guys behind the bar were way cool.*
– PHRASES **across** (Brit. also **over**) **the way** nearby, especially on the opposite side of the street. **be on one's way** have started one's journey. ■ (in imperative (**be**) **on your way**) informal go away: *on your way, and stop wasting my time!* **by a long way** by a great amount; by far. **by the way** incidentally (used to introduce a new, less important topic): *oh, by the way, while you were away I had a message.* **by way of 1** so as to pass through or across; via: *he travelled by way of Canterbury.* **2** constituting; as a form of: *'I can't help it,' shouted Tom by way of apology.* **3** by means of: *non-compliance with the rules is punishable by way of a fine.* **come one's way** happen or become available to one: *he did whatever jobs came his way.* **get** (or **have**) **one's** (**own**) **way** get or do what one wants in spite of opposition. **give way 1** (of a support or structure) be unable to carry a load or withstand a force; collapse or break. ■ yield to someone or something: *he was not a man to **give way to** this kind of pressure.* ■ (**give way to**) allow oneself to be overcome by or to succumb to (an emotion or impulse): *she gave way to a burst of weeping.* **2** (**give way to**) be replaced or superseded by: *Alan's discomfort gave way to anger.* **3** Brit. allow someone or something to be or go first: ***give way to** traffic coming from the right.* **4** (of rowers) row hard. **go all** (or **the whole**) **way** continue a course of action to its conclusion. ■ informal have full sexual intercourse with someone. **go out of one's way** [usu. with infinitive] make a special effort to do something: *Mrs Mott went out of her way to be courteous to Sara.* **go one's own way** act independently or as one wishes, especially against contrary advice. **go one's way 1** (of events, circumstances, etc.) be favourable to one: *I was just hoping things went my way.* **2** leave: *one by one the staff went their way.* **have it your** (**own**) **way** [in imperative] informal used to indicate angrily that although one disagrees with something said or proposed, one is not going to argue further: *have it your way—we'll go to Princetown.* **have a way with** have a particular talent for dealing with or ability in: *she's got a way with animals.* **have a way with one** have a charming and persuasive manner. **have one's way with** humorous have sexual intercourse with (someone) (typically implying that it is against their better judgement). **in more ways than one** used to indicate that a statement has more than one meaning: *Shelley let her hair down in more ways than one.* **in a way** (or **in some ways** or **in one way**) to a certain extent (used to reduce the effect of a statement): *in some ways television is more challenging than theatre.* **in the** (or **one's**) **way** forming an obstacle or hindrance to movement or action: *his head was in the way of my view.* **in the way of** another way of saying **BY WAY OF** (sense 2) above. **in someone/thing's** (**own**) **way** if regarded from a particular standpoint appropriate to that person or thing: *it's a good enough book in its way.* **in no way** not at all. **keep** (or **stay**) **out of someone's way** avoid someone: *he tried to keep out of her way at school.* **know one's way around** (or **about**) be familiar with (an area, procedure, or subject). **lead the way** go first along a route to show someone the way. ■ be a pioneer in a particular activity. **look the other way** deliberately avoid seeing or noticing someone or something. **my way or the highway** N. Amer. informal said to assert the view that there is no alternative (apart from leaving) but to accept the speaker's opinions or policies: *they know no way but the way of the autocrat—it's my way or the highway.* **one way and another** (or **one way or another**) **1** taking most aspects or considerations into account: *it's been quite a day one way and another.* **2** another way of saying **ONE WAY OR THE OTHER** below. **one way or the other** (or **one way and another**) used to indicate that something is the case for any of various unspecified reasons: *one way or another she brought it on herself.* ■ by some means: *he wants to get rid of me one way or another.* ■ whichever of two given alternatives is the case: *the question is not yet decided, one way or the other.* **on the** (or **one's**) **way** in the course of a journey: *I'll tell you on the way home.* **on the** (or **its**) **way** about to arrive or happen: *there's more snow on the way.* ■ informal (of a child) conceived but not yet born. **on the** (or **one's**) **way out** in the process of leaving. ■ informal going out of fashion or favour. ■ informal dying. **the other way round** (or **around**; Brit. also **about**) in the opposite position or direction. ■ the opposite of what is expected or supposed: *it was you who sought me out, not the other way round.* **out of the way 1** (of a place) remote. **2** dealt with or finished: *economic recovery will begin once the election is out of the way.* ■ (of a person) no longer an obstacle or hindrance to someone's plans: *why did Josie want her out of the way?* **3** [usu. with negative] unusual, exceptional, or remarkable: *he'd seen nothing out of the way.* **out of one's way** not on one's intended route. **put someone in the way of** dated give someone the opportunity of. **that way** used euphemistically to indicate that someone is homosexual: *he was a bit that way.* **to one's way of thinking** in one's opinion. **way back** (US also **way back when**) informal long ago. **the way of the Cross** the journey of Jesus to the place of his crucifixion. ■ a set of images representing the Stations of the Cross. ■ the suffering and self-sacrifice of a Christian. **way of life** the typical pattern of behaviour of a person or group: *the rural way of life.* **the way of the world** the manner in which people typically behave or things typically happen: *all those millions of pounds are not going to create many jobs, but that's the way of the world.* **ways and means** methods and resources for achieving something: *the company is seeking ways and means of safeguarding jobs.* **way to go!** N. Amer. informal used to express pleasure, approval, or excitement.
– ORIGIN Old English *weg*, of Germanic origin; related to Dutch *weg* and German *Weg*, from a base meaning 'move, carry'.

-way ▶ suffix equivalent to **-WAYS**.

wayang /ˈwɑːjaŋ/ ▶ noun (in Indonesia and Malaysia) a theatrical performance employing puppets or human dancers.
– ORIGIN Javanese.

waybill ▶ noun a list of passengers or goods being carried on a vehicle.

waybread ▶ noun [mass noun] archaic the Eurasian common plantain, with broad rounded leaves. ● *Plantago major*, family Plantaginaceae.
– ORIGIN Old English *wegbrǣde* (see **WAY, BROAD**).

wayfarer ▶ noun literary a person who travels on foot.

wayfaring literary ▶ adjective (of a person) travelling on foot: *a wayfaring stranger.*
▶ noun [mass noun] the action of travelling by foot.

wayfaring tree ▶ noun a white-flowered Eurasian shrub which has berries at different stages of ripening (green, red, and black) occurring together, growing chiefly on calcareous soils. ● *Viburnum lantana*, family Caprifoliaceae.

Wayland the Smith /ˈweɪlənd/ (also **Weland**) Scandinavian & Anglo-Saxon Mythology a smith with supernatural powers, in English legend supposed to have his forge in a Neolithic chambered tomb (**Wayland's Smithy**) on the downs in SW Oxfordshire.

waylay ▶ verb (past and past participle **waylaid**) [with obj.] stop or interrupt (someone) and detain them in conversation or trouble them in some other way: *he waylaid me on the stairs.*

way leave ▶ noun a right of way granted by a landowner, generally in exchange for payment and typically for purposes such as the erection of telegraph wires or laying of pipes.

waymark ▶ noun (also **waymarker**) a sign forming one of a series used to mark out a route, especially a footpath or bridle path.
▶ verb [with obj.] identify (a route) with a waymark.

Wayne, John (1907–79), American actor; born *Marion Michael Morrison*. Associated with the film director John Ford from 1930, Wayne became a Hollywood star with *Stagecoach* (1939) and appeared in classic westerns such as *The Searchers* (1956) and *True Grit* (1969), for which he won an Oscar.

way-out ▶ adjective informal extremely unconventional, unusual, or avant-garde: *teachers were accused of espousing way-out ideologies and teaching methods.*

waypoint ▶ noun a stopping place on a journey. ■ the computer-checked coordinates of each stage of a flight or sea journey.

-ways ▶ suffix forming adjectives and adverbs of direction or manner: *edgeways* | *lengthways*. Compare with **-WISE**.

wayside ▶ noun the edge of a road.
– PHRASES **fall by the wayside** fail to persist in an endeavour or undertaking: *many readers will fall by the wayside as the terminology becomes more complicated.* [with biblical allusion to Luke 8:5.]

wayside pulpit ▸ noun a board placed outside a place of worship, displaying a religious text or maxim.

way station ▸ noun N. Amer. a stopping point on a journey. ■ a minor station on a railway.

wayward ▸ adjective difficult to control or predict because of wilful or perverse behaviour: *a wayward adolescent* | figurative *his wayward emotions*.
– DERIVATIVES **waywardly** adverb, **waywardness** noun.
– ORIGIN late Middle English: shortening of obsolete *awayward* 'turned away'; compare with **FROWARD**.

way-worn ▸ adjective archaic weary with travelling.

wayzgoose /ˈweɪzguːs/ ▸ noun (pl. **wayzgooses**) Brit. historical an annual summer dinner or outing held by a printing house for its employees.
– ORIGIN mid 18th cent. (earlier *waygoose*): of unknown origin.

wazir /wəˈzɪə/ ▸ noun another term for **VIZIER**.

wazoo /wəˈzuː/ ▸ noun US informal a person's buttocks or anus.
– PHRASES **up** (or **out**) **the wazoo** in great quantities.
– ORIGIN 1960s: of unknown origin.

wazz (also **waz** /waz/) Brit. informal ▸ noun an act of urinating.
▸ verb [no obj.] urinate.
– ORIGIN 1980s: origin uncertain; perhaps an alteration of **WHIZZ**.

wazzock /ˈwazək/ ▸ noun Brit. informal a stupid or annoying person.
– ORIGIN 1980s: of unknown origin.

Wb ▸ abbreviation weber(s).

WBA ▸ abbreviation World Boxing Association.

WBC ▸ abbreviation World Boxing Council.

W boson ▸ noun another term for **W PARTICLE**.

WC ▸ abbreviation ■ Brit. water closet. ■ (of a region) west central.

WCC ▸ abbreviation World Council of Churches.

we ▸ pronoun [first person plural] **1** used by a speaker to refer to himself or herself and one or more other people considered together: *shall we have a drink?* ■ used to refer to the speaker together with other people regarded in the same category: *nobody knows kids better than we teachers do*. ■ people in general: *we should eat as varied and well-balanced a diet as possible*. ■ W. Indian us or our: *thought you wasn't coming to look for we*.
2 used in formal contexts for or by a royal person, or by a writer or editor, to refer to himself or herself: *in this section we discuss the reasons for this decision*.
3 used condescendingly to refer to the person being addressed: *how are we today?*
– ORIGIN Old English, of Germanic origin; related to Dutch *wij* and German *wir*.

WEA ▸ abbreviation (in the UK) Workers' Educational Association.

weak ▸ adjective **1** lacking the power to perform physically demanding tasks; having little physical strength or energy: *she was recovering from flu, and was very weak*. ■ lacking power or influence: *the central government had grown too weak to impose order* | (as plural noun **the weak**) *the new king used his powers to protect the weak*. ■ (of a team or military force) containing too few members or members of insufficient quality. ■ (of a faculty or part of the body) not able to fulfil its functions properly: *he had a weak stomach*. ■ of a low standard; performing or performed badly: *the choruses on this recording are weak*. ■ not convincing or logically forceful: *the argument is an extremely weak one* | *a weak plot*. ■ exerting only a small force: *a weak magnetic field*.
2 liable to break or give way under pressure; easily damaged: *the salamander's tail may be broken off at a weak spot near the base*. ■ lacking the force of character to hold to one's own decisions, beliefs, or principles; irresolute. ■ (of a belief) not held with conviction or intensity: *their commitment to the project is weak*. ■ (of prices or a market) having a downward tendency.
3 lacking intensity or brightness: *a weak light from a single street lamp*. ■ (of a liquid or solution) heavily diluted: *a cup of weak coffee*. ■ displaying or characterized by a lack of enthusiasm or energy: *she managed a weak, nervous smile*. ■ (of features) not striking or strongly marked: *his beard covered a weak chin*. ■ (of a syllable) unstressed.
4 Grammar denoting a class of verbs in Germanic languages that form the past tense and past participle by addition of a suffix (in English, typically *-ed*).
5 Physics relating to or denoting the weakest of the known kinds of force between particles, which acts only at distances less than about 10^{-15} cm, is very much weaker than the electromagnetic and the strong interactions, and conserves neither strangeness, parity, nor isospin.
– PHRASES **the weaker sex** [treated as sing. or pl.] dated women regarded collectively. **weak at the knees** helpless with emotion. **the weakest link** the point at which a system, sequence, or organization is most vulnerable; the least dependable element or member.
– DERIVATIVES **weakish** adjective.
– ORIGIN Old English *wāc* 'pliant', 'of little worth', 'not steadfast', reinforced in Middle English by Old Norse *veikr*, from a Germanic base meaning 'yield, give way'.

weaken ▸ verb make or become weaker in power, resolve, or physical strength: [with obj.] *fault lines had weakened and shattered the rocks* | [no obj.] *his resistance had weakened*.
– DERIVATIVES **weakener** noun.

weak ending ▸ noun Prosody an unstressed syllable in a place at the end of a line of verse that normally receives a stress.

weakfish ▸ noun (pl. **same** or **weakfishes**) a large slender-bodied marine fish living along the east coast of North America, popular as a food fish and for sport. Also called **SEA TROUT**. ● *Cynoscion regalis*, family Sciaenidae.
– ORIGIN late 18th cent.: from obsolete Dutch *weekvisch*, from *week* 'soft' + *visch* 'fish'.

weak interaction ▸ noun Physics interaction at short distances between subatomic particles mediated by the weak force.

weak-kneed ▸ adjective weak and shaky as a result of fear or excitement. ■ lacking in resolve or courage; cowardly.

weakling ▸ noun a person or animal that is physically weak and frail. ■ an ineffectual or cowardly person.

weakly ▸ adverb in a way that lacks strength or force: *she leaned weakly against the wall*.
▸ adjective (**weaklier**, **weakliest**) sickly; not robust.

weak-minded ▸ adjective lacking determination, emotional strength, or intellectual capacity.
– DERIVATIVES **weak-mindedness** noun.

weakness ▸ noun **1** [mass noun] the state or condition of being weak: *the country's weakness in international dealings*.
2 a disadvantage or fault: *you must recognize your product's strengths and weaknesses*.
3 a person or thing that one is unable to resist or likes excessively: *you're his one weakness—he should never have met you*. ■ (**weakness for**) a self-indulgent liking for: *his weakness for prawn cocktails*.

weak sister ▸ noun N. Amer. informal a weak, ineffectual, or unreliable member of a group.

weak-willed ▸ adjective lacking the ability to resist the influence of other people or to control one's own impulses: *he is weak-willed and indecisive*.

weal[1] /wiːl/ (also chiefly Medicine **wheal**) ▸ noun a red, swollen mark left on flesh by a blow or pressure. ■ Medicine an area of the skin which is temporarily raised, typically reddened, and usually accompanied by itching.
▸ verb [with obj.] mark with a weal.
– ORIGIN early 19th cent.: variant of **WALE**, influenced by obsolete *wheal* 'suppurate'.

weal[2] /wiːl/ ▸ noun [mass noun] formal that which is best for someone or something: *I am holding this trial behind closed doors in the public weal*.
– PHRASES **the common weal** the benefit or interests of all members of a country or community: *such things as police protection and national defence are benefits vital to the common weal*.
– ORIGIN Old English *wela* 'wealth, well-being', of West Germanic origin; related to **WELL[1]**.

Weald /wiːld/ a formerly wooded district including parts of Kent, Surrey, and East Sussex.
– ORIGIN Old English, variant of *wald* (see **WOLD**).

Weald clay ▸ noun [mass noun] Geology a series of beds of clay, sandstone, limestone, and ironstone, forming the top of the Wealden strata in southern England and containing abundant fossil remains.

Wealden /ˈwiːld(ə)n/ ▸ adjective Brit. relating to the Weald. ■ denoting a style of timber house built in the Weald in the late medieval and Tudor periods. ■ Geology relating to or denoting a series of Lower Cretaceous estuarine and freshwater deposits best exemplified in the Weald.

wealth ▸ noun [mass noun] **1** an abundance of valuable possessions or money: *he used his considerable wealth to bribe officials*. ■ the state of being rich; material prosperity: *some people buy boats and cars to display their wealth*. ■ plentiful supplies of a particular resource: *the country's mineral wealth*.
2 [in sing.] a plentiful supply of a particular desirable thing: *the tables and maps contain **a wealth of** information*.
3 archaic well-being.
– ORIGIN Middle English *welthe*, from **WELL[1]** or **WEAL[2]**, on the pattern of *health*.

wealth tax ▸ noun a tax levied on personal capital.

wealthy ▸ adjective (**wealthier**, **wealthiest**) having a great deal of money, resources, or assets; rich: *the wealthy nations of the world* | (as plural noun **the wealthy**) *the burden of taxation on the wealthy*.
– DERIVATIVES **wealthily** adverb.

wean[1] ▸ verb [with obj.] accustom (an infant or other young mammal) to food other than its mother's milk. ■ (often **wean someone off**) accustom (someone) to managing without something which they have become dependent on: *the doctor tried to wean her off the sleeping pills*. ■ (**be weaned on**) be strongly influenced by (something), especially from an early age: *I was weaned on a regular diet of Hollywood fantasy*.
– ORIGIN Old English *wenian*, of Germanic origin; related to Dutch *wennen* and German *entwohnen*.

wean[2] ▸ noun Scottish & N. English a young child.
– ORIGIN late 17th cent.: contraction of *wee ane* 'little one'.

weaner ▸ noun a calf, lamb, or pig weaned during the current year.

weanling ▸ noun a newly weaned animal.

weapon ▸ noun a thing designed or used for inflicting bodily harm or physical damage: *nuclear weapons*. ■ a means of gaining an advantage or defending oneself in a conflict or contest: *resignation threats had long been a weapon in his armoury*.
– DERIVATIVES **weaponed** adjective, **weaponless** adjective.
– ORIGIN Old English *wǣp(e)n*, of Germanic origin; related to Dutch *wapen* and German *Waffe*.

weaponize (also **weaponise**) ▸ verb [with obj.] adapt for use as a weapon: *they had produced and weaponized many deadly biological agents, including anthrax* | (as adj. **weaponized**) *weaponized versions of smallpox*.
– DERIVATIVES **weaponization** noun.

weapon of mass destruction ▸ noun a nuclear, biological, or chemical weapon able to cause widespread devastation and loss of life.

weaponry ▸ noun [treated as sing. or pl.] weapons regarded collectively.

weapons-grade ▸ adjective denoting fissile material which is suitable for making nuclear weapons: *weapons-grade plutonium*.

wear[1] ▸ verb (past **wore**; past participle **worn** /wɔːn/)
1 [with obj.] have (something) on one's body as clothing, decoration, or protection: *he was wearing a dark suit* | *firemen wearing breathing apparatus*. ■ habitually have on one's body or be dressed in: *although she was a widow, she didn't wear black*. ■ exhibit or present (a particular facial expression or appearance): *they wear a frozen smile on their faces*. ■ [with obj. and complement or adverbial] have (one's hair or beard) at a specified length or arranged in a specified style: *the students wore their hair long*. ■ Nautical (of a ship) fly (a flag).
2 [with obj. and adverbial or complement] damage, erode, or destroy by friction or use: *the track has been worn down in part to bare rock* | *shells worn smooth by the sea*. ■ [no obj., with adverbial or complement] undergo such damage, erosion, or destruction: *mountains are wearing down with each passing second*. ■ [with obj.] form (a hole, path, etc.) by constant friction or use: *the water was forced up through holes it had worn*. ■ [no obj., with adverbial] withstand continued use or life in a specified way: *a carpet that seems to wear well*.
3 [with obj.] literary pass (a period of time) in some activity: *spinning long stories, wearing half the day*.
4 [with obj.] [usu. with negative] Brit. informal tolerate; accept: *the environmental health people wouldn't wear it*.
▸ noun [mass noun] **1** [with modifier or in combination] clothing suitable for a particular purpose or of a particular type: *evening wear*. ■ the wearing of something or the state of being worn as clothing: *some new tops for wear in the evening*.
2 damage or deterioration sustained from continuous use: *you need to make a deduction for wear*

W

and tear on all your belongings. ■ the capacity for withstanding continuous use without such damage: *the suit has about another 10 years of normal wear left in it.*
– PHRASES **wear one's heart on one's sleeve** see HEART. **wear oneself to a shadow** see SHADOW. **wear thin** be gradually used up or become less convincing or acceptable: *his patience was wearing thin* | *the joke had started to wear thin.* **wear the trousers** see TROUSERS.
– PHRASAL VERBS **wear someone/thing down** overcome someone or something by persistence: *initially, she protested, but he wore down her resistance.* **wear off** lose effectiveness or intensity: *the effects of the drug were wearing off.* **wear on** (of a period of time) pass, especially slowly or tediously: *as the afternoon wore on he began to look unhappy.* **wear something out** (also **wear out**) use or be used until no longer in good condition or working order: *wearing out the stair carpet* | *the type was used again and again until it wore out.* **wear someone/thing out** exhaust or tire someone or something: *an hour of this wandering wore him out.*
– DERIVATIVES **wearability** noun, **wearable** adjective, **wearer** noun.
– ORIGIN Old English *werian*, of Germanic origin, from an Indo-European root shared by Latin *vestis* 'clothing'.

wear² ▶ verb (past and past participle **wore**) [with obj.] Sailing bring (a ship) about by turning its head away from the wind: *Shannon gives the order to **wear ship**.* Compare with TACK¹ (sense 3 of the verb).
– ORIGIN early 17th cent.: of unknown origin.

weariness ▶ noun [mass noun] **1** extreme tiredness; fatigue: *he began to feel weariness.*
2 reluctance to see or experience any more of something: *growing war-weariness.*

wearing ▶ adjective mentally or physically tiring.
– DERIVATIVES **wearingly** adverb.

wearing course ▶ noun the top layer of a road surface which is worn down by traffic.

wearisome ▶ adjective causing one to feel tired or bored.
– DERIVATIVES **wearisomely** adverb, **wearisomeness** noun.

weary ▶ adjective (**wearier**, **weariest**) **1** feeling or showing extreme tiredness, especially as a result of excessive exertion: *he gave a long, weary sigh.* ■ calling for a great amount of energy or endurance; tiring and tedious: *the weary journey began again.*
2 reluctant to see or experience any more of; tired of: *she was **weary of** their constant arguments* | [in combination] *war-weary Americans.*
▶ verb (**wearies**, **wearying**, **wearied**) **1** [with obj.] cause to become tired: *she was wearied by her persistent cough.*
2 [no obj.] (**weary of**) grow tired of or bored with: *she wearied of the sameness of her life.*
3 [no obj.] chiefly Scottish be distressed; fret: *don't think I'm wearying about not being able to paint any more.*
– DERIVATIVES **weariless** adjective, **wearily** adverb.
– ORIGIN Old English *wērig*, *wǣrig*, of West Germanic origin.

wearying ▶ adjective causing tiredness; tiring: *a long, wearying journey.*
– DERIVATIVES **wearyingly** adverb.

weasel ▶ noun **1** a small, slender carnivorous mammal related to, but smaller than, the stoat. ● Genus *Mustela*, family Mustelidae (the **weasel family**): several species, in particular *M. nivalis* of northern Eurasia and northern North America. The family also includes the polecats, minks, martens, skunks, wolverine, otters, and badgers.
■ Irish term for STOAT.
2 a deceitful or treacherous person.
▶ verb (**weasels**, **weaselling**, **weaselled**; US **weasels**, **weaseling**, **weaseled**) [no obj.] achieve something by use of cunning or deceit: *she suspects me of trying to weasel my way into his affections.* ■ chiefly N. Amer. behave or talk evasively.
– PHRASES **weasel words** words or statements that are intentionally ambiguous or misleading.
– DERIVATIVES **weaselly** adjective.
– ORIGIN Old English *wesle*, *wesule*, of West Germanic origin; related to Dutch *wezel* and German *Wiesel*.

weasel-faced ▶ adjective (of a person) having a face with unattractively thin, sharp, or pointed features.

weasel's snout ▶ noun a small wild Eurasian snapdragon with reddish-purple flowers, naturalized in Britain and North America. ● *Misopates* (formerly *Antirrhinum*) *orontium*, family Scrophulariaceae.

W

weather ▶ noun [mass noun] the state of the atmosphere at a particular place and time as regards heat, cloudiness, dryness, sunshine, wind, rain, etc.: *if the weather's good we can go for a walk.* ■ cold, wet, and unpleasant or unpredictable atmospheric conditions: *stone walls provide shelter from wind and weather.*
■ [as modifier] denoting the side from which the wind is blowing, especially on board a ship; windward: *the weather side of the yacht.* Contrasted with LEE.
▶ verb [with obj.] **1** wear away or change the appearance or texture of (something) by long exposure to the atmosphere: [with obj. and complement] *his skin was weathered almost black by his long outdoor life.* ■ [no obj.] (of rock or other material) be worn away or altered by long exposure to the atmosphere: *the ice sheet preserves specimens that would **weather away** more quickly in other regions.*
2 (of a ship) come safely through (a storm). ■ withstand (a difficulty or danger): *this year has tested industry's ability to weather recession.* ■ Sailing get to the windward of (a cape).
3 make (boards or tiles) overlap downwards to keep out rain. ■ (in building) slope or bevel (a surface) to throw off rain.
4 (usu. as noun **weathering**) Falconry allow (a hawk) to spend a period perched in the open air.
– PHRASES **in all weathers** Brit. in every kind of weather, both good and bad. **keep a weather eye on** observe very carefully, especially for changes or developments. **make heavy weather of** informal have unnecessary difficulty in dealing with (a task or problem). [from the nautical phrase *make good* or *bad weather of it*, referring to a ship in a storm.] **under the weather** informal slightly unwell or in low spirits.
– ORIGIN Old English *weder*, of Germanic origin; related to Dutch *weer* and German *Wetter*, probably also to the noun WIND¹.

weather balloon ▶ noun a balloon equipped with meteorological apparatus which is sent into the atmosphere to provide information about the weather.

weather-beaten ▶ adjective damaged or worn by exposure to the weather: *a tiny weather-beaten church.* ■ having skin that is lined and tanned or reddened through prolonged time spent outdoors.

weatherboard chiefly Brit. ▶ noun a sloping board attached to the bottom of an outside door to keep out the rain. ■ each of a series of horizontal boards nailed to outside walls with edges overlapping to keep out the rain.
▶ verb [with obj.] fit or supply with weatherboards.

weatherboarding ▶ noun [mass noun] weatherboards collectively.

weatherbound ▶ adjective prevented by bad weather from travelling or proceeding with a course of action.

weathercock ▶ noun a weathervane in the form of a cockerel.
▶ verb [no obj.] (of a boat or aircraft) tend to turn to head into the wind.

weathered ▶ adjective worn by long exposure to the air; weather-beaten: *weathered rock.*

weatherfish ▶ noun (pl. **same** or **weatherfishes**) a yellowish-brown freshwater loach which is reputed to become restless at the approach of stormy weather. ● Genus *Misgurnus*, family Cobitidae: the European *M. fossilis*, and the Asian *M. anguillicaudatus*, which has also been introduced to North America.

weather forecast ▶ noun an analysis of the state of the weather in an area with an assessment of likely developments.
– DERIVATIVES **weather forecaster** noun, **weather forecasting** noun.

weather gage ▶ noun see GAUGE (sense 3 of the noun).

weathergirl ▶ noun informal a young female weather forecaster.

weather glass ▶ noun dated a barometer.

weather helm ▶ noun [mass noun] Nautical a tendency in a sailing ship to head into the wind if the tiller is released.

weather house ▶ noun a toy hygroscope in the form of a small house with figures of a man and woman standing in two porches, the man coming out of his porch in wet weather and the woman out of hers in dry.

weatherize (also **weatherise**) ▶ verb [with obj.] US make (a house or other building) resistant to cold weather, typically by adding insulation: *the average family could save $350 on their energy bills by weatherizing their home.*
– DERIVATIVES **weatherization** noun.

weatherly ▶ adjective Sailing (of a boat) able to sail close to the wind without drifting to leeward.

weatherman ▶ noun (pl. **weathermen**) a man who broadcasts a description and forecast of weather conditions.

weather map ▶ noun another term for WEATHER CHART.

weatherproof ▶ adjective resistant to the effects of bad weather, especially rain: *the building is structurally sound and weatherproof.*
▶ verb [with obj.] make (something) weatherproof.

weather station ▶ noun an observation post where weather conditions and meteorological data are observed and recorded.

weatherstrip N. Amer. ▶ noun a strip of rubber, metal, or other material used to seal the edges of a door or window against rain and wind.
▶ verb (**weatherstrips**, **weatherstripping**, **weatherstripped**) [with obj.] apply a weatherstrip to (a door or window).
– DERIVATIVES **weatherstripping** noun.

weatherstruck joint ▶ noun another term for STRUCK JOINT.

weathertight ▶ adjective (of a building) sealed against rain and wind.

weather tile ▶ noun each of a series of overlapping tiles used to cover a wall.

weathervane ▶ noun a revolving pointer to show the direction of the wind, typically mounted on top of a building.

weather-worn ▶ adjective eroded or altered by exposure to the weather: *a weather-worn gravestone.*

weave¹ ▶ verb (past **wove** ; past participle **woven** or **wove**) [with obj.] **1** form (fabric or a fabric item) by interlacing long threads passing in one direction with others at a right angle to them: *textiles woven from linen or wool* | (as noun **weaving**) *cotton spinning and weaving was done in mills* | (as adj. **woven**) *woven shawls.* ■ form (thread) into fabric in this way: *some thick mohairs can be difficult to weave.*
2 make (a complex story or pattern) from a number of interconnected elements: *he weaves colourful, cinematic plots.* ■ (**weave something into**) include an element in (such a story or pattern): *interpretative comments are woven into the narrative.*
▶ noun [usu. with adj.] a particular style or manner in which something is woven: *cloth of a very fine weave.*
– ORIGIN Old English *wefan*, of Germanic origin, from an Indo-European root shared by Greek *huphē* 'web' and Sanskrit *ūrṇavābhi* 'spider', literally 'wool-weaver'. The current noun sense dates from the late 19th cent.

weave² ▶ verb [no obj.] twist and turn from side to side while moving somewhere in order to avoid obstructions: *he had to **weave his way** through the crowds.*
■ take evasive action in an aircraft, typically by moving it from side to side. ■ (of a horse) repeatedly swing the head and forepart of the body from side to side (considered to be a vice).
– PHRASES **get weaving** Brit. informal set briskly to work; begin action.
– ORIGIN late 16th cent.: probably from Old Norse *veifa* 'to wave, brandish'.

weaver ▶ noun **1** a person who weaves fabric.
2 (also **weaver bird**) a finch-like songbird of tropical Africa and Asia, related to the sparrows and building elaborately woven nests. ● Family Ploceidae: several genera, in particular *Ploceus*, and numerous species.

weaver ant ▶ noun a tropical ant which builds its nest between leaves that are fastened together using silk secreted by the larvae. ● Genera *Oecophylla* and *Camponotus*, family Formicidae.

weaver's knot ▶ noun a sheet bend used for joining threads in weaving.

web ▶ noun **1** a network of fine threads constructed by a spider from fluid secreted by its spinnerets, used to catch its prey. ■ a similar filmy network spun by some insect larvae, especially communal caterpillars.
2 a complex system of interconnected elements: *he found himself caught up in a web of bureaucracy.*
■ (**the Web**) the World Wide Web or the Internet: *material downloaded from the Web* | [as modifier] *Web publishing.*
3 a membrane between the toes of a swimming bird or other aquatic animal. ■ a thin flat part connecting thicker or more solid parts in machinery.

4 a roll of paper used in a continuous printing process. ■ the endless wire mesh in a papermaking machine on which such paper is made.
5 a piece of woven fabric.
▶ verb (**webs, webbing, webbed**) [with obj.] cover with or as though with a web: *she noticed his tanned skin, webbed with fine creases.*
– DERIVATIVES **web-like** adjective.
– ORIGIN Old English *web(b)* 'woven fabric', of Germanic origin; related to Dutch *web*, also to WEAVE[1].

WORD TRENDS Our lives are now so dominated by the Internet that it is difficult to think of a time when a **web** was simply the realm of lurking spiders and petrified files. **The Web** was first seen in a computing context in 1993, as a shortening of **World Wide Web**, and the word is now widely used as a synonym for 'the Internet'. As the Oxford English Corpus shows, this sense is now the dominant one, with *site*, *page*, and *server* the most frequent collocates, and the verbs *surf*, *use*, and *search* pushing the spider's *weave* and *spin* down the rankings. The Corpus also shows that while **web** and **Internet** have increased in usage since 2000, the full phrase **World Wide Web** has declined.

webbed ▶ adjective **1** (of the feet of a swimming bird or other aquatic animal) having the toes connected by a membrane. ■ Medicine (of fingers or toes) abnormally united by a fold of skin.
2 (of a band or strip of tough material) made from webbing or similar fabric.

webbing ▶ noun [mass noun] **1** strong, closely woven fabric used for making items such as straps and belts. ■ the system of belts, pouches, and straps worn by a soldier as part of his combat uniform.
2 the part of a baseball glove between the thumb and forefinger.

webcam /ˈwɛbkam/ ▶ noun (trademark in the US) a video camera connected to a computer, allowing its images to be seen by Internet users.

webcast /ˈwɛbkɑːst/ ▶ noun a video broadcast of an event transmitted across the Internet.
– DERIVATIVES **webcaster** noun, **webcasting** noun.

Weber[1] /ˈveɪbə/, German /ˈveːbɐ/, Carl Maria (Friedrich Ernst) von (1786–1826), German composer. He is regarded as the founder of the German romantic school of opera. Notable operas: *Der Freischütz* (1817–21), *Euryanthe* (1822–3).

Weber[2] /ˈveɪbə/, German /ˈveːbɐ/, Max (1864–1920), German economist and sociologist, regarded as one of the founders of modern sociology. Notable works: *The Protestant Ethic and the Spirit of Capitalism* (1904) and *Economy and Society* (1922).

Weber[3] /ˈveɪbə/, German /ˈveːbɐ/, Wilhelm Eduard (1804–91), German physicist. He proposed a unified system for electrical units and determined the ratio between the units of electrostatic and electromagnetic charge.

weber /ˈveɪbə/ (abbrev.: **Wb**) ▶ noun the SI unit of magnetic flux, causing the electromotive force of one volt in a circuit of one turn when generated or removed in one second.
– ORIGIN late 19th cent.: named after W. E. *Weber* (see WEBER[3]).

Webern /ˈveɪb(ə)n/, German /ˈveːbɐn/, Anton (Friedrich Ernst) von (1883–1945), Austrian composer, a leading exponent of serialism. His music is marked by its brevity: the atonal *Five Pieces for Orchestra* (1911–13) lasts under a minute.

web-footed ▶ adjective (of a swimming bird or other aquatic animal) having webbed feet.

web hosting ▶ noun [mass noun] the activity or business of providing storage space and access for websites.

webinar /ˈwɛbɪnɑː/ ▶ noun a seminar conducted over the Internet.
– ORIGIN 1990s: blend of WEB and SEMINAR.

weblink ▶ noun Computing another term for HYPERLINK. ■ a printed address of a website in a book, newspaper, etc.

weblog /ˈwɛblɒg/ ▶ noun full form of BLOG.
– DERIVATIVES **weblogger** noun.
– ORIGIN 1990s: from WEB in the sense 'World Wide Web' + LOG[1] in the sense 'regular record of incidents'.

webmail ▶ noun [mass noun] email available for use online and stored in the Internet server mailbox.

webmaster ▶ noun the person who maintains a particular website.

web offset ▶ noun [mass noun] offset printing on continuous paper fed from a reel.

web page ▶ noun a hypertext document connected to the World Wide Web.

web ring ▶ noun a number of websites with related content, offering links to one another in such a way that one may view each of them without returning to a single referring site.

website ▶ noun a location connected to the Internet that maintains one or more web pages.

webspace ▶ noun [mass noun] **1** an amount of disk storage space allowed on an Internet server.
2 the environment in which communication over computer networks occurs; cyberspace.

web-spinner ▶ noun a slender mainly tropical insect with a soft brownish body, living under stones or logs in a tunnel of silk produced by glands on the front legs. ● Order Embioptera: several families.

Webster[1], John (*c.*1580–*c.*1625), English dramatist. Notable works: *The White Devil* (1612) and *The Duchess of Malfi* (1623), both revenge tragedies.

Webster[2], Noah (1758–1843), American lexicographer. His *American Dictionary of the English Language* (1828) was the first dictionary to give comprehensive coverage of American usage.

web wheel ▶ noun a wheel with a plate instead of spokes, or one with rim, spokes, and centre made in one piece, as in the balance wheel of a clock or watch.

webwork ▶ noun a mesh or network of links or connecting pieces: *a webwork of beams and girders.*

webworm ▶ noun N. Amer. a caterpillar which spins a web in which to rest or feed. When present in large numbers it can become a serious pest. ● *Loxostega* and other genera, family Pyralidae.

webzine /ˈwebziːn/ ▶ noun a magazine published electronically on the Internet.

wed ▶ verb (**weds, wedding**; past and past participle **wedded** or **wed**) [with obj.] **1** chiefly formal or archaic get married to: *he was to wed the king's daughter.* ■ [no obj.] get married: *they wed a week after meeting* | (**be wed**) *they were wed in London.* ■ give or join in marriage: *will you wed your daughter to him?* ■ (as adj. **wedded**) of or concerning marriage: *25 years' **wedded bliss**.*
2 combine (two factors or qualities, especially desirable ones): *in this album he weds an excellent programme with a distinctive vocal style.* ■ (**be wedded to**) be obstinately attached or devoted to (an activity, belief, or system): *the government was wedded to budgetary orthodoxy.*
– ORIGIN Old English *weddian*, from the Germanic base of Scots *wed* 'a pledge'; related to Latin *vas* 'surety', also to GAGE[1].

Wed. ▶ abbreviation Wednesday.

we'd ▶ contraction we had: *we'd already been on board.* ■ we should or we would: *we'd like to make you an offer.*

Weddell Sea /ˈwɛd(ə)l/ an arm of the Atlantic Ocean, off the coast of Antarctica.
– ORIGIN named after the British explorer James *Weddell* (1787–1834), who visited it in 1823.

Weddell seal ▶ noun a large mottled grey seal with a small head, ranging farther south than any other seal and breeding on the fast ice of Antarctica. ● *Leptonychotes weddelli*, family Phocidae.
– ORIGIN early 20th cent.: named after James *Weddell* (see WEDDELL SEA).

wedding ▶ noun a marriage ceremony, especially considered as including the associated celebrations.
– ORIGIN Old English *weddung* (see WED, -ING[1]).

wedding band ▶ noun chiefly N. Amer. a wedding ring.

wedding bells ▶ plural noun bells rung to celebrate a wedding (used to allude to the likelihood of marriage between two people): *they were seen everywhere together, and her friends could hear wedding bells.*

wedding breakfast ▶ noun Brit. a celebratory meal eaten just after a wedding (at any time of day) by the couple and their guests.

wedding cake ▶ noun a rich iced cake, typically in two or more tiers, served at a wedding reception. ■ [as modifier] informal denoting a building that is very ornate: *a wedding-cake mansion.*

wedding day ▶ noun the day or anniversary of a wedding.

wedding list ▶ noun a list of items that a couple about to get married have asked to receive as presents.

wedding march ▶ noun a piece of march music played at the entrance of the bride or the exit of the couple at a wedding.

wedding night ▶ noun the night after a wedding (especially with reference to its consummation).

wedding ring ▶ noun a ring worn by a married person, given to them by their spouse at their wedding.

wedding tackle ▶ noun another term for TACKLE (see sense 1 of the noun).

Wedekind /ˈveɪdəkɪnd/, German /ˈveːdəkɪnt/, Frank (1864–1918), German dramatist. A key figure of expressionist drama, he scandalized contemporary German society with the explicit and sardonic portrayal of sexual awakening in *The Awakening of Spring* (1891).

wedge[1] ▶ noun **1** a piece of wood, metal, etc. having one thick end and tapering to a thin edge, that is driven between two objects or parts of an object to secure or separate them. ■ an object or piece of something shaped like a wedge: ***a wedge of** cheese.* ■ a formation of people or animals in the shape of a wedge.
2 a golf club with a low, angled face for maximum loft. ■ a shot made with a wedge.
3 a shoe with a fairly high heel forming a solid block with the sole. ■ a heel on a wedge shoe.
4 [mass noun] Brit. informal money or earnings: *he invested his wedge in stocks and shares.*
▶ verb **1** [with obj.] fix in position using a wedge: [with obj. and complement] *the door was wedged open.*
2 [with obj. and adverbial] force into a narrow space: *she wedged her holdall between two bags.*
– PHRASES **drive a wedge between** separate: *the general aimed to drive a wedge between the city and its northern defences.* ■ cause disagreement or hostility between: *I'm not trying to drive a wedge between you and your father.* **the thin end of the wedge** informal an action or procedure of little importance that is likely to lead to more serious developments.
– DERIVATIVES **wedge-like** adjective.
– ORIGIN Old English *wecg* (noun), of Germanic origin; related to Dutch *wig*.

wedge[2] ▶ verb [with obj.] prepare (pottery clay) for use by cutting, kneading, and throwing down to homogenize it and remove air pockets.
– ORIGIN late 17th cent.: of unknown origin.

wedgebill ▶ noun an Australian songbird of the logrunner family, with a wedge-shaped bill, long tail, and upright crest. ● *Sphenostoma cristatum*, family Orthonychidae.

wedge issue ▶ noun US a very divisive political issue, regarded as a basis for drawing voters away from an opposing party whose supporters have diverging opinions on it.

wedge shell ▶ noun a marine bivalve mollusc which has a somewhat triangular shell. ● Family Donacidae: *Donax* and other genera.

wedgie ▶ noun informal **1** a shoe with a wedge heel.
2 chiefly N. Amer. an act of pulling up the material of someone's underwear tightly between their buttocks as a practical joke.

Wedgwood /ˈwɛdʒwʊd/ ▶ noun [mass noun] trademark ceramic ware made by the English potter Josiah Wedgwood (1730–95) and his successors. Wedgwood is most associated with the powder-blue stoneware pieces with white embossed cameos that first appeared in 1775. ■ a powder-blue colour characteristic of Wedgwood stoneware.

wedlock ▶ noun [mass noun] the state of being married.
PHRASES **born in** (or **out of**) **wedlock** born of married (or unmarried) parents.
– ORIGIN late Old English *wedlāc* 'marriage vow', from *wed* 'pledge' (related to WED) + the suffix *-lāc* (denoting action).

Wednesday ▶ noun the day of the week before Thursday and following Tuesday: *a report goes before the councillors **on Wednesday*** | *they finish early on Wednesdays* | [as modifier] *on a Wednesday morning.*
▶ adverb chiefly N. Amer. on Wednesday: *see you Wednesday.* ■ (**Wednesdays**) on Wednesdays; each Wednesday: *Wednesdays, the jazz DJ hosts a jam session.*
– ORIGIN Old English *Wōdnesdæg*, named after the Germanic god ODIN; translation of late Latin *Mercurii dies*; compare with Dutch *woensdag*.

Weds. ▶ abbreviation Wednesday.

wee[1] ▶ adjective (**weer, weest**) chiefly Scottish little: *when I was just a wee bairn* | *the lyrics are **a wee bit** too sweet and sentimental.*
– ORIGIN Middle English (originally a noun use in Scots, usually as *a little wee* 'a little bit'): from Old English *wēg(e)* (see WEY).

wee[2] informal, chiefly Brit. ▶ noun [usu. in sing.] an act of urinating. ■ [mass noun] urine.
▶ verb (**wees, weeing, weed**) [no obj.] urinate.
– ORIGIN 1930s: imitative.

W

weebill ▶ noun a very small Australian warbler with an olive back, yellow underparts, and a short, stubby bill. ● *Smicrornis brevirostris*, family Acanthizidae.

weed ▶ noun **1** a wild plant growing where it is not wanted and in competition with cultivated plants. ■ [mass noun] any wild plant growing in salt or fresh water. ■ [mass noun] informal cannabis. ■ (**the weed**) informal tobacco.
2 Brit. informal a contemptibly feeble person.
3 informal a leggy, loosely built horse.
▶ verb [with obj.] **1** remove unwanted plants from (an area of ground): *I was weeding a flower bed.*
2 (**weed someone/thing out**) remove an inferior or unwanted component of a group or collection: *we must raise the level of research and weed out the poorest work.*
– DERIVATIVES **weeder** noun, **weedless** adjective.
– ORIGIN Old English *wēod* (noun), *wēodian* (verb), of unknown origin; related to Dutch *wieden* (verb).

weedgrown ▶ adjective overgrown with weeds.

weedicide ▶ noun a chemical weedkiller.

weedkiller ▶ noun a substance used to destroy weeds.

weeds ▶ plural noun short for WIDOW'S WEEDS.

weed whacker ▶ noun chiefly US an electrically powered grass trimmer with a nylon cutting cord that rotates rapidly on a spindle.

weedy ▶ adjective (**weedier**, **weediest**) **1** containing or covered with many weeds: *a weedy path led to the gate.* ■ of the nature of or resembling a weed: *a weedy species of plant.*
2 Brit. informal (of a person) thin and physically weak in appearance.
– DERIVATIVES **weediness** noun.

Wee Free ▶ noun a member of the minority group nicknamed the **Wee Free Kirk** which stood apart from the Free Church of Scotland when the majority amalgamated with the United Presbyterian Church to form the United Free Church in 1900. The group continued to call itself the Free Church of Scotland after this date.

weejuns /ˈwiːdʒənz/ ▶ plural noun (trademark in the US) moccasin-style shoes for casual wear.
– ORIGIN 1950s: an invented word.

week ▶ noun a period of seven days: *the course lasts sixteen weeks | he'd cut the grass a week ago.* ■ the period of seven days generally reckoned from and to midnight on Saturday night: *she has an art class twice a week.* ■ workdays as opposed to the weekend; the five days from Monday to Friday: *I work during the week, so I can only get to this shop on Saturdays.* ■ the time spent working in this period: *she works a 48-hour week.* ■ Brit. informal used after the name of a day to indicate that something will happen seven days after that day: *the programme will be broadcast on Sunday week.*
– PHRASES **a week on ——** seven days after the specified day or date: *we'll be back a week on Friday.* **week in, week out** every week without exception.
– ORIGIN Old English *wice*, of Germanic origin; related to Dutch *week* and German *Woche*, from a base probably meaning 'sequence, series'.

weekday ▶ noun a day of the week other than Sunday or Saturday.

weekend ▶ noun Saturday and Sunday, especially regarded as a time for leisure: *she spent the weekend camping* | [as modifier] *a weekend break.*
▶ verb [no obj., with adverbial] informal spend a weekend somewhere: *he was weekending in the country.*

weekender ▶ noun a person who spends time in a particular place only at weekends. ■ Austral. informal a holiday cottage. ■ a small pleasure boat.

weekend warrior ▶ noun N. Amer. informal a person who participates in an activity only in their spare time.

weekly ▶ adjective done, produced, or occurring once a week: *there was a weekly dance on Wednesdays.* ■ relating to or calculated in terms of a week: *the difference in weekly income is £29.10.*
▶ adverb once a week: *interviews were given weekly.*
▶ noun (pl. **weeklies**) a newspaper or periodical issued every week.

weel ▶ adverb, adjective, & exclamation Scottish form of WELL[1].

ween ▶ verb [no obj.] archaic be of the opinion; think or suppose: *he, I ween, is no sacred personage.*
– ORIGIN Old English *wēnan*, of Germanic origin; related to Dutch *wanen* 'imagine', German *wähnen* 'suppose wrongly', also to WISH.

weenie ▶ noun another term for WIENER.

weeny ▶ adjective (**weenier**, **weeniest**) informal tiny.
– ORIGIN late 18th cent.: from WEE[1], on the pattern of *tiny*; compare with TEENY.

weep ▶ verb (past and past participle **wept**) [no obj.] **1** shed tears: *a grieving mother wept over the body of her daughter* | [with obj.] *he wept bitter tears at her cruelty* | (as adj. **weeping**) *the weeping figure of a woman.* ■ utter or express with tears: [with direct speech] *'No!' she wept.* ■ [with obj.] archaic mourn for; shed tears over: *a young widow weeping her lost lord.*
2 (as adj. **weeping**) used in names of tree and shrub varieties with drooping branches, e.g. **weeping cherry**.
3 exude liquid: *she rubbed the sore, making it weep.*
▶ noun [in sing.] a fit or period of weeping.
– DERIVATIVES **weepingly** adverb.
– ORIGIN Old English *wēpan* (verb), of Germanic origin, probably imitative.

weeper ▶ noun **1** a person who weeps. ■ historical a hired mourner at a funeral. ■ a small image of a mourner on a monument.
2 N. Amer. another term for WEEPY.
3 (**weepers**) historical mourning clothes, in particular a man's crape hatband or a widow's black crape veil and white cuffs.
4 (**weepers**) dated long side whiskers worn without a beard.

weepie ▶ noun (pl. **weepies**) variant spelling of WEEPY.

Weeping Cross ▶ noun historical a wayside cross for penitents to pray at.

weeping widow ▶ noun a mushroom which has a buff cap with purplish-black gills that appear to secrete drops of fluid when damp, found commonly in both Eurasia and North America. ● *Lacrymaria velutina*, family Coprinaceae, class Hymenomycetes.

weeping willow ▶ noun a Eurasian willow with trailing branches and foliage reaching down to the ground, widely grown as an ornamental in waterside settings. ● Genus *Salix*, family Salicaceae: several species and hybrids, in particular *S.* × *chrysocoma*.

weepy informal ▶ adjective (**weepier**, **weepiest**) tearful; inclined to weep: *seeing a bride always made her feel weepy.* ■ sentimental: *a weepy made-for-TV movie.*
▶ noun a sentimental film, book, or song.
– DERIVATIVES **weepily** adverb, **weepiness** noun.

weever (also **weever fish**) ▶ noun a small, long-bodied fish with eyes at the top of the head and venomous dorsal spines. It occurs along East Atlantic coasts, typically buried in the sand with just the eyes and spines protruding. ● Family Trachinidae: several genera and species.
– ORIGIN early 17th cent.: perhaps a transferred use of Old French *wivre* 'serpent, dragon', from Latin *vipera* 'viper'.

weevil /ˈwiːv(ə)l, ˈwiːvɪl/ ▶ noun a small beetle with an elongated snout, the larvae of which typically develop inside seeds, stems, or other plant parts. Many are pests of crops or stored foodstuffs. ● Curculionidae and other families in the superfamily Curculionoidea: numerous genera.
■ informal any small insect that damages stored grain.
– DERIVATIVES **weevily** adjective.
– ORIGIN Old English *wifel* 'beetle', from a Germanic base meaning 'move briskly'.

wee-wee informal, chiefly Brit. ▶ noun a child's word for urine.
▶ verb [no obj.] urinate.
– ORIGIN 1930s: imitative.

w.e.f. ▶ abbreviation Brit. with effect from: *a budget to allocate w.e.f. 1st April.*

weft[1] ▶ noun [in sing.] (in weaving) the crosswise threads on a loom that are passed over and under the warp threads to make cloth.
– ORIGIN Old English *weft(a)*, of Germanic origin; related to WEAVE[1].

weft[2] ▶ noun variant spelling of WAFT (sense 2 of the noun).

Wegener /ˈveɪɡənə/, German /ˈveːɡənɐ/, Alfred Lothar (1880–1930), German meteorologist and geologist. He was the first serious proponent of the theory of continental drift.

Wehrmacht /ˈveːrmɑːxt/, German /ˈveːɐmaxt/ the German armed forces, especially the army, from 1921 to 1945.
– ORIGIN German, literally 'defensive force'.

Wei /weɪ/ the name of several dynasties which ruled in China, especially that of AD 386–535.

wei ch'i /weɪ ˈtʃiː/ ▶ noun [mass noun] a traditional Chinese board game of territorial possession and capture.
– ORIGIN Chinese, from *wei* 'surround' + *ch'i* 'chess'.

Weichsel /ˈvʌɪks(ə)l/ ▶ noun [usu. as modifier] Geology the final Pleistocene glaciation in northern Europe, corresponding to the Devensian of Britain (and possibly the Würm of the Alps). ■ the system of deposits laid down at the time of the Weichsel glaciation.
– DERIVATIVES **Weichselian** /vʌɪkˈsiːlɪən/ adjective & noun.
– ORIGIN 1930s: from the German name of the River Vistula in Poland.

Weifang /weɪˈfaŋ/ a city in Shandong province, eastern China; pop. 975,300 (est. 2006). Former name WEIHSIEN.

weigela /wʌɪˈdʒiːlə/ ▶ noun an Asian flowering shrub of the honeysuckle family, which has pink, red, or yellow flowers and is a popular ornamental. ● Genus *Weigela*, family Caprifoliaceae: several species, in particular *W. florida*.
– ORIGIN modern Latin, named after Christian E. *Weigel* (1748–1831), German physician.

weigh[1] ▶ verb [with obj.] **1** find out how heavy (someone or something) is, typically using scales: *weigh yourself on the day you begin the diet | the vendor weighed the vegetables.* ■ have a specified weight: *when the twins were born they weighed ten pounds.* ■ balance in the hands to guess or as if to guess the weight of: *she picked up the brick and weighed it in her right hand.* ■ (**weigh something out**) measure and take from a larger quantity of a substance a portion of a particular weight: *she weighed out two ounces of loose tobacco.*
2 assess the nature or importance of, especially with a view to a decision or action: *the consequences of the move would need to be very carefully weighed.* ■ (**weigh something against**) compare the importance of one factor with that of (another): *they need to weigh benefit against risk.* ■ [no obj.] influence a decision or action; be considered important: *arguments which weighed in favour of publication | the evidence weighed against him.*
– PHRASES **weigh anchor** see ANCHOR. **weigh one's words** carefully choose the way one expresses something.
– PHRASAL VERBS **weigh someone down** be heavy and cumbersome to someone: *my waders and fishing gear weighed me down.* ■ be oppressive or burdensome to someone: *she was weighed down by the responsibility of looking after her sisters.* **weigh in 1** (of a boxer or jockey) be officially weighed before or after a contest. **2** informal make a forceful contribution to a competition or argument: *the dispute turned nastier when Steward weighed in | the paper's editor weighed in with criticism of the president.* **weigh in at** be of (a specified weight). ■ cost (a specified amount). **weigh into** informal join in forcefully or enthusiastically: *they weighed into the election campaign.* ■ attack physically or verbally: *he weighed into the companies for their high costs.* **weigh on** be depressing or burdensome to: *his unhappiness would weigh on my mind so much.* **weigh out** (of a jockey) be weighed before a race. **weigh someone/thing up** carefully assess someone or something: *the coach weighed up his team's opponents.*
– DERIVATIVES **weighable** adjective, **weigher** noun.
– ORIGIN Old English *wegan*, of Germanic origin; related to Dutch *wegen* 'weigh', German *bewegen* 'move', from an Indo-European root shared by Latin *vehere* 'convey'. Early senses included 'transport from one place to another' and 'raise up'.

weigh[2] ▶ noun (in phrase **under weigh**) Nautical another way of saying UNDER WAY.
– ORIGIN late 18th cent.: from an erroneous association with *weigh anchor* (see ANCHOR).

weighbridge ▶ noun a machine for weighing vehicles, set into the ground to be driven on to.

weigh-in ▶ noun an official or regular weighing of something or someone, for example of boxers before a fight.

weight ▶ noun **1** [mass noun] a body's relative mass or the quantity of matter contained by it, giving rise to a downward force; the heaviness of a person or thing: *he was at least fifteen stone in weight.* ■ Physics the force exerted on the mass of a body by a gravitational field. ■ the quality of being heavy: *as he came upstairs the boards creaked under his weight.* ■ [count noun] a unit or system of units used for expressing how much an object or quantity of matter weighs: *weights and measures.*

2 a piece of metal known to weigh a definite amount and used on scales to determine how heavy an object or quantity of a substance is. ■ a heavy object, especially one being lifted or carried. ■ a heavy object used to give an impulse or act as a counterpoise in a mechanism. ■ a heavy object thrown by a shot-putter. ■ (**weights**) blocks or discs of metal or other heavy material used in weightlifting or weight training. ■ [mass noun] the amount that a jockey is expected or required to weigh, or the amount that a horse can easily carry.
3 [mass noun] the ability of someone or something to influence decisions or actions: *a recommendation by the committee will carry great weight.* ■ the importance attributed to something: *individuals differ in the weight they attach to various aspects of a job.* ■ Statistics a factor associated with one of a set of numerical quantities, used to represent its importance relative to the other members of the set.
4 the surface density of cloth, used as a measure of its quality.
▶ **verb** [with obj.] **1** hold (something) down by placing a heavy object on top of it: *a mug half filled with coffee* ***weighted down*** *a stack of papers.* ■ attach a heavy object to (something), especially so as to make it stay in place: *the jugs were covered with muslin veils weighted with coloured beads.*
2 attribute importance or value to: *speaking, reading, and writing should be weighted equally in the assessment.* ■ (**be weighted**) be planned or arranged so as to put a specified person, group, or factor in a position of advantage or disadvantage: *the balance of power is weighted in favour of the government.* ■ Statistics multiply the components of (an average) by factors to take account of their importance.
3 assign a handicap weight to (a horse).
4 treat (a fabric) with a mineral to make it seem thicker and heavier.
– PHRASES **put on** (or **lose**) **weight** become fatter (or thinner). **throw one's weight about** (or **around**) informal be unpleasantly self-assertive. **throw one's weight behind** informal use one's influence to help support. **the weight of the world** used in reference to a very heavy burden of worry or responsibility: *he continues to carry the weight of the world on his shoulders.* **be a weight off one's mind** come as a great relief after one has been worried. **be worth one's weight in gold** be extremely useful or helpful.
– ORIGIN Old English *(ge)wiht*, of Germanic origin; related to Dutch *wicht* and German *Gewicht*. The form of the word has been influenced by **WEIGH**[1].

weight belt ▶ **noun** a belt to which weights are attached, designed to help divers stay submerged.

weighted average ▶ **noun** Statistics an average resulting from the multiplication of each component by a factor reflecting its importance.

weighting ▶ **noun** [mass noun] **1** allowance or adjustment made in order to take account of special circumstances or compensate for a distorting factor. ■ Brit. an extra amount of wages or salary paid especially to allow for a higher cost of living in a particular area: *London weighting of £1,750 is payable.*
2 emphasis or priority: *they will give due weighting to quality as well as price.*

weightless ▶ **adjective** (of a body, especially in an orbiting spacecraft) not apparently acted on by gravity.
– DERIVATIVES **weightlessly** adverb, **weightlessness** noun.

weightlifting ▶ **noun** [mass noun] the sport or activity of lifting barbells or other heavy weights. There are two standard lifts in modern weightlifting: the single-movement lift from floor to extended position (the **snatch**), and the two-movement lift from floor to shoulder position, and from shoulders to extended position (the **clean and jerk**).
– DERIVATIVES **weightlifter** noun.

weight training ▶ **noun** [mass noun] physical training that involves lifting weights.

weight-watcher ▶ **noun** a person who is concerned about their weight, especially one who diets.
– DERIVATIVES **weight-watching** noun & adjective.
– ORIGIN from the proprietary name *Weight Watchers*, an organization for slimmers.

weighty ▶ **adjective** (**weightier**, **weightiest**) weighing a great deal; heavy: *a weighty tome.* ■ of great seriousness and importance: *he threw off all weighty considerations of state.* ■ having a great deal of influence on events or decisions.
– DERIVATIVES **weightily** adverb, **weightiness** noun.

Weihsien /weɪˈʃjɛn/ former name for **WEIFANG**.

Weil /vʌɪl/, French /vɛj/, Simone (1909–43), French essayist, philosopher, and mystic. During the Second World War she joined the resistance movement in England and died of tuberculosis while weakened by voluntary starvation in identification with her French compatriots.

Weill /vʌɪl/, Kurt (1900–50), German composer, resident in the US from 1935. He is best known for the operas he wrote with Bertolt Brecht, political satires including *The Threepenny Opera* (1928).

Weil's disease /vʌɪlz/ ▶ **noun** [mass noun] a severe, sometimes fatal, form of leptospirosis transmitted by rats via contaminated water.
– ORIGIN late 19th cent.: named after H. Adolf *Weil* (1848–1916), German physician.

Weimar /ˈvʌɪmɑː/, German /ˈvaɪmar/ a city in Thuringia, central Germany; pop. 64,500 (est. 2006). It was famous in the late 18th and early 19th century for its intellectual and cultural life.

Weimaraner /ˈvʌɪmə,rɑːnə, ˈwʌɪ-/ ▶ **noun** a dog of a thin-coated, typically grey breed of pointer used as a gun dog.
– ORIGIN 1940s: from German, from **WEIMAR** in Germany, where the breed was developed.

Weimar Republic the German republic of 1919–33, so called because its constitution was drawn up at Weimar. The republic was faced with huge reparation costs deriving from the Treaty of Versailles as well as soaring inflation and high unemployment. The 1920s saw a growth in support for right-wing groups and the Republic was eventually overthrown by the Nazi Party of Adolf Hitler.

Weinberg /ˈwʌɪnbəːg/, Steven (b.1933), American theoretical physicist. He devised a theory to unify electromagnetic interactions and the weak forces within the nucleus of an atom, for which he was awarded the Nobel Prize for Physics in 1979, shared with Sheldon Lee Glashow and Abdus Salam.

Weinstube /ˈvʌɪn,ʃtuːbə, -stuːbə/, German /ˈvaɪn,ʃtuːbə/ ▶ **noun** (pl. **Weinstuben** /-,ʃtuːb(ə)n, -stuːb(ə)n/, German /-,ʃtuːbn/) a small German wine bar or tavern.
– ORIGIN German, literally 'wine room'.

weir ▶ **noun** a low dam built across a river to raise the level of water upstream or regulate its flow. ■ an enclosure of stakes set in a stream as a trap for fish.
– ORIGIN Old English *wer*, from *werian* 'dam up'.

weird ▶ **adjective** **1** suggesting something supernatural; unearthly: *weird, inhuman sounds.* ■ informal very strange; bizarre: *a weird coincidence | all sorts of* ***weird and wonderful*** *characters.*
2 archaic connected with fate.
▶ **noun** archaic, chiefly Scottish a person's destiny.
▶ **verb** [with obj.] (**weird someone out**) N. Amer. informal induce a sense of disbelief or alienation in someone.
– DERIVATIVES **weirdly** adverb, **weirdness** noun.
– ORIGIN Old English *wyrd* 'destiny', of Germanic origin. The adjective (late Middle English) originally meant 'having the power to control destiny', and was used especially in *the Weird Sisters*, originally referring to the Fates, later the witches in Shakespeare's *Macbeth*; the latter use gave rise to the sense 'unearthly' (early 19th cent.).

weirdie (also **weirdy**) ▶ **noun** (pl. **weirdies**) another term for **WEIRDO**.

weirdo ▶ **noun** (pl. **weirdos**) informal a person whose dress or behaviour seems strange or eccentric.

weird sisters ▶ **plural noun** (usu. **the weird sisters**) the Fates. ■ witches, especially those in Shakespeare's *Macbeth*.

Weismann /ˈvʌɪsmən/, German /ˈvaɪsman/, August Friedrich Leopold (1834–1914), German biologist, one of the founders of modern genetics. He expounded the theory of germ plasm, which ruled out the transmission of acquired characteristics, and suggested that variability in individuals came from the recombination of chromosomes during reproduction.
– DERIVATIVES **Weismannism** noun.

Weissmuller /ˈwʌɪs,mʊlə/, Johnny (1904–84), American swimmer and actor; full name *John Peter Weissmuller*. He won three Olympic gold medals in 1924 and two in 1928. In the 1930s and 1940s he was the star of the Tarzan films.

Weisswurst /ˈvʌɪsvəːst/ (also **weisswurst**) ▶ **noun** [mass noun] whitish German sausage made chiefly of veal.
– ORIGIN German, literally 'white sausage'.

Weizmann /ˈvʌɪtsmən, ˈwʌɪzmən/, Chaim (Azriel) (1874–1952), Russian-born Israeli statesman, President 1949–52. He played an important role in persuading the US government to recognize the new state of Israel (1948) and became its first President.

weka /ˈwɛkə/ ▶ **noun** a large flightless New Zealand rail with heavily built legs and feet. ● *Gallirallus australis*, family Rallidae.
– ORIGIN mid 19th cent.: from Maori, imitative of its cry.

Weland /ˈwɛlənd/ variant of **WAYLAND THE SMITH**.

welch /wɛltʃ/ ▶ **verb** variant spelling of **WELSH**.

welcome ▶ **noun** an instance or manner of greeting someone: *you will receive a warm welcome* | [mass noun] *he went to meet them with his hand stretched out in welcome.* ■ a pleased or approving reaction: *the announcement received an immediate welcome from childcare agencies.*
▶ **exclamation** used to greet someone in a polite or friendly way: ***welcome to*** *the Wildlife Park.*
▶ **verb** [with obj.] greet (someone arriving) in a polite or friendly way: *hotels should welcome guests in their own language* | (as adj. **welcoming**) *a welcoming smile.* ■ be glad to entertain (someone) or receive (something): *we welcome any comments.* ■ react with pleasure or approval to (an event or development): *the bank's decision to cut its rates was widely welcomed.*
▶ **adjective** **1** (of a guest or new arrival) gladly received: *I'm pleased to see you, lad—you're welcome.*
2 very pleasing because much needed or desired: *after your walk, the tea room serves a welcome cuppa* | *the news will be most* ***welcome to*** *those whose jobs will now be safeguarded.*
3 [predic., with infinitive] allowed or invited to do a specified thing: *we arrange a framework of activities which you are welcome to join.* ■ (**welcome to**) used to indicate relief at relinquishing the control or possession of something to someone else: *the job is all yours and you're welcome to it!*
– PHRASES **make someone welcome** receive and treat someone hospitably. **outstay** (or **overstay**) **one's welcome** stay as a visitor longer than one is wanted. **you are welcome** used as a polite response to thanks.
– DERIVATIVES **welcomely** adverb, **welcomeness** noun, **welcomer** noun, **welcomingly** adverb.
– ORIGIN Old English *wilcuma* 'a person whose coming is pleasing', *wilcumian* (verb), from *wil-* 'desire, pleasure' + *cuman* 'come'. The first element was later changed to *wel-* 'well', influenced by Old French *bien venu* or Old Norse *velkominn*.

Welcome Wagon ▶ **noun** N. Amer. trademark a vehicle bringing gifts and samples from local merchants to newcomers in a community.

weld[1] ▶ **verb** [with obj.] **1** join together (metal parts) by heating the surfaces to the point of melting with a blowpipe, electric arc, or other means, and uniting them by pressing, hammering, etc.: *steel plates were being welded | the truck had spikes welded to the back.* ■ forge (an article) by welding. ■ unite (pieces of plastic or other material) by melting or softening of surfaces in contact.
2 cause to combine and form a harmonious or effective whole: *cross-curricular themes would* ***weld*** *the curriculum* ***together.***
▶ **noun** a welded joint.
– DERIVATIVES **weldability** noun, **weldable** adjective, **welder** noun.
– ORIGIN late 16th cent. (in the sense 'become united'): alteration (probably influenced by the past participle) of **WELL**[2] in the obsolete sense 'melt or weld heated metal'.

weld[2] ▶ **noun** a widely distributed plant related to mignonette, yielding a yellow dye. ● *Reseda luteola*, family Resedaceae.
■ [mass noun] the yellow dye made from weld, which has been used since Neolithic times and was a popular colour for Roman wedding garments.
– ORIGIN late Middle English: related to Dutch *wouw*, perhaps also to **WOLD**.

weldmesh ▶ **noun** [mass noun] trademark wire mesh formed by welding together two series of parallel wires crossing at right angles.

welfare ▶ **noun** [mass noun] **1** the health, happiness, and fortunes of a person or group: *they don't give a damn about the welfare of their families.*
2 statutory procedure or social effort designed to promote the basic physical and material well-being of people in need: *the protection of rights to education, housing, and welfare.* ■ chiefly N. Amer. financial support given to those who are unemployed or otherwise in need.
– ORIGIN Middle English: from the adverb **WELL**[1] + the verb **FARE**.

welfare state ▸ noun a system whereby the state undertakes to protect the health and well-being of its citizens, especially those in financial or social need, by means of grants, pensions, and other benefits. The foundations for the modern welfare state in the UK were laid by the Beveridge Report of 1942; proposals such as the establishment of a National Health Service and the National Insurance Scheme were implemented by the Labour administration in 1948. ■ a country practising such a system.

welfare to work ▸ noun [mass noun] (in the UK) the government policy of encouraging unemployed people and others receiving state benefits to find a job, for example by paying a fee to their new employers.

welfare work ▸ noun [mass noun] organized effort to promote the basic physical and material well-being of people in need.
– DERIVATIVES **welfare worker** noun.

welfarism ▸ noun [mass noun] the principles or policies associated with a welfare state.
– DERIVATIVES **welfarist** noun & adjective.

welkin /ˈwɛlkɪn/ ▸ noun literary the sky or heaven.
– PHRASES **make the welkin ring** make a very loud sound: *the crew made the welkin ring with their hurrahs.*
– ORIGIN Old English *wolcen* 'cloud, sky', of West Germanic origin; related to Dutch *wolk* and German *Wolke*.

Welkom /ˈvɛlkəm/ a town in central South Africa, in Free State; pop. 584,700 (est. 2009).

well[1] ▸ adverb (**better, best**) **1** in a good or satisfactory way: *the whole team played well.* ■ in a way that is appropriate to the facts or circumstances: *you did well to come and tell me* | [as submodifier, in combination] *a well-timed exit.* ■ so as to have a fortunate outcome: *his campaign was not going well.* ■ in a kind way: *the animals will remain loyal to humans if treated well.* ■ with praise or approval: *people spoke well of him* | *the film was quite well reviewed at the time.* ■ with equanimity: *she took it very well, all things considered.* ■ profitably; advantageously: *she would marry well or not at all.* ■ in a condition of prosperity or comfort: *they lived well and were generous with their money.* ■ archaic luckily; opportunely: *hail fellow, well met.*
2 in a thorough manner: *add the mustard and lemon juice and mix well.* ■ to a great extent or degree (often used for emphasis): *the visit had been planned well in advance* | [as submodifier, in combination] *a well-loved colleague* | *a well-deserved reputation.* ■ intimately; closely: *he knew my father very well.* ■ [as submodifier] Brit. informal very; extremely: *he was well out of order.* ■ [with submodifier] used as an intensifier: *I should jolly well hope so.*
3 [with modal] very probably; in all likelihood: *being short of breath may well be the first sign of asthma.* ■ without difficulty: *she could well afford to pay for the reception herself.* ■ with good reason: *'What are we doing here?' 'You may well ask.'*
▸ adjective (**better, best**) [predic.] **1** in good health; free or recovered from illness: *I don't feel very well* | *it would be some time before Sarah was completely well* | [attrib.] informal *I am not a well man.* ■ in a satisfactory state or position: *I do hope all is well with you and your family.*
2 sensible; advisable: *it would be well to know just what this suggestion entails.*
▸ exclamation used to express a range of emotions including surprise, anger, resignation, or relief: *Well, really! The manners of some people!* ■ used when pausing to consider one's next words, to mark the resumption or end of a conversation, etc.: *well, I suppose I could fit you in at 3.45* | *well, cheers, Tom—I must fly.* ■ used to indicate that one is waiting for an answer or explanation from someone: *Well? You promised to tell me all about it.*
– PHRASES **as well 1** in addition; too: *the museum provides hours of fun and a few surprises as well.* **2** (**as well** or **just as well**) with equal reason or an equally good result: *I may as well have a look.* ■ sensible, appropriate, or desirable: *it would be as well to let him go.* **as well as** and in addition; and also: *a shop that sold books as well as newspapers.* **as well he** (or **she** etc.) **might** (or **may**) used to convey the speaker's opinion that a reaction is appropriate or unsurprising: *she sounded rather chipper, as well she might, given her bright prospects.* **be well away** Brit. informal having made considerable or easy progress: *if we got Terry to do that, we'd be well away.* **be well in with** informal have a good relationship with (someone in a position of influence or authority): *you're well in with O'Brien aren't you.* **be well out of** Brit. informal be fortunate to be no longer involved in (a situation). **be well up on** (or **in**) know a great deal about (a particular thing): *I'm not all that well up in musical matters.* **do well for oneself** be successful in material or financial terms. **leave** (or **let**) **well** (N. Amer. **enough**) **alone** refrain from interfering with or trying to improve something. **very well** used to express agreement or understanding: *oh very well then, come in.* **(all) well and good** used to express acceptance of a first statement before introducing a contradictory or confirming second statement: *that's all well and good, but why didn't he phone her to say so?* **well and truly** completely: *Leith was well and truly rattled.* **well enough** to a reasonable degree: *he liked Isobel well enough, but wouldn't want to make a close friend of her.* **well worth** certainly worth: *Salzburg is well worth a visit.*
– DERIVATIVES **wellness** noun.
– ORIGIN Old English *wel(l)*, of Germanic origin; related to Dutch *wel* and German *wohl*; probably also to the verb WILL[1]. Vowel lengthening in Middle English gave rise to the current Scots form WEEL.

> **USAGE** The adverb **well** is often used in combination with past participles to form adjectival compounds: **well adjusted, well intentioned, well known,** and so on. As far as hyphenation is concerned, the general stylistic principle is that if the adjectival compound is placed attributively (i.e. it comes before the noun), it should be hyphenated (*a well-intentioned remark*) but that if it is placed predicatively (i.e. standing alone after the verb), it should not be hyphenated (*her remarks were **well intentioned***). In this dictionary the unhyphenated form is generally the only one given, although the hyphenated form may be seen in illustrative examples.

well[2] ▸ noun **1** a shaft sunk into the ground to obtain water, oil, or gas. ■ archaic a water spring or fountain. ■ (**Wells**) [in place names] a place where there are mineral springs: *Tunbridge Wells.* ■ a depression made to hold liquid: *put the flour on a flat surface and make a well to hold the eggs.*
2 a plentiful source or supply: *she could feel a deep well of sympathy and compassion.*
3 an enclosed space in the middle of a building, giving room for stairs or a lift, or to allow light or ventilation. ■ Brit. the place in a law court where the clerks and ushers sit.
4 Physics a region of minimum potential: *a gravity well.*
▸ verb [no obj., with adverbial] (often **well up**) (of a liquid) rise up to the surface and spill or be about to spill: *tears were beginning to well up in her eyes.* ■ (of an emotion) develop and become more intense: *all the old bitterness began to well up inside her again.*
– ORIGIN Old English *wella*, of Germanic origin; related to Dutch *wel* and German *Welle* 'a wave'.

we'll ▸ contraction we shall; we will.

well acquainted ▸ adjective having a good knowledge of something: *both are very **well acquainted with** the area.*

well adjusted ▸ adjective (of a person) mentally and emotionally stable.

well advised ▸ adjective [with infinitive] sensible; wise: *you would be well advised to obtain legal advice.*

Welland Canal /ˈwɛlənd/ (also **Welland Ship Canal**) a canal in southern Canada, 42 km (26 miles) long, linking Lake Erie with Lake Ontario, bypassing Niagara Falls and forming part of the St Lawrence Seaway.

well appointed ▸ adjective (of a building or room) having a high standard of equipment or furnishing.

well attended ▸ adjective (of an event) attended by a large number of people: *a well-attended conference.*

well balanced ▸ adjective (of a person) emotionally stable.

well behaved ▸ adjective conducting oneself in an appropriate manner: *the crowd was very well behaved.* ■ (of a computer program) communicating with hardware via standard operating system calls rather than directly and therefore able to be used on different machines.

well-being ▸ noun [mass noun] the state of being comfortable, healthy, or happy: *an improvement in the patient's well-being.*

well born ▸ adjective from a noble or wealthy family.

well bred ▸ adjective having or showing good breeding or manners.

well built ▸ adjective (of a person) having a strong, sturdy physique.

well chosen ▸ adjective carefully selected, especially for a particular effect: *he would sum up any situation with a few well-chosen words.*

well conducted ▸ adjective **1** properly organized or carried out: *responsible, well-conducted businesses.*
2 archaic well behaved.

well connected ▸ adjective acquainted with or related to people with prestige or influence.

well covered ▸ adjective Brit. informal slightly plump.

well deck ▸ noun an open space on the main deck of a ship, lying at a lower level between the forecastle and poop.

well disposed ▸ adjective having a positive, sympathetic, or friendly attitude towards someone or something: *the company is **well disposed to** the idea of partnership.*

well done ▸ adjective **1** carried out successfully or satisfactorily: *the decoration was very well done* | *the satisfaction of **a job well done**.*
2 (of meat) thoroughly cooked.
▸ exclamation used to express congratulations or approval: *Well done—you've worked very hard!*

well dressed ▸ adjective wearing smart or fashionable clothes.

well dressing ▸ noun [mass noun] the decoration of wells with flowers at Whitsuntide, especially in Derbyshire, as an ancient custom originally associated with the belief in water deities.

well earned ▸ adjective fully merited or deserved: *a well-earned rest.*

well endowed ▸ adjective having plentiful supplies of a resource: *the country is **well endowed with** mineral resources.* ■ well provided with money; wealthy. ■ informal, humorous (of a man) having large genitals. ■ informal, humorous (of a woman) large-breasted.

Welles /wɛlz/, (George) Orson (1915–85), American film director and actor. His realistic radio dramatization in 1938 of H. G. Wells's *The War of the Worlds* persuaded many listeners that a Martian invasion was really happening. Notable films as director and actor include *Citizen Kane* (1941) and as actor *The Third Man* (1949).

well established ▸ adjective firmly established, especially because of a long existence: *his father was now well established in his career* | *a well-established tradition.*

well favoured (US **well favored**) ▸ adjective having special advantages, especially good looks.

well fed ▸ adjective having good meals regularly.

well formed ▸ adjective correctly or attractively proportioned or shaped. ■ (especially of a sentence or phrase) constructed according to grammatical rules. ■ Logic conforming to the formation rules of a logical system.

well found ▸ adjective (chiefly of a boat) well equipped and maintained.

well founded ▸ adjective (especially of a suspicion or belief) based on good evidence or reasons: *their apprehensions were well founded.*

well groomed ▸ adjective (especially of a person) clean, tidy, and smart.

well grounded ▸ adjective **1** based on good evidence or reasons: *her fears were well grounded.*
2 having a good training in or knowledge of a subject: *boys who are **well grounded in** traditional academic subjects.*

well head ▸ noun **1** the place where a spring comes out of the ground.
2 the structure over a well, typically an oil or gas well.

well heeled ▸ adjective informal wealthy.

well house ▸ noun a small building or room enclosing a well and its apparatus.

well hung ▸ adjective **1** informal, humorous (of a man) having large genitals.
2 (of meat or game) hung until sufficiently dry, tender, or high before cooking.

wellie ▸ noun variant spelling of WELLY.

well informed ▸ adjective having or showing much knowledge about a wide range of subjects, or about one particular subject.

Wellington[1] the capital of New Zealand, situated at the southern tip of the North Island; pop. 179,463 (2006). It became the capital in 1865, when the seat of government was moved from Auckland.

Wellington[2], Arthur Wellesley, 1st Duke of (1769–1852), British soldier and Tory statesman,

W

Prime Minister 1828–30 and 1834; known as **the Iron Duke**. He served as commander of the British forces in the Peninsular War (1808–14) and in 1815 defeated Napoleon at the Battle of Waterloo, so ending the Napoleonic Wars.

wellington (also **wellington boot**) ▶ **noun** Brit. a knee-length waterproof rubber or plastic boot.
– ORIGIN early 19th cent.: named after the 1st Duke of *Wellington* (see **WELLINGTON**²).

wellingtonia /ˌwɛlɪŋˈtəʊnɪə/ ▶ **noun** the giant redwood.
– ORIGIN mid 19th cent.: modern Latin, from the former binomial *Wellingtonia gigantea* (from **WELLINGTON**²).

well intentioned ▶ **adjective** having or showing good intentions despite a lack of success or fortunate results: *well-intentioned advice*.

well judged ▶ **adjective** showing careful consideration or much skill.

well kept ▶ **adjective 1** (especially of property) kept clean, tidy, and in good condition.
2 (of a secret) not told to anyone or made widely known.

well knit ▶ **adjective** (of a person) strongly and compactly built.

well known ▶ **adjective** known widely or thoroughly: *a well-known television personality*.

well liked ▶ **adjective** regarded with much affection; popular with many people: *he is efficient, fair-minded, and well liked by his colleagues*.

well made ▶ **adjective** strongly or skilfully constructed: *a well-made film*. ■ (of a person) having a good, strong build.

well mannered ▶ **adjective** having or showing good manners; polite: *they were well mannered and eager to please*.

well matched ▶ **adjective** (of two or more people or items) appropriate for or very similar to each other: *a fiercely contested semi-final between two well-matched sides*.

well meaning (also **well meant**) ▶ **adjective** well intentioned: *well-meaning friends*.

well-nigh ▶ **adverb** almost: *a task that is well-nigh impossible*.

well off ▶ **adjective** wealthy: *her family are quite well off* | (as plural noun **the well-off**) *tax rises for the well-off*. ■ in a favourable situation or circumstances: *they were well off without her*.

well oiled ▶ **adjective 1** (especially of an organization) operating smoothly: *the ruling party's well-oiled political machine*.
2 informal drunk.

well ordered ▶ **adjective** arranged or organized in an orderly way: *the only rash decision of his well-ordered life*.

well paid ▶ **adjective** earning or providing good pay: *a well-paid job*.

well placed ▶ **adjective** cleverly or judiciously positioned or deployed: *I obtained the information through well-placed questions*. ■ having a fortunate or advantageous position: *the country is well placed to take advantage of the single market*.

well pleased ▶ **adjective** highly gratified or satisfied: *Moore paused, well pleased with the effect*.

well preserved ▶ **adjective** (of something old) having remained in good condition. ■ (of an old person) showing little sign of ageing.

well read ▶ **adjective** having a lot of knowledge from reading widely; knowledgeable: *I am very well read in the classics*.

well rounded ▶ **adjective 1** (of a person) plump or curvaceous.
2 (of a person) having a personality that is fully developed in all aspects.
3 (of a phrase or sentence) carefully composed and balanced.

Wells, H. G. (1866–1946), English novelist; full name *Herbert George Wells*. He wrote some of the earliest science-fiction novels, such as *The War of the Worlds* (1898), which combined political satire with warnings about the powers of science.

well set ▶ **adjective** (of a construction) firmly established; solidly fixed or arranged. ■ (also **well-set-up**) (of a person) strongly built.

Wells, Fargo & Co. /ˈfɑːɡəʊ/ a US transportation company founded in 1852 by the businessmen Henry Wells (1805–78) and William Fargo (1818–81) and others. It carried mail to and from the newly developed West, founded a San Francisco bank, and later ran a stagecoach service.

well spent ▶ **adjective** (of money or time) usefully or profitably expended: *time spent in taking stock is time well spent*.

well spoken ▶ **adjective** (of a person) speaking in an educated and refined manner.

wellspring ▶ **noun 1** literary term for **WELL HEAD** (sense 1).
2 an abundant source of something: *a wellspring of ideas*.

well stocked ▶ **adjective** filled with a plentiful supply of something: *a well-stocked bar*.

well tempered ▶ **adjective 1** having a cheerful or emotionally stable disposition.
2 (of a process or activity) properly regulated, controlled, or moderated.

well thought of ▶ **adjective** having a good reputation; admired or respected by others: *he was very well thought of within the club*.

well thought out ▶ **adjective** carefully considered and planned: *an excellent and well-thought-out presentation*.

well thumbed ▶ **adjective** (of a book, magazine, etc.) having been read often and bearing marks of frequent handling.

well timed ▶ **adjective** occurring at an appropriate time; timely: *a well-timed exit*.

well-to-do ▶ **adjective** wealthy; prosperous: *a well-to-do family*.

well travelled (US **well traveled**) ▶ **adjective 1** (of a person) having travelled widely.
2 (of a route) much frequented by travellers.

well tried ▶ **adjective** having been used often and therefore known to be reliable: *well-tried tactics*.

well trodden ▶ **adjective** much frequented by travellers: *a well-trodden path*.

well turned ▶ **adjective 1** (of a compliment, phrase, or verse) elegantly expressed.
2 (especially of a person's ankle or leg) having an elegant and attractive shape.

well upholstered ▶ **adjective** (of a chair or sofa) having plenty of padding. ■ humorous (of a person) fat.

well used ▶ **adjective** much used: *a well-used wax jacket*.

well-wisher ▶ **noun** a person who desires happiness or success for another, or who expresses such a desire.

well woman ▶ **noun** [as modifier] Brit. denoting a clinic or other establishment providing health advice and check-ups for problems specific to women.

well worn ▶ **adjective** showing the signs of extensive use or wear: *a well-worn leather armchair*. ■ (of a phrase, idea, or joke) used or repeated so often that it no longer has interest or significance.

well wrought ▶ **adjective** skilfully constructed or put together: *a well-wrought argument*.

welly (also **wellie**) Brit. informal ▶ **noun** (pl. **wellies**)
1 short for **WELLINGTON**.
2 [mass noun] power or vigour: *I like big, fat voices with plenty of welly*.
▶ **verb** (**wellies**, **wellying**, **wellied**) [with obj.] hit or kick (something) hard: *Francis wellied the ball upfield*.

wels /wɛls, vɛls/ ▶ **noun** (pl. **same**) a large freshwater catfish that occurs from central Europe to central Asia. It has been known to reach a length of 5 m and a weight of over 300 kg. Also called **SHEATFISH**. ● *Silurus glanis*, family Siluridae.
– ORIGIN late 19th cent.: from German *Wels*.

Welsbach /ˈwɛlzbak/, German /ˈvɛlsbax/, Carl Auer von, see **AUER**.

Welsh ▶ **adjective** relating to Wales, its people, or their language.
▶ **noun 1** [mass noun] the Celtic language of Wales, spoken by about 500,000 people (mainly bilingual in English). Descended from the Brythonic language spoken in most of Roman Britain, it has been strongly revived after a long decline.
2 (as plural noun **the Welsh**) the people of Wales collectively.
– DERIVATIVES **Welshness** noun.
– ORIGIN Old English *Welisc*, *Wælisc*, from a Germanic word meaning 'foreigner', from Latin *Volcae*, the name of a Celtic people.

welsh (also **welch**) ▶ **verb** [no obj.] (**welsh on**) fail to honour (a debt or obligation incurred through a promise or agreement): *banks began welshing on their agreement not to convert dollar reserves into gold*.
– DERIVATIVES **welsher** noun.
– ORIGIN mid 19th cent.: of unknown origin.

Welsh Black ▶ **noun** an animal of a black-coated breed of cattle developed in North Wales, now generally kept for both meat and milk production.

Welsh corgi ▶ **noun** see **CORGI**.

Welsh dragon ▶ **noun** a red heraldic dragon as the emblem of Wales.

Welsh dresser ▶ **noun** Brit. a piece of wooden furniture with cupboards and drawers in the lower part and open shelves in the upper part.

Welsh harp ▶ **noun** another term for **TRIPLE HARP**. Compare with **CELTIC HARP**.

Welshman ▶ **noun** (pl. **Welshmen**) a male native or inhabitant of Wales, or a man of Welsh descent.

Welsh mountain pony ▶ **noun** a small, strong, slender pony of a hardy breed, used as a riding pony or in harness.

Welsh mountain sheep ▶ **noun** a sheep of a small hardy breed developed in the uplands of Wales.

Welsh onion ▶ **noun** an Asian onion that forms clusters of slender bulbs which resemble salad (spring) onions. It is the onion most commonly used in SE Asia. ● *Allium fistulosum*, family Liliaceae (or Alliaceae).
– ORIGIN early 18th cent. (as *Welch onion*): *Welsh* from German *welsch* 'foreign'.

Welsh poppy ▶ **noun** a yellow- or orange-flowered European poppy of shady rocky places. ● *Meconopsis cambrica*, family Papaveraceae.

Welsh rarebit (also **Welsh rabbit**) ▶ **noun** another term for **RAREBIT**.

Welsh springer ▶ **noun** see **SPRINGER** (sense 1).

Welsh terrier ▶ **noun** a stocky, rough-coated, typically black-and-tan terrier of a breed with a square muzzle and drop ears.

Welshwoman ▶ **noun** (pl. **Welshwomen**) a female native or inhabitant of Wales, or a woman of Welsh descent.

welt ▶ **noun 1** a leather rim sewn round the edge of a shoe upper to which the sole is attached. ■ a ribbed, reinforced, or decorative border of a garment or pocket.
2 a red, raised mark or scar; a weal.
3 a heavy blow.
▶ **verb** [with obj.] **1** provide with a welt.
2 strike (someone or something) hard and heavily: *I could have welted him*.
3 [no obj.] develop a raised scar or weal: *his lip was beginning to thicken and welt from the blow*.
– ORIGIN late Middle English: of unknown origin.

Weltanschauung /ˈvɛltˌanʃaʊʊŋ/ ▶ **noun** (pl. **Weltanschauungen** /-(ə)n/) a particular philosophy or view of life; the world view of an individual or group.
– ORIGIN German, from *Welt* 'world' + *Anschauung* 'perception'.

welter¹ ▶ **verb** [no obj.] literary **1** move in a turbulent fashion: *the streams foam and welter*.
2 lie soaked in blood.
▶ **noun** a large number of items in no order; a confused mass: *there's such a welter of conflicting rules*. ■ a state of general disorder: *the attack petered out in a welter of bloody, confused fighting*.
– ORIGIN Middle English (in the sense 'writhe, wallow'): from Middle Dutch, Middle Low German *welteren*.

welter² ▶ **noun** short for **WELTERWEIGHT**.

welterweight ▶ **noun** [mass noun] a weight in boxing and other sports intermediate between lightweight and middleweight. In the amateur boxing scale it ranges from 63.5–67 kg. ■ [count noun] a boxer or other competitor of this weight.
– ORIGIN early 19th cent.: *welter* of unknown origin.

Weltschmerz /ˈvɛltˌʃmɛːts/, German /ˈvɛltˌʃmɛrts/ ▶ **noun** [mass noun] a feeling of melancholy and world-weariness.
– ORIGIN German, from *Welt* 'world' + *Schmerz* 'pain'.

Welty /ˈwɛlti/, Eudora (1909–2001), American novelist, short-story writer, and critic. Welty's novels chiefly focus on life in the Southern states of the US and contain Gothic elements; they include *The Optimist's Daughter* (1972), which won the Pulitzer Prize.

welwitschia /wɛlˈwɪtʃɪə/ ▶ **noun** a gymnospermous plant of desert regions in SW Africa, which has a

dwarf, massive trunk, two long strap-shaped leaves, and male and female flowers in the scales of scarlet cones. ● *Welwitschia mirabilis*, family Welwitschiaceae.
– ORIGIN mid 19th cent.: modern Latin, named after Friedrich *Welwitsch* (1806–72), Austrian botanist.

Wembley Stadium a sports stadium in Wembley, NW London. The FA Cup Final and the England football team's home matches are traditionally played there.

wen¹ ▸ **noun 1** a boil or other swelling or growth on the skin, especially a sebaceous cyst.
2 archaic a very large or overcrowded city: *the great wen of London*.
– ORIGIN Old English *wen(n)*, of unknown origin; compare with Low German *wehne* 'tumour, wart'.

wen² ▸ **noun** variant spelling of **WYNN**.

Wenceslas /ˈwɛnsɪsləs, ˈwɛnsəslas/ (also **Wenceslaus** /-laʊs/) (1361–1419), king of Bohemia (as Wenceslas IV) 1378–1419. He became king of Germany, Holy Roman emperor, and King of Bohemia in the same year, but was deposed by the German Electors in 1400.

Wenceslas, St (also **Wenceslaus**) (*c.*907–29), Duke of Bohemia and patron saint of the Czech Republic; also known as **Good King Wenceslas**. He worked to Christianize the people of Bohemia but was murdered by his brother; he later became venerated as a martyr. Feast day, 28 September.

wench /wɛn(t)ʃ/ ▸ **noun 1** archaic or humorous a girl or young woman.
2 archaic a prostitute.
▸ **verb** [no obj.] archaic (of a man) habitually associate with prostitutes.
– DERIVATIVES **wencher** noun.
– ORIGIN Middle English: abbreviation of obsolete *wenchel* 'child, servant, prostitute'; perhaps related to Old English *wancol* 'unsteady, inconstant'.

Wen-Chou /wɛnˈtʃəʊ/ variant of **WENZHOU**.

Wend /wɛnd/ ▸ **noun** another term for **SORB**.
– ORIGIN from German *Wende*, of unknown origin.

wend ▸ **verb** [no obj., with adverbial] (**wend one's way**) go in a specified direction, typically slowly or by an indirect route: *they wended their way across the city*.
– ORIGIN Old English *wendan* 'to turn, depart', of Germanic origin; related to Dutch and German *wenden*, also to **WIND²**.

wendigo /ˈwɛndɪɡəʊ/ ▸ **noun** variant spelling of **WINDIGO**.

Wendish /ˈwɛndɪʃ/ ▸ **adjective & noun** another term for **SORBIAN**.

Wendy house ▸ **noun** Brit. a toy house large enough for children to play in.
– ORIGIN named after the house built around *Wendy* in J. M. Barrie's play *Peter Pan*.

Wensleydale /ˈwɛnzlɪdeɪl/ ▸ **noun 1** [mass noun] a type of white cheese with a crumbly texture.
2 a sheep of a breed with long wool.
– ORIGIN named after *Wensleydale* in Yorkshire.

went past of **GO¹**.

wentletrap /ˈwɛnt(ə)ltrap/ ▸ **noun** a marine mollusc which has a tall spiral shell with many whorls that are ringed with oblique ridges. Also called **STAIRCASE SHELL**. ● Family Epitoniidae, class Gastropoda: numerous species, including the European **common wentletrap** (*Clathrus clathrus*).
– ORIGIN mid 18th cent.: from Dutch *wenteltrap*, literally 'winding stair'.

Wenzhou /wɛnˈdʒəʊ/ (also **Wen-Chou**) an industrial city in Zhejiang province, eastern China; pop. 633,600 (est. 2006).

wept past and past participle of **WEEP**.

were second person singular past, plural past, and past subjunctive of **BE**.

we're ▸ **contraction** we are.

weren't ▸ **contraction** were not.

W

werewolf /ˈwɛːwʊlf, ˈwɪə-, ˈwəː-/ ▸ **noun** (pl. **werewolves**) (in folklore) a person who changes for periods of time into a wolf, typically when there is a full moon.
– ORIGIN late Old English *werewulf*; the first element has usually been identified with Old English *wer* 'man'. In modern use the word has been revived through folklore studies.

werf /vɛrf/ ▸ **noun** (pl. **werfs** or **werven**) S. African a farm homestead and farmyard.
– ORIGIN from archaic and dialect Dutch, literally 'raised ground on which a house is built'.

Werner¹ /ˈvɛːnə/, German /ˈvɛrnɐ/, Abraham Gottlob (1749–1817), German geologist. He was the chief exponent of the theory of Neptunism, eventually shown to be incorrect, and attempted to establish a universal stratigraphic sequence.

Werner² /ˈvɛːnə/, French /vɛʀnɛʀ/, Alfred (1866–1919), French-born Swiss chemist. He showed that stereochemistry was general to the whole of chemistry and was a pioneer in the study of coordination compounds. Nobel Prize for Chemistry (1913).

Werner's syndrome /ˈwəːnəz, ˈvɛː-/ ▸ **noun** [mass noun] Medicine a rare hereditary syndrome causing rapid premature ageing, susceptibility to cancer, and other disorders.
– ORIGIN 1930s: named after Carl O. *Werner* (1879–1936), German physician.

Wernicke's area /ˈwəːnɪkəz, ˈvɛː-/ ▸ **noun** Anatomy a region of the brain concerned with the comprehension of language, located in the cortex of the dominant temporal lobe. Damage in this area causes **Wernicke's aphasia**, characterized by superficially fluent, grammatical speech but an inability to use or understand more than the most basic nouns and verbs.
– ORIGIN late 19th cent.: named after Karl *Wernicke* (1848–1905), German neuropsychiatrist.

Wernicke's encephalopathy (also **Wernicke's syndrome**) ▸ **noun** [mass noun] Medicine a neurological disorder caused by thiamine deficiency, typically from chronic alcoholism or persistent vomiting, and marked by mental confusion, abnormal eye movements, and unsteady gait.
– ORIGIN late 19th cent.: named after Karl *Wernicke* (see **WERNICKE'S AREA**).

wert /wəːt/ archaic second person singular past of **BE**.

Wesak /ˈvɛsak/ ▸ **noun** variant spelling of **VESAK**.

Weser /ˈveɪzə/, German /ˈveːzɐ/ a river of NW Germany, which is formed at the junction of the Werra and Fulda Rivers in Lower Saxony and flows 292 km (182 miles) northwards to the North Sea near Bremerhaven.

Wesker /ˈwɛskə/, Sir Arnold (b.1932), English dramatist. His writing is associated with the British kitchen-sink drama of the 1950s. Notable plays: *Roots* (1959) and *Chips with Everything* (1962).

Wesley /ˈwɛzli/, John (1703–91), English preacher and co-founder of Methodism. Wesley was a committed Christian evangelist who won many working-class converts, often through open-air preaching. The opposition they encountered from the Church establishment led to the Methodists forming a separate denomination in 1791. His brother **Charles** (1707–88) was also a founding Methodist, and both wrote many hymns.

Wesleyan ▸ **adjective** relating to or denoting the teachings of John Wesley or the main branch of the Methodist Church which he founded.
▸ **noun** a follower of Wesley or adherent of the main Methodist tradition.
– DERIVATIVES **Wesleyanism** noun.

Wessex the kingdom of the West Saxons, established in Hampshire in the early 6th century and gradually extended by conquest to include much of southern England. The name was revived in the 19th century by Thomas Hardy to designate the south-western counties of England (especially Dorset) in which his novels are set.

West¹, Benjamin (1738–1820), American painter, resident in Britain from 1763. He became historical painter to George III in 1769 and the second president of the Royal Academy in 1792. Notable works: *The Death of General Wolfe* (1771).

West², Mae (1892–1980), American actress and dramatist. She made her name on Broadway in her own comedies *Sex* (1926) and *Diamond Lil* (1928), memorable for their spirited approach to sexual matters, before embarking on her successful Hollywood career in the 1930s.

West³, Dame Rebecca (1892–1983), Irish-born British writer and feminist; born *Cicily Isabel Fairfield*. She is best remembered for her study of the Nuremberg trials *The Meaning of Treason* (1949). Other notable works: *The Fountain Overflows* (novel, 1957).

west ▸ **noun** (usu. **the west**) **1** the direction towards the point of the horizon where the sun sets at the equinoxes, on the left-hand side of a person facing north: *the evening sun glowed from the west* | *a patrol aimed to create a diversion to the west of the city*. ■ the compass point corresponding to this.
2 the western part of the world or of a specified country, region, or town: *it will become windy in the west*. ■ (usu. **the West**) Europe and North America seen in contrast to other civilizations. ■ (**the West**) historical the non-Communist states of Europe and North America, contrasted with the former Communist states of eastern Europe. ■ (usu. **the West**) the western part of the United States, especially the states west of the Mississippi.
3 (**West**) [as name] Bridge the player sitting to the right of North and partnering East.
▸ **adjective 1** [attrib.] lying towards, near, or facing the west: *the west coast*. ■ (of a wind) blowing from the west.
2 of or denoting the western part of a specified area, city, or country or its inhabitants: *West Africa*.
▸ **adverb** to or towards the west: *he faced west and watched the sunset* | *the accident happened a mile west of Bowes*.
– PHRASES **go west** Brit. informal be killed or lost; meet with disaster.
– ORIGIN Old English, of Germanic origin; related to Dutch and German *west*, from an Indo-European root shared by Greek *hesperos*, Latin *vesper* 'evening'.

West Africa the western part of the African continent, especially the countries bounded by and including Mauritania, Mali, and Niger in the north and Gabon in the south.

West Bank a region west of the River Jordan and north-west of the Dead Sea; pop. 2,461,300 (est. 2009). It contains Jericho, Hebron, Nablus, Bethlehem, and other settlements. It became part of Jordan in 1948 and was occupied by Israel following the Six Day War of 1967. In 1993 an agreement was signed which granted limited autonomy to the Palestinians, who comprise 97 per cent of its inhabitants; withdrawal of Israeli troops began in 1994 but conflict in the area continues.

West Bengal a state in eastern India; capital, Kolkata (Calcutta). It was formed in 1947 from the predominantly Hindu area of former Bengal.

westbound ▸ **adjective** leading or travelling towards the west: *a westbound train*.

West Briton ▸ **noun** Irish, derogatory an Irish person who greatly admires England or Britain.

West Bromwich /ˈbrɒmɪtʃ/ an industrial town in the west Midlands; pop. 127,000 (est. 2009).

West Country the south-western counties of England.

West End the entertainment and shopping area of London to the west of the City.

westering ▸ **adjective** literary (especially of the sun) nearing the west.
– ORIGIN mid 17th cent.: from the literary verb *wester*, from **WEST**.

westerly ▸ **adjective & adverb** in a westward position or direction: [as adj.] *he stumbled slowly along in a westerly direction* | [as adv.] *our plan was to keep westerly*. ■ (of a wind) blowing from the west: [as adj.] *a stiff westerly breeze*.
▸ **noun** a wind blowing from the west. ■ (**westerlies**) the belt of prevailing westerly winds in medium latitudes in the southern hemisphere.
– ORIGIN late 15th cent.: from obsolete *wester* 'western' + **-LY¹**.

western ▸ **adjective 1** [attrib.] situated in the west, or directed towards or facing the west: *there will be showers in some western areas*. ■ (of a wind) blowing from the west.
2 (**Western**) living in or originating from the West, in particular Europe or the United States: *Western society*. ■ relating to or characteristic of the West or its inhabitants: *the history of Western art*. ■ historical of or originating from the non-Communist states of Europe and North America in contrast to the Eastern bloc.
▸ **noun** a film, television drama, or novel about cowboys in western North America, set especially in the late 19th and early 20th centuries.
– DERIVATIVES **westernmost** adjective.
– ORIGIN Old English *westerne* (see **WEST**, **-ERN**).

Western Australia a state comprising the western part of Australia; pop. 2,171,197 (2008); capital, Perth. It was colonized by the British in 1826, and was federated with the other states of Australia in 1901.

Western blot ▸ **noun** Biochemistry an adaptation of the Southern blot procedure, used to identify specific amino-acid sequences in proteins.
– ORIGIN suggested by **SOUTHERN BLOT**.

Western Cape a province of south-western South Africa, formerly part of Cape Province; capital, Cape Town.

Western Church the part of the Christian Church historically originating in the Latin Church of the Western Roman Empire, including the Roman Catholic Church and the Anglican, Lutheran, and Reformed Churches, especially as distinct from the Eastern Orthodox Church.

Western Empire the western part of the Roman Empire, after its division in AD 395.

westerner ▶ **noun** a native or inhabitant of the west, especially of western Europe or North America.

Western European Union (abbrev.: **WEU**) an association formed in 1955 from the former Western Union, with the addition of Italy and West Germany, chiefly in order to coordinate defence and promote economic cooperation.

Western Front the zone of fighting in western Europe in the First World War, in which the German army engaged the armies to its west, i.e. France, the UK (and its dominions), and, from 1917, the US. For most of the war the front line stretched from the Vosges mountains in eastern France through Amiens to Ostend in Belgium.

Western Ghats see **GHATS**.

western hemisphere the half of the earth containing the Americas.

western hemlock ▶ **noun** a large coniferous North American tree with flattened needles of two different sizes, grown for pulp and as an ornamental.
● *Tsuga heterophylla*, family Pinaceae.

Western Isles another name for the Outer Hebrides (see **HEBRIDES**). ■ a council area of Scotland, consisting of the Outer Hebrides; administrative centre, Stornoway.

westernize (also **westernise**) ▶ **verb** [with obj.] cause (a country, person, or system) to adopt or be influenced by the cultural, economic, or political systems of Europe and North America: *the agreement provided for the legal system to be westernized* | (as adj. **westernized**) *the more westernized parts of the city*. ■ [no obj.] be in the process of adopting or being influenced by the systems of the West: (as adj. **westernizing**) *a westernizing tribe*.
– DERIVATIVES **westernization** noun, **westernizer** noun.

Western Ocean former term for **ATLANTIC OCEAN**.

Western Roman Empire see **ROMAN EMPIRE**.

Western saddle ▶ **noun** a saddle with a deep seat, high pommel and cantle, and broad stirrups.

Western Sahara a region of NW Africa, on the Atlantic coast between Morocco and Mauritania; pop. 405,200 (est. 2009); capital, Laayoune.

> The region was formerly an overseas Spanish province, called Spanish Sahara. After the Spanish withdrew in 1976 it was renamed and annexed by Morocco and Mauritania. Mauritania withdrew in 1979 and Morocco extended its control over the entire region. A liberation movement, the Polisario Front, which had launched a guerrilla war against the Spanish in 1973, continued its struggle against Morocco in an attempt to establish an independent Saharawi Arab Democratic Republic; a ceasefire came into effect in 1991.

Western Samoa see **SAMOA**.

western sandwich ▶ **noun** N. Amer. a sandwich having an omelette filling containing onion, green pepper, and ham.

western swing ▶ **noun** [mass noun] a style of country music influenced by jazz, popular in the 1930s.

Western Union an association of western European nations (Belgium, France, Luxembourg, the Netherlands, and the UK) formed in 1948 with similar aims to, and later superseded by, the Western European Union.

Western Wall another name for **WAILING WALL**.

Western Zhou see **ZHOU**.

Westfalen /vɛst'fa:lən/ German name for **WESTPHALIA**.

West Flanders a province of NW Belgium; capital, Bruges.

West Frisian Islands see **FRISIAN ISLANDS**.

West Germanic ▶ **noun** [mass noun] the western group of Germanic languages, comprising High and Low German, Dutch, Frisian, and English.
▶ **adjective** relating to West Germanic.

West Germany see **GERMANY**.

West Glamorgan a former county of South Wales, formed in 1974 and dissolved in 1996.

West Highland terrier ▶ **noun** a dog of a small, short-legged breed of terrier with a white coat and erect ears and tail, developed in the West Highlands.

Westie ▶ **noun** (pl. **Westies**) informal a West Highland terrier.

West Indian ▶ **noun** a native or inhabitant of any of the islands of the West Indies. ■ a person of West Indian descent.
▶ **adjective** relating to the West Indies or its people.

West Indies a chain of islands extending from the Florida peninsula to the coast of Venezuela, lying between the Caribbean and the Atlantic.

> They consist of three main island groups, the Greater and Lesser Antilles and the Bahamas, with Bermuda lying further to the north. Originally inhabited by Arawak and Carib Indians, the islands were visited by Columbus in 1492 and named by him in the belief that he had reached the coast of India.

westing ▶ **noun** [mass noun] distance travelled or measured westward, especially at sea. ■ [count noun] a figure or line representing westward distance on a map.

Westinghouse, George (1846–1914), American engineer. His achievements covered several fields but he is best known for developing vacuum operated safety brakes and electrically controlled signals for railways. He built up a huge company to manufacture his products.

West Irian another name for **IRIAN JAYA**.

Westmann Islands /'vɛstmən, 'wɛst-/ a group of fifteen volcanic islands off the south coast of Iceland. Icelandic name **VESTMANNAEYJAR**.

Westmeath /wɛst'mi:θ/ a county of the Republic of Ireland, in the province of Leinster; county town, Mullingar.

West Midlands a former metropolitan county of central England.

Westminster an inner London borough which contains the Houses of Parliament and many government offices. Full name **City of Westminster**. ■ used in reference to the British Parliament: *Westminster must become more effective in holding the government to account*.

Westminster, Palace of the building in Westminster in which the British Parliament meets; the Houses of Parliament. The present building, designed by Sir Charles Barry, was formally opened in 1852. The original palace, a royal residence until it was damaged by fire in 1512, was destroyed by a fire in 1834.

Westminster, Statute of a statute of 1931 recognizing the equality of status of the dominions as autonomous communities within the British Empire, and giving their legislatures independence from British control.

Westminster Abbey the collegiate church of St Peter in Westminster, originally the abbey church of a Benedictine monastery. Nearly all the kings and queens of England have been crowned in Westminster Abbey; it is also the burial place of many of England's monarchs and of some of the nation's leading figures.

Westminster Confession a Calvinist doctrinal statement which was issued by the synod appointed to reform the English and Scottish Churches in 1643, and became widely accepted among Presbyterian Churches.

Westmorland /'wɛstmələnd/ a former county of NW England. In 1974 it was united with Cumberland and northern parts of Lancashire to form the county of Cumbria.

west-north-west ▶ **noun** the direction or compass point midway between west and north-west.

Weston-super-Mare /ˌwɛstən,su:pə'mɛ:, -ˌsju:pə-/ a resort in SW England, on the Bristol Channel; pop. 79,500 (est. 2009).

West Papua a province of Indonesia in the western part of the island of New Guinea.

Westphalia /wɛst'feɪlɪə/ a former province of NW Germany. Previously a duchy of the archbishop of Cologne, it became a province of Prussia in 1815. In 1946 the major part was incorporated in the state of North Rhine–Westphalia, the northern portion becoming part of Lower Saxony. German name **WESTFALEN**.
– DERIVATIVES **Westphalian** adjective & noun.

Westphalia, Treaty of the peace accord (1648) which ended the Thirty Years War, signed simultaneously in Osnabrück and Münster.

West Point (in full **West Point Academy**) the US Military Academy, founded in 1802, located on the site of a former strategic fort on the west bank of the Hudson River in New York State.

West Saxon ▶ **noun 1** a native or inhabitant of the Anglo-Saxon kingdom of Wessex.
2 [mass noun] the dialect of Old English used by the West Saxons.
▶ **adjective** relating to the West Saxons or their dialect.

West Side the western part of any of several North American cities or boroughs, especially the island borough of Manhattan, New York.

west-south-west ▶ **noun** the direction or compass point midway between west and south-west.

West Sussex a county of SE England; county town, Chichester.

West Virginia a state of the eastern US; pop. 1,814,468 (est. 2008); capital, Charleston. It separated from Virginia during the American Civil War (1861) and became the 35th state of the US in 1863.
– DERIVATIVES **West Virginian** noun & adjective.

westward ▶ **adjective** towards the west: *the journey covers eight time zones in a westward direction*.
▶ **adverb** (also **westwards**) in a westerly direction: *a track leads westwards through the glen*.
▶ **noun** (**the westward**) a direction or region towards the west: *he sees a light to the westward*.
– DERIVATIVES **westwardly** adverb.

West Yorkshire a metropolitan county of northern England.

wet ▶ **adjective** (**wetter**, **wettest**) **1** covered or saturated with water or another liquid: *she followed, slipping on the wet rock*. ■ (of the weather) rainy: *a wet, windy evening*. ■ (of paint, ink, plaster, or a similar substance) not yet having dried or hardened. ■ (of a baby or young child) having urinated in its nappy or underwear. ■ involving the use of water or liquid: *wet methods of photography*. ■ Nautical (of a ship) liable to take in water over her bows or sides.
2 Brit. informal showing a lack of forcefulness or strength of character; feeble: *they thought the cadets were a bit wet*. ■ Conservative with liberal tendencies, especially as regarded by right-wing Conservatives.
3 informal (of a country or region or of its legislation) allowing the free sale of alcoholic drink. ■ (of a person) addicted to or drinking alcohol.
▶ **verb** (**wets**, **wetting**; past and past participle **wet** or **wetted**) [with obj.] cover or touch with liquid; moisten: *he wetted a finger and flicked through the pages* | (as noun **wetting**) *it was a velvet cap, and a wetting would ruin it*. ■ (especially of a baby or young child) urinate in or on: *while dreaming the child wet the bed*. ■ (**wet oneself**) urinate involuntarily. ■ dialect infuse (tea) by pouring on boiling water.
▶ **noun 1** [mass noun] liquid that makes something damp: *I could feel the wet of his tears*. ■ (**the wet**) rainy weather: *the race was held in the wet*. ■ [count noun] Brit. informal a drink: *I took a wet from my bottle*.
2 Brit. informal a person lacking forcefulness or strength of character. ■ a Conservative with liberal tendencies.
3 US a person opposed to the prohibition of alcohol.
– PHRASES **all wet** N. Amer. completely wrong. **wet the baby's head** Brit. informal celebrate a baby's birth with a drink, typically an alcoholic one. **wet behind the ears** informal lacking experience; immature. **wet through** (or **to the skin**) with one's clothes soaked; completely drenched. **wet one's whistle** informal have a drink.
– DERIVATIVES **wetly** adverb, **wetness** noun, **wettable** adjective, **wettish** adjective.
– ORIGIN Old English *wǣt* (adjective and noun), *wǣtan* (verb); related to **WATER**.

weta /'wɛtə/ ▶ **noun** a large brown wingless insect related to the grasshoppers, with long spiny legs and wood-boring larvae, found only in New Zealand.
● Family Stenopelmatidae: several genera, including *Deinacrida* (the **giant wetas**).
– ORIGIN mid 19th cent.: from Maori.

wetback ▶ **noun** US informal, derogatory a Mexican living in the US, especially one who is an illegal immigrant.
– ORIGIN 1920s: so named from the practice of swimming the Rio Grande to reach the US.

wet bar ▶ **noun** N. Amer. a bar or counter in the home for serving alcoholic drinks.

wet blanket ▸ noun informal a person who spoils other people's fun by failing to join in with or by disapproving of their activities.

wet bulb ▸ noun one of the two thermometers of a psychrometer, the bulb of which is enclosed in wetted material so that water is constantly evaporating from it and cooling the bulb.

wet cell ▸ noun a primary electric cell in which the electrolyte is a liquid.

wet dock ▸ noun a dock in which water is maintained at a level at which a ship is able to float.

wet dream ▸ noun an erotic dream that causes involuntary ejaculation of semen.

wet fish ▸ noun [mass noun] fresh fish, as opposed to fish which has been frozen, cooked, or dried.

wet fly ▸ noun an artificial fishing fly designed to sink below the surface of the water.

wether /ˈwɛðə/ ▸ noun a castrated ram.
– ORIGIN Old English, of Germanic origin; related to Dutch *weer* and German *Widder*.

wetland ▸ noun [mass noun] (also **wetlands**) land consisting of marshes or swamps; saturated land.

wet lease ▸ noun an arrangement covering the hire of an aircraft including the provision of a flight crew and sometimes fuel.
▸ verb (**wet-lease**) [with obj.] hire (an aircraft) on the basis of a wet lease.

wet look ▸ noun a wet or shiny appearance given to a fabric or achieved by applying a type of gel to the hair.

wet nurse ▸ noun chiefly historical a woman employed to suckle another woman's child.
▸ verb (**wet-nurse**) [with obj.] act as a wet nurse to.
■ informal look after (someone) as though they were a helpless infant.

wet pack ▸ noun **1** a session of hydrotherapy in which the body is wrapped in wet cloth.
2 a washbag.

wet plate ▸ noun Photography a sensitized collodion plate exposed in the camera while the collodion is moist.

wet room ▸ noun a bathroom in which the shower is open or set behind a single wall, its floor area being flush with the floor of the rest of the room and the water draining away through an outlet set into the floor.

wet rot ▸ noun [mass noun] **1** a brown fungal rot affecting timber with a high moisture content.
2 (also **wet rot fungus**) the fungus that causes wet rot. ● *Coniophora puteana*, family Coniophoraceae, class Hymenomycetes, and other species.

wetsuit ▸ noun a close-fitting rubber garment typically covering the entire body, worn for warmth in water sports or diving.

wetting agent ▸ noun a chemical that can be added to a liquid to reduce its surface tension and make it more effective in spreading over and penetrating surfaces.

wetware ▸ noun [mass noun] human brain cells or thought processes regarded as analogous to, or in contrast with, computer systems. ■ (chiefly in science fiction) computer technology in which the brain is linked to artificial systems, or used as a model for artificial systems based on biochemical processes.

WEU ▸ abbreviation Western European Union.

we've ▸ contraction we have.

Wexford /ˈwɛksfəd/ a county of the Republic of Ireland, in the south-east in the province of Leinster. ■ the county town of Wexford, a port on the Irish Sea; pop. 8,894 (2006).

wey /weɪ/ ▸ noun a former unit of weight or volume varying with different kinds of goods, e.g. 3 cwt of cheese.
– ORIGIN Old English *wǣg(e)*, *wēg(e)* 'balance, weight', of Germanic origin; related to WEIGH[1].

W

Weyden /ˈveɪd(ə)n/, Rogier van der (*c.*1400–64), Flemish painter; French name *Rogier de la Pasture*. He was particularly influential in the development of Dutch portrait painting. Notable works: *The Last Judgement* and *The Deposition in the Tomb* (both *c.*1450).

Weymouth[1] /ˈweɪməθ/ a resort and port on the coast of Dorset, southern England; pop. 50,100 (est. 2009).

Weymouth[2] /ˈweɪməθ/ ▸ noun (also **Weymouth bit**) a simple curb bit, used especially in a double bridle. ■ (also **Weymouth bridle**) a double bridle in which the curb bit is a Weymouth bit.
– ORIGIN late 18th cent.: of unknown origin.

w.f. ▸ abbreviation Printing wrong font (used as a proofreading mark).

WFTU ▸ abbreviation World Federation of Trade Unions.

Wg Cdr ▸ abbreviation Wing Commander.

whack informal ▸ verb [with obj.] strike forcefully with a sharp blow: *his attacker whacked him on the head* | [no obj.] *she found a stick to* **whack at** *the branches.* ■ defeat in a contest: [with obj. and complement] *the team were whacked six-nil.* ■ [with obj. and adverbial] put or push (something) roughly or carelessly in a specified place or direction: *he whacks a tape into the cassette recorder.* ■ N. Amer. murder: *he was whacked while sitting in his car.*
▸ noun **1** a sharp or resounding blow.
2 a try or attempt: *we decided to* **take a whack at** *spotting the decade's trends.*
3 Brit. a specified share of or contribution to something: *motorists* **pay a fair whack** *for the use of the roads through taxes.*
4 N. Amer. a large quantity or amount.
– PHRASES **out of whack** N. Amer. & Austral./NZ out of order; not working: *all their calculations were out of whack.* **top** (or **full**) **whack** chiefly Brit. the maximum price or rate: *the car has a top whack of 107 mph.*
– PHRASAL VERBS **whack off** vulgar slang masturbate.
– DERIVATIVES **whacker** noun.
– ORIGIN early 18th cent.: imitative, or perhaps an alteration of THWACK.

whacked (also **wacked**) ▸ adjective **1** Brit. informal completely exhausted: *I'm not staying long—I'm whacked.*
2 N. Amer. informal under the influence of drugs: *a sixteen-year-old* **whacked out** *on acid.*

whacking ▸ adjective [attrib.] Brit. informal very large: *she poured us two whacking drinks* | [as submodifier] *he dug a whacking great hole.*

whacko[1] ▸ exclamation Brit. informal, dated used to express delight and enthusiasm: *Home on Friday. Whacko!*

whacko[2] ▸ adjective & noun (pl. **whackos**) variant spelling of WACKO.

whacky ▸ adjective variant spelling of WACKY.

whale[1] ▸ noun (pl. **same** or **whales**) a very large marine mammal with a streamlined hairless body, a horizontal tail fin, and a blowhole on top of the head for breathing. ● Order Cetacea. See BALEEN WHALE and TOOTHED WHALE.
– PHRASES **a whale of a ——** informal an extremely good example of a particular thing: *you've been doing a whale of a job.* **have a whale of a time** enjoy oneself very much.
– ORIGIN Old English *hwæl*, of Germanic origin.

whale[2] ▸ verb [with obj.] informal, chiefly N. Amer. beat; hit: *Dad came upstairs and whaled me* | [no obj.] *they* **whaled at** *the water with their paddles.*
– ORIGIN late 18th cent.: variant of WALE.

whaleback ▸ noun a thing that is shaped like a whale's back, especially an arched structure over the bow or stern part of the deck of a steamer, or a large elongated hill: [as modifier] *a whaleback ridge.*

whalebird ▸ noun a prion (seabird) (so called because often found in the vicinity of whales or whaling vessels).

whaleboat ▸ noun a long rowing boat with a bow at either end for easy manoeuvrability, formerly used in whaling.

whalebone ▸ noun [mass noun] an elastic horny substance which grows in a series of thin parallel plates in the upper jaw of some whales and is used by them to strain plankton from the seawater. Also called BALEEN. ■ strips of whalebone, formerly used as stays in corsets and dresses: [as modifier] *a whalebone bodice.*

whalebone whale ▸ noun another term for BALEEN WHALE.

whale-headed stork ▸ noun an African stork with grey plumage and a very large bill shaped like a clog. Also called SHOEBILL. ● *Balaeniceps rex*, the only member of the family Balaenicipitidae.

whale oil ▸ noun [mass noun] oil obtained from the blubber of a whale, formerly used in oil lamps or for making soap.

whaler ▸ noun **1** a whaling ship. ■ a seaman engaged in whaling.
2 any of a number of large slender-bodied sharks: ● a shark that typically occurs inshore and is sometimes found in rivers (genus *Carcharhinus*, family Carcharhinidae), including the Australasian *C. brachyurus*. ● another term for BLUE SHARK.

whale shark ▸ noun a very large tropical shark which typically swims close to the surface, where it feeds chiefly on plankton. It is the largest known fish. ● *Rhincodon typus*, the sole member of the family Rhincodontidae.

whaling ▸ noun [mass noun] the practice or industry of hunting and killing whales for their oil, meat, or whalebone.

wham informal ▸ exclamation used to express the sound of a forcible impact: *the bombs landed—wham!—right on target.* ■ used to express the idea of a sudden and dramatic occurrence: *he asked me out for a drink, and—wham!—that was it.*
▸ verb (**whams**, **whamming**, **whammed**) [no obj., with adverbial] strike something forcefully: *trucks whammed into each other.* ■ make a loud sound as of a forceful impact: *my heart was whamming away like a drum.*
– ORIGIN 1920s: imitative.

wham-bam ▸ adjective informal characterized by quick or violent action: *Hollywood wanted a wham-bam end to the plot.*
– PHRASES **wham-bam-thank-you-ma'am** used in reference to sexual activity conducted roughly and quickly, without tenderness.
– ORIGIN 1950s (as *wham-bang*): from WHAM + BAM or the verb BANG[1].

whammo ▸ exclamation another word for WHAM.

whammy ▸ noun (pl. **whammies**) informal **1** an event with a powerful and unpleasant effect; a blow: *the third whammy was the degradation of the financial system.* See also DOUBLE WHAMMY.
2 chiefly US an evil or unlucky influence: *I've come to* **put the whammy on** *them.*
– ORIGIN 1940s: from the noun WHAM + -Y[1]; associated from the 1950s with the cartoon strip *Li'l Abner*, in which the hillbilly Evil-Eye Fleegle could 'shoot a whammy' (to put a curse on somebody) by pointing a finger with one eye open, and a 'double whammy' with both eyes open.

whammy bar ▸ noun informal a tremolo arm on an electric guitar.

whanau /ˈfɑːnaʊ/ ▸ noun (pl. **same**) NZ an extended family or community of related families who live together in the same area.
– ORIGIN Maori.

whang informal ▸ verb [no obj., with adverbial] make or produce a loud noise: *the cheerleader whanged on a tambourine.* ■ [with obj.] strike or throw heavily and loudly: *he whanged down the receiver.* ■ [no obj.] drive at speed: *we whanged round the bend.*
▸ noun **1** a noisy blow: *he gave a whang with his hammer.*
2 variant form of WHANGER.
– ORIGIN late 17th cent. (in the sense 'strike as if with a thong'): variant of THONG; senses describing noise are imitative.

Whangarei /ˌwɒŋəˈreɪ/ a port on the NE coast of the North Island, New Zealand; pop. 49,100 (est. 2006).

whanger (also **whang**) ▸ noun informal a man's penis.

whap ▸ verb (**whaps**, **whapping**, **whapped**) & noun chiefly N. Amer. variant spelling of WHOP.

whare /ˈwɒri/ ▸ noun a Maori hut or house.
– ORIGIN Maori.

wharf /wɔːf/ ▸ noun (pl. **wharves** or **wharfs**) a level quayside area to which a ship may be moored to load and unload.
– ORIGIN late Old English *hwearf*, of Germanic origin.

wharfage ▸ noun [mass noun] accommodation provided at a wharf for the loading, unloading, or storage of goods.

wharfie ▸ noun Austral./NZ informal a person who works at a wharf; a waterside worker or labourer.

wharfinger /ˈwɔːfɪn(d)ʒə/ ▸ noun an owner or keeper of a wharf.
– ORIGIN Middle English: from WHARFAGE + -ER[1].

Wharton /ˈwɔːt(ə)n/, Edith (Newbold) (1862–1937), American novelist and short-story writer, resident in France from 1907. Her novels are concerned with the conflict between social and individual fulfilment. They include *The Age of Innocence* (1920), which won a Pulitzer Prize.

wharves plural form of WHARF.

what ▸ pronoun **1** [interrogative pronoun] asking for information specifying something: *what is your name?* | *I'm not sure what you mean.* ■ asking for repetition of something not heard or confirmation of something not understood: *what? I can't hear you* | *you did what?*

2 [relative pronoun] the thing or things that (used in specifying something): *what we need is a commitment.* ■ (referring to the whole of an amount) whatever: *I want to do what I can to make a difference.*
3 (in exclamations) emphasizing something surprising or remarkable: *what some people do for a crust!*
▶ **determiner 1** [interrogative determiner] asking for information specifying something: *what time is it?* | *do you know what excuse he gave?*
2 [relative determiner] (referring to the whole of an amount) whatever: *he had been robbed of what little money he had.*
3 (in exclamations) how great or remarkable: [as determiner] *what luck!* | [as predeterminer] *what a fool she was.*
▶ **interrogative adverb 1** to what extent?: *what does it matter?*
2 used to indicate an estimate or approximation: *see you, what, about four?*
3 informal, dated used for emphasis or to invite agreement: *pretty poor show, what?*
– PHRASES **and** (or **or**) **what have you** informal and/or anything else similar: *all these home-made sweets and cakes and what have you.* **and what not** informal and other similar things. **what about ——? 1** used when asking for information or an opinion on something: *what about the practical angle?* **2** used to make a suggestion: *what about a walk?* **what-d'you-call-it** (or **what's-its-name**) informal used as a substitute for a name not recalled. **what for?** informal for what reason? **what if ——? 1** what would result if ——?: *what if nobody shows up?* **2** what does it matter if ——?: *what if our house is a mess? I'm clean.* **what is more** and as an additional point; moreover. **what next** see **NEXT**. **what of ——?** what is the news concerning ——? **what of it?** why should that be considered significant? **what's-his** (or **-its**) **-name** another term for **WHAT-D'YOU-CALL-IT**. **what say ——?** used to make a suggestion: *what say we call a tea break?* **what's what** informal what is useful or important: *I'll teach her what's what.* **what with** because of (used typically to introduce several causes of something): *what with the drought and the neglect, the garden is in a sad condition.*
– ORIGIN Old English *hwæt*, of Germanic origin; related to Dutch *wat* and German *was*, from an Indo-European root shared by Latin *quod*.

whatchamacallit /ˈwɒtʃəməˌkɔːlɪt/ ▶ **noun** another word for **WHATSIT**.

whate'er /wɒtˈɛː/ literary ▶ **contraction** whatever.

whatever ▶ **relative pronoun & determiner** used to emphasize a lack of restriction in referring to any thing or amount, no matter what: [as pronoun] *do whatever you like* | [as determiner] *take whatever action is needed.* ■ regardless of what: [as pronoun] *you have our support, whatever you decide* | [as determiner] *whatever decision he made I would support it.*
▶ **interrogative pronoun** used for emphasis instead of 'what' in questions, typically expressing surprise or confusion: *whatever is the matter?*
▶ **adverb 1** [with negative] at all; of any kind (used for emphasis): *they received no help whatever.*
2 informal no matter what happens: *we told him we'd back him whatever.*
▶ **exclamation** informal said as a response indicating a reluctance to discuss something, often implying indifference: *'I'll call you later.' I shrugged. 'Whatever.'*
– PHRASES **or whatever** informal or anything similar: *use chopped herbs, nuts, garlic, or whatever.* **what ever next** see **NEXT**.

> **WORD TRENDS** The exclamation **whatever** is disliked intensely by many for the attitude of indifference and contempt it conveys. Popularized by the affluent Valley Girls of 1980s California, **whatever** has grown in use as a powerfully dismissive way to end a conversation ever since: *'Whatever,' he said and pulled his hood up and swaggered off.* It can also be used to imply disagreement with a preceding statement (*They are telling me it's about time I earned my own money, and everything will taste sweeter for it. Whatever!*) or disbelief (*we found out later that she was casting for a major motion picture, and we were all like 'Oh, yeah, whatever!'*), and is even used as shorthand for everything seen to be wrong with the modern world, embodying apathy and refusal to accept responsibility: *the chancellor will probably brush this off, and say, 'hey, whatever!'.* See also usage at **HOWEVER**.

whatnot ▶ **noun 1** informal used to refer to an item or items that are not identified but are felt to have something in common with items already named: *little flashing digital displays, electric zooms and whatnots* | *pictures and books and manuscripts and whatnot.*
2 a stand with shelves for small objects.

whatsit ▶ **noun** informal, chiefly Brit. a person or thing whose name one cannot recall, does not know, or does not wish to specify: *Let's say two o'clock on the whatsit of May?* | *he's a right old interfering whatsit.*

whatso ▶ **pronoun & determiner** archaic whatever: [as pronoun] *whatso goes into their brain comes out as prose.*
– ORIGIN Middle English: reduced form of Old English *swā hwæt swā* 'so what so'.

whatsoe'er /ˌwɒtsəʊˈɛː/ literary ▶ **contraction** whatsoever.

whatsoever ▶ **adverb** [with negative] at all (used for emphasis): *I have no doubt whatsoever.*
▶ **determiner & pronoun** archaic whatever.

what-you-see-is-what-you-get ▶ **adjective** see **WYSIWYG**.

whaup /(h)wɔːp/ ▶ **noun** chiefly Scottish a curlew.
– ORIGIN mid 16th cent.: imitative of the bird's cry.

wheal ▶ **noun** variant spelling of **WEAL**[1].

wheat ▶ **noun** [mass noun] a cereal which is the most important kind grown in temperate countries, the grain of which is ground to make flour for bread, pasta, pastry, etc. ● Genus *Triticum*, family Gramineae: several species, including **bread wheat** (*T. aestivum*) and **durum wheat**, and many distinctive cultivars.
■ the grain of wheat.
– PHRASES **separate the wheat from the chaff** see **CHAFF**[1].
– ORIGIN Old English *hwǣte* of Germanic origin; related to Dutch *weit*, German *Weizen*, also to **WHITE**.

wheat belt ▶ **noun** a region where wheat is the chief agricultural product.

wheat bunt ▶ **noun** see **BUNT**[2].

wheatear ▶ **noun** a mainly Eurasian and African songbird related to the chats, with black and buff or black and white plumage and a white rump. ● Genus *Oenanthe*, family Turdidae: several species, in particular the grey-backed (**northern**) **wheatear** (*O. oenanthe*) of Eurasia and NE Canada.
– ORIGIN late 16th cent.: apparently from **WHITE** (assimilated to **WHEAT**) + **ARSE** (assimilated to **EAR**[2]).

wheaten ▶ **adjective** made from the grains or flour of wheat: *a wheaten loaf.* ■ of a colour resembling that of wheat; a pale yellow-beige.

wheaten terrier ▶ **noun** a terrier of a breed with a soft, wavy pale golden coat.

wheatgerm ▶ **noun** [mass noun] a nutritious foodstuff of a dry floury consistency consisting of the extracted embryos of grains of wheat.

wheatgrass ▶ **noun** another term for **COUCH**[2].

wheatish ▶ **adjective** Indian (of the complexion) of the pale golden colour of ripe wheat; light brown.

wheatmeal ▶ **noun** [mass noun] flour made from wheat from which some of the bran and germ has been removed.

Wheatstone /ˈwiːtstən/, Sir Charles (1802–75), English physicist and inventor. He is best known for his electrical inventions which included an electric clock, the Wheatstone bridge, the rheostat, and with Sir W. F. Cooke, the electric telegraph.

Wheatstone bridge ▶ **noun** a simple circuit for measuring an unknown resistance by connecting it so as to form a quadrilateral with three known resistances and applying a voltage between a pair of opposite corners.

whee ▶ **exclamation** used to express delight, excitement, or exhilaration: *as the car began to bump down the track he felt a lightening of his spirits—whee!*
– ORIGIN natural exclamation: first recorded in English in the 1920s.

wheech /hwiːx, hwiːk/ ▶ **verb** [with obj.] Scottish snatch or remove (something) quickly: *I wheeched the duvet off Gavin's bed.* ■ [no obj., with adverbial of direction] rush; dash.
– ORIGIN early 19th cent.: symbolic.

wheedle ▶ **verb** [no obj.] use endearments or flattery to persuade someone to do something or give one something: *she* **wheedled her way** *on to the guest list* | [with obj.] *she had* **wheedled** *us* **into** *employing her brother* | [with direct speech] *'Please, for my sake,' he wheedled.*
– DERIVATIVES **wheedler** noun, **wheedlingly** adverb.
– ORIGIN mid 17th cent.: perhaps from German *wedeln* 'cringe, fawn', from *Wedel* 'tail, fan'.

wheel ▶ **noun 1** a circular object that revolves on an axle and is fixed below a vehicle or other object to enable it to move over the ground. ■ a circular object that revolves on an axle and forms part of a machine. ■ (**the wheel**) used in reference to the cycle of a specified condition or set of events: *the final release from the wheel of life.* ■ (**the wheel**) historical a large wheel used as an instrument of punishment or torture, especially by binding someone to it and breaking their limbs: *a man sentenced to be* **broken on the wheel**.
2 a machine or structure having a wheel as its essential part. ■ (**the wheel**) the steering wheel of a vehicle or vessel: *his crew know when he wants to* **take the wheel**. ■ a device with a revolving disc or drum used in various games of chance. ■ a system, or a part of a system, regarded as a relentlessly moving machine: *the wheels of justice.*
3 (**wheels**) informal a car: *she's got wheels now.*
4 a thing resembling a wheel, in particular a cheese made in the form of a shallow disc.
5 an instance of wheeling; a turn or rotation.
6 N. Amer. informal short for **BIG WHEEL** (sense 2).
7 a set of short lines, typically five in number and rhyming, concluding the stanza of a poem.
▶ **verb 1** [with obj.] push or pull (a vehicle with wheels): *the tea trolley was* **wheeled out**. ■ [with obj. and adverbial of direction] carry in or on a vehicle with wheels: *a young woman is wheeled into the operating theatre.* ■ (**wheel something on/out**) informal produce something that is unimpressive because it has been frequently seen or heard before: *the old journalistic arguments have been wheeled out.*
2 [no obj.] (of a bird or aircraft) fly in a wide circle or curve: *the birds wheeled and dived.* ■ turn round quickly so as to face another way: *Robert* **wheeled round** *to see the face of Mr Mafouz.*
– PHRASES **on someone's wheel** close behind someone when they are driving or cycling: *I had dominated the race early on and he sat on my wheel.* **on wheels 1** by, or travelling by, car or bicycle: *a journey on wheels.* ■ Brit. informal smoothly: *the business ran on wheels.* **2** Brit. informal used to emphasize one's distaste or dislike of the person or thing mentioned: *she was a bitch on wheels.* **silly as a wheel** Austral. very silly. **wheel and deal** engage in commercial or political scheming, especially unscrupulously: (as noun **wheeling and dealing**) *the wheeling and dealing of the Wall Street boom years.* **the wheel of Fortune** the wheel which the deity Fortune is represented as turning as a symbol of random luck or change. **wheels within wheels** used to indicate that a situation is complicated and affected by secret or indirect influences.
– DERIVATIVES **wheeled** adjective [in combination] *a four-wheeled cart*, **wheelless** adjective.
– ORIGIN Old English *hwēol* (noun), of Germanic origin, from an Indo-European root shared by Sanskrit *cakra* 'wheel, circle' and Greek *kuklos* 'circle'.

wheel and axle ▶ **noun** a simple lifting machine consisting of a rope which unwinds from a wheel on to a cylindrical drum or shaft joined to the wheel to provide mechanical advantage.

wheel arch ▶ **noun** an arch-shaped cavity in the body of a vehicle, which houses a wheel.

wheelback ▶ **adjective** (of a chair) with a back incorporating the design of a wheel.

wheelbarrow ▶ **noun** a small cart with a single wheel at the front and two supporting legs and two handles at the rear, used typically for carrying loads in building work or gardening.

wheelbase ▶ **noun** the distance between the front and rear axles of a vehicle: [in combination] *a short-wheelbase model.*

wheel brace ▶ **noun 1** a tool for screwing and unscrewing nuts on the wheel of a vehicle.
2 a hand drill worked by turning a wheel.

wheelchair ▶ **noun** a chair built on wheels for an invalid or disabled person, either pushed by another person or propelled by the occupant.

wheel clamp Brit. ▶ **noun** a device for immobilizing an illegally parked car.
▶ **verb** (**wheel-clamp**) [with obj.] immobilize (an illegally parked car) with a wheel clamp.

wheel dog ▶ **noun** the dog harnessed nearest to the sleigh in a dog team.

Wheeler, John Archibald (1911–2008), American theoretical physicist. Wheeler worked with Niels Bohr on nuclear fission, and collaborated with Richard Feynman on problems concerning the retarded effects of action at a distance. He coined the term **black hole** in 1967.

wheeler ▶ **noun 1** [in combination] a vehicle having a specified number of wheels: *a huge sixteen-wheeler truck.*
2 a wheelwright.

W

3 a horse harnessed next to the wheels of a cart and behind a leading horse.

wheeler-dealer (also **wheeler and dealer**) ▶ **noun** a person who engages in commercial or political scheming.
– DERIVATIVES **wheeler-dealing** noun.

wheel horse ▶ **noun** a horse harnessed nearest the wheels of a vehicle. ■ US a responsible and hard-working person, especially an experienced member of a political party.

wheelhouse ▶ **noun 1** a part of a boat or ship serving as a shelter for the person at the wheel.
2 Archaeology a stone-built circular house with inner partition walls radiating like the spokes of a wheel, found in western and northern Scotland and dating chiefly from about 100 BC to AD 100.

wheelie ▶ **noun** informal a trick or manoeuvre whereby a bicycle or motorcycle is ridden for a short distance with the front wheel raised off the ground.

wheelie bin (also **wheely bin**) ▶ **noun** Brit. informal a large refuse bin set on wheels.

wheel lock ▶ **noun** historical a kind of gun with a lock in which a steel wheel rubbed against a flint.

wheelman ▶ **noun** (pl. **wheelmen**) N. Amer. informal **1** a driver, in particular the driver of a getaway vehicle.
2 a cyclist.

wheel set ▶ **noun** a pair of wheels attached to an axle.

wheelsman ▶ **noun** (pl. **wheelsmen**) N. Amer. a person who steers a ship or boat.

wheelspin ▶ **noun** [mass noun] rotation of a vehicle's wheels without traction.

wheel well ▶ **noun** a recess in a vehicle in which a wheel is located.

wheelwright ▶ **noun** chiefly historical a person who makes or repairs wooden wheels.

wheely bin ▶ **noun** variant spelling of WHEELIE BIN.

wheen /wiːn/ ▶ **noun** [in sing.] chiefly Scottish a considerable amount or number: ***a wheen of** pennies.*
– ORIGIN late Middle English: from Old English *hwēne* 'in some degree'.

wheesht /wiːʃt/ ▶ **exclamation** variant of WHISHT.

wheeze ▶ **verb** [no obj.] breathe with a whistling or rattling sound in the chest, as a result of obstruction in the air passages: *the illness often leaves her wheezing* | (as adj. **wheezing**) *his wheezing old father.* ■ [with obj.] say (something) with a wheezing sound: *he could barely wheeze out his pleas for a handout* | [with direct speech] *'Don't worry son,' he wheezed.* ■ [no obj., with adverbial of direction] walk or move slowly making a wheezing sound: *she wheezed up the hill towards them.* ■ (of a device) make an irregular rattling or spluttering sound: *the engine coughed, wheezed, and shrieked into life.*
▶ **noun 1** a wheezing sound.
2 Brit. informal a clever or amusing scheme, idea, or trick: *a new wheeze to help farmers.*
– DERIVATIVES **wheezer** noun.
– ORIGIN late Middle English: probably from Old Norse *hvæsa* 'to hiss'.

wheezy ▶ **adjective** (**wheezier**, **wheeziest**) making the sound of a person wheezing: *a wheezy laugh.*
– DERIVATIVES **wheezily** adverb, **wheeziness** noun.

whelk[1] /wɛlk/ ▶ **noun** a predatory marine mollusc with a heavy pointed spiral shell, some kinds of which are edible. ● Family Buccinidae, class Gastropoda: *Buccinum* and other genera.
– ORIGIN Old English *wioloc*, *weoloc*, of unknown origin; the spelling with *wh-* was perhaps influenced by WHELK[3].

whelk[2] /wɛlk/ ▶ **noun** archaic a pimple.
– ORIGIN Old English *hwylca*, related to *hwelian* 'suppurate'.

whelm /wɛlm/ archaic ▶ **verb** [with obj.] engulf, submerge, or bury: *a swimmer whelmed in a raging storm.* ■ [no obj.] well up or flow: *the brook whelmed up from its source.*
▶ **noun** an act or instance of flowing or heaping up abundantly; a surge: *the whelm of the tide.*
– ORIGIN Middle English: representing an Old English form parallel to *hwelfan* 'overturn (a vessel)'.

whelp ▶ **noun** chiefly archaic **1** a puppy. ■ a cub: *let the lioness suckle her whelps.*
2 a boy or young man (often as a disparaging form of address).
3 (**whelps**) Nautical a set of projections on the barrel of a capstan or windlass.
▶ **verb** [with obj.] (of a female dog) give birth to (a puppy): *Copper whelped seven puppies* | [no obj.] *a bitch due to whelp.*
– PHRASES **in whelp** (of a female dog) pregnant.
– ORIGIN Old English *hwelp* (noun), of Germanic origin; related to Dutch *welp* and German *Welf.*

when ▶ **interrogative adverb** at what time: *when did you last see him?* | [with prep.] *since when have you been interested?* ■ how soon: *when can I see you?* ■ in what circumstances: *when would such a rule be justifiable?*
▶ **relative adverb** at or on which (referring to a time or circumstance): *Saturday is the day when I get my hair done.*
▶ **conjunction 1** at or during the time that: *I loved maths when I was at school.* ■ after: *call me when you've finished.* ■ at any time that; whenever: *can you spare five minutes when it's convenient?*
2 after which; and just then (implying suddenness): *he had just drifted off to sleep when the phone rang.*
3 in view of the fact that; considering that: *why bother to paint it when you can photograph it with the same effect?*
4 although; whereas: *I'm saying it now when I should have told you long ago.*
– ORIGIN Old English *hwanne*, *hwenne*; of Germanic origin; related to German *wenn* 'if', *wann* 'when'.

whence (also **from whence**) formal or archaic ▶ **interrogative adverb** from what place or source: *whence does Parliament derive this power?*
▶ **relative adverb** from which; from where: *the Ural mountains, whence the ore is procured.* ■ to the place from which: *he will be sent back whence he came.* ■ as a consequence of which: *whence it followed that the strategies were obsolete.*
– ORIGIN Middle English *whennes*, from earlier *whenne* (from Old English *hwanon*, of Germanic origin) + -s[3] (later respelled *-ce* to denote the unvoiced sound).

> **USAGE** Strictly speaking, **whence** means 'from what place', as in ***whence** did you come?* Thus, the preposition **from** in ***from whence** did you come?* is redundant, and its use is considered incorrect by some. The use with **from** is very common, though, and has been used by reputable writers since the 14th century. It is now broadly accepted in standard English.

whencesoever ▶ **relative adverb** formal or archaic from whatever place or source.

whene'er /wɛnˈɛː/ literary ▶ **contraction** whenever.

whenever ▶ **conjunction** at whatever time; on whatever occasion (emphasizing a lack of restriction): *you can ask for help whenever you need it.* ■ every time that: *the springs in the armchair creak whenever I change position.*
▶ **interrogative adverb** used for emphasis instead of 'when' in questions, typically expressing surprise or confusion: *whenever shall we get there?*
– PHRASES **or whenever** informal or at any time: *if you lay eyes on him, either tonight or tomorrow or whenever, call me straight away.*

> **USAGE** See USAGE at HOWEVER.

when-issued ▶ **adjective** Finance, chiefly US relating to trading in securities which have not yet been issued.

whensoe'er /ˌwɛnsəʊˈɛː/ literary ▶ **contraction** whensoever.

whensoever ▶ **conjunction & adverb** formal word for WHENEVER.

whenua /ˈfɛnʊə/ ▶ **noun** [mass noun] NZ land.
– ORIGIN Maori.

where ▶ **interrogative adverb** in or to what place or position: *where do you live?* | [with prep.] *where do you come from?* ■ in what direction or respect: *where does the argument lead?* ■ in or from what source: *where did you read that?* ■ in or to what situation or condition: *just where is all this leading us?*
▶ **relative adverb 1** at, in, or to which (used after reference to a place or situation): *I first saw him in Paris, where I lived in the early sixties.*
2 the place or situation in which: *this is where I live.* ■ in or to a place or situation in which: *sit where I can see you* | *where people were concerned, his threshold of boredom was low.* ■ in or to any place in which; wherever: *he was free to go where he liked.*
– ORIGIN Old English *hwǣr*, of Germanic origin; related to Dutch *waar* and German *wo.*

whereabouts ▶ **interrogative adverb** where or approximately where: *whereabouts do you come from?*
▶ **noun** [treated as sing. or pl.] the place where someone or something is: *his whereabouts remain secret.*

whereafter ▶ **relative adverb** formal after which: *dinner was taken at a long wooden table, whereafter we sipped liqueurs in front of a roaring fire.*

whereas ▶ **conjunction** in contrast or comparison with the fact that: *you treat the matter lightly, whereas I myself was never more serious.* ■ (especially in legal preambles) taking into consideration the fact that.

whereat ▶ **relative adverb & conjunction** archaic or formal at which: *they demanded an equal share in the high command, whereat negotiations broke down.*

whereby ▶ **relative adverb** by which: *a system whereby people could vote by telephone.*

where'er /wɛːrˈɛː/ literary ▶ **contraction** wherever.

wherefore archaic ▶ **interrogative adverb** for what reason: *she took an ill turn, but wherefore I cannot say.*
▶ **relative adverb & conjunction** as a result of which: [as conjunction] *truly he cared for me, wherefore I title him with all respect.*

wherefrom ▶ **relative adverb** archaic from which or from where: *one day you may lose this pride of place wherefrom you now dominate.*

wherein formal ▶ **adverb 1** [relative adverb] in which: *the situation wherein the information will eventually be used.*
2 [interrogative adverb] in what place or respect?: *so wherein lies the difference?*

whereof /wɛːrˈɒv/ ▶ **relative adverb** formal of what or which: *I know whereof I speak.*

whereon ▶ **relative adverb** archaic on which: *the cliff side whereon I walked.*

wheresoe'er /ˌwɛːsəʊˈɛː/ literary ▶ **contraction** wheresoever.

wheresoever ▶ **adverb & conjunction** formal word for WHEREVER.

whereto /wɛːˈtuː/ ▶ **relative adverb** archaic or formal to which: *young ambition's ladder, whereto the climber upward turns his face.*

whereupon ▶ **conjunction** immediately after which: *he qualified in February, whereupon he was promoted to Sergeant.*

wherever ▶ **relative adverb** in or to whatever place (emphasizing a lack of restriction): *meet me wherever you like.* ■ in all places; regardless of where: *it should be available wherever you go to shop.*
▶ **interrogative adverb** used for emphasis instead of 'where' in questions, typically expressing surprise or confusion: *wherever can he have gone to?*
▶ **conjunction** in every case when: *use wholegrain breakfast cereals wherever possible.*
– PHRASES **or wherever** informal or any similar place: *they need to keep in touch with their editors in New York or Washington or wherever.*

> **USAGE** See USAGE at HOWEVER.

wherewith ▶ **relative adverb** formal or archaic with or by which: *the instrumental means wherewith the action is performed.*

wherewithal ▶ **noun** [usu. with infinitive] (**the wherewithal**) the money or other means needed for a particular purpose: *they lacked the wherewithal to pay.*

wherry /ˈwɛri/ ▶ **noun** (pl. **wherries**) a light rowing boat used chiefly for carrying passengers. ■ Brit. a large light barge.
– ORIGIN late Middle English: of unknown origin.

whet /wɛt/ ▶ **verb** (**whets**, **whetting**, **whetted**) [with obj.] **1** sharpen the blade of (a tool or weapon): *her husband is whetting his knife.*
2 excite or stimulate (someone's desire, interest, or appetite): *here's an extract to whet your appetite.*
▶ **noun** archaic a thing that stimulates appetite or desire: *he swallowed his two dozen oysters as a whet.*
– DERIVATIVES **whetter** noun.
– ORIGIN Old English *hwettan*, of Germanic origin; related to German *wetzen*, based on an adjective meaning 'sharp'.

whether ▶ **conjunction** expressing a doubt or choice between alternatives: *he seemed undecided **whether** to go **or** stay* | *it is still not clear **whether or not** he realizes.* ■ expressing an enquiry or investigation (often used in indirect questions): *I'll see whether she's at home.* ■ indicating that a statement applies whichever of the alternatives mentioned is the case: *I'm going **whether** you like it **or not**.*
– PHRASES **whether or no 1** whether or not: *the only issue arising would be whether or no the publication was defamatory.* **2** archaic in any case: *God help us, whether or no!*
– ORIGIN Old English *hwæther*, *hwether*, of Germanic origin; related to German *weder* 'neither'.